BECKETT is registered trademark of

BECKETT PUBLICATIONS
DALLAS, TX

Manufactured in the United States of America
First Printing
ISBN 1-887432-84-1

# BECKETT

**Includes prices and listings from 1910 to present!**

# HOCKEY CARD PRICE GUIDE & ALPHABETICAL CHECKLIST #9

**ALL NEW ALPHABETICAL PLAYER CHECKLIST**

Edited by

## DR. JAMES BECKETT & BILL SUTHERLAND

with the price guide staff of
*Beckett Hockey Monthly*

BECKETT PUBLICATIONS • DALLAS, TEXAS

# Beckett Hockey Card Price Guide
## Table of Contents

# About the Author

Jim Beckett, the leading authority on sports card values in the United States, maintains a wide range of activities in the world of sports. He possesses one of the finest collections of sports cards and autographs in the world, has made numerous appearances on radio and television, and has been frequently cited in many national publications. He was awarded the first "Special Achievement Award" for Contributions to the Hobby by the National Sports Collectors Convention in 1980, the "Jock-Jaspersen Award" for Hobby Dedication in 1983, and the "Buck Barker, Spirit of the Hobby" Award in 1991.

Dr. Beckett is the author of *Beckett Baseball Card Price Guide*, *The Official Price Guide to Baseball Cards*, *The Beckett Almanac of Baseball Cards and Beckett Cardholders*, *Beckett Football Card Price Guide*, *The Official Price Guide to Football Cards*, *Beckett Hockey Card Price Guide*, *Beckett Basketball Card Price Guide*, and *The Official Price Guide to Basketball Cards*, *Beckett Football Card Alphabetical Checklist*, and *Beckett Basketball Card Alphabetical Checklist*. In addition, he is the founder, publisher, and editor of *Beckett Baseball Card Monthly*, *Beckett Basketball Monthly*, *Beckett Football Card Monthly*, *Beckett Hockey Collector*, *Beckett Racing & Motorsports Marketplace* and *Beckett Sports Collectibles and Autographs* magazines dedicated to advancing the card collecting hobby.

Jim Beckett received his Ph.D. in Statistics from Southern Methodist University in 1975. Prior to starting Beckett Publications in 1984, Dr. Beckett served as an Associate Professor of Statistics at Bowling Green State University and as a Vice President of a consulting firm in Dallas, Texas. He currently resides in Dallas.

*Jim Beckett*

# Special Acknowledgements

This volume of the Beckett Hockey Annual Price Guide and Alphabetical Checklist is even bigger and better than last year's effort which is pretty amazing considering the amount of information and listings crammed into the previous edition. And while we do acknowledge our many contributors for their work on this edition in the back of the book, we believe this is the proper time and place to single out those people who have worked especially hard on this project and those before it. In pricing: The pricing task was deftly coordinated by Bill Sutherland (Beckett Hockey Collector Price Guide Editor). The Price Guide analysts for this volume were Al Muir, whose encyclopedic knowledge of junior and foreign hockey is invaluable to this publication and Lon Levitan, and Rob Springs (Kenner). Many of the checklists included in this edition were entered by Jeany Finch and Beverly Mills. Those two also wrote most of the informational blurbs that accompany the checklists, and this book is as much their work as anyone's at this office. Paul Kerutis laid out the typesetting you see in this edition. His

work is the reason why the book looks as good as it does. Daniel Moscoso Jr., with help from Andrea Paul and Clark Palomino, were responsible for scanning the majority of card photos you see in this book. Louise Bird was responsible for coordinating the advertisements in this title and did a great job with her typical exuberance. Eric Best worked as chief programmer for the computer improvements which make our voluminous pricing tasks easier. And of course, to all our contributors, both those who we spend hours on the phone or e-mail with to those whose notes change a seemingly insignificant detail - believe us, nothing is insignificant - we thank each and every one of you. For without your help, this book simply could not have made the quantum improvements it has made since the first volume in 1991. A steady release of new sets in recent weeks means new listings are already in the works for the 1999 volume. But we've got time for that. Right now, enjoy this volume of the Beckett Hockey Card Price Guide and Alphabetical Checklist.

# How to Use This Book

Isn't it great? Every year this book gets bigger and bigger, packed with all the new sets coming out. But even more exciting is that every year there are more attractive choices and, subsequently, more interest in the cards we love so much. This edition has been enhanced and expanded from the previous edition. The cards you collect — who they depict, what they look like, where they are from, and (most importantly to many of you) what their current values are — are enumerated within. Many of the features contained in the other Beckett Price Guides have been incorporated into this volume since condition grading, terminology, and many other aspects of collecting are common to the card hobby in general. We hope you find the book both interesting and useful in your collecting pursuits.

The Beckett Guide has been successful where other attempts have failed because it is complete, current and valid. This price guide contains not just one, but three prices by condition for all the hockey cards listed. These account for most of the hockey cards in existence. The prices were added to the card lists just prior to printing and reflect not the author's opinions or desires but the going retail prices for each card, based on the marketplace (sports memorabilia conventions and shows, sports card shops, hobby papers, current mail-order catalogs, local club meetings, auction results, and other firsthand reportings of actually realized prices).

What is the BEST Price Guide available on the market today? Of course card sellers will prefer the Price Guide with the highest prices, while card buyers will naturally prefer the one with the lowest prices. Accuracy, however, is the true test. Use the Price Guide used by more collectors and dealers than all the others combined. Look for the Beckett name. I won't put my name on anything I won't stake my reputation on. Not the lowest and not the highest — but the most accurate, with integrity.

To facilitate your use of this book, read the complete introductory section on the following pages before going to the pricing pages. Every collectible field has its own terminology; we've tried to capture most of these terms and definitions in our glossary. Please read carefully the section on grading and the

condition of your cards, as you will not be able to determine which price column is appropriate for a given card without first knowing its condition.

# Introduction

Welcome to the exciting world of sports card collecting, America's fastest growing avocation. You have made a good choice in buying this book, since it will open up to you the entire panorama of this field in the simplest, most concise way.

The growth of *Beckett Baseball Card Monthly, Beckett Basketball Monthly, Beckett Football Card Monthly, Beckett Hockey Collector, Beckett Sports Collectibles and Autographs,* and *Beckett Racing & Motorsports Marketplace* is an indication of this rising crescendo of popularity for sports cards. Founded in 1984 by Dr. James Beckett, the author of this Price Guide, *Beckett Baseball Card Monthly* contains the most extensive and accepted monthly Price Guide, collectible glossy superstar covers, colorful feature articles, "Hot List," Convention calendar, tips for beginners, "Readers Write" letters to and responses from the editor, information on errors and varieties, autograph collecting tips and profiles of the sports Hottest stars. Published every month, *BBCM* is the hobby's largest paid circulation periodical. The other five magazines were built on the success of *BBCM*.

So collecting sports cards — while still pursued as a hobby with youthful exuberance by kids in the neighborhood — also has taken on the trappings of an industry, with thousands of full- and part-time card dealers, as well as vendors of supplies, clubs and conventions. In fact, each year since 1980, thousands of hobbyists have assembled for a National Sports Collectors Convention, at which hundreds of dealers have displayed their wares, seminars have been conducted, autographs have been penned by sports notables, and millions of cards have changed hands.The Beckett Guide is the best annual guide available to this exciting world of sports cards. Read it and use it. May your enjoyment and your card collection increase in the coming months and years.

# How to Collect

Each collection is personal and reflects the individuality of its owner. There are no set rules on how to collect cards. Since card collecting is a hobby or leisure pastime, what you collect, how much you collect, and how much time and money you spend collecting are entirely up to you. The funds you have available for collecting and your own personal taste should determine how you collect. Information and ideas presented here are intended to help you get the most enjoyment from this hobby.

It is impossible to collect every card ever produced. Therefore, beginners as well as intermediate and advanced collectors usually specialize in some way. One of the most popular aspects of this hobby is that individual collectors can define and tailor their collecting methods to match their own tastes. To give you some ideas of the various approaches to collecting, we will list some of the more popular areas of specialization.

Many collectors select complete sets from particular years. For example, they may concentrate on assembling complete sets from all the years since their birth or since they became avid sports fans. They may try to collect a card for every player during that specified period of time.

Many others wish to acquire only certain players. Usually such players are the superstars of the sport, but occasionally collectors will specialize in all the cards of players who attended a particular college or came from a certain town. Some collectors are only interested in the first cards or Rookie Cards of certain players.

Another fun way to collect cards is by team. Most fans have a favorite team, and it is natural for that loyalty to be translated into a desire for cards of the players on that favorite team. For most of the recent years, team sets (all the cards from a given team for that year) are readily available at a reasonable price.

## Obtaining Cards

Several avenues are open to card collectors. Cards can still be purchased in the traditional way: by the pack at the local discount, grocery and convenience stores. But there are also thousands of card shops across the country that specialize in selling cards individually or by the pack, box, or set. Another alternative is the thousands of card shows held each month around the country, which feature anywhere from five to 800 tables of sports cards and memorabilia for sale. For many years, it has been possible to purchase complete sets of sports cards through mail-order advertisers found in traditional sports media publications, such as *The Sporting News, Hockey Digest, The Hockey News,* and others. These sets also are advertised in card collecting periodicals. Many collectors will begin by subscribing to at least one of the hobby periodicals. In fact, subscription offers can be found in the advertising section of this book.

Most serious card collectors obtain old (and new) cards from one or more of several main sources: (1) trading or buying from other collectors or dealers; (2) responding to sale or auction ads in the hobby publications; (3) buying at a local hobby store; and/or (4) attending sports collectibles shows or conventions. We advise that you try all four methods since each has its own distinct advantages: (1) trading is a great way to make new friends; (2) hobby periodicals help you keep up with what's going on in the hobby (including when and where the conventions are happening); (3) stores provide the opportunity to enjoy personalized service and consider a great diversity of material in a relaxed sports-oriented atmosphere; and (4) shows allow you to choose from multiple dealers and thousands of cards under one roof in a competitive situation.

## Preserving Your Cards

Cards are fragile. They must be handled properly in order to retain their value. Careless handling can easily result in creased or bent cards. It is, however, not recommended that tweezers or tongs be used to pick up your cards, since such utensils might mar or indent card surfaces and thus reduce

those cards' conditions and values. In general, your cards should be handled directly as little as possible. This is sometimes easier to say than to do.

Although there are still many who use custom boxes, storage trays, or even shoe boxes, plastic sheets are the preferred method of many collectors for storing cards. A collection stored in plastic pages in a three-ring album allows you to view your collection at any time without the need to touch the card itself.

Cards also can be kept in single holders (of various types and thickness) designed for the enjoyment of each card individually. For a large collection, some collectors may use a combination of the above methods. When purchasing plastic sheets for your cards, be sure that you find the pocket size that fits the cards snugly. Don't put your 1954-55 Topps in a sheet designed to fit 1996-97 Fleer. Most hobby and collectibles shops and virtually all collectors' conventions will have these plastic pages available in quantity for the various sizes offered, or you can purchase them directly from the advertisers in this book. Also, remember that pocket size isn't the only factor to consider when looking for plastic sheets. Other factors such as safety, economy, appearance, availability, or personal preference also may indicate which types of sheets a collector may want to buy.

Damp, sunny and/or hot conditions — no, this is not a weather forecast — are three elements to avoid in extremes if you are interested in preserving your collection. Too much (or too little) humidity can cause gradual deterioration of a card. Direct, bright sun (or fluorescent light) over time will bleach out the color of a card. Extreme heat accelerates the decomposition of the card. On the other hand, many cards have lasted more than 50 years without much scientific intervention. So be cautious, even if the above factors typically present a problem only when present in the extreme. It never hurts to be prudent.

## Collecting vs. Investing

Collecting individual players and collecting complete sets are both popular vehicles for investment and speculation. Most investors and speculators stock up on complete sets or on quantities of players they think have good investment potential. There is obviously no guarantee in this book, or anywhere else for that matter, that cards will outperform the stock market or other investment alternatives in the future. After all, sports cards do not pay quarterly dividends and cards cannot be sold at their "current values" as easily as stocks and bonds. Nevertheless, investors have noticed a favorable long-term trend in the past performance of sports collectibles, and certain cards and sets have outperformed just about any other investments in some years.

Some of the obvious questions are: Which cards? When to buy? When to sell? The best investment you can make is in your own education. The more you know about your collection and the hobby, the more informed the decisions you will be able to make. We're not selling investment tips. We're selling information about the current value of hockey cards. It's up to you to use that information to your best advantage.

# Terminology

Each hobby has its own language to describe its area of interest. The terminology traditionally used for trading cards is derived from the *American Card Catalog*, published in 1960 by Nostalgia Press. That catalog, written by Jefferson Burdick (who is called the "Father of Card Collecting" for his pioneering work), uses letter and number designations for each separate set of cards. The letter used in the ACC designation refers to the generic type of card. While both sport and non-sport issues are classified in the ACC, we shall confine ourselves to the sport issues. The following list defines the letters and their meanings as used by the *American Card Catalog*.

**(none) or N** - 19th Century U.S. Tobacco
**B** - Blankets
**C** - Canadian Tobacco
**D** - Bakery Inserts Including Bread
**E** - Early Candy and Gum
**F** - Food Inserts
**H** - Advertising
**M** - Periodicals
**PC** - Postcards
**R** - Candy and Gum since 1930
**V** - Canadian Candy

Following the letter prefix and an optional hyphen are one-, two-, or three-digit numbers, R(-)999. These typically represent the company or entity issuing the cards. In several cases, the ACC number is extended by an additional hyphen and another one- or two-digit numerical suffix. For example, the 1933-34 Canadian Gum hockey card issue carries an ACC designation of V252. The "V" indicates a Canadian candy. The "252" is the ACC designation for Canadian Gum.

Like other traditional methods of identification, this system provides order to the process of cataloging cards; however, most serious collectors learn the ACC designation of the popular sets by repetition and familiarity, rather than by attempting to "figure out" what they might or should be.

From 1951 forward, collectors and dealers commonly refer to all sets by their year, maker, type of issue and any other distinguishing characteristic. For example, such a characteristic could be an unusual issue or one of several regular issues put out by a specific maker in a single year. Regional issues are usually referred to by year, maker, and sometimes, by title or theme of the set.

# Glossary/Legend

Our glossary defines terms frequently used in the card collecting hobby. Many of these terms also are common to other types of sports memorabilia collecting. Some terms may have several meanings, depending on use and context.
**ACETATE** - A transparent plastic.

**ACO** - Assistant Coach.

**ACO/GM** - Assistant Coach/General Manager.

**ACTION SCENES CARD** - a special type of card showing an action photo of a player or players with a description.

**ADAMS** - Trophy awarded to NHL's coach of the year.

**AGM** - Assistant General Manager.

**AHL** - American Hockey League.

**AS1** - First Team All-Star.

**AS2** - Second Team All-Star.

**ATG** - All-Time Great card.

**AUTO** - An autographed card.

**BRICK** - A group of cards, usually 50 or more, having common characteristics, that is intended to be bought, sold, or traded as a unit. Dealers usually place a star or superstar card on top as a selling tool.

**BYNG** - Lady Byng trophy, award for NHL's most gentlemanly player.

**CALDER** - Trophy awarded to NHL's Rookie of the Year.

**CAMPBELL** - Campbell Trophy winner.

**CAN** - Canada or Team Canada.

**CAPT** - Captain.

**CHC** - Chairman Hockey Committee.

**CHECKLIST** - A list of the cards contained in a particular set. The list is always in numerical order if the cards are numbered. Some unnumbered sets are artificially numbered in alphabetical order, or by team and alphabetically within the team for convenience.

**CHL** - Central Hockey League or Canadian Hockey League (also known as the Junior Leagues).

**CL** - Checklist card. A card that lists in order the cards and players in the set or series. Older checklist cards in Mint condition that have not been checked off are very desirable.

**CLANCY** - Trophy awarded for humanitarian contributions.

**CO/MG** - Coach/Manager.

**COLLECTOR ISSUE** - A set produced for the sake of the card itself with no product or service sponsor. It derives its name from the fact that most of these sets are produced for sale directly to the hobby market.

**COMBINATION CARD** - A single card depicting two or more players (but not a team card).

**COMMON CARD** - The typical card of any set; it has no premium value accruing from subject matter, numerical scarcity, popular demand, or anomaly.

**COR** - Corrected card.

**COUNTERFEIT** - An unauthorized reproduction of a card. Sometimes only very close inspection reveals the difference between a real and a fake card.

**COUPON** - See Tab.

**CZE** - Czechoslovakia.

**DECKLE EDGE** - Jagged edge found on a special OPC 1970-71 set.

**DIE-CUT** - A card with part of its stock partially cut, allowing one or more parts to be folded or removed. After removal or appropriate folding, the remaining part of the card frequently can be made to stand up.

**DIR** - Director of Player Personnel.

**DISC** - A circular-shaped card.

**DISPLAY CARD** - A sheet, usually containing three to nine cards, that is printed and used by the manufacturer to advertise and/or display the packages containing his products and cards. The backs of display cards are blank or contain advertisements.

**DISPLAY SHEET** - A clear, plastic page that is punched for insertion into a binder (with standard three-ring spacing) contain-ing pockets for displaying cards. Many different styles of sheets exist with pockets of varying sizes to hold the many differing card formats. The vast majority of current cards measure 2-1/2 by 3-1/2 inches and fit in nine-pocket sheets.

**DOUBLE** - Two-trophy card.

**DP** - Double Print (a card that was printed in double the quantity compared to the other cards in the same series).

**DUFEX** - A method of card manufacturing technology patented by Pinnacle Brands, Inc. It involves a refractive quality to a card with a foil coating.

**EJ** - Euro Junior.

**EJC** - European Junior Championships.

**EMBOSSED** - A raised surface; features of a card that are projected from a flat background.

**ERR** - Error card. A card with erroneous information, spelling, or depiction on either side of the card. Most errors are never corrected by the producing card company.

**ETCHED** - Impressions within the surface of a card.

**EXHIBIT** - The generic name given to thick stock, postcard-size cards with single color obverse pictures. The name is derived from the Exhibit Supply Co. of Chicago, the principal manufacturer of this type of card. These are also known as Arcade cards since they were found in many arcades.

**FULL-BLEED** - A borderless card; a card containing a photo that encompasses the entire card.

**FULL SHEET** - A complete sheet of cards that has not been cut up into individual cards by the manufacturer. Also called an uncut sheet.

**GAME CARD** - Scarce special insert cards issued in 1962-63 Parkhurst.

**GLOSS** - A card with luster; a shiny finish as in a card with UV coating.

**GM** - General Manager.

**GOALIE CARD** - Cards of goalies, even average ones, command slight premiums.

**HALL OF FAMER** - (HOFer) A card that portrays a player who has been inducted into the Hall of Fame.

**HART** - Hart Trophy, awarded to the NHL's Most Valuable Player.

**HERO** - Upper Deck Heroes of Hockey.

**HIGH NUMBER** - The cards in the last series of numbers in a year in which such higher-numbered cards were printed or distributed in significantly lesser quantities than the lower-numbered cards. The high-number designation refers to a scarcity of the high-numbered cards. Not all years have high numbers in terms of this definition.

**HOB** - Hobey Baker Award, given annually to the collegiate Player of the Year.

**HOF** - Acronym for Hall of Fame.

**HOLOGRAM** - A three-dimensional photographic image.

**HOR** - Horizontal pose on card as opposed to the standard

# ALL STAR HOCKEY

*Buy • Sell • Trade*

*Rookies & Stars • 1980–Present*
*Wheaties Boxes • Inserts • Memorabilia*

Joe & Chris -- (516) 669-0726
539 Empire Ave. , N. Babylon, N.Y. 11703
Store Hours: M-SAT 12-9

---

## CARDBOARD INVESTMENTS SIX

**Tom Nunn**

*a division of Cardboard Investments,*
*specializing in "Original Six" hockey singles from 1951 to 1968*

Always buying pre-1970 Hockey cards in all conditions.
Want Lists Welcome: 1951 to 1999

Ph/Fax: (570) 435-2589 • Hrs: M-Sun 10-8 pm EST
94 Caraway Drive, Cogan Station PA 17728

---

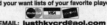

### CARTOMANIA

JOSEPH E. FILION, PROPRIETOR

Open Daily 8 - 8

*We are experienced with customers from all countries in Europe, Japan, Australia, New Zealand*
Cards from 1951/52 to Present
Also Bee Hive • Quaker Oats • Kraft • Post • Esso and much more
Cards by Singles • Packs • Boxes
- FREE CATALOGUE ON REQUEST -
*Cartomania has been recognized for over 25 years of fully satisfied customers.*
Cartomania • 82 Principale, Cheneville, Que J0V 1E0
Tel: 819-428-7053 • FAX: 819-428-1241
E-Mail: cartomania.jsjf@sympatico.ca

---

639 Southdale Rd.
London, Ontario
N6E 3M2

**FSC**

FRESHER SPORTS CARDS

Fred Lacroix
Phone/Fax: 519-649-6116
fresher@golden.net

www.golden.net/~fresher

Hockey Cards • Baseball Cards • Magic Cards • Memorabilia
**Visit us on-line @ www.golden.net/~fresher**
E-Mail us @ fresher@golden.net
Phone or Fax us @ 1-519-649-6116
**WANT LISTS WELCOME**
Thousands of Other Singles Available – Please Call, Fax or E-Mail for Avail. Or Check
*Beckett Online* for a listing of Available Singles – Seller: Fresher
**Ordering Instructions:**
1 – All prices in U.S. Funds • 2 – We accept Personal Checks,
Money Orders, MasterCard & American Express

---

Buy • Sell    (773) 594-1925    Fax:(773) 594-9446

## GRAF BASEBALL CARD CO.

Baseball • Football • Hockey • Basketball
*"Everything For The Card Collector"*
We carry a giant selection of commons
for your hard-to-complete sets.
*"One of the most complete card inventories in Chicago"*
INSERT CARDS OUR SPECIALTY
★ Send or Fax Us Your Want Lists ★
Web: http://www.grafcard.com • E-Mail: sports@graf.com
M-F 12-7                    5754 N. Milwaukee Avenue
Sat.10:30-6 • Sun. 1-5            Chicago, IL 60646

---

## Harvey's COLLECTORS CORNER

### MEMORABILIA & COLLECTABLES

► Harvey Davids            ► Ross Kekewich

Deerfoot Mall
901 - 64th Avenue N.E.
Calgary, Alberta T2E 7P4

Mailing Address:
Box 6712, Postal Stn. D.
Calgary, Alberta T2P 2E6

Email: davids@netway.ab.ca
Phone: (403) 275-4006   Fax: (403) 278-1494

---

## JUST HOCKEY CARDS

Specializing in the Players YOU collect!
375+ NHL/AHL players stocked!
Send your want lists of your favorite players!

EMAIL: justhkycrd@aol.com

A. Scott Dean Phone/Fax (860) 872-6825
P.O. Box 826, Tolland, CT 06084
Hrs:  11-9 Mon-Sat

---

## 1 if by cards 2 if by comics

CARDS ▪ COMICS ▪ HOCKEY JERSEYS
MEMORABILIA ▪ RANGERS STUFF

1107 Central Park Avenue        (914) 725-2225
Scarsdale, NY 10583              Hrs: M-F 11-8
www.1ifbycards.com              Sat. 11-7 ▪ Sun. 12-6

---

## SLAPSHOT Sports Cards

Largest Wax Pack Selection In New England
Sports Cards • Collecting Supplies • Beanie Babies

# 781-231-1800

184 Broadway, Saugus, Rte 1 North (Godfried's Plaza)
Open Mon-Fri 10-8 • Sat 10-7 • Sun 12-6

**BUY • SELL • TRADE • CARDS**

---

# REACH MORE COLLECTORS!

A Business Card Ad In
***Beckett Hockey Collector***
Reaches More Collectors Than All Other Card Publications Combined!
Find out more by calling (972) 991-6657.

---

# SCOTT CCM

## I DEAL IN THE FOLLOWING:

**PUCKS, PROGRAMS, MEDIA GUIDES, MAGAZINES, BOOKS, SCHEDULES, CALENDARS, PUZZLES, PHOTOS, PINS, COINS, CARDS, CAPS, AUTOGRAPHED ITEMS AND MORE!**

IF YOU WOULD LIKE TO BE ONE OF MY SATISFIED CUSTOMERS,
I INVITE YOU TO CALL, WRITE, OR BETTER YET, E-MAIL ME
TO TELL ME WHAT YOU ARE AFTER.

**C**ARDS

**C**OLLECTIBLES

**M**EMORABILIA

SCOTT COATES
**SCOTT CCM**
2123 WAY'S MILLS ROAD
AYER'S CLIFF, QUEBEC J0B 1C0
819-838-4454
E-Mail: scottccm@abacom.com
Beckett ID:  **scottccm**
Ebay ID:  **kid4life**

---

# BECKETT. GRADING SERVICES

## www.beckett.com

The Hobby's Finest Third-Party Grading

vertical orientation found on most cards.

**IA** - In Action card. A special type of card depicting a player in an action photo. Denoted in the Price Guide as "IA".

**IHL** - International Hockey League.

**INSERT** - A special card or other collectible (often a poster or sticker) contained and sold in the same package along with cards of a major set. Sometimes called a BONUS or CHASE CARD.

**INTERACTIVE** - A concept that involves collector participation.

**ISSUE** - Synonymous with set, but usually used in conjunction with a manufacturer, e.g., a Topps issue.

**JENN** - Jennings Trophy awarded to team with most outstanding goaltending.

**LAYERING** - The separation or peeling of one or more layers of the card stock, usually at the corner of the card.

**LID** - A circular-shaped card (possibly with tab) that forms the top of the container for the product being promoted.

**MAJOR SET** - A set produced by a national manufacturer of cards containing a large number of cards. Usually 132 or more different cards comprise a major set.

**MAST** - Masterson Trophy, awarded for perseverance, sportsmanship and dedication.

**MD** - Managing Director.

**MEM** - Memorial card.

**MEMORIAL CUP** - Award given to the overall champions of the Junior Leagues.

**METALLIC** - A glossy design method that enhances card features.

**MG** - Manager card.

**MINI** - A small card or stamp (for example, the 1988-89 O-Pee-Chee mini-set).

**MVP** - Most Valuable Player.

**NHL** - National Hockey League.

**NNO** - No number on card.

**NOBIO** - No Biography.

**NOR** - Norris Trophy, awarded to NHL's outstanding defenseman.

**NYI** - New York Islanders.

**NYR** - New York Rangers.

**OBVERSE** - The front, face, or pictured side of the card.

**OHL** - Ontario Hockey League.

**OII** - On Ice Insights.

**OLY** - Olympic card.

**OPC** - O-Pee-Chee.

**OTG** - Old Time Great.

**P1** - First Printing.

**P2** - Second Printing.

**P3** - Third Printing.

**PACKS** - A means with which cards are issued in terms of pack type (wax, cello, foil, rack, etc.) and channels of distribution (hobby, retail, etc.).

**PANEL** - An extended card that is composed of two or more individual cards. Often the panel forms the back part of the container for the product being promoted.

**PARALLEL** - A card that is similar in design to its counterpart from a basic set, but offers a distinguishing quality.

**PATRICK** - Patrick Trophy, awarded for outstanding service to U.S. hockey.

**PEARSON** - Lester B. Pearson Award, given to NHL's

Outstanding Player as voted on by the Players Association.

**PLATINUM** - A metallic element used in the process of creating a glossy card.

**POY** - Player of the Year.

**PR** - President or public relations.

**PREMIUM** - A card, sometimes on photographic stock, that is purchased or obtained in conjunction with (or redeemed for) another card or product. This term applies mainly to older products, as newer cards distributed in this manner generally are lumped together as peripheral sets.

**PREMIUM CARDS** - A class of products introduced recently that are intended to have higher quality card stock and photography than regular cards, but more limited production and higher cost. Defining what is and isn't a premium card is somewhat subjective.

**PROMOTIONAL SET** - A set, usually containing a small number of cards, issued by a national card producer and distributed in limited quantities or to a select group of people such as major show attendees or dealers with wholesale accounts. Presumably, the purpose of a promo set is to stir up demand for an upcoming set. Also called a preview, prototype or test set.

**PT** - Point.

**PUZ** - Puzzle.

**QMJHL** - Quebec Major Junior Hockey League.

**RARE** - A card or series of cards of very limited availability. Unfortunately, "rare" is a subjective term sometimes used indiscriminately. Rare cards are harder to obtain than scarce cards.

**REDEMPTION** - A program established by card manufacturers that allows collectors to mail in a special card (usually a random insert) in return for special cards, sets or other prizes not available through conventional channels.

**REFRACTORS** - A card that features a design element which enhances (distorts) its color/appearance through deflecting light.

**REGIONAL** - A card issued and distributed only in a limited geographical area of the country. The producer is not a major, national producer of trading cards.

**REPLICA** - An identical copy or reproduction.

**RET** - Retired player.

**REVERSE** - The back or narrative side of the card.

**REV NEG** - Reversed or flopped photo side of the card. This is a major type of error card, but only some are corrected.

**ROOKIE CARD** - A player's first appearance on a regular-issue card from one of the major card companies. Each company has only one regular-issue set, and that is the traditional set that is widely available. Until the recent growth of the hockey card market, which saw several manufacturers begin producing NHL cards, each player had only one Rookie Card (RC). A Rookie Card cannot be a Record Breaker, All-Star, Action Scenes, trophy winner or other special card.

**ROSS** - Art Ross trophy, awarded to NHL's points scoring leader.

**ROY** - Acronym for Rookie of the Year.

**RS** - Russian Star or Rookie Sensation.

**SA** - Super Action (1981-82 O-Pee-Chee and Topps).

**SCARCE** - A card or series of cards of limited availability. This subjective term is sometimes used indiscriminately to

# Centering

**Well-centered**

**Slightly Off-centered**

**Off-centered**

**Badly Off-centered**

**Miscut**

# Corner Wear

The partial cards shown at right have been photographed at 300%. This was done in order to magnify each card's corner wear to such a degree that differences could be shown on a printed page.

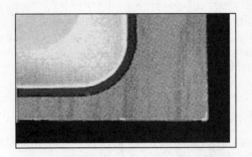

*This 1966-67 Topps Paul Henderson card has a slight touch of wear. The corner is still sharp, but the woodgrain borders shows extremely slight fraying.*

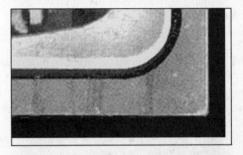

*This 1966-67 Topps Gordie Howe All-Star card has a fuzzy corner. Although it still comes to a point, the corner has begun to fray. A slightly dinged corner is considered the same as a fuzzy corner.*

*This 1966-67 Topps Gordie Howe All-Star card has a slightly rounded corner, evident by the lack of a point and flaking on both edges. A "dinged" corner is considered the same as a slightly rounded corner.*

*This 1966-67 Topps Gordie Howe All-Star card displays a badly rounded corner. Notice the heavy wear and excessive fraying.*

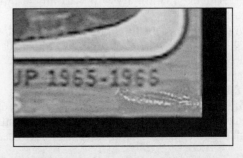

*This 1966-67 Topps Montreal Canadians Team card displays creasing. Notice the slight hairline creases, as well as the thick crease in the corner.*

promote or hype value. Scarce cards are not as difficult to obtain as rare cards.

**SELKE** - Frank J. Selke Trophy, awarded to NHL's best defensive forward.

**SEMI-HIGH** - A card from the next to last series of a sequentially issued set. It has more value than an average card and generally less value than a high number. A card is not called semihigh unless the next to last series in which it exists has an additional premium attached to it.

**SERIES** - The entire set of cards issued by a particular producer in a particular year, e.g., the 1971-72 Topps series. Also, within a particular set, series can refer to a group of (consecutively numbered) cards printed at the same time, e.g., the last series of the 1972-73 O-Pee-Chee issue (#'s 290 through 341) encompasses the WHA subset.

**SET** - One each of the entire run of cards of the same type produced by a particular manufacturer during a single season. In other words, if you have a complete set of 1985-86 Topps cards, then you have every card from #1 up to and including #165; i.e., all the different cards that were produced.

**SHEEN** - Brightness or luster emitted by a card.

**SMART** - Play Smart.

**SMYTHE** - Conn Smythe Trophy, awarded to most outstanding player in the NHL playoffs.

**SP** - Single or Short Print (a card which was printed in lesser quantity compared to the other cards in the same series; see also DP and TP).

**SPECIAL CARD** - A card that portrays something other than a single player or team; for example, a card that portrays the previous year's statistical leaders or the results from the previous year's postseason action.

**STAMP** - Adhesive-backed papers depicting a player. The stamp may be individual or in a sheet of many stamps. Moisture must be applied to the adhesive in order for the stamp to be attached to another surface.

**STANLEY CUP** - Trophy awarded to NHL championship team.

**STAR CARD** - A card that portrays a player of some repute, usually determined by his ability, but sometimes referring to sheer popularity.

**STICKER** - A card with a removable layer that can be affixed to (stuck onto) another surface.

**STOCK** - The cardboard or paper on which the card is printed.

**SUPER ACTION** - Card type similar to In Action. Abbreviated in the Price Guide as SA.

**SUPERIMPOSED** - To be affixed on top of something, i.e., a player photo over a solid background.

**SUPERSTAR CARD** - A card that portrays a superstar, e.g., a Hall of Fame member or a player whose current performance eventually will warrant Hall of Fame consideration.

**TAB** - A card portion set off from the rest of the card, usually with perforations, that may be removed without damaging the central character or event depicted by the card.

**TC** - Team Checklist.

**TEAM CARD** - A card that depicts an entire team.

**TEST SET** - A set, usually containing a small number of cards, issued by a national card producer and distributed in a limited section or sections of the country. Presumably, the purpose of a test set is to measure market appeal for a particular type of card.

**THER** - Athletic therapists.

**THN** - The Hockey News.

**THREE-DIMENSIONAL (3D)** - A visual image that provides an illusion depth and perspective.

**TL** - Team Leader card.

**TOPICAL** - a subset or group of cards that have a common theme, i.e., MVP award winners.

**TP** - Triple Print (a card that was printed in triple the quantity compared to the other cards in the same series).

**TR** - Trade or Traded or Trainer.

**TRANSPARENT** - Clear, see through.

**TRIMMED** - A card cut down from its original size. Trimmed cards are undesirable to most collectors, and are, therefore, much less valuable than otherwise identical untrimmed cards.

**TRIPLE** - Three-trophy card.

**TTG** - Through The Glass.

**TW** - Trophy Winners.

**UER** - Uncorrected error.

**UV** - Ultraviolet, a glossy coating used in producing cards.

**VARIATION** - One of two or more cards from the same series with the same card number (or player with identical pose if the series is unnumbered) differing from one another in some aspect, from the printing, stock or other feature of the card. This is most often caused when the manufacturer of the cards notices an error in a particular card, corrects the error and then resumes the print run. In this case there will be two versions or variations of the same card. Sometimes one of the variations is relatively scarce. Variations also can result from accidental or deliberate design changes, information updates, photo substitutions, etc.

**VERT** - Vertical pose on card.

**VEZINA** - Trophy awarded to NHL's outstanding goaltender.

**VP** - Vice president.

**W** - West.

**WALES** - Prince of Wales Trophy Winner.

**WB** - World Junior Best.

**WHA** - World Hockey Association.

**WHL** - Western Hockey League.

**WJC** - World Junior Championship.

**4X** - Quadruple exposure card.

**50/50** - 50 goals in 50 games.

**\*** - Multi-sport set.

# Understanding Card Values

### Determining Value

Why are some cards more valuable than others? Obviously, the economic laws of supply and demand are applicable to sports card collecting, just as they are to any other field where a commodity is bought, sold or traded in a free, unregulated market.

Supply (the number of cards available on the market) is less than the total number of cards originally produced, since attrition diminishes that original quantity. Each year a percentage of cards is typically thrown away, destroyed or otherwise lost to collectors. This percentage is much, much

smaller today than it was in the past because more and more people have become increasingly aware of the value of sports cards.

For those who collect only Mint condition cards, the supply of older cards can be quite small indeed. Until recently, collectors were not so conscious of the need to preserve the condition of their cards. For this reason, it is difficult to know exactly how many 1957-58 Topps hockey cards are currently available, Mint condition or otherwise. It is generally accepted that there are fewer 1957-58 Topps available than 1967-68, 1977-78, or 1987-88 Topps hockey cards. If demand was equal for each of these sets, the law of supply and demand would increase the price for the least available sets. Demand, however, is never equal for all sets, so price correlations can be complicated.

The demand for a card is influenced by many factors. These include: (1) the age of the card; (2) the number of cards printed; (3) the player(s) portrayed on the card; (4) the attractiveness and popularity of the set; and (5) the physical condition of the card.

In general, (1) the older the card, (2) the fewer the number of the cards printed, (3) the more famous, popular and talented the player, (4) the more attractive and popular the set, and (5) the better the condition of the card, the higher the value of the card will be. There are exceptions to all but one of these factors: the condition of the card. Given two cards similar in all respects except condition, the one in the best condition will always be valued higher.

While those guidelines help to establish the value of a card, the countless exceptions and peculiarities make any simple, direct mathematical formula to determine card values impossible.

## Regional Variation

Since the market varies from region to region, card prices of local players may be higher. This is known as a regional premium. How significant the premium is — and if there is any premium at all — depends on the local popularity of the team and the player.

The largest regional premiums usually do not apply to superstars, who often are so well known nationwide that the prices of their key cards are too high for local dealers to realize a premium.

Lesser stars often command the strongest premiums. Their popularity is concentrated in their home region, creating local demand that greatly exceeds overall demand.

Regional premiums can apply to popular retired players and sometimes can be found in the areas where the players grew up or starred in college.

A regional discount is the converse of a regional premium. Regional discounts occur when a player has been so popular in his region for so long that local collectors and dealers have accumulated quantities of his key cards. The abundant supply may make the cards available in that area at the lowest prices anywhere.

## Set Prices

A somewhat paradoxical situation exists in the price of a complete set vs. the combined cost of the individual cards in the set. In nearly every case, the sum of the prices for the individual cards is higher than the cost for the complete set. This is prevalent especially in the cards of the last few years. The reasons for this apparent anomaly stem from the habits of collectors and from the carrying costs to dealers. Today, each card in a set normally is produced in the same quantity as all others in its set.

Many collectors pick up only stars, superstars and particular teams. As a result, the dealer is left with a shortage of certain player cards and an abundance of others. He therefore incurs an expense in simply "carrying" these less desirable cards in stock. On the other hand, if he sells a complete set, he gets rid of large numbers of cards at one time. For this reason, he generally is willing to receive less money for a complete set. By doing this, he recovers all of his costs and also makes a profit.

The disparity between the price of the complete set and the sum of the individual cards also has been influenced by the fact that some of the major manufacturers now are pre-collating card sets. Since "pulling" individual cards from the sets of all three manufacturers involves a specific type of labor (and cost), the singles or star card market is not affected significantly by pre-collation.

Set prices also do not include rare card varieties, unless specifically stated. Of course, the prices for sets do include one example of each type for the given set, but this is the least expensive variety.

## Scarce Series

Scarce series occur because certain O-Pee-Chee and Topps sets were made available to the public each year in more than one series of finite numbers of cards, as opposed to all cards of the set being available for purchase at one time. At some point during the season, interest in the current year's cards usually waned. Consequently, the manufacturers produced smaller numbers of these later-series cards. Specific series information, if any, is included above the price list for each set.

We are always looking for information or photographs of printing sheets of cards for research. Each year, we try to update the hobby's knowledge of distribution anomalies. Please let us know at the address in this book if you have firsthand knowledge that would be helpful in this pursuit.

# Grading Your Cards

Each hobby has its own grading terminology — stamps, coins, comic books, record collecting, etc. Collectors of sports cards are no exception. The one invariable criterion for determining the value of a card is its condition: The better the condition of the card, the more valuable it is. Condition grading, however, is subjective. Individual card dealers and collectors differ in the strictness of their grading, but the stated

condition of a card should be determined without regard to whether it is being bought or sold.

No allowance is made for age. A 1955-56 card is judged by the same standards as a 1995-96 card.

## Centering

Current centering terminology uses numbers representing the percentage of border on either side of the main design. Obviously, centering is diminished in importance for borderless cards such as Stadium Club.

**Slightly Off-Center (60/40):** A slightly off-center card is one that upon close inspection is found to have one border bigger than the opposite border. This degree once was offensive only to purists, but now some hobbyists try to avoid cards that are anything other than perfectly centered.

**Off-Center (70/30):** An off-center card has one border that is noticeably more than twice as wide as the opposite border.

**Badly Off-Center (80/20 or worse):** A badly off-center card has virtually no border on one side of the card.

**Miscut:** A miscut card actually shows part of the adjacent card in its larger border and consequently a corresponding amount of its card is cut off.

## Corner Wear

Corner wear is the most scrutinized grading criteria in the hobby. These are the major categories of corner wear:

**Corner with a slight touch of wear:** The corner still is sharp, but there is a slight touch of wear showing. On a dark-bordered card, this shows as a dot of white.

**Fuzzy corner:** The corner still comes to a point, but the point has just begun to fray. A slightly "dinged" corner is considered the same as a fuzzy corner.

**Slightly rounded corner:** The fraying of the corner has increased to where there is only a hint of a point. Mild layering may be evident. A "dinged" corner is considered the same as a slightly rounded corner.

**Rounded corner:** The point is completely gone. Some layering is noticeable.

**Badly rounded corner:** The corner is completely round and rough. Severe layering is evident.

## Creases

A third common defect is the crease. The degree of creasing in a card is difficult to show in a drawing or picture. On giving the specific condition of an expensive card for sale, the seller should note any creases additionally. Creases can be categorized as to severity according to the following scale.

**Light Crease:** A light crease is a crease that is barely noticeable upon close inspection. In fact, when cards are in plastic sheets or holders, a light crease may not be seen (until the card is taken out of the holder). A light crease on the front is much more serious than a light crease on the card back only.

**Medium Crease:** A medium crease is noticeable when held and studied at arm's length by the naked eye, but does not overly detract from the appearance of the card. It is an obvious crease, but not one that breaks the picture surface of the card.

**Heavy Crease:** A heavy crease is one that has torn or broken through the card's picture surface, e.g., puts a tear in the photo surface.

## Alterations

**Deceptive Trimming:** This occurs when someone alters the card in order (1) to shave off edge wear, (2) to improve the sharpness of the corners, or (3) to improve centering — obviously their objective is to falsely increase the perceived value of the card to an unsuspecting buyer. The shrinkage usually is evident only if the trimmed card is compared to an adjacent full-sized card or if the trimmed card is itself measured.

**Obvious Trimming:** Obvious trimming is noticeable and unfortunate. It is usually performed by non-collectors who give no thought to the present or future value of their cards.

**Deceptively Retouched Borders:** This occurs when the borders (especially on those cards with dark borders) are touched up on the edges and corners with magic marker or crayons of appropriate color in order to make the card appear to be Mint.

## Categorization of Defects— Miscellaneous Flaws

The following are common minor flaws that, depending on severity, lower a card's condition by one to four grades and often render it no better than Excellent-Mint: bubbles (lumps in surface), gum and wax stains, diamond cutting (slanted borders), notching, off-centered backs, paper wrinkles, scratched-off cartoons or puzzles, rubber band marks, scratches, surface impressions and warping.

The following are common serious flaws that, depending on severity, lower a card's condition at least four grades and often render it no better than Good: chemical or sun fading, erasure marks, mildew, miscutting (severe off-centering), holes, bleached or retouched borders, tape marks, tears, trimming, water or coffee stains and writing.

# Condition Guide

### Grades

**Mint** (Mt) - A card with no flaws or wear. The card has four perfect corners, 60/40 or better centering from top to bottom and from left to right, original gloss, smooth edges and original color borders. A Mint card does not have print spots, color or focus imperfections.

**Near Mint-Mint (NrMt-Mt)** - A card with one minor flaw. Any one of the following would lower a Mint card to Near Mint-Mint: one corner with a slight touch of wear, barely noticeable print spots, color or focus imperfections. The card must have 60/40 or better centering in both directions, original gloss, smooth edges and original color borders.

**Near Mint** (NrMt) - A card with one minor flaw. Any one of the following would lower a Mint card to Near Mint: one fuzzy corner, or two to four corners with slight touches of wear, 70/30 to 60/40 centering, slightly rough edges, minor print

spots, color or focus imperfections. The card must have original gloss and original color borders.

**Excellent-Mint** (ExMt) - A card with two or three fuzzy, but not rounded, corners and centering no worse than 80/20. The card may have no more than two of the following: slightly rough edges, very slightly discolored borders, minor print spots, color or focus imperfections. The card must have original gloss.

**Excellent** (Ex) - A card with four fuzzy but definitely not rounded corners and centering no worse than 80/20. The card may have a small amount of original gloss lost, rough edges, slightly discolored borders and minor print spots, color or focus imperfections.

**Very Good** (Vg) - A card that has been handled but not abused: slightly rounded corners with slight layering, slight notching on edges, a significant amount of gloss lost from the surface but no scuffing and moderate discoloration of borders. The card may have a few light creases.

**Good** (G), **Fair** (F), **Poor** (P) - A well-worn, mishandled or abused card: badly rounded and layered corners, scuffing, most or all original gloss missing, seriously discolored borders, moderate or heavy creases, and one or more serious flaws. The grade of Good, Fair or Poor depends on the severity of wear and flaws. Good, Fair and Poor cards generally are used only as fillers.

The most widely used grades are defined above. Obviously, many cards will not perfectly fit one of the definitions.

Therefore, categories between the major grades known as in-between grades are used, such as Good to Very Good (G-Vg), Very Good to Excellent (VgEx), and Excellent-Mint to Near Mint (ExMt-NrMt). Such grades indicate a card with all qualities of the lower category but with at least a few qualities of the higher category.

The Beckett Guide lists each card and set in three grades, with the middle grade valued at about 40%-45% of the top grade, and the bottom grade valued at about 10%-15% of the top grade.

The value of cards that fall between the listed columns can also be calculated using a percentage of the top grade. For example, a card that falls between the top and middle grades (Ex, ExMt or NrMt in most cases) generally will be valued at anywhere from 50% to 90% of the top grade.

Similarly, a card that falls between the middle and bottom grades (G-Vg, Vg or VgEx in most cases) generally will be valued at anywhere from 20% to 40% of the top grade.

There are also cases where cards are in better condition than the top grade or worse than the bottom grade. Cards that grade worse than the lowest grade generally are valued at 5%-10% of the top grade.

When a card exceeds the top grade by one — such as NrMt-Mt when the top grade is NrMt, or Mint when the top grade is NrMt-Mt — a premium of up to 50% is possible, with 10%-20% the usual norm.

When a card exceeds the top grade by two — such as Mint when the top grade is NrMt, or NrMt-Mt when the top grade is ExMt — a premium of 25%-50% is the usual norm. But certain condition sensitive cards or sets, particularly those from the pre-war era, can bring premiums of up to 100% or even more.

Unopened packs, boxes and factory-collated sets are considered Mint in their unknown (and presumed perfect) state. Once opened, however, each card can be graded (and valued) in its own right by taking into account any defects that may be present in spite of the fact that the card has never been handled.

# Selling Your Cards

Just about every collector sells cards or will sell cards eventually. Someday, you may be interested in selling your duplicates or maybe even your whole collection. You may sell to other collectors, friends or dealers. You may even sell cards you purchased from a certain dealer back to that same dealer. In any event, it helps to know some of the mechanics of the typical transaction between buyer and seller.

Dealers will buy cards in order to resell them to other collectors who are interested in the cards. Dealers will always pay a higher percentage for items that (in their opinion) can be resold quickly, and a much lower percentage for those items that are perceived as having low demand and hence are slow moving. In either case, dealers must buy at a price that allows for the expense of doing business and a margin for profit.

If you have cards for sale, the best advice we can give is that you get several offers for your cards — either from card shops or at a card show — and take the best offer, all things considered. Note, the "best" offer may not be the one for the highest amount. And remember, if a dealer really wants your cards, he won't let you get away without making his best competitive offer. Another alternative is to place your cards in an auction as one or several lots.

Many people think nothing of going into a department store and paying $15 for an item of clothing for which the store paid $5. But if you were selling your $15 card to a dealer and he offered you $5 for it, you might think his mark-up unreasonable. To complete the analogy: most department stores (and card dealers) that consistently pay $10 for $15 items eventually go out of business. An exception is when the dealer has lined up a willing buyer for the item(s) you are attempting to sell, or if the cards are so Hot that it's likely he'll have to hold the cards for only a short period of time.

In those cases, an offer of up to 75 percent of book value still will allow the dealer to make a reasonable profit considering the short time he will need to hold the merchandise. In general, however, most cards and collections will bring offers in the range of 25 to 50 percent of retail price. Also consider that most material from the last five to 10 years is plentiful. If that's what you're selling, don't be surprised if your best offer is well below that range.

# Interesting Notes

The first card numerically of an issue is the single card most likely to obtain excessive wear. Consequently, you typically will find the price on the #1 card (in NrMt or Mint condition) somewhat higher than might otherwise be the case. Similarly, but to a lesser extent (because normally the less important, reverse side of the card is the one exposed), the last card numerically in an issue also is prone to abnormal wear. This extra wear and tear occurs because the first and last cards are exposed to the elements (human element included) more than any other cards. They generally are end cards in any brick formations, rubber bandings, stackings on wet surfaces, and like activities.

Sports cards have no intrinsic value. The value of a card, like the value of other collectibles, can be determined only by you and your enjoyment in viewing and possessing these cardboard treasures.

Remember, the buyer ultimately determines the price of each card. You are the determining price factor because you have the ability to say "No" to the price of any card by not exchanging your hard-earned money for a given card. When the cost of a trading card exceeds the enjoyment you will receive from it, your answer should be "No." We assess and report the prices. You set them!

We are always interested in receiving the price input of collectors and dealers from around the country. We happily credit major contributors. We welcome your opinions, since your contributions assist us in ensuring a better guide each year. If you would like to join our survey list for the next editions of this book and others authored by Dr. Beckett, please send your name and address to Dr. James Beckett, 15850 Dallas Parkway, Dallas, TX 75248.

# Advertising

Within this Price Guide, you will find advertisements for sports memo-rabilia material, mail-order and retail sports collectibles establishments. All advertisements were accepted in good faith based on the reputation of the advertiser; however, neither the author, the publisher, the distributors nor the other advertisers in this Price Guide accept any responsibility for any particular advertiser not complying with the terms of his or her ad.

Readers also should be aware that prices in advertisements are subject to change over the annual period before a new edition of this volume is issued each spring. When replying to an advertisement late in the hockey year, the reader should take this into account, and contact the dealer by phone or in writing for up-to-date price information. Should you come into contact with any of the advertisers in this guide as a result of their advertisement herein, please mention this source as your contact.

# Additional Reading

Each year Beckett Publications produces comprehensive annual price guides for each of the four major sports: *Beckett Baseball Card Price Guide*, *Beckett Football Card Price Guide*, *Beckett Basketball Card Price Guide*, and *Beckett Hockey Card Price Guide*. The aim of these annual guides is to provide information and accurate pricing on a wide array of sports cards, ranging from main issues by the major card manufacturers to various regional, promotional, and food issues. Also alphabetical checklists, such as *Sport Americana Baseball Card Alphabetical Checklist #6*, are published to assist the collector in identifying all the cards of any particular player. The seasoned collector will find these tools valuable sources of information that will enable him to pursue his hobby interests.

In addition, abridged editions of the Beckett Price Guides have been published for each of the other major sports as part of the House of Collectibles series: *The Official Price Guide to Baseball Cards*, *The Official Price Guide to Football Cards*, and *The Official Price Guide to Basketball Cards*. Published in a convenient mass-market paperback format, these price guides provide information and accurate pricing on all the main issues by the major card manufacturers.

# Prices in this Guide

Prices found in this guide reflect current retail rates just prior to the printing of this book. They do not reflect the FOR SALE prices of the author, the publisher, the distributors, the advertisers, or any card dealers associated with this guide. No one is obligated in any way to buy, sell or trade his or her cards based on these prices. The price listings were compiled by the author from actual buy/sell transactions at sports conventions, sports card shops, buy/sell advertisements in the hobby papers, for sale prices from dealer catalogs and price lists, and discussions with leading hobbyists in the United States and Canada. All prices are in U.S. dollars.

# History of Hockey Cards

Hockey cards have been produced for much longer periods than football or basketball cards — a fact no doubt influenced by hockey's predominance in Canada as its national pastime. Cigarette companies issued hockey cards from 1910 to 1913. While three distinct cigarette card sets have been identified, the manufacturers of these sets have not been determined. During the 1920s, four candy hockey sets and one cigarette hockey set were issued; none were in color. It was not until the 1930s that the Canadian gum companies started issuing card premiums with their chewing gum. World Wide Gum Co. and the familiar O-Pee-Chee were among these early Canadian hockey issuers. Bee Hive photos made their first appearance during the 1930s also. This Canadian chewing-gum card awakening parallels Goudey and

National Chicle emerging as gum card issuers in the United States.

The recent history of hockey cards begins with the post-World War II Parkhurst issues of the 1950s and early 1960s. Parkhurst issued hockey card sets from 1951 through 1964, except for the 1956-57 season. Topps started issuing hockey cards in 1954. Then after a two-year hiatus, it issued cards regularly from the 1957-58 season to the present with the exception of a break for the 1982-83 and 1983-84 seasons. During the 1950s, Topps typically issued cards of players from American teams while Parkhurst issued cards with players from the two Canadian teams existing at the time, Montreal and Toronto. From the 1960-61 season until its demise after the 1963-64 season, Parkhurst issued cards of the two Canadian teams plus Detroit, while Topps issued cards of the remaining three American teams. Beginning with the 1964-65 season, Topps issued players from all teams in the NHL.

Topps attempted to produce a 66-card set aimed strictly at the American market, with no French on the cards, in 1966-67. This test issue, now quite scarce, is very similar to the regular 1966-67 Topps set and includes a Bobby Orr card.

O-Pee-Chee re-entered the hockey card market in 1968, and has issued sets from the 1968-69 season to the present. O-Pee-Chee sets are larger in size compared to Topps sets, perhaps a reflection of the relative popularity of hockey in Canada as compared to the United States. O-Pee-Chee also issued separate card sets containing World Hockey Association players for a four-year period between the 1974-75 and 1977-78 seasons. During recent years, beginning with the 1974-75 season, the Topps cards have been nearly identical to the O-Pee-Chee cards (the OPCs have white backs, the Topps gray).

In 1990-91, the NHL card market saw five new major sets: Bowman, O-Pee-Chee Premier, Pro Set, Score and Upper Deck. Most represented significant improvements over the quality of previous sets, and all enjoyed moderate to superb levels of success. Needless to say, this reflects the growing interest in hockey cards. Score and Upper Deck issued Canadian and French sets, respectively, which drew attention from collectors due to their perceived relative scarcity. Score's debut sets were partially fueled by the inclusion of ultratalented prospect Eric Lindros. Upper Deck matched Score by including a Canadian National Junior Championship subset (featuring Lindros, Pat Falloon and Scott Niedermayer, who were the top three picks, respectively, in the 1991 NHL draft) in its high number set.

The 1991-92 hockey card season saw the decline in interest in Canadian and French versions. Overall, the hockey card market enjoyed further growth, at least in the area of supply. All seven major 1990-91 sets returned, and four new "premium" sets made their debuts: Pro Set Platinum, Parkhurst (also produced by Pro Set), Score Pinnacle and Topps Stadium Club. Overall, the values of the new sets generally remained stable or decreased because of overproduction. It will be interesting to see how the card companies respond to what appears to be a saturated new card market.

The 1992-93 hockey card season will be remembered for two things: the pervasiveness of insert card sets and the come-from-behind success of Bowman. The five returning licensees joined with newcomer Fleer to produce 12 regular sets and a staggering 31 insert sets. In reaction to the overproduction of recent years, Topps drastically curtailed its shipments of Bowman hockey. This reduction of supply, along with a number of shortprinted insert cards, made the set wildly popular with collectors, and may signal the start of a new direction in card manufacturing.

The 1993-94 card season was drastically affected by a joint decision from the NHL and the NHLPA to limit licensees to two brands each. The new regulations were particularly tough on Topps, which released five sets in 1992-93 (including two through sublicensee, OPC). The company responded by dropping both base products and the Bowman line, leaving only Stadium Club, Topps and OPC Premier.

After experiencing financial troubles, Pro Set was denied a new license. The rights to the Parkhurst brand, which had served as Pro Set's premium product, were sold to Upper Deck. The company continued the revival of that grand old name as a super-premium line in late 1993. Upper Deck also broke with tradition by issuing its base brand set in two distinct series. And in the place of Pro Set, the NHL and NHLPA awarded the fifth license to Leaf Brands, which released a two series, super-premium product, as well as a premium series under the Donruss imprint.

The 1994-95 card season was as memorable as the lockout which curtailed the NHL schedule to a mere 48 games. Collectors were given a total of sixteen separate sets from which to choose, as well as more than ninety insert issues; both were new highs for the hockey hobby. The explosion was made possible by the relaxing of the two brand limit imposed the previous year. Companies were allowed to drop the second series of one brand each in favor of a new product. This move was made by the licensing bodies in an effort to spur sales when the season finally got underway in January, 1995. The second series of Donruss, Flair, Parkhurst, Score and Stadium Club were replaced by Leaf Limited, Fleer, SP, Select and Finest, respectively. Upper Deck also produced a set in conjunction with the NHLPA called Be A Player. Each pack contained one card bearing an authentic signature from an NHL player, setting a standard likely to be mimicked by the other major sports.

With so many options, single player and team collecting became the predominant styles. Many hobbyists limited their pursuits to the various insert issues. Following the path established by the other sports, manufacturers courted collectors with a melange of interactive inserts based on game performances, such as the Stadium Club Super Teams and Upper Deck Predictors series, and multi-level parallel and redemption issues.

In a bold marketing move, UD released a second Parkhurst series, entitled SE, solely in eleven European countries, in an attempt to gain a foothold in that burgeoning hobby segment. That expanding market served to alleviate any contraction on the domestic side.

Of course, the most dramatic announcement of the season came in November when O-Pee-Chee, the venerable Canadian card manufacturer, revealed that the 1994-95 series II product would be its last. The company cited declining sales, a changing marketplace and internal goal revisions as the reasons for the move.

1995-96 saw more cards produced than ever before (150 sets, including parallels). Topps declined to renew its licence, and Pinnacle bought Leaf/Donruss. The most popular sets of the year were the new breed of Canadian-only inserts from

Topps, Home Grown Canada and OPC parallel, both of which benefitted from the presence of short prints. While the market was expanding, so was Beckett, with the launch of home grown versions of BHCM for both Finland and Sweden.

1996-97 again saw a huge increase in sets produced, with parallel sets and serial numbering taking center stage. Several products had production runs limited to 150 copies of each card, or less. The big winners in this race were the Select Certified Mirror parallels; reportedly, just 24 copies of the Gold Mirrors were produced. While insert cards played a large role in the market, Rookie Cards began a pronounced march back to respectability led to three Upper Deck products. Collectors pursued such hyped prospects as Joe Thornton, Patrick Marleau and Dainius Zubrus with a vigor usually reserved for elite superstars.

1997-98 will be remembered as the debut year for Pacific Trading Cards and the finale of Pinnacle/Donruss. Pinnacle's history will be noted for its tremendous number of parallel sets, and Pinnacle/Donruss will be noted for filing for Bankruptcy protection. 1997-98 will also be known for its innovations: cards in a can (and parallels of the cans as well), cards in a tin, superb die-cut technology, stamp sets, the fusing of plastic and cardboard, the meshing of jerseys, sticks, gloves, and stirrups with cardboard, etc. This was also the first year in which an entire base set was issued with serial numbers (Pinnacle Totally Certified). 1997-98 also saw the re-emergence of the Beehive line, chock full of young talent and veterans alike. Autograph cards also played a large part in this past hockey card season, with Upper Deck's SP Authentic leading the way with over 40 different autograph cards available in boxes.

With Topps re-entering the market for 1998-99, and the possibility of others entering the market, the hockey card market is expected to produce another wide variety of sets and innovations. Enjoy the ride, for like the game, the world of Hockey Cards is fast paced and exciting.

# Finding Out More

The above has been a thumbnail sketch of card collecting from its inception to the present. It is difficult to tell the whole story in just a few pages — there are several other good sources of information. Serious collectors should subscribe to at least one of the excellent hobby periodicals. We also suggest that collectors visit their local card shop(s) and also attend a sports collectibles show in their area. Card collecting is still a young and informal hobby. You can learn more about it in either place. After all, smart dealers realize that spending a few minutes teaching beginners about the hobby often pays off for them in the long run.

# Acknowledgments

A great deal of diligence, hard work, and dedicated effort went into this year's volume. The high standards to which we hold ourselves, however, could not have been met without the expert input and generous amount of time contributed by many people. Our sincere thanks are extended to each and every one of you.

A complete list of these invaluable contributors appears after the Price Guide section.

## 1989-90 Action Packed Prototypes

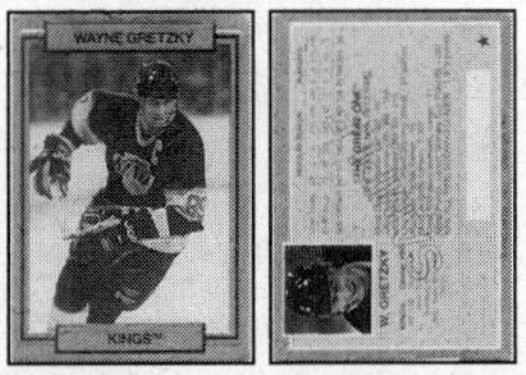

This three-card set was produced by Action Packed to show the NHL and NHLPA a sample in order to obtain a license for hockey cards. The cards are unnumbered and listed below in alphabetical order. Reportedly only 1000 cards of Gretzky and Lemieux were produced and only 300 of Yzerman. These cards are standard size with the rounded corners.

| | MINT | NRMT |
|---|---|---|
| COMPLETE SET (3) | 600.00 | 275.00 |
| COMMON CARD (1-3) | 150.00 | 70.00 |
| ❑ 1 Wayne Gretzky | 175.00 | 80.00 |
| ❑ 2 Mario Lemieux | 150.00 | 70.00 |
| ❑ 3 Mario Lemieux<br>White border | 150.00 | 70.00 |
| ❑ 4 Steve Yzerman | 250.00 | 110.00 |

## 1993 Action Packed HOF Induction

This special limited edition standard-size set was produced by Action Packed to commemorate the 1993 Hockey Hall Of Fame induction on November 16, 1993, and honors the ten inductees. It was given to attendees at the induction and was on sale at the Hockey Hall of Fame. The fronts feature embossed color and black-and-white borderless photos, a silver embossed Stanley Cup, and the words "Action Packed." The horizontal backs carry the inductee's name, a short biography, the date "November 16, 1993," and a brief career summary in French and English. This set was released in a special black cardboard display featuring all ten cards (in two rows of five) and which could be placed in a black cardboard sleeve with the Hall of Fame logo and the words "1993 Hockey Hall of Fame Induction, November 16, 1993" printed in silver letters on the front. The back of the sleeve gives the set serial number out of a total of 5,000 sets produced.

| | MINT | NRMT |
|---|---|---|
| COMPLETE SET (10) | 35.00 | 16.00 |
| COMMON CARD (1-10) | 2.00 | .90 |
| ❑ 1 Edgar Laprade | 5.00 | 2.20 |
| ❑ 2 Guy Lapointe | 8.00 | 3.60 |
| ❑ 3 Billy Smith | 10.00 | 4.50 |
| ❑ 4 Steve Shutt | 8.00 | 3.60 |
| ❑ 5 John D'Amico | 2.00 | .90 |
| ❑ 6 Al Shaver | 2.00 | .90 |
| ❑ 7 Seymour Knox III | 2.00 | .90 |
| ❑ 8 Frank Griffiths | 2.00 | .90 |
| ❑ 9 Fred Page | 2.00 | .90 |
| ❑ 10 Al Strachan | 2.00 | .90 |

## 1993 Action Packed Prototypes

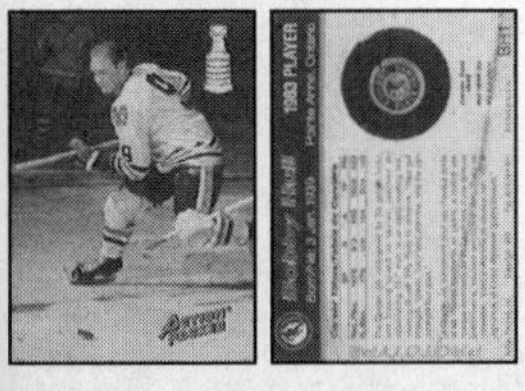

Both prototype cards measure the standard size and feature Bobby Hull. The first card has a borderless embossed color photo, while the second card has the same design but is all in gold. Both cards feature a silver Stanley Cup in the upper right corner. The horizontal backs carry biographical (in English and French) and statistical information, the Blackhawks logo on a puck, and the word "Prototype" printed vertically on the left. The cards are numbered on the back with a "BH" prefix.

| | MINT | NRMT |
|---|---|---|
| COMPLETE SET (2) | 8.00 | 3.60 |
| COMMON CARD (1-2) | 4.00 | 1.80 |
| ❑ 1 Bobby Hull<br>(Color) | 4.00 | 1.80 |
| ❑ 2 Bobby Hull<br>(Gold) | 5.00 | 2.20 |

## 1994 Action Packed Badge of Honor Promos

Issued to herald the release of a new product, each of these four pins measures approximately 1 1/2" by 1". They were packaged together in a cardboard sleeve which carries a checklist on its back. On a bronze background, the fronts feature color player portraits with a gold border. The player's last name appears in gold lettering at the bottom. The Action Packed logo is above the picture, while the year 1994 inside a puck and hockey sticks icon is below. The backs carry the copyrights "Action Packed 1994" and "NHL 1994", and "NHLPA 1994." The pins are unnumbered and checklisted below in alphabetical order. By all accounts, the actual set these pins were designed to promote never was released.

| | MINT | NRMT |
|---|---|---|
| COMPLETE SET (4) | 20.00 | 9.00 |
| COMMON CARD (1-4) | 4.00 | 1.80 |
| ❑ 1 Sergei Fedorov | 6.00 | 2.70 |
| ❑ 2 Doug Gilmour | 4.00 | 1.80 |
| ❑ 3 Mike Modano | 5.00 | 2.20 |
| ❑ 4 Patrick Roy | 10.00 | 4.50 |

## 1994-95 Action Packed Big Picture Promos

These four standard-size cards were issued to preview a proposed (but never released) Action Packed product, "Big Picture" cards. The fronts have borderless embossed color action photos. On a team color-coded background, the backs have a color close-up inside a gold foil circle, the player's name and team in gold foil lettering, and player profile. The front and back are hinged at the top, and the card opens up to reveal a 5 3/4" by 6 1/2" mini-poster, with a movie-frame design.

| | MINT | NRMT |
|---|---|---|
| COMPLETE SET (4) | 15.00 | 6.75 |
| COMMON CARD (BP1-BP4) | 3.00 | 1.35 |
| ❑ BP1 Jeremy Roenick | 3.00 | 1.35 |
| ❑ BP2 John Vanbiesbrouck | 4.00 | 1.80 |
| ❑ BP3 Jaromir Jagr | 6.00 | 2.70 |
| ❑ BP4 Steve Yzerman | 6.00 | 2.70 |

## 1990-91 Alberta International Team Canada

This 24-card set features the Canadian National Team and a bonus card of Vladislav Tretiak, the honorary captain of the Soviet Olympic team during the Pre-Olympic Hockey Tour. The cards are slightly smaller than standard size, measuring approximately 2 7/16" by 3 1/2". The front design has color head shots against a blue background, with no borders on the sides of the picture. A black stripe with the words "Collector's Edition" in orange and a white stripe border the picture above, and white and gray stripes border the picture below. Red and white diagonals overlay the gray stripe, and the player's name appears in an orange box that casts a black shadow. The backs have a similar design, with biography and statistics replacing the player photo. The cards are numbered on both sides in the lower right corner.

| | MINT | NRMT |
|---|---|---|
| COMPLETE SET (24) | 15.00 | 6.75 |
| COMMON CARD (1-23) | .25 | .11 |
| ❑ 1 Craig Billington | .75 | .35 |
| ❑ 2 Doug Dadswell | .50 | .23 |
| ❑ 3 Greg Andrusak | .50 | .23 |
| ❑ 4 Karl Dykhuis | .60 | .25 |
| ❑ 5 Gord Hynes | .50 | .23 |
| ❑ 6 Ken MacArthur | .50 | .23 |
| ❑ 7 Jim Paek | .50 | .23 |
| ❑ 8 Brad Schlegel | .50 | .23 |
| ❑ 9 Dave Archibald | .50 | .23 |
| ❑ 10 Stu Barnes | .75 | .35 |
| ❑ 11 Brad Bennett | .50 | .23 |
| ❑ 12 Todd Brost | .50 | .23 |
| ❑ 13 Jose Charbonneau | .50 | .23 |
| ❑ 14 Jason Lafreniere | .50 | .23 |
| ❑ 15 Chris Lindberg | .50 | .23 |
| ❑ 16 Ken Priestlay | .50 | .23 |
| ❑ 17 Stephane Roy | .60 | .25 |
| ❑ 18 Randy Smith | .50 | .23 |
| ❑ 19 Todd Strueby | .50 | .23 |
| ❑ 20 Vladislav Tretiak | 2.50 | 1.10 |
| ❑ 21 Dave King CO | .75 | .35 |
| ❑ 22 Wayne Fleming | .25 | .11 |
| ❑ 23 Checklist Card | .25 | .11 |
| ❑ NNO Title Card | .50 | .23 |

## 1991-92 Alberta International Team Canada

Sponsored by Alberta Lotteries, this 24-card standard-size set features the Canadian National Team. The fronts feature posed player photos on the ice that are full-bleed on the left and bottom. The pictures are bordered by a white bar with five thin red stripes on top carrying the player's name and number, and by a blue stripe on the right carrying the words "Canada's National Team" and the player's position. The backs carry biographical information, player profile, season-by-season stats, and team and sponsor logos. The cards are unnumbered and checklisted below in alphabetical order.

| | MINT | NRMT |
|---|---|---|
| COMPLETE SET (24) | 15.00 | 6.75 |
| COMMON CARD (1-24) | .25 | .11 |
| ❑ 1 Dave Archibald | .50 | .23 |
| ❑ 2 Todd Brost | .50 | .23 |
| ❑ 3 Sean Burke | 2.00 | .90 |
| ❑ 4 Terry Crisp ACO | .50 | .23 |
| ❑ 5 Kevin Dahl | .50 | .23 |
| ❑ 6 Karl Dykhuis | .50 | .23 |
| ❑ 7 Wayne Fleming AGM/ACO | .25 | .11 |
| ❑ 8 Curt Giles | .50 | .23 |
| ❑ 9 Gord Hynes | .50 | .23 |
| ❑ 10 Fabian Joseph | .50 | .23 |
| ❑ 11 Joe Juneau | 2.00 | .90 |
| ❑ 12 Trevor Kidd | 1.50 | .70 |
| ❑ 13 Dave King GM/CO | .50 | .23 |
| ❑ 14 Chris Kontos | .50 | .23 |
| ❑ 15 Chris Lindberg | .50 | .23 |
| ❑ 16 Kent Manderville | .50 | .23 |
| ❑ 17 Adrien Plavsic | .50 | .23 |
| ❑ 18 Dan Ratushny | .50 | .23 |
| ❑ 19 Stephane Roy | .50 | .23 |
| ❑ 20 Brad Schlegel | .50 | .23 |
| ❑ 21 Scott Scissons | .50 | .23 |
| ❑ 22 Randy Smith | .50 | .23 |
| ❑ 23 Jason Woolley | .75 | .35 |
| ❑ 24 Title Card | .25 | .11 |

## 1992-93 Alberta International Team Canada

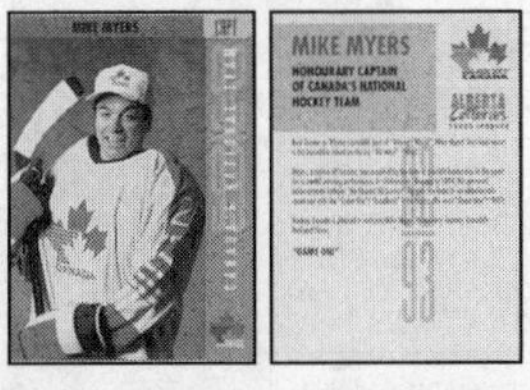

This 22-card set features the Canadian National Team as well as bonus cards of Mike Myers, honorary captain of the team, and of Vladislav Tretiak, honorary captain of Russia's National Team. The cards are slightly smaller than standard size, measuring 2 1/2" by 3 7/16". The fronts feature posed action shots that are full-bleed on the left and bottom. The pictures are bordered by a red stripe on top carrying the player's name, and by a blue stripe on the right carrying the year and "Canada's National Team." At the intersection of the two stripes in the upper right corner is a yellow block displaying the player's uniform number. The backs carry biographical information (on a yellow panel), player profile, and season-by-season statistics. The cards are unnumbered and checklisted below in alphabetical order.

| | MINT | NRMT |
|---|---|---|
| COMPLETE SET (22) | 15.00 | 6.75 |
| COMMON CARD (1-22) | .25 | .11 |
| ❑ 1 Dominic Amodeo | .50 | .23 |
| ❑ 2 Mark Astley | .50 | .23 |
| ❑ 3 Adrian Aucoin | .60 | .25 |
| ❑ 4 Mark Bassen | .50 | .23 |
| ❑ 5 Eric Bellerose | .50 | .23 |
| ❑ 6 Mike Brewer | .50 | .23 |
| ❑ 7 Dany Dube CO | .25 | .11 |
| ❑ 8 Mike Fountain | .75 | .35 |
| ❑ 9 Todd Hlushko | .50 | .23 |
| ❑ 10 Hank Lammens | .50 | .23 |
| ❑ 11 Derek Laxdal | .50 | .23 |
| ❑ 12 Derek Mayer | .50 | .23 |
| ❑ 13 Keith Morris | .50 | .23 |
| ❑ 14 Mike Myers SNL | 5.00 | 2.20 |
| ❑ 15 Jackson Penney | .50 | .23 |
| ❑ 16 Garth Premak | .50 | .23 |
| ❑ 17 Tom Renney CO | .50 | .23 |
| ❑ 18 Allain Roy | .75 | .35 |
| ❑ 19 Stephane Roy | .50 | .23 |
| ❑ 20 Trevor Sim | .50 | .23 |
| ❑ 21 Vladislav Tretiak | 1.50 | .70 |
| ❑ 22 Title Card | .50 | .23 |

## 1993-94 Alberta International Team Canada

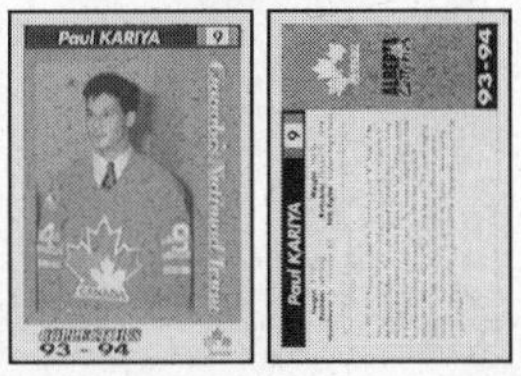

This 23-card standard-size set features players on the 1994 Canadian National Hockey Team. The white-bordered fronts feature posed black-and-white photos of the players on ice. The photo is set on a gold-colored background that bleeds through to highlight the suited-up player. The player's name and uniform number appear within the black stripe at the top; the logo for the team rests at the lower right. The white horizontal backs carry the player's name and uniform number at the top, followed below by biography, statistics, and career highlights. The logo for the sponsor, Alberta Lotteries, appears with the team logo in the gold-colored stripe on the right. The cards are unnumbered and checklisted below in alphabetical order.

| | MINT | NRMT |
|---|---|---|
| COMPLETE SET (23) | 25.00 | 11.00 |
| COMMON CARD (1-23) | .25 | .11 |
| ❑ 1 Adrian Aucoin | .50 | .23 |
| ❑ 2 Todd Brost | .50 | .23 |
| ❑ 3 Dany Dube ACO | .25 | .11 |
| ❑ 4 David Harlock | .50 | .23 |
| ❑ 5 Corey Hirsch | 1.50 | .70 |
| ❑ 6 Todd Hlushko | .50 | .23 |
| ❑ 7 Fabian Joseph | .50 | .23 |
| ❑ 8 Paul Kariya | 15.00 | 6.75 |
| ❑ 9 Chris Kontos | .50 | .23 |
| ❑ 10 Manny Legace | .75 | .35 |
| ❑ 11 Brett Lindros | .75 | .35 |
| ❑ 12 Ken Lovsin | .50 | .23 |
| ❑ 13 Jason Marshall | .50 | .23 |
| ❑ 14 Derek Mayer | .50 | .23 |
| ❑ 15 Dwayne Norris | .50 | .23 |
| ❑ 16 Tom Renney CO | .50 | .23 |
| ❑ 17 Russ Romaniuk | .50 | .23 |
| ❑ 18 Brian Savage | 1.00 | .45 |
| ❑ 19 Trevor Sim | .50 | .23 |
| ❑ 20 Chris Therien | .75 | .35 |
| ❑ 21 Todd Warriner | 1.00 | .45 |
| ❑ 22 Craig Woodcroft | .50 | .23 |
| ❑ 23 Title Card | .25 | .11 |

## 1992-93 All World Mario Lemieux Promos

This set consists of six standard-size cards. All cards feature the same color action photo of Mario Lemieux, skating with stick in both hands. On the first three cards, the top of the photo is oval-shaped and framed by yellow stripes. The space above the oval as well as the stripe at the bottom carrying player information are purple. The outer border is green. Inside green borders, the horizontal

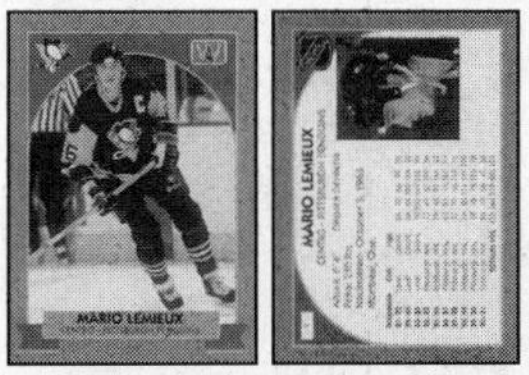

back has a color close-up photo, biography and statistics. On the second three cards listed below, the player photo is tilted slightly to the right and framed by a thin green border. Yellow stripes above and below the picture carry information, and the outer border is black-and-white speckled. The back has a similar design and displays a close-up color head shot and biographical and statistical information on a pastel green panel. All cards are numbered as number 1. The cards were issued three different ways, in Spanish, French, and English. The design and concept of these cards is very similar to the 1992 All World Troy Aikman promos.

| | MINT | NRMT |
|---|---|---|
| COMPLETE SET (6) | 20.00 | 9.00 |
| COMMON CARD (1A-1F) | 5.00 | 2.20 |
| ❑ 1A Mario Lemieux<br>(Green border;<br>English) | 5.00 | 2.20 |
| ❑ 1B Mario Lemieux<br>(Green border;<br>French) | 5.00 | 2.20 |
| ❑ 1C Mario Lemieux<br>(Green border;<br>Spanish) | 5.00 | 2.20 |
| ❑ 1D Mario Lemieux<br>(Speckled border;<br>English) | 5.00 | 2.20 |
| ❑ 1E Mario Lemieux<br>(Speckled border;<br>French) | 5.00 | 2.20 |
| ❑ 1F Mario Lemieux<br>(Speckled border;<br>Spanish) | 5.00 | 2.20 |

## 1993 American Licorice Sour Punch Caps

Printed in Canada and sponsored by the American Licorice Co., these individually wrapped cards were inserted in specially-marked packages of 4 1/2 oz. Sour Punch Candy Straws. Each package contained one card, measuring the standard size with two punch-out caps, each measuring 1 1/2" in diameter. One cap carries the Sour Punch logo and where appropriate, a flavor, while the other cap features a color player portrait with a black border. The cards are numbered on the front, and the backs are blank. There is a special promotion cap featuring Bobby Hull with no number, but the letter "P." This promo cap was used by the American Licorice sales brokerage as a sales sample.

| | MINT | NRMT |
|---|---|---|
| COMPLETE SET (8) | 12.00 | 5.50 |
| COMMON CARD (1-8) | .25 | .11 |
| ❑ 1 Theoren Fleury<br>Sour Apple Cap | 1.00 | .45 |
| ❑ 2 Guy Lafleur<br>Blue Raspberry Cap | 2.50 | 1.10 |
| ❑ 3 Chris Chelios<br>Strawberry Cap | 1.50 | .70 |
| ❑ 4 Stan Mikita<br>Sour Apple Cap | 1.25 | .55 |
| ❑ 5 Rocket Richard<br>Strawberry Cap | 2.50 | 1.10 |
| ❑ 6 Steve Thomas<br>Blue Raspberry Cap | .50 | .23 |
| ❑ 7 Checklist 1<br>Sour Punch Cap Logo | .25 | .11 |
| ❑ 8 Checklist 2<br>Sour Punch Cap Logo | .25 | .11 |
| ❑ P Bobby Hull<br>Sour Punch Cap Logo | 2.50 | 1.10 |

## 1997 Avalanche Pins

Sponsored by Denver Post. Set checklist is not complete.

| | MINT | NRMT |
|---|---|---|
| COMPLETE SET (3) | 10.00 | 4.50 |
| COMMON PIN (1-3) | 1.00 | .45 |
| ❑ 1 Marc Crawford CO | 1.00 | .45 |

❑ 2 Patrick Roy 5.00 2.20
❑ 3 Joe Sakic 4.00 1.80

## 1991-92 BayBank Bobby Orr

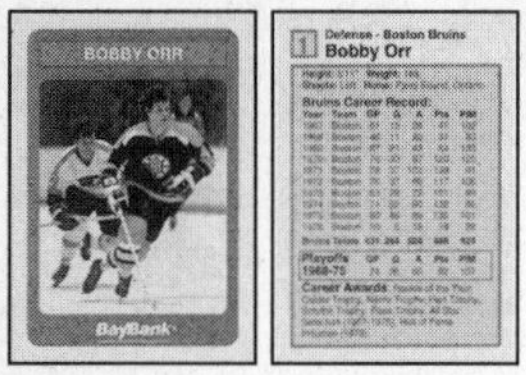

These promotional cards were sponsored by BayBank and measure approximately 2 1/2" by 3 1/2". A player card and a sponsor advertisement were packaged inside a hockey puck-shaped holder (bearing the Bruin logo) and passed out to ticket holders on BayBank Night at the Bruins game. The fronts of the first two cards have a color action player photo framed by a blue and green inner border design. The white outer border on card 1 is slightly thicker than on card 2, and the positions of the player's name and the sponsor name are reversed when one compares the two cards. The third card has a green border. Against a pale green background, the back presents biography, statistics (career and playoffs), and career awards. The card number appears in a green box in the upper left corner.

| | MINT | NRMT |
|---|---|---|
| COMPLETE SET (4) | 30.00 | 13.50 |
| COMMON CARD (1-3) | 8.00 | 3.60 |

❑ 1 Bobby Orr 8.00 3.60
(Skating with Flyer in pursuit)
❑ 2 Bobby Orr 8.00 3.60
(Skating alone with puck)
❑ 3 Bobby Orr 8.00 3.60
(Skating behind the net)
❑ NNO Bobby Orr 10.00 4.50
(8 1/2" by 11")
(Skating without puck)

## 1995 BayBank Bobby Orr

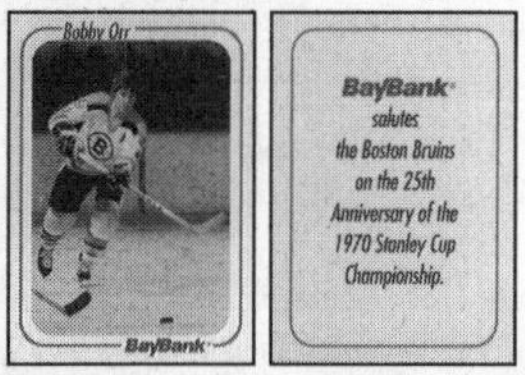


This set consists of a 10" by 8" sheet, featuring a color action photo of Bobby Orr, and a standard-size card carrying the same picture. The sheet has a blank back; the card back salutes the Boston Bruins on the 25th Anniversary of the 1970 Stanley Cup Championship.

| | MINT | NRMT |
|---|---|---|
| COMPLETE SET (2) | 15.00 | 6.75 |
| COMMON CARD (1-2) | 5.00 | 2.20 |

❑ 1 Bobby Orr 10.00 4.50
(Oversized card)
❑ 2 Bobby Orr 5.00 2.20
(Regular size card)

## 1971-72 Bazooka

The 1971-72 Bazooka set contains 36 cards. The cards, nearly identical in design to the 1971-72 Topps and O-Pee-Chee hockey cards, were distributed in 12 three-card panels as the bottoms of Bazooka bubble gum boxes. The cards are numbered at the bottom of each obverse. The cards are blank backed and are about 2/3 the size of standard cards. The panels of three are in numerical order, e.g., cards 1-3 are a panel, cards 4-6 form a panel, etc. The prices below refer to cut-apart individual cards; values for panels are 50 percent more than the values below.

| | NRMT-MT | EXC |
|---|---|---|
| COMPLETE SET (36) | 4500.00 | 2000.00 |
| COMMON CARD (1-36) | 40.00 | 18.00 |

❑ 1 Phil Esposito 300.00 135.00
❑ 2 Frank Mahovlich 150.00 70.00
❑ 3 Ed Van Impe 40.00 18.00
❑ 4 Bobby Hull 500.00 220.00
❑ 5 Henri Richard 150.00 70.00
❑ 6 Gilbert Perreault 300.00 135.00
❑ 7 Alex Delvecchio 100.00 45.00
❑ 8 Denis DeJordy 50.00 22.00
❑ 9 Ted Harris 40.00 18.00
❑ 10 Gilles Villemure 50.00 22.00
❑ 11 Dave Keon 100.00 45.00
❑ 12 Derek Sanderson 150.00 70.00
❑ 13 Orland Kurtenbach 40.00 18.00
❑ 14 Bob Nevin 40.00 18.00
❑ 15 Yvan Cournoyer 100.00 45.00
❑ 16 Andre Boudrias 40.00 18.00
❑ 17 Frank St.Marseille 40.00 18.00
❑ 18 Norm Ullman 125.00 55.00
❑ 19 Garry Unger 50.00 22.00
❑ 20 Pierre Bouchard 40.00 18.00
❑ 21 Roy Edwards 50.00 22.00
❑ 22 Ralph Backstrom 40.00 18.00
❑ 23 Guy Trottier 40.00 18.00
❑ 24 Serge Bernier 40.00 18.00
❑ 25 Bert Marshall 40.00 18.00
❑ 26 Wayne Hillman 40.00 18.00
❑ 27 Tim Ecclestone 40.00 18.00
❑ 28 Walt McKechnie 40.00 18.00
❑ 29 Tony Esposito 400.00 180.00
❑ 30 Rod Gilbert 100.00 45.00
❑ 31 Walt Tkaczuk 40.00 18.00
❑ 32 Roger Crozier 80.00 36.00
❑ 33 Ken Schinkel 40.00 18.00
❑ 34 Ron Ellis 40.00 18.00
❑ 35 Stan Mikita 300.00 135.00
❑ 36 Bobby Orr 1200.00 550.00

## 1994-95 Be A Player

This set was issued by Upper Deck in conjunction with the NHL Players Association. The set contains 180 standard-size cards, each numbered with an "R" prefix. The card backs contain text and personal information. The set was released in hobby (blue) and retail (purple) packaging. Production total for both was announced at 1,995 cases. Each box is individually numbered on the side. Each pack includes 11 cards and one autographed card. Suggested retail was $5.95 per pack. The NNO Wayne Gretzky promo card was included as a premium in an NHLPA hockey tips video. The card is slightly different from his R99 regular issue card. This set is not licensed by the National Hockey League and does not use any NHL team logos.

| | MINT | NRMT |
|---|---|---|
| COMPLETE SET (180) | 40.00 | 18.00 |
| COMMON CARD (R1-R180) | .10 | .05 |

❑ R1 Doug Gilmour .40 .18
❑ R2 Joel Otto .10 .05
❑ R3 Kirk Muller .10 .05
❑ R4 Marty McInnis .10 .05
❑ R5 Dave Gagner .20 .09
❑ R6 Geoff Courtnall .10 .05
❑ R7 Dale Hawerchuk .20 .09
❑ R8 Mike Modano .50 .23
❑ R9 Roman Hamrlik .20 .09
❑ R10 Marty McSorley .10 .05
❑ R11 Teemu Selanne .75 .35
❑ R12 Jeremy Roenick .40 .18
❑ R13 Glenn Healy .20 .09
❑ R14 Darren Turcotte .10 .05
❑ R15 Derian Hatcher .10 .05
❑ R16 Enrico Ciccone .10 .05
❑ R17 Tony Amonte .20 .09
❑ R18 Mark Recchi .20 .09
❑ R19 Eric Weinrich .10 .05
❑ R20 John Vanbiesbrouck .60 .25
❑ R21 Nick Kypreos .10 .05
❑ R22 Gilbert Dionne .10 .05
❑ R23 Theoren Fleury .20 .09
❑ R24 Todd Gill .10 .05
❑ R25 Jari Kurri .20 .09
❑ R26 Brad May .20 .09
❑ R27 Russ Courtnall .10 .05
❑ R28 Bill Ranford .20 .09
❑ R29 Steve Yzerman 1.25 .55
❑ R30 Alexandre Daigle .10 .05
❑ R31 Mike Hudson .10 .05
❑ R32 Ray Bourque .40 .18
❑ R33 Dave Andreychuk .20 .09
❑ R34 Jason Arnott .40 .18
❑ R35 Pavel Bure 1.00 .45
❑ R36 Keith Tkachuk .50 .23
❑ R37 Scott Niedermayer .10 .05
❑ R38 Johan Garpenlov .10 .05
❑ R39 Dino Ciccarelli .20 .09
❑ R40 Rob Blake .10 .05
❑ R41 Dave Manson .10 .05
❑ R42 Adam Foote .10 .05
❑ R43 Chris Pronger .20 .09
❑ R44 Scott Lachance .10 .05
❑ R45 Adam Oates .20 .09
❑ R46 Brian Leetch .40 .18
❑ R47 Guy Hebert .20 .09
❑ R48 Brett Hull .50 .23
❑ R49 Mike Ricci .10 .05
❑ R50 Dave Ellett .10 .05
❑ R51 Owen Nolan UER .20 .09
(Birthdate 9/22/71; should be 2/12/72)
❑ R52 Craig Janney .20 .09
❑ R53 Trevor Linden .20 .09
❑ R54 Ray Sheppard .20 .09
❑ R55 Rob Niedermayer .20 .09
❑ R56 Kevin Haller .10 .05
❑ R57 Jeff Norton .10 .05
❑ R58 Martin Brodeur 1.00 .45
❑ R59 Robb Stauber .20 .09
❑ R60 Sylvain Turgeon .10 .05
❑ R61 Pat Verbeek .10 .05
❑ R62 Steve Smith .10 .05
❑ R63 Jaromir Jagr 1.25 .55
❑ R64 Steve Duchesne .10 .05
❑ R65 Tie Domi .20 .09
❑ R66 Sylvain Lefebvre .10 .05
❑ R67 Guy Carbonneau .10 .05
❑ R68 Alexander Mogilny .20 .09
❑ R69 Mario Lemieux 3.00 1.35
❑ R70 Neil Wilkinson .10 .05
❑ R71 Curtis Joseph .40 .18
❑ R72 Wendel Clark .20 .09
❑ R73 Kirk McLean .20 .09
❑ R74 Mikael Renberg .20 .09
❑ R75 Shawn McEachern .10 .05
❑ R76 Mats Sundin .20 .09
❑ R77 Craig Simpson .10 .05
❑ R78 Phil Housley .20 .09
❑ R79 Pat LaFontaine .20 .09
❑ R80 Pierre Turgeon .20 .09
❑ R81 Felix Potvin .40 .18
❑ R82 Kevin Stevens .10 .05
❑ R83 Steve Chiasson .10 .05
❑ R84 Robert Petrovicky .10 .05
❑ R85 Joe Juneau .20 .09
❑ R86 Brendan Shanahan 1.00 .45
❑ R87 Joe Sacco .10 .05
❑ R88 David Reid .10 .05
❑ R89 Louie DeBrusk .10 .05
❑ R90 Darryl Sydor .10 .05
❑ R91 Paul Coffey .40 .18
❑ R92 Alexei Yashin .20 .09
❑ R93 Jason Arnott .20 .09
❑ R94 Gary Suter .10 .05
❑ R95 Luc Robitaille .20 .09
❑ R96 Joe Sakic .75 .35
❑ R97 Chris Chelios .40 .18
❑ R98 Tony Granato .10 .05
❑ R99 Wayne Gretzky 4.00 1.80
❑ R100 Joe Juneau .20 .09
❑ R101 Curtis Joseph .40 .18
❑ R102 Vincent Damphousse .20 .09
❑ R103 Paul Kariya 2.00 .90
❑ R104 Brendan Shanahan 1.00 .45
❑ R105 Eric Desjardins .10 .05
❑ R106 Eric Lindros 2.50 1.10
❑ R107 Kirk McLean .20 .09
❑ R108 Mike Ricci .10 .05
❑ R109 Chris Chelios .40 .18
❑ R110 Chris Gratton .20 .09
❑ R111 Doug Gilmour .40 .18
❑ R112 Vincent Damphousse .20 .09
❑ R113 Mark Osborne .10 .05
❑ R114 Mike Modano .20 .09
❑ R115 Steve Yzerman 1.25 .55
❑ R116 Garry Valk .10 .05
❑ R117 Adam Graves .20 .09
❑ R118 Doug Weight .20 .09
❑ R119 Rob Niedermayer .20 .09
❑ R120 Craig Simpson .10 .05
❑ R121 Patrick Roy 3.00 1.35
❑ R122 Ronnie Stern .10 .05
❑ R123 Jiri Slegr .10 .05
❑ R124 Darren Turcotte .10 .05
❑ R125 Vladimir Malakhov .10 .05
❑ R126 Paul Kariya 1.00 .45
❑ R127 Mike Gartner .20 .09
❑ R128 Scott Niedermayer .10 .05
❑ R129 Dino Ciccarelli .20 .09
❑ R130 Martin Brodeur .50 .23
❑ R131 Kevin Hatcher .10 .05
❑ R132 Pat LaFontaine .20 .09
❑ R133 Joel Otto .10 .05
❑ R134 Jason Arnott .20 .09
❑ R135 John Vanbiesbrouck .40 .18
❑ R136 Derian Hatcher .10 .05
❑ R137 Brendan Shanahan .40 .18
❑ R138 Felix Potvin .40 .18
❑ R139 Trevor Linden .20 .09
❑ R140 Ken Baumgartner .10 .05
❑ R141 Denis Leary .10 .05
❑ R142 Wendel Clark .20 .09
❑ R143 Cam Neely .20 .09
❑ R144 Jeremy Roenick .40 .18
❑ R145 Sergei Fedorov .75 .35
❑ R146 Scott Stevens .20 .09
❑ R147 Wayne Gretzky 4.00 1.80
❑ R148 Darius Kasparaitis .10 .05
❑ R149 Brian Leetch .40 .18
❑ R150 Marty McSorley .10 .05
❑ R151 Paul Kariya 2.00 .90
❑ R152 Peter Forsberg 1.50 .70
❑ R153 Brett Lindros .10 .05
❑ R154 Kenny Jonsson .10 .05
❑ R155 Jason Allison .10 .05
❑ R156 Aaron Gavey .10 .05
❑ R157 Jamie Storr .20 .09
❑ R158 Viktor Kozlov .10 .05
❑ R159 Valeri Bure .20 .09
❑ R160 Oleg Tverdovsky .20 .09
❑ R161 Brent Gretzky .10 .05
❑ R162 Todd Harvey .10 .05
❑ R163 Todd Warriner .10 .05
❑ R164 Jeff Friesen .20 .09
❑ R165 Adam Deadmarsh .20 .09
❑ R166 Ken Baumgartner .10 .05
❑ R167 Terry Carkner .10 .05
❑ R168 Tie Domi .20 .09
❑ R169 Steve Larmer .20 .09
❑ R170 Larry Murphy .20 .09
❑ R171 Steve Thomas .10 .05
❑ R172 Alexei Yashin .20 .09
❑ R173 Felix Potvin .40 .18
❑ R174 Curtis Joseph .40 .18
❑ R175 Rob Zamuner .10 .05
❑ R176 Wayne Gretzky 5.00 2.20
❑ R177 Pavel Bure 1.00 .45
❑ R178 Eric Lindros 2.50 1.10
❑ R179 Patrick Roy 3.00 1.35
❑ R180 Doug Gilmour .40 .18
❑ NNO Wayne Gretzky promo 10.00 4.50

## 1994-95 Be A Player 99 All-Stars

This 19-card set was inserted at rates of one per 16-pack hobby box and two per 16-pack retail box. The set commemorates the tour of Wayne Gretzky's All-Star team through Europe during the NHL lockout of 1994. The players are shown in action photos wearing their red and white Ninety Nine All-Star uniforms that are styled after the Red Wings of the prewar era. The back has a brief text about the player and a team photo. The card numbers contain a "G" prefix.

| | MINT | NRMT |
|---|---|---|
| COMPLETE SET (19) | 150.00 | 70.00 |
| COMMON CARD (G1-G19) | 4.00 | 1.80 |

❑ G1 Wayne Gretzky 60.00 27.00
❑ G2 Paul Coffey 10.00 4.50
❑ G3 Rob Blake 4.00 1.80
❑ G4 Pat Conacher 4.00 1.80
❑ G5 Russ Courtnall 4.00 1.80
❑ G6 Sergei Fedorov 20.00 9.00
❑ G7 Grant Fuhr 6.00 2.70
❑ G8 Todd Gill 4.00 1.80
❑ G9 Tony Granato 4.00 1.80
❑ G10 Brett Hull 12.00 5.50
❑ G11 Charlie Huddy 4.00 1.80
❑ G12 Steve Larmer 4.00 1.80
❑ G13 Kelly Hrudey 4.00 1.80
❑ G14 Al MacInnis 4.00 1.80
❑ G15 Marty McSorley 4.00 1.80
❑ G16 Jari Kurri 4.00 1.80
❑ G17 Kirk Muller 4.00 1.80
❑ G18 Rick Tocchet 6.00 2.70
❑ G19 Steve Yzerman 30.00 13.50

## 1994-95 Be A Player Signature Cards

These authentic signature cards were issued one in every foil pack. All autographs were guaranteed by the National Hockey League Players Association. The Jiri Slegr card (#119) was only available through a mail-in offer. The set is considered complete without it. Reportedly, most players signed approximately 2,400 of each card (including Slegr). Players who signed fewer are indicated below with parenthesis indicating approximately how many cards they signed.

| | MINT | NRMT |
|---|---|---|
| COMPLETE SET (177) | 3400.00 | 1500.00 |
| COMMON CARD (1-178) | 5.00 | 2.20 |

❑ 1 Doug Gilmour (1250) 40.00 18.00
❑ 2 Adam Foote 5.00 2.20
❑ 3 Martin Brodeur 60.00 27.00
❑ 4 Alexander Semak 5.00 2.20
❑ 5 Dale Hawerchuk 10.00 4.50
❑ 6 Derek King 5.00 2.20
❑ 7 Mark Recchi 10.00 4.50
❑ 8 Fredrik Olausson 5.00 2.20
❑ 9 Dave McLlwain 5.00 2.20
❑ 10 Marc Bergevin 5.00 2.20
❑ 11 Teemu Selanne (600) 200.00 90.00
❑ 12 Jeremy Roenick (600) 100.00 45.00
❑ 13 Eric Lacroix 5.00 2.20
❑ 14 Marty McInnis 5.00 2.20
❑ 15 Kris King 5.00 2.20
❑ 16 Bill Ranford 10.00 4.50
❑ 17 Gary Roberts 5.00 2.20
❑ 18 Mark Osborne 5.00 2.20
❑ 19 Dmitri Mironov 5.00 2.20
❑ 20 John Vanbiesbrouck (600) 200.00 90.00
❑ 21 Alexei Zhamnov 10.00 4.50
❑ 22 Brad May 8.00 3.60
❑ 23 Doug Lidster 5.00 2.20
❑ 24 Mikael Renberg 15.00 6.75
❑ 25 Kris Draper 5.00 2.20
❑ 26 Darryl Sydor 5.00 2.20
❑ 27 Claude Lemieux 10.00 4.50
❑ 28 Doug Brown 5.00 2.20
❑ 29 Louie DeBrusk 5.00 2.20
❑ 30 Andy Moog 10.00 4.50
❑ 31 Donald Audette 5.00 2.20
❑ 32 Ray Bourque (600) 150.00 70.00
❑ 33 Brian Rolston 5.00 2.20
❑ 34 Ted Drury 5.00 2.20
❑ 35 Darren Turcotte 5.00 2.20
❑ 36 Gary Shuchuk 5.00 2.20
❑ 37 Mike Ricci 10.00 4.50
❑ 38 Kirk Maltby 5.00 2.20
❑ 39 Doug Bodger 5.00 2.20
❑ 40 Kirk Muller 10.00 4.50
❑ 41 Sylvain Lefebvre 5.00 2.20
❑ 42 Brent Grieve 5.00 2.20
❑ 43 Bill Houlder 5.00 2.20
❑ 44 Neil Wilkinson 5.00 2.20
❑ 45 Donald Dufresne 5.00 2.20
❑ 46 Brian Leetch (600) 150.00 70.00
❑ 47 Bryan Smolinski 10.00 4.50
❑ 48 Kevin Hatcher 5.00 2.20
❑ 49 Steven Rice 5.00 2.20
❑ 50 Bill Guerin 5.00 2.20
❑ 51 Grant Jennings 5.00 2.20
❑ 52 Dave Andreychuk 10.00 4.50
❑ 53 Sean Burke 10.00 4.50
❑ 54 Nick Kypreos 5.00 2.20
❑ 55 Drake Berehowsky 5.00 2.20
❑ 56 Kevin Haller 5.00 2.20
❑ 57 Bill Berg 5.00 2.20
❑ 58 Chris Simon 5.00 2.20
❑ 59 Owen Nolan 10.00 4.50
Wrong birthdate blacked out on back)
❑ 60 Don Sweeney 5.00 2.20
❑ 61 Johan Garpenlov 5.00 2.20
❑ 62 Garry Galley 5.00 2.20
❑ 63 Pat LaFontaine 10.00 4.50
❑ 64 Craig Berube 5.00 2.20
❑ 65 Dave Ellett 5.00 2.20
❑ 66 Robert Kron 5.00 2.20
❑ 67 Alexander Godynyuk 5.00 2.20
❑ 68 Markus Naslund 5.00 2.20
❑ 69 Joel Otto 5.00 2.20
❑ 70 Igor Ulanov 5.00 2.20
❑ 71 Pat Verbeek 10.00 4.50
❑ 72 Craig MacTavish 5.00 2.20
❑ 73 Gary Leeman 5.00 2.20
❑ 74 Kevin Todd 5.00 2.20
❑ 75 Mike Sullivan 5.00 2.20
❑ 76 Rob Pearson 5.00 2.20
❑ 77 Dave Gagner 5.00 2.20
❑ 78 Dirk Graham 5.00 2.20
❑ 79 Joe Sacco 5.00 2.20
❑ 80 Jassen Cullimore 5.00 2.20
❑ 81 Glen Featherstone 5.00 2.20
❑ 82 Scott Lachance 5.00 2.20
❑ 83 Kerry Huffman 5.00 2.20
❑ 84 Troy Loney 5.00 2.20
❑ 85 Rob Gaudreau 5.00 2.20
❑ 86 Brendan Shanahan (600) 200.00 90.00
❑ 87 Joe Murphy 10.00 4.50
❑ 88 Scott Niedermayer 10.00 4.50
❑ 89 Dan Quinn 5.00 2.20
❑ 90 Jeff Norton 5.00 2.20
❑ 91 Jim Dowd 5.00 2.20
❑ 92 Ray Ferraro 10.00 4.50
❑ 93 Shawn Burr 5.00 2.20
❑ 94 Denis Savard 10.00 4.50
❑ 95 Dave Manson 5.00 2.20
❑ 96 Joe Nieuwendyk 10.00 4.50
❑ 97 Tony Amonte 10.00 4.50
❑ 98 James Patrick 5.00 2.20
❑ 99 Guy Hebert 10.00 4.50
❑ 100 Peter Zezel 5.00 2.20
❑ 101 Shawn McEachern 5.00 2.20
❑ 102 Dave Lowry 5.00 2.20
❑ 103 David Reid 5.00 2.20
❑ 104 Todd Gill 5.00 2.20
❑ 105 John Cullen 5.00 2.20
❑ 106 Guy Carbonneau 5.00 2.20
❑ 107 Jeff Beukeboom 5.00 2.20
❑ 108 Wayne Gretzky (300) 800.00 350.00
❑ 109 Curtis Joseph 20.00 9.00
❑ 110 Jason Arnott 15.00 6.75
❑ 112 Gary Suter 5.00 2.20
❑ 113 Luc Robitaille 10.00 4.50
❑ 114 Tony Granato 5.00 2.20
❑ 115 Steve Yzerman (600) 400.00 180.00
❑ 116 Chris Gratton 10.00 4.50
❑ 117 Doug Weight 10.00 4.50
❑ 118 Garry Valk 5.00 2.20
❑ 119 Jiri Slegr MAIL IN 50.00 22.00
❑ 120 Vincent Damphousse 10.00 4.50
❑ 121 Vladimir Malakhov 5.00 2.20
❑ 122 Craig Simpson 5.00 2.20
❑ 123 Theoren Fleury 10.00 4.50

❑ 124 Dave Poulin 5.00 2.20
❑ 125 Derian Hatcher 5.00 2.20
❑ 126 Jimmy Waite 10.00 4.50
❑ 127 Norm Maciver 5.00 2.20
❑ 128 Glenn Healy 10.00 4.50
❑ 129 Jocelyn Lemieux 5.00 2.20
❑ 130 Steve Chiasson 5.00 2.20
❑ 131 Keith Jones 5.00 2.20
❑ 132 Enrico Ciccone 5.00 2.20
❑ 133 Martin Lapointe 5.00 2.20
❑ 134 John MacLean 10.00 4.50
❑ 135 Geoff Courtnall 5.00 2.20
❑ 136 David Shaw 5.00 2.20
❑ 137 Steve Duchesne 5.00 2.20
❑ 138 Dean Evason 5.00 2.20
❑ 139 Eric Weinrich 5.00 2.20
❑ 140 Kelly Hrudey 10.00 4.50
❑ 141 Ted Donato 5.00 2.20
❑ 142 Darius Kasparaitis 5.00 2.20
❑ 143 Tie Domi 10.00 4.50
❑ 144 Terry Carkner 5.00 2.20
❑ 145 Steve Thomas 10.00 4.50
❑ 146 Steve Larmer 10.00 4.50
❑ 147 Rob Zamuner 5.00 2.20
❑ 148 Larry Murphy 10.00 4.50
❑ 149 Ken Baumgartner 5.00 2.20
❑ 150 Alexei Yashin (600) 80.00 36.00
❑ 151 Paul Kariya (600) 400.00 180.00
❑ 152 Todd Harvey 10.00 4.50
❑ 153A Viktor Kozlov 10.00 4.50
(VK variation)
❑ 153B Viktor Kozlov 200.00 90.00
(Full Signature)
❑ 154 Brent Gretzky 5.00 2.20
❑ 155 Petr Klima 5.00 2.20
❑ 156 Kent Manderville 5.00 2.20
❑ 157 Mike Eagles 5.00 2.20
❑ 158 Valeri Kamensky 10.00 4.50
❑ 159 Thomas Steen 5.00 2.20
❑ 160 Michal Pivonka 5.00 2.20
❑ 161 Steve Heinze 5.00 2.20
❑ 162 Nicklas Lidstrom 10.00 4.50
❑ 163 Uwe Krupp 5.00 2.20
❑ 164 Pat Elynuik 5.00 2.20
❑ 165 Mike Peca 10.00 4.50
❑ 166 Sylvain Cote 5.00 2.20
❑ 167 Trevor Kidd 10.00 4.50
❑ 168 Patrick Poulin 5.00 2.20
❑ 169 Shane Churla 5.00 2.20
❑ 170 Scott Mellanby 10.00 4.50
❑ 171 Mike Sillinger 5.00 2.20
❑ 172 Shayne Corson 5.00 2.20
❑ 173 Micah Aivazoff 5.00 2.20
❑ 174 Robert Lang 5.00 2.20
❑ 175 Rod Brind'Amour 10.00 4.50
❑ 176 Troy Murray 5.00 2.20
❑ 177 Mike Krushelnyski 5.00 2.20
❑ 178 Sergio Momesso 5.00 2.20

## 1994-95 Be A Player Up Close and Personal

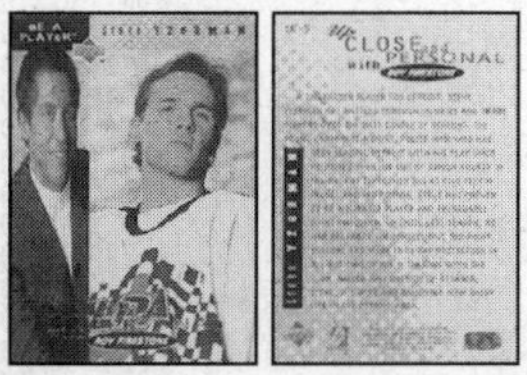

This 10-card set was inserted two per box (1:8 packs) in Be A Player product. The cards feature an "Up Close" photo of the player and Roy Firestone, a popular ESPN show host. The text on the back was written by Firestone. The cards are numbered with an "UC" prefix.

| | MINT | NRMT |
|---|---|---|
| COMPLETE SET (10) | 100.00 | 45.00 |
| COMMON CARD (UC1-UC10) | 4.00 | 1.80 |

❑ UC1 Wayne Gretzky 20.00 9.00
❑ UC2 Eric Lindros 12.00 5.50
❑ UC3 Pavel Bure 6.00 2.70
❑ UC4 Teemu Selanne 6.00 2.70
❑ UC5 Steve Yzerman 10.00 4.50
❑ UC6 Jeremy Roenick 4.00 1.80
❑ UC7 Sergei Fedorov 6.00 2.70
❑ UC8 Patrick Roy 15.00 6.75
❑ UC9 Paul Kariya 15.00 6.75
❑ UC10 Doug Gilmour 4.00 1.80

## 1995-96 Be A Player

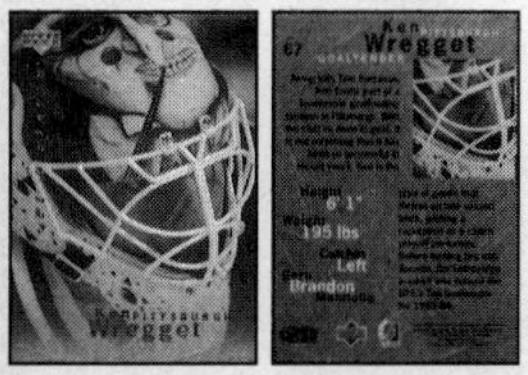

This 225-card set was released in June, 1996. It was released by Upper Deck, in conjunction with the NHLPA. The set was not licensed by the NHL, hence the absence of logos and insignia from player uniforms, and the color changes on the sweaters of players from Colorado and the Islanders. Suggested retail was $7.99 per ten-card pack, although packs tended to sell for more due to the allure of the one-per-pack autographs.

| | MINT | NRMT |
|---|---|---|
| COMPLETE SET (225) | 40.00 | 18.00 |
| COMMON CARD (1-225) | .15 | .07 |

❑ 1 Brett Hull 1.00 .45
❑ 2 Jyrki Lumme .15 .07
❑ 3 Shean Donovan .15 .07
❑ 4 Yuri Khmylev .15 .07
❑ 5 Stephane Matteau .15 .07
❑ 6 Basil McRae .15 .07
❑ 7 Dimitri Yushkevich .15 .07
❑ 8 Ron Francis .30 .14
❑ 9 Keith Carney .15 .07
❑ 10 Brad Dalgarno .15 .07
❑ 11 Bob Carpenter .15 .07
❑ 12 Kevin Stevens .15 .07
❑ 13 Patrick Flatley .15 .07
❑ 14 Craig Muni .15 .07
❑ 15 Travis Green .30 .14
❑ 16 Derek Plante .15 .07
❑ 17 Mike Craig .15 .07
❑ 18 Chris Pronger .30 .14
❑ 19 Bret Hedican .15 .07
❑ 20 Mathieu Schneider .15 .07
❑ 21 Chris Therien .15 .07
❑ 22 Greg Adams .15 .07
❑ 23 Arturs Irbe .30 .14
❑ 24 Zigmund Palffy .30 .14
❑ 25 Peter Douris .15 .07
❑ 26 Bob Sweeney .15 .07
❑ 27 Chris Terreri .30 .14
❑ 28 Alexei Zhitnik .15 .07
❑ 29 Jay Wells .15 .07
❑ 30 Andrew Cassels .15 .07
❑ 31 Radek Bonk .15 .07
❑ 32 Brian Bellows .30 .14
❑ 33 Frantisek Kucera .15 .07
❑ 34 Valeri Bure .30 .14
❑ 35 Randy Wood .15 .07
❑ 36 Dimitri Khristich .15 .07
❑ 37 Randy Ladouceur .15 .07
❑ 38 Nelson Emerson .15 .07
❑ 39 Bryan Marchment .15 .07
❑ 40 Kevin Lowe .15 .07
❑ 41 Trevor Linden .30 .14
❑ 42 Neal Broten .30 .14
❑ 43 Tom Chorske .15 .07
❑ 44 Patrice Brisebois .15 .07
❑ 45 Wayne Presley .15 .07
❑ 46 Murray Craven .15 .07
❑ 47 Craig Janney .30 .14
❑ 48 Ken Daneyko .15 .07
❑ 49 Dino Ciccarelli .30 .14
❑ 50 Jason Dawe .15 .07
❑ 51 Brad McCrimmon .15 .07
❑ 52 Randy McKay .15 .07
❑ 53 Rudy Poeschek .15 .07
❑ 54 Calle Johansson .15 .07
❑ 55 Wendel Clark .30 .14
❑ 56 Rob Ray .15 .07
❑ 57 Garth Snow .30 .14
❑ 58 Joe Juneau .15 .07
❑ 59 Craig Wolanin .15 .07
❑ 60 Ray Sheppard .30 .14
❑ 61 Oleg Tverdovsky .30 .14
❑ 62 Geoff Sanderson .30 .14
❑ 63 Mike Ridley .15 .07
❑ 64 David Oliver .15 .07
❑ 65 Russ Courtnall .15 .07
❑ 66 Joe Reekie .15 .07
❑ 67 Ken Wregget .30 .14
❑ 68 Teppo Numminen .15 .07
❑ 69 Mikhail Shtalenkov .15 .07
❑ 70 Luke Richardson .15 .07
❑ 71 Brent Gilchrist .15 .07
❑ 72 Phil Housley .30 .14
❑ 73 Greg Johnson .15 .07
❑ 74 Sean Hill .15 .07
❑ 75 Karl Dykhuis .15 .07
❑ 76 Tim Cheveldae .30 .14
❑ 77 Shjon Podein .15 .07
❑ 78 Rene Corbet .15 .07
❑ 79 Ronnie Stern .15 .07
❑ 80 Mike Donnelly .15 .07
❑ 81 Randy Cunneyworth .15 .07
❑ 82 Rick Tocchet .30 .14
❑ 83 Dallas Drake .15 .07
❑ 84 Cam Russell .15 .07
❑ 85 Daren Puppa .30 .14
❑ 86 Benoit Brunet .15 .07
❑ 87 Paul Ranheim .15 .07
❑ 88 Bob Rouse .15 .07
❑ 89 Todd Elik .15 .07
❑ 90 Darcy Wakaluk .30 .14
❑ 91 Cliff Ronning .15 .07
❑ 92 Pat Conacher .15 .07
❑ 93 Todd Krygier .15 .07
❑ 94 Dave Babych .15 .07
❑ 95 Pat Falloon .15 .07
❑ 96 Don Beaupre .30 .14
❑ 97 Wayne Gretzky 6.00 2.70
❑ 98 Chris Joseph .15 .07
❑ 99 Vyacheslav Kozlov .15 .07
❑ 100 Brent Fedyk .15 .07
❑ 101 Tim Taylor .15 .07
❑ 102 Mike Eastwood .15 .07
❑ 103 Mike Keane .15 .07
❑ 104 Grant Ledyard .15 .07
❑ 105 Rob Dimaio .15 .07
❑ 106 Martin Straka .15 .07
❑ 107 Scott Young .15 .07
❑ 108 Zarley Zalapski .15 .07
❑ 109 Steve Leach .15 .07
❑ 110 Jody Hull .15 .07
❑ 111 Lyle Odelein .15 .07
❑ 112 Bob Corkum .15 .07
❑ 113 Rob Blake .15 .07
❑ 114 Randy Burridge .15 .07
❑ 115 Keith Primeau .30 .14
❑ 116 Glen Wesley .15 .07
❑ 117 Brian Bradley .15 .07
❑ 118 Andrei Kovalenko .15 .07
❑ 119 Patrik Juhlin .15 .07
❑ 120 John Tucker .15 .07
❑ 121 Stephane Fiset .30 .14
❑ 122 Mike Hough .15 .07
❑ 123 Steve Smith .15 .07
❑ 124 Tom Barrasso .30 .14
❑ 125 Ray Whitney .15 .07
❑ 126 Benoit Hogue .15 .07
❑ 127 Stu Barnes .15 .07
❑ 128 Craig Ludwig .15 .07
❑ 129 Curtis Leschyshyn .15 .07
❑ 130 John LeClair 1.00 .45
❑ 131 Dennis Vial .15 .07
❑ 132 Cory Stillman .15 .07
❑ 133 Roman Hamrlik .30 .14
❑ 134 Al MacInnis .30 .14
❑ 135 Igor Korolev .15 .07
❑ 136 Rick Zombo .15 .07
❑ 137 Zdeno Ciger .15 .07
❑ 138 Brian Savage .15 .07
❑ 139 Paul Ysebaert .15 .07
❑ 140 Brent Sutter .15 .07
❑ 141 Ed Olczyk .15 .07
❑ 142 Adam Creighton .15 .07
❑ 143 Jesse Belanger .15 .07
❑ 144 Glen Murray .15 .07
❑ 145 Alexander Selivanov .15 .07
❑ 146 Trent Yawney .15 .07
❑ 147 Bruce Driver .15 .07
❑ 148 Michael Nylander .15 .07
❑ 149 Martin Gelinas .15 .07
❑ 150 Yanic Perreault .15 .07
❑ 151 Craig Billington .30 .14
❑ 152 Pierre Turgeon .30 .14
❑ 153 Mike Modano 1.00 .45
❑ 154 Joe Mullen .30 .14
❑ 155 Todd Ewen .15 .07
❑ 156 Petr Nedved .30 .14
❑ 157 Dominic Roussel .30 .14
❑ 158 Murray Baron .15 .07
❑ 159 Robert Dirk .15 .07
❑ 160 Tomas Sandstrom .15 .07
❑ 161 Brian Holzinger .60 .25
❑ 162 Ken Klee .15 .07
❑ 163 Radek Dvorak .30 .14
❑ 164 Marcus Ragnarsson .15 .07
❑ 165 Aaron Gavey .15 .07
❑ 166 Jeff O'Neill .30 .14
❑ 167 Chad Kilger .30 .14
❑ 168 Todd Bertuzzi .30 .14
❑ 169 Robert Svehla .15 .07
❑ 170 Eric Daze .60 .25
❑ 171 Daniel Alfredsson 1.00 .45
❑ 172 Shane Doan .30 .14
❑ 173 Kyle McLaren .30 .14
❑ 174 Saku Koivu 1.25 .55
❑ 175 Jere Lehtinen .15 .07
❑ 176 Nikolai Khabibulin .30 .14
❑ 177 Niklas Sundstrom .30 .14
❑ 178 Ed Jovanovski .60 .25
❑ 179 Jason Bonsignore .15 .07
❑ 180 Kenny Jonsson .15 .07
❑ 181 Vitali Yachmenev .15 .07
❑ 182 Alexei Kovalev .15 .07
❑ 183 Sandis Ozolinsh .30 .14
❑ 184 Rob Niedermayer .30 .14
❑ 185 Richard Park .15 .07
❑ 186 Adam Deadmarsh .30 .14
❑ 187 Sergei Krivokrasov .15 .07
❑ 188 Alexandre Daigle .15 .07
❑ 189 Jim Carey .60 .25
❑ 190 Todd Marchant .15 .07
❑ 191 Mike Richter .60 .25
❑ 192 Dominik Hasek 1.25 .55
❑ 193 Chris Osgood .60 .25
❑ 194 Ed Belfour .75 .35
❑ 195 Felix Potvin .60 .25
❑ 196 Grant Fuhr .30 .14
❑ 197 Patrick Roy 3.00 1.35
❑ 198 Ron Hextall .30 .14
❑ 199 Jocelyn Thibault .60 .25
❑ 200 Kirk McLean .30 .14
❑ 201 Jari Kurri .30 .14
❑ 202 Bobby Holik .15 .07
❑ 203 Mats Sundin .30 .14
❑ 204 Alexander Mogilny .30 .14
❑ 205 Valeri Karpov .15 .07
❑ 206 Igor Larionov .15 .07
❑ 207 Valeri Zelepukin .15 .07
❑ 208 Jozef Stumpel .15 .07
❑ 209 Sergei Nemchinov .15 .07
❑ 210 Peter Bondra .60 .25
❑ 211 Chris Chelios .60 .25
❑ 212 Adam Graves .30 .14
❑ 213 Dale Hunter .15 .07
❑ 214 Tony Twist .15 .07
❑ 215 Keith Tkachuk .60 .25
❑ 216 Vladimir Konstantinov .15 .07
❑ 217 Sandy McCarthy .15 .07
❑ 218 Jamie Macoun .15 .07
❑ 219 Scott Stevens .30 .14
❑ 220 Mark Tinordi .15 .07
❑ 221 Bob Probert .30 .14
❑ 222 Gino Odjick .15 .07
❑ 223 Ulf Samuelsson .15 .07
❑ 224 Stu Grimson .15 .07
❑ 225 Marty McSorley .15 .07

## 1995-96 Be A Player Signatures

These authentic signed cards were inserted at a rate of one per pack. Every seventh pack featured a special signed card which was distinguished by unique die-cut corners. Because these cards were tougher to pull, they command a premium; multipliers for these cards are listed below. The card fronts are the same as the regular cards, but the backs of the signed cards feature a certificate of authenticity. Although production numbers were not officially revealed, documents suggest approximately 3,000 regular and 400 die-cut versions of each signed card were released. The quantities of the Wayne Gretzky cards (#S97) were intially reported at 802 signed and 99 die-cut copies. Upper Deck later announced the actual numbers as being 648 regular and 234 die-cut. The Mike Richter card (#191) was not inserted in packs, but was made available through a mail-in offer. The set is considered complete without this card.

| | MINT | NRMT |
|---|---|---|
| COMPLETE SET (224) | 1800.00 | 800.00 |
| COMMON CARD (S1-S225) | 4.00 | 1.80 |
| COMPLETE DIE-CUT SET (224) | 5000.00 | 2200.00 |
| COMMON DIE CUT (S1-S225) | 8.00 | 3.60 |

*DIE CUT STARS: 1X TO 2X BASIC SIGNATURES

❑ S1 Brett Hull 30.00 13.50
❑ S2 Jyrki Lumme 4.00 1.80
❑ S3 Shean Donovan 4.00 1.80
❑ S4 Yuri Khmylev 4.00 1.80
❑ S5 Stephane Matteau 4.00 1.80
❑ S6 Basil McRae 4.00 1.80
❑ S7 Dimitri Yushkevich 4.00 1.80
❑ S8 Ron Francis 12.00 5.50
❑ S9 Keith Carney 4.00 1.80
❑ S10 Brad Dalgarno 4.00 1.80
❑ S11 Bob Carpenter 4.00 1.80
❑ S12 Kevin Stevens 15.00 6.75
❑ S13 Pat Flatley 4.00 1.80
❑ S14 Craig Muni 4.00 1.80
❑ S15 Travis Green 4.00 1.80
❑ S16 Derek Plante 4.00 1.80
❑ S17 Mike Craig 4.00 1.80
❑ S18 Chris Pronger 15.00 6.75
❑ S19 Bret Hedican 4.00 1.80
❑ S20 Mathieu Schneider 4.00 1.80
❑ S21 Chris Therien 4.00 1.80
❑ S22 Greg Adams 4.00 1.80
❑ S23 Arturs Irbe 15.00 6.75
❑ S24 Zigmund Palffy 25.00 11.00
❑ S25 Peter Douris 4.00 1.80
❑ S26 Bob Sweeney 4.00 1.80
❑ S27 Chris Terreri 15.00 6.75
❑ S28 Alexei Zhitnik 4.00 1.80
❑ S29 Jay Wells 4.00 1.80
❑ S30 Andrew Cassels 4.00 1.80
❑ S31 Radek Bonk 15.00 6.75
❑ S32 Brian Bellows 15.00 6.75
❑ S33 Frantisek Kucera 4.00 1.80
❑ S34 Valeri Bure 15.00 6.75
❑ S35 Randy Wood 4.00 1.80
❑ S36 Dimitri Khristich 4.00 1.80
❑ S37 Randy Ladouceur 4.00 1.80
❑ S38 Nelson Emerson 15.00 6.75
❑ S39 Bryan Marchment 4.00 1.80
❑ S40 Kevin Lowe 4.00 1.80
❑ S41 Trevor Linden 15.00 6.75
❑ S42 Neal Broten 4.00 1.80
❑ S43 Tom Chorske 4.00 1.80
❑ S44 Patrice Brisebois 4.00 1.80
❑ S45 Wayne Presley 4.00 1.80
❑ S46 Murray Craven 4.00 1.80
❑ S47 Craig Janney 15.00 6.75
❑ S48 Ken Daneyko 4.00 1.80
❑ S49 Dino Ciccarelli 15.00 6.75
❑ S50 Jason Dawe 4.00 1.80
❑ S51 Brad McCrimmon 4.00 1.80
❑ S52 Randy McKay 4.00 1.80
❑ S53 Rudy Poeschek 4.00 1.80
❑ S54 Calle Johansson 4.00 1.80
❑ S55 Wendel Clark 15.00 6.75
❑ S56 Rob Ray 8.00 3.60
❑ S57 Garth Snow 15.00 6.75
❑ S58 Joe Juneau 15.00 6.75
❑ S59 Craig Wolanin 4.00 1.80
❑ S60 Ray Sheppard 4.00 1.80
❑ S61 Oleg Tverdovsky 15.00 6.75
❑ S62 Geoff Sanderson 15.00 6.75
❑ S63 Mike Ridley 4.00 1.80
❑ S64 David Oliver 4.00 1.80
❑ S65 Russ Courtnall 15.00 6.75
❑ S66 Joe Reekie 4.00 1.80
❑ S67 Ken Wregget 15.00 6.75
❑ S68 Teppo Numminen 4.00 1.80
❑ S69 Mikhail Shtalenkov 15.00 6.75
❑ S70 Luke Richardson 4.00 1.80
❑ S71 Brent Gilchrist 4.00 1.80
❑ S72 Phil Housley 15.00 6.75
❑ S73 Greg Johnson 4.00 1.80
❑ S74 Sean Hill 4.00 1.80
❑ S75 Karl Dykhuis 4.00 1.80
❑ S76 Tim Cheveldae 15.00 6.75
❑ S77 Shjon Podein 4.00 1.80
❑ S78 Rene Corbet 4.00 1.80
❑ S79 Ron Stern 4.00 1.80
❑ S80 Mike Donnelly 4.00 1.80
❑ S81 Randy Cunneyworth 4.00 1.80
❑ S82 Rick Tocchet 15.00 6.75
❑ S83 Dallas Drake 4.00 1.80
❑ S84 Cam Russell 4.00 1.80
❑ S85 Daren Puppa 15.00 6.75
❑ S86 Benoit Brunet 4.00 1.80
❑ S87 Paul Ranheim 4.00 1.80
❑ S88 Bob Rouse 4.00 1.80
❑ S89 Todd Elik 4.00 1.80
❑ S90 Darcy Wakaluk 15.00 6.75
❑ S91 Cliff Ronning 4.00 1.80
❑ S92 Pat Conacher 4.00 1.80
❑ S93 Todd Krygier 4.00 1.80
❑ S94 Dave Babych 4.00 1.80
❑ S95 Pat Falloon 15.00 6.75
❑ S96 Don Beaupre 15.00 6.75
❑ S97 Wayne Gretzky (648) 600.00 275.00
❑ S98 Chris Joseph 4.00 1.80
❑ S99 Vyacheslav Kozlov 15.00 6.75
❑ S100 Brent Fedyk 4.00 1.80
❑ S101 Tim Taylor 4.00 1.80
❑ S102 Mike Eastwood 4.00 1.80
❑ S103 Mike Keane 4.00 1.80
❑ S104 Grant Ledyard 4.00 1.80
❑ S105 Rob Dimaio 4.00 1.80
❑ S106 Martin Straka 4.00 1.80
❑ S107 Scott Young 4.00 1.80
❑ S108 Zarley Zalapski 4.00 1.80
❑ S109 Steve Leach 4.00 1.80
❑ S110 Jody Hull 4.00 1.80
❑ S111 Lyle Odelein 4.00 1.80
❑ S112 Bob Corkum 4.00 1.80
❑ S113 Rob Blake 4.00 1.80
❑ S114 Randy Burridge 4.00 1.80
❑ S115 Keith Primeau 15.00 6.75
❑ S116 Glen Wesley 4.00 1.80
❑ S117 Brian Bradley 4.00 1.80
❑ S118 Andrei Kovalenko 4.00 1.80
❑ S119 Patrik Juhlin 4.00 1.80
❑ S120 John Tucker 4.00 1.80
❑ S121 Stephane Fiset 15.00 6.75
❑ S122 Mike Hough 4.00 1.80
❑ S123 Steve Smith 4.00 1.80
❑ S124 Tom Barrasso 15.00 6.75
❑ S125 Ray Whitney 4.00 1.80
❑ S126 Benoit Hogue 4.00 1.80
❑ S127 Stu Barnes 4.00 1.80
❑ S128 Craig Ludwig 4.00 1.80
❑ S129 Curtis Leschyshyn 4.00 1.80
❑ S130 John LeClair 40.00 18.00
❑ S131 Dennis Vial 4.00 1.80
❑ S132 Cory Stillman 4.00 1.80
❑ S133 Roman Hamrlik 15.00 6.75
❑ S134 Al MacInnis 15.00 6.75
❑ S135 Igor Korolev 4.00 1.80
❑ S136 Rick Zombo 4.00 1.80
❑ S137 Zdeno Ciger 4.00 1.80
❑ S138 Brian Savage 4.00 1.80
❑ S139 Paul Ysebaert 4.00 1.80
❑ S140 Brent Sutter 4.00 1.80
❑ S141 Ed Olczyk 4.00 1.80
❑ S142 Adam Creighton 4.00 1.80
❑ S143 Jesse Belanger 4.00 1.80
❑ S144 Glen Murray 4.00 1.80
❑ S145 Alexander Selivanov 15.00 6.75
❑ S146 Trent Yawney 4.00 1.80
❑ S147 Bruce Driver 4.00 1.80
❑ S148 Michael Nylander 4.00 1.80
❑ S149 Martin Gelinas 4.00 1.80
❑ S150 Yanic Perreault 4.00 1.80
❑ S151 Craig Billington 15.00 6.75
❑ S152 Pierre Turgeon 15.00 6.75
❑ S153 Mike Modano 30.00 13.50
❑ S154 Joe Mullen 15.00 6.75
❑ S155 Todd Ewen 4.00 1.80
❑ S156 Petr Nedved 15.00 6.75
❑ S157 Dominic Roussel 15.00 6.75
❑ S158 Murray Baron 4.00 1.80
❑ S159 Robert Dirk 4.00 1.80
❑ S160 Tomas Sandstrom 15.00 6.75
❑ S161 Brian Holzinger 15.00 6.75
❑ S162 Ken Klee 4.00 1.80
❑ S163 Radek Dvorak 15.00 6.75
❑ S164 Marcus Ragnarsson 15.00 6.75
❑ S165 Aaron Gavey 15.00 6.75
❑ S166 Jeff O'Neill 15.00 6.75
❑ S167 Chad Kilger 15.00 6.75
❑ S168 Todd Bertuzzi 15.00 6.75
❑ S169 Robert Svehla 4.00 1.80
❑ S170 Eric Daze 12.00 5.50
❑ S171 Daniel Alfredsson 12.00 5.50
❑ S172 Shane Doan 15.00 6.75
❑ S173 Kyle McLaren 15.00 6.75
❑ S174 Saku Koivu 30.00 13.50
❑ S175 Jere Lehtinen 4.00 1.80
❑ S176 Nikolai Khabibulin 12.00 5.50
❑ S177 Niklas Sundstrom 15.00 6.75
❑ S178 Ed Jovanovski 12.00 5.50
❑ S179 Jason Bonsignore 4.00 1.80
❑ S180 Kenny Jonsson 15.00 6.75
❑ S181 Vitali Yachmenev 4.00 1.80
❑ S182 Alexei Kovalev 15.00 6.75
❑ S183 Sandis Ozolinsh 12.00 5.50

| | | |
|---|---|---|
| ❑ S184 Rob Niedermayer | 4.00 | 1.80 |
| ❑ S185 Richard Park | 4.00 | 1.80 |
| ❑ S186 Adam Deadmarsh | 12.00 | 5.50 |
| ❑ S187 Sergei Krivokrasov | 4.00 | 1.80 |
| ❑ S188 Alexandre Daigle | 4.00 | 1.80 |
| ❑ S189 Jim Carey | 12.00 | 5.50 |
| ❑ S190 Todd Marchant | 15.00 | 6.75 |
| ❑ S191 Mike Richter MAIL-IN | 150.00 | 70.00 |
| ❑ S192 Dominik Hasek | 50.00 | 22.00 |
| ❑ S193 Chris Osgood | 30.00 | 13.50 |
| ❑ S194 Ed Belfour | 30.00 | 13.50 |
| ❑ S195 Felix Potvin | 12.00 | 5.50 |
| ❑ S196 Grant Fuhr | 12.00 | 5.50 |
| ❑ S197 Patrick Roy | 120.00 | 55.00 |
| ❑ S198 Ron Hextall | 12.00 | 5.50 |
| ❑ S199 Jocelyn Thibault | 12.00 | 5.50 |
| ❑ S200 Kirk McLean | 15.00 | 6.75 |
| ❑ S201 Jari Kurri | 12.00 | 5.50 |
| ❑ S202 Bobby Holik | 4.00 | 1.80 |
| ❑ S203 Mats Sundin | 25.00 | 11.00 |
| ❑ S204 Alexander Mogilny | 12.00 | 5.50 |
| ❑ S205 Valeri Karpov | 4.00 | 1.80 |
| ❑ S206 Igor Larionov | 15.00 | 6.75 |
| ❑ S207 Valeri Zelepukin | 4.00 | 1.80 |
| ❑ S208 Jozef Stumpel | 4.00 | 1.80 |
| ❑ S209 Sergei Nemchinov | 4.00 | 1.80 |
| ❑ S210 Peter Bondra | 25.00 | 11.00 |
| ❑ S211 Chris Chelios | 25.00 | 11.00 |
| ❑ S212 Adam Graves | 15.00 | 6.75 |
| ❑ S213 Dale Hunter | 15.00 | 6.75 |
| ❑ S214 Tony Twist | 15.00 | 6.75 |
| ❑ S215 Keith Tkachuk | 40.00 | 18.00 |
| ❑ S216 Vladimir Konstantinov | 70.00 | 32.00 |
| ❑ S217 Sandy McCarthy | 4.00 | 1.80 |
| ❑ S218 Jamie Macoun | 4.00 | 1.80 |
| ❑ S219 Scott Stevens | 15.00 | 6.75 |
| ❑ S220 Mark Tinordi | 4.00 | 1.80 |
| ❑ S221 Bob Probert | 15.00 | 6.75 |
| ❑ S222 Gino Odjick | 4.00 | 1.80 |
| ❑ S223 Ulf Samuelsson | 4.00 | 1.80 |
| ❑ S224 Stu Grimson | 4.00 | 1.80 |
| ❑ S225 Marty McSorley | 15.00 | 6.75 |
| ❑ *S97 W.Gretzky DC (234) | 1200.00 | 550.00 |

## 1995-96 Be A Player Gretzky's Great Memories

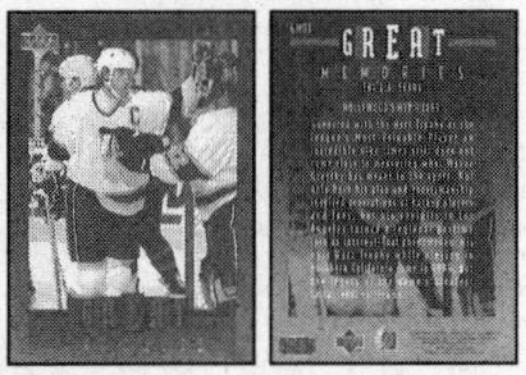

This ten-card set shines the spotlight on but a few of the many memorable happenstances in the career of Wayne Gretzky. The cards were randomly inserted at the rate of 1:15 packs.

| | MINT | NRMT |
|---|---|---|
| COMPLETE SET (10) | 100.00 | 45.00 |
| COMMON GRETZKY (GM1-GM10) | 10.00 | 4.50 |

| | | |
|---|---|---|
| ❑ GM1 The First Game in L.A. | 10.00 | 4.50 |
| ❑ GM2 Going Back to Edmonton | 10.00 | 4.50 |
| ❑ GM3 Hollywood's MVP | 10.00 | 4.50 |
| ❑ GM4 Point Number 1,851 | 10.00 | 4.50 |
| ❑ GM5 23-Game Assist Streak | 10.00 | 4.50 |
| ❑ GM6 Goal Number 802 | 10.00 | 4.50 |
| ❑ GM7 The Tenth Art Ross Trophy | 10.00 | 4.50 |
| ❑ GM8 Conference Champions | 10.00 | 4.50 |
| ❑ GM9 Stanley Cup Finalists | 10.00 | 4.50 |
| ❑ GM10 Reaching 2,500 Points | 10.00 | 4.50 |

## 1995-96 Be A Player Lethal Lines

Although the title may appear to be a misnomer for this set of single player cards, each one actually utilizes a unique die-cut format allowing a series of three players to be linked to form a "lethal line". The cards were inserted at a rate of 1:7 packs.

| | MINT | NRMT |
|---|---|---|
| COMPLETE SET (15) | 80.00 | 36.00 |
| COMMON CARD (LL1-LL15) | 3.00 | 1.35 |

| | | |
|---|---|---|
| ❑ LL1 Keith Tkachuk | 4.00 | 1.80 |
| ❑ LL2 Wayne Gretzky | 15.00 | 6.75 |
| ❑ LL3 Brett Hull | 4.00 | 1.80 |
| ❑ LL4 Eric Daze | 6.00 | 2.70 |
| ❑ LL5 Saku Koivu | 4.00 | 1.80 |
| ❑ LL6 Daniel Alfredsson | 6.00 | 2.70 |
| ❑ LL7 Pavel Bure | 5.00 | 2.20 |
| ❑ LL8 Sergei Fedorov | 5.00 | 2.20 |
| ❑ LL9 Alexander Mogilny | 6.00 | 2.70 |
| ❑ LL10 Paul Kariya | 10.00 | 4.50 |
| ❑ LL11 Mario Lemieux | 12.00 | 5.50 |
| ❑ LL12 Jaromir Jagr | 8.00 | 3.60 |
| ❑ LL13 Brendan Shanahan | 5.00 | 2.20 |
| ❑ LL14 Eric Lindros | 8.00 | 3.60 |
| ❑ LL15 Alexei Kovalev | 3.00 | 1.35 |

## 1996-97 Be A Player

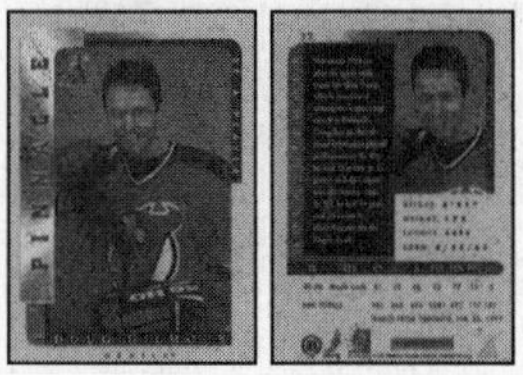

This 220-card set was issued by Pinnacle in two series and was distributed in eight-card packs with a suggested retail price of $6.99. For the first time, the series was licensed by the NHL, as well as the NHLPA, and thus the players were allowed to be seen in their own uniforms.The fronts feature color action player photos with white borders. Rookie cards in this set include Mike Grier and Kevin Hodson. Promotional cards were issued to dealers in six-card and two-card packs. These cards mirror those in the regular set save for the addition of the word PROMO written on the card back. The numbering, however, is the same as the base cards. The P prefix has been added for checklist purposes only.

| | MINT | NRMT |
|---|---|---|
| COMPLETE SET (220) | 30.00 | 13.50 |
| COMPLETE SERIES 1 (110) | 15.00 | 6.75 |
| COMPLETE SERIES 2 (110) | 15.00 | 6.75 |
| COMMON CARD (1-220) | .25 | .11 |

| | | |
|---|---|---|
| ❑ 1 Todd Gill | .25 | .11 |
| ❑ 2 Dave Andreychuk | .25 | .11 |
| ❑ 3 Igor Kravchuk | .25 | .11 |
| ❑ 4 Tom Fitzgerald | .25 | .11 |
| ❑ 5 Jeremy Roenick | .75 | .35 |
| ❑ 6 Peter Popovic | .25 | .11 |
| ❑ 7 Andy Moog | .60 | .25 |
| ❑ 8 Steven Rice | .25 | .11 |
| ❑ 9 Darren Langdon | .25 | .11 |
| ❑ 10 Mark Fitzpatrick | .50 | .23 |
| ❑ 11 Alexei Zhamnov | .50 | .23 |
| ❑ 12 Luc Robitaille | .60 | .25 |
| ❑ 13 Michal Pivonka | .25 | .11 |
| ❑ 14 Kevin Hatcher | .25 | .11 |
| ❑ 15 Stephane Yelle | .25 | .11 |
| ❑ 16 Bill Ranford | .60 | .25 |
| ❑ 17 Jamie Baker | .25 | .11 |
| ❑ 18 Sean Burke | .50 | .23 |
| ❑ 19 Al Iafrate | .25 | .11 |
| ❑ 20 Mark Recchi | .60 | .25 |
| ❑ 21 Rod Brind'Amour | .60 | .25 |
| ❑ 22 Doug Gilmour | .75 | .35 |
| ❑ 23 Mike Wilson | .25 | .11 |
| ❑ 24 Barry Potomski | .25 | .11 |
| ❑ 25 Mike Gartner | .60 | .25 |
| ❑ 26 Jason Wiemer | .25 | .11 |
| ❑ 27 Scott Lachance | .25 | .11 |
| ❑ 28 Joe Murphy | .25 | .11 |
| ❑ 29 Bill Guerin | .25 | .11 |
| ❑ 30 Byron Dafoe | .50 | .23 |
| ❑ 31 Esa Tikkanen | .25 | .11 |
| ❑ 32 Ken Baumgartner | .25 | .11 |
| ❑ 33 Valeri Kamensky | .60 | .25 |
| ❑ 34 J.J. Daigneault | .25 | .11 |
| ❑ 35 Ulf Dahlen | .25 | .11 |
| ❑ 36 Jason Allison | .25 | .11 |
| ❑ 37 Ted Donato | .25 | .11 |
| ❑ 38 Pat Verbeek | .25 | .11 |
| ❑ 39 Miroslav Satan | .25 | .11 |
| ❑ 40 Eric Desjardins | .25 | .11 |
| ❑ 41 Dave Karpa | .25 | .11 |
| ❑ 42 Jeff Hackett | .60 | .25 |
| ❑ 43 Doug Brown | .25 | .11 |
| ❑ 44 Gord Murphy | .25 | .11 |
| ❑ 45 Kelly Hrudey | .60 | .25 |
| ❑ 46 Kelly Miller | .25 | .11 |
| ❑ 47 Tie Domi | .25 | .11 |
| ❑ 48 Alexei Yashin | .60 | .25 |
| ❑ 49 German Titov | .25 | .11 |
| ❑ 50 Stephane Richer | .50 | .23 |
| ❑ 51 Corey Hirsch | .60 | .25 |
| ❑ 52 Brad May | .60 | .25 |
| ❑ 53 Joe Nieuwendyk | .60 | .25 |
| ❑ 54 Sylvain Lefebvre | .25 | .11 |
| ❑ 55 Brian Leetch | .75 | .35 |
| ❑ 56 Petr Svoboda | .25 | .11 |
| ❑ 57 Dave Manson | .25 | .11 |
| ❑ 58 Jason Woolley | .25 | .11 |
| ❑ 59 Scott Niedermayer | .25 | .11 |
| ❑ 60 Kelly Chase | .25 | .11 |
| ❑ 61 Guy Hebert | .60 | .25 |
| ❑ 62 Shayne Corson | .25 | .11 |
| ❑ 63 Jon Casey | .50 | .23 |
| ❑ 64 Rob Zettler | .25 | .11 |
| ❑ 65 Mikael Andersson | .25 | .11 |
| ❑ 66 Tony Amonte | .60 | .25 |
| ❑ 67 Johan Garpenlov | .25 | .11 |
| ❑ 68 Denny Lambert | .25 | .11 |
| ❑ 69 Jim McKenzie | .25 | .11 |
| ❑ 70 Darren Turcotte | .25 | .11 |
| ❑ 71 Eric Weinrich | .25 | .11 |
| ❑ 72 Troy Mallette | .25 | .11 |
| ❑ 73 Donald Audette | .25 | .11 |
| ❑ 74 Philippe Boucher | .25 | .11 |
| ❑ 75 Shawn Chambers | .25 | .11 |
| ❑ 76 Joel Otto | .25 | .11 |
| ❑ 77 Tommy Salo | .50 | .23 |
| ❑ 78 Olaf Kolzig | .50 | .23 |
| ❑ 79 Adrian Aucoin | .25 | .11 |
| ❑ 80 Alek Stojanov | .25 | .11 |
| ❑ 81 Robert Reichel | .25 | .11 |
| ❑ 82 Marc Bureau | .25 | .11 |
| ❑ 83 Alexander Godynyuk | .25 | .11 |
| ❑ 84 Bill Berg | .25 | .11 |
| ❑ 85 Marc Bergevin | .25 | .11 |
| ❑ 86 Kevin Kaminski | .25 | .11 |
| ❑ 87 Uwe Krupp | .25 | .11 |
| ❑ 88 Boris Mironov | .25 | .11 |
| ❑ 89 Bob Bassen | .25 | .11 |
| ❑ 90 Darryl Shannon | .25 | .11 |
| ❑ 91 Mikael Renberg | .60 | .25 |
| ❑ 92 Mike Stapleton | .25 | .11 |
| ❑ 93 David Roberts | .25 | .11 |
| ❑ 94 Peter Zezel | .25 | .11 |
| ❑ 95 Mathieu Dandenault | .25 | .11 |
| ❑ 96 Bobby Dollas | .25 | .11 |
| ❑ 97 Don Sweeney | .25 | .11 |
| ❑ 98 Niklas Andersson | .25 | .11 |
| ❑ 99 Pat Jablonski | .50 | .23 |
| ❑ 100 John Slaney | .25 | .11 |
| ❑ 101 Kevin Todd | .25 | .11 |
| ❑ 102 Jamie Pushor | .25 | .11 |
| ❑ 103 Andreas Johansson | .25 | .11 |
| ❑ 104 Corey Schwab | .50 | .23 |
| ❑ 105 Todd Simpson | .25 | .11 |
| ❑ 106 Landon Wilson | .25 | .11 |
| ❑ 107 Daniel Goneau | .50 | .23 |
| ❑ 108 David Wilkie | .25 | .11 |
| ❑ 109 Andreas Dackell | .25 | .11 |
| ❑ 110 Marek Malik | .25 | .11 |
| ❑ 111 Mark Messier | .75 | .35 |
| ❑ 112 Francois Leroux | .25 | .11 |
| ❑ 113 Michal Sykora | .25 | .11 |
| ❑ 114 Rob Zamuner | .25 | .11 |
| ❑ 115 Craig Berube | .25 | .11 |
| ❑ 116 Mike Ricci | .25 | .11 |
| ❑ 117 Adam Burt | .25 | .11 |
| ❑ 118 Alexander Karpovtsev | .25 | .11 |
| ❑ 119 Shawn McEachern | .25 | .11 |
| ❑ 120 Shawn Antoski | .25 | .11 |
| ❑ 121 Dave Reid | .25 | .11 |
| ❑ 122 Todd Warriner | .25 | .11 |
| ❑ 123 Markus Naslund | .25 | .11 |
| ❑ 124 Martin Rucinsky | .25 | .11 |
| ❑ 125 Bob Carpenter | .25 | .11 |
| ❑ 126 Dean McAmmond | .25 | .11 |
| ❑ 127 Trevor Kidd | .60 | .25 |
| ❑ 128 Martin Lapointe | .25 | .11 |
| ❑ 129 Enrico Ciccone | .25 | .11 |
| ❑ 130 Dixon Ward | .25 | .11 |
| ❑ 131 Jason Muzzatti | .50 | .23 |
| ❑ 132 Bryan Smolinski | .25 | .11 |
| ❑ 133 Norm Maciver | .25 | .11 |
| ❑ 134 Fredrik Olausson | .25 | .11 |
| ❑ 135 Daniel Lacroix | .25 | .11 |
| ❑ 136 Mike Peluso | .25 | .11 |
| ❑ 137 Andrei Nikolishin | .25 | .11 |
| ❑ 138 Rhett Warrener | .25 | .11 |
| ❑ 139 Ray Ferraro | .25 | .11 |
| ❑ 140 Glenn Healy | .50 | .23 |
| ❑ 141 Steve Duchesne | .25 | .11 |
| ❑ 142 Tony Granato | .25 | .11 |
| ❑ 143 Cory Cross | .25 | .11 |
| ❑ 144 Jon Klemm | .25 | .11 |
| ❑ 145 Sami Kapanen | .25 | .11 |
| ❑ 146 Grant Marshall | .25 | .11 |
| ❑ 147 Matthew Barnaby | .25 | .11 |
| ❑ 148 Lyle Odelein | .25 | .11 |
| ❑ 149 Joe Dziedzic | .25 | .11 |
| ❑ 150 Sergei Gonchar | .25 | .11 |
| ❑ 151 Doug Zmolek | .25 | .11 |
| ❑ 152 Sean O'Donnell | .25 | .11 |
| ❑ 153 Scott Thornton | .25 | .11 |
| ❑ 154 Steve Heinze | .25 | .11 |
| ❑ 155 Garry Valk | .25 | .11 |
| ❑ 156 Jeff Finley | .25 | .11 |
| ❑ 157 Trent Klatt | .25 | .11 |
| ❑ 158 Jeff Beukeboom | .25 | .11 |
| ❑ 159 Theoren Fleury | .60 | .25 |
| ❑ 160 Dana Murzyn | .25 | .11 |
| ❑ 161 Tommy Albelin | .50 | .23 |
| ❑ 162 Bryan McCabe | .25 | .11 |
| ❑ 163 Shaun Van Allen | .25 | .11 |
| ❑ 164 Rick Tabaracci | .50 | .23 |
| ❑ 165 Kevin Miller | .25 | .11 |
| ❑ 166 Mariusz Czerkawski | .25 | .11 |
| ❑ 167 Gerald Diduck | .25 | .11 |
| ❑ 168 Brad McCrimmon | .25 | .11 |
| ❑ 169 Stephane Matteau | .25 | .11 |
| ❑ 170 Scott Daniels | .25 | .11 |
| ❑ 171 Scott Mellanby | .50 | .23 |
| ❑ 172 Sandy Moger | .25 | .11 |
| ❑ 173 Steve Konowalchuk | .25 | .11 |
| ❑ 174 Doug Weight | .60 | .25 |
| ❑ 175 Darren McCarty | .25 | .11 |
| ❑ 176 Darryl Sydor | .25 | .11 |
| ❑ 177 Dave Ellett | .25 | .11 |
| ❑ 178 Bob Boughner | .25 | .11 |
| ❑ 179 Derek Armstrong | .25 | .11 |
| ❑ 180 Gary Suter | .25 | .11 |
| ❑ 181 Donald Brashear | .25 | .11 |
| ❑ 182 Chris Tamer | .25 | .11 |
| ❑ 183 Darrin Shannon | .25 | .11 |
| ❑ 184 Stanislav Neckar | .25 | .11 |
| ❑ 185 Brent Severyn | .25 | .11 |
| ❑ 186 Steve Rucchin | .25 | .11 |
| ❑ 187 Jeff Norton | .25 | .11 |
| ❑ 188 Steven Finn | .25 | .11 |
| ❑ 189 Kjell Samuelsson | .25 | .11 |
| ❑ 190 Jeff Friesen | .50 | .23 |
| ❑ 191 Shawn Burr | .25 | .11 |
| ❑ 192 Paul Laus | .25 | .11 |
| ❑ 193 Jeff Odgers | .25 | .11 |
| ❑ 194 Keith Jones | .25 | .11 |
| ❑ 195 Richard Matvichuk | .25 | .11 |
| ❑ 196 Adam Foote | .25 | .11 |
| ❑ 197 Bob Errey | .25 | .11 |
| ❑ 198 Ryan Smyth | .60 | .25 |
| ❑ 199 Mark Janssens | .25 | .11 |
| ❑ 200 Claude Lapointe | .25 | .11 |
| ❑ 201 Brian Noonan | .25 | .11 |
| ❑ 202 Damian Rhodes | .50 | .23 |
| ❑ 203 Dale Hawerchuk | .60 | .25 |
| ❑ 204 Bill Lindsay | .25 | .11 |
| ❑ 205 Brian Skrudland | .25 | .11 |
| ❑ 206 Curtis Joseph | .75 | .35 |
| ❑ 207 Jon Rohloff | .25 | .11 |
| ❑ 208 Doug Bodger | .25 | .11 |
| ❑ 209 Steve Sullivan | .50 | .23 |
| ❑ 210 Ricard Persson | .25 | .11 |
| ❑ 211 Dwayne Roloson | .50 | .23 |
| ❑ 212 Mike Dunham | .60 | .25 |
| ❑ 213 Marcel Cousineau | .25 | .11 |
| ❑ 214 Eric Fichaud | .60 | .25 |
| ❑ 215 Matt Johnson | .25 | .11 |
| ❑ 216 Fredrik Modin | .50 | .23 |
| ❑ 217 Denis Pederson | .25 | .11 |
| ❑ 218 Kevin Hodson | .60 | .25 |
| ❑ 219 Drew Bannister | .25 | .11 |
| ❑ 220 Mike Grier | 1.25 | .55 |
| ❑ P52 Brad May promo | .50 | .23 |
| ❑ P55 Brian Leetch promo | 2.00 | .90 |
| ❑ P89 Bob Bassen promo | .50 | .23 |
| ❑ P91 Mikael Renberg promo | 2.00 | .90 |
| ❑ P176 Darryl Sydor promo | .50 | .23 |
| ❑ P217 Denis Pederson promo | .50 | .23 |
| ❑ P218 Kevin Hodson promo | 2.00 | .90 |
| ❑ P219 Drew Bannister promo | .50 | .23 |

## 1996-97 Be A Player Autographs

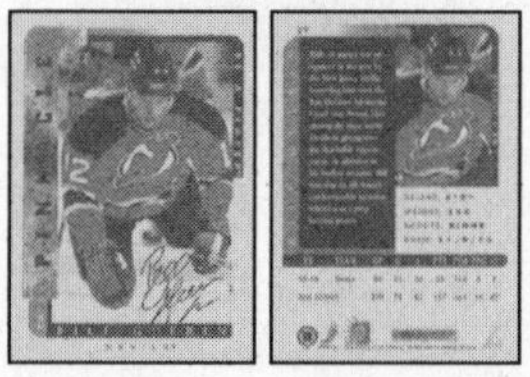

Randomly inserted one per Series 1 and Series 2 pack, cards from this 219-card issue parallel the regular set. Gold foil and an autograph distinguish these cards from their regular counterparts. Alexei Zhamnov has a regular card, but no autographed version exists; the set is considered complete without it at 219 cards. A silver parallel version of the autograph set exists as well. The cards are distinguishable by the silver foil backing on the card fronts. Although no odds were published, these cards were inserted at a rate of about 1:30 packs.

| | MINT | NRMT |
|---|---|---|
| COMPLETE SET (219) | 1000.00 | 450.00 |
| COMMON CARD | 4.00 | 1.80 |
| COMP.SILVER SET (219) | 2500.00 | 1100.00 |
| COMMON SILVER | 8.00 | 3.60 |

*SILVER AU's: 1X TO 2X BASIC CARDS

| | | |
|---|---|---|
| ❑ 1 Todd Gill | 4.00 | 1.80 |
| ❑ 2 Dave Andreychuk | 4.00 | 1.80 |
| ❑ 3 Igor Kravchuk | 4.00 | 1.80 |
| ❑ 4 Tom Fitzgerald | 4.00 | 1.80 |
| ❑ 5 Jeremy Roenick | 25.00 | 11.00 |
| ❑ 6 Peter Popovic | 4.00 | 1.80 |
| ❑ 7 Andy Moog | 20.00 | 9.00 |
| ❑ 8 Steven Rice | 4.00 | 1.80 |
| ❑ 9 Darren Langdon | 4.00 | 1.80 |
| ❑ 10 Mark Fitzpatrick | 10.00 | 4.50 |
| ❑ 12 Luc Robitaille | 4.00 | 1.80 |
| ❑ 13 Michal Pivonka | 4.00 | 1.80 |
| ❑ 14 Kevin Hatcher | 4.00 | 1.80 |
| ❑ 15 Stephane Yelle | 4.00 | 1.80 |
| ❑ 16 Bill Ranford | 4.00 | 1.80 |
| ❑ 17 Jamie Baker | 4.00 | 1.80 |
| ❑ 18 Sean Burke | 10.00 | 4.50 |
| ❑ 19 Al Iafrate | 4.00 | 1.80 |
| ❑ 20 Mark Recchi | 4.00 | 1.80 |
| ❑ 21 Rob Brind'Amour | 4.00 | 1.80 |
| ❑ 22 Doug Gilmour | 25.00 | 11.00 |
| ❑ 23 Mike Wilson | 4.00 | 1.80 |
| ❑ 24 Barry Potomski | 4.00 | 1.80 |
| ❑ 25 Mike Gartner | 4.00 | 1.80 |
| ❑ 26 Jason Wiemer | 4.00 | 1.80 |
| ❑ 27 Scott Lachance | 4.00 | 1.80 |
| ❑ 28 Joe Murphy | 4.00 | 1.80 |
| ❑ 29 Bill Guerin | 4.00 | 1.80 |
| ❑ 30 Byron Dafoe | 10.00 | 4.50 |
| ❑ 31 Esa Tikkanen | 10.00 | 4.50 |
| ❑ 32 Ken Baumgartner | 4.00 | 1.80 |
| ❑ 34 J.J. Daigneault | 4.00 | 1.80 |
| ❑ 35 Ulf Dahlen | 4.00 | 1.80 |
| ❑ 36 Jason Allison | 6.00 | 2.70 |
| ❑ 37 Ted Donato | 4.00 | 1.80 |
| ❑ 38 Pat Verbeek | 4.00 | 1.80 |
| ❑ 39 Miroslav Satan | 4.00 | 1.80 |
| ❑ 40 Eric Desjardins | 4.00 | 1.80 |
| ❑ 41 Dave Karpa | 4.00 | 1.80 |
| ❑ 42 Jeff Hackett | 10.00 | 4.50 |
| ❑ 43 Doug Brown | 4.00 | 1.80 |
| ❑ 44 Gord Murphy | 4.00 | 1.80 |
| ❑ 45 Kelly Hrudey | 4.00 | 1.80 |
| ❑ 46 Kelly Miller | 4.00 | 1.80 |
| ❑ 47 Tie Domi | 10.00 | 4.50 |
| ❑ 48 Alexei Yashin | 4.00 | 1.80 |
| ❑ 49 German Titov | 4.00 | 1.80 |
| ❑ 50 Stephane Richer | 4.00 | 1.80 |
| ❑ 51 Corey Hirsch | 8.00 | 3.60 |
| ❑ 52 Brad May | 8.00 | 3.60 |
| ❑ 53 Joe Nieuwendyk | 10.00 | 4.50 |
| ❑ 54 Sylvain Lefebvre | 4.00 | 1.80 |
| ❑ 55 Brian Leetch | 25.00 | 11.00 |
| ❑ 56 Petr Svoboda | 4.00 | 1.80 |
| ❑ 57 Dave Manson | 4.00 | 1.80 |
| ❑ 58 Jason Woolley | 4.00 | 1.80 |
| ❑ 59 Scott Niedermayer | 4.00 | 1.80 |
| ❑ 60 Kelly Chase | 4.00 | 1.80 |
| ❑ 61 Guy Hebert | 4.00 | 1.80 |
| ❑ 62 Shayne Corson | 4.00 | 1.80 |
| ❑ 63 Jon Casey | 10.00 | 4.50 |
| ❑ 64 Rob Zettler | 4.00 | 1.80 |
| ❑ 65 Mikael Andersson | 4.00 | 1.80 |
| ❑ 66 Tony Amonte | 4.00 | 1.80 |
| ❑ 67 Johan Garpenlov | 4.00 | 1.80 |
| ❑ 68 Denny Lambert | 4.00 | 1.80 |
| ❑ 69 Jim McKenzie | 4.00 | 1.80 |
| ❑ 70 Darren Turcotte | 4.00 | 1.80 |
| ❑ 71 Eric Weinrich | 4.00 | 1.80 |
| ❑ 72 Troy Mallette | 4.00 | 1.80 |
| ❑ 73 Donald Audette | 10.00 | 4.50 |
| ❑ 74 Philippe Boucher | 4.00 | 1.80 |
| ❑ 75 Shawn Chambers | 4.00 | 1.80 |
| ❑ 76 Joel Otto | 4.00 | 1.80 |
| ❑ 77 Tommy Salo | 10.00 | 4.50 |
| ❑ 78 Olaf Kolzig | 20.00 | 9.00 |
| ❑ 79 Adrian Aucoin | 4.00 | 1.80 |
| ❑ 80 Alek Stojanov | 4.00 | 1.80 |
| ❑ 81 Robert Reichel | 6.00 | 2.70 |
| ❑ 82 Marc Bureau | 4.00 | 1.80 |
| ❑ 83 Alexander Godynyuk | 4.00 | 1.80 |
| ❑ 84 Bill Berg | 4.00 | 1.80 |
| ❑ 85 Marc Bergevin | 4.00 | 1.80 |
| ❑ 86 Kevin Kaminski | 4.00 | 1.80 |
| ❑ 87 Uwe Krupp | 4.00 | 1.80 |
| ❑ 88 Boris Mironov | 4.00 | 1.80 |
| ❑ 89 Bob Bassen | 4.00 | 1.80 |
| ❑ 90 Darryl Shannon | 4.00 | 1.80 |
| ❑ 91 Mikael Renberg | 4.00 | 1.80 |
| ❑ 92 Mike Stapleton | 4.00 | 1.80 |
| ❑ 93 David Roberts | 4.00 | 1.80 |
| ❑ 94 Peter Zezel | 4.00 | 1.80 |
| ❑ 95 Mathieu Dandenault | 4.00 | 1.80 |
| ❑ 96 Bobby Dollas | 4.00 | 1.80 |
| ❑ 97 Don Sweeney | 4.00 | 1.80 |
| ❑ 98 Niklas Andersson | 4.00 | 1.80 |
| ❑ 99 Pat Jablonski | 8.00 | 3.60 |
| ❑ 100 John Slaney | 4.00 | 1.80 |
| ❑ 101 Kevin Todd | 4.00 | 1.80 |
| ❑ 102 Jamie Pushor | 4.00 | 1.80 |
| ❑ 103 Andreas Johansson | 4.00 | 1.80 |
| ❑ 104 Corey Schwab | 4.00 | 1.80 |
| ❑ 105 Todd Simpson | 4.00 | 1.80 |
| ❑ 106 Landon Wilson | 4.00 | 1.80 |
| ❑ 107 Daniel Goneau | 10.00 | 4.50 |
| ❑ 108 David Wilkie | 4.00 | 1.80 |
| ❑ 109 Andreas Dackell | 4.00 | 1.80 |
| ❑ 110 Marek Malik | 4.00 | 1.80 |
| ❑ 111 Mark Messier | 60.00 | 27.00 |
| ❑ 112 Francois Leroux | 4.00 | 1.80 |
| ❑ 113 Michal Sykora | 4.00 | 1.80 |
| ❑ 114 Rob Zamuner | 4.00 | 1.80 |
| ❑ 115 Craig Berube | 4.00 | 1.80 |
| ❑ 116 Mike Ricci | 8.00 | 3.60 |
| ❑ 117 Adam Burt | 4.00 | 1.80 |
| ❑ 118 Alexander Karpovtsev | 4.00 | 1.80 |
| ❑ 119 Shawn McEachern | 4.00 | 1.80 |
| ❑ 120 Shawn Antoski | 4.00 | 1.80 |
| ❑ 121 Dave Reid | 4.00 | 1.80 |
| ❑ 122 Todd Warriner | 4.00 | 1.80 |
| ❑ 123 Markus Naslund | 4.00 | 1.80 |
| ❑ 124 Martin Rucinsky | 4.00 | 1.80 |
| ❑ 125 Bob Carpenter | 4.00 | 1.80 |
| ❑ 126 Dean McAmmond | 4.00 | 1.80 |
| ❑ 127 Trevor Kidd | 10.00 | 4.50 |
| ❑ 128 Martin Lapointe | 4.00 | 1.80 |
| ❑ 129 Enrico Ciccone | 4.00 | 1.80 |
| ❑ 130 Dixon Ward | 4.00 | 1.80 |
| ❑ 131 Jason Muzzatti | 8.00 | 3.60 |
| ❑ 132 Bryan Smolinski | 4.00 | 1.80 |
| ❑ 133 Norm Maciver | 4.00 | 1.80 |
| ❑ 134 Fredrik Olausson | 4.00 | 1.80 |
| ❑ 135 Daniel Lacroix | 4.00 | 1.80 |
| ❑ 136 Mike Peluso | 4.00 | 1.80 |
| ❑ 137 Andrei Nikolishin | 4.00 | 1.80 |
| ❑ 138 Rhett Warrener | 4.00 | 1.80 |
| ❑ 139 Ray Ferraro | 4.00 | 1.80 |
| ❑ 140 Glenn Healy | 4.00 | 1.80 |
| ❑ 141 Steve Duchesne | 4.00 | 1.80 |
| ❑ 142 Tony Granato | 4.00 | 1.80 |
| ❑ 143 Cory Cross | 4.00 | 1.80 |
| ❑ 144 Jon Klemm | 4.00 | 1.80 |
| ❑ 145 Sami Kapanen | 4.00 | 1.80 |
| ❑ 146 Grant Marshall | 4.00 | 1.80 |
| ❑ 147 Matthew Barnaby | 10.00 | 4.50 |
| ❑ 148 Lyle Odelein | 4.00 | 1.80 |
| ❑ 149 Joe Dziedzic | 4.00 | 1.80 |
| ❑ 150 Sergei Gonchar | 4.00 | 1.80 |
| ❑ 151 Doug Zmolek | 4.00 | 1.80 |
| ❑ 152 Sean O'Donnell | 4.00 | 1.80 |
| ❑ 153 Scott Thornton | 4.00 | 1.80 |
| ❑ 154 Steve Heinze | 4.00 | 1.80 |
| ❑ 155 Garry Valk | 4.00 | 1.80 |
| ❑ 156 Jeff Finley | 4.00 | 1.80 |

❑ 157 Trent Klatt 4.00 1.80
❑ 158 Jeff Beukeboom 4.00 1.80
❑ 159 Theoren Fleury 4.00 1.80
❑ 160 Dana Murzyn 4.00 1.80
❑ 161 Tommy Albelin 4.00 1.80
❑ 162 Bryan McCabe 4.00 1.80
❑ 163 Shaun Van Allen 4.00 1.80
❑ 164 Rick Tabaracci 8.00 3.60
❑ 165 Kevin Miller 4.00 1.80
❑ 166 Mariusz Czerkawski 4.00 1.80
❑ 167 Gerald Diduck 4.00 1.80
❑ 168 Brad McCrimmon 4.00 1.80
❑ 169 Stephane Matteau 4.00 1.80
❑ 170 Scott Daniels 4.00 1.80
❑ 171 Scott Mellanby 8.00 3.60
❑ 172 Sandy Moger 4.00 1.80
❑ 173 Steve Konowalchuk 4.00 1.80
❑ 174 Doug Weight 15.00 6.75
❑ 175 Darren McCarty 10.00 4.50
❑ 176 Darryl Sydor 4.00 1.80
❑ 177 Dave Ellett 4.00 1.80
❑ 178 Bob Boughner 4.00 1.80
❑ 179 Derek Armstrong 4.00 1.80
❑ 180 Gary Suter 4.00 1.80
❑ 181 Donald Brashear 4.00 1.80
❑ 182 Chris Tamer 4.00 1.80
❑ 183 Darrin Shannon 4.00 1.80
❑ 184 Stanislav Neckar 4.00 1.80
❑ 185 Brent Severyn 4.00 1.80
❑ 186 Steve Rucchin 8.00 3.60
❑ 187 Jeff Norton 4.00 1.80
❑ 188 Steven Finn 4.00 1.80
❑ 189 Kjell Samuelsson 4.00 1.80
❑ 190 Jeff Friesen 10.00 4.50
❑ 191 Shawn Burr 4.00 1.80
❑ 192 Paul Laus 4.00 1.80
❑ 193 Jeff Odgers 4.00 1.80
❑ 194 Keith Jones 8.00 3.60
❑ 195 Richard Matvichuk 4.00 1.80
❑ 196 Adam Foote 4.00 1.80
❑ 197 Bob Errey 4.00 1.80
❑ 198 Ryan Smyth 4.00 1.80
❑ 199 Mark Janssens 4.00 1.80
❑ 200 Claude Lapointe 4.00 1.80
❑ 201 Brian Noonan 4.00 1.80
❑ 202 Damian Rhodes 10.00 4.50
❑ 203 Dale Hawerchuk 10.00 4.50
❑ 204 Bill Lindsay 4.00 1.80
❑ 205 Brian Skrudland 4.00 1.80
❑ 206 Curtis Joseph 25.00 11.00
❑ 207 Jon Rohloff 4.00 1.80
❑ 208 Doug Bodger 4.00 1.80
❑ 209 Steve Sullivan 6.00 2.70
❑ 210 Ricard Persson 4.00 1.80
❑ 211 Dwayne Roloson 8.00 3.60
❑ 212 Mike Dunham 10.00 4.50
❑ 213 Marcel Cousineau 8.00 3.60
❑ 214 Eric Fichaud 4.00 1.80
❑ 215 Matt Johnson 4.00 1.80
❑ 216 Fredrik Modin 6.00 2.70
❑ 217 Denis Pederson 4.00 1.80
❑ 218 Kevin Hodson 10.00 4.50
❑ 219 Drew Bannister 4.00 1.80
❑ 220 Mike Grier 4.00 1.80

## 1996-97 Be A Player Biscuit In The Basket

Randomly inserted in series 1 and 2 packs at a rate of one in 17, this 25-card set features color photos of the top scorers in the league captured on Pinnacle's exclusive all-foil Dufex print technology. The backs carry a small player head shot along with player information.

| | MINT | NRMT |
|---|---|---|
| COMPLETE SET (25) | 200.00 | 90.00 |
| COMMON CARD (1-25) | 3.00 | 1.35 |

❑ 1 Wayne Gretzky 25.00 11.00
❑ 2 Mario Lemieux 20.00 9.00
❑ 3 Eric Lindros 12.00 5.50
❑ 4 Theoren Fleury 4.00 1.80
❑ 5 Peter Forsberg 12.00 5.50
❑ 6 Keith Tkachuk 5.00 2.20
❑ 7 Sergei Fedorov 8.00 3.60
❑ 8 Mike Modano 5.00 2.20
❑ 9 Jaromir Jagr 12.00 5.50
❑ 10 Brendan Shanahan 8.00 3.60
❑ 11 Teemu Selanne 8.00 3.60
❑ 12 Mats Sundin 4.00 1.80
❑ 13 Steve Yzerman 12.00 5.50
❑ 14 Brett Hull 5.00 2.20
❑ 15 Zigmund Palffy 4.00 1.80
❑ 16 Joe Sakic 8.00 3.60
❑ 17 John LeClair 6.00 2.70
❑ 18 Pavel Bure 8.00 3.60
❑ 19 Mark Messier 5.00 2.20
❑ 20 Paul Kariya 15.00 6.75
❑ 21 Jason Arnott 3.00 1.35
❑ 22 Saku Koivu 6.00 2.70
❑ 23 Daniel Alfredsson 3.00 1.35
❑ 24 Alexander Mogilny 3.00 1.35
❑ 25 Owen Nolan 3.00 1.35

## 1996-97 Be A Player Link to History

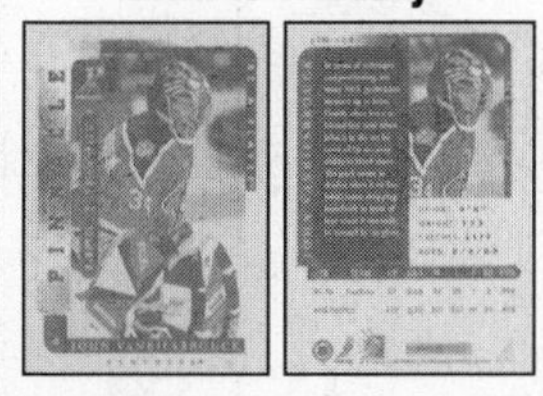

Randomly inserted at an approximate rate of 1:2 packs, cards from this 20-card set feature ten top rookie standouts matched with their 10 mega-star veteran counterparts. The first five rookie "Links" appeared in series 1 with the second five veteran "Links" and featured silver foil with blue accents. The second five rookie "Links" appeared in series 2 with the first five veteran "Links" and featured silver foil with red accents.

| | MINT | NRMT |
|---|---|---|
| COMPLETE SET (20) | 30.00 | 13.50 |
| COMPLETE SERIES 1 (10) | 15.00 | 6.75 |
| COMPLETE SERIES 2 (10) | 15.00 | 6.75 |
| COMMON CARD (1A-10B) | .50 | .23 |

❑ 1A Jarome Iginla 1.00 .45
❑ 1B Teemu Selanne 2.00 .90
❑ 2A Harry York .50 .23
❑ 2B Peter Forsberg 3.00 1.35
❑ 3A Sergei Berezin 1.00 .45
❑ 3B Brendan Shanahan 2.00 .90
❑ 4A Ethan Moreau 1.00 .45
❑ 4B Pavel Bure 2.00 .90
❑ 5A Rem Murray .50 .23
❑ 5B Jason Arnott 1.00 .45
❑ 6A Jamie Langenbrunner .50 .23
❑ 6B Paul Kariya 4.00 1.80
❑ 7A Jim Campbell 1.00 .45
❑ 7B Eric Lindros 4.00 1.80
❑ 8A Jonas Hoglund .50 .23
❑ 8B Pat LaFontaine 1.00 .45
❑ 9A Wade Redden 1.00 .45
❑ 9B Steve Yzerman 3.00 1.35
❑ 10A Patrick Lalime 1.00 .45
❑ 10B John Vanbiesbrouck 1.50 .70

## 1996-97 Be A Player Link to History Autographs

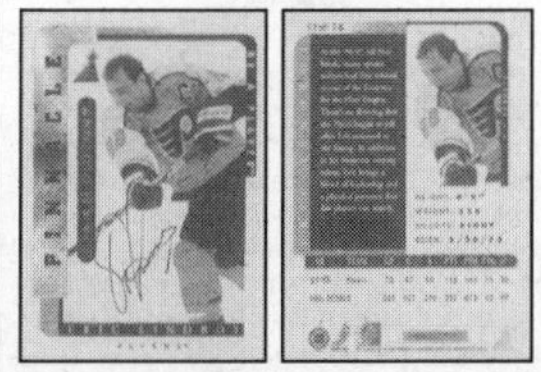

An authentic autograph and gold foil on each card front make these parallel cards easy to identify from their more common Link to History counterparts. Exact odds per pack were not released, but they're significantly tougher to pull than the non-autographed cards. Because of a delayed return, Ethan Moreau's cards were inserted in series 2 packs only; Teemu Selanne's autographed cards replaced them in series 1 packs. A silver parallel version of the autograph set exists as well. The cards are distinguishable by the silver foil backing on the card fronts. Although no odds were published, these cards were inserted at a rate of about 1:30 packs.

| | MINT | NRMT |
|---|---|---|
| COMPLETE SET (20) | 500.00 | 220.00 |
| COMMON CARD (1A-10B) | 8.00 | 3.60 |
| COMP.SILVER SET (20) | 1200.00 | 550.00 |
| COMMON SILVER (1A-10B) | 20.00 | 9.00 |

*SILVER AUs: 1X TO 2X BASIC CARDS

❑ 1A Jarome Iginla 15.00 6.75
❑ 1B Teemu Selanne 30.00 13.50
❑ 2A Harry York 8.00 3.60
❑ 2B Peter Forsberg 60.00 27.00
❑ 3A Sergei Berezin 15.00 6.75
❑ 3B Brendan Shanahan 50.00 22.00
❑ 4A Ethan Moreau 8.00 3.60
❑ 4B Pavel Bure 30.00 13.50
❑ 5A Rem Murray 8.00 3.60
❑ 5B Jason Arnott 15.00 6.75
❑ 6A Jamie Langenbrunner 8.00 3.60
❑ 6B Paul Kariya 60.00 27.00
❑ 7A Jim Campbell 8.00 3.60
❑ 7B Eric Lindros 50.00 22.00
❑ 8A Jonas Hoglund 8.00 3.60
❑ 8B Pat LaFontaine 15.00 6.75
❑ 9A Wade Redden 8.00 3.60
❑ 9B Steve Yzerman 60.00 27.00
❑ 10A Patrick Lalime 15.00 6.75
❑ 10B John Vanbiesbrouck 30.00 13.50

## 1996-97 Be A Player Stacking the Pads

Randomly inserted in series 1 and 2 packs at a rate of one in 35, this 15-card set honors the league's top goalies. Utilizing Pinnacle's Dufex all-foil print technology, the fronts feature color action player photos in a white border. The backs carry another photo and player information.

| | MINT | NRMT |
|---|---|---|
| COMPLETE SET (15) | 250.00 | 110.00 |
| COMMON CARD (1-15) | 8.00 | 3.60 |

❑ 1 Patrick Lalime 10.00 4.50
❑ 2 Chris Osgood 15.00 6.75
❑ 3 Ron Hextall 8.00 3.60
❑ 4 John Vanbiesbrouck 15.00 6.75
❑ 5 Martin Brodeur 25.00 11.00
❑ 6 Felix Potvin 15.00 6.75
❑ 7 Nikolai Khabibulin 8.00 3.60
❑ 8 Jim Carey 15.00 6.75
❑ 9 Grant Fuhr 8.00 3.60
❑ 10 Mike Richter 15.00 6.75
❑ 11 Dominik Hasek 20.00 9.00
❑ 12 Andy Moog 8.00 3.60
❑ 13 Patrick Roy 50.00 22.00
❑ 14 Curtis Joseph 15.00 6.75
❑ 15 Jocelyn Thibault 15.00 6.75

## 1997-98 Be A Player

The 1997-98 Be A Player set was issued by Pinnacle in two series totalling 250 cards and was distributed in eight-card packs with a suggested retail price of $6.99. The fronts feature color action photos of players with a heavy emphasis on rookies and Calder Trophy candidates in a white and net-shadow border. The backs carry a head photo with player information and career statistics.

| | MINT | NRMT |
|---|---|---|
| COMPLETE SET (250) | 30.00 | 13.50 |
| COMMON CARD (1-250) | .25 | .11 |

❑ 1 Eric Lindros 2.00 .90
❑ 2 Martin Brodeur 1.50 .70
❑ 3 Saku Koivu 1.00 .45
❑ 4 Felix Potvin .60 .25
❑ 5 Adam Oates .50 .23
❑ 6 Rob DiMaio .25 .11
❑ 7 Jari Kurri .50 .23
❑ 8 Andrew Cassels .25 .11
❑ 9 Trevor Linden .50 .23
❑ 10 Jocelyn Thibault .50 .23
❑ 11 Chris Chelios .60 .25
❑ 12 Paul Coffey .60 .25
❑ 13 Nikolai Khabibulin .50 .23
❑ 14 Robert Lang .25 .11
❑ 15 Brett Hull .75 .35
❑ 16 Mike Sillinger .25 .11
❑ 17 Lyle Odelein .25 .11
❑ 18 Bryan Berard .25 .11
❑ 19 Craig Muni .25 .11
❑ 20 Kris Draper .25 .11
❑ 21 Ed Jovanovski .50 .23
❑ 22 Keith Tkachuk .75 .35
❑ 23 Dean Malkoc .25 .11
❑ 24 Cory Stillman .25 .11
❑ 25 Chris Osgood .60 .25
❑ 26 Dainius Zubrus .25 .11
❑ 27 Yves Racine .25 .11
❑ 28 Eric Cairns RC .25 .11
❑ 29 Dan Bylsma .25 .11
❑ 30 Chris Terreri .25 .11
❑ 31 Bill Huard .25 .11
❑ 32 Warren Rychel .25 .11
❑ 33 Scott Walker .25 .11
❑ 34 Brian Holzinger .25 .11
❑ 35 Roman Turek .50 .23
❑ 36 Ron Tugnutt .50 .23
❑ 37 Mike Richter .60 .25
❑ 38 Mattias Norstrom .25 .11
❑ 39 Joe Sacco .25 .11
❑ 40 Derek King .25 .11
❑ 41 Brad Werenka .25 .11
❑ 42 Paul Kruse .25 .11
❑ 43 Mike Knuble .25 .11
❑ 44 Mike Peca .25 .11
❑ 45 Jean-Yves Leroux .25 .11
❑ 46 Ray Sheppard .25 .11
❑ 47 Reid Simpson .25 .11
❑ 48 Rob Brown .25 .11
❑ 49 Dave Babych .25 .11
❑ 50 Scott Pellerin .25 .11
❑ 51 Bruce Gardiner .25 .11
❑ 52 Adam Deadmarsh .50 .23
❑ 53 Curtis Brown .25 .11
❑ 54 Jason Marshall .25 .11
❑ 55 Gerald Diduck .25 .11
❑ 56 Mick Vukota .25 .11
❑ 57 Kevin Dean .25 .11
❑ 58 Adam Graves .50 .23
❑ 59 Craig Conroy .25 .11
❑ 60 Cale Hulse .25 .11
❑ 61 Dimitri Khristich .25 .11
❑ 62 Chris Wells .25 .11
❑ 63 Travis Green .25 .11
❑ 64 Tyler Wright .25 .11
❑ 65 Chris Simon .25 .11
❑ 66 Mikhail Shtalenkov .25 .11
❑ 67 Anson Carter .25 .11
❑ 68 Zarley Zalapski .25 .11
❑ 69 Per Gustafsson .25 .11
❑ 70 Jayson More .25 .11
❑ 71 Steve Thomas .25 .11
❑ 72 Todd Marchant .25 .11
❑ 73 Gary Roberts .25 .11
❑ 74 Richard Smehlik .25 .11
❑ 75 Aaron Miller .25 .11
❑ 76 Daren Puppa .25 .11
❑ 77 Garth Snow .50 .23
❑ 78 Greg DeVries .25 .11
❑ 79 Randy Burridge .25 .11
❑ 80 Jim Cummins .25 .11
❑ 81 Richard Pilon .25 .11
❑ 82 Chris McAlpine .25 .11
❑ 83 Joe Sakic 1.25 .55
❑ 84 Ted Drury .25 .11
❑ 85 Brent Gilchrist .25 .11
❑ 86 Dallas Eakins .25 .11
❑ 87 Bruce Driver .25 .11
❑ 88 Jamie Huscroft .25 .11
❑ 89 Jeff Brown .25 .11
❑ 90 Janne Laukkanen .25 .11
❑ 91 Ken Klee .25 .11
❑ 92 Peter Bondra .60 .25
❑ 93 Ian Moran .25 .11
❑ 94 Stephane Quintal .25 .11
❑ 95 Jason York .25 .11
❑ 96 Todd Harvey .25 .11
❑ 97 Slava Kozlov .25 .11
❑ 98 Kevin Haller .25 .11
❑ 99 Alexei Zhamnov .25 .11
❑ 100 Craig Johnson .25 .11
❑ 101 Mike Keane .25 .11
❑ 102 Craig Rivet .25 .11
❑ 103 Roman Vopat .25 .11
❑ 104 Jim Johnson .25 .11
❑ 105 Ray Whitney .25 .11
❑ 106 Ron Sutter .25 .11
❑ 107 Jamie McLennan .25 .11
❑ 108 Kris King .25 .11
❑ 109 Lance Pitlick .25 .11
❑ 110 Mike Dunham .50 .23
❑ 111 Jim Dowd .25 .11
❑ 112 Geoff Sanderson .50 .23
❑ 113 Vladimir Vujtek .25 .11
❑ 114 Tim Taylor .25 .11
❑ 115 Sandis Ozolinsh .50 .23
❑ 116 Scott Daniels .25 .11
❑ 117 Bob Corkum .25 .11
❑ 118 Kirk McLean .50 .23
❑ 119 Darcy Tucker .25 .11
❑ 120 Dennis Vaske .25 .11
❑ 121 Kirk Muller .25 .11
❑ 122 Jay McKee .25 .11
❑ 123 Jere Lehtinen .25 .11
❑ 124 Ruslan Salei .25 .11
❑ 125 Al MacInnis .25 .11
❑ 126 Ulf Samuelsson .25 .11
❑ 127 Rick Tocchet .50 .23
❑ 128 Nick Kypreos .25 .11
❑ 129 Joel Bouchard .25 .11
❑ 130 Jeff O'Neill .25 .11
❑ 131 Daniel McGillis .25 .11
❑ 132 Sean Pronger .25 .11
❑ 133 Vladimir Malakhov .25 .11
❑ 134 Petr Sykora .25 .11
❑ 135 Zigmund Palffy .75 .35
❑ 136 Joe Reekie .25 .11
❑ 137 Chris Gratton .25 .11
❑ 138 Craig Billington .50 .23
❑ 139 Steve Washburn .25 .11
❑ 140 Robert Kron .25 .11
❑ 141 Larry Murphy .25 .11
❑ 142 Shean Donovan .25 .11
❑ 143 Scott Young .25 .11
❑ 144 Janne Niinimaa .50 .23
❑ 145 Ken Belanger .25 .11
❑ 146 Pavol Demitra .25 .11
❑ 147 Roman Hamrlik .25 .11
❑ 148 Lonny Bohonos .25 .11
❑ 149 Mike Eagles .25 .11
❑ 150 Kelly Buchberger .25 .11
❑ 151 Mattias Timander .25 .11
❑ 152 Benoit Hogue .25 .11
❑ 153 Joey Kocur .25 .11
❑ 154 Mats Lindgren .25 .11
❑ 155 Aki Berg .25 .11
❑ 156 Tim Sweeney .25 .11
❑ 157 Vincent Damphousse .50 .23
❑ 158 Dan Kordic .25 .11
❑ 159 Darius Kasparaitis .25 .11
❑ 160 Randy McKay .25 .11
❑ 161 Steve Staios .25 .11
❑ 162 Brendan Witt .25 .11
❑ 163 Paul Ysebaert .25 .11
❑ 164 Greg Adams .25 .11
❑ 165 Kent Manderville .25 .11
❑ 166 Steve Dubinsky .25 .11
❑ 167 David Nemirovsky .25 .11
❑ 168 Todd Bertuzzi .25 .11
❑ 169 Frederic Chabot .25 .11
❑ 170 Dmitri Mironov .25 .11
❑ 171 Pat Peake .25 .11
❑ 172 Ed Ward .25 .11
❑ 173 Jeff Shantz .25 .11
❑ 174 Dave Gagner .25 .11
❑ 175 Randy Cunneyworth .25 .11
❑ 176 Daymond Langkow .25 .11
❑ 177 Alex Hicks .25 .11
❑ 178 Darby Hendrickson .25 .11
❑ 179 Mike Sullivan .25 .11
❑ 180 Anders Eriksson .25 .11
❑ 181 Turner Stevenson .25 .11
❑ 182 Shane Churla .25 .11
❑ 183 Dave Lowry .25 .11
❑ 184 Joe Juneau .25 .11
❑ 185 Bob Essensa .25 .11
❑ 186 James Black .25 .11
❑ 187 Michal Grosek .25 .11
❑ 188 Tomas Holmstrom .25 .11
❑ 189 Ian Laperriere .25 .11
❑ 190 Terry Yake .25 .11
❑ 191 Jason Smith .25 .11
❑ 192 Sergei Zholtok .25 .11
❑ 193 Doug Houda .25 .11
❑ 194 Guy Carbonneau .25 .11
❑ 195 Terry Carkner .25 .11
❑ 196 Alexei Gusarov .25 .11
❑ 197 Vladimir Tsyplakov .25 .11
❑ 198 Jarrod Skalde .25 .11
❑ 199 Marty Murray .25 .11
❑ 200 Aaron Ward .25 .11
❑ 201 Bobby Holik .25 .11
❑ 202 Steve Chiasson .25 .11
❑ 203 Brantt Myhres .25 .11
❑ 204 Eric Messier .50 .23
❑ 205 Rene Corbet .25 .11
❑ 206 Mathieu Schneider .25 .11
❑ 207 Tom Chorske .25 .11
❑ 208 Doug Lidster .25 .11
❑ 209 Igor Ulanov .25 .11
❑ 210 Blair Atcheynum .25 .11
❑ 211 Sebastien Bordeleau .25 .11
❑ 212 Alexei Morozov .60 .25
❑ 213 Vaclav Prospal 1.00 .45
❑ 214 Brad Bombardir .25 .11
❑ 215 Mattias Ohlund .60 .25
❑ 216 Chris Dingman .25 .11
❑ 217 Erik Rasmussen .25 .11
❑ 218 Mike Johnson .50 .23
❑ 219 Chris Phillips .25 .11
❑ 220 Sergei Samsonov 2.00 .90
❑ 221 Patrick Marleau 1.25 .55
❑ 222 Alyn McCauley .50 .23
❑ 223 Ryan Vandenbussche .25 .11
❑ 224 Daniel Cleary .50 .23
❑ 225 Magnus Arvedson .25 .11
❑ 226 Brad Isbister .25 .11
❑ 227 Pascal Rheaume .25 .11
❑ 228 Patrik Elias .75 .35
❑ 229 Krzysztof Oliwa .25 .11
❑ 230 Tyler Moss .25 .11
❑ 231 Jamie Rivers .25 .11
❑ 232 Joe Thornton 1.25 .55
❑ 233 Steve Shields .50 .23
❑ 234 Dave Scatchard .25 .11
❑ 235 Patrick Cote .25 .11
❑ 236 Rich Brennan .25 .11
❑ 237 Boyd Devereaux .25 .11
❑ 238 Per Johan Axelsson .25 .11
❑ 239 Craig Millar .25 .11
❑ 240 Juha Ylonen .25 .11
❑ 241 Donald MacLean .25 .11
❑ 242 Jaroslav Svejkovsky .50 .23
❑ 243 Marco Sturm 1.00 .45
❑ 244 Steve McKenna .25 .11
❑ 245 Derek Morris .25 .11
❑ 246 Dean Chynoweth .25 .11
❑ 247 Alexander Mogilny .50 .23
❑ 248 Ray Bourque .60 .25
❑ 249 Ed Belfour .60 .25
❑ 250 John LeClair 1.00 .45
❑ P3 Saku Koivu PROMO 2.00 .90

## 1997-98 Be A Player Autographs

Randomly inserted one in every pack, this 250-card set is an autographed gold foil enhanced parallel version of the base set. Die-cut and limited prismatic die-cut parallel autographed versions of the base set were also produced.

| | MINT | NRMT |
|---|---|---|
| COMPLETE SET (250) | 2800.00 | 1250.00 |
| COMMON CARD (1-250) | 5.00 | 2.20 |

SEMISTARS/GOALIES 12.00 5.50
UNLISTED STARS 15.00 6.75
COMMON DIE CUT (1-250) 10.00 4.50
*DIE CUT STARS: 1X TO 2X BASIC AUTO
*DIE CUT SP's: .75X TO 1.5X BASIC AUTO
*DIE CUT YOUNG STARS: .75X TO 1.5X BASIC AUTOGRAPHS
DIE CUT STATED ODDS 1:7
COMMON PRISMATIC (1-250) 25.00 11.00
*PRISMATIC STARS: 2.5X TO 5X BASIC AUTO
*PRISMATIC SP's: 1X TO 2X BASIC AUTO
*PRISMATIC YOUNG STARS:2 X TO 2X BASIC AUTO
PRISMATIC STATED PRINT RUN 100 SETS

2 Martin Brodeur SP 200.00 90.00
3 Saku Koivu 25.00 11.00
4 Felix Potvin 25.00 11.00
5 Adam Oates 20.00 9.00
6 Rob DiMaio 5.00 2.20
7 Jari Kurri 20.00 9.00
8 Andrew Cassels 5.00 2.20
9 Trevor Linden 12.00 5.50
10 Jocelyn Thibault 12.00 5.50
11 Chris Chelios 25.00 11.00
12 Paul Coffey 20.00 9.00
13 Nikolai Khabibulin 12.00 5.50
14 Robert Lang 5.00 2.20
15 Brett Hull SP 125.00 55.00
16 Mike Sillinger 5.00 2.20
17 Lyle Odelein 5.00 2.20
18 Bryan Berard 5.00 2.20
19 Craig Muni 5.00 2.20
20 Kris Draper 5.00 2.20
21 Ed Jovanovski 12.00 5.50
22 Keith Tkachuk 40.00 18.00
23 Dean Malkoc 5.00 2.20
24 Cory Stillman 5.00 2.20
25 Chris Osgood 30.00 13.50
26 Dainius Zubrus 5.00 2.20
27 Yves Racine 5.00 2.20
28 Eric Cairns 5.00 2.20
29 Dan Bylsma 5.00 2.20
30 Chris Terreri 5.00 2.20
31 Bill Huard 5.00 2.20
32 Warren Rychel 5.00 2.20
33 Scott Walker 5.00 2.20
34 Brian Holzinger 5.00 2.20
35 Roman Turek 12.00 5.50
36 Ron Tugnutt 12.00 5.50
37 Mike Richter 25.00 11.00
38 Mattias Norstrom 5.00 2.20
39 Joe Sacco 5.00 2.20
40 Derek King 5.00 2.20
41 Brad Werenka 5.00 2.20
42 Paul Kruse 5.00 2.20
43 Mike Knuble 12.00 5.50
44 Mike Peca 12.00 5.50
45 Jean-Yves Leroux 5.00 2.20
46 Ray Sheppard 5.00 2.20
47 Reid Simpson 5.00 2.20
48 Rob Brown 5.00 2.20
49 Dave Babych 5.00 2.20
50 Scott Pellerin 5.00 2.20
51 Bruce Gardiner 5.00 2.20
52 Adam Deadmarsh 12.00 5.50
53 Curtis Brown 5.00 2.20
54 Jason Marshall 5.00 2.20
55 Gerald Diduck 5.00 2.20
56 Mick Vukota 5.00 2.20
57 Kevin Dean 5.00 2.20
58 Adam Graves 12.00 5.50
59 Craig Conroy 5.00 2.20
60 Cale Hulse 5.00 2.20
61 Dimitri Khristich 5.00 2.20
62 Chris Wells 5.00 2.20
63 Travis Green 5.00 2.20
64 Tyler Wright 5.00 2.20
65 Chris Simon 5.00 2.20
66 Mikhail Shtalenkov 5.00 2.20
67 Anson Carter 5.00 2.20
68 Zarley Zalapski 5.00 2.20
69 Per Gustafsson 5.00 2.20
70 Jayson More 5.00 2.20
71 Steve Thomas 5.00 2.20
72 Todd Marchant 5.00 2.20
73 Gary Roberts 5.00 2.20
74 Richard Smehlik 5.00 2.20
75 Aaron Miller 5.00 2.20
76 Daren Puppa 12.00 5.50
77 Garth Snow 12.00 5.50
78 Greg DeVries 5.00 2.20
79 Randy Burridge 5.00 2.20
80 Jim Cummins 5.00 2.20
81 Richard Pilon 5.00 2.20
82 Chris McAlpine 5.00 2.20
83 Joe Sakic SP 200.00 90.00
84 Ted Drury 5.00 2.20
85 Brent Gilchrist 5.00 2.20
86 Dallas Eakins 5.00 2.20
87 Bruce Driver 5.00 2.20
88 Jamie Huscroft 5.00 2.20
89 Jeff Brown 5.00 2.20
90 Janne Laukkanen 5.00 2.20
91 Ken Klee 5.00 2.20
92 Peter Bondra 25.00 11.00
93 Ian Moran 5.00 2.20
94 Stephane Quintal 5.00 2.20
95 Jason York 5.00 2.20
96 Todd Harvey 5.00 2.20
97 Slava Kozlov 12.00 5.50
98 Kevin Haller 5.00 2.20
99 Alexei Zhamnov 5.00 2.20
100 Craig Johnson 5.00 2.20
101 Mike Keane 5.00 2.20
102 Craig Rivet 5.00 2.20
103 Roman Vopat 5.00 2.20
104 Jim Johnson 5.00 2.20
105 Ray Whitney 5.00 2.20
106 Ron Sutter 5.00 2.20
107 Jamie McLennan 5.00 2.20
108 Kris King 5.00 2.20
109 Lance Pitlick 5.00 2.20
110 Mike Dunham 12.00 5.50
111 Jim Dowd 5.00 2.20
112 Geoff Sanderson 12.00 5.50
113 Vladimir Vujtek 5.00 2.20
114 Tim Taylor 5.00 2.20
115 Sandis Ozolinsh 12.00 5.50
116 Scott Daniels 5.00 2.20
117 Bob Corkum 5.00 2.20
118 Kirk McLean 12.00 5.50
119 Darcy Tucker 5.00 2.20
120 Dennis Vaske 5.00 2.20
121 Kirk Muller 5.00 2.20
122 Jay McKee 5.00 2.20
123 Jere Lehtinen 5.00 2.20
124 Ruslan Salei 5.00 2.20
125 Al MacInnis SP 80.00 36.00
126 Ulf Samuelsson 5.00 2.20
127 Rick Tocchet 12.00 5.50
128 Nick Kypreos 5.00 2.20
129 Joel Bouchard 5.00 2.20
130 Jeff O'Neill 5.00 2.20
131 Daniel McGillis 5.00 2.20
132 Sean Pronger 5.00 2.20
133 Vladimir Malakhov 5.00 2.20
134 Petr Sykora 5.00 2.20
135 Zigmund Palffy 25.00 11.00
136 Joe Reekie 5.00 2.20
137 Chris Gratton 12.00 5.50
138 Craig Billington 12.00 5.50
139 Steve Washburn 5.00 2.20
140 Robert Kron 5.00 2.20
141 Larry Murphy 5.00 2.20
142 Shean Donovan 5.00 2.20
143 Scott Young 5.00 2.20
144 Janne Niinimaa 12.00 5.50
145 Ken Belanger 5.00 2.20
146 Pavol Demitra 20.00 9.00
147 Roman Hamrlik 5.00 2.20
148 Lonny Bohonos 5.00 2.20
149 Mike Eagles 5.00 2.20
150 Kelly Buchberger 5.00 2.20
151 Mattias Timander 5.00 2.20
152 Benoit Hogue 5.00 2.20
153 Joey Kocur 12.00 5.50
154 Mats Lindgren 5.00 2.20
155 Aki Berg 5.00 2.20
156 Tim Sweeney 5.00 2.20
157 Vincent Damphousse 12.00 5.50
158 Dan Kordic 5.00 2.20
159 Darius Kasparaitis 12.00 5.50
160 Randy McKay 5.00 2.20
161 Steve Staios 5.00 2.20
162 Brendan Witt 5.00 2.20
163 Paul Ysebaert 5.00 2.20
164 Greg Adams 5.00 2.20
165 Kent Manderville 5.00 2.20
166 Steve Dubinsky 5.00 2.20
167 David Nemirovsky 5.00 2.20
168 Todd Bertuzzi 5.00 2.20
169 Frederic Chabot 5.00 2.20
170 Dmitri Mironov 5.00 2.20
171 Pat Peake 5.00 2.20
172 Ed Ward 5.00 2.20
173 Jeff Shantz 5.00 2.20
174 Dave Gagner 5.00 2.20
175 Randy Cunneyworth 5.00 2.20
176 Daymond Langkow 5.00 2.20
177 Alex Hicks 5.00 2.20
178 Darby Hendrickson 5.00 2.20
179 Mike Sullivan 5.00 2.20
180 Anders Eriksson 5.00 2.20
181 Turner Stevenson 5.00 2.20
182 Shane Churla 5.00 2.20
183 Dave Lowry 5.00 2.20
184 Joe Juneau 5.00 2.20
185 Bob Essensa 5.00 2.20
186 James Black 5.00 2.20
187 Michal Grosek 5.00 2.20
188 Tomas Holmstrom 5.00 2.20
189 Ian Laperriere 5.00 2.20
190 Terry Yake 5.00 2.20
191 Jason Smith 5.00 2.20
192 Sergei Zholtok 5.00 2.20
193 Doug Houda 5.00 2.20
194 Guy Carbonneau 5.00 2.20
195 Terry Carkner 5.00 2.20
196 Alexei Gusarov 5.00 2.20
197 Vladimir Tsyplakov 5.00 2.20
198 Jarrod Skalde 5.00 2.20
199 Marty Murray 5.00 2.20
200 Aaron Ward 5.00 2.20
201 Bobby Holik 5.00 2.20
202 Steve Chiasson 5.00 2.20
203 Brantt Myhres 5.00 2.20
204 Eric Messier 12.00 5.50
205 Rene Corbet 5.00 2.20
206 Mathieu Schneider 5.00 2.20
207 Tom Chorske 5.00 2.20
208 Doug Lidster 5.00 2.20
209 Igor Ulanov 5.00 2.20
210 Blair Atcheynum 5.00 2.20
211 Sebastien Bordeleau 5.00 2.20
212 Alexei Morozov 15.00 6.75
213 Vaclav Prospal 15.00 6.75
214 Brad Bombardir 5.00 2.20
215 Mattias Ohlund 12.00 5.50
216 Chris Dingman 5.00 2.20
217 Erik Rasmussen 5.00 2.20
218 Mike Johnson 15.00 6.75
219 Chris Phillips 5.00 2.20
220 Sergei Samsonov 40.00 18.00
221 Patrick Marleau 30.00 13.50
222 Alyn McCauley 12.00 5.50
223 Ryan Vandenbussche 5.00 2.20
224 Daniel Cleary 12.00 5.50
225 Magnus Arvedson 5.00 2.20
226 Brad Isbister 5.00 2.20
227 Pascal Rheaume 5.00 2.20
228 Patrik Elias 15.00 6.75
229 Krzysztof Oliwa 5.00 2.20
230 Tyler Moss 5.00 2.20
231 Jamie Rivers 5.00 2.20
232 Joe Thornton 30.00 13.50
233 Steve Shields 12.00 5.50
234 Dave Scatchard 5.00 2.20
235 Patrick Cote 5.00 2.20
236 Rich Brennan 5.00 2.20
237 Boyd Devereaux 12.00 5.50
238 Per Johan Axelsson 5.00 2.20
239 Craig Millar 5.00 2.20
240 Juha Ylonen 5.00 2.20
241 Donald MacLean 5.00 2.20
242 Jaroslav Svejkovsky 12.00 5.50
243 Marco Sturm 15.00 6.75
244 Steve McKenna 5.00 2.20
245 Derek Morris 5.00 2.20
246 Dean Chynoweth 5.00 2.20
247 Alexander Mogilny SP 80.00 36.00
248 Ray Bourque SP 125.00 55.00
249 Ed Belfour SP 125.00 55.00
250 John LeClair SP 200.00 90.00

## 1997-98 Be A Player One Timers

Randomly inserted in packs at the rate of one in seven, this 20-card set features color action photos of Hockey's most dangerous slot shooters printed on flashy foil.

| | MINT | NRMT |
|---|---|---|
| COMPLETE SET (20) | 100.00 | 45.00 |
| COMMON CARD (1-20) | 1.25 | .55 |

1 Wayne Gretzky 15.00 6.75
2 Keith Tkachuk 3.00 1.35
3 Eric Lindros 8.00 3.60
4 Brendan Shanahan 5.00 2.20
5 Paul Kariya 10.00 4.50
6 Brett Hull 3.00 1.35
7 Jaromir Jagr 8.00 3.60
8 Teemu Selanne 5.00 2.20
9 John LeClair 4.00 1.80
10 Mike Modano 3.00 1.35
11 Peter Forsberg 8.00 3.60
12 Pavel Bure 5.00 2.20
13 Peter Bondra 2.50 1.10
14 Saku Koivu 4.00 1.80
15 Pat LaFontaine 2.00 .90
16 Patrik Elias 2.50 1.10
17 Richard Zednik 1.25 .55
18 Mike Johnson 2.50 1.10
19 Marco Sturm 3.00 1.35
20 Joe Thornton 4.00 1.80

## 1997-98 Be A Player Stacking the Pads

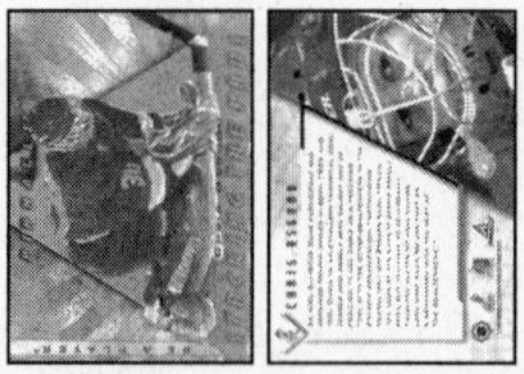

Randomly inserted in packs at the rate of one in 15, this 15-card set features color action photos of Hockey's greatest goaltenders printed on cards using dufex technology.

| | MINT | NRMT |
|---|---|---|
| COMPLETE SET (15) | 150.00 | 70.00 |
| COMMON CARD (1-15) | 6.00 | 2.70 |

1 Guy Hebert 6.00 2.70
2 Dominik Hasek 15.00 6.75
3 Felix Potvin 8.00 3.60
4 Patrick Roy 40.00 18.00
5 Ed Belfour 8.00 3.60
6 Chris Osgood 8.00 3.60
7 Curtis Joseph 8.00 3.60
8 John Vanbiesbrouck 12.00 5.50
9 Jocelyn Thibault 6.00 2.70
10 Mike Richter 8.00 3.60
11 Martin Brodeur 20.00 9.00
12 Garth Snow 6.00 2.70
13 Nikolai Khabibulin 6.00 2.70
14 Tommy Salo 6.00 2.70
15 Byron Dafoe 6.00 2.70

## 1997-98 Be A Player Take A Number

Randomly inserted in packs at the rate of one in 15, this 20-card set features color action photos of some of Hockey's top stars printed using Pinnacle's famous dufex technology. The backs carry the explanation of why they wear certain jersey numbers.

| | MINT | NRMT |
|---|---|---|
| COMPLETE SET (20) | 200.00 | 90.00 |
| COMMON CARD (1-20) | 2.00 | .90 |

1 Ray Bourque 6.00 2.70
2 Eric Daze 2.00 .90
3 Ed Belfour 6.00 2.70
4 Patrick Roy 30.00 13.50
5 Sergei Fedorov 12.00 5.50
6 John Vanbiesbrouck 10.00 4.50
7 Doug Gilmour 6.00 2.70
8 Wayne Gretzky 40.00 18.00
9 Bryan Berard 2.00 .90
10 Eric Lindros 20.00 9.00
11 Paul Coffey 6.00 2.70
12 Jeremy Roenick 6.00 2.70
13 Brett Hull 8.00 3.60
14 Pierre Turgeon 2.00 .90
15 Keith Primeau 2.00 .90
16 Daren Puppa 2.00 .90
17 Mark Messier 8.00 3.60
18 Alexander Mogilny 2.00 .90
19 Joe Sakic 12.00 5.50
20 Jaromir Jagr 20.00 9.00

## 1998-99 Be A Player

The 1998-99 Be A Player set was issued in two series totalling 300 cards and was distributed in eight-card packs with a suggested retail price of $6.99. The fronts feature color action photos of players with a heavy emphasis on rookies and Calder Trophy candidates printed on 30 pt. card stock with a full foil treatment. The backs carry a head photo with player information and career statistics.

| | MINT | NRMT |
|---|---|---|
| COMPLETE SET (300) | 180.00 | 80.00 |
| COMP.SERIES 1 (150) | 100.00 | 45.00 |
| COMP.SERIES 2 (150) | 80.00 | 36.00 |
| COMMON CARD (1-300) | .40 | .18 |

1 Jason Marshall .40 .18
2 Paul Kariya 6.00 2.70
3 Teemu Selanne 3.00 1.35
4 Guy Hebert 1.25 .55
5 Ted Drury .40 .18
6 Byron Dafoe 1.25 .55
7 Rob Dimaio .40 .18
8 Ray Bourque .40 .18
9 Joe Thornton 1.50 .70
10 Sergei Samsonov 2.50 1.10
11 Dimitri Khristich .40 .18
12 Michael Peca .40 .18
13 Jason Woolley .40 .18
14 Matthew Barnaby .40 .18
15 Brian Holzinger .40 .18
16 Dixon Ward .40 .18
17 Tyler Moss .40 .18
18 Jarome Iginla .40 .18
19 Marty McInnis .40 .18
20 Andrew Cassels .40 .18
21 Jason Wiemer .40 .18
22 Trevor Kidd .40 .18
23 Keith Primeau 1.25 .55
24 Sami Kapanen .40 .18
25 Robert Kron .40 .18
26 Glen Wesley .40 .18
27 Jeff Hackett 1.25 .55
28 Tony Amonte .40 .18
29 Alexei Zhamnov .40 .18
30 Eric Weinrich .40 .18
31 Jeff Shantz .40 .18
32 Christian Laflamme .40 .18
33 Adam Foote .40 .18
34 Patrick Roy 8.00 3.60
35 Peter Forsberg 5.00 2.20
36 Adam Deadmarsh 1.25 .55
37 Joe Sakic 3.00 1.35
38 Eric Lacroix .40 .18
39 Guy Carbonneau .40 .18
40 Mike Modano 2.00 .90
41 Roman Turek .40 .18
42 Mike Keane .40 .18
43 Sergei Zubov .40 .18
44 Jere Lehtinen .40 .18
45 Sergei Fedorov 3.00 1.35
46 Steve Yzerman 5.00 2.20
47 Chris Osgood 1.50 .70
48 Larry Murphy .40 .18
49 Vyacheslav Kozlov .40 .18
50 Darren McCarty .40 .18
51 Boris Mironov .40 .18
52 Roman Hamrlik .40 .18
53 Bill Guerin 1.25 .55
54 Mike Grier .40 .18
55 Todd Marchant .40 .18
56 Ray Whitney .40 .18
57 Dave Gagner .40 .18
58 Scott Mellanby .40 .18
59 Robert Svehla .40 .18
60 Viktor Kozlov .40 .18
61 Luc Robitaille 1.25 .55
62 Yanic Perreault .40 .18
63 Jozef Stumpel 1.25 .55
64 Sandy Moger .40 .18
65 Ian Laperriere .40 .18
66 Jocelyn Thibault 1.25 .55
67 Dave Manson .40 .18
68 Mark Recchi 1.25 .55
69 Patrick Poulin .40 .18
70 Benoit Brunet .40 .18
71 Turner Stevenson .40 .18
72 Mike Dunham 1.25 .55
73 Tom Fitzgerald .40 .18
74 Darren Turcotte .40 .18
75 Brad Smyth .40 .18
76 J.J. Daigneault .40 .18
77 Dave Andreychuk 1.25 .55
78 Jason Arnott 1.25 .55
79 Martin Brodeur 4.00 1.80
80 Randy McKay .40 .18
81 Patrik Elias .75 .35
82 Kevin Dean .40 .18
83 Tommy Salo .40 .18
84 Scott Lachance .40 .18
85 Bryan Berard 1.25 .55
86 Robert Reichel .40 .18
87 Kenny Jonsson .40 .18
88 Kevin Stevens .40 .18
89 Mike Richter 1.50 .70
90 Wayne Gretzky 10.00 4.50
91 Adam Graves 1.25 .55
92 Alexei Kovalev .40 .18
93 Ulf Samuelsson .40 .18
94 Radek Bonk .40 .18
95 Wade Redden .40 .18
96 Damian Rhodes 1.25 .55
97 Bruce Gardiner .40 .18
98 Daniel Alfredsson 1.25 .55
99 Ron Hextall .40 .18
100 Eric Lindros 5.00 2.20
101 Chris Gratton 1.25 .55
102 Dainius Zubrus .40 .18
103 Luke Richardson .40 .18
104 Petr Svoboda .40 .18
105 Rick Tocchet .40 .18
106 Teppo Numminen .40 .18
107 Jeremy Roenick 1.50 .70
108 Nikolai Khabibulin 1.25 .55
109 Brad Isbister .40 .18
110 Peter Skudra .40 .18
111 Alexei Morozov .40 .18
112 Kevin Hatcher .40 .18
113 Darius Kasparaitis .40 .18
114 Stu Barnes .40 .18
115 Martin Straka .40 .18
116 Andrei Zyuzin .40 .18
117 Marcus Ragnarsson .40 .18
118 Murray Craven .40 .18
119 Marco Sturm .40 .18
120 Patrick Marleau .40 .18
121 Shawn Burr .40 .18
122 Grant Fuhr 1.25 .55
123 Chris Pronger 1.25 .55
124 Geoff Courtnall .40 .18
125 Jim Campbell .40 .18
126 Pavol Demitra .40 .18
127 Todd Gill .40 .18
128 Cory Cross .40 .18
129 Daymond Langkow .40 .18
130 Alexander Selivanov .40 .18
131 Mikael Renberg 1.25 .55
132 Rob Zamuner .40 .18
133 Stephane Richer .40 .18
134 Fredrik Modin .40 .18
135 Derek King .40 .18
136 Mats Sundin 1.50 .70
137 Mike Johnson .40 .18
138 Alyn McCauley .40 .18
139 Jason Smith .40 .18
140 Markus Naslund .40 .18
141 Alexander Mogilny 1.25 .55
142 Mattias Ohlund .40 .18
143 Donald Brashear .40 .18
144 Garth Snow 1.25 .55
145 Brian Bellows .40 .18
146 Peter Bondra .40 .18
147 Joe Juneau 1.25 .55
148 Steve Konowalchuk .40 .18
149 Ken Klee .40 .18
150 Michal Pivonka .40 .18
151 Steve Rucchin .40 .18
152 Stu Grimson .40 .18
153 Tomas Sandstrom .40 .18

| | | |
|---|---|---|
| □ 154 Fredrik Olausson | .40 | .18 |
| □ 155 Travis Green | .40 | .18 |
| □ 156 Jason Allison | .40 | .18 |
| □ 157 Steve Heinze | .40 | .18 |
| □ 158 Rob Tallas | .40 | .18 |
| □ 159 Darren Van Impe | .40 | .18 |
| □ 160 Ken Baumgartner | .40 | .18 |
| □ 161 Peter Ferraro | .40 | .18 |
| □ 162 Dominik Hasek | 3.00 | 1.35 |
| □ 163 Geoff Sanderson | .40 | .18 |
| □ 164 Miroslav Satan | .40 | .18 |
| □ 165 Rob Ray | .40 | .18 |
| □ 166 Alexei Zhitnik | .40 | .18 |
| □ 167 Phil Housley | .40 | .18 |
| □ 168 Theo Fleury | .40 | .18 |
| □ 169 Ken Wregget | .40 | .18 |
| □ 170 Valeri Bure | .40 | .18 |
| □ 171 Rico Fata | .40 | .18 |
| □ 172 Arturs Irbe | .40 | .18 |
| □ 173 Sean Hill | .40 | .18 |
| □ 174 Ron Francis | .40 | .18 |
| □ 175 Jeff O'Neill | .40 | .18 |
| □ 176 Paul Ranheim | .40 | .18 |
| □ 177 Paul Coffey | .40 | .18 |
| □ 178 Doug Gilmour | .40 | .18 |
| □ 179 Eric Daze | .40 | .18 |
| □ 180 Chris Chelios | .40 | .18 |
| □ 181 Bob Probert | .40 | .18 |
| □ 182 Mark Fitzpatrick | .40 | .18 |
| □ 183 Alexei Gusarov | .40 | .18 |
| □ 184 Sylvain Lefebvre | .40 | .18 |
| □ 185 Craig Billington | .40 | .18 |
| □ 186 Valeri Kamensky | .40 | .18 |
| □ 187 Milan Hejduk RC | 2.50 | 1.10 |
| □ 188 Sandis Ozolinsh | .40 | .18 |
| □ 189 Brett Hull | 2.00 | .90 |
| □ 190 Ed Belfour | .40 | .18 |
| □ 191 Darryl Sydor | .40 | .18 |
| □ 192 Sergei Gusev | .40 | .18 |
| □ 193 Joe Nieuwendyk | .40 | .18 |
| □ 194 Derian Hatcher | .40 | .18 |
| □ 195 Brendan Shanahan | 3.00 | 1.35 |
| □ 196 Tomas Holmstrom | .40 | .18 |
| □ 197 Nicklas Lidstrom | .40 | .18 |
| □ 198 Martin Lapointe | .40 | .18 |
| □ 199 Igor Larionov | .40 | .18 |
| □ 200 Kris Draper | .40 | .18 |
| □ 201 Kelly Buchberger | .40 | .18 |
| □ 202 Andrei Kovalenko | .40 | .18 |
| □ 203 Josef Beranek | .40 | .18 |
| □ 204 Mikhail Shtalenkov | .40 | .18 |
| □ 205 Pat Falloon | .40 | .18 |
| □ 206 Mark Parrish RC | 2.50 | 1.10 |
| □ 207 Terry Carkner | .40 | .18 |
| □ 208 Rob Niedermayer | .40 | .18 |
| □ 209 Sean Burke | .40 | .18 |
| □ 210 Oleg Kvasha RC | 1.50 | .70 |
| □ 211 Pavel Bure | 3.00 | 1.35 |
| □ 212 Rob Blake | .40 | .18 |
| □ 213 Vladimir Tsyplakov | .40 | .18 |
| □ 214 Stephane Fiset | .40 | .18 |
| □ 215 Steve Duchesne | .40 | .18 |
| □ 216 Patrice Brisebois | .40 | .18 |
| □ 217 Vincent Damphousse | .40 | .18 |
| □ 218 Saku Koivu | 2.50 | 1.10 |
| □ 219 Jose Theodore | .40 | .18 |
| □ 220 Brett Clark | .40 | .18 |
| □ 221 Martin Rucinsky | .40 | .18 |
| □ 222 Vladimir Malakhov | .40 | .18 |
| □ 223 Sergei Krivokrasov | .40 | .18 |
| □ 224 Scott Walker | .40 | .18 |
| □ 225 Greg Johnson | .40 | .18 |
| □ 226 Cliff Ronning | .40 | .18 |
| □ 227 Eric Fichaud | .40 | .18 |
| □ 228 Bob Carpenter | .40 | .18 |
| □ 229 Scott Daniels | .40 | .18 |
| □ 230 Brian Rolston | .40 | .18 |
| □ 231 Sergei Brylin | .40 | .18 |
| □ 232 Scott Niedermayer | .40 | .18 |
| □ 233 Bryan Smolinski | .40 | .18 |
| □ 234 Trevor Linden | .40 | .18 |
| □ 235 Eric Brewer | .40 | .18 |
| □ 236 Zigmund Palffy | .40 | .18 |
| □ 237 Sergei Nemchinov | .40 | .18 |
| □ 238 Brian Leetch | .40 | .18 |
| □ 239 Mathieu Schneider | .40 | .18 |
| □ 240 Niklas Sundstrom | .40 | .18 |
| □ 241 Manny Malhotra | .40 | .18 |
| □ 242 Jeff Beukeboom | .40 | .18 |
| □ 243 Petr Nedved | .40 | .18 |
| □ 244 Ron Tugnutt | .40 | .18 |
| □ 245 Shawn Van Allen | .40 | .18 |
| □ 246 Alexei Yashin | .40 | .18 |
| □ 247 Jason York | .40 | .18 |
| □ 248 Shawn McEachern | .40 | .18 |
| □ 249 Marian Hossa | .40 | .18 |
| □ 250 John LeClair | 2.50 | 1.10 |
| □ 251 Rod Brind'Amour | .40 | .18 |
| □ 252 John Vanbiesbrouck | 2.50 | 1.10 |
| □ 253 Eric Desjardins | .40 | .18 |
| □ 254 Valeri Zelepukin | .40 | .18 |
| □ 255 Karl Dykhuis | .40 | .18 |
| □ 256 Keith Tkachuk | 2.00 | .90 |
| □ 257 Dallas Drake | .40 | .18 |
| □ 258 Oleg Tverdovsky | .40 | .18 |
| □ 259 Jyrki Lumme | .40 | .18 |
| □ 260 Jimmy Waite | .40 | .18 |
| □ 261 Jaromir Jagr | 5.00 | 2.20 |
| □ 262 German Titov | .40 | .18 |
| □ 263 Robert Lang | .40 | .18 |
| □ 264 Brad Werenka | .40 | .18 |
| □ 265 Rob Brown | .40 | .18 |
| □ 266 Bobby Dollas | .40 | .18 |
| □ 267 Jeff Friesen | .40 | .18 |
| □ 268 Andy Sutton | .40 | .18 |
| □ 269 Steve Shields | .40 | .18 |
| □ 270 Mike Ricci | .40 | .18 |
| □ 271 Joe Murphy | .40 | .18 |
| □ 272 Tony Granato | .40 | .18 |
| □ 273 Jamie McLennan | .40 | .18 |
| □ 274 Al MacInnis | .40 | .18 |
| □ 275 Pierre Turgeon | .40 | .18 |
| □ 276 Kelly Chase | .40 | .18 |
| □ 277 Craig Conroy | .40 | .18 |
| □ 278 Scott Young | .40 | .18 |
| □ 279 Vincent Lecavalier | 3.00 | 1.35 |
| □ 280 Wendel Clark | .40 | .18 |
| □ 281 Daren Puppa | .40 | .18 |
| □ 282 Sandy McCarthy | .40 | .18 |
| □ 283 Daniil Markov | .40 | .18 |
| □ 284 Curtis Joseph | .40 | .18 |
| □ 285 Sergei Berezin | 1.25 | .55 |
| □ 286 Steve Sullivan | .40 | .18 |
| □ 287 Tomas Kaberle RC | .40 | .18 |
| □ 288 Kris King | .40 | .18 |
| □ 289 Igor Korolev | .40 | .18 |
| □ 290 Mark Messier | .40 | .18 |
| □ 291 Bill Muckalt RC | 2.00 | .90 |
| □ 292 Todd Bertuzzi | .40 | .18 |
| □ 293 Brad May | .40 | .18 |
| □ 294 Peter Zezel | .40 | .18 |
| □ 295 Dmitri Mironov | .40 | .18 |
| □ 296 Adam Oates | .40 | .18 |
| □ 297 Calle Johansson | .40 | .18 |
| □ 298 Craig Berube | .40 | .18 |
| □ 299 Sergei Gonchar | .40 | .18 |
| □ 300 Andrei Nikolishin | .40 | .18 |

## 1998-99 Be A Player Gold

Randomly inserted into packs, this 300-card set is a gold foil parallel version of the base set.

| | MINT | NRMT |
|---|---|---|
| COMPLETE SET (300) | 700.00 | 325.00 |
| COMMON CARD (1-300) | 2.50 | 1.10 |

*STARS: 3X TO 6X BASIC CARD

## 1998-99 Be A Player Autographs

Inserted one per pack, this 300-card set is an autographed gold foil enhanced parallel version of the base set.

| | MINT | NRMT |
|---|---|---|
| COMMON CARD (1-300) | 5.00 | 2.20 |
| □ 1 Jason Marshall | 5.00 | 2.20 |
| □ 2 Paul Kariya SP | 200.00 | 90.00 |
| □ 3 Teemu Selanne SP | 120.00 | 55.00 |
| □ 4 Guy Hebert | 12.00 | 5.50 |
| □ 5 Ted Drury | 5.00 | 2.20 |
| □ 6 Byron Dafoe | 12.00 | 5.50 |
| □ 7 Rob Dimaio | 5.00 | 2.20 |
| □ 8 Ray Bourque SP | 80.00 | 36.00 |
| □ 9 Joe Thornton | 25.00 | 11.00 |
| □ 10 Sergei Samsonov | 40.00 | 18.00 |
| □ 11 Dimitri Khristich | 5.00 | 2.20 |
| □ 12 Michael Peca | 5.00 | 2.20 |
| □ 13 Jason Woolley | 5.00 | 2.20 |
| □ 14 Matthew Barnaby | 5.00 | 2.20 |
| □ 15 Brian Holzinger | 5.00 | 2.20 |
| □ 16 Dixon Ward | 5.00 | 2.20 |
| □ 17 Tyler Moss | 5.00 | 2.20 |
| □ 18 Jarome Iginla | 5.00 | 2.20 |
| □ 19 Marty McInnis | 5.00 | 2.20 |
| □ 20 Andrew Cassels | 5.00 | 2.20 |
| □ 21 Jason Wiemer | 5.00 | 2.20 |
| □ 22 Trevor Kidd | 5.00 | 2.20 |
| □ 23 Keith Primeau | 12.00 | 5.50 |
| □ 24 Sami Kapanen | 5.00 | 2.20 |
| □ 25 Robert Kron | 5.00 | 2.20 |
| □ 26 Glen Wesley | 5.00 | 2.20 |
| □ 27 Jeff Hackett | 12.00 | 5.50 |
| □ 28 Tony Amonte SP | 40.00 | 18.00 |
| □ 29 Alexei Zhamnov | 5.00 | 2.20 |
| □ 30 Eric Weinrich | 5.00 | 2.20 |
| □ 31 Jeff Shantz | 5.00 | 2.20 |
| □ 32 Christian Laflamme | 5.00 | 2.20 |
| □ 33 Adam Foote | 5.00 | 2.20 |
| □ 34 Patrick Roy SP | 200.00 | 90.00 |
| □ 35 Peter Forsberg SP | 175.00 | 80.00 |
| □ 36 Adam Deadmarsh | 12.00 | 5.50 |
| □ 37 Joe Sakic SP | 100.00 | 45.00 |
| □ 38 Eric Lacroix | 5.00 | 2.20 |
| □ 39 Guy Carbonneau | 5.00 | 2.20 |
| □ 40 Mike Modano SP | 80.00 | 36.00 |
| □ 41 Roman Turek | 5.00 | 2.20 |
| □ 42 Mike Keane | 5.00 | 2.20 |
| □ 43 Sergei Zubov | 5.00 | 2.20 |
| □ 44 Jere Lehtinen | 5.00 | 2.20 |
| □ 45 Sergei Fedorov SP | 100.00 | 45.00 |
| □ 46 Steve Yzerman SP | 175.00 | 80.00 |
| □ 47 Chris Osgood | 25.00 | 11.00 |
| □ 48 Larry Murphy | 5.00 | 2.20 |
| □ 49 Vyacheslav Kozlov | 5.00 | 2.20 |
| □ 50 Darren McCarty | 5.00 | 2.20 |
| □ 51 Boris Mironov | 5.00 | 2.20 |
| □ 52 Roman Hamrlik | 5.00 | 2.20 |
| □ 53 Bill Guerin | 12.00 | 5.50 |
| □ 54 Mike Grier | 5.00 | 2.20 |
| □ 55 Todd Marchant | 5.00 | 2.20 |
| □ 56 Ray Whitney | 5.00 | 2.20 |
| □ 57 Dave Gagner | 5.00 | 2.20 |
| □ 58 Scott Mellanby | 5.00 | 2.20 |
| □ 59 Robert Svehla | 5.00 | 2.20 |
| □ 60 Viktor Kozlov | 5.00 | 2.20 |
| □ 61 Luc Robitaille | 12.00 | 5.50 |
| □ 62 Yanic Perreault | 5.00 | 2.20 |
| □ 63 Jozef Stumpel | 12.00 | 5.50 |
| □ 64 Sandy Moger | 5.00 | 2.20 |
| □ 65 Ian Laperriere | 5.00 | 2.20 |
| □ 66 Jocelyn Thibault | 12.00 | 5.50 |
| □ 67 Dave Manson | 5.00 | 2.20 |
| □ 68 Mark Recchi SP | 40.00 | 18.00 |
| □ 69 Patrick Poulin | 5.00 | 2.20 |
| □ 70 Benoit Brunet | 5.00 | 2.20 |
| □ 71 Turner Stevenson | 5.00 | 2.20 |
| □ 72 Mike Dunham | 12.00 | 5.50 |
| □ 73 Tom Fitzgerald | 5.00 | 2.20 |
| □ 74 Darren Turcotte | 5.00 | 2.20 |
| □ 75 Brad Smyth | 5.00 | 2.20 |
| □ 76 J.J. Daigneault | 5.00 | 2.20 |
| □ 77 Dave Andreychuk | 12.00 | 5.50 |
| □ 78 Jason Arnott | 12.00 | 5.50 |
| □ 79 Martin Brodeur SP | 150.00 | 70.00 |
| □ 80 Randy McKay | 5.00 | 2.20 |
| □ 81 Patrik Elias | .75 | .35 |
| □ 82 Kevin Dean | 5.00 | 2.20 |
| □ 83 Tommy Salo | 5.00 | 2.20 |
| □ 84 Scott Lachance | 5.00 | 2.20 |
| □ 85 Bryan Berard | 12.00 | 5.50 |
| □ 86 Robert Reichel | 5.00 | 2.20 |
| □ 87 Kenny Jonsson | 5.00 | 2.20 |
| □ 88 Kevin Stevens | 5.00 | 2.20 |
| □ 89 Mike Richter SP | 50.00 | 22.00 |
| □ 90 Wayne Gretzky SP | 1000.00 | 450.00 |
| □ 91 Adam Graves | 12.00 | 5.50 |
| □ 92 Alexei Kovalev | 5.00 | 2.20 |
| □ 93 Ulf Samuelsson | 5.00 | 2.20 |
| □ 94 Radek Bonk | 5.00 | 2.20 |
| □ 95 Wade Redden | 5.00 | 2.20 |
| □ 96 Damian Rhodes | 12.00 | 5.50 |
| □ 97 Bruce Gardiner | 5.00 | 2.20 |
| □ 98 Daniel Alfredsson | 12.00 | 5.50 |
| □ 99 Ron Hextall | 5.00 | 2.20 |
| □ 100 Eric Lindros SP | 150.00 | 70.00 |
| □ 101 Chris Gratton | 12.00 | 5.50 |
| □ 102 Dainius Zubrus | 5.00 | 2.20 |
| □ 103 Luke Richardson | 5.00 | 2.20 |
| □ 104 Petr Svoboda | 5.00 | 2.20 |
| □ 105 Rick Tocchet | 5.00 | 2.20 |
| □ 106 Teppo Numminen | 5.00 | 2.20 |
| □ 107 Jeremy Roenick SP | 40.00 | 18.00 |
| □ 108 Nikolai Khabibulin | 12.00 | 5.50 |
| □ 109 Brad Isbister | 5.00 | 2.20 |
| □ 110 Peter Skudra | 5.00 | 2.20 |
| □ 111 Alexei Morozov | 5.00 | 2.20 |
| □ 112 Kevin Hatcher | 5.00 | 2.20 |
| □ 113 Darius Kasparaitis | 5.00 | 2.20 |
| □ 114 Stu Barnes | 5.00 | 2.20 |
| □ 115 Martin Straka | 5.00 | 2.20 |
| □ 116 Andrei Zyuzin | 5.00 | 2.20 |
| □ 117 Marcus Ragnarsson | 5.00 | 2.20 |
| □ 118 Murray Craven | 5.00 | 2.20 |
| □ 119 Marco Sturm | 5.00 | 2.20 |
| □ 120 Patrick Marleau | 5.00 | 2.20 |
| □ 121 Shawn Burr | 5.00 | 2.20 |
| □ 122 Grant Fuhr | 12.00 | 5.50 |
| □ 123 Chris Pronger | 12.00 | 5.50 |
| □ 124 Geoff Courtnall | 5.00 | 2.20 |
| □ 125 Jim Campbell | 5.00 | 2.20 |
| □ 126 Pavol Demitra | 30.00 | 13.50 |
| □ 127 Todd Gill | 5.00 | 2.20 |
| □ 128 Cory Cross | 5.00 | 2.20 |
| □ 129 Daymond Langkow | 5.00 | 2.20 |
| □ 130 Alexander Selivanov | 5.00 | 2.20 |
| □ 131 Mikael Renberg | 12.00 | 5.50 |
| □ 132 Rob Zamuner | 5.00 | 2.20 |
| □ 133 Stephane Richer | 5.00 | 2.20 |
| □ 134 Fredrik Modin | 5.00 | 2.20 |
| □ 135 Derek King | 5.00 | 2.20 |
| □ 136 Mats Sundin SP | 80.00 | 36.00 |
| □ 137 Mike Johnson | 5.00 | 2.20 |
| □ 138 Alyn McCauley | 5.00 | 2.20 |
| □ 139 Jason Smith | 5.00 | 2.20 |
| □ 140 Markus Naslund | 5.00 | 2.20 |
| □ 141 Alexander Mogilny SP | 50.00 | 22.00 |
| □ 142 Mattias Ohlund | 5.00 | 2.20 |
| □ 143 Donald Brashear | 5.00 | 2.20 |
| □ 144 Garth Snow | 12.00 | 5.50 |
| □ 145 Brian Bellows | 5.00 | 2.20 |
| □ 146 Peter Bondra SP | 50.00 | 22.00 |
| □ 147 Joe Juneau | 12.00 | 5.50 |
| □ 148 Steve Konowalchuk | 5.00 | 2.20 |
| □ 149 Ken Klee | 5.00 | 2.20 |
| □ 150 Michal Pivonka | 5.00 | 2.20 |
| □ 151 Steve Rucchin | 5.00 | 2.20 |
| □ 152 Stu Grimson | 5.00 | 2.20 |
| □ 153 Tomas Sandstrom | 5.00 | 2.20 |
| □ 154 Fredrik Olausson | 5.00 | 2.20 |
| □ 155 Travis Green | 5.00 | 2.20 |
| □ 156 Jason Allison | 12.00 | 5.50 |
| □ 157 Steve Heinze | 5.00 | 2.20 |
| □ 158 Rob Tallas | 5.00 | 2.20 |
| □ 159 Darren Van Impe | 5.00 | 2.20 |
| □ 160 Ken Baumgartner | 5.00 | 2.20 |
| □ 161 Peter Ferraro | 5.00 | 2.20 |
| □ 162 Dominik Hasek SP | 120.00 | 55.00 |
| □ 163 Geoff Sanderson | 12.00 | 5.50 |
| □ 164 Miroslav Satan | 12.00 | 5.50 |
| □ 165 Rob Ray | 5.00 | 2.20 |
| □ 166 Alexei Zhitnik | 5.00 | 2.20 |
| □ 167 Phil Housley | 12.00 | 5.50 |
| □ 168 Theo Fleury SP | 60.00 | 27.00 |
| □ 169 Ken Wregget | 12.00 | 5.50 |
| □ 170 Valeri Bure | 5.00 | 2.20 |
| □ 171 Rico Fata | 12.00 | 5.50 |
| □ 172 Arturs Irbe | 12.00 | 5.50 |
| □ 173 Sean Hill | 5.00 | 2.20 |
| □ 174 Ron Francis SP | 30.00 | 13.50 |
| □ 175 Jeff O'Neill | 5.00 | 2.20 |
| □ 176 Paul Ranheim | 5.00 | 2.20 |
| □ 177 Paul Coffey SP | 30.00 | 13.50 |
| □ 178 Doug Gilmour SP | 30.00 | 13.50 |
| □ 179 Eric Daze | 5.00 | 2.20 |
| □ 180 Chris Chelios SP | 60.00 | 27.00 |
| □ 181 Bob Probert | 5.00 | 2.20 |
| □ 182 Mark Fitzpatrick | 12.00 | 5.50 |
| □ 183 Alexei Gusarov | 5.00 | 2.20 |
| □ 184 Sylvain Lefebvre | 5.00 | 2.20 |
| □ 185 Craig Billington | 12.00 | 5.50 |
| □ 186 Valeri Kamensky | 12.00 | 5.50 |
| □ 187 Milan Hejduk | 40.00 | 18.00 |
| □ 188 Sandis Ozolinsh | 12.00 | 5.50 |
| □ 189 Brett Hull SP | 60.00 | 27.00 |
| □ 190 Ed Belfour SP | 60.00 | 27.00 |
| □ 191 Darryl Sydor | 5.00 | 2.20 |
| □ 192 Sergei Gusev | 5.00 | 2.20 |
| □ 193 Joe Nieuwendyk SP | 30.00 | 13.50 |
| □ 194 Derian Hatcher | 5.00 | 2.20 |
| □ 195 Brendan Shanahan SP | 80.00 | 36.00 |
| □ 196 Tomas Holmstrom | 5.00 | 2.20 |
| □ 197 Nicklas Lidstrom | 12.00 | 5.50 |
| □ 198 Martin Lapointe | 5.00 | 2.20 |
| □ 199 Igor Larionov | 5.00 | 2.20 |
| □ 200 Kris Draper | 5.00 | 2.20 |
| □ 201 Kelly Buchberger | 5.00 | 2.20 |
| □ 202 Andrei Kovalenko | 5.00 | 2.20 |
| □ 203 Josef Beranek | 5.00 | 2.20 |
| □ 204 Mikhail Shtalenkov | 5.00 | 2.20 |
| □ 205 Pat Falloon | 5.00 | 2.20 |
| □ 206 Mark Parrish | 5.00 | 2.20 |
| □ 207 Terry Carkner | 5.00 | 2.20 |
| □ 208 Rob Niedermayer | 5.00 | 2.20 |
| □ 209 Sean Burke | 12.00 | 5.50 |
| □ 210 Oleg Kvasha | 12.00 | 5.50 |
| □ 211 Pavel Bure SP | 120.00 | 55.00 |
| □ 212 Rob Blake | 12.00 | 5.50 |
| □ 213 Vladimir Tsyplakov | 5.00 | 2.20 |
| □ 214 Stephane Fiset | 12.00 | 5.50 |
| □ 215 Steve Duchesne | 12.00 | 5.50 |
| □ 216 Patrice Brisebois | 5.00 | 2.20 |
| □ 217 Vincent Damphousse | 12.00 | 5.50 |
| □ 218 Saku Koivu | 30.00 | 13.50 |
| □ 219 Jose Theodore | 12.00 | 5.50 |
| □ 220 Brett Clark | 5.00 | 2.20 |
| □ 221 Martin Rucinsky | 5.00 | 2.20 |
| □ 222 Vladimir Malakhov | 5.00 | 2.20 |
| □ 223 Sergei Krivokrasov | 5.00 | 2.20 |
| □ 224 Scott Walker | 5.00 | 2.20 |
| □ 225 Greg Johnson | 5.00 | 2.20 |
| □ 226 Cliff Ronning | 5.00 | 2.20 |
| □ 227 Eric Fichaud | 12.00 | 5.50 |
| □ 228 Bob Carpenter | 5.00 | 2.20 |
| □ 229 Scott Daniels | 5.00 | 2.20 |
| □ 230 Brian Rolston | 5.00 | 2.20 |
| □ 231 Sergei Brylin | 5.00 | 2.20 |
| □ 232 Scott Niedermayer | 5.00 | 2.20 |
| □ 233 Bryan Smolinski | 5.00 | 2.20 |
| □ 234 Trevor Linden | 12.00 | 5.50 |
| □ 235 Eric Brewer | 12.00 | 5.50 |
| □ 236 Zigmund Palffy SP | 50.00 | 22.00 |
| □ 237 Sergei Nemchinov | 5.00 | 2.20 |
| □ 238 Brian Leetch SP | 30.00 | 13.50 |
| □ 239 Mathieu Schneider | 5.00 | 2.20 |
| □ 240 Niklas Sundstrom | 5.00 | 2.20 |
| □ 241 Manny Malhotra | 12.00 | 5.50 |
| □ 242 Jeff Beukeboom | 5.00 | 2.20 |
| □ 243 Petr Nedved | 12.00 | 5.50 |
| □ 244 Ron Tugnutt | 12.00 | 5.50 |
| □ 245 Shawn Van Allen | 5.00 | 2.20 |
| □ 246 Alexei Yashin | 30.00 | 13.50 |
| □ 247 Jason York | 5.00 | 2.20 |
| □ 248 Shawn McEachern | 5.00 | 2.20 |
| □ 249 Marian Hossa | 12.00 | 5.50 |
| □ 250 John LeClair SP | 80.00 | 36.00 |
| □ 251 Rod Brind'Amour | 12.00 | 5.50 |
| □ 252 John Vanbiesbrouck | 50.00 | 22.00 |
| □ 253 Eric Desjardins | 5.00 | 2.20 |
| □ 254 Valeri Zelepukin | 5.00 | 2.20 |
| □ 255 Karl Dykhuis | 5.00 | 2.20 |
| □ 256 Keith Tkachuk SP | 80.00 | 36.00 |
| □ 257 Dallas Drake | 5.00 | 2.20 |
| □ 258 Oleg Tverdovsky | 5.00 | 2.20 |
| □ 259 Jyrki Lumme | 5.00 | 2.20 |
| □ 260 Jimmy Waite | 12.00 | 5.50 |
| □ 261 Jaromir Jagr SP | 175.00 | 80.00 |
| □ 262 German Titov | 5.00 | 2.20 |
| □ 263 Robert Lang | 5.00 | 2.20 |
| □ 264 Brad Werenka | 5.00 | 2.20 |
| □ 265 Rob Brown | 5.00 | 2.20 |
| □ 266 Bobby Dollas | 5.00 | 2.20 |
| □ 267 Jeff Friesen | 12.00 | 5.50 |
| □ 268 Andy Sutton | 5.00 | 2.20 |
| □ 269 Steve Shields | 12.00 | 5.50 |
| □ 270 Mike Ricci | 12.00 | 5.50 |
| □ 271 Joe Murphy | 5.00 | 2.20 |
| □ 272 Tony Granato | 5.00 | 2.20 |
| □ 273 Jamie McLennan | 5.00 | 2.20 |
| □ 274 Al MacInnis SP | 30.00 | 13.50 |
| □ 275 Pierre Turgeon | 12.00 | 5.50 |
| □ 276 Kelly Chase | 5.00 | 2.20 |
| □ 277 Craig Conroy | 5.00 | 2.20 |
| □ 278 Scott Young | 5.00 | 2.20 |
| □ 279 Vincent Lecavalier | 50.00 | 22.00 |
| □ 280 Wendel Clark | 12.00 | 5.50 |
| □ 281 Daren Puppa | 12.00 | 5.50 |
| □ 282 Sandy McCarthy | 5.00 | 2.20 |
| □ 283 Daniil Markov | 5.00 | 2.20 |
| □ 284 Curtis Joseph SP | 30.00 | 13.50 |
| □ 285 Sergei Berezin | 12.00 | 5.50 |
| □ 286 Steve Sullivan | 5.00 | 2.20 |
| □ 287 Tomas Kaberle | 5.00 | 2.20 |
| □ 288 Kris King | 5.00 | 2.20 |
| □ 289 Igor Korolev | 5.00 | 2.20 |
| □ 290 Mark Messier SP | 60.00 | 27.00 |
| □ 291 Bill Muckalt | 12.00 | 5.50 |
| □ 292 Todd Bertuzzi | 5.00 | 2.20 |
| □ 293 Brad May | 5.00 | 2.20 |
| □ 294 Peter Zezel | 5.00 | 2.20 |
| □ 295 Dmitri Mironov | 5.00 | 2.20 |
| □ 296 Adam Oates SP | 30.00 | 13.50 |
| □ 297 Calle Johansson | 5.00 | 2.20 |
| □ 298 Craig Berube | 5.00 | 2.20 |
| □ 299 Sergei Gonchar | 5.00 | 2.20 |
| □ 300 Andrei Nikolishin | 5.00 | 2.20 |
| □ *90 W.Gretzky GOLD/9... | 6000.00 | 2700.00 |

## 1998-99 Be A Player Autograph Gold

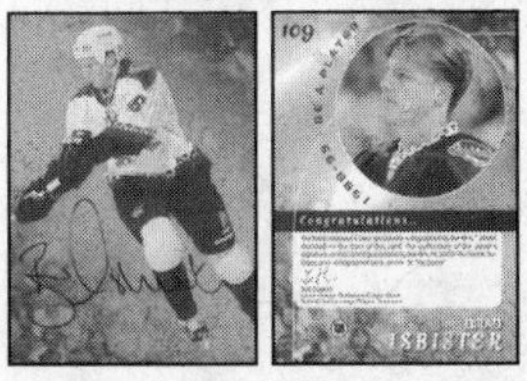

Randomly inserted in packs, this 300-card set is a gold all-foil parallel version of the regular Autograph parallel set.

| | MINT | NRMT |
|---|---|---|
| COMMON CARD (1-300) | 15.00 | 6.75 |

*STARS: 1.5X TO 3X BASE CARD

## 1998-99 Be A Player All-Star Game Used Stick Cards

Randomly inserted in packs, this 24-card set features color action player photos with a piece of a game-used stick of the superstars of the NHL embedded in the card. Only 100 sets were produced.

| | MINT | NRMT |
|---|---|---|
| COMPLETE SET (23) | 4000.00 | 1800.00 |
| COMMON CARD (S1-S23) | 80.00 | 36.00 |
| □ S1 Eric Lindros | 250.00 | 110.00 |
| □ S2 Peter Forsberg | 250.00 | 110.00 |
| □ S3 Teemu Selanne | 150.00 | 70.00 |
| □ S4 Mike Modano | 120.00 | 55.00 |
| □ S5 Mats Sundin | 100.00 | 45.00 |
| □ S6 Patrick Roy | 400.00 | 180.00 |
| □ S7 Paul Kariya | 300.00 | 135.00 |
| □ S8 Martin Brodeur | 200.00 | 90.00 |
| □ S9 Steve Yzerman | 250.00 | 110.00 |
| □ S10 Mark Messier | 100.00 | 45.00 |
| □ S11 Brett Hull | 100.00 | 45.00 |
| □ S12 Joe Sakic | 175.00 | 80.00 |
| □ S13 Alexander Mogilny | 80.00 | 36.00 |
| □ S14 Sergei Fedorov | 150.00 | 70.00 |
| □ S15 Ray Bourque | 100.00 | 45.00 |
| □ S16 Jeremy Roenick | 80.00 | 36.00 |
| □ S17 Jaromir Jagr | 250.00 | 110.00 |
| □ S18 Dominik Hasek | 150.00 | 70.00 |
| □ S19 Chris Chelios | 100.00 | 45.00 |
| □ S20 John LeClair | 150.00 | 70.00 |
| □ S21 Brendan Shanahan | 150.00 | 70.00 |
| □ S22 Ed Belfour | 120.00 | 55.00 |
| □ S23 Wayne Gretzky | 500.00 | 220.00 |

## 1998-99 Be A Player All-Star Game Used Jersey Cards

Randomly inserted in packs, this 25-card set features color action player photos with a piece of a game-worn jersey of the All-Star games in New York (1994), Boston (1995), San Jose (1997) and Vancouver (1998) embedded in the card. Only 100 sets were produced.

| | MINT | NRMT |
|---|---|---|
| COMPLETE SET (25) | 8000.00 | 3600.00 |
| COMMON CARD (AS1-AS25) | 150.00 | 70.00 |
| □ AS1 Eric Lindros | 500.00 | 220.00 |
| □ AS2 Peter Forsberg | 500.00 | 220.00 |
| □ AS3 Teemu Selanne | 300.00 | 135.00 |
| □ AS4 Mike Modano | 250.00 | 110.00 |

❑ AS5 Mats Sundin 200.00 90.00
❑ AS6 Patrick Roy 600.00 275.00
❑ AS7 Paul Kariya 600.00 275.00
❑ AS8 Martin Brodeur 400.00 180.00
❑ AS9 Steve Yzerman 500.00 220.00
❑ AS10 Mark Messier 200.00 90.00
❑ AS11 Paul Coffey 150.00 70.00
❑ AS12 Brett Hull 200.00 90.00
❑ AS13 Joe Sakic 300.00 135.00
❑ AS14 Alexander Mogilny 150.00 70.00
❑ AS15 Sergei Fedorov 300.00 135.00
❑ AS16 Ray Bourque 150.00 70.00
❑ AS17 Jeremy Roenick 150.00 70.00
❑ AS18 Jaromir Jagr 500.00 220.00
❑ AS19 Pavel Bure 300.00 135.00
❑ AS20 Dominik Hasek 300.00 135.00
❑ AS21 Chris Chelios 150.00 70.00
❑ AS22 John LeClair 300.00 135.00
❑ AS23 Brendan Shanahan 300.00 135.00
❑ AS24 Ed Belfour 250.00 110.00
❑ AS25 Wayne Gretzky 800.00 350.00

## 1998-99 Be A Player All-Star Legend Gordie Howe

Randomly inserted in packs, this two-card set features pieces of game-used Gordie Howe Detroit Red Wing jerseys embedded in the cards. Each card is autographed by Gordie Howe.

| | MINT | NRMT |
|---|---|---|
| COMPLETE SET (2) | 3000.00 | 1350.00 |
| COMMON CARD (GH1-GH2) | 1000.00 | 450.00 |

❑ GH1 G.Howe GJ AU 2000.00 900.00
❑ GH2 Gordie Howe AU 1000.00 450.00

## 1998-99 Be A Player All-Star Milestones

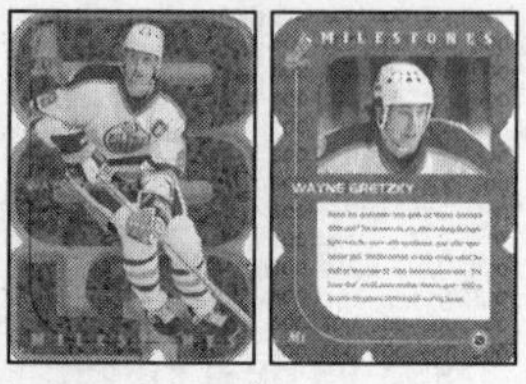

Randomly inserted in packs, this 22-card set features color action photos of the league's current five hundred goal scorers and one thousand point achievers printed on die-cut cards.

| | MINT | NRMT |
|---|---|---|
| COMPLETE SET (22) | 150.00 | 70.00 |
| COMMON CARD (M1-M22) | 4.00 | 1.80 |

❑ M1 Wayne Gretzky 30.00 13.50
❑ M2 Mark Messier 6.00 2.70
❑ M3 Dino Ciccarelli 4.00 1.80
❑ M4 Steve Yzerman 15.00 6.75
❑ M5 Dave Andreychuk 4.00 1.80
❑ M6 Brett Hull 6.00 2.70
❑ M7 Wayne Gretzky 30.00 13.50
❑ M8 Mark Messier 6.00 2.70
❑ M9 Dino Ciccarelli 4.00 1.80
❑ M10 Steve Yzerman 15.00 6.75
❑ M11 Bernie Nicholls 4.00 1.80
❑ M12 Ron Francis 4.00 1.80
❑ M13 Ray Bourque 5.00 2.20
❑ M14 Paul Coffey 5.00 2.20
❑ M15 Adam Oates 4.00 1.80
❑ M16 Phil Housley 4.00 1.80
❑ M17 Dale Hunter 4.00 1.80
❑ M18 Luc Robitaille 4.00 1.80
❑ M19 Doug Gilmour 5.00 2.20
❑ M20 Larry Murphy 4.00 1.80
❑ M21 Dave Andreychuk 4.00 1.80
❑ M22 Al MacInnis 4.00 1.80

## 1998-99 Be A Player Playoff Game Used Jersey Cards

Randomly inserted into packs, this 24-card set features color action player photos with pieces of game-used jerseys embedded in the cards.

| | MINT | NRMT |
|---|---|---|
| COMPLETE SET (24) | 8000.00 | 3600.00 |
| COMMON CARD (J1-J24) | 150.00 | 70.00 |

❑ G1 Wayne Gretzky 1000.00 450.00
❑ G2 Mats Sundin 200.00 90.00
❑ G3 Jeremy Roenick 150.00 70.00
❑ G4 Eric Lindros 500.00 220.00
❑ G5 John LeClair 300.00 135.00
❑ G6 Joe Sakic 300.00 135.00
❑ G7 Peter Forsberg 500.00 220.00
❑ G8 Patrick Roy 600.00 275.00
❑ G9 Martin Brodeur 400.00 180.00
❑ G10 Pavel Bure 300.00 135.00
❑ G11 Teemu Selanne 300.00 135.00
❑ G12 Paul Kariya 600.00 275.00
❑ G13 Ray Bourque 200.00 90.00
❑ G14 Brendan Shanahan 300.00 135.00
❑ G15 Steve Yzerman 500.00 220.00
❑ G16 Sergei Fedorov 300.00 135.00
❑ G17 Mike Modano 250.00 110.00
❑ G18 Brett Hull 200.00 90.00
❑ G19 Ed Belfour 250.00 110.00
❑ G20 Mark Messier 200.00 90.00
❑ G21 Alexander Mogilny 150.00 70.00
❑ G22 Tony Amonte 150.00 70.00
❑ G23 Jaromir Jagr 500.00 220.00
❑ G24 Alexei Yashin 150.00 70.00

## 1998-99 Be A Player Playoff Game Used Jersey Cards Autographed

Randomly inserted into packs, this 14-card set is a partial parallel version of the Game Used Jersey Card set and features the same cards as the regular insert set, only autographed. Each card is serial numbered out of 10, and guaranteed authentic by the NHLPA and Be A Player.

| | MINT | NRMT |
|---|---|---|
| COMPLETE SET (14) | 30000.00 | 13500.00 |
| COMMON CARD | 800.00 | 350.00 |

❑ G1 Wayne Gretzky 8000.00 3600.00
❑ G2 Mats Sundin 800.00 350.00
❑ G4 Eric Lindros 2500.00 1100.00
❑ G5 John LeClair 1200.00 550.00
❑ G6 Joe Sakic 1500.00 700.00
❑ G8 Patrick Roy 4000.00 1800.00
❑ G9 Martin Brodeur 2000.00 900.00
❑ G10 Pavel Bure 1500.00 700.00
❑ G11 Teemu Selanne 1500.00 700.00
❑ G12 Paul Kariya 3000.00 1350.00
❑ G14 Brendan Shanahan 1500.00 700.00
❑ G15 Steve Yzerman 2500.00 1100.00
❑ G16 Sergei Fedorov 1500.00 700.00
❑ G22 Alexei Yashin 800.00 350.00

## 1998-99 Be A Player Playoff Highlights

| | MINT | NRMT |
|---|---|---|
| COMPLETE SET (18) | 175.00 | 80.00 |
| COMMON CARD (P1-P18) | 5.00 | 2.20 |

❑ H1 Mark Messier 6.00 2.70
❑ H2 Peter Forsberg 15.00 6.75
❑ H3 Wayne Gretzky 30.00 13.50
❑ H4 Martin Brodeur 12.00 5.50
❑ H5 Jaromir Jagr 15.00 6.75
❑ H6 Mike Richter 5.00 2.20
❑ H7 Steve Yzerman 15.00 6.75
❑ H8 Patrick Roy 25.00 11.00
❑ H9 Paul Coffey 5.00 2.20
❑ H10 Joe Sakic 10.00 4.50
❑ H11 John Vanbiesbrouck 8.00 3.60
❑ H12 Pavel Bure 10.00 4.50
❑ H13 Chris Osgood 5.00 2.20
❑ H14 Chris Chelios 5.00 2.20
❑ H15 Curtis Joseph 5.00 2.20
❑ H16 Brian Leetch 5.00 2.20
❑ H17 Sergei Fedorov 10.00 4.50
❑ H18 Doug Gilmour 5.00 2.20

## 1998-99 Be A Player Playoff Legend Mario Lemieux

| | MINT | NRMT |
|---|---|---|
| COMPLETE SET (4) | 8000.00 | 3600.00 |
| COMMON CARD (L1-L4) | 2000.00 | 900.00 |

❑ L1 Mario Lemieux 2000.00 900.00
All-Star Jersey Card
❑ L2 Mario Lemieux 2000.00 900.00
Penguins Jersey Card
❑ L3 Mario Lemieux 2400.00 1100.00
All-Star Jersey/Stick Card
❑ L4 Mario Lemieux 2400.00 1100.00
Penguins Jersey/Stick Card

## 1998-99 Be A Player Playoff Practice Used Jersey Cards

Randomly inserted in packs, this 24-card set features color action player photos with actual pieces of practice-used jerseys embedded in the cards. Only 100 sets were printed.

| | MINT | NRMT |
|---|---|---|
| COMPLETE SET (24) | 6000.00 | 2700.00 |
| COMMON CARD (P1-P24) | 120.00 | 55.00 |

❑ P1 Brett Hull 150.00 70.00
❑ P2 Alexander Mogilny 120.00 55.00
❑ P3 Ray Bourque 150.00 70.00
❑ P4 Pavel Bure 250.00 110.00
❑ P5 Steve Yzerman 400.00 180.00
❑ P6 Ed Belfour 150.00 70.00
❑ P7 Jaromir Jagr 400.00 180.00
❑ P8 Sergei Fedorov 250.00 110.00
❑ P9 Teemu Selanne 250.00 110.00
❑ P10 Eric Lindros 400.00 180.00
❑ P11 Tony Amonte 120.00 55.00
❑ P12 Jeremy Roenick 120.00 55.00
❑ P13 John LeClair 200.00 90.00
❑ P14 Mike Modano 200.00 90.00
❑ P15 Joe Sakic 250.00 110.00
❑ P16 Patrick Roy 500.00 220.00
❑ P17 Mark Messier 150.00 70.00
❑ P18 Paul Kariya 500.00 220.00
❑ P19 Martin Brodeur 300.00 135.00
❑ P20 Mats Sundin 150.00 70.00
❑ P21 Brendan Shanahan 250.00 110.00
❑ P22 Peter Forsberg 300.00 135.00
❑ P23 Alexei Yashin 120.00 55.00
❑ P24 Wayne Gretzky 800.00 350.00

## 1998-99 Be A Player Spring Expo

Available via wrapper redemption at the Be A Player booth during the 1999 Toronto Spring Expo Show. Each wrapper was exchanged for one random card from the Be A Player Playoff Series that was serially #'d and embossed with the Spring Expo logo. Each card is #'d/25.

| | MINT | NRMT |
|---|---|---|
| COMPLETE SET (150) | 9000.00 | 4000.00 |
| COMMON CARD (151-300) | 15.00 | 6.75 |

*STARS: 25X TO 50X BASE CARDS

## 1998-99 Be A Player Tampa Bay All Star Game

| | MINT | NRMT |
|---|---|---|
| COMPLETE SET (150) | 7000.00 | 3200.00 |
| COMMON CARD (1-150) | 8.00 | 3.60 |

*STARS: 20X TO 40X BASE CARDS

## 1934-44 Beehive Group I Photos

The 1934-44 Beehive photos are the first of three groups. Production was suspended in 1944 due to wartime priorities. The photos include a facsimile autograph, small script or occasionally block letters, and are subdivided according to team as follows: Boston Bruins (1-37), Chicago Blackhawks (38-85), Detroit Red Wings (86-132), Montreal Canadiens (133-188), Montreal Maroons (189-210), New York Americans (211-260), New York Rangers (261-297), and Toronto Maple Leafs (298-354). The set concludes with the following categories: Miscellaneous Photos (355-357), Trophies (358-365), and Not Dated Blank Back (366-373). Complete set price is not given due to an ongoing debate over what constitutes a complete set. A number of unconfirmed photos are scattered throughout the checklist below. Though there has been no confirmation of these photos, they were a part of the master Beehive checklist. If anyone has information to corroborate the existence of any of these cards, please forward it to Beckett Publications.

| | EX-MT | VG-E |
|---|---|---|
| COMMON PHOTO | 10.00 | 4.50 |

❑ 1 Bobby Bauer 12.00 5.50
❑ 2 Red Beattie 20.00 9.00
❑ 3 Buzz Boll
(Unconfirmed)
❑ 4 Yank Boyd 120.00 55.00
❑ 5A Frankie Brimsek 20.00 9.00
(With Net)
❑ 5B Frankie Brimsek 25.00 11.00
(Without Net)
❑ 6 Herb Cain
(Unconfirmed)
❑ 7 Murph Chamberlain
(Unconfirmed)
❑ 8 Dit Clapper 15.00 6.75
❑ 9 Roy Conacher 15.00 6.75
❑ 10 Bun Cook 15.00 6.75
❑ 11 Bill Cowley 15.00 6.75
❑ 12 John Crawford 12.00 5.50
❑ 13 Woody Dumart 20.00 9.00
❑ 14 Don Gallinger 150.00 70.00
❑ 15 Ray Getiffe 25.00 11.00
❑ 16 Leroy Goldsworthy
(Unconfirmed)
❑ 17 Bep Guidolin 80.00 36.00
❑ 18 Red Hamill 25.00 11.00
❑ 19 Mel Hill 15.00 6.75
❑ 20 Frank Hollett
(Unconfirmed)
❑ 21 Art Jackson
(Unconfirmed)
❑ 22 Harvey Jackson
(Unconfirmed)
❑ 23 Bill Jennings
(Unconfirmed)
❑ 24 Pat McReavy 10.00 4.50
❑ 25 Alex Motter 25.00 11.00
❑ 26 Peggy O'Neil 15.00 6.75
❑ 27 Gord Pettinger
(Unconfirmed)
❑ 28 Jack Portland
(Unconfirmed)
❑ 29 Charlie Sands 15.00 6.75
❑ 30 Jackie Schmidt 150.00 70.00
❑ 31 Milt Schmidt 15.00 6.75
❑ 32 Jack Shewchuk 15.00 6.75
❑ 33 Eddie Shore 80.00 36.00
❑ 34 Des Smith
(Unconfirmed)
❑ 35 Tiny Thompson 40.00 18.00
❑ 36 Cooney Weiland 15.00 6.75
❑ 37 Eddie Wiseman
(Unconfirmed)
❑ 38 George Allen 20.00 9.00
❑ 39 Doug Bentley 25.00 11.00
❑ 40 Max Bentley 30.00 13.50
❑ 41 Russ Blinco
(Unconfirmed)
❑ 42 Glenn Brydson 100.00 45.00
❑ 43 Marty Burke 12.00 5.50
❑ 44 Bill Carse 10.00 4.50
❑ 45 Bob Carse 10.00 4.50
❑ 46 Lorne Chabot 40.00 18.00
❑ 47 John Chad 25.00 11.00
❑ 48 Joe Cooper
(Unconfirmed)
❑ 49 Les Cunningham 25.00 11.00
❑ 50 Cully Dahlstrom 15.00 6.75
❑ 51 Joffre Desilets
(Unconfirmed)
❑ 52 Bert Gardiner
(Unconfirmed)
❑ 53 Leroy Goldsworthy 20.00 9.00
❑ 54 Paul Goodman 30.00 13.50
❑ 55 Johnny Gottselig 20.00 9.00
❑ 56 Philip Hergesheimer 12.00 5.50
❑ 57 Roger Jenkins
(Unconfirmed)
❑ 58 George(Wingy) Johnston 150.00 70.00
❑ 59 Alex Kaleta 25.00 11.00
❑ 60 Mike Karakas 25.00 11.00
❑ 61 Reg Kelly
(Unconfirmed)
❑ 62 William Kendall
(Unconfirmed)
❑ 63 Alex Levinsky 20.00 9.00
❑ 64 Sam LoPresti 40.00 18.00
❑ 65 Dave Mackay 200.00 90.00
❑ 66 Bill MacKenzie
(Unconfirmed)
❑ 67 Mush March 12.00 5.50
❑ 68 John Mariucci 40.00 18.00
❑ 69 Joe Matte 100.00 45.00
❑ 70 Red Mitchell UER 150.00 70.00
(Name misspelled Mitchel)
❑ 71 Baldy Northcott
(Unconfirmed)
❑ 72 Peter Palangio 60.00 27.00
❑ 73 Joe Papike 80.00 36.00
❑ 74 Jack Portland
(Unconfirmed)
❑ 75 Cliff Purpur 150.00 70.00
❑ 76 Earl Robinson
(Unconfirmed)
❑ 77 Doc Romnes 40.00 18.00
❑ 78 Earl Seibert 15.00 6.75
❑ 79 Jack Shill
(Unconfirmed)
❑ 80 Des Smith
(Unconfirmed)
❑ 81 Paul Thompson 25.00 11.00
❑ 82 Bill Thoms
(Unconfirmed)
❑ 83 Louis Trudel UER 30.00 13.50
(Name misspelled Trudell)
❑ 84 Audley Tuten 150.00 70.00
❑ 85 Art Wiebe 20.00 9.00
❑ 86 Sid Abel 25.00 11.00
❑ 87 Larry Aurie 10.00 4.50
❑ 88 Marty Barry 20.00 9.00
❑ 89 Ralph Bowman 20.00 9.00
❑ 90 Adam Brown 60.00 27.00
❑ 91 Connie Brown 80.00 36.00
❑ 92 Jerry Brown 250.00 110.00
❑ 93 Mud Bruneteau 15.00 6.75
❑ 94 Eddie Bush 200.00 90.00
❑ 95 Joe Carveth 10.00 4.50
❑ 96 Charlie Conacher
(Unconfirmed)
❑ 97 Doug Deacon
(Unconfirmed)
❑ 98 Cecil Dillon
(Unconfirmed)
❑ 99 Les Douglas 80.00 36.00
❑ 100 Gus Biesebrecht UER 12.00 5.50
(Name misspelled Geisebrech)
❑ 101 Ebbie Goodfellow 15.00 6.75
❑ 102 Don Grosso 12.00 5.50
❑ 103 Dutch Hiller
(Unconfirmed)
❑ 104 Syd Howe 15.00 6.75
❑ 105 Bill Jennings 60.00 27.00
❑ 106 Jack Keating 25.00 11.00
❑ 107 Pete Kelly 15.00 6.75
❑ 108 Hec Kilrea 15.00 6.75
❑ 109 Ken Kilrea 15.00 6.75
❑ 110 Wally Kilrea 15.00 6.75
❑ 111 Herb Lewis 15.00 6.75
❑ 112 Carl Liscombe 12.00 5.50
❑ 113 Charley Mason
(Unconfirmed)
❑ 114 Douglas McCaig 60.00 27.00
❑ 115A Bucko McDonald 90.00 40.00
(Ice photo)
❑ 115B Bucko McDonald 80.00 36.00
(Dressing room photo)
❑ 116 Pat McReavy 60.00 27.00
❑ 117 Alex Motter
(Unconfirmed)
❑ 118 Johnny Mowers 20.00 9.00
❑ 119 Jimmy Orlando 12.00 5.50
❑ 120 Gord Pettinger 35.00 16.00
❑ 121 John Sherf 30.00 13.50
❑ 122 Cully Simon
(Unconfirmed)
❑ 123 Norm Smith 25.00 11.00
❑ 124 John Sorrell 20.00 9.00
❑ 125 Jack Stewart 30.00 13.50
❑ 126 Harvey Teno
(Unconfirmed)
❑ 127 Tiny Thompson
(Unconfirmed)
❑ 128 Carl Voss 80.00 36.00
❑ 129 Eddie Wares 200.00 90.00
❑ 130 Harry Watson
(Unconfirmed)
❑ 131 Arch Wilder 20.00 9.00
❑ 132 Douglas Young 20.00 9.00
❑ 133 Jack Adams 20.00 9.00
❑ 134 Marty Barry 400.00 180.00
❑ 135 Joe Benoit 15.00 6.75
❑ 136 Paul Bibeault 40.00 18.00
❑ 137 Toe Blake 25.00 11.00
❑ 138 Butch Bouchard 10.00 4.50
❑ 139 Claude Bourque 35.00 16.00
❑ 140 George Allan Brown 100.00 45.00
❑ 141 Walt Buswell 30.00 13.50
❑ 142 Herb Cain
(Unconfirmed)
❑ 143 Murph Chamberlain 40.00 18.00
❑ 144 Wilf Cude 25.00 11.00
❑ 145 Bunny Dame 40.00 18.00
❑ 146 Tony DeMeres UER 12.00 5.50
(Name misspelled Dremers)
❑ 147 Joffre Desilets 15.00 6.75
❑ 148 Gordie Drillon 700.00 325.00
❑ 149 Polly Drouin 12.00 5.50
❑ 150 Stewart Evans
(Unconfirmed)
❑ 151 Johnny Gagnon 12.00 5.50
❑ 152 Bert Gardiner 25.00 11.00
❑ 153 Ray Getiffe 60.00 27.00
❑ 154 Red Goupille 15.00 6.75
❑ 155 Tony Graboski 15.00 6.75
❑ 156 Bob Gracie
(Unconfirmed)
❑ 157 Paul Haynes 12.00 5.50
❑ 158 Gerry Heffernan 125.00 55.00
❑ 159 Dutch Hiller
(Unconfirmed)
❑ 160 Roger Jenkins 50.00 22.00
❑ 161 Aurel Joliat 30.00 13.50
❑ 162 Elmer Lach 30.00 13.50
❑ 163 Leo Lamoreux UER 100.00 45.00
(Name misspelled Camoreaux)
❑ 164 Pit Lepine 12.00 5.50
❑ 165 Rod Lorraine 25.00 11.00
❑ 166 Georges Mantha 15.00 6.75
❑ 167 Sylvio Mantha 15.00 6.75
❑ 168 Bill McKenzie
(Unconfirmed)
❑ 169 Armand Mondou 10.00 4.50
❑ 170 Howie Morenz 750.00 350.00
❑ 171 Pete Morin 125.00 55.00
❑ 172 Buddy O'Connor 125.00 55.00
❑ 173 Peggy O'Neil
(Unconfirmed)
❑ 174 Charles Phillippe
(Unconfirmed)
❑ 175 Jack Portland 12.00 5.50
❑ 176 John Quilty 20.00 9.00
❑ 177 Ken Reardon 30.00 13.50
❑ 178 Terry Reardon 90.00 40.00
❑ 179 Maurice Richard 35.00 16.00
❑ 180 Earl Robinson 400.00 180.00
❑ 181 Charlie Sands 50.00 22.00
❑ 182 Babe Siebert 30.00 13.50
❑ 183 Alex Singbush 80.00 36.00
❑ 184 Bill Summerhill 150.00 70.00
❑ 185 Louis Trudel 60.00 27.00
❑ 186 Jimmy Ward
(Unconfirmed)
❑ 187 Cy Wentworth 3000.00 1350.00
❑ 188 Douglas Young 80.00 36.00
❑ 189 Bill Beveridge 50.00 22.00
❑ 190 Russ Blinco 30.00 13.50
❑ 191 Herb Cain 50.00 22.00
❑ 192 Gerry Carson UER 150.00 70.00

(Name misspelled Jerry)
❑ 193 King Clancy (Unconfirmed)
❑ 194 Alex Connell.................. 50.00 22.00
❑ 195 Tom Cook..................... 30.00 13.50
❑ 196 Stewart Evans.............. 25.00 11.00
❑ 197 Bob Gracie.................... 80.00 36.00
❑ 198 Max Kaminsky........... 150.00 70.00
❑ 199 Bill MacKenzie.......... 100.00 45.00
❑ 200 Gus Marker................ 175.00 80.00
❑ 201 Baldy Northcott............ 50.00 22.00
❑ 202 Earl Robinson.............. 40.00 18.00
❑ 203 Paul Runge................ 150.00 70.00
❑ 204 Gerry Shannon UER.... 150.00 70.00
(Name misspelled Jerry)
❑ 205 Al Shields (Unconfirmed)
❑ 206 Des Smith..................... 35.00 16.00
❑ 207 Hooley Smith................ 30.00 13.50
❑ 208 Dave Trottier................ 90.00 40.00
❑ 209 Jimmy Ward.................. 35.00 16.00
❑ 210 Cy Wentworth.............. 40.00 18.00
❑ 211 Viv Allen....................... 50.00 22.00
❑ 212 Tom Anderson.............. 30.00 13.50
❑ 213 Murray Armstrong (Unconfirmed)
❑ 214 Red Beattie (Unconfirmed)
❑ 215 Bill Benson.................. 40.00 18.00
❑ 216 Buzz Boll (Unconfirmed)
❑ 217 Andy Brannigan (Unconfirmed)
❑ 218 Lorne Carr.................. 45.00 20.00
❑ 219 Art Chapman................ 30.00 13.50
❑ 220 Charlie Conacher (Unconfirmed)
❑ 221 Hap Day (Unconfirmed)
❑ 222 Red Dutton.................. 40.00 18.00
❑ 223 Pat Egan....................... 35.00 16.00
❑ 224 Hap Emms.................... 60.00 27.00
❑ 225 Wilf Field..................... 30.00 13.50
❑ 226 John Gallagher............ 35.00 16.00
❑ 227 Leroy Goldsworthy (Unconfirmed)
❑ 228 Red Heron (Unconfirmed)
❑ 229 Mel Hill (Unconfirmed)
❑ 230 Art Jackson (Unconfirmed)
❑ 231 Harvey Jackson (Unconfirmed)
❑ 232 Joe Jerwa..................... 40.00 18.00
❑ 233 Pete Kelly (Unconfirmed)
❑ 234 Jim Klein....................... 80.00 36.00
❑ 235 Nick Knott (Unconfirmed)
❑ 236 Joe Krol.................... 1250.00 550.00
❑ 237 Joe Lamb...................... 60.00 27.00
❑ 238 Red Heron.................... 30.00 13.50
❑ 239 Gus Marker (Unconfirmed)
❑ 240 Ron Martin (Unconfirmed)
❑ 241 Hazen McAndrew...... 1500.00 700.00
❑ 242 Charley McVeigh (Unconfirmed)
❑ 243 Ken Mosdell............... 400.00 180.00
❑ 244 Al Murray...................... 25.00 11.00
❑ 245 John O'Flaherty........... 50.00 22.00
❑ 246 Chuck Rayner............ 175.00 80.00
❑ 247 Earl Robertson............. 45.00 20.00
❑ 248 Doc Romnes (Unconfirmed)
❑ 249 Sweeny Schriner.......... 35.00 16.00
❑ 250 Al Shields.................... 80.00 36.00
❑ 251 Jack Shill (Unconfirmed)
❑ 252 Pete Slobodzian UER.... 50.00 22.00
(Name misspelled Slobodian)
❑ 253 Hooley Smith (Unconfirmed)
❑ 254 John Sorrell (Unconfirmed)
❑ 255 Nels Stewart................ 45.00 20.00
❑ 256 Fred Thurier............... 125.00 55.00
❑ 257 Harry Watson............. 200.00 90.00
❑ 258 Eddie Wiseman............ 25.00 11.00
❑ 259 Roy Worters................. 50.00 22.00
❑ 260 Ralph Wycherly........... 50.00 22.00
❑ 261 Frank Boucher............. 30.00 13.50
❑ 262 Doug Brennan (Unconfirmed)
❑ 263 Norm Burns.................. 80.00 36.00
❑ 264 Angus Cameron (Unconfirmed)
❑ 265 Mac Colville................. 12.00 5.50
❑ 266 Neil Colville.................. 15.00 6.75
❑ 267 Bill Cook....................... 20.00 9.00
❑ 268 Joe Cooper.................... 10.00 4.50
❑ 269 Art Coulter.................... 12.00 5.50
❑ 270 Gord Davidson............. 50.00 22.00
❑ 271 Cecil Dillon.................. 15.00 6.75
❑ 272 Jim Franks................. 175.00 80.00
❑ 273 Red Garrett................ 125.00 55.00
❑ 274 Hank Goldup (Unconfirmed)
❑ 275 Ott Heller..................... 10.00 4.50
❑ 276A Jim Henry.................. 80.00 36.00
(Vertical photo)
❑ 276B Jim Henry.................. 50.00 22.00
(Horizontal photo)
❑ 277 Bryan Hextall Sr........... 25.00 11.00
❑ 278 Dutch Hiller.................. 15.00 6.75
❑ 279 Ching Johnson............ 20.00 9.00
❑ 280 Bill Juzda..................... 15.00 6.75
❑ 281 Butch Keeling.............. 15.00 6.75
❑ 282 Davey Kerr.................... 25.00 11.00
❑ 283 Bobby Kirk.................... 80.00 36.00
❑ 284 Bob Kirkpatrick............ 80.00 36.00
❑ 285 Kilby MacDonald.......... 15.00 6.75
❑ 286 Larry Molyneaux.......... 25.00 11.00
❑ 287 John Murray Murdoch.. 35.00 16.00
❑ 288 Vic Myles................... 150.00 70.00
❑ 289 Lynn Patrick................. 15.00 6.75
❑ 290 Murray Patrick............. 12.00 5.50
❑ 291 Alf Pike......................... 10.00 4.50
❑ 292 Babe Pratt.................... 20.00 9.00
❑ 293 Alex Shibicky................ 12.00 5.50
❑ 294 Clint Smith.................... 12.00 5.50
❑ 295 Norman Tustin............. 80.00 36.00
❑ 296 Grant Warwick............. 80.00 36.00
❑ 297 Phil Watson.................. 10.00 4.50
❑ 298 Syl Apps Sr................... 20.00 9.00
❑ 299 Murray Armstrong........ 10.00 4.50
❑ 300 Andy Blair..................... 15.00 6.75
❑ 301 Buzz Boll...................... 15.00 6.75
❑ 302 George Boothman....... 200.00 90.00
❑ 303 Turk Broda................... 20.00 9.00
❑ 304 Lorne Carr.................... 50.00 22.00
❑ 305 Murph Chamberlain...... 12.00 5.50
❑ 306 Lex Chisholm................ 15.00 6.75
❑ 307 Jack Church.................. 15.00 6.75
❑ 308 Francis Clancy............. 25.00 11.00
❑ 309 Charlie Conacher.......... 20.00 9.00
❑ 310 Bob Copp...................... 50.00 22.00
❑ 311 Baldy Cotton................. 15.00 6.75
❑ 312 Bob Davidson............... 12.00 5.50
❑ 313 Hap Day........................ 12.00 5.50
❑ 314 Ernie Dickens............. 175.00 80.00
❑ 315 Gordie Drillon............... 12.00 5.50
❑ 316 Frank Finnigan............. 20.00 9.00
❑ 317 Jack Forsey................ 175.00 80.00
❑ 318 Jimmy Fowler UER....... 12.00 5.50
(Name misspelled Jimmie)
❑ 319 Bob Goldham.............. 175.00 80.00
❑ 320 Hank Goldup................ 12.00 5.50
❑ 321 George Hainsworth....... 35.00 16.00
❑ 322 Reg Hamilton................ 12.00 5.50
❑ 323 Red Heron..................... 15.00 6.75
❑ 324 Mel Hill....................... 200.00 90.00
❑ 325 Frank Hollett................ 12.00 5.50
❑ 326 Red Horner................... 15.00 6.75
❑ 327 Art Jackson.................. 10.00 4.50
❑ 328 Harvey Jackson............ 10.00 4.50
❑ 329 Bingo Kampman............ 30.00 13.50
❑ 330 Reg Kelly...................... 15.00 6.75
❑ 331 William Kendall............ 60.00 27.00
❑ 332 Hec Kilrea..................... 45.00 20.00
❑ 333 Pete Langelle............... 15.00 6.75
❑ 334 Bucko McDonald.......... 15.00 6.75
❑ 335A Norm Mann................ 20.00 9.00
❑ 335B Norm Mann............. 150.00 70.00
(Name overlaps stick)
❑ 336 Gus Marker................... 12.00 5.50
❑ 337 Johnny McCreedy......... 30.00 13.50
❑ 338 Jack McLean................ 80.00 36.00
❑ 339 Don Metz...................... 10.00 4.50
❑ 340 Nick Metz...................... 10.00 4.50
❑ 341 George Parsons........... 20.00 9.00
❑ 342 Bud Poile.................... 150.00 70.00
❑ 343 Babe Pratt.................. 225.00 100.00
❑ 344 Joe Primeau.................. 20.00 9.00
❑ 345 Doc Romnes................. 40.00 18.00
❑ 346 Sweeny Schriner.......... 25.00 11.00
❑ 347 Jack Shill...................... 20.00 9.00
❑ 348 Wally Stanowski UER... 12.00 5.50
(Name misspelled Stanowsky)
❑ 349 Phil Stein...................... 40.00 18.00
❑ 350A Gaye Stewart.......... 300.00 135.00
(Home Sweater)
❑ 350B Gaye Stewart.......... 175.00 80.00
(Away Sweater)
❑ 351 Billy Taylor................... 12.00 5.50
❑ 352 Rhys Thompson......... 350.00 160.00
❑ 353 Bill Thoms.................... 12.00 5.50
❑ 354 1944-45 Maple Leafs.. 250.00 110.00
❑ 355 1937 Winnipeg Monarchs 125.00 55.00
❑ 356 Foster Hewitt................ 60.00 27.00
❑ 357 Wes McKnight............ 100.00 45.00
❑ 358A Allan Cup................... 50.00 22.00
(Dated on back)
❑ 358B Allan Cup................. 100.00 45.00
(Blank Back)
❑ 359A Lady Byng Trophy...... 50.00 22.00
(Dated on back)
❑ 359B Lady Byng Trophy.... 100.00 45.00
(Blank back)
❑ 360A Calder Trophy........... 50.00 22.00
(Dated on back)
❑ 360B Calder Trophy......... 100.00 45.00
(Blank back)
❑ 361A Hart Trophy.............. 50.00 22.00
(Dated on back)
❑ 361B Hart Trophy............ 100.00 45.00
(Blank back)
❑ 362A Memorial Cup............ 60.00 27.00
(Dated on back)
❑ 362B Memorial Cup.......... 125.00 55.00
(Blank back)
❑ 363A Prince of Wales Trophy 150.00 70.00
(Dated on back)
❑ 363B Prince of Wales Trophy 175.00 80.00
(Blank back)
❑ 364A Stanley Cup.............. 50.00 22.00
(Dated on back)
❑ 364B Stanley Cup.............. 80.00 36.00
(Blank back)
❑ 364C Stanley Cup.............. 80.00 36.00
(Name horizontal)
❑ 365A Georges Vezina Trophy 50.00 22.00
(Dated on back)
❑ 365B Georges Vezina Trophy 100.00 45.00
(Blank back)

## 1944-63 Beehive Group II Photos

The 1944-63 Beehive photos are the second of three groups. Issued after World War II, this group generally had new photos and a larger script than was typical of Group I. Facsimile autographs were again featured. The set is subdivided as follows: Boston Bruins (1-74), Chicago Blackhawks (75-148), Detroit Red Wings (149-219), Montreal Canadiens (220-294), New York Rangers (295-369), Toronto Maple Leafs (370-461), Four White Border Trophies (462A-464A), and Bottom White Border Trophies (462B-469B). Complete set price is not given due to an ongoing debate over what constitutes a complete set. There are a number of unconfirmed photos that are indicated as such in the checklist below. These photos appeared on the Beehive checklist, but confirmation of their existence is lacking. Among these are the Allan and Memorial Cup trophies in either of their varieties. Anyone with information regarding the existence of any of these unconfirmed photos is asked to forward it to Beckett Publications.

EX-MT VG-E
COMMON PHOTO.................... 5.00 2.20

❑ 1 Bob Armstrong.................. 8.00 3.60
❑ 2 Pete Babando.................. 45.00 20.00
❑ 3 Ray Barry......................... 40.00 18.00
❑ 4 Gus Bodnar...................... 60.00 27.00
❑ 5 Leo Boivin........................ 10.00 4.50
❑ 6 Frankie Brimsek............... 20.00 9.00
❑ 7 Adam Brown (Unconfirmed)
❑ 8 John Bucyk....................... 12.00 5.50
❑ 9 Charlie Burns..................... 8.00 3.60
❑ 10 Jack Caffery.................... 50.00 22.00
❑ 11 Real Chevrefils.................. 5.00 2.20
❑ 12A Wayne Connelly........... 15.00 6.75
❑ 12B Wayne Connelly........... 50.00 22.00
(Name overlaps skate)
❑ 14 John Crawford................. 15.00 6.75
❑ 15A Dave Creighton............ 10.00 4.50
(White sweater)
❑ 15B Dave Creighton............ 50.00 22.00
(Photo on ice)
❑ 16 Woody Dumart................. 20.00 9.00
❑ 17 Pat Egan......................... 25.00 11.00
❑ 18 Bill Ezinicki (Unconfirmed)
❑ 19 Lorne Ferguson............... 10.00 4.50
❑ 20 Fern Flaman...................... 8.00 3.60
❑ 21 Bruce Gamble................. 10.00 4.50
❑ 22 Cal Gardner..................... 10.00 4.50
❑ 23 Ray Gariepy.................... 15.00 6.75
❑ 24 Jack Gelineau.................. 20.00 9.00
❑ 25 Jean-Guy Gendron............. 5.00 2.20
❑ 26A Warren Godfrey............ 10.00 4.50
(A on sweater)
❑ 26B Warren Godfrey............ 50.00 22.00
(With puck)
❑ 26C Warren Godfrey............ 90.00 40.00
(Without puck)
❑ 27 Ed Harrison........................ 5.00 2.20
❑ 28 Don Head........................... 8.00 3.60
❑ 29 Andy Hebenton................ 12.00 5.50
❑ 30 Murray Henderson........... 12.00 5.50
❑ 31 Jim Henry......................... 25.00 11.00
❑ 32 Larry Hillman.................. 25.00 11.00
❑ 33 Pete Horeck..................... 15.00 6.75
❑ 34 Bronco Horvath.................. 8.00 3.60
❑ 35 Tom Johnson................... 10.00 4.50
❑ 36 Eddie Johnston................ 12.00 5.50
❑ 37 Forbes Kennedy (Unconfirmed)
❑ 38 Joe Klukay..................... 150.00 70.00
❑ 39 Edward Kryznowski......... 10.00 4.50
❑ 40 Orland Kurtenbach.......... 30.00 13.50
❑ 41 Leo Labine......................... 5.00 2.20
❑ 42 Hal Laycoe......................... 8.00 3.60
❑ 43 Harry Lumley................... 12.00 5.50
❑ 44 Pentti Lund................. 1000.00 450.00
❑ 45 Fleming Mackell................ 5.00 2.20
❑ 46 Phil Maloney.................... 15.00 6.75
❑ 47 Frank Martin.................... 15.00 6.75
❑ 48 Jack McIntyre.................. 15.00 6.75
❑ 49 Don McKenney................... 5.00 2.20
❑ 50 Dick Meissner.................... 5.00 2.20
❑ 51 Doug Mohns...................... 5.00 2.20
❑ 52 Murray Oliver..................... 5.00 2.20
❑ 53 Willie O'Ree..................... 12.00 5.50
❑ 54A John Peirson................ 10.00 4.50
❑ 54B Johnny Peirson............. 75.00 34.00
❑ 55A Cliff Pennington............ 15.00 6.75
(Name away from skate)
❑ 55B Cliff Pennington............ 75.00 34.00
(Name near skate)
❑ 56A Bob Perreault............... 15.00 6.75
(Name away from skate)
❑ 56B Bob Perreault............... 75.00 34.00
(Name overlaps skate)
❑ 57 Jim Peters....................... 15.00 6.75
❑ 58 Dean Prentice.................. 10.00 4.50
❑ 59 Andre Pronovost................ 8.00 3.60
❑ 60 Bill Quackenbush............ 15.00 6.75
❑ 61 Larry Regan.................... 40.00 18.00
❑ 62 Earl Reibel....................... 30.00 13.50
❑ 63 Paul Ronty....................... 10.00 4.50
❑ 64 Ed Sandford....................... 8.00 3.60
❑ 65 Terry Sawchuk............. 110.00 50.00
❑ 66A Don Simmons ERR.... 150.00 70.00
(Photo of Norm Defelice)
❑ 66B Don Simmons COR........ 8.00 3.60
❑ 67 Kenny Smith.................... 10.00 4.50
❑ 68A Pat Stapleton................ 15.00 6.75
(Name away from skate)
❑ 68B Pat Stapleton................ 75.00 34.00
(Name near skate)
❑ 69 Vic Stasiuk......................... 5.00 2.20
❑ 70 Red Sullivan.................... 20.00 9.00
❑ 71 Jerry Toppazzini................. 5.00 2.20
❑ 72 Zellio Toppazzini............. 10.00 4.50
❑ 73 Grant Warwick................. 35.00 16.00
❑ 74 Tom Williams..................... 8.00 3.60
❑ 75 Al Arbour......................... 10.00 4.50
❑ 76 Pete Babando.................. 15.00 6.75
❑ 77 Earl Balfour........................ 5.00 2.20
❑ 78 Murray Balfour................... 5.00 2.20
❑ 79 Jim Bedard...................... 15.00 6.75
❑ 80 Doug Bentley................... 20.00 9.00
❑ 81 Gus Bodnar...................... 10.00 4.50
❑ 82 Frankie Brimsek.............. 30.00 13.50
❑ 83 Adam Brown.................... 15.00 6.75
❑ 84 Hank Ciesla..................... 35.00 16.00
❑ 85 Jim Conacher................... 12.00 5.50
❑ 86 Pete Conacher.................... 8.00 3.60
❑ 87 Roy Conacher..................... 8.00 3.60
❑ 88 Joe Conn......................... 60.00 27.00
❑ 89 Murray Costello................ 60.00 27.00
❑ 90 Gerry Couture................. 20.00 9.00
❑ 91 Al Dewsbury..................... 10.00 4.50
❑ 92 Ernie Dickens..................... 8.00 3.60
❑ 93 Jack Evans......................... 5.00 2.20
❑ 94 Reggie Fleming................... 5.00 2.20
❑ 95 Lee Fogolin...................... 12.00 5.50
❑ 96 Bill Gadsby......................... 8.00 3.60
❑ 97 George Gee...................... 10.00 4.50
❑ 98 Bob Goldham................... 20.00 9.00
❑ 99 Bep Guidolin.................... 10.00 4.50
❑ 100 Glenn Hall..................... 10.00 4.50
❑ 101 Murray Hall................... 25.00 11.00
❑ 102 Red Hamill.................... 25.00 11.00
❑ 103 Billy Hay.......................... 5.00 2.20
❑ 104 Jim Henry...................... 25.00 11.00
❑ 105 Wayne Hillman.............. 20.00 9.00
❑ 106 Pete Horeck (Unconfirmed)
❑ 107 Bronco Horvath.............. 10.00 4.50
❑ 108 Fred Hucul..................... 20.00 9.00
❑ 109A Bobby Hull............... 200.00 90.00
(Jersey 9)
❑ 109B Bobby Hull................. 25.00 11.00
(Jersey 16)
❑ 110 Lou Jankowski................ 20.00 9.00
❑ 111 Forbes Kennedy............. 50.00 22.00
❑ 112 Ted Lindsay.................... 12.00 5.50
❑ 113 Ed Litzenberger................ 5.00 2.20
❑ 114 Harry Lumley................. 30.00 13.50
Goalie
❑ 115A Len Lunde.................. 50.00 22.00
(Name away from stick)
❑ 115B Len Lunde.................. 15.00 6.75
(Name overlaps stick)
❑ 116 Pat Lundy...................... 12.00 5.50
❑ 117 Vic Lynn (Unconfirmed)
❑ 118A Al MacNeil................. 30.00 13.50
(Name overlaps stick and skate)
❑ 118B Al MacNeil................. 10.00 4.50
(Name overlaps stick)
❑ 119A Chico Maki................. 12.00 5.50
(Name away from stick)
❑ 119B Chico Maki............... 100.00 45.00
(Name overlaps stick)
❑ 120 Doug McCaig.................. 20.00 9.00
❑ 121 Ab McDonald................... 5.00 2.20
❑ 122 Jim McFadden............... 30.00 13.50
❑ 123 Max McNab (Unconfirmed)
❑ 124 Gerry Melnyk UER.......... 5.00 2.20
(Name misspelled Jerry)
❑ 125 Stan Mikita.................... 10.00 4.50
❑ 126 Don Morrison (Unconfirmed)
❑ 127 Gus Mortson.................... 5.00 2.20
❑ 128 Bill Mosienko................. 12.00 5.50
❑ 129 Ron Murphy..................... 5.00 2.20
❑ 130 Ralph Nattrass............... 20.00 9.00
❑ 131 Eric Nesterenko................ 5.00 2.20
❑ 132 Bert Olmstead................ 20.00 9.00
❑ 133 Jim Peters...................... 30.00 13.50
❑ 134 Pierre Pilote.................... 8.00 3.60
❑ 135 Metro Prystai................. 10.00 4.50
❑ 136 Max Quackenbush (Unconfirmed)
❑ 137 Clare Raglan.................. 25.00 11.00
❑ 138A Al Rollins................... 80.00 36.00
(Vertical photo)
❑ 138B Al Rollins................... 25.00 11.00
(Horizontal photo)
❑ 139 Tod Sloan........................ 5.00 2.20
❑ 140 Dollard St. Laurent......... 5.00 2.20
❑ 141 Gaye Stewart................. 15.00 6.75
❑ 142 Jack Stewart.................. 30.00 13.50
❑ 143A Bob Turner................. 40.00 18.00
(Name away from stick)
❑ 143B Bob Turner................. 25.00 11.00
(Name overlaps stick)
❑ 144 Elmer Vasko..................... 5.00 2.20
❑ 145 Kenny Wharram............... 5.00 2.20
❑ 146 Larry Wilson.................. 15.00 6.75
❑ 147 Howie Young.................. 20.00 9.00
❑ 148 Larry Zeidel (Unconfirmed)
❑ 149 Sid Abel......................... 15.00 6.75
❑ 150 Al Arbour....................... 35.00 16.00
❑ 151 Pete Babando................ 20.00 9.00
❑ 152A Doug Barkley............. 50.00 22.00
(Stick blade showing)
❑ 152B Doug Barkley............. 15.00 6.75
(No blade showing)
❑ 153 Hank Bassen.................. 10.00 4.50
❑ 154 Stephen Black................ 25.00 11.00
❑ 155 Marcel Bonin.................. 12.00 5.50
❑ 156 John Bucyk..................... 50.00 22.00
❑ 157 John Conacher........... 175.00 80.00
❑ 158 Gerry Couture UER....... 10.00 4.50
(Name misspelled Jerry)
❑ 159 Billy Dea........................ 20.00 9.00
❑ 160 Alex Delvecchio............... 8.00 3.60
❑ 161 Al Dewsbury (Unconfirmed)
❑ 162 Bill Dineen....................... 5.00 2.20
❑ 163 Jim Enio........................ 50.00 22.00
❑ 164 Alex Faulkner................. 40.00 18.00
❑ 165 Lee Fogolin.................... 10.00 4.50
❑ 166 Val Fonteyne.................... 5.00 2.20
❑ 167 Bill Gadsby..................... 12.00 5.50
❑ 168 Fern Gauthier................. 30.00 13.50
❑ 169 George Gee................... 12.00 5.50
❑ 170 Fred Glover..................... 8.00 3.60
❑ 171 Howie Glover................... 5.00 2.20
❑ 172 Warren Godfrey................ 5.00 2.20
❑ 173 Peter Goegan................... 5.00 2.20
❑ 174 Bob Goldham.................. 10.00 4.50
❑ 175 Glenn Hall...................... 60.00 27.00
❑ 176 Larry Hillman................. 40.00 18.00
❑ 177 Pete Horeck................... 35.00 16.00
❑ 178A Gordie Howe............... 40.00 18.00
❑ 178B Gordie Howe............... 60.00 27.00
(C on sweater)
❑ 179 Ron Ingram.................... 30.00 13.50
❑ 180 Larry Jeffrey.................. 25.00 11.00
❑ 181 Al Johnson...................... 5.00 2.20
❑ 182 Red Kelly......................... 8.00 3.60
❑ 183 Forbes Kennedy............... 6.00 2.70
❑ 184 Leo Labine...................... 5.00 2.20
❑ 185 Tony Leswick................... 8.00 3.60
❑ 186 Ted Lindsay.................. 10.00 4.50
❑ 187 Ed Litzenberger............. 25.00 11.00
❑ 188 Harry Lumley................. 20.00 9.00
❑ 189 Len Lunde........................ 5.00 2.20
❑ 190 Parker MacDonald............ 5.00 2.20
❑ 191 Bruce MacGregor............. 8.00 3.60
❑ 192 Clare Martin.................. 20.00 9.00
❑ 193 Jim McFadden................ 12.00 5.50
❑ 194 Max McNab.................... 20.00 9.00
❑ 195 Gerry Melnyk UER........... 5.00 2.20
(Name misspelled Jerry)
❑ 196 Don Morrison.................. 20.00 9.00
❑ 197 Rod Morrison................. 40.00 18.00
❑ 198 Gerry Odrowski................ 5.00 2.20
❑ 199 Murray Oliver.................. 8.00 3.60
❑ 200 Marty Pavelich................ 5.00 2.20
❑ 201 Jim Peters..................... 40.00 18.00
❑ 202 Bud Poile..................... 125.00 55.00
❑ 203 Andre Pronovost............ 10.00 4.50
❑ 204 Marcel Pronovost............ 5.00 2.20
❑ 205 Metro Prystai................... 8.00 3.60
❑ 206 Bill Quackenbush........... 50.00 22.00
❑ 207 Earl Reibel....................... 8.00 3.60
❑ 208 Leo Reise Jr................... 10.00 4.50
❑ 209 Terry Sawchuk.............. 25.00 11.00
❑ 210 Glen Skov........................ 5.00 2.20
❑ 211 Floyd Smith................... 10.00 4.50
❑ 212A Vic Stasiuk................. 20.00 9.00
(Home sweater; full stick showing)
❑ 212B Vic Stasiuk................. 35.00 16.00
(Home sweater; partial stick showing)
❑ 212C Vic Stasiuk................... 5.00 2.20
(Away sweater)
❑ 213 Gaye Stewart................ 25.00 11.00
❑ 214 Jack Stewart.................. 25.00 11.00
❑ 215 Norm Ullman................... 8.00 3.60
❑ 216 Johnny Wilson................. 5.00 2.20
❑ 217 Benny Woit...................... 8.00 3.60
❑ 218 Howie Young.................. 10.00 4.50
❑ 219 Larry Zeidel................... 20.00 9.00
❑ 220 Ralph Backstrom.............. 8.00 3.60
❑ 221 Dave Balon....................... 8.00 3.60
❑ 222 Jean Beliveau................ 15.00 6.75
❑ 223A Red Berenson.............. 20.00 9.00
(White script)
❑ 223B Red Berenson........... 175.00 80.00
(Black script)
❑ 224 Marcel Bonin.................... 8.00 3.60
❑ 225 Butch Bouchard................ 8.00 3.60
❑ 226 Tod Campeau................ 75.00 34.00

❑ 227 Joe Carveth 10.00 4.50
❑ 228 Murph Chamberlain 40.00 18.00
❑ 229 Doc Couture 35.00 16.00
❑ 230 Floyd Curry UER 5.00 2.20
(Name misspelled Currie)
❑ 231 Ian Cushenan 12.00 5.50
❑ 232 Lorne Davis 10.00 4.50
❑ 233 Eddie Dorohoy 20.00 9.00
❑ 234 Gilles Dube 50.00 22.00
❑ 235 Bill Durnan 30.00 13.50
❑ 236 Norm Dussault 20.00 9.00
❑ 237 John Ferguson 10.00 4.50
❑ 238 Bob Fillion 12.00 5.50
❑ 239 Louie Fontinato 8.00 3.60
❑ 240 Dick Gamble 15.00 6.75
❑ 241 Bernard Geoffrion 12.00 5.50
❑ 242 Phil Goyette 8.00 3.60
❑ 243 Leo Gravelle 20.00 9.00
❑ 244 John Hanna 50.00 22.00
❑ 245 Glen Harmon 15.00 6.75
❑ 246 Terry Harper 8.00 3.60
❑ 247 Doug Harvey 12.00 5.50
❑ 248 Bill Hicke 6.00 2.70
❑ 249 Ike Hildebrand
(Unconfirmed)
❑ 250 Bert Hirschfeld
(Unconfirmed)
❑ 251A Charlie Hodge 60.00 27.00
(White script)
❑ 251B Charlie Hodge 10.00 4.50
(Black script)
❑ 252 Tom Johnson 10.00 4.50
❑ 253 Vern Kaiser 35.00 16.00
❑ 254 Frank King 35.00 16.00
❑ 255 Elmer Lach 10.00 4.50
❑ 256 Al Langlois 6.00 2.70
❑ 257 Jacques Laperriere 8.00 3.60
❑ 258 Hal Laycoe 10.00 4.50
❑ 259 Jackie Leclair 6.00 2.70
❑ 260 Roger Leger 15.00 6.75
❑ 261 Ed Litzenberger 20.00 9.00
❑ 262 Ross Lowe 35.00 16.00
❑ 263 Al MacNeil 8.00 3.60
❑ 264 Bud MacPherson 8.00 3.60
❑ 265 Cesare Maniago 10.00 4.50
❑ 266 Don Marshall 8.00 3.60
❑ 267 Paul Masnick 8.00 3.60
❑ 268 Eddie Mazur 15.00 6.75
❑ 269 John McCormack 10.00 4.50
❑ 270 Alvin McDonald 6.00 2.70
❑ 271 Calum MacKay 10.00 4.50
❑ 272 Gerry McNeil 12.00 5.50
❑ 273 Paul Meger 15.00 6.75
❑ 274 Dickie Moore 10.00 4.50
❑ 275 Kenny Mosdell 15.00 6.75
❑ 276 Bert Olmstead 8.00 3.60
❑ 277 Gerry Plamondon 15.00 6.75
❑ 278 Jacques Plante 30.00 13.50
❑ 279 Andre Pronovost 8.00 3.60
❑ 280 Claude Provost 8.00 3.60
❑ 281 Ken Reardon 20.00 9.00
❑ 282 Billy Reay 10.00 4.50
❑ 283 Henri Richard 15.00 6.75
❑ 284 Maurice Richard 25.00 11.00
❑ 285 Rip Riopelle 25.00 11.00
❑ 286 George Robertson 80.00 36.00
❑ 287 Bobby Rousseau 8.00 3.60
❑ 288 Dollard St. Laurent 8.00 3.60
❑ 289 Jean-Guy Talbot 5.00 2.20
❑ 290A Gilles Tremblay 5.00 2.20
(Dark background)
❑ 290B Gilles Tremblay 175.00 80.00
(Light background)
❑ 291A J.C. Tremblay 8.00 3.60
(Dark background)
❑ 291B J.C. Tremblay 200.00 90.00
(Light background)
❑ 292 Bob Turner 8.00 3.60
❑ 293 Grant Warwick 35.00 16.00
❑ 294 Gump Worsley 20.00 9.00
❑ 295 Clint Albright 10.00 4.50
❑ 296A Dave Balon 20.00 9.00
(Name high on photo)
❑ 296B Dave Balon 8.00 3.60
(Name low on photo)
❑ 297A Andy Bathgate 10.00 4.50
(Home sweater)
❑ 297B Andy Bathgate 15.00 6.75
(Away sweater)
❑ 298 Max Bentley 40.00 18.00
❑ 299 Johnny Bower 50.00 22.00
❑ 300 Hy Buller 15.00 6.75
❑ 301A Larry Cahan 10.00 4.50
(Home sweater)
❑ 301B Larry Cahan 20.00 9.00
(Away sweater)
❑ 302 Bob Crystal 25.00 11.00
❑ 303 Jim Conacher
(Unconfirmed)
❑ 304 Brian Cullen 5.00 2.20
❑ 305 Ian Cushenan 5.00 2.20
❑ 306 Billy Dea 25.00 11.00
❑ 307 Frank Eddolls 5.00 2.20
❑ 308 Pat Egan 30.00 13.50
❑ 309A Jack Evans 5.00 2.20
(Name parallel to bottom)
❑ 309B Jack Evans 35.00 16.00
(Name printed diagonally)
❑ 310 Dunc Fisher 12.00 5.50
❑ 311 Louie Fontinato 8.00 3.60
❑ 312 Bill Gadsby 5.00 2.20
❑ 313 Jean-Guy Gendron 5.00 2.20
❑ 314 Rod Gilbert 10.00 4.50
❑ 315 Howie Glover 35.00 16.00
❑ 316 Jackie Gordon
(Unconfirmed)
❑ 317 Phil Goyette 5.00 2.20
❑ 318 Aldo Guidolin 40.00 18.00
❑ 319 Vic Hadfield 10.00 4.50
❑ 320 Ted Hampson 5.00 2.20
❑ 321 Doug Harvey 10.00 4.50
❑ 322 Andy Hebenton 8.00 3.60
❑ 323 Camille Henry 5.00 2.20
❑ 324 Wally Hergesheimer 5.00 2.20
❑ 325 Ike Hildebrand 25.00 11.00
❑ 326 Bronco Horvath 10.00 4.50
❑ 327 Harry Howell 5.00 2.20
❑ 328A Earl Ingarfield Sr. 8.00 3.60
(Name away from stick)
❑ 328B Earl Ingarfield Sr. 20.00 9.00
(Name near stick)
❑ 329 Bing Juckes 25.00 11.00
❑ 330 Alex Kaleta 12.00 5.50
❑ 331 Stephen Kraftcheck 30.00 13.50
❑ 332 Eddie Kullman 12.00 5.50
❑ 333 Gus Kyle 10.00 4.50
❑ 334 Gord Labossiere 40.00 18.00
❑ 335 Al Langlois 5.00 2.20
❑ 336 Edgar Laprade 12.00 5.50
❑ 337 Tony Leswick 10.00 4.50
❑ 338 Danny Lewicki 5.00 2.20
❑ 339 Pentti Lund 15.00 6.75
❑ 340 Don Marshall 20.00 9.00
❑ 341 Jack McCartan 10.00 4.50
❑ 342 Bill McDonagh 20.00 9.00
❑ 343 Don McKenney 15.00 6.75
❑ 344 Jackie McLeod 15.00 6.75
❑ 345 Nick Mickoski 10.00 4.50
❑ 346 Billy Moe 12.00 5.50
❑ 347 Elwyn Morris
(Unconfirmed)
❑ 348 Ron Murphy 5.00 2.20
❑ 349 Buddy O'Connor 12.00 5.50
❑ 350 Marcel Paille 80.00 36.00
❑ 351 Jacques Plante 80.00 36.00
❑ 352 Bud Poile 30.00 13.50
❑ 353 Larry Popein 5.00 2.20
❑ 354A Dean Prentice 5.00 2.20
(Home sweater)
❑ 354B Dean Prentice 12.00 5.50
(Away sweater)
❑ 355 Don Raleigh 12.00 5.50
❑ 356A Jean Ratelle ERR 50.00 22.00
(Name misspelled John)
❑ 356B Jean Ratelle COR 35.00 16.00
❑ 357 Chuck Rayner 20.00 9.00
❑ 358 Leo Reise Jr. 10.00 4.50
❑ 359 Paul Ronty 10.00 4.50
❑ 360 Ken Schinkel 5.00 2.20
❑ 361 Eddie Shack 25.00 11.00
❑ 362 Fred Shero 25.00 11.00
❑ 363 Reg Sinclair 30.00 13.50
❑ 364 Eddie Slowinski 12.00 5.50
❑ 365 Allan Stanley 6.00 2.70
❑ 366 Wally Stanowski 10.00 4.50
❑ 367 Red Sullivan 5.00 2.20
❑ 368 Zellio Toppazzini
(Unconfirmed)
❑ 369 Gump Worsley 8.00 3.60
❑ 370 Gary Aldcorn 15.00 6.75
❑ 371 Syl Apps Sr. 150.00 70.00
❑ 372 Al Arbour 5.00 2.20
❑ 373A George Armstrong 10.00 4.50
❑ 373B George Armstrong 20.00 9.00
(Dark background)
❑ 373C George Armstrong 200.00 90.00
(Light background)
❑ 374 Bob Bailey 30.00 13.50
❑ 375 Earl Balfour 15.00 6.75
❑ 376 Bill Barilko 40.00 18.00
❑ 377 Andy Bathgate 40.00 18.00
❑ 378 Bob Baun 8.00 3.60
❑ 379 Max Bentley 20.00 9.00
❑ 380 Jack Bionda 125.00 55.00
❑ 381 Garth Boesch 10.00 4.50
❑ 382 Leo Boivin 12.00 5.50
❑ 383 Hugh Bolton 6.00 2.70
❑ 384 Johnny Bower 15.00 6.75
❑ 385 Carl Brewer 5.00 2.20
❑ 386 Turk Broda 20.00 9.00
❑ 387 Larry Cahan 12.00 5.50
❑ 388 Ray Ceresino 60.00 27.00
❑ 389 Ed Chadwick 10.00 4.50
❑ 390 Pete Conacher 80.00 36.00
❑ 391 Les Costello 30.00 13.50
❑ 392 Dave Creighton 15.00 6.75
❑ 393 Barry Cullen 20.00 9.00
❑ 394 Brian Cullen 8.00 3.60
❑ 395 Robert Dawes 20.00 9.00
❑ 396 Kent Douglas 5.00 2.20
❑ 397 Dick Duff 8.00 3.60
❑ 398 Gary Edmundson 5.00 2.20
❑ 399 Gerry Ehman 5.00 2.20
❑ 400 Bill Ezinicki 15.00 6.75
❑ 401 Fern Flaman 50.00 22.00
❑ 402 Cal Gardner 15.00 6.75
❑ 403 Ted Hampson 8.00 3.60
❑ 404 Gord Hannigan 15.00 6.75
❑ 405 Billy Harris 5.00 2.20
❑ 406 Bob Hassard 60.00 27.00
❑ 407 Larry Hillman 5.00 2.20
❑ 408 Tim Horton 20.00 9.00
❑ 409 Bronco Horvath 15.00 6.75
❑ 410 Ron Hurst 125.00 55.00
❑ 411 Gerry James UER 25.00 11.00
(Name misspelled Jerry)
❑ 412 Bill Juzda 12.00 5.50
❑ 413A Red Kelly 10.00 4.50
(Bare-headed)
❑ 413B Red Kelly 25.00 11.00
(Wearing helmet)
❑ 414 Ted Kennedy 15.00 6.75
❑ 415 Dave Keon 12.00 5.50
❑ 416 Joe Klukay 10.00 4.50
❑ 417 Stephen Kraftcheck 30.00 13.50
❑ 418 Danny Lewicki 20.00 9.00
❑ 419 Ed Litzenberger 10.00 4.50
❑ 420 Harry Lumley 20.00 9.00
❑ 421 Vic Lynn 10.00 4.50
❑ 422 Fleming MacKell 12.00 5.50
❑ 423 John MacMillan 5.00 2.20
❑ 424 Al MacNeil 15.00 6.75
❑ 425 Frank Mahovlich 20.00 9.00
❑ 426 Phil Maloney 125.00 55.00
❑ 427 Cesare Maniago 10.00 4.50
❑ 428 Frank Mathers 30.00 13.50
❑ 429 John McCormack 50.00 22.00
❑ 430 Parker MacDonald 20.00 9.00
❑ 431 Don McKenney 30.00 13.50
❑ 432 Howie Meeker 12.00 5.50
❑ 433 Don Metz 250.00 110.00
❑ 434 Nick Metz 200.00 90.00
❑ 435 Rudy Migay 5.00 2.20
❑ 436 Jim Mikol 5.00 2.20
❑ 437 Jim Morrison 5.00 2.20
❑ 438 Gus Mortson 10.00 4.50
❑ 439 Eric Nesterenko 12.00 5.50
❑ 440 Bob Nevin 5.00 2.20
❑ 441 Mike Nykoluk 40.00 18.00
❑ 442 Bert Olmstead 10.00 4.50
❑ 443 Bob Pulford 8.00 3.60
❑ 444 Marc Reaume 12.00 5.50
❑ 445 Larry Regan 5.00 2.20
❑ 446 Dave Reid 125.00 55.00
❑ 447 Al Rollins 25.00 11.00
❑ 448A Eddie Shack 250.00 110.00
(Dark background)
❑ 449 Don Simmons 10.00 4.50
❑ 450 Tod Sloan 5.00 2.20
❑ 451 Sid Smith 5.00 2.20
❑ 452 Bob Solinger 50.00 22.00
❑ 453A Allan Stanley ERR 10.00 4.50
(Name misspelled Alan;
dark background)
❑ 453B Allan Stanley COR 20.00 9.00
(Light background)
❑ 454 Wally Stanowski 400.00 180.00
❑ 455 Ron Stewart 5.00 2.20
❑ 456 Harry Taylor 30.00 13.50
❑ 457 Jim Thomson 10.00 4.50
❑ 458 Ray Timgren 12.00 5.50
❑ 459 Harry Watson 10.00 4.50
❑ 460 Johnny Wilson 5.00 2.20
❑ 461 1962-63 Maple Leafs.. 450.00 200.00
(Team picture)
❑ 462A Lady Byng Trophy .... 300.00 135.00
(Four white borders)
❑ 462B Lady Byng Trophy .... 100.00 45.00
(White bottom
border only)
❑ 463A Calder Memorial Trophy 300.00135.00
(Four white borders)
❑ 463B Calder Memorial Trophy 100.00 45.00
(White bottom
border only)
❑ 464A Hart Trophy 300.00 135.00
(Four white borders)
❑ 464B Hart Trophy 100.00 45.00
(White bottom
border only)
❑ 465A James Norris 300.00 135.00
Memorial Trophy
(Four white borders)
❑ 465B James Norris 100.00 45.00
Memorial Trophy
(White bottom
border only)
❑ 466A Prince of Wales Trophy 300.00 135.00
(Four white borders)
❑ 466B Prince of Wales Trophy 100.00 45.00
(White bottom
border only)
❑ 467A Art Ross Trophy 300.00 135.00
(Four white borders)
❑ 467B Art Ross Trophy 100.00 45.00
(White bottom
border only)
❑ 468A Stanley Cup 300.00 135.00
(Four white borders)
❑ 468B Stanley Cup 100.00 45.00
(White bottom
border only)
❑ 469A Georges Vezina Trophy 300.00 135.00
(Four white borders)
❑ 469B Georges Vezina Trophy 100.00 45.00
(White bottom
border only)

## 1964-67 Beehive Group III Photos

The 1964-67 Beehive photo set is the third of three groups. These photos were issued by St. Lawrence Starch and measure 5 3/8" by 8". The fronts display black-and-white action poses inside a white inner border and a simulated wood-grain outer border. The player's name is displayed on an plaque in the lower wooden border. The backs are blank. The set is subdivided as follows: Boston Bruins (1-29), Chicago Blackhawks (30-60), Detroit Red Wings (61-96), Montreal Canadiens (97-119), New York Rangers (120-149), Toronto Maple Leafs (150-188), Trophies and Miscellaneous (189-197). Complete set price is not given due to an ongoing debate over what constitutes a complete set. A number of unconfirmed photos are scattered throughout the checklist and indicated as such. These photos were part of the Beehive checklist, but have yet to be confirmed. Unnumbered, the checklist is in alphabetical order by team.

NRMT VG-E
COMMON PHOTO 10.00 4.50

❑ 1 Murray Balfour 20.00 9.00
❑ 2 Leo Boivin 10.00 4.50
❑ 3 John Bucyk 12.00 5.50
❑ 4 Wayne Connelly 150.00 70.00
❑ 5 Bob Dillabough 10.00 4.50
❑ 6 Gary Dornhoefer 12.00 5.50
❑ 7 Reggie Fleming 10.00 4.50
❑ 8 Guy Gendron 100.00 45.00
❑ 9 Warren Godfrey 250.00 110.00
❑ 10 Ted Green 10.00 4.50
❑ 11 Andy Hebenton 150.00 70.00
❑ 12 Eddie Johnston 12.00 5.50
❑ 13 Tom Johnson 12.00 5.50
❑ 14 Forbes Kennedy 10.00 4.50
❑ 15 Orland Kurtenbach 30.00 13.50
❑ 16 Bobby Leiter 10.00 4.50
❑ 17 Parker MacDonald 10.00 4.50
❑ 18 Bob McCord 10.00 4.50
❑ 19 Ab McDonald 10.00 4.50
❑ 20 Murray Oliver 10.00 4.50
❑ 21 Bernie Parent 60.00 27.00
❑ 22 Cliff Pennington 200.00 90.00
❑ 23 Bob Perreault 300.00 135.00
❑ 24 Dean Prentice 10.00 4.50
❑ 25 Ron Schock UER 10.00 4.50
(Name misspelled Shock)
❑ 26 Pat Stapleton 40.00 18.00
❑ 27 Ron Stewart 12.00 5.50
❑ 28 Ed Westfall 10.00 4.50
❑ 29 Tom Williams 10.00 4.50
❑ 30 Lou Angotti 10.00 4.50
❑ 31 Wally Boyer 10.00 4.50
❑ 32 Denis DeJordy 12.00 5.50
❑ 33 Dave Dryden 12.00 5.50
❑ 34A Phil Esposito 60.00 27.00
(Blade showing)
❑ 34B Phil Esposito 15.00 6.75
(No blade showing)
❑ 35 Glenn Hall ERR 15.00 6.75
(Name misspelled Glen)
❑ 36 Murray Hall 200.00 90.00
❑ 37 Billy Hay 10.00 4.50
❑ 38 Camille Henry 15.00 6.75
❑ 39 Wayne Hillman 125.00 55.00
❑ 40 Ken Hodge Sr. 12.00 5.50
❑ 41A Bobby Hull 200.00 90.00
(Home sweater)
❑ 41B Bobby Hull 350.00 160.00
(Home sweater;
negative reversed)
❑ 41C Bobby Hull 25.00 11.00
(Away sweater;
blade showing)
❑ 41D Bobby Hull 25.00 11.00
(Away sweater;
no blade showing)
❑ 41E Bobby Hull 400.00 180.00
(Home portrait)
❑ 41F Bobby Hull 25.00 11.00
(Promotional portrait)
❑ 42 Dennis Hull 10.00 4.50
❑ 43 Doug Jarrett 10.00 4.50
❑ 44 Len Lunde 10.00 4.50
❑ 45 Al MacNeil 10.00 4.50
❑ 46A Chico Maki 75.00 34.00
(In action)
❑ 46B Chico Maki 10.00 4.50
(Portrait)
❑ 47 John McKenzie 10.00 4.50
❑ 48 Gerry Melnyk
(Unconfirmed)
❑ 49 Stan Mikita 15.00 6.75
❑ 50 Doug Mohns 10.00 4.50
❑ 51A Eric Nesterenko 200.00 90.00
(Light background)
❑ 51B Eric Nesterenko 10.00 4.50
(Dark background)
❑ 52A Pierre Pilote 225.00 100.00
(Home sweater)
❑ 52B Pierre Pilote 12.00 5.50
(Away sweater)
❑ 53 Matt Ravlich 10.00 4.50
❑ 54 Dollard St. Laurent
(Unconfirmed)
❑ 55A Fred Stanfield 125.00 55.00
❑ 55B Fred Stanfield 85.00 38.00
(Reversed negative)
❑ 56 Pat Stapleton 10.00 4.50
❑ 57 Bob Turner 225.00 100.00
❑ 58 Ed Van Impe 10.00 4.50
❑ 59 Elmer Vasko 12.00 5.50
❑ 60 Kenny Wharram 10.00 4.50
❑ 61 Doug Barkley 10.00 4.50
❑ 62 Hank Bassen 12.00 5.50
❑ 63A Andy Bathgate 10.00 4.50
(Number visible
on sleeve)
❑ 63B Andy Bathgate 10.00 4.50
(Partial number visible)
❑ 64 Gary Bergman 10.00 4.50
❑ 65 Leo Boivin 12.00 5.50
❑ 66 Roger Crozier 12.00 5.50
❑ 67A Alex Delvecchio 15.00 6.75
(Home sweater)
❑ 67B Alex Delvecchio 250.00 110.00
(Away sweater)
❑ 68 Alex Faulkner 300.00 135.00
❑ 69 Val Fonteyne 10.00 4.50
❑ 70 Bill Gadsby 10.00 4.50
❑ 71 Warren Godfrey 20.00 9.00
❑ 72 Pete Goegan 22.00 10.00
❑ 73 Murray Hall 10.00 4.50
❑ 74 Ted Hampson 10.00 4.50
❑ 75 Billy Harris 25.00 11.00
❑ 76 Paul Henderson 15.00 6.75
❑ 77A Gordie Howe 30.00 13.50
❑ 77B Gordie Howe 200.00 90.00
(C on sweater)
❑ 78 Ron Ingram 250.00 110.00
❑ 79A Larry Jeffrey 75.00 34.00
(Home sweater)
❑ 79B Larry Jeffrey 50.00 22.00
(Away sweater)
❑ 80A Eddie Joyal 20.00 9.00
❑ 80B Eddie Joyal 200.00 90.00
(Reversed negative)
❑ 81 Al Langlois 10.00 4.50
❑ 82 Ted Lindsay 15.00 6.75
❑ 83 Parker MacDonald 10.00 4.50
❑ 84A Bruce MacGregor 12.00 5.50
(Home sweater)
❑ 84B Bruce MacGregor 75.00 34.00
(Away sweater)
❑ 85 Pete Mahovlich 10.00 4.50
❑ 86 Bert Marshall 10.00 4.50
❑ 87 Pit Martin 10.00 4.50
❑ 88 Bob McCord
(Unconfirmed)
❑ 89 Ab McDonald 10.00 4.50
❑ 90 Ron Murphy 10.00 4.50
❑ 91 Dean Prentice 10.00 4.50
❑ 92 Andre Pronovost 15.00 6.75
❑ 93 Marcel Pronovost
(Unconfirmed)
❑ 94A Floyd Smith 12.00 5.50
(Home sweater)
❑ 94B Floyd Smith 200.00 90.00
(Home sweater;
reversed negative)
❑ 94C Floyd Smith 150.00 70.00
(Away sweater)
❑ 95 Norm Ullman 15.00 6.75
❑ 96 Bob Wall 10.00 4.50
❑ 97 Ralph Backstrom 10.00 4.50
❑ 98 Dave Balon 10.00 4.50
❑ 99 Jean Beliveau 20.00 9.00
❑ 100 Red Berenson 10.00 4.50
❑ 101 Yvan Cournoyer 15.00 6.75
❑ 102 Dick Duff 12.00 5.50
❑ 103 John Ferguson 10.00 4.50
❑ 104 John Hanna 175.00 80.00
❑ 105A Terry Harper 10.00 4.50
(Posed)
❑ 105B Terry Harper 200.00 90.00
(In action)
❑ 106 Ted Harris 10.00 4.50
❑ 107 Bill Hicke 12.00 5.50
❑ 108 Charlie Hodge 15.00 6.75
❑ 109 Jacques Laperriere 10.00 4.50
❑ 110A Claude Larose 10.00 4.50
❑ 110B Claude Larose 450.00 200.00
(Reversed negative)
❑ 111 Claude Provost 10.00 4.50
❑ 112 Henri Richard 20.00 9.00
❑ 113 Maurice Richard 40.00 18.00
❑ 114 Jim Roberts 10.00 4.50
❑ 115 Bobby Rousseau 10.00 4.50
❑ 116 Jean-Guy Talbot 10.00 4.50
❑ 117A Gilles Tremblay 10.00 4.50
(Sweater 21)
❑ 117B Gilles Tremblay 80.00 36.00
(Sweater 24)
❑ 118 J.C. Tremblay 10.00 4.50
❑ 119 Gump Worsley 15.00 6.75
❑ 120 Lou Angotti 10.00 4.50
❑ 121 Arnie Brown 10.00 4.50
❑ 122 Larry Cahan 250.00 110.00
❑ 123 Dick Duff
(Unconfirmed)
❑ 124 Reggie Fleming 10.00 4.50
❑ 125 Bernie Geoffrion 15.00 6.75
❑ 126 Ed Giacomin 15.00 6.75
❑ 127 Rod Gilbert 15.00 6.75
❑ 128 Phil Goyette 10.00 4.50
❑ 129 Vic Hadfield 12.00 5.50
❑ 130 Doug Harvey
(Unconfirmed)
❑ 131 Camille Henry 135.00 60.00
❑ 132 Bill Hicke 10.00 4.50
❑ 133 Wayne Hillman 10.00 4.50
❑ 134 Harry Howell 12.00 5.50
❑ 135 Earl Ingarfield Sr. 10.00 4.50
❑ 136 Don Johns
(Unconfirmed)
❑ 137 Orland Kurtenbach 10.00 4.50
❑ 138 Gord Labossiere 125.00 55.00
❑ 139 Al MacNeil 10.00 4.50
❑ 140 Cesare Maniago 12.00 5.50
❑ 141 Don Marshall 10.00 4.50
❑ 142 Jim Mikol
(Unconfirmed)
❑ 143 Jim Neilson 10.00 4.50
❑ 144 Bob Nevin 10.00 4.50
❑ 145 Marcel Paille 35.00 16.00
❑ 146 Jacques Plante 60.00 27.00
❑ 147 Jean Ratelle 20.00 9.00
❑ 148 Rod Seiling 10.00 4.50
❑ 149 Red Sullivan
(Unconfirmed)
❑ 150 Al Arbour
(Unconfirmed)
❑ 151 George Armstrong 15.00 6.75

□ 152 Andy Bathgate 15.00 6.75
□ 153A Bob Baun 100.00 45.00
(Number visible)
□ 153B Bob Baun 15.00 6.75
(No number visible)
□ 154A Johnny Bower 150.00 70.00
(Number visible)
□ 154B Johnny Bower 20.00 9.00
(No number visible)
□ 155 Wally Boyer 25.00 11.00
□ 156 John Brenneman 10.00 4.50
□ 157 Carl Brewer 20.00 9.00
□ 158 Turk Broda 25.00 11.00
□ 159 Brian Conacher 10.00 4.50
□ 160 Kent Douglas 10.00 4.50
□ 161 Ron Ellis 10.00 4.50
□ 162 Bruce Gamble 15.00 6.75
□ 163A Billy Harris 75.00 34.00
(Number visible)
□ 163B Billy Harris 200.00 90.00
(No number visible)
□ 164 Larry Hillman 20.00 9.00
□ 165A Tim Horton 150.00 70.00
(Number visible)
□ 165B Tim Horton 25.00 11.00
(No number visible)
□ 166 Bronco Horvath 150.00 70.00
□ 167 Larry Jeffrey 25.00 11.00
□ 168 Eddie Joyal 35.00 16.00
□ 169 Red Kelly 15.00 6.75
□ 170 Ted Kennedy 15.00 6.75
□ 171A Dave Keon 125.00 55.00
(Number visible)
□ 171B Dave Keon 20.00 9.00
(No number visible)
□ 172 Orland Kurtenbach 12.00 5.50
□ 173 Ed Litzenberger 15.00 6.75
□ 174A Frank Mahovlich 150.00 70.00
(Number visible)
□ 174B Frank Mahovlich 25.00 11.00
(No number visible)
□ 175A Don McKenney 75.00 34.00
(Small photo)
□ 175B Don McKenney 15.00 6.75
(Large photo)
□ 176 Dickie Moore 15.00 6.75
□ 177 Jim Pappin 10.00 4.50
□ 178A Marcel Pronovost 12.00 5.50
(Blade showing)
□ 178B Marcel Pronovost 25.00 11.00
(No Blade showing)
□ 180A Bob Pulford 75.00 34.00
(Number visible)
□ 180B Bob Pulford 15.00 6.75
(No number visible)
□ 181 Terry Sawchuk 25.00 11.00
□ 182 Brit Selby 10.00 4.50
□ 183 Eddie Shack 20.00 9.00
□ 184 Don Simmons 20.00 9.00
□ 185 Allan Stanley 15.00 6.75
□ 186 Pete Stemkowski 10.00 4.50
□ 187A Ron Stewart 150.00 70.00
(Number visible)
□ 187B Ron Stewart 50.00 22.00
(No number visible)
□ 188 Mike Walton 25.00 11.00
□ 189 Bernie Geoffrion 40.00 18.00
□ 190 Lady Byng Trophy 100.00 45.00
□ 191 Calder Memorial 100.00 45.00
Trophy
□ 192 Hart Trophy 100.00 45.00
□ 193 Prince of Wales 100.00 45.00
Trophy
□ 194 James Norris 100.00 45.00
Memorial Trophy
□ 195 Art Ross Trophy 100.00 45.00
□ 196 Stanley Cup 100.00 45.00
□ 197 Vezina Trophy 100.00 45.00

## 1997-98 Beehive

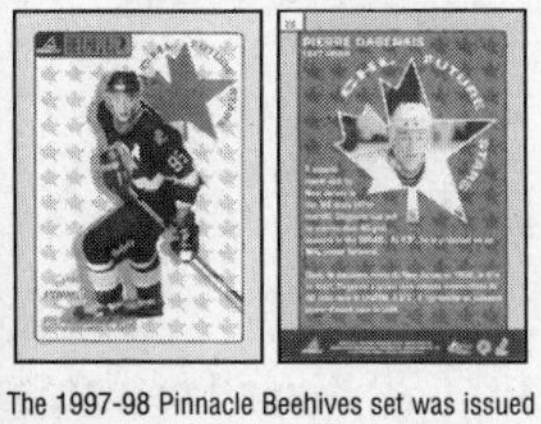

The 1997-98 Pinnacle Beehives set was issued in one series totalling 75 cards and was distributed in four-card packs with a suggested retail price of $4.99. This set is a revival of the 1934-67 Beehive Photos sets produced by the St. Lawrence Starch Co. of Port Credit, Ontario. This new version features color player portraits printed on 5" by 7" cards. The backs carry a black-and-white action player photos with player information and career statistics. The player information as well as a trivia question is printed in both French and English. The set contains the topical subsets: Golden Originals (57-62), and Junior League Stars (63-74).

| | MINT | NRMT |
|---|---|---|
| COMPLETE SET (75) | 70.00 | 32.00 |
| COMMON CARD (1-75) | .25 | .11 |

□ 1 Eric Lindros 2.50 1.10
□ 2 Teemu Selanne 1.50 .70
□ 3 Brendan Shanahan 1.50 .70
□ 4 Joe Sakic 1.50 .70
□ 5 John LeClair 1.25 .55
□ 6 Brett Hull 1.00 .45
□ 7 Jaromir Jagr 2.50 1.10
□ 8 Bryan Berard .60 .25
□ 9 Peter Forsberg 2.50 1.10
□ 10 Ed Belfour .75 .35
□ 11 Steve Yzerman 2.50 1.10
□ 12 Curtis Joseph .75 .35
□ 13 Saku Koivu 1.25 .55
□ 14 Keith Tkachuk 1.00 .45
□ 15 Pavel Bure 1.50 .70
□ 16 Felix Potvin .75 .35
□ 17 Ray Bourque .75 .35
□ 18 Theoren Fleury .60 .25
□ 19 Patrick Roy 4.00 1.80
□ 20 Joe Nieuwendyk .60 .25
□ 21 Alexei Yashin .60 .25
□ 22 Owen Nolan .60 .25
□ 23 Mark Recchi .60 .25
□ 24 Dominik Hasek 1.50 .70
□ 25 Chris Chelios .75 .35
□ 26 Mike Modano 1.00 .45
□ 27 John Vanbiesbrouck 1.50 .70
□ 28 Brian Leetch .75 .35
□ 29 Dino Ciccarelli .25 .11
□ 30 Mark Messier 1.00 .45
□ 31 Paul Kariya 3.00 1.35
□ 32 Jocelyn Thibault .60 .25
□ 33 Wayne Gretzky 5.00 2.20
□ 34 Doug Weight .60 .25
□ 35 Yanic Perreault .25 .11
□ 36 Luc Robitaille .60 .25
□ 37 Chris Osgood .75 .35
□ 38 Adam Oates .60 .25
□ 39 Mats Sundin .75 .35
□ 40 Trevor Linden .60 .25
□ 41 Mike Richter .75 .35
□ 42 Zigmund Palffy .75 .35
□ 43 Pat LaFontaine .60 .25
□ 44 Grant Fuhr .60 .25
□ 45 Martin Brodeur 2.00 .90
□ 46 Sergei Fedorov 1.50 .70
□ 47 Doug Gilmour .75 .35
□ 48 Daniel Alfredsson .60 .25
□ 49 Ron Francis .60 .25
□ 50 Geoff Sanderson .60 .25
□ 51 Joe Thornton 1.50 .70
□ 52 Vaclav Prospal 1.50 .70
□ 53 Patrik Elias 1.50 .70
□ 54 Mike Johnson 1.50 .70
□ 55 Alyn McCauley .60 .25
□ 56 Brendan Morrison 1.50 .70
□ 57 Johnny Bower GO 1.00 .45
□ 58 John Bucyk GO 1.00 .45
□ 59 Stan Mikita GO 1.00 .45
□ 60 Ted Lindsay GO 1.00 .45
□ 61 Maurice Richard GO 3.00 1.35
□ 62 Andy Bathgate GO 1.00 .45
□ 63 Stefan Cherneski JLS 1.25 .55
□ 64 Craig Hillier JLS 1.25 .55
□ 65 Daniel Tkaczuk JLS .75 .35
□ 66 Josh Holden JLS .60 .25
□ 67 Marian Cisar JLS .60 .25
□ 68 J.P. Dumont JLS 1.25 .55
□ 69 Roberto Luongo JLS 5.00 2.20
□ 70 Aren Miller JLS .60 .25
□ 71 Mathieu Garon JLS .75 .35
□ 72 Charlie Stephens JLS .75 .35
□ 73 Sergei Varlamov JLS 1.50 .70
□ 74 Pierre Dagenais JLS 1.50 .70
□ 75 Willie O'Ree CC 1.50 .70
□ P1 Eric Lindros PROMO 3.00 1.35
□ R1 Redemption 40.00 18.00

## 1997-98 Beehive Authentic Autographs

Randomly inserted in packs at the rate of one in 12, this 19-card set features autographed cards of CHL stars that seem to have an outstanding chance of becoming NHL stars as well as some of the NHL's top rookies.

| | MINT | NRMT |
|---|---|---|
| COMPLETE SET (17) | 400.00 | 180.00 |
| COMMON CARD | 15.00 | 6.75 |

□ 51 Joe Thornton 30.00 13.50
□ 52 Vaclav Prospal 25.00 11.00
□ 53 Patrik Elias 25.00 11.00
□ 54 Mike Johnson 25.00 11.00
□ 55 Alyn McCauley 25.00 11.00
□ 56 Brendan Morrison 25.00 11.00
□ 63 Stefan Cherneski 20.00 9.00
□ 64 Craig Hillier 20.00 9.00
□ 65 Daniel Tkaczuk 20.00 9.00
□ 66 Josh Holden 20.00 9.00
□ 67 Marian Cisar 15.00 6.75
□ 68 J.P. Dumont 20.00 9.00
□ 69 Roberto Luongo 40.00 18.00
□ 70 Aren Miller 15.00 6.75
□ 71 Mathieu Garon 20.00 9.00
□ 72 Charlie Stephens 20.00 9.00
□ 73 Sergei Varlamov 20.00 9.00
□ 74 Pierre Dagenais 20.00 9.00
□ 75 Willie O'Ree 25.00 11.00

## 1997-98 Beehive Golden Portraits

Randomly inserted in packs at the rate of one in three, this 75-card set is a gold-foil parallel version of the base set.

| | MINT | NRMT |
|---|---|---|
| COMPLETE SET (75) | 400.00 | 180.00 |
| COMMON CARD (1-75) | 1.25 | .55 |

*STARS: 2.5X TO 5X BASIC CARD
*YOUNG STARS: 2X TO 4X BASIC CARD
*RC's: 1.5X TO 3X BASIC CARD

## 1997-98 Beehive Golden Originals Autographs

Randomly inserted in packs at the rate of one in 36, this six-card set features autographed color photos of six top retired players.

| | MINT | NRMT |
|---|---|---|
| COMPLETE SET (6) | 200.00 | 90.00 |
| COMMON CARD | 30.00 | 13.50 |

□ 57 Johnny Bower 30.00 13.50
□ 58 John Bucyk 30.00 13.50
□ 59 Stan Mikita 40.00 18.00
□ 60 Ted Lindsay 30.00 13.50
□ 61 Maurice Richard 60.00 27.00
□ 62 Andy Bathgate 30.00 13.50

## 1997-98 Beehive Team

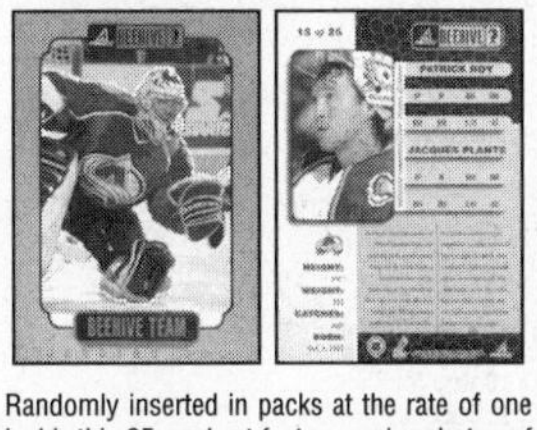

Randomly inserted in packs at the rate of one in 11, this 25-card set features color photos of some of Hockey's best players. The backs carry player information. A Beehive Gold Team set was also produced which is a parallel version to this insert set and has an insertion rate of 1:49.

| | MINT | NRMT |
|---|---|---|
| COMPLETE SET (25) | 300.00 | 135.00 |
| COMMON CARD (1-25) | 5.00 | 2.20 |
| COMP.GOLD TEAM (25) | 600.00 | 275.00 |
| COMMON GOLD TEAM (1-25) | 10.00 | 4.50 |

*GOLD TEAM STARS: 1X TO 2X BASIC CARDS

□ 1 Paul Kariya 25.00 11.00
□ 2 Mark Messier 8.00 3.60
□ 3 Mike Modano 8.00 3.60
□ 4 Brendan Shanahan 12.00 5.50
□ 5 John Vanbiesbrouck 10.00 4.50
□ 6 Martin Brodeur 15.00 6.75
□ 7 Wayne Gretzky 40.00 18.00
□ 8 Eric Lindros 20.00 9.00
□ 9 Peter Forsberg 20.00 9.00
□ 10 Jaromir Jagr 20.00 9.00
□ 11 Teemu Selanne 12.00 5.50
□ 12 John LeClair 10.00 4.50
□ 13 Saku Koivu 10.00 4.50
□ 14 Brett Hull 8.00 3.60
□ 15 Patrick Roy 30.00 13.50
□ 16 Steve Yzerman 20.00 9.00
□ 17 Keith Tkachuk 8.00 3.60
□ 18 Pat LaFontaine 5.00 2.20
□ 19 Joe Sakic 12.00 5.50
□ 20 Patrik Elias 6.00 2.70
□ 21 Vaclav Prospal 6.00 2.70
□ 22 Joe Thornton 10.00 4.50
□ 23 Sergei Samsonov 12.00 5.50
□ 24 Alexei Morozov 5.00 2.20
□ 25 Marco Sturm 8.00 3.60

## 1968-69 Blackhawks

This 8-card set measures approximately 4" by 6" and features the Chicago Blackhawks. The fronts carry borderless, posed, color player photos except at the bottom, where a white bar carries the player's name. The backs are blank. The cards are unnumbered and checklisted below in alphabetical order.

| | NRMT-MT | EXC |
|---|---|---|
| COMPLETE SET (8) | 40.00 | 18.00 |
| COMMON CARD | 5.00 | 2.20 |

□ 1 Dennis Hull 8.00 3.60
□ 2 Doug Jarrett 5.00 2.20
□ 3 Chico Maki 6.00 2.70
□ 4 Gilles Marotte 5.00 2.20
□ 5 Stan Mikita 15.00 6.75
□ 6 Jim Pappin 5.00 2.20
□ 7 Pat Stapleton 5.00 2.20
□ 8 Ken Wharram 6.00 2.70

## 1970-71 Blackhawks Borderless

This 14-card set measures approximately 4" by 6". The fronts feature borderless posed color player photos except at the bottom, where a white bar carries the player's name. The backs are blank. The cards are unnumbered and checklisted below in alphabetical order.

| | NRMT-MT | EXC |
|---|---|---|
| COMPLETE SET (14) | 50.00 | 22.00 |
| COMMON CARD (1-14) | 3.00 | 1.35 |

□ 1 Lou Angotti 3.00 1.35
□ 2 Bryan Campbell 3.00 1.35
□ 3 Bobby Hull 15.00 6.75
Bill Wirtz OWN
Stan Mikita
□ 4 Dennis Hull 6.00 2.70
□ 5 Tommy Ivan GM 3.00 1.35
Billy Reay CO
□ 6 Doug Jarrett 3.00 1.35
□ 7 Keith Magnuson 5.00 2.20
□ 8 Pit Martin 3.00 1.35
□ 9 Stan Mikita 10.00 4.50
□ 10 Eric Nesterenko 5.00 2.20
□ 11 Jim Pappin 4.00 1.80
□ 12 Allan Pinder 3.00 1.35
□ 13 Paul Shmyr 3.00 1.35
□ 14 Bill White 4.00 1.80

## 1980-81 Blackhawks Brown Background

These postcard-size cards measure approximately 4" by 6" and feature borderless posed color player photos with brown backgrounds. The plain white back carries the player's name, position, and biography. The cards are unnumbered and checklisted below in alphabetical order.

| | NRMT-MT | EXC |
|---|---|---|
| COMPLETE SET (16) | 20.00 | 9.00 |
| COMMON CARD | 1.00 | .45 |

□ 1 Keith Brown 2.00 .90
□ 2 Greg Fox 1.00 .45
□ 3 Dave Hutchison 1.00 .45
□ 4 Cliff Koroll ACO 1.00 .45
□ 5 Keith Magnuson CO 1.50 .70
□ 6 Peter Marsh 1.50 .70
□ 7 Grant Mulvey 1.50 .70
□ 8 Rich Preston 1.00 .45
□ 9 Florent Robidoux 1.00 .45
□ 10 Terry Ruskowski 1.50 .70
□ 11 Denis Savard 5.00 2.20
□ 12 Al Secord 2.00 .90
□ 13 Ron Sedlbauer 1.00 .45
□ 14 Glen Sharpley 1.00 .45
□ 15 Darryl Sutter 2.00 .90
□ 16 Miles Zaharko 1.00 .45

## 1980-81 Blackhawks White Border

These 14 blank-backed photos measure approximately 5 1/2" by 8 1/2" and feature posed black-and-white player photos on their white-bordered fronts. The player's name appears in black lettering within the lower white margin. The photos are unnumbered and checklisted below in alphabetical order.

| | NRMT-MT | EXC |
|---|---|---|
| COMPLETE SET (14) | 20.00 | 9.00 |
| COMMON CARD | 1.00 | .45 |

□ 1 Murray Bannerman 1.50 .70
□ 2 J.P. Bordeleau 1.00 .45
□ 3 Keith Brown 2.00 .90
□ 4 Tony Esposito 5.00 2.20
□ 5 Greg Fox 1.00 .45
□ 6 Tim Higgins 1.00 .45
□ 7 Doug Lecuyer 1.00 .45
□ 8 John Marks 1.00 .45
□ 9 Grant Mulvey 1.50 .70
□ 10 Rich Preston 1.00 .45
□ 11 Terry Ruskowski 1.50 .70
□ 12 Denis Savard 5.00 2.20
□ 13 Darryl Sutter 2.00 .90
□ 14 Tim Trimper 1.00 .45

## 1981-82 Blackhawks Borderless Postcards

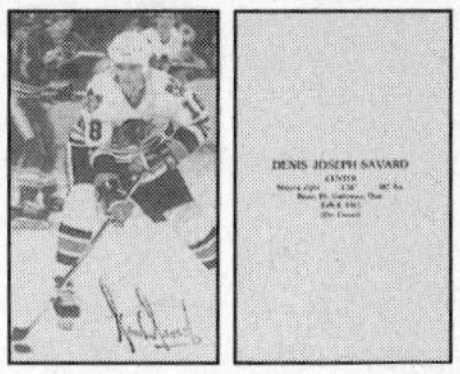

These 28 postcards measure approximately 3 1/2" by 5 1/2" and feature color action player photos on their borderless fronts. A facsimile player autograph rests near the bottom. The backs carry the player's name, position and brief biography. The postcards are unnumbered and checklisted below in alphabetical order.

| | NRMT-MT | EXC |
|---|---|---|
| COMPLETE SET (28) | 30.00 | 13.50 |
| COMMON CARD | .75 | .35 |

□ 1 Murray Bannerman 1.50 .70
□ 2 Keith Brown 1.50 .70
□ 3 Ted Bulley .75 .35
□ 4 Doug Crossman 1.50 .70
□ 5 Jerome Dupont .75 .35
□ 6 Tony Esposito 5.00 2.20
□ 7 Greg Fox .75 .35
□ 8 Bill Gardner .75 .35
□ 9 Tim Higgins .75 .35
□ 10 Dave Hutchison .75 .35
□ 11 Reg Kerr .75 .35
□ 12 Cliff Koroll ACO .75 .35
□ 13 Tom Lysiak 1.50 .70
□ 14 Keith Magnuson CO 1.50 .70
□ 15 John Marks .75 .35
□ 16 Peter Marsh .75 .35
□ 17 Grant Mulvey .75 .35
□ 18 Bob Murray .75 .35
□ 19 Rick Paterson .75 .35
□ 20 Rich Preston .75 .35
□ 21 Bob Pulford GM 1.50 .70
□ 22 Terry Ruskowski .75 .35
□ 23 Denis Savard 5.00 2.20
□ 24 Al Secord 2.00 .90
□ 25 Glen Sharpley .75 .35
□ 26 Darryl Sutter 2.00 .90
□ 27 Toni Tanti 2.00 .90
□ 28 Doug Wilson 3.00 1.35

## 1981-82 Blackhawks Brown Background

These 17 postcards measure approximately 4" by 6" and feature borderless posed color player photos with brown backgrounds. The plain white back carries the player's name, position, and biography. The cards are unnumbered and checklisted below in alphabetical order.

| | NRMT-MT | EXC |
|---|---|---|
| COMPLETE SET (17) | 25.00 | 11.00 |
| COMMON CARD | 1.00 | .45 |

□ 1 Keith Brown 2.00 .90
□ 2 Greg Fox 1.00 .45
□ 3 Dave Hutchison 1.00 .45
□ 4 Cliff Koroll ACO 1.00 .45
□ 5 Keith Magnuson CO 2.00 .90
□ 6 Peter Marsh 2.00 .90
□ 7 Grant Mulvey 2.00 .90
□ 8 Bob Pulford GM/CO 3.00 1.35
□ 9 Rich Preston 1.00 .45
□ 10 Florent Robidoux 1.00 .45
□ 11 Terry Ruskowski 2.00 .90
□ 12 Denis Savard 7.50 3.40
□ 13 Al Secord 2.00 .90
□ 14 Ron Sedlbauer 1.00 .45
□ 15 Glen Sharpley 1.00 .45
□ 16 Darryl Sutter 3.00 1.35
□ 17 Miles Zaharko 1.00 .45

## 1983-84 Blackhawks Borderless Postcards

These 27 postcards measure approximately 3 1/2" by 5 1/2" and feature posed color player portraits on their borderless fronts. The backs carry the player's name, position and brief biography. The postcards are unnumbered and checklisted below in alphabetical order.

| | NRMT-MT | EXC |
|---|---|---|
| COMPLETE SET (27) | 35.00 | 16.00 |
| COMMON CARD | .50 | .23 |
| ❑ 1 Murray Bannerman | 1.50 | .70 |
| ❑ 2 Keith Brown | 1.00 | .45 |
| ❑ 3 Denis Cyr | .75 | .35 |
| ❑ 4 Jerome Dupont | .75 | .35 |
| ❑ 5 Tony Esposito | 4.00 | 1.80 |
| ❑ 6 Dave Feamster | .75 | .35 |
| ❑ 7 Curt Fraser | 1.00 | .45 |
| ❑ 8 Bill Gardner | .75 | .35 |
| ❑ 9 Bob Janecyk | 1.50 | .70 |
| ❑ 10 Cliff Koroll ACO | .50 | .23 |
| ❑ 11 Steve Larmer | 7.00 | 3.10 |
| ❑ 12 Steve Ludzik | 1.50 | .70 |
| ❑ 13 Tom Lysiak | 1.50 | .70 |
| ❑ 14 Peter Marsh | .75 | .35 |
| ❑ 15 Bob Murray | .75 | .35 |
| ❑ 16 Troy Murray | 1.50 | .70 |
| ❑ 17 Jack O'Callahan | .75 | .35 |
| ❑ 18 Rick Paterson | .75 | .35 |
| ❑ 19 Rich Preston | .75 | .35 |
| ❑ 20 Denis Savard | 4.00 | 1.80 |
| ❑ 21 Al Secord | 2.00 | .90 |
| ❑ 22 Darryl Sutter | 2.00 | .90 |
| ❑ 23 Orval Tessier CO | .50 | .23 |
| ❑ 24 Behn Wilson | .75 | .35 |
| ❑ 25 Doug Wilson | 2.50 | 1.10 |
| ❑ 26 Ken Yaremchuk | .75 | .35 |
| ❑ 27 Title Card | .50 | .23 |

## 1986-87 Blackhawks Coke

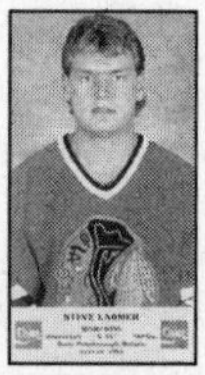

This 24-card set of Chicago Blackhawks was sponsored by Coca-Cola, whose company logo appears at the bottom corner on the card front. The cards measure approximately 3 1/2" by 6 1/2" and feature borderless color posed photos of the players. The player's name and brief biographical information is given beneath the picture between the Coke logos. The backs are blank. The cards are unnumbered and we have checklisted them below in alphabetical order.

| | MINT | NRMT |
|---|---|---|
| COMPLETE SET (24) | 20.00 | 9.00 |
| COMMON CARD | .75 | .35 |
| ❑ 1 Murray Bannerman | 1.00 | .45 |
| ❑ 2 Marc Bergevin | .75 | .35 |
| ❑ 3 Keith Brown | .75 | .35 |
| ❑ 4 Dave Donnelly | .75 | .35 |
| ❑ 5 Curt Fraser | .75 | .35 |
| ❑ 6 Steve Larmer | 3.00 | 1.35 |
| ❑ 7 Steve Ludzik | .75 | .35 |
| ❑ 8 Dave Manson | 1.50 | .70 |
| ❑ 9 Bob Murray | .75 | .35 |
| ❑ 10 Troy Murray | .75 | .35 |
| ❑ 11 Gary Nylund | .75 | .35 |
| ❑ 12 Jack O'Callahan | .75 | .35 |
| ❑ 13 Ed Olczyk | 1.00 | .45 |
| ❑ 14 Rick Paterson | .75 | .35 |
| ❑ 15 Wayne Presley | .75 | .35 |
| ❑ 16 Rich Preston | .75 | .35 |
| ❑ 17 Bob Sauve | 1.00 | .45 |
| ❑ 18 Denis Savard | 3.00 | 1.35 |
| ❑ 19 Al Secord | 1.00 | .45 |
| ❑ 20 Mike Stapleton | .75 | .35 |
| ❑ 21 Darryl Sutter | 1.00 | .45 |
| ❑ 22 Bill Watson | .75 | .35 |
| ❑ 23 Behn Wilson | .75 | .35 |
| ❑ 24 Doug Wilson | 1.50 | .70 |

## 1987-88 Blackhawks Coke

This 30-card set of Chicago Blackhawks was sponsored by Coca-Cola, whose company logo appears at the bottom corner on the card front. The cards measure approximately 3 1/2" by 6 1/2" and feature borderless color posed photos of the players. The player's name and brief biographical information is given beneath the picture between the Coke logos. The backs are blank. The cards are unnumbered and we have checklisted them below in alphabetical order.

| | MINT | NRMT |
|---|---|---|
| COMPLETE SET (30) | 20.00 | 9.00 |
| COMMON CARD (1-30) | .75 | .35 |
| ❑ 1 Murray Bannerman | 1.00 | .45 |
| ❑ 2 Marc Bergevin | .75 | .35 |
| ❑ 3 Keith Brown | .75 | .35 |
| ❑ 4 Glen Cochrane | .75 | .35 |
| ❑ 5 Curt Fraser | .75 | .35 |
| ❑ 6 Steve Larmer | 2.50 | 1.10 |
| ❑ 7 Mark LaVarre | .75 | .35 |
| ❑ 8 Steve Ludzik | .75 | .35 |
| ❑ 9 Dave Manson | 1.50 | .70 |
| ❑ 10 Bob Mason | 1.00 | .45 |
| ❑ 11 Bob McGill | .75 | .35 |
| ❑ 12 Bob Murdoch CO | .75 | .35 |
| ❑ 13 Bob Murray | .75 | .35 |
| ❑ 14 Troy Murray | 1.00 | .45 |
| ❑ 15 Brian Noonan | .75 | .35 |
| ❑ 16 Gary Nylund | .75 | .35 |
| ❑ 17 Darren Pang | 1.50 | .70 |
| ❑ 18 Wayne Presley | .75 | .35 |
| ❑ 19 Everett Sanipass | .75 | .35 |
| ❑ 20 Denis Savard | 2.50 | 1.10 |
| ❑ 21 Mike Stapleton | .75 | .35 |
| ❑ 22 Darryl Sutter CO | .75 | .35 |
| ❑ 23 Duane Sutter | 1.00 | .45 |
| ❑ 24 Steve Thomas | 1.25 | .55 |
| ❑ 25 Wayne Thomas CO | .75 | .35 |
| ❑ 26 Rick Vaive | 1.00 | .45 |
| ❑ 27 Dan Vincelette | .75 | .35 |
| ❑ 28 Bill Watson | .75 | .35 |
| ❑ 29 Behn Wilson | .75 | .35 |
| ❑ 30 Doug Wilson | 1.50 | .70 |

## 1988-89 Blackhawks Coke

This 25-card set of Chicago Blackhawks was sponsored by Coca-Cola, whose company logo appears at the bottom corner on the card front. The cards measure approximately 3 1/2" by 6 1/2" and feature borderless color posed photos of the players. The player's name and brief biographical information is given beneath the picture between the Coke logos. The backs are blank. The cards are unnumbered and we have checklisted them below in alphabetical order. The set features an early card of Ed Belfour pre-dating his Rookie Cards by two years.

| | MINT | NRMT |
|---|---|---|
| COMPLETE SET (25) | 20.00 | 9.00 |
| COMMON CARD (1-25) | .25 | .11 |
| ❑ 1 Ed Belfour | 7.50 | 3.40 |
| ❑ 2 Keith Brown | .50 | .23 |
| ❑ 3 Bruce Cassidy | .50 | .23 |
| ❑ 4 Mike Eagles | .50 | .23 |
| ❑ 5 Dirk Graham | 1.00 | .45 |
| ❑ 6 Mike Hudson | .50 | .23 |
| ❑ 7 Mike Keenan CO | 1.50 | .70 |
| ❑ 8 Steve Larmer | 1.50 | .70 |
| ❑ 9 Dave Manson | 1.00 | .45 |
| ❑ 10 Jacques Martin CO | .25 | .11 |
| ❑ 11 Bob McGill | .50 | .23 |
| ❑ 12 E.J. McGuire CO | .25 | .11 |
| ❑ 13 Troy Murray | 1.00 | .45 |
| ❑ 14 Brian Noonan | .50 | .23 |
| ❑ 15 Darren Pang | .75 | .35 |
| ❑ 16 Wayne Presley | .50 | .23 |
| ❑ 17 Everett Sanipass | .50 | .23 |
| ❑ 18 Denis Savard | 2.00 | .90 |
| ❑ 19 Duane Sutter | .75 | .35 |
| ❑ 20 Steve Thomas | 1.00 | .45 |
| ❑ 21 Rick Vaive | .75 | .35 |
| ❑ 22 Dan Vincelette | .50 | .23 |
| ❑ 23 Jimmy Waite | .75 | .35 |
| ❑ 24 Doug Wilson | 1.00 | .45 |
| ❑ 25 Trent Yawney | .50 | .23 |

## 1989-90 Blackhawks Coke

This 27-card set was sponsored by Coke. The cards were issued in a photo album consisting of five unperforated sheets measuring approximately 12" by 12". The first four sheets have six players each, while the last sheet features the three coaches. If the cards were cut, they would measure approximately 4" by 6". The fronts have posed color player photos, shot from the waist up against a blue background. Biographical information appears below the picture between two Coke logos. The backs are blank. The cards are unnumbered and checklisted below according to the order they appear in the photo album. The set features an early card of Jeremy Roenick pre-dating his Rookie Cards by one year. The set price below is for complete album form; the singles prices are for cut cards.

| | MINT | NRMT |
|---|---|---|
| COMPLETE SET (27) | 20.00 | 9.00 |
| COMMON CARD (1-27) | .25 | .11 |
| ❑ 1 Denis Savard | 2.00 | .90 |
| ❑ 2 Troy Murray | .75 | .35 |
| ❑ 3 Steve Larmer | 1.50 | .70 |
| ❑ 4 Doug Wilson | 1.50 | .70 |
| ❑ 5 Bob Murray | .50 | .23 |
| ❑ 6 Jeremy Roenick | 5.00 | 2.20 |
| ❑ 7 Duane Sutter | .75 | .35 |
| ❑ 8 Greg Gilbert | .50 | .23 |
| ❑ 9 Trent Yawney | .50 | .23 |
| ❑ 10 Bob McGill | .50 | .23 |
| ❑ 11 Jacques Cloutier | .75 | .35 |
| ❑ 12 Bob Bassen | .50 | .23 |
| ❑ 13 Steve Thomas | 1.00 | .45 |
| ❑ 14 Adam Creighton | .75 | .35 |
| ❑ 15 Wayne Van Dorp | .50 | .23 |
| ❑ 16 Dirk Graham | 1.00 | .45 |
| ❑ 17 Mike Hudson | .50 | .23 |
| ❑ 18 Al Secord | .75 | .35 |
| ❑ 19 Alain Chevrier | .75 | .35 |
| ❑ 20 Wayne Presley | .50 | .23 |
| ❑ 21 Steve Konroyd | .50 | .23 |
| ❑ 22 Everett Sanipass | .50 | .23 |
| ❑ 23 Keith Brown | .50 | .23 |
| ❑ 24 Dave Manson | 1.00 | .45 |
| ❑ 25 Mike Keenan CO | 1.00 | .45 |
| ❑ 26 E.J. McGuire CO | .25 | .11 |
| ❑ 27 Jacques Martin CO | .25 | .11 |

## 1990-91 Blackhawks Coke

This 28-card set was sponsored by Coke, and the cards were issued in a photo album consisting of five unperforated sheets measuring approximately 11 3/4" by 12 1/4". The first four sheets have six players each, while the last sheet features the four coaches. If the cards were cut, they would measure approximately 3 1/2" by 6". The fronts have posed color player photos, shot from the waist up against a blue background. Biographical information appears below the picture between two Coke logos. The backs are blank. The cards are unnumbered and checklisted below according to the order they appear in the photo album.

| | MINT | NRMT |
|---|---|---|
| COMPLETE SET (28) | 20.00 | 9.00 |
| COMMON CARD | .25 | .11 |
| ❑ 1 Dirk Graham | .75 | .35 |
| ❑ 2 Troy Murray | .75 | .35 |
| ❑ 3 Steve Larmer | 1.00 | .45 |
| ❑ 4 Doug Wilson | 1.00 | .45 |
| ❑ 5 Chris Chelios | 2.50 | 1.10 |
| ❑ 6 Jeremy Roenick | 3.00 | 1.35 |
| ❑ 7 Steve Thomas | .75 | .35 |
| ❑ 8 Greg Gilbert | .50 | .23 |
| ❑ 9 Trent Yawney | .50 | .23 |
| ❑ 10 Bob McGill | .50 | .23 |
| ❑ 11 Jacques Cloutier | .60 | .25 |
| ❑ 12 Jocelyn Lemieux | .50 | .23 |
| ❑ 13 Michel Goulet | 1.00 | .45 |
| ❑ 14 Adam Creighton | .60 | .25 |
| ❑ 15 Mike McNeill | .50 | .23 |
| ❑ 16 Ed Belfour | 4.00 | 1.80 |
| ❑ 17 Mike Hudson | .50 | .23 |
| ❑ 18 Greg Millen | .75 | .35 |
| ❑ 19 Stu Grimson | .75 | .35 |
| ❑ 20 Wayne Presley | .50 | .23 |
| ❑ 21 Steve Konroyd | .50 | .23 |
| ❑ 22 Mike Peluso | .75 | .35 |
| ❑ 23 Keith Brown | .50 | .23 |
| ❑ 24 Dave Manson | .75 | .35 |
| ❑ 25 Mike Keenan CO | .75 | .35 |
| ❑ 26 Darryl Sutter CO | .75 | .35 |
| ❑ 27 E.J. McGuire CO | .25 | .11 |
| ❑ 28 Vladislav Tretiak CO | 2.50 | 1.10 |

## 1991-92 Blackhawks Coke

The 1991-92 Chicago Blackhawks Photo Album was sponsored by Coke. The album measures approximately 11 5/8" by 12 1/4". The first four glossy pages feature six 3 1/2" by 6" posed color player photos, while the inside of the back cover displays four coaches' photos. The photos are attractive full body shots in Chicago Original Six uniforms. Player information appears below the picture between two Coke logos. The backs are blank. The cards are unnumbered and checklisted below in alphabetical order.

| | MINT | NRMT |
|---|---|---|
| COMPLETE SET (28) | 18.00 | 8.00 |
| COMMON CARD (1-28) | .25 | .11 |
| ❑ 1 Ed Belfour | 3.00 | 1.35 |
| ❑ 2 Keith Brown | .50 | .23 |
| ❑ 3 Rod Buskas | .50 | .23 |
| ❑ 4 Chris Chelios | 1.50 | .70 |
| ❑ 5 Karl Dykhuis | .50 | .23 |
| ❑ 6 Greg Gilbert | .50 | .23 |
| ❑ 7 Michel Goulet | .75 | .35 |
| ❑ 8 Dirk Graham | .75 | .35 |
| ❑ 9 Stu Grimson | .75 | .35 |
| ❑ 10 Mike Hudson | .50 | .23 |
| ❑ 11 Mike Keenan GM/CO | 1.00 | .45 |
| ❑ 12 Steve Konroyd | .50 | .23 |
| ❑ 13 Frantisek Kucera | .50 | .23 |
| ❑ 14 Steve Larmer | 1.00 | .45 |
| ❑ 15 Brad Lauer | .50 | .23 |
| ❑ 16 Jocelyn Lemieux | .50 | .23 |
| ❑ 17 Bryan Marchment | .50 | .23 |
| ❑ 18 Dave McDowall CO | .25 | .11 |
| ❑ 19 Brian Noonan | .50 | .23 |
| ❑ 20 Mike Peluso | .50 | .23 |
| ❑ 21 Rich Preston CO | .25 | .11 |
| ❑ 22 Jeremy Roenick | 2.50 | 1.10 |
| ❑ 23 Steve Smith | .75 | .35 |
| ❑ 24 Mike Stapleton | .50 | .23 |
| ❑ 25 Brent Sutter | .75 | .35 |
| ❑ 26 Darryl Sutter CO | .75 | .35 |
| ❑ 27 John Tonelli | .75 | .35 |
| ❑ 28 Jimmy Waite | .75 | .35 |

## 1993-94 Blackhawks Coke

Sponsored by Coca-Cola, the 1993-94 Chicago Blackhawks Photo Album measures approximately 11 1/2" by 12 1/4". Each of the four glossy pages features two rows with three player cards per row; the final six player cards are printed on the inside of the back cover. The cards are unperforated, but if they were cut, they would measure approximately 3 1/2" by 6". The photos are full-body color shots of the players in action. In the wider bottom border appears player identification between two Coke logos. The backs are blank. The cards are unnumbered and checklisted below according to the order they appear in the photo album.

| | MINT | NRMT |
|---|---|---|
| COMPLETE SET (30) | 15.00 | 6.75 |
| COMMON CARD (1-30) | .25 | .11 |
| ❑ 1 Joe Murphy | .75 | .35 |
| ❑ 2 Chris Chelios | 1.50 | .70 |
| ❑ 3 Rich Sutter | .50 | .23 |
| ❑ 4 Frantisek Kucera | .50 | .23 |
| ❑ 5 Jeff Shantz | .50 | .23 |
| ❑ 6 Brian Noonan | .50 | .23 |
| ❑ 7 Michel Goulet | .75 | .35 |
| ❑ 8 Jeremy Roenick | 1.50 | .70 |
| ❑ 9 Dave Christian | .50 | .23 |
| ❑ 10 Patrick Poulin | .50 | .23 |
| ❑ 11 Brent Sutter | .50 | .23 |
| ❑ 12 Cam Russell | .50 | .23 |
| ❑ 13 Stephane Matteau | .50 | .23 |
| ❑ 14 Ed Belfour | 2.50 | 1.10 |
| ❑ 15 Neil Wilkinson | .50 | .23 |
| ❑ 16 Eric Weinrich | .50 | .23 |
| ❑ 17 Christian Ruuttu | .50 | .23 |
| ❑ 18 Kevin Todd | .50 | .23 |
| ❑ 19 Jeff Hackett | 1.00 | .45 |
| ❑ 20 Steve Smith | .60 | .25 |
| ❑ 21 Jocelyn Lemieux | .50 | .23 |
| ❑ 22 Keith Carney | .50 | .23 |
| ❑ 23 Troy Murray | .50 | .23 |
| ❑ 24 Darin Kimble | .50 | .23 |
| ❑ 25 Dirk Graham | .60 | .25 |
| ❑ 26 Bob Pulford GM | .50 | .23 |
| ❑ 27 Darryl Sutter CO | .50 | .23 |
| ❑ 28 Paul Baxter ACO | .25 | .11 |
| ❑ 29 Rich Preston ACO | .25 | .11 |
| ❑ 30 Phil Myre ACO | .25 | .11 |

## 1998 Blackhawks Legends

Made and distibuted by Pizza Hut in 1998, these cards feature rounded courners, and full color photos on the front. Backs feature statistical information and discount coupons for your next pizza order. Cards are unnumbered and checklisted below in alphabetical order.

| | MINT | NRMT |
|---|---|---|
| COMPLETE SET (5) | 10.00 | 4.50 |
| COMMON CARD (1-5) | 1.50 | .70 |
| ❑ 1 Tony Esposito | 3.00 | 1.35 |
| ❑ 2 Glenn Hall | 2.00 | .90 |
| ❑ 3 Bobby Hull | 4.00 | 1.80 |
| ❑ 4 Steve Larmer | 1.50 | .70 |
| ❑ 5 Denis Savard | 1.50 | .70 |

## 1993 Bleachers 23K Manon Rheaume

This four-card standard-size set features posed and action, color player photos with 23 Karat gold borders. The production run was reportedly 10,000 numbered sets and 1,500 uncut numbered strips. The player's name and the card title appear in a gold oval below the picture. Another gold oval above the picture is printed with "23KT" and is outlined in black. Six black stars accent the top of the card. The backs carry a serial number ("X of 10,000"), biographical information, player profile, career highlights, and a gold foil facsimile autograph within multi-colored blocks.

| | MINT | NRMT |
|---|---|---|
| COMPLETE SET (4) | 30.00 | 13.50 |
| COMMON CARD | 8.00 | 3.60 |
| ❑ 1 Manon Rheaume<br>Trois-Rivieres | 8.00 | 3.60 |
| ❑ 2 Manon Rheaume<br>Atlanta Knights | 8.00 | 3.60 |
| ❑ 3 Manon Rheaume<br>Tampa Bay | 8.00 | 3.60 |
| ❑ NNO Manon Rheaume<br>Title Card | 8.00 | 3.60 |

## 1971-72 Blues Postcards

This 25-card set measures approximately 3 1/2" by 5 1/2" and features full-bleed color action player photos. A facsimile autograph appears near the bottom. The backs are white and carry limited biographical information and the St. Louis Blues logo. The cards are unnumbered and checklisted below in alphabetical order.

| | NRMT-MT | EXC |
|---|---|---|
| COMPLETE SET (25) | 40.00 | 18.00 |

| | | |
|---|---|---|
| COMMON CARD (1-25) | 1.00 | .45 |
| ❑ 1 Al Arbour CO | 5.00 | 2.20 |
| ❑ 2 John Arbour | 1.50 | .70 |
| ❑ 3 Carl Brewer | 3.00 | 1.35 |
| ❑ 4 Jacques Caron | 1.50 | .70 |
| ❑ 5 Terry Crisp | 3.00 | 1.35 |
| ❑ 6 Andre Dupont | 2.00 | .90 |
| ❑ 7 Jack Egers | 1.50 | .70 |
| ❑ 8 Larry Hornung | 1.50 | .70 |
| ❑ 9 Brian Lavender | 1.50 | .70 |
| ❑ 10 Gordon Marchant ATR<br>Alex McPherson ATR | 1.00 | .45 |
| ❑ 11 Mike Murphy | 1.50 | .70 |
| ❑ 12 Gerry Odrowski | 1.50 | .70 |
| ❑ 13 Danny O'Shea | 1.50 | .70 |
| ❑ 14 Mike Parizeau | 1.50 | .70 |
| ❑ 15 Noel Picard | 1.50 | .70 |
| ❑ 16 Barclay Plager | 3.00 | 1.35 |
| ❑ 17 Bill Plager | 2.00 | .90 |
| ❑ 18 Bob Plager | 3.00 | 1.35 |
| ❑ 19 Phil Roberto | 1.50 | .70 |
| ❑ 20 Gary Sabourin | 1.50 | .70 |
| ❑ 21 Frank St. Marseille | 1.50 | .70 |
| ❑ 22 Floyd Thomson | 1.50 | .70 |
| ❑ 23 Garry Unger | 3.00 | 1.35 |
| ❑ 24 Ernie Wakely | 2.00 | .90 |
| ❑ 25 Tom Woodcock TR | 1.00 | .45 |

## 1972-73 Blues White Border

Printed on thin white stock, this set of 22 photos measures approximately 6 7/8" by 8 3/4". The fronts display white-bordered color player action shots. The player's name appears in the lower white margin, and his facsimile autograph is inscribed across the picture. The backs are blank. The photos are unnumbered and checklisted below in alphabetical order.

| | NRMT-MT | EXC |
|---|---|---|
| COMPLETE SET (22) | 30.00 | 13.50 |
| COMMON CARD (1-22) | 1.50 | .70 |
| ❑ 1 Jacques Caron | 1.50 | .70 |
| ❑ 2 Steve Durbano | 2.00 | .90 |
| ❑ 3 Jack Egers | 1.50 | .70 |
| ❑ 4 Chris Evans | 1.50 | .70 |
| ❑ 5 Jean Hamel | 1.50 | .70 |
| ❑ 6 Fran Huck | 1.50 | .70 |
| ❑ 7 Brent Hughes | 1.50 | .70 |
| ❑ 8 Bob Johnson | 3.00 | 1.35 |
| ❑ 9 Mike Lampman | 1.50 | .70 |
| ❑ 10 Bob McCord | 1.50 | .70 |
| ❑ 11 Wayne Merrick | 2.00 | .90 |
| ❑ 12 Mike Murphy | 1.50 | .70 |
| ❑ 13 Danny O'Shea | 1.50 | .70 |
| ❑ 14 Barclay Plager | 3.00 | 1.35 |
| ❑ 15 Bob Plager | 3.00 | 1.35 |
| ❑ 16 Pierre Plante | 1.50 | .70 |
| ❑ 17 Phil Roberto | 2.00 | .90 |
| ❑ 18 Gary Sabourin | 1.50 | .70 |
| ❑ 19 Wayne Stephenson | 2.00 | .90 |
| ❑ 20 Jean-Guy Talbot CO | 1.50 | .70 |
| ❑ 21 Floyd Thomson | 1.50 | .70 |
| ❑ 22 Garry Unger | 3.00 | 1.35 |

## 1973-74 Blues White Border

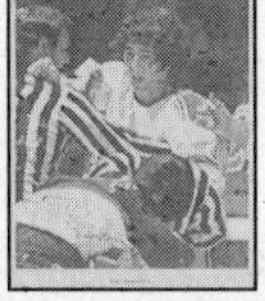

Printed on thin white stock, this set of 24 photos measures approximately 6 7/8" by 8 3/4". The fronts display white-bordered color player action shots. The player's name appears in the lower white margin, and his facsimile autograph is inscribed across the picture. The backs are blank. The photos are unnumbered and checklisted below in alphabetical order. The set is dated by the Glen Sather photo; 1973-74 was his only season with the team.

| | NRMT-MT | EXC |
|---|---|---|
| COMPLETE SET (24) | 40.00 | 18.00 |
| COMMON CARD (1-24) | 1.50 | .70 |
| ❑ 1 Lou Angotti | 1.50 | .70 |
| ❑ 2 Don Awrey | 1.50 | .70 |
| ❑ 3 John Davidson | 5.00 | 2.20 |
| ❑ 4 Ab Demarco | 1.50 | .70 |
| ❑ 5 Steve Durbano | 1.50 | .70 |
| ❑ 6 Chris Evans | 1.50 | .70 |
| ❑ 7 Larry Giroux | 1.50 | .70 |
| ❑ 8 Jean Hamel | 1.50 | .70 |
| ❑ 9 Nick Harbaruk | 1.50 | .70 |
| ❑ 10 J.Bob Kelly | 2.00 | .90 |
| ❑ 11 Mike Lampman | 1.50 | .70 |
| ❑ 12 Wayne Merrick | 1.50 | .70 |
| ❑ 13 Barclay Plager | 3.00 | 1.35 |
| ❑ 14 Bob Plager | 3.00 | 1.35 |
| ❑ 15 Pierre Plante | 3.00 | 1.35 |
| ❑ 16 Phil Roberto | 1.50 | .70 |
| ❑ 17 Gary Sabourin | 1.50 | .70 |
| ❑ 18 Glen Sather | 4.00 | 1.80 |
| ❑ 19 Wayne Stephenson | 2.50 | 1.10 |
| ❑ 20 Jean-Guy Talbot CO | 1.50 | .70 |
| ❑ 21 Floyd Thomson | 1.50 | .70 |
| ❑ 22 Garry Unger | 2.50 | 1.10 |
| ❑ 23 Garry Unger action | 2.50 | 1.10 |
| ❑ 24 Team Photo<br>(1972-73 team) | 3.00 | 1.35 |

## 1978-79 Blues Postcards

This 21-postcard set of the St. Louis Blues measures approximately 3 1/2" by 5 1/2". The fronts feature color posed player portraits. The backs have a postcard format and carry the player's name and biographical information. The cards are unnumbered and checklisted below in alphabetical order.

| | NRMT-MT | EXC |
|---|---|---|
| COMPLETE SET (24) | 25.00 | 11.00 |
| COMMON CARD (1-24) | .25 | .11 |
| ❑ 1 Wayne Babych | 1.50 | .70 |
| ❑ 2 Curt Bennett | 1.50 | .70 |
| ❑ 3 Harvey Bennett | 1.00 | .45 |
| ❑ 4 Red Berenson | .25 | .11 |
| ❑ 5 Blue Angels | 1.00 | .45 |
| ❑ 6 Jack Brownschidle | 1.00 | .45 |
| ❑ 7 Mike Crombeen | 1.00 | .45 |
| ❑ 8 Tony Currie | 1.00 | .45 |
| ❑ 9 Fanvan | .25 | .11 |
| ❑ 10 Bernie Federko | 4.00 | 1.80 |
| ❑ 11 Barry Gibbs | 1.00 | .45 |
| ❑ 12 Larry Giroux | 1.00 | .45 |
| ❑ 13 Inge Hammarstrom | 1.00 | .45 |
| ❑ 14 Neil Labatte | .25 | .11 |
| ❑ 15 Bob Murdoch | .25 | .11 |
| ❑ 16 Phil Myre | 2.00 | .90 |
| ❑ 17 Larry Patey | 1.00 | .45 |
| ❑ 18 Barclay Plager CO | 2.00 | .90 |
| ❑ 19 Rick Shinske | 1.00 | .45 |
| ❑ 20 John Smrke | 1.00 | .45 |
| ❑ 21 Ed Staniowski | 1.00 | .45 |
| ❑ 22 Bob Stewart | 1.00 | .45 |
| ❑ 23 Brian Sutter | 4.00 | 1.80 |
| ❑ 24 Garry Unger | 3.00 | 1.35 |

## 1987-88 Blues Team Photos

The 20 team photos in this set each measure approximately 8 1/2" by 11". Inside white borders, the fronts display color team photos that were shot either on ice or in the stands at the edge of the arena. The year and the players' names (listed by row) appear in black print in the wider white border beneath each photo. The team photos are blank-backed and unnumbered. They are listed below in chronological order.

| | MINT | NRMT |
|---|---|---|
| COMPLETE SET (20) | 15.00 | 6.75 |
| COMMON TEAM (1-20) | 1.00 | .45 |
| ❑ 1 1967-68 Team Photo | 1.50 | .70 |
| ❑ 2 1968-69 Team Photo | 1.00 | .45 |
| ❑ 3 1969-70 Team Photo | 1.00 | .45 |
| ❑ 4 1970-71 Team Photo | 1.00 | .45 |
| ❑ 5 1971-72 Team Photo | 1.00 | .45 |
| ❑ 6 1972-73 Team Photo | 1.00 | .45 |
| ❑ 7 1973-74 Team Photo | 1.00 | .45 |
| ❑ 8 1974-75 Team Photo | 1.00 | .45 |
| ❑ 9 1975-76 Team Photo | 1.00 | .45 |
| ❑ 10 1976-77 Team Photo | 1.00 | .45 |
| ❑ 11 1977-78 Team Photo | 1.00 | .45 |
| ❑ 12 1978-79 Team Photo | 1.00 | .45 |
| ❑ 13 1979-80 Team Photo | 1.00 | .45 |
| ❑ 14 1980-81 Team Photo | 1.00 | .45 |
| ❑ 15 1981-82 Team Photo | 1.00 | .45 |
| ❑ 16 1982-83 Team Photo | 1.00 | .45 |
| ❑ 17 1983-84 Team Photo | 1.00 | .45 |
| ❑ 18 1984-85 Team Photo | 1.00 | .45 |
| ❑ 19 1985-86 Team Photo | 1.00 | .45 |
| ❑ 20 1986-87 Team Photo | 1.00 | .45 |

## 1987-88 Blues Kodak

The 1987-88 St. Louis Blues Team Photo Album was sponsored by Kodak in conjunction with KMOX Radio. The set consists of three large sheets, each measuring approximately 11" by 8 1/4" and joined together to form one

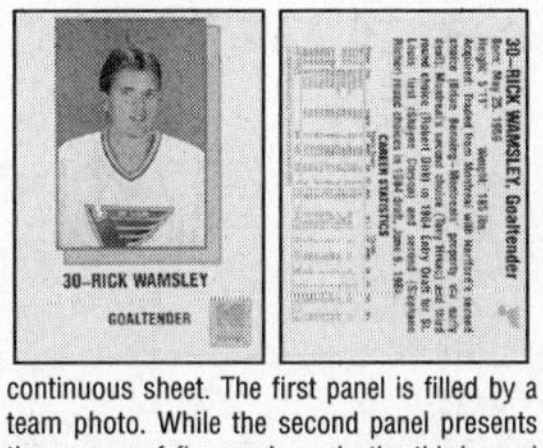


continuous sheet. The first panel is filled by a team photo. While the second panel presents three rows of five cards each, the third panel presents two rows of five cards, with one player card and four Kodak coupons completing the third row of the panel. After perforation, the cards measure approximately 2 3/16" by 3". They feature color posed photos bordered in blue, shadowed by an orange border on the right and bottom of the picture. Player information and a Kodak logo fill the space below the picture. The back has biographical and statistical information in a horizontal format. We have checklisted the names below in alphabetical order, with the uniform number to the right of the name. The set features an early card of Cliff Ronning pre-dating his Rookie Cards by two years.

| | MINT | NRMT |
|---|---|---|
| COMPLETE SET (26) | 30.00 | 13.50 |
| COMMON CARD (1-26) | .75 | .35 |
| ❑ 1 Brian Benning 2 | 1.00 | .45 |
| ❑ 2 Tim Bothwell 6 | .75 | .35 |
| ❑ 3 Charlie Bourgeois 4 | .75 | .35 |
| ❑ 4 Paul Cavallini 14 | 1.00 | .45 |
| ❑ 5 Gino Cavallini 17 | 1.00 | .45 |
| ❑ 6 Michael Dark 26 | .75 | .35 |
| ❑ 7 Doug Evans 32 | .75 | .35 |
| ❑ 8 Todd Ewen 21 | 1.50 | .70 |
| ❑ 9 Bernie Federko 24 | 3.00 | 1.35 |
| ❑ 10 Ron Flockhart 12 | .75 | .35 |
| ❑ 11 Doug Gilmour 9 | 6.00 | 2.70 |
| ❑ 12 Gaston Gingras 23 | .75 | .35 |
| ❑ 13 Tony Hrkac 18 | 1.00 | .45 |
| ❑ 14 Mark Hunter 20 | 1.00 | .45 |
| ❑ 15 Jocelyn Lemieux 16 | .75 | .35 |
| ❑ 16 Tony McKegney 10 | 1.00 | .45 |
| ❑ 17 Rick Meagher 22 | 1.00 | .45 |
| ❑ 18 Greg Millen 29 | 1.50 | .70 |
| ❑ 19 Robert Nordmark 27 | .75 | .35 |
| ❑ 20 Greg Paslawski 28 | .75 | .35 |
| ❑ 21 Herb Raglan 25 | .75 | .35 |
| ❑ 22 Rob Ramage 5 | 1.00 | .45 |
| ❑ 23 Cliff Ronning 7 | 2.50 | 1.10 |
| ❑ 24 Brian Sutter 11 | 1.50 | .70 |
| ❑ 25 Perry Turnbull 19 | .75 | .35 |
| ❑ 26 Rick Wamsley 30 | 1.50 | .70 |

## 1987-88 Blues Team Issue

This 24-card set measures 3 1/2" by 5 1/2". The fronts feature posed color photos with the player's name and jersey number at the top. A facsimile autograph is inscribed across the picture. The backs are blank. The cards are unnumbered and checklisted below in alphabetical order.

| | MINT | NRMT |
|---|---|---|
| COMPLETE SET (24) | 35.00 | 16.00 |
| COMMON CARD (1-24) | .75 | .35 |
| ❑ 1 Brian Benning | 1.00 | .45 |
| ❑ 2 Mike Bullard | 2.00 | .90 |
| ❑ 3 Gino Cavallini | 1.00 | .45 |
| ❑ 4 Paul Cavallini | 1.00 | .45 |
| ❑ 5 Craig Coxe | .75 | .35 |
| ❑ 6 Robert Dirk | .75 | .35 |
| ❑ 7 Doug Evans | .75 | .35 |
| ❑ 8 Todd Ewen | 1.50 | .70 |
| ❑ 9 Bernie Federko | 3.00 | 1.35 |
| ❑ 10 Gaston Gingras | .75 | .35 |
| ❑ 11 Tony Hrkac | 1.00 | .45 |
| ❑ 12 Brett Hull | 15.00 | 6.75 |
| ❑ 13 Tony McKegney | 1.00 | .45 |
| ❑ 14 Rick Meagher | 1.00 | .45 |
| ❑ 15 Greg Millen | 1.50 | .70 |
| ❑ 16 Sergio Momesso | .75 | .35 |
| ❑ 17 Greg Paslawski | .75 | .35 |
| ❑ 18 Herb Raglan | .75 | .35 |
| ❑ 19 Dave Richter | .75 | .35 |
| ❑ 20 Vincent Riendeau | 1.00 | .45 |
| ❑ 21 Gordie Roberts | 1.00 | .45 |
| ❑ 22 Brian Sutter | 1.50 | .70 |
| ❑ 23 Tom Tilley | .75 | .35 |
| ❑ 24 Steve Tuttle | .75 | .35 |

## 1988-89 Blues Kodak

The 1988-89 St. Louis Blues Team Photo Album was sponsored by Kodak. It consists of three large sheets, each measuring approximately 11" by 8 1/4" and joined together to form one continuous sheet. The first panel is filled by a picture of hockey gear intermingled with various Kodak products. While the second panel presents three rows of five cards each, the third panel presents two rows of five cards, with five Kodak coupons completing the left over portion of the panel. After perforation, the cards measure approximately 2 3/16" by 3". They feature color posed photos bordered in yellow, shadowed by a blue border on the right and bottom of the picture. Player information and a Kodak logo fill the space below the picture. The back has biographical and statistical information in a horizontal format. The cards are listed below by sweater number, which is prominently displayed on the card front.

| | MINT | NRMT |
|---|---|---|
| COMPLETE SET (25) | 25.00 | 11.00 |
| COMMON CARD | .75 | .35 |
| ❑ 2 Brian Benning | .75 | .35 |
| ❑ 4 Gordie Roberts | .75 | .35 |
| ❑ 5 Dave Richter | .75 | .35 |
| ❑ 6 Tim Bothwell | .75 | .35 |
| ❑ 7 Cliff Ronning | 1.50 | .70 |
| ❑ 9 Peter Zezel | 1.00 | .45 |
| ❑ 10 Tony McKegney | 1.00 | .45 |
| ❑ 14 Paul Cavallini | .75 | .35 |
| ❑ 15 Craig Coxe | .75 | .35 |
| ❑ 16 Brett Hull | 10.00 | 4.50 |
| ❑ 17 Gino Cavallini | .75 | .35 |
| ❑ 18 Tony Hrkac | 1.00 | .45 |
| ❑ 20 Tom Tilley | .75 | .35 |
| ❑ 21 Todd Ewen | 1.00 | .45 |
| ❑ 22 Rick Meagher | .75 | .35 |
| ❑ 23 Gaston Gingras | .75 | .35 |
| ❑ 24 Bernie Federko | 2.00 | .90 |
| ❑ 25 Herb Raglan | .75 | .35 |
| ❑ 26 Mike Lalor | .75 | .35 |
| ❑ 27 Sergio Momesso | .75 | .35 |
| ❑ 28 Greg Paslawski | .75 | .35 |
| ❑ 29 Greg Millen | 1.00 | .45 |
| ❑ 30 Vincent Riendeau | 1.00 | .45 |
| ❑ 32 Doug Evans | .75 | .35 |
| ❑ 35 Steve Tuttle | .75 | .35 |

## 1988-89 Blues Team Issue

This 24-card set measures approximately 3 1/2" by 5 1/4". The fronts feature borderless posed color portraits with the player's name and jersey number printed in black at the top. The backs are blank. The cards are unnumbered and checklisted below in alphabetical order.

| | MINT | NRMT |
|---|---|---|
| COMPLETE SET (24) | 25.00 | 11.00 |
| COMMON CARD (1-24) | .75 | .35 |
| ❑ 1 Brian Benning | .75 | .35 |
| ❑ 2 Mike Bullard | 1.50 | .70 |
| ❑ 3 Gino Cavallini | .75 | .35 |
| ❑ 4 Paul Cavallini | .75 | .35 |
| ❑ 5 Craig Coxe | .75 | .35 |
| ❑ 6 Robert Dirk | .75 | .35 |
| ❑ 7 Doug Evans | .75 | .35 |
| ❑ 8 Todd Ewen | 1.00 | .45 |
| ❑ 9 Bernie Federko | 2.00 | .90 |
| ❑ 10 Gaston Gingras | .75 | .35 |
| ❑ 11 Tony Hrkac | 1.00 | .45 |
| ❑ 12 Brett Hull | 10.00 | 4.50 |
| ❑ 13 Tony McKegney | 1.00 | .45 |
| ❑ 14 Rick Meagher | .75 | .35 |
| ❑ 15 Greg Millen | 1.00 | .45 |
| ❑ 16 Sergio Momesso | .75 | .35 |
| ❑ 17 Greg Paslawski | .75 | .35 |
| ❑ 18 Herb Raglan | .75 | .35 |
| ❑ 19 Dave Richter | .75 | .35 |
| ❑ 20 Vincent Riendeau | 1.00 | .45 |
| ❑ 21 Gordie Roberts | .75 | .35 |
| ❑ 22 Brian Sutter CO | 1.00 | .45 |
| ❑ 23 Tom Tilley | .75 | .35 |
| ❑ 24 Steve Tuttle | .75 | .35 |

## 1989-90 Blues Kodak

This 25-card set of St. Louis Blues measures approximately 2 3/8" by 3 1/2" and has a portrait shot of the player surrounded by yellow borders. Players pictured in their white home sweaters are shown against a blue background whereas players in their away blue sweaters are shown against a dark yellow background. Only Tony Twist and Kelly Chase

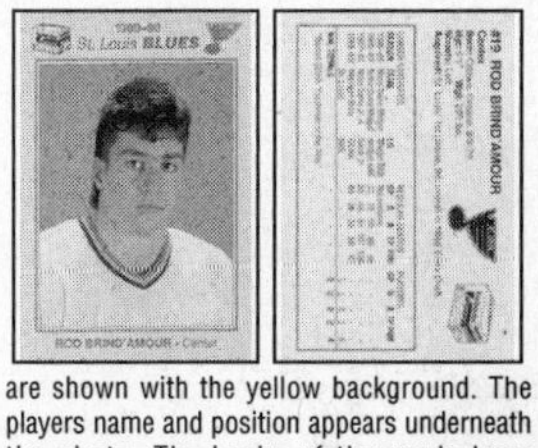


are shown with the yellow background. The players name and position appears underneath the photo. The backs of the cards have biographical and statistical information about the players portrayed. The set is arranged by sweater numbers in the checklist below. Among the stars featured in this set are Brett Hull and Adam Oates. The set features early cards of Rod Brind'Amour and Curtis Joseph pre-dating their Rookie Cards by one year. The set was supposedly passed out to the first 15,000 ticket-holders at the Blues vs. Buffalo Sabres game on February 27th.

| | MINT | NRMT |
|---|---|---|
| COMPLETE SET (25) | 25.00 | 11.00 |
| COMMON CARD | .50 | .23 |
| ❑ 1 Pat Jablonski | 1.00 | .45 |
| ❑ 4 Gordie Roberts | .50 | .23 |
| ❑ 6 Tony Twist | 1.50 | .70 |
| ❑ 9 Peter Zezel | .75 | .35 |
| ❑ 10 Dave Lowry | .50 | .23 |
| ❑ 12 Adam Oates | 3.00 | 1.35 |
| ❑ 14 Paul Cavallini | .50 | .23 |
| ❑ 15 Paul MacLean | .75 | .35 |
| ❑ 16 Brett Hull | 5.00 | 2.20 |
| ❑ 17 Gino Cavallini | .50 | .23 |
| ❑ 19 Rod Brind'Amour | 3.00 | 1.35 |
| ❑ 20 Tom Tilley | .50 | .23 |
| ❑ 21 Jeff Brown | 1.00 | .45 |
| ❑ 22 Rick Meagher | .50 | .23 |
| ❑ 23 Adrien Plavsic | .50 | .23 |
| ❑ 25 Herb Raglan | .50 | .23 |
| ❑ 26 Mike Lalor | .50 | .23 |
| ❑ 27 Sergio Momesso | .50 | .23 |
| ❑ 30 Vincent Riendeau | 1.00 | .45 |
| ❑ 31 Curtis Joseph | 5.00 | 2.20 |
| ❑ 35 Steve Tuttle | .50 | .23 |
| ❑ 38 Dominic Lavoie | .50 | .23 |
| ❑ 39 Kelly Chase | .50 | .23 |
| ❑ 40 Dave Thomlinson | .50 | .23 |
| ❑ NNO Brian Sutter CO | .75 | .35 |

## 1990-91 Blues Kodak

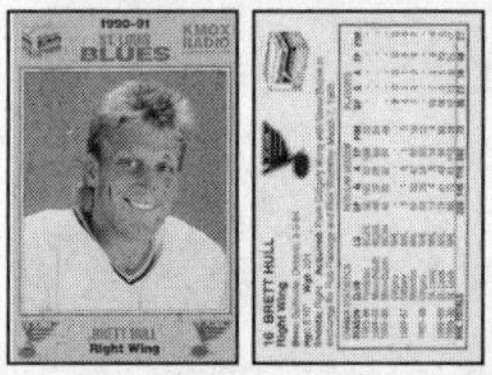


This 25-card standard-size set was sponsored by Kodak in conjunction with KMOX Radio. On an orangish-yellow card face, the fronts feature color head and shoulders shots against a blue background. Thin white and red borders enclose the pictures, and the player's name and position appear at the card bottom between two team logos. The horizontally oriented backs carry biography, career statistics, team logo, and sponsor logo. The cards are unnumbered and checklisted below in alphabetical order.

| | MINT | NRMT |
|---|---|---|
| COMPLETE SET (25) | 25.00 | 11.00 |
| COMMON CARD (1-25) | .50 | .23 |
| ❑ 1 Bob Bassen | .50 | .23 |
| ❑ 2 Rod Brind'Amour | 3.00 | 1.35 |
| ❑ 3 Jeff Brown | .75 | .35 |
| ❑ 4 David Bruce | .50 | .23 |
| ❑ 5 Gino Cavallini | .50 | .23 |
| ❑ 6 Paul Cavallini | .50 | .23 |
| ❑ 7 Geoff Courtnall | 1.00 | .45 |
| ❑ 8 Robert Dirk | .50 | .23 |
| ❑ 9 Glen Featherstone | .50 | .23 |
| ❑ 10 Brett Hull | 5.00 | 2.20 |
| ❑ 11 Curtis Joseph | 3.00 | 1.35 |
| ❑ 12 Dave Lowry | .50 | .23 |
| ❑ 13 Paul MacLean | .50 | .23 |
| ❑ 14 Mario Marois | .50 | .23 |
| ❑ 15 Rick Meagher | .50 | .23 |
| ❑ 16 Sergio Momesso | .50 | .23 |
| ❑ 17 Adam Oates | 3.00 | 1.35 |
| ❑ 18 Vincent Riendeau | .75 | .35 |
| ❑ 19 Cliff Ronning | .75 | .35 |
| ❑ 20 Harold Snepsts | 1.00 | .45 |
| ❑ 21 Scott Stevens | 1.50 | .70 |
| ❑ 22 Brian Sutter CO | .50 | .23 |
| ❑ 23 Rich Sutter | .50 | .23 |
| ❑ 24 Steve Tuttle | .50 | .23 |
| ❑ 25 Ron Wilson | .50 | .23 |

## 1991-92 Blues Postcards

This 22-card set measures approximately 3 1/2" by 5 1/2". The horizontal and vertical

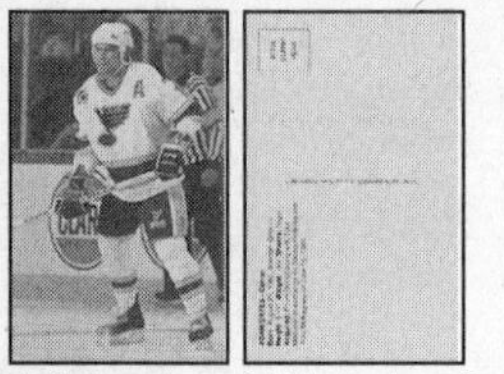

fronts feature glossy, full-bleed color action player photos. The white backs carry the player's name, position and statistics in the upper left corner. The postcards are unnumbered and checklisted below in alphabetical order.

| | MINT | NRMT |
|---|---|---|
| COMPLETE SET (22) | 20.00 | 9.00 |
| COMMON CARD (1-22) | .50 | .23 |

❑ 1 Murray Baron .50 .23
❑ 2 Bob Bassen .50 .23
❑ 3 Jeff Brown 1.00 .45
❑ 4 Garth Butcher .75 .35
❑ 5 Gino Cavallini .50 .23
❑ 6 Paul Cavallini .50 .23
❑ 7 Kelly Chase .60 .25
❑ 8 Dave Christian .75 .35
❑ 9 Nelson Emerson .75 .35
❑ 10 Brett Hull 4.00 1.80
❑ 11 Pat Jablonski .75 .35
❑ 12 Curtis Joseph 2.00 .90
❑ 13 Darin Kimble .50 .23
❑ 14 Dave Lowry .50 .23
❑ 15 Michel Mongeau .50 .23
❑ 16 Adam Oates 2.00 .90
❑ 17 Rob Robinson .50 .23
❑ 18 Brendan Shanahan 4.00 1.80
❑ 19 Rich Sutter .75 .35
❑ 20 Ron Sutter .75 .35
❑ 21 Ron Wilson .50 .23
❑ 22 Rick Zombo .50 .23

## 1992-93 Blues Upper Deck Best of the Blues

This 28-card standard-size set, subtitled "Best of the Blues" was distributed at McDonald's restaurants of St. Louis and Metro East and showcases St. Louis Blues' players from the past 25 years. Proceeds from the cards benefitted Ronald McDonald Children's Charities of St. Louis and Metro East. The cards were available in six-card packs for 99 cents with the purchase of any large sandwich or any breakfast sandwich. The offer was valid through March 4. Also, 100 autographed Brett Hull cards were randomly inserted in the packs. The fronts feature color action player photos. Black-and-white photos appear on the reverse of some cards. On Monday nights beginning on February 15 and running through March 30, "Best of the Blues" trading card nights were held at participating restaurants to enable collectors to assemble complete sets. In conjunction with these events, a giant Brett Hull card was raffled off at each restaurant on the last trading card night (March 30, 1993). Finally, a holder to display the set was available through a mail-in offer for 8.50. The fronts features color action player photos with silver borders that give a shadow effect against the white card face. The player's name is printed in a black stripe across the bottom. The Best of the Blues logo is superimposed over the picture at the upper left. The backs carry a small, shadow-bordered, close-up photo. A player profile appears below the picture. Statistics are printed in a horizontally oriented box.

| | MINT | NRMT |
|---|---|---|
| COMPLETE SET (28) | 35.00 | 16.00 |
| COMMON CARD (1-28) | .75 | .35 |

❑ 1 Glenn Hall 3.00 1.35
❑ 2 Doug Gilmour 4.00 1.80
❑ 3 Al Arbour 1.00 .45
❑ 4 Mike Liut 1.00 .45
❑ 5 Blake Dunlop .75 .35
❑ 6 Noel Picard .75 .35
❑ 7 Bob Plager 1.00 .45
❑ 8 Ab McDonald .75 .35
❑ 9 Curtis Joseph 5.00 2.20
❑ 10 Wayne Babych .75 .35
❑ 11 Red Berenson 1.00 .45
❑ 12 Brett Hull 5.00 2.20
❑ 13 Bob Gassoff 1.00 .45
❑ 14 Bernie Federko 1.50 .70
❑ 15 Gary Sabourin .75 .35
❑ 16 Joe Mullen 1.00 .45
❑ 17 Adam Oates 3.00 1.35
❑ 18 Jorgen Pettersson .75 .35
❑ 19 Frank St. Marseille .75 .35
❑ 20 Scott Stevens 1.50 .70
❑ 21 Rob Ramage 1.00 .45
❑ 22 Jacques Plante 3.00 1.35
❑ 23 Rick Meagher .75 .35
❑ 24 Barclay Plager 1.00 .45
❑ 25 Brian Sutter 1.00 .45
❑ 26 Perry Turnbull .75 .35
❑ 27 Garry Unger 1.00 .45
❑ 28 Checklist SP 5.00 2.20
❑ NNO Brett Hull AU 250.00 110.00

## 1990-91 Bowman

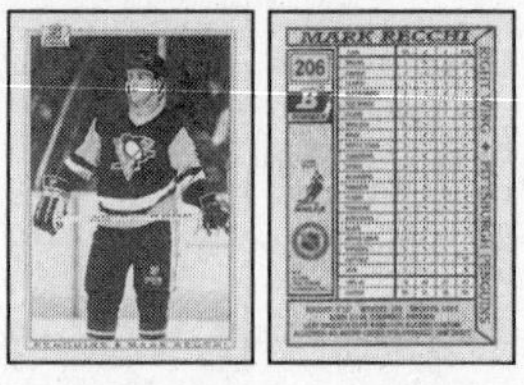

The 1990-91 Bowman set contains 264 standard-size cards. The fronts feature color photos with variegated borders in green, yellow, and red. The team name and player's name appear in black lettering below the picture. The backs are tinted blue with black lettering on gray card stock, and provide biographical information and career statistics. The cards are numbered on the back and are arranged alphabetically according to team name. Rookie Cards include Ed Belfour, Rod Brind'Amour, Mike Modano, Alexander Mogilny, Mark Recchi, Mike Richter, Jeremy Roenick.

| | MINT | NRMT |
|---|---|---|
| COMPLETE SET (264) | 15.00 | 6.75 |
| COMP.FACT.SET (264) | 15.00 | 6.75 |
| COMMON CARD (1-264) | .05 | .02 |

❑ 1 Jeremy Roenick 1.00 .45
❑ 2 Doug Wilson .05 .02
❑ 3 Greg Millen .10 .05
❑ 4 Steve Thomas .05 .02
❑ 5 Steve Larmer .05 .02
❑ 6 Denis Savard .10 .05
❑ 7 Ed Belfour 1.50 .70
❑ 8 Dirk Graham .05 .02
❑ 9 Adam Creighton .05 .02
❑ 10 Keith Brown .05 .02
❑ 11 Jacques Cloutier .10 .05
❑ 12 Al Secord UER .05 .02
(Photo actually Duane Sutter)
❑ 13 Troy Murray .05 .02
❑ 14 Kelly Chase .05 .02
❑ 15 Dave Lowry .05 .02
❑ 16 Adam Oates .10 .05
❑ 17 Sergio Momesso .05 .02
❑ 18 Paul MacLean .05 .02
❑ 19 Peter Zezel .05 .02
❑ 20 Vincent Riendeau .10 .05
❑ 21 Dave Thomlinson .05 .02
❑ 22 Paul Cavallini .05 .02
❑ 23 Rod Brind'Amour .75 .35
❑ 24 Brett Hull .60 .25
❑ 25 Jeff Brown .05 .02
❑ 26 Dominic Lavoie .05 .02
❑ 27 Andy Brickley .05 .02
❑ 28 Bob Sweeney .05 .02
❑ 29 Cam Neely .10 .05
❑ 30 Bob Carpenter .05 .02
❑ 31 Ray Bourque .25 .11
❑ 32 Rejean Lemelin .10 .05
❑ 33 Craig Janney .10 .05
❑ 34 Bob Beers .05 .02
❑ 35 Andy Moog .10 .05
❑ 36 Dave Poulin .05 .02
❑ 37 Brian Propp .05 .02
❑ 38 John Byce .05 .02
❑ 39 John Carter .05 .02
❑ 40 Dave Christian .05 .02
❑ 41 Shayne Corson .05 .02
❑ 42 Chris Chelios .25 .11
❑ 43 Mike McPhee .05 .02
❑ 44 Guy Carbonneau .10 .05
❑ 45 Stephane Richer .10 .05
❑ 46 Petr Svoboda UER .05 .02
(Photo actually Chris Chelios)
❑ 47 Russ Courtnall .05 .02
❑ 48 Sylvain Lefebvre .05 .02
❑ 49 Brian Skrudland .05 .02
❑ 50 Patrick Roy 1.25 .55
❑ 51 Bobby Smith .10 .05
❑ 52 Mathieu Schneider .05 .02
❑ 53 Stephan Lebeau .05 .02
❑ 54 Petri Skriko .05 .02
❑ 55 Jim Sandlak .05 .02
❑ 56 Doug Lidster .05 .02
❑ 57 Kirk McLean .10 .05
❑ 58 Brian Bradley .05 .02
❑ 59 Greg Adams .05 .02
❑ 60 Paul Reinhart .05 .02
❑ 61 Trevor Linden .10 .05
❑ 62 Adrien Plavsic .05 .02
❑ 63 Igor Larionov .50 .23
❑ 64 Steve Bozek .05 .02
❑ 65 Dan Quinn .05 .02
❑ 66 Mike Liut .10 .05
❑ 67 Nick Kypreos .05 .02
❑ 68 Michal Pivonka .05 .02
❑ 69 Dino Ciccarelli .10 .05
❑ 70 Kevin Hatcher .05 .02
❑ 71 Dale Hunter .05 .02
❑ 72 Don Beaupre .10 .05
❑ 73 Geoff Courtnall .05 .02
❑ 74 Rob Murray .05 .02
❑ 75 Calle Johansson .05 .02
❑ 76 Kelly Miller .05 .02
❑ 77 Mike Ridley .05 .02
❑ 78 Alan May .05 .02
❑ 79 Bob Brooke .05 .02
❑ 80 Slava Fetisov .05 .02
❑ 81 Sylvain Turgeon .05 .02
❑ 82 Kirk Muller .05 .02
❑ 83 John MacLean .10 .05
❑ 84 Jon Morris .05 .02
❑ 85 Brendan Shanahan .75 .35
❑ 86 Peter Stastny .10 .05
❑ 87 Bruce Driver .05 .02
❑ 88 Neil Brady .05 .02
❑ 89 Patrik Sundstrom .05 .02
❑ 90 Eric Weinrich .05 .02
❑ 91 Joe Nieuwendyk .10 .05
❑ 92 Sergei Makarov .05 .02
❑ 93 Al MacInnis .10 .05
❑ 94 Mike Vernon .10 .05
❑ 95 Gary Roberts .05 .02
❑ 96 Doug Gilmour .25 .11
❑ 97 Joe Mullen .10 .05
❑ 98 Rick Wamsley .10 .05
❑ 99 Joel Otto .05 .02
❑ 100 Paul Ranheim .05 .02
❑ 101 Gary Suter .05 .02
❑ 102 Theoren Fleury .10 .05
❑ 103 Sergei Priakin .05 .02
❑ 104 Tony Horacek .05 .02
❑ 105 Ron Hextall .10 .05
❑ 106 Gord Murphy .05 .02
❑ 107 Pelle Eklund .05 .02
❑ 108 Rick Tocchet .10 .05
❑ 109 Murray Craven .05 .02
❑ 110 Doug Sulliman .05 .02
❑ 111 Kjell Samuelsson .05 .02
❑ 112 Ilkka Sinisalo .05 .02
❑ 113 Keith Acton .05 .02
❑ 114 Mike Bullard .05 .02
❑ 115 Doug Crossman .05 .02
❑ 116 Tom Fitzgerald .05 .02
❑ 117 Don Maloney .05 .02
❑ 118 Alan Kerr .05 .02
❑ 119 Mark Fitzpatrick .10 .05
❑ 120 Hubie McDonough .05 .02
❑ 121 Randy Wood .05 .02
❑ 122 Jeff Norton .05 .02
❑ 123 Pat LaFontaine .10 .05
❑ 124 Pat Flatley .05 .02
❑ 125 Joe Reekie .05 .02
❑ 126 Brent Sutter .05 .02
❑ 127 David Volek .05 .02
❑ 128 Shawn Cronin .05 .02
❑ 129 Dale Hawerchuk .10 .05
❑ 130 Brent Ashton .05 .02
❑ 131 Bob Essensa .10 .05
❑ 132 Dave Ellett .05 .02
❑ 133 Thomas Steen .05 .02
❑ 134 Doug Smail .05 .02
❑ 135 Fredrik Olausson .05 .02
❑ 136 Dave McLlwain UER .05 .02
(Card says shoots right& should say left)
❑ 137 Pat Elynuik .05 .02
❑ 138 Teppo Numminen .05 .02
❑ 139 Paul Fenton .05 .02
❑ 140 Tony Granato .05 .02
❑ 141 Tomas Sandstrom .05 .02
❑ 142 Rob Blake .30 .14
❑ 143 Wayne Gretzky 1.50 .70
❑ 144 Kelly Hrudey .10 .05
❑ 145 Mike Krushelnyski .05 .02
❑ 146 Steve Duchesne .05 .02
❑ 147 Steve Kasper .05 .02
❑ 148 John Tonelli .05 .02
❑ 149 Dave Taylor .10 .05
❑ 150 Larry Robinson .10 .05
❑ 151 Todd Elik .05 .02
❑ 152 Luc Robitaille .10 .05
❑ 153 Al Iafrate .05 .02
❑ 154 Allan Bester .10 .05
❑ 155 Gary Leeman .05 .02
❑ 156 Mark Osborne .05 .02
❑ 157 Tom Fergus .05 .02
❑ 158 Brad Marsh .05 .02
❑ 159 Wendel Clark .10 .05
❑ 160 Daniel Marois .05 .02
❑ 161 Ed Olczyk .05 .02
❑ 162 Rob Ramage .05 .02
❑ 163 Vincent Damphousse .10 .05
❑ 164 Lou Franceschetti .05 .02
❑ 165 Paul Gillis .05 .02
❑ 166 Craig Wolanin .05 .02
❑ 167 Marc Fortier .05 .02
❑ 168 Tony McKegney .05 .02
❑ 169 Joe Sakic .75 .35
❑ 170 Michel Petit .05 .02
❑ 171 Scott Gordon .05 .02
❑ 172 Tony Hrkac .05 .02
❑ 173 Bryan Fogarty .05 .02
❑ 174 Mike Hough .05 .02
❑ 175 Claude Loiselle .05 .02
❑ 176 Ulf Dahlen .05 .02
❑ 177 Larry Murphy .10 .05
❑ 178 Neal Broten .10 .05
❑ 179 Don Barber .05 .02
❑ 180 Shawn Chambers .05 .02
❑ 181 Clark Donatelli UER .05 .02
(Born 11/22/67& should be 11/22/65; '77-78 U.S. Olympic team)
❑ 182 Brian Bellows .05 .02
❑ 183 Jon Casey .10 .05
❑ 184 Neil Wilkinson .05 .02
❑ 185 Aaron Broten .05 .02
❑ 186 Dave Gagner .10 .05
❑ 187 Basil McRae .05 .02
❑ 188 Mike Modano 1.25 .55
❑ 189 Grant Fuhr .10 .05
❑ 190 Martin Gelinas .40 .18
❑ 191 Jari Kurri .10 .05
❑ 192 Geoff Smith .05 .02
❑ 193 Craig MacTavish .05 .02
❑ 194 Esa Tikkanen .05 .02
❑ 195 Glenn Anderson .10 .05
❑ 196 Joe Murphy .05 .02
❑ 197 Petr Klima .05 .02
❑ 198 Kevin Lowe .05 .02
❑ 199 Mark Messier .40 .18
❑ 200 Steve Smith .05 .02
❑ 201 Craig Simpson .05 .02
❑ 202 Rob Brown .05 .02
❑ 203 Wendell Young .10 .05
❑ 204 Mario Lemieux 1.25 .55
❑ 205 Phil Bourque .05 .02
❑ 206 Mark Recchi UER .50 .23
(Birthplace given as Cornwall, Ontario; should be Kamloops, B.C.)
❑ 207 Zarley Zalapski .05 .02
❑ 208 Kevin Stevens .05 .02
❑ 209 Tom Barrasso .10 .05
❑ 210 John Cullen .05 .02
❑ 211 Paul Coffey .25 .11
❑ 212 Bob Errey .05 .02
❑ 213 Tony Tanti .05 .02
❑ 214 Carey Wilson .05 .02
❑ 215A Brian Leetch ERR .75 .35
(Name spelled eetch)
❑ 215B Brian Leetch COR .40 .18
❑ 216 Darren Turcotte .05 .02
❑ 217 Brian Mullen .05 .02
❑ 218 Mike Richter 1.00 .45
❑ 219 Troy Mallette .05 .02
❑ 220 Mike Gartner .10 .05
❑ 221 Bernie Nicholls .10 .05
❑ 222 John Vanbiesbrouck .50 .23
❑ 223 John Ogrodnick .05 .02
❑ 224 Paul Broten .05 .02
❑ 225 James Patrick .05 .02
❑ 226 Mark Janssens .05 .02
❑ 227 Randy McKay .05 .02
❑ 228 Marc Habscheid .05 .02
❑ 229 Jimmy Carson .05 .02
❑ 230 Yves Racine .05 .02
❑ 231 Dave Barr .05 .02
❑ 232 Shawn Burr .05 .02
❑ 233 Steve Yzerman .75 .35
❑ 234 Steve Chiasson .05 .02
❑ 235 Daniel Shank .05 .02
❑ 236 John Chabot .05 .02
❑ 237 Gerard Gallant .05 .02
❑ 238 Bernie Federko .10 .05
❑ 239 Phil Housley .10 .05
❑ 240 Alexander Mogilny 1.00 .45
❑ 241 Pierre Turgeon .10 .05
❑ 242 Daren Puppa .10 .05
❑ 243 Scott Arniel .05 .02
❑ 244 Christian Ruuttu .05 .02
❑ 245 Doug Bodger .05 .02
❑ 246 Dave Andreychuk .10 .05
❑ 247 Mike Foligno .05 .02
❑ 248 Dean Kennedy .05 .02
❑ 249 Dave Snuggerud .05 .02
❑ 250 Rick Vaive .05 .02
❑ 251 Todd Krygier .05 .02
❑ 252 Adam Burt .05 .02
❑ 253 Scott Young .05 .02
❑ 254 Ron Francis .10 .05
❑ 255 Peter Sidorkiewicz .10 .05
❑ 256 Dave Babych .05 .02
❑ 257 Pat Verbeek .05 .02
❑ 258 Ray Ferraro .05 .02
❑ 259 Chris Govedaris .05 .02
❑ 260 Brad Shaw .05 .02
❑ 261 Kevin Dineen .05 .02
❑ 262 Dean Evason .05 .02
❑ 263 Checklist 1-132 .05 .02
❑ 264 Checklist 133-264 .05 .02

## 1990-91 Bowman Tiffany

Parallel to base set, Topps only produced 3000 sets. Cards can be distinguished by a glossy coating not found on regular issued cards.

| | MINT | NRMT |
|---|---|---|
| COMPLETE SET (264) | 150.00 | 70.00 |
| COMMON CARD (1-264) | 1.25 | .55 |

*STARS: 12.5X TO 25X BASIC CARDS

## 1990-91 Bowman Hat Tricks

This 22-card standard size set was issued as an insert in the 1990-91 Bowman hockey wax packs. This set honored the 14 players (1-14) who scored three or more goals (a hat trick) in a game at least twice during the 1989-90 regular season and the eight players (15-22)

who performed the feat during the 1990 NHL playoffs. The fronts of the cards have a glossy sheen to them while the backs talk about the hat tricks of the players. There are two Mike Gartner cards as he had hat tricks for two different teams.

| | MINT | NRMT |
|---|---|---|
| COMPLETE SET (22) | 6.00 | 2.70 |
| COMMON CARD (1-22) | .15 | .07 |

❑ 1 Brett Hull .50 .23
❑ 2 Mario Lemieux 2.00 .90
❑ 3 Rob Brown .15 .07
❑ 4 Mark Messier .60 .25
❑ 5 Steve Yzerman 1.25 .55
❑ 6 Vincent Damphousse .30 .14
❑ 7 Kevin Dineen .15 .07
❑ 8 Mike Gartner UER .30 .14
(Pictured with Minnesota& identified as Maple Leaf)
❑ 9 Pat LaFontaine .30 .14
❑ 10 Gary Leeman .15 .07
❑ 11 Stephane Richer .15 .07
❑ 12 Luc Robitaille .30 .14
❑ 13 Steve Thomas .15 .07
❑ 14 Rick Tocchet .30 .14
❑ 15 Dino Ciccarelli .30 .14
❑ 16 John Druce .15 .07
❑ 17 Mike Gartner .30 .14
❑ 18 Tony Granato .15 .07
❑ 19 Jari Kurri .30 .14
❑ 20 Bernie Nicholls .30 .14
❑ 21 Tomas Sandstrom .30 .14
❑ 22 Dave Taylor .15 .07

## 1991-92 Bowman

The 1991-92 Bowman hockey set contains 429 standard-size cards. On a white card face, the fronts display color action player photos enclosed by blue and tan border stripes. The player's name appears in a purple stripe below the picture. The backs are colorful (displaying blue, green, and red fading to yellow sections) and present biography and statistics (career and for the 1990-91 season). The season statistics are broken down to show the player's performance against each NHL team. The cards are numbered on the back and checklisted below according to teams. The only Rookie Card worthy of note is John LeClair.

| | MINT | NRMT |
|---|---|---|
| COMPLETE SET (429) | 12.00 | 5.50 |
| COMP.FACT.SET (429) | 15.00 | 6.75 |
| COMMON CARD (1-429) | .05 | .02 |

❑ 1 John Cullen .05 .02
❑ 2 Todd Krygier .05 .02
❑ 3 Kay Whitmore .10 .05
❑ 4 Terry Yake .05 .02
❑ 5 Randy Ladouceur .05 .02
❑ 6 Kevin Dineen .05 .02
❑ 7 Jim McKenzie .05 .02
❑ 8 Brad Shaw .05 .02
❑ 9 Mark Hunter .05 .02
❑ 10 Dean Evason .05 .02
❑ 11 Mikael Andersson .05 .02
❑ 12 Pat Verbeek .05 .02
❑ 13 Peter Sidorkiewicz .10 .05
❑ 14 Mike Tomlak .05 .02
❑ 15 Zarley Zalapski .05 .02
❑ 16 Rob Brown .05 .02
❑ 17 Sylvain Cote .05 .02
❑ 18 Bobby Holik .05 .02
❑ 19 Daryl Reaugh .05 .02
❑ 20 Paul Cyr .05 .02
❑ 21 Doug Bodger .05 .02
❑ 22 Dave Andreychuk .10 .05
❑ 23 Clint Malarchuk .10 .05
❑ 24 Darrin Shannon .05 .02
❑ 25 Christian Ruuttu .05 .02
❑ 26 Uwe Krupp .05 .02
❑ 27 Pierre Turgeon .10 .05
❑ 28 Kevin Haller .05 .02
❑ 29 Dave Snuggerud .05 .02
❑ 30 Alexander Mogilny .10 .05
❑ 31 Dale Hawerchuk .10 .05
❑ 32 Mike Ramsey .05 .02
❑ 33 Darcy Wakaluk .10 .05
❑ 34 Tony Tanti .05 .02

❑ 35 Jay Wells .05 .02
❑ 36 Mikko Makela .05 .02
❑ 37 Daren Puppa .10 .05
❑ 38 Benoit Hogue .05 .02
❑ 39 Rick Vaive .05 .02
❑ 40 Grant Ledyard .05 .02
❑ 41 Steve Yzerman HT .10 .05
❑ 42 Steve Yzerman .50 .23
❑ 43 Shawn Burr .05 .02
❑ 44 Yves Racine .05 .02
❑ 45 Johan Garpenlov .05 .02
❑ 46 Keith Primeau .10 .05
❑ 47 Tim Cheveldae .10 .05
❑ 48 Brad McCrimmon .05 .02
❑ 49 Dave Barr .05 .02
❑ 50 Sergei Fedorov .50 .23
❑ 51 Brent Fedyk .05 .02
❑ 52 Jimmy Carson .05 .02
❑ 53 Paul Ysebaert .05 .02
❑ 54 Rick Zombo .05 .02
❑ 55 Bob Probert .10 .05
❑ 56 Gerard Gallant .05 .02
❑ 57 Kevin Miller .05 .02
❑ 58 Randy Moller .05 .02
❑ 59 Kris King .05 .02
❑ 60 Corey Millen .05 .02
❑ 61 Brian Mullen .05 .02
❑ 62 Darren Turcotte .05 .02
❑ 63 Ray Sheppard .10 .05
❑ 64 David Shaw .05 .02
❑ 65 Troy Mallette .05 .02
❑ 66 James Patrick .05 .02
❑ 67 Mark Janssens .05 .02
❑ 68 John Vanbiesbrouck .30 .14
❑ 69 Joey Kocur .05 .02
❑ 70 Mike Richter .25 .11
❑ 71 John Ogrodnick .05 .02
❑ 72 Kelly Kisio .05 .02
❑ 73 Normand Rochefort .05 .02
❑ 74 Mike Gartner .10 .05
❑ 75 Brian Leetch .25 .11
❑ 76 Bernie Nicholls .10 .05
❑ 77 Jan Erixon .05 .02
❑ 78 Larry Murphy .10 .05
❑ 79 Joe Mullen .10 .05
❑ 80 Tom Barrasso .10 .05
❑ 81 Paul Coffey .25 .11
❑ 82 Jiri Hrdina .05 .02
❑ 83 Mark Recchi .10 .05
❑ 84 Randy Gilhen .05 .02
❑ 85 Bob Errey .05 .02
❑ 86 Scott Young .05 .02
❑ 87 Mario Lemieux .75 .35
❑ 88 Ulf Samuelsson .05 .02
❑ 89 Frank Pietrangelo .10 .05
❑ 90 Ron Francis .10 .05
❑ 91 Paul Stanton .05 .02
❑ 92 Kevin Stevens .05 .02
❑ 93 Bryan Trottier .10 .05
❑ 94 Phil Bourque .05 .02
❑ 95 Jaromir Jagr .50 .23
❑ 96 Petr Klima HT .05 .02
❑ 97 Adam Graves .10 .05
❑ 98 Esa Tikkanen .05 .02
❑ 99 Norm Maciver .05 .02
❑ 100 Craig MacTavish .05 .02
❑ 101 Bill Ranford .10 .05
❑ 102 Martin Gelinas .05 .02
❑ 103 Charlie Huddy .05 .02
❑ 104 Petr Klima .05 .02
❑ 105 Ken Linseman .05 .02
❑ 106 Steve Smith .05 .02
❑ 107 Craig Simpson .05 .02
❑ 108 Chris Joseph .05 .02
❑ 109 Joe Murphy .05 .02
❑ 110 Jeff Beukeboom .05 .02
❑ 111 Grant Fuhr .10 .05
❑ 112 Geoff Smith .05 .02
❑ 113 Anatoli Semenov .05 .02
❑ 114 Mark Messier .25 .11
❑ 115 Kevin Lowe .05 .02
❑ 116 Glenn Anderson .10 .05
❑ 117 Bobby Smith .10 .05
❑ 118 Doug Smail .05 .02
❑ 119 Jon Casey .10 .05
❑ 120 Gaetan Duchesne .05 .02
❑ 121 Neal Broten .10 .05
❑ 122 Brian Hayward .10 .05
❑ 123 Brian Propp .05 .02
❑ 124 Mark Tinordi .05 .02
❑ 125 Mike Modano .25 .11
❑ 126 Marc Bureau .05 .02
❑ 127 Ulf Dahlen .05 .02
❑ 128 Chris Dahlquist .05 .02
❑ 129 Brian Bellows .05 .02
❑ 130 Mike Craig .05 .02
❑ 131 Dave Gagner .10 .05
❑ 132 Brian Glynn .05 .02
❑ 133 Joe Sakic .40 .18
❑ 134 Owen Nolan .10 .05
❑ 135 Everett Sanipass .05 .02
❑ 136 Jamie Baker .05 .02
❑ 137 Mats Sundin .10 .05
❑ 138 Craig Wolanin .05 .02
❑ 139 Kip Miller .05 .02
❑ 140 Steven Finn .05 .02
❑ 141 Tony Hrkac .05 .02
❑ 142 Curtis Leschyshyn .05 .02
❑ 143 Mike McNeil .05 .02
❑ 144 Mike Hough .05 .02
❑ 145 Alexei Gusarov .05 .02
❑ 146 Jacques Cloutier .10 .05
❑ 147 Shawn Anderson .05 .02
❑ 148 Stephane Morin .05 .02
❑ 149 Bryan Fogarty .05 .02
❑ 150 Scott Pearson .05 .02
❑ 151 Ron Tugnutt .10 .05
❑ 152 Randy Velischek .05 .02
❑ 153 David Reid .05 .02
❑ 154 Rob Ramage .05 .02
❑ 155 Dave Hannan .05 .02
❑ 156 Wendel Clark .10 .05
❑ 157 Peter Ing .10 .05
❑ 158 Michel Petit .05 .02
❑ 159 Brian Bradley .05 .02
❑ 160 Rob Cimetta .05 .02
❑ 161 Gary Leeman .05 .02
❑ 162 Aaron Broten .05 .02
❑ 163 Dave Ellett .05 .02
❑ 164 Peter Zezel .05 .02
❑ 165 Daniel Marois .05 .02
❑ 166 Mike Krushelnyski .05 .02
❑ 167 Luke Richardson .05 .02
❑ 168 Scott Thornton .05 .02
❑ 169 Mike Foligno .05 .02
❑ 170 Vincent Damphousse .10 .05
❑ 171 Todd Gill .05 .02
❑ 172 Kevin Maguire .05 .02
❑ 173 Wayne Gretzky HT .50 .23
❑ 174 Tomas Sandstrom HT .05 .02
❑ 175 John Tonelli .05 .02
❑ 176 Wayne Gretzky 1.25 .55
❑ 177 Larry Robinson .10 .05
❑ 178 Jay Miller .05 .02
❑ 179 Tomas Sandstrom .05 .02
❑ 180 John McIntyre .05 .02
❑ 181 Brad Jones .05 .02
❑ 182 Rob Blake .10 .05
❑ 183 Kelly Hrudey .10 .05
❑ 184 Marty McSorley .05 .02
❑ 185 Todd Elik .05 .02
❑ 186 Dave Taylor .10 .05
❑ 187 Steve Kasper .05 .02
❑ 188 Luc Robitaille .10 .05
❑ 189 Bob Kudelski .05 .02
❑ 190 Daniel Berthiaume .10 .05
❑ 191 Steve Duchesne .05 .02
❑ 192 Tony Granato .05 .02
❑ 193 Bob Essensa .10 .05
❑ 194 Phil Sykes .05 .02
❑ 195 Paul MacDermid .05 .02
❑ 196 Dave McLlwain .05 .02
❑ 197 Phil Housley .10 .05
❑ 198 Pat Elynuik .05 .02
❑ 199 Randy Carlyle .05 .02
❑ 200 Thomas Steen .05 .02
❑ 201 Teppo Numminen .05 .02
❑ 202 Danton Cole .05 .02
❑ 203 Doug Evans .05 .02
❑ 204 Ed Olczyk .05 .02
❑ 205 Moe Mantha .05 .02
❑ 206 Scott Arniel .05 .02
❑ 207 Rick Tabaracci .10 .05
❑ 208 Bryan Marchment .05 .02
❑ 209 Mark Osborne .05 .02
❑ 210 Fredrik Olausson .05 .02
❑ 211 Brent Ashton .05 .02
❑ 212 Ray Ferraro .05 .02
❑ 213 Mark Fitzpatrick .10 .05
❑ 214 Hubie McDonough .05 .02
❑ 215 Joe Reekie .05 .02
❑ 216 Bill Berg .05 .02
❑ 217 Wayne McBean .05 .02
❑ 218 Pat Flatley .05 .02
❑ 219 Jeff Hackett .10 .05
❑ 220 Derek King .05 .02
❑ 221 Craig Ludwig .05 .02
❑ 222 Pat LaFontaine .10 .05
❑ 223 David Volek .05 .02
❑ 224 Glenn Healy .10 .05
❑ 225 Jeff Norton .05 .02
❑ 226 Brent Sutter .05 .02
❑ 227 Randy Wood .05 .02
❑ 228 Gary Nylund .05 .02
❑ 229 Dave Chyzowski .05 .02
❑ 230 Rick Tocchet .10 .05
❑ 231 Ken Wregget .10 .05
❑ 232 Terry Carkner .05 .02
❑ 233 Martin Hostak .05 .02
❑ 234 Ron Hextall .10 .05
❑ 235 Gord Murphy .05 .02
❑ 236 Scott Mellanby .05 .02
❑ 237 Pete Peeters .10 .05
❑ 238 Ron Sutter .05 .02
❑ 239 Murray Craven .05 .02
❑ 240 Kjell Samuelsson .05 .02
❑ 241 Pelle Eklund .05 .02
❑ 242 Mark Pederson .05 .02
❑ 243 Murray Baron .05 .02
❑ 244 Keith Acton .05 .02
❑ 245 Derrick Smith .05 .02
❑ 246 Mike Ricci .05 .02
❑ 247 Dale Kushner .05 .02
❑ 248 Normand Lacombe .05 .02
❑ 249 Theoren Fleury HT .10 .05
❑ 250 Sergei Makarov HT .05 .02
❑ 251 Paul Ranheim .05 .02
❑ 252 Joe Nieuwendyk .10 .05
❑ 253 Mike Vernon .10 .05
❑ 254 Gary Suter .05 .02
❑ 255 Doug Gilmour .25 .11
❑ 256 Paul Fenton .05 .02
❑ 257 Roger Johansson .05 .02
❑ 258 Stephane Matteau .05 .02
❑ 259 Frank Musil .05 .02
❑ 260 Joel Otto .05 .02
❑ 261 Tim Sweeney .05 .02
❑ 262 Al MacInnis .10 .05
❑ 263 Gary Roberts .05 .02
❑ 264 Sergei Makarov .05 .02
❑ 265 Carey Wilson .05 .02
❑ 266 Ric Nattress .05 .02
❑ 267 Robert Reichel .05 .02
❑ 268 Rick Wamsley .10 .05
❑ 269 Brian MacLellan .05 .02
❑ 270 Theoren Fleury .10 .05
❑ 271 Claude Lemieux .10 .05
❑ 272 John MacLean .10 .05
❑ 273 Slava Fetisov .05 .02
❑ 274 Kirk Muller .05 .02
❑ 275 Sean Burke .10 .05
❑ 276 Alexei Kasatonov .05 .02
❑ 277 Claude Lemieux .10 .05
❑ 278 Eric Weinrich .05 .02
❑ 279 Patrik Sundstrom .05 .02
❑ 280 Zdeno Ciger .05 .02
❑ 281 Bruce Driver .05 .02
❑ 282 Laurie Boschman .05 .02
❑ 283 Chris Terreri .10 .05
❑ 284 Ken Daneyko .05 .02
❑ 285 Doug Brown .05 .02
❑ 286 Jon Morris .05 .02
❑ 287 Peter Stastny .10 .05
❑ 288 Brendan Shanahan .40 .18
❑ 289 John MacLean .10 .05
❑ 290 Mike Liut .10 .05
❑ 291 Michal Pivonka .05 .02
❑ 292 Kelly Miller .05 .02
❑ 293 John Druce .05 .02
❑ 294 Calle Johansson .05 .02
❑ 295 Alan May .05 .02
❑ 296 Kevin Hatcher .05 .02
❑ 297 Tim Bergland .05 .02
❑ 298 Mikhail Tatarinov .05 .02
❑ 299 Peter Bondra .25 .11
❑ 300 Al Iafrate .10 .05
❑ 301 Nick Kypreos .05 .02
❑ 302 Dino Ciccarelli .10 .05
❑ 303 Dale Hunter .05 .02
❑ 304 Don Beaupre .10 .05
❑ 305 Jim Hrivnak .10 .05
❑ 306 Stephen Leach .05 .02
❑ 307 Dimitri Khristich .05 .02
❑ 308 Mike Ridley .05 .02
❑ 309 Sergio Momesso .05 .02
❑ 310 Kirk McLean .10 .05
❑ 311 Greg Adams .05 .02
❑ 312 Adrien Plavsic .05 .02
❑ 313 Cliff Ronning .05 .02
❑ 314 Garry Valk .05 .02
❑ 315 Troy Gamble .10 .05
❑ 316 Gino Odjick .05 .02
❑ 317 Doug Lidster .05 .02
❑ 318 Geoff Courtnall .05 .02
❑ 319 Tom Kurvers .05 .02
❑ 320 Robert Kron .05 .02
❑ 321 Jyrki Lumme .05 .02
❑ 322 Jay Mazur .05 .02
❑ 323 Dave Capuano .05 .02
❑ 324 Petr Nedved .10 .05
❑ 325 Steve Bozek .05 .02
❑ 326 Igor Larionov .05 .02
❑ 327 Trevor Linden .10 .05
❑ 328 Shayne Corson .05 .02
❑ 329 Eric Desjardins .05 .02
❑ 330 Stephane Richer .10 .05
❑ 331 Brian Skrudland .05 .02
❑ 332 Sylvain Lefebvre .05 .02
❑ 333 Stephan Lebeau .05 .02
❑ 334 Mike Keane .05 .02
❑ 335 Patrick Roy UER .75 .35
(Photo actually
Jean Claude Bergeron)
❑ 336 Brent Gilchrist .05 .02
❑ 337 Andre Racicot .10 .05
❑ 338 Guy Carbonneau .10 .05
❑ 339 Mike McPhee .05 .02
❑ 340 Andrew Cassels .05 .02
❑ 341 Petr Svoboda .05 .02
❑ 342 Denis Savard .10 .05
❑ 343 Mathieu Schneider .05 .02
❑ 344 John LeClair 1.50 .70
❑ 345 Tom Chorske .05 .02
❑ 346 Russ Courtnall .05 .02
❑ 347 Ken Hodge Jr. HT .05 .02
❑ 348 Cam Neely HT .10 .05
❑ 349 Randy Burridge .05 .02
❑ 350 Glen Wesley .05 .02
❑ 351 Chris Nilan .05 .02
❑ 352 Jeff Lazaro .05 .02
❑ 353 Wes Walz .05 .02
❑ 354 Rejean Lemelin .10 .05
❑ 355 Craig Janney .10 .05
❑ 356 Ray Bourque .25 .11
❑ 357 Bob Sweeney .05 .02
❑ 358 Dave Christian .05 .02
❑ 359 Dave Poulin .05 .02
❑ 360 Garry Galley .05 .02
❑ 361 Andy Moog .10 .05
❑ 362 Ken Hodge Jr. .05 .02
❑ 363 Jim Wiemer .05 .02
❑ 364 Petri Skriko .05 .02
❑ 365 Don Sweeney .05 .02
❑ 366 Cam Neely .10 .05
❑ 367 Brett Hull HT .25 .11
❑ 368 Gino Cavallini .05 .02
❑ 369 Scott Stevens .10 .05
❑ 370 Rich Sutter .05 .02
❑ 371 Glen Featherstone .05 .02
❑ 372 Vincent Riendeau .10 .05
❑ 373 Dave Lowry .05 .02
❑ 374 Rod Brind'Amour .10 .05
❑ 375 Brett Hull .30 .14
❑ 376 Dan Quinn .05 .02
❑ 377 Tom Tilley .05 .02
❑ 378 Paul Cavallini .05 .02
❑ 379 Bob Bassen .05 .02
❑ 380 Mario Marois .05 .02
❑ 381 Darin Kimble .05 .02
❑ 382 Ron Wilson .05 .02
❑ 383 Garth Butcher .05 .02
❑ 384 Adam Oates .10 .05
❑ 385 Jeff Brown .05 .02
❑ 386 Jeremy Roenick HT .25 .11
❑ 387 Tony McKegney .05 .02
❑ 388 Troy Murray .05 .02
❑ 389 Dave Manson .05 .02
❑ 390 Ed Belfour .25 .11
❑ 391 Steve Thomas .05 .02
❑ 392 Michel Goulet .10 .05
❑ 393 Trent Yawney .05 .02
❑ 394 Adam Creighton .05 .02
❑ 395 Steve Larmer .10 .05
❑ 396 Jimmy Waite .10 .05
❑ 397 Dirk Graham .05 .02
❑ 398 Chris Chelios .25 .11
❑ 399 Mike Hudson .05 .02
❑ 400 Doug Wilson .10 .05
❑ 401 Greg Gilbert .05 .02
❑ 402 Wayne Presley .05 .02
❑ 403 Jeremy Roenick .25 .11
❑ 404 Frantisek Kucera .05 .02
❑ 405 Blackhawks/North Stars .05 .02
Playoff Photo
❑ 406 Blues/Red Wings .05 .02
Playoff Action (Adam Oates)
❑ 407 Flames/Oilers .05 .02
Playoff Action
❑ 408 Penguins/Devils .05 .02
Playoff Action
❑ 409 Rangers/Capitals .05 .02
Playoff Action
❑ 410 Bruins/Whalers .05 .02
Playoff Action
❑ 411 Canadiens/Sabres .05 .02
Playoff Action
❑ 412 Kings/Canucks .05 .02
Playoff Action
❑ 413 Penguins/Capitals .05 .02
Playoff Action
❑ 414 Bruins/Canadiens .05 .02
Playoff Action
❑ 415 North Stars/Blues .05 .02
Playoff Action
❑ 416 Kings/Oilers .05 .02
Playoff Action
❑ 417 North Stars/Oilers .05 .02
Playoff Action
❑ 418 Bruins/Penguins .05 .02
Playoff Action (Kevin Stevens)
❑ 419 Game 1 Cup Finals .10 .05
❑ 420 Game 2 Cup Finals .10 .05
❑ 421 Game 3 Cup Finals .10 .05
❑ 422 Game 4 Cup Finals .10 .05
(Kevin Stevens)
❑ 423 Game 5 Cup Finals .10 .05
❑ 424 Game 6 Cup Finals .10 .05
❑ 425 Mario Lemieux MVP .40 .18
(Smythe)
❑ 426 Checklist 1-108 .05 .02
❑ 427 Checklist 109-216 .05 .02
❑ 428 Checklist 217-324 .05 .02
❑ 429 Checklist 325-429 .05 .02

## 1992-93 Bowman

The 1992-93 Bowman hockey set contains 442 standard-size cards. Reportedly only 2,000 16-box wax cases were produced. One of 45 gold-foil engraved cards was inserted in each 15-card pack. These gold-foil cards feature 44 All-Stars (Campbell Conference on cards 199-220 and Wales Conference on cards 222-243) and a special card commemorating Mario Lemieux as the winner of the Conn Smythe trophy (440). The 18 gold-foil All-Stars that were single printed are listed in the checklist below as SP. The basic card fronts feature color action player photos with white borders. A magenta bar at the top left corner carries the Bowman "B". A gradated turquoise bar at the bottom right displays the player's name. The backs have a burlap-textured background and carry a close-up photo, a yellow and white statistics box presenting the player's performance vs. other teams, and biography. The only noteworthy Rookie Card in the set is Guy Hebert. There are a number of non glossy Eric Lindros (No. 442) cards on the market. These are unauthorized releases and should be avoided by collectors.

| | MINT | NRMT |
|---|---|---|
| COMPLETE SET (442) | 250.00 | 110.00 |
| COMMON CARD (1-442) | .25 | .11 |

❑ 1 Wayne Gretzky 8.00 3.60
❑ 2 Mike Krushelnyski .25 .11
❑ 3 Ray Bourque 1.25 .55
❑ 4 Keith Brown .25 .11
❑ 5 Bob Sweeney UER .25 .11
(Photo on back
actually Don Sweeney)
❑ 6 Dave Christian .25 .11
❑ 7 Frantisek Kucera .25 .11
❑ 8 John LeClair 2.50 1.10
❑ 9 Jamie Macoun .25 .11
❑ 10 Bob Carpenter .25 .11
❑ 11 Garry Galley .25 .11
❑ 12 Bob Kudelski .25 .11
❑ 13 Doug Bodger .25 .11
❑ 14 Craig Janney .50 .23
❑ 15 Glen Wesley .25 .11
❑ 16 Daren Puppa .50 .23
❑ 17 Andy Brickley .25 .11
❑ 18 Steve Konroyd .25 .11
❑ 19 Dave Poulin .25 .11
❑ 20 Phil Housley .50 .23
❑ 21 Kevin Todd .25 .11
❑ 22 Tomas Sandstrom .25 .11
❑ 23 Pierre Turgeon .50 .23
❑ 24 Steve Smith .25 .11
❑ 25 Ray Sheppard .50 .23
❑ 26 Stu Barnes .25 .11
❑ 27 Grant Ledyard .25 .11
❑ 28 Benoit Hogue UER .25 .11
(Photo of Dennis Vaske on back)
❑ 29 Randy Burridge .25 .11
❑ 30 Clint Malarchuk .50 .23
❑ 31 Steve Duchesne .25 .11
❑ 32 Guy Hebert 2.00 .90
❑ 33 Steve Kasper .25 .11
❑ 34 Alexander Mogilny .50 .23
❑ 35 Marty McSorley .25 .11
❑ 36 Doug Weight 1.25 .55
❑ 37 Dave Taylor .50 .23
❑ 38 Guy Carbonneau .50 .23
❑ 39 Brian Benning .25 .11
❑ 40 Nelson Emerson .25 .11
❑ 41 Craig Wolanin .25 .11
❑ 42 Kelly Hrudey .50 .23
❑ 43 Chris Chelios 1.25 .55
❑ 44 Dave Andreychuk .50 .23
❑ 45 Russ Courtnall .25 .11
❑ 46 Stephane Richer .50 .23
❑ 47 Petr Svoboda .25 .11
❑ 48 Barry Pederson .25 .11
❑ 49 Claude Lemieux .50 .23
❑ 50 Tony Granato .25 .11
❑ 51 Al MacInnis .50 .23
❑ 52 Luciano Borsato .25 .11
❑ 53 Sergei Makarov .25 .11
❑ 54 Bobby Smith .50 .23
❑ 55 Gary Suter .25 .11
❑ 56 Tom Draper .50 .23
❑ 57 Corry Millen .25 .11
❑ 58 Joe Mullen .50 .23
❑ 59 Joe Nieuwendyk .50 .23
❑ 60 Brian Hayward .50 .23
❑ 61 Steve Larmer .50 .23
❑ 62 Cam Neely .50 .23
❑ 63 Ric Nattress .25 .11
❑ 64 Denis Savard .50 .23
❑ 65 Gerald Diduck .25 .11
❑ 66 Pat Jablonski .50 .23
❑ 67 Brad McCrimmon .25 .11
❑ 68 Dirk Graham .25 .11
❑ 69 Joel Otto .25 .11
❑ 70 Luc Robitaille .50 .23
❑ 71 Dana Murzyn .25 .11
❑ 72 Jocelyn Lemieux .25 .11
❑ 73 Mike Hudson .25 .11
❑ 74 Patrick Roy UER 5.00 2.20
(Games played vs. Edmonton was 2& not 32)
❑ 75 Doug Wilson .50 .23
❑ 76 Wayne Presley .25 .11
❑ 77 Felix Potvin UER 1.25 .55
('91-92 season record
was 0-2-1& not 0-3-1)
❑ 78 Jeremy Roenick 1.25 .55
❑ 79 Andy Moog .50 .23
❑ 80 Joe Kocur .50 .23
❑ 81 Neal Broten .50 .23
❑ 82 Shayne Corson .25 .11
❑ 83 Doug Gilmour 1.25 .55
❑ 84 Rob Zettler .25 .11
❑ 85 Bob Probert .50 .23
❑ 86 Mike Vernon .50 .23
❑ 87 Rick Zombo .25 .11
❑ 88 Adam Creighton .25 .11
❑ 89 Mike McPhee .25 .11
❑ 90 Ed Belfour 1.25 .55
❑ 91 Steve Chiasson .25 .11
❑ 92 Dominic Roussel .50 .23
❑ 93 Troy Murray .25 .11
❑ 94 Jari Kurri .50 .23
❑ 95 Geoff Smith .25 .11
❑ 96 Paul Ranheim .25 .11
❑ 97 Rick Wamsley .50 .23
❑ 98 Brian Noonan .25 .11
❑ 99 Kevin Lowe .25 .11
❑ 100 Josef Beranek .25 .11
❑ 101 Michel Petit .25 .11
❑ 102 Craig Billington .50 .23
❑ 103 Steve Yzerman 4.00 1.80
❑ 104 Glenn Anderson .50 .23
❑ 105 Perry Berezan .25 .11
❑ 106 Bill Ranford .50 .23
❑ 107 Randy Ladouceur .25 .11
❑ 108 Jimmy Carson .25 .11
❑ 109 Gary Roberts .25 .11
❑ 110 Checklist 1-110 .25 .11
❑ 111 Brad Shaw .25 .11
❑ 112 Pat Verbeek .25 .11
❑ 113 Mark Messier 2.00 .90
❑ 114 Grant Fuhr .50 .23

❑ 115 Sylvain Cote .25 .11
❑ 116 Mike Sullivan .25 .11
❑ 117 Steve Thomas .25 .11
❑ 118 Craig MacTavish .25 .11
❑ 119 Dave Babych .25 .11
❑ 120 Jim Waite .50 .23
❑ 121 Kevin Dineen .25 .11
❑ 122 Shawn Burr .25 .11
❑ 123 Ron Francis .50 .23
❑ 124 Garth Butcher .25 .11
❑ 125 Jarmo Myllys .25 .11
❑ 126 Doug Brown .25 .11
❑ 127 James Patrick .25 .11
❑ 128 Ray Ferraro .25 .11
❑ 129 Terry Carkner .25 .11
❑ 130 John MacLean .50 .23
❑ 131 Randy Velischek .25 .11
❑ 132 John Vanbiesbrouck 2.00 .90
❑ 133 Dean Evason .25 .11
❑ 134 Patrick Flatley .25 .11
❑ 135 Petr Klima .25 .11
❑ 136 Geoff Sanderson .50 .23
❑ 137 Joe Reekie .25 .11
❑ 138 Kirk Muller .25 .11
❑ 139 Brian Mullen .25 .11
❑ 140 Daniel Berthiaume .50 .23
❑ 141 David Shaw .25 .11
❑ 142 Pat LaFontaine .50 .23
❑ 143 Ulf Dahlen .25 .11
❑ 144 Esa Tikkanen .25 .11
❑ 145 Slava Fetisov .25 .11
❑ 146 Mike Gartner .50 .23
❑ 147 Brent Sutter .25 .11
❑ 148 Darcy Wakaluk .50 .23
❑ 149 Brian Leetch 1.25 .55
❑ 150 Craig Simpson .25 .11
❑ 151 Mike Modano 2.00 .90
❑ 152 Bryan Trottier .50 .23
❑ 153 Larry Murphy .50 .23
❑ 154 Pavel Bure 2.50 1.10
❑ 155 Kay Whitmore .50 .23
❑ 156 Darren Turcotte .25 .11
❑ 157 Frank Musil .25 .11
❑ 158 Mikael Andersson .25 .11
❑ 159 Rick Tocchet .50 .23
❑ 160 Scott Stevens .50 .23
❑ 161 Bernie Nicholls .50 .23
❑ 162 Peter Sidorkiewicz .50 .23
❑ 163 Scott Mellanby .50 .23
❑ 164 Alexander Semak .25 .11
❑ 165 Kjell Samuelsson .25 .11
❑ 166 Kelly Kisio .25 .11
❑ 167 Sylvain Turgeon .25 .11
❑ 168 Rob Brown .25 .11
❑ 169 Gerard Gallant .25 .11
❑ 170 Jyrki Lumme .25 .11
❑ 171 Dave Gagner .50 .23
❑ 172 Tony Tanti .25 .11
❑ 173 Zarley Zalapski .25 .11
❑ 174 Joe Murphy .25 .11
❑ 175 Ron Sutter .25 .11
❑ 176 Dino Ciccarelli .50 .23
❑ 177 Jim Johnson .25 .11
❑ 178 Mike Hough .25 .11
❑ 179 Pelle Eklund .25 .11
❑ 180 John Druce .25 .11
❑ 181 Paul Coffey 1.25 .55
❑ 182 Ken Wregget .50 .23
❑ 183 Brendan Shanahan 2.50 1.10
❑ 184 Keith Acton .25 .11
❑ 185 Steven Finn .25 .11
❑ 186 Brett Hull 2.00 .90
❑ 187 Rollie Melanson .50 .23
❑ 188 Derek King .25 .11
❑ 189 Mario Lemieux 6.00 2.70
❑ 190 Mathieu Schneider .25 .11
❑ 191 Claude Vilgrain .25 .11
❑ 192 Gary Leeman .25 .11
❑ 193 Paul Cavallini .25 .11
❑ 194 John Cullen .25 .11
❑ 195 Ron Hextall .50 .23
(Traded to Quebec)
❑ 196 David Volek .25 .11
❑ 197 Gordie Roberts .25 .11
❑ 198 Dale Craigwell .25 .11
❑ 199 Ed Belfour 4.00 1.80
AS FOIL
❑ 200 Brian Bellows 6.00 2.70
AS FOIL SP
❑ 201 Chris Chelios 3.00 1.35
AS FOIL
❑ 202 Tim Cheveldae 6.00 2.70
AS FOIL SP
❑ 203A Vincent Damphousse ... 3.00 1.35
AS FOIL ERR
(Team name missing
on card back)
❑ 203B Vincent Damphousse ... 3.00 1.35
AS FOIL COR
❑ 204 Dave Ellett 1.50 .70
AS FOIL
❑ 205 Sergei Fedorov 25.00 11.00
AS FOIL SP
❑ 206 Theoren Fleury 3.00 1.35
AS FOIL
❑ 207 Wayne Gretzky 15.00 6.75
AS FOIL
❑ 208 Phil Housley 1.50 .70
AS FOIL
❑ 209 Brett Hull 4.00 1.80
AS FOIL
❑ 210 Trevor Linden 1.25 .55
AS FOIL SP
❑ 211 Al MacInnis 6.00 2.70
AS FOIL SP
❑ 212 Kirk McLean 1.25 .55
AS FOIL SP
❑ 213 Adam Oates 3.00 1.35
AS FOIL
❑ 214 Gary Roberts 6.00 2.70
AS FOIL SP
❑ 215 Larry Robinson 1.50 .70
AS FOIL
❑ 216 Luc Robitaille 3.00 1.35
AS FOIL
❑ 217 Jeremy Roenick 15.00 6.75
AS FOIL SP
❑ 218 Mark Tinordi 1.50 .70
AS FOIL
❑ 219 Doug Wilson 1.50 .70
AS FOIL
❑ 220 Steve Yzerman 8.00 3.60
AS FOIL
❑ 221 Checklist 111-220 .25 .11
❑ 222 Don Beaupre 6.00 2.70
AS FOIL SP
❑ 223 Ray Bourque 3.00 1.35
AS FOIL
❑ 224 Rod Brind'Amour UER 1.25 .55
AS FOIL SP
(Apostrophe in last
name is missing)
❑ 225 Randy Burridge 6.00 2.70
AS FOIL SP
❑ 226 Paul Coffey 10.00 4.50
AS FOIL SP
❑ 227 John Cullen 6.00 2.70
AS FOIL SP
❑ 228 Eric Desjardins 6.00 2.70
AS FOIL SP
❑ 229 Ray Ferraro 6.00 2.70
AS FOIL SP
❑ 230 Kevin Hatcher 1.50 .70
AS FOIL
❑ 231 Jaromir Jagr 8.00 3.60
AS FOIL
❑ 232 Brian Leetch 10.00 4.50
AS FOIL SP
❑ 233 Mario Lemieux 12.00 5.50
AS FOIL
❑ 234 Mark Messier 4.00 1.80
AS FOIL
❑ 235 Alexander Mogilny 1.25 .55
AS FOIL
❑ 236 Kirk Muller 1.50 .70
AS FOIL
❑ 237 Owen Nolan 3.00 1.35
AS FOIL
❑ 238 Mike Richter 3.00 1.35
AS FOIL
❑ 239 Patrick Roy 12.00 5.50
AS FOIL
❑ 240 Joe Sakic 25.00 11.00
AS FOIL SP
❑ 241 Kevin Stevens 1.50 .70
AS FOIL
❑ 242 Scott Stevens 1.50 .70
AS FOIL
❑ 243 Brian Trottier 6.00 2.70
AS FOIL SP
❑ 244 Joe Sakic 3.00 1.35
❑ 245 Daniel Marois .25 .11
❑ 246 Randy Wood .25 .11
❑ 247 Jeff Brown .25 .11
❑ 248 Peter Bondra 1.25 .55
❑ 249 Peter Stastny .50 .23
❑ 250 Tom Barrasso .50 .23
❑ 251 Al Iafrate .50 .23
❑ 252 James Black .25 .11
❑ 253 Jan Erixon .25 .11
❑ 254 Brian Lawton .25 .11
❑ 255 Luke Richardson .25 .11
❑ 256 Rich Sutter .25 .11
❑ 257 Jeff Chychrun UER .25 .11
(Misspelled Chychurn
on card front)
❑ 258 Adam Oates .50 .23
❑ 259 Tom Kurvers .25 .11
❑ 260 Brian Bellows .25 .11
❑ 261 Trevor Linden .50 .23
❑ 262 Vincent Riendeau .50 .23
❑ 263 Peter Zezel .25 .11
❑ 264 Rich Pilon .25 .11
❑ 265 Paul Broten .25 .11
❑ 266 Gaetan Duchesne .25 .11
❑ 267 Doug Lidster .25 .11
❑ 268 Rod Brind'Amour .50 .23
❑ 269 Jon Casey .50 .23
❑ 270 Pat Elynuik .25 .11
❑ 271 Kevin Hatcher .25 .11
❑ 272 Brian Propp .25 .11
❑ 273 Tom Fergus .25 .11
❑ 274 Steve Weeks .50 .23
❑ 275 Calle Johansson .25 .11
❑ 276 Russ Romaniuk .25 .11
❑ 277 Greg Paslawski .25 .11
❑ 278 Ed Olczyk .25 .11
❑ 279 Rod Langway .25 .11
❑ 280 Murray Craven .25 .11
❑ 281 Guy Larose .25 .11
❑ 282 Paul MacDermid .25 .11
❑ 283 Brian Bradley .25 .11
❑ 284 Paul Stanton .25 .11
❑ 285 Kirk McLean .50 .23
❑ 286 Andrei Lomakin .25 .11
❑ 287 Randy Carlyle .25 .11
❑ 288 Donald Audette .50 .23
❑ 289 Dan Quinn .25 .11
❑ 290 Mike Keane .25 .11
❑ 291 Dave Ellett .25 .11
❑ 292 Joe Juneau UER .50 .23
(Card back says shoots
right& should be left)
❑ 293 Phil Bourque .25 .11
❑ 294 Michal Pivonka .25 .11
❑ 295 Fredrik Olausson .25 .11
❑ 296 Randy McKay .25 .11
❑ 297 Don Beaupre .50 .23
❑ 298 Steve Leach .25 .11
❑ 299 Teppo Numminen .25 .11
❑ 300 Slava Kozlov .50 .23
❑ 301 Kevin Haller .25 .11
❑ 302 Jaromir Jagr 4.00 1.80
❑ 303 Dale Hunter .25 .11
❑ 304 Bob Errey .25 .11
❑ 305 Nicklas Lidstrom .50 .23
❑ 306 Bob Essensa .50 .23
❑ 307 Sylvain Lefebvre .25 .11
❑ 308 Dale Hawerchuk .50 .23
❑ 309 Dave Snuggerud .25 .11
❑ 310 Michel Goulet .50 .23
❑ 311 Eric Desjardins .25 .11
❑ 312 Thomas Steen .25 .11
❑ 313 Scott Niedermayer .50 .23
❑ 314 Mark Recchi .50 .23
❑ 315 Gord Murphy .25 .11
❑ 316 Sergio Momesso .25 .11
❑ 317 Todd Elik .25 .11
❑ 318 Louie DeBrusk .25 .11
❑ 319 Mike Lalor .25 .11
❑ 320 Jamie Leach .25 .11
❑ 321 Darryl Sydor .25 .11
❑ 322 Brent Gilchrist .25 .11
❑ 323 Alexei Kasatonov .25 .11
❑ 324 Rick Tabaracci .50 .23
❑ 325 Wendel Clark .50 .23
❑ 326 Vladimir Konstantinov .25 .11
❑ 327 Randy Gilhen .25 .11
❑ 328 Owen Nolan .50 .23
❑ 329 Vincent Damphousse .50 .23
❑ 330 Checklist 221-331 .25 .11
❑ 331 Yves Racine .25 .11
❑ 332 Jacques Cloutier .50 .23
❑ 333 Greg Adams .25 .11
❑ 334 Mike Craig .25 .11
❑ 335 Curtis Leschyshyn .25 .11
❑ 336 John McIntyre .25 .11
❑ 337 Stephane Quintal .25 .11
❑ 338 Kelly Miller .25 .11
❑ 339 Dave Manson .25 .11
❑ 340 Stephane Matteau .25 .11
❑ 341 Christian Ruuttu .25 .11
❑ 342 Mike Donnelly .25 .11
❑ 343 Eric Weinrich .25 .11
❑ 344 Mats Sundin 1.25 .55
❑ 345 Geoff Courtnall .25 .11
❑ 346 Stephan Lebeau .25 .11
❑ 347 Jeff Beukeboom .25 .11
❑ 348 Jeff Hackett .50 .23
❑ 349 Uwe Krupp .25 .11
❑ 350 Igor Larionov .25 .11
❑ 351 Ulf Samuelsson .25 .11
❑ 352 Marty McInnis .25 .11
❑ 353 Peter Ahola .25 .11
❑ 354 Mike Richter 1.25 .55
❑ 355 Theoren Fleury .50 .23
❑ 356 Dan Lambert .25 .11
❑ 357 Brent Ashton .25 .11
❑ 358 David Bruce .25 .11
❑ 359 Chris Dahlquist .25 .11
❑ 360 Mike Ridley .25 .11
❑ 361 Pat Falloon .25 .11
❑ 362 Doug Smail .25 .11
❑ 363 Adrien Plavsic .25 .11
❑ 364 Ron Wilson .25 .11
❑ 365 Derian Hatcher .25 .11
❑ 366 Kevin Stevens .25 .11
❑ 367 Rob Blake .50 .23
❑ 368 Curtis Joseph 1.25 .55
❑ 369 Tom Fitzgerald .25 .11
❑ 370 Dave Lowry .25 .11
❑ 371 J.J. Daigneault .25 .11
❑ 372 Jim Hrivnak .50 .23
❑ 373 Adam Graves .50 .23
❑ 374 Brad May .50 .23
❑ 375 Todd Gill .25 .11
❑ 376 Paul Ysebaert .25 .11
❑ 377 David Williams .25 .11
❑ 378 Bob Bassen .25 .11
❑ 379 Brian Glynn .25 .11
❑ 380 Kris King .25 .11
❑ 381 Rob Pearson .25 .11
❑ 382 Marc Bureau .25 .11
❑ 383 Jim Paek .25 .11
❑ 384 Tomas Forslund .25 .11
❑ 385 Darrin Shannon .25 .11
❑ 386 Chris Terreri .50 .23
❑ 387 Andrew Cassels .25 .11
❑ 388 Jay More .50 .23
❑ 389 Tony Amonte .50 .23
❑ 390 Mark Pederson .25 .11
❑ 391 Kevin Miller .25 .11
❑ 392 Igor Ulanov .25 .11
❑ 393 Kelly Buchberger .25 .11
❑ 394 Mark Fitzpatrick .50 .23
❑ 395 Mikhail Tatarinov .25 .11
❑ 396 Petr Nedved .50 .23
❑ 397 Jeff Odgers .25 .11
❑ 398 Stephane Fiset .50 .23
❑ 399 Mark Tinordi .25 .11
❑ 400 Johan Garpenlov .25 .11
❑ 401 Robert Reichel .25 .11
❑ 402 Don Sweeney UER .25 .11
(Back photo actually
Bob Sweeney)
❑ 403 Rob DiMaio .25 .11
❑ 404 Bill Lindsay .25 .11
❑ 405 Steph Beauregard .50 .23
❑ 406 Mike Ricci .25 .11
❑ 407 Bobby Holik .25 .11
❑ 408 Igor Kravchuk .25 .11
❑ 409 Murray Baron .25 .11
❑ 410 Troy Gamble .50 .23
❑ 411 Cliff Ronning .25 .11
❑ 412 Jeff Reese .25 .11
❑ 413 Robert Kron .25 .11
❑ 414 Benoit Brunet .25 .11
❑ 415 Shawn McEachern .25 .11
❑ 416 Sergei Fedorov 2.50 1.10
❑ 417 Joe Sacco .25 .11
❑ 418 Bryan Marchment .25 .11
❑ 419 John LeBlanc .25 .11
❑ 420 Tim Cheveldae .50 .23
❑ 421 Claude LaPointe .25 .11
❑ 422 Ken Sutton .25 .11
❑ 423 Anatoli Semenov .25 .11
❑ 424 Mike McNeil .25 .11
❑ 425 Norm Maciver .25 .11
❑ 426 Sergei Nemchinov .25 .11
❑ 427 Dimitri Khristich .25 .11
❑ 428 Dominik Hasek 4.00 1.80
❑ 429 Bob McGill .25 .11
❑ 430 Valeri Zelepukin .25 .11
❑ 431 Vladimir Ruzicka .25 .11
❑ 432 Valeri Kamensky .50 .23
❑ 433 Pat MacLeod .25 .11
❑ 434 Glenn Healy .50 .23
❑ 435 Patrice Brisebois .25 .11
❑ 436 James Baker .25 .11
❑ 437 Michel Picard .25 .11
❑ 438 Scott Lachance UER .25 .11
(Back photo actually
Brad Turner)
❑ 439 Gilbert Dionne .25 .11
❑ 440 Mario Lemieux FOIL 10.00 4.50
Conn Smythe Winner
❑ 441 Checklist 332-441 .25 .11
❑ 442 Eric Lindros UER 15.00 6.75
(Acquired 6-30-92&
not 6-20-92 as in bio)

## 1995-96 Bowman

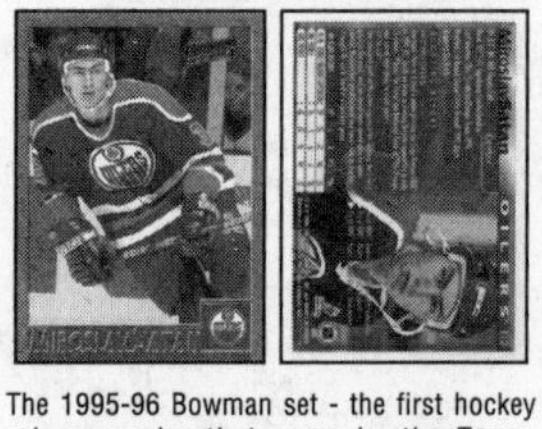

The 1995-96 Bowman set - the first hockey release under that name by the Topps company since 1992-93 - was issued in one series totaling 165 cards. The 9-card packs had a suggested retail price of $2.00. The highlight of the set is an extended Rookies subset (91-165). Rookie Cards in the set include Daniel Alfredsson and Petr Sykora. The Cool Trade redemption offer expired on October 15, 1996.

| | MINT | NRMT |
|---|---|---|
| COMPLETE SET (165) | 25.00 | 11.00 |
| COMMON CARD (1-165) | .10 | .05 |

❑ 1 Wayne Gretzky 2.00 .90
❑ 2 Ray Bourque .30 .14
❑ 3 Craig Janney .15 .07
❑ 4 Andrew Cassels .10 .05
❑ 5 Alexander Mogilny .15 .07
❑ 6 Pierre Turgeon .15 .07
❑ 7 Dave Andreychuk .15 .07
❑ 8 Mark Messier .40 .18
❑ 9 Igor Korolev .10 .05
❑ 10 Tomas Sandstrom .10 .05
❑ 11 Shayne Corson .10 .05
❑ 12 Chris Chelios .30 .14
❑ 13 Claude Lemieux .15 .07
❑ 14 Stephane Richer .15 .07
❑ 15 Patrick Roy 1.50 .70
❑ 16 Al MacInnis .15 .07
❑ 17 Cam Neely .15 .07
❑ 18 Doug Gilmour .30 .14
❑ 19 Steve Thomas .10 .05
❑ 20 Jeremy Roenick .30 .14
❑ 21 Steve Yzerman 1.00 .45
❑ 22 Petr Klima .10 .05
❑ 23 Luc Robitaille .15 .07
❑ 24 Bill Ranford .15 .07
❑ 25 Grant Fuhr .15 .07
❑ 26 Sean Burke .15 .07
❑ 27 John MacLean .15 .07
❑ 28 Brendan Shanahan .60 .25
❑ 29 Pat LaFontaine .15 .07
❑ 30 John Vanbiesbrouck .50 .23
❑ 31 Ron Francis .15 .07
❑ 32 Brian Leetch .30 .14
❑ 33 Dave Gagner .15 .07
❑ 34 Larry Murphy .15 .07
❑ 35 Mike Modano .40 .18
❑ 36 Rick Tocchet .15 .07
❑ 37 Scott Mellanby .15 .07
❑ 38 Ron Hextall .15 .07
❑ 39 Joe Juneau .10 .05
❑ 40 Mario Lemieux 1.50 .70
❑ 41 Paul Coffey .30 .14
❑ 42 Joe Sakic .60 .25
❑ 43 Brett Hull .40 .18
❑ 44 Adam Oates .15 .07
❑ 45 Wendel Clark .15 .07
❑ 46 Trevor Linden .15 .07
❑ 47 Tom Barrasso .15 .07
❑ 48 Kevin Hatcher .10 .05
❑ 49 Mats Sundin .15 .07
❑ 50 Scott Stevens .15 .07
❑ 51 Mark Recchi .15 .07
❑ 52 Theoren Fleury .15 .07
❑ 53 Ed Belfour .30 .14
❑ 54 Adam Graves .15 .07
❑ 55 Peter Bondra .30 .14
❑ 56 Dominik Hasek .60 .25
❑ 57 Jaromir Jagr 1.00 .45
❑ 58 Owen Nolan .15 .07
❑ 59 Kevin Stevens .10 .05
❑ 60 Alexei Zhamnov .15 .07
❑ 61 Dimitri Khristich .10 .05
❑ 62 Chris Pronger .15 .07
❑ 63 John LeClair .50 .23
❑ 64 Scott Niedermayer .10 .05
❑ 65 Pavel Bure .60 .25
❑ 66 Chris Osgood .30 .14
❑ 67 Geoff Sanderson .15 .07
❑ 68 Doug Weight .15 .07
❑ 69 Keith Tkachuk .40 .18
❑ 70 Martin Brodeur .75 .35
❑ 71 Eric Lindros 1.00 .45
❑ 72 Martin Straka .10 .05
❑ 73 Alexander Selivanov .10 .05
❑ 74 Jim Carey .30 .14
❑ 75 Teemu Selanne .60 .25
❑ 76 Rob Niedermayer .15 .07
❑ 77 Vyacheslav Kozlov .10 .05
❑ 78 Todd Harvey .10 .05
❑ 79 Felix Potvin .30 .14
❑ 80 Sergei Fedorov .50 .23
❑ 81 Mathieu Schneider .10 .05
❑ 82 Roman Hamrlik .15 .07
❑ 83 Mikael Renberg .15 .07
❑ 84 Jeff Friesen .15 .07
❑ 85 Peter Forsberg 1.00 .45
❑ 86 Kenny Jonsson .10 .05
❑ 87 Brian Savage .10 .05
❑ 88 Oleg Tverdovsky .15 .07
❑ 89 Nikolai Khabibulin .15 .07
❑ 90 Paul Kariya 1.25 .55
❑ 91 Zdenek Nedved RC .10 .05
❑ 92 Darren Langdon .10 .05
❑ 93 Lonny Bohonos .10 .05
❑ 94 Mike Wilson .10 .05
❑ 95 Landon Wilson .10 .05
❑ 96 Bryan McCabe .10 .05
❑ 97 Byron Dafoe .15 .07
❑ 98 Denny Lambert .10 .05
❑ 99 Craig Mills .10 .05
❑ 100 Ed Jovanovski .30 .14
❑ 101 Jason Bonsignore .10 .05
❑ 102 Clayton Beddoes UER .10 .05
back reads Bleddoes
❑ 103 Jamie Pushor .10 .05
❑ 104 Drew Bannister .10 .05
❑ 105 Ed Ward .10 .05
❑ 106 Todd Warriner .10 .05
❑ 107 Deron Quint .10 .05
❑ 108 Rhett Warrener .10 .05
❑ 109 Marko Kiprusoff .10 .05
❑ 110 Daniel Alfredsson .60 .25
❑ 111 Marcus Ragnarsson UER .10 .05
❑ 112 Miroslav Satan 1.50 .70
❑ 113 Niklas Sundstrom .10 .05
❑ 114 Mathieu Dandenault .10 .05
❑ 115 Vitali Yachmenev .10 .05
❑ 116 Petr Sykora .30 .14
❑ 117 Antti Tormanen .10 .05
❑ 118 Jeff O'Neill .10 .05
❑ 119 David Nemirovsky .10 .05
❑ 120 Jason Doig .10 .05
❑ 121 Aaron Gavey .10 .05
❑ 122 Ladislav Kohn .10 .05
❑ 123 Richard Park .10 .05
❑ 124 Stephane Yelle .10 .05
❑ 125 Eric Daze .30 .14
❑ 126 Niclas Andersson .10 .05
❑ 127 Brendan Witt .10 .05
❑ 128 Jamie Storr .15 .07
❑ 129 Darby Hendrickson .10 .05
❑ 130 Radek Dvorak .10 .05
❑ 131 Cory Stillman .10 .05
❑ 132 Jamie Rivers .10 .05
❑ 133 Ville Peltonen .10 .05
❑ 134 Peter Ferraro .10 .05
❑ 135 Trent McCleary .10 .05
❑ 136 Chris Wells .10 .05
❑ 137 Chad Kilger .10 .05
❑ 138 Denis Pederson .10 .05
❑ 139 Roman Vopat .10 .05
❑ 140 Shean Donovan .10 .05
❑ 141 Alex Stojanov .10 .05
❑ 142 Mark Kolesar .10 .05
❑ 143 Scott Walker .10 .05
❑ 144 Dave Roche .10 .05
❑ 145 Corey Hirsch .15 .07
❑ 146 Aki Berg .10 .05
❑ 147 Stefan Ustorf .10 .05
❑ 148 Saku Koivu .50 .23
❑ 149 Shane Doan .10 .05
❑ 150 Jere Lehtinen .10 .05
❑ 151 Kyle McLaren .10 .05
❑ 152 Marty Murray .10 .05
❑ 153 Sean Pronger .10 .05
❑ 154 Joaquin Gage .10 .05
❑ 155 Eric Fichaud .15 .07
❑ 156 Todd Bertuzzi .10 .05
❑ 157 Wayne Primeau .10 .05
❑ 158 Scott Bailey .10 .05
❑ 159 Viktor Kozlov .10 .05
❑ 160 Valeri Bure .15 .07

❑ 161 Dody Wood .10 .05
❑ 162 Grant Marshall .10 .05
❑ 163 Ken Klee .10 .05
❑ 164 Corey Schwab .15 .07
❑ 165 Brian Holzinger .30 .14
❑ NNO Cool Trade Exchange EXP. 1.00 .45

## 1995-96 Bowman All Foil

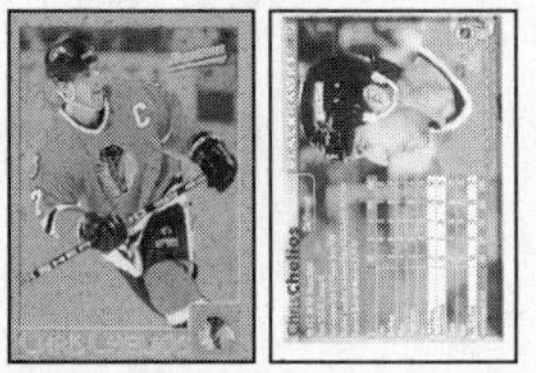

The 1995-96 Bowman All Foil set is a 165-card parallel of the regular version. The cards, which were inserted one per pack, feature a stylish metallicized front, while the backs remain the same as the basic cards.

| | MINT | NRMT |
|---|---|---|
| COMPLETE SET (165) | 150.00 | 70.00 |
| COMMON CARD (1-165) | .25 | .11 |

*VETERAN STARS: 4X TO 8X BASIC CARDS
*YOUNG STARS: 2.5X TO 5X BASIC CARDS
*RCs: 1.5X TO 3X BASIC CARDS

## 1995-96 Bowman Draft Prospects

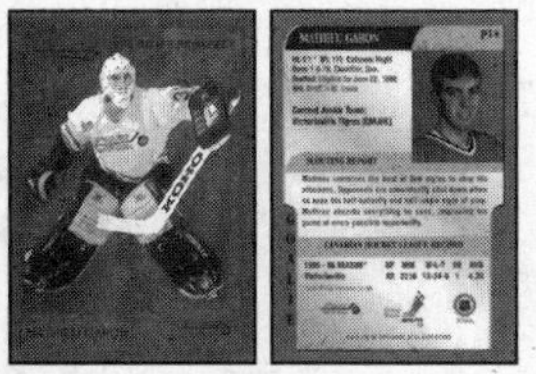

Inserted one in every pack, this 40-card set features the players who participated in the first annual 1996 CHL Draft Prospects game in Toronto. Fourteen of the players pictured went on to become first-round selections in the 1996 NHL entry draft.

| | MINT | NRMT |
|---|---|---|
| COMPLETE SET (40) | 20.00 | 9.00 |
| COMMON CARD (P1-P40) | .40 | .18 |

❑ P1 Johnathan Aitken .60 .25
❑ P2 Chris Allen .40 .18
❑ P3 Matt Bradley .40 .18
❑ P4 Daniel Briere 2.50 1.10
❑ P5 Jeff Brown .40 .18
❑ P6 Jan Bulis 1.25 .55
❑ P7 Daniel Corso .60 .25
❑ P8 Luke Curtin .40 .18
❑ P9 Matthieu Descoteaux .60 .25
❑ P10 Boyd Devereaux 2.00 .90
❑ P11 Jason Doyle .40 .18
❑ P12 Etienne Drapeau .40 .18
❑ P13 Jean-Pierre Dumont 1.00 .45
❑ P14 Mathieu Garon .75 .35
❑ P15 Josh Green .40 .18
❑ P16 Chris Hajt .40 .18
❑ P17 Matt Higgins .40 .18
❑ P18 Craig Hillier 1.00 .45
❑ P19 Josh Holden 1.00 .45
❑ P20 Dan Focht .60 .25
❑ P21 Henry Kuster .40 .18
❑ P22 Francis Larivee .60 .25
❑ P23 Mario Larocque .40 .18
❑ P24 Wes Mason .40 .18
❑ P25 Francois Methot .40 .18
❑ P26 Geoff Peters .40 .18
❑ P27 Randy Petruk .60 .25
❑ P28 Chris Phillips 2.00 .90
❑ P29 Boris Protsenko .40 .18
❑ P30 Remi Royer .40 .18
❑ P31 Cory Sarich 1.25 .55
❑ P32 Jaroslav Svejkovsky 2.00 .90
❑ P33 Curtis Tipler .40 .18
❑ P34 Darren Van Oene .60 .25
❑ P35 Jesse Wallin .60 .25
❑ P36 Kurt Walsh .40 .18
❑ P37 Lance Ward .40 .18
❑ P38 Steve Wasylko .40 .18
❑ P39 Trevor Wasyluk .60 .25
❑ P40 Jon Zukiwsky .40 .18

## 1995-96 Bowman's Best

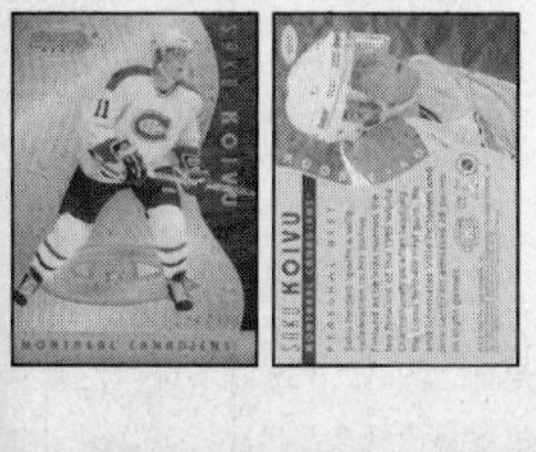

Randomly inserted in packs at a rate of one in 12, this 30-card set is dedicated to the finest stars and up'n'comers in the NHL.

| | MINT | NRMT |
|---|---|---|
| COMPLETE SET (30) | 200.00 | 90.00 |
| COMMON CARD (BB1-BB30) | 2.00 | .90 |
| COMPLETE REFRACTOR SET | 600.00 | 275.00 |
| COMMON REF. (BB1-BB30) | 8.00 | 3.60 |

*VETERAN STARS: 20X TO 40X BASIC CARDS

❑ BB1 Peter Forsberg 12.00 5.50
❑ BB2 Teemu Selanne 8.00 3.60
❑ BB3 Eric Lindros 15.00 6.75
❑ BB4 Scott Stevens 2.00 .90
❑ BB5 Wayne Gretzky 25.00 11.00
❑ BB6 Mark Messier 5.00 2.20
❑ BB7 Jaromir Jagr 12.00 5.50
❑ BB8 Martin Brodeur 10.00 4.50
❑ BB9 Alexander Mogilny 4.00 1.80
❑ BB10 Mario Lemieux 20.00 9.00
❑ BB11 Joe Sakic 10.00 4.50
❑ BB12 Sergei Fedorov 8.00 3.60
❑ BB13 Pavel Bure 8.00 3.60
❑ BB14 Brian Leetch 5.00 2.20
❑ BB15 Paul Kariya 15.00 6.75
❑ BB16 Daniel Alfredsson 4.00 1.80
❑ BB17 Saku Koivu 8.00 3.60
❑ BB18 Eric Daze 4.00 1.80
❑ BB19 Ed Jovanovski 4.00 1.80
❑ BB20 Vitali Yachmenev 2.00 .90
❑ BB21 Niklas Sundstrom 2.00 .90
❑ BB22 Radek Dvorak 2.00 .90
❑ BB23 Byron Dafoe 2.00 .90
❑ BB24 Shane Doan 2.00 .90
❑ BB25 Chad Kilger 2.00 .90
❑ BB26 Jeff O'Neill 2.00 .90
❑ BB27 Cory Stillman 2.00 .90
❑ BB28 Valeri Bure 2.00 .90
❑ BB29 Marcus Ragnarsson 2.00 .90
❑ BB30 Todd Bertuzzi 2.00 .90

## 1998-99 Bowman's Best

This 150-card set was distributed in six-card packs with a suggested retail price of $5. The set features color action photos of 100 key veterans printed on cards with a gold design and 35 top NHL rookies and 14 CHL stars showcased on silver-designed cards. The cards are all printed on thick 26-pt. stock. The backs carry player information and career statistics.

| | MINT | NRMT |
|---|---|---|
| COMPLETE SET (150) | 150.00 | 70.00 |
| COMMON CARD (1-100) | .25 | .11 |
| COMMON SP (101-150) | 2.50 | 1.10 |

❑ 1 Steve Yzerman 2.50 1.10
❑ 2 Paul Kariya 3.00 1.35
❑ 3 Wayne Gretzky 5.00 2.20
❑ 4 Jaromir Jagr 2.50 1.10
❑ 5 Mark Messier 1.00 .45
❑ 6 Keith Tkachuk 1.00 .45
❑ 7 John LeClair 1.25 .55
❑ 8 Martin Brodeur 2.00 .90
❑ 9 Rob Blake .60 .25
❑ 10 Brett Hull 1.00 .45
❑ 11 Dominik Hasek 1.50 .70
❑ 12 Peter Forsberg 2.50 1.10
❑ 13 Doug Gilmour .60 .25
❑ 14 Vincent Damphousse .60 .25
❑ 15 Zigmund Palffy .75 .35
❑ 16 Daniel Alfredsson .60 .25
❑ 17 Mike Vernon .60 .25
❑ 18 Chris Pronger .60 .25
❑ 19 Wendel Clark .60 .25
❑ 20 Curtis Joseph .75 .35
❑ 21 Peter Bondra .75 .35
❑ 22 Grant Fuhr .60 .25
❑ 23 Nikolai Khabibulin .60 .25
❑ 24 Kevin Hatcher .25 .11
❑ 25 Brian Leetch .75 .35
❑ 26 Patrik Elias .25 .11
❑ 27 Chris Osgood .75 .35
❑ 28 Patrick Roy 4.00 1.80
❑ 29 Chris Chelios .75 .35
❑ 30 Trevor Kidd .60 .25
❑ 31 Theoren Fleury .75 .35
❑ 32 Michael Peca .25 .11
❑ 33 Ray Bourque .75 .35
❑ 34 Ed Belfour .75 .35
❑ 35 Sergei Fedorov 1.50 .70
❑ 36 Adrian Aucoin .25 .11
❑ 37 Alexei Yashin .60 .25
❑ 38 Rick Tocchet .60 .25
❑ 39 Mats Sundin .75 .35
❑ 40 Alexander Mogilny .60 .25
❑ 41 Jeff Friesen .60 .25
❑ 42 Eric Lindros 2.50 1.10
❑ 43 Mike Richter .75 .35
❑ 44 Saku Koivu 1.25 .55
❑ 45 Teemu Selanne 1.50 .70
❑ 46 Doug Weight .60 .25
❑ 47 Nicklas Lidstrom .60 .25
❑ 48 Mike Modano 1.00 .45
❑ 49 Joe Sakic 1.50 .70
❑ 50 Ron Francis .60 .25
❑ 51 Jason Allison .60 .25
❑ 52 Brendan Shanahan 1.50 .70
❑ 53 Bobby Holik .25 .11
❑ 54 Damian Rhodes .60 .25
❑ 55 Jeremy Roenick .75 .35
❑ 56 Tom Barrasso .25 .11
❑ 57 Al MacInnis .60 .25
❑ 58 Pavel Bure 1.50 .70
❑ 59 Olaf Kolzig .60 .25
❑ 60 Patrick Marleau .25 .11
❑ 61 Cliff Ronning .25 .11
❑ 62 Joe Nieuwendyk .60 .25
❑ 63 Jeff Hackett .60 .25
❑ 64 Keith Primeau .60 .25
❑ 65 Jarome Iginla .60 .25
❑ 66 Sergei Samsonov 1.25 .55
❑ 67 Rod Brind'Amour .60 .25
❑ 68 Dino Ciccarelli .60 .25
❑ 69 Ryan Smyth .60 .25
❑ 70 Owen Nolan .60 .25
❑ 71 Mike Johnson .25 .11
❑ 72 Adam Oates .60 .25
❑ 73 Mattias Ohlund .60 .25
❑ 74 Jamie Heward .25 .11
❑ 75 Mike Dunham .60 .25
❑ 76 Jere Lehtinen .60 .25
❑ 77 Tony Amonte .60 .25
❑ 78 Derek Morris .25 .11
❑ 79 Darren McCarty .25 .11
❑ 80 Bryan Berard .60 .25
❑ 81 Adam Graves .60 .25
❑ 82 John Vanbiesbrouck 1.25 .55
❑ 83 Marco Sturm .25 .11
❑ 84 Joe Thornton .75 .35
❑ 85 Wade Redden .25 .11
❑ 86 Pierre Turgeon .60 .25
❑ 87 Bill Ranford .60 .25
❑ 88 Alexei Zhitnik .25 .11
❑ 89 Valeri Kamensky .25 .11
❑ 90 Dean McAmmond .25 .11
❑ 91 Jozef Stumpel .60 .25
❑ 92 Jocelyn Thibault .60 .25
❑ 93 Joe Juneau .60 .25
❑ 94 Craig Janney .60 .25
❑ 95 Robert Reichel .60 .25
❑ 96 Mark Recchi .60 .25
❑ 97 Sami Kapanen .60 .25
❑ 98 Shayne Corson .25 .11
❑ 99 Scott Niedermayer .25 .11
❑ 100 Trevor Linden .60 .25
❑ 101 Olli Jokinen SP 2.50 1.10
❑ 102 Chris Drury SP 5.00 2.20
❑ 103 Dan Cleary SP 2.50 1.10
❑ 104 Yan Golubovsky SP 2.50 1.10
❑ 105 Brendan Morrison SP 2.50 1.10
❑ 106 Manny Malhotra SP 2.50 1.10
❑ 107 Marian Hossa SP 2.50 1.10
❑ 108 Daniel Briere SP 2.50 1.10
❑ 109 Vincent Lecavalier SP 12.00 5.50
❑ 110 Milan Hejduk SP 5.00 2.20
❑ 111 Tom Poti SP 2.50 1.10
❑ 112 Mike Maneluk SP 5.00 2.20
❑ 113 Marty Reasoner SP 2.50 1.10
❑ 114 Rico Fata SP 2.50 1.10
❑ 115 Eric Brewer SP 2.50 1.10
❑ 116 Dan Cloutier SP 2.50 1.10
❑ 117 Mike Leclerc SP 2.50 1.10
❑ 118 Dimitri Tertyshny SP 2.50 1.10
❑ 119 Josh Green SP 2.50 1.10
❑ 120 Mark Parrish SP 5.00 2.20
❑ 121 Jamie Wright SP 2.50 1.10
❑ 122 Fred Lindquist SP 2.50 1.10
❑ 123 Daniil Markov SP 2.50 1.10
❑ 124 Bill Muckalt SP 4.00 1.80
❑ 125 Johan Davidsson SP 2.50 1.10
❑ 126 Oleg Kvasha SP 4.00 1.80
❑ 127 Cameron Mann SP 2.50 1.10
❑ 128 Pascal Trepanier SP 2.50 1.10
❑ 129 Clarke Wilm SP 2.50 1.10
❑ 130 Alain Nasreddine SP 2.50 1.10
❑ 131 Bryan Helmer SP 2.50 1.10
❑ 132 Michal Handzus SP 4.00 1.80
❑ 133 Pavel Kubina SP 4.00 1.80
❑ 134 Zdeno Chara SP 2.50 1.10
❑ 135 Matt Higgins SP 2.50 1.10
❑ 136 David Legwand SP 8.00 3.60
❑ 137 Brad Stuart SP 2.50 1.10
❑ 138 Mark Bell SP 8.00 3.60
❑ 139 Eric Chouinard SP 2.50 1.10
❑ 140 Simon Gagne SP 3.00 1.35
❑ 141 Ramzi Abid SP 8.00 3.60
❑ 142 Sergei Varlamov SP 6.00 2.70
❑ 143 Mike Ribiero SP 2.50 1.10
❑ 144 Derrick Walser SP 2.50 1.10
❑ 145 Mathieu Garon SP 2.50 1.10
❑ 146 Daniel Tkaczuk SP 2.50 1.10
❑ 147 Jeff Hereema SP 5.00 2.20
❑ 148 Sebastien Roger SP 2.50 1.10
❑ 149 Bret DeCecco SP 2.50 1.10
❑ 150 Checklist SP 2.50 1.10

## 1998-99 Bowman's Best Refractors

Randomly inserted in packs at the rate of one in 52, this 150-card set is a refractive parallel version of the base set. Only 400 of each card were produced and sequentially numbered.

| | MINT | NRMT |
|---|---|---|
| COMPLETE SET (150) | 2000.00 | 900.00 |
| COMMON CARD (1-150) | 5.00 | 2.20 |

*STARS: 10X TO 20X BASIC CARDS
*YNG.STARS: 7.5X TO 15X
*RC's: 5X TO 10X

## 1998-99 Bowman's Best Atomic Refractors

Randomly inserted into packs at the rate of one in 52, this 150-card set is a parallel version of the base set and is similar in design. The difference is seen in the special sparkling refractive sheen of the cards. Only 100 of each card was produced and sequentially numbered.

| | MINT | NRMT |
|---|---|---|
| COMMON CARD (1-150) | 20.00 | 9.00 |

*STARS: 40X TO 80X BASIC CARDS
*YNG.STARS: 25X TO 50X
*RC's: 10X TO 20X

## 1998-99 Bowman's Best Autographs

Randomly inserted in packs at the rate of one in 97, this 20-card set displays autographed color photos of five rookie and five veteran players each featured in two different photos. Both versions of the rookies carry silver backgrounds, with gold backgrounds for the veterans. Each card is stamped with the Topps "Certified Autograph Issue" logo.

| | MINT | NRMT |
|---|---|---|
| COMPLETE SET (20) | 800.00 | 350.00 |
| COMMON CARD (A1A-A10B) | 25.00 | 11.00 |

❑ A1A Dominik Hasek 60.00 27.00
❑ A1B Dominik Hasek 60.00 27.00
❑ A2A Jaromir Jagr 100.00 45.00
❑ A2B Jaromir Jagr 100.00 45.00
❑ A3A Peter Bondra 40.00 18.00
❑ A3B Peter Bondra 40.00 18.00
❑ A4A Sergei Fedorov 60.00 27.00
❑ A4B Sergei Fedorov 60.00 27.00
❑ A5A Ray Bourque 40.00 18.00
❑ A5B Ray Bourque 40.00 18.00
❑ A6A Bill Muckalt 20.00 9.00
❑ A6B Bill Muckalt 20.00 9.00
❑ A7A Brendan Morrison 25.00 11.00
❑ A7B Brendan Morrison 25.00 11.00
❑ A8A Chris Drury 25.00 11.00
❑ A8B Chris Drury 25.00 11.00
❑ A9A Mark Parrish 25.00 11.00
❑ A9B Mark Parrish 25.00 11.00
❑ A10A Manny Malhotra 30.00 13.50
❑ A10B Manny Malhotra 30.00 13.50

## 1998-99 Bowman's Best Autographs Refractors

Randomly inserted into packs with the rate of one in 516, this 20-card set is a refractive parallel version of the regular autographs insert set.

| | MINT | NRMT |
|---|---|---|
| COMPLETE SET (20) | 2500.00 | 1100.00 |
| COMMON CARD (A1A-A10B) | 80.00 | 36.00 |

*STARS: 1.5X TO 3X BASIC CARDS

## 1998-99 Bowman's Best Autographs Atomic Refractors

Randomly inserted into packs at the rate of one in 1,549, this 20-card set is parallel to the regular autographs insert set and is similar in design. The difference is seen in the special sparkling refractive sheen of the cards.

| | MINT | NRMT |
|---|---|---|
| COMPLETE SET (20) | 4000.00 | 1800.00 |
| COMMON CARD (A1A-A10B) | 120.00 | 55.00 |

*STARS: 2.5X TO 5X BASIC CARDS

## 1998-99 Bowman's Best Mirror Image Fusion

Randomly inserted in packs at the rate of one in 12, this 20-card set features color action photos of Western and Eastern Conference players printed on die-cut, double-sided cards. Each card features a veteran on one side and a rising star on the other and can be married to its die-cut counterpart from the opposite conference.

| | MINT | NRMT |
|---|---|---|
| COMPLETE SET (20) | 200.00 | 90.00 |
| COMMON CARD (F1-F20) | 3.00 | 1.35 |

❑ F1 J.LeClair/B.Battaglia 8.00 3.60
❑ F2 P.Kariya/M.LeClerc 20.00 9.00
❑ F3 J.Jagr/M.Parrish 20.00 9.00
❑ F4 T.Selanne/F.Lindquist 10.00 4.50
❑ F5 E.Lindros/V.LeCavalier 25.00 11.00
❑ F6 P.Forsberg/O.Jokinen 15.00 6.75
❑ F7 B.Leetch/D.Markov 5.00 2.20
❑ F8 N.Lidstrom/Y.Golubovsky 3.00 1.35
❑ F9 D.Hasek/D.Cloutier 10.00 4.50
❑ F10 P.Roy/T.Moss 25.00 11.00
❑ F11 S.Samsonov/M.Watt 8.00 3.60
❑ F12 K.Tkachuk/J.Wright 6.00 2.70
❑ F13 P.Bondra/M.Hossa 6.00 2.70
❑ F14 P.Bure/B.Muckalt 12.00 5.50
❑ F15 W.Gretzky/B.Morrison 30.00 13.50
❑ F16 S.Fedorov/M.Reasoner 10.00 4.50
❑ F17 R.Bourque/E.Brewer 5.00 2.20
❑ F18 C.Pronger/T.Poti 3.00 1.35
❑ F19 M.Brodeur/J.Theodore 12.00 5.50
❑ F20 C.Osgood/J.Storr 5.00 2.20

## 1998-99 Bowman's Best Mirror Image Fusion Refractors

Randomly inserted into packs at the rate of one in 387, this 20-card set is a refractive parallel version of the regular insert set. Each card is sequentially numbered to 100.

| | MINT | NRMT |
|---|---|---|
| COMPLETE SET (20) | 2000.00 | 900.00 |
| COMMON CARD (F1-F20) | 30.00 | 13.50 |

*STARS: 5X TO 10X BASIC CARDS

## 1998-99 Bowman's Best Mirror Image Fusion Atomic Refractors

Randomly inserted into packs at the rate of one in 1,549 packs, this 20-card set is a parallel version of the regular insert set and is similar in design. The difference is found in the special sparkling refractive sheen of the cards. Each card is sequentially numbered to 25.

| | MINT | NRMT |
|---|---|---|
| COMPLETE SET (20) | 5000.00 | 2200.00 |
| COMMON CARD (F1-F20) | 80.00 | 36.00 |

*STARS: 12.5X TO 25X BASIC CARDS

## 1998-99 Bowman's Best Performers

Randomly inserted in packs at the rate of one in 12, this 10-card set features action color photos of top young stars and rookies.

| | MINT | NRMT |
|---|---|---|
| COMPLETE SET (10) | 50.00 | 22.00 |
| COMMON CARD (BP1-BP10) | 3.00 | 1.35 |

❑ BP1 Mike Johnson 4.00 1.80
❑ BP2 Sergei Samsonov 8.00 3.60
❑ BP3 Patrik Elias 4.00 1.80
❑ BP4 Patrick Marleau 6.00 2.70

| | | |
|---|---|---|
| ❑ BP5 Mattias Ohlund | 4.00 | 1.80 |
| ❑ BP6 Manny Malhotra | 3.00 | 1.35 |
| ❑ BP7 Chris Drury | 6.00 | 2.70 |
| ❑ BP8 Daniel Briere | 3.00 | 1.35 |
| ❑ BP9 Brendan Morrison | 5.00 | 2.20 |
| ❑ BP10 Vincent Lecavalier | 10.00 | 4.50 |

## 1998-99 Bowman's Best Performers Refractors

Randomly inserted into packs at the rate of one in 387, this 10-card set is a refractive parallel version of the regular insert set. Only 200 of each card was produced and sequentially numbered.

| | MINT | NRMT |
|---|---|---|
| COMPLETE SET (10) | 500.00 | 220.00 |
| COMMON CARD (BP1-BP10) | 30.00 | 13.50 |
| *STARS: 5X TO 10X BASIC CARDS | | |

## 1998-99 Bowman's Best Performers Atomic Refractors

Randomly inserted in packs at the rate of one in 1,549, this 10-card set is parallel to the regular insert set and is similar in design. The difference is seen in the special sparkling refractive sheen of the cards. Only 50 of each card was produced and sequentially numbered.

| | MINT | NRMT |
|---|---|---|
| COMPLETE SET (10) | 1200.00 | 550.00 |
| COMMON CARD (BP1-BP10) | 80.00 | 36.00 |
| *STARS: 12.5X TO 25X BASIC CARDS | | |

## 1998-99 Bowman's Best Scotty Bowman's Best

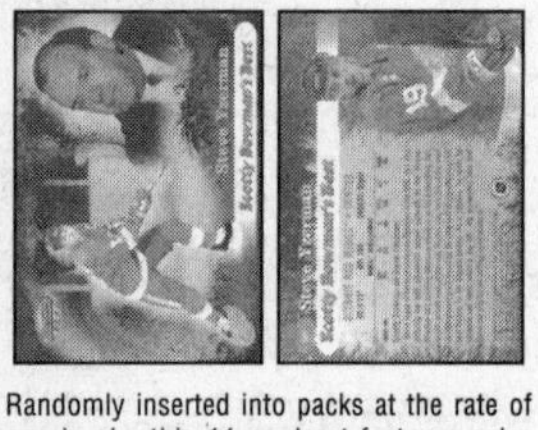

Randomly inserted into packs at the rate of one in six, this 11-card set features color photos of ten of the best present day players in the NHL according to Scotty Bowman who is one of the greates coaches of all time. Card #11 is a card of the coach himself and 100 of these cards were autographed with an insertion rate of 1:7,745.

| | MINT | NRMT |
|---|---|---|
| COMPLETE SET (11) | 100.00 | 45.00 |
| COMMON CARD (SB1-SB11) | 3.00 | 1.35 |
| ❑ SB1 Dominik Hasek | 8.00 | 3.60 |
| ❑ SB2 Martin Brodeur | 10.00 | 4.50 |
| ❑ SB3 Chris Osgood | 4.00 | 1.80 |
| ❑ SB4 Nicklas Lidstrom | 3.00 | 1.35 |
| ❑ SB5 Eric Lindros | 12.00 | 5.50 |
| ❑ SB6 Jaromir Jagr | 12.00 | 5.50 |
| ❑ SB7 Steve Yzerman | 12.00 | 5.50 |
| ❑ SB8 Peter Forsberg | 12.00 | 5.50 |
| ❑ SB9 Paul Kariya | 15.00 | 6.75 |
| ❑ SB10 Ray Bourque | 4.00 | 1.80 |
| ❑ SB11 Scotty Bowman | 4.00 | 1.80 |
| ❑ SB11S Scotty Bowman AU | 150.00 | 70.00 |

## 1998-99 Bowman's Best Scotty Bowman's Best Refractors

Randomly inserted into packs at the rate of one in 352, this set is a refractive parallel version of the regular insert set.

| | MINT | NRMT |
|---|---|---|
| COMPLETE SET (11) | 1000.00 | 450.00 |
| COMMON CARD (SB1-SB11) | 30.00 | 13.50 |
| *STARS: 5X TO 10X BASIC CARDS | | |

## 1998-99 Bowman's Best Scotty Bowman's Best Atomic Refractors

Randomly inserted into packs at the rate of one in 1,408, this set is a parallel version of the regular insert set and is similar in design. The difference is seen in the special sparkling refractive sheen of the cards. The cards are sequentially numbered to 50.

| | MINT | NRMT |
|---|---|---|
| COMPLETE SET (11) | 2000.00 | 900.00 |
| COMMON CARD (SB1-SB11) | 60.00 | 27.00 |
| *STARS: 10X TO 20X BASIC CARDS | | |

## 1938-39 Bruins Garden Magazine Supplement

These large (8 X 10") photos were printed on very thin, sepia-toned stock and inserted in game programs issued at the Boston Gardens. They feature a posed player photo on the front with a simulated autograph. The border which surrounds the photo is broken up at the bottom by the words Supplement to Boston Garden Hockey Magazine. The backs are blank and unnumbered, leading to the alphabetical listing below. The listing below is believed to be incomplete. Any additional information would be appreciated.

| | EX-MT | VG-E |
|---|---|---|
| COMPLETE SET (9) | 650.00 | 300.00 |
| COMMON CARD (1-9) | 35.00 | 15.75 |
| ❑ 1 Red Beattie | 35.00 | 16.00 |
| ❑ 2 Walter Galbraith | 35.00 | 16.00 |
| ❑ 3 Lionel Hitchman | 80.00 | 36.00 |
| ❑ 4 Joseph Lamb | 35.00 | 16.00 |
| ❑ 5 Harry Oliver | 35.00 | 16.00 |
| ❑ 6 Art Ross | 150.00 | 70.00 |
| ❑ 7 Eddie Shore | 250.00 | 110.00 |
| ❑ 8 Nels Stewart | 80.00 | 36.00 |
| ❑ 9 Tiny Thompson | 100.00 | 45.00 |

## 1955-56 Bruins Photos

These black and white photos measure approximately 6" x 8" and feature blank backs. Photos were distributed in an envelope bearing the Bruins logo. Photos are unnumbered and checklisted below alphabetically.

| | MINT | NRMT |
|---|---|---|
| COMPLETE SET (17) | 200.00 | 90.00 |
| COMMON CARD (1-17) | 8.00 | 3.60 |
| ❑ 1 Bob Armstrong | 10.00 | 4.50 |
| ❑ 2 Marcel Bonin | 15.00 | 6.75 |
| ❑ 3 Leo Boivin | 20.00 | 9.00 |
| ❑ 4 Real Chevrefils | 12.00 | 5.50 |
| ❑ 5 Fern Flaman | 15.00 | 6.75 |
| ❑ 6 Cal Gardner | 8.00 | 3.60 |
| ❑ 7 Lionel Heinrich | 8.00 | 3.60 |
| ❑ 8 Leo Labine | 15.00 | 6.75 |
| ❑ 9 Hal Laycoe | 10.00 | 4.50 |
| ❑ 10 Fleming Mackell | 10.00 | 4.50 |
| ❑ 11 Don McKenney | 10.00 | 4.50 |
| ❑ 12 Doug Mohns | 15.00 | 6.75 |
| ❑ 13 Bill Quackenbush | 15.00 | 6.75 |
| ❑ 14 Johnny Peirson | 8.00 | 3.60 |
| ❑ 15 Terry Sawchuk | 40.00 | 18.00 |
| ❑ 16 Vic Stasiuk | 8.00 | 3.60 |
| ❑ 17 Jerry Toppazzini | 8.00 | 3.60 |
| ❑ NNO Envelope | | |

## 1957 Bruins Team Issue

This 14-card set measures approximately 6 5/8" by 8 1/8". The fronts feature black-and-white posed player photos with white borders. The player's facsimile signature appears on the bottom. The backs are blank. The cards are unnumbered and checklisted below in alphabetical order.

| | NRMT | VG-E |
|---|---|---|
| COMPLETE SET (20) | 150.00 | 70.00 |
| COMMON CARD (1-20) | 5.00 | 2.20 |
| ❑ 1 Bob Armstrong | 5.00 | 2.20 |
| ❑ 2 Jack Bionda | 5.00 | 2.20 |
| ❑ 3 Leo Boivin | 10.00 | 4.50 |
| ❑ 4 Johnny Bucyk | 20.00 | 9.00 |
| ❑ 5 Real Chevrefils | 5.00 | 2.20 |
| ❑ 6 Fern Flaman | 10.00 | 4.50 |
| ❑ 7 Jean-Guy Gendron | 10.00 | 4.50 |
| ❑ 8 Larry Hillman | 10.00 | 4.50 |
| ❑ 9 Bronco Horvath | 12.00 | 5.50 |
| ❑ 10 Norm Johnson | 12.00 | 5.50 |
| ❑ 11 Leo Labine | 8.00 | 3.60 |
| ❑ 12 Fleming Mackell | 5.00 | 2.20 |
| ❑ 13 Don McKenney | 8.00 | 3.60 |
| ❑ 14 Doug Mohns | 8.00 | 3.60 |
| ❑ 15 Jim Morrison | 8.00 | 3.60 |
| ❑ 16 Johnny Peirson | 10.00 | 4.50 |
| ❑ 17 Larry Regan | 5.00 | 2.20 |
| ❑ 18 Milt Schmidt | 20.00 | 9.00 |
| ❑ 19 Vic Stasiuk | 8.00 | 3.60 |
| ❑ 20 Jerry Toppazzini | 8.00 | 3.60 |

## 1970-71 Bruins Postcards

Cards are standard postcard size and were issued in a binder with perforations. Card fronts are borderless and card backs feature stats and biographical information. Cards are listed below as they appear in the binder.

| | MINT | NRMT |
|---|---|---|
| COMPLETE SET (21) | 125.00 | 55.00 |
| COMMON CARD (1-21) | 5.00 | 2.20 |
| ❑ 1 Team Photo | 5.00 | 2.20 |
| ❑ 2 Ed Johnston | 10.00 | 4.50 |
| ❑ 3 Gerry Cheevers | 15.00 | 6.75 |
| ❑ 4 Wayne Cashman | 8.00 | 3.60 |
| ❑ 5 Ace Bailey | 5.00 | 2.20 |
| ❑ 6 Don Marcotte | 5.00 | 2.20 |
| ❑ 7 John Bucyk | 10.00 | 4.50 |
| ❑ 8 Wayne Carleton | 5.00 | 2.20 |
| ❑ 9 Reggie Leach | 8.00 | 3.60 |
| ❑ 10 Ken Hodge | 10.00 | 4.50 |
| ❑ 11 Ed Westfall | 5.00 | 2.20 |
| ❑ 12 John McKenzie | 8.00 | 3.60 |
| ❑ 13 Phil Esposito | 15.00 | 6.75 |
| ❑ 14 Fred Stanfield | 5.00 | 2.20 |
| ❑ 15 Derek Sanderson | 15.00 | 6.75 |
| ❑ 16 Bobby Orr | 40.00 | 18.00 |
| ❑ 17 Dallas Smith | 5.00 | 2.20 |
| ❑ 18 Rick Smith | 5.00 | 2.20 |
| ❑ 19 Ted Green | 5.00 | 2.20 |
| ❑ 20 Don Awrey | 5.00 | 2.20 |
| ❑ 21 Tom Johnson CO | 5.00 | 2.20 |

## 1970-71 Bruins Team Issue

This set of 18 team-issue photos commemorates the Boston Bruins as 1970 Stanley Cup Champions. The set was issued in two different photo packs of nine photos each. The photos measure approximately 6" by 8" and feature a non-glossy posed head-and-shoulders shot of the player. The backs are blank. These unnumbered photos are listed below alphabetically by player's name within pack, i.e., 1-9 are from the first pack and 10-18 are found in the second pack.

| | NRMT-MT | EXC |
|---|---|---|
| COMPLETE SET (18) | 90.00 | 40.00 |
| COMMON CARD (1-9) | 3.00 | 1.35 |
| COMMON CARD (10-18) | 3.00 | 1.35 |
| ❑ 1 Garnet Bailey | 3.00 | 1.35 |
| ❑ 2 Johnny Bucyk | 8.00 | 3.60 |
| ❑ 3 Gary Doak | 4.00 | 1.80 |
| ❑ 4 Phil Esposito | 15.00 | 6.75 |
| ❑ 5 Ed Johnston | 4.00 | 1.80 |
| ❑ 6 Don Marcotte | 3.00 | 1.35 |
| ❑ 7 Derek Sanderson | 8.00 | 3.60 |
| ❑ 8 Dallas Smith | 4.00 | 1.80 |
| ❑ 9 Ed Westfall | 4.00 | 1.80 |
| ❑ 10 Don Awrey | 3.00 | 1.35 |
| ❑ 11 Wayne Carleton | 3.00 | 1.35 |
| ❑ 12 Wayne Cashman | 4.00 | 1.80 |
| ❑ 13 Gerry Cheevers | 8.00 | 3.60 |
| ❑ 14 Ken Hodge | 4.00 | 1.80 |
| ❑ 15 John McKenzie | 4.00 | 1.80 |
| ❑ 16 Bobby Orr | 40.00 | 18.00 |
| ❑ 17 Rick Smith | 3.00 | 1.35 |
| ❑ 18 Fred Stanfield | 3.00 | 1.35 |

## 1971-72 Bruins Team Issue

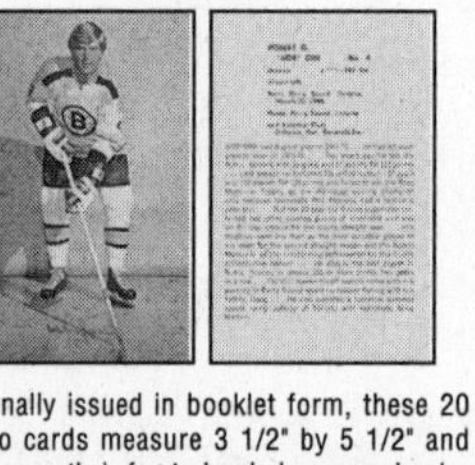

Originally issued in booklet form, these 20 photo cards measure 3 1/2" by 5 1/2" and feature on their fronts borderless posed color shots of the 1971-72 Boston Bruins. The player's facsimile autograph appears near the bottom. The white back carries the player's name and uniform number at the top, followed by position, biography, and personal profile, all in blue lettering. The cards have perforated tops that allow them to be detached from the yellow booklet, which bears the Bruins logo and crossed hockey sticks on its front. The unnumbered cards are listed below as they are organized within the booklet.

| | NRMT-MT | EXC |
|---|---|---|
| COMPLETE SET (20) | 80.00 | 36.00 |
| COMMON CARD (1-20) | 2.00 | .90 |
| ❑ 1 Ed Johnston | 4.00 | 1.80 |
| ❑ 2 Bobby Orr | 40.00 | 18.00 |
| ❑ 3 Teddy Green | 3.00 | 1.35 |
| ❑ 4 Phil Esposito | 20.00 | 9.00 |
| ❑ 5 Ken Hodge | 4.00 | 1.80 |
| ❑ 6 John Bucyk | 6.00 | 2.70 |
| ❑ 7 Rick Smith | 2.00 | .90 |
| ❑ 8 Mike Walton | 3.00 | 1.35 |
| ❑ 9 Wayne Cashman | 4.00 | 1.80 |
| ❑ 10 Ace Bailey | 3.00 | 1.35 |
| ❑ 11 Derek Sanderson | 10.00 | 4.50 |
| ❑ 12 Fred Stanfield | 2.00 | .90 |
| ❑ 13 Ed Westfall | 3.00 | 1.35 |
| ❑ 14 John McKenzie | 3.00 | 1.35 |
| ❑ 15 Dallas Smith | 2.00 | .90 |
| ❑ 16 Don Marcotte | 2.00 | .90 |
| ❑ 17 Garry Peters | 2.00 | .90 |
| ❑ 18 Don Awrey | 2.00 | .90 |
| ❑ 19 Reggie Leach | 4.00 | 1.80 |
| ❑ 20 Gerry Cheevers | 10.00 | 4.50 |

## 1983-84 Bruins Team Issue

This 17-card set measures approximately 3 1/8" by 4 1/8" and features black and white action player photos with white borders. The pictures have irregular centering so that the bottom border is thicker than the top border. The player's name appears in the bottom border. The backs are blank. The cards are unnumbered and checklisted below alphabetically. The Luc Dufour card appears in his RC year.

| | MINT | NRMT |
|---|---|---|
| COMPLETE SET (17) | 25.00 | 11.00 |
| COMMON CARD (1-17) | 1.00 | .45 |
| ❑ 1 Ray Bourque | 7.50 | 3.40 |
| ❑ 2 Bruce Crowder | 1.00 | .45 |
| ❑ 3 Keith Crowder | 1.50 | .70 |
| ❑ 4 Luc Dufour | 1.00 | .45 |
| ❑ 5 Tom Fergus | 1.00 | .45 |
| ❑ 6 Randy Hillier | 1.00 | .45 |
| ❑ 7 Steve Kasper | 1.50 | .70 |
| ❑ 8 Gord Kluzak | 1.50 | .70 |
| ❑ 9 Mike Krushelnyski | 1.00 | .45 |
| ❑ 10 Peter McNab | 1.50 | .70 |
| ❑ 11 Rick Middleton | 3.00 | 1.35 |
| ❑ 12 Mike Milbury | 1.50 | .70 |
| ❑ 13 Mike O'Connell | 1.50 | .70 |
| ❑ 14 Terry O'Reilly | 2.00 | .90 |
| ❑ 15 Brad Palmer | 1.00 | .45 |
| ❑ 16 Barry Pederson | 1.50 | .70 |
| ❑ 17 Pete Peeters | 2.00 | .90 |

## 1988-89 Bruins Sports Action

This 24-card set measures the standard size. This set was issued by Sports Action and features members of the 1988-89 Boston Bruins. The fronts of these cards have the action photo of the player framed by the colors of the Bruins while the backs of the cards contain biographical information. The cards are unnumbered so we have checklisted them below in alphabetical order. The set features an early card of Craig Janney pre-dating his Rookie Cards by one year.

| | MINT | NRMT |
|---|---|---|
| COMPLETE SET (24) | 15.00 | 6.75 |
| COMMON CARD (1-24) | .25 | .11 |
| ❑ 1 Ray Bourque | 2.50 | 1.10 |
| ❑ 2 Randy Burridge | .35 | .16 |
| ❑ 3 Lyndon Byers | .35 | .16 |
| ❑ 4 Keith Crowder | .25 | .11 |
| ❑ 5 Craig Janney | 1.00 | .45 |
| ❑ 6 Bob Joyce | .25 | .11 |
| ❑ 7 Steve Kasper | .50 | .23 |
| ❑ 8 Gord Kluzak | .50 | .23 |
| ❑ 9 Reed Larson | .25 | .11 |
| ❑ 10 Rejean Lemelin | .75 | .35 |
| ❑ 11 Ken Linseman | .50 | .23 |
| ❑ 12 Tom McCarthy | .25 | .11 |
| ❑ 13 Rick Middleton | 1.00 | .45 |
| ❑ 14 Jay Miller | .50 | .23 |
| ❑ 15 Andy Moog | 1.50 | .70 |
| ❑ 16 Cam Neely | 2.50 | 1.10 |
| ❑ 17 Terry O'Reilly CO | .50 | .23 |
| ❑ 18 Allen Pederson | .25 | .11 |
| ❑ 19 Willi Plett | .25 | .11 |
| ❑ 20 Bob Sweeney | .25 | .11 |
| ❑ 21 Michael Thelven | .25 | .11 |
| ❑ 22 Glen Wesley | .75 | .35 |
| ❑ 23 Bob Joyce / Craig Janney | .75 | .35 |
| ❑ 24 Dynamic Duo / Ray Bourque / Cam Neely | 2.00 | .90 |

## 1988-89 Bruins Postcards

This 20-postcard set of the Boston Bruins was produced by Sports Action Marketing anddistributed by the club for promotional purposes. Players were given copies of their own cards to mail out to autograph seekers, and complete sets were sold in the club's gift shop. The fronts feature full-bleed action photography, but no other distinguishing marks. The backs are laid out in typical postcard format, with the subject identified in the upper left corner, and a place for the stamp in the upper right. As the cards are unnumbered, they are listed below in alphabetical order.

| | MINT | NRMT |
|---|---|---|
| COMPLETE SET (20) | 20.00 | 9.00 |
| COMMON CARD (1-20) | .50 | .23 |
| ❑ 1 Ray Bourque | 4.00 | 1.80 |
| ❑ 2 Andy Brickley | .50 | .23 |
| ❑ 3 John Carter | .50 | .23 |
| ❑ 4 Garry Galley | .75 | .35 |
| ❑ 5 Craig Janney | 1.50 | .70 |
| ❑ 6 Greg Johnston | .50 | .23 |
| ❑ 7 Bob Joyce | .50 | .23 |
| ❑ 8 Steve Kasper | .75 | .35 |
| ❑ 9 Gord Kluzak | .75 | .35 |
| ❑ 10 Rejean Lemelin | 1.00 | .45 |
| ❑ 11 Ken Linseman | .75 | .35 |
| ❑ 12 Rick Middleton | 1.50 | .70 |
| ❑ 13 Andy Moog | 2.50 | 1.10 |
| ❑ 14 Cam Neely | 4.00 | 1.80 |
| ❑ 15 Bill O'Dwyer | .50 | .23 |
| ❑ 16 Allen Pedersen | .50 | .23 |
| ❑ 17 Stephane Quintal | .50 | .23 |
| ❑ 18 Bob Sweeney | .50 | .23 |
| ❑ 19 Michael Thelven | .50 | .23 |
| ❑ 20 Glen Wesley | 1.00 | .45 |

## 1989-90 Bruins Sports Action

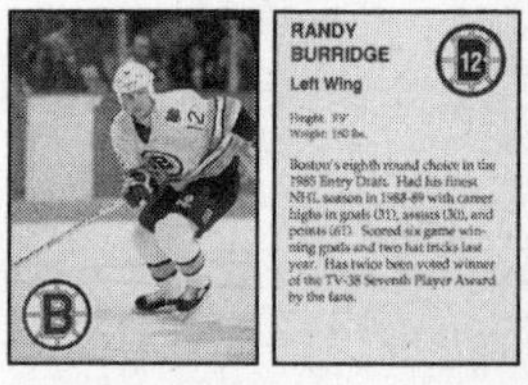


This standard sized 24-card set was issued by Sports Action and features members of the 1989-90 Boston Bruins. The fronts of the cards feature full-color borderless action shots of the Bruins while the backs of the cards have biographical information about the player. Since there is no numerical designation for these players, we have checklisted this set below in alphabetical order.

| | MINT | NRMT |
|---|---|---|
| COMPLETE SET (24) | 12.00 | 5.50 |
| COMMON CARD (1-24) | .50 | .23 |
| ❑ 1 Ray Bourque | 2.00 | .90 |
| ❑ 2 Andy Brickley | .50 | .23 |
| ❑ 3 Randy Burridge | .50 | .23 |
| ❑ 4 Lyndon Byers | .50 | .23 |
| ❑ 5 Bob Carpenter | .50 | .23 |
| ❑ 6 John Carter | .50 | .23 |
| ❑ 7 Rob Cimetta | .50 | .23 |
| ❑ 8 Garry Galley | .75 | .35 |
| ❑ 9 Bob Gould | .50 | .23 |
| ❑ 10 Greg Hawgood | .50 | .23 |
| ❑ 11 Craig Janney | .75 | .35 |
| ❑ 12 Bob Joyce | .50 | .23 |
| ❑ 13 Rejean Lemelin | .75 | .35 |
| ❑ 14 Ken Linseman | .50 | .23 |
| ❑ 15 Andy Moog | 1.00 | .45 |
| ❑ 16 Nevin Markwart | .50 | .23 |
| ❑ 17 Cam Neely | 1.50 | .70 |
| ❑ 18 Allen Pedersen | .50 | .23 |
| ❑ 19 Stephane Quintal | .50 | .23 |
| ❑ 20 Bob Sweeney | .50 | .23 |
| ❑ 21 Michael Thelven | .50 | .23 |
| ❑ 22 Glen Wesley | .75 | .35 |
| ❑ 23 Bruins Top 10 Scorers | 1.00 | .45 |
| ❑ 24 Stanley Cup Champions | 1.00 | .45 |

## 1989-90 Bruins Sports Action Update

This 12-card standard-size set was issued by Sports Action to reflect the changes made by

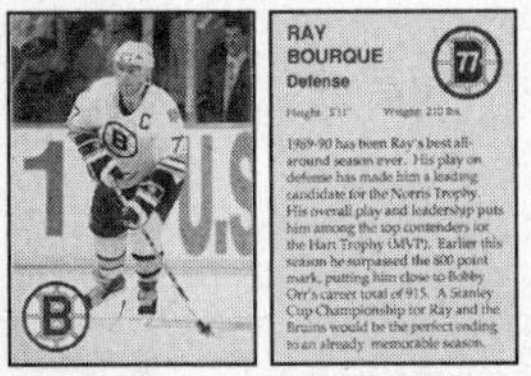


the Boston Bruins during the 1989-90 hockey season. The borderless fronts feature full-color action shots while the backs feature biographical information. Since the cards are unnumbered, they are checklisted in alphabetical order.

| | MINT | NRMT |
|---|---|---|
| COMPLETE SET (12) | 8.00 | 3.60 |
| COMMON CARD (1-12) | .50 | .23 |
| ❑ 1 Ray Bourque | 2.00 | .90 |
| ❑ 2 Dave Christian | .75 | .35 |
| ❑ 3 Peter Douris | .50 | .23 |
| ❑ 4 Gord Kluzak | .75 | .35 |
| ❑ 5 Brian Lawton | .50 | .23 |
| ❑ 6 Mike Millar | .50 | .23 |
| ❑ 7 Dave Poulin | .75 | .35 |
| ❑ 8 Brian Propp | .75 | .35 |
| ❑ 9 Don Sweeney | .75 | .35 |
| ❑ 10 Graeme Townshend | .50 | .23 |
| ❑ 11 Jim Wiemer | .50 | .23 |
| ❑ 12 Bruins Leaders<br>Ray Bourque<br>Rejean Lemelin<br>Cam Neely | 2.00 | .90 |

## 1990-91 Bruins Sports Action

This 26-card standard size set features members of the 1990-91 Boston Bruins. This set features full-color borderless action shots of the Bruins. The back is in a horizontal format with biographical information about the player on the left side of the card and a black-and-white photo on the right. The Markwart and Quintal cards were reportedly only issued in the first print run of 400 24-card sets. In the second and larger print run, these cards were replaced by Byers and Hodge. Consequently, the Markwart and Quintal cards are more difficult to find than the Byers and Hodge cards. We have checklisted this set in alphabetical order below, with the multi-player card listed at the end.

| | MINT | NRMT |
|---|---|---|
| COMPLETE SET (26) | 20.00 | 9.00 |
| COMMON CARD (1-26) | .50 | .23 |
| ❑ 1 Bob Beers | .50 | .23 |
| ❑ 2 Ray Bourque | 2.50 | 1.10 |
| ❑ 3 Andy Brickley | .50 | .23 |
| ❑ 4 Randy Burridge | .60 | .25 |
| ❑ 5 John Byce | .50 | .23 |
| ❑ 6 Lyndon Byers | .75 | .35 |
| ❑ 7 Bob Carpenter | .50 | .23 |
| ❑ 8 John Carter | .50 | .23 |
| ❑ 9 Dave Christian | .60 | .25 |
| ❑ 10 Peter Douris | .50 | .23 |
| ❑ 11 Garry Galley | .50 | .23 |
| ❑ 12 Ken Hodge Jr. | .50 | .23 |
| ❑ 13 Craig Janney | .75 | .35 |
| ❑ 14 Rejean Lemelin | .75 | .35 |
| ❑ 15 Nevin Markwart SP | 3.00 | 1.35 |
| ❑ 16 Andy Moog | 1.50 | .70 |
| ❑ 17 Cam Neely | 2.00 | .90 |
| ❑ 18 Chris Nilan | .60 | .25 |
| ❑ 19 Allen Pedersen | .50 | .23 |
| ❑ 20 Dave Poulin | .60 | .25 |
| ❑ 21 Stephane Quintal SP | 3.00 | 1.35 |
| ❑ 22 Bob Sweeney | .50 | .23 |
| ❑ 23 Don Sweeney | .60 | .25 |
| ❑ 24 Wes Walz | .50 | .23 |
| ❑ 25 Glen Wesley | .75 | .35 |
| ❑ 26 Rejean Lemelin<br>Andy Moog | 1.00 | .45 |

## 1991-92 Bruins Sports Action

This 24-card standard-size set was issued by Sports Action and features members of the 1991-92 Boston Bruins. The cards are printed on thin card stock. The fronts feature full-bleed glossy color action photos. In a horizontal format, the backs carry brief biography, career summary, and the team logo. The cards are unnumbered and checklisted below in alphabetical order.

| | MINT | NRMT |
|---|---|---|
| COMPLETE SET (24) | 14.00 | 6.25 |
| COMMON CARD (1-24) | .40 | .18 |
| ❑ 1 Brent Ashton | .40 | .18 |
| ❑ 2 Bob Beers | .40 | .18 |
| ❑ 3 Daniel Berthiaume | .60 | .25 |
| ❑ 4 Ray Bourque | 2.00 | .90 |
| ❑ 5 Bob Carpenter | .40 | .18 |
| ❑ 6 Peter Douris | .40 | .18 |
| ❑ 7 Glen Featherstone | .40 | .18 |
| ❑ 8 Ken Hodge Jr. | .40 | .18 |
| ❑ 9 Jeff Lazaro | .40 | .18 |
| ❑ 10 Stephen Leach | .40 | .18 |
| ❑ 11 Andy Moog | 1.25 | .55 |
| ❑ 12 Gord Murphy | .50 | .23 |
| ❑ 13 Cam Neely | 1.50 | .70 |
| ❑ 14 Adam Oates | 1.50 | .70 |
| ❑ 15 Dave Poulin | .50 | .23 |
| ❑ 16 David Reid | .60 | .25 |
| ❑ 17 Vladimir Ruzicka | .40 | .18 |
| ❑ 18 Bob Sweeney | .40 | .18 |
| ❑ 19 Don Sweeney | .60 | .25 |
| ❑ 20 Jim Vesey | .40 | .18 |
| ❑ 21 Glen Wesley | .60 | .25 |
| ❑ 22 Jim Wiemer | .40 | .18 |
| ❑ 23 Chris Winnes | .40 | .18 |
| ❑ 24 The Big Three<br>Andy Moog<br>Ray Bourque<br>Cam Neely | 1.50 | .70 |

## 1991-92 Bruins Sports Action Legends

The 1991-92 Bruins Legends hockey set features the outstanding players throughout the history of the Boston Bruins' franchise. The fronts of the standard-size cards feature full-bleed black and white player photos. The backs present the player's name, position, biography, honors received, and career statistics. The cards of players with retired numbers have their number inside the team logo in the upper right corner of the back. Though most of the cards feature one player, the set includes several multi-player cards with brief commentary on their backs. The cards are unnumbered and checklisted below in alphabetical order.

| | MINT | NRMT |
|---|---|---|
| COMPLETE SET (36) | 15.00 | 6.75 |
| COMMON CARD (1-36) | .25 | .11 |
| ❑ 1 Bob Armstrong | .25 | .11 |
| ❑ 2 Leo Boivin | .35 | .16 |
| ❑ 3 Ray Bourque | 1.50 | .70 |
| ❑ 4 Frank Brimsek | .75 | .35 |
| ❑ 5 Johnny Bucyk | 1.00 | .45 |
| ❑ 6 Wayne Cashman | .25 | .11 |
| ❑ 7 Gerry Cheevers | 1.00 | .45 |
| ❑ 8 Dit Clapper | .75 | .35 |
| ❑ 9 Bill Cowley | .25 | .11 |
| ❑ 10 Phil Esposito | 1.25 | .55 |
| ❑ 11 Fernie Flaman | .35 | .16 |
| ❑ 12 Mel Hill<br>Bill Cowley<br>Roy Conacher | .35 | .16 |
| ❑ 13 Lionel Hitchman | .35 | .16 |
| ❑ 14 Fleming Mackell | .25 | .11 |
| ❑ 15 Don Marcotte | .25 | .11 |
| ❑ 16 Don McKenney | .25 | .11 |
| ❑ 17 Rick Middleton | .50 | .23 |
| ❑ 18 Doug Mohns | .25 | .11 |
| ❑ 19 Terry O'Reilly | .35 | .16 |
| ❑ 20 Bobby Orr | 3.00 | 1.35 |
| ❑ 21 Brad Park | .75 | .35 |
| ❑ 22 John Peirson | .25 | .11 |
| ❑ 23 Bill Quackenbush | .50 | .23 |
| ❑ 24 Jean Ratelle | .75 | .35 |
| ❑ 25 Art Ross CO/GM | .50 | .23 |
| ❑ 26 Ed Sandford | .25 | .11 |
| ❑ 27 Terry Sawchuk | 1.50 | .70 |
| ❑ 28 Milt Schmidt | 1.00 | .45 |
| ❑ 29 Milt Schmidt<br>Cooney Weiland<br>Bill Cowley | .50 | .23 |
| ❑ 30 Eddie Shore | 1.00 | .45 |
| ❑ 31 Harry Sinden CO/GM<br>and President | .50 | .23 |
| ❑ 32 Tiny Thompson | .35 | .16 |
| ❑ 33 Cooney Weiland | .35 | .16 |
| ❑ 34 Ed Westfall | .25 | .11 |
| ❑ 35 Bruins Defense<br>1955-56<br>Bill Quackenbush<br>Fern Flaman<br>Terry Sawchuk<br>Bob Armstrong<br>Leo Boivin | .50 | .23 |
| ❑ 36 The Kraut Line<br>Milt Schmidt<br>Woody Dumart<br>Bobby Bauer | .75 | .35 |

## 1992-93 Bruins Postcards

This set measures approximately 3 1/2" by 5 1/2" and are in the postcard format. The horizontal and vertical fronts feature full-bleed color action player photos. The white backs carry the player's name, team name, and jersey number. The cards are unnumbered and checklisted below in alphabetical order.

| | MINT | NRMT |
|---|---|---|
| COMPLETE SET (12) | 10.00 | 4.50 |
| COMMON CARD (1-12) | .50 | .23 |
| ❑ 1 Ray Bourque | 3.00 | 1.35 |
| ❑ 2 Ted Donato | .50 | .23 |
| ❑ 3 Joe Juneau | .75 | .35 |
| ❑ 4 Dimitri Kvartalnov | .50 | .23 |
| ❑ 5 Stephen Leach | .50 | .23 |
| ❑ 6 Andy Moog | 2.00 | .90 |
| ❑ 7 Adam Oates | 2.00 | .90 |
| ❑ 8 Dave Poulin | .75 | .35 |
| ❑ 9 Gordie Roberts | .50 | .23 |
| ❑ 10 Vladimir Ruzicka | .50 | .23 |
| ❑ 11 Don Sweeney | .75 | .35 |
| ❑ 12 Glen Wesley | .75 | .35 |

## 1911-12 C55

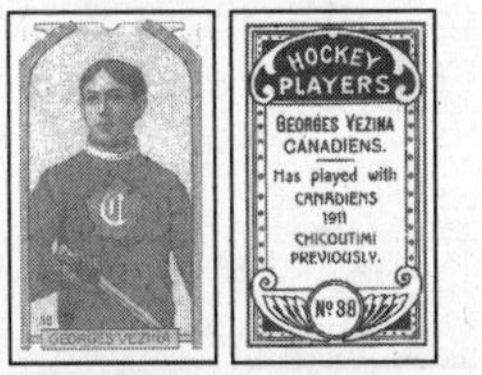


The C55 Hockey set, probably issued during the 1911-12 season, contains 45 numbered cards. Being one of the early Canadian cigarette cards, the issuer of this set is unknown, although there is speculation that it may have been Imperial Tobacco. These small cards measure approximately 1 1/2" by 2 1/2". The line drawing, color portrait on the front of the card is framed by two hockey sticks. The number of the card appears on both the front and back as does the player's name. The players in the set were members of the NHA: Quebec Bulldogs, Ottawa Senators, Montreal Canadiens, Montreal Wanderers, and Renfrew Millionaires. This set is prized highly by collectors but is the easiest of the three early sets (C55, C56, or C57) to find. The complete set price includes either variety of the Smaill variation.

| | EX-MT | VG-E |
|---|---|---|
| COMPLETE SET (45) | 13500.00 | 6800.00 |
| COMMON CARD (1-45) | 125.00 | 60.00 |
| ❑ 1 Paddy Moran | 400.00 | 200.00 |
| ❑ 2 Joe Hall | 250.00 | 125.00 |
| ❑ 3 Barney Holden | 125.00 | 60.00 |
| ❑ 4 Joe Malone | 800.00 | 400.00 |
| ❑ 5 Ed Oatman | 125.00 | 60.00 |
| ❑ 6 Tom Dunderdale | 250.00 | 125.00 |
| ❑ 7 Ken Mallen | 125.00 | 60.00 |
| ❑ 8 Jack MacDonald | 125.00 | 60.00 |
| ❑ 9 Fred Lake | 125.00 | 60.00 |
| ❑ 10 Albert Kerr | 125.00 | 60.00 |
| ❑ 11 Marty Walsh | 250.00 | 125.00 |
| ❑ 12 Hamby Shore | 125.00 | 60.00 |
| ❑ 13 Alex Currie | 125.00 | 60.00 |
| ❑ 14 Bruce Ridpath | 125.00 | 60.00 |
| ❑ 15 Bruce Stuart | 250.00 | 125.00 |
| ❑ 16 Percy Lesueur | 250.00 | 125.00 |
| ❑ 17 Jack Darragh | 250.00 | 125.00 |
| ❑ 18 Steve Vair | 125.00 | 60.00 |
| ❑ 19 Don Smith | 125.00 | 60.00 |
| ❑ 20 Cyclone Taylor | 1200.00 | 600.00 |
| ❑ 21 Bert Lindsay | 200.00 | 100.00 |
| ❑ 22 H.L.(Larry) Gilmour | 250.00 | 125.00 |
| ❑ 23 Bobby Rowe | 125.00 | 60.00 |
| ❑ 24 Sprague Cleghorn | 400.00 | 200.00 |
| ❑ 25 Odie Cleghorn | 200.00 | 100.00 |
| ❑ 26 Skein Ronan | 125.00 | 60.00 |
| ❑ 27A Walter Smaill<br>(Right hand on top<br>of hockey stick) | 400.00 | 200.00 |
| ❑ 27B Walter Smaill<br>(Right hand on hip) | 500.00 | 250.00 |
| ❑ 28 Ernest(Moose) Johnson | 300.00 | 150.00 |
| ❑ 29 Jack Marshall | 250.00 | 125.00 |
| ❑ 30 Harry Hyland | 200.00 | 100.00 |
| ❑ 31 Art Ross | 1200.00 | 600.00 |
| ❑ 32 Riley Hern | 250.00 | 125.00 |
| ❑ 33 Gordon Roberts | 200.00 | 100.00 |
| ❑ 34 Frank Glass | 125.00 | 60.00 |
| ❑ 35 Ernest Russell | 250.00 | 125.00 |
| ❑ 36 James Gardner | 250.00 | 125.00 |
| ❑ 37 Art Bernier | 125.00 | 60.00 |
| ❑ 38 Georges Vezina | 5000.00 | 2500.00 |
| ❑ 39 G.(Henri) Dallaire | 125.00 | 60.00 |
| ❑ 40 R.(Rocket) Power | 125.00 | 60.00 |
| ❑ 41 Didier(Pit) Pitre | 250.00 | 125.00 |
| ❑ 42 Newsy Lalonde | 1200.00 | 600.00 |
| ❑ 43 Eugene Payan | 125.00 | 60.00 |
| ❑ 44 George Poulin | 125.00 | 60.00 |
| ❑ 45 Jack Laviolette | 250.00 | 125.00 |

## 1910-11 C56

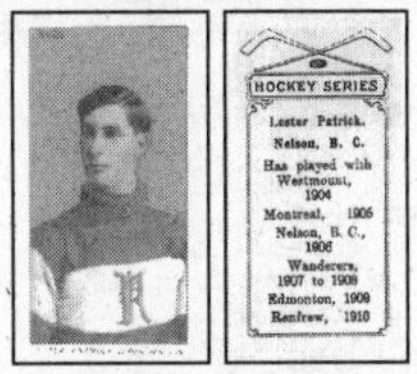


One of the first hockey sets to appear (circa 1910-11), this full-color set of unknown origin (although there is speculation that the issuer was Imperial Tobacco) features 36 cards. The card numbering appears in the upper left part of the front of the card. These small cards measure approximately 1 1/2" by 2 5/8". The player's name and affiliation appear at the bottom within the border. The backs feature the player's name and career affiliations below crossed hockey sticks, a puck and the words "Hockey Series."

| | EX-MT | VG-E |
|---|---|---|
| COMPLETE SET (36) | 10000.00 | 5000.00 |
| COMMON CARD (1-36) | 150.00 | 75.00 |
| ❑ 1 Frank Patrick | 600.00 | 300.00 |
| ❑ 2 Percy Lesueur | 300.00 | 150.00 |
| ❑ 3 Gordon Roberts | 300.00 | 150.00 |
| ❑ 4 Barney Holden | 150.00 | 75.00 |
| ❑ 5 Frank(Pud) Glass | 150.00 | 75.00 |
| ❑ 6 Edgar Dey | 150.00 | 75.00 |
| ❑ 7 Marty Walsh | 250.00 | 125.00 |
| ❑ 8 Art Ross | 1000.00 | 500.00 |
| ❑ 9 Angus Campbell | 250.00 | 125.00 |
| ❑ 10 Harry Hyland | 300.00 | 150.00 |
| ❑ 11 Herb Clark | 150.00 | 75.00 |
| ❑ 12 Art Ross | 1000.00 | 500.00 |
| ❑ 13 Ed Decary | 150.00 | 75.00 |
| ❑ 14 Tom Dunderdale | 300.00 | 150.00 |
| ❑ 15 Cyclone Taylor | 1000.00 | 500.00 |
| ❑ 16 Joseph Cattarinich | 200.00 | 100.00 |
| ❑ 17 Bruce Stuart | 300.00 | 150.00 |
| ❑ 18 Nick Bawlf | 150.00 | 75.00 |
| ❑ 19 Jim Jones | 200.00 | 100.00 |
| ❑ 20 Ernest Russell | 350.00 | 180.00 |
| ❑ 21 Jack Laviolette | 250.00 | 125.00 |
| ❑ 22 Riley Hern | 300.00 | 150.00 |
| ❑ 23 Didier(Pit) Pitre | 300.00 | 150.00 |
| ❑ 24 Skinner Poulin | 150.00 | 75.00 |
| ❑ 25 Art Bernier | 150.00 | 75.00 |
| ❑ 26 Lester Patrick | 700.00 | 350.00 |
| ❑ 27 Fred Lake | 150.00 | 75.00 |
| ❑ 28 Paddy Moran | 500.00 | 250.00 |
| ❑ 29 C.Toms | 150.00 | 75.00 |
| ❑ 30 Ernest(Moose) Johnson | 500.00 | 250.00 |
| ❑ 31 Horace Gaul | 150.00 | 75.00 |
| ❑ 32 Harold McNamara | 150.00 | 75.00 |
| ❑ 33 Jack Marshall | 250.00 | 125.00 |
| ❑ 34 Bruce Ridpath | 150.00 | 75.00 |
| ❑ 35 Jack Marshall | 250.00 | 125.00 |
| ❑ 36 Newsy Lalonde | 1000.00 | 500.00 |

## 1912-13 C57

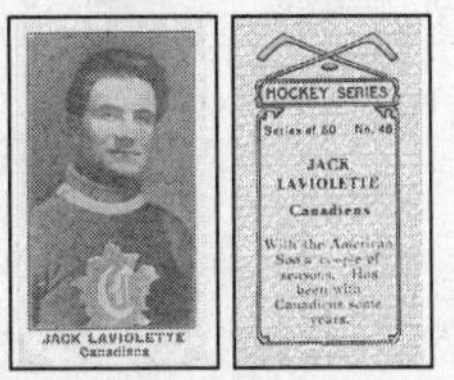


This set of 50 black and white cards was produced circa 1912-13. These small cards measure approximately 1 1/2" by 2 5/8". The player's name and affiliation are printed on both the front and back. The card number appears on the back only with the words "Series of 50." Although the origin of the set is unknown, it is safe to assume that the producer who issued the C56 series issued this as well, as the backs of the cards are quite similar. A brief career outline in English is contained on the back. This set is considered to be the toughest to find of the three early hockey sets.

| | EX-MT | VG-E |
|---|---|---|
| COMPLETE SET (50) | 17500.00 | 8800.00 |
| COMMON CARD (1-50) | 200.00 | 100.00 |
| ❑ 1 Georges Vezina | 2500.00 | 1250.00 |
| ❑ 2 Punch Broadbent | 600.00 | 300.00 |
| ❑ 3 Clint Benedict | 600.00 | 300.00 |
| ❑ 4 A. Atchinson | 200.00 | 100.00 |
| ❑ 5 Tom Dunderdale | 350.00 | 180.00 |
| ❑ 6 Art Bernier | 200.00 | 100.00 |
| ❑ 7 G.(Henri) Dallaire | 200.00 | 100.00 |
| ❑ 8 George Poulin | 200.00 | 100.00 |
| ❑ 9 Eugene Payan | 200.00 | 100.00 |
| ❑ 10 Steve Vair | 200.00 | 100.00 |
| ❑ 11 Bobby Rowe | 200.00 | 100.00 |
| ❑ 12 Don Smith | 200.00 | 100.00 |
| ❑ 13 Bert Lindsay | 250.00 | 125.00 |
| ❑ 14 Skene Ronan | 200.00 | 100.00 |
| ❑ 15 Sprague Cleghorn | 500.00 | 250.00 |
| ❑ 16 Joe Hall | 400.00 | 200.00 |
| ❑ 17 Jack MacDonald | 200.00 | 100.00 |
| ❑ 18 Paddy Moran | 400.00 | 200.00 |
| ❑ 19 Harry Hyland | 300.00 | 150.00 |
| ❑ 20 Art Ross | 1000.00 | 500.00 |
| ❑ 21 Frank(Pud) Glass | 200.00 | 100.00 |
| ❑ 22 Walter Smaill | 200.00 | 100.00 |
| ❑ 23 Gordon Roberts | 300.00 | 150.00 |
| ❑ 24 James Gardner | 350.00 | 180.00 |
| ❑ 25 Ernest(Moose) Johnson | 400.00 | 200.00 |
| ❑ 26 Ernie Russell | 400.00 | 200.00 |
| ❑ 27 Percy Lesueur | 350.00 | 180.00 |
| ❑ 28 Bruce Ridpath | 200.00 | 100.00 |
| ❑ 29 Jack Darragh | 350.00 | 180.00 |
| ❑ 30 Hamby Shore | 200.00 | 100.00 |
| ❑ 31 Fred Lake | 200.00 | 100.00 |
| ❑ 32 Alex Currie | 200.00 | 100.00 |
| ❑ 33 Albert Kerr | 200.00 | 100.00 |
| ❑ 34 Eddie Gerard | 350.00 | 180.00 |
| ❑ 35 Carl Kendall | 200.00 | 100.00 |
| ❑ 36 Jack Fournier | 200.00 | 100.00 |
| ❑ 37 Goldie Prodgers | 200.00 | 100.00 |
| ❑ 38 Jack Marks | 200.00 | 100.00 |
| ❑ 39 George Broughton | 250.00 | 125.00 |
| ❑ 40 Arthur Boyce | 250.00 | 125.00 |
| ❑ 41 Lester Patrick | 750.00 | 375.00 |
| ❑ 42 Joe Dennison | 200.00 | 100.00 |
| ❑ 43 Cyclone Taylor | 1000.00 | 500.00 |
| ❑ 44 Newsy Lalonde | 1000.00 | 500.00 |
| ❑ 45 Didier(Pit) Pitre | 300.00 | 150.00 |
| ❑ 46 Jack Laviolette | 300.00 | 150.00 |
| ❑ 47 Ed Oatman | 200.00 | 100.00 |
| ❑ 48 Joe Malone | 750.00 | 375.00 |
| ❑ 49 Marty Walsh | 350.00 | 180.00 |
| ❑ 50 Odie Cleghorn | 250.00 | 125.00 |

## 1924-25 C144 Champ's Cigarettes

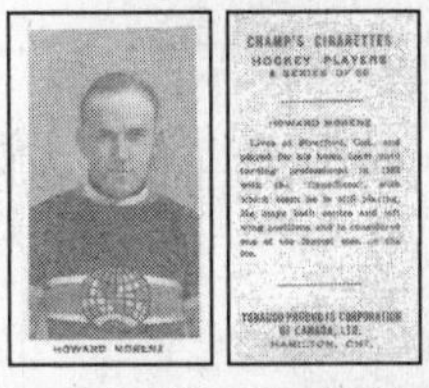


This unnumbered 60-card set was issued during the 1924-25 season by Champ's Cigarettes. There is a brief biography on the card back written in English. The cards are sepia tone and measure approximately 1 1/2" by 2 1/2". Since the cards are unnumbered, they are checklisted in alphabetical order by subject.

| | EX-MT | VG-E |
|---|---|---|
| COMPLETE SET (60) | 20000.00 | 10000.00 |
| COMMON CARD (1-60) | 175.00 | 90.00 |
| ❑ 1 Jack Adams | 250.00 | 125.00 |
| ❑ 2 Lloyd Andrews | 175.00 | 90.00 |
| ❑ 3 Clint Benedict | 400.00 | 200.00 |
| ❑ 4 Louis Berlinquette | 175.00 | 90.00 |
| ❑ 5 Eddie Bouchard | 175.00 | 90.00 |
| ❑ 6 Billy Boucher | 200.00 | 100.00 |
| ❑ 7 Bob Boucher | 175.00 | 90.00 |
| ❑ 8 Punch Broadbent | 350.00 | 180.00 |
| ❑ 9 Billy Burch | 350.00 | 180.00 |
| ❑ 10 Dutch Cain | 175.00 | 90.00 |
| ❑ 11 Earl Campbell | 175.00 | 90.00 |
| ❑ 12 George Carroll | 175.00 | 90.00 |
| ❑ 13 King Clancy | 1750.00 | 900.00 |
| ❑ 14 Odie Cleghorn | 225.00 | 110.00 |
| ❑ 15 Sprague Cleghorn | 400.00 | 200.00 |
| ❑ 16 Alex Connell | 400.00 | 200.00 |
| ❑ 17 Carson Cooper | 175.00 | 90.00 |
| ❑ 18 Bert Corbeau | 200.00 | 100.00 |
| ❑ 19 Billy Coutu | 175.00 | 90.00 |
| ❑ 20 Clarence (Hap) Day | 400.00 | 200.00 |
| ❑ 21 Cy Denneny | 350.00 | 180.00 |
| ❑ 22 Charles A. Dinsmore | 175.00 | 90.00 |
| ❑ 23 Babe Dye | 350.00 | 180.00 |
| ❑ 24 Frank Finnigan | 350.00 | 180.00 |
| ❑ 25 Vernon Forbes | 175.00 | 90.00 |
| ❑ 26 Norman Fowler | 200.00 | 100.00 |
| ❑ 27 Red Green | 175.00 | 90.00 |
| ❑ 28 Shorty Green | 350.00 | 180.00 |
| ❑ 29 Curly Headley | 175.00 | 90.00 |
| ❑ 30 Jim Herberts | 175.00 | 90.00 |
| ❑ 31 Fred Hitchman | 175.00 | 90.00 |
| ❑ 32 Albert Holway | 175.00 | 90.00 |
| ❑ 33 Stan Jackson | 175.00 | 90.00 |
| ❑ 34 Aurel Joliat | 1400.00 | 700.00 |
| ❑ 35 Louis C. Langlois | 175.00 | 90.00 |
| ❑ 36 Fred (Frock) Lowrey | 175.00 | 90.00 |
| ❑ 37 Sylvio Mantha | 350.00 | 180.00 |

| | | |
|---|---|---|
| ❑ 38 Albert McCaffrey | 175.00 | 90.00 |
| ❑ 39 Robert McKinnon | 175.00 | 90.00 |
| ❑ 40 Herbie Mitchell | 175.00 | 90.00 |
| ❑ 41 Howie Morenz | 3500.00 | 1800.00 |
| ❑ 42 Dunc Munro | 225.00 | 110.00 |
| ❑ 43 Gerald J.M. Munro | 175.00 | 90.00 |
| ❑ 44 Frank Nighbor | 400.00 | 200.00 |
| ❑ 45 Reg Noble | 350.00 | 180.00 |
| ❑ 46 Mickey O'Leary | 175.00 | 90.00 |
| ❑ 47 Goldie Prodgers | 175.00 | 90.00 |
| ❑ 48 Ken Randall | 175.00 | 90.00 |
| ❑ 49 George Redding | 175.00 | 90.00 |
| ❑ 50 John Ross Roach | 200.00 | 100.00 |
| ❑ 51 Mickey Roach | 175.00 | 90.00 |
| ❑ 52 Sam Rothschild | 175.00 | 90.00 |
| ❑ 53 Werner Schnarr | 175.00 | 90.00 |
| ❑ 54 Ganton Scott | 175.00 | 90.00 |
| ❑ 55 Alf Skinner | 175.00 | 90.00 |
| ❑ 56 Hooley Smith | 350.00 | 180.00 |
| ❑ 57 Chris Speyers | 175.00 | 90.00 |
| ❑ 58 Jesse Spring | 175.00 | 90.00 |
| ❑ 59 The Stanley Cup | 600.00 | 300.00 |
| ❑ 60 Georges Vezina | 1750.00 | 900.00 |

## 1994-95 Canada Games NHL POGS

Produced by Canada Games Company Limited, this set includes 376 POGS and 8 checklist cards. Each POG measures 1 5/8" in diameter; the checklist cards measure 2 3/8" by 3 1/2". Each cello pack featured 5 POGS and one checklist card; also one in every five packs contained a bonus kini. The fronts display color action head shots framed by foil and color geometric designs. The team name, player's name, and his position are printed on the fronts. In black on white, the backs carry biography, 1993-94 season statistics, NHL totals, and various logos. The POGS are numbered on the back.

| | MINT | NRMT |
|---|---|---|
| COMPLETE SET (376) | 100.00 | 45.00 |
| COMMON POG (1-376) | .10 | .05 |

| | | |
|---|---|---|
| ❑ 1 Kini-Kings | .50 | .23 |
| ❑ 2 Kini-Rangers | .50 | .23 |
| ❑ 3 Kini-Penguins | .50 | .23 |
| ❑ 4 Kini-Stars | .50 | .23 |
| ❑ 5 Kini-Senators | .50 | .23 |
| ❑ 6 Kini-Jets | .50 | .23 |
| ❑ 7 Kini-Canucks | .50 | .23 |
| ❑ 8 Kini-Capitals | .50 | .23 |
| ❑ 9 Kini-Ducks | .50 | .23 |
| ❑ 10 Kini-Bruins | .50 | .23 |
| ❑ 11 Kini-Sabres | .50 | .23 |
| ❑ 12 Kini-Flames | .50 | .23 |
| ❑ 13 Kini-Blackhawks | .50 | .23 |
| ❑ 14 Kini-Red Wings | .50 | .23 |
| ❑ 15 Kini-Oilers | .50 | .23 |
| ❑ 16 Kini-Panthers | .50 | .23 |
| ❑ 17 Kini-Whalers | .50 | .23 |
| ❑ 18 Kini-Canadiens | .50 | .23 |
| ❑ 19 Kini-Devils | .50 | .23 |
| ❑ 20 Kini-Islanders | .50 | .23 |
| ❑ 21 Kini-Flyers | .50 | .23 |
| ❑ 22 Kini-Nordiques | .50 | .23 |
| ❑ 23 Kini-Sharks | .50 | .23 |
| ❑ 24 Kini-Blues | .50 | .23 |
| ❑ 25 Kini-Lightning | .50 | .23 |
| ❑ 26 Kini-Leafs | .50 | .23 |
| ❑ 27 Cliff Ronning | .10 | .05 |
| ❑ 28 Bob Corkum | .10 | .05 |
| ❑ 29 Joe Sacco | .10 | .05 |
| ❑ 30 Peter Douris | .10 | .05 |
| ❑ 31 Shaun Van Allen | .10 | .05 |
| ❑ 32 Stephan Lebeau | .10 | .05 |
| ❑ 33 Stu Grimson | .10 | .05 |
| ❑ 34 Tim Sweeney | .10 | .05 |
| ❑ 35 Adam Oates | .50 | .23 |
| ❑ 36 Al Iafrate | .15 | .07 |
| ❑ 37 Alexei Kastanov | .10 | .05 |
| ❑ 38 Bryan Smolinski | .25 | .11 |
| ❑ 39 Cam Neely | .75 | .35 |
| ❑ 40 Don Sweeney | .10 | .05 |
| ❑ 41 Glen Murray | .10 | .05 |
| ❑ 42 Ray Bourque | 1.00 | .45 |
| ❑ 43 Ted Donato | .10 | .05 |
| ❑ 44 Alexander Mogilny | 1.00 | .45 |
| ❑ 45 Doug Gilmour | 1.00 | .45 |
| ❑ 46 Dale Hawerchuk | .50 | .23 |
| ❑ 47 Derek Plante | .25 | .11 |
| ❑ 48 Donald Audette | .25 | .11 |
| ❑ 49 Doug Bodger | .10 | .05 |
| ❑ 50 Pat LaFontaine | .50 | .23 |
| ❑ 51 Randy Wood | .10 | .05 |
| ❑ 52 Richard Smehlik | .10 | .05 |
| ❑ 53 Yuri Khmylev | .10 | .05 |
| ❑ 54 Theo Fleury | .75 | .35 |
| ❑ 55 Kelly Kisio | .10 | .05 |
| ❑ 56 Joe Nieuwendyk | .25 | .11 |
| ❑ 57 Michael Nylander | .10 | .05 |
| ❑ 58 Joel Otto | .10 | .05 |
| ❑ 59 James Patrick | .10 | .05 |
| ❑ 60 Robert Reichel | .25 | .11 |
| ❑ 61 Gary Roberts | .25 | .11 |
| ❑ 62 Wes Walz | .10 | .05 |
| ❑ 63 Ulf Dahlen | .10 | .05 |
| ❑ 64 Zarley Zalapski | .10 | .05 |
| ❑ 65 Tony Amonte | .75 | .35 |
| ❑ 66 Dirk Graham | .10 | .05 |
| ❑ 67 Joe Murphy | .15 | .07 |
| ❑ 68 Bernie Nicholls | .25 | .11 |
| ❑ 69 Patrick Poulin | .10 | .05 |
| ❑ 70 Jeremy Roenick | 1.00 | .45 |
| ❑ 71 Christian Ruutu | .10 | .05 |
| ❑ 72 Brent Sutter | .10 | .05 |
| ❑ 73 Chris Chelios | 1.50 | .70 |
| ❑ 74 Steve Smith | .10 | .05 |
| ❑ 75 Gary Suter | .10 | .05 |
| ❑ 76 Neal Broten | .15 | .07 |
| ❑ 77 Russ Courtnall | .10 | .05 |
| ❑ 78 Dean Evason | .10 | .05 |
| ❑ 79 Dave Gagner | .15 | .07 |
| ❑ 80 Mike McPhee | .10 | .05 |
| ❑ 81 Mike Modano | .75 | .35 |
| ❑ 82 Paul Cavallini | .10 | .05 |
| ❑ 83 Derian Hatcher | .10 | .05 |
| ❑ 84 Grant Ledyard | .10 | .05 |
| ❑ 85 Mark Tinordi | .10 | .05 |
| ❑ 86 Dino Ciccarelli | .35 | .16 |
| ❑ 87 Sergei Fedorov | 3.00 | 1.35 |
| ❑ 88 Slava Kozlov | .25 | .11 |
| ❑ 89 Darren McCarty | .25 | .11 |
| ❑ 90 Keith Primeau | .25 | .11 |
| ❑ 91 Ray Sheppard | .25 | .11 |
| ❑ 92 Steve Yzerman | 5.00 | 2.20 |
| ❑ 93 Paul Coffey | 1.00 | .45 |
| ❑ 94 Vladimir Konstantinov | .10 | .05 |
| ❑ 95 Nicklas Lidstrom | .35 | .16 |
| ❑ 96 Greg Adams | .10 | .05 |
| ❑ 97 Jason Arnott | .75 | .35 |
| ❑ 98 Kelly Buchberger | .10 | .05 |
| ❑ 99 Shayne Corson | .10 | .05 |
| ❑ 100 Scott Pearson | .10 | .05 |
| ❑ 101 Doug Weight | .50 | .23 |
| ❑ 102 Boris Mironov | .25 | .11 |
| ❑ 103 Fredrik Olausson | .10 | .05 |
| ❑ 104 Stu Barnes | .10 | .05 |
| ❑ 105 Bob Kudelski | .10 | .05 |
| ❑ 106 Andrei Lomakin | .10 | .05 |
| ❑ 107 Dave Lowry | .10 | .05 |
| ❑ 108 Scott Mellanby | .25 | .11 |
| ❑ 109 Rob Niedermayer | .50 | .23 |
| ❑ 110 Brian Skrudland | .10 | .05 |
| ❑ 111 Brian Benning | .10 | .05 |
| ❑ 112 Gord Murphy | .10 | .05 |
| ❑ 113 Andrew Cassels | .10 | .05 |
| ❑ 114 Robert Kron | .10 | .05 |
| ❑ 115 Jocelyn Lemieux | .10 | .05 |
| ❑ 116 Paul Ranheim | .10 | .05 |
| ❑ 117 Geoff Sanderson | .50 | .23 |
| ❑ 118 Jim Sandlak | .10 | .05 |
| ❑ 119 Darren Turcotte | .10 | .05 |
| ❑ 120 Pat Verbeek | .25 | .11 |
| ❑ 121 Chris Pronger | .35 | .16 |
| ❑ 122 Pat Conacher | .10 | .05 |
| ❑ 123 Mike Donnelly | .10 | .05 |
| ❑ 124 John Druce | .10 | .05 |
| ❑ 125 Tony Granato | .15 | .07 |
| ❑ 126 Wayne Gretzky | 10.00 | 4.50 |
| ❑ 127 Jari Kurri | .25 | .11 |
| ❑ 128 Warren Rychel | .10 | .05 |
| ❑ 129 Rob Blake | .20 | .09 |
| ❑ 130 Marty McSorley | .25 | .11 |
| ❑ 131 Alexei Zhitnik | .10 | .05 |
| ❑ 132 Brian Bellows | .10 | .05 |
| ❑ 133 Vince Damphousse | .50 | .23 |
| ❑ 134 Gilbert Dionne | .10 | .05 |
| ❑ 135 Mike Keane | .10 | .05 |
| ❑ 136 John LeClair | 2.50 | 1.10 |
| ❑ 137 Kirk Muller | .25 | .11 |
| ❑ 138 Oleg Petrov | .10 | .05 |
| ❑ 139 Eric Desjardins | .10 | .05 |
| ❑ 140 Lyle Odelein | .10 | .05 |
| ❑ 141 Peter Popovic | .10 | .05 |
| ❑ 142 Mathieu Schneider | .10 | .05 |
| ❑ 143 Trent Klatt | .10 | .05 |
| ❑ 144 Bobby Holik | .10 | .05 |
| ❑ 145 Claude Lemieux | .35 | .16 |
| ❑ 146 John MacLean | .20 | .09 |
| ❑ 147 Corey Millen | .10 | .05 |
| ❑ 148 Stephane Richer | .15 | .07 |
| ❑ 149 Valeri Zelepukin | .10 | .05 |
| ❑ 150 Bruce Driver | .10 | .05 |
| ❑ 151 Gino Odjick | .10 | .05 |
| ❑ 152 Scott Stevens | .25 | .11 |
| ❑ 153 Brad Dalgarno | .10 | .05 |
| ❑ 154 Ray Ferraro | .10 | .05 |
| ❑ 155 Pat Flatley | .10 | .05 |
| ❑ 156 Travis Green | .15 | .07 |
| ❑ 157 Derek King | .10 | .05 |
| ❑ 158 Marty McInnis | .10 | .05 |
| ❑ 159 Steve Thomas | .25 | .11 |
| ❑ 160 Pierre Turgeon | .50 | .23 |
| ❑ 161 Darius Kasparaitis | .10 | .05 |
| ❑ 162 Vladimir Malakhov | .10 | .05 |
| ❑ 163 Alexei Kovalev | .25 | .11 |
| ❑ 164 Steve Larmer | .25 | .11 |
| ❑ 165 Stephane Matteau | .10 | .05 |
| ❑ 166 Mark Messier | 2.00 | .90 |
| ❑ 167 Sergei Nemchinov | .10 | .05 |
| ❑ 168 Brian Noonan | .10 | .05 |
| ❑ 169 Petr Nedved | .25 | .11 |
| ❑ 170 Brian Leetch | 1.50 | .70 |
| ❑ 171 Kevin Lowe | .10 | .05 |
| ❑ 172 Sergei Zubov | .10 | .05 |
| ❑ 173 Sylvain Turgeon | .10 | .05 |
| ❑ 174 Alexei Yashin | .50 | .23 |
| ❑ 175 Norm Maciver | .10 | .05 |
| ❑ 176 Brad Shaw | .10 | .05 |
| ❑ 177 Brent Fedyk | .10 | .05 |
| ❑ 178 Mark Lamb | .10 | .05 |
| ❑ 179 Don McSween | .10 | .05 |
| ❑ 180 Mark Recchi | .50 | .23 |
| ❑ 181 Mikael Renberg | .75 | .35 |
| ❑ 182 Gary Galley | .10 | .05 |
| ❑ 183 Ron Francis | .50 | .23 |
| ❑ 184 Jaromir Jagr | 5.00 | 2.20 |
| ❑ 185 Mario Lemieux | 8.00 | 3.60 |
| ❑ 186 Shawn McEachern | .10 | .05 |
| ❑ 187 Joe Mullen | .20 | .09 |
| ❑ 188 Tomas Sandstrom | .15 | .07 |
| ❑ 189 Kevin Stevens | .20 | .09 |
| ❑ 190 Martin Straka | .10 | .05 |
| ❑ 191 Larry Murphy | .25 | .11 |
| ❑ 192 Kjell Samuelsson | .10 | .05 |
| ❑ 193 Ulf Samuelsson | .10 | .05 |
| ❑ 194 Wendel Clark | .35 | .16 |
| ❑ 195 Valeri Kamensky | .35 | .16 |
| ❑ 196 Andrei Kovalenko | .10 | .05 |
| ❑ 197 Owen Nolan | .50 | .23 |
| ❑ 198 Mike Ricci | .10 | .05 |
| ❑ 199 Joe Sakic | 4.00 | 1.80 |
| ❑ 200 Scott Young | .10 | .05 |
| ❑ 201 Uwe Krupp | .10 | .05 |
| ❑ 202 Curtis Leschyshyn | .10 | .05 |
| ❑ 203 Brett Hull | 2.00 | .90 |
| ❑ 204 Craig Janney | .25 | .11 |
| ❑ 205 Kevin Miller | .10 | .05 |
| ❑ 206 Vitali Prokhorov | .10 | .05 |
| ❑ 207 Brendan Shanahan | 3.00 | 1.35 |
| ❑ 208 Peter Stastny | .25 | .11 |
| ❑ 209 Esa Tikkanen | .20 | .09 |
| ❑ 210 Steve Duchesne | .10 | .05 |
| ❑ 211 Gaeten Duchesne | .10 | .05 |
| ❑ 212 Todd Elik | .10 | .05 |
| ❑ 213 Pogman | .50 | .23 |
| ❑ 214 Pat Falloon | .10 | .05 |
| ❑ 215 Johan Garpenlov | .10 | .05 |
| ❑ 216 Igor Larionov | .25 | .11 |
| ❑ 217 Sergei Makarov | .15 | .07 |
| ❑ 218 Jeff Norton | .10 | .05 |
| ❑ 219 Sandis Ozolinsh | .50 | .23 |
| ❑ 220 Mikael Andersson | .10 | .05 |
| ❑ 221 Brian Bradley | .25 | .11 |
| ❑ 222 Danton Cole | .10 | .05 |
| ❑ 223 Chris Gratton | .50 | .23 |
| ❑ 224 Petr Klima | .10 | .05 |
| ❑ 225 Denis Savard | .25 | .11 |
| ❑ 226 John Tucker | .10 | .05 |
| ❑ 227 Shawn Chambers | .10 | .05 |
| ❑ 228 Chris Joseph | .10 | .05 |
| ❑ 229 Dave Andreychuk | .25 | .11 |
| ❑ 230 Nikolai Borschevsky | .10 | .05 |
| ❑ 231 Mike Craig | .10 | .05 |
| ❑ 232 Mike Eastwood | .10 | .05 |
| ❑ 233 Mike Gartner | .50 | .23 |
| ❑ 234 Doug Gilmour | 1.00 | .45 |
| ❑ 235 Kent Manderville | .10 | .05 |
| ❑ 236 Mike Ridley | .10 | .05 |
| ❑ 237 Mats Sundin | .75 | .35 |
| ❑ 238 Dave Ellett | .10 | .05 |
| ❑ 239 Todd Gill | .10 | .05 |
| ❑ 240 Jamie Macoun | .10 | .05 |
| ❑ 241 Dmitri Mironov | .10 | .05 |
| ❑ 242 Peter Bondra | 1.00 | .45 |
| ❑ 243 Randy Burridge | .10 | .05 |
| ❑ 244 Dale Hunter | .10 | .05 |
| ❑ 245 Joe Juneau | .35 | .16 |
| ❑ 246 Dmitri Khristich | .25 | .11 |
| ❑ 247 Kelly Miller | .10 | .05 |
| ❑ 248 Michal Pivonka | .10 | .05 |
| ❑ 249 Sylvain Cote | .10 | .05 |
| ❑ 250 Tie Domi | .50 | .23 |
| ❑ 251 Dallas Drake | .10 | .05 |
| ❑ 252 Nelson Emerson | .10 | .05 |
| ❑ 253 Teemu Selanne | 3.00 | 1.35 |
| ❑ 254 Darrin Shannon | .10 | .05 |
| ❑ 255 Thomas Steen | .10 | .05 |
| ❑ 256 Keith Tkachuk | 2.00 | .90 |
| ❑ 257 Dave Manson | .10 | .05 |
| ❑ 258 Stephane Quintal | .10 | .05 |
| ❑ 259 Adam Graves AS | .25 | .11 |
| ❑ 260 Brian Leetch AS | 1.00 | .45 |
| ❑ 261 John Vanbiesbrouck AS | 4.00 | 1.80 |
| ❑ 262 Scott Stevens AS | .25 | .11 |
| ❑ 263 Ray Bourque AS | 1.00 | .45 |
| ❑ 264 Al MacInnis AS | .25 | .11 |
| ❑ 265 Brendan Shanahan AS | 2.50 | 1.10 |
| ❑ 266 Pavel Bure AS | 2.50 | 1.10 |
| ❑ 267 Sergei Fedorov AS | 2.50 | 1.10 |
| ❑ 268 Wayne Gretzky AS | 10.00 | 4.50 |
| ❑ 269 Guy Hebert | .50 | .23 |
| ❑ 270 Kirk McLean | .50 | .23 |
| ❑ 271 John Blue | .25 | .11 |
| ❑ 272 Vincent Riendeau | .25 | .11 |
| ❑ 273 Grant Fuhr | .50 | .23 |
| ❑ 274 Dominik Hasek | 3.00 | 1.35 |
| ❑ 275 Trevor Kidd | .35 | .16 |
| ❑ 276 Ed Belfour | 1.50 | .70 |
| ❑ 277 Andy Moog | .50 | .23 |
| ❑ 278 Mike Vernon | .50 | .23 |
| ❑ 279 Bill Ranford | .50 | .23 |
| ❑ 280 John Vanbiesbrouck | 2.50 | 1.10 |
| ❑ 281 Sean Burke | .50 | .23 |
| ❑ 282 Kelly Hrudey | .50 | .23 |
| ❑ 283 Patrick Roy | 8.00 | 3.60 |
| ❑ 284 Martin Brodeur | 4.00 | 1.80 |
| ❑ 285 Chris Terreri | .15 | .07 |
| ❑ 286 Jamie McLennan | .20 | .09 |
| ❑ 287 Glenn Healy | .25 | .11 |
| ❑ 288 Mike Richter | 1.50 | .70 |
| ❑ 289 Craig Billington | .25 | .11 |
| ❑ 290 Dominic Roussel | .20 | .09 |
| ❑ 291 Tom Barrasso | .25 | .11 |
| ❑ 292 Stephane Fiset | .25 | .11 |
| ❑ 293 Curtis Joseph | 1.50 | .70 |
| ❑ 294 Arturs Irbe | 1.00 | .45 |
| ❑ 295 Daren Puppa | .50 | .23 |
| ❑ 296 Felix Potvin | 1.50 | .70 |
| ❑ 297 Tim Cheveldae | .25 | .11 |
| ❑ 298 Don Beaupre | .25 | .11 |
| ❑ 299 Rick Tabaracci | .20 | .09 |
| ❑ 300 Anaheim Mighty Ducks | .35 | .16 |
| ❑ 301 Boston Bruins | .35 | .16 |
| ❑ 302 Buffalo Sabres | .10 | .05 |
| ❑ 303 Calgary Flames | .10 | .05 |
| ❑ 304 Chicago Blackhawks | .25 | .11 |
| ❑ 305 Dallas Stars | .10 | .05 |
| ❑ 306 Detroit Red Wings | .35 | .16 |
| ❑ 307 Edmonton Oilers | .10 | .05 |
| ❑ 308 Florida Panthers | .10 | .05 |
| ❑ 309 Hartford Whalers | .10 | .05 |
| ❑ 310 Los Angeles Kings | .35 | .16 |
| ❑ 311 Montreal Canadiens | .35 | .16 |
| ❑ 312 New Jersey Devils | .10 | .05 |
| ❑ 313 Jeff Brown | .10 | .05 |
| ❑ 314 New York Rangers | .35 | .16 |
| ❑ 315 Ottawa Senators | .10 | .05 |
| ❑ 316 Philadelphia Flyers | .10 | .05 |
| ❑ 317 Pittsburgh Penguins | .10 | .05 |
| ❑ 318 Quebec Nordiques | .10 | .05 |
| ❑ 319 St. Louis Blues | .10 | .05 |
| ❑ 320 San Jose Sharks | .25 | .11 |
| ❑ 321 Tampa Bay Lightning | .10 | .05 |
| ❑ 322 Toronto Maple Leafs | .25 | .11 |
| ❑ 323 Vancouver Canucks | .10 | .05 |
| ❑ 324 Washington Capitals | .10 | .05 |
| ❑ 325 Winnipeg Jets | .10 | .05 |
| ❑ 326 Martin Brodeur AW | 3.00 | 1.35 |
| ❑ 327 Brian Leetch AW | 1.00 | .45 |
| ❑ 328 Cam Neely AW | .75 | .35 |
| ❑ 329 Geoff Courtnall | .10 | .05 |
| ❑ 330 Pogman | .50 | .23 |
| ❑ 331 Sergei Fedorov AW | 2.50 | 1.10 |
| ❑ 332 Dominik Hasek AW | 3.00 | 1.35 |
| ❑ 333 Dominik Hasek Grant Fuhr AW | 1.50 | .70 |
| ❑ 334 Brian Leetch | 1.00 | .45 |
| ❑ 335 Martin Gelinas | .20 | .09 |
| ❑ 336 Cam Neely | .50 | .23 |
| ❑ 337 Mike Richter | 1.50 | .70 |
| ❑ 338 Luke Richardson | .10 | .05 |
| ❑ 339 Jyrki Lumme | .10 | .05 |
| ❑ 340 Nathan Lafayette | .10 | .05 |
| ❑ 341 Pavel Bure | 2.50 | 1.10 |
| ❑ 342 Sergio Momesso | .10 | .05 |
| ❑ 343 Trevor Linden | .50 | .23 |
| ❑ 344 Tie Domi | .35 | .16 |
| ❑ 345 Scott Stevens | .25 | .11 |
| ❑ 346 Teppo Numminen | .10 | .05 |
| ❑ 347 Anatoli Semenov | .10 | .05 |
| ❑ 348 Steve Heinze | .10 | .05 |
| ❑ 349 Tom Chorske | .10 | .05 |
| ❑ 350 Bill Guerin | .20 | .09 |
| ❑ 351 Scott Niedermayer | .25 | .11 |
| ❑ 352 Adam Graves | .25 | .11 |
| ❑ 353 Alexandre Daigle | .50 | .23 |
| ❑ 354 Troy Mallette | .10 | .05 |
| ❑ 355 Dave McLlwain | .10 | .05 |
| ❑ 356 Josef Beranek | .10 | .05 |
| ❑ 357 Kevin Dineen | .10 | .05 |
| ❑ 358 Eric Lindros | 6.00 | 2.70 |
| ❑ 359 Bob Rouse | .10 | .05 |
| ❑ 360 Sergei Fedorov AW | 3.00 | 1.35 |
| ❑ 361 Bob Errey | .10 | .05 |
| ❑ 362 Brad May | .10 | .05 |
| ❑ 363 Kevin Hatcher | .10 | .05 |
| ❑ 364 New York Islanders | .10 | .05 |
| ❑ 365 Randy Ladouceur | .10 | .05 |
| ❑ 366 Bobby Dollas | .10 | .05 |
| ❑ 367 Igor Kravchuk | .10 | .05 |
| ❑ 368 Jesse Belanger | .10 | .05 |
| ❑ 369 Pogman | .50 | .23 |
| ❑ 370 Gary Valk | .10 | .05 |
| ❑ 371 Pogman | .50 | .23 |
| ❑ 372 Ron Hextall | .50 | .23 |
| ❑ 373 Rod Brind'Amour | .50 | .23 |
| ❑ 374 Benoit Hogue | .10 | .05 |
| ❑ 375 Alexei Zhamnov | .25 | .11 |
| ❑ 376 Pavel Bure AW | 2.50 | 1.10 |
| ❑ NNO Checklist 1-47 | .10 | .05 |
| ❑ NNO Checklist 48-94 | .10 | .05 |
| ❑ NNO Checklist 95-141 | .10 | .05 |
| ❑ NNO Checklist 142-188 | .10 | .05 |
| ❑ NNO Checklist 189-235 | .10 | .05 |
| ❑ NNO Checklist 236-282 | .10 | .05 |
| ❑ NNO Checklist 283-329 | .10 | .05 |
| ❑ NNO Checklist 330-376 | .10 | .05 |

## 1995-96 Canada Games NHL POGS

This set of 296 POGS was produced by Canada Games. The POGS were distributed in packs of five, with every fifth pack containing a bonus Kini. These Kinis are listed at the end of the checklist with a K-prefix. They do not picture the trophy mentioned. The POGS themselves feature a colorful action shot of the player, while the backs feature abbreviated stats. The checklist below is incomplete; additional information would be appreciated.

| | MINT | NRMT |
|---|---|---|
| COMPLETE SET (296) | 80.00 | 36.00 |
| COMMON POG (1-296) | .10 | .05 |

| | | |
|---|---|---|
| ❑ 1 Wayne Gretzky | 6.00 | 2.70 |
| ❑ 2 Mario Lemieux | 5.00 | 2.20 |
| ❑ 3 Cam Neely | .50 | .23 |
| ❑ 4 Ray Bourque | 1.00 | .45 |
| ❑ 5 Patrick Roy | 5.00 | 2.20 |
| ❑ 6 Mark Messier | 1.25 | .55 |
| ❑ 7 Brett Hull | 1.25 | .55 |
| ❑ 8 Grant Fuhr | .50 | .23 |
| ❑ 9 Eric Lindros | 4.00 | 1.80 |
| ❑ 10 John LeClair | 1.50 | .70 |
| ❑ 11 Jaromir Jagr | 3.00 | 1.35 |
| ❑ 12 Chris Chelios | 1.00 | .45 |
| ❑ 13 Paul Coffey | 1.00 | .45 |
| ❑ 14 Dominik Hasek | 2.00 | .90 |
| ❑ 15 Alexei Zhamnov | .25 | .11 |
| ❑ 16 Keith Tkachuk | 1.25 | .55 |
| ❑ 17 Theoren Fleury | .50 | .23 |
| ❑ 18 Ray Bourque | 1.00 | .45 |
| ❑ 19 Larry Murphy | .25 | .11 |
| ❑ 20 Ed Belfour | 1.00 | .45 |
| ❑ 21 Pavel Bure | 2.00 | .90 |
| ❑ 22 Doug Gilmour | .75 | .35 |
| ❑ 23 Brett Hull | 1.25 | .55 |
| ❑ 24 Mark Messier | 1.25 | .55 |
| ❑ 25 Cam Neely | .50 | .23 |
| ❑ 26 Jeremy Roenick | 1.00 | .45 |
| ❑ 27 Patrick Roy | 5.00 | 2.20 |
| ❑ 28 Jim Carey | .75 | .35 |
| ❑ 29 Peter Forsberg | 3.00 | 1.35 |
| ❑ 30 Jeff Friesen | .10 | .05 |
| ❑ 31 Kenny Jonsson | .25 | .11 |
| ❑ 32 Paul Kariya | 3.00 | 1.35 |
| ❑ 33 Ian Laperriere | .10 | .05 |
| ❑ 34 David Oliver | .10 | .05 |
| ❑ 35 Kyle McLaren | .50 | .23 |
| ❑ 36 Ray Bourque | 1.00 | .45 |
| ❑ 37 Alexei Kasatonov | .10 | .05 |
| ❑ 38 Blaine Lacher | .50 | .23 |
| ❑ 39 Brian Holzinger | .25 | .11 |
| ❑ 41 Mike Peca | .10 | .05 |
| ❑ 42 Pat LaFontaine | .50 | .23 |
| ❑ 45 Yuri Khmylev | .10 | .05 |
| ❑ 46 Garry Galley | .10 | .05 |
| ❑ 47 Alexei Zhitnik | .10 | .05 |
| ❑ 48 Dominik Hasek | 2.00 | .90 |
| ❑ 49 Joe Nieuwendyk | .25 | .11 |
| ❑ 50 German Titov | .10 | .05 |
| ❑ 51 Cory Stillman | .10 | .05 |
| ❑ 59 Ron Stern | .10 | .05 |
| ❑ 65 Sergei Krivokrasov | .10 | .05 |
| ❑ 66 Joe Murphy | .15 | .07 |
| ❑ 67 Patrick Poulin | .10 | .05 |
| ❑ 68 Bob Probert | .25 | .11 |
| ❑ 69 Gary Suter | .10 | .05 |
| ❑ 70 Chris Chelios | 1.00 | .45 |
| ❑ 71 Ed Belfour | 1.00 | .45 |
| ❑ 72 Joe Sakic | 2.50 | 1.10 |
| ❑ 73 Mike Ricci | .10 | .05 |
| ❑ 74 Valeri Kamensky | .35 | .16 |
| ❑ 75 Andrei Kovalenko | .10 | .05 |
| ❑ 76 Owen Nolan | .50 | .23 |
| ❑ 77 Peter Forsberg | 3.00 | 1.35 |
| ❑ 78 Scott Young | .10 | .05 |
| ❑ 79 Uwe Krupp | .10 | .05 |
| ❑ 80 Curtis Leschyshyn | .10 | .05 |
| ❑ 81 Adam Deadmarsh | .25 | .11 |
| ❑ 82 Stephane Fiset | .25 | .11 |
| ❑ 83 Bob Bassen | .10 | .05 |
| ❑ 84 Corey Millen | .10 | .05 |
| ❑ 85 Mike Modano | 1.25 | .55 |
| ❑ 86 Dave Gagner | .15 | .07 |
| ❑ 87 Mike Donnelly | .10 | .05 |
| ❑ 88 Trent Klatt | .10 | .05 |
| ❑ 89 Kevin Hatcher | .10 | .05 |
| ❑ 90 Grant Ledyard | .10 | .05 |
| ❑ 91 Greg Adams | .10 | .05 |
| ❑ 92 Andy Moog | .50 | .23 |
| ❑ 93 Keith Primeau | .25 | .11 |
| ❑ 94 Kris Draper | .10 | .05 |
| ❑ 95 Sergei Fedorov | 2.00 | .90 |
| ❑ 96 Steve Yzerman | 3.00 | 1.35 |
| ❑ 97 Vyacheslav Kozlov | .10 | .05 |
| ❑ 98 Ray Sheppard | .25 | .11 |
| ❑ 99 Dino Ciccarelli | .25 | .11 |
| ❑ 100 Viacheslav Fetisov | .10 | .05 |
| ❑ 101 Nicklas Lidstrom | .25 | .11 |
| ❑ 102 Paul Coffey | 1.00 | .45 |
| ❑ 103 Darren McCarty | .25 | .11 |
| ❑ 104 Mike Vernon | .50 | .23 |
| ❑ 105 Doug Weight | .50 | .23 |
| ❑ 106 Jason Arnott | .50 | .23 |
| ❑ 107 Todd Marchant | .10 | .05 |
| ❑ 108 David Oliver | .10 | .05 |
| ❑ 109 Igor Kravchuk | .10 | .05 |
| ❑ 110 Jiri Slegr | .10 | .05 |
| ❑ 111 Kelly Buchberger | .10 | .05 |
| ❑ 112 Scott Thornton | .10 | .05 |
| ❑ 113 Bill Ranford | .50 | .23 |
| ❑ 114 Jesse Belanger | .10 | .05 |
| ❑ 115 Stu Barnes | .10 | .05 |
| ❑ 116 Scott Mellanby | .25 | .11 |
| ❑ 117 Bill Lindsay | .10 | .05 |
| ❑ 118 Dave Lowry | .10 | .05 |
| ❑ 119 Gaetan Duchesne | .10 | .05 |
| ❑ 120 Johan Garpenlov | .10 | .05 |
| ❑ 121 Paul Laus | .10 | .05 |
| ❑ 122 Gord Murphy | .10 | .05 |
| ❑ 123 John Vanbiesbrouck | 1.50 | .70 |
| ❑ 124 Andrew Cassels | .10 | .05 |
| ❑ 125 Geoff Sanderson | .50 | .23 |
| ❑ 126 Brendan Shanahan | 2.00 | .90 |
| ❑ 127 Paul Ranheim | .10 | .05 |
| ❑ 128 Steven Rice | .10 | .05 |
| ❑ 129 Frantisek Kucera | .10 | .05 |
| ❑ 130 Glen Wesley | .10 | .05 |
| ❑ 131 Sean Burke | .50 | .23 |
| ❑ 132 Wayne Gretzky | 6.00 | 2.70 |
| ❑ 133 Dimitri Khristich | .10 | .05 |
| ❑ 134 Jari Kurri | .25 | .11 |

| | | |
|---|---|---|
| ☐ 135 John Druce | .10 | .05 |
| ☐ 136 Pat Conacher | .10 | .05 |
| ☐ 137 Rick Tocchet | .20 | .09 |
| ☐ 138 Rob Blake | .20 | .09 |
| ☐ 139 Tony Granato | .15 | .07 |
| ☐ 140 Marty McSorley | .25 | .11 |
| ☐ 141 Darryl Sydor | .10 | .05 |
| ☐ 142 Eric Lacroix | .10 | .05 |
| ☐ 143 Kelly Hrudey | .50 | .23 |
| ☐ 144 Brian Savage | .10 | .05 |
| ☐ 145 Pierre Turgeon | .50 | .23 |
| ☐ 146 Benoit Brunet | .10 | .05 |
| ☐ 147 Valeri Bure | .10 | .05 |
| ☐ 148 Vincent Damphousse | .50 | .23 |
| ☐ 149 Mike Keane | .10 | .05 |
| ☐ 150 Mark Recchi | .50 | .23 |
| ☐ 151 Vladimir Malakhov | .10 | .05 |
| ☐ 152 Patrice Brisebois | .10 | .05 |
| ☐ 153 J.J. Daigneault | .10 | .05 |
| ☐ 154 Yves Racine | .10 | .05 |
| ☐ 155 Patrick Roy | 5.00 | 2.20 |
| ☐ 156 Bob Carpenter | .10 | .05 |
| ☐ 157 Neal Broten | .15 | .07 |
| ☐ 158 Steve Thomas | .25 | .11 |
| ☐ 159 Bobby Holik | .10 | .05 |
| ☐ 160 John MacLean | .20 | .09 |
| ☐ 161 Mike Peluso | .10 | .05 |
| ☐ 162 Randy McKay | .10 | .05 |
| ☐ 163 Stephane Richer | .15 | .07 |
| ☐ 164 Scott Niedermayer | .25 | .11 |
| ☐ 165 Scott Stevens | .25 | .11 |
| ☐ 166 Bill Guerin | .20 | .09 |
| ☐ 167 Martin Brodeur | 2.50 | 1.10 |
| ☐ 168 Kirk Muller | .25 | .11 |
| ☐ 169 Zigmund Palffy | 1.25 | .55 |
| ☐ 170 Travis Green | .15 | .07 |
| ☐ 171 Brett Lindros | .10 | .05 |
| ☐ 172 Derek King | .10 | .05 |
| ☐ 173 Pat Flatley | .10 | .05 |
| ☐ 174 Wendel Clark | .35 | .16 |
| ☐ 175 Bryan McCabe | .10 | .05 |
| ☐ 176 Mathieu Schneider | .10 | .05 |
| ☐ 177 Eric Fichaud | .50 | .23 |
| ☐ 178 Ray Ferraro | .10 | .05 |
| ☐ 179 Adam Graves | .25 | .11 |
| ☐ 180 Mark Messier | 1.25 | .55 |
| ☐ 181 Sergei Nemchinov | .10 | .05 |
| ☐ 182 Pat Verbeek | .25 | .11 |
| ☐ 183 Luc Robitaille | .50 | .23 |
| ☐ 184 Alexei Kovalev | .25 | .11 |
| ☐ 185 Jeff Beukeboom | .10 | .05 |
| ☐ 186 Brian Leetch | 1.00 | .45 |
| ☐ 187 Ulf Samuelsson | .10 | .05 |
| ☐ 188 Alexander Karpovtsev | .10 | .05 |
| ☐ 189 Mike Richter | 1.00 | .45 |
| ☐ 190 Alexandre Daigle | .50 | .23 |
| ☐ 191 Alexei Yashin | .50 | .23 |
| ☐ 192 Dan Quinn | .10 | .05 |
| ☐ 193 Martin Straka | .10 | .05 |
| ☐ 194 Radek Bonk | .10 | .05 |
| ☐ 195 Pavol Demitra | .10 | .05 |
| ☐ 196 Steve Duchesne | .10 | .05 |
| ☐ 197 Chris Dahlquist | .10 | .05 |
| ☐ 198 Sean Hill | .10 | .05 |
| ☐ 199 Stanislav Neckar | .10 | .05 |
| ☐ 200 Don Beaupre | .25 | .11 |
| ☐ 201 Eric Lindros | 4.00 | 1.80 |
| ☐ 202 Rod Brind'Amour | .50 | .23 |
| ☐ 203 Shjon Podein | .10 | .05 |
| ☐ 204 Brent Fedyk | .10 | .05 |
| ☐ 205 Joel Otto | .10 | .05 |
| ☐ 206 John LeClair | 1.50 | .70 |
| ☐ 207 Kevin Dineen | .10 | .05 |
| ☐ 208 Petr Svoboda | .10 | .05 |
| ☐ 209 Eric Desjardins | .10 | .05 |
| ☐ 210 Ron Hextall | .50 | .23 |
| ☐ 211 Mario Lemieux | 5.00 | 2.20 |
| ☐ 212 Petr Nedved | .25 | .11 |
| ☐ 213 Bryan Smolinski | .25 | .11 |
| ☐ 214 Tomas Sandstrom | .15 | .07 |
| ☐ 215 Ron Francis | .50 | .23 |
| ☐ 216 Jaromir Jagr | 3.00 | 1.35 |
| ☐ 217 Sergei Zubov | .10 | .05 |
| ☐ 218 Drake Berehowsky | .10 | .05 |
| ☐ 219 Dmitri Mironov | .10 | .05 |
| ☐ 220 Ken Wregget | .50 | .23 |
| ☐ 221 Tom Barrasso | .25 | .11 |
| ☐ 222 Igor Larionov | .25 | .11 |
| ☐ 223 Jeff Friesen | .10 | .05 |
| ☐ 224 Kevin Miller | .10 | .05 |
| ☐ 225 Ray Whitney | .10 | .05 |
| ☐ 226 Craig Janney | .25 | .11 |
| ☐ 227 Pat Falloon | .10 | .05 |
| ☐ 228 Ulf Dahlen | .10 | .05 |
| ☐ 229 Viktor Kozlov | .10 | .05 |
| ☐ 230 Michal Sykora | .10 | .05 |
| ☐ 231 Sandis Ozolinsh | .50 | .23 |
| ☐ 232 Jamie Baker | .10 | .05 |
| ☐ 233 Arturs Irbe | .50 | .23 |
| ☐ 234 Adam Creighton | .10 | .05 |
| ☐ 235 Ian Laperriere | .10 | .05 |
| ☐ 236 Brett Hull | 1.25 | .55 |
| ☐ 237 Brian Noonan | .10 | .05 |
| ☐ 238 Dale Hawerchuk | .50 | .23 |
| ☐ 239 Esa Tikkanen | .20 | .09 |
| ☐ 240 Geoff Courtnall | .10 | .05 |
| ☐ 241 Shayne Corson | .10 | .05 |
| ☐ 242 Al MacInnis | .25 | .11 |
| ☐ 243 Chris Pronger | .35 | .16 |
| ☐ 244 Jeff Norton | .10 | .05 |
| ☐ 245 Grant Fuhr | .50 | .23 |
| ☐ 246 Brian Bradley | .25 | .11 |
| ☐ 247 Chris Gratton | .50 | .23 |
| ☐ 248 John Cullen | .10 | .05 |
| ☐ 249 John Tucker | .10 | .05 |
| ☐ 250 Paul Ysebaert | .10 | .05 |
| ☐ 251 Petr Klima | .10 | .05 |
| ☐ 252 Alexander Selivanov | .10 | .05 |
| ☐ 253 Brian Bellows | .10 | .05 |
| ☐ 254 Enrico Ciccone | .10 | .05 |
| ☐ 255 Roman Hamrlik | .25 | .11 |
| ☐ 256 Daren Puppa | .50 | .23 |
| ☐ 257 Doug Gilmour | .75 | .35 |
| ☐ 258 Benoit Hogue | .10 | .05 |
| ☐ 259 Mats Sundin | 1.00 | .45 |
| ☐ 260 Dave Andreychuk | .25 | .11 |
| ☐ 261 Mike Gartner | .50 | .23 |
| ☐ 262 Randy Wood | .10 | .05 |
| ☐ 263 Tie Domi | .35 | .16 |
| ☐ 264 Dave Ellett | .10 | .05 |
| ☐ 265 Todd Gill | .10 | .05 |
| ☐ 266 Larry Murphy | .25 | .11 |
| ☐ 267 Kenny Jonsson | .25 | .11 |
| ☐ 268 Felix Potvin | 1.00 | .45 |
| ☐ 269 Cliff Ronning | .10 | .05 |
| ☐ 270 Mike Ridley | .10 | .05 |
| ☐ 271 Trevor Linden | .50 | .23 |
| ☐ 272 Alexander Mogilny | .75 | .35 |
| ☐ 273 Martin Gelinas | .20 | .09 |
| ☐ 274 Pavel Bure | 2.00 | .90 |
| ☐ 275 Russ Courtnall | .10 | .05 |
| ☐ 276 Jeff Brown | .10 | .05 |
| ☐ 277 Jyrki Lumme | .10 | .05 |
| ☐ 278 Kirk McLean | .50 | .23 |
| ☐ 279 Steve Konowalchuk | .10 | .05 |
| ☐ 280 Kelly Miller | .10 | .05 |
| ☐ 281 Peter Bondra | 1.00 | .45 |
| ☐ 282 Keith Jones | .10 | .05 |
| ☐ 283 Joe Juneau | .35 | .16 |
| ☐ 284 Mark Tinordi | .10 | .05 |
| ☐ 285 Calle Johansson | .10 | .05 |
| ☐ 286 Sergei Gonchar | .10 | .05 |
| ☐ 287 Jim Carey | .75 | .35 |
| ☐ 288 Dallas Drake | .10 | .05 |
| ☐ 289 Alexei Zhamnov | .25 | .11 |
| ☐ 290 Mike Eastwood | .10 | .05 |
| ☐ 291 Igor Korolev | .10 | .05 |
| ☐ 292 Teemu Selanne | 2.00 | .90 |
| ☐ 293 Keith Tkachuk | 1.25 | .55 |
| ☐ 294 Teppo Numminen | .10 | .05 |
| ☐ 295 Dave Manson | .10 | .05 |
| ☐ 296 Tim Cheveldae | .25 | .11 |
| ☐ K1 Lester B. Pearson | .50 | .23 |
| ☐ K2 Art Ross | .50 | .23 |
| ☐ K3 Bill Masterton | .50 | .23 |
| ☐ K4 Calder | .50 | .23 |
| ☐ K5 Clarence S. Campbell | .50 | .23 |
| ☐ K6 Conn Smythe | .50 | .23 |
| ☐ K7 Frank J. Selke | .50 | .23 |
| ☐ K8 Hart | .50 | .23 |
| ☐ K9 Jack Adams | .50 | .23 |
| ☐ K10 James Norris | .50 | .23 |
| ☐ K11 King Clancy | .50 | .23 |
| ☐ K12 Lady Byng | .50 | .23 |
| ☐ K13 Prince of Wales | .50 | .23 |
| ☐ K14 Stanley Cup | .50 | .23 |
| ☐ K15 Vezina | .50 | .23 |
| ☐ K16 William M. Jennings | .50 | .23 |

## 1983 Canadian National Juniors

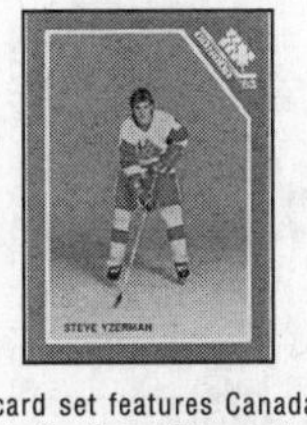

This 21-card set features Canada's 1983 National Junior Team. The cards measure approximately 3 1/2" by 5" and feature on the fronts either color posed action shots or close-up photos, shot against a blue background. On a red card face, the photos are enclosed by white borders, and the upper right corner of the picture is cut off to allow space for the team logo. The backs are blank and the unnumbered cards are checklisted below in alphabetical order. The set includes early cards of Mario Lemieux, Steve Yzerman, Mike Vernon, Dave Andreychuk, and Pat Verbeek. Three other players on the team who were not at the photo session and therefore not represented in the set are Paul Boutillier, Marc Habscheid, and Brad Shaw. A large team card (approximately 5" by 10 1/4") featuring all the players (except Marc Habscheid) and coaches was also produced. A two-thirds size (measuring approximately 5" by 7 1/4") team card entitled Celebration '82 with Troy Murray holding the Memorial Cup as well as a (7 1/4" by 10 1/4") '82 team card were also produced. These special oversized cards are not typically included as part of the complete set as listed and valued below.

| | MINT | NRMT |
|---|---|---|
| COMPLETE SET (21) | 175.00 | 80.00 |
| COMMON CARD (1-21) | 1.00 | .45 |
| | | |
| ☐ 1 Dave Andreychuk | 8.00 | 3.60 |
| ☐ 2 Joe Cirella | 2.00 | .90 |
| ☐ 3 Paul Cyr | 1.00 | .45 |
| ☐ 4 Dale Derkatch | 1.00 | .45 |
| ☐ 5 Mike Eagles | 1.00 | .45 |
| ☐ 6 Pat Flatley UER (Misspelled Flately) | 2.00 | .90 |
| ☐ 7 Mario Gosselin | 2.00 | .90 |
| ☐ 8 Gary Leeman | 2.00 | .90 |
| ☐ 9 Mario Lemieux | 80.00 | 36.00 |
| ☐ 10 Mark Morrison | 1.00 | .45 |
| ☐ 11 James Patrick | 4.00 | 1.80 |
| ☐ 12 Mike Sands | 1.50 | .70 |
| ☐ 13 Gord Sherven | 1.00 | .45 |
| ☐ 14 Tony Tanti | 2.00 | .90 |
| ☐ 15 Larry Trader | 1.00 | .45 |
| ☐ 16 Sylvain Turgeon | 2.00 | .90 |
| ☐ 17 Pat Verbeek | 10.00 | 4.50 |
| ☐ 18 Mike Vernon | 8.00 | 3.60 |
| ☐ 19 Steve Yzerman | 60.00 | 27.00 |
| ☐ 20 Checklist Card | 1.00 | .45 |
| ☐ 21 Title Card | 1.00 | .45 |
| ☐ NNO Team Card (Regular size) | 8.00 | 3.60 |
| ☐ NNO Large Team Card | 20.00 | 9.00 |
| ☐ NNO Team Card '82 | 10.00 | 4.50 |
| ☐ NNO Celebration '82 (Troy Murray) | 10.00 | 4.50 |

## 1964-65 Canadiens Postcards

This 24-postcard set features the Montreal Canadiens. The standard-size postcards feature action, black and white photography on the front, with the player's autograph stamped on in blue ink. The backs are blank.

| | MINT | NRMT |
|---|---|---|
| COMPLETE SET (24) | 200.00 | 90.00 |
| COMMON POSTCARD (1-24) | 3.00 | 1.35 |
| | | |
| ☐ 1 Ralph Backstrom | 5.00 | 2.20 |
| ☐ 2 Jean Beliveau | 20.00 | 9.00 |
| ☐ 3 Toe Blake | 10.00 | 4.50 |
| ☐ 4 Yvan Cournoyer | 20.00 | 9.00 |
| ☐ 5 Dick Duff | 8.00 | 3.60 |
| ☐ 6 John Ferguson | 10.00 | 4.50 |
| ☐ 7 Danny Grant | 5.00 | 2.20 |
| ☐ 8 Terry Harper | 5.00 | 2.20 |
| ☐ 9 Ted Harris | 5.00 | 2.20 |
| ☐ 10 Jacques Laperriere | 8.00 | 3.60 |
| ☐ 11 Claude Larose | 5.00 | 2.20 |
| ☐ 12 Jacques Lemaire | 15.00 | 6.75 |
| ☐ 13 Garry Monahan | 5.00 | 2.20 |
| ☐ 14 Claude Provost | 5.00 | 2.20 |
| ☐ 15 Mickey Redmond | 15.00 | 6.75 |
| ☐ 16 Henri Richard | 15.00 | 6.75 |
| ☐ 17 Bobby Rousseau | 5.00 | 2.20 |
| ☐ 18 Serge Savard | 10.00 | 4.50 |
| ☐ 19 Gilles Tremblay | 5.00 | 2.20 |
| ☐ 20 J.C. Tremblay | 5.00 | 2.20 |
| ☐ 21 Carol Vadnais | 3.00 | 1.35 |
| ☐ 22 Rogatien Vachon | 20.00 | 9.00 |
| ☐ 23 Bryan Watson | 3.00 | 1.35 |
| ☐ 24 Gump Worsley | 10.00 | 4.50 |

## 1965-66 Canadiens Steinberg Glasses

This set of plastic glasses honoring members of the Montreal Canadiens were issued in the mid 1960's. As they are unnumbered, we are sequencing them in alphabetical order.

| | MINT | NRMT |
|---|---|---|
| COMPLETE SET (12) | 150.00 | 70.00 |
| COMMON CARD (1-12) | 10.00 | 4.50 |
| | | |
| ☐ 1 Ralph Backstrom | 10.00 | 4.50 |
| ☐ 2 Jean Beliveau | 30.00 | 13.50 |
| ☐ 3 John Ferguson | 15.00 | 6.75 |
| ☐ 4 Charlie Hodge | 15.00 | 6.75 |
| ☐ 5 Jacques Laperierre | 10.00 | 4.50 |
| ☐ 6 Claude Provost | 10.00 | 4.50 |
| ☐ 7 Henri Richard | 20.00 | 9.00 |
| ☐ 8 Bob Rousseau | 10.00 | 4.50 |
| ☐ 9 Jean Guy Talbot | 10.00 | 4.50 |
| ☐ 10 Gilles Trembley | 10.00 | 4.50 |
| ☐ 11 J.C. Trembley | 12.00 | 5.50 |
| ☐ 12 Gump Worsley | 20.00 | 9.00 |

## 1966-67 Canadiens IGA

The 1966-67 Canadiens IGA set apparently is comprised of 10 small, postage stamp sized (3/4" by 3/4") cards which likely were part of a larger coupon book. With no attention to date on the card, it has been set by the Gilles Tremblay issue. The cards feature a head shot on a pinkish-red background. If anyone knows of other cards in this set, please forward the information to Beckett Publications.

| | NRMT-MT | EXC |
|---|---|---|
| COMPLETE SET (10) | 300.00 | 135.00 |
| COMMON CARD (1-10) | 25.00 | 11.00 |
| | | |
| ☐ 1 J.C. Tremblay | 30.00 | 13.50 |
| ☐ 2 Ralph Backstrom | 30.00 | 13.50 |
| ☐ 3 Dick Duff | 30.00 | 13.50 |
| ☐ 4 Ted Harris | 25.00 | 11.00 |
| ☐ 5 Claude Larose | 25.00 | 11.00 |
| ☐ 6 Bobby Rousseau | 30.00 | 13.50 |
| ☐ 7 Terry Harper | 30.00 | 13.50 |
| ☐ 8 Gilles Tremblay | 25.00 | 11.00 |
| ☐ 9 John Ferguson | 30.00 | 13.50 |
| ☐ 10 Gump Worsley | 80.00 | 36.00 |

## 1967-68 Canadiens IGA

The 1967-68 IGA Montreal Canadiens set includes 23 color cards measuring approximately 1 5/8" by 1 7/8". The cards are unnumbered other than by jersey number which is how they are listed below. The cards were part of a game involving numerous prizes. The card backs contain no personal information about the player (only information about the IGA game) and are written in French and English. The set features early cards of Jacques Lemaire and Rogatien Vachon in their Rookie Card year as well as Serge Savard two years prior to his Rookie Card year.

| | NRMT-MT | EXC |
|---|---|---|
| COMPLETE SET (23) | 650.00 | 300.00 |
| COMMON CARD | 20.00 | 9.00 |
| | | |
| ☐ 1 Gump Worsley | 50.00 | 22.00 |
| ☐ 2 Jacques Laperriere | 30.00 | 13.50 |
| ☐ 3 J.C. Tremblay | 25.00 | 11.00 |
| ☐ 4 Jean Beliveau | 80.00 | 36.00 |
| ☐ 5 Gilles Tremblay | 20.00 | 9.00 |
| ☐ 6 Ralph Backstrom | 20.00 | 9.00 |
| ☐ 8 Dick Duff | 25.00 | 11.00 |
| ☐ 10 Ted Harris | 20.00 | 9.00 |
| ☐ 11 Claude Larose | 20.00 | 9.00 |
| ☐ 12 Yvan Cournoyer | 40.00 | 18.00 |
| ☐ 14 Claude Provost | 20.00 | 9.00 |
| ☐ 15 Bobby Rousseau | 20.00 | 9.00 |
| ☐ 16 Henri Richard | 50.00 | 22.00 |
| ☐ 17 Carol Vadnais | 20.00 | 9.00 |
| ☐ 18 Serge Savard | 50.00 | 22.00 |
| ☐ 19 Terry Harper | 25.00 | 11.00 |
| ☐ 20 Garry Monahan | 20.00 | 9.00 |
| ☐ 22 John Ferguson | 25.00 | 11.00 |
| ☐ 23 Danny Grant | 25.00 | 11.00 |
| ☐ 24 Mickey Redmond | 40.00 | 18.00 |
| ☐ 25 Jacques Lemaire | 60.00 | 27.00 |
| ☐ 30 Rogatien Vachon | 80.00 | 36.00 |
| ☐ NNO Hector(Toe) Blake CO | 30.00 | 13.50 |

## 1968-69 Canadiens IGA

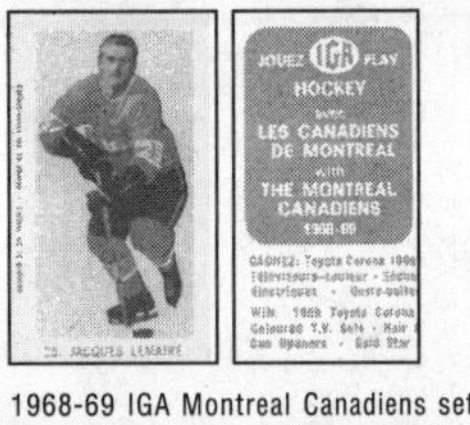

The 1968-69 IGA Montreal Canadiens set includes 19 color cards measuring approximately 1 1/4" by 2 1/4". The cards are unnumbered other than by jersey number which is how they are listed below. The cards were part of a game involving numerous prizes. The card backs contain no personal information about the player (only information about the IGA game) and are written in French and English.

| | NRMT-MT | EXC |
|---|---|---|
| COMPLETE SET (19) | 600.00 | 275.00 |
| COMMON CARD | 20.00 | 9.00 |
| | | |
| ☐ 1 Gump Worsley | 60.00 | 27.00 |
| ☐ 2 Jacques Laperriere | 30.00 | 13.50 |
| ☐ 3 J.C. Tremblay | 25.00 | 11.00 |
| ☐ 4 Jean Beliveau | 80.00 | 36.00 |
| ☐ 5 Gilles Tremblay | 20.00 | 9.00 |
| ☐ 6 Ralph Backstrom | 25.00 | 11.00 |
| ☐ 8 Dick Duff | 25.00 | 11.00 |
| ☐ 10 Ted Harris | 20.00 | 9.00 |
| ☐ 12 Yvan Cournoyer | 50.00 | 22.00 |
| ☐ 14 Claude Provost | 20.00 | 9.00 |
| ☐ 15 Bobby Rousseau | 25.00 | 11.00 |
| ☐ 16 Henri Richard | 50.00 | 22.00 |
| ☐ 18 Serge Savard | 40.00 | 18.00 |
| ☐ 19 Terry Harper | 25.00 | 11.00 |
| ☐ 20 Garry Monahan | 20.00 | 9.00 |
| ☐ 22 John Ferguson | 30.00 | 13.50 |
| ☐ 24 Mickey Redmond | 40.00 | 18.00 |
| ☐ 25 Jacques Lemaire | 60.00 | 27.00 |
| ☐ 30 Rogatien Vachon | 60.00 | 27.00 |

## 1968-69 Canadiens Postcards BW

This 20-card set of black and white postcards features full-bleed posed player photos with facsimile autographs in white. This set marks the last year the Canadiens' organization issued black and white postcards. The cards are unnumbered and checklisted below in alphabetical order. Serge Savard appears in this set prior to his Rookie Card year.

| | NRMT-MT | EXC |
|---|---|---|
| COMPLETE SET (20) | 80.00 | 36.00 |
| COMMON CARD (1-20) | 2.50 | 1.10 |
| | | |
| ☐ 1 Ralph Backstrom | 3.00 | 1.35 |
| ☐ 2 Jean Beliveau | 15.00 | 6.75 |
| ☐ 3 Yvan Cournoyer | 8.00 | 3.60 |
| ☐ 4 Dick Duff | 3.00 | 1.35 |
| ☐ 5 John Ferguson | 4.00 | 1.80 |
| ☐ 6 Terry Harper | 3.00 | 1.35 |
| ☐ 7 Ted Harris | 2.50 | 1.10 |
| ☐ 8 Jacques Laperriere | 4.00 | 1.80 |
| ☐ 9 Jacques Lemaire | 10.00 | 4.50 |
| ☐ 10 Garry Monahan | 2.50 | 1.10 |
| ☐ 11 Claude Provost | 2.50 | 1.10 |
| ☐ 12 Mickey Redmond | 5.00 | 2.20 |
| ☐ 13 Henri Richard | 8.00 | 3.60 |
| ☐ 14 Bobby Rousseau | 3.00 | 1.35 |
| ☐ 15 Claude Ruel CO | 2.50 | 1.10 |
| ☐ 16 Serge Savard | 8.00 | 3.60 |
| ☐ 17 Gilles Tremblay | 2.50 | 1.10 |
| ☐ 18 J.C. Tremblay | 3.00 | 1.35 |
| ☐ 19 Rogatien Vachon | 10.00 | 4.50 |
| ☐ 20 Gump Worsley | 10.00 | 4.50 |

## 1969-71 Canadiens Postcards Color

This 31-card set of postcards features full-bleed posed color player photos with facsimile autographs in black across the bottom of the pictures. These postcards were also issued without facsimile autographs. For the 1969-70, 1970-71, and 1971-72 seasons, many of the same postcards were issued. The cards are unnumbered and checklisted below in alphabetical order.

| | NRMT-MT | EXC |
|---|---|---|
| COMPLETE SET (31) | 100.00 | 45.00 |
| COMMON CARD (1-31) | 2.50 | 1.10 |
| | | |
| ☐ 1 Ralph Backstrom | 3.00 | 1.35 |
| ☐ 2 Jean Beliveau | 12.00 | 5.50 |
| ☐ 3 Chris Bordeleau | 2.50 | 1.10 |
| ☐ 4 Pierre Bouchard | 2.50 | 1.10 |
| ☐ 5 Guy Charron | 2.50 | 1.10 |
| ☐ 6 Bill Collins | 2.50 | 1.10 |
| ☐ 7 Yvan Cournoyer | 8.00 | 3.60 |
| ☐ 8 John Ferguson | 4.00 | 1.80 |
| ☐ 9 Terry Harper | 3.00 | 1.35 |
| ☐ 10 Ted Harris | 2.50 | 1.10 |
| ☐ 11 Rejean Houle | 4.00 | 1.80 |
| ☐ 12 Jacques Laperriere | 4.00 | 1.80 |
| ☐ 13 Guy Lapointe | 6.00 | 2.70 |
| ☐ 14 Claude Larose | 2.50 | 1.10 |
| ☐ 15 Jacques Lemaire | 8.00 | 3.60 |
| ☐ 16 Al MacNeil CO | 2.50 | 1.10 |
| ☐ 17 Frank Mahovlich | 8.00 | 3.60 |
| ☐ 18 Peter Mahovlich | 6.00 | 2.70 |
| ☐ 19 Phil Myre | 4.00 | 1.80 |
| ☐ 20 Larry Pleau | 3.00 | 1.35 |
| ☐ 21 Claude Provost | 3.00 | 1.35 |
| ☐ 22 Mickey Redmond | 8.00 | 3.60 |
| ☐ 23 Henri Richard | 8.00 | 3.60 |
| ☐ 24 Phil Roberto | 2.50 | 1.10 |
| ☐ 25 Jim Roberts | 2.50 | 1.10 |
| ☐ 26 Bobby Rousseau | 3.00 | 1.35 |
| ☐ 27 Claude Ruel CO | 2.50 | 1.10 |
| ☐ 28 Serge Savard | 8.00 | 3.60 |
| ☐ 29 Marc Tardif | 3.00 | 1.35 |
| ☐ 30 J.C. Tremblay | 3.00 | 1.35 |
| ☐ 31 Rogatien Vachon | 10.00 | 4.50 |

## 1970-72 Canadiens Pins

This 22-pin set features members of the Montreal Canadiens. Each pin measures approximately 1 3/4" in diameter and has a black and white picture of the player. With the exception of Guy Lafleur, Frank Mahovlich, and Claude Ruel, who are pictured from the waist up, the other pictures are full body shots. The player's name appears below the picture. The pins are made of metal and have a metal clasp on the back. The pins are undated; since Bobby Rousseau's last season with the Canadiens was 1969-70 and 1971-72 was Ken Dryden, Guy Lafleur, and Frank Mahovlich's first season with Montreal, we have assigned 1970-72 to the set, meaning the set was likely issued over a period of years and may, in fact, comprise two distinct sets entirely.

| | NRMT-MT | EXC |
|---|---|---|
| COMPLETE SET (22) | 150.00 | 70.00 |
| COMMON PIN (1-22) | 4.00 | 1.80 |
| | | |
| ☐ 1 Jean Beliveau | 20.00 | 9.00 |
| ☐ 2 Yvan Cournoyer | 8.00 | 3.60 |
| ☐ 3 Ken Dryden | 40.00 | 18.00 |
| ☐ 4 John Ferguson | 5.00 | 2.20 |
| ☐ 5 Terry Harper | 4.00 | 1.80 |
| ☐ 6 Guy Lafleur | 25.00 | 11.00 |
| ☐ 7 Jacques Laperriere | 5.00 | 2.20 |
| ☐ 8 Guy Lapointe | 5.00 | 2.20 |

❑ 9 Jacques Lemaire 8.00 3.60
❑ 10 Frank Mahovlich 10.00 4.50
❑ 11 Peter Mahovlich 5.00 2.20
❑ 12 Henri Richard 10.00 4.50
❑ 13 Bobby Rousseau 5.00 2.20
❑ 14 Claude Ruel CO 3.00 1.35
❑ 15 Serge Savard 5.00 2.20
❑ 16 J.C. Tremblay 4.00 1.80
❑ 17 Rogatien Vachon 8.00 3.60
❑ 18 Ted Harris 5.00 2.20
❑ 19 Claude Provost 5.00 2.20
❑ 20 Mickey Redmond 6.00 2.70
❑ 21 Ralph Backstrom 5.00 2.20
❑ 22 Gump Worsley 10.00 4.50

## 1971-72 Canadiens Postcards

This 25-card set of postcards features full-bleed posed color player photos with facsimile autographs in black across the pictures. For the 1969-70, 1970-71, and 1971-72 seasons, many of the same poses were issued. The cards are unnumbered and checklisted below in alphabetical order. The key cards in the set are Ken Dryden and Guy Lafleur appearing in their Rookie Card year. Also noteworthy is Coach Scotty Bowman's first card.

NRMT-MT EXC
COMPLETE SET (25) 125.00 55.00
COMMON CARD (1-25) 1.50 .70

❑ 1 Pierre Bouchard 1.50 .70
❑ 2 Scotty Bowman CO 8.00 3.60
❑ 3 Yvan Cournoyer 6.00 2.70
❑ 4 Denis DeJordy 2.50 1.10
❑ 5 Ken Dryden 40.00 18.00
❑ 6 Terry Harper 2.00 .90
❑ 7 Dale Hoganson 1.50 .70
❑ 8 Rejean Houle 2.00 .90
❑ 9 Guy Lafleur 25.00 11.00
❑ 10 Jacques Laperriere 4.00 1.80
❑ 11 Guy Lapointe 4.00 1.80
❑ 12 Claude Larose 1.50 .70
❑ 13 Jacques Lemaire 6.00 2.70
❑ 14 Frank Mahovlich 8.00 3.60
❑ 15 Peter Mahovlich 3.00 1.35
❑ 16 Phil Myre 2.50 1.10
❑ 17 Larry Pleau 2.00 .90
❑ 18 Henri Richard 8.00 3.60
❑ 19 Phil Roberto 1.50 .70
❑ 20 Jim Roberts 1.50 .70
❑ 21 Leon Rochefort 1.50 .70
❑ 22 Serge Savard 4.00 1.80
❑ 23 Marc Tardif 2.50 1.10
❑ 24 J.C. Tremblay 2.50 1.10
❑ 25 Rogatien Vachon 8.00 3.60

## 1972-73 Canadiens Postcards

This 22-card set features white bordered posed color player photos with pale green backgrounds. A facsimile autograph appears across the picture. The words "Pro Star Promotions, Inc." are printed in the border at the bottom. The Scotty Bowman card is the same as in the 1971-72 set. The cards are unnumbered and checklisted below in alphabetical order. The card of Steve Shutt predates his Rookie Card by two years.

NRMT-MT EXC
COMPLETE SET (22) 80.00 36.00
COMMON CARD (1-22) 1.50 .70

❑ 1 Chuck Arnason 1.50 .70
❑ 2 Pierre Bouchard 1.50 .70
❑ 3 Scotty Bowman CO 10.00 4.50
❑ 4 Yvan Cournoyer 5.00 2.20
❑ 5 Ken Dryden 25.00 11.00
❑ 6 Rejean Houle 2.00 .90
❑ 7 Guy Lafleur 15.00 6.75
❑ 8 Jacques Laperriere 3.00 1.35
❑ 9 Guy Lapointe 3.00 1.35
❑ 10 Claude Larose 1.50 .70
❑ 11 Chuck Lefley 1.50 .70
❑ 12 Jacques Lemaire 4.00 1.80
❑ 13 Frank Mahovlich 5.00 2.20
❑ 14 Peter Mahovlich 2.50 1.10
❑ 15 Bob Murdoch 1.50 .70
❑ 16 Michel Plasse 3.00 1.35
❑ 17 Henri Richard 5.00 2.20
❑ 18 Jim Roberts 1.50 .70
❑ 19 Serge Savard 3.00 1.35
❑ 20 Steve Shutt 8.00 3.60
❑ 21 Marc Tardif 2.00 .90
❑ 22 Murray Wilson 1.50 .70

## 1972 Canadiens Great West Life Prints

Cards measure 11" x 14" and were produced by Great West Life Insurance Company. Backs are blank. Cards are unnumbered and checklisted below in alphabetical order.

MINT NRMT
COMPLETE SET (6) 75.00 34.00
COMMON CARD (1-6) 8.00 3.60

❑ 1 Pierre Bouchard 8.00 3.60
❑ 2 Yvan Cournoyer 8.00 3.60
❑ 3 Ken Dryden 30.00 13.50
❑ 4 Pete Mahovlich 8.00 3.60
❑ 5 Guy Lafleur 15.00 6.75
❑ 6 Steve Shutt 8.00 3.60

## 1973-74 Canadiens Postcards

This 24-card set features full-bleed color action player photos. The player's name, number and a facsimile autograph are printed on the back. Reportedly distribution problems limited sales to the public. The cards are unnumbered and checklisted below in alphabetical order. The card of Bob Gainey predates his Rookie Card by one year.

NRMT-MT EXC
COMPLETE SET (24) 80.00 36.00
COMMON CARD (1-24) 1.50 .70

❑ 1 Jean Beliveau 12.00 5.50
(Portrait)
❑ 2 Pierre Bouchard 1.50 .70
❑ 3 Scotty Bowman CO 6.00 2.70
(At bench)
❑ 4 Yvan Cournoyer 5.00 2.20
❑ 5 Bob Gainey 8.00 3.60
❑ 6 Dave Gardner 1.50 .70
❑ 7 Guy Lafleur 10.00 4.50
❑ 8 Yvon Lambert 1.50 .70
❑ 9 Jacques Laperriere 2.50 1.10
❑ 10 Guy Lapointe 2.50 1.10
❑ 11 Michel Larocque 3.00 1.35
❑ 12 Claude Larose SP 5.00 2.20
❑ 13 Chuck Lefley 1.50 .70
❑ 14 Jacques Lemaire 3.00 1.35
❑ 15 Frank Mahovlich 5.00 2.20
❑ 16 Peter Mahovlich 2.50 1.10
❑ 17 Michel Plasse SP 5.00 2.20
❑ 18 Henri Richard 5.00 2.20
❑ 19 Jim Roberts SP 5.00 2.20
❑ 20 Larry Robinson 10.00 4.50
❑ 21 Serge Savard 2.50 1.10
❑ 22 Steve Shutt 5.00 2.20
❑ 23 Wayne Thomas 2.50 1.10
❑ 24 Murray Wilson SP 5.00 2.20

## 1974-75 Canadiens Postcards

This 27-card set features full-bleed color photos of players seated on a bench in the forum. The cards were issued with and without facsimile autographs. Claude Larose (13) and Chuck Lefley (14) went to St. Louis mid-season resulting in limited distribution of their cards. The Mario Tremblay card (25) was issued only without a facsimile autograph. The cards are unnumbered and checklisted below in alphabetical order.

NRMT-MT EXC
COMPLETE SET (27) 75.00 34.00
COMMON CARD (1-27) 1.50 .70

❑ 1 Pierre Bouchard 1.50 .70
❑ 2 Scotty Bowman CO 4.00 1.80
❑ 3 Rick Chartraw 1.50 .70
❑ 4 Yvan Cournoyer 4.00 1.80
❑ 5 Ken Dryden 12.00 5.50
❑ 6 Bob Gainey 8.00 3.60
❑ 7 Glenn Goldup 1.50 .70
❑ 8 Guy Lafleur 8.00 3.60
❑ 9 Yvon Lambert 1.50 .70
❑ 10 Jacques Laperriere 2.00 .90
❑ 11 Guy Lapointe 3.00 1.35
❑ 12 Michel Larocque 2.00 .90
❑ 13 Claude Larose SP 3.00 1.35
❑ 14 Chuck Lefley SP 3.00 1.35
❑ 15 Jacques Lemaire 4.00 1.80
❑ 16 Peter Mahovlich 2.00 .90
❑ 17 Henri Richard 4.00 1.80
❑ 18 Doug Risebrough 2.00 .90
❑ 19 Jim Roberts SP 3.00 1.35
❑ 20 Larry Robinson 8.00 3.60
❑ 21 Glen Sather 3.00 1.35
❑ 22 Serge Savard 2.00 .90
❑ 23 Steve Shutt 4.00 1.80
❑ 24 Wayne Thomas 2.00 .90
❑ 25 Mario Tremblay 2.00 .90
❑ 26 John Van Boxmeer 1.50 .70
❑ 27 Murray Wilson SP 3.00 1.35

## 1975-76 Canadiens Postcards

This 20-card set features posed color photos of players on ice. A facsimile autograph appears in a white bottom border. The cards are unnumbered and checklisted below in alphabetical order. The Doug Jarvis card predates his Rookie Card by one year.

NRMT-MT EXC
COMPLETE SET (20) 50.00 22.00
COMMON CARD (1-20) 1.50 .70

❑ 1 Don Awrey 1.50 .70
❑ 2 Pierre Bouchard 1.50 .70
❑ 3 Scotty Bowman CO 4.00 1.80
(Portrait)
❑ 4 Yvan Cournoyer 4.00 1.80
❑ 5 Ken Dryden 12.00 5.50
❑ 6 Bob Gainey 4.00 1.80
❑ 7 Doug Jarvis 4.00 1.80
(White uniform)
❑ 8 Guy Lafleur 8.00 3.60
❑ 9 Yvon Lambert 1.50 .70
❑ 10 Guy Lapointe 2.50 1.10
❑ 11 Michel Larocque 2.00 .90
❑ 12 Jacques Lemaire 4.00 1.80
❑ 13 Peter Mahovlich 2.00 .90
❑ 14 Doug Risebrough 1.50 .70
❑ 15 Jim Roberts 1.50 .70
❑ 16 Larry Robinson 6.00 2.70
❑ 17 Serge Savard 2.50 1.10
❑ 18 Steve Shutt 4.00 1.80
❑ 19 Mario Tremblay 2.00 .90
❑ 20 Murray Wilson 1.50 .70

## 1976-77 Canadiens Postcards

This 23-card set features posed color photos of players seated in front of a light blue studio background. A facsimile autograph appears in a white bottom border. The cards are unnumbered and checklisted below in alphabetical order.

NRMT-MT EXC
COMPLETE SET (23) 45.00 20.00
COMMON CARD (1-23) 1.00 .45

❑ 1 Pierre Bouchard 1.50 .70
❑ 2 Scotty Bowman CO 4.00 1.80
❑ 3 Rick Chartraw 1.50 .70
❑ 4 Yvan Cournoyer 3.00 1.35
❑ 5 Ken Dryden 10.00 4.50
❑ 6 Bob Gainey 4.00 1.80
❑ 7 Rejean Houle 1.50 .70
❑ 8 Doug Jarvis 2.00 .90
❑ 9 Guy Lafleur 8.00 3.60
❑ 10 Yvon Lambert 1.50 .70
❑ 11 Guy Lapointe 2.00 .90
❑ 12 Michel Larocque 2.50 1.10
❑ 13 Jacques Lemaire 3.00 1.35
❑ 14 Peter Mahovlich 2.00 .90
❑ 15 Bill Nyrop 1.50 .70
❑ 16 Doug Risebrough 1.50 .70
❑ 17 Jim Roberts 1.50 .70
❑ 18 Larry Robinson 5.00 2.20
❑ 19 Claude Ruel CO 1.00 .45
❑ 20 Serge Savard 2.00 .90
❑ 21 Steve Shutt 3.00 1.35
❑ 22 Mario Tremblay 2.00 .90
❑ 23 Murray Wilson 1.50 .70

## 1977-78 Canadiens Postcards

This 25-card set features posed action color photos of players on the ice. A facsimile autograph appears in a white bottom border. New players were photographed from the shoulders up. Many of the cards are the same as in the 1975-76 set. The cards are unnumbered and checklisted below in alphabetical order.

NRMT-MT EXC
COMPLETE SET (25) 40.00 18.00
COMMON CARD (1-25) 1.00 .45

❑ 1 Pierre Bouchard 1.00 .45
❑ 2 Scotty Bowman CO 3.00 1.35
❑ 3 Rick Chartraw 1.00 .45
❑ 4 Yvan Cournoyer 3.00 1.35
❑ 5 Ken Dryden 9.00 4.00
❑ 6 Brian Engblom 1.50 .70
❑ 7 Bob Gainey 3.00 1.35
❑ 8 Rejean Houle 1.00 .45
❑ 9 Doug Jarvis 1.50 .70
❑ 10 Guy Lafleur 6.00 2.70
❑ 11 Yvon Lambert 1.00 .45
❑ 12 Guy Lapointe 2.00 .90
❑ 13 Michel Larocque 1.50 .70
❑ 14 Pierre Larouche 2.00 .90
❑ 15 Jacques Lemaire 2.50 1.10
❑ 16 Gilles Lupien 1.00 .45
❑ 17 Pierre Mondou 1.00 .45
❑ 18 Bill Nyrop 1.00 .45
❑ 19 Doug Risebrough 1.00 .45
❑ 20 Larry Robinson 4.00 1.80
❑ 21 Claude Ruel CO 1.00 .45
❑ 22 Serge Savard 2.00 .90
❑ 23 Steve Shutt 3.00 1.35
❑ 24 Mario Tremblay 1.50 .70
❑ 25 Murray Wilson 1.00 .45

## 1978-79 Canadiens Postcards

This 26-card set features posed color player photos taken from the shoulders up. All the pictures have a red background except for Ruel and Cournoyer who are shown against blue. A facsimile autograph appears in a white bottom border. The cards are unnumbered and checklisted below in alphabetical order. The key card in the set is Rod Langway, appearing two years before his Rookie Card.

NRMT-MT EXC
COMPLETE SET (26) 40.00 18.00
COMMON CARD (1-26) 1.00 .45

❑ 1 Scotty Bowman CO 3.00 1.35
❑ 2 Rick Chartraw 1.00 .45
❑ 3 Cam Connor 1.00 .45
❑ 4 Yvan Cournoyer 3.00 1.35
❑ 5 Ken Dryden 8.00 3.60
❑ 6 Brian Engblom 1.00 .45
❑ 7 Bob Gainey 3.00 1.35
❑ 8 Rejean Houle 1.00 .45
❑ 9 Pat Hughes 1.00 .45
❑ 10 Doug Jarvis 1.50 .70
❑ 11 Guy Lafleur 6.00 2.70
❑ 12 Yvon Lambert 1.00 .45
❑ 13 Rod Langway 4.00 1.80
❑ 14 Guy Lapointe 2.00 .90
❑ 15 Michel Larocque 1.50 .70
❑ 16 Pierre Larouche 2.00 .90
❑ 17 Jacques Lemaire 2.50 1.10
❑ 18 Gilles Lupien 1.00 .45
❑ 19 Pierre Mondou 1.00 .45
❑ 20 Mark Napier 1.00 .45
❑ 21 Doug Risebrough 1.00 .45
❑ 22 Larry Robinson 4.00 1.80
❑ 23 Claude Ruel CO 1.00 .45
❑ 24 Serge Savard 2.00 .90
❑ 25 Steve Shutt 3.00 1.35
❑ 26 Mario Tremblay 1.00 .45

## 1979-80 Canadiens Postcards

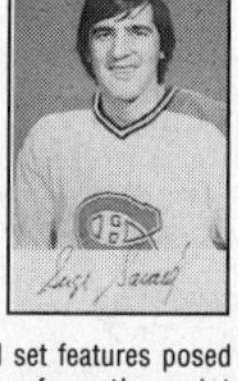

This 25-card set features posed color player photos taken from the waist up. All the pictures have a red background except for Ruel who is shown against blue. A facsimile autograph appears in a white bottom border. Several cards are the same as the 1978-79 issue. Bernie Geoffrion's card was not distributed after he resigned as coach on December 12, 1980. Richard Sevigny's card received limited distribution because of late issue. The cards are unnumbered and checklisted below in alphabetical order. The cards measure approximately 3 1/2" by 5 1/2" and the backs are blank.

NRMT-MT EXC
COMPLETE SET (25) 40.00 18.00
COMMON CARD (1-25) 1.00 .45

❑ 1 Rick Chartraw 1.00 .45
❑ 2 Normand Dupont 1.00 .45
❑ 3 Brian Engblom 1.00 .45
❑ 4 Bob Gainey 3.00 1.35
❑ 5 Bernie Geoffrion CO SP 5.00 2.20
❑ 6 Danny Geoffrion 1.00 .45
❑ 7 Denis Herron 1.50 .70
❑ 8 Rejean Houle 1.00 .45
❑ 9 Doug Jarvis 1.00 .45
❑ 10 Guy Lafleur 5.00 2.20
❑ 11 Yvon Lambert 1.00 .45
❑ 12 Rod Langway 2.00 .90
❑ 13 Guy Lapointe 2.00 .90
❑ 14 Michel Larocque 1.50 .70
❑ 15 Pierre Larouche 2.00 .90
❑ 16 Gilles Lupien 1.00 .45
❑ 17 Pierre Mondou 1.00 .45
❑ 18 Mark Napier 1.50 .70
❑ 19 Doug Risebrough 1.50 .70
❑ 20 Larry Robinson 3.00 1.35
❑ 21 Claude Ruel CO 1.00 .45
❑ 22 Serge Savard 1.50 .70
❑ 23 Richard Sevigny SP 5.00 2.20
❑ 24 Steve Shutt 2.00 .90
❑ 25 Mario Tremblay 1.50 .70

## 1980-81 Canadiens Postcards

This 26-card set features posed color player photos taken from the waist up against a blue background. A facsimile autograph appears in a white bottom border. The cards are unnumbered and checklisted below in alphabetical order. The cards measure approximately 3 1/2" by 5 1/2" and the backs are blank.

NRMT-MT EXC
COMPLETE SET (26) 30.00 13.50
COMMON CARD (1-26) 1.00 .45

❑ 1 Keith Acton 1.50 .70
❑ 2 Bill Baker 1.00 .45
❑ 3 Rick Chartraw 1.00 .45
❑ 4 Brian Engblom 1.00 .45
❑ 5 Bob Gainey 2.00 .90
❑ 6 Gaston Gingras 1.00 .45
❑ 7 Denis Herron 2.00 .90
❑ 8 Rejean Houle 1.50 .70
❑ 9 Doug Jarvis 1.00 .45
❑ 10 Guy Lafleur 5.00 2.20
❑ 11 Yvon Lambert 1.00 .45
❑ 12 Rod Langway 1.50 .70
❑ 13 Guy Lapointe 2.00 .90
❑ 14 Michel Larocque 2.00 .90
❑ 15 Pierre Larouche 1.50 .70
❑ 16 Pierre Mondou 1.00 .45
❑ 17 Mark Napier 1.00 .45
❑ 18 Chris Nilan 2.00 .90
❑ 19 Doug Risebrough 1.00 .45
❑ 20 Larry Robinson 3.00 1.35
❑ 21 Claude Ruel CO 1.00 .45
❑ 22 Serge Savard 1.50 .70
❑ 23 Richard Sevigny 1.00 .45
❑ 24 Steve Shutt 2.00 .90
❑ 25 Mario Tremblay 1.50 .70
❑ 26 Doug Wickenheiser 1.00 .45

## 1981-82 Canadiens Postcards

This 28-card set features posed color player photos taken from the waist up against a blue or blue-white background. A facsimile autograph appears in a white bottom border. Many cards are the same as in the 1980-81 set. The Gilbert Delorme card was short-printed. The cards are unnumbered and checklisted below in alphabetical order.

NRMT-MT EXC
COMPLETE SET (28) 35.00 16.00
COMMON CARD (1-28) .75 .35

❑ 1 Team Photo 3.00 1.35
❑ 2 Keith Acton 1.00 .45

❑ 3 Bob Berry CO .75 .35
❑ 4 Jeff Brubaker .75 .35
❑ 5 Gilbert Delorme SP 4.00 1.80
❑ 6 Brian Engblom .75 .35
❑ 7 Bob Gainey 2.00 .90
❑ 8 Gaston Gingras .75 .35
❑ 9 Denis Herron 1.25 .55
❑ 10 Rejean Houle 1.00 .45
❑ 11 Mark Hunter .75 .35
❑ 12 Doug Jarvis .75 .35
❑ 13 Guy Lafleur 5.00 2.20
❑ 14 Rod Langway 1.50 .70
❑ 15 Jacques Laperriere 1.50 .70
❑ 16 Guy Lapointe 1.50 .70
❑ 17 Craig Laughlin .75 .35
❑ 18 Pierre Mondou .75 .35
❑ 19 Mark Napier 1.00 .45
❑ 20 Chris Nilan 1.00 .45
❑ 21 Robert Picard .75 .35
❑ 22 Doug Risebrough .75 .35
❑ 23 Larry Robinson 3.00 1.35
❑ 24 Richard Sevigny 1.25 .55
❑ 25 Steve Shutt 2.00 .90
❑ 26 Mario Tremblay 1.00 .45
❑ 27 Rick Wamsley 1.25 .55
❑ 28 Doug Wickenheiser .75 .35

## 1982-83 Canadiens Postcards

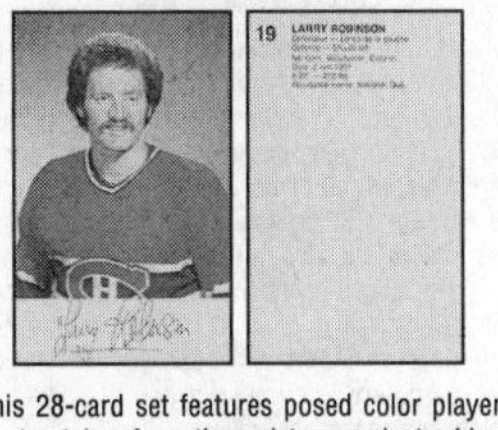

This 28-card set features posed color player photos taken from the waist up against a blue background. A facsimile autograph appears in a white bottom panel. Many photos are the same as in the 1980-81 and 1981-82 sets. Player information, jersey number, and the team logo are on the back. The Richard card has the same style but it is not originally part of the set; it was issued in 1983. The Root card was issued late in the year and thus was limited in its distribution. Some color variations appear in the Gainey and Picard cards. The cards are unnumbered and checklisted below in alphabetical order. Notable cards in the set include Guy Carbonneau and Mats Naslund appearing the year before their Rookie Card.

MINT NRMT
COMPLETE SET (28) 30.00 13.50
COMMON CARD (1-28) .75 .35

❑ 1 Keith Acton .75 .35
❑ 2 Bob Berry CO .75 .35
❑ 3 Guy Carbonneau 4.00 1.80
❑ 4 Dan Daoust .75 .35
❑ 5 Gilbert Delorme .75 .35
❑ 6 Bob Gainey 2.00 .90
❑ 7 Gaston Gingras .75 .35
❑ 8 Rick Green .75 .35
❑ 9 Rejean Houle .75 .35
❑ 10 Mark Hunter .75 .35
❑ 11 Guy Lafleur 5.00 2.20
❑ 12 Jacques Laperriere 1.00 .45
❑ 13 Craig Ludwig 1.50 .70
❑ 14 Pierre Mondou .75 .35
❑ 15 Mark Napier 1.00 .45
❑ 16 Mats Naslund 3.00 1.35
❑ 17 Ric Nattress .75 .35
❑ 18 Chris Nilan 1.00 .45
❑ 19 Robert Picard .75 .35
❑ 20 Henri Richard 3.00 1.35
❑ 21 Larry Robinson 3.00 1.35
❑ 22 Bill Root SP 2.00 .90
❑ 23 Richard Sevigny 1.25 .55
❑ 24 Steve Shutt 2.00 .90
❑ 25 Mario Tremblay 1.00 .45
❑ 26 Ryan Walter 1.00 .45
❑ 27 Rick Wamsley 1.25 .55
❑ 28 Doug Wickenheiser .75 .35

## 1982-83 Canadiens Steinberg

This 24-card set was sponsored by Steinberg and the Montreal Canadiens Hockey Club as the "Follow the Play" promotion. The cards were issued in a small vinyl photo album with one card per binder and measure approximately 3 1/2" by 4 15/16". A full color action photo of the player occupies the entire front of the card, and the player's facsimile signature is inscribed across the bottom of the picture. The back has a full-color posed (head and shoulders) photo of the player, uniform number, Steinberg logo, and basic biographical information. For a few of the players, the biography on the card back is written in French; those players are so noted in the checklist below. We have checklisted the cards below in alphabetical order, with sweater number to the right of the player's name. The cards are thin and glossy.

MINT NRMT
COMPLETE SET (24) 25.00 11.00
COMMON CARD (1-24) .50 .23

❑ 1 Keith Acton 12 .50 .23
❑ 2 Guy Carbonneau 21 3.00 1.35
❑ 3 Gilbert Delorme 27 .50 .23
(French bio)
❑ 4 Bob Gainey 23 1.50 .70
❑ 5 Rick Green 5 .50 .23
❑ 6 Mark Hunter 20 .50 .23
❑ 7 Rejean Houle 15 .50 .23
❑ 8 Guy Lafleur 10 4.00 1.80
❑ 9 Craig Ludwig 17 1.00 .45
❑ 10 Pierre Mondou 6 .50 .23
❑ 11 Mark Napier 31 .75 .35
❑ 12 Mats Naslund 26 2.00 .90
❑ 13 Ric Nattress 3 .50 .23
(French bio)
❑ 14 Chris Nilan 30 .75 .35
❑ 15 Robert Picard 24 .50 .23
❑ 16 Larry Robinson 19 2.00 .90
❑ 17 Bill Root 18 .50 .23
❑ 18 Richard Sevigny 33 1.00 .45
❑ 19 Steve Shutt 22 1.50 .70
❑ 20 Mario Tremblay 14 .75 .35
❑ 21 Ryan Walter 11 .75 .35
❑ 22 Rick Wamsley 1 1.00 .45
(French bio)
❑ 23 Doug Wickenheiser 25 .50 .23
❑ 24 Title Card 1.25 .55
Team photo (Canadiens celebrating on ice)
❑ xx Vinyl Card Album 5.00 2.20

## 1983-84 Canadiens Postcards

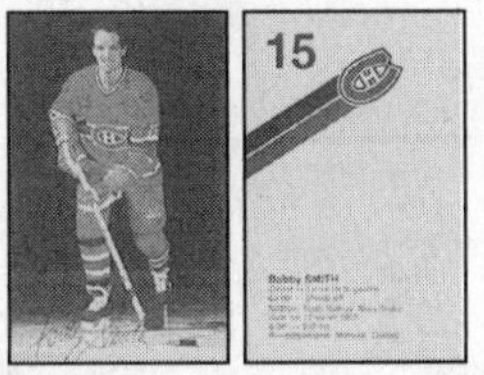

This 33-card set features color photos of players posed on the ice. A facsimile autograph appears at the bottom. Player information, jersey number, and the team logo are on the back. The team continued to issue cards throughout the season, so several card were distributed on a limited basis. The Laperriere card (number 14) is the same card as in the 1982-83 set. The Delorme and Wickenheiser cards were not issued as part of the set because of trade. Issued in 1984, the Beliveau card was not part of the team set but has the same style. The cards are unnumbered and checklisted below in alphabetical order. The key card in the set is Chris Chelios appearing the year before his Rookie Card.

MINT NRMT
COMPLETE SET (33) 40.00 18.00
COMMON CARD (1-33) .75 .35

❑ 1 Jean Beliveau 3.00 1.35
❑ 2 Bob Berry CO .75 .35
❑ 3 Guy Carbonneau 2.00 .90
❑ 4 Kent Carlson .75 .35
❑ 5 John Chabot .75 .35
❑ 6 Chris Chelios 10.00 4.50
❑ 7 Gilbert Delorme SP 3.00 1.35
❑ 8 Bob Gainey 1.50 .70
❑ 9 Rick Green .75 .35
❑ 10 Jean Hamel .75 .35
❑ 11 Mark Hunter .75 .35
❑ 12 Guy Lafleur 4.00 1.80
❑ 13 Jacques Lemaire 1.50 .70
❑ 14 Jacques Laperriere 1.00 .45
(Action shot)
❑ 15 Jacques Laperriere 1.00 .45
(Head shot)
❑ 16 Craig Ludwig 1.00 .45
❑ 17 Pierre Mondou .75 .35
❑ 18 Mats Naslund 2.00 .90
❑ 19 Ric Nattress .75 .35
❑ 20 Chris Nilan 1.00 .45
❑ 21 Steve Penney 1.00 .45
❑ 22 Jacques Plante 3.00 1.35
❑ 23 Larry Robinson 2.50 1.10
❑ 24 Bill Root .75 .35
❑ 25 Richard Sevigny 1.00 .45
❑ 26 Steve Shutt 1.50 .70
❑ 27 Bobby Smith 1.50 .70
❑ 28 Mario Tremblay 1.00 .45
❑ 29 Alfie Turcotte .75 .35
❑ 30 Perry Turnbull .75 .35
❑ 31 Ryan Walter .75 .35
❑ 32 Rick Wamsley 1.25 .55
❑ 33 Doug Wickenheiser SP 3.00 1.35

## 1984-85 Canadiens Postcards

This 31-card set features color photos of players posed on the ice. A facsimile autograph appears at the bottom. Player information, jersey number, and the team logo are on the back. Many cards are the same as in the 1983-84 set. The cards are unnumbered and checklisted below in alphabetical order.

MINT NRMT
COMPLETE SET (31) 30.00 13.50
COMMON CARD (1-31) .75 .35

❑ 1 Guy Carbonneau 1.50 .70
(Action on ice& foot raised& with puck)
❑ 2 Guy Carbonneau 1.50 .70
(Still& both feet on ice& no puck)
❑ 3 Kent Carlson .75 .35
❑ 4 Chris Chelios 6.00 2.70
(Same card as 1983-84& but with autograph on front)
❑ 5 Lucien Deblois .75 .35
❑ 6 Ron Flockhart .75 .35
❑ 7 Bob Gainey 1.50 .70
❑ 8 Rick Green .75 .35
❑ 9 Jean Hamel .75 .35
❑ 10 Mark Hunter .75 .35
❑ 11 Tom Kurvers .75 .35
❑ 12 Guy Lafleur 4.00 1.80
❑ 13 Jacques Laperriere 1.00 .45
❑ 14 Jacques Lemaire 1.50 .70
❑ 15 Craig Ludwig 1.00 .45
❑ 16 Mike McPhee 1.50 .70
❑ 17 Pierre Mondou .75 .35
❑ 18 Mats Naslund 2.00 .90
❑ 19 Ric Nattress .75 .35
❑ 20 Chris Nilan 1.00 .45
❑ 21 Steve Penney 1.00 .45
(Same card as 1983-84)
❑ 22 Steve Penney 1.00 .45
❑ 23 Jean Perron .75 .35
❑ 24 Larry Robinson 2.50 1.10
❑ 25 Bobby Smith 1.50 .70
❑ 26 Doug Soetaert 1.00 .45
❑ 27 Petr Svoboda 1.50 .70
❑ 28 Mario Tremblay .75 .35
❑ 29 Alfie Turcotte .75 .35
(Same card as 1983-84)
❑ 30 Alfie Turcotte .75 .35
(Autograph on front)
❑ 31 Ryan Walter 1.00 .45

## 1985-86 Canadiens Placemats

Sponsored by Pepsi-Cola and 7-Up, this set of seven placemats was issued to commemorate the Montreal Canadiens as the 1984-85 Division Champions. Each placemat measures approximately 11" by 17". On an yellow-orange background with a white border, the front carries a painted portrait, action shot and a facsimile autograph of two different players. Player name, position, and number, date and place of birth, and career statistics in French and English are also found on the front. The sponsors' logos appear in the upper right corner. The backs feature a red-and-white plaid design. The placemats are unnumbered. One placemat shows portraits of all twelve players with their facsimile autographs.

MINT NRMT
COMPLETE SET (7) 20.00 9.00
COMMON CARD (1-7) 2.00 .90

❑ 1 Bob Gainey 4.00 1.80
Guy Carbonneau
❑ 2 Mats Naslund 2.00 .90
Tom Kurvers
❑ 3 Chris Nilan 2.00 .90
Petr Svoboda
❑ 4 Steve Penney 5.00 2.20
Chris Chelios
❑ 5 Larry Robinson 4.00 1.80
Serge Boisvert
❑ 6 Mario Tremblay 2.00 .90
Bobby Smith
❑ 7 Hockey Stars 5.00 2.20
Steve Penney
Chris Chelios
Larry Robinson
Serge Boisvert
Mario Tremblay
Bobby Smith
Mats Naslund
Tom Kurvers
Bob Gainey
Guy Carbonneau
Chris Nilan
Petr Svoboda

## 1985-86 Canadiens Postcards

This 40-card set features color photos of players posed in red uniforms against a white background. A facsimile autograph appears on a red diagonal line in the lower right corner on most cards. However, there is some variation in the autograph location. Player information and the team logo are on the back. Several cards (1, 2, 3, 11, 14, 17, 19) were issued late in the season. The cards are unnumbered and checklisted below in alphabetical order. The key card in this set is Patrick Roy, which predates his Rookie Card by one year. Other notable early cards include Claude Lemieux, Stephane Richer, and Brian Skrudland.

MINT NRMT
COMPLETE SET (40) 60.00 27.00
COMMON CARD (1-40) .50 .23

❑ 1 Serge Boisvert SP 1.50 .70
(No red line or autograph)
❑ 2 Serge Boisvert SP 1.50 .70
(Portrait)
❑ 3 Randy Bucyk SP 1.50 .70
(No red line or autograph)
❑ 4 Guy Carbonneau 1.00 .45
❑ 5 Chris Chelios 4.00 1.80
❑ 6 Kjell Dahlin .50 .23
(J in autograph on stick)
❑ 7 Kjell Dahlin .50 .23
(E in autograph on stick)
❑ 8 Lucien Deblois .50 .23
❑ 9 Bob Gainey 1.50 .70
(B in autograph on stick)
❑ 10 Bob Gainey 1.50 .70
(G in autograph on stick)
❑ 11 Gaston Gingras SP 1.50 .70
❑ 12 Rick Green .50 .23
(No letters on stick)
❑ 13 Rick Green .50 .23
(C in autograph on stick)
❑ 14 John Kordic SP 5.00 2.20
(No red line or autograph)
❑ 15 Tom Kurvers .50 .23
❑ 16 Mike Lalor .50 .23
❑ 17 Claude Lemieux SP 8.00 3.60
(No red line or autograph)
❑ 18 Craig Ludwig .75 .35
❑ 19 David Maley SP 1.50 .70
(No red line or autograph)
❑ 20 Mike McPhee 1.00 .45
❑ 21 Sergio Momesso .75 .35
❑ 22 Mats Naslund 1.50 .70
❑ 23 Chris Nilan .75 .35
(Dot from i in Nilan touching toe)
❑ 24 Chris Nilan .75 .35
(Dot from i in Nilan away from toe)
❑ 25 Steve Penney .75 .35
❑ 26 Jean Perron .50 .23
(Portrait)
❑ 27 Stephane Richer 2.00 .90
❑ 28 Larry Robinson 2.50 1.10
❑ 29 Steve Rooney .50 .23
(Loop in R through skate toe)
❑ 30 Steve Rooney .50 .23
(Loop in R through skate laces)
❑ 31 Patrick Roy 25.00 11.00
❑ 32 Brian Skrudland 2.00 .90
❑ 33 Bobby Smith 1.00 .45
(B in autograph touching stick)
❑ 34 Bobby Smith 1.00 .45
(O in autograph on stick)
❑ 35 Doug Soetaert .75 .35
(T at end of name by pad)
❑ 36 Doug Soetaert .75 .35
(T at end of name away from pad)
❑ 37 Petr Svoboda .75 .35
❑ 38 Mario Tremblay .75 .35
(T in autograph touching blade)
❑ 39 Mario Tremblay .75 .35
(T in autograph away from blade)
❑ 40 Ryan Walter .75 .35

## 1985-86 Canadiens Provigo

This 25-sticker set of the Montreal Canadiens was produced by Provigo. The puffy (styrofoam-backed) stickers measure approximately 1 1/8" by 2 1/4" and feature a color head and shoulders photo of the player, with the player's number and name bordered by star-studded banners across the bottom of the picture. The Canadiens' logo is superimposed over the banner at its right end. The backs are blank. We have checklisted them below in alphabetical order, with the uniform number to the right of the player's name. The 25 stickers were to be attached to a cardboard poster. The poster measures approximately 20" by 11" and has 25 white spaces designated for the stickers on a red background. At the center is a picture of a goalie mask, with the Canadiens' logo above and slightly to the right. The back of the poster has a checklist, stripes in the team's colors, and two team logos. The set features early cards of Stephane Richer and Patrick Roy predating their actual Rookie Cards.

MINT NRMT
COMPLETE SET (25) 40.00 18.00
COMMON CARD (1-25) .50 .23

❑ 1 Guy Carbonneau 21 1.25 .55
❑ 2 Chris Chelios 24 4.00 1.80
❑ 3 Kjell Dahlin 20 .50 .23
❑ 4 Lucien Deblois 27 .50 .23
❑ 5 Bob Gainey 23 1.50 .70
❑ 6 Rick Green 5 .50 .23
❑ 7 Tom Kurvers 18 .50 .23
❑ 8 Mike Lalor 38 .50 .23
❑ 9 Craig Ludwig 17 .75 .35
❑ 10 Mike McPhee 35 1.00 .45
❑ 11 Sergio Momesso 36 .75 .35
❑ 12 Mats Naslund 26 1.50 .70
❑ 13 Chris Nilan 30 .75 .35
❑ 14 Steve Penney 37 .75 .35
❑ 15 Jean Perron CO .50 .23
❑ 16 Stephane Richer 44 2.00 .90
❑ 17 Larry Robinson 19 2.50 1.10
❑ 18 Steve Rooney 28 .50 .23
❑ 19 Patrick Roy 33 25.00 11.00
❑ 20 Brian Skrudland 39 2.00 .90
❑ 21 Bobby Smith 15 1.00 .45
❑ 22 Doug Soetaert 1 .75 .35
❑ 23 Petr Svoboda 25 .75 .35
❑ 24 Mario Tremblay 14 .75 .35
❑ 25 Ryan Walter 11 .75 .35
❑ NNO Provigo Poster 5.00 2.20

## 1986-87 Canadiens Postcards

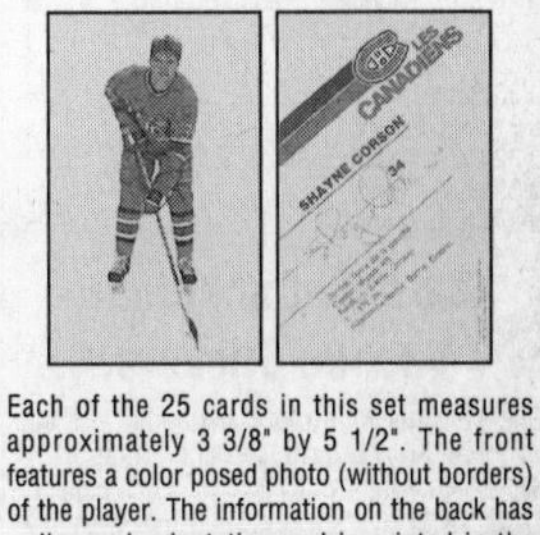

Each of the 25 cards in this set measures approximately 3 3/8" by 5 1/2". The front features a color posed photo (without borders) of the player. The information on the back has a diagonal orientation and is printed in the Canadiens' team colors read and blue. At the top on the back appears the Canadiens' logo,

followed by the player's name, his signature, and brief biographical information (in French and English). Notably, the Shayne Corson card in this set pre-dates his RC by three years.

| | MINT | NRMT |
|---|---|---|
| COMPLETE SET (25) | 35.00 | 16.00 |
| COMMON CARD (1-25) | .50 | .23 |
| ❑ 1 Guy Carbonneau 21 | 1.00 | .45 |
| ❑ 2 Chris Chelios 24 | 3.00 | 1.35 |
| ❑ 3 Shayne Corson 34 | 2.00 | .90 |
| ❑ 4 Kjell Dahlin 20 | .50 | .23 |
| ❑ 5 Bob Gainey 23 | 1.00 | .45 |
| ❑ 6 Rick Green 5 | .50 | .23 |
| ❑ 7 Brian Hayward 1 | 1.00 | .45 |
| ❑ 8 John Kordic 31 | 1.50 | .70 |
| ❑ 9 Mike Lalor 38 | .50 | .23 |
| ❑ 10 Jacques Laperriere ACO | .75 | .35 |
| ❑ 11 Claude Lemieux | 4.00 | 1.80 |
| ❑ 12 Craig Ludwig 17 | .50 | .23 |
| ❑ 13 Mike McPhee 35 | .75 | .35 |
| ❑ 14 Sergio Momesso 36 | .50 | .23 |
| ❑ 15 Mats Naslund 26 | 1.00 | .45 |
| ❑ 16 Chris Nilan 30 | .75 | .35 |
| ❑ 17 Jean Perron CO | .50 | .23 |
| ❑ 18 Stephane Richer 44 | 2.00 | .90 |
| ❑ 19 Larry Robinson 19 | 2.00 | .90 |
| ❑ 20 Patrick Roy 33 | 15.00 | 6.75 |
| ❑ 21 Scott Sandelin 3 | .50 | .23 |
| ❑ 22 Brian Skrudland 39 | 1.50 | .70 |
| ❑ 23 Bobby Smith 15 | .75 | .35 |
| ❑ 24 Petr Svoboda 25 | .50 | .23 |
| ❑ 25 Ryan Walter 11 | .75 | .35 |

## 1987-88 Canadiens Postcards

This 35-card set is in the postcard size format, with each card measuring approximately 3 1/2" by 5 1/2". The fronts feature full-bleed posed color action shots. In a diagonal format at the top of the back appears the team logo, followed by the player's name, his signature, and brief biographical information (in French and English). The cards are unnumbered and checklisted below in alphabetical order. There are two versions of the Stephane Richer postcard (#23); both are included in the complete set price.

| | MINT | NRMT |
|---|---|---|
| COMPLETE SET (35) | 30.00 | 13.50 |
| COMMON CARD (1-34) | .25 | .11 |
| ❑ 1 Francois Allaire ACO | .25 | .11 |
| ❑ 2 Guy Carbonneau | 1.00 | .45 |
| ❑ 3 Jose Charbonneau | .50 | .23 |
| ❑ 4 Chris Chelios | 2.50 | 1.10 |
| ❑ 5 Shayne Corson | 1.00 | .45 |
| ❑ 6 Kjell Dahlin | .50 | .23 |
| ❑ 7 Bob Gainey | 1.25 | .55 |
| ❑ 8 Rick Green | .50 | .23 |
| ❑ 9 Gaston Gringras | .50 | .23 |
| ❑ 10 Brian Hayward | .75 | .35 |
| ❑ 11 John Kordic | 1.50 | .70 |
| ❑ 12 Mike Lalor | .50 | .23 |
| ❑ 13 Jacques Laperriere ACO | .50 | .23 |
| ❑ 14 Claude Lemieux | 3.00 | 1.35 |
| ❑ 15 Craig Ludwig | .50 | .23 |
| ❑ 16 David Maley | .50 | .23 |
| ❑ 17 Mike McPhee | .75 | .35 |
| ❑ 18 Sergio Momesso | .50 | .23 |
| ❑ 19 Claude Mouton ANN | .25 | .11 |
| ❑ 20 Mats Naslund | 1.00 | .45 |
| ❑ 21 Chris Nilan | .75 | .35 |
| ❑ 22 Jean Perron CO | .25 | .11 |
| ❑ 23A Stephane Richer (With moustache) | 1.50 | .70 |
| ❑ 23B Stephane Richer (No moustache) | 1.50 | .70 |
| ❑ 24 Larry Robinson | 2.00 | .90 |
| ❑ 25 Steve Rooney | .50 | .23 |
| ❑ 26 Patrick Roy | 15.00 | 6.75 |
| ❑ 27 Scott Sandelin | .50 | .23 |
| ❑ 28 Serge Savard DIR | .75 | .35 |
| ❑ 29 Brian Skrudland | 1.25 | .55 |
| ❑ 30 Bobby Smith | .75 | .35 |
| ❑ 31 Petr Svoboda | .50 | .23 |
| ❑ 32 Gilles Thibaudeau | .50 | .23 |
| ❑ 33 Larry Trader | .50 | .23 |
| ❑ 34 Ryan Walter | .75 | .35 |

## 1987-88 Canadiens Vachon Stickers

Featuring the Montreal Canadiens, this set consists of 28 panels, each measuring approximately 2 7/8" by 5 9/16". Each panel is made up of five stickers, two that measure approximately 1 1/2" by 2 5/8", and three that measure approximately 1" by 1 11/16". The larger stickers carry color action player photos

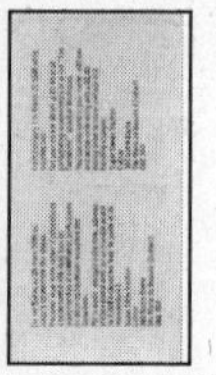

or team pictures. The smaller ones are close-ups of players or action shots. The stickers appear in a variety of combinations on the panels, with one panel showing small player shots and another panel carrying the same player shots but with different action photos. All told, 88 different stickers were printed. The back of the panel explains in French and English that albums are available for 49 cents at participating supermarkets and at "Les Canadiens" souvenir boutiques, and that collectors can send in 2.00 to Super Series Vachon and receive the album through the mail. The first six stickers can be pieced together to form a composite team photo. The stickers are numbered on the front.

| | MINT | NRMT |
|---|---|---|
| COMPLETE SET (88) | 40.00 | 18.00 |
| COMMON CARD (1-88) | .25 | .11 |
| ❑ 1 Canadiens Team Photo (Top left) | .25 | .11 |
| ❑ 2 Canadiens Team Photo (Top middle) | .25 | .11 |
| ❑ 3 Canadiens Team Photo (Top right) | .25 | .11 |
| ❑ 4 Canadiens Team Photo (Bottom left) | .25 | .11 |
| ❑ 5 Canadiens Team Photo (Bottom middle) | .25 | .11 |
| ❑ 6 Canadiens Team Photo (Bottom right) | .25 | .11 |
| ❑ 7 Jean Perron CO | .25 | .11 |
| ❑ 8 Jacques Laperriere ACO | .25 | .11 |
| ❑ 9 Francois Allaire ACO | .25 | .11 |
| ❑ 10 Jean Perron CO | .25 | .11 |
| ❑ 11 Jacques Laperriere | .25 | .11 |
| ❑ 12 Bob Gainey | .75 | .35 |
| ❑ 13 Bob Gainey | .75 | .35 |
| ❑ 14 Guy Carbonneau | .35 | .16 |
| ❑ 15 Guy Carbonneau | .35 | .16 |
| ❑ 16 Guy Carbonneau | .35 | .16 |
| ❑ 17 Michael McPhee | .35 | .16 |
| ❑ 18 Bob Gainey | .75 | .35 |
| ❑ 19 Chris Nilan | .35 | .16 |
| ❑ 20 Chris Nilan | .35 | .16 |
| ❑ 21 Guy Carbonneau | .35 | .16 |
| ❑ 22 Mike Lalor | .25 | .11 |
| ❑ 23 Patrick Roy and Guy Carbonneau | 4.00 | 1.80 |
| ❑ 24 Ryan Walter | .25 | .11 |
| ❑ 25 Ryan Walter | .25 | .11 |
| ❑ 26 Bobby Smith | .35 | .16 |
| ❑ 27 Mats Naslund | .35 | .16 |
| ❑ 28 Bobby Smith | .35 | .16 |
| ❑ 29 Mike McPhee | .35 | .16 |
| ❑ 30 Bobby Smith | .35 | .16 |
| ❑ 31 Claude Lemieux | 2.00 | .90 |
| ❑ 32 Brian Skrudland | .25 | .11 |
| ❑ 33 Craig Ludwig | .35 | .16 |
| ❑ 34 Brian Skrudland | .35 | .16 |
| ❑ 35 Craig Ludwig | .25 | .11 |
| ❑ 36 Brian Skrudland | .35 | .16 |
| ❑ 37 Mike McPhee | .35 | .16 |
| ❑ 38 Mike McPhee | .35 | .16 |
| ❑ 39 Kjell Dahlin | .25 | .11 |
| ❑ 40 Kjell Dahlin | .25 | .11 |
| ❑ 41 Bobby Smith | .35 | .16 |
| ❑ 42 Patrick Roy | 5.00 | 2.20 |
| ❑ 43 Patrick Roy | 5.00 | 2.20 |
| ❑ 44 Larry Trader | .25 | .11 |
| ❑ 45 Mats Naslund | .50 | .23 |
| ❑ 46 Mats Naslund | .50 | .23 |
| ❑ 47 Mats Naslund | .50 | .23 |
| ❑ 48 Mats Naslund | .50 | .23 |
| ❑ 49 Shayne Corson | .50 | .23 |
| ❑ 50 Shayne Corson | .50 | .23 |
| ❑ 51 Stephane Richer | .50 | .23 |
| ❑ 52 Stephane Richer | .50 | .23 |
| ❑ 53 Bob Gainey | .75 | .35 |
| ❑ 54 Stephane Richer | .50 | .23 |
| ❑ 55 Sergio Momesso | .25 | .11 |
| ❑ 56 Sergio Momesso | .25 | .11 |
| ❑ 57 John Kordic | 1.00 | .45 |
| ❑ 58 John Kordic | 1.00 | .45 |
| ❑ 59 Mike Lalor | .25 | .11 |
| ❑ 60 Mike Lalor | .25 | .11 |
| ❑ 61 Brian Hayward | .35 | .16 |
| ❑ 62 Guy Carbonneau | .35 | .16 |
| ❑ 63 Guy Carbonneau | .35 | .16 |
| ❑ 64 Brian Hayward | .35 | .16 |
| ❑ 65 Rick Green | .25 | .11 |
| ❑ 66 Rick Green | .25 | .11 |
| ❑ 67 Brian Hayward | .35 | .16 |
| ❑ 68 Rick Green | .25 | .11 |
| ❑ 69 Patrick Roy | 5.00 | 2.20 |
| ❑ 70 Rick Green | .25 | .11 |
| ❑ 71 Patrick Roy | 5.00 | 2.20 |
| ❑ 72 Larry Robinson | 1.00 | .45 |
| ❑ 73 Larry Robinson | 1.00 | .45 |
| ❑ 74 Patrick Roy | 5.00 | 2.20 |
| ❑ 75 Petr Svoboda | .25 | .11 |
| ❑ 76 Patrick Roy | 5.00 | 2.20 |
| ❑ 77 Petr Svoboda | .25 | .11 |
| ❑ 78 Chris Chelios | 1.50 | .70 |
| ❑ 79 Chris Chelios | 1.50 | .70 |
| ❑ 80 Craig Ludwig | .35 | .16 |
| ❑ 81 Craig Ludwig | .35 | .16 |
| ❑ 82 Chris Chelios | 1.50 | .70 |
| ❑ 83 Chris Chelios | 1.50 | .70 |
| ❑ 84 Brian Hayward | .35 | .16 |
| ❑ 85 Craig Ludwig | .35 | .16 |
| ❑ 86 Bobby Smith | .35 | .16 |
| ❑ 87 Mats Naslund | .35 | .16 |
| ❑ 88 Bob Gainey | .75 | .35 |
| ❑ xx Sticker Album | 5.00 | 2.20 |

## 1988-89 Canadiens Postcards

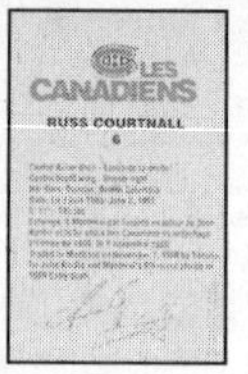


This 30-card, team-issued set measures approximately 3 1/2" by 5 1/2" and features full-bleed color player photos. The players are posed on the ice against a white background. The coaches' cards feature color portraits against a black background. The backs are white and show the team name and logo in large red letters at the top. The player's name, number, and biography are printed in blue. A facsimile autograph at the bottom rounds out the back. The cards are unnumbered and checklisted below in alphabetical order.

| | MINT | NRMT |
|---|---|---|
| COMPLETE SET (30) | 25.00 | 11.00 |
| COMMON CARD (1-30) | .25 | .11 |
| ❑ 1 Francois Allaire ACO | .25 | .11 |
| ❑ 2 Pat Burns CO | 1.00 | .45 |
| ❑ 3 Guy Carbonneau | 1.00 | .45 |
| ❑ 4 Jose Charbonneau | .50 | .23 |
| ❑ 5 Chris Chelios | 2.00 | .90 |
| ❑ 6 Ronald Corey PRES | .25 | .11 |
| ❑ 7 Shayne Corson | 1.00 | .45 |
| ❑ 8 Russ Courtnall | 1.00 | .45 |
| ❑ 9 Eric Desjardins | 1.50 | .70 |
| ❑ 10 Bob Gainey | 1.00 | .45 |
| ❑ 11 Brent Gilchrist | .75 | .35 |
| ❑ 12 Rick Green | .50 | .23 |
| ❑ 13 Brian Hayward | .75 | .35 |
| ❑ 14 Mike Keane | 1.00 | .45 |
| ❑ 15 Mike Lalor | .50 | .23 |
| ❑ 16 Jacques Laperriere ACO | .50 | .23 |
| ❑ 17 Claude Lemieux | 1.50 | .70 |
| ❑ 18 Craig Ludwig | .75 | .35 |
| ❑ 19 Steven Martinson | .50 | .23 |
| ❑ 20 Mike McPhee | .75 | .35 |
| ❑ 21 Mats Naslund | 1.00 | .45 |
| ❑ 22 Stephane Richer | 1.00 | .45 |
| ❑ 23 Larry Robinson | 2.00 | .90 |
| ❑ 24 Patrick Roy | 10.00 | 4.50 |
| ❑ 25 Serge Savard DIR | 1.00 | .45 |
| ❑ 26 Brian Skrudland | 1.00 | .45 |
| ❑ 27 Bobby Smith | .75 | .35 |
| ❑ 28 Petr Svoboda | .50 | .23 |
| ❑ 30 Ryan Walter | .50 | .23 |
| ❑ 39 Gilles Thibaudeau | .50 | .23 |

## 1989-90 Canadiens Kraft

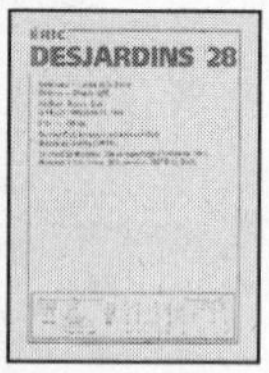


This 24-card set of Montreal Canadiens was sponsored by Le Journal de Montreal and Kraft Foods. The cards were issued as two four-card insert sheets in Les Canadiens magazine. The cards measure approximately 3 3/4" by 5 7/16". The front features a posed color photo of the player on white card stock. Thin red, white, and blue borders outline the card face, and the sponsors' logos appear in the lower corners. The upper right-hand corner of the border is formed by text rather than by the color lines. The back gives the player's name and number in large red print at the top. Brief biographical information is given (in French and English) below the player's name in black lettering. The card back is framed by a thin blue border. The red box at the bottom is filled with statistical information. The cards are unnumbered and hence are listed below in alphabetical order by player name with sweater number after the name.

| | MINT | NRMT |
|---|---|---|
| COMPLETE SET (24) | 25.00 | 11.00 |
| COMMON CARD (1-24) | .75 | .35 |
| ❑ 1 Pat Burns CO | 1.00 | .45 |
| ❑ 2 Guy Carbonneau 21 | 1.00 | .45 |
| ❑ 3 Chris Chelios 24 | 2.50 | 1.10 |
| ❑ 4 Shayne Corson 27 | 1.50 | .70 |
| ❑ 5 Russ Courtnall 6 | 1.00 | .45 |
| ❑ 6 J.J. Daigneault 48 | .75 | .35 |
| ❑ 7 Eric Desjardins 28 | 1.00 | .45 |
| ❑ 8 Todd Ewen 36 | .75 | .35 |
| ❑ 9 Brent Gilchrist 41 | .75 | .35 |
| ❑ 10 Brian Hayward 1 | 1.00 | .45 |
| ❑ 11 Mike Keane 12 | 1.00 | .45 |
| ❑ 12 Stephan Lebeau 47 | 1.50 | .70 |
| ❑ 13 Sylvain Lefebvre 3 | 1.00 | .45 |
| ❑ 14 Claude Lemieux 32 | 2.00 | .90 |
| ❑ 15 Craig Ludwig 17 | .75 | .35 |
| ❑ 16 Mike McPhee 35 | 1.00 | .45 |
| ❑ 17 Mats Naslund 26 | 1.50 | .70 |
| ❑ 18 Stephane Richer 44 | 1.50 | .70 |
| ❑ 19 Patrick Roy 33 | 8.00 | 3.60 |
| ❑ 20 Mathieu Schneider 18 | 2.00 | .90 |
| ❑ 21 Brian Skrudland 39 | 1.00 | .45 |
| ❑ 22 Bobby Smith 15 | 1.00 | .45 |
| ❑ 23 Petr Svoboda 25 | .75 | .35 |
| ❑ 24 Ryan Walter 11 | .75 | .35 |

## 1989-90 Canadiens Postcards

This 32-card set measures approximately 3 7/16" by 5 7/16" and features borderless color player photos. The players are posed on the ice against a white background. The coaches' cards feature color portraits against a black background. The backs are white and carry the team name and logo in large red letters at the top. The player's name, jersey number, and biography are printed in blue. A facsimile autograph at the bottom rounds out the back. The cards are unnumbered and checklisted below in alphabetical order.

| | MINT | NRMT |
|---|---|---|
| COMPLETE SET (32) | 25.00 | 11.00 |
| COMMON CARD (1-32) | .25 | .11 |
| ❑ 1 Francois Allaire ACO | .25 | .11 |
| ❑ 2 Pat Burns CO | 1.00 | .45 |
| ❑ 3 Guy Carbonneau | .75 | .35 |
| ❑ 4 Chris Chelios | 1.50 | .70 |
| ❑ 5 Tom Chorske | .50 | .23 |
| ❑ 6 Ronald Corey PR | .25 | .11 |
| ❑ 7 Shayne Corson | 1.00 | .45 |
| ❑ 8 Russ Courtnall | 1.00 | .45 |
| ❑ 9 Jean-Jacques Daigneault | .50 | .23 |
| ❑ 10 Eric Desjardins | 1.00 | .45 |
| ❑ 11 Martin Desjardins | .50 | .23 |
| ❑ 12 Donald Dufresne | .50 | .23 |
| ❑ 13 Brent Gilchrist | .50 | .23 |
| ❑ 14 Brian Hayward | .75 | .35 |
| ❑ 15 Mike Keane | .75 | .35 |
| ❑ 16 Jacques Laperriere ACO | .50 | .23 |
| ❑ 17 Stephan Lebeau | .75 | .35 |
| ❑ 18 Sylvain Lefebvre | 1.00 | .45 |
| ❑ 19 Claude Lemieux | 1.00 | .45 |
| ❑ 20 Jocelyn Lemieux | .50 | .23 |
| ❑ 21 Craig Ludwig | .50 | .23 |
| ❑ 22 Jyrki Lumme | 1.00 | .45 |
| ❑ 23 Steven Martinson | .50 | .23 |
| ❑ 24 Mike McPhee | .75 | .35 |
| ❑ 25 Mats Naslund | 1.00 | .45 |
| ❑ 26 Stephane Richer | 1.00 | .45 |
| ❑ 27 Patrick Roy | 6.00 | 2.70 |
| ❑ 28 Serge Savard DIR | .50 | .23 |
| ❑ 29 Brian Skrudland | 1.00 | .45 |
| ❑ 30 Bobby Smith | .75 | .35 |
| ❑ 31 Petr Svoboda | .75 | .35 |
| ❑ 32 Ryan Walter | .50 | .23 |

## 1989-90 Canadiens Provigo Figurines

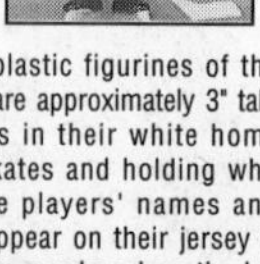

These 13 plastic figurines of the 1989-90 Canadiens are approximately 3" tall and show the players in their white home jerseys, wearing skates and holding white hockey sticks. The players' names and uniform numbers appear on their jersey backs. The figurines are numbered on the backs of the hockey sticks. The original issue price for these figurines was 1.99 Canadian. The figurines were distributed in a package with a coupon booklet.

| | MINT | NRMT |
|---|---|---|
| COMPLETE SET (13) | 60.00 | 27.00 |
| COMMON CARD | 3.00 | 1.35 |
| ❑ 6 Russ Courtnall | 4.00 | 1.80 |
| ❑ 15 Bobby Smith | 4.00 | 1.80 |
| ❑ 17 Craig Ludwig | 3.00 | 1.35 |
| ❑ 21 Guy Carbonneau | 4.00 | 1.80 |
| ❑ 23 Bob Gainey | 5.00 | 2.20 |
| ❑ 24 Chris Chelios | 8.00 | 3.60 |
| ❑ 25 Petr Svoboda | 3.00 | 1.35 |
| ❑ 26 Mats Naslund | 5.00 | 2.20 |
| ❑ 27 Shayne Corson | 5.00 | 2.20 |
| ❑ 33 Patrick Roy | 25.00 | 11.00 |
| ❑ 35 Mike McPhee | 3.00 | 1.35 |
| ❑ 39 Brian Skrudland | 4.00 | 1.80 |
| ❑ 44 Stephane Richer | 5.00 | 2.20 |

## 1990-91 Canadiens Postcards

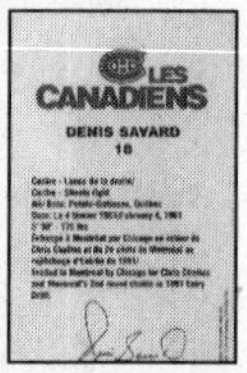


This 33-card set measures approximately 3 1/2" by 5 1/2" and features borderless color player photos. The players are posed on the ice against a white background. The coaches' cards feature color portraits against a black background. The backs are white and carry the team name and logo in large red letters at the top. The player's name, jersey number, and biography are printed in blue. A facsimile autograph at the bottom rounds out the back. The cards are unnumbered and checklisted below in alphabetical order.

| | MINT | NRMT |
|---|---|---|
| COMPLETE SET (33) | 25.00 | 11.00 |
| COMMON CARD (1-33) | .25 | .11 |
| ❑ 1 Francois Allaire ACO | .25 | .11 |
| ❑ 2 Jean-Claude Bergeron | .75 | .35 |
| ❑ 3 Benoit Brunet | .50 | .23 |
| ❑ 4 Pat Burns CO | .75 | .35 |
| ❑ 5 Guy Carbonneau | .75 | .35 |
| ❑ 6 Andrew Cassels | .75 | .35 |
| ❑ 7 Tom Chorske | .50 | .23 |
| ❑ 8 Ronald Corey PR | .25 | .11 |
| ❑ 9 Shayne Corson | 1.00 | .45 |
| ❑ 10 Russ Courtnall | .75 | .35 |
| ❑ 11 Jean-Jacques Daigneault | .50 | .23 |
| ❑ 12 Eric Desjardins | 1.00 | .45 |
| ❑ 13 Gerald Diduck | .50 | .23 |
| ❑ 14 Donald Dufresne | .50 | .23 |
| ❑ 15 Todd Ewen | .60 | .25 |
| ❑ 16 Brent Gilchrist | .50 | .23 |
| ❑ 17 Mike Keane | .75 | .35 |
| ❑ 18 Jacques Laperriere ACO | .50 | .23 |
| ❑ 19 Stephan Lebeau | .50 | .23 |
| ❑ 20 Sylvain Lefebvre | .75 | .35 |
| ❑ 21 Mike McPhee | .75 | .35 |
| ❑ 22 Lyle Odelein | 1.00 | .45 |
| ❑ 23 Mark Pederson | .50 | .23 |
| ❑ 24 Stephane Richer | .75 | .35 |
| ❑ 25 Patrick Roy | 6.00 | 2.70 |
| ❑ 26 Denis Savard | 1.50 | .70 |
| ❑ 27 Serge Savard DIR | .75 | .35 |
| ❑ 28 Mathieu Schneider | 1.00 | .45 |
| ❑ 29 Brian Skrudland | 1.00 | .45 |
| ❑ 30 Petr Svoboda | .75 | .35 |
| ❑ 31 Charles Thiffault ACO | .25 | .11 |
| ❑ 32 Sylvain Turgeon | .50 | .23 |
| ❑ 33 Ryan Walter | .50 | .23 |

## 1991 Canadiens Panini Team Stickers

This 32-sticker set was issued in a plastic bag that contained two 16-sticker sheets (approximately 9" by 12") and a foldout poster, "Super Poster - Hockey 91", on which the stickers could be affixed. The players' names appear only on the poster, not on the stickers. Each sticker measures about 2 1/8" by 2 7/8" and features a color player action shot on its white-bordered front. The back of the white sticker sheet is lined off into 16 panels, each carrying the logos for Panini, the NHL, and the NHLPA, as well as the same number that appears on the front of the sticker. Every Canadian NHL team was featured in this promotion. Each team set was available by mail-order from Panini Canada Ltd. for 2.99 plus 50 cents for shipping and handling.

| | MINT | NRMT |
|---|---|---|
| COMPLETE SET (32) | 5.00 | 2.20 |
| COMMON STICKER (1-24) | .05 | .02 |
| COMMON STICKER (A-H) | .15 | .07 |
| ❑ 1 Jean-Claude Bergeron | .10 | .05 |
| ❑ 2 Guy Carbonneau | .10 | .05 |
| ❑ 3 Andrew Cassels | .15 | .07 |
| ❑ 4 Tom Chorske | .05 | .02 |
| ❑ 5 Shayne Corson | .15 | .07 |
| ❑ 6 Russ Courtnall | .15 | .07 |

| Card | MINT | NRMT |
|---|---|---|
| 7 Jean-Jacques Daigneault | .10 | .05 |
| 8 Eric Desjardins | .10 | .05 |
| 9 Gerald Diduck | .05 | .02 |
| 10 Donald Dufresne | .05 | .02 |
| 11 Todd Ewen | .05 | .02 |
| 12 Brent Gilchrist | .10 | .05 |
| 13 Mike Keane | .10 | .05 |
| 14 Stephan Lebeau | .10 | .05 |
| 15 Sylvain Lefebvre | .10 | .05 |
| 16 Mike McPhee | .10 | .05 |
| 17 Mark Pederson | .05 | .02 |
| 18 Stephane Richer | .25 | .11 |
| 19 Patrick Roy | 2.00 | .90 |
| 20 Denis Savard | .35 | .16 |
| 21 Mathieu Schneider | .10 | .05 |
| 22 Brian Skrudland | .10 | .05 |
| 23 Petr Svoboda | .10 | .05 |
| 24 Ryan Walter | .10 | .05 |
| A Team Logo Left Side | .15 | .07 |
| B Team Logo Right Side | .15 | .07 |
| C Canadiens in Action Upper Left Corner | .15 | .07 |
| D Canadiens in Action Lower Left Corner | .15 | .07 |
| E Game Action Upper Right Corner | .15 | .07 |
| F Game Action Lower Right Corner | .15 | .07 |
| G Patrick Roy | 2.00 | .90 |
| H Game Action | .25 | .11 |

## 1991-92 Canadiens Postcards

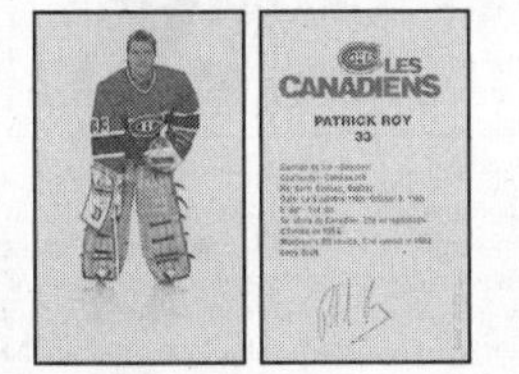

This 31-card team-issued set measures approximately 3 1/2" by 5 1/2". The fronts feature full-bleed color photos, with the players posed in front of a white background. The backs are white and show the team name in large red letters at the top. The player's name, number, and biography (in French and English) are printed in blue. A facsimile autograph at the bottom rounds out the back. The cards are unnumbered and checklisted below in alphabetical order.

| | MINT | NRMT |
|---|---|---|
| COMPLETE SET (31) | 25.00 | 11.00 |
| COMMON CARD (1-31) | .25 | .11 |
| 1 Francois Allaire ACO | .25 | .11 |
| 2 Patrice Brisebois | .75 | .35 |
| 3 Pat Burns CO | .75 | .35 |
| 4 Guy Carbonneau | .75 | .35 |
| 5 Ronald Corey PRES | .25 | .11 |
| 6 Shayne Corson | 1.00 | .45 |
| 7 Alain Cote | .50 | .23 |
| 8 Russ Courtnall | 1.00 | .45 |
| 9 Jean-Jacques Daigneault | .50 | .23 |
| 10 Eric Desjardins | .75 | .35 |
| 11 Donald Dufresne | .50 | .23 |
| 12 Todd Ewen | .50 | .23 |
| 13 Brent Gilchrist | .75 | .35 |
| 14 Mike Keane | .75 | .35 |
| 15 Jacques Laperriere ACO | .50 | .23 |
| 16 Stephan Lebeau | .50 | .23 |
| 17 John LeClair | 6.00 | 2.70 |
| 18 Sylvain Lefebvre | .75 | .35 |
| 19 Mike McPhee | .75 | .35 |
| 20 Kirk Muller | 1.00 | .45 |
| 21 Lyle Odelein | .75 | .35 |
| 22 Andre Racicot | .75 | .35 |
| 23 Mario Roberge | .50 | .23 |
| 24 Patrick Roy | 5.00 | 2.20 |
| 25 Denis Savard | 1.00 | .45 |
| 26 Serge Savard DIR | .75 | .35 |
| 27 Mathieu Schneider | .75 | .35 |
| 28 Brian Skrudland | .75 | .35 |
| 29 Petr Svoboda | .50 | .23 |
| 30 Charles Thiffault ACO | .25 | .11 |
| 31 Sylvain Turgeon | .50 | .23 |

## 1992-93 Canadiens Postcards

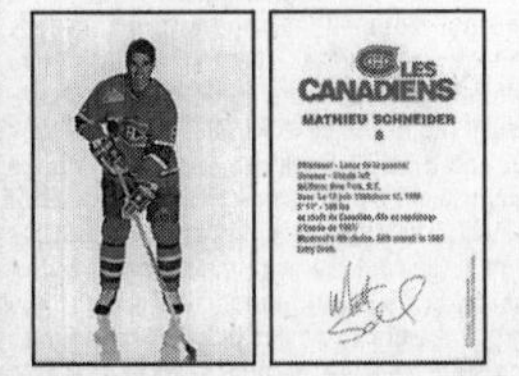

This 27-card team-issued set measures 3 1/2" by 5 1/2" and features full-bleed glossy color player photos. The players are posed on the ice against a white background. The backs are white and show the team name in large red letters at the top. The player's name, number, and biography are printed in blue. A facsimile autograph at the bottom rounds out the back. The cards are unnumbered and checklisted below in alphabetical order.

| | MINT | NRMT |
|---|---|---|
| COMPLETE SET (27) | 18.00 | 8.00 |
| COMMON CARD (1-27) | .50 | .23 |
| 1 Brian Bellows | .75 | .35 |
| 2 Patrice Brisebois | .50 | .23 |
| 3 Benoit Brunet | .50 | .23 |
| 4 Guy Carbonneau | .75 | .35 |
| 5 Jean-Jacques Daigneault | .50 | .23 |
| 6 Vincent Damphousse | 1.00 | .45 |
| 7 Eric Desjardins | .75 | .35 |
| 8 Jacques Demers CO | .75 | .35 |
| 9 Gilbert Dionne | .50 | .23 |
| 10 Donald Dufresne | .50 | .23 |
| 11 Todd Ewen | .50 | .23 |
| 12 Kevin Haller | .50 | .23 |
| 13 Sean Hill | .50 | .23 |
| 14 Mike Keane | .75 | .35 |
| 15 Patric Kjellberg | .50 | .23 |
| 16 Stephan Lebeau | .50 | .23 |
| 17 John LeClair | 3.00 | 1.35 |
| 18 Kirk Muller | 1.00 | .45 |
| 19 Lyle Odelein | .75 | .35 |
| 20 Oleg Petrov | .50 | .23 |
| 21 Andre Racicot | .60 | .25 |
| 22 Mario Roberge | .50 | .23 |
| 23 Ed Ronan | .50 | .23 |
| 24 Patrick Roy | 4.00 | 1.80 |
| 25 Denis Savard | 1.00 | .45 |
| 26 Mathieu Schneider | .75 | .35 |
| 27 Brian Skrudland | .75 | .35 |

## 1993-94 Canadiens Molson

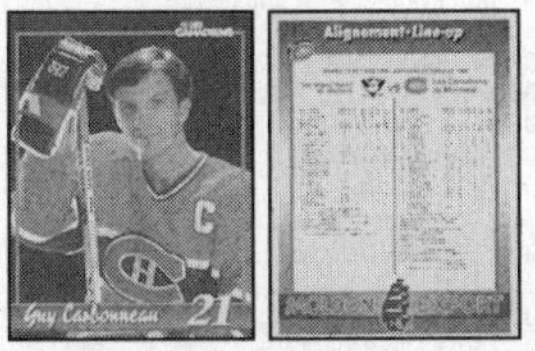

Measuring approximately 8" by 10 1/2", this ten-card set was sponsored by Molson and was apparently distributed in conjunction with certain games throughout the season. The fronts feature full-bleed posed color photos. The photos are accented by a red line on the top and each side; at the bottom, a blue stripe carries the player's name and his uniform number. Inside a white outer border and a fading team color-coded inner border, the backs present team line-ups in English and French for the Canadiens and the respective visiting team. The cards are unnumbered and checklisted below in alphabetical order.

| | MINT | NRMT |
|---|---|---|
| COMPLETE SET (10) | 50.00 | 22.00 |
| COMMON CARD (1-10) | 5.00 | 2.20 |
| 1 Brian Bellows | 6.00 | 2.70 |
| 2 Benoit Brunet | 5.00 | 2.20 |
| 3 Guy Carbonneau | 6.00 | 2.70 |
| 4 Vincent Damphousse | 10.00 | 4.50 |
| 5 Jean-Jacques Daigneault | 8.00 | 3.60 |
| 6 Kevin Haller | 5.00 | 2.20 |
| 7 Mike Keane | 6.00 | 2.70 |
| 8 Kirk Muller | 6.00 | 2.70 |
| 9 Peter Popovic | 5.00 | 2.20 |
| 10 Mathieu Schneider | 6.00 | 2.70 |

## 1993-94 Canadiens Postcards

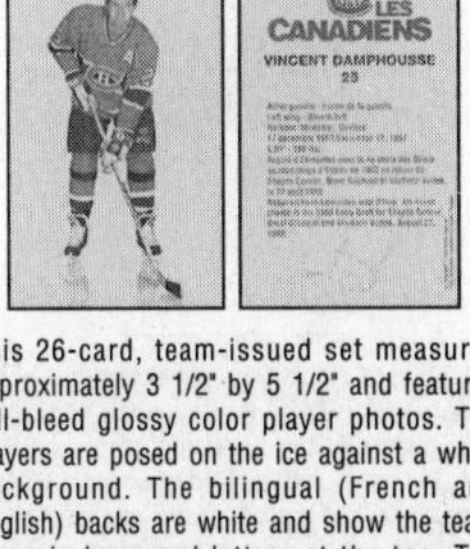

This 26-card, team-issued set measures approximately 3 1/2" by 5 1/2" and features full-bleed glossy color player photos. The players are posed on the ice against a white background. The bilingual (French and English) backs are white and show the team name in large red letters at the top. The player's name, number, and biography are printed in blue. A facsimile autograph at the bottom rounds out the back. The cards are unnumbered and checklisted below in alphabetical order.

| | MINT | NRMT |
|---|---|---|
| COMPLETE SET (26) | 15.00 | 6.75 |
| COMMON CARD (1-26) | .50 | .23 |
| 1 Brian Bellows | .75 | .35 |
| 2 Patrice Brisebois | .60 | .25 |
| 3 Benoit Brunet | .50 | .23 |
| 4 Guy Carbonneau | .75 | .35 |
| 5 Jean-Jacques Daigneault | .50 | .23 |
| 6 Vincent Damphousse | 1.00 | .45 |
| 7 Jacques Demers CO | .50 | .23 |
| 8 Eric Desjardins | .75 | .35 |
| 9 Gilbert Dionne | .50 | .23 |
| 10 Paul DiPietro | .50 | .23 |
| 11 Kevin Haller | .50 | .23 |
| 12 Mike Keane | .60 | .25 |
| 13 Stephan Lebeau | .50 | .23 |
| 14 John LeClair | 2.50 | 1.10 |
| 15 Gary Leeman | .50 | .23 |
| 16 Kirk Muller | .75 | .35 |
| 17 Lyle Odelein | .75 | .35 |
| 18 Peter Popovic | .50 | .23 |
| 19 Andre Racicot | .60 | .25 |
| 20 Rob Ramage | .50 | .23 |
| 21 Mario Roberge | .50 | .23 |
| 22 Ed Ronan | .50 | .23 |
| 23 Patrick Roy | 4.00 | 1.80 |
| 24 Mathieu Schneider | .75 | .35 |
| 25 Pierre Sevigny | .50 | .23 |
| 26 Ron Wilson | .50 | .23 |

## 1994-95 Canadiens Postcards

This 27-card set measures approximately 3 1/2" by 5 1/2" and features borderless color player photos. The players are posed on the ice against a white background. The backs are white and carry the team name and logo in large red letters at the top. The player's name, jersey number, and biography are printed in blue. A facsimile autograph at the bottom rounds out the back. The cards are unnumbered and checklisted below in alphabetical order.

| | MINT | NRMT |
|---|---|---|
| COMPLETE SET (27) | 15.00 | 6.75 |
| COMMON CARD (1-27) | .50 | .23 |
| 1 Brian Bellows | .75 | .35 |
| 2 Donald Brashear | .50 | .23 |
| 3 Patrice Brisebois | .60 | .25 |
| 4 Benoit Brunet | .50 | .23 |
| 5 J.J Daigneault | .50 | .23 |
| 6 Vincent Damphousse | 1.00 | .45 |
| 7 Jacques Demers CO | .50 | .23 |
| 8 Eric Desjardins | .75 | .35 |
| 9 Gilbert Dionne | .50 | .23 |
| 10 Paul DiPietro | .50 | .23 |
| 11 Gerry Fleming | .50 | .23 |
| 12 Bryan Fogarty | .50 | .23 |
| 13 Mike Keane | .60 | .25 |
| 14 John LeClair | 2.00 | .90 |
| 15 Jim Montgomery | .50 | .23 |
| 16 Kirk Muller | .75 | .35 |
| 17 Lyle Odelein | .75 | .35 |
| 18 Oleg Petrov | .50 | .23 |
| 19 Peter Popovic | .50 | .23 |
| 20 Yves Racine | .50 | .23 |
| 21 Ed Ronan | .50 | .23 |
| 22 Patrick Roy | 4.00 | 1.80 |
| 23 Brian Savage | .75 | .35 |
| 24 Mathieu Schneider | .75 | .35 |
| 25 Pierre Sevigny | .50 | .23 |
| 26 Turner Stevenson | .50 | .23 |
| 27 Ron Tugnutt | .75 | .35 |

## 1995-96 Canadiens Postcards

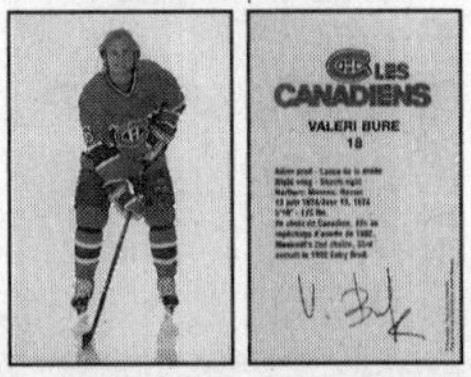

This 20-card set measures approximately 3 1/2" by 5 1/2" and features borderless color player photos. The players are posed on the ice against a white background. The backs are white and carry the team name and logo in large red letters at the top. The player's name, jersey number, and biography are printed in blue. A facsimile autograph at the bottom rounds out the back. The cards are unnumbered and checklisted below in alphabetical order.

| | MINT | NRMT |
|---|---|---|
| COMPLETE SET (20) | 15.00 | 6.75 |
| COMMON CARD (1-20) | .50 | .23 |
| 1 Donald Brashear | .50 | .23 |
| 2 Patrice Brisebois | .50 | .23 |
| 3 Benoit Brunet | .50 | .23 |
| 4 Valeri Bure | .50 | .23 |
| 5 Marc Bureau | .50 | .23 |
| 6 Vincent Damphousse | 1.00 | .45 |
| 7 Mike Keane | .60 | .25 |
| 8 Saku Koivu | 4.00 | 1.80 |
| 9 Vladimir Malakhov | .50 | .23 |
| 10 Lyle Odelein | .50 | .23 |
| 11 Oleg Petrov | .50 | .23 |
| 12 Peter Popovic | .50 | .23 |
| 13 Stephane Quintal | .50 | .23 |
| 14 Yves Racine | .50 | .23 |
| 15 Mark Recchi | 1.00 | .45 |
| 16 Patrick Roy | 4.00 | 1.80 |
| 17 Brian Savage | .60 | .25 |
| 18 Turner Stevenson | .50 | .23 |
| 19 Mario Tremblay CO | .50 | .23 |
| 20 Pierre Turgeon | 1.00 | .45 |

## 1995-96 Canadiens Sheets

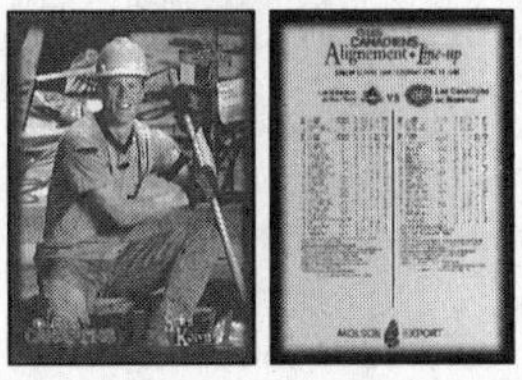

These 12 sheets were inserted in Montreal Canadiens game programs during the 1995-96 season. The fronts of the 8 1/2" by 11" sheets feature black and white photos of Motnreal players in construction gear, while the backs feature lineups for that evening's match. There are reports that the Bure sheet is the toughest to find; hence a premium has been attached. The cards are dated, but unnumbered, and thus have been checklisted alphabetically below.

| | MINT | NRMT |
|---|---|---|
| COMPLETE SET (12) | 120.00 | 55.00 |
| COMMON CARD (1-12) | 10.00 | 4.50 |
| 1 Valeri Bure | 20.00 | 9.00 |
| 2 Benoit Brunet | 10.00 | 4.50 |
| 3 Peter Popovic | 10.00 | 4.50 |
| 4 Saku Koivu | 15.00 | 6.75 |
| 5 Turner Stevenson | 10.00 | 4.50 |
| 6 Mark Recchi | 12.00 | 5.50 |
| 7 Vladimir Malakhov | 10.00 | 4.50 |
| 8 Stephane Quintal | 10.00 | 4.50 |
| 9 Brian Savage | 10.00 | 4.50 |
| 10 Patrice Brisebois | 10.00 | 4.50 |
| 11 Vincent Damphousse | 12.00 | 5.50 |
| 12 Pierre Turgeon | 12.00 | 5.50 |

## 1996-97 Canadiens Postcards

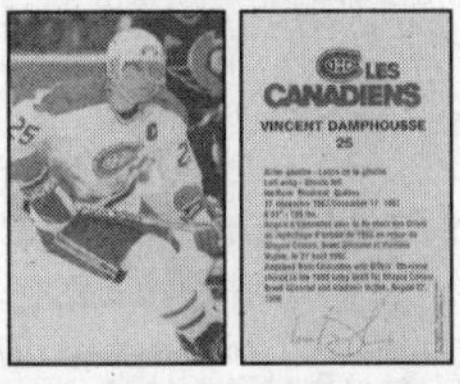

This 33-card postcard set was produced by the team for distribution in set form through the club store, or as autographable handouts by the players. They are standard postcard size and feature full-bleed color photos on the front. The backs include biographical information. The unnumbered cards are listed below alphabetically.

| | MINT | NRMT |
|---|---|---|
| COMPLETE SET (33) | 15.00 | 6.75 |
| COMMON POSTCARD (1-33) | .50 | .23 |
| 1 Murray Baron | .50 | .23 |
| 2 Sebastien Bordeleau | .50 | .23 |
| 3 Patrice Brisebois | .50 | .23 |
| 4 Benoit Brunet | .50 | .23 |
| 5 Valeri Bure | .50 | .23 |
| 6 Marc Bureau | .50 | .23 |
| 7 Ronald Corey | .50 | .23 |
| 8 Shayne Corson | 1.00 | .45 |
| 9 Yvan Cournoyer | 1.50 | .70 |
| 10 Jassen Cullimore | .50 | .23 |
| 11 Vincent Damphousse | 1.00 | .45 |
| 12 Rejean Houle | .50 | .23 |
| 13 Pat Jablonski | .50 | .23 |
| 14 Saku Koivu | 3.00 | 1.35 |
| 15 Jacques Laperierre | .75 | .35 |
| 16 Vladimir Malakhov | .50 | .23 |
| 17 Dave Manson | .50 | .23 |
| 18 Chris Murray | .50 | .23 |
| 19 Peter Popovic | .50 | .23 |
| 20 Stephane Qunital | .50 | .23 |
| 21 Mark Recchi | .75 | .35 |
| 22 Stephane Richer | 1.00 | .45 |
| 23 Craig Rivet | .50 | .23 |
| 24 Martin Rucinsky | .75 | .35 |
| 25 Brian Savage | .75 | .35 |
| 26 Steve Shutt | .75 | .35 |
| 27 Turner Stevenson | .50 | .23 |
| 28 Jose Theodore | 1.00 | .45 |
| 29 Joceyln Thibault | 1.00 | .45 |
| 30 Scott Thornton | .50 | .23 |
| 31 Mario Trembley | .50 | .23 |
| 32 Darcy Tucker | .50 | .23 |
| 33 David Wilkie | .50 | .23 |

## 1996-97 Canadiens Sheets

These large (8.5" X 11") sheets were distributed one per issue of the Montreal Canadiens game program during the exhibition and regular season. The fronts are dominated by a posed head shot, with a smaller action photo superimposed. The player's name and sweater number also appear. The back features the lineups for both teams from that evening's contest, as well as the logo of sponsor Molson Export. Unnumbered, the set is listed below in alphabetical order.

| | MINT | NRMT |
|---|---|---|
| COMPLETE SET (28) | 150.00 | 70.00 |
| COMMON SHEET (1-28) | 5.00 | 2.20 |
| 1 Patrice Brisebois | 5.00 | 2.20 |
| 2 Benoit Brunet | 5.00 | 2.20 |
| 3 Valeri Bure | 5.00 | 2.20 |
| 4 Marc Bureau | 5.00 | 2.20 |
| 5 Shayne Corson | 6.00 | 2.70 |
| 6 Jassen Cullimore | 5.00 | 2.20 |
| 7 Vincent Damphousse | 8.00 | 3.60 |
| 8 Rory Fitzpatrick | 5.00 | 2.20 |
| 9 Saku Koivu | 15.00 | 6.75 |
| 10 Vladimir Malakhov | 5.00 | 2.20 |
| 11 Dave Manson | 5.00 | 2.20 |
| 12 Chris Murray | 5.00 | 2.20 |
| 13 Peter Popovic | 5.00 | 2.20 |
| 14 Stephane Quintal | 5.00 | 2.20 |
| 15 Mark Recchi | 8.00 | 3.60 |
| 16 Stephane Richer | 6.00 | 2.70 |
| 17 Craig Rivet | 5.00 | 2.20 |
| 18 Martin Rucinsky | 6.00 | 2.70 |
| 19 Brian Savage | 6.00 | 2.70 |
| 20 Turner Stevenson | 5.00 | 2.20 |
| 21 Jose Theodore | 10.00 | 4.50 |
| 22 Jocelyn Thibault | 10.00 | 4.50 |
| 23 Scott Thornton | 5.00 | 2.20 |
| 24 Darcy Tucker | 5.00 | 2.20 |
| 25 Pierre Turgeon | 8.00 | 3.60 |
| 26 David Wilkie | 5.00 | 2.20 |
| 27 Centre Molson First Anniversary | 5.00 | 2.20 |
| 28 Canadiens Line-up | 5.00 | 2.20 |

## 1997-98 Canadiens Postcards

This 26-card set was produced by the team and measures the standard postcard size. The fronts feature color player photos. The backs carry player information. The cards are unnumbered and checklisted below in alphabetical order.

| | MINT | NRMT |
|---|---|---|
| COMPLETE SET (26) | 15.00 | 6.75 |
| COMMON CARD | .50 | .23 |
| 1 Sebastien Bordeleau | .50 | .23 |
| 2 Patrice Brisebois | .50 | .23 |
| 3 Benoit Brunet | .50 | .23 |
| 4 Valeri Bure | .50 | .23 |
| 5 Marc Bureau | .50 | .23 |
| 6 Brett Clark | .50 | .23 |
| 7 Shayne Corson | 1.00 | .45 |
| 8 Jassen Cullimore | 1.00 | .45 |
| 9 Vincent Damphousse | 1.00 | .45 |
| 10 Saku Koivu | 3.00 | 1.35 |
| 11 Vladimir Malakhov | .50 | .23 |
| 12 Dave Manson | .50 | .23 |
| 13 Andy Moog | 1.00 | .45 |
| 14 Peter Popovic | .50 | .23 |
| 15 Stephane Quintal | .50 | .23 |
| 16 Mark Recchi | .75 | .35 |
| 17 Stephane Richer | 1.00 | .45 |
| 18 Craig Rivet | .50 | .23 |
| 19 Martin Rucinsky | .75 | .35 |
| 20 Brian Savage | .75 | .35 |
| 21 Turner Stevenson | .50 | .23 |
| 22 Jocelyn Thibault | 1.00 | .45 |
| 23 Scott Thornton | .50 | .23 |
| 24 Darcy Tucker | .50 | .23 |
| 25 Alain Vigneault | .50 | .23 |
| 26 David Wilkie | .50 | .23 |

## 1970-71 Canucks Royal Bank

This 20-card set of Vancouver Canucks was sponsored by Royal Bank, whose company logo appears at the lower left corner on the front. The set is subtitled Royal Bank Leo's Leaders Canucks Player of the Week. The black and white posed player photos measure approximately 5" by 7" and have white borders. The player's signature is inscribed across the bottom of the picture, and the backs are blank. The cards are unnumbered and checklisted below in alphabetical order.

| | NRMT-MT | EXC |
|---|---|---|
| COMPLETE SET (20) | 60.00 | 27.00 |
| COMMON CARD (1-20) | 3.00 | 1.35 |
| ❑ 1 Andre Boudrias | 4.00 | 1.80 |
| ❑ 2 Mike Corrigan | 3.00 | 1.35 |
| ❑ 3 Ray Cullen | 5.00 | 2.20 |
| ❑ 4 Gary Doak | 3.00 | 1.35 |
| ❑ 5 George Gardner | 3.00 | 1.35 |
| ❑ 6 Murray Hall | 3.00 | 1.35 |
| ❑ 7 Charlie Hodge | 7.00 | 3.10 |
| ❑ 8 Danny Johnson | 3.00 | 1.35 |
| ❑ 9 Orland Kurtenbach | 5.00 | 2.20 |
| ❑ 10 Wayne Maki | 3.00 | 1.35 |
| ❑ 11 Rosaire Paiement | 4.00 | 1.80 |
| ❑ 12 Paul Popiel | 4.00 | 1.80 |
| ❑ 13 Pat Quinn | 8.00 | 3.60 |
| ❑ 14 Marc Reaume | 3.00 | 1.35 |
| ❑ 15 Darryl Sly | 3.00 | 1.35 |
| ❑ 16 Dale Tallon | 5.00 | 2.20 |
| ❑ 17 Ted Taylor | 3.00 | 1.35 |
| ❑ 18 Barry Wilkins | 3.00 | 1.35 |
| ❑ 19 Dunc Wilson | 5.00 | 2.20 |
| ❑ 20 Jim Wiste | 3.00 | 1.35 |

## 1971-72 Canucks Royal Bank

This 20-card set of Vancouver Canucks was sponsored by Royal Bank, whose company logo appears at the lower left corner on the front. The set is subtitled Royal Bank Leo's Leaders Canucks Player of the Week. The black and white posed player photos measure approximately 5" by 7" and have white borders. The player's signature is inscribed across the bottom of the picture, and the backs are blank. The cards are numbered by week of issue. Card number 10 is unknown and may have never been issued.

| | NRMT-MT | EXC |
|---|---|---|
| COMPLETE SET (20) | 50.00 | 22.00 |
| COMMON CARD (1-21) | 2.00 | .90 |
| ❑ 1 Bobby Lalonde | 2.00 | .90 |
| ❑ 2 Mike Corrigan | 2.00 | .90 |
| ❑ 3 Murray Hall | 2.00 | .90 |
| ❑ 4 Jocelyn Guevremont | 4.00 | 1.80 |
| ❑ 5 Pat Quinn | 6.00 | 2.70 |
| ❑ 6 Orland Kurtenbach | 4.00 | 1.80 |
| ❑ 7 Paul Popiel | 4.00 | 1.80 |
| ❑ 8 Ron Ward | 2.00 | .90 |
| ❑ 9 Rosaire Paiement | 3.00 | 1.35 |
| ❑ 11 Dale Tallon | 4.00 | 1.80 |
| ❑ 12 Bobby Schmautz | 4.00 | 1.80 |
| ❑ 13 Dennis Kearns | 2.00 | .90 |
| ❑ 14 Barry Wilkins | 2.00 | .90 |
| ❑ 15 Dunc Wilson | 5.00 | 2.20 |
| ❑ 16 Andre Boudrias | 4.00 | 1.80 |
| ❑ 17 Ted Taylor | 3.00 | 1.35 |
| ❑ 18 George Gardner | 2.00 | .90 |
| ❑ 19 John Schella | 2.00 | .90 |
| ❑ 20 Wayne Maki | 3.00 | 1.35 |
| ❑ 21 Gary Doak | 2.00 | .90 |

## 1972-73 Canucks Nalley's

This six-card set was available on the backs of specially marked Nalley's Triple Pak Potato Chips boxes. The back yellow panel has a 6 3/4" by 5 3/8" (approximately) action shot of a Canuck player beside the goalie and net. One

player card is superimposed over the lower left corner of this large action photo. The card is framed by a thin perforated line; if the card were cut out, it would measure about 3" by 3 3/4". The front features a close-up posed color player photo (from the waste up) with white borders. The player's name and position appear in white bottom border. The backs are blank. At the bottom of each back panel are miniature blue-tinted versions of all six player cards. The cards are unnumbered and checklisted below in alphabetical order.

| | NRMT-MT | EXC |
|---|---|---|
| COMPLETE SET (6) | 125.00 | 55.00 |
| COMMON CARD (1-6) | 20.00 | 9.00 |
| ❑ 1 Andre Boudrias | 20.00 | 9.00 |
| ❑ 2 George Gardner | 20.00 | 9.00 |
| ❑ 3 Wayne Maki | 25.00 | 11.00 |
| ❑ 4 Rosaire Paiement | 25.00 | 11.00 |
| ❑ 5 Pat Quinn | 40.00 | 18.00 |
| ❑ 6 Barry Wilkins | 20.00 | 9.00 |

## 1972-73 Canucks Royal Bank

This 21-card set of Vancouver Canucks was sponsored by Royal Bank, whose company logo appears at the lower left corner on the front. The set is subtitled Leo's Leaders Canucks Player of the Week. These colorful full body player photos measure approximately 5" by 7" and have white borders. The background of the photos ranges from light blue to royal blue. The player's facsimile signature is inscribed across the bottom of the picture, and the backs are blank. The cards are unnumbered on the front and checklisted below in alphabetical order.

| | NRMT-MT | EXC |
|---|---|---|
| COMPLETE SET (21) | 40.00 | 18.00 |
| COMMON CARD (1-21) | 2.00 | .90 |
| ❑ 1 Dave Balon | 3.00 | 1.35 |
| ❑ 2 Gregg Boddy | 2.00 | .90 |
| ❑ 3 Larry Bolonchuk | 2.00 | .90 |
| ❑ 4 Andre Boudrias | 2.00 | .90 |
| ❑ 5 Ed Dyck | 2.00 | .90 |
| ❑ 6 Jocelyn Guevremont | 3.00 | 1.35 |
| ❑ 7 James Hargreaves | 2.00 | .90 |
| ❑ 8 Dennis Kearns | 2.00 | .90 |
| ❑ 9 Orland Kurtenbach | 3.00 | 1.35 |
| ❑ 10 Bobby Lalonde | 2.00 | .90 |
| ❑ 11 Richard Lemieux | 2.00 | .90 |
| ❑ 12 Don Lever | 3.00 | 1.35 |
| ❑ 13 Wayne Maki | 3.00 | 1.35 |
| ❑ 14 Bryan McSheffrey | 2.00 | .90 |
| ❑ 15 Gerry O'Flaherty | 2.00 | .90 |
| ❑ 16 Bobby Schmautz | 3.00 | 1.35 |
| ❑ 17 Dale Tallon | 3.00 | 1.35 |
| ❑ 18 Don Tannahill | 2.00 | .90 |
| ❑ 19 Barry Wilkins | 2.00 | .90 |
| ❑ 20 Dunc Wilson | 3.00 | 1.35 |
| ❑ 21 John Wright | 2.00 | .90 |

## 1973-74 Canucks Royal Bank

This 21-card set of Vancouver Canucks was sponsored by Royal Bank, whose company logo appears at the lower left corner on the front. The set is subtitled Royal Leaders Canucks Player of the Week. These colorful full body player photos measure approximately 5" by 7" and have white borders. The background of the photos ranges from yellowish green to green. The player's facsimile signature is inscribed across the bottom of the picture, and the backs are blank. The cards are unnumbered on the front and checklisted below in alphabetical order.

| | NRMT-MT | EXC |
|---|---|---|
| COMPLETE SET (21) | 40.00 | 18.00 |
| COMMON CARD (1-21) | 2.00 | .90 |
| ❑ 1 Paulin Bordeleau | 2.00 | .90 |
| ❑ 2 Andre Boudrias | 2.00 | .90 |
| ❑ 3 Jacques Caron | 2.00 | .90 |
| ❑ 4 Bob Dailey | 2.00 | .90 |
| ❑ 5 Dave Dunn | 2.00 | .90 |
| ❑ 6 Jocelyn Guevremont | 3.00 | 1.35 |
| ❑ 7 Dennis Kearns | 2.00 | .90 |
| ❑ 8 Jerry Korab | 2.00 | .90 |
| ❑ 9 Orland Kurtenbach | 4.00 | 1.80 |
| ❑ 10 Bobby Lalonde | 2.00 | .90 |
| ❑ 11 Richard Lemieux | 2.00 | .90 |
| ❑ 12 Don Lever | 3.00 | 1.35 |
| ❑ 13 Bill McCreary | 2.00 | .90 |
| ❑ 14 Bryan McSheffrey | 2.00 | .90 |
| ❑ 15 Gerry O'Flaherty | 2.00 | .90 |
| ❑ 16 Bobby Schmautz | 4.00 | 1.80 |
| ❑ 17 Gary Smith | 4.00 | 1.80 |
| ❑ 18 Don Tannahill | 2.00 | .90 |
| ❑ 19 Dennis Ververgaert | 3.00 | 1.35 |
| ❑ 20 Barry Wilkins | 2.00 | .90 |
| ❑ 21 John Wright | 2.00 | .90 |

## 1974-75 Canucks Royal Bank

This 20-card set of Vancouver Canucks was sponsored by Royal Bank, whose company logo appears at the lower left corner on the front. The set is subtitled Royal Leaders Player of the Week. These colorful head and shoulders player photos are presented on a white background with a thin black border. The cards measure approximately 5" by 7", have white borders, and are printed on glossy paper. The player's facsimile signature is inscribed across the bottom of the picture, and the backs are blank. The cards are unnumbered on the front and checklisted below in alphabetical order.

| | NRMT-MT | EXC |
|---|---|---|
| COMPLETE SET (20) | 40.00 | 18.00 |
| COMMON CARD (1-20) | 2.00 | .90 |
| ❑ 1 Gregg Boddy | 2.00 | .90 |
| ❑ 2 Paulin Bordeleau | 3.00 | 1.35 |
| ❑ 3 Andre Boudrias | 3.00 | 1.35 |
| ❑ 4 Bob Dailey | 2.00 | .90 |
| ❑ 5 Ab DeMarco | 2.00 | .90 |
| ❑ 6 John Gould | 2.00 | .90 |
| ❑ 7 John Grisdale | 2.00 | .90 |
| ❑ 8 Dennis Kearns | 2.00 | .90 |
| ❑ 9 Bobby Lalonde | 2.00 | .90 |
| ❑ 10 Don Lever | 3.00 | 1.35 |
| ❑ 11 Ken Lockett | 2.00 | .90 |
| ❑ 12 Gerry Meehan | 3.00 | 1.35 |
| ❑ 13 Garry Monahan | 2.00 | .90 |
| ❑ 14 Chris Oddleifson | 2.00 | .90 |
| ❑ 15 Gerry O'Flaherty | 2.00 | .90 |
| ❑ 16 Tracy Pratt | 2.00 | .90 |
| ❑ 17 Mike Robitaille | 2.00 | .90 |
| ❑ 18 Leon Rochefort | 2.00 | .90 |
| ❑ 19 Gary Smith | 3.00 | 1.35 |
| ❑ 20 Dennis Ververgaert | 3.00 | 1.35 |

## 1975-76 Canucks Royal Bank

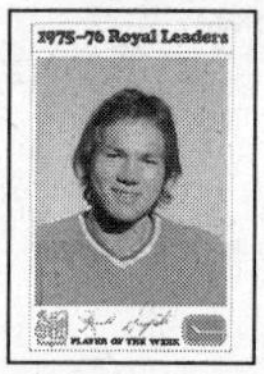

This 22-card set of Vancouver Canucks was sponsored by Royal Bank, whose company logo appears at the lower left corner on the front. The set is subtitled Royal Leaders Player of the Week. The cards measure approximately 4 3/4" by 7 1/4" and are printed on glossy paper. The fronts feature a color head and shoulders shot of the player on white background with a thin black border. The player's facsimile autograph appears below the picture. The backs are blank. The cards are unnumbered and we have checklisted them below in alphabetical order.

| | NRMT-MT | EXC |
|---|---|---|
| COMPLETE SET (22) | 40.00 | 18.00 |
| COMMON CARD (1-22) | 2.00 | .90 |
| ❑ 1 Rick Blight | 2.00 | .90 |
| ❑ 2 Gregg Boddy | 2.00 | .90 |
| ❑ 3 Paulin Bordeleau | 2.00 | .90 |
| ❑ 4 Andre Boudrias | 2.00 | .90 |
| ❑ 5 Bob Dailey | 2.00 | .90 |
| ❑ 6 Ab DeMarco | 2.00 | .90 |
| ❑ 7 John Gould | 2.00 | .90 |
| ❑ 8 John Grisdale | 2.00 | .90 |
| ❑ 9 Dennis Kearns | 2.00 | .90 |
| ❑ 10 Bobby Lalonde | 2.00 | .90 |
| ❑ 11 Don Lever | 3.00 | 1.35 |
| ❑ 12 Ken Lockett | 2.00 | .90 |
| ❑ 13 Garry Monahan | 2.00 | .90 |
| ❑ 14 Bob Murray | 2.00 | .90 |
| ❑ 15 Chris Oddleifson | 2.00 | .90 |
| ❑ 16 Gerry O'Flaherty | 2.00 | .90 |
| ❑ 17 Tracy Pratt | 2.00 | .90 |
| ❑ 18 Mike Robitaille | 2.00 | .90 |
| ❑ 19 Ron Sedlbauer | 2.00 | .90 |
| ❑ 20 Gary Smith | 3.00 | 1.35 |
| ❑ 21 Harold Snepsts | 6.00 | 2.70 |
| ❑ 22 Dennis Ververgaert | 3.00 | 1.35 |

## 1976-77 Canucks Royal Bank

This 23-card set of Vancouver Canucks was sponsored by Royal Bank, whose company logo appears at the lower left corner on the front. The set is subtitled Royal Leaders Player of the Week. The cards measure approximately 4 3/4" by 7 1/4" and are printed on glossy paper. The fronts feature a color head and shoulders shot of the player on white background with a thin black border. The player's facsimile autograph appears below the picture. The backs are blank. The cards are unnumbered and we have checklisted them below in alphabetical order.

| | NRMT-MT | EXC |
|---|---|---|
| COMPLETE SET (23) | 40.00 | 18.00 |
| COMMON CARD (1-23) | 2.00 | .90 |
| ❑ 1 Rick Blight | 2.00 | .90 |
| ❑ 2 Bob Dailey | 2.00 | .90 |
| ❑ 3 Dave Fortier | 2.00 | .90 |
| ❑ 4 Brad Gassoff | 2.00 | .90 |
| ❑ 5 John Gould | 2.00 | .90 |
| ❑ 6 John Grisdale | 2.00 | .90 |
| ❑ 7 Dennis Kearns | 2.00 | .90 |
| ❑ 8 Bobby Lalonde | 2.00 | .90 |
| ❑ 9 Don Lever | 3.00 | 1.35 |
| ❑ 10 Cesare Maniago | 4.00 | 1.80 |
| ❑ 11 Garry Monahan | 2.00 | .90 |
| ❑ 12 Bob Murray | 2.00 | .90 |
| ❑ 13 Chris Oddleifson | 2.00 | .90 |
| ❑ 14 Gerry O'Flaherty | 2.00 | .90 |
| ❑ 15 Curt Ridley | 2.00 | .90 |
| ❑ 16 Mike Robitaille | 2.00 | .90 |
| ❑ 17 Ron Sedlbauer | 2.00 | .90 |
| ❑ 18 Harold Snepsts | 5.00 | 2.20 |
| ❑ 19 Andy Spruce | 2.00 | .90 |
| ❑ 20 Ralph Stewart | 2.00 | .90 |
| ❑ 21 Dennis Ververgaert | 3.00 | 1.35 |
| ❑ 22 Mike Walton | 3.00 | 1.35 |
| ❑ 23 Jim Wiley | 3.00 | 1.35 |

## 1977-78 Canucks Canada Dry Cans

| | MINT | NRMT |
|---|---|---|
| COMPLETE SET (16) | 40.00 | 18.00 |
| COMMON CARD (1-16) | 2.00 | .90 |
| ❑ 1 Rick Blight | 2.00 | .90 |
| ❑ 2 Brad Gassoff | 2.00 | .90 |
| ❑ 3 Jere Gillis | 2.00 | .90 |
| ❑ 4 Larry Goodenough | 2.00 | .90 |
| ❑ 5 Hilliard Graves | 2.00 | .90 |
| ❑ 6 Dennis Kearns | 2.00 | .90 |
| ❑ 7 Don Lever | 2.00 | .90 |
| ❑ 8 Cesare Maniago | 5.00 | 2.20 |
| ❑ 9 Jack Mcilhargey | 2.00 | .90 |
| ❑ 10 Garry Monahan | 2.00 | .90 |
| ❑ 11 Chris Oddleifson | 2.00 | .90 |
| ❑ 12 Curt Ridley | 2.00 | .90 |
| ❑ 13 Derek Sanderson | 5.00 | 2.20 |
| ❑ 14 Harold Snepsts | 4.00 | 1.80 |
| ❑ 15 Mike Walton | 2.00 | .90 |
| ❑ 16 Dennis Ververgaert | 2.00 | .90 |

## 1977-78 Canucks Royal Bank

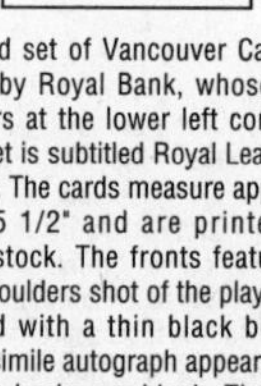

This 21-card set of Vancouver Canucks was sponsored by Royal Bank, whose company logo appears at the lower left corner on the front. The set is subtitled Royal Leaders Player of the Week. The cards measure approximately 4 1/4" by 5 1/2" and are printed on thin cardboard stock. The fronts feature a color head and shoulders shot of the player on white background with a thin black border. The player's facsimile autograph appears below the picture. The backs are blank. The cards are unnumbered; they are checklisted below in alphabetical order.

| | NRMT-MT | EXC |
|---|---|---|
| COMPLETE SET (21) | 40.00 | 18.00 |
| COMMON CARD (1-21) | 2.00 | .90 |
| ❑ 1 Rick Blight | 2.00 | .90 |
| ❑ 2 Larry Carriere | 2.00 | .90 |
| ❑ 3 Rob Flockhart | 2.00 | .90 |
| ❑ 4 Brad Gassoff | 2.00 | .90 |
| ❑ 5 Jere Gillis | 2.00 | .90 |
| ❑ 6 Larry Goodenough | 2.00 | .90 |
| ❑ 7 Hilliard Graves | 2.00 | .90 |
| ❑ 8 John Grisdale | 2.00 | .90 |
| ❑ 9 Dennis Kearns | 2.00 | .90 |
| ❑ 10 Don Lever | 3.00 | 1.35 |
| ❑ 11 Cesare Maniago | 4.00 | 1.80 |
| ❑ 12 Bob Manno | 2.00 | .90 |
| ❑ 13 Jack McIlhargey | 2.00 | .90 |
| ❑ 14 Garry Monahan | 2.00 | .90 |
| ❑ 15 Chris Oddleifson | 2.00 | .90 |
| ❑ 16 Gerry O'Flaherty | 2.00 | .90 |
| ❑ 17 Curt Ridley | 3.00 | 1.35 |
| ❑ 18 Ron Sedlbauer | 2.00 | .90 |
| ❑ 19 Harold Snepsts | 4.00 | 1.80 |
| ❑ 20 Dennis Ververgaert | 3.00 | 1.35 |
| ❑ 21 Mike Walton | 2.00 | .90 |

## 1978-79 Canucks Royal Bank

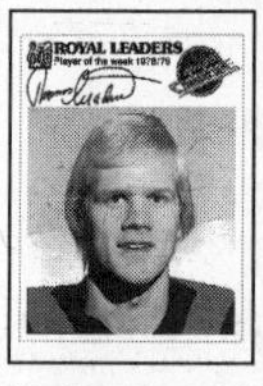

This 23-card set of Vancouver Canucks was sponsored by Royal Bank, whose company logo appears at the upper left corner on the front. The cards measure approximately 4 1/4" by 5 1/2" and are printed on thin cardboard stock. The fronts feature a color head and shoulders shot of the player on white background with a thin blue border. The player's facsimile autograph and the team logo appear above the picture. The backs present biographical and statistical information. The cards are unnumbered; they are checklisted below in alphabetical order.

| | NRMT-MT | EXC |
|---|---|---|
| COMPLETE SET (23) | 40.00 | 18.00 |
| COMMON CARD (1-23) | 1.50 | .70 |
| ❑ 1 Rick Blight | 1.50 | .70 |
| ❑ 2 Gary Bromley | 2.00 | .90 |
| ❑ 3 Bill Derlago | 1.50 | .70 |
| ❑ 4 Roland Eriksson | 1.50 | .70 |
| ❑ 5 Curt Fraser | 2.00 | .90 |
| ❑ 6 Jere Gillis | 1.50 | .70 |
| ❑ 7 Thomas Gradin | 4.00 | 1.80 |
| ❑ 8 Hilliard Graves | 1.50 | .70 |
| ❑ 9 John Grisdale | 1.50 | .70 |
| ❑ 10 Glen Hanlon | 2.50 | 1.10 |
| ❑ 11 Randy Holt | 1.50 | .70 |
| ❑ 12 Dennis Kearns | 1.50 | .70 |
| ❑ 13 Don Lever | 2.00 | .90 |
| ❑ 14 Lars Lindgren | 1.50 | .70 |
| ❑ 15 Bob Manno | 1.50 | .70 |
| ❑ 16 Pit Martin | 2.00 | .90 |
| ❑ 17 Jack McIlhargey | 1.50 | .70 |
| ❑ 18 Chris Oddleifson | 1.50 | .70 |
| ❑ 19 Ron Sedlbauer | 1.50 | .70 |
| ❑ 20 Stan Smyl | 4.00 | 1.80 |
| ❑ 21 Harold Snepsts | 4.00 | 1.80 |
| ❑ 22 Dennis Ververgaert | 2.00 | .90 |
| ❑ 23 Lars Zetterstrom | 1.50 | .70 |

## 1979-80 Canucks Royal Bank

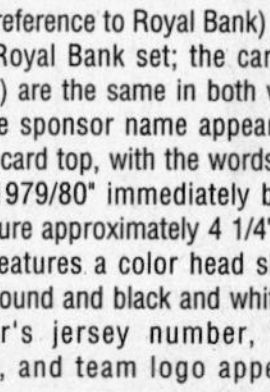

This 22-card set features posed color player photos from the shoulders up of the Vancouver Canucks. There are actually two different sets with the same value, a team-issued (no reference to Royal Bank) blank back set and a Royal Bank set; the card pictures (and values) are the same in both versions of the set. The sponsor name appears in black print at the card top, with the words "Player of the Week 1979/80" immediately below. The cards measure approximately 4 1/4" by 5 1/2". The front features a color head shot with a blue background and black and white borders. The player's jersey number, facsimile autograph, and team logo appear in the

bottom white border. Since this is an unnumbered set, the cards are listed alphabetically. The Royal Bank backs carry biography, career summary, and complete statistical information (season by season, regular schedule, and playoffs).

| | NRMT-MT | EXC |
|---|---|---|
| COMPLETE SET (22) | 30.00 | 13.50 |
| COMMON CARD (1-22) | 1.50 | .70 |
| ❑ 1 Brent Ashton | 2.00 | .90 |
| ❑ 2 Rick Blight | 1.50 | .70 |
| ❑ 3 Gary Bromley | 2.00 | .90 |
| ❑ 4 Drew Callander | 1.50 | .70 |
| ❑ 5 Bill Derlago | 2.00 | .90 |
| ❑ 6 Curt Fraser | 2.00 | .90 |
| ❑ 7 Jere Gillis | 1.50 | .70 |
| ❑ 8 Thomas Gradin | 3.00 | 1.35 |
| ❑ 9 Glen Hanlon | 2.50 | 1.10 |
| ❑ 10 John Hughes | 1.50 | .70 |
| ❑ 11 Dennis Kearns | 1.50 | .70 |
| ❑ 12 Don Lever | 2.00 | .90 |
| ❑ 13 Lars Lindgren | 1.50 | .70 |
| ❑ 14 Bob Manno | 1.50 | .70 |
| ❑ 15 Kevin McCarthy | 1.50 | .70 |
| ❑ 16 Jack McIlhargey | 1.50 | .70 |
| ❑ 17 Chris Oddleifson | 1.50 | .70 |
| ❑ 18 Curt Ridley | 1.50 | .70 |
| ❑ 19 Ron Sedlbauer | 1.50 | .70 |
| ❑ 20 Stan Smyl | 3.00 | 1.35 |
| ❑ 21 Harold Snepsts | 3.00 | 1.35 |
| ❑ 22 Rick Vaive | 2.50 | 1.10 |

## 1980-81 Canucks Silverwood Dairies

This 24-card set of Vancouver Canucks was sponsored by Silverwood Dairies. The cards measure approximately 2 1/2" by 3 1/2" individually but were issued as perforated panels of three. The cards are checklisted below in alphabetical order, with the panel number after the player's name.

| | NRMT-MT | EXC |
|---|---|---|
| COMPLETE SET (24) | 40.00 | 18.00 |
| COMMON CARD (1-24) | 1.50 | .70 |
| ❑ 1 Brent Ashton 6 | 2.00 | .90 |
| ❑ 2 Ivan Boldirev 4 | 2.00 | .90 |
| ❑ 3 Per-Olov Brasar 5 | 1.50 | .70 |
| ❑ 4 Richard Brodeur 3 | 4.00 | 1.80 |
| ❑ 5 Gary Bromley 4 | 2.00 | .90 |
| ❑ 6 Jerry Butler 1 | 1.50 | .70 |
| ❑ 7 Colin Campbell 5 | 2.50 | 1.10 |
| ❑ 8 Curt Fraser 8 | 2.00 | .90 |
| ❑ 9 Thomas Gradin 6 | 2.50 | 1.10 |
| ❑ 10 Glen Hanlon 5 | 2.50 | 1.10 |
| ❑ 11 Dennis Kearns 6 | 1.50 | .70 |
| ❑ 12 Rick Lanz 2 | 1.50 | .70 |
| ❑ 13 Lars Lindgren 7 | 1.50 | .70 |
| ❑ 14 Dave Logan 8 | 1.50 | .70 |
| ❑ 15 Gary Lupul 3 | 1.50 | .70 |
| ❑ 16 Bob Manno 1 | 1.50 | .70 |
| ❑ 17 Kevin McCarthy 3 | 1.50 | .70 |
| ❑ 18 Gerry Minor 2 | 1.50 | .70 |
| ❑ 19 Kevin Primeau 7 | 1.50 | .70 |
| ❑ 20 Darcy Rota 2 | 1.50 | .70 |
| ❑ 21 Stan Smyl 1 | 3.00 | 1.35 |
| ❑ 22 Harold Snepsts 4 | 3.00 | 1.35 |
| ❑ 23 Bobby Schmautz 8 | 1.50 | .70 |
| ❑ 24 Dave(Tiger) Williams 7 | 4.00 | 1.80 |

## 1980-81 Canucks Team Issue

This 22-card set measures approximately 3 3/4" by 4 7/8" and features posed color head and shoulder player photos against a light blue-gray background. The pictures have rounded corners and are enclosed by thick black and thin red border stripes. The player's name, uniform number, position, and the team logo appear in the thicker bottom border. A facsimile autograph runs vertically to the left of the player's head. The backs are blank.

| | NRMT-MT | EXC |
|---|---|---|
| COMPLETE SET (22) | 30.00 | 13.50 |
| COMMON CARD (1-22) | 1.50 | .70 |
| ❑ 1 Brent Ashton | 2.00 | .90 |
| ❑ 2 Ivan Boldirev | 2.00 | .90 |
| ❑ 3 Per-Olov Brasar | 1.50 | .70 |
| ❑ 4 Richard Brodeur | 4.00 | 1.80 |
| ❑ 5 Gary Bromley | 2.00 | .90 |
| ❑ 6 Jerry Butler | 1.50 | .70 |
| ❑ 7 Colin Campbell | 2.50 | 1.10 |
| ❑ 8 Curt Fraser | 2.00 | .90 |
| ❑ 9 Thomas Gradin | 2.50 | 1.10 |
| ❑ 10 Glen Hanlon | 2.50 | 1.10 |
| ❑ 11 Dennis Kearns | 1.50 | .70 |
| ❑ 12 Rick Lanz | 1.50 | .70 |
| ❑ 13 Lars Lindgren | 1.50 | .70 |
| ❑ 14 Dave Logan | 1.50 | .70 |
| ❑ 15 Gary Lupul | 1.50 | .70 |
| ❑ 16 Kevin McCarthy | 1.50 | .70 |
| ❑ 17 Gerry Minor | 1.50 | .70 |
| ❑ 18 Darcy Rota | 1.50 | .70 |
| ❑ 19 Bobby Schmautz | 1.50 | .70 |
| ❑ 20 Stan Smyl | 3.00 | 1.35 |
| ❑ 21 Harold Snepsts | 3.00 | 1.35 |
| ❑ 22 Tiger Williams | 4.00 | 1.80 |

## 1981-82 Canucks Silverwood Dairies

This 24-card set of Vancouver Canucks was sponsored by Silverwood Dairies, and the sponsor's name and logo appear at the top of the card face. The cards measure approximately 2 7/16" by 4 1/16" and feature a color action player photo, with the team logo superimposed at the lower right corner of the picture. The sponsor information above and the player information below the photo are enframed by an orange border (on white cardboard stock). The backs have career summary and statistics, as well as a facsimile autograph of the player at the bottom of the card. The cards are unnumbered and are checklisted by the order they appear on the panels. The panel number is given after the name for each card in the checklist below.

| | NRMT-MT | EXC |
|---|---|---|
| COMPLETE SET (24) | 25.00 | 11.00 |
| COMMON CARD (1-24) | 1.00 | .45 |
| ❑ 1 Rick Lanz 1 | 1.00 | .45 |
| ❑ 2 Curt Fraser 1 | 1.00 | .45 |
| ❑ 3 Marc Crawford 1 | 2.00 | .90 |
| ❑ 4 Ivan Hlinka 2 | 1.00 | .45 |
| ❑ 5 Jerry Butler 2 | 1.00 | .45 |
| ❑ 6 Doug Halward 2 | 1.00 | .45 |
| ❑ 7 Glen Hanlon 3 | 1.50 | .70 |
| ❑ 8 Harold Snepsts 3 | 2.50 | 1.10 |
| ❑ 9 Gerry Minor 3 | 1.00 | .45 |
| ❑ 10 Richard Brodeur 4 | 2.50 | 1.10 |
| ❑ 11 Lars Lindgren 4 | 1.00 | .45 |
| ❑ 12 Darcy Rota 4 | 1.00 | .45 |
| ❑ 13 Stan Smyl 5 | 2.50 | 1.10 |
| ❑ 14 Colin Campbell 5 | 1.50 | .70 |
| ❑ 15 Per-Olov Brasar 5 | 1.00 | .45 |
| ❑ 16 Dave(Tiger) Williams 6 | 2.50 | 1.10 |
| ❑ 17 Anders Eldebrink 6 | 1.00 | .45 |
| ❑ 18 Gary Lupul 6 | 1.00 | .45 |
| ❑ 19 Thomas Gradin 7 | 2.00 | .90 |
| ❑ 20 Jiri Bubla 7 | 1.00 | .45 |
| ❑ 21 Blair MacDonald 7 | 1.00 | .45 |
| ❑ 22 Kevin McCarthy 8 | 1.00 | .45 |
| ❑ 23 Ivan Boldirev 8 | 1.25 | .55 |
| ❑ 24 Lars Molin 8 | 1.00 | .45 |

## 1981-82 Canucks Team Issue

This 20-card set measures approximately 3 3/4" by 4 7/8" and features posed color head and shoulder player photos against a blue background. The pictures have rounded corners and are enclosed by thick black and thin red border stripes. The player's name, uniform number, position, and the team logo appear in the thicker bottom border. A facsimile autograph runs vertically to the left of the player's head. The backs are blank. The card of Richard Brodeur is the same one used in the 1980-81 team-issued set.

| | NRMT-MT | EXC |
|---|---|---|
| COMPLETE SET (20) | 20.00 | 9.00 |
| COMMON CARD (1-20) | 1.00 | .45 |
| ❑ 1 Ivan Boldirev | 1.50 | .70 |
| ❑ 2 Per-Olov Brasar | 1.00 | .45 |
| ❑ 3 Richard Brodeur | 2.50 | 1.10 |
| ❑ 4 Jiri Bubla | 1.00 | .45 |
| ❑ 5 Jerry Butler | 1.00 | .45 |
| ❑ 6 Colin Campbell | 2.50 | 1.10 |
| ❑ 7 Anders Eldebrink | 1.00 | .45 |
| ❑ 8 Curt Fraser | 1.50 | .70 |
| ❑ 9 Thomas Gradin | 2.00 | .90 |
| ❑ 10 Doug Halward | 1.00 | .45 |
| ❑ 11 Glen Hanlon | 1.50 | .70 |
| ❑ 12 Rick Lanz | 1.00 | .45 |
| ❑ 13 Gary Lupul | 1.00 | .45 |
| ❑ 14 Blair MacDonald | 1.00 | .45 |
| ❑ 15 Kevin McCarthy | 1.00 | .45 |
| ❑ 16 Gerry Minor | 1.00 | .45 |
| ❑ 17 Lars Molin | 1.00 | .45 |
| ❑ 18 Darcy Rota | 1.00 | .45 |
| ❑ 19 Stan Smyl | 2.00 | .90 |
| ❑ 20 Tiger Williams | 2.50 | 1.10 |

## 1982-83 Canucks

This 23-card set of the Vancouver Canucks was issued in three panels of six cards each with a fourth panel having five cards because the team photo fills the space of two player cards. The cards measure approximately 3 3/4" by 4 7/8". The fronts feature a color posed photo of the player with rounded corners and surrounded by a thick black and a thin red

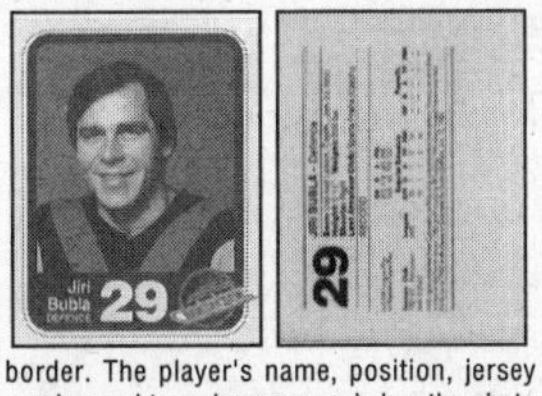

border. The player's name, position, jersey number and team logo appear below the photo in a wide black border. The horizontal backs carry the player's name, postion, jersey number, biographical and statistical information. The cards are unnumbered and checklisted below in alphabetical order.

| | NRMT-MT | EXC |
|---|---|---|
| COMPLETE SET (23) | 20.00 | 9.00 |
| COMMON CARD (1-23) | .75 | .35 |
| ❑ 1 Ivan Boldirev | 1.00 | .45 |
| ❑ 2 Richard Brodeur | 2.50 | 1.10 |
| ❑ 3 Jiri Bubla | .75 | .35 |
| ❑ 4 Garth Butcher | 1.00 | .45 |
| ❑ 5 Ron Delorme | .75 | .35 |
| ❑ 6 Ken Ellacott | .75 | .35 |
| ❑ 7 Curt Fraser | .75 | .35 |
| ❑ 8 Thomas Gradin | 1.50 | .70 |
| ❑ 9 Doug Halward | .75 | .35 |
| ❑ 10 Ivan Hlinka | .75 | .35 |
| ❑ 11 Rick Lanz | .75 | .35 |
| ❑ 12 Moe Lemay | .75 | .35 |
| ❑ 13 Lars Lindgren | .75 | .35 |
| ❑ 14 Kevin McCarthy | .75 | .35 |
| ❑ 15 Gerry Minor | .75 | .35 |
| ❑ 16 Lars Molin | .75 | .35 |
| ❑ 17 Jim Nill | .75 | .35 |
| ❑ 18 Darcy Rota | .75 | .35 |
| ❑ 19 Stan Smyl | 1.50 | .70 |
| ❑ 20 Harold Snepsts | 2.50 | 1.10 |
| ❑ 21 Patrik Sundstrom | 2.00 | .90 |
| ❑ 22 Dave Williams | 2.00 | .90 |
| ❑ 23 Team Photo | .75 | .35 |

## 1983-84 Canucks

This 23-card set of Vancouver Canucks was issued in three panels of six cards each, with the fourth panel having 5 cards (the team photo card fills the space of two player cards). The player cards measure approximately 3 11/16" by 4 5/8". The front features a color posed photo (with rounded corners) of the player, surrounded by a thick black and a thin red border. The Canucks' logo and player information appear below the picture. The back has biographical and statistical information in a horizontal format. We have checklisted the names below in alphabetical order, with the uniform number to the right of the name.

| | MINT | NRMT |
|---|---|---|
| COMPLETE SET (23) | 18.00 | 8.00 |
| COMMON CARD (1-23) | .50 | .23 |
| ❑ 1 Richard Brodeur 35 | 2.00 | .90 |
| ❑ 2 Jiri Bubla 29 | .50 | .23 |
| ❑ 3 Garth Butcher 5 | 1.00 | .45 |
| ❑ 4 Marc Crawford 28 | 1.00 | .45 |
| ❑ 5 Ron Delorme 19 | .50 | .23 |
| ❑ 6 John Garrett 31 | 1.00 | .45 |
| ❑ 7 Jere Gillis 4 | .50 | .23 |
| ❑ 8 Thomas Gradin 23 | 1.50 | .70 |
| ❑ 9 Doug Halward 2 | .50 | .23 |
| ❑ 10 Mark Kirton 16 | .50 | .23 |
| ❑ 11 Rick Lanz 4 | .50 | .23 |
| ❑ 12 Gary Lupul 7 | .50 | .23 |
| ❑ 13 Kevin McCarthy 25 | .50 | .23 |
| ❑ 14 Lars Molin 26 | .50 | .23 |
| ❑ 15 Jim Nill 8 | .50 | .23 |
| ❑ 16 Michel Petit 3 | 1.00 | .45 |
| ❑ 17 Darcy Rota 18 | .50 | .23 |
| ❑ 18 Stan Smyl 12 | 1.50 | .70 |
| ❑ 19 Harold Snepsts 27 | 2.00 | .90 |
| ❑ 20 Patrik Sundstrom 17 | 1.50 | .70 |
| ❑ 21 Tony Tanti 9 | 1.50 | .70 |
| ❑ 22 Dave(Tiger) Williams 22 | 2.00 | .90 |
| ❑ 23 Team Photo | 1.00 | .45 |

## 1984-85 Canucks

This 26-card set of Vancouver Canucks was issued in four six-card panels plus a larger team photo card and an Air Canucks advertisement card (the latter two measure approximately 4 5/8" by 7"). The player cards measure 3 5/16" by 4 1/4". The key card in the set is Cam Neely appearing in his Rookie Card year. The cards are unnumbered and checklisted below in alphabetical order.

| | MINT | NRMT |
|---|---|---|
| COMPLETE SET (26) | 25.00 | 11.00 |
| COMMON CARD (1-26) | .25 | .11 |
| ❑ 1 Neil Belland | .50 | .23 |
| ❑ 2 Richard Brodeur | 1.50 | .70 |
| ❑ 3 Jiri Bubla | .50 | .23 |
| ❑ 4 Garth Butcher | .75 | .35 |
| ❑ 5 Frank Caprice | .75 | .35 |
| ❑ 6 J.J. Daigneault | .75 | .35 |
| ❑ 7 Ron Delorme | .50 | .23 |
| ❑ 8 John Garrett | 1.00 | .45 |
| ❑ 9 Thomas Gradin | 1.50 | .70 |
| ❑ 10 Taylor Hall | .50 | .23 |
| ❑ 11 Doug Halward | .50 | .23 |
| ❑ 12 Rick Lanz | .50 | .23 |
| ❑ 13 Moe Lemay | .50 | .23 |
| ❑ 14 Doug Lidster | .75 | .35 |
| ❑ 15 Gary Lupul | .50 | .23 |
| ❑ 16 Al MacAdam | .50 | .23 |
| ❑ 17 Peter McNab | .75 | .35 |
| ❑ 18 Cam Neely | 10.00 | 4.50 |
| ❑ 19 Michel Petit | .75 | .35 |
| ❑ 20 Darcy Rota | .50 | .23 |
| ❑ 21 Petri Skriko | 1.00 | .45 |
| ❑ 22 Stan Smyl | 1.00 | .45 |
| ❑ 23 Patrik Sundstrom | 1.00 | .45 |
| ❑ 24 Tony Tanti | 1.00 | .45 |
| ❑ 25 Team Photo (Large size) | 1.50 | .70 |
| ❑ 26 Air Canucks (Advertisement) | .25 | .11 |

## 1985-86 Canucks

This 25-card set of Vancouver Canucks was issued in four panels of six cards each, with a separate team photo card. The player cards measure approximately 3 3/8" by 4 1/4". The team photo measures approximately 7" by 4 5/8". The fronts feature color posed player photos (with rounded corners) surrounded by thick black and thin red borders. The Canucks' logo and player information appear below the picture. The backs are blank. The cards are unnumbered and checklisted below in alphabetical order.

| | MINT | NRMT |
|---|---|---|
| COMPLETE SET (25) | 18.00 | 8.00 |
| COMMON CARD (1-25) | .50 | .23 |
| ❑ 1 Richard Brodeur | 1.50 | .70 |
| ❑ 2 Jiri Bubla | .50 | .23 |
| ❑ 3 Garth Butcher | .75 | .35 |
| ❑ 4 Frank Caprice | .75 | .35 |
| ❑ 5 Glen Cochrane | .50 | .23 |
| ❑ 6 Craig Coxe | .50 | .23 |
| ❑ 7 J.J. Daigneault | .75 | .35 |
| ❑ 8 Thomas Gradin | 1.00 | .45 |
| ❑ 9 Taylor Hall | .50 | .23 |
| ❑ 10 Doug Halward | .50 | .23 |
| ❑ 11 Jean-Marc Lanthier | .50 | .23 |
| ❑ 12 Rick Lanz | .50 | .23 |
| ❑ 13 Moe Lemay | .50 | .23 |
| ❑ 14 Doug Lidster | .75 | .35 |
| ❑ 15 Dave Lowry | .50 | .23 |
| ❑ 16 Gary Lupul | .50 | .23 |
| ❑ 17 Cam Neely | 7.50 | 3.40 |
| ❑ 18 Brent Peterson | .50 | .23 |
| ❑ 19 Jim Sandlak | .75 | .35 |
| ❑ 20 Petri Skriko | 1.00 | .45 |
| ❑ 21 Stan Smyl | 1.00 | .45 |
| ❑ 22 Patrik Sundstrom | 1.00 | .45 |
| ❑ 23 Steve Tambellini | .50 | .23 |
| ❑ 24 Tony Tanti | 1.00 | .45 |
| ❑ 25 Team Photo (Large size) | 3.00 | 1.35 |

## 1986-87 Canucks

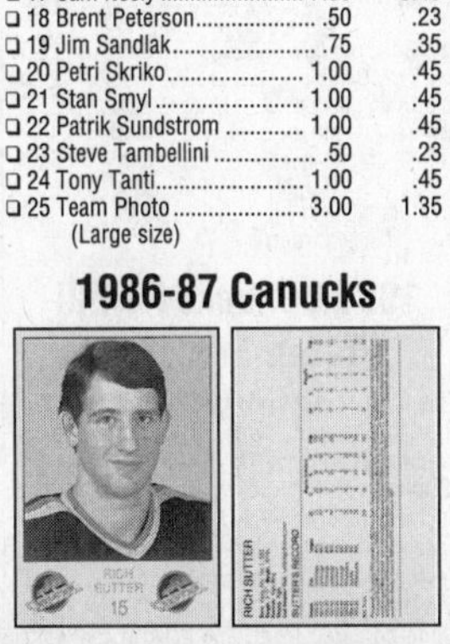

This 24-card set of Vancouver Canucks was issued in four panels of six cards each; after perforation, the cards measure the standard size (2 1/2" by 3 1/2"). The front design has color head and shoulder shots with white borders. Below the picture the player's name and number appear between two team logos. The horizontally oriented backs have biography and career statistics. The cards are unnumbered and checklisted below in alphabetical order, with the uniform number after the name.

| | MINT | NRMT |
|---|---|---|
| COMPLETE SET (24) | 12.00 | 5.50 |
| COMMON CARD (1-24) | .50 | .23 |
| ❑ 1 Richard Brodeur 35 | 1.50 | .70 |
| ❑ 2 Garth Butcher 5 | .75 | .35 |
| ❑ 3 Frank Caprice 30 | .75 | .35 |
| ❑ 4 Glen Cochrane 29 | .50 | .23 |
| ❑ 5 Craig Coxe 32 | .50 | .23 |
| ❑ 6 Taylor Hall 8 | .50 | .23 |
| ❑ 7 Stu Kulak 16 | .50 | .23 |
| ❑ 8 Moe Lemay 14 | .50 | .23 |
| ❑ 9 Dave Lowry 22 | .50 | .23 |
| ❑ 10 Brad Maxwell 27 | .50 | .23 |
| ❑ 11 Petri Skriko 26 | .75 | .35 |
| ❑ 12 Barry Pederson 7 | 1.00 | .45 |
| ❑ 13 Rick Lanz 4 | .50 | .23 |
| ❑ 14 Doug Lidster 3 | .75 | .35 |
| ❑ 15 Brent Peterson 10 | .50 | .23 |
| ❑ 16 Michel Petit 24 | .75 | .35 |
| ❑ 17 Dave Richter 6 | .50 | .23 |
| ❑ 18 Stan Smyl 12 | 1.00 | .45 |
| ❑ 19 Jim Sandlak 33 | .50 | .23 |
| ❑ 20 Patrik Sundstrom 17 | 1.00 | .45 |
| ❑ 21 Rich Sutter 15 | .50 | .23 |
| ❑ 22 Steve Tambellini 20 | .50 | .23 |
| ❑ 23 Tony Tanti 9 | 1.00 | .45 |
| ❑ 24 Wendell Young 1 | 1.00 | .45 |

## 1987-88 Canucks Shell Oil

This 24-card set of Vancouver Canucks was sponsored by Shell Oil and released only in British Columbia. It was issued as eight different three-card panels, with the cards measuring the standard size, 2 1/2" by 3 1/2", after perforation. The cards were distributed as a promotion for Shell Oil, with one panel set per week given out at participating Shell stations. Included with the cards was a coupon offering a 5.00 discount on tickets to the Canucks games. The front features a color head and shoulders shot of the player, with the Canucks' logo superimposed at the upper left hand corner of the picture. The player's name, position, and the "Formula Shell" logo appear below the picture. The back has biographical and career information on the player. The cards are unnumbered and checklisted below in alphabetical order. Kirk McLean's card predates his Rookie Card by two years.

| | MINT | NRMT |
|---|---|---|
| COMPLETE SET (24) | 8.00 | 3.60 |
| COMMON CARD (1-24) | .25 | .11 |
| ❑ 1 Greg Adams | .75 | .35 |
| ❑ 2 Jim Benning | .25 | .11 |
| ❑ 3 Randy Boyd | .25 | .11 |
| ❑ 4 Richard Brodeur | 1.00 | .45 |
| ❑ 5 David Bruce | .25 | .11 |
| ❑ 6 Garth Butcher | .25 | .11 |
| ❑ 7 Frank Caprice | .35 | .16 |
| ❑ 8 Craig Coxe | .25 | .11 |
| ❑ 9 Willie Huber | .25 | .11 |
| ❑ 10 Doug Lidster | .50 | .23 |
| ❑ 11 Dave Lowry | .25 | .11 |
| ❑ 12 Kirk McLean | 2.50 | 1.10 |
| ❑ 13 Larry Melnyk | .25 | .11 |
| ❑ 14 Barry Pederson | .50 | .23 |
| ❑ 15 Dave Richter | .25 | .11 |
| ❑ 16 Jim Sandlak | .25 | .11 |
| ❑ 17 Dave Saunders | .25 | .11 |
| ❑ 18 Petri Skriko | .50 | .23 |
| ❑ 19 Stan Smyl | .75 | .35 |
| ❑ 20 Daryl Stanley | .25 | .11 |
| ❑ 21 Rich Sutter | .25 | .11 |
| ❑ 22 Steve Tambellini | .25 | .11 |
| ❑ 23 Tony Tanti | .75 | .35 |
| ❑ 24 Doug Wickenheiser | .25 | .11 |

## 1988-89 Canucks Mohawk

This 24-card standard-size set of Vancouver Canucks was sponsored by Mohawk and issued in six panels of four cards each. The cards feature on the front a color head and

shoulders shot of the player on white card stock. The Canucks' and Mohawk logos appear at the bottom of the card. The Canucks' name, position, and number are given in black lettering running the bottom to top on the left side of the picture. The backs are blank. We have checklisted the cards below in alphabetical order, with the player's number to the right of his name. The cards of Trevor Linden and Kirk McLean's predate their Rookie Cards by one year.

| | MINT | NRMT |
|---|---|---|
| COMPLETE SET (24) | 15.00 | 6.75 |
| COMMON CARD (1-24) | .50 | .23 |

| | | |
|---|---|---|
| ❑ 1 Greg Adams 8 | 1.00 | .45 |
| ❑ 2 Jim Benning 4 | .50 | .23 |
| ❑ 3 Ken Berry 18 | .50 | .23 |
| ❑ 4 Randy Boyd 29 | .50 | .23 |
| ❑ 5 Steve Bozek 14 | .50 | .23 |
| ❑ 6 Brian Bradley 10 | 1.50 | .70 |
| ❑ 7 David Bruce 25 | .50 | .23 |
| ❑ 8 Garth Butcher 5 | .50 | .23 |
| ❑ 9 Kevan Guy 2 | .50 | .23 |
| ❑ 10 Doug Lidster 3 | .50 | .23 |
| ❑ 11 Trevor Linden 16 | 5.00 | 2.20 |
| ❑ 12 Kirk McLean 1 | 3.00 | 1.35 |
| ❑ 13 Larry Melnyk 24 | .50 | .23 |
| ❑ 14 Robert Nordmark 6 | .50 | .23 |
| ❑ 15 Barry Pederson 7 | .75 | .35 |
| ❑ 16 Paul Reinhart 23 | .75 | .35 |
| ❑ 17 Jim Sandlak 19 | .50 | .23 |
| ❑ 18 Petri Skriko 26 | .75 | .35 |
| ❑ 19 Stan Smyl 12 | .75 | .35 |
| ❑ 20 Harold Snepsts 27 | 1.50 | .70 |
| ❑ 21 Ronnie Stern 20 | .50 | .23 |
| ❑ 22 Rich Sutter 15 | .50 | .23 |
| ❑ 23 Tony Tanti 9 | .75 | .35 |
| ❑ 24 Steve Weeks 31 | .75 | .35 |

## 1989-90 Canucks Mohawk

This 24-card standard-size set was sponsored by Mohawk to commemorate the Vancouver Canucks' 20th year in the NHL and was issued in six panels of four cards each. The cards feature a color head and shoulders shot of the player on white card stock. The Canucks' and Mohawk logos appear at the bottom of the card, and the Canucks' logo has the number "2" before it joining with the circular shape of the logo to suggest "20." The player's name, position, and number are given in black lettering running the bottom to top on the left side of the picture. The backs are blank. We have checklisted the cards below in alphabetical order, with the player's number to the right of his name.

| | MINT | NRMT |
|---|---|---|
| COMPLETE SET (24) | 15.00 | 6.75 |
| COMMON CARD (1-24) | .50 | .23 |

| | | |
|---|---|---|
| ❑ 1 Greg Adams 8 | .75 | .35 |
| ❑ 2 Jim Benning 4 | .50 | .23 |
| ❑ 3 Steve Bozek 14 | .50 | .23 |
| ❑ 4 Brian Bradley 10 | 1.00 | .45 |
| ❑ 5 Garth Butcher 5 | .50 | .23 |
| ❑ 6 Craig Coxe 22 | .50 | .23 |
| ❑ 7 Vladimir Krutov 17 | 1.00 | .45 |
| ❑ 8 Igor Larionov 18 | 2.00 | .90 |
| ❑ 9 Doug Lidster 3 | .50 | .23 |
| ❑ 10 Trevor Linden 16 | 4.00 | 1.80 |
| ❑ 11 Kirk McLean 1 | 2.00 | .90 |
| ❑ 12 Larry Melnyk 24 | .50 | .23 |
| ❑ 13 Robert Nordmark 6 | .50 | .23 |
| ❑ 14 Barry Pederson 7 | .75 | .35 |
| ❑ 15 Paul Reinhart 23 | .75 | .35 |
| ❑ 16 Jim Sandlak 19 | .50 | .23 |
| ❑ 17 Petri Skriko 26 | .75 | .35 |
| ❑ 18 Doug Smith | .50 | .23 |
| ❑ 19 Stan Smyl 12 | 1.00 | .45 |
| ❑ 20 Harold Snepsts 27 | 1.00 | .45 |
| ❑ 21 Daryl Stanley 29 | .50 | .23 |
| ❑ 22 Rich Sutter 15 | .50 | .23 |
| ❑ 23 Tony Tanti 9 | .75 | .35 |
| ❑ 24 Steve Weeks 31 | .75 | .35 |

## 1990-91 Canucks Mohawk

This 29-card set of Vancouver Canucks was sponsored by Mohawk and issued in panels. After perforation, the cards measure the standard size. The front features color mugshots of the players, with thin red borders on a white card face. The player's name and position appear in black lettering above the picture, while the team logo in the lower right corner rounds out the card face. The

horizontally oriented backs have biographical information and statistics (regular season and playoff). The cards are unnumbered and checklisted below in alphabetical order.

| | MINT | NRMT |
|---|---|---|
| COMPLETE SET (29) | 15.00 | 6.75 |
| COMMON CARD (1-29) | .50 | .23 |

| | | |
|---|---|---|
| ❑ 1 Greg Adams | .75 | .35 |
| ❑ 2 Jim Agnew | .50 | .23 |
| ❑ 3 Steve Bozek | .50 | .23 |
| ❑ 4 Garth Butcher | .50 | .23 |
| ❑ 5 Dave Capuano | .50 | .23 |
| ❑ 6 Craig Coxe | .50 | .23 |
| ❑ 7 Gerald Diduck | .50 | .23 |
| ❑ 8 Troy Gamble | .75 | .35 |
| ❑ 9 Don Gibson | .50 | .23 |
| ❑ 10 Kevan Guy | .50 | .23 |
| ❑ 11 Robert Kron | .50 | .23 |
| ❑ 12 Tom Kurvers | .50 | .23 |
| ❑ 13 Igor Larionov | 1.50 | .70 |
| ❑ 14 Doug Lidster | .50 | .23 |
| ❑ 15 Trevor Linden | 2.00 | .90 |
| ❑ 16 Jyrki Lumme | .75 | .35 |
| ❑ 17 Jay Mazur | .50 | .23 |
| ❑ 18 Andrew McBain | .50 | .23 |
| ❑ 19 Kirk McLean | 1.50 | .70 |
| ❑ 20 Rob Murphy | .50 | .23 |
| ❑ 21 Petr Nedved | 1.50 | .70 |
| ❑ 22 Robert Nordmark | .50 | .23 |
| ❑ 23 Gino Odjick | .75 | .35 |
| ❑ 24 Adrien Plavsic | .50 | .23 |
| ❑ 25 Dan Quinn | .50 | .23 |
| ❑ 26 Jim Sandlak | .50 | .23 |
| ❑ 27 Stan Smyl | .75 | .35 |
| ❑ 28 Ronnie Stern | .50 | .23 |
| ❑ 29 Garry Valk | .50 | .23 |

## 1990-91 Canucks Molson

This set features large (approximately 8" by 10") glossy color close-up photos of Canucks, who were honored as the Molson Canadian Player of the Month. The photos are enclosed by a gold border. The player's name appears in the bottom gold border. At the bottom center is a picture of the Molson Cup. The team logo and a Molson logo in the lower corners round out the front. The backs are blank, and the unnumbered photos are checklisted below in alphabetical order.

| | MINT | NRMT |
|---|---|---|
| COMPLETE SET (6) | 40.00 | 18.00 |
| COMMON CARD (1-6) | 5.00 | 2.20 |

| | | |
|---|---|---|
| ❑ 1 Brian Bradley | 5.00 | 2.20 |
| ❑ 2 Troy Gamble | 5.00 | 2.20 |
| ❑ 3 Doug Lidster | 5.00 | 2.20 |
| ❑ 4 Trevor Linden | 10.00 | 4.50 |
| ❑ 5 Kirk McLean (Facing right) | 8.00 | 3.60 |
| ❑ 6 Kirk McLean (Facing front) | 8.00 | 3.60 |

## 1991 Canucks Panini Team Stickers

This 32-sticker set was issued in a plastic bag that contained two 16-sticker sheets (approximately 9" by 12") and a foldout poster, "Super Poster - Hockey 91", on which the stickers could be affixed. The players' names appear only on the poster, not on the stickers. Each sticker measures about 2 1/8" by 2 7/8" and features a color player action shot on its white-bordered front. The back of the white sticker sheet is lined off into 16 panels, each carrying the logos for Panini, the NHL, and the NHLPA, as well as the same number that appears on the front of the sticker. Every Canadian NHL team was featured in this promotion. Each team set was available by mail-order from Panini Canada Ltd. for 2.99 plus 50 cents for shipping and handling.

| | MINT | NRMT |
|---|---|---|
| COMPLETE SET (32) | 4.00 | 1.80 |
| COMMON STICKER (1-24) | .05 | .02 |
| COMMON STICKER (A-H) | .15 | .07 |

| | | |
|---|---|---|
| ❑ 1 Greg Adams | .10 | .05 |
| ❑ 2 Jim Agnew | .05 | .02 |
| ❑ 3 Steve Bozek | .05 | .02 |
| ❑ 4 Brian Bradley | .20 | .09 |
| ❑ 5 Garth Butcher | .05 | .02 |
| ❑ 6 Dave Capuano | .05 | .02 |
| ❑ 7 Craig Coxe | .05 | .02 |
| ❑ 8 Troy Gamble | .10 | .05 |
| ❑ 9 Kevan Guy | .05 | .02 |
| ❑ 10 Robert Kron | .05 | .02 |
| ❑ 11 Igor Larionov | .25 | .11 |
| ❑ 12 Doug Lidster | .10 | .05 |
| ❑ 13 Trevor Linden | .50 | .23 |
| ❑ 14 Jyrki Lumme | .10 | .05 |
| ❑ 15 Andrew McBain | .05 | .02 |
| ❑ 16 Rob Murphy | .05 | .02 |
| ❑ 17 Petr Nedved | .50 | .23 |
| ❑ 18 Robert Nordmark | .05 | .02 |
| ❑ 19 Adrien Plavsic | .05 | .02 |
| ❑ 20 Dan Quinn | .10 | .05 |
| ❑ 21 Jim Sandlak | .05 | .02 |
| ❑ 22 Petri Skriko | .10 | .05 |
| ❑ 23 Stan Smyl | .20 | .09 |
| ❑ 24 Ronnie Stern | .05 | .02 |
| ❑ A Team Logo Left Side | .15 | .07 |
| ❑ B Team Logo Right Side | .15 | .07 |
| ❑ C Canucks in Action Upper Left Corner | .15 | .07 |
| ❑ D Canucks in Action Lower Left Corner | .15 | .07 |
| ❑ E Game Action Upper Right Corner | .15 | .07 |
| ❑ F Game Action Lower Right Corner | .15 | .07 |
| ❑ G Kirk McLean | .50 | .23 |
| ❑ H Trevor Linden | .50 | .23 |

## 1991-92 Canucks Autograph Cards

These autograph cards, each measuring approximately 3 3/4" by 8 1/2", were issued by the team with a large white area at the bottom for the players to sign. The front features a glossy color close-up photo, with the year and the team logo in the white border above the picture. In cursive lettering, the player's name and number appear below the picture, with his position printed in block lettering. The unnumbered cards are blank on the back and checklisted below in alphabetical order.

| | MINT | NRMT |
|---|---|---|
| COMPLETE SET (23) | 25.00 | 11.00 |
| COMMON CARD (1-23) | .50 | .23 |

| | | |
|---|---|---|
| ❑ 1 Greg Adams | 1.00 | .45 |
| ❑ 2 Pavel Bure | 8.00 | 3.60 |
| ❑ 3 Dave Babych | 1.00 | .45 |
| ❑ 4 Geoff Courtnall | 1.00 | .45 |
| ❑ 5 Gerald Diduck | .50 | .23 |
| ❑ 6 Robert Dirk | .50 | .23 |
| ❑ 7 Troy Gamble | .75 | .35 |
| ❑ 8 Randy Gregg | .50 | .23 |
| ❑ 9 Robert Kron | .50 | .23 |
| ❑ 10 Igor Larionov | 1.50 | .70 |
| ❑ 11 Doug Lidster | .50 | .23 |
| ❑ 12 Trevor Linden | 2.50 | 1.10 |
| ❑ 13 Jyrki Lumme | .75 | .35 |
| ❑ 14 Kirk McLean | 2.50 | 1.10 |
| ❑ 15 Sergio Momesso | .50 | .23 |
| ❑ 16 Rob Murphy | .50 | .23 |
| ❑ 17 Dana Murzyn | .50 | .23 |
| ❑ 18 Petr Nedved | 2.50 | 1.10 |
| ❑ 19 Gino Odjick | .75 | .35 |
| ❑ 20 Adrien Plavsic | .50 | .23 |
| ❑ 21 Cliff Ronning | 1.00 | .45 |
| ❑ 22 Jim Sandlak | .50 | .23 |
| ❑ 23 Ryan Walter | .50 | .23 |

## 1991-92 Canucks Molson

This set features large (approximately 8" by 10") glossy color close-up photos of Canucks who were honored as the Molson Canadian Player of the Month or Player of the Year. The photos are enclosed by white, red, and blue border stripes. A gold leaf appear above the picture, while a gold plaque identifying the player appears below the picture. The team logo and a Molson logo appear in the lower corners. The backs are blank, and the unnumbered photos are checklisted below in alphabetical order.

| | MINT | NRMT |
|---|---|---|
| COMPLETE SET (7) | 50.00 | 22.00 |
| COMMON CARD (1-7) | 4.00 | 1.80 |

| | | |
|---|---|---|
| ❑ 1 Greg Adams | 4.00 | 1.80 |
| ❑ 2 Pavel Bure (White uniform) | 15.00 | 6.75 |
| ❑ 3 Pavel Bure POY (Black uniform) | 15.00 | 6.75 |
| ❑ 4 Igor Larionov | 6.00 | 2.70 |
| ❑ 5 Trevor Linden | 7.00 | 3.10 |
| ❑ 6 Kirk McLean | 7.00 | 3.10 |
| ❑ 7 Cliff Ronning | 4.00 | 1.80 |

## 1991-92 Canucks Team Issue 8x10

This set features 8" by 10" glossy color close-up photos of the Vancouver Canucks. The photos are enclosed by a thin black border. In cursive lettering, the player's name and number appear below the picture, with his position printed in block lettering. The team logo in the lower left corner completes the front. The backs carry a black and white head shot, biography, 1990-91 season summary, career highlights, personal information, and complete statistics. The cards are unnumbered and checklisted below in alphabetical order.

| | MINT | NRMT |
|---|---|---|
| COMPLETE SET (23) | 75.00 | 34.00 |
| COMMON CARD (1-23) | 3.00 | 1.35 |

| | | |
|---|---|---|
| ❑ 1 Greg Adams | 4.00 | 1.80 |
| ❑ 2 Pavel Bure | 15.00 | 6.75 |
| ❑ 3 Dave Babych | 3.00 | 1.35 |
| ❑ 4 Geoff Courtnall | 4.00 | 1.80 |
| ❑ 5 Gerald Diduck | 3.00 | 1.35 |
| ❑ 6 Robert Dirk | 3.00 | 1.35 |
| ❑ 7 Troy Gamble | 4.00 | 1.80 |
| ❑ 8 Randy Gregg | 3.00 | 1.35 |
| ❑ 9 Robert Kron | 3.00 | 1.35 |
| ❑ 10 Igor Larionov | 4.00 | 1.80 |
| ❑ 11 Doug Lidster | 3.00 | 1.35 |
| ❑ 12 Trevor Linden | 5.00 | 2.20 |
| ❑ 13 Jyrki Lumme | 3.00 | 1.35 |
| ❑ 14 Kirk McLean | 5.00 | 2.20 |
| ❑ 15 Sergio Momesso | 3.00 | 1.35 |
| ❑ 16 Rob Murphy | 3.00 | 1.35 |
| ❑ 17 Dana Murzyn | 3.00 | 1.35 |
| ❑ 18 Petr Nedved | 5.00 | 2.20 |
| ❑ 19 Gino Odjick | 4.00 | 1.80 |
| ❑ 20 Adrien Plavsic | 3.00 | 1.35 |
| ❑ 21 Cliff Ronning | 4.00 | 1.80 |
| ❑ 22 Jim Sandlak | 3.00 | 1.35 |
| ❑ 23 Ryan Walter | 3.00 | 1.35 |

## 1992-93 Canucks Road Trip Art

Dubbed "Road Trip Art Cards," this set of 25 approximately 4 3/4" by 7" player portraits was available only at Subway and Payless stores. Each week for six weeks, a set of four player portraits was released at a suggested price of 2.29 per pack. Also there was a tab inside each package and one could win a pair of 1993-94 season tickets, autographed Road Trip prints, limited edition Road Trip prints, Road Trip puzzles, and Road Trip coloring books. The photos are black-and-white and picture the Canuck players dressed in western garb. A gold foil facsimile autograph is printed near the bottom. The backs carry the player's name in a wide red stripe at the top. Humorous text in the form of player quotes rests against a white background along with the team logo and the words "Road Trip." A bright yellow stripe accents the bottom of the card and contains manufacturer information. The portraits are listed below in alphabetical order with the week issued denoted.

| | MINT | NRMT |
|---|---|---|
| COMPLETE SET (25) | 15.00 | 6.75 |
| COMMON CARD (1-25) | .50 | .23 |

| | | |
|---|---|---|
| ❑ 1 Greg Adams W1 | .75 | .35 |
| ❑ 2 Shawn Antoski W5 | .50 | .23 |
| ❑ 3 Dave Babych W5 | .75 | .35 |
| ❑ 4 Pavel Bure W3 | 5.00 | 2.20 |
| ❑ 5 Geoff Courtnall W5 | .75 | .35 |
| ❑ 6 Gerald Diduck W4 | .50 | .23 |
| ❑ 7 Robert Dirk W5 | .50 | .23 |
| ❑ 8 Tom Fergus W3 | .50 | .23 |
| ❑ 9 Robert Kron W2 | .50 | .23 |
| ❑ 10 Doug Lidster W2 | .50 | .23 |
| ❑ 11 Trevor Linden W1 | 1.50 | .70 |
| ❑ 12 Jyrki Lumme W1 | .75 | .35 |
| ❑ 13 Kirk McLean W2 | 1.50 | .70 |
| ❑ 14 Sergio Momesso W2 | .50 | .23 |
| ❑ 15 Dana Murzyn W3 | .50 | .23 |
| ❑ 16 Petr Nedved W4 | 1.50 | .70 |
| ❑ 17 Gino Odjick W4 | 1.00 | .45 |
| ❑ 18 Adrien Plavsic W6 | .50 | .23 |
| ❑ 19 Cliff Ronning W6 | .75 | .35 |
| ❑ 20 Jim Sandlak W6 | .50 | .23 |
| ❑ 21 Jiri Slegr W1 | .50 | .23 |
| ❑ 22 Garry Valk W4 | .50 | .23 |
| ❑ 23 Ryan Walter W5 | .50 | .23 |
| ❑ 24 Dixon Ward W3 | .50 | .23 |
| ❑ 25 Kay Whitmore W6 | .75 | .35 |

## 1994-95 Canucks Program Inserts

Measuring approximately 8" by 10 1/2", these program inserts feature the 1994-95 Vancouver Canucks. The fronts have color action player shots with white borders. The player's name, number and position appear on the fronts, along with the words "Canucks Collector Series" in a bar at the top. The backs are blank. The inserts are unnumbered and checklisted below in alphabetical order.

| | MINT | NRMT |
|---|---|---|
| COMPLETE SET (22) | 80.00 | 36.00 |
| COMMON CARD (1-22) | 4.00 | 1.80 |

| | | |
|---|---|---|
| ❑ 1 Greg Adams | 5.00 | 2.20 |
| ❑ 2 Shawn Antoski | 4.00 | 1.80 |
| ❑ 3 Dave Babych | 4.00 | 1.80 |
| ❑ 4 Jeff Brown | 5.00 | 2.20 |
| ❑ 5 Pavel Bure | 12.00 | 5.50 |
| ❑ 6 Geoff Courtnall | 5.00 | 2.20 |
| ❑ 7 Gerald Diduck | 4.00 | 1.80 |
| ❑ 8 Robert Dirk | 4.00 | 1.80 |
| ❑ 9 Martin Gelinas | 5.00 | 2.20 |
| ❑ 10 Brian Glynn | 4.00 | 1.80 |
| ❑ 11 Tim Hunter | 5.00 | 2.20 |
| ❑ 12 Nathan LaFayette | 4.00 | 1.80 |
| ❑ 13 Trevor Linden | 6.00 | 2.70 |
| ❑ 14 Jyrki Lumme | 5.00 | 2.20 |
| ❑ 15 Kirk McLean | 6.00 | 2.70 |
| ❑ 16 Dana Murzyn | 4.00 | 1.80 |
| ❑ 17 Gino Odjick | 5.00 | 2.20 |
| ❑ 18 Adrien Plavsic | 4.00 | 1.80 |
| ❑ 19 Cliff Ronning | 5.00 | 2.20 |
| ❑ 20 Jiri Slegr | 4.00 | 1.80 |
| ❑ 21 Dixon Ward | 4.00 | 1.80 |
| ❑ 22 Kay Whitmore | 5.00 | 2.20 |

## 1995-96 Canucks Building the Dream Art

This 18-card set of the Vancouver Canucks features 5" by 7" borderless black-and-white player photos in construction worker poses with gold facsimile autographs at the bottom. The backs carry player information. This set continues the tradition begun in 1992-93 with the Canucks Road Trip Art set.

| | MINT | NRMT |
|---|---|---|
| COMPLETE SET (18) | 15.00 | 6.75 |
| COMMON CARD (1-18) | .50 | .23 |

| | | |
|---|---|---|
| ❑ 1 Kirk McLean | 1.00 | .45 |
| ❑ 2 Kay Whitmore | .60 | .25 |
| ❑ 3 Bret Hedican | .50 | .23 |
| ❑ 4 Tim Hunter | .50 | .23 |
| ❑ 5 Dana Murzyn | .50 | .23 |
| ❑ 6 Jyrki Lumme | .60 | .25 |
| ❑ 7 Cliff Ronning | .75 | .35 |
| ❑ 8 Jeff Brown | .75 | .35 |
| ❑ 9 Martin Gelinas | 1.00 | .45 |
| ❑ 10 Pavel Bure | 5.00 | 2.20 |
| ❑ 11 Jiri Slegr | .50 | .23 |
| ❑ 12 Sergio Momesso | .50 | .23 |
| ❑ 13 Gino Odjick | 1.00 | .45 |
| ❑ 14 Geoff Courtnall | .50 | .23 |
| ❑ 15 John McIntyre | .50 | .23 |
| ❑ 16 Trevor Linden | 2.00 | .90 |
| ❑ 17 Mike Peca | 1.00 | .45 |
| ❑ 18 Dave Babych | .50 | .23 |

## 1996-97 Canucks Postcards

This extremely attractive, 27-postcard set was produced by the Canucks and sponsored by IGA grocery stores as a promotional giveaway. The highly stylized fronts have an action color photo with the team name above, and a row of team logos to the right. Immediately below the photo is a strip for autographing. The backs are blank. As the postcards are unnumbered, they are listed according to their sweater number, which is displayed on the lower right hand front corner.

| | MINT | NRMT |
|---|---|---|
| COMPLETE SET (27) | 15.00 | 6.75 |
| COMMON POSTCARD | .25 | .11 |
| ❑ 1 Kirk McLean | .75 | .35 |
| ❑ 3 Bret Hedican | .25 | .11 |
| ❑ 4 Mark Wotton | .25 | .11 |
| ❑ 5 Dana Murzyn | .25 | .11 |
| ❑ 6 Adrian Aucoin | .25 | .11 |
| ❑ 7 David Roberts | .25 | .11 |
| ❑ 8 Donald Brashear | .25 | .11 |
| ❑ 9 Russ Courtnall | .50 | .23 |
| ❑ 10 Esa Tikkanen | .50 | .23 |
| ❑ 16 Trevor Linden | .75 | .35 |
| ❑ 17 Mike Ridley | .50 | .23 |
| ❑ 18 Troy Crowder | .25 | .11 |
| ❑ 19 Markus Naslund | .50 | .23 |
| ❑ 20 Alexander Semak | .25 | .11 |
| ❑ 21 Jyrki Lumme | .50 | .23 |
| ❑ 23 Martin Gelinas | .75 | .35 |
| ❑ 24 Scott Walker | .50 | .23 |
| ❑ 26 Mike Sillinger | .25 | .11 |
| ❑ 27 Leif Rohlin | .25 | .11 |
| ❑ 29 Gino Odjick | .75 | .35 |
| ❑ 30 Mike Fountain | .50 | .23 |
| ❑ 31 Corey Hirsch | .75 | .35 |
| ❑ 32 Chris Joseph | .25 | .11 |
| ❑ 44 Dave Babych | .50 | .23 |
| ❑ 89 Alexander Mogilny | 1.50 | .70 |
| ❑ 96 Pavel Bure | 4.00 | 1.80 |
| ❑ NNO Team Photo | .50 | .23 |

## 1974-75 Capitals White Borders

This 25-card set measures approximately 5" by 7" is printed on very thin paper stock. The fronts have black-and-white player portraits with white borders. The player's name and the team logo appear under the photo. The backs are blank. The cards are unnumbered and checklisted below in alphabetical order.

| | NRMT-MT | EXC |
|---|---|---|
| COMPLETE SET (25) | 45.00 | 20.00 |
| COMMON CARD (1-25) | 2.00 | .90 |
| ❑ 1 John Adams | 2.00 | .90 |
| ❑ 2 Jim Anderson CO | 2.00 | .90 |
| ❑ 3 Ron Anderson | 2.00 | .90 |
| ❑ 4 Steve Atkinson | 2.00 | .90 |
| ❑ 5 Michel Belhumeur | 4.00 | 1.80 |
| ❑ 6 Mike Bloom | 2.00 | .90 |
| ❑ 7 Gord Brooks | 2.00 | .90 |
| ❑ 8 Bruce Cowick | 2.00 | .90 |
| ❑ 9 Denis Dupere | 2.00 | .90 |
| ❑ 10 Jack Egers | 2.00 | .90 |
| ❑ 11 Jim Hrycuik | 2.00 | .90 |
| ❑ 12 Greg Joly | 3.00 | 1.35 |
| ❑ 13 Dave Kryskow | 2.00 | .90 |
| ❑ 14 Yvon Labre | 3.00 | 1.35 |
| ❑ 15 Pete Laframboise | 2.00 | .90 |
| ❑ 16 Bill Lesuk | 2.00 | .90 |
| ❑ 17 Ron Low | 4.00 | 1.80 |
| ❑ 18 Joe Lundrigan | 2.00 | .90 |
| ❑ 19 Mike Marson | 3.00 | 1.35 |
| ❑ 20 Bill Mikkelson | 2.00 | .90 |
| ❑ 21 Doug Mohns | 4.00 | 1.80 |
| ❑ 22 Andre Peloffy | 2.00 | .90 |
| ❑ 23 Milt Schmidt GM | 5.00 | 2.20 |
| ❑ 24 Gord Smith | 2.00 | .90 |
| ❑ 25 Tom Williams | 3.00 | 1.35 |

## 1981-82 Capitals

This 21-card set measures approximately 5" by 7". The fronts have black-and-white player portraits with white borders. The player's name, postion, jersey number, and the team logo appear under the photo. The backs are blank. The cards are unnumbered and checklisted below in alphabetical order.

| | NRMT-MT | EXC |
|---|---|---|
| COMPLETE SET (21) | 30.00 | 13.50 |
| COMMON CARD (1-21) | 1.00 | .45 |
| ❑ 1 Timo Blomqvist | 1.00 | .45 |
| ❑ 2 Bobby Carpenter | 3.00 | 1.35 |
| ❑ 3 Glen Currie | 1.00 | .45 |
| ❑ 4 Gaetan Duchesne | 1.50 | .70 |
| ❑ 5 Mike Gartner | 10.00 | 4.50 |
| ❑ 6 Rick Green | 1.50 | .70 |
| ❑ 7 Randy Holt | 1.00 | .45 |
| ❑ 8 Wes Jarvis | 1.00 | .45 |
| ❑ 9 Al Jensen | 1.50 | .70 |
| ❑ 10 Dennis Maruk | 3.00 | 1.35 |
| ❑ 11 Terry Murray | 1.00 | .45 |
| ❑ 12 Lee Norwood | 1.00 | .45 |
| ❑ 13 Mike Palmateer | 3.00 | 1.35 |
| ❑ 14 Dave Parro | 1.50 | .70 |
| ❑ 15 Torrie Robertson | 1.50 | .70 |
| ❑ 16 Greg Theberge | 1.00 | .45 |
| ❑ 17 Chris Valentine | 1.00 | .45 |
| ❑ 18 Darren Veitch | 1.00 | .45 |
| ❑ 20 Howard Walker | 1.00 | .45 |
| ❑ 21 Ryan Walter | 2.00 | .90 |

## 1982-83 Capitals

This 25-card set measures approximately 5" by 7". The fronts have black-and-white player portraits with white borders. The player's name, postion, jersey number, and the team logo appear under the photo. The backs are blank. The cards are unnumbered and checklisted below in alphabetical order. The card of Scot Stevens appears one year before his Rookie Card.

| | NRMT-MT | EXC |
|---|---|---|
| COMPLETE SET (25) | 40.00 | 18.00 |
| COMMON CARD (1-25) | 1.00 | .45 |
| ❑ 1 Timo Blomqvist | 1.00 | .45 |
| ❑ 2 Ted Bulley | 1.00 | .45 |
| ❑ 3 Bobby Carpenter | 2.00 | .90 |
| ❑ 4 Glen Currie | 1.00 | .45 |
| ❑ 5 Brian Engblom | 1.50 | .70 |
| ❑ 6 Mike Gartner | 8.00 | 3.60 |
| ❑ 7 Bob Gould | 1.00 | .45 |
| ❑ 8 Bengt Gustafsson | 2.00 | .90 |
| ❑ 9 Alan Haworth | 1.00 | .45 |
| ❑ 10 Randy Holt | 1.00 | .45 |
| ❑ 11 Ken Houston | 1.00 | .45 |
| ❑ 12 Doug Jarvis | 2.00 | .90 |
| ❑ 13 Rod Langway | 4.00 | 1.80 |
| ❑ 14 Craig Laughlin | 1.00 | .45 |
| ❑ 15 Dennis Maruk | 2.00 | .90 |
| ❑ 16 Bryan Murray CO | 1.00 | .45 |
| ❑ 17 Terry Murray ACO | 1.00 | .45 |
| ❑ 18 Lee Norwood | 1.00 | .45 |
| ❑ 19 Milan Novy | 1.00 | .45 |
| ❑ 20 Dave Parro | 1.50 | .70 |
| ❑ 21 David Poile GM | 1.00 | .45 |
| ❑ 22 Pat Riggin | 2.50 | 1.10 |
| ❑ 23 Scott Stevens | 10.00 | 4.50 |
| ❑ 24 Chris Valentine | 1.00 | .45 |
| ❑ 25 Darren Veitch | 1.00 | .45 |

## 1984-85 Capitals Pizza Hut

These cards of Washington Capitals were given out to members of the Junior Capitals Club and measure approximately 4 1/2" by 6". The front features a color action photo of the player, with three blue stripes on the picture. The back has a small head shot of the player and his career statistics. The cards are unnumbered and hence are listed below alphabetically by player name.

| | MINT | NRMT |
|---|---|---|
| COMPLETE SET (15) | 35.00 | 16.00 |
| COMMON CARD (1-15) | 1.50 | .70 |
| ❑ 1 Bob Carpenter | 2.00 | .90 |
| ❑ 2 Dave Christian | 2.50 | 1.10 |
| ❑ 3 Glen Currie | 1.50 | .70 |
| ❑ 4 Gaetan Duchesne | 1.50 | .70 |
| ❑ 5 Mike Gartner | 7.50 | 3.40 |
| ❑ 6 Bob Gould | 1.50 | .70 |
| ❑ 7 Bengt Gustafsson | 2.00 | .90 |
| ❑ 8 Alan Haworth | 1.50 | .70 |
| ❑ 9 Doug Jarvis | 2.00 | .90 |
| ❑ 10 Al Jensen | 2.00 | .90 |
| ❑ 11 Rod Langway | 3.00 | 1.35 |
| ❑ 12 Craig Laughlin | 1.50 | .70 |
| ❑ 13 Larry Murphy | 5.00 | 2.20 |
| ❑ 14 Pat Riggin | 2.00 | .90 |
| ❑ 15 Scott Stevens | 7.50 | 3.40 |

## 1985-86 Capitals Pizza Hut

These cards of Washington Capitals were mailed three at a time to members of the Junior Capitals Club and measure approximately 4 1/2" by 6". The front features a color action photo of the player, with three red stripes on the picture. The back has a small head shot of the player and his career statistics. When Doug Jarvis, Pat Riggin, and Darren Veitch were traded, supposedly their cards were pulled and never mailed to club members. It is alleged that these cards were destroyed and only a few were kept. Consequently, these player cards are scarce.

| | MINT | NRMT |
|---|---|---|
| COMPLETE SET (15) | 35.00 | 16.00 |
| COMMON CARD (1-15) | 1.50 | .70 |
| ❑ 1 Bob Carpenter | 2.00 | .90 |
| ❑ 2 Dave Christian | 2.50 | 1.10 |
| ❑ 3 Gaetan Duchesne | 1.50 | .70 |
| ❑ 4 Mike Gartner | 6.00 | 2.70 |
| ❑ 5 Bob Gould | 1.50 | .70 |
| ❑ 6 Bengt Gustafsson | 2.00 | .90 |
| ❑ 7 Alan Haworth | 1.50 | .70 |
| ❑ 8 Doug Jarvis SP | 4.00 | 1.80 |
| ❑ 9 Al Jensen | 2.00 | .90 |
| ❑ 10 Rod Langway | 3.00 | 1.35 |
| ❑ 11 Craig Laughlin | 1.50 | .70 |
| ❑ 12 Larry Murphy | 5.00 | 2.20 |
| ❑ 13 Pat Riggin SP | 5.00 | 2.20 |
| ❑ 14 Scott Stevens | 6.00 | 2.70 |
| ❑ 15 Darren Veitch SP | 4.00 | 1.80 |

## 1986-87 Capitals Kodak

The 1986-87 Washington Capitals Team Photo Album was sponsored by Kodak. It consists of three large sheets joined together to form one continuous sheet. The first panel has a team photo measuring approximately 10" by 8". The second and third panels consist of player cards; after perforation, they measure approximately 2" by 2 5/8". The cards feature color posed photos, with player information below. The cards are unnumbered and we have checklisted them below in alphabetical order. Kevin Hatcher's card predates his Rookie Card by one year.

| | MINT | NRMT |
|---|---|---|
| COMPLETE SET (26) | 30.00 | 13.50 |
| COMMON CARD (1-26) | .75 | .35 |
| ❑ 1 Greg Adams | 1.50 | .70 |
| ❑ 2 John Barrett | .75 | .35 |
| ❑ 3 John Blum | .75 | .35 |
| ❑ 4 Dave Christian | 1.00 | .45 |
| ❑ 5 Bob Crawford | .75 | .35 |
| ❑ 6 Gaetan Duchesne | .75 | .35 |
| ❑ 7 Lou Franceschetti | .75 | .35 |
| ❑ 8 Mike Gartner | 4.00 | 1.80 |
| ❑ 9 Bob Gould | .75 | .35 |
| ❑ 10 Jeff Greenlaw | .75 | .35 |
| ❑ 11 Kevin Hatcher | 2.00 | .90 |
| ❑ 12 Alan Haworth | .75 | .35 |
| ❑ 13 David A. Jensen | .75 | .35 |
| ❑ 14 Rod Langway | 2.00 | .90 |
| ❑ 15 Craig Laughlin | .75 | .35 |
| ❑ 16 Bob Mason | 1.00 | .45 |
| ❑ 17 Kelly Miller | 1.00 | .45 |
| ❑ 18 Larry Murphy | 2.50 | 1.10 |
| ❑ 19 Bryan Murray CO | .75 | .35 |
| ❑ 20 Pete Peeters | 2.00 | .90 |
| ❑ 21 Michal Pivonka | 3.00 | 1.35 |
| ❑ 22 Mike Ridley | 2.00 | .90 |
| ❑ 23 Gary Sampson | .75 | .35 |
| ❑ 24 Greg Smith | .75 | .35 |
| ❑ 25 Scott Stevens | 4.00 | 1.80 |
| ❑ 26 Large Team Photo | 2.00 | .90 |

## 1986-87 Capitals Police

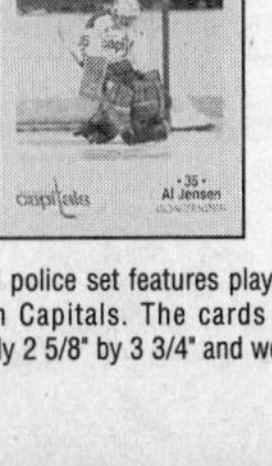

This 24-card police set features players of the Washington Capitals. The cards measure approximately 2 5/8" by 3 3/4" and were issued in two-card panels. The front has a color action photo on white card stock, with player information and the Capitals' logo below the picture. Inside a thin black border the back features a hockey tip ("Caps Tips"), an anti-crime tip, and logos of sponsoring police agenices. The cards are unnumbered and we have checklisted them below in alphabetical order, with the jersey number to the right of the player's name. Kevin Hatcher's card predates his Rookie Card by one year.

| | MINT | NRMT |
|---|---|---|
| COMPLETE SET (24) | 15.00 | 6.75 |
| COMMON CARD (1-24) | .50 | .23 |
| ❑ 1 Greg Adams 22 | 1.00 | .45 |
| ❑ 2 John Barrett 6 | .50 | .23 |
| ❑ 3 Bob Carpenter 10 | .50 | .23 |
| ❑ 4 Dave Christian 27 | .75 | .35 |
| ❑ 5 Yvon Corriveau 26 | .50 | .23 |
| ❑ 6 Gaetan Duchesne 14 | .50 | .23 |
| ❑ 7 Lou Franceschetti 32 | .50 | .23 |
| ❑ 8 Mike Gartner 11 | 3.00 | 1.35 |
| ❑ 9 Bob Gould 23 | .50 | .23 |
| ❑ 10 Kevin Hatcher 4 | 1.50 | .70 |
| ❑ 11 Alan Haworth 15 | .50 | .23 |
| ❑ 12 Al Jensen 35 | .60 | .25 |
| ❑ 13 David A. Jensen 9 | .50 | .23 |
| ❑ 14 Rod Langway 5 | 1.50 | .70 |
| ❑ 15 Craig Laughlin 18 | .50 | .23 |
| ❑ 16 Stephen Leach 21 | .75 | .35 |
| ❑ 17 Larry Murphy 8 | 2.00 | .90 |
| ❑ 18 Bryan Murray CO | .50 | .23 |
| ❑ 19 Pete Peeters 1 | 1.50 | .70 |
| ❑ 20 Jorgen Pettersson 12 | .50 | .23 |
| ❑ 21 Michal Pivonka 17 | 2.00 | .90 |
| ❑ 22 David Poile VP/GM | .50 | .23 |
| ❑ 23 Greg Smith 19 | .50 | .23 |
| ❑ 24 Scott Stevens 3 | 3.00 | 1.35 |

## 1987-88 Capitals Kodak

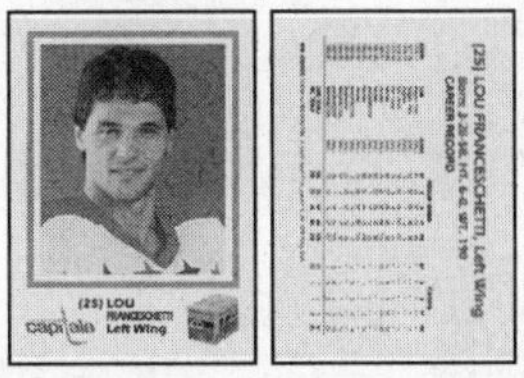

The 1987-88 Washington Capitals Team Photo Album was sponsored by Kodak. It consists of three large sheets, each measuring approximately 11" by 8 1/4" and joined together to form one continuous sheet. The first panel has a team photo, with the players' names listed according to rows below the picture. While the second panel presents three rows of five cards each, the third panel presents two rows of five cards, with five Kodak coupons completing the left over portion of the panel. After perforation, the cards measure approximately 2 3/16" by 2 15/16". They feature color-posed photos bordered in red, with player information below the picture. The Capitals' logo and a picture of a Kodak film box complete the card face. The back has biographical and statistical information in a horizontal format. The cards are checklisted below by sweater number.

| | MINT | NRMT |
|---|---|---|
| COMPLETE SET (26) | 20.00 | 9.00 |
| COMMON CARD | .50 | .23 |
| ❑ 1 Pete Peeters | 1.00 | .45 |
| ❑ 2 Garry Galley | 1.00 | .45 |
| ❑ 3 Scott Stevens | 2.00 | .90 |
| ❑ 4 Kevin Hatcher | 2.00 | .90 |
| ❑ 5 Rod Langway | 1.00 | .45 |
| ❑ 6 John Barrett | .50 | .23 |
| ❑ 8 Larry Murphy | 1.50 | .70 |
| ❑ 10 Kelly Miller | .75 | .35 |
| ❑ 11 Mike Gartner | 2.50 | 1.10 |
| ❑ 12 Peter Sundstrom | .75 | .35 |
| ❑ 16 Bengt Gustafsson | .75 | .35 |
| ❑ 17 Mike Ridley | 1.50 | .70 |
| ❑ 18 Craig Laughlin | .50 | .23 |
| ❑ 19 Greg Smith | .50 | .23 |
| ❑ 20 Michal Pivonka | 1.50 | .70 |
| ❑ 22 Greg Adams | 1.00 | .45 |
| ❑ 23 Bob Gould | .50 | .23 |
| ❑ 25 Lou Franceschetti | .50 | .23 |
| ❑ 27 Dave Christian | 1.00 | .45 |
| ❑ 29 Ed Kastelic | .50 | .23 |
| ❑ 30 Clint Malarchuk | 1.00 | .45 |
| ❑ 32 Dale Hunter | 1.50 | .70 |
| ❑ 34 Bill Houlder | .75 | .35 |
| ❑ XX Team Photo | 1.00 | .45 |
| ❑ xx Bryan Murray CO | .50 | .23 |
| ❑ xx David Poile VP/GM | .50 | .23 |

## 1987-88 Capitals Team Issue

This 23-card set measures 5 1/4" by 8". The fronts feature autographed color action photos. The backs carry a head shot, biography, 1986-87 recap, career highlights, personal information and complete statistics with the player's name, position and jersey number at the top. The cards are unnumbered and checklisted below in alphabetical order.

| | MINT | NRMT |
|---|---|---|
| COMPLETE SET (23) | 25.00 | 11.00 |
| COMMON CARD (1-23) | .75 | .35 |
| ❑ 1 Greg Adams | 1.25 | .55 |
| ❑ 2 John Barrett | .75 | .35 |
| ❑ 3 Dave Christian | 1.25 | .55 |
| ❑ 4 Lou Franceschetti | .75 | .35 |
| ❑ 5 Garry Galley | 1.50 | .70 |
| ❑ 6 Mike Gartner | 3.00 | 1.35 |
| ❑ 7 Bob Gould | .75 | .35 |
| ❑ 8 Bengt Gustafsson | 1.00 | .45 |
| ❑ 9 Kevin Hatcher | 3.00 | 1.35 |
| ❑ 10 Dale Hunter | 2.00 | .90 |
| ❑ 11 David Jensen | .75 | .35 |
| ❑ 12 Ed Kastelic | .75 | .35 |
| ❑ 13 Rod Langway | 1.25 | .55 |
| ❑ 14 Craig Laughlin | .75 | .35 |
| ❑ 15 Clint Malarchuk | 1.25 | .55 |
| ❑ 16 Kelly Miller | 1.00 | .45 |
| ❑ 17 Larry Murphy | 2.00 | .90 |
| ❑ 18 Pete Peeters | 1.50 | .70 |
| ❑ 19 Michal Pivonka | 2.00 | .90 |
| ❑ 20 Mike Ridley | 2.00 | .90 |
| ❑ 21 Greg Smith | .75 | .35 |
| ❑ 22 Scott Stevens | 2.50 | 1.10 |
| ❑ 23 Peter Sundstrom | 1.00 | .45 |

## 1988-89 Capitals Borderless

Measuring approximately 5" by 7", this 21-card set features the 1988-89 Washington Capitals. The fronts have borderless color action player photos. The backs carry player biography and statistics, season and career highlights, and short personal information. The cards are unnumbered and checklisted below in alphabetical order.

| | MINT | NRMT |
|---|---|---|
| COMPLETE SET (21) | 15.00 | 6.75 |
| COMMON CARD (1-21) | .75 | .35 |
| ❑ 1 Dave Christian | 1.00 | .45 |
| ❑ 2 Yvon Corriveau | .75 | .35 |
| ❑ 3 Geoff Courtnall | 2.00 | .90 |
| ❑ 4 Lou Franceschetti | .75 | .35 |
| ❑ 5 Mike Gartner | 2.00 | .90 |
| ❑ 6 Bob Gould | .75 | .35 |
| ❑ 7 Bengt Gustafsson | 1.00 | .45 |
| ❑ 8 Kevin Hatcher | 1.50 | .70 |
| ❑ 9 Dale Hunter | 1.50 | .70 |
| ❑ 10 Rod Langway | 1.50 | .70 |
| ❑ 11 Stephen Leach | .75 | .35 |
| ❑ 12 Grant Ledyard | .75 | .35 |
| ❑ 13 Clint Malarchuk | 1.00 | .45 |
| ❑ 14 Kelly Miller | .75 | .35 |
| ❑ 15 Larry Murphy | 1.50 | .70 |
| ❑ 16 Pete Peeters | 1.00 | .45 |
| ❑ 17 Michal Pivonka | 2.00 | .90 |
| ❑ 18 Mike Ridley | 1.50 | .70 |
| ❑ 19 Neil Sheehy | .75 | .35 |
| ❑ 20 Scott Stevens | 2.00 | .90 |
| ❑ 21 Peter Sundstrom | 1.00 | .45 |

## 1988-89 Capitals Smokey

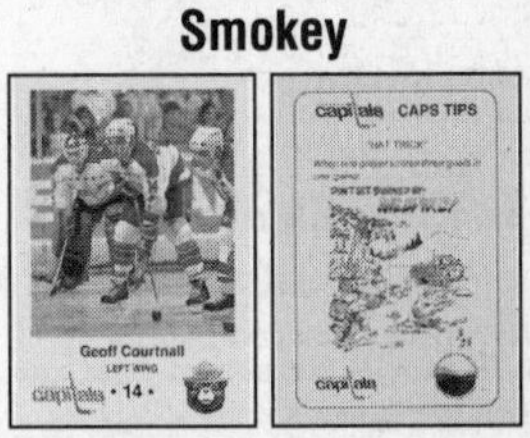


This 24-card safety set features players of the Washington Capitals. The cards measure approximately 2 5/8" by 3 3/4" and were issued in two-card panels. The front has a color action photo on white card stock, with player information and logos below the picture. Inside a thin black border the back features a hockey tip ("Caps Tips") and a fire prevention cartoon starring Smokey. The cards are unnumbered and we have checklisted them below in alphabetical order, with the sweater number to the right of the player's name. Geoff Courtnall's card predates his Rookie Card by a year.

| | MINT | NRMT |
|---|---|---|
| COMPLETE SET (24) | 15.00 | 6.75 |
| COMMON CARD (1-24) | .50 | .23 |

❑ 1 Dave Christian 27 .75 .35
❑ 2 Yvon Corriveau 26 .50 .23
❑ 3 Geoff Courtnall 14 1.50 .70
❑ 4 Lou Franceschetti 25 .50 .23
❑ 5 Mike Gartner 11 1.50 .70
❑ 6 Bob Gould 23 .50 .23
❑ 7 Bengt Gustafsson 16 .75 .35
❑ 8 Kevin Hatcher 4 1.00 .45
❑ 9 Dale Hunter 32 1.00 .45
❑ 10 Rod Langway 5 1.00 .45
❑ 11 Stephen Leach 21 .50 .23
❑ 12 Grant Ledyard 6 .50 .23
❑ 13 Clint Malarchuk 30 .75 .35
❑ 14 Kelly Miller 10 .50 .23
❑ 15 Larry Murphy 8 1.00 .45
❑ 16 Bryan Murray CO .75 .35
❑ 17 Pete Peeters 1 .75 .35
❑ 18 Michal Pivonka 20 1.50 .70
❑ 19 David Poile VP/GM .50 .23
❑ 20 Mike Ridley 17 1.00 .45
❑ 21 Neil Sheehy 15 .50 .23
❑ 22 Scott Stevens 3 1.50 .70
❑ 23 Peter Sundstrom 12 .75 .35
❑ 24 Title Card .50 .23
Smokey the Bear

## 1989-90 Capitals Kodak

The 1989-90 Washington Capitals Team Photo Album was co-sponsored by Kodak and W. Bell and Co. It consists of three large sheets, each measuring approximately 11" by 8 1/4" and joined together to form one continuous sheet. The first panel has a large blue square designated for autographs. While the second panel presents three rows of five cards each, the third panel presents two rows of five cards, with Kodak advertisements completing the left over portion of the panel. After perforation, the cards measure approximately 2 3/16" by 2 1/2". They feature color action photos bordered in red, with player information below the picture. The Capitals' logo and a picture of a Kodak film box complete the card face. The back has biographical and statistical information in a horizontal format. The cards are checklisted below by sweater number.

MINT NRMT
COMPLETE SET (25) 20.00 9.00
COMMON CARD .50 .23

❑ 1 Mike Liut 1.00 .45
❑ 3 Scott Stevens 2.00 .90
❑ 4 Kevin Hatcher 1.50 .70
❑ 5 Rod Langway 1.50 .70
❑ 6 Calle Johansson 1.00 .45
❑ 8 Bob Rouse .75 .35
❑ 10 Kelly Miller 1.00 .45
❑ 11 Tim Bergland .75 .35
❑ 12 John Tucker .75 .35
❑ 14 Geoff Courtnall 1.50 .70
❑ 15 Neil Sheehy .75 .35
❑ 16 Alan May .75 .35
❑ 17 Mike Ridley 1.00 .45
❑ 19 John Druce .75 .35
❑ 20 Michal Pivonka 1.00 .45
❑ 21 Stephen Leach .75 .35
❑ 22 Dino Ciccarelli 2.00 .90
❑ 26 Steve Maltais .75 .35
❑ 27 Bob Joyce .75 .35
❑ 29 Scot Kleinendorst .75 .35
❑ 32 Dale Hunter 1.50 .70
❑ 33 Don Beaupre 1.00 .45
❑ xx Rob Laird ACO .50 .23
❑ xx Terry Murray CO .50 .23
❑ xx David Poile VP/GM .50 .23

## 1989-90 Capitals Team Issue

This 23-card set measures approximately 5" by 7". The fronts feature full-bleed, posed color photos with the player's jersey as a background. The backs are blank. The cards are unnumbered and checklisted below in alphabetical order.

MINT NRMT
COMPLETE SET (23) 18.00 8.00
COMMON CARD (1-23) .50 .23

❑ 1 Don Beaupre .75 .35
❑ 2 Dave Christian .75 .35
❑ 3 Dino Ciccarelli 1.50 .70
❑ 4 Yvon Corriveau .50 .23
❑ 5 Geoff Courtnall 1.00 .45
❑ 6 Kevin Hatcher 1.00 .45
❑ 7 Bill Houlder .75 .35
❑ 8 Dale Hunter 1.00 .45
❑ 9 Calle Johansson .75 .35
❑ 10 Dimitri Khristich 1.50 .70
❑ 11 Scot Kleinendorst .50 .23
❑ 12 Nick Kypreos .50 .23
❑ 13 Rod Langway 1.00 .45
❑ 14 Stephen Leach .50 .23
❑ 15 Bob Mason .75 .35
❑ 16 Alan May .50 .23
❑ 17 Kelly Miller .75 .35
❑ 18 Michal Pivonka .75 .35
❑ 19 Mike Ridley .75 .35
❑ 20 Bob Rouse .50 .23
❑ 21 Neil Sheehy .50 .23
❑ 22 Scott Stevens 1.50 .70
❑ 23 Doug Wickenheiser .50 .23

## 1990-91 Capitals Kodak

The 1990-91 Washington Capitals Team Photo Album was sponsored by Kodak. It consists of three large sheets joined together to form one continuous sheet. The first panel has a team photo measuring approximately 10" by 8". The second and third panels consist of player cards; after perforation, they measure approximately 2" by 2 5/8". The cards feature color posed photos, with player information below. The cards are unnumbered and we have checklisted them below in alphabetical order.

MINT NRMT
COMPLETE SET (25) 15.00 6.75
COMMON CARD (1-25) .25 .11

❑ 1 Don Beaupre 1.00 .45
❑ 2 Tim Bergland .50 .23
❑ 3 Peter Bondra 5.00 2.20
❑ 4 Dino Ciccarelli 1.00 .45
❑ 5 John Druce .50 .23
❑ 6 Kevin Hatcher 1.00 .45
❑ 7 Dale Hunter 1.00 .45
❑ 8 Al Iafrate 1.50 .70
❑ 9 Calle Johansson .75 .35
❑ 10 Dimitri Khristich 1.00 .45
❑ 11 Nick Kypreos .50 .23
❑ 12 Mike Lalor .50 .23
❑ 13 Rod Langway 1.00 .45
❑ 14 Stephen Leach .50 .23
❑ 15 Mike Liut 1.00 .45
❑ 16 Alan May .50 .23
❑ 17 Kelly Miller .50 .23
❑ 18 Terry Murray CO .25 .11
❑ 19 John Perpich .50 .23
❑ 20 Michal Pivonka 1.00 .45
❑ 21 David Poile VP/GM .25 .11
❑ 22 Mike Ridley 1.00 .45
❑ 23 Ken Sabourin .50 .23
❑ 24 Mikhail Tatarinov .50 .23
❑ 25 Dave Tippett .50 .23

## 1990-91 Capitals Postcards

This 5 x 7 set features full color photos on the front and a blank back. Cards are unnumbered and checklisted below in alphabetical order.

MINT NRMT
COMPLETE SET (22) 20.00 9.00
COMMON CARD (1-22) .50 .23

❑ 1 Don Beaupre 1.00 .45
❑ 2 Tim Bergland .50 .23
❑ 3 Peter Bondra 5.00 2.20
❑ 4 Dino Ciccarelli 1.00 .45
❑ 5 John Druce .50 .23
❑ 6 Kevin Hatcher 1.00 .45
❑ 7 Jim Hrivnak .60 .25
❑ 8 Dale Hunter 1.00 .45
❑ 9 Al Iafrate 1.50 .70
❑ 10 Calle Johansson .75 .35
❑ 11 Nick Kypreos .50 .23
❑ 12 Mike Lalor .50 .23
❑ 13 Rod Langway 1.00 .45
❑ 14 Steve Leach .50 .23
❑ 15 Mike Liut 1.00 .45
❑ 16 Alan May .50 .23
❑ 17 Kelly Miller .50 .23
❑ 18 Rob Murray .50 .23
❑ 19 Michal Pivonka 1.00 .45
❑ 20 Mike Ridley 1.00 .45
❑ 21 Neil Sheehy .50 .23
❑ 22 Dave Tippett .50 .23

## 1990-91 Capitals Smokey

This fire safety set contains 22 cards and features members of the Washington Capitals. The cards measure approximately 2 1/2" by 3 3/4" and were issued in two-card panels. The front has a color action photo of the player, with player information below the picture between the Smokey the Bear and team logos. The back includes %%Caps Tips~ and a fire prevention message from Smokey.

MINT NRMT
COMPLETE SET (22) 12.00 5.50
COMMON CARD (1-22) .35 .16

❑ 1 Don Beaupre .75 .35
❑ 2 Tim Bergland .35 .16
❑ 3 Peter Bondra 4.00 1.80
❑ 4 Dino Ciccarelli 1.00 .45
❑ 5 John Druce .35 .16
❑ 6 Kevin Hatcher .75 .35
❑ 7 Jim Hrivnak .50 .23
❑ 8 Dale Hunter .75 .35
❑ 9 Calle Johansson .50 .23
❑ 10 Nick Kypreos .35 .16
❑ 11 Mike Lalor .35 .16
❑ 12 Rod Langway .75 .35
❑ 13 Stephen Leach .50 .23
❑ 14 Mike Liut 1.00 .45
❑ 15 Alan May .35 .16
❑ 16 Kelly Miller .35 .16
❑ 17 Rob Murray .35 .16
❑ 18 Michal Pivonka 1.00 .45
❑ 19 Mike Ridley .75 .35
❑ 20 Neil Sheehy .35 .16
❑ 21 Mikhail Tatarinov .35 .16
❑ 22 Dave Tippett .35 .16

## 1991-92 Capitals Junior 5x7

This 25-card set measures approximately 5" by 7" and features full-bleed glossy action photos; in small black type across the bottom, the uniform number, name, and position are burned in. The backs are blank.

MINT NRMT
COMPLETE SET (25) 18.00 8.00
COMMON CARD (1-25) .50 .23

❑ 1 Don Beaupre 1.00 .45
❑ 2 Tim Bergland .50 .23
❑ 3 Peter Bondra 4.00 1.80
❑ 4 Randy Burridge .75 .35
❑ 5 Shawn Chambers .50 .23
❑ 6 Dino Ciccarelli 1.50 .70
❑ 7 Sylvain Cote .75 .35
❑ 8 John Druce .50 .23
❑ 9 Jeff Greenlaw .50 .23
❑ 10 Kevin Hatcher 1.50 .70
❑ 11 Dale Hunter 1.50 .70
❑ 12 Al Iafrate 1.50 .70
❑ 13 Calle Johansson .75 .35
❑ 14 Dimitri Khristich 1.50 .70
❑ 15 Todd Krygier .50 .23
❑ 16 Nick Kypreos .50 .23
❑ 17 Mike Lalor .50 .23
❑ 18 Rod Langway 1.00 .45
❑ 19 Mike Liut 1.00 .45
❑ 20 Alan May .50 .23
❑ 21 Kelly Miller .50 .23
❑ 22 Michal Pivonka 1.50 .70
❑ 23 Mike Ridley 1.00 .45
❑ 24 Ken Sabourin .50 .23
❑ 25 Dave Tippett .50 .23

## 1991-92 Capitals Kodak

The 1991-92 Washington Capitals Team Photo Album was sponsored by Kodak. It consists of three large sheets joined together to form one continuous sheet. The first panel measures approximately 11" by 8," and it has blank space allotted for autographs. The second panel carries three rows with five player cards each; after perforation, they measure approximately 2 3/16" by 2 3/4." The third panel has two rows with five player cards each, and a final row consisting of two Kodak coupons. The cards feature color head shots, with player information, team logo, and a picture of a Kodak film box below. In a horizontal format, the backs have biographical and statistical information. Though the cards are unnumbered, they are arranged in alphabetical order by players' last names and checklisted below accordingly.

MINT NRMT
COMPLETE SET (25) 12.00 5.50
COMMON CARD (1-25) .35 .16

❑ 1 Don Beaupre .75 .35
❑ 2 Tim Bergland .35 .16
❑ 3 Peter Bondra 2.50 1.10
❑ 4 Randy Burridge .50 .23
❑ 5 Shawn Chambers .35 .16
❑ 6 Dino Ciccarelli 1.00 .45
❑ 7 Sylvain Cote .50 .23
❑ 8 John Druce .35 .16
❑ 9 Kevin Hatcher .75 .35
❑ 10 Jim Hrivnak .50 .23
❑ 11 Dale Hunter .75 .35
❑ 12 Al Iafrate 1.00 .45
❑ 13 Calle Johansson .50 .23
❑ 14 Dimitri Khristich 1.00 .45
❑ 15 Todd Krygier .35 .16
❑ 16 Nick Kypreos .35 .16
❑ 17 Rod Langway .75 .35
❑ 18 Mike Liut .75 .35
❑ 19 Paul MacDermid .35 .16
❑ 20 Alan May .35 .16
❑ 21 Kelly Miller .35 .16
❑ 22 Michal Pivonka 1.00 .45
❑ 23 Mike Ridley .75 .35
❑ 24 Brad Schlegel .35 .16
❑ 25 Dave Tippett .35 .16

## 1992-93 Capitals Kodak

The 1992-93 Washington Capitals Team Photo Album was sponsored by Kodak. It consists of three 8 1/4" by 11" sheets joined together to form one continuous sheet. The first panel has a slot for collecting autographs. The second and third panels consist of player cards; after

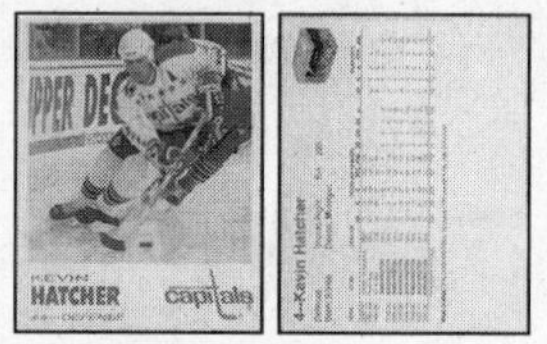


perforation, they measure approximately 2 3/16" by 2 3/4". The fronts feature color action player photos with white borders. Player information and the team logo are printed in the bottom white border. The horizontal backs carry biography and complete statistical information. Though the cards are unnumbered, they are arranged alphabetically on the sheet and checklisted below accordingly.

MINT NRMT
COMPLETE SET (25) 15.00 6.75
COMMON CARD (1-25) .50 .23

❑ 1 Shawn Anderson .50 .23
❑ 2 Don Beaupre 1.00 .45
❑ 3 Peter Bondra 2.50 1.10
❑ 4 Randy Burridge .60 .25
❑ 5 Bobby Carpenter .60 .25
❑ 6 Paul Cavallini .50 .23
❑ 7 Sylvain Cote .50 .23
❑ 8 Pat Elynuik .50 .23
❑ 9 Kevin Hatcher .75 .35
❑ 10 Jim Hrivnak .60 .25
❑ 11 Dale Hunter 1.00 .45
❑ 12 Al Iafrate 1.00 .45
❑ 13 Calle Johansson .60 .25
❑ 14 Keith Jones .60 .25
❑ 15 Dimitri Khristich 1.00 .45
❑ 16 Steve Konowalchuk .75 .35
❑ 17 Todd Krygier .50 .23
❑ 18 Rod Langway .75 .35
❑ 19 Paul MacDermid .50 .23
❑ 20 Alan May .50 .23
❑ 21 Kelly Miller .50 .23
❑ 22 Michal Pivonka 1.00 .45
❑ 23 Mike Ridley .75 .35
❑ 24 Reggie Savage .50 .23
❑ 25 Jason Woolley .60 .25

## 1995-96 Capitals

This 28-card set was given away as a premium in complete sheet form at a game late in the '95-96 season. The cards -- which feature the Caps in their new sweaters -- are perforated to be removed. As the cards are unnumbered, they are listed below in alphabetical order.

MINT NRMT
COMPLETE SET (28) 12.00 5.50
COMMON CARD .10 .05

❑ 1 Jason Allison .75 .35
❑ 2 Craig Berube .35 .16
❑ 3 Peter Bondra 3.00 1.35
❑ 4 Jim Carey 1.00 .45
❑ 5 Sylvain Cote .35 .16
❑ 6 Mike Eagles .35 .16
❑ 7 Martin Gendron .35 .16
❑ 8 Sergei Gonchar .35 .16
❑ 9 Dale Hunter .75 .35
❑ 10 Calle Johansson .50 .23
❑ 11 Jim Johnson .35 .16
❑ 12 Keith Jones .50 .23
❑ 13 Joe Juneau .75 .35
❑ 14 Kevin Kaminski .35 .16
❑ 15 Ken Klee .35 .16
❑ 16 Olaf Kolzig 1.25 .55
❑ 17 Steve Konowalchuk .75 .35
❑ 18 Kelly Miller .35 .16
❑ 19 Jeff Nelson .35 .16
❑ 20 Pat Peake .35 .16
❑ 21 Michal Pivonka .75 .35
❑ 22 Joe Reekie .35 .16
❑ 23 Jim Schoenfeld CO .25 .11
❑ 24 Slapshot .10 .05
Mascot
❑ 25 Slapshot .10 .05
Mascot
❑ 26 Mark Tinordi .35 .16
❑ 27 Stefan Ustorf .35 .16
❑ 28 Brendan Witt .50 .23

## 1997-98 Carolina Hurricanes

The set is unnumbered and checklisted below in alphabetical order.

MINT NRMT
COMPLETE SET (28) 8.00 3.60
COMMON CARD (28) .10 .05

❑ 1 Jeff Brown .20 .09
❑ 2 Sean Burke .75 .35
❑ 3 Adam Burt .20 .09
❑ 4 Steve Chiasson .20 .09
❑ 5 Enrico Ciccone .20 .09
❑ 6 Kevin Dineen .30 .14
❑ 7 Nelson Emerson .30 .14
❑ 8 Martin Gelinas .30 .14
❑ 9 Stu Grimson .30 .14
❑ 10 Steve Halko .20 .09
❑ 11 Kevin Haller .20 .09
❑ 12 Sean Hill .20 .09
❑ 13 Sami Kapanen 1.25 .55
❑ 14 Trevor Kidd .75 .35
❑ 15 Robert Kron .30 .14
❑ 16 Steve Leach .20 .09
❑ 17 Curtis Leschyshyn .20 .09
❑ 18 Kent Manderville .20 .09
❑ 19 Jeff O'Neill .20 .09
❑ 20 Nolan Pratt .20 .09
❑ 21 Keith Primeau .75 .35
❑ 22 Paul Ranheim .20 .09
❑ 23 Steven Rice .30 .14
❑ 24 Gary Roberts .30 .14
❑ 25 Geoff Sanderson .50 .23
❑ 26 Glen Wesley .30 .14
❑ 27 Paul Maurice .20 .09
Tom Webster
Randy Ladouceur CO
❑ 28 Stormy(Mascot) .10 .05

## 1936 Champion Postcards

The set is in the same format as the 1936 Triumph set and was issued in the same manner as the Triumph set, except as an insert in "Boys" magazine published weekly in Great Britain. Three cards were issued in the first week of the promotion in "The Champion" and then one per week in "Boys" magazine. The cards are sepia toned and are postcard size, measuring approximately 3 1/2" by 5 1/2". The set is subtitled "Stars of the Ice Rinks". The cards are unnumbered and hence presented in alphabetical order. The date mentioned below is the issue date as noted on the card back in Canadian style, day/month/year.

EX-MT VG-E
COMPLETE SET (10) 1750.00 900.00
COMMON CARD (1-10) 80.00 40.00

❑ 1 Marty Barry 80.00 40.00
18/1/36
❑ 2 Harold(Mush) March 80.00 40.00
8/2/36
❑ 3 Reg(Hooley) Smith 175.00 90.00
18/1/36
❑ 4 Sweeney Schriner 175.00 90.00
22/2/36
❑ 5 King Clancy 500.00 250.00
18/1/36
❑ 6 Bill Cook 200.00 100.00
1/2/36
❑ 7 Pep Kelly 80.00 40.00
25/1/36
❑ 8 Aurel Joliat 450.00 220.00
15/2/36
❑ 9 Charles Conacher 400.00 200.00
29/2/36
❑ 10 Fred(Bun) Cook 200.00 100.00
7/3/36

## 1963-65 Chex Photos

The 1963-65 Chex Photos measure approximately 5" by 7". This unnumbered set depicts players from four NHL teams, Chicago Blackhawks, Detroit Red Wings, Toronto Maple Leafs, and Montreal Canadiens. These blank-backed, stiff-cardboard photos are thought to have been issued during the 1963-64 (Canadiens and Maple Leafs) and 1964-65 (Blackhawks, Red Wings, and Canadiens again) seasons. Since these photo cards are unnumbered, they are ordered and numbered below alphabetically according to the player's name. There is rumored to be a Denis DeJordy in this set. The complete set price below

includes both varieties of Beliveau and Rousseau.

| | NRMT | VG-E |
|---|---|---|
| COMPLETE SET (60) | 2000.00 | 900.00 |
| COMMON CARD (1-58) | 15.00 | 6.75 |
| ❑ 1 George Armstrong | 40.00 | 18.00 |
| ❑ 2 Ralph Backstrom | 20.00 | 9.00 |
| ❑ 3 Dave Balon | 15.00 | 6.75 |
| ❑ 4 Bob Baun | 25.00 | 11.00 |
| ❑ 5A Jean Beliveau (Looking ahead) | 100.00 | 45.00 |
| ❑ 5B Jean Beliveau (Looking left) | 100.00 | 45.00 |
| ❑ 6 Red Berenson | 20.00 | 9.00 |
| ❑ 7 Hector(Toe) Blake CO | 30.00 | 13.50 |
| ❑ 8 Johnny Bower | 50.00 | 22.00 |
| ❑ 9 Alex Delvecchio | 40.00 | 18.00 |
| ❑ 10 Kent Douglas | 15.00 | 6.75 |
| ❑ 11 Dick Duff | 20.00 | 9.00 |
| ❑ 12 Phil Esposito | 150.00 | 70.00 |
| ❑ 13 John Ferguson | 25.00 | 11.00 |
| ❑ 14 Bill Gadsby | 30.00 | 13.50 |
| ❑ 15 Jean Gauthier | 15.00 | 6.75 |
| ❑ 16 BoomBoom Geoffrion | 50.00 | 22.00 |
| ❑ 17 Glenn Hall | 50.00 | 22.00 |
| ❑ 18 Terry Harper | 20.00 | 9.00 |
| ❑ 19 Billy Harris | 15.00 | 6.75 |
| ❑ 20 Bill(Red) Hay | 15.00 | 6.75 |
| ❑ 21 Paul Henderson | 40.00 | 18.00 |
| ❑ 22 Bill Hicke | 15.00 | 6.75 |
| ❑ 23 Wayne Hillman | 15.00 | 6.75 |
| ❑ 24 Charlie Hodge | 25.00 | 11.00 |
| ❑ 25 Tim Horton | 100.00 | 45.00 |
| ❑ 26 Gordie Howe | 225.00 | 100.00 |
| ❑ 27 Bobby Hull | 200.00 | 90.00 |
| ❑ 28 Punch Imlach CO | 20.00 | 9.00 |
| ❑ 29 Red Kelly | 40.00 | 18.00 |
| ❑ 30 Dave Keon | 60.00 | 27.00 |
| ❑ 31 Jacques Laperriere | 25.00 | 11.00 |
| ❑ 32 Ed Litzenberger | 15.00 | 6.75 |
| ❑ 33 Parker MacDonald | 15.00 | 6.75 |
| ❑ 34 Bruce MacGregor | 15.00 | 6.75 |
| ❑ 35 Frank Mahovlich | 60.00 | 27.00 |
| ❑ 36 Chico Maki | 20.00 | 9.00 |
| ❑ 37 Pit Martin | 20.00 | 9.00 |
| ❑ 38 John MacMillan | 15.00 | 6.75 |
| ❑ 39 Stan Mikita | 60.00 | 27.00 |
| ❑ 40 Bob Nevin | 15.00 | 6.75 |
| ❑ 41 Pierre Pilote | 25.00 | 11.00 |
| ❑ 42 Marcel Pronovost | 30.00 | 13.50 |
| ❑ 43 Claude Provost | 15.00 | 6.75 |
| ❑ 44 Bob Pulford | 30.00 | 13.50 |
| ❑ 45 Marc Reaume | 15.00 | 6.75 |
| ❑ 46 Henri Richard | 60.00 | 27.00 |
| ❑ 47A Bobby Rousseau | 20.00 | 9.00 |
| ❑ 47B Bob Rousseau | 30.00 | 13.50 |
| ❑ 48 Eddie Shack | 40.00 | 18.00 |
| ❑ 49 Don Simmons | 20.00 | 9.00 |
| ❑ 50 Allan Stanley | 30.00 | 13.50 |
| ❑ 51 Ron Stewart | 15.00 | 6.75 |
| ❑ 52 Jean-Guy Talbot | 20.00 | 9.00 |
| ❑ 53 Gilles Tremblay | 15.00 | 6.75 |
| ❑ 54 J.C. Tremblay | 20.00 | 9.00 |
| ❑ 55 Norm Ullman | 40.00 | 18.00 |
| ❑ 56 Elmer(Moose) Vasko | 15.00 | 6.75 |
| ❑ 57 Ken Wharram | 20.00 | 9.00 |
| ❑ 58 Gump Worsley | 50.00 | 22.00 |

## 1992-93 Clark Candy Mario Lemieux

Issued by Clark Candy, this three-card set features three different color player photos of the Pittsburgh Penguins' Mario Lemieux. One card was inserted in each Bun candy bar pack. Each card measures approximately 3" by 3" and has a facsimile autograph in black inscribed across the picture. The pictures have black borders, and a gold stripe carrying the team logo cuts across the bottom of the card. The backs present biographical information, career summary, honors and awards, or career playing record. Only card number 3 listed below has a black-and-white close-up photo on its back. The cards are unnumbered and checklisted below in alphabetical order. There are reports that Lemieux may have signed some cards for insertion; to date, these rumors remain unsubstantiated.

| | MINT | NRMT |
|---|---|---|
| COMPLETE SET (3) | 6.00 | 2.70 |
| COMMON CARD (1-3) | 2.50 | 1.10 |
| ❑ 1 Mario Lemieux (Skating left) | 2.50 | 1.10 |
| ❑ 2 Mario Lemieux (Close-up photo) | 2.50 | 1.10 |
| ❑ 3 Mario Lemieux (Skating right) | 2.50 | 1.10 |

## 1972-73 Cleveland Crusaders WHA

This 15-card set measures 8 1/2" x 11" and features a black and white head shot on the front along with a facsimile autograph, and a Cleveland Crusaders color logo in the lower left corner. Featured portraits were done by Charles Linnett. The cards are unnumbered and checklisted below in alphabetical order.

| | MINT | NRMT |
|---|---|---|
| COMPLETE SET (15) | 40.00 | 18.00 |
| COMMON CARD (1-15) | 3.00 | 1.35 |
| ❑ 1 Ron Buchanan | 3.00 | 1.35 |
| ❑ 2 Ray Clearwater | 3.00 | 1.35 |
| ❑ 3 Bob Dillabough | 3.00 | 1.35 |
| ❑ 4 Grant Erickson | 3.00 | 1.35 |
| ❑ 5 Ted Hodgson | 3.00 | 1.35 |
| ❑ 6 Ralph Hopiavouri | 3.00 | 1.35 |
| ❑ 7 Bill Horton | 3.00 | 1.35 |
| ❑ 8 Gary Jarrett | 3.00 | 1.35 |
| ❑ 9 Skip Krake | 3.00 | 1.35 |
| ❑ 10 Wayne Muloin | 3.00 | 1.35 |
| ❑ 11 Bill Needham CO | 3.00 | 1.35 |
| ❑ 12 Rick Pumple | 4.00 | 1.80 |
| ❑ 13 Paul Shmyr | 3.00 | 1.35 |
| ❑ 14 Robert Whidden | 3.00 | 1.35 |
| ❑ 15 Jim Wiste | 4.00 | 1.80 |

## 1964-65 Coca-Cola Caps

The 1964-65 Coca-Cola Caps set contains 108 bottle caps measuring approximately 1 1/8" in diameter. The caps feature a black and white picture on the tops, and are unnumbered except for uniform numbers (which is listed to the right of the player's name in the checklist below). These caps were issued with both Coke and Sprite. Because Sprite was sold in lesser quantities than Coke, those caps tend to be harder to find. As such, some dealers charge a slight premium for those caps. There are also rumoured to be French variations for both the Coke and the Sprite caps, making a total of four possible ways to put the set together. While no transactions have been reported for these French versions, it's fair to assume that their scarcity alone might earn them a slight premium over the prices listed below.The set numbering below is by teams and numerically within teams as follows: Boston Bruins (1-18), Chicago Blackhawks (19-36), Detroit Red Wings (37-54), Montreal Canadiens (55-72, New York Rangers (73-90), and Toronto Maple Leafs (91-108). A plastic holder (in the shape of a rink) was also available for holding and displaying the caps; the holder is not included in the complete set price below.

| | NRMT | VG-E |
|---|---|---|
| COMPLETE SET (108) | 600.00 | 275.00 |
| COMMON CAP (1-108) | 3.00 | 1.35 |
| ❑ 1 Ed Johnston 1 | 5.00 | 2.20 |
| ❑ 2 Bob McCord 4 | 3.00 | 1.35 |
| ❑ 3 Ted Green 6 | 4.00 | 1.80 |
| ❑ 4 Orland Kurtenbach 7 | 4.00 | 1.80 |
| ❑ 5 Gary Dornhoefer 8 | 4.00 | 1.80 |
| ❑ 6 Johnny Bucyk 9 | 10.00 | 4.50 |
| ❑ 7 Tom Johnson 10 | 4.00 | 1.80 |
| ❑ 8 Tom Williams 11 | 3.00 | 1.35 |
| ❑ 9 Murray Balfour 12 | 3.00 | 1.35 |
| ❑ 10 Forbes Kennedy 14 | 3.00 | 1.35 |
| ❑ 11 Murray Oliver 16 | 3.00 | 1.35 |
| ❑ 12 Dean Prentice 17 | 4.00 | 1.80 |
| ❑ 13 Ed Westfall 18 | 4.00 | 1.80 |
| ❑ 14 Reg Fleming 19 | 3.00 | 1.35 |
| ❑ 15 Leo Boivin 20 | 4.00 | 1.80 |
| ❑ 16 Ab McDonald 21 | 3.00 | 1.35 |
| ❑ 17 Ron Schock 23 | 3.00 | 1.35 |
| ❑ 18 Bob Leiter 24 | 3.00 | 1.35 |
| ❑ 19 Glenn Hall 1 | 12.00 | 5.50 |
| ❑ 20 Doug Mohns 2 | 4.00 | 1.80 |
| ❑ 21 Pierre Pilote 3 | 5.00 | 2.20 |
| ❑ 22 Elmer Vasko 4 | 3.00 | 1.35 |
| ❑ 23 Fred Stanfield 6 | 3.00 | 1.35 |
| ❑ 24 Phil Esposito 7 | 40.00 | 18.00 |
| ❑ 25 Bobby Hull 9 | 50.00 | 22.00 |
| ❑ 26 Bill(Red) Hay 11 | 2.50 | 1.10 |
| ❑ 27 John Brenneman 12 | 2.50 | 1.10 |
| ❑ 28 Doug Robinson 14 | 3.00 | 1.35 |
| ❑ 29 Eric Nesterenko 15 | 4.00 | 1.80 |
| ❑ 30 Chico Maki 16 | 4.00 | 1.80 |
| ❑ 31 Ken Wharram 17 | 3.00 | 1.35 |
| ❑ 32 John McKenzie 18 | 3.00 | 1.35 |
| ❑ 33 Al MacNeil 19 | 3.00 | 1.35 |
| ❑ 34 Wayne Hillman 20 | 3.00 | 1.35 |
| ❑ 35 Stan Mikita 21 | 15.00 | 6.75 |
| ❑ 36 Denis DeJordy 30 | 4.00 | 1.80 |
| ❑ 37 Roger Crozier 1 | 5.00 | 2.20 |
| ❑ 38 Albert Langlois 2 | 3.00 | 1.35 |
| ❑ 39 Marcel Pronovost 3 | 4.00 | 1.80 |
| ❑ 40 Bill Gadsby 4 | 4.00 | 1.80 |
| ❑ 41 Doug Barkley 5 | 3.00 | 1.35 |
| ❑ 42 Norm Ullman 7 | 8.00 | 3.60 |
| ❑ 43 Pit Martin 8 | 4.00 | 1.80 |
| ❑ 44 Gordie Howe 9 | 60.00 | 27.00 |
| ❑ 45A Gordie Howe 10 | 80.00 | 36.00 |
| ❑ 45B Alex Delvecchio 10 | 30.00 | 13.50 |
| ❑ 46 Ron Murphy 12 | 3.00 | 1.35 |
| ❑ 47 Larry Jeffrey 14 | 3.00 | 1.35 |
| ❑ 48 Ted Lindsay 15 | 10.00 | 4.50 |
| ❑ 49 Bruce MacGregor 16 | 3.00 | 1.35 |
| ❑ 50 Floyd Smith 17 | 3.00 | 1.35 |
| ❑ 51 Gary Bergman 18 | 3.00 | 1.35 |
| ❑ 52 Paul Henderson 19 | 6.00 | 2.70 |
| ❑ 53 Parker MacDonald 20 | 3.00 | 1.35 |
| ❑ 54 Eddie Joyal 21 | 3.00 | 1.35 |
| ❑ 55 Charlie Hodge 1 | 4.00 | 1.80 |
| ❑ 56 Jacques Laperriere 2 | 4.00 | 1.80 |
| ❑ 57 J.C. Tremblay 3 | 4.00 | 1.80 |
| ❑ 58 Jean Beliveau 4 | 20.00 | 9.00 |
| ❑ 59 Ralph Backstrom 6 | 4.00 | 1.80 |
| ❑ 60 Bill Hicke 8 | 3.00 | 1.35 |
| ❑ 61 Ted Harris 10 | 3.00 | 1.35 |
| ❑ 62 Claude Larose 11 | 3.00 | 1.35 |
| ❑ 63 Yvan Cournoyer 12 | 15.00 | 6.75 |
| ❑ 64 Claude Provost 14 | 3.00 | 1.35 |
| ❑ 65 Bobby Rousseau 15 | 4.00 | 1.80 |
| ❑ 66 Henri Richard 16 | 12.00 | 5.50 |
| ❑ 67 Jean-Guy Talbot 17 | 4.00 | 1.80 |
| ❑ 68 Terry Harper 19 | 4.00 | 1.80 |
| ❑ 69 Dave Balon 20 | 3.00 | 1.35 |
| ❑ 70 Gilles Tremblay 21 | 3.00 | 1.35 |
| ❑ 71 John Ferguson 22 | 5.00 | 2.20 |
| ❑ 72 Jim Roberts 26 | 3.00 | 1.35 |
| ❑ 73 Jacques Plante 1 | 20.00 | 9.00 |
| ❑ 74 Harry Howell 3 | 4.00 | 1.80 |
| ❑ 75 Arnie Brown 4 | 3.00 | 1.35 |
| ❑ 76 Don Johns 6 | 3.00 | 1.35 |
| ❑ 77 Rod Gilbert 7 | 8.00 | 3.60 |
| ❑ 78 Bob Nevin 8 | 3.00 | 1.35 |
| ❑ 79 Dick Duff 9 | 4.00 | 1.80 |
| ❑ 80 Earl Ingarfield 10 | 3.00 | 1.35 |
| ❑ 81 Vic Hadfield 11 | 4.00 | 1.80 |
| ❑ 82 Jim Mikol 12 | 3.00 | 1.35 |
| ❑ 83 Val Fonteyne 14 | 3.00 | 1.35 |
| ❑ 84 Jim Neilson 15 | 3.00 | 1.35 |
| ❑ 85 Rod Seiling 16 | 3.00 | 1.35 |
| ❑ 86 Lou Angotti 17 | 3.00 | 1.35 |
| ❑ 87 Phil Goyette 20 | 3.00 | 1.35 |
| ❑ 88 Camille Henry 21 | 4.00 | 1.80 |
| ❑ 89 Don Marshall 22 | 4.00 | 1.80 |
| ❑ 90 Marcel Paille 23 | 4.00 | 1.80 |
| ❑ 91 Johnny Bower 1 | 10.00 | 4.50 |
| ❑ 92 Carl Brewer 2 | 4.00 | 1.80 |
| ❑ 93 Red Kelly 4 | 10.00 | 4.50 |
| ❑ 94 Tim Horton 7 | 15.00 | 6.75 |
| ❑ 95 George Armstrong 9 | 8.00 | 3.60 |
| ❑ 96 Andy Bathgate 10 | 8.00 | 3.60 |
| ❑ 97 Ron Ellis 11 | 4.00 | 1.80 |
| ❑ 98 Ralph Stewart 12 | 3.00 | 1.35 |
| ❑ 99 Dave Keon 14 | 8.00 | 3.60 |
| ❑ 100 Dickie Moore 16 | 5.00 | 2.20 |
| ❑ 101 Don McKenney 17 | 3.00 | 1.35 |
| ❑ 102 Kent Douglas 19 | 3.00 | 1.35 |
| ❑ 103 Bob Pulford 20 | 5.00 | 2.20 |
| ❑ 104 Bob Baun 21 | 5.00 | 2.20 |
| ❑ 105 Eddie Shack 23 | 8.00 | 3.60 |
| ❑ 106 Terry Sawchuk 24 | 20.00 | 9.00 |
| ❑ 107 Allan Stanley 26 | 5.00 | 2.20 |
| ❑ 108 Frank Mahovlich | 12.00 | 5.50 |
| ❑ xx Cap Holder (Plastic Rink) | 100.00 | 45.00 |

## 1965-66 Coca-Cola

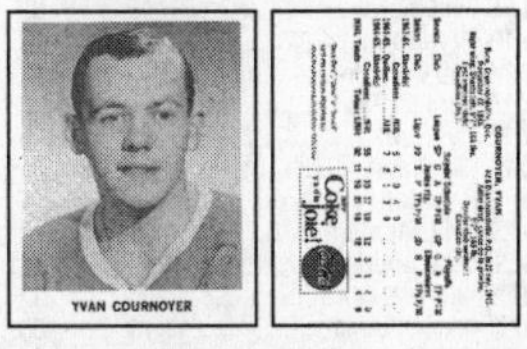

This set contains 108 unnumbered black and white cards featuring 18 players from each of the six NHL teams. The cards were issued in perforated team panels of 18 cards. The cards are priced below as perforated cards; the value of unperforated strips is approximately 20-30 percent more than the sum of the individual prices. The cards are approximately 2 3/4" by 3 1/2" and have bi-lingual (French and English) write-ups on the card backs. An album to hold the cards was available from the company on a mail-order basis. It retails in the $50-$75 range in Near Mint. The set numbering below is by teams and numerically within teams as follows: Boston Bruins (1-18), Chicago Blackhawks (19-36), Detroit Red Wings (37-54), Montreal Canadiens (55-72, New York Rangers (73-90), and Toronto Maple Leafs (91-108).

| | NRMT-MT | EXC |
|---|---|---|
| COMPLETE SET (108) | 400.00 | 180.00 |
| COMMON CARD (1-108) | 1.50 | .70 |
| ❑ 1 Gerry Cheevers | 30.00 | 13.50 |
| ❑ 2 Albert Langlois | 1.50 | .70 |
| ❑ 3 Ted Green | 2.00 | .90 |
| ❑ 4 Ron Stewart | 1.50 | .70 |
| ❑ 5 Bob Woytowich | 1.50 | .70 |
| ❑ 6 Johnny Bucyk | 6.00 | 2.70 |
| ❑ 7 Tom Williams | 1.50 | .70 |
| ❑ 8 Forbes Kennedy | 1.50 | .70 |
| ❑ 9 Murray Oliver | 1.50 | .70 |
| ❑ 10 Dean Prentice | 2.00 | .90 |
| ❑ 11 Ed Westfall | 2.00 | .90 |
| ❑ 12 Reg Fleming | 1.50 | .70 |
| ❑ 13 Leo Boivin | 3.00 | 1.35 |
| ❑ 14 Parker MacDonald | 1.50 | .70 |
| ❑ 15 Bob Dillabough | 1.50 | .70 |
| ❑ 16 Barry Ashbee | 5.00 | 2.20 |
| ❑ 17 Don Awrey | 1.50 | .70 |
| ❑ 18 Bernie Parent | 30.00 | 13.50 |
| ❑ 19 Glenn Hall | 10.00 | 4.50 |
| ❑ 20 Doug Mohns | 2.00 | .90 |
| ❑ 21 Pierre Pilote | 3.00 | 1.35 |
| ❑ 22 Elmer Vasko | 1.50 | .70 |
| ❑ 23 Matt Ravlich | 1.50 | .70 |
| ❑ 24 Fred Stanfield | 1.50 | .70 |
| ❑ 25 Phil Esposito | 40.00 | 18.00 |
| ❑ 26 Bobby Hull | 40.00 | 18.00 |
| ❑ 27 Dennis Hull | 5.00 | 2.20 |
| ❑ 28 Bill(Red) Hay | 2.00 | .90 |
| ❑ 29 Ken Hodge | 3.00 | 1.35 |
| ❑ 30 Eric Nesterenko | 2.00 | .90 |
| ❑ 31 Chico Maki | 2.00 | .90 |
| ❑ 32 Ken Wharram | 2.00 | .90 |
| ❑ 33 Al MacNeil | 1.50 | .70 |
| ❑ 34 Doug Jarrett | 1.50 | .70 |
| ❑ 35 Stan Mikita | 12.00 | 5.50 |
| ❑ 36 Dave Dryden | 2.50 | 1.10 |
| ❑ 37 Roger Crozier | 3.00 | 1.35 |
| ❑ 38 Warren Godfrey | 1.50 | .70 |
| ❑ 39 Bert Marshall | 1.50 | .70 |
| ❑ 40 Bill Gadsby | 3.00 | 1.35 |
| ❑ 41 Doug Barkley | 1.50 | .70 |
| ❑ 42 Norm Ullman | 4.00 | 1.80 |
| ❑ 43 Gordie Howe | 60.00 | 27.00 |
| ❑ 44 Alex Delvecchio | 5.00 | 2.20 |
| ❑ 45 Val Fonteyne | 1.50 | .70 |
| ❑ 46 Ron Murphy | 1.50 | .70 |
| ❑ 47 Billy Harris | 1.50 | .70 |
| ❑ 48 Bruce MacGregor | 1.50 | .70 |
| ❑ 49 Floyd Smith | 1.50 | .70 |
| ❑ 50 Paul Henderson | 8.00 | 3.60 |
| ❑ 51 Andy Bathgate | 3.50 | 1.55 |
| ❑ 52 Ab McDonald | 1.50 | .70 |
| ❑ 53 Gary Bergman | 1.50 | .70 |
| ❑ 54 Hank Bassen | 2.50 | 1.10 |
| ❑ 55 Charlie Hodge | 3.00 | 1.35 |
| ❑ 56 Jacques Laperriere | 3.00 | 1.35 |
| ❑ 57 Jean-Claude Tremblay | 2.00 | .90 |
| ❑ 58 Jean Beliveau | 15.00 | 6.75 |
| ❑ 59 Ralph Backstrom | 2.00 | .90 |
| ❑ 60 Dick Duff | 2.50 | 1.10 |
| ❑ 61 Ted Harris | 2.00 | .90 |
| ❑ 62 Claude Larose | 1.50 | .70 |
| ❑ 63 Yvan Cournoyer | 20.00 | 9.00 |
| ❑ 64 Claude Provost | 2.00 | .90 |
| ❑ 65 Bobby Rousseau | 2.00 | .90 |
| ❑ 66 Henri Richard | 10.00 | 4.50 |
| ❑ 67 Jean-Guy Talbot | 2.50 | 1.10 |
| ❑ 68 Terry Harper | 1.50 | .70 |
| ❑ 69 Gilles Tremblay | 1.50 | .70 |
| ❑ 70 John Ferguson | 2.50 | 1.10 |
| ❑ 71 Jim Roberts | 2.00 | .90 |
| ❑ 72 Gump Worsley | 10.00 | 4.50 |
| ❑ 73 Ed Giacomin | 25.00 | 11.00 |
| ❑ 74 Wayne Hillman | 1.50 | .70 |
| ❑ 75 Harry Howell | 4.00 | 1.80 |
| ❑ 76 Arnie Brown | 1.50 | .70 |
| ❑ 77 Doug Robinson | 1.50 | .70 |
| ❑ 78 Mike McMahon | 1.50 | .70 |
| ❑ 79 Rod Gilbert | 5.00 | 2.20 |
| ❑ 80 Bob Nevin | 1.50 | .70 |
| ❑ 81 Earl Ingarfield | 1.50 | .70 |
| ❑ 82 Vic Hadfield | 2.50 | 1.10 |
| ❑ 83 Bill Hicke | 1.50 | .70 |
| ❑ 84 John McKenzie | 2.00 | .90 |
| ❑ 85 Jim Neilson | 1.50 | .70 |
| ❑ 86 Jean Ratelle | 5.00 | 2.20 |
| ❑ 87 Phil Goyette | 1.50 | .70 |
| ❑ 88 Garry Peters | 1.50 | .70 |
| ❑ 89 Don Marshall | 1.50 | .70 |
| ❑ 90 Don Simmons | 2.50 | 1.10 |
| ❑ 91 Johnny Bower | 10.00 | 4.50 |
| ❑ 92 Marcel Pronovost | 4.00 | 1.80 |
| ❑ 93 Red Kelly | 5.00 | 2.20 |
| ❑ 94 Tim Horton | 15.00 | 6.75 |
| ❑ 95 Ron Ellis | 2.00 | .90 |
| ❑ 96 George Armstrong | 4.00 | 1.80 |
| ❑ 97 Brit Selby | 1.50 | .70 |
| ❑ 98 Pete Stemkowski | 1.50 | .70 |
| ❑ 99 Dave Keon | 10.00 | 4.50 |
| ❑ 100 Mike Walton | 2.00 | .90 |
| ❑ 101 Kent Douglas | 1.50 | .70 |
| ❑ 102 Bob Pulford | 4.00 | 1.80 |
| ❑ 103 Bob Baun | 4.00 | 1.80 |
| ❑ 104 Eddie Shack | 5.00 | 2.20 |
| ❑ 105 Orland Kurtenbach | 2.00 | .90 |
| ❑ 106 Allan Stanley | 3.00 | 1.35 |
| ❑ 107 Frank Mahovlich | 10.00 | 4.50 |
| ❑ 108 Terry Sawchuk | 20.00 | 9.00 |
| ❑ NNO Album | 80.00 | 36.00 |

## 1965-66 Coca-Cola Booklets

These four "How To Play" booklets are illustrated with cartoon-like drawings, each measure approximately 4 7/8" by 3 1/2", and are printed on newsprint. Booklets A and B have yellow covers, while booklets C and D have blue covers. The 31-page booklets could be obtained through a mail-in offer. Under bottle caps of Coke or Sprite (marked with a

hockey stick) were cork liners bearing the name of the player who wrote a booklet. To receive a booklet, the collector had to send in ten cork liners (with name of the player whose booklet was desired), ten cents, and the correct answer to a trivia question. Issued by Coca-Cola to promote hockey among the school-aged, they are designed in comic book fashion showing correct positions and moves for goalie, forward (both defensive and offensive), and defenseman. They are authored by the hockey players listed below. They are lettered rather than numbered and we have checklisted them below accordingly. The booklets were available in both English and French.

| | NRMT-MT | EXC |
|---|---|---|
| COMPLETE SET (4) | 150.00 | 70.00 |
| COMMON CARD (A-D) | 25.00 | 11.00 |
| ❑ A Johnny Bower How To Play Goal | 50.00 | 22.00 |
| ❑ B Dave Keon How To Play Forward (Defensive) | 50.00 | 22.00 |
| ❑ C Jacques Laperriere How To Play Defence | 25.00 | 11.00 |
| ❑ D Henri Richard How To Play Forward (Offensive) | 50.00 | 22.00 |

## 1977-78 Coca-Cola

Each of these mini-cards measures approximately 1 3/8" by 1 3/8". The fronts feature a color "mug shot" of the player, with his name given above the picture. Red and blue lines form the borders on the sides of the picture. The year 1978, the city from which the team hails, and the Coke logo appear below the picture. Inside a black border (with rounded corners) the back has basic biographical information. These unnumbered cards are listed alphabetically below.

| | NRMT-MT | EXC |
|---|---|---|
| COMPLETE SET (30) | 80.00 | 36.00 |
| COMMON CARD (1-30) | 1.50 | .70 |
| ❑ 1 Syl Apps | 1.50 | .70 |
| ❑ 2 Dave Burrows | 1.50 | .70 |
| ❑ 3 Bobby Clarke | 10.00 | 4.50 |
| ❑ 4 Yvan Cournoyer | 4.00 | 1.80 |
| ❑ 5 John Davidson | 3.00 | 1.35 |
| ❑ 6 Marcel Dionne | 6.00 | 2.70 |
| ❑ 7 Doug Favell | 2.50 | 1.10 |
| ❑ 8 Rod Gilbert | 3.00 | 1.35 |
| ❑ 9 Brian Glennie | 1.50 | .70 |
| ❑ 10 Butch Goring | 1.50 | .70 |
| ❑ 11 Lorne Henning | 1.50 | .70 |
| ❑ 12 Cliff Koroll | 1.50 | .70 |
| ❑ 13 Guy Lapointe | 3.00 | 1.35 |
| ❑ 14 Dave Maloney | 1.50 | .70 |
| ❑ 15 Pit Martin | 1.50 | .70 |
| ❑ 16 Lou Nanne | 1.50 | .70 |
| ❑ 17 Bobby Orr | 50.00 | 22.00 |
| ❑ 18 Brad Park | 4.00 | 1.80 |
| ❑ 19 Craig Ramsay | 1.50 | .70 |
| ❑ 20 Larry Robinson | 8.00 | 3.60 |
| ❑ 21 Jim Rutherford | 2.50 | 1.10 |
| ❑ 22 Don Saleski | 1.50 | .70 |
| ❑ 23 Steve Shutt | 4.00 | 1.80 |
| ❑ 24 Darryl Sittler | 6.00 | 2.70 |
| ❑ 25 Billy Smith | 5.00 | 2.20 |
| ❑ 26 Bob Stewart | 1.50 | .70 |
| ❑ 27 Rogatien Vachon | 4.00 | 1.80 |
| ❑ 28 Jimmy Watson | 1.50 | .70 |
| ❑ 29 Joe Watson | 1.50 | .70 |
| ❑ 30 Ed Westfall | 1.50 | .70 |

## 1994 Coke/Mac's Milk Gretzky POGs

This 18-disc set features POGs measuring approximately 1 5/8" in diameter. These cards

were offered through Mac's Milk stores in Canada (primarily Ontario); they were available at the store counter with the purchase of any Coke bottled product from May through middle of June of 1994. Inside a gold-foil holographic border, the fronts feature action color player photos with the words "The Great One" printed in black letters above the photo and a Coca-Cola Future Stars emblem at the bottom. The backs feature Gretzky's most prolific records and accomplishments.

| | MINT | NRMT |
|---|---|---|
| COMPLETE SET (18) | 15.00 | 6.75 |
| COMMON POG (1-18) | 1.00 | .45 |

❑ 1 Wayne Gretzky 1.00 .45
Most Assists& Career
❑ 2 Wayne Gretzky 1.00 .45
Most Points& Career
❑ 3 Wayne Gretzky 1.00 .45
Most 100 Point Seasons
❑ 4 Wayne Gretzky 1.00 .45
Most Three Goal Games& Career
❑ 5 Wayne Gretzky 1.00 .45
Most Goals& Season
❑ 6 Wayne Gretzky 1.00 .45
Most Points& Season
❑ 7 Wayne Gretzky 1.00 .45
Longest Consecutive Point Streak
❑ 8 Wayne Gretzky 1.00 .45
Most Assists& Game
❑ 9 Wayne Gretzky 1.00 .45
Most Goals& One Period
❑ 10 Wayne Gretzky 1.00 .45
Most Playoff Points& Career
❑ 11 Wayne Gretzky 1.00 .45
Most Points In One Playoff Year
❑ 12 Wayne Gretzky 1.00 .45
Most Goals All-Star Game& Career
❑ 13 Wayne Gretzky 1.00 .45
Most Goals& One Period& All-Star Game
❑ 14 Wayne Gretzky 1.00 .45
MVP (Hart Trophy)
❑ 15 Wayne Gretzky 1.00 .45
NHL Leading Scorer (Art Ross Trophy)
❑ 16 Wayne Gretzky 1.00 .45
MVP As Voted By Players (Lester B. Pearson Trophy)
❑ 17 Wayne Gretzky 1.00 .45
Most Game Winning Goals In Playoffs (Career)
❑ 18 Wayne Gretzky 1.00 .45
Most Goals

## 1970-71 Colgate Stamps

The 1970-71 Colgate Stamps set includes 93 small color stamps measuring approximately 1" by 1 1/4". The set was distributed in three sheets of 31. Sheet one featured centers (numbered 1-31) and was available with the giant size of toothpaste, sheet two featured wings (numbered 32-62) and was available with the family size of toothpaste, and sheet three featured goalies and defensemen (numbered 63-93) and was available with king and super size toothpaste. The cards are priced below as individual stamps; the value of a complete sheet would be approximately 20 percent more than the sum of the individual stamp prices. Colgate also issued three calendars so that brushers could stick a stamp on each day for brushing regularly. These calendars retail in the $5-$10 range. The cards were numbered in a star in the upper left corner of the card face.

| | NRMT-MT | EXC |
|---|---|---|
| COMPLETE SET (93) | 150.00 | 70.00 |
| COMMON STAMP (1-93) | .75 | .35 |

❑ 1 Walt McKechnie .75 .35
❑ 2 Bob Pulford 2.00 .90
❑ 3 Mike Walton 1.00 .45
❑ 4 Alex Delvecchio 4.00 1.80
❑ 5 Tom Williams .75 .35
❑ 6 Derek Sanderson 6.00 2.70
❑ 7 Garry Unger 1.50 .70
❑ 8 Lou Angotti .75 .35
❑ 9 Ted Hampson .75 .35
❑ 10 Phil Goyette .75 .35
❑ 11 Juha Widing .75 .35
❑ 12 Norm Ullman 3.00 1.35
❑ 13 Garry Monahan .75 .35
❑ 14 Henri Richard 4.00 1.80
❑ 15 Ray Cullen 1.00 .45
❑ 16 Danny O'Shea .75 .35
❑ 17 Marc Tardif 1.00 .45
❑ 18 Jude Drouin .75 .35
❑ 19 Charlie Burns .75 .35
❑ 20 Gerry Meehan 1.00 .45
❑ 21 Ralph Backstrom 1.00 .45
❑ 22 Frank St.Marseille .75 .35
❑ 23 Orland Kurtenbach 1.00 .45
❑ 24 Red Berenson 1.00 .45
❑ 25 Jean Ratelle 3.00 1.35
❑ 26 Syl Apps 1.00 .45
❑ 27 Don Marshall .75 .35
❑ 28 Gilbert Perreault 8.00 3.60
❑ 29 Andre Lacroix 1.00 .45
❑ 30 Jacques Lemaire 2.50 1.10
❑ 31 Pit Martin 1.00 .45
❑ 32 Dennis Hull 1.25 .55
❑ 33 Dave Balon .75 .35
❑ 34 Keith McCreary .75 .35
❑ 35 Bobby Rousseau 1.00 .45
❑ 36 Danny Grant 1.00 .45
❑ 37 Brit Selby .75 .35
❑ 38 Bob Nevin .75 .35
❑ 39 Rosaire Paiement .75 .35
❑ 40 Gary Dornhoefer 1.50 .70
❑ 41 Eddie Shack 3.00 1.35
❑ 42 Ron Schock .75 .35
❑ 43 Jim Pappin .75 .35
❑ 44 Mickey Redmond 2.00 .90
❑ 45 Vic Hadfield 1.00 .45
❑ 46 Johnny Bucyk 3.00 1.35
❑ 47 Gordie Howe 40.00 18.00
❑ 48 Ron Anderson .75 .35
❑ 49 Gary Jarrett .75 .35
❑ 50 Jean Pronovost 1.00 .45
❑ 51 Simon Nolet .75 .35
❑ 52 Bill Goldsworthy 1.00 .45
❑ 53 Rod Gilbert 3.00 1.35
❑ 54 Ron Ellis 1.00 .45
❑ 55 Mike Byers .75 .35
❑ 56 Norm Ferguson .75 .35
❑ 57 Gary Sabourin .75 .35
❑ 58 Tim Ecclestone .75 .35
❑ 59 John McKenzie .75 .35
❑ 60 Yvan Cournoyer 3.00 1.35
❑ 61 Ken Schinkel .75 .35
❑ 62 Ken Hodge 1.50 .70
❑ 63 Cesare Maniago 2.00 .90
❑ 64 J.C. Tremblay 1.00 .45
❑ 65 Gilles Marotte 1.00 .45
❑ 66 Bob Baun 1.50 .70
❑ 67 Gerry Desjardins 1.50 .70
❑ 68 Charlie Hodge 2.50 1.10
❑ 69 Matt Ravlich .75 .35
❑ 70 Ed Giacomin 5.00 2.20
❑ 71 Gerry Cheevers 6.00 2.70
❑ 72 Pat Quinn 1.25 .55
❑ 73 Gary Bergman 1.00 .45
❑ 74 Serge Savard 1.50 .70
❑ 75 Les Binkley 1.50 .70
❑ 76 Arnie Brown .75 .35
❑ 77 Pat Stapleton 1.00 .45
❑ 78 Ed Van Impe .75 .35
❑ 79 Jim Dorey .75 .35
❑ 80 Dave Dryden 2.00 .90
❑ 81 Dale Tallon 1.00 .45
❑ 82 Bruce Gamble 2.50 1.10
❑ 83 Roger Crozier 2.50 1.10
❑ 84 Denis DeJordy 2.00 .90
❑ 85 Rogatien Vachon 3.00 1.35
❑ 86 Carol Vadnais .75 .35
❑ 87 Bobby Orr 60.00 27.00
❑ 88 Noel Picard .75 .35
❑ 89 Gilles Villemure 2.00 .90
❑ 90 Gary Smith 2.00 .90
❑ 91 Doug Favell 2.00 .90
❑ 92 Ernie Wakely 2.00 .90
❑ 93 Bernie Parent 8.00 3.60
❑ NNO Stamp Calendar Sheet 10.00 4.50

## 1971-72 Colgate Heads

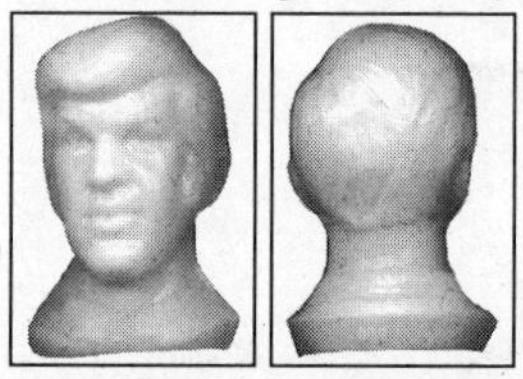

The 16 hockey collectibles in this set measure approximately 1 1/4" in height with a base of 7/8" and are made out of cream-colored or beige plastic. The promotion lasted approximately five months during the winter of 1972. The busts were issued in series of four in the various sizes of Colgate Toothpaste. The player's last name is found only on the back of the base of the head. The Ullmann error is not included in the complete set price below. The heads are unnumbered and checklisted below in alphabetical order.

| | NRMT-MT | EXC |
|---|---|---|
| COMPLETE SET (16) | 200.00 | 90.00 |
| COMMON HEAD (1-16) | 4.00 | 1.80 |

❑ 1 Yvon Cournoyer 8.00 3.60
❑ 2 Marcel Dionne UER 15.00 6.75
(Head actually Stan Mikita)
❑ 3 Ken Dryden 25.00 11.00
❑ 4 Paul Henderson 6.00 2.70
❑ 5 Guy Lafleur 20.00 9.00
❑ 6 Frank Mahovlich 10.00 4.50
❑ 7 Richard Martin SP 30.00 13.50
❑ 8 Bobby Orr 40.00 18.00
❑ 9 Brad Park SP 40.00 18.00
❑ 10 Jacques Plante 15.00 6.75
❑ 11 Jean Ratelle 8.00 3.60
❑ 12 Derek Sanderson 15.00 6.75
❑ 13 Dale Tallon 4.00 1.80
❑ 14 Walt Tkaczuk 4.00 1.80
❑ 15A Norm Ullman ERR 10.00 4.50
(Misspelled Ullmann)
❑ 15B Norm Ullman COR 25.00 11.00
❑ 16 Garry Unger 4.00 1.80

## 1995-96 Collector's Choice

This 396 card standard-size set was issued in 12-card packs with a suggested retail price of 99 cents per pack. The design is similar to the 1995 Collector Choice issues in baseball, basketball and football. Each card features a photo framed by white borders. The player's name and team is identified in the lower right-hand corner. The backs contain another photograph, biographical information and statistics. The last 70 cards of the set are dedicated to the following subsets: 1995 European Junior Championship (325-354), What's Your Game? (355-369), and Hardware Heroes (370-394). Rookie Cards in this set include Teemu Riihijarvi and Marcus Nilsson. In addition, 15-card set was available only to collectors who redeemed through the mail a Young Guns Trade card, which was inserted at a rate of 1:34 packs. The cards were intended to "complete" the Collector's Choice set by including several of the top rookies of 1995-96, and thus bear the same design and continue the numbering from that set.

| | MINT | NRMT |
|---|---|---|
| COMPLETE SET (396) | 20.00 | 9.00 |
| COMMON CARD (1-396) | .05 | .02 |
| COMP.YOUNG GUN SET (15) | 10.00 | 4.50 |
| COMMON CARD (397-411) | .25 | .11 |

❑ 1 Wayne Gretzky 1.50 .70
❑ 2 Darius Kasparaitis .05 .02
❑ 3 Scott Niedermayer .05 .02
❑ 4 Brendan Shanahan .50 .23
Traded to Whalers
❑ 5 Doug Gilmour .25 .11
❑ 6 Lyle Odelein .05 .02
❑ 7 Dave Gagner .10 .05
❑ 8 Gary Suter .05 .02
❑ 9 Sandis Ozolinsh .10 .05
❑ 10 Sergei Zubov .05 .02
❑ 11 Don Beaupre .10 .05
❑ 12 Bill Lindsay .05 .02
❑ 13 David Oliver .05 .02
❑ 14 Bob Corkum .05 .02
❑ 15 German Titov .05 .02
❑ 16 Jari Kurri .10 .05
❑ 17 Cliff Ronning .05 .02
❑ 18 Paul Coffey .25 .11
❑ 19 Ian Laperriere .05 .02
❑ 20 Dave Andreychuk .10 .05
❑ 21 Andrei Nikolishin .05 .02
❑ 22 Blaine Lacher .10 .05
❑ 23 Yuri Khmylev .05 .02
❑ 24 Darren Turcotte .05 .02
❑ 25 Joe Mullen .10 .05
❑ 26 Peter Forsberg .75 .35
❑ 27 Paul Ysebaert .05 .02
❑ 28 Tommy Soderstrom .10 .05
❑ 29 Rod Brind'Amour .10 .05
❑ 30 Jim Carey .25 .11
❑ 31 Geoff Courtnall .05 .02
Signed by Blues
❑ 32 Slava Kozlov .10 .05
❑ 33 Ray Ferraro .05 .02
Signed Rangers
❑ 34 John MacLean .10 .05
❑ 35 Benoit Brunet .05 .02
❑ 36 Trent Klatt .05 .02
❑ 37 Chris Chelios .25 .11
❑ 38 Tom Pederson .05 .02
❑ 39 Pat Elynuik .05 .02
❑ 40 Rob Niedermayer .10 .05
❑ 41 Jason Arnott .10 .05
❑ 42 Patrik Carnback .05 .02
❑ 43 Steve Chiasson .05 .02
❑ 44 Marty McSorley .05 .02
❑ 45 Pavel Bure .50 .23
❑ 46 Glenn Anderson .10 .05
❑ 47 Doug Brown .05 .02
❑ 48 Mike Ridley .05 .02
Traded to Canucks
❑ 49 Alexei Zhamnov .10 .05
❑ 50 Mariusz Czerkawski .05 .02
❑ 51 Derek Plante .05 .02
❑ 52 Andrew Cassels .05 .02
❑ 53 Tom Barrasso .10 .05
❑ 54 Andrei Kovalenko .05 .02
❑ 55 Pat Verbeek .05 .02
❑ 56 Alexander Semak .05 .02
❑ 57 Eric Lindros .75 .35
❑ 58 Peter Bondra .25 .11
❑ 59 Marty McInnis .05 .02
❑ 60 Bill Guerin .05 .02
❑ 61 Patrice Brisebois .05 .02
❑ 62 Andy Moog .10 .05
❑ 63 Eric Weinrich .05 .02
❑ 64 Arturs Irbe .10 .05
❑ 65 Sean Hill .05 .02
❑ 66 Jesse Belanger .05 .02
❑ 67 Bryan Marchment .05 .02
❑ 68 Joe Sacco .05 .02
❑ 69 Trevor Kidd .10 .05
❑ 70 Dan Quinn .05 .02
Signed by Senators
❑ 71 Kirk McLean .10 .05
❑ 72 Benoit Hogue .05 .02
❑ 73 Garry Galley .05 .02
❑ 74 Randy Wood .05 .02
❑ 75 Nikolai Khabibulin .10 .05
❑ 76 Ted Donato .05 .02
❑ 77 Doug Bodger .05 .02
❑ 78 Paul Ranheim .05 .02
❑ 79 Ulf Samuelsson .05 .02
❑ 80 Uwe Krupp .05 .02
❑ 81 Oleg Tverdovsky .10 .05
❑ 82 Kelly Miller .05 .02
❑ 83 Darryl Sydor .05 .02
❑ 84 Brian Bellows .05 .02
❑ 85 Jeremy Roenick .25 .11
❑ 86 Phil Bourque .05 .02
❑ 87 Louie DeBrusk .05 .02
❑ 88 Joel Otto .05 .02
Signed by Flyers
❑ 89 Dino Ciccarelli .10 .05
❑ 90 Mats Sundin .10 .05
❑ 91 Don Sweeney .05 .02
❑ 92 Roman Hamrlik .10 .05
❑ 93 Petr Svoboda .05 .02
❑ 94 Zigmund Palffy .10 .05
❑ 95 Patrick Roy 1.00 .45
❑ 96 Sergei Krivokrasov .05 .02
❑ 97 Wade Flaherty .10 .05
❑ 98 Fredrik Olausson .05 .02
❑ 99 Sergio Momesso .05 .02
Traded to Maple Leafs
❑ 100 Mike Vernon .10 .05
❑ 101 Todd Gill .05 .02
❑ 102 Cam Neely .10 .05
❑ 103 Wendel Clark .10 .05
❑ 104 John Tucker .05 .02
❑ 105 Eric Desjardins .05 .02
❑ 106 Ed Olczyk .05 .02
❑ 107 Bob Beers .05 .02
❑ 108 Mark Recchi .10 .05
❑ 109 Ed Belfour .25 .11
❑ 110 Radek Bonk .05 .02
❑ 111 Cory Stillman .05 .02
❑ 112 Jeff Norton .05 .02
❑ 113 Terry Carkner .05 .02
❑ 114 Felix Potvin .25 .11
❑ 115 Alexei Kasatonov .05 .02
❑ 116 Brian Noonan .05 .02
Signed by Blues
❑ 117 Daren Puppa .10 .05
❑ 118 Joe Juneau .05 .02
❑ 119 Valeri Bure .10 .05
❑ 120 Murray Craven .05 .02
❑ 121 Marko Tuomainen .05 .02
❑ 122 Trevor Linden .10 .05
❑ 123 Zarley Zalapski .05 .02
❑ 124 Jeff Shantz .05 .02
❑ 125 Dmitri Mironov .05 .02
Traded to Penguins
❑ 126 Jamie Huscroft .05 .02
❑ 127 Jaromir Jagr .75 .35
❑ 128 Brian Bradley .05 .02
❑ 129 Brett Lindros .05 .02
❑ 130 Calle Johansson .05 .02
❑ 131 Pierre Turgeon .10 .05
❑ 132 Denis Savard .10 .05
❑ 133 Joe Nieuwendyk .10 .05
❑ 134 Petr Klima .05 .02
❑ 135 John Druce .05 .02
❑ 136 Chris Osgood .25 .11
❑ 137 Kenny Jonsson .05 .02
❑ 138 Jocelyn Lemieux .05 .02
❑ 139 Tomas Sandstrom .05 .02
❑ 140 Chris Gratton .10 .05
❑ 141 Mark Tinordi .05 .02
❑ 142 Kirk Muller .05 .02
❑ 143 Vladimir Malakhov .05 .02
❑ 144 Jiri Slegr .05 .02
❑ 145 Shawn McEachern .05 .02
Traded to Bruins
❑ 146 Shayne Corson .05 .02
Signed by Blues
❑ 147 Kelly Hrudey .10 .05
❑ 148 Sergei Fedorov .40 .18
❑ 149 Mike Gartner .10 .05
❑ 150 Stephane Fiset .10 .05
❑ 151 Larry Murphy .10 .05
Traded to Maple Leafs
❑ 152 Enrico Ciccone .05 .02
❑ 153 Mike Keane .05 .02
❑ 154 Steve Larmer .10 .05
❑ 155 Dale Hunter .05 .02
❑ 156 Joe Murphy .05 .02
❑ 157 Pat LaFontaine .10 .05
❑ 158 Rob Gaudreau .05 .02
❑ 159 Paul Kariya 1.00 .45
❑ 160 Rob Blake .05 .02
❑ 161 Keith Primeau .10 .05
❑ 162 Dave Ellett .05 .02
❑ 163 Alexander Mogilny .10 .05
Traded to Canucks
❑ 164 Luc Robitaille .10 .05
❑ 165 Alexander Selivanov .05 .02
❑ 166 Keith Jones .05 .02
❑ 167 Turner Stevenson .05 .02
❑ 168 Keith Tkachuk .30 .14
❑ 169 Bernie Nicholls .05 .02
❑ 170 Stanislav Neckar .05 .02
❑ 171 Scott Mellanby .10 .05
❑ 172 Doug Weight .10 .05
❑ 173 Shaun Van Allen .05 .02
❑ 174 Gary Roberts .05 .02
❑ 175 Robert Lang .05 .02
❑ 176 Martin Gelinas .05 .02
❑ 177 Ray Sheppard .10 .05
❑ 178 Bryan Smolinski .05 .02
Traded to Penguins
❑ 179 Wayne Presley .05 .02
❑ 180 Jimmy Carson .05 .02
❑ 181 John Cullen .05 .02
❑ 182 Mikael Andersson .05 .02
❑ 183 Dimitri Khristich .05 .02
Traded to Kings
❑ 184 Chris Therien .05 .02
❑ 185 Bobby Holik .05 .02
❑ 186 Kevin Hatcher .05 .02
❑ 187 Patrick Poulin .05 .02
❑ 188 Pat Falloon .05 .02
❑ 189 Alexei Yashin .10 .05
❑ 190 Gord Murphy .05 .02
❑ 191 Kirk Maltby .05 .02
❑ 192 Dave Karpa .05 .02
❑ 193 Kelly Kisio .05 .02
❑ 194 Tony Granato .05 .02
❑ 195 Al Iafrate .05 .02
❑ 196 Nelson Emerson .05 .02
❑ 197 Adam Oates .10 .05
❑ 198 Rob Ray .05 .02
❑ 199 Sean Burke .10 .05
❑ 200 Ron Francis .10 .05
❑ 201 Theoren Fleury .10 .05
❑ 202 Patrick Flatley .05 .02
❑ 203 Ron Hextall .10 .05
❑ 204 Martin Brodeur .60 .25
❑ 205 Mike Kennedy .05 .02
❑ 206 Tony Amonte .10 .05
❑ 207 Sergei Makarov .05 .02
❑ 208 Alexandre Daigle .05 .02
❑ 209 Stu Barnes .05 .02
❑ 210 Todd Marchant .05 .02
❑ 211 Valeri Karpov .05 .02
❑ 212 Phil Housley .10 .05
❑ 213 Jamie Storr .10 .05
❑ 214 Brett Hull .30 .14
❑ 215 Kris King .05 .02
❑ 216 Ray Bourque .25 .11
❑ 217 Donald Audette .10 .05
❑ 218 Steven Rice .05 .02
❑ 219 Kevin Stevens .05 .02
Traded to Bruins
❑ 220 Mark Messier .30 .14
❑ 221 Valeri Kamensky .10 .05
❑ 222 Mikael Renberg .10 .05
❑ 223 Scott Stevens .10 .05
❑ 224 Derian Hatcher .05 .02
❑ 225 Ray Whitney .05 .02
❑ 226 Bob Kudelski .05 .02
❑ 227 Mikhail Shtalenkov .05 .02
❑ 228 Nicklas Lidstrom .10 .05
❑ 229 Adam Creighton .05 .02
Signed by Capitals
❑ 230 Dave Manson .05 .02
❑ 231 Craig Simpson .05 .02
❑ 232 Chris Pronger .10 .05
Traded to Blues
❑ 233 Adrien Plavsic .05 .02
❑ 234 Alexei Kovalev .05 .02
❑ 235 Tommy Salo .30 .14
❑ 236 Patrik Juhlin .05 .02
❑ 237 Tom Chorske .05 .02
❑ 238 Mike Modano .30 .14
❑ 239 Igor Larionov .05 .02
❑ 240 Johan Garpenlov .05 .02
❑ 241 Todd Krygier .05 .02
❑ 242 Tie Domi .10 .05
❑ 243 Bill Houlder .05 .02
Signed by Lightning
❑ 244 Teemu Selanne .50 .23
❑ 245 Dale Hawerchuk .10 .05
Signed by Blues
❑ 246 Bill Ranford .10 .05
❑ 247 Brian Leetch .25 .11
❑ 248 Steve Thomas .05 .02
❑ 249 Dimitri Yushkevich .05 .02
❑ 250 Stephane Richer .10 .05
❑ 251 Todd Harvey .05 .02
❑ 252 Viktor Kozlov .05 .02
❑ 253 John Vanbiesbrouck .40 .18
❑ 254 Rick Tocchet .10 .05
❑ 255 Bret Hedican .05 .02
❑ 256 Mario Lemieux 1.25 .55
❑ 257 Igor Korolev .05 .02
❑ 258 Dominik Hasek .50 .23
❑ 259 Owen Nolan .10 .05
❑ 260 Michal Pivonka .05 .02
❑ 261 John LeClair .40 .18
❑ 262 Claude Lemieux .10 .05
❑ 263 Mike Donnelly .05 .02
❑ 264 Craig Janney .10 .05
❑ 265 Milos Holan .05 .02
❑ 266 Steve Yzerman .75 .35

❑ 267 Russ Courtnall .05 .02
❑ 268 Esa Tikkanen .05 .02
❑ 269 Dallas Drake .05 .02
❑ 270 Norm Maciver .05 .02
❑ 271 Scott Young .05 .02
❑ 272 Glenn Healy .10 .05
❑ 273 Brian Rolston .05 .02
❑ 274 Corey Millen .05 .02
❑ 275 Kevin Miller .05 .02
❑ 276 Eric LaCroix .05 .02
❑ 277 Adam Graves .10 .05
❑ 278 Christian Ruuttu .05 .02
❑ 279 Steve Duchesne .05 .02
Traded to Senators
❑ 280 Stephane Quintal .05 .02
Traded to Canadiens
❑ 281 Brent Gretzky .05 .02
❑ 282 Mike Ricci .05 .02
❑ 283 Sergei Nemchinov .05 .02
❑ 284 Sylvain Cote .05 .02
❑ 285 Neal Broten .10 .05
❑ 286 Greg Adams .05 .02
❑ 287 Guy Hebert .10 .05
❑ 288 Joe Sakic .50 .23
❑ 289 Bobby Dollas .05 .02
❑ 290 Gino Odjick .05 .02
❑ 291 Curtis Joseph .25 .11
Traded to Oilers
❑ 292 Teppo Numminen .05 .02
❑ 293 Geoff Sanderson .10 .05
❑ 294 Adam Deadmarsh .10 .05
❑ 295 Kevin Haller .05 .02
❑ 296 Sergei Brylin .05 .02
❑ 297 Ulf Dahlen .05 .02
❑ 298 Robert Kron .05 .02
❑ 299 Dave Lowry .05 .02
❑ 300 Nikolai Borschevsky .05 .02
❑ 301 Jeff Brown .05 .02
❑ 302 Guy Carbonneau .05 .02
❑ 303 Alexei Zhitnik .05 .02
❑ 304 Frantisek Kucera .05 .02
❑ 305 Curtis Leschyshyn .05 .02
❑ 306 Mike Richter .25 .11
❑ 307 Dean Evason .05 .02
❑ 308 Jozef Stumpel .05 .02
❑ 309 Jeff Friesen .10 .05
❑ 310 Kelly Buchberger .05 .02
❑ 311 Michael Nylander .05 .02
❑ 312 Josef Beranek .05 .02
❑ 313 Al MacInnis .05 .02
❑ 314 Ken Wregget .10 .05
❑ 315 Glen Wesley .05 .02
❑ 316 Jocelyn Thibault .25 .11
❑ 317 Jeff Beukeboom .05 .02
❑ 318 Steve Konowalchuk .05 .02
❑ 319 Tim Cheveldae .10 .05
❑ 320 Vincent Damphousse .10 .05
❑ 321 Mats Naslund .05 .02
❑ 322 Mathieu Schneider .05 .02
❑ 323 Petr Nedved .10 .05
❑ 324 Brent Fedyk .05 .02
❑ 325 Jussi Tie .10 .05
❑ 326 Mikko Markkanen .10 .05
❑ 327 Timo Hakanen .10 .05
❑ 328 Sami Salonen .10 .05
❑ 329 Juha Viinikainen .10 .05
❑ 330 Jani Riihinen .10 .05
❑ 331 Teemu Riihijarvi .10 .05
❑ 332 Jaako Niskavaara .10 .05
❑ 333 Miika Elomo .10 .05
❑ 334 Tomi Kallio .10 .05
❑ 335 Vesa Toskala .10 .05
❑ 336 Tuomas Reijonen .10 .05
❑ 337 Aki-Petteri Berg .05 .02
❑ 338 Tomi Hirvonen .10 .05
❑ 339 Jussi Salminen .10 .05
❑ 340 Andreas Sjolund .10 .05
❑ 341 Johan Ramstedt .05 .02
❑ 342 Bjorn Danielsson .10 .05
❑ 343 Per Gustavsson .10 .05
❑ 344 Niklas Anger .10 .05
❑ 345 Marcus Nilsson .05 .02
❑ 346 Per Anton Lundstrom .10 .05
❑ 347 Henrik Rehnberg .10 .05
❑ 348 Robert Borgqvist .10 .05
❑ 349 Ted Christensen .10 .05
❑ 350 Samuel Phalsson .05 .02
❑ 351 Fredrik Loven .05 .02
❑ 352 Patrik Wallenberg .10 .05
❑ 353 Jan Labraaten .10 .05
❑ 354 Peter Wallin .05 .02
❑ 355 Cam Neely .10 .05
❑ 356 Keith Tkachuk .25 .11
❑ 357 Chris Gratton .10 .05
❑ 358 Adam Graves .10 .05
❑ 359 Doug Gilmour .25 .11
❑ 360 Adam Deadmarsh .10 .05
❑ 361 Wayne Gretzky .75 .35
❑ 362 Joe Sakic .25 .11
❑ 363 Paul Kariya .50 .23
❑ 364 Brett Hull .25 .11
❑ 365 Sergei Fedorov .25 .11
❑ 366 Brian Rolston .05 .02
❑ 367 Dominik Hasek .25 .11
❑ 368 John Vanbiesbrouck .25 .11
❑ 369 Jim Carey .25 .11
❑ 370 Paul Kariya .50 .23
❑ 371 Peter Forsberg .40 .18
❑ 372 Jeff Friesen .10 .05
❑ 373 Kenny Jonsson .05 .02
❑ 374 Chris Therien .05 .02
❑ 375 Jim Carey .25 .11
❑ 376 John LeClair .25 .11
❑ 377 Eric Lindros .40 .18
❑ 378 Jaromir Jagr .40 .18
❑ 379 Paul Coffey .25 .11
❑ 380 Chris Chelios .25 .11
❑ 381 Dominik Hasek .25 .11
❑ 382 Keith Tkachuk .25 .11
❑ 383 Alexei Zhamnov .10 .05
❑ 384 Theoren Fleury .10 .05
❑ 385 Ray Bourque .25 .11
❑ 386 Larry Murphy .10 .05
❑ 387 Ed Belfour .25 .11
❑ 388 Eric Lindros .40 .18
❑ 389 Jaromir Jagr .40 .18
❑ 390 Paul Coffey .25 .11
❑ 391 Peter Forsberg .40 .18
❑ 392 Claude Lemieux .10 .05
❑ 393 Ron Francis .10 .05
❑ 394 Dominik Hasek .25 .11
❑ 395 Checklist 1-200 .30 .14
(Wayne Gretzky)
❑ 396 Checklist 201-396 .30 .14
(Wayne Gretzky)
❑ 397 Saku Koivu TRADE 3.00 1.35
❑ 398 Radek Dvorak TRADE .25 .11
❑ 399 Ed Jovanovski TRADE .25 .11
❑ 400 Brendan Witt TRADE .25 .11
❑ 401 Jeff O'Neill TRADE .25 .11
❑ 402 Daymond Langkow TRADE .50 .23
❑ 403 Shane Doan TRADE .25 .11
❑ 404 Bryan McCabe TRADE .25 .11
❑ 405 Marty Murray TRADE .25 .11
❑ 406 Daniel Alfredsson TRADE 2.50 1.10
❑ 407 Jason Doig TRADE .50 .23
❑ 408 Niklas Sundstrom TRADE .25 .11
❑ 409 Vitali Yachmenev TRADE .25 .11
❑ 410 Aki Berg TRADE .25 .11
❑ 411 Eric Daze TRADE 1.50 .70
❑ NNO Young Guns Trade Card .25 .11

## 1995-96 Collector's Choice Player's Club

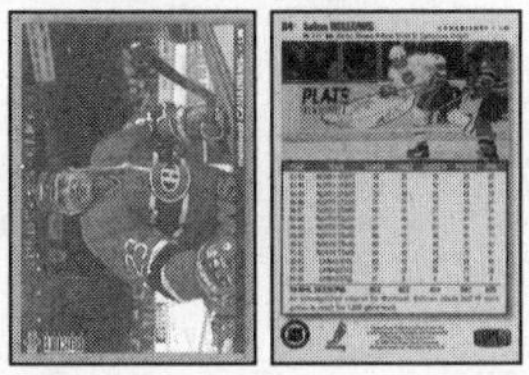

Issued one per pack, this 396 card standard-size set is a parallel to the regular Collector's Choice issue. These cards have silver borders and the words "Players Club" are printed vertically on the left side of the card in silver-foil. Values for these cards can be obtained by using the multipliers below on the values listed for the basic cards.

| | MINT | NRMT |
|---|---|---|
| COMPLETE SET (396) | 100.00 | 45.00 |
| COMMON CARD (1-396) | .25 | .11 |

*STARS: 5X TO 10X BASIC CARDS
*YOUNG STARS: 3X TO 6X BASIC CARDS
*RCs: 2X TO 4X BASIC CARDS

## 1995-96 Collector's Choice Player's Club Platinum

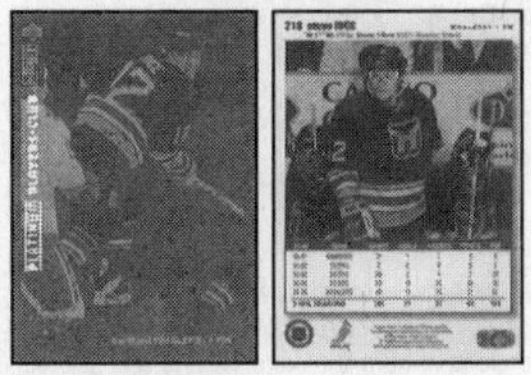

This 396-card standard size set is a parallel to the regular Collector's Choice set. Issued a rate of 1:34 packs, these cards are printed on silver-foil paper stock. Although difficult to pull from packs, many of the cards came over from Europe, where they were readily available from collectors clubs. This added supply dampened demand somewhat for these cards in North America. Values for a few heavily traded singles are listed below; values for the rest can be determined by applying the multipliers below to the base set cards.

| | MINT | NRMT |
|---|---|---|
| COMPLETE SET (396) | 1000.00 | 450.00 |
| COMMON CARD (1-396) | 2.00 | .90 |

*STARS: 30X TO 75X BASIC CARDS
*YOUNG STARS: 20X TO 50X BASIC CARDS
*RCs: 15X TO 40X BASIC CARDS

## 1995-96 Collector's Choice Crash The Game

Consisting of 90 cards, this interactive set features 30 players. Each player has three cards with different dates on the front. If the player scored a goal on either of the dates, the card with the corresponding date could be redeemed for a special 30-card set. Randomly

inserted in packs, these cards come in silver (1:5 packs) and gold (1:34 packs) foil versions. The words "silver" or "gold" are in their respective color foil at bottom left and the date is also done in foil. There are also several parallels of this set, including gold and silver redeemed winner sets, and gold and silver bonus cards awarded of the redeemed player along with the gold or silver set. Multipliers can be found in the header below to determine values for these versions. Because not every player had a winning card, however, the gold and silver bonus sets are considered complete at 23 cards each. It should be noted however that a few copies of the bonus cards have been confirmed to exist of the seven players that did not have winning cards. Also, several erroneous variation cards have been reported featuring game dates on which that player's team did not play. These cards appear to be in short supply, but do not demand exhorbitant premiums. To differentiate between each of the player's three insert cards, they are numbered here with A, B and C suffixes. The expiration date for redeeming cards was July 1st, 1996.

| | MINT | NRMT |
|---|---|---|
| COMPLETE SET (90) | 100.00 | 45.00 |
| COMMON CARD (C1-C30) | .50 | .23 |
| COMP.GOLD SET (90) | 500.00 | 220.00 |
| COMMON GOLD (C1-C30) | 3.00 | 1.35 |
| *GOLD STARS: 2X TO 4X BASIC CARDS | | |
| COMP.EXCH.SET (30) | 8.00 | 3.60 |
| COMMON EXCH. (C1-C30) | .15 | .07 |
| *EXCHANGE CARDS: .1X TO .25X BASIC CARDS | | |
| COMP.GOLD EXCH.SET (30) | 25.00 | 11.00 |
| COMM.GOLD EXCH. (C1-C30) | .40 | .18 |
| *GOLD EXCH.CARDS: .4X TO .8X BASIC CARDS | | |
| COMP.BONUS SET (23) | 50.00 | 22.00 |
| COMMON BONUS (1-30) | 1.00 | .45 |
| *BONUS CARDS: 1X TO 2X BASIC CARDS | | |
| COMP.GOLD.BONUS SET (23) | 125.00 | 55.00 |
| COMM.GOLD BONUS (1-30) | 2.50 | 1.10 |
| *GOLD BONUS CARDS: 2.5X TO 5X BASIC CARDS | | |

❑ C1 Pavel Bure 10/12/95 1.50 .70
❑ C1B Pavel Bure 12/17/95 1.50 .70
❑ C1C Pavel Bure 3/23/96 1.50 .70
❑ C2 Sergei Fedorov 10/19/95 1.50 .70
❑ C2B Sergei Fedorov 12/31/95 1.50 .70
❑ C2C Sergei Fedorov 3/12/96 1.50 .70
❑ C3 Wayne Gretzky 10/7/95 5.00 2.20
❑ C3B Wayne Gretzky 12/31/95 5.00 2.20
❑ C3C Wayne Gretzky 2/10/96 5.00 2.20
❑ C4 Eric Lindros 11/12/95 2.50 1.10
❑ C4B Eric Lindros 1/3/96 3.00 1.35
❑ C4C Eric Lindros 3/3/96 3.00 1.35
❑ C5 Brett Hull 10/10/95 1.25 .55
❑ C5B Brett Hull 12/9/95 1.25 .55
❑ C5C Brett Hull 3/24/96 1.25 .55
❑ C6 Mark Messier 11/8/95 1.25 .55
❑ C6B Mark Messier 1/22/96 1.50 .70
❑ C6C Mark Messier 3/31/96 1.50 .70
❑ C7 Jaromir Jagr 10/14/95 2.50 1.10
❑ C7B Jaromir Jagr 12/17/95 3.00 1.35
❑ C7C Jaromir Jagr 3/5/96 3.00 1.35
❑ C8 Alexei Zhamnov 10/9/95 .75 .35
❑ C8B Alexei Zhamnov 12/28/95 .75 .35
❑ C8C Alexei Zhamnov 2/21/96 .75 .35
❑ C9 Joe Sakic 10/6/95 1.50 .70
❑ C9B Joe Sakic 12/9/95 2.50 1.10
❑ C9C Joe Sakic 2/3/96 2.50 1.10
❑ C10 Paul Kariya 10/18/95 3.00 1.35
❑ C10B Paul Kariya 12/19/95 3.00 1.35
❑ C10C Paul Kariya 3/17/96 3.00 1.35
❑ C11 Theoren Fleury 10/27/95 .75 .35
❑ C11B Theoren Fleury 12/11/95 .75 .35
❑ C11C Theoren Fleury 2/6/96 .75 .35
❑ C12 Owen Nolan 11/1/95 .75 .35
❑ C12B Owen Nolan 1/4/96 .75 .35
❑ C12C Owen Nolan 3/17/96 .75 .35
❑ C13 Peter Bondra 10/13/95 .75 .35
❑ C13B Peter Bondra 12/2/95 .75 .35
❑ C13C Peter Bondra 3/12/96 .75 .35
❑ C14 Cam Neely 11/7/95 .75 .35
❑ C14B Cam Neely 1/11/96 .75 .35
❑ C14C Cam Neely 3/23/96 .75 .35
❑ C15 Pierre Turgeon 10/25/95 .75 .35
❑ C15B Pierre Turgeon 12/23/95 .75 .35
❑ C15C Pierre Turgeon 2/21/96 .75 .35
❑ C16 Mike Modano 11/1/95 .75 .35
❑ C16B Mike Modano 1/5/96 .75 .35
❑ C16C Mike Modano 2/22/96 .75 .35
❑ C17 Bernie Nicholls 10/10/95 .50 .23
❑ C17B Bernie Nicholls 12/15/95 .50 .23
❑ C17C Bernie Nicholls 3/24/96 .50 .23
❑ C18 Alexei Yashin 11/4/95 .75 .35
❑ C18B Alexie Yashin 12/23/95 .75 .35
❑ C18C Alexei Yashin 3/21/96 .75 .35
❑ C19 Jason Arnott 10/27/95 .75 .35
❑ C19B Jason Arnott 12/18/95 .75 .35
❑ C19C Jason Arnott 2/28/96 .75 .35
❑ C20 Peter Forsberg 11/22/95 2.50 1.10
❑ C20B Peter Forsberg 2/15/96 3.00 1.35
❑ C20C Peter Forsberg 3/27/96 3.00 1.35
❑ C21 Doug Gilmour 10/17/95 .75 .35
❑ C21B Doug Gilmour 12/16/95 .75 .35
❑ C21C Doug Gilmour 2/18/96 .75 .35
❑ C22 G. Sanderson 10/11/95 .50 .23
❑ C22B G. Sanderson 12/18/95 .50 .23
❑ C22C G. Sanderson 3/6/96 .50 .23
❑ C23 John LeClair 10/15/95 .75 .35
❑ C23B John LeClair 12/16/95 .75 .35
❑ C23C John LeClair 2/19/96 .75 .35
❑ C24 Ray Bourque 10/11/95 .75 .35
❑ C24B Ray Bourque 12/16/95 .75 .35
❑ C24C Ray Bourque 2/6/96 .75 .35
❑ C25 Mario Lemieux 11/1/95 4.00 1.80
❑ C25B Mario Lemieux 12/1/95 4.00 1.80
❑ C25C Mario Lemieux 2/6/96 4.00 1.80
❑ C26 Steve Yzerman 11/7/95 2.50 1.10
❑ C26B Steve Yzerman 1/24/96 2.50 1.10
❑ C26C Steve Yzerman 2/27/96 2.50 1.10
❑ C27 Pat LaFontaine 10/20/95 .75 .35
❑ C27B Pat LaFontaine 12/27/95 .75 .35
❑ C27C Pat LaFontaine 2/17/96 .75 .35
❑ C28 Claude Lemieux 10/7/95 .75 .35
❑ C28B Claude Lemieux 12/15/95 .75 .35
❑ C28C Claude Lemieux 2/10/96 .75 .35
❑ C29 Paul Coffey 10/15/95 .75 .35
❑ C29B Paul Coffey 12/5/95 .75 .35
❑ C29C Paul Coffey 2/13/96 .75 .35
❑ C30 Mats Sundin 11/7/95 1.00 .45
❑ C30B Mats Sundin 1/3/96 1.00 .45
❑ C30C Mats Sundin 3/15/96 1.00 .45

## 1996-97 Collector's Choice

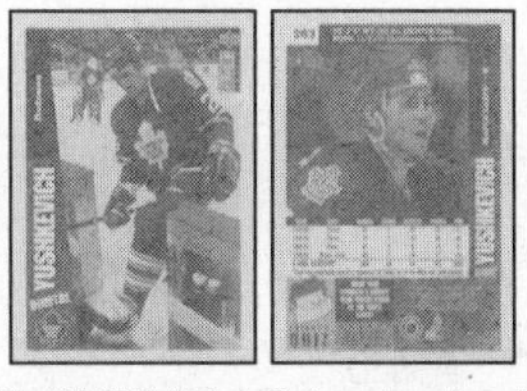

The '96-97 Collector's Choice set was issued in one series totalling 348 cards. The 12-card packs retailed for $.99 each. The set contains three subsets: Scotty Bowman's Winning Formula (289-308), Three-Star Selection (309-336) and Captain Tomorrow (337-346). Fifteen additional Young Guns cards (numbered 349-363) were available via mail in exchange for the randomly inserted Young Guns Trade card (1:35 packs). They are not considered part of the complete set, but are listed below as they are numbered consecutively to the regular set. The Gretzky 4 X 6 cards were received when redeeming winning trivia cards from the Meet the Stars contest.

| | MINT | NRMT |
|---|---|---|
| COMPLETE SET (348) | 25.00 | 11.00 |
| COMMON CARD (1-348) | .05 | .02 |
| COMP.YOUNG GUN SET (15) | 8.00 | 3.60 |
| COMMON CARD (349-363) | .25 | .11 |

❑ 1 Paul Kariya 1.00 .45
❑ 2 Teemu Selanne .50 .23
❑ 3 Steve Rucchin .05 .02
❑ 4 Mikhail Shtalenkov .05 .02
❑ 5 Guy Hebert .10 .05
❑ 6 Shaun Van Allen .05 .02
❑ 7 Anatoli Semenov .05 .02
❑ 8 J.F. Jomphe .05 .02
❑ 9 Alex Hicks .05 .02
❑ 10 Roman Oksiuta .05 .02
❑ 11 Todd Ewen .05 .02
❑ 12 Adam Oates .10 .05
❑ 13 Ray Bourque .25 .11
❑ 14 Don Sweeney .05 .02
❑ 15 Kyle McLaren .05 .02
❑ 16 Cam Neely .10 .05
❑ 17 Bill Ranford .10 .05
❑ 18 Rick Tocchet .10 .05
❑ 19 Ted Donato .05 .02
❑ 20 Shawn McEachern .05 .02
❑ 21 Jon Rohloff .05 .02
❑ 22 Joe Mullen .10 .05
❑ 23 Pat LaFontaine .10 .05
❑ 24 Brian Holzinger .10 .05
❑ 25 Wayne Primeau .05 .02
❑ 26 Alexei Zhitnik .05 .02
❑ 27 Derek Plante .05 .02
❑ 28 Randy Burridge .05 .02
❑ 29 Brad May .10 .05
❑ 30 Dominik Hasek .50 .23
❑ 31 Jason Dawe .05 .02
❑ 32 Mike Peca .05 .02
❑ 33 Matthew Barnaby .10 .05
❑ 34 Trevor Kidd .10 .05
❑ 35 Theoren Fleury .10 .05
❑ 36 Cale Hulse .05 .02
❑ 37 Bob Sweeney .05 .02
❑ 38 Michael Nylander .05 .02
❑ 39 German Titov .05 .02
❑ 40 Cory Stillman .05 .02
❑ 41 Zarley Zalapski .05 .02
❑ 42 Jocelyn Lemieux .05 .02
❑ 43 Sandy McCarthy .05 .02
❑ 44 Gary Roberts .05 .02
❑ 45 Eric Daze .10 .05
❑ 46 Jeremy Roenick .25 .11
❑ 47 Chris Chelios .25 .11
❑ 48 Joe Murphy .05 .02
❑ 49 Tony Amonte .10 .05
❑ 50 Bernie Nicholls .05 .02
❑ 51 Eric Weinrich .05 .02
❑ 52 Gary Suter .05 .02
❑ 53 Jeff Shantz .05 .02
❑ 54 Jeff Hackett .10 .05
❑ 55 Ed Belfour .25 .11
❑ 56 Uwe Krupp .05 .02
❑ 57 Claude Lemieux .10 .05
❑ 58 Adam Deadmarsh .10 .05
❑ 59 Stephane Fiset .10 .05
❑ 60 Sandis Ozolinsh .10 .05
❑ 61 Stephane Yelle .05 .02
❑ 62 Valeri Kamensky .10 .05
❑ 63 Peter Forsberg .75 .35
❑ 64 Joe Sakic .50 .23
❑ 65 Patrick Roy 1.25 .55
❑ 66 Chris Simon .05 .02
❑ 67 Todd Harvey .05 .02
❑ 68 Joe Nieuwendyk .10 .05
❑ 69 Mike Modano .30 .14
❑ 70 Derian Hatcher .05 .02
❑ 71 Kevin Hatcher .05 .02
❑ 72 Benoit Hogue .05 .02
❑ 73 Guy Carbonneau .05 .02
❑ 74 Jamie Langenbrunner .05 .02
❑ 75 Jere Lehtinen .05 .02
❑ 76 Craig Ludwig .05 .02
❑ 77 Grant Marshall .05 .02
❑ 78 Greg Johnson .05 .02
❑ 79 Steve Yzerman .75 .35
❑ 80 Sergei Fedorov .40 .18
❑ 81 Vyacheslav Kozlov .05 .02
❑ 82 Vladimir Konstantinov .05 .02
❑ 83 Igor Larionov .05 .02
❑ 84 Chris Osgood .25 .11
❑ 85 Paul Coffey .25 .11
❑ 86 Nicklas Lidstrom .10 .05
❑ 87 Keith Primeau .10 .05
❑ 88 Dino Ciccarelli .10 .05
❑ 89 Darren McCarty .05 .02
❑ 90 Curtis Joseph .25 .11
❑ 91 Doug Weight .10 .05
❑ 92 Jason Arnott .10 .05
❑ 93 Mariusz Czerkawski .05 .02
❑ 94 Kelly Buchberger .05 .02
❑ 95 Zdeno Ciger .05 .02
❑ 96 David Oliver .05 .02
❑ 97 Todd Marchant .05 .02
❑ 98 Miroslav Satan .05 .02
❑ 99 Bryan Marchment .05 .02
❑ 100 Louie DeBrusk .05 .02
❑ 101 John Vanbiesbrouck .40 .18
❑ 102 Scott Mellanby .10 .05
❑ 103 Rob Niedermayer .10 .05
❑ 104 Robert Svehla .05 .02
❑ 105 Ed Jovanovski .10 .05
❑ 106 Johan Garpenlov .05 .02
❑ 107 Jody Hull .05 .02
❑ 108 Bill Lindsay .05 .02
❑ 109 Terry Carkner .05 .02
❑ 110 Stu Barnes .05 .02
❑ 111 Ray Sheppard .10 .05
❑ 112 Brendan Shanahan .50 .23
❑ 113 Geoff Sanderson .10 .05
❑ 114 Andrei Nikolishin .05 .02
❑ 115 Andrew Cassels .05 .02
❑ 116 Nelson Emerson .05 .02
❑ 117 Jason Muzzatti .10 .05
❑ 118 Marek Malik .05 .02
❑ 119 Sean Burke .10 .05
❑ 120 Jeff Brown .05 .02
❑ 121 Jeff O'Neill .05 .02
❑ 122 Kelly Chase .05 .02
❑ 123 Dimitri Khristich .05 .02
❑ 124 Kevin Stevens .05 .02
❑ 125 Vitali Yachmenev .05 .02
❑ 126 Yanic Perreault .05 .02
❑ 127 Kevin Todd .05 .02
❑ 128 Aki Berg .05 .02
❑ 129 Craig Johnson .05 .02
❑ 130 Mattias Norstrom .05 .02
❑ 131 Ray Ferraro .05 .02
❑ 132 Steven Finn .05 .02
❑ 133 Pierre Turgeon .10 .05
❑ 134 Saku Koivu .40 .18
❑ 135 Mark Recchi .10 .05
❑ 136 Jocelyn Thibault .25 .11
❑ 137 Andrei Kovalenko .05 .02
❑ 138 Vincent Damphousse .10 .05
❑ 139 Vladimir Malakhov .05 .02
❑ 140 Brian Savage .05 .02
❑ 141 Valeri Bure .10 .05
❑ 142 Patrice Brisebois .05 .02
❑ 143 Martin Rucinsky .05 .02
❑ 144 Martin Brodeur .60 .25
❑ 145 Steve Thomas .05 .02
❑ 146 Bill Guerin .05 .02
❑ 147 Petr Sykora .05 .02
❑ 148 Scott Stevens .10 .05
❑ 149 Scott Niedermayer .05 .02
❑ 150 Phil Housley .10 .05
❑ 151 Brian Rolston .05 .02
❑ 152 Neal Broten .10 .05
❑ 153 Dave Andreychuk .10 .05
❑ 154 Randy McKay .05 .02
❑ 155 Eric Fichaud .10 .05
❑ 156 Zigmund Palffy .25 .11
❑ 157 Travis Green .10 .05
❑ 158 Darby Hendrickson .05 .02

❑ 159 Kenny Jonsson .05 .02
❑ 160 Marty McInnis .05 .02
❑ 161 Bryan McCabe .05 .02
❑ 162 Darius Kasparaitis .05 .02
❑ 163 Alexander Semak .05 .02
❑ 164 Todd Bertuzzi .05 .02
❑ 165 Niclas Andersson .05 .02
❑ 166 Mark Messier .30 .14
❑ 167 Mike Richter .25 .11
❑ 168 Niklas Sundstrom .05 .02
❑ 169 Brian Leetch .25 .11
❑ 170 Wayne Gretzky 3.00 1.35
❑ 171 Luc Robitaille .10 .05
❑ 172 Marty McSorley .05 .02
❑ 173 Jari Kurri .10 .05
❑ 174 Adam Graves .10 .05
❑ 175 Sergei Nemchinov .05 .02
❑ 176 Alexei Kovalev .05 .02
❑ 177 Daniel Alfredsson .10 .05
❑ 178 Randy Cunneyworth .05 .02
❑ 179 Alexei Yashin .10 .05
❑ 180 Alexandre Daigle .05 .02
❑ 181 Radek Bonk .05 .02
❑ 182 Steve Duchesne .05 .02
❑ 183 Ted Drury .05 .02
❑ 184 Antti Tormanen .05 .02
❑ 185 Stan Neckar .05 .02
❑ 186 Damian Rhodes .10 .05
❑ 187 Janne Laukkanen .05 .02
❑ 188 Eric Lindros .75 .35
❑ 189 Mikael Renberg .10 .05
❑ 190 John LeClair .40 .18
❑ 191 Ron Hextall .10 .05
❑ 192 Rod Brind'Amour .10 .05
❑ 193 Joel Otto .05 .02
❑ 194 Pat Falloon .05 .02
❑ 195 Eric Desjardins .05 .02
❑ 196 Dale Hawerchuk .10 .05
❑ 197 Chris Therien .05 .02
❑ 198 Dan Quinn .05 .02
❑ 199 Oleg Tverdovsky .10 .05
❑ 200 Chad Kilger .05 .02
❑ 201 Keith Tkachuk .30 .14
❑ 202 Igor Korolev .05 .02
❑ 203 Alexei Zhamnov .10 .05
❑ 204 Nikolai Khabibulin .10 .05
❑ 205 Shane Doan .05 .02
❑ 206 Deron Quint .05 .02
❑ 207 Craig Janney .10 .05
❑ 208 Norm MacIver .05 .02
❑ 209 Teppo Numminen .05 .02
❑ 210 Mario Lemieux 1.25 .55
❑ 211 Jaromir Jagr .75 .35
❑ 212 Ron Francis .10 .05
❑ 213 Tom Barrasso .10 .05
❑ 214 Sergei Zubov .05 .02
❑ 215 Tomas Sandstrom .05 .02
❑ 216 Joe Dziedzic .05 .02
❑ 217 Richard Park .05 .02
❑ 218 Bryan Smolinski .05 .02
❑ 219 Petr Nedved .10 .05
❑ 220 Ken Wregget .10 .05
❑ 221 Dmitri Mironov .05 .02
❑ 222 Peter Zezel .05 .02
❑ 223 Brett Hull .30 .14
❑ 224 Grant Fuhr .10 .05
❑ 225 Shayne Corson .05 .02
❑ 226 Chris Pronger .10 .05
❑ 227 Craig MacTavish .05 .02
❑ 228 Al MacInnis .10 .05
❑ 229 Geoff Courtnall .05 .02
❑ 230 Stephane Matteau .05 .02
❑ 231 Tony Twist .05 .02
❑ 232 Brian Noonan .05 .02
❑ 233 Owen Nolan .10 .05
❑ 234 Shean Donovan .05 .02
❑ 235 Darren Turcotte .05 .02
❑ 236 Marcus Ragnarsson .05 .02
❑ 237 Viktor Kozlov UER .05 .02
(has Slava Kozlov's stats)
❑ 238 Jeff Friesen .10 .05
❑ 239 Chris Terreri .10 .05
❑ 240 Ray Whitney .05 .02
❑ 241 Ville Peltonen .05 .02
❑ 242 Andrei Nazarov .05 .02
❑ 243 Ulf Dahlen .05 .02
❑ 244 Roman Hamrlik .10 .05
❑ 245 Chris Gratton .10 .05
❑ 246 Petr Klima .05 .02
❑ 247 Daren Puppa .10 .05
❑ 248 Rob Zamuner .05 .02
❑ 249 Aaron Gavey .05 .02
❑ 250 Brian Bradley .05 .02
❑ 251 Paul Ysebaert .05 .02
❑ 252 Igor Ulanov .05 .02
❑ 253 Alexander Selivanov .05 .02
❑ 254 Shawn Burr .05 .02
❑ 255 Mats Sundin .10 .05
❑ 256 Doug Gilmour .25 .11
❑ 257 Felix Potvin .25 .11
❑ 258 Wendel Clark .10 .05
❑ 259 Kirk Muller .05 .02
❑ 260 Dave Gagner .10 .05
❑ 261 Tie Domi .10 .05
❑ 262 Mathieu Schneider .05 .02
❑ 263 Dimitri Yushkevich .05 .02
❑ 264 Don Beaupre .10 .05
❑ 265 Larry Murphy .10 .05
❑ 266 Pavel Bure .50 .23
❑ 267 Alexander Mogilny .10 .05
❑ 268 Trevor Linden .10 .05
❑ 269 Jyrki Lumme .05 .02
❑ 270 Cliff Ronning .05 .02
❑ 271 Kirk McLean .10 .05
❑ 272 Corey Hirsch .10 .05
❑ 273 Esa Tikkanen .05 .02
❑ 274 Gino Odjick .05 .02
❑ 275 Markus Naslund .05 .02
❑ 276 Russ Courtnall .05 .02
❑ 277 Joe Juneau .05 .02
❑ 278 Jim Carey .25 .11
❑ 279 Peter Bondra .25 .11
❑ 280 Michal Pivonka .05 .02
❑ 281 Steve Konowalchuk .05 .02
❑ 282 Pat Peake .05 .02
❑ 283 Brendan Witt .05 .02
❑ 284 Stefan Ustorf .05 .02
❑ 285 Keith Jones .05 .02
❑ 286 Sergei Gonchar .05 .02
❑ 287 Sylvain Cote .05 .02
❑ 288 Dale Hunter .05 .02
❑ 289 Paul Kariya SB .25 .11
❑ 290 Wayne Gretzky SB .25 .11
❑ 291 Eric Lindros SB .25 .11
❑ 292 Steve Yzerman SB .25 .11
❑ 293 Mario Lemieux SB .25 .11
❑ 294 Jaromir Jagr SB .25 .11
❑ 295 Keith Tkachuk SB .25 .11
❑ 296 Mark Messier SB .25 .11
❑ 297 Jeremy Roenick SB .25 .11
❑ 298 Peter Forsberg SB .25 .11
❑ 299 Joe Sakic SB .25 .11
❑ 300 Theoren Fleury SB .10 .05
❑ 301 Chris Chelios SB .25 .11
❑ 302 Vlad Konstantinov SB .05 .02
❑ 303 Brian Leetch SB .25 .11
❑ 304 Ray Bourque SB .25 .11
❑ 305 Scott Stevens SB .10 .05
❑ 306 Martin Brodeur SB .25 .11
❑ 307 Patrick Roy SB .25 .11
❑ 308 Scotty Bowman .10 .05
❑ 309 Paul Kariya .50 .23
Teemu Selanne
Guy Hebert
❑ 310 Adam Oates .10 .05
Ray Bourque
Cam Neely
❑ 311 Pat LaFontaine .10 .05
Alexei Zhitnik
Dominik Hasek
❑ 312 Theo Fleury .10 .05
Michael Nylander
Trevor Kidd
❑ 313 Jeremy Roenick .10 .05
Chris Chelios
Eric Daze
❑ 314 Joe Sakic 1.00 .45
Patrick Roy
Peter Forsberg
❑ 315 Mike Modano .10 .05
Joe Nieuwendyk
Todd Harvey
❑ 316 Sergei Fedorov .25 .11
Vladimir Konstantinov
Paul Coffey
❑ 317 Doug Weight .25 .11
Jason Arnott
Curtis Joseph
❑ 318 Ed Jovanovski .10 .05
John Vanbiesbrouck
Rob Niedermayer
❑ 319 Brendan Shanahan .10 .05
Geoff Sanderson
Sean Burke
❑ 320 Vitali Yachmenev .05 .02
Dimitri Khristich
Ray Ferraro
❑ 321 Jocelyn Thibault .25 .11
Pierre Turgeon
Saku Koivu
❑ 322 Martin Brodeur .10 .05
Steve Thomas
Scott Stevens
❑ 323 Todd Bertuzzi .10 .05
Eric Fichaud
Zigmund Palffy
❑ 324 Brian Leetch .25 .11
Adam Graves
Mike Richter
❑ 325 Alexander Daigle .10 .05
Alexei Yashin
Damian Rhodes
❑ 326 Ron Hextall .10 .05
John LeClair
Mikael Renberg
❑ 327 Alexei Zhamnov .10 .05
Keith Tkachuk
Oleg Tverdovsky
❑ 328 Jaromir Jagr .25 .11
Petr Nedved
Ron Francis
❑ 329 Wayne Gretzky 1.00 .45
Brett Hull
Al MacInnis
❑ 330 Owen Nolan .10 .05
Darren Turcotte
Chris Terreri
❑ 331 Roman Hamrlik .10 .05
Chris Gratton
Darren Puppa
❑ 332 Doug Gilmour .10 .05
Felix Potvin
Mats Sundin
❑ 333 Alexander Mogilny .10 .05
Pavel Bure
Trevor Linden
❑ 334 Jim Carey .10 .05
Joe Juneau
Peter Bondra
❑ 335 Mario Lemieux .75 .35
Mark Messier
Eric Lindros
❑ 336 Wayne Gretzky 1.00 .45
Teemu Selanne
Joe Sakic
❑ 337 Chad Kilger .05 .02
❑ 338 Todd Bertuzzi .05 .02
❑ 339 Petr Sykora .05 .02
❑ 340 Ed Jovanovski .10 .05
❑ 341 Kyle McLaren .05 .02
❑ 342 Brian Holzinger .10 .05
❑ 343 Jeff O'Neill .05 .02
❑ 344 Daniel Alfredsson .10 .05
❑ 345 Brendan Witt .05 .02
❑ 346 Daymond Langkow .05 .02
❑ 347 Checklist .05 .02
❑ 348 Checklist .05 .02
❑ 349 Jarome Iginla TRADE .25 .11
❑ 350 Sergei Berezin TRADE 1.50 .70
❑ 351 Jose Theodore TRADE 1.00 .45
❑ 352 Rem Murray TRADE .25 .11
❑ 353 Daniel Goneau TRADE .75 .35
❑ 354 Ethan Moreau TRADE .25 .11
❑ 355 Jonas Hoglund TRADE .25 .11
❑ 356 Anders Eriksson TRADE .25 .11
❑ 357 Christian Dube TRADE .25 .11
❑ 358 Roman Turek TRADE .75 .35
❑ 359 Bryan Berard TRADE 1.00 .45
❑ 360 Jim Campbell TRADE 1.00 .45
❑ 361 Janne Niinimaa TRADE .25 .11
❑ 362 Wade Redden TRADE .25 .11
❑ 363 Marc Denis TRADE 1.50 .70
❑ P222 Wayne Gretzky PROMO 5.00 2.20
❑ NNO Young Guns Trade .50 .23
❑ NNO1 Wayne Gretzky '79-80 5.00 2.20
Meet the Stars 4X6
❑ NNO2 Wayne Gretzky 802 5.00 2.20
Meet the Stars 4X6

## 1996-97 Collector's Choice MVP

This set consists of 45 of the NHL's top stars and rookies. Silver versions are found one per pack, while the tougher gold parallel version is found 1:25 packs. These cards can be differentiated by the color of the foil on the left-hand border. The card fronts feature a color action photo with with abbreviation "MVP" appearing in either silver or gold (depending on the version) at the bottom of the card. Values for the gold cards can be determined by utilizing the multiplier below.

| | MINT | NRMT |
|---|---|---|
| COMPLETE SET (45) | 25.00 | 11.00 |
| COMMON CARD (UD1-UD45) | .25 | .11 |
| COMP.GOLD SET (45) | 150.00 | 67.50 |
| COMMON GOLD (UD1-UD45) | 1.50 | .67 |

*GOLD: 3X TO 6X BASIC CARDS

❑ UD1 Wayne Gretzky 5.00 2.20
❑ UD2 Ron Francis .40 .18
❑ UD3 Peter Forsberg 2.00 .90
❑ UD4 Alexander Mogilny .40 .18
❑ UD5 Joe Sakic 1.25 .55
❑ UD6 Claude Lemieux .40 .18
❑ UD7 Teemu Selanne 1.25 .55
❑ UD8 John LeClair 1.00 .45
❑ UD9 Doug Weight .40 .18
❑ UD10 Paul Kariya 2.50 1.10
❑ UD11 Theoren Fleury .40 .18
❑ UD12 John Vanbiesbrouck 1.00 .45
❑ UD13 Sergei Fedorov 1.00 .45
❑ UD14 Steve Yzerman 2.00 .90
❑ UD15 Adam Oates .40 .18
❑ UD16 Keith Tkachuk .75 .35
❑ UD17 Mike Modano .75 .35
❑ UD18 Jeremy Roenick .60 .25
❑ UD19 Patrick Roy 3.00 1.35
❑ UD20 Felix Potvin .60 .25
❑ UD21 Martin Brodeur 1.50 .70
❑ UD22 Pavel Bure 1.25 .55
❑ UD23 Peter Bondra .40 .18
❑ UD24 Zigmund Palffy .60 .25
❑ UD25 Roman Hamrlik .40 .18
❑ UD26 Brendan Shanahan 1.25 .55
❑ UD27 Ray Bourque .60 .25
❑ UD28 Paul Coffey .60 .25
❑ UD29 Brett Hull .75 .35
❑ UD30 Brian Leetch .60 .25
❑ UD31 Chris Chelios .60 .25
❑ UD32 Vitali Yachmenev .25 .11
❑ UD33 Nicklas Lidstrom .25 .11
❑ UD34 Ed Jovanovski .40 .18
❑ UD35 Sandis Ozolinsh .40 .18
❑ UD36 Scott Stevens .25 .11
❑ UD37 Eric Daze .40 .18
❑ UD38 Saku Koivu 1.00 .45
❑ UD39 Daniel Alfredsson .40 .18
❑ UD40 Pat LaFontaine .25 .11
❑ UD41 Cam Neely .40 .18
❑ UD42 Owen Nolan .40 .18
❑ UD43 Jaromir Jagr 2.00 .90
❑ UD44 Mats Sundin .40 .18
❑ UD45 Doug Gilmour .40 .18

## 1996-97 Collector's Choice Stick'Ums

This unusual set consists of 30 stickers, the first 25 of which feature the NHL's top players. The remaining stickers feature a variety of hockey-oriented doo-daddery. These stickers were randomly inserted at 1:3 packs.

| | MINT | NRMT |
|---|---|---|
| COMPLETE SET (30) | 30.00 | 13.50 |
| COMMON STICKER (S1-S30) | .25 | .11 |

❑ S1 Wayne Gretzky 5.00 2.20
❑ S2 Brett Hull 1.00 .45
❑ S3 Peter Forsberg 2.50 1.10
❑ S4 Patrick Roy 4.00 1.80
❑ S5 Cam Neely .50 .23
❑ S6 Jeremy Roenick .75 .35
❑ S7 Mario Lemieux 4.00 1.80
❑ S8 Jaromir Jagr 2.50 1.10
❑ S9 Eric Lindros 2.50 1.10
❑ S10 Mark Messier 1.00 .45
❑ S11 Felix Potvin .75 .35
❑ S12 Brendan Shanahan 1.50 .70
❑ S13 Teemu Selanne 1.50 .70
❑ S14 Paul Kariya 3.00 1.35
❑ S15 Mike Modano 1.00 .45
❑ S16 Pavel Bure 1.50 .70
❑ S17 Jim Carey .75 .35
❑ S18 Roman Hamrlik .50 .23
❑ S19 Pierre Turgeon .50 .23
❑ S20 Theoren Fleury .50 .23
❑ S21 Pat LaFontaine .25 .11
❑ S22 Steve Yzerman 2.50 1.10
❑ S23 Sergei Fedorov 1.50 .70
❑ S24 Martin Brodeur 2.00 .90
❑ S25 Owen Nolan .50 .23
❑ S26 Ice Machine .25 .11
❑ S27 Champions .25 .11
❑ S28 Slap Shot .25 .11
❑ S29 Stripes .25 .11
❑ S30 Goal .25 .11

## 1996-97 Collector's Choice Crash the Game

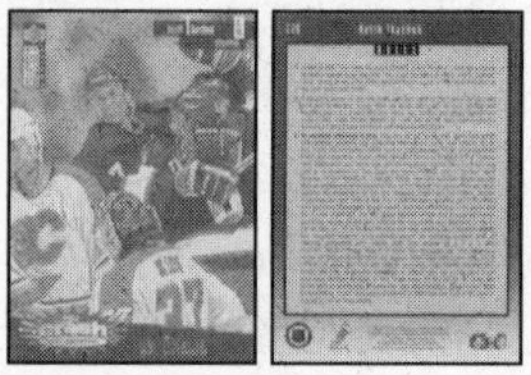

This interactive set features 30 NHL stars on a total of 88 cards. 28 players appear on 3 variations each, while two (Joe Sakic and Adam Oates) are featured on but two by virtue of an error by Upper Deck. Randomly inserted in packs, these cards come in silver (1:5 packs) and gold (1:44 packs) foil versions. If the player scored a goal against the team featured on his card, the winning card could be redeemed for a special exchange card. There are two versions of this set as well. Both versions feature the same design and photos, but they are different from the Crash cards for which they were redeemed. Furthermore, the gold versions of the exchange cards were die-cut. To differentiate between each of the player's three insert cards, they are numbered here with A, B and C suffixes. These suffixes do not appear on the cards themselves. The expiration date for these cards was July 1, 1997.

| | MINT | NRMT |
|---|---|---|
| COMPLETE SET (88) | 80.00 | 36.00 |
| COMMON CARD (C1-30) | .50 | .23 |
| COMPLETE GOLD SET | 250.00 | 110.00 |
| COMMON GOLD (C1-30) | 1.50 | .70 |

*GOLD STARS: 1.5X TO 3X SILVER CRASH

❑ C1A Wayne Gretzky ANA L 5.00 2.20
❑ C1B Wayne Gretzky EDM L 5.00 2.20
❑ C1C Wayne Gretzky LA W 5.00 2.20
❑ C2A Doug Gilmour PHI L .75 .35
❑ C2B Doug Gilmour PIT L .75 .35
❑ C2C Doug Gilmour TB W .75 .35
❑ C3A Alexander Mogilny BUF L .75 .35
❑ C3B Alexander Mogilny NYI .75 .35
❑ C3C Alexander Mogilny OTT L .75 .35
❑ C4A Peter Bondra DET W .50 .23
❑ C4B Peter Bondra LA .50 .23
❑ C4C Peter Bondra PHO W .50 .23
❑ C5A Mario Lemieux CHI W 4.00 1.80
❑ C5B Mario Lemieux COL L 4.00 1.80
❑ C5C Mario Lemieux EDM 4.00 1.80
❑ C6A Jaromir Jagr CAL W 2.50 1.10
❑ C6B Jaromir Jagr DET L 3.00 1.35
❑ C6C Jaromir Jagr TOR W 3.00 1.35
❑ C7A Joe Sakic FLA L 1.50 .70
❑ C7B Joe Sakic PIT 2.00 .90
❑ C8A Vitali Yachmenev HAR W .50 .23
❑ C8B Vitali Yachmenev MON .50 .23
❑ C8C Vitali Yachmenev NJ L .50 .23
❑ C9A Doug Weight BOS L .75 .35
❑ C9B Doug Weight NYI L .75 .35
❑ C9C Doug Weight NYR W .75 .35
❑ C10A Steve Yzerman BOS L 2.50 1.10
❑ C10B Steve Yzerman FLA W 2.50 1.10
❑ C10C Steve Yzerman NJ L 2.50 1.10
❑ C11A Alexei Zhamnov BUF L .50 .23
❑ C11B Alexei Zhamnov HAR W .50 .23
❑ C11C Alexei Zhamnov TB L .50 .23
❑ C12A John LeClair ANA W 1.25 .55
❑ C12B John LeClair DET W 1.00 .45
❑ C12C John LeClair STL W 1.00 .45
❑ C13A Daniel Alfredsson COL L .50 .23
❑ C13B Daniel Alfredsson LA W .50 .23
❑ C13C Daniel Alfredsson VAN L .50 .23
❑ C14A Brendan Shanahan CAL W 1.50 .70
❑ C14B Brendan Shanahan CHI 1.50 .70
❑ C14C Brendan Shanahan TOR W 1.50 .70
❑ C15A Saku Koivu ANA L 1.25 .55
❑ C15B Saku Koivu LA 1.50 .70
❑ C15C Saku Koivu STL L 1.50 .70
❑ C16A Steve Thomas CHI L .50 .23
❑ C16B Steve Thomas PHO W .50 .23
❑ C16C Steve Thomas VAN L .50 .23
❑ C17A Pavel Bure BOS L 1.50 .70
❑ C17B Pavel Bure FLA L 1.50 .70
❑ C17C Pavel Bure NYR W 1.50 .70
❑ C18A Slava Kozlov BUF W .50 .23
❑ C18B Slava Kozlov OTT L .50 .23
❑ C18C Slava Kozlov TB .50 .23
❑ C19A Teemu Selanne HAR W 1.50 .70
❑ C19B Teemu Selanne NYI W 1.50 .70
❑ C19C Teemu Selanne PHI W 1.50 .70
❑ C20A Eric Daze BOS L .50 .23
❑ C20B Eric Daze BUF L .50 .23
❑ C20C Eric Daze PIT L .50 .23
❑ C21A Adam Oates DET L .50 .23
❑ C21B Adam Oates SJ .50 .23
❑ C22A Ray Bourque CHI L .75 .35
❑ C22B Ray Bourque TOR W .75 .35
❑ C22C Ray Bourque VAN L .75 .35
❑ C23A Jason Arnott HAR W .75 .35
❑ C23B Jason Arnott PHI L .75 .35
❑ C23C Jason Arnott TB L .75 .35
❑ C24A Paul Kariya BOS L 3.00 1.35
❑ C24B Paul Kariya FLA L 3.00 1.35
❑ C24C Paul Kariya NYR W 3.00 1.35
❑ C25A Mikael Renberg DET L .50 .23
❑ C25B Mikael Renberg PHO L .50 .23
❑ C25C Mikael Renberg SJ L .50 .23
❑ C26A Keith Tkachuk MON W 1.00 .45
❑ C26B Keith Tkachuk OTT L 1.00 .45
❑ C26C Keith Tkachuk PIT W 1.00 .45
❑ C27A Brian Leetch ANA L .75 .35
❑ C27B Brian Leetch COL L .75 .35
❑ C27C Brian Leetch VAN .75 .35
❑ C28A Eric Lindros CAL L 2.50 1.10
❑ C28B Eric Lindros LA 3.00 1.35
❑ C28C Eric Lindros STL W 3.00 1.35
❑ C29A Mats Sundin BUF W .75 .35
❑ C29B Mats Sundin FLA L .75 .35
❑ C29C Mats Sundin NYI .75 .35
❑ C30A Mark Messier CHI L 1.00 .45
❑ C30B Mark Messier DET W 1.25 .55
❑ C30C Mark Messier TOR W 1.25 .55

## 1996-97 Collector's Choice Crash the Game Exchange

Collectors who redeemed winning Crash the Game cards (randomly seeded into 1:5 Collector's Choice packs) received one of these Exchange cards through mail. The exchange was based on a card-for-card trade out of the respective player mailed in. The deadline for the exchange was July 1st, 1997. Exchange cards feature completely redesigned fronts and backs to the basic Crash inserts. Card fronts feature a burgundy and silver foil background with a color action shot of each player. Of the thirty players featured in the original Crash set, only two (#20 Eric Daze and #25 Mikael Renberg) failed to win a prize. While copies of these cards are reported to exist, they were not widely distributed, and thus the Exchange set is complete at 28 cards.

| | MINT | NRMT |
|---|---|---|
| COMPLETE SET (28) | 80.00 | 36.00 |

*EXCH.STARS: 1.5X TO 3X BASIC CRASH CARDS
COMP.GOLD EXCHANGE SET (28) 250.00

110.00
*GOLD EXCH.STARS: 5X TO 10X BASIC CARDS

## 1996-97 Collector's Choice Blow-Ups

The ten cards in this set were issued one per special retail box of Collector's Choice. The cards are identical in every way to their corresponding regular version, except for the size; these cards measure 4 X 6 inches.

| | MINT | NRMT |
|---|---|---|
| COMPLETE SET (10) | 25.00 | 11.00 |
| COMMON CARD | 1.00 | .45 |
| ❑ 13 Ray Bourque | 2.00 | .90 |
| ❑ 23 Pat LaFontaine | 1.50 | .70 |
| ❑ 35 Theoren Fleury | 1.50 | .70 |
| ❑ 62 Valeri Kamensky | 1.50 | .70 |
| ❑ 69 Mike Modano | 2.50 | 1.10 |
| ❑ 84 Chris Osgood | 2.00 | .90 |
| ❑ 133 Pierre Turgeon | 1.50 | .70 |
| ❑ 170 Wayne Gretzky | 12.00 | 5.50 |
| ❑ 244 Roman Hamrlik | 1.00 | .45 |
| ❑ 257 Felix Potvin | 2.00 | .90 |

## 1996-97 Collector's Choice Blow-ups Bi-Way

These eight oversized (4 by 6 inches) cards mirrored the regular edition Collector's Choice cards, save for the numbering on the back. The cards were inserted one per box sold through the Bi-Way discount chain in Canada.

| | MINT | NRMT |
|---|---|---|
| COMPLETE SET (8) | 30.00 | 13.50 |
| COMMON CARD (1-8) | 2.50 | 1.10 |
| ❑ 1 Wayne Gretzky | 15.00 | 6.75 |
| ❑ 2 Theoren Fleury | 2.50 | 1.10 |
| ❑ 3 Jason Arnott | 2.50 | 1.10 |
| ❑ 4 Saku Koivu | 5.00 | 2.20 |
| ❑ 5 Pierre Turgeon | 2.50 | 1.10 |
| ❑ 6 Daniel Alfredsson | 2.50 | 1.10 |
| ❑ 7 Felix Potvin | 3.00 | 1.35 |
| ❑ 8 Alexander Mogilny | 2.50 | 1.10 |

## 1997-98 Collector's Choice

This 320-card set features color photos of approximately ten players from each of the NHL's 26 teams and was distributed in 14-card packs with a suggested retail price of $1.29. The set contains 275 regular player cards and two subsets: National Heroes (36 cards) which includes some of the most talented junior players, and Chippy's Checklist (9 cards) which highlights nine of the mascot's favorite players on the set's checklist cards. The cards are dual numbered and are checklisted in team order alphabetized by city.

| | MINT | NRMT |
|---|---|---|
| COMPLETE SET (320) | 25.00 | 11.00 |
| COMMON CARD (1-320) | .10 | .05 |
| ❑ 1 Guy Hebert | .25 | .11 |
| ❑ 2 Sean Pronger | .10 | .05 |
| ❑ 3 Dmitri Mironov | .10 | .05 |
| ❑ 4 Darren Van Impe | .10 | .05 |
| ❑ 5 Joe Sacco | .10 | .05 |
| ❑ 6 Ted Drury | .10 | .05 |
| ❑ 7 Steve Rucchin | .10 | .05 |
| ❑ 8 Teemu Selanne | .60 | .25 |
| ❑ 9 Paul Kariya | 1.25 | .55 |
| ❑ 10 Jari Kurri | .25 | .11 |
| ❑ 11 Kevin Todd | .10 | .05 |
| ❑ 12 Ray Bourque | .30 | .14 |
| ❑ 13 Anson Carter | .10 | .05 |
| ❑ 14 Ted Donato | .10 | .05 |
| ❑ 15 Kyle McLaren | .10 | .05 |
| ❑ 16 Jason Allison | .25 | .11 |
| ❑ 17 Jim Carey | .25 | .11 |
| ❑ 18 Jozef Stumpel | .25 | .11 |
| ❑ 19 Jean-Yves Roy | .10 | .05 |
| ❑ 20 Steve Heinze | .10 | .05 |
| ❑ 21 Sheldon Kennedy | .10 | .05 |
| ❑ 22 Dominik Hasek | .60 | .25 |
| ❑ 23 Rob Ray | .10 | .05 |
| ❑ 24 Derek Plante | .10 | .05 |
| ❑ 25 Brian Holzinger | .10 | .05 |
| ❑ 26 Mike Peca | .10 | .05 |
| ❑ 27 Matthew Barnaby | .10 | .05 |
| ❑ 28 Donald Audette | .10 | .05 |
| ❑ 29 Alexei Zhitnik | .10 | .05 |
| ❑ 30 Garry Galley | .10 | .05 |
| ❑ 31 Pat LaFontaine | .25 | .11 |
| ❑ 32 Jason Dawe | .10 | .05 |
| ❑ 33 Hnat Domenichelli | .10 | .05 |
| ❑ 34 Jarome Iginla | .25 | .11 |
| ❑ 35 Chris O'Sullivan | .10 | .05 |
| ❑ 36 Todd Simpson | .10 | .05 |
| ❑ 37 Trevor Kidd | .25 | .11 |
| ❑ 38 Dave Gagner | .10 | .05 |
| ❑ 39 German Titov | .25 | .11 |
| ❑ 40 Theoren Fleury | .25 | .11 |
| ❑ 41 Dwayne Roloson | .10 | .05 |
| ❑ 42 Marty McInnis | .10 | .05 |
| ❑ 43 Jonas Hoglund | .10 | .05 |
| ❑ 44 Tony Amonte | .25 | .11 |
| ❑ 45 Gary Suter | .10 | .05 |
| ❑ 46 Chris Chelios | .30 | .14 |
| ❑ 47 Jeff Hackett | .25 | .11 |
| ❑ 48 Ulf Dahlen | .10 | .05 |
| ❑ 49 Bob Probert | .10 | .05 |
| ❑ 50 Kevin Miller | .10 | .05 |
| ❑ 51 Ethan Moreau | .10 | .05 |
| ❑ 52 Eric Weinrich | .10 | .05 |
| ❑ 53 Eric Daze | .25 | .11 |
| ❑ 54 Peter Forsberg | 1.00 | .45 |
| ❑ 55 Joe Sakic | .60 | .25 |
| ❑ 56 Patrick Roy | 1.50 | .70 |
| ❑ 57 Adam Deadmarsh | .25 | .11 |
| ❑ 58 Valeri Kamensky | .25 | .11 |
| ❑ 59 Keith Jones | .10 | .05 |
| ❑ 60 Sandis Ozolinsh | .25 | .11 |
| ❑ 61 Mike Ricci | .10 | .05 |
| ❑ 62 Claude Lemieux | .25 | .11 |
| ❑ 63 Mike Keane | .10 | .05 |
| ❑ 64 Adam Foote | .10 | .05 |
| ❑ 65 Mike Modano | .40 | .18 |
| ❑ 66 Pat Verbeek | .10 | .05 |
| ❑ 67 Andy Moog | .25 | .11 |
| ❑ 68 Joe Nieuwendyk | .25 | .11 |
| ❑ 69 Jamie Langenbrunner | .10 | .05 |
| ❑ 70 Derian Hatcher | .10 | .05 |
| ❑ 71 Greg Adams | .10 | .05 |
| ❑ 72 Daryll Sydor | .10 | .05 |
| ❑ 73 Dave Reid | .10 | .05 |
| ❑ 74 Jere Lehtinen | .10 | .05 |
| ❑ 75 Todd Harvey | .10 | .05 |
| ❑ 76 Brendan Shanahan | .60 | .25 |
| ❑ 77 Mike Vernon | .25 | .11 |
| ❑ 78 Steve Yzerman | 1.00 | .45 |
| ❑ 79 Sergei Fedorov | .60 | .25 |
| ❑ 80 Chris Osgood | .30 | .14 |
| ❑ 81 Nicklas Lidstrom | .25 | .11 |
| ❑ 82 Vladimir Konstantinov | .10 | .05 |
| ❑ 83 Darren McCarty | .10 | .05 |
| ❑ 84 Kirk Maltby | .10 | .05 |
| ❑ 85 Vyacheslav Kozlov | .10 | .05 |
| ❑ 86 Martin Lapointe | .10 | .05 |
| ❑ 87 Doug Weight | .25 | .11 |
| ❑ 88 Mike Grier | .10 | .05 |
| ❑ 89 Curtis Joseph | .30 | .14 |
| ❑ 90 Andrei Kovalenko | .10 | .05 |
| ❑ 91 Rem Murray | .10 | .05 |
| ❑ 92 Ryan Smyth | .25 | .11 |
| ❑ 93 Mariusz Czerkawski | .10 | .05 |
| ❑ 94 Drew Bannister | .10 | .05 |
| ❑ 95 Jason Arnott | .25 | .11 |
| ❑ 96 Luke Richardson | .10 | .05 |
| ❑ 97 Dean McAmmond | .10 | .05 |
| ❑ 98 Kirk Muller | .10 | .05 |
| ❑ 99 Ray Sheppard | .10 | .05 |
| ❑ 100 Scott Mellanby | .10 | .05 |
| ❑ 101 Ed Jovanovski | .25 | .11 |
| ❑ 102 John Vanbiesbrouck | .50 | .23 |
| ❑ 103 Radek Dvorak | .10 | .05 |
| ❑ 104 Robert Svehla | .10 | .05 |
| ❑ 105 Rob Niedermayer | .10 | .05 |
| ❑ 106 Dave Nemirovsky | .10 | .05 |
| ❑ 107 Steve Washburn | .10 | .05 |
| ❑ 108 Bill Lindsay | .10 | .05 |
| ❑ 109 Kevin Dineen | .10 | .05 |
| ❑ 110 Keith Primeau | .10 | .05 |
| ❑ 111 Sean Burke | .25 | .11 |
| ❑ 112 Derek King | .10 | .05 |
| ❑ 113 Andrew Cassels | .10 | .05 |
| ❑ 114 Glen Wesley | .10 | .05 |
| ❑ 115 Nelson Emerson | .10 | .05 |
| ❑ 116 Geoff Sanderson | .25 | .11 |
| ❑ 117 Jeff O'Neill | .10 | .05 |
| ❑ 118 Kent Manderville | .10 | .05 |
| ❑ 119 Dimitri Khristich | .10 | .05 |
| ❑ 120 Ian Laperriere | .10 | .05 |
| ❑ 121 Aki Berg | .10 | .05 |
| ❑ 122 Vladimir Tsyplakov | .10 | .05 |
| ❑ 123 Vitali Yachmenev | .10 | .05 |
| ❑ 124 Roman Vopat | .10 | .05 |
| ❑ 125 Rob Blake | .10 | .05 |
| ❑ 126 Jan Vopat | .10 | .05 |
| ❑ 127 Jeff Shevalier | .10 | .05 |
| ❑ 128 Byron Dafoe | .25 | .11 |
| ❑ 129 Saku Koivu | .50 | .23 |
| ❑ 130 Vincent Damphousse | .25 | .11 |
| ❑ 131 Brian Savage | .10 | .05 |
| ❑ 132 Valeri Bure | .10 | .05 |
| ❑ 133 Mark Recchi | .25 | .11 |
| ❑ 134 Jocelyn Thibault | .25 | .11 |
| ❑ 135 Jose Theodore | .25 | .11 |
| ❑ 136 Dave Manson | .10 | .05 |
| ❑ 137 Shayne Corson | .10 | .05 |
| ❑ 138 Stephane Richer | .10 | .05 |
| ❑ 139 Doug Gilmour | .30 | .14 |
| ❑ 140 Scott Stevens | .10 | .05 |
| ❑ 141 Martin Brodeur | .75 | .35 |
| ❑ 142 Dave Andreychuk | .10 | .05 |
| ❑ 143 Bobby Holik | .10 | .05 |
| ❑ 144 Brian Rolston | .10 | .05 |
| ❑ 145 Jay Pandolfo | .10 | .05 |
| ❑ 146 John MacLean | .10 | .05 |
| ❑ 147 Bill Guerin | .25 | .11 |
| ❑ 148 Scott Niedermayer | .10 | .05 |
| ❑ 149 Denis Pederson | .10 | .05 |
| ❑ 150 Zigmund Palffy | .30 | .14 |
| ❑ 151 Robert Reichel | .10 | .05 |
| ❑ 152 Bryan Smolinski | .10 | .05 |
| ❑ 153 Eric Fichaud | .25 | .11 |
| ❑ 154 Todd Bertuzzi | .10 | .05 |
| ❑ 155 Bryan Berard | .25 | .11 |
| ❑ 156 Niklas Anderson | .10 | .05 |
| ❑ 157 Bryan McCabe | .10 | .05 |
| ❑ 158 Tommy Salo | .25 | .11 |
| ❑ 159 Kenny Jonsson | .10 | .05 |
| ❑ 160 Travis Green | .10 | .05 |
| ❑ 161 Mike Richter | .30 | .14 |
| ❑ 162 Brian Leetch | .30 | .14 |
| ❑ 163 Adam Graves | .25 | .11 |
| ❑ 164 Vladimir Vorobiev | .10 | .05 |
| ❑ 165 Niklas Sundstrom | .10 | .05 |
| ❑ 166 Russ Courtnall | .10 | .05 |
| ❑ 167 Wayne Gretzky | 2.00 | .90 |
| ❑ 168 Mark Messier | .40 | .18 |
| ❑ 169 Alexander Karpovtsev | .10 | .05 |
| ❑ 170 Luc Robitaille | .25 | .11 |
| ❑ 171 Ulf Samuelsson | .10 | .05 |
| ❑ 172 Daniel Alfredsson | .25 | .11 |
| ❑ 173 Alexei Yashin | .25 | .11 |
| ❑ 174 Alexandre Daigle | .25 | .11 |
| ❑ 175 Andreas Dackell | .10 | .05 |
| ❑ 176 Wade Redden | .10 | .05 |
| ❑ 177 Sergei Zholtok | .10 | .05 |
| ❑ 178 Damian Rhodes | .25 | .11 |
| ❑ 179 Steve Duchesne | .10 | .05 |
| ❑ 180 Shawn McEachern | .10 | .05 |
| ❑ 181 Ron Tugnutt | .25 | .11 |
| ❑ 182 John Leclair | .50 | .23 |
| ❑ 183 Janne Niinimaa | .25 | .11 |
| ❑ 184 Mikael Renberg | .25 | .11 |
| ❑ 185 Vaclav Prospal | .50 | .23 |
| ❑ 186 Eric Lindros | 1.00 | .45 |
| ❑ 187 Dainius Zubrus | .30 | .14 |
| ❑ 188 Ron Hextall | .25 | .11 |
| ❑ 189 Paul Coffey | .30 | .14 |
| ❑ 190 Dale Hawerchuk | .25 | .11 |
| ❑ 191 Trent Klatt | .10 | .05 |
| ❑ 192 Rod Brind'Amour | .25 | .11 |
| ❑ 193 Nikolai Khabibulin | .25 | .11 |
| ❑ 194 Keith Tkachuk | .40 | .18 |
| ❑ 195 Jeremy Roenick | .30 | .14 |
| ❑ 196 Mike Gartner | .25 | .11 |
| ❑ 197 Dallas Drake | .10 | .05 |
| ❑ 198 Oleg Tverdovsky | .10 | .05 |
| ❑ 199 Cliff Ronning | .10 | .05 |
| ❑ 200 Teppo Numminen | .10 | .05 |
| ❑ 201 Craig Janney | .10 | .05 |
| ❑ 202 Deron Quint | .10 | .05 |
| ❑ 203 Jason Wooley | .10 | .05 |
| ❑ 204 Ron Francis | .25 | .11 |
| ❑ 205 Jaromir Jagr | 1.00 | .45 |
| ❑ 206 Greg Johnson | .10 | .05 |
| ❑ 207 Kevin Hatcher | .10 | .05 |
| ❑ 208 Patrick Lalime | .25 | .11 |
| ❑ 209 Petr Nedved | .25 | .11 |
| ❑ 210 Ken Wregget | .25 | .11 |
| ❑ 211 Darius Kasparaitis | .10 | .05 |
| ❑ 212 Stu Barnes | .10 | .05 |
| ❑ 213 Joe Dziedzic | .10 | .05 |
| ❑ 214 Owen Nolan | .25 | .11 |
| ❑ 215 Jeff Friesen | .25 | .11 |
| ❑ 216 Ed Belfour | .30 | .14 |
| ❑ 217 Viktor Kozlov | .10 | .05 |
| ❑ 218 Tony Granato | .10 | .05 |
| ❑ 219 Darren Turcotte | .10 | .05 |
| ❑ 220 Stephen Guolla | .10 | .05 |
| ❑ 221 Marty McSorley | .10 | .05 |
| ❑ 222 Marcus Ragnarsson | .10 | .05 |
| ❑ 223 Al Iafrate | .10 | .05 |
| ❑ 224 Brett Hull | .40 | .18 |
| ❑ 225 Grant Fuhr | .25 | .11 |
| ❑ 226 Pierre Turgeon | .25 | .11 |
| ❑ 227 Geoff Courtnall | .10 | .05 |
| ❑ 228 Jim Campbell | .10 | .05 |
| ❑ 229 Harry York | .10 | .05 |
| ❑ 230 Tony Twist | .25 | .11 |
| ❑ 231 Joe Murphy | .10 | .05 |
| ❑ 232 Pavol Demitra | .10 | .05 |
| ❑ 233 Chris Pronger | .25 | .11 |
| ❑ 234 Al MacInnis | .25 | .11 |
| ❑ 235 Daren Puppa | .25 | .11 |
| ❑ 236 Chris Gratton | .25 | .11 |
| ❑ 237 Dino Ciccarelli | .10 | .05 |
| ❑ 238 Rob Zamuner | .10 | .05 |
| ❑ 239 Igor Ulanov | .10 | .05 |
| ❑ 240 Roman Hamrlik | .10 | .05 |
| ❑ 241 Alexander Selivanov | .10 | .05 |
| ❑ 242 Patrick Poulin | .10 | .05 |
| ❑ 243 Daymond Langkow | .10 | .05 |
| ❑ 244 Corey Schwab | .25 | .11 |
| ❑ 245 Mats Sundin | .30 | .14 |
| ❑ 246 Wendel Clark | .25 | .11 |
| ❑ 247 Sergei Berezin | .10 | .05 |
| ❑ 248 Steve Sullivan | .10 | .05 |
| ❑ 249 Fredrik Modin | .10 | .05 |
| ❑ 250 Darby Hendrickson | .10 | .05 |
| ❑ 251 Jason Podollan | .10 | .05 |
| ❑ 252 Felix Potvin | .30 | .14 |
| ❑ 253 Tie Domi | .10 | .05 |
| ❑ 254 Todd Warriner | .10 | .05 |
| ❑ 255 Pavel Bure | .60 | .25 |
| ❑ 256 Alexander Mogilny | .25 | .11 |
| ❑ 257 Martin Gelinas | .10 | .05 |
| ❑ 258 Corey Hirsch | .25 | .11 |
| ❑ 259 Trevor Linden | .25 | .11 |
| ❑ 260 Mike Sillinger | .10 | .05 |
| ❑ 261 Markus Naslund | .10 | .05 |
| ❑ 262 Jyrki Lumme | .10 | .05 |
| ❑ 263 Gino Odjick | .10 | .05 |
| ❑ 264 Mike Ridley | .10 | .05 |
| ❑ 265 Dave Roberts | .10 | .05 |
| ❑ 266 Adam Oates | .25 | .11 |
| ❑ 267 Bill Ranford | .25 | .11 |
| ❑ 268 Joe Juneau | .25 | .11 |
| ❑ 269 Chris Simon | .10 | .05 |
| ❑ 270 Peter Bondra | .30 | .14 |
| ❑ 271 Dale Hunter | .10 | .05 |
| ❑ 272 Jaroslav Svejkovski | .25 | .11 |
| ❑ 273 Sergei Gonchar | .10 | .05 |
| ❑ 274 Steve Konowalchuk | .10 | .05 |
| ❑ 275 Phil Housley | .10 | .05 |
| ❑ 276 Angela James | .25 | .11 |
| ❑ 277 Nancy Drolet | .10 | .05 |
| ❑ 278 Lesley Reddon | .25 | .11 |
| ❑ 279 Hayley Wickenheiser | .25 | .11 |
| ❑ 280 Vicky Sunohara | .10 | .05 |
| ❑ 281 Cassie Campbell | .25 | .11 |
| ❑ 282 Geraldine Heaney | .10 | .05 |
| ❑ 283 Judy Diduck | .10 | .05 |
| ❑ 284 France St. Louis | .10 | .05 |
| ❑ 285 Danielle Goyette | .10 | .05 |
| ❑ 286 Therese Brisson | .10 | .05 |
| ❑ 287 Stacey Wilson | .10 | .05 |
| ❑ 288 Danielle Dube | .25 | .11 |
| ❑ 289 Jayna Hefford | .10 | .05 |
| ❑ 290 Luce Letendre | .10 | .05 |
| ❑ 291 Lori Dupuis | .10 | .05 |
| ❑ 292 Rebecca Fahey | .10 | .05 |
| ❑ 293 Fiona Smith | .10 | .05 |
| ❑ 294 Laura Schuler | .10 | .05 |
| ❑ 295 Karen Nystrom | .10 | .05 |
| ❑ 296 Joe Thornton | .60 | .25 |
| ❑ 297 Peter Schaefer | .40 | .18 |
| ❑ 298 Daniel Tkaczuk | .40 | .18 |
| ❑ 299 Alyn McCauley | .25 | .11 |
| ❑ 300 Shane Willis | .10 | .05 |
| ❑ 301 Chris Phillips | .10 | .05 |
| ❑ 302 Marc Denis | .25 | .11 |
| ❑ 303 Jason Ward | .10 | .05 |
| ❑ 304 Patrick Marleau | .60 | .25 |
| ❑ 305 Brad Isbister | .10 | .05 |
| ❑ 306 Cameron Mann | .40 | .18 |
| ❑ 307 Daniel Cleary | .25 | .11 |
| ❑ 308 Brad Larsen | .10 | .05 |
| ❑ 309 Nick Boynton | .25 | .11 |
| ❑ 310 Scott Barney | .25 | .11 |
| ❑ 311 Boyd Devereaux | .10 | .05 |
| ❑ 312 Wayne Gretzky CL | .30 | .14 |
| ❑ 313 Steve Yzerman CL | .30 | .14 |
| ❑ 314 Jaromir Jagr CL | .30 | .14 |
| ❑ 315 Jarome Iginla CL | .25 | .11 |
| ❑ 316 Patrick Roy CL | .30 | .14 |
| ❑ 317 John Vanbiesbrouck CL | .25 | .11 |
| ❑ 318 Paul Kariya CL | .30 | .14 |
| ❑ 319 Doug Weight CL | .10 | .05 |
| ❑ 320 Mats Sundin CL | .25 | .11 |

## 1997-98 Collector's Choice Crash the Game

Randomly inserted in packs at the rate of one in five, this 90-card set features color player photos. If the pictured player scores against the designated team, the card could be redeemed for a special high quality redemption card of that player.

| | MINT | NRMT |
|---|---|---|
| COMPLETE SET (90) | 60.00 | 27.00 |
| COMMON CARD (1A-30C) | .20 | .09 |
| CRASH EXPIRATION: 7/1/98 | | |
| COMP.EXCH.SET (30) | 60.00 | 27.00 |
| COMMON EXCH (1-30) | .75 | .35 |
| *EXCH.STARS: 2X TO 4X HI COLUMN | | |
| ❑ C1A Wayne Gretzky | 4.00 | 1.80 |
| ❑ C1B Wayne Gretzky DET L | 4.00 | 1.80 |
| ❑ C1C Wayne Gretzky EDM L | 4.00 | 1.80 |
| ❑ C2A Mike Modano | .75 | .35 |
| ❑ C2B Mike Modano NYI W | .75 | .35 |
| ❑ C2C Mike Modano NYR L | .75 | .35 |
| ❑ C3A Doug Weight BUF L | .50 | .23 |
| ❑ C3B Doug Weight OTT W | .50 | .23 |
| ❑ C3C Doug Weight NYR W | .50 | .23 |
| ❑ C4A Brendan Shanahan | 1.25 | .55 |
| ❑ C4B Brendan Shanahan PIT W | 1.25 | .55 |
| ❑ C4C Brendan Shanahan PHI W | 1.25 | .55 |
| ❑ C5A Ray Sheppard ANA L | .20 | .09 |
| ❑ C5B Ray Sheppard DET L | .20 | .09 |
| ❑ C5C Ray Sheppard PHO | .20 | .09 |
| ❑ C6A Keith Primeau CAL W | .50 | .23 |
| ❑ C6B Keith Primeau DET L | .50 | .23 |
| ❑ C6C Keith Primeau TOR L | .50 | .23 |
| ❑ C7A Ray Bourque CHI L | .60 | .25 |
| ❑ C7B Ray Bourque LA L | .60 | .25 |
| ❑ C7C Ray Bourque VAN W | .60 | .25 |
| ❑ C8A Teemu Selanne | 1.25 | .55 |
| ❑ C8B Teemu Selanne NYI W | 1.25 | .55 |
| ❑ C8C Teemu Selanne WAS W | 1.25 | .55 |
| ❑ C9A Paul Kariya | 2.50 | 1.10 |
| ❑ C9B Paul Kariya PIT L | 2.50 | 1.10 |
| ❑ C9C Paul Kariya TB | 2.50 | 1.10 |
| ❑ C10A Tony Amonte MON L | .50 | .23 |
| ❑ C10B Tony Amonte NYR W | .50 | .23 |
| ❑ C10C Tony Amonte PHI L | .50 | .23 |
| ❑ C11A Saku Koivu | 1.00 | .45 |
| ❑ C11B Saku Koivu PHO L | 1.00 | .45 |
| ❑ C11C Saku Koivu SJ W | 1.00 | .45 |
| ❑ C12A Donald Audette ANA W | .20 | .09 |
| ❑ C12B Donald Audette EDM L | .20 | .09 |
| ❑ C12C Donald Audette STL L | .20 | .09 |
| ❑ C13A Doug Gilmour CAL W | .50 | .23 |
| ❑ C13B Doug Gilmour STL | .50 | .23 |
| ❑ C13C Doug Gilmour TOR W | .50 | .23 |
| ❑ C14A Theoren Fleury BUF L | .60 | .25 |
| ❑ C14B Theoren Fleury FLO | .60 | .25 |
| ❑ C14C Theoren Fleury PHI W | .60 | .25 |
| ❑ C15A Alexei Yashin COL | .50 | .23 |
| ❑ C15B Alexei Yashin LA L | .50 | .23 |
| ❑ C15C Alexei Yashin TOR W | .50 | .23 |
| ❑ C16A Zigmund Palffy CHI W | .50 | .23 |
| ❑ C16B Zigmund Palffy DET W | .50 | .23 |
| ❑ C16C Zigmund Palffy SJ W | .50 | .23 |
| ❑ C17A Dmitri Khristich OTT W | .20 | .09 |
| ❑ C17B Dmitri Khristich TB W | .20 | .09 |
| ❑ C17C Dmitri Khristich WAS W | .20 | .09 |
| ❑ C18A Joe Sakic | 1.25 | .55 |
| ❑ C18B Joe Sakic NYR L | 1.25 | .55 |
| ❑ C18C Joe Sakic PHI W | 1.25 | .55 |
| ❑ C19A Steve Yzerman | 2.00 | .90 |
| ❑ C19B Steve Yzerman MON L | 2.00 | .90 |
| ❑ C19C Steve Yzerman PHI W | 2.00 | .90 |
| ❑ C20A Eric Lindros | 2.00 | .90 |
| ❑ C20B Eric Lindros PHO W | 2.00 | .90 |
| ❑ C20C Eric Lindros TOR L | 2.00 | .90 |
| ❑ C21A Peter Forsberg FLO | 2.00 | .90 |
| ❑ C21B Peter Forsberg PHI L | 2.00 | .90 |
| ❑ C21C Peter Forsberg WAS W | 2.00 | .90 |
| ❑ C22A Dino Ciccarelli DAL W | .20 | .09 |
| ❑ C22B Dino Ciccarelli DET L | .20 | .09 |
| ❑ C22C Dino Ciccarelli EDM L | .20 | .09 |
| ❑ C23A Mats Sundin BUF L | .60 | .25 |
| ❑ C23B Mats Sundin MON L | .60 | .25 |
| ❑ C23C Mats Sundin OTT L | .60 | .25 |
| ❑ C24A Pavel Bure | 1.25 | .55 |
| ❑ C24B Pavel Bure NYR W | 1.25 | .55 |
| ❑ C24C Pavel Bure PIT W | 1.25 | .55 |
| ❑ C25A Peter Bondra CHI | .60 | .25 |
| ❑ C25B Peter Bondra LA W | .60 | .25 |
| ❑ C25C Peter Bondra VAN W | .60 | .25 |
| ❑ C26A Brett Hull | .75 | .35 |
| ❑ C26B Brett Hull NYR L | .75 | .35 |
| ❑ C26C Brett Hull WAS W | .75 | .35 |
| ❑ C27A Keith Tkachuk BOS | .75 | .35 |
| ❑ C27B Keith Tkachuk NJ L | .75 | .35 |
| ❑ C27C Keith Tkachuk TB W | .75 | .35 |
| ❑ C28A Jaromir Jagr | 2.00 | .90 |
| ❑ C28B Jaromir Jagr EDM W | 2.00 | .90 |
| ❑ C28C Jaromir Jagr STL L | 2.00 | .90 |
| ❑ C29A Jarome Iginla MON L | .20 | .09 |
| ❑ C29B Jarome Iginla OTT L | .20 | .09 |
| ❑ C29C Jarome Iginla WAS L | .20 | .09 |
| ❑ C30A Owen Nolan BUF L | .20 | .09 |
| ❑ C30B Owen Nolan FLO L | .20 | .09 |
| ❑ C30C Owen Nolan NYI L | .20 | .09 |

## 1997-98 Collectors Choice Magic Men

Randomly inserted in Canadian packs at the rate of one in 32, this 10-card set features five color photos each of Wayne Gretzky and Patrick Roy.

| | MINT | NRMT |
|---|---|---|
| COMPLETE SET (10) | 80.00 | 36.00 |
| COMMON GRETZKY (MM1-MM5) | 10.00 | 4.50 |
| COMMON ROY (MM6-MM10) | 8.00 | 3.60 |
| ❑ MM1 Wayne Gretzky | 10.00 | 4.50 |
| ❑ MM2 Wayne Gretzky | 10.00 | 4.50 |
| ❑ MM3 Wayne Gretzky | 10.00 | 4.50 |
| ❑ MM4 Wayne Gretzky | 10.00 | 4.50 |
| ❑ MM5 Wayne Gretzky | 10.00 | 4.50 |
| ❑ MM6 Patrick Roy | 8.00 | 3.60 |
| ❑ MM7 Patrick Roy | 8.00 | 3.60 |
| ❑ MM8 Patrick Roy | 8.00 | 3.60 |
| ❑ MM9 Patrick Roy | 8.00 | 3.60 |
| ❑ MM10 Patrick Roy | 8.00 | 3.60 |

## 1997-98 Collector's Choice Star Quest

This 90-card, four-tier insert set features color photos of some of the top NHL Superstars printed using the hobby's top technology. The 45 cards in Tier One (SQ1-SQ45) were randomly inserted one in every pack; the 20 cards in Tier Two (SQ45-SQ65) were randomly inserted one in every 21 packs; the 15 cards of Tier Three (SQ66-SQ80) were randomly inserted one in every 71 packs; the 10 cards of Tier Four were randomly inserted one in every 145 packs.

| | MINT | NRMT |
|---|---|---|
| COMPLETE SET (90) | 500.00 | 220.00 |
| COMP.SER.1 (45) | 8.00 | 3.60 |

| | | |
|---|---|---|
| COMMON CARD (1-45) | .20 | .09 |
| COMP.SER.2 (20) | 50.00 | 22.00 |
| COMMON CARD (46-65) | 1.50 | .70 |
| COMP.SER.3 (15) | 100.00 | 45.00 |
| COMMON CARD (66-80) | 5.00 | 2.20 |
| COMP.SER.4 (10) | 350.00 | 160.00 |
| COMMON CARD (81-90) | 12.00 | 5.50 |

| | | |
|---|---|---|
| ❑ SQ1 Bryan Berard | .40 | .18 |
| ❑ SQ2 Robert Svehla | .20 | .09 |
| ❑ SQ3 Petr Nedved | .40 | .18 |
| ❑ SQ4 Steve Sullivan | .20 | .09 |
| ❑ SQ5 Nicklas Lidstrom | .40 | .18 |
| ❑ SQ6 Wade Redden | .20 | .09 |
| ❑ SQ7 Jason Arnott | .40 | .18 |
| ❑ SQ8 Martin Gelinas | .20 | .09 |
| ❑ SQ9 Mikael Renberg | .20 | .09 |
| ❑ SQ10 Jeff Friesen | .40 | .18 |
| ❑ SQ11 Chris Chelios | .50 | .23 |
| ❑ SQ12 Jarome Iginla | .40 | .18 |
| ❑ SQ13 Vyacheslav Kozlov | .20 | .09 |
| ❑ SQ14 Brian Holzinger | .20 | .09 |
| ❑ SQ15 Eric Daze | .40 | .18 |
| ❑ SQ16 Pat Verbeek | .20 | .09 |
| ❑ SQ17 Jozef Stumpel | .40 | .18 |
| ❑ SQ18 Rob Niedermayer | .40 | .18 |
| ❑ SQ19 Sergei Fedorov | 1.00 | .45 |
| ❑ SQ20 Brian Leetch | .50 | .23 |
| ❑ SQ21 Bill Guerin | .20 | .09 |
| ❑ SQ22 Dino Ciccarelli | .20 | .09 |
| ❑ SQ23 Adam Oates | .40 | .18 |
| ❑ SQ24 Mike Grier | .20 | .09 |
| ❑ SQ25 Alexandre Daigle | .40 | .18 |
| ❑ SQ26 Janne Niinimaa | .40 | .18 |
| ❑ SQ27 Dimitri Khristich | .20 | .09 |
| ❑ SQ28 Oleg Tverdovsky | .20 | .09 |
| ❑ SQ29 Felix Potvin | .50 | .23 |
| ❑ SQ30 Mike Richter | .50 | .23 |
| ❑ SQ31 Curtis Joseph | .50 | .23 |
| ❑ SQ32 Vincent Damphousse | .40 | .18 |
| ❑ SQ33 Vladimir Konstantinov | .20 | .09 |
| ❑ SQ34 Andy Moog | .40 | .18 |
| ❑ SQ35 Nikolai Khabibulin | .40 | .18 |
| ❑ SQ36 Ed Belfour | .50 | .23 |
| ❑ SQ37 Scott Mellanby | .20 | .09 |
| ❑ SQ38 Sandis Ozolinsh | .40 | .18 |
| ❑ SQ39 Travis Green | .20 | .09 |
| ❑ SQ40 Patrick Lalime | .40 | .18 |
| ❑ SQ41 Niklas Sundstrom | .20 | .09 |
| ❑ SQ42 Guy Hebert | .40 | .18 |
| ❑ SQ43 Vitali Yachmenev | .20 | .09 |
| ❑ SQ44 Roman Hamrlik | .20 | .09 |
| ❑ SQ45 Adam Deadmarsh | .40 | .18 |
| ❑ SQ46 Alexei Zhamnov | 1.50 | .70 |
| ❑ SQ47 Saku Koivu | 5.00 | 2.20 |
| ❑ SQ48 Sergei Berezin | 2.50 | 1.10 |
| ❑ SQ49 Mark Messier | 4.00 | 1.80 |
| ❑ SQ50 Martin Brodeur | 8.00 | 3.60 |
| ❑ SQ51 Daniel Alfredsson | 2.50 | 1.10 |
| ❑ SQ52 John LeClair | 5.00 | 2.20 |
| ❑ SQ53 Mike Vernon | 2.50 | 1.10 |
| ❑ SQ54 Ron Francis | 2.50 | 1.10 |
| ❑ SQ55 Keith Primeau | 1.50 | .70 |
| ❑ SQ56 Pierre Turgeon | 2.50 | 1.10 |
| ❑ SQ57 Jim Carey | 2.50 | 1.10 |
| ❑ SQ58 Peter Bondra | 3.00 | 1.35 |
| ❑ SQ59 Pavel Bure | 6.00 | 2.70 |
| ❑ SQ60 Ray Sheppard | 1.50 | .70 |
| ❑ SQ61 Chris Gratton | 2.50 | 1.10 |
| ❑ SQ62 Derek Plante | 1.50 | .70 |
| ❑ SQ63 Joe Sakic | 6.00 | 2.70 |
| ❑ SQ64 Theoren Fleury | 2.50 | 1.10 |
| ❑ SQ65 Tony Amonte | 2.50 | 1.10 |
| ❑ SQ66 Zigmund Palffy | .50 | .23 |
| ❑ SQ67 Steve Yzerman | 20.00 | 9.00 |
| ❑ SQ68 Doug Weight | 5.00 | 2.20 |
| ❑ SQ69 Alexander Mogilny | 5.00 | 2.20 |
| ❑ SQ70 Doug Gilmour | 6.00 | 2.70 |
| ❑ SQ71 Peter Forsberg | 20.00 | 9.00 |
| ❑ SQ72 Alexei Yashin | 5.00 | 2.20 |
| ❑ SQ73 Geoff Sanderson | 5.00 | 2.20 |
| ❑ SQ74 Brendan Shanahan | 12.00 | 5.50 |
| ❑ SQ75 Mark Recchi | 5.00 | 2.20 |
| ❑ SQ76 Brett Hull | 8.00 | 3.60 |
| ❑ SQ77 Ray Bourque | 6.00 | 2.70 |
| ❑ SQ78 Owen Nolan | 5.00 | 2.20 |
| ❑ SQ79 Jeremy Roenick | 6.00 | 2.70 |
| ❑ SQ80 Teemu Selanne | 12.00 | 5.50 |
| ❑ SQ81 Dominik Hasek | 25.00 | 11.00 |
| ❑ SQ82 Mike Modano | 15.00 | 6.75 |
| ❑ SQ83 Mats Sundin | 12.00 | 5.50 |
| ❑ SQ84 John Vanbiesbrouck | 20.00 | 9.00 |
| ❑ SQ85 Paul Kariya | 50.00 | 22.00 |
| ❑ SQ86 Patrick Roy | 60.00 | 27.00 |
| ❑ SQ87 Keith Tkachuk | 15.00 | 6.75 |
| ❑ SQ88 Eric Lindros | 40.00 | 18.00 |
| ❑ SQ89 Jaromir Jagr | 40.00 | 18.00 |
| ❑ SQ90 Wayne Gretzky | 80.00 | 36.00 |

## 1997-98 Collector's Choice Stick'Ums

Randomly inserted in packs at the rate of one in three, this 30-card set features color action player photos printed on re-stickable stickers that stick anywhere.

| | MINT | NRMT |
|---|---|---|
| COMPLETE SET (30) | 30.00 | 13.50 |
| COMMON CARD (S1-S30) | .25 | .11 |

| | | |
|---|---|---|
| ❑ S1 Wayne Gretzky | 5.00 | 2.20 |
| ❑ S2 John Vanbiesbrouck | 1.25 | .55 |
| ❑ S3 Martin Brodeur | 2.00 | .90 |
| ❑ S4 Rob Blake | .50 | .23 |
| ❑ S5 Saku Koivu | 1.25 | .55 |
| ❑ S6 Curtis Joseph | .75 | .35 |
| ❑ S7 Chris Chelios | .75 | .35 |
| ❑ S8 Mike Modano | 1.00 | .45 |
| ❑ S9 Paul Kariya | 3.00 | 1.35 |
| ❑ S10 Eric Lindros | 2.50 | 1.10 |
| ❑ S11 Daniel Alfredsson | .50 | .23 |
| ❑ S12 Jarome Iginla | .50 | .23 |
| ❑ S13 Jeremy Roenick | .75 | .35 |
| ❑ S14 Brendan Shanahan | 1.50 | .70 |
| ❑ S15 Jaromir Jagr | 2.50 | 1.10 |
| ❑ S16 Zigmund Palffy | .75 | .35 |
| ❑ S17 Mats Sundin | .75 | .35 |
| ❑ S18 Teemu Selanne | 1.50 | .70 |
| ❑ S19 Joe Sakic | 1.50 | .70 |
| ❑ S20 Ed Belfour | .75 | .35 |
| ❑ S21 Peter Forsberg | 2.50 | 1.10 |
| ❑ S22 Dino Ciccarelli | .25 | .11 |
| ❑ S23 Patrick Roy | 4.00 | 1.80 |
| ❑ S24 Doug Gilmour | .75 | .35 |
| ❑ S25 Pavel Bure | 1.50 | .70 |
| ❑ S26 Brett Hull | 1.00 | .45 |
| ❑ S27 Ray Bourque | .75 | .35 |
| ❑ S28 Adam Oates | .50 | .23 |
| ❑ S29 Steve Yzerman | 2.50 | 1.10 |
| ❑ S30 Dominik Hasek | 1.50 | .70 |

## 1997-98 Collectors Choice World Domination

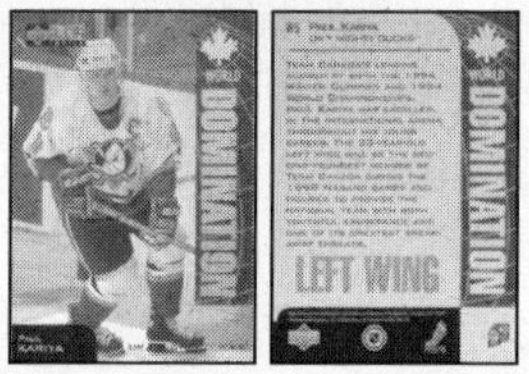

Randomly inserted in Canadian packs at the rate of one in four, this 20-card set features color photos of top players. The backs carry player information.

| | MINT | NRMT |
|---|---|---|
| COMPLETE SET (20) | 70.00 | 32.00 |
| COMMON CARD (1-20) | 1.50 | .70 |

| | | |
|---|---|---|
| ❑ W1 Wayne Gretzky | 12.00 | 5.50 |
| ❑ W2 Mark Messier | 2.50 | 1.10 |
| ❑ W3 Steve Yzerman | 6.00 | 2.70 |
| ❑ W4 Brendan Shanahan | 4.00 | 1.80 |
| ❑ W5 Paul Kariya | 8.00 | 3.60 |
| ❑ W6 Joe Sakic | 4.00 | 1.80 |
| ❑ W7 Eric Lindros | 3.00 | 1.35 |
| ❑ W8 Rod Brind'Amour | 1.50 | .70 |
| ❑ W9 Keith Primeau | 1.50 | .70 |
| ❑ W10 Trevor Linden | 1.50 | .70 |
| ❑ W11 Theo Fleury | 1.50 | .70 |
| ❑ W12 Scott Niedermeyer | 1.50 | .70 |
| ❑ W13 Rob Blake | 1.50 | .70 |
| ❑ W14 Chris Pronger | 1.50 | .70 |
| ❑ W15 Eric Desjardins | 1.50 | .70 |
| ❑ W16 Adam Foote | 1.50 | .70 |
| ❑ W17 Scott Stevens | 1.50 | .70 |
| ❑ W18 Patrick Roy | 10.00 | 4.50 |
| ❑ W19 Curtis Joseph | 2.00 | .90 |
| ❑ W20 Martin Brodeur | 5.00 | 2.20 |

## 1924-25 Crescent Falcon-Tigers

The 1924-25 Crescent Ice Cream Falcon-Tigers set contains 13 black and white cards measuring approximately 1 9/16" by 2 3/8". The back has the card number (at the top) and two offers: 1) a brick of ice cream to any person bringing to the Crescent Ice Cream plant any 14 Crescent Hockey Pictures bearing consecutive numbers; and 2) a hockey stick to anyone bringing to the ice cream plant three sets of Crescent Hockey Pictures bearing consecutive numbers from 1-14. The complete set price below does not include the unknown card 6, which is believed to have been short printed.

| | EX-MT | VG-E |
|---|---|---|
| COMPLETE SET (13) | 2400.00 | 1200.00 |
| COMMON CARD (1-14) | 200.00 | 100.00 |

| | | |
|---|---|---|
| ❑ 1 Bill Cockburn | 225.00 | 110.00 |
| ❑ 2 Wally Byron | 200.00 | 100.00 |
| ❑ 3 Wally Fridfinson | 200.00 | 100.00 |
| ❑ 4 Murray Murdoch | 250.00 | 125.00 |
| ❑ 5 Oliver Redpath | 200.00 | 100.00 |
| ❑ 7 Ward McVey | 200.00 | 100.00 |
| ❑ 8 Tote Mitchell | 200.00 | 100.00 |
| ❑ 9 Lorne Carrol | 200.00 | 100.00 |
| ❑ 10 Tony Wise | 200.00 | 100.00 |
| ❑ 11 Johnny Myres | 200.00 | 100.00 |
| ❑ 12 Gordon McKenzie | 200.00 | 100.00 |
| ❑ 13 Harry Neal | 225.00 | 110.00 |
| ❑ 14 Blake Watson | 225.00 | 110.00 |

## 1923-24 Crescent Selkirks

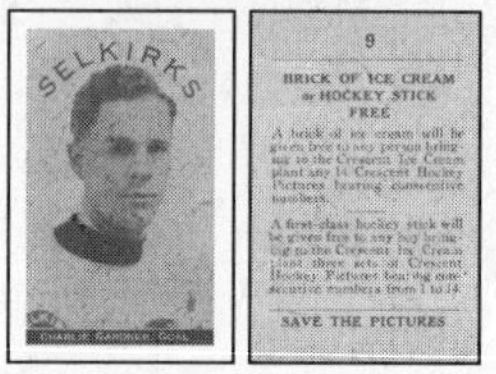

The 1923-24 Crescent Ice Cream set contains 14 cards measuring approximately 1 9/16" by 2 3/8". The set features the Selkirks hockey club and was produced by Crescent Ice Cream of Winnipeg, Manitoba. The front shows a black and white head and shoulders shot of the player, with the team name written in a crescent over the player's head. At the bottom of the picture, the player's name and position appear in white lettering in a black stripe. The back has the card number (at the top) and two offers: 1) a brick of ice cream to any person bringing to the Crescent Ice Cream plant any 14 Crescent Hockey Pictures bearing consecutive numbers; and 2) a hockey stick to anyone bringing to the ice cream plant three sets of Crescent Hockey Pictures bearing consecutive numbers from 1-14. The complete set price below does not include the unknown card number 6.

| | EX-MT | VG-E |
|---|---|---|
| COMPLETE SET (13) | 1000.00 | 500.00 |
| COMMON CARD (1-14) | 90.00 | 45.00 |

| | | |
|---|---|---|
| ❑ 1 Cliff O'Meara | 100.00 | 50.00 |
| ❑ 2 Leo Benard | 90.00 | 45.00 |
| ❑ 3 Pete Speirs | 90.00 | 45.00 |
| ❑ 4 Howard Brandon | 90.00 | 45.00 |
| ❑ 5 George Clark | 90.00 | 45.00 |
| ❑ 7 Cecil Browne | 90.00 | 45.00 |
| ❑ 8 Jack Connelly | 90.00 | 45.00 |
| ❑ 9 Charlie Gardner | 200.00 | 100.00 |
| ❑ 10 Ward Turvey | 90.00 | 45.00 |
| ❑ 11 Connie Johanneson | 90.00 | 45.00 |
| ❑ 12 Frank Woodall | 90.00 | 45.00 |
| ❑ 13 Harold McMunn | 90.00 | 45.00 |
| ❑ 14 Connie Neil | 100.00 | 50.00 |

## 1924-25 Crescent Selkirks

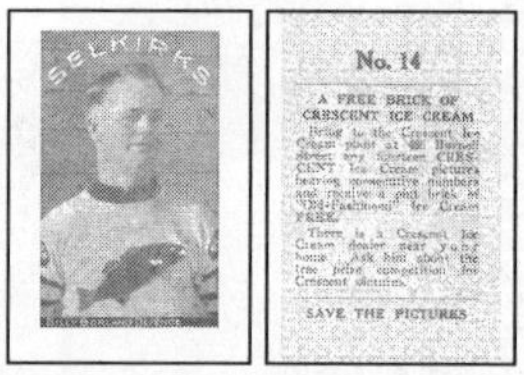

The 1924-25 Crescent Ice Cream Selkirks set contains 14 black and white cards measuring approximately 1 9/16" by 2 3/8". The back has the card number (at the top) and two offers: 1) a brick of ice cream to any person bringing to the Crescent Ice Cream plant any 14 Crescent Hockey Pictures bearing consecutive numbers; and 2) a hockey stick to anyone bringing to the ice cream plant three sets of Crescent Hockey Pictures bearing consecutive numbers from 1-14. Card number 8 of the Selkirks team is perhaps the first hockey team card ever issued.

| | EX-MT | VG-E |
|---|---|---|
| COMPLETE SET (14) | 1700.00 | 850.00 |
| COMMON CARD (1-14) | 90.00 | 45.00 |

| | | |
|---|---|---|
| ❑ 1 Howard Brandon | 100.00 | 50.00 |
| ❑ 2 Jack Hughes | 90.00 | 45.00 |
| ❑ 3 Tony Baril | 90.00 | 45.00 |
| ❑ 4 Bill Bowman | 90.00 | 45.00 |
| ❑ 5 W. Roberts | 90.00 | 45.00 |
| ❑ 6 Cecil Browne SP | 750.00 | 375.00 |
| ❑ 7 Errol Gillis | 100.00 | 50.00 |
| ❑ 8 Selkirks Team On The Ice | 200.00 | 100.00 |
| ❑ 9 Fred Comfort | 100.00 | 50.00 |
| ❑ 10 Cliff O'Meara | 90.00 | 45.00 |
| ❑ 11 Leo Benard | 90.00 | 45.00 |
| ❑ 12 Pete Speirs | 90.00 | 45.00 |
| ❑ 13 Peter Meurer | 90.00 | 45.00 |
| ❑ 14 Bill Borland | 100.00 | 50.00 |

## 1997-98 Crown Royale

The 1997-98 Pacific Crown Royale set was issued in one series totalling 144 cards and was distributed in four-card packs. The fronts

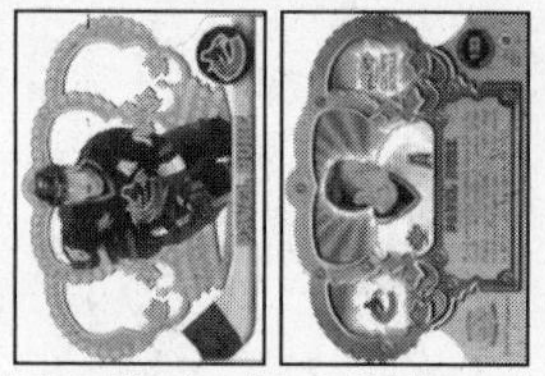

features color player images printed on an all-die-cut crown format. The backs carry player information

| | MINT | NRMT |
|---|---|---|
| COMPLETE SET (144) | 150.00 | 70.00 |
| COMMON CARD (1-144) | .50 | .23 |
| COMP.EMERALD SET (144) | 800.00 | 350.00 |
| COMMON EMERALD (1-144) | 2.50 | 1.10 |

*EMERALD STARS: 2.5X TO 5X BASIC CARDS
*EMERALD YNG STARS: 2X TO 4X BASIC CARDS

| | | |
|---|---|---|
| COMP.SILVER SET (144) | 800.00 | 350.00 |
| COMMON SILVER (1-144) | 2.50 | 1.10 |

*SILVER STARS: 2.5X TO 5X BASIC CARDS
*SILVER YNG.STARS: 2X TO 4X BASIC CARDS

| | | |
|---|---|---|
| ❑ 1 Guy Hebert | 1.25 | .55 |
| ❑ 2 Paul Kariya | 6.00 | 2.70 |
| ❑ 3 Steve Rucchin | .50 | .23 |
| ❑ 4 Tomas Sandstrom | .50 | .23 |
| ❑ 5 Teemu Selanne | 3.00 | 1.35 |
| ❑ 6 Jason Allison | 1.25 | .55 |
| ❑ 7 Ray Bourque | 1.50 | .70 |
| ❑ 8 Anson Carter | .50 | .23 |
| ❑ 9 Byron Dafoe | 1.25 | .55 |
| ❑ 10 Ted Donato | .50 | .23 |
| ❑ 11 Joe Thornton | 3.00 | 1.35 |
| ❑ 12 Jason Dawe | .50 | .23 |
| ❑ 13 Michal Grosek | .50 | .23 |
| ❑ 14 Dominik Hasek | 3.00 | 1.35 |
| ❑ 15 Michael Peca | .50 | .23 |
| ❑ 16 Miroslav Satan | .50 | .23 |
| ❑ 17 Chris Dingman | .50 | .23 |
| ❑ 18 Theoren Fleury | 1.25 | .55 |
| ❑ 19 Jarome Iginla | 1.25 | .55 |
| ❑ 20 Tyler Moss | .50 | .23 |
| ❑ 21 Cory Stillman | .50 | .23 |
| ❑ 22 Kevin Dineen | .50 | .23 |
| ❑ 23 Nelson Emerson | .50 | .23 |
| ❑ 24 Trevor Kidd | 1.25 | .55 |
| ❑ 25 Keith Primeau | .50 | .23 |
| ❑ 26 Geoff Sanderson | 1.25 | .55 |
| ❑ 27 Tony Amonte | 1.25 | .55 |
| ❑ 28 Chris Chelios | 1.50 | .70 |
| ❑ 29 Eric Daze | 1.25 | .55 |
| ❑ 30 Jeff Hackett | 1.25 | .55 |
| ❑ 31 Chris Terreri | 1.25 | .55 |
| ❑ 32 Adam Deadmarsh | 1.25 | .55 |
| ❑ 33 Peter Forsberg | 5.00 | 2.20 |
| ❑ 34 Valeri Kamensky | 1.25 | .55 |
| ❑ 35 Jari Kurri | 1.25 | .55 |
| ❑ 36 Claude Lemieux | 1.25 | .55 |
| ❑ 37 Patrick Roy | 8.00 | 3.60 |
| ❑ 38 Joe Sakic | 3.00 | 1.35 |
| ❑ 39 Ed Belfour | 1.50 | .70 |
| ❑ 40 Derian Hatcher | .50 | .23 |
| ❑ 41 Mike Modano | 2.00 | .90 |
| ❑ 42 Joe Nieuwendyk | 1.25 | .55 |
| ❑ 43 Pat Verbeek | .50 | .23 |
| ❑ 44 Sergei Zubov | .50 | .23 |
| ❑ 45 Sergei Fedorov | 3.00 | 1.35 |
| ❑ 46 Vyacheslav Kozlov | .50 | .23 |
| ❑ 47 Nicklas Lidstrom | 1.25 | .55 |
| ❑ 48 Darren McCarty | .50 | .23 |
| ❑ 49 Chris Osgood | 1.50 | .70 |
| ❑ 50 Brendan Shanahan | 3.00 | 1.35 |
| ❑ 51 Steve Yzerman | 5.00 | 2.20 |
| ❑ 52 Jason Arnott | 1.25 | .55 |
| ❑ 53 Curtis Joseph | 1.50 | .70 |
| ❑ 54 Ryan Smyth | 1.25 | .55 |
| ❑ 55 Doug Weight | 1.25 | .55 |
| ❑ 56 Dave Gagner | .50 | .23 |
| ❑ 57 Ed Jovanovski | 1.25 | .55 |
| ❑ 58 Viktor Kozlov | .50 | .23 |
| ❑ 59 Scott Mellanby | .50 | .23 |
| ❑ 60 John Vanbiesbrouck | 3.00 | 1.35 |
| ❑ 61 Kevin Weekes | .50 | .23 |
| ❑ 62 Rob Blake | .50 | .23 |
| ❑ 63 Donald MacLean | .50 | .23 |
| ❑ 64 Yanic Perreault | .50 | .23 |
| ❑ 65 Luc Robitaille | 1.25 | .55 |
| ❑ 66 Jozef Stumpel | 1.25 | .55 |
| ❑ 67 Shayne Corson | .50 | .23 |
| ❑ 68 Vincent Damphousse | 1.25 | .55 |
| ❑ 69 Saku Koivu | 2.50 | 1.10 |
| ❑ 70 Andy Moog | 1.25 | .55 |
| ❑ 71 Mark Recchi | 1.25 | .55 |
| ❑ 72 Stephane Richer | .50 | .23 |
| ❑ 73 Martin Brodeur | 4.00 | 1.80 |
| ❑ 74 Patrik Elias | 2.00 | .90 |
| ❑ 75 Doug Gilmour | 1.50 | .70 |
| ❑ 76 Bobby Holik | .50 | .23 |
| ❑ 77 Scott Stevens | .50 | .23 |
| ❑ 78 Bryan Berard | 1.25 | .55 |
| ❑ 79 Zigmund Palffy | 1.50 | .70 |
| ❑ 80 Robert Reichel | .50 | .23 |
| ❑ 81 Tommy Salo | 1.25 | .55 |
| ❑ 82 Bryan Smolinski | .50 | .23 |
| ❑ 83 Adam Graves | 1.25 | .55 |
| ❑ 84 Wayne Gretzky | 10.00 | 4.50 |
| ❑ 85 Pat LaFontaine | 1.25 | .55 |
| ❑ 86 Brian Leetch | 1.50 | .70 |
| ❑ 87 Mike Richter | 1.50 | .70 |
| ❑ 88 Niklas Sundstrom | .50 | .23 |
| ❑ 89 Daniel Alfredsson | 1.25 | .55 |
| ❑ 90 Alexandre Daigle | 1.25 | .55 |
| ❑ 91 Shawn McEachern | .50 | .23 |
| ❑ 92 Chris Phillips | .50 | .23 |
| ❑ 93 Ron Tugnutt | 1.25 | .55 |
| ❑ 94 Alexei Yashin | 1.25 | .55 |
| ❑ 95 Rod Brind'Amour | 1.25 | .55 |
| ❑ 96 Chris Gratton | 1.25 | .55 |
| ❑ 97 Ron Hextall | 1.25 | .55 |
| ❑ 98 John LeClair | 2.50 | 1.10 |
| ❑ 99 Eric Lindros | 5.00 | 2.20 |
| ❑ 100 Vaclav Prospal | 2.00 | .90 |
| ❑ 101 Dainius Zubrus | 1.50 | .70 |
| ❑ 102 Mike Gartner | 1.25 | .55 |
| ❑ 103 Brad Isbister | .50 | .23 |
| ❑ 104 Nikolai Khabibulin | 1.25 | .55 |
| ❑ 105 Jeremy Roenick | 1.50 | .70 |
| ❑ 106 Cliff Ronning | .50 | .23 |
| ❑ 107 Keith Tkachuk | 2.00 | .90 |
| ❑ 108 Tom Barrasso | 1.25 | .55 |
| ❑ 109 Ron Francis | 1.25 | .55 |
| ❑ 110 Jaromir Jagr | 5.00 | 2.20 |
| ❑ 111 Alexei Morozov | 1.25 | .55 |
| ❑ 112 Ed Olczyk | .50 | .23 |
| ❑ 113 Jim Campbell | .50 | .23 |
| ❑ 114 Pavol Demitra | .50 | .23 |
| ❑ 115 Steve Duchesne | .50 | .23 |
| ❑ 116 Grant Fuhr | 1.25 | .55 |
| ❑ 117 Brett Hull | 2.00 | .90 |
| ❑ 118 Pierre Turgeon | 1.25 | .55 |
| ❑ 119 Jeff Friesen | 1.25 | .55 |
| ❑ 120 Patrick Marleau | 3.00 | 1.35 |
| ❑ 121 Owen Nolan | 1.25 | .55 |
| ❑ 122 Marco Sturm | 2.50 | 1.10 |
| ❑ 123 Mike Vernon | 1.25 | .55 |
| ❑ 124 Dino Ciccarelli | .50 | .23 |
| ❑ 125 Roman Hamrlik | .50 | .23 |
| ❑ 126 Daren Puppa | 1.25 | .55 |
| ❑ 127 Paul Ysebaert | .50 | .23 |
| ❑ 128 Sergei Berezin | .50 | .23 |
| ❑ 129 Wendel Clark | 1.25 | .55 |
| ❑ 130 Alyn McCauley | 1.25 | .55 |
| ❑ 131 Felix Potvin | 1.50 | .70 |
| ❑ 132 Mats Sundin | 1.50 | .70 |
| ❑ 133 Pavel Bure | 3.00 | 1.35 |
| ❑ 134 Martin Gelinas | .50 | .23 |
| ❑ 135 Trevor Linden | 1.25 | .55 |
| ❑ 136 Mark Messier | 2.00 | .90 |
| ❑ 137 Alexander Mogilny | 1.25 | .55 |
| ❑ 138 Peter Bondra | 1.50 | .70 |
| ❑ 139 Dale Hunter | .50 | .23 |
| ❑ 140 Joe Juneau | 1.25 | .55 |
| ❑ 141 Olaf Kolzig | 1.25 | .55 |
| ❑ 142 Adam Oates | 1.25 | .55 |
| ❑ 143 Jaroslav Svejkovsky | 1.25 | .55 |
| ❑ 144 Richard Zednik | .50 | .23 |

## 1997-98 Crown Royale Ice Blue

Randomly inserted in packs at the rate of one in 25, this 144-card set is a parallel version of the base set with blue foil highlights.

| | MINT | NRMT |
|---|---|---|
| COMMON CARD (1-144) | 15.00 | 6.75 |
| SEMISTARS/GOALIES | 40.00 | 18.00 |
| UNLISTED STARS | 50.00 | 22.00 |

*STARS: 15X TO 30X BASIC CARDS
*YOUNG STARS: 12.5X TO 25X BASIC CARDS

| | | |
|---|---|---|
| ❑ 2 Paul Kariya | 200.00 | 90.00 |
| ❑ 5 Teemu Selanne | 100.00 | 45.00 |
| ❑ 14 Dominik Hasek | 100.00 | 45.00 |
| ❑ 33 Peter Forsberg | 150.00 | 70.00 |
| ❑ 37 Patrick Roy | 250.00 | 110.00 |
| ❑ 38 Joe Sakic | 120.00 | 55.00 |
| ❑ 45 Sergei Fedorov | 100.00 | 45.00 |
| ❑ 50 Brendan Shanahan | 100.00 | 45.00 |
| ❑ 51 Steve Yzerman | 150.00 | 70.00 |
| ❑ 69 Saku Koivu | 100.00 | 45.00 |
| ❑ 73 Martin Brodeur | 120.00 | 55.00 |
| ❑ 84 Wayne Gretzky | 300.00 | 135.00 |
| ❑ 99 Eric Lindros | 200.00 | 90.00 |
| ❑ 110 Jaromir Jagr | 150.00 | 70.00 |
| ❑ 133 Pavel Bure | 100.00 | 45.00 |

## 1997-98 Crown Royale Blades of Steel Die-Cuts

Randomly inserted in packs at the rate of one in 49, this 20-card set features color images of top NHL players on a laser-cut and die-cut skate background.

| | MINT | NRMT |
|---|---|---|
| COMPLETE SET (20) | 600.00 | 275.00 |
| COMMON CARD (1-20) | 10.00 | 4.50 |

| | | |
|---|---|---|
| ❑ 1 Paul Kariya | 50.00 | 22.00 |
| ❑ 2 Teemu Selanne | 25.00 | 11.00 |
| ❑ 3 Joe Thornton | 20.00 | 9.00 |
| ❑ 4 Chris Chelios | 12.00 | 5.50 |
| ❑ 5 Peter Forsberg | 40.00 | 18.00 |

| | MINT | NRMT |
|---|---|---|
| ❑ 6 Patrick Roy | 60.00 | 27.00 |
| ❑ 7 Mike Modano | 15.00 | 6.75 |
| ❑ 8 Sergei Fedorov | 25.00 | 11.00 |
| ❑ 9 Brendan Shanahan | 25.00 | 11.00 |
| ❑ 10 Steve Yzerman | 40.00 | 18.00 |
| ❑ 11 Ryan Smyth | 10.00 | 4.50 |
| ❑ 12 Saku Koivu | 20.00 | 9.00 |
| ❑ 13 Bryan Berard | 10.00 | 4.50 |
| ❑ 14 Wayne Gretzky | 80.00 | 36.00 |
| ❑ 15 Brian Leetch | 12.00 | 5.50 |
| ❑ 16 Eric Lindros | 40.00 | 18.00 |
| ❑ 17 Jaromir Jagr | 40.00 | 18.00 |
| ❑ 18 Brett Hull | 15.00 | 6.75 |
| ❑ 19 Pavel Bure | 25.00 | 11.00 |
| ❑ 20 Mark Messier | 15.00 | 6.75 |

## 1997-98 Crown Royale Cramer's Choice Jumbos

Randomly inserted one per box, this ten-card set features top NHL Hockey players as chosen by Pacific President and CEO, Michael Cramer. The fronts display a color action player cut-out on a pyramid die-cut shaped background printed on a premium-sized card.

| | MINT | NRMT |
|---|---|---|
| COMPLETE SET (10) | 125.00 | 55.00 |
| COMMON CARD (1-10) | 8.00 | 3.60 |
| ❑ 1 Paul Kariya | 15.00 | 6.75 |
| ❑ 2 Teemu Selanne | 8.00 | 3.60 |
| ❑ 3 Joe Thornton | 8.00 | 3.60 |
| ❑ 4 Peter Forsberg | 12.00 | 5.50 |
| ❑ 5 Patrick Roy | 20.00 | 9.00 |
| ❑ 6 Steve Yzerman | 12.00 | 5.50 |
| ❑ 7 Wayne Gretzky | 25.00 | 11.00 |
| ❑ 8 Eric Lindros | 12.00 | 5.50 |
| ❑ 9 Jaromir Jagr | 12.00 | 5.50 |
| ❑ 10 Pavel Bure | 8.00 | 3.60 |

## 1997-98 Crown Royale Freeze Out Die-Cuts

Randomly inserted in packs at the rate of one in 25, this 20-card set features color action photos of top goalies on a background of shattering ice and printed on a die-cut card.

| | MINT | NRMT |
|---|---|---|
| COMPLETE SET (20) | 300.00 | 135.00 |
| COMMON CARD (1-20) | 10.00 | 4.50 |
| ❑ 1 Guy Hebert | 10.00 | 4.50 |
| ❑ 2 Byron Dafoe | 10.00 | 4.50 |
| ❑ 3 Dominik Hasek | 25.00 | 11.00 |
| ❑ 4 Tyler Moss | 10.00 | 4.50 |
| ❑ 5 Patrick Roy | 60.00 | 27.00 |
| ❑ 6 Ed Belfour | 15.00 | 6.75 |
| ❑ 7 Chris Osgood | 15.00 | 6.75 |
| ❑ 8 Curtis Joseph | 15.00 | 6.75 |
| ❑ 9 John Vanbiesbrouck | 20.00 | 9.00 |
| ❑ 10 Andy Moog | 10.00 | 4.50 |
| ❑ 11 Martin Brodeur | 30.00 | 13.50 |
| ❑ 12 Mike Richter | 15.00 | 6.75 |
| ❑ 13 Ron Hextall | 10.00 | 4.50 |
| ❑ 14 Garth Snow | 10.00 | 4.50 |
| ❑ 15 Nikolai Khabibulin | 10.00 | 4.50 |
| ❑ 16 Tom Barrasso | 10.00 | 4.50 |
| ❑ 17 Grant Fuhr | 10.00 | 4.50 |
| ❑ 18 Mike Vernon | 10.00 | 4.50 |
| ❑ 19 Felix Potvin | 15.00 | 6.75 |
| ❑ 20 Olaf Kolzig | 10.00 | 4.50 |

## 1997-98 Crown Royale Hat Tricks Die-Cuts

Randomly inserted in packs at the rate of one in 25, this 20-card set features color photos of top NHL scorers printed on a hat-shaped die-cut card.

| | MINT | NRMT |
|---|---|---|
| COMPLETE SET (20) | 300.00 | 135.00 |
| COMMON CARD (1-20) | 6.00 | 2.70 |
| ❑ 1 Paul Kariya | 30.00 | 13.50 |
| ❑ 2 Teemu Selanne | 15.00 | 6.75 |
| ❑ 3 Joe Thornton | 10.00 | 4.50 |
| ❑ 4 Peter Forsberg | 25.00 | 11.00 |
| ❑ 5 Joe Sakic | 15.00 | 6.75 |
| ❑ 6 Mike Modano | 10.00 | 4.50 |
| ❑ 7 Brendan Shanahan | 15.00 | 6.75 |
| ❑ 8 Steve Yzerman | 25.00 | 11.00 |
| ❑ 9 Ryan Smyth | 6.00 | 2.70 |
| ❑ 10 Zigmund Palffy | 8.00 | 3.60 |
| ❑ 11 Wayne Gretzky | 50.00 | 22.00 |
| ❑ 12 John LeClair | 12.00 | 5.50 |
| ❑ 13 Eric Lindros | 25.00 | 11.00 |
| ❑ 14 Keith Tkachuk | 10.00 | 4.50 |
| ❑ 15 Jaromir Jagr | 25.00 | 11.00 |
| ❑ 16 Brett Hull | 10.00 | 4.50 |
| ❑ 17 Mats Sundin | 8.00 | 3.60 |
| ❑ 18 Pavel Bure | 15.00 | 6.75 |
| ❑ 19 Mark Messier | 10.00 | 4.50 |
| ❑ 20 Peter Bondra | 8.00 | 3.60 |

## 1997-98 Crown Royale Lamplighters Cel-Fusion Die-Cuts

Randomly inserted in packs at the rate of one in 73, this 20-card set features color photos of the NHL's top goal scorers with a net and goal light as background and printed on a die-cut cel-fusion card.

| | MINT | NRMT |
|---|---|---|
| COMPLETE SET (20) | 900.00 | 400.00 |
| COMMON CARD (1-20) | 6.00 | 2.70 |
| ❑ 1 Paul Kariya | 80.00 | 36.00 |
| ❑ 2 Teemu Selanne | 40.00 | 18.00 |
| ❑ 3 Joe Thornton | 25.00 | 11.00 |
| ❑ 4 Michael Peca | 6.00 | 2.70 |
| ❑ 5 Peter Forsberg | 60.00 | 27.00 |
| ❑ 6 Joe Sakic | 40.00 | 18.00 |
| ❑ 7 Mike Modano | 25.00 | 11.00 |
| ❑ 8 Brendan Shanahan | 40.00 | 18.00 |
| ❑ 9 Steve Yzerman | 60.00 | 27.00 |
| ❑ 10 Saku Koivu | 30.00 | 13.50 |
| ❑ 11 Wayne Gretzky | 120.00 | 55.00 |
| ❑ 12 Pat LaFontaine | 15.00 | 6.75 |
| ❑ 13 John LeClair | 30.00 | 13.50 |
| ❑ 14 Eric Lindros | 60.00 | 27.00 |
| ❑ 15 Dainius Zubrus | 15.00 | 6.75 |
| ❑ 16 Keith Tkachuk | 25.00 | 11.00 |
| ❑ 17 Jaromir Jagr | 60.00 | 27.00 |
| ❑ 18 Brett Hull | 25.00 | 11.00 |
| ❑ 19 Pavel Bure | 40.00 | 18.00 |
| ❑ 20 Mark Messier | 25.00 | 11.00 |

## 1998-99 Crown Royale

The 1998-99 Pacific Crown Royale set was issued in one series totalling 144 cards and was distributed in six-card packs with a suggested retail price of $5.99. The set features color action player photos printed on cards with silver and gold foil highlights, dual etching and a die-cut crown as background

| | MINT | NRMT |
|---|---|---|
| COMPLETE SET (144) | 150.00 | 70.00 |
| COMMON CARD (1-144) | .50 | .23 |
| ❑ 1 Travis Green | .50 | .23 |
| ❑ 2 Guy Hebert | 1.25 | .55 |
| ❑ 3 Paul Kariya | 6.00 | 2.70 |
| ❑ 4 Tomas Sandstrom | .50 | .23 |
| ❑ 5 Teemu Selanne | 3.00 | 1.35 |
| ❑ 6 Jason Allison | 1.25 | .55 |
| ❑ 7 Ray Bourque | 1.50 | .70 |
| ❑ 8 Byron Dafoe | 1.25 | .55 |
| ❑ 9 Dimitri Khristich | .50 | .23 |
| ❑ 10 Sergei Samsonov | 2.50 | 1.10 |
| ❑ 11 Matthew Barnaby | .50 | .23 |
| ❑ 12 Michal Grosek | .50 | .23 |
| ❑ 13 Dominik Hasek | 3.00 | 1.35 |
| ❑ 14 Michael Peca | .50 | .23 |
| ❑ 15 Miroslav Satan | .50 | .23 |
| ❑ 16 Andrew Cassels | .50 | .23 |
| ❑ 17 Rico Fata | 1.25 | .55 |
| ❑ 18 Theoren Fleury | 1.50 | .70 |
| ❑ 19 Jarome Iginla | .50 | .23 |
| ❑ 20 Martin St. Louis | 1.25 | .55 |
| ❑ 21 Ken Wregget | 1.25 | .55 |
| ❑ 22 Ron Francis | 1.25 | .55 |
| ❑ 23 Arturs Irbe | 1.25 | .55 |
| ❑ 24 Sami Kapanen | 1.25 | .55 |
| ❑ 25 Trevor Kidd | 1.25 | .55 |
| ❑ 26 Keith Primeau | 1.25 | .55 |
| ❑ 27 Tony Amonte | 1.25 | .55 |
| ❑ 28 Chris Chelios | 1.50 | .70 |
| ❑ 29 Eric Daze | .50 | .23 |
| ❑ 30 Doug Gilmour | 1.50 | .70 |
| ❑ 31 Jocelyn Thibault | 1.25 | .55 |
| ❑ 32 Chris Drury | 2.00 | .90 |
| ❑ 33 Peter Forsberg | 5.00 | 2.20 |
| ❑ 34 Milan Hejduk | 2.50 | 1.10 |
| ❑ 35 Patrick Roy | 8.00 | 3.60 |
| ❑ 36 Joe Sakic | 3.00 | 1.35 |
| ❑ 37 Ed Belfour | 1.50 | .70 |
| ❑ 38 Brett Hull | 2.00 | .90 |
| ❑ 39 Jamie Langenbrunner | .50 | .23 |
| ❑ 40 Jere Lehtinen | 1.25 | .55 |
| ❑ 41 Mike Modano | 2.00 | .90 |
| ❑ 42 Joe Nieuwendyk | 1.25 | .55 |
| ❑ 43 Darryl Sydor | .50 | .23 |
| ❑ 44 Sergei Fedorov | 3.00 | 1.35 |
| ❑ 45 Nicklas Lidstrom | 1.25 | .55 |
| ❑ 46 Darren McCarty | .50 | .23 |
| ❑ 47 Chris Osgood | 1.50 | .70 |
| ❑ 48 Brendan Shanahan | 3.00 | 1.35 |
| ❑ 49 Steve Yzerman | 5.00 | 2.20 |
| ❑ 50 Bob Essensa | 1.25 | .55 |
| ❑ 51 Bill Guerin | 1.25 | .55 |
| ❑ 52 Janne Niinimaa | .50 | .23 |
| ❑ 53 Tom Poti | .50 | .23 |
| ❑ 54 Ryan Smyth | .50 | .23 |
| ❑ 55 Doug Weight | 1.25 | .55 |
| ❑ 56 Sean Burke | 1.25 | .55 |
| ❑ 57 Dino Ciccarelli | 1.25 | .55 |
| ❑ 58 Ed Jovanovski | .50 | .23 |
| ❑ 59 Viktor Kozlov | .50 | .23 |
| ❑ 60 Oleg Kvasha | 1.50 | .70 |
| ❑ 61 Mark Parrish | 2.50 | 1.10 |
| ❑ 62 Rob Blake | .50 | .23 |
| ❑ 63 Manny Legace | .50 | .23 |
| ❑ 64 Yanic Perreault | .50 | .23 |
| ❑ 65 Luc Robitaille | 1.25 | .55 |
| ❑ 66 Jozef Stumpel | 1.25 | .55 |
| ❑ 67 Shayne Corson | .50 | .23 |
| ❑ 68 Vincent Damphousse | 1.25 | .55 |
| ❑ 69 Jeff Hackett | 1.25 | .55 |
| ❑ 70 Saku Koivu | 2.50 | 1.10 |
| ❑ 71 Mark Recchi | 1.25 | .55 |
| ❑ 72 Andrew Brunette | .50 | .23 |
| ❑ 73 Mike Dunham | 1.25 | .55 |
| ❑ 74 Tom Fitzgerald | .50 | .23 |
| ❑ 75 Greg Johnson | .50 | .23 |
| ❑ 76 Sergei Krivokrasov | .50 | .23 |
| ❑ 77 Jason Arnott | 1.25 | .55 |
| ❑ 78 Martin Brodeur | 4.00 | 1.80 |
| ❑ 79 Patrik Elias | 1.25 | .55 |
| ❑ 80 Bobby Holik | .50 | .23 |
| ❑ 81 Brendan Morrison | 1.25 | .55 |
| ❑ 82 Bryan Berard | 1.25 | .55 |
| ❑ 83 Trevor Linden | 1.25 | .55 |
| ❑ 84 Zigmund Palffy | 1.50 | .70 |
| ❑ 85 Robert Reichel | .50 | .23 |
| ❑ 86 Tommy Salo | 1.25 | .55 |
| ❑ 87 Adam Graves | 1.25 | .55 |
| ❑ 88 Wayne Gretzky | 10.00 | 4.50 |
| ❑ 89 Brian Leetch | 1.50 | .70 |
| ❑ 90 Manny Malhotra | .50 | .23 |
| ❑ 91 Mike Richter | 1.50 | .70 |
| ❑ 92 Daniel Alfredsson | 1.25 | .55 |
| ❑ 93 Igor Kravchuk | .50 | .23 |
| ❑ 94 Shawn McEachern | .50 | .23 |
| ❑ 95 Damian Rhodes | 1.25 | .55 |
| ❑ 96 Alexei Yashin | 1.25 | .55 |
| ❑ 97 Rod Brind'Amour | 1.25 | .55 |
| ❑ 98 Ron Hextall | 1.25 | .55 |
| ❑ 99 John LeClair | 2.50 | 1.10 |
| ❑ 100 Eric Lindros | 5.00 | 2.20 |
| ❑ 101 John Vanbiesbrouck | 2.50 | 1.10 |
| ❑ 102 Dainius Zubrus | .50 | .23 |
| ❑ 103 Nikolai Khabibulin | 1.25 | .55 |
| ❑ 104 Jeremy Roenick | 1.50 | .70 |
| ❑ 105 Keith Tkachuk | 2.00 | .90 |
| ❑ 106 Rick Tocchet | 1.25 | .55 |
| ❑ 107 Oleg Tverdovsky | .50 | .23 |
| ❑ 108 Tom Barrasso | 1.25 | .55 |
| ❑ 109 Jan Hrdina | 2.00 | .90 |
| ❑ 110 Jaromir Jagr | 5.00 | 2.20 |
| ❑ 111 Alexei Morozov | .50 | .23 |
| ❑ 112 German Titov | .50 | .23 |
| ❑ 113 Jim Campbell | .50 | .23 |
| ❑ 114 Grant Fuhr | 1.25 | .55 |
| ❑ 115 Al MacInnis | 1.25 | .55 |
| ❑ 116 Chris Pronger | 1.25 | .55 |
| ❑ 117 Pierre Turgeon | 1.25 | .55 |
| ❑ 118 Jeff Friesen | 1.25 | .55 |
| ❑ 119 Patrick Marleau | .50 | .23 |
| ❑ 120 Owen Nolan | 1.25 | .55 |
| ❑ 121 Marco Sturm | .50 | .23 |
| ❑ 122 Mike Vernon | 1.25 | .55 |
| ❑ 123 Wendel Clark | 1.25 | .55 |
| ❑ 124 Vincent Lecavalier | 5.00 | 2.20 |
| ❑ 125 Bill Ranford | 1.25 | .55 |
| ❑ 126 Stephane Richer | 1.25 | .55 |
| ❑ 127 Rob Zamuner | .50 | .23 |
| ❑ 128 Sergei Berezin | 1.25 | .55 |
| ❑ 129 Tie Domi | .50 | .23 |
| ❑ 130 Mike Johnson | 1.25 | .55 |
| ❑ 131 Curtis Joseph | 1.50 | .70 |
| ❑ 132 Mats Sundin | 1.50 | .70 |
| ❑ 133 Donald Brashear | .50 | .23 |
| ❑ 134 Pavel Bure | 3.00 | 1.35 |
| ❑ 135 Mark Messier | 2.00 | .90 |
| ❑ 136 Alexander Mogilny | 1.25 | .55 |
| ❑ 137 Bill Muckalt | 2.00 | .90 |
| ❑ 138 Mattias Ohlund | 1.25 | .55 |
| ❑ 139 Garth Snow | 1.25 | .55 |
| ❑ 140 Peter Bondra | 1.50 | .70 |
| ❑ 141 Matthew Herr | .50 | .23 |
| ❑ 142 Joe Juneau | 1.25 | .55 |
| ❑ 143 Olaf Kolzig | 1.25 | .55 |
| ❑ 144 Adam Oates | 1.25 | .55 |

## 1998-99 Crown Royale Limited Series

Randomly inserted into packs, this 144-card set is a limited parallel edition of the base set printed on 24-point card stock. Only 99 serial-numbered sets were produced.

| | MINT | NRMT |
|---|---|---|
| COMMON CARD (1-144) | 20.00 | 9.00 |
| SEMISTARS/GOALIES | 60.00 | 27.00 |
| UNLISTED STARS | 80.00 | 36.00 |
| ❑ 3 Paul Kariya | 250.00 | 110.00 |
| ❑ 5 Teemu Selanne | 120.00 | 55.00 |
| ❑ 10 Sergei Samsonov | 100.00 | 45.00 |
| ❑ 13 Dominik Hasek | 120.00 | 55.00 |
| ❑ 33 Peter Forsberg | 200.00 | 90.00 |
| ❑ 35 Patrick Roy | 300.00 | 135.00 |
| ❑ 36 Joe Sakic | 120.00 | 55.00 |
| ❑ 38 Brett Hull | 80.00 | 36.00 |
| ❑ 41 Mike Modano | 80.00 | 36.00 |
| ❑ 44 Sergei Fedorov | 120.00 | 55.00 |
| ❑ 48 Brendan Shanahan | 120.00 | 55.00 |
| ❑ 49 Steve Yzerman | 200.00 | 90.00 |
| ❑ 70 Saku Koivu | 100.00 | 45.00 |
| ❑ 78 Martin Brodeur | 150.00 | 70.00 |
| ❑ 88 Wayne Gretzky | 400.00 | 180.00 |
| ❑ 99 John LeClair | 100.00 | 45.00 |
| ❑ 100 Eric Lindros | 200.00 | 90.00 |
| ❑ 101 John Vanbiesbrouck | 100.00 | 45.00 |
| ❑ 105 Keith Tkachuk | 80.00 | 36.00 |
| ❑ 110 Jaromir Jagr | 200.00 | 90.00 |
| ❑ 134 Pavel Bure | 120.00 | 55.00 |
| ❑ 135 Mark Messier | 80.00 | 36.00 |

## 1998-99 Crown Royale Cramer's Choice Awards Jumbos

Inserted one per box, this 10-card set features color action cut-outs of top NHL players as chosen by Pacific President and CEO, Michael Cramer, printed on premium-sized, dual-foiled, die-cut pyramid-shaped cards. Six different serial-numbered parallel sets were also produced: 35 serial-numbered dark blue foil sets, 30 serial-numbered green foil sets, 25 serial-numbered red foil sets, 20 serial-numbered light blue foil sets, 10 serial-numbered gold foil sets, and 1 serial-numbered purple foil set.

| | MINT | NRMT |
|---|---|---|
| COMPLETE SET (10) | 120.00 | 55.00 |
| COMMON CARD (1-10) | 8.00 | 3.60 |

*DARK BLUES: 15X TO 30X HI COLUMN
DARK BLUE PRINT RUN 35 SERIAL #'d SETS
*GOLD: 30X TO 60X HI COLUMN
GOLD PRINT RUN 10 SERIAL #'d SETS
*GREEN: 15X TO 30X HI COLUMN
GREEN PRINT RUN 30 SERIAL #'d SETS
*LT.BLUE: 25X TO 50X HI COLUMN
LT.BLUE PRINT RUN 20 SERIAL #'d SETS
*RED: 20X TO 40X HI COLUMN
RED PRINT RUN 25 SERIAL #'d SETS

| | MINT | NRMT |
|---|---|---|
| ❑ 1 Paul Kariya | 15.00 | 6.75 |
| ❑ 2 Teemu Selanne | 8.00 | 3.60 |
| ❑ 3 Dominik Hasek | 8.00 | 3.60 |
| ❑ 4 Peter Forsberg | 12.00 | 5.50 |
| ❑ 5 Patrick Roy | 20.00 | 9.00 |
| ❑ 6 Steve Yzerman | 12.00 | 5.50 |
| ❑ 7 Martin Brodeur | 10.00 | 4.50 |
| ❑ 8 Wayne Gretzky | 25.00 | 11.00 |
| ❑ 9 Eric Lindros | 12.00 | 5.50 |
| ❑ 10 Jaromir Jagr | 12.00 | 5.50 |

## 1998-99 Crown Royale Living Legends

Randomly inserted in hobby packs at the rate of one in 73, this 10-card set features color action photos of some of the NHL's all-time great players. Only 375 serial-numbered sets were produced.

| | MINT | NRMT |
|---|---|---|
| COMPLETE SET (10) | 600.00 | 275.00 |
| COMMON CARD (1-10) | 40.00 | 18.00 |
| ❑ 1 Paul Kariya | 80.00 | 36.00 |
| ❑ 2 Teemu Selanne | 40.00 | 18.00 |
| ❑ 3 Dominik Hasek | 40.00 | 18.00 |
| ❑ 4 Peter Forsberg | 60.00 | 27.00 |
| ❑ 5 Patrick Roy | 100.00 | 45.00 |
| ❑ 6 Steve Yzerman | 60.00 | 27.00 |
| ❑ 7 Martin Brodeur | 50.00 | 22.00 |
| ❑ 8 Wayne Gretzky | 120.00 | 55.00 |
| ❑ 9 Eric Lindros | 60.00 | 27.00 |
| ❑ 10 Jaromir Jagr | 60.00 | 27.00 |

## 1998-99 Crown Royale Master Performers

Randomly inserted in hobby packs at the rate of 2:25, this 20-card set features color action photos of some of the most popular players printed on fully foiled, etched cards.

| | MINT | NRMT |
|---|---|---|
| COMPLETE SET (20) | 250.00 | 110.00 |
| COMMON CARD (1-20) | 5.00 | 2.20 |
| ❑ 1 Paul Kariya | 20.00 | 9.00 |
| ❑ 2 Teemu Selanne | 10.00 | 4.50 |
| ❑ 3 Dominik Hasek | 10.00 | 4.50 |
| ❑ 4 Peter Forsberg | 15.00 | 6.75 |
| ❑ 5 Patrick Roy | 25.00 | 11.00 |
| ❑ 6 Joe Sakic | 10.00 | 4.50 |
| ❑ 7 Brett Hull | 6.00 | 2.70 |
| ❑ 8 Mike Modano | 6.00 | 2.70 |
| ❑ 9 Sergei Fedorov | 10.00 | 4.50 |
| ❑ 10 Brendan Shanahan | 10.00 | 4.50 |
| ❑ 11 Steve Yzerman | 15.00 | 6.75 |
| ❑ 12 Saku Koivu | 8.00 | 3.60 |
| ❑ 13 Martin Brodeur | 12.00 | 5.50 |
| ❑ 14 Wayne Gretzky | 30.00 | 13.50 |
| ❑ 15 John LeClair | 8.00 | 3.60 |
| ❑ 16 Eric Lindros | 15.00 | 6.75 |
| ❑ 17 Jaromir Jagr | 15.00 | 6.75 |
| ❑ 18 Mats Sundin | 5.00 | 2.20 |
| ❑ 19 Mark Messier | 6.00 | 2.70 |
| ❑ 20 Peter Bondra | 5.00 | 2.20 |

## 1998-99 Crown Royale Pillars of the Game

Inserted one at the bottom of every pack, this 25-card set features color action photos of popular players with a hockey puck in the background and printed on holographic gold foil cards.

| | MINT | NRMT |
|---|---|---|
| COMPLETE SET (25) | 30.00 | 13.50 |
| COMMON CARD (1-25) | .60 | .25 |
| ❑ 1 Teemu Selanne | 1.50 | .70 |
| ❑ 2 Ray Bourque | .75 | .35 |
| ❑ 3 Michael Peca | .60 | .25 |
| ❑ 4 Theoren Fleury | .75 | .35 |
| ❑ 5 Chris Chelios | .75 | .35 |
| ❑ 6 Doug Gilmour | .75 | .35 |
| ❑ 7 Patrick Roy | 4.00 | 1.80 |
| ❑ 8 Joe Sakic | 1.50 | .70 |
| ❑ 9 Ed Belfour | .75 | .35 |
| ❑ 10 Brett Hull | 1.00 | .45 |
| ❑ 11 Mike Modano | 1.00 | .45 |
| ❑ 12 Sergei Fedorov | 1.50 | .70 |
| ❑ 13 Brendan Shanahan | 1.50 | .70 |
| ❑ 14 Steve Yzerman | 2.50 | 1.10 |
| ❑ 15 Saku Koivu | 1.25 | .55 |
| ❑ 16 Martin Brodeur | 2.00 | .90 |
| ❑ 17 John LeClair | 1.25 | .55 |
| ❑ 18 Eric Lindros | 2.50 | 1.10 |
| ❑ 19 John Vanbiesbrouck | 1.25 | .55 |
| ❑ 20 Keith Tkachuk | 1.00 | .45 |
| ❑ 21 Jaromir Jagr | 2.50 | 1.10 |
| ❑ 22 Curtis Joseph | .75 | .35 |
| ❑ 23 Mats Sundin | .75 | .35 |
| ❑ 24 Mark Messier | 1.00 | .45 |
| ❑ 25 Peter Bondra | .75 | .35 |

## 1998-99 Crown Royale Pivotal Players

Inserted one at the top of every pack, this 25-card set features color action photos of top stars and rookies printed on holographic silver foil cards.

| | MINT | NRMT |
|---|---|---|
| COMPLETE SET (25) | 30.00 | 13.50 |
| COMMON CARD (1-25) | .60 | .25 |
| ❑ 1 Paul Kariya | 3.00 | 1.35 |
| ❑ 2 Dominik Hasek | 1.50 | .70 |
| ❑ 3 Michael Peca | .60 | .25 |
| ❑ 4 Peter Forsberg | 2.50 | 1.10 |
| ❑ 5 Joe Sakic | 1.50 | .70 |
| ❑ 6 Brett Hull | 1.00 | .45 |
| ❑ 7 Mike Modano | 1.00 | .45 |
| ❑ 8 Sergei Fedorov | 1.50 | .70 |
| ❑ 9 Chris Osgood | .75 | .35 |
| ❑ 10 Brendan Shanahan | 1.50 | .70 |
| ❑ 11 Ryan Smyth | .60 | .25 |
| ❑ 12 Mark Parrish | 2.50 | 1.10 |
| ❑ 13 Saku Koivu | 1.25 | .55 |
| ❑ 14 Martin Brodeur | 2.00 | .90 |
| ❑ 15 Trevor Linden | .60 | .25 |
| ❑ 16 Wayne Gretzky | 5.00 | 2.20 |
| ❑ 17 Alexei Yashin | .60 | .25 |
| ❑ 18 John LeClair | 1.25 | .55 |
| ❑ 19 John Vanbiesbrouck | 1.25 | .55 |
| ❑ 20 Keith Tkachuk | 1.00 | .45 |
| ❑ 21 Vincent Lecavalier | 1.00 | .45 |
| ❑ 22 Mats Sundin | .75 | .35 |
| ❑ 23 Mark Messier | 1.00 | .45 |
| ❑ 24 Peter Bondra | .75 | .35 |
| ❑ 25 Olaf Kolzig | .60 | .25 |

## 1998-99 Crown Royale Rookie Class

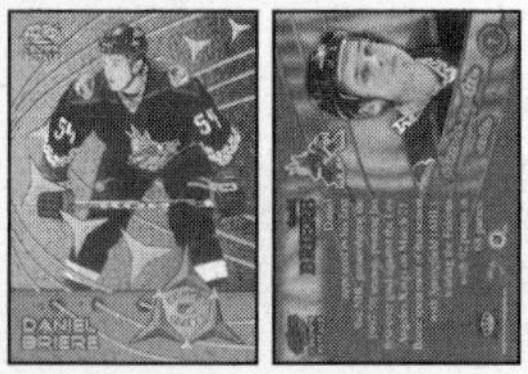

Randomly inserted in packs at the rate of one in 25, this 10-card set features color action photos of top rookies printed on full-foil designed cards.

| | MINT | NRMT |
|---|---|---|
| COMPLETE SET (10) | 150.00 | 70.00 |
| COMMON CARD (1-10) | 10.00 | 4.50 |
| ❑ 1 Chris Drury | 15.00 | 6.75 |
| ❑ 2 Milan Hejduk | 20.00 | 9.00 |
| ❑ 3 Mark Parrish | 20.00 | 9.00 |
| ❑ 4 Manny Legace | 10.00 | 4.50 |
| ❑ 5 Brendan Morrison | 15.00 | 6.75 |
| ❑ 6 Manny Malhotra | 20.00 | 9.00 |
| ❑ 7 Daniel Briere | 10.00 | 4.50 |
| ❑ 8 Vincent Lecavalier | 30.00 | 13.50 |
| ❑ 9 Tomas Kaberle | 10.00 | 4.50 |
| ❑ 10 Bill Muckalt | 15.00 | 6.75 |

## 1972-73 Crusaders Cleveland WHA Linnett

These blank-backed charcoal drawings by Charles Linnett of the 1972-73 Cleveland Crusaders measure approximately 8 1/2" by 11". The textured white paper drawings also carry a facsimile autograph and the Crusaders' logo. The drawings are unnumbered and checklisted below in alphabetical order.

| | NRMT-MT | EXC |
|---|---|---|
| COMPLETE SET (9) | 35.00 | 16.00 |
| COMMON CARD (1-9) | 4.00 | 1.80 |
| ❑ 1 Ron Buchanan | 4.00 | 1.80 |
| ❑ 2 Bob Dillabough | 4.00 | 1.80 |
| ❑ 3 Ted Hodgson | 4.00 | 1.80 |
| ❑ 4 Bill Horton | 4.00 | 1.80 |
| ❑ 5 Ralph Hopiavuori | 4.00 | 1.80 |
| ❑ 6 Jim McMasters | 4.00 | 1.80 |
| ❑ 7 Bill Needham CO | 4.00 | 1.80 |
| ❑ 8 Rick Pumple | 5.00 | 2.20 |
| ❑ 9 Jim Wiste | 5.00 | 2.20 |

## 1970-71 Dad's Cookies

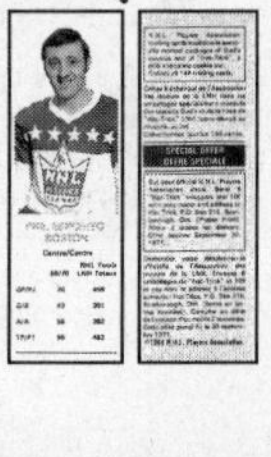

The 1970-71 Dad's Cookies set contains 144 unnumbered color cards. Each card measures approximately 1 7/8" by 5 3/8". Each player is pictured on the front dressed in an "NHL Players" emblazoned jersey. The fronts contain player statistics for the 1969-70 season and for his career. The backs, in both English and French, are the same for all cards. The backs contain an ad for these cards and Dad's Cookies, a special offer for an NHL Players Association decal and a 1969 NHL Players Association copyright line.

| | NRMT-MT | EXC |
|---|---|---|
| COMPLETE SET (144) | 225.00 | 100.00 |
| COMMON CARD (1-144) | .75 | .35 |
| ❑ 1 Lou Angotti | 1.00 | .45 |
| ❑ 2 Don Awrey | .75 | .35 |
| ❑ 3 Bob Baun | 1.00 | .45 |
| ❑ 4 Jean Beliveau | 8.00 | 3.60 |
| ❑ 5 Red Berenson | 1.00 | .45 |
| ❑ 6 Gary Bergman | 1.00 | .45 |
| ❑ 7 Les Binkley | 2.00 | .90 |
| ❑ 8 Andre Boudrias | .75 | .35 |
| ❑ 9 Wally Boyer | .75 | .35 |
| ❑ 10 Arnie Brown | .75 | .35 |
| ❑ 11 Johnny Bucyk | 3.00 | 1.35 |
| ❑ 12 Charlie Burns | .75 | .35 |
| ❑ 13 Larry Cahan | .75 | .35 |
| ❑ 14 Gerry Cheevers | 5.00 | 2.20 |
| ❑ 15 Bobby Clarke | 15.00 | 6.75 |
| ❑ 16 Wayne Connelly | .75 | .35 |
| ❑ 17 Yvan Cournoyer | 3.00 | 1.35 |
| ❑ 18 Roger Crozier | 2.00 | .90 |
| ❑ 19 Ray Cullen | 1.00 | .45 |
| ❑ 20 Denis DeJordy | 2.00 | .90 |
| ❑ 21 Alex Delvecchio | 3.00 | 1.35 |
| ❑ 22 Bob Dillabough | .75 | .35 |
| ❑ 23 Gary Doak | .75 | .35 |
| ❑ 24 Gary Dornhoefer | 2.00 | .90 |
| ❑ 25 Dick Duff | 1.00 | .45 |
| ❑ 26 Tim Ecclestone | .75 | .35 |
| ❑ 27 Roy Edwards | 2.00 | .90 |
| ❑ 28 Gerry Ehman | .75 | .35 |
| ❑ 29 Ron Ellis | 1.00 | .45 |
| ❑ 30 Phil Esposito | 12.00 | 5.50 |
| ❑ 31 Tony Esposito | 12.00 | 5.50 |
| ❑ 32 Doug Favell | 2.00 | .90 |
| ❑ 33 John Ferguson | 2.00 | .90 |
| ❑ 34 Norm Ferguson | .75 | .35 |
| ❑ 35 Reg Fleming | 1.00 | .45 |
| ❑ 36 Bill Flett | 1.00 | .45 |
| ❑ 37 Bruce Gamble | 2.00 | .90 |
| ❑ 38 Jean-Guy Gendron | .75 | .35 |
| ❑ 39 Ed Giacomin | 5.00 | 2.20 |
| ❑ 40 Rod Gilbert | 2.50 | 1.10 |
| ❑ 41 Bill Goldsworthy | 1.00 | .45 |
| ❑ 42 Phil Goyette | .75 | .35 |
| ❑ 43 Danny Grant | 1.00 | .45 |
| ❑ 44 Ted Green | 1.00 | .45 |
| ❑ 45 Vic Hadfield | 1.00 | .45 |
| ❑ 46 Al Hamilton | .75 | .35 |
| ❑ 47 Ted Hampson | .75 | .35 |
| ❑ 48 Terry Harper | 1.00 | .45 |
| ❑ 49 Ted Harris | .75 | .35 |
| ❑ 50 Paul Henderson | 3.00 | 1.35 |
| ❑ 51 Bryan Hextall | 1.00 | .45 |
| ❑ 52 Bill Hicke | .75 | .35 |
| ❑ 53 Larry Hillman | .75 | .35 |
| ❑ 54 Wayne Hillman | .75 | .35 |
| ❑ 55 Charlie Hodge | 2.50 | 1.10 |
| ❑ 56 Ken Hodge | 1.00 | .45 |
| ❑ 57 Gordie Howe | 25.00 | 11.00 |
| ❑ 58 Harry Howell | 2.50 | 1.10 |
| ❑ 59 Bobby Hull | 20.00 | 9.00 |
| ❑ 60 Dennis Hull | 1.50 | .70 |
| ❑ 61 Earl Ingarfield | .75 | .35 |
| ❑ 62 Doug Jarrett | .75 | .35 |
| ❑ 63 Gary Jarrett | .75 | .35 |
| ❑ 64 Ed Johnston | 2.00 | .90 |
| ❑ 65 Dave Keon | 3.00 | 1.35 |
| ❑ 66 Skip Krake | .75 | .35 |
| ❑ 67 Orland Kurtenbach | 1.00 | .45 |
| ❑ 68 Andre Lacroix | 1.00 | .45 |
| ❑ 69 Jacques Laperriere | 1.00 | .45 |
| ❑ 70 Jacques Lemaire | 3.00 | 1.35 |
| ❑ 71 Rick Ley | 1.00 | .45 |
| ❑ 72 Bruce MacGregor | .75 | .35 |
| ❑ 73 Keith Magnuson | 1.00 | .45 |
| ❑ 74 Frank Mahovlich | 5.00 | 2.20 |
| ❑ 75 Chico Maki | 1.00 | .45 |
| ❑ 76 Gilles Marotte | 1.00 | .45 |
| ❑ 77 Bert Marshall | .75 | .35 |
| ❑ 78 Don Marshall | .75 | .35 |
| ❑ 79 Pit Martin | 1.00 | .45 |
| ❑ 80 Keith McCreary | .75 | .35 |
| ❑ 81 Ab McDonald | .75 | .35 |
| ❑ 82 Jim McKenny | 1.00 | .45 |
| ❑ 83 John McKenzie | 1.00 | .45 |
| ❑ 84 Mike McMahon | .75 | .35 |
| ❑ 85 Larry Mickey | .75 | .35 |
| ❑ 86 Stan Mikita | 5.00 | 2.20 |
| ❑ 87 Doug Mohns | 1.00 | .45 |
| ❑ 88 Wayne Muloin | .75 | .35 |
| ❑ 89 Jim Neilson | .75 | .35 |
| ❑ 90 Bob Nevin | .75 | .35 |
| ❑ 91 Murray Oliver | .75 | .35 |
| ❑ 92 Bobby Orr | 50.00 | 22.00 |
| ❑ 93 Danny O'Shea | .75 | .35 |
| ❑ 94 Rosaire Paiement | .75 | .35 |
| ❑ 95 Bernie Parent | 5.00 | 2.20 |
| ❑ 96 Jean-Paul Parise | 1.00 | .45 |
| ❑ 97 Brad Park | 3.00 | 1.35 |
| ❑ 98 Mike Pelyk | .75 | .35 |
| ❑ 99 Gilbert Perreault | 5.00 | 2.20 |
| ❑ 100 Noel Picard | .75 | .35 |
| ❑ 101 Barclay Plager | 1.00 | .45 |
| ❑ 102 Jacques Plante | 12.00 | 5.50 |
| ❑ 103 Tracy Pratt | .75 | .35 |
| ❑ 104 Dean Prentice | 1.00 | .45 |
| ❑ 105 Jean Pronovost | 1.00 | .45 |
| ❑ 106 Bob Pulford | 1.00 | .45 |
| ❑ 107 Pat Quinn | 2.00 | .90 |
| ❑ 108 Jean Ratelle | 2.50 | 1.10 |
| ❑ 109 Matt Ravlich | .75 | .35 |
| ❑ 110 Mickey Redmond | 2.00 | .90 |
| ❑ 111 Henri Richard | 5.00 | 2.20 |
| ❑ 112 Jim Roberts | 1.00 | .45 |
| ❑ 113 Dale Rolfe | .75 | .35 |
| ❑ 114 Bobby Rousseau | 1.00 | .45 |
| ❑ 115 Gary Sabourin | .75 | .35 |
| ❑ 116 Derek Sanderson | 8.00 | 3.60 |
| ❑ 117 Glen Sather | 3.00 | 1.35 |
| ❑ 118 Serge Savard | 2.00 | .90 |
| ❑ 119 Ken Schinkel | .75 | .35 |
| ❑ 120 Rod Seiling | .75 | .35 |
| ❑ 121 Brit Selby | .75 | .35 |
| ❑ 122 Eddie Shack | 3.00 | 1.35 |
| ❑ 123 Floyd Smith | .75 | .35 |
| ❑ 124 Fred Stanfield | .75 | .35 |
| ❑ 125 Pat Stapleton | 1.00 | .45 |
| ❑ 126 Frank St.Marseille | .75 | .35 |
| ❑ 127 Dale Tallon | 1.00 | .45 |
| ❑ 128 Walt Tkaczuk | 1.00 | .45 |
| ❑ 129 J.C. Tremblay | 1.00 | .45 |
| ❑ 130 Norm Ullman | 2.00 | .90 |
| ❑ 131 Garry Unger | 1.00 | .45 |
| ❑ 132 Rogatien Vachon | 4.00 | 1.80 |
| ❑ 133 Carol Vadnais | .75 | .35 |
| ❑ 134 Ed Van Impe | .75 | .35 |
| ❑ 135 Bob Wall | .75 | .35 |
| ❑ 136 Mike Walton | 1.00 | .45 |
| ❑ 137 Bryan Watson | .75 | .35 |
| ❑ 138 Joe Watson | .75 | .35 |
| ❑ 139 Tom Webster | 1.00 | .45 |
| ❑ 140 Juha Widing | 1.00 | .45 |
| ❑ 141 Tom Williams | .75 | .35 |
| ❑ 142 Jim Wiste | .75 | .35 |
| ❑ 143 Gump Worsley | 5.00 | 2.20 |
| ❑ 144 Bob Woytowich | 1.00 | .45 |

## 1984-85 Devils Postcards

This 25-card set of New Jersey Devils features on the front borderless color photos of the players, with two team logos (in green and red) in the white stripe below the picture. The cards measure approximately 3 1/4" by 6 1/8" and are in the postcard type format. On the left half of the back appear a black and white head shot of the player, basic player information, and the Devils' team logo. The cards are checklisted below according to uniform number. The side panel of the package of Colgate Dental Cream listed the checklist of the complete set. The cards of John MacLean and Kirk Muller predate their Rookie Cards.

| | MINT | NRMT |
|---|---|---|
| COMPLETE SET (25) | 20.00 | 9.00 |
| COMMON CARD | .50 | .23 |
| ❑ 1 Chico Resch | 2.00 | .90 |
| ❑ 2 Joe Cirella | .75 | .35 |
| ❑ 4 Bob Lorimer | .50 | .23 |
| ❑ 5 Phil Russell | .50 | .23 |
| ❑ 8 Dave Pichette | .50 | .23 |
| ❑ 9 Don Lever | .75 | .35 |
| ❑ 10 Aaron Broten | 1.00 | .45 |
| ❑ 12 Pat Verbeek | 5.00 | 2.20 |
| ❑ 14 Rich Chernomaz | .50 | .23 |
| ❑ 15 John MacLean | 4.00 | 1.80 |
| ❑ 16 Rick Meagher | .50 | .23 |
| ❑ 17 Paul Gagne | .50 | .23 |
| ❑ 18 Mel Bridgman | .75 | .35 |
| ❑ 19 Rich Preston | .50 | .23 |
| ❑ 20 Tim Higgins | .50 | .23 |
| ❑ 21 Bob Hoffmeyer | .50 | .23 |
| ❑ 22 Doug Sulliman | .50 | .23 |
| ❑ 23 Bruce Driver | 1.00 | .45 |
| ❑ 25 Dave Lewis | .50 | .23 |
| ❑ 27 Kirk Muller | 5.00 | 2.20 |
| ❑ 28 Uli Hiemer | .50 | .23 |
| ❑ 29 Jan Ludvig | .50 | .23 |
| ❑ 30 Ron Low | .75 | .35 |
| ❑ 33 Hannu Kamppurri | .75 | .35 |
| ❑ NNO Doug Carpenter CO | .50 | .23 |

## 1985-86 Devils Postcards

This ten-card set of New Jersey Devils features on the front borderless color player photos. The cards measure approximately 3 5/8" by 5 1/2" and are in the postcard format. The horizontal backs are divided in half by a thin

black line and have the year, biographical information, home town, and a career highlight at the upper left corner. The cards are unnumbered and checklisted below in alphabetical order. Key cards in the set are Kirk Muller in his Rookie Card year and Craig Billington prior to his Rookie Card year.

| | MINT | NRMT |
|---|---|---|
| COMPLETE SET (10) | 14.00 | 6.25 |
| COMMON CARD (1-10) | 1.00 | .45 |
| ❑ 1 Greg Adams | 1.50 | .70 |
| ❑ 2 Perry Anderson | 1.00 | .45 |
| ❑ 3 Craig Billington | 2.00 | .90 |
| ❑ 4 Alain Chevrier | 1.50 | .70 |
| ❑ 5 Paul Gagne | 1.00 | .45 |
| ❑ 6 Mark Johnson | 1.00 | .45 |
| ❑ 7 Kirk Muller | 4.00 | 1.80 |
| ❑ 8 Chico Resch | 2.50 | 1.10 |
| ❑ 9 Randy Velischek | 1.00 | .45 |
| ❑ 10 Craig Wolanin | 1.00 | .45 |

## 1986-87 Devils Police

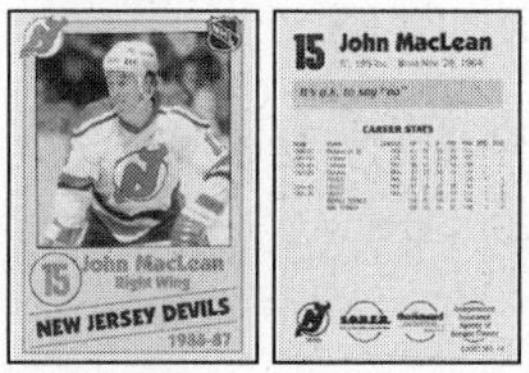

This 20-card set was jointly sponsored by the New Jersey Devils, S.O.B.E.R., Howard Bank, and Independent Insurance Agents of Bergen Country. Logos for these sponsors appear on the bottom of the card back. The front features a color action photo of the player, with the Devils' and NHL logos superimposed over the top corners of the picture. A thin black line and a green line serves as the inner and outer borders respectively; the area in between is yellow, with printing in the team's colors red and black. In addition to sponsors' logos, the back has biographical information, an anti-drug message, and career statistics. We have checklisted the cards below in alphabetical order, with uniform number to the right of the player's name.

| | MINT | NRMT |
|---|---|---|
| COMPLETE SET (20) | 30.00 | 13.50 |
| COMMON CARD (1-20) | 1.00 | .45 |
| ❑ 1 Greg Adams 24 | 1.50 | .70 |
| ❑ 2 Perry Anderson 25 | 1.00 | .45 |
| ❑ 3 Timo Blomqvist 5 | 1.00 | .45 |
| ❑ 4 Andy Brickley 26 | 1.00 | .45 |
| ❑ 5 Mel Bridgman 18 | 1.50 | .70 |
| ❑ 6 Aaron Broten 10 | 1.00 | .45 |
| ❑ 7 Alain Chevrier 30 | 1.50 | .70 |
| ❑ 8 Joe Cirella 2 | 1.50 | .70 |
| ❑ 9 Ken Daneyko 3 | 1.50 | .70 |
| ❑ 10 Bruce Driver 23 | 2.00 | .90 |
| ❑ 11 Uli Hiemer 28 | 1.00 | .45 |
| ❑ 12 Mark Johnson 12 | 1.50 | .70 |
| ❑ 13 Jan Ludvig 29 | 1.00 | .45 |
| ❑ 14 John MacLean 15 | 4.00 | 1.80 |
| ❑ 15 Peter McNab 7 | 1.50 | .70 |
| ❑ 16 Kirk Muller 9 | 5.00 | 2.20 |
| ❑ 17 Doug Sulliman 22 | 1.00 | .45 |
| ❑ 18 Randy Velischek 27 | 1.00 | .45 |
| ❑ 19 Pat Verbeek | 5.00 | 2.20 |
| ❑ 20 Craig Wolanin 6 | 1.00 | .45 |

## 1988-89 Devils Caretta

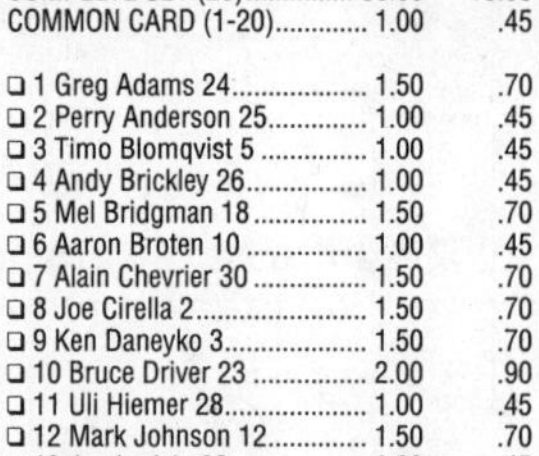

This 30-card set has color action photos of the New Jersey Devils on the front, with a thin black border on white card stock. The cards measure approximately 2 7/8" by 4 1/4". The team name and logo on the top are printed in green and red; the text below the picture, giving player name, uniform number, and position, is printed in black. The horizontally oriented back has career statistics, a team logo, and a Carretta Trucking logo. We have checklisted the cards below in alphabetical order. Brendan Shanahan appears in his Rookie Card year.

| | MINT | NRMT |
|---|---|---|
| COMPLETE SET (30) | 25.00 | 11.00 |
| COMMON CARD (1-30) | .25 | .11 |
| ❑ 1 Perry Anderson 25 | .50 | .23 |
| ❑ 2 Bob Bellemore CO | .50 | .23 |
| ❑ 3 Aaron Broten 10 | .50 | .23 |
| ❑ 4 Doug Brown 24 | .50 | .23 |
| ❑ 5 Sean Burke 1 | 3.00 | 1.35 |
| ❑ 6 Anders Carlsson 20 | .50 | .23 |
| ❑ 7 Joe Cirella 2 | .50 | .23 |
| ❑ 8 Pat Conacher 32 | .50 | .23 |
| ❑ 9 Ken Daneyko 3 | .75 | .35 |
| ❑ 10 Bruce Driver 23 | .75 | .35 |
| ❑ 11 Bob Hoffmeyer CO | .50 | .23 |
| ❑ 12 Jamie Huscroft 4 | .50 | .23 |
| ❑ 13 Mark Johnson 12 | .75 | .35 |
| ❑ 14 Jim Korn 14 | .50 | .23 |
| ❑ 15 Tom Kurvers 5 | .50 | .23 |
| ❑ 16 Lou Lamoriello P/GM | .25 | .11 |
| ❑ 17 Claude Loiselle 19 | .50 | .23 |
| ❑ 18 John MacLean 15 | 2.00 | .90 |
| ❑ 19 David Maley 8 | .50 | .23 |
| ❑ 20 Doug McKay CO | .25 | .11 |
| ❑ 21 Kirk Muller 9 | 2.00 | .90 |
| ❑ 22 Jack O'Callahan 7 | .50 | .23 |
| ❑ 23 Steve Rooney 18 | .50 | .23 |
| ❑ 24 Bob Sauve 28 | .75 | .35 |
| ❑ 25 Jim Schoenfeld CO | 1.00 | .45 |
| ❑ 26 Brendan Shanahan 11 | 15.00 | 6.75 |
| ❑ 27 Patrik Sundstrom 17 | .75 | .35 |
| ❑ 28 Randy Velischek 27 | .50 | .23 |
| ❑ 29 Pat Verbeek 16 | 2.00 | .90 |
| ❑ 30 Craig Wolanin 6 | .50 | .23 |

## 1989-90 Devils Caretta

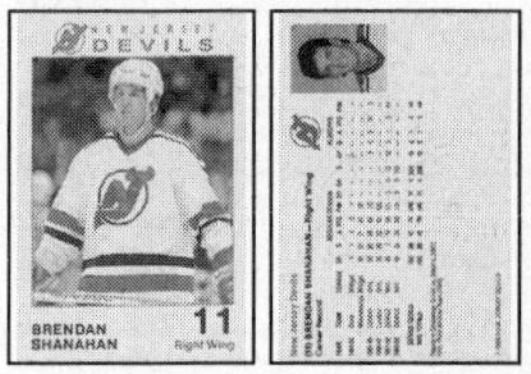

This 29-card set has color action photos of the New Jersey Devils on the front, with a thin red border on white card stock. The team name and logo on the top are printed in green and red; the text below the picture, giving player name, uniform number, and position, is printed in black. The horizontal back provides brief biographical information and career statistics, a black-and-white picture and a Caretta Trucking logo. (The set also was issued without the trucking logo.) The cards measure approximately 2 7/8" by 4 1/4". These unnumbered cards are checklisted below alphabetically with sweater number noted to the right.

| | MINT | NRMT |
|---|---|---|
| COMPLETE SET (29) | 18.00 | 8.00 |
| COMMON CARD (1-29) | .25 | .11 |
| ❑ 1 Tommy Albelin 26 | .50 | .23 |
| ❑ 2 Bob Bellemore CO | .25 | .11 |
| ❑ 3 Neil Brady 19 | .50 | .23 |
| ❑ 4 Aaron Broten 10 | .50 | .23 |
| ❑ 5 Doug Brown 24 | .50 | .23 |
| ❑ 6 Sean Burke 1 | 2.00 | .90 |
| ❑ 7 Pat Conacher 32 | .50 | .23 |
| ❑ 8 John Cunniff CO | .25 | .11 |
| ❑ 9 Ken Daneyko 3 | .50 | .23 |
| ❑ 10 Bruce Driver 23 | 1.00 | .45 |
| ❑ 11 Viacheslav Fetisov 2 | 2.00 | .90 |
| ❑ 12 Mark Johnson 12 | .50 | .23 |
| ❑ 13 Jim Korn 14 | .50 | .23 |
| ❑ 14 Lou Lamoriello P/GM | .25 | .11 |
| ❑ 15 John MacLean 15 | 1.50 | .70 |
| ❑ 16 David Maley 8 | .50 | .23 |
| ❑ 17 Kirk Muller 9 | 2.00 | .90 |
| ❑ 18 Janne Ojanen 22 | .50 | .23 |
| ❑ 19 Walt Poddubny 21 | .50 | .23 |
| ❑ 20 Reijo Ruotsalainen 29 | .50 | .23 |
| ❑ 21 Brendan Shanahan 11 | 5.00 | 2.20 |
| ❑ 22 Sergei Starikov 4 | .50 | .23 |
| ❑ 23 Patrik Sundstrom 17 | .50 | .23 |
| ❑ 24 Peter Sundstrom 20 | .50 | .23 |
| ❑ 25 Chris Terreri 31 | 1.00 | .45 |
| ❑ 26 Sylvain Turgeon 16 | .50 | .23 |
| ❑ 27 Randy Velischek 27 | .50 | .23 |
| ❑ 28 Eric Weinrich 7 | .50 | .23 |
| ❑ 29 Craig Wolanin 6 | .50 | .23 |

## 1990-91 Devils

This set contains 30 standard-size cards and features members of the New Jersey Devils. The front has a color photo of the player, with the team logo in the upper left corner. The back has statistical information. These cards are unnumbered and are checklisted below in alphabetical order.

| | MINT | NRMT |
|---|---|---|
| COMPLETE SET (30) | 15.00 | 6.75 |
| COMMON CARD (1-30) | .25 | .11 |
| ❑ 1 Tommy Albelin | .35 | .16 |

❑ 2 Laurie Boschman .35 .16
❑ 3 Doug Brown .50 .23
❑ 4 Sean Burke 1.50 .70
❑ 5 Tim Burke .35 .16
❑ 6 Zdeno Ciger .50 .23
❑ 7 Pat Conacher .35 .16
❑ 8 Troy Crowder .50 .23
❑ 9 John Cunniff CO .25 .11
❑ 10 Ken Daneyko .75 .35
❑ 11 Bruce Driver .50 .23
❑ 12 Viacheslav Fetisov .75 .35
❑ 13 Alexei Kasatonov .50 .23
❑ 14 Lou Lamoriello P/GM .25 .11
❑ 15 Claude Lemieux 1.00 .45
❑ 16 David Maley .35 .16
❑ 17 John MacLean 1.00 .45
❑ 18 Jon Morris .35 .16
❑ 19 Kirk Muller 1.50 .70
❑ 20 Lee Norwood .35 .16
❑ 21 Myles O'Connor .35 .16
❑ 22 Walt Poddubny .50 .23
❑ 23 Brendan Shanahan 5.00 2.20
❑ 24 Peter Stastny 1.50 .70
❑ 25 Alan Stewart .35 .16
❑ 26 Warren Strelow .35 .16
❑ 27 Doug Sulliman .35 .16
❑ 28 Patrik Sundstrom .50 .23
❑ 29 Chris Terreri .50 .23
❑ 30 Eric Weinrich .50 .23

## 1991-92 Devils Teams Carvel

This ten-card set features team photos of the ten Devils teams from 1982-83 through 1991-92. The cards have a coupon for Carvel Ice Cream with an entry form for the "Shoot to Win" contest. The backs list all the players who are pictured and the statistical leaders from that particular year. The cards are unnumbered and measure approximately 2 1/2" by 6" with coupon. One card was issued per spectator at certain home games during the 1991-92 season.

| | MINT | NRMT |
|---|---|---|
| COMPLETE SET (10) | 20.00 | 9.00 |
| COMMON TEAM (1-10) | 2.50 | 1.10 |

❑ 1 1982-83 Devils Team 3.00 1.35
❑ 2 1983-84 Devils Team 2.50 1.10
❑ 3 1984-85 Devils Team 2.50 1.10
❑ 4 1985-86 Devils Team 2.50 1.10
❑ 5 1986-87 Devils Team 2.50 1.10
❑ 6 1987-88 Devils Team 2.50 1.10
❑ 7 1988-89 Devils Team 2.50 1.10
❑ 8 1989-90 Devils Team 2.50 1.10
❑ 9 1990-91 Devils Team 2.50 1.10
❑ 10 1991-92 Devils Team 2.50 1.10

## 1996-97 Devils

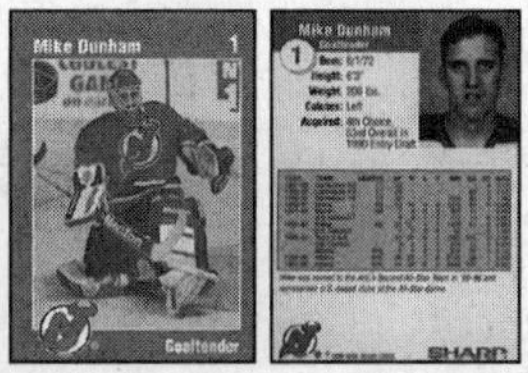


This attractive team-issued set is complete at 30-cards. It was apparently issued as a premium at a game sometime during the '96-97 season and was sponsored by Sharp Electronics. The fronts feature action color photos surrounded by a red border. The player's name and number appear at the top, while his position and team logo grace the bottom. The backs include a black and white head shot as well as comprehensive statistics.

| | MINT | NRMT |
|---|---|---|
| COMPLETE SET (30) | 10.00 | 4.50 |
| COMMON CARD | .10 | .05 |

❑ 1 Mike Dunham .50 .23
❑ 3 Ken Daneyko .25 .11
❑ 4 Scott Stevens .50 .23
❑ 10 Denis Pederson .50 .23
❑ 11 Steve Sullivan .50 .23
❑ 12 Bill Guerin .50 .23
❑ 14 Brian Rolston .35 .16
❑ 15 John MacLean .50 .23
❑ 16 Bobby Holik .25 .11
❑ 17 Petr Sykora .50 .23
❑ 18 Sergei Brylin .25 .11
❑ 19 Bob Carpenter .25 .11
❑ 20 Jay Pandolfo .25 .11
❑ 21 Randy McKay .25 .11
❑ 22 Patrik Elias .35 .16
❑ 23 Dave Andreychuk .50 .23
❑ 24 Lyle Odelein .25 .11
❑ 25 Valeri Zelepukin .25 .11
❑ 26 Jason Smith .25 .11
❑ 27 Scott Niedermayer .50 .23
❑ 28 Kevin Dean .25 .11
❑ 29 Shawn Chambers .25 .11
❑ 30 Martin Brodeur 2.00 .90
❑ 32 Steve Thomas .35 .16
❑ 33 Reid Simpson .25 .11
❑ NNO Jacques Lemaire CO .25 .11
❑ NNO Lou Lamoriello GM .10 .05
❑ NNO John J. McMullen CH .10 .05
❑ NNO Robbie Ftorek ACO .10 .05
❑ NNO Jacques Caron ACO .10 .05

## 1998-99 Devils Power Play

Cards were distributed in a sealed pack and were made available through give-aways at various arenas, in conjunction with Power Play magazine. Each packet contains 4-cards, similar in design to the base set from each manufacturer, but featuring a different card number on the back.

| | MINT | NRMT |
|---|---|---|
| COMPLETE SET (4) | 3.00 | 1.35 |
| COMMON CARD (1-4) | .30 | .14 |

❑ NJD1 Scott Niedermayer .30 .14
❑ NJD2 Scott Stevens .30 .14
❑ NJD3 Martin Brodeur 2.00 .90
❑ NJD4 Bobby Holik .30 .14

## 1934-35 Diamond Matchbooks Silver

Covers from this first hockey matchbook issue generally feature color action shots with a silver background and green and black vertical bars on the cover's left side. "The Diamond Match Co., NYC" imprint appears on a double line below the striker. These matchbooks usually were issued in twin-packs through cigar and drug stores of the day. Complete matchbooks carry a 50 percent premium over the prices listed below.

| | EX-MT | VG-EX |
|---|---|---|
| COMPLETE SET (60) | 1800.00 | 800.00 |
| COMMON MATCHBOOK | 20.00 | 9.00 |

❑ 1 Taffy Abel 20.00 9.00
❑ 2 Marty Barry 20.00 9.00
❑ 3 Red Beattie 20.00 9.00
❑ 4 Frank Boucher 30.00 13.50
❑ 5 Doug Brennan 20.00 9.00
❑ 6 Bill Brydge 20.00 9.00
❑ 7 Eddie Burke 40.00 18.00
❑ 8 Marty Burke 20.00 9.00
❑ 9 Gerald Carson 20.00 9.00
❑ 10 Lorne Chabot 40.00 18.00
❑ 11 Art Chapman 20.00 9.00
❑ 12 Dit Clapper 60.00 27.00
❑ 13 Lionel Conacher 60.00 27.00
❑ 14 Red Conn 20.00 9.00
❑ 15 Bill Cook 40.00 18.00
❑ 16 Bun Cook 40.00 18.00
❑ 17 Thomas Cook 25.00 11.00
❑ 18 Rosario "Lolo" Couture 20.00 9.00
❑ 19 Bob Davie 20.00 9.00
❑ 20 Cecil Dillon 20.00 9.00
❑ 21 Duke Dutkowski 20.00 9.00
❑ 22 Red Dutton 30.00 13.50
❑ 23 Johnny Gagnon 20.00 9.00
❑ 24 Chuck Gardiner 40.00 18.00
❑ 25 Johnny Gottselig 20.00 9.00
❑ 26 Robert Gracie 20.00 9.00
❑ 27 Lloyd Gross 20.00 9.00
❑ 28 Ott Heller 20.00 9.00
❑ 29 Normie Himes 20.00 9.00
❑ 30 Lionel Hitchman 40.00 18.00
❑ 31 Red Jackson 20.00 9.00
❑ 32 Roger Jenkins 20.00 9.00
❑ 33 Aurel Joliat 60.00 27.00
❑ 34 Butch Keeling 20.00 9.00
❑ 35 William Kendall 20.00 9.00
❑ 36 Jim Klein 20.00 9.00
❑ 37 Joe Lamb 20.00 9.00
❑ 38 Wildor Larochelle 25.00 11.00
❑ 39 Pit Lepine 20.00 9.00
❑ 40 Jack Leswick 20.00 9.00
❑ 41 Georges Mantha 40.00 18.00
❑ 42 Sylvio Mantha 40.00 18.00
❑ 43 Mush March 25.00 11.00
❑ 44 Ronnie Martin 20.00 9.00
❑ 45 Rabbitt McVeigh 20.00 9.00
❑ 46 Howie Morenz 300.00 135.00
❑ 47 Murray Murdoch 20.00 9.00
❑ 48 Harold Oliver 30.00 13.50
❑ 49 George Patterson 20.00 9.00
❑ 50 Hal Picketts 20.00 9.00
❑ 51 Victor Ripley 20.00 9.00
❑ 52 Doc Romnes 20.00 9.00
❑ 53 Johnny Sheppard 20.00 9.00
❑ 54 Eddie Shore 100.00 45.00
❑ 55 Art Somers 20.00 9.00
❑ 56 Chris Speyers 20.00 9.00
❑ 57 Nelson Stewart 40.00 18.00
❑ 58 Tiny Thompson 60.00 27.00
❑ 59 Louis Trudel 20.00 9.00
❑ 60 Roy Worters 40.00 18.00

## 1935-36 Diamond Matchbooks Tan 2

The Type 2 covers are similar to the Type 1 tan-bordered set except that the player's position or team affiliation information has been ommitted from the reverse side. "The Diamond Match Co., NYC" imprint appears in a single line. As complete matchbooks are fairly scarce, they carry a premium of 50 percent over the prices below.

| | EX-MT | VG-EX |
|---|---|---|
| COMPLETE SET (63) | 1250.00 | 550.00 |
| COMMON MATCHBOOK | 15.00 | 6.75 |

❑ 1 Tommy Anderson 15.00 6.75
❑ 2 Vern Ayres 15.00 6.75
❑ 3 Frank Boucher 25.00 11.00
❑ 4 Frank Boucher 25.00 11.00
❑ 5 Bill Brydge 15.00 6.75
❑ 6 Marty Burke 15.00 6.75
❑ 7 Lorne Carr 15.00 6.75
❑ 8 Lorne Chabot 30.00 13.50
❑ 9 Art Chapman 15.00 6.75
❑ 10 Bert Connolly 15.00 6.75
❑ 11 Bill Cook 30.00 13.50
❑ 12 Bill Cook 30.00 13.50
❑ 13 Bun Cook 30.00 13.50
❑ 14 Tommy Cook 20.00 9.00
❑ 15 Art Coulter 15.00 6.75
❑ 16 Lolo Couture 15.00 6.75
❑ 17 Wilf Cude 25.00 11.00
❑ 18 Cecil Dillon 15.00 6.75
❑ 19 Cecil Dillon 15.00 6.75
❑ 20 Red Dutton 25.00 11.00
❑ 21 Hap Emms 25.00 11.00
❑ 22 Irv Frew 15.00 6.75
❑ 23 Johnny Gagnon 15.00 6.75
❑ 24 Leroy Goldsworthy 15.00 6.75
❑ 25 Johnny Gottselig 15.00 6.75
❑ 26 Paul Haynes 15.00 6.75
❑ 27 Ott Heller 15.00 6.75
❑ 28 Irving Jaffee
recently confirmed
❑ 29 Joe Jerwa 15.00 6.75
❑ 30 Ching Johnson 30.00 13.50
❑ 31 Aurel Joliat 45.00 20.00
❑ 32 Butch Keeling 15.00 6.75
❑ 33 William Kendall 15.00 6.75
❑ 34 Davey Kerr 25.00 11.00
❑ 35 Lloyd Klein 15.00 6.75
❑ 36 Wildor Larochelle 20.00 9.00
❑ 37 Pit Lepine 15.00 6.75
❑ 38 Arthur Lesieur 15.00 6.75
❑ 39 Alex Levinsky 20.00 9.00
❑ 40 Alex Levinsky 20.00 9.00
❑ 41 Norm Locking 15.00 6.75
❑ 42 Georges Mantha 30.00 13.50
❑ 43 Sylvio Mantha 30.00 13.50
❑ 44 Mush Marsh 20.00 9.00
❑ 45 Charlie Mason 15.00 6.75
❑ 46 Donnie McFadyen 15.00 6.75
❑ 47 Jack McGill 15.00 6.75
❑ 48 Armand Mondou 15.00 6.75
❑ 49 Howie Morenz 250.00 110.00
❑ 50 Murray Murdoch 15.00 6.75
❑ 51 Al Murray 15.00 6.75
❑ 52 Harry Oliver 30.00 13.50
❑ 53 Eddie Ouellette 15.00 6.75
❑ 54 Lynn Patrick 30.00 13.50
❑ 55 Lynn Patrick 30.00 13.50
❑ 56 Paul Runge 15.00 6.75
❑ 57 Sweeney Schriner 30.00 13.50
❑ 58 Art Somers 15.00 6.75
❑ 59 Harold Starr
recently confirmed
❑ 60 Nels Stewart 40.00 18.00
❑ 61 Paul Thompson 15.00 6.75
❑ 62 Louis Trudel 15.00 6.75
❑ 63 Carl Voss 20.00 9.00
❑ 64 Art Wiebe 30.00 13.50
❑ 65 Roy Worters 30.00 13.50

## 1935-36 Diamond Matchbooks Tan 3

The Type 3 matchbook covers are almost identical to the Type 2 covers except that the manufacturer's imprint "Made In The USA/The Diamond Match Co. NYC" is a double line designation. Complete matchbooks are rairly scarce and carry a 50 percent premium over the prices below.

| | EX-MT | VG-EX |
|---|---|---|
| COMPLETE SET (60) | 1200.00 | 550.00 |
| COMMON MATCHBOOK | 15.00 | 6.75 |

❑ 1 Tommy Anderson 15.00 6.75
❑ 2 Vern Ayres 15.00 6.75
❑ 3 Frank Boucher 25.00 11.00
❑ 4 Bill Brydge 15.00 6.75
❑ 5 Marty Burke 15.00 6.75
❑ 6 Walter Buswell 15.00 6.75
❑ 7 Lorne Carr 15.00 6.75
❑ 8 Lorne Chabot 30.00 13.50
❑ 9 Art Chapman 15.00 6.75
❑ 10 Bert Connolly 15.00 6.75
❑ 11 Bill Cook 30.00 13.50
❑ 12 Bun Cook 30.00 13.50
❑ 13 Tommy Cook 20.00 9.00
❑ 14 Art Coulter 15.00 6.75
❑ 15 Lolo Couture 15.00 6.75
❑ 16 Wilf Cude 25.00 11.00
❑ 17 Cecil Dillon 15.00 6.75
❑ 18 Red Dutton 25.00 11.00
❑ 19 Hap Emms 25.00 11.00
❑ 20 Irvin Frew 15.00 6.75
❑ 21 Johnny Gagnon 15.00 6.75
❑ 22 Leroy Goldsworthy 15.00 6.75
❑ 23 Johnny Gottselig 15.00 6.75
❑ 24 Paul Haynes 15.00 6.75
❑ 25 Ott Heller 15.00 6.75
❑ 26 Joe Jerwa 15.00 6.75
❑ 27 Ching Johnson 30.00 13.50
❑ 28 Aurel Joliat 45.00 20.00
❑ 29 Mike Karakas 20.00 9.00
❑ 30 Butch Keeling 15.00 6.75
❑ 31 Dave Kerr 25.00 11.00
❑ 32 Lloyd Klein 15.00 6.75
❑ 33 Wildor Larochelle 20.00 9.00
❑ 34 Pit Lepine 15.00 6.75
❑ 35 Arthur Lesieur 15.00 6.75
❑ 36 Alex Levinsky 20.00 9.00
❑ 37 Norman Locking 15.00 6.75
❑ 38 George Mantha 30.00 13.50
❑ 39 Sylvio Mantha 30.00 13.50
❑ 40 Harold "Mush" March 20.00 9.00
❑ 41 Charlie Mason 15.00 6.75
❑ 42 Charlie Mason 15.00 6.75
❑ 43 Donnie McFadyen 15.00 6.75
❑ 44 Jack McGill 15.00 6.75
❑ 45 Armand Mondou 15.00 6.75
❑ 46 Howie Morenz 250.00 110.00
❑ 47 Murray Murdoch 15.00 6.75
❑ 48 Al Murray 15.00 6.75
❑ 49 Harry Oliver 30.00 13.50
❑ 50 Eddie Ouellette 15.00 6.75
❑ 51 Lynn Patrick 30.00 13.50
❑ 52 Paul Runge 15.00 6.75
❑ 53 Sweeney Schriner 30.00 13.50
❑ 54 Harold Starr
recently confirmed
❑ 55 Nels Stewart 40.00 18.00
❑ 56 Paul Thompson 15.00 6.75
❑ 57 Louis Trudel 15.00 6.75
❑ 58 Carl Voss 25.00 11.00
❑ 59 Art Wiebe 20.00 9.00
❑ 60 Roy Worters 25.00 11.00

## 1935-36 Diamond Matchbooks Tan 4

This tan-bordered issue is comprised only of Chicago Blackhawks players. The set is similar to Type 1 in that the player's team name appears between the player's name and bio on the reverse. The "Made in USA/The Diamond Match Co., NYC" imprint appears on two lines. Complete matchbooks carry a 50 percent premium.

| | MINT | NRMT |
|---|---|---|
| COMPLETE SET (15) | 250.00 | 110.00 |
| COMMON MATCHBOOK | 15.00 | 6.75 |

❑ 1 Andy Blair 15.00 6.75
❑ 2 Glenn Brydson 15.00 6.75
❑ 3 Marty Burke 15.00 6.75
❑ 4 Tommy Cook 20.00 9.00
❑ 5 Johnny Gottselig 15.00 6.75
❑ 6 Harold Jackson 15.00 6.75
❑ 7 Mike Karakas 20.00 9.00
❑ 8 Wildor Larochelle 20.00 9.00
❑ 9 Alex Levinsky 20.00 9.00
❑ 10 Clem Loughlin 15.00 6.75
❑ 11 Harold March 20.00 9.00
❑ 12 Earl Seibert 25.00 11.00
❑ 13 Paul Thompson 15.00 6.75
❑ 14 Louis Trudel 15.00 6.75
❑ 15 Art Wiebe 20.00 9.00

## 1935-36 Diamond Matchbooks Tan 5

This tan-bordered set features only players from the Chicago Blackhawks. This is the hardest matchcover issue to distinguish. The difference is that the team name is not featured between the player's name and his bio on the reverse. Complete matchbooks carry a 50 percent premium over the prices below.

| | EX-MT | VG-EX |
|---|---|---|
| COMPLETE SET (14) | 150.00 | 70.00 |
| COMMON MATCHBOOK | 12.50 | 5.50 |

❑ 1 Glenn Brydson 12.50 5.50
❑ 2 Marty Burke 12.50 5.50
❑ 3 Tommy Cook 15.00 6.75
❑ 4 Cully Dahlstrom 12.50 5.50
❑ 5 Johnny Gottselig 12.50 5.50
❑ 6 Vic Heyliger 12.50 5.50
❑ 7 Mike Karakas 15.00 6.75
❑ 8 Alex Levinsky 15.00 6.75
❑ 9 Harold March 15.00 6.75
❑ 10 Earl Seibert 15.00 6.75
❑ 11 William J. Stewart 12.50 5.50
❑ 12 Paul Thompson 12.50 5.50
❑ 13 Louis Trudel 12.50 5.50
❑ 14 Art Wiebe 15.00 6.75

## 1935-36 Diamond Matchbooks Tan I

The reverse of these tan-colored covers feature a brief player history with the player's name and team affiliation or position appearing at the top. "The Diamond Match Co., NYC" imprint appears below the striker on a single line. Complete matchbookds carry a 50 percent premium over the prices below. A matchbook of Joe Starke is reported to exist, but we cannot officially confirm that at this point in time.

| | EX-MT | VG-EX |
|---|---|---|
| COMPLETE SET (69) | 1250.00 | 550.00 |
| COMMON MATCHBOOK | 15.00 | 6.75 |

❑ 1 Andy Aitkenhead 15.00 6.75
❑ 2 Vern Ayres 15.00 6.75
❑ 3 Bill Beveridge 25.00 11.00
❑ 4 Ralph Bowman 15.00 6.75
❑ 5 Bill Brydge 15.00 6.75
❑ 6 Glenn Brydson 15.00 6.75
❑ 7 Eddie Burke 25.00 11.00
❑ 8 Marty Burke 15.00 6.75
❑ 9 Lorne Carr 15.00 6.75
❑ 10 Gerald Carson 15.00 6.75
❑ 11 Lorne Chabot 35.00 16.00
❑ 12 Art Chapman 15.00 6.75
❑ 13 Red Conn 15.00 6.75
❑ 14 Bert Connoly 15.00 6.75
❑ 15 Bun Cook 30.00 13.50
❑ 16 Tommy Cook 20.00 9.00
❑ 17 Art Coulter 15.00 6.75
❑ 18 Lolo Couture 15.00 6.75
❑ 19 Bill Cowley 25.00 11.00
❑ 20 Wilf Cude 25.00 11.00
❑ 21 Red Dutton 25.00 11.00
❑ 22 Frank Finnigan 20.00 9.00
❑ 23 Irv Frew 15.00 6.75
❑ 24 LeRoy Goldsworthy 15.00 6.75
❑ 25 Johnny Gottselig 15.00 6.75
❑ 26 Bob Gracie 15.00 6.75
❑ 27 Ott Heller 15.00 6.75
❑ 28 Normie Himes 15.00 6.75
❑ 29 Syd Howe 30.00 13.50
❑ 30 Roger Jenkins 15.00 6.75
❑ 31 Ching Johnson 40.00 18.00
❑ 32 Aurel Joliat 50.00 22.00
❑ 33 Max Kaminsky 15.00 6.75
❑ 34 Butch Keeling 15.00 6.75
❑ 35 Bill Kendall 15.00 6.75
❑ 36 Lloyd Klein 15.00 6.75
❑ 37 Joe Lamb 15.00 6.75
❑ 38 Wildor Larochelle 20.00 9.00
❑ 39 Pit Lepine 15.00 6.75
❑ 40 Norman Locking 15.00 6.75
❑ 41 Georges Mantha 30.00 13.50
❑ 42 Sylvio Mantha 30.00 13.50
❑ 43 Harold March 20.00 9.00
❑ 44 Charlie Mason 15.00 6.75
❑ 45 Donnie McFadyen 15.00 6.75
❑ 46 Jack McGill 15.00 6.75
❑ 47 Rabbit McVeigh 15.00 6.75
❑ 48 Armand Mondou 15.00 6.75
❑ 49 Howie Morenz 250.00 110.00
❑ 50 Murray Murdoch 15.00 6.75
❑ 51 Al Murray 15.00 6.75
❑ 52 Harry Oliver 30.00 13.50
❑ 53 Jean Pusie 15.00 6.75
❑ 54 Paul Marcel Raymond 15.00 6.75
❑ 55 Jack Riley 15.00 6.75
❑ 56 Vic Ripley 15.00 6.75
❑ 57 Desse Roche 15.00 6.75
❑ 58 Earl Roche 15.00 6.75
❑ 59 Doc Romnes 15.00 6.75
❑ 60 Sweeney Schriner 40.00 18.00
❑ 61 Earl Seibert 30.00 13.50
❑ 62 Gerald Shannon 15.00 6.75
❑ 63 Alex Smith 15.00 6.75
❑ 64 Joe Starke
recently confirmed
❑ 65 Nels Stewart 40.00 18.00
❑ 66 Paul Thompson 15.00 6.75
❑ 67 Louis Trudel 15.00 6.75
❑ 68 Carl Voss 20.00 9.00
❑ 69 Art Wiebe 20.00 9.00
❑ 70 Roy Worters 30.00 13.50

## 1937 Diamond Matchbooks Tan 6

This 14-matchbook set is actually a reissue of the Type 5 Blackhawks set, and was released one year later. The only difference between the two series is that the reissued matchbooks have black match tips while the Type 5 issue has tan match tips. Complete matchbooks carry a 50 percent premium over the prices listed below.

| | EX-MT | VG-EX |
|---|---|---|
| COMPLETE SET (14) | 200.00 | 90.00 |
| COMMON MATCHBOOK | 15.00 | 6.75 |

❑ 1 Glenn Brydson 15.00 6.75
❑ 2 Marty Burke 15.00 6.75
❑ 3 Tom Cook 20.00 9.00
❑ 4 Cully Dahlstrom 15.00 6.75
❑ 5 Johnny Gottselig 15.00 6.75
❑ 6 Vic Heyliger 15.00 6.75
❑ 7 Mike Karakas 20.00 9.00
❑ 8 Alex Levinsky 20.00 9.00
❑ 9 Harold March 20.00 9.00
❑ 10 Earl Seibert 25.00 11.00
❑ 11 William J. Stewart 15.00 6.75
❑ 12 Paul Thompson 15.00 6.75
❑ 13 Louis Trudel 15.00 6.75
❑ 14 Art Wiebe 20.00 9.00

## 1992 Disney Mighty Ducks Movie

Issued to promote the Walt Disney movie "The Mighty Ducks", this eight-card set measures approximately 3 1/2" by 6" and is designed in the postcard format. Each card is perforated; the left portion, measuring the standard size, displays a full-bleed color photo, while the right portion is a solid neon color with a box for the stamp at the upper right. The back of the trading card portion has a brief player profile, while the other portion has an advertisement for the movie. The cards are unnumbered and checklisted below in alphabetical order. The character's name in the movie is given on the continuation line.

| | MINT | NRMT |
|---|---|---|
| COMPLETE SET (8) | 40.00 | 18.00 |
| COMMON CARD (1-8) | 5.00 | 2.20 |
| ❑ 1 Brandon Adams Jesse | 5.00 | 2.20 |
| ❑ 2 Emilio Estevez Coach Bombay | 6.00 | 2.70 |
| ❑ 3 Joshua Jackson Charlie | 8.00 | 3.60 |
| ❑ 4 Marguerite Moreau Connie | 5.00 | 2.20 |
| ❑ 5 Elden Ratliff Fulton | 5.00 | 2.20 |
| ❑ 6 Shaun Weiss Goldberg | 5.00 | 2.20 |
| ❑ 7 Rollerblading in Shopping Mall | 5.00 | 2.20 |
| ❑ 8 Team Photo | 5.00 | 2.20 |

## 1993-94 Donruss

These 510 standard-size cards feature borderless color player action shots on their fronts. The player's name appears in gold foil within a team-color-coded stripe near the bottom. His team logo rests in a lower corner. The backs, some of which are horizontal, carry another borderless color player action shot. The player's name, team, position, and biography are shown within a black rectangle on the left. His statistics appear in ghosted strips below or alongside. The cards are numbered on the back. Production of the Update set (401-510) was limited to 4,000 cases. Rookie Cards include Jason Arnott, Chris Osgood, Jocelyn Thibault and German Titov.

| | MINT | NRMT |
|---|---|---|
| COMPLETE SET (510) | 30.00 | 13.50 |
| COMPLETE SERIES 1 (400) | 25.00 | 11.00 |
| COMPLETE UPDATE SET (110) | 5.00 | 2.20 |
| COMMON CARD (1-510) | .10 | .05 |
| ❑ 1 Steven King | .10 | .05 |
| ❑ 2 Joe Sacco | .10 | .05 |
| ❑ 3 Anatoli Semenov | .10 | .05 |
| ❑ 4 Terry Yake | .10 | .05 |
| ❑ 5 Alexei Kasatonov | .10 | .05 |
| ❑ 6 Patrik Carnback | .10 | .05 |
| ❑ 7 Sean Hill | .10 | .05 |
| ❑ 8 Bill Houlder | .10 | .05 |
| ❑ 9 Todd Ewen | .10 | .05 |
| ❑ 10 Bob Corkum | .10 | .05 |
| ❑ 11 Tim Sweeney | .10 | .05 |
| ❑ 12 Ron Tugnutt | .15 | .07 |
| ❑ 13 Guy Hebert | .15 | .07 |
| ❑ 14 Shaun Van Allen | .10 | .05 |
| ❑ 15 Stu Grimson | .10 | .05 |
| ❑ 16 Jon Casey | .15 | .07 |
| ❑ 17 Dan Marois | .10 | .05 |
| ❑ 18 Adam Oates | .15 | .07 |
| ❑ 19 Glen Wesley | .10 | .05 |
| ❑ 20 Cam Stewart | .10 | .05 |
| ❑ 21 Don Sweeney | .10 | .05 |
| ❑ 22 Glen Murray | .10 | .05 |
| ❑ 23 Jozef Stumpel | .10 | .05 |
| ❑ 24 Ray Bourque | .30 | .14 |
| ❑ 25 Ted Donato | .10 | .05 |
| ❑ 26 Joe Juneau | .15 | .07 |
| ❑ 27 Dmitri Kvartalnov | .10 | .05 |
| ❑ 28 Steve Leach | .10 | .05 |
| ❑ 29 Cam Neely | .15 | .07 |
| ❑ 30 Bryan Smolinski | .10 | .05 |
| ❑ 31 Craig Simpson | .10 | .05 |
| ❑ 32 Donald Audette | .15 | .07 |
| ❑ 33 Doug Bodger | .10 | .05 |
| ❑ 34 Grant Fuhr | .15 | .07 |
| ❑ 35 Dale Hawerchuk | .15 | .07 |
| ❑ 36 Yuri Khmylev | .10 | .05 |
| ❑ 37 Pat LaFontaine | .15 | .07 |
| ❑ 38 Brad May | .15 | .07 |
| ❑ 39 Alexander Mogilny | .15 | .07 |
| ❑ 40 Richard Smehlik | .10 | .05 |
| ❑ 41 Petr Svoboda | .10 | .05 |
| ❑ 42 Matthew Barnaby | .15 | .07 |
| ❑ 43 Sergei Petrenko | .10 | .05 |
| ❑ 44 Mark Astley | .10 | .05 |
| ❑ 45 Derek Plante | .10 | .05 |
| ❑ 46 Theoren Fleury | .15 | .07 |
| ❑ 47 Al MacInnis | .15 | .07 |
| ❑ 48 Joe Nieuwendyk | .15 | .07 |
| ❑ 49 Joel Otto | .10 | .05 |
| ❑ 50 Paul Ranheim | .10 | .05 |
| ❑ 51 Robert Reichel | .10 | .05 |
| ❑ 52 Gary Roberts | .10 | .05 |
| ❑ 53 Gary Suter | .10 | .05 |
| ❑ 54 Mike Vernon | .15 | .07 |
| ❑ 55 Kelly Kisio | .10 | .05 |
| ❑ 56 German Titov | .10 | .05 |
| ❑ 57 Wes Walz | .10 | .05 |
| ❑ 58 Ted Drury | .10 | .05 |
| ❑ 59 Sandy McCarthy | .10 | .05 |
| ❑ 60 Vesa Viitakoski | .10 | .05 |
| ❑ 61 Jeff Hackett | .15 | .07 |
| ❑ 62 Neil Wilkinson | .10 | .05 |
| ❑ 63 Dirk Graham | .10 | .05 |
| ❑ 64 Ed Belfour | .30 | .14 |
| ❑ 65 Chris Chelios | .30 | .14 |
| ❑ 66 Joe Murphy | .10 | .05 |
| ❑ 67 Jeremy Roenick | .30 | .14 |
| ❑ 68 Steve Smith | .10 | .05 |
| ❑ 69 Brent Sutter | .10 | .05 |
| ❑ 70 Steve Dubinsky | .10 | .05 |
| ❑ 71 Michel Goulet | .15 | .07 |
| ❑ 72 Christian Ruuttu | .10 | .05 |
| ❑ 73 Bryan Marchment | .10 | .05 |
| ❑ 74 Sergei Krivokrasov | .10 | .05 |
| ❑ 75 Jeff Shantz | .10 | .05 |
| ❑ 76 Mike Modano | .40 | .18 |
| ❑ 77 Derian Hatcher | .10 | .05 |
| ❑ 78 Ulf Dahlen | .10 | .05 |
| ❑ 79 Mark Tinordi | .10 | .05 |
| ❑ 80 Russ Courtnall | .10 | .05 |
| ❑ 81 Mike Craig | .10 | .05 |
| ❑ 82 Trent Klatt | .10 | .05 |
| ❑ 83 Dave Gagner | .15 | .07 |
| ❑ 84 Chris Tancill | .10 | .05 |
| ❑ 85 James Black | .10 | .05 |
| ❑ 86 Dean Evason | .10 | .05 |
| ❑ 87 Andy Moog | .15 | .07 |
| ❑ 88 Paul Cavallini | .10 | .05 |
| ❑ 89 Grant Ledyard | .10 | .05 |
| ❑ 90 Jarkko Varvio | .10 | .05 |
| ❑ 91 Slava Kozlov | .15 | .07 |
| ❑ 92 Mike Sillinger | .10 | .05 |
| ❑ 93 Aaron Ward | .10 | .05 |
| ❑ 94 Greg Johnson | .10 | .05 |
| ❑ 95 Steve Yzerman | 1.00 | .45 |
| ❑ 96 Tim Cheveldae | .15 | .07 |
| ❑ 97 Steve Chiasson | .10 | .05 |
| ❑ 98 Dino Ciccarelli | .15 | .07 |
| ❑ 99 Paul Coffey | .30 | .14 |
| ❑ 100 Dallas Drake | .10 | .05 |
| ❑ 101 Sergei Fedorov | .60 | .25 |
| ❑ 102 Nicklas Lidstrom | .15 | .07 |
| ❑ 103 Darren McCarty | .40 | .18 |
| ❑ 104 Bob Probert | .15 | .07 |
| ❑ 105 Ray Sheppard | .15 | .07 |
| ❑ 106 Scott Pearson | .10 | .05 |
| ❑ 107 Steven Rice | .10 | .05 |
| ❑ 108 Louie DeBrusk | .10 | .05 |
| ❑ 109 Dave Manson | .10 | .05 |
| ❑ 110 Dean McAmmond | .10 | .05 |
| ❑ 111 Roman Oksiuta | .10 | .05 |
| ❑ 112 Geoff Smith | .10 | .05 |
| ❑ 113 Zdeno Ciger | .10 | .05 |
| ❑ 114 Shayne Corson | .10 | .05 |
| ❑ 115 Luke Richardson | .10 | .05 |
| ❑ 116 Igor Kravchuk | .10 | .05 |
| ❑ 117 Bill Ranford | .15 | .07 |
| ❑ 118 Doug Weight | .15 | .07 |
| ❑ 119 Fred Brathwaite | .15 | .07 |
| ❑ 120 Jason Arnott | 1.00 | .45 |
| ❑ 121 Tom Fitzgerald | .10 | .05 |
| ❑ 122 Mike Hough | .10 | .05 |
| ❑ 123 Jesse Belanger | .10 | .05 |
| ❑ 124 Brian Skrudland | .10 | .05 |
| ❑ 125 Dave Lowry | .10 | .05 |
| ❑ 126 Scott Mellanby | .15 | .07 |
| ❑ 127 Evgeny Davydov | .10 | .05 |
| ❑ 128 Andrei Lomakin | .10 | .05 |
| ❑ 129 Brian Benning | .10 | .05 |
| ❑ 130 Scott Levins | .10 | .05 |
| ❑ 131 Gord Murphy | .10 | .05 |
| ❑ 132 John Vanbiesbrouck | .50 | .23 |
| ❑ 133 Mark Fitzpatrick | .15 | .07 |
| ❑ 134 Rob Niedermayer | .15 | .07 |
| ❑ 135 Alexander Godynyuk | .10 | .05 |
| ❑ 136 Eric Weinrich | .10 | .05 |
| ❑ 137 Mark Greig | .10 | .05 |
| ❑ 138 Jim Sandlak | .10 | .05 |
| ❑ 139 Adam Burt | .10 | .05 |
| ❑ 140 Nick Kypreos | .10 | .05 |
| ❑ 141 Sean Burke | .15 | .07 |
| ❑ 142 Andrew Cassels | .10 | .05 |
| ❑ 143 Robert Kron | .10 | .05 |
| ❑ 144 Michael Nylander | .10 | .05 |
| ❑ 145 Robert Petrovicky | .10 | .05 |
| ❑ 146 Patrick Poulin | .10 | .05 |
| ❑ 147 Geoff Sanderson | .15 | .07 |
| ❑ 148 Pat Verbeek | .10 | .05 |
| ❑ 149 Zarley Zalapski | .10 | .05 |
| ❑ 150 Chris Pronger | .15 | .07 |
| ❑ 151 Jari Kurri | .15 | .07 |
| ❑ 152 Wayne Gretzky | 2.00 | .90 |
| ❑ 153 Pat Conacher | .10 | .05 |
| ❑ 154 Shawn McEachern | .10 | .05 |
| ❑ 155 Mike Donnelly | .10 | .05 |
| ❑ 156 Warren Rychel | .10 | .05 |
| ❑ 157 Gary Shuchuk | .10 | .05 |
| ❑ 158 Rob Blake | .10 | .05 |
| ❑ 159 Jimmy Carson | .10 | .05 |
| ❑ 160 Tony Granato | .10 | .05 |
| ❑ 161 Kelly Hrudey | .15 | .07 |
| ❑ 162 Luc Robitaille | .15 | .07 |
| ❑ 163 Tomas Sandstrom | .10 | .05 |
| ❑ 164 Darryl Sydor | .10 | .05 |
| ❑ 165 Alexei Zhitnik | .10 | .05 |
| ❑ 166 Benoit Brunet | .10 | .05 |
| ❑ 167 Lyle Odelein | .10 | .05 |
| ❑ 168 Kevin Haller | .10 | .05 |
| ❑ 169 Pierre Sevigny | .10 | .05 |
| ❑ 170 Brian Bellows | .10 | .05 |
| ❑ 171 Patrice Brisebois | .10 | .05 |
| ❑ 172 Vincent Damphousse | .15 | .07 |
| ❑ 173 Eric Desjardins | .10 | .05 |
| ❑ 174 Gilbert Dionne | .10 | .05 |
| ❑ 175 Stephan Lebeau | .10 | .05 |
| ❑ 176 John LeClair | .50 | .23 |
| ❑ 177 Kirk Muller | .10 | .05 |
| ❑ 178 Patrick Roy | 1.50 | .70 |
| ❑ 179 Mathieu Schneider | .10 | .05 |
| ❑ 180 Peter Popovic | .10 | .05 |
| ❑ 181 Corey Millen | .10 | .05 |
| ❑ 182 Jason Smith | .10 | .05 |
| ❑ 183 Bobby Holik | .10 | .05 |
| ❑ 184 John MacLean | .15 | .07 |
| ❑ 185 Bruce Driver | .10 | .05 |
| ❑ 186 Bill Guerin | .10 | .05 |
| ❑ 187 Claude Lemieux | .15 | .07 |
| ❑ 188 Bernie Nicholls | .10 | .05 |
| ❑ 189 Scott Niedermayer | .10 | .05 |
| ❑ 190 Stephane Richer | .15 | .07 |
| ❑ 191 Alexander Semak | .10 | .05 |
| ❑ 192 Scott Stevens | .15 | .07 |
| ❑ 193 Valeri Zelepukin | .10 | .05 |
| ❑ 194 Chris Terreri | .15 | .07 |
| ❑ 195 Martin Brodeur | 1.00 | .45 |
| ❑ 196 Ron Hextall | .15 | .07 |
| ❑ 197 Brad Dalgarno | .10 | .05 |
| ❑ 198 Ray Ferraro | .10 | .05 |
| ❑ 199 Patrick Flatley | .10 | .05 |
| ❑ 200 Travis Green | .15 | .07 |
| ❑ 201 Benoit Hogue | .10 | .05 |
| ❑ 202 Steve Junker | .10 | .05 |
| ❑ 203 Darius Kasparaitis | .10 | .05 |
| ❑ 204 Derek King | .10 | .05 |
| ❑ 205 Uwe Krupp | .10 | .05 |
| ❑ 206 Scott Lachance | .10 | .05 |
| ❑ 207 Vladimir Malakhov | .10 | .05 |
| ❑ 208 Steve Thomas | .10 | .05 |
| ❑ 209 Pierre Turgeon | .15 | .07 |
| ❑ 210 Scott Scissons | .10 | .05 |
| ❑ 211 Glenn Healy | .15 | .07 |
| ❑ 212 Alexander Karpovtsev | .10 | .05 |
| ❑ 213 James Patrick | .10 | .05 |
| ❑ 214 Sergei Nemchinov | .10 | .05 |
| ❑ 215 Esa Tikkanen | .10 | .05 |
| ❑ 216 Corey Hirsch | .15 | .07 |
| ❑ 217 Tony Amonte | .15 | .07 |
| ❑ 218 Mike Gartner | .15 | .07 |
| ❑ 219 Adam Graves | .15 | .07 |
| ❑ 220 Alexei Kovalev | .15 | .07 |
| ❑ 221 Brian Leetch | .30 | .14 |
| ❑ 222 Mark Messier | .40 | .18 |
| ❑ 223 Mike Richter | .30 | .14 |
| ❑ 224 Darren Turcotte | .10 | .05 |
| ❑ 225 Sergei Zubov | .10 | .05 |
| ❑ 226 Craig Billington | .15 | .07 |
| ❑ 227 Troy Mallette | .10 | .05 |
| ❑ 228 Vladimir Ruzicka | .10 | .05 |
| ❑ 229 Darrin Madeley | .10 | .05 |
| ❑ 230 Mark Lamb | .10 | .05 |
| ❑ 231 Dave Archibald | .10 | .05 |
| ❑ 232 Bob Kudelski | .10 | .05 |
| ❑ 233 Norm Maciver | .10 | .05 |
| ❑ 234 Brad Shaw | .10 | .05 |
| ❑ 235 Sylvain Turgeon | .10 | .05 |
| ❑ 236 Brian Glynn | .10 | .05 |
| ❑ 237 Alexandre Daigle | .10 | .05 |
| ❑ 238 Alexei Yashin | .15 | .07 |
| ❑ 239 Dimitri Filimonov | .10 | .05 |
| ❑ 240 Pavol Demitra | .10 | .05 |
| ❑ 241 Jason Bowen | .10 | .05 |
| ❑ 242 Eric Lindros | 1.25 | .55 |
| ❑ 243 Dominic Roussel | .15 | .07 |
| ❑ 244 Milos Holan | .10 | .05 |
| ❑ 245 Greg Hawgood | .10 | .05 |
| ❑ 246 Yves Racine | .10 | .05 |
| ❑ 247 Josef Beranek | .10 | .05 |
| ❑ 248 Rod Brind'Amour | .15 | .07 |
| ❑ 249 Kevin Dineen | .15 | .07 |
| ❑ 250 Pelle Eklund | .10 | .05 |
| ❑ 251 Garry Galley | .10 | .05 |
| ❑ 252 Mark Recchi | .15 | .07 |
| ❑ 253 Tommy Soderstrom | .15 | .07 |
| ❑ 254 Dimitri Yushkevich | .10 | .05 |
| ❑ 255 Mikael Renberg | .30 | .14 |
| ❑ 256 Marty McSorley | .10 | .05 |
| ❑ 257 Joe Mullen | .15 | .07 |
| ❑ 258 Doug Brown | .10 | .05 |
| ❑ 259 Kjell Samuelsson | .10 | .05 |
| ❑ 260 Tom Barrasso | .15 | .07 |
| ❑ 261 Ron Francis | .15 | .07 |
| ❑ 262 Mario Lemieux | 1.50 | .70 |
| ❑ 263 Larry Murphy | .15 | .07 |
| ❑ 264 Ulf Samuelsson | .10 | .05 |
| ❑ 265 Kevin Stevens | .10 | .05 |
| ❑ 266 Martin Straka | .10 | .05 |
| ❑ 267 Rick Tocchet | .15 | .07 |
| ❑ 268 Bryan Trottier | .15 | .07 |
| ❑ 269 Markus Naslund | .10 | .05 |
| ❑ 270 Jaromir Jagr | 1.00 | .45 |
| ❑ 271 Martin Gelinas | .10 | .05 |
| ❑ 272 Adam Foote | .10 | .05 |
| ❑ 273 Curtis Leschyshyn | .10 | .05 |
| ❑ 274 Stephane Fiset | .15 | .07 |
| ❑ 275 Jocelyn Thibault | 1.25 | .55 |
| ❑ 276 Steve Duchesne | .10 | .05 |
| ❑ 277 Valeri Kamensky | .15 | .07 |
| ❑ 278 Andrei Kovalenko | .10 | .05 |
| ❑ 279 Owen Nolan | .15 | .07 |
| ❑ 280 Mike Ricci | .10 | .05 |
| ❑ 281 Martin Rucinsky | .10 | .05 |
| ❑ 282 Joe Sakic | .60 | .25 |
| ❑ 283 Mats Sundin | .15 | .07 |
| ❑ 284 Scott Young | .10 | .05 |
| ❑ 285 Claude Lapointe | .10 | .05 |
| ❑ 286 Brett Hull | .40 | .18 |
| ❑ 287 Vitali Karamnov | .10 | .05 |
| ❑ 288 Ron Sutter | .10 | .05 |
| ❑ 289 Garth Butcher | .10 | .05 |
| ❑ 290 Vitali Prokhorov | .10 | .05 |
| ❑ 291 Bret Hedican | .10 | .05 |
| ❑ 292 Tony Hrkac | .10 | .05 |
| ❑ 293 Jeff Brown | .10 | .05 |
| ❑ 294 Phil Housley | .15 | .07 |
| ❑ 295 Craig Janney | .15 | .07 |
| ❑ 296 Curtis Joseph | .30 | .14 |
| ❑ 297 Igor Korolev | .10 | .05 |
| ❑ 298 Kevin Miller | .10 | .05 |
| ❑ 299 Brendan Shanahan | .60 | .25 |
| ❑ 300 Jim Montgomery | .10 | .05 |
| ❑ 301 Gaetan Duchesne | .10 | .05 |
| ❑ 302 Jimmy Waite | .15 | .07 |
| ❑ 303 Jeff Norton | .10 | .05 |
| ❑ 304 Sergei Makarov | .10 | .05 |
| ❑ 305 Igor Larionov | .10 | .05 |
| ❑ 306 Mike Lalor | .10 | .05 |
| ❑ 307 Michal Sykora | .10 | .05 |
| ❑ 308 Pat Falloon | .10 | .05 |
| ❑ 309 Johan Garpenlov | .10 | .05 |
| ❑ 310 Rob Gaudreau | .10 | .05 |
| ❑ 311 Arturs Irbe | .15 | .07 |
| ❑ 312 Sandis Ozolinsh | .15 | .07 |
| ❑ 313 Doug Zmolek | .10 | .05 |
| ❑ 314 Mike Rathje | .10 | .05 |
| ❑ 315 Vlastimil Kroupa | .10 | .05 |
| ❑ 316 Daren Puppa | .15 | .07 |
| ❑ 317 Petr Klima | .10 | .05 |
| ❑ 318 Brent Gretzky | .10 | .05 |
| ❑ 319 Denis Savard | .15 | .07 |
| ❑ 320 Garard Gallant | .10 | .05 |
| ❑ 321 Joe Reekie | .10 | .05 |
| ❑ 322 Mikael Andersson | .10 | .05 |
| ❑ 323 Bill McDougall | .10 | .05 |
| ❑ 324 Brian Bradley | .10 | .05 |
| ❑ 325 Shawn Chambers | .10 | .05 |
| ❑ 326 Adam Creighton | .10 | .05 |
| ❑ 327 Roman Hamrlik | .15 | .07 |
| ❑ 328 John Tucker | .10 | .05 |
| ❑ 329 Rob Zamuner | .10 | .05 |
| ❑ 330 Chris Gratton | .15 | .07 |
| ❑ 331 Sylvain Lefebvre | .10 | .05 |
| ❑ 332 Nikolai Borschevsky | .10 | .05 |
| ❑ 333 Bob Rouse | .10 | .05 |
| ❑ 334 John Cullen | .10 | .05 |
| ❑ 335 Todd Gill | .10 | .05 |
| ❑ 336 Drake Berehowsky | .10 | .05 |
| ❑ 337 Wendel Clark | .15 | .07 |
| ❑ 338 Peter Zezel | .10 | .05 |
| ❑ 339 Rob Pearson | .10 | .05 |
| ❑ 340 Glenn Anderson | .15 | .07 |
| ❑ 341 Doug Gilmour | .30 | .14 |
| ❑ 342 Dave Andreychuk | .15 | .07 |
| ❑ 343 Felix Potvin | .30 | .14 |
| ❑ 344 David Ellett | .10 | .05 |
| ❑ 345 Alexei Kudashov | .10 | .05 |
| ❑ 346 Gino Odjick | .10 | .05 |
| ❑ 347 Jyrki Lumme | .10 | .05 |
| ❑ 348 Dana Murzyn | .10 | .05 |
| ❑ 349 Sergio Momesso | .10 | .05 |
| ❑ 350 Greg Adams | .10 | .05 |
| ❑ 351 Pavel Bure | .60 | .25 |
| ❑ 352 Geoff Courtnall | .10 | .05 |
| ❑ 353 Murray Craven | .10 | .05 |
| ❑ 354 Trevor Linden | .15 | .07 |
| ❑ 355 Kirk McLean | .15 | .07 |
| ❑ 356 Petr Nedved | .15 | .07 |
| ❑ 357 Cliff Ronning | .10 | .05 |
| ❑ 358 Jiri Slegr | .10 | .05 |
| ❑ 359 Kay Whitmore | .15 | .07 |
| ❑ 360 Gerald Diduck | .10 | .05 |
| ❑ 361 Pat Peake | .10 | .05 |
| ❑ 362 Dave Poulin | .10 | .05 |
| ❑ 363 Rick Tabaracci | .15 | .07 |
| ❑ 364 Jason Woolley | .10 | .05 |
| ❑ 365 Kelly Miller | .10 | .05 |
| ❑ 366 Peter Bondra | .30 | .14 |
| ❑ 367 Sylvain Cote | .10 | .05 |
| ❑ 368 Pat Elynuik | .10 | .05 |
| ❑ 369 Kevin Hatcher | .10 | .05 |
| ❑ 370 Dale Hunter | .10 | .05 |
| ❑ 371 Al Iafrate | .10 | .05 |
| ❑ 372 Calle Johansson | .10 | .05 |
| ❑ 373 Dimitri Khristich | .10 | .05 |
| ❑ 374 Michal Pivonka | .10 | .05 |
| ❑ 375 Mike Ridley | .10 | .05 |
| ❑ 376 Paul Ysebaert | .10 | .05 |
| ❑ 377 Stu Barnes | .10 | .05 |
| ❑ 378 Sergei Bautin | .10 | .05 |
| ❑ 379 Kris King | .10 | .05 |
| ❑ 380 Alexei Zhamnov | .15 | .07 |
| ❑ 381 Tie Domi | .15 | .07 |
| ❑ 382 Bob Essensa | .15 | .07 |
| ❑ 383 Nelson Emerson | .10 | .05 |
| ❑ 384 Boris Mironov | .10 | .05 |
| ❑ 385 Teppo Numminen | .10 | .05 |
| ❑ 386 Fredrik Olausson | .10 | .05 |
| ❑ 387 Teemu Selanne | .75 | .35 |
| ❑ 388 Darrin Shannon | .10 | .05 |
| ❑ 389 Thomas Steen | .10 | .05 |
| ❑ 390 Keith Tkachuk | .40 | .18 |
| ❑ 391 Opening Night Panthers | .75 | .35 |
| ❑ 392 Opening Night-Ducks | .75 | .35 |
| ❑ 393 Alexandre Daigle Chris Pronger Chris Gratton | .15 | .07 |
| ❑ 394 Teemu Selanne Joe Juneau RB | .40 | .18 |
| ❑ 395 Wayne Gretzky Luc Robitaille | .75 | .35 |
| ❑ 396 Inserts Checklist | .10 | .05 |
| ❑ 397 Atlantic Div. Checklist | .10 | .05 |
| ❑ 398 Northeast Div. Checklist | .10 | .05 |
| ❑ 399 Central Div. Checklist | .10 | .05 |
| ❑ 400 Pacific Div. Checklist | .10 | .05 |
| ❑ 401 Garry Valk | .10 | .05 |
| ❑ 402 Al Iarante | .10 | .05 |
| ❑ 403 David Reid | .10 | .05 |
| ❑ 404 Jason Dawe | .10 | .05 |
| ❑ 405 Craig Muni | .10 | .05 |
| ❑ 406 Dan Keczmer | .10 | .05 |
| ❑ 407 Michael Nylander | .10 | .05 |
| ❑ 408 James Patrick | .10 | .05 |
| ❑ 409 Andrei Trefilov | .10 | .05 |
| ❑ 410 Zarley Zalapski | .10 | .05 |
| ❑ 411 Tony Amonte | .15 | .07 |
| ❑ 412 Keith Carney | .10 | .05 |
| ❑ 413 Randy Cunneyworth | .10 | .05 |
| ❑ 414 Ivan Droppa | .10 | .05 |
| ❑ 415 Gary Suter | .10 | .05 |
| ❑ 416 Eric Weinrich | .10 | .05 |
| ❑ 417 Paul Ysebaert | .10 | .05 |
| ❑ 418 Richard Matvichuk | .10 | .05 |
| ❑ 419 Alan May | .10 | .05 |
| ❑ 420 Darcy Wakaluk | .15 | .07 |
| ❑ 421 Micah Aivazoff | .10 | .05 |
| ❑ 422 Terry Carkner | .10 | .05 |
| ❑ 423 Kris Draper | .10 | .05 |
| ❑ 424 Chris Osgood | 2.00 | .90 |
| ❑ 425 Keith Primeau | .15 | .07 |
| ❑ 426 Bob Beers | .10 | .05 |
| ❑ 427 Ilya Byakin | .10 | .05 |
| ❑ 428 Kirk Maltby | .10 | .05 |
| ❑ 429 Boris Mironov | .10 | .05 |
| ❑ 430 Fredrik Olausson | .10 | .05 |
| ❑ 431 Peter White | .10 | .05 |
| ❑ 432 Stu Barnes | .10 | .05 |
| ❑ 433 Mike Foligno | .10 | .05 |
| ❑ 434 Bob Kudelski | .10 | .05 |
| ❑ 435 Geoff Smith | .10 | .05 |
| ❑ 436 Igor Chibirev | .10 | .05 |
| ❑ 437 Ted Drury | .10 | .05 |
| ❑ 438 Alexander Godynyuk | .10 | .05 |
| ❑ 439 Frank Kucera | .10 | .05 |
| ❑ 440 Jocelyn Lemieux | .10 | .05 |
| ❑ 441 Brian Propp | .10 | .05 |
| ❑ 442 Paul Ranheim | .10 | .05 |
| ❑ 443 Jeff Reese | .10 | .05 |
| ❑ 444 Kevin Smyth | .10 | .05 |
| ❑ 445 Jim Storm | .10 | .05 |
| ❑ 446 Phil Crowe | .10 | .05 |
| ❑ 447 Marty McSorley | .10 | .05 |
| ❑ 448 Keith Redmond | .10 | .05 |
| ❑ 449 Dixon Ward | .10 | .05 |
| ❑ 450 Guy Carbonneau | .10 | .05 |
| ❑ 451 Mike Keane | .10 | .05 |
| ❑ 452 Oleg Petrov | .10 | .05 |
| ❑ 453 Ron Tugnutt | .15 | .07 |
| ❑ 454 Randy McKay | .10 | .05 |
| ❑ 455 Jaroslav Modry | .10 | .05 |
| ❑ 456 Yan Kaminsky | .10 | .05 |
| ❑ 457 Marty McInnis | .10 | .05 |
| ❑ 458 Jamie McLennan | .30 | .14 |
| ❑ 459 Zigmund Palffy | .30 | .14 |
| ❑ 460 Glenn Anderson | .15 | .07 |
| ❑ 461 Steve Larmer | .15 | .07 |
| ❑ 462 Craig MacTavish | .10 | .05 |
| ❑ 463 Stephane Matteau | .10 | .05 |
| ❑ 464 Brian Noonan | .10 | .05 |
| ❑ 465 Mattias Norstrom | .10 | .05 |
| ❑ 466 Scott Levins | .10 | .05 |
| ❑ 467 Derek Mayer | .10 | .05 |
| ❑ 468 Andy Schneider | .10 | .05 |
| ❑ 469 Todd Hlushko | .10 | .05 |
| ❑ 470 Stewart Malgunas | .10 | .05 |
| ❑ 471 Justin Duberman | .10 | .05 |
| ❑ 472 Ladislav Karabin | .10 | .05 |
| ❑ 473 Shawn McEachern | .10 | .05 |
| ❑ 474 Ed Patterson | .10 | .05 |
| ❑ 475 Tomas Sandstrom | .10 | .05 |
| ❑ 476 Bob Bassen | .10 | .05 |
| ❑ 477 Garth Butcher | .10 | .05 |
| ❑ 478 Iain Fraser | .10 | .05 |
| ❑ 479 Mike McKee | .10 | .05 |
| ❑ 480 Dwayne Norris | .10 | .05 |
| ❑ 481 Garth Snow | .40 | .18 |
| ❑ 482 Ron Sutter | .10 | .05 |
| ❑ 483 Kelly Chase | .10 | .05 |
| ❑ 484 Steve Duchesne | .10 | .05 |
| ❑ 485 Daniel Laperrire | .10 | .05 |
| ❑ 486 Petr Nedved | .15 | .07 |
| ❑ 487 Peter Stastny | .15 | .07 |

| | | |
|---|---|---|
| ❑ 488 Ulf Dahlen | .10 | .05 |
| ❑ 489 Todd Elik | .10 | .05 |
| ❑ 490 Andrei Nazarov | .10 | .05 |
| ❑ 491 Danton Cole | .10 | .05 |
| ❑ 492 Chris Joseph | .10 | .05 |
| ❑ 493 Chris LiPuma | .10 | .05 |
| ❑ 494 Mike Gartner | .15 | .07 |
| ❑ 495 Mark Greig | .10 | .05 |
| ❑ 496 David Harlock | .10 | .05 |
| ❑ 497 Matt Martin | .10 | .05 |
| ❑ 498 Shawn Antoski | .10 | .05 |
| ❑ 499 Jeff Brown | .10 | .05 |
| ❑ 500 Jimmy Carson | .10 | .05 |
| ❑ 501 Martin Gelinas | .10 | .05 |
| ❑ 502 Yevgeny Namestnikov | .10 | .05 |
| ❑ 503 Randy Burridge | .10 | .05 |
| ❑ 504 Joe Juneau | .15 | .07 |
| ❑ 505 Kevin Kaminski | .10 | .05 |
| ❑ 506 Arto Blomsten | .10 | .05 |
| ❑ 507 Tim Cheveldae | .15 | .07 |
| ❑ 508 Dallas Drake | .10 | .05 |
| ❑ 509 Dave Manson | .10 | .05 |
| ❑ 510 Update Checklist | .10 | .05 |

## 1993-94 Donruss Elite

These 15 cards feature on their fronts color player photos framed by diamond-shaped starburst designs set within dark marbleized inner borders and prismatic foil outer borders. The player's name appears within the lower prismatic foil margin. The back carries the player's name, career highlights, and a color head shot, all set on a dark marbleized background framed by a silver border. The cards are numbered on the back. The 10 first-series Elite cards (1-10) were random inserts in '93-94 Donruss Series 1 packs. The five Elite Update cards (U1-U5) were randomly inserted in Donruss Update packs. All Elite cards are individually numbered on the back and have a production limited to 10,000 of each.

| | MINT | NRMT |
|---|---|---|
| COMPLETE SET (10) | 175.00 | 80.00 |
| COMMON CARD (1-10) | 6.00 | 2.70 |
| COMPLETE UPDATE SET (5) | 50.00 | 22.00 |
| COMMON UPDATE (U1-U5) | 10.00 | 4.50 |

| | | |
|---|---|---|
| ❑ 1 Mario Lemieux | 30.00 | 13.50 |
| ❑ 2 Alexandre Daigle | 6.00 | 2.70 |
| ❑ 3 Teemu Selanne | 20.00 | 9.00 |
| ❑ 4 Eric Lindros | 25.00 | 11.00 |
| ❑ 5 Brett Hull | 10.00 | 4.50 |
| ❑ 6 Jeremy Roenick | 12.00 | 5.50 |
| ❑ 7 Doug Gilmour | 6.00 | 2.70 |
| ❑ 8 Alexander Mogilny | 6.00 | 2.70 |
| ❑ 9 Patrick Roy | 30.00 | 13.50 |
| ❑ 10 Wayne Gretzky | 40.00 | 18.00 |
| ❑ U1 Mikael Renberg | 10.00 | 4.50 |
| ❑ U2 Sergei Fedorov | 20.00 | 9.00 |
| ❑ U3 Felix Potvin | 10.00 | 4.50 |
| ❑ U4 Cam Neely | 10.00 | 4.50 |
| ❑ U5 Alexei Yashin | 10.00 | 4.50 |

## 1993-94 Donruss Ice Kings

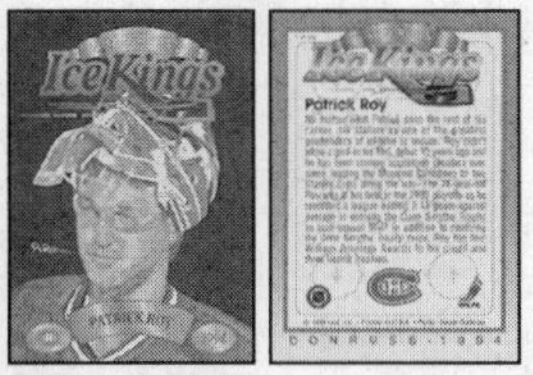

Randomly inserted in Series 1 packs, these 10 cards feature on their fronts borderless color player drawings by noted sports artist Dick Perez. The player's name, his team's logo, and the year, 1994, appear within a blue banner near the bottom. The blue-bordered back carries the player's career highlights on a ghosted representation of a hockey rink. The cards are numbered on the back as "X of 10."

| | MINT | NRMT |
|---|---|---|
| COMPLETE SET (10) | 30.00 | 13.50 |
| COMMON CARD (1-10) | 1.00 | .45 |

| | | |
|---|---|---|
| ❑ 1 Patrick Roy | 5.00 | 2.20 |
| ❑ 2 Pat LaFontaine | 1.00 | .45 |
| ❑ 3 Jaromir Jagr | 3.00 | 1.35 |
| ❑ 4 Wayne Gretzky | 6.00 | 2.70 |
| ❑ 5 Chris Chelios | 2.50 | 1.10 |
| ❑ 6 Felix Potvin | 1.50 | .70 |
| ❑ 7 Mario Lemieux | 5.00 | 2.20 |
| ❑ 8 Pavel Bure | 2.00 | .90 |
| ❑ 9 Eric Lindros | 5.00 | 2.20 |
| ❑ 10 Teemu Selanne | 2.50 | 1.10 |

## 1993-94 Donruss Rated Rookies

Randomly inserted in Series 1 packs, these 15 cards have borderless fronts that feature color player action shots on motion streaked backgrounds. The player's name appears at the top. On its right side, the black horizontal back carries a color player action cutout superposed upon his team's logo. Biography and career highlights are shown alongside on the left. The cards are numbered on the back as "X of 15."

| | MINT | NRMT |
|---|---|---|
| COMPLETE SET (15) | 25.00 | 11.00 |
| COMMON CARD (1-15) | .50 | .23 |

| | | |
|---|---|---|
| ❑ 1 Alexandre Daigle | 2.00 | .90 |
| ❑ 2 Chris Gratton | 2.00 | .90 |
| ❑ 3 Chris Pronger | 2.00 | .90 |
| ❑ 4 Rob Niedermayer | 2.00 | .90 |
| ❑ 5 Mikael Renberg | 2.00 | .90 |
| ❑ 6 Jarkko Varvio | .50 | .23 |
| ❑ 7 Alexei Yashin | 2.00 | .90 |
| ❑ 8 Markus Naslund | .50 | .23 |
| ❑ 9 Boris Mironov | .50 | .23 |
| ❑ 10 Martin Brodeur | 7.00 | 3.10 |
| ❑ 11 Jocelyn Thibault | 5.00 | 2.20 |
| ❑ 12 Jason Arnott | 4.00 | 1.80 |
| ❑ 13 Jim Montgomery | .50 | .23 |
| ❑ 14 Ted Drury | .50 | .23 |
| ❑ 15 Roman Oksiuta | .50 | .23 |

## 1993-94 Donruss Special Print

Randomly inserted in Series 1 packs, these 26 cards feature on their fronts color player action shots that are borderless, except at the bottom, where the black edge carries the player's name in white cursive lettering. The prismatic foil set logo rests in a lower corner. The words "Special Print 1 of 20,000" appear in prismatic foil across the top. The backs, some of which are horizontal, carry another borderless color player action shot. The player's name, team, position, and biography are shown within a black rectangle on one side. His statistics appear in ghosted strips below or alongside. The cards are numbered, or rather lettered (A-Z), on the back. Two additional unnumbered special print cards (Robitaille WC and Lemieux EC) could be found at the rate of 1:360 packs.

| | MINT | NRMT |
|---|---|---|
| COMPLETE SET (26) | 150.00 | 70.00 |
| COMMON CARD (A-Z) | 1.00 | .45 |

| | | |
|---|---|---|
| ❑ A Ron Tugnutt | 1.50 | .70 |
| ❑ B Adam Oates | 1.50 | .70 |
| ❑ C Alexander Mogilny | 1.50 | .70 |
| ❑ D Theoren Fleury | 1.50 | .70 |
| ❑ E Jeremy Roenick | 3.00 | 1.35 |
| ❑ F Mike Modano | 1.50 | .70 |
| ❑ G Steve Yzerman | 3.00 | 1.35 |
| ❑ H Jason Arnott | 3.00 | 1.35 |
| ❑ I Rob Niedermayer | 1.50 | .70 |
| ❑ J Chris Pronger | 1.50 | .70 |
| ❑ K Wayne Gretzky | 3.00 | 1.35 |
| ❑ L Patrick Roy | 3.00 | 1.35 |
| ❑ M Scott Niedermayer | 1.50 | .70 |
| ❑ N Pierre Turgeon | 1.50 | .70 |
| ❑ O Mark Messier | 3.00 | 1.35 |
| ❑ P Alexandre Daigle | 1.50 | .70 |
| ❑ Q Eric Lindros | 3.00 | 1.35 |
| ❑ R Mario Lemieux | 3.00 | 1.35 |
| ❑ S Mats Sundin | 1.50 | .70 |
| ❑ T Pat Falloon | 1.00 | .45 |
| ❑ U Brett Hull | 3.00 | 1.35 |
| ❑ V Chris Gratton | 1.50 | .70 |
| ❑ W Felix Potvin | 3.00 | 1.35 |
| ❑ X Pavel Bure | 3.00 | 1.35 |
| ❑ Y Al Iafrate | 1.00 | .45 |
| ❑ Z Teemu Selanne | 3.00 | 1.35 |
| ❑ NNO Luc Robitaille WC | 8.00 | 3.60 |
| ❑ NNO Mario Lemieux EC | 30.00 | 13.50 |

## 1993-94 Donruss Team Canada

One of these 22 (or one of the 22 Team USA) cards were inserted in every 1993-94 Donruss Update pack. The front of each card features a player action cutout set on a red metallic background highlighted by a world map. The player's name appears at the upper left. The horizontal back carries a color player action shot on the right side. Below the photo are the player's statistics from his 1994 World Junior Championships play. On the left side are the player's name, position, biography, and NHL status. The cards are numbered on the back as "X of 22." The unnumbered checklist carries the 22 Team Canada cards, as well as the 22 Team USA cards.

| | MINT | NRMT |
|---|---|---|
| COMPLETE SET (22) | 10.00 | 4.50 |
| COMMON CARD (1-22) | .50 | .23 |

| | | |
|---|---|---|
| ❑ 1 Jason Allison | 2.50 | 1.10 |
| ❑ 2 Chris Armstrong | .50 | .23 |
| ❑ 3 Drew Bannister | .50 | .23 |
| ❑ 4 Jason Botterill | .50 | .23 |
| ❑ 5 Joel Bouchard | .50 | .23 |
| ❑ 6 Curtis Bowen | .50 | .23 |
| ❑ 7 Anson Carter | 1.00 | .45 |
| ❑ 8 Brandon Convery | .50 | .23 |
| ❑ 9 Yannick Dube | 1.00 | .45 |
| ❑ 10 Manny Fernandez | 1.00 | .45 |
| ❑ 11 Jeff Friesen | 2.00 | .90 |
| ❑ 12 Aaron Gavey | .50 | .23 |
| ❑ 13 Martin Gendron | .50 | .23 |
| ❑ 14 Rick Girard | .50 | .23 |
| ❑ 15 Todd Harvey | 1.00 | .45 |
| ❑ 16 Bryan McCabe | 1.00 | .45 |
| ❑ 17 Marty Murray | 1.00 | .45 |
| ❑ 18 Mike Peca | 1.50 | .70 |
| ❑ 19 Nick Stajduhar | .50 | .23 |
| ❑ 20 Jamie Storr | 1.00 | .45 |
| ❑ 21 Brent Tully | .50 | .23 |
| ❑ 22 Brendan Witt | .75 | .35 |
| ❑ NNO WJC Checklist | 2.00 | .90 |

## 1993-94 Donruss Team USA

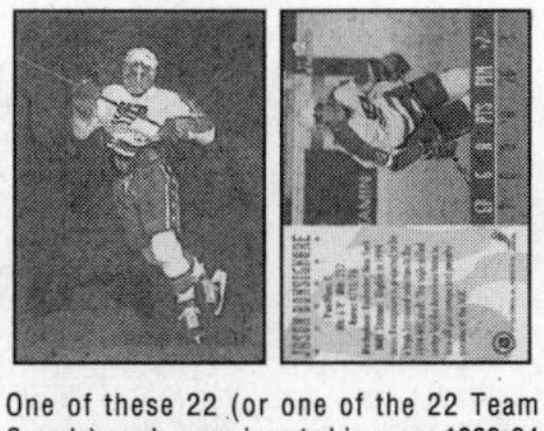

One of these 22 (or one of the 22 Team Canada) cards were inserted in every 1993-94 Donruss Update pack. The front of each card features a player action cutout set on a blue metallic background highlighted by a world map. The player's name appears at the upper left. The horizontal back carries a color player action shot on the right side. Below the photo are the player's statistics from his 1994 World Junior Championships play. On the left side are the player's name, position, biography, and NHL status. The cards are numbered on the back as "X of 22." The unnumbered checklist carries the 22 Team Canada cards, as well as the 22 Team USA cards.

| | MINT | NRMT |
|---|---|---|
| COMPLETE SET (22) | 8.00 | 3.60 |
| COMMON CARD (1-22) | .50 | .23 |

| | | |
|---|---|---|
| ❑ 1 Kevyn Adams | .50 | .23 |
| ❑ 2 Jason Bonsignore | .75 | .35 |
| ❑ 3 Andy Brink | .50 | .23 |
| ❑ 4 Jon Coleman | .50 | .23 |
| ❑ 5 Adam Deadmarsh | 1.50 | .70 |
| ❑ 6 Aaron Ellis | .50 | .23 |
| ❑ 7 John Emmons | .50 | .23 |
| ❑ 8 Ashlin Halfnight | .50 | .23 |
| ❑ 9 Kevin Hilton | .50 | .23 |
| ❑ 10 Jason Karmanos | .50 | .23 |
| ❑ 11 Toby Kvalevog | .50 | .23 |
| ❑ 12 Bob Lachance | .50 | .23 |
| ❑ 13 Jamie Langenbrunner | 1.50 | .70 |
| ❑ 14 Jason McBain | .50 | .23 |
| ❑ 15 Chris O'Sullivan | .50 | .23 |
| ❑ 16 Jay Pandolfo | .50 | .23 |
| ❑ 17 Richard Park | .75 | .35 |
| ❑ 18 Deron Quint | .75 | .35 |
| ❑ 19 Ryan Sittler | .50 | .23 |
| ❑ 20 Blake Sloan | .50 | .23 |
| ❑ 21 John Varga | .50 | .23 |
| ❑ 22 David Wilkie | .75 | .35 |
| ❑ NNO WJC Checklist | 2.00 | .90 |

## 1994-95 Donruss

This 330-card standard-size set was issued in one series. Cards were issued in 12-card hobby packs and 18-card jumbo packs. Fronts feature a near full-bleed design, other than the bottom right corner which displays player name, set name, and position stamped in a silver foil sunburst design. This silver foil area is very difficult to read. Backs feature two additional photos, team logo, and single season stats. Rookie Cards in the set include Mariusz Czerkawski, Mikhail Shtalenkov and John Gruden.

| | MINT | NRMT |
|---|---|---|
| COMPLETE SET (330) | 15.00 | 6.75 |
| COMMON CARD (1-330) | .10 | .05 |

| | | |
|---|---|---|
| ❑ 1 Steve Yzerman | 1.00 | .45 |
| ❑ 2 Paul Ysebaert | .10 | .05 |
| ❑ 3 Doug Weight | .15 | .07 |
| ❑ 4 Trevor Kidd | .15 | .07 |
| ❑ 5 Mario Lemieux | 1.50 | .70 |
| ❑ 6 Andrei Kovalenko | .10 | .05 |
| ❑ 7 Arturs Irbe | .15 | .07 |
| ❑ 8 Doug Gilmour | .30 | .14 |
| ❑ 9 Mark Messier | .40 | .18 |
| ❑ 10 Milos Holan | .10 | .05 |
| ❑ 11 Kevin Miller | .10 | .05 |
| ❑ 12 Felix Potvin | .30 | .14 |
| ❑ 13 Josef Beranek | .10 | .05 |
| ❑ 14 Mikael Andersson | .10 | .05 |
| ❑ 15 Stephane Matteau | .10 | .05 |
| ❑ 16 Todd Simon | .10 | .05 |
| ❑ 17 Darcy Wakaluk | .15 | .07 |
| ❑ 18 Kelly Buchberger | .10 | .05 |
| ❑ 19 Pavel Bure | .60 | .25 |
| ❑ 20 Dave Lowry | .10 | .05 |
| ❑ 21 Bryan Smolinski | .10 | .05 |
| ❑ 22 Kirk McLean | .15 | .07 |
| ❑ 23 Pierre Turgeon | .15 | .07 |
| ❑ 24 Martin Brodeur | .75 | .35 |
| ❑ 25 Jason Arnott | .15 | .07 |
| ❑ 26 Steve Dubinsky | .10 | .05 |
| ❑ 27 Larry Murphy | .15 | .07 |
| ❑ 28 Craig Janney | .15 | .07 |
| ❑ 29 Patrik Carnback | .10 | .05 |
| ❑ 30 Derek King | .10 | .05 |
| ❑ 31 Peter Bondra | .30 | .14 |
| ❑ 32 Jason Bowen | .10 | .05 |
| ❑ 33 Maxim Bets | .10 | .05 |
| ❑ 34 Matt Martin | .10 | .05 |
| ❑ 35 Jeff Hackett | .15 | .07 |
| ❑ 36 Kevin Dineen | .10 | .05 |
| ❑ 37 Trent Klatt | .10 | .05 |
| ❑ 38 Joe Murphy | .10 | .05 |
| ❑ 39 Sandy McCarthy | .10 | .05 |
| ❑ 40 Brian Bradley | .10 | .05 |
| ❑ 41 Scott Lachance | .10 | .05 |
| ❑ 42 Scott Mellanby | .15 | .07 |
| ❑ 43 Adam Graves | .15 | .07 |
| ❑ 44 Dale Hawerchuk | .15 | .07 |
| ❑ 45 Owen Nolan | .15 | .07 |
| ❑ 46 Keith Primeau | .15 | .07 |
| ❑ 47 Jim Dowd | .10 | .05 |
| ❑ 48 Dan Plante | .10 | .05 |
| ❑ 49 Rick Tabaracci | .15 | .07 |
| ❑ 50 Geoff Courtnall | .10 | .05 |
| ❑ 51 Markus Naslund | .10 | .05 |
| ❑ 52 Kelly Miller | .10 | .05 |
| ❑ 53 Kirk Maltby | .10 | .05 |
| ❑ 54 Paul Coffey | .30 | .14 |
| ❑ 55 Gord Murphy | .10 | .05 |
| ❑ 56 Joe Nieuwendyk | .15 | .07 |
| ❑ 57 Ulf Dahlen | .10 | .05 |
| ❑ 58 Dmitri Mironov | .10 | .05 |
| ❑ 59 Kevin Smyth | .10 | .05 |
| ❑ 60 Tie Domi | .15 | .07 |
| ❑ 61 Oleg Petrov | .10 | .05 |
| ❑ 62 Bill Guerin | .10 | .05 |
| ❑ 63 Alexei Yashin | .15 | .07 |
| ❑ 64 Joe Sacco | .10 | .05 |
| ❑ 65 Aris Brimanis | .10 | .05 |
| ❑ 66 Randy Burridge | .10 | .05 |
| ❑ 67 Neal Broten | .15 | .07 |
| ❑ 68 Ray Bourque | .30 | .14 |
| ❑ 69 Ron Tugnutt | .15 | .07 |
| ❑ 70 Darryl Sydor | .10 | .05 |
| ❑ 71 Jocelyn Thibault | .30 | .14 |
| ❑ 72 Shawn Chambers | .10 | .05 |
| ❑ 73 Alexei Zhamnov | .15 | .07 |
| ❑ 74 Michael Nylander | .10 | .05 |
| ❑ 75 Travis Green | .15 | .07 |
| ❑ 76 Brad May | .15 | .07 |
| ❑ 77 Geoff Sanderson | .15 | .07 |
| ❑ 78 Derek Plante | .10 | .05 |
| ❑ 79 Stephane Richer | .15 | .07 |
| ❑ 80 Rod Brind'Amour | .15 | .07 |
| ❑ 81 Guy Hebert | .15 | .07 |
| ❑ 82 Claude Lemieux | .15 | .07 |
| ❑ 83 Pat Falloon | .10 | .05 |
| ❑ 84 Alexei Kudashov | .10 | .05 |
| ❑ 85 Andrei Lomakin | .10 | .05 |
| ❑ 86 Dino Ciccarelli | .15 | .07 |
| ❑ 87 John Tucker | .10 | .05 |
| ❑ 88 Jamie McLennan | .10 | .05 |
| ❑ 89 Peter Taglianetti | .10 | .05 |
| ❑ 90 Bobby Holik | .10 | .05 |
| ❑ 91 Sergei Krivokrasov | .10 | .05 |
| ❑ 92 Alexander Mogilny | .15 | .07 |
| ❑ 93 Jari Kurri | .15 | .07 |
| ❑ 94 Dominik Hasek | .75 | .35 |
| ❑ 95 Shawn McEachern | .10 | .05 |
| ❑ 96 Bob Corkum | .10 | .05 |
| ❑ 97 Dimitri Filimonov | .10 | .05 |
| ❑ 98 John LeClair | .50 | .23 |
| ❑ 99 Theoren Fleury | .15 | .07 |
| ❑ 100 Daren Puppa | .15 | .07 |
| ❑ 101 Greg Adams | .10 | .05 |
| ❑ 102 Joel Otto | .10 | .05 |
| ❑ 103 Sergei Makarov | .10 | .05 |
| ❑ 104 Mike Ricci | .10 | .05 |
| ❑ 105 Sylvain Turgeon | .10 | .05 |
| ❑ 106 Igor Larionov | .10 | .05 |
| ❑ 107 Tony Amonte | .15 | .07 |
| ❑ 108 Andy Moog | .15 | .07 |
| ❑ 109 Jeff Brown | .10 | .05 |
| ❑ 110 Checklist 1-83 | .10 | .05 |
| ❑ 111 Mike Gartner | .15 | .07 |
| ❑ 112 Craig Simpson | .10 | .05 |
| ❑ 113 Rob Niedermayer | .15 | .07 |
| ❑ 114 Robert Kron | .10 | .05 |
| ❑ 115 Jason York | .10 | .05 |
| ❑ 116 Valeri Kamensky | .15 | .07 |
| ❑ 117 Ray Whitney | .10 | .05 |
| ❑ 118 Chris Chelios | .30 | .14 |
| ❑ 119 Scott Levins | .10 | .05 |
| ❑ 120 Sandis Ozolinsh | .15 | .07 |
| ❑ 121 Mark Recchi | .15 | .07 |
| ❑ 122 Ron Francis | .15 | .07 |
| ❑ 123 Dean McAmmond | .10 | .05 |
| ❑ 124 Terry Yake | .10 | .05 |
| ❑ 125 Sergei Nemchinov | .10 | .05 |
| ❑ 126 Vitali Prokhorov | .10 | .05 |
| ❑ 127 Wayne Gretzky | 2.00 | .90 |
| ❑ 128 Roman Hamrlik | .15 | .07 |
| ❑ 129 Jarkko Varvio | .10 | .05 |
| ❑ 130 Brian Skrudland | .10 | .05 |
| ❑ 131 Murray Craven | .10 | .05 |
| ❑ 132 Jeff Norton | .10 | .05 |
| ❑ 133 Pavol Demitra | .10 | .05 |
| ❑ 134 Mike Keane | .10 | .05 |
| ❑ 135 Paul Cavallini | .10 | .05 |
| ❑ 136 Richard Smehlik | .10 | .05 |
| ❑ 137 Eric Lindros | 1.25 | .55 |
| ❑ 138 Mariusz Czerkawski | .10 | .05 |
| ❑ 139 Darrin Shannon | .10 | .05 |
| ❑ 140 Brian Noonan | .10 | .05 |
| ❑ 141 Joe Sakic | .60 | .25 |
| ❑ 142 Steve Thomas | .10 | .05 |
| ❑ 143 Gary Roberts | .10 | .05 |
| ❑ 144 Patrick Poulin | .10 | .05 |
| ❑ 145 Tony Granato | .10 | .05 |
| ❑ 146 Donald Brashear | .10 | .05 |
| ❑ 147 Ron Hextall | .15 | .07 |
| ❑ 148 Corey Millen | .10 | .05 |
| ❑ 149 Dale Hunter | .10 | .05 |
| ❑ 150 Greg Johnson | .10 | .05 |
| ❑ 151 John MacLean | .15 | .07 |
| ❑ 152 Brian Leetch | .30 | .14 |
| ❑ 153 Sylvain Cote | .10 | .05 |
| ❑ 154 Thomas Steen | .10 | .05 |
| ❑ 155 Ted Donato | .10 | .05 |
| ❑ 156 Nathan Lafayette | .10 | .05 |
| ❑ 157 Kelly Chase | .10 | .05 |
| ❑ 158 Sean Burke | .15 | .07 |
| ❑ 159 Jaromir Jagr | 1.00 | .45 |
| ❑ 160 Checklist 84-166 | .10 | .05 |
| ❑ 161 Scott Niedermayer | .10 | .05 |
| ❑ 162 Ray Ferraro | .10 | .05 |
| ❑ 163 Todd Elik | .10 | .05 |
| ❑ 164 Dave Gagner | .15 | .07 |
| ❑ 165 Mike Richter | .30 | .14 |
| ❑ 166 Garry Galley | .10 | .05 |
| ❑ 167 Russ Courtnall | .10 | .05 |
| ❑ 168 Marty McSorley | .10 | .05 |
| ❑ 169 Robert Reichel | .10 | .05 |
| ❑ 170 Mike Rathje | .10 | .05 |
| ❑ 171 Bill Ranford | .15 | .07 |
| ❑ 172 Danton Cole | .10 | .05 |
| ❑ 173 Sergei Fedorov | .60 | .25 |
| ❑ 174 Brendan Shanahan | .60 | .25 |
| ❑ 175 Byron Dafoe | 1.25 | .55 |
| ❑ 176 John Vanbiesbrouck | .50 | .23 |
| ❑ 177 Eric Desjardins | .10 | .05 |
| ❑ 178 Andrew Cassels | .10 | .05 |
| ❑ 179 John Gruden | .10 | .05 |
| ❑ 180 Slava Kozlov | .15 | .07 |
| ❑ 181 Trevor Linden | .15 | .07 |
| ❑ 182 Kris Draper | .10 | .05 |
| ❑ 183 Steve Smith | .10 | .05 |
| ❑ 184 Andre Faust | .10 | .05 |
| ❑ 185 James Patrick | .10 | .05 |
| ❑ 186 Ted Drury | .10 | .05 |
| ❑ 187 Dan Laperriere | .10 | .05 |
| ❑ 188 Benoit Hogue | .10 | .05 |
| ❑ 189 Chris Gratton | .15 | .07 |
| ❑ 190 Jyrki Lumme | .10 | .05 |
| ❑ 191 Peter Stastny | .15 | .07 |
| ❑ 192 Keith Tkachuk | .40 | .18 |
| ❑ 193 Mike Modano | .40 | .18 |
| ❑ 194 Nicklas Lidstrom | .15 | .07 |
| ❑ 195 Pierre Sevigny | .10 | .05 |
| ❑ 196 Scott Pearson | .10 | .05 |
| ❑ 197 Jaroslav Modry | .10 | .05 |

| | | |
|---|---|---|
| ❑ 198 Garry Valk | .10 | .05 |
| ❑ 199 Kevin Hatcher | .10 | .05 |
| ❑ 200 Denis Tsygurov | .10 | .05 |
| ❑ 201 Paul Laus | .10 | .05 |
| ❑ 202 Alexander Godynyuk | .10 | .05 |
| ❑ 203 Brian Bellows | .10 | .05 |
| ❑ 204 Michal Sykora | .10 | .05 |
| ❑ 205 Al Iafrate | .10 | .05 |
| ❑ 206 Mark Tinordi | .10 | .05 |
| ❑ 207 Kelly Hrudey | .15 | .07 |
| ❑ 208 Tom Barrasso | .15 | .07 |
| ❑ 209 Craig Billington | .15 | .07 |
| ❑ 210 Teemu Selanne | .60 | .25 |
| ❑ 211 Alexandre Daigle | .10 | .05 |
| ❑ 212 Grant Fuhr | .15 | .07 |
| ❑ 213 Doug Brown | .10 | .05 |
| ❑ 214 Tim Sweeney | .10 | .05 |
| ❑ 215 Chris Pronger | .15 | .07 |
| ❑ 216 Alexei Gusarov | .10 | .05 |
| ❑ 217 Gary Suter | .10 | .05 |
| ❑ 218 Boris Mironov | .10 | .05 |
| ❑ 219 Sergei Zubov | .10 | .05 |
| ❑ 220 Checklist 167-249 | .10 | .05 |
| ❑ 221 Shayne Corson | .10 | .05 |
| ❑ 222 Jeremy Roenick | .30 | .14 |
| ❑ 223 John Druce | .10 | .05 |
| ❑ 224 Martin Straka | .10 | .05 |
| ❑ 225 Stephane Fiset | .15 | .07 |
| ❑ 226 Vincent Damphousse | .15 | .07 |
| ❑ 227 Bob Kudelski | .10 | .05 |
| ❑ 228 German Titov | .10 | .05 |
| ❑ 229 Kevin Stevens | .10 | .05 |
| ❑ 230 Dave Ellett | .10 | .05 |
| ❑ 231 Steve Larmer | .15 | .07 |
| ❑ 232 Glen Wesley | .10 | .05 |
| ❑ 233 Mathieu Schneider | .10 | .05 |
| ❑ 234 Stephan Lebeau | .10 | .05 |
| ❑ 235 Mark Fitzpatrick | .15 | .07 |
| ❑ 236 Mikael Renberg | .15 | .07 |
| ❑ 237 Darren McCarty | .10 | .05 |
| ❑ 238 Todd Nelson | .10 | .05 |
| ❑ 239 Igor Korolev | .10 | .05 |
| ❑ 240 Warren Rychel | .10 | .05 |
| ❑ 241 Gino Odjick | .10 | .05 |
| ❑ 242 Dave Manson | .10 | .05 |
| ❑ 243 Calle Johansson | .10 | .05 |
| ❑ 244 Andrei Trefilov | .10 | .05 |
| ❑ 245 Jason Dawe | .10 | .05 |
| ❑ 246 Glen Murray | .10 | .05 |
| ❑ 247 Jeff Shantz | .10 | .05 |
| ❑ 248 Zarley Zalapski | .10 | .05 |
| ❑ 249 Petr Klima | .10 | .05 |
| ❑ 250 Patrice Brisebois | .10 | .05 |
| ❑ 251 Chris Osgood | .50 | .23 |
| ❑ 252 Darius Kasparaitis | .10 | .05 |
| ❑ 253 Chris Joseph | .10 | .05 |
| ❑ 254 Glenn Anderson | .15 | .07 |
| ❑ 255 Kirk Muller | .10 | .05 |
| ❑ 256 Jason Smith | .10 | .05 |
| ❑ 257 Bob Bassen | .10 | .05 |
| ❑ 258 Joe Juneau | .15 | .07 |
| ❑ 259 Igor Kravchuk | .10 | .05 |
| ❑ 260 John Lilley | .10 | .05 |
| ❑ 261 Philippe Bozon | .10 | .05 |
| ❑ 262 Scott Stevens | .15 | .07 |
| ❑ 263 Dominic Roussel | .15 | .07 |
| ❑ 264 Dimitri Khristich | .10 | .05 |
| ❑ 265 Ed Patterson | .10 | .05 |
| ❑ 266 Mike Peca | .10 | .05 |
| ❑ 267 Teppo Numminen | .10 | .05 |
| ❑ 268 Alexei Kovalev | .15 | .07 |
| ❑ 269 Cam Neely | .15 | .07 |
| ❑ 270 Iain Fraser | .10 | .05 |
| ❑ 271 Tomas Sandstrom | .10 | .05 |
| ❑ 272 Lyle Odelein | .10 | .05 |
| ❑ 273 Norm Maciver | .10 | .05 |
| ❑ 274 Zdeno Ciger | .10 | .05 |
| ❑ 275 Ed Belfour | .30 | .14 |
| ❑ 276 Brian Savage | .10 | .05 |
| ❑ 277 Vlastimil Kroupa | .10 | .05 |
| ❑ 278 Cliff Ronning | .10 | .05 |
| ❑ 279 Alexei Zhitnik | .10 | .05 |
| ❑ 280 Jim Storm | .10 | .05 |
| ❑ 281 Don Sweeney | .10 | .05 |
| ❑ 282 Mike Donnelly | .10 | .05 |
| ❑ 283 Glenn Healy | .15 | .07 |
| ❑ 284 Denis Savard | .15 | .07 |
| ❑ 285 Chris Terreri | .15 | .07 |
| ❑ 286 Darren Turcotte | .10 | .05 |
| ❑ 287 Curtis Joseph | .30 | .14 |
| ❑ 288 Ken Baumgartner | .10 | .05 |
| ❑ 289 Matthew Barnaby | .15 | .07 |
| ❑ 290 Brent Sutter | .10 | .05 |
| ❑ 291 Valeri Zelepukin | .10 | .05 |
| ❑ 292 Michal Pivonka | .10 | .05 |
| ❑ 293 Ray Sheppard | .15 | .07 |
| ❑ 294 Jiri Slegr | .10 | .05 |
| ❑ 295 Vesa Viitakoski | .10 | .05 |
| ❑ 296 Ulf Samuelsson | .10 | .05 |
| ❑ 297 Nelson Emerson | .10 | .05 |
| ❑ 298 John Slaney | .10 | .05 |
| ❑ 299 Pat Verbeek | .10 | .05 |
| ❑ 300 Pat LaFontaine | .15 | .07 |
| ❑ 301 Johan Garpenlov | .10 | .05 |
| ❑ 302 Eric Weinrich | .10 | .05 |
| ❑ 303 Richard Matvichuk | .10 | .05 |
| ❑ 304 Steve Duchesne | .10 | .05 |
| ❑ 305 Donald Audette | .15 | .07 |
| ❑ 306 Stu Barnes | .10 | .05 |
| ❑ 307 Vladimir Malakhov | .10 | .05 |
| ❑ 308 Dimitri Yushkevich | .10 | .05 |
| ❑ 309 David Sacco | .10 | .05 |
| ❑ 310 Scott Young | .10 | .05 |
| ❑ 311 Marty McInnis | .10 | .05 |
| ❑ 312 Grant Ledyard | .10 | .05 |
| ❑ 313 Peter Popovic | .10 | .05 |
| ❑ 314 Mikhail Shtalenkov | .10 | .05 |
| ❑ 315 Dave McLlwain | .10 | .05 |
| ❑ 316 Cam Stewart | .10 | .05 |
| ❑ 317 Derian Hatcher | .10 | .05 |
| ❑ 318 Pat Peake | .10 | .05 |
| ❑ 319 Wes Walz | .10 | .05 |
| ❑ 320 Fred Brathwaite | .15 | .07 |
| ❑ 321 Jesse Belanger | .10 | .05 |
| ❑ 322 Jozef Stumpel | .10 | .05 |
| ❑ 323 Dave Andreychuk | .15 | .07 |
| ❑ 324 Yuri Khmylev | .10 | .05 |
| ❑ 325 Tim Cheveldae | .15 | .07 |
| ❑ 326 Anatoli Semenov | .10 | .05 |
| ❑ 327 Alexander Karpovtsev | .10 | .05 |
| ❑ 328 Patrick Roy | 1.50 | .70 |
| ❑ 329 Troy Mallette | .10 | .05 |
| ❑ 330 Checklist 250-330 | .10 | .05 |

## 1994-95 Donruss Dominators

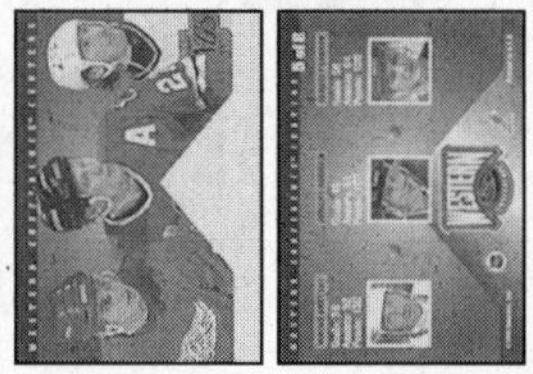

The eight cards in this set were randomly inserted in Donruss product at the rate of one in 36 packs. Each card features head shots of three players, grouped by position and conference, over a silver foil set logo. Individual photos appear on the back with statistical information. Cards are numbered "X of 8."

| | MINT | NRMT |
|---|---|---|
| COMPLETE SET (8) | 80.00 | 36.00 |
| COMMON CARD (1-8) | 4.00 | 1.80 |
| ❑ 1 Eric Lindros<br>Mario Lemieux<br>Mark Messier | 15.00 | 6.75 |
| ❑ 2 Brian Leetch<br>Ray Bourque<br>Scott Stevens | 4.00 | 1.80 |
| ❑ 3 Patrick Roy<br>Dominik Hasek<br>John Vanbiesbrouck | 15.00 | 6.75 |
| ❑ 4 Cam Neely<br>Jaromir Jagr<br>Mikael Renberg | 10.00 | 4.50 |
| ❑ 5 Sergei Fedorov<br>Jeremy Roenick<br>Wayne Gretzky | 20.00 | 9.00 |
| ❑ 6 Chris Chelios<br>Paul Coffey<br>Al MacInnis | 4.00 | 1.80 |
| ❑ 7 Arturs Irbe<br>Ed Belfour<br>Felix Potvin | 8.00 | 3.60 |
| ❑ 8 Brett Hull<br>Pavel Bure<br>Teemu Selanne | 10.00 | 4.50 |

## 1994-95 Donruss Elite

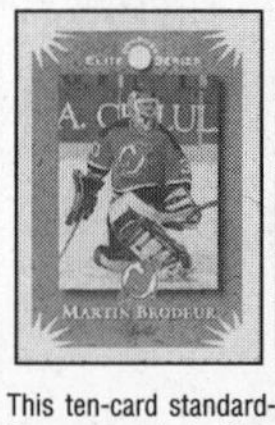

This ten-card standard-size set was issued in Donruss product at the rate of 1:72 packs. The design features a silver border with a deckle edge cut and rounded corners surrounding an action player photo. The set title tops the photo, with team logo, player name and team name below it. Card backs feature a small photo and personal information. Each card is individually numbered out of 10,000 on the back.

| | MINT | NRMT |
|---|---|---|
| COMPLETE SET (10) | 300.00 | 135.00 |
| COMMON CARD (1-10) | 10.00 | 4.50 |
| ❑ 1 Jason Arnott | 10.00 | 4.50 |
| ❑ 2 Martin Brodeur | 25.00 | 11.00 |
| ❑ 3 Pavel Bure | 20.00 | 9.00 |
| ❑ 4 Sergei Fedorov | 20.00 | 9.00 |
| ❑ 5 Wayne Gretzky | 60.00 | 27.00 |
| ❑ 6 Mario Lemieux | 50.00 | 22.00 |
| ❑ 7 Eric Lindros | 30.00 | 13.50 |
| ❑ 8 Felix Potvin | 15.00 | 6.75 |
| ❑ 9 Jeremy Roenick | 12.00 | 5.50 |
| ❑ 10 Patrick Roy | 50.00 | 22.00 |

## 1994-95 Donruss Ice Masters

This ten-card set was produced in the style of

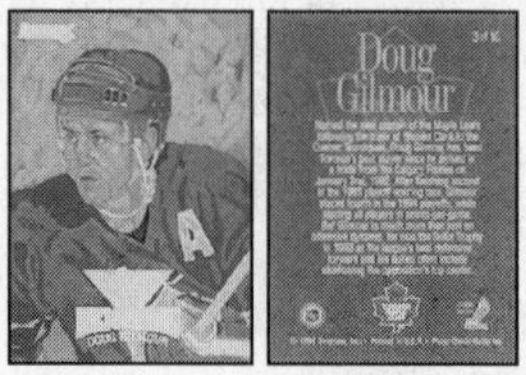

previous Diamond King sets in baseball, featuring the renderings of artist Dick Perez. The cards were randomly inserted at the rate of 1:18 packs. A foil logo and player name are stamped in silver foil on the front. Backs are black and have a brief paragraph of information. Cards are numbered "X of 10."

| | MINT | NRMT |
|---|---|---|
| COMPLETE SET (10) | 30.00 | 13.50 |
| COMMON CARD (1-10) | 1.00 | .45 |
| ❑ 1 Ed Belfour | 1.25 | .55 |
| ❑ 2 Sergei Fedorov | 2.50 | 1.10 |
| ❑ 3 Doug Gilmour | 1.00 | .45 |
| ❑ 4 Wayne Gretzky | 8.00 | 3.60 |
| ❑ 5 Mario Lemieux | 6.00 | 2.70 |
| ❑ 6 Eric Lindros | 6.00 | 2.70 |
| ❑ 7 Mark Messier | 1.50 | .70 |
| ❑ 8 Mike Modano | 1.50 | .70 |
| ❑ 9 Luc Robitaille | 1.00 | .45 |
| ❑ 10 John Vanbiesbrouck | 2.00 | .90 |

## 1994-95 Donruss Masked Marvels

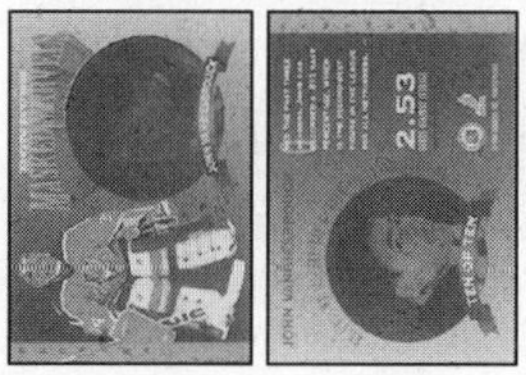

The ten cards in this set of NHL goalies were randomly inserted at a rate of 1:18 packs. The card fronts display a small action photo to the left and a holographic facial image printed in a silver foil disc at right. Cards are numbered X of 10 on the back. These cards feature a removable clear plastic coating on the front which is designed to protect the hologram from scratches. A white sticker reading "Remove Protective Coating" covers a small segment of each card front. Prices below reflect values for cards with the coating intact; collectors are free to preserve their cards with or without this coating.

| | MINT | NRMT |
|---|---|---|
| COMPLETE SET (10) | 50.00 | 22.00 |
| COMMON CARD (1-10) | 3.00 | 1.35 |
| ❑ 1 Ed Belfour | 5.00 | 2.20 |
| ❑ 2 Martin Brodeur | 7.00 | 3.10 |
| ❑ 3 Dominik Hasek | 7.00 | 3.10 |
| ❑ 4 Arturs Irbe | 3.00 | 1.35 |
| ❑ 5 Curtis Joseph | 5.00 | 2.20 |
| ❑ 6 Kirk McLean | 3.00 | 1.35 |
| ❑ 7 Felix Potvin | 6.00 | 2.70 |
| ❑ 8 Mike Richter | 5.00 | 2.20 |
| ❑ 9 Patrick Roy | 12.00 | 5.50 |
| ❑ 10 John Vanbiesbrouck | 5.00 | 2.20 |

## 1995-96 Donruss

These 390 standard-size cards represent the first and second series of the 1995-96 Donruss issue. The fronts feature borderless color action player photos. The player's name and team is identified on the bottom of the card. The borderless backs carry a color action photo with seasonal and career stats as an inset on the right side. Rookie Cards include Daniel Alfredsson and Daymond Langkow.

| | MINT | NRMT |
|---|---|---|
| COMPLETE SET (390) | 30.00 | 13.50 |
| COMPLETE SERIES 1 (205) | 18.00 | 8.00 |
| COMPLETE SERIES 2 (185) | 12.00 | 5.50 |
| COMMON CARD (1-390) | .10 | .05 |
| ❑ 1 Eric Lindros | 1.00 | .45 |
| ❑ 2 Steve Larmer | .15 | .07 |
| ❑ 3 Oleg Tverdovsky | .15 | .07 |
| ❑ 4 Vladimir Malakhov | .10 | .05 |
| ❑ 5 Ian Laperriere | .10 | .05 |
| ❑ 6 Chris Marinucci | .10 | .05 |
| ❑ 7 Nelson Emerson | .10 | .05 |
| ❑ 8 David Oliver | .10 | .05 |
| ❑ 9 Felix Potvin | .30 | .14 |
| ❑ 10 Manny Fernandez | .15 | .07 |
| ❑ 11 Jason Wiemer | .10 | .05 |
| ❑ 12 Dale Hunter | .10 | .05 |
| ❑ 13 Wayne Gretzky | 2.00 | .90 |
| ❑ 14 Todd Gill | .10 | .05 |
| ❑ 15 Radim Bicanek | .10 | .05 |
| ❑ 16 Kirk McLean | .15 | .07 |
| ❑ 17 Esa Tikkanen | .10 | .05 |
| ❑ 18 Yuri Khmylev | .10 | .05 |
| ❑ 19 Peter Bondra | .30 | .14 |
| ❑ 20 Brian Savage | .10 | .05 |
| ❑ 21 Mariusz Czerkawski | .10 | .05 |
| ❑ 22 Rob Blake | .10 | .05 |
| ❑ 23 Chris Osgood | .30 | .14 |
| ❑ 24 Bernie Nicholls | .10 | .05 |
| ❑ 25 Doug Weight | .15 | .07 |
| ❑ 26 Shaun Van Allen | .10 | .05 |
| ❑ 27 Jeremy Roenick | .30 | .14 |
| ❑ 28 Sean Burke | .15 | .07 |
| ❑ 29 Pat Verbeek | .10 | .05 |
| ❑ 30 Dino Ciccarelli | .15 | .07 |
| ❑ 31 Trevor Kidd | .15 | .07 |
| ❑ 32 Steve Thomas | .10 | .05 |
| ❑ 33 Dominik Hasek | .60 | .25 |
| ❑ 34 Sandis Ozolinsh | .15 | .07 |
| ❑ 35 Bill Guerin | .10 | .05 |
| ❑ 36 Scott Young | .10 | .05 |
| ❑ 37 Scott Mellanby | .15 | .07 |
| ❑ 38 Joe Mullen | .15 | .07 |
| ❑ 39 Steve Larouche | .10 | .05 |
| ❑ 40 Joe Nieuwendyk | .15 | .07 |
| ❑ 41 Rick Tocchet | .15 | .07 |
| ❑ 42 Keith Primeau | .15 | .07 |
| ❑ 43 Darren Turcotte | .10 | .05 |
| ❑ 44 Jason Arnott | .15 | .07 |
| ❑ 45 Brantt Myhres | .10 | .05 |
| ❑ 46 Murray Craven | .10 | .05 |
| ❑ 47 Martin Gendron | .10 | .05 |
| ❑ 48 Mark Recchi | .15 | .07 |
| ❑ 49 Uwe Krupp | .10 | .05 |
| ❑ 50 Alexei Zhitnik | .10 | .05 |
| ❑ 51 Rob Niedermayer | .15 | .07 |
| ❑ 52 Sergei Brylin | .10 | .05 |
| ❑ 53 Mats Naslund | .10 | .05 |
| ❑ 54 Glenn Healy | .15 | .07 |
| ❑ 55 Mathieu Schneider | .10 | .05 |
| ❑ 56 Marko Tuomainen | .10 | .05 |
| ❑ 57 Paul Kariya | 1.25 | .55 |
| ❑ 58 Dave Gagner | .15 | .07 |
| ❑ 59 Mike Richter | .30 | .14 |
| ❑ 60 Patrik Juhlin | .10 | .05 |
| ❑ 61 Pierre Turgeon | .15 | .07 |
| ❑ 62 Mike Modano | .40 | .18 |
| ❑ 63 Chris Pronger | .15 | .07 |
| ❑ 64 Chris Joseph | .10 | .05 |
| ❑ 65 Peter Forsberg | 1.00 | .45 |
| ❑ 66 Roman Oksiuta | .10 | .05 |
| ❑ 67 Jamie Storr | .15 | .07 |
| ❑ 68 Brett Hull | .40 | .18 |
| ❑ 69 Steve Chiasson | .10 | .05 |
| ❑ 70 Benoit Hogue | .10 | .05 |
| ❑ 71 Guy Hebert | .15 | .07 |
| ❑ 72 Chris Therien | .10 | .05 |
| ❑ 73 Darryl Sydor | .10 | .05 |
| ❑ 74 Phil Housley | .15 | .07 |
| ❑ 75 Jason Allison | .10 | .05 |
| ❑ 76 Richard Smehlik | .10 | .05 |
| ❑ 77 Shean Donovan | .10 | .05 |
| ❑ 78 Keith Tkachuk | .40 | .18 |
| ❑ 79 Cliff Ronning | .10 | .05 |
| ❑ 80 Mikael Renberg | .15 | .07 |
| ❑ 81 Steven Rice | .10 | .05 |
| ❑ 82 Adam Graves | .15 | .07 |
| ❑ 83 Nicklas Lidstrom | .15 | .07 |
| ❑ 84 Daren Puppa | .15 | .07 |
| ❑ 85 Todd Warriner | .10 | .05 |
| ❑ 86 Jon Rohloff | .10 | .05 |
| ❑ 87 Patrice Tardif | .10 | .05 |
| ❑ 88 John MacLean | .15 | .07 |
| ❑ 89 Ulf Samuelsson | .10 | .05 |
| ❑ 90 Alexander Selivanov | .10 | .05 |
| ❑ 91 Chris Chelios | .30 | .14 |
| ❑ 92 Ulf Dahlen | .10 | .05 |
| ❑ 93 Brad May | .15 | .07 |
| ❑ 94 Ron Francis | .15 | .07 |
| ❑ 95 Kevin Hatcher | .10 | .05 |
| ❑ 96 Steve Yzerman | 1.00 | .45 |
| ❑ 97 Jocelyn Thibault | .30 | .14 |
| ❑ 98 Dave Andreychuk | .15 | .07 |
| ❑ 99 Gary Suter | .10 | .05 |
| ❑ 100 Teemu Selanne | .60 | .25 |
| ❑ 101 Don Sweeney | .10 | .05 |
| ❑ 102 Valeri Bure | .15 | .07 |
| ❑ 103 Todd Harvey | .10 | .05 |
| ❑ 104 Luc Robitaille | .15 | .07 |
| ❑ 105 Scott Niedermayer | .10 | .05 |
| ❑ 106 John Vanbiesbrouck | .50 | .23 |
| ❑ 107 Alexei Yashin | .15 | .07 |
| ❑ 108 Ed Belfour | .30 | .14 |
| ❑ 109 Jyrki Lumme | .10 | .05 |
| ❑ 110 Petr Klima | .10 | .05 |
| ❑ 111 Tony Granato | .10 | .05 |
| ❑ 112 Bob Corkum | .10 | .05 |
| ❑ 113 Chris McAlpine | .10 | .05 |
| ❑ 114 John LeClair | .50 | .23 |
| ❑ 115 Kenny Jonsson | .10 | .05 |
| ❑ 116 Garry Galley | .10 | .05 |
| ❑ 117 Jeff Norton | .10 | .05 |
| ❑ 118 Tomas Sandstrom | .10 | .05 |
| ❑ 119 Paul Coffey | .30 | .14 |
| ❑ 120 Mike Ricci | .10 | .05 |
| ❑ 121 Tony Amonte | .15 | .07 |
| ❑ 122 Chris Gratton | .15 | .07 |
| ❑ 123 Blaine Lacher | .15 | .07 |
| ❑ 124 Andrei Nikolishin | .10 | .05 |
| ❑ 125 Michal Grosek | .10 | .05 |
| ❑ 126 Shawn Chambers | .10 | .05 |
| ❑ 127 Ray Bourque | .30 | .14 |
| ❑ 128 Jeff Nelson | .10 | .05 |
| ❑ 129 Kirk Muller | .10 | .05 |
| ❑ 130 Sergei Zubov | .10 | .05 |
| ❑ 131 Stanislav Neckar | .10 | .05 |
| ❑ 132 Stu Barnes | .10 | .05 |
| ❑ 133 Jari Kurri | .15 | .07 |
| ❑ 134 Slava Kozlov | .15 | .07 |
| ❑ 135 Curtis Joseph | .30 | .14 |
| ❑ 136 Joe Juneau | .10 | .05 |
| ❑ 137 Craig Janney | .15 | .07 |
| ❑ 138 Bryan Smolinski | .10 | .05 |
| ❑ 139 Brian Bradley | .10 | .05 |
| ❑ 140 Steve Rucchin | .10 | .05 |
| ❑ 141 Donald Audette | .15 | .07 |
| ❑ 142 Jaromir Jagr | 1.00 | .45 |
| ❑ 143 Mike Torchia | .15 | .07 |
| ❑ 144 Ray Ferraro | .10 | .05 |
| ❑ 145 Adam Deadmarsh | .15 | .07 |
| ❑ 146 Joe Murphy | .10 | .05 |
| ❑ 147 Ron Hextall | .15 | .07 |
| ❑ 148 Andrew Cassels | .10 | .05 |
| ❑ 149 Martin Brodeur | .75 | .35 |
| ❑ 150 Marek Malik | .10 | .05 |
| ❑ 151 Eric Desjardins | .10 | .05 |
| ❑ 152 Cory Stillman | .10 | .05 |
| ❑ 153 Owen Nolan | .15 | .07 |
| ❑ 154 Randy Wood | .10 | .05 |
| ❑ 155 Alexei Zhamnov | .15 | .07 |
| ❑ 156 John Cullen | .10 | .05 |
| ❑ 157 Zdenek Nedved | .10 | .05 |
| ❑ 158 Greg Adams | .10 | .05 |
| ❑ 159 Kelly Miller | .10 | .05 |
| ❑ 160 Alexandre Daigle | .10 | .05 |
| ❑ 161 Gord Murphy | .10 | .05 |
| ❑ 162 Jeff Friesen | .15 | .07 |
| ❑ 163 Scott Stevens | .15 | .07 |
| ❑ 164 Denis Chasse | .10 | .05 |
| ❑ 165 Cam Neely | .15 | .07 |
| ❑ 166 Magnus Svensson | .10 | .05 |
| ❑ 167 Joe Sakic | .60 | .25 |
| ❑ 168 Kevin Brown | .10 | .05 |
| ❑ 169 Craig Conroy | .10 | .05 |
| ❑ 170 Pavel Bure | .60 | .25 |
| ❑ 171 Viktor Kozlov | .10 | .05 |
| ❑ 172 Pat LaFontaine | .15 | .07 |
| ❑ 173 Sergei Gonchar | .10 | .05 |
| ❑ 174 Brett Lindros | .10 | .05 |
| ❑ 175 Jassen Cullimore | .10 | .05 |
| ❑ 176 Mats Sundin | .15 | .07 |
| ❑ 177 Zarley Zalapski | .10 | .05 |
| ❑ 178 Stephane Richer | .15 | .07 |
| ❑ 179 Steve Smith | .10 | .05 |
| ❑ 180 Brendan Shanahan | .60 | .25 |
| ❑ 181 Brian Leetch | .30 | .14 |
| ❑ 182 Ken Wregget | .15 | .07 |
| ❑ 183 Jeff Brown | .10 | .05 |
| ❑ 184 Darby Hendrickson | .10 | .05 |
| ❑ 185 Nikolai Khabibulin | .15 | .07 |
| ❑ 186 Glen Wesley | .10 | .05 |
| ❑ 187 Andrei Nazarov | .10 | .05 |
| ❑ 188 Rod Brind'Amour | .15 | .07 |
| ❑ 189 Jim Carey | .30 | .14 |
| ❑ 190 Derek Plante | .10 | .05 |
| ❑ 191 Valeri Karpov | .10 | .05 |
| ❑ 192 Mike Kennedy | .10 | .05 |
| ❑ 193 Wendel Clark | .15 | .07 |
| ❑ 194 Radek Bonk | .10 | .05 |
| ❑ 195 Jozef Stumpel | .10 | .05 |
| ❑ 196 Tommy Salo | .40 | .18 |
| ❑ 197 Michal Pivonka | .10 | .05 |
| ❑ 198 Ray Sheppard | .15 | .07 |
| ❑ 199 Russ Courtnall | .10 | .05 |
| ❑ 200 Todd Marchant | .10 | .05 |
| ❑ 201 Geoff Sanderson | .15 | .07 |
| ❑ 202 Vincent Damphousse | .15 | .07 |
| ❑ 203 Sergei Krivokrasov | .10 | .05 |
| ❑ 204 Jesse Belanger | .10 | .05 |
| ❑ 205 Al MacInnis | .15 | .07 |
| ❑ 206 Philippe DeRouville | .10 | .05 |
| ❑ 207 Mike Eastwood | .10 | .05 |
| ❑ 208 Travis Green | .15 | .07 |
| ❑ 209 Jeff Shantz | .10 | .05 |
| ❑ 210 Shane Doan | .10 | .05 |
| ❑ 211 Mike Sullivan | .10 | .05 |
| ❑ 212 Kevin Dineen | .10 | .05 |
| ❑ 213 Pat Falloon | .10 | .05 |
| ❑ 214 Rick Tabaracci | .15 | .07 |
| ❑ 215 Kelly Hrudey | .15 | .07 |
| ❑ 216 Alexei Kovalev | .10 | .05 |
| ❑ 217 Matt Johnson | .10 | .05 |
| ❑ 218 Turner Stevenson | .10 | .05 |
| ❑ 219 Mike Sillinger | .10 | .05 |
| ❑ 220 Bobby Holik | .10 | .05 |
| ❑ 221 Kevin Stevens | .10 | .05 |
| ❑ 222 Dave Lowry | .10 | .05 |
| ❑ 223 Martin Gelinas | .10 | .05 |
| ❑ 224 Darren Langdon | .10 | .05 |
| ❑ 225 Tie Domi | .15 | .07 |
| ❑ 226 Doug Bodger | .10 | .05 |
| ❑ 227 Patrick Flatley | .10 | .05 |
| ❑ 228 Anders Myrvold | .10 | .05 |
| ❑ 229 German Titov | .10 | .05 |
| ❑ 230 Pat Peake | .10 | .05 |
| ❑ 231 Robert Kron | .10 | .05 |
| ❑ 232 Mike Donnelly | .10 | .05 |
| ❑ 233 Denis Savard | .15 | .07 |
| ❑ 234 Mathieu Dandenault | .10 | .05 |
| ❑ 235 Joe Dziedzic | .10 | .05 |
| ❑ 236 Valeri Kamensky | .15 | .07 |
| ❑ 237 Joaquin Gage | .10 | .05 |
| ❑ 238 Geoff Courtnall | .10 | .05 |
| ❑ 239 Arturs Irbe | .15 | .07 |

| | | |
|---|---|---|
| ❑ 240 Dan Quinn | .10 | .05 |
| ❑ 241 J.C. Bergeron | .10 | .05 |
| ❑ 242 Brian Noonan | .10 | .05 |
| ❑ 243 Ulf Samuelsson | .10 | .05 |
| ❑ 244 Jeff O'Neill | .10 | .05 |
| ❑ 245 Sandy Moger | .10 | .05 |
| ❑ 246 Don Beaupre | .15 | .07 |
| ❑ 247 Bob Probert | .15 | .07 |
| ❑ 248 Mattias Norstrom | .10 | .05 |
| ❑ 249 Jason Bonsignore | .10 | .05 |
| ❑ 250 Mike Ridley | .10 | .05 |
| ❑ 251 Joe Mullen | .15 | .07 |
| ❑ 252 Petr Nedved | .15 | .07 |
| ❑ 253 Jason Doig | .10 | .05 |
| ❑ 254 Olaf Kolzig | .15 | .07 |
| ❑ 255 Mark Tinordi | .10 | .05 |
| ❑ 256 Roman Hamrlik | .15 | .07 |
| ❑ 257 Denis Pederson | .10 | .05 |
| ❑ 258 Paul Ysebaert | .10 | .05 |
| ❑ 259 Neal Broten | .15 | .07 |
| ❑ 260 Jason Woolley | .10 | .05 |
| ❑ 261 Teppo Numminen | .10 | .05 |
| ❑ 262 Scott Thornton | .10 | .05 |
| ❑ 263 Ted Donato | .10 | .05 |
| ❑ 264 Marcus Ragnarsson | .10 | .05 |
| ❑ 265 Dimitri Khristich | .10 | .05 |
| ❑ 266 Mike Peca | .10 | .05 |
| ❑ 267 Dominic Roussel | .15 | .07 |
| ❑ 268 Owen Nolan | .15 | .07 |
| ❑ 269 Patrick Poulin | .10 | .05 |
| ❑ 270 Mario Lemieux | 1.50 | .70 |
| ❑ 271 Mark Messier | .40 | .18 |
| ❑ 272 Slava Fetisov | .10 | .05 |
| ❑ 273 Andrei Trefilov | .10 | .05 |
| ❑ 274 Damian Rhodes | .15 | .07 |
| ❑ 275 Alexander Mogilny | .15 | .07 |
| ❑ 276 Ray Sheppard | .15 | .07 |
| ❑ 277 Radek Dvorak | .10 | .05 |
| ❑ 278 Steve Duchesne | .10 | .05 |
| ❑ 279 Jason Smith | .10 | .05 |
| ❑ 280 Wade Flaherty | .15 | .07 |
| ❑ 281 Lyle Odelein | .10 | .05 |
| ❑ 282 Keith Jones | .10 | .05 |
| ❑ 283 Saku Koivu | .50 | .23 |
| ❑ 284 Marty Murray | .10 | .05 |
| ❑ 285 Sergei Fedorov | .50 | .23 |
| ❑ 286 Brian Rolston | .10 | .05 |
| ❑ 287 Dave Roche | .10 | .05 |
| ❑ 288 Sylvain Lefebvre | .10 | .05 |
| ❑ 289 Theoren Fleury | .15 | .07 |
| ❑ 290 Andy Moog | .15 | .07 |
| ❑ 291 Tom Barrasso | .15 | .07 |
| ❑ 292 Craig Mills | .10 | .05 |
| ❑ 293 Mike Gartner | .15 | .07 |
| ❑ 294 Stefan Ustorf | .10 | .05 |
| ❑ 295 Darren Turcotte | .10 | .05 |
| ❑ 296 Steve Konowalchuk | .10 | .05 |
| ❑ 297 Ray Ferraro | .10 | .05 |
| ❑ 298 Brian Holzinger | .30 | .14 |
| ❑ 299 Daniel Alfredsson | .60 | .25 |
| ❑ 300 Derek King | .10 | .05 |
| ❑ 301 Mark Fitzpatrick | .15 | .07 |
| ❑ 302 Joe Sacco | .10 | .05 |
| ❑ 303 Scott Walker | .10 | .05 |
| ❑ 304 Ricard Persson | .10 | .05 |
| ❑ 305 Mike Rathje | .10 | .05 |
| ❑ 306 Petr Svoboda | .10 | .05 |
| ❑ 307 Roman Vopat | .10 | .05 |
| ❑ 308 Ray Whitney | .10 | .05 |
| ❑ 309 Calle Johansson | .10 | .05 |
| ❑ 310 Grant Fuhr | .15 | .07 |
| ❑ 311 John Tucker | .10 | .05 |
| ❑ 312 Anatoli Semenov | .10 | .05 |
| ❑ 313 Darren McCarty | .10 | .05 |
| ❑ 314 Stephane Quintal | .10 | .05 |
| ❑ 315 Jason Dawe | .10 | .05 |
| ❑ 316 Zigmund Palffy | .15 | .07 |
| ❑ 317 Dave Manson | .10 | .05 |
| ❑ 318 Vitali Yachmenev | .10 | .05 |
| ❑ 319 Chris Pronger | .15 | .07 |
| ❑ 320 Valeri Zelepukin | .10 | .05 |
| ❑ 321 Ryan Smyth | .10 | .05 |
| ❑ 322 Johan Garpenlov | .10 | .05 |
| ❑ 323 Bill Ranford | .15 | .07 |
| ❑ 324 Daymond Langkow | .30 | .14 |
| ❑ 325 Aki-Petteri Berg | .10 | .05 |
| ❑ 326 Derian Hatcher | .10 | .05 |
| ❑ 327 Bryan Smolinski | .10 | .05 |
| ❑ 328 Michel Picard | .10 | .05 |
| ❑ 329 Alek Stojanov | .10 | .05 |
| ❑ 330 Trent Klatt | .10 | .05 |
| ❑ 331 Richard Park | .10 | .05 |
| ❑ 332 Jere Lehtinen | .10 | .05 |
| ❑ 333 Bryan McCabe | .10 | .05 |
| ❑ 334 Kyle McLaren | .10 | .05 |
| ❑ 335 Todd Krygier | .10 | .05 |
| ❑ 336 Adam Creighton | .10 | .05 |
| ❑ 337 Jamie Pushor | .10 | .05 |
| ❑ 338 Patrick Roy | 1.50 | .70 |
| ❑ 339 Milos Holan | .10 | .05 |
| ❑ 340 Dave Ellett | .10 | .05 |
| ❑ 341 Brian Bellows | .10 | .05 |
| ❑ 342 Jamie Rivers | .10 | .05 |
| ❑ 343 Claude Lemieux | .15 | .07 |
| ❑ 344 Leif Rohlin | .10 | .05 |
| ❑ 345 Eric Daze | .30 | .14 |
| ❑ 346 Todd Bertuzzi | .15 | .07 |
| ❑ 347 Antti Tormanen | .10 | .05 |
| ❑ 348 Luc Robitaille | .15 | .07 |
| ❑ 349 Tim Taylor | .10 | .05 |
| ❑ 350 Stephane Yelle | .10 | .05 |
| ❑ 351 Marko Kiprusoff | .10 | .05 |
| ❑ 352 Igor Korolev | .10 | .05 |
| ❑ 353 Scott Lachance | .10 | .05 |
| ❑ 354 Marty McSorley | .10 | .05 |
| ❑ 355 Joel Otto | .10 | .05 |
| ❑ 356 Josef Beranek | .10 | .05 |
| ❑ 357 Sergei Zubov | .10 | .05 |
| ❑ 358 Rhett Warrener | .10 | .05 |
| ❑ 359 Jimmy Carson | .10 | .05 |
| ❑ 360 Zdeno Ciger | .10 | .05 |
| ❑ 361 Brendan Witt | .10 | .05 |
| ❑ 362 Byron Dafoe | .15 | .07 |
| ❑ 363 Steve Thomas | .10 | .05 |
| ❑ 364 Deron Quint | .10 | .05 |
| ❑ 365 Nelson Emerson | .10 | .05 |
| ❑ 366 Larry Murphy | .15 | .07 |
| ❑ 367 Benoit Brunet | .10 | .05 |
| ❑ 368 Kjell Samuelsson | .10 | .05 |
| ❑ 369 Aaron Gavey | .10 | .05 |
| ❑ 370 Robert Svehla | .10 | .05 |
| ❑ 371 Rene Corbet | .10 | .05 |
| ❑ 372 Gary Roberts | .10 | .05 |
| ❑ 373 Shawn McEachern | .10 | .05 |
| ❑ 374 Andrei Kovalenko | .10 | .05 |
| ❑ 375 Yanic Perreault | .10 | .05 |
| ❑ 376 Shayne Corson | .10 | .05 |
| ❑ 377 Brendan Shanahan | .60 | .25 |
| ❑ 378 Sergei Nemchinov | .10 | .05 |
| ❑ 379 Chad Kilger | .10 | .05 |
| ❑ 380 Sergio Momesso | .10 | .05 |
| ❑ 381 Craig Billington | .15 | .07 |
| ❑ 382 Niklas Sundstrom | .10 | .05 |
| ❑ 383 Matthew Barnaby | .15 | .07 |
| ❑ 384 Dale Hawerchuk | .15 | .07 |
| ❑ 385 Trevor Linden | .15 | .07 |
| ❑ 386 Adam Oates | .15 | .07 |
| ❑ 387 Dimitri Yushkevich | .10 | .05 |
| ❑ 388 Todd Elik | .10 | .05 |
| ❑ 389 Wendel Clark | .15 | .07 |
| ❑ 390 Stephane Fiset | .15 | .07 |
| ❑ NNO Checklist Card 1 | .15 | .07 |
| ❑ NNO Checklist Card 2 | .15 | .07 |
| ❑ NNO Checklist Card 3 | .15 | .07 |
| ❑ NNO Checklist Card 4 | .15 | .07 |
| ❑ NNO Checklist Card 5 | .15 | .07 |
| ❑ NNO Checklist Card 6 | .15 | .07 |
| ❑ NNO Checklist Card 7 | .15 | .07 |
| ❑ NNO Checklist Card 8 | .15 | .07 |

## 1995-96 Donruss Between The Pipes

Shaped like a goal and outlined in red foil, these ten cards were randomly inserted in series 1 (1-5) and 2 (6-10) packs at a rate of 1:36. The goaltender is pictured within the goal with a solid blue background. The backs feature a brief write-up and career statistics.

| | MINT | NRMT |
|---|---|---|
| COMPLETE SET (10) | 90.00 | 40.00 |
| COMPLETE SERIES 1 (5) | 35.00 | 16.00 |
| COMPLETE SERIES 2 (5) | 55.00 | 25.00 |
| COMMON CARD (1-10) | 6.00 | 2.70 |
| ❑ 1 Blaine Lacher | 6.00 | 2.70 |
| ❑ 2 Dominik Hasek | 15.00 | 6.75 |
| ❑ 3 Mike Vernon | 6.00 | 2.70 |
| ❑ 4 Trevor Kidd | 6.00 | 2.70 |
| ❑ 5 Martin Brodeur | 20.00 | 9.00 |
| ❑ 6 Jim Carey | 6.00 | 2.70 |
| ❑ 7 Patrick Roy | 25.00 | 11.00 |
| ❑ 8 Sean Burke | 6.00 | 2.70 |
| ❑ 9 Felix Potvin | 6.00 | 2.70 |
| ❑ 10 Ed Belfour | 8.00 | 3.60 |

## 1995-96 Donruss Canadian World Junior Team

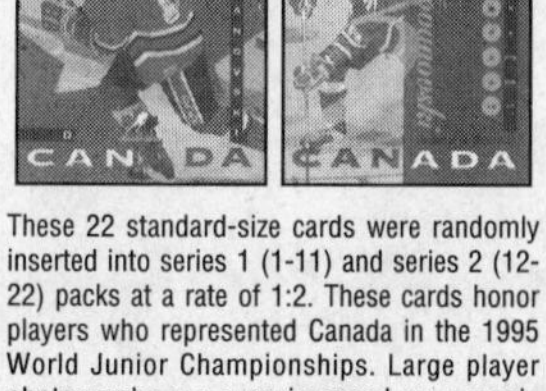

These 22 standard-size cards were randomly inserted into series 1 (1-11) and series 2 (12-22) packs at a rate of 1:2. The cards honor players who represented Canada in the 1995 World Junior Championships. Large player photographs are superimposed on a maple leaf design. The backs feature two player photos. One is an inset photo in a maple leaf and the other on the left side is a black-and-white image. Information about the player is located in the upper left corner while his National Junior Team career stats are printed on the right side of the card. The cards are numbered "X of 22" in the upper right-hand corner.

| | MINT | NRMT |
|---|---|---|
| COMPLETE SET (22) | 16.00 | 7.25 |
| COMPLETE SERIES 1 (11) | 6.00 | 2.70 |
| COMPLETE SERIES 2 (11) | 10.00 | 4.50 |
| COMMON CARD (1-22) | .50 | .23 |
| ❑ 1 Jamie Storr | 1.00 | .45 |
| ❑ 2 Dan Cloutier | .50 | .23 |
| ❑ 3 Nolan Baumgartner | .50 | .23 |
| ❑ 4 Chad Allen | .50 | .23 |
| ❑ 5 Wade Redden | 1.00 | .45 |
| ❑ 6 Ed Jovanovski | 1.50 | .70 |
| ❑ 7 Jamie Rivers | .50 | .23 |
| ❑ 8 Bryan McCabe | 1.00 | .45 |
| ❑ 9 Lee Sorochan | .50 | .23 |
| ❑ 10 Marty Murray | .50 | .23 |
| ❑ 11 Larry Courville | .50 | .23 |
| ❑ 12 Jason Allison | 1.00 | .45 |
| ❑ 13 Darcy Tucker | .50 | .23 |
| ❑ 14 Jeff O'Neill | 1.00 | .45 |
| ❑ 15 Eric Daze | 2.00 | .90 |
| ❑ 16 Alexandre Daigle | 1.50 | .70 |
| ❑ 17 Todd Harvey | 1.00 | .45 |
| ❑ 18 Jason Botterill | .50 | .23 |
| ❑ 19 Shean Donovan | 1.00 | .45 |
| ❑ 20 Denis Pederson | .50 | .23 |
| ❑ 21 Jeff Friesen | 1.50 | .70 |
| ❑ 22 Ryan Smyth | 2.50 | 1.10 |

## 1995-96 Donruss Dominators

The eight cards in this set were randomly inserted in series two hobby packs only at a rate of 1:35. Each features three of the top players at each position from each conference. The cards are individually numbered on the backs out of 5,000.

| | MINT | NRMT |
|---|---|---|
| COMPLETE SET (8) | 175.00 | 80.00 |
| COMMON CARD (1-8) | 10.00 | 4.50 |
| ❑ 1 Peter Forsberg<br>Eric Lindros<br>Mario Lemieux | 40.00 | 18.00 |
| ❑ 2 John LeClair<br>Mikael Renberg<br>Jaromir Jagr | 15.00 | 6.75 |
| ❑ 3 Sergei Zubov<br>Ray Bourque<br>Brian Leetch | 10.00 | 4.50 |
| ❑ 4 Jim Carey<br>Martin Brodeur<br>Dominik Hasek | 25.00 | 11.00 |
| ❑ 5 Doug Gilmour<br>Wayne Gretzky<br>Sergei Fedorov | 40.00 | 18.00 |
| ❑ 6 Brett Hull<br>Paul Kariya<br>Pavel Bure | 30.00 | 13.50 |
| ❑ 7 Paul Coffey<br>Chris Chelios<br>Al MacInnis | 10.00 | 4.50 |
| ❑ 8 Felix Potvin<br>Ed Belfour<br>Trevor Kidd | 10.00 | 4.50 |

## 1995-96 Donruss Elite Inserts

These ten standard-size cards were randomly inserted into first (1-5) and second series (6-10) Donruss at a rate of 1:116 and 1:47 packs respectively. Each card is sequentially numbered out of 10,000. The fronts feature blue holographic foil, layered with copper foil which emphasize the player's name and team logo. The word "Elite" is noted in the upper right-hand corner. The card backs are printed in metallic copper and metallic blue ink silhouetting the player's image. There is a brief blurb about the player on the left side of the card. The cards are numbered "X" of 10 in the upper right corner.

| | MINT | NRMT |
|---|---|---|
| COMPLETE SET (10) | 200.00 | 90.00 |
| COMPLETE SERIES 1 (5) | 50.00 | 22.00 |
| COMPLETE SERIES 2 (5) | 150.00 | 70.00 |
| COMMON CARD (1-10) | 6.00 | 2.70 |
| ❑ 1 Alexei Zhamnov | | |
| ❑ 2 Joe Sakic | 15.00 | 6.75 |
| ❑ 3 Mikael Renberg | 6.00 | 2.70 |
| ❑ 4 Sergei Fedorov | 15.00 | 6.75 |
| ❑ 5 Paul Coffey | 6.00 | 2.70 |
| ❑ 6 Paul Kariya | 30.00 | 13.50 |
| ❑ 7 Wayne Gretzky | 50.00 | 22.00 |
| ❑ 8 Eric Lindros | 25.00 | 11.00 |
| ❑ 9 Mario Lemieux | 40.00 | 18.00 |
| ❑ 10 Jaromir Jagr | 25.00 | 11.00 |

## 1995-96 Donruss Igniters

These 10 standard-size cards were randomly inserted in Series 1 hobby packs. The horizontally-oriented cards feature the player's photo superimposed against the word "Igniters". His name and team are identified on the bottom of the card. The backs are individually numbered out of 5,000.

| | MINT | NRMT |
|---|---|---|
| COMPLETE SET (10) | 120.00 | 55.00 |
| COMMON CARD (1-10) | 8.00 | 3.60 |
| ❑ 1 Adam Oates | 8.00 | 3.60 |
| ❑ 2 Paul Coffey | 12.00 | 5.50 |
| ❑ 3 Doug Gilmour | 8.00 | 3.60 |
| ❑ 4 Pierre Turgeon | 8.00 | 3.60 |
| ❑ 5 Mark Messier | 15.00 | 6.75 |
| ❑ 6 Alexei Zhamnov | 8.00 | 3.60 |
| ❑ 7 Jeremy Roenick | 12.00 | 5.50 |
| ❑ 8 Steve Yzerman | 40.00 | 18.00 |
| ❑ 9 Joe Nieuwendyk | 8.00 | 3.60 |
| ❑ 10 Ron Francis | 8.00 | 3.60 |

## 1995-96 Donruss Marksmen

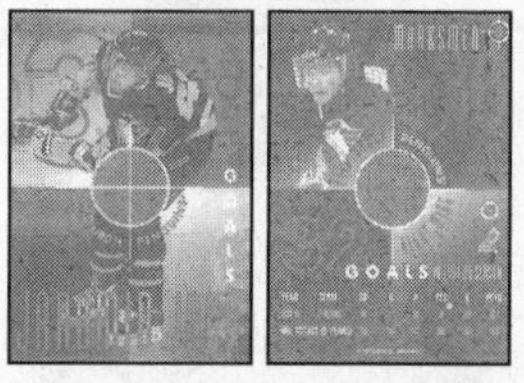

The eight cards in this set were randomly inserted into series one Donruss retail packs only at a rate of 1:24. The cards showcase the top eight goal scorers of the 1994-95 season.

| | MINT | NRMT |
|---|---|---|
| COMPLETE SET (8) | 120.00 | 55.00 |
| COMMON CARD (1-8) | 6.00 | 2.70 |
| ❑ 1 Peter Bondra | 10.00 | 4.50 |
| ❑ 2 Owen Nolan | 10.00 | 4.50 |
| ❑ 3 Eric Lindros | 40.00 | 18.00 |
| ❑ 4 Ray Sheppard | 6.00 | 2.70 |
| ❑ 5 Jaromir Jagr | 40.00 | 18.00 |
| ❑ 6 Theoren Fleury | 10.00 | 4.50 |
| ❑ 7 Brett Hull | 20.00 | 9.00 |
| ❑ 8 Brendan Shanahan | 25.00 | 11.00 |

## 1995-96 Donruss Pro Pointers

Inserted one per series two pack, these twenty cards feature hockey tips from top players born in the United States (1-10) and Canada (11-20).

| | MINT | NRMT |
|---|---|---|
| COMPLETE SET (20) | 6.00 | 2.70 |
| COMMON CARD (1-20) | .10 | .05 |
| ❑ 1 Jeremy Roenick USA | .40 | .18 |
| ❑ 2 Pat LaFontaine USA | .25 | .11 |
| ❑ 3 Jason Bonsignore USA | .10 | .05 |
| ❑ 4 Chris Chelios USA | .40 | .18 |
| ❑ 5 Brian Leetch USA | .40 | .18 |
| ❑ 6 Brett Hull USA | .50 | .23 |
| ❑ 7 Keith Tkachuk USA | .50 | .23 |
| ❑ 8 Mike Modano USA | .50 | .23 |
| ❑ 9 Brian Rolston USA | .10 | .05 |
| ❑ 10 Darren Turcotte USA | .10 | .05 |
| ❑ 11 Jeff Friesen CAN | .25 | .11 |
| ❑ 12 Theoren Fleury CAN | .25 | .11 |
| ❑ 13 Eric Lindros CAN | 1.50 | .70 |
| ❑ 14 Mario Lemieux CAN | 2.00 | .90 |
| ❑ 15 Jamie Storr CAN | .25 | .11 |
| ❑ 16 Trevor Kidd CAN | .25 | .11 |
| ❑ 17 Chris Pronger CAN | .25 | .11 |
| ❑ 18 Brendan Witt CAN | .10 | .05 |
| ❑ 19 Paul Kariya CAN | 1.50 | .70 |
| ❑ 20 Todd Harvey CAN | .25 | .11 |

## 1995-96 Donruss Rated Rookies

Randomly inserted at a rate of 1:24 series two retail packs, this 16-card set features a plethora of players who made their NHL debuts in the 1995-96 season.

| | MINT | NRMT |
|---|---|---|
| COMPLETE SET (16) | 150.00 | 70.00 |
| COMMON CARD (1-16) | 5.00 | 2.20 |
| ❑ 1 Saku Koivu | 25.00 | 11.00 |
| ❑ 2 Todd Bertuzzi | 8.00 | 3.60 |
| ❑ 3 Niklas Sundstrom | 5.00 | 2.20 |
| ❑ 4 Jeff O'Neill | 8.00 | 3.60 |
| ❑ 5 Zdenek Nedved | 5.00 | 2.20 |
| ❑ 6 Eric Daze | 10.00 | 4.50 |
| ❑ 7 Chad Kilger | 8.00 | 3.60 |
| ❑ 8 Shane Doan | 5.00 | 2.20 |
| ❑ 9 Vitali Yachmenev | 8.00 | 3.60 |
| ❑ 10 Radek Dvorak | 12.00 | 5.50 |
| ❑ 11 Marty Murray | 5.00 | 2.20 |
| ❑ 12 Cory Stillman | 5.00 | 2.20 |
| ❑ 13 Marcus Ragnarsson | 8.00 | 3.60 |
| ❑ 14 Daniel Alfredsson | 20.00 | 9.00 |
| ❑ 15 Antti Tormanen | 5.00 | 2.20 |
| ❑ 16 Petr Sykora | 12.00 | 5.50 |

## 1995-96 Donruss Rookie Team

These nine standard-size cards featuring leading rookies from the 1994-95 season were issued in first series packs (1:12). The borderless fronts feature the player's photo blending into various colors which represent his team's color pattern. The player's name and team identification are located on the bottom. The horizontal back features a close-up player photo, along with a brief note. The cards are numbered on the upper right as "X" of 9.

| | MINT | NRMT |
|---|---|---|
| COMPLETE SET (9) | 20.00 | 9.00 |
| COMMON CARD (1-9) | 1.50 | .70 |
| ❑ 1 Jim Carey | 3.00 | 1.35 |
| ❑ 2 Peter Forsberg | 6.00 | 2.70 |
| ❑ 3 Paul Kariya | 8.00 | 3.60 |
| ❑ 4 David Oliver | 1.50 | .70 |
| ❑ 5 Blaine Lacher | 2.00 | .90 |
| ❑ 6 Oleg Tverdovsky | 3.00 | 1.35 |
| ❑ 7 Jeff Friesen | 3.00 | 1.35 |
| ❑ 8 Todd Marchant | 1.50 | .70 |
| ❑ 9 Todd Harvey | 3.00 | 1.35 |

## 1996-97 Donruss

The 1996-97 Donruss set was issued in one series totaling 240 cards. The 10-card packs retailed for $1.89 each. Card fronts feaure a borderless color action photo along with player name at the top and team name and logo at the bottom. Card backs feature another color action photo, along with stats and biographical information. Key Rookie Cards include Ethan Moreau and Kevin Hodson.

| | MINT | NRMT |
|---|---|---|
| COMPLETE SET (240) | 20.00 | 9.00 |
| COMMON CARD (1-240) | .05 | .02 |
| ❑ 1 Joe Sakic | .50 | .23 |
| ❑ 2 Jeremy Roenick | .25 | .11 |
| ❑ 3 Kirk McLean | .10 | .05 |
| ❑ 4 Zarley Zalapski | .05 | .02 |

❑ 5 Jyrki Lumme .05 .02
❑ 6 Owen Nolan .10 .05
❑ 7 Luc Robitaille .10 .05
❑ 8 Bob Probert .10 .05
❑ 9 Ken Baumgartner .05 .02
❑ 10 Rick Tabaracci .10 .05
❑ 11 Alexei Zhitnik .05 .02
❑ 12 Al MacInnis .10 .05
❑ 13 Brian Leetch .25 .11
❑ 14 Valeri Kamensky .10 .05
❑ 15 Todd Gill .05 .02
❑ 16 Mark Messier .30 .14
❑ 17 Pierre Turgeon .10 .05
❑ 18 Mathieu Schneider .05 .02
❑ 19 Vyacheslav Kozlov .05 .02
❑ 20 Milos Holan .05 .02
❑ 21 Yanic Perreault .05 .02
❑ 22 Mike Modano .30 .14
❑ 23 Claude Lemieux .10 .05
❑ 24 Rob Niedermayer .10 .05
❑ 25 Eric Desjardins .05 .02
❑ 26 Alexander Semak .05 .02
❑ 27 Mark Recchi .10 .05
❑ 28 Viacheslav Fetisov .05 .02
❑ 29 Kevin Hatcher .05 .02
❑ 30 Mats Sundin .10 .05
❑ 31 Jeff Reese .10 .05
❑ 32 Alexander Selivanov .05 .02
❑ 33 Jim Carey .25 .11
❑ 34 Daren Puppa .10 .05
❑ 35 Vincent Damphousse .10 .05
❑ 36 John LeClair .40 .18
❑ 37 Jon Casey .10 .05
❑ 38 Chris Terreri .10 .05
❑ 39 Larry Murphy .10 .05
❑ 40 Geoff Sanderson .10 .05
❑ 41 Adam Oates .10 .05
❑ 42 Sandy McCarthy .05 .02
❑ 43 Jaromir Jagr .75 .35
❑ 44 Roman Oksiuta .05 .02
❑ 45 Zigmund Palffy .25 .11
❑ 46 Doug Gilmour .25 .11
❑ 47 Cliff Ronning .05 .02
❑ 48 Curtis Leschyshyn .05 .02
❑ 49 Scott Mellanby .10 .05
❑ 50 Sergei Fedorov .40 .18
❑ 51 Denis Savard .10 .05
❑ 52 Mike Vernon .10 .05
❑ 53 Todd Marchant .05 .02
❑ 54 Geoff Courtnall .05 .02
❑ 55 Shayne Corson .05 .02
❑ 56 Dimitri Khristich .05 .02
❑ 57 Scott Stevens .10 .05
❑ 58 German Titov .05 .02
❑ 59 Darren Turcotte .05 .02
❑ 60 Michal Pivonka .05 .02
❑ 61 Ron Hextall .10 .05
❑ 62 Ed Belfour .25 .11
❑ 63 Chris Pronger .10 .05
❑ 64 Brian Bellows .05 .02
❑ 65 Pavel Bure .50 .23
❑ 66 Adam Graves .10 .05
❑ 67 Tom Barrasso .10 .05
❑ 68 Stu Barnes .05 .02
❑ 69 Norm MacIver .05 .02
❑ 70 Jesse Belanger .05 .02
❑ 71 Chris Chelios .25 .11
❑ 72 Tommy Soderstrom .10 .05
❑ 73 Nelson Emerson .05 .02
❑ 74 Kenny Jonsson .05 .02
❑ 75 Bill Lindsay .05 .02
❑ 76 Petr Nedved .10 .05
❑ 77 Robert Svehla .05 .02
❑ 78 Tomas Sandstrom .05 .02
❑ 79 Jeff Friesen .10 .05
❑ 80 Tony Amonte .10 .05
❑ 81 Sylvain Lefebvre .05 .02
❑ 82 Greg Adams .05 .02
❑ 83 Vladimir Konstantinov .05 .02
❑ 84 Roman Hamrlik .10 .05
❑ 85 Doug Weight .10 .05
❑ 86 Shaun Van Allen .05 .02
❑ 87 Bill Ranford .10 .05
❑ 88 Jeff Hackett .10 .05
❑ 89 Alexei Zhamnov .10 .05
❑ 90 Dale Hawerchuk .10 .05
❑ 91 Sergei Zubov .05 .02
❑ 92 Dan Quinn .05 .02
❑ 93 Wayne Gretzky 2.00 .90
❑ 94 Todd Harvey .05 .02
❑ 95 Chris Osgood .25 .11
❑ 96 Felix Potvin .25 .11
❑ 97 Richard Matvichuk .05 .02
❑ 98 Wendel Clark .10 .05
❑ 99 Bryan Smolinski .05 .02
❑ 100 Rob Blake .05 .02
❑ 101 Jocelyn Thibault .25 .11
❑ 102 Trevor Linden .10 .05
❑ 103 Craig MacTavish .05 .02
❑ 104 Sandis Ozolinsh .10 .05
❑ 105 Oleg Tverdovsky .10 .05
❑ 106 Garry Galley .05 .02
❑ 107 Derek Plante .05 .02
❑ 108 Stephane Richer .10 .05
❑ 109 Dave Andreychuk .10 .05
❑ 110 Curtis Joseph .25 .11
❑ 111 Greg Johnson .05 .02
❑ 112 Patrick Roy 1.25 .55
❑ 113 Pat LaFontaine .10 .05
❑ 114 Uwe Krupp .05 .02
❑ 115 Ulf Dahlen .05 .02
❑ 116 Brian Bradley .05 .02
❑ 117 Grant Fuhr .10 .05
❑ 118 Brian Skrudland .05 .02
❑ 119 Nicklas Lidstrom .10 .05
❑ 120 Steve Chiasson .05 .02
❑ 121 Sean Burke .10 .05
❑ 122 Rick Tocchet .10 .05
❑ 123 Martin Rucinsky .05 .02
❑ 124 Alexei Yashin .10 .05
❑ 125 Mikael Renberg .10 .05
❑ 126 Teppo Numminen .05 .02
❑ 127 Randy Burridge .05 .02
❑ 128 Radek Bonk .05 .02
❑ 129 Scott Young .05 .02
❑ 130 Gary Suter .05 .02
❑ 131 Mario Lemieux 1.25 .55
❑ 132 Ray Bourque .25 .11
❑ 133 Martin Gelinas .05 .02
❑ 134 Keith Tkachuk .30 .14
❑ 135 Benoit Hogue .05 .02
❑ 136 Ken Wregget .10 .05
❑ 137 Eric Lindros .75 .35
❑ 138 Keith Primeau .10 .05
❑ 139 Peter Forsberg .75 .35
❑ 140 Paul Coffey .25 .11
❑ 141 Mike Ridley .05 .02
❑ 142 Paul Kariya 1.00 .45
❑ 143 Jason Arnott .10 .05
❑ 144 Joe Murphy .05 .02
❑ 145 Adam Deadmarsh .10 .05
❑ 146 John MacLean .10 .05
❑ 147 Peter Bondra .25 .11
❑ 148 Martin Brodeur .60 .25
❑ 149 Ron Francis .10 .05
❑ 150 Dino Ciccarelli .10 .05
❑ 151 Joe Juneau .10 .05
❑ 152 Matthew Barnaby .10 .05
❑ 153 Mark Tinordi .05 .02
❑ 154 Craig Janney .10 .05
❑ 155 Rod Brind'Amour .10 .05
❑ 156 Damian Rhodes .10 .05
❑ 157 Teemu Selanne .50 .23
❑ 158 James Patrick .05 .02
❑ 159 Theoren Fleury .10 .05
❑ 160 Trevor Kidd .10 .05
❑ 161 Kirk Muller .05 .02
❑ 162 Andrew Cassels .05 .02
❑ 163 Brent Fedyk .05 .02
❑ 164 Guy Hebert .10 .05
❑ 165 Jason Dawe .05 .02
❑ 166 Andy Moog .10 .05
❑ 167 Igor Larionov .05 .02
❑ 168 Brian Savage .05 .02
❑ 169 Kris Draper .05 .02
❑ 170 Dave Gagner .05 .02
❑ 171 Steve Yzerman .75 .35
❑ 172 Nikolai Khabibulin .10 .05
❑ 173 Chris Gratton .05 .02
❑ 174 Dave Lowry .05 .02
❑ 175 Travis Green .10 .05
❑ 176 Alexei Kovalev .05 .02
❑ 177 Mike Ricci .05 .02
❑ 178 Brendan Shanahan .50 .23
❑ 179 Corey Hirsch .10 .05
❑ 180 Bill Guerin .05 .02
❑ 181 Alexander Mogilny .10 .05
❑ 182 Steve Duchesne .05 .02
❑ 183 Ray Ferraro .05 .02
❑ 184 Mike Richter .25 .11
❑ 185 Yuri Khmylev .05 .02
❑ 186 Stephane Fiset .10 .05
❑ 187 John Vanbiesbrouck .40 .18
❑ 188 Scott Niedermayer .05 .02
❑ 189 Brad May .10 .05
❑ 190 Shawn McEachern .05 .02
❑ 191 Joe Mullen .10 .05
❑ 192 Dominik Hasek .50 .23
❑ 193 Steve Thomas .05 .02
❑ 194 Russ Courtnall .05 .02
❑ 195 Joe Nieuwendyk .10 .05
❑ 196 Petr Klima .05 .02
❑ 197 Brett Hull .30 .14
❑ 198 Bernie Nicholls .05 .02
❑ 199 Dale Hunter .05 .02
❑ 200 Pat Verbeek .05 .02
❑ 201 Phil Housley .10 .05
❑ 202 Todd Krygier .05 .02
❑ 203 Zdeno Ciger .05 .02
❑ 204 Alexandre Daigle .05 .02
❑ 205 Cam Neely .10 .05
❑ 206 Mike Gartner .10 .05
❑ 207 Garth Snow .10 .05
❑ 208 Pat Falloon .05 .02
❑ 209 Kelly Hrudey .10 .05
❑ 210 Ray Sheppard .10 .05
❑ 211 Ted Donato .05 .02
❑ 212 Glenn Healy .10 .05
❑ 213 Radek Dvorak .05 .02
❑ 214 Niclas Andersson .05 .02
❑ 215 Miroslav Satan .05 .02
❑ 216 Roman Vopat .05 .02
❑ 217 Bryan McCabe .05 .02
❑ 218 Jamie Langenbrunner .05 .02
❑ 219 Kyle McLaren .05 .02
❑ 220 Stephane Yelle .05 .02
❑ 221 Byron Dafoe .10 .05
❑ 222 Grant Marshall .05 .02
❑ 223 Ryan Smyth .25 .11
❑ 224 Ville Peltonen .05 .02
❑ 225 Deron Quint .05 .02
❑ 226 Brian Holzinger .10 .05
❑ 227 Jose Theodore .10 .05
❑ 228 Ethan Moreau RC .25 .11
❑ 229 Steve Sullivan .10 .05
❑ 230 Kevin Hodson .25 .11
❑ 231 Cory Stillman .05 .02
❑ 232 Ralph Intranuovo .05 .02
❑ 233 Vitali Yachmenev .05 .02
❑ 234 Marcus Ragnarsson .05 .02
❑ 235 Nolan Baumgartner .05 .02
❑ 236 Chad Kilger .05 .02
❑ 237 Niklas Sundstrom .05 .02
❑ 238 Paul Coffey CL (1-120) .25 .11
❑ 239 Doug Gilmour CL (121-240) .25 .11
❑ 240 Steve Yzerman CL (inserts) .25 .11

## 1996-97 Donruss Press Proofs

This 240-card standard size set is a parallel issue to the regular Donruss set. A cut-out star in the upper right-hand corner, along with the words "First 2,000 Printed, Press Proof" printed above the set logo, along the bottom distinguish these cards from their regular counterparts.

| | MINT | NRMT |
|---|---|---|
| COMPLETE SET (240) | 1000.00 | 450.00 |
| COMMON CARD (1-240) | 2.50 | 1.10 |

*STARS: 20X TO 50X BASIC CARDS
*YOUNG STARS: 12.5X TO 30X BASIC CARDS

## 1996-97 Donruss Between the Pipes

This standard size set features 10 of the NHL's top netminders. The card fronts feature a full color photo with a rounded edge on the right hand corners. The player's name is featured on the left-hand side of the card and the Donruss logo is printed in red foil on the upper right-hand corner. These cards are found only in retail packs and are serially numbered to 4,000.

| | MINT | NRMT |
|---|---|---|
| COMPLETE SET (10) | 150.00 | 70.00 |
| COMMON CARD (1-10) | 8.00 | 3.60 |

❑ 1 Patrick Roy 50.00 22.00
❑ 2 Martin Brodeur 25.00 11.00
❑ 3 Jim Carey 10.00 4.50
❑ 4 John Vanbiesbrouck 15.00 6.75
❑ 5 Chris Osgood 10.00 4.50
❑ 6 Ed Belfour 10.00 4.50
❑ 7 Jocelyn Thibault 10.00 4.50
❑ 8 Curtis Joseph 10.00 4.50
❑ 9 Nikolai Khabibulin 8.00 3.60
❑ 10 Felix Potvin 10.00 4.50

## 1996-97 Donruss Dominators

The ten cards in this set were randomly inserted in hobby packs at indeterminate odds and feature three of the top players at each position. These cards are serially numbered to 5,000 and printed on laminated holographic foil stock.

| | MINT | NRMT |
|---|---|---|
| COMPLETE SET (10) | 150.00 | 70.00 |
| COMMON CARD (1-10) | 8.00 | 3.60 |

❑ 1 Jim Carey 12.00 5.50
Martin Brodeur
John Vanbiesbrouck
❑ 2 Nikolai Khabibulin 15.00 6.75
Chris Osgood
Jocelyn Thibault
❑ 3 Chris Chelios 8.00 3.60
Paul Coffey
Ray Bourque
❑ 4 Mario Lemieux 30.00 13.50
Jaromir Jagr
Ron Francis
❑ 5 Eric Lindros 30.00 13.50
Wayne Gretzky
Jason Arnott
❑ 6 Doug Gilmour 8.00 3.60
Wendel Clark
Pierre Turgeon
❑ 7 Alexander Mogilny 12.00 5.50
Pavel Bure
Trevor Linden
❑ 8 Paul Kariya 25.00 11.00
Teemu Selanne
Keith Tkachuk
❑ 9 Mike Modano 12.00 5.50
Jeremy Roenick
Sergei Fedorov
❑ 10 Eric Daze 15.00 6.75
Saku Koivu
Ed Jovanovski

## 1996-97 Donruss Elite Inserts

These ten standard-size cards were randomly inserted into all varieties of packs. The basic version of the set has silver borders with cards serially numbered to 10,000. The tougher-to-find gold parallel version features, naturally enough, gold borders with serial numbering to 2,000.

| | MINT | NRMT |
|---|---|---|
| COMPLETE SET (10) | 100.00 | 45.00 |
| COMMON CARD (1-10) | 3.00 | 1.35 |
| COMP.GOLD SET (10) | 300.00 | 135.00 |
| COMMON GOLD (1-10) | 10.00 | 4.50 |

*GOLD: 1.5X TO 3X BASIC CARDS

❑ 1 Pavel Bure 8.00 3.60
❑ 2 Wayne Gretzky 25.00 11.00
❑ 3 Doug Weight 3.00 1.35
❑ 4 Brett Hull 5.00 2.20
❑ 5 Mark Messier 5.00 2.20
❑ 6 Brendan Shanahan 8.00 3.60
❑ 7 Joe Sakic 8.00 3.60
❑ 8 Sergei Fedorov 8.00 3.60
❑ 9 Eric Lindros 12.00 5.50
❑ 10 Patrick Roy 20.00 9.00

## 1996-97 Donruss Go Top Shelf

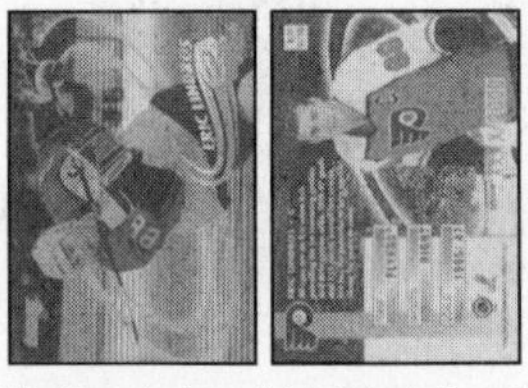

This 10-card set was distributed only through magazine packs, with each card numbered out of 2,000. Card fronts feature a color player photo over a holographic silver background. Card backs feature another color photo along with biographical information.

| | MINT | NRMT |
|---|---|---|
| COMPLETE SET (10) | 400.00 | 180.00 |
| COMMON CARD (1-10) | 12.00 | 5.50 |

❑ 1 Mario Lemieux 60.00 27.00
❑ 2 Teemu Selanne 25.00 11.00
❑ 3 Joe Sakic 25.00 11.00
❑ 4 Alexander Mogilny 12.00 5.50
❑ 5 Jaromir Jagr 40.00 18.00
❑ 6 Brett Hull 15.00 6.75
❑ 7 Mike Modano 15.00 6.75
❑ 8 Paul Kariya 50.00 22.00
❑ 9 Eric Lindros 40.00 18.00
❑ 10 Peter Forsberg 40.00 18.00

## 1996-97 Donruss Hit List

This set features 20 of the NHL's top bangers and crashers. Individually numbered to 10,000, these cards feature an internal die-cut with a color photo, and the player's name and position in silver foil on the front.

| | MINT | NRMT |
|---|---|---|
| COMPLETE SET (20) | 80.00 | 36.00 |
| COMMON CARD (1-20) | 1.50 | .70 |

❑ 1 Eric Lindros 10.00 4.50
❑ 2 Wendel Clark 4.00 1.80
❑ 3 Ed Jovanovski 4.00 1.80
❑ 4 Jeremy Roenick 3.00 1.35
❑ 5 Doug Weight 4.00 1.80
❑ 6 Chris Chelios 3.00 1.35
❑ 7 Brendan Shanahan 6.00 2.70
❑ 8 Mark Messier 4.00 1.80
❑ 9 Scott Stevens 1.50 .70
❑ 10 Keith Tkachuk 4.00 1.80
❑ 11 Trevor Linden 4.00 1.80
❑ 12 Eric Daze 4.00 1.80
❑ 13 John LeClair 5.00 2.20
❑ 14 Peter Forsberg 10.00 4.50
❑ 15 Doug Gilmour 4.00 1.80
❑ 16 Roman Hamrlik 4.00 1.80
❑ 17 Owen Nolan 4.00 1.80
❑ 18 Claude Lemieux 4.00 1.80
❑ 19 Saku Koivu 5.00 2.20
❑ 20 Theoren Fleury 4.00 1.80
❑ P1 Eric Lindros PROMO 5.00 2.20

## 1996-97 Donruss Rated Rookies

This set features ten top young superstars. Card fronts feature full color action photos with the player's name and team printed in silver foil. Card backs feature a portrait and biographical information. A rare press proof version of these cards exists, though little about them, including quantity of production, is unknown. They are not mentioned on any product literature, nor are they widely available. They are fairly easy to distinguish by virtue of their gold foil finish. The press proof versions, when seen, have been trading with a multiplier of 5X to 10X the value of the basic cards.

| | MINT | NRMT |
|---|---|---|
| COMPLETE SET (10) | 30.00 | 13.50 |
| COMMON CARD (1-10) | 2.00 | .90 |

❑ 1 Eric Daze 5.00 2.20
❑ 2 Petr Sykora 2.00 .90
❑ 3 Valeri Bure 2.00 .90
❑ 4 Jere Lehtinen 2.00 .90
❑ 5 Jeff O'Neill 3.00 1.35
❑ 6 Saku Koivu 8.00 3.60
❑ 7 Ed Jovanovski 5.00 2.20
❑ 8 Eric Fichaud 3.00 1.35
❑ 9 Todd Bertuzzi 3.00 1.35
❑ 10 Daniel Alfredsson 4.00 1.80

## 1997-98 Donruss

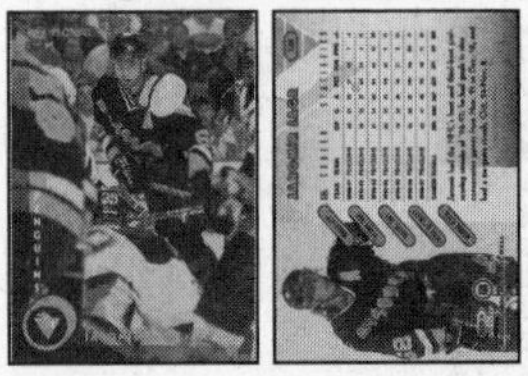

The 1997-98 Donruss set was issued in one series totalling 230 cards and distributed in 10-card packs. The fronts freature color action player photos. The backs carry player information.

| | MINT | NRMT |
|---|---|---|
| COMPLETE SET (230) | 25.00 | 11.00 |
| COMMON CARD (1-230) | .10 | .05 |

❑ 1 Peter Forsberg 1.00 .45
❑ 2 Steve Yzerman 1.00 .45
❑ 3 Eric Lindros 1.00 .45
❑ 4 Mark Messier .40 .18
❑ 5 Patrick Roy 1.50 .70
❑ 6 Jeremy Roenick .30 .14
❑ 7 Paul Kariya 1.25 .55
❑ 8 Valeri Bure .10 .05
❑ 9 Dominik Hasek .60 .25
❑ 10 Doug Gilmour .30 .14
❑ 11 Garth Snow .20 .09
❑ 12 Todd Bertuzzi .10 .05
❑ 13 Chris Osgood .30 .14
❑ 14 Jarome Iginla .20 .09
❑ 15 Lonny Bohonos .10 .05
❑ 16 Jeff O'Neill .10 .05
❑ 17 Daniel Alfredsson .20 .09
❑ 18 Daymond Langkow .10 .05
❑ 19 Alexei Yashin .20 .09
❑ 20 Byron Dafoe .20 .09
❑ 21 Mike Peca .10 .05
❑ 22 Jim Carey .20 .09
❑ 23 Pat Verbeek .10 .05

❑ 24 Terry Ryan .10 .05
❑ 25 Adam Oates .20 .09
❑ 26 Kevin Hatcher .10 .05
❑ 27 Ken Wregget .20 .09
❑ 28 Pierre Turgeon .20 .09
❑ 29 John LeClair .50 .23
❑ 30 Jere Lehtinen .10 .05
❑ 31 Jamie Storr .20 .09
❑ 32 Doug Weight .20 .09
❑ 33 Tommy Salo .20 .09
❑ 34 Bernie Nicholls .10 .05
❑ 35 Jocelyn Thibault .20 .09
❑ 36 Dale Hawerchuk .20 .09
UER front Dave
❑ 37 Chris Chelios .30 .14
❑ 38 Kirk Muller .10 .05
❑ 39 Steve Sullivan .10 .05
❑ 40 Andy Moog .20 .09
❑ 41 Martin Gelinas .10 .05
❑ 42 Shayne Corson .10 .05
❑ 43 Curtis Joseph .30 .14
❑ 44 Donald Audette .10 .05
❑ 45 Rick Tocchet .20 .09
❑ 46 Craig Janney .10 .05
❑ 47 Geoff Courtnall .10 .05
❑ 48 Wade Redden .10 .05
❑ 49 Steve Rucchin .10 .05
❑ 50 Ethan Moreau .10 .05
❑ 51 Steve Shields .20 .09
❑ 52 Jamie Pushor .10 .05
❑ 53 Saku Koivu .50 .23
❑ 54 Oleg Tverdovsky .10 .05
❑ 55 Jeff Friesen .20 .09
❑ 56 Chris Gratton .20 .09
❑ 57 Wendel Clark .20 .09
❑ 58 John Vanbiesbrouck .50 .23
❑ 59 Trevor Kidd .20 .09
❑ 60 Sandis Ozolinsh .20 .09
❑ 61 Dave Andreychuk .10 .05
❑ 62 Travis Green .10 .05
❑ 63 Paul Coffey .30 .14
❑ 64 Roman Turek .20 .09
❑ 65 Vladimir Konstantinov .10 .05
❑ 66 Ray Bourque .30 .14
❑ 67 Wayne Primeau .10 .05
❑ 68 Todd Harvey .10 .05
❑ 69 Derek King .10 .05
❑ 70 Adam Graves .20 .09
❑ 71 Brett Hull .40 .18
❑ 72 Scott Niedermayer .10 .05
❑ 73 Mike Vernon .20 .09
❑ 74 Brian Holzinger .10 .05
❑ 75 Dainius Zubrus .30 .14
❑ 76 Patrick Lalime .20 .09
❑ 77 Corey Schwab .20 .09
❑ 78 Alexandre Daigle .20 .09
❑ 79 Geoff Sanderson .20 .09
❑ 80 Dave Gagner .10 .05
❑ 81 Jose Theodore .20 .09
❑ 82 Sergei Fedorov .60 .25
❑ 83 Keith Tkachuk .40 .18
❑ 84 Owen Nolan .20 .09
❑ 85 Brandon Convery .10 .05
❑ 86 Trevor Linden .20 .09
❑ 87 Landon Wilson .10 .05
❑ 88 Claude Lemieux .20 .09
❑ 89 Dimitri Khristich .10 .05
❑ 90 Luc Robitaille .20 .09
❑ 91 Todd Warriner .10 .05
❑ 92 Kelly Hrudey .20 .09
❑ 93 Mike Dunham .20 .09
❑ 94 Mike Grier .10 .05
❑ 95 Joe Juneau .20 .09
❑ 96 Alexei Zhamnov .10 .05
❑ 97 Jamie Langenbrunner .10 .05
❑ 98 Sean Pronger .10 .05
❑ 99 Janne Niinimaa .20 .09
❑ 100 Chris Pronger .20 .09
❑ 101 Ray Sheppard .10 .05
❑ 102 Tony Amonte .20 .09
❑ 103 Ron Tugnutt .20 .09
❑ 104 Mike Modano .40 .18
❑ 105 Dan Trebil .10 .05
❑ 106 Alexander Mogilny .20 .09
❑ 107 Darren McCarty .10 .05
❑ 108 Ted Donato .10 .05
❑ 109 Brian Savage .10 .05
❑ 110 Mike Gartner .20 .09
❑ 111 Jim Campbell .10 .05
❑ 112 Roman Hamrlik .10 .05
❑ 113 Andreas Dackell .10 .05
❑ 114 Ron Hextall .20 .09
❑ 115 Steve Washburn .10 .05
❑ 116 Jeff Hackett .20 .09
❑ 117 Joe Sakic .60 .25
❑ 118 Anson Carter .10 .05
❑ 119 Vyacheslav Kozlov .10 .05
❑ 120 Nikolai Khabibulin .20 .09
❑ 121 Tony Granato .10 .05
❑ 122 Al MacInnis .20 .09
❑ 123 Daren Puppa .20 .09
❑ 124 Mike Richter .30 .14
❑ 125 Zigmund Palffy .30 .14
❑ 126 Martin Brodeur .75 .35
❑ 127 Rem Murray .10 .05
❑ 128 Sean Burke .20 .09
❑ 129 Aki Berg .10 .05
❑ 130 Dmitri Mironov .10 .05
❑ 131 Jamie Allison .10 .05
❑ 132 Valeri Kamensky .20 .09
❑ 133 Pat LaFontaine .20 .09
❑ 134 Jozef Stumpel .20 .09
❑ 135 Peter Bondra .30 .14
❑ 136 Mark Recchi .20 .09
❑ 137 Ron Francis .20 .09
❑ 138 Harry York .10 .05
❑ 139 Mats Sundin .30 .14
❑ 140 Bobby Holik .10 .05
❑ 141 Eric Desjardins .10 .05
❑ 142 Scott Lachance .10 .05
❑ 143 Wayne Gretzky 2.00 .90
❑ 144 Ed Jovanovski .20 .09
❑ 145 Jason Arnott .20 .09
❑ 146 Andrew Cassels .10 .05
❑ 147 Roman Vopat .10 .05
❑ 148 Dwayne Roloson .10 .05
❑ 149 Derek Plante .10 .05
❑ 150 Phil Housley .10 .05
❑ 151 Mikael Renberg .20 .09
❑ 152 Petr Nedved .20 .09
❑ 153 Grant Fuhr .20 .09
❑ 154 Felix Potvin .30 .14
❑ 155 John MacLean .10 .05
❑ 156 Brian Leetch .30 .14
❑ 157 Rod Brind'Amour .20 .09
❑ 158 Ryan Smyth .20 .09
❑ 159 Teemu Selanne .60 .25
❑ 160 Theoren Fleury .20 .09
❑ 161 Adam Deadmarsh .20 .09
❑ 162 Corey Hirsch .20 .09
❑ 163 Bryan Berard .20 .09
❑ 164 Ed Belfour .30 .14
❑ 165 Sergei Berezin .10 .05
❑ 166 Damian Rhodes .20 .09
❑ 167 Guy Hebert .20 .09
❑ 168 Derian Hatcher .10 .05
❑ 169 Jonas Hoglund .10 .05
❑ 170 Matthew Barnaby .10 .05
❑ 171 Scott Mellanby .10 .05
❑ 172 Bill Ranford .20 .09
❑ 173 Vincent Damphousse .20 .09
❑ 174 Anders Eriksson .10 .05
❑ 175 Chad Kilger .10 .05
❑ 176 Darren Turcotte .10 .05
❑ 177 Dino Ciccarelli .10 .05
❑ 178 Niklas Sundstrom .10 .05
❑ 179 Stephane Fiset .20 .09
❑ 180 Mike Ricci .10 .05
❑ 181 Brendan Shanahan .60 .25
❑ 182 Darcy Tucker .10 .05
❑ 183 Eric Fichaud .20 .09
❑ 184 Todd Marchant .10 .05
❑ 185 Keith Primeau .10 .05
❑ 186 Joe Nieuwendyk .20 .09
❑ 187 Pavel Bure .60 .25
❑ 188 Jaromir Jagr 1.00 .45
❑ 189 Kirk McLean .20 .09
❑ 190 Daniel Goneau .10 .05
❑ 191 Rob Niedermayer .10 .05
❑ 192 Eric Daze .20 .09
❑ 193 Richard Matvichuk .10 .05
❑ 194 Scott Stevens .10 .05
❑ 195 Dale Hunter .10 .05
❑ 196 Hnat Domenichelli .10 .05
❑ 197 Philippe DeRouville .10 .05
❑ 198 Marcel Cousineau .20 .09
❑ 199 Kevin Hodson .20 .09
❑ 200 Jean-Sebastien Giguere .20 .09
❑ 201 Paxton Schafer .20 .09
❑ 202 Marc Denis .20 .09
❑ 203 Frank Banham .10 .05
❑ 204 Vadim Sharifijanov .10 .05
❑ 205 Paul Healey .10 .05
❑ 206 D.J. Smith .10 .05
❑ 207 Christian Matte .10 .05
❑ 208 Sean Brown .10 .05
❑ 209 Tomas Vokoun .10 .05
❑ 210 Vladimir Vorobiev .10 .05
❑ 211 Jean-Yves Leroux .10 .05
❑ 212 Domenic Pittis .10 .05
❑ 213 Derek Wilkinson .10 .05
❑ 214 Jason Holland .10 .05
❑ 215 Pascal Rheaume .10 .05
❑ 216 Steve Kelly .10 .05
❑ 217 Vaclav Varada .10 .05
❑ 218 Mike Fountain .10 .05
❑ 219 Vaclav Prospal .50 .23
❑ 220 Jaroslav Svejkovsky .20 .09
❑ 221 Marty Murray .10 .05
❑ 222 Wade Belak .20 .09
❑ 223 Jamal Mayers .10 .05
❑ 224 Shayne Toporowski .10 .05
❑ 225 Mike Knuble .20 .09
❑ 226 Jarome Iginla CL (1-60) .10 .05
❑ 227 Keith Tkachuk CL (61-120) .20 .09
❑ 228 Adam Oates CL (121-180) .10 .05
❑ 229 John LeClair CL (181-230) .25 .11
❑ 230 Brian Leetch CL (inserts) .20 .09

## 1997-98 Donruss Press Proofs Silver

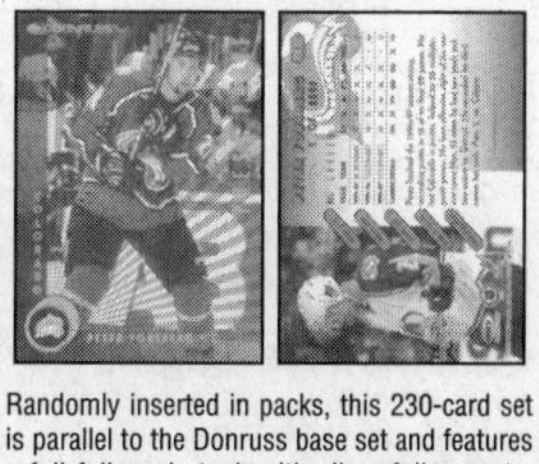

Randomly inserted in packs, this 230-card set is parallel to the Donruss base set and features a full foil card stock with silver foil accents. Only 1500 of this set were produced and are sequentially numbered.

| | MINT | NRMT |
|---|---|---|
| COMPLETE SET (230) | 1200.00 | 550.00 |
| COMMON CARD (1-230) | 3.00 | 1.35 |

*STARS: 20X TO 40X BASIC CARDS
*YOUNG STARS: 12.5X TO 25X BASIC CARDS

## 1997-98 Donruss Press Proofs Gold

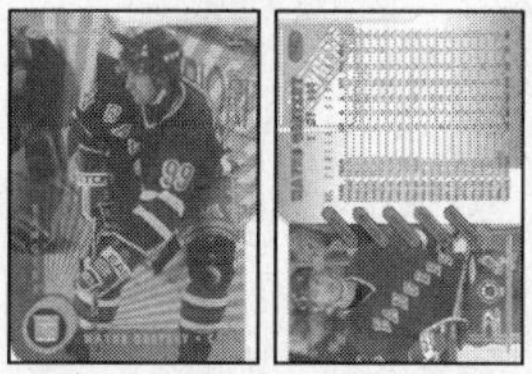

Randomly inserted in packs, this 230-card set is parallel to the Donruss base set and features a unique die cut design with gold foil stamping. Only 500 of this set were produced and are sequentially numbered.

| | MINT | NRMT |
|---|---|---|
| COMPLETE SET (230) | 2500.00 | 1100.00 |
| COMMON CARD (1-230) | 10.00 | 4.50 |

*STARS: 40X TO 100X BASIC CARDS
*YOUNG STARS: 40X TO 80X BASIC CARDS

❑ 1 Peter Forsberg 100.00 45.00
❑ 2 Steve Yzerman 100.00 45.00
❑ 3 Eric Lindros 120.00 55.00
❑ 5 Patrick Roy 150.00 70.00
❑ 7 Paul Kariya 120.00 55.00
❑ 117 Joe Sakic 75.00 34.00
❑ 143 Wayne Gretzky 200.00 90.00
❑ 188 Jaromir Jagr 100.00 45.00

## 1997-98 Donruss Between The Pipes

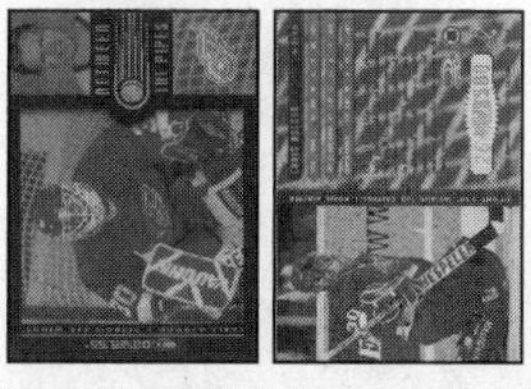

Randomly inserted in hobby packs only, this 10-card set features color photos of the league's top defensive players printed on an etched, full foil card stock with foil stamped accents. Only 3000 of this set were produced and are sequentially numbered.

| | MINT | NRMT |
|---|---|---|
| COMPLETE SET (10) | 200.00 | 90.00 |
| COMMON CARD (1-10) | 10.00 | 4.50 |

❑ 1 Patrick Roy 60.00 27.00
❑ 2 Martin Brodeur 30.00 13.50
❑ 3 John Vanbiesbrouck 20.00 9.00
❑ 4 Dominik Hasek 25.00 11.00
❑ 5 Chris Osgood 12.00 5.50
❑ 6 Jose Theodore 10.00 4.50
❑ 7 Garth Snow 10.00 4.50
❑ 8 Curtis Joseph 12.00 5.50
❑ 9 Felix Potvin 10.00 4.50
❑ 10 Jocelyn Thibault 10.00 4.50

## 1997-98 Donruss Elite Inserts

Randomly inserted in packs, this 12-card set features color photos of the league's most dominant superstars printed on card stock utilizing a double treatment of gold and holographic gold foils. Only 2500 of each card were produced and are sequentially numbered.

| | MINT | NRMT |
|---|---|---|
| COMPLETE SET (12) | 300.00 | 135.00 |
| COMMON CARD (1-12) | 12.00 | 5.50 |

❑ 1 Wayne Gretzky 50.00 22.00
❑ 2 Jaromir Jagr 25.00 11.00
❑ 3 Eric Lindros 25.00 11.00
❑ 4 Paul Kariya 30.00 13.50
❑ 5 Patrick Roy 40.00 18.00
❑ 6 Steve Yzerman 25.00 11.00
❑ 7 Peter Forsberg 25.00 11.00
❑ 8 John Vanbiesbrouck 12.00 5.50
❑ 9 Brendan Shanahan 15.00 6.75
❑ 10 Martin Brodeur 20.00 9.00
❑ 11 Dominik Hasek 15.00 6.75
❑ 12 Teemu Selanne 15.00 6.75

## 1997-98 Donruss Line 2 Line

Randomly inserted in packs, this 24-card fractured insert set contains three levels of scarcity with each level printed on foil card stocks. Level one is "Red Line" which features color photos of 12 players with red foil enhancements and each card sequentially numbered to 4000; Level two is "Blue Line" which features color photos of eight players with blue foil enhancements and each sequentially numbered to 2000; Level three is "Gold Line" which features color photos of four players with each sequentailly numbered to 1000. The first 250 of each Line two card features a unique die-cut design.

| | MINT | NRMT |
|---|---|---|
| COMPLETE SET (24) | 600.00 | 275.00 |
| COMMON CARD (1-24) | 6.00 | 2.70 |

*RED DIE CUTS: 2.5X TO 5X BASIC RED
*BLUE DIE CUTS: 1.5X TO 3X BASIC BLUE
*GOLD DIE CUTS: 1.5X TO 3X BASIC GOLD

❑ 1 Wayne Gretzky G 100.00 45.00
❑ 2 Teemu Selanne R 15.00 6.75
❑ 3 Brian Leetch B 12.00 5.50
❑ 4 Peter Forsberg R 25.00 11.00
❑ 5 Steve Yzerman R 25.00 11.00
❑ 6 Oleg Tverdovsky B 6.00 2.70
❑ 7 Doug Gilmour R 6.00 2.70
❑ 8 Eric Lindros G 50.00 22.00
❑ 9 Bryan Berard B 12.00 5.50
❑ 10 Brendan Shanahan R 15.00 6.75
❑ 11 Pavel Bure R 15.00 6.75
❑ 12 Joe Sakic R 15.00 6.75
❑ 13 Chris Chelios B 12.00 5.50
❑ 14 Mike Modano R 10.00 4.50
❑ 15 Paul Coffey B 12.00 5.50
❑ 16 Jaromir Jagr G 50.00 22.00
❑ 17 Jarome Iginla R 6.00 2.70
❑ 18 Brett Hull R 10.00 4.50
❑ 19 Wade Redden B 6.00 2.70
❑ 20 Paul Kariya G 60.00 27.00
❑ 21 Ray Bourque B 12.00 5.50
❑ 22 Ryan Smyth R 6.00 2.70
❑ 23 Mark Messier R 10.00 4.50
❑ 24 Sandis Ozolinsh B 10.00 4.50

## 1997-98 Donruss Rated Rookies

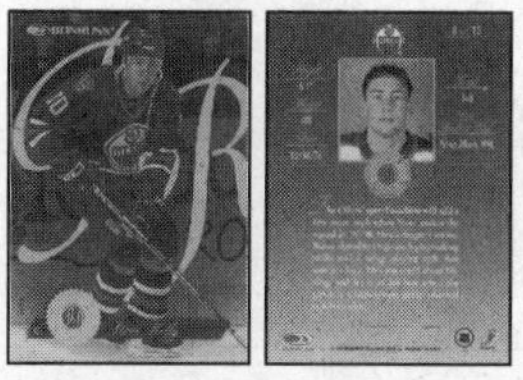

Randomly inserted in packs, this 10-card set features color action photos of the hottest young rookie prospects printed on a background with the letters "RR."

| | MINT | NRMT |
|---|---|---|
| COMPLETE SET (10) | 50.00 | 22.00 |
| COMMON CARD (1-10) | 3.00 | 1.35 |
| COMP.MEDALIST SET (10) | 800.00 | 350.00 |
| COMMON MEDALIST (1-10) | 50.00 | 22.00 |

❑ 1 Tomas Vokoun 5.00 2.20
❑ 2 Paxton Schafer 5.00 2.20
❑ 3 Vaclav Prospal 8.00 3.60
❑ 4 Marc Denis 8.00 3.60
❑ 5 Domenic Pittis 3.00 1.35
❑ 6 Christian Matte 3.00 1.35
❑ 7 Marcel Cousineau 5.00 2.20
❑ 8 Steve Kelly 5.00 2.20
❑ 9 Jaroslav Svejkovsky 5.00 2.20
❑ 10 Jean-Sebastien Giguere 5.00 2.20

## 1997-98 Donruss Red Alert

Randomly inserted in retail packs only, this 10-card set features color photos of the league's top goal scorers printed on thick plastic card stock, die cut in the shape of a goal light and highlighted with red holographic foil treatments. Only 5,000 of the set were produced and are sequentially numbered.

| | MINT | NRMT |
|---|---|---|
| COMPLETE SET (10) | 150.00 | 70.00 |
| COMMON CARD (1-10) | 12.00 | 5.50 |

❑ 1 Adam Deadmarsh 12.00 5.50
❑ 2 Ryan Smyth 12.00 5.50
❑ 3 Sergei Fedorov 30.00 13.50
❑ 4 Keith Tkachuk 20.00 9.00
❑ 5 Brett Hull 20.00 9.00
❑ 6 Pavel Bure 30.00 13.50
❑ 7 John LeClair 25.00 11.00
❑ 8 Zigmund Palffy 12.00 5.50
❑ 9 Mats Sundin 15.00 6.75
❑ 10 Peter Bondra 15.00 6.75

## 1996-97 Donruss Canadian Ice

This 150-card set was issued eight cards per pack with a suggested retail price of $2.99. While these sets were initially made for distribution to Canada, a large amount of the product was shipped to the United States. Card fronts feature a full color action photo with the player's name and team appearing near the bottom of the card. Key rookies in this set include Mike Grier, Kevin Hodson, Ethan Moreau, and Dainius Zubrus.

| | MINT | NRMT |
|---|---|---|
| COMPLETE SET (150) | 30.00 | 13.50 |
| COMMON CARD (1-150) | .10 | .05 |

❑ 1 Jaromir Jagr 1.50 .70
❑ 2 Jocelyn Thibault .50 .23
❑ 3 Paul Kariya 2.00 .90
❑ 4 Derian Hatcher .10 .05
❑ 5 Wayne Gretzky 3.00 1.35
❑ 6 Peter Forsberg 1.50 .70
❑ 7 Eric Lindros 1.50 .70
❑ 8 Adam Oates .25 .11
❑ 9 Paul Coffey .50 .23
❑ 10 Chris Osgood .50 .23
❑ 11 Pat LaFontaine .25 .11
❑ 12 Mats Sundin .25 .11
❑ 13 Rob Niedermayer .25 .11
❑ 14 Doug Weight .25 .11
❑ 15 Al MacInnis .25 .11
❑ 16 Damian Rhodes .25 .11
❑ 17 Stephane Fiset .25 .11
❑ 18 Mike Gartner .25 .11
❑ 19 Patrick Roy 2.50 1.10
❑ 20 Eric Daze .25 .11
❑ 21 Ray Bourque .50 .23
❑ 22 Keith Tkachuk .60 .25
❑ 23 Mark Recchi .25 .11
❑ 24 Peter Bondra .50 .23
❑ 25 Mike Modano .60 .25
❑ 26 Mike Richter .50 .23
❑ 27 Keith Primeau .25 .11
❑ 28 Todd Bertuzzi .10 .05
❑ 29 Wendel Clark .25 .11
❑ 30 Scott Young .10 .05
❑ 31 Mario Lemieux 2.50 1.10
❑ 32 Valeri Kamensky .25 .11
❑ 33 Kirk McLean .25 .11
❑ 34 Daniel Alfredsson .25 .11
❑ 35 Ed Jovanovski .25 .11
❑ 36 Kelly Hrudey .25 .11
❑ 37 Trevor Kidd .25 .11
❑ 38 Joe Juneau .25 .11
❑ 39 Steve Yzerman 1.50 .70
❑ 40 Saku Koivu .75 .35
❑ 41 Alexei Kovalev .10 .05
❑ 42 Rob Blake .10 .05
❑ 43 Shayne Corson .10 .05
❑ 44 Roman Hamrlik .25 .11
❑ 45 Stephane Yelle .10 .05
❑ 46 Martin Brodeur 1.25 .55
❑ 47 Kirk Muller .10 .05
❑ 48 Pat Verbeek .10 .05
❑ 49 Jari Kurri .25 .11
❑ 50 Michal Pivonka .10 .05
❑ 51 Ron Hextall .25 .11
❑ 52 Trevor Linden .25 .11
❑ 53 Vincent Damphousse .25 .11
❑ 54 Owen Nolan .25 .11
❑ 55 Sergei Fedorov 1.00 .45
❑ 56 Chris Chelios .50 .23
❑ 57 Jeremy Roenick .50 .23
❑ 58 Zigmund Palffy .50 .23
❑ 59 Pavel Bure 1.00 .45
❑ 60 Dominik Hasek 1.00 .45
❑ 61 Alexei Yashin .25 .11
❑ 62 Chris Gratton .25 .11
❑ 63 Joe Nieuwendyk .25 .11

❑ 64 Luc Robitaille .25 .11
❑ 65 Brett Hull .60 .25
❑ 66 Sean Burke .25 .11
❑ 67 Felix Potvin .50 .23
❑ 68 Jason Arnott .25 .11
❑ 69 Valeri Bure .25 .11
❑ 70 Tom Barrasso .25 .11
❑ 71 Vyacheslav Kozlov .10 .05
❑ 72 Petr Sykora .10 .05
❑ 73 Corey Hirsch .25 .11
❑ 74 Joe Sakic 1.00 .45
❑ 75 Bill Ranford .25 .11
❑ 76 Yanic Perreault .10 .05
❑ 77 Mikael Renberg .25 .11
❑ 78 Theoren Fleury .25 .11
❑ 79 Jim Carey .50 .23
❑ 80 Vitali Yachmenev .10 .05
❑ 81 Martin Rucinsky .10 .05
❑ 82 Jeff O'Neill .10 .05
❑ 83 Marcus Ragnarsson .10 .05
❑ 84 John Vanbiesbrouck .75 .35
❑ 85 Teemu Selanne 1.00 .45
❑ 86 Larry Murphy .25 .11
❑ 87 Mark Messier .60 .25
❑ 88 Alexei Zhamnov .25 .11
❑ 89 Ryan Smyth .50 .23
❑ 90 Andy Moog .25 .11
❑ 91 Alexander Mogilny .25 .11
❑ 92 Kris Draper .10 .05
❑ 93 Ron Francis .25 .11
❑ 94 Mike Vernon .25 .11
❑ 95 Nikolai Khabibulin .25 .11
❑ 96 Mariusz Czerkawski .10 .05
❑ 97 Mathieu Schneider .10 .05
❑ 98 Stephane Richer .25 .11
❑ 99 Mike Ricci .10 .05
❑ 100 John LeClair .75 .35
❑ 101 Brendan Shanahan 1.00 .45
❑ 102 Daren Puppa .25 .11
❑ 103 Scott Stevens .25 .11
❑ 104 Alexandre Daigle .10 .05
❑ 105 Dimitri Khristich .10 .05
❑ 106 Bernie Nicholls .10 .05
❑ 107 Scott Mellanby .25 .11
❑ 108 Brian Leetch .50 .23
❑ 109 Grant Fuhr .25 .11
❑ 110 Pierre Turgeon .25 .11
❑ 111 Jere Lehtinen .10 .05
❑ 112 Doug Gilmour .50 .23
❑ 113 Ed Belfour .50 .23
❑ 114 Geoff Sanderson .25 .11
❑ 115 Claude Lemieux .25 .11
❑ 116 Curtis Joseph .50 .23
❑ 117 Igor Larionov .10 .05
❑ 118 Jamie Pushor .10 .05
❑ 119 Sergei Berezin .75 .35
❑ 120 Eric Fichaud .25 .11
❑ 121 Wade Redden .10 .05
❑ 122 Hnat Domenichelli .10 .05
❑ 123 Rem Murray .10 .05
❑ 124 Jarome Iginla .50 .23
❑ 125 Richard Zednik .10 .05
❑ 126 Daniel Goneau .10 .05
❑ 127 Ethan Moreau .50 .23
❑ 128 Janne Niinimaa .50 .23
❑ 129 Tomas Holmstrom .10 .05
❑ 130 Fredrik Modin .10 .05
❑ 131 Bryan Berard .50 .23
❑ 132 Jim Campbell .10 .05
❑ 133 Chris O'Sullivan .10 .05
❑ 134 Andreas Dackell .10 .05
❑ 135 Daymond Langkow .10 .05
❑ 136 Kevin Hodson .50 .23
❑ 137 Jamie Langenbrunner .10 .05
❑ 138 Mattias Timander .10 .05
❑ 139 Tuomas Gronman .10 .05
❑ 140 Jonas Hoglund .10 .05
❑ 141 Mike Grier 1.00 .45
❑ 142 Terry Ryan .10 .05
❑ 143 Darcy Tucker .10 .05
❑ 144 Brandon Convery .10 .05
❑ 145 Anders Eriksson .10 .05
❑ 146 Christian Dube .10 .05
❑ 147 Dainius Zubrus 1.00 .45
❑ 148 Grant Fuhr CL .10 .05
❑ 149 Paul Coffey CL .25 .11
❑ 150 Ray Bourque CL .25 .11

## 1996-97 Donruss Canadian Ice Gold Press Proofs

This 150-card set is the tougher of two parallels to the base set. Production of these cards is limited to 150 sets, a fact which is noted on the card. The words Canadian Gold appear on the top of the card, and a gold foil treatment is used to enhance the appearance. No complete set price is listed below, as few, if any, sets have been completed due to the limited press run of the individual cards.

| | MINT | NRMT |
|---|---|---|
| COMMON CARD (1-150) | 8.00 | 3.60 |

*STARS: 50X TO 100X BASIC CARDS
*YOUNG STARS: 30X TO 60X BASIC CARDS
*RCs: 20X TO 40X BASIC CARDS

❑ 1 Jaromir Jagr 200.00 90.00
❑ 3 Paul Kariya 250.00 110.00
❑ 5 Wayne Gretzky 400.00 180.00
❑ 6 Peter Forsberg 200.00 90.00
❑ 7 Eric Lindros 250.00 110.00
❑ 19 Patrick Roy 300.00 135.00
❑ 31 Mario Lemieux 300.00 135.00

## 1996-97 Donruss Canadian Ice Red Press Proofs

This 150-card set is the easier of two parallels to the base set. Production of these cards is limited to 750 sets, a fact noted on the card. The fronts feature silver and red foil enhancements, along with the words Canadian Red.

| | MINT | NRMT |
|---|---|---|
| COMPLETE SET (150) | 1500.00 | 700.00 |
| COMMON CARD (1-150) | 3.00 | 1.35 |
| SEMISTARS/GOALIES | 8.00 | 3.60 |
| UNLISTED STARS | 15.00 | 6.75 |

*STARS: 12X TO 30X BASIC CARDS
*YOUNG STARS: 8X TO 20X

## 1996-97 Donruss Canadian Ice Les Gardiens

This bronze foil set features 10 of the NHL's top netminders, each of whom were born in Quebec. A full-color portrait of each player adorns the card fronts, along with the skyline of Montreal in the background. The player's name and team are printed in gold foil along the bottom of these cards. Each card is serially numbered out of 1,500.

| | MINT | NRMT |
|---|---|---|
| COMPLETE SET (10) | 300.00 | 135.00 |
| COMMON CARD (1-10) | 15.00 | 6.75 |

❑ 1 Patrick Roy 80.00 36.00
❑ 2 Jocelyn Thibault 20.00 9.00
❑ 3 Felix Potvin 20.00 9.00
❑ 4 Martin Brodeur 50.00 22.00
❑ 5 Stephane Fiset 15.00 6.75
❑ 6 Eric Fichaud 15.00 6.75
❑ 7 Dominic Roussel 15.00 6.75
❑ 8 Emmanuel Fernandez 15.00 6.75
❑ 9 Martin Biron 15.00 6.75
❑ 10 Jose Theodore 20.00 9.00

## 1996-97 Donruss Canadian Ice Mario Lemieux Scrapbook

This 25-card set was made as a tribute to Mario Lemieux. Each card depicts a different highlight from the storied career of the Penguins' great. Only 1,966 individually numbered copies of each card were produced. Mario also hand signed a number of these cards, and there are two distinct versions of this card. The first, numbered out of 1200, was randomly inserted into packs. The second, numbered out of 500, was available in a framed version of the set available directly through an in-pack offer from Donruss.

| | MINT | NRMT |
|---|---|---|
| COMPLETE SET (25) | 250.00 | 110.00 |
| COMMON CARD (1-25) | 10.00 | 4.50 |
| CERTIFIED AUTO/1200 | 200.00 | 90.00 |
| CERTIFIED AUTO/500 | 250.00 | 110.00 |

## 1996-97 Donruss Canadian Ice O Canada

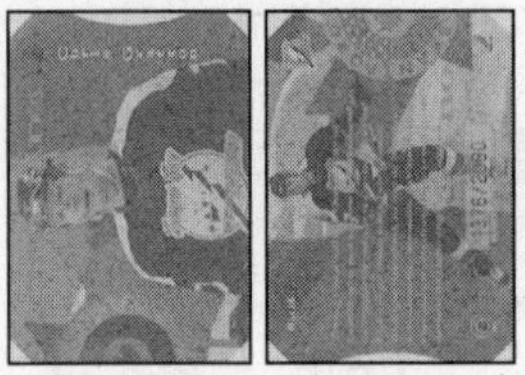

This 16-card set features some of the top players born in Canada. Card fronts contain a color action photo, with the Canadian flag in the background. Each card has die-cut corners and features gold and red foil printing. Just 2,000 individually numbered copies of each of these cards were produced.

| | MINT | NRMT |
|---|---|---|
| COMPLETE SET (16) | 300.00 | 135.00 |
| COMMON CARD (1-16) | 6.00 | 2.70 |

❑ 1 Joe Sakic 20.00 9.00
❑ 2 Paul Kariya 40.00 18.00
❑ 3 Mark Messier 12.00 5.50
❑ 4 Jarome Iginla 12.00 5.50
❑ 5 Theoren Fleury 8.00 3.60
❑ 6 Ed Belfour 12.00 5.50
❑ 7 Wayne Gretzky 60.00 27.00
❑ 8 Chris Gratton 6.00 2.70
❑ 9 Doug Gilmour 8.00 3.60
❑ 10 Kirk Muller 6.00 2.70
❑ 11 Eric Lindros 30.00 13.50
❑ 12 Brendan Shanahan 20.00 9.00
❑ 13 Mario Lemieux 50.00 22.00
❑ 14 Eric Daze 8.00 3.60
❑ 15 Geoff Sanderson 8.00 3.60
❑ 16 Terry Ryan 6.00 2.70

## 1997-98 Donruss Canadian Ice

The 1997-98 Donruss Canadian Ice set was issued in one series totalling 150 cards and distributed in eight-card packs. The fronts feature color action player photos. The backs carry player information.

| | MINT | NRMT |
|---|---|---|
| COMPLETE SET (150) | 30.00 | 13.50 |
| COMMON CARD (1-150) | .10 | .05 |

❑ 1 Patrick Roy 2.50 1.10
❑ 2 Paul Kariya 2.00 .90
❑ 3 Eric Lindros 1.50 .70
❑ 4 Steve Yzerman 1.50 .70
❑ 5 Wayne Gretzky 3.00 1.35
❑ 6 Peter Forsberg 1.50 .70
❑ 7 John Vanbiesbrouck .75 .35
❑ 8 Jaromir Jagr 1.50 .70
❑ 9 Jim Campbell .10 .05
❑ 10 Dominik Hasek 1.00 .45
❑ 11 Ray Bourque .50 .23
❑ 12 Jarome Iginla .25 .11
❑ 13 Mike Modano .60 .25
❑ 14 Ed Jovanovski .25 .11
❑ 15 Jocelyn Thibault .25 .11
❑ 16 Keith Tkachuk .60 .25
❑ 17 Brett Hull .60 .25
❑ 18 Pavel Bure 1.00 .45
❑ 19 Saku Koivu .75 .35
❑ 20 Curtis Joseph .50 .23
❑ 21 Eric Daze .25 .11
❑ 22 Keith Primeau .10 .05
❑ 23 Theoren Fleury .25 .11
❑ 24 Pierre Turgeon .25 .11
❑ 25 Peter Bondra .50 .23
❑ 26 Ed Belfour .50 .23
❑ 27 Pat Verbeek .10 .05
❑ 28 Chris Osgood .50 .23
❑ 29 Ray Sheppard .10 .05
❑ 30 Stephane Fiset .25 .11
❑ 31 Wade Redden .10 .05
❑ 32 Trevor Linden .25 .11
❑ 33 Zigmund Palffy .50 .23
❑ 34 Tony Amonte .25 .11
❑ 35 Derek Plante .10 .05
❑ 36 Jonas Hoglund .10 .05
❑ 37 Guy Hebert .25 .11
❑ 38 Garth Snow .25 .11
❑ 39 Chris Gratton .25 .11
❑ 40 Mats Sundin .50 .23
❑ 41 Geoff Sanderson .25 .11
❑ 42 Martin Brodeur 1.25 .55
❑ 43 Jozef Stumpel .25 .11
❑ 44 Ron Francis .25 .11
❑ 45 Alexander Mogilny .25 .11
❑ 46 Bill Ranford .25 .11
❑ 47 Kirk Muller .10 .05
❑ 48 Ron Hextall .25 .11
❑ 49 Doug Gilmour .50 .23
❑ 50 Mark Messier .60 .25
❑ 51 Joe Nieuwendyk .25 .11
❑ 52 Ryan Smyth .25 .11
❑ 53 Mark Recchi .25 .11
❑ 54 Mike Gartner .25 .11
❑ 55 Al MacInnis .25 .11
❑ 56 Felix Potvin .50 .23
❑ 57 Rob Blake .10 .05
❑ 58 Dimitri Khristich .10 .05
❑ 59 Jim Carey .25 .11
❑ 60 Trevor Kidd .25 .11
❑ 61 Martin Gelinas .10 .05
❑ 62 Oleg Tverdovsky .10 .05
❑ 63 Ron Tugnutt .25 .11
❑ 64 Paul Coffey .50 .23
❑ 65 Travis Green .10 .05
❑ 66 Andrew Cassels .10 .05
❑ 67 Brendan Shanahan 1.00 .45
❑ 68 Luc Robitaille .25 .11
❑ 69 Pat LaFontaine .25 .11
❑ 70 Daymond Langkow .10 .05
❑ 71 Petr Nedved .25 .11
❑ 72 Sergei Fedorov 1.00 .45
❑ 73 Anson Carter .10 .05
❑ 74 Teemu Selanne 1.00 .45
❑ 75 Nikolai Khabibulin .25 .11
❑ 76 Ken Wregget .25 .11
❑ 77 Dino Ciccarelli .10 .05
❑ 78 Adam Oates .25 .11
❑ 79 Kirk McLean .25 .11
❑ 80 Wendel Clark .25 .11
❑ 81 Jeff Friesen .25 .11
❑ 82 Valeri Kamensky .25 .11
❑ 83 Ethan Moreau .10 .05
❑ 84 Matthew Barnaby .10 .05
❑ 85 Andy Moog .25 .11
❑ 86 Doug Weight .25 .11
❑ 87 Mike Dunham .25 .11
❑ 88 Brian Leetch .50 .23
❑ 89 Mike Peca .10 .05
❑ 90 Chris Pronger .25 .11
❑ 91 Alexei Zhamnov .10 .05
❑ 92 Bryan Berard .25 .11
❑ 93 John LeClair .50 .23
❑ 94 Steve Sullivan .10 .05
❑ 95 Grant Fuhr .25 .11
❑ 96 Mikael Renberg .25 .11
❑ 97 Adam Graves .25 .11
❑ 98 Ray Ferraro .10 .05
❑ 99 Sean Burke .25 .11
❑ 100 Jeremy Roenick .50 .23
❑ 101 Jeff Hackett .25 .11
❑ 102 Joe Sakic 1.00 .45
❑ 103 Jamie Langenbrunner .10 .05
❑ 104 Stephane Richer .10 .05
❑ 105 Dave Andreychuk .10 .05
❑ 106 Tommy Salo .25 .11
❑ 107 Mike Richter .50 .23
❑ 108 Owen Nolan .25 .11
❑ 109 Corey Hirsch .25 .11
❑ 110 Daren Puppa .25 .11
❑ 111 Darcy Tucker .10 .05
❑ 112 Daniel Alfredsson .25 .11
❑ 113 Rod Brind'Amour .25 .11
❑ 114 Scott Stevens .10 .05
❑ 115 Vincent Damphousse .25 .11
❑ 116 Mathieu Schneider .10 .05
❑ 117 Jason Arnott .25 .11
❑ 118 Mike Vernon .25 .11
❑ 119 Sandis Ozolinsh .25 .11
❑ 120 Chris Chelios .50 .23
❑ 121 Mike Grier .10 .05
❑ 122 Alexandre Daigle .25 .11
❑ 123 Roman Hamrlik .10 .05
❑ 124 Derian Hatcher .10 .05
❑ 125 Damian Rhodes .25 .11
❑ 126 Adam Deadmarsh .25 .11
❑ 127 Alexei Yashin .25 .11
❑ 128 Terry Ryan .10 .05
❑ 129 Jeff Ware .10 .05
❑ 130 Steve Kelly .10 .05
❑ 131 Hnat Domenichelli .10 .05
❑ 132 Steve Shields .25 .11
❑ 133 Paxton Schafer .25 .11
❑ 134 Vadim Sharifijanov .10 .05
❑ 135 Vaclav Prospal .75 .35
❑ 136 Mike Fountain .10 .05
❑ 137 Christian Matte .10 .05
❑ 138 Tomas Vokoun .10 .05
❑ 139 Vladimir Vorobiev .10 .05
❑ 140 Domenic Pittis .10 .05
❑ 141 Vaclav Varada .10 .05
❑ 142 D.J. Smith .10 .05
❑ 143 Jaroslav Svejkovsky .25 .11
❑ 144 Jason Holland .10 .05
❑ 145 Marc Denis .25 .11
❑ 146 Jean-Sebastien Giguere .25 .11
❑ 147 Marcel Cousineau .25 .11
❑ 148 Dave Andreychuk CL (1-75) .10 .05
❑ 149 Mike Gartner CL (76-150) .10 .05
❑ 150 Stanley Cup .10 .05
Team Picture CL (inserts)

## 1997-98 Donruss Canadian Ice Dominion Series

This 150-card set is parallel to the base set and is similar in design. Only 150 of each card were produced.

| | MINT | NRMT |
|---|---|---|
| COMPLETE SET (150) | 5500.00 | 2500.00 |
| COMMON CARD (1-150) | 8.00 | 3.60 |

*DOMINION STARS: 50X TO 125X BASIC CARDS
*DOMINION YOUNG STARS: 30X TO 75X BASIC CARDS
SERIAL #'d/NON SERIAL #'d: SAME VALUE

## 1997-98 Donruss Canadian Ice Provincial Series

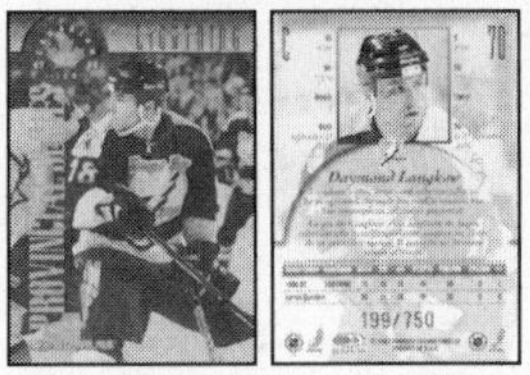

This 150-card set is parallel to the base set and is similar in design. Only 750 of each card were produced, and are sequentially numbered.

| | MINT | NRMT |
|---|---|---|
| COMPLETE SET (150) | 1200.00 | 550.00 |
| COMMON CARD (1-150) | 4.00 | 1.80 |

*PROV.STARS: 15X TO 30X BASIC CARDS
*PROV. YNG STARS: 10X TO 20X BASIC CARDS

## 1997-98 Donruss Canadian Ice Les Gardiens

Randomly inserted in packs, this 12-card set features color photos honoring great goaltenders from Quebec printed on micro-etched foil board. Only 1500 of each card were produced and are sequentially numbered.

| | MINT | NRMT |
|---|---|---|
| COMPLETE SET (12) | 200.00 | 90.00 |
| COMMON CARD (1-12) | 10.00 | 4.50 |

❑ 1 Patrick Roy 60.00 27.00
❑ 2 Felix Potvin 12.00 5.50
❑ 3 Martin Brodeur 30.00 13.50
❑ 4 Jean-Sebastien Giguere 10.00 4.50
❑ 5 Stephane Fiset 10.00 4.50
❑ 6 Jose Theodore 10.00 4.50
❑ 7 Jocelyn Thibault 20.00 9.00
❑ 8 Eric Fichaud 10.00 4.50
❑ 9 Patrick Lalime 20.00 9.00
❑ 10 Marcel Cousineau 10.00 4.50
❑ 11 Philippe DeRouville 10.00 4.50
❑ 12 Marc Denis 10.00 4.50

## 1997-98 Donruss Canadian Ice National Pride

Randomly inserted in packs, this 30-card set features color photos of the most prominent native Canadian players printed on a die cut plastic card in the shape of a maple leaf and with gold foil highlights.

| | MINT | NRMT |
|---|---|---|
| COMPLETE SET (30) | 250.00 | 110.00 |
| COMMON CARD (1-30) | 3.00 | 1.35 |

❑ 1 Wayne Gretzky 50.00 22.00

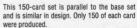

| Card | MINT | NRMT |
|---|---|---|
| ❑ 2 Mark Messier | 10.00 | 4.50 |
| ❑ 3 Paul Kariya | 30.00 | 13.50 |
| ❑ 4 Steve Yzerman | 25.00 | 11.00 |
| ❑ 5 Brendan Shanahan | 15.00 | 6.75 |
| ❑ 6 Chris Osgood | 10.00 | 4.50 |
| ❑ 7 Adam Oates | 5.00 | 2.20 |
| ❑ 8 Eric Lindros | 25.00 | 11.00 |
| ❑ 9 Doug Gilmour | 10.00 | 4.50 |
| ❑ 10 Ryan Smyth | 5.00 | 2.20 |
| ❑ 11 Ray Bourque | 10.00 | 4.50 |
| ❑ 12 Jason Arnott | 5.00 | 2.20 |
| ❑ 13 Jarome Iginla | 5.00 | 2.20 |
| ❑ 14 Geoff Sanderson | 5.00 | 2.20 |
| ❑ 15 Alexandre Daigle | 5.00 | 2.20 |
| ❑ 16 Trevor Linden | 5.00 | 2.20 |
| ❑ 17 Joe Sakic | 15.00 | 6.75 |
| ❑ 18 Mark Recchi | 5.00 | 2.20 |
| ❑ 19 Theoren Fleury | 5.00 | 2.20 |
| ❑ 20 Ron Francis | 5.00 | 2.20 |
| ❑ 21 Daymond Langkow | 3.00 | 1.35 |
| ❑ 22 Ed Belfour | 10.00 | 4.50 |
| ❑ 23 Paul Coffey | 10.00 | 4.50 |
| ❑ 24 Pierre Turgeon | 5.00 | 2.20 |
| ❑ 25 Claude Lemieux | 5.00 | 2.20 |
| ❑ 26 Ron Hextall | 5.00 | 2.20 |
| ❑ 27 Curtis Joseph | 10.00 | 4.50 |
| ❑ 28 Mike Vernon | 5.00 | 2.20 |
| ❑ 29 Vincent Damphousse | 5.00 | 2.20 |
| ❑ 30 Owen Nolan | 5.00 | 2.20 |

## 1997-98 Donruss Canadian Ice Stanley Cup Scrapbook

Randomly inserted in packs, this 33-card set is a fractured chase set which features color photos of players from each round of the 1997 Stanley Cup Playoffs. Only 2000 of the 16 Quarterfinals cards were produced and are sequentially numbered; 1500 of the eight sequentially numbered Conference Semifinals cards were produced; 1000 of the six sequentially numbered Conference Finals cards were produced; 750 of the two sequentially numbered Stanley Cup Finals cards were produced; only 250 of the one Stanley Cup Champions cards were produced and are sequentially numbered. Mike Vernon and Eric Lindros each autographed 750 of the Stanley Cup Finals cards, and Brendan Shanahan autographed 250 of the Stanley Cup Champions cards.

| | MINT | NRMT |
|---|---|---|
| COMPLETE SET (33) | 1200.00 | 550.00 |
| COMP.QRTRFINALS SET (16) | 10.00 | 4.50 |
| COMMON QRTRFINALS | 8.00 | 3.60 |
| COMP.CONF.SEMIFINALS SET (8) | 10.00 | 4.50 |
| COMMON CONF.SEMIFINALS | 10.00 | 4.50 |
| COMP.CONF.FINALS SET (6) | 10.00 | 4.50 |
| COMMON CONF.FINALS | 10.00 | 4.50 |

| Card | MINT | NRMT |
|---|---|---|
| ❑ 1 Mike Modano Q | 8.00 | 3.60 |
| ❑ 2 Curtis Joseph Q | 10.00 | 4.50 |
| ❑ 3 Joe Sakic Q | 20.00 | 9.00 |
| ❑ 4 Chris Chelios Q | 10.00 | 4.50 |
| ❑ 5 Chris Osgood Q | 10.00 | 4.50 |
| ❑ 6 Brett Hull Q | 12.00 | 5.50 |
| ❑ 7 Jeremy Roenick Q | 10.00 | 4.50 |
| ❑ 8 Teemu Selanne Q | 20.00 | 9.00 |
| ❑ 9 Jaromir Jagr Q | 30.00 | 13.50 |
| ❑ 10 Garth Snow Q | 8.00 | 3.60 |
| ❑ 11 Alexei Yashin Q | 8.00 | 3.60 |
| ❑ 12 Steve Shields Q | 8.00 | 3.60 |
| ❑ 13 Doug Gilmour Q | 8.00 | 3.60 |
| ❑ 14 Jose Theodore Q | 8.00 | 3.60 |
| ❑ 15 Mike Richter Q | 10.00 | 4.50 |
| ❑ 16 John Vanbiesbrouck Q | 15.00 | 6.75 |
| ❑ 17 Ryan Smyth CS | 8.00 | 3.60 |
| ❑ 18 Peter Forsberg CS | 40.00 | 18.00 |
| ❑ 19 Steve Yzerman CS | 40.00 | 18.00 |
| ❑ 20 Paul Kariya CS | 50.00 | 22.00 |
| ❑ 21 Janne Niinimaa CS | 8.00 | 3.60 |
| ❑ 22 Dominik Hasek CS | 25.00 | 11.00 |
| ❑ 23 Mark Messier CS | 15.00 | 6.75 |
| ❑ 24 Martin Brodeur CS | 30.00 | 13.50 |
| ❑ 25 Slava Kozlov CF | 8.00 | 3.60 |
| ❑ 26 Sergei Fedorov CF | 40.00 | 18.00 |
| ❑ 27 Patrick Roy CF | 100.00 | 45.00 |
| ❑ 28 Wayne Gretzky CF | 120.00 | 55.00 |
| ❑ 29 John LeClair CF | 30.00 | 13.50 |
| ❑ 30 Paul Coffey CF | 20.00 | 9.00 |
| ❑ 31 M.Vernon SCF/AU 750 | 40.00 | 18.00 |
| ❑ 32 E.Lindros SCF/AU 750 | 120.00 | 55.00 |
| ❑ 33 B.Shanahan SCC/AU 250 | 150.00 | 70.00 |

## 1995-96 Donruss Elite

This 110-card super premium set was the last mainstream release of the 1995-96 card season. The product was distributed by Pinnacle Brands, which purchased Donruss

and all of its sports licenses just prior to the set's debut. The eight-card packs had a suggested retail of $2.99. The Cool Trade Exchange card was randomly inserted 1:48 packs, although there were numerous reports of collectors finding up to eight copies per box. When found, it could be redeemed for parallel versions of the four Donruss Elite cards found in the NHL Cool Trade wrapper redemption set. This offer expired on September 30, 1996. Rookie Cards include Daniel Alfredsson, Todd Bertuzzi, Radek Dvorak, Chad Kilger and Marcus Ragnarsson.

| | MINT | NRMT |
|---|---|---|
| COMPLETE SET (110) | 25.00 | 11.00 |
| COMMON CARD (1-110) | .15 | .07 |

| Card | MINT | NRMT |
|---|---|---|
| ❑ 1 Jocelyn Thibault | .50 | .23 |
| ❑ 2 Nicklas Lidstrom | .25 | .11 |
| ❑ 3 Brendan Shanahan | 1.00 | .45 |
| ❑ 4 Kenny Jonsson | .15 | .07 |
| ❑ 5 Doug Weight | .25 | .11 |
| ❑ 6 Oleg Tverdovsky | .25 | .11 |
| ❑ 7 Brett Hull | .75 | .35 |
| ❑ 8 Larry Murphy | .25 | .11 |
| ❑ 9 Ray Bourque | .50 | .23 |
| ❑ 10 Adam Graves | .25 | .11 |
| ❑ 11 Gary Suter | .15 | .07 |
| ❑ 12 Bill Ranford | .25 | .11 |
| ❑ 13 Zigmund Palffy | .50 | .23 |
| ❑ 14 Cam Neely | .25 | .11 |
| ❑ 15 Al MacInnis | .25 | .11 |
| ❑ 16 Joe Sakic | 1.00 | .45 |
| ❑ 17 Kevin Hatcher | .15 | .07 |
| ❑ 18 Alexander Mogilny | .25 | .11 |
| ❑ 19 Radek Dvorak | .15 | .07 |
| ❑ 20 Ed Belfour | .50 | .23 |
| ❑ 21 Jeff O'Neill | .15 | .07 |
| ❑ 22 Valeri Kamensky | .25 | .11 |
| ❑ 23 John MacLean | .25 | .11 |
| ❑ 24 Zdeno Ciger | .15 | .07 |
| ❑ 25 Daniel Alfredsson | 1.00 | .45 |
| ❑ 26 Owen Nolan | .25 | .11 |
| ❑ 27 Wendel Clark | .25 | .11 |
| ❑ 28 Brian Savage | .15 | .07 |
| ❑ 29 Alexei Zhamnov | .25 | .11 |
| ❑ 30 Dominik Hasek | 1.00 | .45 |
| ❑ 31 Paul Kariya | 2.00 | .90 |
| ❑ 32 Mike Modano | .75 | .35 |
| ❑ 33 Craig Janney | .25 | .11 |
| ❑ 34 Todd Harvey | .15 | .07 |
| ❑ 35 Jaromir Jagr | 1.50 | .70 |
| ❑ 36 Roman Hamrlik | .25 | .11 |
| ❑ 37 Sergei Zubov | .15 | .07 |
| ❑ 38 Marcus Ragnarsson | .15 | .07 |
| ❑ 39 Peter Forsberg | 1.50 | .70 |
| ❑ 40 Ron Francis | .25 | .11 |
| ❑ 41 German Titov | .15 | .07 |
| ❑ 42 Grant Fuhr | .25 | .11 |
| ❑ 43 Martin Brodeur | 1.25 | .55 |
| ❑ 44 Claude Lemieux | .25 | .11 |
| ❑ 45 Trevor Linden | .25 | .11 |
| ❑ 46 Mark Messier | .75 | .35 |
| ❑ 47 Jeremy Roenick | .50 | .23 |
| ❑ 48 Peter Bondra | .50 | .23 |
| ❑ 49 Donald Audette | .25 | .11 |
| ❑ 50 Joe Nieuwendyk | .25 | .11 |
| ❑ 51 Mario Lemieux CL | .75 | .35 |
| ❑ 52 Vitali Yachmenev | .15 | .07 |
| ❑ 53 Sergei Fedorov | 1.00 | .45 |
| ❑ 54 Kirk Muller | .15 | .07 |
| ❑ 55 Chad Kilger | .15 | .07 |
| ❑ 56 John LeClair | .75 | .35 |
| ❑ 57 Todd Bertuzzi | .25 | .11 |
| ❑ 58 Wayne Gretzky | 4.00 | 1.80 |
| ❑ 59 Curtis Joseph | .50 | .23 |
| ❑ 60 Niklas Sundstrom | .15 | .07 |
| ❑ 61 Chris Chelios | .50 | .23 |
| ❑ 62 Radek Bonk | .15 | .07 |
| ❑ 63 Eric Daze | .50 | .23 |
| ❑ 64 Patrick Roy | 2.50 | 1.10 |
| ❑ 65 Rob Niedermayer | .25 | .11 |
| ❑ 66 Mario Lemieux | 2.50 | 1.10 |
| ❑ 67 Saku Koivu | .75 | .35 |
| ❑ 68 Ed Jovanovski | .50 | .23 |
| ❑ 69 Jim Carey | .50 | .23 |
| ❑ 70 Scott Stevens | .25 | .11 |
| ❑ 71 Steve Thomas | .15 | .07 |
| ❑ 72 Mats Sundin | .25 | .11 |
| ❑ 73 Teemu Selanne | 1.00 | .45 |
| ❑ 74 Tomas Sandstrom | .15 | .07 |
| ❑ 75 Pat LaFontaine | .25 | .11 |
| ❑ 76 Pat Verbeek | .15 | .07 |
| ❑ 77 Pavel Bure | 1.00 | .45 |
| ❑ 78 Jeff Brown | .15 | .07 |
| ❑ 79 Alexei Yashin | .25 | .11 |
| ❑ 80 Adam Oates | .25 | .11 |
| ❑ 81 Keith Tkachuk | .60 | .25 |
| ❑ 82 Brian Bradley | .15 | .07 |
| ❑ 83 John Vanbiesbrouck | .75 | .35 |
| ❑ 84 Alexander Selivanov | .15 | .07 |
| ❑ 85 Paul Coffey | .50 | .23 |
| ❑ 86 Scott Mellanby | .25 | .11 |
| ❑ 87 Slava Kozlov | .25 | .11 |
| ❑ 88 Eric Lindros | 1.50 | .70 |
| ❑ 89 Deron Quint | .15 | .07 |
| ❑ 90 Pierre Turgeon | .25 | .11 |
| ❑ 91 Rod Brind'Amour | .25 | .11 |
| ❑ 92 Doug Gilmour | .50 | .23 |
| ❑ 93 Sandis Ozolinsh | .25 | .11 |
| ❑ 94 Mikael Renberg | .25 | .11 |
| ❑ 95 Kevin Stevens | .15 | .07 |
| ❑ 96 Vincent Damphousse | .25 | .11 |
| ❑ 97 Felix Potvin | .50 | .23 |
| ❑ 98 Brian Leetch | .50 | .23 |
| ❑ 99 Steve Yzerman | 1.50 | .70 |
| ❑ 100 Dale Hawerchuk | .25 | .11 |
| ❑ 101 Jason Arnott | .25 | .11 |
| ❑ 102 Ray Sheppard | .25 | .11 |
| ❑ 103 Mark Recchi | .25 | .11 |
| ❑ 104 Joe Juneau | .15 | .07 |
| ❑ 105 Luc Robitaille | .25 | .11 |
| ❑ 106 Theoren Fleury | .25 | .11 |
| ❑ 107 Sean Burke | .25 | .11 |
| ❑ 108 Ron Hextall | .25 | .11 |
| ❑ 109 Shane Doan | .15 | .07 |
| ❑ 110 Eric Lindros CL | .50 | .23 |
| ❑ NNO Cool Trade Exchange | .50 | .23 |

## 1995-96 Donruss Elite Die Cut Stars

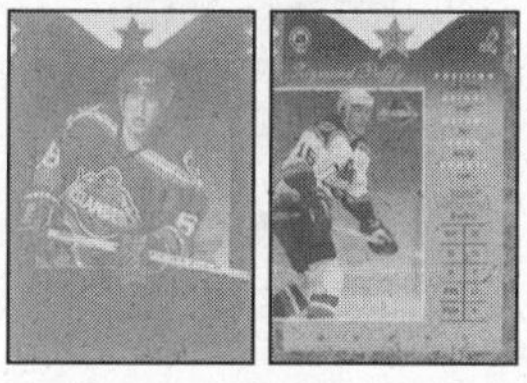

This die-cut set parallelled the main Donruss Elite set. The first 500 cards off the press had the die-cut pattern. Interestingly, boxes from early in the production run contained cards intended to be die-cut which weren't. These cards were unintentionally released, and thus are considered variations, rather than a separate set. These cards are discernible from regular issue cards by a curvilinear pattern which runs across the top of the card just above the photo. Although some collectors have speculated that these cards are in shorter supply than the regular die-cuts, that is unverifiable by the company, and unsubstantiated by market evidence. Multipliers can be found in the header below to determine values for these.

| | MINT | NRMT |
|---|---|---|
| COMPLETE SET (110) | 800.00 | 350.00 |
| COMMON CARD (1-110) | 2.00 | .90 |

*STARS: 12.5X TO 30X BASIC CARDS
*YOUNG STARS: 8X TO 20X BASIC CARDS
*UN-CUT CARDS: .25X TO .75X DIE CUTS

## 1995-96 Donruss Elite Cutting Edge

This 15-card insert set celebrates the top performers of the 1995-96 season. The cards were printed and embossed on laminated polycarbonate material that simulates brushed steel. Each card was serially numbered out of 2,500. The cards were randomly inserted at a rate of 1:32 packs.

| | MINT | NRMT |
|---|---|---|
| COMPLETE SET (15) | 200.00 | 90.00 |
| COMMON CARD (1-15) | 6.00 | 2.70 |

| Card | MINT | NRMT |
|---|---|---|
| ❑ 1 Eric Lindros | 15.00 | 6.75 |
| ❑ 2 Mario Lemieux | 25.00 | 11.00 |
| ❑ 3 Wayne Gretzky | 30.00 | 13.50 |
| ❑ 4 Peter Forsberg | 15.00 | 6.75 |
| ❑ 5 Paul Kariya | 20.00 | 9.00 |
| ❑ 6 Jaromir Jagr | 15.00 | 6.75 |
| ❑ 7 Alexander Mogilny | 6.00 | 2.70 |
| ❑ 8 Mark Messier | 8.00 | 3.60 |
| ❑ 9 Sergei Fedorov | 10.00 | 4.50 |
| ❑ 10 Pierre Turgeon | 6.00 | 2.70 |
| ❑ 11 Mats Sundin | 12.00 | 5.50 |
| ❑ 12 Brett Hull | 8.00 | 3.60 |
| ❑ 13 Paul Coffey | 15.00 | 6.75 |
| ❑ 14 Jeremy Roenick | 15.00 | 6.75 |
| ❑ 15 Teemu Selanne | 10.00 | 4.50 |

## 1995-96 Donruss Elite Lemieux/Lindros Series

These two seven-card sets recognize two of the most dominating players in the game today, Eric Lindros and Mario Lemieux, who also happen to be Donruss spokesmen. The cards were printed on gold holographic foil, with the Lindros cards serially numbered up to 1,088 and the Lemieux cards to 1,066. The seventh card in each series is autographed, giving it a considerably higher value. The seven cards were inserted at a rate of 1:160. There also was a card signed by both Lindros and Lemieux, which is not considered part of either complete set. Both this card and the Lemieux autograph were available only through redemption cards; Lemieux was unable to sign them in time for random insertion. The dual signed card was limited to 500 copies and was inserted in 1:2400 packs. Expired, unredeemed redemption cards are valued at $5-$10. The Lindros cards have been assigned an E suffix for cataloguing purposes only.

| | MINT | NRMT |
|---|---|---|
| COMP.LEMIEUX SET (7) | 550.00 | 250.00 |
| COMMON LEMIEUX (1-6) | 40.00 | 18.00 |
| COMP.LINDROS SET (7) | 500.00 | 220.00 |
| COMMON LINDROS (1-6) | 35.00 | 16.00 |

| Card | MINT | NRMT |
|---|---|---|
| ❑ 1 Mario Lemieux | 40.00 | 18.00 |
| ❑ 1E Eric Lindros | 35.00 | 16.00 |
| ❑ 2 Mario Lemieux | 40.00 | 18.00 |
| ❑ 2E Eric Lindros | 35.00 | 16.00 |
| ❑ 3 Mario Lemieux | 40.00 | 18.00 |
| ❑ 3E Eric Lindros | 35.00 | 16.00 |
| ❑ 4 Mario Lemieux | 40.00 | 18.00 |
| ❑ 4E Eric Lindros | 35.00 | 16.00 |
| ❑ 5 Mario Lemieux | 40.00 | 18.00 |
| ❑ 5E Eric Lindros | 35.00 | 16.00 |
| ❑ 6 Mario Lemieux | 40.00 | 18.00 |
| ❑ 6E Eric Lindros | 35.00 | 16.00 |
| ❑ 7 Mario Lemieux AU | 300.00 | 135.00 |
| ❑ 7E Eric Lindros AU | 275.00 | 125.00 |
| ❑ NNO Lemieux/Lindros AU | 500.00 | 220.00 |

## 1995-96 Donruss Elite Painted Warriors

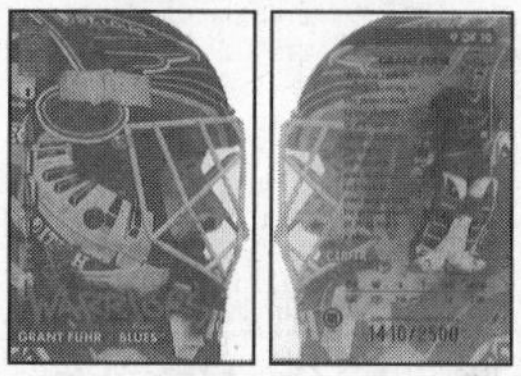

This ten card insert set focuses on top goalies and their brightly painted headgear. Each card is printed on clear plastic and then die-cut around the face mask. The cards are individually numbered out of 2,500. The cards were inserted at a rate of 1:48 packs.

| | MINT | NRMT |
|---|---|---|
| COMPLETE SET (10) | 120.00 | 55.00 |
| COMMON CARD (1-10) | 6.00 | 2.70 |

| Card | MINT | NRMT |
|---|---|---|
| ❑ 1 Patrick Roy | 40.00 | 18.00 |
| ❑ 2 Felix Potvin | 6.00 | 2.70 |
| ❑ 3 Martin Brodeur | 20.00 | 9.00 |
| ❑ 4 Ed Belfour | 8.00 | 3.60 |
| ❑ 5 Guy Hebert | 12.00 | 5.50 |
| ❑ 6 John Vanbiesbrouck | 12.00 | 5.50 |
| ❑ 7 Jocelyn Thibault | 6.00 | 2.70 |
| ❑ 8 Ron Hextall | 6.00 | 2.70 |
| ❑ 9 Grant Fuhr | 6.00 | 2.70 |
| ❑ 10 Jim Carey | 6.00 | 2.70 |
| ❑ P4 Ed Belfour | 20.00 | 9.00 |
| ❑ P9 Grant Fuhr | 15.00 | 6.75 |

## 1995-96 Donruss Elite Rookies

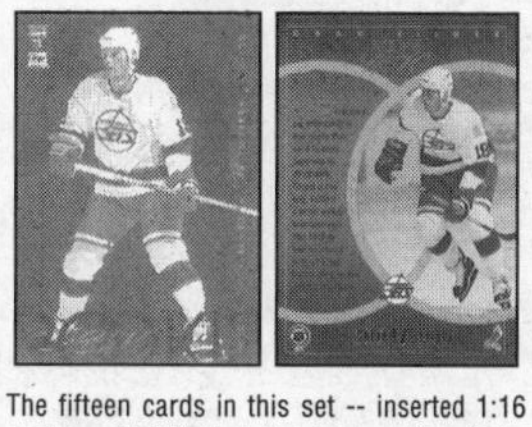

The fifteen cards in this set -- inserted 1:16 packs -- highlighted the top rookies of the 1995-96 season. The cards were printed on an icy silver foil background and detailed with gold trim. The cards were individually numbered out of 5,000.

| | MINT | NRMT |
|---|---|---|
| COMPLETE SET (15) | 100.00 | 45.00 |
| COMMON CARD (1-15) | 5.00 | 2.20 |

| Card | MINT | NRMT |
|---|---|---|
| ❑ 1 Eric Daze | 8.00 | 3.60 |
| ❑ 2 Vitali Yachmenev | 5.00 | 2.20 |
| ❑ 3 Daniel Alfredsson | 12.00 | 5.50 |
| ❑ 4 Todd Bertuzzi | 5.00 | 2.20 |
| ❑ 5 Byron Dafoe | 5.00 | 2.20 |
| ❑ 6 Eric Fichaud | 8.00 | 3.60 |
| ❑ 7 Marcus Ragnarsson | 8.00 | 3.60 |
| ❑ 8 Saku Koivu | 15.00 | 6.75 |
| ❑ 9 Chad Kilger | 5.00 | 2.20 |
| ❑ 10 Radek Dvorak | 5.00 | 2.20 |
| ❑ 11 Ed Jovanovski | 8.00 | 3.60 |
| ❑ 12 Jeff O'Neill | 8.00 | 3.60 |
| ❑ 13 Shane Doan | 5.00 | 2.20 |
| ❑ 14 Niklas Sundstrom | 8.00 | 3.60 |
| ❑ 15 Kyle McLaren | 5.00 | 2.20 |

## 1995-96 Donruss Elite World Juniors

This 44-card insert set features the top Canadian and US players from the 1996 World Junior Championships. The cards were printed on canvas stock that simulated the flag of the player's home country. Each card is individually numbered out of 1,000. The cards were inserted 1:30 packs.

| | MINT | NRMT |
|---|---|---|
| COMPLETE SET (44) | 500.00 | 220.00 |
| COMMON CARD (1-44) | 8.00 | 3.60 |

| Card | MINT | NRMT |
|---|---|---|
| ❑ 1 Marc Denis | 25.00 | 11.00 |
| ❑ 2 Jose Theodore | 20.00 | 9.00 |
| ❑ 3 Chad Allan | 15.00 | 6.75 |
| ❑ 4 Nolan Baumgartner | 10.00 | 4.50 |
| ❑ 5 Denis Gauthier | 8.00 | 3.60 |
| ❑ 6 Jason Holland | 8.00 | 3.60 |
| ❑ 7 Chris Phillips | 15.00 | 6.75 |
| ❑ 8 Wade Redden | 15.00 | 6.75 |
| ❑ 9 Rhett Warrener | 12.00 | 5.50 |
| ❑ 10 Jason Botterill | 8.00 | 3.60 |
| ❑ 11 Curtis Brown | 15.00 | 6.75 |
| ❑ 12 Hnat Domenichelli | 12.00 | 5.50 |
| ❑ 13 Christian Dube | 15.00 | 6.75 |
| ❑ 14 Robb Gordon | 8.00 | 3.60 |
| ❑ 15 Jarome Iginla | 15.00 | 6.75 |
| ❑ 16 Daymond Langkow | 15.00 | 6.75 |
| ❑ 17 Brad Larsen | 8.00 | 3.60 |
| ❑ 18 Alyn McCauley | 20.00 | 9.00 |
| ❑ 19 Craig Mills | 8.00 | 3.60 |
| ❑ 20 Jason Podollan | 15.00 | 6.75 |
| ❑ 21 Mike Watt | 8.00 | 3.60 |
| ❑ 22 Jamie Wright | 8.00 | 3.60 |
| ❑ 23 Brian Boucher | 20.00 | 9.00 |
| ❑ 24 Marc Magliarditi | 10.00 | 4.50 |
| ❑ 25 Bryan Berard | 20.00 | 9.00 |
| ❑ 26 Chris Bogas | 8.00 | 3.60 |
| ❑ 27 Ben Clymer | 8.00 | 3.60 |
| ❑ 28 Jeff Kealty | 8.00 | 3.60 |
| ❑ 29 Mike McBain | 8.00 | 3.60 |
| ❑ 30 Jeremiah McCarthy | 8.00 | 3.60 |
| ❑ 31 Tom Poti | 8.00 | 3.60 |
| ❑ 32 Reg Berg | 8.00 | 3.60 |
| ❑ 33 Matt Cullen | 8.00 | 3.60 |
| ❑ 34 Chris Drury | 40.00 | 18.00 |
| ❑ 35 Jeff Farkas | 8.00 | 3.60 |
| ❑ 36 Casey Hankinson | 8.00 | 3.60 |
| ❑ 37 Matt Herr | 8.00 | 3.60 |
| ❑ 38 Mark Parrish | 30.00 | 13.50 |
| ❑ 39 Erik Rasmussen | 20.00 | 9.00 |
| ❑ 40 Marty Reasoner | 15.00 | 6.75 |
| ❑ 41 Wyatt Smith | 8.00 | 3.60 |
| ❑ 42 Brian Swanson | 8.00 | 3.60 |
| ❑ 43 Mike Sylvia | 8.00 | 3.60 |
| ❑ 44 Mike York | 15.00 | 6.75 |

## 1996-97 Donruss Elite

The 1996-97 Donruss Elite set was issued in one series totaling 150 cards. Packs contained eight cards for a suggested retail price of $3.99, and were distributed as a hobby-only product. Card fronts feature a color action photo with a foil background. A 20-card rookie subset is found at the end of the set (#128-147). Key rookies include Sergei Berezin, Patrick Lalime, Ethan Moreau, and Dainius Zubrus.

| | MINT | NRMT |
|---|---|---|
| COMPLETE SET (150) | 25.00 | 11.00 |
| COMMON CARD (1-150) | .15 | .07 |

| Card | MINT | NRMT |
|---|---|---|
| ❑ 1 Paul Kariya | 2.50 | 1.10 |
| ❑ 2 Ron Hextall | .30 | .14 |
| ❑ 3 Andy Moog | .30 | .14 |
| ❑ 4 Brett Hull | .75 | .35 |
| ❑ 5 Felix Potvin | .60 | .25 |
| ❑ 6 Jocelyn Thibault | .60 | .25 |
| ❑ 7 Eric Lindros | 2.00 | .90 |

| | | |
|---|---|---|
| ❑ 8 Jaromir Jagr | 2.00 | .90 |
| ❑ 9 Sergei Fedorov | 1.00 | .45 |
| ❑ 10 Wayne Gretzky | 4.00 | 1.80 |
| ❑ 11 Peter Bondra | .60 | .25 |
| ❑ 12 Peter Forsberg | 2.00 | .90 |
| ❑ 13 Stephane Fiset | .30 | .14 |
| ❑ 14 Owen Nolan | .30 | .14 |
| ❑ 15 Rob Niedermayer | .30 | .14 |
| ❑ 16 Martin Brodeur | 1.50 | .70 |
| ❑ 17 Ray Bourque | .60 | .25 |
| ❑ 18 Todd Bertuzzi | .15 | .07 |
| ❑ 19 Jim Carey | .60 | .25 |
| ❑ 20 Chris Chelios | .60 | .25 |
| ❑ 21 Chris Osgood | .60 | .25 |
| ❑ 22 Mark Messier | .75 | .35 |
| ❑ 23 Roman Hamrlik | .30 | .14 |
| ❑ 24 Kevin Hatcher | .15 | .07 |
| ❑ 25 Doug Weight | .30 | .14 |
| ❑ 26 Mark Recchi | .30 | .14 |
| ❑ 27 Jeremy Roenick | .60 | .25 |
| ❑ 28 Derian Hatcher | .15 | .07 |
| ❑ 29 Grant Fuhr | .30 | .14 |
| ❑ 30 Scott Stevens | .30 | .14 |
| ❑ 31 Adam Oates | .30 | .14 |
| ❑ 32 Scott Mellanby | .30 | .14 |
| ❑ 33 Mikael Renberg | .30 | .14 |
| ❑ 34 Corey Hirsch | .30 | .14 |
| ❑ 35 Michal Pivonka | .15 | .07 |
| ❑ 36 Stephane Richer | .30 | .14 |
| ❑ 37 Dominik Hasek | 1.25 | .55 |
| ❑ 38 Steve Yzerman | 2.00 | .90 |
| ❑ 39 Jeff O'Neill | .15 | .07 |
| ❑ 40 Ron Francis | .30 | .14 |
| ❑ 41 Alexei Yashin | .30 | .14 |
| ❑ 42 Pat Verbeek | .15 | .07 |
| ❑ 43 Geoff Courtnall | .15 | .07 |
| ❑ 44 Doug Gilmour | .60 | .25 |
| ❑ 45 Trevor Kidd | .30 | .14 |
| ❑ 46 Jason Arnott | .30 | .14 |
| ❑ 47 Niklas Sundstrom | .15 | .07 |
| ❑ 48 Rob Blake | .15 | .07 |
| ❑ 49 Nikolai Khabibulin | .30 | .14 |
| ❑ 50 Igor Larionov | .15 | .07 |
| ❑ 51 Sean Burke | .30 | .14 |
| ❑ 52 Zigmund Palffy | .60 | .25 |
| ❑ 53 Jeff Friesen | .30 | .14 |
| ❑ 54 Theoren Fleury | .30 | .14 |
| ❑ 55 Mats Sundin | .30 | .14 |
| ❑ 56 Alexander Mogilny | .30 | .14 |
| ❑ 57 John LeClair | 1.00 | .45 |
| ❑ 58 Shayne Corson | .15 | .07 |
| ❑ 59 Teemu Selanne | 1.25 | .55 |
| ❑ 60 Kelly Hrudey | .30 | .14 |
| ❑ 61 Keith Tkachuk | .75 | .35 |
| ❑ 62 Joe Nieuwendyk | .30 | .14 |
| ❑ 63 Tom Barrasso | .30 | .14 |
| ❑ 64 Aaron Gavey | .15 | .07 |
| ❑ 65 Alexei Zhamnov | .30 | .14 |
| ❑ 66 Patrick Roy | 3.00 | 1.35 |
| ❑ 67 Al MacInnis | .30 | .14 |
| ❑ 68 Trevor Linden | .30 | .14 |
| ❑ 69 Bill Guerin | .15 | .07 |
| ❑ 70 Dimitri Khristich | .15 | .07 |
| ❑ 71 Eric Daze | .30 | .14 |
| ❑ 72 Paul Coffey | .60 | .25 |
| ❑ 73 Keith Primeau | .30 | .14 |
| ❑ 74 John Vanbiesbrouck | 1.00 | .45 |
| ❑ 75 Bernie Nicholls | .15 | .07 |
| ❑ 76 Yanic Perreault | .15 | .07 |
| ❑ 77 Jere Lehtinen | .15 | .07 |
| ❑ 78 Luc Robitaille | .30 | .14 |
| ❑ 79 Todd Gill | .15 | .07 |
| ❑ 80 Saku Koivu | 1.00 | .45 |
| ❑ 81 Vyacheslav Kozlov | .15 | .07 |
| ❑ 82 Ed Jovanovski | .30 | .14 |
| ❑ 83 Brendan Witt | .15 | .07 |
| ❑ 84 Alexandre Daigle | .15 | .07 |
| ❑ 85 Jari Kurri | .30 | .14 |
| ❑ 86 Mike Vernon | .30 | .14 |
| ❑ 87 Jeff Beukeboom | .15 | .07 |
| ❑ 88 Mathieu Schneider | .15 | .07 |
| ❑ 89 Niklas Andersson | .15 | .07 |
| ❑ 90 Joe Juneau | .15 | .07 |
| ❑ 91 Ed Belfour | .60 | .25 |
| ❑ 92 Curtis Joseph | .60 | .25 |
| ❑ 93 Rod Brind'Amour | .30 | .14 |
| ❑ 94 Vitali Yachmenev | .15 | .07 |
| ❑ 95 Alexander Selivanov | .15 | .07 |
| ❑ 96 Mike Richter | .60 | .25 |
| ❑ 97 Bill Ranford | .30 | .14 |
| ❑ 98 Wendel Clark | .30 | .14 |
| ❑ 99 Viacheslav Fetisov | .15 | .07 |
| ❑ 100 Daniel Alfredsson | .30 | .14 |
| ❑ 101 Pat LaFontaine | .30 | .14 |
| ❑ 102 Joe Murphy | .15 | .07 |
| ❑ 103 Pavel Bure | 1.25 | .55 |
| ❑ 104 Craig Janney | .30 | .14 |
| ❑ 105 Radek Dvorak | .15 | .07 |
| ❑ 106 Cory Stillman | .15 | .07 |
| ❑ 107 Adam Graves | .30 | .14 |
| ❑ 108 Aki Berg | .15 | .07 |
| ❑ 109 Mario Lemieux | 3.00 | 1.35 |
| ❑ 110 Claude Lemieux | .30 | .14 |
| ❑ 111 Sergei Zubov | .15 | .07 |
| ❑ 112 Pierre Turgeon | .30 | .14 |
| ❑ 113 Damian Rhodes | .30 | .14 |
| ❑ 114 Daren Puppa | .30 | .14 |
| ❑ 115 Alexei Zhitnik | .15 | .07 |
| ❑ 116 Mike Modano | .75 | .35 |
| ❑ 117 Kenny Jonsson | .15 | .07 |
| ❑ 118 Valeri Kamensky | .30 | .14 |
| ❑ 119 Valeri Bure | .30 | .14 |
| ❑ 120 Joe Sakic | 1.25 | .55 |
| ❑ 121 Kirk McLean | .30 | .14 |
| ❑ 122 Petr Sykora | .15 | .07 |
| ❑ 123 Mike Gartner | .30 | .14 |
| ❑ 124 Ryan Smyth | .60 | .25 |
| ❑ 125 Brian Leetch | .60 | .25 |
| ❑ 126 Brendan Shanahan | 1.25 | .55 |
| ❑ 127 Geoff Sanderson | .30 | .14 |
| ❑ 128 Corey Schwab | .30 | .14 |
| ❑ 129 Anders Eriksson | .15 | .07 |
| ❑ 130 Harry York | .60 | .25 |
| ❑ 131 Jarome Iginla | .60 | .25 |
| ❑ 132 Eric Fichaud | .30 | .14 |
| ❑ 133 Patrick Lalime | .60 | .25 |
| ❑ 134 Daymond Langkow | .15 | .07 |
| ❑ 135 Mattias Timander | .15 | .07 |
| ❑ 136 Ethan Moreau | .60 | .25 |
| ❑ 137 Christian Dube | .15 | .07 |
| ❑ 138 Sergei Berezin | 1.00 | .45 |
| ❑ 139 Jose Theodore | .30 | .14 |
| ❑ 140 Wade Redden | .15 | .07 |
| ❑ 141 Dainius Zubrus | 1.25 | .55 |
| ❑ 142 Jim Campbell | .15 | .07 |
| ❑ 143 Daniel Goneau | .50 | .23 |
| ❑ 144 Jamie Langenbrunner | .15 | .07 |
| ❑ 145 Rem Murray | .15 | .07 |
| ❑ 146 Jonas Hoglund | .15 | .07 |
| ❑ 147 Bryan Berard | .60 | .25 |
| ❑ 148 Chris Osgood CL (1-75) | .30 | .14 |
| ❑ 149 Eric Lindros CL (76-150) | .60 | .25 |
| ❑ 150 Jason Arnott CL (inserts) | .30 | .14 |

## 1996-97 Donruss Elite Die Cut Stars

This die-cut set paralleled the main Donruss Elite set. Card fronts feature a die-cut, silver-poly laminate foil to distinguish them from their base counterparts. Only the most active cards are listed individually below; all other values can be determined by using the multipliers in the header line.

| | MINT | NRMT |
|---|---|---|
| COMMON CARD (1-150) | 4.00 | 1.80 |

*STARS: 15X TO 40X BASIC CARDS
*YOUNG STARS: 8X TO 20X BASIC CARDS
*RCs: 6X TO 12X BASIC CARDS

## 1996-97 Donruss Elite Aspirations

This set features twenty-five of the NHL's top rookies and young superstars. Each card is serially numbered out of 3,000. Card fronts feature a color action photo with blue and silver foil surrounding the photo.

| | MINT | NRMT |
|---|---|---|
| COMPLETE SET (25) | 120.00 | 55.00 |
| COMMON CARD (1-25) | 4.00 | 1.80 |
| ❑ 1 Eric Daze | 15.00 | 6.75 |
| ❑ 2 Daniel Alfredsson | 10.00 | 4.50 |
| ❑ 3 Petr Sykora | 4.00 | 1.80 |
| ❑ 4 Todd Bertuzzi | 4.00 | 1.80 |
| ❑ 5 Saku Koivu | 20.00 | 9.00 |
| ❑ 6 Ed Jovanovski | 15.00 | 6.75 |
| ❑ 7 Jim Campbell | 8.00 | 3.60 |
| ❑ 8 Valeri Bure | 4.00 | 1.80 |
| ❑ 9 Jeff O'Neill | 4.00 | 1.80 |
| ❑ 10 Jere Lehtinen | 4.00 | 1.80 |
| ❑ 11 Terry Ryan | 4.00 | 1.80 |
| ❑ 12 Jonas Hoglund | 4.00 | 1.80 |
| ❑ 13 Daymond Langkow | 4.00 | 1.80 |
| ❑ 14 Eric Fichaud | 10.00 | 4.50 |
| ❑ 15 Dainius Zubrus | 15.00 | 6.75 |
| ❑ 16 Janne Niinimaa | 15.00 | 6.75 |
| ❑ 17 Sergei Berezin | 6.00 | 2.70 |
| ❑ 18 Daniel Goneau | 10.00 | 4.50 |
| ❑ 19 Jarome Iginla | 15.00 | 6.75 |
| ❑ 20 Ethan Moreau | 10.00 | 4.50 |
| ❑ 21 Jamie Langenbrunner | 4.00 | 1.80 |
| ❑ 22 Rem Murray | 4.00 | 1.80 |
| ❑ 23 Bryan Berard | 12.00 | 5.50 |
| ❑ 24 Wade Redden | 10.00 | 4.50 |
| ❑ 25 Christian Dube | 8.00 | 3.60 |

## 1996-97 Donruss Elite Painted Warriors

This 10-card insert set focuses on top goalies and their brightly painted headgear. Each card is printed on clear plastic and then die-cut around the mask. The cards are individually numbered out of 2,500. A complete promotional version of this set also was available. The cards mirror the regular versions except in the serial number box on the back, where the number reads PROMO/2500. The Brodeur is the most readily available of these cards.

| | MINT | NRMT |
|---|---|---|
| COMPLETE SET (10) | 200.00 | 90.00 |
| COMMON CARD (1-10) | 12.00 | 5.50 |
| ❑ 1 Patrick Roy | 80.00 | 36.00 |
| ❑ 2 Mike Richter | 15.00 | 6.75 |
| ❑ 3 Jim Carey | 15.00 | 6.75 |
| ❑ 4 John Vanbiesbrouck | 25.00 | 11.00 |
| ❑ 5 Jocelyn Thibault | 15.00 | 6.75 |
| ❑ 6 Felix Potvin | 15.00 | 6.75 |
| ❑ 7 Ed Belfour | 15.00 | 6.75 |
| ❑ 8 Martin Brodeur | 40.00 | 18.00 |
| ❑ 9 Nikolai Khabibulin | 12.00 | 5.50 |
| ❑ 10 Stephane Fiset | 12.00 | 5.50 |
| ❑ P1 Patrick Roy PROMO | 40.00 | 18.00 |
| ❑ P2 Mike Richter PROMO | 8.00 | 3.60 |
| ❑ P3 Jim Carey PROMO | 8.00 | 3.60 |
| ❑ P4 John Vanbiesbrouck PROMO | 25.00 | 11.00 |
| ❑ P5 Jocelyn Thibault PROMO | 8.00 | 3.60 |
| ❑ P6 Felix Potvin PROMO | 12.00 | 5.50 |
| ❑ P7 Ed Belfour PROMO | 8.00 | 3.60 |
| ❑ P8 Martin Brodeur PROMO | 5.00 | 2.20 |
| ❑ P9 Nikolai Khabibulin PROMO | 5.00 | 2.20 |
| ❑ P10 Stephane Fiset PROMO | 5.00 | 2.20 |

## 1996-97 Donruss Elite Perspective

This 12-card set focuses on the NHL's veteran stars. Card fronts feature a die-cut, micro-etched, foil design. Each card is individually numbered out of 500.

| | MINT | NRMT |
|---|---|---|
| COMPLETE SET (12) | 1000.00 | 450.00 |
| COMMON CARD (1-12) | 40.00 | 18.00 |
| ❑ 1 Wayne Gretzky | 250.00 | 110.00 |
| ❑ 2 Mark Messier | 50.00 | 22.00 |
| ❑ 3 Steve Yzerman | 120.00 | 55.00 |
| ❑ 4 Mario Lemieux | 200.00 | 90.00 |
| ❑ 5 Paul Coffey | 40.00 | 18.00 |
| ❑ 6 Doug Gilmour | 40.00 | 18.00 |
| ❑ 7 Brendan Shanahan | 80.00 | 36.00 |
| ❑ 8 Jaromir Jagr | 120.00 | 55.00 |
| ❑ 9 Brett Hull | 50.00 | 22.00 |
| ❑ 10 Pat LaFontaine | 40.00 | 18.00 |
| ❑ 11 Chris Chelios | 40.00 | 18.00 |
| ❑ 12 Grant Fuhr | 40.00 | 18.00 |

## 1996-97 Donruss Elite Status

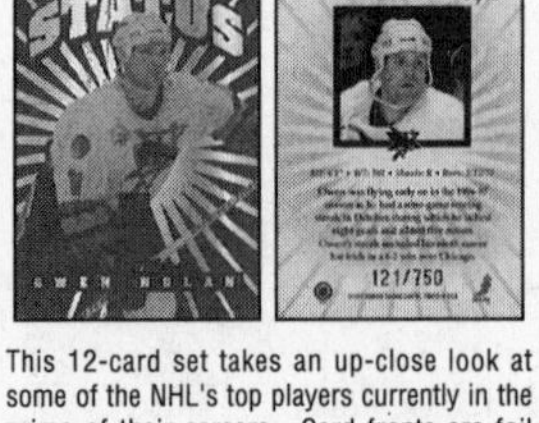


This 12-card set takes an up-close look at some of the NHL's top players currently in the prime of their careers. Card fronts are foil laminate and feature a full-color photo. Each card is serially numbered out of 750.

| | MINT | NRMT |
|---|---|---|
| COMPLETE SET (12) | 600.00 | 275.00 |
| COMMON CARD (1-12) | 15.00 | 6.75 |
| ❑ 1 Pavel Bure | 50.00 | 22.00 |
| ❑ 2 Keith Tkachuk | 30.00 | 13.50 |
| ❑ 3 Sergei Fedorov | 50.00 | 22.00 |
| ❑ 4 Doug Weight | 15.00 | 6.75 |
| ❑ 5 Paul Kariya | 100.00 | 45.00 |
| ❑ 6 Owen Nolan | 15.00 | 6.75 |
| ❑ 7 Peter Forsberg | 80.00 | 36.00 |
| ❑ 8 Eric Lindros | 80.00 | 36.00 |
| ❑ 9 Alexander Mogilny | 15.00 | 6.75 |
| ❑ 10 Teemu Selanne | 50.00 | 22.00 |
| ❑ 11 Joe Sakic | 50.00 | 22.00 |
| ❑ 12 Jeremy Roenick | 25.00 | 11.00 |

## 1997-98 Donruss Elite

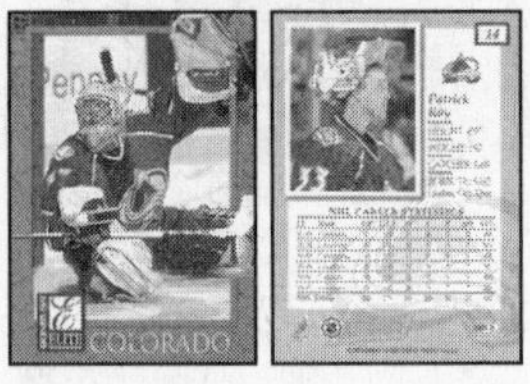


The 1997-98 Donruss Elite hobby exclusive set was issued in one series totalling 150 cards and was distributed in five-card packs with a suggested retail price of $3.99. The fronts feature color player photos printed on thick foil card stock. The backs carry player information. The set contains the topical subset: Elite Generations (115-144).

| | MINT | NRMT |
|---|---|---|
| COMPLETE SET (150) | 40.00 | 18.00 |
| COMMON CARD (1-150) | .20 | .09 |
| ❑ 1 Peter Forsberg | 2.00 | .90 |
| ❑ 2 Mike Modano | .75 | .35 |
| ❑ 3 John Vanbiesbrouck | 1.00 | .45 |
| ❑ 4 Pavel Bure | 1.25 | .55 |
| ❑ 5 Mark Messier | .75 | .35 |
| ❑ 6 Joe Thornton | 1.25 | .55 |
| ❑ 7 Paul Kariya | 2.50 | 1.10 |
| ❑ 8 Martin Brodeur | 1.50 | .70 |
| ❑ 9 Wayne Gretzky | 4.00 | 1.80 |
| ❑ 10 Eric Lindros | 2.00 | .90 |
| ❑ 11 Jaromir Jagr | 2.00 | .90 |
| ❑ 12 Brett Hull | .75 | .35 |
| ❑ 13 Jarome Iginla | .50 | .23 |
| ❑ 14 Patrick Roy | 3.00 | 1.35 |
| ❑ 15 Steve Yzerman | 2.00 | .90 |
| ❑ 16 Sergei Samsonov | 1.50 | .70 |
| ❑ 17 Teemu Selanne | 1.25 | .55 |
| ❑ 18 Brendan Shanahan | 1.25 | .55 |
| ❑ 19 Curtis Joseph | .60 | .25 |
| ❑ 20 Saku Koivu | 1.00 | .45 |
| ❑ 21 Ray Bourque | .60 | .25 |
| ❑ 22 Jaroslav Svejkovsky | .50 | .23 |
| ❑ 23 Keith Primeau | .20 | .09 |
| ❑ 24 Alexandre Daigle | .50 | .23 |
| ❑ 25 Vyacheslav Kozlov | .20 | .09 |
| ❑ 26 Jozef Stumpel | .20 | .09 |
| ❑ 27 Alexei Yashin | .50 | .23 |
| ❑ 28 Marian Hossa | 3.00 | 1.35 |
| ❑ 29 Bryan Berard | .50 | .23 |
| ❑ 30 Dominik Hasek | 1.25 | .55 |
| ❑ 31 Chris Chelios | .60 | .25 |
| ❑ 32 Derian Hatcher | .20 | .09 |
| ❑ 33 Ed Jovanovski | .50 | .23 |
| ❑ 34 Zigmund Palffy | .60 | .25 |
| ❑ 35 Ron Hextall | .50 | .23 |
| ❑ 36 Daymond Langkow | .20 | .09 |
| ❑ 37 Daniel Cleary | .50 | .23 |
| ❑ 38 Alyn McCauley | .50 | .23 |
| ❑ 39 Sean Burke | .50 | .23 |
| ❑ 40 Brian Leetch | .60 | .25 |
| ❑ 41 Joe Juneau | .50 | .23 |
| ❑ 42 Damian Rhodes | .50 | .23 |
| ❑ 43 Dino Ciccarelli | .20 | .09 |
| ❑ 44 Valeri Kamensky | .50 | .23 |
| ❑ 45 Guy Hebert | .50 | .23 |
| ❑ 46 Brad Isbister | .20 | .09 |
| ❑ 47 Adam Graves | .50 | .23 |
| ❑ 48 Andrew Cassels | .20 | .09 |
| ❑ 49 Joe Sakic | 1.25 | .55 |
| ❑ 50 Dainius Zubrus | .60 | .25 |
| ❑ 51 Roberto Luongo | 2.50 | 1.10 |
| ❑ 52 Ethan Moreau | .20 | .09 |
| ❑ 53 Chris Osgood | .60 | .25 |
| ❑ 54 Stephane Fiset | .50 | .23 |
| ❑ 55 Sergei Berezin | .20 | .09 |
| ❑ 56 Mike Richter | .60 | .25 |
| ❑ 57 Valeri Bure | .20 | .09 |
| ❑ 58 Mats Sundin | .60 | .25 |
| ❑ 59 Mike Dunham | .50 | .23 |
| ❑ 60 Byron Dafoe | .50 | .23 |
| ❑ 61 Joe Nieuwendyk | .50 | .23 |
| ❑ 62 Mike Grier | .20 | .09 |
| ❑ 63 Paul Coffey | .60 | .25 |
| ❑ 64 Chris Phillips | .20 | .09 |
| ❑ 65 Patrik Elias | .75 | .35 |
| ❑ 66 Andy Moog | .50 | .23 |
| ❑ 67 Geoff Sanderson | .50 | .23 |
| ❑ 68 Jere Lehtinen | .20 | .09 |
| ❑ 69 Alexander Mogilny | .50 | .23 |
| ❑ 70 Ryan Smyth | .50 | .23 |
| ❑ 71 John LeClair | 1.00 | .45 |
| ❑ 72 Olli Jokinen | 1.00 | .45 |
| ❑ 73 Doug Gilmour | .60 | .25 |
| ❑ 74 Theoren Fleury | .50 | .23 |
| ❑ 75 Adam Deadmarsh | .50 | .23 |
| ❑ 76 Scott Mellanby | .50 | .23 |
| ❑ 77 Jeremy Roenick | .60 | .25 |
| ❑ 78 Jim Campbell | .20 | .09 |
| ❑ 79 Daren Puppa | .50 | .23 |
| ❑ 80 Vaclav Prospal | .75 | .35 |
| ❑ 81 Vincent Damphousse | .50 | .23 |
| ❑ 82 Derek Plante | .20 | .09 |
| ❑ 83 Sandis Ozolinsh | .50 | .23 |
| ❑ 84 Darren McCarty | .20 | .09 |
| ❑ 85 Luc Robitaille | .50 | .23 |
| ❑ 86 Wade Redden | .20 | .09 |
| ❑ 87 Eric Fichaud | .50 | .23 |
| ❑ 88 Jocelyn Thibault | .50 | .23 |
| ❑ 89 Trevor Linden | .50 | .23 |
| ❑ 90 Boyd Devereaux | .20 | .09 |
| ❑ 91 Chris Gratton | .50 | .23 |
| ❑ 92 Janne Niinimaa | .50 | .23 |
| ❑ 93 Jeff Friesen | .50 | .23 |
| ❑ 94 Roman Hamrlik | .20 | .09 |
| ❑ 95 Jason Arnott | .50 | .23 |
| ❑ 96 Sergei Fedorov | 1.25 | .55 |
| ❑ 97 Tony Amonte | .50 | .23 |
| ❑ 98 Mattias Ohlund | .50 | .23 |
| ❑ 99 Patrick Marleau | 1.25 | .55 |
| ❑ 100 Felix Potvin | .60 | .25 |
| ❑ 101 Tommy Salo | .50 | .23 |
| ❑ 102 Ed Belfour | .60 | .25 |
| ❑ 103 Doug Weight | .50 | .23 |
| ❑ 104 Daniel Alfredsson | .50 | .23 |
| ❑ 105 Pierre Turgeon | .50 | .23 |
| ❑ 106 Espen Knutsen | .20 | .09 |
| ❑ 107 Trevor Kidd | .50 | .23 |
| ❑ 108 Alexei Morozov | .50 | .23 |
| ❑ 109 Oleg Tverdovsky | .20 | .09 |
| ❑ 110 Grant Fuhr | .50 | .23 |
| ❑ 111 Pat LaFontaine | .50 | .23 |
| ❑ 112 Keith Tkachuk | .75 | .35 |
| ❑ 113 Ron Francis | .50 | .23 |
| ❑ 114 Derek Morris | .20 | .09 |
| ❑ 115 Joe Sakic G | .60 | .25 |
| ❑ 116 Brian Leetch G | .30 | .14 |
| ❑ 117 Alyn McCauley G | .20 | .09 |
| ❑ 118 Pavel Bure G | .60 | .25 |
| ❑ 119 Eric Lindros G | 1.00 | .45 |
| ❑ 120 Teemu Selanne G | .60 | .25 |
| ❑ 121 Jarome Iginla G | .25 | .11 |
| ❑ 122 Steve Yzerman G | 1.00 | .45 |
| ❑ 123 Daniel Cleary G | .20 | .09 |
| ❑ 124 Bryan Berard G | .20 | .09 |
| ❑ 125 Jaromir Jagr G | 1.00 | .45 |
| ❑ 126 John Vanbiesbrouck G | .50 | .23 |
| ❑ 127 Mark Messier G | .40 | .18 |
| ❑ 128 Patrick Marleau G | .60 | .25 |
| ❑ 129 Mike Modano G | .40 | .18 |
| ❑ 130 Zigmund Palffy G | .40 | .18 |
| ❑ 131 Felix Potvin G | .30 | .14 |
| ❑ 132 Derek Morris G | .20 | .09 |
| ❑ 133 Brendan Shanahan G | .60 | .25 |
| ❑ 134 Sergei Samsonov G | .60 | .25 |
| ❑ 135 Dainius Zubrus G | .25 | .11 |
| ❑ 136 Paul Kariya G | 1.25 | .55 |
| ❑ 137 Martin Brodeur G | .75 | .35 |
| ❑ 138 Joe Thornton G | .60 | .25 |
| ❑ 139 Mattias Ohlund G | .20 | .09 |
| ❑ 140 Ryan Smyth G | .20 | .09 |
| ❑ 141 Jaroslav Svejkovsky G | .20 | .09 |
| ❑ 142 Patrick Roy G | 1.50 | .70 |
| ❑ 143 Wayne Gretzky G | 2.00 | .90 |
| ❑ 144 Espen Knutsen G | .20 | .09 |
| ❑ 145 Patrick Marleau CL | .60 | .25 |
| ❑ 146 Pat Lafontaine CL | .20 | .09 |
| ❑ 147 Mike Gartner CL | .20 | .09 |
| ❑ 148 Joe Thornton CL | .60 | .25 |
| ❑ 149 Teemu Selanne CL | .60 | .25 |
| ❑ 150 Mark Messier CL | .40 | .18 |

## 1997-98 Donruss Elite Aspirations

Randomly inserted in packs, this 150-card set is a die-cut parallel version of the base set printed on foil board. Each card is numbered 1 of 750.

| | MINT | NRMT |
|---|---|---|
| COMPLETE SET (150) | 1000.00 | 450.00 |
| COMMON CARD (1-150) | 3.00 | 1.35 |

*STARS: 6X TO 15X BASIC CARDS
*YOUNG STARS: 5X TO 12 X BASIC CARDS

## 1997-98 Donruss Elite Status

Randomly inserted in packs, this 150-card set is a die-cut parallel version of the base set printed on holofoil board. Each card is sequentially numbered to 100.

| | MINT | NRMT |
|---|---|---|
| COMPLETE SET (150) | 9000.00 | 4000.00 |
| COMMON CARD (1-150) | 20.00 | 9.00 |
| SEMISTARS/GOALIES | 50.00 | 22.00 |
| UNLISTED STARS | 60.00 | 27.00 |

*STARS: 40X TO 100X BASIC CARDS
*YOUNG STARS: 30X TO 80X

## 1997-98 Donruss Elite Back to the Future

Randomly inserted in packs, this eight-card set features color player photos printed on double-sided cards. One side displays a veteran star or Hockey HOF member while the

other side highlights a younger talent. The first 100 of each card was autographed by both of the featured players.

| | MINT | NRMT |
|---|---|---|
| COMPLETE SET (8) | 150.00 | 70.00 |
| COMMON CARD (1-8) | 8.00 | 3.60 |
| ❑ 1 Eric Lindros / Joe Thornton | 20.00 | 9.00 |
| ❑ 2 Jocelyn Thibault / Marc Denis | 8.00 | 3.60 |
| ❑ 3 Teemu Selanne / Patrick Marleau | 20.00 | 9.00 |
| ❑ 4 Jaromir Jagr / Daniel Cleary | 20.00 | 9.00 |
| ❑ 5 Sergei Fedorov / Peter Forsberg | 25.00 | 11.00 |
| ❑ 6 Brett Hull / Bobby Hull | 20.00 | 9.00 |
| ❑ 7 Martin Brodeur / Roberto Luongo | 20.00 | 9.00 |
| ❑ 8 Gordie Howe / Steve Yzerman | 30.00 | 13.50 |

## 1997-98 Donruss Elite Back to the Future Autographs

Randomly inserted in packs, this eight-card set if parallel to the regular Back to the Future insert set and consists of the first 100 cards of the regular set autographed by both players.

| | MINT | NRMT |
|---|---|---|
| COMPLETE SET (8) | 2800.00 | 1250.00 |
| COMMON CARD (1-8) | 150.00 | 70.00 |
| ❑ 1 Eric Lindros / Joe Thornton | 300.00 | 135.00 |
| ❑ 2 Jocelyn Thibault / Marc Denis | 150.00 | 70.00 |
| ❑ 3 Teemu Selanne / Patrick Marleau | 250.00 | 110.00 |
| ❑ 4 Jaromir Jagr / Daniel Cleary | 300.00 | 135.00 |
| ❑ 5 Sergei Fedorov / Peter Forsberg | 400.00 | 180.00 |
| ❑ 6 Brett Hull / Bobby Hull | 300.00 | 135.00 |
| ❑ 7 Martin Brodeur / Roberto Luongo | 300.00 | 135.00 |
| ❑ 8 Gordie Howe / Steve Yzerman | 600.00 | 275.00 |

## 1997-98 Donruss Elite Craftsmen

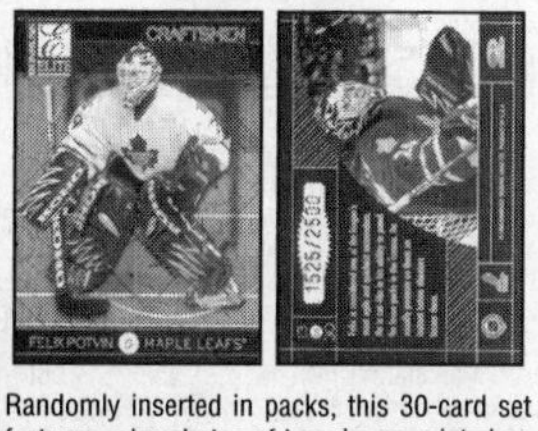

Randomly inserted in packs, this 30-card set features color photos of top players printed on full foil board and micro-etched. The cards are sequentially numbered to 2,500.

| | MINT | NRMT |
|---|---|---|
| COMPLETE SET (30) | 250.00 | 110.00 |
| COMMON CARD (1-30) | 2.50 | 1.10 |
| ❑ 1 John Vanbiesbrouck | 6.00 | 2.70 |
| ❑ 2 Eric Lindros | 12.00 | 5.50 |
| ❑ 3 Joe Sakic | 8.00 | 3.60 |
| ❑ 4 Mark Messier | 5.00 | 2.20 |
| ❑ 5 Jaroslav Svejkovsky | 3.00 | 1.35 |
| ❑ 6 Dominik Hasek | 8.00 | 3.60 |
| ❑ 7 Chris Osgood | 2.50 | 1.10 |
| ❑ 8 Martin Brodeur | 10.00 | 4.50 |
| ❑ 9 Sergei Fedorov | 8.00 | 3.60 |
| ❑ 10 Daniel Cleary | 2.50 | 1.10 |
| ❑ 11 Patrick Marleau | 5.00 | 2.20 |
| ❑ 12 Sergei Samsonov | 5.00 | 2.20 |
| ❑ 13 Felix Potvin | 4.00 | 1.80 |
| ❑ 14 Patrick Roy | 20.00 | 9.00 |
| ❑ 15 Teemu Selanne | 8.00 | 3.60 |
| ❑ 16 Steve Yzerman | 12.00 | 5.50 |
| ❑ 17 Jarome Iginla | 3.00 | 1.35 |
| ❑ 18 Mike Modano | 5.00 | 2.20 |
| ❑ 19 Wayne Gretzky | 25.00 | 11.00 |
| ❑ 20 Pavel Bure | 8.00 | 3.60 |
| ❑ 21 Ryan Smyth | 3.00 | 1.35 |
| ❑ 22 Paul Kariya | 15.00 | 6.75 |
| ❑ 23 Peter Forsberg | 12.00 | 5.50 |
| ❑ 24 Joe Thornton | 5.00 | 2.20 |
| ❑ 25 Jaromir Jagr | 12.00 | 5.50 |
| ❑ 26 Bryan Berard | 2.50 | 1.10 |
| ❑ 27 Brendan Shanahan | 8.00 | 3.60 |
| ❑ 28 Keith Tkachuk | 5.00 | 2.20 |
| ❑ 29 Curtis Joseph | 4.00 | 1.80 |
| ❑ 30 Brian Leetch | 4.00 | 1.80 |

## 1997-98 Donruss Elite Master Craftsmen

Randomly inserted in packs, this 30-card set is parallel to the regular Craftsmen insert set and

is printed on holofoil board. The set is sequentailly numbered to 100.

| | MINT | NRMT |
|---|---|---|
| COMPLETE SET (30) | 4000.00 | 1800.00 |
| COMMON CARD (1-30) | 40.00 | 18.00 |
| *STARS: 8X TO 16X BASIC CARDS 40.00 18.00 | | |

## 1997-98 Donruss Elite Prime Numbers

Randomly inserted in packs, this 36-card set features color photos of 12 top stars with a number in the background. Each star appears on three cards which, when linked together in the right order, display a significant career statistic. Each card in the set is sequentially numbered to the career statistic.

| | MINT | NRMT |
|---|---|---|
| COMMON CARD (1A-12C) | 20.00 | 9.00 |
| PRINT RUNS IN PARENTHESIS BELOW | | |
| ❑ 1A Peter Forsberg 2 (54) | 200.00 | 90.00 |
| ❑ 1B Peter Forsberg 5 (204) | 50.00 | 22.00 |
| ❑ 1C Peter Forsberg 4 (250) | 50.00 | 22.00 |
| ❑ 2A Patrick Roy 3 (49) | 300.00 | 135.00 |
| ❑ 2B Patrick Roy 4 (309) | 60.00 | 27.00 |
| ❑ 2C Patrick Roy 9 (340) | 60.00 | 27.00 |
| ❑ 3A Mark Messier 2 (95) | 60.00 | 27.00 |
| ❑ 3B Mark Messier 9 (205) | 25.00 | 11.00 |
| ❑ 3C Mark Messier 5 (290) | 20.00 | 9.00 |
| ❑ 4A Eric Lindros 4 (36) | 300.00 | 135.00 |
| ❑ 4B Eric Lindros 3 (406) | 40.00 | 18.00 |
| ❑ 4C Eric Lindros 6 (430) | 40.00 | 18.00 |
| ❑ 5A Paul Kariya 2 (46) | 250.00 | 110.00 |
| ❑ 5B Paul Kariya 4 (206) | 60.00 | 27.00 |
| ❑ 5C Paul Kariya 6 (240) | 60.00 | 27.00 |
| ❑ 6A Jaromir Jagr 2 (66) | 150.00 | 70.00 |
| ❑ 6B Jaromir Jagr 6 (206) | 50.00 | 22.00 |
| ❑ 6C Jaromir Jagr 6 (260) | 50.00 | 22.00 |
| ❑ 7A Teemu Selanne 2 (37) | 150.00 | 70.00 |
| ❑ 7B Teemu Selanne 3 (207) | 30.00 | 13.50 |
| ❑ 7C Teemu Selanne 7 (230) | 30.00 | 13.50 |
| ❑ 8A John Vanbiesbrouck 2 (88) | 60.00 | 27.00 |
| ❑ 8B John Vanbiesbrouck 8 (208) | 25.00 | 11.00 |
| ❑ 8C John Vanbiesbrouck 8 (280) | 20.00 | 9.00 |
| ❑ 9A Brendan Shanahan 3 (35) | 150.00 | 70.00 |
| ❑ 9B Brendan Shanahan 3 (305) | 25.00 | 11.00 |
| ❑ 9C Brendan Shanahan 5 (330) | 25.00 | 11.00 |
| ❑ 10A Steve Yzerman 5 (39) | 300.00 | 135.00 |
| ❑ 10B Steve Yzerman 3 (509) | 30.00 | 13.50 |
| ❑ 10C Steve Yzerman 9 (530) | 30.00 | 13.50 |
| ❑ 11A Joe Sakic 3 (7) | | |
| ❑ 11B Joe Sakic 0 (307) | 25.00 | 11.00 |
| ❑ 11C Joe Sakic 7 (300) | 25.00 | 11.00 |
| ❑ 12A Pavel Bure 3 (88) | 80.00 | 36.00 |
| ❑ 12B Pavel Bure 8 (308) | 25.00 | 11.00 |
| ❑ 12C Pavel Bure 8 (380) | 20.00 | 9.00 |

## 1997-98 Donruss Elite Prime Numbers Die-Cuts

Randomly inserted in packs, this 36-card set is a die-cut parallel version of the regular Prime Numbers set. How many of each card was produced depended on the specified statistical number the card represented.

| | MINT | NRMT |
|---|---|---|
| COMMON CARD (1A-12C) | 25.00 | 11.00 |
| RANDOM INSERTS IN PACKS | | |
| PRINT RUN IN PARENTHESIS BELOW | | |
| ❑ 1A Peter Forsberg 2 (200) | 50.00 | 22.00 |
| ❑ 1B Peter Forsberg 5 (50) | 200.00 | 90.00 |
| ❑ 1C Peter Forsberg 4 (4) | | |
| ❑ 2A Patrick Roy 3 (300) | 60.00 | 27.00 |
| ❑ 2B Patrick Roy 4 (40) | 300.00 | 135.00 |
| ❑ 2C Patrick Roy 9 (9) | | |
| ❑ 3A Mark Messier 2 (200) | 25.00 | 11.00 |
| ❑ 3B Mark Messier 9 (90) | 60.00 | 27.00 |
| ❑ 3C Mark Messier 5 (5) | | |
| ❑ 4A Eric Lindros 4 (400) | 40.00 | 18.00 |
| ❑ 4B Eric Lindros 3 (30) | 300.00 | 135.00 |
| ❑ 4C Eric Lindros 6 (6) | | |
| ❑ 5A Paul Kariya 2 (200) | 60.00 | 27.00 |
| ❑ 5B Paul Kariya 4 (40) | 250.00 | 110.00 |
| ❑ 5C Paul Kariya 6 (6) | | |
| ❑ 6A Jaromir Jagr 2 (200) | 50.00 | 22.00 |
| ❑ 6B Jaromir Jagr 6 (60) | 150.00 | 70.00 |
| ❑ 6C Jaromir Jagr 6 (6) | | |
| ❑ 7A Teemu Selanne 2 (200) | 30.00 | 13.50 |
| ❑ 7B Teemu Selanne 3 (30) | 200.00 | 90.00 |
| ❑ 7C Teemu Selanne 7 (7) | | |
| ❑ 8A John Vanbiesbrouck 2 (200) | 25.00 | 11.00 |
| ❑ 8B John Vanbiesbrouck 8 (80) | 60.00 | 27.00 |
| ❑ 8C John Vanbiesbrouck 8 (8) | | |
| ❑ 9A Brendan Shanahan 3 (300) | 25.00 | 11.00 |
| ❑ 9B Brendan Shanahan 3 (30) | 150.00 | 70.00 |
| ❑ 9C Brendan Shanahan 5 (5) | | |
| ❑ 10A Steve Yzerman 5 (500) | 30.00 | 13.50 |
| ❑ 10B Steve Yzerman 3 (30) | 300.00 | 135.00 |
| ❑ 10C Steve Yzerman 9 (9) | | |
| ❑ 11A Joe Sakic 3 (300) | 25.00 | 11.00 |
| ❑ 11B Joe Sakic 0 (0) | | |
| ❑ 11C Joe Sakic 7 (7) | | |
| ❑ 12A Pavel Bure 3 (300) | 25.00 | 11.00 |
| ❑ 12B Pavel Bure 8 (80) | 80.00 | 36.00 |
| ❑ 12C Pavel Bure 8 (8) | | |

## 1997-98 Donruss Limited

This 200-card set was distributed in five-card packs with a suggested retail price of $4.99 and features full-bleed player photographs printed on double-sided cards. The set contains the following subsets: Counterparts, which displays photos of two superstar players connected by their positions utilizing a Poly-Chromium print technology; Double Team, which features two formidable teammates back-to-back; Star Factor, which highlights the top stars using a different photo of the same star on each side; and Unlimited Potential/Talent, which combines a photo of a young rookie on one side and a veteran star's photo on the other.

| | MINT | NRMT |
|---|---|---|
| COMPLETE SET (200) | 2000.00 | 900.00 |
| COMP.COUNTERPART.SET (100) | 40.00 | 18.00 |
| COMMON COUNTERPART | .25 | .11 |
| COMP.DBLE.TEAM SET (40) | 200.00 | 90.00 |
| COMMON DOUBLE TEAM | 1.50 | .70 |
| COMP.STAR FACT.SET (40) | 1000.00 | 450.00 |
| COMMON STAR FACTOR | 5.00 | 2.20 |
| COMP.UNLIMITED SET (20) | 800.00 | 350.00 |
| UNLIMITED COMMONS | 4.00 | 1.80 |
| ❑ 1 Brendan Shanahan / Harry York C | 1.50 | .70 |
| ❑ 2 Peter Forsberg / Michael Knuble C | 2.50 | 1.10 |
| ❑ 3 Chris Osgood / Kirk McLean C | .75 | .35 |
| ❑ 4 Wayne Gretzky S | 100.00 | 45.00 |
| ❑ 5 John Vanbiesbrouck / Ed Jovanovski D | 6.00 | 2.70 |
| ❑ 6 Paul Coffey / Darryl Sydor C | .75 | .35 |
| ❑ 7 Pavel Bure / Valeri Bure C | 1.50 | .70 |
| ❑ 8 Sergei Berezin / Jaromir Jagr U | 50.00 | 22.00 |
| ❑ 9 Saku Koivu / Mats Sundin C | 1.25 | .55 |
| ❑ 10 Trevor Kidd / Corey Hirsch C | .60 | .25 |
| ❑ 11 Teemu Selanne S | 30.00 | 13.50 |
| ❑ 12 Zigmund Palffy / Radek Bonk C | .75 | .35 |
| ❑ 13 Mats Sundin / Sergei Berezin D | 5.00 | 2.20 |
| ❑ 14 Jim Carey / Bill Ranford C | .60 | .25 |
| ❑ 15 John LeClair / Claude Lemieux C | 1.25 | .55 |
| ❑ 16 Janne Niinimaa / Chris Chelios U | 12.00 | 5.50 |
| ❑ 17 Kevin Hodson / Michael Knuble D | 4.00 | 1.80 |
| ❑ 18 Adam Graves / Keith Jones C | .60 | .25 |
| ❑ 19 Mike Modano / Trevor Linden C | 1.00 | .45 |
| ❑ 20 Brett Hull S | 20.00 | 9.00 |
| ❑ 21 Derian Hatcher / Kevin Hatcher C | .25 | .11 |
| ❑ 22 Daniel Alfredsson / Dave Andreychuk C | .60 | .25 |
| ❑ 23 Steve Shields / Vaclav Varada D | 4.00 | 1.80 |
| ❑ 24 Theo Fleury / Geoff Courtnall C | .60 | .25 |
| ❑ 25 Mark Messier / Dino Ciccarelli C | 1.00 | .45 |
| ❑ 26 Ryan Smyth S | 12.00 | 5.50 |
| ❑ 27 Mike Grier / Jason Arnott D | 4.00 | 1.80 |
| ❑ 28 Ed Belfour / Andy Moog C | .75 | .35 |
| ❑ 29 Jean-Sebastian Giguere / Felix Potvin U | 12.00 | 5.50 |
| ❑ 30 Eric Lindros / Todd Bertuzzi C | 2.50 | 1.10 |
| ❑ 31 Daymond Langkow / David Roberts C | .25 | .11 |
| ❑ 32 Mike Richter / Grant Fuhr C | .75 | .35 |
| ❑ 33 Adam Oates / Jaroslav Svejkovsky D | 4.00 | 1.80 |
| ❑ 34 Saku Koivu / Darcy Tucker D | 8.00 | 3.60 |
| ❑ 35 Paul Kariya S | 60.00 | 27.00 |
| ❑ 36 Joe Sakic / Bernie Nicholls C | 1.50 | .70 |
| ❑ 37 Ed Jovanovski / D.J.Smith C | .60 | .25 |
| ❑ 38 Vaclav Prospal / Brendan Shanahan U | 40.00 | 18.00 |
| ❑ 39 Mike Peca / Marty Murray C | .25 | .11 |
| ❑ 40 Mike Gartner / Wendel Clark C | .60 | .25 |
| ❑ 41 Steve Yzerman S | 50.00 | 22.00 |
| ❑ 42 Mike Modano / Roman Turek D | 6.00 | 2.70 |
| ❑ 43 Joe Nieuwendyk / Jarome Iginla C | .60 | .25 |
| ❑ 44 Patrick Roy / Jocelyn Thibault C | 4.00 | 1.80 |
| ❑ 45 Hnat Domenichelli / Andrew Cassels C | .25 | .11 |
| ❑ 46 Christian Dube / Steve Sullivan C | .25 | .11 |
| ❑ 47 Marc Denis / Valeri Kamensky D | 4.00 | 1.80 |
| ❑ 48 Peter Forsberg S | 50.00 | 22.00 |
| ❑ 49 Derek Plante / Todd Harvey C | .25 | .11 |
| ❑ 50 Mike Grier / Eric Lindros U | 50.00 | 22.00 |
| ❑ 51 Brett Hull / Jim Campbell D | 6.00 | 2.70 |
| ❑ 52 Mark Recchi / Landon Wilson C | .25 | .11 |
| ❑ 53 Darcy Tucker / Pascal Rheaume C | .25 | .11 |
| ❑ 54 Chris O'Sullivan / Anders Eriksson C | .25 | .11 |
| ❑ 55 Jaromir Jagr S | 50.00 | 22.00 |
| ❑ 56 Paul Kariya / Teemu Selanne D | 30.00 | 13.50 |
| ❑ 57 Felix Potvin / Damian Rhodes C | .75 | .35 |
| ❑ 58 Brian Holzinger / Mike Ricci C | .60 | .25 |
| ❑ 59 Eric Fichaud / Travis Green D | 4.00 | 1.80 |
| ❑ 60 Ethan Moreau / John MacLean C | .25 | .11 |
| ❑ 61 Joe Juneau / Jeff O'Neill C | .25 | .11 |
| ❑ 62 John Vanbiesbrouck S | 25.00 | 11.00 |
| ❑ 63 Byron Dafoe / Steve Shields C | .60 | .25 |
| ❑ 64 Mikael Renberg / Niklas Sundstrom C | .25 | .11 |
| ❑ 65 Ryan Smyth / Eric Daze C | .60 | .25 |
| ❑ 66 Doug Gilmour / Pascal Rheaume D | 4.00 | 1.80 |
| ❑ 67 Jim Campbell / Craig Janney C | .25 | .11 |
| ❑ 68 Alexander Mogilny / Mathew Barnaby C | .60 | .25 |
| ❑ 69 Alexei Yashin S | 5.00 | 2.20 |
| ❑ 70 Bryan Berard / Brian Leetch U | 12.00 | 5.50 |
| ❑ 71 Alexei Yashin / Brain Savage C | .60 | .25 |
| ❑ 72 Jeff Friesen / Darren McCarty C | .60 | .25 |
| ❑ 73 Dimitri Khristich / Chad Kilger C | .25 | .11 |
| ❑ 74 Martin Brodeur / Dave Andreychuk D | 12.00 | 5.50 |
| ❑ 75 Luc Robitaille / Pat Verbeek C | .60 | .25 |
| ❑ 76 Dominik Hasek / Jamie Storr C | 1.50 | .70 |
| ❑ 77 Felix Potvin S | 15.00 | 6.75 |
| ❑ 78 Mike Dunham / Vadim Sharifijanov D | 4.00 | 1.80 |
| ❑ 79 Jason Arnott / Rob Niedermayer C | .60 | .25 |
| ❑ 80 Eric Desjardins / Chris Phillips C | .25 | .11 |
| ❑ 81 Curtis Joseph / Jose Theodore C | .75 | .35 |
| ❑ 82 Doug Gilmour / Rod Brind'Amour C | .75 | .35 |
| ❑ 83 Keith Tkachuk / Rick Tocchet C | 1.00 | .45 |
| ❑ 84 Mark Messier S | 20.00 | 9.00 |
| ❑ 85 Chris Pronger / Aki Berg C | .60 | .25 |
| ❑ 86 Marcel Cousineau / Dominik Hasek U | 25.00 | 11.00 |
| ❑ 87 Ethan Moreau / Chris Chelios D | 5.00 | 2.20 |
| ❑ 88 Jonas Hoglund / Rob Zamuner C | .25 | .11 |
| ❑ 89 Ron Hextall / Kevin Hodson C | .60 | .25 |
| ❑ 90 John LeClair S | 25.00 | 11.00 |
| ❑ 91 Vaclav Prospal RC / Viktor Kozlov C | 1.25 | .55 |
| ❑ 92 Ray Bourque / Joe Thornton D | 12.00 | 5.50 |
| ❑ 93 Oleg Tverdovsky / Sergei Zubov C | .25 | .11 |
| ❑ 94 Ethan Moreau / John LeClair U | 25.00 | 11.00 |
| ❑ 95 Adam Deadmarsh S | 12.00 | 5.50 |
| ❑ 96 Jaroslav Svejkovsky / Jozef Stumpel C | .60 | .25 |
| ❑ 97 Wayne Gretzky / Vladimir Vorobiev D | 30.00 | 13.50 |
| ❑ 98 Sergei Fedorov S | 30.00 | 13.50 |
| ❑ 99 Jim Campbell / Ryan Smyth U | 10.00 | 4.50 |
| ❑ 100 Vaclav Prospal / Paul Coffey D | 5.00 | 2.20 |
| ❑ 101 Wayne Primeau / Sean Pronger C | .60 | .25 |
| ❑ 102 Jean-Sebastian Giguere / Guy Hebert C | .60 | .25 |
| ❑ 103 Curtis Joseph S | 15.00 | 6.75 |
| ❑ 104 Pavel Bure / Alexander Mogilny D | 10.00 | 4.50 |
| ❑ 105 Jeremy Roenick / Tony Amonte C | .60 | .25 |
| ❑ 106 Sandis Ozolinsh / Kirk McLaren C | .60 | .25 |
| ❑ 107 Anson Carter / Steve Kelly C | .25 | .11 |
| ❑ 108 Paul Coffey S | 15.00 | 6.75 |
| ❑ 109 Dainius Zubrus / Peter Forsberg U | 50.00 | 22.00 |
| ❑ 110 Travis Green / Scott Mellanby C | .25 | .11 |
| ❑ 111 Pat LaFontaine / Valeri Kamensky C | .60 | .25 |
| ❑ 112 Adam Oates S | 12.00 | 5.50 |
| ❑ 113 John Vanbiesbrouck / Roman Turek C | 1.25 | .55 |
| ❑ 114 Jarome Iginla / Paul Kariya U | 60.00 | 27.00 |
| ❑ 115 Steve Yzerman / Chris Osgood D | 15.00 | 6.75 |
| ❑ 116 Marcel Cousineau / Steve Sullivan D | 4.00 | 1.80 |
| ❑ 117 Owen Nolan / Steve Rucchin C | .60 | .25 |
| ❑ 118 Donald Audette / Ted Donato C | .25 | .11 |
| ❑ 119 Geoff Sanderson / Sean Burke D | 4.00 | 1.80 |
| ❑ 120 Jeremy Roenick S | 12.00 | 5.50 |
| ❑ 121 Vladimir Vorobiev / Andreas Johansson | .25 | .11 |
| ❑ 122 Alexander Mogilny S | 12.00 | 5.50 |
| ❑ 123 Jocelyn Thibault / Terry Ryan D | 4.00 | 1.80 |
| ❑ 124 Eric Fichaud / Nikolai Khabibulin C | .60 | .25 |
| ❑ 125 Ray Bourque / Eric Messier C | .75 | .35 |
| ❑ 126 Sergei Fedorov / Keith Primeau C | 1.50 | .70 |
| ❑ 127 Marc Denis / Martin Brodeur U | 40.00 | 18.00 |
| ❑ 128 Mats Sundin S | 15.00 | 6.75 |
| ❑ 129 Peter Bondra / Roman Vopat C | .75 | .35 |
| ❑ 130 Tommy Salo / Corey Schwab C | .60 | .25 |
| ❑ 131 Sergei Samsonov / Jim Carey D | 12.00 | 5.50 |
| ❑ 132 Adam Deadmarsh / Joe Sakic D | 10.00 | 4.50 |
| ❑ 133 Daymond Langkow / Keith Tkachuk U | 15.00 | 6.75 |
| ❑ 134 Mike Richter S | 15.00 | 6.75 |
| ❑ 135 Geoff Sanderson / Jere Lehtinen C | .60 | .25 |
| ❑ 136 Janne Niinimaa / Jamie Pushor C | .60 | .25 |
| ❑ 137 Andreas Dackell / Vincent Damphousse C | .60 | .25 |
| ❑ 138 Keith Tkachuk S | 20.00 | 9.00 |
| ❑ 139 Ray Bourque S | 15.00 | 6.75 |
| ❑ 140 Keith Tkachuk / Jeremy Roenick D | 6.00 | 2.70 |
| ❑ 141 Rem Murray / Ray Sheppard C | .25 | .11 |
| ❑ 142 Peter Schafer / Patrick Lalime C | .60 | .25 |
| ❑ 143 Jaroslav Svejkovsky / Teemu Selanne U | 30.00 | 13.50 |
| ❑ 144 Todd Marchant / Tony Granato C | .25 | .11 |
| ❑ 145 Sandis Ozolinsh S | 12.00 | 5.50 |
| ❑ 146 Roman Hamrlik / Nicklas Lidstrom C | .60 | .25 |
| ❑ 147 Dominik Hasek S | 30.00 | 13.50 |
| ❑ 148 Chris Gratton / Daniel Goneau C | .60 | .25 |
| ❑ 149 Martin Brodeur S | 40.00 | 18.00 |
| ❑ 150 Martin Brodeur / Stephane Fiset C | 2.00 | .90 |
| ❑ 151 Jose Theodore / Patrick Roy U | 60.00 | 27.00 |
| ❑ 152 Jose Theodore / Mark Recchi D | 4.00 | 1.80 |
| ❑ 153 Pavel Bure S | 30.00 | 13.50 |
| ❑ 154 Sergei Berezin / Denis Pederson C | .25 | .11 |
| ❑ 155 Doug Gilmour S | 15.00 | 6.75 |
| ❑ 156 Peter Nedved / Kirk Muller C | .25 | .11 |
| ❑ 157 Theoren Fleury S | 12.00 | 5.50 |
| ❑ 158 Harry York / Pierre Turgeon D | 4.00 | 1.80 |
| ❑ 159 Andreas Johansson / Patrick Lalime D | 4.00 | 1.80 |
| ❑ 160 Marcel Cousineau / Jeff Hackett C | .60 | .25 |
| ❑ 161 Adam Deadmarsh / Alexandre Daigle C | .60 | .25 |
| ❑ 162 Adam Oates / Todd Warriner C | .60 | .25 |
| ❑ 163 Zigmund Palffy S | 15.00 | 6.75 |
| ❑ 164 Ed Belfour S | 15.00 | 6.75 |
| ❑ 165 Saku Koivu / Steve Yzerman U | 50.00 | 22.00 |

☐ 166 Chris Chelios .75 .35
Scott Lachance C
☐ 167 Jamie Langenbrunner .25 .11
Brandon Convery C
☐ 168 Janne Niinimaa 8.00 3.60
John LeClair D
☐ 169 Brendan Shanahan S 30.00 13.50
☐ 170 Darren Puppa .60 .25
Garth Snow C
☐ 171 Chris Osgood S 15.00 6.75
☐ 172 Pierre Turgeon .60 .25
Shane Corson C
☐ 173 Doug Weight 4.00 1.80
Rem Murray D
☐ 174 Eric Fichaud 12.00 5.50
Curtis Joseph U
☐ 175 Chris Chelios S 15.00 6.75
☐ 176 Wade Redden .25 .11
Scott Stevens C
☐ 177 Jarome Iginla 4.00 1.80
Theo Fleury D
☐ 178 Vaclav Varada .25 .11
Igor Larionov C
☐ 179 Brian Leetch S 15.00 6.75
☐ 180 Stephane Fiset 4.00 1.80
Roman Vopat D
☐ 181 Zigmund Palffy 5.00 2.20
Bryan Berard D
☐ 182 Bryan Berard .75 .35
Brian Leetch
☐ 183 Eric Lindros S 50.00 22.00
☐ 184 Derek Plante 4.00 1.80
Brian Holzinger D
☐ 185 Brett Hull 2.00 .90
Martin Gelinas C
☐ 186 Daniel Alfredsson 4.00 1.80
Damian Rhodes D
☐ 187 Joe Thornton 30.00 13.50
Mark Messier U
☐ 188 Mike Vernon .60 .25
Ken Wregget C
☐ 189 Alexei Yashin 1.50 .70
Wade Redden D
☐ 190 Joe Sakic S 30.00 13.50
☐ 191 Doug Weight .60 .25
Darren Turcotte C
☐ 192 Daymond Langkow .25 .11
Darren Puppa C
☐ 193 Mike Modano S 20.00 9.00
☐ 194 Sean Burke .60 .25
Mike Dunham C
☐ 195 Dainius Zubrus .60 .25
Sebastien Bordeleau C
☐ 196 Owen Nolan 4.00 1.80
Jeff Friesen D
☐ 197 Vladimir Vorobiev 30.00 13.50
Sergei Fedorov U
☐ 198 Patrick Roy S 80.00 36.00
☐ 199 Mike Grier .60 .25
Ron Francis C
☐ 200 Patrick Marleau 100.00 45.00
Wayne Gretzky U
☐ P183 Eric Lindros PROMO 5.00 2.20

## 1997-98 Donruss Limited Exposure

Randomly inserted in packs, this 200-card set is parallel to the base set and features holographic poly-chromium technology on both sides. The set is designated by an exclusive "Limited Exposure" stamp. Less than 25 sets were produced.

| | MINT | NRMT |
|---|---|---|
| COMPLETE SET (200) | 22000.00 | 9900.00 |
| COMP.CNTRPART.SET (100) | 1000.00 | 450.00 |
| COMMON COUNTERPART | 4.00 | 1.80 |
| COUNTER.SEMISTARS | 10.00 | 4.50 |
| COUNTER.UNLISTED STARS | 12.00 | 5.50 |
| COMP.DBL.TEAM SET (40) | 4000.00 | 1800.00 |
| COMMON DOUBLE TEAM | 25.00 | 11.00 |
| DBL.TEAM SEMISTARS | 60.00 | 27.00 |
| DBL.TEAM UNLISTED STARS | 80.00 | 36.00 |
| COMP.STAR FACT.SET (40) | 12000.00 | 5400.00 |
| COMMON STAR FACTOR | 60.00 | 27.00 |
| ST.FACT.SEMISTARS | 150.00 | 70.00 |
| ST.FACT.UNLISTED STARS | 200.00 | 90.00 |
| COMP.UNLIMITED SET (20) | 5000.00 | 2200.00 |
| COMMON UNLIMITED | 30.00 | 13.50 |

25 OF EACH STAR FACTOR MADE
LESS THAN 40 OF EACH UNLIMITED MADE

☐ 1 Brendan Shanahan 25.00 11.00
Harry York C
☐ 2 Peter Forsberg 40.00 18.00
Michael Knuble C
☐ 3 Chris Osgood 12.00 5.50
Kirk McLean C
☐ 4 Wayne Gretzky S 1200.00 550.00
☐ 5 John Vanbiesbrouck 100.00 45.00
Ed Jovanovski D
☐ 6 Paul Coffey 12.00 5.50
Darryl Sydor C
☐ 7 Pavel Bure 25.00 11.00
Valeri Bure C
☐ 8 Sergei Berezin 300.00 135.00
Jaromir Jagr U
☐ 9 Saku Koivu 20.00 9.00
Mats Sundin C
☐ 10 Trevor Kidd 10.00 4.50
Corey Hirsch C
☐ 11 Teemu Selanne S 400.00 180.00
☐ 12 Zigmund Palffy 12.00 5.50
Radek Bonk C
☐ 13 Mats Sundin 80.00 36.00
Sergei Berezin D
☐ 14 Jim Carey 10.00 4.50
Bill Ranford C
☐ 15 John LeClair 20.00 9.00
Claude Lemieux C
☐ 16 Janne Niinimaa 100.00 45.00
Chris Chelios U
☐ 17 Kevin Hodson 60.00 27.00
Michael Knuble D
☐ 18 Adam Graves 10.00 4.50
Keith Jones C
☐ 19 Mike Modano 15.00 6.75
Trevor Linden C
☐ 20 Brett Hull S 250.00 110.00
☐ 21 Derian Hatcher 4.00 1.80
Kevin Hatcher C
☐ 22 Daniel Alfredsson 10.00 4.50
Dave Andreychuk C
☐ 23 Steve Shields 60.00 27.00
Vaclav Varada D
☐ 24 Theo Fleury 10.00 4.50
Geoff Courtnall C
☐ 25 Mark Messier 15.00 6.75
Dino Ciccarelli C
☐ 26 Ryan Smyth S 150.00 70.00
☐ 27 Mike Grier 60.00 27.00
Jason Arnott D
☐ 28 Ed Belfour 12.00 5.50
Andy Moog C
☐ 29 Jean-Sebastian Giguere 100.00 45.00
Felix Potvin U
☐ 30 Eric Lindros 40.00 18.00
Todd Bertuzzi C
☐ 31 Daymond Langkow 4.00 1.80
David Roberts C
☐ 32 Mike Richter 12.00 5.50
Grant Fuhr C
☐ 33 Adam Oates 60.00 27.00
Jarslav Svejkovsky D
☐ 34 Saku Koivu 120.00 55.00
Darcy Tucker D
☐ 35 Paul Kariya S 800.00 350.00
☐ 36 Joe Sakic 25.00 11.00
Bernie Nicholls C
☐ 37 Ed Jovanovski 10.00 4.50
D.J.Smith C
☐ 38 Vaclav Prospal 250.00 110.00
Brendan Shanahan U
☐ 39 Mike Peca 4.00 1.80
Marty Murray C
☐ 40 Mike Gartner 10.00 4.50
Wendal Clark C
☐ 41 Steve Yzerman S 600.00 275.00
☐ 42 Mike Modano 100.00 45.00
Roman Turek D
☐ 43 Joe Nieuwendyk 10.00 4.50
Jarome Iginla C
☐ 44 Patrick Roy 60.00 27.00
Jocelyn Thibault C
☐ 45 Hnat Domenichelli 4.00 1.80
Andrew Cassels C
☐ 46 Christian Dube 4.00 1.80
Steve Sullivan C
☐ 47 Marc Denis 60.00 27.00
Valeri Kamensky D
☐ 48 Peter Forsberg S 600.00 275.00
☐ 49 Derek Plante 4.00 1.80
Todd Harvey C
☐ 50 Mike Grier 300.00 135.00
Eric Lindros U
☐ 51 Brett Hull 100.00 45.00
Jim Campbell D
☐ 52 Mark Recchi 4.00 1.80
Landon Wilson C
☐ 53 Darcy Tucker 4.00 1.80
Pascal Rheaume C
☐ 54 Chris O'Sullivan 4.00 1.80
Anders Eriksson C
☐ 55 Jaromir Jagr S 600.00 275.00
☐ 56 Paul Kariya 500.00 220.00
Teemu Selanne D
☐ 57 Felix Potvin 12.00 5.50
Damian Rhodes C
☐ 58 Brian Holzinger 10.00 4.50
Mike Ricci C
☐ 59 Eric Fichaud 60.00 27.00
Travis Green D
☐ 60 Ethan Moreau 4.00 1.80
John MacLean C
☐ 61 Joe Juneau 4.00 1.80
Jeff O'Neill C
☐ 62 John Vanbiesbrouck S 300.00 135.00
☐ 63 Byron Dafoe 10.00 4.50
Steve Shields C
☐ 64 Mikael Renberg 4.00 1.80
Niklas Sundstrom C
☐ 65 Ryan Smyth 10.00 4.50
Eric Daze C
☐ 66 Doug Gilmour 60.00 27.00
Pascal Rheaume D
☐ 67 Jim Campbell 4.00 1.80
Craig Janney C
☐ 68 Alexander Mogilny 10.00 4.50
Mathew Barnaby C
☐ 69 Alexei Yashin S 60.00 27.00
☐ 70 Bryan Berard 100.00 45.00
Brian Leetch U
☐ 71 Alexei Yashin 10.00 4.50
Brian Savage C
☐ 72 Jeff Friesen 10.00 4.50
Darren McCarty C
☐ 73 Dimitri Khristich 4.00 1.80
Chad Kilger C
☐ 74 Martin Brodeur 200.00 90.00
Dave Andreychuk D
☐ 75 Luc Robitaille 10.00 4.50
Pat Verbeek C
☐ 76 Dominik Hasek 25.00 11.00
Jamie Storr C
☐ 77 Felix Potvin S 200.00 90.00
☐ 78 Mike Dunham 60.00 27.00
Vadim Sharifijanov D
☐ 79 Jason Arnott 10.00 4.50
Rob Niedermayer C
☐ 80 Eric Desjardins 4.00 1.80
Chris Phillips C
☐ 81 Curtis Joseph 12.00 5.50
Jose Theodore C
☐ 82 Doug Gilmour 12.00 5.50
Rod Brind'Amour C
☐ 83 Keith Tkachuk 15.00 6.75
Rick Tocchet C
☐ 84 Mark Messier S 250.00 110.00
☐ 85 Chris Pronger 10.00 4.50
Aki Berg C
☐ 86 Marcel Cousineau 200.00 90.00
Dominik Hasek U
☐ 87 Ethan Moreau 80.00 36.00
Chris Chelios D
☐ 88 Jonas Hoglund 4.00 1.80
Rob Zamuner C
☐ 89 Ron Hextall 10.00 4.50
Kevin Hodson C
☐ 90 John LeClair S 300.00 135.00
☐ 91 Vaclav Prospal 12.00 5.50
Viktor Kozlov C
☐ 92 Ray Bourque 150.00 70.00
Joe Thornton D
☐ 93 Oleg Tverdovsky 4.00 1.80
Sergei Zubov C
☐ 94 Ethan Moreau 250.00 110.00
John LeClair U
☐ 95 Adam Deadmarsh S 150.00 70.00
☐ 96 Jasoslav Svejkovsky 10.00 4.50
Jozef Stumpel C
☐ 97 Wayne Gretzky 500.00 220.00
Vladimir Vorobiev D
☐ 98 Sergei Fedorov S 400.00 180.00
☐ 99 Jim Campbell 80.00 36.00
Ryan Smyth U
☐ 100 Vaclav Prospal 80.00 36.00
Paul Coffey D
☐ 101 Wayne Primeau 10.00 4.50
Sean Pronger C
☐ 102 Jean-Sebastian Giguere 10.00 4.50
Guy Hebert C
☐ 103 Curtis Joseph S 200.00 90.00
☐ 104 Pavel Bure 150.00 70.00
Alexander Mogilny D
☐ 105 Jeremy Roenick 10.00 4.50
Tony Amonte C
☐ 106 Sandis Ozolinsh 10.00 4.50
Kirk McLaren C
☐ 107 Anson Carter 4.00 1.80
Steve Kelly C
☐ 108 Paul Coffey S 200.00 90.00
☐ 109 Dainius Zubrus 250.00 110.00
Peter Forsberg U
☐ 110 Travis Green 4.00 1.80
Scott Mellanby C
☐ 111 Pat LaFontaine 10.00 4.50
Valeri Kamensky C
☐ 112 Adam Oates S 150.00 70.00
☐ 113 John Vanbiesbrouck 20.00 9.00
Roman Turek C
☐ 114 Jarome Iginla 400.00 180.00
Paul Kariya U
☐ 115 Steve Yzerman 250.00 110.00
Chris Osgood D
☐ 116 Marcel Cousineau 60.00 27.00
Steve Sullivan D
☐ 117 Owen Nolan 10.00 4.50
Steve Rucchin C
☐ 118 Donald Audette 4.00 1.80
Ted Donato C
☐ 119 Geoff Sanderson 60.00 27.00
Sean Burke D
☐ 120 Jeremy Roenick S 150.00 70.00
☐ 121 Vladimir Vorobiev 4.00 1.80
Andreas Johansson C
☐ 122 Alexander Mogilny S 150.00 70.00
☐ 123 Jocelyn Thibault 60.00 27.00
Terry Ryan D
☐ 124 Eric Fichaud 10.00 4.50
Nikolai Khabibulin C
☐ 125 Ray Bourque 12.00 5.50
Eric Messier C
☐ 126 Sergei Fedorov 25.00 11.00
Keith Primeau C
☐ 127 Marc Denis 250.00 110.00
Martin Brodeur U
☐ 128 Mats Sundin S 200.00 90.00
☐ 129 Peter Bondra 12.00 5.50
Roman Vopat C
☐ 130 Tommy Salo 10.00 4.50
Corey Schwab C
☐ 131 Sergei Samsonov 150.00 70.00
Jim Carey D
☐ 132 Adam Deadmarsh 150.00 70.00
Joe Sakic D
☐ 133 Daymond Langkow 120.00 55.00
Keith Tkachuk U
☐ 134 Mike Richter S 200.00 90.00
☐ 135 Geoff Sanderson 10.00 4.50
Jere Lehtinen C
☐ 136 Janne Niinimaa 10.00 4.50
Jamie Pushor C
☐ 137 Andreas Dackell 10.00 4.50
Vincent Damphousse C
☐ 138 Keith Tkachuk S 250.00 110.00
☐ 139 Ray Bourque S 200.00 90.00
☐ 140 Keith Tkachuk 100.00 45.00
Jeremy Roenick D
☐ 141 Rem Murray 4.00 1.80
Ray Sheppard C
☐ 142 Peter Schafer 10.00 4.50
Patrick Lalime C
☐ 143 Jaroslav Svejkovsky 250.00 110.00
Teemu Selanne U
☐ 144 Todd Marchant 4.00 1.80
Tony Granato C
☐ 145 Sandis Ozolinsh S 150.00 70.00
☐ 146 Roman Hamrlik 10.00 4.50
Nicklas Lidstrom C
☐ 147 Dominik Hasek S 400.00 180.00
☐ 148 Chris Gratton 10.00 4.50
Daniel Goneau C
☐ 149 Martin Brodeur S 500.00 220.00
☐ 150 Martin Brodeur 30.00 13.50
Stephane Fiset C
☐ 151 Jose Theodore 500.00 220.00
Patrick Roy U
☐ 152 Jose Theodore 60.00 27.00
Mark Recchi D
☐ 153 Pavel Bure S 400.00 180.00
☐ 154 Sergei Berezin 4.00 1.80
Denis Pederson C
☐ 155 Doug Gilmour S 200.00 90.00
☐ 156 Peter Nedved 4.00 1.80
Kirk Muller C
☐ 157 Theoren Fleury S 150.00 70.00
☐ 158 Harry York 60.00 27.00
Pierre Turgeon D
☐ 159 Andreas Johansson 60.00 27.00
Patrick Lalime D
☐ 160 Marcel Cousineau 10.00 4.50
Jeff Hackett C
☐ 161 Adam Deadmarsh 10.00 4.50
Alexandre Daigle C
☐ 162 Adam Oates 10.00 4.50
Todd Warriner C
☐ 163 Zigmund Palffy S 200.00 90.00
☐ 164 Ed Belfour S 200.00 90.00
☐ 165 Saku Koivu 400.00 180.00
Steve Yzerman U
☐ 166 Chris Chelios 12.00 5.50
Scott Lachance C
☐ 167 Jamie Langenbrunner 4.00 1.80
Brandon Convery C
☐ 168 Janne Niinimaa 150.00 70.00
John LeClair D
☐ 169 Brendan Shanahan S 400.00 180.00
☐ 170 Darren Puppa 10.00 4.50
Garth Snow C
☐ 171 Chris Osgood S 200.00 90.00
☐ 172 Pierre Turgeon 10.00 4.50
Shane Corson C
☐ 173 Doug Weight 60.00 27.00
Rem Murray D
☐ 174 Eric Fichaud 100.00 45.00
Curtis Joseph U
☐ 175 Chris Chelios S 200.00 90.00
☐ 176 Wade Redden 4.00 1.80
Steve Stevens C
☐ 177 Jarome Iginla 60.00 27.00
Theo Fleury D
☐ 178 Vaclav Varada 4.00 1.80
Igor Larinov C
☐ 179 Brian Leetch S 200.00 90.00
☐ 180 Stephane Fiset 60.00 27.00
Roman Vopat D
☐ 181 Zigmund Palffy 80.00 36.00
Bryan Berard D
☐ 182 Bryan Berard 12.00 5.50
Brian Leetch
☐ 183 Eric Lindros S 600.00 275.00
☐ 184 Derek Plante 60.00 27.00
Brian Holzinger D
☐ 185 Brett Hull 15.00 6.75
Martin Gelinas C
☐ 186 Daniel Alfredsson 60.00 27.00
Damian Rhodes D
☐ 187 Joe Thornton 150.00 70.00
Mark Messier U
☐ 188 Mike Vernon 10.00 4.50
Ken Wregget C
☐ 189 Alexei Yashin 25.00 11.00
Wade Redden D
☐ 190 Joe Sakic S 300.00 135.00
☐ 191 Doug Weight 10.00 4.50
Darren Turcott C
☐ 192 Daymond Langkow 4.00 1.80
Darren Puppa D
☐ 193 Mike Modano S 200.00 90.00
☐ 194 Sean Burke 10.00 4.50
Mike Dunham C
☐ 195 Dainius Zubrus 10.00 4.50
Sebastien Bordeleau C
☐ 196 Owen Nolan 60.00 27.00
Jeff Friesen D
☐ 197 Vladimir Vorobiev 200.00 90.00
Sergei Fedorov U
☐ 198 Patrick Roy S 1000.00 450.00
☐ 199 Mike Grier 10.00 4.50
Ron Francis C
☐ 200 Patrick Marleau 1000.00 450.00
Wayne Gretzky U

## 1997-98 Donruss Limited Fabric of the Game

Randomly inserted in packs, this 72-card partial multi-fractured set features color player photos distinguised by using three different technologies, each of which represents a

different statistical category: Embossed Canvas (Wins), Leather (Goals), and Wood (Assists). Five more levels cross the sections and are sequentially numbered: Legendary Material (numbered to 100), Hall of Fame Material (numbered to 250), Superstar Material (numbered to 500), Star Material (numbered to 750), and Major Material (numbered to 1000)

| | MINT | NRMT |
|---|---|---|
| COMPLETE SET (72) | 4500.00 | 2000.00 |
| COMMON MAJOR LEAGUE | 3.00 | 1.35 |
| COMMON STAR | 12.00 | 5.50 |
| COMMON SUPERSTAR | 20.00 | 9.00 |
| COMMON HOF | 40.00 | 18.00 |
| HOF SEMISTARS | 50.00 | 22.00 |
| HOF UNLISTED STARS | 60.00 | 27.00 |
| COMMON LEGENDARY | 100.00 | 45.00 |

ALL MATERIALS EQUAL VALUE

☐ 1 Wayne Gretzky HF 300.00 135.00
☐ 2 Martin Brodeur S 40.00 18.00
☐ 3 Dainius Zubrus M 10.00 4.50
☐ 4 Joe Sakic SS 40.00 18.00
☐ 5 Joe Sakic HF 100.00 45.00
☐ 6 Sergei Fedorov S 30.00 13.50
☐ 7 John Vanbiesbrouck HF 80.00 36.00
☐ 8 Saku Koivu M 15.00 6.75
☐ 9 Jean-Sebastien Giguere M 8.00 3.60
☐ 10 Paul Kariya S 60.00 27.00
☐ 11 Mike Richter SS 30.00 13.50
☐ 12 Paul Coffey L 100.00 45.00
☐ 13 Brendan Shanahan L 200.00 90.00
☐ 14 Jaromir Jagr SS 60.00 27.00
☐ 15 Felix Potvin SS 30.00 13.50
☐ 16 Mats Sundin SS 30.00 13.50
☐ 17 Mike Vernon HF 50.00 22.00
☐ 18 Keith Tkachuk S 20.00 9.00
☐ 19 Doug Gilmour HF 60.00 27.00
☐ 20 Patrick Roy L 600.00 275.00
☐ 21 Sergei Samsonov M 25.00 11.00
☐ 22 Mike Grier M 3.00 1.35
☐ 23 Curtis Joseph SS 30.00 13.50
☐ 24 Zigmund Palffy S 15.00 6.75
☐ 25 Chris Osgood S 15.00 6.75
☐ 26 Mats Sundin S 15.00 6.75
☐ 27 Kelly Hrudey HF 50.00 22.00
☐ 28 Brett Hull L 150.00 70.00
☐ 29 Ray Bourque HF 60.00 27.00
☐ 30 Nikolai Khabibulin S 12.00 5.50
☐ 31 Bryan Berard M 3.00 1.35
☐ 32 Jaroslav Svejkovsky M 8.00 3.60
☐ 33 Ed Belfour SS 30.00 13.50
☐ 34 Wayne Gretzky L 800.00 350.00
☐ 35 Jeremy Roenick SS 25.00 11.00
☐ 36 Andy Moog L 100.00 45.00
☐ 37 Eric Lindros S 50.00 22.00
☐ 38 Brett Hull SS 25.00 11.00
☐ 39 Marcel Cousineau M 8.00 3.60
☐ 40 Paul Kariya M 40.00 18.00
☐ 41 Mike Dunham M 8.00 3.60
☐ 42 Chris Phillips M 3.00 1.35
☐ 43 Teemu Selanne SS 40.00 18.00
☐ 44 Mark Messier L 150.00 70.00
☐ 45 Grant Fuhr L 100.00 45.00
☐ 46 Daniel Alfredsson M 8.00 3.60
☐ 47 Marc Denis M 8.00 3.60
☐ 48 Daymond Langkow M 3.00 1.35
☐ 49 Steve Yzerman HF 150.00 70.00
☐ 50 Ryan Smyth S 12.00 5.50
☐ 51 Alexander Mogilny HF 50.00 22.00
☐ 52 Ron Hextall HF 50.00 22.00
☐ 53 Brendan Shanahan S 30.00 13.50
☐ 54 Jim Carey S 12.00 5.50
☐ 55 Eric Lindros S 50.00 22.00
☐ 56 Eric Fichaud M 8.00 3.60
☐ 57 Sergei Berezin M 3.00 1.35
☐ 58 Chris Chelios HF 60.00 27.00
☐ 59 Mark Messier HF 60.00 27.00
☐ 60 Damian Rhodes M 8.00 3.60
☐ 61 Jarome Iginla M 8.00 3.60
☐ 62 Jocelyn Thibault S 12.00 5.50
☐ 63 John LeClair S 25.00 11.00
☐ 64 Brian Leetch SS 30.00 13.50
☐ 65 Dominik Hasek S 30.00 13.50
☐ 66 Pavel Bure SS 40.00 18.00
☐ 67 Mike Modano S 20.00 9.00
☐ 68 Daniel Cleary M 8.00 3.60
☐ 69 Janne Niinimaa M 8.00 3.60
☐ 70 Steve Yzerman L 400.00 180.00
☐ 71 Jose Theodore M 8.00 3.60
☐ 72 Peter Forsberg S 50.00 22.00

## 1997-98 Donruss Preferred

The 1997-98 Donruss Preferred set was issued in one series totalling 200 cards and distributed in five-card packs inside collectible tins. The set features color player photos on an all micro-etched foil board card with bronze, silver, gold, and platinum finishes.

| | MINT | NRMT |
|---|---|---|
| COMPLETE SET (200) | 1200.00 | 550.00 |
| COMP.BRONZE SET (100) | 30.00 | 13.50 |
| COMMON BRONZE | .25 | .11 |
| COMP.SILVER SET (60) | 300.00 | 135.00 |
| COMMON SILVER | 1.50 | .70 |
| COMP.GOLD SET (30) | 400.00 | 180.00 |
| COMMON GOLD | 3.00 | 1.35 |
| COMP.PLATINUM SET (10) | 500.00 | 220.00 |
| COMMON PLATINUM | 20.00 | 9.00 |

| | | |
|---|---|---|
| ❑ 1 Dominik Hasek G | 20.00 | 9.00 |
| ❑ 2 Peter Forsberg G | 30.00 | 13.50 |
| ❑ 3 Brendan Shanahan P | 30.00 | 13.50 |
| ❑ 4 Wayne Gretzky P | 100.00 | 45.00 |
| ❑ 5 Eric Lindros P | 50.00 | 22.00 |
| ❑ 6 Keith Tkachuk G | 12.00 | 5.50 |
| ❑ 7 Mark Messier P | 20.00 | 9.00 |
| ❑ 8 Mike Modano G | 12.00 | 5.50 |
| ❑ 9 John Vanbiesbrouck P | 25.00 | 11.00 |
| ❑ 10 Paul Kariya P | 60.00 | 27.00 |
| ❑ 11 Saku Koivu G | 15.00 | 6.75 |
| ❑ 12 Paul Coffey B | .60 | .25 |
| ❑ 13 Joe Juneau B | .50 | .23 |
| ❑ 14 Jeff Friesen S | 4.00 | 1.80 |
| ❑ 15 Brett Hull G | 12.00 | 5.50 |
| ❑ 16 Martin Brodeur G | 25.00 | 11.00 |
| ❑ 17 Jarome Iginla G | 8.00 | 3.60 |
| ❑ 18 Keith Primeau S | 4.00 | 1.80 |
| ❑ 19 Ed Jovanovski B | .50 | .23 |
| ❑ 20 Jamie Langenbrunner B | .50 | .23 |
| ❑ 21 Derian Hatcher S | 1.50 | .70 |
| ❑ 22 Brian Leetch G | 10.00 | 4.50 |
| ❑ 23 Daymond Langkow S | 1.50 | .70 |
| ❑ 24 Ray Bourque S | 5.00 | 2.20 |
| ❑ 25 Pavel Bure G | 20.00 | 9.00 |
| ❑ 26 Janne Niinimaa S | 4.00 | 1.80 |
| ❑ 27 Jamie Storr S | 4.00 | 1.80 |
| ❑ 28 Darcy Tucker B | .25 | .11 |
| ❑ 29 Anson Carter B | .25 | .11 |
| ❑ 30 Jeff O'Neill B | .25 | .11 |
| ❑ 31 Jason Arnott G | 8.00 | 3.60 |
| ❑ 32 Tommy Salo B | .50 | .23 |
| ❑ 33 Petr Nedved B | .50 | .23 |
| ❑ 34 Mike Peca B | .50 | .23 |
| ❑ 35 Ethan Moreau S | 1.50 | .70 |
| ❑ 36 Ray Sheppard B | .50 | .23 |
| ❑ 37 Damian Rhodes B | .50 | .23 |
| ❑ 38 Mats Sundin S | 5.00 | 2.20 |
| ❑ 39 Alexander Mogilny G | 8.00 | 3.60 |
| ❑ 40 Mike Dunham S | 4.00 | 1.80 |
| ❑ 41 Steve Yzerman P | 50.00 | 22.00 |
| ❑ 42 Alexei Yashin S | 4.00 | 1.80 |
| ❑ 43 Jim Carey S | 4.00 | 1.80 |
| ❑ 44 Mike Grier S | 1.50 | .70 |
| ❑ 45 Steve Rucchin B | .25 | .11 |
| ❑ 46 Mark Recchi S | 1.50 | .70 |
| ❑ 47 Mike Gartner B | .50 | .23 |
| ❑ 48 Alexandre Daigle S | 4.00 | 1.80 |
| ❑ 49 Eric Fichaud G | 8.00 | 3.60 |
| ❑ 50 Harry York B | .25 | .11 |
| ❑ 51 Dino Ciccarelli B | .50 | .23 |
| ❑ 52 Bill Ranford B | .50 | .23 |
| ❑ 53 Adam Deadmarsh G | 8.00 | 3.60 |
| ❑ 54 Ed Belfour B | .60 | .25 |
| ❑ 55 Jozef Stumpel S | 4.00 | 1.80 |
| ❑ 56 Rem Murray B | .25 | .11 |
| ❑ 57 Pat Verbeek B | .50 | .23 |
| ❑ 58 Pat LaFontaine S | 4.00 | 1.80 |
| ❑ 59 Dainius Zubrus S | 4.00 | 1.80 |
| ❑ 60 Grant Fuhr B | .50 | .23 |
| ❑ 61 Rob Niedermayer B | .50 | .23 |
| ❑ 62 Brian Savage B | .25 | .11 |
| ❑ 63 Gary Roberts B | .25 | .11 |
| ❑ 64 Tony Amonte B | .50 | .23 |
| ❑ 65 Jere Lehtinen B | .50 | .23 |
| ❑ 66 Dave Andreychuk B | .50 | .23 |
| ❑ 67 Rod Brind'Amour B | .50 | .23 |
| ❑ 68 Mikael Renberg B | .50 | .23 |
| ❑ 69 Doug Gilmour S | 5.00 | 2.20 |
| ❑ 70 Kevin Hatcher B | .25 | .11 |
| ❑ 71 Byron Dafoe B | .50 | .23 |
| ❑ 72 Derek Plante S | 1.50 | .70 |
| ❑ 73 Trevor Kidd B | .50 | .23 |
| ❑ 74 Doug Weight S | 4.00 | 1.80 |
| ❑ 75 Valeri Bure B | .50 | .23 |
| ❑ 76 John LeClair G | 15.00 | 6.75 |
| ❑ 77 Sergei Berezin B | .50 | .23 |
| ❑ 78 Peter Bondra S | 5.00 | 2.20 |
| ❑ 79 Bryan Berard G | 8.00 | 3.60 |
| ❑ 80 Steve Shields B | .50 | .23 |
| ❑ 81 Chris Osgood G | 10.00 | 4.50 |
| ❑ 82 Mike Vernon B | .50 | .23 |
| ❑ 83 Martin Gelinas B | .50 | .23 |
| ❑ 84 Curtis Joseph S | 5.00 | 2.20 |
| ❑ 85 Geoff Sanderson S | 4.00 | 1.80 |
| ❑ 86 Patrick Roy P | 80.00 | 36.00 |
| ❑ 87 Jocelyn Thibault G | 8.00 | 3.60 |
| ❑ 88 Jeremy Roenick S | 4.00 | 1.80 |
| ❑ 89 Trevor Linden B | .50 | .23 |
| ❑ 90 Daniel Alfredsson S | 4.00 | 1.80 |
| ❑ 91 Sergei Zubov B | .25 | .11 |
| ❑ 92 Dimitri Khristich S | 1.50 | .70 |
| ❑ 93 Brian Holzinger B | .25 | .11 |
| ❑ 94 Andrew Cassels B | .25 | .11 |
| ❑ 95 Teemu Selanne G | 20.00 | 9.00 |
| ❑ 96 Ron Hextall B | .50 | .23 |
| ❑ 97 Wade Redden B | .25 | .11 |
| ❑ 98 Jim Campbell B | .25 | .11 |
| ❑ 99 Felix Potvin G | 10.00 | 4.50 |
| ❑ 100 Adam Oates S | 4.00 | 1.80 |
| ❑ 101 Nikolai Khabibulin B | .50 | .23 |
| ❑ 102 Jose Theodore S | 4.00 | 1.80 |
| ❑ 103 Sandis Ozolinsh S | 4.00 | 1.80 |
| ❑ 104 Sean Burke B | .50 | .23 |
| ❑ 105 Vaclav Prospal G | 12.00 | 5.50 |
| ❑ 106 Zigmund Palffy G | 10.00 | 4.50 |
| ❑ 107 Kyle McLaren B | .25 | .11 |
| ❑ 108 Owen Nolan S | 4.00 | 1.80 |
| ❑ 109 Chris Pronger S | 4.00 | 1.80 |
| ❑ 110 Daren Puppa B | .50 | .23 |
| ❑ 111 Garth Snow B | .50 | .23 |
| ❑ 112 Aki Berg B | .25 | .11 |
| ❑ 113 Andy Moog B | .50 | .23 |
| ❑ 114 Darren McCarty B | .25 | .11 |
| ❑ 115 Joe Nieuwendyk B | .50 | .23 |
| ❑ 116 Eric Daze S | 1.50 | .70 |
| ❑ 117 Pierre Turgeon S | 4.00 | 1.80 |
| ❑ 118 Ken Wregget B | .50 | .23 |
| ❑ 119 Ryan Smyth G | 8.00 | 3.60 |
| ❑ 120 Kirk Muller B | .25 | .11 |
| ❑ 121 Luc Robitaille B | .50 | .23 |
| ❑ 122 Sergei Fedorov G | 20.00 | 9.00 |
| ❑ 123 Sean Pronger B | .25 | .11 |
| ❑ 124 Mike Richter S | 5.00 | 2.20 |
| ❑ 125 Jaromir Jagr P | 50.00 | 22.00 |
| ❑ 126 Claude Lemieux B | .50 | .23 |
| ❑ 127 Chris Chelios S | 5.00 | 2.20 |
| ❑ 128 Joe Sakic P | 30.00 | 13.50 |
| ❑ 129 Guy Hebert S | 4.00 | 1.80 |
| ❑ 130 Chris Gratton S | 4.00 | 1.80 |
| ❑ 131 Steve Sullivan B | .25 | .11 |
| ❑ 132 Al MacInnis B | .50 | .23 |
| ❑ 133 Adam Graves S | 4.00 | 1.80 |
| ❑ 134 Vyacheslav Kozlov B | .25 | .11 |
| ❑ 135 Scott Mellanby S | 1.50 | .70 |
| ❑ 136 Stephane Fiset B | .50 | .23 |
| ❑ 137 Oleg Tverdovsky S | 1.50 | .70 |
| ❑ 138 Theoren Fleury S | 4.00 | 1.80 |
| ❑ 139 Jeff Hackett B | .50 | .23 |
| ❑ 140 Vincent Damphousse B | .50 | .23 |
| ❑ 141 Roman Hamrlik S | 1.50 | .70 |
| ❑ 142 Ron Francis S | 4.00 | 1.80 |
| ❑ 143 Scott Lachance B | .25 | .11 |
| ❑ 144 Todd Harvey B | .25 | .11 |
| ❑ 145 Marc Denis S | 4.00 | 1.80 |
| ❑ 146 Jaroslav Svejkovsky G | 8.00 | 3.60 |
| ❑ 147 Olli Jokinen S | 4.00 | 1.80 |
| ❑ 148 Sergei Samsonov G | 25.00 | 11.00 |
| ❑ 149 Chris Phillips G | 3.00 | 1.35 |
| ❑ 150 Patrick Marleau G | 25.00 | 11.00 |
| ❑ 151 Joe Thornton G | 25.00 | 11.00 |
| ❑ 152 Daniel Cleary S | 4.00 | 1.80 |
| ❑ 153 Alyn McCauley G | 8.00 | 3.60 |
| ❑ 154 Brad Isbister S | 1.50 | .70 |
| ❑ 155 Alexei Morozov S | 5.00 | 2.20 |
| ❑ 156 Shawn Bates B | .25 | .11 |
| ❑ 157 Jean-Yves Leroux B | .25 | .11 |
| ❑ 158 Marcel Cousineau B | .50 | .23 |
| ❑ 159 Vaclav Varada B | .25 | .11 |
| ❑ 160 Jean-Sebastien Giguere S | 4.00 | 1.80 |
| ❑ 161 Espen Knutsen B | .50 | .23 |
| ❑ 162 Marian Hossa S | 20.00 | 9.00 |
| ❑ 163 Robert Dome B | .25 | .11 |
| ❑ 164 Juha Lind B | .25 | .11 |
| ❑ 165 Sergei Fedorov NT B | 1.25 | .55 |
| ❑ 166 Jarome Iginla NT B | .50 | .23 |
| ❑ 167 Jaroslav Svejkovsky NT B | .50 | .23 |
| ❑ 168 Patrick Roy NT S | 25.00 | 11.00 |
| ❑ 169 Dominik Hasek NT B | 1.25 | .55 |
| ❑ 170 Alexander Mogilny NT B | .50 | .23 |
| ❑ 171 Chris Chelios NT B | .60 | .25 |
| ❑ 172 Wayne Gretzky NT S | 30.00 | 13.50 |
| ❑ 173 Peter Forsberg NT B | 2.00 | .90 |
| ❑ 174 Ray Bourque NT B | .60 | .25 |
| ❑ 175 Joe Sakic NT S | 10.00 | 4.50 |
| ❑ 176 Mike Modano NT B | .60 | .25 |
| ❑ 177 Mark Messier NT B | .75 | .35 |
| ❑ 178 Teemu Selanne NT B | 1.25 | .55 |
| ❑ 179 Steve Yzerman NT S | 15.00 | 6.75 |
| ❑ 180 Eric Lindros NT S | 15.00 | 6.75 |
| ❑ 181 Doug Weight NT B | .50 | .23 |
| ❑ 182 John Vanbiesbrouck NT B | 1.00 | .45 |
| ❑ 183 Paul Kariya NT S | 20.00 | 9.00 |
| ❑ 184 Brendan Shanahan NT S | 10.00 | 4.50 |
| ❑ 185 Martin Brodeur NT B | 1.50 | .70 |
| ❑ 186 Bryan Berard NT B | .50 | .23 |
| ❑ 187 Marc Denis NT B | .50 | .23 |
| ❑ 188 Brian Leetch NT B | .60 | .25 |
| ❑ 189 Ryan Smyth NT S | 5.00 | 2.20 |
| ❑ 190 Dainius Zubrus NT B | .50 | .23 |
| ❑ 191 Keith Tkachuk NT B | .75 | .35 |
| ❑ 192 Jaromir Jagr NT S | 15.00 | 6.75 |
| ❑ 193 Brett Hull NT B | .75 | .35 |
| ❑ 194 Pavel Bure NT B | 1.25 | .55 |
| ❑ 195 Sergei Samsonov B | 1.50 | .70 |
| ❑ 196 Olli Jokinen B | 1.00 | .45 |
| ❑ 197 Chris Phillips B | .50 | .23 |
| ❑ 198 Patrick Marleau B | 1.50 | .70 |
| ❑ 199 Daniel Cleary B | .50 | .23 |
| ❑ 200 Joe Thornton B | 1.50 | .70 |

## 1997-98 Donruss Preferred Cut to the Chase

Randomly inserted in packs, this 200-card set is a die-cut parallel version of the base set.

Each card features a background of bronze, silver gold, or platinum.

| | MINT | NRMT |
|---|---|---|
| COMPLETE SET (200) | 4200.00 | 1900.00 |
| COMP.BRONZE SET (100) | 400.00 | 180.00 |
| COMMON BRONZE | 2.00 | .90 |
| COMP.SILVER SET (60) | 1200.00 | 550.00 |
| COMMON SILVER | 6.00 | 2.70 |
| COMP.GOLD SET (30) | 1000.00 | 450.00 |
| COMMON GOLD | 10.00 | 4.50 |
| COMP.PLATINUM SET (10) | 1600.00 | 700.00 |
| COMMON PLATINUM | 80.00 | 36.00 |

| | | |
|---|---|---|
| ❑ 1 Dominik Hasek G | 60.00 | 27.00 |
| ❑ 2 Peter Forsberg G | 100.00 | 45.00 |
| ❑ 3 Brendan Shanahan P | 100.00 | 45.00 |
| ❑ 4 Wayne Gretzky P | 300.00 | 135.00 |
| ❑ 5 Eric Lindros P | 150.00 | 70.00 |
| ❑ 6 Keith Tkachuk G | 40.00 | 18.00 |
| ❑ 7 Mark Messier P | 60.00 | 27.00 |
| ❑ 8 Mike Modano G | 40.00 | 18.00 |
| ❑ 9 John Vanbiesbrouck P | 80.00 | 36.00 |
| ❑ 10 Paul Kariya P | 200.00 | 90.00 |
| ❑ 11 Saku Koivu G | 50.00 | 22.00 |
| ❑ 12 Paul Coffey B | 6.00 | 2.70 |
| ❑ 13 Joe Juneau B | 5.00 | 2.20 |
| ❑ 14 Jeff Friesen S | 15.00 | 6.75 |
| ❑ 15 Brett Hull G | 40.00 | 18.00 |
| ❑ 16 Martin Brodeur G | 80.00 | 36.00 |
| ❑ 17 Jarome Iginla G | 25.00 | 11.00 |
| ❑ 18 Keith Primeau S | 15.00 | 6.75 |
| ❑ 19 Ed Jovanovski B | 5.00 | 2.20 |
| ❑ 20 Jamie Langenbrunner B | 5.00 | 2.20 |
| ❑ 21 Derian Hatcher S | 6.00 | 2.70 |
| ❑ 22 Brian Leetch G | 30.00 | 13.50 |
| ❑ 23 Daymond Langkow S | 6.00 | 2.70 |
| ❑ 24 Ray Bourque S | 20.00 | 9.00 |
| ❑ 25 Pavel Bure G | 60.00 | 27.00 |
| ❑ 26 Janne Niinimaa S | 15.00 | 6.75 |
| ❑ 27 Jamie Storr S | 15.00 | 6.75 |
| ❑ 28 Darcy Tucker B | 2.00 | .90 |
| ❑ 29 Anson Carter B | 2.00 | .90 |
| ❑ 30 Jeff O'Neill B | 2.00 | .90 |
| ❑ 31 Jason Arnott G | 25.00 | 11.00 |
| ❑ 32 Tommy Salo B | 5.00 | 2.20 |
| ❑ 33 Petr Nedved B | 5.00 | 2.20 |
| ❑ 34 Mike Peca B | 5.00 | 2.20 |
| ❑ 35 Ethan Moreau S | 6.00 | 2.70 |
| ❑ 36 Ray Sheppard B | 5.00 | 2.20 |
| ❑ 37 Damian Rhodes B | 5.00 | 2.20 |
| ❑ 38 Mats Sundin S | 20.00 | 9.00 |
| ❑ 39 Alexander Mogilny G | 25.00 | 11.00 |
| ❑ 40 Mike Dunham S | 15.00 | 6.75 |
| ❑ 41 Steve Yzerman P | 150.00 | 70.00 |
| ❑ 42 Alexei Yashin S | 15.00 | 6.75 |
| ❑ 43 Jim Carey S | 15.00 | 6.75 |
| ❑ 44 Mike Grier S | 6.00 | 2.70 |
| ❑ 45 Steve Rucchin B | 2.00 | .90 |
| ❑ 46 Mark Recchi S | 6.00 | 2.70 |
| ❑ 47 Mike Gartner B | 5.00 | 2.20 |
| ❑ 48 Alexandre Daigle S | 15.00 | 6.75 |
| ❑ 49 Eric Fichaud G | 25.00 | 11.00 |
| ❑ 50 Harry York B | 2.00 | .90 |
| ❑ 51 Dino Ciccarelli B | 5.00 | 2.20 |
| ❑ 52 Bill Ranford B | 5.00 | 2.20 |
| ❑ 53 Adam Deadmarsh G | 25.00 | 11.00 |
| ❑ 54 Ed Belfour B | 6.00 | 2.70 |
| ❑ 55 Jozef Stumpel S | 15.00 | 6.75 |
| ❑ 56 Rem Murray B | 2.00 | .90 |
| ❑ 57 Pat Verbeek B | 5.00 | 2.20 |
| ❑ 58 Pat LaFontaine S | 15.00 | 6.75 |
| ❑ 59 Dainius Zubrus S | 15.00 | 6.75 |
| ❑ 60 Grant Fuhr B | 5.00 | 2.20 |
| ❑ 61 Rob Niedermayer B | 5.00 | 2.20 |
| ❑ 62 Brian Savage B | 2.00 | .90 |
| ❑ 63 Gary Roberts B | 2.00 | .90 |
| ❑ 64 Tony Amonte B | 5.00 | 2.20 |
| ❑ 65 Jere Lehtinen B | 5.00 | 2.20 |
| ❑ 66 Dave Andreychuk B | 5.00 | 2.20 |
| ❑ 67 Rod Brind'Amour B | 5.00 | 2.20 |
| ❑ 68 Mikael Renberg B | 5.00 | 2.20 |
| ❑ 69 Doug Gilmour S | 20.00 | 9.00 |
| ❑ 70 Kevin Hatcher B | 2.00 | .90 |
| ❑ 71 Byron Dafoe B | 5.00 | 2.20 |
| ❑ 72 Derek Plante S | 6.00 | 2.70 |
| ❑ 73 Trevor Kidd B | 5.00 | 2.20 |
| ❑ 74 Doug Weight S | 15.00 | 6.75 |
| ❑ 75 Valeri Bure B | 5.00 | 2.20 |
| ❑ 76 John LeClair G | 50.00 | 22.00 |
| ❑ 77 Sergei Berezin B | 5.00 | 2.20 |
| ❑ 78 Peter Bondra S | 20.00 | 9.00 |
| ❑ 79 Bryan Berard G | 25.00 | 11.00 |
| ❑ 80 Steve Shields B | 5.00 | 2.20 |
| ❑ 81 Chris Osgood G | 30.00 | 13.50 |
| ❑ 82 Mike Vernon B | 5.00 | 2.20 |
| ❑ 83 Martin Gelinas B | 5.00 | 2.20 |
| ❑ 84 Curtis Joseph S | 20.00 | 9.00 |
| ❑ 85 Geoff Sanderson S | 15.00 | 6.75 |
| ❑ 86 Patrick Roy P | 250.00 | 110.00 |
| ❑ 87 Jocelyn Thibault G | 25.00 | 11.00 |
| ❑ 88 Jeremy Roenick S | 15.00 | 6.75 |
| ❑ 89 Trevor Linden B | 5.00 | 2.20 |
| ❑ 90 Daniel Alfredsson S | 15.00 | 6.75 |
| ❑ 91 Sergei Zubov B | 2.00 | .90 |
| ❑ 92 Dimitri Khristich S | 6.00 | 2.70 |
| ❑ 93 Brian Holzinger B | 2.00 | .90 |
| ❑ 94 Andrew Cassels B | 2.00 | .90 |
| ❑ 95 Teemu Selanne G | 60.00 | 27.00 |
| ❑ 96 Ron Hextall B | 5.00 | 2.20 |
| ❑ 97 Wade Redden B | 2.00 | .90 |
| ❑ 98 Jim Campbell B | 2.00 | .90 |
| ❑ 99 Felix Potvin G | 30.00 | 13.50 |
| ❑ 100 Adam Oates S | 15.00 | 6.75 |
| ❑ 101 Nikolai Khabibulin B | 5.00 | 2.20 |
| ❑ 102 Jose Theodore S | 15.00 | 6.75 |
| ❑ 103 Sandis Ozolinsh S | 15.00 | 6.75 |
| ❑ 104 Sean Burke B | 5.00 | 2.20 |
| ❑ 105 Vaclav Prospal G | 20.00 | 9.00 |
| ❑ 106 Zigmund Palffy G | 30.00 | 13.50 |
| ❑ 107 Kyle McLaren B | 2.00 | .90 |
| ❑ 108 Owen Nolan S | 15.00 | 6.75 |
| ❑ 109 Chris Pronger S | 15.00 | 6.75 |
| ❑ 110 Daren Puppa B | 5.00 | 2.20 |
| ❑ 111 Garth Snow B | 5.00 | 2.20 |
| ❑ 112 Aki Berg B | 2.00 | .90 |
| ❑ 113 Andy Moog B | 5.00 | 2.20 |
| ❑ 114 Darren McCarty B | 2.00 | .90 |
| ❑ 115 Joe Nieuwendyk B | 5.00 | 2.20 |
| ❑ 116 Eric Daze S | 6.00 | 2.70 |
| ❑ 117 Pierre Turgeon S | 15.00 | 6.75 |
| ❑ 118 Ken Wregget B | 5.00 | 2.20 |
| ❑ 119 Ryan Smyth G | 25.00 | 11.00 |
| ❑ 120 Kirk Muller B | 2.00 | .90 |
| ❑ 121 Luc Robitaille B | 5.00 | 2.20 |
| ❑ 122 Sergei Fedorov G | 60.00 | 27.00 |
| ❑ 123 Sean Pronger B | 2.00 | .90 |
| ❑ 124 Mike Richter S | 20.00 | 9.00 |
| ❑ 125 Jaromir Jagr P | 150.00 | 70.00 |
| ❑ 126 Claude Lemieux B | 5.00 | 2.20 |
| ❑ 127 Chris Chelios S | 20.00 | 9.00 |
| ❑ 128 Joe Sakic P | 100.00 | 45.00 |
| ❑ 129 Guy Hebert S | 15.00 | 6.75 |
| ❑ 130 Chris Gratton S | 15.00 | 6.75 |
| ❑ 131 Steve Sullivan B | 2.00 | .90 |
| ❑ 132 Al MacInnis B | 5.00 | 2.20 |
| ❑ 133 Adam Graves S | 15.00 | 6.75 |
| ❑ 134 Vyacheslav Kozlov B | 2.00 | .90 |
| ❑ 135 Scott Mellanby S | 6.00 | 2.70 |
| ❑ 136 Stephane Fiset B | 5.00 | 2.20 |
| ❑ 137 Oleg Tverdovsky S | 6.00 | 2.70 |
| ❑ 138 Theoren Fleury S | 15.00 | 6.75 |
| ❑ 139 Jeff Hackett B | 5.00 | 2.20 |
| ❑ 140 Vincent Damphousse B | 5.00 | 2.20 |
| ❑ 141 Roman Hamrlik S | 6.00 | 2.70 |
| ❑ 142 Ron Francis S | 15.00 | 6.75 |
| ❑ 143 Scott Lachance B | 2.00 | .90 |
| ❑ 144 Todd Harvey B | 2.00 | .90 |
| ❑ 145 Marc Denis S | 15.00 | 6.75 |
| ❑ 146 Jaroslav Svejkovsky G | 25.00 | 11.00 |
| ❑ 147 Olli Jokinen S | 25.00 | 11.00 |
| ❑ 148 Sergei Samsonov G | 30.00 | 13.50 |
| ❑ 149 Chris Phillips G | 10.00 | 4.50 |
| ❑ 150 Patrick Marleau G | 40.00 | 18.00 |
| ❑ 151 Joe Thornton G | 40.00 | 18.00 |
| ❑ 152 Daniel Cleary S | 15.00 | 6.75 |
| ❑ 153 Alyn McCauley G | 25.00 | 11.00 |
| ❑ 154 Brad Isbister S | 6.00 | 2.70 |
| ❑ 155 Alexei Morozov S | 20.00 | 9.00 |
| ❑ 156 Shawn Bates B | 2.00 | .90 |
| ❑ 157 Jean-Yves Leroux B | 2.00 | .90 |
| ❑ 158 Marcel Cousineau B | 5.00 | 2.20 |
| ❑ 159 Vaclav Varada B | 2.00 | .90 |
| ❑ 160 Jean-Sebastien Giguere S | 15.00 | 6.75 |
| ❑ 161 Espen Knutsen B | 5.00 | 2.20 |
| ❑ 162 Marian Hossa S | 20.00 | 9.00 |
| ❑ 163 Robert Dome B | 2.00 | .90 |
| ❑ 164 Juha Lind B | 2.00 | .90 |
| ❑ 165 Sergei Fedorov NT B | 12.00 | 5.50 |
| ❑ 166 Jarome Iginla B | 5.00 | 2.20 |
| ❑ 167 Jaroslav Svejkovsky B | 5.00 | 2.20 |
| ❑ 168 Patrick Roy NT S | 100.00 | 45.00 |
| ❑ 169 Dominik Hasek NT B | 12.00 | 5.50 |
| ❑ 170 Alexander Mogilny B | 5.00 | 2.20 |
| ❑ 171 Chris Chelios B | 6.00 | 2.70 |
| ❑ 172 Wayne Gretzky NT S | 120.00 | 55.00 |
| ❑ 173 Peter Forsberg NT B | 20.00 | 9.00 |
| ❑ 174 Ray Bourque B | 6.00 | 2.70 |
| ❑ 175 Joe Sakic NT S | 40.00 | 18.00 |
| ❑ 176 Mike Modano B | 6.00 | 2.70 |
| ❑ 177 Mark Messier NT B | 8.00 | 3.60 |
| ❑ 178 Teemu Selanne NT B | 12.00 | 5.50 |
| ❑ 179 Steve Yzerman NT S | 60.00 | 27.00 |
| ❑ 180 Eric Lindros NT S | 60.00 | 27.00 |
| ❑ 181 Doug Weight NT B | 5.00 | 2.20 |
| ❑ 182 John Vanbiesbrouck NT B | 10.00 | 4.50 |
| ❑ 183 Paul Kariya NT S | 80.00 | 36.00 |
| ❑ 184 Brendan ShanahanNT S | 40.00 | 18.00 |
| ❑ 185 Martin Brodeur NT B | 15.00 | 6.75 |
| ❑ 186 Bryan Berard NT B | 6.00 | 2.70 |
| ❑ 187 Marc Denis B | 5.00 | 2.20 |
| ❑ 188 Brian Leetch B | 5.00 | 2.20 |
| ❑ 189 Ryan Smyth S | 6.00 | 2.70 |
| ❑ 190 Dainius Zubrus NT B | 20.00 | 9.00 |
| ❑ 191 Keith Tkachuk NT B | 8.00 | 3.60 |
| ❑ 192 Jaromir Jagr NT S | 60.00 | 27.00 |
| ❑ 193 Brett Hull NT B | 8.00 | 3.60 |
| ❑ 194 Pavel Bure NT B | 12.00 | 5.50 |
| ❑ 195 Sergei Samsonov B | 6.00 | 2.70 |
| ❑ 196 Olli Jokinen B | 6.00 | 2.70 |
| ❑ 197 Chris Phillips B | 6.00 | 2.70 |
| ❑ 198 Patrick Marleau B | 6.00 | 2.70 |
| ❑ 199 Daniel Cleary B | 5.00 | 2.20 |
| ❑ 200 Joe Thornton B | 12.00 | 5.50 |

## 1997-98 Donruss Preferred Color Guard

Randomly inserted in packs, this 18-card set features color images of top puckstoppers printed on die-cut plastic cards with the player's team colors in the background. The set is sequentially numbered to 1,500.

| | MINT | NRMT |
|---|---|---|
| COMPLETE SET (18) | 300.00 | 135.00 |
| COMMON CARD (1-18) | 12.00 | 5.50 |
| ❑ 1 Patrick Roy | 80.00 | 36.00 |
| ❑ 2 Martin Brodeur | 40.00 | 18.00 |
| ❑ 3 Curtis Joseph | 20.00 | 9.00 |
| ❑ 4 John Vanbiesbrouck | 25.00 | 11.00 |
| ❑ 5 Felix Potvin | 20.00 | 9.00 |
| ❑ 6 Dominik Hasek | 30.00 | 13.50 |
| ❑ 7 Chris Osgood | 20.00 | 9.00 |
| ❑ 8 Eric Fichaud | 12.00 | 5.50 |
| ❑ 9 Jocelyn Thibault | 12.00 | 5.50 |
| ❑ 10 Marc Denis | 12.00 | 5.50 |
| ❑ 11 Jose Theodore | 12.00 | 5.50 |
| ❑ 12 Mike Vernon | 12.00 | 5.50 |
| ❑ 13 Jim Carey | 12.00 | 5.50 |
| ❑ 14 Ron Hextall | 12.00 | 5.50 |
| ❑ 15 Mike Richter | 20.00 | 9.00 |
| ❑ 16 Ed Belfour | 20.00 | 9.00 |
| ❑ 17 Mike Dunham | 12.00 | 5.50 |
| ❑ 18 Damian Rhodes | 12.00 | 5.50 |
| ❑ P18 Damian Rhodes PROMO | 3.00 | 1.35 |

## 1997-98 Donruss Preferred Line of the Times

Randomly inserted in packs, this 24-card set features color photos of star players printed on die-cut cards and utilizing micro-etching technology. Three cards were made to be placed side by side to form one interactive card which spelled out a particular word in the background. The set is sequentially numbered to 2,500.

| | MINT | NRMT |
|---|---|---|
| COMPLETE SET (24) | 600.00 | 275.00 |
| COMMON CARD (1A-8C) | 6.00 | 2.70 |
| ❑ 1A Ryan Smyth | 8.00 | 3.60 |
| ❑ 1B Sergei Fedorov | 20.00 | 9.00 |
| ❑ 1C Jaromir Jagr | 30.00 | 13.50 |
| ❑ 2A Eric Lindros | 30.00 | 13.50 |
| ❑ 2B Joe Thornton | 12.00 | 5.50 |
| ❑ 2C Brendan Shanahan | 20.00 | 9.00 |
| ❑ 3A John LeClair | 15.00 | 6.75 |
| ❑ 3B Keith Tkachuk | 12.00 | 5.50 |
| ❑ 3C Brett Hull | 12.00 | 5.50 |
| ❑ 4A Pavel Bure | 20.00 | 9.00 |
| ❑ 4B Sergei Samsonov | 8.00 | 3.60 |
| ❑ 4C Paul Kariya | 40.00 | 18.00 |
| ❑ 5A Mike Modano | 12.00 | 5.50 |
| ❑ 5B Teemu Selanne | 20.00 | 9.00 |
| ❑ 5C Patrick Marleau | 12.00 | 5.50 |
| ❑ 6A Wayne Gretzky | 60.00 | 27.00 |
| ❑ 6B Steve Yzerman | 30.00 | 13.50 |
| ❑ 6C Daniel Cleary | 8.00 | 3.60 |
| ❑ 7A Jarome Iginla | 8.00 | 3.60 |
| ❑ 7B Peter Forsberg | 30.00 | 13.50 |
| ❑ 7C Mark Messier | 12.00 | 5.50 |
| ❑ 8A Joe Sakic | 20.00 | 9.00 |
| ❑ 8B Jaroslav Svejkovsky | 8.00 | 3.60 |
| ❑ 8C Dainius Zubrus | 10.00 | 4.50 |

## 1997-98 Donruss Preferred Precious Metals

Randomly inserted in packs, this 15-card set is a partial parallel version of the base set. The cards are printed on card stock consisting of 1 gram of real gold or platinum. Only 100 of each card was produced.

| | MINT | NRMT |
|---|---|---|
| COMPLETE SET (15) | 4000.00 | 1800.00 |
| COMMON CARD (1-15) | 120.00 | 55.00 |
| ONE GRAM OF PRECIOUS METAL PER CARD | | |
| ❑ 1 Brendan Shanahan P | 200.00 | 90.00 |
| ❑ 2 Joe Thornton G | 120.00 | 55.00 |
| ❑ 3 Wayne Gretzky P | 600.00 | 275.00 |
| ❑ 4 Mark Messier P | 120.00 | 55.00 |
| ❑ 5 Patrick Roy P | 500.00 | 220.00 |
| ❑ 6 Martin Brodeur G | 250.00 | 110.00 |
| ❑ 7 Eric Lindros P | 300.00 | 135.00 |

❑ 8 Paul Kariya P 400.00 180.00
❑ 9 Teemu Selanne G 200.00 90.00
❑ 10 Jaromir Jagr P 300.00 135.00
❑ 11 Joe Sakic P 200.00 90.00
❑ 12 Peter Forsberg G 300.00 135.00
❑ 13 John Vanbiesbrouck P 150.00 70.00
❑ 14 Steve Yzerman P 300.00 135.00
❑ 15 Sergei Samsonov G 120.00 55.00

## 1997-98 Donruss Preferred Tin Packs

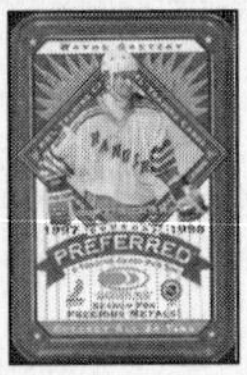

This 24-card set features color images printed on special tin containers of the NHL players who played in the 1998 Winter Olympic Games on either the Canadian or United States teams. The U.S. tins are highlighted in blue, and the Canadian version is highlighted in red. There was also a gold version of this set which were originally slated to be included in boxes, but was later available only through the manufacturer.

MINT NRMT
COMPLETE SET (24) 20.00 9.00
COMMON PACK (1-24) .50 .23
COMMON SEALED PACK 5.00 2.20
*SEALED: 1.5X TO 3X ON 2.00+ PACKS
COMP.GOLD SET (24) 200.00 90.00
COMMON GOLD PACK (1-24) 5.00 2.20
*GOLD PACKS: 4X TO 10X BASIC TIN PACKS
*GOLD SEALED PACKS: 7.5X TO 15X BASIC TIN PACKS
GOLD PACKS: 499 SERIAL #'d SETS
COMP.BLUE BOX SET (24) 120.00 55.00
*BLUE BOXES: 3X TO 6X BASIC TIN PACKS
BLUE BOXES: 499 SERIAL #'d SETS
BLUE BOXES: U.S. HOBBY
COMP.RED BOX SET (24) 120.00 55.00
*RED BOXES: 3X TO 6X BASIC TIN PACKS
RED BOXES: 499 SERIAL #'d SETS
RED BOXES: CANADIAN HOBBY

❑ 1 Eric Lindros 1.25 .55
❑ 2 Paul Kariya 1.50 .70
❑ 3 Wayne Gretzky 2.50 1.10
❑ 4 Teemu Selanne .75 .35
❑ 5 Patrick Roy 2.00 .90
❑ 6 John Vanbiesbrouck .60 .25
❑ 7 Mike Modano .50 .23
❑ 8 Joe Sakic .75 .35
❑ 9 Peter Forsberg 1.25 .55
❑ 10 Martin Brodeur 1.00 .45
❑ 11 Sergei Samsonov 1.00 .45
❑ 12 Brendan Shanahan .75 .35
❑ 13 Steve Yzerman 1.25 .55
❑ 14 Jaromir Jagr 1.25 .55
❑ 15 Mark Messier .50 .23
❑ 16 Joe Thornton 1.00 .45
❑ 17 Pavel Bure .75 .35
❑ 18 Brett Hull .50 .23
❑ 19 Brendan Shanahan MC .75 .35
❑ 20 Jaromir Jagr MC 1.25 .55
❑ 21 Eric Lindros MC 1.25 .55
❑ 22 Paul Kariya MC 1.50 .70
❑ 23 Wayne Gretzky MC 2.50 1.10
❑ 24 Patrick Roy MC 2.00 .90

## 1997-98 Donruss Preferred Tin Packs Double Wide

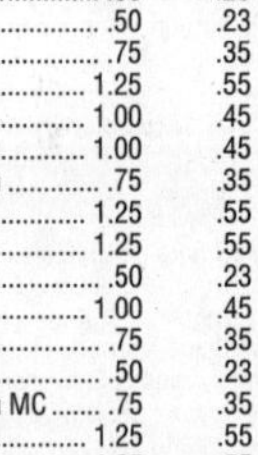

This 12-card set features color images of the NHL players who played in the 1998 Winter Olympic Games on either the Canadian or United States teams and are printed on special retail only tin containers.

MINT NRMT
COMPLETE SET (12) 25.00 11.00
COMMON CARD (1-12) 1.00 .45

❑ 1 Wayne Gretzky 3.00 1.35
Joe Thornton
❑ 2 Paul Kariya 1.50 .70
Brett Hull
❑ 3 Eric Lindros 2.00 .90
Joe Sakic
❑ 4 Teemu Selanne 2.00 .90
Peter Forsberg
❑ 5 Pavel Bure 1.00 .45
Mike Modano
❑ 6 Sergei Samsonov 3.00 1.35
Steve Yzerman
❑ 7 Jaromir Jagr 1.50 .70
Brendan Shanahan
❑ 8 Mark Messier 1.00 .45
John Vanbiesbrouck
❑ 9 Patrick Roy 3.00 1.35
Martin Brodeur
❑ 10 Brendan Shanahan 1.50 .70
Eric Lindros
❑ 11 Jaromir Jagr 3.00 1.35
Paul Kariya
❑ 12 Wayne Gretzky 4.00 1.80
Patrick Roy

## 1997-98 Donruss Priority

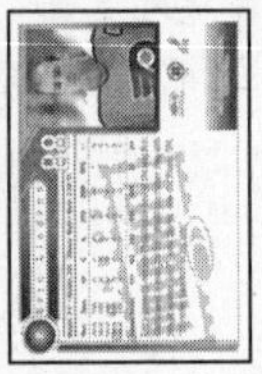

The 1997-98 Donruss Priority hobby only set was issued in one series totalling 220 cards and was distributed in two-types of five-card packs--postcard and stamp packs--with a suggested retail price of $4.99. Postcard packs had a 5" by 7" horizontal format and contained only even numbered cards from the set. The odd numbered cards were twice as scarce and could be found only in the stamp packs. The fronts features color action player photos printed with foil treatments, while the backs carry player information. The set contains the topical subset: 1st Class Package (185-214). The set was released towards the end of the 97-98 NHL season.

MINT NRMT
COMPLETE SET (220) 50.00 22.00
COMMON EVEN # (2-220) .20 .09
COMMON ODD# (1-219) .30 .14

❑ 1 Patrick Roy SP 3.00 1.35
❑ 2 Eric Lindros 1.25 .55
❑ 3 Keith Tkachuk SP .75 .35
❑ 4 Steve Yzerman 1.25 .55
❑ 5 John Vanbiesbrouck SP 1.00 .45
❑ 6 Teemu Selanne .75 .35
❑ 7 Martin Brodeur SP 1.50 .70
❑ 8 Peter Forsberg 1.25 .55
❑ 9 Brett Hull SP .75 .35
❑ 10 Wayne Gretzky 2.50 1.10
❑ 11 Mike Modano SP .75 .35
❑ 12 Sergei Fedorov .75 .35
❑ 13 Paul Kariya SP 2.50 1.10
❑ 14 Saku Koivu .60 .25
❑ 15 Pavel Bure SP 1.25 .55
❑ 16 Mark Messier .50 .23
❑ 17 Joe Sakic SP 1.25 .55
❑ 18 Jaromir Jagr 1.25 .55
❑ 19 Brendan Shanahan SP 1.25 .55
❑ 20 Ray Bourque .40 .18
❑ 21 Daymond Langkow SP .30 .14
❑ 22 Alexandre Daigle .20 .09
❑ 23 Dainius Zubrus SP .20 .09
❑ 24 Ryan Smyth .30 .14
❑ 25 Derek Plante SP .30 .14
❑ 26 Eric Daze .20 .09
❑ 27 Ed Jovanovski SP .30 .14
❑ 28 Sergei Berezin .20 .09
❑ 29 Roman Turek SP .40 .18
❑ 30 Derian Hatcher .20 .09
❑ 31 Jarome Iginla SP .30 .14
❑ 32 Luc Robitaille .30 .14
❑ 33 Rod Brind'Amour SP .40 .18
❑ 34 Mathieu Schneider .20 .09
❑ 35 Olaf Kolzig SP .40 .18
❑ 36 Nikolai Khabibulin .30 .14
❑ 37 Scott Niedermayer SP .30 .14
❑ 38 Keith Primeau .30 .14
❑ 39 Dimitri Khristich SP .30 .14
❑ 40 Eric Fichaud .30 .14
❑ 41 Pierre Turgeon SP .40 .18
❑ 42 Kevin Stevens .20 .09
❑ 43 Nicklas Lidstrom SP .30 .14
❑ 44 Sean Burke .30 .14
❑ 45 Sandis Ozolinsh SP .40 .18
❑ 46 Owen Nolan .30 .14
❑ 47 Peter Bondra SP .60 .25
❑ 48 Ron Hextall .30 .14
❑ 49 Rob Blake SP .30 .14
❑ 50 Geoff Sanderson .30 .14
❑ 51 Sergei Zubov SP .30 .14
❑ 52 Doug Gilmour .40 .18
❑ 53 Oleg Tverdovsky SP .30 .14
❑ 54 Bryan Berard .20 .09
❑ 55 Bill Ranford SP .40 .18
❑ 56 Mats Sundin .40 .18
❑ 57 Damian Rhodes SP .40 .18
❑ 58 Zigmund Palffy .40 .18
❑ 59 Mike Grier SP .30 .14
❑ 60 Jozef Stumpel .30 .14
❑ 61 Mark Recchi SP .30 .14
❑ 62 Alexei Zhamnov .20 .09
❑ 63 Jere Lehtinen SP .30 .14
❑ 64 Andrew Cassels .20 .09
❑ 65 Kevin Hodson SP .40 .18
❑ 66 Dino Ciccarelli .30 .14
❑ 67 Niklas Sundstrom SP .30 .14
❑ 68 Jeff Hackett .30 .14
❑ 69 Brian Holzinger SP .40 .18
❑ 70 Jeff Friesen .30 .14
❑ 71 Ed Belfour SP .60 .25
❑ 72 Wayne Primeau .20 .09
❑ 73 Sami Kapanen SP .40 .18
❑ 74 Brian Leetch .40 .18
❑ 75 Mikael Renberg SP .40 .18
❑ 76 Ron Tugnutt .30 .14
❑ 77 Ron Francis SP .40 .18
❑ 78 Jocelyn Thibault .30 .14
❑ 79 Jamie Langenbrunner SP .40 .18
❑ 80 Dominik Hasek .75 .35
❑ 81 Chris Osgood SP .60 .25
❑ 82 Grant Fuhr .30 .14
❑ 83 Adam Graves SP .40 .18
❑ 84 Janne Niinimaa .30 .14
❑ 85 Kelly Hrudey SP .40 .18
❑ 86 Mike Dunham .30 .14
❑ 87 Valeri Kamensky SP .40 .18
❑ 88 Cory Stillman .20 .09
❑ 89 Anson Carter SP .30 .14
❑ 90 Igor Larionov .20 .09
❑ 91 Chris Pronger SP .40 .18
❑ 92 Steve Sullivan .20 .09
❑ 93 Mike Gartner SP .40 .18
❑ 94 Jim Campbell .30 .14
❑ 95 Valeri Bure SP .30 .14
❑ 96 Stephane Fiset .30 .14
❑ 97 Jason Arnott SP .40 .18
❑ 98 Trevor Kidd .30 .14
❑ 99 Chris Chelios SP .60 .25
❑ 100 Kevin Hatcher .20 .09
❑ 101 Felix Potvin SP .60 .25
❑ 102 Travis Green .20 .09
❑ 103 Dave Gagner SP .30 .14
❑ 104 Byron Dafoe .30 .14
❑ 105 Rick Tabaracci SP .40 .18
❑ 106 Gary Roberts .20 .09
❑ 107 Mike Ricci SP .30 .14
❑ 108 Andy Moog .30 .14
❑ 109 Sean Pronger SP .30 .14
❑ 110 Paul Coffey .40 .18
❑ 111 Trevor Linden SP .40 .18
❑ 112 Rob Zamuner .20 .09
❑ 113 Daniel Alfredsson SP .40 .18
❑ 114 Ray Sheppard .30 .14
❑ 115 Steve Shields SP .40 .18
❑ 116 Ethan Moreau .20 .09
❑ 117 Tomas Sandstrom SP .30 .14
❑ 118 Chris Gratton .30 .14
❑ 119 Alexander Mogilny SP .40 .18
❑ 120 Roman Hamrlik .20 .09
❑ 121 Tommy Salo SP .30 .14
❑ 122 Jason Allison .30 .14
❑ 123 Curtis Joseph SP .60 .25
❑ 124 Guy Hebert .30 .14
❑ 125 Jeff O'Neill SP .30 .14
❑ 126 Donald Audette .20 .09
❑ 127 Claude Lemieux SP .40 .18
❑ 128 Brian Savage .20 .09
❑ 129 Scott Mellanby SP .30 .14
❑ 130 Vyacheslav Kozlov .30 .14
❑ 131 Wade Redden SP .30 .14
❑ 132 John LeClair .60 .25
❑ 133 Jeremy Roenick SP .60 .25
❑ 134 Andreas Johansson .20 .09
❑ 135 Nelson Emerson SP .30 .14
❑ 136 Daren Puppa .30 .14
❑ 137 Joe Juneau SP .40 .18
❑ 138 Garth Snow .30 .14
❑ 139 Tom Barrasso SP .40 .18
❑ 140 Joe Nieuwendyk .30 .14
❑ 141 Theoren Fleury SP .40 .18
❑ 142 Yanic Perreault .20 .09
❑ 143 Mike Richter SP .60 .25
❑ 144 Al MacInnis .30 .14
❑ 145 Mike Peca SP .40 .18
❑ 146 Darren McCarty .30 .14
❑ 147 Alexei Yashin SP .40 .18
❑ 148 Rick Tocchet .30 .14
❑ 149 Adam Oates SP .40 .18
❑ 150 Wendel Clark .20 .09
❑ 151 Tony Amonte SP .40 .18
❑ 152 Dave Andreychuk .20 .09
❑ 153 Jamie Storr SP .40 .18
❑ 154 Craig Janney .30 .14
❑ 155 Todd Bertuzzi SP .30 .14
❑ 156 Harry York .20 .09
❑ 157 Todd Harvey SP .40 .18
❑ 158 Bobby Holik .20 .09
❑ 159 Mike Vernon SP .40 .18
❑ 160 Pat LaFontaine .30 .14
❑ 161 Doug Weight SP .40 .18
❑ 162 Kirk McLean .30 .14
❑ 163 Adam Deadmarsh SP .40 .18
❑ 164 Vincent Damphousse .30 .14
❑ 165 Vaclav Prospal SP .60 .25
❑ 166 Daniel Cleary .30 .14
❑ 167 Jaroslav Svejkovsky SP .40 .18
❑ 168 Marco Sturm .60 .25
❑ 169 Robert Dome SP .30 .14
❑ 170 Patrik Elias .50 .23
❑ 171 Mattias Ohlund SP .40 .18
❑ 172 Espen Knutsen .30 .14
❑ 173 Joe Thornton SP 1.25 .55
❑ 174 Jan Bulis .20 .09
❑ 175 Patrick Marleau SP 1.25 .55
❑ 176 Brad Isbister .20 .09
❑ 177 Kevin Weekes SP .30 .14
❑ 178 Sergei Samsonov 1.00 .45
❑ 179 Tyler Moss SP .30 .14
❑ 180 Chris Phillips .20 .09
❑ 181 Alyn McCauley SP .30 .14
❑ 182 Derek Morris .20 .09
❑ 183 Alexei Morozov SP .60 .25
❑ 184 Boyd Devereaux .20 .09
❑ 185 Peter Forsberg SP 1.00 .45
❑ 186 Brendan Shanahan .30 .14
❑ 187 Teemu Selanne SP .60 .25
❑ 188 Eric Lindros .30 .14
❑ 189 Mark Messier SP .25 .11
❑ 190 Vaclav Prospal .30 .14
❑ 191 Jarome Iginla SP .30 .14
❑ 192 Mike Modano .30 .14
❑ 193 John Vanbiesbrouck SP .50 .23
❑ 194 Bryan Berard .20 .09
❑ 195 Patrick Marleau SP .75 .35
❑ 196 Martin Brodeur .30 .14
❑ 197 Patrick Roy SP 1.50 .70
❑ 198 Felix Potvin .30 .14
❑ 199 Wayne Gretzky SP 4.00 1.80
❑ 200 Sergei Samsonov .30 .14
❑ 201 Ryan Smyth SP .40 .18
❑ 202 Keith Tkachuk .30 .14
❑ 203 Chris Osgood SP .40 .18
❑ 204 Paul Kariya .30 .14
❑ 205 John LeClair SP 1.00 .45
❑ 206 Alyn McCauley .30 .14
❑ 207 Joe Thornton SP .75 .35
❑ 208 Joe Sakic .30 .14
❑ 209 Steve Yzerman SP 2.00 .90
❑ 210 Saku Koivu .30 .14
❑ 211 Pavel Bure SP 1.25 .55
❑ 212 Zigmund Palffy .30 .14
❑ 213 Alexei Yashin SP .40 .18
❑ 214 Sergei Fedorov .30 .14
❑ 215 Joe Thornton CL SP .75 .35
❑ 216 Patrick Marleau CL .30 .14
❑ 217 Daniel Cleary CL SP .30 .14
❑ 218 Sergei Samsonov CL .30 .14
❑ 219 Jaroslav Svejkovsky CL SP .30 .14
❑ 220 Alyn McCauley CL .20 .09
❑ NNO E.Lindros puck (1000) 60.00 27.00
❑ NNO E.Lindros jersey (25) 800.00 350.00
❑ NNO E.Lindros stick (15) 250.00 110.00

## 1997-98 Donruss Priority Stamp of Approval

This 220-card set is parallel to the base set. Each card is randomly inserted into packs and is serial numbered out of 100. Card design features a deckle edge similar to a postage stamp, and design front is different from that of the base set.

MINT NRMT
COMMON CARD (1-220) 25.00 11.00
SEMISTARS/GOALIES 60.00 27.00
UNLISTED STARS 80.00 36.00
*STARS: 100X TO 200 X BASIC CARDS
*SP STARS: 60X TO 120X HI
*YNG.STARS: 75X TO 150X BASIC CARDS

❑ 1 Patrick Roy 400.00 180.00
❑ 2 Eric Lindros 300.00 135.00
❑ 4 Steve Yzerman 250.00 110.00
❑ 5 John Vanbiesbrouck 120.00 55.00
❑ 6 Teemu Selanne 150.00 70.00
❑ 7 Martin Brodeur 200.00 90.00
❑ 8 Peter Forsberg 250.00 110.00
❑ 10 Wayne Gretzky 500.00 220.00
❑ 12 Sergei Fedorov 150.00 70.00
❑ 13 Paul Kariya 300.00 135.00
❑ 14 Saku Koivu 150.00 70.00
❑ 15 Pavel Bure 150.00 70.00
❑ 17 Joe Sakic 200.00 90.00
❑ 18 Jaromir Jagr 250.00 110.00
❑ 19 Brendan Shanahan 150.00 70.00
❑ 80 Dominik Hasek 150.00 70.00
❑ 199 Wayne Gretzky 250.00 110.00
❑ 209 Steve Yzerman 120.00 55.00

## 1997-98 Donruss Priority Direct Deposit

Randomly inserted in packs, this 30-card set features color action photos of top goal scorers printed on swirled-look foil board with micro etching. The cards are sequentially numbered to just 3,000.

MINT NRMT
COMPLETE SET (30) 350.00 160.00
COMMON CARD (1-30) 4.00 1.80

❑ 1 Brendan Shanahan 12.00 5.50
❑ 2 Steve Yzerman 20.00 9.00
❑ 3 Pavel Bure 12.00 5.50
❑ 4 Jaromir Jagr 20.00 9.00
❑ 5 Ryan Smyth 4.00 1.80
❑ 6 Sergei Samsonov 15.00 6.75
❑ 7 Mark Messier 8.00 3.60
❑ 8 Wayne Gretzky 40.00 18.00
❑ 9 Jarome Iginla 4.00 1.80
❑ 10 Peter Forsberg 20.00 9.00
❑ 11 Joe Sakic 12.00 5.50
❑ 12 Sergei Fedorov 12.00 5.50
❑ 13 Mike Modano 8.00 3.60
❑ 14 Paul Kariya 25.00 11.00
❑ 15 Teemu Selanne 12.00 5.50
❑ 16 Eric Lindros 20.00 9.00
❑ 17 Keith Tkachuk 8.00 3.60
❑ 18 Patrick Marleau 12.00 5.50
❑ 19 Jaroslav Svejkovsky 4.00 1.80
❑ 20 Alyn McCauley 4.00 1.80
❑ 21 Saku Koivu 10.00 4.50
❑ 22 Zigmund Palffy 4.00 1.80
❑ 23 Brett Hull 8.00 3.60
❑ 24 Patrik Elias 8.00 3.60
❑ 25 Joe Thornton 12.00 5.50
❑ 26 Espen Knutsen 4.00 1.80
❑ 27 Daniel Alfredsson 4.00 1.80
❑ 28 John LeClair 10.00 4.50
❑ 29 Dainius Zubrus 4.00 1.80
❑ 30 Jason Arnott 4.00 1.80
❑ P22 Zigmund Palffy PROMO 2.00 .90

## 1997-98 Donruss Priority Postcards

MINT NRMT
COMPLETE SET (360 80.00 36.00
COMMON CARD (1-36) 1.00 .45
ONE PER LARGE PACK

❑ 1 Patrick Roy 6.00 2.70
❑ 2 Brendan Shanahan 2.50 1.10
❑ 3 Steve Yzerman 4.00 1.80
❑ 4 Jaromir Jagr 4.00 1.80
❑ 5 Pavel Bure 2.50 1.10
❑ 6 Mark Messier 1.50 .70
❑ 7 Wayne Gretzky 8.00 3.60
❑ 8 Eric Lindros 4.00 1.80
❑ 9 Joe Sakic 2.50 1.10
❑ 10 Peter Forsberg 4.00 1.80
❑ 11 John Vanbiesbrouck 2.00 .90
❑ 12 Mike Modano 1.50 .70
❑ 13 Paul Kariya 5.00 2.20
❑ 14 Teemu Selanne 2.50 1.10
❑ 15 Sergei Fedorov 2.50 1.10
❑ 16 Joe Thornton 2.50 1.10
❑ 17 Sergei Samsonov 3.00 1.35
❑ 18 Patrick Marleau 2.50 1.10
❑ 19 Ryan Smyth 1.00 .45
❑ 20 Jarome Iginla 1.00 .45
❑ 21 John LeClair 2.00 .90
❑ 22 Brian Leetch 1.25 .55
❑ 23 Chris Chelios 1.25 .55
❑ 24 Martin Brodeur 3.00 1.35
❑ 25 Bryan Berard 1.00 .45
❑ 26 Keith Tkachuk 1.50 .70
❑ 27 Saku Koivu 2.00 .90
❑ 28 Brett Hull 1.50 .70
❑ 29 Felix Potvin 1.25 .55
❑ 30 Chris Osgood 1.25 .55
❑ 31 Dominik Hasek 2.50 1.10
❑ 32 Zigmund Palffy 1.25 .55
❑ 33 Jeremy Roenick 1.25 .55
❑ 34 Dainius Zubrus 1.00 .45
❑ 35 Ray Bourque 1.25 .55
❑ 36 Jocelyn Thibault 1.00 .45

## 1997-98 Donruss Priority Postcards Opening Day Issues

Randomly inserted in packs, this 30-card set features color player photos on an all-foil postcard with gold-foil stamping and slits for the corresponding Donruss Priority Stamp card or Donruss Priority trading card with a stamp and a commemorative cancel. Each card is numbered just 1 of 1,000.

MINT NRMT
COMPLETE SET (30) 800.00 350.00
COMMON CARD (1-30) 10.00 4.50

❑ 1 Patrick Roy 60.00 27.00
❑ 2 Eric Lindros 40.00 18.00
❑ 3 Keith Tkachuk 15.00 6.75
❑ 4 Steve Yzerman 40.00 18.00
❑ 5 John Vanbiesbrouck 20.00 9.00
❑ 6 Teemu Selanne 25.00 11.00
❑ 7 Martin Brodeur 30.00 13.50

❑ 8 Peter Forsberg 40.00 18.00
❑ 9 Brett Hull 15.00 6.75
❑ 10 Wayne Gretzky 80.00 36.00
❑ 11 Mike Modano 15.00 6.75
❑ 12 Paul Kariya 50.00 22.00
❑ 13 Pavel Bure 25.00 11.00
❑ 14 Mark Messier 15.00 6.75
❑ 15 Joe Sakic 25.00 11.00
❑ 16 Jaromir Jagr 40.00 18.00
❑ 17 Brendan Shanahan 25.00 11.00
❑ 18 Ryan Smyth 10.00 4.50
❑ 19 Jarome Iginla 10.00 4.50
❑ 20 Bryan Berard 10.00 4.50
❑ 21 Jocelyn Thibault 10.00 4.50
❑ 22 Dominik Hasek 25.00 11.00
❑ 23 Chris Osgood 10.00 4.50
❑ 24 Chris Chelios 10.00 4.50
❑ 25 Felix Potvin 10.00 4.50
❑ 26 John LeClair 20.00 9.00
❑ 27 Saku Koivu 20.00 9.00
❑ 28 Joe Thornton 25.00 11.00
❑ 29 Patrick Marleau 25.00 11.00
❑ 30 Sergei Samsonov 25.00 11.00

## 1997-98 Donruss Priority Postmaster General

Randomly inserted in packs, this 20-card set features color photos of top goalies printed on all-foil board with foil stamping. Only 1,500 of each card were produced and sequentially numbered.

| | MINT | NRMT |
|---|---|---|
| COMPLETE SET (20) | 300.00 | 135.00 |
| COMMON CARD (1-20) | 12.00 | 5.50 |

❑ 1 Patrick Roy 80.00 36.00
❑ 2 John Vanbiesbrouck 25.00 11.00
❑ 3 Felix Potvin 15.00 6.75
❑ 4 Curtis Joseph 15.00 6.75
❑ 5 Mike Richter 15.00 6.75
❑ 6 Jocelyn Thibault 12.00 5.50
❑ 7 Ed Belfour 15.00 6.75
❑ 8 Chris Osgood 15.00 6.75
❑ 9 Ron Hextall 12.00 5.50
❑ 10 Martin Brodeur 40.00 18.00
❑ 11 Mike Vernon 12.00 5.50
❑ 12 Eric Fichaud 12.00 5.50
❑ 13 Dominik Hasek 30.00 13.50
❑ 14 Byron Dafoe 12.00 5.50
❑ 15 Tommy Salo 12.00 5.50
❑ 16 Garth Snow 12.00 5.50
❑ 17 Tom Barrasso 12.00 5.50
❑ 18 Marc Denis 12.00 5.50
❑ 19 Grant Fuhr 12.00 5.50
❑ 20 Guy Hebert 12.00 5.50
❑ P16 Garth Snow PROMO 12.00 5.50

## 1997-98 Donruss Priority Stamps

Randomly inserted one per small pack, this 36-card set features color photos of top NHL players printed on real currency stamps. Printed in the country of Grenada, each stamp comes protected in a stamp holder card. Bronze, silver, and gold parallel versions of this set were also produced with an insertion rate of 1:6.

| | MINT | NRMT |
|---|---|---|
| COMPLETE SET (36) | 80.00 | 36.00 |
| COMMON STAMP (1-36) | 1.00 | .45 |
| COMP.BRONZE SET (36) | 150.00 | 70.00 |
| COMMON BRONZE (1-36) | 2.00 | .90 |
| *BRONZE STARS: 1X TO 2X BASIC CARDS | | |
| COMP.SILVER SET (36) | 300.00 | 135.00 |
| COMMON SILVER (1-36) | 4.00 | 1.80 |
| *SILVER STARS: 2X TO 4X BASIC CARDS | | |
| COMP.GOLD SET (36) | 600.00 | 275.00 |
| COMMON GOLD (1-36) | 8.00 | 3.60 |
| *GOLD STARS: 4X TO 8X BASIC CARDS | | |

❑ 1 Patrick Roy 6.00 2.70
❑ 2 Brendan Shanahan 2.50 1.10
❑ 3 Steve Yzerman 4.00 1.80
❑ 4 Jaromir Jagr 4.00 1.80
❑ 5 Pavel Bure 2.50 1.10
❑ 6 Mark Messier 1.50 .70
❑ 7 Wayne Gretzky 8.00 3.60
❑ 8 Eric Lindros 4.00 1.80
❑ 9 Joe Sakic 2.50 1.10
❑ 10 Peter Forsberg 4.00 1.80
❑ 11 John Vanbiesbrouck 2.00 .90
❑ 12 Mike Modano 1.50 .70
❑ 13 Paul Kariya 5.00 2.20
❑ 14 Teemu Selanne 2.50 1.10
❑ 15 Sergei Fedorov 2.50 1.10
❑ 16 Joe Thornton 2.50 1.10
❑ 17 Sergei Samsonov 3.00 1.35
❑ 18 Patrick Marleau 2.50 1.10
❑ 19 Ryan Smyth 1.00 .45
❑ 20 Jarome Iginla 1.00 .45
❑ 21 John LeClair 2.00 .90
❑ 22 Brian Leetch 1.00 .45
❑ 23 Chris Chelios 1.00 .45
❑ 24 Martin Brodeur 3.00 1.35
❑ 25 Bryan Berard 1.00 .45
❑ 26 Keith Tkachuk 1.50 .70
❑ 27 Saku Koivu 2.00 .90
❑ 28 Brett Hull 1.50 .70
❑ 29 Felix Potvin 1.00 .45
❑ 30 Chris Osgood 1.00 .45
❑ 31 Dominik Hasek 2.50 1.10
❑ 32 Zigmund Palffy 1.00 .45
❑ 33 Jeremy Roenick 1.00 .45
❑ 34 Dainius Zubrus 1.00 .45
❑ 35 Ray Bourque 1.00 .45
❑ 36 Jocelyn Thibault 1.00 .45

## 1993-94 Ducks Milk Caps

This set of six milk caps measures approximately 1 1/2" in diameter and features the Mighty Ducks of Anaheim. The fronts show a color player headshot set against a teal green background with a neon yellow stripe. The player's name appears at the bottom, along with the production figures "One of 15,000". The backs are solid white. The milk caps are numbered on the front.

| | MINT | NRMT |
|---|---|---|
| COMPLETE SET (6) | 5.00 | 2.20 |
| COMMON CAP (1-5) | 1.00 | .45 |

❑ 1 Tim Sweeney 1.00 .45
❑ 2 Bobby Dollas 1.00 .45
❑ 3 Stu Grimson 1.50 .70
❑ 4 Terry Yake 1.00 .45
❑ 5 Bob Corkum 1.00 .45
❑ NNO Inaugural Season 1.00 .45
First Win

## 1994-95 Ducks Carl's Jr.

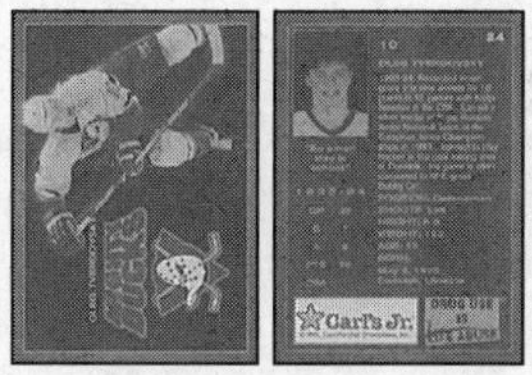

The 28-card standard-size set is sponsored by Carl's Jr. The fronts feature a color action player photo on a back ground with a purple border. The player's name and team logo is at the left. The backs carry a head shot of the player, biographical information, statistics, and jersey number. The sponsor name and logo is at the bottom with a saying against drug use.

| | MINT | NRMT |
|---|---|---|
| COMPLETE SET (28) | 15.00 | 6.75 |
| COMMON CARD (1-28) | .10 | .05 |

❑ 1 Patrik Carnback .35 .16
❑ 2 Bob Corkum .35 .16
❑ 3 Robert Dirk .35 .16
❑ 4 Bobby Dollas .35 .16
❑ 5 Peter Douris .35 .16
❑ 6 Todd Ewen .35 .16
❑ 7 Shaun Van Allen .35 .16
❑ 8 Garry Valk .35 .16
❑ 9 Guy Hebert 1.50 .70
❑ 10 Paul Kariya 10.00 4.50
❑ 11 Valeri Karpov .50 .23
❑ 12 Steven King .35 .16
❑ 13 Todd Krygier .35 .16
❑ 14 Tom Kurvers .35 .16
❑ 15 Randy Ladouceur .35 .16
❑ 16 Stephan Lebeau .35 .16
❑ 17 John Lilley .35 .16
❑ 18 Don McSween .35 .16
❑ 19 Steve Rucchin .75 .35
❑ 20 David Sacco .35 .16
❑ 21 Joe Sacco .35 .16
❑ 22 Mikhail Shtalenkov .75 .35
❑ 23 Jim Thomson .35 .16
❑ 24 Oleg Tverdovsky 1.00 .45
❑ 25 David Williams .35 .16
❑ 26 Wild Wing (Mascot) .25 .11
❑ 27 Carl Karcher .10 .05
(Sponsor Owner)
❑ 28 Happy Star .10 .05
(Sponsor Logo)

## 1995-96 Ducks

These five oversized (5" X 7") black and white photos picture members of the '95-96 Mighty Ducks of Anaheim. The cards feature a posed head shot, with the player's name and a pair of team logos along the bottom. The backs are blank. The photos are unnumbered, and are listed below alphabetically. It's highly unlikely that the checklist is complete as listed below. Additional information would be appreciated and can be forwarded to Beckett Publications.

| | MINT | NRMT |
|---|---|---|
| COMPLETE SET (5) | 3.00 | 1.35 |
| COMMON CARD (1-5) | .50 | .23 |

❑ 1 Bobby Dollas .50 .23
❑ 2 David Karpa .50 .23
❑ 3 Steve Rucchin .75 .35
❑ 4 Mikhail Shtalenkov .75 .35
❑ 5 Garry Valk .50 .23

## 1996-97 Ducks

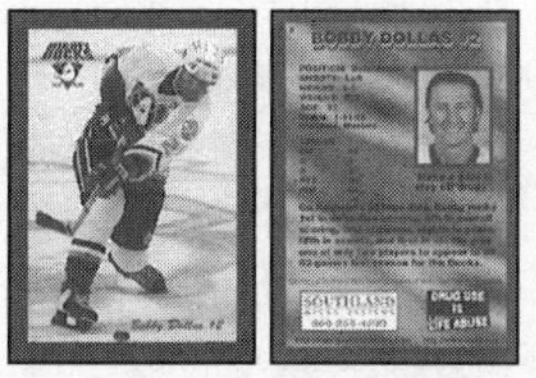

This unique 26-card set was produced by Up Front Sports and sponsored by Southland Micro Systems. The first twenty cards in the set follow the standard design of action photo on the front and stats on the back. Cards 21-24, however, are die-cut pop-up cards. Reports indicate a card originally was produced for Garry Valk. Valk was traded, however, before the set's release, which apparently led to all of his cards being pulled from the sets and destroyed. A few copies may still exist, but this has yet to be confirmed.

| | MINT | NRMT |
|---|---|---|
| COMPLETE SET (26) | 20.00 | 9.00 |
| COMMON CARD (1-27) | .10 | .05 |

❑ 1 Mikhail Shtalenkov .50 .23
❑ 2 Bobby Dollas .40 .18
❑ 3 Roman Oksiuta .40 .18
❑ 4 Kevin Todd .40 .18
❑ 5 Ted Drury .40 .18
❑ 6 Joe Sacco .40 .18
❑ 7 Dmitri Mironov .50 .23
❑ 8 Warren Rychel .50 .23
❑ 10 Shawn Antoski .40 .18
❑ 11 Steve Rucchin .50 .23
❑ 12 Ken Baumgartner .40 .18
❑ 13 Brian Bellows .40 .18
❑ 14 Nikolai Tsulygin .40 .18
❑ 15 Jason Marshall .40 .18
❑ 16 Darren Van Impe .40 .18
❑ 17 David Karpa .40 .18
❑ 18 Wild Wing .40 .18
❑ 19 J.F. Jomphe .40 .18
❑ 20 Sean Pronger .40 .18
❑ 21 Guy Hebert 2.00 .90
❑ 22 Paul Kariya 6.00 2.70
❑ 23 Jari Kurri 2.00 .90
❑ 24 Teemu Selanne 4.00 1.80
❑ 25 Southland .10 .05
❑ 26 Southland .10 .05
❑ 27 Ron Wilson CO .25 .11

## 1992-93 Durivage Panini

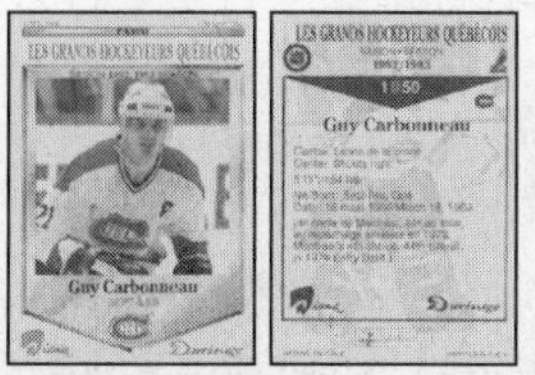


This 50-card standard-size set showcases hockey stars who were born in Quebec. The cards, which were inserted in loaves of bread, feature color, action player photos set on a gold plaque design. The player's name appears below the photo on the plaque. The words "Les Grands Hockeyeurs Quebecois" are printed in red at the top of the card. The backs have a ghosted black-and-white player photo with biography and career summary printed in French over the picture. The Patrick Roy signed card was randomly inserted. It is believed he signed 500 copies, although that has not been confirmed.

| | MINT | NRMT |
|---|---|---|
| COMPLETE SET (50) | 35.00 | 16.00 |
| COMMON CARD (1-50) | .35 | .16 |

❑ 1 Guy Carbonneau .50 .23
❑ 2 Lucien Deblois .35 .16
❑ 3 Benoit Hogue .35 .16
❑ 4 Steve Kasper .35 .16
❑ 5 Mike Krushelnyski .35 .16
❑ 6 Claude Lapointe .35 .16
❑ 7 Stephan Lebeau .35 .16
❑ 8 Mario Lemieux 8.00 3.60
❑ 9 Stephane Morin .35 .16
❑ 10 Denis Savard .50 .23
❑ 11 Pierre Turgeon .50 .23
❑ 12 Kevin Dineen .35 .16
❑ 13 Gord Donnelly .35 .16
❑ 14 Claude Lemieux .50 .23
❑ 15 Jocelyn Lemieux .35 .16
❑ 16 Daniel Marois .35 .16
❑ 17 Scott Mellanby .35 .16
❑ 18 Stephane Richer .50 .23
❑ 19 Benoit Brunet .35 .16
❑ 20 Vincent Damphousse .50 .23
❑ 21 Gilbert Dionne .35 .16
❑ 22 Gaetan Duchesne .35 .16
❑ 23 Bob Errey .35 .16
❑ 24 Michel Goulet .50 .23
❑ 25 Mike Hough .35 .16
❑ 26 Sergio Momesso .35 .16
❑ 27 Mario Roberge .35 .16
❑ 28 Luc Robitaille .50 .23
❑ 29 Sylvain Turgeon .35 .16
❑ 30 Marc Bergevin .35 .16
❑ 31 Raymond Bourque .75 .35
❑ 32 Patrice Brisebois .35 .16
❑ 33 Jeff Chychrun .35 .16
❑ 34 Sylvain Cote .35 .16
❑ 35 J.J. Daigneault .35 .16
❑ 36 Eric Desjardins .35 .16
❑ 37 Gord Dineen .35 .16
❑ 38 Steve Duchesne .50 .23
❑ 39 Donald Dufresne .35 .16
❑ 40 Steven Finn .35 .16
❑ 41 Garry Galley .35 .16
❑ 42 Kevin Lowe .35 .16
❑ 43 Michel Petit .35 .16
❑ 44 Normand Rochefort .35 .16
❑ 45 Randy Velischek .35 .16
❑ 46 Jacques Cloutier .50 .23
❑ 47 Stephane Fiset .50 .23
❑ 48 Rejean Lemelin .50 .23
❑ 49 Andre Racicot .50 .23
❑ 50 Patrick Roy 8.00 3.60
❑ NNO Patrick Roy AU 200.00 90.00

## 1993-94 Durivage Score

These 50 standard-size white-bordered cards feature color player action shots "mounted" on golden plaque designs. The player's name and hometown appear within a black stripe below the photo. All the players in the set are from the province of Quebec. His team's logo appears further below. The white-bordered back carries a color player action photo on the right and, on the left, bilingual biography and statistics. Cards 1-6 belong to a "Special Edition" subset and have gold-foil highlights on their fronts. The cards are numbered on the back as "X of 50."

| | MINT | NRMT |
|---|---|---|
| COMPLETE SET (50) | 25.00 | 11.00 |
| COMMON CARD (1-50) | .35 | .16 |

❑ 1 Alexandre Daigle .75 .35
❑ 2 Pierre Sevigny .50 .23
❑ 3 Jocelyn Thibault 2.00 .90
❑ 4 Philippe Boucher .50 .23
❑ 5 Martin Brodeur 5.00 2.20
❑ 6 Martin Lapointe .50 .23
❑ 7 Patrice Brisebois .50 .23
❑ 8 Benoit Brunet .35 .16
❑ 9 Guy Carbonneau .50 .23
❑ 10 Jean-Jacques Daigneault .35 .16
❑ 11 Vincent Damphousse .75 .35
❑ 12 Eric Desjardins .60 .25
❑ 13 Gilbert Dionne .35 .16
❑ 14 Stephan Lebeau .35 .16
❑ 15 Andre Racicot .50 .23
❑ 16 Mario Roberge .35 .16
❑ 17 Patrick Roy 7.00 3.10
❑ 18 Jacques Cloutier .50 .23
❑ 19 Alain Cote .35 .16
❑ 20 Steven Finn .35 .16
❑ 21 Stephane Fiset .75 .35
❑ 22 Martin Gelinas .50 .23
❑ 23 Reggie Savage .35 .16
❑ 24 Claude Lapointe .35 .16
❑ 25 Denis Savard .75 .35
❑ 26 Ray Bourque 1.50 .70
❑ 27 Joe Juneau .75 .35
❑ 28 Ron Stern .35 .16
❑ 29 Benoit Hogue .35 .16
❑ 30 Pierre Turgeon 1.00 .45
❑ 31 Mike Krushelnyski .35 .16
❑ 32 Felix Potvin 1.50 .70
❑ 33 Sergio Momesso .35 .16
❑ 34 Yves Racine .35 .16
❑ 35 Sylvain Cote .35 .16
❑ 36 Sylvain Turgeon .35 .16
❑ 37 Kevin Dineen .50 .23
❑ 38 Garry Galley .50 .23
❑ 39 Dominic Roussel .50 .23
❑ 40 Gaetan Duchesne .35 .16
❑ 41 Luc Robitaille 1.00 .45
❑ 42 Michel Goulet .75 .35
❑ 43 Jocelyn Lemieux .35 .16
❑ 44 Stephane Matteau .35 .16
❑ 45 Mike Hough .35 .16
❑ 46 Scott Mellanby .75 .35
❑ 47 Claude Lemieux .75 .35
❑ 48 Stephane Richer .50 .23
❑ 49 Jimmy Waite .50 .23
❑ 50 Patrick Poulin .35 .16
❑ NNO Patrick Roy AU 200.00 90.00
❑ NNO Jocelyn Thibault AU 100.00 45.00

## 1996-97 Duracell All-Cherry Team

This 22-card set was available in three-card packs with the purchase of specially-marked packages of Duracell batteries in English-speaking Canada and was produced by Pinnacle Brands. The players featured in the set were chosen by CBC commentator and fashion doyenne Don Cherry. The card fronts feature a color action photo, along with manufacturer logos. The backs include a brief resume. Interestingly, the player's stats could only be revealed by pressing a trio of heat-sensitive strips. There were rumored to be short printed cards in the set, but no confirmation of this has become available.

| | MINT | NRMT |
|---|---|---|
| COMPLETE SET (22) | 20.00 | 9.00 |
| COMMON CARD (DC1-DC22) | .25 | .11 |

❑ DC1 Paul Coffey .75 .35
❑ DC2 Lyle Odelein .25 .11
❑ DC3 Joe Sakic 1.50 .70
❑ DC4 Curtis Joseph .75 .35
❑ DC5 Brett Hull 1.00 .45
❑ DC6 Eric Lindros 2.50 1.10
❑ DC7 Doug Gilmour .75 .35
❑ DC8 Chris Chelios .75 .35
❑ DC9 Marty McSorley .25 .11
❑ DC10 Kirk Muller .35 .16
❑ DC11 Trevor Linden .35 .16
❑ DC12 Brendan Shanahan 1.50 .70
❑ DC13 Tie Domi .35 .16
❑ DC14 Rick Tocchet .35 .16
❑ DC15 Steve Yzerman 2.50 1.10
❑ DC16 Scott Stevens .25 .11
❑ DC17 Patrick Roy 4.00 1.80
❑ DC18 Keith Tkachuk 1.00 .45
❑ DC19 Owen Nolan .50 .23
❑ DC20 Dale Hunter .25 .11
❑ DC21 Don Cherry 1.00 .45
❑ DC22 Don Cherry 1.00 .45

## 1996-97 Duracell L'Equipe Beliveau

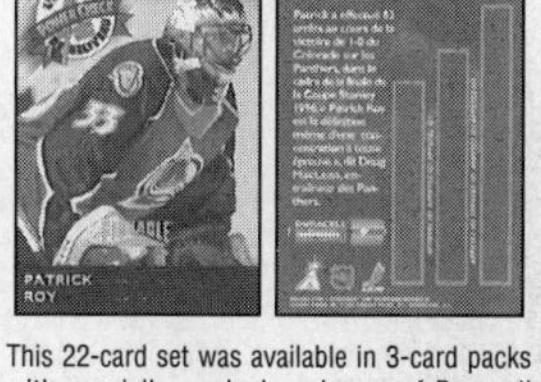

This 22-card set was available in 3-card packs with specially marked packages of Duracell batteries in French-speaking Canada. The set was produced by Pinnacle. The design is the same as that of the All-Cherry team cards, save for the different logo in the upper left corner of the front; also the text on the back of these cards is French. As the team was

selected by former Habs great Jean Beliveau, the player composition is slightly different, with a notable increase in the francophone content. As this series was produced in more limited quantities than the Cherry set, the French version of the singles which appear in both sets carry a slight premium.

| | MINT | NRMT |
|---|---|---|
| COMPLETE SET (22) | 35.00 | 16.00 |
| COMMON CARD (JB1-JB22) | .35 | .16 |

| | | |
|---|---|---|
| ❑ JB1 Paul Coffey | 1.00 | .45 |
| ❑ JB2 Lyle Odelein | .35 | .16 |
| ❑ JB3 Joe Sakic | 3.00 | 1.35 |
| ❑ JB4 Eric Daze | .75 | .35 |
| ❑ JB5 Brett Hull | 2.00 | .90 |
| ❑ JB6 Martin Brodeur | 3.00 | 1.35 |
| ❑ JB7 Doug Gilmour | 1.00 | .45 |
| ❑ JB8 Peter Forsberg | 4.00 | 1.80 |
| ❑ JB9 Mike Gartner | .50 | .23 |
| ❑ JB10 Saku Koivu | 2.50 | 1.10 |
| ❑ JB11 Trevor Linden | .50 | .23 |
| ❑ JB12 Felix Potvin | 1.00 | .45 |
| ❑ JB13 Mats Sundin | 1.00 | .45 |
| ❑ JB14 Pierre Turgeon | .50 | .23 |
| ❑ JB15 Vincent Damphousse | .50 | .23 |
| ❑ JB16 Scott Stevens | .35 | .16 |
| ❑ JB17 Patrick Roy | 6.00 | 2.70 |
| ❑ JB18 Keith Tkachuk | 1.50 | .70 |
| ❑ JB19 Ray Bourque | 1.00 | .45 |
| ❑ JB20 Paul Kariya | 5.00 | 2.20 |
| ❑ JB21 Jean Beliveau | 1.00 | .45 |
| ❑ JB22 Jean Beliveau | 1.00 | .45 |

## 1994 EA Sports

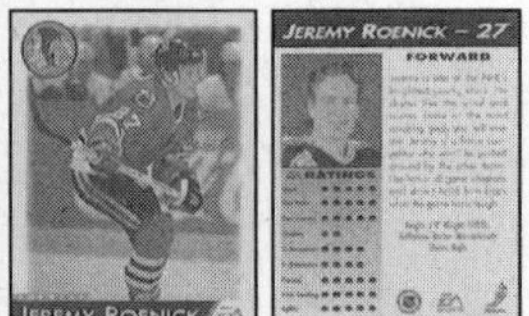


This 225-card boxed set was issued by Electronic Arts Sports as a premium within packages of its NHLPA '94 video game. Two cards were included with each game. In addition, an order form for a complete set was found inside the game box; the original price was 24.95 direct. The fronts are white with action player photos that have airbrushed edges. The team logo appears in the upper left corner with the player's name printed on a black bar across the bottom edge. The player's position is on a team color-coded stripe above the player's name. The borderless backs display a head shot in the upper left corner with player performance rating below. A brief biography and career summary appear to the right.

| | MINT | NRMT |
|---|---|---|
| COMPLETE SET (225) | 80.00 | 36.00 |
| COMMON CARD (1-225) | .05 | .02 |
| SEMISTARS/GOALIES | .15 | .07 |
| UNLISTED STARS | .25 | .11 |

| | | |
|---|---|---|
| ❑ 1 Alexei Kasatonov | .05 | .02 |
| ❑ 2 Randy Ladouceur | .05 | .02 |
| ❑ 3 Terry Yake | .05 | .02 |
| ❑ 4 Troy Loney | .05 | .02 |
| ❑ 5 Anatoli Semenov | .05 | .02 |
| ❑ 6 Guy Hebert | .25 | .11 |
| ❑ 7 Ray Bourque | 1.50 | .70 |
| ❑ 8 Don Sweeney | .05 | .02 |
| ❑ 9 Adam Oates | .50 | .23 |
| ❑ 10 Joe Juneau | .35 | .16 |
| ❑ 11 Cam Neely | 1.00 | .45 |
| ❑ 12 Andy Moog | .25 | .11 |
| ❑ 13 Doug Bodger | .05 | .02 |
| ❑ 14 Petr Svoboda | .05 | .02 |
| ❑ 15 Pat LaFontaine | .50 | .23 |
| ❑ 16 Dale Hawerchuk | .15 | .07 |
| ❑ 17 Alexander Mogilny | .75 | .35 |
| ❑ 18 Grant Fuhr | .35 | .16 |
| ❑ 19 Gary Suter | .05 | .02 |
| ❑ 20 Al MacInnis | .15 | .07 |
| ❑ 21 Joe Nieuwendyk | .20 | .09 |
| ❑ 22 Gary Roberts | .10 | .05 |
| ❑ 23 Theoren Fleury | 1.50 | .70 |
| ❑ 24 Mike Vernon | .15 | .07 |
| ❑ 25 Chris Chelios | 1.50 | .70 |
| ❑ 26 Steve Smith | .05 | .02 |
| ❑ 27 Jeremy Roenick | 1.50 | .70 |
| ❑ 28 Michel Goulet | .10 | .05 |
| ❑ 29 Steve Larmer | .15 | .07 |
| ❑ 30 Ed Belfour | 1.50 | .70 |
| ❑ 31 Mark Tinordi | .05 | .02 |
| ❑ 32 Tommy Sjodin | .05 | .02 |
| ❑ 33 Mike Modano | 2.00 | .90 |
| ❑ 34 Dave Gagner | .10 | .05 |
| ❑ 35 Russ Courtnall | .10 | .05 |
| ❑ 36 Jon Casey | .10 | .05 |
| ❑ 37 Paul Coffey | 1.50 | .70 |
| ❑ 38 Steve Chiasson | .05 | .02 |
| ❑ 39 Steve Yzerman | 5.00 | 2.20 |
| ❑ 40 Sergei Fedorov | 3.00 | 1.35 |
| ❑ 41 Dino Ciccarelli | .10 | .05 |
| ❑ 42 Tim Cheveldae | .10 | .05 |
| ❑ 43 Dave Manson | .05 | .02 |
| ❑ 44 Igor Kravchuk | .05 | .02 |
| ❑ 45 Doug Weight | .35 | .16 |
| ❑ 46 Shayne Corson | .10 | .05 |
| ❑ 47 Petr Klima | .05 | .02 |
| ❑ 48 Bill Ranford | .20 | .09 |
| ❑ 49 Joe Cirella | .05 | .02 |
| ❑ 50 Gord Murphy | .05 | .02 |
| ❑ 51 Brian Skrudland | .05 | .02 |
| ❑ 52 Andrei Lomakin | .05 | .02 |
| ❑ 53 Scott Mellanby | .15 | .07 |
| ❑ 54 John Vanbiesbrouck | 2.50 | 1.10 |
| ❑ 55 Zarley Zalapski | .05 | .02 |
| ❑ 56 Eric Weinrich | .05 | .02 |
| ❑ 57 Andrew Cassels | .05 | .02 |
| ❑ 58 Geoff Sanderson | .15 | .07 |
| ❑ 59 Pat Verbeek | .10 | .05 |
| ❑ 60 Sean Burke | .15 | .07 |
| ❑ 61 Rob Blake | .10 | .05 |
| ❑ 62 Marty McSorley | .10 | .05 |
| ❑ 63 Wayne Gretzky | 10.00 | 4.50 |
| ❑ 64 Luc Robitaille | .50 | .23 |
| ❑ 65 Tomas Sandstrom | .10 | .05 |
| ❑ 66 Kelly Hrudey | .15 | .07 |
| ❑ 67 Eric Desjardins | .05 | .02 |
| ❑ 68 Mathieu Schneider | .10 | .05 |
| ❑ 69 Kirk Muller | .10 | .05 |
| ❑ 70 Vincent Damphousse | .25 | .11 |
| ❑ 71 Brian Bellows | .10 | .05 |
| ❑ 72 Patrick Roy | 8.00 | 3.60 |
| ❑ 73 Scott Stevens | .15 | .07 |
| ❑ 74 Viacheslav Fetisov | .10 | .05 |
| ❑ 75 Alexander Semak | .05 | .02 |
| ❑ 76 Stephane Richer | .10 | .05 |
| ❑ 77 Claude Lemieux | .15 | .07 |
| ❑ 78 Chris Terreri | .10 | .05 |
| ❑ 79 Vladimir Malakhov | .05 | .02 |
| ❑ 80 Darius Kasparaitis | .05 | .02 |
| ❑ 81 Pierre Turgeon | .50 | .23 |
| ❑ 82 Steve Thomas | .10 | .05 |
| ❑ 83 Benoit Hogue | .05 | .02 |
| ❑ 84 Glenn Healy | .10 | .05 |
| ❑ 85 Brian Leetch | 1.50 | .70 |
| ❑ 86 James Patrick | .05 | .02 |
| ❑ 87 Mark Messier | 2.00 | .90 |
| ❑ 88 Designer Tip | .05 | .02 |
| ❑ 89 Mike Gartner | .15 | .07 |
| ❑ 90 Mike Richter | 1.50 | .70 |
| ❑ 91 Norm Maciver | .05 | .02 |
| ❑ 92 Brad Shaw | .05 | .02 |
| ❑ 93 Jamie Baker | .05 | .02 |
| ❑ 94 Sylvain Turgeon | .05 | .02 |
| ❑ 95 Bob Kudelski | .05 | .02 |
| ❑ 96 Peter Sidorkiewicz | .10 | .05 |
| ❑ 97 Garry Galley | .05 | .02 |
| ❑ 98 Dimitri Yushkevich | .05 | .02 |
| ❑ 99 Eric Lindros | 5.00 | 2.20 |
| ❑ 100 Rod Brind'Amour | .15 | .07 |
| ❑ 101 Mark Recchi | .50 | .23 |
| ❑ 102 Tommy Soderstrom | .10 | .05 |
| ❑ 103 Larry Murphy | .15 | .07 |
| ❑ 104 Ulf Samuelsson | .10 | .05 |
| ❑ 105 Mario Lemieux | 8.00 | 3.60 |
| ❑ 106 Kevin Stevens | .10 | .05 |
| ❑ 107 Jaromir Jagr | 5.00 | 2.20 |
| ❑ 108 Tom Barrasso | .15 | .07 |
| ❑ 109 Steve Duchesne | .10 | .05 |
| ❑ 110 Curtis Leschyshyn | .05 | .02 |
| ❑ 111 Mats Sundin | 1.50 | .70 |
| ❑ 112 Joe Sakic | 3.00 | 1.35 |
| ❑ 113 Owen Nolan | .50 | .23 |
| ❑ 114 Ron Hextall | .25 | .11 |
| ❑ 115 Doug Wilson | .10 | .05 |
| ❑ 116 Neil Wilkinson | .05 | .02 |
| ❑ 117 Kelly Kisio | .05 | .02 |
| ❑ 118 Johan Garpenlov | .05 | .02 |
| ❑ 119 Pat Falloon | .10 | .05 |
| ❑ 120 Arturs Irbe | .35 | .16 |
| ❑ 121 Jeff Brown | .10 | .05 |
| ❑ 122 Garth Butcher UER (Ray Bourque photo on card back) | .10 | .05 |
| ❑ 123 Craig Janney | .10 | .05 |
| ❑ 124 Brendan Shanahan | 3.00 | 1.35 |
| ❑ 125 Brett Hull | 2.00 | .90 |
| ❑ 126 Curtis Joseph | 1.50 | .70 |
| ❑ 127 Bob Beers | .05 | .02 |
| ❑ 128 Roman Hamrlik | .15 | .07 |
| ❑ 129 Brian Bradley | .10 | .05 |
| ❑ 130 Mikael Andersson | .05 | .02 |
| ❑ 131 Chris Kontos | .05 | .02 |
| ❑ 132 Wendell Young | .05 | .02 |
| ❑ 133 Todd Gill | .05 | .02 |
| ❑ 134 Dave Ellett | .05 | .02 |
| ❑ 135 Doug Gilmour | 1.50 | .70 |
| ❑ 136 Dave Andreychuk | .10 | .05 |
| ❑ 137 Nikolai Borschevsky | .05 | .02 |
| ❑ 138 Felix Potvin | 1.50 | .70 |
| ❑ 139 Jyrki Lumme | .05 | .02 |
| ❑ 140 Doug Lidster | .05 | .02 |
| ❑ 141 Cliff Ronning | .10 | .05 |
| ❑ 142 Geoff Courtnall | .05 | .02 |
| ❑ 143 Pavel Bure | 3.00 | 1.35 |
| ❑ 144 Kirk McLean | .10 | .05 |
| ❑ 145 Phil Housley | .10 | .05 |
| ❑ 146 Teppo Numminen | .05 | .02 |
| ❑ 147 Alexei Zhamnov | .25 | .11 |
| ❑ 148 Thomas Steen | .05 | .02 |
| ❑ 149 Teemu Selanne | 3.00 | 1.35 |
| ❑ 150 Bob Essensa | .05 | .02 |
| ❑ 151 Kevin Hatcher | .05 | .02 |
| ❑ 152 Al Iafrate | .10 | .05 |
| ❑ 153 Mike Ridley | .05 | .02 |
| ❑ 154 Dimitri Khristich | .10 | .05 |
| ❑ 155 Peter Bondra | 1.50 | .70 |
| ❑ 156 Don Beaupre | .10 | .05 |
| ❑ 157 All Stars East CL | .10 | .05 |
| ❑ 158 All Stars West CL | .10 | .05 |
| ❑ 159 Mighty Ducks Team CL | .10 | .05 |
| ❑ 160 Bruins Team CL | .10 | .05 |
| ❑ 161 Sabres Team CL | .10 | .05 |
| ❑ 162 Flames Team CL | .10 | .05 |
| ❑ 163 Blackhawks Team CL | .10 | .05 |
| ❑ 164 Red Wings Team CL | .10 | .05 |
| ❑ 165 Oilers Team CL | .10 | .05 |
| ❑ 166 Panthers Team CL | .10 | .05 |
| ❑ 167 Whalers Team CL | .10 | .05 |
| ❑ 168 Kings Team CL | .10 | .05 |
| ❑ 169 Stars Team CL | .10 | .05 |
| ❑ 170 Canadiens Team CL | .10 | .05 |
| ❑ 171 Devils Team CL | .10 | .05 |
| ❑ 172 Islanders Team CL | .10 | .05 |
| ❑ 173 Rangers Team CL | .10 | .05 |
| ❑ 174 Senators Team CL | .10 | .05 |
| ❑ 175 Flyers Team CL | .10 | .05 |
| ❑ 176 Penguins Team CL | .10 | .05 |
| ❑ 177 Nordiques Team CL | .10 | .05 |
| ❑ 178 Sharks Team CL | .10 | .05 |
| ❑ 179 Blues Team CL | .10 | .05 |
| ❑ 180 Lightning Team CL | .10 | .05 |
| ❑ 181 Leafs Team CL | .10 | .05 |
| ❑ 182 Canucks Team CL | .10 | .05 |
| ❑ 183 Capitals Team CL | .10 | .05 |
| ❑ 184 Jets Team CL | .10 | .05 |
| ❑ 185 Ray Bourque SL | .50 | .23 |
| ❑ 186 Chris Chelios SL | .50 | .23 |
| ❑ 187 Ed Belfour SL | .75 | .35 |
| ❑ 188 Adam Oates SL | .25 | .11 |
| ❑ 189 Mario Lemieux SL | 4.00 | 1.80 |
| ❑ 190 Al Iafrate SL | .10 | .05 |
| ❑ 191 Alexander Mogilny SL | .50 | .23 |
| ❑ 192 Wayne Gretzky SL | 5.00 | 2.20 |
| ❑ 193 New Feature | .05 | .02 |
| ❑ 194 Derian Hatcher | .05 | .02 |
| ❑ 195 Dmitri Kvartalnov | .05 | .02 |
| ❑ 196 Randy Wood | .05 | .02 |
| ❑ 197 Gord Murphy | .05 | .02 |
| ❑ 198 New Feature | .05 | .02 |
| ❑ 199 Ducks/Panthers Team Logo | .10 | .05 |
| ❑ 200 Luc Robitaille | .50 | .23 |
| ❑ 201 Terry Yake | .05 | .02 |
| ❑ 202 Mark Fitzpatrick | .15 | .07 |
| ❑ 203 Brad Shaw | .05 | .02 |
| ❑ 204 NHL Logos | .05 | .02 |
| ❑ 205 Jyrki Lumme | .05 | .02 |
| ❑ 206 Peter Sidorkiewicz | .10 | .05 |
| ❑ 207 Gord Murphy | .05 | .02 |
| ❑ 208 Viacheslav Fetisov | .10 | .05 |
| ❑ 209 Stephan LeBeau | .05 | .02 |
| ❑ 210 Gord Murphy | .05 | .02 |
| ❑ 211 Dominik Hasek | 3.00 | 1.35 |
| ❑ 212 Cam Neely | 1.00 | .45 |
| ❑ 213 Designer Tips | .05 | .02 |
| ❑ 214 Designer Tips | .05 | .02 |
| ❑ 215 Designer Tips | .05 | .02 |
| ❑ 216 Designer Tips | .05 | .02 |
| ❑ 217 Designer Tips | .05 | .02 |
| ❑ 218 Designer Tips | .05 | .02 |
| ❑ 219 Designer Tips | .05 | .02 |
| ❑ 220 Designer Tips | .05 | .02 |
| ❑ 221 Designer Tips | .05 | .02 |
| ❑ 222 Designer Tips | .05 | .02 |
| ❑ 223 Designer Tips | .05 | .02 |
| ❑ 224 Designer Tips | .05 | .02 |
| ❑ 225 Designer Tips | .05 | .02 |

## 1962-63 El Producto Discs

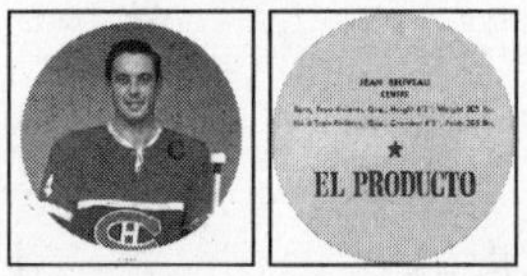


The six discs in this set measure approximately 3" in diameter. They were issued as a strip of six connected in a fragile manner and are in full color. The discs are unnumbered and checklisted below in alphabetical order. The set in unperforated form is valued 25 percent greater than the value below.

| | NRMT | VG-E |
|---|---|---|
| COMPLETE SET (6) | 300.00 | 135.00 |
| COMMON DISC (1-6) | 50.00 | 22.00 |

| | | |
|---|---|---|
| ❑ 1 Jean Beliveau | 60.00 | 27.00 |
| ❑ 2 Glenn Hall | 50.00 | 22.00 |
| ❑ 3 Gordie Howe | 150.00 | 70.00 |
| ❑ 4 Dave Keon | 60.00 | 27.00 |
| ❑ 5 Frank Mahovlich | 50.00 | 22.00 |
| ❑ 6 Henri Richard | 50.00 | 22.00 |

## 1995-96 Emotion Sample

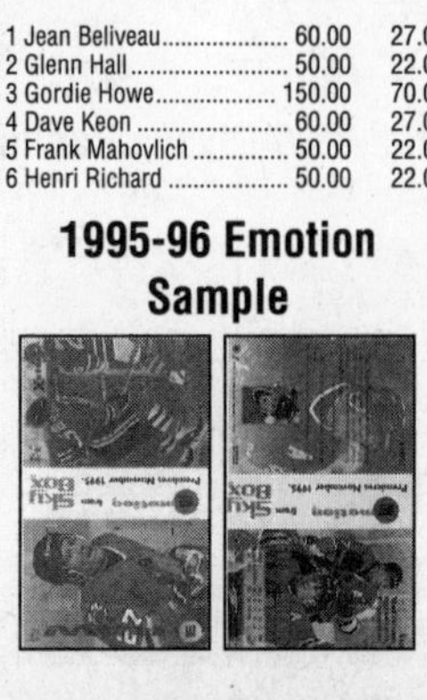

This 6" by 3" strip was distributed by Skybox to introduce its Emotion line of cards. The front features two cards of Jeremy Roenick of the Chicago Blackhawks: his basic Emotion issue and his X-Cited insert. They are identical to the regularly issued cards, except for the word sample found in the back upper right corner. They are separated by a white bar with the sponsor logo horizontally printed in gold and date cards premier in black.

| | MINT | NRMT |
|---|---|---|
| COMPLETE SET (1) | 1.00 | .45 |
| COMMON CARD (1) | 1.00 | .45 |

| | | |
|---|---|---|
| ❑ 1 Jeremy Roenick | 1.00 | .45 |

## 1995-96 Emotion

This 200-card high end set was released in 8-card packs with an SRP of $4.99. The set was distinguished by its use of an "emotional" term to describe the action on the card face. The Jeremy Roenick SkyMotion card was obtainable in exchange for three wrappers and $25. The unique card featured three seconds of actual game footage. The offer for this card expired on June 30, 1996. The only Rookie Card of note in this set is Todd Bertuzzi.

| | MINT | NRMT |
|---|---|---|
| COMPLETE SET (200) | 40.00 | 18.00 |
| COMMON CARD (1-200) | .15 | .07 |

| | | |
|---|---|---|
| ❑ 1 Bobby Dollas | .15 | .07 |
| ❑ 2 Guy Hebert | .30 | .14 |
| ❑ 3 Paul Kariya | 2.00 | .90 |
| ❑ 4 Oleg Tverdovsky | .30 | .14 |
| ❑ 5 Shaun Van Allen | .15 | .07 |
| ❑ 6 Ray Bourque | .50 | .23 |
| ❑ 7 Al Iafrate | .15 | .07 |
| ❑ 8 Blaine Lacher | .30 | .14 |
| ❑ 9 Joe Mullen | .30 | .14 |
| ❑ 10 Cam Neely | .30 | .14 |
| ❑ 11 Adam Oates | .30 | .14 |
| ❑ 12 Kevin Stevens | .15 | .07 |
| ❑ 13 Don Sweeney | .15 | .07 |
| ❑ 14 Donald Audette | .30 | .14 |
| ❑ 15 Garry Galley | .15 | .07 |
| ❑ 16 Dominik Hasek | 1.00 | .45 |
| ❑ 17 Brian Holzinger | .50 | .23 |
| ❑ 18 Pat LaFontaine | .30 | .14 |
| ❑ 19 Alexei Zhitnik | .15 | .07 |
| ❑ 20 Steve Chiasson | .15 | .07 |
| ❑ 21 Theoren Fleury | .30 | .14 |
| ❑ 22 Phil Housley | .30 | .14 |
| ❑ 23 Trevor Kidd | .30 | .14 |
| ❑ 24 Joe Nieuwendyk | .30 | .14 |
| ❑ 25 Gary Roberts | .15 | .07 |
| ❑ 26 Zarley Zalapski | .15 | .07 |
| ❑ 27 Ed Belfour | .50 | .23 |
| ❑ 28 Chris Chelios | .50 | .23 |
| ❑ 29 Sergei Krivokrasov | .15 | .07 |
| ❑ 30 Joe Murphy | .15 | .07 |
| ❑ 31 Bernie Nicholls | .15 | .07 |
| ❑ 32 Patrick Poulin | .15 | .07 |
| ❑ 33 Jeremy Roenick | .50 | .23 |
| ❑ 34 Gary Suter | .15 | .07 |
| ❑ 35 Rene Corbet | .15 | .07 |
| ❑ 36 Peter Forsberg | 1.50 | .70 |
| ❑ 37 Valeri Kamensky | .30 | .14 |
| ❑ 38 Uwe Krupp | .15 | .07 |
| ❑ 39 Curtis Leschyshyn | .15 | .07 |
| ❑ 40 Owen Nolan | .30 | .14 |
| ❑ 41 Mike Ricci | .15 | .07 |
| ❑ 42 Joe Sakic | 1.00 | .45 |
| ❑ 43 Jocelyn Thibault | .50 | .23 |
| ❑ 44 Bob Bassen | .15 | .07 |
| ❑ 45 Dave Gagner | .30 | .14 |
| ❑ 46 Todd Harvey | .15 | .07 |
| ❑ 47 Derian Hatcher | .15 | .07 |
| ❑ 48 Kevin Hatcher | .15 | .07 |
| ❑ 49 Mike Modano | .75 | .35 |
| ❑ 50 Andy Moog | .30 | .14 |
| ❑ 51 Dino Ciccarelli | .30 | .14 |
| ❑ 52 Paul Coffey | .50 | .23 |
| ❑ 53 Sergei Fedorov | 1.00 | .45 |
| ❑ 54 Vladimir Konstantinov | .15 | .07 |
| ❑ 55 Slava Kozlov | .30 | .14 |
| ❑ 56 Nicklas Lidstrom | .30 | .14 |
| ❑ 57 Keith Primeau | .30 | .14 |
| ❑ 58 Ray Sheppard | .30 | .14 |
| ❑ 59 Mike Vernon | .30 | .14 |
| ❑ 60 Steve Yzerman | 1.50 | .70 |
| ❑ 61 Jason Arnott | .30 | .14 |
| ❑ 62 Curtis Joseph | .50 | .23 |
| ❑ 63 Igor Kravchuk | .15 | .07 |
| ❑ 64 Todd Marchant | .15 | .07 |
| ❑ 65 David Oliver | .15 | .07 |
| ❑ 66 Bill Ranford | .30 | .14 |
| ❑ 67 Doug Weight | .30 | .14 |
| ❑ 68 Stu Barnes | .15 | .07 |
| ❑ 69 Jesse Belanger | .15 | .07 |
| ❑ 70 Gord Murphy | .15 | .07 |
| ❑ 71 Magnus Svensson | .15 | .07 |
| ❑ 72 John Vanbiesbrouck | .75 | .35 |
| ❑ 73 Sean Burke | .30 | .14 |
| ❑ 74 Andrew Cassels | .15 | .07 |
| ❑ 75 Frantisek Kucera | .15 | .07 |
| ❑ 76 Andrei Nikolishin | .15 | .07 |
| ❑ 77 Geoff Sanderson | .30 | .14 |
| ❑ 78 Brendan Shanahan | 1.00 | .45 |
| ❑ 79 Darren Turcotte | .15 | .07 |
| ❑ 80 Rob Blake | .15 | .07 |
| ❑ 81 Wayne Gretzky | 4.00 | 1.80 |
| ❑ 82 Dimitri Khristich | .15 | .07 |
| ❑ 83 Jari Kurri | .30 | .14 |
| ❑ 84 Jamie Storr | .30 | .14 |
| ❑ 85 Darryl Sydor | .15 | .07 |
| ❑ 86 Rick Tocchet | .30 | .14 |
| ❑ 87 Vincent Damphousse | .30 | .14 |
| ❑ 88 Vladimir Malakhov | .15 | .07 |
| ❑ 89 Stephane Quintal | .15 | .07 |
| ❑ 90 Mark Recchi | .30 | .14 |
| ❑ 91 Patrick Roy | 2.50 | 1.10 |
| ❑ 92 Brian Savage | .15 | .07 |
| ❑ 93 Pierre Turgeon | .30 | .14 |
| ❑ 94 Martin Brodeur | 1.25 | .55 |
| ❑ 95 Neal Broten | .30 | .14 |
| ❑ 96 Shawn Chambers | .15 | .07 |
| ❑ 97 Claude Lemieux | .30 | .14 |
| ❑ 98 John MacLean | .30 | .14 |
| ❑ 99 Randy McKay | .15 | .07 |
| ❑ 100 Scott Niedermayer | .15 | .07 |
| ❑ 101 Stephane Richer | .30 | .14 |
| ❑ 102 Scott Stevens | .30 | .14 |
| ❑ 103 Todd Bertuzzi | .30 | .14 |
| ❑ 104 Patrick Flatley | .15 | .07 |
| ❑ 105 Brett Lindros | .15 | .07 |
| ❑ 106 Kirk Muller | .15 | .07 |
| ❑ 107 Tommy Salo | .75 | .35 |
| ❑ 108 Mathieu Schneider | .15 | .07 |
| ❑ 109 Alexander Semak | .15 | .07 |
| ❑ 110 Dennis Vaske | .15 | .07 |
| ❑ 111 Ray Ferraro | .15 | .07 |
| ❑ 112 Adam Graves | .30 | .14 |
| ❑ 113 Alexei Kovalev | .15 | .07 |
| ❑ 114 Steve Larmer | .30 | .14 |
| ❑ 115 Brian Leetch | .50 | .23 |
| ❑ 116 Mark Messier | .75 | .35 |
| ❑ 117 Mike Richter | .50 | .23 |
| ❑ 118 Luc Robitaille | .30 | .14 |
| ❑ 119 Ulf Samuelsson | .15 | .07 |
| ❑ 120 Pat Verbeek | .15 | .07 |
| ❑ 121 Don Beaupre | .30 | .14 |
| ❑ 122 Radek Bonk | .15 | .07 |
| ❑ 123 Alexandre Daigle | .15 | .07 |
| ❑ 124 Steve Duchesne | .15 | .07 |
| ❑ 125 Steve Larouche | .15 | .07 |
| ❑ 126 Dan Quinn | .15 | .07 |
| ❑ 127 Martin Straka | .15 | .07 |
| ❑ 128 Alexei Yashin | .30 | .14 |
| ❑ 129 Rod Brind'Amour | .30 | .14 |
| ❑ 130 Eric Desjardins | .15 | .07 |
| ❑ 131 Ron Hextall | .30 | .14 |
| ❑ 132 John LeClair | .75 | .35 |
| ❑ 133 Eric Lindros | 1.50 | .70 |
| ❑ 134 Mikael Renberg | .30 | .14 |
| ❑ 135 Chris Therien | .15 | .07 |
| ❑ 136 Ron Francis | .30 | .14 |
| ❑ 137 Jaromir Jagr | 1.50 | .70 |
| ❑ 138 Mario Lemieux | 2.50 | 1.10 |
| ❑ 139 Dmitri Mironov | .15 | .07 |
| ❑ 140 Petr Nedved | .30 | .14 |
| ❑ 141 Tomas Sandstrom | .15 | .07 |
| ❑ 142 Bryan Smolinski | .15 | .07 |
| ❑ 143 Ken Wregget | .30 | .14 |
| ❑ 144 Sergei Zubov | .15 | .07 |
| ❑ 145 Shayne Corson | .15 | .07 |
| ❑ 146 Geoff Courtnall | .15 | .07 |
| ❑ 147 Dale Hawerchuk | .30 | .14 |
| ❑ 148 Brett Hull | .75 | .35 |
| ❑ 149 Ian Laperriere | .15 | .07 |
| ❑ 150 Al MacInnis | .30 | .14 |
| ❑ 151 Chris Pronger | .30 | .14 |
| ❑ 152 David Roberts | .15 | .07 |
| ❑ 153 Esa Tikkanen | .15 | .07 |
| ❑ 154 Ulf Dahlen | .15 | .07 |
| ❑ 155 Jeff Friesen | .30 | .14 |
| ❑ 156 Arturs Irbe | .30 | .14 |
| ❑ 157 Craig Janney | .30 | .14 |
| ❑ 158 Sergei Makarov | .15 | .07 |
| ❑ 159 Sandis Ozolinsh | .30 | .14 |
| ❑ 160 Mike Rathje | .15 | .07 |
| ❑ 161 Ray Whitney | .15 | .07 |
| ❑ 162 Brian Bradley | .15 | .07 |
| ❑ 163 Chris Gratton | .30 | .14 |
| ❑ 164 Roman Hamrlik | .30 | .14 |
| ❑ 165 Petr Klima | .15 | .07 |
| ❑ 166 Daren Puppa | .30 | .14 |
| ❑ 167 Paul Ysebaert | .15 | .07 |
| ❑ 168 Dave Andreychuk | .30 | .14 |
| ❑ 169 Mike Gartner | .30 | .14 |
| ❑ 170 Todd Gill | .15 | .07 |
| ❑ 171 Doug Gilmour | .50 | .23 |
| ❑ 172 Kenny Jonsson | .15 | .07 |
| ❑ 173 Larry Murphy | .30 | .14 |
| ❑ 174 Felix Potvin | .50 | .23 |
| ❑ 175 Mats Sundin | .30 | .14 |
| ❑ 176 Josef Beranek | .15 | .07 |
| ❑ 177 Jeff Brown | .15 | .07 |
| ❑ 178 Pavel Bure | 1.00 | .45 |
| ❑ 179 Russ Courtnall | .15 | .07 |
| ❑ 180 Trevor Linden | .30 | .14 |
| ❑ 181 Kirk McLean | .30 | .14 |
| ❑ 182 Alexander Mogilny | .30 | .14 |
| ❑ 183 Roman Oksiuta | .15 | .07 |
| ❑ 184 Mike Ridley | .15 | .07 |
| ❑ 185 Jason Allison | .15 | .07 |
| ❑ 186 Jim Carey | .50 | .23 |
| ❑ 187 Sergei Gonchar | .15 | .07 |

| | | |
|---|---|---|
| ❑ 188 Dale Hunter | .15 | .07 |
| ❑ 189 Calle Johansson | .15 | .07 |
| ❑ 190 Joe Juneau | .15 | .07 |
| ❑ 191 Joe Reekie | .15 | .07 |
| ❑ 192 Nelson Emerson | .15 | .07 |
| ❑ 193 Nikolai Khabibulin | .30 | .14 |
| ❑ 194 Dave Manson | .15 | .07 |
| ❑ 195 Teppo Numminen | .15 | .07 |
| ❑ 196 Teemu Selanne | 1.00 | .45 |
| ❑ 197 Keith Tkachuk | .60 | .25 |
| ❑ 198 Alexei Zhamnov | .30 | .14 |
| ❑ 199 Checklist #1 | .15 | .07 |
| ❑ 200 Checklist #2 | .15 | .07 |
| ❑ NNO J.Roenick SkyMotion | 30.00 | 13.50 |

## 1995-96 Emotion generatioNext

This ten-card set takes a look at those players thought to be the stars of tomorrow. The cards, which feature a player bust over a fiery metallic foil background were inserted at a rate of 1:10 packs. The cards are numbered "X of 10" on the back.

| | MINT | NRMT |
|---|---|---|
| COMPLETE SET (10) | 40.00 | 18.00 |
| COMMON CARD (1-10) | 2.50 | 1.10 |
| ❑ 1 Brian Holzinger | 4.00 | 1.80 |
| ❑ 2 Eric Daze | 5.00 | 2.20 |
| ❑ 3 Jason Bonsignore | 4.00 | 1.80 |
| ❑ 4 Jamie Storr | 4.00 | 1.80 |
| ❑ 5 Tommy Salo | 4.00 | 1.80 |
| ❑ 6 Brendan Witt | 2.50 | 1.10 |
| ❑ 7 Saku Koivu | 10.00 | 4.50 |
| ❑ 8 Todd Bertuzzi | 2.50 | 1.10 |
| ❑ 9 Ed Jovanovski | 5.00 | 2.20 |
| ❑ 10 Chad Kilger | 2.50 | 1.10 |

## 1995-96 Emotion Ntense Power

This ten-card set highlights the game's top power forwards. Utilizing a design element similar to the previous set using this name, the cards feature a cut-out player photo over a swirling foil background. The cards were randomly inserted 1:30 packs, and are numbered "X of 10" on the back.

| | MINT | NRMT |
|---|---|---|
| COMPLETE SET (10) | 80.00 | 36.00 |
| COMMON CARD (1-10) | 6.00 | 2.70 |
| ❑ 1 Cam Neely | 8.00 | 3.60 |
| ❑ 2 Keith Primeau | 6.00 | 2.70 |
| ❑ 3 Mark Messier | 10.00 | 4.50 |
| ❑ 4 Eric Lindros | 30.00 | 13.50 |
| ❑ 5 Mikael Renberg | 8.00 | 3.60 |
| ❑ 6 Owen Nolan | 8.00 | 3.60 |
| ❑ 7 Brendan Shanahan | 15.00 | 6.75 |
| ❑ 8 Kevin Stevens | 6.00 | 2.70 |
| ❑ 9 Keith Tkachuk | 10.00 | 4.50 |
| ❑ 10 Rick Tocchet | 8.00 | 3.60 |

## 1995-96 Emotion Xcel

This ten-card set features the top ten players in the league as chosen by the Fleer staff. The cards were issued randomly in packs at the rate of 1:72 packs. It was apparent, however, that a significant quantity of these cards entered the market through non-pack distribution, making them significantly easier to acquire than the long pack odds would suggest. This additional supply dampened the demand -- and hence, the prices -- for these cards.

| | MINT | NRMT |
|---|---|---|
| COMPLETE SET (10) | 200.00 | 90.00 |
| COMMON CARD (1-10) | 6.00 | 2.70 |
| ❑ 1 Adam Oates | 8.00 | 3.60 |
| ❑ 2 Jeremy Roenick | 10.00 | 4.50 |
| ❑ 3 Sergei Fedorov | 20.00 | 9.00 |
| ❑ 4 Wayne Gretzky | 60.00 | 27.00 |
| ❑ 5 Alexei Yashin | 6.00 | 2.70 |
| ❑ 6 Eric Lindros | 30.00 | 13.50 |
| ❑ 7 Ron Francis | 8.00 | 3.60 |
| ❑ 8 Mario Lemieux | 50.00 | 22.00 |
| ❑ 9 Joe Sakic | 20.00 | 9.00 |
| ❑ 10 Alexei Zhamnov | 8.00 | 3.60 |

## 1995-96 Emotion Xcited

This twenty-card set was the easiest pull from this issue, randomly inserted 1:3 packs. The set included many of the top offensive players in the game.

| | MINT | NRMT |
|---|---|---|
| COMPLETE SET (20) | 50.00 | 22.00 |
| COMMON CARD (1-20) | .50 | .23 |
| ❑ 1 Theoren Fleury | .75 | .35 |
| ❑ 2 Jeremy Roenick | 1.00 | .45 |
| ❑ 3 Mike Modano | 2.00 | .90 |
| ❑ 4 Sergei Fedorov | 3.00 | 1.35 |
| ❑ 5 Wayne Gretzky | 10.00 | 4.50 |
| ❑ 6 Brian Leetch | 1.00 | .45 |
| ❑ 7 Alexei Yashin | .50 | .23 |
| ❑ 8 Brett Hull | 2.00 | .90 |
| ❑ 9 Jaromir Jagr | 5.00 | 2.20 |
| ❑ 10 Mario Lemieux | 8.00 | 3.60 |
| ❑ 11 Ron Francis | .75 | .35 |
| ❑ 12 Keith Primeau | .75 | .35 |
| ❑ 13 Joe Sakic | 4.00 | 1.80 |
| ❑ 14 Peter Forsberg | 5.00 | 2.20 |
| ❑ 15 Paul Kariya | 6.00 | 2.70 |
| ❑ 16 Pavel Bure | 3.00 | 1.35 |
| ❑ 17 Alexei Zhamnov | .75 | .35 |
| ❑ 18 Martin Brodeur | 4.00 | 1.80 |
| ❑ 19 Jim Carey | .75 | .35 |
| ❑ 20 Chris Chelios | 1.00 | .45 |

## 1992-93 Enor Mark Messier

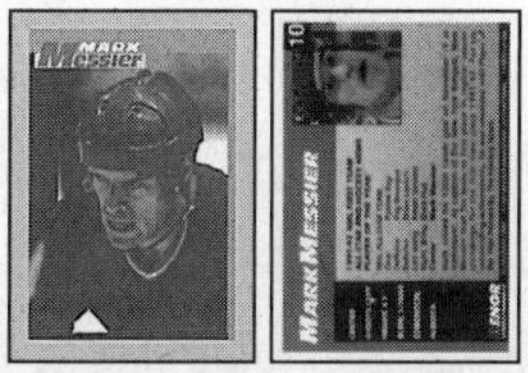

One card from this ten-card standard-size set was included in each specially marked package of Enor Progard Plus sportscard pages. The cards feature color player photos with silver borders. A red stripe that runs along the right edge and top of the photo accents the card face and provides a backdrop for the player's name, which is printed in white and blue. The horizontal back shows a close-up player photo that overlaps a red border stripe similar to the one on the front and a pale blue panel. The red stripe contains the player's name. The blue panel contains player information. A black vertical bar runs along the left edge of the panel and contains biographical information.

| | MINT | NRMT |
|---|---|---|
| COMPLETE SET (10) | 5.00 | 2.20 |
| COMMON MESSIER (1-10) | .50 | .23 |
| ❑ 1 Mark Messier | .50 | .23 |
| ❑ 2 Mark Messier | .50 | .23 |
| ❑ 3 Mark Messier | .50 | .23 |
| ❑ 4 Mark Messier | .50 | .23 |
| ❑ 5 Mark Messier | .50 | .23 |
| ❑ 6 Mark Messier | .50 | .23 |
| ❑ 7 Mark Messier | .50 | .23 |
| ❑ 8 Mark Messier | .50 | .23 |
| ❑ 9 Mark Messier | .50 | .23 |
| ❑ 10 Mark Messier | .50 | .23 |

## 1970-71 Esso Power Players

The 1970-71 Esso Power Players set includes 252 color stamps measuring approximately 1 1/2" by 2". The stamps were issued in six-stamp sheets and given away free with a minimum purchase of 3.00 of Esso gasoline. There were 18 stamps for each of the 14 teams then in the NHL. The stamps are

unnumbered except for jersey (uniform) number. The set was issued with an album, which can be found in either a soft or hard bound version. The hard cover album supposedly had extra pages with additional players. The stamps and albums are available in both French and English language versions. The set is numbered below numerically within each team as follows: Montreal Canadiens (1-18), Toronto Maple Leafs (19-36), Vancouver Canucks (37-54), Boston Bruins (55-72), Buffalo Sabres (73-90), California Golden Seals (91-108), Chicago Blackhawks (109-126), Detroit Red Wings (127-144), Los Angeles Kings (145-162), Minnesota North Stars (163-180), New York Rangers (181-198), Philadelphia Flyers (199-216), Pittsburgh Penguins (217-234), and St. Louis Blues (235-252). Supposedly there are 59 stamps which are tougher to find than the others. The short-printed stamps are apparently those players who were pre-printed into the soft-cover album and hence not included in the first stamp printing.

| | NRMT-MT | EXC |
|---|---|---|
| COMPLETE SET (252) | 200.00 | 90.00 |
| COMMON STAMP (1-252) | .40 | .18 |
| ❑ 1 Rogatien Vachon 1 | 3.00 | 1.35 |
| ❑ 2 Jacques Laperriere 2 | .75 | .35 |
| ❑ 3 J.C. Tremblay 3 | .50 | .23 |
| ❑ 4 Jean Beliveau 4 | 8.00 | 3.60 |
| ❑ 5 Guy Lapointe 5 | 1.00 | .45 |
| ❑ 6 Fran Huck 6 | .40 | .18 |
| ❑ 7 Bill Collins 10 | .40 | .18 |
| ❑ 8 Marc Tardif 11 | .50 | .23 |
| ❑ 9 Yvan Cournoyer 12 | 1.50 | .70 |
| ❑ 10 Claude Larose 15 | .40 | .18 |
| ❑ 11 Henri Richard 16 | 4.00 | 1.80 |
| ❑ 12 Serge Savard 18 | .75 | .35 |
| ❑ 13 Terry Harper 19 | .50 | .23 |
| ❑ 14 Pete Mahovlich 20 | .75 | .35 |
| ❑ 15 John Ferguson 22 | 1.00 | .45 |
| ❑ 16 Mickey Redmond 24 | 1.25 | .55 |
| ❑ 17 Jacques Lemaire 25 | 1.25 | .55 |
| ❑ 18 Phil Myre 30 | .75 | .35 |
| ❑ 19 Jacques Plante 1 | 8.00 | 3.60 |
| ❑ 20 Rick Ley 2 | .50 | .23 |
| ❑ 21 Mike Pelyk 4 | .40 | .18 |
| ❑ 22 Ron Ellis 6 | .50 | .23 |
| ❑ 23 Jim Dorey 8 | .40 | .18 |
| ❑ 24 Norm Ullman 9 | 2.00 | .90 |
| ❑ 25 Guy Trottier 11 | .40 | .18 |
| ❑ 26 Jim Harrison 12 | .40 | .18 |
| ❑ 27 Dave Keon 14 | 2.00 | .90 |
| ❑ 28 Mike Walton 16 | .50 | .23 |
| ❑ 29 Jim McKenny 18 | .40 | .18 |
| ❑ 30 Paul Henderson 19 | 1.00 | .45 |
| ❑ 31 Garry Monahan 20 SP | 1.00 | .45 |
| ❑ 32 Bob Baun 21 | .75 | .35 |
| ❑ 33 Bill MacMillan 23 | .40 | .18 |
| ❑ 34 Brian Glennie 24 | .40 | .18 |
| ❑ 35 Darryl Sittler 27 | 10.00 | 4.50 |
| ❑ 36 Bruce Gamble 30 | 1.00 | .45 |
| ❑ 37 Charlie Hodge 1 | 1.25 | .55 |
| ❑ 38 Gary Doak 2 | .40 | .18 |
| ❑ 39 Pat Quinn 3 | .75 | .35 |
| ❑ 40 Barry Wilkins 4 | .40 | .18 |
| ❑ 41 Darryl Sly 5 SP | 1.00 | .45 |
| ❑ 42 Marc Reaume 6 | .40 | .18 |
| ❑ 43 Andre Boudrias 7 | .40 | .18 |
| ❑ 44 Danny Johnson 8 | .40 | .18 |
| ❑ 45 Ray Cullen 10 SP | 1.00 | .45 |
| ❑ 46 Wayne Maki 11 | .40 | .18 |
| ❑ 47 Mike Corrigan 12 | .40 | .18 |
| ❑ 48 Rosaire Paiement 15 | .40 | .18 |
| ❑ 49 Paul Popiel 18 SP | .75 | .35 |
| ❑ 50 Dale Tallon 19 | .50 | .23 |
| ❑ 51 Murray Hall 23 SP | 1.00 | .45 |
| ❑ 52 Len Lunde 24 | .40 | .18 |
| ❑ 53 Orland Kurtenbach 25 | .50 | .23 |
| ❑ 54 Dunc Wilson 30 SP | 1.00 | .45 |
| ❑ 55 Ed Johnston 1 | 1.00 | .45 |
| ❑ 56 Bobby Orr 4 | 25.00 | 11.00 |
| ❑ 57 Ted Green 6 | .50 | .23 |
| ❑ 58 Phil Esposito 7 | 5.00 | 2.20 |
| ❑ 59 Ken Hodge 8 | .75 | .35 |
| ❑ 60 Johnny Bucyk 9 | 2.00 | .90 |
| ❑ 61 Rick Smith 10 SP | 1.00 | .45 |
| ❑ 62 Wayne Carleton 11 SP | 1.00 | .45 |
| ❑ 63 Wayne Cashman 12 SP | 1.50 | .70 |
| ❑ 64 Garnet Bailey 14 | .40 | .18 |
| ❑ 65 Derek Sanderson 16 | 4.00 | 1.80 |
| ❑ 66 Fred Stanfield 17 SP | 1.00 | .45 |
| ❑ 67 Ed Westfall 18 | .50 | .23 |
| ❑ 68 John McKenzie 19 | .40 | .18 |
| ❑ 69 Dallas Smith 20 | .40 | .18 |
| ❑ 70 Don Marcotte 21 | .40 | .18 |
| ❑ 71 Don Awrey 26 SP | 1.00 | .45 |
| ❑ 72 Gerry Cheevers 30 | 3.00 | 1.35 |
| ❑ 73 Roger Crozier 1 | 1.50 | .70 |
| ❑ 74 Jim Watson 2 | .50 | .23 |
| ❑ 75 Tracy Pratt 3 | .40 | .18 |
| ❑ 76 Doug Barrie 5 SP | 1.00 | .45 |
| ❑ 77 Al Hamilton 6 | .50 | .23 |
| ❑ 78 Cliff Schmautz 7 SP | 1.00 | .45 |
| ❑ 79 Reg Fleming 9 | .40 | .18 |
| ❑ 80 Phil Goyette 10 | .40 | .18 |
| ❑ 81 Gilbert Perreault 11 | 5.00 | 2.20 |
| ❑ 82 Skip Krake 12 | .40 | .18 |
| ❑ 83 Gerry Meehan 15 | .50 | .23 |
| ❑ 84 Ron Anderson 16 | .40 | .18 |
| ❑ 85 Floyd Smith 17 SP | 1.00 | .45 |
| ❑ 86 Steve Atkinson 19 | .40 | .18 |
| ❑ 87 Paul Andrea 21 SP | 1.00 | .45 |
| ❑ 88 Don Marshall 22 | .40 | .18 |
| ❑ 89 Eddie Shack 23 SP | 3.00 | 1.35 |
| ❑ 90 Larry Keenan 26 | .40 | .18 |
| ❑ 91 Gary Smith 1 | 1.00 | .45 |
| ❑ 92 Doug Roberts 2 | .40 | .18 |
| ❑ 93 Harry Howell 3 | 1.25 | .55 |
| ❑ 94 Wayne Muloin 4 | .40 | .18 |
| ❑ 95 Carol Vadnais 5 | .40 | .18 |
| ❑ 96 Dick Mattiussi 6 | .40 | .18 |
| ❑ 97 Earl Ingarfield 7 | .40 | .18 |
| ❑ 98 Gerry Ehman 8 | .40 | .18 |
| ❑ 99 Bill Hicke 9 | .40 | .18 |
| ❑ 100 Ted Hampson 10 | .40 | .18 |
| ❑ 101 Gary Jarrett 12 | .40 | .18 |
| ❑ 102 Joe Hardy 14 SP | 1.00 | .45 |
| ❑ 103 Tony Featherstone 16 SP | 1.00 | .45 |
| ❑ 104 Gary Croteau 18 | .40 | .18 |
| ❑ 105 Ernie Hicke 20 SP | 1.00 | .45 |
| ❑ 106 Ron Stackhouse 21 | .40 | .18 |
| ❑ 107 Dennis Hextall 22 SP | 1.50 | .70 |
| ❑ 108 Bob Sneddon 30 SP | 1.00 | .45 |
| ❑ 109 Gerry Desjardins 1 SP | 1.50 | .70 |
| ❑ 110 Bill White 2 | .50 | .23 |
| ❑ 111 Keith Magnuson 3 | .50 | .23 |
| ❑ 112 Doug Jarrett 4 SP | 1.00 | .45 |
| ❑ 113 Lou Angotti 6 | .40 | .18 |
| ❑ 114 Pit Martin 7 | .50 | .23 |
| ❑ 115 Jim Pappin 8 | .40 | .18 |
| ❑ 116 Bobby Hull 9 | 10.00 | 4.50 |
| ❑ 117 Dennis Hull 10 SP | 2.00 | .90 |
| ❑ 118 Doug Mohns 11 | .50 | .23 |
| ❑ 119 Pat Stapleton 12 | .50 | .23 |
| ❑ 120 Bryan Campbell 14 SP | 1.00 | .45 |
| ❑ 121 Eric Nesterenko 15 | .50 | .23 |
| ❑ 122 Chico Maki 16 | .50 | .23 |
| ❑ 123 Gerry Pinder 18 | .50 | .23 |
| ❑ 124 Cliff Koroll 20 | .40 | .18 |
| ❑ 125 Stan Mikita 21 | 6.00 | 2.70 |
| ❑ 126 Tony Esposito 35 | 6.00 | 2.70 |
| ❑ 127 Jim Rutherford 1 SP | 2.00 | .90 |
| ❑ 128 Gary Bergman 2 | .50 | .23 |
| ❑ 129 Dale Rolfe 3 | .40 | .18 |
| ❑ 130 Larry Brown 4 SP | 1.00 | .45 |
| ❑ 131 Serge Lajeunesse 5 | .40 | .18 |
| ❑ 132 Garry Unger 7 | .75 | .35 |
| ❑ 133 Tom Webster 8 | .50 | .23 |
| ❑ 134 Gordie Howe 9 | 15.00 | 6.75 |
| ❑ 135 Alex Delvecchio 10 | 2.00 | .90 |
| ❑ 136 Don Luce 11 SP | 1.00 | .45 |
| ❑ 137 Bruce MacGregor 12 | .40 | .18 |
| ❑ 138 Nick Libett 14 | .50 | .23 |
| ❑ 139 Al Karlander 15 | .40 | .18 |
| ❑ 140 Ron Harris 16 | .40 | .18 |
| ❑ 141 Wayne Connelly 17 SP | 1.00 | .45 |
| ❑ 142 Billy Dea 21 SP | 1.00 | .45 |
| ❑ 143 Frank Mahovlich 27 | 4.00 | 1.80 |
| ❑ 144 Roy Edwards 30 | .75 | .35 |
| ❑ 145 Jack Norris 1 | .40 | .18 |
| ❑ 146 Dale Hoganson 2 | .40 | .18 |
| ❑ 147 Larry Cahan 3 | .40 | .18 |
| ❑ 148 Gilles Marotte 4 SP | 1.00 | .45 |
| ❑ 149 Noel Price 5 SP | 1.00 | .45 |
| ❑ 150 Paul Curtis 6 SP | 1.00 | .45 |
| ❑ 151 Ross Lonsberry 8 | .40 | .18 |
| ❑ 152 Gord Labossiere 9 | .40 | .18 |
| ❑ 153 Doug Robinson 11 SP | 1.00 | .45 |
| ❑ 154 Larry Mickey 12 | .40 | .18 |
| ❑ 155 Juha Widing 15 | .40 | .18 |
| ❑ 156 Eddie Joyal 16 | .40 | .18 |
| ❑ 157 Bill Flett 17 | .40 | .18 |
| ❑ 158 Bob Berry 18 | .50 | .23 |
| ❑ 159 Bob Pulford 20 | .75 | .35 |
| ❑ 160 Matt Ravlich 21 | .40 | .18 |
| ❑ 161 Mike Byers 24 SP | 1.00 | .45 |
| ❑ 162 Denis DeJordy 30 | 1.00 | .45 |
| ❑ 163 Gump Worsley 1 | 4.00 | 1.80 |
| ❑ 164 Barry Gibbs 2 SP | 1.00 | .45 |
| ❑ 165 Fred Barrett 3 | .40 | .18 |
| ❑ 166 Ted Harris 4 | .40 | .18 |
| ❑ 167 Danny O'Shea 7 | .40 | .18 |
| ❑ 168 Bill Goldsworthy 8 | .50 | .23 |
| ❑ 169 Charlie Burns 9 | .40 | .18 |
| ❑ 170 Murray Oliver 10 | .40 | .18 |
| ❑ 171 Jean-Paul Parise 11 | .50 | .23 |
| ❑ 172 Tom Williams 12 SP | 1.00 | .45 |
| ❑ 173 Bobby Rousseau 15 | .50 | .23 |
| ❑ 174 Buster Harvey 18 SP | 1.00 | .45 |
| ❑ 175 Tom Reid 20 SP | 1.00 | .45 |
| ❑ 176 Danny Grant 21 | .50 | .23 |
| ❑ 177 Walt McKechnie 22 | .40 | .18 |
| ❑ 178 Lou Nanne 23 | .50 | .23 |
| ❑ 179 Danny Lawson 24 SP | 1.00 | .45 |
| ❑ 180 Cesare Maniago 30 | 1.00 | .45 |
| ❑ 181 Ed Giacomin 1 | 3.00 | 1.35 |
| ❑ 182 Brad Park 2 | 5.00 | 2.20 |
| ❑ 183 Tim Horton 3 | 5.00 | 2.20 |
| ❑ 184 Arnie Brown 4 | .40 | .18 |
| ❑ 185 Rod Gilbert 7 | 1.50 | .70 |
| ❑ 186 Bob Nevin 8 | .40 | .18 |
| ❑ 187 Bill Fairbairn 10 SP | 1.00 | .45 |
| ❑ 188 Vic Hadfield 11 | .50 | .23 |
| ❑ 189 Ron Stewart 12 | .50 | .23 |
| ❑ 190 Jim Neilson 15 | .50 | .23 |
| ❑ 191 Rod Seiling 16 SP | 1.00 | .45 |
| ❑ 192 Dave Balon 17 SP | 1.00 | .45 |
| ❑ 193 Walt Tkaczuk 18 | .50 | .23 |
| ❑ 194 Jean Ratelle 19 | 1.50 | .70 |
| ❑ 195 Jack Egers 20 | .40 | .18 |
| ❑ 196 Pete Stemkowski 21 SP | 1.00 | .45 |
| ❑ 197 Ted Irvine 27 | .40 | .18 |
| ❑ 198 Gilles Villemure 30 | 1.00 | .45 |
| ❑ 199 Doug Favell 1 | 1.50 | .70 |
| ❑ 200 Ed Van Impe 2 | .40 | .18 |
| ❑ 201 Larry Hillman 3 | .40 | .18 |
| ❑ 202 Barry Ashbee 4 | .75 | .35 |
| ❑ 203 Wayne Hillman 6 SP | 1.00 | .45 |
| ❑ 204 Andre Lacroix 7 | .50 | .23 |
| ❑ 205 Lew Morrison 8 | .40 | .18 |
| ❑ 206 Bob Kelly 9 SP | 1.00 | .45 |
| ❑ 207 Jean-Guy Gendron 11 | .40 | .18 |
| ❑ 208 Gary Dornhoefer 12 | .75 | .35 |
| ❑ 209 Joe Watson 14 | .40 | .18 |
| ❑ 210 Garry Peters 15 SP | 1.00 | .45 |
| ❑ 211 Bobby Clarke 16 | 10.00 | 4.50 |
| ❑ 212 Earl Heiskala 19 SP | 1.00 | .45 |
| ❑ 213 Jim Johnson 20 | .40 | .18 |
| ❑ 214 Serge Bernier 21 | .40 | .18 |
| ❑ 215 Larry Hale 23 SP | 1.00 | .45 |
| ❑ 216 Bernie Parent 30 | 5.00 | 2.20 |
| ❑ 217 Al Smith 1 | .75 | .35 |
| ❑ 218 Duane Rupp 2 | .40 | .18 |
| ❑ 219 Bob Woytowich 3 | .40 | .18 |
| ❑ 220 Bob Blackburn 4 | .40 | .18 |
| ❑ 221 Bryan Watson 5 SP | 1.00 | .45 |
| ❑ 222 Dunc McCallum 6 | .50 | .23 |
| ❑ 223 Bryan Hextall 7 | .50 | .23 |
| ❑ 224 Andy Bathgate 9 SP | 2.50 | 1.10 |
| ❑ 225 Keith McCreary 10 SP | 1.00 | .45 |
| ❑ 226 Nick Harbaruk 11 | .40 | .18 |
| ❑ 227 Ken Schinkel 12 | .40 | .18 |
| ❑ 228 Glen Sather 16 SP | 2.50 | 1.10 |
| ❑ 229 Ron Schock 17 | .40 | .18 |
| ❑ 230 Wally Boyer 18 | .40 | .18 |
| ❑ 231 Jean Pronovost 19 | .50 | .23 |
| ❑ 232 Dean Prentice 20 | .50 | .23 |
| ❑ 233 Jim Morrison 27 | .40 | .18 |
| ❑ 234 Les Binkley 30 SP | 1.50 | .70 |
| ❑ 235 Glenn Hall 1 | 4.00 | 1.80 |
| ❑ 236 Bob Wall 2 | .40 | .18 |
| ❑ 237 Noel Picard 4 | .40 | .18 |
| ❑ 238 Bob Plager 5 | .50 | .23 |
| ❑ 239 Jim Roberts 6 | .50 | .23 |
| ❑ 240 Red Berenson 7 | .50 | .23 |
| ❑ 241 Barclay Plager 8 | .50 | .23 |
| ❑ 242 Frank St.Marseille 9 | .40 | .18 |
| ❑ 243 George Morrison 10 SP | 1.00 | .45 |
| ❑ 244 Gary Sabourin 11 | .40 | .18 |
| ❑ 245 Terry Crisp 12 SP | 2.00 | .90 |
| ❑ 246 Tim Ecclestone 14 | .40 | .18 |
| ❑ 247 Bill McCreary 15 | .40 | .18 |
| ❑ 248 Brit Selby 18 SP | 1.00 | .45 |
| ❑ 249 Jim Lorentz 19 SP | 1.00 | .45 |
| ❑ 250 Ab McDonald 20 | .40 | .18 |
| ❑ 251 Chris Bordeleau 21 SP | 1.00 | .45 |
| ❑ 252 Ernie Wakely 31 | 1.00 | .45 |
| ❑ xx Soft Cover Album | 15.00 | 6.75 |
| ❑ xx Hard Cover Album | 50.00 | 22.00 |

## 1983-84 Esso

The 1983-84 Esso set contains 21 color cards measuring approximately 4 1/2" by 3" although the player photo portion of the card is only 2" by 3". There are actually two different sets, one in French and one in English. The cards are actually part of a lottery-type game where 5000.00 cash could be won instantly via a scratch-off. The card backs contain information about the contest on the back of the contest portion and player statistics on the back of the player photo portion of the card. The cards are unnumbered and hence they are checklisted below alphabetically. There is very little difference in availability of the English set as opposed to the French set; however there seems to be a slight premium on the French set over the English set of about 20 percent over the prices listed below.

| | MINT | NRMT |
|---|---|---|
| COMPLETE SET (21) | 15.00 | 6.75 |
| COMMON CARD (1-21) | .50 | .23 |
| ❑ 1 Glenn Anderson | 1.00 | .45 |
| ❑ 2 John Anderson | .50 | .23 |
| ❑ 3 Dave Babych | .50 | .23 |
| ❑ 4 Richard Brodeur | 1.00 | .45 |
| ❑ 5 Paul Coffey | 4.00 | 1.80 |
| ❑ 6 Bill Derlago | .50 | .23 |
| ❑ 7 Bob Gainey | 1.50 | .70 |
| ❑ 8 Michel Goulet | 1.00 | .45 |
| ❑ 9 Dale Hawerchuk | 2.00 | .90 |
| ❑ 10 Dale Hunter | .75 | .35 |
| ❑ 11 Morris Lukowich | .50 | .23 |
| ❑ 12 Lanny McDonald | 1.50 | .70 |
| ❑ 13 Mark Messier | 5.00 | 2.20 |
| ❑ 14 Jim Peplinski | .50 | .23 |
| ❑ 15 Paul Reinhart | .50 | .23 |

| | | |
|---|---|---|
| ❑ 16 Larry Robinson | 1.25 | .55 |
| ❑ 17 Stan Smyl | .75 | .35 |
| ❑ 18 Harold Snepsts | .75 | .35 |
| ❑ 19 Marc Tardif | .50 | .23 |
| ❑ 20 Mario Tremblay | .50 | .23 |
| ❑ 21 Rick Vaive | .75 | .35 |

## 1988-89 Esso All-Stars

The 1988-89 Esso All-Stars set contains 48 color cards (actually adhesive-backed "stickers") measuring approximately 2 1/8" by 3 1/4". The fronts feature borderless color action photos with facsimile autographs. The backs have complete checklists for the whole set. The players depicted include hockey greats from the past and present. The cards (stickers) are unnumbered and hence are checklisted below in alphabetical order. There is a 32-page album (8 1/2" by 11") available in either English or French, which was intended to hold the stickers. In fact each album already contains five pasted-in cards, Ed Giacomin, Al MacInnis, Rick Middleton, Bernie Parent, and Pierre Pilote. The cards were distributed in Canada in packs of six with a purchase of gasoline at participating Esso service stations. The complete set price below includes the album.

| | MINT | NRMT |
|---|---|---|
| COMPLETE SET (48) | 15.00 | 6.75 |
| COMMON CARD (1-48) | .20 | .09 |
| ❑ 1 Jean Beliveau | .75 | .35 |
| ❑ 2 Mike Bossy | .75 | .35 |
| ❑ 3 Ray Bourque | .75 | .35 |
| ❑ 4 Johnny Bower | .35 | .16 |
| ❑ 5 Bobby Clarke | .50 | .23 |
| ❑ 6 Paul Coffey | .75 | .35 |
| ❑ 7 Yvan Cournoyer | .25 | .11 |
| ❑ 8 Marcel Dionne | .35 | .16 |
| ❑ 9 Ken Dryden | 1.00 | .45 |
| ❑ 10 Phil Esposito | .75 | .35 |
| ❑ 11 Tony Esposito | .50 | .23 |
| ❑ 12 Grant Fuhr | .35 | .16 |
| ❑ 13 Clark Gillies | .20 | .09 |
| ❑ 14 Michel Goulet | .25 | .11 |
| ❑ 15 Wayne Gretzky | 4.00 | 1.80 |
| ❑ 16 Dale Hawerchuk | .25 | .11 |
| ❑ 17 Ron Hextall | .35 | .16 |
| ❑ 18 Gordie Howe | 1.50 | .70 |
| ❑ 19 Mark Howe | .20 | .09 |
| ❑ 20 Bobby Hull | .75 | .35 |
| ❑ 21 Tim Kerr | .20 | .09 |
| ❑ 22 Jari Kurri | .25 | .11 |
| ❑ 23 Guy Lafleur | .75 | .35 |
| ❑ 24 Rod Langway | .20 | .09 |
| ❑ 25 Jacques Laperriere | .20 | .09 |
| ❑ 26 Guy Lapointe | .25 | .11 |
| ❑ 27 Mario Lemieux | 2.50 | 1.10 |
| ❑ 28 Frank Mahovlich | .50 | .23 |
| ❑ 29 Lanny McDonald | .25 | .11 |
| ❑ 30 Mark Messier | 1.00 | .45 |
| ❑ 31 Stan Mikita | .50 | .23 |
| ❑ 32 Mats Naslund | .20 | .09 |
| ❑ 33 Bobby Orr | 2.00 | .90 |
| ❑ 34 Brad Park | .25 | .11 |
| ❑ 35 Gilbert Perreault | .25 | .11 |
| ❑ 36 Denis Potvin | .25 | .11 |
| ❑ 37 Larry Robinson | .25 | .11 |
| ❑ 38 Luc Robitaille | .50 | .23 |
| ❑ 39 Borje Salming | .20 | .09 |
| ❑ 40 Denis Savard | .25 | .11 |
| ❑ 41 Serge Savard | .25 | .11 |
| ❑ 42 Steve Shutt | .25 | .11 |
| ❑ 43 Darryl Sittler | .25 | .11 |
| ❑ 44 Billy Smith | .25 | .11 |
| ❑ 45 John Tonelli | .20 | .09 |
| ❑ 46 Bryan Trottier | .25 | .11 |
| ❑ 47 Norm Ullman | .25 | .11 |
| ❑ 48 Gump Worsley | .50 | .23 |
| ❑ xx Album | 3.00 | 1.35 |

## 1997-98 Esso Olympic Hockey Heroes

These oversized cards feature color action photos on the front, along with biographical information on the back. Each player is pictured in his or her respective olympic uniform. The set was available in six series from Esso gas stations and comes complete with a black binder.

| | MINT | NRMT |
|---|---|---|
| COMPLETE SET (60) | 25.00 | 11.00 |
| COMMON CARD (1-60) | .10 | .05 |
| *FRENCH VERSION: 1X TO 1.5X BASIC CARDS | | |
| ❑ 1 Header Card | .10 | .05 |
| ❑ 2 Olympic Hockey History | .10 | .05 |
| ❑ 3 CBC Broadcast Guide | .10 | .05 |
| ❑ 4 Olympic Hockey Bracket | .10 | .05 |
| ❑ 5 Team Canada | .10 | .05 |
| ❑ 6 Eric Lindros | 2.00 | .90 |
| ❑ 7 Joe Sakic | 1.50 | .70 |
| ❑ 8 Trevor Linden | .40 | .18 |
| ❑ 9 Paul Kariya | 2.00 | .90 |
| ❑ 10 Brendan Shanahan | 1.00 | .45 |
| ❑ 11 Rod Brind'Amour | .40 | .18 |
| ❑ 12 Theoren Fleury | .40 | .18 |
| ❑ 13 Eric Desjardins | .25 | .11 |
| ❑ 14 Scott Niedermayer | .25 | .11 |
| ❑ 15 Chris Pronger | .40 | .18 |
| ❑ 16 Rob Blake | .25 | .11 |
| ❑ 17 Patrick Roy | 2.50 | 1.10 |
| ❑ 18 Curtis Joseph | .50 | .23 |
| ❑ 19 Keith Primeau | .40 | .18 |
| ❑ 20 Mark Messier | .75 | .35 |
| ❑ 21 Adam Foote | .25 | .11 |
| ❑ 22 Team USA | .10 | .05 |
| ❑ 23 Keith Tkachuk | .60 | .25 |
| ❑ 24 Mike Modano | .50 | .23 |
| ❑ 25 John LeClair | .75 | .35 |
| ❑ 26 Doug Weight | .40 | .18 |
| ❑ 27 Brett Hull | .60 | .25 |
| ❑ 28 Jeremy Roenick | .50 | .23 |
| ❑ 29 Brian Leetch | .50 | .23 |
| ❑ 30 Chris Chelios | .50 | .23 |
| ❑ 31 Kevin Hatcher | .25 | .11 |
| ❑ 32 Derian Hatcher | .25 | .11 |
| ❑ 33 Mike Richter | .50 | .23 |
| ❑ 34 John Vanbiesbrouck | 1.00 | .45 |
| ❑ 35 Team Russia | .10 | .05 |
| ❑ 36 Sergei Fedorov | 1.00 | .45 |
| ❑ 37 Alexei Yashin | .40 | .18 |
| ❑ 38 Pavel Bure | 1.00 | .45 |
| ❑ 39 Alexander Mogilny | .40 | .18 |
| ❑ 40 Nikolai Khabibulin | .40 | .18 |
| ❑ 41 Team Sweden | .10 | .05 |
| ❑ 42 Mats Sundin | .50 | .23 |
| ❑ 43 Peter Forsberg | 1.50 | .70 |
| ❑ 44 Daniel Alfredsson | .40 | .18 |
| ❑ 45 Nicklas Lidstrom | .40 | .18 |
| ❑ 46 Kenny Jonsson | .25 | .11 |
| ❑ 47 Team Finland | .10 | .05 |
| ❑ 48 Saku Koivu | 1.00 | .45 |
| ❑ 49 Esa Tikkanen | .40 | .18 |
| ❑ 50 Teemu Selanne | 1.00 | .45 |
| ❑ 51 Team Czech Republic | .10 | .05 |
| ❑ 52 Jaromir Jagr | 1.50 | .70 |
| ❑ 53 Roman Hamrlik | .40 | .18 |
| ❑ 54 Dominik Hasek | 1.00 | .45 |
| ❑ 55 Women's Team Canada | .10 | .05 |
| ❑ 56 Nancy Drolet | .40 | .18 |
| ❑ 57 Geraldine Heaney | .40 | .18 |
| ❑ 58 Hayley Wickenheiser | .40 | .18 |
| ❑ 59 Cassie Campbell | .40 | .18 |
| ❑ 60 Stacy Wilson | .40 | .18 |
| ❑ NNO E.Lindros AU | .10 | .05 |

## 1948-52 Exhibits Canadian

These cards measure approximately 3 1/4" by 5 1/4" and were issued on heavy cardboard stock. The cards show full-bleed photos with the player's name burned in toward the bottom. The hockey exhibit cards are generally considered more scarce than their baseball exhibit counterparts. Since the cards are unnumbered, the set is arranged below alphabetically within teams as follows: Montreal (1-27), Toronto (28-42), Detroit (43-46), Boston (47-48), Chicago (49-50), and New York (51). The set closes with an Action subset (52-65).

| | EX-MT | VG-E |
|---|---|---|
| COMPLETE SET (65) | 1500.00 | 700.00 |
| COMMON CARD (1-65) | 10.00 | 4.50 |
| ❑ 1 Reggie Abbott | 10.00 | 4.50 |
| ❑ 2 Jean Beliveau | 75.00 | 34.00 |
| ❑ 3 Jean Beliveau (Aces' captain) | 100.00 | 45.00 |
| ❑ 4 Toe Blake | 40.00 | 18.00 |
| ❑ 5 Butch Bouchard | 20.00 | 9.00 |
| ❑ 6 Bob Fillion | 10.00 | 4.50 |
| ❑ 7 Dick Gamble | 15.00 | 6.75 |
| ❑ 8 Bernie Geoffrion | 50.00 | 22.00 |
| ❑ 9 Doug Harvey | 40.00 | 18.00 |
| ❑ 10 Tom Johnson | 20.00 | 9.00 |
| ❑ 11 Elmer Lach | 40.00 | 18.00 |
| ❑ 12 Hal Laycoe | 10.00 | 4.50 |
| ❑ 13 Jacques Locas | 10.00 | 4.50 |
| ❑ 14 Bud McPherson | 10.00 | 4.50 |
| ❑ 15 Paul Maznick | 10.00 | 4.50 |
| ❑ 16 Gerry McNeil | 40.00 | 18.00 |
| ❑ 17 Paul Meger | 10.00 | 4.50 |
| ❑ 18 Dickie Moore | 40.00 | 18.00 |
| ❑ 19 Ken Mosdell | 12.00 | 5.50 |
| ❑ 20 Bert Olmstead | 20.00 | 9.00 |
| ❑ 21 Ken Reardon | 25.00 | 11.00 |
| ❑ 22 Billy Reay | 15.00 | 6.75 |
| ❑ 23 Maurice Richard (Stick on ice) | 80.00 | 36.00 |
| ❑ 24 Maurice Richard (Stairs in back ground) | 80.00 | 36.00 |
| ❑ 25 Dollard St.Laurent | 15.00 | 6.75 |
| ❑ 26 Grant Warwick | 10.00 | 4.50 |
| ❑ 27 Floyd Curry | 15.00 | 6.75 |
| ❑ 28 Bill Barilko | 40.00 | 18.00 |
| ❑ 29 Turk Broda | 40.00 | 18.00 |
| ❑ 30 Cal Gardner | 20.00 | 9.00 |
| ❑ 31 Bill Juzda | 10.00 | 4.50 |
| ❑ 32 Ted Kennedy | 40.00 | 18.00 |
| ❑ 33 Joe Klukay | 10.00 | 4.50 |
| ❑ 34 Fleming Mackell | 12.00 | 5.50 |
| ❑ 35 Howie Meeker | 30.00 | 13.50 |
| ❑ 36 Gus Mortson | 10.00 | 4.50 |
| ❑ 37 Al Rollins | 25.00 | 11.00 |
| ❑ 38 Sid Smith | 15.00 | 6.75 |
| ❑ 39 Tod Sloan | 10.00 | 4.50 |
| ❑ 40 Ray Timgren | 10.00 | 4.50 |
| ❑ 41 Jim Thomson | 10.00 | 4.50 |
| ❑ 42 Max Bentley | 25.00 | 11.00 |
| ❑ 43 Sid Abel | 20.00 | 9.00 |
| ❑ 44 Gordie Howe | 125.00 | 55.00 |
| ❑ 45 Ted Lindsay | 50.00 | 22.00 |
| ❑ 46 Harry Lumley | 40.00 | 18.00 |
| ❑ 47 Jack Gelineau | 10.00 | 4.50 |
| ❑ 48 Paul Ronty | 10.00 | 4.50 |
| ❑ 49 Doug Bentley | 25.00 | 11.00 |
| ❑ 50 Roy Conacher | 15.00 | 6.75 |
| ❑ 51 Chuck Rayner | 25.00 | 11.00 |
| ❑ 52 Boston vs. Montreal (In front of net; 23 of Boston visible) | 20.00 | 9.00 |
| ❑ 53 Detroit vs. New York (Howe and Ranger on goal line on ice) | 60.00 | 27.00 |
| ❑ 54 Montreal vs. Toronto (Richard shooting puck past Toronto goalie) | 50.00 | 22.00 |
| ❑ 55 New York vs. Montreal (Richard is on goalie) | 50.00 | 22.00 |
| ❑ 56 New York vs. Montreal (Open net; 9 of Rangers on ice) | 20.00 | 9.00 |
| ❑ 57 Montreal vs. Boston (Ref and several players in front of Boston goal) | 20.00 | 9.00 |
| ❑ 58 Detroit vs. Montreal (Two Canadiens in front of Detroit goalie) | 20.00 | 9.00 |
| ❑ 59 Chicago vs. Montreal (5 Blackhawks and 2 Canadiens on ice in front of goalie) | 20.00 | 9.00 |
| ❑ 60 New York vs. Montreal (Richard and Elmer Lach in front of Ranger and Rayner) | 40.00 | 18.00 |
| ❑ 61 Chicago vs. Montreal (5 Geoffrion shooting at Chicago goalie) | 30.00 | 13.50 |
| ❑ 62 Detroit vs. Montreal (Sawchuk saves against 8) | 40.00 | 18.00 |
| ❑ 63 Detroit vs. Montreal (Canadiens score) | 20.00 | 9.00 |
| ❑ 64 Toronto vs. Montreal (Canadiens score) | 20.00 | 9.00 |
| ❑ 65 Chicago vs. Montreal (Canadiens score) | 20.00 | 9.00 |

## 1995-96 Fanfest Phil Esposito

This five-card set was sponsored by the five licensed card companies (Donruss, Fleer/Skybox, Pinnacle, Topps, and Upper Deck) who each produced one card for distribution at the 1996 All-Star Game Fanfest, which was held in Boston. The fronts feature color action photos of Phil Esposito in designs unique to each manufacturer. The backs carry information about the legendary Bruin great.

| | MINT | NRMT |
|---|---|---|
| COMPLETE SET (5) | 30.00 | 13.50 |
| COMMON ESPO (1-5) | 6.00 | 2.70 |
| ❑ 1 Phil Esposito Donruss | 6.00 | 2.70 |
| ❑ 2 Phil Esposito Emotion | 6.00 | 2.70 |
| ❑ 3 Phil Esposito Pinnacle | 6.00 | 2.70 |
| ❑ 4 Phil Esposito Topps | 6.00 | 2.70 |
| ❑ 5 Phil Esposito Upper Deck | 6.00 | 2.70 |

## 1972-73 Fighting Saints Postcards WHA

Borderless postcards featuring action photos on the front. Cards also features players name and biographical information.

| | MINT | NRMT |
|---|---|---|
| COMPLETE SET (25) | 70.00 | 32.00 |
| COMMON CARD | 3.00 | 1.35 |
| ❑ 1 Mike Antonovich | 4.00 | 1.80 |
| ❑ 2 John Arbour | 3.00 | 1.35 |
| ❑ 3 Terry Ball | 3.00 | 1.35 |
| ❑ 4 Keith Christiansen | 3.00 | 1.35 |
| ❑ 5 Wayne Connelly | 5.00 | 2.20 |
| ❑ 6 Mike Curran | 3.00 | 1.35 |
| ❑ 7 Craig Falkman | 3.00 | 1.35 |
| ❑ 8 Ted Hampson | 4.00 | 1.80 |
| ❑ 9 Jimmy Johnson | 3.00 | 1.35 |
| ❑ 10 Bill Klatt | 3.00 | 1.35 |
| ❑ 11 George Konik | 3.00 | 1.35 |
| ❑ 12 Leonard Lilyholm | 3.00 | 1.35 |
| ❑ 13 Bob MacMillan | 3.00 | 1.35 |
| ❑ 14 Jack McCartan | 5.00 | 2.20 |
| ❑ 15 Mike McMahon | 3.00 | 1.35 |
| ❑ 16 George Morrison | 3.00 | 1.35 |
| ❑ 17 Dick Paradise | 3.00 | 1.35 |
| ❑ 18 Mel Pearson | 3.00 | 1.35 |
| ❑ 19 Terry Ryan | 3.00 | 1.35 |
| ❑ 20 Blaine Rydman | 3.00 | 1.35 |
| ❑ 21 Frank Sanders | 3.00 | 1.35 |
| ❑ 22 Glen Sonmor CO | 3.00 | 1.35 |
| ❑ 23 Fred Speck | 3.00 | 1.35 |
| ❑ 24 Bill Young | 3.00 | 1.35 |
| ❑ 25 Carl Wetzel | 3.00 | 1.35 |

## 1974-75 Fighting Saints WHA

This 23 card set measures 3 1/2" x 5 1/2" and features borderless color action photos on the front. Backs feature a head shot and statistics, along with the players position. The Saints logo can be found in black along the top of card back.

| | MINT | NRMT |
|---|---|---|
| COMPLETE SET (23) | 50.00 | 22.00 |
| COMMON CARD (1-23) | 3.00 | 1.35 |
| ❑ 1 Mike Antonovich | 4.00 | 1.80 |
| ❑ 2 John Arbour | 3.00 | 1.35 |
| ❑ 3 Terry Ball (unconfirmed) | | |
| ❑ 4 Bob Boyd (unconfirmed) | | |
| ❑ 5 Ron Busniuk | 3.00 | 1.35 |
| ❑ 6 Wayne Connelly | 4.00 | 1.80 |
| ❑ 7 Mike Curran | 3.00 | 1.35 |
| ❑ 8 Gord Gallant | 4.00 | 1.80 |
| ❑ 9 Gary Gambucci | 3.00 | 1.35 |
| ❑ 10 John Garrett | 10.00 | 4.50 |
| ❑ 11 Ted Hampson | 4.00 | 1.80 |
| ❑ 12 Murray Heatley | 3.00 | 1.35 |
| ❑ 13 Fran Huck | 3.00 | 1.35 |
| ❑ 14 Jim Johnson | 3.00 | 1.35 |
| ❑ 15 Jack McCartan (unconfirmed) | | |
| ❑ 16 Mike McMahon | 3.00 | 1.35 |
| ❑ 17 George Morrison (unconfirmed) | | |
| ❑ 18 Harry Neale (unconfirmed) | | |
| ❑ 19 Danny O'Shea (unconfirmed) | | |
| ❑ 20 Rich Smith | 3.00 | 1.35 |
| ❑ 21 Glen Sonmor (unconfirmed) | | |
| ❑ 22 Don Tannahill (unconfirmed) | | |
| ❑ 23 Mike Walton | 5.00 | 2.20 |

## 1994-95 Finest

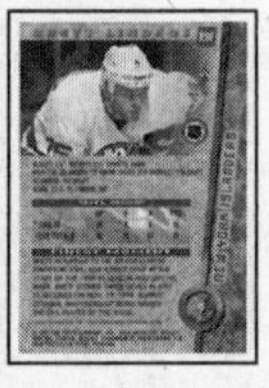

This 165-card super-premium set was issued in seven-card packs, in 24-pack boxes. The cards feature a blue marbleized foil border with a centered player photo. The player's last name only, along with the Finest logo, dominates the top of the front. The card fronts also feature a clear protective peel-off coating which was designed to prevent scratches and other damage to the card. Values below reflect unpeeled cards, although hobby opinions on whether to leave the coating intact or remove it vary. Collectors are advised to make a decision based on their own preference. Card backs have player photos, brief stats, and a recap of that player's finest moment. Card numbers 5, 56, 68, and 99 have wrong photos and player names on the back. These were corrected only in the '94-95 Finest Super Team Stanley Cup Winner Redemption set. A World Junior players subset is included (112-165). Rookie cards in the set include Bryan Berard, Radek Bonk, Eric Daze, Miikka Elomo, Eric Fichaud, Sean Haggerty, Ed Jovanovski, Ryan Smyth, Jeff O'Neill and Wade Redden.

| | MINT | NRMT |
|---|---|---|
| COMPLETE SET (165) | 70.00 | 32.00 |
| COMMON CARD (1-165) | .25 | .11 |
| ❑ 1 Peter Forsberg | 5.00 | 2.20 |
| ❑ 2 Oleg Tverdovsky | 1.25 | .55 |
| ❑ 3 Radek Bonk | .75 | .35 |
| ❑ 4 Brian Rolston | .25 | .11 |
| ❑ 5 Kenny Jonsson UER (Alexei Yashin photo on back) | .25 | .11 |
| ❑ 6 Patrik Juhlin | .25 | .11 |
| ❑ 7 Paul Kariya | 5.00 | 2.20 |
| ❑ 8 Janne Laukkanen | .25 | .11 |
| ❑ 9 Brett Lindros | .25 | .11 |
| ❑ 10 Andrei Nikolishin | .25 | .11 |
| ❑ 11 Jeff Friesen | .50 | .23 |
| ❑ 12 Jamie Storr | .50 | .23 |
| ❑ 13 Chris Therien | .25 | .11 |
| ❑ 14 Alexander Cherbayev | .25 | .11 |
| ❑ 15 Kevin Brown | .25 | .11 |
| ❑ 16 Mark Messier | 2.00 | .90 |
| ❑ 17 Kevin Hatcher | .25 | .11 |
| ❑ 18 Scott Stevens | .50 | .23 |
| ❑ 19 Keith Tkachuk | 1.50 | .70 |
| ❑ 20 Guy Hebert | .50 | .23 |
| ❑ 21 Jason Arnott | 1.25 | .55 |
| ❑ 22 Cam Neely | .50 | .23 |
| ❑ 23 Adam Graves | .50 | .23 |
| ❑ 24 Pavel Bure | 2.50 | 1.10 |
| ❑ 25 Mark Tinordi | .25 | .11 |
| ❑ 26 Felix Potvin | 1.25 | .55 |
| ❑ 27 Nikolai Khabibulin | .50 | .23 |
| ❑ 28 Theoren Fleury | .50 | .23 |
| ❑ 29 Curtis Joseph | 1.25 | .55 |
| ❑ 30 Patrick Roy | 6.00 | 2.70 |
| ❑ 31 Adam Deadmarsh | .50 | .23 |
| ❑ 32 Pat Falloon | .25 | .11 |
| ❑ 33 Jaromir Jagr | 4.00 | 1.80 |
| ❑ 34 Chris Chelios | 1.25 | .55 |
| ❑ 35 Ray Bourque | 1.25 | .55 |
| ❑ 36 Mike Vernon | .50 | .23 |
| ❑ 37 Steve Thomas | .25 | .11 |
| ❑ 38 Eric Lindros | 4.00 | 1.80 |
| ❑ 39 Dave Andreychuk | .50 | .23 |
| ❑ 40 John Vanbiesbrouck | 2.00 | .90 |
| ❑ 41 Wayne Gretzky | 8.00 | 3.60 |
| ❑ 42 Brett Hull | 2.00 | .90 |
| ❑ 43 Dominik Hasek | 3.00 | 1.35 |
| ❑ 44 Kirk Muller | .25 | .11 |
| ❑ 45 Rob Blake | .25 | .11 |
| ❑ 46 Viktor Kozlov | .25 | .11 |
| ❑ 47 Todd Harvey | .50 | .23 |
| ❑ 48 Valeri Bure | .50 | .23 |
| ❑ 49 Brian Leetch | 1.25 | .55 |
| ❑ 50 Ray Sheppard | .50 | .23 |
| ❑ 51 Ed Belfour | 1.25 | .55 |
| ❑ 52 Rick Tocchet | .50 | .23 |
| ❑ 53 Daren Puppa | .50 | .23 |
| ❑ 54 Russ Courtnall | .25 | .11 |
| ❑ 55 Jason Allison | .25 | .11 |
| ❑ 56 Alexei Yashin UER (Kenny Jonsson photo on back) | .50 | .23 |
| ❑ 57 Sandis Ozolinsh | .50 | .23 |
| ❑ 58 Chris Gratton | .50 | .23 |
| ❑ 59 Mike Peca | .25 | .11 |
| ❑ 60 Glen Wesley | .25 | .11 |
| ❑ 61 Kirk McLean | .50 | .23 |
| ❑ 62 Chris Pronger | .50 | .23 |
| ❑ 63 Steve Larmer | .50 | .23 |
| ❑ 64 Michal Grosek | .25 | .11 |
| ❑ 65 Sergei Fedorov | 2.50 | 1.10 |
| ❑ 66 Stu Barnes | .25 | .11 |
| ❑ 67 Adam Oates | .50 | .23 |
| ❑ 68 Paul Coffey UER (Alexander Mogilny photo on back) | 1.25 | .55 |
| ❑ 69 Joe Sakic | 2.50 | 1.10 |
| ❑ 70 Pat LaFontaine | .50 | .23 |
| ❑ 71 Martin Brodeur | 3.00 | 1.35 |
| ❑ 72 Bob Corkum | .25 | .11 |
| ❑ 73 Jeremy Roenick | 1.25 | .55 |
| ❑ 74 Shayne Corson | .25 | .11 |
| ❑ 75 German Titov | .25 | .11 |
| ❑ 76 Teemu Selanne | 2.50 | 1.10 |
| ❑ 77 Eric Fichaud | 2.50 | 1.10 |
| ❑ 78 Pierre Turgeon | .50 | .23 |
| ❑ 79 Alexander Selivanov | .25 | .11 |
| ❑ 80 Kevin Stevens | .25 | .11 |
| ❑ 81 Jari Kurri | .50 | .23 |
| ❑ 82 Gary Roberts | .25 | .11 |
| ❑ 83 Geoff Courtnall | .25 | .11 |
| ❑ 84 Steve Yzerman | 4.00 | 1.80 |
| ❑ 85 Rod Brind'Amour | .50 | .23 |
| ❑ 86 Mike Richter | 1.25 | .55 |
| ❑ 87 Bernie Nicholls | .25 | .11 |
| ❑ 88 Alexandre Daigle | .25 | .11 |
| ❑ 89 Luc Robitaille | .50 | .23 |
| ❑ 90 John MacLean | .50 | .23 |
| ❑ 91 Phil Housley | .50 | .23 |
| ❑ 92 Brendan Shanahan | 2.50 | 1.10 |
| ❑ 93 Joe Juneau | .50 | .23 |
| ❑ 94 Stephane Richer | .50 | .23 |
| ❑ 95 Blaine Lacher | .50 | .23 |
| ❑ 96 Mike Gartner | .50 | .23 |
| ❑ 97 Rene Corbet | .25 | .11 |
| ❑ 98 Vincent Damphousse | .50 | .23 |
| ❑ 99 Alexander Mogilny UER (Paul Coffey photo on back) | .50 | .23 |
| ❑ 100 Doug Gilmour | 1.25 | .55 |
| ❑ 101 Petr Nedved | .50 | .23 |
| ❑ 102 Alexei Zhamnov | .50 | .23 |

| | MINT | NRMT |
|---|---|---|
| 103 Wendel Clark | .50 | .23 |
| 104 Arturs Irbe | .50 | .23 |
| 105 Brian Bellows | .25 | .11 |
| 106 Mike Modano | 2.00 | .90 |
| 107 Ravil Gusmanov | .25 | .11 |
| 108 Geoff Sanderson | .50 | .23 |
| 109 Mark Recchi | .50 | .23 |
| 110 Mats Sundin | .50 | .23 |
| 111 Pavol Demitra | .25 | .11 |
| 112 Richard Park | .25 | .11 |
| 113 Doug Bonner | .25 | .11 |
| 114 Bryan Berard | 6.00 | 2.70 |
| 115 Rory Fitzpatrick | .25 | .11 |
| 116 Deron Quint | .25 | .11 |
| 117 Jason Bonsignore | .25 | .11 |
| 118 Adam Deadmarsh | .50 | .23 |
| 119 Sean Haggerty | .50 | .23 |
| 120 Jamie Langenbrunner | .50 | .23 |
| 121 Jeff Mitchell | .25 | .11 |
| 122 Antti Aalto | .50 | .23 |
| 123 Tommi Rajamaki | .50 | .23 |
| 124 Jussi Markkanen UER | .50 | .23 |
| 125 Miikka Kiprusoff | .50 | .23 |
| 126 Jere Karalahti | .50 | .23 |
| 127 Petri Kokko | .25 | .11 |
| 128 Janne Niinimaa | 2.00 | .90 |
| 129 Kimmo Timonen | .50 | .23 |
| 130 Martti Jarventie | .50 | .23 |
| 131 Mikko Helisten | .50 | .23 |
| 132 Niko Halttunen | .50 | .23 |
| 133 Tommi Miettinen | .50 | .23 |
| 134 Miska Kangasniemi | .50 | .23 |
| 135 Veli-Pekka Nutikka | .50 | .23 |
| 136 Jani Hassinen | .50 | .23 |
| 137 Timo Salonen | .50 | .23 |
| 138 Tommi Sova | .50 | .23 |
| 139 Toni Makiaho | .50 | .23 |
| 140 Tommi Hamalainen | .50 | .23 |
| 141 Juha Vuorivirta | .50 | .23 |
| 142 Jussi Tarvainen | .50 | .23 |
| 143 Miikka Elomo | .50 | .23 |
| 144 Jason Botterill | .25 | .11 |
| 145 Dan Cloutier | 1.00 | .45 |
| 146 Jamie Storr | .50 | .23 |
| 147 Chad Allan | .25 | .11 |
| 148 Nolan Baumgartner | .25 | .11 |
| 149 Ed Jovanovski | 1.25 | .55 |
| 150 Bryan McCabe | .25 | .11 |
| 151 Wade Redden | 1.25 | .55 |
| 152 Jamie Rivers | .25 | .11 |
| 153 Lee Sorochan | .25 | .11 |
| 154 Jason Allison | .25 | .11 |
| 155 Alexandre Daigle | .25 | .11 |
| 156 Larry Courville | .25 | .11 |
| 157 Eric Daze | 4.00 | 1.80 |
| 158 Shean Donovan | .25 | .11 |
| 159 Jeff Friesen | .50 | .23 |
| 160 Todd Harvey | .50 | .23 |
| 161 Marty Murray | .25 | .11 |
| 162 Jeff O'Neill | .75 | .35 |
| 163 Denis Pederson | .75 | .35 |
| 164 Darcy Tucker | .50 | .23 |
| 165 Ryan Smyth | 6.00 | 2.70 |

## 1994-95 Finest Super Team Winners

This 165-card set was awarded to collectors who redeemed the winning New Jersey Devils team card. The cards are the same as the regular Finest cards save for the Super Team Winner embossed logo. Values for the cards can be determined by applying the multipliers below to the values listed for the regular cards.

| | MINT | NRMT |
|---|---|---|
| COMPLETE SET (165) | 200.00 | 90.00 |
| COMMON CARD (1-165) | .75 | .35 |

*STARS: 2X TO 4X BASIC CARDS
*YOUNG STARS: 2X TO 3X BASIC CARDS

## 1994-95 Finest Refractors

The cards in this set are parallel to the Finest set. They were randomly inserted at the rate of 1:12 packs. These cards appear identical to the regular issue; careful examination in the proper light reveals a reflective, rainbow-like sheen to the foil on the front. If in doubt, we recommend comparing to other cards from the set; in this setting, a refractor truly stands out. These cards also came with the clear protective peel-off coating. Multipliers can be found in the header below to determine value for these.

| | MINT | NRMT |
|---|---|---|
| COMPLETE SET (165) | 1700.00 | 750.00 |
| COMMON CARD (1-165) | 5.00 | 2.20 |

*VETERAN STARS: 10X TO 25X BASIC CARDS
*YOUNG STARS: 6X TO 15X BASIC CARDS
*RCs: 3X TO 8X BASIC CARDS

| | MINT | NRMT |
|---|---|---|
| 1 Peter Forsberg | 150.00 | 70.00 |
| 7 Paul Kariya | 150.00 | 70.00 |
| 24 Pavel Bure | 60.00 | 27.00 |
| 30 Patrick Roy | 150.00 | 70.00 |
| 33 Jaromir Jagr | 120.00 | 55.00 |
| 38 Eric Lindros | 150.00 | 70.00 |
| 40 John Vanbiesbrouck | 60.00 | 27.00 |
| 41 Wayne Gretzky | 250.00 | 110.00 |
| 43 Dominik Hasek | 60.00 | 27.00 |
| 65 Sergei Fedorov | 60.00 | 27.00 |
| 69 Joe Sakic | 80.00 | 36.00 |
| 71 Martin Brodeur | 80.00 | 36.00 |
| 76 Teemu Selanne | 60.00 | 27.00 |
| 84 Steve Yzerman | 100.00 | 45.00 |
| 92 Brendan Shanahan | 60.00 | 27.00 |
| 114 Bryan Berard WJC | 40.00 | 18.00 |
| 149 Ed Jovanovski WJC | 40.00 | 18.00 |
| 157 Eric Daze WJC | 40.00 | 18.00 |
| 165 Ryan Smyth WJC | 60.00 | 27.00 |

## 1994-95 Finest Bowman's Best

This 45-card set was randomly inserted in Finest packs at the rate of 1:4. Card fronts feature a cut-out player photo over a blue or red hi-tech half moon background utilizing the Finest printing technology. The first twenty cards in the set feature NHL veterans. The second twenty consists of NHL rookies. The last five cards pair a star veteran and a top rookie in a horizontal format. The card fronts have the clear protective peel-off coating. The backs of the first forty cards have brief text information outlining the player's strong points, and a small portrait photo. The final five cards simply feature text comparing the two players. Cards are numbered with a B (1-20) prefix for veterans, R (1-20) for rookies, and X (21-25) for dual player cards.

| | MINT | NRMT |
|---|---|---|
| COMPLETE SET (45) | 150.00 | 70.00 |
| COMMON CARD (B1-B20) | 3.00 | 1.35 |
| COMMON CARD (R1-R20) | 3.00 | 1.35 |
| COMMON CARD (X21-X25) | 4.00 | 1.80 |
| B1 Ray Bourque | 5.00 | 2.20 |
| B2 Mark Messier | 5.00 | 2.20 |
| B3 Cam Neely | 4.00 | 1.80 |
| B4 Theoren Fleury | 4.00 | 1.80 |
| B5 Jeremy Roenick | 5.00 | 2.20 |
| B6 Mike Modano | 5.00 | 2.20 |
| B7 Sergei Fedorov | 8.00 | 3.60 |
| B8 John Vanbiesbrouck | 6.00 | 2.70 |
| B9 Pierre Turgeon | 4.00 | 1.80 |
| B10 Kirk Muller | 3.00 | 1.35 |
| B11 Pavel Bure | 8.00 | 3.60 |
| B12 Brian Leetch | 5.00 | 2.20 |
| B13 Mike Richter | 5.00 | 2.20 |
| B14 Teemu Selanne | 8.00 | 3.60 |
| B15 Brett Hull | 5.00 | 2.20 |
| B16 Eric Lindros | 12.00 | 5.50 |
| B17 Keith Tkachuk | 5.00 | 2.20 |
| B18 Joe Sakic | 8.00 | 3.60 |
| B19 Doug Gilmour | 4.00 | 1.80 |
| B20 Jaromir Jagr | 12.00 | 5.50 |
| R1 Paul Kariya | 15.00 | 6.75 |
| R2 Oleg Tverdovsky | 3.00 | 1.35 |
| R3 Blaine Lacher | 3.00 | 1.35 |
| R4 Todd Harvey | 3.00 | 1.35 |
| R5 Roman Oksiuta | 3.00 | 1.35 |
| R6 David Oliver | 3.00 | 1.35 |
| R7 Jamie Storr | 3.00 | 1.35 |
| R8 Brian Savage | 3.00 | 1.35 |
| R9 Brian Rolston | 3.00 | 1.35 |
| R10 Brett Lindros | 3.00 | 1.35 |
| R11 Radek Bonk | 3.00 | 1.35 |
| R12 Peter Forsberg | 15.00 | 6.75 |
| R13 Adam Deadmarsh | 4.00 | 1.80 |
| R14 Jeff Friesen | 3.00 | 1.35 |
| R15 Denis Chasse | 3.00 | 1.35 |
| R16 Jason Wiemer | 3.00 | 1.35 |
| R17 Alexander Selivanov | 3.00 | 1.35 |
| R18 Kenny Jonsson | 3.00 | 1.35 |
| R19 Todd Marchant | 3.00 | 1.35 |
| R20 Mariusz Czerkawski | 3.00 | 1.35 |
| X21 Theoren Fleury<br>Paul Kariya | 10.00 | 4.50 |
| X22 Doug Gilmour<br>Peter Forsberg | 10.00 | 4.50 |
| X23 Joe Sakic<br>Radek Bonk | 4.00 | 1.80 |
| X24 Brian Leetch<br>Oleg Tverdovsky | 4.00 | 1.80 |
| X25 Cam Neely<br>Jason Wiemer | 4.00 | 1.80 |

## 1994-95 Finest Division's Finest Clear Cut

The 20 cards in this set were randomly inserted in Finest packs at the rate of 1:12. The cards feature a color action photo over a clear acetate design. Player name appears in a red bar along the right-hand side, with the set title directly below it. Due to the nature of the acetate design, the cards have very limited information on the back, with the card number and one sentence of text down the side.

| | MINT | NRMT |
|---|---|---|
| COMPLETE SET (20) | 100.00 | 45.00 |
| COMMON CARD (1-20) | 2.00 | .90 |
| 1 Patrick Roy | 20.00 | 9.00 |
| 2 Ray Bourque | 4.00 | 1.80 |
| 3 Adam Oates | 3.00 | 1.35 |
| 4 Luc Robitaille | 3.00 | 1.35 |
| 5 Mark Recchi | 2.00 | .90 |
| 6 Mike Richter | 4.00 | 1.80 |
| 7 Scott Stevens | 2.00 | .90 |
| 8 Eric Lindros | 12.00 | 5.50 |
| 9 Adam Graves | 3.00 | 1.35 |
| 10 Stephane Richer | 2.00 | .90 |
| 11 Ed Belfour | 4.00 | 1.80 |
| 12 Al MacInnis | 2.00 | .90 |
| 13 Sergei Fedorov | 8.00 | 3.60 |
| 14 Brendan Shanahan | 8.00 | 3.60 |
| 15 Brett Hull | 5.00 | 2.20 |
| 16 Arturs Irbe | 3.00 | 1.35 |
| 17 Sandis Ozolinsh | 2.00 | .90 |
| 18 Wayne Gretzky | 25.00 | 11.00 |
| 19 Gary Roberts | 2.00 | .90 |
| 20 Pavel Bure | 8.00 | 3.60 |

## 1994-95 Finest Ring Leaders

This 20-card set is comprised of players who have earned at least two Stanley Cup rings. The cards were randomly inserted in Finest product at a rate of 1:24 packs. The fronts have an action player photo beside photos of the Stanley Cup and a ring, over a power matrix background. The backs have simple information about the player's Cup appearances next to a photo. The cards are numbered of 20. Unlike other Finest cards, these did not come with a peel-off coating.

| | MINT | NRMT |
|---|---|---|
| COMPLETE SET (20) | 120.00 | 55.00 |
| COMMON CARD (1-20) | 2.50 | 1.10 |
| 1 Mark Messier | 10.00 | 4.50 |
| 2 Kevin Lowe | 2.50 | 1.10 |
| 3 Jari Kurri | 6.00 | 2.70 |
| 4 Grant Fuhr | 6.00 | 2.70 |
| 5 Wayne Gretzky | 50.00 | 22.00 |
| 6 Paul Coffey | 8.00 | 3.60 |
| 7 Craig Simpson | 2.50 | 1.10 |
| 8 Craig MacTavish | 2.50 | 1.10 |
| 9 Jeff Beukeboom | 2.50 | 1.10 |
| 10 Joe Mullen | 2.50 | 1.10 |
| 11 Marty McSorley | 2.50 | 1.10 |
| 12 Steve Smith | 2.50 | 1.10 |
| 13 Kevin Stevens | 6.00 | 2.70 |
| 14 Patrick Roy | 40.00 | 18.00 |
| 15 Jaromir Jagr | 25.00 | 11.00 |
| 16 Ron Francis | 6.00 | 2.70 |
| 17 Bill Ranford | 6.00 | 2.70 |
| 18 Larry Murphy | 6.00 | 2.70 |
| 19 Tom Barrasso | 6.00 | 2.70 |
| 20 Adam Graves | 6.00 | 2.70 |

## 1995-96 Finest

The 1995-96 Finest set was issued in one series totaling 191 cards. The 6-card hobby packs had an SRP of $5.00 each. The players were featured across three themes: Finest Rookies, Finest Performers and Finest Defenders. Within those themes, cards were produced in different quantities: some players were common, some uncommon and some

rare. The breakdown for the player selection of common (bronze), uncommon (silver) and rare (gold) cards was supposedly random with no consideration given to the status of each player in the set, although many of the gold cards did feature upper-echelon stars. Odds of finding an uncommon silver card were 1:4 packs, while golds were found 1:24 packs. Because of the difficulty in acquiring the tough gold cards, many collectors and dealers simply built sets of the bronze and silver cards. Values for these sets are included below.

| | MINT | NRMT |
|---|---|---|
| COMPLETE SET (191) | 1000.00 | 450.00 |
| COMP.BRONZE SET (110) | 40.00 | 18.00 |
| COMMON BRONZE | .25 | .11 |
| COMP.SILVER SET (55) | 125.00 | 55.00 |
| COMMON SILVER | 2.50 | 1.10 |
| COMP.GOLD SET (26) | 900.00 | 400.00 |
| COMMON GOLD | 10.00 | 4.50 |
| 1 Eric Lindros B | 3.00 | 1.35 |
| 2 Ray Bourque G | 20.00 | 9.00 |
| 3 Eric Daze B | 1.00 | .45 |
| 4 Craig Janney S | 2.50 | 1.10 |
| 5 Wayne Gretzky B | 6.00 | 2.70 |
| 6 Dave Andreychuk B | .50 | .23 |
| 7 Phil Housley B | .50 | .23 |
| 8 Mike Gartner B | .50 | .23 |
| 9 Cam Neely B | 1.00 | .45 |
| 10 Brett Hull B | 1.50 | .70 |
| 11 Daren Puppa S | 4.00 | 1.80 |
| 12 Tomas Sandstrom S | 2.50 | 1.10 |
| 13 Patrick Roy G | 100.00 | 45.00 |
| 14 Steve Thomas B | .25 | .11 |
| 15 Joe Sakic B | 2.00 | .90 |
| 16 Ray Sheppard S | 2.50 | 1.10 |
| 17 Steve Duchesne B | .25 | .11 |
| 18 Shayne Corson S | 2.50 | 1.10 |
| 19 Chris Chelios G | 20.00 | 9.00 |
| 20 John Vanbiesbrouck B | 1.50 | .70 |
| 21 Randy Burridge B | .25 | .11 |
| 22 Shane Doan B | .25 | .11 |
| 23 Brian Savage B | .25 | .11 |
| 24 Luc Robitaille B | .50 | .23 |
| 25 Jeremy Roenick G | 20.00 | 9.00 |
| 26 Peter Forsberg B | 3.00 | 1.35 |
| 27 Jeff Friesen S | 2.50 | 1.10 |
| 28 Aaron Gavey S | 2.50 | 1.10 |
| 29 Kenny Jonsson S | 2.50 | 1.10 |
| 30 Theoren Fleury G | 10.00 | 4.50 |
| 31 Dave Gagner S | 2.50 | 1.10 |
| 32 Alexander Selivanov S | 2.50 | 1.10 |
| 33 Scott Stevens B | .50 | .23 |
| 34 Valeri Bure B | .25 | .11 |
| 35 Teemu Selanne G | 40.00 | 18.00 |
| 36 Ray Ferraro S | 2.50 | 1.10 |
| 37 Sylvain Cote S | 2.50 | 1.10 |
| 38 John MacLean B | .50 | .23 |
| 39 Brendan Shanahan B | 2.00 | .90 |
| 40 Pat LaFontaine B | .50 | .23 |
| 41 Brian Leetch G | 20.00 | 9.00 |
| 42 Larry Murphy B | .50 | .23 |
| 43 Adam Oates B | .50 | .23 |
| 44 Rod Brind'Amour B | .50 | .23 |
| 45 Martin Brodeur G | 50.00 | 22.00 |
| 46 Pierre Turgeon B | .50 | .23 |
| 47 Claude Lemieux B | .50 | .23 |
| 48 Al MacInnis S | 4.00 | 1.80 |
| 49 Geoff Courtnall S | 2.50 | 1.10 |
| 50 Mark Messier B | 1.50 | .70 |
| 51 Bill Ranford B | .50 | .23 |
| 52 Vincent Damphousse S | 2.50 | 1.10 |
| 53 Jere Lehtinen B | .25 | .11 |
| 54 Bryan McCabe S | 2.50 | 1.10 |
| 55 Doug Gilmour G | 20.00 | 9.00 |
| 56 Mathieu Schneider S | 2.50 | 1.10 |
| 57 Igor Larionov S | 2.50 | 1.10 |
| 58 Joe Murphy S | 2.50 | 1.10 |
| 59 Niklas Sundstrom B | .25 | .11 |
| 60 John LeClair B | 1.50 | .70 |
| 61 Cory Stillman B | .25 | .11 |
| 62 David Oliver B | .25 | .11 |
| 63 Nikolai Khabibulin B | .50 | .23 |
| 64 Steve Rucchin B | .25 | .11 |
| 65 Brendan Shanahan S | 10.00 | 4.50 |
| 66 Jim Carey B | 1.00 | .45 |
| 67 Brian Holzinger S | 4.00 | 1.80 |
| 68 Stu Barnes S | 2.50 | 1.10 |
| 69 Nicklas Lidstrom B | .50 | .23 |
| 70 Jaromir Jagr B | 3.00 | 1.35 |
| 71 Donald Audette S | 4.00 | 1.80 |
| 72 Dominik Hasek B | 2.00 | .90 |
| 73 Peter Bondra S | 4.00 | 1.80 |
| 74 Andrew Cassels B | .25 | .11 |
| 75 Pavel Bure B | 2.00 | .90 |
| 76 Marcus Ragnarsson B | .25 | .11 |
| 77 Ray Bourque S | 4.00 | 1.80 |
| 78 Alexei Zhamnov B | .25 | .11 |
| 79 Travis Green S | 2.50 | 1.10 |
| 80 Joe Sakic B | 2.00 | .90 |
| 81 Chad Kilger B | .25 | .11 |
| 82 Bill Guerin S | 2.50 | 1.10 |
| 83 Vyacheslav Kozlov B | .25 | .11 |
| 84 Igor Korolev S | 2.50 | 1.10 |
| 85 Saku Koivu G | 30.00 | 13.50 |
| 86 Ron Hextall B | .50 | .23 |
| 87 Wendel Clark S | 2.50 | 1.10 |
| 88 Eric Lindros G | 60.00 | 27.00 |
| 89 Richard Park B | .25 | .11 |
| 90 Dominik Hasek S | 12.00 | 5.50 |
| 91 Shawn McEachern B | .25 | .11 |
| 92 Martin Straka S | 2.50 | 1.10 |
| 93 Roman Hamrlik B | .25 | .11 |
| 94 Roman Oksiuta S | 2.50 | 1.10 |
| 95 Sergei Fedorov B | 2.00 | .90 |
| 96 Jeff O'Neill S | 2.50 | 1.10 |
| 97 Todd Harvey S | 2.50 | 1.10 |
| 98 Rob Niedermayer B | .25 | .11 |
| 99 Mark Messier G | 20.00 | 9.00 |
| 100 Peter Forsberg G | 60.00 | 27.00 |
| 101 Deron Quint B | .25 | .11 |
| 102 Nelson Emerson S | 2.50 | 1.10 |
| 103 Scott Niedermayer B | .25 | .11 |
| 104 Doug Weight S | 4.00 | 1.80 |
| 105 Felix Potvin B | 1.00 | .45 |
| 106 Brendan Witt B | .25 | .11 |
| 107 Zdeno Ciger B | .25 | .11 |
| 108 Ed Belfour S | 4.00 | 1.80 |
| 109 Jody Hull B | .25 | .11 |
| 110 Cam Neely S | 4.00 | 1.80 |
| 111 Kyle McLaren B | .25 | .11 |
| 112 Petr Klima S | 2.50 | 1.10 |
| 113 Grant Fuhr B | .50 | .23 |
| 114 Todd Krygier B | .25 | .11 |
| 115 Brian Leetch B | 1.00 | .45 |
| 116 Daniel Alfredsson S | 10.00 | 4.50 |
| 117 Zigmund Palffy B | .25 | .11 |
| 118 Antti Tormanen B | .25 | .11 |
| 119 Mark Recchi B | .25 | .11 |
| 120 Mikael Renberg B | .50 | .23 |
| 121 Chris Chelios B | 1.00 | .45 |
| 122 Guy Hebert B | .50 | .23 |
| 123 Keith Tkachuk G | 25.00 | 11.00 |
| 124 Joe Juneau S | 2.50 | 1.10 |
| 125 Radek Dvorak S | 2.50 | 1.10 |
| 126 Gary Suter B | .25 | .11 |
| 127 Ron Francis B | .50 | .23 |
| 128 Mike Modano G | 20.00 | 9.00 |
| 129 Tom Barrasso B | .50 | .23 |
| 130 Pat LaFontaine B | .50 | .23 |
| 131 Pat Verbeek B | .25 | .11 |
| 132 Sean Burke S | 4.00 | 1.80 |
| 133 Rick Tocchet B | .50 | .23 |
| 134 Petr Sykora B | .75 | .35 |
| 135 Felix Potvin B | 1.00 | .45 |
| 136 Scott Mellanby B | .25 | .11 |
| 137 Paul Coffey B | 1.00 | .45 |
| 138 Aki Berg G | 10.00 | 4.50 |
| 139 Jason Arnott B | .50 | .23 |
| 140 Alexander Mogilny G | 20.00 | 9.00 |
| 141 Sandis Ozolinsh B | .50 | .23 |
| 142 Owen Nolan S | 2.50 | 1.10 |
| 143 Brian Bradley B | .25 | .11 |
| 144 Trevor Linden B | .25 | .11 |
| 145 Patrick Roy B | 5.00 | 2.20 |
| 146 Todd Bertuzzi B | .25 | .11 |
| 147 Michal Pivonka B | .25 | .11 |
| 148 Kevin Hatcher S | 2.50 | 1.10 |
| 149 Chris Terreri B | .50 | .23 |
| 150 Mario Lemieux B | 5.00 | 2.20 |
| 151 Alexei Yashin S | 4.00 | 1.80 |
| 152 Scott Stevens S | 2.50 | 1.10 |
| 153 Dale Hawerchuk B | .50 | .23 |
| 154 Markus Naslund B | .25 | .11 |
| 155 Teemu Selanne B | 2.00 | .90 |
| 156 Darcy Wakaluk S | 4.00 | 1.80 |
| 157 Vitali Yachmenev B | .25 | .11 |
| 158 Jason Dawe B | .25 | .11 |
| 159 Chris Osgood B | 1.00 | .45 |
| 160 Alexander Mogilny B | 1.00 | .45 |
| 161 Kirk McLean S | 4.00 | 1.80 |
| 162 Steve Yzerman G | 60.00 | 27.00 |
| 163 Shean Donovan B | .25 | .11 |
| 164 Valeri Kamensky S | 4.00 | 1.80 |
| 165 Paul Kariya B | 4.00 | 1.80 |
| 166 Dimitri Khristich S | 2.50 | 1.10 |
| 167 Teppo Numminen B | .25 | .11 |
| 168 Joe Nieuwendyk S | 4.00 | 1.80 |
| 169 Mike Richter S | 4.00 | 1.80 |
| 170 Doug Gilmour B | 1.00 | .45 |
| 171 Sergei Zubov B | .25 | .11 |
| 172 Michael Nylander B | .25 | .11 |
| 173 Geoff Sanderson B | .25 | .11 |
| 174 Eric Desjardins S | 2.50 | 1.10 |
| 175 Jeremy Roenick B | 1.00 | .45 |
| 176 Ed Jovanovski G | 20.00 | 9.00 |
| 177 Mats Sundin B | .50 | .23 |
| 178 Martin Brodeur B | 2.50 | 1.10 |
| 179 John LeClair G | 30.00 | 13.50 |
| 180 Wayne Gretzky G | 125.00 | 55.00 |
| 181 Theoren Fleury B | 1.00 | .45 |
| 182 Pierre Turgeon S | 4.00 | 1.80 |
| 183 Robert Svehla B | .25 | .11 |
| 184 Brett Hull G | 20.00 | 9.00 |
| 185 Jaromir Jagr G | 60.00 | 27.00 |
| 186 Sergei Fedorov B | 2.00 | .90 |
| 187 Pavel Bure G | 40.00 | 18.00 |
| 188 John Vanbiesbrouck B | 1.50 | .70 |
| 189 Paul Kariya B | 4.00 | 1.80 |
| 190 Mario Lemieux G | 100.00 | 45.00 |
| 191 Checklist UER G | 10.00 | 4.50 |

## 1995-96 Finest Refractors

The 1995-96 Finest Refractors set was issued as a parallel to the Finest set. Mirroring it's three levels of difficulty, the cards were

inserted at varying rates. Common refractors could be found 1:12 packs. Uncommon refractors were 1:48, while the rare refractors were hidden 1:288 packs. It is believed there were less than 150 rare refractors, less than 450 uncommon and less than 1,000 common refractors available.

| | MINT | NRMT |
|---|---|---|
| COMPLETE SET (191) | 5000.00 | 2200.00 |
| COMP.BRONZE SET (110) | 1000.00 | 450.00 |
| COMMON BRONZE | 3.00 | 1.35 |
| COMP.SILVER SET (55) | 800.00 | 350.00 |
| COMMON SILVER | 6.00 | 2.70 |
| COMP.GOLD SET (26) | 3500.00 | 1600.00 |
| COMMON GOLD | 20.00 | 9.00 |

| | | |
|---|---|---|
| ❑ 1 Eric Lindros B | 40.00 | 18.00 |
| ❑ 2 Ray Bourque G | 50.00 | 22.00 |
| ❑ 5 Wayne Gretzky B | 100.00 | 45.00 |
| ❑ 13 Patrick Roy G | 250.00 | 110.00 |
| ❑ 19 Chris Chelios G | 50.00 | 22.00 |
| ❑ 25 Jeremy Roenick G | 50.00 | 22.00 |
| ❑ 35 Teemu Selanne G | 100.00 | 45.00 |
| ❑ 41 Brian Leetch G | 50.00 | 22.00 |
| ❑ 45 Martin Brodeur G | 120.00 | 55.00 |
| ❑ 55 Doug Gilmour G | 50.00 | 22.00 |
| ❑ 65 Brendan Shanahan S | 50.00 | 22.00 |
| ❑ 70 Jaromir Jagr B | 12.00 | 5.50 |
| ❑ 85 Saku Koivu G | 80.00 | 36.00 |
| ❑ 88 Eric Lindros G | 150.00 | 70.00 |
| ❑ 90 Dominik Hasek S | 50.00 | 22.00 |
| ❑ 99 Mark Messier G | 60.00 | 27.00 |
| ❑ 100 Peter Forsberg G | 150.00 | 70.00 |
| ❑ 123 Keith Tkachuk G | 60.00 | 27.00 |
| ❑ 140 Alexander Mogilny G | 40.00 | 18.00 |
| ❑ 145 Patrick Roy B | 60.00 | 27.00 |
| ❑ 150 Mario Lemieux B | 60.00 | 27.00 |
| ❑ 162 Steve Yzerman G | 150.00 | 70.00 |
| ❑ 165 Paul Kariya B | 50.00 | 22.00 |
| ❑ 176 Ed Jovanovski G | 60.00 | 27.00 |
| ❑ 179 John LeClair G | 100.00 | 45.00 |
| ❑ 180 Wayne Gretzky G | 400.00 | 180.00 |
| ❑ 184 Brett Hull G | 60.00 | 27.00 |
| ❑ 185 Jaromir Jagr G | 300.00 | 135.00 |
| ❑ 187 Pavel Bure G | 100.00 | 45.00 |
| ❑ 189 Paul Kariya B | 50.00 | 22.00 |
| ❑ 190 Mario Lemieux G | 250.00 | 110.00 |

## 1998-99 Finest

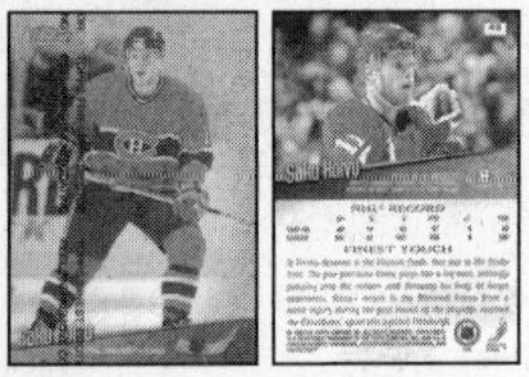

The 1998-99 Finest set was issued in one series totalling 150 cards and was distributed in six-card packs with a suggested retail price of $5. The fronts feature color action player photos printed on 29-pt. stock and identified by a different graphic according to the player's position. The backs carry player information and career statistics.

| | MINT | NRMT |
|---|---|---|
| COMPLETE SET (150) | 60.00 | 27.00 |
| COMMON CARD (1-150) | .30 | .14 |

| | | |
|---|---|---|
| ❑ 1 Teemu Selanne | 1.50 | .70 |
| ❑ 2 Theoren Fleury | .75 | .35 |
| ❑ 3 Ed Belfour | .75 | .35 |
| ❑ 4 Dominik Hasek | 1.50 | .70 |
| ❑ 5 Dino Ciccarelli | .60 | .25 |
| ❑ 6 Peter Forsberg | 2.50 | 1.10 |
| ❑ 7 Rob Blake | .60 | .25 |
| ❑ 8 Martin Gelinas | .30 | .14 |
| ❑ 9 Vincent Damphousse | .60 | .25 |
| ❑ 10 Doug Brown | .30 | .14 |
| ❑ 11 Dave Andreychuk | .60 | .25 |
| ❑ 12 Bill Guerin | .60 | .25 |
| ❑ 13 Daniel Alfredsson | .60 | .25 |
| ❑ 14 Dainius Zubrus | .30 | .14 |
| ❑ 15 Nikolai Khabibulin | .60 | .25 |
| ❑ 16 Sergei Nemchinov | .30 | .14 |
| ❑ 17 Rod Brind'Amour | .60 | .25 |
| ❑ 18 Patrick Marleau | .30 | .14 |
| ❑ 19 Brett Hull | 1.00 | .45 |
| ❑ 20 Rob Zamuner | .30 | .14 |
| ❑ 21 Anson Carter | .30 | .14 |
| ❑ 22 Chris Pronger | .60 | .25 |
| ❑ 23 Owen Nolan | .60 | .25 |
| ❑ 24 Alexandre Daigle | .30 | .14 |
| ❑ 25 Darius Kasparaitis | .30 | .14 |
| ❑ 26 Steve Rucchin | .30 | .14 |
| ❑ 27 Grant Fuhr | .60 | .25 |
| ❑ 28 Mike Sillinger | .30 | .14 |
| ❑ 29 Tony Amonte | .60 | .25 |
| ❑ 30 Jeremy Roenick | .75 | .35 |
| ❑ 31 Garry Galley | .30 | .14 |
| ❑ 32 Jeff Friesen | .60 | .25 |
| ❑ 33 Alexei Zhitnik | .30 | .14 |
| ❑ 34 Sergei Fedorov | 1.50 | .70 |
| ❑ 35 Martin Brodeur | 2.00 | .90 |
| ❑ 36 Curtis Joseph | .75 | .35 |
| ❑ 37 Mike Johnson | .30 | .14 |
| ❑ 38 Mattias Ohlund | .60 | .25 |
| ❑ 39 Derian Hatcher | .30 | .14 |
| ❑ 40 Zigmund Palffy | .75 | .35 |
| ❑ 41 Rob Niedermayer | .30 | .14 |
| ❑ 42 Keith Primeau | .60 | .25 |
| ❑ 43 Valeri Kamensky | .30 | .14 |
| ❑ 44 Cliff Ronning | .30 | .14 |
| ❑ 45 Saku Koivu | 1.25 | .55 |
| ❑ 46 Jiri Slegr | .30 | .14 |
| ❑ 47 Igor Korolev | .30 | .14 |
| ❑ 48 Sergei Samsonov | 1.25 | .55 |
| ❑ 49 Vaclav Prospal | .30 | .14 |
| ❑ 50 Ron Francis | .60 | .25 |
| ❑ 51 John LeClair | 1.25 | .55 |
| ❑ 52 Peter Bondra | .75 | .35 |
| ❑ 53 Matt Cullen | .30 | .14 |
| ❑ 54 Doug Gilmour | .75 | .35 |
| ❑ 55 John Vanbiesbrouck | 1.25 | .55 |
| ❑ 56 Kevin Stevens | .60 | .25 |
| ❑ 57 Vladimir Malakhov | .30 | .14 |
| ❑ 58 Guy Hebert | .60 | .25 |
| ❑ 59 Patrik Elias | .60 | .25 |
| ❑ 60 Boris Mironov | .30 | .14 |
| ❑ 61 Rob DiMaio | .30 | .14 |
| ❑ 62 Pavol Demitra | .60 | .25 |
| ❑ 63 Michael Nylander | .30 | .14 |
| ❑ 64 Wayne Gretzky | 5.00 | 2.20 |
| ❑ 65 Miroslav Satan | .30 | .14 |
| ❑ 66 Eric Daze | .30 | .14 |
| ❑ 67 Jozef Stumpel | .60 | .25 |
| ❑ 68 Mark Messier | 1.00 | .45 |
| ❑ 69 Pat Verbeek | .60 | .25 |
| ❑ 70 Felix Potvin | .75 | .35 |
| ❑ 71 Ethan Moreau | .30 | .14 |
| ❑ 72 Steve Yzerman | 2.50 | 1.10 |
| ❑ 73 Paul Ysebaert | .30 | .14 |
| ❑ 74 Jaromir Jagr | 2.50 | 1.10 |
| ❑ 75 Mike Modano | 1.00 | .45 |
| ❑ 76 Chris Osgood | .75 | .35 |
| ❑ 77 Robert Svehla | .30 | .14 |
| ❑ 78 Joe Juneau | .60 | .25 |
| ❑ 79 Adam Deadmarsh | .60 | .25 |
| ❑ 80 Keith Tkachuk | 1.00 | .45 |
| ❑ 81 Mark Recchi | .60 | .25 |
| ❑ 82 Andrew Cassels | .30 | .14 |
| ❑ 83 Mike Hough | .30 | .14 |
| ❑ 84 Rem Murray | .30 | .14 |
| ❑ 85 Trevor Kidd | .60 | .25 |
| ❑ 86 Jeff Hackett | .60 | .25 |
| ❑ 87 Mikael Renberg | .60 | .25 |
| ❑ 88 Al MacInnis | .60 | .25 |
| ❑ 89 Mike Richter | .75 | .35 |
| ❑ 90 Markus Naslund | .30 | .14 |
| ❑ 91 Joe Sakic | 1.50 | .70 |
| ❑ 92 Michael Peca | .30 | .14 |
| ❑ 93 Scott Thornton | .30 | .14 |
| ❑ 94 Vyacheslav Kozlov | .60 | .25 |
| ❑ 95 Bobby Holik | .30 | .14 |
| ❑ 96 Alexei Yashin | .60 | .25 |
| ❑ 97 Robert Kron | .30 | .14 |
| ❑ 98 Adam Oates | .60 | .25 |
| ❑ 99 Chris Simon | .30 | .14 |
| ❑ 100 Paul Kariya | 3.00 | 1.35 |
| ❑ 101 Ray Bourque | .75 | .35 |
| ❑ 102 Eric Desjardins | .30 | .14 |
| ❑ 103 Glen Murray | .30 | .14 |
| ❑ 104 Oleg Tverdovsky | .30 | .14 |
| ❑ 105 Pavel Bure | 1.50 | .70 |
| ❑ 106 Mats Sundin | .75 | .35 |
| ❑ 107 Bryan Berard | .60 | .25 |
| ❑ 108 Janne Niinimaa | .30 | .14 |
| ❑ 109 Wade Redden | .30 | .14 |
| ❑ 110 Trevor Linden | .60 | .25 |
| ❑ 111 Jarome Iginla | .30 | .14 |
| ❑ 112 Joe Nieuwendyk | .60 | .25 |
| ❑ 113 Alexei Kovalev | .30 | .14 |
| ❑ 114 Dave Gagner | .30 | .14 |
| ❑ 115 Dimitri Yushkevich | .30 | .14 |
| ❑ 116 Sandis Ozolinsh | .60 | .25 |
| ❑ 117 Dimitri Khristich | .30 | .14 |
| ❑ 118 Jim Campbell | .30 | .14 |
| ❑ 119 Nicklas Lidstrom | .60 | .25 |
| ❑ 120 Scott Niedermayer | .30 | .14 |
| ❑ 121 Niklas Sundstrom | .30 | .14 |
| ❑ 122 Karl Dykhuis | .30 | .14 |
| ❑ 123 Brendan Shanahan | 1.50 | .70 |
| ❑ 124 Sandy McCarthy | .30 | .14 |
| ❑ 125 Pierre Turgeon | .60 | .25 |
| ❑ 126 Olaf Kolzig | .60 | .25 |
| ❑ 127 Chris Chelios | .75 | .35 |
| ❑ 128 Luc Robitaille | .60 | .25 |
| ❑ 129 Alexander Mogilny | .60 | .25 |
| ❑ 130 Sami Kapanen | .60 | .25 |
| ❑ 131 Stu Barnes | .30 | .14 |
| ❑ 132 Scott Stevens | .60 | .25 |
| ❑ 133 Doug Weight | .60 | .25 |
| ❑ 134 Alexei Zhamnov | .30 | .14 |
| ❑ 135 Mike Vernon | .60 | .25 |
| ❑ 136 Derek Morris | .60 | .25 |
| ❑ 137 Brian Leetch | .75 | .35 |
| ❑ 138 Ray Whitney | .30 | .14 |
| ❑ 139 Chris Gratton | .60 | .25 |
| ❑ 140 Patrick Roy | 4.00 | 1.80 |
| ❑ 141 Jason Allison | .60 | .25 |
| ❑ 142 Tom Barrasso | .60 | .25 |
| ❑ 143 Derek Plante | .30 | .14 |
| ❑ 144 Denis Pederson | .30 | .14 |
| ❑ 145 Mike Ricci | .30 | .14 |
| ❑ 146 Damian Rhodes | .60 | .25 |
| ❑ 147 Marco Sturm | .30 | .14 |
| ❑ 148 Darryl Sydor | .30 | .14 |
| ❑ 149 Eric Lindros | 2.50 | 1.10 |
| ❑ 150 Checklist | .30 | .14 |

## 1998-99 Finest No Protectors

Randomly inserted into packs at the rate of one in four, this 150-card set is parallel to the

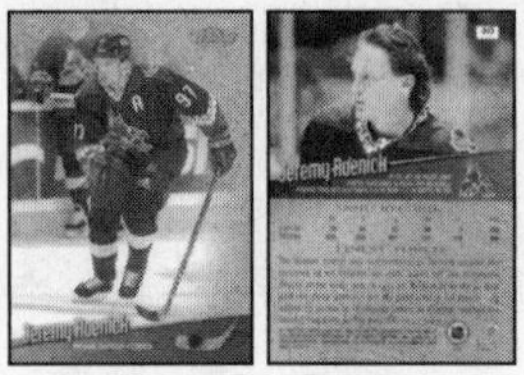

base set without the Finest Protector.

| | MINT | NRMT |
|---|---|---|
| COMPLETE SET (150) | 200.00 | 90.00 |
| COMMON CARD (1-150) | 1.00 | .45 |

*STARS: 1.5X TO 3X BASIC CARDS

## 1998-99 Finest No Protectors Refractors

Randomly inserted into packs at the rate of one in 24, this 150-card set is parallel to the regular refractor set without the Finest protector.

| | MINT | NRMT |
|---|---|---|
| COMPLETE SET (150) | 1200.00 | 550.00 |
| COMMON CARD (1-150) | 6.00 | 2.70 |

*STARS: 10X TO 20X BASIC CARDS

## 1998-99 Finest Refractors

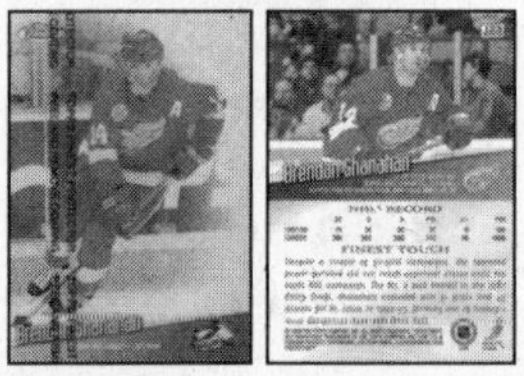

Randomly inserted into packs at the rate of one in 12, this 150-card set is parallel to the base set and is distinguished by the refractive quality of the card.

| | MINT | NRMT |
|---|---|---|
| COMPLETE SET (150) | 600.00 | 275.00 |
| COMMON CARD (1-150) | 4.00 | 1.80 |

*STARS: 5X TO 10X BASIC CARDS

## 1998-99 Finest Centurion

Randomly inserted into packs at the rate of one in 72, this 20-card set features color action photos of rising NHL stars. Only 500 serial-numbered sets were produced.

| | MINT | NRMT |
|---|---|---|
| COMPLETE SET (20) | 400.00 | 180.00 |
| COMMON CARD (C1-C20) | 8.00 | 3.60 |

| | | |
|---|---|---|
| ❑ C1 Patrik Elias | 12.00 | 5.50 |
| ❑ C2 Bryan Berard | 12.00 | 5.50 |
| ❑ C3 Chris Osgood | 15.00 | 6.75 |
| ❑ C4 Saku Koivu | 25.00 | 11.00 |
| ❑ C5 Alexei Yashin | 12.00 | 5.50 |
| ❑ C6 Zigmund Palffy | 15.00 | 6.75 |
| ❑ C7 Peter Forsberg | 50.00 | 22.00 |
| ❑ C8 Jason Allison | 12.00 | 5.50 |
| ❑ C9 Wade Redden | 8.00 | 3.60 |
| ❑ C10 Paul Kariya | 60.00 | 27.00 |
| ❑ C11 Martin Brodeur | 40.00 | 18.00 |
| ❑ C12 Patrick Marleau | 8.00 | 3.60 |
| ❑ C13 Jaromir Jagr | 50.00 | 22.00 |
| ❑ C14 Mattias Ohlund | 12.00 | 5.50 |
| ❑ C15 Teemu Selanne | 30.00 | 13.50 |
| ❑ C16 Mike Johnson | 12.00 | 5.50 |
| ❑ C17 Joe Thornton | 8.00 | 3.60 |
| ❑ C18 Jocelyn Thibault | 12.00 | 5.50 |
| ❑ C19 Daniel Alfredsson | 12.00 | 5.50 |
| ❑ C20 Sergei Samsonov | 25.00 | 11.00 |

## 1998-99 Finest Centurion Refractors

Randomly inserted into packs at the rate of one in 477, this 20-card set is a refractive parallel version of the regular insert set. Only 75 sequentially numbered sets were produced.

| | MINT | NRMT |
|---|---|---|
| COMPLETE SET (20) | 1600.00 | 700.00 |
| COMMON CARD (C1-C20) | 30.00 | 13.50 |

*STARS: 2X TO 4X BASIC CARDS

## 1998-99 Finest Double Sided Mystery Finest

Randomly inserted into packs at the rate of one in 36, this 50-card set features color action photos of 20 players printed on double-sided cards with one of three other players on the back or the same player on both sides. The opaque Finest Protector had to be peeled off in order to view the card.

| | MINT | NRMT |
|---|---|---|
| COMPLETE SET (50) | 1000.00 | 450.00 |
| COMMON CARD (M1-M50) | 12.00 | 5.50 |

| | | |
|---|---|---|
| ❑ M1 Jaromir Jagr<br>Wayne Gretzky | 40.00 | 18.00 |
| ❑ M2 Jaromir Jagr<br>Dominik Hasek | 20.00 | 9.00 |
| ❑ M3 Jaromir Jagr<br>Eric Lindros | 20.00 | 9.00 |
| ❑ M4 Jaromir Jagr<br>Jaromir Jagr | 25.00 | 11.00 |
| ❑ M5 Dominik Hasek<br>Wayne Gretzky | 30.00 | 13.50 |
| ❑ M6 Dominik Hasek<br>Eric Lindros | 20.00 | 9.00 |
| ❑ M7 Dominik Hasek<br>Dominik Hasek | 15.00 | 6.75 |
| ❑ M8 Wayne Gretzky<br>Eric Lindros | 30.00 | 13.50 |
| ❑ M9 Wayne Gretzky<br>Wayne Gretzky | 50.00 | 22.00 |
| ❑ M10 Eric Lindros<br>Eric Lindros | 25.00 | 11.00 |
| ❑ M11 Paul Kariya<br>Teemu Selanne | 25.00 | 11.00 |
| ❑ M12 Paul Kariya<br>Ray Bourque | 20.00 | 9.00 |
| ❑ M13 Paul Kariya<br>Sergei Samsonov | 20.00 | 9.00 |
| ❑ M14 Paul Kariya<br>Paul Kariya | 30.00 | 13.50 |
| ❑ M15 Teemu Selanne<br>Ray Bourque | 15.00 | 6.75 |
| ❑ M16 Teemu Selanne<br>Sergei Samsonov | 15.00 | 6.75 |
| ❑ M17 Teemu Selanne<br>Teemu Selanne | 15.00 | 6.75 |
| ❑ M18 Ray Bourque<br>Sergei Samsonov | 12.00 | 5.50 |
| ❑ M19 Ray Bourque<br>Ray Bourque | 12.00 | 5.50 |
| ❑ M20 Sergei Samsonov<br>Sergei Samsonov | 12.00 | 5.50 |
| ❑ M21 Martin Brodeur<br>Peter Forsberg | 25.00 | 11.00 |
| ❑ M22 Martin Brodeur<br>Patrick Roy | 25.00 | 11.00 |
| ❑ M23 Martin Brodeur<br>Joe Sakic | 20.00 | 9.00 |
| ❑ M24 Martin Brodeur<br>Martin Brodeur | 20.00 | 9.00 |
| ❑ M25 Peter Forsberg<br>Patrick Roy | 30.00 | 13.50 |
| ❑ M26 Peter Forsberg<br>Joe Sakic | 25.00 | 11.00 |
| ❑ M27 Peter Forsberg<br>Peter Forsberg | 25.00 | 11.00 |
| ❑ M28 Patrick Roy<br>Joe Sakic | 30.00 | 13.50 |
| ❑ M29 Patrick Roy<br>Patrick Roy | 40.00 | 18.00 |
| ❑ M30 Joe Sakic<br>Joe Sakic | 15.00 | 6.75 |
| ❑ M31 Mike Modano<br>Steve Yzerman | 20.00 | 9.00 |
| ❑ M32 Mike Modano<br>Sergei Fedorov | 15.00 | 6.75 |
| ❑ M33 Mike Modano<br>Brendan Shanahan | 15.00 | 6.75 |
| ❑ M34 Mike Modano<br>Mike Modano | 12.00 | 5.50 |
| ❑ M35 Steve Yzerman<br>Sergei Fedorov | 20.00 | 9.00 |
| ❑ M36 Steve Yzerman<br>Brendan Shanahan | 20.00 | 9.00 |
| ❑ M37 Steve Yzerman<br>Steve Yzerman | 25.00 | 11.00 |
| ❑ M38 Sergei Fedorov<br>Brendan Shanahan | 15.00 | 6.75 |
| ❑ M39 Sergei Fedorov<br>Sergei Fedorov | 15.00 | 6.75 |
| ❑ M40 Brendan Shanahan<br>Brendan Shanahan | 15.00 | 6.75 |
| ❑ M41 Mark Messier<br>John Leclair | 12.00 | 5.50 |
| ❑ M42 Mark Messier<br>Keith Tkachuk | 12.00 | 5.50 |
| ❑ M43 Mark Messier<br>Pavel Bure | 12.00 | 5.50 |
| ❑ M44 Mark Messier<br>Mark Messier | 12.00 | 5.50 |
| ❑ M45 John Leclair<br>Keith Tkachuk | 12.00 | 5.50 |
| ❑ M46 John Leclair<br>Pavel Bure | 12.00 | 5.50 |
| ❑ M47 John Leclair<br>John Leclair | 12.00 | 5.50 |
| ❑ M48 Pavel Bure<br>Keith Tkachuk | 12.00 | 5.50 |
| ❑ M49 Pavel Bure<br>Pavel Bure | 15.00 | 6.75 |
| ❑ M50 Keith Tkachuk<br>Keith Tkachuk | 12.00 | 5.50 |

## 1998-99 Finest Double Sided Mystery Finest Refractors

Randomly inserted in packs at the rate of one in 144, this 50-card set is a refractive parallel version of the regular insert set.

| | MINT | NRMT |
|---|---|---|
| COMPLETE SET (50) | 2000.00 | 900.00 |
| COMMON CARD (M1-M50) | 25.00 | 11.00 |

*STARS: 1X TO 2X BASIC CARDS

## 1998-99 Finest Futures Finest

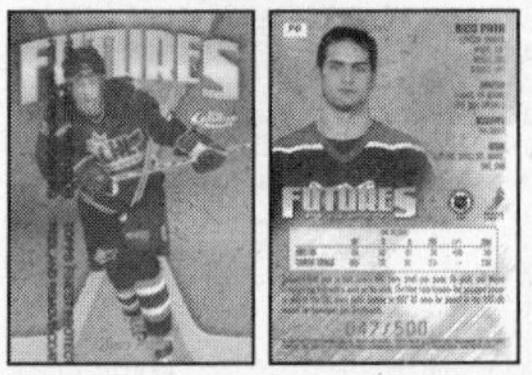

Randomly inserted into packs at the rate of one in 72, this 20-card set features color action photos of hard-charging NHL prospects and CHL players. Only 500 serial-numbered sets were produced.

| | MINT | NRMT |
|---|---|---|
| COMPLETE SET (20) | 250.00 | 110.00 |
| COMMON CARD (F1-F20) | 4.00 | 1.80 |

| | | |
|---|---|---|
| ❑ F1 David Legwand | 30.00 | 13.50 |
| ❑ F2 Manny Malhotra | 20.00 | 9.00 |
| ❑ F3 Vincent Lecavalier | 50.00 | 22.00 |
| ❑ F4 Brad Stuart | 8.00 | 3.60 |
| ❑ F5 Bryan Allen | 6.00 | 2.70 |
| ❑ F6 Rico Fata | 25.00 | 11.00 |
| ❑ F7 Mark Bell | 15.00 | 6.75 |
| ❑ F8 Michael Rupp | 12.00 | 5.50 |
| ❑ F9 Jeff Heerema | 10.00 | 4.50 |
| ❑ F10 Alex Tanguay | 30.00 | 13.50 |
| ❑ F11 Patrick Desrochers | 15.00 | 6.75 |
| ❑ F12 Mathieu Chouinard | 15.00 | 6.75 |
| ❑ F13 Eric Chouinard | 6.00 | 2.70 |
| ❑ F14 Martin Skoula | 6.00 | 2.70 |
| ❑ F15 Robyn Regehr | 4.00 | 1.80 |
| ❑ F16 Marian Hossa | 15.00 | 6.75 |
| ❑ F17 Dan Cleary | 6.00 | 2.70 |
| ❑ F18 Olli Jokinen | 6.00 | 2.70 |
| ❑ F19 Brendan Morrison | 25.00 | 11.00 |
| ❑ F20 Erik Rasmussen | 6.00 | 2.70 |

## 1998-99 Finest Futures Finest Refractors

Randomly inserted into packs at the rate of one in 238, this 20-card set is a refractive version of the regular insert set. Only 150 of each card were produced and sequentially numbered.

| | MINT | NRMT |
|---|---|---|
| COMPLETE SET (20) | 500.00 | 220.00 |
| COMMON CARD (F1-F20) | 8.00 | 3.60 |

*STARS: 1X TO 2X BASIC CARDS

## 1998-99 Finest Oversize

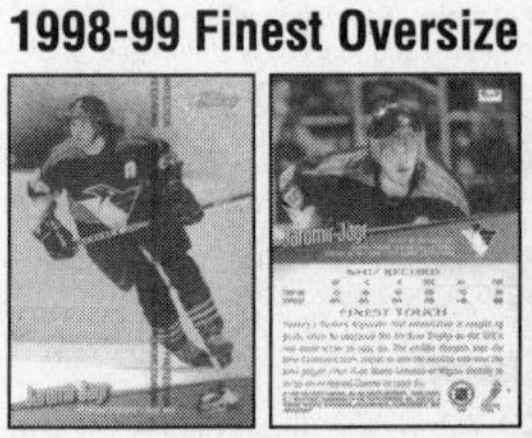

Inserted one per hobby box, this seven-card set features color action photos of top NHL players printed on oversized cards measuring

approximately 3 1/4" by 4 9/16".

| | MINT | NRMT |
|---|---|---|
| COMPLETE SET (7) | 40.00 | 18.00 |
| COMMON CARD (1-7) | 4.00 | 1.80 |
| ❑ 1 Teemu Selanne | 4.00 | 1.80 |
| ❑ 2 Dominik Hasek | 4.00 | 1.80 |
| ❑ 3 Martin Brodeur | 5.00 | 2.20 |
| ❑ 4 Wayne Gretzky | 12.00 | 5.50 |
| ❑ 5 Steve Yzerman | 6.00 | 2.70 |
| ❑ 6 Jaromir Jagr | 6.00 | 2.70 |
| ❑ 7 Eric Lindros | 6.00 | 2.70 |

## 1998-99 Finest Oversize Refractors

Randomly inserted one in every six hobby boxes, this seven-card set is a refractive parallel version of the regular oversized insert set.

| | MINT | NRMT |
|---|---|---|
| COMPLETE SET (7) | 120.00 | 55.00 |
| COMMON CARD (1-7) | 12.00 | 5.50 |

*STARS: 1.5X TO 3X BASIC CARDS

## 1998-99 Finest Promos

This six-card set features color action player photos printed on an embossed card with faint skating marks in the background. The fronts are covered with the Finest Protector film. The backs carry another player photos, biographical information, and season and career statistics. The cards are numbered with a "PP" prefix on the backs.

| | MINT | NRMT |
|---|---|---|
| COMPLETE SET (6) | | |
| COMMON CARD (PP1-PP6) | | |
| ❑ PP1 Scott Stevens | 1.00 | .45 |
| ❑ PP2 Michael Nylander | 1.00 | .45 |
| ❑ PP3 Brendan Shanahan | 4.00 | 1.80 |
| ❑ PP4 Trevor Kidd | 2.00 | .90 |
| ❑ PP5 Bill Guerin | 2.00 | .90 |
| ❑ PP6 Brian Leetch | 2.50 | 1.10 |

## 1998-99 Finest Red Lighters

Randomly inserted in packs at the rate of one in 24, this 20-card set features color action photos of top NHL scorers printed on die-cut chromium cards.

| | MINT | NRMT |
|---|---|---|
| COMPLETE SET (20) | 200.00 | 90.00 |
| COMMON CARD (R1-R20) | 4.00 | 1.80 |
| ❑ R1 Jaromir Jagr | 15.00 | 6.75 |
| ❑ R2 Mike Modano | 6.00 | 2.70 |
| ❑ R3 Paul Kariya | 20.00 | 9.00 |
| ❑ R4 Pavel Bure | 10.00 | 4.50 |
| ❑ R5 Peter Bondra | 5.00 | 2.20 |
| ❑ R6 Sergei Fedorov | 10.00 | 4.50 |
| ❑ R7 Steve Yzerman | 15.00 | 6.75 |
| ❑ R8 Teemu Selanne | 10.00 | 4.50 |
| ❑ R9 Wayne Gretzky | 30.00 | 13.50 |
| ❑ R10 Brendan Shanahan | 10.00 | 4.50 |
| ❑ R11 Eric Lindros | 15.00 | 6.75 |
| ❑ R12 Alexei Yashin | 4.00 | 1.80 |
| ❑ R13 Jason Allison | 4.00 | 1.80 |
| ❑ R14 Joe Nieuwendyk | 4.00 | 1.80 |
| ❑ R15 Joe Sakic | 10.00 | 4.50 |
| ❑ R16 John Leclair | 8.00 | 3.60 |
| ❑ R17 Keith Tkachuk | 6.00 | 2.70 |
| ❑ R18 Mark Messier | 6.00 | 2.70 |
| ❑ R19 Mats Sundin | 5.00 | 2.20 |
| ❑ R20 Zigmund Palffy | 5.00 | 2.20 |

## 1998-99 Finest Red Lighters Refractors

Randomly inserted in packs at the rate of one in 72, this 20-card set is a refractive parallel version of the regular Finest Red Lighters insert set.

| | MINT | NRMT |
|---|---|---|
| COMPLETE SET (20) | 400.00 | 180.00 |
| COMMON CARD (R1-R20) | 8.00 | 3.60 |

*STARS: 1X TO 2X BASIC CARDS

## 1994-95 Flair

This 225-card super premium set was issued in 10-card packs with a suggested retail price of $3.99. The cards feature a full-bleed design with dual action photos on the front and gold foil printing. The card stock is thicker than any basic issue. Yearly stats appear on back in silver, printed over one more photo. The cards

are arranged alphabetically within teams. Rookie cards in this set include Mariusz Czerkawski, David Oliver, Eric Fichaud and Jason Wiemer. To prevent tampering or searching, Fleer employed an innovative packaging design: the packs are actually a cello-wrapped, two-piece silver foil box, with the cards inside wrapped again in a sealed cello pouch.

| | MINT | NRMT |
|---|---|---|
| COMPLETE SET (225) | 50.00 | 22.00 |
| COMMON CARD (1-225) | .20 | .09 |
| ❑ 1 Bob Corkum | .20 | .09 |
| ❑ 2 Bobby Dollas | .20 | .09 |
| ❑ 3 Guy Hebert | .40 | .18 |
| ❑ 4 Paul Kariya | 3.50 | 1.55 |
| ❑ 5 Anatoli Semenov | .20 | .09 |
| ❑ 6 Tim Sweeney | .20 | .09 |
| ❑ 7 Garry Valk | .20 | .09 |
| ❑ 8 Ray Bourque | .75 | .35 |
| ❑ 9 Mariusz Czerkawski | .20 | .09 |
| ❑ 10 Al Iafrate | .20 | .09 |
| ❑ 11 Cam Neely | .40 | .18 |
| ❑ 12 Adam Oates | .40 | .18 |
| ❑ 13 Vincent Riendeau | .40 | .18 |
| ❑ 14 Don Sweeney | .20 | .09 |
| ❑ 15 Donald Audette | .40 | .18 |
| ❑ 16 Doug Bodger | .20 | .09 |
| ❑ 17 Dominik Hasek | 2.00 | .90 |
| ❑ 18 Dale Hawerchuk | .40 | .18 |
| ❑ 19 Pat LaFontaine | .40 | .18 |
| ❑ 20 Alexander Mogilny | .40 | .18 |
| ❑ 21 Craig Muni | .20 | .09 |
| ❑ 22 Richard Smehlik | .20 | .09 |
| ❑ 23 Denis Tsygurov | .20 | .09 |
| ❑ 24 Theoren Fleury | .40 | .18 |
| ❑ 25 Trevor Kidd | .40 | .18 |
| ❑ 26 James Patrick | .20 | .09 |
| ❑ 27 Robert Reichel | .20 | .09 |
| ❑ 28 Gary Roberts | .20 | .09 |
| ❑ 29 German Titov | .20 | .09 |
| ❑ 30 Zarley Zalapski | .20 | .09 |
| ❑ 31 Ed Belfour | .75 | .35 |
| ❑ 32 Chris Chelios | .75 | .35 |
| ❑ 33 Dirk Graham | .20 | .09 |
| ❑ 34 Joe Murphy | .20 | .09 |
| ❑ 35 Bernie Nicholls | .20 | .09 |
| ❑ 36 Jeremy Roenick | .75 | .35 |
| ❑ 37 Steve Smith | .20 | .09 |
| ❑ 38 Gary Suter | .20 | .09 |
| ❑ 39 Neal Broten | .40 | .18 |
| ❑ 40 Russ Courtnall | .20 | .09 |
| ❑ 41 Todd Harvey | .20 | .09 |
| ❑ 42 Grant Ledyard | .20 | .09 |
| ❑ 43 Mike Modano | 1.00 | .45 |
| ❑ 44 Andy Moog | .40 | .18 |
| ❑ 45 Mark Tinordi | .20 | .09 |
| ❑ 46 Dino Ciccarelli | .40 | .18 |
| ❑ 47 Paul Coffey | .75 | .35 |
| ❑ 48 Sergei Fedorov | 1.50 | .70 |
| ❑ 49 Vladimir Konstantinov | .20 | .09 |
| ❑ 50 Slava Kozlov | .40 | .18 |
| ❑ 51 Keith Primeau | .40 | .18 |
| ❑ 52 Ray Sheppard | .40 | .18 |
| ❑ 53 Mike Vernon | .40 | .18 |
| ❑ 54 Jason York | .20 | .09 |
| ❑ 55 Steve Yzerman | 2.50 | 1.10 |
| ❑ 56 Jason Arnott | .75 | .35 |
| ❑ 57 Shayne Corson | .20 | .09 |
| ❑ 58 Igor Kravchuk | .20 | .09 |
| ❑ 59 Dean McAmmond | .20 | .09 |
| ❑ 60 David Oliver | .20 | .09 |
| ❑ 61 Bill Ranford | .40 | .18 |
| ❑ 62 Doug Weight | .40 | .18 |
| ❑ 63 Jesse Belanger | .20 | .09 |
| ❑ 64 Bob Kudelski | .20 | .09 |
| ❑ 65 Scott Mellanby | .40 | .18 |
| ❑ 66 Gord Murphy | .20 | .09 |
| ❑ 67 Rob Niedermayer | .40 | .18 |
| ❑ 68 Brian Skrudland | .20 | .09 |
| ❑ 69 John Vanbiesbrouck | 1.25 | .55 |
| ❑ 70 Sean Burke | .40 | .18 |
| ❑ 71 Andrew Cassels | .20 | .09 |
| ❑ 72 Alexander Godynyuk | .20 | .09 |
| ❑ 73 Chris Pronger | .40 | .18 |
| ❑ 74 Geoff Sanderson | .40 | .18 |
| ❑ 75 Darren Turcotte | .20 | .09 |
| ❑ 76 Pat Verbeek | .20 | .09 |
| ❑ 77 Rob Blake | .20 | .09 |
| ❑ 78 Mike Donnelly | .20 | .09 |
| ❑ 79 Wayne Gretzky | 5.00 | 2.20 |
| ❑ 80 Kelly Hrudey | .40 | .18 |
| ❑ 81 Jari Kurri | .40 | .18 |
| ❑ 82 Marty McSorley | .20 | .09 |
| ❑ 83 Rick Tocchet | .40 | .18 |
| ❑ 84 Brian Bellows | .20 | .09 |
| ❑ 85 Patrice Brisebois | .20 | .09 |
| ❑ 86 Valeri Bure | .40 | .18 |
| ❑ 87 Vincent Damphousse | .40 | .18 |
| ❑ 88 Eric Desjardins | .20 | .09 |
| ❑ 89 Kirk Muller | .20 | .09 |
| ❑ 90 Oleg Petrov | .20 | .09 |
| ❑ 91 Patrick Roy | 4.00 | 1.80 |
| ❑ 92 Martin Brodeur | 2.00 | .90 |
| ❑ 93 David Emma | .20 | .09 |
| ❑ 94 Bill Guerin | .20 | .09 |
| ❑ 95 John MacLean | .40 | .18 |
| ❑ 96 Scott Niedermayer | .20 | .09 |
| ❑ 97 Stephane Richer | .40 | .18 |
| ❑ 98 Brian Rolston | .20 | .09 |
| ❑ 99 Alexander Semak | .20 | .09 |
| ❑ 100 Scott Stevens | .40 | .18 |
| ❑ 101 Valeri Zelepukin | .20 | .09 |
| ❑ 102 Patrick Flatley | .20 | .09 |
| ❑ 103 Derek King | .20 | .09 |
| ❑ 104 Brett Lindros | .20 | .09 |
| ❑ 105 Vladimir Malakhov | .20 | .09 |
| ❑ 106 Marty McInnis | .20 | .09 |
| ❑ 107 Jamie McLennan | .20 | .09 |
| ❑ 108 Steve Thomas | .20 | .09 |
| ❑ 109 Pierre Turgeon | .40 | .18 |
| ❑ 110 Jeff Beukeboom | .20 | .09 |
| ❑ 111 Adam Graves | .40 | .18 |
| ❑ 112 Alexei Kovalev | .40 | .18 |
| ❑ 113 Steve Larmer | .40 | .18 |
| ❑ 114 Brian Leetch | .75 | .35 |
| ❑ 115 Mark Messier | 1.00 | .45 |
| ❑ 116 Sergei Nemchinov | .20 | .09 |
| ❑ 117 Mike Richter | .75 | .35 |
| ❑ 118 Sergei Zubov | .20 | .09 |
| ❑ 119 Craig Billington | .40 | .18 |
| ❑ 120 Alexandre Daigle | .20 | .09 |
| ❑ 121 Sean Hill | .20 | .09 |
| ❑ 122 Norm Maciver | .20 | .09 |
| ❑ 123 Dave McLlwain | .20 | .09 |
| ❑ 124 Alexei Yashin | .40 | .18 |
| ❑ 125 Vladislav Boulin | .20 | .09 |
| ❑ 126 Rod Brind'Amour | .40 | .18 |
| ❑ 127 Ron Hextall | .40 | .18 |
| ❑ 128 Patrik Juhlin | .20 | .09 |
| ❑ 129 Eric Lindros | 3.00 | 1.35 |
| ❑ 130 Mark Recchi | .40 | .18 |
| ❑ 131 Mikael Renberg | .40 | .18 |
| ❑ 132 Chris Therien | .20 | .09 |
| ❑ 133 Tom Barrasso | .40 | .18 |
| ❑ 134 Ron Francis | .40 | .18 |
| ❑ 135 Mario Lemieux | 4.00 | 1.80 |
| ❑ 136 Shawn McEachern | .20 | .09 |
| ❑ 137 Larry Murphy | .40 | .18 |
| ❑ 138 Luc Robitaille | .40 | .18 |
| ❑ 139 Ulf Samuelsson | .20 | .09 |
| ❑ 140 Kevin Stevens | .20 | .09 |
| ❑ 141 Martin Straka | .20 | .09 |
| ❑ 142 Wendel Clark | .40 | .18 |
| ❑ 143 Rene Corbet | .20 | .09 |
| ❑ 144 Adam Deadmarsh | .40 | .18 |
| ❑ 145 Stephane Fiset | .40 | .18 |
| ❑ 146 Peter Forsberg | 3.00 | 1.35 |
| ❑ 147 Valeri Kamensky | .40 | .18 |
| ❑ 148 Janne Laukkanen | .20 | .09 |
| ❑ 149 Sylvain Lefebvre | .20 | .09 |
| ❑ 150 Mike Ricci | .20 | .09 |
| ❑ 151 Joe Sakic | 1.50 | .70 |
| ❑ 152 Steve Duchesne | .20 | .09 |
| ❑ 153 Brett Hull | 1.00 | .45 |
| ❑ 154 Craig Janney | .40 | .18 |
| ❑ 155 Craig Johnson | .20 | .09 |
| ❑ 156 Curtis Joseph | .75 | .35 |
| ❑ 157 Al MacInnis | .40 | .18 |
| ❑ 158 Brendan Shanahan | 1.50 | .70 |
| ❑ 159 Peter Stastny | .40 | .18 |
| ❑ 160 Esa Tikkanen | .20 | .09 |
| ❑ 161 Ulf Dahlen | .20 | .09 |
| ❑ 162 Todd Elik | .20 | .09 |
| ❑ 163 Pat Falloon | .20 | .09 |
| ❑ 164 Jeff Friesen | .40 | .18 |
| ❑ 165 Johan Garpenlov | .20 | .09 |
| ❑ 166 Arturs Irbe | .40 | .18 |
| ❑ 167 Sergei Makarov | .20 | .09 |
| ❑ 168 Jeff Norton | .20 | .09 |
| ❑ 169 Sandis Ozolinsh | .40 | .18 |
| ❑ 170 Brian Bradley | .20 | .09 |
| ❑ 171 Shawn Chambers | .20 | .09 |
| ❑ 172 Aaron Gavey | .20 | .09 |
| ❑ 173 Chris Gratton | .40 | .18 |
| ❑ 174 Petr Klima | .20 | .09 |
| ❑ 175 Daren Puppa | .40 | .18 |
| ❑ 176 Jason Wiemer | .20 | .09 |
| ❑ 177 Dave Andreychuk | .40 | .18 |
| ❑ 178 Dave Ellett | .20 | .09 |
| ❑ 179 Eric Fichaud | 1.25 | .55 |
| ❑ 180 Mike Gartner | .40 | .18 |
| ❑ 181 Doug Gilmour | .75 | .35 |
| ❑ 182 Kenny Jonsson | .20 | .09 |
| ❑ 183 Dmitri Mironov | .20 | .09 |
| ❑ 184 Felix Potvin | .75 | .35 |
| ❑ 185 Mike Ridley | .20 | .09 |
| ❑ 186 Mats Sundin | .40 | .18 |
| ❑ 187 Greg Adams | .20 | .09 |
| ❑ 188 Jeff Brown | .20 | .09 |
| ❑ 189 Pavel Bure | 1.50 | .70 |
| ❑ 190 Nathan Lafayette | .20 | .09 |
| ❑ 191 Trevor Linden | .40 | .18 |
| ❑ 192 Jyrki Lumme | .20 | .09 |
| ❑ 193 Kirk McLean | .40 | .18 |
| ❑ 194 Cliff Ronning | .20 | .09 |
| ❑ 195 Jason Allison | .20 | .09 |
| ❑ 196 Peter Bondra | .75 | .35 |
| ❑ 197 Randy Burridge | .20 | .09 |
| ❑ 198 Sylvain Cote | .20 | .09 |
| ❑ 199 Dale Hunter | .20 | .09 |
| ❑ 200 Joe Juneau | .40 | .18 |
| ❑ 201 Dimitri Khristich | .20 | .09 |
| ❑ 202 Todd Nelson | .20 | .09 |
| ❑ 203 Pat Peake | .20 | .09 |
| ❑ 204 Rick Tabaracci | .40 | .18 |
| ❑ 205 Tim Cheveldae | .40 | .18 |
| ❑ 206 Dallas Drake | .20 | .09 |
| ❑ 207 Dave Manson | .20 | .09 |
| ❑ 208 Teppo Numminen | .20 | .09 |
| ❑ 209 Teemu Selanne | 1.50 | .70 |
| ❑ 210 Darrin Shannon | .20 | .09 |
| ❑ 211 Keith Tkachuk | 1.00 | .45 |
| ❑ 212 Alexei Zhamnov | .40 | .18 |
| ❑ 213 Sergei Fedorov | .75 | .35 |
| ❑ 214 Sergei Fedorov | .75 | .35 |
| ❑ 215 Sergei Fedorov | .75 | .35 |
| ❑ 216 Sergei Fedorov | .75 | .35 |
| ❑ 217 Sergei Fedorov | .75 | .35 |
| ❑ 218 Sergei Fedorov | .75 | .35 |
| ❑ 219 Sergei Fedorov | .75 | .35 |
| ❑ 220 Sergei Fedorov | .75 | .35 |
| ❑ 221 Sergei Fedorov | .75 | .35 |
| ❑ 222 Sergei Fedorov | .75 | .35 |
| ❑ 223 Checklist | .20 | .09 |
| ❑ 224 Checklist | .20 | .09 |
| ❑ 225 Checklist | .20 | .09 |

## 1994-95 Flair Center Spotlight

The 10 cards in this set, which highlight some of the league's top centers, were randomly inserted in Flair product at the rate of 1:4 packs. The cards feature an action shot with two spotlights defining the background. Backs feature another action photo, along with a player profile. The cards are numbered on the back as "X of 10".

| | MINT | NRMT |
|---|---|---|
| COMPLETE SET (10) | 30.00 | 13.50 |
| COMMON CARD (1-10) | 1.00 | .45 |
| ❑ 1 Jason Arnott | 1.00 | .45 |
| ❑ 2 Sergei Fedorov | 3.00 | 1.35 |
| ❑ 3 Doug Gilmour | 1.00 | .45 |
| ❑ 4 Wayne Gretzky | 10.00 | 4.50 |
| ❑ 5 Pat LaFontaine | 1.00 | .45 |
| ❑ 6 Mario Lemieux | 8.00 | 3.60 |
| ❑ 7 Eric Lindros | 6.00 | 2.70 |
| ❑ 8 Mark Messier | 2.00 | .90 |
| ❑ 9 Mike Modano | 2.00 | .90 |
| ❑ 10 Jeremy Roenick | 1.00 | .45 |

## 1994-95 Flair Hot Numbers

The ten cards in this set, which highlight some of the game's deadliest snipers, were randomly inserted in Flair product at the rate of 1:16 packs. The cards feature an action shot over a black background featuring a scribble of neon colors. The player, team, and set name appear vertically along the left border of the card. Card backs have a similar style as the front and are numbered as "X of 10".

| | MINT | NRMT |
|---|---|---|
| COMPLETE SET (10) | 100.00 | 45.00 |
| COMMON CARD (1-10) | 4.00 | 1.80 |
| ❑ 1 Pavel Bure | 8.00 | 3.60 |
| ❑ 2 Wayne Gretzky | 25.00 | 11.00 |
| ❑ 3 Dominik Hasek | 8.00 | 3.60 |
| ❑ 4 Brett Hull | 5.00 | 2.20 |
| ❑ 5 Mario Lemieux | 20.00 | 9.00 |
| ❑ 6 Adam Oates | 4.00 | 1.80 |
| ❑ 7 Luc Robitaille | 4.00 | 1.80 |
| ❑ 8 Patrick Roy | 20.00 | 9.00 |
| ❑ 9 Brendan Shanahan | 8.00 | 3.60 |
| ❑ 10 Steve Yzerman | 12.00 | 5.50 |

## 1994-95 Flair Scoring Power

This 10-card standard-size set was inserted in packs at a rate of 1:8. The fronts have a color action photo on the right side and the player's name and the word "Power" going down the left side in silver-foil. The background consists of many multi-color lines scrawled about. The backs have a color photo with player information and the player's name and "Scoring Power" in silver-foil at the top. The background is similar to the front and they are numbered "X of 10" at the bottom.

| | MINT | NRMT |
|---|---|---|
| COMPLETE SET (10) | 30.00 | 13.50 |
| COMMON CARD (1-10) | 1.50 | .70 |
| ❑ 1 Pavel Bure | 2.50 | 1.10 |
| ❑ 2 Alexandre Daigle | 1.50 | .70 |
| ❑ 3 Sergei Fedorov | 2.50 | 1.10 |
| ❑ 4 Alexei Kovalev | 1.50 | .70 |
| ❑ 5 Brian Leetch | 2.50 | 1.10 |
| ❑ 6 Eric Lindros | 10.00 | 4.50 |
| ❑ 7 Mike Modano | 2.50 | 1.10 |
| ❑ 8 Alexander Mogilny | 2.00 | .90 |
| ❑ 9 Jeremy Roenick | 2.50 | 1.10 |
| ❑ 10 Alexei Yashin | 1.50 | .70 |

## 1996-97 Flair

The 1996-97 Flair set was issued in one series totaling 125 cards. The set contains the Wave of the Future subset (101-125). Although numbered as part of the set, these cards were shortprinted and inserted at a rate of 1:4 packs. Card fronts feature a color action photo, and a background portrait of the player. Card backs contained a color action photo and statistics. Cards were distributed in four-card packs and carried a suggested retail price of $3.99. Key rookies include Sergei Berezin, Mike Grier, Patrick Lalime, Ethan Moreau and Dainius Zubrus.

| | MINT | NRMT |
|---|---|---|
| COMPLETE SET (125) | 120.00 | 55.00 |
| COMP.BASE SET (100) | 40.00 | 18.00 |
| COMMON CARD (1-100) | .25 | .11 |
| COMP.WAVE SET (25) | 80.00 | 36.00 |
| COMMON WAVE (101-125) | 2.00 | .90 |
| ❑ 1 Guy Hebert | .50 | .23 |
| ❑ 2 Paul Kariya | 3.00 | 1.35 |
| ❑ 3 Teemu Selanne | 1.50 | .70 |
| ❑ 4 Ray Bourque | .75 | .35 |
| ❑ 5 Adam Oates | .50 | .23 |
| ❑ 6 Bill Ranford | .50 | .23 |
| ❑ 7 Jozef Stumpel | .25 | .11 |
| ❑ 8 Dominik Hasek | 1.50 | .70 |
| ❑ 9 Pat LaFontaine | .50 | .23 |
| ❑ 10 Alexei Zhitnik | .25 | .11 |
| ❑ 11 Theoren Fleury | .50 | .23 |
| ❑ 12 Dave Gagner | .50 | .23 |
| ❑ 13 Trevor Kidd | .50 | .23 |
| ❑ 14 Tony Amonte | .50 | .23 |
| ❑ 15 Chris Chelios | .75 | .35 |
| ❑ 16 Eric Daze | .50 | .23 |
| ❑ 17 Alexei Zhamnov | .50 | .23 |
| ❑ 18 Peter Forsberg | 2.50 | 1.10 |
| ❑ 19 Sandis Ozolinsh | .50 | .23 |
| ❑ 20 Patrick Roy | 4.00 | 1.80 |
| ❑ 21 Joe Sakic | 1.50 | .70 |
| ❑ 22 Derian Hatcher | .25 | .11 |
| ❑ 23 Mike Modano | 1.00 | .45 |
| ❑ 24 Andy Moog | .50 | .23 |
| ❑ 25 Pat Verbeek | .25 | .11 |
| ❑ 26 Sergei Fedorov | 1.50 | .70 |
| ❑ 27 Viacheslav Fetisov | .25 | .11 |
| ❑ 28 Nicklas Lidstrom | .50 | .23 |
| ❑ 29 Chris Osgood | .75 | .35 |
| ❑ 30 Brendan Shanahan | 1.50 | .70 |
| ❑ 31 Steve Yzerman | 2.50 | 1.10 |
| ❑ 32 Jason Arnott | .50 | .23 |
| ❑ 33 Curtis Joseph | .75 | .35 |
| ❑ 34 Boris Mironov | .25 | .11 |
| ❑ 35 Ryan Smyth | .75 | .35 |
| ❑ 36 Doug Weight | .50 | .23 |
| ❑ 37 Ed Jovanovski | .50 | .23 |
| ❑ 38 Ray Sheppard | .50 | .23 |
| ❑ 39 Robert Svehla | .25 | .11 |
| ❑ 40 John Vanbiesbrouck | 1.25 | .55 |
| ❑ 41 Andrew Cassels | .25 | .11 |
| ❑ 42 Jason Muzzatti | .50 | .23 |
| ❑ 43 Keith Primeau | .50 | .23 |
| ❑ 44 Geoff Sanderson | .50 | .23 |
| ❑ 45 Rob Blake | .25 | .11 |
| ❑ 46 Dimitri Khristich | .25 | .11 |
| ❑ 47 Vincent Damphousse | .50 | .23 |
| ❑ 48 Saku Koivu | 1.25 | .55 |
| ❑ 49 Mark Recchi | .50 | .23 |
| ❑ 50 Martin Rucinsky | .25 | .11 |
| ❑ 51 Jocelyn Thibault | .75 | .35 |
| ❑ 52 Martin Brodeur | 2.00 | .90 |
| ❑ 53 Bill Guerin | .25 | .11 |
| ❑ 54 Scott Stevens | .50 | .23 |
| ❑ 55 Scott Lachance | .25 | .11 |
| ❑ 56 Zigmund Palffy | .75 | .35 |

| | MINT | NRMT |
|---|---|---|
| ❑ 57 Tommy Salo | .50 | .23 |
| ❑ 58 Bryan Smolinski | .25 | .11 |
| ❑ 59 Wayne Gretzky | 6.00 | 2.70 |
| ❑ 60 Brian Leetch | .75 | .35 |
| ❑ 61 Mark Messier | 1.00 | .45 |
| ❑ 62 Mike Richter | .75 | .35 |
| ❑ 63 Daniel Alfredsson | .50 | .23 |
| ❑ 64 Damian Rhodes | .50 | .23 |
| ❑ 65 Alexei Yashin | .50 | .23 |
| ❑ 66 Paul Coffey | .75 | .35 |
| ❑ 67 Dale Hawerchuk | .50 | .23 |
| ❑ 68 Ron Hextall | .50 | .23 |
| ❑ 69 John LeClair | 1.25 | .55 |
| ❑ 70 Eric Lindros | 2.50 | 1.10 |
| ❑ 71 Nikolai Khabibulin | .50 | .23 |
| ❑ 72 Jeremy Roenick | .75 | .35 |
| ❑ 73 Keith Tkachuk | 1.00 | .45 |
| ❑ 74 Oleg Tverdovsky | .50 | .23 |
| ❑ 75 Ron Francis | .50 | .23 |
| ❑ 76 Kevin Hatcher | .25 | .11 |
| ❑ 77 Jaromir Jagr | 2.50 | 1.10 |
| ❑ 78 Mario Lemieux | 4.00 | 1.80 |
| ❑ 79 Petr Nedved | .50 | .23 |
| ❑ 80 Grant Fuhr | .50 | .23 |
| ❑ 81 Brett Hull | 1.00 | .45 |
| ❑ 82 Al MacInnis | .50 | .23 |
| ❑ 83 Ed Belfour | .75 | .35 |
| ❑ 84 Tony Granato | .25 | .11 |
| ❑ 85 Owen Nolan | .50 | .23 |
| ❑ 86 Dino Ciccarelli | .50 | .23 |
| ❑ 87 John Cullen | .25 | .11 |
| ❑ 88 Roman Hamrlik | .50 | .23 |
| ❑ 89 Wendel Clark | .50 | .23 |
| ❑ 90 Doug Gilmour | .75 | .35 |
| ❑ 91 Felix Potvin | .75 | .35 |
| ❑ 92 Mats Sundin | .50 | .23 |
| ❑ 93 Pavel Bure | 1.50 | .70 |
| ❑ 94 Corey Hirsch | .50 | .23 |
| ❑ 95 Trevor Linden | .50 | .23 |
| ❑ 96 Alexander Mogilny | .50 | .23 |
| ❑ 97 Peter Bondra | .75 | .35 |
| ❑ 98 Jim Carey | .75 | .35 |
| ❑ 99 Dale Hunter | .25 | .11 |
| ❑ 100 Chris Simon | .25 | .11 |
| ❑ 101 Mattias Timander SP | 2.00 | .90 |
| ❑ 102 Vaclav Varada SP | 2.00 | .90 |
| ❑ 103 Jarome Iginla SP | .75 | .35 |
| ❑ 104 Ethan Moreau SP | .75 | .35 |
| ❑ 105 Jamie Langenbrunner SP | 2.00 | .90 |
| ❑ 106 Roman Turek SP | 5.00 | 2.20 |
| ❑ 107 Tomas Holmstrom SP | 2.00 | .90 |
| ❑ 108 Kevin Hodson SP | 4.00 | 1.80 |
| ❑ 109 Mats Lindgren SP | 2.00 | .90 |
| ❑ 110 Mike Grier SP | 6.00 | 2.70 |
| ❑ 111 Rem Murray SP | 2.00 | .90 |
| ❑ 112 Jose Theodore SP | 4.00 | 1.80 |
| ❑ 113 David Wilkie SP | 2.00 | .90 |
| ❑ 114 Bryan Berard SP | 5.00 | 2.20 |
| ❑ 115 Eric Fichaud SP | 2.00 | .90 |
| ❑ 116 Daniel Goneau SP | 2.00 | .90 |
| ❑ 117 Andreas Dackell SP | 2.00 | .90 |
| ❑ 118 Wade Redden SP | 2.00 | .90 |
| ❑ 119 Dainius Zubrus SP | 5.00 | 2.20 |
| ❑ 120 Janne Niinimaa SP | .75 | .35 |
| ❑ 121 Patrick Lalime SP | .75 | .35 |
| ❑ 122 Harry York SP | 2.00 | .90 |
| ❑ 123 Jim Campbell SP | 4.00 | 1.80 |
| ❑ 124 Sergei Berezin SP | 5.00 | 2.20 |
| ❑ 125 Jaro. Svejkovsky SP | 3.00 | 1.35 |

## 1996-97 Flair Blue Ice

This 125-card set paralleled the basic Flair set. The cards were randomly inserted in packs at a rate of one in 20, though many dealers suggest they were harder to obtain than the odds suggest. Each card is serial numbered to 250, and card fronts carry a blue foil background along with the words BLUE ICE. No complete set price is listed below due to the extremely short print run of the set, and the lack of market activity in complete set form. Prices for a few of the most heavily traded singles are listed below. Values for other cards can be detemined by applying the multipliers below to the prices for the corresponding regular card.

| | MINT | NRMT |
|---|---|---|
| COMPLETE SET (125) | 4000.00 | 1800.00 |
| COMMON CARD (1-125) | 8.00 | 3.60 |
| SEMISTARS/GOALIES | 20.00 | 9.00 |
| UNLISTED STARS | 50.00 | 22.00 |

*STARS: 25X TO 50X BASIC CARDS
*YOUNG STARS: 15X TO 30X BASIC CARDS
*WAVE/FUTURE: 1.5X TO 3X BASIC CARDS

## 1996-97 Flair Center Ice Spotlight

This set features ten of the NHL's top players. Card fronts feature a color action photo, with purple, red and yellow spotlights highlighting

the background. The cards were randomly inserted in packs at a rate of one in 30.

| | MINT | NRMT |
|---|---|---|
| COMPLETE SET (10) | 200.00 | 90.00 |
| COMMON CARD (1-10) | 8.00 | 3.60 |
| ❑ 1 Pavel Bure | 20.00 | 9.00 |
| ❑ 2 Sergei Fedorov | 15.00 | 6.75 |
| ❑ 3 Peter Forsberg | 30.00 | 13.50 |
| ❑ 4 Brett Hull | 12.00 | 5.50 |
| ❑ 5 Jaromir Jagr | 30.00 | 13.50 |
| ❑ 6 Paul Kariya | 40.00 | 18.00 |
| ❑ 7 Joe Sakic | 20.00 | 9.00 |
| ❑ 8 Teemu Selanne | 20.00 | 9.00 |
| ❑ 9 Mats Sundin | 8.00 | 3.60 |
| ❑ 10 Steve Yzerman | 30.00 | 13.50 |

## 1996-97 Flair Hot Gloves

This insert set focuses on twelve of the NHL's best netminders. Card fronts feature a color action photo with the mesh of a goalie glove in the background. Card backs contain a player photo and biographical information. Each card is die-cut and randomly inserted in packs at a rate of one in 40.

| | MINT | NRMT |
|---|---|---|
| COMPLETE SET (12) | 300.00 | 135.00 |
| COMMON CARD (1-12) | 10.00 | 4.50 |
| ❑ 1 Ed Belfour | 12.00 | 5.50 |
| ❑ 2 Martin Brodeur | 30.00 | 13.50 |
| ❑ 3 Jim Carey | 10.00 | 4.50 |
| ❑ 4 Dominik Hasek | 25.00 | 11.00 |
| ❑ 5 Curtis Joseph | 12.00 | 5.50 |
| ❑ 6 Patrick Lalime | 40.00 | 18.00 |
| ❑ 7 Chris Osgood | 25.00 | 11.00 |
| ❑ 8 Felix Potvin | 30.00 | 13.50 |
| ❑ 9 Mike Richter | 12.00 | 5.50 |
| ❑ 10 Patrick Roy | 60.00 | 27.00 |
| ❑ 11 Jocelyn Thibault | 15.00 | 6.75 |
| ❑ 12 John Vanbiesbrouck | 20.00 | 9.00 |

## 1996-97 Flair Hot Numbers

This 10-card insert set features NHL superstars who wear double numbers on their jerseys. Card fronts feature a color photo with an orange/red background and their jersey number along the top of the card. The cards were randomly inserted in packs at a rate of one in 72.

| | MINT | NRMT |
|---|---|---|
| COMPLETE SET (10) | 150.00 | 70.00 |
| COMMON CARD (1-10) | 8.00 | 3.60 |
| ❑ 1 Ray Bourque | 10.00 | 4.50 |
| ❑ 2 Paul Coffey | 10.00 | 4.50 |
| ❑ 3 Eric Daze | 8.00 | 3.60 |
| ❑ 4 Wayne Gretzky | 50.00 | 22.00 |
| ❑ 5 Ed Jovanovski | 8.00 | 3.60 |
| ❑ 6 Saku Koivu | 12.00 | 5.50 |
| ❑ 7 Mario Lemieux | 40.00 | 18.00 |
| ❑ 8 Eric Lindros | 25.00 | 11.00 |
| ❑ 9 Mark Messier | 10.00 | 4.50 |
| ❑ 10 Owen Nolan | 8.00 | 3.60 |

## 1996-97 Flair Now And Then

Each card in this set features three players who share a common bond. They are pictured in their rookie seasons on the front, while the back gives an up-to-date look. The cards were randomly inserted in packs at a rate of one in 400.

| | MINT | NRMT |
|---|---|---|
| COMPLETE SET (3) | 400.00 | 180.00 |
| COMMON CARD (1-3) | 125.00 | 55.00 |
| ❑ 1 Wayne Gretzky<br>Mark Messier<br>Mike Gartner | 200.00 | 90.00 |
| ❑ 2 Mario Lemieux<br>Patrick Roy<br>Kirk Muller | 150.00 | 70.00 |
| ❑ 3 Eric Lindros<br>Peter Forsberg<br>Scott Niedermayer | 100.00 | 45.00 |

## 1972-73 Flames

This 20-card set of the Atlanta Flames measures 3 1/2" by 5 1/2". The fronts feature color action player photos with a white border. The player's autograph is across the bottom of the photo. The backs are blank. The cards are unnumbered and checklisted below in alphabetical order.

| | NRMT-MT | EXC |
|---|---|---|
| COMPLETE SET (20) | 50.00 | 22.00 |
| COMMON CARD (1-20) | 2.00 | .90 |
| ❑ 1 Curt Bennett | 2.00 | .90 |
| ❑ 2 Dan Bouchard | 5.00 | 2.20 |
| ❑ 3 Rey Comeau | 2.00 | .90 |
| ❑ 4 BoomBoom Geoffrion CO | 8.00 | 3.60 |
| ❑ 5 Bob Leiter | 2.00 | .90 |
| ❑ 6 Kerry Ketter | 2.00 | .90 |
| ❑ 7 Billy MacMillan | 2.00 | .90 |
| ❑ 8 Randy Manery | 2.00 | .90 |
| ❑ 9 Keith McCreary | 2.00 | .90 |
| ❑ 10 Lew Morrison | 2.00 | .90 |
| ❑ 11 Phil Myre | 5.00 | 2.20 |
| ❑ 12 Bob Paradise | 2.00 | .90 |
| ❑ 13 Noel Picard | 2.00 | .90 |
| ❑ 14 Bill Plager | 3.00 | 1.35 |
| ❑ 15 Noel Price | 3.00 | 1.35 |
| ❑ 16 Pat Quinn | 5.00 | 2.20 |
| ❑ 17 Jacques Richard | 3.00 | 1.35 |
| ❑ 18 Leon Rochefort | 2.00 | .90 |
| ❑ 19 Larry Romanchych | 2.00 | .90 |
| ❑ 20 John Stewart | 2.00 | .90 |

## 1979-80 Flames Postcards

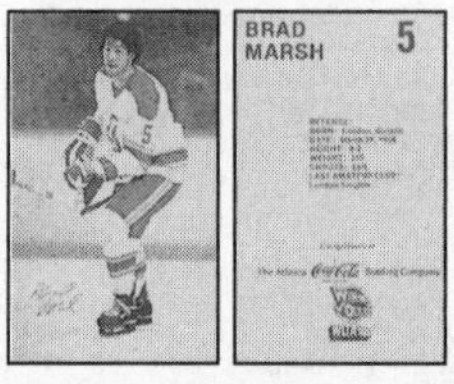


This 20-card set was sponsored by the Atlanta Coca-Cola Bottling Company, Winn Dixie, and radio station WLTA-100. The set is in the postcard format, with each card measuring approximately 3 1/2" by 5 1/2". The fronts feature full-bleed color action shots; a facsimile autograph is inscribed across the lower portion of the pictures. The backs carry the player's name, uniform number, biography, and sponsor logos. The cards are unnumbered and checklisted below in alphabetical order.

| | NRMT-MT | EXC |
|---|---|---|
| COMPLETE SET (20) | 30.00 | 13.50 |
| COMMON CARD (1-20) | 1.00 | .45 |
| ❑ 1 Curt Bennett | 1.00 | .45 |
| ❑ 2 Dan Bouchard | 3.00 | 1.35 |
| ❑ 3 Guy Chouinard | 2.00 | .90 |
| ❑ 4 Bill Clement | 2.50 | 1.10 |
| ❑ 5 Jim Craig | 4.00 | 1.80 |
| ❑ 6 Ken Houston | 1.00 | .45 |
| ❑ 7 Don Lever | 1.00 | .45 |
| ❑ 8 Bob MacMillan | 1.00 | .45 |
| ❑ 9 Brad Marsh | 4.00 | 1.80 |
| ❑ 10 Bob Murdoch | 1.50 | .70 |
| ❑ 11 Kent Nilsson | 4.00 | 1.80 |
| ❑ 12 Willi Plett | 2.00 | .90 |
| ❑ 13 Jean Pronovost | 1.50 | .70 |
| ❑ 14 Pekka Rautakallio | 1.00 | .45 |
| ❑ 15 Paul Reinhart | 1.50 | .70 |
| ❑ 16 Pat Riggin | 2.00 | .90 |
| ❑ 17 Phil Russell | 1.00 | .45 |
| ❑ 18 David Shand | 1.00 | .45 |
| ❑ 19 Garry Unger | 2.50 | 1.10 |
| ❑ 20 Eric Vail | 1.50 | .70 |

## 1979-80 Flames Team Issue

Cards measure 3 3/4 x 5 1/4 and feature black and white action photos on the front along with a facsimile signature. Backs are blank. Cards are unnumbered and checklisted below in alphabetical order.

| | MINT | NRMT |
|---|---|---|
| COMPLETE SET (22) | 40.00 | 18.00 |
| COMMON CARD (1-22) | 1.00 | .45 |
| ❑ 1 Curt Bennett | 1.00 | .45 |
| ❑ 2 Ivan Boldirev | 1.00 | .45 |
| ❑ 3 Dan Bouchard | 3.00 | 1.35 |
| ❑ 4 Guy Chouinard | 2.00 | .90 |
| ❑ 5 Bill Clement | 2.50 | 1.10 |
| ❑ 6 Jim Craig | 4.00 | 1.80 |
| ❑ 7 Ken Houston | 1.00 | .45 |
| ❑ 8 Brad Marsh | 4.00 | 1.80 |
| ❑ 9 Bob MacMillan | 1.00 | .45 |
| ❑ 10 Al McNeil | 1.00 | .45 |
| ❑ 11 Bob Murdoch | 1.50 | .70 |
| ❑ 12 Kent Nilsson | 4.00 | 1.80 |
| ❑ 13 Willi Plett | 2.00 | .90 |
| ❑ 14 Jean Pronovost | 1.50 | .70 |
| ❑ 15 Pekka Rautakallio | 1.00 | .45 |
| ❑ 16 Paul Reinhart | 1.50 | .70 |
| ❑ 17 Pat Riggin | 2.00 | .90 |
| ❑ 18 Darcy Rota | 1.00 | .45 |
| ❑ 19 Phil Russell | 1.00 | .45 |
| ❑ 20 David Shand | 1.00 | .45 |
| ❑ 21 Garry Unger | 2.50 | 1.10 |
| ❑ 22 Eric Vail | 1.50 | .70 |

## 1980-81 Flames Postcards

This 24-postcard set measures approximately 3 3/4" by 5". The fronts feature borderless posed color player photos. The backs are blank. The cards are unnumbered and checklisted below in alphabetical order.

| | NRMT-MT | EXC |
|---|---|---|
| COMPLETE SET (24) | 40.00 | 18.00 |
| COMMON CARD (1-24) | 1.00 | .45 |
| ❑ 1 Daniel Bouchard | 3.00 | 1.35 |
| ❑ 2 Guy Chouinard | 2.00 | .90 |
| ❑ 3 Bill Clement | 2.00 | .90 |
| ❑ 4 Denis Cyr | 1.00 | .45 |
| ❑ 5 Randy Holt | 1.00 | .45 |
| ❑ 6 Ken Houston | 1.00 | .45 |
| ❑ 7 Rejean Lemelin | 5.00 | 2.20 |
| ❑ 8 Kevin Lavallee | 1.00 | .45 |
| ❑ 9 Don Lever | 1.00 | .45 |
| ❑ 10 Bob MacMillan | 1.00 | .45 |
| ❑ 11 Bob Murdoch | 1.00 | .45 |
| ❑ 12 Brad Marsh | 2.50 | 1.10 |
| ❑ 13 Kent Nilsson | 4.00 | 1.80 |
| ❑ 14 Willi Plett | 1.50 | .70 |
| ❑ 15 Jim Peplinski | 2.50 | 1.10 |
| ❑ 16 Pekka Rautakallio | 2.00 | .90 |
| ❑ 17 Paul Reinhart | 2.50 | 1.10 |
| ❑ 18 Pat Riggin | 2.00 | .90 |
| ❑ 19 Phil Russell | 1.00 | .45 |
| ❑ 20 Brad Smith | 1.00 | .45 |
| ❑ 21 Jay Soleway | 1.00 | .45 |
| ❑ 22 Eric Vail | 1.50 | .70 |
| ❑ 23 Bert Wilson | 1.00 | .45 |
| ❑ 24 Team Photo | 1.50 | .70 |

## 1981-82 Flames Postcards

This 20-postcard set measures approximately 3 3/4" by 5". The fronts feature borderless posed color player photos. The backs are blank. The cards are unnumbered and checklisted below in alphabetical order.

| | NRMT-MT | EXC |
|---|---|---|
| COMPLETE SET (20) | 25.00 | 11.00 |
| COMMON CARD (1-20) | .75 | .35 |
| ❑ 1 Charlie Bourgeois | .75 | .35 |
| ❑ 2 Mel Bridgman | 1.00 | .45 |
| ❑ 3 Guy Chouinard | 1.50 | .70 |
| ❑ 4 Bill Clement | 1.50 | .70 |
| ❑ 5 Denis Cyr | .75 | .35 |
| ❑ 6 Jamie Hislop | .75 | .35 |
| ❑ 7 Ken Houston | .75 | .35 |
| ❑ 8 Steve Konroyd | .75 | .35 |
| ❑ 9 Dan Labraaten | .75 | .35 |
| ❑ 10 Kevin Lavallee | .75 | .35 |
| ❑ 11 Rejean Lemelin | 3.00 | 1.35 |
| ❑ 12 Lanny McDonald | 3.00 | 1.35 |
| ❑ 13 Gary McAdam | .75 | .35 |
| ❑ 14 Bob Murdoch | 1.00 | .45 |
| ❑ 15 Jim Peplinski | 2.00 | .90 |
| ❑ 16 Willi Plett | 1.50 | .70 |
| ❑ 17 Pekka Rautakallio | 1.00 | .45 |
| ❑ 18 Paul Reinhart | 1.50 | .70 |
| ❑ 19 Pat Riggin | 1.50 | .70 |
| ❑ 20 Phil Russell | .75 | .35 |

## 1982-83 Flames Dollars

These six cards, measuring approximately 3" by 5" and perforated on each end, were issued with "Hockey Dollars" or what may be better described as silver-colored coins. Each coin (measuring approximately 1 1/4" in diameter) displayed an engraving of the player's face on the obverse and the team logo on the reverse. The card fronts are gray with tan lettering. They have the player's name, number, year, team logo, and a picture of the coin. In a horizontal format, the backs carry biography, career highlights, and career statistics. The cards are numbered on the back in the upper right corner. The prices below refer to the coin-card combination intact.

| | MINT | NRMT |
|---|---|---|
| COMPLETE SET (6) | 25.00 | 11.00 |
| COMMON CARD (1-6) | 4.00 | 1.80 |
| ❑ 1 Mel Bridgman | 4.00 | 1.80 |
| ❑ 2 Don Edwards | 4.00 | 1.80 |
| ❑ 3 Lanny McDonald DP | 8.00 | 3.60 |
| ❑ 4 Kent Nilsson | 6.00 | 2.70 |
| ❑ 5 Jim Peplinski | 4.00 | 1.80 |
| ❑ 6 Paul Reinhart | 5.00 | 2.20 |

## 1985-86 Flames Red Rooster Police

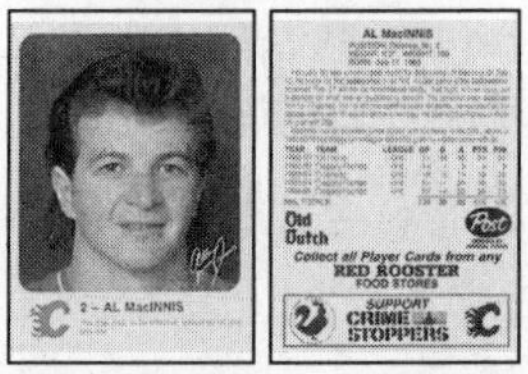


This 30-card set of Calgary Flames was sponsored by Red Rooster Food Stores, Old Dutch Potato Chips, and Post Cereals. The player cards could be collected from any Red Rooster Food Stores. The cards measure approximately 2 3/4" by 3 5/8" and feature on the front a color posed head shot (with rounded corners) of the player, with a facsimile autograph in white ink in the lower right-hand corner of the picture. The player's name, uniform number, the Calgary Flames' logo, and a hockey tip appear below the picture. The back has biographical and statistical information on the top portion, while the bottom has sponsor advertisements and the anti-crime slogan "Support Crime Stoppers." The set includes two different cards of Lanny McDonald and Doug Risebrough. Al MacInnis appears in his Rookie Card year whereas Mike Vernon's appearance predates his Rookie Card by two years.

| | MINT | NRMT |
|---|---|---|
| COMPLETE SET (30) | 25.00 | 11.00 |
| COMMON CARD (1-30) | .35 | .16 |
| ❑ 1 Paul Baxter | .35 | .16 |
| ❑ 2 Ed Beers | .35 | .16 |
| ❑ 3 Perry Berezan | .35 | .16 |
| ❑ 4 Charlie Bourgeois | .35 | .16 |
| ❑ 5 Steve Bozek | .35 | .16 |
| ❑ 6 Gino Cavallini | .35 | .16 |
| ❑ 7 Marc D'Amour | .50 | .23 |
| ❑ 8 Tim Hunter | 1.00 | .45 |
| ❑ 9 Bob Johnson CO | 2.50 | 1.10 |
| ❑ 10 Steve Konroyd | .35 | .16 |
| ❑ 11 Richard Kromm | .35 | .16 |
| ❑ 12 Rejean Lemelin | 1.00 | .45 |
| ❑ 13 Hakan Loob | 1.00 | .45 |
| ❑ 14 Lanny McDonald | 2.00 | .90 |
| ❑ 15 Lanny McDonald | 2.00 | .90 |
| ❑ 16 Al MacInnis | 6.00 | 2.70 |
| ❑ 17 Jamie Macoun | .50 | .23 |
| ❑ 18 Bob Murdoch CO | .35 | .16 |
| ❑ 19 Joel Otto | 1.50 | .70 |
| ❑ 20 Pierre Page CO | .50 | .23 |
| ❑ 21 Colin Patterson | .35 | .16 |
| ❑ 22 Jim Peplinski | .75 | .35 |
| ❑ 23 Dan Quinn | .50 | .23 |
| ❑ 24 Paul Reinhart | .75 | .35 |
| ❑ 25 Doug Risebrough | .35 | .16 |
| ❑ 26 Doug Risebrough | .35 | .16 |
| ❑ 27 Neil Sheehy | .35 | .16 |
| ❑ 28 Gary Suter | 1.00 | .45 |
| ❑ 29 Mike Vernon<br>(No facsimile autograph) | 6.00 | 2.70 |

on card front)
❑ 30 Carey Wilson .35 .16

## 1986-87 Flames Red Rooster

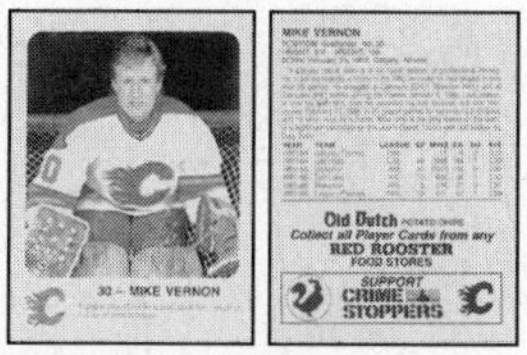

This 30-card set of Calgary Flames was sponsored by Red Rooster Food Stores in conjunction with Old Dutch Potato Chips. The player cards could be collected from any Red Rooster Food Stores. The cards measure approximately 2 3/4" by 3 5/8" and feature a color posed photo (with rounded corners) of the player, with a facsimile autograph in blue ink across the bottom of the picture. The player's name, uniform number, the Calgary Flames' logo, and a hockey tip appear below the picture. The back has biographical and statistical information on the top portion, while the bottom has sponsor advertisements and the anti-crime slogan "Support Crime Stoppers." The set includes two different cards of Lanny McDonald, Joe Mullen, and Paul Reinhart. Gary Roberts' card predates his Rookie Card year by three years.

| | MINT | NRMT |
|---|---|---|
| COMPLETE SET (30) | 20.00 | 9.00 |
| COMMON CARD (1-30) | .50 | .23 |

| | | |
|---|---|---|
| ❑ 1 Paul Baxter | .50 | .23 |
| ❑ 2 Perry Berezan | .50 | .23 |
| ❑ 3 Steve Bozek | .50 | .23 |
| ❑ 4 Brian Bradley | 1.00 | .45 |
| ❑ 5 Brian Engblom | .50 | .23 |
| ❑ 6 Nick Fotiu | .50 | .23 |
| ❑ 7 Tim Hunter | .75 | .35 |
| ❑ 8 Bob Johnson CO | 2.00 | .90 |
| ❑ 9 Rejean Lemelin | 1.00 | .45 |
| ❑ 10 Hakan Loob | 1.00 | .45 |
| ❑ 11 Al MacInnis | 3.00 | 1.35 |
| ❑ 12 Jamie Macoun | .50 | .23 |
| ❑ 13 Lanny McDonald | 1.50 | .70 |
| ❑ 14 Lanny McDonald | 1.50 | .70 |
| ❑ 15 Joe Mullen | 1.50 | .70 |
| ❑ 16 Joe Mullen | 1.50 | .70 |
| ❑ 17 Bob Murdoch CO | .50 | .23 |
| ❑ 18 Joel Otto | 1.00 | .45 |
| ❑ 19 Pierre Page CO | .50 | .23 |
| ❑ 20 Colin Patterson | .50 | .23 |
| ❑ 21 Jim Peplinski | .50 | .23 |
| ❑ 22 Paul Reinhart | .50 | .23 |
| ❑ 23 Paul Reinhart | .50 | .23 |
| ❑ 24 Doug Risebrough | .50 | .23 |
| ❑ 25 Gary Roberts | 4.00 | 1.80 |
| ❑ 26 Neil Sheehy | .50 | .23 |
| ❑ 27 Gary Suter | .75 | .35 |
| ❑ 28 John Tonelli | .75 | .35 |
| ❑ 29 Mike Vernon | 3.00 | 1.35 |
| ❑ 30 Carey Wilson | .50 | .23 |

## 1987-88 Flames Red Rooster Police

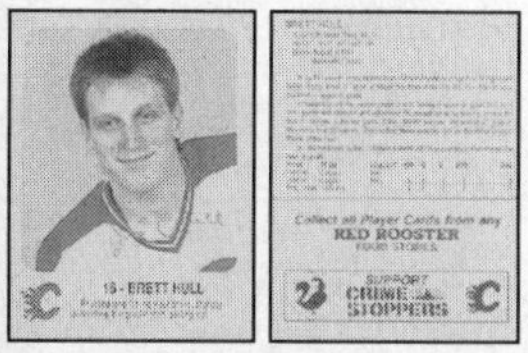

This 30-card set of Calgary Flames was sponsored by Red Rooster Food Stores, and the player cards could be collected from any of these stores. The cards measure 2 11/16" by 3 9/16" and feature on the front a color posed head-and-shoulders shot (with rounded corners) of the player, with a facsimile autograph in blue ink across the bottom of the picture. The player's name, uniform number, the Calgary Flames' logo, and a hockey tip appear below the picture. The back has biographical and statistical information on the top portion, while the bottom has a sponsor advertisement and the anti-crime slogan "Support Crime Stoppers." The set includes two different cards of Hakan Loob, Lanny McDonald, and Joe Nieuwendyk. The Brett Hull and Joe Nieuwendyk cards are the key cards in the set since they pre-date their O-Pee-Chee and Topps Rookie Cards by one year.

| | MINT | NRMT |
|---|---|---|
| COMPLETE SET (30) | 40.00 | 18.00 |
| COMMON CARD (1-30) | .35 | .16 |

| | | |
|---|---|---|
| ❑ 1 Perry Berezan | .35 | .16 |
| ❑ 2 Steve Bozek | .35 | .16 |
| ❑ 3 Mike Bullard | .50 | .23 |
| ❑ 4 Shane Churla | .75 | .35 |
| ❑ 5 Terry Crisp CO | .35 | .16 |
| ❑ 6 Doug Dadswell | .50 | .23 |
| ❑ 7 Brian Glynn | .35 | .16 |
| ❑ 8 Brett Hull | 20.00 | 9.00 |
| ❑ 9 Tim Hunter | .50 | .23 |
| ❑ 10 Hakan Loob | .75 | .35 |
| ❑ 11 Hakan Loob | .75 | .35 |
| ❑ 12 Al MacInnis | 2.00 | .90 |
| ❑ 13 Brad McCrimmon | .50 | .23 |
| ❑ 14 Lanny McDonald | 1.00 | .45 |
| ❑ 15 Lanny McDonald | 1.00 | .45 |
| ❑ 16 Joe Mullen | 1.00 | .45 |
| ❑ 17 Dana Murzyn | .35 | .16 |
| ❑ 18 Ric Nattress | .35 | .16 |
| ❑ 19 Joe Nieuwendyk | 6.00 | 2.70 |
| ❑ 20 Joe Nieuwendyk | 6.00 | 2.70 |
| ❑ 21 Joel Otto | .75 | .35 |
| ❑ 22 Pierre Page CO | .35 | .16 |
| ❑ 23 Colin Patterson | .35 | .16 |
| ❑ 24 Jim Peplinski | .50 | .23 |
| ❑ 25 Paul Reinhart | .50 | .23 |
| ❑ 26 Doug Risebrough CO | .35 | .16 |
| ❑ 27 Gary Roberts | 2.00 | .90 |
| ❑ 28 Gary Suter | .75 | .35 |
| ❑ 29 John Tonelli | .50 | .23 |
| ❑ 30 Mike Vernon | 2.00 | .90 |

## 1990-91 Flames IGA/McGavin's

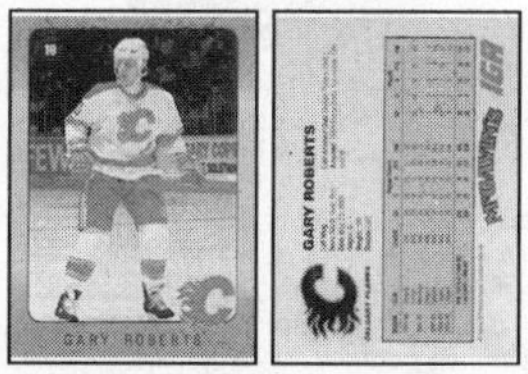

This 30-card standard-size set was sponsored by IGA food stores in conjunction with McGavin's, a distributor of bread and other products in Alberta. Protected by a cello pack, one card was inserted in bread loaves distributed by McGavin's to IGA stores in Calgary and Edmonton. Calgary consumers received a Flames' card, while Edmonton consumers received an Oilers' card. Checklist and coaches cards were not inserted in the loaves but were included on five hundred individually numbered and uncut sheets not offered to the general public. The cards are printed on thin card stock. The fronts have posed color player photos, with a border that shades from red to orange and back to red. The player's name is printed in the bottom border, and his uniform number is printed in a circle in the upper left corner of each picture. The horizontally oriented backs feature biographical information, with year-by-year statistics presented in a pink rectangle. Sponsor logos at the bottom round out the back. The cards are unnumbered and checklisted below in alphabetical order.

| | MINT | NRMT |
|---|---|---|
| COMPLETE SET (30) | 35.00 | 16.00 |
| COMMON CARD (1-30) | .50 | .23 |

| | | |
|---|---|---|
| ❑ 1 Paul Baxter CO SP | 3.00 | 1.35 |
| ❑ 2 Guy Charron CO SP | 4.00 | 1.80 |
| ❑ 3 Theoren Fleury | 5.00 | 2.20 |
| ❑ 4 Doug Gilmour | 5.00 | 2.20 |
| ❑ 5 Jiri Hrdina | .50 | .23 |
| ❑ 6 Mark Hunter | .50 | .23 |
| ❑ 7 Tim Hunter | 1.00 | .45 |
| ❑ 8 Roger Johansson | .50 | .23 |
| ❑ 9 Al MacInnis | 2.00 | .90 |
| ❑ 10 Brian MacLellan | .50 | .23 |
| ❑ 11 Jamie Macoun | .75 | .35 |
| ❑ 12 Sergei Makarov | 1.50 | .70 |
| ❑ 13 Sergei Makarov (Calder Trophy Winner) and Al MacInnis (NHL First AS Team& Defence 1989-90) | 1.50 | .70 |
| ❑ 14 Stephane Matteau | .75 | .35 |
| ❑ 15 Dana Murzyn | .50 | .23 |
| ❑ 16 Frantisek Musil | .50 | .23 |
| ❑ 17 Ric Nattress | .50 | .23 |
| ❑ 18 Joe Nieuwendyk | 3.00 | 1.35 |
| ❑ 19 Joel Otto | 1.00 | .45 |
| ❑ 20 Colin Patterson | .50 | .23 |
| ❑ 21 Sergei Priakin | .50 | .23 |
| ❑ 22 Paul Ranheim | .75 | .35 |
| ❑ 23 Robert Reichel | 1.50 | .70 |
| ❑ 24 Doug Risebrough SP CO/GM | 3.00 | 1.35 |
| ❑ 25 Gary Roberts | 2.00 | .90 |
| ❑ 26 Gary Suter | 1.00 | .45 |
| ❑ 27 Tim Sweeney | .50 | .23 |
| ❑ 28 Mike Vernon | 2.00 | .90 |
| ❑ 29 Rick Wamsley | 1.00 | .45 |
| ❑ 30 Checklist Card SP | 3.00 | 1.35 |

## 1991 Flames Panini Team Stickers

This 32-sticker set was issued in a plastic bag that contained two 16-sticker sheets (approximately 9" by 12") and a foldout poster, "Super Poster - Hockey 91", on which the stickers could be affixed. The players' names appear only on the poster, not on the stickers. Each sticker measures about 2 1/8" by 2 7/8" and features a color player action shot on its white-bordered front. The back of the white sticker sheet is lined off into 16 panels, each carrying the logos for Panini, the NHL, and the NHLPA, as well as the same number that appears on the front of the sticker. Every Canadian NHL team was featured in this promotion. Each team set was available by mail-order from Panini Canada Ltd. for 2.99 plus 50 cents for shipping and handling.

| | MINT | NRMT |
|---|---|---|
| COMPLETE SET (32) | 4.00 | 1.80 |
| COMMON STICKER (1-24) | .05 | .02 |
| COMMON STICKER (A-H) | .05 | .02 |

| | | |
|---|---|---|
| ❑ 1 Theoren Fleury | .75 | .35 |
| ❑ 2 Doug Gilmour | .75 | .35 |
| ❑ 3 Jiri Hrdina | .05 | .02 |
| ❑ 4 Mark Hunter | .05 | .02 |
| ❑ 5 Tim Hunter | .10 | .05 |
| ❑ 6 Roger Johansson | .05 | .02 |
| ❑ 7 Al MacInnis | .35 | .16 |
| ❑ 8 Brian MacLellan | .05 | .02 |
| ❑ 9 Jamie Macoun | .05 | .02 |
| ❑ 10 Sergei Makarov | .25 | .11 |
| ❑ 11 Stephane Matteau | .05 | .02 |
| ❑ 12 Dana Murzyn | .05 | .02 |
| ❑ 13 Ric Nattress | .05 | .02 |
| ❑ 14 Joe Nieuwendyk | .40 | .18 |
| ❑ 15 Joel Otto | .15 | .07 |
| ❑ 16 Colin Patterson | .05 | .02 |
| ❑ 17 Sergei Priakin | .05 | .02 |
| ❑ 18 Paul Ranheim | .10 | .05 |
| ❑ 19 Gary Roberts | .35 | .16 |
| ❑ 20 Ken Sabourin | .05 | .02 |
| ❑ 21 Gary Suter | .10 | .05 |
| ❑ 22 Tim Sweeney | .05 | .02 |
| ❑ 23 Mike Vernon | .35 | .16 |
| ❑ 24 Rick Wamsley | .10 | .05 |
| ❑ A Team Logo Left Side | .05 | .02 |
| ❑ B Team Logo Right Side | .05 | .02 |
| ❑ C Flames' Time Out Upper Left Corner | .05 | .02 |
| ❑ D Flames' Time Out Lower Left Corner | .05 | .02 |
| ❑ E Flames' Time Out Upper Right Corner | .05 | .02 |
| ❑ F Flames' Time Out Lower Right Corner | .05 | .02 |
| ❑ G Joel Otto Roger Johansson | .10 | .05 |
| ❑ H Gary Suter | .10 | .05 |

## 1991-92 Flames IGA

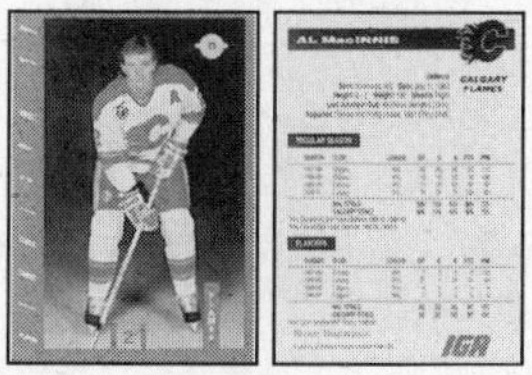

This 30-card standard-size set of Calgary Flames was sponsored by IGA food stores and included manufacturers' discount coupons. One pack of cards was distributed in Calgary and Edmonton IGA stores with any grocery purchase of 10.00 or more. The cards are printed on thin card stock. The fronts have posed color action photos bordered in red. The player's name is printed vertically in the wider left border, and his uniform number and the team name appear at the bottom of the picture. In black print on a white background, the backs present biography and statistics (regular season and playoff). Packs were kept under the cash drawer, and therefore many of the cards were creased. Each pack contained three Oilers and two Flames cards. The checklist and coaches cards for both teams were not included in the packs but were available on a very limited basis through an uncut team sheet offer. Also the Osiecki card seemed to be in short supply, either because of short printing or short distribution. The cards are unnumbered and checklisted below in alphabetical order, with the coaches cards listed after the players.

| | MINT | NRMT |
|---|---|---|
| COMPLETE SET (30) | 25.00 | 11.00 |
| COMMON CARD (1-30) | .40 | .18 |

| | | |
|---|---|---|
| ❑ 1 Theoren Fleury | 2.50 | 1.10 |
| ❑ 2 Tomas Forslund | .40 | .18 |
| ❑ 3 Doug Gilmour | 2.50 | 1.10 |
| ❑ 4 Marc Habscheid | .40 | .18 |
| ❑ 5 Tim Hunter | .60 | .25 |
| ❑ 6 Jim Kyte | .40 | .18 |
| ❑ 7 Al MacInnis | 1.00 | .45 |
| ❑ 8 Jamie Macoun | .40 | .18 |
| ❑ 9 Sergei Makarov | 1.00 | .45 |
| ❑ 10 Stephane Matteau | .40 | .18 |
| ❑ 11 Frantisek Musil | .40 | .18 |
| ❑ 12 Ric Nattress | .40 | .18 |
| ❑ 13 Joe Nieuwendyk | 1.25 | .55 |
| ❑ 14 Mark Osiecki | 2.00 | .90 |
| ❑ 15 Joel Otto | .60 | .25 |
| ❑ 16 Paul Ranheim | .40 | .18 |
| ❑ 17 Robert Reichel | .75 | .35 |
| ❑ 18 Gary Roberts | 1.00 | .45 |
| ❑ 19 Neil Sheehy | .40 | .18 |
| ❑ 20 Martin Simard | .40 | .18 |
| ❑ 21 Ronnie Stern | .40 | .18 |
| ❑ 22 Gary Suter | .75 | .35 |
| ❑ 23 Tim Sweeney | .40 | .18 |
| ❑ 24 Mike Vernon | 1.00 | .45 |
| ❑ 25 Rick Wamsley | .75 | .35 |
| ❑ 26 Carey Wilson | .40 | .18 |
| ❑ 27 Paul Baxter CO SP | 2.50 | 1.10 |
| ❑ 28 Guy Charron CO SP | 2.50 | 1.10 |
| ❑ 29 Doug Risebrough CO SP | 2.50 | 1.10 |
| ❑ 30 Checklist Card SP | 2.50 | 1.10 |

## 1992-93 Flames IGA

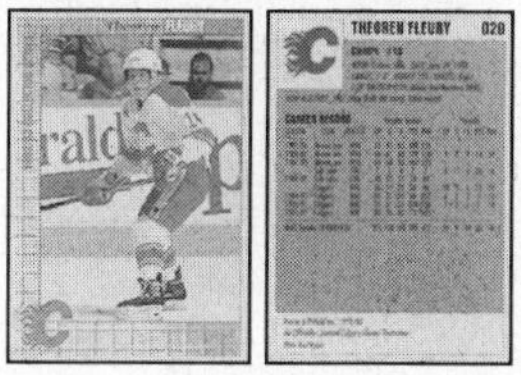

Sponsored by IGA food stores, the 30 standard-size cards comprising this Special Edition Collector Series set feature color player action shots on their fronts. Each photo is trimmed with a black line and offset flush with the thin white border on the right, which surrounds the card. On the remaining three sides, the picture is edged with a gray and white netlike pattern. The player's name appears in the upper right and the Flames logo rests in the lower left. The back carries the player's name at the top, with his position, uniform number, biography, and stat table set within a reddish-gray screened background. The Flames logo in the upper right rounds out the card.

| | MINT | NRMT |
|---|---|---|
| COMPLETE SET (30) | 15.00 | 6.75 |
| COMMON CARD (1-30) | .25 | .11 |

| | | |
|---|---|---|
| ❑ 1 Checklist | .40 | .18 |
| ❑ 2 Craig Berube | .40 | .18 |
| ❑ 3 Gary Leeman | .40 | .18 |
| ❑ 4 Joel Otto | .75 | .35 |
| ❑ 5 Robert Reichel | 1.00 | .45 |
| ❑ 6 Gary Roberts | 1.50 | .70 |
| ❑ 7 Greg Smyth | .40 | .18 |
| ❑ 8 Gary Suter | .75 | .35 |
| ❑ 9 Jeff Reese | .60 | .25 |
| ❑ 10 Mike Vernon | 1.50 | .70 |
| ❑ 11 Carey Wilson | .40 | .18 |
| ❑ 12 Trent Yawney | .40 | .18 |
| ❑ 13 Michel Petit | .40 | .18 |
| ❑ 14 Paul Ranheim | .40 | .18 |
| ❑ 15 Sergei Makarov | 1.00 | .45 |
| ❑ 16 Frantisek Musil | .40 | .18 |
| ❑ 17 Joe Nieuwendyk | 1.75 | .80 |
| ❑ 18 Alexander Godynyuk | .40 | .18 |
| ❑ 19 Roger Johansson | .40 | .18 |
| ❑ 20 Theoren Fleury | 2.50 | 1.10 |
| ❑ 21 Chris Lindberg | .40 | .18 |
| ❑ 22 Al MacInnis | 1.50 | .70 |
| ❑ 23 Kevin Dahl | .40 | .18 |
| ❑ 24 Chris Dahlquist | .40 | .18 |
| ❑ 25 Ronnie Stern | .50 | .23 |
| ❑ 26 Dave King CO | .50 | .23 |
| ❑ 27 Guy Charron CO | .25 | .11 |
| ❑ 28 Slavomir Lener CO | .25 | .11 |
| ❑ 29 Jamie Hislop CO | .25 | .11 |
| ❑ 30 Franchise History | .40 | .18 |

## 1994-95 Fleer

This set was issued in a single 250-card series. Cards were issued in 12-card hobby and 18-card jumbo packs. There are four different card front designs, one unique to each of the NHL's divisions. Each card front has personal information in varying positions on the card. The card backs are all similar as they feature two photos, the player's name and expanded statistics. Rookie Cards include Mariusz Czerkawski, Blaine Lacher, David Oliver, Radek Bonk and Jim Carey.

| | MINT | NRMT |
|---|---|---|
| COMPLETE SET (250) | 25.00 | 11.00 |
| COMMON CARD (1-250) | .10 | .05 |

| | | |
|---|---|---|
| ❑ 1 Patrik Carnback | .10 | .05 |
| ❑ 2 Bob Corkum | .10 | .05 |
| ❑ 3 Paul Kariya | 1.50 | .70 |
| ❑ 4 Valeri Karpov | .10 | .05 |
| ❑ 5 Tom Kurvers | .10 | .05 |
| ❑ 6 John Lilley | .10 | .05 |
| ❑ 7 Mikhail Shtalenkov | .10 | .05 |
| ❑ 8 Oleg Tverdovsky | .15 | .07 |
| ❑ 9 Ray Bourque | .30 | .14 |
| ❑ 10 Mariusz Czerkawski | .10 | .05 |
| ❑ 11 John Gruden | .10 | .05 |
| ❑ 12 Al Iafrate | .10 | .05 |
| ❑ 13 Blaine Lacher | .15 | .07 |
| ❑ 14 Mats Naslund | .10 | .05 |
| ❑ 15 Cam Neely | .15 | .07 |
| ❑ 16 Adam Oates | .15 | .07 |
| ❑ 17 Bryan Smolinski | .10 | .05 |
| ❑ 18 Don Sweeney | .10 | .05 |
| ❑ 19 Donald Audette | .15 | .07 |
| ❑ 20 Dominik Hasek | .60 | .25 |
| ❑ 21 Dale Hawerchuk | .15 | .07 |
| ❑ 22 Yuri Khmylev | .10 | .05 |
| ❑ 23 Pat LaFontaine | .15 | .07 |
| ❑ 24 Brad May | .15 | .07 |
| ❑ 25 Alexander Mogilny | .15 | .07 |
| ❑ 26 Derek Plante | .10 | .05 |
| ❑ 27 Richard Smehlik | .10 | .05 |
| ❑ 28 Steve Chiasson | .10 | .05 |
| ❑ 29 Theoren Fleury | .15 | .07 |
| ❑ 30 Phil Housley | .15 | .07 |
| ❑ 31 Trevor Kidd | .15 | .07 |
| ❑ 32 Joe Nieuwendyk | .15 | .07 |
| ❑ 33 James Patrick | .10 | .05 |
| ❑ 34 Robert Reichel | .10 | .05 |
| ❑ 35 Gary Roberts | .10 | .05 |
| ❑ 36 German Titov | .10 | .05 |
| ❑ 37 Tony Amonte | .15 | .07 |
| ❑ 38 Ed Belfour | .30 | .14 |
| ❑ 39 Chris Chelios | .30 | .14 |
| ❑ 40 Dirk Graham | .10 | .05 |
| ❑ 41 Sergei Krivokrasov | .10 | .05 |
| ❑ 42 Joe Murphy | .10 | .05 |
| ❑ 43 Bernie Nicholls | .10 | .05 |
| ❑ 44 Patrick Poulin | .10 | .05 |
| ❑ 45 Jeremy Roenick | .30 | .14 |
| ❑ 46 Steve Smith | .10 | .05 |
| ❑ 47 Gary Suter | .10 | .05 |
| ❑ 48 Russ Courtnall | .10 | .05 |
| ❑ 49 Dave Gagner | .15 | .07 |
| ❑ 50 Brent Gilchrist | .10 | .05 |
| ❑ 51 Todd Harvey | .15 | .07 |
| ❑ 52 Derian Hatcher | .10 | .05 |
| ❑ 53 Kevin Hatcher | .10 | .05 |
| ❑ 54 Mike Kennedy | .10 | .05 |
| ❑ 55 Mike Modano | .15 | .07 |
| ❑ 56 Andy Moog | .15 | .07 |
| ❑ 57 Dino Ciccarelli | .15 | .07 |
| ❑ 58 Paul Coffey | .30 | .14 |
| ❑ 59 Sergei Fedorov | .50 | .23 |
| ❑ 60 Vladimir Konstantinov | .10 | .05 |
| ❑ 61 Slava Kozlov | .15 | .07 |
| ❑ 62 Nicklas Lidstrom | .15 | .07 |
| ❑ 63 Chris Osgood | .50 | .23 |
| ❑ 64 Keith Primeau | .15 | .07 |
| ❑ 65 Ray Sheppard | .15 | .07 |
| ❑ 66 Mike Vernon | .15 | .07 |
| ❑ 67 Steve Yzerman | 1.00 | .45 |
| ❑ 68 Jason Arnott | .15 | .07 |
| ❑ 69 Shayne Corson | .10 | .05 |
| ❑ 70 Igor Kravchuk | .10 | .05 |
| ❑ 71 Todd Marchant | .10 | .05 |
| ❑ 72 Roman Oksiuta | .10 | .05 |
| ❑ 73 Fredrik Olausson | .10 | .05 |
| ❑ 74 David Oliver | .10 | .05 |
| ❑ 75 Bill Ranford | .15 | .07 |
| ❑ 76 Stu Barnes | .10 | .05 |
| ❑ 77 Jesse Belanger | .10 | .05 |
| ❑ 78 Keith Brown | .10 | .05 |
| ❑ 79 Bob Kudelski | .10 | .05 |
| ❑ 80 Scott Mellanby | .15 | .07 |
| ❑ 81 Gord Murphy | .10 | .05 |
| ❑ 82 Rob Niedermayer | .15 | .07 |
| ❑ 83 John Vanbiesbrouck | .50 | .23 |
| ❑ 84 Sean Burke | .15 | .07 |
| ❑ 85 Jimmy Carson | .10 | .05 |
| ❑ 86 Andrew Cassels | .10 | .05 |
| ❑ 87 Andrei Nikolishin | .10 | .05 |
| ❑ 88 Chris Pronger | .15 | .07 |
| ❑ 89 Geoff Sanderson | .15 | .07 |
| ❑ 90 Darren Turcotte | .10 | .05 |
| ❑ 91 Pat Verbeek | .10 | .05 |
| ❑ 92 Glen Wesley | .10 | .05 |
| ❑ 93 Rob Blake | .10 | .05 |
| ❑ 94 Wayne Gretzky | 2.00 | .90 |
| ❑ 95 Kelly Hrudey | .15 | .07 |
| ❑ 96 Jari Kurri | .15 | .07 |
| ❑ 97 Eric Lacroix | .10 | .05 |
| ❑ 98 Marty McSorley | .10 | .05 |
| ❑ 99 Jamie Storr | .15 | .07 |
| ❑ 100 Rick Tocchet | .15 | .07 |
| ❑ 101 Brian Bellows | .10 | .05 |
| ❑ 102 Patrice Brisebois | .10 | .05 |
| ❑ 103 Vincent Damphousse | .15 | .07 |
| ❑ 104 Kirk Muller | .10 | .05 |
| ❑ 105 Lyle Odelein | .10 | .05 |
| ❑ 106 Mark Recchi | .15 | .07 |
| ❑ 107 Patrick Roy | 1.50 | .70 |
| ❑ 108 Brian Savage | .10 | .05 |
| ❑ 109 Mathieu Schneider | .10 | .05 |

| | | |
|---|---|---|
| ❑ 110 Turner Stevenson | .10 | .05 |
| ❑ 111 Martin Brodeur | .75 | .35 |
| ❑ 112 Bill Guerin | .10 | .05 |
| ❑ 113 Claude Lemieux | .15 | .07 |
| ❑ 114 John MacLean | .15 | .07 |
| ❑ 115 Scott Niedermayer | .10 | .05 |
| ❑ 116 Stephane Richer | .15 | .07 |
| ❑ 117 Brian Rolston | .10 | .05 |
| ❑ 118 Alexander Semak | .10 | .05 |
| ❑ 119 Scott Stevens | .15 | .07 |
| ❑ 120 Ray Ferraro | .10 | .05 |
| ❑ 121 Patrick Flatley | .10 | .05 |
| ❑ 122 Darius Kasparaitis | .10 | .05 |
| ❑ 123 Derek King | .10 | .05 |
| ❑ 124 Scott Lachance | .10 | .05 |
| ❑ 125 Brett Lindros | .10 | .05 |
| ❑ 126 Vladimir Malakhov | .10 | .05 |
| ❑ 127 Jamie McLennan | .10 | .05 |
| ❑ 128 Zigmund Palffy | .30 | .14 |
| ❑ 129 Steve Thomas | .10 | .05 |
| ❑ 130 Pierre Turgeon | .15 | .07 |
| ❑ 131 Jeff Beukeboom | .10 | .05 |
| ❑ 132 Adam Graves | .15 | .07 |
| ❑ 133 Alexei Kovalev | .15 | .07 |
| ❑ 134 Steve Larmer | .15 | .07 |
| ❑ 135 Brian Leetch | .30 | .14 |
| ❑ 136 Mark Messier | .40 | .18 |
| ❑ 137 Petr Nedved | .15 | .07 |
| ❑ 138 Sergei Nemchinov | .10 | .05 |
| ❑ 139 Mike Richter | .30 | .14 |
| ❑ 140 Sergei Zubov | .10 | .05 |
| ❑ 141 Don Beaupre | .15 | .07 |
| ❑ 142 Radek Bonk | .10 | .05 |
| ❑ 143 Alexandre Daigle | .10 | .05 |
| ❑ 144 Pavol Demitra | .10 | .05 |
| ❑ 145 Pat Elynuik | .10 | .05 |
| ❑ 146 Rob Gaudreau | .10 | .05 |
| ❑ 147 Sean Hill | .10 | .05 |
| ❑ 148 Sylvain Turgeon | .10 | .05 |
| ❑ 149 Alexei Yashin | .15 | .07 |
| ❑ 150 Rod Brind'Amour | .15 | .07 |
| ❑ 151 Eric Desjardins | .10 | .05 |
| ❑ 152 Gilbert Dionne | .10 | .05 |
| ❑ 153 Garry Galley | .10 | .05 |
| ❑ 154 Ron Hextall | .15 | .07 |
| ❑ 155 Patrik Juhlin | .10 | .05 |
| ❑ 156 John LeClair | .50 | .23 |
| ❑ 157 Eric Lindros | 1.25 | .55 |
| ❑ 158 Mikael Renberg | .15 | .07 |
| ❑ 159 Chris Therien | .10 | .05 |
| ❑ 160 Dimitri Yushkevich | .10 | .05 |
| ❑ 161 Len Barrie | .10 | .05 |
| ❑ 162 Ron Francis | .15 | .07 |
| ❑ 163 Jaromir Jagr | 1.00 | .45 |
| ❑ 164 Shawn McEachern | .10 | .05 |
| ❑ 165 Joe Mullen | .15 | .07 |
| ❑ 166 Larry Murphy | .15 | .07 |
| ❑ 167 Luc Robitaille | .15 | .07 |
| ❑ 168 Ulf Samuelsson | .10 | .05 |
| ❑ 169 Tomas Sandstrom | .10 | .05 |
| ❑ 170 Kevin Stevens | .10 | .05 |
| ❑ 171 Martin Straka | .10 | .05 |
| ❑ 172 Ken Wregget | .15 | .07 |
| ❑ 173 Wendel Clark | .15 | .07 |
| ❑ 174 Adam Deadmarsh | .15 | .07 |
| ❑ 175 Stephane Fiset | .15 | .07 |
| ❑ 176 Peter Forsberg | 1.25 | .55 |
| ❑ 177 Valeri Kamensky | .15 | .07 |
| ❑ 178 Andrei Kovalenko | .10 | .05 |
| ❑ 179 Uwe Krupp | .10 | .05 |
| ❑ 180 Sylvain Lefebvre | .10 | .05 |
| ❑ 181 Owen Nolan | .15 | .07 |
| ❑ 182 Mike Ricci | .10 | .05 |
| ❑ 183 Joe Sakic | .60 | .25 |
| ❑ 184 Denis Chasse | .10 | .05 |
| ❑ 185 Adam Creighton | .10 | .05 |
| ❑ 186 Steve Duchesne | .10 | .05 |
| ❑ 187 Brett Hull | .40 | .18 |
| ❑ 188 Curtis Joseph | .30 | .14 |
| ❑ 189 Ian Laperriere | .10 | .05 |
| ❑ 190 Al MacInnis | .15 | .07 |
| ❑ 191 Brendan Shanahan | .60 | .25 |
| ❑ 192 Patrice Tardif | .10 | .05 |
| ❑ 193 Esa Tikkanen | .10 | .05 |
| ❑ 194 Ulf Dahlen | .10 | .05 |
| ❑ 195 Pat Falloon | .10 | .05 |
| ❑ 196 Jeff Friesen | .15 | .07 |
| ❑ 197 Arturs Irbe | .15 | .07 |
| ❑ 198 Sergei Makarov | .10 | .05 |
| ❑ 199 Andrei Nazarov | .10 | .05 |
| ❑ 200 Sandis Ozolinsh | .15 | .07 |
| ❑ 201 Michal Sykora | .10 | .05 |
| ❑ 202 Ray Whitney | .10 | .05 |
| ❑ 203 Brian Bradley | .10 | .05 |
| ❑ 204 Shawn Chambers | .10 | .05 |
| ❑ 205 Eric Charron | .10 | .05 |
| ❑ 206 Chris Gratton | .15 | .07 |
| ❑ 207 Roman Hamrlik | .15 | .07 |
| ❑ 208 Petr Klima | .10 | .05 |
| ❑ 209 Daren Puppa | .15 | .07 |
| ❑ 210 Alexander Selivanov | .10 | .05 |
| ❑ 211 Jason Wiemer | .10 | .05 |
| ❑ 212 Dave Andreychuk | .15 | .07 |
| ❑ 213 Dave Ellett | .10 | .05 |
| ❑ 214 Mike Gartner | .15 | .07 |
| ❑ 215 Doug Gilmour | .30 | .14 |
| ❑ 216 Kenny Jonsson | .10 | .05 |
| ❑ 217 Dmitri Mironov | .10 | .05 |
| ❑ 218 Felix Potvin | .30 | .14 |
| ❑ 219 Mike Ridley | .10 | .05 |
| ❑ 220 Mats Sundin | .15 | .07 |
| ❑ 221 Josef Beranek | .10 | .05 |
| ❑ 222 Jeff Brown | .10 | .05 |
| ❑ 223 Pavel Bure | .60 | .25 |
| ❑ 224 Geoff Courtnall | .10 | .05 |
| ❑ 225 Trevor Linden | .15 | .07 |
| ❑ 226 Jyrki Lumme | .10 | .05 |
| ❑ 227 Kirk McLean | .15 | .07 |
| ❑ 228 Gino Odjick | .10 | .05 |
| ❑ 229 Mike Peca | .10 | .05 |
| ❑ 230 Cliff Ronning | .10 | .05 |
| ❑ 231 Jason Allison | .10 | .05 |
| ❑ 232 Peter Bondra | .30 | .14 |
| ❑ 233 Jim Carey | .75 | .35 |
| ❑ 234 Sylvain Cote | .10 | .05 |
| ❑ 235 Dale Hunter | .10 | .05 |
| ❑ 236 Joe Juneau | .15 | .07 |
| ❑ 237 Dimitri Khristich | .10 | .05 |
| ❑ 238 Pat Peake | .10 | .05 |
| ❑ 239 Mark Tinordi | .10 | .05 |
| ❑ 240 Nelson Emerson | .10 | .05 |
| ❑ 241 Michal Grosek | .10 | .05 |
| ❑ 242 Nikolai Khabibulin | .15 | .07 |
| ❑ 243 Dave Manson | .10 | .05 |
| ❑ 244 Stephane Quintal | .10 | .05 |
| ❑ 245 Teemu Selanne | .50 | .23 |
| ❑ 246 Keith Tkachuk | .40 | .18 |
| ❑ 247 Alexei Zhamnov | .15 | .07 |
| ❑ 248 Checklist | .10 | .05 |
| ❑ 249 Checklist | .10 | .05 |
| ❑ 250 Checklist | .10 | .05 |

## 1994-95 Fleer Franchise Futures

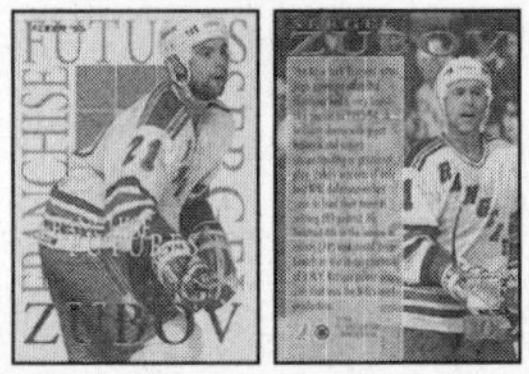

The 10-card set was randomly inserted at a rate of 1:7 12-card hobby packs. The set features young stars of the NHL in action photos positioned over the card title. The background is in the color of the team. The back has a photo and player information.

| | MINT | NRMT |
|---|---|---|
| COMPLETE SET (10) | 10.00 | 4.50 |
| COMMON CARD (1-10) | .50 | .23 |
| ❑ 1 Jason Arnott | 3.00 | 1.35 |
| ❑ 2 Rob Blake | .50 | .23 |
| ❑ 3 Adam Graves | .50 | .23 |
| ❑ 4 Arturs Irbe | .50 | .23 |
| ❑ 5 Joe Juneau | .50 | .23 |
| ❑ 6 Sandis Ozolinsh | .75 | .35 |
| ❑ 7 Mikael Renberg | 2.00 | .90 |
| ❑ 8 Keith Tkachuk | 4.00 | 1.80 |
| ❑ 9 Alexei Yashin | .75 | .35 |
| ❑ 10 Sergei Zubov | .50 | .23 |

## 1994-95 Fleer Headliners

This 10-card set was randomly inserted in packs at the rate of 1:4. The set features the superstars of the league in a borderless design. The word "Headliner", the player's name and team are printed in silver foil on the lower portion of the card front. A photo and informative text are on the back.

| | MINT | NRMT |
|---|---|---|
| COMPLETE SET (10) | 15.00 | 6.75 |
| COMMON CARD (1-10) | .50 | .23 |
| ❑ 1 Pavel Bure | 1.50 | .70 |
| ❑ 2 Sergei Fedorov | 1.50 | .70 |
| ❑ 3 Doug Gilmour | .75 | .35 |
| ❑ 4 Wayne Gretzky | 5.00 | 2.20 |
| ❑ 5 Brian Leetch | .75 | .35 |
| ❑ 6 Eric Lindros | 3.00 | 1.35 |
| ❑ 7 Mark Messier | 1.00 | .45 |
| ❑ 8 Cam Neely | .50 | .23 |
| ❑ 9 Mark Recchi | .50 | .23 |
| ❑ 10 Brendan Shanahan | 1.50 | .70 |

## 1994-95 Fleer Netminders

The easiest of the Fleer insert sets, these 10-card set was found at the rate of 1:2 packs. The set features the top goalies in the league in a silhouetted design. The word "Netminder" and the player's name are printed in gold foil on the front side portion of the card front. A portrait photo and player information are on the back.

| | MINT | NRMT |
|---|---|---|
| COMPLETE SET (10) | 8.00 | 3.60 |
| COMMON CARD (1-10) | .50 | .23 |
| ❑ 1 Ed Belfour | .75 | .35 |
| ❑ 2 Martin Brodeur | 1.50 | .70 |
| ❑ 3 Dominik Hasek | 1.25 | .55 |
| ❑ 4 Arturs Irbe | .50 | .23 |
| ❑ 5 Curtis Joseph | .75 | .35 |
| ❑ 6 Kirk McLean | .50 | .23 |
| ❑ 7 Felix Potvin | .75 | .35 |
| ❑ 8 Mike Richter | .75 | .35 |
| ❑ 9 Patrick Roy | 3.00 | 1.35 |
| ❑ 10 John Vanbiesbrouck | 1.00 | .45 |

## 1994-95 Fleer Rookie Sensations

This 10-card set was randomly inserted at a rate of 1:7 jumbo retail packs. The set features the top first-year stars of the league over a water-splashed design. The phrase "Rookie Sensation" along with the player's name are printed in silver foil in the center portion of the card front. A photo and text information are on the back.

| | MINT | NRMT |
|---|---|---|
| COMPLETE SET (10) | 75.00 | 34.00 |
| COMMON CARD (1-10) | 2.00 | .90 |
| ❑ 1 Radek Bonk | 5.00 | 2.20 |
| ❑ 2 Peter Forsberg | 25.00 | 11.00 |
| ❑ 3 Jeff Friesen | 6.00 | 2.70 |
| ❑ 4 Todd Harvey | 2.00 | .90 |
| ❑ 5 Paul Kariya | 25.00 | 11.00 |
| ❑ 6 Blaine Lacher | 5.00 | 2.20 |
| ❑ 7 Brett Lindros | 2.00 | .90 |
| ❑ 8 Mike Peca | 2.00 | .90 |
| ❑ 9 Jamie Storr | 5.00 | 2.20 |
| ❑ 10 Oleg Tverdovsky | 5.00 | 2.20 |

## 1994-95 Fleer Slapshot Artists

The most difficult of the Fleer inserts, the ten cards in this set were inserted at the rate of 1:12 packs. The cards feature a silhouetted player photo surrounded by three smaller cut-out versions of the same photo. The background is in the team's color. The back has the player's photo and career information.

| | MINT | NRMT |
|---|---|---|
| COMPLETE SET (10) | 30.00 | 13.50 |
| COMMON CARD (1-10) | 1.00 | .45 |
| ❑ 1 Wendel Clark | 2.00 | .90 |
| ❑ 2 Brett Hull | 5.00 | 2.20 |
| ❑ 3 Al Iafrate | 1.00 | .45 |
| ❑ 4 Jaromir Jagr | 12.00 | 5.50 |
| ❑ 5 Al MacInnis | 1.00 | .45 |
| ❑ 6 Mike Modano | 5.00 | 2.20 |
| ❑ 7 Stephane Richer | 1.00 | .45 |
| ❑ 8 Jeremy Roenick | 3.00 | 1.35 |
| ❑ 9 Geoff Sanderson | 2.00 | .90 |
| ❑ 10 Steve Thomas | 1.00 | .45 |

## 1995-96 Fleer Metal Promo Panel

Measuring 7" by 7", this promo panel was issued to preview the 1995-96 Fleer Metal series. Its left side consists of a 2" by 7" strip with ad copy; to the right are four standard-size perforated cards. The fronts display color action cutouts on a silver metallic background. On a background consisting of a closeup photo and a jagged ice design, the backs carry biography and a bar graph presenting statistics. The cards are numbered "SAMPLE X" in the upper left corner.

| | MINT | NRMT |
|---|---|---|
| COMPLETE SHEET | 2.00 | .90 |
| COMMON CARD | .25 | .11 |
| ❑ 1 Felix Potvin | 1.00 | .45 |
| ❑ 2 Jeremy Roenick | .75 | .35 |
| ❑ 3 Theoren Fleury | .50 | .23 |
| ❑ 4 Richard Park | .25 | .11 |

## 1996-97 Fleer Promo Sheet

This sheet, which features samples of John LeClair and Peter Ferraro regular cards, as well as a John LeClair Art Ross insert card, contains product and release date information for '96-97 Fleer. The cards are unnumbered, and would bear perforation marks if removed, distinguishing them from their regular counterparts. They are listed below as they appear on the sheet.

| | MINT | NRMT |
|---|---|---|
| COMPLETE SET (3) | 1.00 | .45 |
| COMMON CARD (1-3) | .10 | .05 |
| ❑ 1 John LeClair | .25 | .11 |
| ❑ 2 John LeClair<br>Art Ross insert | .75 | .35 |
| ❑ 3 Peter Ferraro | .10 | .05 |

## 1996-97 Fleer

This 150-card set was released in one series in 10-card packs for both the hobby and retail markets with an SRP of $1.49. Although rarely delving past first-line players, the set boasts a strong player selection. All major stars are represented, among them Wayne Gretzky's first card in a New York Rangers sweater. The only Rookie Card of note is Martin Biron.

| | MINT | NRMT |
|---|---|---|
| COMPLETE SET (150) | 15.00 | 6.75 |
| COMMON CARD (1-150) | .10 | .05 |
| ❑ 1 Guy Hebert | .15 | .07 |
| ❑ 2 Paul Kariya | 1.25 | .55 |
| ❑ 3 Teemu Selanne | .60 | .25 |
| ❑ 4 Ray Bourque | .30 | .14 |
| ❑ 5 Kyle McLaren | .10 | .05 |
| ❑ 6 Adam Oates | .15 | .07 |
| ❑ 7 Bill Ranford | .15 | .07 |
| ❑ 8 Rick Tocchet | .15 | .07 |
| ❑ 9 Jason Dawe | .10 | .05 |
| ❑ 10 Dominik Hasek | .60 | .25 |
| ❑ 11 Pat LaFontaine | .15 | .07 |
| ❑ 12 Theoren Fleury | .15 | .07 |
| ❑ 13 Trevor Kidd | .15 | .07 |
| ❑ 14 German Titov | .10 | .05 |
| ❑ 15 Ed Belfour | .30 | .14 |
| ❑ 16 Chris Chelios | .30 | .14 |
| ❑ 17 Eric Daze | .15 | .07 |
| ❑ 18 Jeremy Roenick | .30 | .14 |
| ❑ 19 Gary Suter | .10 | .05 |
| ❑ 20 Peter Forsberg | 1.00 | .45 |
| ❑ 21 Valeri Kamensky | .15 | .07 |
| ❑ 22 Claude Lemieux | .15 | .07 |
| ❑ 23 Sandis Ozolinsh | .15 | .07 |
| ❑ 24 Patrick Roy | 1.50 | .70 |
| ❑ 25 Joe Sakic | .60 | .25 |
| ❑ 26 Derian Hatcher | .10 | .05 |
| ❑ 27 Mike Modano | .40 | .18 |
| ❑ 28 Sergei Zubov | .10 | .05 |
| ❑ 29 Paul Coffey | .30 | .14 |
| ❑ 30 Sergei Fedorov | .50 | .23 |
| ❑ 31 Vladimir Konstantinov | .10 | .05 |
| ❑ 32 Slava Kozlov | .15 | .07 |
| ❑ 33 Chris Osgood | .30 | .14 |
| ❑ 34 Keith Primeau | .15 | .07 |
| ❑ 35 Steve Yzerman | 1.00 | .45 |
| ❑ 36 Jason Arnott | .15 | .07 |
| ❑ 37 Curtis Joseph | .30 | .14 |
| ❑ 38 Doug Weight | .15 | .07 |
| ❑ 39 Ed Jovanovski | .15 | .07 |
| ❑ 40 Scott Mellanby | .15 | .07 |
| ❑ 41 Rob Niedermayer | .15 | .07 |
| ❑ 42 Ray Sheppard | .15 | .07 |
| ❑ 43 Robert Svehla | .10 | .05 |
| ❑ 44 John Vanbiesbrouck | .50 | .23 |
| ❑ 45 Sean Burke | .15 | .07 |
| ❑ 46 Andrew Cassels | .10 | .05 |
| ❑ 47 Geoff Sanderson | .15 | .07 |
| ❑ 48 Brendan Shanahan | .60 | .25 |
| ❑ 49 Ray Ferraro | .10 | .05 |
| ❑ 50 Dimitri Khristich | .10 | .05 |
| ❑ 51 Vitali Yachmenev | .10 | .05 |
| ❑ 52 Valeri Bure | .15 | .07 |
| ❑ 53 Vincent Damphousse | .15 | .07 |
| ❑ 54 Saku Koivu | .50 | .23 |
| ❑ 55 Mark Recchi | .15 | .07 |
| ❑ 56 Jocelyn Thibault | .30 | .14 |
| ❑ 57 Pierre Turgeon | .15 | .07 |
| ❑ 58 Martin Brodeur | .75 | .35 |
| ❑ 59 Phil Housley | .15 | .07 |
| ❑ 60 Scott Niedermayer | .10 | .05 |
| ❑ 61 Scott Stevens | .15 | .07 |
| ❑ 62 Steve Thomas | .10 | .05 |
| ❑ 63 Todd Bertuzzi | .10 | .05 |
| ❑ 64 Travis Green | .15 | .07 |
| ❑ 65 Kenny Jonsson | .10 | .05 |
| ❑ 66 Zigmund Palffy | .10 | .05 |
| ❑ 67 Adam Graves | .15 | .07 |
| ❑ 68 Wayne Gretzky | 3.00 | 1.35 |
| ❑ 69 Alexei Kovalev | .10 | .05 |
| ❑ 70 Brian Leetch | .30 | .14 |
| ❑ 71 Mark Messier | .40 | .18 |
| ❑ 72 Niklas Sundstrom | .10 | .05 |
| ❑ 73 Daniel Alfredsson | .15 | .07 |
| ❑ 74 Radek Bonk | .10 | .05 |
| ❑ 75 Steve Duchesne | .10 | .05 |
| ❑ 76 Damian Rhodes | .15 | .07 |
| ❑ 77 Alexei Yashin | .15 | .07 |
| ❑ 78 Rod Brind'Amour | .15 | .07 |
| ❑ 79 Eric Desjardins | .10 | .05 |
| ❑ 80 Ron Hextall | .15 | .07 |
| ❑ 81 John LeClair | .50 | .23 |
| ❑ 82 Eric Lindros | 1.00 | .45 |
| ❑ 83 Mikael Renberg | .15 | .07 |
| ❑ 84 Tom Barrasso | .15 | .07 |
| ❑ 85 Ron Francis | .15 | .07 |
| ❑ 86 Jaromir Jagr | 1.00 | .45 |
| ❑ 87 Mario Lemieux | 1.50 | .70 |
| ❑ 88 Petr Nedved | .15 | .07 |
| ❑ 89 Bryan Smolinski | .10 | .05 |
| ❑ 90 Nikolai Khabibulin | .15 | .07 |
| ❑ 91 Teppo Numminen | .10 | .05 |
| ❑ 92 Keith Tkachuk | .40 | .18 |
| ❑ 93 Oleg Tverdovsky | .15 | .07 |
| ❑ 94 Alexei Zhamnov | .15 | .07 |
| ❑ 95 Shayne Corson | .10 | .05 |
| ❑ 96 Grant Fuhr | .15 | .07 |
| ❑ 97 Brett Hull | .40 | .18 |
| ❑ 98 Al MacInnis | .15 | .07 |
| ❑ 99 Chris Pronger | .15 | .07 |
| ❑ 100 Owen Nolan | .15 | .07 |
| ❑ 101 Marcus Ragnarsson | .10 | .05 |
| ❑ 102 Chris Terreri | .15 | .07 |
| ❑ 103 Brian Bradley | .10 | .05 |
| ❑ 104 Roman Hamrlik | .15 | .07 |
| ❑ 105 Daren Puppa | .15 | .07 |
| ❑ 106 Alexander Selivanov | .10 | .05 |
| ❑ 107 Doug Gilmour | .30 | .14 |
| ❑ 108 Larry Murphy | .15 | .07 |
| ❑ 109 Felix Potvin | .30 | .14 |
| ❑ 110 Mats Sundin | .15 | .07 |
| ❑ 111 Pavel Bure | .60 | .25 |
| ❑ 112 Trevor Linden | .15 | .07 |
| ❑ 113 Kirk McLean | .15 | .07 |
| ❑ 114 Alexander Mogilny | .15 | .07 |
| ❑ 115 Peter Bondra | .30 | .14 |
| ❑ 116 Jim Carey | .30 | .14 |
| ❑ 117 Sergei Gonchar | .10 | .05 |
| ❑ 118 Joe Juneau | .10 | .05 |
| ❑ 119 Michal Pivonka | .10 | .05 |
| ❑ 120 Brendan Witt | .10 | .05 |
| ❑ 121 Nolan Baumgartner | .10 | .05 |
| ❑ 122 Martin Biron | .15 | .07 |
| ❑ 123 Jason Bonsignore | .10 | .05 |
| ❑ 124 Andrew Brunette | .10 | .05 |
| ❑ 125 Jason Doig | .10 | .05 |
| ❑ 126 Peter Ferraro | .10 | .05 |
| ❑ 127 Eric Fichaud | .15 | .07 |
| ❑ 128 Ladislav Kohn | .10 | .05 |
| ❑ 129 Jamie Langenbrunner | .10 | .05 |
| ❑ 130 Daymond Langkow | .10 | .05 |
| ❑ 131 Jay McKee | .10 | .05 |
| ❑ 132 Wayne Primeau | .10 | .05 |
| ❑ 133 Jamie Storr | .15 | .07 |
| ❑ 134 Jose Theodore | .15 | .07 |
| ❑ 135 Roman Vopat | .10 | .05 |
| ❑ 136 Rookie Scoring Leaders<br>Daniel Alfredsson<br>Valeri Bure<br>Eric Daze<br>Saku Koivu | .30 | .14 |
| ❑ 137 Points Leaders<br>Ron Francis<br>Jaromir Jagr<br>Mario Lemieux<br>Joe Sakic | .30 | .14 |
| ❑ 138 Goals Leaders<br>Peter Bondra<br>Jaromir Jagr<br>Mario Lemieux | .30 | .14 |

| | | |
|---|---|---|
| Alexander Mogilny | | |
| ❑ 139 Assists Leaders | .30 | .14 |
| Peter Forsberg | | |
| Ron Francis | | |
| Jaromir Jagr | | |
| Mario Lemieux | | |
| ❑ 140 Defensive Points Leaders | .30 | .14 |
| Ray Bourque | | |
| Chris Chelios | | |
| Paul Coffey | | |
| Brian Leetch | | |
| ❑ 141 Mario Lemieux | .30 | .14 |
| Jaromir Jagr | | |
| Paul Kariya | | |
| Keith Tkachuk | | |
| ❑ 142 Jaromir Jagr | .30 | .14 |
| Sergei Fedorov | | |
| John LeClair | | |
| Claude Lemieux | | |
| ❑ 143 Plus/Minus Leaders | .10 | .05 |
| Sergei Federov | | |
| Slava Fetisov | | |
| Vladimir Konstantinov | | |
| Petr Nedved | | |
| ❑ 144 Goals Against Ave. Leaders | .30 | .14 |
| Jim Carey | | |
| Ron Hextall | | |
| Chris Osgood | | |
| Mike Vernon | | |
| ❑ 145 Games Won Leaders | .30 | .14 |
| Martin Brodeur | | |
| Jim Carey | | |
| Ron Hextall | | |
| Chris Osgood | | |
| ❑ 146 Shutouts Leaders | .30 | .14 |
| Martin Brodeur | | |
| Jim Carey | | |
| Chris Osgood | | |
| Daren Puppa | | |
| ❑ 147 Dominik Hasek | .15 | .07 |
| Daren Puppa | | |
| Jeff Hackett | | |
| Guy Hebert | | |
| ❑ 148 Checklist (1-72) | .10 | .05 |
| ❑ 149 Checklist (73-150) | .10 | .05 |
| ❑ 150 Checklist (Inserts) | .10 | .05 |

## 1996-97 Fleer Art Ross

Randomly inserted in packs at a rate of 1:6, this 25-card set features players in contention for the Art Ross trophy as the league's leading scorer.

| | MINT | NRMT |
|---|---|---|
| COMPLETE SET (25) | 50.00 | 22.00 |
| COMMON CARD (1-25) | 1.00 | .45 |
| ❑ 1 Pavel Bure | 3.00 | 1.35 |
| ❑ 2 Sergei Fedorov | 3.00 | 1.35 |
| ❑ 3 Theoren Fleury | 1.25 | .55 |
| ❑ 4 Peter Forsberg | 5.00 | 2.20 |
| ❑ 5 Ron Francis | 1.25 | .55 |
| ❑ 6 Wayne Gretzky | 10.00 | 4.50 |
| ❑ 7 Brett Hull | 2.00 | .90 |
| ❑ 8 Jaromir Jagr | 5.00 | 2.20 |
| ❑ 9 Valeri Kamensky | 1.00 | .45 |
| ❑ 10 Paul Kariya | 6.00 | 2.70 |
| ❑ 11 Pat LaFontaine | 1.00 | .45 |
| ❑ 12 John LeClair | 2.50 | 1.10 |
| ❑ 13 Mario Lemieux | 8.00 | 3.60 |
| ❑ 14 Eric Lindros | 5.00 | 2.20 |
| ❑ 15 Mark Messier | 1.50 | .70 |
| ❑ 16 Alexander Mogilny | 1.25 | .55 |
| ❑ 17 Petr Nedved | 1.00 | .45 |
| ❑ 18 Adam Oates | 1.00 | .45 |
| ❑ 19 Jeremy Roenick | 1.50 | .70 |
| ❑ 20 Joe Sakic | 3.00 | 1.35 |
| ❑ 21 Teemu Selanne | 3.00 | 1.35 |
| ❑ 22 Keith Tkachuk | 2.50 | 1.10 |
| ❑ 23 Pierre Turgeon | 1.00 | .45 |
| ❑ 24 Doug Weight | 1.00 | .45 |
| ❑ 25 Steve Yzerman | 5.00 | 2.20 |

## 1996-97 Fleer Calder Candidates

Randomly inserted in packs at a rate of 1:96, this 10-card set features up-and-comers poised to make a run at the Calder trophy, which is awarded to the NHL's rookie of the year.

| | MINT | NRMT |
|---|---|---|
| COMPLETE SET (10) | 40.00 | 18.00 |
| COMMON CARD (1-10) | 4.00 | 1.80 |
| ❑ 1 Andrew Brunette | 4.00 | 1.80 |
| ❑ 2 Jason Doig | 4.00 | 1.80 |
| ❑ 3 Peter Ferraro | 4.00 | 1.80 |
| ❑ 4 Eric Fichaud | 12.00 | 5.50 |
| ❑ 5 Ladislav Kohn | 4.00 | 1.80 |
| ❑ 6 Jamie Langenbrunner | 4.00 | 1.80 |
| ❑ 7 Daymond Langkow | 10.00 | 4.50 |
| ❑ 8 Jamie Storr | 7.50 | 3.40 |
| ❑ 9 Jose Theodore | 15.00 | 6.75 |
| ❑ 10 Roman Vopat | 4.00 | 1.80 |

## 1996-97 Fleer Norris

Randomly inserted in retail packs only at a rate of 1:36, this 10-card set features veteran rearguards in contention for recognition as the game's top blueliner.

| | MINT | NRMT |
|---|---|---|
| COMPLETE SET (10) | 40.00 | 18.00 |
| COMMON CARD (1-10) | 3.00 | 1.35 |
| ❑ 1 Ray Bourque | 10.00 | 4.50 |
| ❑ 2 Chris Chelios | 10.00 | 4.50 |
| ❑ 3 Paul Coffey | 10.00 | 4.50 |
| ❑ 4 Eric Desjardins | 3.00 | 1.35 |
| ❑ 5 Phil Housley | 3.00 | 1.35 |
| ❑ 6 Vladimir Konstantinov | 6.00 | 2.70 |
| ❑ 7 Brian Leetch | 10.00 | 4.50 |
| ❑ 8 Teppo Numminen | 3.00 | 1.35 |
| ❑ 9 Larry Murphy | 3.00 | 1.35 |
| ❑ 10 Sandis Ozolinsh | 6.00 | 2.70 |

## 1996-97 Fleer Pearson

Randomly inserted in packs at a rate of 1:144, this 10-card set is the most difficult to come by of this year's Fleer offering, and also the most star-studded. Gracing this set are ten top stars worthy of consideration for the NHLPA MVP award.

| | MINT | NRMT |
|---|---|---|
| COMPLETE SET (10) | 400.00 | 180.00 |
| COMMON CARD (1-10) | 25.00 | 11.00 |
| ❑ 1 Pavel Bure | 25.00 | 11.00 |
| ❑ 2 Sergei Fedorov | 25.00 | 11.00 |
| ❑ 3 Peter Forsberg | 40.00 | 18.00 |
| ❑ 4 Wayne Gretzky | 80.00 | 36.00 |
| ❑ 5 Jaromir Jagr | 40.00 | 18.00 |
| ❑ 6 Paul Kariya | 50.00 | 22.00 |
| ❑ 7 Mario Lemieux | 60.00 | 27.00 |
| ❑ 8 Eric Lindros | 40.00 | 18.00 |
| ❑ 9 Patrick Roy | 60.00 | 27.00 |
| ❑ 10 Joe Sakic | 25.00 | 11.00 |

## 1996-97 Fleer Rookie Sensations

Randomly inserted in hobby packs only at a rate of 1:20, this 10-card set features some of the top rookie attractions of the '95-96 campaign.

| | MINT | NRMT |
|---|---|---|
| COMPLETE SET (10) | 60.00 | 27.00 |
| COMMON CARD (1-10) | 4.00 | 1.80 |
| ❑ 1 Daniel Alfredsson | 8.00 | 3.60 |
| ❑ 2 Todd Bertuzzi | 4.00 | 1.80 |
| ❑ 3 Valeri Bure | 4.00 | 1.80 |
| ❑ 4 Eric Daze | 8.00 | 3.60 |
| ❑ 5 Sergei Gonchar | 4.00 | 1.80 |
| ❑ 6 Ed Jovanovski | 8.00 | 3.60 |
| ❑ 7 Saku Koivu | 15.00 | 6.75 |
| ❑ 8 Marcus Ragnarsson | 4.00 | 1.80 |
| ❑ 9 Petr Sykora | 4.00 | 1.80 |
| ❑ 10 Vitali Yachmenev | 4.00 | 1.80 |

## 1996-97 Fleer Vezina

Randomly inserted in packs at a rate of 1:60, this set features ten netminders who are perennial favorites to win the Vezina award.

| | MINT | NRMT |
|---|---|---|
| COMPLETE SET (10) | 120.00 | 55.00 |
| COMMON CARD (1-10) | 8.00 | 3.60 |
| ❑ 1 Ed Belfour | 10.00 | 4.50 |
| ❑ 2 Sean Burke | 8.00 | 3.60 |
| ❑ 3 Jim Carey | 12.00 | 5.50 |
| ❑ 4 Dominik Hasek | 20.00 | 9.00 |
| ❑ 5 Ron Hextall | 8.00 | 3.60 |
| ❑ 6 Chris Osgood | 10.00 | 4.50 |
| ❑ 7 Felix Potvin | 12.00 | 5.50 |
| ❑ 8 Daren Puppa | 8.00 | 3.60 |
| ❑ 9 Patrick Roy | 40.00 | 18.00 |
| ❑ 10 John Vanbiesbrouck | 15.00 | 6.75 |

## 1996-97 Fleer Picks

This 90-card set was a joint venture with Topps and was skip-numbered. All cards in this set have even numbers, while the Topps Picks set has the odds. The cards were issued in seven-card packs with a suggested retail price of $.99. The two card companies held a fantasy-style draft with each picking 56 forwards, 28 defensemen and six goaltenders to be included in their half of the set. The fronts feature color action player photos in a bordered design with the backs displaying projected stats for the 1996-97 season.

| | MINT | NRMT |
|---|---|---|
| COMPLETE SET (92) | 10.00 | 4.50 |
| COMMON CARD | .05 | .02 |
| ❑ 2 Joe Sakic | .50 | .23 |
| ❑ 4 Eric Lindros | .75 | .35 |
| ❑ 6 Paul Kariya | 1.00 | .45 |
| ❑ 8 Wayne Gretzky | 3.50 | 1.55 |
| ❑ 10 Chris Osgood | .25 | .11 |
| ❑ 12 Brian Leetch | .25 | .11 |
| ❑ 14 Ray Bourque | .25 | .11 |
| ❑ 16 Ron Francis | .10 | .05 |
| ❑ 18 Keith Tkachuk | .30 | .14 |
| ❑ 20 Paul Coffey | .25 | .11 |
| ❑ 22 Phil Housley | .10 | .05 |
| ❑ 24 Theoren Fleury | .10 | .05 |
| ❑ 26 Sergei Zubov | .05 | .02 |
| ❑ 28 Adam Oates | .10 | .05 |
| ❑ 30 John LeClair | .40 | .18 |
| ❑ 32 Pierre Turgeon | .10 | .05 |
| ❑ 34 Nicklas Lidstrom | .10 | .05 |
| ❑ 36 Vincent Damphousse | .10 | .05 |
| ❑ 38 Pat LaFontaine | .10 | .05 |
| ❑ 40 Brendan Shanahan | .50 | .23 |
| ❑ 42 Robert Svehla | .05 | .02 |
| ❑ 44 Peter Bondra | .25 | .11 |
| ❑ 46 Mikael Renberg | .10 | .05 |
| ❑ 48 Alexei Yashin | .10 | .05 |
| ❑ 50 Zigmund Palffy | .25 | .11 |
| ❑ 52 Larry Murphy | .10 | .05 |
| ❑ 54 Rod Brind'Amour | .10 | .05 |
| ❑ 56 Alexei Zhamnov | .10 | .05 |
| ❑ 58 Jason Arnott | .10 | .05 |
| ❑ 60 Craig Janney | .10 | .05 |
| ❑ 62 Jason Woolley | .05 | .02 |
| ❑ 64 Jeff Brown | .05 | .02 |
| ❑ 66 Tomas Sandstrom | .05 | .02 |
| ❑ 68 Doug Gilmour | .25 | .11 |
| ❑ 70 Travis Green | .10 | .05 |
| ❑ 72 Teppo Numminen | .05 | .02 |
| ❑ 74 Petr Sykora | .05 | .02 |
| ❑ 76 Saku Koivu | .40 | .18 |
| ❑ 78 Daniel Alfredsson | .10 | .05 |
| ❑ 80 Ron Hextall | .10 | .05 |
| ❑ 82 Jocelyn Thibault | .25 | .11 |
| ❑ 84 Mike Richter | .25 | .11 |
| ❑ 86 Nikolai Khabibulin | .10 | .05 |
| ❑ 88 John Vanbiesbrouck | .40 | .18 |
| ❑ 90 Adam Graves | .10 | .05 |
| ❑ 92 Kenny Jonsson | .05 | .02 |
| ❑ 94 Jyrki Lumme | .05 | .02 |
| ❑ 96 Zdeno Ciger | .05 | .02 |
| ❑ 98 Ed Jovanovski | .10 | .05 |
| ❑ 100 Greg Johnson | .05 | .02 |
| ❑ 102 Pat Falloon | .05 | .02 |
| ❑ 104 Andrew Cassels | .05 | .02 |
| ❑ 106 German Titov | .05 | .02 |
| ❑ 108 Joe Juneau | .05 | .02 |
| ❑ 110 Igor Larionov | .05 | .02 |
| ❑ 112 Norm Maciver | .05 | .02 |
| ❑ 114 Chris Pronger | .10 | .05 |
| ❑ 116 Scott Niedermayer | .05 | .02 |
| ❑ 118 Vladimir Malakhov | .05 | .02 |
| ❑ 120 Dale Hawerchuk | .10 | .05 |
| ❑ 122 Jason Dawe | .05 | .02 |
| ❑ 124 Valeri Bure | .10 | .05 |
| ❑ 126 Marcus Ragnarsson | .05 | .02 |
| ❑ 128 Stephane Richer | .10 | .05 |
| ❑ 130 Wendel Clark | .10 | .05 |
| ❑ 132 Bryan Smolinski | .05 | .02 |
| ❑ 134 Dimitri Khristich | .05 | .02 |
| ❑ 136 Benoit Hogue | .05 | .02 |
| ❑ 138 Kirk Muller | .05 | .02 |
| ❑ 140 Peter Ferraro | .05 | .02 |
| ❑ 142 Vitali Yachmenev | .05 | .02 |
| ❑ 144 Jere Lehtinen | .05 | .02 |
| ❑ 146 Brandon Convery | .05 | .02 |
| ❑ 148 Darcy Tucker | .05 | .02 |
| ❑ 150 Curtis Brown | .05 | .02 |
| ❑ 152 Alexei Zhitnik | .05 | .02 |
| ❑ 154 John Slaney | .05 | .02 |
| ❑ 156 Bruce Driver | .05 | .02 |
| ❑ 158 Jeff O'Neill | .05 | .02 |
| ❑ 160 Patrice Brisebois | .05 | .02 |
| ❑ 162 Gord Murphy | .05 | .02 |
| ❑ 164 Doug Bodger | .05 | .02 |
| ❑ 166 Marty McSorley | .05 | .02 |
| ❑ 168 Nolan Baumgartner | .05 | .02 |
| ❑ 170 Mike Gartner | .10 | .05 |
| ❑ 172 Andrei Nikolishin | .05 | .02 |
| ❑ 174 Alexei Yegorov | .05 | .02 |
| ❑ 176 Dave Reid | .05 | .02 |
| ❑ 178 Marty Murray | .05 | .02 |
| ❑ 180 Anders Eriksson | .05 | .02 |
| ❑ 182 Checklist (2-180) | .05 | .02 |
| ❑ 184 Checklist (inserts) | .05 | .02 |

## 1996-97 Fleer Picks Captain's Choice

Randomly inserted in packs at a rate of one in 360, this set featured ten top team captains. The fronts carried borderless color action player photos while the backs displayed player information.

| | MINT | NRMT |
|---|---|---|
| COMPLETE SET (10) | 600.00 | 275.00 |
| COMMON CARD (1-10) | 12.00 | 5.50 |
| ❑ 1 Eric Lindros | 80.00 | 36.00 |
| ❑ 2 Steve Yzerman | 80.00 | 36.00 |
| ❑ 3 Mario Lemieux | 120.00 | 55.00 |
| ❑ 4 Wayne Gretzky | 150.00 | 70.00 |
| ❑ 5 Mark Messier | 30.00 | 13.50 |
| ❑ 6 Joe Sakic | 50.00 | 22.00 |
| ❑ 7 Keith Tkachuk | 30.00 | 13.50 |
| ❑ 8 Doug Gilmour | 25.00 | 11.00 |
| ❑ 9 Trevor Linden | 12.00 | 5.50 |
| ❑ 10 Brendan Shanahan | 50.00 | 22.00 |

## 1996-97 Fleer Picks Dream Lines

Randomly inserted in packs at a rate of one in 70, this 10-card set featured three star players sharing some connection on each card.

| | MINT | NRMT |
|---|---|---|
| COMPLETE SET (10) | 200.00 | 90.00 |
| COMMON CARD (1-10) | 8.00 | 3.60 |
| ❑ 1 Wayne Gretzky | 30.00 | 13.50 |
| Mario Lemieux | | |
| Eric Lindros | | |
| ❑ 2 Jeremy Roenick | 8.00 | 3.60 |
| Chris Chelios | | |
| Mike Richter | | |
| ❑ 3 Daniel Alfredsson | 15.00 | 6.75 |
| Peter Forsberg | | |
| Martin Brodeur | | |
| ❑ 4 Sergei Fedorov | 12.00 | 5.50 |
| Alexander Mogilny | | |
| Pavel Bure | | |
| ❑ 5 Teemu Selanne | 20.00 | 9.00 |
| Paul Kariya | | |
| Keith Tkachuk | | |
| ❑ 6 Jaromir Jagr | 15.00 | 6.75 |
| Dominik Hasek | | |
| Roman Hamrlik | | |
| ❑ 7 John LeClair | 10.00 | 4.50 |
| Brendan Shanahan | | |
| Mike Modano | | |
| ❑ 8 Patrick Roy | 30.00 | 13.50 |
| Ed Belfour | | |
| John Vanbiesbrouck | | |
| ❑ 9 Joe Sakic | 8.00 | 3.60 |
| Valeri Kamensky | | |
| Sandis Ozolinsh | | |
| ❑ 10 Brett Hull | 8.00 | 3.60 |
| Pat Verbeek | | |
| Pat LaFontaine | | |

## 1996-97 Fleer Picks Fabulous 50

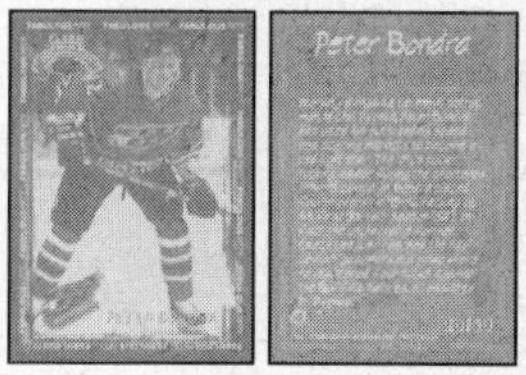

Inserted one in every pack, this 50-card set featured color action photos of the best players in the NHL. The nature of this set allowed Fleer to include players they were unable to select in the draft, thus giving a more complete feel to the entire product.

| | MINT | NRMT |
|---|---|---|
| COMPLETE SET (50) | 30.00 | 13.50 |
| COMMON CARD (1-50) | .20 | .09 |
| ❑ 1 Daniel Alfredsson | .50 | .23 |
| ❑ 2 Peter Bondra | .50 | .23 |
| ❑ 3 Ray Bourque | .75 | .35 |
| ❑ 4 Martin Brodeur | 2.00 | .90 |
| ❑ 5 Pavel Bure | 1.50 | .70 |
| ❑ 6 Jim Carey | .75 | .35 |
| ❑ 7 Chris Chelios | .75 | .35 |
| ❑ 8 Paul Coffey | .75 | .35 |
| ❑ 9 Eric Daze | .50 | .23 |
| ❑ 10 Sergei Fedorov | 1.25 | .55 |
| ❑ 11 Theoren Fleury | .50 | .23 |
| ❑ 12 Peter Forsberg | 2.50 | 1.10 |
| ❑ 13 Ron Francis | .50 | .23 |
| ❑ 14 Sergei Gonchar | .20 | .09 |
| ❑ 15 Wayne Gretzky | 5.00 | 2.20 |
| ❑ 16 Roman Hamrlik | .50 | .23 |
| ❑ 17 Kevin Hatcher | .20 | .09 |
| ❑ 18 Ron Hextall | .20 | .09 |
| ❑ 19 Brett Hull | 1.00 | .45 |
| ❑ 20 Jaromir Jagr | 2.50 | 1.10 |
| ❑ 21 Ed Jovanovski | .50 | .23 |
| ❑ 22 Valeri Kamensky | .20 | .09 |
| ❑ 23 Paul Kariya | 3.00 | 1.35 |
| ❑ 24 John LeClair | 1.25 | .55 |
| ❑ 25 Brian Leetch | .75 | .35 |
| ❑ 26 Mario Lemieux | 4.00 | 1.80 |
| ❑ 27 Trevor Linden | .20 | .09 |
| ❑ 28 Eric Lindros | 2.50 | 1.10 |
| ❑ 29 Mark Messier | 1.00 | .45 |
| ❑ 30 Mike Modano | 1.00 | .45 |
| ❑ 31 Alexander Mogilny | .50 | .23 |
| ❑ 32 Petr Nedved | .20 | .09 |
| ❑ 33 Joe Nieuwendyk | .20 | .09 |
| ❑ 34 Owen Nolan | .50 | .23 |
| ❑ 35 Adam Oates | .20 | .09 |
| ❑ 36 Chris Osgood | .75 | .35 |
| ❑ 37 Sandis Ozolinsh | .20 | .09 |
| ❑ 38 Zigmund Palffy | .75 | .35 |
| ❑ 39 Jeremy Roenick | .75 | .35 |
| ❑ 40 Patrick Roy | 4.00 | 1.80 |
| ❑ 41 Joe Sakic | 1.50 | .70 |
| ❑ 42 Teemu Selanne | 1.50 | .70 |
| ❑ 43 Brendan Shanahan | 1.50 | .70 |
| ❑ 44 Keith Tkachuk | 1.00 | .45 |
| ❑ 45 Pierre Turgeon | .20 | .09 |
| ❑ 46 John Vanbiesbrouck | 1.25 | .55 |
| ❑ 47 Doug Weight | .20 | .09 |
| ❑ 48 Alexei Yashin | .20 | .09 |
| ❑ 49 Steve Yzerman | 2.50 | 1.10 |
| ❑ 50 Alexei Zhamnov | .50 | .23 |

## 1996-97 Fleer Picks Fantasy Force

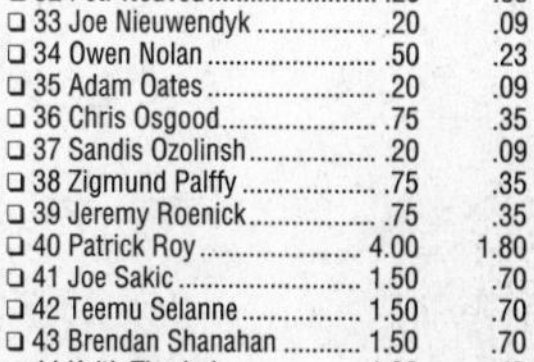

Randomly inserted in packs at a rate of one in 50, this 10-card set featured color action photos of ten of the league's most valuable assets to fantasy league owners.

| | MINT | NRMT |
|---|---|---|
| COMPLETE SET (10) | 60.00 | 27.00 |
| COMMON CARD (1-10) | 4.00 | 1.80 |
| ❑ 1 John LeClair | 12.00 | 5.50 |
| ❑ 2 Chris Osgood | 8.00 | 3.60 |
| ❑ 3 Ron Hextall | 6.00 | 2.70 |
| ❑ 4 Eric Daze | 6.00 | 2.70 |
| ❑ 5 Jaromir Jagr | 25.00 | 11.00 |
| ❑ 6 Brett Hull | 10.00 | 4.50 |
| ❑ 7 Ron Francis | 6.00 | 2.70 |
| ❑ 8 Martin Brodeur | 20.00 | 9.00 |
| ❑ 9 Sergei Fedorov | 15.00 | 6.75 |
| ❑ 10 Petr Nedved | 4.00 | 1.80 |

## 1996-97 Fleer Picks Jagged Edge

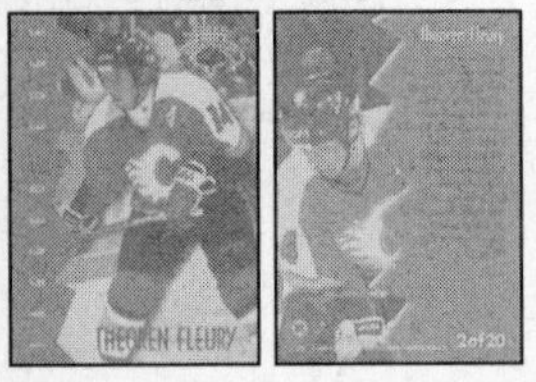

Randomly inserted in packs at a rate of one in 18, this 20-card set featured color action photos of players with a propensity for the dramatic.

| | MINT | NRMT |
|---|---|---|
| COMPLETE SET (20) | 50.00 | 22.00 |
| COMMON CARD (1-20) | 2.00 | .90 |
| ❑ 1 Daniel Alfredsson | 3.00 | 1.35 |
| ❑ 2 Theoren Fleury | 3.00 | 1.35 |
| ❑ 3 Alexander Mogilny | 3.00 | 1.35 |
| ❑ 4 Doug Weight | 2.00 | .90 |
| ❑ 5 Alexei Yashin | 2.00 | .90 |
| ❑ 6 Paul Kariya | 12.00 | 5.50 |
| ❑ 7 Saku Koivu | 5.00 | 2.20 |
| ❑ 8 Sandis Ozolinsh | 2.00 | .90 |
| ❑ 9 Petr Nedved | 2.00 | .90 |
| ❑ 10 Jeremy Roenick | 3.00 | 1.35 |
| ❑ 11 Mike Modano | 4.00 | 1.80 |
| ❑ 12 Jim Carey | 3.00 | 1.35 |
| ❑ 13 Ed Jovanovski | 3.00 | 1.35 |
| ❑ 14 Alexei Zhamnov | 3.00 | 1.35 |
| ❑ 15 Adam Oates | 2.00 | .90 |
| ❑ 16 Ron Francis | 3.00 | 1.35 |
| ❑ 17 Brian Leetch | 3.00 | 1.35 |
| ❑ 18 Paul Coffey | 3.00 | 1.35 |
| ❑ 19 Eric Daze | 3.00 | 1.35 |
| ❑ 20 Zigmund Palffy | 3.00 | 1.35 |

## 1994 Fleury Hockey Tips

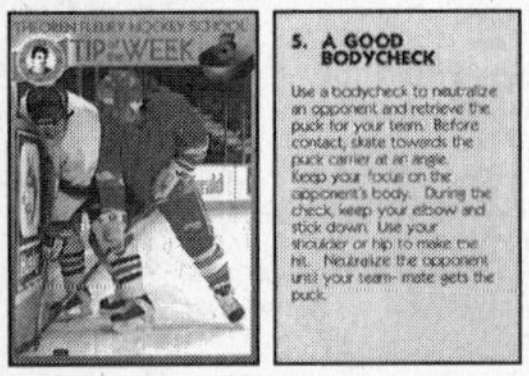


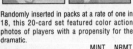

Titled "Theoren Fleury Hockey School Tip of the Week," this 14-card set measures the standard size. The lavender-bordered fronts have color action photos illustrating each hockey tip. The backs carry the "Tip of the Week" in black lettering followed by discussion. The cards are numbered on both sides.

| | MINT | NRMT |
|---|---|---|
| COMPLETE SET (14) | 5.00 | 2.20 |
| COMMON CARD (1-14) | .50 | .23 |
| ❑ 1 Stickhandling | .50 | .23 |
| ❑ 2 An Explosive Start | .50 | .23 |
| ❑ 3 Shoot To Score | .50 | .23 |
| ❑ 4 Passing Accurately | .50 | .23 |
| ❑ 5 A Good Bodycheck | .50 | .23 |
| ❑ 6 The Backhand Shot | .50 | .23 |
| ❑ 7 Receiving A Pass | .50 | .23 |
| ❑ 8 Stopping | .50 | .23 |
| ❑ 9 At The Opponent's Net | .50 | .23 |
| ❑ 10 Protecting The Puck | .50 | .23 |
| ❑ 11 Playing In The Defensive Zone | .50 | .23 |
| ❑ 12 Supporting My Defenseman | .50 | .23 |
| ❑ 13 Winning The Face Off | .50 | .23 |
| ❑ 14 The One-Timer | .50 | .23 |

## 1970-71 Flyers Postcards

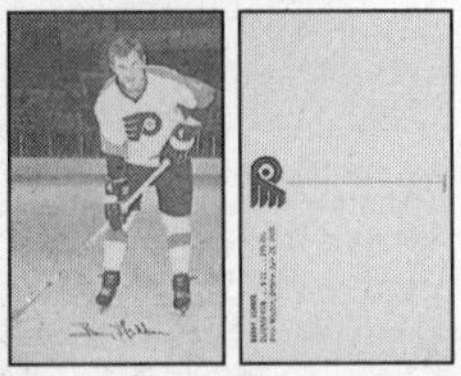

This 12-card, team-issued set measures 3 1/2" by 5 1/2" and is in the postcard format. The fronts feature full-bleed color photos, with the players posed on ice at the skating rink. A facsimile autograph is inscribed across the bottom. The white backs carry player information and team logo across the top. The cards are unnumbered and checklisted below in alphabetical order.

| | NRMT-MT | EXC |
|---|---|---|
| COMPLETE SET (12) | 40.00 | 18.00 |
| COMMON CARD (1-12) | 2.00 | .90 |
| ❑ 1 Barry Ashbee | 6.00 | 2.70 |
| ❑ 2 Gary Dornhoefer | 6.00 | 2.70 |
| ❑ 3 Warren Elliott, Frank Leurs | 2.00 | .90 |
| ❑ 4 Doug Favell | 6.00 | 2.70 |
| ❑ 5 Earl Heiskala | 3.00 | 1.35 |
| ❑ 6 Larry Hillman | 5.00 | 2.20 |
| ❑ 7 Andre Lacroix | 5.00 | 2.20 |
| ❑ 8 Lew Morrison | 3.00 | 1.35 |
| ❑ 9 Simon Nolet | 4.00 | 1.80 |
| ❑ 10 Garry Peters | 3.00 | 1.35 |
| ❑ 11 Vic Stasiuk CO | 3.00 | 1.35 |
| ❑ 12 George Swarbrick | 3.00 | 1.35 |

## 1972 Flyers Mighty Milk

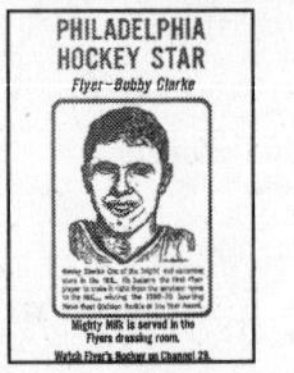


These seven panels, which were issued on the sides of half gallon cartons of Mighty Milk, feature members of the Philadelphia Flyers. After cutting, the panels measure approximately 3 5/8" by 7 1/2". All lettering and the portrait itself are in blue. Inside a frame with rounded corners, each panel displays a portrait of the player and a player profile. The words "Philadelphia Hockey Star" and the player's name appear above the frame, while an advertisement for Mighty Milk and another for TV Channel 29 appear immediately below. The backs are blank. The panels are unnumbered and checklisted below in alphabetical order.

| | NRMT-MT | EXC |
|---|---|---|
| COMPLETE SET (7) | 175.00 | 80.00 |
| COMMON CARD (1-7) | 15.00 | 6.75 |
| ❑ 1 Serge Bernier | 15.00 | 6.75 |
| ❑ 2 Bobby Clarke | 80.00 | 36.00 |
| ❑ 3 Gary Dornhoefer | 20.00 | 9.00 |
| ❑ 4 Doug Favell | 30.00 | 13.50 |
| ❑ 5 Jean-Guy Gendron | 15.00 | 6.75 |
| ❑ 6 Bill Lesuk | 15.00 | 6.75 |
| ❑ 7 Ed Van Impe | 20.00 | 9.00 |

## 1973-74 Flyers Linnett

These oversize cards were produce by Charles Linnett Studios. Cards are done in black and white and feature a facsimile signature. Original price per piece was only 50 cents. Cards measure 8 1/2 x 11. They are unnumbered and checklisted below in alphabetical order.

| | MINT | NRMT |
|---|---|---|
| COMPLETE SET (1-18) | 80.00 | 36.00 |
| COMMON CARD (1-) | 3.00 | 1.35 |
| ❑ 1 Barry Ashbee | 3.00 | 1.35 |
| ❑ 2 Bill Barber | 10.00 | 4.50 |
| ❑ 3 Tom Bladon | 3.00 | 1.35 |
| ❑ 4 Bob Clarke | 10.00 | 4.50 |
| ❑ 5 Bill Clement | 6.00 | 2.70 |
| ❑ 6 Terry Crisp | 5.00 | 2.20 |
| ❑ 7 Bill Flett | 4.00 | 1.80 |
| ❑ 8 Bob Kelly | 3.00 | 1.35 |
| ❑ 9 Orest Kindrachuk | 3.00 | 1.35 |
| ❑ 10 Ross Lonsberry | 3.00 | 1.35 |
| ❑ 11 Rick Macleish | 4.00 | 1.80 |
| ❑ 12 Simon Nolet | 4.00 | 1.80 |
| ❑ 13 Bernard Parent | 10.00 | 4.50 |
| ❑ 14 Don Saleski | 3.00 | 1.35 |
| ❑ 15 Dave Schultz | 6.00 | 2.70 |
| ❑ 16 Ed Van Impe | 3.00 | 1.35 |
| ❑ 17 Jim Watson | 4.00 | 1.80 |
| ❑ 18 Joe Watson | 4.00 | 1.80 |

## 1983-84 Flyers J.C. Penney

Sponsored by J.C. Penney, this 22-card set measures approximately 4" by 6". The fronts feature color posed action shots of the players on ice. Beneath the picture are the team name, logo, player's name, and the phrase "Compliments of J.C. Penney Stores in the Delaware Valley." The backs are blank. The cards are unnumbered and checklisted below in alphabetical order.

| | MINT | NRMT |
|---|---|---|
| COMPLETE SET (22) | 35.00 | 16.00 |
| COMMON CARD (1-22) | 1.00 | .45 |
| ❑ 1 Ray Allison | 1.00 | .45 |
| ❑ 2 Bill Barber | 2.00 | .90 |
| ❑ 3 Frank Bathe | 1.00 | .45 |
| ❑ 4 Lindsay Carson | 1.00 | .45 |
| ❑ 5 Bobby Clarke | 5.00 | 2.20 |
| ❑ 6 Glen Cochrane | 1.00 | .45 |
| ❑ 7 Doug Crossman | 1.50 | .70 |
| ❑ 8 Miroslav Dvorak | 1.00 | .45 |
| ❑ 9 Thomas Eriksson | 1.00 | .45 |
| ❑ 10 Bob Froese | 1.50 | .70 |
| ❑ 11 Randy Holt | 1.00 | .45 |
| ❑ 12 Mark Howe | 2.00 | .90 |
| ❑ 13 Tim Kerr | 2.00 | .90 |
| ❑ 14 Pelle Lindbergh | 12.00 | 5.50 |
| ❑ 15 Brad Marsh | 1.50 | .70 |
| ❑ 16 Brad McCrimmon | 1.50 | .70 |
| ❑ 17 Dave Poulin | 1.50 | .70 |
| ❑ 18 Brian Propp | 2.00 | .90 |
| ❑ 19 Ilkka Sinisalo | 1.50 | .70 |
| ❑ 20 Darryl Sittler | 4.00 | 1.80 |
| ❑ 21 Rich Sutter | 1.00 | .45 |
| ❑ 22 Ron Sutter | 1.00 | .45 |

## 1985-86 Flyers Postcards

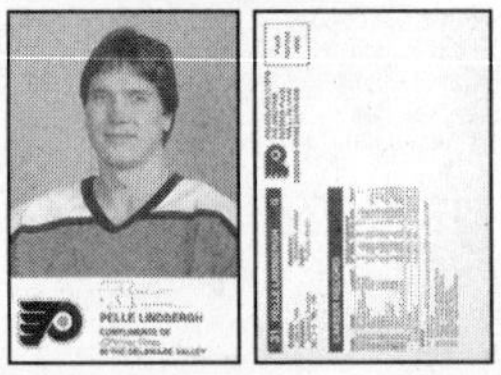

This 31 card set features aciton photos on the front, and comes complete with player name, number and statistics.

| | MINT | NRMT |
|---|---|---|
| COMPLETE SET (31) | 25.00 | 11.00 |
| COMMON CARD | .25 | .11 |
| ❑ 1 Bill Barber | 1.00 | .45 |
| ❑ 2 Dave Brown | .75 | .35 |
| ❑ 3 Lindsay Carson | .50 | .23 |
| ❑ 4 Bob Clarke | 2.00 | .90 |
| ❑ 5 Murray Craven | .50 | .23 |
| ❑ 6 Pat Croce | .25 | .11 |
| ❑ 7 Doug Crossman | .50 | .23 |
| ❑ 8 Per-Erik Eklund | .50 | .23 |
| ❑ 9 Thomas Eriksson | .50 | .23 |
| ❑ 10 Bob Froese | .75 | .35 |
| ❑ 11 Len Lachborn | .25 | .11 |
| ❑ 12 Paul Holmgren | .50 | .23 |
| ❑ 13 Ed Hospodar | .50 | .23 |
| ❑ 14 Mark Howe | .75 | .35 |
| ❑ 15 Mike Keenan | 1.00 | .45 |
| ❑ 16 Tim Kerr | .75 | .35 |
| ❑ 17 Pelle Lindbergh | 8.00 | 3.60 |
| ❑ 18 Brad Marsh | .50 | .23 |
| ❑ 19 Brad McCrimmon | .75 | .35 |
| ❑ 20 E.J. McGuire CO | .25 | .11 |
| ❑ 21 Bernie Parent CO | 1.00 | .45 |
| ❑ 22 Joe Paterson | .25 | .11 |
| ❑ 23 Dave Poulin | .50 | .23 |
| ❑ 24 Brian Propp | 1.00 | .45 |
| ❑ 25 Ilkka Sinisalo | .50 | .23 |
| ❑ 26 Derrick Smith | .50 | .23 |
| ❑ 27 Rich Sutter | .50 | .23 |
| ❑ 28 Ron Sutter | .50 | .23 |
| ❑ 29 Rick Tocchet | 6.00 | 2.70 |
| ❑ 30 Peter Zezel | 2.00 | .90 |
| ❑ 31 Team Photo | 2.00 | .90 |

## 1986-87 Flyers Postcards

This 29-card set of Philadelphia Flyers features full-bleed, color action and posed photos. The cards measure approximately 4 1/8" by 6" and are in a postcard format. A player's autograph facsimile is printed on the front. A diagonal black stripe cuts across the lower portion of the picture. Within the black stripe appear narrow orange stripes, the Flyers logo, and player information. The horizontal white backs carry career statistics and biography on the left, and the postcard format mailing address space on the right. The cards are unnumbered and checklisted below in alphabetical order.

| | MINT | NRMT |
|---|---|---|
| COMPLETE SET (29) | 25.00 | 11.00 |
| COMMON CARD (1-29) | .25 | .11 |
| ❑ 1 Bill Barber CO | 1.00 | .45 |
| ❑ 2 Dave Brown | .75 | .35 |
| ❑ 3 Lindsay Carson | .50 | .23 |
| ❑ 4 Murray Craven | .50 | .23 |
| ❑ 5 Pat Croce TR | .25 | .11 |
| ❑ 6 Doug Crossman | .50 | .23 |
| ❑ 7 Jean-Jacques Daigneault | .50 | .23 |
| ❑ 8 Pelle Eklund | .75 | .35 |
| ❑ 9 Ron Hextall | 4.00 | 1.80 |
| ❑ 10 Paul Holmgren CO | .50 | .23 |
| ❑ 11 Ed Hospodar | .50 | .23 |
| ❑ 12 Mark Howe | 1.50 | .70 |
| ❑ 13 Mike Keenan CO | 1.00 | .45 |
| ❑ 14 Tim Kerr | 1.50 | .70 |
| ❑ 15 Brad Marsh | .50 | .23 |
| ❑ 16 Brad McCrimmon | .75 | .35 |
| ❑ 17 E.J. McGuire CO | .25 | .11 |
| ❑ 18 Scott Mellanby | 1.50 | .70 |
| ❑ 19 Bernie Parent CO | 1.00 | .45 |
| ❑ 20 Dave Poulin | .75 | .35 |
| ❑ 21 Brian Propp | 1.00 | .45 |
| ❑ 22 Glenn Resch | 1.00 | .45 |
| ❑ 23 Ilkka Sinisalo | .50 | .23 |
| ❑ 24 Derrick Smith | .50 | .23 |
| ❑ 25 Daryl Stanley | .50 | .23 |
| ❑ 26 Ron Sutter | .50 | .23 |
| ❑ 27 Rick Tocchet | 5.00 | 2.20 |
| ❑ 28 Peter Zezel | 1.00 | .45 |
| ❑ 29 Team Photo | 2.00 | .90 |

## 1989-90 Flyers Postcards

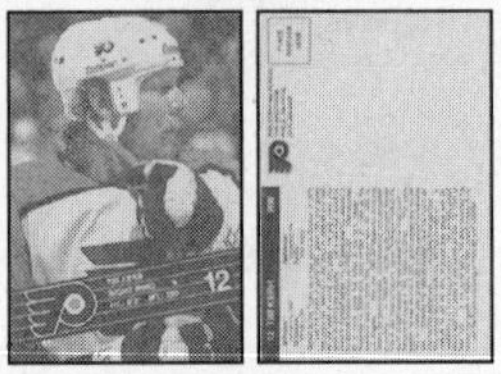

This 29-card set measures 4 1/8" by 6" and is in the postcard format. The fronts feature full-bleed color action player photos. A team color-coded (black with thin orange stripes) diagonal stripe cuts across the bottom portion and carries the team logo, biographical information, and jersey number. The white horizonal backs carry the team logo, biography, and career summary. The cards are unnumbered and checklisted below in alphabetical order.

| | MINT | NRMT |
|---|---|---|
| COMPLETE SET (29) | 20.00 | 9.00 |
| COMMON CARD (1-29) | .25 | .11 |
| ❑ 1 Keith Acton | .50 | .23 |
| ❑ 2 Craig Berube | .50 | .23 |
| ❑ 3 Mike Bullard | .50 | .23 |
| ❑ 4 Terry Carkner | .50 | .23 |
| ❑ 5 Jeff Chychrun | .50 | .23 |
| ❑ 6 Bob Clarke VP/GM | 2.00 | .90 |
| ❑ 7 Murray Craven | .50 | .23 |
| ❑ 8 Mike Eaves ACO | .25 | .11 |
| ❑ 9 Pelle Eklund | .75 | .35 |
| ❑ 10 Ron Hextall | 2.00 | .90 |
| ❑ 11 Paul Holmgren CO | .50 | .23 |
| ❑ 12 Mark Howe | 1.00 | .45 |
| ❑ 13 Kerry Huffman | .50 | .23 |
| ❑ 14 Tim Kerr | 1.00 | .45 |
| ❑ 15 Scott Mellanby | 1.00 | .45 |
| ❑ 16 Gord Murphy | .50 | .23 |
| ❑ 17 Andy Murray ACO | .25 | .11 |
| ❑ 18 Pete Peeters | 1.00 | .45 |
| ❑ 19 Dave Poulin | 1.00 | .45 |
| ❑ 20 Brian Propp | 1.00 | .45 |
| ❑ 21 Kjell Samuelsson | 1.00 | .45 |
| ❑ 22 Ilkka Sinisalo | .50 | .23 |
| ❑ 23 Derrick Smith | .50 | .23 |
| ❑ 24 Doug Sulliman | .50 | .23 |
| ❑ 25 Ron Sutter | .50 | .23 |
| ❑ 26 Rick Tocchet | 2.00 | .90 |
| ❑ 27 Jay Wells | .50 | .23 |
| ❑ 28 Ken Wregget | 2.00 | .90 |
| ❑ 29 Team Photo | 2.00 | .90 |

## 1990-91 Flyers Postcards

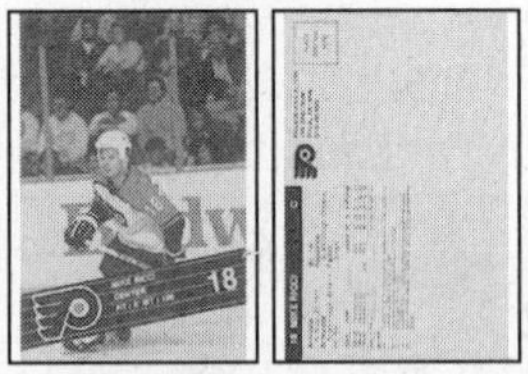

This 26-card set was issued by the Philadelphia Flyers. Each card measures approximately 4 1/8" by 6". The fronts display full-bleed color action photos. A team color-coded (black with thin orange stripes) diagonal stripe cuts across the bottom portion and carries the team logo, biographical information, and jersey number. The horizontal backs are postcard design and, on the left, present biography, statistics, and notes. The cards are unnumbered and checklisted below in alphabetical order.

| | MINT | NRMT |
|---|---|---|
| COMPLETE SET (26) | 15.00 | 6.75 |
| COMMON CARD (1-26) | .50 | .23 |
| ❑ 1 Keith Acton | .75 | .35 |
| ❑ 2 Murray Baron | .50 | .23 |
| ❑ 3 Craig Berube | .50 | .23 |
| ❑ 4 Terry Carkner | .50 | .23 |
| ❑ 5 Jeff Chychrun | .50 | .23 |
| ❑ 6 Murray Craven | .75 | .35 |
| ❑ 7 Pelle Eklund | .75 | .35 |
| ❑ 8 Ron Hextall | 1.50 | .70 |
| ❑ 9 Tony Horacek | .50 | .23 |
| ❑ 10 Martin Hostak | .50 | .23 |
| ❑ 11 Mark Howe | 1.00 | .45 |
| ❑ 12 Kerry Huffman | .50 | .23 |
| ❑ 13 Tim Kerr | 1.00 | .45 |
| ❑ 14 Dale Kushner | .50 | .23 |
| ❑ 15 Norman Lacombe | .50 | .23 |
| ❑ 16 Jiri Latal | .50 | .23 |
| ❑ 17 Scott Mellanby | 1.00 | .45 |
| ❑ 18 Gord Murphy | .50 | .23 |
| ❑ 19 Pete Peeters | .75 | .35 |
| ❑ 20 Mike Ricci | 1.50 | .70 |
| ❑ 21 Kjell Samuelsson | .75 | .35 |
| ❑ 22 Derrick Smith | .50 | .23 |
| ❑ 23 Ron Sutter | .50 | .23 |
| ❑ 24 Rick Tocchet | 2.00 | .90 |
| ❑ 25 Ken Wregget | 1.00 | .45 |
| ❑ 26 Team Photo | 2.00 | .90 |

## 1991-92 Flyers J.C. Penney

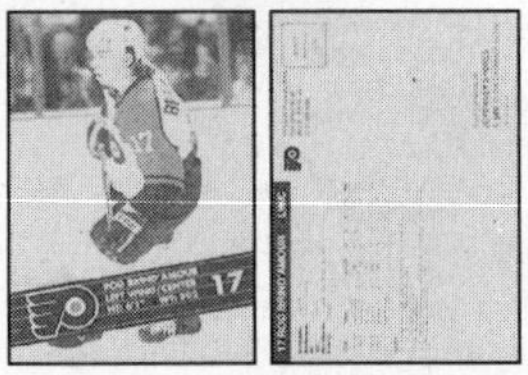

This 26-card set was issued by the Flyers in conjunction with J.C. Penney Stores and Lee. Each card measures approximately 4 1/8" by 6". The fronts display full-bleed color action photos. A team color-coded (black with thin orange stripes) diagonal stripe cuts across the bottom portion and carries the team logo, biographical information, and jersey number. The horizontal backs are postcard design and, on the left, present biography, statistics, and notes. The cards are unnumbered and checklisted below in alphabetical order.

| | MINT | NRMT |
|---|---|---|
| COMPLETE SET (26) | 15.00 | 6.75 |
| COMMON CARD (1-26) | .50 | .23 |
| ❑ 1 Keith Acton | .75 | .35 |
| ❑ 2 Rod Brind'Amour | 1.50 | .70 |
| ❑ 3 Dave Brown | .75 | .35 |
| ❑ 4 Terry Carkner | .50 | .23 |
| ❑ 5 Kimbi Daniels | .50 | .23 |
| ❑ 6 Kevin Dineen | 1.00 | .45 |
| ❑ 7 Steve Duchesne | .75 | .35 |
| ❑ 8 Pelle Eklund | .50 | .23 |
| ❑ 9 Corey Foster | .50 | .23 |
| ❑ 10 Ron Hextall | 1.50 | .70 |
| ❑ 11 Tony Horacek | .50 | .23 |
| ❑ 12 Mark Howe | 1.00 | .45 |
| ❑ 13 Kerry Huffman | .50 | .23 |
| ❑ 14 Brad Jones | .50 | .23 |
| ❑ 15 Steve Kasper UER (Misspelled Kaspar on front) | .50 | .23 |
| ❑ 16 Dan Kordic | .50 | .23 |
| ❑ 17 Jiri Latal | .50 | .23 |
| ❑ 18 Andrei Lomakin | .50 | .23 |
| ❑ 19 Gord Murphy | .50 | .23 |
| ❑ 20 Mark Pederson | .50 | .23 |
| ❑ 21 Dan Quinn | .50 | .23 |
| ❑ 22 Mike Ricci | 1.00 | .45 |
| ❑ 23 Kjell Samuelsson | .60 | .25 |
| ❑ 24 Rick Tocchet | 1.50 | .70 |
| ❑ 25 Ken Wregget | 1.00 | .45 |
| ❑ 26 Team Photo | 1.50 | .70 |

## 1992-93 Flyers J.C. Penney

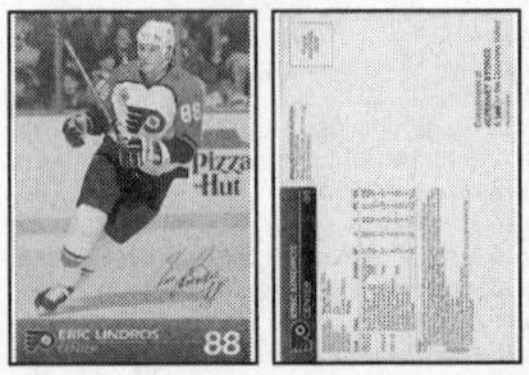

This 23-card set was sponsored by J.C. Penney Stores and Lee in the Delaware Valley. The cards measure approximately 4 1/8" by 6" and feature color, action player photos with facsimile autographs near the bottom of each picture. A gray border stripe across the bottom carries the team logo, player's name, position, and jersey number. The horizontal backs display biographical information, statistics, and career notes within a postcard-type format. The cards are unnumbered and checklisted below in alphabetical order.

| | MINT | NRMT |
|---|---|---|
| COMPLETE SET (23) | 20.00 | 9.00 |
| COMMON CARD (1-23) | .50 | .23 |
| ❑ 1 Keith Acton | .60 | .25 |
| ❑ 2 Stephane Beauregard | .60 | .25 |
| ❑ 3 Brian Benning | .50 | .23 |
| ❑ 4 Rod Brind'Amour | 1.50 | .70 |
| ❑ 5 Claude Boivin | .50 | .23 |
| ❑ 6 Dave Brown | .75 | .35 |
| ❑ 7 Terry Carkner | .50 | .23 |
| ❑ 8 Shawn Cronin | .50 | .23 |
| ❑ 9 Kevin Dineen | .75 | .35 |
| ❑ 10 Pelle Eklund | .50 | .23 |
| ❑ 11 Doug Evans | .50 | .23 |

❑ 12 Brent Fedyk .50 .23
❑ 13 Garry Galley .75 .35
❑ 14 Gord Hynes .50 .23
❑ 15 Eric Lindros 10.00 4.50
❑ 16 Andrei Lomakin .50 .23
❑ 17 Ryan McGill .50 .23
❑ 18 Ric Nattress .50 .23
❑ 19 Greg Paslawski .50 .23
❑ 20 Mark Recchi 2.00 .90
❑ 21 Dominic Roussel .75 .35
❑ 22 Dimitri Yushkevich .50 .23
❑ 23 Team Photo 1.50 .70

## 1992-93 Flyers Upper Deck Sheets

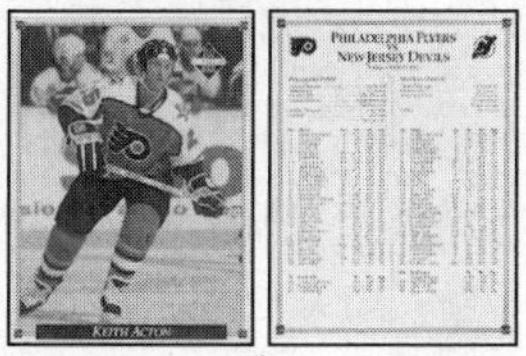

The 44 commemorative sheets in this set were distributed individually in game programs at Philadelphia Flyers home games during the 1992-93 season in Flyer magazine. The sheets measure approximately 8 1/2" by 11" and feature color, posed and action, player photos with orange and white borders. A black bar with an orange accent stripe above it carries either the player's name or a picture title. On sheets with a title, the player's name is printed on the photo in either orange or white lettering. A black diamond design is printed with the individual sheet number and the production run. The backs display the game date and teams playing. All sheets are the Flyers versus another NHL team. The roster and management of each team is also given. The sheets are unnumbered and checklisted below in chronological order. There was a second team photo issued March 13th. Due to a violent winter storm, only a few thousand spectators made it to the Spectrum. Play was halted when a severe wind blew out a few windows in the concourse area causing debris to scatter out into the seats. The sheets were distributed again during the make-up game on April 1.

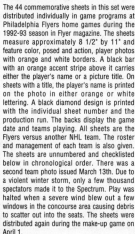

| | MINT | NRMT |
|---|---|---|
| COMPLETE SET (44) | 250.00 | 110.00 |
| COMMON SHEET (1-44) | 3.00 | 1.35 |

❑ 1 Quebec Nordiques 5.00 2.20
Sept. 19& 1992 (4&500)
Kevin Dineen
❑ 2 New Jersey Devils 3.00 1.35
Sept. 24& 1992 (4&500)
Brian Benning
❑ 3 Washington Capitals 8.00 3.60
Oct. 3& 1992 (4&500)
Mark Recchi
❑ 4 New Jersey Devils 4.00 1.80
Oct. 9& 1992 (7&500)
Keith Acton
❑ 5 New York Islanders 8.00 3.60
Oct. 15& 1992 (4&500)
Rod Brind'Amour
❑ 6 Winnipeg Jets 4.00 1.80
Oct. 18& 1992 (4&500)
Dave Brown
❑ 7 Vancouver Canucks 5.00 2.20
Oct. 22& 1992 (4&500)
Dominic Roussel
❑ 8 Montreal Canadiens 3.00 1.35
Oct. 24& 1992 (4&500)
Gord Hynes
❑ 9 St. Louis Blues 3.00 1.35
Nov. 7& 1992 (4&500)
Claude Boivin
❑ 10 New York Islanders 3.00 1.35
Nov. 12& 1992 (4&500)
Dimitri Yushkevich
❑ 11 Ottawa Senators 40.00 18.00
Nov. 15& 1992 (5&500)
Eric Lindros
❑ 12 New York Rangers 4.00 1.80
Nov. 19& 1992 (4&500)
Steve Kasper
❑ 13A Buffalo Sabres 12.00 5.50
Nov. 22& 1992 (4&500)
1992-93 Team Picture
❑ 13B Buffalo Sabres 10.00 4.50
Nov. 22& 1992
1992-93 Team Picture
(Pizza Hut logo on front
and Citation Graphics
Ad on back)
❑ 14 New York Islanders 3.00 1.35
Nov. 27& 1992 (5&500)
Greg Paslawski
❑ 15 Quebec Nordiques 4.00 1.80
Dec. 3& 1992 (4&500)
Terry Carkner
❑ 16 Boston Bruins 3.00 1.35
Dec. 6& 1992 (4&500)
Shawn Cronin
❑ 17 Washington Capitals 3.00 1.35
Dec. 12& 1992 (4&500)
Brent Fedyk
❑ 18 Pittsburgh Penguins 4.00 1.80
Dec. 17& 1992 (4&500)
Garry Galley
❑ 19 Chicago Blackhawks 3.00 1.35
Dec. 19& 1992 (5&000)
Andrei Lomakin
❑ 20 Pittsburgh Penguins 5.00 2.20
Dec. 23& 1992 (5&500)
Bill and Kevin Dineen
❑ 21 Washington Capitals 4.00 1.80
Jan. 7& 1993 (4&500)
Stephane Beauregard
❑ 22 New York Rangers 8.00 3.60
Jan. 9& 1993 (6&000)
Mark Recchi
❑ 23 Edmonton Oilers 3.00 1.35
Jan. 10& 1993 (5&000)
Ryan McGill
❑ 24 Calgary Flames 3.00 1.35
Jan. 14& 1993 (6&500)
Doug Evans
❑ 25 Detroit Red Wings 5.00 2.20
Jan. 17& 1993 (5&000)
The Captains
Kevin Dineen
Keith Acton
Terry Carkner
❑ 26 Boston Bruins 3.00 1.35
Jan. 21& 1993 (5&000)
Ric Nattress
❑ 27 Hartford Whalers 8.00 3.60
Jan. 24& 1993 (5&000)
Rod Brind'Amour
❑ 28 Buffalo Sabres 5.00 2.20
Jan. 26& 1993 (5&000)
Tommy Soderstrom
❑ 29 Quebec Nordiques 4.00 1.80
Jan. 28& 1993 (5&000)
Pelle Eklund
❑ 30 Ottawa Senators 4.00 1.80
Feb. 9& 1993 (5&000)
Dave Brown
❑ 31 Montreal Canadiens 25.00 11.00
Feb. 11& 1993 (5&500)
The Rookies
Tommy Soderstrom
Dimitri Yushkevich
Dominic Roussel
Ryan McGill
Eric Lindros
❑ 32 New Jersey Devils 3.00 1.35
Feb. 14& 1993 (5&000)
Josef Beranek
❑ 33 New Jersey Devils 3.00 1.35
Feb. 25& 1993 (6&000)
Greg Paslawski
❑ 34 New York Islanders 4.00 1.80
Feb. 27& 1993 (5&000)
The Coaches
Craig Hartsburg
Bill Dineen
Ken Hitchcock
❑ 35 Pittsburgh Penguins 4.00 1.80
Mar. 2& 1993 (5&000)
Keith Acton
❑ 36 Washington Capitals 8.00 3.60
Mar. 11& 1993 (5&500)
NHL All-Star
Mark Recchi
❑ 37A Los Angeles Kings 4.00 1.80
Mar. 13& 1993 (5&500)
Garry Galley
❑ 37B Los Angeles Kings 7.50 3.40
Make-up Game
1992-93 Team Picture
❑ 38 Minnesota North Stars 4.00 1.80
Mar. 16& 1993 (5&000)
Terry Carkner
❑ 39 New Jersey Devils 5.00 2.20
Mar. 21& 1993 (5&000)
Dominic Roussel
❑ 40 San Jose Sharks 3.00 1.35
Mar. 25& 1993 (5&000)
Greg Hawgood
❑ 41 Tampa Bay Lightning 3.00 1.35
Apr. 3& 1993 (5&500)
Viacheslav Butsayev
❑ 42 Toronto Maple Leafs 25.00 11.00
Apr. 4& 1993 (6&000)
Crazy 8's
Mark Recchi
Eric Lindros
Brent Fedyk
❑ 43 Washington Capitals 5.00 2.20
Apr. 8& 1993 (5&500)
European Style
Andrei Lomakin
Dimitri Yushkevich
Viacheslav Butsayev
❑ 44 New York Rangers 10.00 4.50
Apr. 12& 1993 (5&500)
Hockey Hall of Famers
Bob Clarke
Ed Snider
Bill Barber
Bernie Parent
Keith Allen

## 1996-97 Flyers Postcards

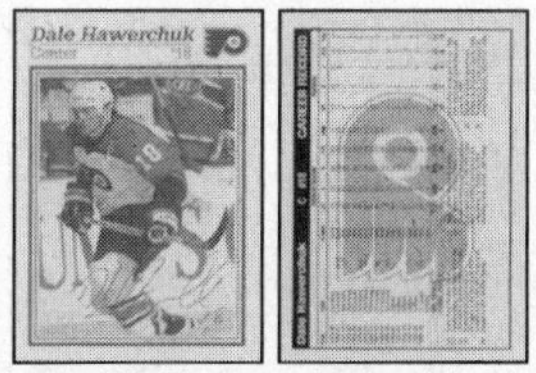


This attractive 24-card set was produced late in the '96-97 season by the club. The standard-sized postcards feature an action photo on the front, along with the player's name, position and jersey number. The back contains a remarkably thorough stats package, including career numbers, awards and transaction info. Unnumbered, the cards are listed below in alphabetical order.

| | MINT | NRMT |
|---|---|---|
| COMPLETE SET (24) | 15.00 | 6.75 |
| COMMON CARD | .25 | .11 |

❑ 1 Team Photo .50 .23
❑ 2 Rod Brind'Amour .75 .35
❑ 3 Paul Coffey 1.00 .45
❑ 4 Scott Daniels .25 .11
❑ 5 Eric Desjardins .40 .18
❑ 6 John Druce .25 .11
❑ 7 Karl Dykhuis .25 .11
❑ 8 Pat Falloon .25 .11
❑ 9 Dale Hawerchuk .75 .35
❑ 10 Ron Hextall .75 .35
❑ 11 Trent Klatt .25 .11
❑ 12 Dan Kordic .25 .11
❑ 13 Daniel Lacroix .25 .11
❑ 14 John LeClair 2.00 .90
❑ 15 Eric Lindros 5.00 2.20
❑ 16 Janne Niinimaa 1.50 .70
❑ 17 Joel Otto .25 .11
❑ 18 Shjon Podein .25 .11
❑ 19 Mikael Renberg .75 .35
❑ 20 Kjell Samuelsson .25 .11
❑ 21 Garth Snow .50 .23
❑ 22 Petr Svoboda .25 .11
❑ 23 Chris Therien .25 .11
❑ 24 Dainius Zubrus 2.00 .90

## 1971-72 Frito Lay

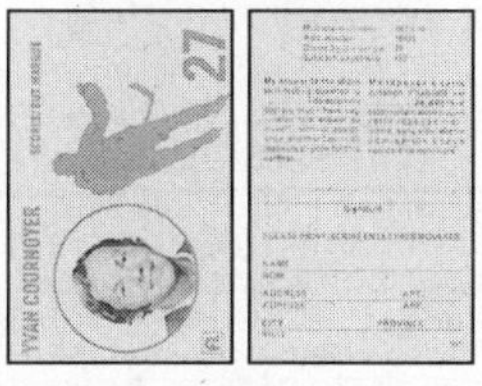

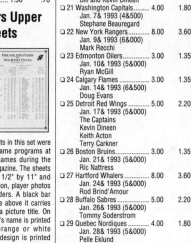

This ten-card set features members of the Toronto Maple Leafs and Montreal Canadiens. Since the cards are unnumbered, they have been listed below in alphabetical order within team, Montreal (1-5) and Toronto (6-10). The cards are paper thin, each measuring approximately 1 1/2" by 2".

| | NRMT-MT | EXC |
|---|---|---|
| COMPLETE SET (10) | 100.00 | 45.00 |
| COMMON CARD (1-10) | 4.00 | 1.80 |

❑ 1 Yvan Cournoyer 8.00 3.60
❑ 2 Ken Dryden 50.00 22.00
❑ 3 Frank Mahovlich 10.00 4.50
❑ 4 Henri Richard 10.00 4.50
❑ 5 J.C. Tremblay 4.00 1.80
❑ 6 Bobby Baun 4.00 1.80
❑ 7 Ron Ellis 4.00 1.80
❑ 8 Paul Henderson 6.00 2.70
❑ 9 Jacques Plante 20.00 9.00
❑ 10 Norm Ullman 6.00 2.70

## 1988-89 Frito-Lay Stickers

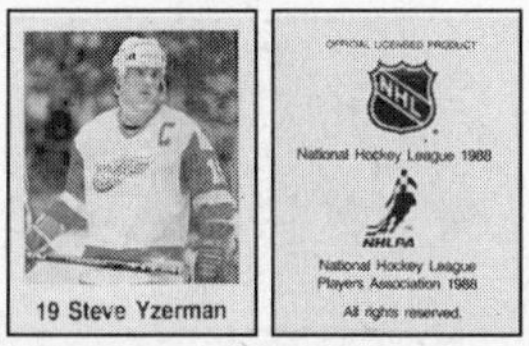


The 1988-89 Frito-Lay Hockey Stickers set includes 42 small (1 3/8" by 1 3/4") stickers. The fronts are dominated by color photos, but also have each player's name and uniform number. The stickers were distributed in sealed plastic, and packaged one per special Frito-Lay snack bag. Reportedly distribution was via 35 million bags of Ruffles, O'Gradys, Dulac, Lays, Doritos, Fritos, Tostitos, Cheetos, and Chester Popcorn -- each containing one of the 42 players in the set. Since they are actually stickers, there is very little information on the backing. The checklist below also gives the player's uniform number as listed on each card. A poster was also available from the company by sending in 2.00 and one UPC symbol from any Frito-Lay product.

| | MINT | NRMT |
|---|---|---|
| COMPLETE SET (42) | 30.00 | 13.50 |
| COMMON STICKER (1-42) | .25 | .11 |

❑ 1 Mario Lemieux 66 6.00 2.70
❑ 2 Bryan Trottier 19 .75 .35
❑ 3 Steve Yzerman 19 4.00 1.80
❑ 4 Bernie Federko 24 .35 .16
❑ 5 Brian Bellows 23 .35 .16
❑ 6 Denis Savard 18 .50 .23
❑ 7 Neal Broten 7 .35 .16
❑ 8 Doug Gilmour 9 1.50 .70
❑ 9 Dale Hawerchuk 10 .50 .23
❑ 10 Luc Robitaille 20 1.50 .70
❑ 11 Ed Olczyk 16 .25 .11
❑ 12 Andrew McBain 20 .25 .11
❑ 13 Mike Gartner 11 1.00 .45
❑ 14 Pat LaFontaine 16 1.50 .70
❑ 15 Scott Stevens 3 .50 .23
❑ 16 Ray Bourque 77 1.50 .70
❑ 17 Cam Neely 8 1.50 .70
❑ 18 Mike Foligno 17 .25 .11
❑ 19 Tom Barrasso 30 .50 .23
❑ 20 Ron Francis 10 .75 .35
❑ 21 Peter Stastny 26 .50 .23
❑ 22 Michel Goulet 16 .50 .23
❑ 23 Bernie Nicholls 9 .50 .23
❑ 24 Paul Coffey 77 1.50 .70
❑ 25 Mats Naslund 26 .35 .16
❑ 26 Glenn Anderson 9 .50 .23
❑ 27 Dave Poulin 20 .35 .16
❑ 28 Kevin Dineen 11 .35 .16
❑ 29 Wendel Clark 17 .75 .35
❑ 30 James Patrick 3 .25 .11
❑ 31 Al MacInnis 2 .75 .35
❑ 32 Troy Murray 19 .25 .11
❑ 33 Kirk Muller 9 .75 .35
❑ 34 Marcel Dionne 16 .50 .23
❑ 35 Mark Messier 11 2.00 .90
❑ 36 Joe Nieuwendyk 25 1.50 .70
❑ 37 Ron Hextall 27 .75 .35
❑ 38 Sean Burke 1 .50 .23
❑ 39 Barry Pederson 7 .25 .11
❑ 40 Stephane Richer 44 .50 .23
❑ 41 Bob Probert 24 1.50 .70
❑ 42 Tony Tanti 9 .35 .16
❑ NNO Set Poster 3.00 1.35

## 1996-97 Frosted Flakes Masks

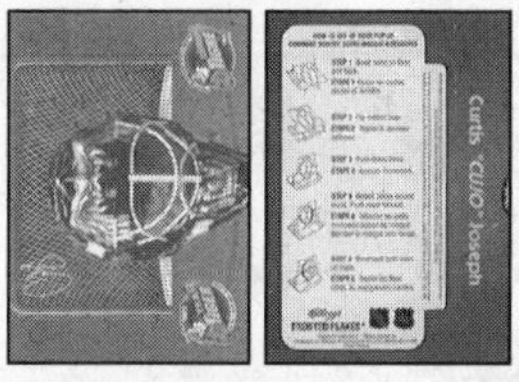


One of thse 7 cards was inserted into specially marked boxes of Frosted Flakes in Canada early in the season. These unique die-cut cards featured a net design and a goalie mask, which could be popped up on display in front of the net. Just two of the cards feature the actual faces and mask designs of individual goalies (#1-2). Cards 3-6 feature generic masks with the design of the team logo, while the seventh features a Tony the Tiger mask. The complete set was available by mail for $2.50 plus three proofs of purchase.

| | MINT | NRMT |
|---|---|---|
| COMPLETE SET (7) | 20.00 | 9.00 |
| COMMON MASK | 3.00 | 1.35 |

❑ 1 Felix Potvin 3.00 1.35
❑ 2 Curtis Joseph 4.00 1.80
❑ 3 Montreal Canadiens 3.00 1.35
❑ 4 Ottawa Senators 3.00 1.35
❑ 5 Calgary Flames 3.00 1.35
❑ 6 Vancouver Canucks 3.00 1.35
❑ 7 Tony the Tiger 3.00 1.35

## 1991-92 Future Trends Canada '72 Promos

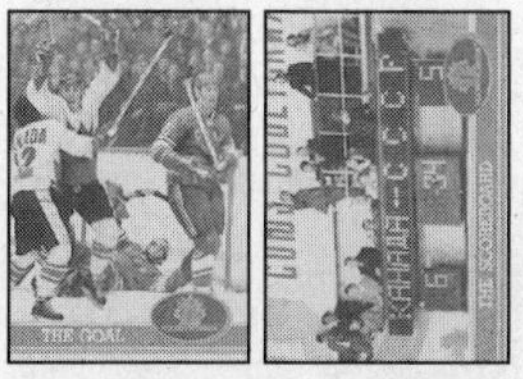


This standard-size three-card set was issued to promote the release of Future Trends' Team Canada '72 set. To commemorate Team Canada of 1972, 7200 of each promotional card were offered for sale at Canada's Hudson Bay Stores. The fronts feature full-bleed black-and-white action shots from a game between Team Canada and the Soviet team. The card title appears in white lettering within a red stripe across the bottom of the picture. The '72 Hockey Canada logo appears in the lower right. Except for their horizontal orientation, the backs are similar to the fronts, with full-bleed black-and-white photos, white lettering within a red stripe at the bottom, and logo in the lower right. The cards are unnumbered and checklisted below in alphabetical order by title. These promos were issued in English and French versions.

| | MINT | NRMT |
|---|---|---|
| COMPLETE SET (3) | 18.00 | 8.00 |
| COMMON CARD (1-3) | 6.00 | 2.70 |

❑ 1 The Goal 8.00 3.60
The Scoreboard
❑ 2 The Leader 9.00 4.00
Phil Esposito
❑ 3 The Legend 6.00 2.70
The Kid

## 1991-92 Future Trends Canada '72

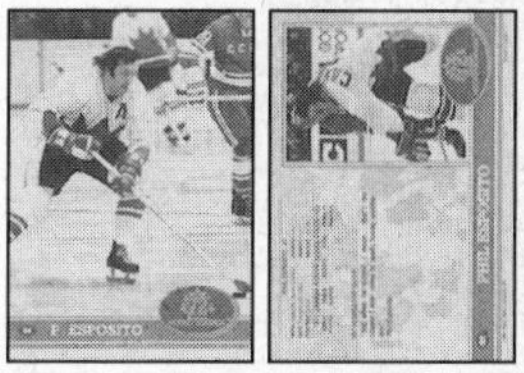


Future Trends Experience Ltd. produced this 101-card standard-size set to celebrate the 20th anniversary of the 1972 Summit Series between the Soviets and the Canadians. The cards were available initially only at the Bay and were sold in ten-card foil packs with no factory sets. The 70 players of the Canadian and Russian teams are represented, and 30 additional special cards capture unforgettable moments from the series. Between one and two special cards, signed in gold paint pen by living Canadian players, were randomly inserted into each foil case. Only one non-Canadian, Vladislav Tretiak, signed cards. Supposedly each of the signers signed only 750 cards for insertion and distribution within the packs. These cards were specially coated with a swirl pattern over the autograph. Reportedly, The Bay also issued 2500 autographed sets without the special coating, but we have no confirmation of this at this time. The cards feature on the fronts borderless black-and-white, action or posed pictures. A white, red, and gold stripe cuts across the bottom of the card face and intersects the '72 Hockey Canada logo at the lower right corner. The backs carry additional photos, biographical information, series statistics, sportswriters' editorial comments, and/or player quotes. Card number 40 features Phil Esposito's September 8, 1972, address to the nation. The card number appears in a blue oblong design within the bottom red stripe on both sides. The '72 Hockey Canada logo also appears in the lower right corner of the back. The set was issued in both an English and a French version. The production quantities were reportedly 9,000 English and 1,000 French 12-box cases. Also released were 1972 uncut sheet sets. Signed cards generally command 100 to 150 times the values below.

| | MINT | NRMT |
|---|---|---|
| COMPLETE SET (101) | 6.00 | 2.70 |
| COMMON CARD (1-101) | .05 | .02 |

❑ 1 In The Beginning .15 .07
❑ 2 The Backyard Rink .05 .02
❑ 3 It Didn't Take Long .05 .02
❑ 4 The Patriarch .15 .07
Anatoli Tarasov
❑ 5 More Hours a Day .50 .23
Vladislav Tretiak
❑ 6 Coming Out Party .15 .07
❑ 7 Never In Doubt .05 .02
❑ 8 Team Canada .25 .11
❑ 9 Pat Stapleton .05 .02
❑ 10 Vsevolod Bobrov .05 .02
❑ 11 Vladislav Tretiak .50 .23
❑ 12 Faceoff .05 .02
Game 1& Montreal (9/2/72)
❑ 13 30 Seconds .10 .05
Game 1& Montreal (9/2/72)
❑ 14 Yevgeny Zimin .05 .02
❑ 15 Bill White .05 .02
❑ 16 7-3 .05 .02
Game 1 Statistics
❑ 17 Don Awrey .05 .02
❑ 18 Mickey Redmond .20 .09
❑ 19 Alexander Gusev .15 .07
❑ 20 Alexander Maltsev .25 .11
❑ 21 Rod Seiling .05 .02
❑ 22 Dale Tallon .05 .02
❑ 23 Coming Back .05 .02
Game 2& Toronto (9/4/72)

| | | |
|---|---|---|
| ❑ 24 Unforgettable | .05 | .02 |
| Game 2 Statistics | | |
| ❑ 25 Wayne Cashman | .15 | .07 |
| ❑ 26 Frank Mahovlich | .25 | .11 |
| ❑ 27 Peter Mahovlich | .05 | .02 |
| ❑ 28 Vyacheslav Solodukhin | .15 | .07 |
| Alexander Sidelnikov | | |
| ❑ 29 Yuri Shatalov | .15 | .07 |
| ❑ 30 Brothers | .15 | .07 |
| Frank Mahovlich | | |
| Peter Mahovlich | | |
| ❑ 31 The Goalies | .50 | .23 |
| ❑ 32 Alexander Bodunov | .05 | .02 |
| ❑ 33 All Even | .05 | .02 |
| Game 3 Statistics | | |
| ❑ 34 Yuri Blinov | .05 | .02 |
| ❑ 35 Jocelyn Guevremont | .05 | .02 |
| ❑ 36 Vic Hadfield | .05 | .02 |
| ❑ 37 Yuri Lebedev | .05 | .02 |
| ❑ 38 Yevgeny Poladiev | .15 | .07 |
| Vyacheslav Starshinov | | |
| ❑ 39 Disaster | .05 | .02 |
| Game 4 Statistics | | |
| ❑ 40 Address to The Nation | .25 | .11 |
| Phil Esposito | | |
| ❑ 41 Victor Kuzkin | .05 | .02 |
| ❑ 42 Vladimir Lutchenko | .25 | .11 |
| ❑ 43 Boris Mikhailov | .35 | .16 |
| ❑ 44 Grace Under Pressure | .05 | .02 |
| Game 5& Moscow (9/22/72) | | |
| ❑ 45 Afraid to Lose | .05 | .02 |
| ❑ 46 Ready To Win | .05 | .02 |
| Game 5 Statistics | | |
| ❑ 47 Vladimir Vikulov | .05 | .02 |
| ❑ 48 Red Berenson | .05 | .02 |
| ❑ 49 Richard Martin | .05 | .02 |
| ❑ 50 Alexander Martynyuk | .05 | .02 |
| ❑ 51 Gilbert Perreault | .25 | .11 |
| ❑ 52 Vladimir Petrov | .35 | .16 |
| ❑ 53 Serge Savard | .15 | .07 |
| ❑ 54 Vladimir Shadrin | .05 | .02 |
| ❑ 55 DA DA KA-NA-DA | .05 | .02 |
| Game 6& Moscow (9/24/72) | | |
| ❑ 56 One Step Back | .05 | .02 |
| Game 6 Statistics | | |
| ❑ 57 Bobby Clarke | .35 | .16 |
| ❑ 58 Valeri Kharlamov | .50 | .23 |
| ❑ 59 Alexander Volchkov | .15 | .07 |
| ❑ 60 Standing Guard | .15 | .07 |
| ❑ 61 Stan Mikita | .35 | .16 |
| ❑ 62 One More To Go | .05 | .02 |
| Game 7 Statistics | | |
| Moscow (9/26/72) | | |
| ❑ 63 The Winner | .05 | .02 |
| ❑ 64 The Fans Go Wild | .05 | .02 |
| ❑ 65 Alexander Ragulin | .15 | .07 |
| ❑ 66 Jean Ratelle | .15 | .07 |
| ❑ 67 Gennady Tsygankov | .15 | .07 |
| ❑ 68 Valeri Vasiliev | .35 | .16 |
| ❑ 69 International Dialogue | .05 | .02 |
| ❑ 70 Series Stars | .35 | .16 |
| Phil Esposito | | |
| Alexander Yakushev | | |
| ❑ 71 Series Stars | .35 | .16 |
| Paul Henderson | | |
| Vladislav Tretiak | | |
| ❑ 72 No Solitudes | .05 | .02 |
| Game 8& Moscow (9/28/72) | | |
| The Telegrams | | |
| ❑ 73 2-2 | .05 | .02 |
| Game 8& Moscow (9/28/72) | | |
| ❑ 74 Rod Gilbert | .15 | .07 |
| ❑ 75 Yevgeny Mishokov | .15 | .07 |
| ❑ 76 Ron Ellis | .05 | .02 |
| ❑ 77 5-4 | .05 | .02 |
| ❑ 78 Different Games | .05 | .02 |
| Game 8& Moscow (9/28/72) | | |
| Interlude | | |
| ❑ 79 Bill Goldsworthy | .05 | .02 |
| ❑ 80 The Huddle | .05 | .02 |
| ❑ 81 The Moment | .50 | .23 |
| ❑ 82 Yvan Cournoyer | .25 | .11 |
| ❑ 83 Yuri Liapkin | .05 | .02 |
| ❑ 84 Phil Esposito | .35 | .16 |
| ❑ 85 Ken Dryden | .50 | .23 |
| ❑ 86 Peace | .05 | .02 |
| Game 8 Statistics | | |
| ❑ 87 Gary Bergman | .05 | .02 |
| ❑ 88 Brian Glennie | .05 | .02 |
| ❑ 89 Dennis Hull | .05 | .02 |
| ❑ 90 Vyacheslav Anisin | .05 | .02 |
| ❑ 91 Marcel Dionne | .25 | .11 |
| ❑ 92 Guy Lapointe | .15 | .07 |
| ❑ 93 Ed Johnston | .10 | .05 |
| ❑ 94 Harry Sinden GM | .05 | .02 |
| ❑ 95 Brad Park | .25 | .11 |
| ❑ 96 Tony Esposito | .25 | .11 |
| ❑ 97 Alexander Yakushev | .35 | .16 |
| ❑ 98 Paul Henderson | .50 | .23 |
| ❑ 99 J.P. Parise | .05 | .02 |
| ❑ 100 Valeri Kharlamov | .50 | .23 |
| Alex Kharlamov on back | | |
| ❑ 101 Checklist | .15 | .07 |

## 1992 Future Trends '76 Canada Cup

This 100-card, standard-size set was produced by The Future Trends Experience Ltd. and licensed by Hockey Canada. Commemorating the 1976 Canada Cup, the card numbering picks up where the '72 Team Canada set left off by tracing the growth of international hockey. According to the company the production run was 50,000 numbered display

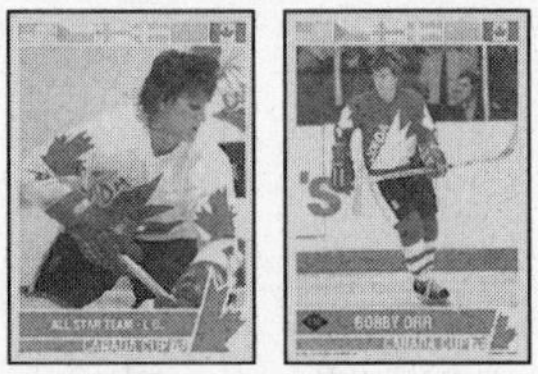

boxes. Randomly inserted in the packs were 3,750 gold-foil stamped signature cards; five players (Bobby Orr, Bobby Hull, Rogatien Vachon, Darryl Sittler, and Bobby Clarke) signed 750 cards each. These cards are valued generally 75 to 100 times the values below. The cards feature vertical and horizontal color action and posed player and team photos. Some shots are of game action with several players pictured. The bottom of each is accented by red and gold border stripes with a red Canada Cup logo in the right corner. Most cards are bordered in white, but some are bordered on the top by the national flags of the various teams in the set. The horizontal backs carry the same flag pattern ghosted behind information about the pictured player or team. A color photo of the players or player is displayed to the right of the copy. Red and gold border stripes similar to the front appear below. Topical subsets featured are '72 Retrospective (102-106), 1974 Russian team vs. WHA (107-110), a 6-card training camp subset (111-116), MVPs (184-190), and the first ever Canada Cup All-Star team (195-200). The cards are numbered on the back. An 8 1/2" by 11" sheet was also issued; it has an artist's color painting of the players on the front and a checklist on its back.

| | MINT | NRMT |
|---|---|---|
| COMPLETE SET (100) | 8.00 | 3.60 |
| COMMON CARD (102-201) | .05 | .02 |
| ❑ 102 Phil Esposito | .35 | .16 |
| ❑ 103 Vladislav Tretiak | .50 | .23 |
| ❑ 104 Bobby Orr | .75 | .35 |
| ❑ 105 Paul Henderson | .15 | .07 |
| The Goal | | |
| ❑ 106 Alexander Yakushev | .15 | .07 |
| ❑ 107 Bobby Hull | .50 | .23 |
| ❑ 108 Valeri Kharlamov | .35 | .16 |
| ❑ 109 Gerry Cheevers | .25 | .11 |
| Vladislav Tretiak | | |
| ❑ 110 Bobby Hull | .50 | .23 |
| Vladislav Tretiak | | |
| ❑ 111 Soviet on-ice workout | .10 | .05 |
| ❑ 112 Czech on-ice workout | .05 | .02 |
| ❑ 113 Finn on-ice workout | .05 | .02 |
| ❑ 114 Swedes take the ice | .05 | .02 |
| ❑ 115 USA on-ice workout | .10 | .05 |
| ❑ 116 Darryl Sittler | .25 | .11 |
| ❑ 117 Serge Savard | .15 | .07 |
| ❑ 118 Team Finland | .05 | .02 |
| ❑ 119 Team Sweden | .05 | .02 |
| ❑ 120 Team Czechoslavakia | .05 | .02 |
| ❑ 121 Soviets | .15 | .07 |
| ❑ 122 Team USA | .15 | .07 |
| ❑ 123 Team Canada | .15 | .07 |
| ❑ 124 The Opening Barrage | .05 | .02 |
| ❑ 125 Richard Martin | .05 | .02 |
| ❑ 126 Bobby Orr | .75 | .35 |
| ❑ 127 Sweden vs. USA | .05 | .02 |
| ❑ 128 Ivan Hlinka | .05 | .02 |
| ❑ 129 CSSR 5 - CCCP 3 | .05 | .02 |
| ❑ 130 Helmut Balderis | .15 | .07 |
| ❑ 131 Peter Stastny | .20 | .09 |
| ❑ 132 Valeri Vasiliev | .15 | .07 |
| ❑ 133 Out of Contention | .05 | .02 |
| ❑ 134 Standing Alone | .05 | .02 |
| ❑ 135 The Miracle On Ice | .05 | .02 |
| ❑ 136 Josef Augusta | .05 | .02 |
| ❑ 137 A Soviet Rout | .05 | .02 |
| ❑ 138 Vicktor Zhluktov | .10 | .05 |
| ❑ 139 Bobby Hull | .35 | .16 |
| Phil Esposito | | |
| Marcel Dionne | | |
| ❑ 140 Bob Gainey | .15 | .07 |
| ❑ 141 Anders Hedberg | .15 | .07 |
| ❑ 142 Bobby Hull | .50 | .23 |
| ❑ 143 Ulf Nilsson | .15 | .07 |
| ❑ 144 Sergei Kapustin | .15 | .07 |
| ❑ 145 Borje Salming | .15 | .07 |
| ❑ 146 Well Enough To Win | .05 | .02 |
| ❑ 147 Biggest Upset | .05 | .02 |
| ❑ 148 Matti Hagman | .05 | .02 |
| ❑ 149 Unbeatable | .05 | .02 |
| ❑ 150 Boris Alexandrov | .15 | .07 |
| ❑ 151 A Goal Tending Duel | .10 | .05 |
| ❑ 152 Vladimir Dzurilla | .10 | .05 |
| ❑ 153 Phil Esposito | .35 | .16 |
| ❑ 154 Rogatien Vachon | .15 | .07 |
| ❑ 155 Milan Novy | .05 | .02 |
| ❑ 156 Vladimir Martinec | .10 | .05 |
| ❑ 157 Good For Hockey | .05 | .02 |
| ❑ 158 Bill Nyrop | .05 | .02 |
| ❑ 159 Pride | .05 | .02 |
| ❑ 160 Another Summit | .05 | .02 |
| ❑ 161 Alexander Maltsev | .15 | .07 |
| ❑ 162 Gilbert Perreault | .25 | .11 |
| ❑ 163 Vladislav Tretiak | .50 | .23 |
| ❑ 164 Vladimir Vikulov | .10 | .05 |
| ❑ 165 Canada Cup Final | .05 | .02 |
| Game 1 | | |
| ❑ 166 Not There Yet | .05 | .02 |
| ❑ 167 Fast and Furious | .05 | .02 |
| ❑ 168 4 - 3 | .05 | .02 |
| 4 - 4 | | |
| ❑ 169 Bill Barber | .15 | .07 |
| ❑ 170 The Grapevine | .10 | .05 |
| ❑ 171 Guy Lapointe | .15 | .07 |
| ❑ 172 Reggie Leach | .05 | .02 |
| ❑ 173 Sittler's Goal | .25 | .11 |
| ❑ 174 Lanny McDonald | .25 | .11 |
| ❑ 175 Darryl Sittler | .25 | .11 |
| ❑ 176 The Canada Cup | .15 | .07 |
| ❑ 177 Bobby Clarke | .25 | .11 |
| ❑ 178 Last Time for No. 9 | .25 | .11 |
| ❑ 179 Marcel Dionne | .25 | .11 |
| ❑ 180 Peter Mahovlich | .05 | .02 |
| ❑ 181 Denis Potvin | .25 | .11 |
| ❑ 182 Larry Robinson | .25 | .11 |
| ❑ 183 Steve Shutt | .15 | .07 |
| ❑ 184 Bobby Orr | .75 | .35 |
| Tournament MVP | | |
| ❑ 185 Rogatien Vachon | .15 | .07 |
| ❑ 186 Milan Novy | .10 | .05 |
| ❑ 187 Matti Hagman | .05 | .02 |
| ❑ 188 Borje Salming | .15 | .07 |
| ❑ 189 Robbie Ftorek | .05 | .02 |
| ❑ 190 Alexander Maltsev | .15 | .07 |
| ❑ 191 Canada Final Series | .05 | .02 |
| ❑ 192 Canada Series Totals | .05 | .02 |
| ❑ 193 CSSR Final Series | .05 | .02 |
| ❑ 194 CSSR Series Totals | .05 | .02 |
| ❑ 195 Rogatien Vachon AS | .15 | .07 |
| ❑ 196 Bobby Orr AS | .75 | .35 |
| ❑ 197 Borje Salming AS | .15 | .07 |
| ❑ 198 Milan Novy AS | .05 | .02 |
| ❑ 199 Darryl Sittler AS | .15 | .07 |
| ❑ 200 Alexander Maltsev AS | .15 | .07 |
| ❑ 201 Canada Cup Checklist | .10 | .05 |
| ❑ NNO Checklist Sheet | 2.00 | .90 |
| (8 1/2~ by 11~; artist rendition on front) | | |

## 1992 Future Trends Promo Sheet

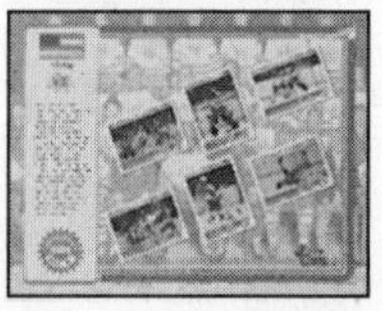

Produced by The Future Trends Experience Ltd., this limited edition sample sheet commemorates the 1976 U.S. Olympic Team. The front of this 11" by 8 1/2" sheet features a full-bleed ghosted team photo as the background for six Canada Cup cards. The cards are placed in two rows diagonally across the sheet. Red and gold stripes form a border surrounding the cards and intersecting a white panel on the left side of the sheet. The panel has a thin red, gold, and blue border and contains an American flag icon, the Team USA emblem, text about the team, and a gold limited edition stamp with the production run total (10,000). The back is blank. The cards are unnumbered and checklisted below as they appear from left to right starting with the first row.

| | MINT | NRMT |
|---|---|---|
| COMPLETE SET (1) | 4.00 | 1.80 |
| COMMON SHEET | 4.00 | 1.80 |
| ❑ 1 Team USA Sheet | 4.00 | 1.80 |
| Anticipation | | |
| Vladislav Tretiak | | |
| Gary Sargent | | |
| Defending the Crease | | |
| Maltsev vs. Milbury | | |
| Mike Curran | | |

## 1967-68 General Mills

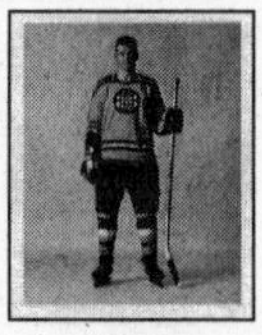

Little is known about this recently catalogued five-card set, save for it measures approximately 2 5/16" by 2 13/16" and features color player photos in a white border. It appears the cards were cut-outs from boxes of General Mills cereal, as a full box back picturing Harry Howell with a checklist listing these cards is known to exist. Further information would be appreciated. The backs are blank. The cards are unnumbered and checklisted below in alphabetical order.

| | MINT | NRMT |
|---|---|---|
| COMPLETE SET (5) | 1000.00 | 450.00 |
| COMMON CARD (1-5) | 80.00 | 36.00 |
| ❑ 1 Jean Beliveau | 125.00 | 55.00 |
| ❑ 2 Gordie Howe | 300.00 | 135.00 |
| ❑ 3 Harry Howell | 80.00 | 36.00 |
| ❑ 4 Stan Mikita | 125.00 | 55.00 |
| ❑ 5 Bobby Orr | 500.00 | 220.00 |

## 1991-92 Gillette

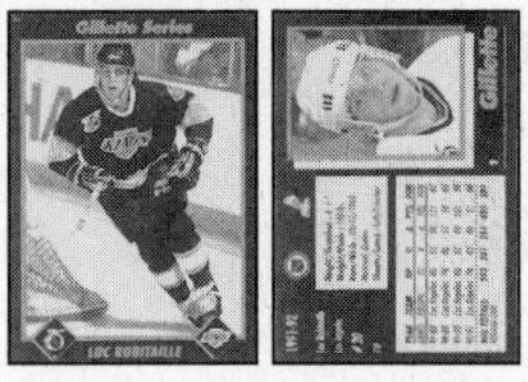

This 48-card standard-size set, sponsored by Gillette, features players ifrom the old four divisions of the NHL: Smythe (1-10), Norris (11-20), Adams (21-30), and Patrick (31-40). Each ten-card pack came with a trivia card and a checklist card. To receive one ten-card pack, collectors were required to send to Gillette of Canada one UPC symbol from any Canadian Gillette product, the dated receipt with purchase price circled, and 2.00 for shipping and handling. The entire set could be obtained by sending in three UPC symbols plus 5.00. Reportedly just 30,000 sets were produced, and the offer expired on August 28, 1992. On a black card face, the fronts carry a full-color action photo enclosed by a gold border. The title "Gillette Series" appears in gold lettering at the top, while the player's name appears at the bottom between the 75th NHL Anniversary logo and the team logo. Some of the cards have the words "Rookie Card" in the bottom gold border (numbers 3, 10, 20, 30, 40). In a horizontal format, the backs have biography and statistics (1987-91) in English and French, as well as a color head shot. The player cards are numbered on the back. Although the backs of the four unnumbered checklist cards are identical (each one lists all 40 cards), a different division name appears on the front of each checklist card: Smythe, Norris, Adams, and Patrick. The fronts of each of the four unnumbered trivia card are identical, while their backs features two different questions and answers.

| | MINT | NRMT |
|---|---|---|
| COMPLETE SET (48) | 25.00 | 11.00 |
| COMMON CARD (1-48) | .10 | .05 |
| ❑ 1 Luc Robitaille | .50 | .23 |
| ❑ 2 Esa Tikkanen | .25 | .11 |
| ❑ 3 Pat Falloon | .15 | .07 |
| ❑ 4 Theoren Fleury | .50 | .23 |
| ❑ 5 Trevor Linden | .35 | .16 |
| ❑ 6 Rob Blake | .25 | .11 |
| ❑ 7 Al MacInnis | .35 | .16 |
| ❑ 8 Bob Essensa | .25 | .11 |
| ❑ 9 Bill Ranford | .35 | .16 |
| ❑ 10 Pavel Bure | 2.00 | .90 |
| ❑ 11 Wendel Clark | .50 | .23 |
| ❑ 12 Sergei Fedorov | 2.00 | .90 |
| ❑ 13 Jeremy Roenick | .75 | .35 |
| ❑ 14 Brett Hull | 1.00 | .45 |
| ❑ 15 Mike Modano | .50 | .23 |
| ❑ 16 Chris Chelios | .75 | .35 |
| ❑ 17 Dave Ellett | .15 | .07 |
| ❑ 18 Ed Belfour | .75 | .35 |
| ❑ 19 Grant Fuhr | .35 | .16 |
| ❑ 20 Martin Lapointe | .15 | .07 |
| ❑ 21 Kirk Muller | .25 | .11 |
| ❑ 22 Joe Sakic | 1.50 | .70 |
| ❑ 23 Pat LaFontaine | .35 | .16 |
| ❑ 24 Pat Verbeek | .25 | .11 |
| ❑ 25 Owen Nolan | .50 | .23 |
| ❑ 26 Ray Bourque | .75 | .35 |
| ❑ 27 Eric Desjardins | .25 | .11 |
| ❑ 28 Patrick Roy | 4.00 | 1.80 |
| ❑ 29 Andy Moog | .25 | .11 |
| ❑ 30 Valeri Kamensky | .35 | .16 |
| ❑ 31 Mark Messier | 1.00 | .45 |
| ❑ 32 Mike Ricci | .25 | .11 |
| ❑ 33 Mario Lemieux | 4.00 | 1.80 |
| ❑ 34 Jaromir Jagr | 3.00 | 1.35 |
| ❑ 35 Pierre Turgeon | .35 | .16 |
| ❑ 36 Kevin Hatcher | .15 | .07 |
| ❑ 37 Paul Coffey | .75 | .35 |
| ❑ 38 Chris Terreri | .25 | .11 |
| ❑ 39 Mike Richter | .75 | .35 |
| ❑ 40 Kevin Todd | .15 | .07 |
| ❑ NNO Norris Checklist | .10 | .05 |
| ❑ NNO Adams Checklist | .10 | .05 |
| ❑ NNO Patrick Trivia | .10 | .05 |
| ❑ NNO Adams Trivia | .10 | .05 |
| ❑ NNO Patrick Checklist | .10 | .05 |
| ❑ NNO Norris Trivia | .10 | .05 |
| ❑ NNO Smythe Checklist | .10 | .05 |
| ❑ NNO Smythe Trivia | .10 | .05 |

## 1983 Hall of Fame Postcards

These postcard-sized (approximately 4" by 6") cards were distributed by complete sub-series.

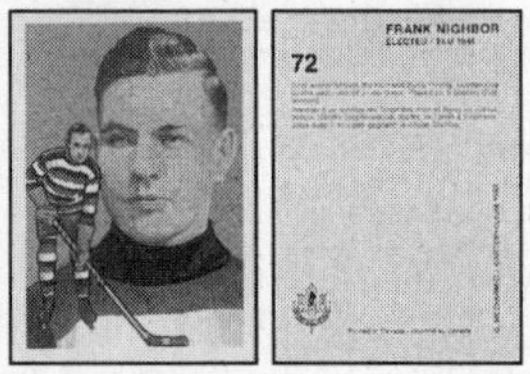

The set is complete at 15 series totalling 240 members of the Hockey Hall of Fame. Cards are listed alphabetically within each sub-series in the checklist below. The cards in this imperial postcard-sized set feature full-color art work by Carlton McDiarmid. The set was produced by the Hockey Hall of Fame, McDiarmid, and Cartophilium. The postcard backs contain the player's name and the year he was elected to the Hockey Hall of Fame. Career milestones or significant accomplishments of the player are listed in both French and English.

| | MINT | NRMT |
|---|---|---|
| COMPLETE SET (240) | 350.00 | 160.00 |
| COMMON CARD | 1.00 | .45 |
| ❑ A1 Sid Abel | 2.00 | .90 |
| ❑ A2 Punch Broadbent | 1.00 | .45 |
| ❑ A3 Clarence Campbell | 1.00 | .45 |
| ❑ A4 Neil Colville | 1.00 | .45 |
| ❑ A5 Charlie Conacher | 3.00 | 1.35 |
| ❑ A6 Mervyn(Red) Dutton | 1.00 | .45 |
| ❑ A7 Foster Hewitt | 3.00 | 1.35 |
| ❑ A8 Fred Hume | 1.00 | .45 |
| ❑ A9 Mickey Ion | 1.00 | .45 |
| ❑ A10 Ernest(Moose) Johnson | 1.00 | .45 |
| ❑ A11 Bill Mosienko | 1.00 | .45 |
| ❑ A12 Maurice Richard | 10.00 | 4.50 |
| ❑ A13 Barney Stanley | 1.00 | .45 |
| ❑ A14 Lord Stanley | 2.00 | .90 |
| ❑ A15 Cyclone Taylor | 2.50 | 1.10 |
| ❑ A16 Tiny Thompson | 3.00 | 1.35 |
| ❑ B1 Dan Bain | 1.00 | .45 |
| ❑ B2 Hobey Baker | 2.00 | .90 |
| ❑ B3 Frank Calder | 1.00 | .45 |
| ❑ B4 Frank Foyston | 1.00 | .45 |
| ❑ B5 James Hendy | 1.00 | .45 |
| ❑ B6 Gordie Howe | 15.00 | 6.75 |
| ❑ B7 Harry Lumley | 3.00 | 1.35 |
| ❑ B8 Reg Noble | 1.00 | .45 |
| ❑ B9 Frank Patrick | 1.00 | .45 |
| ❑ B10 Harvey Pulford | 1.00 | .45 |
| ❑ B11 Ken Reardon | 1.50 | .70 |
| ❑ B12 Bullet Joe Simpson | 1.50 | .70 |
| ❑ B13 Conn Smythe | 2.00 | .90 |
| ❑ B14 Red Storey | 1.00 | .45 |
| ❑ B15 Lloyd Turner | 1.00 | .45 |
| ❑ B16 Georges Vezina | 7.50 | 3.40 |
| ❑ C1 Jean Beliveau | 7.50 | 3.40 |
| ❑ C2 Max Bentley | 1.50 | .70 |
| ❑ C3 King Clancy | 3.00 | 1.35 |
| ❑ C4 Babe Dye | 1.00 | .45 |
| ❑ C5 Ebbie Goodfellow | 1.00 | .45 |
| ❑ C6 Charles Hay | 1.00 | .45 |
| ❑ C7 Percy Lesueur | 1.50 | .70 |
| ❑ C8 Tommy Lockhart | 1.00 | .45 |
| ❑ C9 Jack Marshall | 1.00 | .45 |
| ❑ C10 Lester Patrick | 2.00 | .90 |
| ❑ C11 Bill Quackenbush | 1.50 | .70 |
| ❑ C12 Frank Selke | 1.50 | .70 |
| ❑ C13 Cooper Smeaton | 1.00 | .45 |
| ❑ C14 Hooley Smith | 1.00 | .45 |
| ❑ C15 Capt.J.T.Sutherland | 1.00 | .45 |
| ❑ C16 Fred Whitcroft | 1.00 | .45 |
| ❑ D1 Charles F. Adams | 1.00 | .45 |
| ❑ D2 Russell Bowie | 1.00 | .45 |
| ❑ D3 Frank Frederickson | 1.00 | .45 |
| ❑ D4 Billy Gilmour | 1.00 | .45 |
| ❑ D5 Ching Johnson | 1.50 | .70 |
| ❑ D6 Tom Johnson | 1.50 | .70 |
| ❑ D7 Aurel Joliat | 4.00 | 1.80 |
| ❑ D8 Duke Keats | 1.00 | .45 |
| ❑ D9 Red Kelly | 3.00 | 1.35 |
| ❑ D10 Frank McGee | 1.00 | .45 |
| ❑ D11 James D. Norris | 1.50 | .70 |
| ❑ D12 Philip D. Ross | 1.00 | .45 |
| ❑ D13 Terry Sawchuk | 7.50 | 3.40 |
| ❑ D14 Babe Siebert | 1.50 | .70 |
| ❑ D15 Anatoli V. Tarasov | 1.50 | .70 |
| ❑ D16 Roy Worters | 2.00 | .90 |
| ❑ E1 T. Franklin Ahearn | 1.00 | .45 |
| ❑ E2 Harold E. Ballard | 2.00 | .90 |
| ❑ E3 Billy Burch | 1.00 | .45 |
| ❑ E4 Bill Chadwick | 1.00 | .45 |
| ❑ E5 Sprague Cleghorn | 2.00 | .90 |
| ❑ E6 Rusty Crawford | 1.00 | .45 |
| ❑ E7 Alex Delvecchio | 3.00 | 1.35 |
| ❑ E8 George S. Dudley | 1.00 | .45 |
| ❑ E9 Ted Kennedy | 2.00 | .90 |
| ❑ E10 Newsy Lalonde | 2.50 | 1.10 |
| ❑ E11 Billy McGimsie | 1.00 | .45 |
| ❑ E12 Frank Nighbor | 1.50 | .70 |
| ❑ E13 Bobby Orr | 15.00 | 6.75 |
| ❑ E14 Sen. Donat Raymond | 1.00 | .45 |
| ❑ E15 Art Ross | 2.50 | 1.10 |
| ❑ E16 Jack Walker | 1.00 | .45 |
| ❑ F1 Doug Bentley | 1.50 | .70 |
| ❑ F2 Walter A. Brown | 1.00 | .45 |
| ❑ F3 Dit Clapper | 2.50 | 1.10 |
| ❑ F4 Hap Day | 1.00 | .45 |
| ❑ F5 Frank Dilio | 1.00 | .45 |
| ❑ F6 Bobby Hewitson | 1.00 | .45 |
| ❑ F7 Harry Howell | 1.00 | .45 |

❑ F8 Paul Loicq 1.00 .45
❑ F9 Sylvio Mantha 1.50 .70
❑ F10 Jacques Plante 8.00 3.60
❑ F11 George Richardson 1.00 .45
❑ F12 Nels Stewart 2.00 .90
❑ F13 Hod Stuart 1.00 .45
❑ F14 Harry Trihey 1.00 .45
❑ F15 Marty Walsh 1.00 .45
❑ F16 Arthur M. Wirtz 1.00 .45
❑ G1 Toe Blake 3.00 1.35
❑ G2 Frank Boucher 1.50 .70
❑ G3 Turk Broda 4.00 1.80
❑ G4 Harry Cameron 1.00 .45
❑ G5 Leo Dandurand 1.00 .45
❑ G6 Joe Hall 1.00 .45
❑ G7 George Hay 1.00 .45
❑ G8 William A. Hewitt 1.00 .45
❑ G9 Bouse Hutton 1.00 .45
❑ G10 Dick Irvin 2.00 .90
❑ G11 Henri Richard 3.00 1.35
❑ G12 John Ross Robertson 1.00 .45
❑ G13 Frank D. Smith 1.00 .45
❑ G14 Allan Stanley 1.00 .45
❑ G15 Norm Ullman 1.00 .45
❑ G16 Harry Watson 1.00 .45
❑ H1 Clint Benedict 3.00 1.35
❑ H2 Dickie Boon 1.00 .45
❑ H3 Gordie Drillon 1.50 .70
❑ H4 Bill Gadsby 1.00 .45
❑ H5 Rod Gilbert 1.00 .45
❑ H6 Moose Goheen 1.00 .45
❑ H7 Tommy Gorman 1.00 .45
❑ H8 Glenn Hall 3.00 1.35
❑ H9 Red Horner 1.00 .45
❑ H10 Gen.J.R.Kilpatrick 1.00 .45
❑ H11 Robert Lebel 1.00 .45
❑ H12 Howie Morenz 7.50 3.40
❑ H13 Fred Scanlan 1.00 .45
❑ H14 Tommy Smith 1.00 .45
❑ H15 Fred C. Waghorne 1.00 .45
❑ H16 Cooney Weiland 2.00 .90
❑ I1 Weston Adams 1.00 .45
❑ I2 Sir Montagu Allan 1.00 .45
❑ I3 Frank Brimsek 3.00 1.35
❑ I4 Angus Campbell 1.00 .45
❑ I5 Bill Cook 2.00 .90
❑ I6 Tom Dunderdale 1.00 .45
❑ I7 Emile Francis 1.00 .45
❑ I8 Charlie Gardiner 1.50 .70
❑ I9 Elmer Lach 1.50 .70
❑ I10 Frank Mahovlich 3.00 1.35
❑ I11 Didier Pitre 1.00 .45
❑ I12 Joe Primeau 3.00 1.35
❑ I13 Frank Rankin 1.00 .45
❑ I14 Ernie Russell 1.00 .45
❑ I15 Thayer Tutt 1.00 .45
❑ I16 Harry Westwick 1.00 .45
❑ J1 Jack Adams 1.00 .45
❑ J2 Bunny Ahearne 1.00 .45
❑ J3 J.P. Bickell 1.00 .45
❑ J4 Johnny Bucyk 1.50 .70
❑ J5 Art Coulter 1.00 .45
❑ J6 C.G. Drinkwater 1.00 .45
❑ J7 George Hainsworth 3.00 1.35
❑ J8 Tim Horton 5.00 2.20
❑ J9 Maj. F. McLaughlin 1.00 .45
❑ J10 Dickie Moore 2.00 .90
❑ J11 Pierre Pilote 1.00 .45
❑ J12 Claude C. Robinson 1.00 .45
❑ J13 Sweeney Schriner 1.00 .45
❑ J14 Oliver Seibert 1.00 .45
❑ J15 Alfred Smith 1.00 .45
❑ J16 Phat Wilson 1.50 .70
❑ K1 Yvan Cournoyer 1.50 .70
❑ K2 Scotty Davidson 1.00 .45
❑ K3 Cy Denneny 1.50 .70
❑ K4 Bill Durnan 2.50 1.10
❑ K5 Shorty Green 1.00 .45
❑ K6 Riley Hern 1.00 .45
❑ K7 Bryan Hextall 1.00 .45
❑ K8 Bill Jennings 1.00 .45
❑ K9 Gordon W. Juckes 1.00 .45
❑ K10 Paddy Moran 1.50 .70
❑ K11 James Norris 1.00 .45
❑ K12 Harry Oliver 1.00 .45
❑ K13 Sam Pollock 1.00 .45
❑ K14 Marcel Pronovost 1.00 .45
❑ K15 Jack Ruttan 1.00 .45
❑ K16 Earl Seibert 1.00 .45
❑ L1 Buck Boucher 1.00 .45
❑ L2 George V. Brown 1.00 .45
❑ L3 Arthur F. Farrell 1.00 .45
❑ L4 Herb Gardiner 1.00 .45
❑ L5 Si Griffis 1.00 .45
❑ L6 Hap Holmes 1.00 .45
❑ L7 Harry Hyland 1.00 .45
❑ L8 Tommy Ivan 1.00 .45
❑ L9 Jack Laviolette 1.00 .45
❑ L10 Ted Lindsay 3.00 1.35
❑ L11 Francis Nelson 1.00 .45
❑ L12 William M. Northey 1.00 .45
❑ L13 Babe Pratt 1.00 .45
❑ L14 Chuck Rayner 2.00 .90
❑ L15 Milt Rodden 1.00 .45
❑ L16 Milt Schmidt 2.50 1.10
❑ M1 Butch Bouchard 1.50 .70
❑ M2 Jack Butterfield 1.00 .45
❑ M3 Joseph Cattarinich 1.00 .45
❑ M4 Alex Connell 2.00 .90
❑ M5 Bill Cowley 1.50 .70
❑ M6 Chaucer Elliott 1.00 .45
❑ M7 Jimmy Gardner 1.00 .45
❑ M8 Boom Boom Geoffrion 4.00 1.80
❑ M9 Tom Hooper 1.00 .45
❑ M10 Syd Howe 1.00 .45
❑ M11 Harvey(Busher)Jackson 1.50 .70
❑ M12 Al Leader 1.00 .45
❑ M13 Steamer Maxwell 1.00 .45
❑ M14 Blair Russell 1.00 .45
❑ M15 William W. Wirtz 1.00 .45
❑ M16 Gump Worsley 3.00 1.35
❑ N1 George Armstrong 2.00 .90
❑ N2 Ace Bailey 3.00 1.35
❑ N3 Jack Darragh 1.00 .45
❑ N4 Ken Dryden 8.00 3.60
❑ N5 Eddie Gerard 1.00 .45
❑ N6 Jack Gibson 1.00 .45
❑ N7 Hugh Lehman 1.00 .45
❑ N8 Mickey MacKay 1.00 .45
❑ N9 Joe Malone 3.00 1.35
❑ N10 Bruce A. Norris 1.00 .45
❑ N11 J. Ambrose O'Brien 1.00 .45
❑ N12 Lynn Patrick 1.50 .70
❑ N13 Tommy Phillips 1.00 .45
❑ N14 Allan W. Pickard 1.00 .45
❑ N15 Jack Stewart 1.00 .45
❑ N16 Frank Udvari 1.00 .45
❑ O1 Syl Apps 2.00 .90
❑ O2 John G. Ashley 1.00 .45
❑ O3 Marty Barry 1.00 .45
❑ O4 Andy Bathgate 1.50 .70
❑ O5 Johnny Bower 3.00 1.35
❑ O6 Frank Buckland 1.00 .45
❑ O7 Jimmy Dunn 1.00 .45
❑ O8 Michael Grant 1.00 .45
❑ O9 Doug Harvey 3.00 1.35
❑ O10 George McNamara 1.00 .45
❑ O11 Stan Mikita 3.00 1.35
❑ O12 Sen.H.de M. Molson 1.00 .45
❑ O13 Gordon Roberts 1.00 .45
❑ O14 Eddie Shore 7.50 3.40
❑ O15 Bruce Stuart 1.00 .45
❑ O16 Carl P. Voss 1.00 .45
❑ NNO Binder 20.00 9.00

## 1985-87 Hall of Fame Cards

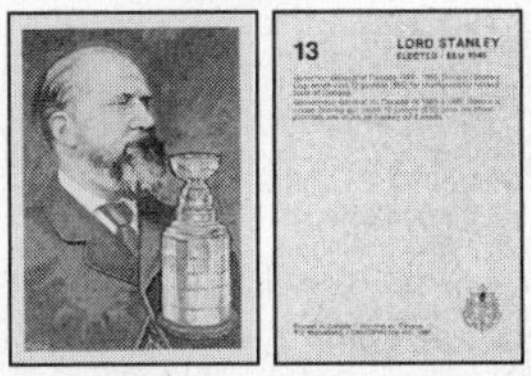

This 261-card standard-size set is basically two different sets but the second set is merely a reissue of the first Hall of Fame set done two years before, adding the new inductees since that time. The only difference in the first 240 cards in this later 1987 set and the prior set is the different copyright year at the bottom of each reverse in this set. Note however that the copyright line for the 1985 set confusingly shows a 1983 copyright date (apparently referring back to the post card set) vertically printed on the card back. One exception is Gordie Howe; his career was so long that his season-by-season statistics fill up the entire card back leaving no room for a copyright line. The set features members of the Hockey Hall of Fame portrayed by the artwork of Carlton McDiarmid. Backs are written in both French and English. The set was originally sold in the Canadian Sears 1985 Christmas Catalog.

| | MINT | NRMT |
|---|---|---|
| COMPLETE SET (261) | 100.00 | 45.00 |
| COMMON CARD (1-240) | .35 | .16 |
| COMMON CARD (241-261) | .60 | .25 |

❑ 1 Maurice Richard 5.00 2.20
❑ 2 Sid Abel .75 .35
❑ 3 Punch Broadbent .35 .16
❑ 4 Clarence S. Campbell .35 .16
❑ 5 Neil Colville .35 .16
❑ 6 Charlie Conacher 1.00 .45
❑ 7 Mervyn(Red) Dutton .35 .16
❑ 8 Foster W. Hewitt 1.00 .45
❑ 9 Mickey Ion .35 .16
❑ 10 Ernest(Moose) Johnson .35 .16
❑ 11 Bill Mosienko .35 .16
❑ 12 Russell Stanley .35 .16
❑ 13 Lord Stanley .75 .35
❑ 14 Cyclone Taylor .75 .35
❑ 15 Tiny Thompson .75 .35
❑ 16 Gordie Howe 7.50 3.40
❑ 17 Hobey Baker .75 .35
❑ 18 Frank Calder .35 .16
❑ 19 Jim Hendy .35 .16
❑ 20 Frank Foyston .35 .16
❑ 21 Harry Lumley 1.00 .45
❑ 22 Reg Noble .35 .16
❑ 23 Frank A. Patrick .35 .16
❑ 24 Harvey Pulford .35 .16
❑ 25 Ken Reardon .50 .23
❑ 26 Bullet Joe Simpson .50 .23
❑ 27 Conn Smythe .75 .35
❑ 28 Red Storey .35 .16
❑ 29 Lloyd Turner .35 .16
❑ 30 Georges Vezina 2.50 1.10
❑ 31 Jean Beliveau 2.50 1.10
❑ 32 Max Bentley .50 .23
❑ 33 King Clancy 1.00 .45
❑ 34 Babe Dye .35 .16
❑ 35 Ebbie Goodfellow .35 .16
❑ 36 Charles Hay .35 .16
❑ 37 Percy Lesueur .50 .23
❑ 38 Tommy Lockhart .35 .16
❑ 39 Jack Marshall .35 .16
❑ 40 Lester Patrick .75 .35
❑ 41 Frank Selke .50 .23
❑ 42 J. Cooper Smeaton .35 .16
❑ 43 Hooley Smith .35 .16
❑ 44 Capt.J.T. Sutherland .35 .16
❑ 45 Fred Whitcroft .35 .16
❑ 46 Terry Sawchuk 4.00 1.80
❑ 47 Charles F. Adams .35 .16
❑ 48 Russell Bowie .35 .16
❑ 49 Frank Frederickson .35 .16
❑ 50 Billy Gilmour .35 .16
❑ 51 Ching Johnson .50 .23
❑ 52 Tom Johnson .75 .35
❑ 53 Aurel Joliat 1.50 .70
❑ 54 Duke Keats .35 .16
❑ 55 Red Kelly 1.00 .45
❑ 56 Frank McGee .35 .16
❑ 57 James D. Norris .35 .16
❑ 58 Philip D. Ross .35 .16
❑ 59 Babe Siebert .50 .23
❑ 60 Roy Worters .75 .35
❑ 61 Bobby Orr 7.50 3.40
❑ 62 T. Franklin Ahearn .35 .16
❑ 63 Harold E. Ballard .75 .35
❑ 64 Billy Burch .35 .16
❑ 65 Bill Chadwick .35 .16
❑ 66 Sprague Cleghorn .75 .35
❑ 67 Rusty Crawford .35 .16
❑ 68 George S. Dudley .35 .16
❑ 69 Teeder Kennedy .75 .35
❑ 70 Newsy Lalonde 1.00 .45
❑ 71 Billy McGimsie .35 .16
❑ 72 Frank Nighbor .50 .23
❑ 73 Sen. Donat Raymond .35 .16
❑ 74 Art Ross 1.00 .45
❑ 75 Jack Walker .35 .16
❑ 76 Jacques Plante 4.00 1.80
❑ 77 Doug Bentley .50 .23
❑ 78 Walter A. Brown .35 .16
❑ 79 Dit Clapper 1.00 .45
❑ 80 Hap Day .35 .16
❑ 81 Frank Dilio .35 .16
❑ 82 Bobby Hewitson .35 .16
❑ 83 Harry Howell .35 .16
❑ 84 Sylvio Mantha .50 .23
❑ 85 George Richardson .35 .16
❑ 86 Nels Stewart .75 .35
❑ 87 Hod Stuart .35 .16
❑ 88 Harry Trihey .35 .16
❑ 89 Marty Walsh .35 .16
❑ 90 Arthur M. Wirtz .35 .16
❑ 91 Henri Richard 1.50 .70
❑ 92 Toe Blake 1.00 .45
❑ 93 Frank Boucher .50 .23
❑ 94 Turk Broda 1.50 .70
❑ 95 Harry Cameron .35 .16
❑ 96 Leo J.V. Dandurand .35 .16
❑ 97 Joe Hall .35 .16
❑ 98 George W. Hay .35 .16
❑ 99 William A. Hewitt .35 .16
❑ 100 Bouse Hutton .35 .16
❑ 101 Dick Irvin .50 .23
❑ 102 John Ross Robertson .35 .16
❑ 103 Frank D. Smith .35 .16
❑ 104 Norm Ullman .35 .16
❑ 105 Moose Watson .35 .16
❑ 106 Howie Morenz 2.50 1.10
❑ 107 Clint Benedict 1.00 .45
❑ 108 Dickie Boon .35 .16
❑ 109 Gordon Drillon .50 .23
❑ 110 Bill Gadsby .35 .16
❑ 111 Rod Gilbert .35 .16
❑ 112 Moose Goheen .35 .16
❑ 113 Tommy Gorman .35 .16
❑ 114 Glenn Hall 1.00 .45
❑ 115 Red Horner .35 .16
❑ 116 Gen.J.R. Kilpatrick .35 .16
❑ 117 Robert Lebel .35 .16
❑ 118 Fred Scanlan .35 .16
❑ 119 Fred C. Waghorne .35 .16
❑ 120 Cooney Weiland .75 .35
❑ 121 Frank Mahovlich 1.00 .45
❑ 122 Weston Adams Sr. .35 .16
❑ 123 Sir Montagu Allan .35 .16
❑ 124 Frank Brimsek 1.00 .45
❑ 125 Angus D. Campbell .35 .16
❑ 126 Bill Cook .75 .35
❑ 127 Tom Dunderdale .35 .16
❑ 128 Chuck Gardiner .35 .16
❑ 129 Elmer Lach .50 .23
❑ 130 Didier Pitre .35 .16
❑ 131 Joe Primeau 1.00 .45
❑ 132 Frank Rankin .35 .16
❑ 133 Ernie Russell .35 .16
❑ 134 W. Thayer Tutt .35 .16
❑ 135 Harry Westwick .35 .16
❑ 136 Yvan Cournoyer .50 .23
❑ 137 Scotty Davidson .35 .16
❑ 138 Cy Denneny .50 .23
❑ 139 Bill Durnan 1.00 .45
❑ 140 Shorty Green .35 .16
❑ 141 Bryan Hextall .35 .16
❑ 142 Bill Jennings .35 .16
❑ 143 Gordon W. Juckes .35 .16
❑ 144 Paddy Moran .50 .23
❑ 145 James Norris .35 .16
❑ 146 Harold Oliver .35 .16
❑ 147 Sam Pollock .35 .16
❑ 148 Marcel Pronovost .35 .16
❑ 149 Jack Ruttan .35 .16
❑ 150 Earl W. Seibert .35 .16
❑ 151 Ted Lindsay 1.00 .45
❑ 152 George V. Brown .35 .16
❑ 153 Arthur F. Farrell .35 .16
❑ 154 Herb Gardiner .35 .16
❑ 155 Si Griffis .35 .16
❑ 156 Hap Holmes .35 .16
❑ 157 Harry Hyland .35 .16
❑ 158 Tommy Ivan .35 .16
❑ 159 Jack Laviolette .35 .16
❑ 160 Francis Nelson .35 .16
❑ 161 William M. Northey .35 .16
❑ 162 Babe Pratt .35 .16
❑ 163 Chuck Rayner .75 .35
❑ 164 Mike Rodden .35 .16
❑ 165 Milt Schmidt 1.00 .45
❑ 166 Boom Boom Geoffrion 1.50 .70
❑ 167 Jack Butterfield .35 .16
❑ 168 Joseph Cattarinich .35 .16
❑ 169 Alex Connell .75 .35
❑ 170 Bill Cowley .50 .23
❑ 171 Chaucer Eliott .35 .16
❑ 172 Jimmy Gardner .35 .16
❑ 173 Tom Hooper .35 .16
❑ 174 Syd Howe .35 .16
❑ 175 Harvey(Busher) Jackson .50 .23
❑ 176 Al Leader .35 .16
❑ 177 Steamer Maxwell .35 .16
❑ 178 Blair Russell .35 .16
❑ 179 William W. Wirtz .35 .16
❑ 180 Gump Worsley 1.00 .45
❑ 181 Johnny Bucyk .50 .23
❑ 182 Jack Adams .35 .16
❑ 183 Bunny Ahearne .35 .16
❑ 184 J.P. Bickell .35 .16
❑ 185 Art Coulter .35 .16
❑ 186 C.G. Drinkwater .35 .16
❑ 187 George Hainsworth 1.00 .45
❑ 188 Tim Horton 2.50 1.10
❑ 189 Maj.F. McLaughlin .35 .16
❑ 190 Dickie Moore .75 .35
❑ 191 Pierre Pilote .35 .16
❑ 192 Claude C. Robinson .35 .16
❑ 193 Oliver L. Seibert .35 .16
❑ 194 Alfred E. Smith .35 .16
❑ 195 Phat Wilson .35 .16
❑ 196 Ken Dryden 4.00 1.80
❑ 197 George Armstrong .75 .35
❑ 198 Ace Bailey 1.00 .45
❑ 199 Jack Darragh .35 .16
❑ 200 Eddie Gerard .35 .16
❑ 201 Jack Gibson .35 .16
❑ 202 Hugh Lehman .35 .16
❑ 203 Mickey MacKay .35 .16
❑ 204 Joe Malone .75 .35
❑ 205 Bruce A. Norris .35 .16
❑ 206 J.Ambrose O'Brien .35 .16
❑ 207 Lynn Patrick .50 .23
❑ 208 Tommy Phillips .35 .16
❑ 209 Allan W. Pickard .35 .16
❑ 210 Jack Stewart .35 .16
❑ 211 Johnny Bower 1.00 .45
❑ 212 Syl Apps .75 .35
❑ 213 John G. Ashley .35 .16
❑ 214 Marty Barry .35 .16
❑ 215 Andy Bathgate .50 .23
❑ 216 Frank Buckland .35 .16
❑ 217 Jimmy Dunn .35 .16
❑ 218 Michael Grant .35 .16
❑ 219 Doug Harvey 1.00 .45
❑ 220 George McNamara .35 .16
❑ 221 Sen.H.deM. Molson .35 .16
❑ 222 Gordon Roberts .35 .16
❑ 223 Eddie Shore 2.50 1.10
❑ 224 Bruce Stuart .35 .16
❑ 225 Carl P. Voss .35 .16
❑ 226 Stan Mikita 1.00 .45
❑ 227 Dan Bain .35 .16
❑ 228 Butch Bouchard .50 .23
❑ 229 Buck Boucher .35 .16
❑ 230 Alex Delvecchio 1.00 .45
❑ 231 Emile P. Francis .35 .16
❑ 232 Riley Hern .35 .16
❑ 233 Fred J. Hume .35 .16
❑ 234 Paul Loicq .35 .16
❑ 235 Bill Quackenbush .50 .23
❑ 236 Sweeney Schriner .35 .16
❑ 237 Tommy Smith .35 .16
❑ 238 Allan Stanley .35 .16
❑ 239 Anatoli V. Tarasov .50 .23
❑ 240 Frank Udvari .35 .16
❑ 241 Harry Sinden .75 .35
❑ 242 Bobby Hull 4.00 1.80
❑ 243 Punch Imlach .60 .25
❑ 244 Phil Esposito 2.00 .90
❑ 245 Jacques Lemaire .75 .35
❑ 246 Bernie Parent 1.00 .45
❑ 247 Rudy Pilous .60 .25
❑ 248 Bert Olmstead .60 .25
❑ 249 Jean Ratelle 1.00 .45
❑ 250 Gerry Cheevers 1.00 .45
❑ 251 William Hanley .60 .25
❑ 252 Leo Boivin .60 .25
❑ 253 Jake Milford .60 .25
❑ 254 John Mariucci .60 .25
❑ 255 Dave Keon 1.00 .45
❑ 256 Serge Savard .60 .25
❑ 257 John A. Ziegler Jr. .60 .25
❑ 258 Bobby Clarke 1.50 .70
❑ 259 Ed Giacomin 1.00 .45
❑ 260 Jacques Laperriere .60 .25
❑ 261 Matt Pavelich .60 .25

## 1992-93 Hall of Fame Legends

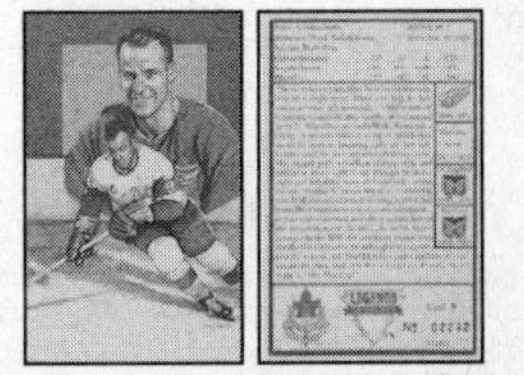

The Hockey Hall of Fame in association with the Diamond Connection and the Sports Gallery of Art produced this 18-card set as the first of three series to be released each year. Over a four year period, all members and builders of Hockey's Hall of Fame will be featured. Production was limited to 10,000 numbered sets, and buyers retained exclusive rights to their assigned number throughout the duration of the project. Issued in a cardboard box, the cards measure approximately 3 1/2" by 5 1/2" and feature the work of noted sports artist Doug West. The front displays a color reproduction of the artist's original painting. The back has a parchment background with navy blue borders and includes biographical information, a player profile, career statistics, each team played for, and the years played. A registration form and an ownership transfer form were included with each set. The card number and set serial number are in the lower right corner.

| | MINT | NRMT |
|---|---|---|
| COMPLETE SET (36) | 150.00 | 70.00 |
| COMMON CARD (1-18) | 4.00 | 1.80 |
| COMMON CARD (19-36) | 4.00 | 1.80 |

❑ 1 Harry Lumley 5.00 2.20
❑ 2 Conn Smythe CO 4.00 1.80
❑ 3 Maurice Richard 10.00 4.50
❑ 4 Bobby Orr 20.00 9.00
❑ 5 Bernie Geoffrion 6.00 2.70
❑ 6 Hobey Baker 5.00 2.20
❑ 7 Phil Esposito 6.00 2.70
❑ 8 King Clancy 6.00 2.70
❑ 9 Gordie Howe 15.00 6.75
❑ 10 Emile Francis 4.00 1.80
❑ 11 Jacques Plante 8.00 3.60
❑ 12 Sid Abel 4.00 1.80
❑ 13 Foster Hewitt 5.00 2.20
❑ 14 Charlie Conacher 5.00 2.20
❑ 15 Stan Mikita 6.00 2.70
❑ 16 Bobby Clarke 5.00 2.20
❑ 17 Norm Ullman 4.00 1.80
❑ 18 Lord Stanley of Preston 5.00 2.20
❑ 19 Ted Lindsay 5.00 2.20
❑ 20 Duke Keats 4.00 1.80
❑ 21 Jack Adams 4.00 1.80
❑ 22 Bill Mosienko 4.00 1.80
❑ 23 Johnny Bower 5.00 2.20
❑ 24 Tim Horton 8.00 3.60
❑ 25 Punch Imlach 4.00 1.80
❑ 26 Georges Vezina 10.00 4.50
❑ 27 Earl Seibert 4.00 1.80
❑ 28 Bryan Hextall Sr. 4.00 1.80
❑ 29 Babe Pratt 4.00 1.80
❑ 30 Gump Worsley 5.00 2.20
❑ 31 Ed Giacomin 5.00 2.20
❑ 32 Ace Bailey 5.00 2.20
❑ 33 Harry Sinden 4.00 1.80
❑ 34 Lanny McDonald 5.00 2.20
❑ 35 Tommy Ivan 4.00 1.80
❑ 36 Frank Calder 4.00 1.80

## 1994 Hall of Fame Tickets

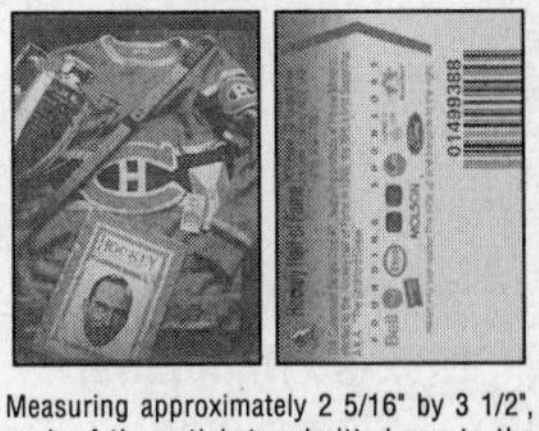

Measuring approximately 2 5/16" by 3 1/2", each of these tickets admitted one to the Hockey Hall of Fame in Toronto. Each ticket is printed on thin cardboard stock and features a full-bleed photo on its front. On a background that shades from blue to white, the horizontal backs carry the Hall of Fame's street address, a description of the front picture, founding sponsors' logos, and a barcode. The tickets are numbered on the back.

| | MINT | NRMT |
|---|---|---|
| COMPLETE SET (12) | 45.00 | 20.00 |
| COMMON CARD (1-12) | 3.00 | 1.35 |

❑ 1 Stanley Cup 4.00 1.80
❑ 2 O'Brien Trophy 3.00 1.35
❑ 3 Dan Bain Artifacts 3.00 1.35
❑ 4 Art Ross Artifacts 4.00 1.80
❑ 5 Ace Bailey Artifacts 4.00 1.80
❑ 6 Clint Benedict Artifacts 5.00 2.20
❑ 7 Howie Morenz Artifacts 7.00 3.10
❑ 8 Roy Worters Artifacts 4.00 1.80
❑ 9 Andy Bathgate Artifacts 3.00 1.35

| | | |
|---|---|---|
| ❑ 10 Jacques Plante Artifacts | 7.00 | 3.10 |
| ❑ 11 Terry Sawchuk Artifacts | 7.00 | 3.10 |
| ❑ 12 Milt Schmidt Artifacts | 4.00 | 1.80 |

## 1998 Hall of Fame Medallions

Issued only in Canada, these medallions were mounted on a a clear plastic holder and featured statistical and biographical information on the back.

| | MINT | NRMT |
|---|---|---|
| COMPLETE SET (2) | 15.00 | 6.75 |
| COMMON CARD (1-2) | 8.00 | 3.60 |
| ❑ 1 Michel Goulet | 8.00 | 3.60 |
| ❑ 2 Peter Stastny | 8.00 | 3.60 |

## 1975-76 Heroes Stand-Ups

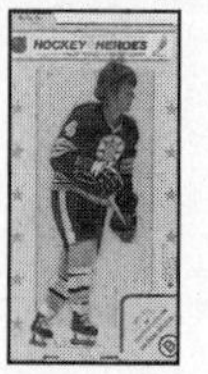

These 31 "Hockey Heroes Autographed Pin-up/Stand-Up Sportrophies" feature NHL players from five different teams. The stand-ups come in two different sizes. The Bruins and Flyers stand-ups are approximately 15 1/2" by 8/3/4", while the Islanders stand-ups are approximately 13 1/2" by 7 1/2" and were issued three to a strip. The stand-ups are made of laminated cardboard, and the yellow frame is decorated with red stars. Each stand-up features a color action shot of the player. A facsimile autograph is inscribed across the bottom of the stand-up. The stand-ups are unnumbered and checklisted below alphabetically according to and within teams as follows: Boston Bruins (1-7), Montreal Canadiens (8-13), New York Islanders (14-19), Philadelphia Flyers (20-25), and Toronto Maple Leafs (26-31).

| | NRMT-MT | EXC |
|---|---|---|
| COMPLETE SET (31) | 200.00 | 90.00 |
| COMMON CARD (1-31) | 5.00 | 2.20 |
| ❑ 1 Gerry Cheevers | 10.00 | 4.50 |
| ❑ 2 Terry O'Reilly | 6.00 | 2.70 |
| ❑ 3 Bobby Orr | 40.00 | 18.00 |
| ❑ 4 Brad Park | 8.00 | 3.60 |
| ❑ 5 Jean Ratelle | 8.00 | 3.60 |
| ❑ 6 Andre Savard | 5.00 | 2.20 |
| ❑ 7 Gregg Sheppard | 5.00 | 2.20 |
| ❑ 8 Yvan Cournoyer | 8.00 | 3.60 |
| ❑ 9 Guy Lafleur | 15.00 | 6.75 |
| ❑ 10 Jacques Lemaire | 8.00 | 3.60 |
| ❑ 11 Peter Mahovlich | 5.00 | 2.20 |
| ❑ 12 Doug Risebrough | 5.00 | 2.20 |
| ❑ 13 Larry Robinson | 10.00 | 4.50 |
| ❑ 14 Billy Harris | 5.00 | 2.20 |
| ❑ 15 Gerry Hart | 5.00 | 2.20 |
| ❑ 16 Denis Potvin | 10.00 | 4.50 |
| ❑ 17 Glenn Resch | 8.00 | 3.60 |
| ❑ 18 Bryan Trottier | 10.00 | 4.50 |
| ❑ 19 Ed Westfall | 5.00 | 2.20 |
| ❑ 20 Bill Barber | 8.00 | 3.60 |
| ❑ 21 Bobby Clarke | 10.00 | 4.50 |
| ❑ 22 Reggie Leach | 5.00 | 2.20 |
| ❑ 23 Rick MacLeish | 5.00 | 2.20 |
| ❑ 24 Bernie Parent | 10.00 | 4.50 |
| ❑ 25 Dave Schultz | 8.00 | 3.60 |
| ❑ 26 Lanny McDonald | 8.00 | 3.60 |
| ❑ 27 Borje Salming | 6.00 | 2.70 |
| ❑ 28 Darryl Sittler | 8.00 | 3.60 |
| ❑ 29 Wayne Thomas | 6.00 | 2.70 |
| ❑ 30 Errol Thompson | 5.00 | 2.20 |
| ❑ 31 Dave(Tiger) Williams | 6.00 | 2.70 |

## 1992-93 High Liner Stanley Cup

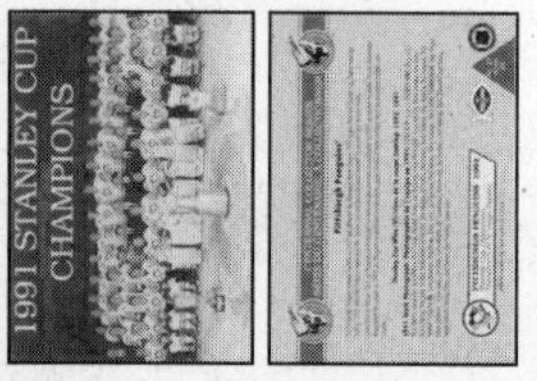


National Sea Products Ltd., producer and manufacturer of High Liner brand fish products, produced a 28-card, standard-size set to celebrate the Centennial of the Stanley Cup (1893-1993). Specially marked packages of High Liner frozen fish products contained two cards. Collectors could also order additional cards by clipping the order form from the box, checking the cards desired, and sending it in with six UPC symbols from any High Liner brand product plus 3.99. The form limited requests to one card request per card number. The fronts feature full-bleed black-and-white and color team pictures of Stanley Cup champions. The pale blue, horizontal backs present a French and English summary of the championship season and a list of the players pictured. A darker blue stripe across the top displays the Stanley Cup logo and the set name in French and English. The team name and the year they won the Stanley Cup appear in the lower left corner.

| | MINT | NRMT |
|---|---|---|
| COMPLETE SET (28) | 40.00 | 18.00 |
| COMMON TEAM (1-28) | 1.50 | .70 |
| ❑ 1 Montreal AAA | 2.50 | 1.10 |
| ❑ 2 Winnipeg Victorias | 1.50 | .70 |
| ❑ 3 Montreal Victorias | 2.50 | 1.10 |
| ❑ 4 Montreal Shamrocks | 2.50 | 1.10 |
| ❑ 5 Ottawa Silver Seven | 1.50 | .70 |
| ❑ 6 Kenora Thistles | 1.50 | .70 |
| ❑ 7 Montreal Wanderers | 2.50 | 1.10 |
| ❑ 8 Quebec Bulldogs | 1.50 | .70 |
| ❑ 9 Toronto Blueshirts | 2.50 | 1.10 |
| ❑ 10 Vancouver Millionaires | 2.50 | 1.10 |
| ❑ 11 Seattle Metropolitans | 2.50 | 1.10 |
| ❑ 12 Toronto Arenas | 2.50 | 1.10 |
| ❑ 13 Toronto St. Patricks | 2.50 | 1.10 |
| ❑ 14 Victoria Cougars | 1.50 | .70 |
| ❑ 15 Ottawa Senators | 1.50 | .70 |
| ❑ 16 Montreal Maroons | 2.50 | 1.10 |
| ❑ 17 New York Rangers | 1.50 | .70 |
| ❑ 18 Detroit Red Wings | 3.00 | 1.35 |
| ❑ 19 Montreal Canadiens | 4.00 | 1.80 |
| ❑ 20 Chicago Blackhawks | 1.50 | .70 |
| ❑ 21 Toronto Maple Leafs | 3.00 | 1.35 |
| ❑ 22 Boston Bruins | 3.00 | 1.35 |
| ❑ 23 Philadelphia Flyers | 1.50 | .70 |
| ❑ 24 New York Islanders | 1.50 | .70 |
| ❑ 25 Edmonton Oilers | 5.00 | 2.20 |
| ❑ 26 Calgary Flames | 1.50 | .70 |
| ❑ 27 Pittsburgh Penguins | 2.50 | 1.10 |
| ❑ 28 Checklist Card | 2.50 | 1.10 |

## 1993-94 High Liner Greatest Goalies

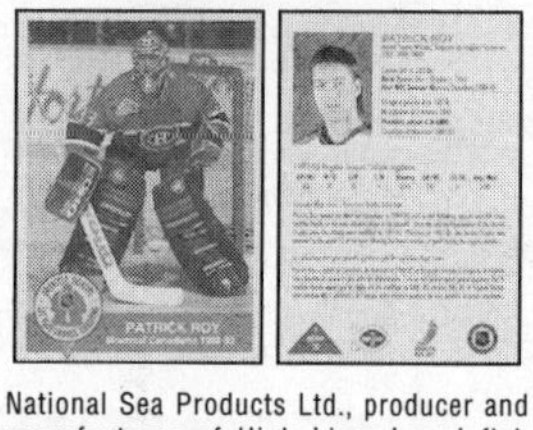

National Sea Products Ltd., producer and manufacturer of High Liner brand fish products, produced a 15-card, standard-size set of the Greatest Goalies of the NHL, a follow-up to High Liner's 28-card 1992-93 Stanley Cup Centennial set. Specially marked packages of High Liner frozen fish products contained one card. Collectors could also order the complete set through a mail-in offer as outlined on the inside of the specially marked High Liner packages. The set is made from white card stock and is primarily devoted to goalies that have won the Vezina Trophy, the NHL's top annual award for goaltenders. The fronts feature white-bordered color player action shots, with the player's name, team and, season printed in white within a blue band at the bottom. The logo, with Greatest Goalies printed in French and English, appears in the lower left. The white back has a color posed player head shot in the upper left, with the player's name in orange lettering alongside to the right. A biography, stat table, and career highlights are printed in English and French. The High Liner, NHLPA, and NHL logos on the bottom round out the card.

| | MINT | NRMT |
|---|---|---|
| COMPLETE SET (15) | 20.00 | 9.00 |
| COMMON CARD (1-15) | 1.00 | .45 |
| ❑ 1 Patrick Roy | 7.00 | 3.10 |
| ❑ 2 Ed Belfour | 3.00 | 1.35 |
| ❑ 3 Grant Fuhr | 1.50 | .70 |
| ❑ 4 Ron Hextall | 1.50 | .70 |
| ❑ 5 John Vanbiesbrouck | 4.00 | 1.80 |
| ❑ 6 Tom Barrasso | 1.00 | .45 |
| ❑ 7 Bernie Parent | 1.25 | .55 |
| ❑ 8 Tony Esposito | 1.50 | .70 |
| ❑ 9 Johnny Bower | 1.50 | .70 |
| ❑ 10 Jacques Plante | 2.50 | 1.10 |
| ❑ 11 Terry Sawchuk | 2.50 | 1.10 |
| ❑ 12 Bill Durnan | 1.25 | .55 |
| ❑ 13 Felix Potvin | 1.50 | .70 |
| ❑ 14 The Evolution of the Goalie Mask | 2.50 | 1.10 |
| ❑ 15 Vezina Trophy Checklist | 1.00 | .45 |

## 1992 High-5 Previews

These six cards feature color action player

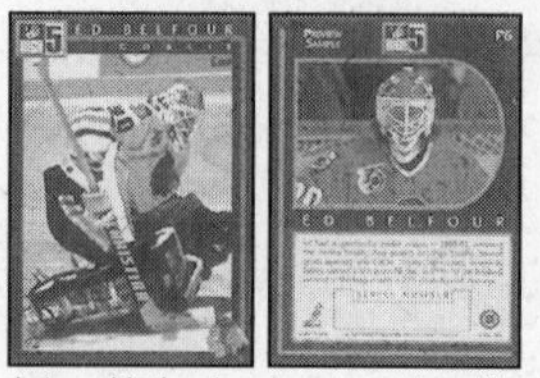

photos with the player's name and position printed above the photo. The backs carry another color player photo, with the player's name and career highlights on a white panel. The words "Preview Sample" appear in the top left corner. The cards are numbered on the back with a "P" prefix. Bourque and Belfour were produced in larger quantities. The cards were originally distributed as promo items at the 1992 National which led to extremely high values. In 1996, an additional supply of these cards was inserted into boxes of Collector's Edge Future Legends product in three-card sleeves. The additional quantities severely dampened demand. A signed version of the Belfour card also was included as a random insert in these packs, and as a promotional giveaway direct from Collector's Edge. This card was serially numbered out of 1500.

| | MINT | NRMT |
|---|---|---|
| COMPLETE SET (6) | 100.00 | 45.00 |
| COMMON CARD (P1-P6) | 4.00 | 1.80 |
| ❑ P1 Ray Bourque DP | 5.00 | 2.20 |
| ❑ P2 Brett Hull | 10.00 | 4.50 |
| ❑ P3 Wayne Gretzky | 40.00 | 18.00 |
| ❑ P4 Mark Messier | 10.00 | 4.50 |
| ❑ P5 Mario Lemieux | 30.00 | 13.50 |
| ❑ P6 Ed Belfour DP | 4.00 | 1.80 |
| ❑ *P6 Ed Belfour AU/1500 | 40.00 | 18.00 |

## 1994 Hockey Wit

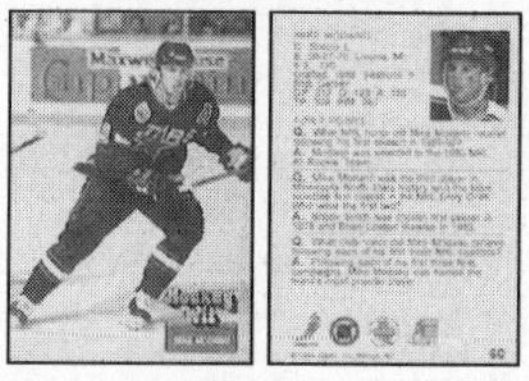

Seventh in a series of "WIT" trivia games, this Hockey Wit card set features 108 standard-size cards and includes hockey players of the past and present. The fronts feature full-bleed color action player photos, with the player's name inside a blue box with a gold-foil border and the words "Hockey Wit". On a white background, the backs carry a small color headshot, player biography and trivia questions and answers. Inserted in each mastercase of 72 games was a bonus card which collectors could redeem for one of 500 limited edition sets of uncut flat sheets. The production run was reportedly limited to 30,000 sets, and a portion of the proceeds from the sale benefited amateur hockey in Canada and the United States. The set includes 21 Hall of Famers. The collector who answers all the questions on the backs achieved a perfect score of 801, the total number of goals scored in the NHL by Gordie Howe. The cards are numbered on the back at the lower right corner.

| | MINT | NRMT |
|---|---|---|
| COMPLETE SET (108) | 20.00 | 9.00 |
| COMMON CARD (1-108) | .10 | .05 |
| ❑ 1 Mike Richter | .50 | .23 |
| ❑ 2 Tony Amonte | .25 | .11 |
| ❑ 3 Patrick Roy | 3.00 | 1.35 |
| ❑ 4 Craig Janney | .10 | .05 |
| ❑ 5 Adam Oates | .25 | .11 |
| ❑ 6 Geoff Sanderson | .20 | .09 |
| ❑ 7 Pavel Bure | 1.00 | .45 |
| ❑ 8 Steve Duchesne | .10 | .05 |
| ❑ 9 Gordie Howe | 1.00 | .45 |
| ❑ 10 Brad Park | .20 | .09 |
| ❑ 11 Brian Bellows | .10 | .05 |
| ❑ 12 Chris Chelios | .50 | .23 |
| ❑ 13 Bill Barber | .15 | .07 |
| ❑ 14 Gump Worsley | .20 | .09 |
| ❑ 15 The Stanley Cup | .20 | .09 |
| ❑ 16 Maurice Richard | .50 | .23 |
| ❑ 17 Kevin Hatcher | .10 | .05 |
| ❑ 18 Ed Belfour | .50 | .23 |
| ❑ 19 Kirk Muller | .15 | .07 |
| ❑ 20 Kevin Stevens | .15 | .07 |
| ❑ 21 Dave Taylor | .10 | .05 |
| ❑ 22 Dale Hawerchuk | .25 | .11 |
| ❑ 23 Jean Beliveau | .35 | .16 |
| ❑ 24 Rogatien Vachon | .20 | .09 |
| ❑ 25 Tom Barrasso | .15 | .07 |
| ❑ 26 Rod Langway | .10 | .05 |
| ❑ 27 Pierre Turgeon | .25 | .11 |
| ❑ 28 Derek King | .10 | .05 |
| ❑ 29 Brendan Shanahan | 1.00 | .45 |
| ❑ 30 Darren Turcotte | .10 | .05 |
| ❑ 31 Chris Terreri | .15 | .07 |
| ❑ 32 Tony Granato | .10 | .05 |
| ❑ 33 Michel Goulet | .15 | .07 |
| ❑ 34 Felix Potvin | .35 | .16 |
| ❑ 35 Curtis Joseph | .50 | .23 |
| ❑ 36 Cam Neely | .35 | .16 |
| ❑ 37 Borje Salming | .20 | .09 |
| ❑ 38 Denis Savard | .20 | .09 |
| ❑ 39 Stan Mikita | .35 | .16 |
| ❑ 40 Grant Fuhr | .20 | .09 |
| ❑ 41 Gary Suter | .10 | .05 |
| ❑ 42 Serge Savard | .10 | .05 |
| ❑ 43 Steve Larmer | .15 | .07 |
| ❑ 44 Bryan Trottier | .20 | .09 |
| ❑ 45 Mike Vernon | .25 | .11 |
| ❑ 46 Paul Coffey | .35 | .16 |
| ❑ 47 Bernie Federko | .10 | .05 |
| ❑ 48 Larry Murphy | .15 | .07 |
| ❑ 49 Scotty Bowman CO | .15 | .07 |
| ❑ 50 Glenn Anderson | .15 | .07 |
| ❑ 51 Mats Sundin | .50 | .23 |
| ❑ 52 Henri Richard | .25 | .11 |
| ❑ 53 Ron Francis | .25 | .11 |
| ❑ 54 Scott Niedermayer | .15 | .07 |
| ❑ 55 Teemu Selanne | 1.00 | .45 |
| ❑ 56 Frank Mahovlich | .25 | .11 |
| ❑ 57 Owen Nolan | .20 | .09 |
| ❑ 58 Rick Tocchet | .20 | .09 |
| ❑ 59 Rod Brind'Amour | .20 | .09 |
| ❑ 60 Mike Modano | .75 | .35 |
| ❑ 61 Doug Gilmour | .35 | .16 |
| ❑ 62 Jimmy Carson | .10 | .05 |
| ❑ 63 Mike Keane | .10 | .05 |
| ❑ 64 Bernie Nicholls | .15 | .07 |
| ❑ 65 Scott Stevens | .15 | .07 |
| ❑ 66 Mario Lemieux | 3.00 | 1.35 |
| ❑ 67 Keith Primeau | .15 | .07 |
| ❑ 68 Bobby Carpenter | .10 | .05 |
| ❑ 69 Sergei Fedorov | 1.00 | .45 |
| ❑ 70 Peter Stastny | .20 | .09 |
| ❑ 71 Brian Leetch | .35 | .16 |
| ❑ 72 Vincent Damphousse | .20 | .09 |
| ❑ 73 Darryl Sitter | .20 | .09 |
| ❑ 74 Al Iafrate | .15 | .07 |
| ❑ 75 Alexander Mogilny | .35 | .16 |
| ❑ 76 Bill Ranford | .25 | .11 |
| ❑ 77 Raymond Bourque | .50 | .23 |
| ❑ 78 Joey Mullen | .10 | .05 |
| ❑ 79 Mike Ricci | .15 | .07 |
| ❑ 80 Bobby Clarke | .25 | .11 |
| ❑ 81 Gerry Cheevers | .20 | .09 |
| ❑ 82 Joe Nieuwendyk | .35 | .16 |
| ❑ 83 Terry Sawchuk | .25 | .11 |
| ❑ 84 Ray Ferraro | .10 | .05 |
| ❑ 85 Lanny McDonald | .20 | .09 |
| ❑ 86 Adam Graves | .20 | .09 |
| ❑ 87 Tomas Sandstrom | .10 | .05 |
| ❑ 88 Eric Lindros | 2.50 | 1.10 |
| ❑ 89 Jari Kurri | .25 | .11 |
| ❑ 90 Al MacInnis | .20 | .09 |
| ❑ 91 Alexandre Daigle | .25 | .11 |
| ❑ 92 Larry Robinson | .25 | .11 |
| ❑ 93 Kelly Hrudey | .20 | .09 |
| ❑ 94 Theoren Fleury | .50 | .23 |
| ❑ 95 Billy Smith | .20 | .09 |
| ❑ 96 Luc Robitaille | .25 | .11 |
| ❑ 97 Brett Hull | .75 | .35 |
| ❑ 98 Pat Falloon | .10 | .05 |
| ❑ 99 Wayne Gretzky | 4.00 | 1.80 |
| ❑ 100 Joe Sakic | 1.00 | .45 |
| ❑ 101 Phil Housley | .15 | .07 |
| ❑ 102 Mark Messier | .75 | .35 |
| ❑ 103 Jeremy Roenick | .35 | .16 |
| ❑ 104 Mark Recchi | .25 | .11 |
| ❑ 105 Pat LaFontaine | .25 | .11 |
| ❑ 106 Trevor Linden | .20 | .09 |
| ❑ 107 Jaromir Jagr | 2.50 | 1.10 |
| ❑ 108 Steve Yzerman | 2.50 | 1.10 |

## 1996-97 Hockey Greats Coins

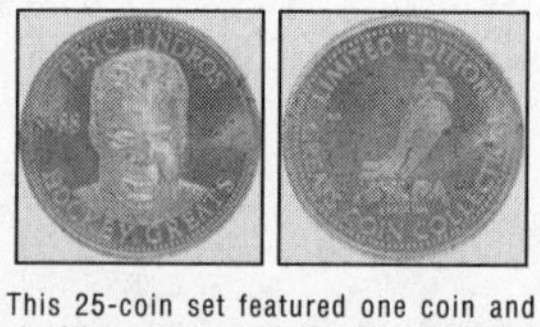

This 25-coin set featured one coin and checklist card per pack. Each box -- with a suggested retail price of $149.95 contained 80 packs. The coins were silver in color, about the size of a half dollar and featured a bust of the player on the obverse. A Collectors Album also was available for $5.49. The Chris Chelios coin (#4) was believed to be shortprinted, and thus earns the sizable premium noted below. A gold parallel version of the set exists as well. These coins were inserted at a rate of 1:150 packs. The gold coins are valued at 15 to 25 times the prices below, except for the Chelios, which goes for 3 to 5 times.

| | MINT | NRMT |
|---|---|---|
| COMPLETE SET (25) | 75.00 | 34.00 |
| COMMON COIN (1-25) | 1.00 | .45 |
| ❑ 1 Ed Belfour | 1.50 | .70 |
| ❑ 2 Raymond Bourque | 1.50 | .70 |
| ❑ 3 Pavel Bure | 3.00 | 1.35 |
| ❑ 4 Chris Chelios | 15.00 | 6.75 |
| ❑ 5 Vincent Damphousse | 1.25 | .55 |
| ❑ 6 Sergei Fedorov | 3.00 | 1.35 |
| ❑ 7 Theoren Fleury | 1.50 | .70 |
| ❑ 8 Doug Gilmour | 1.50 | .70 |
| ❑ 9 Wayne Gretzky | 10.00 | 4.50 |
| ❑ 10 Brett Hull | 2.00 | .90 |
| ❑ 11 Jaromir Jagr | 5.00 | 2.20 |
| ❑ 12 Paul Kariya | 6.00 | 2.70 |
| ❑ 13 Mario Lemieux | 8.00 | 3.60 |
| ❑ 14 Eric Lindros | 5.00 | 2.20 |
| ❑ 15 Mark Messier | 2.00 | .90 |
| ❑ 16 Alexander Mogilny | 1.00 | .45 |
| ❑ 17 Jeremy Roenick | 1.50 | .70 |
| ❑ 18 Patrick Roy | 8.00 | 3.60 |
| ❑ 19 Joe Sakic | 3.00 | 1.35 |
| ❑ 20 Steve Yzerman | 5.00 | 2.20 |
| ❑ 21 Sergei Berezin | 1.25 | .55 |
| ❑ 22 Jim Campbell | 1.00 | .45 |
| ❑ 23 Jarome Iginla | 1.25 | .55 |
| ❑ 24 Rem Murray | 1.00 | .45 |
| ❑ 25 David Wilkie | 1.00 | .45 |
| ❑ NNO Album | 5.00 | 2.20 |

## 1924-25 Holland Creameries

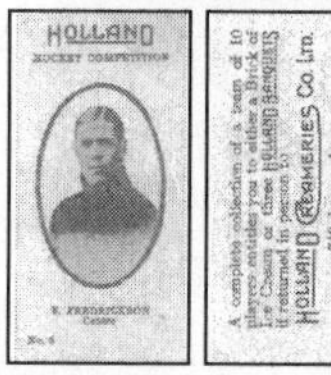

The 1924-25 Holland Creameries set contains ten black and white cards measuring approximately 1 1/2" by 3". The front has a black and white head and shoulders shot of the player, in an oval-shaped black frame on white card stock. The words %%Holland Hockey Competition~ appear above the picture, with the player's name and position below. The cards are numbered in the lower left corner on the front. The horizontally formatted card back has an offer to exchange one complete collection of ten players for either a brick of ice cream or three Holland Banquets. Supposedly the difficult card in the set was Connie Neil, marked as SP in the checklist below.

| | EX-MT | VG-E |
|---|---|---|
| COMPLETE SET (10) | 1200.00 | 600.00 |
| COMMON CARD (1-10) | 90.00 | 45.00 |
| ❑ 1 Wally Fridfinson | 100.00 | 50.00 |
| ❑ 2 Harold McMunn | 90.00 | 45.00 |
| ❑ 3 Art Somers | 90.00 | 45.00 |
| ❑ 4 Frank Woodall | 90.00 | 45.00 |
| ❑ 5 Frank Frederickson | 250.00 | 125.00 |
| ❑ 6 Bobbie Benson | 90.00 | 45.00 |
| ❑ 7 Harry Neal | 90.00 | 45.00 |
| ❑ 8 Wally Byron | 90.00 | 45.00 |
| ❑ 9 Connie Neil SP | 500.00 | 250.00 |
| ❑ 10 J. Austman | 100.00 | 50.00 |

## 1992-93 Humpty Dumpty I

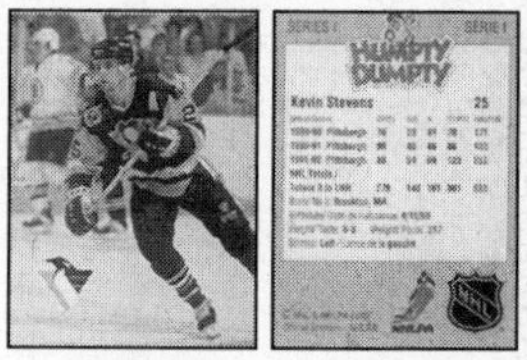

This 26-card set was sponsored by Humpty Dumpty Foods Ltd., a snack food company located in Eastern Canada and owned by Borden Inc. This promotion consisted of one cello-wrapped (approximately) 1 7/16" by 1 15/16" mini-hockey card, which was inserted into specially marked bags of Humpty Dumpty Chips and Snacks. Two series of cards were produced, and complete sets could be obtained only by collecting the cards through the promotion. The promotion lasted from October 1992 to March 1993. A total of 11,000,000 series I cards were produced, or 423,077 of each card, and they were evenly distributed between Ontario, Quebec, and the Atlantic provinces. The fronts display glossy color action photos, with the team logo superimposed toward the bottom of the picture. On a white panel framed by gray, the back presents 1991-92 season statistics and biography in French and English. The cards are unnumbered and checklisted below in alphabetical order.

| | MINT | NRMT |
|---|---|---|
| COMPLETE SET (26) | 20.00 | 9.00 |
| COMMON CARD (1-26) | .25 | .11 |
| ❑ 1 Ray Bourque | .75 | .35 |
| ❑ 2 Rod Brind'Amour | .50 | .23 |
| ❑ 3 Chris Chelios | .75 | .35 |

❑ 4 Wendel Clark .50 .23
❑ 5 Gilbert Dionne .25 .11
❑ 6 Pat Falloon .35 .16
❑ 7 Ray Ferraro .35 .16
❑ 8 Theoren Fleury .60 .25
❑ 9 Grant Fuhr .50 .23
❑ 10 Wayne Gretzky 5.00 2.20
❑ 11 Kevin Hatcher .25 .11
❑ 12 Valeri Kamensky .50 .23
❑ 13 Mike Keane .25 .11
❑ 14 Brian Leetch .75 .35
❑ 15 Kirk McLean .50 .23
❑ 16 Alexander Mogilny .60 .25
❑ 17 Troy Murray .25 .11
❑ 18 Patrick Roy 4.00 1.80
❑ 19 Joe Sakic 2.00 .90
❑ 20 Brendan Shanahan 1.50 .70
❑ 21 Kevin Stevens .35 .16
❑ 22 Scott Stevens .50 .23
❑ 23 Mark Tinordi .25 .11
❑ 24 Steve Yzerman 2.00 .90
❑ 25 Zarley Zalapski .25 .11
❑ 26 Checklist .50 .23

## 1992-93 Humpty Dumpty II

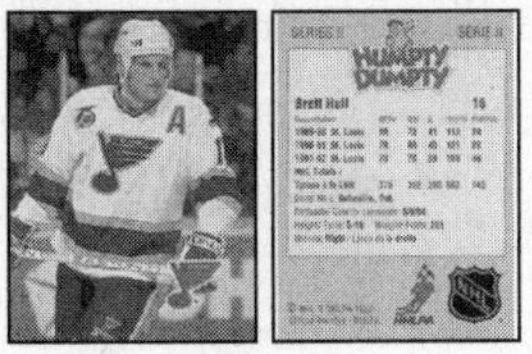

This 26-card set was sponsored by Humpty Dumpty Foods Ltd., a snack food company located in Eastern Canada and owned by Borden Inc. This promotion consisted of one cello-wrapped approximately 1 7/16" by 1 15/16" mini-hockey card randomly inserted into specially marked bags of Humpty Dumpty Chips and Snacks. Two series of cards were produced, and complete sets could be obtained only by collecting the cards through the promotion. The promotion lasted from October 1992 to March 1993. A total of 18,000,000 series II cards were produced, or 692,307 of each card, and they were evenly distributed between Ontario, Quebec, and the Atlantic provinces. The fronts display glossy color action photos, with the team logo superimposed toward the bottom of the picture. On a white panel framed by beige, the back presents 1991-92 season statistics and biography in French and English. The cards are unnumbered and checklisted below in alphabetical order.

| | MINT | NRMT |
|---|---|---|
| COMPLETE SET (26) | 20.00 | 9.00 |
| COMMON CARD (1-26) | .25 | .11 |

❑ 1 Drake Berehowsky .25 .11
❑ 2 Shayne Corson .35 .16
❑ 3 Russ Courtnall .35 .16
❑ 4 Dave Ellett .25 .11
❑ 5 Sergei Fedorov 1.50 .70
❑ 6 Dave Gagner .35 .16
❑ 7 Doug Gilmour .75 .35
❑ 8 Phil Housley .35 .16
❑ 9 Brett Hull 1.00 .45
❑ 10 Jaromir Jagr 2.50 1.10
❑ 11 Pat LaFontaine .50 .23
❑ 12 Mario Lemieux 4.00 1.80
❑ 13 Trevor Linden .35 .16
❑ 14 Al MacInnis .50 .23
❑ 15 Mark Messier 1.00 .45
❑ 16 Cam Neely .75 .35
❑ 17 Owen Nolan .50 .23
❑ 18 Bill Ranford .50 .23
❑ 19 Luc Robitaille .60 .25
❑ 20 Jeremy Roenick .75 .35
❑ 21 Mats Sundin .75 .35
❑ 22 Chris Terreri .35 .16
❑ 23 Steve Thomas .35 .16
❑ 24 Pat Verbeek .35 .16
❑ 25 Neil Wilkinson .25 .11
❑ 26 Checklist .50 .23

## 1995-96 Imperial Stickers

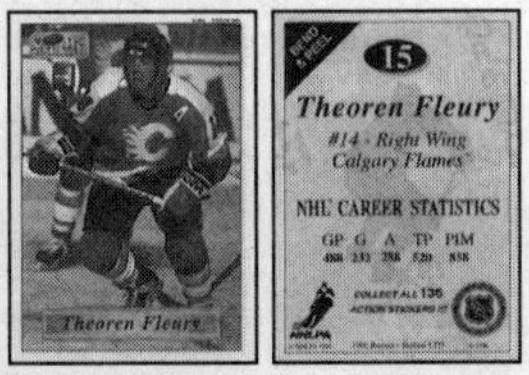

This set of 136 stickers was released in five-sticker packs (plus one stick of tasty gum!) late in the 1995-96 season. The stickers measure the standard size and feature color player photos and name on the front, and playing information on the back. Collation of this product was extremely poor, making set building somewhat arduous.

| | MINT | NRMT |
|---|---|---|
| COMPLETE SET (136) | 35.00 | 16.00 |
| COMMON CARD (1-136) | .05 | .02 |

❑ 1 Ducks Logo .15 .07
❑ 2 Paul Kariya 2.50 1.10
❑ 3 Chad Kilger .15 .07
❑ 4 Oleg Tverdovsky .10 .05
❑ 5 Bruins Logo .15 .07
❑ 6 Raymond Bourque .50 .23
❑ 7 Cam Neely .25 .11
❑ 8 Adam Oates .20 .09
❑ 9 Kevin Stevens .10 .05
❑ 10 Sabres Logo .15 .07
❑ 11 Pat LaFontaine .20 .09
❑ 12 Dominik Hasek 1.25 .55
❑ 13 Alexei Zhitnik .05 .02
❑ 14 Flames Logo .15 .07
❑ 15 Theoren Fleury .50 .23
❑ 16 Phil Housley .10 .05
❑ 17 Trevor Kidd .10 .05
❑ 18 Joe Nieuwendyk .35 .16
❑ 19 Zarley Zalapski .05 .02
❑ 20 Blackhawks Logo .15 .07
❑ 21 Jeremy Roenick .35 .16
❑ 22 Chris Chelios .50 .23
❑ 23 Ed Belfour .50 .23
❑ 24 Joe Murphy .10 .05
❑ 25 Patrick Poulin .05 .02
❑ 26 Avalanche Logo .15 .07
❑ 27 Joe Sakic 1.50 .70
❑ 28 Peter Forsberg 2.00 .90
❑ 29 Sandis Ozolinsh .15 .07
❑ 30 Mike Ricci .10 .05
❑ 31 Valeri Kamensky .15 .07
❑ 32 Stars Logo .15 .07
❑ 33 Mike Modano 1.00 .45
❑ 34 Kevin Hatcher .05 .02
❑ 35 Andy Moog .20 .09
❑ 36 Red Wings Logo .15 .07
❑ 37 Steve Yzerman 2.00 .90
❑ 38 Sergei Fedorov 1.25 .55
❑ 39 Paul Coffey .50 .23
❑ 40 Keith Primeau .10 .05
❑ 41 Nicklas Lidstrom .15 .07
❑ 42 Oilers Logo .15 .07
❑ 43 Doug Weight .20 .09
❑ 44 Jason Arnott .25 .11
❑ 45 Bill Ranford .15 .07
❑ 46 Panthers Logo .15 .07
❑ 47 John Vanbiesbrouck 1.00 .45
❑ 48 Stu Barnes .10 .05
❑ 49 Scott Mellanby .10 .05
❑ 50 Rob Niedermayer .20 .09
❑ 51 Whalers Logo .15 .07
❑ 52 Brendan Shanahan 1.25 .55
❑ 53 Geoff Sanderson .15 .07
❑ 54 Sean Burke .10 .05
❑ 55 Jeff O'Neill .10 .05
❑ 56 Kings Logo .15 .07
❑ 57 Wayne Gretzky 4.00 1.80
❑ 58 Rob Blake .10 .05
❑ 59 Rick Tocchet .10 .05
❑ 60 Dimitri Khristich .05 .02
❑ 61 Kelly Hrudey .15 .07
❑ 62 Canadiens Logo .15 .07
❑ 63 Pierre Turgeon .20 .09
❑ 64 Mark Recchi .20 .09
❑ 65 Saku Koivu 1.00 .45
❑ 66 Patrick Roy 3.00 1.35
❑ 67 Vincent Damphousse .15 .07
❑ 68 Devils Logo .15 .07
❑ 69 Stephane Richer .05 .02
❑ 70 Martin Brodeur 1.50 .70
❑ 71 Scott Niedermayer .20 .09
❑ 72 Scott Stevens .10 .05
❑ 73 Islander Logo .15 .07
❑ 74 Kirk Muller .10 .05
❑ 75 Mathieu Schneider .05 .02
❑ 76 Wendel Clark .25 .11
❑ 77 Derek King .05 .02
❑ 78 Ranger Logo .15 .07
❑ 79 Brian Leetch .50 .23
❑ 80 Mark Messier 1.00 .45
❑ 81 Alexei Kovalev .15 .07
❑ 82 Luc Robitaille .20 .09
❑ 83 Mike Richter .50 .23
❑ 84 Senators Logo .15 .07
❑ 85 Dan Quinn .05 .02
❑ 86 Alexandre Daigle .10 .05
❑ 87 Steve Duchesne .05 .02
❑ 88 Radek Bonk .10 .05
❑ 89 Flyers Logo .15 .07
❑ 90 Eric Lindros 2.00 .90
❑ 91 Mikael Renberg .25 .11
❑ 92 John LeClair 1.00 .45
❑ 93 Eric Desjardins .05 .02
❑ 94 Rod Brind'Amour .15 .07
❑ 95 Penguins Logo .15 .07
❑ 96 Jaromir Jagr 2.00 .90
❑ 97 Mario Lemieux 3.00 1.35
❑ 98 Ron Francis .25 .11
❑ 99 Sergei Zubov .10 .05
❑ 100 Blues Logo .15 .07
❑ 101 Brett Hull 1.00 .45
❑ 102 Al MacInnis .15 .07
❑ 103 Dale Hawerchuk .15 .07
❑ 104 Chris Pronger .15 .07
❑ 105 Sharks Logo .15 .07
❑ 106 Craig Janney .10 .05
❑ 107 Pat Falloon .05 .02
❑ 108 Arturs Irbe .15 .07
❑ 109 Ulf Dahlen .05 .02
❑ 110 Owen Nolan .20 .09
❑ 111 Lightning Logo .15 .07
❑ 112 Roman Hamrlik .15 .07
❑ 113 Brian Bradley .10 .05
❑ 114 Chris Gratton .15 .07
❑ 115 Brian Bellows .05 .02
❑ 116 Maple Leafs Logo .15 .07
❑ 117 Doug Gilmour .50 .23
❑ 118 Mats Sundin .50 .23
❑ 119 Dave Andreychuk .10 .05
❑ 120 Felix Potvin .50 .23
❑ 121 Larry Murphy .10 .05
❑ 122 Canucks Logo .15 .07
❑ 123 Pavel Bure 1.25 .55
❑ 124 Alexander Mogilny .35 .16
❑ 125 Trevor Linden .10 .05
❑ 126 Jeff Brown .05 .02
❑ 127 Kirk McLean .15 .07
❑ 128 Capitals Logo .15 .07
❑ 129 Joe Juneau .10 .05
❑ 130 Peter Bondra .50 .23
❑ 131 Jim Carey .35 .16
❑ 132 Calle Johansson .05 .02
❑ 133 Jets Logo .15 .07
❑ 134 Teemu Selanne 1.25 .55
❑ 135 Alexei Zhamnov .15 .07
❑ 136 Keith Tkachuk 1.00 .45

## 1995-96 Imperial Stickers Die Cut Superstars

These die-cut stickers were randomly inserted in packs at indeterminate odds. They feature player images over a starburst background. Backs are blank.

| | MINT | NRMT |
|---|---|---|
| COMPLETE SET (25) | 30.00 | 13.50 |
| COMMON CARD (1-25) | .15 | .07 |

❑ 1 Pierre Turgeon .35 .16
❑ 2 Patrick Roy 4.00 1.80
❑ 3 Pat LaFontaine .35 .16
❑ 4 Joe Sakic 1.50 .70
❑ 5 Paul Coffey .50 .23
❑ 6 Ray Bourque .50 .23
❑ 7 Brian Leetch .50 .23
❑ 8 Joe Juneau .25 .11
❑ 9 Jeremy Roenick .50 .23
❑ 10 Chris Chelios .50 .23
❑ 11 Brett Hull 1.00 .45
❑ 12 Paul Kariya 3.00 1.35
❑ 13 Jason Arnott .25 .11
❑ 14 Pavel Bure 1.25 .55
❑ 15 Steve Duchesne .15 .07
❑ 16 Martin Brodeur 2.00 .90
❑ 17 Eric Lindros 2.50 1.10
❑ 18 Mikael Renberg .35 .16
❑ 19 Felix Potvin .50 .23
❑ 20 Roman Hamrlik .25 .11
❑ 21 Wayne Gretzky 5.00 2.20
❑ 22 Brendan Shanahan 1.25 .55
❑ 23 Jaromir Jagr 2.50 1.10
❑ 24 Mario Lemieux 4.00 1.80
❑ 25 Steve Yzerman 2.50 1.10

## 1979-80 Islanders Transparencies

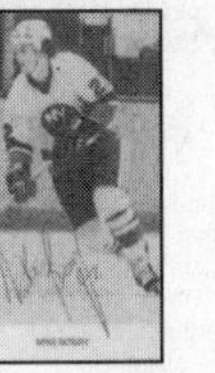

These standard postcard size cards feature black and white posed photos on a thin, transparent paper stock. Cards are unnumbered and checklisted below alphabetically.

| | MINT | NRMT |
|---|---|---|
| COMPLETE SET (22) | 40.00 | 18.00 |
| COMMON CARD | .60 | .25 |

❑ 1 Mike Bossy 15.00 6.75
❑ 2 Bob Bourne .75 .35
❑ 3 Clark Gillies .75 .35
❑ 4 Billy Harris .75 .35
❑ 5 Lerne Henning .75 .35
❑ 6 Anders Kallur .75 .35
❑ 7 Mike Kaszycki .75 .35
❑ 8 Dave Langevin .75 .35
❑ 9 Dave Lewis .75 .35
❑ 10 Bob Lorimer .75 .35
❑ 11 Wayne Merrick .75 .35
❑ 12 Bob Nystrom 2.00 .90
❑ 13 Stefan Persson .75 .35
❑ 14 Denis Potvin 2.00 .90
❑ 15 Jean Potvin .75 .35
❑ 16 Garry Howatt .75 .35
❑ 17 Glenn Resch 5.00 2.20
❑ 18 Bill Smith 5.00 2.20
❑ 19 Steven Tambellini .75 .35
❑ 20 John Tonelli 1.50 .70
❑ 21 Bryan Trottier 4.00 1.80
❑ 22 Header Card .60 .25

## 1983-84 Islanders Team Issue

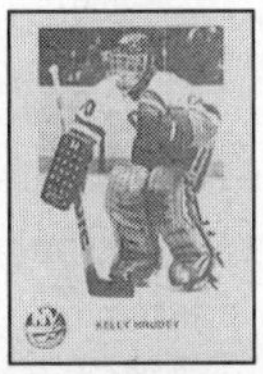

This 19-card set measures approximately 4" by 5 1/2" and features the 1983-84 New York Islanders. The cards are printed on thin paper stock. The fronts have black-and-white action player photos with white borders. The player's name and the team logo appear below the photo. The cards are unnumbered and checklisted below in alphabetical order. The set features an early card of Kelly Hrudey predating his O-Pee-Chee and Topps Rookie Cards by two years.

| | MINT | NRMT |
|---|---|---|
| COMPLETE SET (19) | 30.00 | 13.50 |
| COMMON CARD (1-19) | 1.00 | .45 |

❑ 1 Mike Bossy 5.00 2.20
❑ 2 Bob Bourne 1.00 .45
❑ 3 Billy Carroll 1.00 .45
❑ 4 Clark Gillies 2.00 .90
❑ 5 Mats Hallin 1.00 .45
❑ 6 Kelly Hrudey 4.00 1.80
❑ 7 Tomas Jonsson 1.00 .45
❑ 8 Dave Langevin 1.00 .45
❑ 9 Roland Melanson 1.50 .70
❑ 10 Wayne Merrick 1.00 .45
❑ 11 Ken Morrow 1.50 .70
❑ 12 Bob Nystrom 1.50 .70
❑ 13 Denis Potvin 4.00 1.80
❑ 14 Billy Smith 4.00 1.80
❑ 15 Brent Sutter 2.00 .90
❑ 16 Duane Sutter 1.50 .70
❑ 17 John Tonelli 2.00 .90
❑ 18 Bryan Trottier 4.00 1.80
❑ 19 Team Photo 2.00 .90

## 1984 Islanders Islander News

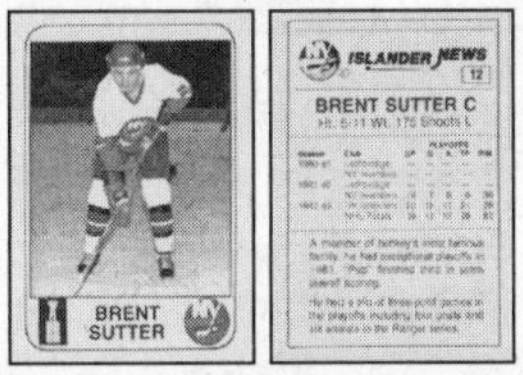

This 38-card standard-size set of New York Islanders was sponsored by Islander News and issued during the summer of 1984 to commemorate the Islanders' fourth consecutive Stanley Cup victory. The color photo on the front is framed by a thin black border. Another thin black border (with rounded corners) outlines the card front, and the space in between is pale blue. The player's name is given below the picture and sandwiched between a trophy cup icon and the New York Islanders' logo. The back has biographical information and a career summary on the player.

| | MINT | NRMT |
|---|---|---|
| COMPLETE SET (38) | 25.00 | 11.00 |
| COMMON CARD (1-38) | .25 | .11 |

❑ 1 Checklist Card .50 .23
❑ 2 Mike Bossy 4.00 1.80
❑ 3 Bob Bourne .50 .23
❑ 4 Billy Carroll .50 .23
❑ 5 Greg Gilbert .50 .23
❑ 6 Clark Gillies 1.25 .55
❑ 7 Butch Goring 1.00 .45
❑ 8 Mats Hallin .50 .23
❑ 9 Anders Kallur .50 .23
❑ 10 Wayne Merrick .50 .23
❑ 11 Bob Nystrom .75 .35
❑ 12 Brent Sutter 1.25 .55
❑ 13 Duane Sutter 1.00 .45
❑ 14 John Tonelli 1.25 .55
❑ 15 Bryan Trottier 3.00 1.35
❑ 16 Tomas Jonsson .50 .23
❑ 17 Gordie Lane .50 .23
❑ 18 Dave Langevin .50 .23
❑ 19 Ken Morrow 1.00 .45
❑ 20 Stefan Persson .50 .23
❑ 21 Denis Potvin 2.50 1.10
❑ 22 Roland Melanson .75 .35
❑ 23 Billy Smith 2.00 .90
❑ 24 Cup Number 1 .50 .23
❑ 25 Cup Number 2 .50 .23
❑ 26 Cup Number 4 .50 .23
❑ 27 Lorne Henning CO .50 .23
❑ 28 Bill Torrey GM .50 .23
❑ 29 Al Arbour CO 1.00 .45
❑ 30 Waske-Pickard .25 .11
Two Trainers
❑ 31 1979-80 Team Photo 1.00 .45
❑ 32 1980-81 Team Photo 1.00 .45
❑ 33 1981-82 Team Photo 1.00 .45
❑ 34 1982-83 Team Photo 1.00 .45
❑ 35 Mike Bossy 2.00 .90
'82 Conn Smythe Winner
❑ 36 Billy Smith 1.25 .55
'83 Conn Smythe Winner
❑ 37 Bryan Trottier 1.50 .70
'80 Conn Smythe Winner
❑ 38 Butch Goring .75 .35
'81 Conn Smythe Winner

## 1985 Islanders Islander News

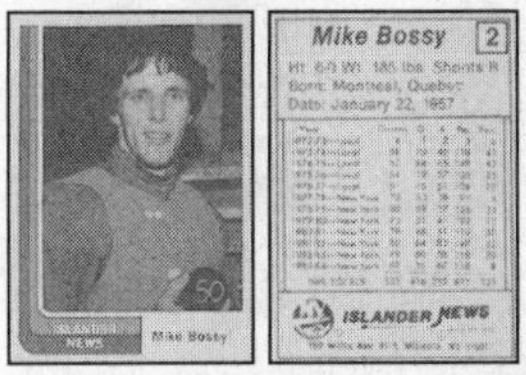

This 37-card standard-size set of New York Islanders was sponsored by Islander News and issued during the summer of 1985. The color photo on the front is enframed by a thin black border. A red and blue hockey stick forms the border on the left side of the picture, with the end of the stick below the picture. The words "Islander News" appears on the end of the stick, and the player's name is given to the right. The back has biographical information including a career summary on the player as well as the notation "Second Series". The key card in the set is the Pat LaFontaine card as it was issued concurrently with his O-Pee-Chee and Topps Rookie Cards.

| | MINT | NRMT |
|---|---|---|
| COMPLETE SET (37) | 30.00 | 13.50 |
| COMMON CARD (1-37) | .25 | .11 |

❑ 1 Checklist Card .50 .23
❑ 2 Mike Bossy 4.00 1.80
❑ 3 Bob Bourne .50 .23
❑ 4 Pat Flatley .75 .35
❑ 5 Greg Gilbert .50 .23
❑ 6 Clark Gillies 1.00 .45
❑ 7 Mats Hallin .50 .23
❑ 8 Anders Kallur .50 .23
❑ 9 Alan Kerr .50 .23
❑ 10 Roger Kortko .50 .23
❑ 11 Pat LaFontaine 8.00 3.60
❑ 12 Bob Nystrom .75 .35
❑ 13 Brent Sutter 1.00 .45
❑ 14 Duane Sutter .75 .35
❑ 15 John Tonelli 1.00 .45
❑ 16 Bryan Trottier 3.00 1.35
❑ 17 Paul Boutilier .50 .23
❑ 18 Gerald Diduck .50 .23
❑ 19 Gord Dineen .50 .23
❑ 20 Tomas Jonsson .75 .35
❑ 21 Gordie Lane .50 .23
❑ 22 Dave Langevin .50 .23
❑ 23 Ken Morrow .75 .35
❑ 24 Stefan Persson .50 .23
❑ 25 Denis Potvin 2.50 1.10
❑ 26 Kelly Hrudey 3.00 1.35
❑ 27 Billy Smith 2.00 .90
❑ 28 Bill Torrey GM/P .75 .35
❑ 29 Al Arbour CO 1.00 .45
❑ 30 Brian Kilrea CO .25 .11
❑ 31 Pickard/Smith .25 .11
Two Trainers
❑ 32 Mike Bossy 2.00 .90
Milestone-400 Goals
❑ 33 Denis Potvin 1.50 .70
Milestone-600 Assists
❑ 34 Billy Smith 1.00 .45
Milestone-500 Games
❑ 35 Bryan Trottier 1.50 .70
Milestone-1000 Points
❑ 36 1984-85 Team 1.00 .45
❑ 37 Wales Champs .75 .35

## 1985 Islanders Islander News Trottier

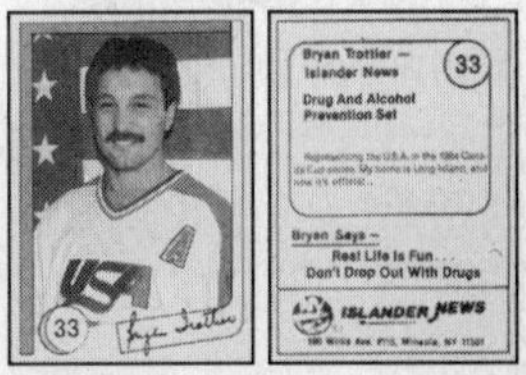

This 33-card standard-size set was sponsored by the New York Islander News and issued during the summer of 1985 supposedly by the Port Washington Police Department. It highlights the early career of then-Islander, Bryan Trottier, who is credited with writing the drug and alcohol prevention tips on the back

of the cards. The cards feature color or black and white photos of Trottier on the front. They are framed by a red border on two sides, and white border; the white border is in the shape of a hockey stick, with Trottier's signature across the bottom of the stick. The cards are numbered on both sides. In addition to the anti-drug or alcohol message, the back also has Trottier's own comments about each photo.

| | MINT | NRMT |
|---|---|---|
| COMPLETE SET (33) | 25.00 | 11.00 |
| COMMON CARD (1-33) | .50 | .23 |
| ❑ 1 Penalty box | 1.00 | .45 |
| ❑ 2 Swift Current Broncos | 1.00 | .45 |
| ❑ 3 Three goals in first game at Nassau Coliseum | .50 | .23 |
| ❑ 4 All-Star game | .75 | .35 |
| ❑ 5 Four goals vs. Atlanta | .50 | .23 |
| ❑ 6 Ross and Hart Trophies | .75 | .35 |
| ❑ 7 Street hockey equipment | .50 | .23 |
| ❑ 8 Bearing down on the draw against Maruk | .75 | .35 |
| ❑ 9 Pleading with referee | .50 | .23 |
| ❑ 10 Trottier/Rangers action | .50 | .23 |
| ❑ 11 Trottier/Holmgren action | .75 | .35 |
| ❑ 12 Trottier/Canadiens action | .75 | .35 |
| ❑ 13 1980 Boston playoff | .75 | .35 |
| ❑ 14 1980 Final Game vs. Flyers | .75 | .35 |
| ❑ 15 NHL Awards Luncheon | .50 | .23 |
| ❑ 16 Trottier/Rangers action | .75 | .35 |
| ❑ 17 Watching action in resting area | .50 | .23 |
| ❑ 18 Warm-up time | .50 | .23 |
| ❑ 19 Debating with referee | .50 | .23 |
| ❑ 20 1981 Playoff with Oilers | .75 | .35 |
| ❑ 21 Trottier/Gretzky action | 10.00 | 4.50 |
| ❑ 22 Trottier/North Stars action | .75 | .35 |
| ❑ 23 Congratulating Don Beaupre | .75 | .35 |
| ❑ 24 Second Stanley Cup Championship | .50 | .23 |
| ❑ 25 Trottier/Sutter celebrate | .75 | .35 |
| ❑ 26 Trottier psyching himself | .50 | .23 |
| ❑ 27 Trottier/Devils action | .75 | .35 |
| ❑ 28 1983 All-Star | .75 | .35 |
| ❑ 29 Trottier defending goal (Gretzky behind net) | 7.50 | 3.40 |
| ❑ 30 Fourth Stanley Cup Championship | .50 | .23 |
| ❑ 31 Trottier and Denis Potvin celebrate | 1.50 | .70 |
| ❑ 32 Trottier and Mike Bossy celebrate | 2.00 | .90 |
| ❑ 33 1984 Canada Cup Series | 1.00 | .45 |

## 1989-90 Islanders

This 22-card set measures approximately 3 7/8" by 7 1/8". The fronts feature autographed color action photos. The player's name, jersey number, position, team logo and team name are printed in the wider bottom border. The cards are unnumbered and checklisted below in alphabetical order.

| | MINT | NRMT |
|---|---|---|
| COMPLETE SET (22) | 12.00 | 5.50 |
| COMMON CARD (1-22) | .50 | .23 |
| ❑ 1 Al Arbour CO | .75 | .35 |
| ❑ 2 Dean Chynoweth | .50 | .23 |
| ❑ 3 Dave Chyzowski | .50 | .23 |
| ❑ 4 Doug Crossman | .50 | .23 |
| ❑ 5 Gerald Diduck | .50 | .23 |
| ❑ 6 Tom Fitzgerald | .50 | .23 |
| ❑ 7 Mark Fitzpatrick | 1.50 | .70 |
| ❑ 8 Patrick Flatley | .75 | .35 |
| ❑ 9 Glenn Healy | 1.00 | .45 |
| ❑ 10 Alan Kerr | .50 | .23 |
| ❑ 11 Pat LaFontaine | 2.50 | 1.10 |
| ❑ 12 Mikko Makela | .50 | .23 |
| ❑ 13 Don Maloney | .50 | .23 |
| ❑ 14 Jeff Norton | .50 | .23 |
| ❑ 15 Gary Nylund | .50 | .23 |
| ❑ 16 Rich Pilon | .50 | .23 |
| ❑ 17 Brent Sutter | .75 | .35 |
| ❑ 18 Gilles Thibaudeau | .50 | .23 |
| ❑ 19 Bryan Trottier | 2.00 | .90 |
| ❑ 20 David Volek | .50 | .23 |
| ❑ 21 Mick Vukota | .50 | .23 |
| ❑ 22 Randy Wood | .50 | .23 |

## 1993-94 Islanders Chemical Bank Alumni

This ten-card set was issued as a promotional giveaway to honor prestigious members of the Islanders alumni on January 28, 1994. The cards are standard size and feature color action photos surrounded by an orange border. The logos of Chemical Bank and the Isles adorn the corners, and the player name appears along the bottom. The two-color backs include career highlights. As the cards are unnumbered, they are listed in alphabetical order.

| | MINT | NRMT |
|---|---|---|
| COMPLETE SET (10) | 8.00 | 3.60 |
| COMMON CARD (1-10) | .25 | .11 |
| ❑ 1 Title Card | .25 | .11 |
| ❑ 2 Mike Bossy | 2.00 | .90 |
| ❑ 3 Clark Gillies | .75 | .35 |
| ❑ 4 Gerry Hart | .50 | .23 |
| ❑ 5 Wayne Merrick | .50 | .23 |
| ❑ 6 Bob Nystrom | .75 | .35 |
| ❑ 7 Denis Potvin | 1.50 | .70 |
| ❑ 8 Bill Smith | 1.50 | .70 |
| ❑ 9 John Tonelli | .75 | .35 |
| ❑ 10 Eddie Westfall | .50 | .23 |

## 1996-97 Islander Postcards

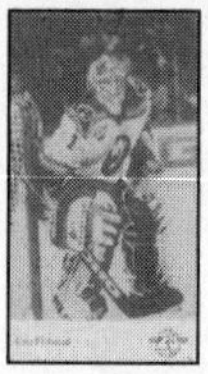

This 23-postcard set was produced by the Islanders for promotional giveaways and autograph signings. They feature black and white action photos on the front, with a white border along the bottom containing the players's name and the club's special 25th anniversary logo. The backs are blank and unnumbered, hence the alphabetical listing below.

| | MINT | NRMT |
|---|---|---|
| COMPLETE SET (23) | 15.00 | 6.75 |
| COMMON CARD (1-23) | .50 | .23 |
| ❑ 1 Niclas Andersson | .50 | .23 |
| ❑ 2 Derek Armstrong | .50 | .23 |
| ❑ 3 Todd Bertuzzi | .75 | .35 |
| ❑ 4 Eric Fichaud | 2.00 | .90 |
| ❑ 5 Travis Green | .75 | .35 |
| ❑ 6 Doug Houda | .50 | .23 |
| ❑ 7 Brent Hughes | .50 | .23 |
| ❑ 8 Kenny Jonsson | .75 | .35 |
| ❑ 9 Derek King | .75 | .35 |
| ❑ 10 Paul Kruse | .50 | .23 |
| ❑ 11 Claude Lapointe | .50 | .23 |
| ❑ 12 Scott Lachance | .50 | .23 |
| ❑ 13 Bryan McCabe | .50 | .23 |
| ❑ 14 Marty McInnis | .50 | .23 |
| ❑ 15 Mike Milbury CO | .50 | .23 |
| ❑ 16 Zigmund Palffy | 3.00 | 1.35 |
| ❑ 17 Dan Plante | .50 | .23 |
| ❑ 18 Richard Pilon | .50 | .23 |
| ❑ 19 Tommy Salo | 1.50 | .70 |
| ❑ 20 Bryan Smolinski | .75 | .35 |
| ❑ 21 Dennis Vaske | .50 | .23 |
| ❑ 22 Mick Vukota | .50 | .23 |
| ❑ 23 Randy Wood | .50 | .23 |

## 1998-99 Islanders Power Play

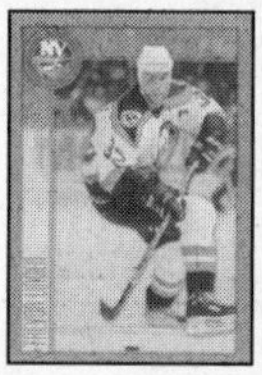

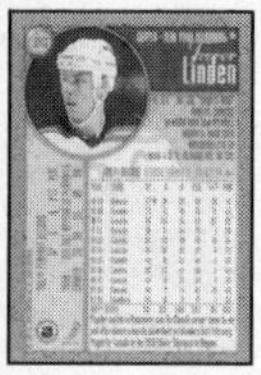

Cards were distributed in a sealed pack and were made available through give-aways at various arenas, in conjunction with Power Play magazine. Each packet contains 4-cards, similar in design to the base set from each manufacturer, but featuring a different card number on the back.

| | MINT | NRMT |
|---|---|---|
| COMPLETE SET (4) | 2.00 | .90 |
| COMMON CARD (1-4) | .30 | .14 |
| ❑ NYI1 Trevor Linden | .30 | .14 |
| ❑ NYI2 Bryan Smolinski | .30 | .14 |
| ❑ NYI3 Mike Watt | .30 | .14 |
| ❑ NYI4 Zigmund Palffy | 1.00 | .45 |

## 1998 Jello Spoons

Available one per pack in select boxes of Jello Pudding mix. These small stickers feature a head shot of the selected player.

| | MINT | NRMT |
|---|---|---|
| COMPLETE SET (8) | 15.00 | 6.75 |
| COMMON SPOON (1-8) | .60 | .25 |
| ❑ 1 Rod Brind'Amour | .60 | .25 |
| ❑ 2 Theo Fleury | .75 | .35 |
| ❑ 3 Wayne Gretzky | 4.00 | 1.80 |
| ❑ 4 Curtis Joseph | .75 | .35 |
| ❑ 5 Paul Kariya | 2.50 | 1.10 |
| ❑ 6 Eric Lindros | 2.00 | .90 |
| ❑ 7 Patrick Roy | 3.00 | 1.35 |
| ❑ 8 Joe Sakic | 1.50 | .70 |

## 1978-79 Jets Postcards

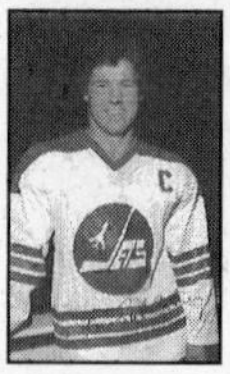

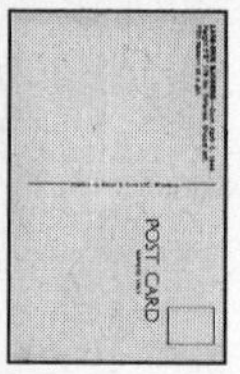

This 23-postcard set measures approximately 3 1/2" by 5 1/2". The fronts feature posed-on-ice borderless color player photos with a facsimile player autograph near the bottom. The backs have a postcard format and carry the player's name and a brief biography. The postcards are unnumbered and checklisted below in alphabetical order.

| | NRMT-MT | EXC |
|---|---|---|
| COMPLETE SET (23) | 25.00 | 11.00 |
| COMMON CARD (1-23) | .75 | .35 |
| ❑ 1 Mike Amodeo | .75 | .35 |
| ❑ 2 Scott Campbell | .75 | .35 |
| ❑ 3 Kim Clackson | 1.00 | .45 |
| ❑ 4 Joe Daley | 2.00 | .90 |
| ❑ 5 John Gray | .75 | .35 |
| ❑ 6 Ted Green | 2.00 | .90 |
| ❑ 7 Robert Guindon | .75 | .35 |
| ❑ 8 Glenn Hicks | .75 | .35 |
| ❑ 9 Larry Hillman | .75 | .35 |
| ❑ 10 Bill Lesuk | 1.00 | .45 |
| ❑ 11 Willy Lindstrom | 1.50 | .70 |
| ❑ 12 Barry Long | .75 | .35 |
| ❑ 13 Morris Lukowich | 1.50 | .70 |
| ❑ 14 Paul MacKinnon | .75 | .35 |
| ❑ 15 Markus Mattsson | 1.50 | .70 |
| ❑ 16 Lyle Moffat | .75 | .35 |
| ❑ 17 Kent Nilsson | 5.00 | 2.20 |
| ❑ 18 Rich Preston | 1.00 | .45 |
| ❑ 19 Terry Ruskowski | 2.50 | 1.10 |
| ❑ 20 Lars-Erik Sjoberg | 2.50 | 1.10 |
| ❑ 21 Peter Sullivan | .75 | .35 |
| ❑ 22 Paul Terbenche | .75 | .35 |
| ❑ 23 Steve West | .75 | .35 |

## 1979-80 Jets Postcards

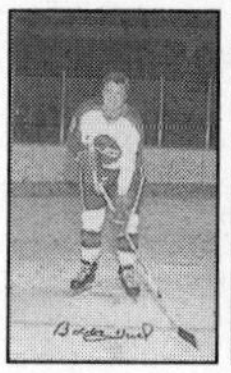

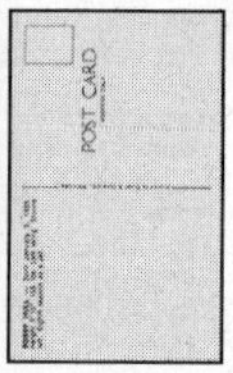

These 28 postcards measure approximately 3 1/2" by 5 1/2" and feature posed-on-ice color player photos on their borderless fronts. A facsimile player autograph rests near the bottom. The backs have a postcard format and carry the player's name and brief biography. The postcards are unnumbered and checklisted below in alphabetical order.

| | NRMT-MT | EXC |
|---|---|---|
| COMPLETE SET (28) | 25.00 | 11.00 |
| COMMON CARD (1-28) | .50 | .23 |
| ❑ 1 Mike Amodeo | .75 | .35 |
| ❑ 2 Al Cameron | .75 | .35 |
| ❑ 3 Scott Campbell | .75 | .35 |
| ❑ 4 Wayne Dillon | .75 | .35 |
| ❑ 5 Jude Drouin | .75 | .35 |
| ❑ 6 John Ferguson GM | 1.00 | .45 |
| ❑ 7 Hilliard Graves | .75 | .35 |
| ❑ 8 Pierre Hamel | .75 | .35 |
| ❑ 9 Dave Hoyda | .75 | .35 |
| ❑ 10 Bobby Hull | 8.00 | 3.60 |
| ❑ 11 Bill Lesuk | .75 | .35 |
| ❑ 12 Willy Lindstrom | 1.50 | .70 |
| ❑ 13 Morris Lukowich | 1.50 | .70 |
| ❑ 14 Jimmy Mann | 1.50 | .70 |
| ❑ 15 Peter Marsh | 1.00 | .45 |
| ❑ 16 Gord McTavish | .75 | .35 |
| ❑ 17 Tom McVie CO | .75 | .35 |
| ❑ 18 Barry Melrose | 3.00 | 1.35 |
| ❑ 19 Lyle Moffat | .75 | .35 |
| ❑ 20 Craig Norwich | .75 | .35 |
| ❑ 21 Lars-Erik Sjoberg | 2.50 | 1.10 |
| ❑ 22 Gary Smith | 1.00 | .45 |
| ❑ 23 Gordon Smith | .75 | .35 |
| ❑ 24 Lorne Stamler | .75 | .35 |
| ❑ 25 Peter Sullivan | .75 | .35 |
| ❑ 26 Bill Sutherland ACO | .50 | .23 |
| ❑ 27 Ron Wilson | 1.00 | .45 |
| ❑ 28 Title Card | .50 | .23 |

## 1980-81 Jets Postcards

This 23-card set of the Winnipeg Jets measures approximately 3 1/2" by 5 1/2". The fronts feature borderless black-and-white action player photos. A facsimile autograph rounds out the front. The backs are blank. The cards are unnumbered and checklisted below in alphabetical order.

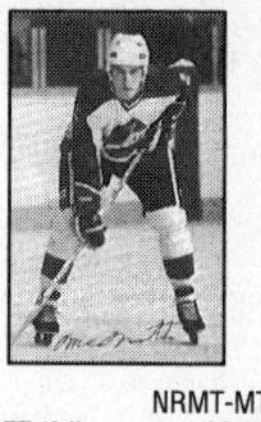

| | NRMT-MT | EXC |
|---|---|---|
| COMPLETE SET (24) | 20.00 | 9.00 |
| COMMON CARD (1-24) | 1.00 | .45 |
| ❑ 1 David Babych | 2.50 | 1.10 |
| ❑ 2 Al Cameron | 1.00 | .45 |
| ❑ 3 Scott Campbell | 1.00 | .45 |
| ❑ 4 Dave Chartier | 1.00 | .45 |
| ❑ 5 Dave Christian | 1.00 | .45 |
| ❑ 6 Jude Drouin | 1.00 | .45 |
| ❑ 7 Norm Dupont | 1.00 | .45 |
| ❑ 8 Dan Geoffrion | 1.00 | .45 |
| ❑ 9 Pierre Hamel | 1.00 | .45 |
| ❑ 10 Barry Legge | 1.00 | .45 |
| ❑ 11 Willy Lindstrom | 1.50 | .70 |
| ❑ 12 Barry Long | 1.50 | .70 |
| ❑ 13 Morris Lukowich | 1.00 | .45 |
| ❑ 14 Kris Manery | 1.00 | .45 |
| ❑ 15 Jimmy Mann | 1.50 | .70 |
| ❑ 16 Moe Mantha | 1.50 | .70 |
| ❑ 17 Markus Mattsson | 1.50 | .70 |
| ❑ 18 Richard Mulhern | 1.00 | .45 |
| ❑ 19 Doug Smail | 1.50 | .70 |
| ❑ 20 Don Spring | 1.00 | .45 |
| ❑ 21 Anders Steen | 1.00 | .45 |
| ❑ 22 Pete Sullivan | 1.00 | .45 |
| ❑ 23 Tim Trimper | 1.00 | .45 |
| ❑ 24 Ron Wilson | 1.50 | .70 |

## 1981-82 Jets Postcards

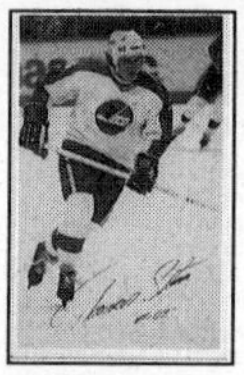

This 24-card set of the Winnipeg Jets measures approximately 3 1/2" by 5 1/2". The fronts feature black-and-white action player photos with a white border and a facsimile autograph near the bottom. The backs are blank. The cards are unnumbered and checklisted below in alphabetical order. This set features a postcard of Dale Hawerchuk that predates his RC by one year.

| | MINT | NRMT |
|---|---|---|
| COMPLETE SET (24) | 30.00 | 13.50 |
| COMMON CARD (1-24) | .75 | .35 |
| ❑ 1 Scott Arniel | 1.00 | .45 |
| ❑ 2 Dave Babych | 1.50 | .70 |
| ❑ 3 Dave Christian | 1.50 | .70 |
| ❑ 4 Lucien Deblois | 1.00 | .45 |
| ❑ 5 Normand Dupont | .75 | .35 |
| ❑ 6 Dale Hawerchuk | 10.00 | 4.50 |
| ❑ 7 Larry Hopkins | .75 | .35 |
| ❑ 8 Craig Levie | .75 | .35 |
| ❑ 9 Willy Lindstrom | 1.00 | .45 |
| ❑ 10 Morris Lukowich | 1.00 | .45 |
| ❑ 11 Bengt Lundholm | .75 | .35 |
| ❑ 12 Paul MacLean | 1.50 | .70 |
| ❑ 13 Jimmy Mann | 1.00 | .45 |
| ❑ 14 Bryan Maxwell | .75 | .35 |
| ❑ 15 Serge Savard | 1.25 | .55 |
| ❑ 16 Doug Smail | 1.50 | .70 |
| ❑ 17 Doug Soetaert | 1.50 | .70 |
| ❑ 18 Don Spring | .75 | .35 |
| ❑ 19 Ed Staniowski | .75 | .35 |
| ❑ 20 Thomas Steen | 2.00 | .90 |
| ❑ 21 Bill Sutherland CO | .75 | .35 |
| ❑ 22 Tim Trimper | .75 | .35 |
| ❑ 23 Tom Watt CO | .75 | .35 |
| ❑ 24 Tim Watters | .75 | .35 |

## 1982-83 Jets

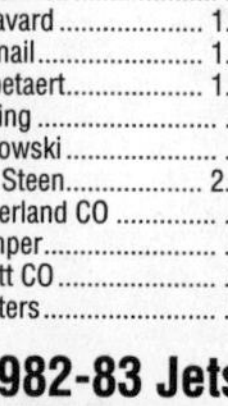

This 28-card set measures approximately 3 1/2" by 5 1/2". The fronts feature white-bordered posed color player photos with the player's name and jersey number printed in blue inside a white bar at the bottom. The backs are blank. The cards are unnumbered and checklisted below in alphabetical order.

| | MINT | NRMT |
|---|---|---|
| COMPLETE SET (28) | 25.00 | 11.00 |
| COMMON CARD (1-28) | .50 | .23 |
| ❑ 1 Scott Arniel | .75 | .35 |
| ❑ 2 Dave Babych | 1.00 | .45 |
| ❑ 3 Jerry Butler | .50 | .23 |
| ❑ 4 Wade Campbell | .50 | .23 |
| ❑ 5 Dave Christian | 1.00 | .45 |
| ❑ 6 Lucien DeBlois | .75 | .35 |
| ❑ 7 Norm Dupont | .50 | .23 |
| ❑ 8 Dale Hawerchuk (Sitting holding trophy) | 7.00 | 3.10 |
| ❑ 9 Dale Hawerchuk | 7.00 | 3.10 |
| ❑ 10 Jim Kyte | .50 | .23 |
| ❑ 11 Craig Levie | .50 | .23 |
| ❑ 12 Willy Lindstrom | .75 | .35 |
| ❑ 13 Morris Lukowich | .50 | .23 |
| ❑ 14 Bengt Lundholm | .75 | .35 |
| ❑ 15 Paul MacLean | .75 | .35 |
| ❑ 16 Jimmy Mann | .50 | .23 |
| ❑ 17 Bryan Maxwell | .50 | .23 |
| ❑ 18 Brian Mullen | .50 | .23 |
| ❑ 19 Serge Savard | 1.00 | .45 |
| ❑ 20 Doug Smail | 1.00 | .45 |
| ❑ 21 Doug Soetaert | .75 | .35 |
| ❑ 22 Don Spring | .50 | .23 |
| ❑ 23 Ed Staniowski | .50 | .23 |
| ❑ 24 Thomas Steen | 1.50 | .70 |
| ❑ 25 Bill Sutherland ACO | .50 | .23 |
| ❑ 26 Tom Watt CO | .50 | .23 |
| ❑ 27 Tim Watters | .50 | .23 |
| ❑ 28 Team Photo | .50 | .23 |

## 1983-84 Jets

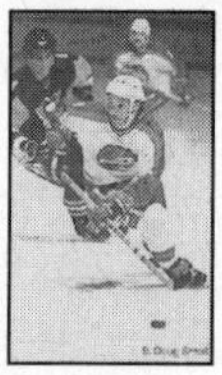

This 25-card set measures 3 1/4" by 5 1/4". The fronts feature full-bleed color action photos with the player's name and jersey number at the lower right corner. The backs are blank. The cards are unnumbered and checklisted below in alphabetical order.

| | MINT | NRMT |
|---|---|---|
| COMPLETE SET (25) | 15.00 | 6.75 |
| COMMON CARD (1-25) | .50 | .23 |
| ❑ 1 Scott Arniel | .50 | .23 |
| ❑ 2 Dave Babych | .75 | .35 |
| ❑ 3 Laurie Boschman | .50 | .23 |
| ❑ 4 Wade Campbell | .50 | .23 |
| ❑ 5 Lucien DeBlois | .75 | .35 |
| ❑ 6 John Ferguson VP/GM | .75 | .35 |
| ❑ 7 John Gibson | .50 | .23 |
| ❑ 8 Dale Hawerchuk | 4.00 | 1.80 |
| ❑ 9 Brian Hayward | 1.00 | .45 |
| ❑ 10 Jim Kyte | .75 | .35 |
| ❑ 11 Barry Long CO | .50 | .23 |
| ❑ 12 Morris Lukowich | .50 | .23 |
| ❑ 13 Bengt Lundholm | .50 | .23 |
| ❑ 14 Paul MacLean | .75 | .35 |
| ❑ 15 Jimmy Mann | .50 | .23 |
| ❑ 16 Moe Mantha | .50 | .23 |
| ❑ 17 Andrew McBain | .50 | .23 |
| ❑ 18 Brian Mullen | .50 | .23 |
| ❑ 19 Robert Picard | .50 | .23 |
| ❑ 20 Doug Smail | .75 | .35 |
| ❑ 21 Doug Soetaert | .75 | .35 |
| ❑ 22 Thomas Steen | .75 | .35 |
| ❑ 23 Tim Watters | .50 | .23 |
| ❑ 24 Ron Wilson | .50 | .23 |
| ❑ 25 Tim Young | .50 | .23 |

## 1984-85 Jets Police

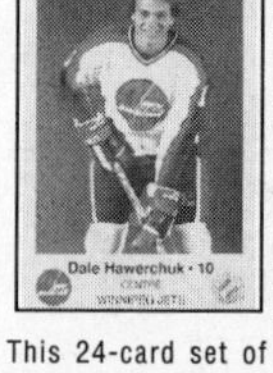

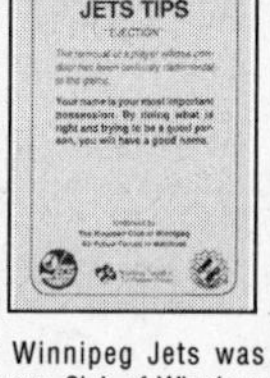


This 24-card set of Winnipeg Jets was sponsored by The Kinsmen Club of Winnipeg and all police forces in Manitoba. The cards measure approximately 2 5/8" by 3 11/16" and were issued in panels of two cards each. The front features a color posed photo of the player shot against a blue background. The borders are white, and the player information beneath the picture is sandwiched between the Jets' and the Kinsmen logos. The back has "Jets Tips" in the form of a hockey tip paralleled by an anti-crime or safety tip. We have checklisted the cards below in alphabetical order, with the uniform number to the right of the player's name.

| | MINT | NRMT |
|---|---|---|
| COMPLETE SET (24) | 8.00 | 3.60 |
| COMMON CARD (1-24) | .25 | .11 |

❑ 1 Scott Arniel 11 .25 .11
❑ 2 Dave Babych 44 .75 .35
❑ 3 Marc Behrend 29 .50 .23
❑ 4 Laurie Boschman 16 .50 .23
❑ 5 Randy Carlyle 8 .75 .35
❑ 6 Dave Ellett 2 1.00 .45
❑ 7 John Ferguson VP/GM .75 .35
❑ 8 Dale Hawerchuk 10 2.00 .90
❑ 9 Brian Hayward 1 1.00 .45
❑ 10 Jim Kyte 6 .25 .11
❑ 11 Morris Lukowich 12 .50 .23
❑ 12 Bengt Lundholm 22 .25 .11
❑ 13 Paul MacLean 15 .75 .35
❑ 14 Andrew McBain 20 .25 .11
❑ 15 Brian Mullen 19 .50 .23
❑ 16 Robert Picard 3 .25 .11
❑ 17 Paul Pooley 23 .25 .11
❑ 18 Doug Smail 9 .75 .35
❑ 19 Thomas Steen 25 1.25 .55
❑ 20 Perry Turnbull 27 .25 .11
❑ 21 Tim Watters 7 .25 .11
❑ 22 Ron Wilson 24 .25 .11
❑ 23 Assistant Coaches .25 .11
Bill Sutherland
Barry Long
Rick Bowness
❑ 24 Team Photo .75 .35

## 1985-86 Jets Police

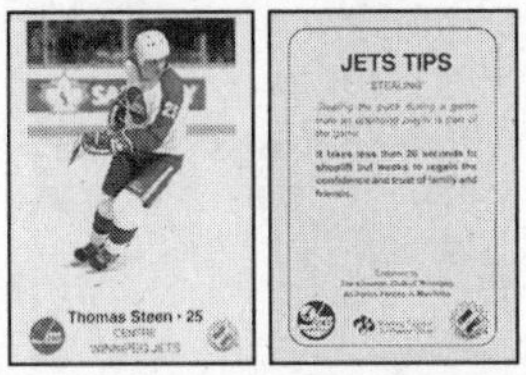


This 24-card set of Winnipeg Jets was sponsored by The Kinsmen Club of Winnipeg and all police forces in Manitoba. The cards measure approximately 2 5/8" by 3 3/4" and were issued in panels of two cards each. The front features a color action shot of the player. The borders are white, and the player information beneath the picture is sandwiched between the Jets' and the Kinsmen logos. The back has "Jets Tips" in the form of a hockey tip paralleled by an anti-crime or safety tip. We have checklisted the cards below in alphabetical order, with the uniform number to the right of the player's name.

| | MINT | NRMT |
|---|---|---|
| COMPLETE SET (24) | 8.00 | 3.60 |
| COMMON CARD (1-24) | .25 | .11 |

❑ 1 Scott Arniel 11 .25 .11
❑ 2 Laurie Boschman 16 .50 .23
❑ 3 Dan Bouchard 35 .50 .23
❑ 4 Randy Carlyle 8 .75 .35
❑ 5 Dave Ellett 2 1.00 .45
❑ 6 John Ferguson VP/GM .50 .23
❑ 7 Dale Hawerchuk 10 2.00 .90
❑ 8 Brian Hayward 1 1.00 .45
❑ 9 Jim Kyte 6 .25 .11
❑ 10 Paul MacLean 15 .75 .35
❑ 11 Mario Marois 22 .25 .11
❑ 12 Andrew McBain 20 .25 .11
❑ 13 Anssi Melametsa 14 .25 .11
❑ 14 Brian Mullen 19 .50 .23
❑ 15 Ray Neufeld 28 .25 .11
❑ 16 Jim Nill 17 .25 .11
❑ 17 Dave Silk 34 .25 .11
❑ 18 Doug Smail 9 .75 .35
❑ 19 Thomas Steen 25 1.25 .55
❑ 20 Perry Turnbull 27 .25 .11
❑ 21 Tim Watters 7 .50 .23
❑ 22 Ron Wilson 24 .50 .23
❑ 23 Assistant Coaches .25 .11
Bill Sutherland
Barry Long
Rick Bowness
❑ 24 Team Photo .50 .23

## 1985-86 Jets Silverwood Dairy

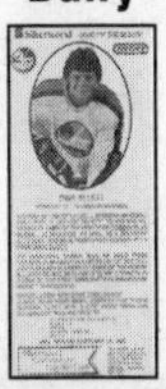

This six-panel set of Winnipeg Jets was issued by Silverwood Dairy on the side of half-gallon milk cartons. The picture and text are printed in blue. The top of the panel features an oval-shaped head and shoulders shot of the player, with his name immediately below the picture. The bottom of the panel presents the instructions for the Silverwood Game of the Month contest, in which ten lucky winners would win a pair of tickets to see the featured game of the month. The panels are unnumbered and checklisted below in alphabetical order.

| | MINT | NRMT |
|---|---|---|
| COMPLETE SET (6) | 60.00 | 27.00 |
| COMMON CARD (1-6) | 10.00 | 4.50 |

❑ 1 Laurie Boschman 10.00 4.50
❑ 2 Randy Carlyle 12.00 5.50
❑ 3 Dave Ellett 12.00 5.50
❑ 4 Dale Hawerchuk 25.00 11.00
❑ 5 Paul MacLean 10.00 4.50
❑ 6 Brian Mullen 12.00 5.50

## 1986-87 Jets Borderless

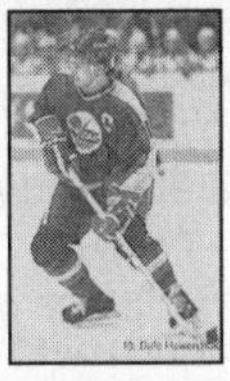

This blank-backed 26-card set measures approximately 3 1/4" by 5 1/4". The fronts have borderless color action player photos. The player's name and uniform number appear on the bottom. The cards are unnumbered and checklisted below in alphabetical order.

| | MINT | NRMT |
|---|---|---|
| COMPLETE SET (26) | 20.00 | 9.00 |
| COMMON CARD (1-26) | .50 | .23 |

❑ 1 Brad Berry .75 .35
❑ 2 Laurie Boschman 1.00 .45
❑ 3 Rick Bowness ACO .50 .23
Dan Maloney CO
Bill Sutherland ACO
❑ 4 Randy Carlyle 2.00 .90
❑ 5 Bill Derlago 1.00 .45
❑ 6 Dave Ellett 1.50 .70
❑ 7 John Ferguson GM 1.00 .45
❑ 8 Gilles Hamel .75 .35
❑ 9 Dale Hawerchuk 4.00 1.80
❑ 10 Hannu Jarvenpaa .75 .35
❑ 11 Jim Kyte .75 .35
❑ 12 Paul MacLean 1.00 .45
❑ 13 Mario Marois .75 .35
❑ 14 Andrew McBain .75 .35
❑ 15 Brian Mullen 1.00 .45
❑ 16 Ray Neufeld .75 .35
❑ 17 Jim Nill .75 .35
❑ 18 Fredrik Olausson 1.50 .70
❑ 19 Steve Penney 1.00 .45
❑ 20 Eldon Reddick 1.00 .45
❑ 21 Doug Smail 1.00 .45
❑ 22 Thomas Steen 1.50 .70
❑ 23 Perry Turnbull .75 .35
❑ 24 Tim Watters .75 .35
❑ 25 Ron Wilson .75 .35
❑ 26 Team Photo 2.00 .90

## 1987-88 Jets

This 24-card set measures approximately 3 1/4" by 5 1/4". The fronts feature autographed color action player photos with the player's jersey number and name in the lower right. The backs are blank. The cards are unnumbered and checklisted below in alphabetical order.

| | MINT | NRMT |
|---|---|---|
| COMPLETE SET (24) | 12.00 | 5.50 |
| COMMON CARD (1-24) | .50 | .23 |

❑ 1 Brad Berry .50 .23
❑ 2 Daniel Berthiaume .75 .35
❑ 3 Laurie Boschman .50 .23
❑ 4 Randy Carlyle .75 .35
❑ 5 Iain Duncan .50 .23
❑ 6 Dave Ellett .75 .35
❑ 7 Pat Elynuik .50 .23
❑ 8 Gilles Hamel .50 .23
❑ 9 Dale Hawerchuk 1.50 .70
❑ 10 Hannu Jarvenpaa .50 .23
❑ 11 Jim Kyte .50 .23
❑ 12 Paul MacLean .75 .35
❑ 13 Mario Marois .50 .23
❑ 14 Andrew McBain .50 .23
❑ 15 Ray Neufeld .50 .23
❑ 16 Fredrik Olausson 1.00 .45
❑ 17 Eldon Reddick .75 .35
❑ 18 Steve Rooney .75 .35
❑ 19 Doug Smail .75 .35
❑ 20 Thomas Steen 1.00 .45
❑ 21 Peter Taglianetti .50 .23
❑ 22 Tim Watters .50 .23
❑ 23 Ron Wilson .50 .23
❑ 24 Team Photo 1.00 .45

## 1988-89 Jets Police

This 24-card set of Winnipeg Jets was sponsored by The Kinsmen Club of Winnipeg and all police forces in Manitoba. The cards measure approximately 2 5/8" by 3 3/4" and were issued as 12 panels of two cards each. By uniform numbers, the panel pairs are CO/TEAM, 39/ACO, 23/4, 6/10, 16/20, 25/32, 19/22, 8/7, 27/28, 2/34, 9/12, and 31/33. The front features a color action shot of the player.

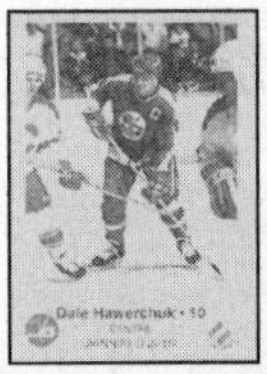


The borders are white, and the player information beneath the picture is sandwiched between the Jets' and the Kinsmen logos. The back has "Jets Tips" in the form of a hockey tip paralleled by an anti-crime or safety tip. We have checklisted the cards below in alphabetical order, with the uniform number to the right of the player's name.

| | MINT | NRMT |
|---|---|---|
| COMPLETE SET (24) | 8.00 | 3.60 |
| COMMON CARD (1-24) | .25 | .11 |

❑ 1 Brent Ashton 7 .25 .11
❑ 2 Laurie Boschman 16 .50 .23
❑ 3 Randy Carlyle 8 .75 .35
❑ 4 Alain Chevrier 31 .50 .23
❑ 5 Iain Duncan 19 .25 .11
❑ 6 Dave Ellett 2 .75 .35
❑ 7 Pat Elynuik 34 .25 .11
❑ 8 Randy Gilhen 39 .25 .11
❑ 9 Dale Hawerchuk 10 1.50 .70
❑ 10 Dave Hunter 12 .25 .11
❑ 11 Hannu Jarvenpaa 23 .25 .11
❑ 12 Jim Kyte 6 .25 .11
❑ 13 Dan Maloney CO .25 .11
❑ 14 Mario Marois 22 .25 .11
❑ 15 Andrew McBain 20 .25 .11
❑ 16 Ray Neufeld 28 .25 .11
❑ 17 Teppo Numminen 27 .75 .35
❑ 18 Fredrik Olausson 4 .50 .23
❑ 19 Eldon Reddick 33 .50 .23
❑ 20 Doug Smail 9 .50 .23
❑ 21 Thomas Steen 25 .75 .35
❑ 22 Peter Taglianetti 32 .25 .11
❑ 23 Assistant Coaches .25 .11
Bill Sutherland
Bruce Southern
Rick St.Croix
❑ 24 Team Photo .75 .35

## 1989-90 Jets Safeway

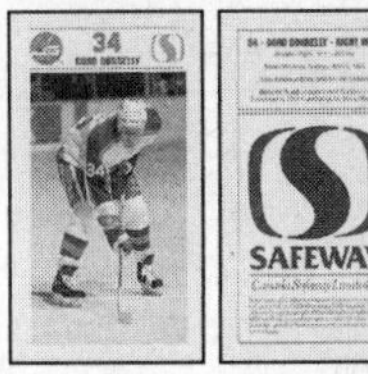


This 30-card set was sponsored by Safeway Limited of Canada and features players from the Winnipeg Jets. The cards measure approximately 3 3/4" by 6 7/8". The front has a color action photo of the player, with his number and name above the picture between the Jets' and Safeway logos. The back is outlined in black boxes and includes player information as well as a oversized Safeway logo and advertisement. Since the cards are unnumbered, they are listed below in alphabetical order with the player's sweater number after the name.

| | MINT | NRMT |
|---|---|---|
| COMPLETE SET (30) | 12.00 | 5.50 |
| COMMON CARD (1-30) | .25 | .11 |

❑ 1 Brent Ashton 7 .50 .23
❑ 2 Stu Barnes 14 .75 .35
❑ 3 Brad Berry 29 .50 .23
❑ 4 Daniel Berthiaume 30 .75 .35
❑ 5 Laurie Boschman 16 .50 .23
❑ 6 Randy Carlyle 8 .75 .35
❑ 7 Shawn Cronin 44 .50 .23
❑ 8 Randy Cunneyworth 18 .50 .23
❑ 9 Gord Donnelly 34 .50 .23
❑ 10 Tom Draper 37 .75 .35
❑ 11 Iain Duncan 19 .50 .23
❑ 12 Dave Ellett 2 .75 .35
❑ 13 Pat Elynuik 15 .50 .23
❑ 14 Bob Essensa 35 .75 .35
❑ 15 Paul Fenton 11 .50 .23
❑ 16 Dale Hawerchuk 10 1.50 .70
❑ 17 Brent Hughes 46 .50 .23
❑ 18 Mark Kumpel 21 .50 .23
❑ 19 Moe Mantha 22 .50 .23
❑ 20 Dave McLlwain 20 .50 .23
❑ 21 Brian McReynolds 26 .50 .23
❑ 22 Teppo Numminen 27 .75 .35
❑ 23 Fredrik Olausson 4 .75 .35
❑ 24 Greg Paslawski 28 .50 .23
❑ 25 Doug Smail 12 .75 .35
❑ 26 Thomas Steen 25 .75 .35
❑ 27 Peter Taglianetti 32 .50 .23
❑ 28 Benny 00 (Mascot) .25 .11
❑ 29 Coaches Card .25 .11
Alpo Suhonen
Bob Murdoch
Clare Drake
❑ 30 Team Photo 1.00 .45

## 1990-91 Jets IGA

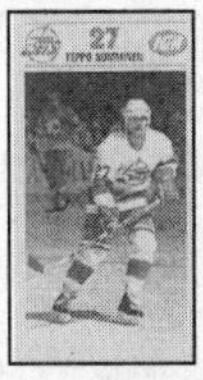


This 35-card set measures approximately 3 1/2" by 6 1/2" and features color action player photos with white borders. The team logo, sweater number, player's name, and sponsor logo appear at the card top between two thin purple stripes. The back is divided into two sections; in the upper appears player information, while in the lower appears a GreenCare advertisement (environmentally safe and carried in IGA stores). The cards are unnumbered and checklisted below in alphabetical order.

| | MINT | NRMT |
|---|---|---|
| COMPLETE SET (35) | 10.00 | 4.50 |
| COMMON CARD (1-35) | .25 | .11 |

❑ 1 Scott Arniel .35 .16
❑ 2 Brent Ashton .35 .16
❑ 3 Don Barber .35 .16
❑ 4 Stephane Beauregard .50 .23
❑ 5 Randy Carlyle .75 .35
❑ 6 Danton Cole .35 .16
❑ 7 Shawn Cronin .35 .16
❑ 8 Gord Donnelly .35 .16
❑ 9 Clare Drake CO .25 .11
❑ 10 Kris Draper 1.00 .45
❑ 11 Iain Duncan .35 .16
❑ 12 Pat Elynuik .35 .16
❑ 13 Bob Essensa .50 .23
❑ 14 Doug Evans .35 .16
❑ 15 Phil Housley 1.00 .45
❑ 16 Sergei Kharin .35 .16
❑ 17 Mark Kumpel .35 .16
❑ 18 Guy Larose .35 .16
❑ 19 Paul MacDermid .35 .16
❑ 20 Moe Mantha .35 .16
❑ 21 Brian Marchment .50 .23
❑ 22 Dave McLlwain .35 .16
❑ 23 Bob Murdoch CO .25 .11
❑ 24 Teppo Numminen .75 .35
❑ 25 Fredrik Olausson .50 .23
❑ 26 Ed Olczyk .50 .23
❑ 27 Mark Osborne .35 .16
❑ 28 Greg Paslawski .35 .16
❑ 29 Terry Simpson CO .25 .11
❑ 30 Thomas Steen .75 .35
❑ 31 Phil Sykes .35 .16
❑ 32 Rick Tabaracci .60 .25
❑ 33 Simon Wheeldon .35 .16
❑ 34 Benny (Mascot) .25 .11
❑ 35 Team Photo 1.00 .45

## 1991 Jets Panini Team Stickers

This 32-sticker set was issued in a plastic bag that contained two 16-sticker sheets (approximately 9" by 12") and a foldout poster, "Super Poster - Hockey 91", on which the stickers could be affixed. The players' names appear only on the poster, not on the stickers. Each sticker measures about 2 1/8" by 2 7/8" and features a color player action shot on its white-bordered front. The back of the white sticker sheet is lined off into 16 panels, each carrying the logos for Panini, the NHL, and the NHLPA, as well as the same number that appears on the front of the sticker. Every Canadian NHL team was featured in this promotion. Each team set was available by mail-order from Panini Canada Ltd. for 2.99 plus 50 cents for shipping and handling.

| | MINT | NRMT |
|---|---|---|
| COMPLETE SET (32) | 2.50 | 1.10 |
| COMMON STICKER (1-24) | .05 | .02 |
| COMMON STICKER (A-H) | .05 | .02 |

❑ 1 Scott Arniel .10 .05
❑ 2 Brent Ashton .10 .05
❑ 3 Stephane Beauregard .10 .05
❑ 4 Randy Carlyle .10 .05
❑ 5 Danton Cole .05 .02
❑ 6 Shawn Cronin .05 .02
❑ 7 Gord Donnelly .05 .02
❑ 8 Kris Draper .15 .07
❑ 9 Dave Ellett .10 .05
❑ 10 Pat Elynuik .05 .02
❑ 11 Doug Evans .05 .02
❑ 12 Paul Fenton .05 .02
❑ 13 Phil Housley .25 .11
❑ 14 Mark Kumpel .05 .02
❑ 15 Paul MacDermid .05 .02
❑ 16 Moe Mantha .05 .02
❑ 17 Dave McLlwain .05 .02
❑ 18 Teppo Numminen .15 .07
❑ 19 Fredrik Olausson .10 .05
❑ 20 Greg Paslawski .05 .02
❑ 21 Doug Smail .05 .02
❑ 22 Thomas Steen .10 .05
❑ 23 Phil Sykes .05 .02
❑ 24 Rick Tabaracci .15 .07
❑ A Team Logo .05 .02
Left Side
❑ B Team Logo .05 .02
Right Side
❑ C Jets in Action .05 .02
Upper Left Corner
❑ D Jets in Action .05 .02
Lower Left Corner
❑ E Jets in Action .05 .02
Upper Right Corner
❑ F Jets in Action .05 .02
Lower Right Corner
❑ G Paul Fenton .05 .02
❑ H Phil Housley .25 .11

## 1991-92 Jets IGA

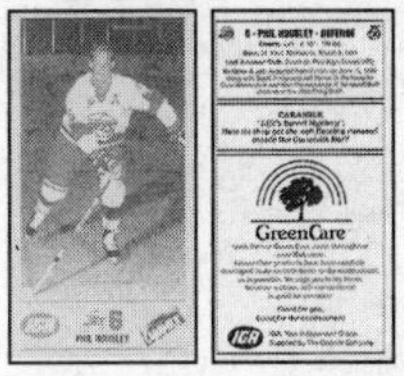


This 35-card set measures approximately 3 1/2" by 6 1/2" and features color action player photos with white borders. The IGA logo, sweater number, player's name, and a picture of Cadbury's Caramilk candy appear at the card bottom between two thin purple stripes. The back is divided into three sections; in the top appears player information; in the middle and bottom appear ads for Caramilk and GreenCare, respectively. The front of the Thomas Steen card shows (in lower right corner) another Cadbury candy bar/product, "Crunchie". The cards are unnumbered and checklisted below in alphabetical order.

| | MINT | NRMT |
|---|---|---|
| COMPLETE SET (35) | 10.00 | 4.50 |
| COMMON CARD (1-35) | .25 | .11 |

❑ 1 Stu Barnes .50 .23
❑ 2 Stephane Beauregard .50 .23
❑ 3 Luciano Borsato .35 .16
❑ 4 Randy Carlyle .50 .23
❑ 5 Danton Cole .35 .16
❑ 6 Shawn Cronin .35 .16
❑ 7 Burton Cummings .50 .23
❑ 8 Mike Eagles .35 .16
❑ 9 Pat Elynuik .35 .16
❑ 10 Bryan Erickson .35 .16
❑ 11 Bob Essensa .50 .23
❑ 12 Doug Evans .35 .16
❑ 13 Mike Hartman .35 .16
❑ 14 Phil Housley .75 .35
❑ 15 Dean Kennedy .35 .16
❑ 16 Paul MacDermid .35 .16
❑ 17 Moe Mantha .35 .16
❑ 18 Rob Murray .35 .16
❑ 19 Troy Murray .35 .16
❑ 20 Teppo Numminen .50 .23
❑ 21 Fredrik Olausson .50 .23
❑ 22 Ed Olczyk .35 .16
❑ 23 Mark Osborne .35 .16
❑ 24 John Paddock CO .25 .11
❑ 25 Kent Paynter .35 .16
❑ 26 Dave Prior .35 .16
❑ 27 Russ Romaniuk .35 .16
❑ 28 Darrin Shannon .50 .23
❑ 29 Terry Simpson CO .25 .11
❑ 30 Thomas Steen .50 .23
❑ 31 Phil Sykes .35 .16
❑ 32 Rick Tabaracci .50 .23
❑ 33 Glen Williamson CO .25 .11
❑ 34 Benny (Mascot) .25 .11
❑ 35 Team Photo UER .75 .35
(Incorrectly
marked 1990-91)

## 1993-94 Jets Ruffles

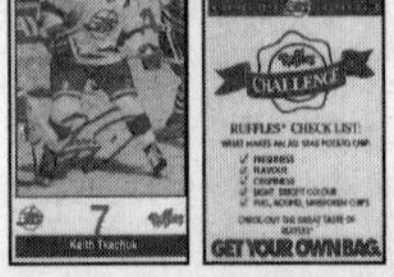


This 29-postcard set measures approximately 3 1/2" by 6 1/2" and features color action player photos with a thin black border on a white background. The player's name is printed in white in a black bar across the bottom in the wide white border with the team logo, jersey number and sponsor logo printed in red and blue above the bar. The backs carry the player's name, jersey number, position, and biographical information in black print on a white background above a Ruffles Challenge logo and checklist for an all-star potato chip.

The cards are unnumbered and checklisted below in alphabetical order.

| | MINT | NRMT |
|---|---|---|
| COMPLETE SET (29) | 15.00 | 6.75 |
| COMMON CARD (1-29) | .25 | .11 |
| ❑ 1 Stu Barnes | .75 | .35 |
| ❑ 2 Sergei Bautin | .35 | .16 |
| ❑ 3 Stephane Beauregard | .50 | .23 |
| ❑ 4 Benny (Mascot) | .25 | .11 |
| ❑ 5 Zinetula Bilyaletdinov ACO | .25 | .11 |
| ❑ 6 Arto Blomsten | .35 | .16 |
| ❑ 7 Luciano Borsato | .35 | .16 |
| ❑ 8 Tie Domi | 1.00 | .45 |
| ❑ 9 Mike Eagles | .35 | .16 |
| ❑ 10 Nelson Emerson | .75 | .35 |
| ❑ 11 Bryan Erickson | .35 | .16 |
| ❑ 12 Bob Essensa | .50 | .23 |
| ❑ 13 Yan Kaminsky | .35 | .16 |
| ❑ 14 Dean Kennedy | .35 | .16 |
| ❑ 15 Kris King | .35 | .16 |
| ❑ 16 Boris Mironov | .60 | .25 |
| ❑ 17 Andy Murray ACO | .25 | .11 |
| ❑ 18 Teppo Numminen | .60 | .25 |
| ❑ 19 Fredrik Olausson | .35 | .16 |
| ❑ 20 John Paddock CO | .25 | .11 |
| ❑ 21 Stephane Quintal | .35 | .16 |
| ❑ 22 Teemu Selanne | 5.00 | 2.20 |
| ❑ 23 Darrin Shannon | .35 | .16 |
| ❑ 24 Thomas Steen | .75 | .35 |
| ❑ 25 Keith Tkachuk | 2.50 | 1.10 |
| ❑ 26 Igor Ulanov | .35 | .16 |
| ❑ 27 Paul Ysebaert | .35 | .16 |
| ❑ 28 Alexei Zhamnov | 1.00 | .45 |
| ❑ 29 Team Picture | .50 | .23 |

## 1995-96 Jets Readers Club

This set of 12 bookmarks features the Winnipeg Jets. The top of the front features a player photo, his name and jersey number along with a quote on the importance of reading and a pre-printed autograph. The backs display the logos of the various corporate sponsors of this program. The bookmarks were distributed to children who successfully read a number of books.

| | MINT | NRMT |
|---|---|---|
| COMPLETE SET (12) | 8.00 | 3.60 |
| COMMON CARD (1-12) | .25 | .11 |
| ❑ 1 Tim Cheveldae | .50 | .23 |
| ❑ 2 Dallas Drake | .25 | .11 |
| ❑ 3 Mike Eastwood | .25 | .11 |
| ❑ 4 Nikolai Khabibulin | 1.00 | .45 |
| ❑ 5 Kris King | .50 | .23 |
| ❑ 6 Igor Korolev | .25 | .11 |
| ❑ 7 Dave Manson | .25 | .11 |
| ❑ 8 Teppo Numminen | .50 | .23 |
| ❑ 9 Teemu Selanne | 3.00 | 1.35 |
| ❑ 10 Darrin Shannon | .25 | .11 |
| ❑ 11 Keith Tkachuk | 1.50 | .70 |
| ❑ 12 Alexei Zhamnov | 1.00 | .45 |

## 1995-96 Jets Team Issue

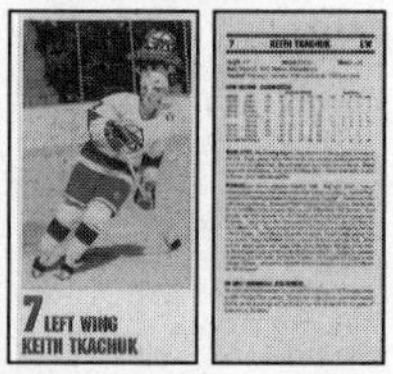


This 26-card set measures approximately 3 1/2" by 6 1/2" and features color action player photos in a white border. The player's name, position, and jersey number are printed in the wide bottom margin. The backs carry player information. The cards are unnumbered and checklisted below in alphabetical order.

| | MINT | NRMT |
|---|---|---|
| COMPLETE SET (26) | 10.00 | 4.50 |
| COMMON CARD (1-26) | .10 | .05 |
| ❑ 1 Title Card | .35 | .16 |
| ❑ 2 Benny (Mascot) | .10 | .05 |
| ❑ 3 Tim Cheveldae | .50 | .23 |
| ❑ 4 Coaches Card | .25 | .11 |
| Terry Simpson CO | | |
| Perry Pearn ACO | | |
| Randy Carlyle ACO | | |
| ❑ 5 Shane Doan | .50 | .23 |
| ❑ 6 Jason Doig | .35 | .16 |
| ❑ 7 Dallas Drake | .35 | .16 |
| ❑ 8 Mike Eastwood | .35 | .16 |
| ❑ 9 Randy Gilhen | .35 | .16 |
| ❑ 10 Nikolai Khabibulin | 1.50 | .70 |
| ❑ 11 Kris King | .35 | .16 |
| ❑ 12 Igor Korolev | .35 | .16 |
| ❑ 13 Stewart Malgunas | .35 | .16 |
| ❑ 14 Dave Manson | .35 | .16 |
| ❑ 15 Jim McKenzie | .35 | .16 |
| ❑ 16 Teppo Numminen | .35 | .16 |
| ❑ 17 Eddie Olczyk | .35 | .16 |
| ❑ 18 Deron Quint | .50 | .23 |
| ❑ 19 Ed Ronan | .35 | .16 |
| ❑ 20 Teemu Selanne | 3.00 | 1.35 |
| ❑ 21 Darrin Shannon | .35 | .16 |
| ❑ 22 Darryl Shannon | .35 | .16 |
| ❑ 23 Mike Stapleton | .35 | .16 |
| ❑ 24 Keith Tkachuk | 1.50 | .70 |
| ❑ 25 Darren Turcotte | .35 | .16 |
| ❑ 26 Alexei Zhamnov | .75 | .35 |

## 1992 Jofa/Koho

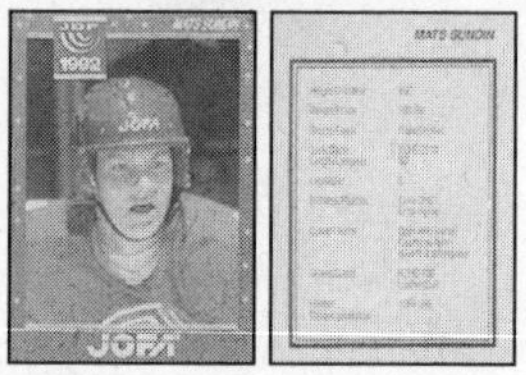

This six-card standard-size set was apparently sponsored by four major brands of hockey equipment: Jofa, Koho, Titan, and Canadien. The set is also known as "The Endorsers" and features six famous current players who endorse their respective products. The cards are printed on thin card stock. The fronts feature color close-up player photos. The borders shade from one color to another and are studded with miniature stars. On various pastel-colored backs, biographical information is presented inside black border stripes. The cards are unnumbered and checklisted below in alphabetical order. The manufacturer's name that appears at the bottom of the card front is listed below beneath the player's name.

| | MINT | NRMT |
|---|---|---|
| COMPLETE SET (6) | 12.00 | 5.50 |
| COMMON CARD (1-6) | 1.00 | .45 |
| ❑ 1 Theoren Fleury | 2.00 | .90 |
| Jofa | | |
| ❑ 2 Jari Kurri | 1.00 | .45 |
| Koho | | |
| ❑ 3 Mario Lemieux | 5.00 | 2.20 |
| Koho | | |
| ❑ 4 Eric Lindros | 4.00 | 1.80 |
| Titan | | |
| ❑ 5 Denis Savard | 1.00 | .45 |
| Canadien | | |
| ❑ 6 Mats Sundin | 1.50 | .70 |
| Jofa | | |

## 1972 Kellogg's Iron-On Transfers

These six iron-on transfers each measure approximately 6 1/2" by 10". Each transfer consists of a cartoon drawing of the player's body with an oversized head. The puck is comically portrayed with human characteristics (face, arms, and legs). A facsimile player autograph appears below the drawing. At the bottom are instructions in English and French for applying the iron-on to clothing; these are to be cut off before application. These iron-on transfers are unnumbered and checklisted below in alphabetical order.

| | NRMT-MT | EXC |
|---|---|---|
| COMPLETE SET (6) | 300.00 | 135.00 |
| COMMON TRANSFER (1-6) | 25.00 | 11.00 |
| ❑ 1 Ron Ellis | 25.00 | 11.00 |
| ❑ 2 Phil Esposito | 75.00 | 34.00 |
| ❑ 3 Rod Gilbert | 40.00 | 18.00 |
| ❑ 4 Bobby Hull | 125.00 | 55.00 |
| ❑ 5 Frank Mahovlich | 40.00 | 18.00 |
| ❑ 6 Stan Mikita | 50.00 | 22.00 |

## 1984-85 Kellogg's Accordion Discs

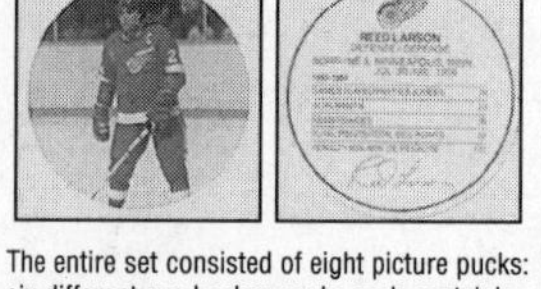

The entire set consisted of eight picture pucks: six different pro hockey pucks each containing action shots and personal records for six NHL players, and two different sports pucks each featuring achievements of six famous female athletes. Each puck came with a stick-on NHL Team Emblem or Sports Crest. The pucks were inserted in specially marked packages of Kellogg's Cereals in Canada. By finding instant prize messages inside the picture pucks, one could win sports equipment, such as hockey jerseys, skates, sport bags, or hockey sticks. The promotion also included a mail-in offer for a plastic collector's shield that would hold all the picture pucks and be mounted on a wall.

This set of thin cardboard discs measure approximately 2" in diameter. Six discs are joined together at their sides (like the bellows of an accordion) and were issued in a thin black plastic case. The front features a round-shaped color action photo with white border. The back provides biographical and statistical information in French and English, with the team logo at the top and a facsimile autograph at the bottom. The complete set price below includes only one of the variation pairs.

| | MINT | NRMT |
|---|---|---|
| COMPLETE SET (8) | 40.00 | 18.00 |
| COMMON PANEL (1-8) | 4.00 | 1.80 |
| ❑ 1 Dino Ciccarelli | 7.00 | 3.10 |
| Mike Bossy | | |
| Richard Brodeur | | |
| Michel Goulet | | |
| Jari Kurri | | |
| Paul Reinhart | | |
| ❑ 2 Reed Larson | 5.00 | 2.20 |
| Marcel Dionne | | |
| Peter Statsny | | |
| Paul MacLean | | |
| Doug Risebrough | | |
| Larry Robinson | | |
| ❑ 3A Stanley Cup | 6.00 | 2.70 |
| Gilbert Perreault | | |
| Rick Middleton | | |
| Bob Gainey | | |
| Kevin Lowe | | |
| Borje Salming | | |
| ❑ 3B Stanley Cup | 6.00 | 2.70 |
| Gilbert Perreault | | |
| Rick Middleton | | |
| Guy Lafleur | | |
| Kevin Lowe | | |
| Borje Salming | | |
| ❑ 4 Bernie Federko | 6.00 | 2.70 |
| Ron Francis | | |
| Stan Smyl | | |
| Mike Gartner | | |
| Dave Babych | | |
| Lanny McDonald | | |
| ❑ 5A Barry Beck | 5.00 | 2.20 |
| Rick Kehoe | | |
| Dale Hawerchuk | | |
| John Anderson | | |
| Mario Tremblay | | |
| Paul Coffey | | |
| ❑ 5B Barry Beck | 5.00 | 2.20 |
| Denis Herron | | |
| Dale Hawerchuk | | |
| Dan Daoust | | |
| Mario Tremblay | | |
| Paul Coffey | | |
| ❑ 6 Thomas Gradin | 5.00 | 2.20 |
| Dale Hunter | | |
| Doug Wilson | | |
| Darryl Sittler | | |
| Glenn Resch | | |
| Rick Vaive | | |
| ❑ 7 Tracy Austin | 4.00 | 1.80 |
| Tennis | | |
| Olga Korbut | | |
| Gymnastics | | |
| Kathy Kreiner | | |
| Alpine Skiing | | |
| Angela Taylor | | |
| Track and Field | | |
| Anne Ottenbrite | | |
| Swimming | | |
| Paul Martini | | |
| Skating | | |
| Barbara Underhill | | |
| Skating | | |
| ❑ 8 Tatiana Kolpakova | 4.00 | 1.80 |
| Long Jump | | |
| Kay Thompson | | |
| Skating | | |
| Kornelia Ender | | |
| Swimming | | |
| Melanie Smith | | |
| Equestrian | | |
| Nadia Comaneci | | |
| Gymnastics | | |
| Carling Bassett | | |
| Tennis | | |

## 1992 Kellogg's Trophies

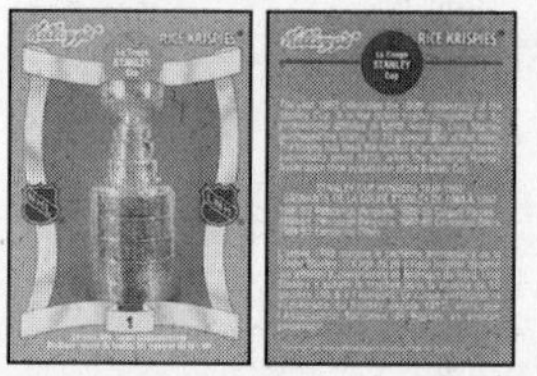

Protected by a clear plastic cello pack, these 11 cards were inserted into Kellogg's Rice Krispies cereal boxes in Canada. The cards measure approximately 2 3/8" by 3 1/4" and are printed on thin card stock. The fronts feature a color photo of the trophy inside a gold border on a turquoise card face. The name of the trophy appears in a red circle at the center of the top. The backs are red and carry text in white print about the trophy. All text on both sides is in English and French.

The cards are numbered on the front at the bottom center.

| | MINT | NRMT |
|---|---|---|
| COMPLETE SET (11) | 20.00 | 9.00 |
| COMMON CARD (1-11) | 2.00 | .90 |
| ❑ 1 Stanley Cup | 3.00 | 1.35 |
| ❑ 2 Presidents' Trophy | 2.00 | .90 |
| ❑ 3 Hart Memorial Trophy | 2.00 | .90 |
| ❑ 4 Conn Smythe Trophy | 2.00 | .90 |
| ❑ 5 Vezina Trophy | 2.00 | .90 |
| ❑ 6 James Norris Memorial Trophy | 2.00 | .90 |
| ❑ 7 Calder Memorial Trophy | 2.00 | .90 |
| ❑ 8 Frank J. Selke Trophy | 2.00 | .90 |
| ❑ 9 Lady Byng Memorial Trophy | 2.00 | .90 |
| ❑ 10 Art Ross Trophy | 2.00 | .90 |
| ❑ 11 Jack Adams Trophy | 2.00 | .90 |

## 1992-93 Kellogg's Posters

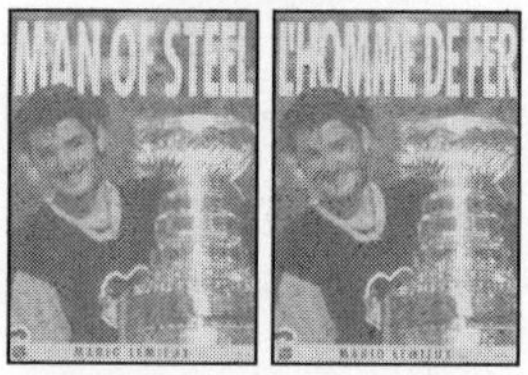


These 9 1/4" by 14" posters were inserted inside specially marked Kellogg's products. The two-sided posters each bear the same photo, with the descriptive legend at the top written in French on one side and English on the other. The bottom of the poster features the player's name, along with the logos of the NHL and Kellogg's. The posters were folded into card-sized squares and then placed into a protective cellophane seal. All posters, therefore, are subject to extreme creasing, and are considered in top condition in this form. The checklist below may be incomplete. Collectors with additional information are encouraged to forward it to the publisher.

| | MINT | NRMT |
|---|---|---|
| COMPLETE SET | 40.00 | 18.00 |
| COMMON POSTER | 3.00 | 1.35 |
| ❑ 1 Mario Lemieux | 20.00 | 9.00 |
| ❑ 2 Mark Messier | 5.00 | 2.20 |
| ❑ 3 Luc Robitaille | 3.00 | 1.35 |
| ❑ 4 Patrick Roy | 15.00 | 6.75 |
| ❑ 5 Cornelius Rooster | 3.00 | 1.35 |
| Mascot | | |

## 1995-96 Kellogg's Donruss

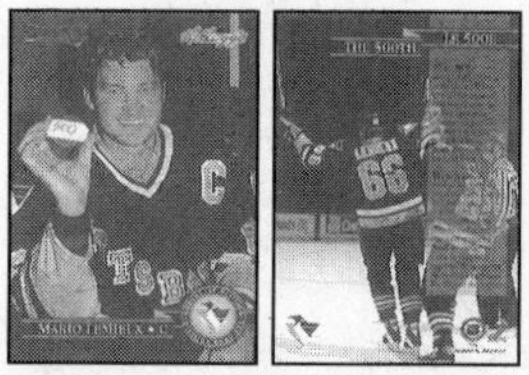

This six-card set was distributed in specially-marked boxes of Kellogg's Cereal in Canada and features color photos of hockey stars Mario Lemieux and Brett Hull. The backs carry another color player photo with the card title and explanation of the title. The cards are unnumbered and listed below as Mario Lemieux (1-4) and Brett Hull (5-6).

| | MINT | NRMT |
|---|---|---|
| COMPLETE SET (6) | 30.00 | 13.50 |
| COMMON CARD (1-6) | 3.00 | 1.35 |
| ❑ 1 Mario Lemieux | 7.50 | 3.40 |
| The Fiver | | |
| ❑ 2 Mario Lemieux | 7.50 | 3.40 |
| The Cup | | |
| ❑ 3 Mario Lemieux | 7.50 | 3.40 |
| The 500th | | |
| ❑ 4 Mario Lemieux | 7.50 | 3.40 |
| The Comeback | | |
| ❑ 5 Brett Hull | 3.00 | 1.35 |
| 50 in 49 | | |
| ❑ 6 Brett Hull | 3.00 | 1.35 |
| The MVP | | |

## 1980-81 Kings Card Night

The cards in this 14-card set are in color and are standard size. The set was produced during the 1980-81 season by All-Star Cards Ltd. for the Los Angeles Kings at the request of owner Jerry Buss. Reportedly 5000 sets were produced, virtually all of which were given away at the Kings' "Card Night." The

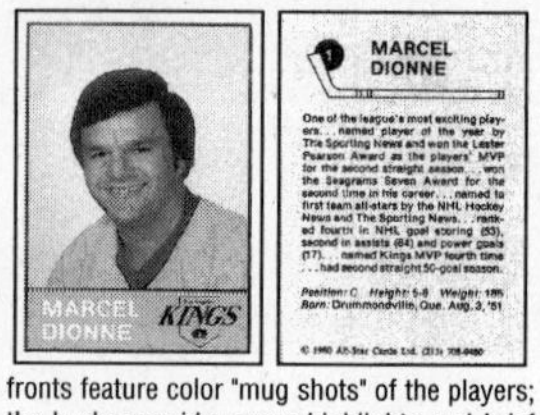


fronts feature color "mug shots" of the players; the backs provide career highlights and brief biographical information.

| | NRMT-MT | EXC |
|---|---|---|
| COMPLETE SET (14) | 15.00 | 6.75 |
| COMMON CARD (1-14) | .75 | .35 |
| ❑ 1 Marcel Dionne | 6.00 | 2.70 |
| ❑ 2 Glenn Goldup | .75 | .35 |
| ❑ 3 Doug Halward | .75 | .35 |
| ❑ 4 Billy Harris | 1.00 | .45 |
| ❑ 5 Steve Jensen | 1.00 | .45 |
| ❑ 6 Jerry Korab | .75 | .35 |
| ❑ 7 Mario Lessard | 1.50 | .70 |
| ❑ 8 Dave Lewis | 1.00 | .45 |
| ❑ 9 Mike Murphy | .75 | .35 |
| ❑ 10 Rob Palmer | .75 | .35 |
| ❑ 11 Charlie Simmer | 2.00 | .90 |
| ❑ 12 Dave Taylor | 3.00 | 1.35 |
| ❑ 13 Garry Unger | 1.50 | .70 |
| ❑ 14 Jay Wells | 1.00 | .45 |

## 1984-85 Kings Smokey

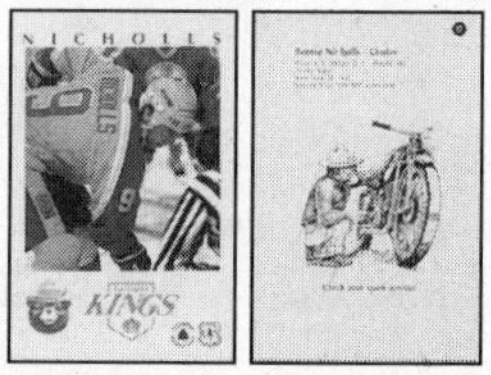

This fire safety set contains 23 cards which are numbered on the back. Players in the set are members of the Los Angeles Kings hockey team. The cards measure approximately 2 15/16" by 4 3/8" and are numbered on the back in the upper right corner. Card backs contain a fire safety cartoon and minimal information about the player. The set was sponsored by the California Department of Forestry.

| | MINT | NRMT |
|---|---|---|
| COMPLETE SET (23) | 15.00 | 6.75 |
| COMMON CARD (1-23) | .50 | .23 |
| ❑ 1 Russ Anderson | .50 | .23 |
| ❑ 2 Marcel Dionne | 5.00 | 2.20 |
| ❑ 3 Brian Engblom | .75 | .35 |
| ❑ 4 Daryl Evans | .50 | .23 |
| ❑ 5 Jim Fox | .75 | .35 |
| ❑ 6 Garry Galley | 1.50 | .70 |
| ❑ 7 Anders Hakansson | .50 | .23 |
| ❑ 8 Mark Hardy | .50 | .23 |
| ❑ 9 Bob Janecyk | .75 | .35 |
| ❑ 10 John Paul Kelly | .50 | .23 |
| ❑ 11 Brian MacLellan | .50 | .23 |
| ❑ 12 Bernie Nicholls | 2.50 | 1.10 |
| ❑ 13 Craig Redmond | .50 | .23 |
| ❑ 14 Terry Ruskowski | .75 | .35 |
| ❑ 15 Doug Smith | .50 | .23 |
| ❑ 16 Dave Taylor | 2.00 | .90 |
| ❑ 17 Jay Wells | .50 | .23 |
| ❑ 18 Darren Eliot | .75 | .35 |
| ❑ 19 Rick Lapointe | .50 | .23 |
| ❑ 20 Bob Miller | .50 | .23 |
| ❑ 21 Steve Seguin | .50 | .23 |
| ❑ 22 Phil Sykes | .50 | .23 |
| ❑ 23 Pat Quinn CO | .50 | .23 |

## 1986-87 Kings 20th Anniversary Team Issue

Cards measure 4" x 6 1/4" and feature black and white photos on the front along with player name and 20th anniversary logo. Backs are blank.

| | MINT | NRMT |
|---|---|---|
| COMPLETE SET (23) | 20.00 | 9.00 |
| COMMON CARD (1-23) | .25 | .11 |
| ❑ 1 Bob Bourne | .25 | .11 |
| ❑ 2 Jimmy Carson | 2.00 | .90 |
| ❑ 3 Steve Duchesne | 2.00 | .90 |
| ❑ 4 Darren Eliot | .25 | .11 |
| ❑ 5 Bryan Erickson | .25 | .11 |
| ❑ 6 Jim Fox | .25 | .11 |
| ❑ 7 Garry Galley | 1.00 | .45 |
| ❑ 8 Paul Guay | .25 | .11 |
| ❑ 9 Mark Hardy | .25 | .11 |
| ❑ 10 Bob Janecyk | .75 | .35 |
| ❑ 11 Dean Kennedy | .25 | .11 |
| ❑ 12 Grant Ledyard | .50 | .23 |
| ❑ 13 Morris Lukowich | .25 | .11 |
| ❑ 14 Sean McKenna | .25 | .11 |
| ❑ 15 Roland Melanson | .75 | .35 |
| ❑ 16 Bernie Nicholls | 2.00 | .90 |
| ❑ 17 Joe Paterson | .25 | .11 |
| ❑ 18 Larry Playfair | .25 | .11 |
| ❑ 19 Luc Robitaille | 8.00 | 3.60 |

| | MINT | NRMT |
|---|---|---|
| ❑ 20 Phil Sykes | .25 | .11 |
| ❑ 21 Dave Taylor | .75 | .35 |
| ❑ 22 Jay Wells | .25 | .11 |
| ❑ 23 Dave Williams | .75 | .35 |

## 1987-88 Kings Team Issue 4x6

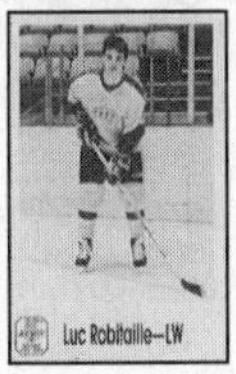


Issued to commemorate the Kings' 20th season, the 23 blank-backed photos comprising this set measure approximately 4" by 6 1/4" and feature white-bordered, black-and-white photos of Kings player's suited-up and posed on the ice. The player's name, along with the 20th Kings Season logo, appear in black lettering within the lower margin. The photos are unnumbered and checklisted below in alphabetical order. The set features early cards of Jimmy Carson, Steve Duchesne, and Luc Robitaille.

| | MINT | NRMT |
|---|---|---|
| COMPLETE SET (23) | 25.00 | 11.00 |
| COMMON CARD (1-23) | .50 | .23 |
| ❑ 1 Bob Bourne | .75 | .35 |
| ❑ 2 Jimmy Carson | 1.00 | .45 |
| ❑ 3 Steve Duchesne | 3.00 | 1.35 |
| ❑ 4 Darren Eliot | 1.00 | .45 |
| ❑ 5 Bryan Erickson | .50 | .23 |
| ❑ 6 Jim Fox | .75 | .35 |
| ❑ 7 Garry Galley | 1.50 | .70 |
| ❑ 8 Paul Guay | .50 | .23 |
| ❑ 9 Mark Hardy | .75 | .35 |
| ❑ 10 Bob Janecyk | 1.00 | .45 |
| ❑ 11 Dean Kennedy | .50 | .23 |
| ❑ 12 Grant Ledyard | .75 | .35 |
| ❑ 13 Morris Lukowich | .50 | .23 |
| ❑ 14 Sean McKenna | .50 | .23 |
| ❑ 15 Roland Melanson | 1.00 | .45 |
| ❑ 16 Bernie Nicholls | 3.00 | 1.35 |
| ❑ 17 Joe Paterson | .50 | .23 |
| ❑ 18 Larry Playfair | .50 | .23 |
| ❑ 19 Luc Robitaille | 8.00 | 3.60 |
| ❑ 20 Phil Sykes | .50 | .23 |
| ❑ 21 Dave Taylor | 2.00 | .90 |
| ❑ 22 Jay Wells | .50 | .23 |
| ❑ 23 Dave(Tiger) Williams | 1.50 | .70 |

## 1988-89 Kings Smokey

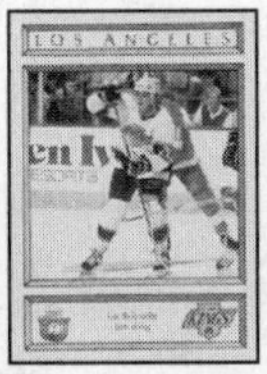

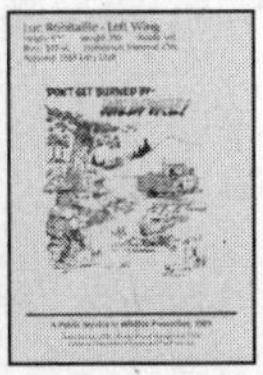

This fire safety set contains 25 cards and features members of the Los Angeles Kings hockey team in their then-new silver and black colors. The cards are unnumbered; not even the player's uniform number is given on the card. The players are listed below alphabetically by name. The cards measure approximately 2 1/2" by 3 1/2". Card backs contain a fire safety cartoon and minimal information about the player. The set was sponsored by the California Department of Forestry and Fire Protection.

| | MINT | NRMT |
|---|---|---|
| COMPLETE SET (25) | 30.00 | 13.50 |
| COMMON CARD (1-25) | .25 | .11 |
| ❑ 1 Mike Allison | .50 | .23 |
| ❑ 2 Ken Baumgartner | .75 | .35 |
| ❑ 3 Bob Carpenter | .50 | .23 |
| ❑ 4 Doug Crossman | .50 | .23 |
| ❑ 5 Dale DeGray | .50 | .23 |
| ❑ 6 Steve Duchesne | 1.50 | .70 |
| ❑ 7 Ron Duguay | .75 | .35 |
| ❑ 8 Mark Fitzpatrick | 1.00 | .45 |
| ❑ 9 Jim Fox | .50 | .23 |
| ❑ 10 Robbie Ftorek CO | .50 | .23 |
| ❑ 11 Wayne Gretzky | 15.00 | 6.75 |
| ❑ 12 Gilles Hamel | .50 | .23 |
| ❑ 13 Glenn Healy | 1.00 | .45 |
| ❑ 14 Mike Krushelnyski | .50 | .23 |
| ❑ 15 Tom Laidlaw | .50 | .23 |
| ❑ 16 Bryan Maxwell CO | .25 | .11 |
| ❑ 17 Wayne McBean | .50 | .23 |
| ❑ 18 Marty McSorley | 3.00 | 1.35 |
| ❑ 19 Bernie Nicholls | 1.50 | .70 |
| ❑ 20 Cap Raeder CO | .25 | .11 |
| ❑ 21 Luc Robitaille | 4.00 | 1.80 |
| ❑ 22 Dave Taylor | 1.50 | .70 |
| ❑ 23 John Tonelli | .75 | .35 |
| ❑ 24 Tim Watters | .50 | .23 |
| ❑ 25 Title Card (Checklist on back) | .50 | .23 |

## 1989-90 Kings Smokey

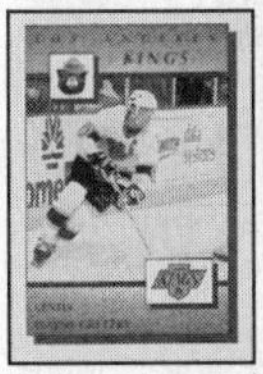

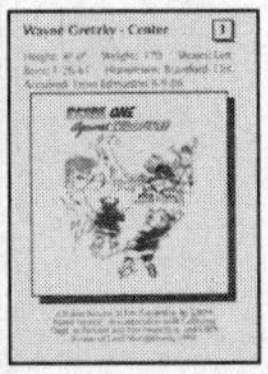

This 24-card standard-size set of Los Angeles Kings was sponsored by the USDA Forest Service in cooperation with other agencies. The front features a color action photo, banded above and below with gray stripes. The Smokey the Bear logo appears in the upper left-hand corner, and the Los Angeles Kings logo in the lower right-hand corner. A black border below and on the right of the picture creates the impression of a shadow. The back provides player information, card number, and a fire prevention cartoon. The cards are numbered in the upper right corner of the reverse.

| | MINT | NRMT |
|---|---|---|
| COMPLETE SET (24) | 25.00 | 11.00 |
| COMMON CARD (1-24) | .50 | .23 |
| ❑ 1 Wayne Gretzky | 12.00 | 5.50 |
| ❑ 2 Tim Watters | .50 | .23 |
| ❑ 3 Mikael Lindholm | .50 | .23 |
| ❑ 4 Mike Allison | .50 | .23 |
| ❑ 5 Steve Kasper | .50 | .23 |
| ❑ 6 Dave Taylor | 1.00 | .45 |
| ❑ 7 Larry Robinson | 2.00 | .90 |
| ❑ 8 Luc Robitaille | 3.00 | 1.35 |
| ❑ 9 Barry Beck | .75 | .35 |
| ❑ 10 Keith Crowder | .50 | .23 |
| ❑ 11 Petr Prajsler | .50 | .23 |
| ❑ 12 Mike Krushelnyski | .50 | .23 |
| ❑ 13 John Tonelli | .75 | .35 |
| ❑ 14 Steve Duchesne | 1.00 | .45 |
| ❑ 15 Jay Miller | .50 | .23 |
| ❑ 16 Kelly Hrudey | 1.50 | .70 |
| ❑ 17 Marty McSorley | 2.00 | .90 |
| ❑ 18 Mario Gosselin | .75 | .35 |
| ❑ 19 Craig Duncanson | .50 | .23 |
| ❑ 20 Bob Kudelski | .50 | .23 |
| ❑ 21 Brian Benning | .50 | .23 |
| ❑ 22 Mikko Makela | .50 | .23 |
| ❑ 23 Tom Laidlaw | .50 | .23 |
| ❑ 24 Checklist Card | .50 | .23 |

## 1989-90 Kings Smokey Gretzky 8x10

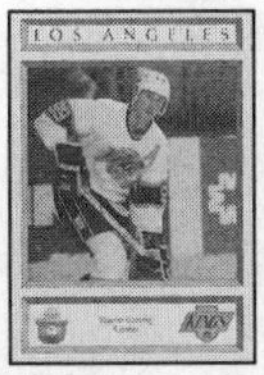

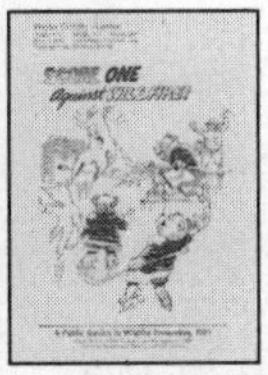

This 8" by 10" blowup of Wayne Gretzky's regular Smokey issue features a white-bordered color action shot of him on the front. The team name appears at the top, and his name and position, along with the Kings and Smokey logos, are shown at the bottom. The black-and-white back has his name and biography in the upper left corner and features a cartoon of bears on skates scoring a goal against a wildfire goalie while Smokey looks on. The card is unnumbered.

| | MINT | NRMT |
|---|---|---|
| COMPLETE SET (1) | 15.00 | 6.75 |
| COMMON CARD | 15.00 | 6.75 |
| ❑ NNO Wayne Gretzky | 15.00 | 6.75 |

## 1990-91 Kings Smokey

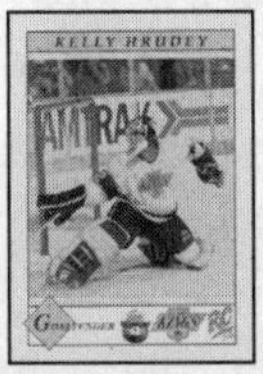


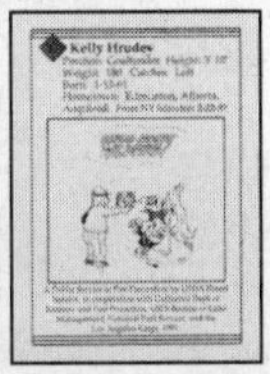

This 25-card set of Los Angeles Kings was sponsored by Royal Crown Cola in cooperation with the USDA Forest Service and other agencies and features members of the Los Angeles Kings. The cards measure the standard size (2 1/2" by 3 1/2"). The fronts feature color action player photos with white borders. The player's name appears in a silver-gray stripe above the picture, while his position and several logos appear in a white rectangle below the picture. The backs have biographical information and a fire prevention cartoon starring Smokey, enframed by thin black borders. The cards are numbered on the back in the upper left corner. The mascot card has a checklist on its reverse.

| | MINT | NRMT |
|---|---|---|
| COMPLETE SET (25) | 15.00 | 6.75 |
| COMMON CARD (1-24) | .10 | .05 |
| ❑ 1 Wayne Gretzky | 8.00 | 3.60 |
| ❑ 2 Brian Benning | .25 | .11 |
| ❑ 3 Rob Blake | 1.00 | .45 |
| ❑ 4 Tim Watters | .25 | .11 |
| ❑ 5 Todd Elik | .25 | .11 |
| ❑ 6 Tomas Sandstrom | .50 | .23 |
| ❑ 7 Steve Kasper | .25 | .11 |
| ❑ 8 Dave Taylor | 1.00 | .45 |
| ❑ 9 Larry Robinson | 1.00 | .45 |
| ❑ 10 Luc Robitaille | 1.50 | .70 |
| ❑ 11 Tony Granato | .50 | .23 |
| ❑ 12 Tom Laidlaw | .25 | .11 |
| ❑ 13 Francois Breault | .25 | .11 |
| ❑ 14 John Tonelli | .50 | .23 |
| ❑ 15 Steve Duchesne | .50 | .23 |
| ❑ 16 Jay Miller | .25 | .11 |
| ❑ 17 Kelly Hrudey | 1.50 | .70 |
| ❑ 18 Marty McSorley | 1.00 | .45 |
| ❑ 19 Daniel Berthiaume | .50 | .23 |
| ❑ 20 Bob Kudelski | .25 | .11 |
| ❑ 21 Brad Jones | .25 | .11 |
| ❑ 22 John McIntyre | .25 | .11 |
| ❑ 23 Rod Buskas | .25 | .11 |
| ❑ 24 Kingston (Mascot) (Checklist on back) | .10 | .05 |
| ❑ NNO RC Cola Challenge | .10 | .05 |

## 1991-92 Kings Upper Deck Season Ticket

This approximately 5" by 3 1/2" horizontally oriented card was sent out to 7,000 Los Angeles Kings season ticket holders along with a Christmas card from Upper Deck in December 1991 celebrating the Kings' 25th anniversary. The front features a borderless color action shot of several Kings players and opponent(s) in a pileup in front of the Kings' net with Kings' goalie Kelly Hrudey. The limited edition seal with production number is placed in the upper left. The Upper Deck Hockey logo is in the upper right. The horizontal back carries a drawing of Wayne Gretzky, Rogie Vachon, Bruce McNall, Marcel Dionne, and Luc Robitaille.

| | MINT | NRMT |
|---|---|---|
| COMPLETE SET (1) | 100.00 | 45.00 |
| COMMON CARD | 100.00 | 45.00 |
| ❑ NNO Los Angeles Kings Season Ticket Holders 25th Anniversary Kelly Hrudey | 100.00 | 45.00 |

## 1992-93 Kings Upper Deck Season Ticket

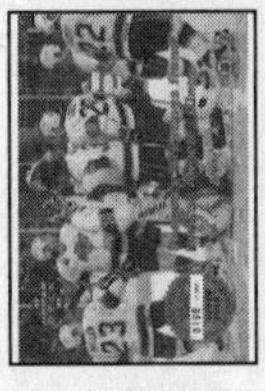

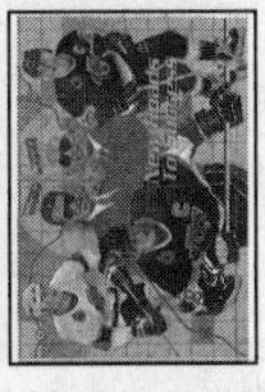

This approximately 5" by 3 1/2" horizontally oriented card was sent out to Los Angeles Kings season ticket holders along with a Christmas card from Upper Deck in December 1992. The card is numbered out of 10,000.

| | MINT | NRMT |
|---|---|---|
| COMPLETE SET (1) | 75.00 | 34.00 |
| COMMON CARD | 75.00 | 34.00 |
| ❑ NNO Los Angeles Kings Season Ticket Holders | 75.00 | 34.00 |

## 1993-94 Kings Upper Deck Season Ticket

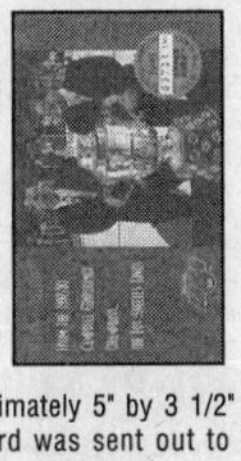

This approximately 5" by 3 1/2" horizontally oriented card was sent out to 10,000 Los Angeles Kings season ticket holders along with a Christmas card from Upper Deck in December 1993.

| | MINT | NRMT |
|---|---|---|
| COMPLETE SET (1) | 75.00 | 34.00 |
| COMMON CARD | 75.00 | 34.00 |
| ❑ NNO Los Angeles Kings Season Ticket Holders | 75.00 | 34.00 |

## 1994-95 Kings Upper Deck Season Ticket

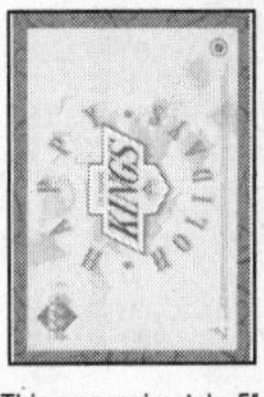

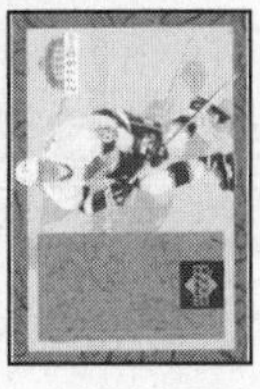

This approximately 5" by 3 1/2" horizontally oriented card was sent out to Los Angeles Kings season ticket holders as a seasonal greeting from the Kings and Upper Deck in December 1994. The front of the card carries a yuletide message over a ghoseted image of Wayne Gretzky. The back has another message, a color photo of Gretzky, and the individual serial number out of 45,000.

| | MINT | NRMT |
|---|---|---|
| COMPLETE SET (1) | 25.00 | 11.00 |
| COMMON CARD | 25.00 | 11.00 |
| ❑ NNO Los Angeles Kings Season Ticket Holders Wayne Gretzky | 25.00 | 11.00 |

## 1998-99 Kings LA Times Coins

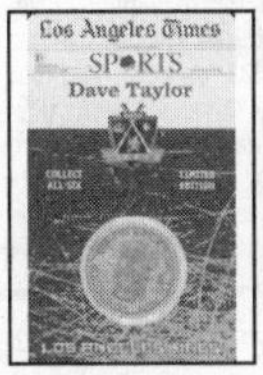


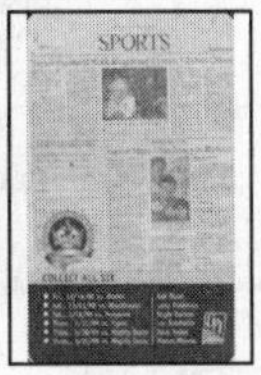

| | MINT | NRMT |
|---|---|---|
| COMPLETE SET (6) | 15.00 | 6.75 |
| COMMON CARD (1-6) | 1.00 | .45 |
| ❑ 1 Rob Blake | 1.00 | .45 |
| ❑ 2 Marcel Dionne | 5.00 | 2.20 |
| ❑ 3 Larry Robinson | 3.00 | 1.35 |
| ❑ 4 Luc Robitaille | 5.00 | 2.20 |
| ❑ 5 Dave Taylor | 1.00 | .45 |
| ❑ 6 Rogie Vachon | 2.00 | .90 |

## 1998-99 Kings Power Play

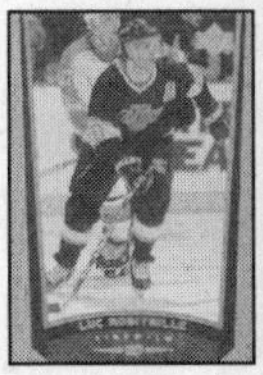

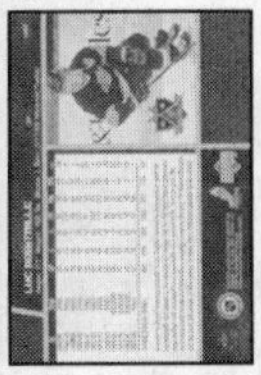

Cards were distributed in a sealed pack and were made available through give-aways at various arenas, in conjunction with Power Play magazine. Each packet contains 4-cards, similar in design to the base set from each manufacturer, but featuring a different card number on the back.

| | MINT | NRMT |
|---|---|---|
| COMPLETE SET (4) | 2.00 | .90 |
| COMMON CARD (1-4) | .30 | .14 |
| ❑ LAK1 Rob Blake | .40 | .18 |
| ❑ LAK2 Jozef Stumpel | .40 | .18 |
| ❑ LAK3 Luc Robitaille | 1.00 | .45 |
| ❑ LAK4 Yanic Perreault | .30 | .14 |

## 1994 Kollectorfest

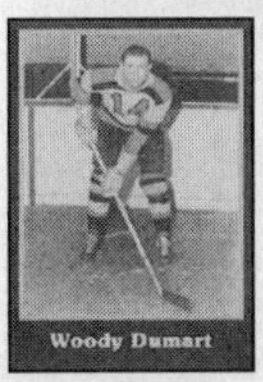


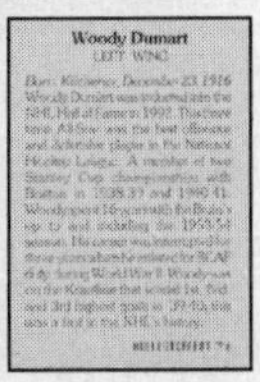


This five-card standard-size set was issued in conjuction with a collectibles show on October 9, 1994 in Kitchener, Ontario. The three players in this set are all Kitchener natives and donated their time for this show. Reportedly only 3,000 sets were produced, and each set has its own serial number on a title card. The fronts feature black-and-white posed player photos with team color-coded borders and the player's name on the bottom. The players' uniforms have been colorized. The backs carry player profiles. The cards are unnumbered and checklisted below in alphabetical order.

| | MINT | NRMT |
|---|---|---|
| COMPLETE SET (5) | 5.00 | 2.20 |
| COMMON CARD (1-5) | .50 | .23 |
| ❑ 1 Woody Dumart | 1.50 | .70 |
| ❑ 2 Dutch Hiller | 1.00 | .45 |
| ❑ 3 Milt Schmidt | 2.50 | 1.10 |
| ❑ 4 Title Card Kollectorfest '94 | .50 | .23 |
| ❑ 5 Title Card Oktoberfest 1994 | .50 | .23 |

## 1986-87 Kraft Drawings

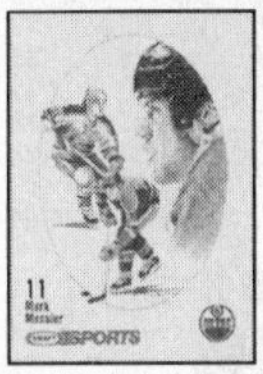

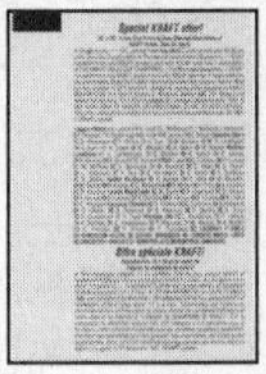

The 1986-87 Kraft Hockey Drawings set contains 81 standard-size unnumbered cards featuring players from Canadian-based NHL teams. The fronts feature black and white drawings of the players in action, along with each player's team logo. Each back shows the entire checklist for the set. Noted sports artists Jerry Hersh and Carlton McDiarmid drew 42 and 30, respectively, of the 81 cards in the set. The cards are unnumbered and so they are presented below in alphabetical order. Prints of these cards were available through an offer detailed on the card backs. These tend to sell in the two to five times the values listed below. Dealers have reported the existence of a John Kordic print, which apparently is was not released to the public. This print sells for $5-$10. An album for the cards was also offered. The set features early cards of Wendel Clark, Stephane Richer, Patrick Roy, and Mike Vernon.

| | MINT | NRMT |
|---|---|---|
| COMPLETE SET (81) | 90.00 | 40.00 |
| COMPLETE FACT.SET (81) | 125.00 | 55.00 |
| COMMON CARD (1-81) | .50 | .23 |
| ❑ 1 Glenn Anderson | 1.00 | .45 |
| ❑ 2 Brent Ashton | .50 | .23 |
| ❑ 3 Laurie Boschman | .50 | .23 |
| ❑ 4 Richard Brodeur | .75 | .35 |
| ❑ 5 Guy Carbonneau | .75 | .35 |
| ❑ 6 Randy Carlyle | .75 | .35 |
| ❑ 7 Chris Chelios | 3.00 | 1.35 |
| ❑ 8 Wendel Clark | 8.00 | 3.60 |
| ❑ 9 Glen Cochrane | .50 | .23 |
| ❑ 10 Paul Coffey | 3.00 | 1.35 |
| ❑ 11 Alain Cote | .50 | .23 |
| ❑ 12 Russ Courtnall | 1.00 | .45 |
| ❑ 13 Kjell Dahlin | .50 | .23 |
| ❑ 14 Dan Daoust | .50 | .23 |
| ❑ 15 Bill Derlago | .50 | .23 |
| ❑ 16 Tom Fergus | .50 | .23 |
| ❑ 17 Grant Fuhr | 2.00 | .90 |
| ❑ 18 Bob Gainey | 1.00 | .45 |
| ❑ 19 Gaston Gingras | .50 | .23 |
| ❑ 20 Mario Gosselin | .75 | .35 |
| ❑ 21 Michel Goulet | 1.00 | .45 |
| ❑ 22 Rick Green | .50 | .23 |
| ❑ 23 Wayne Gretzky | 40.00 | 18.00 |
| ❑ 24 Doug Halward | .50 | .23 |
| ❑ 25 Dale Hawerchuk | 1.50 | .70 |
| ❑ 26 Brian Hayward | .75 | .35 |
| ❑ 27 Dale Hunter | 1.00 | .45 |
| ❑ 28 Mike Krushelnyski | .50 | .23 |
| ❑ 29 Jari Kurri | 2.50 | 1.10 |
| ❑ 30 Mike Lalor | .50 | .23 |
| ❑ 31 Gary Leeman | .50 | .23 |
| ❑ 32 Rejean Lemelin | 1.00 | .45 |
| ❑ 33 Claude Lemieux | 5.00 | 2.20 |
| ❑ 34 Doug Lidster | .50 | .23 |
| ❑ 35 Hakan Loob | .75 | .35 |
| ❑ 36 Kevin Lowe | .75 | .35 |
| ❑ 37 Craig Ludwig | .50 | .23 |
| ❑ 38 Paul MacLean | .50 | .23 |
| ❑ 39 Clint Malarchuk | .75 | .35 |
| ❑ 40 Mario Marois | .50 | .23 |
| ❑ 41 Lanny McDonald | 1.00 | .45 |
| ❑ 42 Mike McPhee | .75 | .35 |
| ❑ 43 Mark Messier | 7.50 | 3.40 |
| ❑ 44 Randy Moller | .50 | .23 |
| ❑ 45 Sergio Momesso | .50 | .23 |
| ❑ 46 Andy Moog | 2.00 | .90 |
| ❑ 47 Brian Mullen | .50 | .23 |
| ❑ 48 Joe Mullen | 1.00 | .45 |
| ❑ 49 Mark Napier | .50 | .23 |

❑ 50 Mats Naslund 1.00 .45
❑ 51 Chris Nilan .75 .35
❑ 52 Barry Pederson .75 .35
❑ 53 Steve Penney .75 .35
❑ 54 Jim Peplinski .50 .23
❑ 55 Brent Peterson .50 .23
❑ 56 Pat Price .50 .23
❑ 57 Paul Reinhart .50 .23
❑ 58 Stephane Richer 1.50 .70
❑ 59 Doug Risebrough .50 .23
❑ 60 Larry Robinson 1.00 .45
❑ 61 Patrick Roy 40.00 18.00
❑ 62 Borje Salming 1.00 .45
❑ 63 Petri Skriko .50 .23
❑ 64 Brian Skrudland .75 .35
❑ 65 Bobby Smith .75 .35
❑ 66 Stan Smyl UER .75 .35
(Misspelled Syml on card front)
❑ 67 Anton Stastny .50 .23
❑ 68 Peter Stastny 1.00 .45
❑ 69 Thomas Steen .75 .35
❑ 70 Patrik Sundstrom .50 .23
❑ 71 Gary Suter 1.00 .45
❑ 72 Petr Svoboda .75 .35
❑ 73 Tony Tanti .75 .35
❑ 74 Greg Terrion .50 .23
❑ 75 Steve Thomas 1.00 .45
❑ 76 Perry Turnbull .50 .23
❑ 77 Rick Vaive .75 .35
❑ 78 Mike Vernon 3.00 1.35
❑ 79 Ryan Walter .50 .23
❑ 80 Carey Wilson .50 .23
❑ 81 Ken Wregget 1.50 .70
❑ x Album 25.00 11.00

## 1989-90 Kraft

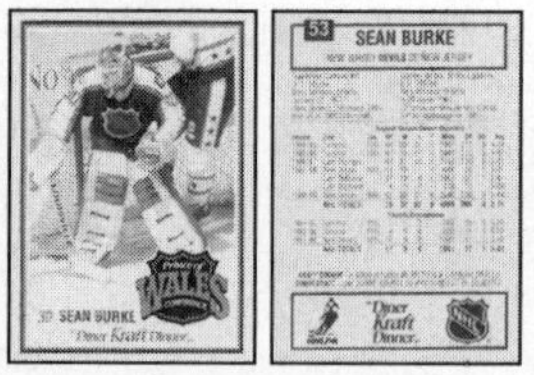

This set of 64 standard-size cards featuring players from Canadian-based NHL teams was available on the package backs of specially marked boxes of Kraft Dinner, Spirals, and Egg Noodles. Also specially marked boxes of Jello Puddings and Pie Fillings and Kraft Singles featured additional NHL hockey cards. Each card featured a color action photo of the player, with his name, number, and team logo in different color strips running across the bottom of the picture. Kraft also issued a special album to house the cards. The cards were distributed in a variety of ways. There were 26 different Kraft boxes each with two cards on the package back. A sheet of six All-Star cards was packed in each unopened case of Kraft Dinners. Sticker sheets were found in specially marked 500g packages of Kraft Singles. Cards could also be obtained in exchange for UPCs and a small handling fee. The set numbering is listed below according to the company's checklist.

| | MINT | NRMT |
|---|---|---|
| COMPLETE SET (64) | 90.00 | 40.00 |
| COMPLETE FACT.SET (64) | 125.00 | 55.00 |
| COMMON CARD (1-51) | .50 | .23 |
| COMMON ALL-STARS (52-64) | .50 | .23 |

❑ 1 Doug Gilmour 2.00 .90
❑ 2 Theoren Fleury 5.00 2.20
❑ 3 Al MacInnis 1.00 .45
❑ 4 Sergei Makarov .75 .35
❑ 5 Joe Nieuwendyk 1.00 .45
❑ 6 Joel Otto .50 .23
❑ 7 Colin Patterson .50 .23
❑ 8 Sergei Priakin .50 .23
❑ 9 Paul Ranheim .50 .23
❑ 10 Glenn Anderson 1.00 .45
❑ 11 Grant Fuhr 1.00 .45
❑ 12 Charlie Huddy .50 .23
❑ 13 Jari Kurri 2.00 .90
❑ 14 Kevin Lowe .50 .23
❑ 15 Mark Messier 3.00 1.35
❑ 16 Craig Simpson .50 .23
❑ 17 Steve Smith .50 .23
❑ 18 Esa Tikkanen 1.00 .45
❑ 19 Guy Carbonneau .75 .35
❑ 20 Chris Chelios 2.00 .90
❑ 21 Shayne Corson 1.00 .45
❑ 22 Russ Courtnall .75 .35
❑ 23 Mats Naslund .75 .35
❑ 24 Stephane Richer .75 .35
❑ 25 Patrick Roy 8.00 3.60
❑ 26 Bobby Smith .75 .35
❑ 27 Petr Svoboda .50 .23
❑ 28 Jeff Brown .50 .23
❑ 29 Paul Gillis .50 .23
❑ 30 Michel Goulet .75 .35
❑ 31 Guy Lafleur 2.00 .90
❑ 32 Joe Sakic 5.00 2.20
❑ 33 Peter Stastny .75 .35
❑ 34 Wendel Clark 1.00 .45
❑ 35 Vincent Damphousse 1.00 .45
❑ 36 Gary Leeman .50 .23
❑ 37 Daniel Marois .50 .23
❑ 38 Ed Olczyk .50 .23
❑ 39 Rob Ramage .50 .23
❑ 40 Vladimir Krutov .50 .23
❑ 41 Igor Larionov 1.00 .45
❑ 42 Trevor Linden 1.00 .45
❑ 43 Kirk McLean 1.00 .45
❑ 44 Paul Reinhart .50 .23
❑ 45 Tony Tanti .50 .23
❑ 46 Brent Ashton .50 .23
❑ 47 Randy Carlyle .50 .23
❑ 48 Randy Cunneyworth .50 .23
❑ 49 Dave Ellett .50 .23
❑ 50 Dale Hawerchuk 1.00 .45
❑ 51 Fredrik Olausson .50 .23
❑ 52 Ray Bourque AS 2.00 .90
❑ 53 Sean Burke AS 1.00 .45
❑ 54 Paul Coffey AS 2.00 .90
❑ 55 Mario Lemieux AS 8.00 3.60
❑ 56 Cam Neely AS 2.00 .90
❑ 57 Rick Tocchet AS 1.00 .45
❑ 58 Steve Duchesne AS .50 .23
❑ 59 Wayne Gretzky AS 10.00 4.50
❑ 60 Joe Mullen AS 1.00 .45
❑ 61 Gary Suter AS .50 .23
❑ 62 Mike Vernon AS 1.00 .45
❑ 63 Steve Yzerman AS 5.00 2.20
❑ 64 Checklist Card .50 .23
❑ xx Album 25.00 11.00

## 1989-90 Kraft All-Stars Stickers

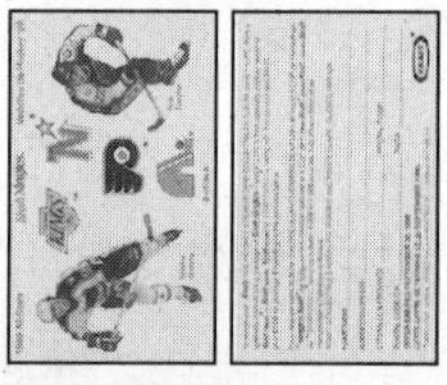

Distributed by Kraft General Foods Canada in packages of Kraft Singles, these six bilingual sticker-sheets measure approximately 4 1/2" by 2 3/4" and each features stickers of two players in their NHL All-Star uniforms and four NHL team logo stickers. The sheets are white, with color player action shots and color team logos on the peel-away stickers. The white back of each sticker-sheet carries a bilingual order form for the Kraft NHL Hockey sticker/card album. The stickers are numbered on the front.

| | MINT | NRMT |
|---|---|---|
| COMPLETE SET (6) | 20.00 | 9.00 |
| COMMON PANEL (1-6) | 1.00 | .45 |

❑ 1 Mike McPhee 1.00 .45
and Paul Reinhart
❑ 2 Wayne Gretzky 12.00 5.50
and Rick Tocchet
❑ 3 Paul Coffey 6.00 2.70
and Steve Yzerman
❑ 4 Mike Vernon 3.00 1.35
and Ray Bourque
❑ 5 Jari Kurri 8.00 3.60
and Mario Lemieux
❑ 6 Kevin Lowe 1.00 .45
and Sean Burke

## 1990-91 Kraft

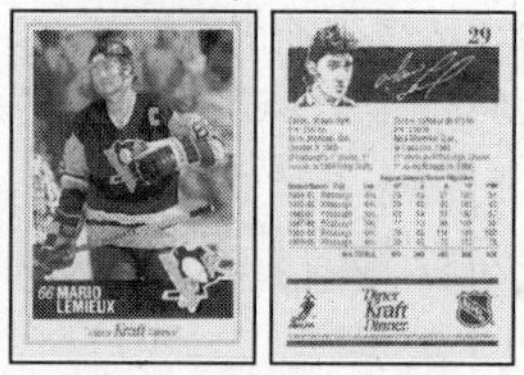

This 115-card standard-size set was issued by Kraft to honor some of the stars of the NHL. There was also a special album, which included advertisements for various Kraft products, issued to store all the cards. The set is divided into three parts: Cards 1-64 are NHL star players listed alphabetically while 65-91 are the Conference All-Stars (Campbell 65-78 and Wales 79-91). Card numbers 92-115 are team photos along with three unnumbered team checklist cards. To complete the set, the consumer had to purchase items from eight different Kraft product groups. Only card number 66 (Wayne Gretzky) was available in two different product groups: Jello Instant Pudding (four servings) and Jello Lemon Pie Filling (tri-portion).

| | MINT | NRMT |
|---|---|---|
| COMPLETE SET (115) | 125.00 | 55.00 |
| COMPLETE FACT.SET (115) | 140.00 | 65.00 |
| COMMON CARD (1-115) | .25 | .11 |

❑ 1 Dave Babych .50 .23
❑ 2 Brian Bellows .75 .35
❑ 3 Ray Bourque 1.50 .70
❑ 4 Sean Burke 1.00 .45
❑ 5 Jimmy Carson .50 .23
❑ 6 Chris Chelios 1.50 .70
❑ 7 Dino Ciccarelli .75 .35
❑ 8 Paul Coffey 1.50 .70
❑ 9 Geoff Courtnall .75 .35
❑ 10 Doug Crossman .50 .23
❑ 11 Kevin Dineen .50 .23
❑ 12 Pat Elynuik .50 .23
❑ 13 Ron Francis 1.00 .45
❑ 14 Gerard Gallant .50 .23
❑ 15 Wayne Gretzky 10.00 4.50
❑ 16 Dale Hawerchuk 1.00 .45
❑ 17 Ron Hextall 1.00 .45
❑ 18 Phil Housley .75 .35
❑ 19 Mark Howe .75 .35
❑ 20 Brett Hull 2.50 1.10
❑ 21 Al Iafrate .60 .25
❑ 22 Guy Lafleur 1.50 .70
❑ 23 Pat LaFontaine 1.00 .45
❑ 24 Rod Langway .50 .23
❑ 25 Igor Larionov 1.00 .45
❑ 26 Steve Larmer .75 .35
❑ 27 Gary Leeman .50 .23
❑ 28 Brian Leetch 1.50 .70
❑ 29 Mario Lemieux 7.00 3.10
❑ 30 Trevor Linden 1.00 .45
❑ 31 Mike Liut .60 .25
❑ 32 Mark Messier 2.50 1.10
❑ 33 Al MacInnis .75 .35
❑ 34 Mike Modano 3.00 1.35
❑ 35 Andy Moog 1.00 .45
❑ 36 Joe Mullen .75 .35
❑ 37 Kirk Muller .75 .35
❑ 38 Petr Nedved 1.25 .55
❑ 39 Cam Neely 1.50 .70
❑ 40 Bernie Nicholls .75 .35
❑ 41 Joe Nieuwendyk .75 .35
❑ 42 Mats Sundin 2.00 .90
❑ 43 Daren Puppa .75 .35
❑ 44 Rob Ramage .50 .23
❑ 45 Bill Ranford 1.00 .45
❑ 46 Stephane Richer .75 .35
❑ 47 Larry Robinson 1.00 .45
❑ 48 Luc Robitaille 1.00 .45
❑ 49 Patrick Roy 7.00 3.10
❑ 50 Joe Sakic 4.00 1.80
❑ 51 Denis Savard 1.00 .45
❑ 52 Craig Simpson .50 .23
❑ 53 Bobby Smith .60 .25
❑ 54 Peter Stastny 1.00 .45
❑ 55 Thomas Steen .50 .23
❑ 56 Scott Stevens .75 .35
❑ 57 Brent Sutter .50 .23
❑ 58 Rick Tocchet 1.00 .45
❑ 59 Pierre Turgeon 1.00 .45
❑ 60 John Vanbiesbrouck 3.00 1.35
❑ 61 Mike Vernon 1.00 .45
❑ 62 Doug Wilson .75 .35
❑ 63 Steve Yzerman 5.00 2.20
❑ 64 Checklist Card .50 .23
❑ 65 Steve Duchesne AS .50 .23
❑ 66 Wayne Gretzky AS 6.00 2.70
❑ 67 Brett Hull AS 2.50 1.10
❑ 68 Jari Kurri AS 1.00 .45
❑ 69 Mike Gartner AS .75 .35
❑ 70 Kirk McLean AS 1.00 .45
❑ 71 Mark Messier AS 2.00 .90
❑ 72 Joe Mullen AS .60 .25
❑ 73 Bernie Nicholls AS .60 .25
❑ 74 Joe Nieuwendyk AS .60 .25
❑ 75 Luc Robitaille AS 1.00 .45
❑ 76 Mario Vernon AS .75 .35
❑ 77 Doug Wilson AS .50 .23
❑ 78 Steve Yzerman AS 4.00 1.80
❑ 79 Joe Sakic AS 3.00 1.35
❑ 80 Ray Bourque AS 1.50 .70
❑ 81 Chris Chelios AS 1.50 .70
❑ 82 Paul Coffey AS 1.50 .70
❑ 83 Ron Francis AS 1.00 .45
❑ 84 Cam Neely AS 1.00 .45
❑ 85 Phil Housley AS .60 .25
❑ 86 Pat LaFontaine AS 1.00 .45
❑ 87 Mario Lemieux AS 5.00 2.20
❑ 88 Kirk Muller AS .60 .25
❑ 89 Stephane Richer AS .60 .25
❑ 90 Patrick Roy AS 5.00 2.20
❑ 91 Pierre Turgeon AS 1.00 .45
❑ 92 Boston Bruins .60 .25
❑ 93 Buffalo Sabres .50 .23
❑ 94 Calgary Flames .50 .23
❑ 95 Chicago Blackhawks .60 .25
❑ 96 Detroit Red Wings .60 .25
❑ 97 Edmonton Oilers .50 .23
❑ 98 Hartford Whalers .50 .23
❑ 99 Los Angeles Kings .60 .25
❑ 100 Minnesota North Stars .50 .23
❑ 101 Montreal Canadiens .60 .25
❑ 102 New Jersey Devils .50 .23
❑ 103 New York Islanders .50 .23
❑ 104 New York Rangers .60 .25
❑ 105 Philadelphia Flyers .50 .23
❑ 106 Pittsburgh Penguins .50 .23
❑ 107 Quebec Nordiques .50 .23
❑ 108 St. Louis Blues .50 .23
❑ 109 Toronto Maple Leafs .60 .25
❑ 110 Vancouver Canucks .50 .23
❑ 111 Washington Capitals .50 .23
❑ 112 Winnipeg Jets .50 .23
❑ 113 Unnumbered Checklist .25 .11
❑ 114 Unnumbered Checklist .25 .11
❑ 115 Unnumbered Checklist .25 .11
❑ xx Album 25.00 11.00

## 1991-92 Kraft

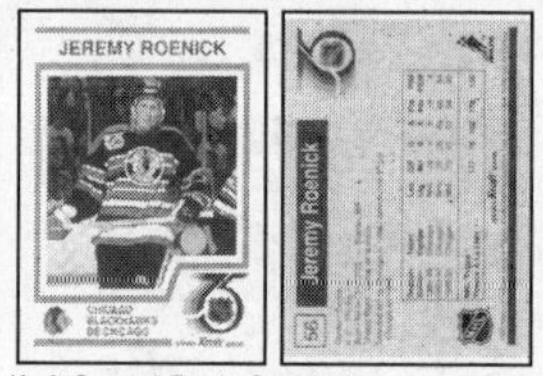

This set of 92 collectibles was sponsored by Kraft-General Foods Canada to commemorate the 75th anniversary of the NHL. It consists of 68 standard-size cards and 24 discs. To store the set, a 75th Anniversary NHL hockey card album could be purchased. Kraft also provided the opportunity for the collector to purchase any combination of ten cards or discs through the mail to complete the set. Cards 1-40 were issued in Kraft Dinners, cards 41-56 in Kraft Spirals, and cards 57-64 in Kraft Noodles. An eight-card subset highlights "Great Moments" in NHL history. The fronts feature action player photos framed inside a team color border. The player's name is printed in black lettering across the top while the team name, team logo, and 75th NHL Anniversary logo appear below the picture. The horizontally oriented backs are light gray with red print and carry biography, career statistics, and logos. Measuring 2 3/4" in diameter, the discs (65-88) were available under the caps of Kraft Peanut Butter. They feature action cut-out photos of two players (superimposed on a blue background), pairing today's All-Stars with legends of the past. Players' names and their teams appear in a white semi-circular margin. The bilingual disc backs are bright yellow with black print and carry biographical and statistical information. Both discs and cards are numbered on the back.

| | MINT | NRMT |
|---|---|---|
| COMPLETE SET (92) | 100.00 | 45.00 |
| COMPLETE FACT.SET (92) | 125.00 | 55.00 |
| COMMON CARD (1-64) | .50 | .23 |
| COMMON DISC (65-88) | .75 | .35 |
| COMMON LOGO (89-92) | .50 | .23 |

❑ 1 Mario Lemieux 7.00 3.10
❑ 2 Mark Recchi 1.00 .45
❑ 3 Jaromir Jagr 7.00 3.10
❑ 4 Mats Sundin 2.00 .90
❑ 5 Adam Oates 1.50 .70
❑ 6 Great Moments 1.50 .70
Canadien Dynasty
Maurice Richard
Jacques Plante
❑ 7 Brendan Shanahan 2.50 1.10
❑ 8 Pat Falloon .50 .23
❑ 9 Grant Fuhr 1.00 .45
❑ 10 Gary Leeman .50 .23
❑ 11 Petr Nedved 1.25 .55
❑ 12 Kirk Muller .75 .35
❑ 13 Theoren Fleury 2.00 .90
❑ 14 Dino Ciccarelli .60 .25
❑ 15 Geoff Courtnall .50 .23
❑ 16 Mark Messier 2.50 1.10
❑ 17 Ken Hodge Jr. .50 .23
❑ 18 Chris Chelios 2.00 .90
❑ 19 Mike Vernon .75 .35
❑ 20 Kevin Hatcher .60 .25
❑ 21 Stephane Richer .50 .23
❑ 22 Mark Tinordi .50 .23
❑ 23 Pat Verbeek .60 .25
❑ 24 John Cullen .50 .23
❑ 25 Pat LaFontaine 1.00 .45
❑ 26 Stephan Lebeau .50 .23
❑ 27 Mike Gartner .75 .35
❑ 28 Great Moments .75 .35
Last Leaf Dynasty
Bobby Baun
❑ 29 Shayne Corson .60 .25
❑ 30 Trevor Linden 1.00 .45
❑ 31 Craig Janney .60 .25
❑ 32 Al MacInnis .75 .35
❑ 33 Phil Housley .60 .25
❑ 34 Doug Wilson .50 .23
❑ 35 Tony Granato .50 .23
❑ 36 Dale Hawerchuk .75 .35
❑ 37 Bill Durnan 2.00 .90
Turk Broda
❑ 38 Brian Bellows .50 .23
❑ 39 Great Moments .75 .35
Number 23 with number 23
Bob Gainey
❑ 40 Great Moments .75 .35
A Night to Remember
Darryl Sittler
❑ 41 Joe Sakic 4.00 1.80
❑ 42 Wendel Clark 1.00 .45
❑ 43 Brent Sutter .50 .23
❑ 44 Bill Ranford .75 .35
❑ 45 Rick Tocchet .60 .25
❑ 46 Paul Ysebaert .50 .23
❑ 47 Adam Creighton .50 .23
❑ 48 Mike Modano 2.50 1.10
❑ 49 Russ Courtnall .50 .23
❑ 50 Great Moments .50 .23
Evolution of Stanley Cup
Syl Apps
❑ 51 Sergei Fedorov 5.00 2.20
❑ 52 Mike Ricci .60 .25
❑ 53 Scott Stevens .60 .25
❑ 54 Great Moments 1.00 .45
The Ultimate Expansion
Bobby Clarke
❑ 55 Owen Nolan .75 .35
❑ 56 Jeremy Roenick 2.00 .90
❑ 57 Ray Bourque 2.00 .90
❑ 58 Gerard Gallant .50 .23
❑ 59 Andy Moog 1.00 .45
❑ 60 Alexander Mogilny 1.25 .55
❑ 61 Great Moments .50 .23
Islander Tradition
Denis Potvin
❑ 62 Ed Olczyk .50 .23
❑ 63 Tomas Sandstrom .50 .23
❑ 64 Checklist .50 .23
❑ 65 Wayne Gretzky 10.00 4.50
Maurice Richard
❑ 66 Brett Hull 2.50 1.10
Guy Lafleur
❑ 67 Jari Kurri 1.00 .45
Bobby Clarke
❑ 68 Steve Yzerman 5.00 2.20
Jean Beliveau
❑ 69 Steve Larmer .60 .25
Pat Stapleton
❑ 70 Luc Robitaille 1.50 .70
Ted Lindsay
❑ 71 Larry Murphy 1.00 .45
Doug Harvey
❑ 72 Denis Potvin .75 .35
Gary Suter
❑ 73 Brian Leetch 2.00 .90
Harry Howell
❑ 74 Paul Coffey 2.00 .90
Bill Gadsby
❑ 75 Jon Casey 1.50 .70
Terry Sawchuk
❑ 76 Patrick Roy 7.00 3.10
Jacques Plante
❑ 77 Denis Savard 1.00 .45
Serge Savard
❑ 78 Doug Gilmour 2.00 .90
Bob Baun
❑ 79 Guy Carbonneau .75 .35
Yvan Cournoyer
❑ 80 Gilbert Perreault 1.00 .45
Larry Robinson
❑ 81 Red Kelly .75 .35
Craig Simpson
❑ 82 Bobby Smith .75 .35
Rod Gilbert
❑ 83 Syl Apps .75 .35
Peter Stastny
❑ 84 BoomBoom Geoffrion 1.50 .70
Vincent Damphousse
❑ 85 Marcel Dionne .75 .35
Steve Smith
❑ 86 Tim Horton 2.00 .90
Kevin Dineen
❑ 87 Michel Goulet 1.00 .45
Frank Mahovlich
❑ 88 Mike Richter 1.50 .70
Henri Richard
❑ 89 Boston Bruins logo .50 .23
New York Rangers logo
Original Six
(Unnumbered)
❑ 90 Montreal Canadiens logo .50 .23
Toronto Maple Leafs logo
Original Six
(Unnumbered)
❑ 91 Chicago Blackhawks logo .50 .23
Detroit Red Wings logo
Original Six
(Unnumbered)
❑ 92 Stanley Cup 1.00 .45
(Unnumbered)
❑ xx Album 25.00 11.00

## 1992-93 Kraft

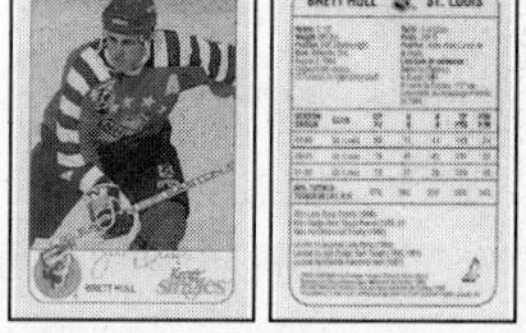

This set of 48 collectibles was sponsored by Kraft General Foods Canada to commemorate the 100th anniversary of the Stanley Cup. It consists of 24 team cards, 12 discs, and 12 All-Star cards. To store the set, a Stanley Cup 100th anniversary album could be purchased by sending in three UPC symbols from Kraft Dinner, one UPC symbol from both Kraft Peanut Butter and Kraft Singles, and 12.99 along with sales tax and shipping and handling charges. The album included special storage sheets for the cards, the history of the Stanley Cup, and team autographs. The team cards, which measure approximately 5 3/16" by 3 7/16" and were distributed on the back of Kraft Dinner boxes, show players in their centennial uniforms. The team name and logo appear in a team color-coded stripe at the bottom. The backs are plain cardboard with the team history in red print. The discs, which measure approximately 2 3/4" in diameter and were distributed under the lids of Kraft Peanut

Butter jars, are double-sided and feature 24 NHL goaltenders. The goalies are shown in action in a three-quarter-moon shaped picture against a team color-coded background. Statistics are included on the disc. The 12 All-Star cards, which measure approximately 1 3/4" by 2 1/2" and were distributed in groups of four in packages of Kraft Singles, carry color action player photos with white borders. A facsimile autograph is near the bottom of the picture. The player's name is printed in the wider bottom border between sponsor logos. The backs are white and include biographical information, statistics, and career highlights. Collectors who did not complete the series by purchasing the products could obtain any combination of eight cards or discs by sending the same UPC symbols, 3.00, plus shipping and handling charges. The cards are unnumbered and checklisted below in alphabetical order within each subset. The factory set price includes the album.

| | MINT | NRMT |
|---|---|---|
| COMPLETE SET (48) | 70.00 | 32.00 |
| COMPLETE FACT.SET (48) | 85.00 | 38.00 |
| COMMON TEAM CARD (1-24) | 1.00 | .45 |
| COMMON DISC (25-36) | 1.00 | .45 |
| COMMON ALL-STAR (37-48) | .75 | .35 |
| ❑ 1 Boston Bruins | 1.50 | .70 |
| ❑ 2 Buffalo Sabres | 1.00 | .45 |
| ❑ 3 Calgary Flames | 1.00 | .45 |
| ❑ 4 Chicago Blackhawks | 1.50 | .70 |
| ❑ 5 Detroit Red Wings | 1.50 | .70 |
| ❑ 6 Edmonton Oilers | 1.00 | .45 |
| ❑ 7 Hartford Whalers | 1.00 | .45 |
| ❑ 8 Los Angeles Kings | 1.50 | .70 |
| ❑ 9 Minnesota North Stars | 1.00 | .45 |
| ❑ 10 Montreal Canadiens | 1.50 | .70 |
| ❑ 11 New Jersey Devils | 1.00 | .45 |
| ❑ 12 New York Islanders | 1.00 | .45 |
| ❑ 13 New York Rangers | 1.50 | .70 |
| ❑ 14 Ottawa Senators | 1.00 | .45 |
| ❑ 15 Philadelphia Flyers | 1.00 | .45 |
| ❑ 16 Pittsburgh Penguins | 1.50 | .70 |
| ❑ 17 Quebec Nordiques | 1.00 | .45 |
| ❑ 18 San Jose Sharks | 1.00 | .45 |
| ❑ 19 St. Louis Blues | 1.00 | .45 |
| ❑ 20 Tampa Bay Lightning | 1.00 | .45 |
| ❑ 21 Toronto Maple Leafs | 1.50 | .70 |
| ❑ 22 Vancouver Canucks | 1.00 | .45 |
| ❑ 23 Washington Capitals | 1.00 | .45 |
| ❑ 24 Winnipeg Jets | 1.00 | .45 |
| ❑ 25 Tom Barrasso<br>Wendell Young | 1.00 | .45 |
| ❑ 26 Don Beaupre<br>Bob Essensa | 1.00 | .45 |
| ❑ 27 Jon Casey<br>Dominic Roussel | 1.00 | .45 |
| ❑ 28 Tim Cheveldae<br>Sean Burke | 1.00 | .45 |
| ❑ 29 Jeff Hackett<br>Kirk McLean | 1.50 | .70 |
| ❑ 30 Dominik Hasek<br>Chris Terreri | 3.00 | 1.35 |
| ❑ 31 Ron Hextall<br>Curtis Joseph | 2.00 | .90 |
| ❑ 32 Andy Moog<br>Mark Fitzpatrick | 1.50 | .70 |
| ❑ 33 Bill Ranford<br>Kelly Hrudey | 1.50 | .70 |
| ❑ 34 Patrick Roy<br>John Vanbiesbrouck | 10.00 | 4.50 |
| ❑ 35 Peter Sidorkiewicz<br>Grant Fuhr | 1.50 | .70 |
| ❑ 36 Mike Vernon<br>Ed Belfour | 2.00 | .90 |
| ❑ 37 Ray Bourque AS | 1.50 | .70 |
| ❑ 38 Chris Chelios AS | 1.50 | .70 |
| ❑ 39 Paul Coffey AS | 1.50 | .70 |
| ❑ 40 Wayne Gretzky AS | 7.00 | 3.10 |
| ❑ 41 Brett Hull AS | 2.00 | .90 |
| ❑ 42 Jaromir Jagr AS | 4.00 | 1.80 |
| ❑ 43 Mario Lemieux AS | 5.00 | 2.20 |
| ❑ 44 Trevor Linden AS | .75 | .35 |
| ❑ 45 Mark Messier AS | 2.00 | .90 |
| ❑ 46 Jeremy Roenick AS | 1.50 | .70 |
| ❑ 47 Patrick Roy AS | 5.00 | 2.20 |
| ❑ 48 Steve Yzerman AS | 3.00 | 1.35 |
| ❑ xx Album | 15.00 | 6.75 |

## 1993-94 Kraft

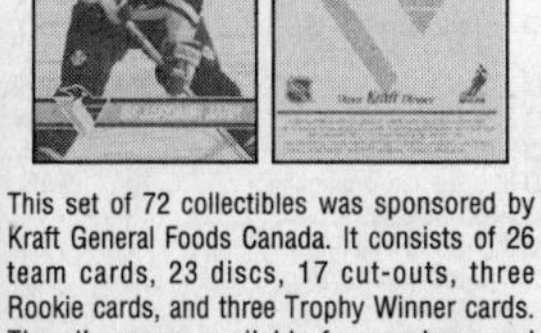

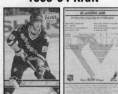

This set of 72 collectibles was sponsored by Kraft General Foods Canada. It consists of 26 team cards, 23 discs, 17 cut-outs, three Rookie cards, and three Trophy Winner cards. The album was available for purchase and contained special storage sheets for all the collectibles. It is organized by team and also includes information (both in French and English) and a picture of the teams' stadiums. The team cards measure approximately 3 1/2" by 5 1/8" and were distributed on the back of Kraft Dinner boxes. The fronts show a color action player photo with the player's name and number, and the team logo printed in a team color-coded stripe at the bottom. The backs have a ghosted light red team logo with biography (both in French and English) and statistics printed over the team logo. The discs, which measure approximately 3 3/4" in diameter and were distributed under the lids of Kraft Peanut Butter Jars, feature NHL captains and coaches. The captains' cards are double-sided and feature a blue border, while the double-sided coaches' cards have a gray border around the photo. The cut-outs, which were distributed in Jello boxes, feature color action poses. Also distributed in Kraft dinner boxes, the Rookie and Trophy Winner cards measure the same size as the team cards. The Trophy Winner cards show the players with their respective trophies. The cards are unnumbered and checklisted below in alphabetical order within each subset. The factory set price includes the album.

| | MINT | NRMT |
|---|---|---|
| COMPLETE SET (72) | 100.00 | 45.00 |
| COMPLETE FACT.SET (72) | 125.00 | 55.00 |
| COMMON CARD (1-26) | .50 | .23 |
| COMMON DISC (27-49) | 2.00 | .90 |
| COMMON CUT-OUT (50-66) | .50 | .23 |
| COMMON ROOKIE (67-69) | .75 | .35 |
| COMMON AWARD WINNER(70-72) | .75 | .35 |
| ❑ 1 Ed Belfour | 1.50 | .70 |
| ❑ 2 Brian Bradley | .50 | .23 |
| ❑ 3 Pavel Bure | 2.00 | .90 |
| ❑ 4 Paul Coffey | 1.00 | .45 |
| ❑ 5 Russ Courtnall | .50 | .23 |
| ❑ 6 Alexandre Daigle | .75 | .35 |
| ❑ 7 Pat Falloon | .50 | .23 |
| ❑ 8 Theoren Fleury | 1.00 | .45 |
| ❑ 9 Doug Gilmour | 1.00 | .45 |
| ❑ 10 Adam Graves | .75 | .35 |
| ❑ 11 Stu Grimson | .50 | .23 |
| ❑ 12 Al Iafrate | .50 | .23 |
| ❑ 13 Jaromir Jagr | 3.00 | 1.35 |
| ❑ 14 Joe Juneau | .75 | .35 |
| ❑ 15 Eric Lindros | 3.00 | 1.35 |
| ❑ 16 Alexander Mogilny | 1.50 | .70 |
| ❑ 17 Kirk Muller | .50 | .23 |
| ❑ 18 Bill Ranford | .75 | .35 |
| ❑ 19 Mike Ricci | .50 | .23 |
| ❑ 20 Luc Robitaille | 1.00 | .45 |
| ❑ 21 Geoff Sanderson | .60 | .25 |
| ❑ 22 Teemu Selanne | 2.50 | 1.10 |
| ❑ 23 Brendan Shanahan | 2.50 | 1.10 |
| ❑ 24 Pierre Turgeon | 1.00 | .45 |
| ❑ 25 John Vanbiesbrouck | 2.00 | .90 |
| ❑ 26 Valeri Zelepukin | .50 | .23 |
| ❑ 27 Al Arbour CO | 2.00 | .90 |
| ❑ 28 Bob Berry CO | 2.00 | .90 |
| ❑ 29 Ray Bourque<br>Patrick Flatley | 3.00 | 1.35 |
| ❑ 30 Scott Bowman CO | 3.00 | 1.35 |
| ❑ 31 Pat Burns CO | 2.00 | .90 |
| ❑ 32 Jacques Demers CO | 2.00 | .90 |
| ❑ 33 Kevin Dineen<br>Kevin Hatcher | 2.00 | .90 |
| ❑ 34 Wayne Gretzky<br>Wendel Clark | 8.00 | 3.60 |
| ❑ 35 Brett Hull<br>Brad Shaw | 3.00 | 1.35 |
| ❑ 36 Eddie Johnston CO | 2.00 | .90 |
| ❑ 37 Dean Kennedy<br>Denis Savard | 2.00 | .90 |
| ❑ 38 Dave King CO | 2.00 | .90 |
| ❑ 39 Pat LaFontaine<br>Pat Verbeek | 2.50 | 1.10 |
| ❑ 40 Mike Lalor<br>Mark Tinordi | 2.00 | .90 |
| ❑ 41 Trevor Linden<br>Troy Loney | 1.25 | .55 |
| ❑ 42 Barry Melrose CO | 2.00 | .90 |
| ❑ 43 Mark Messier<br>Mario Lemieux | 7.00 | 3.10 |
| ❑ 44 John Muckler CO | 2.00 | .90 |
| ❑ 45 Joe Nieuwendyk<br>Joe Sakic | 2.50 | 1.10 |
| ❑ 46 Pierre Page CO | 2.00 | .90 |
| ❑ 47 Jeremy Roenick<br>Guy Carbonneau | 3.00 | 1.35 |
| ❑ 48 Brian Skrudland<br>Craig MacTavish | 2.00 | .90 |
| ❑ 49 Scott Stevens<br>Steve Yzerman | 4.00 | 1.80 |
| ❑ 50 Tom Barrasso | .75 | .35 |
| ❑ 51 Pavel Bure | 2.00 | .90 |
| ❑ 52 Stephane Fiset | .75 | .35 |
| ❑ 53 Doug Gilmour | 1.00 | .45 |
| ❑ 54 Wayne Gretzky | 6.00 | 2.70 |
| ❑ 55 Kelly Hrudey | .60 | .25 |
| ❑ 56 Mario Lemieux | 4.00 | 1.80 |
| ❑ 57 Eric Lindros | 3.00 | 1.35 |
| ❑ 58 Kirk McLean | .75 | .35 |
| ❑ 59 Kirk Muller | .50 | .23 |
| ❑ 60 Joe Nieuwendyk | .75 | .35 |
| ❑ 61 Felix Potvin | 1.00 | .45 |
| ❑ 63 Dominic Roussel | .60 | .25 |
| ❑ 64 Patrick Roy | 4.00 | 1.80 |
| ❑ 65 Joe Sakic | 2.50 | 1.10 |
| ❑ 66 Mike Vernon | .75 | .35 |
| ❑ 67 Jason Arnott | 1.00 | .45 |
| ❑ 68 Rob Niedermayer | 1.50 | .70 |
| ❑ 69 Chris Pronger | .75 | .35 |
| ❑ 70 Chris Chelios | 1.00 | .45 |
| ❑ 71 Mario Lemieux | 4.00 | 1.80 |
| ❑ 72 Patrick Roy | 4.00 | 1.80 |
| ❑ xx Album | 25.00 | 11.00 |

## 1993-94 Kraft Recipes

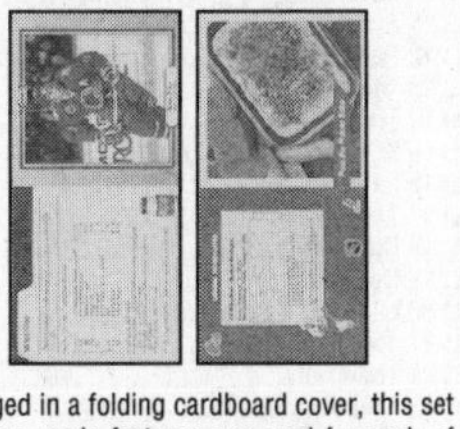

Packaged in a folding cardboard cover, this set of recipe cards features one card for each of the Canadian NHL teams. Each card features a favorite recipe of a Canadian hockey star. The cards measure approximately 4 3/4" by 4 3/4" and consist of two pages bound by a perforated hinge. The front page displays a color picture of the prepared food item, while its inside presents the recipe. On the page opposite the recipe appears a color action player photo with a white-and-red inner border and a ice-blue outer border. The back page carries in its center a color panel displaying biography, statistics, and career summary; the wide surrounding border is a bright color (blue, green, orange, or red) and carries a player cutout as well as team and league logos. The recipe cards are unnumbered and checklisted below in alphabetical order. A Manufacturer's Rebate Coupon was also included in the package but is not considered part of the card set.

| | MINT | NRMT |
|---|---|---|
| COMPLETE SET (8) | 5.00 | 2.20 |
| COMMON CARD (1-8) | .50 | .23 |
| ❑ 1 Vincent Damphousse | .75 | .35 |
| ❑ 2 Bob Essensa | .50 | .23 |
| ❑ 3 Doug Gilmour | 1.25 | .55 |
| ❑ 4 Trevor Linden | .75 | .35 |
| ❑ 5 Al MacInnis | .75 | .35 |
| ❑ 6 Bill Ranford | .75 | .35 |
| ❑ 7 Mike Ricci | .50 | .23 |
| ❑ 8 Brad Shaw | .50 | .23 |

## 1994-95 Kraft

This set of 72 collectibles was sponsored by Kraft General Foods of Canada. Available from January to March 1995, it consists of five distinct series: 14 Hockey Heroes cards, 16 Sharp Shooter cards, 26 Masked Defender cards, ten Award Winner discs, and six All-Star discs. Back panels of the seven different Jello Instant Pudding flavors showcase 14 Hockey Hero Action cards measuring 4 5/8" by 1 1/8". The horizontal fronts feature borderless color action player photos with the player's name, uniform number and team logo in a team color-coded bar alongside the left or right. The horizontal backs carry player biography, stats and sponsor logos, both in English and French. Measuring approximately 2 1/2" by 3 3/4", a pair of Sharp Shooter action cards together with an NHL team logo were inserted in Jello Pudding Snacks. The fronts feature borderless color action player photos on computerized backgrounds. The player's name and uniform number appear in a team color-coded bar alongside the left or right. The backs carry player biography, stats and sponsor logos, both in English and French. Kraft Dinner boxes feature 26 oversized Masked Defenders goalie cards, measuring 3 1/2" by 5", on back panels of boxes. The fronts show color action player photos on team color-coded backgrounds, with the player's name and uniform number in a team color-coded bar alongside the left or right, along with his nickname in stylized script. The backs carry player biography and stats, both in English and French, along with sponsor logos. Finally, two discs of 1994 Award Winners and the All-Star team were placed under each lid of Kraft Peanut Butter jars. The discs measure 2 3/4" in diameter. The Award Winner fronts have color action player photos with the player's name and uniform number, while the backs show the trophy on a blue background. The All-Star fronts have color action player photos with the player's name and uniform number. On a ghosted player background, the backs carry player biography, season and NHL career totals. A collectible album to house all the cards was offered for 21.99. The cards are unnumbered and checklisted below in alphabetical order within each subset.

| | MINT | NRMT |
|---|---|---|
| COMPLETE SET (72) | 100.00 | 45.00 |
| COMM.HOCKEY HERO (1-14) | .50 | .23 |
| COMM.SHARPSHOOTER (15-30) | .50 | .23 |
| COMM.MASKED DEF.(31-56) | .50 | .23 |
| COMM.AWARD WINNER (57-66) | 1.00 | .45 |
| COMM.ALL-STAR (67-72) | 1.00 | .45 |
| ❑ 1 Dave Andreychuk | .50 | .23 |
| ❑ 2 Chris Chelios | 1.50 | .70 |
| ❑ 3 Wendel Clark | .60 | .25 |
| ❑ 4 Theoren Fleury | 1.50 | .70 |
| ❑ 5 Wayne Gretzky | 6.00 | 2.70 |
| ❑ 6 Brett Hull | 1.75 | .80 |
| ❑ 7 Al Iafrate | .50 | .23 |
| ❑ 8 Jaromir Jagr | 3.00 | 1.35 |
| ❑ 9 Kirk Muller | .50 | .23 |
| ❑ 10 Pat LaFontaine | .75 | .35 |
| ❑ 11 Mark Recchi | .75 | .35 |
| ❑ 12 Gary Roberts | .50 | .23 |
| ❑ 13 Mats Sundin | 1.50 | .70 |
| ❑ 14 Steve Yzerman | 3.00 | 1.35 |
| ❑ 15 Jason Arnott | .75 | .35 |
| ❑ 16 Vincent Damphousse | .50 | .23 |
| ❑ 17 Doug Gilmour | 1.50 | .70 |
| ❑ 18 Craig Janney | .50 | .23 |
| ❑ 19 Joe Juneau | .50 | .23 |
| ❑ 20 Trevor Linden | .50 | .23 |
| ❑ 21 Eric Lindros | 3.00 | 1.35 |
| ❑ 22 Mark Messier | 1.75 | .80 |
| ❑ 23 Mike Modano | 1.75 | .80 |
| ❑ 24 Alexander Mogilny | 1.00 | .45 |
| ❑ 25 Adam Oates | .60 | .25 |
| ❑ 26 Robert Reichel | .50 | .23 |
| ❑ 27 Jeremy Roenick | 1.00 | .45 |
| ❑ 28 Joe Sakic | 2.50 | 1.10 |
| ❑ 29 Keith Tkachuk | 1.75 | .80 |
| ❑ 30 Alexei Yashin | 1.50 | .70 |
| ❑ 31 Tom Barrasso | .50 | .23 |
| ❑ 32 Don Beaupre | .50 | .23 |
| ❑ 33 Ed Belfour | 1.50 | .70 |
| ❑ 34 Craig Billington | .50 | .23 |
| ❑ 35 Martin Brodeur | 3.00 | 1.35 |
| ❑ 36 Sean Burke | .75 | .35 |
| ❑ 37 Tim Cheveldae | .50 | .23 |
| ❑ 38 Stephane Fiset | .50 | .23 |
| ❑ 39 Dominik Hasek | 3.00 | 1.35 |
| ❑ 40 Guy Hebert | .75 | .35 |
| ❑ 41 Ron Hextall | .75 | .35 |
| ❑ 42 Kelly Hrudey | .50 | .23 |
| ❑ 43 Arturs Irbe | .50 | .23 |
| ❑ 44 Curtis Joseph | 1.50 | .70 |
| ❑ 45 Trevor Kidd | .75 | .35 |
| ❑ 46 Kirk McLean | .75 | .35 |
| ❑ 47 Jamie McLennan | .50 | .23 |
| ❑ 48 Andy Moog | 1.00 | .45 |
| ❑ 49 Felix Potvin | 2.00 | .90 |
| ❑ 50 Daren Puppa | .75 | .35 |
| ❑ 51 Bill Ranford | .75 | .35 |
| ❑ 52 Mike Richter | 1.50 | .70 |
| ❑ 53 Vincent Riendeau | .50 | .23 |
| ❑ 54 Patrick Roy | 5.00 | 2.20 |
| ❑ 55 John Vanbiesbrouck | 2.50 | 1.10 |
| ❑ 56 Mike Vernon | .75 | .35 |
| ❑ 57 Ray Bourque | 1.50 | .70 |
| ❑ 58 Martin Brodeur | 3.00 | 1.35 |
| ❑ 59 Sergei Fedorov | 3.00 | 1.35 |
| ❑ 60 Dominik Hasek | 4.00 | 1.80 |
| ❑ 61 Jacques Lemaire | 1.00 | .45 |
| ❑ 62 Adam Graves | 1.00 | .45 |
| ❑ 63 Wayne Gretzky | 10.00 | 4.50 |
| ❑ 64 Brian Leetch | 1.50 | .70 |
| ❑ 65 Cam Neely | 1.50 | .70 |
| ❑ 66 New York Rangers<br>Stanley Cup Winners | 3.00 | 1.35 |
| ❑ 67 Ray Bourque | 1.50 | .70 |
| ❑ 68 Pavel Bure | 3.00 | 1.35 |
| ❑ 69 Sergei Fedorov | 3.00 | 1.35 |
| ❑ 70 Dominik Hasek | 4.00 | 1.80 |
| ❑ 71 Brendan Shanahan | 3.00 | 1.35 |
| ❑ 72 Scott Stevens | 1.00 | .45 |
| ❑ NNO Collector's Album | 25.00 | 11.00 |

## 1994-95 Kraft Goalie Masks

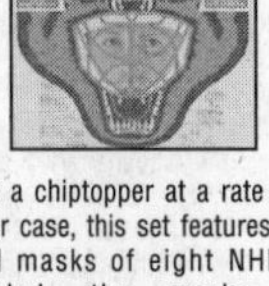

Inserted as a chiptopper at a rate of one per Kraft Dinner case, this set features perforated cardboard masks of eight NHL goalies. Unassembled, the masks measure approximately 14" by 13 1/4". The fronts carry the goalie's mask with a photo of his face, along with his name, team name, and instructions on how to assemble the mask. All text is in French and English. The backs are blank. Additional masks could be ordered by mailing in three UPC's from Kraft dinner cartons plus 3.00 for shipping and handling. The masks are unnumbered and checklisted below in alphabetical order.

| | MINT | NRMT |
|---|---|---|
| COMPLETE SET (8) | 20.00 | 9.00 |
| COMMON CARD (1-8) | 1.50 | .70 |
| ❑ 1 Ed Belfour | 3.00 | 1.35 |
| ❑ 2 Guy Hebert | 1.50 | .70 |
| ❑ 3 Curtis Joseph | 3.00 | 1.35 |
| ❑ 4 Andy Moog | 2.00 | .90 |
| ❑ 5 Felix Potvin | 2.00 | .90 |
| ❑ 6 Vincent Riendeau | 1.50 | .70 |
| ❑ 7 Patrick Roy | 8.00 | 3.60 |
| ❑ 8 John Vanbiesbrouck | 3.00 | 1.35 |

## 1995-96 Kraft

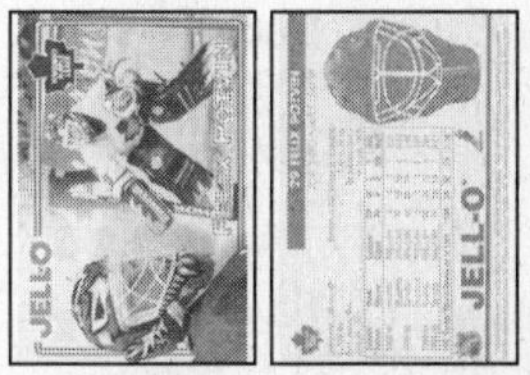

This 79-card set continues the fine tradition of Kraft hockey series. The cards were issued in several sizes and over several Kraft products. The Hottest Ticket were issued with Jell-O Pudding, while Crease Keepers were issued with Jell-O gelatin. The first group were standard card size, while the second group of eight were about half-standard size. 12 All-Stars discs were issued with Kraft Peanut Butter, while 26 Star cards were found on the back of Kraft Dinner boxes. Th 79th card was a disc picturing Conn Smythe winner Claude Lemieux and honoring the Cup champ NJ Devils. The cards are unnumbered, and so are listed below in the order in which they appeared in the factory version of the set.

| | MINT | NRMT |
|---|---|---|
| C OMPLETE SET (79) | 125.00 | 55.00 |
| COMMON CARD (1-79) | .50 | .23 |
| ❑ 1 Sergei Fedorov | 2.50 | 1.10 |
| ❑ 2 Jason Arnott | .75 | .35 |
| ❑ 3 Teemu Selanne | 2.50 | 1.10 |
| ❑ 4 Pierre Turgeon | .50 | .23 |
| ❑ 5 Joe Juneau | .50 | .23 |
| ❑ 6 Scott Stevens | .50 | .23 |
| ❑ 7 Cam Neely | .75 | .35 |
| ❑ 8 Mario Lemieux | 5.00 | 2.20 |
| ❑ 9 Wendel Clark | .75 | .35 |
| ❑ 10 Alexandre Daigle | .50 | .23 |
| ❑ 11 Peter Forsberg | 4.00 | 1.80 |
| ❑ 12 Trevor Linden | .75 | .35 |
| ❑ 13 Phil Housley | .50 | .23 |
| ❑ 14 Doug Gilmour | 1.00 | .45 |
| ❑ 15 Sean Burke | .50 | .23 |
| ❑ 16 Dominik Hasek | 3.00 | 1.35 |
| ❑ 17 Patrick Roy | 5.00 | 2.20 |
| ❑ 18 Kirk McLean | .50 | .23 |
| ❑ 19 Blaine Lacher | .50 | .23 |
| ❑ 20 Jim Carey | 1.00 | .45 |
| ❑ 21 Martin Brodeur | 3.00 | 1.35 |
| ❑ 22 Mike Richter | 2.00 | .90 |
| ❑ 23 Felix Potvin | 1.50 | .70 |
| ❑ 24 Trevor Kidd | .50 | .23 |
| ❑ 25 Ed Belfour | 1.50 | .70 |
| ❑ 26 Stephane Fiset | .50 | .23 |
| ❑ 27 Ron Hextall | .75 | .35 |
| ❑ 28 Grant Fuhr | .75 | .35 |
| ❑ 29 Daren Puppa | .75 | .35 |
| ❑ 30 Andy Moog | .75 | .35 |
| ❑ 31 Mike Vernon | .75 | .35 |
| ❑ 32 John Vanbiesbrouck | 3.00 | 1.35 |
| ❑ 33 Bill Ranford | .75 | .35 |
| ❑ 34 Tommy Soderstrom | .50 | .23 |
| ❑ 35 Tom Barrasso | .50 | .23 |
| ❑ 36 Kelly Hrudey | .50 | .23 |
| ❑ 37 Guy Hebert | .75 | .35 |
| ❑ 38 Arturs Irbe | .50 | .23 |
| ❑ 39 Tim Cheveldae | .50 | .23 |
| ❑ 40 Don Beaupre | .50 | .23 |
| ❑ 41 Eric Lindros | 4.00 | 1.80 |
| ❑ 42 Jaromir Jagr | 4.00 | 1.80 |
| ❑ 43 Paul Coffey | 1.50 | .70 |
| ❑ 44 Chris Chelios | 1.50 | .70 |
| ❑ 45 Dominik Hasek | 3.00 | 1.35 |
| ❑ 46 John LeClair | 2.00 | .90 |
| ❑ 47 Alexei Zhamnov | 1.00 | .45 |
| ❑ 48 Keith Tkachuk | 2.00 | .90 |
| ❑ 49 Theoren Fleury | 1.50 | .70 |
| ❑ 50 Larry Murphy | 1.00 | .45 |
| ❑ 51 Ray Bourque | 1.50 | .70 |
| ❑ 52 Ed Belfour | 2.00 | .90 |
| ❑ 53 Wayne Gretzky | 6.00 | 2.70 |
| ❑ 54 Adam Oates | .75 | .35 |
| ❑ 55 Paul Kariya | 4.00 | 1.80 |
| ❑ 56 Alexander Mogilny | 1.00 | .45 |
| ❑ 57 Dave Gagner | .50 | .23 |
| ❑ 58 Theoren Fleury | 1.00 | .45 |
| ❑ 59 Jesse Belanger | .50 | .23 |
| ❑ 60 Joe Sakic | 3.00 | 1.35 |
| ❑ 61 Peter Bondra | 1.00 | .45 |
| ❑ 62 Andrew Cassels | .50 | .23 |
| ❑ 63 Alexandre Daigle | .50 | .23 |
| ❑ 64 Paul Coffey | .75 | .35 |
| ❑ 65 Ulf Dahlen | .50 | .23 |
| ❑ 66 Brett Hull | 2.00 | .90 |
| ❑ 67 Bernie Nicholls | .50 | .23 |
| ❑ 68 Doug Weight | .75 | .35 |
| ❑ 69 Brian Bradley | .50 | .23 |
| ❑ 70 Mark Messier | 2.00 | .90 |
| ❑ 71 Stephane Richer | .50 | .23 |
| ❑ 72 Eric Lindros | 4.00 | 1.80 |
| ❑ 73 Mark Recchi | .75 | .35 |
| ❑ 74 Ray Ferraro | .50 | .23 |
| ❑ 75 Mats Sundin | .75 | .35 |
| ❑ 76 Alexei Zhamnov | .50 | .23 |
| ❑ 77 Pavel Bure | 2.50 | 1.10 |
| ❑ 78 Jaromir Jagr | 4.00 | 1.80 |

| | | |
|---|---|---|
| ❑ 79 Claude Lemieux | 25.00 | 11.00 |
| ❑ NNO Binder | 20.00 | 9.00 |

## 1996-97 Kraft Upper Deck

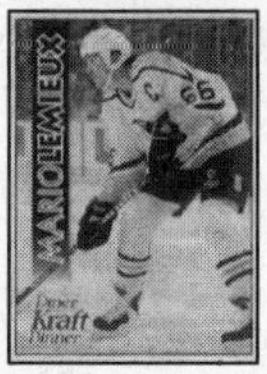


MVP (1-26) were found on the backs of specially marked boxes of Kraft Dinner regular or specialty flavours. All-Stars (27-32) were found on the backs of Jell-O instant pudding. Team Rivals (33-39) were available through a redemtpion offer found on specially marked jars of Kraft Peanut Butter. Award Winners (40-59) were found on specially marked 4 cup packs of Jell-O pudding snacks. Mascots (60-64) were found in 85g boxes of Jell-O jelly powder packs. Magnets (65-72) were found one per unopened case of Kraft Dinner. The existence of a Wayne Gretzky magnet has been reported, but not confirmed.

| | MINT | NRMT |
|---|---|---|
| COMPLETE SET (72) | 125.00 | 55.00 |
| COMMON CARD | .50 | .23 |
| ❑ 1 Brian Leetch | 1.00 | .45 |
| ❑ 2 Keith Tkachuk | 1.50 | .70 |
| ❑ 3 Geoff Sanderson | .75 | .35 |
| ❑ 4 Owen Nolan | .75 | .35 |
| ❑ 5 Saku Koivu | 1.50 | .70 |
| ❑ 6 Adam Oates | .75 | .35 |
| ❑ 7 Mats Sundin | 1.00 | .45 |
| ❑ 8 Theoren Fleury | .75 | .35 |
| ❑ 9 Zigmund Palffy | 1.00 | .45 |
| ❑ 10 Alexei Yashin | .75 | .35 |
| ❑ 11 Brett Hull | 1.00 | .45 |
| ❑ 12 Michal Pivonka | .50 | .23 |
| ❑ 13 Joe Nieuwendyk | .75 | .35 |
| ❑ 14 Martin Brodeur | 2.00 | .90 |
| ❑ 15 Ed Belfour | 1.00 | .45 |
| ❑ 16 Guy Hebert | .75 | .35 |
| ❑ 17 Patrick Roy | 4.00 | 1.80 |
| ❑ 18 Dominik Hasek | 2.00 | .90 |
| ❑ 19 John Vanbiesbrouck | 1.50 | .70 |
| ❑ 20 Yanic Perreault | .50 | .23 |
| ❑ 21 Doug Weight | .75 | .35 |
| ❑ 22 Mario Lemieux | 4.00 | 1.80 |
| ❑ 23 Eric Lindros | 2.50 | 1.10 |
| ❑ 24 Alexander Mogilny | 1.00 | .45 |
| ❑ 25 Sergei Fedorov | 2.00 | .90 |
| ❑ 26 Daren Puppa | .75 | .35 |
| ❑ 27 Chris Chelios | 1.00 | .45 |
| ❑ 28 Mario Lemieux | 4.00 | 1.80 |
| ❑ 29 Paul Kariya | 3.00 | 1.35 |
| ❑ 30 Ray Bourque | 1.00 | .45 |
| ❑ 31 Chris Osgood | 1.00 | .45 |
| ❑ 32 Jaromir Jagr | 3.00 | 1.35 |
| ❑ 33 Rob Blake | 4.00 | 1.80 |
| Paul Kariya | | |
| Kevin Dineen | | |
| Peter Bondra | | |
| ❑ 34 Ray Bourque | 2.50 | 1.10 |
| Adam Graves | | |
| Randy Cunneyworth | | |
| Pat LaFontaine | | |
| ❑ 35 Al MacInnis | 2.50 | 1.10 |
| Trevor Linden | | |
| Kris King | | |
| Mike Modano | | |
| ❑ 36 Paul Ysebaert | 2.50 | 1.10 |
| Owen Nolan | | |
| Theo Fleury | | |
| Kelly Buchberger | | |
| ❑ 37 Vince Damphousse | 8.00 | 3.60 |
| Doug Gilmour | | |
| Mario Lemieux | | |
| Eric Lindros | | |
| ❑ 38 Ziggy Palffy | 4.00 | 1.80 |
| Scott Stevens | | |
| Steve Yzerman | | |
| Chris Chelios | | |
| ❑ 39 Brian Skrudland | 4.00 | 1.80 |
| Joe Sakic | | |
| ❑ 40 Scott Bowman | 1.00 | .45 |
| ❑ 41 Marc Crawford CO | .75 | .35 |
| ❑ 42 Chris Chelios | 1.00 | .45 |
| ❑ 43 Paul Kariya | 3.00 | 1.35 |
| ❑ 44 Ron Francis | .75 | .35 |
| ❑ 45 Daniel Alfredsson | .75 | .35 |
| ❑ 46 Adam Oates | .75 | .35 |
| ❑ 47 Joe Sakic | 2.00 | .90 |
| ❑ 48 Peter Forsberg | 2.50 | 1.10 |
| ❑ 49 Jarome Iginla | .75 | .35 |
| ❑ 50 Jim Carey | .75 | .35 |
| ❑ 51 C.Osgood/M.Vernon | 1.00 | .45 |
| ❑ 52 Mike Richter | 1.00 | .45 |
| ❑ 53 Jocelyn Thibault | .75 | .35 |
| ❑ 54 Mario Lemieux | 4.00 | 1.80 |
| ❑ 55 Ed Jovanovski | .75 | .35 |
| ❑ 56 Mario Lemieux | 4.00 | 1.80 |
| ❑ 57 J.LeClair/B.Shanahan/J.Jagr | 3.00 | 1.35 |
| ❑ 58 Eric Lindros | 2.50 | 1.10 |
| ❑ 59 Sergei Fedorov | 2.00 | .90 |
| ❑ 60 Teemu Selanne | 3.00 | 1.35 |
| Wild Wing | | |
| ❑ 61 Felix Potvin | 1.00 | .45 |
| Carlton the Bear | | |
| ❑ 62 Marty McSorley | .75 | .35 |
| S.J. Sharkie | | |
| ❑ 63 Rob Niedermayer | .75 | .35 |
| Stanley C. Panther | | |
| ❑ 64 Dave Gagner | .50 | .23 |
| Harvey the Hound | | |
| ❑ 65 Theoren Fleury | 2.00 | .90 |
| ❑ 66 Saku Koivu | 3.00 | 1.35 |
| ❑ 67 Mario Lemieux | 10.00 | 4.50 |
| ❑ 68 Eric Lindros | 8.00 | 3.60 |
| ❑ 69 Alexander Mogilny | 1.50 | .70 |
| ❑ 70 Mats Sundin | 2.50 | 1.10 |
| ❑ 71 Doug Weight | 1.50 | .70 |
| ❑ 72 Alexei Yashin | 1.50 | .70 |

## 1927-28 La Patrie

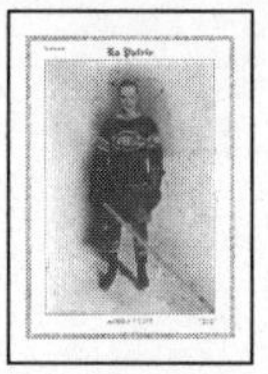


The 1927-28 La Patrie set contains 21 notebook paper-sized (approximately 8 1/2" by 11") photos. The front has a sepia-toned posed photo of the player, enframed by a thin black border. The words "La Patrie" appear above the picture, with the player's name below it. The photo number and year appear at the lower right corner of the picture. A patterned border completes the front. The back is blank. Reports indicate a folder may have been issued to hold the photos.

| | EX-MT | VG-E |
|---|---|---|
| COMPLETE SET (21) | 2500.00 | 1250.00 |
| COMMON CARD (1-21) | 50.00 | 25.00 |
| ❑ 1 Sylvio Mantha | 100.00 | 50.00 |
| ❑ 2 Art Gagne | 60.00 | 30.00 |
| ❑ 3 Leo Lafrance | 60.00 | 30.00 |
| ❑ 4 Aurel Joliat | 300.00 | 150.00 |
| ❑ 5 Pit Lepine | 80.00 | 40.00 |
| ❑ 6 Gizzy Hart | 60.00 | 30.00 |
| ❑ 7 Wildor Larochelle | 80.00 | 40.00 |
| ❑ 8 Georges Hainsworth | 200.00 | 100.00 |
| ❑ 9 Herb Gardiner | 80.00 | 40.00 |
| ❑ 10 Albert Leduc | 60.00 | 30.00 |
| ❑ 11 Marty Burke | 80.00 | 40.00 |
| ❑ 12 Charlie Langlois | 50.00 | 25.00 |
| ❑ 13 Leonard Gaudreault | 50.00 | 25.00 |
| ❑ 14 Howie Morenz | 600.00 | 300.00 |
| ❑ 15 Cecil M. Hart | 80.00 | 40.00 |
| ❑ 16 Leo Dandurand | 50.00 | 25.00 |
| ❑ 17 Newsy Lalonde | 300.00 | 150.00 |
| ❑ 18 Didier Pitre | 50.00 | 25.00 |
| ❑ 19 Jack Laviolette | 100.00 | 50.00 |
| ❑ 20 Georges Patterson | 50.00 | 25.00 |
| ❑ 21 George Vezina | 500.00 | 250.00 |

## 1993-94 Leaf

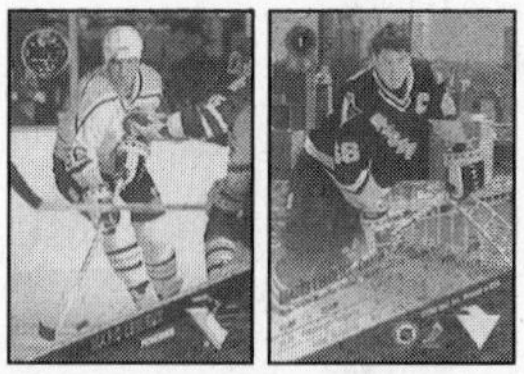

The 1993-94 Leaf hockey set consists of 440 standard-size cards that were issued in two series of 220. The fronts display color action player photos that are full-bleed except at the bottom, where a red diagonal edges the picture. Below the diagonal are a black stripe carrying the player's name in gold foil lettering, and a team color-coded triangle displaying the team logo. Against the background of the home team's skyline or another prominent architectural landmark, the backs carry a color action player cut-out overprinted at the bottom with biographical and statistical information. A holographic team logo appears in the lower right corner. Rookie Cards include Jason Arnott, Damian Rhodes and Jocelyn Thibault. An oversized (8" by 11 3/4") blowup of Mario Lemieux's card #1 was distributed as a promotional item in advance of the release of the set. The card was primarily handed out at the National Convention in Chicago.

| | MINT | NRMT |
|---|---|---|
| COMPLETE SET (440) | 30.00 | 13.50 |
| COMPLETE SERIES 1 (220) | 15.00 | 6.75 |
| COMPLETE SERIES 2 (220) | 15.00 | 6.75 |
| COMMON CARD (1-440) | .10 | .05 |
| ❑ 1 Mario Lemieux | 1.50 | .70 |
| ❑ 2 Curtis Joseph | .30 | .14 |
| ❑ 3 Steve Leach | .10 | .05 |
| ❑ 4 Vincent Damphousse | .15 | .07 |
| ❑ 5 Murray Craven | .10 | .05 |
| ❑ 6 Pat Elynuik | .10 | .05 |
| ❑ 7 Bill Guerin | .10 | .05 |
| ❑ 8 Zarley Zalapski | .10 | .05 |
| ❑ 9 Rob Gaudreau | .10 | .05 |
| ❑ 10 Pavel Bure | .60 | .25 |
| ❑ 11 Brad Shaw | .10 | .05 |
| ❑ 12 Pat LaFontaine | .15 | .07 |
| ❑ 13 Teemu Selanne | .75 | .35 |
| ❑ 14 Trent Klatt | .10 | .05 |
| ❑ 15 Kevin Todd | .10 | .05 |
| ❑ 16 Larry Murphy | .15 | .07 |
| ❑ 17 Tony Amonte | .15 | .07 |
| ❑ 18 Dino Ciccarelli | .15 | .07 |
| ❑ 19 Doug Bodger | .10 | .05 |
| ❑ 20 Luc Robitaille | .15 | .07 |
| ❑ 21 John Tucker | .10 | .05 |
| ❑ 22 Todd Gill | .10 | .05 |
| ❑ 23 Mike Ricci | .10 | .05 |
| ❑ 24 Evgeny Davydov | .10 | .05 |
| ❑ 25 Pierre Turgeon | .15 | .07 |
| ❑ 26 Rod Brind'Amour | .15 | .07 |
| ❑ 27 Jeremy Roenick | .30 | .14 |
| ❑ 28 Joel Otto | .10 | .05 |
| ❑ 29 Jeff Brown | .10 | .05 |
| ❑ 30 Brendan Shanahan | .60 | .25 |
| ❑ 31 Jiri Slegr | .10 | .05 |
| ❑ 32 Vladimir Malakhov | .10 | .05 |
| ❑ 33 Patrick Roy | 1.50 | .70 |
| ❑ 34 Kevin Hatcher | .10 | .05 |
| ❑ 35 Alexander Semak | .10 | .05 |
| ❑ 36 Gary Roberts | .10 | .05 |
| ❑ 37 Tommy Soderstrom | .15 | .07 |
| ❑ 38 Bob Essensa | .15 | .07 |
| ❑ 39 Kelly Hrudey | .15 | .07 |
| ❑ 40 Shawn Chambers | .10 | .05 |
| ❑ 41 Glenn Anderson | .15 | .07 |
| ❑ 42 Owen Nolan | .15 | .07 |
| ❑ 43 Patrick Flatley | .10 | .05 |
| ❑ 44 Ray Sheppard | .15 | .07 |
| ❑ 45 Darren Turcotte | .10 | .05 |
| ❑ 46 Shayne Corson | .10 | .05 |
| ❑ 47 Brad May | .15 | .07 |
| ❑ 48 Bob Kudelski | .10 | .05 |
| ❑ 49 Pat Falloon | .10 | .05 |
| ❑ 50 Andrew Cassels | .10 | .05 |
| ❑ 51 Chris Chelios | .30 | .14 |
| ❑ 52 Sylvain Cote | .10 | .05 |
| ❑ 53 Mathieu Schneider | .10 | .05 |
| ❑ 54 Ted Donato | .10 | .05 |
| ❑ 55 Kirk McLean | .15 | .07 |
| ❑ 56 Bruce Driver | .10 | .05 |
| ❑ 57 Uwe Krupp | .10 | .05 |
| ❑ 58 Brent Fedyk | .10 | .05 |
| ❑ 59 Robert Reichel | .10 | .05 |
| ❑ 60 Scott Stevens | .15 | .07 |
| ❑ 61 Phil Housley | .15 | .07 |
| ❑ 62 Ed Belfour | .30 | .14 |
| ❑ 63 Dave Andreychuk | .15 | .07 |
| ❑ 64 Claude Lapointe | .10 | .05 |
| ❑ 65 Russ Courtnall | .10 | .05 |
| ❑ 66 Grant Fuhr | .15 | .07 |
| ❑ 67 Paul Coffey | .30 | .14 |
| ❑ 68 Bill Ranford | .15 | .07 |
| ❑ 69 Kevin Stevens | .10 | .05 |
| ❑ 70 Brian Leetch | .30 | .14 |
| ❑ 71 Dale Hawerchuk | .15 | .07 |
| ❑ 72 Geoff Courtnall | .10 | .05 |
| ❑ 73 Sandis Ozolinsh | .15 | .07 |
| ❑ 74 Sylvain Turgeon | .10 | .05 |
| ❑ 75 Nelson Emerson | .10 | .05 |
| ❑ 76 Brian Bellows | .10 | .05 |
| ❑ 77 Geoff Sanderson | .15 | .07 |
| ❑ 78 Petr Nedved | .15 | .07 |
| ❑ 79 Peter Bondra | .30 | .14 |
| ❑ 80 Scott Niedermayer | .10 | .05 |
| ❑ 81 Steve Thomas | .10 | .05 |
| ❑ 82 Dimitri Yushkevich | .10 | .05 |
| ❑ 83 Mike Vernon | .15 | .07 |
| ❑ 84 Alexei Zhamnov | .15 | .07 |
| ❑ 85 Adam Creighton | .10 | .05 |
| ❑ 86 Dave Ellett | .10 | .05 |
| ❑ 87 Joe Sakic | .60 | .25 |
| ❑ 88 Mike Craig | .10 | .05 |
| ❑ 89 Nicklas Lidstrom | .15 | .07 |
| ❑ 90 Ed Olczyk | .10 | .05 |
| ❑ 91 Alexander Mogilny | .15 | .07 |
| ❑ 92 Ulf Samuelsson | .10 | .05 |
| ❑ 93 Doug Gilmour | .30 | .14 |
| ❑ 94 Michael Nylander | .10 | .05 |
| ❑ 95 Steve Smith | .10 | .05 |
| ❑ 96 Igor Korolev | .10 | .05 |
| ❑ 97 Dixon Ward | .10 | .05 |
| ❑ 98 John LeClair | .50 | .23 |
| ❑ 99 Cam Neely | .15 | .07 |
| ❑ 100 Patrick Roy/Cup Champs | 1.50 | .70 |
| ❑ 101 Darius Kasparaitis | .10 | .05 |
| ❑ 102 Mike Ridley | .10 | .05 |
| ❑ 103 Josef Beranek | .10 | .05 |
| ❑ 104 Valeri Zelepukin | .10 | .05 |
| ❑ 105 Keith Tkachuk | .40 | .18 |
| ❑ 106 Tomas Sandstrom | .10 | .05 |
| ❑ 107 Peter Zezel | .10 | .05 |
| ❑ 108 Scott Young | .10 | .05 |
| ❑ 109 Rick Tocchet | .15 | .07 |
| ❑ 110 Teemu Selanne CL | .30 | .14 |
| ❑ 111 Steve Chiasson | .10 | .05 |
| ❑ 112 Doug Zmolek | .10 | .05 |
| ❑ 113 Patrick Poulin | .10 | .05 |
| ❑ 114 Stephane Matteau | .10 | .05 |
| ❑ 115 Yves Racine | .10 | .05 |
| ❑ 116 Steve Heinze | .10 | .05 |
| ❑ 117 Gilbert Dionne | .10 | .05 |
| ❑ 118 Dale Hunter | .10 | .05 |
| ❑ 119 Derek King | .10 | .05 |
| ❑ 120 Garry Galley | .10 | .05 |
| ❑ 121 Ray Ferraro | .10 | .05 |
| ❑ 122 Andrei Kovalenko | .10 | .05 |
| ❑ 123 Alexei Zhitnik | .10 | .05 |
| ❑ 124 Fredrik Olausson | .10 | .05 |
| ❑ 125 Claude Lemieux | .15 | .07 |
| ❑ 126 Joe Nieuwendyk | .15 | .07 |
| ❑ 127 Travis Green | .15 | .07 |
| ❑ 128 Dave Gagner | .15 | .07 |
| ❑ 129 Sergei Fedorov | .60 | .25 |
| ❑ 130 Adam Graves | .15 | .07 |
| ❑ 131 Petr Svoboda | .10 | .05 |
| ❑ 132 Sean Burke | .15 | .07 |
| ❑ 133 Johan Garpenlov | .10 | .05 |
| ❑ 134 Jamie Baker | .10 | .05 |
| ❑ 135 Teppo Numminen | .10 | .05 |
| ❑ 136 Mats Sundin | .15 | .07 |
| ❑ 137 Nikolai Borschevsky | .10 | .05 |
| ❑ 138 Stephane Richer | .15 | .07 |
| ❑ 139 Scott Lachance | .10 | .05 |
| ❑ 140 Gary Suter | .10 | .05 |
| ❑ 141 Al Iafrate | .10 | .05 |
| ❑ 142 Brent Sutter | .10 | .05 |
| ❑ 143 Dmitri Kvartalnov | .10 | .05 |
| ❑ 144 Pat Verbeek | .10 | .05 |
| ❑ 145 Ed Courtenay | .10 | .05 |
| ❑ 146 Mark Tinordi | .10 | .05 |
| ❑ 147 Alexei Kovalev | .15 | .07 |
| ❑ 148 Dallas Drake | .10 | .05 |
| ❑ 149 Jimmy Carson | .10 | .05 |
| ❑ 150 Florida Panthers Logo | .50 | .23 |
| ❑ 151 Roman Hamrlik | .15 | .07 |
| ❑ 152 Martin Rucinsky | .10 | .05 |
| ❑ 153 Calle Johansson | .10 | .05 |
| ❑ 154 Theoren Fleury | .15 | .07 |
| ❑ 155 Benoit Hogue | .10 | .05 |
| ❑ 156 Kevin Dineen | .10 | .05 |
| ❑ 157 Jody Hull | .10 | .05 |
| ❑ 158 Mark Messier | .40 | .18 |
| ❑ 159 Dave Manson | .10 | .05 |
| ❑ 160 Chris Kontos | .10 | .05 |
| ❑ 161 Ron Francis | .15 | .07 |
| ❑ 162 Steve Yzerman | 1.00 | .45 |
| ❑ 163 Igor Kravchuk | .10 | .05 |
| ❑ 164 Sergei Zubov | .10 | .05 |
| ❑ 165 Thomas Steen | .10 | .05 |
| ❑ 166 Wendel Clark | .15 | .07 |
| ❑ 167 Scott Pellerin | .10 | .05 |
| ❑ 168 Dimitri Khristich | .10 | .05 |
| ❑ 169 Bernie Nicholls | .10 | .05 |
| ❑ 170 Paul Ranheim | .10 | .05 |
| ❑ 171 Robert Kron | .10 | .05 |
| ❑ 172 Rob Blake | .10 | .05 |
| ❑ 173 Rob Zamuner | .10 | .05 |
| ❑ 174 Rob Pearson | .10 | .05 |
| ❑ 175 Ed Belfour CL | .30 | .14 |
| ❑ 176 Steve Duchesne | .10 | .05 |
| ❑ 177 Pelle Eklund | .10 | .05 |
| ❑ 178 Michal Pivonka | .10 | .05 |
| ❑ 179 Joe Murphy | .10 | .05 |
| ❑ 180 Al MacInnis | .15 | .07 |
| ❑ 181 Craig Janney | .15 | .07 |
| ❑ 182 Kirk Muller | .10 | .05 |
| ❑ 183 Cliff Ronning | .10 | .05 |
| ❑ 184 Doug Weight | .15 | .07 |
| ❑ 185 Mike Richter | .30 | .14 |
| ❑ 186 Bob Probert | .15 | .07 |
| ❑ 187 Robert Petrovicky | .10 | .05 |
| ❑ 188 Richard Smehlik | .10 | .05 |
| ❑ 189 Norm Maciver | .10 | .05 |
| ❑ 190 Stephan Lebeau | .10 | .05 |
| ❑ 191 Patrice Brisebois | .10 | .05 |
| ❑ 192 Kevin Miller | .10 | .05 |
| ❑ 193 Trevor Linden | .15 | .07 |
| ❑ 194 Darrin Shannon | .10 | .05 |
| ❑ 195 Tim Cheveldae | .15 | .07 |
| ❑ 196 Tom Barrasso | .15 | .07 |
| ❑ 197 Zdeno Ciger | .10 | .05 |
| ❑ 198 Ulf Dahlen | .10 | .05 |
| ❑ 199 Arturs Irbe | .15 | .07 |
| ❑ 200 Anaheim Mighty Ducks Logo | .50 | .23 |
| ❑ 201 Tony Granato | .10 | .05 |
| ❑ 202 Mike Modano | .40 | .18 |
| ❑ 203 Eric Desjardins | .10 | .05 |
| ❑ 204 Bryan Smolinski | .10 | .05 |
| ❑ 205 Mark Recchi | .15 | .07 |
| ❑ 206 Darryl Sydor | .10 | .05 |
| ❑ 207 Valeri Kamensky | .15 | .07 |
| ❑ 208 Kelly Kisio | .10 | .05 |
| ❑ 209 Brian Bradley | .10 | .05 |
| ❑ 210 Mario Lemieux CL | .50 | .23 |
| ❑ 211 Yuri Khmylev | .10 | .05 |
| ❑ 212 Derian Hatcher | .10 | .05 |
| ❑ 213 Mike Gartner | .15 | .07 |
| ❑ 214 Mike Needham UER | .10 | .05 |
| (Grant Jennings on back) | | |
| ❑ 215 Ray Bourque | .30 | .14 |
| ❑ 216 Tie Domi | .15 | .07 |
| ❑ 217 Shawn McEachern | .10 | .05 |
| ❑ 218 Joe Juneau | .15 | .07 |
| ❑ 219 Greg Adams | .10 | .05 |
| ❑ 220 Martin Straka | .10 | .05 |
| ❑ 221 Tom Fitzgerald | .10 | .05 |
| ❑ 222 Gary Shuchuk | .10 | .05 |
| ❑ 223 Kevin Haller | .10 | .05 |
| ❑ 224 Bryan Marchment | .10 | .05 |
| ❑ 225 Louie DeBrusk | .10 | .05 |
| ❑ 226 Randy Wood | .10 | .05 |
| ❑ 227 Bobby Holik | .10 | .05 |
| ❑ 228 Troy Mallette | .10 | .05 |
| ❑ 229 Adam Foote | .10 | .05 |
| ❑ 230 Bob Rouse | .10 | .05 |
| ❑ 231 Jyrki Lumme | .10 | .05 |
| ❑ 232 James Patrick | .10 | .05 |
| ❑ 233 Eric Lindros | 1.25 | .55 |
| ❑ 234 Joe Reekie | .10 | .05 |
| ❑ 235 Adam Oates | .15 | .07 |
| ❑ 236 Frank Musil | .10 | .05 |
| ❑ 237 Vladimir Konstantinov | .10 | .05 |
| ❑ 238 Dave Lowry | .10 | .05 |
| ❑ 239 Garth Butcher | .10 | .05 |
| ❑ 240 Jari Kurri | .15 | .07 |
| ❑ 241 Rick Tabaracci | .15 | .07 |
| ❑ 242 Sergei Bautin | .10 | .05 |
| ❑ 243 Scott Scissons | .10 | .05 |
| ❑ 244 Dominic Roussel | .15 | .07 |
| ❑ 245 John Cullen | .10 | .05 |
| ❑ 246 Sheldon Kennedy | .10 | .05 |
| ❑ 247 Mike Hough | .10 | .05 |
| ❑ 248 Paul DiPietro | .10 | .05 |
| ❑ 249 David Shaw | .10 | .05 |
| ❑ 250 Sergio Momesso | .10 | .05 |
| ❑ 251 Jeff Daniels | .10 | .05 |
| ❑ 252 Sergei Nemchinov | .10 | .05 |
| ❑ 253 Kris King | .10 | .05 |
| ❑ 254 Kelly Miller | .10 | .05 |
| ❑ 255 Brett Hull | .40 | .18 |
| ❑ 256 Dominik Hasek | 1.00 | .45 |
| ❑ 257 Chris Pronger | .15 | .07 |
| ❑ 258 Derek Plante | .10 | .05 |
| ❑ 259 Mark Howe | .10 | .05 |
| ❑ 260 Oleg Petrov | .10 | .05 |
| ❑ 261 Ronnie Stern | .10 | .05 |
| ❑ 262 Scott Mellanby | .15 | .07 |
| ❑ 263 Warren Rychel | .10 | .05 |
| ❑ 264 John MacLean | .15 | .07 |
| ❑ 265 Radek Hamr | .10 | .05 |
| ❑ 266 Greg Hawgood | .10 | .05 |
| ❑ 267 Sylvain Lefebvre | .10 | .05 |
| ❑ 268 Glen Wesley | .10 | .05 |
| ❑ 269 Joe Cirella | .10 | .05 |
| ❑ 270 Dirk Graham | .10 | .05 |
| ❑ 271 Eric Weinrich | .10 | .05 |
| ❑ 272 Donald Audette | .15 | .07 |
| ❑ 273 Jason Woolley | .10 | .05 |
| ❑ 274 Kjell Samuelsson | .10 | .05 |
| ❑ 275 Ron Sutter | .10 | .05 |
| ❑ 276 Keith Primeau | .10 | .05 |
| ❑ 277 Ron Tugnutt | .15 | .07 |
| ❑ 278 Jesse Belanger | .10 | .05 |
| ❑ 279 Mike Keane | .10 | .05 |
| ❑ 280 Adam Burt | .10 | .05 |
| ❑ 281 Don Sweeney | .10 | .05 |
| ❑ 282 Mike Donnelly | .10 | .05 |
| ❑ 283 Lyle Odelein | .10 | .05 |
| ❑ 284 Gord Murphy | .10 | .05 |
| ❑ 285 Mikael Andersson | .10 | .05 |
| ❑ 286 Bret Hedican | .10 | .05 |
| ❑ 287 Bill Berg | .10 | .05 |
| ❑ 288 Esa Tikkanen | .10 | .05 |
| ❑ 289 Markus Naslund | .10 | .05 |
| ❑ 290 Checklist | .10 | .05 |
| ❑ 291 Kerry Huffman | .10 | .05 |
| ❑ 292 Dana Murzyn | .10 | .05 |
| ❑ 293 Rob Niedermayer | .15 | .07 |
| ❑ 294 Andre Racicot | .15 | .07 |
| ❑ 295 Ken Sutton | .10 | .05 |
| ❑ 296 Shawn Burr | .10 | .05 |
| ❑ 297 Scott Pearson | .10 | .05 |
| ❑ 298 Joby Messier | .10 | .05 |
| ❑ 299 Darrin Madeley | .10 | .05 |
| ❑ 300 Joe Mullen | .15 | .07 |
| ❑ 301 Stephane Fiset | .15 | .07 |
| ❑ 302 Geoff Smith | .10 | .05 |
| ❑ 303 Vyacheslav Kozlov | .15 | .07 |
| ❑ 304 Wayne Gretzky | 2.00 | .90 |
| ❑ 305 Curtis Leschyshyn | .10 | .05 |
| ❑ 306 Mike Sillinger | .10 | .05 |
| ❑ 307 Vyacheslav Butsayev | .10 | .05 |
| ❑ 308 Mark Lamb | .10 | .05 |
| ❑ 309 German Titov | .10 | .05 |
| ❑ 310 Gerard Gallant | .10 | .05 |
| ❑ 311 Alexandre Daigle | .10 | .05 |
| ❑ 312 Jim Hrivnak | .15 | .07 |
| ❑ 313 Corey Hirsch | .15 | .07 |
| ❑ 314 Craig Berube | .10 | .05 |
| ❑ 315 Bill Houlder | .10 | .05 |
| ❑ 316 Ron Wilson | .10 | .05 |
| ❑ 317 Glen Murray | .10 | .05 |
| ❑ 318 Bryan Trottier | .15 | .07 |
| ❑ 319 Jeff Hackett | .15 | .07 |
| ❑ 320 Brad Dalgarno | .10 | .05 |
| ❑ 321 Petr Klima | .10 | .05 |
| ❑ 322 Jon Casey | .15 | .07 |
| ❑ 323 Mikael Renberg | .30 | .14 |
| ❑ 324 Jimmy Waite | .15 | .07 |
| ❑ 325 Brian Skrudland | .10 | .05 |
| ❑ 326 Vitali Prokhorov | .10 | .05 |
| ❑ 327 Glenn Healy | .15 | .07 |
| ❑ 328 Brian Benning | .10 | .05 |
| ❑ 329 Tony Hrkac | .10 | .05 |
| ❑ 330 Stu Grimson | .10 | .05 |
| ❑ 331 Chris Gratton | .15 | .07 |
| ❑ 332 Dave Poulin | .10 | .05 |
| ❑ 333 Jarrod Skalde | .10 | .05 |
| ❑ 334 Christian Ruuttu | .10 | .05 |
| ❑ 335 Mark Fitzpatrick | .15 | .07 |
| ❑ 336 Martin Lapointe | .10 | .05 |
| ❑ 337 Cam Stewart | .10 | .05 |
| ❑ 338 Anatoli Semenov | .10 | .05 |
| ❑ 339 Gaetan Duchesne | .10 | .05 |
| ❑ 340 Checklist | .10 | .05 |
| ❑ 341 Ron Hextall | .15 | .07 |
| ❑ 342 Mikhail Tatarinov | .10 | .05 |
| ❑ 343 Danny Lorenz | .10 | .05 |
| ❑ 344 Craig Simpson | .10 | .05 |
| ❑ 345 Martin Brodeur | 1.00 | .45 |
| ❑ 346 Jaromir Jagr | 1.00 | .45 |
| ❑ 347 Tyler Wright | .10 | .05 |
| ❑ 348 Greg Gilbert | .10 | .05 |

❏ 349 Dave Tippett ..................10 .05
❏ 350 Stu Barnes .....................10 .05
❏ 351 Daniel Lacroix ...............10 .05
❏ 352 Marty McSorley ..............10 .05
❏ 353 Sean Hill ........................15 .07
❏ 354 Craig Billington ..............15 .07
❏ 355 Donald Dufresne .............10 .05
❏ 356 Guy Hebert .....................15 .07
❏ 357 Neil Wilkinson ................10 .05
❏ 358 Sandy McCarthy .............10 .05
❏ 359 Aaron Ward ....................10 .05
❏ 360 Scott Thomas .................10 .05
❏ 361 Corey Millen ...................15 .07
❏ 362 Matthew Barnaby ............15 .07
❏ 363 Benoit Brunet .................10 .05
❏ 364 Boris Mironov .................10 .05
❏ 365 Doug Lidster ...................10 .05
❏ 366 Pavol Demitra .................10 .05
❏ 367 Damian Rhodes ...............15 .07
❏ 368 Shawn Antoski ................10 .05
❏ 369 Andy Moog .....................15 .07
❏ 370 Greg Johnson .................10 .05
❏ 371 John Vanbiesbrouck .........50 .23
❏ 372 Denis Savard ..................15 .07
❏ 373 Michel Goulet .................15 .07
❏ 374 Dave Taylor .....................15 .07
❏ 375 Enrico Ciccone ...............10 .05
❏ 376 Sergei Zholtok ................10 .05
❏ 377 Bob Errey ........................10 .05
❏ 378 Doug Brown .....................10 .05
❏ 379 Bill McDougall .................10 .05
❏ 380 Pat Conacher ..................10 .05
❏ 381 Alexei Kasatonov ............10 .05
❏ 382 Jason Arnott ................1.00 .45
❏ 383 Jarkko Varvio ..................10 .05
❏ 384 Sergei Makarov ...............10 .05
❏ 385 Trevor Kidd .....................15 .07
❏ 386 Alexei Yashin ..................15 .07
❏ 387 Gerald Diduck .................10 .05
❏ 388 Paul Ysebaert .................10 .05
❏ 389 Jason Smith ....................10 .05
❏ 390 Jeff Norton .....................10 .05
❏ 391 Igor Larionov ..................10 .05
❏ 392 Pierre Sevigny ................10 .05
❏ 393 Wes Walz ........................10 .05
❏ 394 Grant Ledyard .................10 .05
❏ 395 Brad McCrimmon .............10 .05
❏ 396 Martin Gelinas ................10 .05
❏ 397 Paul Cavallini ..................10 .05
❏ 398 Brian Noonan ..................10 .05
❏ 399 Mike Lalor .......................10 .05
❏ 400 Dimitri Filimonov ............10 .05
❏ 401 Andrei Lomakin ...............10 .05
❏ 402 Steve Junker ...................10 .05
❏ 403 Darin Puppa ....................15 .07
❏ 404 Jozef Stumpel .................10 .05
❏ 405 Jeff Shantz .....................10 .05
❏ 406 Terry Yake ......................10 .05
❏ 407 Mike Peluso .....................10 .05
❏ 408 Vitali Karamnov ..............10 .05
❏ 409 Felix Potvin .....................30 .14
❏ 410 Steven King ....................10 .05
❏ 411 Roman Oksiuta ...............10 .05
❏ 412 Mark Greig ......................10 .05
❏ 413 Wayne McBean ................10 .05
❏ 414 Nick Kypreos ...................10 .05
❏ 415 Dominic Lavoie ................10 .05
❏ 416 Chris Simon ....................10 .05
❏ 417 Peter Popovic ..................10 .05
❏ 418 Gino Odjick .....................10 .05
❏ 419 Mike Rathje .....................10 .05
❏ 420 Keith Acton .....................10 .05
❏ 421 Bob Carpenter .................10 .05
❏ 422 Steven Finn ....................10 .05
❏ 423 Ian Herbers .....................10 .05
❏ 424 Ted Drury ........................10 .05
❏ 425 Sergei Petrenko ..............10 .05
❏ 426 Mattias Norstrom ............10 .05
❏ 427 Todd Ewen ......................10 .05
❏ 428 Jocelyn Thibault ...........1.25 .55
❏ 429 Robert Burakovsky ..........10 .05
❏ 430 Chris Terreri ...................15 .07
❏ 431 Michal Sykora ..................10 .05
❏ 432 Craig Ludwig ...................10 .05
❏ 433 Vesa Vitakoski ................10 .05
❏ 434 Sergei Krivokrasov ..........10 .05
❏ 435 Darren McCarty ...............40 .18
❏ 436 Dean McAmmond .............10 .05
❏ 437 J.J. Daigneault ................10 .05
❏ 438 Vladimir Ruzicka ..............10 .05
❏ 439 Vlastimil Kroupa ..............10 .05
❏ 440 Checklist ........................10 .05
❏ NNO Mario Lemieux ..........10.00 4.50
     oversized promo

## 1993-94 Leaf Freshman Phenoms

Randomly inserted in Series II packs, these ten standard-size cards feature borderless color player action shots on their fronts. The player's name appears in white lettering beneath the set's title in the darkened area at the bottom of the player photo. The horizontal back carries a color player action shot on one side, and player information within a black rectangle on the other.

|                          | MINT  | NRMT |
|--------------------------|-------|------|
| COMPLETE SET (10) ...... | 20.00 | 9.00 |
| COMMON CARD (1-10) ... | .50   | .23  |

❏ 1 Alexandre Daigle .............2.50 1.10
❏ 2 Chris Pronger ..................2.50 1.10
❏ 3 Chris Gratton ..................2.50 1.10
❏ 4 Markus Naslund .................50 .23
❏ 5 Mikael Renberg ................2.50 1.10
❏ 6 Rob Niedermayer ..............2.50 1.10
❏ 7 Jason Arnott ....................4.00 1.80
❏ 8 Jarkko Varvio ....................50 .23
❏ 9 Alexei Yashin ...................2.50 1.10
❏ 10 Jocelyn Thibault .............4.00 1.80

## 1993-94 Leaf Gold All-Stars

This 10-card set was randomly inserted in first (1-5) and second (6-10) series foil packs. These standard-size cards feature the NHL's top players at each position, with one player portrayed on each card side.

|                             | MINT  | NRMT  |
|-----------------------------|-------|-------|
| COMPLETE SET (10) ......... | 60.00 | 27.00 |
| COMPLETE SERIES 1 (5) ... | 30.00 | 13.50 |
| COMPLETE SERIES 2 (5) ... | 30.00 | 13.50 |
| COMMON CARD (1-10) ..... | 3.00  | 1.35  |

❏ 1 Mario Lemieux ...............10.00 4.50
     Pat LaFontaine
❏ 2 Chris Chelios ...................3.00 1.35
     Larry Murphy
❏ 3 Brett Hull .......................5.00 2.20
     Teemu Selanne
❏ 4 Kevin Stevens .................3.00 1.35
     Dave Andreychuk
❏ 5 Patrick Roy ...................10.00 4.50
     Tom Barrasso
❏ 6 Wayne Gretzky ..............15.00 6.75
     Doug Gilmour
❏ 7 Ray Bourque ...................3.00 1.35
     Paul Coffey
❏ 8 Alexander Mogilny ...........5.00 2.20
     Pavel Bure
❏ 9 Luc Robitaille ..................5.00 2.20
     Brendan Shanahan
❏ 10 Ed Belfour .....................3.00 1.35
     Felix Potvin

## 1993-94 Leaf Gold Rookies

Randomly inserted in first series foil packs, this 15-card standard-size set showcases top rookies from the 1992-93 season. Borderless horizontal fronts have a photo of the player along with "Gold Leaf Rookie 1992-93" prominent on the front. Red backs carry a player photo and rookie year highlights. The cards are numbered on back as "X of 15".

|                          | MINT  | NRMT  |
|--------------------------|-------|-------|
| COMPLETE SET (15) ...... | 25.00 | 11.00 |
| COMMON CARD (1-15) ... | 1.00  | .45   |

❏ 1 Teemu Selanne ...............4.00 1.80
❏ 2 Joe Juneau ......................1.50 .70
❏ 3 Eric Lindros .....................8.00 3.60
❏ 4 Felix Potvin ....................2.00 .90
❏ 5 Alexei Zhamnov ...............1.50 .70
❏ 6 Andrei Kovalenko .............1.00 .45
❏ 7 Shawn McEachern .............1.00 .45
❏ 8 Alexei Zhitnik .................1.00 .45
❏ 9 Vladimir Malakhov .............1.00 .45
❏ 10 Patrick Poulin .................1.00 .45
❏ 11 Keith Tkachuk .................2.00 .90
❏ 12 Tommy Soderstrom ..........1.50 .70
❏ 13 Darius Kasparaitis ...........1.00 .45
❏ 14 Scott Niedermayer ...........1.00 .45
❏ 15 Darryl Sydor ...................1.00 .45

## 1993-94 Leaf Hat Trick Artists

This 10-card set was randomly inserted in first (1-5) and second (6-10) series U.S. foil and magazine distribution packs. These standard-size cards honor players who scored three or more hat tricks in the 1992-93 season.

|                             | MINT  | NRMT |
|-----------------------------|-------|------|
| COMPLETE SET (10) ......... | 20.00 | 9.00 |
| COMPLETE SERIES 1 (5) ... | 10.00 | 4.50 |
| COMPLETE SERIES 2 (5) ... | 10.00 | 4.50 |
| COMMON CARD (1-10) ..... | 1.25  | .55  |

❏ 1 Mario Lemieux .................4.00 1.80
     Title Card
❏ 2 Alexander Mogilny ...........2.00 .90
❏ 3 Teemu Selanne ...............3.00 1.35
❏ 4 Mario Lemieux .................8.00 3.60
❏ 5 Pierre Turgeon ................2.00 .90
❏ 6 Kevin Dineen ...................1.25 .55
❏ 7 Eric Lindros .....................6.00 2.70
❏ 8 Adam Oates .....................2.00 .90
❏ 9 Kevin Stevens .................2.00 .90
❏ 10 Steve Yzerman ...............4.00 1.80

## 1993-94 Leaf Mario Lemieux

As part of a 10-card subset randomly inserted in first (1-5) and second (6-10) series foil packs, these standard-size cards trace Lemieux's illustrious career. Mario Lemieux personally autographed 2,000 of his cards.

|                              | MINT   | NRMT   |
|------------------------------|--------|--------|
| COMPLETE SET (10) ......... | 20.00  | 9.00   |
| COMPLETE SERIES 1 (5) ... | 10.00  | 4.50   |
| COMPLETE SERIES 2 (5) ... | 10.00  | 4.50   |
| COMMON LEMIEUX (1-10) ... | 2.50   | 1.10   |
| CERTIFIED AUTO .............. | 300.00 | 135.00 |

❏ 1 Mario Lemieux .................2.50 1.10
     Title Card
❏ 2 Mario Lemieux .................2.50 1.10
     1st Pick in
     1984 NHL Draft
❏ 3 Mario Lemieux .................2.50 1.10
     1984 QMJHL POY
❏ 4 Mario Lemieux .................2.50 1.10
     1984-85 Calder Trophy
     Winner
❏ 5 Mario Lemieux .................2.50 1.10
     1987-88 Hart Trophy
     and Art Ross Trophy
     Winner
❏ 6 Two Time Conn Smythe .....2.50 1.10
     Trophy Winner
❏ 7 Six Time .........................2.50 1.10
     NHL All-Star
❏ 8 Penguins Capture .............2.50 1.10
     First Stanley Cup
❏ 9 1992-93; ..........................2.50 1.10
     Mario Lemieux
     Best Season Ever
❏ 10 Mario's ..........................2.50 1.10
     Magnificent Career

## 1993-94 Leaf Painted Warriors

As part of a 10-card subset randomly inserted in first (1-5) and second (6-10) series foil packs, these standard-size cards feature up-close shots of NHL goalies with emphasis on mask design. The back has a small color photo, biography and career highlights.

|                             | MINT  | NRMT |
|-----------------------------|-------|------|
| COMPLETE SET (10) ......... | 25.00 | 11.00 |
| COMPLETE SERIES 1 (5) ... | 15.00 | 6.75 |
| COMPLETE SERIES 2 (5) ... | 10.00 | 4.50 |
| COMMON CARD (1-10) ..... | 2.00  | .90  |

❏ 1 Felix Potvin ....................3.00 1.35
❏ 2 Curtis Joseph ..................3.00 1.35
❏ 3 Kirk McLean ....................2.00 .90
❏ 4 Patrick Roy .....................3.00 1.35
❏ 5 Grant Fuhr ......................3.00 1.35
❏ 6 Ed Belfour .......................3.00 1.35
❏ 7 Mike Vernon ....................2.50 1.10
❏ 8 John Vanbiesbrouck ..........3.00 1.35
❏ 9 Tom Barrasso UER ...........3.00 1.35
     (Notes he was traded to
     Pittsburgh in 1968 instead of '88)
❏ 10 Bill Ranford ...................2.50 1.10

## 1993-94 Leaf Studio Signature

As part of a 10-card subset randomly inserted in first (1-5) and second (6-10) series Canadian and magazine distribution foil packs, these standard-size cards spotlight the NHL's top players. Against a colorful background of the team's uniform, the fronts display a cut out player photo with his gold foil signature stamped across the bottom. The backs carry a full-bleed color close-up photo and text that defines the player's personal style.

|                             | MINT  | NRMT  |
|-----------------------------|-------|-------|
| COMPLETE SET (10) ......... | 40.00 | 18.00 |
| COMPLETE SERIES 1 (5) ... | 20.00 | 9.00  |
| COMPLETE SERIES 2 (5) ... | 20.00 | 9.00  |
| COMMON CARD (1-10) ..... | 2.00  | .90   |

❏ 1 Doug Gilmour ..................2.50 1.10
❏ 2 Pat Falloon .....................2.00 .90
❏ 3 Pat LaFontaine ................2.50 1.10
❏ 4 Wayne Gretzky ..............12.00 5.50
❏ 5 Steve Yzerman ................6.00 2.70
❏ 6 Patrick Roy ...................10.00 4.50
❏ 7 Jeremy Roenick ...............2.50 1.10
❏ 8 Brett Hull .......................2.50 1.10
❏ 9 Alexandre Daigle ..............2.00 .90
❏ 10 Eric Lindros ..................10.00 4.50

## 1994-95 Leaf

This 550-card standard-size set was released in two series. Series 1 was 330 cards while series 2 contained 220 cards. Each came in 12-card hobby and 18-card retail packs. These full-bleed cards carry a small Leaf logo above the player's name in gold foil along the bottom. The team name is stamped across the top, also in gold foil. Card backs feature four photos with brief personal and statistical information. The set contains no subsets. Rookie Cards include Mariusz Czerkaswki, Byron Dafoe, Eric Fichaud, Ian Laperriere and Jason Wiemer.

|                              | MINT  | NRMT  |
|------------------------------|-------|-------|
| COMPLETE SET (550) ....... | 35.00 | 16.00 |
| COMPLETE SERIES 1 (330) ... | 20.00 | 9.00 |
| COMPLETE SERIES 2 (220) ... | 15.00 | 6.75 |
| COMMON CARD (1-550) ..... | .10   | .05   |

❏ 1 Mario Lemieux ................1.50 .70
❏ 2 Tony Amonte ...................15 .07
❏ 3 Steve Duchesne ...............10 .05
❏ 4 Glen Murray ....................10 .05
❏ 5 John LeClair ....................50 .23
❏ 6 Glen Wesley ....................10 .05
❏ 7 Chris Chelios ...................30 .14
❏ 8 Alexei Zhitnik .................10 .05
❏ 9 Mike Modano ...................40 .18
❏ 10 Pavel Bure ......................60 .25
❏ 11 Mark Messier ..................50 .23
❏ 12 Rob Blake ........................10 .05
❏ 13 Tony Twist .......................10 .05
❏ 14 Glenn Anderson ..............15 .07
❏ 15 Keith Redmond .................10 .05
❏ 16 Brett Hull .......................50 .23
❏ 17 Valeri Zelepukin ..............10 .05
❏ 18 Mike Richter .....................30 .14
❏ 19 Alexei Yashin ..................15 .07
❏ 20 Luc Robitaille ..................15 .07

❏ 21 Tim Sweeney ...................10 .05
❏ 22 Ted Drury ........................10 .05
❏ 23 Guy Carbonneau ..............10 .05
❏ 24 Stephane Richer ..............15 .07
❏ 25 Ulf Dahlen .......................10 .05
❏ 26 Fred Brathwaite ...............15 .07
❏ 27 Darius Kasparaitis ............10 .05
❏ 28 Kris Draper ......................10 .05
❏ 29 Alexander Godynyuk ..........10 .05
❏ 30 Brent Sutter ....................10 .05
❏ 31 Josef Beranek ..................10 .05
❏ 32 Stephane Matteau .............10 .05
❏ 33 Derek Plante ....................10 .05
❏ 34 Vesa Viitakoski ................10 .05
❏ 35 Dave Ellett ......................10 .05
❏ 36 Martin Straka ...................10 .05
❏ 37 Dimitri Yushkevich ............10 .05
❏ 38 John Tucker .....................10 .05
❏ 39 Rob Gaudreau ..................10 .05
❏ 40 Doug Weight ....................15 .07
❏ 41 Patrick Roy ...................1.50 .70
❏ 42 Brian Bradley ...................10 .05
❏ 43 Bob Beers ........................10 .05
❏ 44 Dino Ciccarelli .................15 .07
❏ 45 Dean Evason ....................10 .05
❏ 46 Ron Tugnutt ....................15 .07
❏ 47 Andy Moog .......................15 .07
❏ 48 Jason Dawe ......................10 .05
❏ 49 Ted Donato ......................10 .05
❏ 50 Ron Hextall ......................15 .07
❏ 51 Derek Armstrong ..............10 .05
❏ 52 Craig James .....................15 .07
❏ 53 Geoff Courtnall ................15 .07
❏ 54 Mikael Renberg ................15 .07
❏ 55 Theoren Fleury .................15 .07
❏ 56 Martin Brodeur .................75 .35
❏ 57 Mattias Norstrom ..............10 .05
❏ 58 David Sacco .....................10 .05
❏ 59 Jeff Reese .......................10 .05
❏ 60 Bill Ranford ......................15 .07
❏ 61 Dan Quinn ........................10 .05
❏ 62 Joe Juneau ......................15 .07
❏ 63 Jeremy Roenick .................30 .14
❏ 64 Donald Audette .................15 .07
❏ 65 Zdeno Ciger .....................10 .05
❏ 66 Cliff Ronning ....................10 .05
❏ 67 Steve Thomas ..................10 .05
❏ 68 Norm Maciver ...................10 .05
❏ 69 Vincent Damphousse .........15 .07
❏ 70 John Vanbiesbrouck ...........50 .23
❏ 71 Andrei Kovalenko ..............10 .05
❏ 72 Dave Andreychuk ..............15 .07
❏ 73 Stu Barnes .......................10 .05
❏ 74 Jamie McLennan ................15 .07
❏ 75 Rudy Poeschek .................10 .05
❏ 76 Ken Wregget ....................15 .07
❏ 77 Ray Bourque .....................30 .14
❏ 78 Grant Fuhr .......................15 .07
❏ 79 Paul Cavallini ...................10 .05
❏ 80 Nelson Emerson ...............10 .05
❏ 81 Tim Cheveldae ..................15 .07
❏ 82 Mariusz Czerkawski ...........15 .07
❏ 83 Pat Peake ........................15 .07
❏ 84 Craig Billington .................15 .07
❏ 85 Sean Burke .......................15 .07
❏ 86 Chris Gratton ...................15 .07
❏ 87 Andrei Trefilov .................10 .05
❏ 88 Terry Yake .......................10 .05
❏ 89 Mark Recchi .....................15 .07
❏ 90 Igor Korolev .....................10 .05
❏ 91 Mark Tinordi .....................10 .05
❏ 92 Alexei Kovalev ..................15 .07
❏ 93 Bob Essensa .....................15 .07
❏ 94 Keith Tkachuk ..................40 .18
❏ 95 Pat Falloon .......................10 .05
❏ 96 John Slaney ......................10 .05
❏ 97 Alexei Zhamnov ................15 .07
❏ 98 Jeff Norton ......................10 .05
❏ 99 Doug Gilmour ....................30 .14
❏ 100 Rick Tocchet ...................15 .07
❏ 101 Robert Kron .....................10 .05
❏ 102 Patrik Carnback ................10 .05
❏ 103 Tom Barrasso ...................15 .07
❏ 104 Jari Kurri ........................15 .07
❏ 105 Iain Fraser ......................10 .05
❏ 106 Mike Donnelly ..................10 .05
❏ 107 Ray Sheppard ...................15 .07
❏ 108 Scott Young .....................10 .05
❏ 109 Kirk McLean .....................15 .07
❏ 110 Checklist .........................10 .05
❏ 111 Sergei Zubov ...................10 .05
❏ 112 Ivan Droppa .....................10 .05
❏ 113 Brendan Shanahan ............60 .25
❏ 114 Michal Pivonka .................10 .05
❏ 115 Pavol Demitra ..................10 .05
❏ 116 Doug Brown .....................10 .05
❏ 117 Valeri Kamensky ...............15 .07
❏ 118 Alexander Karpovtsev .......10 .05
❏ 119 Alexandre Daigle ..............15 .07
❏ 120 Dominik Hasek ..................60 .25
❏ 121 Murray Craven ..................10 .05
❏ 122 Michal Sykora ...................10 .05
❏ 123 Aris Brimanis ...................10 .05
❏ 124 Benoit Hogue ...................10 .05
❏ 125 Arto Blomsten ..................10 .05
❏ 126 Russ Courtnall .................10 .05
❏ 127 Bryan Marchment ..............10 .05
❏ 128 Jeff Hackett ....................15 .07
❏ 129 Kevin Miller .....................10 .05
❏ 130 Bryan Smolinski ................10 .05
❏ 131 John Druce ......................10 .05
❏ 132 Roman Hamrlik ..................15 .07
❏ 133 Jason Arnott .....................15 .07
❏ 134 Chris Terreri ....................15 .07
❏ 135 Mike Gartner ....................15 .07
❏ 136 Darryl Sydor .....................10 .05

| | | |
|---|---|---|
| ❑ 137 Lyle Odelein | .10 | .05 |
| ❑ 138 Martin Gelinas | .10 | .05 |
| ❑ 139 Mike Rathje | .10 | .05 |
| ❑ 140 Sylvain Cote | .10 | .05 |
| ❑ 141 Nicklas Lidstrom | .15 | .07 |
| ❑ 142 Guy Hebert | .15 | .07 |
| ❑ 143 Jozef Stumpel | .10 | .05 |
| ❑ 144 Owen Nolan | .15 | .07 |
| ❑ 145 Jesse Belanger | .10 | .05 |
| ❑ 146 Bill Guerin | .10 | .05 |
| ❑ 147 Mike Stapleton | .10 | .05 |
| ❑ 148 Steve Yzerman | 1.00 | .45 |
| ❑ 149 Michael Nylander | .10 | .05 |
| ❑ 150 Rod Brind'Amour | .15 | .07 |
| ❑ 151 Jaromir Jagr | 1.00 | .45 |
| ❑ 152 Darcy Wakaluk | .15 | .07 |
| ❑ 153 Sergei Nemchinov | .10 | .05 |
| ❑ 154 Wes Walz | .10 | .05 |
| ❑ 155 Sergei Fedorov | .60 | .25 |
| ❑ 156 Dan Laperriere | .10 | .05 |
| ❑ 157 Marty McInnis | .10 | .05 |
| ❑ 158 Chris Joseph | .10 | .05 |
| ❑ 159 Matt Martin | .10 | .05 |
| ❑ 160 Checklist | .10 | .05 |
| ❑ 161 Denis Tsygurov | .10 | .05 |
| ❑ 162 Stephan Lebeau | .10 | .05 |
| ❑ 163 Kirk Muller | .10 | .05 |
| ❑ 164 Shayne Corson | .10 | .05 |
| ❑ 165 Joe Sakic | .60 | .25 |
| ❑ 166 Denis Savard | .15 | .07 |
| ❑ 167 Kevin Dineen | .10 | .05 |
| ❑ 168 Paul Coffey | .30 | .14 |
| ❑ 169 Sandis Ozolinsh | .15 | .07 |
| ❑ 170 Stewart Malgunas | .10 | .05 |
| ❑ 171 Petr Klima | .10 | .05 |
| ❑ 172 Pat Verbeek | .10 | .05 |
| ❑ 173 Yan Kaminsky | .10 | .05 |
| ❑ 174 Marty McSorley | .10 | .05 |
| ❑ 175 Arturs Irbe | .15 | .07 |
| ❑ 176 Peter Popovic | .10 | .05 |
| ❑ 177 Brian Skrudland | .10 | .05 |
| ❑ 178 John Lilley | .10 | .05 |
| ❑ 179 Boris Mironov | .10 | .05 |
| ❑ 180 Garth Snow | .15 | .07 |
| ❑ 181 Alexei Kudashov | .10 | .05 |
| ❑ 182 Scott Mellanby | .15 | .07 |
| ❑ 183 Dale Hunter | .10 | .05 |
| ❑ 184 Tommy Soderstrom | .15 | .07 |
| ❑ 185 Claude Lemieux | .15 | .07 |
| ❑ 186 Felix Potvin | .30 | .14 |
| ❑ 187 Corey Millen | .10 | .05 |
| ❑ 188 Derek King | .10 | .05 |
| ❑ 189 Kelly Hrudey | .15 | .07 |
| ❑ 190 Dimitri Khristich | .10 | .05 |
| ❑ 191 Sylvain Turgeon | .10 | .05 |
| ❑ 192 John Gruden | .10 | .05 |
| ❑ 193 Mike Peca | .10 | .05 |
| ❑ 194 Vladimir Malakhov | .10 | .05 |
| ❑ 195 Mathieu Schneider | .10 | .05 |
| ❑ 196 Jeff Shantz | .10 | .05 |
| ❑ 197 Darren McCarty | .10 | .05 |
| ❑ 198 Craig Simpson | .10 | .05 |
| ❑ 199 Jarkko Varvio | .10 | .05 |
| ❑ 200 Gino Odjick | .10 | .05 |
| ❑ 201 Martin Lapointe | .10 | .05 |
| ❑ 202 Paul Ysebaert | .10 | .05 |
| ❑ 203 Mike McPhee | .10 | .05 |
| ❑ 204 John MacLean | .15 | .07 |
| ❑ 205 Ulf Samuelsson | .10 | .05 |
| ❑ 206 Garry Valk | .10 | .05 |
| ❑ 207 Tomas Sandstrom | .10 | .05 |
| ❑ 208 Curtis Joseph | .30 | .14 |
| ❑ 209 Mikhail Shtalenkov | .10 | .05 |
| ❑ 210 Darren Turcotte | .10 | .05 |
| ❑ 211 Markus Naslund | .10 | .05 |
| ❑ 212 Al Iafrate | .10 | .05 |
| ❑ 213 Jim Storm | .10 | .05 |
| ❑ 214 Dan Plante | .10 | .05 |
| ❑ 215 Brad May | .15 | .07 |
| ❑ 216 Nathan Lafayette | .10 | .05 |
| ❑ 217 Brian Noonan | .10 | .05 |
| ❑ 218 Brent Hughes | .10 | .05 |
| ❑ 219 Geoff Sanderson | .15 | .07 |
| ❑ 220 Checklist | .10 | .05 |
| ❑ 221 Eric Weinrich | .10 | .05 |
| ❑ 222 Greg Adams | .10 | .05 |
| ❑ 223 Dominic Roussel | .15 | .07 |
| ❑ 224 Daren Puppa | .15 | .07 |
| ❑ 225 Rob Niedermayer | .15 | .07 |
| ❑ 226 Todd Elik | .10 | .05 |
| ❑ 227 Donald Brashear | .10 | .05 |
| ❑ 228 Joe Nieuwendyk | .15 | .07 |
| ❑ 229 Tony Granato | .10 | .05 |
| ❑ 230 Kirk Maltby | .10 | .05 |
| ❑ 231 Jocelyn Thibault | .30 | .14 |
| ❑ 232 Shawn McEachern | .10 | .05 |
| ❑ 233 Teppo Numminen | .10 | .05 |
| ❑ 234 Johan Garpenlov | .10 | .05 |
| ❑ 235 Ron Francis | .15 | .07 |
| ❑ 236 Slava Kozlov | .15 | .07 |
| ❑ 237 Scott Niedermayer | .10 | .05 |
| ❑ 238 Sergei Krivokrasov | .10 | .05 |
| ❑ 239 Dave Manson | .10 | .05 |
| ❑ 240 Mike Ricci | .10 | .05 |
| ❑ 241 Chad Penney | .10 | .05 |
| ❑ 242 Calle Johansson | .10 | .05 |
| ❑ 243 Robert Reichel | .10 | .05 |
| ❑ 244 Igor Kravchuk | .10 | .05 |
| ❑ 245 Jason Smith | .10 | .05 |
| ❑ 246 Neal Broten | .15 | .07 |
| ❑ 247 Jeff Brown | .10 | .05 |
| ❑ 248 Jason Bowen | .10 | .05 |
| ❑ 249 Larry Murphy | .15 | .07 |
| ❑ 250 Gord Murphy | .10 | .05 |
| ❑ 251 Darrin Shannon | .10 | .05 |
| ❑ 252 Bobby Holik | .10 | .05 |
| ❑ 253 Zigmund Palffy | .30 | .14 |
| ❑ 254 Dmitri Mironov | .10 | .05 |
| ❑ 255 Adam Graves | .15 | .07 |
| ❑ 256 Alexander Mogilny | .15 | .07 |
| ❑ 257 Steve Smith | .10 | .05 |
| ❑ 258 Jim Montgomery | .10 | .05 |
| ❑ 259 Danton Cole | .10 | .05 |
| ❑ 260 Dave McLlwain | .10 | .05 |
| ❑ 261 German Titov | .10 | .05 |
| ❑ 262 Tom Chorske | .10 | .05 |
| ❑ 263 Grant Ledyard | .10 | .05 |
| ❑ 264 Garry Galley | .10 | .05 |
| ❑ 265 Vlastimil Kroupa | .10 | .05 |
| ❑ 266 Keith Primeau | .10 | .05 |
| ❑ 267 Cam Neely | .15 | .07 |
| ❑ 268 Chris Pronger | .15 | .07 |
| ❑ 269 Richard Matvichuk | .10 | .05 |
| ❑ 270 Steve Larmer | .15 | .07 |
| ❑ 271 James Patrick | .10 | .05 |
| ❑ 272 Joel Otto | .10 | .05 |
| ❑ 273 Todd Nelson | .10 | .05 |
| ❑ 274 Joe Sacco | .10 | .05 |
| ❑ 275 Jason York | .10 | .05 |
| ❑ 276 Andrew Cassels | .10 | .05 |
| ❑ 277 Peter Bondra | .30 | .14 |
| ❑ 278 Pat LaFontaine | .15 | .07 |
| ❑ 279 Nikolai Borschevsky | .10 | .05 |
| ❑ 280 Dave Mackey | .10 | .05 |
| ❑ 281 Cam Stewart | .10 | .05 |
| ❑ 282 Sergei Makarov | .10 | .05 |
| ❑ 283 Byron Dafoe | 1.25 | .55 |
| ❑ 284 Joe Murphy | .10 | .05 |
| ❑ 285 Matthew Barnaby | .15 | .07 |
| ❑ 286 Derian Hatcher | .10 | .05 |
| ❑ 287 Jyrki Lumme | .10 | .05 |
| ❑ 288 Travis Green | .15 | .07 |
| ❑ 289 Milos Holan | .10 | .05 |
| ❑ 290 Ed Patterson | .10 | .05 |
| ❑ 291 Randy Burridge | .10 | .05 |
| ❑ 292 Brian Savage | .10 | .05 |
| ❑ 293 Stephane Quintal | .10 | .05 |
| ❑ 294 Zarley Zalapski | .10 | .05 |
| ❑ 295 Vitali Prokhorov | .10 | .05 |
| ❑ 296 Ed Belfour | .30 | .14 |
| ❑ 297 Yuri Khmylev | .10 | .05 |
| ❑ 298 Dean McAmmond | .10 | .05 |
| ❑ 299 Bob Corkum | .10 | .05 |
| ❑ 300 Darrin Madeley | .10 | .05 |
| ❑ 301 Brian Bellows | .10 | .05 |
| ❑ 302 Andrei Lomakin | .10 | .05 |
| ❑ 303 Anatoli Semenov | .10 | .05 |
| ❑ 304 Claude Lapointe | .10 | .05 |
| ❑ 305 Adam Oates | .15 | .07 |
| ❑ 306 Richard Smehlik | .10 | .05 |
| ❑ 307 Jim Dowd | .10 | .05 |
| ❑ 308 Mark Fitzpatrick | .15 | .07 |
| ❑ 309 Pierre Sevigny | .10 | .05 |
| ❑ 310 Glenn Healy | .15 | .07 |
| ❑ 311 Igor Larionov | .10 | .05 |
| ❑ 312 Aaron Ward | .10 | .05 |
| ❑ 313 Dale Hawerchuk | .15 | .07 |
| ❑ 314 Bob Kudelski | .10 | .05 |
| ❑ 315 Chris Osgood | .50 | .23 |
| ❑ 316 Trent Klatt | .10 | .05 |
| ❑ 317 Gary Suter | .10 | .05 |
| ❑ 318 Tie Domi | .15 | .07 |
| ❑ 319 Dave Gagner | .15 | .07 |
| ❑ 320 Kevin Smyth | .10 | .05 |
| ❑ 321 Philippe Bozon | .10 | .05 |
| ❑ 322 Trevor Kidd | .15 | .07 |
| ❑ 323 Warren Rychel | .10 | .05 |
| ❑ 324 Steven Rice | .10 | .05 |
| ❑ 325 Patrice Brisebois | .10 | .05 |
| ❑ 326 Gary Roberts | .10 | .05 |
| ❑ 327 Fredrik Olausson | .10 | .05 |
| ❑ 328 Andrei Nazarov | .10 | .05 |
| ❑ 329 Stephane Fiset | .15 | .07 |
| ❑ 330 Checklist | .10 | .05 |
| ❑ 331 Fred Knipscheer | .10 | .05 |
| ❑ 332 Shawn Chambers | .10 | .05 |
| ❑ 333 Kelly Buchberger | .10 | .05 |
| ❑ 334 Ray Ferraro | .10 | .05 |
| ❑ 335 Dirk Graham | .10 | .05 |
| ❑ 336 Ken Daneyko | .10 | .05 |
| ❑ 337 Mark Lamb | .10 | .05 |
| ❑ 338 Shaun Van Allen | .10 | .05 |
| ❑ 339 Chris Simon | .15 | .07 |
| ❑ 340 Brent Gilchrist | .10 | .05 |
| ❑ 341 Greg Gilbert | .15 | .07 |
| ❑ 342 Brent Severyn | .10 | .05 |
| ❑ 343 Craig Berube | .10 | .05 |
| ❑ 344 Randy Moller | .10 | .05 |
| ❑ 345 Wayne Gretzky | 2.00 | .90 |
| ❑ 346 Shawn Anderson | .10 | .05 |
| ❑ 347 Mikael Andersson | .10 | .05 |
| ❑ 348 Jim Montgomery | .10 | .05 |
| ❑ 349 Scott Pearson | .10 | .05 |
| ❑ 350 Kevin Todd | .10 | .05 |
| ❑ 351 Ron Sutter | .10 | .05 |
| ❑ 352 Paul Kruse | .10 | .05 |
| ❑ 353 Doug Lidster | .10 | .05 |
| ❑ 354 Oleg Petrov | .10 | .05 |
| ❑ 355 Greg Johnson | .10 | .05 |
| ❑ 356 Kevin Stevens | .10 | .05 |
| ❑ 357 Doug Bodger | .10 | .05 |
| ❑ 358 Troy Mallette | .10 | .05 |
| ❑ 359 Keith Carney | .10 | .05 |
| ❑ 360 Petr Nedved | .15 | .07 |
| ❑ 361 Mark Janssens | .10 | .05 |
| ❑ 362 Teemu Selanne | .60 | .25 |
| ❑ 363 Scott Stevens | .15 | .07 |
| ❑ 364 Shane Churla | .10 | .05 |
| ❑ 365 John McIntyre | .10 | .05 |
| ❑ 366 Geoff Smith | .10 | .05 |
| ❑ 367 Pierre Turgeon | .15 | .07 |
| ❑ 368 Shawn Burr | .10 | .05 |
| ❑ 369 Kevin Hatcher | .10 | .05 |
| ❑ 370 Paul Ranheim | .10 | .05 |
| ❑ 371 Kevin Haller | .10 | .05 |
| ❑ 372 Scott Lachance | .10 | .05 |
| ❑ 373 Craig Muni | .10 | .05 |
| ❑ 374 Mike Ridley | .10 | .05 |
| ❑ 375 Joby Messier | .10 | .05 |
| ❑ 376 Thomas Steen | .10 | .05 |
| ❑ 377 Bruce Driver | .10 | .05 |
| ❑ 378 Mike Eastwood | .10 | .05 |
| ❑ 379 Brian Benning | .10 | .05 |
| ❑ 380 Dallas Drake | .10 | .05 |
| ❑ 381 Patrick Flatley | .10 | .05 |
| ❑ 382 Cam Russell | .10 | .05 |
| ❑ 383 Bobby Dollas | .10 | .05 |
| ❑ 384 Marc Bergevin | .10 | .05 |
| ❑ 385 Joe Mullen | .15 | .07 |
| ❑ 386 Chris Dahlquist | .10 | .05 |
| ❑ 387 Robert Petrovicky | .10 | .05 |
| ❑ 388 Yves Racine | .10 | .05 |
| ❑ 389 Adam Bennett | .10 | .05 |
| ❑ 390 Patrick Poulin | .10 | .05 |
| ❑ 391 Vladimir Konstantinov | .10 | .05 |
| ❑ 392 Frank Kucera | .10 | .05 |
| ❑ 393 Petr Svoboda | .10 | .05 |
| ❑ 394 Mike Sillinger | .10 | .05 |
| ❑ 395 Kris King | .10 | .05 |
| ❑ 396 Kelly Chase | .10 | .05 |
| ❑ 397 Peter Douris | .10 | .05 |
| ❑ 398 Bob Errey | .10 | .05 |
| ❑ 399 Ronnie Stern | .10 | .05 |
| ❑ 400 Randy McKay | .10 | .05 |
| ❑ 401 Benoit Brunet | .10 | .05 |
| ❑ 402 Gerald Diduck | .10 | .05 |
| ❑ 403 Brian Leetch | .30 | .14 |
| ❑ 404 Steve Heinze | .10 | .05 |
| ❑ 405 Jimmy Waite | .15 | .07 |
| ❑ 406 Nick Kypreos | .10 | .05 |
| ❑ 407 J.J. Daigneault | .10 | .05 |
| ❑ 408 Alexei Gusarov | .10 | .05 |
| ❑ 409 Paul Broten | .10 | .05 |
| ❑ 410 Drake Berehowsky | .10 | .05 |
| ❑ 411 Sandy McCarthy | .10 | .05 |
| ❑ 412 John Cullen | .10 | .05 |
| ❑ 413 Dan Quinn | .10 | .05 |
| ❑ 414 Dave Lowry | .10 | .05 |
| ❑ 415 Eric Lindros | 1.00 | .45 |
| ❑ 416 Igor Ulanov | .10 | .05 |
| ❑ 417 Bob Sweeney | .10 | .05 |
| ❑ 418 Jamie Macoun | .10 | .05 |
| ❑ 419 Brian Mullen | .10 | .05 |
| ❑ 420 Steve Leach | .10 | .05 |
| ❑ 421 Jamie Baker | .10 | .05 |
| ❑ 422 Uwe Krupp | .10 | .05 |
| ❑ 423 Steve Konowalchuk | .10 | .05 |
| ❑ 424 Craig Ludwig | .10 | .05 |
| ❑ 425 Bret Hedican | .10 | .05 |
| ❑ 426 Steve Dubinsky | .10 | .05 |
| ❑ 427 Rob Zamuner | .10 | .05 |
| ❑ 428 Dave Brown | .10 | .05 |
| ❑ 429 Robert Lang | .10 | .05 |
| ❑ 430 Dave Babych | .10 | .05 |
| ❑ 431 Scott Thornton | .10 | .05 |
| ❑ 432 Dave Archibald | .10 | .05 |
| ❑ 433 Eric Desjardins | .10 | .05 |
| ❑ 434 Jim Cummins | .10 | .05 |
| ❑ 435 Troy Loney | .10 | .05 |
| ❑ 436 Bob Carpenter | .10 | .05 |
| ❑ 437 Joe Reekie | .10 | .05 |
| ❑ 438 Mike Krushelnyski | .10 | .05 |
| ❑ 439 Jeff Odgers | .10 | .05 |
| ❑ 440 Checklist | .10 | .05 |
| ❑ 441 Brian Rolston | .10 | .05 |
| ❑ 442 Adam Deadmarsh | .15 | .07 |
| ❑ 443 Eric Fichaud | .75 | .35 |
| ❑ 444 Michel Petit | .10 | .05 |
| ❑ 445 Brett Lindros | .10 | .05 |
| ❑ 446 Pat Jablonski | .15 | .07 |
| ❑ 447 Janne Laukkanen | .10 | .05 |
| ❑ 448 Ray Whitney | .10 | .05 |
| ❑ 449 Tom Kurvers | .10 | .05 |
| ❑ 450 Phil Housley | .15 | .07 |
| ❑ 451 Viktor Kozlov | .10 | .05 |
| ❑ 452 Aaron Gavey | .10 | .05 |
| ❑ 453 Doug Zmolek | .10 | .05 |
| ❑ 454 Tony Twist | .10 | .05 |
| ❑ 455 Paul Kariya | 1.75 | .80 |
| ❑ 456 Vladislav Boulin | .10 | .05 |
| ❑ 457 Kevin Brown | .10 | .05 |
| ❑ 458 David Wilkie | .10 | .05 |
| ❑ 459 Jamie Pushor | .10 | .05 |
| ❑ 460 Glen Wesley | .10 | .05 |
| ❑ 461 Al MacInnis | .15 | .07 |
| ❑ 462 Bernie Nicholls | .10 | .05 |
| ❑ 463 Luc Robitaille | .15 | .07 |
| ❑ 464 Mike Vernon | .15 | .07 |
| ❑ 465 Alex Cherbayev | .10 | .05 |
| ❑ 466 Garth Butcher | .10 | .05 |
| ❑ 467 Todd Harvey | .10 | .05 |
| ❑ 468 Viktor Gordiouk | .10 | .05 |
| ❑ 469 Pat Neaton | .10 | .05 |
| ❑ 470 Jason Muzzatti | .15 | .07 |
| ❑ 471 Valeri Bure | .15 | .07 |
| ❑ 472 Kenny Jonsson | .10 | .05 |
| ❑ 473 Alexei Kasatonov | .10 | .05 |
| ❑ 474 Rick Tocchet | .15 | .07 |
| ❑ 475 Peter Forsberg | 1.50 | .70 |
| ❑ 476 Sean Hill | .10 | .05 |
| ❑ 477 Steven Rice | .10 | .05 |
| ❑ 478 David Roberts | .10 | .05 |
| ❑ 479 Justin Hocking | .10 | .05 |
| ❑ 480 Chris Therien | .10 | .05 |
| ❑ 481 Cale Hulse | .10 | .05 |
| ❑ 482 Jeff Friesen | .15 | .07 |
| ❑ 483 Brandon Convery | .10 | .05 |
| ❑ 484 Ian Laperriere | .10 | .05 |
| ❑ 485 Brent Grieve | .10 | .05 |
| ❑ 486 Valeri Karpov | .10 | .05 |
| ❑ 487 Steve Chiasson | .10 | .05 |
| ❑ 488 Jassen Cullimore | .10 | .05 |
| ❑ 489 Jason Wiemer | .10 | .05 |
| ❑ 490 Checklist | .10 | .05 |
| ❑ 491 Len Barrie | .10 | .05 |
| ❑ 492 Turner Stevenson | .10 | .05 |
| ❑ 493 Kelly Kisio | .10 | .05 |
| ❑ 494 Dwayne Norris | .10 | .05 |
| ❑ 495 Ron Hextall | .15 | .07 |
| ❑ 496 Jaroslav Modry | .10 | .05 |
| ❑ 497 Todd Gill | .10 | .05 |
| ❑ 498 Ken Sutton | .10 | .05 |
| ❑ 499 Sergio Momesso | .10 | .05 |
| ❑ 500 Dean Kennedy | .10 | .05 |
| ❑ 501 David Reid | .10 | .05 |
| ❑ 502 Jocelyn Lemieux | .10 | .05 |
| ❑ 503 Mark Osborne | .10 | .05 |
| ❑ 504 Mike Hough | .10 | .05 |
| ❑ 505 Todd Marchant | .10 | .05 |
| ❑ 506 Keith Jones | .10 | .05 |
| ❑ 507 Sylvain Lefebvre | .10 | .05 |
| ❑ 508 Sergei Zholtok | .10 | .05 |
| ❑ 509 Jay More | .10 | .05 |
| ❑ 510 Mike Craig | .10 | .05 |
| ❑ 511 Jason Allison | .10 | .05 |
| ❑ 512 Jim Paek | .10 | .05 |
| ❑ 513 Chris Tamer | .10 | .05 |
| ❑ 514 Craig MacTavish | .10 | .05 |
| ❑ 515 Mikko Makela | .10 | .05 |
| ❑ 516 Tom Fitzgerald | .10 | .05 |
| ❑ 517 Brent Fedyk | .10 | .05 |
| ❑ 518 Don Sweeney | .10 | .05 |
| ❑ 519 Kelly Miller | .10 | .05 |
| ❑ 520 Jiri Slegr | .10 | .05 |
| ❑ 521 Wayne Presley | .10 | .05 |
| ❑ 522 Mark Greig | .10 | .05 |
| ❑ 523 Doug Houda | .10 | .05 |
| ❑ 524 Kay Whitmore | .15 | .07 |
| ❑ 525 Craig Ferguson | .10 | .05 |
| ❑ 526 Kent Manderville | .10 | .05 |
| ❑ 527 Trevor Linden | .15 | .07 |
| ❑ 528 Jeff Beukeboom | .10 | .05 |
| ❑ 529 Adam Foote | .10 | .05 |
| ❑ 530 Mats Sundin | .15 | .07 |
| ❑ 531 Shjon Podein | .10 | .05 |
| ❑ 532 Louie DeBrusk | .10 | .05 |
| ❑ 533 Peter Zezel | .10 | .05 |
| ❑ 534 Greg Hawgood | .10 | .05 |
| ❑ 535 Pat Elynuik | .10 | .05 |
| ❑ 536 Mike Ramsey | .10 | .05 |
| ❑ 537 Bob Beers | .10 | .05 |
| ❑ 538 David Williams | .10 | .05 |
| ❑ 539 Philippe Boucher | .10 | .05 |
| ❑ 540 Rob Brown | .10 | .05 |
| ❑ 541 Marc Potvin | .10 | .05 |
| ❑ 542 Wendel Clark | .15 | .07 |
| ❑ 543 Alexander Semak | .10 | .05 |
| ❑ 544 Randy Wood | .10 | .05 |
| ❑ 545 Frank Musil | .10 | .05 |
| ❑ 546 Mike Peluso | .10 | .05 |
| ❑ 547 Gaetan Duchesne | .10 | .05 |
| ❑ 548 Curtis Leschyshyn | .10 | .05 |
| ❑ 549 Rob DiMaio | .10 | .05 |
| ❑ 550 Checklist | .10 | .05 |

## 1994-95 Leaf Crease Patrol

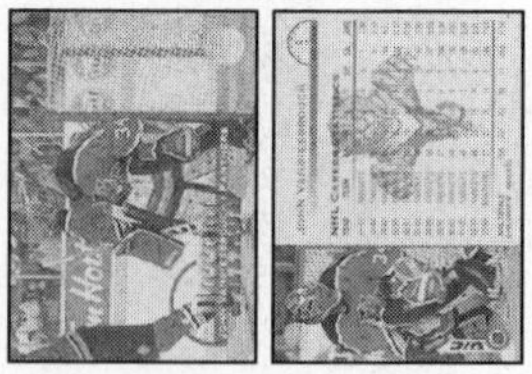

The ten cards in this set were randomly inserted in Leaf series 2 product at the rate of 1:9 packs. Complete sets also were available in randomly inserted Super-Packs. Cards feature a full bleed, horizontally-oriented front, with the set name, player name and logo along the bottom. Backs have a standard card look, with full stats, text, and small player photo. Cards are numbered "X of ten".

| | MINT | NRMT |
|---|---|---|
| COMPLETE SET (10) | 8.00 | 3.60 |
| COMMON CARD (1-10) | .50 | .23 |
| ❑ 1 Patrick Roy | 3.00 | 1.35 |
| ❑ 2 Ed Belfour | .75 | .35 |
| ❑ 3 Curtis Joseph | .75 | .35 |
| ❑ 4 Felix Potvin | .75 | .35 |
| ❑ 5 John Vanbiesbrouck | 1.00 | .45 |
| ❑ 6 Dominik Hasek | 1.25 | .55 |
| ❑ 7 Kirk McLean | .50 | .23 |
| ❑ 8 Mike Richter | .75 | .35 |
| ❑ 9 Martin Brodeur | 1.50 | .70 |
| ❑ 10 Bill Ranford | .75 | .35 |

## 1994-95 Leaf Fire on Ice

This 12-card set was inserted in Leaf series one packs at the rate of 1:18. Cards feature a cutout player image over the words "Fire On Ice", which embellishes the silver foil background. The player name is at the bottom of the card next to the Leaf logo. Card backs

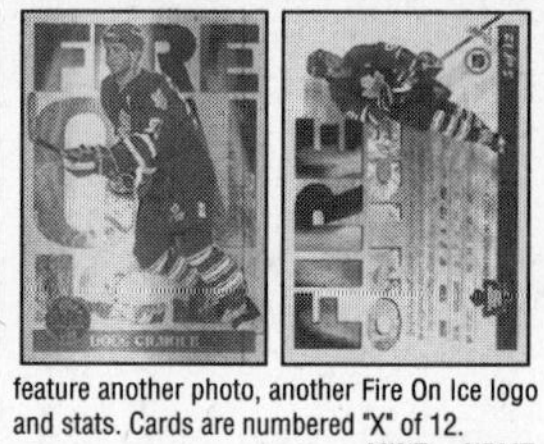

feature another photo, another Fire On Ice logo and stats. Cards are numbered "X" of 12.

| | MINT | NRMT |
|---|---|---|
| COMPLETE SET (12) | 50.00 | 22.00 |
| COMMON CARD (1-12) | 1.00 | .45 |
| ❑ 1 Sergei Fedorov | 3.00 | 1.35 |
| ❑ 2 Jeremy Roenick | 1.50 | .70 |
| ❑ 3 Pavel Bure | 3.00 | 1.35 |
| ❑ 4 Wayne Gretzky | 10.00 | 4.50 |
| ❑ 5 Doug Gilmour | 1.25 | .55 |
| ❑ 6 Eric Lindros | 6.00 | 2.70 |
| ❑ 7 Joe Juneau | 1.25 | .55 |
| ❑ 8 Paul Coffey | 1.50 | .70 |
| ❑ 9 Mario Lemieux | 8.00 | 3.60 |
| ❑ 10 Alexander Mogilny | 1.25 | .55 |
| ❑ 11 Mike Gartner | 1.00 | .45 |
| ❑ 12 Teemu Selanne | 3.00 | 1.35 |

## 1994-95 Leaf Gold Rookies

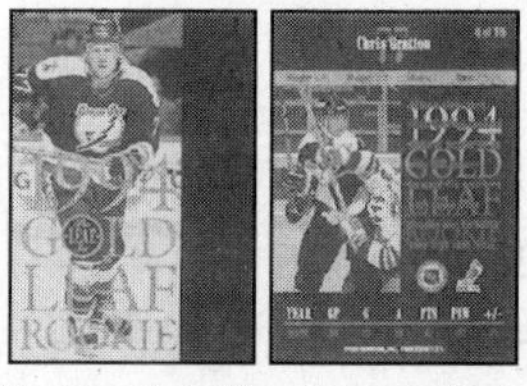

The 15 cards in this set were randomly inserted in Leaf series 1 product at the rate of 1:18 packs. Card fronts are very crowded, featuring one large color photo and three black-and-white photos. The set title is written in speckled gold foil over the large color shot. The team logo, team name and player name appear on the right-hand side with the black and white shots. Card backs feature another photo, along with personal info and stats as well as a short blurb. The cards are numbered "X of 15".

| | MINT | NRMT |
|---|---|---|
| COMPLETE SET (15) | 40.00 | 18.00 |
| COMMON CARD (1-15) | 2.00 | .90 |
| ❑ 1 Martin Brodeur | 10.00 | 4.50 |
| ❑ 2 Jason Arnott | 4.00 | 1.80 |
| ❑ 3 Alexei Yashin | 3.00 | 1.35 |
| ❑ 4 Chris Gratton | 3.00 | 1.35 |
| ❑ 5 Alexandre Daigle | 3.00 | 1.35 |
| ❑ 6 Mikael Renberg | 3.00 | 1.35 |
| ❑ 7 Rob Niedermayer | 3.00 | 1.35 |
| ❑ 8 Boris Mironov | 2.00 | .90 |
| ❑ 9 Chris Pronger | 3.00 | 1.35 |
| ❑ 10 Chris Osgood | 6.00 | 2.70 |
| ❑ 11 Derek Plante | 2.00 | .90 |
| ❑ 12 Pat Peake | 2.00 | .90 |
| ❑ 13 Jason Allison | 2.00 | .90 |
| ❑ 14 Bryan Smolinski | 2.00 | .90 |
| ❑ 15 Jocelyn Thibault | 4.00 | 1.80 |

## 1994-95 Leaf Gold Stars

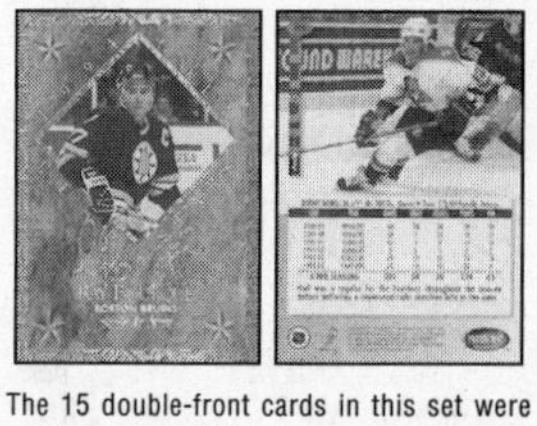

The 15 double-front cards in this set were randomly inserted in Leaf series 1 and 2 product at the rate of 1:72 packs. Cards 1-10 appeared in series 1, 11-15 in series 2. Cards feature a gold prismatic border. The player photo is in a diamond shaped gold prismatic border, surrounded by the set title. A gold foil facsimile autograph appears under the gold diamond, just over the player name and team affiliation. One side of each card bears a serial number out of 10,000. Cards are numbered "X of 15".

| | MINT | NRMT |
|---|---|---|
| COMPLETE SET (15) | 400.00 | 180.00 |
| COMPLETE SERIES 1 (10) | 250.00 | 110.00 |
| COMPLETE SERIES 2 (5) | 150.00 | 70.00 |
| COMMON CARD (1-15) | 20.00 | 9.00 |
| ❑ 1 Sergei Fedorov<br>Wayne Gretzky | 80.00 | 36.00 |
| ❑ 2 Doug Gilmour<br>Jeremy Roenick | 30.00 | 13.50 |

| | MINT | NRMT |
|---|---|---|
| ❑ 3 Patrick Roy / Mike Richter | 60.00 | 27.00 |
| ❑ 4 Brett Hull / Pavel Bure | 40.00 | 18.00 |
| ❑ 5 Mark Messier / Alexei Yashin | 30.00 | 13.50 |
| ❑ 6 Ray Bourque / Brian Leetch | 30.00 | 13.50 |
| ❑ 7 Chris Joseph / Ed Belfour | 30.00 | 13.50 |
| ❑ 8 Martin Brodeur / Dominik Hasek | 40.00 | 18.00 |
| ❑ 9 Cam Neely / Mikael Renberg | 20.00 | 9.00 |
| ❑ 10 Mike Modano / Jason Arnott | 30.00 | 13.50 |
| ❑ 11 Mario Lemieux / Eric Lindros | 60.00 | 27.00 |
| ❑ 12 Scott Stevens / Rob Blake | 20.00 | 9.00 |
| ❑ 13 John Vanbiesbrouck / Felix Potvin | 30.00 | 13.50 |
| ❑ 14 Adam Oates / Pat LaFontaine | 25.00 | 11.00 |
| ❑ 15 Jaromir Jagr / Mark Recchi | 40.00 | 18.00 |

## 1994-95 Leaf Limited Inserts

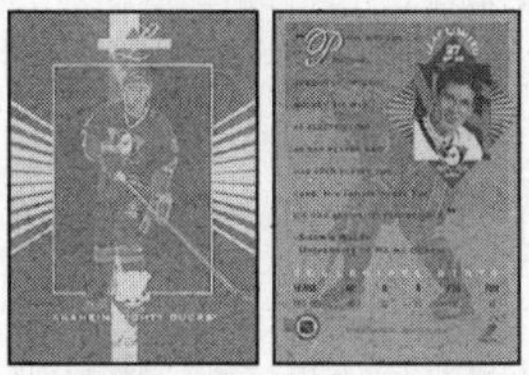

This 28-card insert set was issued in two series of 18 and 10 cards, in first and second series Leaf packs, respectively. Cards were randomly inserted at the rate of 1:18 packs, while series two could also be found randomly inserted into Super Packs. The cards are notable for the reflective silver border with rainbow lines coming out of the centered player photo. Player name is written in black at the base of the card below the team name printed in silver foil. The card backs have a ghosted photo covered by text and a small color portrait. These cards are identical in design to the Leaf Limited set issued in packs later in the season. Although the photos are different, the easiest way to determine which set your card belongs to is the numbering system. The inserts are numbered out of 28, while the regular issue cards simply bear a number.

| | MINT | NRMT |
|---|---|---|
| COMPLETE SET (28) | 140.00 | 65.00 |
| COMPLETE SERIES 1 (18) | 100.00 | 45.00 |
| COMPLETE SERIES 2 (10) | 40.00 | 18.00 |
| COMMON CARD (1-28) | 1.50 | .70 |
| ❑ 1 Guy Hebert | 2.00 | .90 |
| ❑ 2 Adam Oates | 2.50 | 1.10 |
| ❑ 3 Dominik Hasek | 6.00 | 2.70 |
| ❑ 4 Robert Reichel | 1.50 | .70 |
| ❑ 5 Jeremy Roenick | 2.50 | 1.10 |
| ❑ 6 Mike Modano | 3.00 | 1.35 |
| ❑ 7 Sergei Fedorov | 6.00 | 2.70 |
| ❑ 8 Jason Arnott | 2.00 | .90 |
| ❑ 9 John Vanbiesbrouck | 4.00 | 1.80 |
| ❑ 10 Chris Pronger | 2.00 | .90 |
| ❑ 11 Wayne Gretzky | 15.00 | 6.75 |
| ❑ 12 Patrick Roy | 12.00 | 5.50 |
| ❑ 13 Martin Brodeur | 6.00 | 2.70 |
| ❑ 14 Pierre Turgeon | 1.50 | .70 |
| ❑ 15 Mark Messier | 3.00 | 1.35 |
| ❑ 16 Alexei Yashin | 2.00 | .90 |
| ❑ 17 Eric Lindros | 10.00 | 4.50 |
| ❑ 18 Mario Lemieux | 12.00 | 5.50 |
| ❑ 19 Joe Sakic | 5.00 | 2.20 |
| ❑ 20 Brendan Shanahan | 5.00 | 2.20 |
| ❑ 21 Arturs Irbe | 2.00 | .90 |
| ❑ 22 Chris Gratton | 1.50 | .70 |
| ❑ 23 Doug Gilmour | 2.50 | 1.10 |
| ❑ 24 Pavel Bure | 5.00 | 2.20 |
| ❑ 25 Joe Juneau | 2.00 | .90 |
| ❑ 26 Teemu Selanne | 5.00 | 2.20 |
| ❑ 27 Paul Kariya | 10.00 | 4.50 |
| ❑ 28 Peter Forsberg | 10.00 | 4.50 |

## 1994-95 Leaf Phenoms

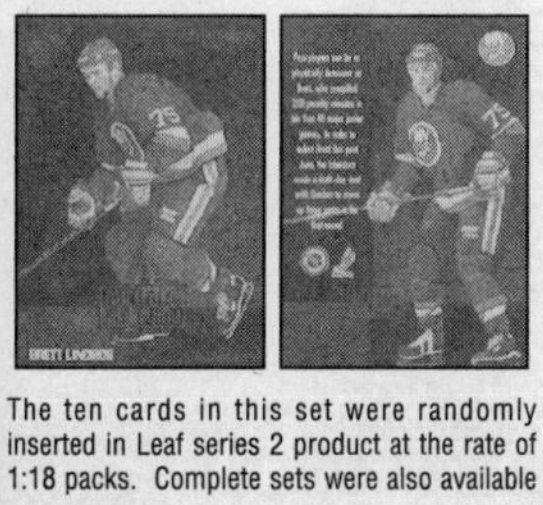

The ten cards in this set were randomly inserted in Leaf series 2 product at the rate of 1:18 packs. Complete sets were also available in random Super Packs. The card fronts come out of packs with a translucent protective film as well as a white sticker which read "Remove Protective Film". the cards are of a thick Mylar-type stock, and feature a player action photo superimposed over a black background. Set logo and player name appear at the bottom. The back carries a brief paragraph of information over a cut-out action photo. Cards are numbered "X of 10".

| | MINT | NRMT |
|---|---|---|
| COMPLETE SET (10) | 25.00 | 11.00 |
| COMMON CARD (1-10) | 2.00 | .90 |
| SEMISTARS/GOALIES | 3.00 | 1.35 |
| ❑ 1 Jamie Storr | 2.00 | .90 |
| ❑ 2 Brett Lindros | 2.00 | .90 |
| ❑ 3 Peter Forsberg | 10.00 | 4.50 |
| ❑ 4 Jason Wiemer | 2.00 | .90 |
| ❑ 5 Paul Kariya | 10.00 | 4.50 |
| ❑ 6 Oleg Tverdovsky | 2.00 | .90 |
| ❑ 7 Eric Fichaud | 5.00 | 2.20 |
| ❑ 8 Viktor Kozlov | 2.00 | .90 |
| ❑ 9 Jeff Friesen | 2.00 | .90 |
| ❑ 10 Valeri Karpov | 2.00 | .90 |

## 1994-95 Leaf Limited

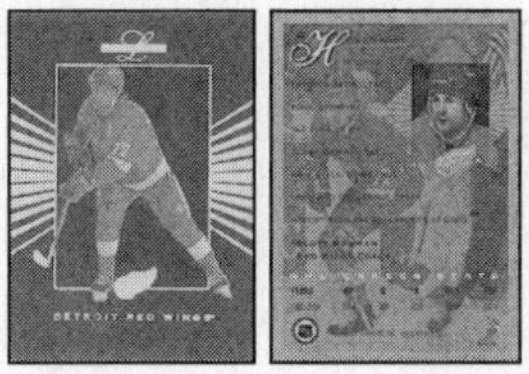

This 120-card super-premium set was issued in five-card packs, in 20 pack boxes, which were individually numbered out of 60,000. The card designs were identical to the Limited Inserts which were randomly inserted in Leaf product earlier in the season. The cards have a large reflective silver border with rainbow lines coming out of the centered player photo. The player name is in black at the base of the card below the team name, which is printed in silver foil. The card backs have a ghosted photo covered by text and a small color portrait. Cards are numbered in silver foil. Rookie cards in the set include Mariusz Czerkawski, Eric Fichaud and Jason Wiemer. Although different photos are used, it is often difficult to distinguish a Leaf Limited card from a Leaf Limited Insert. The best way to differentiate between these cards and the Leaf Limited Inserts is the numbering system. These cards are numbered 1-120, while the inserts are numbered out of 28.

| | MINT | NRMT |
|---|---|---|
| COMPLETE SET (120) | 50.00 | 22.00 |
| COMMON CARD (1-120) | .25 | .11 |
| ❑ 1 Mario Lemieux | 6.00 | 2.70 |
| ❑ 2 Brett Hull | 1.50 | .70 |
| ❑ 3 Ed Belfour | 1.25 | .55 |
| ❑ 4 Brian Rolston | .25 | .11 |
| ❑ 5 Garry Galley | .25 | .11 |
| ❑ 6 Steve Thomas | .25 | .11 |
| ❑ 7 Kevin Brown | .25 | .11 |
| ❑ 8 Doug Gilmour | 1.25 | .55 |
| ❑ 9 Bill Ranford | .50 | .23 |
| ❑ 10 Wayne Gretzky | 8.00 | 3.60 |
| ❑ 11 Rob Niedermayer | .50 | .23 |
| ❑ 12 Larry Murphy | .50 | .23 |
| ❑ 13 Glen Wesley | .25 | .11 |
| ❑ 14 Pat Falloon | .25 | .11 |
| ❑ 15 Jocelyn Thibault | 1.25 | .55 |
| ❑ 16 Felix Potvin | 1.25 | .55 |
| ❑ 17 Mike Richter | 1.25 | .55 |
| ❑ 18 Jeff Brown | .25 | .11 |
| ❑ 19 Jesse Belanger | .25 | .11 |
| ❑ 20 Benoit Hogue | .25 | .11 |
| ❑ 21 Viktor Kozlov | .25 | .11 |
| ❑ 22 Chris Pronger | .50 | .23 |
| ❑ 23 Kirk McLean | .50 | .23 |
| ❑ 24 Oleg Tverdovsky | .50 | .23 |
| ❑ 25 Derian Hatcher | .25 | .11 |
| ❑ 26 Ray Sheppard | .50 | .23 |
| ❑ 27 Pat Verbeek | .25 | .11 |
| ❑ 28 Patrick Roy | 5.00 | 2.20 |
| ❑ 29 Mariusz Czerkawski | .25 | .11 |
| ❑ 30 Ron Francis | .50 | .23 |
| ❑ 31 Wendel Clark | .50 | .23 |
| ❑ 32 Rob Blake | .25 | .11 |
| ❑ 33 Brian Leetch | 1.25 | .55 |
| ❑ 34 Dave Andreychuk | .50 | .23 |
| ❑ 35 Russ Courtnall | .25 | .11 |
| ❑ 36 Alexander Mogilny | .50 | .23 |
| ❑ 37 Kirk Muller | .25 | .11 |
| ❑ 38 Joe Juneau | .50 | .23 |
| ❑ 39 Robert Reichel | .25 | .11 |
| ❑ 40 Scott Niedermayer | .25 | .11 |
| ❑ 41 Owen Nolan | .50 | .23 |
| ❑ 42 Mats Sundin | .50 | .23 |
| ❑ 43 Sandis Ozolinsh | .50 | .23 |
| ❑ 44 Derek Plante | .25 | .11 |
| ❑ 45 Eric Fichaud | 1.50 | .70 |
| ❑ 46 Kevin Stevens | .25 | .11 |
| ❑ 47 Igor Larionov | .25 | .11 |
| ❑ 48 Mikael Renberg | .50 | .23 |
| ❑ 49 Cam Neely | .50 | .23 |
| ❑ 50 Brett Lindros | .25 | .11 |
| ❑ 51 Valeri Karpov | .25 | .11 |
| ❑ 52 Pierre Turgeon | .50 | .23 |
| ❑ 53 Doug Weight | .50 | .23 |
| ❑ 54 Geoff Sanderson | .50 | .23 |
| ❑ 55 Slava Kozlov | .50 | .23 |
| ❑ 56 Chris Gratton | .50 | .23 |
| ❑ 57 Bryan Smolinski | .25 | .11 |
| ❑ 58 Eric Lindros | 4.00 | 1.80 |
| ❑ 59 Alexei Kovalev | .50 | .23 |
| ❑ 60 Mike Modano | 1.50 | .70 |
| ❑ 61 Jeremy Roenick | 1.25 | .55 |
| ❑ 62 Martin Straka | .25 | .11 |
| ❑ 63 Pat LaFontaine | .50 | .23 |
| ❑ 64 Vlastimil Kroupa | .25 | .11 |
| ❑ 65 Sergei Zubov | .25 | .11 |
| ❑ 66 Jason Arnott | .50 | .23 |
| ❑ 67 Petr Nedved | .50 | .23 |
| ❑ 68 Teemu Selanne | 2.50 | 1.10 |
| ❑ 69 Geoff Courtnall | .25 | .11 |
| ❑ 70 Martin Brodeur | 3.00 | 1.35 |
| ❑ 71 Mark Recchi | .50 | .23 |
| ❑ 72 John Vanbiesbrouck | 2.00 | .90 |
| ❑ 73 Adam Graves | .50 | .23 |
| ❑ 74 Arturs Irbe | .50 | .23 |
| ❑ 75 Paul Coffey | 1.25 | .55 |
| ❑ 76 Ulf Dahlen | .25 | .11 |
| ❑ 77 Phil Housley | .50 | .23 |
| ❑ 78 Rod Brind'Amour | .50 | .23 |
| ❑ 79 Al MacInnis | .50 | .23 |
| ❑ 80 Alexei Yashin | .50 | .23 |
| ❑ 81 Sergei Fedorov | 2.50 | 1.10 |
| ❑ 82 Joe Nieuwendyk | .50 | .23 |
| ❑ 83 Chris Chelios | 1.25 | .55 |
| ❑ 84 Ray Bourque | 1.25 | .55 |
| ❑ 85 Scott Stevens | .50 | .23 |
| ❑ 86 Jaromir Jagr | 4.00 | 1.80 |
| ❑ 87 Alexandre Daigle | .25 | .11 |
| ❑ 88 Luc Robitaille | .50 | .23 |
| ❑ 89 Mark Messier | 1.50 | .70 |
| ❑ 90 Vincent Damphousse | .50 | .23 |
| ❑ 91 Craig Janney | .50 | .23 |
| ❑ 92 John MacLean | .50 | .23 |
| ❑ 93 Steve Duchesne | .25 | .11 |
| ❑ 94 Dale Hawerchuk | .50 | .23 |
| ❑ 95 Curtis Joseph | 1.25 | .55 |
| ❑ 96 Chris Osgood | 2.00 | .90 |
| ❑ 97 Brendan Shanahan | 2.50 | 1.10 |
| ❑ 98 Jason Allison | .25 | .11 |
| ❑ 99 Theoren Fleury | .50 | .23 |
| ❑ 100 Pavel Bure | 2.50 | 1.10 |
| ❑ 101 Mathieu Schneider | .25 | .11 |
| ❑ 102 Dominik Hasek | 2.50 | 1.10 |
| ❑ 103 Scott Mellanby | .50 | .23 |
| ❑ 104 Adam Oates | .50 | .23 |
| ❑ 105 Jari Kurri | .50 | .23 |
| ❑ 106 Joe Sakic | 2.50 | 1.10 |
| ❑ 107 Paul Kariya | 5.00 | 2.20 |
| ❑ 108 Keith Tkachuk | 1.50 | .70 |
| ❑ 109 Daren Puppa | .50 | .23 |
| ❑ 110 Keith Primeau | .50 | .23 |
| ❑ 111 Alexei Zhitnik | .25 | .11 |
| ❑ 112 Trevor Linden | .50 | .23 |
| ❑ 113 Alexei Zhamnov | .50 | .23 |
| ❑ 114 Gary Roberts | .25 | .11 |
| ❑ 115 Kenny Jonsson | .25 | .11 |
| ❑ 116 Peter Forsberg | 5.00 | 2.20 |
| ❑ 117 Rick Tocchet | .50 | .23 |
| ❑ 118 Aaron Gavey | .25 | .11 |
| ❑ 119 Jason Wiemer | .25 | .11 |
| ❑ 120 Steve Yzerman | 4.00 | 1.80 |

## 1994-95 Leaf Limited Gold

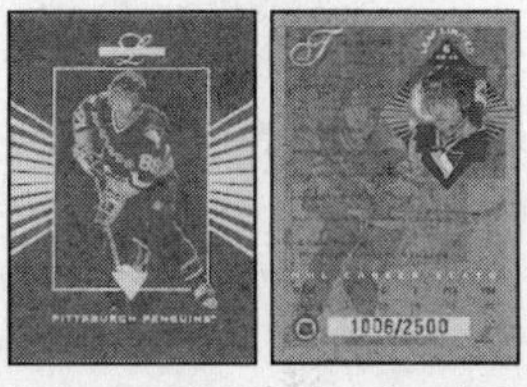

The ten cards in this set were randomly inserted into Limited packs at the rate of 1:48 packs. The cards are designed identically to Limited except for being gold in color rather than silver and feature some of the league's most exciting players. The card backs have a ghosted photo background and feature a player profile and a small color portrait. The cards are individually numbered on the back out of 2,500.

| | MINT | NRMT |
|---|---|---|
| COMPLETE SET (10) | 450.00 | 200.00 |
| COMMON CARD (1-10) | 15.00 | 6.75 |
| ❑ 1 Mario Lemieux | 80.00 | 36.00 |
| ❑ 2 Brett Hull | 20.00 | 9.00 |
| ❑ 3 Doug Gilmour | 15.00 | 6.75 |
| ❑ 4 Eric Lindros | 50.00 | 22.00 |
| ❑ 5 Paul Kariya | 60.00 | 27.00 |
| ❑ 6 Jaromir Jagr | 50.00 | 22.00 |
| ❑ 7 Wayne Gretzky | 100.00 | 45.00 |
| ❑ 8 Jeremy Roenick | 50.00 | 22.00 |
| ❑ 9 Sergei Fedorov | 30.00 | 13.50 |
| ❑ 10 Pavel Bure | 30.00 | 13.50 |

## 1994-95 Leaf Limited World Juniors Canada

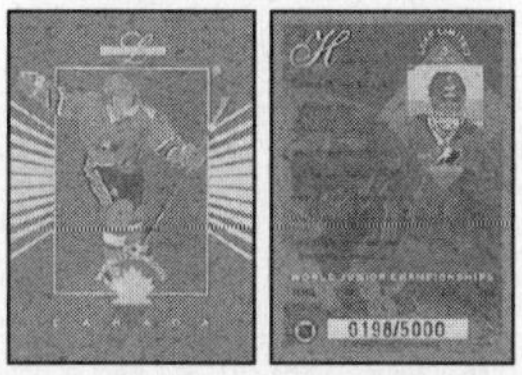

The ten cards in this set were randomly inserted into Limited packs; cards from either the Canadian or U.S. World Juniors could be found at the rate of 1:12 packs. The card fronts are designed identically to Limited except for being bronze in color rather than silver. The cards feature top Canadian players who competed in the 1995 World Junior Championships. The cards are individually numbered on the back out of 5,000. Card backs also contain a small up-close photo and a brief scouting report.

| | MINT | NRMT |
|---|---|---|
| COMPLETE SET (10) | 125.00 | 55.00 |
| COMMON CARD (1-10) | 10.00 | 4.50 |
| ❑ 1 Nolan Baumgartner | 10.00 | 4.50 |
| ❑ 2 Eric Daze | 15.00 | 6.75 |
| ❑ 3 Jeff Friesen | 12.00 | 5.50 |
| ❑ 4 Todd Harvey | 10.00 | 4.50 |
| ❑ 5 Ed Jovanovski | 20.00 | 9.00 |
| ❑ 6 Jeff O'Neill | 12.00 | 5.50 |
| ❑ 7 Wade Redden | 15.00 | 6.75 |
| ❑ 8 Jamie Rivers | 10.00 | 4.50 |
| ❑ 9 Ryan Smyth | 25.00 | 11.00 |
| ❑ 10 Jamie Storr | 10.00 | 4.50 |

## 1994-95 Leaf Limited World Juniors USA

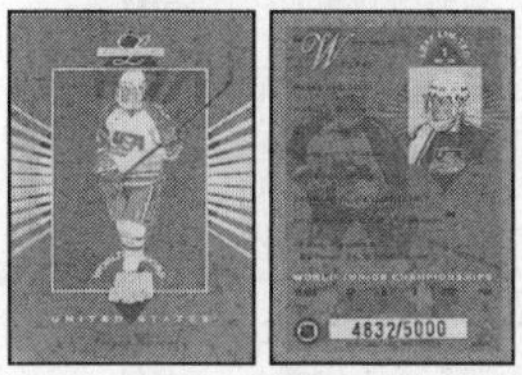

The 10 cards in this set were randomly inserted into Limited packs; cards from either the U.S. or Canadian World Juniors could be found at the rate of 1:12 packs. The card fronts are designed identically to Limited save for being bronze in color rather than silver. The cards feature top American players who competed in the 1995 World Junior Championships. The cards are individually numbered on the back out of 5,000. Card backs also contain a small headshot and a brief scouting report.

| | MINT | NRMT |
|---|---|---|
| COMPLETE SET (10) | 100.00 | 45.00 |
| COMMON CARD (1-10) | 10.00 | 4.50 |
| ❑ 1 Bryan Berard | 15.00 | 6.75 |
| ❑ 2 Doug Bonner | 12.00 | 5.50 |
| ❑ 3 Jason Bonsignore | 10.00 | 4.50 |
| ❑ 4 Adam Deadmarsh | 15.00 | 6.75 |
| ❑ 5 Rory Fitzpatrick | 10.00 | 4.50 |
| ❑ 6 Sean Haggerty | 10.00 | 4.50 |
| ❑ 7 Jamie Langenbrunner | 10.00 | 4.50 |
| ❑ 8 Jeff Mitchell | 12.00 | 5.50 |
| ❑ 9 Richard Park | 10.00 | 4.50 |
| ❑ 10 Deron Quint | 10.00 | 4.50 |

## 1995-96 Leaf

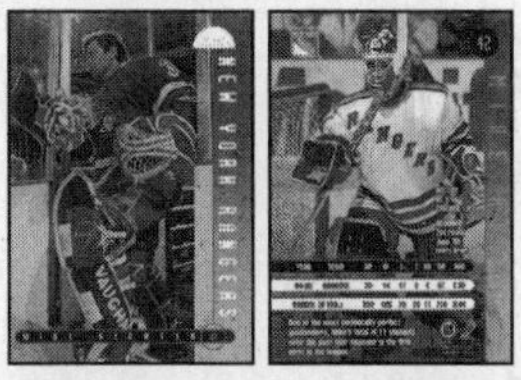

The 1995-96 Leaf set was released in one series of 330-cards. The 12-card packs had an SRP of $1.99. The cards boasted a simple design featuring an action photo with the team name in reflective foil along the right border. A wrapper offer on the packs gave collectors the chance to redeem two wrappers and $9.95 for a special Mario Lemieux Tribute card limited to 15,000 sequentially numbered copies. There are no key Rookie Cards in this set.

| | MINT | NRMT |
|---|---|---|
| COMPLETE SET (330) | 25.00 | 11.00 |
| COMMON CARD (1-330) | .10 | .05 |
| ❑ 1 Mario Lemieux | 1.50 | .70 |
| ❑ 2 Todd Harvey | .10 | .05 |
| ❑ 3 Blaine Lacher | .15 | .07 |
| ❑ 4 Alexei Zhitnik | .10 | .05 |
| ❑ 5 Cory Stillman | .10 | .05 |
| ❑ 6 Murray Craven | .10 | .05 |
| ❑ 7 Mike Kennedy | .10 | .05 |
| ❑ 8 Mike Vernon | .15 | .07 |
| ❑ 9 David Oliver | .10 | .05 |
| ❑ 10 Magnus Svensson | .10 | .05 |
| ❑ 11 Andrei Nikolishin | .10 | .05 |
| ❑ 12 Jamie Storr | .15 | .07 |
| ❑ 13 David Roberts | .10 | .05 |
| ❑ 14 Chris McAlpine | .10 | .05 |
| ❑ 15 Brett Lindros | .10 | .05 |
| ❑ 16 Pat Verbeek | .10 | .05 |
| ❑ 17 Tony Amonte | .15 | .07 |
| ❑ 18 Chris Therien | .10 | .05 |
| ❑ 19 Ken Wregget | .15 | .07 |
| ❑ 20 Peter Forsberg | 1.00 | .45 |
| ❑ 21 Jeff Friesen | .15 | .07 |
| ❑ 22 Patrice Tardif | .10 | .05 |
| ❑ 23 Jason Wiemer | .10 | .05 |
| ❑ 24 Kenny Jonsson | .10 | .05 |
| ❑ 25 Jassen Cullimore | .10 | .05 |
| ❑ 26 Sergei Gonchar | .10 | .05 |
| ❑ 27 Nikolai Khabibulin | .15 | .07 |
| ❑ 28 Oleg Tverdovsky | .15 | .07 |
| ❑ 29 Rick Tocchet | .15 | .07 |
| ❑ 30 Garry Galley | .10 | .05 |
| ❑ 31 German Titov | .10 | .05 |
| ❑ 32 Sergei Krivokrasov | .10 | .05 |
| ❑ 33 Sylvain Turgeon | .10 | .05 |
| ❑ 34 Sergei Fedorov | .50 | .23 |
| ❑ 35 Ralph Intranuovo | .10 | .05 |
| ❑ 36 Stu Barnes | .10 | .05 |
| ❑ 37 Mike Gartner | .15 | .07 |
| ❑ 38 Kevin Brown | .10 | .05 |
| ❑ 39 Valeri Bure | .15 | .07 |
| ❑ 40 Sergei Brylin | .10 | .05 |
| ❑ 41 Kirk Muller | .10 | .05 |
| ❑ 42 Mike Richter | .30 | .14 |
| ❑ 43 Stanislav Neckar | .10 | .05 |
| ❑ 44 Patrik Juhlin | .10 | .05 |
| ❑ 45 Ron Francis | .15 | .07 |
| ❑ 46 Janne Laukkanen | .10 | .05 |
| ❑ 47 Shean Donovan | .10 | .05 |
| ❑ 48 Igor Korolev | .10 | .05 |
| ❑ 49 Alexander Selivanov | .10 | .05 |
| ❑ 50 Frantisek Kucera | .10 | .05 |
| ❑ 51 Russ Courtnall | .10 | .05 |
| ❑ 52 Don Beaupre | .15 | .07 |
| ❑ 53 Michal Grosek | .10 | .05 |
| ❑ 54 Steve Rucchin | .10 | .05 |
| ❑ 55 Mariusz Czerkawski | .10 | .05 |
| ❑ 56 Dominik Hasek | .60 | .25 |
| ❑ 57 Trent Klatt | .10 | .05 |
| ❑ 58 Sergio Momesso | .10 | .05 |
| ❑ 59 Mark Lawrence | .10 | .05 |
| ❑ 60 Steve Yzerman | 1.00 | .45 |
| ❑ 61 Todd Marchant | .10 | .05 |
| ❑ 62 Jesse Belanger | .10 | .05 |
| ❑ 63 Sean Burke | .15 | .07 |
| ❑ 64 Matt Johnson | .10 | .05 |
| ❑ 65 Mark Recchi | .15 | .07 |
| ❑ 66 Martin Brodeur | .75 | .35 |
| ❑ 67 Mathieu Schneider | .10 | .05 |
| ❑ 68 Mark Messier | .40 | .18 |
| ❑ 69 Radim Bicanek | .10 | .05 |
| ❑ 70 Eric Desjardins | .10 | .05 |
| ❑ 71 Jaromir Jagr | 1.00 | .45 |
| ❑ 72 Adam Deadmarsh | .15 | .07 |
| ❑ 73 Viktor Kozlov | .10 | .05 |
| ❑ 74 Jeff Norton | .10 | .05 |
| ❑ 75 Brantt Myhres | .10 | .05 |
| ❑ 76 Darby Hendrickson | .10 | .05 |
| ❑ 77 Roman Oksiuta | .10 | .05 |
| ❑ 78 Jim Carey | .30 | .14 |
| ❑ 79 Keith Tkachuk | .40 | .18 |
| ❑ 80 Valeri Karpov | .10 | .05 |
| ❑ 81 Adam Oates | .15 | .07 |
| ❑ 82 Eric Lindros | 1.00 | .45 |
| ❑ 83 Trevor Kidd | .15 | .07 |
| ❑ 84 Bernie Nicholls | .10 | .05 |
| ❑ 85 Craig Conroy | .10 | .05 |
| ❑ 86 Bill Ranford | .15 | .07 |
| ❑ 87 Scott Mellanby | .15 | .07 |
| ❑ 88 Geoff Sanderson | .15 | .07 |
| ❑ 89 Wayne Gretzky | 2.00 | .90 |
| ❑ 90 Pierre Turgeon | .15 | .07 |
| ❑ 91 Stephane Richer | .15 | .07 |
| ❑ 92 Chris Marinucci | .10 | .05 |
| ❑ 93 Brian Leetch | .30 | .14 |
| ❑ 94 Steve Larouche | .10 | .05 |
| ❑ 95 John LeClair | .50 | .23 |
| ❑ 96 Dmitri Mironov | .10 | .05 |
| ❑ 97 Jocelyn Thibault | .30 | .14 |
| ❑ 98 Craig Janney | .15 | .07 |
| ❑ 99 Ian Laperriere | .10 | .05 |
| ❑ 100 Dino Ciccarelli | .15 | .07 |
| ❑ 101 Todd Warriner | .10 | .05 |
| ❑ 102 Kirk McLean | .15 | .07 |
| ❑ 103 Jason Allison | .10 | .05 |
| ❑ 104 Alexei Zhamnov | .15 | .07 |
| ❑ 105 Keith Jones | .10 | .05 |
| ❑ 106 Ray Bourque | .30 | .14 |
| ❑ 107 John Druce | .10 | .05 |
| ❑ 108 Scott Walker | .10 | .05 |
| ❑ 109 Joe Murphy | .10 | .05 |
| ❑ 110 Checklist (1-110) | .10 | .05 |
| ❑ 111 Philippe DeRouville | .15 | .07 |
| ❑ 112 Greg Adams | .10 | .05 |
| ❑ 113 Cam Neely | .15 | .07 |
| ❑ 114 Mike Peca | .10 | .05 |
| ❑ 115 Theoren Fleury | .15 | .07 |
| ❑ 116 Jeremy Roenick | .30 | .14 |

| | | |
|---|---|---|
| 117 Kevin Hatcher | .10 | .05 |
| 118 Ray Sheppard | .15 | .07 |
| 119 Jason Arnott | .15 | .07 |
| 120 Mark Fitzpatrick | .15 | .07 |
| 121 Brendan Shanahan | .60 | .25 |
| 122 Jari Kurri | .15 | .07 |
| 123 Shayne Corson | .10 | .05 |
| 124 Scott Stevens | .15 | .07 |
| 125 Steve Thomas | .10 | .05 |
| 126 Sergei Zubov | .10 | .05 |
| 127 Denis Savard | .15 | .07 |
| 128 Mikael Renberg | .15 | .07 |
| 129 Luc Robitaille | .15 | .07 |
| 130 Andrei Kovalenko | .10 | .05 |
| 131 Andrei Nazarov | .10 | .05 |
| 132 Denis Chasse | .10 | .05 |
| 133 Chris Gratton | .15 | .07 |
| 134 Benoit Hogue | .10 | .05 |
| 135 Pavel Bure | .60 | .25 |
| 136 Peter Bondra | .30 | .14 |
| 137 Teemu Selanne | .60 | .25 |
| 138 Darren Van Impe | .10 | .05 |
| 139 Dimitri Khristich | .10 | .05 |
| 140 Pat LaFontaine | .15 | .07 |
| 141 Phil Housley | .15 | .07 |
| 142 Chris Chelios | .30 | .14 |
| 143 Steve Duchesne | .10 | .05 |
| 144 Paul Coffey | .30 | .14 |
| 145 Doug Weight | .15 | .07 |
| 146 Gord Murphy | .10 | .05 |
| 147 Andrew Cassels | .10 | .05 |
| 148 Rob Blake | .10 | .05 |
| 149 Vladimir Malakhov | .10 | .05 |
| 150 Scott Niedermayer | .10 | .05 |
| 151 Patrick Flatley | .10 | .05 |
| 152 Adam Graves | .15 | .07 |
| 153 Alexei Yashin | .15 | .07 |
| 154 Rod Brind'Amour | .15 | .07 |
| 155 Joe Mullen | .15 | .07 |
| 156 Mike Ricci | .10 | .05 |
| 157 Ulf Dahlen | .10 | .05 |
| 158 Dave Manson | .10 | .05 |
| 159 Brian Bradley | .10 | .05 |
| 160 Felix Potvin | .30 | .14 |
| 161 Trevor Linden | .15 | .07 |
| 162 Michal Pivonka | .10 | .05 |
| 163 Nelson Emerson | .10 | .05 |
| 164 Joe Sacco | .10 | .05 |
| 165 Todd Elik | .10 | .05 |
| 166 Derek Plante | .10 | .05 |
| 167 Mike Sullivan | .10 | .05 |
| 168 Randy Wood | .10 | .05 |
| 169 Manny Fernandez | .15 | .07 |
| 170 Keith Primeau | .15 | .07 |
| 171 Marko Tuomainen | .10 | .05 |
| 172 John Vanbiesbrouck | .50 | .23 |
| 173 Darren Turcotte | .10 | .05 |
| 174 Tony Granato | .10 | .05 |
| 175 Brian Savage | .10 | .05 |
| 176 John MacLean | .15 | .07 |
| 177 Tommy Salo | .40 | .18 |
| 178 Steve Larmer | .15 | .07 |
| 179 Alexandre Daigle | .10 | .05 |
| 180 Petr Svoboda | .10 | .05 |
| 181 John Cullen | .10 | .05 |
| 182 Joe Sakic | .60 | .25 |
| 183 Sandis Ozolinsh | .15 | .07 |
| 184 Dale Hawerchuk | .15 | .07 |
| 185 Paul Ysebaert | .10 | .05 |
| 186 Larry Murphy | .15 | .07 |
| 187 Alexander Mogilny | .15 | .07 |
| 188 Joe Juneau | .10 | .05 |
| 189 Craig Martin | .10 | .05 |
| 190 Jason Marshall | .10 | .05 |
| 191 Don Sweeney | .10 | .05 |
| 192 Ron Hextall | .15 | .07 |
| 193 Steve Chiasson | .10 | .05 |
| 194 Steve Smith | .10 | .05 |
| 195 Lyle Odelein | .10 | .05 |
| 196 Ryan Smyth | .10 | .05 |
| 197 Rob Niedermayer | .15 | .07 |
| 198 Steven Rice | .10 | .05 |
| 199 Darryl Sydor | .10 | .05 |
| 200 Patrick Roy | 1.50 | .70 |
| 201 Bill Guerin | .10 | .05 |
| 202 Scott Lachance | .10 | .05 |
| 203 Alexei Kovalev | .10 | .05 |
| 204 Ronnie Stern | .10 | .05 |
| 205 Kevin Dineen | .10 | .05 |
| 206 Ulf Samuelsson | .10 | .05 |
| 207 Wendel Clark | .15 | .07 |
| 208 Ray Whitney | .10 | .05 |
| 209 Brett Hull | .40 | .18 |
| 210 Slava Kozlov | .15 | .07 |
| 211 Doug Gilmour | .30 | .14 |
| 212 Mike Ridley | .10 | .05 |
| 213 Mike Torchia | .15 | .07 |
| 214 Tavis Hansen | .15 | .07 |
| 215 Dale Hunter | .10 | .05 |
| 216 Kevin Stevens | .10 | .05 |
| 217 Mike Donnelly | .10 | .05 |
| 218 Sylvain Cote | .10 | .05 |
| 219 Gary Suter | .10 | .05 |
| 220 Checklist (111-120) | .10 | .05 |
| 221 Richard Park | .10 | .05 |
| 222 Dave Gagner | .15 | .07 |
| 223 Jozef Stumpel | .10 | .05 |
| 224 Brad May | .15 | .07 |
| 225 Zarley Zalapski | .10 | .05 |
| 226 Eric Daze | .30 | .14 |
| 227 Mike Modano | .40 | .18 |
| 228 Nicklas Lidstrom | .15 | .07 |
| 229 Jason Bonsignore | .10 | .05 |
| 230 Robert Svehla | .10 | .05 |
| 231 Glen Wesley | .10 | .05 |
| 232 Josef Beranek | .10 | .05 |
| 233 Geoff Courtnall | .10 | .05 |
| 234 Shawn Chambers | .10 | .05 |
| 235 Darius Kasparaitis | .10 | .05 |
| 236 Sergei Nemchinov | .10 | .05 |
| 237 Patrick Poulin | .10 | .05 |
| 238 Anatoli Semenov | .10 | .05 |
| 239 Bryan Smolinski | .10 | .05 |
| 240 Owen Nolan | .15 | .07 |
| 241 Pat Falloon | .10 | .05 |
| 242 Chris Pronger | .15 | .07 |
| 243 Daren Puppa | .15 | .07 |
| 244 Mats Sundin | .30 | .14 |
| 245 Jeff Brown | .10 | .05 |
| 246 Jeff Nelson | .10 | .05 |
| 247 Teppo Numminen | .10 | .05 |
| 248 Shaun Van Allen | .10 | .05 |
| 249 Yanic Perreault | .10 | .05 |
| 250 Brian Holzinger | .30 | .14 |
| 251 Paul Kruse | .10 | .05 |
| 252 Jeff Shantz | .10 | .05 |
| 253 Martin Straka | .10 | .05 |
| 254 Chris Osgood | .30 | .14 |
| 255 Joaquin Gage | .10 | .05 |
| 256 Dave Lowry | .10 | .05 |
| 257 Robert Kron | .10 | .05 |
| 258 Dan Quinn | .10 | .05 |
| 259 David Wilkie | .10 | .05 |
| 260 Valeri Zelepukin | .10 | .05 |
| 261 Derek King | .10 | .05 |
| 262 Darren Langdon | .10 | .05 |
| 263 Radek Bonk | .10 | .05 |
| 264 Karl Dykhuis | .10 | .05 |
| 265 Tomas Sandstrom | .10 | .05 |
| 266 Uwe Krupp | .10 | .05 |
| 267 Arturs Irbe | .15 | .07 |
| 268 Dallas Drake | .10 | .05 |
| 269 John Tucker | .10 | .05 |
| 270 Dave Andreychuk | .15 | .07 |
| 271 Guy Hebert | .15 | .07 |
| 272 Sandy Moger | .10 | .05 |
| 273 Craig Johnson | .10 | .05 |
| 274 Donald Audette | .15 | .07 |
| 275 Cory Cross | .10 | .05 |
| 276 Richard Smehlik | .10 | .05 |
| 277 Gary Roberts | .10 | .05 |
| 278 Todd Gill | .10 | .05 |
| 279 Derian Hatcher | .10 | .05 |
| 280 Slava Fetisov | .10 | .05 |
| 281 Curtis Joseph | .30 | .14 |
| 282 Johan Garpenlov | .10 | .05 |
| 283 Vladimir Konstantinov | .10 | .05 |
| 284 Ray Ferraro | .10 | .05 |
| 285 Turner Stevenson | .10 | .05 |
| 286 Neal Broten | .15 | .07 |
| 287 Jason Wiemer | .10 | .05 |
| 288 Mattias Norstrom | .10 | .05 |
| 289 Michel Picard | .10 | .05 |
| 290 Brent Fedyk | .10 | .05 |
| 291 Dimitri Yushkevich | .10 | .05 |
| 292 Sylvain Lefebvre | .10 | .05 |
| 293 Sergei Makarov | .10 | .05 |
| 294 Brian Rolston | .10 | .05 |
| 295 Roman Hamrlik | .15 | .07 |
| 296 Mark Wotton | .10 | .05 |
| 297 Alek Stojanov | .10 | .05 |
| 298 Calle Johansson | .10 | .05 |
| 299 Mike Eastwood | .10 | .05 |
| 300 Bob Corkum | .10 | .05 |
| 301 Petr Nedved | .15 | .07 |
| 302 Vincent Damphousse | .15 | .07 |
| 303 Brett Harkins | .10 | .05 |
| 304 Paul Kariya | 1.25 | .55 |
| 305 Joe Nieuwendyk | .15 | .07 |
| 306 Dennis Bonvie | .15 | .07 |
| 307 Jason Woolley | .10 | .05 |
| 308 Jimmy Carson | .10 | .05 |
| 309 Marty McSorley | .10 | .05 |
| 310 Craig Rivet | .10 | .05 |
| 311 Claude Lemieux | .15 | .07 |
| 312 Al MacInnis | .15 | .07 |
| 313 Gerald Diduck | .10 | .05 |
| 314 Randy McKay | .10 | .05 |
| 315 Bob Errey | .10 | .05 |
| 316 Rusty Fitzgerald | .10 | .05 |
| 317 Scott Young | .10 | .05 |
| 318 Igor Larionov | .10 | .05 |
| 319 Esa Tikkanen | .10 | .05 |
| 320 Darren McCarty | .10 | .05 |
| 321 Petr Klima | .10 | .05 |
| 322 Jon Rohloff | .10 | .05 |
| 323 Steve Konowalchuk | .10 | .05 |
| 324 Milos Holan | .10 | .05 |
| 325 Checklist (221-330) | .10 | .05 |
| 326 Ted Donato | .10 | .05 |
| 327 Grant Marshall | .10 | .05 |
| 328 Jyrki Lumme | .10 | .05 |
| 329 Ed Belfour | .30 | .14 |
| 330 Checklist (inserts) | .10 | .05 |
| NNO Mario Lemieux<br>wrapper redemption | 15.00 | 6.75 |

## 1995-96 Leaf Fire On Ice

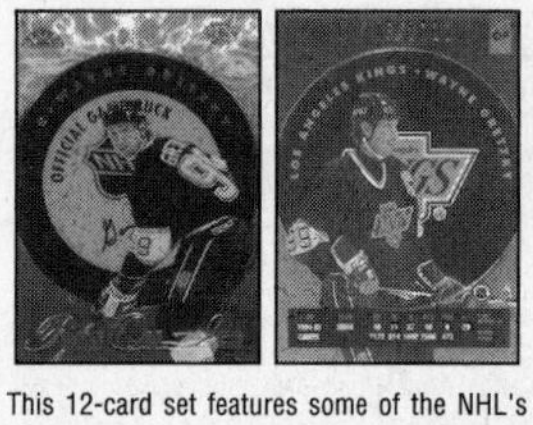

This 12-card set features some of the NHL's most dangerous snipers. The cards were sequentially numbered out of 10,000 and were randomly inserted at a rate of about 1:48 packs.

| | MINT | NRMT |
|---|---|---|
| COMPLETE SET (12) | 200.00 | 90.00 |
| COMMON CARD (1-12) | 5.00 | 2.20 |
| 1 Pavel Bure | 15.00 | 6.75 |
| 2 Eric Lindros | 25.00 | 11.00 |
| 3 Alexei Zhamnov | 6.00 | 2.70 |
| 4 Paul Coffey | 8.00 | 3.60 |
| 5 Theoren Fleury | 6.00 | 2.70 |
| 6 Peter Forsberg | 25.00 | 11.00 |
| 7 Sergei Fedorov | 15.00 | 6.75 |
| 8 Mats Sundin | 6.00 | 2.70 |
| 9 Brett Hull | 12.00 | 5.50 |
| 10 Wayne Gretzky | 50.00 | 22.00 |
| 11 Paul Kariya | 30.00 | 13.50 |
| 12 Mikael Renberg | 5.00 | 2.20 |

## 1995-96 Leaf Freeze Frame

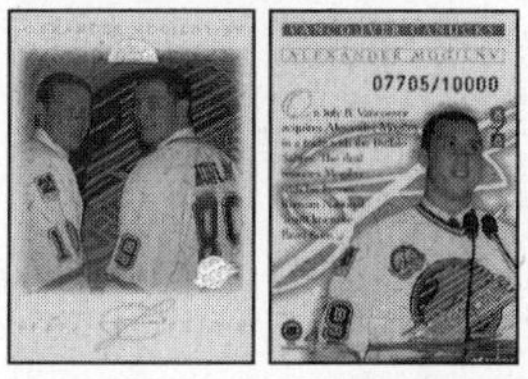

These eight cards, which focus on special moments for a team or player form the 1994-95 season, were randomly inserted at indeterminate odds (estimated at around 1:72). The cards are serially numbered out of 10,000.

| | MINT | NRMT |
|---|---|---|
| COMPLETE SET (8) | 150.00 | 70.00 |
| COMMON CARD (1-8) | 8.00 | 3.60 |
| 1 Jim Carey | 12.00 | 5.50 |
| 2 Pierre Turgeon | 10.00 | 4.50 |
| 3 Mikael Renberg | 10.00 | 4.50 |
| 4 Jaromir Jagr | 40.00 | 18.00 |
| 5 Alexei Zhamnov | 10.00 | 4.50 |
| 6 New Jersey Devils | 8.00 | 3.60 |
| 7 Mario Lemieux | 60.00 | 27.00 |
| 8 A.Mogilny/P.Bure | 20.00 | 9.00 |

## 1995-96 Leaf Gold Stars

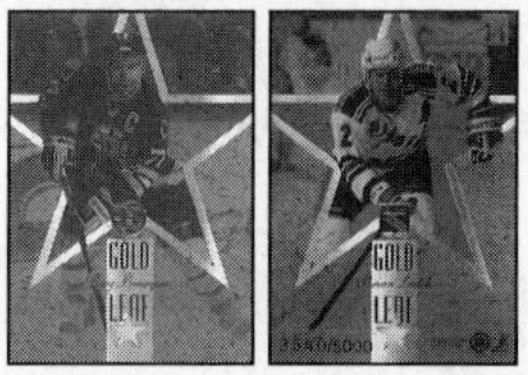

The twelve players featured in this six-card set were the tops at their position in 1994-95. The cards were individually numbered out of 5,000 and were randomly inserted in retail packs at indeterminate odds (estimated at around 1:90).

| | MINT | NRMT |
|---|---|---|
| COMPLETE SET (6) | 100.00 | 45.00 |
| COMMON CARD (1-6) | 8.00 | 3.60 |
| 1 Dominik Hasek<br>Jim Carey | 25.00 | 11.00 |
| 2 Paul Coffey<br>Chris Chelios | 8.00 | 3.60 |
| 3 Ray Bourque<br>Brian Leetch | 8.00 | 3.60 |
| 4 Eric Lindros<br>Alexei Zhamnov | 30.00 | 13.50 |
| 5 Jaromir Jagr<br>Theoren Fleury | 25.00 | 11.00 |
| 6 Brett Hull<br>Mikael Renberg | 15.00 | 6.75 |

## 1995-96 Leaf Lemieux's Best

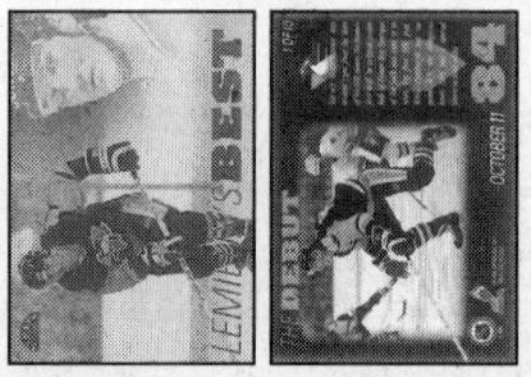

This set captures ten of the greatest moments in the career of one of the greatest players ever, Mario Lemieux. The cards were randomly inserted at indeterminate odds (estimated at around 1:18).

| | MINT | NRMT |
|---|---|---|
| COMPLETE SET (10) | 60.00 | 27.00 |
| COMMON CARD (1-10) | 6.00 | 2.70 |
| 1 Mario Lemieux<br>The Debut | 6.00 | 2.70 |
| 2 Mario Lemieux<br>The Clincher | 6.00 | 2.70 |
| 3 Mario Lemieux<br>The Star | 6.00 | 2.70 |
| 4 Mario Lemieux<br>The Fiver | 6.00 | 2.70 |
| 5 Mario Lemieux<br>The Points | 6.00 | 2.70 |
| 6 Mario Lemieux<br>The Record | 6.00 | 2.70 |
| 7 Mario Lemieux<br>The Star | 6.00 | 2.70 |
| 8 Mario Lemieux<br>The Cup | 6.00 | 2.70 |
| 9 Mario Lemieux<br>The Repeat | 6.00 | 2.70 |
| 10 Mario Lemieux<br>The Comeback | 6.00 | 2.70 |

## 1995-96 Leaf Road To The Cup

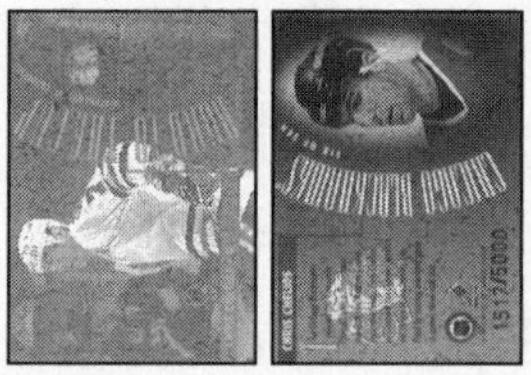

This ten-card set recognizes several key moments from the 1994-95 Stanley Cup playoffs. The cards were serially numbered out of 5,000, and were randomly inserted into hobby packs only at indeterminate odds (estimated at around 1:90).

| | MINT | NRMT |
|---|---|---|
| COMPLETE SET (10) | 200.00 | 90.00 |
| COMMON CARD (1-10) | 5.00 | 2.20 |
| 1 Ray Whitney | 5.00 | 2.20 |
| 2 Martin Brodeur | 30.00 | 13.50 |
| 3 Jaromir Jagr | 40.00 | 18.00 |
| 4 Eric Lindros | 50.00 | 22.00 |
| 5 Paul Coffey | 12.00 | 5.50 |
| 6 Chris Chelios | 12.00 | 5.50 |
| 7 Neal Broten | 5.00 | 2.20 |
| 8 Slava Kozlov | 5.00 | 2.20 |
| 9 Scott Niedermayer | 5.00 | 2.20 |
| 10 Claude Lemieux | 8.00 | 3.60 |

## 1995-96 Leaf Studio Rookies

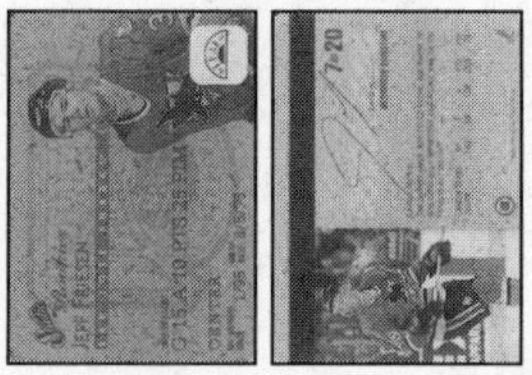

This 20-card set resembles credit cards, down to the shape, the embossed membership data on the front and the signature and metallic data strips on the back. The cards were randomly inserted into packs at indeterminate odds, estimated to be around 1:12.

| | MINT | NRMT |
|---|---|---|
| COMPLETE SET (20) | 50.00 | 22.00 |
| COMMON CARD (1-20) | 2.00 | .90 |
| 1 Jim Carey | 4.00 | 1.80 |
| 2 Peter Forsberg | 8.00 | 3.60 |
| 3 Paul Kariya | 10.00 | 4.50 |
| 4 David Oliver | 2.00 | .90 |
| 5 Blaine Lacher | 2.50 | 1.10 |
| 6 Oleg Tverdovsky | 2.50 | 1.10 |
| 7 Jeff Friesen | 2.50 | 1.10 |
| 8 Todd Marchant | 2.50 | 1.10 |
| 9 Todd Harvey | 2.50 | 1.10 |
| 10 Ian Laperriere | 2.00 | .90 |
| 11 Eric Daze | 4.00 | 1.80 |
| 12 Jason Bonsignore | 2.00 | .90 |
| 13 Jamie Storr | 2.50 | 1.10 |
| 14 Brian Holzinger | 4.00 | 1.80 |
| 15 Brian Savage | 2.00 | .90 |
| 16 Roman Oksiuta | 2.00 | .90 |
| 17 Mariusz Czerkawski | 2.00 | .90 |
| 18 Sergei Krivokrasov | 2.00 | .90 |
| 19 Jason Wiemer | 2.00 | .90 |
| 20 Radek Bonk | 2.00 | .90 |

## 1996-97 Leaf

The 1996-97 Leaf set, consisting of 240 cards, was distributed in 10-card packs with a suggested retail price of $2.99. The fronts featured a color action player photo printed on

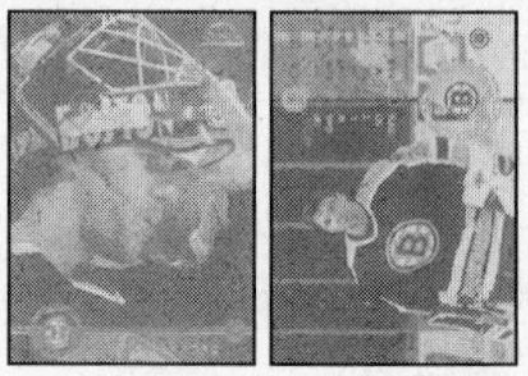

common card stock with silver foil. The backs carried another player photo with season and career statistics. Marin Biron is the only rookie of note.

| | MINT | NRMT |
|---|---|---|
| COMPLETE SET (240) | 30.00 | 13.50 |
| COMMON CARD (1-240) | .10 | .05 |
| 1 Sergei Fedorov | .60 | .25 |
| 2 Bill Ranford | .20 | .09 |
| 3 Oleg Tverdovsky | .20 | .09 |
| 4 Brad May | .20 | .09 |
| 5 Chris Pronger | .20 | .09 |
| 6 Martin Brodeur | 1.00 | .45 |
| 7 Yanic Perreault | .10 | .05 |
| 8 Garry Galley | .10 | .05 |
| 9 Shawn McEachern | .10 | .05 |
| 10 Brian Bellows | .10 | .05 |
| 11 Ron Francis | .20 | .09 |
| 12 Mike Modano | .50 | .23 |
| 13 Steve Yzerman | 1.25 | .55 |
| 14 Joe Mullen | .20 | .09 |
| 15 Pavel Bure | .75 | .35 |
| 16 Dino Ciccarelli | .20 | .09 |
| 17 Claude Lemieux | .20 | .09 |
| 18 Stephane Richer | .20 | .09 |
| 19 Dominik Hasek | .75 | .35 |
| 20 Adam Graves | .20 | .09 |
| 21 Joe Juneau | .10 | .05 |
| 22 Rob Niedermayer | .20 | .09 |
| 23 Zigmund Palffy | .40 | .18 |
| 24 Dave Andreychuk | .20 | .09 |
| 25 Steve Thomas | .10 | .05 |
| 26 Tom Barrasso | .20 | .09 |
| 27 Eric Desjardins | .10 | .05 |
| 28 Curtis Joseph | .40 | .18 |
| 29 Russ Courtnall | .10 | .05 |
| 30 Stu Barnes | .10 | .05 |
| 31 Mark Tinordi | .10 | .05 |
| 32 Gary Suter | .10 | .05 |
| 33 Greg Johnson | .10 | .05 |
| 34 Joe Nieuwendyk | .20 | .09 |
| 35 Norm Maciver | .10 | .05 |
| 36 Craig Janney | .20 | .09 |
| 37 Mark Recchi | .20 | .09 |
| 38 Patrick Roy | 2.00 | .90 |
| 39 Petr Klima | .10 | .05 |
| 40 Ken Wregget | .20 | .09 |
| 41 Rod Brind'Amour | .20 | .09 |
| 42 Viacheslav Fetisov | .10 | .05 |
| 43 Kirk McLean | .20 | .09 |
| 44 Pat LaFontaine | .20 | .09 |
| 45 Brett Hull | .50 | .23 |
| 46 Chris Chelios | .40 | .18 |
| 47 Damian Rhodes | .20 | .09 |
| 48 Kevin Hatcher | .10 | .05 |
| 49 Uwe Krupp | .10 | .05 |
| 50 Bernie Nicholls | .10 | .05 |
| 51 Tommy Soderstrom | .20 | .09 |
| 52 Teemu Selanne | .75 | .35 |
| 53 Mats Sundin | .20 | .09 |
| 54 Jeff Hackett | .20 | .09 |
| 55 Ulf Dahlen | .10 | .05 |
| 56 Dale Hunter | .10 | .05 |
| 57 Robert Kron | .10 | .05 |
| 58 Brian Bradley | .10 | .05 |
| 59 Pat Verbeek | .10 | .05 |
| 60 Kenny Jonsson | .10 | .05 |
| 61 Theoren Fleury | .20 | .09 |
| 62 Alexander Selivanov | .10 | .05 |
| 63 Nikolai Khabibulin | .20 | .09 |
| 64 Grant Fuhr | .20 | .09 |
| 65 Phil Housley | .20 | .09 |
| 66 Bill Lindsay | .10 | .05 |
| 67 Trevor Kidd | .20 | .09 |
| 68 Jim Carey | .40 | .18 |
| 69 Brian Skrudland | .10 | .05 |
| 70 Todd Krygier | .10 | .05 |
| 71 Petr Nedved | .20 | .09 |
| 72 Kirk Muller | .10 | .05 |
| 73 Daren Puppa | .20 | .09 |
| 74 Doug Gilmour | .40 | .18 |
| 75 Nicklas Lidstrom | .20 | .09 |
| 76 Zdeno Ciger | .10 | .05 |
| 77 Robert Svehla | .10 | .05 |
| 78 Andrew Cassels | .10 | .05 |
| 79 Vincent Damphousse | .20 | .09 |
| 80 Alexandre Daigle | .10 | .05 |
| 81 Tomas Sandstrom | .10 | .05 |
| 82 Brent Fedyk | .10 | .05 |
| 83 John LeClair | .60 | .25 |
| 84 Mario Lemieux | 2.00 | .90 |
| 85 Sean Burke | .20 | .09 |
| 86 Cam Neely | .20 | .09 |
| 87 Jeff Friesen | .20 | .09 |
| 88 Guy Hebert | .20 | .09 |
| 89 Jon Casey | .20 | .09 |
| 90 Rick Tocchet | .20 | .09 |
| 91 Mike Gartner | .20 | .09 |
| 92 Tony Amonte | .20 | .09 |
| 93 Jason Dawe | .10 | .05 |
| 94 Chris Terreri | .20 | .09 |
| 95 Zarley Zalapski | .10 | .05 |
| 96 Martin Rucinsky | .10 | .05 |
| 97 Garth Snow | .20 | .09 |

❑ 98 Sylvain Lefebvre .10 .05
❑ 99 Andy Moog .20 .09
❑ 100 Larry Murphy .20 .09
❑ 101 Alexei Yashin .20 .09
❑ 102 Pat Falloon .10 .05
❑ 103 Greg Adams .10 .05
❑ 104 Igor Larionov .10 .05
❑ 105 Geoff Sanderson .20 .09
❑ 106 Jaromir Jagr 1.25 .55
❑ 107 Alexei Zhamnov .20 .09
❑ 108 Mikael Renberg .20 .09
❑ 109 Kelly Hrudey .20 .09
❑ 110 Vladimir Konstantinov .10 .05
❑ 111 Brian Savage .10 .05
❑ 112 Adam Oates .20 .09
❑ 113 Teppo Numminen .10 .05
❑ 114 Ray Sheppard .20 .09
❑ 115 Michael Nylander .10 .05
❑ 116 Jozef Stumpel .10 .05
❑ 117 Ed Olczyk .10 .05
❑ 118 Roman Hamrlik .20 .09
❑ 119 Kris Draper .10 .05
❑ 120 Chris Gratton .20 .09
❑ 121 Randy Burridge .10 .05
❑ 122 Ray Bourque .40 .18
❑ 123 Jyrki Lumme .10 .05
❑ 124 Dale Hawerchuk .20 .09
❑ 125 Dave Lowry .10 .05
❑ 126 Curtis Leschyshyn .10 .05
❑ 127 Martin Gelinas .10 .05
❑ 128 Owen Nolan .20 .09
❑ 129 Radek Bonk .10 .05
❑ 130 Sergei Zubov .10 .05
❑ 131 Travis Green .20 .09
❑ 132 Scott Mellanby .20 .09
❑ 133 Keith Tkachuk .50 .23
❑ 134 Luc Robitaille .20 .09
❑ 135 Alexei Kovalev .10 .05
❑ 136 Doug Weight .20 .09
❑ 137 Benoit Hogue .10 .05
❑ 138 Cory Stillman .10 .05
❑ 139 Joe Sakic .75 .35
❑ 140 Wayne Gretzky 3.00 1.35
❑ 141 Mike Ricci .10 .05
❑ 142 Kyle McLaren .10 .05
❑ 143 Deron Quint .10 .05
❑ 144 Ville Peltonen .10 .05
❑ 145 Todd Harvey .10 .05
❑ 146 Brendan Shanahan .75 .35
❑ 147 Mike Vernon .20 .09
❑ 148 Eric Lindros 1.25 .55
❑ 149 Rick Tabaracci .20 .09
❑ 150 Stephane Yelle .10 .05
❑ 151 Chris Osgood .40 .18
❑ 152 Corey Hirsch .20 .09
❑ 153 Todd Marchant .10 .05
❑ 154 Keith Primeau .20 .09
❑ 155 Alexei Zhitnik .10 .05
❑ 156 Felix Potvin .40 .18
❑ 157 Vitali Yachmenev .10 .05
❑ 158 Geoff Courtnall .10 .05
❑ 159 Peter Forsberg 1.25 .55
❑ 160 Radek Dvorak .10 .05
❑ 161 Bryan McCabe .10 .05
❑ 162 Alexander Mogilny .20 .09
❑ 163 Shayne Corson .10 .05
❑ 164 Paul Coffey .40 .18
❑ 165 Brian Leetch .40 .18
❑ 166 Wendel Clark .20 .09
❑ 167 Aaron Gavey .10 .05
❑ 168 Dimitri Khristich .10 .05
❑ 169 Grant Marshall .10 .05
❑ 170 Valeri Kamensky .20 .09
❑ 171 Ryan Smyth .40 .18
❑ 172 Niklas Sundstrom .10 .05
❑ 173 Cliff Ronning .10 .05
❑ 174 Al MacInnis .20 .09
❑ 175 Scott Stevens .20 .09
❑ 176 Paul Kariya 1.50 .70
❑ 177 Rob Blake .10 .05
❑ 178 Mike Richter .40 .18
❑ 179 Jason Arnott .20 .09
❑ 180 Mark Messier .50 .23
❑ 181 Scott Young .10 .05
❑ 182 Jocelyn Thibault .40 .18
❑ 183 Marcus Ragnarsson .10 .05
❑ 184 Darren Turcotte .10 .05
❑ 185 Joe Murphy .10 .05
❑ 186 Pierre Turgeon .20 .09
❑ 187 Trevor Linden .20 .09
❑ 188 Stephane Fiset .20 .09
❑ 189 Miroslav Satan .10 .05
❑ 190 Mathieu Schneider .10 .05
❑ 191 Jeremy Roenick .40 .18
❑ 192 Craig MacTavish .10 .05
❑ 193 John Vanbiesbrouck .60 .25
❑ 194 Ron Hextall .20 .09
❑ 195 John MacLean .20 .09
❑ 196 Vyacheslav Kozlov .10 .05
❑ 197 Sandis Ozolinsh .20 .09
❑ 198 Scott Niedermayer .10 .05
❑ 199 Ed Belfour .40 .18
❑ 200 Peter Bondra .40 .18
❑ 201 Jere Lehtinen .10 .05
❑ 202 Eric Daze .20 .09
❑ 203 Chad Kilger .10 .05
❑ 204 Saku Koivu .60 .25
❑ 205 Todd Bertuzzi .10 .05
❑ 206 Petr Sykora .10 .05
❑ 207 Valeri Bure .20 .09
❑ 208 Ed Jovanovski .20 .09
❑ 209 Jeff O'Neill .10 .05
❑ 210 Daniel Alfredsson .20 .09
❑ 211 Byron Dafoe .20 .09
❑ 212 Brian Holzinger .20 .09
❑ 213 Martin Biron .20 .09
❑ 214 Anders Eriksson .10 .05
❑ 215 Landon Wilson .10 .05
❑ 216 Alexei Yegorov .10 .05
❑ 217 Jan Caloun .10 .05
❑ 218 David Sacco .10 .05
❑ 219 David Nemirovsky .10 .05
❑ 220 Anders Myrvold .10 .05
❑ 221 Tommy Salo .20 .09
❑ 222 Jan Vopat .10 .05
❑ 223 Steve Staios .10 .05
❑ 224 Patrick Labrecque .10 .05
❑ 225 Jamie Langenbrunner .10 .05
❑ 226 Denis Pederson .10 .05
❑ 227 Marek Malik .10 .05
❑ 228 Geoff Sarjeant .10 .05
❑ 229 Chris Ferraro .10 .05
❑ 230 Zdenek Nedved .10 .05
❑ 231 Wayne Primeau .10 .05
❑ 232 Daymond Langkow .10 .05
❑ 233 Marko Kiprusoff .10 .05
❑ 234 Niklas Sundblad .10 .05
❑ 235 Jamie Ram .10 .05
❑ 236 Jamie Rivers .10 .05
❑ 237 Steve Washburn .10 .05
❑ 238 Teemu Selanne CL .40 .18
❑ 239 Steve Yzerman CL .40 .18
❑ 240 Eric Lindros CL .40 .18

## 1996-97 Leaf Press Proofs

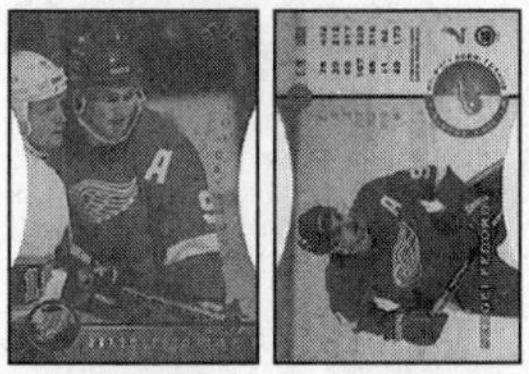

This 240-card set was a die-cut parallel rendition of the regular Leaf set. Only 1,500 sets were produced, with each card sequentially numbered. The words "Press Proof" appear on the card front in gold foil.

| | MINT | NRMT |
|---|---|---|
| COMPLETE SET (240) | 1500.00 | 700.00 |
| COMMON CARD (1-240) | 4.00 | 1.80 |

*STARS: 20X TO 50X BASIC CARDS
*YOUNG STARS:30X TO 30X

## 1996-97 Leaf Fire On Ice

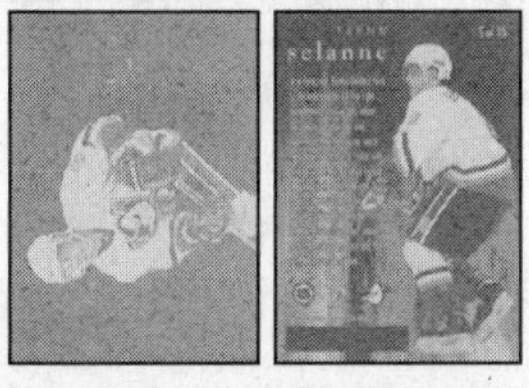

This 15-card insert set, found only in retail packs, featured megastar players who heated up the ice with their play. Color player photos were printed on foil-laminated, micro-etched card stock. Only 2,500 sets were produced, with each card sequentially numbered.

| | MINT | NRMT |
|---|---|---|
| COMPLETE SET (15) | 550.00 | 250.00 |
| COMMON CARD (1-15) | 10.00 | 4.50 |

❑ 1 Mario Lemieux 80.00 36.00
❑ 2 Alexander Mogilny 12.00 5.50
❑ 3 Joe Sakic 40.00 18.00
❑ 4 Paul Kariya 60.00 27.00
❑ 5 Wayne Gretzky 120.00 55.00
❑ 6 Doug Weight 12.00 5.50
❑ 7 Zigmund Palffy 15.00 6.75
❑ 8 Eric Lindros 50.00 22.00
❑ 9 Teemu Selanne 40.00 18.00
❑ 10 Doug Gilmour 12.00 5.50
❑ 11 Jeremy Roenick 15.00 6.75
❑ 12 Steve Yzerman 50.00 22.00
❑ 13 Ed Jovanovski 10.00 4.50
❑ 14 Mike Modano 25.00 11.00
❑ 15 Mark Messier 25.00 11.00

## 1996-97 Leaf Gold Rookies

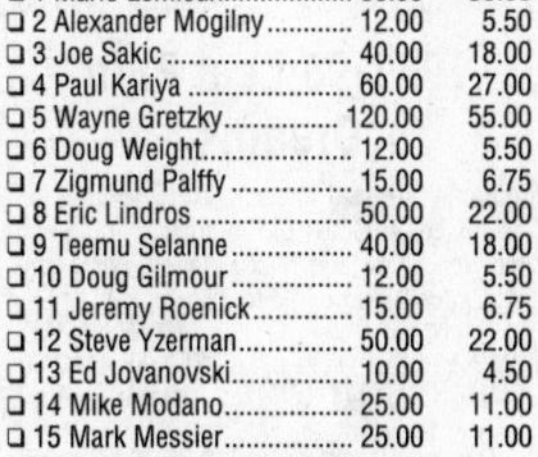

This insert set featured ten of the top NHL rookies from the '95-96 season. The cards displayed color action player photos, with player information on the back.

| | MINT | NRMT |
|---|---|---|
| COMPLETE SET (10) | 60.00 | 27.00 |
| COMMON CARD (1-10) | 4.00 | 1.80 |

❑ 1 Ethan Moreau 8.00 3.60
❑ 2 Kevin Hodson 8.00 3.60
❑ 3 Jose Theodore 8.00 3.60
❑ 4 Peter Ferraro 4.00 1.80
❑ 5 Ralph Intranuovo 4.00 1.80
❑ 6 Nolan Baumgartner 4.00 1.80
❑ 7 Brandon Convery 4.00 1.80
❑ 8 Darcy Tucker 4.00 1.80
❑ 9 Eric Fichaud 8.00 3.60
❑ 10 Steve Sullivan 8.00 3.60

## 1996-97 Leaf Leather And Laces Promos

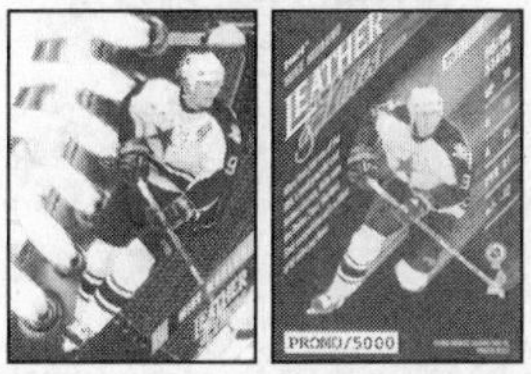

This 20 card set was intended to promote the upcoming Leather and Lace insert set. Unlike the regular set in which 5,000 serial numbered sets were issued, these cards were issued as Promo/5000 in the serial numbered box. Forsberg and Modano were the two most commonly found cards in this set

| | MINT | NRMT |
|---|---|---|
| COMPLETE SET (20) | 100.00 | 45.00 |
| COMMON CARD (1-20) | 3.00 | 1.35 |

❑ P1 Joe Sakic 10.00 4.50
❑ P2 Keith Tkachuk 5.00 2.20
❑ P3 Brett Hull 5.00 2.20
❑ P4 Paul Coffey 3.00 1.35
❑ P5 Jaromir Jagr 15.00 6.75
❑ P6 Peter Forsberg 5.00 2.20
❑ P7 Zigmund Palffy 5.00 2.20
❑ P8 Wayne Gretzky 20.00 9.00
❑ P9 Pavel Bure 7.50 3.40
❑ P10 Eric Lindros 15.00 6.75
❑ P11 Alexander Mogilny 3.00 1.35
❑ P12 Trevor Linden 3.00 1.35
❑ P13 Jeremy Roenick 3.00 1.35
❑ P14 Doug Gilmour 3.00 1.35
❑ P15 Mike Modano 3.00 1.35
❑ P16 Sergei Fedorov 5.00 2.20
❑ P17 Brendan Shanahan 5.00 2.20
❑ P18 Pierre Turgeon 3.00 1.35
❑ P19 Ed Jovanovski 3.00 1.35
❑ P20 Saku Koivu 5.00 2.20

## 1996-97 Leaf Leather And Laces

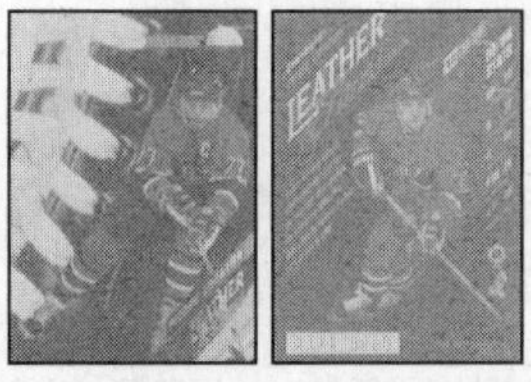

This 20-card set featured color action player photos of the NHL's top skaters printed on embossed leather cards with skate laces in the background and gold foil stamping. The backs carried another player photo and player statistics on a black background. Only 5,000 of these sets were produced and were sequentially numbered. A complete set of promotional cards also was produced by Leaf to hype interest in the product. These cards are numbered the same as the regular cards, but are listed as PROMO/5000 in the serial number box. The P-prefix on the numbering below has been added for checklisting purposes only and does not appear on the card. The Forsberg and Modano promos were the most widely distributed of the group.

| | MINT | NRMT |
|---|---|---|
| COMPLETE SET (20) | 300.00 | 135.00 |
| COMMON CARD (1-20) | 5.00 | 2.20 |

❑ 1 Joe Sakic 25.00 11.00
❑ 2 Keith Tkachuk 12.00 5.50
❑ 3 Brett Hull 12.00 5.50
❑ 4 Paul Coffey 10.00 4.50
❑ 5 Jaromir Jagr 30.00 13.50
❑ 6 Peter Forsberg 30.00 13.50
❑ 7 Zigmund Palffy 12.00 5.50
❑ 8 Wayne Gretzky 60.00 27.00
❑ 9 Pavel Bure 20.00 9.00
❑ 10 Eric Lindros 40.00 18.00
❑ 11 Alexander Mogilny 8.00 3.60
❑ 12 Trevor Linden 5.00 2.20
❑ 13 Jeremy Roenick 10.00 4.50
❑ 14 Doug Gilmour 10.00 4.50
❑ 15 Mike Modano 12.00 5.50
❑ 16 Sergei Fedorov 20.00 9.00
❑ 17 Brendan Shanahan 20.00 9.00
❑ 18 Pierre Turgeon 5.00 2.20
❑ 19 Ed Jovanovski 8.00 3.60
❑ 20 Saku Koivu 20.00 9.00

## 1996-97 Leaf Shut Down

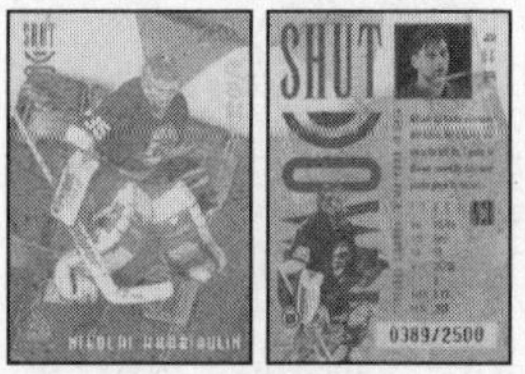

The dominant goaltenders of the NHL (as a group averaging 27 wins in 95-96), were the focus of this 15-card hobby-only chase set. The fronts featured color player photos printed on sailcloth canvas card stock while the backs carried player information. Only 2,500 of this set were produced, with each card sequentially numbered.

| | MINT | NRMT |
|---|---|---|
| COMPLETE SET (15) | 350.00 | 160.00 |
| COMMON CARD (1-15) | 15.00 | 6.75 |

❑ 1 Patrick Roy 80.00 36.00
❑ 2 John Vanbiesbrouck 30.00 13.50
❑ 3 Jocelyn Thibault 20.00 9.00
❑ 4 Ed Belfour 20.00 9.00
❑ 5 Curtis Joseph 20.00 9.00
❑ 6 Martin Brodeur 50.00 22.00
❑ 7 Damian Rhodes 15.00 6.75
❑ 8 Felix Potvin 30.00 13.50
❑ 9 Nikolai Khabibulin 15.00 6.75
❑ 10 Jim Carey 20.00 9.00
❑ 11 Mike Richter 20.00 9.00
❑ 12 Corey Hirsch 15.00 6.75
❑ 13 Chris Osgood 20.00 9.00
❑ 14 Ron Hextall 15.00 6.75
❑ 15 Daren Puppa 15.00 6.75

## 1996-97 Leaf Sweaters Away

This 15-card insert set was printed on embossed, nylon jersey-style card stock in colors simulating the road uniforms of the league's superstars. The fronts displayed color player photos while the backs carried player information. Just 5,000 of these sets were produced and each card was sequentially numbered.

| | MINT | NRMT |
|---|---|---|
| COMPLETE SET (15) | 350.00 | 160.00 |
| COMMON CARD (1-15) | 10.00 | 4.50 |

❑ 1 Mario Lemieux 50.00 22.00
❑ 2 Patrick Roy 50.00 22.00
❑ 3 Eric Lindros 30.00 13.50
❑ 4 John Vanbiesbrouck 15.00 6.75
❑ 5 Paul Kariya 40.00 18.00
❑ 6 Martin Brodeur 25.00 11.00
❑ 7 Eric Daze 10.00 4.50
❑ 8 Mark Messier 12.00 5.50
❑ 9 Jim Carey 10.00 4.50
❑ 10 Brendan Shanahan 20.00 9.00
❑ 11 Sergei Fedorov 20.00 9.00
❑ 12 Brett Hull 12.00 5.50
❑ 13 Pavel Bure 20.00 9.00
❑ 14 Daniel Alfredsson 10.00 4.50
❑ 15 Saku Koivu 15.00 6.75

## 1996-97 Leaf Sweaters Home

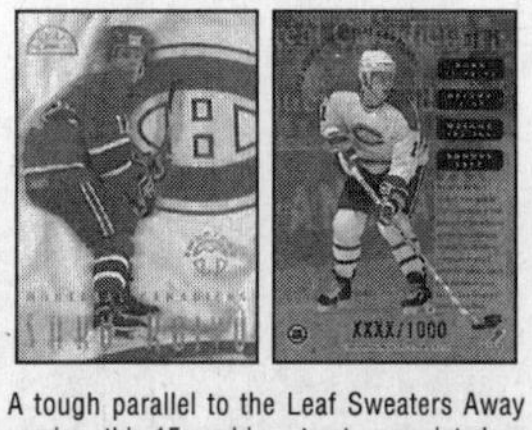

A tough parallel to the Leaf Sweaters Away version, this 15-card insert set was printed on embossed, nylon jersey-style card stock in colors simulating the home uniforms of many of the league's superstars. The fronts displayed color player photos while the backs carried player information. Only 1,000 of these sets were produced, with each card sequentially numbered.

| | MINT | NRMT |
|---|---|---|
| COMPLETE SET (15) | 1400.00 | 650.00 |
| COMMON CARD (1-15) | 40.00 | 18.00 |

*HOME: 2X TO 4X BASIC AWAY SWEATERS

## 1996-97 Leaf The Best Of ...

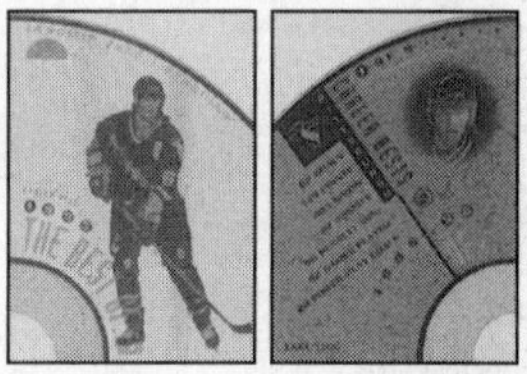

This nine-card insert set featured NHL record breakers and was found exclusively in pre-priced retail packs. Printed on clear plastic with holographic foil, just 1,500 of this die-cut insert set were produced, with each card sequentially numbered.

| | MINT | NRMT |
|---|---|---|
| COMPLETE SET (9) | 400.00 | 180.00 |
| COMMON CARD (1-9) | 15.00 | 6.75 |

❑ 1 Jaromir Jagr 80.00 36.00
❑ 2 Eric Daze 25.00 11.00
❑ 3 Eric Lindros 80.00 36.00
❑ 4 Chris Osgood 25.00 11.00
❑ 5 Keith Tkachuk 30.00 13.50
❑ 6 Nikolai Khabibulin 15.00 6.75
❑ 7 Doug Weight 25.00 11.00
❑ 8 Peter Forsberg 80.00 36.00
❑ 9 Jocelyn Thibault 30.00 13.50

## 1997-98 Leaf

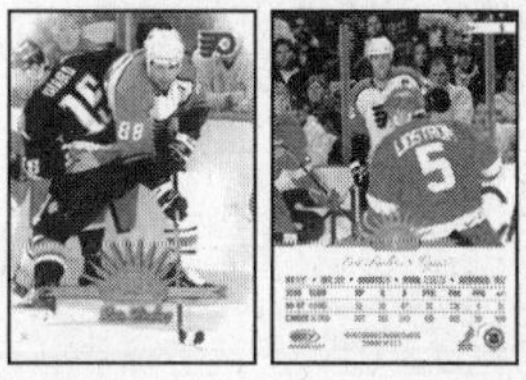

The 1997-98 Leaf set was issued in one series totalling 200 cards and was distributed in 10-card packs with a suggested retail price of $2.99. The fronts freature borderless color action player photos. The backs carry player information. The set contains the topical subsets: Gold Leaf Rookies (148-167), Gamers (168-187), and Day in the Life (188-197).

| | MINT | NRMT |
|---|---|---|
| COMPLETE SET (200) | 150.00 | 70.00 |
| COMMON CARD (1-200) | .15 | .07 |
| COMMON GLR (148-167) | .75 | .35 |
| COMMON GM (168-187) | 1.25 | .55 |
| COMMON DIL (188-197) | 1.00 | .45 |

❑ 1 Eric Lindros 1.50 .70
❑ 2 Dominik Hasek 1.00 .45
❑ 3 Peter Forsberg 1.50 .70
❑ 4 Steve Yzerman 1.50 .70
❑ 5 John Vanbiesbrouck .75 .35
❑ 6 Paul Kariya 2.00 .90
❑ 7 Martin Brodeur 1.25 .55
❑ 8 Wayne Gretzky 3.00 1.35
❑ 9 Mark Messier .60 .25
❑ 10 Jaromir Jagr 1.50 .70
❑ 11 Brett Hull .60 .25
❑ 12 Brendan Shanahan 1.00 .45
❑ 13 Ray Bourque .50 .23
❑ 14 Jarome Iginla .40 .18
❑ 15 Mike Modano .60 .25
❑ 16 Curtis Joseph .50 .23
❑ 17 Ed Jovanovski .40 .18
❑ 18 Teemu Selanne 1.00 .45
❑ 19 Saku Koivu .75 .35
❑ 20 Eric Fichaud .40 .18
❑ 21 Paul Coffey .50 .23
❑ 22 Jeremy Roenick .50 .23
❑ 23 Owen Nolan .40 .18
❑ 24 Felix Potvin .50 .23
❑ 25 Alexander Mogilny .40 .18
❑ 26 Alexandre Daigle .40 .18
❑ 27 Chris Gratton .40 .18
❑ 28 Geoff Sanderson .40 .18
❑ 29 Dimitri Khristich .15 .07
❑ 30 Bryan Berard .15 .07
❑ 31 Vyacheslav Kozlov .15 .07
❑ 32 Jeff Hackett .40 .18
❑ 33 Bill Ranford .40 .18
❑ 34 Pat LaFontaine .40 .18
❑ 35 Joe Sakic 1.00 .45
❑ 36 Niklas Sundstrom .15 .07
❑ 37 Martin Gelinas .15 .07
❑ 38 Mikael Renberg .15 .07
❑ 39 Trevor Linden .40 .18
❑ 40 Jozef Stumpel .40 .18
❑ 41 Joe Thornton CL .50 .23
❑ 42 Jocelyn Thibault .40 .18

❑ 43 Pierre Turgeon .40 .18
❑ 44 Ron Francis .40 .18
❑ 45 Damian Rhodes .40 .18
❑ 46 Jamie Langenbrunner .15 .07
❑ 47 Chris Osgood .50 .23
❑ 48 Vaclav Varada .15 .07
❑ 49 Ryan Smyth .40 .18
❑ 50 Daren Puppa .40 .18
❑ 51 Petr Nedved .40 .18
❑ 52 Ron Hextall .40 .18
❑ 53 Joe Juneau .40 .18
❑ 54 Jim Campbell .15 .07
❑ 55 Zigmund Palffy .50 .23
❑ 56 Roman Turek .40 .18
❑ 57 Adam Deadmarsh .40 .18
❑ 58 Rob Niedermayer .40 .18
❑ 59 Alexei Yashin .40 .18
❑ 60 Pavel Bure 1.00 .45
❑ 61 Jason Arnott .40 .18
❑ 62 Nikolai Khabibulin .40 .18
❑ 63 Sean Burke .40 .18
❑ 64 Chris Chelios .50 .23
❑ 65 Mike Ricci .40 .18
❑ 66 Sergei Berezin .15 .07
❑ 67 Jaroslav Svejkovsky CL .40 .18
❑ 68 Brian Savage .15 .07
❑ 69 Roman Vopat .15 .07
❑ 70 Mike Richter .50 .23
❑ 71 Jim Carey .40 .18
❑ 72 Guy Hebert .40 .18
❑ 73 Keith Tkachuk .60 .25
❑ 74 Kirk McLean .40 .18
❑ 75 Janne Niinimaa .15 .07
❑ 76 Roman Hamrlik .15 .07
❑ 77 Darcy Tucker .15 .07
❑ 78 Pat Verbeek .15 .07
❑ 79 Hnat Domenichelli .15 .07
❑ 80 Doug Gilmour .50 .23
❑ 81 Mike Grier .15 .07
❑ 82 Ken Wregget .40 .18
❑ 83 Dino Ciccarelli .15 .07
❑ 84 Steve Sullivan .15 .07
❑ 85 Anson Carter .15 .07
❑ 86 Steve Shields .40 .18
❑ 87 Ed Belfour .50 .23
❑ 88 Darren McCarty .15 .07
❑ 89 Adam Graves .40 .18
❑ 90 Chris Pronger .40 .18
❑ 91 Peter Bondra .50 .23
❑ 92 Oleg Tverdovsky .15 .07
❑ 93 Stephane Fiset .40 .18
❑ 94 Mike Vernon .40 .18
❑ 95 Scott Lachance .15 .07
❑ 96 Corey Schwab .40 .18
❑ 97 Eric Daze .40 .18
❑ 98 Jere Lehtinen .15 .07
❑ 99 Donald Audette .15 .07
❑ 100 John LeClair .75 .35
❑ 101 Steve Rucchin .15 .07
❑ 102 Jeff Friesen .40 .18
❑ 103 Daymond Langkow .15 .07
❑ 104 Mike Dunham .40 .18
❑ 105 Marc Denis CL .15 .07
❑ 106 Andrew Cassels .15 .07
❑ 107 Mike Peca .15 .07
❑ 108 Joe Nieuwendyk .40 .18
❑ 109 Vincent Damphousse .40 .18
❑ 110 Scott Mellanby .15 .07
❑ 111 Patrick Lalime .40 .18
❑ 112 Derek Plante .15 .07
❑ 113 Wade Redden .15 .07
❑ 114 Marcel Cousineau .40 .18
❑ 115 Ray Sheppard .40 .18
❑ 116 Dave Andreychuk .40 .18
❑ 117 Brian Leetch .50 .23
❑ 118 Sandis Ozolinsh .40 .18
❑ 119 Keith Primeau .15 .07
❑ 120 Brian Holzinger .15 .07
❑ 121 Luc Robitaille .40 .18
❑ 122 Jose Theodore .40 .18
❑ 123 Grant Fuhr .40 .18
❑ 124 Dainius Zubrus .50 .23
❑ 125 Rod Brind'Amour .40 .18
❑ 126 Trevor Kidd .40 .18
❑ 127 Mark Recchi .40 .18
❑ 128 Patrick Roy 2.50 1.10
❑ 129 Kevin Hatcher .15 .07
❑ 130 Adam Oates .40 .18
❑ 131 Doug Weight .40 .18
❑ 132 Vaclav Prospal .60 .25
UER front & back Vinny
❑ 133 Harry York .15 .07
❑ 134 Todd Bertuzzi .15 .07
❑ 135 Sergei Fedorov 1.00 .45
❑ 136 Theoren Fleury .40 .18
❑ 137 Chad Kilger .15 .07
❑ 138 Jamie Storr .40 .18
❑ 139 Tony Amonte .40 .18
❑ 140 Rem Murray .15 .07
❑ 141 Chris O'Sullivan .15 .07
❑ 142 Mats Sundin .50 .23
❑ 143 Ethan Moreau .15 .07
❑ 144 Derian Hatcher .15 .07
❑ 145 Daniel Alfredsson .40 .18
❑ 146 Corey Hirsch .15 .07
❑ 147 Landon Wilson .15 .07
❑ 148 Marc Denis GLR .75 .35
❑ 149 Boyd Devereaux GLR .75 .35
❑ 150 Joe Thornton GLR 3.00 1.35
❑ 151 Sergei Samsonov GLR 4.00 1.80
❑ 152 Alyn McCauley GLR .75 .35
❑ 153 Erik Rasmussen GLR .75 .35
❑ 154 Patrick Marleau GLR 3.00 1.35
❑ 155 Olli Jokinen GLR 2.50 1.10
❑ 156 Chris Phillips GLR .75 .35
❑ 157 Tomas Vokoun GLR .75 .35
❑ 158 Chris Dingman GLR .75 .35
❑ 159 Daniel Cleary GLR 2.00 .90
❑ 160 Juha Lind GLR .75 .35
❑ 161 Jean-Yves Leroux RC GLR .75 .35
❑ 162 Brad Isbister GLR .75 .35
❑ 163 Vadim Sharifijanov GLR .75 .35
❑ 164 Alexei Morozov GLR .75 .35
❑ 165 Vaclav Prospal GLR 2.00 .90
UER front & back Vinny
❑ 166 Vaclav Varada GLR .75 .35
❑ 167 Jaroslav Svejkovsky GLR .75 .35
❑ 168 Eric Lindros GM 8.00 3.60
❑ 169 Dominik Hasek GM 5.00 2.20
❑ 170 Peter Forsberg GM 8.00 3.60
❑ 171 Steve Yzerman GM 8.00 3.60
❑ 172 John Vanbiesbrouck GM 4.00 1.80
❑ 173 Paul Kariya GM 10.00 4.50
❑ 174 Martin Brodeur GM 6.00 2.70
❑ 175 Wayne Gretzky GM 15.00 6.75
❑ 176 Mark Messier GM 3.00 1.35
❑ 177 Jaromir Jagr GM 8.00 3.60
❑ 178 Brett Hull GM 3.00 1.35
❑ 179 Brendan Shanahan GM 5.00 2.20
❑ 180 Jarome Iginla GM 1.25 .55
❑ 181 Mike Modano GM 1.25 .55
❑ 182 Teemu Selanne GM 5.00 2.20
❑ 183 Bryan Berard GM 1.25 .55
❑ 184 Ryan Smyth GM 1.25 .55
❑ 185 Keith Tkachuk GM 3.00 1.35
❑ 186 Dainius Zubrus GM 1.25 .55
❑ 187 Patrick Roy GM 12.00 5.50
❑ 188 Trevor Linden DIL 1.00 .45
❑ 189 Trevor Linden DIL 1.00 .45
❑ 190 Trevor Linden DIL 1.00 .45
❑ 191 Trevor Linden DIL 1.00 .45
❑ 192 Trevor Linden DIL 1.00 .45
❑ 193 Trevor Linden DIL 1.00 .45
❑ 194 Trevor Linden DIL 1.00 .45
❑ 195 Trevor Linden DIL 1.00 .45
❑ 196 Trevor Linden DIL 1.00 .45
❑ 197 Trevor Linden DIL 1.00 .45
❑ 198 Chris Phillips CL .15 .07
❑ 199 Sergei Samsonov CL .40 .18
❑ 200 Daniel Cleary CL .15 .07
❑ P5 Felix Potvin PROMO 1.00 .45
❑ P6 Martin Brodeur PROMO 2.00 .90
❑ P10 Jim Carey PROMO 1.00 .45
❑ NNO Trevor Linden AU/500 30.00 13.50

## 1997-98 Leaf Fractal Matrix

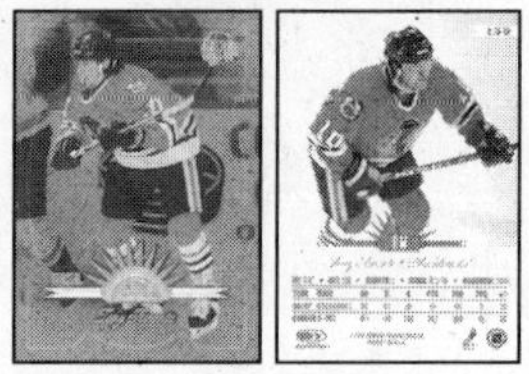

This 200-card set is parallel to the base set and features color player photos with either a bronze, silver or gold finish. Only 100 cards are bronze, 60 cards are silver, and 40 cards are gold. No card is available in more than one of the color.

| | MINT | NRMT |
|---|---|---|
| COMMON BRONZE | 1.25 | .55 |
| BRONZE-X STATED PRINT RUN 1400 SETS | | |
| BRONZE-Y STATED PRINT RUN 1600 SETS | | |
| BRONZE-Z STATED PRINT RUN 1700 SETS | | |
| COMMON SILVER | 4.00 | 1.80 |
| SILVER-X STATED PRINT RUN 500 SETS | | |
| SILVER-Y STATED PRINT RUN 700 SETS | | |
| SILVER-Z STATED PRINT RUN 800 SETS | | |
| COMMON GOLD | 6.00 | 2.70 |
| GOLD-X STATED PRINT RUN 50 SETS | | |
| GOLD-Y STATED PRINT RUN 250 SETS | | |
| GOLD-Z STATED PRINT RUN 350 SETS | | |

❑ 1 Eric Lindros GX 250.00 110.00
❑ 2 Dominik Hasek GZ 40.00 18.00
❑ 3 Peter Forsberg GZ 60.00 27.00
❑ 4 Steve Yzerman GZ 60.00 27.00
❑ 5 John Vanbiesbrouck GZ 30.00 13.50
❑ 6 Paul Kariya GX 300.00 135.00
❑ 7 Martin Brodeur GZ 50.00 22.00
❑ 8 Wayne Gretzky GX 500.00 220.00
❑ 9 Mark Messier GY 30.00 13.50
❑ 10 Jaromir Jagr GZ 30.00 13.50
❑ 11 Brett Hull GY 30.00 13.50
❑ 12 Brendan Shanahan GZ 40.00 18.00
❑ 15 Mike Modano GY 30.00 13.50
❑ 18 Teemu Selanne GZ 40.00 18.00
❑ 19 Saku Koivu GY 40.00 18.00
❑ 35 Joe Sakic GY 50.00 22.00
❑ 41 Joe Thornton CL SZ 15.00 6.75
❑ 60 Pavel Bure GY 50.00 22.00
❑ 73 Keith Tkachuk GY 30.00 13.50
❑ 100 John LeClair GY 40.00 18.00
❑ 128 Patrick Roy GY 120.00 55.00
❑ 132 Vaclav Prospal RC 15.00 6.75
UER front & back Vinny
❑ 135 Sergei Fedorov GY 50.00 22.00
❑ 150 Joe Thornton GLR GX 60.00 27.00
❑ 151 Sergei Samsonov GLR GZ 30.00 13.50
❑ 154 Patrick Marleau GLR SX 30.00 13.50
❑ 155 Olli Jokinen GLR BX 8.00 3.60
❑ 165 Vaclav Prospal GLR BX 6.00 2.70
UER front & back Vinny
❑ 168 Eric Lindros GM SY 30.00 13.50
❑ 169 Dominik Hasek GM BY 8.00 3.60
❑ 170 Peter Forsberg GM BY 12.00 5.50
❑ 171 Steve Yzerman GM SY 30.00 13.50
❑ 172 J.Vanbiesbrouck GM BX 8.00 3.60
❑ 173 Paul Kariya GM SY 40.00 18.00
❑ 174 Martin Brodeur GM BZ 10.00 4.50
❑ 175 Wayne Gretzky GM SY 60.00 27.00
❑ 176 Mark Messier GM BX 6.00 2.70
❑ 177 Jaromir Jagr GM BZ 12.00 5.50
❑ 178 Brett Hull GM BX 6.00 2.70
❑ 179 Brendan Shanahan GM BY 8.00 3.60
❑ 181 Mike Modano GM BY 5.00 2.20
❑ 182 Teemu Selanne GM BY 8.00 3.60
❑ 185 Keith Tkachuk GM BX 6.00 2.70
❑ 187 Patrick Roy GM BX 25.00 11.00
❑ 199 Sergei Samsonov BX CL 10.00 4.50

## 1997-98 Leaf Fractal Matrix Die Cuts

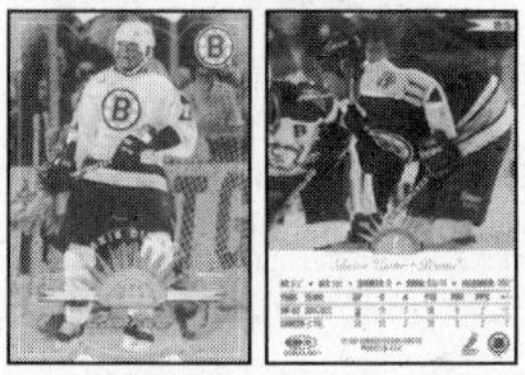

Randomly inserted in packs, this 200-card set is parallel to the base set and features three different die-cut versions in three different finishes. Only 100 cards of the set were produced in the X-Axis cut with 75 of those bronze, 20 silver, and five gold. Only 60 were produced in the Y-Axis cut with 20 of those bronze, 30 silver and 10 gold. Only 40 were produced in the Z-Axis cut with five bronze, 10 silver, and 25 gold. No card was available in more than one color nor in more than one die-cut version.

| | MINT | NRMT |
|---|---|---|
| COMMON X-AXIS | 5.00 | 2.20 |
| X-AXIS STATED PRINT RUN 400 SETS | | |
| COMMON Y-AXIS | 8.00 | 3.60 |
| Y-AXIS STATED PRINT RUN 200 SETS | | |
| COMMON Z-AXIS | 12.00 | 5.50 |
| Z-AXIS STATED PRINT RUN 100 SETS | | |

❑ 1 Eric Lindros GX 50.00 22.00
❑ 2 Dominik Hasek GZ 80.00 36.00
❑ 3 Peter Forsberg GZ 120.00 55.00
❑ 4 Steve Yzerman GZ 120.00 55.00
❑ 5 John Vanbiesbrouck GZ 60.00 27.00
❑ 6 Paul Kariya GX 60.00 27.00
❑ 7 Martin Brodeur GZ 100.00 45.00
❑ 8 Wayne Gretzky GX 100.00 45.00
❑ 9 Mark Messier GY 30.00 13.50
❑ 10 Jaromir Jagr GZ 120.00 55.00
❑ 11 Brett Hull GY 30.00 13.50
❑ 12 Brendan Shanahan GZ 80.00 36.00
❑ 15 Mike Modano GY 30.00 13.50
❑ 18 Teemu Selanne GZ 80.00 36.00
❑ 19 Saku Koivu GY 40.00 18.00
❑ 35 Joe Sakic GY 50.00 22.00
❑ 41 Joe Thornton CL SZ 50.00 22.00
❑ 60 Pavel Bure GY 50.00 22.00
❑ 73 Keith Tkachuk GY 30.00 13.50
❑ 100 John LeClair GY 40.00 18.00
❑ 128 Patrick Roy GY 120.00 55.00
❑ 135 Sergei Fedorov GY 50.00 22.00
❑ 150 Joe Thornton GLR GX 15.00 6.75
❑ 151 Sergei Samsonov GLR GZ 50.00 22.00
❑ 154 Patrick Marleau GLR SX 20.00 9.00
❑ 155 Olli Jokinen GLR BX 12.00 5.50
❑ 165 Vaclav Prospal GLR BX 10.00 4.50
UER front & back Vinny
❑ 168 Eric Lindros GM SY 80.00 36.00
❑ 169 Dominik Hasek GM BY 50.00 22.00
❑ 170 Peter Forsberg GM BY 80.00 36.00
❑ 171 Steve Yzerman GM SY 80.00 36.00
❑ 172 J.Vanbiesbrouck GM BX 25.00 11.00
❑ 173 Paul Kariya GM SY 100.00 45.00
❑ 174 Martin Brodeur GM BZ 100.00 45.00
❑ 175 Wayne Gretzky GM SY 150.00 70.00
❑ 176 Mark Messier GM BX 20.00 9.00
❑ 177 Jaromir Jagr GM BZ 120.00 55.00
❑ 178 Brett Hull GM BX 20.00 9.00
❑ 179 Brendan Shanahan GM BY 50.00 22.00
❑ 181 Mike Modano GM BY 30.00 13.50
❑ 182 Teemu Selanne GM BY 50.00 22.00
❑ 185 Keith Tkachuk GM BX 20.00 9.00
❑ 187 Patrick Roy GM BX 80.00 36.00
❑ 199 Sergei Samsonov BX CL 15.00 6.75

## 1997-98 Leaf Banner Season

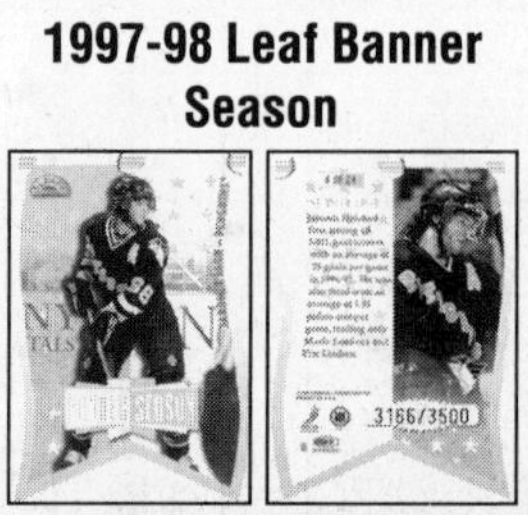

Randomly inserted in packs, this 24-card set features color player photos of top players printed on die-cut banner-shaped canvas card stock. Each card is individually numbered to 3,500.

| | MINT | NRMT |
|---|---|---|
| COMPLETE SET (24) | 150.00 | 70.00 |
| COMMON CARD (1-24) | 2.50 | 1.10 |

❑ 1 Paul Kariya 15.00 6.75
❑ 2 Eric Lindros 12.00 5.50
❑ 3 Wayne Gretzky 25.00 11.00
❑ 4 Jaromir Jagr 12.00 5.50
❑ 5 Steve Yzerman 12.00 5.50
❑ 6 Brendan Shanahan 8.00 3.60
❑ 7 John LeClair 6.00 2.70
❑ 8 Teemu Selanne 8.00 3.60
❑ 9 Mike Modano 5.00 2.20
❑ 10 Ryan Smyth 3.00 1.35
❑ 11 Brett Hull 5.00 2.20
❑ 12 Zigmund Palffy 4.00 1.80
❑ 13 Peter Forsberg 12.00 5.50
❑ 14 Keith Tkachuk 5.00 2.20
❑ 15 Saku Koivu 6.00 2.70
❑ 16 Sergei Fedorov 8.00 3.60
❑ 17 Brian Leetch 4.00 1.80
❑ 18 Bryan Berard 3.00 1.35
❑ 19 Mats Sundin 4.00 1.80
❑ 20 Jarome Iginla 3.00 1.35
❑ 21 Sergei Berezin 3.00 1.35
❑ 22 Dainius Zubrus 4.00 1.80
❑ 23 Mike Grier 2.50 1.10
❑ 24 Joe Sakic 8.00 3.60

## 1997-98 Leaf Fire On Ice

Randomly inserted in packs, this 16-card set features color photos of top players on a background of fire and ice printed using dot matrix hologram technology. Each card is individually numbered to 1,000.

| | MINT | NRMT |
|---|---|---|
| COMPLETE SET (16) | 700.00 | 325.00 |
| COMMON CARD (1-16) | 12.00 | 5.50 |

❑ 1 Wayne Gretzky 100.00 45.00
❑ 2 Eric Lindros 50.00 22.00
❑ 3 Jaromir Jagr 50.00 22.00
❑ 4 Steve Yzerman 50.00 22.00
❑ 5 Brendan Shanahan 30.00 13.50
❑ 6 Mike Modano 20.00 9.00
❑ 7 Joe Sakic 30.00 13.50
❑ 8 Pavel Bure 30.00 13.50
❑ 9 Ryan Smyth 12.00 5.50
❑ 10 Teemu Selanne 30.00 13.50
❑ 11 Mark Messier 20.00 9.00
❑ 12 Peter Forsberg 50.00 22.00
❑ 13 Dainius Zubrus 12.00 5.50
❑ 14 Joe Thornton 20.00 9.00
❑ 15 Sergei Samsonov 20.00 9.00
❑ 16 Paul Kariya 60.00 27.00

## 1997-98 Leaf Lindros Collection

Randomly inserted in packs, this five-card set features color photos of Eric Lindros with actual pieces of game used equipment inserted into the cards. Pieces of his game-used jerseys, sticks, stirrups, and gloves were used. Each card is individually numbered to 100.

| | MINT | NRMT |
|---|---|---|
| COMPLETE SET (5) | 2000.00 | 900.00 |
| COMMON CARD (1-5) | 300.00 | 135.00 |

❑ 1 E.Lindros Home Jersey 600.00 275.00
❑ 2 E.Lindros Away Jersey 600.00 275.00
❑ 3 E.Lindros Stick 300.00 135.00
❑ 4 E.Lindros Glove 300.00 135.00
❑ 5 E.Lindros Stirrups 300.00 135.00

## 1997-98 Leaf Pipe Dreams

Randomly inserted in packs, this 16-card set features color photos of top goalies printed on silver foil board and micro-etched. Each card is individually numbered to 2,500.

| | MINT | NRMT |
|---|---|---|
| COMPLETE SET (16) | 250.00 | 110.00 |
| COMMON CARD (1-16) | 10.00 | 4.50 |

❑ 1 Dominik Hasek 25.00 11.00
❑ 2 John Vanbiesbrouck 20.00 9.00
❑ 3 Patrick Roy 60.00 27.00
❑ 4 Curtis Joseph 12.00 5.50
❑ 5 Felix Potvin 12.00 5.50
❑ 6 Martin Brodeur 30.00 13.50
❑ 7 Guy Hebert 10.00 4.50
❑ 8 Mike Richter 12.00 5.50
❑ 9 Jose Theodore 10.00 4.50
❑ 10 Jim Carey 10.00 4.50
❑ 11 Damian Rhodes 10.00 4.50
❑ 12 Jocelyn Thibault 12.00 5.50
❑ 13 Nikolai Khabibulin 10.00 4.50
❑ 14 Chris Osgood 12.00 5.50
❑ 15 Eric Fichaud 10.00 4.50
❑ 16 Mike Dunham 10.00 4.50

## 1995-96 Leaf Limited

This 120-card super-premium set was released in five-card packs with a suggested retail price of $4.99 per pack. The product was

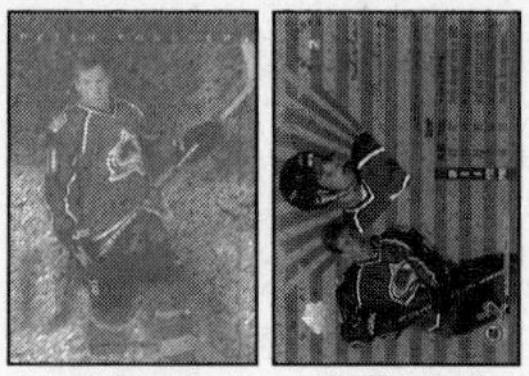

produced to order; hence 25,722 individually numbered boxes were produced, much less than the initially announced figure of 60,000. This reduction wreaked havoc with insertion ratios on the chase cards, which initially hampered interest in the product. It has since recovered nicely. Rookie Cards in this set include Daniel Alfredsson, Todd Bertuzzi, Radek Dvorak, Daymond Langkow and Marcus Ragnarsson.

| | MINT | NRMT |
|---|---|---|
| COMPLETE SET (120) | 50.00 | 22.00 |
| COMMON CARD (1-120) | .25 | .11 |

❑ 1 Mario Lemieux 6.00 2.70
❑ 2 Peter Forsberg 4.00 1.80
❑ 3 Geoff Courtnall .25 .11
❑ 4 Vincent Damphousse .40 .18
❑ 5 Jason Allison .25 .11
❑ 6 Theoren Fleury .40 .18
❑ 7 Shane Doan .25 .11
❑ 8 Chris Gratton .40 .18
❑ 9 Paul Kariya 5.00 2.20
❑ 10 Radek Dvorak .25 .11
❑ 11 Adam Graves .40 .18
❑ 12 Donald Audette .40 .18
❑ 13 Craig Janney .40 .18
❑ 14 Sean Burke .40 .18
❑ 15 Ed Belfour .75 .35
❑ 16 Ray Bourque .75 .35
❑ 17 Pavel Bure 2.50 1.10
❑ 18 Martin Brodeur 3.00 1.35
❑ 19 Todd Bertuzzi .40 .18
❑ 20 Aki-Petteri Berg .25 .11
❑ 21 Dave Andreychuk .40 .18
❑ 22 Jason Arnott .40 .18
❑ 23 Ron Francis .40 .18
❑ 24 Paul Coffey .75 .35
❑ 25 Daniel Alfredsson 2.00 .90
❑ 26 Todd Harvey .25 .11
❑ 27 Claude Lemieux .40 .18
❑ 28 Brett Hull 1.50 .70
❑ 29 Felix Potvin .75 .35
❑ 30 Peter Bondra .75 .35
❑ 31 Trevor Kidd .40 .18
❑ 32 Igor Korolev .25 .11
❑ 33 Roman Hamrlik .40 .18
❑ 34 Chad Kilger .25 .11
❑ 35 Rob Niedermayer .40 .18
❑ 36 Richard Park .25 .11
❑ 37 Mathieu Dandenault .25 .11
❑ 38 Alexander Daigle .25 .11
❑ 39 Jere Lehtinen .25 .11
❑ 40 Chris Chelios .75 .35
❑ 41 Blaine Lacher .40 .18
❑ 42 Trevor Linden .40 .18
❑ 43 Scott Niedermayer .25 .11
❑ 44 Teemu Selanne 2.50 1.10
❑ 45 Daymond Langkow .75 .35
❑ 46 Oleg Tverdovsky .40 .18
❑ 47 John Vanbiesbrouck 2.00 .90
❑ 48 Alexei Kovalev .25 .11
❑ 49 Sergei Fedorov 2.00 .90
❑ 50 Alexei Yashin .40 .18
❑ 51 Mike Modano 1.50 .70
❑ 52 Sandis Ozolinsh .40 .18
❑ 53 Ian Laperriere .25 .11
❑ 54 Mark Recchi .40 .18
❑ 55 Jim Carey .75 .35
❑ 56 Joe Nieuwendyk .40 .18
❑ 57 Keith Tkachuk 1.50 .70
❑ 58 Daren Puppa .40 .18
❑ 59 Jason Bonsignore .25 .11
❑ 60 Tomas Sandstrom .25 .11
❑ 61 Chris Osgood .75 .35
❑ 62 Jeff Friesen .40 .18
❑ 63 Jeff O'Neill .25 .11
❑ 64 Joe Sakic 2.50 1.10
❑ 65 Eric Daze .75 .35
❑ 66 Patrick Roy 6.00 2.70
❑ 67 Kirk McLean .40 .18
❑ 68 Stephane Richer .40 .18
❑ 69 Rod Brind'Amour .40 .18
❑ 70 Wendel Clark .40 .18
❑ 71 Rob Blake .25 .11
❑ 72 Doug Gilmour .75 .35
❑ 73 Jaromir Jagr 4.00 1.80
❑ 74 Sergei Zubov .25 .11
❑ 75 Mark Messier 1.50 .70
❑ 76 Dominik Hasek 2.50 1.10
❑ 77 Viktor Kozlov .25 .11
❑ 78 Marcus Ragnarsson .25 .11
❑ 79 Jocelyn Thibault .75 .35
❑ 80 Jeremy Roenick .75 .35
❑ 81 Cam Neely .40 .18
❑ 82 Brian Savage .25 .11
❑ 83 Alexander Mogilny .40 .18
❑ 84 Steve Thomas .25 .11
❑ 85 John LeClair 2.00 .90
❑ 86 Brett Lindros .25 .11
❑ 87 Wayne Gretzky 8.00 3.60
❑ 88 Kenny Jonsson .25 .11
❑ 89 David Oliver .25 .11
❑ 90 Brian Leetch .75 .35

| | MINT | NRMT |
|---|---|---|
| ❑ 91 Luc Robitaille | .40 | .18 |
| ❑ 92 Keith Primeau | .40 | .18 |
| ❑ 93 Owen Nolan | .40 | .18 |
| ❑ 94 Brendan Shanahan | 2.50 | 1.10 |
| ❑ 95 Al MacInnis | .40 | .18 |
| ❑ 96 Kevin Stevens | .25 | .11 |
| ❑ 97 Larry Murphy | .40 | .18 |
| ❑ 98 Joe Juneau | .25 | .11 |
| ❑ 99 Eric Lindros | 4.00 | 1.80 |
| ❑ 100 Travis Green | .40 | .18 |
| ❑ 101 Jamie Storr | .40 | .18 |
| ❑ 102 Pierre Turgeon | .40 | .18 |
| ❑ 103 Bill Ranford | .40 | .18 |
| ❑ 104 Niklas Sundstrom | .25 | .11 |
| ❑ 105 Steve Yzerman | 4.00 | 1.80 |
| ❑ 106 Ray Sheppard | .40 | .18 |
| ❑ 107 Chris Pronger | .40 | .18 |
| ❑ 108 Adam Oates | .40 | .18 |
| ❑ 109 Mike Gartner | .40 | .18 |
| ❑ 110 Doug Weight | .40 | .18 |
| ❑ 111 Jason Dawe | .25 | .11 |
| ❑ 112 Rick Tocchet | .40 | .18 |
| ❑ 113 Pat LaFontaine | .40 | .18 |
| ❑ 114 Scott Mellanby | .40 | .18 |
| ❑ 115 Vitali Yachmenev | .25 | .11 |
| ❑ 116 Alexei Zhamnov | .40 | .18 |
| ❑ 117 Brendan Witt | .25 | .11 |
| ❑ 118 Saku Koivu | 2.00 | .90 |
| ❑ 119 Mikael Renberg | .40 | .18 |
| ❑ 120 Mats Sundin | .40 | .18 |

## 1995-96 Leaf Limited Rookie Phenoms

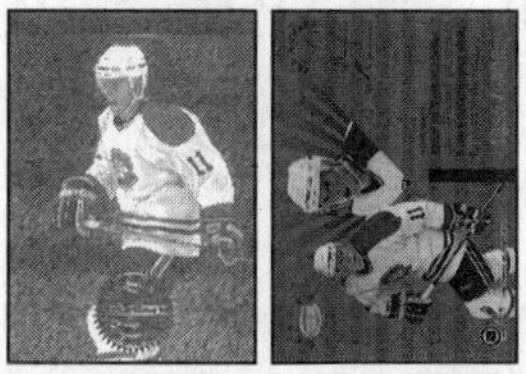

This ten-card set salutes some of the league's top first year players. Each card is printed on gold patterned holographic foil and is individually numbered out of 5,000. The odds were announced at 1:24, but the reduction in production altered those somewhat; the actual odds were closer to 1:12.

| | MINT | NRMT |
|---|---|---|
| COMPLETE SET (10) | 80.00 | 36.00 |
| COMMON CARD (1-10) | 4.00 | 1.80 |
| ❑ 1 Marcus Ragnarsson | 8.00 | 3.60 |
| ❑ 2 Daniel Alfredsson | 20.00 | 9.00 |
| ❑ 3 Chad Kilger | 4.00 | 1.80 |
| ❑ 4 Niklas Sundstrom | 4.00 | 1.80 |
| ❑ 5 Vitali Yachmenev | 4.00 | 1.80 |
| ❑ 6 Eric Daze | 8.00 | 3.60 |
| ❑ 7 Radek Dvorak | 4.00 | 1.80 |
| ❑ 8 Jeff O'Neill | 4.00 | 1.80 |
| ❑ 9 Saku Koivu | 15.00 | 6.75 |
| ❑ 10 Todd Bertuzzi | 4.00 | 1.80 |

## 1995-96 Leaf Limited Stars of the Game

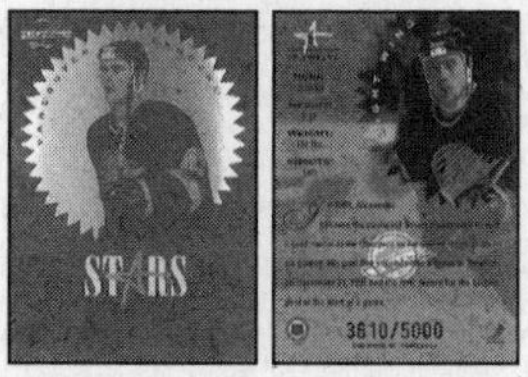

This twelve-card set celebrates some of the biggest stars playing the game. Every card features a photo on micro-etched silver holographic foil. Each card is sequentially numbered of 5,000. The announced odds were 1:20 packs, but the reduced production totals made the real odds closer to 1:10.

| | MINT | NRMT |
|---|---|---|
| COMPLETE SET (12) | 150.00 | 70.00 |
| COMMON CARD (1-12) | 4.00 | 1.80 |
| ❑ 1 Mario Lemieux | 25.00 | 11.00 |
| ❑ 2 Eric Lindros | 15.00 | 6.75 |
| ❑ 3 Wayne Gretzky | 30.00 | 13.50 |
| ❑ 4 Peter Forsberg | 15.00 | 6.75 |
| ❑ 5 Paul Kariya | 20.00 | 9.00 |
| ❑ 6 Alexander Mogilny | 4.00 | 1.80 |
| ❑ 7 Teemu Selanne | 10.00 | 4.50 |
| ❑ 8 Jaromir Jagr | 15.00 | 6.75 |
| ❑ 9 Mats Sundin | 4.00 | 1.80 |
| ❑ 10 Brett Hull | 6.00 | 2.70 |
| ❑ 11 Sergei Fedorov | 10.00 | 4.50 |
| ❑ 12 Jeremy Roenick | 5.00 | 2.20 |

## 1995-96 Leaf Limited Stick Side

This eight-card set was printed on an unusual wood veneer stock and features some of the

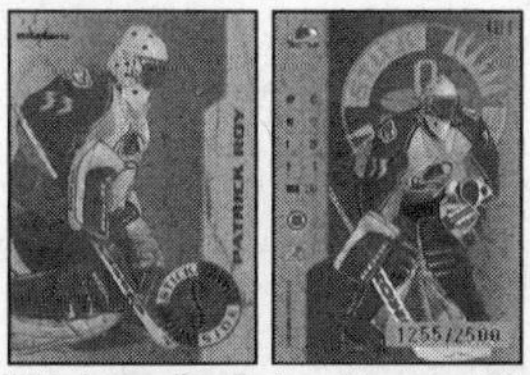

NHL's top goalies. Each card is sequentially numbered out of 2,500. The announced odds were 1:60, but the reduced production run meant the actual odds were closer to 1:30.

| | MINT | NRMT |
|---|---|---|
| COMPLETE SET (8) | 300.00 | 135.00 |
| COMMON CARD (1-8) | 15.00 | 6.75 |
| ❑ 1 Jim Carey | 15.00 | 6.75 |
| ❑ 2 Martin Brodeur | 50.00 | 22.00 |
| ❑ 3 Felix Potvin | 15.00 | 6.75 |
| ❑ 4 Patrick Roy | 80.00 | 36.00 |
| ❑ 5 Dominik Hasek | 40.00 | 18.00 |
| ❑ 6 John Vanbiesbrouck | 30.00 | 13.50 |
| ❑ 7 Ron Hextall | 15.00 | 6.75 |
| ❑ 8 Ed Belfour | 20.00 | 9.00 |

## 1996-97 Leaf Limited

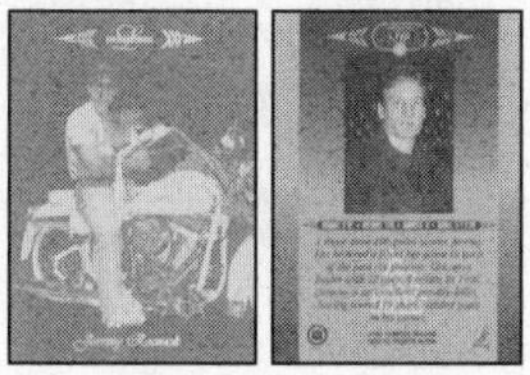

Leaf Limited was a 90-card set featuring the best players in the NHL. The product was hobby-only, with production limited to 27,000 boxes. The cards featured a dazzling silver foil effect. Each sealed box also contained an Eric Lindros card measuring 3 3/4" by 3 3/4". This card featured Lindros on the front, along with a serial number out of 27,000, while the reverse held a series checklist.

| | MINT | NRMT |
|---|---|---|
| COMPLETE SET (90) | 50.00 | 22.00 |
| COMMON CARD (1-90) | .25 | .11 |
| ❑ 1 Chris Chelios | 1.25 | .55 |
| ❑ 2 Brendan Shanahan | 2.50 | 1.10 |
| ❑ 3 Keith Tkachuk | 1.50 | .70 |
| ❑ 4 Roman Hamrlik | .50 | .23 |
| ❑ 5 Adam Oates | .50 | .23 |
| ❑ 6 Chris Osgood | 1.25 | .55 |
| ❑ 7 Wayne Gretzky | 8.00 | 3.60 |
| ❑ 8 Alexander Mogilny | .50 | .23 |
| ❑ 9 Patrick Roy | 6.00 | 2.70 |
| ❑ 10 Saku Koivu | 2.00 | .90 |
| ❑ 11 Jaromir Jagr | 4.00 | 1.80 |
| ❑ 12 Wendel Clark | .50 | .23 |
| ❑ 13 Mike Modano | 1.50 | .70 |
| ❑ 14 Ed Jovanovski | .50 | .23 |
| ❑ 15 John LeClair | 2.00 | .90 |
| ❑ 16 Jim Carey | 1.25 | .55 |
| ❑ 17 Paul Kariya | 5.00 | 2.20 |
| ❑ 18 Paul Coffey | 1.25 | .55 |
| ❑ 19 Todd Bertuzzi | .25 | .11 |
| ❑ 20 Owen Nolan | .50 | .23 |
| ❑ 21 Dominik Hasek | 2.50 | 1.10 |
| ❑ 22 Bill Ranford | .50 | .23 |
| ❑ 23 Scott Stevens | .50 | .23 |
| ❑ 24 Brett Hull | 1.50 | .70 |
| ❑ 25 Trevor Kidd | .50 | .23 |
| ❑ 26 Slava Fetisov | .25 | .11 |
| ❑ 27 Luc Robitaille | .50 | .23 |
| ❑ 28 Mats Sundin | .50 | .23 |
| ❑ 29 Peter Forsberg | 4.00 | 1.80 |
| ❑ 30 John Vanbiesbrouck | 2.00 | .90 |
| ❑ 31 Alexei Yashin | .50 | .23 |
| ❑ 32 Pavel Bure | 2.50 | 1.10 |
| ❑ 33 Pat Verbeek | .25 | .11 |
| ❑ 34 Vitali Yachmenev | .25 | .11 |
| ❑ 35 Ron Hextall | .50 | .23 |
| ❑ 36 Michal Pivonka | .25 | .11 |
| ❑ 37 Eric Daze | .50 | .23 |
| ❑ 38 Pierre Turgeon | .50 | .23 |
| ❑ 39 Petr Nedved | .50 | .23 |
| ❑ 40 Steve Yzerman | 4.00 | 1.80 |
| ❑ 41 Mike Richter | 1.25 | .55 |
| ❑ 42 Marcus Ragnarsson | .25 | .11 |
| ❑ 43 Jason Arnott | .50 | .23 |
| ❑ 44 Jocelyn Thibault | 1.25 | .55 |
| ❑ 45 Alexander Selivanov | .25 | .11 |
| ❑ 46 Claude Lemieux | .50 | .23 |
| ❑ 47 Eric Lindros | 4.00 | 1.80 |
| ❑ 48 Grant Fuhr | .50 | .23 |
| ❑ 49 Ray Bourque | 1.25 | .55 |
| ❑ 50 Scott Mellanby | .50 | .23 |
| ❑ 51 Craig Janney | .50 | .23 |
| ❑ 52 Ron Francis | .50 | .23 |
| ❑ 53 Ed Belfour | 1.25 | .55 |
| ❑ 54 Petr Sykora | .25 | .11 |
| ❑ 55 Damian Rhodes | .50 | .23 |
| ❑ 56 Joe Sakic | 2.50 | 1.10 |
| ❑ 57 Zigmund Palffy | 1.25 | .55 |
| ❑ 58 Daren Puppa | .50 | .23 |
| ❑ 59 Pat LaFontaine | .50 | .23 |
| ❑ 60 Nikolai Khabibulin | .50 | .23 |
| ❑ 61 Sergei Fedorov | 2.50 | 1.10 |
| ❑ 62 Valeri Bure | .50 | .23 |
| ❑ 63 Peter Bondra | 1.25 | .55 |
| ❑ 64 Teemu Selanne | 2.50 | 1.10 |
| ❑ 65 Mark Messier | 1.50 | .70 |
| ❑ 66 Shayne Corson | .25 | .11 |
| ❑ 67 Theoren Fleury | .50 | .23 |
| ❑ 68 Jeff O'Neill | .25 | .11 |
| ❑ 69 Eric Fichaud | .50 | .23 |
| ❑ 70 Doug Gilmour | 1.25 | .55 |
| ❑ 71 Doug Weight | .50 | .23 |
| ❑ 72 Stephane Fiset | .50 | .23 |
| ❑ 73 Daniel Alfredsson | .50 | .23 |
| ❑ 74 Trevor Linden | .50 | .23 |
| ❑ 75 Joe Nieuwendyk | .50 | .23 |
| ❑ 76 Brian Bradley | .25 | .11 |
| ❑ 77 Jere Lehtinen | .25 | .11 |
| ❑ 78 Rob Niedermayer | .50 | .23 |
| ❑ 79 Mikael Renberg | .50 | .23 |
| ❑ 80 Felix Potvin | 1.25 | .55 |
| ❑ 81 Valeri Kamensky | .50 | .23 |
| ❑ 82 Brian Leetch | 1.25 | .55 |
| ❑ 83 Jeff Friesen | .50 | .23 |
| ❑ 84 Vincent Damphousse | .50 | .23 |
| ❑ 85 Mario Lemieux | 6.00 | 2.70 |
| ❑ 86 Jeremy Roenick | 1.25 | .55 |
| ❑ 87 Martin Brodeur | 3.00 | 1.35 |
| ❑ 88 Vyacheslav Kozlov | .25 | .11 |
| ❑ 89 Corey Hirsch | .50 | .23 |
| ❑ 90 Curtis Joseph | 1.25 | .55 |
| ❑ NNO Eric Lindros jumbo | 1.00 | .45 |

## 1996-97 Leaf Limited Gold

A 90-card parallel of the regular Leaf Limited set, this gold version was randomly inserted in packs at an indeterminate rate. Only the values for the most heavily traded cards are listed below. Values for the remaining cards may be determined by using the multipliers below on the values of the regular counterparts.

| | MINT | NRMT |
|---|---|---|
| COMPLETE SET (90) | 600.00 | 275.00 |
| COMMON CARD (1-90) | 4.00 | 1.80 |

*STARS: 6X TO 12X BASIC CARDS
*YOUNG STARS: 5X TO 10X BASIC CARDS

## 1996-97 Leaf Limited Bash the Boards Promos

This 10-card set was intended to promote the Leaf Limited Bash the Boards insert set. Unlike the regular set which is serial numbered to 3500, these cards are numbered as Promo/2500. Doug Gilmour is the most readily found of these cards.

| | MINT | NRMT |
|---|---|---|
| COMPLETE SET (10) | 125.00 | 55.00 |
| COMMON CARD (1-10) | 5.00 | 2.20 |
| ❑ P1 Eric Lindros | 40.00 | 18.00 |
| ❑ P2 Mark Messier | 10.00 | 4.50 |
| ❑ P3 Owen Nolan | 5.00 | 2.20 |
| ❑ P4 Doug Gilmour | 8.00 | 3.60 |
| ❑ P5 Keith Tkachuk | 10.00 | 4.50 |
| ❑ P6 Claude Lemieux | 5.00 | 2.20 |
| ❑ P7 Ed Jovanovski | 8.00 | 3.60 |
| ❑ P8 Peter Forsberg | 30.00 | 13.50 |
| ❑ P9 Brendan Shanahan | 15.00 | 6.75 |
| ❑ P10 Eric Daze | 5.00 | 2.20 |

## 1996-97 Leaf Limited Bash The Boards

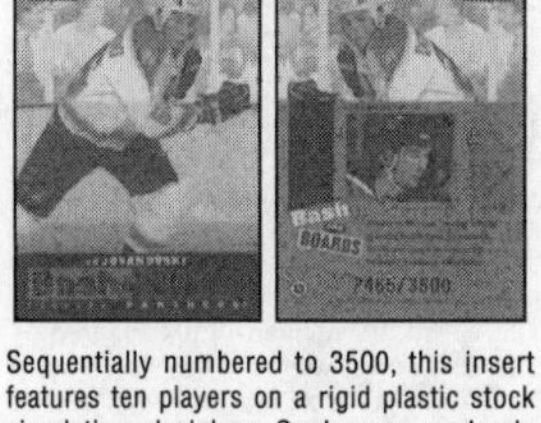

Sequentially numbered to 3500, this insert features ten players on a rigid plastic stock simulating plexiglass. Cards were randomly inserted in packs. A complete version of the set also was available in promotional form. The cards mirror the pack-inserted cards in every way save for the serial numbering on the back: these cards are listed as PROMO/2500. The Doug Gilmour is the most readily available of these.

| | MINT | NRMT |
|---|---|---|
| COMPLETE SET (10) | 150.00 | 70.00 |
| COMMON CARD (1-10) | 8.00 | 3.60 |
| COMP.LTD.ED.SET (10) | 600.00 | 275.00 |
| COMMON LTD.ED. (1-10) | 30.00 | 13.50 |

*LIMITED EDITION: 2.5X TO 4X BASIC CARDS

| | MINT | NRMT |
|---|---|---|
| ❑ 1 Eric Lindros | 60.00 | 27.00 |
| ❑ 2 Mark Messier | 15.00 | 6.75 |
| ❑ 3 Owen Nolan | 10.00 | 4.50 |
| ❑ 4 Doug Gilmour | 12.00 | 5.50 |
| ❑ 5 Keith Tkachuk | 15.00 | 6.75 |
| ❑ 6 Claude Lemieux | 10.00 | 4.50 |
| ❑ 7 Ed Jovanovski | 15.00 | 6.75 |
| ❑ 8 Peter Forsberg | 40.00 | 18.00 |
| ❑ 9 Brendan Shanahan | 25.00 | 11.00 |
| ❑ 10 Eric Daze | 8.00 | 3.60 |

## 1996-97 Leaf Limited Rookies

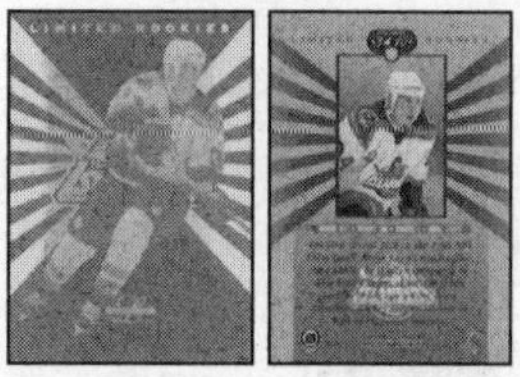

A ten-card random insert, this set consisted of top rookie prospects. Fronts featured a team logo with rays of holographic foil shooting from behind a player photo, while the backs add another photo and a brief player biography. A gold parallel version of this set is known to exist, though quantity produced and distribution source is not entirely clear. Dealers report using a multiplier of 5X to 8X basic cards for these rare parallels.

| | MINT | NRMT |
|---|---|---|
| COMPLETE SET (10) | 100.00 | 45.00 |
| COMMON CARD (1-10) | 8.00 | 3.60 |
| ❑ 1 Ethan Moreau | 10.00 | 4.50 |
| ❑ 2 Jarome Iginla | 25.00 | 11.00 |
| ❑ 3 Bryan Berard | 12.00 | 5.50 |
| ❑ 4 Hnat Domenichelli | 8.00 | 3.60 |
| ❑ 5 Wade Redden | 8.00 | 3.60 |
| ❑ 6 Dainius Zubrus | 30.00 | 13.50 |
| ❑ 7 Sergei Berezin | 10.00 | 4.50 |
| ❑ 8 Jamie Langenbrunner | 8.00 | 3.60 |
| ❑ 9 Tomas Holmstrom | 8.00 | 3.60 |
| ❑ 10 Jonas Hoglund | 8.00 | 3.60 |

## 1996-97 Leaf Limited Stubble

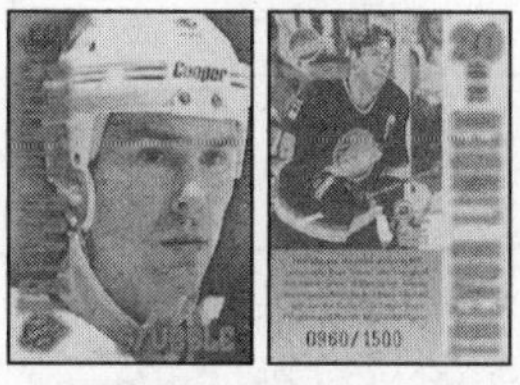

Based upon the old NHL superstition of not shaving while winning during the playoffs, Stubble is a randomly-inserted set highlighted by a felt-like treatment in the beard area. The 20 cards in the set are sequentially numbered to 1000.

| | MINT | NRMT |
|---|---|---|
| COMPLETE SET (20) | 750.00 | 350.00 |
| COMMON CARD (1-20) | 15.00 | 6.75 |
| ❑ 1 Patrick Roy | 100.00 | 45.00 |
| ❑ 2 Eric Lindros | 60.00 | 27.00 |
| ❑ 3 Wayne Gretzky | 150.00 | 70.00 |
| ❑ 4 Paul Coffey | 20.00 | 9.00 |
| ❑ 5 Jim Carey | 20.00 | 9.00 |
| ❑ 6 Ed Belfour | 20.00 | 9.00 |
| ❑ 7 Mario Lemieux | 100.00 | 45.00 |
| ❑ 8 Mike Modano | 25.00 | 11.00 |
| ❑ 9 Todd Bertuzzi | 15.00 | 6.75 |
| ❑ 10 Pavel Bure | 40.00 | 18.00 |
| ❑ 11 Martin Brodeur | 50.00 | 22.00 |
| ❑ 12 Petr Nedved | 15.00 | 6.75 |
| ❑ 13 Alexander Mogilny | 20.00 | 9.00 |
| ❑ 14 Steve Yzerman | 60.00 | 27.00 |
| ❑ 15 Brett Hull | 25.00 | 11.00 |
| ❑ 16 Joe Sakic | 40.00 | 18.00 |
| ❑ 17 Scott Mellanby | 15.00 | 6.75 |
| ❑ 18 Trevor Linden | 15.00 | 6.75 |
| ❑ 19 Rob Niedermayer | 15.00 | 6.75 |
| ❑ 20 Wendel Clark | 15.00 | 6.75 |

## 1996-97 Leaf Preferred

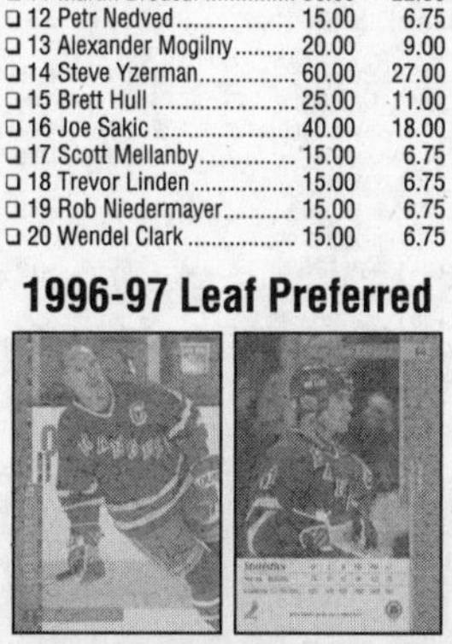

The 1996-97 Leaf Preferred set was issued in one series totaling 150 cards. Suggested retail on packs was $3.49, which included five standard cards and one metal card. Card fronts feature color action photos, a small team logo, and the player's name in team colors. One edge is also enhanced with etched silver foil with the Leaf Preferred logo. Key RCs include Dainus Zubrus and Sergei Berezin.

| | MINT | NRMT |
|---|---|---|
| COMPLETE SET (150) | 30.00 | 13.50 |
| COMMON CARD (1-150) | .10 | .05 |
| ❑ 1 Patrick Roy | 2.00 | .90 |
| ❑ 2 Alexander Mogilny | .25 | .11 |
| ❑ 3 Bill Ranford | .25 | .11 |
| ❑ 4 Jeremy Roenick | .40 | .18 |
| ❑ 5 Travis Green | .25 | .11 |
| ❑ 6 Owen Nolan | .25 | .11 |
| ❑ 7 Paul Kariya | 1.50 | .70 |
| ❑ 8 Pat Verbeek | .10 | .05 |
| ❑ 9 Jeff O'Neill | .10 | .05 |
| ❑ 10 Nikolai Khabibulin | .25 | .11 |
| ❑ 11 Pat LaFontaine | .25 | .11 |
| ❑ 12 Rob Niedermayer | .25 | .11 |
| ❑ 13 Luc Robitaille | .25 | .11 |
| ❑ 14 Mats Sundin | .25 | .11 |
| ❑ 15 Cory Stillman | .10 | .05 |
| ❑ 16 Ray Ferraro | .10 | .05 |
| ❑ 17 Alexei Yashin | .25 | .11 |
| ❑ 18 Brian Bradley | .10 | .05 |
| ❑ 19 Chris Chelios | .40 | .18 |
| ❑ 20 Jason Arnott | .25 | .11 |
| ❑ 21 Petr Sykora | .10 | .05 |
| ❑ 22 Jaromir Jagr | 1.25 | .55 |
| ❑ 23 Jim Carey | .40 | .18 |
| ❑ 24 Claude Lemieux | .25 | .11 |
| ❑ 25 Vincent Damphousse | .25 | .11 |
| ❑ 26 Shayne Corson | .10 | .05 |
| ❑ 27 Joe Nieuwendyk | .25 | .11 |
| ❑ 28 Kenny Jonsson | .10 | .05 |
| ❑ 29 Peter Bondra | .40 | .18 |
| ❑ 30 Ed Belfour | .40 | .18 |
| ❑ 31 Brendan Shanahan | .75 | .35 |
| ❑ 32 Eric Desjardins | .10 | .05 |
| ❑ 33 Corey Hirsch | .25 | .11 |
| ❑ 34 Viacheslav Fetisov | .10 | .05 |
| ❑ 35 Craig Janney | .25 | .11 |
| ❑ 36 Felix Potvin | .40 | .18 |
| ❑ 37 Joe Sakic | .75 | .35 |
| ❑ 38 Scott Stevens | .25 | .11 |
| ❑ 39 Kelly Hrudey | .25 | .11 |
| ❑ 40 Adam Oates | .25 | .11 |
| ❑ 41 John Vanbiesbrouck | .60 | .25 |
| ❑ 42 Brian Leetch | .40 | .18 |
| ❑ 43 Alexander Selivanov | .10 | .05 |
| ❑ 44 Mike Modano | .50 | .23 |
| ❑ 45 Saku Koivu | .60 | .25 |
| ❑ 46 Tom Barrasso | .25 | .11 |
| ❑ 47 Jere Lehtinen | .10 | .05 |
| ❑ 48 Daniel Alfredsson | .25 | .11 |
| ❑ 49 Joe Juneau | .10 | .05 |
| ❑ 50 Chris Osgood | .40 | .18 |
| ❑ 51 Dave Andreychuk | .25 | .11 |
| ❑ 52 Marcus Ragnarsson | .10 | .05 |
| ❑ 53 Valeri Kamensky | .25 | .11 |
| ❑ 54 Doug Weight | .25 | .11 |
| ❑ 55 Mike Richter | .40 | .18 |
| ❑ 56 Teemu Selanne | .75 | .35 |
| ❑ 57 Stephane Fiset | .25 | .11 |
| ❑ 58 Mikael Renberg | .25 | .11 |
| ❑ 59 Trevor Linden | .25 | .11 |
| ❑ 60 Bernie Nicholls | .10 | .05 |
| ❑ 61 Eric Daze | .25 | .11 |
| ❑ 62 Ron Francis | .25 | .11 |
| ❑ 63 Sergei Zubov | .10 | .05 |
| ❑ 64 Rod Brind'Amour | .25 | .11 |
| ❑ 65 Sergei Fedorov | .60 | .25 |
| ❑ 66 Mark Messier | .50 | .23 |
| ❑ 67 Theoren Fleury | .25 | .11 |
| ❑ 68 Ed Jovanovski | .25 | .11 |
| ❑ 69 Daren Puppa | .25 | .11 |
| ❑ 70 Pierre Turgeon | .25 | .11 |
| ❑ 71 Oleg Tverdovsky | .25 | .11 |
| ❑ 72 Ryan Smyth | .40 | .18 |
| ❑ 73 Jocelyn Thibault | .40 | .18 |
| ❑ 74 Brendan Witt | .10 | .05 |
| ❑ 75 Igor Larionov | .10 | .05 |
| ❑ 76 Stephane Richer | .25 | .11 |
| ❑ 77 Ron Hextall | .25 | .11 |
| ❑ 78 Mike Ricci | .10 | .05 |
| ❑ 79 Dimitri Khristich | .10 | .05 |
| ❑ 80 Derian Hatcher | .10 | .05 |
| ❑ 81 Martin Brodeur | 1.00 | .45 |
| ❑ 82 Petr Nedved | .25 | .11 |
| ❑ 83 Ray Bourque | .40 | .18 |
| ❑ 84 Keith Primeau | .25 | .11 |
| ❑ 85 Sean Burke | .25 | .11 |
| ❑ 86 Geoff Sanderson | .25 | .11 |
| ❑ 87 Wendel Clark | .25 | .11 |
| ❑ 88 Valeri Bure | .25 | .11 |
| ❑ 89 Keith Tkachuk | .50 | .23 |
| ❑ 90 Roman Hamrlik | .25 | .11 |
| ❑ 91 Dominik Hasek | .75 | .35 |
| ❑ 92 Ray Sheppard | .25 | .11 |
| ❑ 93 Todd Bertuzzi | .10 | .05 |
| ❑ 94 Pavel Bure | .75 | .35 |
| ❑ 95 Alexei Zhamnov | .25 | .11 |
| ❑ 96 Alexei Kovalev | .10 | .05 |
| ❑ 97 Jeff Friesen | .25 | .11 |
| ❑ 98 Scott Young | .10 | .05 |
| ❑ 99 Vitali Yachmenev | .10 | .05 |
| ❑ 100 Michal Pivonka | .10 | .05 |
| ❑ 101 Paul Coffey | .40 | .18 |
| ❑ 102 Steve Yzerman | 1.25 | .55 |
| ❑ 103 Zigmund Palffy | .40 | .18 |
| ❑ 104 Doug Gilmour | .40 | .18 |
| ❑ 105 John LeClair | .60 | .25 |
| ❑ 106 Brett Hull | .50 | .23 |
| ❑ 107 Yanic Perreault | .10 | .05 |
| ❑ 108 Bill Guerin | .10 | .05 |
| ❑ 109 Damian Rhodes | .25 | .11 |
| ❑ 110 Peter Forsberg | 1.25 | .55 |
| ❑ 111 Scott Mellanby | .25 | .11 |
| ❑ 112 Wayne Gretzky | 2.50 | 1.10 |

| | | |
|---|---|---|
| ❑ 113 Mario Lemieux | 2.00 | .90 |
| ❑ 114 Todd Harvey | .10 | .05 |
| ❑ 115 Mark Recchi | .25 | .11 |
| ❑ 116 Trevor Kidd | .25 | .11 |
| ❑ 117 Eric Lindros | 1.25 | .55 |
| ❑ 118 Jarome Iginla | .40 | .18 |
| ❑ 119 Eric Fichaud | .25 | .11 |
| ❑ 120 Mattias Timander | .10 | .05 |
| ❑ 121 Hnat Domenichelli | .10 | .05 |
| ❑ 122 Chris O'Sullivan | .10 | .05 |
| ❑ 123 Sergei Berezin | .60 | .25 |
| ❑ 124 Jonas Hoglund | .10 | .05 |
| ❑ 125 Anders Eriksson | .10 | .05 |
| ❑ 126 Corey Schwab | .25 | .11 |
| ❑ 127 Janne Niinimaa | .40 | .18 |
| ❑ 128 Dainius Zubrus | .75 | .35 |
| ❑ 129 Bryan Berard | .40 | .18 |
| ❑ 130 Wade Redden | .10 | .05 |
| ❑ 131 Wayne Primeau | .10 | .05 |
| ❑ 132 Brandon Convery | .10 | .05 |
| ❑ 133 Richard Zednik | .10 | .05 |
| ❑ 134 Darcy Tucker | .10 | .05 |
| ❑ 135 Christian Dube | .10 | .05 |
| ❑ 136 Rem Murray | .10 | .05 |
| ❑ 137 Kevin Hodson | .40 | .18 |
| ❑ 138 Steve Washburn | .10 | .05 |
| ❑ 139 Ethan Moreau | .40 | .18 |
| ❑ 140 Daymond Langkow | .10 | .05 |
| ❑ 141 Terry Ryan | .10 | .05 |
| ❑ 142 Curtis Brown | .10 | .05 |
| ❑ 143 Steve Sullivan | .10 | .05 |
| ❑ 144 Jamie Langenbrunner | .10 | .05 |
| ❑ 145 Daniel Goneau | .10 | .05 |
| ❑ 146 Anson Carter | .10 | .05 |
| ❑ 147 Jim Campbell | .10 | .05 |
| ❑ 148 Keith Tkachuk CL (1-76) | .40 | .18 |
| ❑ 149 Eric Daze CL (77-150) | .25 | .11 |
| ❑ 150 Mike Modano CL (inserts) | .25 | .11 |

## 1996-97 Leaf Preferred Press Proofs

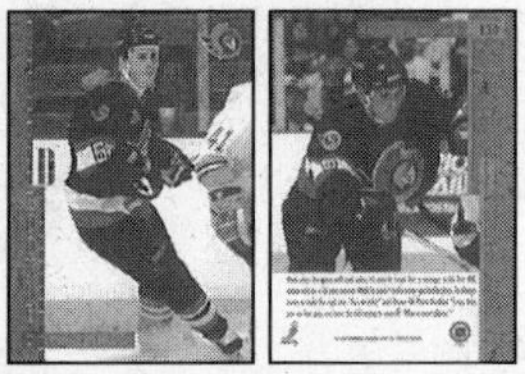

Paralleling the standard 150-card Leaf Preferred set, the randomly inserted Press Proofs were limited to a production run of 250. A gold strip on the lefthand side of the card distinguishes this version from its regular counterpart.

| | MINT | NRMT |
|---|---|---|
| COMPLETE SET (150) | 2500.00 | 1100.00 |
| COMMON CARD (1-150) | 4.00 | 1.80 |

*STARS: 50X TO 80X BASIC CARDS
*YOUNG STARS: 25X TO 40X BASIC CARDS
*RCs: 15X TO 25X BASIC CARDS

| | | |
|---|---|---|
| ❑ 1 Patrick Roy | 150.00 | 70.00 |
| ❑ 7 Paul Kariya | 120.00 | 55.00 |
| ❑ 22 Jaromir Jagr | 100.00 | 45.00 |
| ❑ 102 Steve Yzerman | 100.00 | 45.00 |
| ❑ 110 Peter Forsberg | 100.00 | 45.00 |
| ❑ 112 Wayne Gretzky | 200.00 | 90.00 |
| ❑ 113 Mario Lemieux | 150.00 | 70.00 |
| ❑ 117 Eric Lindros | 150.00 | 70.00 |

## 1996-97 Leaf Preferred Steel

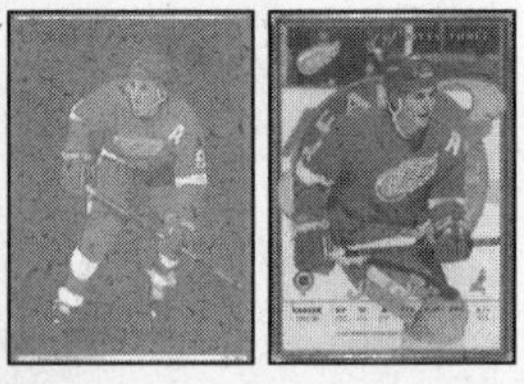

Inserted one per pack, this 63-card set is the first standard-sized, all-metal hockey set. Cards are silver-colored and come with a protective covering. A gold parallel version also exists; values for these cards can be determined by using the multipliers below. Furthermore, an Eric Lindros promo card was created. It is easy to differentiate from the regular version as it is numbered 77 of 77, and includes the word SAMPLE on the back.

| | MINT | NRMT |
|---|---|---|
| COMPLETE SET (63) | 125.00 | 55.00 |
| COMMON CARD (1-63) | 1.00 | .45 |
| COMP.GOLD SET (63) | 1000.00 | 450.00 |
| COMMON GOLD (1-63) | 8.00 | 3.60 |

*GOLD STARS: 4X TO 8X BASIC CARDS

| | | |
|---|---|---|
| ❑ 1 Sergei Fedorov | 5.00 | 2.20 |
| ❑ 2 Martin Brodeur | 6.00 | 2.70 |
| ❑ 3 Corey Hirsch | 1.50 | .70 |
| ❑ 4 Ray Bourque | 2.50 | 1.10 |
| ❑ 5 Saku Koivu | 4.00 | 1.80 |
| ❑ 6 Ron Francis | 1.50 | .70 |
| ❑ 7 Chris Chelios | 2.50 | 1.10 |
| ❑ 8 Scott Mellanby | 1.50 | .70 |
| ❑ 9 Ron Hextall | 1.50 | .70 |
| ❑ 10 Doug Gilmour | 1.50 | .70 |
| ❑ 11 Joe Sakic | 5.00 | 2.20 |
| ❑ 12 Petr Sykora | 1.00 | .45 |
| ❑ 13 Marcus Ragnarsson | 1.00 | .45 |
| ❑ 14 Pat Verbeek | 1.00 | .45 |
| ❑ 15 Stephane Fiset | 1.50 | .70 |
| ❑ 16 Alexei Yashin | 1.00 | .45 |
| ❑ 17 Daren Puppa | 1.50 | .70 |
| ❑ 18 Eric Lindros | 8.00 | 3.60 |
| ❑ 19 Jason Arnott | 1.50 | .70 |
| ❑ 20 Todd Bertuzzi | 1.00 | .45 |
| ❑ 21 Jim Carey | 2.50 | 1.10 |
| ❑ 22 Pat LaFontaine | 1.50 | .70 |
| ❑ 23 Brian Leetch | 2.50 | 1.10 |
| ❑ 24 Trevor Linden | 1.50 | .70 |
| ❑ 25 Eric Daze | 1.50 | .70 |
| ❑ 26 Pierre Turgeon | 1.50 | .70 |
| ❑ 27 Tom Barrasso | 1.50 | .70 |
| ❑ 28 Mike Modano | 3.00 | 1.35 |
| ❑ 29 Brendan Shanahan | 5.00 | 2.20 |
| ❑ 30 Nikolai Khabibulin | 1.50 | .70 |
| ❑ 31 Claude Lemieux | 1.50 | .70 |
| ❑ 32 Zigmund Palffy | 2.50 | 1.10 |
| ❑ 33 Mats Sundin | 1.50 | .70 |
| ❑ 34 Paul Kariya | 10.00 | 4.50 |
| ❑ 35 Daniel Alfredsson | 1.50 | .70 |
| ❑ 36 Patrick Roy | 12.00 | 5.50 |
| ❑ 37 Jaromir Jagr | 8.00 | 3.60 |
| ❑ 38 Vyacheslav Kozlov | 1.00 | .45 |
| ❑ 39 John LeClair | 4.00 | 1.80 |
| ❑ 40 Bill Ranford | 1.50 | .70 |
| ❑ 41 Vitali Yachmenev | 1.00 | .45 |
| ❑ 42 Mark Messier | 3.00 | 1.35 |
| ❑ 43 Valeri Bure | 1.00 | .45 |
| ❑ 44 Roman Hamrlik | 1.50 | .70 |
| ❑ 45 Joe Nieuwendyk | 1.00 | .45 |
| ❑ 46 Mike Richter | 2.50 | 1.10 |
| ❑ 47 Theoren Fleury | 1.50 | .70 |
| ❑ 48 Wendel Clark | 1.50 | .70 |
| ❑ 49 Doug Weight | 1.50 | .70 |
| ❑ 50 Damian Rhodes | 1.50 | .70 |
| ❑ 51 Alexander Mogilny | 1.50 | .70 |
| ❑ 52 Dominik Hasek | 5.00 | 2.20 |
| ❑ 53 Eric Fichaud | 1.50 | .70 |
| ❑ 54 Adam Oates | 1.50 | .70 |
| ❑ 55 Jocelyn Thibault | 2.50 | 1.10 |
| ❑ 56 Petr Nedved | 1.00 | .45 |
| ❑ 57 Mike Vernon | 1.50 | .70 |
| ❑ 58 Mikael Renberg | 1.50 | .70 |
| ❑ 59 Valeri Kamensky | 1.00 | .45 |
| ❑ 60 Peter Forsberg | 8.00 | 3.60 |
| ❑ 61 Rob Niedermayer | 1.00 | .45 |
| ❑ 62 Owen Nolan | 1.50 | .70 |
| ❑ 63 Jere Lehtinen | 1.00 | .45 |
| ❑ 77 Eric Lindros promo | 2.00 | .90 |

## 1996-97 Leaf Preferred Masked Marauders

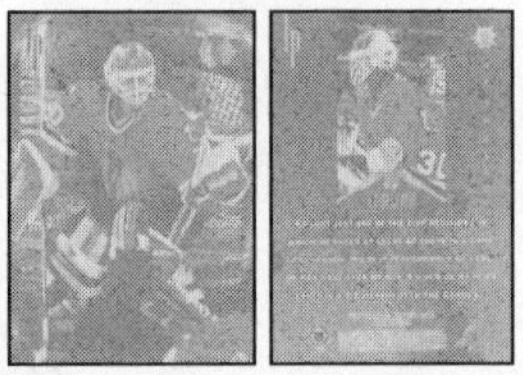

Featuring twelve of the game's top goaltenders, the Masked Marauders were randomly inserted in Leaf Preferred packs and were sequentially numbered to 2500.

| | MINT | NRMT |
|---|---|---|
| COMPLETE SET (12) | 250.00 | 110.00 |
| COMMON CARD (1-12) | 12.00 | 5.50 |

| | | |
|---|---|---|
| ❑ 1 Jim Carey | 15.00 | 6.75 |
| ❑ 2 Martin Brodeur | 40.00 | 18.00 |
| ❑ 3 John Vanbiesbrouck | 25.00 | 11.00 |
| ❑ 4 Patrick Roy | 80.00 | 36.00 |
| ❑ 5 Felix Potvin | 15.00 | 6.75 |
| ❑ 6 Chris Osgood | 15.00 | 6.75 |
| ❑ 7 Dominik Hasek | 30.00 | 13.50 |
| ❑ 8 Jocelyn Thibault | 15.00 | 6.75 |
| ❑ 9 Nikolai Khabibulin | 12.00 | 5.50 |
| ❑ 10 Curtis Joseph | 15.00 | 6.75 |
| ❑ 11 Mike Richter | 15.00 | 6.75 |
| ❑ 12 Ed Belfour | 15.00 | 6.75 |

## 1996-97 Leaf Preferred Steel Power

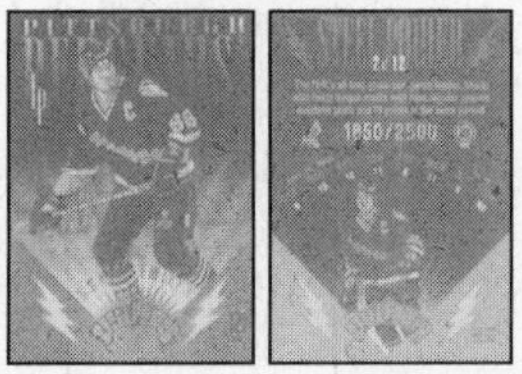

With a stated print run of 2500 serial-numbered sets, the Steel Power set consists of a dozen of the top offensive players. Card fronts feature a color action photo with silver foil at the bottom, and two lightining bolt die-cuts.

| | MINT | NRMT |
|---|---|---|
| COMPLETE SET (12) | 450.00 | 200.00 |
| COMMON CARD (1-12) | 15.00 | 6.75 |

| | | |
|---|---|---|
| ❑ 1 Joe Sakic | 25.00 | 11.00 |
| ❑ 2 Mario Lemieux | 60.00 | 27.00 |
| ❑ 3 Pavel Bure | 20.00 | 9.00 |
| ❑ 4 Mark Messier | 15.00 | 6.75 |
| ❑ 5 Wayne Gretzky | 80.00 | 36.00 |
| ❑ 6 Peter Forsberg | 40.00 | 18.00 |
| ❑ 7 Sergei Fedorov | 20.00 | 9.00 |
| ❑ 8 Jaromir Jagr | 40.00 | 18.00 |
| ❑ 9 Brett Hull | 15.00 | 6.75 |
| ❑ 10 Teemu Selanne | 25.00 | 11.00 |
| ❑ 11 Paul Kariya | 50.00 | 22.00 |
| ❑ 12 Eric Lindros | 40.00 | 18.00 |

## 1996-97 Leaf Preferred Vanity Plates

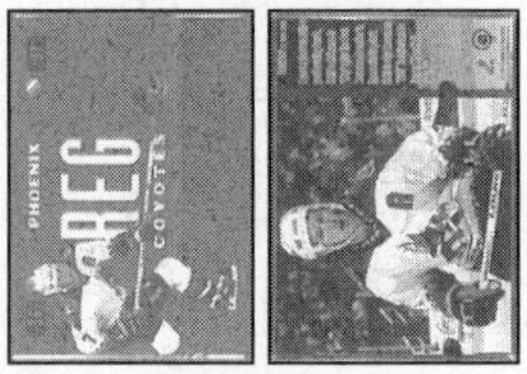

Patterned after the theme of vanity license plates, these 14 cards sport the player's nickname, team, and facsimile signature along with a photo on the front. Card backs include a brief player biography and photo. A protective coating covers the silver-colored metal cards, which were inserted randomly into packs. A tougher gold parallel version also was available. Values for these cards can be determined through the use of the multipliers on the values below.

| | MINT | NRMT |
|---|---|---|
| COMPLETE SET (14) | 150.00 | 70.00 |
| COMMON CARD (1-14) | 4.00 | 1.80 |
| COMP.GOLD SET (14) | 400.00 | 180.00 |
| COMMON GOLD (1-14) | 10.00 | 4.50 |

*GOLD: 1X TO 2.5X BASIC CARDS

| | | |
|---|---|---|
| ❑ 1 Wayne Gretzky | 30.00 | 13.50 |
| ❑ 2 John Vanbiesbrouck | 8.00 | 3.60 |
| ❑ 3 Chris Osgood | 5.00 | 2.20 |
| ❑ 4 Steve Yzerman | 15.00 | 6.75 |
| ❑ 5 Brett Hull | 6.00 | 2.70 |
| ❑ 6 Mario Lemieux | 25.00 | 11.00 |
| ❑ 7 Eric Lindros | 15.00 | 6.75 |
| ❑ 8 Ed Jovanovski | 4.00 | 1.80 |
| ❑ 9 Pavel Bure | 10.00 | 4.50 |
| ❑ 10 Felix Potvin | 5.00 | 2.20 |
| ❑ 11 Teemu Selanne | 10.00 | 4.50 |
| ❑ 12 Keith Tkachuk | 6.00 | 2.70 |
| ❑ 13 Curtis Joseph | 5.00 | 2.20 |
| ❑ 14 Ed Belfour | 5.00 | 2.20 |

## 1997-98 Leaf International

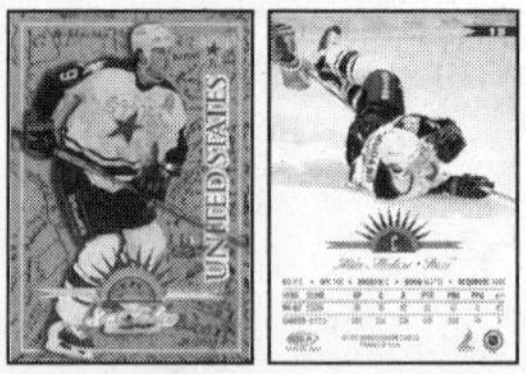

This 150-card set features color player images with a map of their home country in the background and printed on full foil board with heliogram technology and puff ink treatment. The cards are divided into Canadian or U.S./Euro packs, with only Canadian players being found in Canadian packs and the rest of the set in the U.S./Euro version.

| | MINT | NRMT |
|---|---|---|
| COMPLETE SET (150) | 70.00 | 32.00 |
| COMMON CARD (1-150) | .30 | .14 |
| COMP.UNIV.ICE SET (150) | | |

| | | |
|---|---|---|
| ❑ 1 Eric Lindros | 2.00 | .90 |
| ❑ 2 Dominik Hasek | 1.25 | .55 |
| ❑ 3 Peter Forsberg | 2.00 | .90 |
| ❑ 4 Steve Yzerman | 2.00 | .90 |
| ❑ 5 John Vanbiesbrouck | 1.00 | .45 |
| ❑ 6 Paul Kariya | 2.50 | 1.10 |
| ❑ 7 Martin Brodeur | 1.50 | .70 |
| ❑ 8 Wayne Gretzky | 4.00 | 1.80 |
| ❑ 9 Mark Messier | .75 | .35 |
| ❑ 10 Jaromir Jagr | 2.00 | .90 |
| ❑ 11 Brett Hull | .75 | .35 |
| ❑ 12 Brendan Shanahan | 1.25 | .55 |
| ❑ 13 Ray Bourque | .60 | .25 |
| ❑ 14 Jarome Iginla | .50 | .23 |
| ❑ 15 Mike Modano | .75 | .35 |
| ❑ 16 Curtis Joseph | .60 | .25 |
| ❑ 17 Ed Jovanovski | .50 | .23 |
| ❑ 18 Teemu Selanne | 1.25 | .55 |
| ❑ 19 Saku Koivu | 1.00 | .45 |
| ❑ 20 Eric Fichaud | .50 | .23 |
| ❑ 21 Paul Coffey | .60 | .25 |
| ❑ 22 Jeremy Roenick | .60 | .25 |
| ❑ 23 Owen Nolan | .50 | .23 |
| ❑ 24 Felix Potvin | .60 | .25 |
| ❑ 25 Alexander Mogilny | .50 | .23 |
| ❑ 26 Alexandre Daigle | .50 | .23 |
| ❑ 27 Chris Gratton | .50 | .23 |
| ❑ 28 Geoff Sanderson | .50 | .23 |
| ❑ 29 Dimitri Khristich | .30 | .14 |
| ❑ 30 Bryan Berard | .30 | .14 |
| ❑ 31 Vyacheslav Kozlov | .30 | .14 |
| ❑ 32 Jeff Hackett | .50 | .23 |
| ❑ 33 Bill Ranford | .50 | .23 |
| ❑ 34 Pat LaFontaine | .50 | .23 |
| ❑ 35 Joe Sakic | 1.25 | .55 |
| ❑ 36 Niklas Sundstrom | .30 | .14 |
| ❑ 37 Martin Gelinas | .30 | .14 |
| ❑ 38 Mikael Renberg | .30 | .14 |
| ❑ 39 Trevor Linden | .50 | .23 |
| ❑ 40 Jozef Stumpel | .50 | .23 |
| ❑ 41 Joe Thornton CL | 1.00 | .45 |
| ❑ 42 Jocelyn Thibault | .50 | .23 |
| ❑ 43 Pierre Turgeon | .50 | .23 |
| ❑ 44 Ron Francis | .50 | .23 |
| ❑ 45 Damian Rhodes | .50 | .23 |
| ❑ 46 Jamie Langenbrunner | .30 | .14 |
| ❑ 47 Chris Osgood | .60 | .25 |
| ❑ 48 Vaclav Varada | .50 | .23 |
| ❑ 49 Ryan Smyth | .50 | .23 |
| ❑ 50 Daren Puppa | .50 | .23 |
| ❑ 51 Petr Nedved | .50 | .23 |
| ❑ 52 Ron Hextall | .50 | .23 |
| ❑ 53 Joe Juneau | .50 | .23 |
| ❑ 54 Jim Campbell | .30 | .14 |
| ❑ 55 Zigmund Palffy | .60 | .25 |
| ❑ 56 Roman Turek | .50 | .23 |
| ❑ 57 Adam Deadmarsh | .50 | .23 |
| ❑ 58 Rob Niedermayer | .50 | .23 |
| ❑ 59 Alexei Yashin | .50 | .23 |
| ❑ 60 Pavel Bure | 1.25 | .55 |
| ❑ 61 Jason Arnott | .50 | .23 |
| ❑ 62 Nikolai Khabibulin | .50 | .23 |
| ❑ 63 Sean Burke | .50 | .23 |
| ❑ 64 Chris Chelios | .60 | .25 |
| ❑ 65 Mike Ricci | .50 | .23 |
| ❑ 66 Sergei Berezin | .30 | .14 |
| ❑ 67 Jaroslav Svejkovsky CL | .30 | .14 |
| ❑ 68 Brian Savage | .30 | .14 |
| ❑ 69 Roman Vopat | .30 | .14 |
| ❑ 70 Mike Richter | .60 | .25 |
| ❑ 71 Jim Carey | .50 | .23 |
| ❑ 72 Guy Hebert | .50 | .23 |
| ❑ 73 Keith Tkachuk | .75 | .35 |
| ❑ 74 Kirk McLean | .50 | .23 |
| ❑ 75 Janne Niinimaa | .50 | .23 |
| ❑ 76 Roman Hamrlik | .30 | .14 |
| ❑ 77 Darcy Tucker | .30 | .14 |
| ❑ 78 Pat Verbeek | .30 | .14 |
| ❑ 79 Hnat Domenichelli | .30 | .14 |
| ❑ 80 Doug Gilmour | .60 | .25 |
| ❑ 81 Mike Grier | .30 | .14 |
| ❑ 82 Ken Wregget | .30 | .14 |
| ❑ 83 Dino Ciccarelli | .30 | .14 |
| ❑ 84 Steve Sullivan | .30 | .14 |
| ❑ 85 Anson Carter | .30 | .14 |
| ❑ 86 Steve Shields | .50 | .23 |
| ❑ 87 Ed Belfour | .60 | .25 |
| ❑ 88 Darren McCarty | .30 | .14 |
| ❑ 89 Adam Graves | .30 | .14 |
| ❑ 90 Chris Pronger | .50 | .23 |
| ❑ 91 Peter Bondra | .60 | .25 |
| ❑ 92 Oleg Tverdovsky | .30 | .14 |
| ❑ 93 Stephane Fiset | .50 | .23 |
| ❑ 94 Mike Vernon | .50 | .23 |
| ❑ 95 Scott Lachance | .30 | .14 |
| ❑ 96 Corey Schwab | .30 | .14 |
| ❑ 97 Eric Daze | .50 | .23 |
| ❑ 98 Jere Lehtinen | .30 | .14 |
| ❑ 99 Donald Audette | .30 | .14 |
| ❑ 100 John LeClair | 1.00 | .45 |
| ❑ 101 Steve Rucchin | .30 | .14 |
| ❑ 102 Jeff Friesen | .50 | .23 |
| ❑ 103 Daymond Langkow | .30 | .14 |
| ❑ 104 Mike Dunham | .50 | .23 |
| ❑ 105 Marc Denis CL | .30 | .14 |
| ❑ 106 Andrew Cassels | .30 | .14 |
| ❑ 107 Mike Peca | .30 | .14 |
| ❑ 108 Joe Nieuwendyk | .50 | .23 |
| ❑ 109 Vincent Damphousse | .50 | .23 |
| ❑ 110 Scott Mellanby | .30 | .14 |
| ❑ 111 Patrick Lalime | .50 | .23 |
| ❑ 112 Derek Plante | .30 | .14 |
| ❑ 113 Wade Redden | .30 | .14 |
| ❑ 114 Marcel Cousineau | .50 | .23 |
| ❑ 115 Ray Sheppard | .30 | .14 |
| ❑ 116 Dave Andreychuk | .30 | .14 |
| ❑ 117 Brian Leetch | .60 | .25 |
| ❑ 118 Sandis Ozolinsh | .50 | .23 |
| ❑ 119 Keith Primeau | .30 | .14 |
| ❑ 120 Brian Holzinger | .30 | .14 |
| ❑ 121 Luc Robitaille | .50 | .23 |
| ❑ 122 Jose Theodore | .50 | .23 |
| ❑ 123 Grant Fuhr | .50 | .23 |
| ❑ 124 Dainius Zubrus | .60 | .25 |
| ❑ 125 Rod Brind'Amour | .50 | .23 |
| ❑ 126 Trevor Kidd | .50 | .23 |
| ❑ 127 Mark Recchi | .50 | .23 |
| ❑ 128 Patrick Roy | 3.00 | 1.35 |
| ❑ 129 Kevin Hatcher | .30 | .14 |
| ❑ 130 Adam Oates | .50 | .23 |
| ❑ 131 Doug Weight | .50 | .23 |
| ❑ 132 Vaclav Prospal<br>UER front & back Vinny | 1.00 | .45 |
| ❑ 133 Harry York | .30 | .14 |
| ❑ 134 Todd Bertuzzi | .30 | .14 |
| ❑ 135 Sergei Fedorov | 1.25 | .55 |
| ❑ 136 Theoren Fleury | .50 | .23 |
| ❑ 137 Chad Kilger | .30 | .14 |
| ❑ 138 Jamie Storr | .50 | .23 |
| ❑ 139 Tony Amonte | .50 | .23 |
| ❑ 140 Rem Murray | .30 | .14 |
| ❑ 141 Chris O'Sullivan | .30 | .14 |
| ❑ 142 Mats Sundin | .60 | .25 |
| ❑ 143 Ethan Moreau | .30 | .14 |
| ❑ 144 Derian Hatcher | .30 | .14 |
| ❑ 145 Daniel Alfredsson | .50 | .23 |
| ❑ 146 Corey Hirsch | .50 | .23 |
| ❑ 147 Landon Wilson | .30 | .14 |
| ❑ 148 Chris Phillips CL | .30 | .14 |
| ❑ 149 Sergei Samsonov CL | .50 | .23 |
| ❑ 150 Daniel Cleary CL | .30 | .14 |

## 1997-98 Leaf International Universal Ice

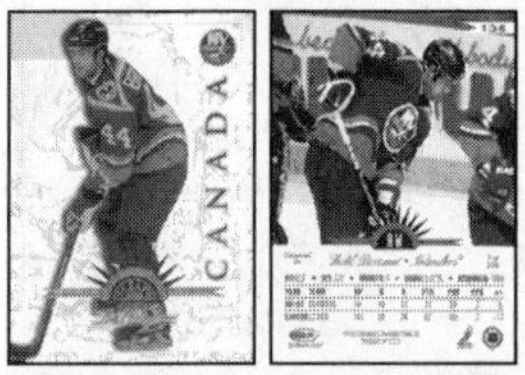

This 150-card set is parallel to the base set and is printed on holofoil board. Only 250 of each card was produced and numbered. All cards of this parallel set appear in both Canadian packs and U.S./Euro packs.

| | MINT | NRMT |
|---|---|---|
| COMMON CARD (1-150) | 15.00 | 6.75 |
| SEMISTARS/GOALIES | 40.00 | 18.00 |
| UNLISTED STARS | 50.00 | 22.00 |

*STARS: 40X TO 80X BASIC CARDS
*YOUNG STARS: 30X TO 60X BASIC CARDS

## 1971-72 Letraset Action Replays

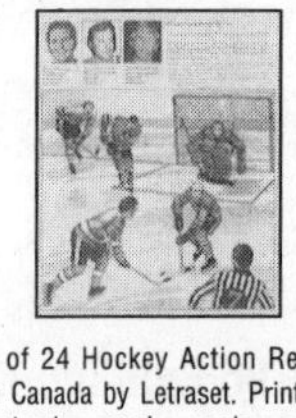

This set of 24 Hockey Action Replays was issued in Canada by Letraset. Printed on thin paper stock, each replay measures approximately 5 1/4" by 6 1/4" and is folded in the center. All replays have a common front consisting of a color photo of a faceoff between Danny O'Shea of the Hawks and Jean Ratelle of the Rangers. On the reverse side, a "Know Your Signals" series illustrates arm signals used by hockey referees. The inside unfolds to display a 5" by 4 1/2" color drawings of NHL action shots. Immediately above is a description of the play plus slots for photos of the players involved in the action. The center photos and some of the players needed to complete the play are missing and supplied on a separate run-on transfer sheet. The action scene could be completed by rubbing the players on the transfer sheet onto the action scene. The replays are numbered in the white panel that presents the referee arm signals, and checklisted below accordingly.

| | NRMT-MT | EXC |
|---|---|---|
| COMPLETE SET (24) | 200.00 | 90.00 |
| COMMON CARD (1-24) | 8.00 | 3.60 |

| | | |
|---|---|---|
| ❑ 1 Rogatien Vachon<br>Dave Keon<br>Gilles Marotte | 10.00 | 4.50 |
| ❑ 2 Ken Dryden<br>Chico Maki<br>Jacques Laperriere | 20.00 | 9.00 |
| ❑ 3 Gary Dornhoefer<br>Roger Crozier<br>Tracy Pratt | 8.00 | 3.60 |
| ❑ 4 Walt Tkaczuk<br>Gump Worsley<br>Vic Hadfield | 8.00 | 3.60 |
| ❑ 5 Dallas Smith<br>Bobby Orr<br>Walt McKechnie | 35.00 | 16.00 |
| ❑ 6 Ab McDonald<br>Gary Sabourin<br>Garry Unger | 8.00 | 3.60 |
| ❑ 7 Jim Rutherford | 8.00 | 3.60 |

| | | |
|---|---|---|
| Orland Kurtenbach | | |
| Bob Woytovich | | |
| ❑ 8 Gerry Cheevers | 12.00 | 5.50 |
| Frank Mahovlich | | |
| Don Awrey | | |
| ❑ 9 Tim Ecclestone | 10.00 | 4.50 |
| Bob Baun | | |
| Jacques Plante | | |
| ❑ 10 Stan Mikita | 12.00 | 5.50 |
| Ed Giacomin | | |
| Jim Pappin | | |
| ❑ 11 Doug Favell | 8.00 | 3.60 |
| Danny Grant | | |
| Ed Van Impe | | |
| ❑ 12 Ernie Wakely | 8.00 | 3.60 |
| Barclay Plager | | |
| Gary Croteau | | |
| ❑ 13 Bryan Hextall | 10.00 | 4.50 |
| Tony Esposito | | |
| Pat Stapleton | | |
| ❑ 14 Jean Ratelle | 10.00 | 4.50 |
| Rod Gilbert | | |
| Jim Roberts | | |
| ❑ 15 Jacques Lemaire | 12.00 | 5.50 |
| Henri Richard | | |
| Yvan Cournoyer | | |
| ❑ 16 George Gardiner | 8.00 | 3.60 |
| Dennis Hull | | |
| Lou Angotti | | |
| ❑ 17 Ed Johnston | 35.00 | 16.00 |
| Norm Ullman | | |
| Bobby Orr | | |
| ❑ 18 Gilles Meloche | 8.00 | 3.60 |
| Wayne Carleton | | |
| Dick Redmond | | |
| ❑ 19 Al Smith | 8.00 | 3.60 |
| Gary Bergman | | |
| Stan Gilbertson | | |
| ❑ 20 Dunc Wilson | 8.00 | 3.60 |
| Brad Park | | |
| Dale Tallon | | |
| ❑ 21 Jude Drouin | 8.00 | 3.60 |
| Doug Favell | | |
| Barry Ashbee | | |
| ❑ 22 Ron Ellis | 20.00 | 9.00 |
| Ken Dryden | | |
| Paul Henderson | | |
| ❑ 23 Gary Edwards | 8.00 | 3.60 |
| Jean Pronovost | | |
| Ron Shock | | |
| ❑ 24 Cesare Maniago | 8.00 | 3.60 |
| Chris Bordeleau | | |
| Ted Harris | | |

## 1992-93 Lightning Sheraton

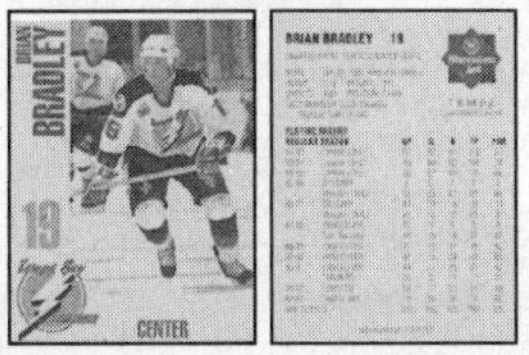

Sponsored by the Sheraton Inn Tampa Conference Center, this album and its 28 perforated cards commemorate the Tampa Bay Lightning's inaugural season. Folded closed, the album measures 10" by 13". The 28 standard-size cards fold out and feature color player action shots on their fronts. These photos are borderless on their top and right sides, and white-bordered on the left and bottom edges. The player's name appears vertically in blue lettering in the margin on the left side, his position appears in blue in the bottom margin, and his uniform number is shown in silver, just above the Lightning logo in the lower left. The white backs display the player's name, uniform number, and biography in the upper left. Below are stats from the player's previous seasons. In the upper right, the Sheraton logo rounds out the card. The cards are unnumbered and checklisted below in alphabetical order.

| | MINT | NRMT |
|---|---|---|
| COMPLETE SET (28) | 20.00 | 9.00 |
| COMMON CARD (1-28) | .25 | .11 |
| ❑ 1 Mikael Andersson | .50 | .23 |
| ❑ 2 Bob Beers | .50 | .23 |
| ❑ 3 J.C. Bergeron | .75 | .35 |
| ❑ 4 Marc Bergevin | .50 | .23 |
| ❑ 5 Tim Bergland | .50 | .23 |
| ❑ 6 Brian Bradley | 1.50 | .70 |
| ❑ 7 Marc Bureau | .50 | .23 |
| ❑ 8 Wayne Cashman CO | .50 | .23 |
| ❑ 9 Shawn Chambers | .50 | .23 |
| ❑ 10 Danton Cole | .50 | .23 |
| ❑ 11 Adam Creighton | .75 | .35 |
| ❑ 12 Terry Crisp CO | .50 | .23 |
| ❑ 13 Rob DiMaio | .75 | .35 |
| ❑ 14 Phil Esposito GM | 2.00 | .90 |
| ❑ 15 Tony Esposito DIR | 1.50 | .70 |
| ❑ 16 Roman Hamrlik | 2.00 | .90 |
| ❑ 17 Pat Jablonski | .75 | .35 |
| ❑ 18 Steve Kasper | .50 | .23 |
| ❑ 19 Chris Kontos | .50 | .23 |
| ❑ 20 Steve Maltais | .50 | .23 |
| ❑ 21 Joe Reekie | .50 | .23 |
| ❑ 22 Thunderbug (Mascot) | .25 | .11 |
| ❑ 23 John Tucker | .75 | .35 |
| ❑ 24 Wendell Young | .75 | .35 |
| ❑ 25 Rob Zamuner | .75 | .35 |
| ❑ 26 Title card | .50 | .23 |
| ❑ 27 Inaugural season card | .25 | .11 |
| ❑ 28 Sheraton logo card | .25 | .11 |

## 1993-94 Lightning Kash n'Karry

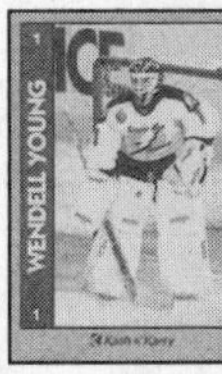

Sponsored by Kash n'Karry, this six-card set measures approximately 5" by 7". Inside gray borders, the fronts feature color action player photos. A blue bar on the left side carries the player's name and number. The sponsor's logo appears in the bottom gray border. The horizontal backs have a postcard design, with the player's name, position, a short biography, and career highlights on the left side. The cards are unnumbered and checklisted below in alphabetical order. The checklist below is incomplete.

| | MINT | NRMT |
|---|---|---|
| COMPLETE SET (6) | 10.00 | 4.50 |
| COMMON CARD (1-6) | 1.00 | .45 |
| ❑ 1 Brian Bradley | 2.00 | .90 |
| ❑ 2 Shawn Chambers | 1.00 | .45 |
| ❑ 3 Chris Gratton | 4.00 | 1.80 |
| ❑ 4 Adam Creighton | 1.00 | .45 |
| ❑ 5 Rob DiMaio | 1.00 | .45 |
| ❑ 6 Wendell Young | 1.50 | .70 |

## 1993-94 Lightning Season in Review

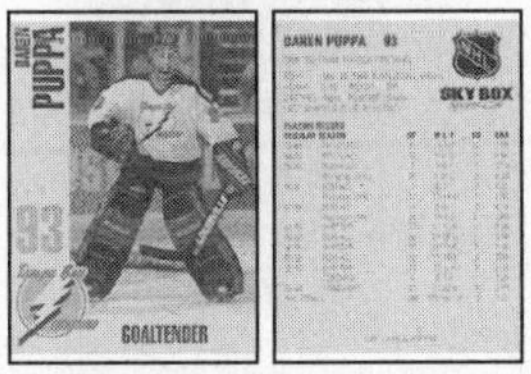

Subtitled "1993-94 Season in Review," the 28 cards comprising this set of the Tampa Bay Lightning were issued in a perforated sheet, which also included a 10" by 13" title page. Each card measures approximately 2 1/2" by 3 1/4" and features on its front a color player action shot, which is borderless at the top and right. The player's name appears vertically within the white margin to the left of the photo; his position appears within the white margin below. His uniform number and the team logo appear at the lower left. The white back carries the player's name and uniform number at the top, followed below by biography and statistics. Logos for the NHL and The Sky Box Sports Cafe at the upper right round out the card. The cards are unnumbered and checklisted below in alphabetical order.

| | MINT | NRMT |
|---|---|---|
| COMPLETE SET (28) | 15.00 | 6.75 |
| COMMON CARD (1-28) | .25 | .11 |
| ❑ 1 Mikael Andersson | .50 | .23 |
| ❑ 2 Marc Bergevin | .50 | .23 |
| ❑ 3 Brian Bradley | .75 | .35 |
| ❑ 4 Marc Bureau | .50 | .23 |
| ❑ 5 Wayne Cashman ACO | .50 | .23 |
| ❑ 6 Shawn Chambers | .50 | .23 |
| ❑ 7 Enrico Ciccone | .50 | .23 |
| ❑ 8 Danton Cole | .50 | .23 |
| ❑ 9 Adam Creighton | .50 | .23 |
| ❑ 10 Terry Crisp CO | .50 | .23 |
| ❑ 11 Jim Cummins | .50 | .23 |
| ❑ 12 Pat Elynuik | .50 | .23 |
| ❑ 13 Phil Esposito GM | 1.50 | .70 |
| ❑ 14 Tony Esposito DIR | 1.00 | .45 |
| ❑ 15 Gerard Gallant | .50 | .23 |
| ❑ 16 Danny Gare ACO | .25 | .11 |
| ❑ 17 Chris Gratton | 1.50 | .70 |
| ❑ 18 Roman Hamrlik | 1.50 | .70 |
| ❑ 19 Chris Joseph | .50 | .23 |
| ❑ 20 Petr Klima | .50 | .23 |
| ❑ 21 Chris LiPuma | .50 | .23 |
| ❑ 22 Rudy Poeschek | .75 | .35 |
| ❑ 23 Daren Puppa | 1.50 | .70 |
| ❑ 24 Denis Savard | 1.00 | .45 |
| ❑ 25 Thunderbug MASCOT | .25 | .11 |
| ❑ 26 John Tucker | .50 | .23 |
| ❑ 27 Wendell Young | .60 | .25 |
| ❑ 28 Rob Zamuner | .50 | .23 |

## 1994-95 Lightning Health Plan

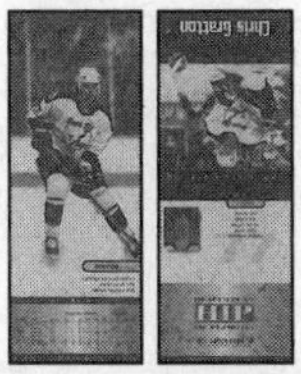

This two-card set was sponsored by Health Plan of Florida and the Tampa Tribune. Twenty thousand sets were produced. The front and back panels are connected at their tops and each measure 4" by 5". The front displays a blue-tinted action photo edged by black stripes, while the back carries a color head shot, biography, and sponsor logos. When unfolded, the inside panel measures 4" by 10" and features a pop-up color player photo and statistics. The cards are numbered on the back at the bottom.

| | MINT | NRMT |
|---|---|---|
| COMPLETE SET (2) | 6.00 | 2.70 |
| COMMON CARD (1-2) | 3.00 | 1.35 |
| ❑ 1 Daren Puppa | 4.00 | 1.80 |
| ❑ 2 Chris Gratton | 3.00 | 1.35 |

## 1994-95 Lightning Photo Album

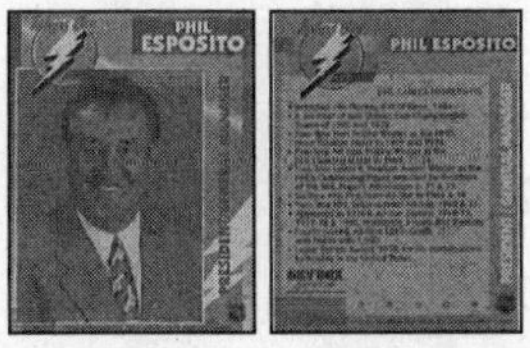

The 1994-95 Tampa Bay Lightning Commemorative Photo Album was sponsored by the Sky Box Sports Cafe at the Sheraton Inn in Tampa. It consists of three perforated sheets, each measuring 12 1/2" by 9 3/4" and joined together to form one continuous sheet. The first panel has an array different size color shots, capturing the Lightning off and on the ice. The second and third panels each display three rows of player cards; if perforated, the cards would measure the standard size. The fronts feature color action photos with team color-coded borders. The team logo, player's name, position, and number are printed in the borders. On a team color-coded background, the backs carry a color head shot, biography, statistics, and career highlights. The cards are unnumbered and checklisted below in alphabetical order.

| | MINT | NRMT |
|---|---|---|
| COMPLETE SET (29) | 12.00 | 5.50 |
| COMMON CARD (1-29) | .35 | .16 |
| ❑ 1 Mikael Andersson | .35 | .16 |
| ❑ 2 J.C. Bergeron | .50 | .23 |
| ❑ 3 Marc Bergevin | .35 | .16 |
| ❑ 4 Brian Bradley | .75 | .35 |
| ❑ 5 Marc Bureau | .35 | .16 |
| ❑ 6 Wayne Cashman ACO | .35 | .16 |
| ❑ 7 Eric Charron | .35 | .16 |
| ❑ 8 Enrico Ciccone | .50 | .23 |
| ❑ 9 Terry Crisp CO | .35 | .16 |
| ❑ 10 Cory Cross | .35 | .16 |
| ❑ 11 Phil Esposito PRES/GM | 1.00 | .45 |
| ❑ 12 Tony Esposito DIR | .50 | .23 |
| ❑ 13 Danny Gare ACO | .25 | .11 |
| ❑ 14 Chris Gratton | .75 | .35 |
| ❑ 15 Bob Halkidis | .35 | .16 |
| ❑ 16 Roman Hamrlik | 1.00 | .45 |
| ❑ 17 Ben Hankinson | .35 | .16 |
| ❑ 18 Petr Klima | .35 | .16 |
| ❑ 19 Brantt Myhres | .35 | .16 |
| ❑ 20 Adrien Plavsic | .35 | .16 |
| ❑ 21 Rudy Poeschek | .50 | .23 |
| ❑ 22 Daren Puppa | 1.25 | .55 |
| ❑ 23 Alexander Selivanov | 1.00 | .45 |
| ❑ 24 Alexander Semak | .35 | .16 |
| ❑ 25 John Tucker | .50 | .23 |
| ❑ 26 Jason Wiemer | .75 | .35 |
| ❑ 27 Paul Ysebaert | .35 | .16 |
| ❑ 28 Rob Zamuner | .35 | .16 |
| ❑ 29 Team Photo | 1.00 | .45 |

## 1994-95 Lightning Postcards

These oversized postcards were issued by The Lightning as promotional giveaways at team events. The postcard are unnumbered, and thus are listed below in alphabetical order.

| | MINT | NRMT |
|---|---|---|
| COMPLETE SET (20) | 25.00 | 11.00 |
| COMMON CARD | 1.00 | .45 |
| ❑ 1 Mikael Andersson | 1.00 | .45 |
| ❑ 2 Brian Bradley | 2.00 | .90 |
| ❑ 3 Shawn Burr | 1.00 | .45 |
| ❑ 4 Terry Crisp CO | 1.00 | .45 |
| ❑ 5 Cory Cross | 1.00 | .45 |
| ❑ 6 John Cullen | 1.00 | .45 |
| ❑ 7 Phil Esposito PRES/GM | 2.00 | .90 |
| ❑ 8 Tony Esposito DIR | 2.00 | .90 |
| ❑ 9 Chris Gratton | 2.00 | .90 |
| ❑ 10 Roman Hamrlik | 2.00 | .90 |
| ❑ 11 Bill Houlder | 1.00 | .45 |
| ❑ 12 Daymond Langkow | 2.00 | .90 |
| ❑ 13 Brantt Myhres | 1.00 | .45 |
| ❑ 14 Daren Puppa | 2.00 | .90 |
| ❑ 15 Chris Reichart | 1.00 | .45 |
| ❑ 16 Alexander Selivanov | 2.00 | .90 |
| ❑ 17 David Shaw | 1.00 | .45 |
| ❑ 18 Jason Wiemer | 1.50 | .70 |
| ❑ 19 Paul Ysebaert | 1.00 | .45 |
| ❑ 20 Rob Zamuner | 2.00 | .90 |

## 1995-96 Lightning Team Issue

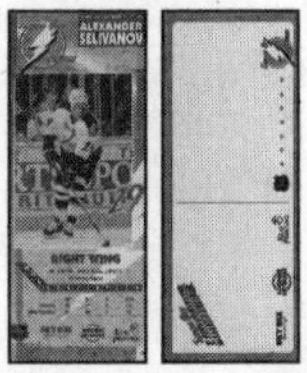

This 21-card set of the Tampa Bay Lightning measures approximately 3 3/4" by 9" and features color action player photos with player information printed below. The cards are unnumbered and checklisted below in alphabetical order.

| | MINT | NRMT |
|---|---|---|
| COMPLETE SET (21) | 20.00 | 9.00 |
| COMMON CARD | 1.00 | .45 |
| ❑ 1 Mikael Andersson | 1.00 | .45 |
| ❑ 2 Brian Bellows | 1.00 | .45 |
| ❑ 3 J.C. Bergeron | 1.50 | .70 |
| ❑ 4 Brian Bradley | 1.50 | .70 |
| ❑ 5 Shawn Burr | 1.00 | .45 |
| ❑ 6 Enrico Ciccone | 1.25 | .55 |
| ❑ 7 Cory Cross | 1.00 | .45 |
| ❑ 8 John Cullen | 1.00 | .45 |
| ❑ 9 Aaron Gavey | 1.00 | .45 |
| ❑ 10 Chris Gratton | 1.50 | .70 |
| ❑ 11 Roman Hamrlik | 2.50 | 1.10 |
| ❑ 12 Bill Houlder | 1.00 | .45 |
| ❑ 13 Petr Klima | 1.00 | .45 |
| ❑ 14 Rudy Poeschek | 1.25 | .55 |
| ❑ 15 Daren Puppa | 2.00 | .90 |
| ❑ 16 Alexander Selivanov | 2.00 | .90 |
| ❑ 17 David Shaw | 1.00 | .45 |
| ❑ 18 John Tucker | 1.00 | .45 |
| ❑ 19 Jason Wiemer | 1.50 | .70 |
| ❑ 20 Paul Ysebaert | 1.00 | .45 |
| ❑ 21 Rob Zamuner | 1.00 | .45 |

## 1974-75 Lipton Soup

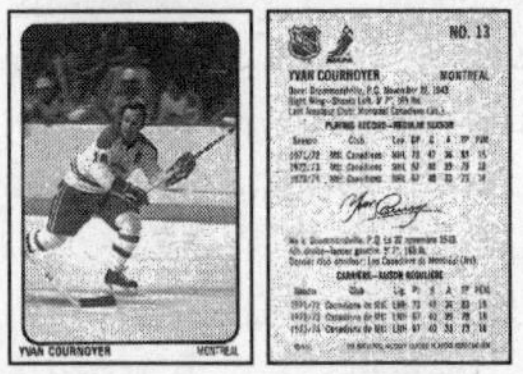

The 1974-75 Lipton Soup NHL set contains 50 color cards measuring approximately 2 1/4" by 3 1/4". The set was issued in two-card panels on the back of Lipton Soup packages. The backs feature statistics in French and English. Both varieties of Salming are included in the complete set below.

| | NRMT-MT | EXC |
|---|---|---|
| COMPLETE SET (51) | 300.00 | 135.00 |
| COMMON CARD (1-50) | 3.00 | 1.35 |
| ❑ 1 Norm Ullman | 8.00 | 3.60 |
| ❑ 2 Gilbert Perreault | 8.00 | 3.60 |
| ❑ 3 Darryl Sittler | 12.00 | 5.50 |
| ❑ 4 Jean-Paul Parise | 4.00 | 1.80 |
| ❑ 5 Garry Unger | 4.00 | 1.80 |
| ❑ 6 Ron Ellis | 5.00 | 2.20 |
| ❑ 7 Rogatien Vachon | 8.00 | 3.60 |
| ❑ 8 Bobby Orr | 60.00 | 27.00 |
| ❑ 9 Wayne Cashman | 5.00 | 2.20 |
| ❑ 10 Brad Park | 6.00 | 2.70 |
| ❑ 11 Serge Savard | 5.00 | 2.20 |
| ❑ 12 Walt Tkaczuk | 4.00 | 1.80 |
| ❑ 13 Yvan Cournoyer | 8.00 | 3.60 |
| ❑ 14 Andre Boudrias | 3.00 | 1.35 |
| ❑ 15 Gary Smith | 5.00 | 2.20 |
| ❑ 16 Guy Lapointe | 4.00 | 1.80 |
| ❑ 17 Dennis Hull | 5.00 | 2.20 |
| ❑ 18 Bernie Parent | 8.00 | 3.60 |
| ❑ 19 Ken Dryden | 40.00 | 18.00 |
| ❑ 20 Rick MacLeish | 5.00 | 2.20 |
| ❑ 21 Bobby Clarke | 15.00 | 6.75 |
| ❑ 22 Dale Tallon | 4.00 | 1.80 |
| ❑ 23 Jim McKenny | 3.00 | 1.35 |
| ❑ 24 Rene Robert | 5.00 | 2.20 |
| ❑ 25 Red Berenson | 4.00 | 1.80 |
| ❑ 26 Ed Giacomin | 8.00 | 3.60 |
| ❑ 27 Cesare Maniago | 6.00 | 2.70 |
| ❑ 28 Ken Hodge | 5.00 | 2.20 |
| ❑ 29 Gregg Sheppard | 3.00 | 1.35 |
| ❑ 30 Dave Schultz | 6.00 | 2.70 |
| ❑ 31 Bill Barber | 8.00 | 3.60 |
| ❑ 32 Henry Boucha | 4.00 | 1.80 |
| ❑ 33 Richard Martin | 5.00 | 2.20 |
| ❑ 34 Steve Vickers | 4.00 | 1.80 |
| ❑ 35 Billy Harris | 3.00 | 1.35 |
| ❑ 36 Jim Pappin | 3.00 | 1.35 |
| ❑ 37 Pit Martin | 3.00 | 1.35 |
| ❑ 38 Jacques Lemaire | 8.00 | 3.60 |
| ❑ 39 Peter Mahovlich | 5.00 | 2.20 |
| ❑ 40 Rod Gilbert | 8.00 | 3.60 |
| ❑ 41A Borje Salming (Horizontal pose) | 12.00 | 5.50 |
| ❑ 41B Borje Salming (Vertical pose) | 12.00 | 5.50 |
| ❑ 42 Pete Stemkowski | 3.00 | 1.35 |
| ❑ 43 Ron Schock | 3.00 | 1.35 |
| ❑ 44 Dan Bouchard | 6.00 | 2.70 |
| ❑ 45 Tony Esposito | 10.00 | 4.50 |
| ❑ 46 Craig Patrick | 4.00 | 1.80 |
| ❑ 47 Ed Westfall | 3.00 | 1.35 |
| ❑ 48 Jocelyn Guevremont | 3.00 | 1.35 |
| ❑ 49 Syl Apps | 4.00 | 1.80 |
| ❑ 50 Dave Keon | 8.00 | 3.60 |

## 1998 Lunchables Goalie Greats

Available only as a premium found in select packs of Lunchables lunch products. Color action photos are featured on the front while backs are blank.

| | MINT | NRMT |
|---|---|---|
| COMPLETE SET (8) | 10.00 | 4.50 |
| COMMON PANEL (1-8) | .60 | .25 |
| ❑ 1 Ed Belfour | .75 | .35 |
| ❑ 2 Martin Brodeur | 2.00 | .90 |
| ❑ 3 Dominik Hasek | 1.50 | .70 |
| ❑ 4 Olaf Kolzig | .60 | .25 |
| ❑ 5 Chris Osgood | .75 | .35 |
| ❑ 6 Damian Rhodes | .60 | .25 |
| ❑ 7 Mike Richter | .75 | .35 |
| ❑ 8 Patrick Roy | 4.00 | 1.80 |

## 1998 Lunchables Goalie Greats Squares

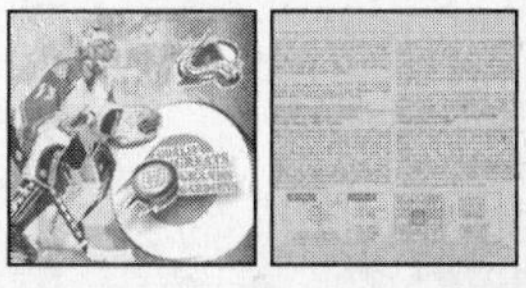

Available only as a premium found in select packs of Lunchables lunch products. Color action photos are featured on the front while backs are blank.

| | MINT | NRMT |
|---|---|---|
| COMPLETE SET (8) | 10.00 | 4.50 |
| COMMON PANEL (1-8) | .60 | .25 |
| ❑ 1 Ed Belfour | .75 | .35 |
| ❑ 2 Martin Brodeur | 2.00 | .90 |
| ❑ 3 Dominik Hasek | 1.50 | .70 |
| ❑ 4 Olaf Kolzig | .60 | .25 |
| ❑ 5 Chris Osgood | .75 | .35 |
| ❑ 6 Damian Rhodes | .60 | .25 |
| ❑ 7 Mike Richter | .75 | .35 |
| ❑ 8 Patrick Roy | 4.00 | 1.80 |

## 1973-74 Mac's Milk

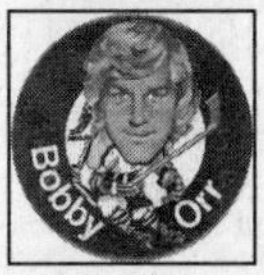


The 1973-74 Mac's Milk set contains 30 unnumbered discs measuring approximately 3" in diameter. These round discs are actually cloth stickers with a peel-off back. They are unnumbered and feature popular players in the National Hockey League. There is no identifying mark anywhere on the discs identifying the sponsor as Mac's Milk. They are checklisted below in alphabetical order by player's name.

| | NRMT-MT | EXC |
|---|---|---|
| COMPLETE SET (30) | 150.00 | 70.00 |
| COMMON CARD (1-30) | 3.00 | 1.35 |
| ❑ 1 Gary Bergman | 3.00 | 1.35 |
| ❑ 2 Johnny Bucyk | 5.00 | 2.20 |
| ❑ 3 Wayne Cashman | 4.00 | 1.80 |
| ❑ 4 Bobby Clarke | 15.00 | 6.75 |
| ❑ 5 Yvan Cournoyer | 6.00 | 2.70 |

❑ 6 Ron Ellis 3.00 1.35
❑ 7 Rod Gilbert 5.00 2.20
❑ 8 Brian Glennie 3.00 1.35
❑ 9 Paul Henderson 5.00 2.20
❑ 10 Ed Johnston 5.00 2.20
❑ 11 Rick Kehoe 3.00 1.35
❑ 12 Orland Kurtenbach 3.00 1.35
❑ 13 Guy Lapointe 5.00 2.20
❑ 14 Jacques Lemaire 5.00 2.20
❑ 15 Frank Mahovlich 10.00 4.50
❑ 16 Pete Mahovlich 5.00 2.20
❑ 17 Richard Martin 4.00 1.80
❑ 18 Jim McKenny 3.00 1.35
❑ 19 Bobby Orr 40.00 18.00
❑ 20 Jean-Paul Parise 3.00 1.35
❑ 21 Brad Park 8.00 3.60
❑ 22 Jacques Plante 15.00 6.75
❑ 23 Jean Ratelle 5.00 2.20
❑ 24 Mickey Redmond 5.00 2.20
❑ 25 Serge Savard 5.00 2.20
❑ 26 Darryl Sittler 10.00 4.50
❑ 27 Pat Stapleton 3.00 1.35
❑ 28 Dale Tallon 3.00 1.35
❑ 29 Norm Ullman 5.00 2.20
❑ 30 Bill White 4.00 1.80

## 1963-64 Maple Leafs White Border

This 22-card set of postcards measures approximately 3 1/2" by 5 1/2" and features black and white action and posed player photos with white borders. The old Toronto Maple Leafs logo is in the bottom right corner. The player's name and position appear at the bottom. The backs are blank. The cards are unnumbered and checklisted below in alphabetical order.

| | NRMT | VG-E |
|---|---|---|
| COMPLETE SET (22) | 125.00 | 55.00 |
| COMMON CARD (1-22) | 3.00 | 1.35 |

❑ 1 Bob Baun 5.00 2.20
(Posed)
❑ 2 Bob Baun 5.00 2.20
(Posed in white uniform& position not listed)
❑ 3 Carl Brewer 5.00 2.20
(White uniform)
❑ 4 Carl Brewer 5.00 2.20
(Dark uniform)
❑ 5 Kent Douglas 3.00 1.35
❑ 6 Dick Duff 4.00 1.80
❑ 7 Ron Ellis 4.00 1.80
❑ 8 Billy Harris 3.00 1.35
(Portrait)
❑ 9 Billy Harris 3.00 1.35
(Action)
❑ 10 Larry Hillman 3.00 1.35
❑ 11 Red Kelly 8.00 3.60
❑ 12 Dave Keon 15.00 6.75
(No number)
❑ 13 Dave Keon 15.00 6.75
(Number 14)
❑ 14 Frank Mahovlich 15.00 6.75
(Dark uniform)
❑ 15 Frank Mahovlich 15.00 6.75
(Dark uniform with added line NHL All-Star)
❑ 16 Don McKenney 3.00 1.35
❑ 17 Dickie Moore 8.00 3.60
❑ 18 Bob Nevin 4.00 1.80
❑ 19 Bert Olmstead 5.00 2.20
❑ 20 Eddie Shack 10.00 4.50
❑ 21 Don Simmons 4.00 1.80
❑ 22 Allan Stanley 6.00 2.70

## 1965-66 Maple Leafs White Border

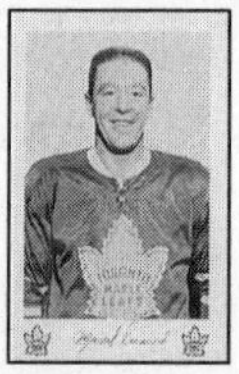

This 17-card set of postcards measures approximately 3 1/2" by 5 1/2" and features black and white portrait and full length photos with white borders. The Toronto Maple Leafs logo is printed in both bottom corners. A facsimile autograph appears at the bottom between the logos. The backs are blank. The cards are unnumbered and checklisted below in alphabetical order.

| | NRMT-MT | EXC |
|---|---|---|
| COMPLETE SET (17) | 60.00 | 27.00 |
| COMMON CARD (1-17) | 3.00 | 1.35 |

❑ 1 George Armstrong 8.00 3.60
❑ 2 Bob Baun 4.00 1.80
❑ 3 Johnny Bower 8.00 3.60
❑ 4 John Brenneman 3.00 1.35
❑ 5 Brian Conacher 3.00 1.35
❑ 6 Ron Ellis 4.00 1.80
(Portrait)
❑ 7 Ron Ellis 4.00 1.80
(Full length; name in print)
❑ 8 Larry Hillman 3.00 1.35
❑ 9 Larry Jeffrey 3.00 1.35
❑ 10 Bruce Gamble 4.00 1.80
❑ 11 Red Kelly 8.00 3.60
❑ 12 Dave Keon 10.00 4.50
❑ 13 Orland Kurtenbach 4.00 1.80
❑ 14 Jim Pappin 3.00 1.35
❑ 15 Marcel Pronovost 6.00 2.70
❑ 16 Eddie Shack 8.00 3.60
❑ 17 Allan Stanley 6.00 2.70

## 1968-69 Maple Leafs White Border

This 11-card set of postcards measures approximately 3 1/2" by 5 1/2" and features black and white player photos with white borders. The Pelyk and Smith cards are portraits while the other cards have posed action shots. The Maple Leafs logo is at the bottom left corner. A facsimile autograph appears at the bottom. The backs are blank. The cards are unnumbered and checklisted below in alphabetical order.

| | NRMT-MT | EXC |
|---|---|---|
| COMPLETE SET (11) | 40.00 | 18.00 |
| COMMON CARD (1-11) | 3.00 | 1.35 |

❑ 1 Johnny Bower 8.00 3.60
❑ 2 Jim Dorey 3.00 1.35
❑ 3 Paul Henderson 4.00 1.80
❑ 4 Tim Horton 10.00 4.50
❑ 5 Rick Ley 3.00 1.35
❑ 6 Murray Oliver 3.00 1.35
❑ 7 Mike Pelyk 3.00 1.35
❑ 8 Pierre Pilote 6.00 2.70
❑ 9 Darryl Sly 3.00 1.35
❑ 10 Floyd Smith 3.00 1.35
❑ 11 Bill Sutherland 3.00 1.35

## 1969-70 Maple Leafs White Border Glossy

This 40-card set of postcards measures approximately 3 1/2" by 5 1/2" and features glossy black and white player photos (posed action or portraits) with white borders. The Maple Leafs logo is printed in black in the bottom left corner. The player's name appears at the bottom in block letters. The backs are blank. The cards are unnumbered and checklisted below in alphabetical order.

| | NRMT-MT | EXC |
|---|---|---|
| COMPLETE SET (40) | 150.00 | 70.00 |
| COMMON CARD (1-40) | 2.00 | .90 |

❑ 1 George Armstrong 6.00 2.70
❑ 2 Johnny Bower 8.00 3.60
❑ 3 Wayne Carleton 2.00 .90
❑ 4 King Clancy 6.00 2.70
❑ 5 Terry Clancy 2.00 .90
❑ 6 Brian Conacher 2.00 .90
❑ 7 Marv Edwards 3.00 1.35
❑ 8 Ron Ellis 3.00 1.35
(Number 6)
❑ 9 Ron Ellis 3.00 1.35
(Number 8)
❑ 10 Ron Ellis 3.00 1.35
(No number)
❑ 11 Bruce Gamble 3.00 1.35
(Front view)
❑ 12 Bruce Gamble 3.00 1.35
(Side view)
❑ 13 Brian Glennie 3.00 1.35
(Portrait)
❑ 14 Brian Glennie 3.00 1.35
(Full length)
❑ 15 Jim Harrison 2.00 .90
❑ 16 Larry Hillman 2.00 .90
❑ 17 Tim Horton 10.00 4.50
❑ 18 Dave Keon 6.00 2.70
(A on sweater)
❑ 19 Dave Keon 6.00 2.70
(C on sweater)
❑ 20 Rick Ley 3.00 1.35
❑ 21 Frank Mahovlich 10.00 4.50
❑ 22 Jim McKenny 2.00 .90
❑ 23 Larry Mickey 2.00 .90
❑ 24 Murray Oliver 2.00 .90
❑ 25 Jim Pappin 2.00 .90
❑ 26 Mike Pelyk 2.00 .90
❑ 27 Marcel Pronovost 4.00 1.80
❑ 28 Bob Pulford 5.00 2.20
(Number on gloves)
❑ 29 Bob Pulford 5.00 2.20
(No number on gloves)
❑ 30 Pat Quinn 4.00 1.80
❑ 31 Brit Selby 2.00 .90
❑ 32 Al Smith 2.00 .90
❑ 33 Floyd Smith 2.00 .90
❑ 34 Allan Stanley 5.00 2.20
❑ 35 Norm Ullman 5.00 2.20
❑ 36 Mike Walton 3.00 1.35
(Stick touching border)
❑ 37 Mike Walton 3.00 1.35
(Stick away from border)
❑ 38 Ron Ward 2.00 .90
❑ 39 Team Photo 1966-67 6.00 2.70
❑ 40 Punch Imlach and King Clancy 6.00 2.70

## 1969-70 Maple Leafs White Border Matte

This six-card set of postcards measures approximately 3 1/2" by 5 1/2" and features matte black and white player photos with white borders. The Toronto Maple Leafs logo is printed in black in the bottom left corner. The player's name appears at the bottom in block letters. The backs are blank. The cards are unnumbered and checklisted below in alphabetical order.

| | NRMT-MT | EXC |
|---|---|---|
| COMPLETE SET (6) | 20.00 | 9.00 |
| COMMON CARD (1-6) | 2.50 | 1.10 |

❑ 1 Brian Glennie 3.00 1.35
❑ 2 Dave Keon 8.00 3.60
❑ 3 Bill MacMillan 2.50 1.10
❑ 4 Larry McIntyre 2.50 1.10
❑ 5 Brian Spencer 5.00 2.20
❑ 6 Norm Ullman 6.00 2.70

## 1970-71 Maple Leafs Postcards

This 15-card set measures approximately 3 1/2" by 5 1/2" and features matte black and white player photos with white borders. The Maple Leafs logo is printed in the bottom left corner. The player's name appears in block letters, and a facsimile autograph is printed in black. The backs are blank. The cards are unnumbered and checklisted below in alphabetical order. Key card in the set is Darryl Sittler appearing in his Rookie Card year.

| | NRMT-MT | EXC |
|---|---|---|
| COMPLETE SET (15) | 50.00 | 22.00 |
| COMMON CARD (1-15) | 2.00 | .90 |

❑ 1 Jim Dorey 2.00 .90
❑ 2 Ron Ellis 3.00 1.35
❑ 3 Bruce Gamble 3.00 1.35
❑ 4 Jim Harrison 2.00 .90
❑ 5 Paul Henderson 3.00 1.35
❑ 6 Rick Ley 2.50 1.10
❑ 7 Bob Liddington 2.00 .90
❑ 8 Jim McKenny 2.00 .90
❑ 9 Garry Monahan 2.00 .90
❑ 10 Mike Pelyk 2.00 .90
❑ 11 Jacques Plante 12.00 5.50
❑ 12 Brad Selwood 2.00 .90
❑ 13 Darryl Sittler 25.00 11.00
❑ 14 Guy Trottier 2.00 .90
❑ 15 Mike Walton 3.00 1.35

## 1971-72 Maple Leafs Postcards

This 21-card set measures approximately 3 1/2" by 5 1/2" and features posed color player photos with black backgrounds. (The sweaters have lace-style neck.) The cards feature a facsimile autograph. The backs are blank. The cards are unnumbered and checklisted below in alphabetical order.

| | NRMT-MT | EXC |
|---|---|---|
| COMPLETE SET (21) | 50.00 | 22.00 |
| COMMON CARD (1-21) | 2.00 | .90 |

❑ 1 Bob Baun 3.00 1.35
❑ 2 Jim Dorey 2.00 .90
❑ 3 Denis Dupere 2.00 .90
❑ 4 Ron Ellis 3.00 1.35
❑ 5 Brian Glennie 2.00 .90
❑ 6 Jim Harrison 2.00 .90
❑ 7 Paul Henderson 3.00 1.35
❑ 8 Dave Keon 5.00 2.20
❑ 9 Rick Ley 2.00 .90
❑ 10 Billy MacMillan 2.00 .90
❑ 11 Don Marshall 2.00 .90
❑ 12 Jim McKenny 2.00 .90
❑ 13 Garry Monahan 2.00 .90
❑ 14 Bernie Parent 8.00 3.60
❑ 15 Mike Pelyk 2.00 .90
❑ 16 Jacques Plante 8.00 3.60
❑ 17 Brad Selwood 2.00 .90
❑ 18 Darryl Sittler 10.00 4.50
❑ 19 Brian Spencer 3.00 1.35
❑ 20 Guy Trottier 2.00 .90
❑ 21 Norm Ullman 4.00 1.80

## 1972-73 Maple Leafs Postcards

This 30-card set measures approximately 3 1/2" by 5 1/2" and features posed color player photos with a black background. The players are pictured wearing "V-neck" sweaters. The cards feature a facsimile autograph. The backs are blank. The cards are unnumbered and checklisted below in alphabetical order.

| | NRMT-MT | EXC |
|---|---|---|
| COMPLETE SET (30) | 80.00 | 36.00 |
| COMMON CARD (1-30) | 1.50 | .70 |

❑ 1 Bob Baun 2.50 1.10
❑ 2 Terry Clancy 1.50 .70
❑ 3 Denis Dupere 1.50 .70
❑ 4 Ron Ellis 2.50 1.10
(Dark print)
❑ 5 Ron Ellis 2.50 1.10
(Light print)
❑ 6 George Ferguson 1.50 .70
❑ 7 Brian Glennie 1.50 .70
(Autograph touches stick)
❑ 8 Brian Glennie 1.50 .70
(Autograph away from stick)
❑ 9 John Grisdale 1.50 .70
❑ 10 Paul Henderson 2.50 1.10
(Light print)
❑ 11 Paul Henderson 2.50 1.10
(Dark print)
❑ 12 Pierre Jarry 1.50 .70
❑ 13 Rick Kehoe 2.50 1.10
❑ 14 Dave Keon 5.00 2.20
(Autograph touches skate)
❑ 15 Dave Keon 5.00 2.20
(Autograph away from skate)
❑ 16 Ron Low 2.50 1.10
❑ 17 Joe Lundrigan 1.50 .70
❑ 18 Larry McIntyre 1.50 .70
❑ 19 Jim McKenny 1.50 .70
(Blue tinge)
❑ 20 Jim McKenny 1.50 .70
(Red tinge)
❑ 21 Garry Monahan 1.50 .70
❑ 22 Randy Osburn 1.50 .70
❑ 23 Mike Pelyk 1.50 .70
❑ 24 Jacques Plante 10.00 4.50
(Autograph through tape)
❑ 25 Jacques Plante 10.00 4.50
(Autograph under tape)
❑ 26 Darryl Sittler 10.00 4.50
(Autograph over stick)
❑ 27 Darryl Sittler 10.00 4.50
(Autograph away from stick)
❑ 28 Errol Thompson 1.50 .70
❑ 29 Norm Ullman 4.00 1.80
(Best Wishes above blueline)
❑ 30 Norm Ullman 4.00 1.80
(Best Wishes across blueline)

## 1973-74 Maple Leafs Postcards

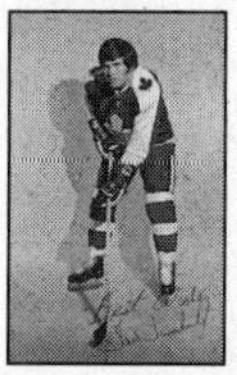

This 29-card set measures approximately 3 1/2" by 5 1/2" and features posed color player photos with a blue-green background. The cards feature a facsimile autograph. The backs are blank. The cards are unnumbered and checklisted below in alphabetical order. The key card in the set is Lanny McDonald, whose card predates his Rookie Card.

| | NRMT-MT | EXC |
|---|---|---|
| COMPLETE SET (29) | 80.00 | 36.00 |
| COMMON CARD (1-29) | 1.50 | .70 |

❑ 1 Johnny Bower 5.00 2.20
❑ 2 Willie Brossart 1.50 .70
❑ 3 Denis Dupere 1.50 .70
❑ 4 Ron Ellis 2.50 1.10
❑ 5 Doug Favell 3.00 1.35
(Standing)
❑ 6 Doug Favell 3.00 1.35
(Bending)
❑ 7 Brian Glennie 1.50 .70
❑ 8 Jim Gregory 1.50 .70
❑ 9 Inge Hammarstrom 1.50 .70
❑ 10 Paul Henderson 2.50 1.10
❑ 11 Eddie Johnston 3.00 1.35
❑ 12 Rick Kehoe 3.00 1.35
(Same as 1972-73 set)
❑ 13 Rick Kehoe 3.00 1.35
(Bending)
❑ 14 Rick Kehoe 3.00 1.35
(Standing)
❑ 15 Red Kelly 6.00 2.70
❑ 16 Dave Keon 6.00 2.70
❑ 17 Lanny McDonald 12.00 5.50
❑ 18 Jim McKenny 1.50 .70
❑ 19 Garry Monahan 1.50 .70
❑ 20 Bob Neely 1.50 .70
❑ 21 Mike Pelyk 1.50 .70
❑ 22 Borje Salming 8.00 3.60
❑ 23 Eddie Shack 6.00 2.70
❑ 24 Darryl Sittler 6.00 2.70
(Bending)
❑ 25 Darryl Sittler 6.00 2.70
(Standing)
❑ 26 Errol Thompson 1.50 .70
❑ 27 Ian Turnbull 1.50 .70
❑ 28 Norm Ullman 3.50 1.55
❑ 29 Dunc Wilson 2.50 1.10

## 1974-75 Maple Leafs Postcards

This 27-card set measures approximately 3 1/2" by 5 1/2" and features posed color player photos with a pale-blue background and a "venetian blind" effect. The cards feature facsimile autographs. The backs are blank. The cards are unnumbered and are checklisted below in alphabetical order.

| | NRMT-MT | EXC |
|---|---|---|
| COMPLETE SET (27) | 50.00 | 22.00 |
| COMMON CARD (1-27) | 1.50 | .70 |

❑ 1 Claire Alexander 1.50 .70
❑ 2 Dave Dunn 1.50 .70
❑ 3 Ron Ellis 2.00 .90
❑ 4 George Ferguson 1.50 .70
(Bending)
❑ 5 George Ferguson 1.50 .70
(Standing)
❑ 6 Bill Flett 1.50 .70
(Front view)
❑ 7 Bill Flett 1.50 .70
(Side view)
❑ 8 Brian Glennie 1.50 .70
❑ 9 Inge Hammarstrom 1.50 .70
❑ 10 Dave Keon 4.00 1.80
(Bending)
❑ 11 Dave Keon 4.00 1.80
(Standing)
❑ 12 Lanny McDonald 6.00 2.70
❑ 13 Jim McKenny 1.50 .70
❑ 14 Gord McRae 1.50 .70
❑ 15 Lyle Moffat 1.50 .70
❑ 16 Bob Neely 1.50 .70
❑ 17 Gary Sabourin 1.50 .70
❑ 18 Borje Salming 4.00 1.80
❑ 19 Rod Seiling 1.50 .70
❑ 20 Eddie Shack 4.00 1.80
❑ 21 Darryl Sittler 4.00 1.80
❑ 22 Blaine Stoughton 2.00 .90
❑ 23 Errol Thompson 1.50 .70
❑ 24 Ian Turnbull 2.00 .90
❑ 25 Norm Ullman 3.00 1.35
❑ 26 Dave(Tiger) Williams 4.00 1.80
❑ 27 Dunc Wilson 2.00 .90

## 1975-76 Maple Leafs Postcards

This 30-card set of postcards measures approximately 3 1/2" by 5 1/2" and features posed color photos of players in blue uniforms. The Maple Leafs logo, the player's name, and number appear inn a white panel at the bottom. A facsimile autograph is inscribed across the picture. The backs have player information. The cards are unnumbered and are checklisted below in alphabetical order.

| | NRMT-MT | EXC |
|---|---|---|
| COMPLETE SET (30) | 50.00 | 22.00 |
| COMMON CARD (1-30) | 1.50 | .70 |

❑ 1 Claire Alexander 1.50 .70
❑ 2 Don Ashby 1.50 .70
(Bending)
❑ 3 Don Ashby 1.50 .70
(Standing)
❑ 4 Pat Boutette 1.50 .70
❑ 5 Dave Dunn 1.50 .70
❑ 6 Doug Favell 2.00 .90
❑ 7 George Ferguson 1.50 .70
❑ 8 Brian Glennie 1.50 .70
❑ 9 Inge Hammarstrom 1.50 .70
(Bending)
❑ 10 Inge Hammarstrom 1.50 .70
(Standing)
❑ 11 Greg Hubick 1.50 .70
❑ 12 Lanny McDonald 5.00 2.20
❑ 13 Jim McKenny 1.50 .70
❑ 14 Gord McRae 1.50 .70
❑ 15 Bob Neely 1.50 .70
❑ 16 Borje Salming 4.00 1.80
(Side view)
❑ 17 Borje Salming 4.00 1.80
(Front view)
❑ 18 Rod Seiling 1.50 .70
❑ 19 Darryl Sittler 4.00 1.80
(Bending)
❑ 20 Darryl Sittler 5.00 2.20
(Standing)
❑ 21 Blaine Stoughton 2.00 .90
❑ 22 Wayne Thomas 2.50 1.10
(Crouching)
❑ 23 Wayne Thomas 2.50 1.10
(Standing)
❑ 24 Errol Thompson 1.50 .70
❑ 25 Ian Turnbull 2.00 .90
(Bending)
❑ 26 Ian Turnbull 2.00 .90
(Standing)
❑ 27 Stan Weir 1.50 .70
❑ 28 Dave(Tiger) Williams 2.50 1.10
(Bending)
❑ 29 Dave(Tiger) Williams 2.50 1.10
(Standing)
❑ 30 Maple Leaf Gardens 2.00 .90
(Painting)

## 1976-77 Maple Leafs Postcards

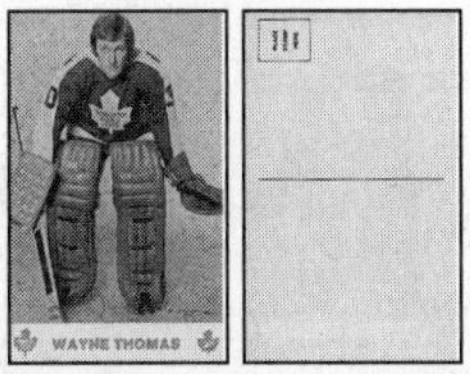


This 24-card set in the postcard format measures approximately 3 1/2" by 5 1/2" and features posed color photos of players in blue uniforms. A white panel at the bottom contains the Maple Leafs logo in each corner, the player's name, and uniform number. A facsimile autograph is inscribed across the picture. The cards are unnumbered and checklisted below in alphabetical order. Key card in the set is Randy Carlyle appearing prior to his Rookie Card year.

| | NRMT-MT | EXC |
|---|---|---|
| COMPLETE SET (24) | 40.00 | 18.00 |
| COMMON CARD (1-24) | 1.25 | .55 |
| ❑ 1 Claire Alexander | 1.25 | .55 |
| ❑ 2 Don Ashby | 1.25 | .55 |
| ❑ 3 Pat Boutette | 1.25 | .55 |
| ❑ 4 Randy Carlyle | 3.00 | 1.35 |
| ❑ 5 George Ferguson | 1.25 | .55 |
| ❑ 6 Scott Garland | 1.25 | .55 |
| ❑ 7 Brian Glennie | 1.25 | .55 |
| ❑ 8 Inge Hammarstrom | 1.25 | .55 |
| ❑ 9 Lanny McDonald | 4.00 | 1.80 |
| ❑ 10 Jim McKenny | 1.25 | .55 |
| ❑ 11 Gord McRae | 1.25 | .55 |
| ❑ 12 Bob Neely | 1.25 | .55 |
| ❑ 13 Mike Palmateer | 4.00 | 1.80 |
| ❑ 14 Mike Pelyk | 1.25 | .55 |
| ❑ 15 Borje Salming | 3.00 | 1.35 |
| ❑ 16 Darryl Sittler | 4.00 | 1.80 |
| ❑ 17 Wayne Thomas | 2.00 | .90 |
| ❑ 18 Errol Thompson | 1.25 | .55 |
| ❑ 19 Ian Turnbull (Dark printing) | 1.50 | .70 |
| ❑ 20 Ian Turnbull (Light printing) | 1.50 | .70 |
| ❑ 21 Jack Valiquette | 1.25 | .55 |
| ❑ 22 Kurt Walker | 1.25 | .55 |
| ❑ 23 Stan Weir | 1.25 | .55 |
| ❑ 24 Dave(Tiger) Williams | 4.00 | 1.80 |

## 1977-78 Maple Leafs Postcards

This 19-card set measures approximately 3 1/2" by 5 1/2" and features posed color photos of players in white uniforms. At the bottom are the Toronto Maple Leafs logo in each corner, the player's uniform number, and the player's name in blue print. The backs are blank. The cards are unnumbered and checklisted below in alphabetical order.

| | NRMT-MT | EXC |
|---|---|---|
| COMPLETE SET (19) | 25.00 | 11.00 |
| COMMON CARD (1-19) | 1.00 | .45 |
| ❑ 1 Pat Boutette | 1.00 | .45 |
| ❑ 2 Randy Carlyle | 2.00 | .90 |
| ❑ 3 Ron Ellis | 1.50 | .70 |
| ❑ 4 George Ferguson | 1.00 | .45 |
| ❑ 5 Brian Glennie | 1.00 | .45 |
| ❑ 6 Inge Hammarstrom | 1.00 | .45 |
| ❑ 7 Trevor Johansen | 1.00 | .45 |
| ❑ 8 Jim Jones | 1.00 | .45 |
| ❑ 9 Lanny McDonald | 4.00 | 1.80 |
| ❑ 10 Jim McKenny | 1.00 | .45 |
| ❑ 11 Gord McRae | 1.00 | .45 |
| ❑ 12 Mike Palmateer | 3.00 | 1.35 |
| ❑ 13 Borje Salming | 3.00 | 1.35 |
| ❑ 14 Darryl Sittler | 4.00 | 1.80 |
| ❑ 15 Errol Thompson | 1.00 | .45 |
| ❑ 16 Ian Turnbull | 1.00 | .45 |
| ❑ 17 Jack Valiquette | 1.00 | .45 |
| ❑ 18 Kurt Walker | 1.00 | .45 |
| ❑ 19 Dave(Tiger) Williams | 3.00 | 1.35 |

## 1978-79 Maple Leafs Postcards

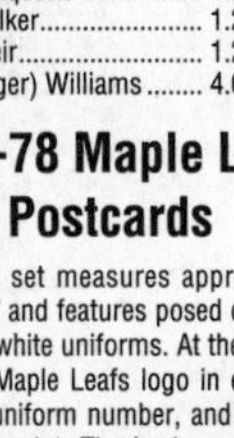


This 25-card set in the postcard format measures approximately 3 1/2" by 5 1/2" and features posed color player photos. At the bottom are the Toronto Maple Leafs logo in each corner, the player's uniform number in the logo at the bottom right, and the player's name in blue print. The cards are unnumbered and checklisted below in alphabetical order.

| | NRMT-MT | EXC |
|---|---|---|
| COMPLETE SET (25) | 30.00 | 13.50 |
| COMMON CARD (1-25) | 1.00 | .45 |
| ❑ 1 John Anderson | 1.50 | .70 |
| ❑ 2 Bruce Boudreau (Black and white) | 1.00 | .45 |
| ❑ 3 Pat Boutette | 1.00 | .45 |
| ❑ 4 Pat Boutette | 1.00 | .45 |
| ❑ 5 Dave Burrows | 1.00 | .45 |
| ❑ 6 Jerry Butler | 1.00 | .45 |
| ❑ 7 Ron Ellis | 1.50 | .70 |
| ❑ 8 Paul Harrison | 1.00 | .45 |
| ❑ 9 Dave Hutchison | 1.00 | .45 |
| ❑ 10 Trevor Johansen | 1.00 | .45 |
| ❑ 11 Jimmy Jones | 1.00 | .45 |
| ❑ 12 Dan Maloney | 1.50 | .70 |
| ❑ 13 Lanny McDonald | 4.00 | 1.80 |
| ❑ 14 Walt McKechnie | 1.00 | .45 |
| ❑ 15 Garry Monahan | 1.00 | .45 |
| ❑ 16 Roger Neilson | 2.00 | .90 |
| ❑ 17 Mike Palmateer | 2.50 | 1.10 |
| ❑ 18 Borje Salming | 2.50 | 1.10 |
| ❑ 19 Darryl Sittler | 4.00 | 1.80 |
| ❑ 20 Lorne Stamler | 1.00 | .45 |
| ❑ 21 Ian Turnbull | 1.00 | .45 |
| ❑ 22 Dave(Tiger) Williams | 2.50 | 1.10 |
| ❑ 23 Ron Wilson | 1.00 | .45 |
| ❑ 24 Harold Ballard and King Clancy | 2.00 | .90 |
| ❑ 25 Team Photo | 2.50 | 1.10 |

## 1979-80 Maple Leafs Postcards

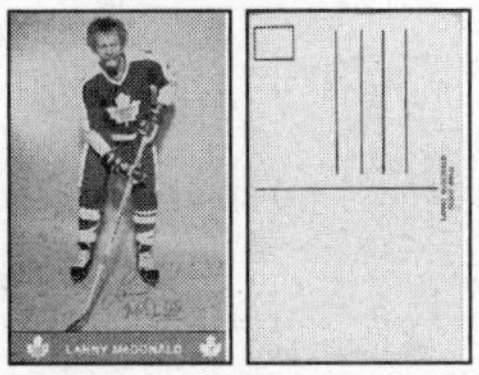


This 34-card set in the postcard format measures approximately 3 1/2" by 5 1/2" and features posed color photos of players in blue uniforms. The Toronto Maple Leafs logo is in each bottom corner. A blue panel across the bottom contains the player's name in white print. The player's uniform number is printed in the logo at the bottom right. Most of the pictures have a light blue tint and are taken against a studio background. These cards also feature facsimile autographs on the lower portion of the picture. The backs are printed with a light blue postcard design and carry the player's name and position. The cards are unnumbered and checklisted below in alphabetical order.

| | NRMT-MT | EXC |
|---|---|---|
| COMPLETE SET (34) | 40.00 | 18.00 |
| COMMON CARD (1-34) | .75 | .35 |
| ❑ 1 John Anderson | 1.00 | .45 |
| ❑ 2 Harold Ballard | 1.50 | .70 |
| ❑ 3 Laurie Boschman | 1.00 | .45 |
| ❑ 4 Pat Boutette | .75 | .35 |
| ❑ 5 Carl Brewer (Action shot taken at rink; borderless; no facsimile autograph; black print on back) | 1.50 | .70 |
| ❑ 6 Dave Burrows | .75 | .35 |
| ❑ 7 Jerry Butler | .75 | .35 |
| ❑ 8 Jiri Crha | 1.50 | .70 |
| ❑ 9 Ron Ellis | 1.00 | .45 |
| ❑ 10 Paul Gardner | .75 | .35 |
| ❑ 11 Paul Harrison | .75 | .35 |
| ❑ 12 Greg Hotham | .75 | .35 |
| ❑ 13 Dave Hutchison | .75 | .35 |
| ❑ 14 Punch Imlach CO | 2.00 | .90 |
| ❑ 15 Jimmy Jones | .75 | .35 |
| ❑ 16 Mark Kirton | .75 | .35 |
| ❑ 17 Dan Maloney | .75 | .35 |
| ❑ 18 Terry Martin (Action shot taken at rink; borderless; no facsimile autograph; black print on back) | 1.00 | .45 |
| ❑ 19 Lanny McDonald | 4.00 | 1.80 |
| ❑ 20 Walt McKechnie | .75 | .35 |
| ❑ 21 Mike Palmateer | 2.00 | .90 |
| ❑ 22 Mike Palmateer (Autograph at different angle) | 2.00 | .90 |
| ❑ 23 Joel Quenneville | 1.00 | .45 |
| ❑ 24 Rocky Saganiuk | .75 | .35 |
| ❑ 25 Borje Salming (Autograph touches blue panel) | 2.50 | 1.10 |
| ❑ 26 Borje Salming (Autograph away from blue panel) | 2.50 | 1.10 |
| ❑ 27 Darryl Sittler (Autograph closer to blue panel) | 4.00 | 1.80 |
| ❑ 28 Darryl Sittler | 4.00 | 1.80 |
| ❑ 29 Floyd Smith | .75 | .35 |
| ❑ 30 Bob Stephenson (Action shot taken at rink; borderless; no facsimile autograph; black print on back) | 1.00 | .45 |
| ❑ 31 Ian Turnbull | .75 | .35 |
| ❑ 32 Dave(Tiger) Williams | 2.00 | .90 |
| ❑ 33 Ron Wilson | .75 | .35 |
| ❑ 34 Faceoff with Cardinal Carter | 1.25 | .55 |

## 1980-81 Maple Leafs Postcards

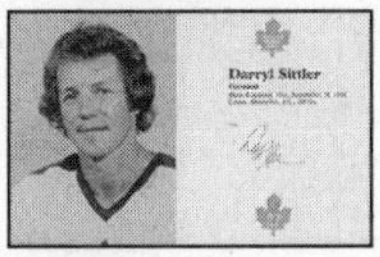


This 28-card set measures approximately 3 1/2" by 5 1/2" and features horizontally oriented color player photos on the left half of the card. The right half displays player information, blue logos, and a facsimile autograph printed in sky blue along with the team logo and a maple leaf carrying the player's jersey number. The backs are blank. The cards are unnumbered and checklisted below in alphabetical order.

| | NRMT-MT | EXC |
|---|---|---|
| COMPLETE SET (28) | 25.00 | 11.00 |
| COMMON CARD (1-28) | .75 | .35 |
| ❑ 1 John Anderson | 1.00 | .45 |
| ❑ 2 Harold Ballard | 1.50 | .70 |
| ❑ 3 Laurie Boschman (Portrait) | 1.00 | .45 |
| ❑ 4 Laurie Boschman (Action) | 1.00 | .45 |
| ❑ 5 Johnny Bower | 3.00 | 1.35 |
| ❑ 6 King Clancy | 2.00 | .90 |
| ❑ 7 Jiri Crha | 1.50 | .70 |
| ❑ 8 Joe Crozier CO | .75 | .35 |
| ❑ 9 Bill Derlago | 1.00 | .45 |
| ❑ 10 Dick Duff | 1.00 | .45 |
| ❑ 11 Vitezslav Duris | .75 | .35 |
| ❑ 12 Dave Farrish | .75 | .35 |
| ❑ 13 Stewart Gavin | 1.00 | .45 |
| ❑ 14 Paul Harrison | .75 | .35 |
| ❑ 15 Pat Hickey | .75 | .35 |
| ❑ 16 Mark Kirton | .75 | .35 |
| ❑ 17 Terry Martin | .75 | .35 |
| ❑ 18 Gerry McNamara | .75 | .35 |
| ❑ 19 Wilf Paiement | 1.00 | .45 |
| ❑ 20 Robert Picard | .75 | .35 |
| ❑ 21 Curt Ridley | .75 | .35 |
| ❑ 22 Rocky Saganiuk | .75 | .35 |
| ❑ 23 Borje Salming | 2.00 | .90 |
| ❑ 24 Dave Shand | .75 | .35 |
| ❑ 25 Darryl Sittler (Portrait) | 4.00 | 1.80 |
| ❑ 26 Darryl Sittler (Action) | 4.00 | 1.80 |
| ❑ 27 Ian Turnbull | .75 | .35 |
| ❑ 28 Rick Vaive | 1.50 | .70 |

## 1981-82 Maple Leafs Postcards

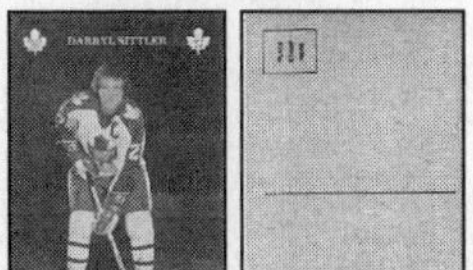


This 26-card set in the postcard format measures approximately 3 1/2" by 5 1/2" and features full-bleed color photos of players posed on the ice against a dark background. A white Maple Leafs logo appears in each top corner and the player's name in white between the logos. The player's number is printed in the right top logo. These cards also feature facsimile autographs. The backs are white and have a basic postcard design printed in light blue. The cards are unnumbered and checklisted below in alphabetical order.

| | NRMT-MT | EXC |
|---|---|---|
| COMPLETE SET (26) | 25.00 | 11.00 |
| COMMON CARD (1-26) | .75 | .35 |
| ❑ 1 John Anderson | 1.00 | .45 |
| ❑ 2 Harold Ballard (Painting) | 2.00 | .90 |
| ❑ 3 Jim Benning | .75 | .35 |
| ❑ 4 Fred Boimistruck | .75 | .35 |
| ❑ 5 Laurie Boschman | .75 | .35 |
| ❑ 6 Bill Derlago | 1.00 | .45 |
| ❑ 7 Stewart Gavin | 1.00 | .45 |
| ❑ 8 Bunny Larocque | 1.50 | .70 |
| ❑ 9 Don Luce | .75 | .35 |
| ❑ 10 Dan Maloney | .75 | .35 |
| ❑ 11 Bob Manno | .75 | .35 |
| ❑ 12 Paul Marshall | .75 | .35 |
| ❑ 13 Terry Martin | .75 | .35 |
| ❑ 14 Bob McGill | .75 | .35 |
| ❑ 15 Barry Melrose | 1.50 | .70 |
| ❑ 16 Mike Nykoluk CO | .75 | .35 |
| ❑ 17 Wilf Paiement | 1.00 | .45 |
| ❑ 18 Rene Robert | 1.00 | .45 |
| ❑ 19 Rocky Saganiuk | .75 | .35 |
| ❑ 20 Borje Salming | 2.00 | .90 |
| ❑ 21 Darryl Sittler | 4.00 | 1.80 |
| ❑ 22 Vincent Tremblay | .75 | .35 |
| ❑ 23 Rick Vaive | 1.50 | .70 |
| ❑ 24 Gary Yaremchuk | .75 | .35 |
| ❑ 25 Ron Zanussi | .75 | .35 |
| ❑ 26 Frank J. Selke and Harold Ballard | 1.50 | .70 |

## 1982-83 Maple Leafs Postcards

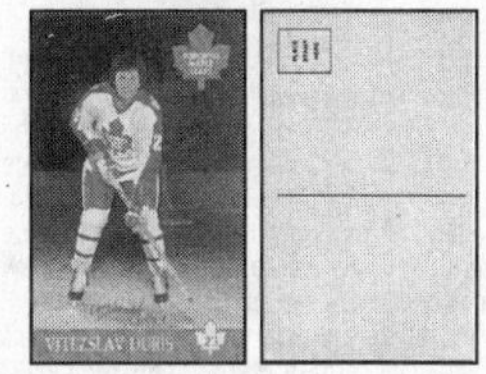


This 37-card set in the postcard format measures approximately 3 1/2" by 5 1/2" and features color photos of players on the ice against a dark background. A white Maple Leafs logo, the sweater number, and the player's name appear in a blue panel at the bottom. A facsimile autograph appears near the bottom of the picture. A blue Maple Leafs logo is printed in one of the top corners. The postcard backs are printed in light blue, in contrast to the 1984-85 issue, which features black print on the back. The cards are unnumbered and checklisted below in alphabetical order.

| | MINT | NRMT |
|---|---|---|
| COMPLETE SET (37) | 25.00 | 11.00 |
| COMMON CARD (1-37) | .75 | .35 |
| ❑ 1 Russ Adam | .75 | .35 |
| ❑ 2 John Anderson | 1.00 | .45 |
| ❑ 3 Normand Aubin | .75 | .35 |
| ❑ 4 Jim Benning | .75 | .35 |
| ❑ 5 Fred Boimistruck | .75 | .35 |
| ❑ 6 Serge Boisvert | .75 | .35 |
| ❑ 7 Dan Daoust | .75 | .35 |
| ❑ 8 Bill Derlago (Autograph 1/8~ from border) | 1.00 | .45 |
| ❑ 9 Bill Derlago (Autograph 1/4~ from border) | 1.00 | .45 |
| ❑ 10 Vitezslav Duris | .75 | .35 |
| ❑ 11 Miroslav Frycer (Autograph touching skate blade) | .75 | .35 |
| ❑ 12 Miroslav Frycer (Autograph away from skate blade) | .75 | .35 |
| ❑ 13 Stewart Gavin | 1.00 | .45 |
| ❑ 14 Gaston Gingras (Dark background) | .75 | .35 |
| ❑ 15 Gaston Gingras (Light background) | .75 | .35 |
| ❑ 16 Billy Harris | .75 | .35 |
| ❑ 17 Paul Higgins | .75 | .35 |
| ❑ 18 Peter Inhacak | .75 | .35 |
| ❑ 19 Jim Korn | .75 | .35 |
| ❑ 20 Bunny Larocque (Bunny touching stick) | 1.00 | .45 |
| ❑ 21 Bunny Larocque (Bunny touching goalie pad) | 1.00 | .45 |
| ❑ 22 Dan Maloney | 1.00 | .45 |
| ❑ 23 Terry Martin | .75 | .35 |
| ❑ 24 Bob McGill | .75 | .35 |
| ❑ 25 Frank Nigro | .75 | .35 |
| ❑ 26 Mike Nykoluk CO | .75 | .35 |
| ❑ 27 Gary Nylund | .75 | .35 |
| ❑ 28 Mike Palmateer | 2.00 | .90 |
| ❑ 29 Walt Poddubny | 1.00 | .45 |
| ❑ 30 Borje Salming (Autograph 1/8~ from skate) | 2.00 | .90 |
| ❑ 31 Borje Salming (Autograph 1/4~ from skate) | 2.00 | .90 |
| ❑ 32 Rick St. Croix | 1.00 | .45 |
| ❑ 33 Greg Terrion (Dark background) | .75 | .35 |
| ❑ 34 Greg Terrion (Light background) | .75 | .35 |
| ❑ 35 Vincent Tremblay | .75 | .35 |
| ❑ 36 Rick Vaive (Autograph touching blade) | 1.25 | .55 |
| ❑ 37 Rick Vaive (Autograph touching toe of skate) | 1.25 | .55 |

## 1983-84 Maple Leafs Postcards

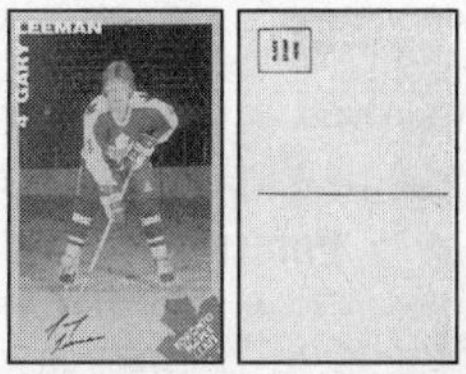


This 26-card set in the postcard format measures approximately 3 1/2" by 5 1/2" and features posed color photos of players on the ice. A pale blue border contains a blue Maple Leafs logo in the bottom right corner. The player's name and number is printed running up the left side and across the top in the left corner. A facsimile autograph is printed in black on the front near the bottom of the photo. The backs are white and carry a basic postcard design in light blue. The cards are unnumbered and checklisted below in alphabetical order.

| | MINT | NRMT |
|---|---|---|
| COMPLETE SET (26) | 20.00 | 9.00 |
| COMMON CARD (1-26) | .75 | .35 |
| ❑ 1 John Anderson | 1.00 | .45 |
| ❑ 2 Jim Benning | .75 | .35 |
| ❑ 3 Dan Daoust | .75 | .35 |
| ❑ 4 Bill Derlago | 1.00 | .45 |
| ❑ 5 Dave Farrish | .75 | .35 |
| ❑ 6 Miroslav Frycer | .75 | .35 |
| ❑ 7 Stewart Gavin | 1.00 | .45 |
| ❑ 8 Gaston Gingras | .75 | .35 |
| ❑ 9 Pat Graham | .75 | .35 |
| ❑ 10 Billy Harris | .75 | .35 |
| ❑ 11 Peter Inhacak | .75 | .35 |
| ❑ 12 Jim Korn | .75 | .35 |
| ❑ 13 Gary Leeman | 1.00 | .45 |
| ❑ 14 Dan Maloney | .75 | .35 |
| ❑ 15 Terry Martin | .75 | .35 |
| ❑ 16 Basil McRae | 1.00 | .45 |
| ❑ 17 Frank Nigro | .75 | .35 |
| ❑ 18 Mike Nykoluk CO | .75 | .35 |
| ❑ 19 Gary Nylund | .75 | .35 |
| ❑ 20 Mike Palmateer | 1.50 | .70 |
| ❑ 21 Walt Poddubny | 1.00 | .45 |
| ❑ 22 Borje Salming | 2.00 | .90 |
| ❑ 23 Bill Stewart | .75 | .35 |
| ❑ 24 Rick St. Croix | 1.00 | .45 |
| ❑ 25 Greg Terrion | .75 | .35 |
| ❑ 26 Rick Vaive | 1.25 | .55 |

## 1984-85 Maple Leafs Postcards

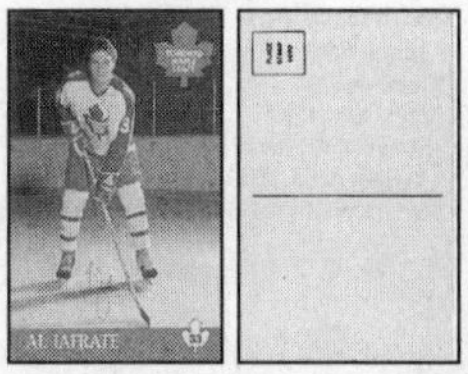


This 25-card set in the postcard format measures approximately 3 1/2" by 5 1/2" and features posed color photos of players on the ice with facsimile autographs. A blue panel at the bottom contains the player's name, sweater number, and a white Maple Leafs logo. A blue Toronto Maple Leafs logo appears in one of the top corners. The backs have a basic postcard design printed in black. The cards are unnumbered and checklisted below in alphabetical order. Both Russ Courtnall and Al Iafrate appear in this set prior to their Rookie Card year. This set can be distinguished from the similarly designed 1982-83 postcard set by the black jersey number and black outline around the team logo in the bottom border stripe.

| | MINT | NRMT |
|---|---|---|
| COMPLETE SET (25) | 25.00 | 11.00 |
| COMMON CARD (1-25) | .75 | .35 |
| ❑ 1 John Anderson | 1.00 | .45 |
| ❑ 2 Jim Benning | .75 | .35 |
| ❑ 3 Allan Bester | 1.25 | .55 |
| ❑ 4 John Brophy CO | 1.00 | .45 |
| ❑ 5 Jeff Brubaker | .75 | .35 |
| ❑ 6 Russ Courtnall | 3.00 | 1.35 |
| ❑ 7 Dan Daoust | .75 | .35 |
| ❑ 8 Bill Derlago | .75 | .35 |
| ❑ 9 Miroslav Frycer | .75 | .35 |
| ❑ 10 Stewart Gavin | 1.00 | .45 |
| ❑ 11 Al Iafrate | 4.00 | 1.80 |
| ❑ 12 Peter Inhacak | .75 | .35 |
| ❑ 13 Jeff Jackson | .75 | .35 |
| ❑ 14 Jim Korn | .75 | .35 |
| ❑ 15 Gary Leeman | 1.00 | .45 |
| ❑ 16 Dan Maloney CO | .75 | .35 |
| ❑ 17 Bob McGill | .75 | .35 |

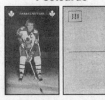

| | MINT | NRMT |
|---|---|---|
| ❑ 18 Gary Nylund | .75 | .35 |
| ❑ 19 Walt Poddubny | 1.00 | .45 |
| ❑ 20 Bill Root | .75 | .35 |
| ❑ 21 Borje Salming | 2.00 | .90 |
| ❑ 22 Bill Stewart | .75 | .35 |
| ❑ 23 Greg Terrion | .75 | .35 |
| ❑ 24 Rick Vaive | 1.25 | .55 |
| ❑ 25 Ken Wregget | 2.50 | 1.10 |

## 1985-86 Maple Leafs Postcards

This 34-card set in the postcard format measures approximately 3 1/2" by 5 1/2" and features color action photos of players on the ice. A blue panel at the bottom contains the player's name, number, and a white Maple Leafs logo. The cards are unnumbered and checklisted below in alphabetical order. Wendel Clark appears in this set the year before his Rookie Card. In addition to the regular set, a special John Bower card was also available.

| | MINT | NRMT |
|---|---|---|
| COMPLETE SET (35) | 30.00 | 13.50 |
| COMMON CARD (1-35) | .75 | .35 |
| ❑ 1 Harold Ballard PRES | 1.00 | .45 |
| ❑ 2 Jim Benning | .75 | .35 |
| ❑ 3 Tim Bernhardt | 1.00 | .45 |
| ❑ 4 Johnny Bower ACO | 1.50 | .70 |
| ❑ 5 Jeff Brubaker | .75 | .35 |
| ❑ 6 Wendel Clark | 10.00 | 4.50 |
| ❑ 7 Russ Courtnall (Dark uniform) | 2.00 | .90 |
| ❑ 8 Russ Courtnall (Light uniform) | 2.00 | .90 |
| ❑ 9 Dan Daoust | .75 | .35 |
| ❑ 10 Don Edwards | 1.50 | .70 |
| ❑ 11 Tom Fergus | .75 | .35 |
| ❑ 12 Miroslav Frycer | .75 | .35 |
| ❑ 13 Dan Hodgson | .75 | .35 |
| ❑ 14 Al Iafrate | 3.00 | 1.35 |
| ❑ 15 Miroslav Inhacak | .75 | .35 |
| ❑ 16 Peter Inhacak | .75 | .35 |
| ❑ 17 Jim Korn | .75 | .35 |
| ❑ 18 Chris Kotsopoulos | .75 | .35 |
| ❑ 19 Gary Leeman | .75 | .35 |
| ❑ 20 Brad Maxwell (Dark uniform) | 1.00 | .45 |
| ❑ 21 Brad Maxwell (Light uniform) | 1.00 | .45 |
| ❑ 22 Bob McGill | .75 | .35 |
| ❑ 23 Gary Nylund | .75 | .35 |
| ❑ 24 Walt Poddubny | 1.00 | .45 |
| ❑ 25 Bill Root | .75 | .35 |
| ❑ 26 Borje Salming | 2.00 | .90 |
| ❑ 27 Marian Stastny | .75 | .35 |
| ❑ 28 Greg Terrion | .75 | .35 |
| ❑ 29 Steve Thomas | 2.50 | 1.10 |
| ❑ 30 Rick Vaive (Taking slapshot& visor on helmet) | 1.00 | .45 |
| ❑ 31 Rick Vaive (Light uniform) | 1.00 | .45 |
| ❑ 32 Blake Wesley | .75 | .35 |
| ❑ 33 Ken Wregget | 1.50 | .70 |
| ❑ 34 Team Photo (5 1/2~ by 8 1/2~) | 3.00 | 1.35 |
| ❑ 35 John Bower SPECIAL | .75 | .35 |

## 1986-87 Maple Leafs Postcards

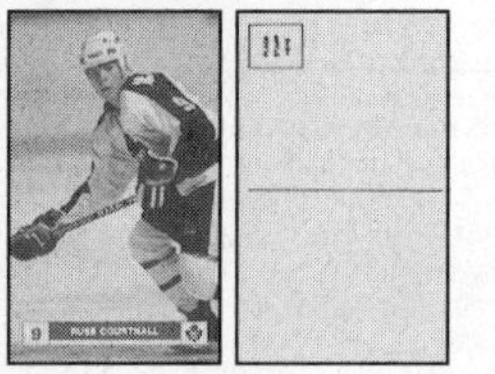

This 22-card set measures approximately 3 1/2" by 5 1/2". The fronts feature full-bleed color action player photos; the player's name, number and team logo are printed in a blue-and-white bar at the top or bottom. The backs are white and show a postcard design. The cards are unnumbered and checklisted below in alphabetical order.

| | MINT | NRMT |
|---|---|---|
| COMPLETE SET (22) | 25.00 | 11.00 |
| COMMON CARD (1-22) | .75 | .35 |
| ❑ 1 Mike Allison | .75 | .35 |
| ❑ 2 Harold Ballard PR | 1.50 | .70 |
| ❑ 3 Tim Bernhardt | 1.00 | .45 |
| ❑ 4 Wendel Clark | 5.00 | 2.20 |
| ❑ 5 Russ Courtnall | 2.00 | .90 |
| ❑ 6 Vincent Damphousse | 5.00 | 2.20 |
| ❑ 7 Jerome Dupont | .75 | .35 |
| ❑ 8 Tom Fergus | .75 | .35 |
| ❑ 9 Miroslav Frycer | .75 | .35 |
| ❑ 10 Todd Gill | .75 | .35 |
| ❑ 11 Al Iafrate | 3.00 | 1.35 |
| ❑ 12 Peter Ihnacak | .75 | .35 |
| ❑ 13 Jeff Jackson | .75 | .35 |
| ❑ 14 Terry Johnson | .75 | .35 |
| ❑ 15 Chris Kotsopoulos | .75 | .35 |
| ❑ 16 Gary Leeman | .75 | .35 |
| ❑ 17 Borje Salming | 2.00 | .90 |
| ❑ 18 Brad Smith | 1.00 | .45 |
| ❑ 19 Greg Terrion | .75 | .35 |
| ❑ 20 Steve Thomas | 1.50 | .70 |
| ❑ 21 Rick Vaive | 1.00 | .45 |
| ❑ 22 Ken Wregget | 2.50 | 1.10 |

## 1987-88 Maple Leafs PLAY

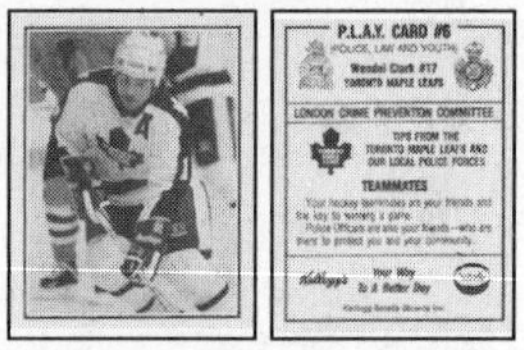


This set contains 30 P.L.A.Y. (Police, Law and Youth) cards, and it was sponsored by Kellogg Salada Canada Inc. in conjunction with the Toronto Maple Leafs and various police agencies. The cards could be collected from members of the London City Police and the Ontario Provincial Police, at a rate of three new cards per week. Three special "make-up weeks" were held to acquire any cards that were missed. The cards measure approximately 2 3/4" by 3 1/4".

| | MINT | NRMT |
|---|---|---|
| COMPLETE SET (30) | 20.00 | 9.00 |
| COMMON CARD (1-30) | .10 | .05 |
| ❑ 1 N.Laverne Shipley (Police Chief) | .10 | .05 |
| ❑ 2 Tom Gosnell (Mayor) | .10 | .05 |
| ❑ 3 Sponsor's Card Kellogg Salada Canada& Inc. | .10 | .05 |
| ❑ 4 Harold E. Ballard PR | .50 | .23 |
| ❑ 5 D. Almond (Police Superintendent) | .10 | .05 |
| ❑ 6 Wendel Clark 17 | 5.00 | 2.20 |
| ❑ 7 Tom Fergus 19 | .75 | .35 |
| ❑ 8 Borje Salming 21 | 1.50 | .70 |
| ❑ 9 Ed Olczyk 16 | .75 | .35 |
| ❑ 10 Gary Leeman 11 | .75 | .35 |
| ❑ 11 Rick Lanz 4 | .50 | .23 |
| ❑ 12 Allan Bester 30 | .75 | .35 |
| ❑ 13 Todd Gill 23 | .75 | .35 |
| ❑ 14 Al Secord 20 | .75 | .35 |
| ❑ 15 Miroslav Frycer 14 | .50 | .23 |
| ❑ 16 Chris Kotsopoulos 26 | .50 | .23 |
| ❑ 17 Vincent Damphousse 10 | 4.00 | 1.80 |
| ❑ 18 Mike Allison 8 | .50 | .23 |
| ❑ 19 Al Iafrate 33 | 2.00 | .90 |
| ❑ 20 Dan Daoust 24 | .50 | .23 |
| ❑ 21 Greg Terrion 7 | .50 | .23 |
| ❑ 22 Brad Smith 29 | .75 | .35 |
| ❑ 23 Mark Osborne 12 | .50 | .23 |
| ❑ 24 Peter Ihnacak 18 | .50 | .23 |
| ❑ 25 Dale Degray 3 | .50 | .23 |
| ❑ 26 Dave Semenko 27 | .75 | .35 |
| ❑ 27 Luke Richardson 2 | .75 | .35 |
| ❑ 28 John Brophy CO | .50 | .23 |
| ❑ 29 Ken Wregget 31 | 1.50 | .70 |
| ❑ 30 Russ Courtnall 9 | 1.00 | .45 |

## 1987-88 Maple Leafs Postcards

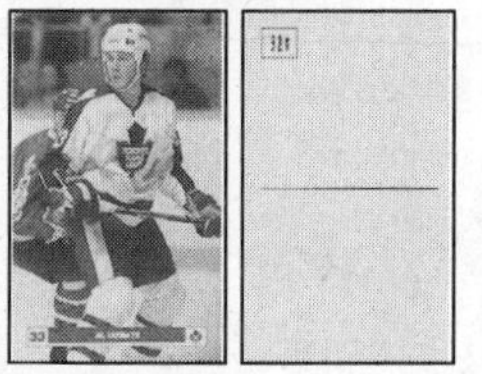

Measuring approximately 5" by 8", this set of oversized postcards features the Toronto Maple Leafs. The fronts have full-bleed color action player photos; the player's name, number, and team logo are printed in a blue-and-white bar at the bottom. The backs are white and show a postcard design. The cards are unnumbered and checklisted below in alphabetical order.

| | MINT | NRMT |
|---|---|---|
| COMPLETE SET (21) | 20.00 | 9.00 |
| COMMON CARD (1-21) | .50 | .23 |
| ❑ 1 Allan Bester | .75 | .35 |
| ❑ 2 Wendel Clark | 5.00 | 2.20 |
| ❑ 3 Russ Courtnall | 1.00 | .45 |
| ❑ 4 Vincent Damphousse | 4.00 | 1.80 |
| ❑ 5 Dan Daoust | .50 | .23 |
| ❑ 6 Tom Fergus | .75 | .35 |
| ❑ 7 Miroslav Frycer | .50 | .23 |
| ❑ 8 Todd Gill | .75 | .35 |
| ❑ 9 Al Iafrate | 2.00 | .90 |
| ❑ 10 Peter Ihnacak | .50 | .23 |
| ❑ 11 Chris Kotsopoulos | .50 | .23 |
| ❑ 12 Rick Lanz | .50 | .23 |
| ❑ 13 Gary Leeman | .75 | .35 |
| ❑ 14 Ed Olczyk | .75 | .35 |
| ❑ 15 Mark Osborne | .50 | .23 |
| ❑ 16 Luke Richardson | .75 | .35 |
| ❑ 17 Borje Salming | 1.50 | .70 |
| ❑ 18 Al Secord | .75 | .35 |
| ❑ 19 Dave Semenko | .75 | .35 |
| ❑ 20 Ken Wregget | 1.50 | .70 |
| ❑ 21 Team Photo | 2.00 | .90 |

## 1987-88 Maple Leafs Postcards Oversized

This set is similar in design and checklist to the regular size set, yet measures 6" x 10".

| | MINT | NRMT |
|---|---|---|
| COMPLETE SET (21) | 20.00 | 9.00 |
| COMMON CARD (1-21) | .50 | .23 |
| ❑ 1 Allan Bester | .75 | .35 |
| ❑ 2 Wendel Clark | 5.00 | 2.20 |
| ❑ 3 Russ Courtnall | 1.00 | .45 |
| ❑ 4 Vincent Damphousse | 4.00 | 1.80 |
| ❑ 5 Dan Daoust | .50 | .23 |
| ❑ 6 Tom Fergus | .75 | .35 |
| ❑ 7 Miroslav Frycer | .50 | .23 |
| ❑ 8 Todd Gill | .75 | .35 |
| ❑ 9 Al Iafrate | 2.00 | .90 |
| ❑ 10 Peter Ihnacak | .50 | .23 |
| ❑ 11 Chris Kotsopoulos | .50 | .23 |
| ❑ 12 Rick Lanz | .50 | .23 |
| ❑ 13 Gary Leeman | .75 | .35 |
| ❑ 14 Ed Olczyk | .75 | .35 |
| ❑ 15 Mark Osborne | .50 | .23 |
| ❑ 16 Luke Richardson | .75 | .35 |
| ❑ 17 Borje Salming | 1.50 | .70 |
| ❑ 18 Al Secord | .75 | .35 |
| ❑ 19 Dave Semenko | .75 | .35 |
| ❑ 20 Ken Wregget | 1.50 | .70 |
| ❑ 21 Team Photo | 2.00 | .90 |

## 1988-89 Maple Leafs PLAY

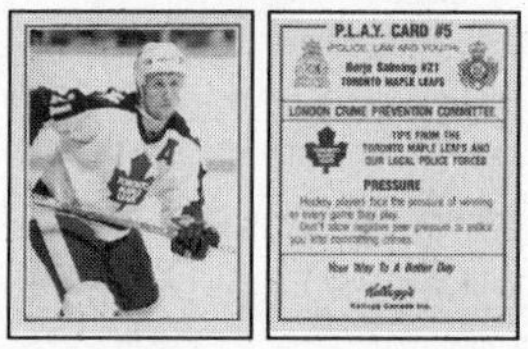


This set contains 30 P.L.A.Y. (Police, Law and Youth) cards, and it was sponsored by Kellogg's in conjunction with Toronto Maple Leafs and various police agencies. The cards could be collected from members of the London City Police and the Ontario Provincial Police, at a rate of three new cards per week. Three special "make-up weeks" were held to acquire any cards that were missed. After collecting the first 12 cards, they were to be brought to police stations in order to obtain the collector album, which measured approximately 7" by 10". The P.L.A.Y. cards measure 2 3/4" by 3 1/2" and the album has three slots per page in a horizontal format. Below each picture the album has the player's name, number, and a hockey tip paralleled by an anti-crime message.

| | MINT | NRMT |
|---|---|---|
| COMPLETE SET (30) | 12.00 | 5.50 |
| COMMON CARD (1-30) | .25 | .11 |
| ❑ 1 Rules and Tips | .25 | .11 |
| ❑ 2 Wendel Clark 17 | 2.00 | .90 |
| ❑ 3 Tom Fergus 19 | .50 | .23 |
| ❑ 4 D. Almond (Superintendent) | .25 | .11 |
| ❑ 5 Borje Salming 21 | 1.50 | .70 |
| ❑ 6 Ed Olczyk 16 | .50 | .23 |
| ❑ 7 Sponsor's Card Kellogg Canada& Inc. | .25 | .11 |
| ❑ 8 Gary Leeman 11 | .50 | .23 |
| ❑ 9 Rick Lanz 4 | .50 | .23 |
| ❑ 10 N.LaVerne Shipley (Chief of Police) | .25 | .11 |
| ❑ 11 Allan Bester 30 | .75 | .35 |
| ❑ 12 Todd Gill 23 | .50 | .23 |
| ❑ 13 Harold E. Ballard PR | 1.00 | .45 |
| ❑ 14 Al Secord 20 | .75 | .35 |
| ❑ 15 Daniel Marois 32 | .50 | .23 |
| ❑ 16 Chris Kotsopoulos 26 | .50 | .23 |
| ❑ 17 Vincent Damphousse 10 | 2.00 | .90 |
| ❑ 18 Craig Laughlin 14 | .50 | .23 |
| ❑ 19 Al Iafrate 33 | 1.00 | .45 |
| ❑ 20 Dan Daoust 24 | .50 | .23 |
| ❑ 21 Derek Laxdal 35 | .50 | .23 |
| ❑ 22 Darren Veitch 25 | .50 | .23 |
| ❑ 23 Mark Osborne 12 | .50 | .23 |
| ❑ 24 David Reid 34 | .75 | .35 |
| ❑ 25 Brad Marsh 3 | .75 | .35 |
| ❑ 26 Brian Curran 28 | .50 | .23 |
| ❑ 27 Sean McKenna 8 | .50 | .23 |
| ❑ 28 John Brophy CO | .50 | .23 |
| ❑ 29 Ken Wregget 31 | 1.00 | .45 |
| ❑ 30 Russ Courtnall 9 | 1.00 | .45 |

## 1991 Maple Leafs Panini Team Stickers

This 32-sticker set was issued in a plastic bag that contained two 16-sticker sheets (approximately 9" by 12") and a foldout poster, "Super Poster - Hockey 91", on which the stickers could be affixed. The players' names appear only on the poster, not on the stickers. Each sticker measures about 2 1/8" by 2 7/8" and features a color player action shot on its white-bordered front. The back of the white sticker sheet is lined off into 16 panels, each carrying the logos for Panini, the NHL, and the NHLPA, as well as the same number that appears on the front of the sticker. Every Canadian NHL team was featured in this promotion. Each team set was available by mail-order from Panini Canada Ltd. for 2.99 plus 50 cents for shipping and handling.

| | MINT | NRMT |
|---|---|---|
| COMPLETE SET (32) | 3.00 | 1.35 |
| COMMON STICKER (1-24) | .05 | .02 |
| COMMON STICKER (A-H) | .05 | .02 |
| ❑ 1 Drake Berehowsky | .05 | .02 |
| ❑ 2 Allan Bester | .10 | .05 |
| ❑ 3 Wendel Clark | .50 | .23 |
| ❑ 4 Brian Curran | .05 | .02 |
| ❑ 5 Vincent Damphousse | .50 | .23 |
| ❑ 6 Lou Franceschetti | .05 | .02 |
| ❑ 7 Todd Gill | .05 | .02 |
| ❑ 8 Dave Hannan | .05 | .02 |
| ❑ 9 Al Iafrate | .10 | .05 |
| ❑ 10 Peter Ing | .10 | .05 |
| ❑ 11 Tom Kurvers | .05 | .02 |
| ❑ 12 Gary Leeman | .05 | .02 |
| ❑ 13 Kevin Maguire | .05 | .02 |
| ❑ 14 Daniel Marois | .05 | .02 |
| ❑ 15 Brad Marsh | .10 | .05 |
| ❑ 16 John McIntyre | .05 | .02 |
| ❑ 17 Ed Olczyk | .05 | .02 |
| ❑ 18 Mark Osborne | .05 | .02 |
| ❑ 19 Scott Pearson | .05 | .02 |
| ❑ 20 Rob Ramage | .10 | .05 |
| ❑ 21 Jeff Reese | .10 | .05 |
| ❑ 22 Dave Reid | .10 | .05 |
| ❑ 23 Luke Richardson | .05 | .02 |
| ❑ 24 Maple Leafs in Action | .05 | .02 |
| ❑ A Team Logo Left Side | .05 | .02 |
| ❑ B Team Logo Right Side | .05 | .02 |
| ❑ C Maple Leafs in Action Upper Left Corner Al Iafrate Dave Reid | .05 | .02 |
| ❑ D Maple Leafs in Action Lower Left Corner Al Iafrate Dave Reid | .05 | .02 |
| ❑ E Maple Leafs in Action Upper Right Corner Al Iafrate Dave Reid | .05 | .02 |
| ❑ F Maple Leafs in Action Lower Right Corner Al Iafrate Dave Reid | .05 | .02 |
| ❑ G Al Iafrate Ken Wregget | .15 | .07 |
| ❑ H Gary Leeman John Kordic | .25 | .11 |

## 1991-92 Maple Leafs Police

| | MINT | NRMT |
|---|---|---|
| COMPLETE SET (30) | 7.00 | 3.10 |
| COMMON CARD (1-30) | .10 | .05 |
| ❑ 1 Glenn Anderson | .40 | .18 |
| ❑ 2 Craig Berube | .25 | .11 |
| ❑ 3 Brian Bradley | .25 | .11 |
| ❑ 4 Mike Bullard | .20 | .09 |
| ❑ 5 Rob Cimetta | .20 | .09 |
| ❑ 6 Wendel Clark | 1.00 | .45 |
| ❑ 7 Bryan Cousineau | .25 | .11 |
| ❑ 8 Lucien Deblois | .25 | .11 |
| ❑ 9 Dave Ellett | .20 | .09 |
| ❑ 10 Tom Fergus | .20 | .09 |
| ❑ 11 Cliff Fletcher | .20 | .09 |
| ❑ 12 Mike Foligno | .20 | .09 |
| ❑ 13 Grant Fuhr | .75 | .35 |
| ❑ 14 Todd Gill | .20 | .09 |
| ❑ 15 Alexander Godynyuk | .25 | .11 |
| ❑ 16 Bob Halkidis | .25 | .11 |
| ❑ 17 Dave Hannan | .20 | .09 |
| ❑ 19 Mike Krushelnyski | .30 | .14 |
| ❑ 20 Lanny the Police Dog | .10 | .05 |
| ❑ 21 Gary Leeman | .20 | .09 |
| ❑ 22 Claude Loiselle | .25 | .11 |
| ❑ 23 Daniel Marois | .20 | .09 |
| ❑ 24 Rob Pearson | .20 | .09 |
| ❑ 25 Michel Petit | .20 | .09 |
| ❑ 26 Jeff Reese | .30 | .14 |
| ❑ 27 Bob Rouse | .25 | .11 |
| ❑ 28 Darryl Shannon | .20 | .09 |
| ❑ 29 Tom Watt | .20 | .09 |
| ❑ 30 Peter Zezel | .30 | .14 |

## 1992-93 Maple Leafs Kodak

| | MINT | NRMT |
|---|---|---|
| COMPLETE SET (22) | 8.00 | 3.60 |
| COMMON CARD (1-22) | .25 | .11 |
| ❑ 1 Glenn Anderson | .40 | .18 |
| ❑ 2 Dave Andreychuk | .50 | .23 |
| ❑ 3 Dave Andreychuk-net | .50 | .23 |
| ❑ 4 Ken Baumgartner | .25 | .11 |
| ❑ 5 Drake Berehowsky | .25 | .11 |
| ❑ 6 Bill Berg | .25 | .11 |
| ❑ 7 Nikolai Borschevsky | .25 | .11 |
| ❑ 8 Wendel Clark | 1.00 | .45 |
| ❑ 9 John Cullen | .25 | .11 |
| ❑ 10 Mike Eastwood | .25 | .11 |
| ❑ 11 Dave Ellett | .25 | .11 |
| ❑ 12 Doug Gilmour | 1.00 | .45 |
| ❑ 13 Sylvain Lefebvre | .25 | .11 |
| ❑ 14 Jamie Macoun | .25 | .11 |
| ❑ 15 Kent Manderville | .25 | .11 |
| ❑ 16 Dave McIlwain | .25 | .11 |
| ❑ 17 Dmitri Mironov | .25 | .11 |
| ❑ 18 Mark Osborne | .25 | .11 |
| ❑ 19 Rob Pearson | .25 | .11 |
| ❑ 20 Felix Potvin | 1.50 | .70 |
| ❑ 21 Bob Rouse | .25 | .11 |
| ❑ 22 Peter Zezel | .40 | .18 |

## 1993-94 Maple Leafs Score Black's

This 24-card, standard-size Toronto Maple Leafs team set was produced by Score and sponsored by Black's Photography. The cards were distributed free in four-card packs, when a customer brought in film for developing, or with a second order of prints, or when purchasing two rolls of Black's P.I. film. The fronts feature a pop-up photo cut-out. The pop-up is accomplished by gently bending the card to pop up the player's head and then pulling a tab at the top to stand the player up. The fronts have an white outer border with a wider purple inner border overlaid with a thin red and purple line. The words "Collector's Edition" are printed in white at the top of the picture. The logo for Black's Photography is printed on the upper left vertical side. Player identification appears under the action photo. The purple backs have a white border with a second player portrait and biography. The Black's Photography logo is printed in the upper left corner. The cards are numbered on the front. There was also an album available for this set; it is not included in the complete set price below.

| | MINT | NRMT |
|---|---|---|
| COMPLETE SET (24) | 30.00 | 13.50 |
| COMMON CARD (1-24) | .50 | .23 |
| ❑ 1 Wendel Clark | 3.50 | 1.55 |
| ❑ 2 Doug Gilmour | 5.00 | 2.20 |
| ❑ 3 Glenn Anderson | 1.50 | .70 |
| ❑ 4 Peter Zezel | .75 | .35 |
| ❑ 5 Bob Rouse | .50 | .23 |
| ❑ 6 Rob Pearson | .50 | .23 |
| ❑ 7 Mark Osborne | .50 | .23 |
| ❑ 8 Dmitri Mironov | 1.00 | .45 |
| ❑ 9 Dave McLlwain | .50 | .23 |
| ❑ 10 Kent Manderville | .50 | .23 |
| ❑ 11 Jamie Macoun | .50 | .23 |
| ❑ 12 Sylvain Lefebvre | .75 | .35 |
| ❑ 13 Dave Andreychuk | 2.00 | .90 |
| ❑ 14 Drake Berehowsky | .50 | .23 |
| ❑ 15 Bill Berg | .50 | .23 |
| ❑ 16 John Cullen | .75 | .35 |
| ❑ 17 Ken Baumgartner | .75 | .35 |
| ❑ 18 Nikolai Borschevsky | .50 | .23 |
| ❑ 19 Mike Eastwood | .50 | .23 |
| ❑ 20 Dave Ellett | .75 | .35 |
| ❑ 21 Mike Foligno | .75 | .35 |
| ❑ 22 Todd Gill | .50 | .23 |
| ❑ 23 Mike Krushelnyski | .50 | .23 |
| ❑ 24 Felix Potvin | 7.50 | 3.40 |
| ❑ xx Album | 5.00 | 2.20 |

## 1994-95 Maple Leafs Gangsters

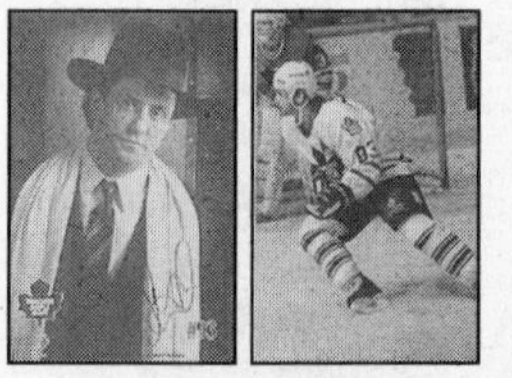

This 17-card set measures approximately 4 3/4" by 7". The fronts have borderless color action player photos. The backs carry black-and-white player portraits with a 1920's style gangster motif.

| | MINT | NRMT |
|---|---|---|
| COMPLETE SET (17) | 12.00 | 5.50 |
| COMMON CARD (1-17) | .25 | .11 |

❑ 1 Dave Andreychuk 1.00 .45
❑ 2 Ken Baumgartner .50 .23
❑ 3 Bill Berg .50 .23
❑ 4 Nikolai Borschevsky .50 .23
❑ 5 Mike Eastwood .50 .23
❑ 6 Dave Ellett .75 .35
❑ 7 Mike Gartner 1.00 .45
❑ 8 Todd Gill .75 .35
❑ 9 Doug Gilmour 2.00 .90
❑ 10 Alexei Kudashov .50 .23
❑ 11 Jamie Macoun .50 .23
❑ 12 Kent Manderville .50 .23
❑ 13 Dmitri Mironov .50 .23
❑ 14 Mark Osborne .50 .23
❑ 15 Felix Potvin 2.00 .90
❑ 16 Damian Rhodes 1.00 .45
❑ 17 Title Card .25 .11

## 1994-95 Maple Leafs Kodak

This set measures approximately 4" x 6" and features full color action photos on the front. Cards feature blank backs and are checklisted below in alphabetical order.

| | MINT | NRMT |
|---|---|---|
| COMPLETE SET (30) | 15.00 | 6.75 |
| COMMON CARD (1-30) | .25 | .11 |

❑ 1 Dave Andreychuk 1.00 .45
❑ 2 Ken Baumgartner .50 .23
❑ 3 Drake Berehowsky .50 .23
❑ 4 Bill Berg .50 .23
❑ 5 Nikolai Borschevsky .50 .23
❑ 6 Pat Burns .25 .11
❑ 7 Garth Butcher .50 .23
❑ 8 Mike Craig .50 .23
❑ 9 Paul Dipietro .25 .11
❑ 10 Tie Domi .75 .35
❑ 11 Mike Gartner 1.00 .45
❑ 12 Todd Gill .75 .35
❑ 13 Doug Gilmour 2.00 .90
❑ 14 David Harlock .75 .35
❑ 15 Benoit Hogue .50 .23
❑ 16 Grant Jennings .25 .11
❑ 17 Kenny Jonsson .75 .35
❑ 18 Jamie Macoun .50 .23
❑ 19 Terry Martin .25 .11
❑ 20 Dmitri Mironov .50 .23
❑ 21 Felix Potvin 3.00 1.35
❑ 22 Damian Rhodes 1.00 .45
❑ 23 Mike Ridley .50 .23
❑ 24 Warren Rychel .25 .11
❑ 25 Mats Sundin 2.00 .90
❑ 26 Rich Sutter .25 .11
❑ 27 Dixon Ward .50 .23
❑ 28 Todd Warriner .50 .23
❑ 29 Randy Wood .25 .11
❑ 30 Terry Yake .25 .11

## 1994-95 Maple Leafs Pin-up Posters

Cards measure 11 1/2" x 15" and were issued in Saturday and Sunday Toronto Sun newspapers. 1995 MAPLE LEAFS appears in red at the bottom of the pin-up.

| | MINT | NRMT |
|---|---|---|
| COMPLETE SET (30) | 15.00 | 6.75 |
| COMMON CARD (1-30) | .25 | .11 |

❑ 1 Mats Sundin 2.00 .90
❑ 2 Doug Gilmour 2.00 .90
❑ 3 Dave Ellett .50 .23
❑ 4 Mike Eastland .50 .23
❑ 5 Garth Butcher .50 .23
❑ 6 Nikolai Borschevsky .50 .23
❑ 7 Kenny Jonsson .75 .35
❑ 8 Todd Gill .75 .35
❑ 9 Bill Berg .50 .23
❑ 10 Jamie Macoun .50 .23
❑ 11 Damian Rhodes 1.00 .45
❑ 12 Mike Ridley .50 .23
❑ 13 Terry Yake .25 .11
❑ 14 Felix Potvin 3.00 1.35
❑ 15 Warren Rychel .25 .11
❑ 16 Randy Wood .25 .11
❑ 17 Kent Manderville .50 .23
❑ 18 Dave Andreychuk 1.00 .45
❑ 19 Ken Baumgartner .50 .23
❑ 20 Dmitri Mironov .50 .23
❑ 21 Mike Craig .50 .23
❑ 21A Mike Gartner 1.00 .45
❑ 23 Matt Martin .50 .23
❑ 24 Tie Domi .75 .35
❑ 25 Paul DiPietro .25 .11
❑ 26 Rich Sutter .25 .11
❑ 27 Grant Jennings .25 .11
❑ 28 Benoit Hogue .50 .23
❑ 29 Darby Hendrickson .50 .23
❑ 30 Pat Burns CL .25 .11

## 1994-95 Maple Leafs Postcards

Sponsored by Coca-Cola, this four-card set measures approximately 5 3/4" by 4". The horizontal and vertical fronts feature borderless color action player photos. The words "1995 Collector Postcard" and Coca-Cola's logo appear on the bottom. The backs have a postcard format and carry a short

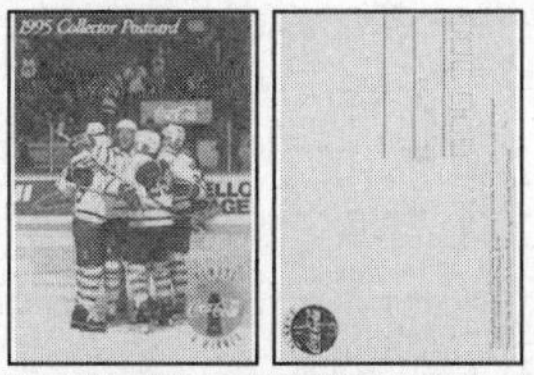

description of the scene depicted on the front. The cards were distributed to fans at Maple Leaf Gardens before a game in March, 1995, and came attached to a series of coupons for Beckers convenience stores. The cards are unnumbered and checklisted below in alphabetical order.

| | MINT | NRMT |
|---|---|---|
| COMPLETE SET (4) | 8.00 | 3.60 |
| COMMON CARD (1-4) | 1.50 | .70 |

❑ 1 Dave Andreychuk 2.50 1.10
Todd Gill
Doug Gilmour
Jamie Macoun
Mats Sundin
❑ 2 Garth Butcher 3.00 1.35
Doug Gilmour
Felix Potvin
Mats Sundin
❑ 3 Dmitri Mironov 1.50 .70
Mike Ridley
Mats Sundin
❑ 4 Felix Potvin 2.50 1.10

## 1996-97 Maple Leafs Postcards

| | MINT | NRMT |
|---|---|---|
| COMPLETE SET (4) | 6.00 | 2.70 |
| COMMON CARD (1-4) | 1.00 | .45 |

❑ 1 Mats Sundin 2.00 .90
Wendel Clark
Doug Gilmour
❑ 2 Felix Potvin 3.00 1.35
Lemieux
❑ 3 Wendel Clark 2.00 .90
❑ 4 Tie Domi 1.00 .45
Berezin

## 1998 Maple Leaf Gardens Postcards

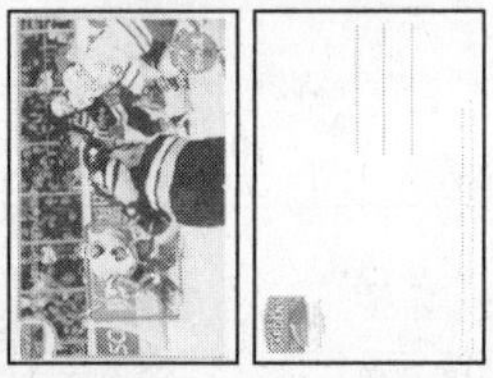

A limited edition of postcards, only 10,000 made, produced and distributed by Beckers to commemorate the 65th Anniversary of MLG.

| | MINT | NRMT |
|---|---|---|
| COMPLETE SET | 10.00 | 4.50 |
| COMMON CARD | 2.50 | 1.10 |

❑ 1 Mats Sundin 2.50 1.10
❑ 2 Felix Potvin 2.50 1.10
❑ 3 Wendel Clark 2.50 1.10
❑ 4 Tie Domi/Sergei Berezin 2.50 1.10

## 1974-75 Mariners San Diego WHA

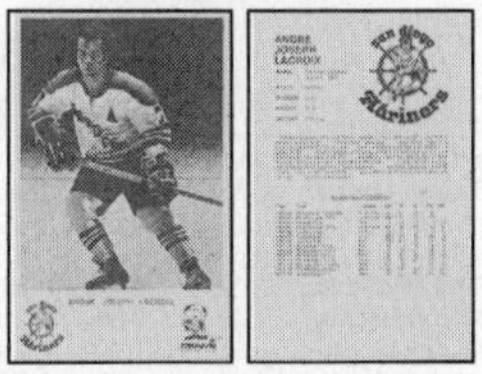

Sponsored by Dean's Photo Service Inc., this set of seven photos measures approximately 5 3/8" by 8 1/2" and features black-and-white action pictures against a white background on thin paper stock. The player's name appears in the white margin below the photo along with the team and sponsor logos. The backs feature biographical information, career highlights, and statistics. The cards came in a light blue paper "picture pack" with the team and sponsor logos and game dates suggested for acquiring autographs. The cards are unnumbered and checklisted below in alphabetical order. This set may be incomplete; additions to the checklist would be welcome.

| | NRMT-MT | EXC |
|---|---|---|
| COMPLETE SET (7) | 40.00 | 18.00 |
| COMMON CARD (1-7) | 5.00 | 2.20 |

❑ 1 Andre Lacroix 10.00 4.50
❑ 2 Mike Laughton 5.00 2.20
❑ 3 Brian Morenz 5.00 2.20
❑ 4 Kevin Morrison 5.00 2.20
❑ 5 Gene Peacosh 5.00 2.20
❑ 6 Ron Plumb 8.00 3.60
❑ 7 Craig Reichmuth 5.00 2.20

## 1971 Mattel Mini-Records

This eight-disc set was designed to be played on a special Mattel mini-record player, which is not included in the complete set price. Measuring roughly 2 1/2" in diameter, the discs were packaged in sets of four. In contrast to basketball and football, hockey only double-sided discs are unknown. The discs are unnumbered and checklisted below in alphabetical order.

| | NRMT-MT | EXC |
|---|---|---|
| COMPLETE SET (8) | 150.00 | 70.00 |
| COMMON CARD (1-8) | 10.00 | 4.50 |

❑ 1 Yvan Cournoyer 10.00 4.50
❑ 2 Tony Esposito 12.00 5.50
❑ 3 Phil Esposito 15.00 6.75
❑ 4 Ed Giacomin 10.00 4.50
❑ 5 Gordie Howe 40.00 18.00
❑ 6 Frank Mahovlich 12.00 5.50
❑ 7 Bobby Orr 50.00 22.00
❑ 8 Jacques Plante 25.00 11.00
❑ NNO Record Player 100.00 45.00

## 1982-83 McDonald's Stickers

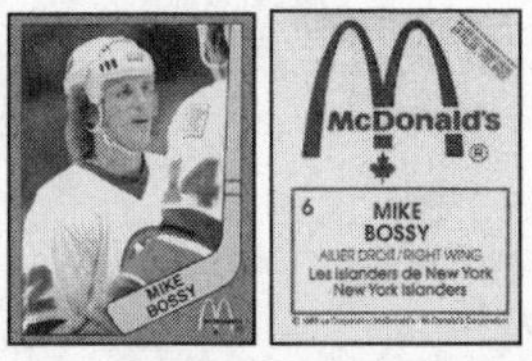

This set consists of 36 full-color stickers measuring 2" by 2 1/2". A 12-page album was also available. The stickers were only issued in the province of Quebec. The stickers are numbered on the front and on the back. The sticker numbering is by position, i.e., goalies (1-5), right wings (6-10), left wings (11-15), all-stars (16-21), centers (22-26), and defensemen (27-36). The all-star stickers are gold foils; the other stickers all have a distinctive red border and show the McDonald's logo in the lower right corner.

| | MINT | NRMT |
|---|---|---|
| COMPLETE SET (36) | 35.00 | 16.00 |
| COMMON CARD (1-36) | .40 | .18 |

❑ 1 Dan Bouchard .50 .23
❑ 2 Richard Brodeur .60 .25
❑ 3 Gilles Meloche .50 .23
❑ 4 Billy Smith 1.00 .45
❑ 5 Rick Wamsley .50 .23
❑ 6 Mike Bossy 2.00 .90
❑ 7 Dino Ciccarelli .75 .35
❑ 8 Guy Lafleur 2.00 .90
❑ 9 Rick Middleton .75 .35
❑ 10 Marian Stastny .40 .18
❑ 11 Bill Barber .60 .25
❑ 12 Bob Gainey 1.00 .45
❑ 13 Clark Gillies .50 .23
❑ 14 Michel Goulet .75 .35
❑ 15 Mark Messier 4.00 1.80
❑ 16 Billy Smith AS .60 .25
❑ 17 Larry Robinson AS .60 .25
❑ 18 Denis Potvin AS .60 .25
❑ 19 Michel Goulet AS .60 .25
❑ 20 Wayne Gretzky AS 8.00 3.60
❑ 21 Mike Bossy AS .75 .35
❑ 22 Wayne Gretzky 10.00 4.50
❑ 23 Denis Savard .75 .35
❑ 24 Peter Stastny .75 .35
❑ 25 Bryan Trottier 1.00 .45
❑ 26 Doug Wickenheiser .40 .18
❑ 27 Barry Beck .40 .18
❑ 28 Ray Bourque 2.50 1.10
❑ 29 Brian Engblom .40 .18
❑ 30 Craig Hartsburg .50 .23
❑ 31 Mark Howe .60 .25
❑ 32 Rod Langway .50 .23
❑ 33 Denis Potvin .75 .35
❑ 34 Larry Robinson 1.00 .45
❑ 35 Normand Rochefort .40 .18
❑ 36 Doug Wilson .60 .25
❑ NNO Album 5.00 2.20

## 1991-92 McDonald's Upper Deck

This 31-card standard-size set, which features 25 regular cards and six hologram cards and

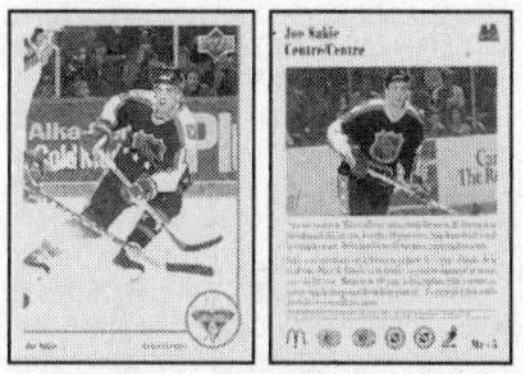

was produced by Upper Deck for McDonald's Restaurants across Canada to honor NHL All-Stars. For 29 cents plus tax, with the purchase of any soft drink, customers could receive a pack with three regular cards and one hologram sticker card. The fronts feature a mix of posed and action pictures enclosed in red and white borders. The Upper Deck logo appears in the upper right corner while the McDonald's All-Stars logo appears in a red circle in the lower right corner. The player's name and position appear in the bottom white border. The backs carry a second color photo and career summary is presented in English and French. Upper Deck's unique anti-counterfeiting device appears in the upper right corner in the shape of McDonald's golden arches. Six players wearing their 1991 All-Star uniforms on the regular cards appear on the hologram cards in their regular team uniforms. The holograms have blank backs and are numbered on the front. The card numbers show a "Mc" prefix.

| | MINT | NRMT |
|---|---|---|
| COMPLETE SET (31) | 15.00 | 6.75 |
| COMMON CARD (1-25) | .25 | .11 |
| COMMON HOLOGRAM (H1-H6) | .75 | .35 |

❑ 1 Cam Neely .50 .23
❑ 2 Rick Tocchet .50 .23
❑ 3 Kevin Stevens .25 .11
❑ 4 Mark Recchi .50 .23
❑ 5 Joe Sakic 1.25 .55
❑ 6 Pat LaFontaine .50 .23
❑ 7 Darren Turcotte .25 .11
❑ 8 Patrick Roy 2.00 .90
❑ 9 Andy Moog .50 .23
❑ 10 Ray Bourque .60 .25
❑ 11 Paul Coffey .60 .25
❑ 12 Brian Leetch .60 .25
❑ 13 Brett Hull .75 .35
❑ 14 Luc Robitaille .50 .23
❑ 15 Steve Larmer .25 .11
❑ 16 Vincent Damphousse .50 .23
❑ 17 Wayne Gretzky 3.00 1.35
❑ 18 Theoren Fleury .60 .25
❑ 19 Steve Yzerman 1.50 .70
❑ 20 Mike Vernon .50 .23
❑ 21 Bill Ranford .50 .23
❑ 22 Chris Chelios .60 .25
❑ 23 Al MacInnis .25 .11
❑ 24 Scott Stevens .25 .11
❑ 25 Checklist .25 .11
❑ H1 Wayne Gretzky 4.00 1.80
❑ H2 Chris Chelios .60 .25
❑ H3 Ray Bourque .60 .25
❑ H4 Brett Hull .75 .35
❑ H5 Cam Neely .60 .25
❑ H6 Patrick Roy 3.00 1.35

## 1992-93 McDonald's Iron-Ons

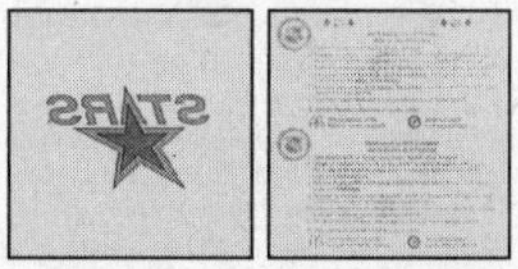

Printed in Canada, these 26 iron-on transfers measure approximately 3" by 3". They feature the NHL team logos and commemorate the 44th All-Star Game in Montreal. The backs carry ironing instructions. These iron-ons were a test issue to be distributed along with the McDonald's All-Star cards, and surfaced just in parts of Quebec. The iron-ons are unnumbered and checklisted below in alphabetical order.

| | MINT | NRMT |
|---|---|---|
| COMPLETE SET (26) | 40.00 | 18.00 |
| COMMON CARD (1-26) | 2.00 | .90 |

❑ 1 Boston Bruins 2.00 .90
❑ 2 Buffalo Sabres 2.00 .90
❑ 3 Calgary Flames 2.00 .90
❑ 4 Chicago Blackhawks 2.00 .90
❑ 5 Minnesota North Stars 2.00 .90
❑ 6 Detroit Red Wings 2.00 .90
❑ 7 Edmonton Oilers 2.00 .90
❑ 8 Hartford Whalers 2.00 .90
❑ 9 Los Angeles Kings 2.00 .90
❑ 10 Montreal Canadiens 2.00 .90
❑ 11 New Jersey Devils 2.00 .90
❑ 12 New York Islanders 2.00 .90
❑ 13 New York Rangers 2.00 .90
❑ 14 Ottawa Senators 2.00 .90
❑ 15 Philadelphia Flyers 2.00 .90
❑ 16 Pittsburgh Penguins 2.00 .90
❑ 17 Quebec Nordiques 2.00 .90
❑ 18 St. Louis Blues 2.00 .90
❑ 19 San Jose Sharks 2.00 .90
❑ 20 Tampa Bay Lightning 2.00 .90
❑ 21 Toronto Maple Leafs 2.00 .90
❑ 22 Vancouver Canucks 2.00 .90
❑ 23 Washington Capitals 2.00 .90
❑ 24 Winnipeg Jets 2.00 .90
❑ 25 All-Stars Logo 2.00 .90
❑ 26 44th NHL All-Star Game Logo 5.00 2.20

## 1992-93 McDonald's Upper Deck

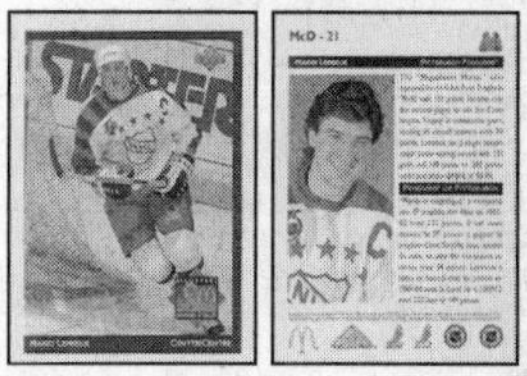

Produced by Upper Deck for McDonald's of Canada, this set consists of 27 regular cards and six hologram cards in honor of 33 of hockey's most exciting players. Four-card packs were available for 39 cents plus tax with a purchase at participating McDonald's restaurants. All cards measure the standard size. The regular cards feature color action photos of the players in their 1992 All-Star uniforms. A black border, which edges the photo on three sides, contains the player's name and position. Featuring six NHL post-season First Team All-Stars, the six hologram cards were randomly inserted in a limited number of card packs. The full-bleed cards feature a small, cut-out action player photos against a facial shot. The player's name appears in a stripe across the bottom. The backs of the regular cards and holograms are identical, each showing a narrow, vertical player photo against a white background with a bilingual (English and French) player profile to the right. The regular cards are arranged according to conference: Campbell (1-14) and Wales (15-27). The cards are numbered on the back with an "McD" prefix.

| | MINT | NRMT |
|---|---|---|
| COMPLETE SET (34) | 20.00 | 9.00 |
| COMMON CARD (1-27) | .25 | .11 |
| COMMON HOLOGRAM (H1-H6) | .50 | .23 |

❑ 1 Ed Belfour 1.00 .45
❑ 2 Brian Bellows .25 .11
❑ 3 Chris Chelios .75 .35
❑ 4 Vincent Damphousse .35 .16
❑ 5 Dave Ellett .25 .11
❑ 6 Sergei Fedorov 1.50 .70
❑ 7 Theoren Fleury .75 .35
❑ 8 Phil Housley .25 .11
❑ 9 Trevor Linden .35 .16
❑ 10 Al MacInnis .35 .16
❑ 11 Adam Oates .50 .23
❑ 12 Luc Robitaille .50 .23
❑ 13 Jeremy Roenick 1.00 .45
❑ 14 Steve Yzerman 2.00 .90
❑ 15 Don Beaupre .35 .16
❑ 16 Rod Brind'Amour .35 .16
❑ 17 Paul Coffey .75 .35
❑ 18 John Cullen .25 .11
❑ 19 Kevin Hatcher .25 .11
❑ 20 Jaromir Jagr 2.00 .90
❑ 21 Mario Lemieux 2.50 1.10
❑ 22 Alexander Mogilny .75 .35
❑ 23 Kirk Muller .25 .11
❑ 24 Owen Nolan .35 .16
❑ 25 Mike Richter .75 .35
❑ 26 Joe Sakic 1.50 .70
❑ 27 Scott Stevens .35 .16
❑ H1 Mark Messier HOLO 1.25 .55
❑ H2 Brett Hull HOLO 1.50 .70
❑ H3 Kevin Stevens HOLO .50 .23
❑ H4 Brian Leetch HOLO .75 .35
❑ H5 Ray Bourque HOLO 1.00 .45
❑ H6 Patrick Roy HOLO 4.00 1.80
❑ NNO Checklist UER SP 2.00 .90
(Bourque listed as 4 and Leetch as 5)

## 1993-94 McDonald's Upper Deck

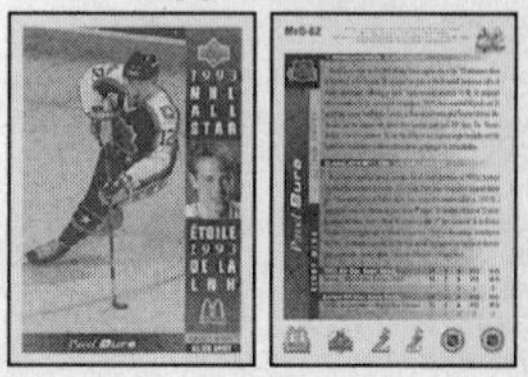

Produced by Upper Deck for McDonald's of

Canada, this set is similar in concept to the previous year's Upper Deck McDonald's set. The 27 regular cards and six hologram-type cards honor 33 of the NHL's most exciting players. The holograms were random inserts in the four-card packs. An oversized (4" by 5 1/2") Patrick Roy card (23) was also available via a redemption card randomly inserted in packs. The redemption card could be redeemed at McDonald's or throught the mail. A number of redemption cards for other prizes, such as trips to games, autographed pucks and sticks, etc, also were included. These cards obviously are extremely difficult to locate, but also experience limited demand from collectors at this point. Most would be valued in the $10-$20 range. Also, Upper Deck has confirmed that the unnumbered checklist card was short-printed. All cards measure the standard size. The regular cards feature on their fronts white-bordered color action shots of players in their 1993 All-Star uniforms. The hologram cards are horizontal on their fronts and backs. The front of each card features a hologram-type action photo of a first team All-Star on the right and a posed closeup on the left. The player's name and position appear within blue, black, and gray stripes near the bottom. The back carries the player's All-Star highlights in both English and French. Variations of the cards with incorrect backs are known to exist. The regular cards are arranged according to conference: Campbell (1-13) and Wales (14-27). The regular cards are numbered on the back with an "McD" prefix; the hologram-types are numbered with an "McH" prefix.

| | MINT | NRMT |
|---|---|---|
| COMPLETE SET (34) | 15.00 | 6.75 |
| COMMON CARD (1-27) | .25 | .11 |
| COMMON HOLOGRAM (H1-H6) | .75 | .35 |

| | MINT | NRMT |
|---|---|---|
| ❑ 1 Brian Bradley | .25 | .11 |
| ❑ 2 Pavel Bure | 1.25 | .55 |
| ❑ 3 Jon Casey | .30 | .14 |
| ❑ 4 Paul Coffey | .60 | .25 |
| ❑ 5 Doug Gilmour | .60 | .25 |
| ❑ 6 Phil Housley | .25 | .11 |
| ❑ 7 Brett Hull | 1.00 | .45 |
| ❑ 8 Jari Kurri | .30 | .14 |
| ❑ 9 Dave Manson | .25 | .11 |
| ❑ 10 Mike Modano | 1.00 | .45 |
| ❑ 11 Gary Roberts | .25 | .11 |
| ❑ 12 Jeremy Roenick | .60 | .25 |
| ❑ 13 Steve Yzerman | 1.50 | .70 |
| ❑ 14 Steve Duchesne | .25 | .11 |
| ❑ 15 Mike Gartner | .35 | .16 |
| ❑ 16 Al Iafrate | .25 | .11 |
| ❑ 17 Jaromir Jagr | 1.50 | .70 |
| ❑ 18 Pat LaFontaine | .35 | .16 |
| ❑ 19 Alexander Mogilny | .50 | .23 |
| ❑ 20A Kirk Muller (Full stick blade showing) | .25 | .11 |
| ❑ 20B Kirk Muller (Stick blade partly cut off by cropping) | .25 | .11 |
| ❑ 21 Adam Oates | .35 | .16 |
| ❑ 22 Mark Recchi | .35 | .16 |
| ❑ 23 Patrick Roy | 2.50 | 1.10 |
| ❑ 23L Patrick Roy Large (4~ by 5 1/2~; only available from redemption card) | 10.00 | 4.50 |
| ❑ 24 Joe Sakic | 1.25 | .55 |
| ❑ 25 Kevin Stevens | .30 | .14 |
| ❑ 26 Scott Stevens | .25 | .11 |
| ❑ 27 Pierre Turgeon | .35 | .16 |
| ❑ H1 Mario Lemieux | 3.00 | 1.35 |
| ❑ H2 Teemu Selanne | 2.00 | .90 |
| ❑ H3 Luc Robitaille | .75 | .35 |
| ❑ H4 Ray Bourque | 1.00 | .45 |
| ❑ H5 Chris Chelios | 1.00 | .45 |
| ❑ H6 Ed Belfour | 1.00 | .45 |
| ❑ NNO Checklist SP | 2.50 | 1.10 |

## 1994-95 McDonald's Upper Deck

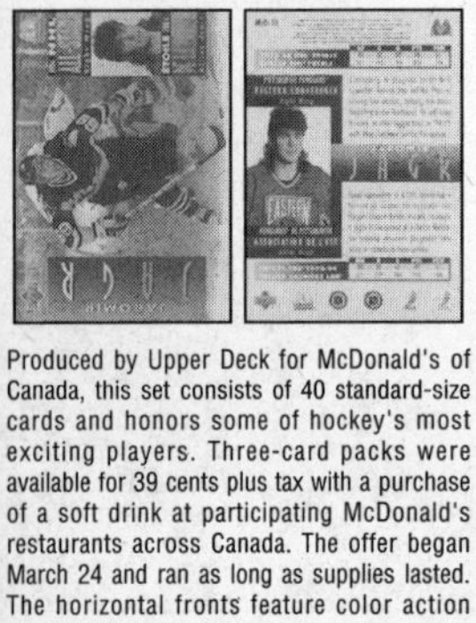

Produced by Upper Deck for McDonald's of Canada, this set consists of 40 standard-size cards and honors some of hockey's most exciting players. Three-card packs were available for 39 cents plus tax with a purchase of a soft drink at participating McDonald's restaurants across Canada. The offer began March 24 and ran as long as supplies lasted. The horizontal fronts feature color action player cutouts on holographic backgrounds. The player's name appears in a team color-coded bar alongside the left, while a small color player portrait in his 1994 All-Star uniform is on the right. The bilingual backs carry another small color player portrait, with profile and statistics. The cards are arranged as follows: 1994 NHL All-Stars Eastern Conference (1-10), 1994 NHL All-Stars Western Conference (11-20), Hat Tricks Eastern Conference (21-25), Hat Tricks Western Conference (26-30), Future NHL All-Stars Eastern Conference (31-35), and Future NHL All-Stars Western Conference (36-39). An unnumbered checklist card featuring All-Star Game MVP Mike Richter completes the set. This card is thought by some to be shortprinted. Since we cannot confirm this, we have not applied this designation.

| | MINT | NRMT |
|---|---|---|
| COMPLETE SET (40) | 25.00 | 11.00 |
| COMMON CARD (McD1-McD39) | .25 | .11 |

| | MINT | NRMT |
|---|---|---|
| ❑ McD1 Joe Sakic | 1.25 | .55 |
| ❑ McD2 Adam Graves | .25 | .11 |
| ❑ McD3 Alexei Yashin | .60 | .25 |
| ❑ McD4 Patrick Roy | 4.00 | 1.80 |
| ❑ McD5 Ray Bourque | .60 | .25 |
| ❑ McD6 Brian Leetch | .60 | .25 |
| ❑ McD7 Scott Stevens | .25 | .11 |
| ❑ McD8 Alexander Mogilny | .50 | .23 |
| ❑ McD9 Eric Lindros | 3.00 | 1.35 |
| ❑ McD10 Jaromir Jagr | 3.00 | 1.35 |
| ❑ McD11 Sandis Ozonlish | .25 | .11 |
| ❑ McD12 Sergei Fedorov | 1.25 | .55 |
| ❑ McD13 Brett Hull | 1.00 | .45 |
| ❑ McD14 Felix Potvin | .60 | .25 |
| ❑ McD15 Al MacInnis | .25 | .11 |
| ❑ McD16 Chris Chelios | .60 | .25 |
| ❑ McD17 Rob Blake | .25 | .11 |
| ❑ McD18 Dave Andreychuk | .25 | .11 |
| ❑ McD19 Paul Coffey | .60 | .25 |
| ❑ McD20 Jeremy Roenick | .60 | .25 |
| ❑ McD21 Joe Nieuwendyk | .40 | .18 |
| ❑ McD22 Cam Neely | .40 | .18 |
| ❑ McD23 Pavel Bure | 1.25 | .55 |
| ❑ McD24 Wendel Clark | .35 | .16 |
| ❑ McD25 Teemu Selanne | 1.25 | .55 |
| ❑ McD26 Pierre Turgeon | .40 | .18 |
| ❑ McD27 Alexei Zhamnov | .25 | .11 |
| ❑ McD28 Doug Gilmour | .60 | .25 |
| ❑ McD29 Vincent Damphousse | .25 | .11 |
| ❑ McD30 Brendan Shanahan | 1.25 | .55 |
| ❑ McD31 Peter Forsberg | 3.00 | 1.35 |
| ❑ McD32 Paul Kariya | 4.00 | 1.80 |
| ❑ McD33 Viktor Kozlov | .25 | .11 |
| ❑ McD34 Brett Lindros | .25 | .11 |
| ❑ McD35 Martin Brodeur | 1.50 | .70 |
| ❑ McD36 Alexandre Daigle | .25 | .11 |
| ❑ McD37 Jason Arnott | .50 | .23 |
| ❑ McD38 Alexei Kovalev | .25 | .11 |
| ❑ McD39 Mikael Renberg | .50 | .23 |
| ❑ NNO Mike Richter CL | .60 | .25 |

## 1995-96 McDonald's Pinnacle

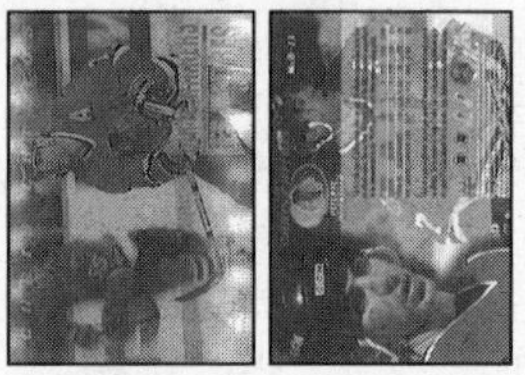

This 41-card set features borderless color player cut-out photos on a 3-D, lenticular background. The backs carry information about the player in both English and French. The cards are divided into three categories as follows: Game Winners (McD-1-McD-24), Game Savers (McD-25-McD-30), and Future Game Winners (McD-31-McD-40). They were available in 3-card packs for 79 cents (with purchase) at participating McDonald's restaurants in Canada.

| | MINT | NRMT |
|---|---|---|
| COMPLETE SET (41) | 25.00 | 11.00 |
| COMMON CARD (MCD1-MCD40) | .25 | .11 |

| | MINT | NRMT |
|---|---|---|
| ❑ MCD-1 Jaromir Jagr | 2.00 | .90 |
| ❑ MCD-2 Eric Lindros | 2.00 | .90 |
| ❑ MCD-3 Alexei Zhamnov | .35 | .16 |
| ❑ MCD-4 Paul Coffey | .60 | .25 |
| ❑ MCD-5 Mark Messier | .75 | .35 |
| ❑ MCD-6 Brett Hull | .75 | .35 |
| ❑ MCD-7 Peter Forsberg | 2.00 | .90 |
| ❑ MCD-8 Pavel Bure | 1.50 | .70 |
| ❑ MCD-9 Doug Gilmour | .60 | .25 |
| ❑ MCD-10 Owen Nolan | .25 | .11 |
| ❑ MCD-11 Paul Kariya | 2.50 | 1.10 |
| ❑ MCD-12 Joe Nieuwendyk | .35 | .16 |
| ❑ MCD-13 Pierre Turgeon | .35 | .16 |
| ❑ MCD-14 Jason Arnott | .25 | .11 |
| ❑ MCD-15 Mario Lemieux | 3.00 | 1.35 |
| ❑ MCD-16 Jeremy Roenick | .60 | .25 |
| ❑ MCD-17 Sergei Fedorov | 1.50 | .70 |
| ❑ MCD-18 Mats Sundin | .60 | .25 |
| ❑ MCD-19 Teemu Selanne | 1.50 | .70 |
| ❑ MCD-20 John LeClair | 1.00 | .45 |
| ❑ MCD-21 Alexander Mogilny | .50 | .23 |
| ❑ MCD-22 Mikael Renberg | .35 | .16 |
| ❑ MCD-23 Chris Chelios | .60 | .25 |
| ❑ MCD-24 Mark Recchi | .35 | .16 |
| ❑ MCD-25 Patrick Roy | 3.00 | 1.35 |
| ❑ MCD-26 Felix Potvin | .60 | .25 |
| ❑ MCD-27 Martin Brodeur | 1.75 | .80 |
| ❑ MCD-28 Dominik Hasek | 1.50 | .70 |
| ❑ MCD-29 Ed Belfour | .60 | .25 |
| ❑ MCD-30 Kirk McLean | .35 | .16 |
| ❑ MCD-31 Jeff Friesen | .25 | .11 |
| ❑ MCD-32 Todd Harvey | .25 | .11 |
| ❑ MCD-33 Brett Lindros | .25 | .11 |
| ❑ MCD-34 Valeri Bure | .25 | .11 |
| ❑ MCD-35 Oleg Tverdovsky | .25 | .11 |
| ❑ MCD-36 Kenny Jonsson | .25 | .11 |
| ❑ MCD-37 Mariusz Czerkawski | .25 | .11 |
| ❑ MCD-38 Alexandre Daigle | .25 | .11 |
| ❑ MCD-39 Saku Koivu | 1.25 | .55 |
| ❑ MCD-40 Jim Carey | .50 | .23 |
| ❑ NNO Joe Sakic CL | 1.00 | .45 |

## 1996-97 McDonald's

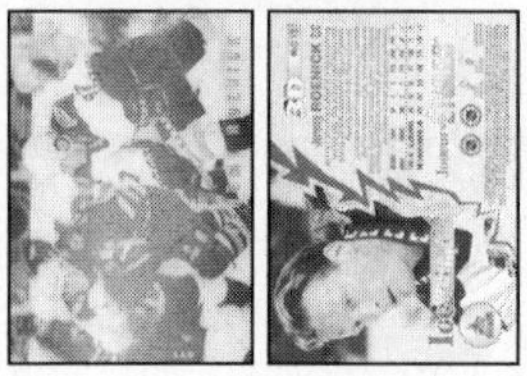

This 40-card set was available through McDonald's Restaurants of Canada and featured advanced 3D technology and Full-Motion Video technology. The set contained three subsets: IceBreakers (3D Cards #1-20 which consisted of 20 of the top NHL players), Premier IceBreakers (Full-Motion Video Cards #21-31 which showcased approximately three seconds of live footage of 11 outstanding NHL players), and Caged IceBreakers (3D Cards #32-40 which featured nine of the league's best goaltenders).

| | MINT | NRMT |
|---|---|---|
| COMPLETE SET (40) | 30.00 | 13.50 |
| COMMON CARD (1-20) | .25 | .11 |
| COMMON CARD (21-31) | 1.00 | .45 |
| COMMON CARD (32-40) | .35 | .16 |

| | MINT | NRMT |
|---|---|---|
| ❑ 1 Paul Coffey | .30 | .14 |
| ❑ 2 Teemu Selanne | 1.00 | .45 |
| ❑ 3 Eric Daze | .25 | .11 |
| ❑ 4 John LeClair | 1.00 | .45 |
| ❑ 5 Saku Koivu | .75 | .35 |
| ❑ 6 Ed Jovanovski | .60 | .25 |
| ❑ 7 Chris Osgood | .75 | .35 |
| ❑ 8 Chris Chelios | .30 | .14 |
| ❑ 9 Daniel Alfredsson | .25 | .11 |
| ❑ 10 Joe Sakic | 1.25 | .55 |
| ❑ 11 Alexander Mogilny | .25 | .11 |
| ❑ 12 Jeremy Roenick | .30 | .14 |
| ❑ 13 Keith Thachuk | .50 | .23 |
| ❑ 14 Doug Gilmour | .30 | .14 |
| ❑ 15 Theoren Fleury | .60 | .25 |
| ❑ 16 Doug Weight | .25 | .11 |
| ❑ 17 Steve Yzerman | 1.50 | .70 |
| ❑ 18 Zigmund Palffy | .40 | .18 |
| ❑ 19 Pierre Turgeon | .25 | .11 |
| ❑ 20 Brian Leetch | .30 | .14 |
| ❑ 21 Mario Lemieux SP | 5.00 | 2.20 |
| ❑ 22 Mark Messier SP | 1.50 | .70 |
| ❑ 23 Jaromir Jagr SP | 3.50 | 1.55 |
| ❑ 24 Brett Hull SP | 1.50 | .70 |
| ❑ 25 Eric Lindros SP | 3.50 | 1.55 |
| ❑ 26 Sergei Fedorov SP | 2.00 | .90 |
| ❑ 27 Pavel Bure SP | 2.00 | .90 |
| ❑ 28 Peter Forsberg SP | 3.50 | 1.55 |
| ❑ 29 Paul Kariya SP | 4.00 | 1.80 |
| ❑ 30 Patrick Roy SP | 5.00 | 2.20 |
| ❑ 31 Ray Bourque SP | 1.00 | .45 |
| ❑ 32 Jim Carey | .50 | .23 |
| ❑ 33 Martin Brodeur | 1.50 | .70 |
| ❑ 34 Trevor Kidd | .35 | .16 |
| ❑ 35 John Vanbiesbrouck | 1.25 | .55 |
| ❑ 36 Jocelyn Thibault | .50 | .23 |
| ❑ 37 Ed Belfour | .60 | .25 |
| ❑ 38 Felix Potvin | .60 | .25 |
| ❑ 39 Damian Rhodes | .35 | .16 |
| ❑ 40 Curtis Joseph | .60 | .25 |
| ❑ NNO Checklist | .05 | .02 |

## 1997-98 McDonald's

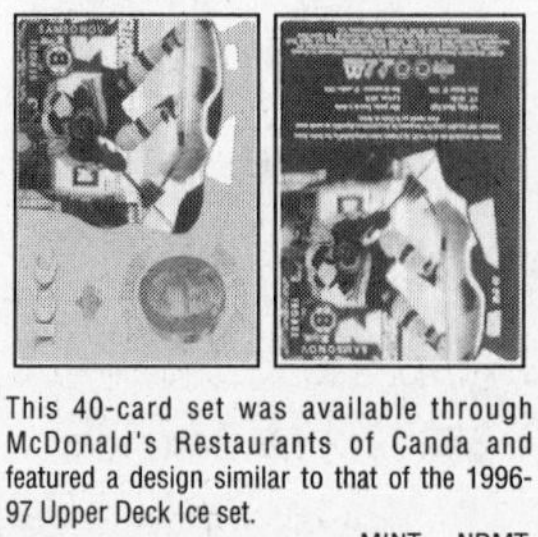

This 40-card set was available through McDonald's Restaurants of Canda and featured a design similar to that of the 1996-97 Upper Deck Ice set.

| | MINT | NRMT |
|---|---|---|
| COMPLETE SET (40) | 25.00 | 11.00 |
| COMMON CARD (1-40) | .25 | .11 |

| | MINT | NRMT |
|---|---|---|
| ❑ 1 Wayne Gretzky | 4.00 | 1.80 |
| ❑ 2 Theoren Fleury | .50 | .23 |
| ❑ 3 Pavel Bure | 1.25 | .55 |
| ❑ 4 Saku Koivu | 1.00 | .45 |
| ❑ 5 Joe Sakic | 1.25 | .55 |
| ❑ 6 Wade Redden | .25 | .11 |
| ❑ 7 Keith Tkachuk | .75 | .35 |
| ❑ 8 Eric Lindros | 2.00 | .90 |
| ❑ 9 Paul Kariya | 2.50 | 1.10 |
| ❑ 10 Bryan Berard | .40 | .18 |
| ❑ 11 Teemu Selanne | 1.25 | .55 |
| ❑ 12 Jarome Iginla | .40 | .18 |
| ❑ 13 Mats Sundin | .50 | .23 |
| ❑ 14 Brendan Shanahan | 1.25 | .55 |
| ❑ 15 Peter Forsberg | 2.00 | .90 |
| ❑ 16 Brett Hull | .75 | .35 |
| ❑ 17 Ray Bourque | .50 | .23 |
| ❑ 18 Doug Weight | .40 | .18 |
| ❑ 19 Steve Yzerman | 2.00 | .90 |
| ❑ 20 Jaromir Jagr | 2.00 | .90 |
| ❑ 21 Vincent Damphousse | .40 | .18 |
| ❑ 22 Trevor Linden | .35 | .16 |
| ❑ 23 Patrick Roy | 3.00 | 1.35 |
| ❑ 24 John Vanbiesbrouck | 1.00 | .45 |
| ❑ 25 Martin Brodeur | 1.50 | .70 |
| ❑ 26 Dominik Hasek | 1.25 | .55 |
| ❑ 27 Curtis Joseph | .50 | .23 |
| ❑ 28 Andy Moog | .40 | .18 |
| ❑ 29 Mike Richter | .50 | .23 |
| ❑ 30 Damian Rhodes | .40 | .18 |
| ❑ 31 Felix Potvin | .50 | .23 |
| ❑ 32 Chris Osgood | .50 | .23 |
| ❑ 33 Joe Thornton | 1.50 | .70 |
| ❑ 34 Patrick Marleau | 1.50 | .70 |
| ❑ 35 Jaroslav Svejkovsky | .60 | .25 |
| ❑ 36 Dan Cleary | .60 | .25 |
| ❑ 37 Chris Phillips | .25 | .11 |
| ❑ 38 Alexei Morozov | .50 | .23 |
| ❑ 39 Vaclav Prospal | 1.00 | .45 |
| ❑ 40 Sergei Samsonov | 1.50 | .70 |

## 1997-98 McDonald's Game Film

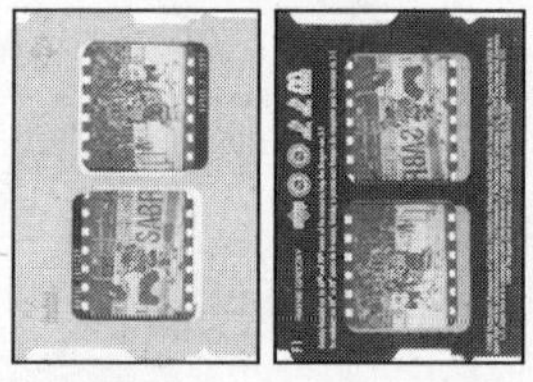

This 10-card set was randomly inserted into packs of McDonalds hockey cards. Each set feaured a design similar to a strip of film.

| | MINT | NRMT |
|---|---|---|
| COMPLETE SET (10) | 120.00 | 55.00 |
| COMMON CARD (1-10) | 4.00 | 1.80 |

| | MINT | NRMT |
|---|---|---|
| ❑ 1 Wayne Gretzky | 30.00 | 13.50 |
| ❑ 2 Alexander Mogilny | 4.00 | 1.80 |
| ❑ 3 Steve Yzerman | 15.00 | 6.75 |
| ❑ 4 Eric Lindros | 15.00 | 6.75 |
| ❑ 5 Patrick Roy | 25.00 | 11.00 |
| ❑ 6 Paul Kariya | 20.00 | 9.00 |
| ❑ 7 Ray Bourque | 5.00 | 2.20 |
| ❑ 8 Saku Koivu | 8.00 | 3.60 |
| ❑ 9 Theo Fleury | 5.00 | 2.20 |
| ❑ 10 Mats Sundin | 5.00 | 2.20 |

## 1998-99 McDonald's

Issued by McDonalds of Canada, these cards were available with any french fry purchase for 79 cents. Cards feature color action photos and statistical information.

| | MINT | NRMT |
|---|---|---|
| COMPLETE SET (28) | 30.00 | 13.50 |
| COMMON CARD (1-28) | .40 | .18 |

| | MINT | NRMT |
|---|---|---|
| ❑ 1 Wayne Gretzky | 5.00 | 2.20 |
| ❑ 2 Theoren Fleury | .75 | .35 |
| ❑ 3 Joe Sakic | 1.75 | .80 |
| ❑ 4 Saku Koivu | 1.50 | .70 |
| ❑ 5 Brendan Shanahan | 1.75 | .80 |
| ❑ 6 Steve Yzerman | 2.50 | 1.10 |
| ❑ 7 Peter Forsberg | 2.50 | 1.10 |
| ❑ 8 Paul Kariya | 3.00 | 1.35 |
| ❑ 9 Alexei Yashin | .75 | .35 |
| ❑ 10 Eric Lindros | 2.50 | 1.10 |
| ❑ 11 Jaromir Jagr | 2.50 | 1.10 |
| ❑ 12 Mats Sundin | .75 | .35 |
| ❑ 13 Sergei Samsonov | 1.50 | .70 |
| ❑ 14 Pavel Bure | 1.75 | .80 |
| ❑ 15 Patrick Roy | 4.00 | 1.80 |
| ❑ 16 Dominik Hasek | 1.75 | .80 |
| ❑ 17 Martin Brodeur | 2.00 | .90 |
| ❑ 18 Curtis Joseph | .75 | .35 |
| ❑ 19 Jocelyn Thibault | .60 | .25 |
| ❑ 20 Chris Osgood | .75 | .35 |
| ❑ 21 Ed Belfour | .75 | .35 |
| ❑ 22 Mattias Ohlund | .60 | .25 |
| ❑ 23 Marian Hossa | .75 | .35 |
| ❑ 24 Brendan Morrison | .50 | .23 |
| ❑ 25 Jason Botterill | .40 | .18 |
| ❑ 26 Cameron Mann | .40 | .18 |
| ❑ 27 Daniel Briere | .40 | .18 |
| ❑ 28 Terry Ryan | .40 | .18 |

## 1998-99 McDonald's Gretzky's Moments

Random inserts in packs of McDonalds cards. Entire set features some of Gretzkys greatest accomplishments.

| | MINT | NRMT |
|---|---|---|
| COMPLETE SET (9) | 40.00 | 18.00 |
| COMMON CARD (1-9) | 4.00 | 1.80 |

| | MINT | NRMT |
|---|---|---|
| ❑ M1 Wayne Gretzky | 4.00 | 1.80 |
| ❑ M2 Wayne Gretzky | 4.00 | 1.80 |
| ❑ M3 Wayne Gretzky | 4.00 | 1.80 |
| ❑ M4 Wayne Gretzky | 4.00 | 1.80 |
| ❑ M5 Wayne Gretzky | 4.00 | 1.80 |
| ❑ M6 Wayne Gretzky | 4.00 | 1.80 |
| ❑ M7 Wayne Gretzky | 4.00 | 1.80 |
| ❑ M8 Wayne Gretzky | 4.00 | 1.80 |
| ❑ M9 Wayne Gretzky | 4.00 | 1.80 |
| ❑ M10 Wayne Gretzky | 4.00 | 1.80 |

## 1998-99 McDonald's Gretzky's Teammates

Random inserts in packs of McDonalds cards. Each card featured Gretzky along with a past or present teammate.

| | MINT | NRMT |
|---|---|---|
| COMPLETE SET (13) | 8.00 | 3.60 |
| COMMON CARD (1-13) | .30 | .14 |

| | MINT | NRMT |
|---|---|---|
| ❑ T1 Walter Gretzky | .50 | .23 |
| ❑ T2 Gordie Howe | 2.00 | .90 |
| ❑ T3 Marty McSorley | .30 | .14 |
| ❑ T4 Brian Leetch | .60 | .25 |
| ❑ T5 Brett Hull | .75 | .35 |
| ❑ T6 Esa Tikkanen | .30 | .14 |
| ❑ T7 Grant Fuhr | .50 | .23 |
| ❑ T8 Mike Richter | .60 | .25 |
| ❑ T9 Jari Kurri | .50 | .23 |
| ❑ T10 Paul Coffey | .60 | .25 |
| ❑ T11 Rob Blake | .50 | .23 |
| ❑ T12 Mario Lemieux | 2.00 | .90 |
| ❑ T13 Luc Robitaille | .50 | .23 |

## 1995-96 Metal

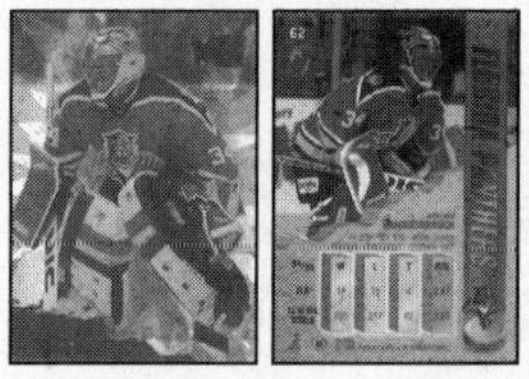

The 1995-96 Fleer Metal set was issued in one series totaling 200 cards. The 8-card packs had a suggested retail of $2.49 each. The hand-engraved etched cards each feature a colorful action photo with the player cutting through a unique metallic foil background. The cards are grouped alphabetically within teams. The Joe Sakic SkyMint Exchange card was randomly inserted 1:360 packs. When exchanged collectors received a unique card with a dime-sized coin featuring the Avalanche star embedded in the corner. The exchange offer expired January 1, 1997. Rookie Cards in this set include Daniel Alfredsson, Radek Dvorak, Chad Kilger, Daymond Langkow, and Kyle McLaren.

| | MINT | NRMT |
|---|---|---|
| COMPLETE SET (200) | 30.00 | 13.50 |
| COMMON CARD (1-200) | .15 | .07 |

| | MINT | NRMT |
|---|---|---|
| ❑ 1 Guy Hebert | .30 | .14 |
| ❑ 2 Paul Kariya | 2.00 | .90 |
| ❑ 3 Todd Krygier | .15 | .07 |
| ❑ 4 Steve Rucchin | .15 | .07 |
| ❑ 5 Oleg Tverdovsky | .30 | .14 |
| ❑ 6 Ray Bourque | .50 | .23 |
| ❑ 7 Blaine Lacher | .30 | .14 |
| ❑ 8 Shawn McEachern | .15 | .07 |
| ❑ 9 Cam Neely | .30 | .14 |
| ❑ 10 Adam Oates | .30 | .14 |
| ❑ 11 Kevin Stevens | .15 | .07 |
| ❑ 12 Donald Audette | .30 | .14 |
| ❑ 13 Randy Burridge | .15 | .07 |
| ❑ 14 Jason Dawe | .15 | .07 |
| ❑ 15 Dominik Hasek | 1.00 | .45 |
| ❑ 16 Pat LaFontaine | .30 | .14 |
| ❑ 17 Alexei Zhitnik | .15 | .07 |
| ❑ 18 Theoren Fleury | .30 | .14 |
| ❑ 19 Phil Housley | .30 | .14 |
| ❑ 20 Trevor Kidd | .30 | .14 |
| ❑ 21 Joe Nieuwendyk | .30 | .14 |
| ❑ 22 Michael Nylander | .15 | .07 |
| ❑ 23 Ed Belfour | .50 | .23 |
| ❑ 24 Chris Chelios | .50 | .23 |
| ❑ 25 Joe Murphy | .15 | .07 |
| ❑ 26 Bernie Nicholls | .15 | .07 |
| ❑ 27 Patrick Poulin | .15 | .07 |
| ❑ 28 Jeremy Roenick | .50 | .23 |
| ❑ 29 Gary Suter | .15 | .07 |
| ❑ 30 Adam Deadmarsh | .30 | .14 |
| ❑ 31 Stephane Fiset | .30 | .14 |
| ❑ 32 Peter Forsberg | 1.50 | .70 |
| ❑ 33 Valeri Kamensky | .30 | .14 |
| ❑ 34 Claude Lemieux | .30 | .14 |

❑ 35 Sandis Ozolinsh .30 .14
❑ 36 Joe Sakic 1.00 .45
❑ 37 Greg Adams .15 .07
❑ 38 Dave Gagner .30 .14
❑ 39 Todd Harvey .15 .07
❑ 40 Derian Hatcher .15 .07
❑ 41 Kevin Hatcher .15 .07
❑ 42 Mike Modano .60 .25
❑ 43 Andy Moog .30 .14
❑ 44 Paul Coffey .50 .23
❑ 45 Sergei Fedorov 1.00 .45
❑ 46 Vladimir Konstantinov .15 .07
❑ 47 Slava Kozlov .30 .14
❑ 48 Nicklas Lidstrom .30 .14
❑ 49 Chris Osgood .50 .23
❑ 50 Keith Primeau .30 .14
❑ 51 Steve Yzerman 1.50 .70
❑ 52 Jason Arnott .30 .14
❑ 53 Zdeno Ciger .15 .07
❑ 54 Todd Marchant .15 .07
❑ 55 David Oliver .15 .07
❑ 56 Bill Ranford .30 .14
❑ 57 Doug Weight .30 .14
❑ 58 Stu Barnes .15 .07
❑ 59 Jody Hull .15 .07
❑ 60 Scott Mellanby .30 .14
❑ 61 Rob Niedermayer .30 .14
❑ 62 John Vanbiesbrouck .75 .35
❑ 63 Sean Burke .30 .14
❑ 64 Andrew Cassels .15 .07
❑ 65 Nelson Emerson .15 .07
❑ 66 Geoff Sanderson .30 .14
❑ 67 Brendan Shanahan 1.00 .45
❑ 68 Glen Wesley .15 .07
❑ 69 Rob Blake .15 .07
❑ 70 Tony Granato .15 .07
❑ 71 Wayne Gretzky 3.00 1.35
❑ 72 Dimitri Khristich .15 .07
❑ 73 Yanic Perreault .15 .07
❑ 74 Rick Tocchet .30 .14
❑ 75 Benoit Brunet .15 .07
❑ 76 Vincent Damphousse .30 .14
❑ 77 Mark Recchi .30 .14
❑ 78 Patrick Roy 2.50 1.10
❑ 79 Brian Savage .15 .07
❑ 80 Pierre Turgeon .30 .14
❑ 81 Martin Brodeur 1.25 .55
❑ 82 Neal Broten .30 .14
❑ 83 John MacLean .30 .14
❑ 84 Scott Niedermayer .15 .07
❑ 85 Scott Stevens .30 .14
❑ 86 Stephane Richer .30 .14
❑ 87 Esa Tikkanen .15 .07
❑ 88 Steve Thomas .15 .07
❑ 89 Wendel Clark .30 .14
❑ 90 Travis Green .30 .14
❑ 91 Kirk Muller .15 .07
❑ 92 Zigmund Palffy .30 .14
❑ 93 Mathieu Schneider .15 .07
❑ 94 Ray Ferraro .15 .07
❑ 95 Alexei Kovalev .15 .07
❑ 96 Brian Leetch .50 .23
❑ 97 Mark Messier .60 .25
❑ 98 Mike Richter .50 .23
❑ 99 Luc Robitaille .30 .14
❑ 100 Ulf Samuelsson .15 .07
❑ 101 Pat Verbeek .15 .07
❑ 102 Radek Bonk .15 .07
❑ 103 Don Beaupre .30 .14
❑ 104 Alexandre Daigle .15 .07
❑ 105 Steve Duchesne .15 .07
❑ 106 Dan Quinn .15 .07
❑ 107 Martin Straka .15 .07
❑ 108 Rod Brind'Amour .30 .14
❑ 109 Eric Desjardins .15 .07
❑ 110 Ron Hextall .30 .14
❑ 111 John LeClair .75 .35
❑ 112 Eric Lindros 1.50 .70
❑ 113 Mikael Renberg .30 .14
❑ 114 Chris Therien .15 .07
❑ 115 Tom Barrasso .30 .14
❑ 116 Ron Francis .30 .14
❑ 117 Jaromir Jagr 1.50 .70
❑ 118 Mario Lemieux 2.50 1.10
❑ 119 Tomas Sandstrom .15 .07
❑ 120 Bryan Smolinski .15 .07
❑ 121 Sergei Zubov .15 .07
❑ 122 Shayne Corson .15 .07
❑ 123 Grant Fuhr .30 .14
❑ 124 Dale Hawerchuk .30 .14
❑ 125 Brett Hull .60 .25
❑ 126 Al MacInnis .30 .14
❑ 127 Chris Pronger .30 .14
❑ 128 Ulf Dahlen .15 .07
❑ 129 Jeff Friesen .30 .14
❑ 130 Arturs Irbe .30 .14
❑ 131 Craig Janney .30 .14
❑ 132 Andrei Nazarov .15 .07
❑ 133 Owen Nolan .30 .14
❑ 134 Ray Sheppard .30 .14
❑ 135 Brian Bradley .15 .07
❑ 136 Chris Gratton .30 .14
❑ 137 Roman Hamrlik .30 .14
❑ 138 Petr Klima .15 .07
❑ 139 Daren Puppa .30 .14
❑ 140 Alexander Selivanov .15 .07
❑ 141 Dave Andreychuk .30 .14
❑ 142 Mike Gartner .30 .14
❑ 143 Doug Gilmour .50 .23
❑ 144 Kenny Jonsson .15 .07
❑ 145 Larry Murphy .30 .14
❑ 146 Felix Potvin .50 .23
❑ 147 Mats Sundin .30 .14
❑ 148 Jeff Brown .15 .07
❑ 149 Pavel Bure 1.00 .45
❑ 150 Russ Courtnall .15 .07
❑ 151 Trevor Linden .30 .14
❑ 152 Kirk McLean .30 .14
❑ 153 Alexander Mogilny .30 .14
❑ 154 Roman Oksiuta .15 .07
❑ 155 Mike Ridley .15 .07
❑ 156 Peter Bondra .50 .23
❑ 157 Jim Carey .50 .23
❑ 158 Sylvain Cote .15 .07
❑ 159 Sergei Gonchar .15 .07
❑ 160 Keith Jones .15 .07
❑ 161 Joe Juneau .15 .07
❑ 162 Nikolai Khabibulin .30 .14
❑ 163 Igor Korolev .15 .07
❑ 164 Teppo Numminen .15 .07
❑ 165 Teemu Selanne 1.00 .45
❑ 166 Keith Tkachuk .60 .25
❑ 167 Darren Turcotte .15 .07
❑ 168 Alexei Zhamnov .30 .14
❑ 169 Daniel Alfredsson .75 .35
❑ 170 Aki-Petteri Berg .15 .07
❑ 171 Todd Bertuzzi .30 .14
❑ 172 Jason Bonsignore .15 .07
❑ 173 Byron Dafoe .30 .14
❑ 174 Eric Daze .50 .23
❑ 175 Shane Doan .15 .07
❑ 176 Radek Dvorak .15 .07
❑ 177 Brian Holzinger .50 .23
❑ 178 Ed Jovanovski .50 .23
❑ 179 Chad Kilger .30 .14
❑ 180 Saku Koivu .75 .35
❑ 181 Darren Langdon .15 .07
❑ 182 Daymond Langkow .50 .23
❑ 183 Jere Lehtinen .15 .07
❑ 184 Kyle McLaren .30 .14
❑ 185 Marty Murray .15 .07
❑ 186 Jeff O'Neill .15 .07
❑ 187 Richard Park .15 .07
❑ 188 Deron Quint .15 .07
❑ 189 Marcus Ragnarsson .15 .07
❑ 190 Miroslav Satan 1.50 .70
❑ 191 Tommy Salo .60 .25
❑ 192 Jamie Storr .30 .14
❑ 193 Niklas Sundstrom .15 .07
❑ 194 Robert Svehla .15 .07
❑ 195 Denis Pederson .15 .07
❑ 196 Antti Tormanen .15 .07
❑ 197 Brendan Witt .15 .07
❑ 198 Vitali Yachmenev .15 .07
❑ 199 Checklist (1-114) .15 .07
❑ 200 Checklist (115-200/inserts) .15 .07
UER Bure is Number 1 in International Steel, not Berg
❑ NNO Joe Sakic Coin/Card 30.00 13.50
❑ NNO Joe Sakic EXCH 2.00 .90

## 1995-96 Metal Heavy Metal

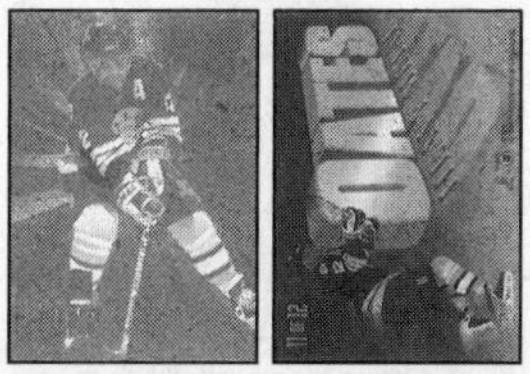

Randomly inserted in packs at a rate of 1:30 packs, this 12-card set highlights some of the league's top players. The fronts feature an isolated player photo over a dynamic starburst metallic background. The backs include another photo, and the card number out of 12.

| | MINT | NRMT |
|---|---|---|
| COMPLETE SET (12) | 150.00 | 70.00 |
| COMMON CARD (1-12) | 5.00 | 2.20 |

❑ 1 Pavel Bure 10.00 4.50
❑ 2 Sergei Fedorov 10.00 4.50
❑ 3 Theoren Fleury 5.00 2.20
❑ 4 Wayne Gretzky 30.00 13.50
❑ 5 Brett Hull 6.00 2.70
❑ 6 Jaromir Jagr 15.00 6.75
❑ 7 Paul Kariya 20.00 9.00
❑ 8 Brian Leetch 8.00 3.60
❑ 9 Mario Lemieux 25.00 11.00
❑ 10 Mike Modano 6.00 2.70
❑ 11 Adam Oates 5.00 2.20
❑ 12 Joe Sakic 10.00 4.50

## 1995-96 Metal International Steel

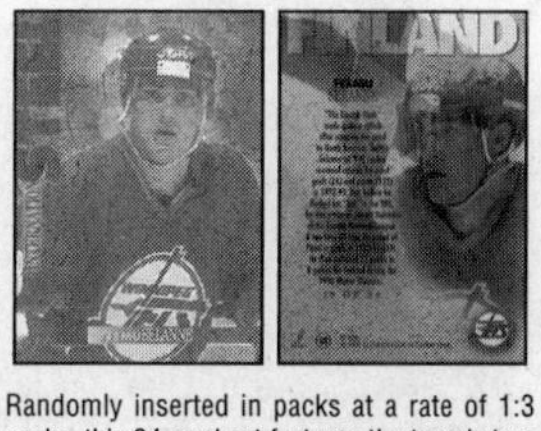

Randomly inserted in packs at a rate of 1:3 packs, this 24-card set features the top skaters from around the globe. The checklist card for this set found in the regular Fleer Metal series suggests that card number one is Aki-Petteri Berg. This is incorrect as this card does not exist. The remaining cards exist as checklisted, save for their number being one less than listed.

| | MINT | NRMT |
|---|---|---|
| COMPLETE SET (24) | 45.00 | 20.00 |
| COMMON CARD (1-24) | .50 | .23 |

❑ 1 Pavel Bure 3.00 1.35
❑ 2 Chris Chelios 1.50 .70
❑ 3 Sergei Fedorov 3.00 1.35
❑ 4 Peter Forsberg 5.00 2.20
❑ 5 Wayne Gretzky 10.00 4.50
❑ 6 Roman Hamrlik 1.00 .45
❑ 7 Dominik Hasek 3.00 1.35
❑ 8 Brett Hull 2.00 .90
❑ 9 Jaromir Jagr 5.00 2.20
❑ 10 Saku Koivu 3.00 1.35
❑ 11 Pat LaFontaine 1.00 .45
❑ 12 Brian Leetch 1.50 .70
❑ 13 Jere Lehtinen .50 .23
❑ 14 Mario Lemieux 8.00 3.60
❑ 15 Alexander Mogilny 1.00 .45
❑ 16 Mikael Renberg 1.00 .45
❑ 17 Jeremy Roenick 1.50 .70
❑ 18 Joe Sakic 4.00 1.80
❑ 19 Teemu Selanne 3.00 1.35
❑ 20 Mats Sundin 1.50 .70
❑ 21 Niklas Sundstrom 1.00 .45
❑ 22 Vitali Yachmenev .50 .23
❑ 23 Alexei Zhamnov 1.00 .45
❑ 24 Sergei Zubov .50 .23

## 1995-96 Metal Iron Warriors

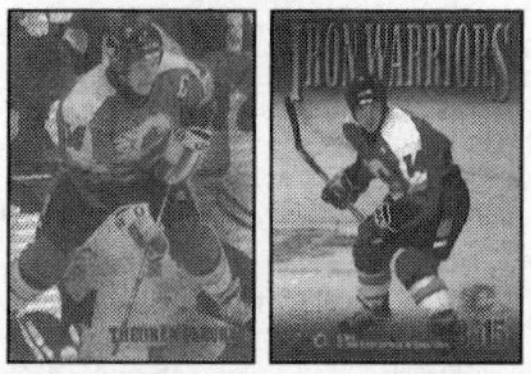

Randomly inserted in packs at a rate of 1:12 packs, this 15-card set has a razor-sharp design and features the NHL's toughest competitors.

| | MINT | NRMT |
|---|---|---|
| COMPLETE SET (15) | 60.00 | 27.00 |
| COMMON CARD (1-15) | 2.00 | .90 |

❑ 1 Jason Arnott 3.00 1.35
❑ 2 Ed Belfour 5.00 2.20
❑ 3 Theoren Fleury 3.00 1.35
❑ 4 Ron Francis 3.00 1.35
❑ 5 John LeClair 8.00 3.60
❑ 6 Claude Lemieux 3.00 1.35
❑ 7 Eric Lindros 20.00 9.00
❑ 8 Mark Messier 6.00 2.70
❑ 9 Cam Neely 3.00 1.35
❑ 10 Keith Primeau 3.00 1.35
❑ 11 Kevin Stevens 2.00 .90
❑ 12 Scott Stevens 2.00 .90
❑ 13 Brendan Shanahan 10.00 4.50
❑ 14 Keith Tkachuk 6.00 2.70
❑ 15 Rick Tocchet 3.00 1.35

## 1995-96 Metal Winners

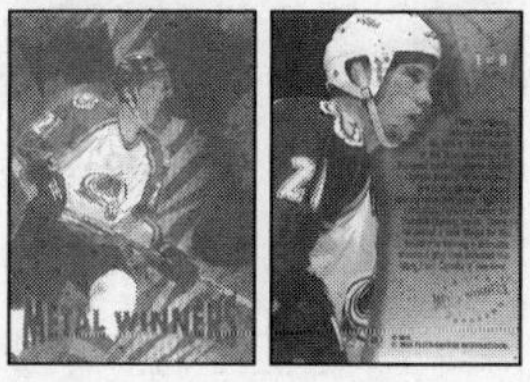

Randomly inserted in packs at a rate of 1:60 packs , this 9-card set emblazoned on a high-tech design, shows players who have won medals in international competitions such as the Olympics or World Championships.

| | MINT | NRMT |
|---|---|---|
| COMPLETE SET (9) | 80.00 | 36.00 |
| COMMON CARD (1-9) | 3.00 | 1.35 |

❑ 1 Peter Forsberg 30.00 13.50
❑ 2 Saku Koivu 20.00 9.00
❑ 3 Alexei Kovalev 3.00 1.35
❑ 4 Eric Lindros 40.00 18.00
❑ 5 Alexander Mogilny 8.00 3.60
❑ 6 Tommy Salo 3.00 1.35
❑ 7 Brian Savage 3.00 1.35
❑ 8 Sergei Zubov 3.00 1.35
❑ 9 Alexei Zhamnov 8.00 3.60

## 1996-97 Metal Universe

Issued in eight-card packs with a SRP of $2.49, this single-series set consisted of 200 cards. The design is comprised of a cutout player photo placed atop a surrealistic, etched-metal backgroud. Key rookies include Dainus Zubrus, Mike Grier, and Sergei Berezin.

| | MINT | NRMT |
|---|---|---|
| COMPLETE SET (200) | 40.00 | 18.00 |

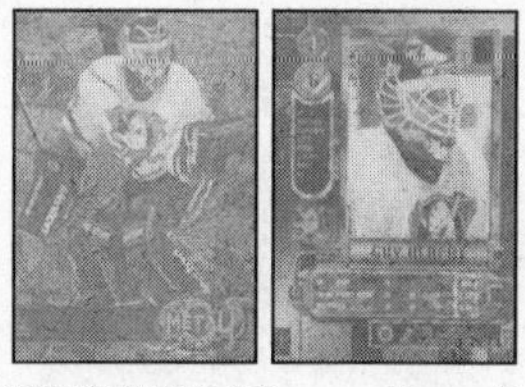

| | | |
|---|---|---|
| COMMON CARD (1-200) | .15 | .07 |

❑ 1 Guy Hebert .25 .11
❑ 2 Paul Kariya 2.00 .90
❑ 3 Jari Kurri .25 .11
❑ 4 Roman Oksiuta .15 .07
❑ 5 Steve Rucchin .15 .07
❑ 6 Teemu Selanne 1.00 .45
❑ 7 Ray Bourque .50 .23
❑ 8 Kyle McLaren .15 .07
❑ 9 Adam Oates .25 .11
❑ 10 Bill Ranford .25 .11
❑ 11 Rick Tocchet .25 .11
❑ 12 Donald Audette .25 .11
❑ 13 Jason Dawe .15 .07
❑ 14 Dominik Hasek 1.00 .45
❑ 15 Pat LaFontaine .25 .11
❑ 16 Derek Plante .15 .07
❑ 17 Wayne Primeau .15 .07
❑ 18 Theoren Fleury .25 .11
❑ 19 Dave Gagner .25 .11
❑ 20 Trevor Kidd .25 .11
❑ 21 James Patrick .15 .07
❑ 22 Robert Reichel .15 .07
❑ 23 German Titov .15 .07
❑ 24 Tony Amonte .25 .11
❑ 25 Ed Belfour .50 .23
❑ 26 Chris Chelios .50 .23
❑ 27 Eric Daze .25 .11
❑ 28 Gary Suter .15 .07
❑ 29 Alexei Zhamnov .15 .07
❑ 30 Adam Deadmarsh .25 .11
❑ 31 Adam Foote .15 .07
❑ 32 Peter Forsberg 1.50 .70
❑ 33 Valeri Kamensky .25 .11
❑ 34 Uwe Krupp .15 .07
❑ 35 Claude Lemieux .25 .11
❑ 36 Sandis Ozolinsh .25 .11
❑ 37 Patrick Roy 2.50 1.10
❑ 38 Joe Sakic 1.00 .45
❑ 39 Derian Hatcher .15 .07
❑ 40 Mike Modano .60 .25
❑ 41 Andy Moog .25 .11
❑ 42 Joe Nieuwendyk .25 .11
❑ 43 Pat Verbeek .15 .07
❑ 44 Sergei Zubov .15 .07
❑ 45 Sergei Fedorov 1.00 .45
❑ 46 Vladimir Konstantinov .15 .07
❑ 47 Slava Kozlov .25 .11
❑ 48 Nicklas Lidstrom .25 .11
❑ 49 Chris Osgood .50 .23
❑ 50 Brendan Shanahan 1.00 .45
❑ 51 Steve Yzerman 1.50 .70
❑ 52 Jason Arnott .25 .11
❑ 53 Curtis Joseph .50 .23
❑ 54 Andrei Kovalenko .15 .07
❑ 55 Miroslav Satan .15 .07
❑ 56 Doug Weight .25 .11
❑ 57 Radek Dvorak .15 .07
❑ 58 Per Gustafsson .25 .11
❑ 59 Ed Jovanovski .25 .11
❑ 60 Scott Mellanby .25 .11
❑ 61 Rob Niedermayer .25 .11
❑ 62 Ray Sheppard .25 .11
❑ 63 Robert Svehla .15 .07
❑ 64 John Vanbiesbrouck .75 .35
❑ 65 Jeff Brown .15 .07
❑ 66 Sean Burke .25 .11
❑ 67 Paul Coffey .50 .23
❑ 68 Nelson Emerson .15 .07
❑ 69 Jeff O'Neill .15 .07
❑ 70 Keith Primeau .25 .11
❑ 71 Geoff Sanderson .25 .11
❑ 72 Aki Berg .15 .07
❑ 73 Rob Blake .15 .07
❑ 74 Stephane Fiset .25 .11
❑ 75 Dimitri Khristich .15 .07
❑ 76 Petr Klima .15 .07
❑ 77 Ed Olczyk .15 .07
❑ 78 Vitali Yachmenev .15 .07
❑ 79 Vincent Damphousse .15 .07
❑ 80 Saku Koivu .75 .35
❑ 81 Mark Recchi .25 .11
❑ 82 Stephane Richer .25 .11
❑ 83 Jocelyn Thibault .50 .23
❑ 84 Pierre Turgeon .25 .11
❑ 85 Dave Andreychuk .25 .11
❑ 86 Martin Brodeur 1.25 .55
❑ 87 Scott Niedermayer .15 .07
❑ 88 Scott Stevens .25 .11
❑ 89 Petr Sykora .15 .07
❑ 90 Steve Thomas .15 .07
❑ 91 Todd Bertuzzi .15 .07
❑ 92 Travis Green .25 .11
❑ 93 Kenny Jonsson .15 .07
❑ 94 Bryan McCabe .15 .07
❑ 95 Zigmund Palffy .50 .23
❑ 96 Wayne Gretzky 4.00 1.80
❑ 97 Alexei Kovalev .15 .07
❑ 98 Brian Leetch .50 .23
❑ 99 Mark Messier .60 .25
❑ 100 Mike Richter .50 .23
❑ 101 Luc Robitaille .25 .11
❑ 102 Niklas Sundstrom .15 .07
❑ 103 Daniel Alfredsson .25 .11
❑ 104 Radek Bonk .15 .07
❑ 105 Alexandre Daigle .15 .07
❑ 106 Steve Duchesne .15 .07
❑ 107 Damian Rhodes .25 .11
❑ 108 Alexei Yashin .25 .11
❑ 109 Rod Brind'Amour .25 .11
❑ 110 Eric Desjardins .15 .07
❑ 111 Dale Hawerchuk .25 .11
❑ 112 Ron Hextall .25 .11
❑ 113 John LeClair .75 .35
❑ 114 Eric Lindros 1.50 .70
❑ 115 Mikael Renberg .25 .11
❑ 116 Mike Gartner .25 .11
❑ 117 Craig Janney .25 .11
❑ 118 Nikolai Khabibulin .25 .11
❑ 119 Dave Manson .15 .07
❑ 120 Teppo Numminen .15 .07
❑ 121 Jeremy Roenick .50 .23
❑ 122 Keith Tkachuk .60 .25
❑ 123 Oleg Tverdovsky .25 .11
❑ 124 Tom Barrasso .25 .11
❑ 125 Ron Francis .25 .11
❑ 126 Kevin Hatcher .15 .07
❑ 127 Jaromir Jagr 1.50 .70
❑ 128 Mario Lemieux 2.50 1.10
❑ 129 Petr Nedved .25 .11
❑ 130 Shayne Corson .15 .07
❑ 131 Grant Fuhr .25 .11
❑ 132 Brett Hull .60 .25
❑ 133 Al MacInnis .25 .11
❑ 134 Joe Murphy .15 .07
❑ 135 Chris Pronger .25 .11
❑ 136 Kelly Hrudey .25 .11
❑ 137 Al Iafrate .15 .07
❑ 138 Bernie Nicholls .15 .07
❑ 139 Owen Nolan .25 .11
❑ 140 Marcus Ragnarsson .15 .07
❑ 141 Darren Turcotte .15 .07
❑ 142 Brian Bradley .15 .07
❑ 143 Dino Ciccarelli .25 .11
❑ 144 Chris Gratton .25 .11
❑ 145 Roman Hamrlik .25 .11
❑ 146 Daren Puppa .25 .11
❑ 147 Alexander Selivanov .15 .07
❑ 148 Wendel Clark .25 .11
❑ 149 Doug Gilmour .50 .23
❑ 150 Kirk Muller .15 .07
❑ 151 Larry Murphy .25 .11
❑ 152 Felix Potvin .50 .23
❑ 153 Mathieu Schneider .15 .07
❑ 154 Mats Sundin .25 .11
❑ 155 Pavel Bure 1.00 .45
❑ 156 Russ Courtnall .15 .07
❑ 157 Trevor Linden .25 .11
❑ 158 Kirk McLean .25 .11
❑ 159 Alexander Mogilny .25 .11
❑ 160 Esa Tikkanen .15 .07
❑ 161 Peter Bondra .50 .23
❑ 162 Jim Carey .50 .23
❑ 163 Sergei Gonchar .15 .07
❑ 164 Phil Housley .25 .11
❑ 165 Calle Johansson .15 .07
❑ 166 Joe Juneau .15 .07
❑ 167 Michal Pivonka .15 .07
❑ 168 Brendan Witt .15 .07
❑ 169 Nolan Baumgartner .15 .07
❑ 170 Bryan Berard .50 .23
❑ 171 Sergei Berezin .75 .35
❑ 172 Curtis Brown .15 .07
❑ 173 Jan Caloun .15 .07
❑ 174 Andreas Dackell .15 .07
❑ 175 Hnat Domenichelli .15 .07
❑ 176 Christian Dube .15 .07
❑ 177 Anders Eriksson .15 .07
❑ 178 Peter Ferraro .15 .07
❑ 179 Eric Fichaud .25 .11
❑ 180 Daniel Goneau .15 .07
❑ 181 Mike Grier 1.00 .45
❑ 182 Jarome Iginla .50 .23
❑ 183 Steve Kelly .15 .07
❑ 184 Jamie Langenbrunner .15 .07
❑ 185 Daymond Langkow .15 .07
❑ 186 Jay McKee .15 .07
❑ 187 Ethan Moreau .50 .23
❑ 188 Rem Murray .15 .07
❑ 189 Janne Niinimaa .50 .23
❑ 190 Wade Redden .15 .07
❑ 191 Ruslan Salei .15 .07
❑ 192 Jamie Storr .25 .11
❑ 193 Darren Van Impe .15 .07
❑ 194 Roman Vopat .15 .07
❑ 195 David Wilkie .15 .07
❑ 196 Landon Wilson .15 .07
❑ 197 Richard Zednik .15 .07
❑ 198 Dainius Zubrus 1.00 .45
❑ 199 Checklist (1-118) .15 .07
❑ 200 Checklist (119-200/inserts) .15 .07

## 1996-97 Metal Universe Armor Plate

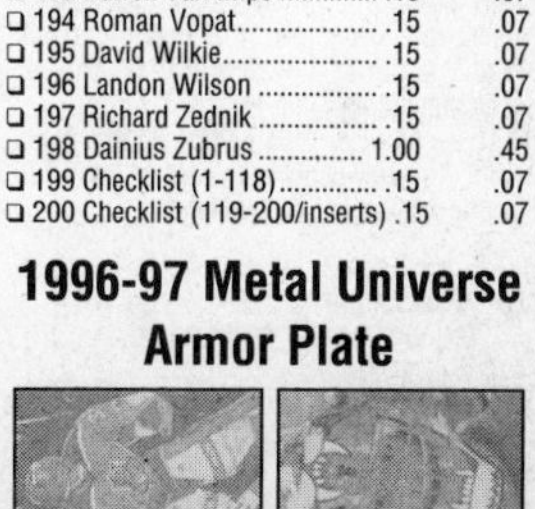

Randomly inserted in packs at a rate of one in

72, this 12-card set is comprised of hockey's top netminders. Cutout player photos are placed over a bubbled metallic surface, with a short write-up and photo on the reverse. A Super Power parallel with enhanced holographic foil backgrounds was inserted one per 720 packs. There is no distinction other than the special holofoil treatment.

| | MINT | NRMT |
|---|---|---|
| COMPLETE SET (12) | 125.00 | 55.00 |
| COMMON CARD (1-12) | 5.00 | 2.20 |
| *SUPER POWER: 1.5X TO 4X BASIC CARDS | | |

| | | |
|---|---|---|
| ❑ 1 Ed Belfour | 8.00 | 3.60 |
| ❑ 2 Martin Brodeur | 20.00 | 9.00 |
| ❑ 3 Jim Carey | 8.00 | 3.60 |
| ❑ 4 Dominik Hasek | 15.00 | 6.75 |
| ❑ 5 Ron Hextall | 5.00 | 2.20 |
| ❑ 6 Chris Osgood | 8.00 | 3.60 |
| ❑ 7 Felix Potvin | 8.00 | 3.60 |
| ❑ 8 Daren Puppa | 5.00 | 2.20 |
| ❑ 9 Damian Rhodes | 5.00 | 2.20 |
| ❑ 10 Mike Richter | 8.00 | 3.60 |
| ❑ 11 Patrick Roy | 40.00 | 18.00 |
| ❑ 12 John Vanbiesbrouck | 12.00 | 5.50 |

## 1996-97 Metal Universe Cool Steel

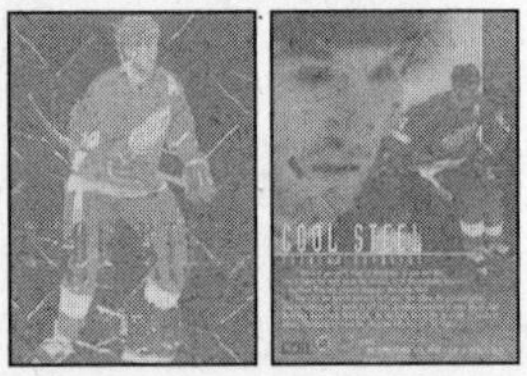

Randomly inserted in packs at a rate of one in 48, this 12-card set features cutout player photos on a brushed metal background. Two photos grace the reverse, including an extreme face closeup, as well as a description of each player's strengths. A Super Power parallel with an enhanced holographic foil background was inserted one per 480 packs. There is no distinction between the two versions other than the special holofoil treatment.

| | MINT | NRMT |
|---|---|---|
| COMPLETE SET (12) | 100.00 | 45.00 |
| COMMON CARD (1-12) | 2.50 | 1.10 |
| *SUPER POWER: 1.5X TO 4X BASIC CARDS | | |

| | | |
|---|---|---|
| ❑ 1 Chris Chelios | 5.00 | 2.20 |
| ❑ 2 Peter Forsberg | 15.00 | 6.75 |
| ❑ 3 Ron Francis | 6.00 | 2.70 |
| ❑ 4 Dominik Hasek | 10.00 | 4.50 |
| ❑ 5 Ed Jovanovski | 6.00 | 2.70 |
| ❑ 6 Vladimir Konstantinov | 2.50 | 1.10 |
| ❑ 7 Eric Lindros | 15.00 | 6.75 |
| ❑ 8 Mark Messier | 6.00 | 2.70 |
| ❑ 9 Patrick Roy | 25.00 | 11.00 |
| ❑ 10 Brendan Shanahan | 10.00 | 4.50 |
| ❑ 11 Keith Tkachuk | 6.00 | 2.70 |
| ❑ 12 John Vanbiesbrouck | 8.00 | 3.60 |

## 1996-97 Metal Universe Ice Carvings

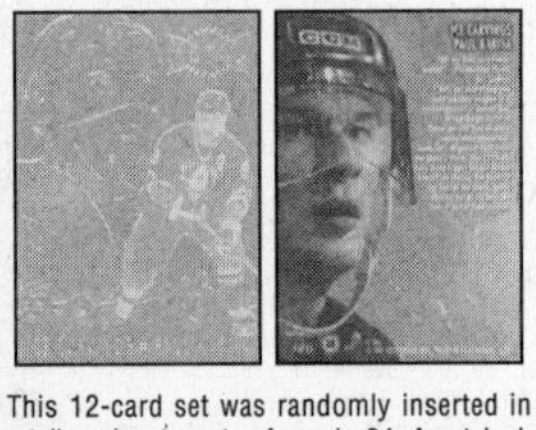

This 12-card set was randomly inserted in retail packs at a rate of one in 24. An etched, blue-foil player image accompanies a cutout photo on the front, while the flip side adds a closeup photo and interesting text on each player. A Super Power parallel with an enhanced holographic foil background was inserted one per 240 packs. There is no distinction between the two versions other than the special holofoil treatment.

| | MINT | NRMT |
|---|---|---|
| COMPLETE SET (12) | 100.00 | 45.00 |
| COMMON CARD (1-12) | 5.00 | 2.20 |
| *SUPER POWER: 1.5X TO 4X BASIC CARDS | | |

| | | |
|---|---|---|
| ❑ 1 Martin Brodeur | 12.00 | 5.50 |
| ❑ 2 Pavel Bure | 10.00 | 4.50 |
| ❑ 3 Jim Carey | 10.00 | 4.50 |
| ❑ 4 Paul Coffey | 10.00 | 4.50 |
| ❑ 5 Sergei Fedorov | 10.00 | 4.50 |
| ❑ 6 Jaromir Jagr | 15.00 | 6.75 |
| ❑ 7 Paul Kariya | 20.00 | 9.00 |
| ❑ 8 Pat LaFontaine | 5.00 | 2.20 |
| ❑ 9 Brian Leetch | 10.00 | 4.50 |
| ❑ 10 Mario Lemieux | 25.00 | 11.00 |
| ❑ 11 Alexander Mogilny | 5.00 | 2.20 |
| ❑ 12 Joe Sakic | 10.00 | 4.50 |

## 1996-97 Metal Universe Lethal Weapons

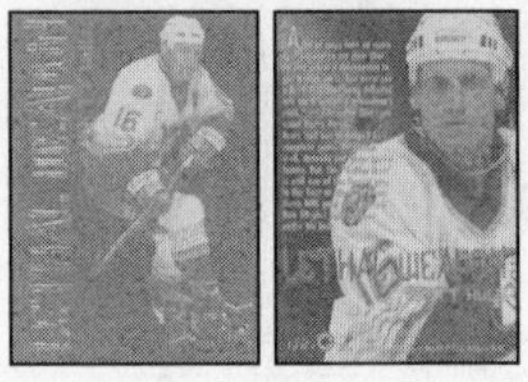

The most common of the Metal inserts, this 20-card set was randomly inserted one per 12 packs and features the top scorers in the NHL. Cutout player photos leap off of bronze metallic backgrounds with a second photo on the card back as well as a description of each player's scoring prowess. Super Power parallels were inserted every 120 packs and differed only by an enhanced holographic foil background.

| | MINT | NRMT |
|---|---|---|
| COMPLETE SET (20) | 100.00 | 45.00 |
| COMMON CARD (1-20) | 2.50 | 1.10 |
| *SUPER POWER: 1.5X TO 4X BASIC CARDS | | |

| | | |
|---|---|---|
| ❑ 1 Peter Bondra | 2.50 | 1.10 |
| ❑ 2 Pavel Bure | 5.00 | 2.20 |
| ❑ 3 Sergei Fedorov | 5.00 | 2.20 |
| ❑ 4 Peter Forsberg | 8.00 | 3.60 |
| ❑ 5 Ron Francis | 4.00 | 1.80 |
| ❑ 6 Wayne Gretzky | 15.00 | 6.75 |
| ❑ 7 Brett Hull | 3.00 | 1.35 |
| ❑ 8 Jaromir Jagr | 8.00 | 3.60 |
| ❑ 9 Paul Kariya | 10.00 | 4.50 |
| ❑ 10 John LeClair | 4.00 | 1.80 |
| ❑ 11 Mario Lemieux | 12.00 | 5.50 |
| ❑ 12 Eric Lindros | 8.00 | 3.60 |
| ❑ 13 Mark Messier | 3.00 | 1.35 |
| ❑ 14 Alexander Mogilny | 2.50 | 1.10 |
| ❑ 15 Adam Oates | 2.50 | 1.10 |
| ❑ 16 Joe Sakic | 5.00 | 2.20 |
| ❑ 17 Teemu Selanne | 5.00 | 2.20 |
| ❑ 18 Brendan Shanahan | 5.00 | 2.20 |
| ❑ 19 Keith Tkachuk | 3.00 | 1.35 |
| ❑ 20 Doug Weight | 4.00 | 1.80 |

## 1972-73 Nationals Ottawa WHA

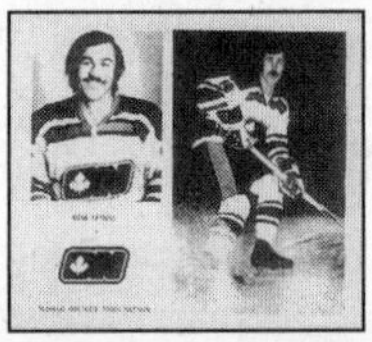

This 23-card set measures approximately 4 3/4" by 4 1/8" and features two black-and-white player photos on a white card face. The left side of the card shows a small, close-up picture above the team logo. The right side of the card is devoted to a full length posed action shot. The words "World Hockey Association" are printed in black at the lower left corner. The backs are blank. The cards are unnumbered and checklisted below in alphabetical order.

| | NRMT-MT | EXC |
|---|---|---|
| COMPLETE SET (23) | 30.00 | 13.50 |
| COMMON CARD (1-23) | 1.50 | .70 |

| | | |
|---|---|---|
| ❑ 1 Mike Amodeo | 1.50 | .70 |
| ❑ 2 Les Binkley | 4.00 | 1.80 |
| ❑ 3 Mike Boland | 1.50 | .70 |
| ❑ 4 Wayne Carleton | 2.50 | 1.10 |
| ❑ 5 Bob Charlebois | 1.50 | .70 |
| ❑ 6 Ron Climie | 2.00 | .90 |
| ❑ 7 Brian Conacher | 1.50 | .70 |
| ❑ 8 Rick Cunningham | 1.50 | .70 |
| ❑ 9 John Donnelly | 1.50 | .70 |
| ❑ 10 Brian Gibbons | 1.50 | .70 |
| ❑ 11 Jack Gibson | 1.50 | .70 |
| ❑ 12 Gilles Gratton | 4.00 | 1.80 |
| ❑ 13 Steve King | 1.50 | .70 |
| ❑ 14 Gavin Kirk | 1.50 | .70 |
| ❑ 15 Bob Leduc | 2.00 | .90 |
| ❑ 16 Tom Martin | 1.50 | .70 |
| ❑ 17 Chris Meloff | 1.50 | .70 |
| ❑ 18 Ron Riley | 1.50 | .70 |
| ❑ 19 Rick Sentes | 1.50 | .70 |
| ❑ 20 Tom Simpson | 1.50 | .70 |
| ❑ 21 Ken Stephanson | 1.50 | .70 |
| ❑ 22 Guy Trottier | 2.00 | .90 |
| ❑ 23 Steve Warr | 1.50 | .70 |

## 1982-83 Neilson's Gretzky

This 50-card set was issued to honor one of hockey's all-time great players, Wayne Gretzky. The cards measure 2 1/2" by 3 1/2". The first nine cards feature vintage black and

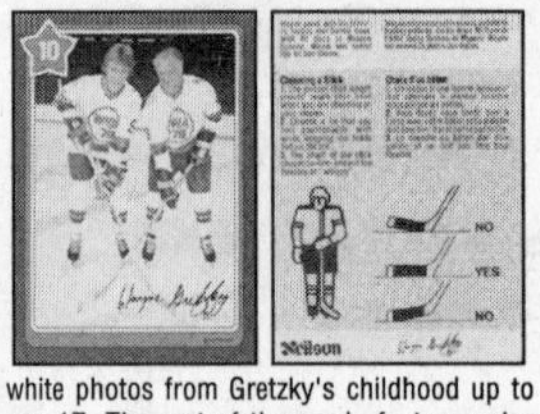

white photos from Gretzky's childhood up to age 17. The rest of the cards feature color action photos highlighting Gretzky's pro career. All the pictures on the cards are framed by white and orange borders on a dark blue background. The card number appears in a star at the upper left hand corner of the card face. A facsimile autograph is inscribed across the bottom of each picture. The card backs have captions to the pictures and include a discussion of some aspect of the game. The card backs are bilingual, i.e., French and English. Many of these discussions are accompanied by illustrations. The cards were issued as inserts with Neilson's candy bars.

| | MINT | NRMT |
|---|---|---|
| COMPLETE SET (50) | 200.00 | 90.00 |
| COMMON CARD (1-50) | 5.00 | 2.20 |

| | | |
|---|---|---|
| ❑ 1 Discard Broken Stick | 10.00 | 4.50 |
| ❑ 2 Handling the Puck | 5.00 | 2.20 |
| ❑ 3 Offsides | 5.00 | 2.20 |
| ❑ 4 Penalty Shot | 5.00 | 2.20 |
| ❑ 5 Icing the Puck | 5.00 | 2.20 |
| ❑ 6 Taping your Stick | 5.00 | 2.20 |
| ❑ 7 Skates | 5.00 | 2.20 |
| ❑ 8 The Helmet | 5.00 | 2.20 |
| ❑ 9 Selecting Skates | 5.00 | 2.20 |
| ❑ 10 Choosing a Stick | 25.00 | 11.00 |
| (with Gordie Howe) | | |
| ❑ 11 General Equipment Care | 5.00 | 2.20 |
| ❑ 12 The Hook Check | 8.00 | 3.60 |
| (with Marcel Dionne) | | |
| ❑ 13 The Hip Check | 5.00 | 2.20 |
| ❑ 14 Forward Skating | 10.00 | 4.50 |
| (With Mike Gartner) | | |
| ❑ 15 Stopping | 5.00 | 2.20 |
| ❑ 16 Sharp Turning | 5.00 | 2.20 |
| ❑ 17 Fast Starts | 5.00 | 2.20 |
| ❑ 18 Backward Skating | 5.00 | 2.20 |
| ❑ 19 The Grip | 5.00 | 2.20 |
| ❑ 20 The Wrist Shot | 5.00 | 2.20 |
| ❑ 21 The Back Hand Shot | 5.00 | 2.20 |
| ❑ 22 The Slap Shot | 5.00 | 2.20 |
| ❑ 23 The Flip Shot | 5.00 | 2.20 |
| ❑ 24 Pass Receiving | 5.00 | 2.20 |
| ❑ 25 Faking | 5.00 | 2.20 |
| ❑ 26 Puck Handling | 5.00 | 2.20 |
| ❑ 27 Deflecting Shots | 5.00 | 2.20 |
| ❑ 28 One On One | 5.00 | 2.20 |
| ❑ 29 Keep Your Head Up | 5.00 | 2.20 |
| ❑ 30 Passing to the Slot | 5.00 | 2.20 |
| ❑ 31 Winning Face-Offs | 12.00 | 5.50 |
| (with Guy Lafleur and Mike Bossy) | | |
| ❑ 32 Forechecking | 5.00 | 2.20 |
| ❑ 33 Body Checking | 5.00 | 2.20 |
| ❑ 34 Breaking Out | 5.00 | 2.20 |
| ❑ 35 The Drop Pass | 5.00 | 2.20 |
| ❑ 36 Backchecking | 10.00 | 4.50 |
| (with Phil Esposito) | | |
| ❑ 37 Using the Boards | 5.00 | 2.20 |
| ❑ 38 The Power Play | 7.00 | 3.10 |
| ❑ 39 Passing the Puck | 5.00 | 2.20 |
| ❑ 40 Clear the Slot | 5.00 | 2.20 |
| ❑ 41 Leg Lifts | 5.00 | 2.20 |
| ❑ 42 Balance Exercise | 5.00 | 2.20 |
| ❑ 43 Leg Stretches | 5.00 | 2.20 |
| ❑ 44 Hip and Groin Stretch | 5.00 | 2.20 |
| ❑ 45 Toe Touches | 10.00 | 4.50 |
| (With Mark Messier) | | |
| ❑ 46 Goalie Warm Up Drill | 5.00 | 2.20 |
| ❑ 47 Leg Exercises | 5.00 | 2.20 |
| ❑ 48 Arm Exercises | 5.00 | 2.20 |
| ❑ 49 Wrist Exercises | 5.00 | 2.20 |
| ❑ 50 Flip Pass | 5.00 | 2.20 |

## 1974-75 NHL Action Stamps

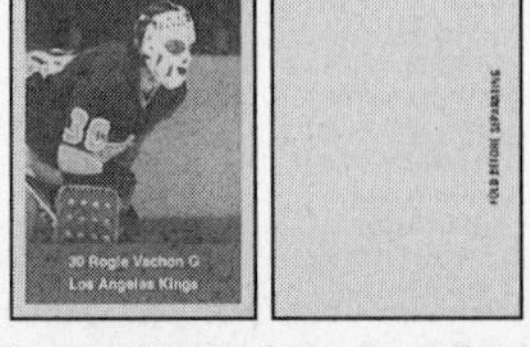

This set of NHL Action Stamps was distributed throughout North America in large grocery chains such as Loblaw's, IGA, A&P, and Acme. Some of these small stickers (or stamps) mention the particular grocery store on back; others have blank backs. A strip of eight player stamps was given out with a grocery purchase. The stamps measure approximately 1 5/8" by 2 1/8". These unnumbered stamps are ordered below alphabetically by teams as follows, Atlanta Flames (1-18), Boston Bruins (19-36), Buffalo Sabres (37-54), California Golden Seals (55-72), Chicago Blackhawks (73-90), Detroit Red Wings (91-108), Kansas City Scouts (109-126), Los Angeles Kings (127-144), Minnesota North Stars (145-162), Montreal Canadiens (163-180), New York Islanders (181-198), New York Rangers (199-216), Philadelphia Flyers (217-234), Pittsburgh Penguins (235-252), St. Louis Blues (253-270), Toronto Maple Leafs (271-288), Vancouver Canucks (289-306), and Washington Capitals (307-324). An album was available for this set which included 20 stamps in the back. Some of the stamps (29, 57, 94, and 164) were only available in the album. Intact strips would be valued at 50 to 75 percent more than the sum of the respective player prices listed below.

| | NRMT-MT | EXC |
|---|---|---|
| COMPLETE SET (324) | 175.00 | 80.00 |
| COMMON STAMP (1-324) | .35 | .16 |

| | | |
|---|---|---|
| ❑ 1 Eric Vail | .50 | .23 |
| ❑ 2 Jerry Byers | .35 | .16 |
| ❑ 3 Rey Comeau | .35 | .16 |
| ❑ 4 Curt Bennett | .35 | .16 |
| ❑ 5 Bob Murray | .35 | .16 |
| ❑ 6 Dan Bouchard | 1.00 | .45 |
| ❑ 7 Pat Quinn | 1.00 | .45 |
| ❑ 8 Larry Romanchych | .35 | .16 |
| ❑ 9 Randy Manery | .35 | .16 |
| ❑ 10 Phil Myre | 1.00 | .45 |
| ❑ 11 Buster Harvey | .35 | .16 |
| ❑ 12 Keith McCreary | .35 | .16 |
| ❑ 13 Jean Lemieux | .35 | .16 |
| ❑ 14 Arnie Brown | .35 | .16 |
| ❑ 15 Bob Leiter | .35 | .16 |
| ❑ 16 Jacques Richard | .50 | .23 |
| ❑ 17 Noel Price | .35 | .16 |
| ❑ 18 Tom Lysiak | .75 | .35 |
| ❑ 19 Bobby Orr | 20.00 | 9.00 |
| ❑ 20 Al Sims | .50 | .23 |
| ❑ 21 Don Marcotte | .35 | .16 |
| ❑ 22 Terry O'Reilly | 1.00 | .45 |
| ❑ 23 Carol Vadnais | .35 | .16 |
| ❑ 24 Gilles Gilbert | 1.50 | .70 |
| ❑ 25 Bobby Schmautz | .50 | .23 |
| ❑ 26 Phil Esposito | 5.00 | 2.20 |
| ❑ 27 Walt McKechnie | .50 | .23 |
| ❑ 28 Ken Hodge | .75 | .35 |
| ❑ 29 Dave Forbes | .35 | .16 |
| ❑ 30 Wayne Cashman | .75 | .35 |
| ❑ 31 Johnny Bucyk | 1.50 | .70 |
| ❑ 32 Ross Brooks | .50 | .23 |
| ❑ 33 Dallas Smith | .35 | .16 |
| ❑ 34 Darryl Edestrand | .35 | .16 |
| ❑ 35 Gregg Sheppard | .35 | .16 |
| ❑ 36 Andre Savard | .50 | .23 |
| ❑ 37 Jim Schoenfeld | .75 | .35 |
| ❑ 38 Brian Spencer | .75 | .35 |
| ❑ 39 Rick Dudley | .50 | .23 |
| ❑ 40 Craig Ramsay | .35 | .16 |
| ❑ 41 Gary Bromley | .75 | .35 |
| ❑ 42 Lee Fogolin | .35 | .16 |
| ❑ 43 Jerry Korab | .35 | .16 |
| ❑ 44 Larry Mickey | .35 | .16 |
| ❑ 45 Roger Crozier | 1.00 | .45 |
| ❑ 46 Larry Carriere | .35 | .16 |
| ❑ 47 Norm Gratton | .35 | .16 |
| ❑ 48 Jim Lorentz | .35 | .16 |
| ❑ 49 Rene Robert | .75 | .35 |
| ❑ 50 Gilbert Perreault | 4.00 | 1.80 |
| (74/75 season on back) | | |
| ❑ 51 Mike Robitaille | .35 | .16 |
| ❑ 52 Don Luce | .35 | .16 |
| ❑ 53 Richard Martin | .75 | .35 |
| ❑ 54 Gerry Meehan | .50 | .23 |
| ❑ 55 Bruce Affleck | .35 | .16 |
| ❑ 56 Wayne King | .35 | .16 |
| ❑ 57 Joseph Johnston | .35 | .16 |
| ❑ 58 Ron Huston | .35 | .16 |
| ❑ 59 Dave Hrechkosy | .35 | .16 |
| ❑ 60 Stan Gilbertson | .35 | .16 |
| ❑ 61 Mike Christie | .35 | .16 |
| ❑ 62 Larry Wright | .35 | .16 |
| ❑ 63 Stan Weir | .35 | .16 |
| ❑ 64 Larry Patey | .35 | .16 |
| ❑ 65 Al MacAdam | .50 | .23 |
| ❑ 66 Ted McAneeley | .35 | .16 |
| ❑ 67 Jim Neilson | .35 | .16 |
| ❑ 68 Rick Hampton | .35 | .16 |
| ❑ 69 Len Frig | .35 | .16 |
| ❑ 70 Gilles Meloche | .75 | .35 |
| ❑ 71 Robert Stewart | .35 | .16 |
| ❑ 72 Craig Patrick | .75 | .35 |
| ❑ 73 Dennis Hull | .75 | .35 |
| ❑ 74 Dale Tallon | .50 | .23 |
| ❑ 75 Bill White | .50 | .23 |
| ❑ 76 Jim Pappin | .35 | .16 |
| ❑ 77 Cliff Koroll | .35 | .16 |
| ❑ 78 Tony Esposito | 5.00 | 2.20 |
| ❑ 79 Doug Jarrett | .35 | .16 |
| ❑ 80 John Marks | .35 | .16 |
| ❑ 81 Stan Mikita | 4.00 | 1.80 |
| ❑ 82 Darcy Rota | .35 | .16 |
| ❑ 83 J.P. Bordeleau | .35 | .16 |
| ❑ 84 Ivan Boldirev | .35 | .16 |
| ❑ 85 Germaine Gagnon UER | .35 | .16 |
| ❑ 86 Dick Redmond | .35 | .16 |
| ❑ 87 Pit Martin | .35 | .16 |
| ❑ 88 Keith Magnuson | .50 | .23 |
| ❑ 89 Phil Russell | .35 | .16 |
| ❑ 90 Chico Maki | .50 | .23 |
| ❑ 91 Jean Hamel | .35 | .16 |
| ❑ 92 Nick Libett | .50 | .23 |
| ❑ 93 Hank Nowak | .35 | .16 |
| ❑ 94 Guy Charron | .50 | .23 |
| ❑ 95 Bryan Watson | .35 | .16 |
| ❑ 96 Nelson Pyatt | .35 | .16 |
| ❑ 97 Billy Lochead | .35 | .16 |
| ❑ 98 Danny Grant | .50 | .23 |
| ❑ 99 Bill Hogaboam | .35 | .16 |
| ❑ 100 Jim Rutherford | 1.00 | .45 |
| ❑ 101 Doug Grant | .35 | .16 |
| ❑ 102 Pierre Jarry | .35 | .16 |
| ❑ 103 Doug Roberts | .35 | .16 |
| ❑ 104 Red Berenson | .75 | .35 |
| ❑ 105 Marcel Dionne | 3.50 | 1.55 |
| ❑ 106 Mickey Redmond | 1.50 | .70 |
| ❑ 107 Jack Lynch | .35 | .16 |
| ❑ 108 Thommie Bergman | .35 | .16 |
| ❑ 109 Mike Corrigan | .35 | .16 |
| ❑ 110 Frank St.Marseille | .35 | .16 |
| ❑ 111 Gene Carr | .35 | .16 |
| ❑ 112 Neil Komadoski | .35 | .16 |
| ❑ 113 Gary Edwards | .75 | .35 |
| ❑ 114 Sheldon Kannegiesser | .35 | .16 |
| ❑ 115 Bob Murdoch | .35 | .16 |
| ❑ 116 Rogatien Vachon | 2.50 | 1.10 |
| ❑ 117 Dave Hutchinson | .35 | .16 |
| ❑ 118 Tom Williams | .35 | .16 |
| ❑ 119 Butch Goring | .75 | .35 |
| ❑ 120 Bob Berry | .50 | .23 |
| ❑ 121 Dan Maloney | .50 | .23 |
| ❑ 122 Mike Murphy | .35 | .16 |
| ❑ 123 Juha Widing | .50 | .23 |
| ❑ 124 Don Kozak | .35 | .16 |
| ❑ 125 Bob Nevin | .35 | .16 |
| ❑ 126 Terry Harper | .50 | .23 |
| ❑ 127 Bill Goldsworthy | .75 | .35 |
| ❑ 128 Dennis O'Brien | .35 | .16 |
| ❑ 129 Dennis Hextall | .50 | .23 |
| ❑ 130 Murray Oliver | .35 | .16 |
| ❑ 131 Lou Nanne | .50 | .23 |
| ❑ 132 Fred Stanfield | .35 | .16 |
| ❑ 133 Jean-Paul Parise | .50 | .23 |
| ❑ 134 Tom Reid | .35 | .16 |
| ❑ 135 Fred Barrett | .35 | .16 |
| ❑ 136 Gary Bergman | .35 | .16 |
| ❑ 137 Barry Gibbs | .35 | .16 |
| ❑ 138 Cesare Maniago | 1.00 | .45 |
| ❑ 139 Jude Drouin | .35 | .16 |
| ❑ 140 Blake Dunlop | .35 | .16 |
| ❑ 141 Henry Boucha | .50 | .23 |
| ❑ 142 Fern Rivard | .35 | .16 |
| ❑ 143 Chris Ahrens | .35 | .16 |
| ❑ 144 Don Martineau | .35 | .16 |
| ❑ 145 Jacques Lemaire | 1.50 | .70 |
| ❑ 146 Peter Mahovlich | .75 | .35 |
| ❑ 147 Yvon Lambert | .35 | .16 |
| ❑ 148 Yvan Cournoyer | 2.50 | 1.10 |
| ❑ 149 Michel Larocque | .75 | .35 |
| ❑ 150 Guy Lapointe | 1.00 | .45 |
| ❑ 151 Steve Shutt | 3.00 | 1.35 |
| ❑ 152 Guy Lafleur | 7.00 | 3.10 |
| ❑ 153 Larry Robinson | 2.00 | .90 |
| ❑ 154 Jacques Laperriere | .75 | .35 |
| ❑ 155 Chuck Lefley | .35 | .16 |
| ❑ 156 Henri Richard | 2.50 | 1.10 |
| ❑ 157 Claude Larose | .35 | .16 |
| ❑ 158 Ken Dryden | 12.00 | 5.50 |
| ❑ 159 Pierre Bouchard | .35 | .16 |
| ❑ 160 Murray Wilson | .35 | .16 |
| ❑ 161 Jim Roberts | .50 | .23 |
| ❑ 162 Serge Savard | 1.00 | .45 |
| ❑ 163 Clark Gillies | 2.50 | 1.10 |
| ❑ 164 Garry Howatt | .35 | .16 |
| ❑ 165 Ernie Hicke | .35 | .16 |
| ❑ 166 Craig Cameron | .35 | .16 |
| ❑ 167 Ralph Stewart | .35 | .16 |
| ❑ 168 Lorne Henning | .35 | .16 |
| ❑ 169 Glenn Resch | 1.00 | .45 |
| ❑ 170 Bill MacMillan | .35 | .16 |
| ❑ 171 Doug Rombough | .35 | .16 |
| ❑ 172 Jean Potvin | .35 | .16 |
| ❑ 173 Gerry Hart | .35 | .16 |
| ❑ 174 Bert Marshall | .35 | .16 |
| ❑ 175 Billy Harris | .35 | .16 |
| ❑ 176 Bob Nystrom | .75 | .35 |
| ❑ 177 Dave Lewis | .35 | .16 |
| ❑ 178 Billy Smith | 2.00 | .90 |
| ❑ 179 Denis Potvin | 8.00 | 3.60 |
| ❑ 180 Ed Westfall | .50 | .23 |
| ❑ 181 Jerry Butler | .35 | .16 |
| ❑ 182 Bobby Rousseau | .50 | .23 |
| ❑ 183 Ron Harris | .35 | .16 |
| ❑ 184 Bill Fairbairn | .35 | .16 |
| ❑ 185 Derek Sanderson | 3.00 | 1.35 |
| ❑ 186 Jean Ratelle | 2.00 | .90 |
| ❑ 187 Greg Polis | .35 | .16 |
| ❑ 188 Rod Gilbert | 2.00 | .90 |
| ❑ 189 Ed Giacomin | 2.00 | .90 |
| ❑ 190 Rod Seiling | .35 | .16 |
| ❑ 191 Dale Rolfe | .35 | .16 |
| ❑ 192 Walt Tkaczuk | .50 | .23 |
| ❑ 193 Pete Stemkowski | .50 | .23 |
| ❑ 194 Gilles Villemure | .75 | .35 |
| ❑ 195 Ted Irvine | .35 | .16 |
| ❑ 196 Brad Park | 2.00 | .90 |
| ❑ 197 Gilles Marotte | .50 | .23 |
| ❑ 198 Steve Vickers | .50 | .23 |
| ❑ 199 Ross Lonsberry | .35 | .16 |
| ❑ 200 Bob Kelly | .50 | .23 |
| ❑ 201 Reggie Leach | .75 | .35 |
| ❑ 202 Bernie Parent | 3.50 | 1.55 |
| ❑ 203 Terry Crisp | .75 | .35 |
| ❑ 204 Bill Clement | 1.00 | .45 |
| ❑ 205 Bill Barber | 1.00 | .45 |
| ❑ 206 Dave Schultz | 1.00 | .45 |
| ❑ 207 Ed Van Impe | .35 | .16 |

❑ 208 Jimmy Watson .50 .23
❑ 209 Tom Bladon .35 .16
❑ 210 Rick MacLeish .75 .35
❑ 211 Andre Dupont .50 .23
❑ 212 Orest Kindrachuk .50 .23
❑ 213 Gary Dornhoefer .75 .35
❑ 214 Joe Watson .50 .23
❑ 215 Don Saleski .35 .16
❑ 216 Bobby Clarke 6.00 2.70
❑ 217 Jean Pronovost .75 .35
❑ 218 Ab DeMarco .35 .16
❑ 219 Wayne Bianchin .35 .16
❑ 220 Dave Burrows .35 .16
❑ 221 Ron Lalonde .35 .16
❑ 222 Syl Apps .75 .35
❑ 223 Bob Kelly .35 .16
❑ 224 Chuck Arnason .35 .16
❑ 225 Steve Durbano .35 .16
❑ 226 Ron Schock .35 .16
❑ 227 Bob Paradise .35 .16
❑ 228 Ron Stackhouse .35 .16
❑ 229 Lowell MacDonald .50 .23
❑ 230 Bob Johnson .35 .16
❑ 231 Rick Kehoe .75 .35
❑ 232 Nelson Debenedet .35 .16
❑ 233 Vic Hadfield .50 .23
❑ 234 Denis Herron 1.00 .45
❑ 235 Phil Roberto .35 .16
❑ 236 Floyd Thomson .35 .16
❑ 237 Don Awrey .35 .16
❑ 238 Rick Wilson .35 .16
❑ 239 John Davidson 3.00 1.35
❑ 240 Pierre Plante .35 .16
❑ 241 Barclay Plager .75 .35
❑ 242 Larry Giroux .35 .16
❑ 243 Bob Gassoff .75 .35
❑ 244 Dave Gardner .35 .16
❑ 245 Brian Ogilvie .35 .16
❑ 246 Ed Johnston 1.00 .45
❑ 247 Bob Plager .50 .23
❑ 248 Wayne Merrick .35 .16
❑ 249 Larry Sacharuk .35 .16
❑ 250 Bill Collins .35 .16
❑ 251 Garnet Bailey .35 .16
❑ 252 Garry Unger .75 .35
❑ 253 Gary Sabourin .35 .16
❑ 254 Willie Brossart .35 .16
❑ 255 Tim Ecclestone .35 .16
❑ 256 Dave Keon 1.50 .70
❑ 257 Darryl Sittler 3.00 1.35
❑ 258 Inge Hammarstrom .35 .16
❑ 259 Ian Turnbull .50 .23
❑ 260 Jim McKenny .35 .16
❑ 261 Norm Ullman 1.50 .70
❑ 262 Doug Favell 1.00 .45
❑ 263 Bob Neely .35 .16
❑ 264 Lanny McDonald 3.00 1.35
❑ 265 Dunc Wilson .75 .35
❑ 266 Errol Thompson .35 .16
❑ 267 Brian Glennie .35 .16
❑ 268 Bill Flett .35 .16
❑ 269 Borje Salming 1.50 .70
❑ 270 Ron Ellis .50 .23
❑ 271 Dave Dunn .35 .16
❑ 272 Chris Oddleifson .35 .16
❑ 273 Barry Wilkins .35 .16
❑ 274 Gary Smith .75 .35
❑ 275 Dennis Ververgaert .35 .16
❑ 276 Jocelyn Guevremont .35 .16
❑ 277 Andre Boudrias .50 .23
❑ 278 John Gould .35 .16
❑ 279 Jim Wiley .35 .16
❑ 280 Bob Dailey .35 .16
❑ 281 Tracy Pratt .35 .16
❑ 282 Ken Lockett .35 .16
❑ 283 Paulin Bordeleau .35 .16
❑ 284 Gerry O'Flaherty .35 .16
❑ 285 Bryan McSheffrey .35 .16
❑ 286 Gregg Boddy .35 .16
❑ 287 Don Lever .50 .23
❑ 288 Dennis Kearns .35 .16
❑ 289 Robin Burns .35 .16
❑ 290 Gary Coalter .35 .16
❑ 291 John Wright .35 .16
❑ 292 Peter McDuffe .75 .35
❑ 293 Simon Nolet .35 .16
❑ 294 Ted Snell .35 .16
❑ 295 Gary Croteau .35 .16
❑ 296 Lynn Powis .35 .16
❑ 297 Dave Hudson .35 .16
❑ 298 Richard Lemieux .35 .16
❑ 299 Bryan Lefley .35 .16
❑ 300 Doug Horbul .35 .16
❑ 301 Brent Hughes .35 .16
❑ 302 Ed Gilbert .35 .16
❑ 303 Michel Plasse .75 .35
❑ 304 Dennis Patterson .35 .16
❑ 305 Randy Rota .35 .16
❑ 306 Chris Evans .35 .16
❑ 307 Bill Mikkelson .35 .16
❑ 308 Ron Low 1.00 .45
❑ 309 Doug Mohns .50 .23
❑ 310 Joe Lundrigan .35 .16
❑ 311 Steve Atkinson .35 .16
❑ 312 Ron Anderson .35 .16
❑ 313 Mike Marson .75 .35
❑ 314 Lew Morrison .35 .16
❑ 315 Jack Egers .35 .16
❑ 316 Gordy Brooks .35 .16
❑ 317 Pete Laframboise .35 .16
❑ 318 Mike Bloom .35 .16
❑ 319 Bob Collyard .35 .16
❑ 320 Dave Kryskow .35 .16
❑ 321 Greg Joly .35 .16
❑ 322 Jim Hrycuik .35 .16
❑ 323 Bob Gryp .35 .16
❑ 324 Larry Fullan .35 .16
❑ NNO Album 20.00 9.00

## 1974-75 NHL Action Stamps Update

A group of 43 previously uncatalogued NHL Action (Loblaw) stamps has been reported. Thirty-six of these stamps are recropped or airbrushed versions of original stamps listing the player's new team. The remaining seven are completely new stamps to replace nine originals dropped from the set. The discrepancy between the seven added and the nine dropped stamps has led some to speculate that there were at least two other stamps in the set, all the more so since two teams (Islanders and Vancouver) have one less player than all the other teams. These stamps are grouped alphabetically within teams and checklisted below alphabetically according to teams as follows: Atlanta Flames (1), Boston Bruins (2), Buffalo Sabres (3-5), California Golden Seals (6-8), Detroit Red Wings (9-13), Kansas City Scouts (14-16), Minnesota North Stars (17-21), Montreal Canadiens (22-23), New York Islanders (24-25), New York Rangers (26), Pittsburgh Penguins (27-29), St. Louis Blues (30-34), Toronto Maple Leafs (35-37), Vancouver Canucks (38-40), and Washington Capitals (41-43).

| | NRMT-MT | EXC |
|---|---|---|
| COMPLETE SET (43) | 50.00 | 22.00 |
| COMMON CARD (1-43) | 1.00 | .45 |

❑ 1 Barry Gibbs 1.00 .45
(Replaces Arnie Brown)
❑ 2 Henry Nowak 1.00 .45
❑ 3 Jocelyn Guevremont 1.00 .45
❑ 4 Bryan McSheffrey 1.00 .45
❑ 5 Fred Stanfield 1.00 .45
❑ 6 Dave Gardner 1.00 .45
(Replaces Stan Gilbertson)
❑ 7 Morris Mott NEW 1.00 .45
(Replaces Bruce Affleck)
❑ 8 Gary Simmons NEW 4.00 1.80
❑ 9 Gary Bergman 1.50 .70
❑ 10 Dave Kryskow 1.00 .45
❑ 11 Walt McKechnie 1.00 .45
❑ 12 Phil Roberto 1.00 .45
❑ 13 Ted Snell 1.00 .45
(Replaces Thommie Bergman)
❑ 14 Guy Charron 1.50 .70
❑ 15 Jean-Guy Lagace NEW 1.00 .45
❑ 16 Denis Herron 4.00 1.80
❑ 17 Craig Cameron 1.00 .45
❑ 18 John Flesch NEW 1.00 .45
❑ 19 Norm Gratton 1.00 .45
❑ 20 Ernie Hicke 1.00 .45
❑ 21 Doug Rombough 1.00 .45
❑ 22 Don Awrey 1.00 .45
❑ 23 Wayne Thomas NEW 4.00 1.80
❑ 24 Jude Drouin 1.00 .45
❑ 25 Jean Paul Parise 1.00 .45
❑ 26 Rick Middleton NEW 5.00 2.20
❑ 27 Lew Morrison 1.00 .45
❑ 28 Michel Plasse 4.00 1.80
❑ 29 Barry Wilkins 1.00 .45
❑ 30 Red Berenson 1.50 .70
❑ 31 Chris Evans 1.00 .45
(Replaces Ace Bailey)
❑ 32 Claude Larose 1.00 .45
❑ 33 Chuck Lefley 1.00 .45
❑ 34 Craig Patrick 1.50 .70
(Replaces Larry Giroux)
❑ 35 Dave Dunn 1.00 .45
❑ 36 George Ferguson NEW 1.00 .45
(Replaces Dunc Wilson)
❑ 37 Rod Seiling 1.00 .45
(Replaces Tim Ecclestone)
❑ 38 Ab Demarco 1.00 .45
❑ 39 Gerry Meehan 1.00 .45
❑ 40 Mike Robitaille 1.00 .45
❑ 41 Willie Brossart 1.00 .45
❑ 42 Ron Lalonde 1.00 .45
(Replaces Pete Laframboise)
❑ 43 Jack Lynch 1.00 .45

## 1995-96 NHL Aces Playing Cards

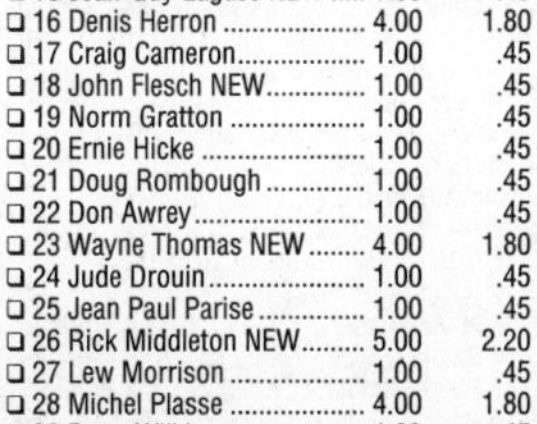


This 55 standard-size playing card set features National Hockey League players. The fronts of these rounded-corner cards feature full-color action player shots. The team logo appears in the upper right of each picture. The player's name and position appear in either a blue or aqua stripe at the bottom. The backs have the NHL Aces design and sponsor logos on a black background. Since this set is similar to a playing card set, the set is checklisted below as if it were a playing card deck. In the checklist C means Clubs, D means Diamonds, H means Hearts and S means Spades. The cards are checklisted in playing order by suits and numbers are assigned to Aces (1), Jacks (11), Queens (12) and Kings (13).

| | MINT | NRMT |
|---|---|---|
| COMPLETE SET (55) | 15.00 | 6.75 |
| COMMON CARD (1-52) | .05 | .02 |

❑ 1C Paul Coffey .30 .14
❑ 1D Wayne Gretzky 3.00 1.35
❑ 1H Eric Lindros 1.50 .70
❑ 1S Patrick Roy 2.00 .90
❑ 2C Scott Stevens .05 .02
❑ 2D Al Macinnis .05 .02
❑ 2H Craig Janney .05 .02
❑ 2S Kirk Muller .05 .02
❑ 3C Bill Ranford .15 .07
❑ 3D Mike Modano .50 .23
❑ 3H Doug Gilmour .30 .14
❑ 3S Steve Yzerman 1.50 .70
❑ 4C Brian Bradley .05 .02
❑ 4D Alexandre Daigle .05 .02
❑ 4H Claude Lemieux .15 .07
❑ 4S Felix Potvin .30 .14
❑ 5C Ed Belfour .30 .14
❑ 5D Jeremy Roenick .30 .14
❑ 5H Trevor Linden .10 .05
❑ 5S Pat Lafontaine .15 .07
❑ 6C Brian Leetch .30 .14
❑ 6D Jason Arnott .10 .05
❑ 6H Geoff Sanderson .05 .02
❑ 6S Jim Carey .30 .14
❑ 7C Ron Francis .15 .07
❑ 7D Peter Bondra .30 .14
❑ 7H Paul Kariya 1.75 .80
❑ 7S John Vanbiesbrouck .50 .23
❑ 8C Teemu Selanne .75 .35
❑ 8D Ray Bourque .30 .14
❑ 8H Pierre Turgeon .15 .07
❑ 8S Alexei Yashin .30 .14
❑ 9C Martin Brodeur 1.00 .45
❑ 9D Pavel Bure .75 .35
❑ 9H Peter Forsberg 1.50 .70
❑ 9S Chris Chelios .30 .14
❑ 10C Joe Nieuwendyk .20 .09
❑ 10D Mats Sundin .30 .14
❑ 10H Adam Oates .15 .07
❑ 10S Cam Neely .20 .09
❑ 11C Mark Messier .50 .23
❑ 11D Brett Hull .50 .23
❑ 11H Sergei Fedorov .75 .35
❑ 11S Keith Tkachuk .50 .23
❑ 12C Mikael Renberg .15 .07
❑ 12D Jaromir Jagr 1.50 .70
❑ 12H Mario Lemieux 2.00 .90
❑ 12S John LeClair .60 .25
❑ 13C Joe Sakic .75 .35
❑ 13D Dominik Hasek .75 .35
❑ 13H Alexei Zhamnov .10 .05
❑ 13S Theoren Fleury .30 .14
❑ NNO Checklist of Players in Deck .05 .02
❑ NNO Western Conference Logo .05 .02
❑ NNO Eastern Conference Logo .05 .02

## 1996-97 NHL Aces Playing Cards

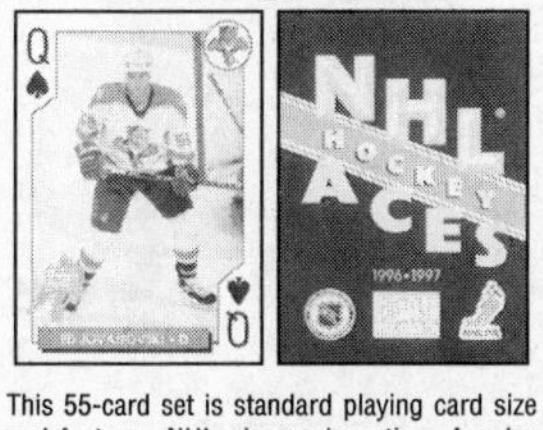


This 55-card set is standard playing card size and features NHL players in action. A color action photo takes up the bulk of the front, with the team logo in the upper right corner. The suits and numbers are located in the upper left and lower right hand corners. Player name and position can be found along the bottom. If the player was a finalist for or winner of any major NHL award, that achievement is noted with a golden icon in the lower left corner. The backs carry a uniformly indistinguishable NHL Hockey Aces logo.

| | MINT | NRMT |
|---|---|---|
| COMPLETE SET (55) | 12.00 | 5.50 |
| COMMON CARD (1-52) | .10 | .05 |

❑ 1 Daniel Alfredsson .20 .09
❑ 2 Jason Arnott .20 .09
❑ 3 Ray Bourque .30 .14
❑ 4 Rod Brind'Amour .20 .09
❑ 5 Martin Brodeur 1.00 .45
❑ 6 Pavel Bure .75 .35
❑ 7 Jim Carey .25 .11
❑ 8 Chris Chelios .30 .14
❑ 9 Vincent Damphousse .15 .07
❑ 10 Eric Daze .25 .11
❑ 11 Sergei Fedorov .75 .35
❑ 12 Ray Ferraro .10 .05
❑ 13 Theoren Fleury .30 .14
❑ 14 Peter Forsberg 1.00 .45
❑ 15 Ron Francis .20 .09
❑ 16 Grant Fuhr .20 .09
❑ 17 Mike Gartner .15 .07
❑ 18 Doug Gilmour .30 .14
❑ 19 Travis Green .10 .05
❑ 20 Wayne Gretzky 2.00 .90
❑ 21 Roman Hamrlik .15 .07
❑ 22 Brett Hull .50 .23
❑ 23 Jaromir Jagr 1.00 .45
❑ 24 Ed Jovanovski .20 .09
❑ 25 Joe Juneau .20 .09
❑ 26 Paul Kariya 1.25 .55
❑ 27 Pat LaFontaine .25 .11
❑ 28 Brian Leetch .30 .14
❑ 29 Mario Lemieux 1.50 .70
❑ 30 Trevor Linden .20 .09
❑ 31 Eric Lindros 1.00 .45
❑ 32 Mark Messier .50 .23
❑ 33 Mike Modano .50 .23
❑ 34 Alexander Mogilny .25 .11
❑ 35 Owen Nolan .15 .07
❑ 36 Adam Oates .25 .11
❑ 37 Chris Osgood .30 .14
❑ 38 Daren Puppa .15 .07
❑ 39 Gary Roberts .15 .07
❑ 40 Jeremy Roenick .30 .14
❑ 41 Patrick Roy 1.50 .70
❑ 42 Joe Sakic .75 .35
❑ 43 Teemu Selanne .75 .35
❑ 44 Brendan Shanahan .75 .35
❑ 45 Mats Sundin .30 .14
❑ 46 Jocelyn Thibault .25 .11
❑ 47 Keith Tkachuk .50 .23
❑ 48 Pierre Turgeon .25 .11
❑ 49 John Vanbiesbrouck .60 .25
❑ 50 Doug Weight .20 .09
❑ 51 Alexei Yashin .30 .14
❑ 52 Steve Yzerman 1.00 .45
❑ NNO Western Conference .10 .05
❑ NNO Eastern Conference .10 .05
❑ NNO Checklist .10 .05

## 1995-96 NHL Cool Trade

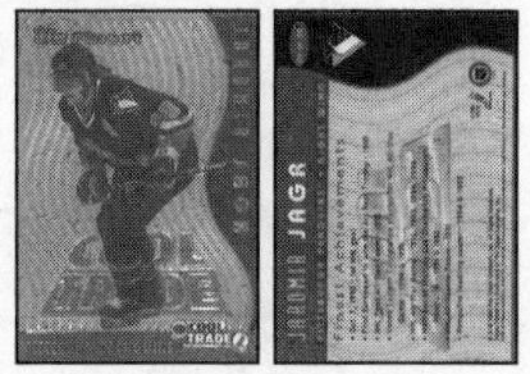


This 20-card standard-size set is the result of a unique collaboration between the NHL, the NHLPA and the five card manufacturers. Each of the latter created four cards for inclusion in the set, which was available to collectors who sent in 20 wrappers plus postage and handling to a mailing address. The set also was available at the NHLPA booth at the 1996 National Convention for between five and ten wrappers, depending upon when you went to the booth. The set includes five different designs, one unique to each contributing manufacturer. There also was the possibility of acquiring limited-edition upgrade versions of the cards. Cool Trade exchange cards were randomly inserted in packs of Bowman, Donruss Elite, Summit, Ultra series 2, and Upper Deck series 2. These could be mailed in to the participating licensee for redemption. The Emotion exchange card inserted in '95-96 Ultra series two was by far the most difficult to acquire. The redemption cards are priced individually below, and have an RP prefix amended to them for cataloguing purposes.

| | MINT | NRMT |
|---|---|---|
| COMPLETE SET (20) | 10.00 | 4.50 |
| COMMON CARD (1-20) | .40 | .18 |
| COMMON RP CARD | 2.00 | .90 |

❑ 1 Cam Neely .40 .18
❑ 2 Wayne Gretzky 4.00 1.80
❑ 3 Jeremy Roenick 1.00 .45
❑ 4 Mario Lemieux 3.00 1.35
❑ 5 Mark Messier 1.00 .45
❑ 6 Ray Bourque .75 .35
❑ 7 Sergei Fedorov 1.25 .55
❑ 8 Paul Kariya 2.50 1.10
❑ 9 Eric Lindros 2.50 1.10
❑ 10 Pavel Bure 1.25 .55
❑ 11 Chris Chelios .75 .35
❑ 12 Peter Forsberg 2.00 .90
❑ 13 Saku Koivu 1.25 .55
❑ 14 Ed Belfour 1.00 .45
❑ 15 Brett Hull .75 .35
❑ 16 Patrick Roy 3.00 1.35
❑ 17 Doug Gilmour .75 .35
❑ 18 Martin Brodeur 1.00 .45
❑ 19 Alexander Mogilny .75 .35
❑ 20 Jaromir Jagr 2.00 .90
❑ RP1 Cam Neely 2.00 .90
❑ RP2 Wayne Gretzky 20.00 9.00
❑ RP3 Jeremy Roenick 6.00 2.70
❑ RP4 Mario Lemieux 6.00 2.70
❑ RP5 Mark Messier 6.00 2.70
❑ RP6 Ray Bourque 2.00 .90
❑ RP7 Sergei Fedorov 5.00 2.20
❑ RP8 Paul Kariya 50.00 22.00
❑ RP9 Eric Lindros 5.00 2.20
❑ RP10 Pavel Bure 10.00 4.50
❑ RP11 Chris Chelios 2.00 .90
❑ RP12 Peter Forsberg 5.00 2.20
❑ RP13 Saku Koivu 12.00 5.50
❑ RP14 Ed Belfour 2.50 1.10
❑ RP15 Brett Hull 6.00 2.70
❑ RP16 Patrick Roy 10.00 4.50
❑ RP17 Doug Gilmour 2.00 .90
❑ RP18 Martin Brodeur 20.00 9.00
❑ RP19 Alexander Mogilny 2.00 .90
❑ RP20 Jaromir Jagr 12.00 5.50

## 1995-96 No Fear Ad Cards

These large (6X9") photocards feature close-up color photos of Fuhr and Fleury, two spokesman for the No Fear company. It is not known whether these were the only cards issued, nor how exactly they were distributed. Any additional information would be appreciate.

| | MINT | NRMT |
|---|---|---|
| COMPLETE SET (2) | 8.00 | 3.60 |
| COMMON CARD (1-2) | 5.00 | 2.20 |

❑ 1 Grant Fuhr 5.00 2.20
❑ 2 Theoren Fleury 6.00 2.70

## 1996-97 NHL Pro Stamps

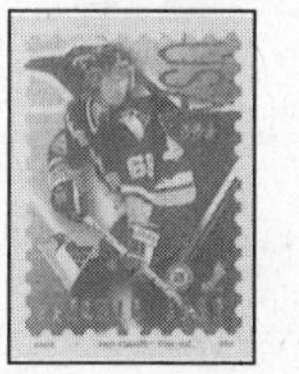

This set of 130 postage stamp-style collectibles was released by Chris Martin Enterprises. The series was issued in 12 numbered sheets of 12 stamps each. There were several double prints-they are noted below with a DP suffix.

| | MINT | NRMT |
|---|---|---|
| COMPLETE SET (130) | 18.00 | 8.00 |
| COMMON STAMP (1-130) | .10 | .05 |

❑ 1 Stephane Fiset .15 .07
❑ 2 Peter Forsberg .60 .25
❑ 3 Claude Lemieux DP .15 .07
❑ 4 Mike Ricci .10 .05
❑ 5 Joe Sakic .50 .23
❑ 6 Ed Belfour .25 .11
❑ 7 Chris Chelios .25 .11
❑ 8 Joe Murphy .10 .05
❑ 9 Bernie Nicholls .10 .05
❑ 10 Jeremy Roenick DP .25 .11
❑ 11 Geoff Courtnall .10 .05
❑ 12 Brett Hull .35 .16
❑ 13 Al MacInnis .15 .07
❑ 14 Chris Pronger .15 .07
❑ 15 Esa Tikkanen .15 .07
❑ 16 Ray Bourque .25 .11
❑ 17 Blaine Lacher .15 .07
❑ 18 Cam Neely .20 .09
❑ 19 Adam Oates DP .20 .09
❑ 20 Kevin Stevens .10 .05
❑ 21 Valeri Bure .10 .05
❑ 22 Vincent Damphousse .15 .07
❑ 23 Mark Recchi .15 .07
❑ 24 Patrick Roy .75 .35
❑ 25 Pierre Turgeon .20 .09
❑ 26 Pavel Bure .40 .18
❑ 27 Trevor Linden .15 .07
❑ 28 Kirk McLean .15 .07
❑ 29 Alexander Mogilny .25 .11
❑ 30 Cliff Ronning .10 .05
❑ 31 Jason Allison .10 .05
❑ 32 Jim Carey .30 .14
❑ 33 Dale Hunter .10 .05
❑ 34 Joe Juneau DP .20 .09
❑ 35 Brendan Witt .10 .05
❑ 36 Martin Brodeur DP .40 .18
❑ 37 John MacLean .15 .07
❑ 38 Scott Niedermayer .15 .07
❑ 39 Stephane Richer .10 .05
❑ 40 Scott Stevens .10 .05
❑ 41 Patrik Carnback .10 .05
❑ 42 Guy Hebert .20 .09
❑ 43 Paul Kariya .60 .25
❑ 44 Oleg Tverdovsky .15 .07
❑ 45 Garry Valk .10 .05
❑ 46 Theoren Fleury .20 .09
❑ 47 Trevor Kidd .15 .07
❑ 48 Joe Nieuwendyk .15 .07
❑ 49 Gary Roberts .10 .05
❑ 50 German Titov .10 .05
❑ 51 Rod Brind'Amour .15 .07
❑ 52 Ron Hextall .15 .07
❑ 53 John LeClair .30 .14
❑ 54 Eric Lindros .60 .25
❑ 55 Mikael Renberg .20 .09
❑ 56 Brett Lindros .10 .05

| | | |
|---|---|---|
| □ 57 Wendel Clark | .15 | .07 |
| □ 58 Patrick Flatley | .10 | .05 |
| □ 59 Kirk Muller | .10 | .05 |
| □ 60 Mathieu Schneider | .10 | .05 |
| □ 61 Tim Cheveldae | .15 | .07 |
| □ 62 Dallas Drake | .10 | .05 |
| □ 63 Teemu Selanne | .40 | .18 |
| □ 64 Keith Tkachuk | .30 | .14 |
| □ 65 Alexei Zhamnov | .15 | .07 |
| □ 66 Rob Blake | .15 | .07 |
| □ 67 Wayne Gretzky DP | 1.00 | .45 |
| □ 68 Jari Kurri | .15 | .07 |
| □ 69 Jamie Storr | .15 | .07 |
| □ 70 Rick Tocchet | .15 | .07 |
| □ 71 Brian Bradley | .10 | .05 |
| □ 72 Chris Gratton | .15 | .07 |
| □ 73 Roman Hamrlik | .15 | .07 |
| □ 74 Paul Ysebaert | .10 | .05 |
| □ 75 Rob Zamuner | .10 | .05 |
| □ 76 Dave Andreychuk | .15 | .07 |
| □ 77 Doug Gilmour | .25 | .11 |
| □ 78 Kenny Jonsson | .15 | .07 |
| □ 79 Felix Potvin | .30 | .14 |
| □ 80 Mats Sundin | .20 | .09 |
| □ 81 Jason Arnott | .20 | .09 |
| □ 82 Jason Bonsignore | .10 | .05 |
| □ 83 Todd Marchant | .10 | .05 |
| □ 84 Bill Ranford | .20 | .09 |
| □ 85 Doug Weight | .20 | .09 |
| □ 86 Jody Hull | .10 | .05 |
| □ 87 Bob Kudelski | .10 | .05 |
| □ 88 Scott Mellanby | .15 | .07 |
| □ 89 Rob Niedermayer | .15 | .07 |
| □ 90 John Vanbiesbrouck | .50 | .23 |
| □ 91 Ron Francis | .20 | .09 |
| □ 92 Jaromir Jagr | .60 | .25 |
| □ 93 Mario Lemieux DP | .75 | .35 |
| □ 94 Bryan Smolinski | .10 | .05 |
| □ 95 Sergei Zubov | .10 | .05 |
| □ 96 Adam Graves | .15 | .07 |
| □ 97 Brian Leetch | .20 | .09 |
| □ 98 Mark Messier DP | .35 | .16 |
| □ 99 Mike Richter | .25 | .11 |
| □ 100 Luc Robitaille | .20 | .09 |
| □ 101 Paul Coffey | .20 | .09 |
| □ 102 Sergei Fedorov DP | .40 | .18 |
| □ 103 Nicklas Lidstrom | .15 | .07 |
| □ 104 Ray Sheppard | .10 | .05 |
| □ 105 Steve Yzerman | .50 | .23 |
| □ 106 Donald Audette | .10 | .05 |
| □ 107 Dominik Hasek DP | .40 | .18 |
| □ 108 Yuri Khmylev | .10 | .05 |
| □ 109 Pat LaFontaine | .15 | .07 |
| □ 110 Alexei Zhitnik | .10 | .05 |
| □ 111 Radek Bonk | .10 | .05 |
| □ 112 Randy Cunneyworth | .10 | .05 |
| □ 113 Alexandre Daigle | .15 | .07 |
| □ 114 Steve Larouche | .10 | .05 |
| □ 115 Martin Straka | .10 | .05 |
| □ 116 Ulf Dahlen | .10 | .05 |
| □ 117 Pat Falloon | .10 | .05 |
| □ 118 Jeff Friesen | .15 | .07 |
| □ 119 Arturs Irbe DP | .15 | .07 |
| □ 120 Craig Janney | .10 | .05 |
| □ 121 Shane Churla | .10 | .05 |
| □ 122 Todd Harvey | .10 | .05 |
| □ 123 Derian Hatcher | .10 | .05 |
| □ 124 Mike Modano | .20 | .09 |
| □ 125 Andy Moog | .20 | .09 |
| □ 126 Sean Burke | .15 | .07 |
| □ 127 Andrew Cassels | .10 | .05 |
| □ 128 Geoff Sanderson | .15 | .07 |
| □ 129 Brendan Shanahan | .35 | .16 |
| □ 130 Darren Turcotte | .10 | .05 |

## 1972-73 Nordiques Postcards

This standard size postcard features color photos surrounded by a white border. Card fronts feature a facsimile autograph and were issued by Pro Star Promotions. Backs are blank. The postcards are unnumbered and checklisted below in alphabetical order.

| | MINT | NRMT |
|---|---|---|
| COMPLETE SET (22) | 40.00 | 18.00 |
| COMMON CARD | 1.00 | .45 |

| | | |
|---|---|---|
| □ 1 Michel Archambeault | 2.00 | .90 |
| □ 2 Serge Aubry | 2.00 | .90 |
| □ 3 Yves Bergeron | 2.00 | .90 |
| □ 4 Jacques Blain | 2.00 | .90 |
| □ 5 Alain Caron | 2.00 | .90 |
| □ 6 Ken Desjardine | 2.00 | .90 |
| □ 7 Maurice Filion | 2.00 | .90 |
| □ 8 Andre Gaudette | 2.00 | .90 |
| □ 9 Jean-Guy Gendron | 2.00 | .90 |
| □ 10 Rejean Giroux | 2.00 | .90 |
| □ 11 Frank Golembrosky | 2.00 | .90 |
| □ 12 Robert Guindon | 2.00 | .90 |
| □ 13 Pierre Guite | 2.00 | .90 |
| □ 14 Francois Lacombe | 2.00 | .90 |
| □ 15 Paul Larose | 2.00 | .90 |
| □ 16 Jacques Lemelin | 2.00 | .90 |
| □ 17 Michel Parizeau | 2.00 | .90 |
| □ 18 Jean Payette | 2.00 | .90 |
| □ 19 Michel Rouleau | 2.00 | .90 |
| □ 20 Pierre Roy | 2.00 | .90 |
| □ 21 J.C. Tremblay | 3.00 | 1.35 |
| □ NNO Header Card | 1.00 | .45 |

## 1973-74 Nordiques Team Issue

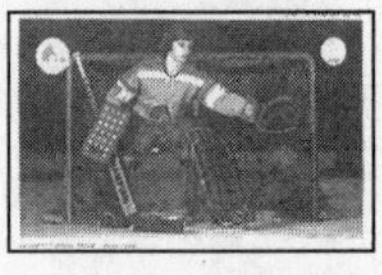

This 21-card team issue set features the 1973-74 Quebec Nordiques of the World Hockey Association. The oversized cards measure approximately 3 1/2" by 5 1/2". The fronts feature glossy color posed photos with white borders. The team and WHA logos are superimposed in the upper corners of the picture. A facsimile autograph is inscribed across the bottom of the picture. The backs are blank. The cards are unnumbered and checklisted below in alphabetical order.

| | NRMT-MT | EXC |
|---|---|---|
| COMPLETE SET (21) | 40.00 | 18.00 |
| COMMON CARD (1-21) | 2.00 | .90 |

| | | |
|---|---|---|
| □ 1 Mike Archambault | 2.00 | .90 |
| □ 2 Serge Aubry | 2.00 | .90 |
| □ 3 Yves Bergeron | 2.00 | .90 |
| □ 4 Jacques Blain | 2.00 | .90 |
| □ 5 Richard Brodeur | 6.00 | 2.70 |
| □ 6 Alain Caron | 2.00 | .90 |
| □ 7 Ken Desjardine | 2.00 | .90 |
| □ 8 Maurice Filion | 2.00 | .90 |
| □ 9 Andre Gaudette | 2.00 | .90 |
| □ 10 Jean-Guy Gendron | 3.00 | 1.35 |
| □ 11 Rejean Giroux | 2.00 | .90 |
| □ 12 Frank Golembrosky | 2.00 | .90 |
| □ 13 Bob Guindon | 2.00 | .90 |
| □ 14 Pierre Guite | 2.00 | .90 |
| □ 15 Frank Lacombe | 2.00 | .90 |
| □ 16 Paul Larose | 2.00 | .90 |
| □ 17 Michel Parizeau | 2.00 | .90 |
| □ 18 Jean Payette | 2.00 | .90 |
| □ 19 Michel Rouleau | 2.00 | .90 |
| □ 20 Pierre Roy | 2.00 | .90 |
| □ 21 J.C. Tremblay | 3.00 | 1.35 |

## 1976 Nordiques Marie Antoinette

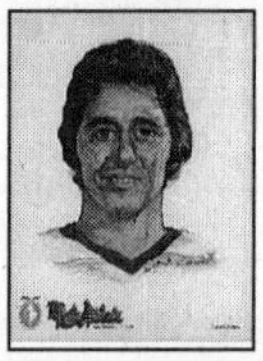

This 14-card set measures approximately 8" by 10 1/2" and features on the fronts color player portraits of the Quebec Nordiques by the artist Claude Laroche. The player's name is printed in black in the lower right with the card logo on the left. The backs are blank. The cards are unnumbered and checklisted below in alphabetical order.

| | NRMT-MT | EXC |
|---|---|---|
| COMPLETE SET (14) | 60.00 | 27.00 |
| COMMON CARD (1-14) | 4.00 | 1.80 |

| | | |
|---|---|---|
| □ 1 Paul Baxter | 4.00 | 1.80 |
| □ 2 Serge Bernier | 4.00 | 1.80 |
| □ 3 Paulin Bordeleau | 4.00 | 1.80 |
| □ 4 Andre Boudrias | 5.00 | 2.20 |
| □ 5 Curt Brackenbury | 4.00 | 1.80 |
| □ 6 Richard Brodeur | 8.00 | 3.60 |
| □ 7 Real Cloutier | 6.00 | 2.70 |
| □ 8 Charles Constantin | 4.00 | 1.80 |
| □ 9 Bob Fitchner | 4.00 | 1.80 |
| □ 10 Richard Grenier | 4.00 | 1.80 |
| □ 11 Marc Tardif | 6.00 | 2.70 |
| □ 12 Jean-Claude Tremblay | 6.00 | 2.70 |
| □ 13 Steve Sutherland | 4.00 | 1.80 |
| □ 14 Wally Weir | 4.00 | 1.80 |

## 1976-77 Nordiques Postcards

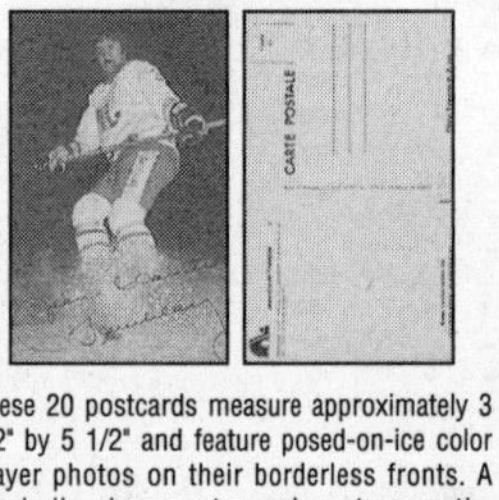

These 20 postcards measure approximately 3 1/2" by 5 1/2" and feature posed-on-ice color player photos on their borderless fronts. A facsimile player autograph rests near the bottom. The backs carry the player's name, uniform number, brief biography, and Nordiques team logo at the upper left. Places for stamp and address appear on the right. All text is in French. The postcards are unnumbered and checklisted below in alphabetical order.

| | NRMT-MT | EXC |
|---|---|---|
| COMPLETE SET (20) | 30.00 | 13.50 |
| COMMON CARD (1-20) | 1.50 | .70 |

| | | |
|---|---|---|
| □ 1 Serge Aubry | 1.50 | .70 |
| □ 2 Paul Baxter | 2.00 | .90 |
| □ 3 Jean Bernier | 1.50 | .70 |
| □ 4 Serge Bernier | 3.00 | 1.35 |
| □ 5 Christian Bordeleau | 1.50 | .70 |
| □ 6 Paulin Bordeleau | 2.00 | .90 |
| □ 7 Andre Boudrias | 2.00 | .90 |
| □ 8 Curt Brackenbury | 1.50 | .70 |
| □ 9 Richard Brodeur | 4.00 | 1.80 |
| □ 10 Real Cloutier | 3.00 | 1.35 |
| □ 11 Charles Constantin | 1.50 | .70 |
| □ 12 Jim Dorey | 2.00 | .90 |
| □ 13 Robert Fitchner | 1.50 | .70 |
| □ 14 Richard Grenier | 1.50 | .70 |
| □ 15 Francois Lacombe | 1.50 | .70 |
| □ 16 Pierre Roy | 1.50 | .70 |
| □ 17 Steve Sutherland | 1.50 | .70 |
| □ 18 Marc Tardif | 3.00 | 1.35 |
| □ 19 J.C. Tremblay | 3.00 | 1.35 |
| □ 20 Wally Weir | 1.50 | .70 |

## 1980-81 Nordiques Postcards

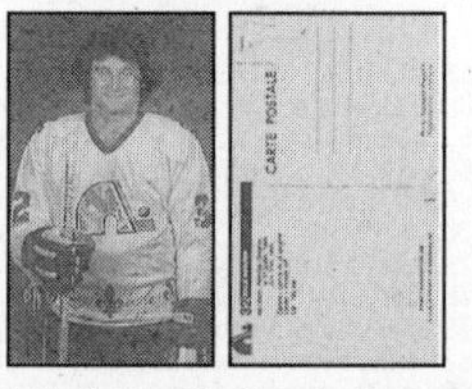

Printed in Canada, this 24-card set measures approximately 3" by 5 1/2" and features members of the 1980-81 Quebec Nordiques. The fronts have borderless, posed color player photos. The backs are in postcard format with a short player biography both in French and in English. The text on some cards is printed in royal blue and on other cards in turquoise. The cards are unnumbered and checklisted below in alphabetical order.

| | NRMT-MT | EXC |
|---|---|---|
| COMPLETE SET (29) | 40.00 | 18.00 |
| COMMON CARD (1-29) | 1.00 | .45 |

| | | |
|---|---|---|
| □ 1 Michel Bergeron | 1.00 | .45 |
| □ 2 Serge Bernier | 2.00 | .90 |
| □ 3 Daniel Bouchard | 1.00 | .45 |
| □ 4 Ron Chipperfield | 1.00 | .45 |
| □ 5 Kim Clackson | 1.50 | .70 |
| □ 6 Real Cloutier | 2.00 | .90 |
| □ 7 Alain Cote | 1.50 | .70 |
| □ 8 Michel Dion | 1.50 | .70 |
| □ 9 Andre Dupont | 1.50 | .70 |
| □ 10 Robbie Ftorek | 2.00 | .90 |
| □ 11 Michel Goulet | 5.00 | 2.20 |
| □ 12 Ron Grahame | 1.00 | .45 |
| □ 13 Jamie Hislop | 1.00 | .45 |
| □ 14 Dale Hoganson | 1.00 | .45 |
| □ 15 Dale Hunter | 5.00 | 2.20 |
| □ 16 Pierre Lacroix | 1.00 | .45 |
| □ 17 Garry Lariviere | 1.00 | .45 |
| □ 18 Richard Leduc | 1.00 | .45 |
| □ 19 Lee Norwood | 1.50 | .70 |
| □ 20 John Paddock | 1.50 | .70 |
| □ 21 Dave Pichette | 1.00 | .45 |
| □ 22 Michel Plasse | 2.00 | .90 |
| □ 23 Jacques Richard | 1.50 | .70 |
| □ 24 Normand Rochefort | 1.00 | .45 |
| □ 25 Anton Stastny | 2.00 | .90 |
| □ 26 Peter Stastny | 8.00 | 3.60 |
| □ 27 Marc Tardif | 2.00 | .90 |
| □ 28 Wally Weir | 1.00 | .45 |
| □ 29 John Wensink | 1.50 | .70 |

## 1981-82 Nordiques Postcards

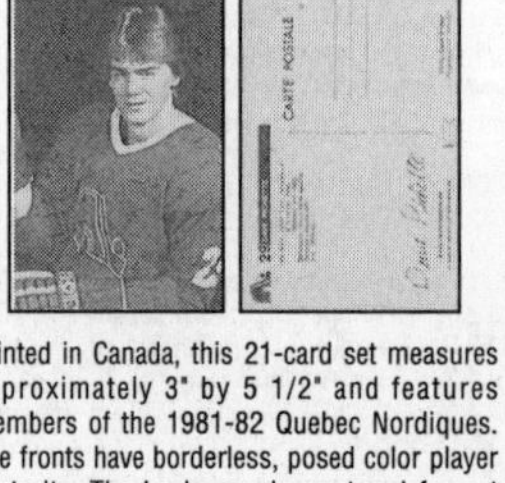

Printed in Canada, this 21-card set measures approximately 3" by 5 1/2" and features members of the 1981-82 Quebec Nordiques. The fronts have borderless, posed color player portraits. The backs are in postcard format with a short player biography both in French and in English. The cards are unnumbered and checklisted below in alphabetical order.

| | NRMT-MT | EXC |
|---|---|---|
| COMPLETE SET (21) | 25.00 | 11.00 |
| COMMON CARD (1-21) | .75 | .35 |

| | | |
|---|---|---|
| □ 1 Pierre Aubry | 1.00 | .45 |
| □ 2 Michel Bergeron CO | 1.50 | .70 |
| □ 3 Daniel Bouchard | 2.00 | .90 |
| □ 4 Real Cloutier | 2.00 | .90 |
| □ 5 Alain Cote | 1.00 | .45 |
| □ 6 Andre Dupont | 1.00 | .45 |
| □ 7 Miroslav Frycer UER (Last and first names are reversed) | 1.00 | .45 |
| □ 8 Michel Goulet | 4.00 | 1.80 |
| □ 9 Dale Hunter | 3.00 | 1.35 |
| □ 10 Pierre Lacroix | 1.00 | .45 |
| □ 11 Mario Marois | 1.00 | .45 |
| □ 12 Dave Pichette | 1.00 | .45 |
| □ 13 Michel Plasse | 1.50 | .70 |
| □ 14 Jacques Richard | 1.50 | .70 |
| □ 15 Normand Rochefort | 1.00 | .45 |
| □ 16 Anton Stastny | 1.50 | .70 |
| □ 17 Peter Stastny | 5.00 | 2.20 |
| □ 18 Marian Stastny | 2.50 | 1.10 |
| □ 19 Marc Tardif | 1.50 | .70 |
| □ 20 Charles Thiffault CO | .75 | .35 |
| □ 21 Wally Weir | 1.00 | .45 |

## 1982-83 Nordiques Postcards

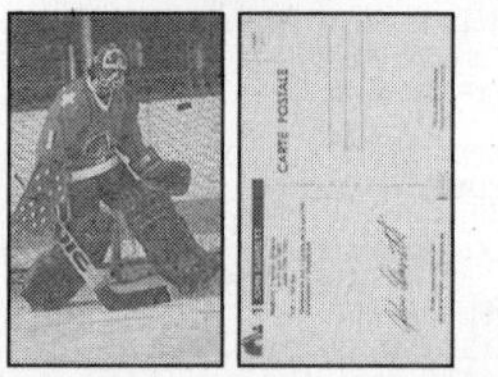

This 24-card set measures approximately 3" by 5 1/2" and features members of the 1982-83 Quebec Nordiques. The fronts have borderless color action player photos. The backs are in postcard format with a short player biography both in French and in English and a facsimile player autograph on the bottom. The cards are unnumbered and checklisted below in alphabetical order.

| | MINT | NRMT |
|---|---|---|
| COMPLETE SET (25) | 25.00 | 11.00 |
| COMMON CARD (1-25) | .50 | .23 |

| | | |
|---|---|---|
| □ 1 Pierre Aubry | .75 | .35 |
| □ 2 Michel Bergeron CO | 1.50 | .70 |
| □ 3 Daniel Bouchard | .50 | .23 |
| □ 4 Real Cloutier | 2.00 | .90 |
| □ 5 Alain Cote | .75 | .35 |
| □ 6 Andre Dupont | 1.00 | .45 |
| □ 7 John Garrett | 1.50 | .70 |
| □ 8 Michel Goulet | 3.00 | 1.35 |
| □ 9 Jean Hamel | .75 | .35 |
| □ 10 Dale Hunter | 2.50 | 1.10 |
| □ 11 Rick Lapointe | 1.00 | .45 |
| □ 12 Clint Malarchuk | 2.00 | .90 |
| □ 13 Mario Marois | .75 | .35 |
| □ 14 Randy Moller | .75 | .35 |
| □ 15 Wilf Paiement | 1.00 | .45 |
| □ 16 Dave Pichette | .75 | .35 |
| □ 17 Jacques Richard | 1.50 | .70 |
| □ 18 Normand Rochefort | .75 | .35 |
| □ 19 Louis Sleigher | .75 | .35 |
| □ 20 Anton Stastny | 1.50 | .70 |
| □ 21 Marian Stastny | 1.50 | .70 |
| □ 22 Peter Stastny | 3.00 | 1.35 |
| □ 23 Marc Tardif | 1.50 | .70 |
| □ 24 Charles Thiffault ACO | .50 | .23 |
| □ 25 Wally Weir | .75 | .35 |

## 1983-84 Nordiques Postcards

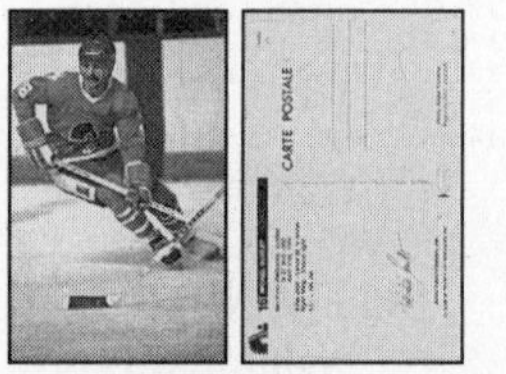

This 32-card set measures approximately 3 1/2" by 5 1/2" and features members of the 1983-84 Quebec Nordiques. This set features borderless full-color action shots on the front. The back is in postcard format with a brief identification of the player written in blue ink. This unnumbered set has been checklisted in alphabetical order.

| | MINT | NRMT |
|---|---|---|
| COMPLETE SET (32) | 25.00 | 11.00 |
| COMMON CARD (1-32) | .75 | .35 |

| | | |
|---|---|---|
| □ 1 Pierre Aubry | .75 | .35 |
| □ 2 Michel Bergeron CO | 1.00 | .45 |
| □ 3 Dan Bouchard | 1.25 | .55 |
| □ 4 Real Cloutier | 1.50 | .70 |
| □ 5 Alain Cote | .75 | .35 |
| □ 6 Andre Dore | .75 | .35 |
| □ 7 Andre Dupont | 1.00 | .45 |
| □ 8 John Garrett | 1.25 | .55 |
| □ 9 Paul Gillis | .75 | .35 |
| □ 10 Mario Gosselin | 1.25 | .55 |
| □ 11 Michel Goulet | 2.50 | 1.10 |
| □ 12 Jean Hamel | .75 | .35 |
| □ 13 Dale Hunter | 1.50 | .70 |
| □ 14 Rick Lapointe | .75 | .35 |
| □ 15 Clint Malarchuk | 1.50 | .70 |
| □ 16 Jimmy Mann | 1.00 | .45 |
| □ 17 Mario Marois | 1.00 | .45 |
| □ 18 Randy Moller | 1.00 | .45 |
| □ 19 Wilf Paiement | 1.00 | .45 |
| □ 20 Dave Pichette | .75 | .35 |
| □ 21 Pat Price | .75 | .35 |
| □ 22 Jacques Richard | 1.00 | .45 |
| □ 23 Normand Rochefort | .75 | .35 |
| □ 24 Jean-Francois Sauve | .75 | .35 |
| □ 25 Andre Savard | .75 | .35 |
| □ 26 Louis Sleigher | .75 | .35 |
| □ 27 Anton Stastny | 1.00 | .45 |
| □ 28 Marian Stastny | 1.00 | .45 |
| □ 29 Peter Stastny | 2.50 | 1.10 |
| □ 30 Marc Tardif | 1.25 | .55 |
| □ 31 Wally Weir | .75 | .35 |
| □ 32 Blake Wesley | .75 | .35 |

## 1984-85 Nordiques Postcards

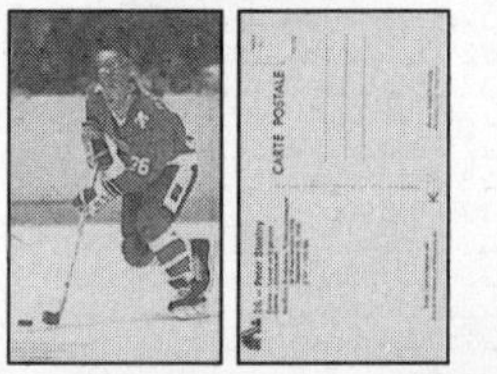

This 27-card set measures approximately 3" by 5 1/2" and features members of the 1984-85 Quebec Nordiques. The fronts have borderless color action player photos. The backs are in postcard format with a short player biography both in French and in English. The years "84-85" appears in the spot where the stamp is supposed to go. The cards are unnumbered and checklisted below in alphabetical order.

| | MINT | NRMT |
|---|---|---|
| COMPLETE SET (27) | 20.00 | 9.00 |
| COMMON CARD (1-27) | .75 | .35 |

| | | |
|---|---|---|
| □ 1 Brent Ashton | .75 | .35 |
| □ 2 Bruce Bell | .75 | .35 |
| □ 3 Michel Bergeron CO | 1.00 | .45 |
| □ 4 Daniel Bouchard | 1.00 | .45 |
| □ 5 Alain Cote | .75 | .35 |
| □ 6 Gord Donnelly | .75 | .35 |
| □ 7 Luc Dufour | .75 | .35 |
| □ 8 Jean-Marc Gaulin | .75 | .35 |
| □ 9 Paul Gillis | .75 | .35 |
| □ 10 Mario Gosselin | 1.00 | .45 |
| □ 11 Michel Goulet | 2.50 | 1.10 |
| □ 12 Dale Hunter | 1.50 | .70 |
| □ 13 Guy Lapointe ACO | 1.00 | .45 |
| □ 14 Jimmy Mann | .75 | .35 |
| □ 15 Mario Marois | .75 | .35 |
| □ 16 Brad Maxwell | .75 | .35 |
| □ 17 Randy Moller | .75 | .35 |
| □ 18 Simon Nolet ACO | .75 | .35 |
| □ 19 Wilf Paiement | 1.00 | .45 |
| □ 20 Pat Price | .75 | .35 |
| □ 21 Normand Rochefort | 1.00 | .45 |
| □ 22 Jean-Francois Sauve | .75 | .35 |
| □ 23 Andre Savard | .75 | .35 |
| □ 24 Richard Sevigny | 1.00 | .45 |
| □ 25 Anton Stastny | 1.00 | .45 |
| □ 26 Marian Stastny | 1.00 | .45 |
| □ 27 Peter Stastny | 2.50 | 1.10 |

## 1985-86 Nordiques General Foods

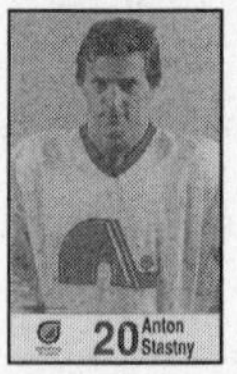


These 27 cards measure approximately 3 1/2" by 5 1/2". The fronts feature color close-ups of the players against a light background. The pictures are full-bleed, except at the bottom where the player's number, name and the sponsor's logo appear in a white bar. The backs are blank. The cards are unnumbered and checklisted below in alphabetical order.

| | MINT | NRMT |
|---|---|---|
| COMPLETE SET (27) | 30.00 | 13.50 |
| COMMON CARD (1-27) | .50 | .23 |

| | | |
|---|---|---|
| □ 1 John Anderson | 1.00 | .45 |

❑ 2 Brent Ashton 1.00 .45
❑ 3 Michel Bergeron CO 1.00 .45
❑ 4 Alain Cote 1.00 .45
❑ 5 Gilbert Delorme 1.00 .45
❑ 6 Mike Eagles 1.00 .45
❑ 7 Steven Finn 1.00 .45
❑ 8 Jean-Marc Gaulin 1.00 .45
❑ 9 Paul Gillis 1.00 .45
❑ 10 Mario Gosselin 1.50 .70
❑ 11 Michel Goulet 2.50 1.10
❑ 12 Ron Harris CO .50 .23
❑ 13 Dale Hunter 2.50 1.10
❑ 14 Mark Kumpel 1.00 .45
❑ 15 Clint Malarchuk 1.50 .70
❑ 16 Jimmy Mann 1.00 .45
❑ 17 Mario Marois 1.00 .45
❑ 18 Randy Moller 1.00 .45
❑ 19 Simon Nolet CO .50 .23
❑ 20 Pat Price 1.00 .45
❑ 21 Normand Rochefort 1.00 .45
❑ 22 Jean-Francois Sauve 1.00 .45
❑ 23 Richard Sevigny 1.50 .70
❑ 24 David Shaw 1.00 .45
❑ 25 Anton Stastny 1.50 .70
❑ 26 Peter Stastny 4.00 1.80
❑ 27 Trevor Stienburg 1.00 .45

## 1985-86 Nordiques McDonald's

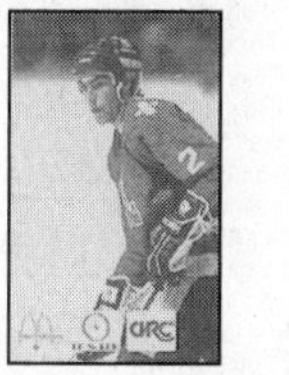

This 22-card set measures approximately 3 1/2" by 5 1/2" and features members of the 1985-86 Quebec Nordiques. The fronts feature borderless color action player photos. The sponsors' logos (McDonald's, Le Soleil and CHRC 80) appear across the bottom; there are no player names on the fronts. The backs are blank. The cards are unnumbered and checklisted below in alphabetical order.

| | MINT | NRMT |
|---|---|---|
| COMPLETE SET (22) | 25.00 | 11.00 |
| COMMON CARD (1-22) | 1.00 | .45 |

❑ 1 Brent Ashton 1.00 .45
❑ 2 Jeff Brown 2.50 1.10
❑ 3 Alain Cote 1.00 .45
❑ 4 Gilbert Delorme 1.00 .45
❑ 5 Gord Donnelly 1.00 .45
❑ 6 Mike Eagles 1.00 .45
❑ 7 Paul Gillis 1.00 .45
❑ 8 Mario Gosselin 1.50 .70
❑ 9 Michel Goulet 2.50 1.10
❑ 10 Dale Hunter 2.50 1.10
❑ 11 Mark Kumpel 1.00 .45
❑ 12 Jason Lafreniere 1.00 .45
❑ 13 Clint Malarchuk 1.50 .70
❑ 14 Randy Moller 1.00 .45
❑ 15 Robert Picard 1.00 .45
❑ 16 Pat Price 1.00 .45
❑ 17 Normand Rochefort 1.00 .45
❑ 18 Richard Sevigny 1.50 .70
❑ 19 David Shaw 1.00 .45
❑ 20 Risto Siltanen 1.00 .45
❑ 21 Anton Stastny 1.50 .70
❑ 22 Peter Stastny 4.00 1.80

## 1985-86 Nordiques Placemats

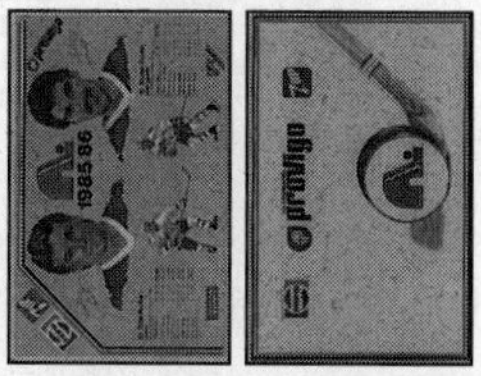

This 6-card placemat set of the Quebec Nordiques is sponsored by Pepsi-Cola and Seven-up and measures approximately 11" by 17". The fronts feature a painted portrait, action shot, and facsimile autograph on a yellow background with white border. The player's name, position, jersey number, date and place of birth, and career statistics in French are also found on the front. The sponsors' logos appear in the upper right corner. The backs carry the sponsors' and team logos on a white background with thin blue, white, and purple borders. The mats are unnumbered, and one placemat shows portraits of all twelve players with their facsimile autographs.

| | MINT | NRMT |
|---|---|---|
| COMPLETE SET (6) | 20.00 | 9.00 |
| COMMON CARD (1-6) | 3.00 | 1.35 |

❑ 1 Brent Ashton 3.00 1.35
Randy Moller
❑ 2 Mario Gosselin 4.00 1.80
Clint Malarchuk
❑ 3 Dale Hunter 5.00 2.20
Michel Goulet
❑ 4 Pat Price 3.00 1.35
Robert Picard
❑ 5 Peter Stastny 5.00 2.20
Anton Stastny
❑ 6 Player Portraits 5.00 2.20
Dale Hunter
Michel Goulet
Peter Stastny
Anton Stastny
Brent Ashton
Randy Moller
Pat Price
Robert Picard
Mario Gosselin
Clint Malarchuk
Alain Cote
John Anderson

## 1985-86 Nordiques Provigo

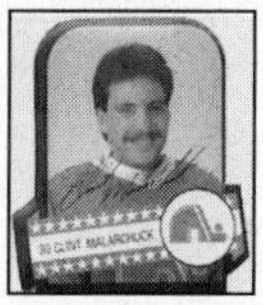

This 25-sticker set of Quebec Nordiques was released through Provigo. The puffy stickers measure approximately 1 1/8" by 2 1/4" and feature a color head and shoulders photo of the player, with the player's number and name bordered by star-studded banners across the bottom of the picture. The player's signature is inscribed just above the banner. The Nordiques' logo is superimposed over the banner at its right end. The backs are blank. We have checklisted them below in alphabetical order, with the uniform number to the right of the player's name. The 25 styrofoam stickers were to be attached to a cardboard poster. The poster measures approximately 20" by 11" and has 25 white spaces (designated for the stickers) on blue background. At the center is a picture of a goalie mask, with the Nordiques' logo above and slightly to the right. The back of the poster has a checklist, stripes in the team's colors, and two team logos.

| | MINT | NRMT |
|---|---|---|
| COMPLETE SET (25) | 20.00 | 9.00 |
| COMMON CARD (1-25) | .75 | .35 |

❑ 1 John Anderson 14 1.00 .45
❑ 2 Brent Ashton 9 .75 .35
❑ 3 Wayne Babych 18 1.00 .45
❑ 4 Michel Bergeron CO .75 .35
❑ 5 Alain Cote 19 .75 .35
❑ 6 Gilbert Delorme 6 .75 .35
❑ 7 Mike Eagles 11 .75 .35
❑ 8 Steven Finn 25 .75 .35
❑ 9 Paul Gillis 23 .75 .35
❑ 10 Mario Gosselin 33 1.00 .45
❑ 11 Michel Goulet 16 2.00 .90
❑ 12 Dale Hunter 32 2.00 .90
❑ 13 Mark Kumpel 17 .75 .35
❑ 14 Clint Malarchuk 30 1.00 .45
❑ 15 Jimmy Mann 10 1.00 .45
❑ 16 Mario Marois 22 1.00 .45
❑ 17 Randy Moller 21 .75 .35
❑ 18 Wilf Paiement 27 1.00 .45
❑ 19 Pat Price 7 .75 .35
❑ 20 Normand Rochefort 5 .75 .35
❑ 21 J.F. Sauve 15 .75 .35
❑ 22 Richard Sevigny 1 1.00 .45
❑ 23 David Shaw 4 .75 .35
❑ 24 Anton Stastny 20 1.00 .45
❑ 25 Peter Stastny 26 3.00 1.35
❑ NNO Poster 5.00 2.20

## 1985-86 Nordiques Team Issue

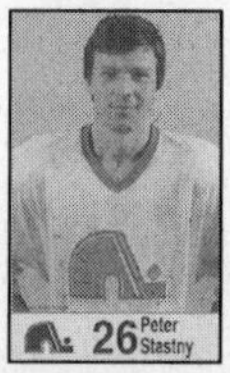

This 27-card set measures approximately 3 1/2" by 5 1/2" and features members of the 1985-86 Quebec Nordiques. The fronts feature posed color close-up shots of the players against a light background. The pictures are borderless except at the bottom, where the player's name, uniform number and the team logo appear in a white bar. The backs are blank. The cards are unnumbered and checklisted below in alphabetical order.

| | MINT | NRMT |
|---|---|---|
| COMPLETE SET (27) | 25.00 | 11.00 |
| COMMON CARD (1-27) | 1.00 | .45 |

❑ 1 Brent Ashton 1.00 .45
❑ 2 Michel Bergeron CO 1.00 .45
❑ 3 Jeff Brown 2.50 1.10
❑ 4 Alain Cote 1.00 .45
❑ 5 Gilbert Delorme 1.00 .45
❑ 6 Gord Donnelly 1.00 .45
❑ 7 Mike Eagles 1.00 .45
❑ 8 Paul Gillis 1.00 .45
❑ 9 Mario Gosselin 1.50 .70
❑ 10 Michel Goulet 2.50 1.10
❑ 11 Dale Hunter 2.50 1.10
❑ 12 Mark Kumpel 1.00 .45
❑ 13 Jason Lafreniere 1.00 .45
❑ 14 Clint Malarchuk 1.50 .70
❑ 15 Randy Moller 1.00 .45
❑ 16 Simon Nolet CO .50 .23
❑ 17 Robert Picard 1.00 .45
❑ 18 Pat Price 1.00 .45
❑ 19 Ken Quinney 1.00 .45
❑ 20 Normand Rochefort 1.00 .45
❑ 21 Richard Sevigny 1.50 .70
❑ 22 David Shaw 1.00 .45
❑ 23 Risto Siltanen 1.00 .45
❑ 24 Anton Stastny 1.50 .70
❑ 25 Peter Stastny 4.00 1.80
❑ 26 Charles Thiffault CO .50 .23
❑ 27 Richard Zemlak 1.00 .45

## 1986-87 Nordiques General Foods

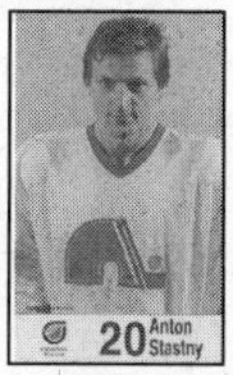

This 28-card set measures approximately 3 1/2" by 5 1/2" and features members of the 1986-87 Quebec Nordiques. The fronts feature posed color close-up shots of the players against a light background. The pictures are borderless except at the bottom, where the player's name, uniform number and the sponsor's logo appear in a white bar. The backs are blank. The cards are unnumbered and checklisted below in alphabetical order.

| | MINT | NRMT |
|---|---|---|
| COMPLETE SET (28) | 25.00 | 11.00 |
| COMMON CARD (1-28) | .50 | .23 |

❑ 1 Brent Ashton .75 .35
❑ 2 Michel Bergeron CO 1.50 .70
❑ 3 Jeff Brown 1.50 .70
❑ 4 Alain Cote .75 .35
❑ 5 Gilbert Delorme .75 .35
❑ 6 Gord Donnelly .75 .35
❑ 7 Mike Eagles .75 .35
❑ 8 Paul Gillis .75 .35
❑ 9 Mario Gosselin 1.50 .70
❑ 10 Michel Goulet 2.00 .90
❑ 11 Mike Hough .75 .35
❑ 12 Dale Hunter 1.50 .70
❑ 13 Mark Kumpel .75 .35
❑ 14 Jason Lafreniere .75 .35
❑ 15 Clint Malarchuk 1.25 .55
❑ 16 Randy Moller .75 .35
❑ 17 Simon Nolet CO .50 .23
❑ 18 Robert Picard .75 .35
❑ 19 Pat Price .75 .35
❑ 20 Ken Quinney .75 .35
❑ 21 Normand Rochefort .75 .35
❑ 22 Richard Sevigny 1.25 .55
❑ 23 David Shaw .75 .35
❑ 24 Risto Siltanen .75 .35
❑ 25 Anton Stastny 1.00 .45
❑ 26 Peter Stastny 3.00 1.35
❑ 27 Charles Thiffault CO .50 .23
❑ 28 Richard Zemlak 1.00 .45

## 1986-87 Nordiques McDonald's

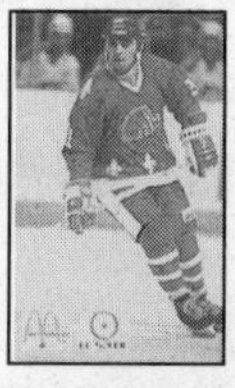

This 25-card set measures approximately 3 1/2" by 5 1/2" and features members of the 1986-87 Quebec Nordiques. The fronts feature borderless color action player photos. The sponsors' logos (McDonald's and Le Soleil) appear across the bottom; there are no player names on the fronts. The backs are blank. The cards are unnumbered and checklisted below in alphabetical order.

| | MINT | NRMT |
|---|---|---|
| COMPLETE SET (25) | 30.00 | 13.50 |
| COMMON CARD (1-25) | 1.00 | .45 |

❑ 1 John Anderson 1.50 .70
❑ 2 Brent Ashton 1.00 .45
❑ 3 Jeff Brown 2.00 .90
❑ 4 Alain Cote 1.00 .45
❑ 5 Gilbert Delorme 1.00 .45
❑ 6 Mike Eagles 1.00 .45
❑ 7 Steven Finn 1.00 .45
❑ 8 Paul Gillis 1.00 .45
❑ 9 Mario Gosselin 1.50 .70
❑ 10 Michel Goulet 2.50 1.10
❑ 11 Mike Hough 1.00 .45
❑ 12 Dale Hunter 2.00 .90
❑ 13 Mark Kumpel 1.00 .45
❑ 14 Alain Lemieux 1.00 .45
❑ 15 Clint Malarchuk 1.50 .70
❑ 16 Jimmy Mann 1.50 .70
❑ 17 Randy Moller 1.00 .45
❑ 18 Wilf Paiement 1.50 .70
❑ 19 Pat Price 1.00 .45
❑ 20 Normand Rochefort 1.00 .45
❑ 21 Jean-Francois Sauve 1.00 .45
❑ 22 Richard Sevigny 1.50 .70
❑ 23 David Shaw 1.00 .45
❑ 24 Anton Stastny 1.50 .70
❑ 25 Peter Stastny 4.00 1.80

## 1986-87 Nordiques Team Issue

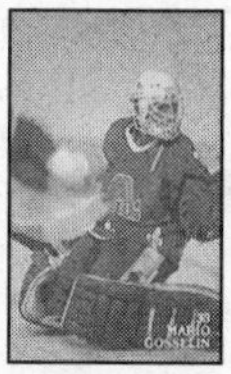

This 29-card set measures approximately 3 1/2" by 5 1/2" and features members of the 1986-87 Quebec Nordiques. The fronts feature borderless color action photos. The player's name and number appear in white or black lettering at the lower right corner. The backs are blank. The cards are unnumbered and checklisted below in alphabetical order.

| | MINT | NRMT |
|---|---|---|
| COMPLETE SET (29) | 20.00 | 9.00 |
| COMMON CARD (1-29) | .75 | .35 |

❑ 1 Jeff Brown 1.75 .80
❑ 2 Alain Cote .75 .35
❑ 3 Bill Derlago .75 .35
❑ 4 Gord Donnelly .75 .35
❑ 5 Mike Eagles .75 .35
❑ 6 Steven Finn .75 .35
❑ 7 Paul Gillis .75 .35
❑ 8 Mario Gosselin 1.00 .45
❑ 9 Michel Goulet 2.00 .90
❑ 10 Mike Hough .75 .35
❑ 11 Dale Hunter 1.50 .70
❑ 12 Jason Lafreniere .75 .35
❑ 13 Clint Malarchuk 1.25 .55
❑ 14 Basil McRae 1.00 .45
❑ 15 Randy Moller .75 .35
❑ 16 John Ogrodnick 1.00 .45
❑ 17 Robert Picard .75 .35
❑ 18 Pat Price .75 .35
❑ 19 Normand Rochefort .75 .35
❑ 20 Richard Sevigny 1.25 .55
❑ 21 David Shaw .75 .35
❑ 22 Doug Shedden .75 .35
❑ 23 Risto Siltanen .75 .35
❑ 24 Anton Stastny 1.00 .45
❑ 25 Peter Stastny 3.00 1.35

## 1986-87 Nordiques Yum-Yum

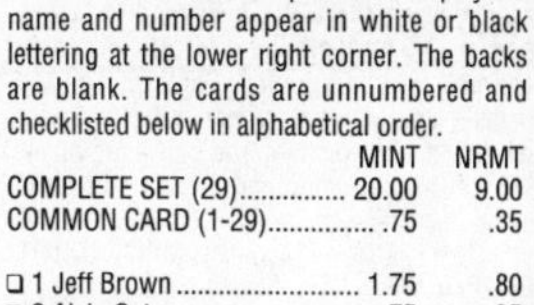

Each card in this ten-card set measures approximately 2" by 2 1/2". The fronts feature color action player photos with blue, white, and red borders. The player's name and number, along with sponsor and team logos, appear on the front. The backs carry a team checklist. The cards are unnumbered and checklisted below in alphabetical order.

| | MINT | NRMT |
|---|---|---|
| COMPLETE SET (10) | 25.00 | 11.00 |
| COMMON CARD (1-10) | 2.00 | .90 |

❑ 1 Alain Cote 2.00 .90
❑ 2 Gilbert Delorme 2.00 .90
❑ 3 Paul Gillis 2.00 .90
❑ 4 Michel Goulet 5.00 2.20
❑ 5 Dale Hunter 4.00 1.80
❑ 6 Clint Malarchuk 3.00 1.35
❑ 7 Robert Picard 2.00 .90
❑ 8 Normand Rochefort 2.00 .90
❑ 9 Anton Stastny 2.50 1.10
❑ 10 Peter Stastny 6.00 2.70

## 1987-88 Nordiques General Foods

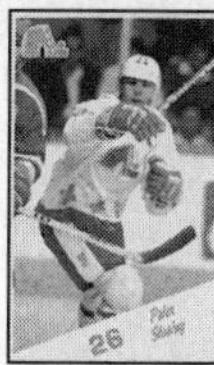

Each card in this 32-card set measures approximately 3 3/4" by 5 5/8". The fronts feature a full color action photo of the player, with the Quebec Nordiques' logo superimposed at the upper left-hand corner of the picture. At the bottom the player's number and name are given in the white triangle. The backs are blank. The set was issued in two versions, one with and one without the General Foods logo at the lower right corner. Both versions are valued equally. The set features an early card of Ron Tugnutt pre-dating his O-Pee-Chee rookie card by two years.

| | MINT | NRMT |
|---|---|---|
| COMPLETE SET (32) | 20.00 | 9.00 |
| COMMON CARD (1-32) | .25 | .11 |

❑ 1 Tommy Albelin 28 .50 .23
❑ 2 Jeff Brown 22 1.25 .55
❑ 3 Mario Brunetta 30 .75 .35
❑ 4 Terry Carkner 4 .75 .35
❑ 5 Alain Cote 19 .50 .23
❑ 6 Gord Donnelly 34 .50 .23
❑ 7 Gaetan Duchesne 14 .75 .35
❑ 8 Mike Eagles 11 .50 .23
❑ 9 Steven Finn 29 .50 .23
❑ 10 Paul Gillis 23 .50 .23
❑ 11 Mario Gosselin 33 1.00 .45
❑ 12 Michel Goulet 16 2.00 .90
❑ 13 Stephane Guerard 46 .50 .23
❑ 14 Alan Haworth 15 .50 .23
❑ 15 Mike Hough 18 .50 .23
❑ 16 Jeff Jackson 25 .50 .23
❑ 17 Stu Kulak 17 .50 .23
❑ 18 Jason Lafreniere 10 .50 .23
❑ 19 Lane Lambert 7 .50 .23
❑ 20 David Latta 27 .50 .23
❑ 21 Max Middendorf 12 .50 .23
❑ 22 Randy Moller 21 .50 .23
❑ 23 Robert Picard 24 .50 .23
❑ 24 Daniel Poudrier 2 .50 .23
❑ 25 Ken Quinney 54 .50 .23
❑ 26 Normand Rochefort 5 .50 .23
❑ 27 Richard Sevigny 1 .75 .35
❑ 28 Anton Stastny 20 .75 .35
❑ 29 Peter Stastny 26 3.00 1.35
❑ 30 Ron Tugnutt 50 4.00 1.80
❑ 31 Alain Chainey .25 .11
Andre Savard
Guy Lapointe
❑ 32 Badaboum (Mascot) .25 .11

## 1987-88 Nordiques Yum-Yum

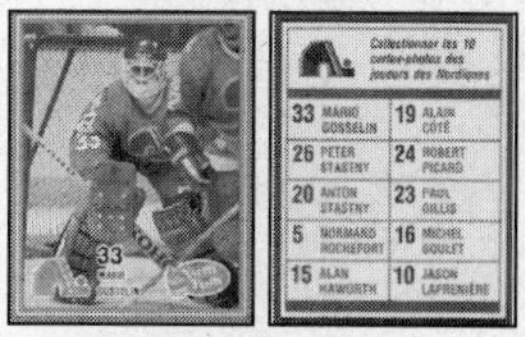

Each card in this ten-card set measures approximately 2" by 2 1/2". The front has a color action photo of the player, enframed by red, white, and blue borders. At the bottom the player's number and name are sandwiched between the Nordiques' logo and the Yum-Yum potato chips logo. The back is printed in red, white, and blue, and presents in two columns a checklist of the ten players. We have checklisted the cards below in alphabetical order, with the uniform number to the right of the player's name.

| | MINT | NRMT |
|---|---|---|
| COMPLETE SET (10) | 20.00 | 9.00 |
| COMMON CARD (1-10) | 1.50 | .70 |

❑ 1 Alain Cote 19 1.50 .70
❑ 2 Paul Gillis 23 1.50 .70
❑ 3A Mario Gosselin 33 ERR 3.00 1.35
(Reverse has 83 for sweater number; three

numbers messed up)
❑ 3B Mario Gosselin 33 COR .... 3.00 1.35
❑ 4 Michel Goulet 16 .... 4.00 1.80
❑ 5 Alan Haworth 15 UER .... 1.50 .70
(Reverse has 38 for sweater number)
❑ 6 Jason Lefreniere 10 UER .... 1.50 .70
(Reverse has 30 for sweater number)
❑ 7 Robert Picard 24 .... 1.50 .70
❑ 8 Normand Rochefort 5 .... 1.50 .70
❑ 9 Anton Stastny 20 .... 2.00 .90
❑ 10 Peter Stastny 26 .... 5.00 2.20

## 1988-89 Nordiques General Foods

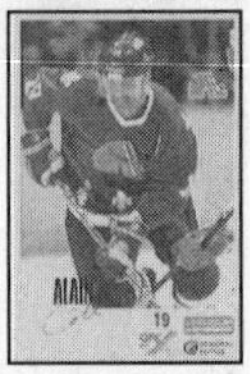

The 31 blank-backed cards comprising this set measure approximately 3 3/4" by 5 5/8" and feature white-bordered color player action shots. The Nordiques logo is displayed at the upper right. The player's first name appears at the lower left of the photo. His last name appears in cursive lettering in the wide white margin below. The player's uniform number and the logos for General Foods, Le Journal de Quebec, and CHRC Sport Radio appear at the bottom right. The cards are unnumbered and checklisted below in alphabetical order. Joe Sakic's card predates his Rookie Card by one year.

| | MINT | NRMT |
|---|---|---|
| COMPLETE SET (31) | 25.00 | 11.00 |
| COMMON CARD (1-31) | .50 | .23 |

❑ 1 Tommy Albelin .... .50 .23
❑ 2 Joel Baillargeon .... .50 .23
❑ 3 Jeff Brown .... 1.25 .55
❑ 4 Mario Brunetta .... .75 .35
❑ 5 Coaches .... .50 .23
Serge Aubry
Ron Lapointe
Guy Lapointe
Alain Chainey
❑ 6 Alain Cote .... .50 .23
❑ 7 Gord Donnelly .... .75 .35
❑ 8 Daniel Dore .... .50 .23
❑ 9 Gaetan Duchesne .... .75 .35
❑ 10 Steven Finn .... .50 .23
❑ 11 Marc Fortier .... .50 .23
❑ 12 Paul Gillis .... .50 .23
❑ 13 Mario Gosselin .... .75 .35
❑ 14 Michel Goulet .... 2.00 .90
❑ 15 Jari Gronstrand .... .50 .23
❑ 16 Stephane Guerard .... .50 .23
❑ 17 Jeff Jackson .... .50 .23
❑ 18 Iiro Jarvi .... .50 .23
❑ 19 Lane Lambert .... .50 .23
❑ 20 David Latta .... .50 .23
❑ 21 Curtis Leschyshyn .... 1.00 .45
❑ 22 Bob Mason .... .75 .35
❑ 23 Randy Moller .... .50 .23
❑ 24 Robert Picard .... .50 .23
❑ 25 Walt Poddubny .... .75 .35
❑ 26 Joe Sakic .... 15.00 6.75
❑ 27 Greg Smyth .... .50 .23
❑ 28 Anton Stastny .... .75 .35
❑ 29 Peter Stastny .... 2.50 1.10
❑ 30 Trevor Steinberg .... .50 .23
❑ 31 Mark Vermette .... .50 .23

## 1988-89 Nordiques Team Issue

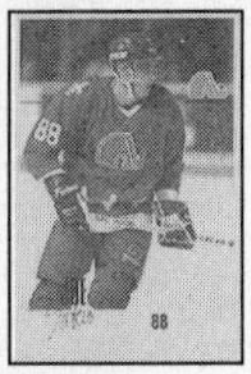

The 33 blank-backed cards comprising this set measure approximately 3 3/4" by 5 5/8" and feature white-bordered player action shots. The team logo is displayed at the upper right. The player's first name in all capital letters appears at the lower left of the photo. His last name is a facsimile autograph in the wide white margin right below, with his uniform number next to it. The cards are unnumbered and checklisted below in alphabetical order. The Joe Sakic issue predates his RC by one year.

| | MINT | NRMT |
|---|---|---|
| COMPLETE SET (33) | 30.00 | 13.50 |
| COMMON CARD (1-33) | .25 | .11 |

❑ 1 Tommy Albelin .... .50 .23
❑ 2 Serge Aubry CO .... .75 .35
Ron Lapointe CO
Guy Lapointe CO
Alain Chainey CO
❑ 3 Badaboum (Mascot) .... .25 .11
❑ 4 Joel Baillargeon .... .50 .23
❑ 5 Jeff Brown .... 1.50 .70
❑ 6 Mario Brunetta .... .75 .35
❑ 7 Alain Cote .... .50 .23
❑ 8 Gord Donnelly .... .75 .35
❑ 9 Daniel Dore .... .50 .23
❑ 10 Gaetan Duchesne .... .75 .35
❑ 11 Steven Finn .... .50 .23
❑ 12 Marc Fortier .... .50 .23
❑ 13 Paul Gillis .... .50 .23
❑ 14 Mario Gosselin .... .75 .35
❑ 15 Michel Goulet .... 2.00 .90
❑ 16 Jari Gronstrand .... .50 .23
❑ 17 Stephane Guerard .... .50 .23
❑ 18 Jeff Jackson .... .50 .23
❑ 19 Iiro Jarvi .... .50 .23
❑ 20 Lane Lambert .... .50 .23
❑ 21 David Latta .... .50 .23
❑ 22 Curtis Leschyshyn .... 1.00 .45
❑ 23 Bob Mason .... .75 .35
❑ 24 Randy Moller .... .50 .23
❑ 25 Robert Picard .... .50 .23
❑ 26 Walt Poddubny .... .75 .35
❑ 27 Joe Sakic .... 15.00 6.75
❑ 28 Greg Smyth .... .50 .23
❑ 29 Anton Stastny .... .75 .35
❑ 30 Peter Stastny .... 2.50 1.10
❑ 31 Trevor Steinburg .... .50 .23
❑ 32 Mark Vermette .... .50 .23
❑ 33 Team Photo .... 2.00 .90

## 1989-90 Nordiques

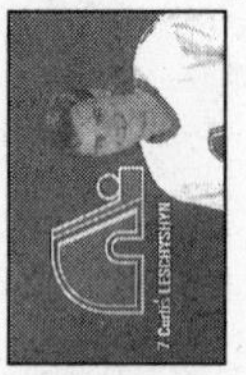

This 39-card set of the Quebec Nordiques printed on white card stock measures approximately 5 5/8" by 3 3/4" and features a borderless posed head shot of the player against a blue background. The team logo and the player's name and jersey number appear to the left of each picture. The backs are blank. The cards are unnumbered and checklisted below in alphabetical order.

| | MINT | NRMT |
|---|---|---|
| COMPLETE SET (39) | 25.00 | 11.00 |
| COMMON CARD (1-39) | .50 | .23 |

❑ 1 Serge Aubry .... .50 .23
❑ 2 Michel Bergeron CO .... .50 .23
❑ 3 Jeff Brown .... .75 .35
❑ 4 Alain Chainey .... .50 .23
❑ 5 Joe Cirella .... .50 .23
❑ 6 Lucien DeBlois .... .50 .23
❑ 7 Daniel Dore .... .50 .23
❑ 8 Steven Finn .... .50 .23
❑ 9 Stephane Fiset .... 1.50 .70
❑ 10 Bryan Fogarty .... .50 .23
❑ 11 Marc Fortier .... .50 .23
❑ 12 Paul Gillis .... .50 .23
❑ 13 Michel Goulet .... 1.00 .45
❑ 14 Jari Gronstrand .... .50 .23
❑ 15 Stephane Guerard .... .50 .23
❑ 16 Mike Hough .... .50 .23
❑ 17 Tony Hrkac .... .50 .23
❑ 18 Jeff Jackson .... .50 .23
❑ 19 Iiro Jarvi .... .50 .23
❑ 20 Kevin Kaminski .... .50 .23
❑ 21 Darin Kimble .... .50 .23
❑ 22 Guy Lafleur .... 2.50 1.10
❑ 23 Guy Lapointe .... .50 .23
❑ 24 David Latta .... .50 .23
❑ 25 Brian Lawton .... .50 .23
❑ 26 Curtis Leschyshyn .... .75 .35
❑ 27 Claude Loiselle .... .50 .23
❑ 28 Mario Marois .... .50 .23
❑ 29 Tony McKegney .... .50 .23
❑ 30 Ken McRae .... .50 .23
❑ 31 Greg Millen .... .75 .35
❑ 32 Randy Moller .... .50 .23
❑ 33 Sergei Mylnikov .... .75 .35
❑ 34 Michel Petit .... .50 .23
❑ 35 Robert Picard .... .50 .23
❑ 36 Joe Sakic .... 10.00 4.50
❑ 37 Peter Stastny .... 1.50 .70
❑ 38 Ron Tugnutt .... 1.50 .70
❑ 39 Team Picture .... .50 .23

## 1989-90 Nordiques General Foods

This 30-card set of Quebec Nordiques printed on white card stock measures approximately 5 5/8" by 3 3/4" and features a borderless posed head shot of the player against a blue background. It is essentially the same as the 1989-90 Quebec Nordiques set save for the

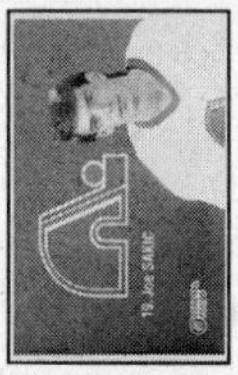

smaller set size and the appearance of a General Foods logo in the lower left corner. Card backs are blank and unnumbered; thus the cards are listed below aphabetically. Joe Sakic's card appears during his Rookie Card year.

| | MINT | NRMT |
|---|---|---|
| COMPLETE SET (30) | 20.00 | 9.00 |
| COMMON CARD (1-30) | .50 | .23 |

❑ 1 Michel Bergeron CO .... .50 .23
❑ 2 Jeff Brown .... .75 .35
❑ 3 Joe Cirella .... .50 .23
❑ 4 Lucien DeBlois .... .50 .23
❑ 5 Daniel Dore .... .50 .23
❑ 6 Steven Finn .... .50 .23
❑ 7 Stephane Fiset .... 1.50 .70
❑ 8 Marc Fortier .... .50 .23
❑ 9 Paul Gillis .... .50 .23
❑ 10 Michel Goulet .... 1.00 .45
❑ 11 Jari Gronstrand .... .50 .23
❑ 12 Stephane Guerard .... .50 .23
❑ 13 Mike Hough .... .50 .23
❑ 14 Jeff Jackson .... .50 .23
❑ 15 Iiro Jarvi .... .50 .23
❑ 16 Kevin Kaminski .... .50 .23
❑ 17 Darin Kimble .... .50 .23
❑ 18 Guy Lafleur .... 2.50 1.10
❑ 19 David Latta .... .50 .23
❑ 20 Curtis Leschyshyn .... .75 .35
❑ 21 Claude Loiselle .... .50 .23
❑ 22 Mario Marois .... .50 .23
❑ 23 Ken McRae .... .50 .23
❑ 24 Sergei Mylnikov .... .75 .35
❑ 25 Michel Petit .... .50 .23
❑ 26 Robert Picard .... .50 .23
❑ 27 Joe Sakic .... 10.00 4.50
❑ 28 Peter Stastny .... 1.50 .70
❑ 29 Ron Tugnutt .... 1.50 .70
❑ 30 Team Photo .... 1.50 .70

## 1989-90 Nordiques Police

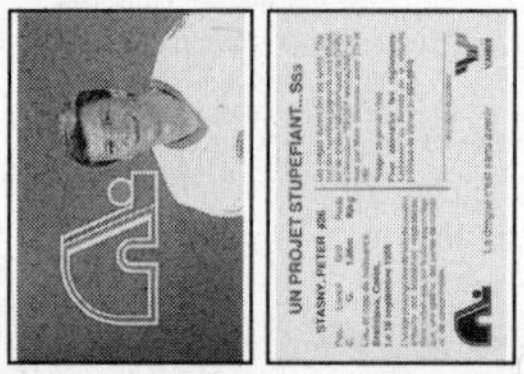

This 27-card police set of Quebec Nordiques was sponsored by the city of Vanier. The cards measure approximately 4" by 2 3/4" and feature a borderless posed head and shoulders photo against a blue background. The team logo appears to the left of each player picture. The backs, which read "Un Project Stupefiant..Sss" across the top, are printed in French and present biography and an anti-drug or alcohol message on the left side. The right side has a local police number and slot for a police officer's signature. The cards are unnumbered and checklisted below in alphabetical order. Joe Sakic's card appears during his Rookie Card year.

| | MINT | NRMT |
|---|---|---|
| COMPLETE SET (27) | 20.00 | 9.00 |
| COMMON CARD (1-27) | .50 | .23 |

❑ 1 Jeff Brown .... .75 .35
❑ 2 Joe Cirella .... .50 .23
❑ 3 Lucien DeBlois .... .50 .23
❑ 4 Daniel Dore .... .50 .23
❑ 5 Steven Finn .... .50 .23
❑ 6 Stephane Fiset .... 1.50 .70
❑ 7 Marc Fortier .... .50 .23
❑ 8 Paul Gillis .... .50 .23
❑ 9 Michel Goulet .... 1.00 .45
❑ 10 Stephane Guerard .... .50 .23
❑ 11 Mike Hough .... .50 .23
❑ 12 Jeff Jackson .... .50 .23
❑ 13 Iiro Jarvi .... .50 .23
❑ 14 Darin Kimble .... .50 .23
❑ 15 Guy Lafleur .... 2.50 1.10
❑ 16 David Latta .... .50 .23
❑ 17 Curtis Leschyshyn .... .75 .35
❑ 18 Claude Loiselle .... .50 .23
❑ 19 Mario Marois .... .50 .23
❑ 20 Ken McRae .... .50 .23
❑ 21 Sergei Mylnikov .... .75 .35
❑ 22 Michel Petit .... .50 .23
❑ 23 Robert Picard .... .50 .23
❑ 24 Jean-Marc Routhier .... .50 .23
❑ 25 Joe Sakic .... 10.00 4.50
❑ 26 Peter Stastny .... 1.50 .70
❑ 27 Ron Tugnutt .... 1.50 .70

## 1990-91 Nordiques Petro-Canada

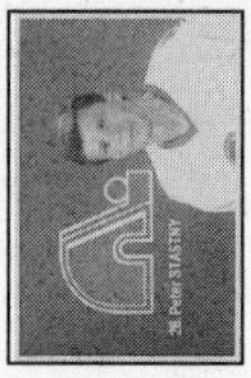

These blank-backed cards measure approximately 3 3/4" by 5 5/8" and feature white-bordered color player action shots. The player's name, uniform number, Nordiques logo, and Petro-Canada logo appear on the bottom. The words "Les Nordiques" in blue letters is printed in the upper right corner. The cards are unnumbered and checklisted below in alphabetical order.

| | MINT | NRMT |
|---|---|---|
| COMPLETE SET (28) | 20.00 | 9.00 |
| COMMON CARD (1-28) | .50 | .23 |

❑ 1 Aaron Broten .... .50 .23
❑ 2 Dave Chambers CO .... .50 .23
❑ 3 Joe Cirella .... .60 .25
❑ 4 Lucien DeBlois .... .50 .23
❑ 5 Steven Finn .... .50 .23
❑ 6 Bryan Fogarty .... .50 .23
❑ 7 Marc Fortier .... .50 .23
❑ 8 Robbie Ftorek ACO .... .50 .23
❑ 9 Paul Gillis .... .50 .23
❑ 10 Scott Gordon .... .60 .25
❑ 11 Mike Hough .... .50 .23
❑ 12 Tony Hrkac .... .60 .25
❑ 13 Darin Kimble .... .60 .25
❑ 14 Guy Lafleur .... 2.00 .90
❑ 15 Curtis Leschyshyn .... .50 .23
❑ 16 Claude Loiselle .... .50 .23
❑ 17 Jacques Martin ACO .... .50 .23
❑ 18 Tony McKegney .... .50 .23
❑ 19 Owen Nolan .... 2.50 1.10
❑ 20 Michel Petit .... .50 .23
❑ 21 Joe Sakic .... 5.00 2.20
❑ 22 Everett Sanipass .... .50 .23
❑ 23 Mats Sundin .... 3.00 1.35
❑ 24 John Tanner .... .75 .35
❑ 25 Ron Tugnutt .... 1.00 .45
❑ 26 Daniel Vincelette .... .50 .23
❑ 27 Craig Wolanin .... .50 .23
❑ 28 Team Photo .... .75 .35

## 1990-91 Nordiques Team Issue

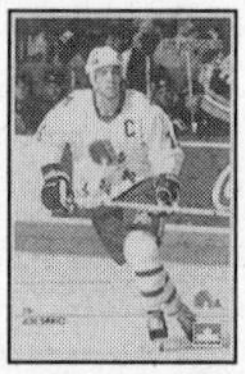

The 25 blank-backed cards comprising this set measure approximately 5 5/8" by 3 3/4" and feature white-bordered posed color player head shots against blue backgrounds. The Quebec Nordiques logo is prominently displayed to the left of the player. The player's name and uniform number appear in white lettering below the logo. The cards are unnumbered and checklisted below in alphabetical order.

| | MINT | NRMT |
|---|---|---|
| COMPLETE SET (25) | 15.00 | 6.75 |
| COMMON CARD (1-25) | .50 | .23 |

❑ 1 Joe Cirella .... .50 .23
❑ 2 Lucien DeBlois .... .50 .23
❑ 3 Daniel Dore .... .50 .23
❑ 4 Steven Finn .... .50 .23
❑ 5 Stephane Fiset .... 1.50 .70
❑ 6 Bryan Fogarty .... .50 .23
❑ 7 Marc Fortier .... .50 .23
❑ 8 Paul Gillis .... .50 .23
❑ 9 Michel Goulet .... 1.25 .55
❑ 10 Stephane Guerard .... .50 .23
❑ 11 Mike Hough .... .50 .23
❑ 12 Tony Hrkac .... .60 .25
❑ 13 Jeff Jackson .... .50 .23
❑ 14 Iiro Jarvi .... .50 .23
❑ 15 Kevin Kaminski .... .50 .23
❑ 16 Darin Kimble .... .60 .25
❑ 17 David Latta .... .50 .23
❑ 18 Curtis Leschyshyn .... .50 .23
❑ 19 Claude Loiselle .... .50 .23
❑ 20 Mario Marois .... .50 .23
❑ 21 Tony McKegney .... .50 .23
❑ 22 Ken McRae .... .50 .23
❑ 23 Michel Petit .... .50 .23
❑ 24 Peter Stastny .... 1.50 .70
❑ 25 Ron Tugnutt .... 1.00 .45

## 1991 Nordiques Panini Team Stickers

This 32-sticker set was issued in a plastic bag that contained two 16-sticker sheets (approximately 9" by 12") and a foldout poster, "Super Poster - Hockey 91", on which the stickers could be affixed. The players' names appear only on the poster, not on the stickers. Each sticker measures about 2 1/8" by 2 7/8" and features a color player action shot on its white-bordered front. The back of the white sticker sheet is lined off into 16 panels, each carrying the logos for Panini, the NHL, and the NHLPA, as well as the same number that appears on the front of the sticker. Every Canadian NHL team was featured in this promotion. Each team set was available by mail-order from Panini Canada Ltd. for 2.99 plus 50 cents for shipping and handling.

| | MINT | NRMT |
|---|---|---|
| COMPLETE SET (32) | 5.00 | 2.20 |
| COMMON STICKER (1-24) | .05 | .02 |
| COMMON STICKER (A-H) | .05 | .02 |

❑ 1 Joe Cirella .... .05 .02
❑ 2 Daniel Dore .... .05 .02
❑ 3 Steven Finn .... .05 .02
❑ 4 Bryan Fogarty .... .05 .02
❑ 5 Marc Fortier .... .05 .02
❑ 6 Paul Gillis .... .05 .02
❑ 7 Scott Gordon .... .10 .05
❑ 8 Stephane Guerard .... .05 .02
❑ 9 Mike Hough .... .05 .02
❑ 10 Tony Hrkac .... .05 .02
❑ 11 Darin Kimble .... .05 .02
❑ 12 Guy Lafleur .... .50 .23
❑ 13 Curtis Leschyshyn .... .10 .05
❑ 14 Claude Loiselle .... .05 .02
❑ 15 Tony McKegney .... .05 .02
❑ 16 Ken McRae .... .05 .02
❑ 17 Owen Nolan .... .50 .23
❑ 18 Joe Sakic .... 1.25 .55
❑ 19 Everett Sanipass .... .05 .02
❑ 20 Mats Sundin .... .75 .35
❑ 21 John Tanner .... .10 .05
❑ 22 Ron Tugnutt .... .15 .07
❑ 23 Randy Velischek .... .05 .02
❑ 24 Craig Wolanin .... .05 .02
❑ A Team Logo .... .05 .02
Left Side
❑ B Team Logo .... .05 .02
Right Side
❑ C Guy Lafleur .... .25 .11
Upper Left Corner
❑ D Guy Lafleur .... .25 .11
Lower Left Corner
❑ E Benoit Hogue .... .10 .05
Upper Right Corner
❑ F Benoit Hogue .... .10 .05
Lower Right Corner
❑ G Guy Lafleur .... .50 .23
❑ H Mats Sundin .... .75 .35

## 1991-92 Nordiques Petro-Canada

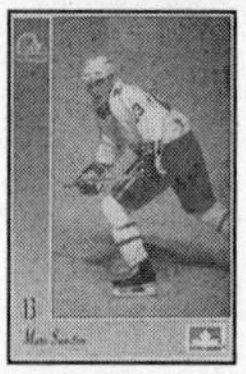

These blank-backed cards measure approximately 3 1/2" by 5 5/8" and feature white-bordered color player action shots. The player's name, uniform number, Nordiques logo, and Petro-Canada logo appear within the purplish margin on the left and below the photo. The cards are unnumbered and checklisted below in alphabetical order.

| | MINT | NRMT |
|---|---|---|
| COMPLETE SET (35) | 20.00 | 9.00 |
| COMMON CARD (1-35) | .25 | .11 |

❑ 1 Badaboum (Mascot) .... .25 .11
❑ 2 Don Barber .... .50 .23
❑ 3 Jacques Cloutier .... .75 .35
❑ 4 Steven Finn .... .50 .23
❑ 5 Stephane Fiset .... 1.25 .55
❑ 6 Bryan Fogarty .... .50 .23
❑ 7 Adam Foote .... 1.00 .45
❑ 8 Marc Fortier .... .50 .23
❑ 9 Alexei Gusarov .... .50 .23
❑ 10 Mike Hough .... .50 .23
❑ 11 Don Jackson ACO .... .25 .11
❑ 12 Valeri Kamensky .... 1.50 .70
❑ 13 John Kordic .... .75 .35
❑ 14 Claude Lapointe .... .50 .23
❑ 15 Curtis Leschyshyn .... .60 .25
❑ 16 Jacques Martin ACO .... .50 .23
❑ 17 Mike McNeill .... .50 .23
❑ 18 Ken McRae .... .50 .23
❑ 19 Kip Miller .... .50 .23
❑ 20 Stephane Morin .... .50 .23
❑ 21 Owen Nolan .... 1.50 .70

| | | |
|---|---|---|
| ❑ 22 Pierre Page GM/CO | .50 | .23 |
| ❑ 23 Greg Paslawski | .50 | .23 |
| ❑ 24 Herb Raglan | .50 | .23 |
| ❑ 25 Joe Sakic | 4.00 | 1.80 |
| ❑ 26 Doug Smail | .50 | .23 |
| ❑ 27 Greg Smyth | .50 | .23 |
| ❑ 28 Mats Sundin | 2.00 | .90 |
| ❑ 29 Mikhail Tatarinov | .50 | .23 |
| ❑ 30 Ron Tugnutt | .75 | .35 |
| ❑ 31 Tony Twist | 1.25 | .55 |
| ❑ 32 Wayne Van Dorp | .50 | .23 |
| ❑ 33 Randy Velischek | .50 | .23 |
| ❑ 34 Mark Vermette | .50 | .23 |
| ❑ 35 Craig Wolanin | .50 | .23 |

## 1992-93 Nordiques Petro-Canada

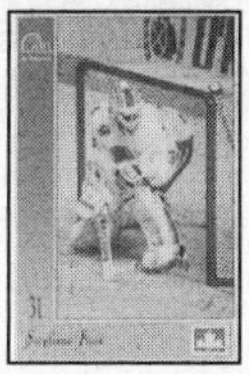

These blank-backed cards measure approximately 3 1/2" by 5 5/8" and feature white-bordered color player action shots. The player's name, uniform number, Nordiques logo, and Petro-Canada logo appear within the purplish margin on the left and below the photo. The cards are unnumbered and checklisted below in alphabetical order.

| | MINT | NRMT |
|---|---|---|
| COMPLETE SET (39) | 20.00 | 9.00 |
| COMMON CARD (1-39) | .25 | .11 |
| ❑ 1 Badaboum (Mascot) | .25 | .11 |
| ❑ 2 Daniel Bouchard CO | .50 | .23 |
| ❑ 3 Gino Cavallini | .50 | .23 |
| ❑ 4 Jacques Cloutier | .75 | .35 |
| ❑ 5 Steve Duchesne | .75 | .35 |
| ❑ 6 Steven Finn | .50 | .23 |
| ❑ 7 Stephane Fiset | 1.00 | .45 |
| ❑ 8 Adam Foote | .75 | .35 |
| ❑ 9 Alexei Gusarov | .50 | .23 |
| ❑ 10 Ron Hextall | 1.25 | .55 |
| ❑ 11 Mike Hough | .50 | .23 |
| ❑ 12 Kerry Huffman | .50 | .23 |
| ❑ 13 Tim Hunter | .50 | .23 |
| ❑ 14 Don Jackson ACO | .25 | .11 |
| ❑ 15 Valeri Kamensky | 1.00 | .45 |
| ❑ 16 David Karpa | .50 | .23 |
| ❑ 17 Andrei Kovalenko | .75 | .35 |
| ❑ 18 Claude Lapointe | .50 | .23 |
| ❑ 19 Curtis Leschyshyn | .60 | .25 |
| ❑ 20 Bill Lindsay | .50 | .23 |
| ❑ 21 Jacques Martin ACO | .50 | .23 |
| ❑ 22 Owen Nolan | 1.25 | .55 |
| ❑ 23 Pierre Page GM/CO | .50 | .23 |
| ❑ 24 Scott Pearson | .50 | .23 |
| ❑ 25 Herb Raglan | .50 | .23 |
| ❑ 26 Mike Ricci | 1.00 | .45 |
| ❑ 27 Martin Rucinsky | .75 | .35 |
| ❑ 28 Joe Sakic | 4.00 | 1.80 |
| ❑ 29 Andre Savard ACO | .25 | .11 |
| ❑ 30 Chris Simon | 1.00 | .45 |
| ❑ 31 Mats Sundin | 2.00 | .90 |
| ❑ 32 John Tanner | .60 | .25 |
| ❑ 33 Mikhail Tatarinov | .50 | .23 |
| ❑ 34 Tony Twist | .75 | .35 |
| ❑ 35 Wayne Van Dorp | .50 | .23 |
| ❑ 36 Mark Vermette | .50 | .23 |
| ❑ 37 Craig Wolanin | .50 | .23 |
| ❑ 38 Scott Young | .75 | .35 |
| ❑ 39 Team Photo | 1.00 | .45 |

## 1994-95 Nordiques Burger King

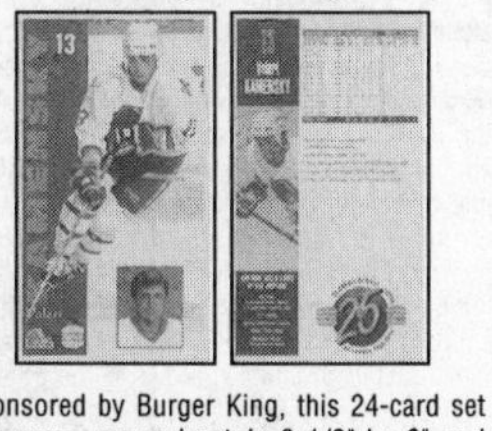

Sponsored by Burger King, this 24-card set measures approximately 3 1/2" by 6" and features members of the 1994-95 Quebec Nordiques. The fronts have white-bordered color action player shots, with the player's name and uniform number is a team color-coded bar alongside the left or right. A small color player portrait with red borders appears on the bottom. The backs carry another small blue-toned action shot, along with biography, career statistics and highlights (both in English and French) and the sponsor logo. The cards are unnumbered and checklisted below in alphabetical order.

| | MINT | NRMT |
|---|---|---|
| COMPLETE SET (28) | 20.00 | 9.00 |
| COMMON CARD (1-28) | .50 | .23 |
| ❑ 1 Badaboum | .50 | .23 |
| ❑ 2 Bob Bassen | .50 | .23 |
| ❑ 3 Wendel Clark | 1.00 | .45 |
| ❑ 4 Adam Deadmarsh | 1.50 | .70 |
| ❑ 5 Steven Finn | .50 | .23 |
| ❑ 6 Stephane Fiset | 1.25 | .55 |
| ❑ 7 Adam Foote | .75 | .35 |
| ❑ 8 Peter Forsberg | 5.00 | 2.20 |
| ❑ 9 Alexei Gusarov | .50 | .23 |
| ❑ 10 Valeri Kamensky | 1.00 | .45 |
| ❑ 11 Jon Klemm | .50 | .23 |
| ❑ 12 Andrei Kovalenko | .75 | .35 |
| ❑ 13 Uwe Krupp | .60 | .25 |
| ❑ 14 Claude Lapointe | .50 | .23 |
| ❑ 15 Janne Laukkanen | .60 | .25 |
| ❑ 16 Sylvain Lefebvre | .50 | .23 |
| ❑ 17 Curtis Leschyshyn | .50 | .23 |
| ❑ 18 Paul MacDermid | .50 | .23 |
| ❑ 19 Owen Nolan | 1.50 | .70 |
| ❑ 20 Mike Ricci | .75 | .35 |
| ❑ 21 Martin Rucinsky | .75 | .35 |
| ❑ 22 Joe Sakic | 3.50 | 1.55 |
| ❑ 23 Reggie Savage | .50 | .23 |
| ❑ 24 Chris Simon | .60 | .25 |
| ❑ 25 Jocelyn Thibault | 2.00 | .90 |
| ❑ 26 Craig Wolanin | .50 | .23 |
| ❑ 27 Scott Young | .75 | .35 |
| ❑ 28 Team Card | .50 | .23 |

## 1970-71 North Stars Postcards

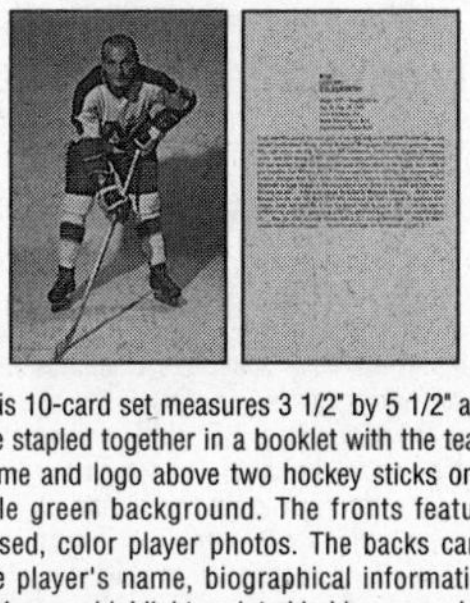

This 10-card set measures 3 1/2" by 5 1/2" and are stapled together in a booklet with the team name and logo above two hockey sticks on a pale green background. The fronts feature posed, color player photos. The backs carry the player's name, biographical information and career highlights printed in blue on a white background. The cards are unnumbered and checklisted below in alphabetical order.

| | NRMT-MT | EXC |
|---|---|---|
| COMPLETE SET (10) | 35.00 | 16.00 |
| COMMON CARD (1-10) | 2.00 | .90 |
| ❑ 1 Barry Gibbs | 2.00 | .90 |
| ❑ 2 Bill Goldsworthy | 5.00 | 2.20 |
| ❑ 3 Danny Grant | 4.00 | 1.80 |
| ❑ 4 Ted Harris | 2.00 | .90 |
| ❑ 5 Cesare Maniago | 6.00 | 2.70 |
| ❑ 6 Jean Paul Parise | 3.00 | 1.35 |
| ❑ 7 Tom Reid | 2.00 | .90 |
| ❑ 8 Bobby Rousseau | 2.00 | .90 |
| ❑ 9 Tom Williams | 2.00 | .90 |
| ❑ 10 Lorne Worsley | 10.00 | 4.50 |

## 1972-73 North Stars Glossy Photos

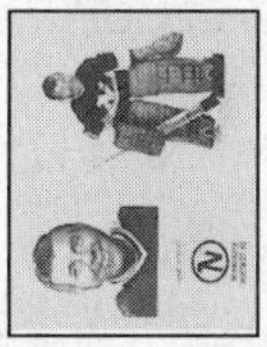

These 20 blank-backed approximately 8" by 10" glossy white-bordered black-and-white photo sheets feature a suited-up posed player photo on the right and, on the left, a posed player head shot. Below the head shot appears the player's name and the Minnesota North Stars name and logo. The photos are unnumbered and checklisted below in alphabetical order.

| | NRMT-MT | EXC |
|---|---|---|
| COMPLETE SET (20) | 20.00 | 9.00 |
| COMMON CARD (1-20) | 1.00 | .45 |
| ❑ 1 Fred Barrett | 1.00 | .45 |
| ❑ 2 Charlie Burns | 1.00 | .45 |
| ❑ 3 Jude Drouin | 1.00 | .45 |
| ❑ 4 Barry Gibbs | 1.00 | .45 |
| ❑ 5 Bill Goldsworthy | 2.50 | 1.10 |
| ❑ 6 Danny Grant | 1.50 | .70 |
| ❑ 7 Ted Harris | 1.00 | .45 |
| ❑ 8 Fred(Buster) Harvey | 1.00 | .45 |
| ❑ 9 Dennis Hextall | 1.50 | .70 |
| ❑ 10 Cesare Maniago | 2.00 | .90 |
| ❑ 11 Doug Mohns | 1.50 | .70 |
| ❑ 12 Lou Nanne | 1.50 | .70 |
| ❑ 13 Bob Nevin | 1.00 | .45 |
| ❑ 14 Dennis O'Brien | 1.00 | .45 |
| ❑ 15 Murray Oliver | 1.00 | .45 |
| ❑ 16 J.P. Parise | 1.00 | .45 |
| ❑ 17 Dean Prentice | 1.50 | .70 |
| ❑ 18 Tom Reid | 1.00 | .45 |
| ❑ 19 Gump Worsley | 5.00 | 2.20 |
| ❑ 20 Wren Blair GM<br>Jack Gordon CO | 1.00 | .45 |

## 1973-74 North Stars Action Posters

These 14 x 20 color action posters were distributed by Mr. Steak restaurants in the Minneapolis area. They were distributed one every two weeks for twenty weeks.

| | MINT | NRMT |
|---|---|---|
| COMPLETE SET (10) | 20.00 | 9.00 |
| COMMON POSTER | 2.00 | .90 |
| ❑ 1 Henry Boucha | 2.00 | .90 |
| ❑ 2 Jude Drouin | 2.00 | .90 |
| ❑ 3 Barry Gibbs | 2.00 | .90 |
| ❑ 4 Bill Goldsworthy | 3.00 | 1.35 |
| ❑ 5 Dennis Hextall | 2.00 | .90 |
| ❑ 6 Cesare Maniago | 3.00 | 1.35 |
| ❑ 7 Lou Nanne | 3.00 | 1.35 |
| ❑ 8 Dennis O'Brien | 2.00 | .90 |
| ❑ 9 J.P. Parise | 3.00 | 1.35 |
| ❑ 10 Tom Reid | 2.00 | .90 |

## 1973-74 North Stars Postcards

These postcard sized cards feature black and white posed photos on the front, and are blank backed. Cards are unnumbered and checklisted below alphabetically.

| | MINT | NRMT |
|---|---|---|
| COMPLETE SET (20) | 20.00 | 9.00 |
| COMMON CARD | .75 | .35 |
| ❑ 1 Fred Barrett | .75 | .35 |
| ❑ 2 Gary Bergman | .75 | .35 |
| ❑ 3 Jude Drouin | .75 | .35 |
| ❑ 4 Tony Featherstone | .75 | .35 |
| ❑ 5 Barry Gibbs | .75 | .35 |
| ❑ 6 Bill Goldsworthy | 1.25 | .55 |
| ❑ 7 Danny Grant | .75 | .35 |
| ❑ 8 Buster Harvey | .75 | .35 |
| ❑ 9 Dennis Hextall | 1.00 | .45 |
| ❑ 10 Parker MacDonald | .75 | .35 |
| ❑ 11 Cesare Maniago | 1.00 | .45 |
| ❑ 12 Lou Nanne | 1.00 | .45 |
| ❑ 13 Rod Norrish | .75 | .35 |
| ❑ 14 Dennis O'Brien | .75 | .35 |
| ❑ 15 Murray Oliver | .75 | .35 |
| ❑ 16 Jean-Paul Parise | .75 | .35 |
| ❑ 17 Dean Prentice | 1.00 | .45 |
| ❑ 18 Tom Reid | .75 | .35 |
| ❑ 19 Fred Stanfield | 1.25 | .55 |
| ❑ 20 Lorne Worsley | 3.00 | 1.35 |

## 1978-79 North Stars Cloverleaf Dairy

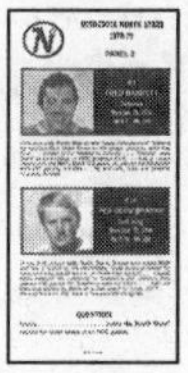

This ten-panel set of Minnesota North Stars was issued on the side of half gallon milk cartons as part of a sweepstakes. The picture and text are printed in either red or purple. The panels measure approximately 3 3/4" by 7 5/8", with two players per panel. The North Stars' logo, the team name, year, and panel number appear at the top of each panel. Each panel features a "mug shot" and brief biographical information on two players. A North Stars question was included at the bottom of each panel. There were ten questions in all: one per panel, and a tenth question on the final entry panel, which also included a list of all ten questions and gave complete entry information. The unnumbered panel describes the sweepstakes promotion and lists the prizes.

| | NRMT-MT | EXC |
|---|---|---|
| COMPLETE SET (11) | 125.00 | 55.00 |
| COMMON PANEL (1-10) | 12.00 | 5.50 |
| ❑ 1 Gilles Meloche and<br>Gary Sargent | 15.00 | 6.75 |
| ❑ 2 Fred Barrett and<br>Per-Olov Brasar | 12.00 | 5.50 |
| ❑ 3 Jean-Paul Parise and<br>Greg Smith | 12.00 | 5.50 |
| ❑ 4 Al MacAdam and<br>Kent-Erik Andersson | 12.00 | 5.50 |
| ❑ 5 Gary Edwards and<br>Bobby Smith | 25.00 | 11.00 |
| ❑ 6 Mike Polich and<br>Brad Maxwell | 12.00 | 5.50 |
| ❑ 7 Steve Payne and<br>Glen Sharpley | 12.00 | 5.50 |
| ❑ 8 Tim Young and<br>Kris Manery | 12.00 | 5.50 |
| ❑ 9 Ron Zanussi and<br>Tom Younghans | 12.00 | 5.50 |
| ❑ 10 Final Entry Panel | 12.00 | 5.50 |
| ❑ NNO Sweepstakes Promotion | 5.00 | 2.20 |

## 1979-80 North Stars Postcards

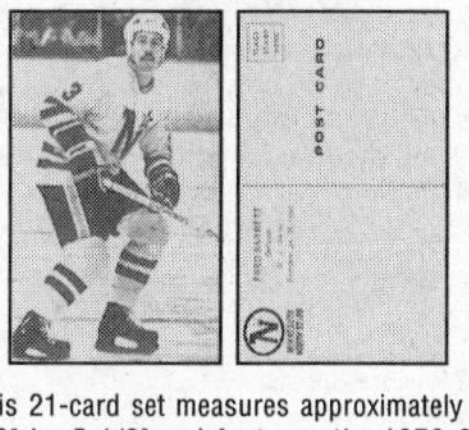

This 21-card set measures approximately 3 1/2" by 5 1/2" and features the 1979-80 Minnesota North Stars. The fronts have borderless black-and-white player action photos. The backs have a postcard format and carry the player's name, position, short biography, and the team logo. The cards are unnumbered and checklisted below in alphabetical order.

| | NRMT-MT | EXC |
|---|---|---|
| COMPLETE SET (21) | 20.00 | 9.00 |
| COMMON CARD (1-21) | .75 | .35 |
| ❑ 1 Kent-Erik Andersson | .75 | .35 |
| ❑ 2 Fred Barrett | .75 | .35 |
| ❑ 3 Gary Edwards | 1.50 | .70 |
| ❑ 4 Mike Fidler | .75 | .35 |
| ❑ 5 Craig Hartsburg | 2.00 | .90 |
| ❑ 6 Al MacAdam | 1.00 | .45 |
| ❑ 7 Kris Manery | .75 | .35 |
| ❑ 8 Brad Maxwell | .75 | .35 |
| ❑ 9 Tom McCarthy | 1.00 | .45 |
| ❑ 10 Gilles Meloche | 2.00 | .90 |
| ❑ 11 Steve Payne | 1.00 | .45 |
| ❑ 12 Mike Polich | .75 | .35 |
| ❑ 13 Gary Sargent | 1.00 | .45 |
| ❑ 14 Glen Sharpley | .75 | .35 |
| ❑ 15 Paul Shmyr | .75 | .35 |
| ❑ 16 Bobby Smith | 3.00 | 1.35 |
| ❑ 17 Greg Smith | .75 | .35 |
| ❑ 18 Glen Sonmor CO | .75 | .35 |
| ❑ 19 Tim Young | 1.00 | .45 |
| ❑ 20 Tom Younghans | .75 | .35 |
| ❑ 21 Ron Zanussi | .75 | .35 |

## 1980-81 North Stars Postcards

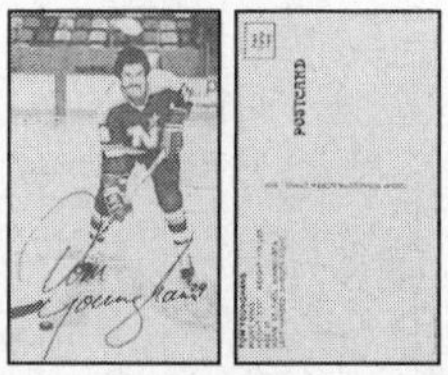

This 24-card set measures approximately 3 1/2" by 5 1/2" and features the 1980-81 Minnesota North Stars. The fronts have borderless color posed player photos with facsimile autographs across the bottom. The backs have a postcard format and carry a short player biography and the team logo in green print. The cards are unnumbered and checklisted below in alphabetical order.

| | NRMT-MT | EXC |
|---|---|---|
| COMPLETE SET (24) | 18.00 | 8.00 |
| COMMON CARD (1-24) | .75 | .35 |
| ❑ 1 Kent-Erik Andersson | .75 | .35 |
| ❑ 2 Fred Barrett | .75 | .35 |
| ❑ 3 Don Beaupre | 2.50 | 1.10 |
| ❑ 4 Jack Carlson | 2.50 | 1.10 |
| ❑ 5 Steve Christoff | 1.00 | .45 |
| ❑ 6 Mike Eaves | .75 | .35 |
| ❑ 7 Gary Edwards | 1.50 | .70 |
| ❑ 8 Curt Giles | 1.00 | .45 |
| ❑ 9 Craig Hartsburg | 2.00 | .90 |
| ❑ 10 Al MacAdam | 1.00 | .45 |
| ❑ 11 Brad Maxwell | .75 | .35 |
| ❑ 12 Tom McCarthy | .75 | .35 |
| ❑ 13 Gilles Meloche | 1.50 | .70 |
| ❑ 14 Murray Oliver ACO<br>J.P. Parise ACO<br>Glen Sonmor CO | .75 | .35 |
| ❑ 15 Steve Payne | .75 | .35 |
| ❑ 16 Mike Polich | .75 | .35 |
| ❑ 17 Gary Sargent | 1.00 | .45 |
| ❑ 18 Glen Sharpley | .75 | .35 |
| ❑ 19 Paul Shmyr | .75 | .35 |
| ❑ 20 Bobby Smith | 2.50 | 1.10 |
| ❑ 21 Greg Smith | .75 | .35 |
| ❑ 22 Tim Young | .75 | .35 |
| ❑ 23 Tom Younghans | .75 | .35 |
| ❑ 24 Ron Zanussi | .75 | .35 |

## 1981-82 North Stars Postcards

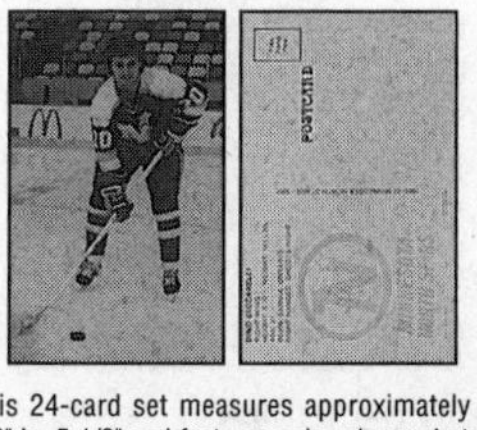

This 24-card set measures approximately 3 1/2" by 5 1/2" and features color player photos on the fronts. The backs have a green postcard design with the North Stars' logo printed in pale green on the left side. The player's name, position, and biographical information appear in the upper left corner. The season and team name appear vertically in the middle, bisecting the cards. The cards are unnumbered and checklisted below in alphabetical order.

| | NRMT-MT | EXC |
|---|---|---|
| COMPLETE SET (24) | 25.00 | 11.00 |
| COMMON CARD (1-24) | .75 | .35 |
| ❑ 1 Kent-Erik Andersson | .75 | .35 |
| ❑ 2 Fred Barrett | .75 | .35 |
| ❑ 3 Don Beaupre | 2.50 | 1.10 |
| ❑ 4 Neal Broten | 4.00 | 1.80 |
| ❑ 5 Jack Carlson | 2.00 | .90 |
| ❑ 6 Steve Christoff | .75 | .35 |
| ❑ 7 Dino Ciccarelli | 6.00 | 2.70 |
| ❑ 8 Mike Eaves | .75 | .35 |
| ❑ 9 Curt Giles | 1.00 | .45 |
| ❑ 10 Anders Hakansson | .75 | .35 |
| ❑ 11 Craig Hartsburg | 1.50 | .70 |
| ❑ 12 Al Macadam | .75 | .35 |
| ❑ 13 Brad Maxwell | .75 | .35 |
| ❑ 14 Kevin Maxwell | .75 | .35 |
| ❑ 15 Tom McCarthy | .75 | .35 |
| ❑ 16 Gilles Meloche | 1.50 | .70 |
| ❑ 17 Bill Nyrop | .75 | .35 |
| ❑ 18 Steve Payne | .75 | .35 |
| ❑ 19 Brad Palmer | .75 | .35 |
| ❑ 20 Gordie Roberts | .75 | .35 |
| ❑ 21 Gary Sargent | .75 | .35 |
| ❑ 22 Bobby Smith | 2.00 | .90 |
| ❑ 23 Glen Sonmor CO<br>J.P. Parise ACO<br>Murray Oliver ACO | .75 | .35 |
| ❑ 24 Tim Young | .75 | .35 |

## 1982-83 North Stars Postcards

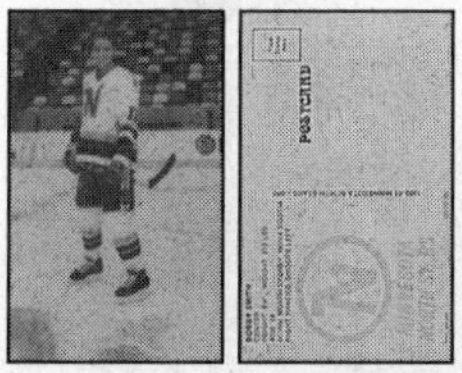

This 25-card set measures approximately 3 1/2" by 5 1/2" and features color player photos on the fronts. The backs have a green postcard design with the North Stars' logo printed in pale green on the left side. The player's name, position, and biographical information appear in the upper left corner. The season and team name appear vertically in the middle, bisecting the cards. The cards are unnumbered and checklisted below in alphabetical order.

| | MINT | NRMT |
|---|---|---|
| COMPLETE SET (24) | 25.00 | 11.00 |
| COMMON CARD (1-24) | .75 | .35 |
| ❑ 1 Fred Barrett | .75 | .35 |
| ❑ 2 Don Beaupre | 1.50 | .70 |
| ❑ 3 Brian Bellows | 3.00 | 1.35 |
| ❑ 4 Neal Broten | 2.50 | 1.10 |
| ❑ 5 Dino Ciccarelli | 4.00 | 1.80 |
| ❑ 6 Dino Ciccarelli<br>Neal Broten | 2.50 | 1.10 |
| ❑ 7 Jordy Douglas | .75 | .35 |
| ❑ 8 Mike Eaves | .75 | .35 |
| ❑ 9 George Ferguson | .75 | .35 |
| ❑ 10 Ron Friest | .75 | .35 |
| ❑ 11 Curt Giles | 1.00 | .45 |
| ❑ 12 Craig Hartsburg | 1.50 | .70 |
| ❑ 13 Al MacAdam | .75 | .35 |
| ❑ 14 Dan Mandich | .75 | .35 |
| ❑ 15 Brad Maxwell | .75 | .35 |
| ❑ 16 Tom McCarthy | .75 | .35 |
| ❑ 17 Gilles Meloche | 1.50 | .70 |
| ❑ 18 Steve Payne | .75 | .35 |
| ❑ 19 Willi Plett | 1.00 | .45 |
| ❑ 20 Gordie Roberts | .75 | .35 |
| ❑ 21 Gary Sargent | .75 | .35 |
| ❑ 22 Bobby Smith | 2.00 | .90 |
| ❑ 23 Ken Solheim | .75 | .35 |
| ❑ 24 Tim Young | .75 | .35 |
| ❑ 25 Team Photo | 1.50 | .70 |

## 1983-84 North Stars Postcards

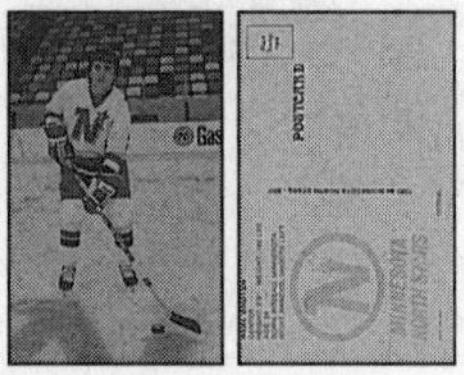

This 27-card set measures approximately 3 1/2" by 5 1/2" and features color player photos on the fronts. The backs have a green postcard design with the North Stars' logo printed in pale green on the left side. The player's name, position, and biographical information appear in the upper left corner. The season and team name appear vertically in the middle, bisecting the cards. The cards are unnumbered and checklisted below in alphabetical order.

| | MINT | NRMT |
|---|---|---|
| COMPLETE SET (27) | 20.00 | 9.00 |
| COMMON CARD (1-27) | .50 | .23 |
| □ 1 Keith Acton | .75 | .35 |
| □ 2 Brent Ashton | .75 | .35 |
| □ 3 Don Beaupre | 1.50 | .70 |
| □ 4 Brian Bellows | 2.00 | .90 |
| □ 5 Neal Broten | 2.00 | .90 |
| □ 6 Dino Ciccarelli | 2.50 | 1.10 |
| □ 7 Jordy Douglas | .75 | .35 |
| □ 8 George Ferguson | .75 | .35 |
| □ 9 Curt Giles | 1.00 | .45 |
| □ 10 Craig Hartsburg | 1.00 | .45 |
| □ 11 Brian Lawton | .75 | .35 |
| □ 12 Craig Levie | .75 | .35 |
| □ 13 Lars Lindgren | .75 | .35 |
| □ 14 Al MacAdam | .75 | .35 |
| □ 15 Bill Mahoney CO | .50 | .23 |
| □ 16 Dan Mandich | .75 | .35 |
| □ 17 Dennis Maruk | 1.25 | .55 |
| □ 18 Brad Maxwell | .75 | .35 |
| □ 19 Tom McCarthy | .75 | .35 |
| □ 20 Gilles Meloche | 1.00 | .45 |
| □ 21 Mark Napier | .75 | .35 |
| □ 22 Steve Payne | .75 | .35 |
| □ 23 Willi Plett | 1.00 | .45 |
| □ 24 Dave Richter | .75 | .35 |
| □ 25 Gordie Roberts | .75 | .35 |
| □ 26 Randy Velischek | .75 | .35 |
| □ 27 Team Photo | 1.50 | .70 |

## 1984-85 North Stars 7-Eleven

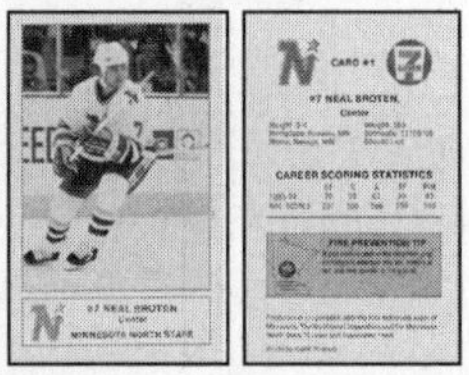

This 12-card safety set was sponsored by the Southland Corporation in cooperation with the Fire Marshalls Assn. of Minnesota and the Minnesota North Stars. The cards measure 2 5/8" by 4 1/8". The front has a color action photo enframed by a thin green border on white card stock. The green box below the picture gives the uniform number, player's name, position, the team name, and team logo. The card number on the back is sandwiched between the North Stars' and 7-Eleven logos. The back also has basic biographical information, career scoring statistics, and a fire prevention tip in a yellow box on the lower portion of the card back.

| | MINT | NRMT |
|---|---|---|
| COMPLETE SET (12) | 7.00 | 3.10 |
| COMMON CARD (1-12) | .50 | .23 |
| □ 1 Neal Broten | 1.25 | .55 |
| □ 2 Willi Plett | .75 | .35 |
| □ 3 Craig Hartsburg | 1.25 | .55 |
| □ 4 Brian Bellows | 2.00 | .90 |
| □ 5 Gordie Roberts | .50 | .23 |
| □ 6 Keith Acton | .75 | .35 |
| □ 7 Paul Holmgren | .75 | .35 |
| □ 8 Gilles Meloche | .75 | .35 |
| □ 9 Dennis Maruk | 1.25 | .55 |
| □ 10 Tom McCarthy | .50 | .23 |
| □ 11 Steve Payne | .75 | .35 |
| □ 12 Dino Ciccarelli | 2.00 | .90 |

## 1984-85 North Stars Postcards

This 25-card set measures approximately 3 1/2" by 5 1/2" and features full-bleed, posed, color player photos. The backs have a green postcard design. The North Stars' logo is

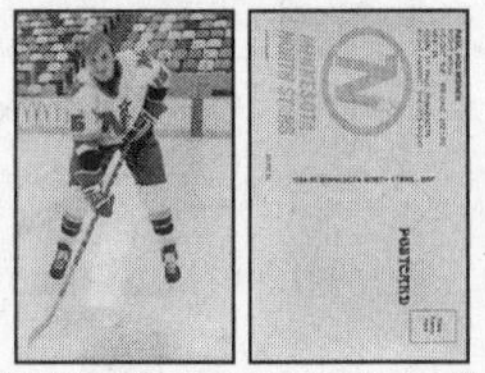

printed in pale green on the left side. The player's name and biographical information appears in the upper left corner. The season and team name appear vertically in the middle, bisecting the cards. The cards are unnumbered and checklisted below in alphabetical order.

| | MINT | NRMT |
|---|---|---|
| COMPLETE SET (29) | 15.00 | 6.75 |
| COMMON CARD (1-29) | .50 | .23 |
| □ 1 Keith Acton | .75 | .35 |
| □ 2 Don Beaupre | 1.50 | .70 |
| □ 3 Brian Bellows | 2.00 | .90 |
| □ 4 Scott Bjugstad | .50 | .23 |
| □ 5 Neal Broten | 1.50 | .70 |
| □ 6 Dino Ciccarelli | 2.00 | .90 |
| □ 7 Curt Giles | .75 | .35 |
| □ 8 Curt Giles w/captains C | .50 | .23 |
| □ 9 Craig Hartsburg | 1.50 | .70 |
| □ 10 Tom Hirsch | .50 | .23 |
| □ 11 Paul Holmgren | 1.00 | .45 |
| □ 12 Brian Lawton | .50 | .23 |
| □ 13 Dan Mandich | .50 | .23 |
| □ 14 Dennis Maruk | 1.50 | .70 |
| □ 15 Brad Maxwell | .50 | .23 |
| □ 16 Tom McCarthy | .50 | .23 |
| □ 17 Tony McKegney | .50 | .23 |
| □ 18 Roland Melanson | .75 | .35 |
| □ 19 Gilles Meloche | .75 | .35 |
| □ 20 Mark Napier | .75 | .35 |
| □ 21 Steve Payne | .75 | .35 |
| □ 22 Willi Plett | .75 | .35 |
| □ 23 Dave Richter | .50 | .23 |
| □ 24 Gordie Roberts | .50 | .23 |
| □ 25 Bob Rouse | .50 | .23 |
| □ 26 Gord Sherven | .50 | .23 |
| □ 27 Harold Snepsts | 1.00 | .45 |
| □ 28 Ken Solheim | .50 | .23 |
| □ 29 Randy Velischek | .50 | .23 |

## 1985-86 North Stars 7-Eleven

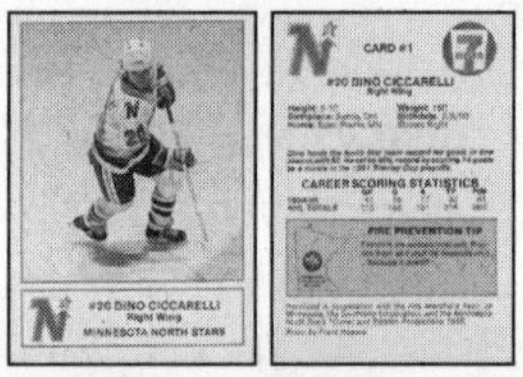

This 12-card safety set was sponsored by the Southland Corporation in cooperation with the Fire Marshalls Assn. of Minnesota and the Minnesota North Stars. The cards measure the standard size, 2 1/2" by 3 1/2". The front has a color action photo enframed by a thin green border on white card stock. The green box below the picture gives the uniform number, player's name, position, the team name, and team logo. The card number on the back is sandwiched between the North Stars' and 7-Eleven logos. The back also has basic biographical information, career scoring statistics, and a fire prevention tip in a yellow box on the lower portion of the card back.

| | MINT | NRMT |
|---|---|---|
| COMPLETE SET (12) | 7.00 | 3.10 |
| COMMON CARD (1-12) | .50 | .23 |
| □ 1 Dino Ciccarelli | 2.00 | .90 |
| □ 2 Scott Bjugstad | .50 | .23 |
| □ 3 Curt Giles | .75 | .35 |
| □ 4 Don Beaupre | 1.00 | .45 |
| □ 5 Tony McKegney | .50 | .23 |
| □ 6 Neal Broten | 1.50 | .70 |
| □ 7 Willi Plett | .75 | .35 |
| □ 8 Craig Hartsburg | 1.00 | .45 |
| □ 9 Brian Bellows | 1.00 | .45 |
| □ 10 Keith Acton | .75 | .35 |
| □ 11 Dave Langevin | .50 | .23 |
| □ 12 Dirk Graham | 1.50 | .70 |

## 1985-86 North Stars Postcards

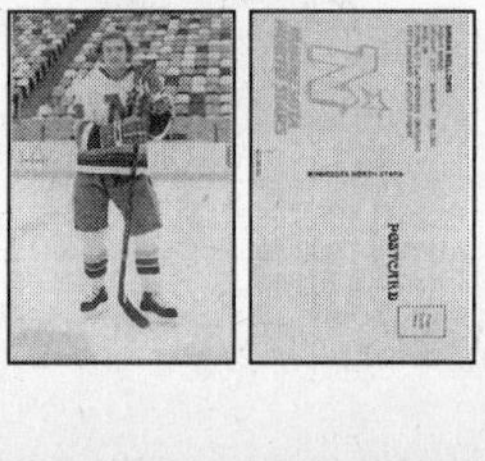

This 27-card set measures 3 1/2" by 5 1/2" and features full-bleed, posed, color player photos on thin card stock. The backs have a green postcard design. The North Stars' logo is printed in pale green outline lettering on the left side. The player's name and biographical information appears in the upper left corner. The cards are unnumbered and checklisted below in alphabetical order. The year of the set is established by the Dave Langevin card; he played with the North Stars only during the 1985-86 season.

| | MINT | NRMT |
|---|---|---|
| COMPLETE SET (27) | 15.00 | 6.75 |
| COMMON CARD (1-27) | .50 | .23 |
| □ 1 Keith Acton | .75 | .35 |
| □ 2 Don Beaupre | 1.00 | .45 |
| □ 3 Brian Bellows | 1.00 | .45 |
| □ 4 Bo Berglund | .50 | .23 |
| □ 5 Scott Bjugstad | .50 | .23 |
| □ 6 Neal Broten | 1.50 | .70 |
| □ 7 Jon Casey | 1.50 | .70 |
| □ 8 Dino Ciccarelli | 2.00 | .90 |
| □ 9 Tim Coulis | .50 | .23 |
| □ 10 Curt Giles | .75 | .35 |
| □ 11 Dirk Graham | 1.50 | .70 |
| □ 12 Mats Hallin | .50 | .23 |
| □ 13 Craig Hartsburg | 1.00 | .45 |
| □ 14 Tom Hirsch | .50 | .23 |
| □ 15 Dave Langevin | .50 | .23 |
| □ 16 Brian Lawton | .50 | .23 |
| □ 17 Craig Levie | .50 | .23 |
| □ 18 Dan Mandich | .50 | .23 |
| □ 19 Dennis Maruk | 1.00 | .45 |
| □ 20 Tom McCarthy | .50 | .23 |
| □ 21 Tony McKegney | .50 | .23 |
| □ 22 Roland Melanson | .75 | .35 |
| □ 23 Steve Payne | .75 | .35 |
| □ 24 Willi Plett | .75 | .35 |
| □ 25 Gordie Roberts | .50 | .23 |
| □ 26 Bob Rouse | .75 | .35 |
| □ 27 Gord Sherven | .50 | .23 |

## 1986-87 North Stars 7-Eleven

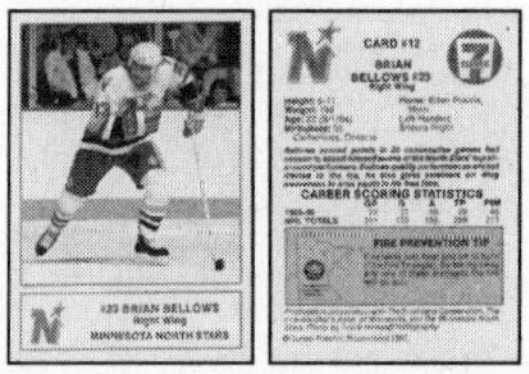

This 12-card safety set was sponsored by the Southland Corporation in cooperation with the Fire Marshalls Assn. of Minnesota and the Minnesota North Stars. The cards measure the standard size, 2 1/2" by 3 1/2". The front has a color action photo enframed by a thin green border on white card stock. The green box below the picture gives the uniform number, player's name, position, the team name, and team logo. The card number on the back is sandwiched between the North Stars' and 7-Eleven logos. The back also has basic biographical information, career scoring statistics, and a fire prevention tip in a yellow box on the lower portion of the card back. The copyright notice on the back says 1987.

| | MINT | NRMT |
|---|---|---|
| COMPLETE SET (12) | 7.00 | 3.10 |
| COMMON CARD (1-12) | .50 | .23 |
| □ 1 Neal Broten | 1.00 | .45 |
| □ 2 Brian MacLellan | .50 | .23 |
| □ 3 Willi Plett | .75 | .35 |
| □ 4 Scott Bjugstad | .50 | .23 |
| □ 5 Don Beaupre | 1.00 | .45 |
| □ 6 Dino Ciccarelli | 2.00 | .90 |
| □ 7 Craig Hartsburg | 1.00 | .45 |
| □ 8 Dennis Maruk | 1.50 | .70 |
| □ 9 Bob Rouse | .50 | .23 |
| □ 10 Gordie Roberts | .50 | .23 |
| □ 11 Bob Brooke | .50 | .23 |
| □ 12 Brian Bellows | 1.50 | .70 |

## 1987-88 North Stars Postcards

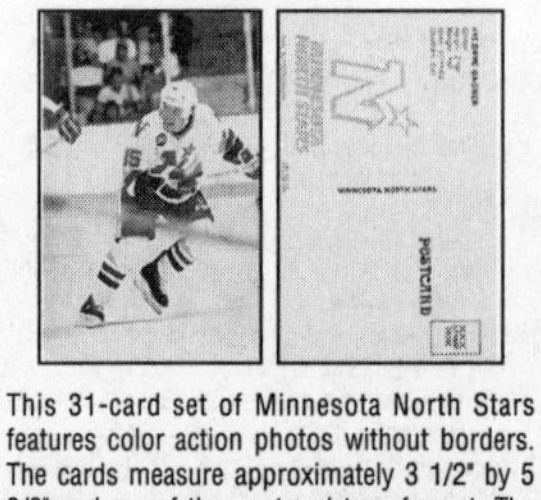

This 31-card set of Minnesota North Stars features color action photos without borders. The cards measure approximately 3 1/2" by 5 3/8" and are of the postcard type format. The backs are printed in green, provide brief biographical information, and have the North Stars' logo on the left-hand portion. These cards are unnumbered and we have checklisted them below in alphabetical order.

| | MINT | NRMT |
|---|---|---|
| COMPLETE SET (31) | 18.00 | 8.00 |
| COMMON CARD (1-31) | .50 | .23 |
| □ 1 Keith Acton | .60 | .25 |
| □ 2 Dave Archibald | .50 | .23 |
| □ 3 Warren Babe | .50 | .23 |
| □ 4 Don Beaupre | 1.00 | .45 |
| □ 5 Brian Bellows | 1.00 | .45 |
| □ 6 Mike Berger | .50 | .23 |
| □ 7 Scott Bjugstad | .50 | .23 |
| □ 8 Bob Brooke | .50 | .23 |
| □ 9 Herb Brooks CO | .75 | .35 |
| □ 10 Neal Broten | 1.00 | .45 |
| □ 11 Dino Ciccarelli | 1.50 | .70 |
| □ 12 Larry DePalma | .50 | .23 |
| □ 13 Dave Gagner | 2.50 | 1.10 |
| □ 14 Curt Giles | .75 | .35 |
| □ 15 Dirk Graham | 1.00 | .45 |
| □ 16 Craig Hartsburg | 1.00 | .45 |
| □ 17 Tom Hirsch | .50 | .23 |
| □ 18 Brian Lawton | .50 | .23 |
| □ 19 Brian MacLellan | .50 | .23 |
| □ 20 Dennis Maruk | .75 | .35 |
| □ 21 Basil McRae | .75 | .35 |
| □ 22 Frantisek Musil | .50 | .23 |
| □ 23 Steve Payne | .60 | .25 |
| □ 24 Pat Price | .50 | .23 |
| □ 25 Chris Pryor | .50 | .23 |
| □ 26 Gordie Roberts | .50 | .23 |
| □ 27 Bob Rouse | .60 | .25 |
| □ 28 Terry Ruskowski | .60 | .25 |
| □ 29 Kari Takko | .75 | .35 |
| □ 30 Ron Wilson | .50 | .23 |
| □ 31 Richard Zemlak | .50 | .23 |

## 1988-89 North Stars ADA

This 23-card set measures 3 1/2" by 7 1/8" and was sponsored by the American Dairy Association and Pro Ex Photo Systems. The fronts feature color action player photos with the team logo, player's name, and sponsors' logos at the bottom in the wide white margin. On the horizontal backs, the left box carries the team logo and player information. The right box displays a nutrition tip from the American Dairy Association of Minnesota. The cards are unnumbered and checklisted below in alphabetical order.

| | MINT | NRMT |
|---|---|---|
| COMPLETE SET (23) | 12.00 | 5.50 |
| COMMON CARD (1-23) | .50 | .23 |
| □ 1 Brian Bellows | 1.00 | .45 |
| □ 2 Bob Brooke | .50 | .23 |
| □ 3 Neal Broten | 1.00 | .45 |
| □ 4 Jon Casey | 1.50 | .70 |
| □ 5 Shawn Chambers | .50 | .23 |
| □ 6 Dino Ciccarelli | 2.00 | .90 |
| □ 7 Larry DePalma | .50 | .23 |
| □ 8 Curt Fraser | .50 | .23 |
| □ 9 Link Gaetz | .75 | .35 |
| □ 10 Dave Gagner | 2.00 | .90 |
| □ 11 Stewart Gavin | .50 | .23 |
| □ 12 Curt Giles | .50 | .23 |
| □ 13 Marc Habscheid | .50 | .23 |
| □ 14 Mark Hardy | .50 | .23 |
| □ 15 Craig Hartsburg | 1.00 | .45 |
| □ 16 Brian MacLellan | .50 | .23 |
| □ 17 Moe Mantha | .50 | .23 |
| □ 18 Basil McRae | .75 | .35 |
| □ 19 Frantisek Musil | .50 | .23 |
| □ 20 Dusan Pasek | .50 | .23 |
| □ 21 Bob Rouse | .50 | .23 |
| □ 22 Terry Ruskowski | .50 | .23 |
| □ 23 Kari Takko | .75 | .35 |

## 1989-90 North Stars ADA

| | MINT | NRMT |
|---|---|---|
| COMPLETE SET (23) | 14.00 | 6.25 |
| COMMON CARD (1-23) | .25 | .11 |
| □ 1 Brian Bellows | .25 | .11 |
| □ 2 Perry Berezan | .25 | .11 |
| □ 3 Bob Brooke | .25 | .11 |
| □ 4 Neal Broten | .25 | .11 |
| □ 5 Jon Casey | .50 | .23 |
| □ 6 Shawn Chambers | .25 | .11 |
| □ 7 Shane Churla | .25 | .11 |
| □ 8 Clark Donatelli | .25 | .11 |
| □ 9 Gaetan Duchesne | .25 | .11 |
| □ 10 Curt Fraser | .25 | .11 |
| □ 11 Dave Gagner | .25 | .11 |
| □ 12 Mike Gartner | .60 | .25 |
| □ 13 Stewart Gavin | .25 | .11 |
| □ 14 Curt Giles | .25 | .11 |
| □ 15 Ken Leiter | .25 | .11 |
| □ 16 Basil McRae | .25 | .11 |
| □ 17 Mike Modano | 8.00 | 3.60 |
| □ 18 Larry Murphy | .50 | .23 |
| □ 19 Frantisek Musil | .25 | .11 |
| □ 20 Pierre Page | .25 | .11 |
| □ 21 Ville Siren | .25 | .11 |
| □ 22 Kari Takko | .40 | .18 |
| □ 23 Mark Tinordi | .25 | .11 |

## 1979-80 Oilers Postcards

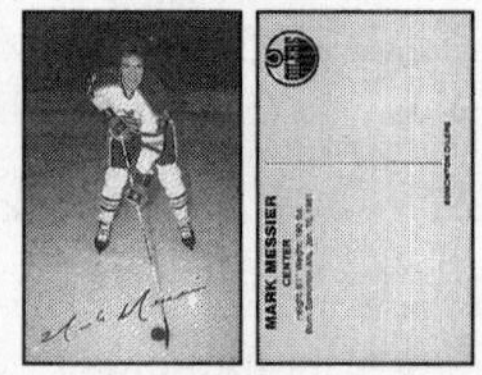

Measuring approximately 3 1/2" by 5 1/4", this 24-card set features borderless posed-on-ice photos of the Edmonton Oilers on the fronts. The postcard format has each of the horizontal backs bisected by a vertical line, with the player's name, position, and biography on the left side, and the team logo on the right. The cards are unnumbered and checklisted below in alphabetical order. Early cards of Wayne Gretzky, Kevin Lowe, and Mark Messier are featured in this set. The complete set price includes both Mio variations.

| | NRMT-MT | EXC |
|---|---|---|
| COMPLETE SET (24) | 100.00 | 45.00 |
| COMMON CARD (1-23) | 1.00 | .45 |
| □ 1 Brett Callighen | 1.00 | .45 |
| □ 2 Colin Campbell | 2.00 | .90 |
| □ 3 Ron Chipperfield | 1.00 | .45 |
| □ 4 Cam Connor | 1.00 | .45 |
| □ 5 Peter Driscoll | 1.00 | .45 |
| □ 6 Dave Dryden | 2.00 | .90 |
| □ 7 Bill Flett | 1.00 | .45 |
| □ 8 Lee Fogolin | 1.00 | .45 |
| □ 9 Wayne Gretzky | 60.00 | 27.00 |
| □ 10 Al Hamilton | 1.00 | .45 |
| □ 11 Doug Hicks | 1.00 | .45 |
| □ 12 Dave Hunter | 1.00 | .45 |
| □ 13 Kevin Lowe | 4.00 | 1.80 |
| □ 14 Dave Lumley | 1.00 | .45 |
| □ 15 Blair MacDonald | 1.00 | .45 |
| □ 16 Kari Makkonen | 1.00 | .45 |
| □ 17 Mark Messier | 25.00 | 11.00 |
| □ 18A Ed Mio ERR (Back says DOB Jan. 31, 1979) | 2.00 | .90 |
| □ 18B Ed Mio COR (Back says DOB Jan. 31, 1954) | 2.00 | .90 |
| □ 19 Pat Price | 1.00 | .45 |
| □ 20 Dave Semenko | 2.00 | .90 |
| □ 21 Bobby Schmautz | 1.00 | .45 |
| □ 22 Risto Siltanen | 1.50 | .70 |
| □ 23 Stan Weir | 1.00 | .45 |

## 1981-82 Oilers Red Rooster

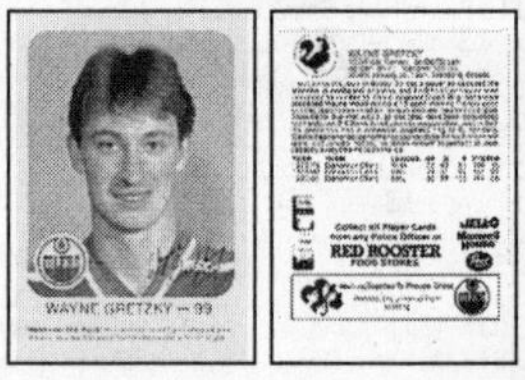

This 30-card set of Edmonton Oilers was sponsored by Red Rooster Food Stores in conjunction with Sun-Rype, Jello, Maxwell House, and Post. The player cards could be collected from any police officer or Red Rooster store. The cards measure approximately 2 3/4" by 3 9/16". The front has a color photo (with rounded corners) of the player, with the Oilers' logo and player's signature across the bottom of the picture. The player's name, uniform number, and a hockey tip are given below the photo. The back has the Red Rooster logo at the upper left-hand corner as well as biographical and statistical information on the player. The bottom includes logos of the sponsors and an anti-crime message. The original printing included four "long-hair" Gretzky cards as well as coaches' cards of Billy Harris and Ted Green. Reportedly those involved didn't approve of the photos and thus most of the offending pictures were destroyed. Consequently, the new poses are much more common and the old ones more scarce. The mass-produced second printing produced six variations so that the total possible cards is 36. These (original) other six cards are very hard to find as they were apparently not released to the general collecting public. The set is checklisted below using sweater numbers for reference.

| | NRMT-MT | EXC |
|---|---|---|
| COMPLETE SET (30) | 60.00 | 27.00 |
| COMMON CARD | .50 | .23 |
| □ 1 Grant Fuhr | 4.00 | 1.80 |
| □ 2 Lee Fogolin | .50 | .23 |

❑ 4 Kevin Lowe 1.50 .70
❑ 5 Doug Hicks .50 .23
❑ 6 Garry Lariviere .50 .23
❑ 7 Paul Coffey 7.00 3.10
❑ 8 Risto Siltanen .50 .23
❑ 9 Glenn Anderson 3.00 1.35
❑ 10 Matti Hagman .50 .23
❑ 11 Mark Messier 8.00 3.60
❑ 12 Dave Hunter .50 .23
❑ 15 Curt Brackenbury .50 .23
❑ 16 Pat Hughes .50 .23
❑ 17 Jari Kurri 5.00 2.20
❑ 18 Brett Callighen .50 .23
❑ 20 Dave Lumley .50 .23
❑ 21 Stan Weir .50 .23
❑ 26 Mike Forbes .50 .23
❑ 27 Dave Semenko 1.00 .45
❑ 30 Ron Low 1.00 .45
❑ 35 Andy Moog 4.00 1.80
❑ 77 Garry Unger .75 .35
❑ 99 Wayne Gretzky-long hair 60.00 27.00
❑ 99 Wayne Gretzky 12.00 5.50
❑ 99 Wayne Gretzky 12.00 5.50
❑ 99 Wayne Gretzky 12.00 5.50
❑ 99 Wayne Gretzky 12.00 5.50
❑ xx Team Autographs 1.00 .45
❑ xx Glen Sather CO .75 .35
❑ xx Billy Harris CO .50 .23
❑ xx Ted Green CO .50 .23

## 1981-82 Oilers West Edmonton Mall

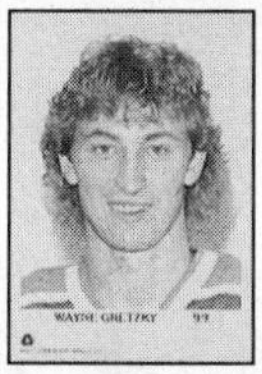

These nine blank-backed photos measure approximately 5" by 7" and feature white-bordered black-and-white player head shots. The player's name and uniform number, along with the name and logo of the West Edmonton Mall, appear in the wide bottom white margin. The photos are unnumbered and checklisted below in alphabetical order.

| | NRMT-MT | EXC |
|---|---|---|
| COMPLETE SET (9) | 100.00 | 45.00 |
| COMMON CARD (1-9) | 4.00 | 1.80 |

❑ 1 Lee Fogolin 4.00 1.80
❑ 2 Grant Fuhr 15.00 6.75
❑ 3 Wayne Gretzky 80.00 36.00
❑ 4 Billy Harris ACO 4.00 1.80
❑ 5 Charlie Huddy 5.00 2.20
❑ 6 Gary Lariviere 4.00 1.80
❑ 7 Dave Lumley 4.00 1.80
❑ 8 Risto Siltanen 4.00 1.80
❑ 9 Stan Weir 4.00 1.80

## 1982-83 Oilers Red Rooster

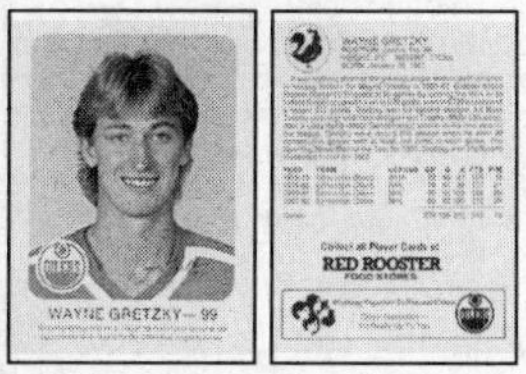

This 30-card set of Edmonton Oilers was sponsored by Red Rooster Food Stores, and the player cards could be collected at any of these stores. The cards measure approximately 2 3/4" by 3 9/16" and the set includes four different cards of Wayne Gretzky. The front has a color photo (with rounded corners) of the player, with the Edmonton Oilers' logo and player's signature across the bottom of the picture. The player's name, uniform number, and a hockey tip are given below the photo. The back has the Red Rooster logo at the upper left-hand corner as well as biographical and statistical information on the player. The bottom has an anti-crime message. The set is checklisted below using sweater numbers for reference.

| | MINT | NRMT |
|---|---|---|
| COMPLETE SET (30) | 40.00 | 18.00 |
| COMMON CARD | .50 | .23 |

❑ 2 Lee Fogolin .50 .23
❑ 4 Kevin Lowe 1.00 .45
❑ 6 Garry Lariviere .50 .23
❑ 7 Paul Coffey 4.00 1.80
❑ 9 Glenn Anderson 1.25 .55
❑ 10 Jaroslav Pouzar .50 .23
❑ 11 Mark Messier 5.00 2.20
❑ 12 Dave Hunter .50 .23
❑ 13 Ken Linseman .50 .23
❑ 14 Laurie Boschman .50 .23
❑ 16 Pat Hughes .50 .23
❑ 17 Jari Kurri 3.00 1.35
❑ 20 Dave Lumley .50 .23
❑ 21 Randy Gregg .50 .23
❑ 22 Charlie Huddy .75 .35
❑ 23 Marc Habscheid .50 .23
❑ 24 Tom Roulston .50 .23
❑ 27 Dave Semenko .75 .35
❑ 29 Don Jackson .50 .23
❑ 30 Ron Low .75 .35
❑ 31 Grant Fuhr 2.50 1.10
❑ 35 Andy Moog 2.50 1.10
❑ 77 Garry Unger .75 .35
❑ 99 Wayne Gretzky 10.00 4.50
❑ 99 Wayne Gretzky 10.00 4.50
❑ 99 Wayne Gretzky 10.00 4.50
❑ 99 Wayne Gretzky 10.00 4.50
❑ NNO Glen Sather CO .75 .35
❑ NNO John Muckler ACO .50 .23
❑ NNO Ted Green ACO .50 .23

## 1983-84 Oilers Dollars

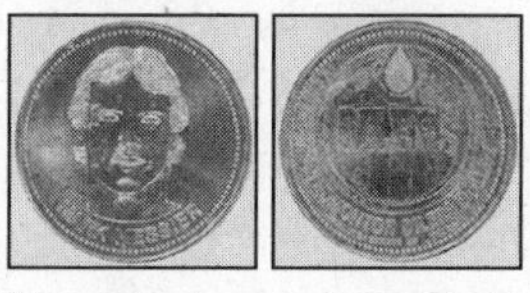

These seven cards, measuring approximately 3" by 5" and perforated on each end, were issued with Hockey Dollars or what may be better described as silver-colored coins. Each coin displayed an engraving of the player's face on the obverse and the team logo on the reverse. The card fronts are gray with tan lettering. They have the player's name, number, year, team logo, and a picture of the coin. In a horizontal format, the backs carry biography, career highlights, and career statistics. The cards are numbered on the back in the upper right corner. The prices below refer to the coin-card combination intact.

| | MINT | NRMT |
|---|---|---|
| COMPLETE SET (7) | 75.00 | 34.00 |
| COMMON CARD (H14-H20) | 3.00 | 1.35 |

❑ H14 Wayne Gretzky 10.00 4.50
❑ H15 Andy Moog 5.00 2.20
❑ H16 Dave Hunter 3.00 1.35
❑ H17 Ken Linseman SP 30.00 13.50
❑ H18 Lee Fogolin SP 30.00 13.50
❑ H19 Dave Semenko 5.00 2.20
❑ H20 Mark Messier 7.50 3.40

## 1983-84 Oilers McDonald's

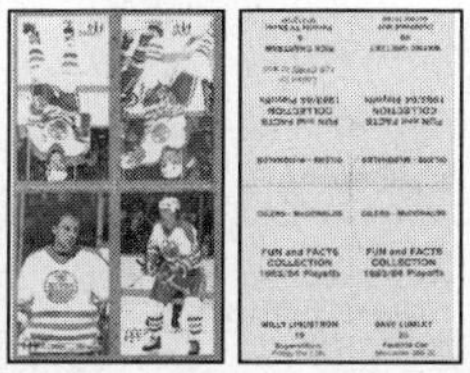

This 25-card set of Edmonton Oilers (entitled McDonald's Playoff Action Album) was issued in seven panels. After perforation, the standard issue cards measure 1 1/2" by 2 1/2" and number 22; three cards (3, 19, and 20) are oversized and measure 3" by 2 1/2". The card fronts feature color action photos with dark blue borders. The card backs give the player's name and number and often include a bit of trivia about player's career or preferences. Cards could be collected from participating McDonald's restaurants and pasted in a playoff album. An adhesive strip on the back could be used to stick the card in a special album. We have checklisted the names below according to the order of the album.

| | MINT | NRMT |
|---|---|---|
| COMPLETE SET (25) | 25.00 | 11.00 |
| COMMON CARD (1-25) | .40 | .18 |

❑ 1 Ken Linseman 13 .50 .23
❑ 2 Dave Semenko 27 .50 .23
❑ 3 Andy Moog 35 2.00 .90
❑ 4 Raimo Summanen 25 .40 .18
❑ 5 Jari Kurri 17 2.00 .90
❑ 6 Rick Chartraw 6 .40 .18
❑ 7 Don Jackson 29 .40 .18
❑ 8 Dave Hunter 12 .40 .18
❑ 9 Charlie Huddy 22 .50 .23
❑ 10 Emery Award .40 .18
❑ 11 Pat Conacher 15 .40 .18
❑ 12 Lee Fogolin 2 .40 .18
❑ 13 Kevin Lowe 4 .75 .35
❑ 14 Randy Gregg 21 .50 .23
❑ 15 Pat Hughes 16 .40 .18
❑ 16 Kevin McClelland 24 .40 .18
❑ 17 Willy Lindstrom 19 .40 .18
❑ 18 Mark Messier 11 4.00 1.80
❑ 19 Grant Fuhr 31 2.00 .90
❑ 20 Coaches .75 .35
Ted Green
Glen Sather
John Muckler
❑ 21 Wayne Gretzky 99 10.00 4.50
❑ 22 Dave Lumley 20 .40 .18
❑ 23 Jaroslav Pouzar 10 .40 .18
❑ 24 Glenn Anderson 9 1.00 .45
❑ 25 Paul Coffey 7 2.50 1.10
❑ xx Playoff Album 3.00 1.35

## 1984-85 Oilers Red Rooster

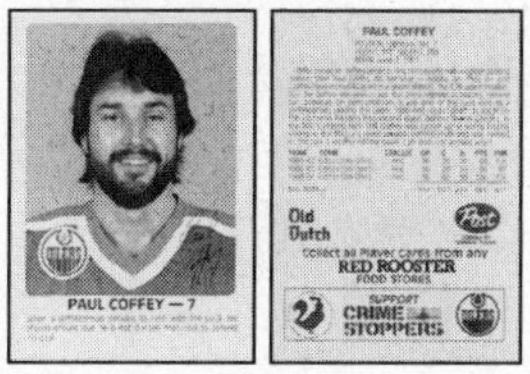

This 30-card set of Edmonton Oilers was sponsored by Red Rooster Food Stores in conjunction with Old Dutch Potato Chips and Post. The player cards could be collected at Red Rooster stores. The cards measure approximately 2 3/4" by 3 9/16" and the set includes four different cards of Wayne Gretzky. The front has a color photo of the player, with the Oilers' logo and player's signature across the bottom of the picture. The player's name, uniform number, and a hockey tip are given below the photo. The top half of the back has biographical and statistical information on the player, while the bottom half has company logos and an anti-crime message. There is a second print version of Glen Sather, which color corrects his first print card to reduce the redness in his face. The set is checklisted below using sweater numbers for reference.

| | MINT | NRMT |
|---|---|---|
| COMPLETE SET (30) | 35.00 | 16.00 |
| COMMON CARD (1-30) | .35 | .16 |

❑ 2 Lee Fogolin .35 .16
❑ 4 Kevin Lowe .50 .23
❑ 7 Paul Coffey 2.50 1.10
❑ 8 Dave Lumley .35 .16
❑ 9 Glenn Anderson 1.00 .45
❑ 10 Jaroslav Pouzar .35 .16
❑ 11 Mark Messier 4.00 1.80
❑ 12 Dave Hunter .35 .16
❑ 16 Pat Hughes .35 .16
❑ 17 Jari Kurri 2.00 .90
❑ 18 Mark Napier .35 .16
❑ 19 Willy Lindstrom .35 .16
❑ 20 Billy Carroll .35 .16
❑ 21 Randy Gregg .35 .16
❑ 22 Charlie Huddy .35 .16
❑ 23 Marc Habscheid .35 .16
❑ 24 Kevin McClelland .35 .16
❑ 26 Mike Krushelnyski .35 .16
❑ 27 Dave Semenko .50 .23
❑ 28 Larry Melnyk .35 .16
❑ 29 Don Jackson .35 .16
❑ 31 Grant Fuhr 2.00 .90
❑ 35 Andy Moog 2.00 .90
❑ 99 Wayne Gretzky 8.00 3.60
❑ 99 Wayne Gretzky 8.00 3.60
❑ 99 Wayne Gretzky 8.00 3.60
❑ 99 Wayne Gretzky 8.00 3.60
❑ NNO Ted Green ACO .35 .16
❑ NNO John Muckler ACO .35 .16
❑ NNO Glen Sather CO P1 .50 .23
(Facsimile autograph on front, redness in face)
❑ NNO Glen Sather CO P2 5.00 2.20
(No facsimile autograph on front, softer colors)

## 1984-85 Oilers Team Issue

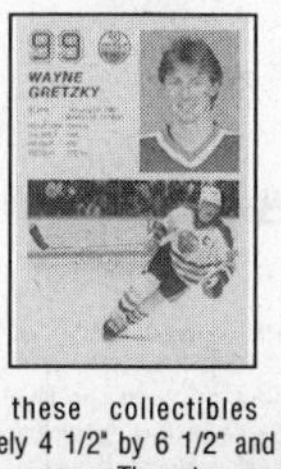

Each of these collectibles measure approximately 4 1/2" by 6 1/2" and is printed on thin glossy paper. The set was packaged in a plastic bag that included three small stickers. Two of the stickers ("Go 2 It Oilers" and "do it again Oilers") determine the date of the set as 1984-85, the season following the Oilers' 1983-84 championship. On the top half, the front features player information on the left and a color portrait with a light blue studio background on the right. On the bottom half, a white-bordered 4" by 3" color action player photo appears. The backs are blank. The cards are unnumbered and checklisted below in alphabetical order.

| | MINT | NRMT |
|---|---|---|
| COMPLETE SET (23) | 30.00 | 13.50 |
| COMMON CARD (1-23) | .50 | .23 |

❑ 1 Glenn Anderson 1.25 .55
❑ 2 Billy Carroll .50 .23
❑ 3 Paul Coffey 3.00 1.35
❑ 4 Lee Fogolin .50 .23
❑ 5 Grant Fuhr 2.00 .90
❑ 6 Randy Gregg .50 .23
❑ 7 Wayne Gretzky 10.00 4.50
❑ 8 Charlie Huddy .50 .23
❑ 9 Pat Hughes .50 .23
❑ 10 Dave Hunter .50 .23
❑ 11 Don Jackson .50 .23
❑ 12 Mike Krushelnyski .75 .35
❑ 13 Jari Kurri 2.00 .90
❑ 14 Willy Lindstrom .50 .23
❑ 15 Kevin Lowe 1.00 .45
❑ 16 Dave Lumley .50 .23
❑ 17 Kevin McClelland .50 .23
❑ 18 Larry Melnyk .50 .23
❑ 19 Mark Messier 5.00 2.20
❑ 20 Andy Moog 2.00 .90
❑ 21 Mark Napier .50 .23
❑ 22 Jaroslav Pouzar .50 .23
❑ 23 Dave Semenko .75 .35

## 1985-86 Oilers Red Rooster

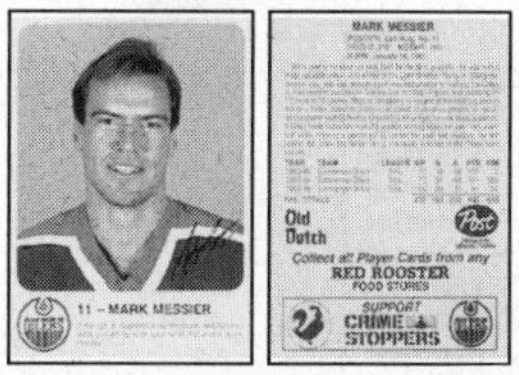

This 30-card set of Edmonton Oilers was sponsored by Red Rooster Food Stores in conjunction with Old Dutch Potato Chips and Post. The player cards could be collected from any Red Rooster stores. The cards measure approximately 2 3/4" by 3 9/16" and the set includes three different cards of Wayne Gretzky. The front has a color photo (with rounded corners) of the player, with the player's signature across the bottom of the picture. The player's name, uniform number, and a hockey tip are given below the photo. In contrast to earlier issues, the team logo now appears beneath the picture. The top half of the back has biographical and statistical information on the player, while the bottom half has company logos and an anti-crime message. The cards of Marty McSorley, Steve Smith, and Esa Tikkanen predate their O-Pee-Chee Rookie Cards by at least a year. The set is checklisted below using sweater numbers for reference.

| | MINT | NRMT |
|---|---|---|
| COMPLETE SET (30) | 35.00 | 16.00 |
| COMMON CARD (1-30) | .35 | .16 |

❑ 2 Lee Fogolin .35 .16
❑ 4 Kevin Lowe .50 .23
❑ 5 Steve Smith 1.50 .70
❑ 7 Paul Coffey 2.50 1.10
❑ 8 Gord Sherven .35 .16
❑ 9 Glenn Anderson .75 .35
❑ 10 Esa Tikkanen 3.00 1.35
❑ 11 Mark Messier 4.00 1.80
❑ 12 Dave Hunter .35 .16
❑ 14 Craig MacTavish .75 .35
❑ 17 Jari Kurri 2.00 .90
❑ 18 Mark Napier .50 .23
❑ 19 Mike Rogers .35 .16
❑ 20 Dave Lumley .35 .16
❑ 21 Randy Gregg .35 .16
❑ 22 Charlie Huddy .35 .16
❑ 24 Kevin McClelland .35 .16
❑ 25 Raimo Summanen .35 .16
❑ 26 Mike Krushelnyski .35 .16
❑ 27 Dave Semenko .50 .23
❑ 29 Don Jackson .35 .16
❑ 31 Grant Fuhr 2.00 .90
❑ 33 Marty McSorley 2.50 1.10
❑ 35 Andy Moog 2.00 .90
❑ 99 Wayne Gretzky 8.00 3.60
❑ 99 Wayne Gretzky 8.00 3.60
❑ 99 Wayne Gretzky 8.00 3.60
❑ NNO Bob McCammon ACO .35 .16
❑ NNO John Muckler ACO .35 .16
❑ NNO Glen Sather CO .50 .23

## 1986-87 Oilers Red Rooster

This 30-card set of Edmonton Oilers was sponsored by Red Rooster Food Stores in conjunction with Old Dutch Potato Chips. The player cards could be collected from any Red Rooster stores. The cards measure approximately 2 3/4" by 3 9/16" and the set includes two different cards of Wayne Gretzky

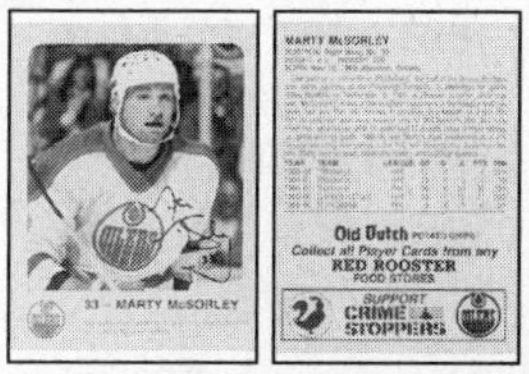

and of Andy Moog. The front has a color photo (with rounded corners) of the player, with the player's signature across the bottom of the picture. The player's name, uniform number, the team logo, and a safety tip are given below the photo. The top half of the back has biographical and statistical information on the player, while the bottom half has the sponsor's advertisements and the anti-crime slogan "Support Crime Stoppers." The set is checklisted below using sweater numbers for reference.

| | MINT | NRMT |
|---|---|---|
| COMPLETE SET (30) | 25.00 | 11.00 |
| COMMON CARD (1-30) | .25 | .11 |

❑ 2 Lee Fogolin .35 .16
❑ 4 Kevin Lowe .50 .23
❑ 5 Steve Smith .75 .35
❑ 6 Jeff Beukeboom .50 .23
❑ 7 Paul Coffey 2.00 .90
❑ 8 Stu Kulak .35 .16
❑ 9 Glenn Anderson .75 .35
❑ 10 Esa Tikkanen 2.00 .90
❑ 11 Mark Messier 3.00 1.35
❑ 12 Dave Hunter .35 .16
❑ 14 Craig MacTavish 1.00 .45
❑ 15 Steve Graves .35 .16
❑ 17 Jari Kurri 1.50 .70
❑ 18 Danny Gare .50 .23
❑ 21 Randy Gregg .35 .16
❑ 22 Charlie Huddy .50 .23
❑ 24 Kevin McClelland .35 .16
❑ 25 Raimo Summanen .35 .16
❑ 26 Mike Krushelnyski .35 .16
❑ 28 Craig Muni .35 .16
❑ 31 Grant Fuhr 1.50 .70
❑ 33 Marty McSorley 2.00 .90
❑ 35 Andy Moog 1.50 .70
❑ 35 Andy Moog 1.50 .70
❑ 65 Mark Napier .50 .23
❑ 99 Wayne Gretzky 8.00 3.60
❑ 99 Wayne Gretzky 8.00 3.60
❑ NNO Ted Green ACO 8.25 3.70
❑ NNO John Muckler ACO .25 .11
❑ NNO Glen Sather CO .50 .23

## 1986-87 Oilers Team Issue

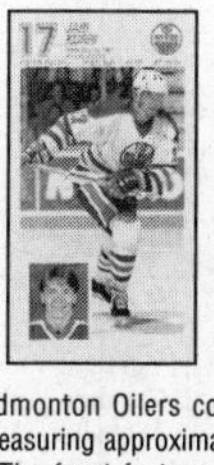

This set of Edmonton Oilers consists of 24 cards, each measuring approximately 3 11/16" by 6 13/16". The front features a full color action shot of the player on white card stock, with a color "mug shot" superimposed for the most part at one of the lower corners of the picture. The player's uniform number, name, Oilers' logo, and brief biographical information are given above the photo. The back of each card is blank. The set is checklisted below using sweater numbers for reference.

| | MINT | NRMT |
|---|---|---|
| COMPLETE SET (24) | 35.00 | 16.00 |
| COMMON CARD (1-24) | .50 | .23 |

❑ 2 Lee Fogolin .50 .23
❑ 4 Kevin Lowe .75 .35
❑ 5 Steve Smith .75 .35
❑ 6 Jeff Beukeboom .75 .35
❑ 7 Paul Coffey 3.00 1.35
❑ 8 Stu Kulak .50 .23
❑ 9 Glenn Anderson 1.00 .45
❑ 10 Esa Tikkanen 3.00 1.35
❑ 11 Mark Messier 5.00 2.20
❑ 12 Dave Hunter .50 .23
❑ 14 Craig MacTavish 1.00 .45
❑ 17 Jari Kurri 2.50 1.10
❑ 20 Jaroslav Pouzar .50 .23
❑ 21 Randy Gregg .50 .23
❑ 22 Charlie Huddy .50 .23
❑ 24 Kevin McClelland .50 .23
❑ 25 Raimo Summanen .50 .23
❑ 26 Mike Krushelnyski .50 .23
❑ 28 Craig Muni .50 .23
❑ 31 Grant Fuhr 2.50 1.10
❑ 33 Marty McSorley 3.00 1.35
❑ 35 Andy Moog 2.50 1.10
❑ 65 Mark Napier .75 .35
❑ 99 Wayne Gretzky 15.00 6.75

## 1987-88 Oilers Team Issue

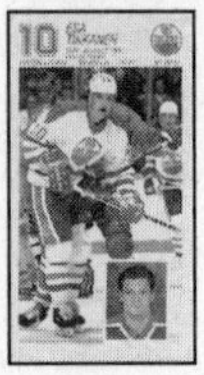

This set of Edmonton Oilers consists of 22 cards, each measuring approximately 3 11/16" by 6 13/16". The front features a full color action shot of the player on white card stock, with a color "mug shot" superimposed for the most part at one of the lower corners of the picture. The player's uniform number, name, Oilers' logo, and brief biographical information are given above the photo. The back of each card is blank. The set is checklisted below using sweater numbers for reference.

| | MINT | NRMT |
|---|---|---|
| COMPLETE SET (22) | 30.00 | 13.50 |
| COMMON CARD (1-22) | .50 | .23 |
| ❑ 4 Kevin Lowe | .75 | .35 |
| ❑ 5 Steve Smith | 1.00 | .45 |
| ❑ 6 Jeff Beukeboom | 1.00 | .45 |
| ❑ 9 Glenn Anderson | 1.00 | .45 |
| ❑ 10 Esa Tikkanen | 1.50 | .70 |
| ❑ 11 Mark Messier | 4.00 | 1.80 |
| ❑ 12 Dave Hannan | .50 | .23 |
| ❑ 14 Craig MacTavish | .75 | .35 |
| ❑ 17 Jari Kurri | 2.00 | .90 |
| ❑ 18 Craig Simpson | 1.00 | .45 |
| ❑ 19 Normand Lacombe | .50 | .23 |
| ❑ 22 Charlie Huddy | .50 | .23 |
| ❑ 23 Keith Acton | .75 | .35 |
| ❑ 24 Kevin McClelland | .50 | .23 |
| ❑ 26 Mike Krushelnyski | .50 | .23 |
| ❑ 28 Craig Muni | .50 | .23 |
| ❑ 29 Daryl Reaugh | .75 | .35 |
| ❑ 30 Warren Skorodenski | .75 | .35 |
| ❑ 31 Grant Fuhr | 2.00 | .90 |
| ❑ 33 Marty McSorley | 1.50 | .70 |
| ❑ 36 Selmar Odelein | .50 | .23 |
| ❑ 99 Wayne Gretzky | 15.00 | 6.75 |

## 1988-89 Oilers Tenth Anniversary

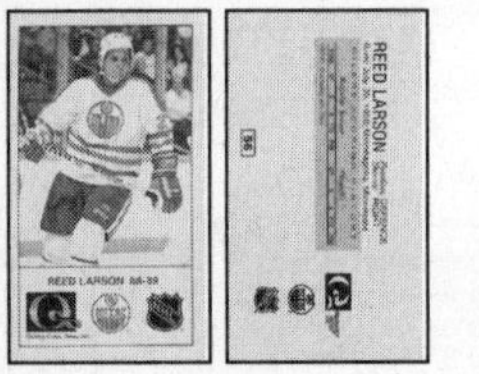

This set contains 164 cards and commemorates the tenth anniversary of the Edmonton Oilers. The cards were issued in four card panels, and each regular season edition of Action Magazine (Edmonton Oilers game program) contained one panel. The panels measured approximately 9 1/4 by 7 7/16", and the horizontally oriented cards were in between a gray stripe at the top and card information at the bottom. The cards were not perforated, but after cutting they measure approximately 2 9/16" by 4 5/16". The front features a color action photo of the player, with a thin black border on white card stock. The box below the picture has player identification and three logos. The back has biographical and statistical information in a horizontal format concerning the player's history with the Oilers.

| | MINT | NRMT |
|---|---|---|
| COMPLETE SET (164) | 125.00 | 55.00 |
| COMMON CARD (1-164) | .50 | .23 |
| ❑ 1 Garry Unger | 1.00 | .45 |
| ❑ 2 Chris Joseph | .50 | .23 |
| ❑ 3 Raimo Summanen | .50 | .23 |
| ❑ 4 Mike Zanier | .75 | .35 |
| ❑ 5 Kevin Lowe | 1.50 | .70 |
| ❑ 6 Dave Semenko | 1.00 | .45 |
| ❑ 7 Peter Driscoll | .50 | .23 |
| ❑ 8 Ken Solheim | .50 | .23 |
| ❑ 9 Glenn Anderson | 2.50 | 1.10 |
| ❑ 10 Curt Brackenbury | .50 | .23 |
| ❑ 11 Ron Shudra | .50 | .23 |
| ❑ 12 Gord Sherven | .50 | .23 |
| ❑ 13 Randy Gregg | .75 | .35 |
| ❑ 14 Larry Melnyk | .50 | .23 |
| ❑ 15 Tom Roulston | .50 | .23 |
| ❑ 16 Billy Carroll | .50 | .23 |
| ❑ 17 Jeff Beukeboom | .75 | .35 |
| ❑ 18 Jaroslav Pouzar | .50 | .23 |
| ❑ 19 Jeff Brubaker | .50 | .23 |
| ❑ 20 Danny Gare | .75 | .35 |
| ❑ 21 Craig MacTavish | .75 | .35 |
| ❑ 22 Reijo Routsalainen | .75 | .35 |
| ❑ 23 Willy Lindstrom | .50 | .23 |
| ❑ 24 Pat Hughes | .50 | .23 |
| ❑ 25 Jim Wiemer | .50 | .23 |
| ❑ 26 Selmar Odelein | .50 | .23 |
| ❑ 27 Kent Nilsson | 1.00 | .45 |
| ❑ 28 Mark Napier | .75 | .35 |
| ❑ 29 Esa Tikkanen | 2.50 | 1.10 |
| ❑ 30 John Miner | .50 | .23 |
| ❑ 31 Tom McMurchy | .50 | .23 |
| ❑ 32 Steve Graves | .50 | .23 |
| ❑ 33 Craig Muni | .50 | .23 |
| ❑ 34 Moe Mantha | .50 | .23 |
| ❑ 35 Dave Lumley | .75 | .35 |
| ❑ 36 Ron Low | .75 | .35 |
| ❑ 37 Marty McSorley | 2.50 | 1.10 |
| ❑ 38 Steve Dykstra | .50 | .23 |
| ❑ 39 Risto Jalo | .50 | .23 |
| ❑ 40 Dave Hunter | .50 | .23 |
| ❑ 41 Jari Kurri | 5.00 | 2.20 |
| ❑ 42 Lee Fogolin | .50 | .23 |
| ❑ 43 Moe Lemay | .50 | .23 |
| ❑ 44 Stu Kulak | .50 | .23 |
| ❑ 45 Charlie Huddy | .75 | .35 |
| ❑ 46 Wayne Gretzky | 25.00 | 11.00 |
| ❑ 47 Ken Linseman | .75 | .35 |
| ❑ 48 Risto Siltanen | .75 | .35 |
| ❑ 49 Glen Sather | 1.00 | .45 |
| ❑ 50 Brett Callighen | .50 | .23 |
| ❑ 51 Eddie Mio | .75 | .35 |
| ❑ 52 Ken Hammond | .50 | .23 |
| ❑ 53 Jimmy Carson | .75 | .35 |
| ❑ 54 Paul Coffey | 5.00 | 2.20 |
| ❑ 55 Wayne Gretzky 1050th | 20.00 | 9.00 |
| ❑ 56 Reed Larson | .50 | .23 |
| ❑ 57 Ted Green | .75 | .35 |
| ❑ 58 Matti Hagman | .50 | .23 |
| ❑ 59 Marc Habscheid | .50 | .23 |
| ❑ 60 Bill Ranford | 5.00 | 2.20 |
| ❑ 61 Mark Lamb | .50 | .23 |
| ❑ 62 Daryl Reaugh | .75 | .35 |
| ❑ 63 Al Hamilton | .50 | .23 |
| ❑ 64 Paul Coffey's 47th | 3.00 | 1.35 |
| ❑ 65 Grant Fuhr | 4.00 | 1.80 |
| ❑ 66 Stan Weir | .50 | .23 |
| ❑ 67 Ken Berry | .50 | .23 |
| ❑ 68 John Muckler CO | .75 | .35 |
| ❑ 69 Doug Smith | .50 | .23 |
| ❑ 70 Lance Nethery | .50 | .23 |
| ❑ 71 Bill Flett | .50 | .23 |
| ❑ 72 Mike Forbes | .50 | .23 |
| ❑ 73 Martin Gelinas | 1.00 | .45 |
| ❑ 74 Ron Chipperfield | .50 | .23 |
| ❑ 75 Reg Kerr | .50 | .23 |
| ❑ 76 Don Jackson | .50 | .23 |
| ❑ 77 Keith Acton | .75 | .35 |
| ❑ 78 Gary Edwards | .75 | .35 |
| ❑ 79 Mike Krushelnyski | .75 | .35 |
| ❑ 80 Trainers | .50 | .23 |
| Lyle Kulchisky | | |
| Peter Millar | | |
| Barrie Stafford | | |
| ❑ 81 Normand Lacombe | .50 | .23 |
| ❑ 82 Pat Price | .50 | .23 |
| ❑ 83 Dave Hannan | .50 | .23 |
| ❑ 84 Garry Lariviere | .50 | .23 |
| ❑ 85 Greg Adams | .50 | .23 |
| ❑ 86 Poul Popiel | .50 | .23 |
| ❑ 87 Tom Gorence | .50 | .23 |
| ❑ 88 Geoff Courtnall | 2.00 | .90 |
| ❑ 89 Mark Messier | 7.50 | 3.40 |
| ❑ 90 Dave Dryden | .75 | .35 |
| ❑ 91 Andy Moog | 4.00 | 1.80 |
| ❑ 92 Jim Ennis | .50 | .23 |
| ❑ 93 Craig Simpson | 1.00 | .45 |
| ❑ 94 Laurie Boschman | .50 | .23 |
| ❑ 95 Doug Hicks | .50 | .23 |
| ❑ 96 Rick Chartraw | .50 | .23 |
| ❑ 97 1984 Stanley Cup Champs | 1.00 | .45 |
| ❑ 98 Ron Carter | .50 | .23 |
| ❑ 99 Blair MacDonald | .50 | .23 |
| ❑ 100 Dean Clark | .50 | .23 |
| ❑ 101 Glen Cochrane | .50 | .23 |
| ❑ 102 Lindsay Middlebrook | .50 | .23 |
| ❑ 103 Ron Areshenkoff | .50 | .23 |
| ❑ 104 Billy Harris CO | .50 | .23 |
| ❑ 105 Conn Smythe Trophy | .75 | .35 |
| ❑ 106 John Blum | .50 | .23 |
| ❑ 107 Wayne Bianchin | .50 | .23 |
| ❑ 108 Tom Bladon | .50 | .23 |
| ❑ 109 Kevin McClelland | .50 | .23 |
| ❑ 110 Roy Sommer | .50 | .23 |
| ❑ 111 Mike Toal | .50 | .23 |
| ❑ 112 Don Ashby | .50 | .23 |
| ❑ 113 Don Nachbaur | .50 | .23 |
| ❑ 114 1985 Stanley Cup Champions | 1.00 | .45 |
| ❑ 115 Jim Corsi | .50 | .23 |
| ❑ 116 John Hughes | .50 | .23 |
| ❑ 117 Coach of the Year Glen Sather | 1.00 | .45 |
| ❑ 118 Bob Dupuis | .50 | .23 |
| ❑ 119 Jim Harrison | .50 | .23 |
| ❑ 120 Don Murdoch | .50 | .23 |
| ❑ 121 Steve Smith | 1.00 | .45 |
| ❑ 122 Pete Lopresti | .50 | .23 |
| ❑ 123 Colin Campbell | 1.00 | .45 |
| ❑ 124 Bryan Watson | .50 | .23 |
| ❑ 125 John Bednarski | .50 | .23 |
| ❑ 126 1987 Stanley Cup Champions | 1.00 | .45 |
| ❑ 127 Scott Metcalfe | .50 | .23 |
| ❑ 128 Mike Rogers | .50 | .23 |
| ❑ 129 Dan Newman | .50 | .23 |
| ❑ 130 Fuhr's 75th | 2.00 | .90 |
| ❑ 131 Warren Skorodenski | .75 | .35 |
| ❑ 132 Todd Strueby | .50 | .23 |
| ❑ 133 Kelly Buchberger | 1.00 | .45 |
| ❑ 134 Cam Connor | .50 | .23 |
| ❑ 135 Dean Hopkins | .50 | .23 |
| ❑ 136 Mike Moller | .50 | .23 |
| ❑ 137 1988 Stanley Cup Champions (Wayne Gretzky) | 7.50 | 3.40 |
| ❑ 138 Bryon Baltimore | .50 | .23 |
| ❑ 139 Pat Conacher | .50 | .23 |
| ❑ 140 Ray Cote | .50 | .23 |
| ❑ 141 Walt Poddubny | .50 | .23 |
| ❑ 142 Jim Playfair | .50 | .23 |
| ❑ 143 Nick Fotiu | .50 | .23 |
| ❑ 144 Kari Makkonen | .50 | .23 |
| ❑ 145 Dave Brown | .75 | .35 |
| ❑ 146 Terry Martin | .50 | .23 |
| ❑ 147 Francois Leroux | .50 | .23 |
| ❑ 148 Kari Jalonen | .50 | .23 |
| ❑ 149 Tomas Jonsson | .75 | .35 |
| ❑ 150 Dave Donnelly | .50 | .23 |
| ❑ 151 Mike Ware | .50 | .23 |
| ❑ 152 Don Cutts | .50 | .23 |
| ❑ 153 Miroslav Frycer | .50 | .23 |
| ❑ 154 Bruce MacGregor GM | .50 | .23 |
| ❑ 155 Kim Issel | .50 | .23 |
| ❑ 156 Marco Baron | .75 | .35 |
| ❑ 157 Doug Halward | .50 | .23 |
| ❑ 158 Barry Fraser DIR | .50 | .23 |
| ❑ 159 Alan May | .50 | .23 |
| ❑ 160 Bobby Schmautz | .50 | .23 |
| ❑ 161 Craig Redmond | .50 | .23 |
| ❑ 162 Oilers Host '89 All-Star Game | .75 | .35 |
| ❑ 163 Alex Tidey | .50 | .23 |
| ❑ 164 Wayne Van Dorp | .50 | .23 |

## 1988-89 Oilers Team Issue

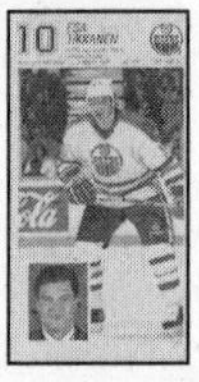

This 27-card set measures approximately 3 3/4" by 6 7/8". On a white background, the fronts feature a color action player photo with a color player portrait superimposed in one of the corners. The player's name, uniform number, a short biography, and the team logo appear above the picture. The backs are blank. The cards are unnumbered and checklisted below in alphabetical order.

| | MINT | NRMT |
|---|---|---|
| COMPLETE SET (27) | 20.00 | 9.00 |
| COMMON CARD (1-27) | .50 | .23 |
| ❑ 1 Glenn Anderson | 1.00 | .45 |
| ❑ 2 Jeff Beukeboom | 1.00 | .45 |
| ❑ 3 Dave Brown | .75 | .35 |
| ❑ 4 Kelly Buchberger | 1.00 | .45 |
| ❑ 5 Jimmy Carson | .75 | .35 |
| ❑ 6 Miroslav Frycer | .50 | .23 |
| ❑ 7 Grant Fuhr | 2.00 | .90 |
| ❑ 8 Randy Gregg | .75 | .35 |
| ❑ 9 Doug Halward | .50 | .23 |
| ❑ 10 Charlie Huddy | .75 | .35 |
| ❑ 11 Dave Hunter | .50 | .23 |
| ❑ 12 Tomas Jonsson | .75 | .35 |
| ❑ 13 Chris Joseph | .50 | .23 |
| ❑ 14 Jari Kurri | 1.50 | .70 |
| ❑ 15 Normand Lacombe | .50 | .23 |
| ❑ 16 Mark Lamb | .50 | .23 |
| ❑ 17 John LeBlanc | .50 | .23 |
| ❑ 18 Kevin Lowe | .75 | .35 |
| ❑ 19 Craig MacTavish | .75 | .35 |
| ❑ 20 Kevin McClelland | .50 | .23 |
| ❑ 21 Mark Messier | 4.00 | 1.80 |
| ❑ 22 Craig Muni | .50 | .23 |
| ❑ 23 Bill Ranford | 3.00 | 1.35 |
| ❑ 24 Craig Redmond | .50 | .23 |
| ❑ 25 Craig Simpson | .75 | .35 |
| ❑ 26 Steve Smith | 1.00 | .45 |
| ❑ 27 Esa Tikkanen | 1.50 | .70 |

## 1989-90 Oilers Team Issue

This standard size set features color action photos on a white background. Players name, number, and a short bio appear at the top of the card. Cards feature blank backs and are checklisted below alphabetically.

| | MINT | NRMT |
|---|---|---|
| COMPLETE SET (24) | 25.00 | 11.00 |
| COMMON CARD (1-24) | .40 | .18 |
| ❑ 1 Glenn Anderson | .75 | .35 |
| ❑ 2 Jeff Beukeboom | .60 | .25 |
| ❑ 3 Dave Brown | .60 | .25 |
| ❑ 4 Kelly Buchberger | .60 | .25 |
| ❑ 5 Peter Eriksson | .40 | .18 |
| ❑ 6 Grant Fuhr | 1.50 | .70 |
| ❑ 7 Martin Gelinas | 2.00 | .90 |
| ❑ 8 Adam Graves | 4.00 | 1.80 |
| ❑ 9 Randy Gregg | .60 | .25 |
| ❑ 10 Charlie Huddy | .60 | .25 |
| ❑ 11 Petr Klima | .75 | .35 |
| ❑ 12 Jari Kurri | 1.50 | .70 |
| ❑ 13 Normand Lacombe | .40 | .18 |
| ❑ 14 Mark Lamb | .40 | .18 |
| ❑ 15 Kevin Lowe | .60 | .25 |
| ❑ 16 Craig Mactavish | .60 | .25 |
| ❑ 17 Mark Messier | 3.00 | 1.35 |
| ❑ 18 Craig Muni | .40 | .18 |
| ❑ 19 Joe Murphy | 2.00 | .90 |
| ❑ 20 Bill Ranford | 2.00 | .90 |
| ❑ 21 Craig Simpson | .60 | .25 |
| ❑ 22 Geoff Smith | .60 | .25 |
| ❑ 23 Steve Smith | .75 | .35 |
| ❑ 24 Esa Tikkanen | .75 | .35 |

## 1990-91 Oilers IGA

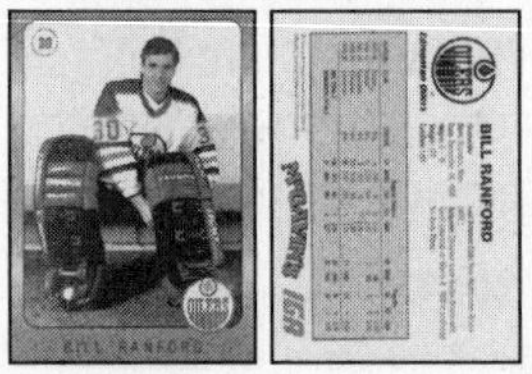

This 30-card standard-size set was sponsored by IGA food stores in conjunction with McGavin's, a distributor of bread and other products in Alberta. Protected by a cello pack, one card was inserted in bread loaves distributed by McGavin's to IGA stores in Calgary and Edmonton. Calgary consumers received a Flames' card, while Edmonton consumers received an Oilers' card. Checklist and coaches cards were not inserted in the loaves but were included on five hundred individually numbered and uncut sheets not offered to the general public. The cards are printed on thin card stock. The fronts have posed color player photos, with a border that shades from blue to orange and back to blue. Most of the photos are shot against the background of the equipment room or dressing room. The player's name is printed in the bottom border, and his uniform number is printed in a circle in the upper left corner of each picture. The horizontally oriented backs feature biographical information, with year-by-year statistics presented in a pink rectangle. Sponsor logos at the bottom round out the back. The cards are unnumbered and checklisted below in alphabetical order. Adam Graves appears during his Rookie Card year.

| | MINT | NRMT |
|---|---|---|
| COMPLETE SET (30) | 35.00 | 16.00 |
| COMMON CARD (1-30) | .50 | .23 |
| ❑ 1 Glenn Anderson | 1.50 | .70 |
| ❑ 2 Jeff Beukeboom | .75 | .35 |
| ❑ 3 Dave Brown | 1.00 | .45 |
| ❑ 4 Kelly Buchberger | 1.00 | .45 |
| ❑ 5 Martin Gelinas | 1.00 | .45 |
| ❑ 6 Adam Graves | 4.00 | 1.80 |
| ❑ 7 Ted Green CO SP | 3.00 | 1.35 |
| ❑ 8 Charlie Huddy | .75 | .35 |
| ❑ 9 Chris Joseph | .75 | .35 |
| ❑ 10 Petr Klima | .50 | .23 |
| ❑ 11 Mark Lamb | .50 | .23 |
| ❑ 12 Ken Linseman | .75 | .35 |
| ❑ 13 Ron Low CO SP | 3.00 | 1.35 |
| ❑ 14 Kevin Lowe | 1.25 | .55 |
| ❑ 15 Craig MacTavish | .75 | .35 |
| ❑ 16 Mark Messier | 6.00 | 2.70 |
| ❑ 17 Joey Moss | .50 | .23 |
| ❑ 18 John Muckler CO SP | 3.00 | 1.35 |
| ❑ 19 Craig Muni | .50 | .23 |
| ❑ 20 Joe Murphy | .75 | .35 |
| ❑ 21 Bill Ranford | 3.00 | 1.35 |
| ❑ 22 Anatoli Semenov | .50 | .23 |
| ❑ 23 Craig Simpson | .50 | .23 |
| ❑ 24 Geoff Smith | .50 | .23 |
| ❑ 25 Steve Smith | 1.00 | .45 |
| ❑ 26 Kari Takko | .75 | .35 |
| ❑ 27 Esa Tikkanen | 1.50 | .70 |
| ❑ 28 Training Staff SP | 1.50 | .70 |
| Ken Low TR/THER | | |
| Lyle Kulchisky TR | | |
| Barrie Stafford TR | | |
| Stewart Poirier THER | | |
| ❑ 29 Edmonton Oilers Year-by-Year Record | .50 | .23 |
| ❑ 30 Checklist Card SP | 3.00 | 1.35 |

## 1991 Oilers Panini Team Stickers

This 32-sticker set was issued in a plastic bag that contained two 16-sticker sheets (approximately 9" by 12") and a foldout poster, "Super Poster - Hockey 91", on which the stickers could be affixed. The players' names appear only on the poster, not on the stickers. Each sticker measures about 2 1/8" by 2 7/8" and features a color player action shot on its white-bordered front. The back of the white sticker sheet is lined off into 16 panels, each carrying the logos for Panini, the NHL, and the NHLPA, as well as the same number that appears on the front of the sticker. Every Canadian NHL team was featured in this promotion. Each team set was available by mail-order from Panini Canada Ltd. for 2.99 plus 50 cents for shipping and handling.

| | MINT | NRMT |
|---|---|---|
| COMPLETE SET (32) | 4.00 | 1.80 |
| COMMON STICKER (1-24) | .05 | .02 |
| COMMON STICKER (A-H) | .05 | .02 |
| ❑ 1 Glenn Anderson | .20 | .09 |
| ❑ 2 Jeff Beukeboom | .05 | .02 |
| ❑ 3 Dave Brown | .05 | .02 |
| ❑ 4 Kelly Buchberger | .10 | .05 |
| ❑ 5 Martin Gelinas | .10 | .05 |
| ❑ 6 Adam Graves | .35 | .16 |
| ❑ 7 Charlie Huddy | .05 | .02 |
| ❑ 8 Chris Joseph | .05 | .02 |
| ❑ 9 Petr Klima | .10 | .05 |
| ❑ 10 Mark Lamb | .05 | .02 |
| ❑ 11 Ken Linesman | .05 | .02 |
| ❑ 12 Kevin Lowe | .15 | .07 |
| ❑ 13 Craig MacTavish | .10 | .05 |
| ❑ 14 Mark Messier | .50 | .23 |
| ❑ 15 Craig Muni | .05 | .02 |
| ❑ 16 Joe Murphy | .10 | .05 |
| ❑ 17 Bill Ranford | .35 | .16 |
| ❑ 18 Eldon Reddick | .10 | .05 |
| ❑ 19 Anatoli Semenov | .05 | .02 |
| ❑ 20 Craig Simpson | .10 | .05 |
| ❑ 21 Geoff Smith | .05 | .02 |
| ❑ 22 Steve Smith | .10 | .05 |
| ❑ 23 Esa Tikkanen | .20 | .09 |
| ❑ 24 Oilers In Action | .15 | .07 |
| ❑ A Team Logo Left Side | .05 | .02 |
| ❑ B Team Logo Right Side | .05 | .02 |
| ❑ C Oilers in Action Upper Left Corner | .05 | .02 |
| ❑ D Oilers in Action Lower Left Corner | .05 | .02 |
| ❑ E Bill Ranford Upper Right Corner | .25 | .11 |
| ❑ F Bill Ranford Lower Right Corner | .25 | .11 |
| ❑ G Mark Messier | .50 | .23 |
| ❑ H Action in the Crease | .15 | .07 |

## 1991-92 Oilers IGA

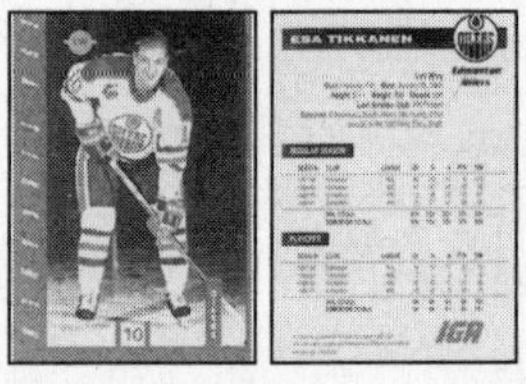

This 30-card standard-size set of Edmonton Oilers was sponsored by IGA food stores and included manufacturers' discount coupons. One pack of cards was distributed in Calgary and Edmonton IGA stores with any grocery purchase of 10.00 or more. The cards are printed on thin card stock. The fronts have posed color action photos bordered in dark blue. The player's name is printed vertically in the wider left border, and his uniform number and the team name appear at the bottom of the picture. In black print on a white background, the backs present biography and statistics (regular season and playoff). Packs were kept under the cash till drawer, and therefore many of the cards were creased. Each pack contained three Oiler and two Flame cards. The checklist and coaches cards for both teams were not included in the packs but were available on a very limited basis through an uncut team sheet offer. The cards are unnumbered and checklisted below in alphabetical order, with the coaches cards listed after the players.

| | MINT | NRMT |
|---|---|---|
| COMPLETE SET (30) | 20.00 | 9.00 |
| COMMON CARD (1-30) | .50 | .23 |
| ❑ 1 Josef Beranek | .50 | .23 |
| ❑ 2 Kelly Buchberger | .75 | .35 |
| ❑ 3 Vincent Damphousse | 1.50 | .70 |
| ❑ 4 Louie DeBrusk | .50 | .23 |
| ❑ 5 Martin Gelinas | .75 | .35 |
| ❑ 6 Peter Ing | .60 | .25 |
| ❑ 7 Petr Klima | .50 | .23 |
| ❑ 8 Mark Lamb | .50 | .23 |
| ❑ 9 Kevin Lowe | .75 | .35 |
| ❑ 10 Norm Maciver | .50 | .23 |
| ❑ 11 Craig MacTavish | .75 | .35 |
| ❑ 12 Troy Mallette | .50 | .23 |
| ❑ 13 Dave Manson | 1.00 | .45 |
| ❑ 14 Scott Mellanby | 1.00 | .45 |
| ❑ 15 Craig Muni | .50 | .23 |
| ❑ 16 Joe Murphy | .75 | .35 |
| ❑ 17 Bill Ranford | 2.00 | .90 |
| ❑ 18 Steven Rice | .50 | .23 |
| ❑ 19 Luke Richardson | .50 | .23 |
| ❑ 20 Anatoli Semenov | .50 | .23 |

❑ 21 David Shaw .50 .23
❑ 22 Craig Simpson .75 .35
❑ 23 Geoff Smith .50 .23
❑ 24 Scott Thornton .50 .23
❑ 25 Esa Tikkanen 1.00 .45
❑ 26 Training Staff SP 1.50 .70
❑ 27 Ted Green CO SP 2.50 1.10
❑ 28 Ron Low CO SP 2.50 1.10
❑ 29 Kevin Primeau CO SP 2.50 1.10
❑ 30 Checklist Card SP 2.50 1.10

## 1991-92 Oilers Team Issue

Printed on thin card stock, this 28-card set measures approximately 3 3/4" by 6 7/8". On the fronts, the white-bordered color action shots have player information and team logo in the top white border. The backs are blank. The cards are unnumbered and checklisted below in alphabetical order.

| | MINT | NRMT |
|---|---|---|
| COMPLETE SET (28) | 15.00 | 6.75 |
| COMMON CARD (1-28) | .50 | .23 |

❑ 1 Josef Beranek .50 .23
❑ 2 Jeff Beukeboom .50 .23
❑ 3 Kelly Buchberger .75 .35
❑ 4 Vincent Damphousse 1.50 .70
❑ 5 Louie DeBrusk .50 .23
❑ 6 Martin Gelinas .50 .23
❑ 7 Peter Ing .60 .25
❑ 8 Chris Joseph .50 .23
❑ 9 Petr Klima .50 .23
❑ 10 Mark Lamb .50 .23
❑ 11 Kevin Lowe .75 .35
❑ 12 Norm Maciver .50 .23
❑ 13 Craig MacTavish .50 .23
❑ 14 Troy Mallette .50 .23
❑ 15 Dave Manson 1.00 .45
❑ 16 Scott Mellanby 1.00 .45
❑ 17 Craig Muni .50 .23
❑ 18 Joe Murphy .75 .35
❑ 19 Bill Ranford 2.00 .90
❑ 20 Eldon(Pokey) Reddick .75 .35
❑ 21 Steve Rice .50 .23
❑ 22 Luke Richardson .50 .23
❑ 23 Martin Rucinsky 1.50 .70
❑ 24 Anatoli Semenov .50 .23
❑ 25 Craig Simpson .50 .23
❑ 26 Geoff Smith .50 .23
❑ 27 Scott Thornton .50 .23
❑ 28 Esa Tikkanen 1.00 .45

## 1992-93 Oilers IGA

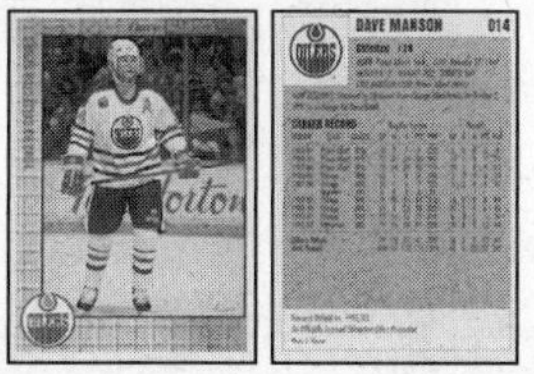

Sponsored by IGA food stores, the 30 standard-size cards comprising this Special Edition Collector Series set feature color player action shots on their fronts. Each photo is trimmed with a black line and offset flush with the thin white border on the right, which surrounds the card. On the remaining three sides, the picture is edged with a gray and white netlike pattern. The player's name appears in the upper right and the Oilers logo rests in the lower left. The back carries the player's name at the top, with his position, uniform number, biography, and stat table set within a bluish-gray screened background. The Oilers logo in the upper right rounds out the card.

| | MINT | NRMT |
|---|---|---|
| COMPLETE SET (30) | 15.00 | 6.75 |
| COMMON CARD (1-30) | .25 | .11 |

❑ 1 Checklist .50 .23
❑ 2 Joseph Beranek .50 .23
❑ 3 Kelly Buchberger .75 .35
❑ 4 Shayne Corson 1.00 .45
❑ 5 Louie DeBrusk .50 .23
❑ 6 Martin Gelinas .75 .35
❑ 7 Brent Gilchrist .50 .23
❑ 8 Brian Glynn .50 .23
❑ 9 Greg Hawgood .50 .23
❑ 10 Petr Klima .50 .23
❑ 11 Chris Joseph .50 .23
❑ 12 Craig MacTavish .50 .23
❑ 13 Dan Currie .50 .23
❑ 14 Dave Manson 1.00 .45
❑ 15 Scott Mellanby .75 .35
❑ 16 Craig Muni .50 .23
❑ 17 Bernie Nicholls 1.00 .45
❑ 18 Bill Ranford 2.00 .90
❑ 19 Luke Richardson .60 .25
❑ 20 Craig Simpson .60 .25
❑ 21 Geoff Smith .50 .23
❑ 22 Vladimir Vujtek .50 .23
❑ 23 Esa Tikkanen 1.00 .45
❑ 24 Ron Tugnutt .75 .35
❑ 25 Shaun Van Allen .50 .23

❑ 26 Glen Sather GM .75 .35
❑ 27 Ted Green CO .50 .23
❑ 28 Ron Low CO .50 .23
❑ 29 Kevin Primeau CO .25 .11
❑ 30 Oilers Yearly Record .50 .23

## 1992-93 Oilers Team Issue

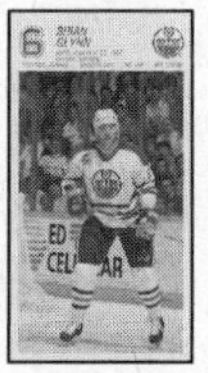

The 22 blank-backed cards comprising this set are printed on thin white card stock and measure approximately 3 3/4" by 6 7/8". They feature white-bordered color player action photos and display the Oilers logo, the player's name, jersey number, and brief biography within the broad white border at the top. The cards are unnumbered and checklisted below in alphabetical order.

| | MINT | NRMT |
|---|---|---|
| COMPLETE SET (22) | 12.00 | 5.50 |
| COMMON CARD (1-22) | .50 | .23 |

❑ 1 Kelly Buchberger .60 .25
❑ 2 Zdeno Ciger .60 .25
❑ 3 Shayne Corson 1.00 .45
❑ 4 Louie DeBrusk .50 .23
❑ 5 Todd Elik .50 .23
❑ 6 Brian Glynn .50 .23
❑ 7 Mike Hudson .50 .23
❑ 8 Chris Joseph .50 .23
❑ 9 Igor Kravchuk .50 .23
❑ 10 Francois Leroux .50 .23
❑ 11 Craig MacTavish .75 .35
❑ 12 Dave Manson 1.00 .45
❑ 13 Shjon Podein .75 .35
❑ 14 Bill Ranford 2.00 .90
❑ 15 Steve Rice .50 .23
❑ 16 Luke Richardson .60 .25
❑ 17 Craig Simpson .60 .25
❑ 18 Geoff Smith .50 .23
❑ 19 Kevin Todd .50 .23
❑ 20 Vladimir Vujtek .50 .23
❑ 21 Doug Weight 2.50 1.10
❑ 22 Brad Werenka .50 .23

## 1996-97 Oilers Postcards

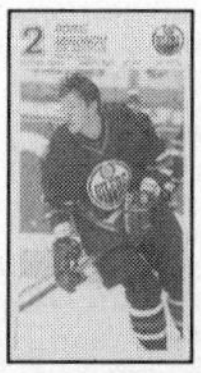

This 27-card set of Oilers postcards was the first to picture the team in their new sweaters. These odd size postcards (3 3/4" by 6 7/8") feature sharp action photography on the front, along with team logo, player name and biographical data. The backs are blank. As the players' jersey numbers are displayed prominently on the upper left corner, they are listed below accordingly.

| | MINT | NRMT |
|---|---|---|
| COMPLETE SET (27) | 15.00 | 6.75 |
| COMMON CARD | .35 | .16 |

❑ 2 Boris Mironov .50 .23
❑ 4 Kevin Lowe .50 .23
❑ 5 Greg de Vries .50 .23
❑ 6 Jeff Norton .35 .16
❑ 7 Jason Arnott 1.00 .45
❑ 8 Sean Brown .35 .16
❑ 10 Steve Kelly .75 .35
❑ 14 Mats Lindgren .50 .23
❑ 16 Kelly Buchberger .50 .23
❑ 17 Rem Murray .75 .35
❑ 18 Miroslav Satan 1.50 .70
❑ 19 Boyd Devereaux 1.00 .45
❑ 21 Mariusz Czerkawski .50 .23
❑ 22 Luke Richardson .50 .23
❑ 23 Dan McGillis .50 .23
❑ 24 Bryan Marchment .50 .23
❑ 25 Mike Grier 1.75 .80
❑ 26 Todd Marchant .50 .23
❑ 29 Louie DeBrusk .35 .16
❑ 30 Bob Essensa .50 .23
❑ 31 Curtis Joseph 1.50 .70
❑ 34 Donald Dufresne .35 .16
❑ 37 Dean McAmmond .35 .16
❑ 39 Doug Weight 1.00 .45
❑ 51 Andrei Kovalenko .50 .23
❑ 85 Petr Klima .35 .16
❑ 94 Ryan Smyth 1.50 .70

## 1932-33 O'Keefe Maple Leafs

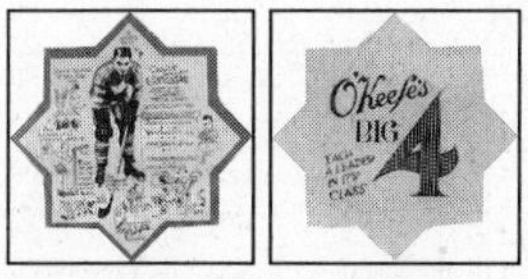

This 20-card set was issued by O'Keefe's Beverages and features the Toronto Maple Leafs, 1931-32 Stanley Cup Champions. Each was designed for use as a coaster. The shape of each card is an eight-pointed star, which measures approximately 5" from one point across to its opposite. Inside a blue border, the front has a black and blue ink portrait or drawing of the player, which is surrounded by cartoons and captions presenting player information. The backs read "O'Keefe's Big 4" and "Each a Leader in its Class." The coasters are numbered on the front near the top and are checklisted below accordingly. Card numbers 13 and 15 are unknown, although many collectors believe it likely that the NNO Doraty and Thoms cards were slated to fill those slots.

| | EX-MT | VG-E |
|---|---|---|
| COMPLETE SET (20) | 8500.00 | 4200.00 |
| COMMON CARD (1-20) | 200.00 | 100.00 |

❑ 1 Lorne Chabot 400.00 200.00
❑ 2 Red Horner 400.00 200.00
❑ 3 Alex Levinsky 300.00 150.00
❑ 4 Hap Day 400.00 200.00
❑ 5 Andy Blair 200.00 100.00
❑ 6 Ace Bailey 750.00 375.00
❑ 7 King Clancy 1000.00 500.00
❑ 8 Harold Cotton 400.00 200.00
❑ 9 Charlie Conacher 600.00 300.00
❑ 10 Joe Primeau 500.00 250.00
❑ 11 Harvey Jackson 750.00 375.00
❑ 12 Frank Finnigan 200.00 100.00
❑ 14 Bob Gracie 200.00 100.00
❑ 16 Harold Darragh 200.00 100.00
❑ 17 Benny Grant 200.00 100.00
❑ 18 Fred Robertson 200.00 100.00
❑ 19 Conn Smythe 1000.00 500.00
❑ 20 Dick Irvin 600.00 300.00
❑ NNO Ken Doraty 500.00 250.00
❑ NNO Bill Thoms 500.00 250.00

## 1933-34 O-Pee-Chee V304A

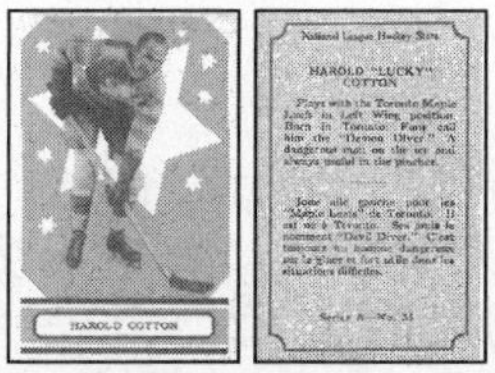

This first of five O-Pee-Chee 1930's hockey card issues features a black and white photo of the player portrayed on a colored field of stars. The cards in the set are approximately 2 5/16" by 3 9/16". The player's name appears in a rectangle at the bottom of the front of the card. Four possible color background fields exist, red, blue, orange and green. The cards are numbered on the back, and a short biography in both English and French is also contained on the back. The catalog designation for this set is V304A. The existence of an album designed to store the cards has been confirmed. It is valued at approximately $250.

| | EX-MT | VG-E |
|---|---|---|
| COMPLETE SET (48) | 11000.00 | 5500.00 |
| COMMON CARD (1-48) | 90.00 | 45.00 |
| WRAPPER (1-CENT) | 350.00 | 180.00 |

❑ 1 Danny Cox 150.00 75.00
❑ 2 Joe Lamb 90.00 45.00
❑ 3 Eddie Shore 1500.00 750.00
❑ 4 Ken Doraty 90.00 45.00
❑ 5 Fred Hitchman 90.00 45.00
❑ 6 Nels Stewart 600.00 300.00
❑ 7 Walter Galbraith 100.00 50.00
❑ 8 Dit Clapper 400.00 200.00
❑ 9 Harry Oliver 175.00 90.00
❑ 10 Red Horner 250.00 125.00
❑ 11 Alex Levinsky 125.00 60.00
❑ 12 Joe Primeau 400.00 200.00
❑ 13 Ace Bailey 400.00 200.00
❑ 14 George Patterson 90.00 45.00
❑ 15 George Hainsworth 300.00 150.00
❑ 16 Ott Heller 90.00 45.00
❑ 17 Art Somers 90.00 45.00
❑ 18 Lorne Chabot 200.00 100.00
❑ 19 Johnny Gagnon 90.00 45.00
❑ 20 Pit Lepine 90.00 45.00
❑ 21 Wildor Larochelle 125.00 60.00
❑ 22 Georges Mantha 125.00 60.00
❑ 23 Howie Morenz 2000.00 1000.00
❑ 24 Syd Howe 250.00 125.00
❑ 25 Frank Finnigan 125.00 60.00
❑ 26 Bill Touhey 90.00 45.00
❑ 27 Cooney Weiland 250.00 125.00
❑ 28 Leo Bourgeault 100.00 50.00
❑ 29 Normie Himes 125.00 60.00
❑ 30 Johnny Sheppard 90.00 45.00
❑ 31 King Clancy 900.00 450.00
❑ 32 Clarence(Hap) Day 175.00 90.00
❑ 33 Harvey(Busher) Jackson 400.00 200.00
❑ 34 Charlie Conacher 900.00 450.00
❑ 35 Harold Cotton 150.00 75.00
❑ 36 Butch Keeling 90.00 45.00
❑ 37 Murray Murdoch 90.00 45.00
❑ 38 Bill Cook 175.00 90.00
❑ 39 Ivan(Ching) Johnson 350.00 180.00
❑ 40 Happy Emms 125.00 60.00
❑ 41 Bert McInenly 90.00 45.00
❑ 42 John Sorrell 90.00 45.00
❑ 43 Bill Phillips 90.00 45.00
❑ 44 Charley McVeigh 100.00 50.00
❑ 45 Roy Worters 300.00 150.00
❑ 46 Albert Leduc 125.00 60.00
❑ 47 Nick Wasnie 90.00 45.00
❑ 48 Armand Mondou 125.00 60.00

## 1933-34 O-Pee-Chee V304B

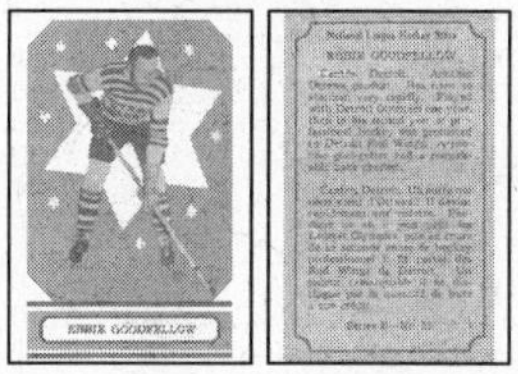

The second O-Pee-Chee hockey series of the 1930's contains 24 cards and continues the numbering sequence of the Series A cards. The format is exactly the same as the cards of Series A. The cards in the set measure approximately 2 5/16" by 3 9/16". The catalog designation for this set is V304B.

| | EX-MT | VG-E |
|---|---|---|
| COMPLETE SET (24) | 3500.00 | 1800.00 |
| COMMON CARD (49-72) | 100.00 | 50.00 |
| WRAPPER (1-CENT) | 350.00 | 180.00 |

❑ 49 Babe Siebert 300.00 150.00
❑ 50 Aurel Joliat 750.00 375.00
❑ 51 Larry Aurie 150.00 75.00
❑ 52 Ebbie Goodfellow 200.00 100.00
❑ 53 John Ross Roach 125.00 60.00
❑ 54 Bill Beveridge 125.00 60.00
❑ 55 Earl Robinson 100.00 50.00
❑ 56 Jimmy Ward 100.00 50.00
❑ 57 Archie Wilcox 100.00 50.00
❑ 58 Lorne Duguid 100.00 50.00
❑ 59 Dave Kerr 150.00 75.00
❑ 60 Baldy Northcott 125.00 60.00
❑ 61 Marvin Wentworth 125.00 60.00
❑ 62 Dave Trottier 100.00 50.00
❑ 63 Wally Kilrea 100.00 50.00
❑ 64 Glen Brydson 100.00 50.00
❑ 65 Vernon Ayers 100.00 50.00
❑ 66 Bob Gracie 100.00 50.00
❑ 67 Vic Ripley 100.00 50.00
❑ 68 Tiny Thompson 250.00 125.00
❑ 69 Alex Smith 100.00 50.00
❑ 70 Andy Blair 100.00 50.00
❑ 71 Cecil Dillon 100.00 50.00
❑ 72 Bun Cook 275.00 140.00

## 1935-36 O-Pee-Chee V304C

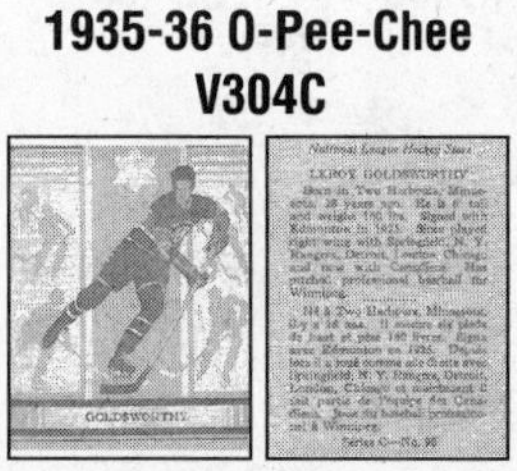

While Series C in the O-Pee-Chee 1930's hockey card set continues the numbering sequence of the previous two years, this 24-card set differs significantly in both format and size. The cards in this set measure approximately 2 3/8" by 2 7/8". Each black and white photo portraying the player on the front can be found on four possible color fields, green, orange, maroon, or yellow. The field consists of a star in the center and cartooned hockey players flanking the center of the card. The backs contain the player's name, the card number, and biographical data in both English and French. The catalog designation for this set is V304C.

| | EX-MT | VG-E |
|---|---|---|
| COMPLETE SET (24) | 3000.00 | 1500.00 |
| COMMON CARD (73-96) | 100.00 | 50.00 |
| WRAPPER (1-CENT) | 350.00 | 180.00 |

❑ 73 Wilfred Cude 250.00 125.00
❑ 74 Jack McGill 100.00 50.00
❑ 75 Russ Blinco 100.00 50.00
❑ 76 Hooley Smith 200.00 100.00
❑ 77 Herb Cain 150.00 75.00
❑ 78 Gus Marker 100.00 50.00
❑ 79 Lynn Patrick 250.00 125.00
❑ 80 Johnny Gottselig 100.00 50.00
❑ 81 Marty Barry 200.00 100.00
❑ 82 Sylvio Mantha 200.00 100.00
❑ 83 Flash Hollett 100.00 50.00
❑ 84 Nick Metz 100.00 50.00
❑ 85 Bill Thoms 100.00 50.00
❑ 86 Hec Kilrea 100.00 50.00
❑ 87 Pep Kelly 100.00 50.00
❑ 88 Art Jackson 100.00 50.00
❑ 89 Allan Shields 100.00 50.00
❑ 90 Buzz Boll 100.00 50.00
❑ 91 Jean Pusie 100.00 50.00
❑ 92 Roger Jenkins 100.00 50.00
❑ 93 Arthur Coulter 200.00 100.00
❑ 94 Art Chapman 100.00 50.00
❑ 95 Paul Haynes 100.00 50.00
❑ 96 Leroy Goldsworthy 175.00 90.00

## 1936-37 O-Pee-Chee V304D

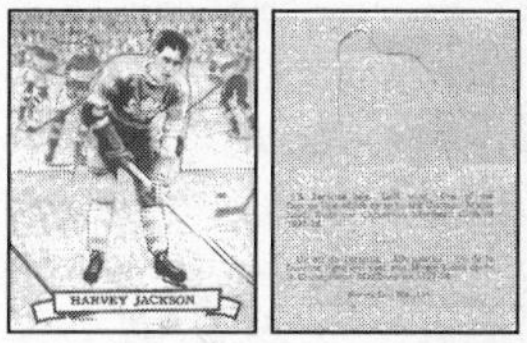

The most significant difference between Series D cards and cards from the previous three O-Pee-Chee sets is the fact that these cards are die-cut and could be folded to give a stand-up figure, like the 1934-36 Batter-Up baseball cards. The cards are in black and white with no colored background field. The cards in the set measure approximately 2 3/8" by 2 15/16". As these cards are difficult to find without the backs missing, this set is the most valuable of the 1930's O-Pee-Chee sets. The backs contain the card number and biographical data in English and French. The player's name is given on the front of the card only. The catalog designation for this set is V304D.

| | EX-MT | VG-E |
|---|---|---|
| COMPLETE SET (36) | 12500.00 | 6200.00 |
| COMMON CARD (97-132) | 150.00 | 75.00 |
| WRAPPER (1-CENT) | 350.00 | 180.00 |

❑ 97 Turk Broda 1000.00 500.00
❑ 98 Sweeney Schriner 350.00 180.00
❑ 99 Jack Shill 150.00 75.00
❑ 100 Bob Davidson 150.00 75.00
❑ 101 Syl Apps 600.00 300.00
❑ 102 Lionel Conacher 500.00 250.00
❑ 103 Jimmy Fowler 150.00 75.00
❑ 104 Al Murray 150.00 75.00
❑ 105 Neil Colville 250.00 125.00
❑ 106 Paul Runge 150.00 75.00
❑ 107 Mike Karakas 175.00 90.00
❑ 108 John Gallagher 150.00 75.00
❑ 109 Alex Shibicky 200.00 100.00
❑ 110 Herb Cain 200.00 100.00
❑ 111 Bill McKenzie 150.00 75.00
❑ 112 Harold Jackson 150.00 75.00
❑ 113 Art Wiebe 150.00 75.00
❑ 114 Joffre Desilets 150.00 75.00
❑ 115 Earl Robinson 150.00 75.00
❑ 116 Cy Wentworth 200.00 100.00
❑ 117 Ebbie Goodfellow 250.00 125.00
❑ 118 Eddie Shore 1500.00 750.00
❑ 119 Buzz Boll 150.00 75.00
❑ 120 Wilfred Cude 175.00 90.00
❑ 121 Howie Morenz 2000.00 1000.00
❑ 122 Red Horner 300.00 150.00
❑ 123 Charlie Conacher 750.00 375.00
❑ 124 Harvey(Busher)Jackson 400.00 200.00
❑ 125 King Clancy 900.00 450.00
❑ 126 Dave Trottier 150.00 75.00
❑ 127 Russ Blinco 150.00 75.00
❑ 128 Lynn Patrick 300.00 150.00
❑ 129 Aurel Joliat 750.00 375.00
❑ 130 Baldy Northcott 175.00 90.00
❑ 131 Larry Aurie 150.00 75.00
❑ 132 Hooley Smith 350.00 180.00

## 1937-38 O-Pee-Chee V304E

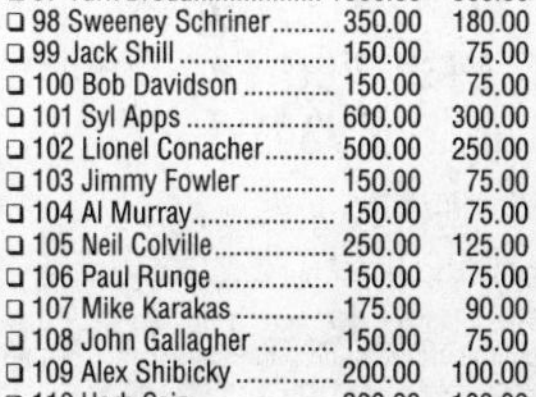

Series E cards continue the numerical series of the 1930's O-Pee-Chee sets and feature a black and white photo of the player within a serrated, colored (blue or purple) frame. A

facsimile autograph and a cartooned hockey player appear on the front in the same color as the frame. The cards in the set measure approximately 2 3/8" by 2 7/8". The backs contain the card number, the player's name, and biographical data in both English and French. The catalog designation for this set is V304E.

| | EX-MT | VG-E |
|---|---|---|
| COMPLETE SET (48) | 6000.00 | 3000.00 |
| COMMON CARD (133-180) | 80.00 | 40.00 |
| WRAPPER (1-CENT) | 300.00 | 150.00 |
| ❑ 133 Turk Broda | 500.00 | 250.00 |
| ❑ 134 Red Horner | 175.00 | 90.00 |
| ❑ 135 Jimmy Fowler | 80.00 | 40.00 |
| ❑ 136 Bob Davidson | 80.00 | 40.00 |
| ❑ 137 Reg. Hamilton | 80.00 | 40.00 |
| ❑ 138 Charlie Conacher | 400.00 | 200.00 |
| ❑ 139 Harvey(Busher)Jackson | 250.00 | 125.00 |
| ❑ 140 Buzz Boll | 80.00 | 40.00 |
| ❑ 141 Syl Apps | 325.00 | 160.00 |
| ❑ 142 Gordie Drillon | 250.00 | 125.00 |
| ❑ 143 Bill Thoms | 90.00 | 45.00 |
| ❑ 144 Nick Metz | 80.00 | 40.00 |
| ❑ 145 Pep Kelly | 80.00 | 40.00 |
| ❑ 146 Murray Armstrong | 80.00 | 40.00 |
| ❑ 147 Murph Chamberlain | 80.00 | 40.00 |
| ❑ 148 Des Smith | 80.00 | 40.00 |
| ❑ 149 Wilfred Cude | 100.00 | 50.00 |
| ❑ 150 Babe Siebert | 175.00 | 90.00 |
| ❑ 151 Bill MacKenzie | 80.00 | 40.00 |
| ❑ 152 Aurel Joliat | 450.00 | 220.00 |
| ❑ 153 Georges Mantha | 80.00 | 40.00 |
| ❑ 154 Johnny Gagnon | 80.00 | 40.00 |
| ❑ 155 Paul Haynes | 80.00 | 40.00 |
| ❑ 156 Joffre Desilets | 80.00 | 40.00 |
| ❑ 157 George Allen Brown | 80.00 | 40.00 |
| ❑ 158 Paul Drouin | 80.00 | 40.00 |
| ❑ 159 Pit Lepine | 80.00 | 40.00 |
| ❑ 160 Toe Blake | 750.00 | 375.00 |
| ❑ 161 Bill Beveridge | 100.00 | 50.00 |
| ❑ 162 Allan Shields | 80.00 | 40.00 |
| ❑ 163 Cy Wentworth | 90.00 | 45.00 |
| ❑ 164 Stew Evans | 80.00 | 40.00 |
| ❑ 165 Earl Robinson | 80.00 | 40.00 |
| ❑ 166 Baldy Northcott | 90.00 | 45.00 |
| ❑ 167 Paul Runge | 80.00 | 40.00 |
| ❑ 168 Dave Trottier | 80.00 | 40.00 |
| ❑ 169 Russ Blinco | 80.00 | 40.00 |
| ❑ 170 Jimmy Ward | 80.00 | 40.00 |
| ❑ 171 Bob Gracie | 80.00 | 40.00 |
| ❑ 172 Herb Cain | 100.00 | 50.00 |
| ❑ 173 Gus Marker | 80.00 | 40.00 |
| ❑ 174 Walter Buswell | 80.00 | 40.00 |
| ❑ 175 Carl Voss | 150.00 | 75.00 |
| ❑ 176 Rod Lorraine | 80.00 | 40.00 |
| ❑ 177 Armand Mondou | 80.00 | 40.00 |
| ❑ 178 Cliff(Red) Goupille | 80.00 | 40.00 |
| ❑ 179 Jerry Shannon | 80.00 | 40.00 |
| ❑ 180 Tom Cook | 175.00 | 90.00 |

## 1939-40 O-Pee-Chee V301-1

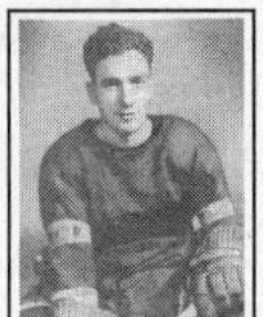

This O-Pee-Chee set of 100 large cards was apparently issued during the 1939-40 season. The catalog designation for this set is V301-1. The cards are black and white and measure approximately 5" by 7". The card backs are blank. The cards are numbered on the front in the lower right corner. Cards in the set are identified on the front by name, team, and position. These cards were premiums and were issued one per cello pack.

| | EX-MT | VG-E |
|---|---|---|
| COMPLETE SET (100) | 5000.00 | 2500.00 |
| COMMON CARD (1-100) | 35.00 | 17.50 |
| ❑ 1 Reg Hamilton | 45.00 | 22.00 |
| ❑ 2 Turk Broda | 250.00 | 125.00 |
| ❑ 3 Bingo Kampman | 35.00 | 17.50 |
| ❑ 4 Gordie Drillon | 60.00 | 30.00 |
| ❑ 5 Bob Davidson | 35.00 | 17.50 |
| ❑ 6 Syl Apps | 175.00 | 90.00 |
| ❑ 7 Pete Langelle | 35.00 | 17.50 |
| ❑ 8 Don Metz | 35.00 | 17.50 |
| ❑ 9 Pep Kelly | 35.00 | 17.50 |
| ❑ 10 Red Horner | 80.00 | 40.00 |
| ❑ 11 Wally Stanowsky | 35.00 | 17.50 |
| ❑ 12 Murph Chamberlain | 35.00 | 17.50 |
| ❑ 13 Bucko MacDonald | 35.00 | 17.50 |
| ❑ 14 Sweeney Schriner | 80.00 | 40.00 |
| ❑ 15 Billy Taylor | 35.00 | 17.50 |
| ❑ 16 Gus Marker | 35.00 | 17.50 |
| ❑ 17 Hooley Smith | 80.00 | 40.00 |
| ❑ 18 Art Chapman | 35.00 | 17.50 |
| ❑ 19 Murray Armstrong | 35.00 | 17.50 |
| ❑ 20 Harvey(Busher) Jackson | 125.00 | 60.00 |
| ❑ 21 Buzz Boll | 35.00 | 17.50 |
| ❑ 22 Cliff(Red) Goupille | 35.00 | 17.50 |
| ❑ 23 Rod Lorraine | 35.00 | 17.50 |
| ❑ 24 Paul Drouin | 35.00 | 17.50 |
| ❑ 25 Johnny Gagnon | 35.00 | 17.50 |
| ❑ 26 Georges Mantha | 35.00 | 17.50 |
| ❑ 27 Armand Mondou | 35.00 | 17.50 |
| ❑ 28 Claude Bourque | 35.00 | 17.50 |
| ❑ 29 Ray Getliffe | 35.00 | 17.50 |
| ❑ 30 Cy Wentworth | 45.00 | 22.00 |
| ❑ 31 Paul Haynes | 35.00 | 17.50 |
| ❑ 32 Walter Buswell | 35.00 | 17.50 |
| ❑ 33 Ott Heller | 35.00 | 17.50 |
| ❑ 34 Arthur Coulter | 60.00 | 30.00 |
| ❑ 35 Clint Smith | 80.00 | 40.00 |
| ❑ 36 Lynn Patrick | 80.00 | 40.00 |
| ❑ 37 Dave Kerr | 60.00 | 30.00 |
| ❑ 38 Murray Patrick | 45.00 | 22.00 |
| ❑ 39 Neil Colville | 80.00 | 40.00 |
| ❑ 40 Jack Portland | 35.00 | 17.50 |
| ❑ 41 Flash Hollett | 35.00 | 17.50 |
| ❑ 42 Herb Cain | 45.00 | 22.00 |
| ❑ 43 Mud Bruneteau | 45.00 | 22.00 |
| ❑ 44 Cully Dahlstrom | 35.00 | 17.50 |
| ❑ 45 Harold(Mush) March | 40.00 | 20.00 |
| ❑ 46 Cully Dahlstrom | 35.00 | 17.50 |
| ❑ 47 Mike Karakas | 45.00 | 22.00 |
| ❑ 48 Bill Thoms | 35.00 | 17.50 |
| ❑ 49 Art Wiebe | 35.00 | 17.50 |
| ❑ 50 Johnny Gottselig | 35.00 | 17.50 |
| ❑ 51 Nick Metz | 35.00 | 17.50 |
| ❑ 52 Jack Church | 35.00 | 17.50 |
| ❑ 53 Bob(Red) Heron | 35.00 | 17.50 |
| ❑ 54 Hank Goldup | 35.00 | 17.50 |
| ❑ 55 Jimmy Fowler | 35.00 | 17.50 |
| ❑ 56 Charlie Sands | 35.00 | 17.50 |
| ❑ 57 Marty Barry | 60.00 | 30.00 |
| ❑ 58 Doug Young | 35.00 | 17.50 |
| ❑ 59 Charlie Conacher | 200.00 | 100.00 |
| ❑ 60 John Sorrell | 35.00 | 17.50 |
| ❑ 61 Tommy Anderson | 35.00 | 17.50 |
| ❑ 62 Lorne Carr | 35.00 | 17.50 |
| ❑ 63 Earl Robertson | 35.00 | 17.50 |
| ❑ 64 Wilfy Field | 35.00 | 17.50 |
| ❑ 65 Jimmy Orlando | 35.00 | 17.50 |
| ❑ 66 Ebbie Goodfellow | 60.00 | 30.00 |
| ❑ 67 Jack Keating | 35.00 | 17.50 |
| ❑ 68 Sid Abel | 300.00 | 150.00 |
| ❑ 69 Gus Giesebrecht | 35.00 | 17.50 |
| ❑ 70 Don Deacon | 35.00 | 17.50 |
| ❑ 71 Hec Kilrea | 35.00 | 17.50 |
| ❑ 72 Syd Howe | 80.00 | 40.00 |
| ❑ 73 Eddie Wares | 35.00 | 17.50 |
| ❑ 74 Carl Liscombe | 35.00 | 17.50 |
| ❑ 75 Tiny Thompson | 125.00 | 60.00 |
| ❑ 76 Earl Seibert | 80.00 | 40.00 |
| ❑ 77 Des Smith | 35.00 | 17.50 |
| ❑ 78 Les Cunningham | 35.00 | 17.50 |
| ❑ 79 Geo.Allen | 35.00 | 17.50 |
| ❑ 80 Bill Carse | 35.00 | 17.50 |
| ❑ 81 Bill McKenzie | 35.00 | 17.50 |
| ❑ 82 Ab DeMarco | 35.00 | 17.50 |
| ❑ 83 Phil Watson | 45.00 | 22.00 |
| ❑ 84 Alf Pike | 35.00 | 17.50 |
| ❑ 85 Babe Pratt | 60.00 | 30.00 |
| ❑ 86 Bryan Hextall | 60.00 | 30.00 |
| ❑ 87 Kilby MacDonald | 35.00 | 17.50 |
| ❑ 88 Alex Shibicky | 40.00 | 20.00 |
| ❑ 89 Dutch Hiller | 35.00 | 17.50 |
| ❑ 90 Mac Colville | 35.00 | 17.50 |
| ❑ 91 Roy Conacher | 80.00 | 40.00 |
| ❑ 92 Cooney Weiland | 80.00 | 40.00 |
| ❑ 93 Art Jackson | 35.00 | 17.50 |
| ❑ 94 Porky Dumart | 100.00 | 50.00 |
| ❑ 95 Dit Clapper | 150.00 | 75.00 |
| ❑ 96 Mel Hill | 45.00 | 22.00 |
| ❑ 97 Frank Brimsek | 200.00 | 100.00 |
| ❑ 98 Bill Cowley | 100.00 | 50.00 |
| ❑ 99 Bobby Bauer | 60.00 | 30.00 |
| ❑ 100 Eddie Shore | 500.00 | 250.00 |

## 1940-41 O-Pee-Chee V301-2

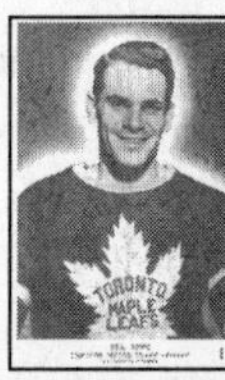

This O-Pee-Chee set is continuously numbered from the 1939-40 O-Pee-Chee set. These large cards were apparently issued during the 1940-41 season. The catalog designation for this set is V301-2. The cards are sepia and measure approximately 5" by 7". The second series numbers are somewhat larger than the numbers used for the first series. The card backs are blank. The cards are numbered on the front in the lower right corner. Cards in the set are identified on the front by name, team, and position. These cards were premiums and were issued one per cello pack.

| | EX-MT | VG-E |
|---|---|---|
| COMPLETE SET (50) | 4000.00 | 2000.00 |
| COMMON CARD (101-125) | 45.00 | 22.00 |
| COMMON CARD (126-150) | 60.00 | 30.00 |
| ❑ 101 Toe Blake | 250.00 | 125.00 |
| ❑ 102 Charlie Sands | 45.00 | 22.00 |
| ❑ 103 Wally Stanowski | 45.00 | 22.00 |
| ❑ 104 Jack Adams | 90.00 | 45.00 |
| ❑ 105 Johnny Mowers | 45.00 | 22.00 |
| ❑ 106 Johnny Quilty | 45.00 | 22.00 |
| ❑ 107 Billy Taylor | 45.00 | 22.00 |
| ❑ 108 Turk Broda | 250.00 | 125.00 |
| ❑ 109 Bingo Kampman | 45.00 | 22.00 |
| ❑ 110 Gordie Drillon | 90.00 | 45.00 |
| ❑ 111 Don Metz | 45.00 | 22.00 |
| ❑ 112 Paul Haynes | 45.00 | 22.00 |
| ❑ 113 Gus Marker | 45.00 | 22.00 |
| ❑ 114 Alex Singbush | 45.00 | 22.00 |
| ❑ 115 Alex Motter | 45.00 | 22.00 |
| ❑ 116 Ken Reardon | 125.00 | 60.00 |
| ❑ 117 Pete Langelle | 45.00 | 22.00 |
| ❑ 118 Syl Apps | 150.00 | 75.00 |
| ❑ 119 Reg. Hamilton | 45.00 | 22.00 |
| ❑ 120 Cliff(Red) Goupille | 45.00 | 22.00 |
| ❑ 121 Joe Benoit | 45.00 | 22.00 |
| ❑ 122 Dave Schriner | 90.00 | 45.00 |
| ❑ 123 Joe Carveth | 45.00 | 22.00 |
| ❑ 124 Jack Stewart | 90.00 | 45.00 |
| ❑ 125 Elmer Lach | 150.00 | 75.00 |
| ❑ 126 Jack Schewchuk | 60.00 | 30.00 |
| ❑ 127 Norman Larson | 60.00 | 30.00 |
| ❑ 128 Don Grosso | 60.00 | 30.00 |
| ❑ 129 Lester Douglas | 60.00 | 30.00 |
| ❑ 130 Turk Broda | 350.00 | 180.00 |
| ❑ 131 Max Bentley | 250.00 | 125.00 |
| ❑ 132 Milt Schmidt | 300.00 | 150.00 |
| ❑ 133 Nick Metz | 60.00 | 30.00 |
| ❑ 134 Jack Crawford | 60.00 | 30.00 |
| ❑ 135 Bill Benson | 60.00 | 30.00 |
| ❑ 136 Lynn Patrick | 125.00 | 60.00 |
| ❑ 137 Cully Dahlstrom | 60.00 | 30.00 |
| ❑ 138 Mud Bruneteau | 80.00 | 40.00 |
| ❑ 139 Dave Kerr | 80.00 | 40.00 |
| ❑ 140 Bob(Red) Heron | 60.00 | 30.00 |
| ❑ 141 Nick Metz | 60.00 | 30.00 |
| ❑ 142 Ott Heller | 60.00 | 30.00 |
| ❑ 143 Phil Hergesheimer | 60.00 | 30.00 |
| ❑ 144 Tony Demers | 60.00 | 30.00 |
| ❑ 145 Archie Wilder | 60.00 | 30.00 |
| ❑ 146 Syl Apps | 200.00 | 100.00 |
| ❑ 147 Ray Getliffe | 60.00 | 30.00 |
| ❑ 148 Lex Chisholm | 60.00 | 30.00 |
| ❑ 149 Eddie Wiseman | 60.00 | 30.00 |
| ❑ 150 Paul Goodman | 80.00 | 40.00 |

## 1968-69 O-Pee-Chee

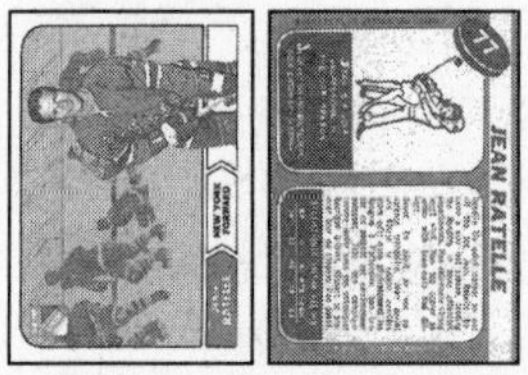

The 1968-69 O-Pee-Chee set contains 216 standard-size color cards. Included are players from the six expansion teams: Philadelphia, Pittsburgh, St. Louis, Minnesota, Los Angeles and Oakland. The cards were originally sold in five-cent wax packs. The horizontally oriented fronts feature the player in the foreground with an artistically rendered hockey scene in the background. The bilingual backs are printed in red and black ink. The player's 1967-68 and career statistics, a short biography, and a cartoon-illustrated fact about the player are included on the back. The cards were printed in Canada and were issued by O-Pee-Chee, even though the Topps Gum copyright is found on the reverse. For the most part, the cards are grouped by teams. However, numerous cards are updated to reflect off-season transactions. The O-Pee-Chee set features many different poses from the corresponding Topps cards. Card No. 193 can be found either numbered or unnumbered. Rookie Cards in this set include Bernie Parent, Mickey Redmond, Gary Smith and Garry Unger.

| | NRMT-MT | EXC |
|---|---|---|
| COMPLETE SET (216) | 2500.00 | 1100.00 |
| COMMON CARD (1-216) | 8.00 | 3.60 |
| ❑ 1 Doug Harvey | 40.00 | 10.00 |
| ❑ 2 Bobby Orr | 350.00 | 160.00 |
| ❑ 3 Don Awrey UER (Photo actually Skip Krake) | 8.00 | 3.60 |
| ❑ 4 Ted Green | 9.00 | 4.00 |
| ❑ 5 Johnny Bucyk | 10.00 | 4.50 |
| ❑ 6 Derek Sanderson | 40.00 | 18.00 |
| ❑ 7 Phil Esposito | 40.00 | 18.00 |
| ❑ 8 Ken Hodge | 9.00 | 4.00 |
| ❑ 9 John McKenzie | 9.00 | 4.00 |
| ❑ 10 Fred Stanfield | 8.00 | 3.60 |
| ❑ 11 Tom Williams | 8.00 | 3.60 |
| ❑ 12 Denis DeJordy | 9.00 | 4.00 |
| ❑ 13 Doug Jarrett | 8.00 | 3.60 |
| ❑ 14 Gilles Marotte | 8.00 | 3.60 |
| ❑ 15 Pat Stapleton | 9.00 | 4.00 |
| ❑ 16 Bobby Hull | 75.00 | 34.00 |
| ❑ 17 Chico Maki | 8.00 | 3.60 |
| ❑ 18 Pit Martin | 9.00 | 4.00 |
| ❑ 19 Doug Mohns | 8.00 | 3.60 |
| ❑ 20 John Ferguson | 9.00 | 4.00 |
| ❑ 21 Jim Pappin | 8.00 | 3.60 |
| ❑ 22 Ken Wharram | 8.00 | 3.60 |
| ❑ 23 Roger Crozier | 9.00 | 4.00 |
| ❑ 24 Bob Baun | 9.00 | 4.00 |
| ❑ 25 Gary Bergman | 8.00 | 3.60 |
| ❑ 26 Kent Douglas | 8.00 | 3.60 |
| ❑ 27 Ron Harris | 8.00 | 3.60 |
| ❑ 28 Alex Delvecchio | 10.00 | 4.50 |
| ❑ 29 Gordie Howe | 100.00 | 45.00 |
| ❑ 30 Bruce MacGregor | 8.00 | 3.60 |
| ❑ 31 Frank Mahovlich | 20.00 | 9.00 |
| ❑ 32 Dean Prentice | 8.00 | 3.60 |
| ❑ 33 Pete Stemkowski | 8.00 | 3.60 |
| ❑ 34 Terry Sawchuk | 50.00 | 22.00 |
| ❑ 35 Larry Cahan | 8.00 | 3.60 |
| ❑ 36 Real Lemieux | 8.00 | 3.60 |
| ❑ 37 Bill White | 12.00 | 5.50 |
| ❑ 38 Gord Labossiere RC | 8.00 | 3.60 |
| ❑ 39 Ted Irvine RC | 8.00 | 3.60 |
| ❑ 40 Eddie Joyal | 8.00 | 3.60 |
| ❑ 41 Dale Rolfe | 8.00 | 3.60 |
| ❑ 42 Lowell MacDonald | 12.00 | 5.50 |
| ❑ 43 Skip Krake UER (Photo actually Don Awrey) | 8.00 | 3.60 |
| ❑ 44 Terry Gray | 8.00 | 3.60 |
| ❑ 45 Cesare Maniago | 9.00 | 4.00 |
| ❑ 46 Mike McMahon | 8.00 | 3.60 |
| ❑ 47 Wayne Hillman | 8.00 | 3.60 |
| ❑ 48 Larry Hillman | 8.00 | 3.60 |
| ❑ 49 Bob Woytowich | 8.00 | 3.60 |
| ❑ 50 Wayne Connelly | 8.00 | 3.60 |
| ❑ 51 Claude Larose | 8.00 | 3.60 |
| ❑ 52 Danny Grant | 12.00 | 5.50 |
| ❑ 53 Andre Boudrias | 8.00 | 3.60 |
| ❑ 54 Ray Cullen | 9.00 | 4.00 |
| ❑ 55 Parker MacDonald | 8.00 | 3.60 |
| ❑ 56 Gump Worsley | 15.00 | 6.75 |
| ❑ 57 Terry Harper | 8.00 | 3.60 |
| ❑ 58 Jacques Laperriere | 9.00 | 4.00 |
| ❑ 59 J.C. Tremblay | 9.00 | 4.00 |
| ❑ 60 Ralph Backstrom | 9.00 | 4.00 |
| ❑ 61 Checklist 1 | 175.00 | 45.00 |
| ❑ 62 Yvan Cournoyer | 20.00 | 9.00 |
| ❑ 63 Jacques Lemaire | 25.00 | 11.00 |
| ❑ 64 Mickey Redmond | 50.00 | 22.00 |
| ❑ 65 Bobby Rousseau | 8.00 | 3.60 |
| ❑ 66 Gilles Tremblay | 8.00 | 3.60 |
| ❑ 67 Ed Giacomin | 20.00 | 9.00 |
| ❑ 68 Arnie Brown | 8.00 | 3.60 |
| ❑ 69 Harry Howell | 9.00 | 4.00 |
| ❑ 70 Al Hamilton | 8.00 | 3.60 |
| ❑ 71 Rod Seiling | 8.00 | 3.60 |
| ❑ 72 Rod Gilbert | 10.00 | 4.50 |
| ❑ 73 Phil Goyette | 8.00 | 3.60 |
| ❑ 74 Larry Jeffrey | 8.00 | 3.60 |
| ❑ 75 Don Marshall | 8.00 | 3.60 |
| ❑ 76 Bob Nevin | 9.00 | 4.00 |
| ❑ 77 Jean Ratelle | 10.00 | 4.50 |
| ❑ 78 Charlie Hodge | 9.00 | 4.00 |
| ❑ 79 Bert Marshall | 8.00 | 3.60 |
| ❑ 80 Billy Harris | 8.00 | 3.60 |
| ❑ 81 Carol Vadnais | 9.00 | 4.00 |
| ❑ 82 Howie Young | 8.00 | 3.60 |
| ❑ 83 John Brenneman | 8.00 | 3.60 |
| ❑ 84 Gerry Ehman | 8.00 | 3.60 |
| ❑ 85 Ted Hampson | 8.00 | 3.60 |
| ❑ 86 Bill Hicke | 8.00 | 3.60 |
| ❑ 87 Gary Jarrett | 8.00 | 3.60 |
| ❑ 88 Doug Roberts | 8.00 | 3.60 |
| ❑ 89 Bernie Parent | 100.00 | 45.00 |
| ❑ 90 Joe Watson | 8.00 | 3.60 |
| ❑ 91 Ed Van Impe | 8.00 | 3.60 |
| ❑ 92 Larry Zeidel | 8.00 | 3.60 |
| ❑ 93 John Miszuk | 8.00 | 3.60 |
| ❑ 94 Gary Dornhoefer | 9.00 | 4.00 |
| ❑ 95 Leon Rochefort | 8.00 | 3.60 |
| ❑ 96 Brit Selby | 8.00 | 3.60 |
| ❑ 97 Forbes Kennedy | 8.00 | 3.60 |
| ❑ 98 Ed Hoekstra | 8.00 | 3.60 |
| ❑ 99 Garry Peters | 8.00 | 3.60 |
| ❑ 100 Les Binkley | 15.00 | 6.75 |
| ❑ 101 Leo Boivin | 9.00 | 4.00 |
| ❑ 102 Earl Ingarfield | 8.00 | 3.60 |
| ❑ 103 Lou Angotti | 8.00 | 3.60 |
| ❑ 104 Andy Bathgate | 9.00 | 4.00 |
| ❑ 105 Wally Boyer | 8.00 | 3.60 |
| ❑ 106 Ken Schinkel | 8.00 | 3.60 |
| ❑ 107 Ab McDonald | 8.00 | 3.60 |
| ❑ 108 Charlie Burns | 8.00 | 3.60 |
| ❑ 109 Val Fonteyne | 8.00 | 3.60 |
| ❑ 110 Noel Price | 8.00 | 3.60 |
| ❑ 111 Glenn Hall | 20.00 | 9.00 |
| ❑ 112 Bob Plager | 12.00 | 5.50 |
| ❑ 113 Jim Roberts | 8.00 | 3.60 |
| ❑ 114 Red Berenson | 9.00 | 4.00 |
| ❑ 115 Larry Keenan | 8.00 | 3.60 |
| ❑ 116 Camille Henry | 8.00 | 3.60 |
| ❑ 117 Gary Sabourin | 8.00 | 3.60 |
| ❑ 118 Ron Schock | 8.00 | 3.60 |
| ❑ 119 Gary Veneruzzo | 8.00 | 3.60 |
| ❑ 120 Gerry Melnyk | 8.00 | 3.60 |
| ❑ 121 Checklist 2 | 150.00 | 38.00 |
| ❑ 122 Johnny Bower | 15.00 | 6.75 |
| ❑ 123 Tim Horton | 25.00 | 11.00 |
| ❑ 124 Pierre Pilote | 9.00 | 4.00 |
| ❑ 125 Marcel Pronovost | 8.00 | 3.60 |
| ❑ 126 Ron Ellis | 9.00 | 4.00 |
| ❑ 127 Paul Henderson | 9.00 | 4.00 |
| ❑ 128 Al Arbour | 9.00 | 4.00 |
| ❑ 129 Bob Pulford | 9.00 | 4.00 |
| ❑ 130 Floyd Smith | 8.00 | 3.60 |
| ❑ 131 Norm Ullman | 10.00 | 4.50 |
| ❑ 132 Mike Walton | 9.00 | 4.00 |
| ❑ 133 Ed Johnston | 9.00 | 4.00 |
| ❑ 134 Glen Sather | 12.00 | 5.50 |
| ❑ 135 Ed Westfall | 9.00 | 4.00 |
| ❑ 136 Dallas Smith | 8.00 | 3.60 |
| ❑ 137 Eddie Shack | 15.00 | 6.75 |
| ❑ 138 Gary Doak | 8.00 | 3.60 |
| ❑ 139 Ron Murphy | 8.00 | 3.60 |
| ❑ 140 Gerry Cheevers | 20.00 | 9.00 |
| ❑ 141 Bob Falkenberg | 8.00 | 3.60 |
| ❑ 142 Garry Unger | 25.00 | 11.00 |
| ❑ 143 Peter Mahovlich | 9.00 | 4.00 |
| ❑ 144 Roy Edwards | 9.00 | 4.00 |
| ❑ 145 Gary Bauman | 8.00 | 3.60 |
| ❑ 146 Bob McCord | 8.00 | 3.60 |
| ❑ 147 Elmer Vasko | 8.00 | 3.60 |
| ❑ 148 Bill Goldsworthy | 12.00 | 5.50 |
| ❑ 149 Jean-Paul Parise | 12.00 | 5.50 |
| ❑ 150 Dave Dryden | 9.00 | 4.00 |
| ❑ 151 Howie Young | 8.00 | 3.60 |
| ❑ 152 Matt Ravlich | 8.00 | 3.60 |
| ❑ 153 Dennis Hull | 9.00 | 4.00 |
| ❑ 154 Eric Nesterenko | 9.00 | 4.00 |
| ❑ 155 Stan Mikita | 30.00 | 13.50 |
| ❑ 156 Bob Wall | 8.00 | 3.60 |
| ❑ 157 Dave Amadio | 8.00 | 3.60 |
| ❑ 158 Howie Hughes | 8.00 | 3.60 |
| ❑ 159 Bill Flett | 12.00 | 5.50 |
| ❑ 160 Doug Robinson | 8.00 | 3.60 |
| ❑ 161 Dick Duff | 9.00 | 4.00 |
| ❑ 162 Ted Harris | 8.00 | 3.60 |
| ❑ 163 Claude Provost | 8.00 | 3.60 |
| ❑ 164 Rogatien Vachon | 40.00 | 18.00 |
| ❑ 165 Henri Richard | 20.00 | 9.00 |
| ❑ 166 Jean Beliveau | 25.00 | 11.00 |
| ❑ 167 Reg Fleming | 8.00 | 3.60 |
| ❑ 168 Ron Stewart | 8.00 | 3.60 |
| ❑ 169 Dave Balon | 8.00 | 3.60 |
| ❑ 170 Orland Kurtenbach | 8.00 | 3.60 |
| ❑ 171 Vic Hadfield | 9.00 | 4.00 |
| ❑ 172 Jim Neilson | 8.00 | 3.60 |
| ❑ 173 Bryan Watson | 8.00 | 3.60 |
| ❑ 174 George Swarbrick | 8.00 | 3.60 |
| ❑ 175 Joe Szura | 8.00 | 3.60 |
| ❑ 176 Gary Smith | 15.00 | 6.75 |
| ❑ 177 Barclay Plager UER (Photo actually Bob Plager) | 15.00 | 6.75 |
| ❑ 178 Tim Ecclestone | 8.00 | 3.60 |
| ❑ 179 Jean-Guy Talbot | 8.00 | 3.60 |
| ❑ 180 Ab McDonald | 8.00 | 3.60 |
| ❑ 181 Jacques Plante | 50.00 | 22.00 |
| ❑ 182 Bill McCreary | 8.00 | 3.60 |
| ❑ 183 Allan Stanley | 9.00 | 4.00 |
| ❑ 184 Andre Lacroix | 12.00 | 5.50 |
| ❑ 185 Jean-Guy Gendron | 8.00 | 3.60 |
| ❑ 186 Jim Johnson | 8.00 | 3.60 |
| ❑ 187 Simon Nolet | 12.00 | 5.50 |
| ❑ 188 Joe Daley | 12.00 | 5.50 |
| ❑ 189 John Arbour | 8.00 | 3.60 |
| ❑ 190 Billy Dea | 8.00 | 3.60 |
| ❑ 191 Bob Dillabough | 8.00 | 3.60 |
| ❑ 192 Bob Woytowich | 8.00 | 3.60 |
| ❑ 193A Keith McCreary ERR (No number) | 40.00 | 18.00 |
| ❑ 193B Keith McCreary COR | 8.00 | 3.60 |
| ❑ 194 Murray Oliver | 8.00 | 3.60 |
| ❑ 195 Larry Mickey | 8.00 | 3.60 |
| ❑ 196 Bill Sutherland | 8.00 | 3.60 |
| ❑ 197 Bruce Gamble | 9.00 | 4.00 |
| ❑ 198 Dave Keon | 12.00 | 5.50 |
| ❑ 199 Gump Worsley AS1 | 10.00 | 4.50 |
| ❑ 200 Bobby Orr AS1 | 125.00 | 55.00 |
| ❑ 201 Tim Horton AS1 | 15.00 | 6.75 |
| ❑ 202 Stan Mikita AS1 | 15.00 | 6.75 |
| ❑ 203 Gordie Howe AS1 | 60.00 | 27.00 |
| ❑ 204 Bobby Hull AS1 | 50.00 | 22.00 |
| ❑ 205 Ed Giacomin AS2 | 15.00 | 6.75 |
| ❑ 206 J.C. Tremblay AS2 | 9.00 | 4.00 |
| ❑ 207 Jim Neilson AS2 | 8.00 | 3.60 |
| ❑ 208 Phil Esposito AS2 | 25.00 | 11.00 |
| ❑ 209 Rod Gilbert AS2 | 9.00 | 4.00 |
| ❑ 210 Johnny Bucyk AS2 | 9.00 | 4.00 |
| ❑ 211 Stan Mikita Hart Trophy Ross Trophy Lady Byng Trophy | 15.00 | 6.75 |
| ❑ 212 Worsley/Vachon Vezina Trophy | 30.00 | 13.50 |
| ❑ 213 Derek Sanderson Calder Trophy | 40.00 | 18.00 |
| ❑ 214 Bobby Orr Norris Trophy | 125.00 | 55.00 |
| ❑ 215 Glenn Hall Conn Smythe Trophy | 12.00 | 5.50 |
| ❑ 216 Claude Provost Masterson Trophy | 15.00 | 3.70 |

## 1968-69 O-Pee-Chee Puck Stickers

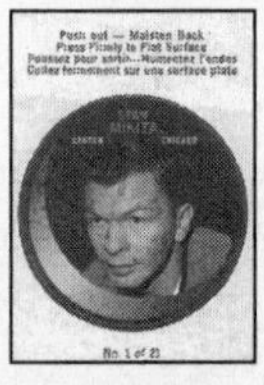

This set consists of 22 numbered (on the front), full-color stickers measuring 2 1/2" by 3 1/2". The card backs are blank and contain an adhesive. These stickers were printed in Canada and were inserted one per pack in 1968-69 O-Pee-Chee regular issue hockey

packs. The pucks were perforated so that they could be punched out. This is obviously not recommended. Sticker card 22 is a special card honoring Gordie Howe's 700th goal.

| | NRMT-MT | EXC |
|---|---|---|
| COMPLETE SET (22) | 400.00 | 180.00 |
| COMMON CARD (1-22) | 4.00 | 1.80 |
| ❑ 1 Stan Mikita | 20.00 | 9.00 |
| ❑ 2 Frank Mahovlich | 10.00 | 4.50 |
| ❑ 3 Bobby Hull | 50.00 | 22.00 |
| ❑ 4 Bobby Orr | 100.00 | 45.00 |
| ❑ 5 Phil Esposito | 20.00 | 9.00 |
| ❑ 6 Gump Worsley | 10.00 | 4.50 |
| ❑ 7 Jean Beliveau | 20.00 | 9.00 |
| ❑ 8 Elmer Vasko | 4.00 | 1.80 |
| ❑ 9 Rod Gilbert | 8.00 | 3.60 |
| ❑ 10 Roger Crozier | 6.00 | 2.70 |
| ❑ 11 Lou Angotti | 4.00 | 1.80 |
| ❑ 12 Charlie Hodge | 6.00 | 2.70 |
| ❑ 13 Glenn Hall | 10.00 | 4.50 |
| ❑ 14 Doug Harvey | 10.00 | 4.50 |
| ❑ 15 Jacques Plante | 30.00 | 13.50 |
| ❑ 16 Allan Stanley | 8.00 | 3.60 |
| ❑ 17 Johnny Bower | 8.00 | 3.60 |
| ❑ 18 Tim Horton | 20.00 | 9.00 |
| ❑ 19 Dave Keon | 8.00 | 3.60 |
| ❑ 20 Terry Sawchuk | 25.00 | 11.00 |
| ❑ 21 Henri Richard | 10.00 | 4.50 |
| ❑ 22 Gordie Howe Special (700th Goal) | 60.00 | 27.00 |

## 1969-70 O-Pee-Chee

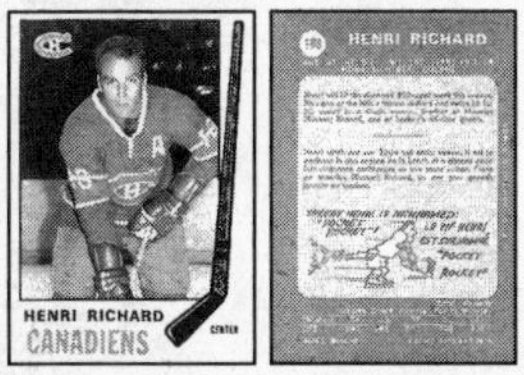


The 1969-70 O-Pee-Chee set contains 231 standard-size cards issued in two series of 132 and 99. The cards were issued in ten-cent wax packs. Bilingual backs contain 1968-69 and career statistics, a short biography and a cartoon-illustrated fact about the player. The cards were printed in Canada with the Topps Gum Company copyright appearing on the reverse. Many player poses in this set are different from the corresponding player poses of the Topps set of this year. Card 193, Gordie Howe "Mr. Hockey" exists with or without the card number. Stamps inserted in wax packs could be placed on the back of the corresponding player's regular-issue cards in a space provided. A card with a stamp on the back is considered to be of less value than one without the stamp. Rookie Cards include Tony Esposito and Serge Savard.

| | NRMT-MT | EXC |
|---|---|---|
| COMPLETE SET (231) | 2000.00 | 900.00 |
| COMMON CARD (1-231) | 5.00 | 2.20 |
| ❑ 1 Gump Worsley | 30.00 | 7.50 |
| ❑ 2 Ted Harris | 5.00 | 2.20 |
| ❑ 3 Jacques Laperriere | 6.00 | 2.70 |
| ❑ 4 Serge Savard | 30.00 | 13.50 |
| ❑ 5 J.C. Tremblay | 6.00 | 2.70 |
| ❑ 6 Yvan Cournoyer | 12.00 | 5.50 |
| ❑ 7 John Ferguson | 6.00 | 2.70 |
| ❑ 8 Jacques Lemaire | 15.00 | 6.75 |
| ❑ 9 Bobby Rousseau | 5.00 | 2.20 |
| ❑ 10 Jean Beliveau | 20.00 | 9.00 |
| ❑ 11 Dick Duff | 6.00 | 2.70 |
| ❑ 12 Glenn Hall | 12.00 | 5.50 |
| ❑ 13 Bob Plager | 6.00 | 2.70 |
| ❑ 14 Ron Anderson | 5.00 | 2.20 |
| ❑ 15 Jean-Guy Talbot | 5.00 | 2.20 |
| ❑ 16 Andre Boudrias | 5.00 | 2.20 |
| ❑ 17 Camille Henry | 5.00 | 2.20 |
| ❑ 18 Ab McDonald | 5.00 | 2.20 |
| ❑ 19 Gary Sabourin | 5.00 | 2.20 |
| ❑ 20 Red Berenson | 6.00 | 2.70 |
| ❑ 21 Phil Goyette | 5.00 | 2.20 |
| ❑ 22 Gerry Cheevers | 15.00 | 6.75 |
| ❑ 23 Ted Green | 6.00 | 2.70 |
| ❑ 24 Bobby Orr | 175.00 | 80.00 |
| ❑ 25 Dallas Smith | 5.00 | 2.20 |
| ❑ 26 Johnny Bucyk | 8.00 | 3.60 |
| ❑ 27 Ken Hodge | 6.00 | 2.70 |
| ❑ 28 John McKenzie | 6.00 | 2.70 |
| ❑ 29 Ed Westfall | 6.00 | 2.70 |
| ❑ 30 Phil Esposito | 30.00 | 13.50 |
| ❑ 31 Checklist 1 | 125.00 | 31.00 |
| ❑ 32 Fred Stanfield | 5.00 | 2.20 |
| ❑ 33 Ed Giacomin | 15.00 | 6.75 |
| ❑ 34 Arnie Brown | 5.00 | 2.20 |
| ❑ 35 Jim Neilson | 5.00 | 2.20 |
| ❑ 36 Rod Seiling | 5.00 | 2.20 |
| ❑ 37 Rod Gilbert | 8.00 | 3.60 |
| ❑ 38 Vic Hadfield | 6.00 | 2.70 |
| ❑ 39 Don Marshall | 6.00 | 2.70 |
| ❑ 40 Bob Nevin | 6.00 | 2.70 |
| ❑ 41 Ron Stewart | 5.00 | 2.20 |
| ❑ 42 Jean Ratelle | 8.00 | 3.60 |
| ❑ 43 Walt Tkaczuk | 8.00 | 3.60 |
| ❑ 44 Bruce Gamble | 6.00 | 2.70 |
| ❑ 45 Jim Dorey | 5.00 | 2.20 |
| ❑ 46 Ron Ellis | 6.00 | 2.70 |
| ❑ 47 Paul Henderson | 6.00 | 2.70 |
| ❑ 48 Brit Selby | 5.00 | 2.20 |
| ❑ 49 Floyd Smith | 5.00 | 2.20 |
| ❑ 50 Mike Walton | 6.00 | 2.70 |
| ❑ 51 Dave Keon | 8.00 | 3.60 |
| ❑ 52 Murray Oliver | 5.00 | 2.20 |
| ❑ 53 Bob Pulford | 6.00 | 2.70 |
| ❑ 54 Norm Ullman | 8.00 | 3.60 |
| ❑ 55 Roger Crozier | 6.00 | 2.70 |
| ❑ 56 Roy Edwards | 6.00 | 2.70 |
| ❑ 57 Bob Baun | 6.00 | 2.70 |
| ❑ 58 Gary Bergman | 5.00 | 2.20 |
| ❑ 59 Carl Brewer | 6.00 | 2.70 |
| ❑ 60 Wayne Connelly | 5.00 | 2.20 |
| ❑ 61 Gordie Howe | 80.00 | 36.00 |
| ❑ 62 Frank Mahovlich | 12.00 | 5.50 |
| ❑ 63 Bruce MacGregor | 5.00 | 2.20 |
| ❑ 64 Ron Harris | 5.00 | 2.20 |
| ❑ 65 Pete Stemkowski | 5.00 | 2.20 |
| ❑ 66 Denis DeJordy | 6.00 | 2.70 |
| ❑ 67 Doug Jarrett | 5.00 | 2.20 |
| ❑ 68 Gilles Marotte | 5.00 | 2.20 |
| ❑ 69 Pat Stapleton | 6.00 | 2.70 |
| ❑ 70 Bobby Hull | 60.00 | 27.00 |
| ❑ 71 Dennis Hull | 6.00 | 2.70 |
| ❑ 72 Doug Mohns | 5.00 | 2.20 |
| ❑ 73 Howie Menard | 5.00 | 2.20 |
| ❑ 74 Ken Wharram | 5.00 | 2.20 |
| ❑ 75 Pit Martin | 6.00 | 2.70 |
| ❑ 76 Stan Mikita | 20.00 | 9.00 |
| ❑ 77 Charlie Hodge | 6.00 | 2.70 |
| ❑ 78 Gary Smith | 6.00 | 2.70 |
| ❑ 79 Harry Howell | 6.00 | 2.70 |
| ❑ 80 Bert Marshall | 5.00 | 2.20 |
| ❑ 81 Doug Roberts | 5.00 | 2.20 |
| ❑ 82 Carol Vadnais | 6.00 | 2.70 |
| ❑ 83 Gerry Ehman | 5.00 | 2.20 |
| ❑ 84 Brian Perry | 5.00 | 2.20 |
| ❑ 85 Gary Jarrett | 5.00 | 2.20 |
| ❑ 86 Ted Hampson | 5.00 | 2.20 |
| ❑ 87 Earl Ingarfield | 5.00 | 2.20 |
| ❑ 88 Doug Favell | 15.00 | 6.75 |
| ❑ 89 Bernie Parent | 40.00 | 18.00 |
| ❑ 90 Larry Hillman | 5.00 | 2.20 |
| ❑ 91 Wayne Hillman | 5.00 | 2.20 |
| ❑ 92 Ed Van Impe | 5.00 | 2.20 |
| ❑ 93 Joe Watson | 5.00 | 2.20 |
| ❑ 94 Gary Dornhoefer | 6.00 | 2.70 |
| ❑ 95 Reg Fleming | 5.00 | 2.20 |
| ❑ 96 Ralph McSweyn | 5.00 | 2.20 |
| ❑ 97 Jim Johnson | 5.00 | 2.20 |
| ❑ 98 Andre Lacroix | 6.00 | 2.70 |
| ❑ 99 Gerry Desjardins | 12.00 | 5.50 |
| ❑ 100 Dale Rolfe | 5.00 | 2.20 |
| ❑ 101 Bill White | 5.00 | 2.20 |
| ❑ 102 Bill Flett | 5.00 | 2.20 |
| ❑ 103 Ted Irvine | 5.00 | 2.20 |
| ❑ 104 Ross Lonsberry | 6.00 | 2.70 |
| ❑ 105 Leon Rochefort | 5.00 | 2.20 |
| ❑ 106 Bryan Campbell | 5.00 | 2.20 |
| ❑ 107 Dennis Hextall | 6.00 | 2.70 |
| ❑ 108 Eddie Joyal | 5.00 | 2.20 |
| ❑ 109 Gord Labossiere | 5.00 | 2.20 |
| ❑ 110 Les Binkley | 6.00 | 2.70 |
| ❑ 111 Tracy Pratt | 5.00 | 2.20 |
| ❑ 112 Bryan Watson | 5.00 | 2.20 |
| ❑ 113 Bob Blackburn | 5.00 | 2.20 |
| ❑ 114 Keith McCreary | 5.00 | 2.20 |
| ❑ 115 Dean Prentice | 5.00 | 2.20 |
| ❑ 116 Glen Sather | 8.00 | 3.60 |
| ❑ 117 Ken Schinkel | 5.00 | 2.20 |
| ❑ 118 Wally Boyer | 5.00 | 2.20 |
| ❑ 119 Val Fonteyne | 5.00 | 2.20 |
| ❑ 120 Ron Schock | 5.00 | 2.20 |
| ❑ 121 Cesare Maniago | 6.00 | 2.70 |
| ❑ 122 Leo Boivin | 6.00 | 2.70 |
| ❑ 123 Bob McCord | 5.00 | 2.20 |
| ❑ 124 John Miszuk | 5.00 | 2.20 |
| ❑ 125 Danny Grant | 6.00 | 2.70 |
| ❑ 126 Bill Collins | 5.00 | 2.20 |
| ❑ 127 Jean-Paul Parise | 6.00 | 2.70 |
| ❑ 128 Tom Williams | 5.00 | 2.20 |
| ❑ 129 Charlie Burns | 5.00 | 2.20 |
| ❑ 130 Ray Cullen | 5.00 | 2.20 |
| ❑ 131 Danny O'Shea | 5.00 | 2.20 |
| ❑ 132 Checklist 2 | 150.00 | 38.00 |
| ❑ 133 Jim Pappin | 6.00 | 2.70 |
| ❑ 134 Lou Angotti | 6.00 | 2.70 |
| ❑ 135 Terry Cafery | 6.00 | 2.70 |
| ❑ 136 Eric Nesterenko | 6.00 | 2.70 |
| ❑ 137 Chico Maki | 6.00 | 2.70 |
| ❑ 138 Tony Esposito | 150.00 | 70.00 |
| ❑ 139 Eddie Shack | 12.00 | 5.50 |
| ❑ 140 Bob Wall | 6.00 | 2.70 |
| ❑ 141 Skip Krake | 6.00 | 2.70 |
| ❑ 142 Howie Hughes | 6.00 | 2.70 |
| ❑ 143 Jimmy Peters | 6.00 | 2.70 |
| ❑ 144 Brent Hughes | 6.00 | 2.70 |
| ❑ 145 Bill Hicke | 5.00 | 2.20 |
| ❑ 146 Norm Ferguson | 6.00 | 2.70 |
| ❑ 147 Dick Mattiussi | 6.00 | 2.70 |
| ❑ 148 Mike Laughton | 6.00 | 2.70 |
| ❑ 149 Gene Ubriaco | 6.00 | 2.70 |
| ❑ 150 Bob Dillabough | 6.00 | 2.70 |
| ❑ 151 Bob Woytowich | 6.00 | 2.70 |
| ❑ 152 Joe Daley | 6.00 | 2.70 |
| ❑ 153 Duane Rupp | 6.00 | 2.70 |
| ❑ 154 Bryan Hextall | 8.00 | 3.60 |
| ❑ 155 Jean Pronovost | 6.00 | 2.70 |
| ❑ 156 Jim Morrison | 6.00 | 2.70 |
| ❑ 157 Alex Delvecchio | 8.00 | 3.60 |
| ❑ 158 Paul Popiel | 6.00 | 2.70 |
| ❑ 159 Garry Unger | 8.00 | 3.60 |
| ❑ 160 Garry Monahan | 6.00 | 2.70 |
| ❑ 161 Matt Ravlich | 6.00 | 2.70 |
| ❑ 162 Nick Libett | 6.00 | 2.70 |
| ❑ 163 Henri Richard | 12.00 | 5.50 |
| ❑ 164 Terry Harper | 6.00 | 2.70 |
| ❑ 165 Rogatien Vachon | 18.00 | 8.00 |
| ❑ 166 Ralph Backstrom | 6.00 | 2.70 |
| ❑ 167 Claude Provost | 6.00 | 2.70 |
| ❑ 168 Gilles Tremblay | 6.00 | 2.70 |
| ❑ 169 Jean-Guy Gendron | 6.00 | 2.70 |
| ❑ 170 Earl Heiskala | 6.00 | 2.70 |
| ❑ 171 Garry Peters | 6.00 | 2.70 |
| ❑ 172 Bill Sutherland | 5.00 | 2.20 |
| ❑ 173 Dick Cherry | 6.00 | 2.70 |
| ❑ 174 Jim Roberts | 6.00 | 2.70 |
| ❑ 175 Noel Picard | 6.00 | 2.70 |
| ❑ 176 Barclay Plager | 6.00 | 2.70 |
| ❑ 177 Frank St. Marseille | 6.00 | 2.70 |
| ❑ 178 Al Arbour | 8.00 | 3.60 |
| ❑ 179 Tim Ecclestone | 6.00 | 2.70 |
| ❑ 180 Jacques Plante | 40.00 | 18.00 |
| ❑ 181 Bill McCreary | 6.00 | 2.70 |
| ❑ 182 Tim Horton | 20.00 | 9.00 |
| ❑ 183 Rick Ley | 6.00 | 2.70 |
| ❑ 184 Wayne Carleton | 6.00 | 2.70 |
| ❑ 185 Marv Edwards | 8.00 | 3.60 |
| ❑ 186 Pat Quinn | 15.00 | 6.75 |
| ❑ 187 Johnny Bower | 12.00 | 5.50 |
| ❑ 188 Orland Kurtenbach | 6.00 | 2.70 |
| ❑ 189 Terry Sawchuk | 40.00 | 18.00 |
| ❑ 190 Real Lemieux | 6.00 | 2.70 |
| ❑ 191 Dave Balon | 6.00 | 2.70 |
| ❑ 192 Al Hamilton | 5.00 | 2.20 |
| ❑ 193A Gordie Howe ERR Mr. Hockey (No number) | 150.00 | 70.00 |
| ❑ 193B Gordie Howe COR Mr. Hockey | 175.00 | 80.00 |
| ❑ 194 Claude Larose | 6.00 | 2.70 |
| ❑ 195 Bill Goldsworthy | 6.00 | 2.70 |
| ❑ 196 Bob Barlow | 6.00 | 2.70 |
| ❑ 197 Ken Broderick | 6.00 | 2.70 |
| ❑ 198 Lou Nanne | 6.00 | 2.70 |
| ❑ 199 Tom Polonic | 6.00 | 2.70 |
| ❑ 200 Ed Johnston | 6.00 | 2.70 |
| ❑ 201 Derek Sanderson | 25.00 | 11.00 |
| ❑ 202 Gary Doak | 5.00 | 2.20 |
| ❑ 203 Don Awrey | 6.00 | 2.70 |
| ❑ 204 Ron Murphy | 6.00 | 2.70 |
| ❑ 205A Phil Esposito Art Ross Trophy Hart Trophy (214 on back and no number on front) | 25.00 | 11.00 |
| ❑ 205B Phil Esposito Art Ross Trophy Hart Trophy (214 on back and 205 on front) | 20.00 | 9.00 |
| ❑ 206 Alex Delvecchio Lady Byng | 6.00 | 2.70 |
| ❑ 207 Jacques Plante Glenn Hall Vezina Trophy | 50.00 | 22.00 |
| ❑ 208 Danny Grant Calder Trophy | 6.00 | 2.70 |
| ❑ 209 Bobby Orr Norris Trophy | 80.00 | 36.00 |
| ❑ 210 Serge Savard Conn Smythe Trophy | 10.00 | 4.50 |
| ❑ 211 Glenn Hall AS | 12.00 | 5.50 |
| ❑ 212 Bobby Orr AS | 80.00 | 36.00 |
| ❑ 213 Tim Horton AS | 15.00 | 6.75 |
| ❑ 214 Phil Esposito AS | 20.00 | 9.00 |
| ❑ 215 Gordie Howe AS | 50.00 | 22.00 |
| ❑ 216 Bobby Hull AS | 35.00 | 16.00 |
| ❑ 217 Ed Giacomin AS | 12.00 | 5.50 |
| ❑ 218 Ted Green AS | 5.00 | 2.20 |
| ❑ 219 Ted Harris AS | 5.00 | 2.20 |
| ❑ 220 Jean Beliveau AS | 15.00 | 6.75 |
| ❑ 221 Yvan Cournoyer AS | 8.00 | 3.60 |
| ❑ 222 Frank Mahovlich AS | 8.00 | 3.60 |
| ❑ 223 Art Ross Trophy | 6.00 | 2.70 |
| ❑ 224 Hart Trophy | 6.00 | 2.70 |
| ❑ 225 Lady Byng Trophy | 6.00 | 2.70 |
| ❑ 226 Vezina Trophy | 8.00 | 3.60 |
| ❑ 227 Calder Trophy | 6.00 | 2.70 |
| ❑ 228 James Norris Trophy | 6.00 | 2.70 |
| ❑ 229 Conn Smythe Trophy | 6.00 | 2.70 |
| ❑ 230 Prince of Wales Trophy | 6.00 | 2.70 |
| ❑ 231 The Stanley Cup | 60.00 | 15.00 |

## 1969-70 O-Pee-Chee Four-in-One

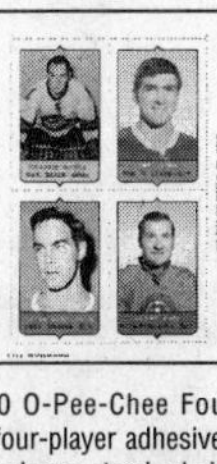

The 1969-70 O-Pee-Chee Four-in-One set contains 18 four-player adhesive-backed color cards. The cards are standard size, 2 1/2" by 3 1/2", whereas the individual mini-cards are approximately 1" by 1 1/2". These small cards could be separated and then stuck in a small team album/booklet that was also available that year from O-Pee-Chee. This set was distributed as an insert with the second series of regular 1969-70 O-Pee-Chee cards. Cards that have been separated into the mini-cards have very little value. The cards are unnumbered and so they are checklisted below alphabetically by the (upper left corner) player's name.

| | NRMT-MT | EXC |
|---|---|---|
| COMPLETE SET (18) | 800.00 | 350.00 |
| COMMON CARD (1-18) | 20.00 | 9.00 |
| ❑ 1 Bob Baun | 40.00 | 18.00 |
| Ken Schinkel | | |
| Tim Horton | | |
| Bernie Parent | | |
| ❑ 2 Les Binkley | 25.00 | 11.00 |
| Ken Hodge | | |
| Reg Fleming | | |
| Jacques Laperriere | | |
| ❑ 3 Yvan Cournoyer | 25.00 | 11.00 |
| Jim Neilson | | |
| Gary Sabourin | | |
| John Miszuk | | |
| ❑ 4 Bruce Gamble | 40.00 | 18.00 |
| Carol Vadnais | | |
| Frank Mahovlich | | |
| Larry Hillman | | |
| ❑ 5 Ed Giacomin | 50.00 | 22.00 |
| Jean Beliveau | | |
| Eddie Joyal | | |
| Leo Boivin | | |
| ❑ 6 Phil Goyette | 20.00 | 9.00 |
| Doug Jarrett | | |
| Ted Green | | |
| Bill Hicke | | |
| ❑ 7 Ted Hampson | 25.00 | 11.00 |
| Carl Brewer | | |
| Denis DeJordy | | |
| Leon Rochefort | | |
| ❑ 8 Charlie Hodge | 40.00 | 18.00 |
| Pat Quinn | | |
| Derek Sanderson | | |
| Duane Rupp | | |
| ❑ 9 Earl Ingarfield | 100.00 | 45.00 |
| Jim Roberts | | |
| Gump Worsley | | |
| Bobby Hull | | |
| ❑ 10 Andre Lacroix | 25.00 | 11.00 |
| Bob Wall | | |
| Serge Savard | | |
| Roger Crozier | | |
| ❑ 11 Cesare Maniago | 200.00 | 90.00 |
| Bobby Orr | | |
| Dave Keon | | |
| Jean-Guy Gendron | | |
| ❑ 12 Keith McCreary | 40.00 | 18.00 |
| Claude Larose | | |
| Rod Gilbert | | |
| Gerry Cheevers | | |
| ❑ 13 Stan Mikita | 40.00 | 18.00 |
| Al Arbour | | |
| Rod Seiling | | |
| Ron Schock | | |
| ❑ 14 Doug Mohns | 150.00 | 70.00 |
| Bob Woytowich | | |
| Gordie Howe | | |
| Gerry Desjardins | | |
| ❑ 15 Bob Nevin | 40.00 | 18.00 |
| Jacques Plante | | |
| Mike Walton | | |
| Ray Cullen | | |
| ❑ 16 Bob Pulford | 60.00 | 27.00 |
| Henri Richard | | |
| Red Berenson | | |
| Eddie Shack | | |
| ❑ 17 Pat Stapleton | 20.00 | 9.00 |
| Danny Grant | | |
| Bert Marshall | | |
| Jean Ratelle | | |
| ❑ 18 Ed Van Impe | 50.00 | 22.00 |
| Dale Rolfe | | |
| Alex Delvecchio | | |
| Phil Esposito | | |

## 1969-70 O-Pee-Chee Stamps

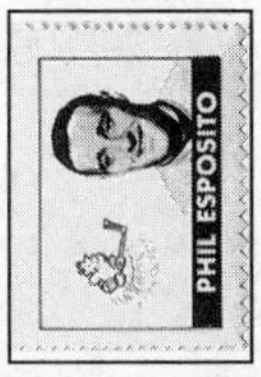


The 1969-70 O-Pee-Chee Stamps set contains 26 black and white stamps measuring approximately 1 1/2" by 1 1/4". The stamps were distributed with the first series of regular 1969-70 O-Pee-Chee hockey cards and may also have been available in some of the Topps wax packs of that year as well. The stamps are unnumbered and hence are checklisted below alphabetically for convenience. OPC intended for the stamps to be stuck on the blank space provided on the backs of the corresponding regular card; collectors are strongly encouraged NOT to follow that procedure. The stamps were produced as pairs; intact pairs are now valued at 1.5 to 2 times the sum of the individual player prices listed below.

| | NRMT-MT | EXC |
|---|---|---|
| COMPLETE SET (26) | 200.00 | 90.00 |
| COMMON CARD (1-26) | 2.50 | 1.10 |
| ❑ 1 Jean Beliveau | 10.00 | 4.50 |
| ❑ 2 Red Berenson | 4.00 | 1.80 |
| ❑ 3 Les Binkley | 4.00 | 1.80 |
| ❑ 4 Yvan Cournoyer | 8.00 | 3.60 |
| ❑ 5 Ray Cullen | 2.50 | 1.10 |
| ❑ 6 Gerry Desjardins | 4.00 | 1.80 |
| ❑ 7 Phil Esposito | 12.00 | 5.50 |
| ❑ 8 Ed Giacomin | 8.00 | 3.60 |
| ❑ 9 Rod Gilbert | 8.00 | 3.60 |
| ❑ 10 Danny Grant | 4.00 | 1.80 |
| ❑ 11 Glenn Hall | 10.00 | 4.50 |
| ❑ 12 Ted Hampson | 2.50 | 1.10 |
| ❑ 13 Ken Hodge | 4.00 | 1.80 |
| ❑ 14 Gordie Howe | 30.00 | 13.50 |
| ❑ 15 Bobby Hull | 20.00 | 9.00 |
| ❑ 16 Eddie Joyal | 2.50 | 1.10 |
| ❑ 17 Dave Keon | 8.00 | 3.60 |
| ❑ 18 Andre Lacroix | 4.00 | 1.80 |
| ❑ 19 Frank Mahovlich | 10.00 | 4.50 |
| ❑ 20 Keith McCreary | 2.50 | 1.10 |
| ❑ 21 Stan Mikita | 10.00 | 4.50 |
| ❑ 22 Bobby Orr | 40.00 | 18.00 |
| ❑ 23 Bernie Parent | 10.00 | 4.50 |
| ❑ 24 Jean Ratelle | 8.00 | 3.60 |
| ❑ 25 Norm Ullman | 5.00 | 2.20 |
| ❑ 26 Carol Vadnais | 2.50 | 1.10 |

## 1969-70 O-Pee-Chee Team Booklets

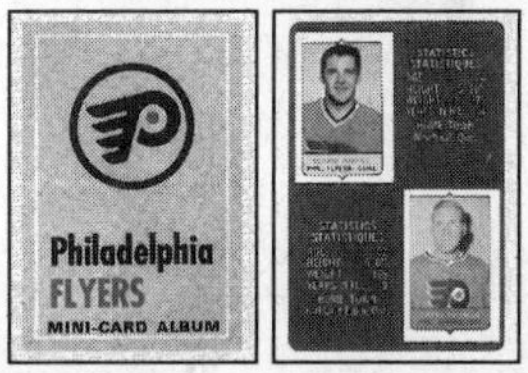


The 1969-70 O-Pee-Chee Team Booklets were issued in order to hold the individual mini-cards of the four-in-one insert set. These small team albums/booklets measure approximately 2 1/2" by 3 1/2". There were 12 albums in the set, one album per team. The team booklets are light green in color. There were four pages in each little booklet with spaces for six stickers (two per page after the front title page) to be placed within.

| | NRMT-MT | EXC |
|---|---|---|
| COMPLETE SET (12) | 75.00 | 34.00 |
| COMMON CARD (1-12) | 8.00 | 3.60 |
| ❑ 1 Boston Bruins | 10.00 | 4.50 |
| ❑ 2 Chicago Blackhawks | 10.00 | 4.50 |
| ❑ 3 Detroit Red Wings | 10.00 | 4.50 |
| ❑ 4 Los Angeles Kings | 8.00 | 3.60 |
| ❑ 5 Minnesota North Stars | 8.00 | 3.60 |
| ❑ 6 Montreal Canadiens | 10.00 | 4.50 |
| ❑ 7 New York Rangers | 10.00 | 4.50 |
| ❑ 8 Oakland Seals | 10.00 | 4.50 |
| ❑ 9 Philadelphia Flyers | 10.00 | 4.50 |
| ❑ 10 Pittsburgh Penguins | 8.00 | 3.60 |
| ❑ 11 St. Louis Blues | 8.00 | 3.60 |
| ❑ 12 Toronto Maple Leafs | 10.00 | 4.50 |

## 1970-71 O-Pee-Chee

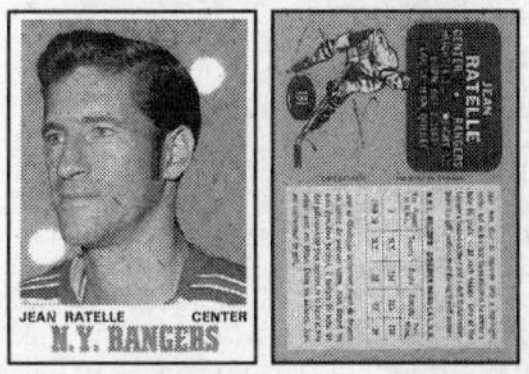


The 1970-71 O-Pee-Chee set contains 264 standard-size cards. Players from expansion Buffalo and Vancouver are included. Bilingual backs feature a short biography as well as the player's 1969-70 and career statistics. The cards were printed in Canada, and the O-Pee-Chee copyright, and not the Topps, appears on the back for the first time. Many player poses are different from the Topps set of this year. Cards are grouped by teams. However, there are a number of cards that have updated team names reflecting off-season trades. Card no. 231 is a special memorial to Terry Sawchuk, who passed away in 1970. Card nos. 111, Brit Selby, and 175 Mickey Redmond, can be found with or without a line of text acknowledging trades. Rookie Cards include Wayne Cashman, Bobby Clarke, Brad Park, Guy Lapointe, Gilbert Perreault, and Darryl Sittler.

| | NRMT-MT | EXC |
|---|---|---|
| COMPLETE SET (264) | 1500.00 | 700.00 |
| COMMON CARD (1-264) | 4.00 | 1.80 |
| ❑ 1 Gerry Cheevers | 25.00 | 6.25 |
| ❑ 2 Johnny Bucyk | 6.00 | 2.70 |

| | | |
|---|---|---|
| ❑ 3 Bobby Orr | 125.00 | 55.00 |
| ❑ 4 Don Awrey | 4.00 | 1.80 |
| ❑ 5 Fred Stanfield | 4.00 | 1.80 |
| ❑ 6 John McKenzie | 5.00 | 2.20 |
| ❑ 7 Wayne Cashman | 15.00 | 6.75 |
| ❑ 8 Ken Hodge | 5.00 | 2.20 |
| ❑ 9 Wayne Carleton | 4.00 | 1.80 |
| ❑ 10 Garnet Bailey | 4.00 | 1.80 |
| ❑ 11 Phil Esposito | 25.00 | 11.00 |
| ❑ 12 Lou Angotti | 4.00 | 1.80 |
| ❑ 13 Jim Pappin | 4.00 | 1.80 |
| ❑ 14 Dennis Hull | 5.00 | 2.20 |
| ❑ 15 Bobby Hull | 50.00 | 22.00 |
| ❑ 16 Doug Mohns | 4.00 | 1.80 |
| ❑ 17 Pat Stapleton | 5.00 | 2.20 |
| ❑ 18 Pit Martin | 5.00 | 2.20 |
| ❑ 19 Eric Nesterenko | 5.00 | 2.20 |
| ❑ 20 Stan Mikita | 20.00 | 9.00 |
| ❑ 21 Roy Edwards | 5.00 | 2.20 |
| ❑ 22 Frank Mahovlich | 10.00 | 4.50 |
| ❑ 23 Ron Harris | 4.00 | 1.80 |
| ❑ 24 Checklist 1 | 150.00 | 38.00 |
| ❑ 25 Pete Stemkowski | 4.00 | 1.80 |
| ❑ 26 Garry Unger | 4.00 | 1.80 |
| ❑ 27 Bruce MacGregor | 4.00 | 1.80 |
| ❑ 28 Larry Jeffrey | 4.00 | 1.80 |
| ❑ 29 Gordie Howe | 80.00 | 36.00 |
| ❑ 30 Billy Dea | 4.00 | 1.80 |
| ❑ 31 Denis DeJordy | 5.00 | 2.20 |
| ❑ 32 Matt Ravlich | 4.00 | 1.80 |
| ❑ 33 Dave Amadio | 4.00 | 1.80 |
| ❑ 34 Gilles Marotte | 4.00 | 1.80 |
| ❑ 35 Eddie Shack | 10.00 | 4.50 |
| ❑ 36 Bob Pulford | 5.00 | 2.20 |
| ❑ 37 Ross Lonsberry | 5.00 | 2.20 |
| ❑ 38 Gord Labossiere | 4.00 | 1.80 |
| ❑ 39 Eddie Joyal | 4.00 | 1.80 |
| ❑ 40 Gump Worsley | 10.00 | 4.50 |
| ❑ 41 Bob McCord | 4.00 | 1.80 |
| ❑ 42 Leo Boivin | 5.00 | 2.20 |
| ❑ 43 Tom Reid | 4.00 | 1.80 |
| ❑ 44 Charlie Burns | 4.00 | 1.80 |
| ❑ 45 Bob Barlow | 4.00 | 1.80 |
| ❑ 46 Bill Goldsworthy | 5.00 | 2.20 |
| ❑ 47 Danny Grant | 5.00 | 2.20 |
| ❑ 48 Norm Beaudin | 4.00 | 1.80 |
| ❑ 49 Rogatien Vachon | 12.00 | 5.50 |
| ❑ 50 Yvan Cournoyer | 8.00 | 3.60 |
| ❑ 51 Serge Savard | 10.00 | 4.50 |
| ❑ 52 Jacques Laperriere | 5.00 | 2.20 |
| ❑ 53 Terry Harper | 4.00 | 1.80 |
| ❑ 54 Ralph Backstrom | 5.00 | 2.20 |
| ❑ 55 Jean Beliveau | 15.00 | 6.75 |
| ❑ 56 Claude Larose | 4.00 | 1.80 |
| ❑ 57 Jacques Lemaire | 10.00 | 4.50 |
| ❑ 58 Peter Mahovlich | 5.00 | 2.20 |
| ❑ 59 Tim Horton | 15.00 | 6.75 |
| ❑ 60 Bob Nevin | 4.00 | 1.80 |
| ❑ 61 Dave Balon | 4.00 | 1.80 |
| ❑ 62 Vic Hadfield | 5.00 | 2.20 |
| ❑ 63 Rod Gilbert | 7.00 | 3.10 |
| ❑ 64 Ron Stewart | 4.00 | 1.80 |
| ❑ 65 Ted Irvine | 4.00 | 1.80 |
| ❑ 66 Arnie Brown | 4.00 | 1.80 |
| ❑ 67 Brad Park | 40.00 | 18.00 |
| ❑ 68 Ed Giacomin | 12.00 | 5.50 |
| ❑ 69 Gary Smith | 5.00 | 2.20 |
| ❑ 70 Carol Vadnais | 5.00 | 2.20 |
| ❑ 71 Doug Roberts | 4.00 | 1.80 |
| ❑ 72 Harry Howell | 5.00 | 2.20 |
| ❑ 73 Joe Szura | 4.00 | 1.80 |
| ❑ 74 Mike Laughton | 4.00 | 1.80 |
| ❑ 75 Gary Jarrett | 4.00 | 1.80 |
| ❑ 76 Bill Hicke | 4.00 | 1.80 |
| ❑ 77 Paul Andrea | 4.00 | 1.80 |
| ❑ 78 Bernie Parent | 25.00 | 11.00 |
| ❑ 79 Joe Watson | 4.00 | 1.80 |
| ❑ 80 Ed Van Impe | 4.00 | 1.80 |
| ❑ 81 Larry Hillman | 4.00 | 1.80 |
| ❑ 82 George Swarbrick | 4.00 | 1.80 |
| ❑ 83 Bill Sutherland | 4.00 | 1.80 |
| ❑ 84 Andre Lacroix | 5.00 | 2.20 |
| ❑ 85 Gary Dornhoefer | 5.00 | 2.20 |
| ❑ 86 Jean-Guy Gendron | 4.00 | 1.80 |
| ❑ 87 Al Smith | 5.00 | 2.20 |
| ❑ 88 Bob Woytowich | 4.00 | 1.80 |
| ❑ 89 Duane Rupp | 4.00 | 1.80 |
| ❑ 90 Jim Morrison | 4.00 | 1.80 |
| ❑ 91 Ron Schock | 4.00 | 1.80 |
| ❑ 92 Ken Schinkel | 4.00 | 1.80 |
| ❑ 93 Keith McCreary | 4.00 | 1.80 |
| ❑ 94 Bryan Hextall | 5.00 | 2.20 |
| ❑ 95 Wayne Hicks | 4.00 | 1.80 |
| ❑ 96 Gary Sabourin | 4.00 | 1.80 |
| ❑ 97 Ernie Wakely | 5.00 | 2.20 |
| ❑ 98 Bob Wall | 4.00 | 1.80 |
| ❑ 99 Barclay Plager | 5.00 | 2.20 |
| ❑ 100 Jean-Guy Talbot | 4.00 | 1.80 |
| ❑ 101 Gary Veneruzzo | 4.00 | 1.80 |
| ❑ 102 Tim Ecclestone | 4.00 | 1.80 |
| ❑ 103 Red Berenson | 5.00 | 2.20 |
| ❑ 104 Larry Keenan | 4.00 | 1.80 |
| ❑ 105 Bruce Gamble | 5.00 | 2.20 |
| ❑ 106 Jim Dorey | 4.00 | 1.80 |
| ❑ 107 Mike Pelyk | 4.00 | 1.80 |
| ❑ 108 Rick Ley | 4.00 | 1.80 |
| ❑ 109 Mike Walton | 4.00 | 1.80 |
| ❑ 110 Norm Ullman | 7.00 | 3.10 |
| ❑ 111A Brit Selby (No mention of trade) | 4.00 | 1.80 |
| ❑ 111B Brit Selby (Trade noted) | 20.00 | 9.00 |
| ❑ 112 Garry Monahan | 4.00 | 1.80 |
| ❑ 113 George Armstrong | 5.00 | 2.20 |
| ❑ 114 Gary Doak | 4.00 | 1.80 |
| ❑ 115 Darryl Sly | 4.00 | 1.80 |
| ❑ 116 Wayne Maki | 4.00 | 1.80 |
| ❑ 117 Orland Kurtenbach | 4.00 | 1.80 |
| ❑ 118 Murray Hall | 4.00 | 1.80 |
| ❑ 119 Marc Reaume | 4.00 | 1.80 |
| ❑ 120 Pat Quinn | 6.00 | 2.70 |
| ❑ 121 Andre Boudrias | 4.00 | 1.80 |
| ❑ 122 Paul Popiel | 4.00 | 1.80 |
| ❑ 123 Paul Terbenche | 4.00 | 1.80 |
| ❑ 124 Howie Menard | 4.00 | 1.80 |
| ❑ 125 Gerry Meehan | 5.00 | 2.20 |
| ❑ 126 Skip Krake | 4.00 | 1.80 |
| ❑ 127 Phil Goyette | 5.00 | 2.20 |
| ❑ 128 Reg Fleming | 4.00 | 1.80 |
| ❑ 129 Don Marshall | 5.00 | 2.20 |
| ❑ 130 Bill Inglis | 4.00 | 1.80 |
| ❑ 131 Gilbert Perreault | 80.00 | 36.00 |
| ❑ 132 Checklist 2 | 125.00 | 31.00 |
| ❑ 133 Ed Johnston | 5.00 | 2.20 |
| ❑ 134 Ted Green | 5.00 | 2.20 |
| ❑ 135 Rick Smith | 4.00 | 1.80 |
| ❑ 136 Derek Sanderson | 15.00 | 6.75 |
| ❑ 137 Dallas Smith | 4.00 | 1.80 |
| ❑ 138 Don Marcotte | 5.00 | 2.20 |
| ❑ 139 Ed Westfall | 5.00 | 2.20 |
| ❑ 140 Floyd Smith | 4.00 | 1.80 |
| ❑ 141 Randy Wyrozub | 4.00 | 1.80 |
| ❑ 142 Cliff Schmautz | 4.00 | 1.80 |
| ❑ 143 Mike McMahon | 4.00 | 1.80 |
| ❑ 144 Jim Watson | 4.00 | 1.80 |
| ❑ 145 Roger Crozier | 5.00 | 2.20 |
| ❑ 146 Tracy Pratt | 4.00 | 1.80 |
| ❑ 147 Cliff Koroll | 5.00 | 2.20 |
| ❑ 148 Gerry Pinder | 5.00 | 2.20 |
| ❑ 149 Chico Maki | 4.00 | 1.80 |
| ❑ 150 Doug Jarrett | 4.00 | 1.80 |
| ❑ 151 Keith Magnuson | 10.00 | 4.50 |
| ❑ 152 Gerry Desjardins | 5.00 | 2.20 |
| ❑ 153 Tony Esposito | 50.00 | 22.00 |
| ❑ 154 Gary Bergman | 4.00 | 1.80 |
| ❑ 155 Tom Webster | 5.00 | 2.20 |
| ❑ 156 Dale Rolfe | 4.00 | 1.80 |
| ❑ 157 Alex Delvecchio | 7.00 | 3.10 |
| ❑ 158 Nick Libett | 4.00 | 1.80 |
| ❑ 159 Wayne Connelly | 4.00 | 1.80 |
| ❑ 160 Mike Byers | 4.00 | 1.80 |
| ❑ 161 Bill Flett | 4.00 | 1.80 |
| ❑ 162 Larry Mickey | 4.00 | 1.80 |
| ❑ 163 Noel Price | 4.00 | 1.80 |
| ❑ 164 Larry Cahan | 4.00 | 1.80 |
| ❑ 165 Jack Norris | 5.00 | 2.20 |
| ❑ 166 Ted Harris | 4.00 | 1.80 |
| ❑ 167 Murray Oliver | 4.00 | 1.80 |
| ❑ 168 Jean-Paul Parise | 5.00 | 2.20 |
| ❑ 169 Tom Williams | 4.00 | 1.80 |
| ❑ 170 Bobby Rousseau | 4.00 | 1.80 |
| ❑ 171 Judo Drouin | 5.00 | 2.20 |
| ❑ 172 Walt McKechnie | 5.00 | 2.20 |
| ❑ 173 Cesare Maniago | 5.00 | 2.20 |
| ❑ 174 Rejean Houle | 8.00 | 3.60 |
| ❑ 175A Mickey Redmond (No mention of trade) | 7.00 | 3.10 |
| ❑ 175B Mickey Redmond (Trade noted) | 15.00 | 6.75 |
| ❑ 176 Henri Richard | 10.00 | 4.50 |
| ❑ 177 Guy Lapointe | 20.00 | 9.00 |
| ❑ 178 J.C. Tremblay | 5.00 | 2.20 |
| ❑ 179 Marc Tardif | 8.00 | 3.60 |
| ❑ 180 Walt Tkaczuk | 5.00 | 2.20 |
| ❑ 181 Jean Ratelle | 6.00 | 2.70 |
| ❑ 182 Pete Stemkowski | 4.00 | 1.80 |
| ❑ 183 Gilles Villemure | 5.00 | 2.20 |
| ❑ 184 Rod Seiling | 4.00 | 1.80 |
| ❑ 185 Jim Neilson | 4.00 | 1.80 |
| ❑ 186 Dennis Hextall | 5.00 | 2.20 |
| ❑ 187 Gerry Ehman | 4.00 | 1.80 |
| ❑ 188 Bert Marshall | 4.00 | 1.80 |
| ❑ 189 Gary Croteau | 4.00 | 1.80 |
| ❑ 190 Ted Hampson | 4.00 | 1.80 |
| ❑ 191 Earl Ingarfield | 4.00 | 1.80 |
| ❑ 192 Dick Mattiussi | 4.00 | 1.80 |
| ❑ 193 Earl Heiskala | 4.00 | 1.80 |
| ❑ 194 Simon Nolet | 4.00 | 1.80 |
| ❑ 195 Bobby Clarke | 150.00 | 70.00 |
| ❑ 196 Garry Peters | 4.00 | 1.80 |
| ❑ 197 Lew Morrison | 4.00 | 1.80 |
| ❑ 198 Wayne Hillman | 4.00 | 1.80 |
| ❑ 199 Doug Favell | 6.00 | 2.70 |
| ❑ 200 Les Binkley | 5.00 | 2.20 |
| ❑ 201 Dean Prentice | 4.00 | 1.80 |
| ❑ 202 Jean Pronovost | 5.00 | 2.20 |
| ❑ 203 Wally Boyer | 4.00 | 1.80 |
| ❑ 204 Bryan Watson | 4.00 | 1.80 |
| ❑ 205 Glen Sather | 5.00 | 2.20 |
| ❑ 206 Lowell MacDonald | 4.00 | 1.80 |
| ❑ 207 Andy Bathgate | 5.00 | 2.20 |
| ❑ 208 Val Fonteyne | 4.00 | 1.80 |
| ❑ 209 Jim Lorentz | 4.00 | 1.80 |
| ❑ 210 Glenn Hall | 10.00 | 4.50 |
| ❑ 211 Bob Plager | 5.00 | 2.20 |
| ❑ 212 Noel Picard | 4.00 | 1.80 |
| ❑ 213 Jim Roberts | 5.00 | 2.20 |
| ❑ 214 Frank St.Marseille | 4.00 | 1.80 |
| ❑ 215 Ab McDonald | 4.00 | 1.80 |
| ❑ 216 Brian Glennie | 4.00 | 1.80 |
| ❑ 217 Paul Henderson | 5.00 | 2.20 |
| ❑ 218 Darryl Sittler | 100.00 | 45.00 |
| ❑ 219 Dave Keon | 6.00 | 2.70 |
| ❑ 220 Jim Harrison | 4.00 | 1.80 |
| ❑ 221 Ron Ellis | 5.00 | 2.20 |
| ❑ 222 Jacques Plante | 25.00 | 11.00 |
| ❑ 223 Bob Baun | 5.00 | 2.20 |
| ❑ 224 George Gardner | 4.00 | 1.80 |
| ❑ 225 Dale Tallon | 5.00 | 2.20 |
| ❑ 226 Rosaire Paiement | 4.00 | 1.80 |
| ❑ 227 Mike Corrigan | 4.00 | 1.80 |
| ❑ 228 Ray Cullen | 4.00 | 1.80 |
| ❑ 229 Charlie Hodge | 5.00 | 2.20 |
| ❑ 230 Len Lunde | 4.00 | 1.80 |
| ❑ 231 Terry Sawchuk Memorial | 60.00 | 27.00 |
| ❑ 232 Boston Bruins Team Stanley Cup Champs | 12.00 | 5.50 |
| ❑ 233 Esposito line: Cashman/Hodge | 20.00 | 9.00 |
| ❑ 234 Tony Esposito AS1 | 25.00 | 11.00 |
| ❑ 235 Bobby Hull AS1 | 25.00 | 11.00 |
| ❑ 236 Bobby Orr AS1 | 50.00 | 22.00 |
| ❑ 237 Phil Esposito AS1 | 15.00 | 6.75 |
| ❑ 238 Gordie Howe AS1 | 40.00 | 18.00 |
| ❑ 239 Brad Park AS1 | 15.00 | 6.75 |
| ❑ 240 Stan Mikita AS2 | 10.00 | 4.50 |
| ❑ 241 John McKenzie AS2 | 5.00 | 2.20 |
| ❑ 242 Frank Mahovlich AS2 | 6.00 | 2.70 |
| ❑ 243 Carl Brewer AS2 | 4.00 | 1.80 |
| ❑ 244 Ed Giacomin AS2 | 7.00 | 3.10 |
| ❑ 245 Jacques Laperriere AS2 | 4.00 | 1.80 |
| ❑ 246 Bobby Orr Hart Trophy | 50.00 | 22.00 |
| ❑ 247 Tony Esposito Calder Trophy | 25.00 | 11.00 |
| ❑ 248A Bobby Orr Norris Trophy (No mention of Howe as NHL all-time leading scorer) | 50.00 | 22.00 |
| ❑ 248B Bobby Orr Norris Trophy (Mentions Howe as NHL all-time leading scorer) | 50.00 | 22.00 |
| ❑ 249 Bobby Orr Art Ross Trophy | 50.00 | 22.00 |
| ❑ 250 Tony Esposito Vezina Trophy | 25.00 | 11.00 |
| ❑ 251 Phil Goyette Lady Byng Trophy | 4.00 | 1.80 |
| ❑ 252 Bobby Orr Conn Smythe | 50.00 | 22.00 |
| ❑ 253 Pit Martin Bill Masterton Trophy | 4.00 | 1.80 |
| ❑ 254 The Stanley Cup | 15.00 | 6.75 |
| ❑ 255 Prince of Wales Trophy | 5.00 | 2.20 |
| ❑ 256 Conn Smythe Trophy | 5.00 | 2.20 |
| ❑ 257 James Norris Trophy | 5.00 | 2.20 |
| ❑ 258 Calder Trophy | 5.00 | 2.20 |
| ❑ 259 Vezina Trophy | 5.00 | 2.20 |
| ❑ 260 Lady Byng Trophy | 5.00 | 2.20 |
| ❑ 261 Hart Trophy | 5.00 | 2.20 |
| ❑ 262 Art Ross Trophy | 5.00 | 2.20 |
| ❑ 263 Clarence S. Campbell Bowl | 5.00 | 2.20 |
| ❑ 264 John Ferguson | 10.00 | 2.50 |

## 1970-71 O-Pee-Chee Deckle

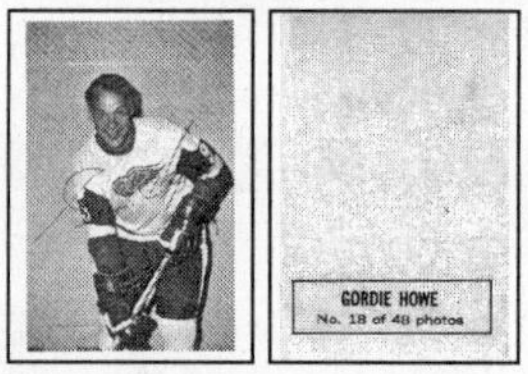


This set consists of 48 numbered black and white deckle edge cards measuring approximately 2 1/8" by 3 1/8". The set was issued as an insert with the second series regular issue of the same year. The cards are numbered on the backs. The set was printed in Canada.

| | NRMT-MT | EXC |
|---|---|---|
| COMPLETE SET (48) | 400.00 | 180.00 |
| COMMON CARD (1-48) | 3.00 | 1.35 |
| ❑ 1 Pat Quinn | 4.00 | 1.80 |
| ❑ 2 Eddie Shack | 6.00 | 2.70 |
| ❑ 3 Eddie Joyal | 3.00 | 1.35 |
| ❑ 4 Bobby Orr | 80.00 | 36.00 |
| ❑ 5 Derek Sanderson | 12.00 | 5.50 |
| ❑ 6 Phil Esposito | 15.00 | 6.75 |
| ❑ 7 Fred Stanfield | 3.00 | 1.35 |
| ❑ 8 Bob Woytowich | 3.00 | 1.35 |
| ❑ 9 Ron Schock | 3.00 | 1.35 |
| ❑ 10 Les Binkley | 4.00 | 1.80 |
| ❑ 11 Roger Crozier | 5.00 | 2.20 |
| ❑ 12 Reg Fleming | 3.00 | 1.35 |
| ❑ 13 Charlie Burns | 3.00 | 1.35 |
| ❑ 14 Bobby Rousseau | 3.00 | 1.35 |
| ❑ 15 Leo Boivin | 4.00 | 1.80 |
| ❑ 16 Garry Unger | 4.00 | 1.80 |
| ❑ 17 Frank Mahovlich | 12.00 | 5.50 |
| ❑ 18 Gordie Howe | 60.00 | 27.00 |
| ❑ 19 Jacques Lemaire | 6.00 | 2.70 |
| ❑ 20 Jacques Laperriere | 4.00 | 1.80 |
| ❑ 21 Jean Beliveau | 20.00 | 9.00 |
| ❑ 22 Rogatien Vachon | 6.00 | 2.70 |
| ❑ 23 Yvan Cournoyer | 5.00 | 2.20 |
| ❑ 24 Henri Richard | 12.00 | 5.50 |
| ❑ 25 Red Berenson | 4.00 | 1.80 |
| ❑ 26 Frank St.Marseille | 3.00 | 1.35 |
| ❑ 27 Glenn Hall | 10.00 | 4.50 |
| ❑ 28 Gary Sabourin | 3.00 | 1.35 |
| ❑ 29 Doug Mohns | 3.00 | 1.35 |
| ❑ 30 Bobby Hull | 40.00 | 18.00 |
| ❑ 31 Ray Cullen | 3.00 | 1.35 |
| ❑ 32 Tony Esposito | 20.00 | 9.00 |
| ❑ 33 Gary Dornhoefer | 4.00 | 1.80 |
| ❑ 34 Ed Van Impe | 3.00 | 1.35 |
| ❑ 35 Doug Favell | 4.00 | 1.80 |
| ❑ 36 Carol Vadnais | 3.00 | 1.35 |
| ❑ 37 Harry Howell | 4.00 | 1.80 |
| ❑ 38 Bill Hicke | 3.00 | 1.35 |
| ❑ 39 Rod Gilbert | 6.00 | 2.70 |
| ❑ 40 Jean Ratelle | 6.00 | 2.70 |
| ❑ 41 Walt Tkaczuk | 3.00 | 1.35 |
| ❑ 42 Ed Giacomin | 6.00 | 2.70 |
| ❑ 43 Brad Park | 10.00 | 4.50 |
| ❑ 44 Bruce Gamble | 4.00 | 1.80 |
| ❑ 45 Orland Kurtenbach | 4.00 | 1.80 |
| ❑ 46 Ron Ellis | 4.00 | 1.80 |
| ❑ 47 Dave Keon | 6.00 | 2.70 |
| ❑ 48 Norm Ullman | 5.00 | 2.20 |

## 1971-72 O-Pee-Chee

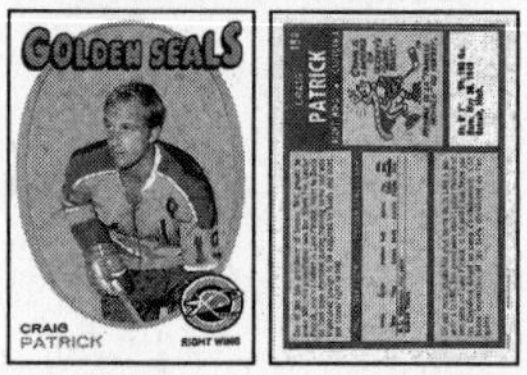


The 1971-72 O-Pee-Chee set contains 264 standard-size cards. The unopened wax packs consisted of eight cards plus a piece of bubble gum. Player photos are framed in an oval. Bilingual backs feature a short biography, year-by-year statistics and a cartoon-illustrated fact about the player. Rookie Cards in this set include Marcel Dionne, Ken Dryden, Butch Goring, Guy Lafleur, Reggie Leach, Richard Martin, and Rick MacLeish.

| | NRMT-MT | EXC |
|---|---|---|
| COMPLETE SET (264) | 1700.00 | 750.00 |
| COMMON CARD (1-132) | 3.00 | 1.35 |
| COMMON CARD (133-264) | 3.50 | 1.55 |
| ❑ 1 Paul Popiel | 7.00 | 1.75 |
| ❑ 2 Pierre Bouchard | 4.00 | 1.80 |
| ❑ 3 Don Awrey | 3.00 | 1.35 |
| ❑ 4 Paul Curtis | 3.00 | 1.35 |
| ❑ 5 Guy Trottier | 3.00 | 1.35 |
| ❑ 6 Paul Shmyr | 3.00 | 1.35 |
| ❑ 7 Fred Stanfield | 3.00 | 1.35 |
| ❑ 8 Mike Robitaille | 3.00 | 1.35 |
| ❑ 9 Vic Hadfield | 4.00 | 1.80 |
| ❑ 10 Jim Harrison | 3.00 | 1.35 |
| ❑ 11 Bill White | 3.00 | 1.35 |
| ❑ 12 Andre Boudrias | 3.00 | 1.35 |
| ❑ 13 Gary Sabourin | 3.00 | 1.35 |
| ❑ 14 Arnie Brown | 3.00 | 1.35 |
| ❑ 15 Yvan Cournoyer | 7.00 | 3.10 |
| ❑ 16 Bryan Hextall | 4.00 | 1.80 |
| ❑ 17 Gary Croteau | 3.00 | 1.35 |
| ❑ 18 Gilles Villemure | 4.00 | 1.80 |
| ❑ 19 Serge Bernier | 4.00 | 1.80 |
| ❑ 20 Phil Esposito | 20.00 | 9.00 |
| ❑ 21 Tom Reid | 3.00 | 1.35 |
| ❑ 22 Doug Barrie | 3.00 | 1.35 |
| ❑ 23 Eddie Joyal | 3.00 | 1.35 |
| ❑ 24 Dunc Wilson | 5.00 | 2.20 |
| ❑ 25 Pat Stapleton | 4.00 | 1.80 |
| ❑ 26 Garry Unger | 4.00 | 1.80 |
| ❑ 27 Al Smith | 4.00 | 1.80 |
| ❑ 28 Bob Woytowich | 3.00 | 1.35 |
| ❑ 29 Marc Tardif | 4.00 | 1.80 |
| ❑ 30 Norm Ullman | 6.00 | 2.70 |
| ❑ 31 Tom Williams | 3.00 | 1.35 |
| ❑ 32 Ted Harris | 3.00 | 1.35 |
| ❑ 33 Andre Lacroix | 4.00 | 1.80 |
| ❑ 34 Mike Byers | 3.00 | 1.35 |
| ❑ 35 Johnny Bucyk | 5.00 | 2.20 |
| ❑ 36 Roger Crozier | 4.00 | 1.80 |
| ❑ 37 Alex Delvecchio | 6.00 | 2.70 |
| ❑ 38 Frank St.Marseille | 3.00 | 1.35 |
| ❑ 39 Pit Martin | 4.00 | 1.80 |
| ❑ 40 Brad Park | 15.00 | 6.75 |
| ❑ 41 Greg Polis | 3.00 | 1.35 |
| ❑ 42 Orland Kurtenbach | 3.00 | 1.35 |
| ❑ 43 Jim McKenny | 3.00 | 1.35 |
| ❑ 44 Bob Nevin | 3.00 | 1.35 |
| ❑ 45 Ken Dryden | 350.00 | 160.00 |
| ❑ 46 Carol Vadnais | 4.00 | 1.80 |
| ❑ 47 Bill Flett | 3.00 | 1.35 |
| ❑ 48 Jim Johnson | 3.00 | 1.35 |
| ❑ 49 Al Hamilton | 3.00 | 1.35 |
| ❑ 50 Bobby Hull | 40.00 | 18.00 |
| ❑ 51 Chris Bordeleau | 3.00 | 1.35 |
| ❑ 52 Tim Ecclestone | 3.00 | 1.35 |
| ❑ 53 Rod Seiling | 3.00 | 1.35 |
| ❑ 54 Gerry Cheevers | 10.00 | 4.50 |
| ❑ 55 Bill Goldsworthy | 4.00 | 1.80 |
| ❑ 56 Ron Schock | 3.00 | 1.35 |
| ❑ 57 Jim Dorey | 3.00 | 1.35 |
| ❑ 58 Wayne Maki | 3.00 | 1.35 |
| ❑ 59 Terry Harper | 3.00 | 1.35 |
| ❑ 60 Gilbert Perreault | 25.00 | 11.00 |
| ❑ 61 Ernie Hicke | 3.00 | 1.35 |
| ❑ 62 Wayne Hillman | 3.00 | 1.35 |
| ❑ 63 Denis DeJordy | 4.00 | 1.80 |
| ❑ 64 Ken Schinkel | 3.00 | 1.35 |
| ❑ 65 Derek Sanderson | 12.00 | 5.50 |
| ❑ 66 Barclay Plager | 4.00 | 1.80 |
| ❑ 67 Paul Henderson | 4.00 | 1.80 |
| ❑ 68 Jude Drouin | 3.00 | 1.35 |
| ❑ 69 Keith Magnuson | 4.00 | 1.80 |
| ❑ 70 Ron Harris | 3.00 | 1.35 |
| ❑ 71 Jacques Lemaire | 6.00 | 2.70 |
| ❑ 72 Doug Favell | 4.00 | 1.80 |
| ❑ 73 Bert Marshall | 3.00 | 1.35 |
| ❑ 74 Ted Irvine | 3.00 | 1.35 |
| ❑ 75 Walt Tkaczuk | 4.00 | 1.80 |
| ❑ 76 Bob Berry | 5.00 | 2.20 |
| ❑ 77 Syl Apps | 5.00 | 2.20 |
| ❑ 78 Tom Webster | 4.00 | 1.80 |
| ❑ 79 Danny Grant | 4.00 | 1.80 |
| ❑ 80 Dave Keon | 5.00 | 2.20 |
| ❑ 81 Ernie Wakely | 4.00 | 1.80 |
| ❑ 82 John McKenzie | 4.00 | 1.80 |
| ❑ 83 Ron Stackhouse | 3.00 | 1.35 |
| ❑ 84 Peter Mahovlich | 4.00 | 1.80 |
| ❑ 85 Dennis Hull | 4.00 | 1.80 |
| ❑ 86 Juha Widing | 3.00 | 1.35 |
| ❑ 87 Gary Doak | 3.00 | 1.35 |
| ❑ 88 Phil Goyette | 3.00 | 1.35 |
| ❑ 89 Lew Morrison | 3.00 | 1.35 |
| ❑ 90 Ab DeMarco | 3.00 | 1.35 |
| ❑ 91 Red Berenson | 4.00 | 1.80 |
| ❑ 92 Mike Pelyk | 3.00 | 1.35 |
| ❑ 93 Gary Jarrett | 3.00 | 1.35 |
| ❑ 94 Bob Pulford | 4.00 | 1.80 |
| ❑ 95 Dan Johnson | 3.00 | 1.35 |
| ❑ 96 Eddie Shack | 8.00 | 3.60 |
| ❑ 97 Jean Ratelle | 5.00 | 2.20 |
| ❑ 98 Jim Pappin | 3.00 | 1.35 |
| ❑ 99 Roy Edwards | 4.00 | 1.80 |
| ❑ 100 Bobby Orr | 100.00 | 45.00 |
| ❑ 101 Ted Hampson | 3.00 | 1.35 |
| ❑ 102 Mickey Redmond | 5.00 | 2.20 |
| ❑ 103 Bob Plager | 4.00 | 1.80 |
| ❑ 104 Barry Ashbee | 4.00 | 1.80 |
| ❑ 105 Frank Mahovlich | 8.00 | 3.60 |
| ❑ 106 Dick Redmond | 3.00 | 1.35 |
| ❑ 107 Tracy Pratt | 3.00 | 1.35 |
| ❑ 108 Ralph Backstrom | 4.00 | 1.80 |
| ❑ 109 Murray Hall | 3.00 | 1.35 |
| ❑ 110 Tony Esposito | 35.00 | 16.00 |
| ❑ 111 Checklist Card | 500.00 | 125.00 |
| ❑ 112 Jim Neilson | 3.00 | 1.35 |
| ❑ 113 Ron Ellis | 4.00 | 1.80 |
| ❑ 114 Bobby Clarke | 60.00 | 27.00 |
| ❑ 115 Ken Hodge | 4.00 | 1.80 |
| ❑ 116 Jim Roberts | 4.00 | 1.80 |
| ❑ 117 Cesare Maniago | 4.00 | 1.80 |
| ❑ 118 Jean Pronovost | 4.00 | 1.80 |
| ❑ 119 Gary Bergman | 3.00 | 1.35 |
| ❑ 120 Henri Richard | 8.00 | 3.60 |
| ❑ 121 Ross Lonsberry | 3.00 | 1.35 |
| ❑ 122 Pat Quinn | 4.00 | 1.80 |
| ❑ 123 Rod Gilbert | 6.00 | 2.70 |
| ❑ 124 Walt McKechnie | 4.00 | 1.80 |
| ❑ 125 Stan Mikita | 15.00 | 6.75 |
| ❑ 126 Ed Van Impe | 3.00 | 1.35 |
| ❑ 127 Terry Crisp | 10.00 | 4.50 |
| ❑ 128 Fred Barrett | 3.00 | 1.35 |
| ❑ 129 Wayne Cashman | 5.00 | 2.20 |
| ❑ 130 J.C. Tremblay | 4.00 | 1.80 |
| ❑ 131 Bernie Parent | 20.00 | 9.00 |
| ❑ 132 Bryan Watson | 4.00 | 1.80 |
| ❑ 133 Marcel Dionne | 200.00 | 90.00 |
| ❑ 134 Ab McDonald | 3.50 | 1.55 |
| ❑ 135 Leon Rochefort | 3.50 | 1.55 |
| ❑ 136 Serge Lajeunesse | 3.50 | 1.55 |
| ❑ 137 Joe Daley | 5.00 | 2.20 |
| ❑ 138 Brian Conacher | 3.50 | 1.55 |
| ❑ 139 Bill Collins | 3.50 | 1.55 |
| ❑ 140 Nick Libett | 3.50 | 1.55 |
| ❑ 141 Bill Sutherland | 3.50 | 1.55 |
| ❑ 142 Bill Hicke | 3.50 | 1.55 |
| ❑ 143 Serge Savard | 5.00 | 2.20 |
| ❑ 144 Jacques Laperriere | 5.00 | 2.20 |
| ❑ 145 Guy Lapointe | 6.00 | 2.70 |
| ❑ 146 Claude Larose UER (Misspelled La Rose on both sides) | 3.50 | 1.55 |
| ❑ 147 Rejean Houle | 5.00 | 2.20 |
| ❑ 148 Guy Lafleur UER (Misspelled La Fleur on both sides) | 200.00 | 90.00 |
| ❑ 149 Dale Hoganson | 3.50 | 1.55 |
| ❑ 150 Al McDonough | 3.50 | 1.55 |
| ❑ 151 Gilles Marotte | 3.50 | 1.55 |
| ❑ 152 Butch Goring | 10.00 | 4.50 |
| ❑ 153 Harry Howell | 5.00 | 2.20 |
| ❑ 154 Real Lemieux | 3.50 | 1.55 |
| ❑ 155 Gary Edwards | 5.00 | 2.20 |
| ❑ 156 Rogatien Vachon | 10.00 | 4.50 |
| ❑ 157 Mike Corrigan | 3.50 | 1.55 |
| ❑ 158 Floyd Smith | 3.50 | 1.55 |
| ❑ 159 Dave Dryden | 5.00 | 2.20 |
| ❑ 160 Gerry Meehan | 5.00 | 2.20 |
| ❑ 161 Richard Martin | 15.00 | 6.75 |
| ❑ 162 Steve Atkinson | 3.50 | 1.55 |
| ❑ 163 Ron Anderson | 3.50 | 1.55 |
| ❑ 164 Dick Duff | 5.00 | 2.20 |
| ❑ 165 Jim Watson | 3.50 | 1.55 |
| ❑ 166 Don Luce | 4.00 | 1.80 |
| ❑ 167 Larry Mickey | 3.50 | 1.55 |
| ❑ 168 Larry Hillman | 3.50 | 1.55 |
| ❑ 169 Ed Westfall | 5.00 | 2.20 |
| ❑ 170 Dallas Smith | 3.50 | 1.55 |
| ❑ 171 Mike Walton | 3.50 | 1.55 |
| ❑ 172 Ed Johnston | 5.00 | 2.20 |
| ❑ 173 Ted Green | 5.00 | 2.20 |
| ❑ 174 Rick Smith | 3.50 | 1.55 |
| ❑ 175 Reggie Leach | 15.00 | 6.75 |
| ❑ 176 Don Marcotte | 3.50 | 1.55 |
| ❑ 177 Bobby Sheehan | 3.50 | 1.55 |
| ❑ 178 Wayne Carleton | 3.50 | 1.55 |
| ❑ 179 Norm Ferguson | 3.50 | 1.55 |
| ❑ 180 Don O'Donoghue | 3.50 | 1.55 |
| ❑ 181 Gary Kurt | 5.00 | 2.20 |

❑ 182 Joey Johnston 3.50 1.55
❑ 183 Stan Gilbertson 3.50 1.55
❑ 184 Craig Patrick 10.00 4.50
❑ 185 Gerry Pinder 3.50 1.55
❑ 186 Tim Horton 12.00 5.50
❑ 187 Darryl Edestrand 3.50 1.55
❑ 188 Keith McCreary 3.50 1.55
❑ 189 Val Fonteyne 3.50 1.55
❑ 190 Sheldon Kannegiesser 3.50 1.55
❑ 191 Nick Harbaruk 3.50 1.55
❑ 192 Les Binkley 5.00 2.20
❑ 193 Darryl Sittler 40.00 18.00
❑ 194 Rick Ley 3.50 1.55
❑ 195 Jacques Plante 25.00 11.00
❑ 196 Bob Baun 5.00 2.20
❑ 197 Brian Glennie 3.50 1.55
❑ 198 Brian Spencer 8.00 3.60
❑ 199 Don Marshall 5.00 2.20
❑ 200 Denis Dupere 3.50 1.55
❑ 201 Bruce Gamble 5.00 2.20
❑ 202 Gary Dornhoefer 3.50 1.55
❑ 203 Bob Kelly 6.00 2.70
❑ 204 Jean-Guy Gendron 3.50 1.55
❑ 205 Brent Hughes 3.50 1.55
❑ 206 Simon Nolet 3.50 1.55
❑ 207 Rick MacLeish 15.00 6.75
❑ 208 Doug Jarrett 3.50 1.55
❑ 209 Cliff Koroll 3.50 1.55
❑ 210 Chico Maki 3.50 1.55
❑ 211 Danny O'Shea 3.50 1.55
❑ 212 Lou Angotti 3.50 1.55
❑ 213 Eric Nesterenko 5.00 2.20
❑ 214 Bryan Campbell 3.50 1.55
❑ 215 Bill Fairbairn 3.50 1.55
❑ 216 Bruce MacGregor 3.50 1.55
❑ 217 Pete Stemkowski 3.50 1.55
❑ 218 Bobby Rousseau 3.50 1.55
❑ 219 Dale Rolfe 3.50 1.55
❑ 220 Ed Giacomin 10.00 4.50
❑ 221 Glen Sather 5.00 2.20
❑ 222 Carl Brewer 5.00 2.20
❑ 223 George Morrison 3.50 1.55
❑ 224 Noel Picard 3.50 1.55
❑ 225 Peter McDuffe 5.00 2.20
❑ 226 Brit Selby 3.50 1.55
❑ 227 Jim Lorentz 3.50 1.55
❑ 228 Phil Roberto 3.50 1.55
❑ 229 Dave Balon 3.50 1.55
❑ 230 Barry Wilkins 3.50 1.55
❑ 231 Dennis Kearns 3.50 1.55
❑ 232 Jocelyn Guevremont 5.00 2.20
❑ 233 Rosaire Paiement 3.50 1.55
❑ 234 Dale Tallon 3.50 1.55
❑ 235 George Gardner 3.50 1.55
❑ 236 Ron Stewart 3.50 1.55
❑ 237 Wayne Connelly 3.50 1.55
❑ 238 Charlie Burns 3.50 1.55
❑ 239 Murray Oliver 3.50 1.55
❑ 240 Lou Nanne 5.00 2.20
❑ 241 Gump Worsley 8.00 3.60
❑ 242 Doug Mohns 3.50 1.55
❑ 243 Jean-Paul Parise 3.50 1.55
❑ 244 Dennis Hextall 5.00 2.20
❑ 245 Bobby Orr 50.00 22.00
Hart Trophy
Norris Trophy
❑ 246 Gilbert Perreault 15.00 6.75
Calder Trophy
❑ 247 Phil Esposito 10.00 4.50
Ross Trophy
❑ 248 Ed Giacomin and 6.00 2.70
Gilles Villemure
Vezina Trophy
❑ 249 Johnny Bucyk 4.00 1.80
Lady Byng Trophy
❑ 250 Ed Giacomin AS1 5.00 2.20
❑ 251 Bobby Orr AS1 50.00 22.00
❑ 252 J.C. Tremblay AS1 4.00 1.80
❑ 253 Phil Esposito AS1 UER 12.00 5.50
(Back reads Phil., shouldn't be a period after Phil)
❑ 254 Ken Hodge AS1 4.00 1.80
❑ 255 Johnny Bucyk AS1 4.00 1.80
❑ 256 Jacques Plante AS2 UER 15.00 6.75
(63 shutouts, should be 77 shutouts)
❑ 257 Brad Park AS2 7.00 3.10
❑ 258 Pat Stapleton AS2 4.00 1.80
❑ 259 Dave Keon AS2 4.00 1.80
❑ 260 Yvan Cournoyer AS2 4.00 1.80
❑ 261 Bobby Hull AS2 25.00 11.00
❑ 262 Gordie Howe 100.00 45.00
(Retirement Special)
❑ 263 Jean Beliveau 80.00 36.00
(Retirement Special)
❑ 264 Checklist Card 150.00 38.00

## 1971-72 O-Pee-Chee/Topps Booklets

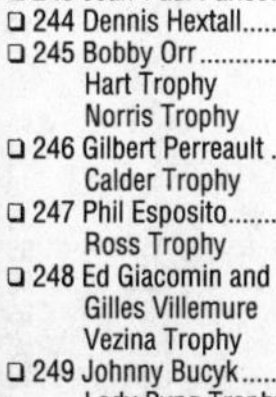

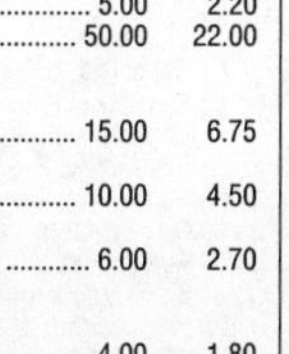


This set consists of 24 colorful comic booklets (eight pages in format) each measuring 2 1/2" by 3 1/2". The booklets were included as an insert with the regular issue of the same year and give a mini-biography of the player. These booklets were also put out by Topps and were printed in the United States. They can be found in either French or English language versions. The booklets are numbered on the fronts with a complete set checklist on the backs. The prices below are valid as well for the 1971-72 Topps version of these booklets although the English version is probably a little easier to find.

| | NRMT-MT | EXC |
|---|---|---|
| COMPLETE SET (24) | 100.00 | 45.00 |
| COMMON CARD (1-24) | 1.00 | .45 |

❑ 1 Bobby Hull 15.00 6.75
❑ 2 Phil Esposito 8.00 3.60
❑ 3 Dale Tallon 1.00 .45
❑ 4 Jacques Plante 8.00 3.60
❑ 5 Roger Crozier 2.00 .90
❑ 6 Henri Richard 3.00 1.35
❑ 7 Ed Giacomin 4.00 1.80
❑ 8 Gilbert Perreault 4.00 1.80
❑ 9 Greg Polis 1.00 .45
❑ 10 Bobby Clarke 10.00 4.50
❑ 11 Danny Grant 1.00 .45
❑ 12 Alex Delvecchio 2.00 .90
❑ 13 Tony Esposito 5.00 2.20
❑ 14 Garry Unger 1.50 .70
❑ 15 Frank St.Marseille 1.00 .45
❑ 16 Dave Keon 3.00 1.35
❑ 17 Ken Dryden 20.00 9.00
❑ 18 Rod Gilbert 2.00 .90
❑ 19 Juha Widing 1.00 .45
❑ 20 Orland Kurtenbach 1.00 .45
❑ 21 Jude Drouin 1.00 .45
❑ 22 Gary Smith 2.00 .90
❑ 23 Gordie Howe 20.00 9.00
❑ 24 Bobby Orr 20.00 9.00

## 1971-72 O-Pee-Chee Posters

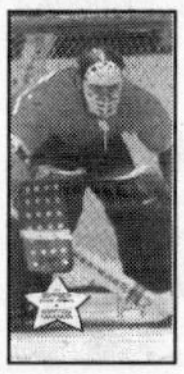

The 1971-72 O-Pee-Chee Posters set contains 24 color pictures measuring approximately 10" by 18". They were originally issued (as a separate issue) in folded form, two to a wax pack. Attached pairs are still sometimes found; these pairs are valued at 25 percent greater than the sum of the individual players included in the pair. The current scarcity of these posters suggests that they may have been a test issue. These posters are numbered and blank backed.

| | EX-MT | VG-EX |
|---|---|---|
| COMPLETE SET (24) | 1000.00 | 450.00 |
| COMMON CARD (1-24) | 12.00 | 5.50 |

❑ 1 Bobby Orr 225.00 100.00
❑ 2 Bob Pulford 30.00 13.50
❑ 3 Dave Keon 30.00 13.50
❑ 4 Yvan Cournoyer 30.00 13.50
❑ 5 Dale Tallon 12.00 5.50
❑ 6 Richard Martin 15.00 6.75
❑ 7 Rod Gilbert 30.00 13.50
❑ 8 Tony Esposito 50.00 22.00
❑ 9 Bobby Hull 80.00 36.00
❑ 10 Red Berenson 15.00 6.75
❑ 11 Norm Ullman 30.00 13.50
❑ 12 Orland Kurtenbach 12.00 5.50
❑ 13 Guy Lafleur 100.00 45.00
❑ 14 Gilbert Perreault 40.00 18.00
❑ 15 Jacques Plante 50.00 22.00
❑ 16 Bruce Gamble 20.00 9.00
❑ 17 Walt McKechnie 12.00 5.50
❑ 18 Tim Horton 60.00 27.00
❑ 19 Jean Ratelle 30.00 13.50
❑ 20 Garry Unger 15.00 6.75
❑ 21 Phil Esposito 50.00 22.00
❑ 22 Ken Dryden 125.00 55.00
❑ 23 Gump Worsley 40.00 18.00
❑ 24 Montreal Canadiens 40.00 18.00
Team Photo

## 1972-73 O-Pee-Chee

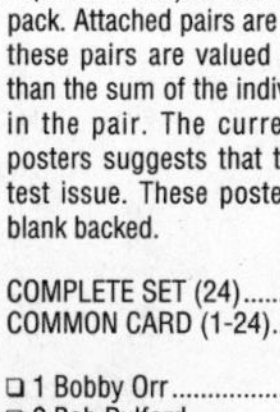

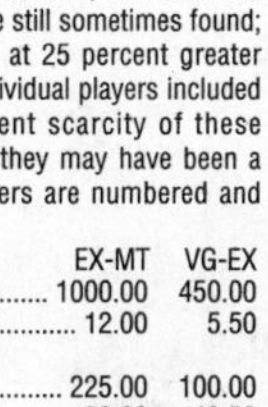

The 1972-73 O-Pee-Chee set features 340 standard-size cards that were printed in Canada. The set features players from the expansion New York Islanders and Atlanta Flames. Unopened packs consisted of eight cards plus a bubble-gum piece. Tan borders on the front include the team name on the left-hand side. Bilingual backs feature a year-by-year record of the player's career, a short biography and a cartoon-illustrated fact about the player. There are a number of In-Action (IA) cards of popular players distributed throughout the set. Card number 208 was never issued. The last series (290-341), which was printed in lesser quantities, features players from the newly formed World Hockey Association. There are apparently 22 double-printed cards in the first series (1-110), but the identity of these 22 is not known at this time except for card no.1 Johnny Bucyk, and no.102, Frank Mahovlich. There are also 22 known double-printed cards in the second series (111-209). These cards are identified by DP in the checklist below.

| | NRMT-MT | EXC |
|---|---|---|
| COMPLETE SET (340) | 1500.00 | 700.00 |
| COMMON CARD (1-110) | 2.00 | .90 |
| COMMON CARD (111-209) | 2.50 | 1.10 |
| COMMON CARD (210-289) | 4.00 | 1.80 |
| COMMON CARD (290-341) | 8.00 | 3.60 |

❑ 1 Johnny Bucyk DP 7.00 1.75
❑ 2 Rene Robert 5.00 2.20
❑ 3 Gary Croteau 2.00 .90
❑ 4 Pat Stapleton 2.50 1.10
❑ 5 Ron Harris 2.00 .90
❑ 6 Checklist 1 45.00 11.00
❑ 7 Playoff Game 1 1.50 .70
Bruins 6
Rangers 5
❑ 8 Marcel Dionne 25.00 11.00
❑ 9 Bob Berry 2.50 1.10
❑ 10 Lou Nanne 2.50 1.10
❑ 11 Marc Tardif 2.00 .90
❑ 12 Jean Ratelle 5.00 2.20
❑ 13 Craig Cameron 2.00 .90
❑ 14 Bobby Clarke 30.00 13.50
❑ 15 Jim Rutherford 10.00 4.50
❑ 16 Andre Dupont 4.00 1.80
❑ 17 Mike Pelyk 2.00 .90
❑ 18 Dunc Wilson 2.50 1.10
❑ 19 Checklist 2 45.00 20.00
(See also card 190; 160 is Bill Harris)
❑ 20 Playoff Game 2 1.50 .70
Bruins 2
Rangers 1
❑ 21 Dallas Smith 2.00 .90
❑ 22 Gerry Meehan 2.50 1.10
❑ 23 Rick Smith UER 2.00 .90
(Wrong total games, should be 262, not 265)
❑ 24 Pit Martin 2.50 1.10
❑ 25 Keith McCreary 2.00 .90
❑ 26 Alex Delvecchio 4.00 1.80
❑ 27 Gilles Marotte 2.00 .90
❑ 28 Gump Worsley 6.00 2.70
❑ 29 Yvan Cournoyer 5.00 2.20
❑ 30 Playoff Game 3 1.50 .70
Rangers 5
Bruins 2
❑ 31 Vic Hadfield 2.50 1.10
❑ 32 Tom Miller 2.00 .90
❑ 33 Ed Van Impe 2.00 .90
❑ 34 Greg Polis 2.00 .90
❑ 35 Barclay Plager 2.50 1.10
❑ 36 Ron Ellis 2.50 1.10
❑ 37 Jocelyn Guevremont 2.00 .90
❑ 38 Playoff Game 4 1.50 .70
Bruins 3
Rangers 2
❑ 39 Carol Vadnais 2.00 .90
❑ 40 Steve Atkinson 2.00 .90
❑ 41 Ivan Boldirev 3.50 1.55
❑ 42 Jim Pappin 2.00 .90
❑ 43 Phil Myre 8.00 3.60
❑ 44 Yvan Cournoyer IA 3.00 1.35
❑ 45 Nick Libett 2.00 .90
❑ 46 Juha Widing 2.00 .90
❑ 47 Jude Drouin 2.00 .90
❑ 48A Jean Ratelle IA ERR 5.00 2.20
(Defense on back)
❑ 48B Jean Ratelle IA COR 3.00 1.35
(Center on back)
❑ 49 Ken Hodge 2.50 1.10
❑ 50 Roger Crozier 2.50 1.10
❑ 51 Reggie Leach 4.00 1.80
❑ 52 Dennis Hull 2.50 1.10
❑ 53 Larry Hale 2.00 .90
❑ 54 Playoff Game 5 1.50 .70
Rangers 3
Bruins 2
❑ 55 Tim Ecclestone 2.00 .90
❑ 56 Butch Goring 4.00 1.80
❑ 57 Danny Grant 2.50 1.10
❑ 58 Bobby Orr IA 40.00 18.00
❑ 59 Guy Lafleur 50.00 22.00
❑ 60 Jim Neilson 2.00 .90
❑ 61 Brian Spencer 2.50 1.10
❑ 62 Joe Watson 2.00 .90
❑ 63 Playoff Game 6 1.50 .70
Bruins 3
Rangers 0
❑ 64 Jean Pronovost 2.50 1.10
❑ 65 Frank St.Marseille 2.00 .90
❑ 66 Bob Baun 2.50 1.10
❑ 67 Paul Popiel 2.00 .90
❑ 68 Wayne Cashman 2.50 1.10
❑ 69 Tracy Pratt 2.00 .90
❑ 70 Stan Gilbertson 2.00 .90
❑ 71 Keith Magnuson 2.50 1.10
❑ 72 Ernie Hicke 2.00 .90
❑ 73 Gary Doak 2.00 .90
❑ 74 Mike Corrigan 2.00 .90
❑ 75 Doug Mohns 2.00 .90
❑ 76 Phil Esposito IA 7.00 3.10
❑ 77 Jacques Lemaire 5.00 2.20
❑ 78 Pete Stemkowski 2.00 .90
❑ 79 Bill Mikkelson 2.00 .90
❑ 80 Rick Foley 2.00 .90
❑ 81 Ron Schock 2.00 .90
❑ 82 Phil Roberto 2.00 .90
❑ 83 Jim McKenny 2.00 .90
❑ 84 Wayne Maki 2.00 .90
❑ 85A Brad Park IA ERR 7.00 3.10
(Center on back)
❑ 85B Brad Park IA COR 5.00 2.20
(Defense on back)
❑ 86 Guy Lapointe 3.00 1.35
❑ 87 Bill Fairbairn 2.00 .90
❑ 88 Terry Crisp 2.50 1.10
❑ 89 Doug Favell 2.50 1.10
❑ 90 Bryan Watson 2.00 .90
❑ 91 Gary Sabourin 2.00 .90
❑ 92 Jacques Plante 20.00 9.00
❑ 93 Andre Boudrias 2.00 .90
❑ 94 Mike Walton 2.00 .90
❑ 95 Don Luce 2.50 1.10
❑ 96 Joey Johnston 2.00 .90
❑ 97 Doug Jarrett 2.00 .90
❑ 98 Bill MacMillan 2.00 .90
❑ 99 Mickey Redmond 3.00 1.35
❑ 100 Rogatien Vachon UER 6.00 2.70
(Misspelled Ragatien on card back)
❑ 101 Barry Gibbs 2.00 .90
❑ 102 Frank Mahovlich DP 4.00 1.80
❑ 103 Bruce MacGregor 2.00 .90
❑ 104 Ed Westfall 2.50 1.10
❑ 105 Rick MacLeish 5.00 2.20
❑ 106 Nick Harbaruk 2.00 .90
❑ 107 Jack Egers 2.00 .90
❑ 108 Dave Keon 4.00 1.80
❑ 109 Barry Wilkins 2.00 .90
❑ 110 Walt Tkaczuk 2.50 1.10
❑ 111 Phil Esposito 15.00 6.75
❑ 112 Gilles Meloche 8.00 3.60
❑ 113 Gary Edwards 2.50 1.10
❑ 114 Brad Park 10.00 4.50
❑ 115 Syl Apps DP 1.00 .45
❑ 116 Jim Lorentz 2.50 1.10
❑ 117 Gary Smith 3.00 1.35
❑ 118 Ted Harris 2.50 1.10
❑ 119 Gerry Desjardins DP 1.00 .45
❑ 120 Garry Unger 3.00 1.35
❑ 121 Dale Tallon 2.50 1.10
❑ 122 Bill Plager 3.00 1.35
❑ 123 Red Berenson DP 1.00 .45
❑ 124 Peter Mahovlich DP 1.00 .45
❑ 125 Simon Nolet 2.50 1.10
❑ 126 Paul Henderson 3.00 1.35
❑ 127 Hart Trophy Winners 2.50 1.10
❑ 128 Frank Mahovlich IA 3.00 1.35
❑ 129 Bobby Orr 75.00 34.00
❑ 130 Bert Marshall 2.50 1.10
❑ 131 Ralph Backstrom 3.00 1.35
❑ 132 Gilles Villemure 3.00 1.35
❑ 133 Dave Burrows 2.50 1.10
❑ 134 Calder Trophy Winners 2.50 1.10
❑ 135 Dallas Smith IA 2.50 1.10
❑ 136 Gilbert Perreault DP 12.00 5.50
❑ 137 Tony Esposito DP 20.00 9.00
❑ 138 Cesare Maniago DP 1.00 .45
❑ 139 Gerry Hart 2.50 1.10
❑ 140 Jacques Caron 2.50 1.10
❑ 141 Orland Kurtenbach 2.50 1.10
❑ 142 Norris Trophy Winners 2.50 1.10
❑ 143 Lew Morrison 2.50 1.10
❑ 144 Arnie Brown 2.50 1.10
❑ 145 Ken Dryden DP 50.00 22.00
❑ 146 Gary Dornhoefer 2.50 1.10
❑ 147 Norm Ullman 4.00 1.80
❑ 148 Art Ross Trophy 2.50 1.10
Winners
❑ 149 Orland Kurtenbach IA 2.50 1.10
❑ 150 Fred Stanfield 2.50 1.10
❑ 151 Dick Redmond DP 1.00 .45
❑ 152 Serge Bernier 3.00 1.35
❑ 153 Rod Gilbert 5.00 2.20
❑ 154 Duane Rupp 2.50 1.10
❑ 155 Vezina Trophy Winners 2.50 1.10
❑ 156 Stan Mikita IA 5.00 2.20
❑ 157 Richard Martin DP 5.00 2.20
❑ 158 Bill White DP 1.00 .45
❑ 159 Bill Goldsworthy DP 1.00 .45
❑ 160 Jack Lynch 2.50 1.10
❑ 161 Bob Plager DP 1.00 .45
❑ 162 Dave Balon UER 2.50 1.10
(Misspelled Ballon on card back)
❑ 163 Noel Price 2.50 1.10
❑ 164 Gary Bergman DP 1.00 .45
❑ 165 Pierre Bouchard 3.00 1.35
❑ 166 Ross Lonsberry 2.50 1.10
❑ 167 Denis Dupere 2.50 1.10
❑ 168 Byng Trophy Winners DP 1.00 .45
❑ 169 Ken Hodge 3.00 1.35
❑ 170 Don Awrey DP 1.00 .45
❑ 171 Marshall Johnston DP 1.00 .45
❑ 172 Terry Harper 2.50 1.10
❑ 173 Ed Giacomin 5.00 2.20
❑ 174 Bryan Hextall DP 1.00 .45
❑ 175 Conn Smythe 2.50 1.10
Trophy Winners
❑ 176 Larry Hillman 2.50 1.10
❑ 177 Stan Mikita DP 8.00 3.60
❑ 178 Charlie Burns 2.50 1.10
❑ 179 Brian Marchinko 2.50 1.10
❑ 180 Noel Picard DP 1.00 .45
❑ 181 Bobby Schmautz 4.00 1.80
❑ 182 Richard Martin IA UER 3.50 1.55
(Photo actually Gilbert Perreault)
❑ 183 Pat Quinn 3.00 1.35
❑ 184 Denis DeJordy UER 3.00 1.35
(Back says plays for Flames, should be Red Wings)
❑ 185 Serge Savard 3.00 1.35
❑ 186 Eddie Shack 4.00 1.80
❑ 187 Bill Flett 2.50 1.10
❑ 188 Darryl Sittler 20.00 9.00
❑ 189 Gump Worsley IA 4.00 1.80
❑ 190 Checklist 2 60.00 15.00
(See also card 19; 160 is Jack Lynch)
❑ 191 Garnet Bailey DP 1.00 .45
❑ 192 Walt McKechnie 3.00 1.35
❑ 193 Harry Howell 3.00 1.35
❑ 194 Rod Seiling 2.50 1.10
❑ 195 Darryl Edestrand 2.50 1.10
❑ 196 Tony Esposito IA 8.00 3.60
❑ 197 Tim Horton 8.00 3.60
❑ 198 Chico Maki DP 1.00 .45
❑ 199 Jean-Paul Parise 2.50 1.10
❑ 200 Germaine Gagnon UER 2.50 1.10
❑ 201 Danny O'Shea 2.50 1.10
❑ 202 Richard Lemieux 2.50 1.10
❑ 203 Dan Bouchard 10.00 4.50
❑ 204 Leon Rochefort 2.50 1.10
❑ 205 Jacques Laperriere 3.00 1.35
❑ 206 Barry Ashbee 3.00 1.35
❑ 207 Garry Monahan 2.50 1.10
❑ 208 Never Issued
❑ 209 Dave Keon IA 4.00 1.80
❑ 210 Rejean Houle 5.00 2.20
❑ 211 Dave Hudson 4.00 1.80
❑ 212 Ted Irvine 4.00 1.80
❑ 213 Don Saleski 5.00 2.20
❑ 214 Lowell MacDonald 4.00 1.80
❑ 215 Mike Murphy 5.00 2.20
❑ 216 Brian Glennie 4.00 1.80
❑ 217 Bobby Lalonde 4.00 1.80
❑ 218 Bob Leiter 4.00 1.80
❑ 219 Don Marcotte 4.00 1.80
❑ 220 Jim Schoenfeld 12.00 5.50
❑ 221 Craig Patrick 5.00 2.20
❑ 222 Cliff Koroll 4.00 1.80
❑ 223 Guy Charron 5.00 2.20
❑ 224 Jim Peters 4.00 1.80
❑ 225 Dennis Hextall 4.00 1.80
❑ 226 Tony Esposito AS1 15.00 6.75
❑ 227 Orr/Park AS1 40.00 18.00
❑ 228 Bobby Hull AS1 25.00 11.00
❑ 229 Rod Gilbert AS1 5.00 2.20
❑ 230 Phil Esposito AS1 10.00 4.50
(Brother Tony pictured in background)
❑ 231 Claude Larose UER 4.00 1.80
(Misspelled La Rose on both sides)
❑ 232 Jim Mair 4.00 1.80
❑ 233 Bobby Rousseau 4.00 1.80
❑ 234 Brent Hughes 4.00 1.80
❑ 235 Al McDonough 4.00 1.80
❑ 236 Chris Evans 4.00 1.80
❑ 237 Pierre Jarry 4.00 1.80
❑ 238 Don Tannahill 4.00 1.80
❑ 239 Rey Comeau 4.00 1.80
❑ 240 Gregg Sheppard UER 4.00 1.80
(Misspelled Shepherd on card front)
❑ 241 Dave Dryden 5.00 2.20
❑ 242 Ted McAneeley 4.00 1.80
❑ 243 Lou Angotti 4.00 1.80
❑ 244 Len Fontaine 4.00 1.80
❑ 245 Bill Lesuk 4.00 1.80
❑ 246 Fred Harvey 4.00 1.80
❑ 247 Ken Dryden AS2 30.00 13.50
❑ 248 Bill White AS2 4.00 1.80
❑ 249 Pat Stapleton AS2 4.00 1.80
❑ 250 Ratelle/Cournoyer/ 6.00 2.70
Hadfield AS2
❑ 251 Henri Richard 7.00 3.10
❑ 252 Bryan Lefley 4.00 1.80
❑ 253 Stanley Cup Trophy 15.00 6.75
❑ 254 Steve Vickers 8.00 3.60
❑ 255 Wayne Hillman 4.00 1.80
❑ 256 Ken Schinkel UER 4.00 1.80
(Misspelled Shinkel on card front)
❑ 257 Kevin O'Shea 4.00 1.80
❑ 258 Ron Low 15.00 6.75
❑ 259 Don Lever 5.00 2.20
❑ 260 Randy Manery 4.00 1.80
❑ 261 Ed Johnston 5.00 2.20
❑ 262 Craig Ramsay 6.00 2.70
❑ 263 Pete Laframboise 4.00 1.80
❑ 264 Dan Maloney 5.00 2.20
❑ 265 Bill Collins 4.00 1.80
❑ 266 Paul Curtis 4.00 1.80
❑ 267 Bob Nevin 4.00 1.80
❑ 268 Penalty Min. Leaders 4.00 1.80
Bryan Watson
Keith Magnuson
Gary Dornhoefer
❑ 269 Jim Roberts 4.00 1.80
❑ 270 Brian Lavender 4.00 1.80
❑ 271 Dale Rolfe 4.00 1.80
❑ 272 Goals Leaders 20.00 9.00

Phil Esposito
Vic Hadfield
Bobby Hull
❑ 273 Michel Belhumeur 8.00 3.60
❑ 274 Eddie Shack 7.00 3.10
❑ 275 Wayne Stephenson UER 10.00 4.50
(Back has Forward stats instead of Goalie stats)
❑ 276 Stanley Cup Winner 8.00 3.60
Boston Bruins Team
❑ 277 Rick Kehoe 8.00 3.60
❑ 278 Gerry O'Flaherty 4.00 1.80
❑ 279 Jacques Richard 4.00 1.80
❑ 280 Scoring Leaders 25.00 11.00
Phil Esposito
Bobby Orr
Jean Ratelle
❑ 281 Nick Beverley 6.00 2.70
❑ 282 Larry Carriere 4.00 1.80
❑ 283 Assists Leaders 25.00 11.00
Bobby Orr
Phil Esposito
Jean Ratelle
❑ 284 Rick Smith IA 4.00 1.80
❑ 285 Jerry Korab 5.00 2.20
❑ 286 Goals Against 12.00 5.50
Average Leaders
Tony Esposito
Gilles Villemure
Gump Worsley
❑ 287 Ron Stackhouse 4.00 1.80
❑ 288 Barry Long 4.00 1.80
❑ 289 Dean Prentice 4.00 1.80
❑ 290 Norm Beaudin 8.00 3.60
❑ 291 Mike Amodeo 8.00 3.60
❑ 292 Jim Harrison 8.00 3.60
❑ 293 J.C. Tremblay 10.00 4.50
❑ 294 Murray Hall 8.00 3.60
❑ 295 Bart Crashley 10.00 4.50
❑ 296 Wayne Connelly 10.00 4.50
❑ 297 Bobby Sheehan 8.00 3.60
❑ 298 Ron Anderson 8.00 3.60
❑ 299 Chris Bordeleau 8.00 3.60
❑ 300 Les Binkley 10.00 4.50
❑ 301 Ron Walters 8.00 3.60
❑ 302 Jean-Guy Gendron 8.00 3.60
❑ 303 Gord Labossiere 8.00 3.60
❑ 304 Gerry Odrowski 8.00 3.60
❑ 305 Mike McMahon 8.00 3.60
❑ 306 Gary Kurt 10.00 4.50
❑ 307 Larry Cahan 8.00 3.60
❑ 308 Wally Boyer 8.00 3.60
❑ 309 Bob Charlebois 8.00 3.60
❑ 310 Bob Falkenberg 8.00 3.60
❑ 311 Jean Payette 8.00 3.60
❑ 312 Ted Taylor 8.00 3.60
❑ 313 Joe Szura 8.00 3.60
❑ 314 George Morrison 8.00 3.60
❑ 315 Wayne Rivers 8.00 3.60
❑ 316 Reg Fleming 8.00 3.60
❑ 317 Larry Hornung 8.00 3.60
❑ 318 Ron Climie 8.00 3.60
❑ 319 Val Fonteyne 8.00 3.60
❑ 320 Michel Archambault 8.00 3.60
❑ 321 Ab McDonald 8.00 3.60
❑ 322 Bob Leduc 8.00 3.60
❑ 323 Bob Wall 8.00 3.60
❑ 324 Alain Caron 8.00 3.60
❑ 325 Bob Woytowich 8.00 3.60
❑ 326 Guy Trottier 8.00 3.60
❑ 327 Bill Hicke 8.00 3.60
❑ 328 Guy Dufour 8.00 3.60
❑ 329 Wayne Rutledge 10.00 4.50
❑ 330 Gary Veneruzzo 8.00 3.60
❑ 331 Fred Speck 8.00 3.60
❑ 332 Ron Ward 8.00 3.60
❑ 333 Rosaire Paiement 10.00 4.50
❑ 334A Checklist 3 80.00 20.00
(Numbers 335-341 listed as More WHA Stars)
❑ 334B Checklist 3 70.00 17.50
(Numbers 335-341 listed correctly)
❑ 335 Michel Parizeau 8.00 3.60
❑ 336 Bobby Hull 60.00 27.00
❑ 337 Wayne Carleton 8.00 3.60
❑ 338 John McKenzie 10.00 4.50
❑ 339 Jim Dorey 8.00 3.60
❑ 340 Gerry Cheevers 30.00 13.50
❑ 341 Gerry Pinder 20.00 5.00

## 1972-73 O-Pee-Chee Player Crests

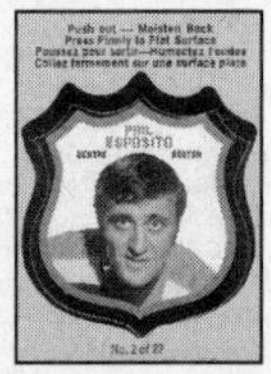

This set consists of 22 full-color cardboard stickers measuring 2 1/2" by 3 1/2". The set was issued as an insert with the regular issue of the same year in with the first series wax packs. Cards are numbered on the front and have a blank adhesive back. Although the cards were designed so that the crest could be popped out, this is strongly discouraged. These stickers were printed in Canada.

| | NRMT-MT | EXC |
|---|---|---|
| COMPLETE SET (22) | 125.00 | 55.00 |
| COMMON CARD (1-22) | 2.00 | .90 |

❑ 1 Pat Quinn 3.00 1.35
❑ 2 Phil Esposito 15.00 6.75
❑ 3 Bobby Orr 40.00 18.00
❑ 4 Richard Martin 3.00 1.35
❑ 5 Stan Mikita 10.00 4.50
❑ 6 Bill White 2.00 .90
❑ 7 Red Berenson 3.00 1.35
❑ 8 Gary Bergman 2.00 .90
❑ 9 Gary Edwards 4.00 1.80
❑ 10 Bill Goldsworthy 3.00 1.35
❑ 11 Jacques Laperriere 3.00 1.35
❑ 12 Ken Dryden 25.00 11.00
❑ 13 Ed Westfall 2.00 .90
❑ 14 Walt Tkaczuk 2.00 .90
❑ 15 Brad Park 6.00 2.70
❑ 16 Doug Favell 4.00 1.80
❑ 17 Eddie Shack 6.00 2.70
❑ 18 Jacques Caron 2.00 .90
❑ 19 Paul Henderson 4.00 1.80
❑ 20 Jim Harrison 2.00 .90
❑ 21 Dale Tallon 2.00 .90
❑ 22 Orland Kurtenbach 2.00 .90

## 1972-73 O-Pee-Chee Team Canada

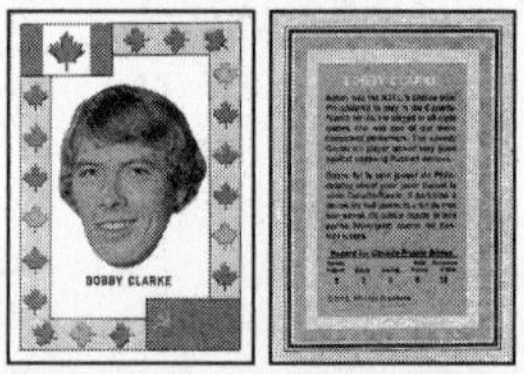

This attractive set consists of 28 unnumbered color cards measuring 2 1/2" by 3 1/2". The 28 players are those who represented Team Canada against Russia in the 1972 Summit Series. Only the players' heads are shown surrounded by a border of maple leaves with a Canadian and Russian flag in each corner. The card back provides a summary of that player's performance in the eight-game series. The set was issued as an insert with the second series of the 1972-73 O-Pee-Chee regular issue. Backs are written in both French and English. The cards were printed in Canada.

| | NRMT-MT | EXC |
|---|---|---|
| COMPLETE SET (28) | 300.00 | 135.00 |
| COMMON CARD (1-28) | 4.00 | 1.80 |

❑ 1 Don Awrey 4.00 1.80
❑ 2 Red Berenson 5.00 2.20
❑ 3 Gary Bergman 4.00 1.80
❑ 4 Wayne Cashman 5.00 2.20
❑ 5 Bobby Clarke 25.00 11.00
❑ 6 Yvan Cournoyer 15.00 6.75
❑ 7 Ken Dryden 50.00 22.00
❑ 8 Ron Ellis 5.00 2.20
❑ 9 Phil Esposito 30.00 13.50
❑ 10 Tony Esposito 25.00 11.00
❑ 11 Rod Gilbert 10.00 4.50
❑ 12 Bill Goldsworthy 5.00 2.20
❑ 13 Vic Hadfield 4.00 1.80
❑ 14 Paul Henderson 20.00 9.00
❑ 15 Dennis Hull 5.00 2.20
❑ 16 Guy Lapointe 6.00 2.70
❑ 17 Frank Mahovlich 20.00 9.00
❑ 18 Pete Mahovlich 6.00 2.70
❑ 19 Stan Mikita 20.00 9.00
❑ 20 Jean-Paul Parise 4.00 1.80
❑ 21 Brad Park 15.00 6.75
❑ 22 Gilbert Perreault 6.00 2.70
❑ 23 Jean Ratelle 10.00 4.50
❑ 24 Mickey Redmond 10.00 4.50
❑ 25 Serge Savard 6.00 2.70
❑ 26 Rod Seiling 4.00 1.80
❑ 27 Pat Stapleton 4.00 1.80
❑ 28 Bill White 4.00 1.80

## 1972-73 O-Pee-Chee Team Logos

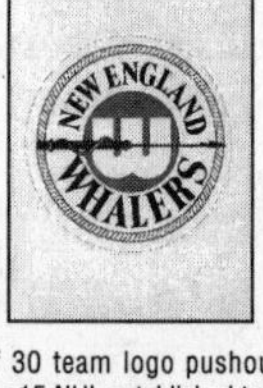

This set of 30 team logo pushouts include logos for the 15 NHL established teams as well as the two new NHL teams, the 12 WHA teams, and the WHA League emblem. The cards are die-cut and adhesive backed. They were inserted in with the third series of the 1972-73 O-Pee-Chee wax packs. The expansion and WHA emblems are more difficult to find and are listed as SP in the checklist below. These inserts are standard size, 2 1/2" by 3 1/2". These team logos cards are distinguished by their lack of instructions on the front.

| | NRMT-MT | EXC |
|---|---|---|
| COMPLETE SET (30) | 200.00 | 90.00 |
| COMMON LOGO (1-30) | 2.00 | .90 |
| COMMON LOGO SP | 12.00 | 5.50 |

❑ 1 NHL Logo 5.00 2.20
❑ 2 Atlanta Flames SP 12.00 5.50
❑ 3 Boston Bruins 4.00 1.80
❑ 4 Buffalo Sabres 2.00 .90
❑ 5 California Seals 5.00 2.20
❑ 6 Chicago Blackhawks 4.00 1.80
❑ 7 Detroit Red Wings 4.00 1.80
❑ 8 Los Angeles Kings 2.00 .90
❑ 9 Minnesota North Stars 2.00 .90
❑ 10 Montreal Canadiens 4.00 1.80
❑ 11 New York Islanders SP 12.00 5.50
❑ 12 New York Rangers 4.00 1.80
❑ 13 Philadelphia Flyers 3.00 1.35
❑ 14 Pittsburgh Penguins 2.00 .90
❑ 15 St. Louis Blues 2.00 .90
❑ 16 Toronto Maple Leafs 4.00 1.80
❑ 17 Vancouver Canucks 3.00 1.35
❑ 18 WHA Logo SP 20.00 9.00
❑ 19 Chicago Cougars SP 15.00 6.75
❑ 20 Cleveland Crusaders SP 15.00 6.75
❑ 21 Edmonton Oilers SP 12.00 5.50
❑ 22 Houston Aeros SP 15.00 6.75
❑ 23 Los Angeles Sharks SP 15.00 6.75
❑ 24 Minnesota Fighting Saints SP 15.00 6.75
❑ 25 New England Whalers SP 12.00 5.50
❑ 26 New York Raiders SP 15.00 6.75
❑ 27 Ottawa Nationals SP 15.00 6.75
❑ 28 Phila. Blazers SP 15.00 6.75
❑ 29 Quebec Nordiques SP 12.00 5.50
❑ 30 Winnipeg Jets SP 12.00 5.50

## 1973-74 O-Pee-Chee

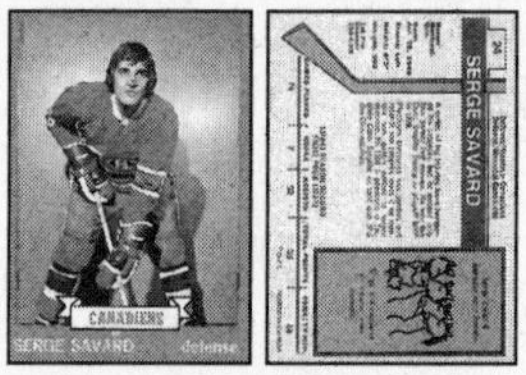

The 1973-74 O-Pee-Chee NHL set features 264 standard-size cards. The cards measure 2 1/2" by 3 1/2". The border color on the fronts differs from the Topps set. Cards 1-198 have a red border and cards 199-264 have a green border. Topps cards are a mix of blue and green. Bilingual backs contain 1972-73 and career statistics, a short biography and a cartoon-illustrated fact about the player. Team cards (92-107) contain team and player records on the back. The cards were printed in Canada on cream or gray card stock. Rookie Cards in this set include Bill Barber, Terry O'Reilly, Larry Robinson, Dave Schultz, and Billy Smith.

| | NRMT-MT | EXC |
|---|---|---|
| COMPLETE SET (264) | 500.00 | 220.00 |
| COMMON CARD (1-264) | 1.50 | .70 |

❑ 1 Alex Delvecchio 5.00 1.25
❑ 2 Gilles Meloche 1.50 .70
❑ 3 Phil Roberto 1.50 .70
❑ 4 Orland Kurtenbach 1.50 .70
❑ 5 Gilles Marotte 1.50 .70
❑ 6 Stan Mikita 8.00 3.60
❑ 7 Paul Henderson 1.50 .70
❑ 8 Gregg Sheppard 1.50 .70
❑ 9 Rod Seiling 1.50 .70
❑ 10 Red Berenson 1.50 .70
❑ 11 Jean Pronovost 1.50 .70
❑ 12 Dick Redmond 1.50 .70
❑ 13 Keith McCreary 1.50 .70
❑ 14 Bryan Watson 1.50 .70
❑ 15 Garry Unger 1.50 .70
❑ 16 Neil Komadoski 1.50 .70
❑ 17 Marcel Dionne 15.00 6.75
❑ 18 Ernie Hicke 1.50 .70
❑ 19 Andre Boudrias 1.50 .70
❑ 20 Bill Flett 1.50 .70
❑ 21 Marshall Johnston 1.50 .70
❑ 22 Gerry Meehan 1.50 .70
❑ 23 Ed Johnston 1.50 .70
❑ 24 Serge Savard 1.50 .70
❑ 25 Walt Tkaczuk 1.50 .70
❑ 26 Ken Hodge 1.50 .70
❑ 27 Norm Ullman 3.00 1.35
❑ 28 Cliff Koroll 1.50 .70
❑ 29 Rey Comeau 1.50 .70
❑ 30 Bobby Orr 50.00 22.00
❑ 31 Wayne Stephenson 1.50 .70
❑ 32 Dan Maloney 1.50 .70
❑ 33 Henry Boucha 1.50 .70
❑ 34 Gerry Hart 1.50 .70
❑ 35 Bobby Schmautz 1.50 .70
❑ 36 Ross Lonsberry 1.50 .70
❑ 37 Ted McAneeley 1.50 .70
❑ 38 Don Luce 1.50 .70
❑ 39 Jim McKenny 1.50 .70
❑ 40 Jacques Laperriere 1.50 .70
❑ 41 Bill Fairbairn 1.50 .70
❑ 42 Craig Cameron 1.50 .70
❑ 43 Bryan Hextall 1.50 .70
❑ 44 Chuck Lefley 1.50 .70
❑ 45 Dan Bouchard 1.50 .70
❑ 46 Jean-Paul Parise 1.50 .70
❑ 47 Barclay Plager 1.50 .70
❑ 48 Mike Corrigan 1.50 .70
❑ 49 Nick Libett 1.50 .70
❑ 50 Bobby Clarke 20.00 9.00
❑ 51 Bert Marshall 1.50 .70
❑ 52 Craig Patrick 1.50 .70
❑ 53 Richard Lemieux 1.50 .70
❑ 54 Tracy Pratt 1.50 .70
❑ 55 Ron Ellis 1.50 .70
❑ 56 Jacques Lemaire 3.00 1.35
❑ 57 Steve Vickers 1.50 .70
❑ 58 Carol Vadnais 1.50 .70
❑ 59 Jim Rutherford 1.50 .70
❑ 60 Rick Kehoe 1.50 .70
❑ 61 Pat Quinn 1.50 .70
❑ 62 Bill Goldsworthy 1.50 .70
❑ 63 Dave Dryden 1.50 .70
❑ 64 Rogatien Vachon 5.00 2.20
❑ 65 Gary Bergman 1.50 .70
❑ 66 Bernie Parent 10.00 4.50
❑ 67 Ed Westfall 1.50 .70
❑ 68 Ivan Boldirev 1.50 .70
❑ 69 Don Tannahill 1.50 .70
❑ 70 Gilbert Perreault 12.00 5.50
❑ 71 Mike Pelyk 1.50 .70
❑ 72 Guy Lafleur 25.00 11.00
❑ 73 Pit Martin 1.50 .70
❑ 74 Gilles Gilbert 8.00 3.60
❑ 75 Jim Lorentz 1.50 .70
❑ 76 Syl Apps 1.50 .70
❑ 77 Phil Myre 1.50 .70
❑ 78 Bill White 1.50 .70
❑ 79 Jack Egers 1.50 .70
❑ 80 Terry Harper 1.50 .70
❑ 81 Bill Barber 20.00 9.00
❑ 82 Roy Edwards 1.50 .70
❑ 83 Brian Spencer 1.50 .70
❑ 84 Reggie Leach 2.50 1.10
❑ 85 Wayne Cashman 1.50 .70
❑ 86 Jim Schoenfeld 3.00 1.35
❑ 87 Henri Richard 6.00 2.70
❑ 88 Dennis O'Brien 1.50 .70
❑ 89 Al McDonough 1.50 .70
❑ 90 Tony Esposito 12.00 5.50
❑ 91 Joe Watson 1.50 .70
❑ 92 Flames Team 4.00 1.80
❑ 93 Bruins Team 4.00 1.80
❑ 94 Sabres Team 4.00 1.80
❑ 95 Golden Seals Team 4.00 1.80
❑ 96 Blackhawks Team 4.00 1.80
❑ 97 Red Wings Team 4.00 1.80
❑ 98 Kings Team 4.00 1.80
❑ 99 North Stars Team 4.00 1.80
❑ 100 Canadiens Team 4.00 1.80
❑ 101 Islanders Team 4.00 1.80
❑ 102 Rangers Team 4.00 1.80
❑ 103 Flyers Team 4.00 1.80
❑ 104 Penguins Team 4.00 1.80
❑ 105 Blues Team 4.00 1.80
❑ 106 Maple Leafs Team 4.00 1.80
❑ 107 Canucks Team 4.00 1.80
❑ 108 Vic Hadfield 1.50 .70
❑ 109 Tom Reid 1.50 .70
❑ 110 Hilliard Graves 1.50 .70
❑ 111 Don Lever 1.50 .70
❑ 112 Jim Pappin 1.50 .70
❑ 113 Andre Dupont 1.50 .70
❑ 114 Guy Lapointe 1.50 .70
❑ 115 Dennis Hextall 1.50 .70
❑ 116 Checklist 1 35.00 8.75
❑ 117 Bob Leiter 1.50 .70
❑ 118 Ab DeMarco 1.50 .70
❑ 119 Gilles Villemure 1.50 .70
❑ 120 Phil Esposito 10.00 4.50
❑ 121 Mike Robitaille 1.50 .70
❑ 122 Real Lemieux 1.50 .70
❑ 123 Jim Neilson 1.50 .70
❑ 124 Steve Durbano 1.50 .70
❑ 125 Jude Drouin 1.50 .70
❑ 126 Gary Smith 1.50 .70
❑ 127 Cesare Maniago 1.50 .70
❑ 128 Lowell MacDonald 1.50 .70
❑ 129 Checklist 2 35.00 8.75
❑ 130 Billy Harris 1.50 .70
❑ 131 Randy Manery 1.50 .70
❑ 132 Darryl Sittler 15.00 6.75
❑ 133 Goals Leaders 4.00 1.80
Phil Esposito
Rick MacLeish
❑ 134 Assists Leaders 6.00 2.70
Phil Esposito
Bobby Clarke
❑ 135 Scoring Leaders 6.00 2.70
Phil Esposito
Bobby Clarke
❑ 136 Goals Against 10.00 4.50
Average Leaders
Ken Dryden
Tony Esposito
❑ 137 Penalty Min. Leaders 3.00 1.35
Jim Schoenfeld
Dave Schultz
❑ 138 Power Play Goal 4.00 1.80
Leaders
Phil Esposito
Rick MacLeish
❑ 139 Rene Robert 1.50 .70
❑ 140 Dave Burrows 1.50 .70
❑ 141 Jean Ratelle 4.00 1.80
❑ 142 Billy Smith 40.00 18.00
❑ 143 Jocelyn Guevremont 1.50 .70
❑ 144 Tim Ecclestone 1.50 .70
❑ 145 Frank Mahovlich 6.00 2.70
❑ 146 Rick MacLeish 3.00 1.35
❑ 147 Johnny Bucyk 3.00 1.35
❑ 148 Bob Plager 1.50 .70
❑ 149 Curt Bennett 1.50 .70
❑ 150 Dave Keon 4.00 1.80
❑ 151 Keith Magnuson 1.50 .70
❑ 152 Walt McKechnie 1.50 .70
❑ 153 Roger Crozier 1.50 .70
❑ 154 Ted Harris 1.50 .70
❑ 155 Butch Goring 1.50 .70
❑ 156 Rod Gilbert 3.00 1.35
❑ 157 Yvan Cournoyer 4.00 1.80
❑ 158 Doug Favell 1.50 .70
❑ 159 Juha Widing 1.50 .70
❑ 160 Ed Giacomin 5.00 2.20
❑ 161 Germaine Gagnon UER 1.50 .70
❑ 162 Dennis Kearns 1.50 .70
❑ 163 Bill Collins 1.50 .70
❑ 164 Peter Mahovlich 1.50 .70
❑ 165 Brad Park 6.00 2.70
❑ 166 Dave Schultz 15.00 6.75
❑ 167 Dallas Smith 1.50 .70
❑ 168 Gary Sabourin 1.50 .70
❑ 169 Jacques Richard 1.50 .70
❑ 170 Brian Glennie 1.50 .70
❑ 171 Dennis Hull 1.50 .70
❑ 172 Joey Johnston 1.50 .70
❑ 173 Richard Martin 3.00 1.35
❑ 174 Barry Gibbs 1.50 .70
❑ 175 Bob Berry 1.50 .70
❑ 176 Greg Polis 1.50 .70
❑ 177 Dale Rolfe 1.50 .70
❑ 178 Gerry Desjardins 1.50 .70
❑ 179 Bobby Lalonde 1.50 .70
❑ 180 Mickey Redmond 1.50 .70
❑ 181 Jim Roberts 1.50 .70
❑ 182 Gary Dornhoefer 1.50 .70
❑ 183 Derek Sanderson 5.00 2.20
❑ 184 Brent Hughes 1.50 .70
❑ 185 Larry Romanchych 1.50 .70
❑ 186 Pierre Jarry 1.50 .70
❑ 187 Doug Jarrett 1.50 .70
❑ 188 Bob Stewart 1.50 .70
❑ 189 Tim Horton 6.00 2.70
❑ 190 Fred Harvey 1.50 .70
❑ 191 Series A 1.50 .70
Canadiens 4
Sabres 2
❑ 192 Series B 1.50 .70
Flyers 4
North Stars 2
❑ 193 Series C 1.50 .70
Blackhawks 4
Blues 1
❑ 194 Series D 1.50 .70
Rangers 4
Bruins
❑ 195 Series E 1.50 .70
Canadiens 4
Flyers 1
❑ 196 Series F 1.50 .70
Blackhawks 4
Rangers 1
❑ 197 Series G 1.50 .70
Canadiens 4
Blackhawks 2
❑ 198 Stanley Cup Champs 4.00 1.80
❑ 199 Gary Edwards 1.50 .70
❑ 200 Ron Schock 1.50 .70
❑ 201 Bruce MacGregor 1.50 .70
❑ 202 Bob Nystrom 5.00 2.20
❑ 203 Jerry Korab 1.50 .70
❑ 204 Thommie Bergman 1.50 .70
❑ 205 Bill Lesuk 1.50 .70
❑ 206 Ed Van Impe 1.50 .70
❑ 207 Doug Roberts 1.50 .70
❑ 208 Chris Evans 1.50 .70
❑ 209 Lynn Powis 1.50 .70
❑ 210 Denis Dupere 1.50 .70
❑ 211 Dale Tallon 1.50 .70
❑ 212 Stan Gilbertson 1.50 .70
❑ 213 Craig Ramsay 1.50 .70
❑ 214 Danny Grant 1.50 .70
❑ 215 Doug Volmar 1.50 .70
❑ 216 Darryl Edestrand 1.50 .70
❑ 217 Pete Stemkowski 1.50 .70
❑ 218 Lorne Henning 1.50 .70
❑ 219 Bryan McSheffrey 1.50 .70
❑ 220 Guy Charron 1.50 .70
❑ 221 Wayne Thomas 5.00 2.20
❑ 222 Simon Nolet 1.50 .70
❑ 223 Fred O'Donnell 1.50 .70
❑ 224 Lou Angotti 1.50 .70
❑ 225 Arnie Brown 1.50 .70
❑ 226 Garry Monahan 1.50 .70
❑ 227 Chico Maki 1.50 .70
❑ 228 Gary Croteau 1.50 .70
❑ 229 Paul Terbenche 1.50 .70
❑ 230 Gump Worsley 4.00 1.80
❑ 231 Jim Peters 1.50 .70
❑ 232 Jack Lynch 1.50 .70
❑ 233 Bobby Rousseau 1.50 .70
❑ 234 Dave Hudson 1.50 .70
❑ 235 Gregg Boddy 1.50 .70
❑ 236 Ron Stackhouse 1.50 .70
❑ 237 Larry Robinson 50.00 22.00
❑ 238 Bobby Taylor 1.50 .70
❑ 239 Nick Beverley 1.50 .70
❑ 240 Don Awrey 1.50 .70
❑ 241 Doug Mohns 1.50 .70
❑ 242 Eddie Shack 5.00 2.20
❑ 243 Phil Russell 1.50 .70
❑ 244 Pete Laframboise 1.50 .70
❑ 245 Steve Atkinson 1.50 .70

❑ 246 Lou Nanne 1.50 .70
❑ 247 Yvon Labre 1.50 .70
❑ 248 Ted Irvine 1.50 .70
❑ 249 Tom Miller 1.50 .70
❑ 250 Gerry O'Flaherty 1.50 .70
❑ 251 Larry Johnston 1.50 .70
❑ 252 Michel Plasse 5.00 2.20
❑ 253 Bob Kelly 1.50 .70
❑ 254 Terry O'Reilly 10.00 4.50
❑ 255 Pierre Plante 1.50 .70
❑ 256 Noel Price 1.50 .70
❑ 257 Dunc Wilson 1.50 .70
❑ 258 J.P. Bordeleau 1.50 .70
❑ 259 Terry Murray 2.50 1.10
❑ 260 Larry Carriere 1.50 .70
❑ 261 Pierre Bouchard 1.50 .70
❑ 262 Frank St.Marseille 1.50 .70
❑ 263 Checklist 3 35.00 8.75
❑ 264 Fred Barrett 2.50 .60

## 1973-74 O-Pee-Chee Rings

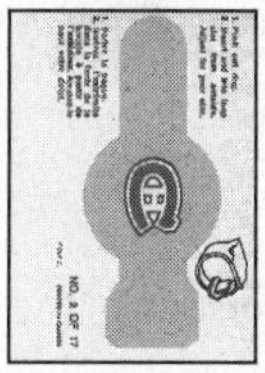

The 1973-74 O-Pee-Chee Rings set contains 17 standard-size cards, featuring the NHL league and team logos. The fronts have a push-out cardboard ring and instructions in English and French. The rings are yellow-colored and feature a NHL team logo in the team's colors. The cards are numbered on the front and the backs are blank.

| | NRMT-MT | EXC |
|---|---|---|
| COMPLETE SET (17) | 80.00 | 36.00 |
| COMMON RING CARD (1-17) | 5.00 | 2.20 |

❑ 1 Vancouver Canucks 6.00 2.70
❑ 2 Montreal Canadiens 6.00 2.70
❑ 3 Toronto Maple Leafs 6.00 2.70
❑ 4 NHL Logo 6.00 2.70
❑ 5 Minnesota North Stars 5.00 2.20
❑ 6 New York Rangers 6.00 2.70
❑ 7 California Seals 6.00 2.70
❑ 8 Pittsburgh Penguins 5.00 2.20
❑ 9 Philadelphia Flyers 5.00 2.20
❑ 10 Chicago Blackhawks 6.00 2.70
❑ 11 Boston Bruins 6.00 2.70
❑ 12 Los Angeles Kings 5.00 2.20
❑ 13 Detroit Red Wings 6.00 2.70
❑ 14 St. Louis Blues 5.00 2.20
❑ 15 Buffalo Sabres 5.00 2.20
❑ 16 Atlanta Flames 6.00 2.70
❑ 17 New York Islanders 5.00 2.20

## 1973-74 O-Pee-Chee Team Logos

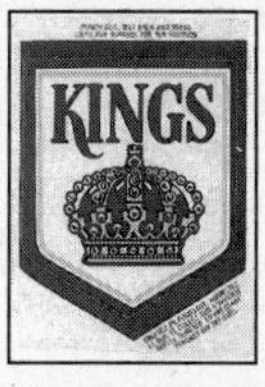

The 1973-74 O-Pee-Chee Team Logos set contains 17 unnumbered, standard-size color stickers, featuring the NHL league and team logos. The cards are die-cut and adhesive backed. After the NHL logo, they are ordered below alphabetically by team city/location. This set is distinguished from the similar set of the previous year by the presence of written instructions on the fronts.

| | NRMT-MT | EXC |
|---|---|---|
| COMPLETE SET (17) | 40.00 | 18.00 |
| COMMON CARD (1-17) | 3.00 | 1.35 |

❑ 1 NHL Logo 4.00 1.80
❑ 2 Atlanta Flames 4.00 1.80
❑ 3 Boston Bruins 4.00 1.80
❑ 4 Buffalo Sabres 3.00 1.35
❑ 5 California Seals 4.00 1.80
❑ 6 Chicago Blackhawks 4.00 1.80
❑ 7 Detroit Red Wings 4.00 1.80
❑ 8 Los Angeles Kings 3.00 1.35
❑ 9 Minnesota North Stars 3.00 1.35
❑ 10 Montreal Canadiens 4.00 1.80
❑ 11 New York Islanders 3.00 1.35
❑ 12 New York Rangers 4.00 1.80
❑ 13 Philadelphia Flyers 3.00 1.35
❑ 14 Pittsburgh Penguins 3.00 1.35
❑ 15 St. Louis Blues 3.00 1.35
❑ 16 Toronto Maple Leafs 4.00 1.80
❑ 17 Vancouver Canucks 3.00 1.35

## 1973-74 O-Pee-Chee WHA Posters

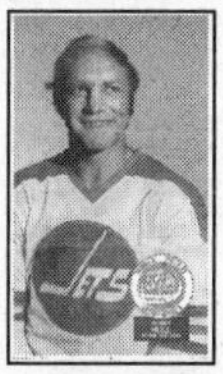

Players featured in this set are from the World Hockey Association (WHA). The set consists of 20 large posters each measuring approximately 7 1/2" by 13 3/4" and was a separate issue in wax packs. The packs contained two posters and gum; gum stains are frequently seen. Posters are numbered on the front and were issued folded. As a result, folded copies are accepted as being in near mint condition. The posters are blank backed.

| | NRMT-MT | EXC |
|---|---|---|
| COMPLETE SET (20) | 100.00 | 45.00 |
| COMMON CARD (1-20) | 3.00 | 1.35 |

❑ 1 Al Smith 5.00 2.20
❑ 2 J.C. Tremblay 5.00 2.20
❑ 3 Guy Dufour 3.00 1.35
❑ 4 Pat Stapleton 5.00 2.20
❑ 5 Rosaire Paiement 3.00 1.35
❑ 6 Gerry Cheevers 10.00 4.50
❑ 7 Gerry Pinder 4.00 1.80
❑ 8 Wayne Carleton 3.00 1.35
❑ 9 Bob Leduc 3.00 1.35
❑ 10 Andre Lacroix 5.00 2.20
❑ 11 Jim Harrison 3.00 1.35
❑ 12 Ron Climie 3.00 1.35
❑ 13 Gordie Howe 25.00 11.00
❑ 14 The Howe Family 25.00 11.00
Gordie/Mark/Marty
❑ 15 Mike Walton 4.00 1.80
❑ 16 Bobby Hull 20.00 9.00
❑ 17 Chris Bordeleau 3.00 1.35
❑ 18 Claude St.Sauveur 3.00 1.35
❑ 19 Bryan Campbell 3.00 1.35
❑ 20 Marc Tardif 5.00 2.20

## 1974-75 O-Pee-Chee NHL

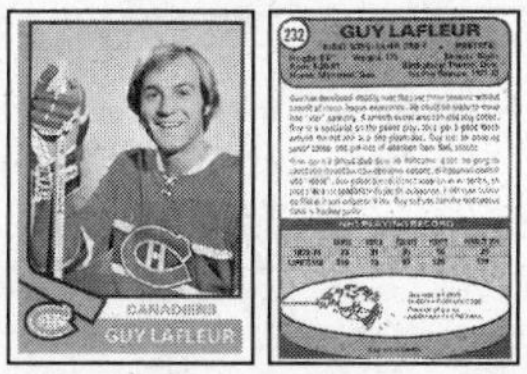


The 1974-75 O-Pee-Chee NHL set contains 396 standard-size cards. The first 264 cards are identical to those of Topps in terms of numbering and photos. Wax packs consisted of eight cards plus a piece of bubble gum. Bilingual backs feature the player's 1973-74 and career statistics, a short biography and a cartoon-illustrated fact about the player. The first six cards in the set (1-6) feature league leaders of the previous season. The set includes players from the expansion Washington Capitals and Kansas City Scouts (presently New Jersey Devils). The set marks the return of coach cards, including Rookie Cards of Don Cherry and Scotty Bowman. Other Rookie Cards include Bill Clement, John Davidson, Bob Gainey, Lanny McDonald, Rick Middleton, Denis Potvin, Glenn "Chico" Resch, Steve Shutt and Borje Salming.

| | NRMT-MT | EXC |
|---|---|---|
| COMPLETE SET (396) | 500.00 | 220.00 |
| COMMON CARD (1-396) | 1.25 | .55 |

❑ 1 Goal Leaders 5.00 1.25
Phil Esposito
Bill Goldsworthy
❑ 2 Assists Leaders 8.00 3.60
Bobby Orr
Dennis Hextall
❑ 3 Scoring Leaders 6.00 2.70
Phil Esposito
Bobby Clarke
❑ 4 Goals Against Leaders 2.50 1.10
Doug Favell
Bernie Parent
❑ 5 Penalty Min. Leaders 1.25 .55
Bryan Watson
Dave Schultz
❑ 6 Power Play Goal 1.25 .55
Leaders
Mickey Redmond
Rick MacLeish
❑ 7 Gary Bromley 1.25 .55
❑ 8 Bill Barber 6.00 2.70
❑ 9 Emile Francis CO 1.25 .55
❑ 10 Gilles Gilbert 2.00 .90
❑ 11 John Davidson 15.00 6.75
❑ 12 Ron Ellis 1.25 .55
❑ 13 Syl Apps 1.25 .55
❑ 14 Flames Leaders 1.25 .55
Jacques Richard
Tom Lysiak
Tom Lysiak
Keith McCreary
❑ 15 Dan Bouchard 1.25 .55
❑ 16 Ivan Boldirev 1.25 .55
❑ 17 Gary Coalter 1.25 .55
❑ 18 Bob Berry 1.25 .55
❑ 19 Red Berenson 1.25 .55
❑ 20 Stan Mikita 6.00 2.70
❑ 21 Fred Shero CO 4.00 1.80
❑ 22 Gary Smith 1.25 .55
❑ 23 Bill Mikkelson 1.25 .55
❑ 24 Jacques Lemaire UER 3.00 1.35
(Pictured in
Sabres sweater)
❑ 25 Gilbert Perreault 8.00 3.60
❑ 26 Cesare Maniago 1.25 .55
❑ 27 Bobby Schmautz 1.25 .55
❑ 28 Bruins Leaders 10.00 4.50
Phil Esposito
Bobby Orr
Phil Esposito
Johnny Bucyk
❑ 29 Steve Vickers 1.25 .55
❑ 30 Lowell MacDonald UER 1.25 .55
(Home: Thornburn,
should be Thorburn)
❑ 31 Fred Stanfield 1.25 .55
❑ 32 Ed Westfall 1.25 .55
❑ 33 Curt Bennett 1.25 .55
❑ 34 Bep Guidolin CO 1.25 .55
❑ 35 Cliff Koroll 1.25 .55
❑ 36 Gary Croteau 1.25 .55
❑ 37 Mike Corrigan 1.25 .55
❑ 38 Henry Boucha 1.25 .55
❑ 39 Ron Low 1.25 .55
❑ 40 Darryl Sittler 10.00 4.50
❑ 41 Tracy Pratt 1.25 .55
❑ 42 Sabres Leaders 1.25 .55
Richard Martin
Rene Robert
Richard Martin
Richard Martin
❑ 43 Larry Carriere 1.25 .55
❑ 44 Gary Dornhoefer 1.25 .55
❑ 45 Denis Herron 5.00 2.20
❑ 46 Doug Favell 1.25 .55
❑ 47 Dave Gardner 1.25 .55
❑ 48 Morris Mott 1.25 .55
❑ 49 Marc Boileau CO 1.25 .55
❑ 50 Brad Park 5.00 2.20
❑ 51 Bob Leiter 1.25 .55
❑ 52 Tom Reid 1.25 .55
❑ 53 Serge Savard 1.25 .55
❑ 54 Checklist 1-132 UER 30.00 7.50
(73 Brent Hughes, should
be 73 Butch Deadmarsh)
❑ 55 Terry Harper 1.25 .55
❑ 56 Golden Seals 1.25 .55
Leaders
Joey Johnston
Joey Johnston
Joey Johnston
Walt McKechnie
❑ 57 Guy Charron 1.25 .55
❑ 58 Pit Martin 1.25 .55
❑ 59 Chris Evans 1.25 .55
❑ 60 Bernie Parent 6.00 2.70
❑ 61 Jim Lorentz 1.25 .55
❑ 62 Dave Kryskow 1.25 .55
❑ 63 Lou Angotti CO 1.25 .55
❑ 64 Bill Flett 1.25 .55
❑ 65 Vic Hadfield 1.25 .55
❑ 66 Wayne Merrick 1.25 .55
❑ 67 Andre Dupont 1.25 .55
❑ 68 Tom Lysiak 2.50 1.10
❑ 69 Blackhawks Leaders 1.25 .55
Jim Pappin
Stan Mikita
Stan Mikita
J.P. Bordeleau
❑ 70 Guy Lapointe 1.25 .55
❑ 71 Gerry O'Flaherty 1.25 .55
❑ 72 Marcel Dionne 10.00 4.50
❑ 73 Butch Deadmarsh 1.25 .55
❑ 74 Butch Goring 1.25 .55
❑ 75 Keith Magnuson 1.25 .55
❑ 76 Red Kelly CO 1.25 .55
❑ 77 Pete Stemkowski 1.25 .55
❑ 78 Jim Roberts 1.25 .55
❑ 79 Don Luce 1.25 .55
❑ 80 Don Awrey 1.25 .55
❑ 81 Rick Kehoe 1.25 .55
❑ 82 Billy Smith 10.00 4.50
❑ 83 Jean-Paul Parise 1.25 .55
❑ 84 Red Wings Leaders 2.00 .90
Mickey Redmond
Marcel Dionne
Marcel Dionne
Bill Hogaboam
❑ 85 Ed Van Impe 1.25 .55
❑ 86 Randy Manery 1.25 .55
❑ 87 Barclay Plager 1.25 .55
❑ 88 Inge Hammarstrom 1.25 .55
❑ 89 Ab DeMarco 1.25 .55
❑ 90 Bill White 1.25 .55
❑ 91 Al Arbour CO 2.50 1.10
❑ 92 Bob Stewart 1.25 .55
❑ 93 Jack Egers 1.25 .55
❑ 94 Don Lever 1.25 .55
❑ 95 Reggie Leach 1.25 .55
❑ 96 Dennis O'Brien 1.25 .55
❑ 97 Peter Mahovlich 1.25 .55
❑ 98 Kings Leaders 1.25 .55
Butch Goring
Frank St.Marseille
Butch Goring
Don Kozak
❑ 99 Gerry Meehan 1.25 .55
❑ 100 Bobby Orr 40.00 18.00
❑ 101 Jean Potvin 1.25 .55
❑ 102 Rod Seiling 1.25 .55
❑ 103 Keith McCreary 1.25 .55
❑ 104 Phil Maloney CO 1.25 .55
❑ 105 Denis Dupere 1.25 .55
❑ 106 Steve Durbano 1.25 .55
❑ 107 Bob Plager UER 1.25 .55
(Photo actually
Barclay Plager)
❑ 108 Chris Oddleifson 1.25 .55
❑ 109 Jim Neilson 1.25 .55
❑ 110 Jean Pronovost 1.25 .55
❑ 111 Don Kozak 1.25 .55
❑ 112 North Stars Leaders 1.25 .55
Bill Goldsworthy
Dennis Hextall
Dennis Hextall
Danny Grant
❑ 113 Jim Pappin 1.25 .55
❑ 114 Richard Lemieux 1.25 .55
❑ 115 Dennis Hextall 1.25 .55
❑ 116 Bill Hogaboam 1.25 .55
❑ 117 Canucks Leaders 1.25 .55
Dennis Ververgaert
Bobby Schmautz
Andre Boudrias
Andre Boudrias
Don Tannahill
❑ 118 Jimmy Anderson CO 1.25 .55
❑ 119 Walt Tkaczuk 1.25 .55
❑ 120 Mickey Redmond 1.25 .55
❑ 121 Jim Schoenfeld 2.00 .90
❑ 122 Jocelyn Guevremont 1.25 .55
❑ 123 Bob Nystrom 2.00 .90
❑ 124 Canadiens Leaders 2.50 1.10
Yvan Cournoyer
Frank Mahovlich
Frank Mahovlich
Claude Larose
❑ 125 Lew Morrison 1.25 .55
❑ 126 Terry Murray 1.25 .55
❑ 127 Richard Martin AS 1.25 .55
❑ 128 Ken Hodge AS 1.00 .45
❑ 129 Phil Esposito AS 4.00 1.80
❑ 130 Bobby Orr AS 20.00 9.00
❑ 131 Brad Park AS 2.50 1.10
❑ 132 Gilles Gilbert AS 1.25 .55
❑ 133 Lowell MacDonald AS 1.00 .45
❑ 134 Bill Goldsworthy AS 1.00 .45
❑ 135 Bobby Clarke AS 6.00 2.70
❑ 136 Bill White AS 1.00 .45
❑ 137 Dave Burrows AS 1.00 .45
❑ 138 Bernie Parent AS 2.50 1.10
❑ 139 Jacques Richard 1.25 .55
❑ 140 Yvan Cournoyer 3.00 1.35
❑ 141 Rangers Leaders 2.50 1.10
Rod Gilbert
Brad Park
Brad Park
Rod Gilbert
❑ 142 Rene Robert 1.25 .55
❑ 143 J. Bob Kelly 1.25 .55
❑ 144 Ross Lonsberry 1.25 .55
❑ 145 Jean Ratelle 2.50 1.10
❑ 146 Dallas Smith 1.25 .55
❑ 147 Bernie Geoffrion CO 3.00 1.35
❑ 148 Ted McAneeley 1.25 .55
❑ 149 Pierre Plante 1.25 .55
❑ 150 Dennis Hull 1.25 .55
❑ 151 Dave Keon 1.25 .55
❑ 152 Dave Dunn 1.25 .55
❑ 153 Michel Belhumeur 1.25 .55
❑ 154 Flyers Leaders 4.00 1.80
Bobby Clarke
Bobby Clarke
Bobby Clarke
Dave Schultz
❑ 155 Ken Dryden 25.00 11.00
❑ 156 John Wright 1.25 .55
❑ 157 Larry Romanchych 1.25 .55
❑ 158 Ralph Stewart 1.25 .55
❑ 159 Mike Robitaille 1.25 .55
❑ 160 Ed Giacomin 3.00 1.35
❑ 161 Don Cherry CO 50.00 22.00
❑ 162 Checklist 133-264 30.00 7.50
❑ 163 Rick MacLeish 2.00 .90
❑ 164 Greg Polis 1.25 .55
❑ 165 Carol Vadnais 1.25 .55
❑ 166 Pete Laframboise 1.25 .55
❑ 167 Ron Schock 1.25 .55
❑ 168 Lanny McDonald 20.00 9.00
❑ 169 Scouts Emblem 2.50 1.10
(Draft Selections
on back)
❑ 170 Tony Esposito 8.00 3.60
❑ 171 Pierre Jarry 1.25 .55
❑ 172 Dan Maloney 1.25 .55
❑ 173 Peter McDuffe 1.25 .55
❑ 174 Danny Grant 1.25 .55
❑ 175 John Stewart 1.25 .55
❑ 176 Floyd Smith CO 1.25 .55
❑ 177 Bert Marshall 1.25 .55
❑ 178 Chuck Lefley UER 1.25 .55
(Photo actually
Pierre Bouchard)
❑ 179 Gilles Villemure 1.25 .55
❑ 180 Borje Salming 25.00 11.00
❑ 181 Doug Mohns 1.25 .55
❑ 182 Barry Wilkins 1.25 .55
❑ 183 Penguins Leaders 1.25 .55
Lowell MacDonald
Syl Apps
Syl Apps
Lowell MacDonald
❑ 184 Gregg Sheppard 1.25 .55
❑ 185 Joey Johnston 1.25 .55
❑ 186 Dick Redmond 1.25 .55
❑ 187 Simon Nolet 1.25 .55
❑ 188 Ron Stackhouse 1.25 .55
❑ 189 Marshall Johnston 1.25 .55
❑ 190 Richard Martin 1.25 .55
❑ 191 Andre Boudrias 1.25 .55
❑ 192 Steve Atkinson 1.25 .55
❑ 193 Nick Libett 1.25 .55
❑ 194 Bob Murdoch 1.25 .55
❑ 195 Denis Potvin 40.00 18.00
❑ 196 Dave Schultz 3.00 1.35
❑ 197 Blues Leaders 1.25 .55
Garry Unger
Garry Unger
Garry Unger
Pierre Plante
❑ 198 Jim McKenny 1.25 .55
❑ 199 Gerry Hart 1.25 .55
❑ 200 Phil Esposito 6.00 2.70
❑ 201 Rod Gilbert 2.50 1.10
❑ 202 Jacques Laperriere 1.25 .55
❑ 203 Barry Gibbs 1.25 .55
❑ 204 Billy Reay CO 1.25 .55
❑ 205 Gilles Meloche 1.25 .55
❑ 206 Wayne Cashman 1.50 .70
❑ 207 Dennis Ververgaert 1.25 .55
❑ 208 Phil Roberto 1.25 .55
❑ 209 Quarter Finals 1.25 .55
Flyers sweep
Flames
❑ 210 Quarter Finals 1.25 .55
Rangers over
Canadiens
❑ 211 Quarter Finals 1.25 .55
Bruins sweep
Maple Leafs
❑ 212 Quarter Finals 1.25 .55
Blackhawks over
L.A. Kings
❑ 213 Semi-Finals 1.25 .55
Flyers over Rangers
❑ 214 Semi-Finals 1.25 .55
Bruins over
Blackhawks
❑ 215 '73-'74 Finals 1.25 .55
Flyers over Bruins
❑ 216 Cup Champions 2.00 .90
❑ 217 Joe Watson 1.25 .55
❑ 218 Wayne Stephenson 1.25 .55
❑ 219 Maple Leaf Leaders 2.00 .90
Darryl Sittler
Norm Ullman
Darryl Sittler
Paul Henderson
Denis Dupere
❑ 220 Bill Goldsworthy 1.25 .55
❑ 221 Don Marcotte 1.25 .55
❑ 222 Alex Delvecchio CO 1.25 .55
❑ 223 Stan Gilbertson 1.25 .55
❑ 224 Mike Murphy 1.25 .55
❑ 225 Jim Rutherford 1.25 .55
❑ 226 Phil Russell 1.25 .55
❑ 227 Lynn Powis 1.25 .55
❑ 228 Billy Harris 1.25 .55
❑ 229 Bob Pulford CO 1.25 .55
L.A. Kings Coach
❑ 230 Ken Hodge 1.25 .55
❑ 231 Bill Fairbairn 1.25 .55
❑ 232 Guy Lafleur 15.00 6.75
❑ 233 Islanders Leaders UER 3.00 1.35
Billy Harris
Ralph Stewart
Denis Potvin
Denis Potvin
Ralph Stewart
(Steward on front)
❑ 234 Fred Barrett 1.25 .55
❑ 235 Rogatien Vachon 4.00 1.80
❑ 236 Norm Ullman 2.50 1.10
❑ 237 Garry Unger 1.25 .55
❑ 238 Jack Gordon CO 1.25 .55
❑ 239 Johnny Bucyk 2.50 1.10
❑ 240 Bob Dailey 1.25 .55
❑ 241 Dave Burrows 1.25 .55
❑ 242 Len Frig 1.25 .55
❑ 243 Masterson Trophy 2.00 .90
Henri Richard
❑ 244 Hart Trophy 4.00 1.80
Phil Esposito
❑ 245 Byng Trophy 1.25 .55
Johnny Bucyk
❑ 246 Ross Trophy 4.00 1.80
Phil Esposito
❑ 247 Prince of Wales 1.50 .70
Trophy
❑ 248 Norris Trophy 20.00 9.00
Bobby Orr
❑ 249 Vezina Trophy 2.50 1.10
Bernie Parent
❑ 250 Stanley Cup 2.00 .90
❑ 251 Smythe Trophy 2.50 1.10
Bernie Parent
❑ 252 Calder Trophy 10.00 4.50
Denis Potvin
❑ 253 Campbell Trophy 1.50 .70
❑ 254 Pierre Bouchard 1.25 .55
❑ 255 Jude Drouin 1.25 .55
❑ 256 Capitals Emblem 2.50 1.10

(Draft Selections
on back)
□ 257 Michel Plasse ................. 1.25 .55
□ 258 Juha Widing ................. 1.25 .55
□ 259 Bryan Watson ................. 1.25 .55
□ 260 Bobby Clarke UER ........ 12.00 5.50
Back mentions Art Ross
Trophy. Should be Hart
Trophy
□ 261 Scotty Bowman CO ....... 40.00 18.00
□ 262 Craig Patrick ................. 1.25 .55
□ 263 Craig Cameron ................. 1.25 .55
□ 264 Ted Irvine ................. 1.25 .55
□ 265 Ed Johnston ................. 1.25 .55
□ 266 Dave Forbes ................. 1.25 .55
□ 267 Detroit Red Wings .......... 4.00 1.80
Team Card
(checklist back)
□ 268 Rick Dudley ................. 1.25 .55
□ 269 Darcy Rota ................. 1.25 .55
□ 270 Phil Myre ................. 1.25 .55
□ 271 Larry Brown ................. 1.25 .55
□ 272 Bob Neely ................. 1.25 .55
□ 273 Jerry Byers ................. 1.25 .55
□ 274 Pittsburgh Penguins ....... 4.00 1.80
Team Card
(checklist back)
□ 275 Glenn Goldup ................. 1.25 .55
□ 276 Ron Harris ................. 1.25 .55
□ 277 Joe Lundrigan ................. 1.25 .55
□ 278 Mike Christie ................. 1.25 .55
□ 279 Doug Rombough ................. 1.25 .55
□ 280 Larry Robinson ............ 20.00 9.00
□ 281 St. Louis Blues .............. 4.00 1.80
Team Card
(checklist back)
□ 282 John Marks ................. 1.25 .55
□ 283 Don Saleski ................. 1.25 .55
□ 284 Rick Wilson ................. 1.25 .55
□ 285 Andre Savard ................. 1.25 .55
□ 286 Pat Quinn ................. 1.25 .55
□ 287 Los Angeles Kings .......... 4.00 1.80
Team Card
(checklist back)
□ 288 Norm Gratton ................. 1.25 .55
□ 289 Ian Turnbull ................. 1.25 .55
□ 290 Derek Sanderson ........... 4.00 1.80
□ 291 Murray Oliver ................. 1.25 .55
□ 292 Wilf Paiement UER ......... 2.50 1.10
(Misspelled Paiemont
on card front)
□ 293 Nelson Debenedet .......... 1.25 .55
□ 294 Greg Joly ................. 1.25 .55
□ 295 Terry O'Reilly ................. 3.00 1.35
□ 296 Rey Comeau ................. 1.25 .55
□ 297 Michel Larocque ............ 5.00 2.20
□ 298 Floyd Thomson ................. 1.25 .55
□ 299 Jean-Guy Lagace ........... 1.25 .55
□ 300 Philadelphia Flyers ......... 4.00 1.80
Team Card
(checklist back)
□ 301 Al MacAdam ................. 2.50 1.10
□ 302 George Ferguson ............ 1.25 .55
□ 303 Jim Watson ................. 2.50 1.10
□ 304 Rick Middleton ............. 15.00 6.75
□ 305 Craig Ramsay UER .......... 1.25 .55
(Name on front is "Graig")
□ 306 Hilliard Graves ................. 1.25 .55
□ 307 New York Islanders ........ 4.00 1.80
Team Card
(checklist back)
□ 308 Blake Dunlop ................. 1.25 .55
□ 309 J.P. Bordeleau ................. 1.25 .55
□ 310 Brian Glennie ................. 1.25 .55
□ 311 Checklist 265-396 UER. 30.00 7.50
(373 Gilies Marotte,
should be Gilles)
□ 312 Doug Roberts ................. 1.25 .55
□ 313 Darryl Edestrand ............. 1.25 .55
□ 314 Ron Anderson ................. 1.25 .55
□ 315 Chicago Blackhawks ....... 4.00 1.80
Team Card
(checklist back)
□ 316 Steve Shutt ................. 15.00 6.75
□ 317 Doug Horbul ................. 1.25 .55
□ 318 Billy Lochead ................. 1.25 .55
□ 319 Fred Harvey ................. 1.25 .55
□ 320 Gene Carr ................. 1.25 .55
□ 321 Henri Richard ................. 4.00 1.80
□ 322 Vancouver Canucks ........ 4.00 1.80
Team Card
(checklist back)
□ 323 Tim Ecclestone ................. 1.25 .55
□ 324 Dave Lewis ................. 1.25 .55
□ 325 Lou Nanne ................. 1.25 .55
□ 326 Bobby Rousseau ............. 1.25 .55
□ 327 Dunc Wilson ................. 1.25 .55
□ 328 Brian Spencer ................. 1.25 .55
□ 329 Rick Hampton ................. 1.25 .55
□ 330 Montreal Canadiens ........ 4.00 1.80
Team Card UER
(checklist back;
275 Glen Holdup,
should be Goldup)
□ 331 Jack Lynch ................. 1.25 .55
□ 332 Garnet Bailey ................. 1.25 .55
□ 333 Al Sims RC ................. 1.25 .55
□ 334 Orest Kindrachuk ............ 2.00 .90
□ 335 Dave Hudson ................. 1.25 .55
□ 336 Bob Murray ................. 1.25 .55
□ 337 Buffalo Sabres ................. 4.00 1.80
Team Card
(checklist back)
□ 338 Sheldon Kannegiesser .... 1.25 .55
□ 339 Bill MacMillan ................. 1.25 .55
□ 340 Paulin Bordeleau ............ 1.25 .55
□ 341 Dale Rolfe ................. 1.25 .55
□ 342 Yvon Lambert ................. 2.00 .90
□ 343 Bob Paradise ................. 1.25 .55
□ 344 Germaine Gagnon UER ... 1.25 .55
□ 345 Yvon Labre ................. 1.25 .55
□ 346 Chris Ahrens ................. 1.25 .55
□ 347 Doug Grant ................. 1.25 .55
□ 348 Blaine Stoughton ............ 4.00 1.80
□ 349 Gregg Boddy ................. 1.25 .55
□ 350 Boston Bruins ................. 4.00 1.80
Team Card
(checklist back)
□ 351 Doug Jarrett ................. 1.25 .55
□ 352 Terry Crisp ................. 1.25 .55
□ 353 Glenn Resch ................. 15.00 6.75
□ 354 Jerry Korab ................. 1.25 .55
□ 355 Stan Weir ................. 1.25 .55
□ 356 Noel Price ................. 1.25 .55
□ 357 Bill Clement ................. 12.00 5.50
□ 358 Neil Komadoski ................. 1.25 .55
□ 359 Murray Wilson ................. 1.25 .55
□ 360 Dale Tallon UER ............. 1.25 .55
(Misspelled Talon
on card front)
□ 361 Gary Doak ................. 1.25 .55
□ 362 Randy Rota ................. 1.25 .55
□ 363 Minnesota North Stars .... 4.00 1.80
Team Card
(checklist back)
□ 364 Bill Collins ................. 1.25 .55
□ 365 Thommie Bergman UER . 1.25 .55
(Misspelled Tommie
on card front)
□ 366 Dennis Kearns ................. 1.25 .55
□ 367 Lorne Henning ................. 1.25 .55
□ 368 Gary Sabourin ................. 1.25 .55
□ 369 Mike Bloom ................. 1.25 .55
□ 370 New York Rangers .......... 4.00 1.80
Team Card
(checklist back)
□ 371 Gary Simmons ................. 4.00 1.80
□ 372 Dwight Bialowas ............. 1.25 .55
□ 373 Gilles Marotte ................. 1.25 .55
□ 374 Frank St.Marseille ........... 1.25 .55
□ 375 Garry Howatt ................. 1.25 .55
□ 376 Ross Brooks ................. 1.25 .55
□ 377 Atlanta Flames ................. 4.00 1.80
Team Card
(checklist back)
□ 378 Bob Nevin ................. 1.25 .55
□ 379 Lyle Moffat ................. 1.25 .55
□ 380 Bob Kelly ................. 1.25 .55
□ 381 John Gould ................. 1.25 .55
□ 382 Dave Fortier ................. 1.25 .55
□ 383 Jean Hamel ................. 1.25 .55
□ 384 Bert Wilson ................. 1.25 .55
□ 385 Chuck Arnason ................. 1.25 .55
□ 386 Bruce Cowick ................. 1.25 .55
□ 387 Ernie Hicke ................. 1.25 .55
□ 388 Bob Gainey ................. 20.00 9.00
□ 389 Vic Venasky ................. 1.25 .55
□ 390 Toronto Maple Leafs ....... 4.00 1.80
Team Card
(checklist back)
□ 391 Eric Vail ................. 1.25 .55
□ 392 Bobby Lalonde ................. 1.25 .55
□ 393 Jerry Butler ................. 1.25 .55
□ 394 Tom Williams ................. 1.25 .55
□ 395 Chico Maki ................. 1.25 .55
□ 396 Tom Bladon ................. 4.00 1.00

## 1974-75 O-Pee-Chee WHA

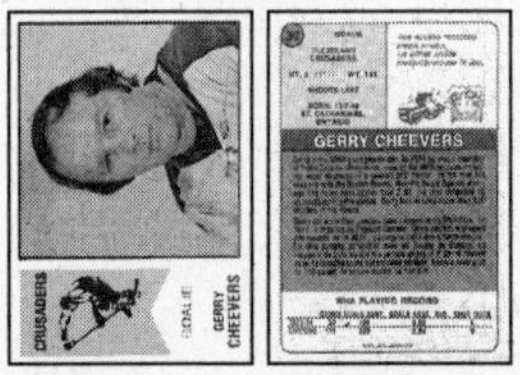


The 1974-75 O-Pee-Chee WHA set consists of 66 color standard-size cards. The cards were originally sold in eight-card ten-cent wax packs. Bilingual backs feature a short biography, the player's 1973-74 and career WHA statistics as well as a cartoon-illustrated hockey fact or interpretation of a referee's signal. Rookie Cards in this set include Anders Hedberg and Ulf Nilsson, although some collectors and dealers consider the Howe Family card to be the Rookie Card for Mark and Marty Howe.

| | NRMT-MT | EXC |
|---|---|---|
| COMPLETE SET (66) | 200.00 | 90.00 |
| COMMON CARD (1-66) | 3.00 | 1.35 |

□ 1 The Howes ................. 75.00 19.00
Gordie Howe
Mark Howe
Marty Howe
□ 2 Bruce MacGregor ............. 3.00 1.35
□ 3 Wayne Dillon ................. 3.00 1.35
□ 4 Ulf Nilsson ................. 12.00 5.50
□ 5 Serge Bernier ................. 4.00 1.80
□ 6 Bryan Campbell ................. 3.00 1.35
□ 7 Rosaire Paiement ............. 3.00 1.35
□ 8 Tom Webster ................. 4.00 1.80
□ 9 Gerry Pinder ................. 3.00 1.35
□ 10 Mike Walton ................. 3.00 1.35
□ 11 Norm Beaudin ................. 3.00 1.35
□ 12 Bob Whitlock ................. 3.00 1.35
□ 13 Wayne Rivers ................. 3.00 1.35
□ 14 Gerry Odrowski ................. 3.00 1.35
□ 15 Ron Climie ................. 3.00 1.35
□ 16 Tom Simpson ................. 3.00 1.35
□ 17 Anders Hedberg ............. 12.00 5.50
□ 18 J.C. Tremblay ................. 3.00 1.35
□ 19 Mike Pelyk ................. 3.00 1.35
□ 20 Dave Dryden ................. 4.00 1.80
□ 21 Ron Ward ................. 3.00 1.35
□ 22 Larry Lund ................. 3.00 1.35
□ 23 Ron Buchanan ................. 3.00 1.35
□ 24 Pat Hickey ................. 4.00 1.80
□ 25 Danny Lawson ................. 4.00 1.80
□ 26 Bob Guindon ................. 3.00 1.35
□ 27 Gene Peacosh ................. 3.00 1.35
□ 28 Fran Huck ................. 3.00 1.35
□ 29 Al Hamilton ................. 3.00 1.35
□ 30 Gerry Cheevers ............. 15.00 6.75
□ 31 Heikki Riihiranta ............. 4.00 1.80
□ 32 Don Burgess ................. 3.00 1.35
□ 33 John French ................. 3.00 1.35
□ 34 Jim Wiste ................. 3.00 1.35
□ 35 Pat Stapleton ................. 4.00 1.80
□ 36 J.P. LeBlanc ................. 3.00 1.35
□ 37 Mike Antonovich ............. 3.00 1.35
□ 38 Joe Daley ................. 4.00 1.80
□ 39 Ross Perkins ................. 3.00 1.35
□ 40 Frank Mahovlich ............ 12.00 5.50
□ 41 Rejean Houle ................. 3.00 1.35
□ 42 Ron Chipperfield ............. 3.00 1.35
□ 43 Marc Tardif ................. 5.00 2.20
□ 44 Murray Keogan ................. 3.00 1.35
□ 45 Wayne Carleton ................. 3.00 1.35
□ 46 Andre Gaudette ................. 3.00 1.35
□ 47 Ralph Backstrom ............. 4.00 1.80
□ 48 Don McLeod ................. 4.00 1.80
□ 49 Vaclav Nedomansky ......... 4.00 1.80
□ 50 Bobby Hull ................. 40.00 18.00
□ 51 Rusty Patenaude ............. 3.00 1.35
□ 52 Michel Parizeau ............. 3.00 1.35
□ 53 Checklist ................. 30.00 7.50
□ 54 Wayne Connelly ............. 4.00 1.80
□ 55 Gary Veneruzzo ............. 3.00 1.35
□ 56 Dennis Sobchuk ............. 3.00 1.35
□ 57 Paul Henderson ............. 4.00 1.80
□ 58 Andy Brown ................. 4.00 1.80
□ 59 Paul Popiel ................. 3.00 1.35
□ 60 Andre Lacroix ................. 4.00 1.80
□ 61 Gary Jarrett ................. 3.00 1.35
□ 62 Claude St.Sauveur ........... 3.00 1.35
□ 63 Real Cloutier ................. 5.00 2.20
□ 64 Jacques Plante ............. 40.00 18.00
□ 65 Gilles Gratton ................. 7.00 3.10
□ 66 Lars-Erik Sjoberg ............. 8.00 2.00

## 1975-76 O-Pee-Chee NHL

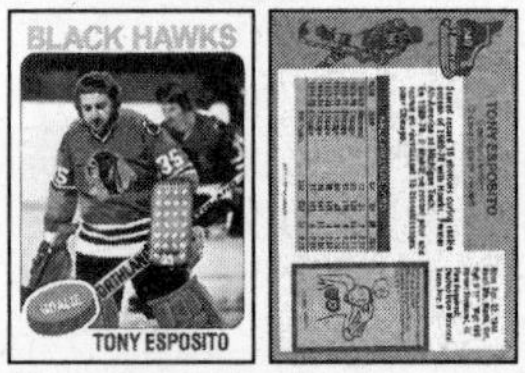


The 1975-76 O-Pee-Chee NHL set consists of 396 color standard-size cards. The cards were originally sold in ten-cent wax packs. The first 330 cards have identical fronts (except perhaps for a short traded line) to the Topps set of this year. Number 395 was not issued; however, the set contains two of number 267, which are checklist cards. Cards 26, 27, 200, 236, 243, 260, and 359 come with or without a traded line. Team cards (81-98) have a team checklist on the back. Bilingual backs contain year-by-year and career statistics, a short biography and a cartoon-illustrated NHL fact or interpretation of a referee's signal. The key Rookie Cards in this set are Clark Gillies, Pierre Larouche and Harold Snepsts. Snepsts, the last card in the set, is considered very difficult to find in top grades.

| | NRMT-MT | EXC |
|---|---|---|
| COMPLETE SET (396) | 350.00 | 160.00 |
| COMMON CARD (1-396) | .75 | .35 |

□ 1 Stanley Cup Finals ............ 3.00 .75
Philadelphia 4
Buffalo 2
□ 2 Semi-Finals ................. 1.00 .45
Philadelphia 4
N.Y. Islanders 3
□ 3 Semi-Finals ................. 1.00 .45
Buffalo 4
Montreal
□ 4 Quarter Finals ................. 1.00 .45
N.Y. Islanders 4
Pittsburgh 2
□ 5 Quarter Finals ................. 1.00 .45
Montreal 4
Vancouver 1
□ 6 Quarter Finals ................. 1.00 .45
Buffalo 4
Chicago 1
□ 7 Quarter Finals ................. 1.00 .45
Philadelphia 4
Toronto 0
□ 8 Curt Bennett ................. .75 .35
□ 9 Johnny Bucyk ................. 2.00 .90
□ 10 Gilbert Perreault ............. 6.00 2.70
□ 11 Darryl Edestrand ............. .75 .35
□ 12 Ivan Boldirev ................. .75 .35
□ 13 Nick Libett ................. .75 .35
□ 14 Jim McElmury ................. .75 .35
□ 15 Frank St.Marseille ............. .75 .35
□ 16 Blake Dunlop ................. .75 .35
□ 17 Yvon Lambert ................. 1.50 .70
□ 18 Gerry Hart ................. .75 .35
□ 19 Steve Vickers ................. .75 .35
□ 20 Rick MacLeish ................. 1.50 .70
□ 21 Bob Paradise ................. .75 .35
□ 22 Red Berenson ................. 1.50 .70
□ 23 Lanny McDonald ............. 7.00 3.10
□ 24 Mike Robitaille ................. .75 .35
□ 25 Ron Low ................. 1.50 .70
□ 26A Bryan Hextall ................. 1.25 .55
(No mention of trade)
□ 26B Bryan Hextall ................. 1.00 .45
(Trade noted)
□ 27A Carol Vadnais ................. 1.25 .55
(No mention of trade)
□ 27B Carol Vadnais ................. 1.00 .45
(Trade noted)
□ 28 Jim Lorentz ................. .75 .35
□ 29 Gary Simmons ................. 1.50 .70
□ 30 Stan Mikita ................. 5.00 2.20
□ 31 Bryan Watson ................. .75 .35
□ 32 Guy Charron ................. .75 .35
□ 33 Bob Murdoch ................. .75 .35
□ 34 Norm Gratton ................. .75 .35
□ 35 Ken Dryden ................. 20.00 9.00
□ 36 Jean Potvin ................. .75 .35
□ 37 Rick Middleton ................. 5.00 2.20
□ 38 Ed Van Impe ................. .75 .35
□ 39 Rick Kehoe ................. 1.50 .70
□ 40 Garry Unger ................. 1.50 .70
□ 41 Ian Turnbull ................. 1.50 .70
□ 42 Dennis Ververgaert ........... .75 .35
□ 43 Mike Marson ................. 1.50 .70
□ 44 Randy Manery ................. .75 .35
□ 45 Gilles Gilbert ................. 1.50 .70
□ 46 Rene Robert ................. 1.50 .70
□ 47 Bob Stewart ................. .75 .35
□ 48 Pit Martin ................. .75 .35
□ 49 Danny Grant ................. 1.50 .70
□ 50 Peter Mahovlich ............. 1.50 .70
□ 51 Dennis Patterson ............. .75 .35
□ 52 Mike Murphy ................. .75 .35
□ 53 Dennis O'Brien ................. .75 .35
□ 54 Garry Howatt ................. .75 .35
□ 55 Ed Giacomin ................. 2.50 1.10
□ 56 Andre Dupont ................. .75 .35
□ 57 Chuck Arnason ................. .75 .35
□ 58 Bob Gassoff ................. .75 .35
□ 59 Ron Ellis ................. 1.50 .70
□ 60 Andre Boudrias ................. .75 .35
□ 61 Yvon Labre ................. .75 .35
□ 62 Hilliard Graves ................. .75 .35
□ 63 Wayne Cashman ............. 1.50 .70
□ 64 Danny Gare ................. 3.00 1.35
□ 65 Rick Hampton ................. .75 .35
□ 66 Darcy Rota ................. .75 .35
□ 67 Bill Hogaboam ................. .75 .35
□ 68 Denis Herron ................. 1.50 .70
□ 69 Sheldon Kannegiesser ....... .75 .35
□ 70 Yvan Cournoyer ............. 2.50 1.10
□ 71 Ernie Hicke ................. .75 .35
□ 72 Bert Marshall ................. .75 .35
□ 73 Derek Sanderson ............. 4.00 1.80
□ 74 Tom Bladon ................. .75 .35
□ 75 Ron Schock ................. .75 .35
□ 76 Larry Sacharuk ................. .75 .35
□ 77 George Ferguson ............. .75 .35
□ 78 Ab DeMarco ................. .75 .35
□ 79 Tom Williams ................. .75 .35
□ 80 Phil Roberto ................. .75 .35
□ 81 Bruins Team ................. 4.00 1.80
(checklist back)
□ 82 Seals Team ................. 4.00 1.80
(checklist back)
□ 83 Sabres Team ................. 4.00 1.80
(checklist back)
□ 84 Blackhawks Team ............. 4.00 1.80
(checklist back)
□ 85 Flames Team ................. 4.00 1.80
(checklist back)
□ 86 Kings Team ................. 4.00 1.80
(checklist back)
□ 87 Red Wings Team ............. 4.00 1.80
(checklist back)
□ 88 Scouts Team ................. 4.00 1.80
(checklist back)
□ 89 North Stars Team ............. 4.00 1.80
(checklist back)
□ 90 Canadiens Team ............. 4.00 1.80
(checklist back)
□ 91 Maple Leafs Team ............. 4.00 1.80
(checklist back)
□ 92 Islanders Team ................. 4.00 1.80
(checklist back)
□ 93 Penguins Team ................. 4.00 1.80
(checklist back)
□ 94 Rangers Team ................. 4.00 1.80
(checklist back)
□ 95 Flyers Team ................. 4.00 1.80
(checklist back)
□ 96 Blues Team ................. 4.00 1.80
(checklist back)
□ 97 Canucks Team ................. 4.00 1.80
(checklist back)
□ 98 Capitals Team ................. 4.00 1.80
(checklist back)
□ 99 Checklist 1-110 ............. 15.00 3.70
□ 100 Bobby Orr ................. 30.00 13.50
□ 101 Germain Gagnon UER ....... .75 .35
(First name spelled Germaine)
□ 102 Phil Russell ................. .75 .35
□ 103 Billy Lochead ................. .75 .35
□ 104 Robin Burns ................. .75 .35
□ 105 Gary Edwards ................. 1.50 .70
□ 106 Dwight Bialowas ............. .75 .35
□ 107 Doug Risebrough UER .... 3.00 1.35
(Photo actually
Bob Gainey)
□ 108 Dave Lewis ................. .75 .35
□ 109 Bill Fairbairn ................. .75 .35
□ 110 Ross Lonsberry ................. .75 .35
□ 111 Ron Stackhouse ............. .75 .35
□ 112 Claude Larose ................. .75 .35
□ 113 Don Luce ................. .75 .35
□ 114 Errol Thompson ............. .75 .35
□ 115 Gary Smith ................. 1.50 .70
□ 116 Jack Lynch ................. .75 .35
□ 117 Jacques Richard ............. .75 .35
□ 118 Dallas Smith ................. .75 .35
□ 119 Dave Gardner ................. .75 .35
□ 120 Mickey Redmond ............. 1.50 .70
□ 121 John Marks ................. .75 .35
□ 122 Dave Hudson ................. .75 .35
□ 123 Bob Nevin ................. .75 .35
□ 124 Fred Barrett ................. .75 .35
□ 125 Gerry Desjardins ............. 1.50 .70
□ 126 Guy Lafleur UER ............. 15.00 6.75
(Shown as Defenseman
on card front)
□ 127 Jean-Paul Parise ............. .75 .35
□ 128 Walt Tkaczuk ................. 1.50 .70
□ 129 Gary Dornhoefer ............. 1.50 .70
□ 130 Syl Apps ................. .75 .35
□ 131 Bob Plager ................. 1.50 .70
□ 132 Stan Weir ................. .75 .35
□ 133 Tracy Pratt ................. .75 .35
□ 134 Jack Egers ................. .75 .35
□ 135 Eric Vail ................. .75 .35
□ 136 Al Sims ................. .75 .35
□ 137 Larry Patey ................. .75 .35
□ 138 Jim Schoenfeld ............. 1.50 .70
□ 139 Cliff Koroll ................. .75 .35
□ 140 Marcel Dionne ................. 7.00 3.10
□ 141 Jean-Guy Lagace ............. .75 .35
□ 142 Juha Widing ................. .75 .35
□ 143 Lou Nanne ................. 1.50 .70
□ 144 Serge Savard ................. 1.50 .70
□ 145 Glenn Resch ................. 5.00 2.20
□ 146 Ron Greschner ................. 3.00 1.35
□ 147 Dave Schultz ................. 2.00 .90
□ 148 Barry Wilkins ................. .75 .35
□ 149 Floyd Thomson ................. .75 .35
□ 150 Darryl Sittler ................. 8.00 3.60
□ 151 Paulin Bordeleau ............. .75 .35
□ 152 Ron Lalonde ................. .75 .35
□ 153 Larry Romanchych ........... .75 .35
□ 154 Larry Carriere ................. .75 .35
□ 155 Andre Savard ................. .75 .35
□ 156 Dave Hrechkosy ............. .75 .35
□ 157 Bill White ................. .75 .35
□ 158 Dave Kryskow ................. .75 .35
□ 159 Denis Dupere ................. .75 .35
□ 160 Rogatien Vachon ............. 3.00 1.35
□ 161 Doug Rombough ............. .75 .35
□ 162 Murray Wilson ................. .75 .35
□ 163 Bob Bourne ................. 3.00 1.35
□ 164 Gilles Marotte ................. .75 .35
□ 165 Vic Hadfield ................. 1.50 .70
□ 166 Reggie Leach ................. 1.50 .70
□ 167 Jerry Butler ................. .75 .35
□ 168 Inge Hammarstrom ........... .75 .35
□ 169 Chris Oddleifson ............. .75 .35
□ 170 Greg Joly ................. .75 .35
□ 171 Checklist 111-220 ........ 15.00 3.70
□ 172 Pat Quinn ................. 1.50 .70
□ 173 Dave Forbes ................. .75 .35
□ 174 Len Frig ................. .75 .35
□ 175 Richard Martin ................. 1.50 .70
□ 176 Keith Magnuson ............. .75 .35
□ 177 Dan Maloney ................. .75 .35
□ 178 Craig Patrick ................. 1.50 .70
□ 179 Tom Williams ................. .75 .35
□ 180 Bill Goldsworthy ............. 1.50 .70
□ 181 Steve Shutt ................. 5.00 2.20
□ 182 Ralph Stewart ................. .75 .35
□ 183 John Davidson ................. 5.00 2.20
□ 184 Bob Kelly ................. .75 .35
□ 185 Ed Johnston ................. 1.50 .70
□ 186 Dave Burrows ................. .75 .35
□ 187 Dave Dunn ................. .75 .35
□ 188 Dennis Kearns ................. .75 .35
□ 189 Bill Clement ................. 4.00 1.80
□ 190 Gilles Meloche ................. 1.50 .70
□ 191 Bob Leiter ................. .75 .35
□ 192 Jerry Korab ................. .75 .35
□ 193 Joey Johnston ................. .75 .35
□ 194 Walt McKechnie ............. .75 .35
□ 195 Wilf Paiement ................. 1.50 .70
□ 196 Bob Berry ................. .75 .35
□ 197 Dean Talafous ................. .75 .35
□ 198 Guy Lapointe ................. 1.50 .70
□ 199 Clark Gillies ................. 8.00 3.60
□ 200A Phil Esposito ................. 8.00 3.60
(No mention of trade)
□ 200B Phil Esposito ................. 5.00 2.20
(Trade noted)
□ 201 Greg Polis ................. .75 .35
□ 202 Jim Watson ................. 1.50 .70
□ 203 Gord McRae ................. 1.50 .70
□ 204 Lowell MacDonald ........... .75 .35
□ 205 Barclay Plager ................. 1.50 .70

❑ 206 Don Lever .75 .35
❑ 207 Bill Mikkelson .75 .35
❑ 208 Goals Leaders 5.00 2.20
Phil Esposito
Guy Lafleur
Richard Martin
❑ 209 Assists Leaders 8.00 3.60
Bobby Clarke
Bobby Orr
Pete Mahovlich
❑ 210 Scoring Leaders 8.00 3.60
Bobby Orr
Phil Esposito
Marcel Dionne
❑ 211 Penalty Min. Leaders .75 .35
Dave Schultz
Andre Dupont
Phil Russell
❑ 212 Power Play 3.00 1.35
Goal Leaders
Phil Esposito
Richard Martin
Danny Grant
❑ 213 Goals Against 8.00 3.60
Average Leaders
Bernie Parent
Rogatien Vachon
Ken Dryden
❑ 214 Barry Gibbs .75 .35
❑ 215 Ken Hodge 1.50 .70
❑ 216 Jocelyn Guevremont .75 .35
❑ 217 Warren Williams .75 .35
❑ 218 Dick Redmond .75 .35
❑ 219 Jim Rutherford 1.50 .70
❑ 220 Simon Nolet .75 .35
❑ 221 Butch Goring 1.50 .70
❑ 222 Glen Sather 1.50 .70
❑ 223 Mario Tremblay UER 5.00 2.20
(Photo not him)
❑ 224 Jude Drouin .75 .35
❑ 225 Rod Gilbert 2.00 .90
❑ 226 Bill Barber 4.00 1.80
❑ 227 Gary Inness 1.50 .70
❑ 228 Wayne Merrick .75 .35
❑ 229 Rod Seiling .75 .35
❑ 230 Tom Lysiak 1.50 .70
❑ 231 Bob Dailey .75 .35
❑ 232 Michel Belhumeur 1.50 .70
❑ 233 Bill Hajt .75 .35
❑ 234 Jim Pappin .75 .35
❑ 235 Gregg Sheppard .75 .35
❑ 236A Gary Bergman 1.25 .55
(No mention of trade)
❑ 236B Gary Bergman 1.00 .45
(Trade noted)
❑ 237 Randy Rota .75 .35
❑ 238 Neil Komadoski .75 .35
❑ 239 Craig Cameron .75 .35
❑ 240 Tony Esposito 6.00 2.70
❑ 241 Larry Robinson 12.00 5.50
❑ 242 Billy Harris .75 .35
❑ 243A Jean Ratelle 3.00 1.35
(No mention of trade)
❑ 243B Jean Ratelle 2.00 .90
(Trade noted)
❑ 244 Ted Irvine UER .75 .35
(Photo actually
Ted Harris)
❑ 245 Bob Neely .75 .35
❑ 246 Bobby Lalonde .75 .35
❑ 247 Ron Jones .75 .35
❑ 248 Rey Comeau .75 .35
❑ 249 Michel Plasse 1.50 .70
❑ 250 Bobby Clarke 10.00 4.50
❑ 251 Bobby Schmautz .75 .35
❑ 252 Peter McNab 4.00 1.80
❑ 253 Al MacAdam .75 .35
❑ 254 Dennis Hull 1.50 .70
❑ 255 Terry Harper .75 .35
❑ 256 Peter McDuffe 1.50 .70
❑ 257 Jean Hamel .75 .35
❑ 258 Jacques Lemaire 2.00 .90
❑ 259 Bob Nystrom 1.50 .70
❑ 260A Brad Park 4.00 1.80
(No mention of trade)
❑ 260B Brad Park 3.00 1.35
(Trade noted)
❑ 261 Cesare Maniago 1.50 .70
❑ 262 Don Saleski .75 .35
❑ 263 J. Bob Kelly .75 .35
❑ 264 Bob Hess .75 .35
❑ 265 Blaine Stoughton 1.50 .70
❑ 266 John Gould .75 .35
❑ 267A Checklist 221-330 15.00 3.70
(See number 395)
❑ 267B Checklist 331-396 15.00 3.70
❑ 268 Dan Bouchard 1.50 .70
❑ 269 Don Marcotte .75 .35
❑ 270 Jim Neilson .75 .35
❑ 271 Craig Ramsay .75 .35
❑ 272 Grant Mulvey 1.50 .70
❑ 273 Larry Giroux .75 .35
❑ 274 Real Lemieux .75 .35
❑ 275 Denis Potvin 12.00 5.50
❑ 276 Don Kozak .75 .35
❑ 277 Tom Reid .75 .35
❑ 278 Bob Gainey 7.00 3.10
❑ 279 Nick Beverley .75 .35
❑ 280 Jean Pronovost 1.50 .70
❑ 281 Joe Watson .75 .35
❑ 282 Chuck Lefley .75 .35
❑ 283 Borje Salming 8.00 3.60
❑ 284 Garnet Bailey .75 .35
❑ 285 Gregg Boddy .75 .35
❑ 286 Bobby Clarke AS1 5.00 2.20
❑ 287 Denis Potvin AS1 5.00 2.20
❑ 288 Bobby Orr AS1 15.00 6.75
❑ 289 Richard Martin AS1 1.50 .70
❑ 290 Guy Lafleur AS1 6.00 2.70
❑ 291 Bernie Parent AS1 2.00 .90
❑ 292 Phil Esposito AS2 4.00 1.80
❑ 293 Guy Lapointe AS2 .75 .35
❑ 294 Borje Salming AS2 4.00 1.80
❑ 295 Steve Vickers AS2 .75 .35
❑ 296 Rene Robert AS2 .75 .35
❑ 297 Rogatien Vachon AS2 2.50 1.10
❑ 298 Buster Harvey .75 .35
❑ 299 Gary Sabourin .75 .35
❑ 300 Bernie Parent 4.00 1.80
❑ 301 Terry O'Reilly 2.00 .90
❑ 302 Ed Westfall 1.50 .70
❑ 303 Pete Stemkowski .75 .35
❑ 304 Pierre Bouchard .75 .35
❑ 305 Pierre Larouche 8.00 3.60
❑ 306 Lee Fogolin .75 .35
❑ 307 Gerry O'Flaherty .75 .35
❑ 308 Phil Myre 1.50 .70
❑ 309 Pierre Plante .75 .35
❑ 310 Dennis Hextall .75 .35
❑ 311 Jim McKenny .75 .35
❑ 312 Vic Venasky .75 .35
❑ 313 Flames Leaders .75 .35
Eric Vail
Tom Lysiak
❑ 314 Bruins Leaders 8.00 3.60
Phil Esposito
Bobby Orr
Johnny Bucyk
❑ 315 Sabres Leaders 1.50 .70
Richard Martin
Rene Robert
❑ 316 Seals Leaders .75 .35
Dave Hrechkosy
Larry Patey
Stan Weir
❑ 317 Blackhawks Leaders 2.50 1.10
Stan Mikita
Jim Pappin
❑ 318 Red Wings Leaders 2.50 1.10
Danny Grant
Marcel Dionne
❑ 319 Scouts Leaders .75 .35
Simon Nolet
Wilf Paiement
Guy Charron
❑ 320 Kings Leaders .75 .35
Bob Nevin
Juha Widing
Bob Berry
❑ 321 North Stars Leaders .75 .35
Bill Goldsworthy
Dennis Hextall
❑ 322 Canadiens Leaders 3.00 1.35
Guy Lafleur
Pete Mahovlich
❑ 323 Islanders Leaders 2.50 1.10
Bob Nystrom
Denis Potvin
Denis Potvin
Clark Gillies
❑ 324 Rangers Leaders 2.50 1.10
Steve Vickers
Rod Gilbert
Jean Ratelle
❑ 325 Flyers Leaders 2.00 .90
Reggie Leach
Bobby Clarke
❑ 326 Penguins Leaders .75 .35
Jean Pronovost
Ron Schock
❑ 327 Blues Leaders 1.50 .70
Garry Unger
Larry Sacharuk
❑ 328 Maple Leafs Leaders 2.50 1.10
Darryl Sittler
❑ 329 Canucks Leaders .75 .35
Don Lever
Andre Boudrias
❑ 330 Capitals Leaders .75 .35
Tommy Williams
Garnet Bailey
❑ 331 Noel Price .75 .35
❑ 332 Fred Stanfield .75 .35
❑ 333 Doug Jarrett .75 .35
❑ 334 Gary Coalter .75 .35
❑ 335 Murray Oliver .75 .35
❑ 336 Dave Fortier .75 .35
❑ 337 Terry Crisp UER .75 .35
(Photo actually
Don Saleski)
❑ 338 Bert Wilson .75 .35
❑ 339 John Grisdale .75 .35
❑ 340 Ken Broderick 1.50 .70
❑ 341 Frank Spring .75 .35
❑ 342 Mike Korney .75 .35
❑ 343 Gene Carr .75 .35
❑ 344 Don Awrey .75 .35
❑ 345 Pat Hickey .75 .35
❑ 346 Colin Campbell 2.50 1.10
❑ 347 Wayne Thomas 1.50 .70
❑ 348 Bob Gryp .75 .35
❑ 349 Bill Flett .75 .35
❑ 350 Roger Crozier 1.50 .70
❑ 351 Dale Tallon .75 .35
❑ 352 Larry Johnston .75 .35
❑ 353 John Flesch .75 .35
❑ 354 Lorne Henning .75 .35
❑ 355 Wayne Stephenson 1.50 .70
❑ 356 Rick Wilson .75 .35
❑ 357 Garry Monahan .75 .35
❑ 358 Gary Doak .75 .35
❑ 359A Pierre Jarry 1.25 .55
(No mention of trade)
❑ 359B Pierre Jarry 1.00 .45
(Trade noted)
❑ 360 George Pesut .75 .35
❑ 361 Mike Corrigan .75 .35
❑ 362 Michel Larocque 2.00 .90
❑ 363 Wayne Dillon .75 .35
❑ 364 Pete Laframboise .75 .35
❑ 365 Brian Glennie .75 .35
❑ 366 Mike Christie .75 .35
❑ 367 Jean Lemieux .75 .35
❑ 368 Gary Bromley 1.50 .70
❑ 369 J.P. Bordeleau .75 .35
❑ 370 Ed Gilbert .75 .35
❑ 371 Chris Ahrens .75 .35
❑ 372 Billy Smith 7.00 3.10
❑ 373 Larry Goodenough .75 .35
❑ 374 Leon Rochefort .75 .35
❑ 375 Doug Gibson .75 .35
❑ 376 Mike Bloom .75 .35
❑ 377 Larry Brown .75 .35
❑ 378 Jim Roberts .75 .35
❑ 379 Gilles Villemure 1.50 .70
❑ 380 Dennis Owchar .75 .35
❑ 381 Doug Favell 1.50 .70
❑ 382 Stan Gilbertson UER .75 .35
(Photo actually
Denis Dupere)
❑ 383 Ed Kea .75 .35
❑ 384 Brian Spencer .75 .35
❑ 385 Mike Veisor 1.50 .70
❑ 386 Bob Murray .75 .35
❑ 387 Andre St.Laurent .75 .35
❑ 388 Rick Chartraw .75 .35
❑ 389 Orest Kindrachuk .75 .35
❑ 390 Dave Hutchinson .75 .35
❑ 391 Glenn Goldup .75 .35
❑ 392 Jerry Holland .75 .35
❑ 393 Peter Sturgeon .75 .35
❑ 394 Alain Daigle .75 .35
❑ 395 Never Issued
(Checklist 330-396,
numbered as 267
and listed as 267B)
❑ 396 Harold Snepsts 20.00 5.00

## 1975-76 O-Pee-Chee WHA

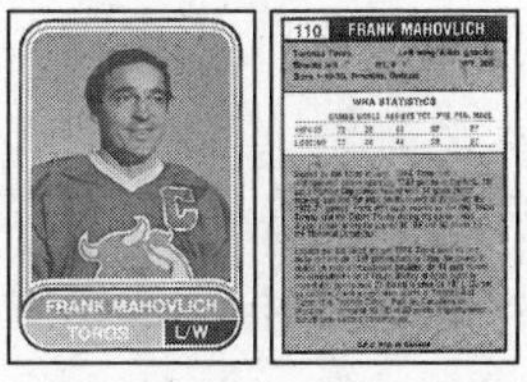

The 1975-76 O-Pee-Chee WHA set consists of 132 color cards. Printed in Canada, the cards measure 2 1/2" by 3 1/2". Bilingual backs feature 1974-75 and career WHA statistics as well as a short biography. Rookie Cards include Richard Brodeur, Nick Fotiu, Robbie Ftorek, John Garrett, Mark Howe, and Mike Rogers.

| | NRMT-MT | EXC |
|---|---|---|
| COMPLETE SET (132) | 450.00 | 200.00 |
| COMMON CARD (1-132) | 3.50 | 1.55 |

❑ 1 Bobby Hull 50.00 12.50
❑ 2 Dale Hoganson 5.00 2.20
❑ 3 Serge Aubry 3.50 1.55
❑ 4 Ron Chipperfield 3.50 1.55
❑ 5 Paul Shmyr 3.50 1.55
❑ 6 Perry Miller 3.50 1.55
❑ 7 Mark Howe 40.00 18.00
❑ 8 Mike Rogers 6.00 2.70
❑ 9 Bryon Baltimore 3.50 1.55
❑ 10 Andre Lacroix 5.00 2.20
❑ 11 Nick Harbaruk 3.50 1.55
❑ 12 John Garrett 12.00 5.50
❑ 13 Lou Nistico 3.50 1.55
❑ 14 Rick Ley 3.50 1.55
❑ 15 Veli-Pekka Ketola 5.00 2.20
❑ 16 Real Cloutier 5.00 2.20
❑ 17 Pierre Guite 3.50 1.55
❑ 18 Duane Rupp 3.50 1.55
❑ 19 Robbie Ftorek 15.00 6.75
❑ 20 Gerry Cheevers 15.00 6.75
❑ 21 John Schella 3.50 1.55
❑ 22 Bruce MacGregor 3.50 1.55
❑ 23 Ralph Backstrom 5.00 2.20
❑ 24 Gene Peacosh 3.50 1.55
❑ 25 Pierre Roy 3.50 1.55
❑ 26 Mike Walton 3.50 1.55
❑ 27 Vaclav Nedomansky 5.00 2.20
❑ 28 Christer Abrahamsson 6.00 2.70
❑ 29 Thommie Bergman 3.50 1.55
❑ 30 Marc Tardif 5.00 2.20
❑ 31 Bryan Campbell 3.50 1.55
❑ 32 Don McLeod 5.00 2.20
❑ 33 Al McDonough 3.50 1.55
❑ 34 Jacques Plante 40.00 18.00
❑ 35 Andre Hinse 3.50 1.55
❑ 36 Eddie Joyal 3.50 1.55
❑ 37 Ken Baird 3.50 1.55
❑ 38 Wayne Rivers 3.50 1.55
❑ 39 Ron Buchanan 3.50 1.55
❑ 40 Anders Hedberg 6.00 2.70
❑ 41 Rick Smith 3.50 1.55
❑ 42 Paul Henderson 5.00 2.20
❑ 43 Wayne Carleton 5.00 2.20
❑ 44 Richard Brodeur 12.00 5.50
❑ 45 John Hughes 3.50 1.55
❑ 46 Larry Israelson 3.50 1.55
❑ 47 Jim Harrison 3.50 1.55
❑ 48 Cam Connor 3.50 1.55
❑ 49 Al Hamilton 5.00 2.20
❑ 50 Ron Grahame 5.00 2.20
❑ 51 Frank Rochon 3.50 1.55
❑ 52 Ron Climie 3.50 1.55
❑ 53 Murray Heatley 3.50 1.55
❑ 54 John Arbour 3.50 1.55
❑ 55 Jim Shaw 5.00 2.20
❑ 56 Larry Pleau 3.50 1.55
❑ 57 Ted Green 6.00 2.70
❑ 58 Rick Dudley 3.50 1.55
❑ 59 Butch Deadmarsh 3.50 1.55
❑ 60 Serge Bernier 5.00 2.20
❑ 61 Ron Grahame AS 4.00 1.80
❑ 62 J.C. Tremblay AS 3.50 1.55
❑ 63 Kevin Morrison AS 3.50 1.55
❑ 64 Andre Lacroix AS 3.50 1.55
❑ 65 Bobby Hull AS 20.00 9.00
❑ 66 Gordie Howe AS 30.00 13.50
❑ 67 Gerry Cheevers AS 8.00 3.60
❑ 68 Poul Popiel AS 3.50 1.55
❑ 69 Barry Long AS 3.50 1.55
❑ 70 Serge Bernier AS 3.50 1.55
❑ 71 Marc Tardif AS 3.50 1.55
❑ 72 Anders Hedberg AS 3.50 1.55
❑ 73 Ron Ward 3.50 1.55
❑ 74 Michel Cormier 3.50 1.55
❑ 75 Marty Howe 6.00 2.70
❑ 76 Rusty Patenaude 3.50 1.55
❑ 77 John McKenzie 5.00 2.20
❑ 78 Mark Napier 6.00 2.70
❑ 79 Henry Boucha 3.50 1.55
❑ 80 Kevin Morrison 3.50 1.55
❑ 81 Tom Simpson 3.50 1.55
❑ 82 Brad Selwood 3.50 1.55
❑ 83 Ulf Nilsson 6.00 2.70
❑ 84 Rejean Houle 5.00 2.20
❑ 85 Normand Lapointe UER 3.50 1.55
(Misspelled Lapoint
on card back)
❑ 86 Danny Lawson 5.00 2.20
❑ 87 Gary Jarrett 3.50 1.55
❑ 88 Al McLeod 3.50 1.55
❑ 89 Gord Labossiere 3.50 1.55
❑ 90 Barry Long 5.00 2.20
❑ 91 Rick Morris 3.50 1.55
❑ 92 Norm Ferguson 3.50 1.55
❑ 93 Bob Whitlock 3.50 1.55
❑ 94 Jim Dorey 3.50 1.55
❑ 95 Tom Webster 5.00 2.20
❑ 96 Gordie Gallant 3.50 1.55
❑ 97 Dave Keon 8.00 3.60
❑ 98 Ron Plumb 3.50 1.55
❑ 99 Rick Jodzio 3.50 1.55
❑ 100 Gordie Howe 50.00 22.00
❑ 101 Joe Daley 6.00 2.70
❑ 102 Wayne Muloin 3.50 1.55
❑ 103 Gavin Kirk 3.50 1.55
❑ 104 Dave Dryden 5.00 2.20
❑ 105 Bob Liddington 3.50 1.55
❑ 106 Rosaire Paiement 3.50 1.55
❑ 107 John Sheridan 3.50 1.55
❑ 108 Nick Fotiu 10.00 4.50
❑ 109 Lars-Erik Sjoberg 3.50 1.55
❑ 110 Frank Mahovlich 12.00 5.50
❑ 111 Mike Antonovich 3.50 1.55
❑ 112 Paul Terbenche 3.50 1.55
❑ 113 Rich Leduc 3.50 1.55
❑ 114 Jack Norris 5.00 2.20
❑ 115 Dennis Sobchuk 3.50 1.55
❑ 116 Chris Bordeleau 3.50 1.55
❑ 117 Doug Barrie 3.50 1.55
❑ 118 Hugh Harris 3.50 1.55
❑ 119 Cam Newton 3.50 1.55
❑ 120 Poul Popiel 3.50 1.55
❑ 121 Fran Huck 3.50 1.55
❑ 122 Tony Featherstone 3.50 1.55
❑ 123 Bob Woytowich 3.50 1.55
❑ 124 Claude St.Sauveur 3.50 1.55
❑ 125 Heikki Riihiranta 5.00 2.20
❑ 126 Gary Kurt 5.00 2.20
❑ 127 Thommy Abrahamsson 5.00 2.20
❑ 128 Danny Gruen 3.50 1.55
❑ 129 Jacques Locas 3.50 1.55
❑ 130 J.C. Tremblay 3.50 1.55
❑ 131 Checklist Card 30.00 7.50
❑ 132 Ernie Wakely 8.00 2.00

## 1976-77 O-Pee-Chee NHL

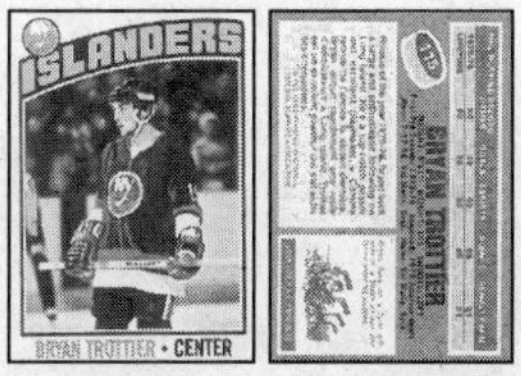

The 1976-77 O-Pee-Chee NHL set consists of 396 color standard-size cards. Printed in Canada, the cards contain both the O-Pee-Chee and the NHL Players Association copyright. The wax packs issued contained eight cards in ten-cent packs along with a bubble-gum slab. Several Record Breaker (RB) cards feature achievements from the previous season. Team cards (132-149) have a team checklist on the back. Bilingual backs contain the player's statistics from the 1975-76 season, career numbers, a short biography and a cartoon-illustrated fact about the player. Cards that feature California players in the 1976-77 Topps set have been updated in this set to show them with the Cleveland Barons. One of those is card 176 Gary Simmons. There are reportedly three variations of the Simmons card. In addition to the basic card, one version has "Team transferred to Colorado" on front. This is an error in itself because the Barons disbanded with players going to Minnesota. The other version has the text shaded or airbrushed out. Information on values and scarcities is not known at this time. Rookie Cards include Bryan Trottier and Dave "Tiger" Williams.

| | NRMT-MT | EXC |
|---|---|---|
| COMPLETE SET (396) | 200.00 | 90.00 |
| COMMON CARD (1-396) | .50 | .23 |

❑ 1 Goals Leaders 3.00 .75
Reggie Leach
Guy Lafleur
Pierre Larouche
❑ 2 Assists Leaders 3.00 1.35
Bobby Clarke
Peter Mahovlich
Guy Lafleur
Gilbert Perrault
Jean Ratelle
❑ 3 Scoring Leaders 3.00 1.35
Guy Lafleur
Bobby Clarke
Gilbert Perreault
❑ 4 Penalty Min. Leaders .50 .23
Steve Durbano
Bryan Watson
Dave Schultz
❑ 5 Power Play Goals 3.00 1.35
Leaders
Phil Esposito
Guy Lafleur
Richard Martin
Pierre Larouche
Denis Potvin
❑ 6 Goals Against 5.00 2.20
Average Leaders
Ken Dryden
Glenn Resch
Michel Larocque
❑ 7 Gary Doak .50 .23
❑ 8 Jacques Richard .50 .23
❑ 9 Wayne Dillon .50 .23
❑ 10 Bernie Parent 3.00 1.35
❑ 11 Ed Westfall .75 .35
❑ 12 Dick Redmond .50 .23
❑ 13 Bryan Hextall .50 .23
❑ 14 Jean Pronovost .50 .23
❑ 15 Peter Mahovlich .75 .35
❑ 16 Danny Grant .50 .23
❑ 17 Phil Myre .50 .23
❑ 18 Wayne Merrick .50 .23
❑ 19 Steve Durbano .50 .23
❑ 20 Derek Sanderson 2.50 1.10
❑ 21 Mike Murphy .50 .23
❑ 22 Borje Salming 5.00 2.20
❑ 23 Mike Walton .50 .23
❑ 24 Randy Manery .50 .23
❑ 25 Ken Hodge .50 .23
❑ 26 Mel Bridgman 2.50 1.10
❑ 27 Jerry Korab .50 .23
❑ 28 Gilles Gratton .50 .23
❑ 29 Andre St.Laurent .50 .23
❑ 30 Yvan Cournoyer 2.50 1.10
❑ 31 Phil Russell .50 .23
❑ 32 Dennis Hextall .50 .23
❑ 33 Lowell MacDonald .50 .23
❑ 34 Dennis O'Brien .50 .23
❑ 35 Gerry Meehan .50 .23
❑ 36 Gilles Meloche .75 .35
❑ 37 Wilf Paiement .50 .23
❑ 38 Bob MacMillan 1.50 .70
❑ 39 Ian Turnbull .50 .23
❑ 40 Rogatien Vachon 2.00 .90
❑ 41 Nick Beverley .50 .23
❑ 42 Rene Robert .75 .35
❑ 43 Andre Savard .50 .23
❑ 44 Bob Gainey 4.00 1.80
❑ 45 Joe Watson .50 .23
❑ 46 Billy Smith 5.00 2.20
❑ 47 Darcy Rota .50 .23
❑ 48 Rick Lapointe .50 .23
❑ 49 Pierre Jarry .50 .23
❑ 50 Syl Apps .50 .23
❑ 51 Eric Vail .50 .23
❑ 52 Greg Joly .50 .23
❑ 53 Don Lever .50 .23
❑ 54 Bob Murdoch .50 .23
Seals Right Wing
❑ 55 Denis Herron .50 .23
❑ 56 Mike Bloom .50 .23
❑ 57 Bill Fairbairn .50 .23
❑ 58 Fred Stanfield .50 .23
❑ 59 Steve Shutt 3.00 1.35
❑ 60 Brad Park 2.50 1.10
❑ 61 Gilles Villemure .50 .23
❑ 62 Bert Marshall .50 .23
❑ 63 Chuck Lefley .50 .23
❑ 64 Simon Nolet .50 .23
❑ 65 Reggie Leach RB .50 .23
Most Goals, Playoffs

❑ 66 Darryl Sittler RB 1.50 .70
Most Points, Game
❑ 67 Bryan Trottier RB 6.00 2.70
Most Points,
Season, Rookie
❑ 68 Garry Unger RB .50 .23
Most Consecutive
Games, Lifetime
❑ 69 Ron Low .50 .23
❑ 70 Bobby Clarke 6.00 2.70
❑ 71 Michel Bergeron .50 .23
❑ 72 Ron Stackhouse .50 .23
❑ 73 Bill Hogaboam .50 .23
❑ 74 Bob Murdoch .50 .23
Kings Defenseman
❑ 75 Steve Vickers .50 .23
❑ 76 Pit Martin .50 .23
❑ 77 Gerry Hart .50 .23
❑ 78 Craig Ramsay .50 .23
❑ 79 Michel Larocque .50 .23
❑ 80 Jean Ratelle 1.50 .70
❑ 81 Don Saleski .50 .23
❑ 82 Bill Clement 1.50 .70
❑ 83 Dave Burrows .50 .23
❑ 84 Wayne Thomas .50 .23
❑ 85 John Gould .50 .23
❑ 86 Dennis Maruk 3.00 1.35
❑ 87 Ernie Hicke .50 .23
❑ 88 Jim Rutherford .50 .23
❑ 89 Dale Tallon .50 .23
❑ 90 Rod Gilbert 1.50 .70
❑ 91 Marcel Dionne 6.00 2.70
❑ 92 Chuck Arnason .50 .23
❑ 93 Jean Potvin .50 .23
❑ 94 Don Luce .50 .23
❑ 95 Johnny Bucyk 1.50 .70
❑ 96 Larry Goodenough .50 .23
❑ 97 Mario Tremblay .75 .35
❑ 98 Nelson Pyatt .50 .23
❑ 99 Brian Glennie .50 .23
❑ 100 Tony Esposito 4.00 1.80
❑ 101 Dan Maloney .50 .23
❑ 102 Dunc Wilson .50 .23
❑ 103 Dean Talafous .50 .23
❑ 104 Ed Staniowski .50 .23
❑ 105 Dallas Smith .50 .23
❑ 106 Jude Drouin .50 .23
❑ 107 Pat Hickey .50 .23
❑ 108 Jocelyn Guevremont .50 .23
❑ 109 Doug Risebrough 1.50 .70
❑ 110 Reggie Leach .75 .35
❑ 111 Dan Bouchard .75 .35
❑ 112 Chris Oddleifson .50 .23
❑ 113 Rick Hampton .50 .23
❑ 114 John Marks .50 .23
❑ 115 Bryan Trottier 50.00 22.00
❑ 116 Checklist 1-132 10.00 2.50
❑ 117 Greg Polis .50 .23
❑ 118 Peter McNab 1.50 .70
❑ 119 Jim Roberts .50 .23
❑ 120 Gerry Cheevers 3.00 1.35
❑ 121 Rick MacLeish .75 .35
❑ 122 Billy Lochead .50 .23
❑ 123 Tom Reid .50 .23
❑ 124 Rick Kehoe .50 .23
❑ 125 Keith Magnuson .50 .23
❑ 126 Clark Gillies 1.50 .70
❑ 127 Rick Middleton 3.00 1.35
❑ 128 Bill Hajt .50 .23
❑ 129 Jacques Lemaire 1.50 .70
❑ 130 Terry O'Reilly 1.50 .70
❑ 131 Andre Dupont .50 .23
❑ 132 Flames Team 3.00 1.35
❑ 133 Bruins Team 3.00 1.35
❑ 134 Sabres Team 3.00 1.35
❑ 135 Seals Team 3.00 1.35
❑ 136 Blackhawks Team 3.00 1.35
❑ 137 Red Wings Team 3.00 1.35
❑ 138 Scouts Team 3.00 1.35
❑ 139 Kings Team 3.00 1.35
❑ 140 North Stars Team 3.00 1.35
❑ 141 Canadiens Team 3.00 1.35
❑ 142 Islanders Team 3.00 1.35
❑ 143 Rangers Team 3.00 1.35
❑ 144 Flyers Team 3.00 1.35
❑ 145 Penguins Team 3.00 1.35
❑ 146 Blues Team 3.00 1.35
❑ 147 Maple Leafs Team 3.00 1.35
❑ 148 Canucks Team 3.00 1.35
❑ 149 Capitals Team 3.00 1.35
❑ 150 Dave Schultz 1.50 .70
❑ 151 Larry Robinson 6.00 2.70
❑ 152 Al Smith .75 .35
❑ 153 Bob Nystrom .75 .35
❑ 154 Ron Greschner .75 .35
❑ 155 Gregg Sheppard .50 .23
❑ 156 Alain Daigle .50 .23
❑ 157 Ed Van Impe .50 .23
❑ 158 Tim Young .75 .35
❑ 159 Bryan Lefley .50 .23
❑ 160 Ed Giacomin 2.50 1.10
❑ 161 Yvon Labre .50 .23
❑ 162 Jim Lorentz .50 .23
❑ 163 Guy Lafleur 12.00 5.50
❑ 164 Tom Bladon .50 .23
❑ 165 Wayne Cashman .75 .35
❑ 166 Pete Stemkowski .50 .23
❑ 167 Grant Mulvey .50 .23
❑ 168 Yves Belanger .50 .23
❑ 169 Bill Goldsworthy .75 .35
❑ 170 Denis Potvin 6.00 2.70
❑ 171 Nick Libett .50 .23
❑ 172 Michel Plasse .50 .23
❑ 173 Lou Nanne .50 .23
❑ 174 Tom Lysiak .50 .23
❑ 175 Dennis Ververgaert .50 .23
❑ 176 Gary Simmons .75 .35
❑ 177 Pierre Bouchard .50 .23
❑ 178 Bill Barber 2.50 1.10
❑ 179 Darryl Edestrand .50 .23
❑ 180 Gilbert Perreault 3.00 1.35
❑ 181 Dave Maloney 1.50 .70
❑ 182 Jean-Paul Parise .50 .23
❑ 183 Jim Harrison .50 .23
❑ 184 Pete Lopresti .50 .23
❑ 185 Don Kozak .50 .23
❑ 186 Guy Charron .50 .23
❑ 187 Stan Gilbertson .50 .23
❑ 188 Bill Nyrop .50 .23
❑ 189 Bobby Schmautz .50 .23
❑ 190 Wayne Stephenson .50 .23
❑ 191 Brian Spencer .50 .23
❑ 192 Gilles Marotte .50 .23
❑ 193 Lorne Henning .50 .23
❑ 194 Bob Neely .50 .23
❑ 195 Dennis Hull .50 .23
❑ 196 Walt McKechnie .50 .23
❑ 197 Curt Ridley .50 .23
❑ 198 Dwight Bialowas .50 .23
❑ 199 Pierre Larouche 1.50 .70
❑ 200 Ken Dryden 20.00 9.00
❑ 201 Ross Lonsberry .50 .23
❑ 202 Curt Bennett .50 .23
❑ 203 Hartland Monahan .50 .23
❑ 204 John Davidson 3.00 1.35
❑ 205 Serge Savard .50 .23
❑ 206 Garry Howatt .50 .23
❑ 207 Darryl Sittler 5.00 2.20
❑ 208 J.P. Bordeleau .50 .23
❑ 209 Henry Boucha .50 .23
❑ 210 Richard Martin .75 .35
❑ 211 Vic Venasky .50 .23
❑ 212 Buster Harvey .50 .23
❑ 213 Bobby Orr 25.00 11.00
❑ 214 French Connection 3.00 1.35
Richard Martin
Gilbert Perreault
Rene Robert
❑ 215 LCB Line 4.00 1.80
Reggie Leach
Bobby Clarke
Bill Barber
❑ 216 Long Island Lightning 5.00 2.20
Clark Gillies
Bryan Trottier
Billy Harris
❑ 217 Checking Line 1.50 .70
Bob Gainey
Doug Jarvis
Jim Roberts
❑ 218 Bicentennial Line .50 .23
Lowell MacDonald
Syl Apps
Jean Pronovost
❑ 219 Bob Kelly .50 .23
❑ 220 Walt Tkaczuk .50 .23
❑ 221 Dave Lewis .50 .23
❑ 222 Danny Gare 1.50 .70
❑ 223 Guy Lapointe .50 .23
❑ 224 Hank Nowak .50 .23
❑ 225 Stan Mikita 4.00 1.80
❑ 226 Vic Hadfield .50 .23
❑ 227 Bernie Wolfe .75 .35
❑ 228 Bryan Watson .50 .23
❑ 229 Ralph Stewart .50 .23
❑ 230 Gerry Desjardins .75 .35
❑ 231 John Bednarski .50 .23
❑ 232 Yvon Lambert .50 .23
❑ 233 Orest Kindrachuk .50 .23
❑ 234 Don Marcotte .50 .23
❑ 235 Bill White .50 .23
❑ 236 Red Berenson .50 .23
❑ 237 Al MacAdam .50 .23
❑ 238 Rick Blight .50 .23
❑ 239 Butch Goring .75 .35
❑ 240 Cesare Maniago .75 .35
❑ 241 Jim Schoenfeld .75 .35
❑ 242 Cliff Koroll .50 .23
❑ 243 Scott Garland .50 .23
❑ 244 Rick Chartraw .50 .23
❑ 245 Phil Esposito 4.00 1.80
❑ 246 Dave Forbes .50 .23
❑ 247 Joe Watson .50 .23
❑ 248 Ron Schock .50 .23
❑ 249 Fred Barrett .50 .23
❑ 250 Glenn Resch 3.00 1.35
❑ 251 Ivan Boldirev .50 .23
❑ 252 Billy Harris .50 .23
❑ 253 Lee Fogolin .50 .23
❑ 254 Murray Wilson .50 .23
❑ 255 Gilles Gilbert .75 .35
❑ 256 Gary Dornhoefer .75 .35
❑ 257 Carol Vadnais .50 .23
❑ 258 Checklist 133-264 10.00 2.50
❑ 259 Errol Thompson .50 .23
❑ 260 Garry Unger .75 .35
❑ 261 J. Bob Kelly .50 .23
❑ 262 Terry Harper .50 .23
❑ 263 Blake Dunlop .50 .23
❑ 264 Stanley Cup Champs 1.50 .70
❑ 265 Richard Mulhern .50 .23
❑ 266 Gary Sabourin .50 .23
❑ 267 Bill McKenzie UER .50 .23
(Spelled KcKenzie on front)
❑ 268 Mike Corrigan .50 .23
❑ 269 Rick Smith .50 .23
❑ 270 Stan Weir .50 .23
❑ 271 Ron Sedlbauer .50 .23
❑ 272 Jean Lemieux .50 .23
❑ 273 Hilliard Graves .50 .23
❑ 274 Dave Gardner .50 .23
❑ 275 Tracy Pratt .50 .23
❑ 276 Frank St.Marseille .50 .23
❑ 277 Bob Hess .50 .23
❑ 278 Bobby Lalonde .50 .23
❑ 279 Tony White .50 .23
❑ 280 Rod Seiling .50 .23
❑ 281 Larry Romanchych .50 .23
❑ 282 Ralph Klassen .50 .23
❑ 283 Gary Croteau .50 .23
❑ 284 Neil Komadoski .50 .23
❑ 285 Ed Johnston .50 .23
❑ 286 George Ferguson .50 .23
❑ 287 Gerry O'Flaherty .50 .23
❑ 288 Jack Lynch .50 .23
❑ 289 Pat Quinn .75 .35
❑ 290 Gene Carr .50 .23
❑ 291 Bob Stewart .50 .23
❑ 292 Doug Favell .75 .35
❑ 293 Rick Wilson .50 .23
❑ 294 Jack Valiquette .50 .23
❑ 295 Garry Monahan .50 .23
❑ 296 Michel Belhumeur .50 .23
❑ 297 Larry Carriere .50 .23
❑ 298 Fred Ahern .50 .23
❑ 299 Dave Hudson .50 .23
❑ 300 Bob Berry .50 .23
❑ 301 Bob Gassoff .50 .23
❑ 302 Jim McKenny .50 .23
❑ 303 Gord Smith .50 .23
❑ 304 Garnet Bailey .50 .23
❑ 305 Bruce Affleck .50 .23
❑ 306 Doug Halward .50 .23
❑ 307 Lew Morrison .50 .23
❑ 308 Bob Sauve 3.00 1.35
❑ 309 Bob Murray (Chicago) .50 .23
❑ 310 Claude Larose .50 .23
❑ 311 Don Awrey .50 .23
❑ 312 Bill MacMillan .50 .23
❑ 313 Doug Jarvis 2.50 1.10
❑ 314 Dennis Owchar .50 .23
❑ 315 Jerry Holland .50 .23
❑ 316 Guy Chouinard 1.50 .70
❑ 317 Gary Smith .75 .35
❑ 318 Pat Price .50 .23
❑ 319 Tom Williams .50 .23
❑ 320 Larry Patey .50 .23
❑ 321 Claire Alexander .50 .23
❑ 322 Larry Bolonchuk .50 .23
❑ 323 Bob Sirois .50 .23
❑ 324 Joe Zanussi .50 .23
❑ 325 Joey Johnston .50 .23
❑ 326 J.P. LeBlanc .50 .23
❑ 327 Craig Cameron .50 .23
❑ 328 Dave Fortier .50 .23
❑ 329 Ed Gilbert .50 .23
❑ 330 John Van Boxmeer .50 .23
❑ 331 Gary Inness .75 .35
❑ 332 Bill Flett .50 .23
❑ 333 Mike Christie .50 .23
❑ 334 Denis Dupere .50 .23
❑ 335 Sheldon Kannegiesser .50 .23
❑ 336 Jerry Butler .50 .23
❑ 337 Gord McRae .50 .23
❑ 338 Dennis Kearns .50 .23
❑ 339 Ron Lalonde .50 .23
❑ 340 Jean Hamel .50 .23
❑ 341 Barry Gibbs .50 .23
❑ 342 Mike Pelyk .50 .23
❑ 343 Rey Comeau .50 .23
❑ 344 Jim Neilson .50 .23
❑ 345 Phil Roberto .50 .23
❑ 346 Dave Hutchinson .50 .23
❑ 347 Ted Irvine .50 .23
❑ 348 Lanny McDonald 4.00 1.80
❑ 349 Jim Moxey .50 .23
❑ 350 Bob Dailey .50 .23
❑ 351 Tim Ecclestone .50 .23
❑ 352 Len Frig .50 .23
❑ 353 Randy Rota .50 .23
❑ 354 Juha Widing .50 .23
❑ 355 Larry Brown .50 .23
❑ 356 Floyd Thomson .50 .23
❑ 357 Richard Nantais .50 .23
❑ 358 Inge Hammarstrom .50 .23
❑ 359 Mike Robitaille .50 .23
❑ 360 Rejean Houle .50 .23
❑ 361 Ed Kea .50 .23
❑ 362 Bob Girard .50 .23
❑ 363 Bob Murray (Vancouver) .50 .23
❑ 364 Dave Hrechkosy .50 .23
❑ 365 Gary Edwards .50 .23
❑ 366 Harold Snepsts 4.00 1.80
❑ 367 Pat Boutette 1.50 .70
❑ 368 Bob Paradise .50 .23
❑ 369 Bob Plager .75 .35
❑ 370 Tim Jacobs .50 .23
❑ 371 Pierre Plante .50 .23
❑ 372 Colin Campbell .75 .35
❑ 373 Dave(Tiger) Williams 25.00 11.00
❑ 374 Ab DeMarco .50 .23
❑ 375 Mike Lampman .50 .23
❑ 376 Mark Heaslip .50 .23
❑ 377 Checklist Card 10.00 2.50
❑ 378 Bert Wilson .50 .23
❑ 379 Flames Leaders .50 .23
Curt Bennett
Tom Lysiak
Pat Quinn
Claude St.Sauveur
❑ 380 Sabres Leaders .50 .23
Danny Gare
Gilbert Perreault
Richard Martin
❑ 381 Bruins Leaders 2.00 .90
Johnny Bucyk
Jean Ratelle
Terry O'Reilly
❑ 382 Blackhawks Leaders .50 .23
Pit Martin
Dale Tallon
Phil Russell
Cliff Koroll
❑ 383 Seals Leaders .50 .23
Wayne Merrick
Al MacAdam
Rick Hampton
Mike Christie
Bob Murdoch
❑ 384 Scouts Leaders .50 .23
Guy Charron
Steve Durbano
❑ 385 Red Wings Leaders .50 .23
Michel Bergeron
Walt McKechnie
Bryan Watson
❑ 386 Kings Leaders .50 .23
Marcel Dionne
Dave Hutchison
Mike Corrigan
❑ 387 North Stars Leaders .50 .23
Bill Hogaboam
Tim Young
Dennis O'Brien
❑ 388 Canadiens Leaders 3.00 1.35
Guy Lafleur
Pete Mahovlich
Doug Risebrough
❑ 389 Islanders Leaders 1.50 .70
Clark Gillies
Denis Potvin
Garry Howatt
❑ 390 Rangers Leaders 2.00 .90
Rod Gilbert
Steve Vickers
Carol Vadnais
Phil Esposito
❑ 391 Flyers Leaders 2.00 .90
Reggie Leach
Bobby Clarke
Dave Schultz
Bill Barber
❑ 392 Penguins Leaders .50 .23
Pierre Larouche
Syl Apps
Ron Schock
❑ 393 Blues Leaders .50 .23
Chuck Lefley
Garry Unger
Bob Gassoff
❑ 394 Maple Leafs Leaders .50 .23
Errol Thompson
Darryl Sittler
Dave(Tiger) Williams
❑ 395 Canucks Leaders .50 .23
Dennis Ververgaert
Chris Oddleifson
Dennis Kearns
Harold Snepsts
❑ 396 Capitals Leaders .50 .12
Nelson Pyatt
Gerry Meehan
Yvon Labre
Tony White

## 1976-77 O-Pee-Chee WHA

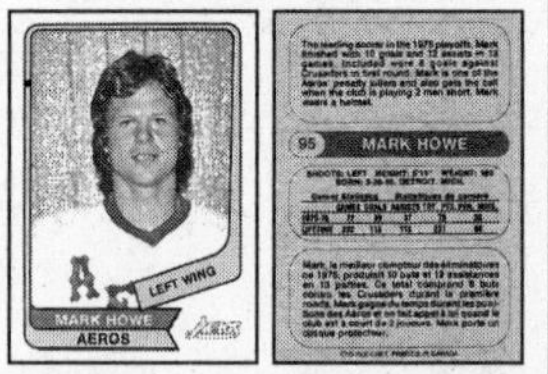

The 1976-77 O-Pee-Chee WHA set consists of 132 color cards featuring WHA players. Cards are 2 1/2" by 3 1/2". The cards were originally sold in ten-cent wax packs. The backs, in both French and English, a short biography of the player and career statistics. The cards were printed in Canada. Cards 1-6 feature the league leaders from the previous season in various statistical categories. The backs of cards 62-65, 67, and 71 form a puzzle of Gordie Howe. A puzzle of Bobby Hull is derived from the backs of cards 61, 66, 68-70 and 72. These cards (61-72) comprise the All-Star subset.

| | NRMT-MT | EXC |
|---|---|---|
| COMPLETE SET (132) | 150.00 | 70.00 |
| COMMON CARD (1-132) | 1.50 | .70 |

❑ 1 Goals Leaders 4.00 1.00
Marc Tardif
Real Cloutier
Vaclav Nedomansky
❑ 2 Assists Leaders 3.00 1.35
J.C. Tremblay
Marc Tardif
Ulf Nilsson
❑ 3 Scoring Leaders 8.00 3.60
Marc Tardif
Bobby Hull
Real Cloutier
Ulf Nilsson
❑ 4 Penalties Leaders 2.00 .90
Curt Brackenbury
Gord Gallant
❑ 5 Points Leaders 8.00 3.60
Marc Tardif
Bobby Hull
Ulf Nilsson
❑ 6 Goals Against 2.00 .90
Average Leaders
Michel Dion
Joe Daley
Wayne Rutledge
❑ 7 Barry Long 1.50 .70
❑ 8 Danny Lawson 1.50 .70
❑ 9 Ulf Nilsson 2.50 1.10
❑ 10 Kevin Morrison 1.50 .70
❑ 11 Gerry Pinder 1.50 .70
❑ 12 Richard Brodeur 5.00 2.20
❑ 13 Robbie Ftorek 6.00 2.70
❑ 14 Tom Webster 2.00 .90
❑ 15 Marty Howe 3.00 1.35
❑ 16 Bryan Campbell 1.50 .70
❑ 17 Rick Dudley 1.50 .70
❑ 18 Jim Turkiewicz 1.50 .70
❑ 19 Rusty Patenaude 1.50 .70
❑ 20 Joe Daley 2.00 .90
❑ 21 Gary Veneruzzo 1.50 .70
❑ 22 Chris Evans 1.50 .70
❑ 23 Mike Antonovich 1.50 .70
❑ 24 Jim Dorey 1.50 .70
❑ 25 John Gray 1.50 .70
❑ 26 Larry Pleau 1.50 .70
❑ 27 Poul Popiel 1.50 .70
❑ 28 Renald Leclerc 1.50 .70
❑ 29 Dennis Sobchuk 1.50 .70
❑ 30 Lars-Erik Sjoberg 1.50 .70
❑ 31 Wayne Wood 2.00 .90
❑ 32 Ron Chipperfield 1.50 .70
❑ 33 Tim Sheehy 1.50 .70
❑ 34 Brent Hughes 1.50 .70
❑ 35 Ron Ward 1.50 .70
❑ 36 Ron Huston 1.50 .70
❑ 37 Rosaire Paiement 1.50 .70
❑ 38 Terry Ruskowski 5.00 2.20
❑ 39 Hugh Harris 1.50 .70
❑ 40 J.C. Tremblay 1.50 .70
❑ 41 Rich Leduc 1.50 .70
❑ 42 Peter Sullivan 1.50 .70
❑ 43 Jerry Rollins 1.50 .70
❑ 44 Ken Broderick 2.00 .90
❑ 45 Peter Driscoll 1.50 .70
❑ 46 Joe Noris 1.50 .70
❑ 47 Al McLeod 1.50 .70
❑ 48 Bruce Landon 2.00 .90
❑ 49 Chris Bordeleau 1.50 .70
❑ 50 Gordie Howe 35.00 16.00
❑ 51 Thommie Bergman 1.50 .70
❑ 52 Dave Keon 4.00 1.80
❑ 53 Butch Deadmarsh 1.50 .70
❑ 54 Bryan Maxwell 1.50 .70
❑ 55 John Garrett 2.00 .90
❑ 56 Glen Sather 2.00 .90
❑ 57 John Miszuk 1.50 .70
❑ 58 Heikki Riihiranta 2.00 .90
❑ 59 Richard Grenier 1.50 .70
❑ 60 Gene Peacosh 1.50 .70
❑ 61 Joe Daley AS 2.00 .90
❑ 62 J.C. Tremblay AS 1.50 .70
❑ 63 Lars-Erik Sjoberg AS 1.50 .70
❑ 64 Vaclav Nedomansky AS 1.50 .70
❑ 65 Bobby Hull AS 18.00 8.00
❑ 66 Anders Hedberg AS 2.00 .90
❑ 67 Chris Abrahamsson AS 2.00 .90
❑ 68 Kevin Morrison AS 1.50 .70
❑ 69 Paul Shmyr AS 1.50 .70
❑ 70 Andre Lacroix AS 1.50 .70
❑ 71 Gene Peacosh AS 1.50 .70
❑ 72 Gordie Howe AS 25.00 11.00
❑ 73 Bob Nevin 1.50 .70
❑ 74 Richard Lemieux 1.50 .70
❑ 75 Mike Ford 1.50 .70
❑ 76 Real Cloutier 2.00 .90
❑ 77 Al McDonough 1.50 .70
❑ 78 Del Hall 1.50 .70
❑ 79 Thommy Abrahamsson 2.00 .90
❑ 80 Andre Lacroix 2.00 .90
❑ 81 Frank Hughes 1.50 .70
❑ 82 Reg Thomas 1.50 .70
❑ 83 Dave Inkpen 1.50 .70
❑ 84 Paul Henderson 2.00 .90
❑ 85 Dave Dryden 2.00 .90
❑ 86 Lynn Powis 1.50 .70
❑ 87 Andre Boudrias 1.50 .70
❑ 88 Veli-Pekka Ketola 2.00 .90
❑ 89 Cam Connor 1.50 .70
❑ 90 Claude St.Sauveur 1.50 .70
❑ 91 Garry Swain 1.50 .70
❑ 92 Ernie Wakely 2.00 .90
❑ 93 Blair MacDonald 1.50 .70
❑ 94 Ron Plumb 1.50 .70
❑ 95 Mark Howe 12.00 5.50
❑ 96 Peter Marrin 1.50 .70
❑ 97 Al Hamilton 2.00 .90
❑ 98 Paulin Bordeleau 1.50 .70
❑ 99 Gavin Kirk 1.50 .70
❑ 100 Bobby Hull 30.00 13.50
❑ 101 Rick Ley 1.50 .70
❑ 102 Gary Kurt 2.00 .90
❑ 103 John McKenzie 2.00 .90
❑ 104 Al Karlander 1.50 .70
❑ 105 John French 1.50 .70
❑ 106 John Hughes 1.50 .70
❑ 107 Ron Grahame 2.00 .90
❑ 108 Mark Napier 2.00 .90
❑ 109 Serge Bernier 2.00 .90
❑ 110 Christer Abrahamsson 2.00 .90
❑ 111 Frank Mahovlich 6.00 2.70
❑ 112 Ted Green 2.00 .90

❑ 113 Rick Jodzio 1.50 .70
❑ 114 Michel Dion 5.00 2.20
❑ 115 Rich Preston 1.50 .70
❑ 116 Pekka Rautakallio 2.00 .90
❑ 117 Checklist Card 30.00 7.50
❑ 118 Marc Tardif 2.00 .90
❑ 119 Doug Barrie 1.50 .70
❑ 120 Vaclav Nedomansky 2.00 .90
❑ 121 Bill Lesuk 1.50 .70
❑ 122 Wayne Connelly 1.50 .70
❑ 123 Pierre Guite 1.50 .70
❑ 124 Ralph Backstrom 2.00 .90
❑ 125 Anders Hedberg 2.50 1.10
❑ 126 Norm Ullman 3.00 1.35
❑ 127 Steve Sutherland 1.50 .70
❑ 128 John Schella 1.50 .70
❑ 129 Don McLeod 2.00 .90
❑ 130 Canadian Finals 2.00 .90
❑ 131 U.S. Finals 2.00 .90
❑ 132 World Trophy Final 8.00 2.00

## 1977-78 O-Pee-Chee NHL

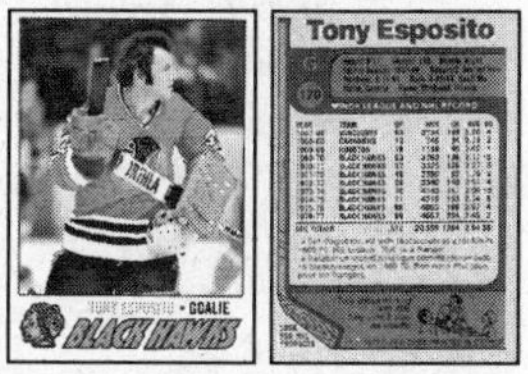


The 1977-78 O-Pee-Chee NHL set consists of 396 color standard-size cards. Unopened packs consisted of 12 cards plus a bubble-gum stick. Cards 203 and 255 feature different players than corresponding Topps cards. Bilingual backs contain yearly statistics and a cartoon-illustrated fact about the player. Cards 322-339 have a team logo on the front with team records on the back. Rookie Cards include Mike Milbury, Mike Palmateer and Paul Holmgren. The Rick Bourbonnais card (312) actually depicts Bernie Federko, predating his Rookie Card by one year.

| | NRMT-MT | EXC |
|---|---|---|
| COMPLETE SET (396) | 125.00 | 55.00 |
| COMMON CARD (1-396) | .35 | .16 |

❑ 1 Goals Leaders 3.00 .75
Steve Shutt
Guy Lafleur
Marcel Dionne
❑ 2 Assists Leaders 2.00 .90
Guy Lafleur
Marcel Dionne
Larry Robinson
Borje Salming
Tim Young
❑ 3 Scoring Leaders 2.50 1.10
Guy Lafleur
Marcel Dionne
Steve Shutt
❑ 4 Penalty Min. Leaders .50 .23
Dave(Tiger) Williams
Dennis Polonich
Bob Gassoff
❑ 5 Power Play Goals 1.00 .45
Leaders
Lanny McDonald
Phil Esposito
Tom Williams
❑ 6 Goals Against 4.00 1.80
Average Leaders
Michel Larocque
Ken Dryden
Glenn Resch
❑ 7 Game Winning 2.50 1.10
Goals Leaders
Gilbert Perreault
Steve Shutt
Guy Lafleur
Rick MacLeish
Peter McNab
❑ 8 Shutouts Leaders 5.00 2.20
Ken Dryden
Rogatien Vachon
Bernie Parent
Dunc Wilson
❑ 9 Brian Spencer .35 .16
❑ 10 Denis Potvin AS2 4.00 1.80
❑ 11 Nick Fotiu 1.00 .45
❑ 12 Bob Murray .35 .16
❑ 13 Pete Lopresti .50 .23
❑ 14 J. Bob Kelly .35 .16
❑ 15 Rick MacLeish .50 .23
❑ 16 Terry Harper .35 .16
❑ 17 Willi Plett 3.00 1.35
❑ 18 Peter McNab .50 .23
❑ 19 Wayne Thomas .50 .23
❑ 20 Pierre Bouchard .35 .16
❑ 21 Dennis Maruk 1.00 .45
❑ 22 Mike Murphy .35 .16
❑ 23 Cesare Maniago .50 .23
❑ 24 Paul Gardner .35 .16
❑ 25 Rod Gilbert 1.00 .45
❑ 26 Orest Kindrachuk .35 .16
❑ 27 Bill Hajt .35 .16
❑ 28 John Davidson 1.50 .70
❑ 29 Jean-Paul Parise .35 .16
❑ 30 Larry Robinson AS1 5.00 2.20
❑ 31 Yvon Labre .35 .16
❑ 32 Walt McKechnie .35 .16
❑ 33 Rick Kehoe .50 .23
❑ 34 Randy Holt .35 .16
❑ 35 Garry Unger .50 .23
❑ 36 Lou Nanne .35 .16
❑ 37 Dan Bouchard .50 .23
❑ 38 Darryl Sittler 3.00 1.35
❑ 39 Bob Murdoch .35 .16
❑ 40 Jean Ratelle 1.00 .45
❑ 41 Dave Maloney .35 .16
❑ 42 Danny Gare .50 .23
❑ 43 Jim Watson .35 .16
❑ 44 Tom Williams .35 .16
❑ 45 Serge Savard .35 .16
❑ 46 Derek Sanderson 2.00 .90
❑ 47 John Marks .35 .16
❑ 48 Al Cameron .35 .16
❑ 49 Dean Talafous .35 .16
❑ 50 Glenn Resch 2.00 .90
❑ 51 Ron Schock .35 .16
❑ 52 Gary Croteau .35 .16
❑ 53 Gerry Meehan .35 .16
❑ 54 Ed Staniowski .35 .16
❑ 55 Phil Esposito UER 3.00 1.35
(Goal total reads 78, should be 55)
❑ 56 Dennis Ververgaert .35 .16
❑ 57 Rick Wilson .35 .16
❑ 58 Jim Lorentz .35 .16
❑ 59 Bobby Schmautz .35 .16
❑ 60 Guy Lapointe AS2 .50 .23
❑ 61 Ivan Boldirev .35 .16
❑ 62 Bob Nystrom .35 .16
❑ 63 Rick Hampton .35 .16
❑ 64 Jack Valiquette .35 .16
❑ 65 Bernie Parent 2.50 1.10
❑ 66 Dave Burrows .35 .16
❑ 67 Butch Goring .50 .23
❑ 68 Checklist 1-132 8.00 2.00
❑ 69 Murray Wilson .35 .16
❑ 70 Ed Giacomin 1.50 .70
❑ 71 Flames Team 2.00 .90
(checklist back)
❑ 72 Bruins Team 2.00 .90
(checklist back)
❑ 73 Sabres Team 2.00 .90
(checklist back)
❑ 74 Blackhawks Team 2.00 .90
(checklist back)
❑ 75 Barons Team 2.00 .90
(checklist back)
❑ 76 Rockies Team 2.00 .90
(checklist back)
❑ 77 Red Wings Team 2.00 .90
(checklist back)
❑ 78 Kings Team 2.00 .90
(checklist back)
❑ 79 North Stars Team 2.00 .90
(checklist back)
❑ 80 Canadiens Team 2.00 .90
(checklist back)
❑ 81 Islanders Team 2.00 .90
(checklist back)
❑ 82 Rangers Team 2.00 .90
(checklist back)
❑ 83 Flyers Team 2.00 .90
(checklist back)
❑ 84 Penguins Team 2.00 .90
(checklist back)
❑ 85 Blues Team 2.00 .90
(checklist back)
❑ 86 Maple Leafs Team 2.00 .90
(checklist back)
❑ 87 Canucks Team 2.00 .90
(checklist back)
❑ 88 Capitals Team 2.00 .90
(checklist back)
❑ 89 Keith Magnuson .35 .16
❑ 90 Walt Tkaczuk .50 .23
❑ 91 Bill Nyrop .35 .16
❑ 92 Michel Plasse .50 .23
❑ 93 Bob Bourne .50 .23
❑ 94 Lee Fogolin .35 .16
❑ 95 Gregg Sheppard .35 .16
❑ 96 Hartland Monahan .35 .16
❑ 97 Curt Bennett .35 .16
❑ 98 Bob Dailey .35 .16
❑ 99 Bill Goldsworthy .50 .23
❑ 100 Ken Dryden AS1 15.00 6.75
❑ 101 Grant Mulvey .35 .16
❑ 102 Pierre Larouche 1.00 .45
❑ 103 Nick Libett .35 .16
❑ 104 Rick Smith .35 .16
❑ 105 Bryan Trottier 15.00 6.75
❑ 106 Pierre Jarry .35 .16
❑ 107 Red Berenson .50 .23
❑ 108 Jim Schoenfeld .50 .23
❑ 109 Gilles Meloche .50 .23
❑ 110 Lanny McDonald AS2 2.50 1.10
❑ 111 Don Lever .35 .16
❑ 112 Greg Polis .35 .16
❑ 113 Gary Sargent .35 .16
❑ 114 Earl Anderson .35 .16
❑ 115 Bobby Clarke 5.00 2.20
❑ 116 Dave Lewis .35 .16
❑ 117 Darcy Rota .35 .16
❑ 118 Andre Savard .35 .16
❑ 119 Denis Herron .50 .23
❑ 120 Steve Shutt AS1 2.00 .90
❑ 121 Mel Bridgman .35 .16
❑ 122 Buster Harvey .35 .16
❑ 123 Roland Eriksson .35 .16
❑ 124 Dale Tallon .35 .16
❑ 125 Gilles Gilbert .50 .23
❑ 126 Billy Harris .35 .16
❑ 127 Tom Lysiak .50 .23
❑ 128 Jerry Korab .35 .16
❑ 129 Bob Gainey 2.50 1.10
❑ 130 Wilf Paiement .50 .23
❑ 131 Tom Bladon .35 .16
❑ 132 Ernie Hicke .35 .16
❑ 133 J.P. LeBlanc .35 .16
❑ 134 Mike Milbury 8.00 3.60
❑ 135 Pit Martin .35 .16
❑ 136 Steve Vickers .35 .16
❑ 137 Don Awrey .35 .16
❑ 138 Bernie Wolfe .50 .23
❑ 139 Doug Jarvis .50 .23
❑ 140 Borje Salming AS1 3.00 1.35
❑ 141 Bob MacMillan .35 .16
❑ 142 Wayne Stephenson .50 .23
❑ 143 Dave Forbes .35 .16
❑ 144 Jean Potvin .35 .16
❑ 145 Guy Charron .35 .16
❑ 146 Cliff Koroll .35 .16
❑ 147 Danny Grant .50 .23
❑ 148 Bill Hogaboam .35 .16
❑ 149 Al MacAdam .35 .16
❑ 150 Gerry Desjardins .50 .23
❑ 151 Yvon Lambert .35 .16
❑ 152 Rick Lapointe .35 .16
❑ 153 Ed Westfall .50 .23
❑ 154 Carol Vadnais .35 .16
❑ 155 Johnny Bucyk 1.00 .45
❑ 156 J.P. Bordeleau .35 .16
❑ 157 Ron Stackhouse .35 .16
❑ 158 Glen Sharpley .35 .16
❑ 159 Michel Bergeron .35 .16
❑ 160 Rogatien Vachon AS2 1.50 .70
❑ 161 Fred Stanfield .35 .16
❑ 162 Gerry Hart .35 .16
❑ 163 Mario Tremblay .50 .23
❑ 164 Andre Dupont .35 .16
❑ 165 Don Marcotte .35 .16
❑ 166 Wayne Dillon .35 .16
❑ 167 Claude Larose .35 .16
❑ 168 Eric Vail .35 .16
❑ 169 Tom Edur .35 .16
❑ 170 Tony Esposito 3.00 1.35
❑ 171 Andre St.Laurent .35 .16
❑ 172 Dan Maloney .35 .16
❑ 173 Dennis O'Brien .35 .16
❑ 174 Blair Chapman .35 .16
❑ 175 Dennis Kearns .35 .16
❑ 176 Wayne Merrick .35 .16
❑ 177 Michel Larocque .50 .23
❑ 178 Bob Kelly .35 .16
❑ 179 Dave Farrish .35 .16
❑ 180 Richard Martin AS2 .50 .23
❑ 181 Gary Doak .35 .16
❑ 182 Jude Drouin .35 .16
❑ 183 Barry Dean .35 .16
❑ 184 Gary Smith .50 .23
❑ 185 Reggie Leach .50 .23
❑ 186 Ian Turnbull .50 .23
❑ 187 Vic Venasky .35 .16
❑ 188 Wayne Bianchin .35 .16
❑ 189 Doug Risebrough .50 .23
❑ 190 Brad Park 2.00 .90
❑ 191 Craig Ramsay .35 .16
❑ 192 Ken Hodge .50 .23
❑ 193 Phil Myre .50 .23
❑ 194 Garry Howatt .35 .16
❑ 195 Stan Mikita 3.00 1.35
❑ 196 Garnet Bailey .35 .16
❑ 197 Dennis Hextall .35 .16
❑ 198 Nick Beverley .35 .16
❑ 199 Larry Patey .35 .16
❑ 200 Guy Lafleur AS1 10.00 4.50
❑ 201 Don Edwards 4.00 1.80
❑ 202 Gary Dornhoefer .50 .23
❑ 203 Bob Paradise .35 .16
❑ 204 Alex Pirus .35 .16
❑ 205 Peter Mahovlich .50 .23
❑ 206 Bert Marshall .35 .16
❑ 207 Gilles Gratton .50 .23
❑ 208 Alain Daigle .35 .16
❑ 209 Chris Oddleifson .35 .16
❑ 210 Gilbert Perreault AS2 2.50 1.10
❑ 211 Mike Palmateer 8.00 3.60
❑ 212 Billy Lochead .35 .16
❑ 213 Dick Redmond .35 .16
❑ 214 Guy Lafleur RB 2.50 1.10
Most Points,
RW, Season
❑ 215 Ian Turnbull RB .35 .16
Most Goals,
Defenseman, Game
❑ 216 Guy Lafleur RB 2.50 1.10
Longest Point
Scoring Streak
❑ 217 Steve Shutt RB .50 .23
Most Goals,
LW, Season
❑ 218 Guy Lafleur RB 2.50 1.10
Most Assists,
RW, Season
❑ 219 Lorne Henning .35 .16
❑ 220 Terry O'Reilly .50 .23
❑ 221 Pat Hickey .35 .16
❑ 222 Rene Robert .50 .23
❑ 223 Tim Young .35 .16
❑ 224 Dunc Wilson .50 .23
❑ 225 Dennis Hull .50 .23
❑ 226 Rod Seiling .35 .16
❑ 227 Bill Barber 1.00 .45
❑ 228 Dennis Polonich .35 .16
❑ 229 Billy Smith 2.50 1.10
❑ 230 Yvan Cournoyer 1.50 .70
❑ 231 Don Luce .35 .16
❑ 232 Mike McEwen .35 .16
❑ 233 Don Saleski .35 .16
❑ 234 Wayne Cashman .50 .23
❑ 235 Phil Russell .35 .16
❑ 236 Mike Corrigan .35 .16
❑ 237 Guy Chouinard .50 .23
❑ 238 Steve Jensen .35 .16
❑ 239 Jim Rutherford .50 .23
❑ 240 Marcel Dionne AS1 4.00 1.80
❑ 241 Rejean Houle .35 .16
❑ 242 Jocelyn Guevremont .35 .16
❑ 243 Jim Harrison .35 .16
❑ 244 Don Murdoch .35 .16
❑ 245 Rick Green 1.00 .45
❑ 246 Rick Middleton 2.00 .90
❑ 247 Joe Watson .35 .16
❑ 248 Syl Apps .35 .16
❑ 249 Checklist 133-264 8.00 2.00
❑ 250 Clark Gillies .50 .23
❑ 251 Bobby Orr 25.00 11.00
❑ 252 Nelson Pyatt .35 .16
❑ 253 Gary McAdam .35 .16
❑ 254 Jacques Lemaire 1.00 .45
❑ 255 Bob Girard .35 .16
❑ 256 Ron Greschner .50 .23
❑ 257 Ross Lonsberry .35 .16
❑ 258 Dave Gardner .35 .16
❑ 259 Rick Blight .35 .16
❑ 260 Gerry Cheevers 2.00 .90
❑ 261 Jean Pronovost .50 .23
❑ 262 Cup Semi-Finals .50 .23
Canadiens skate
Past Islanders
❑ 263 Cup Semi-Finals .50 .23
Bruins Advance
to Finals
❑ 264 Stanley Cup Finals 1.00 .45
Canadiens Win
20th Stanley Cup
❑ 265 Rick Bowness .50 .23
❑ 266 George Ferguson .35 .16
❑ 267 Mike Kitchen .35 .16
❑ 268 Bob Berry .35 .16
❑ 269 Greg Smith .35 .16
❑ 270 Stan Jonathan 3.00 1.35
❑ 271 Dwight Bialowas .35 .16
❑ 272 Pete Stemkowski .35 .16
❑ 273 Greg Joly .35 .16
❑ 274 Ken Houston .35 .16
❑ 275 Brian Glennie .35 .16
❑ 276 Ed Johnston .50 .23
❑ 277 John Grisdale .35 .16
❑ 278 Craig Patrick .50 .23
❑ 279 Ken Breitenbach .35 .16
❑ 280 Fred Ahern .35 .16
❑ 281 Jim Roberts .35 .16
❑ 282 Harvey Bennett .35 .16
❑ 283 Ab DeMarco .35 .16
❑ 284 Pat Boutette .50 .23
❑ 285 Bob Plager .50 .23
❑ 286 Hilliard Graves .35 .16
❑ 287 Gordie Lane .35 .16
❑ 288 Ron Andruff .35 .16
❑ 289 Larry Brown .35 .16
❑ 290 Mike Fidler .35 .16
❑ 291 Fred Barrett .35 .16
❑ 292 Bill Clement .50 .23
❑ 293 Errol Thompson .35 .16
❑ 294 Doug Grant .50 .23
❑ 295 Harold Snepsts 2.00 .90
❑ 296 Rick Bragnalo .35 .16
❑ 297 Bryan Lefley .35 .16
❑ 298 Gene Carr .35 .16
❑ 299 Bob Stewart .35 .16
❑ 300 Lew Morrison .35 .16
❑ 301 Ed Kea .35 .16
❑ 302 Scott Garland .35 .16
❑ 303 Bill Fairbairn .35 .16
❑ 304 Larry Carriere .35 .16
❑ 305 Ron Low .50 .23
❑ 306 Tom Reid .35 .16
❑ 307 Paul Holmgren 4.00 1.80
❑ 308 Pat Price .35 .16
❑ 309 Kirk Bowman .35 .16
❑ 310 Bobby Simpson .35 .16
❑ 311 Ron Ellis .50 .23
❑ 312 Rick Bourbonnais UER 1.00 .45
(Photo actually
Bernie Federko)
❑ 313 Bobby Lalonde .35 .16
❑ 314 Tony White .35 .16
❑ 315 John Van Boxmeer .50 .23
❑ 316 Don Kozak .35 .16
❑ 317 Jim Neilson .35 .16
❑ 318 Terry Martin .35 .16
❑ 319 Barry Gibbs .35 .16
❑ 320 Inge Hammarstrom .35 .16
❑ 321 Darryl Edestrand .35 .16
❑ 322 Flames Logo 2.00 .90
❑ 323 Bruins Logo 2.00 .90
❑ 324 Sabres Logo 2.00 .90
❑ 325 Blackhawks Logo 2.00 .90
❑ 326 Barons Logo 2.00 .90
❑ 327 Rockies Logo 2.00 .90
❑ 328 Red Wings Logo 2.00 .90
❑ 329 Kings Logo 2.00 .90
❑ 330 North Stars Logo 2.00 .90
❑ 331 Canadiens Logo 2.00 .90
❑ 332 Islanders Logo 2.00 .90
❑ 333 Rangers Logo 2.00 .90
❑ 334 Flyers Logo 2.00 .90
❑ 335 Penguins Logo 2.00 .90
❑ 336 Blues Logo 2.00 .90
❑ 337 Maple Leafs Logo 2.00 .90
❑ 338 Canucks Logo 2.00 .90
❑ 339 Capitals Logo 2.00 .90
❑ 340 Chuck Lefley .35 .16
❑ 341 Garry Monahan .35 .16
❑ 342 Bryan Watson .35 .16
❑ 343 Dave Hudson .35 .16
❑ 344 Neil Komadoski .35 .16
❑ 345 Gary Edwards .50 .23
❑ 346 Rey Comeau .35 .16
❑ 347 Bob Neely .35 .16
❑ 348 Jean Hamel .35 .16
❑ 349 Jerry Butler .35 .16
❑ 350 Mike Walton .35 .16
❑ 351 Bob Sirois .35 .16
❑ 352 Jim McElmury .35 .16
❑ 353 Dave Schultz .50 .23
❑ 354 Doug Palazzari .35 .16
❑ 355 David Shand .35 .16
❑ 356 Stan Weir .35 .16
❑ 357 Mike Christie .35 .16
❑ 358 Floyd Thomson .35 .16
❑ 359 Larry Goodenough .35 .16
❑ 360 Bill Riley .35 .16
❑ 361 Doug Hicks .35 .16
❑ 362 Dan Newman .35 .16
❑ 363 Rick Chartraw .35 .16
❑ 364 Tim Ecclestone .35 .16
❑ 365 Don Ashby .35 .16
❑ 366 Jacques Richard .35 .16
❑ 367 Yves Belanger .35 .16
❑ 368 Ron Sedlbauer .35 .16
❑ 369 Jack Lynch UER .35 .16
(Photo actually
Bill Collins)
❑ 370 Doug Favell .50 .23
❑ 371 Bob Murdoch .35 .16
❑ 372 Ralph Klassen .35 .16
❑ 373 Richard Mulhern .35 .16
❑ 374 Jim McKenny .35 .16
❑ 375 Mike Bloom .35 .16
❑ 376 Bruce Affleck .35 .16
❑ 377 Gerry O'Flaherty .35 .16
❑ 378 Ron Lalonde .35 .16
❑ 379 Chuck Arnason .35 .16
❑ 380 Dave Hutchinson .35 .16
❑ 381A Checklist ERR 8.00 2.00
(Topps heading)
❑ 381B Checklist COR 8.00 2.00
(No Topps heading)
❑ 382 John Gould .35 .16
❑ 383 Dave(Tiger) Williams 4.00 1.80
❑ 384 Len Frig .35 .16
❑ 385 Pierre Plante .35 .16
❑ 386 Ralph Stewart .35 .16
❑ 387 Gord Smith .35 .16
❑ 388 Denis Dupere .35 .16
❑ 389 Randy Manery .35 .16
❑ 390 Lowell MacDonald .35 .16
❑ 391 Dennis Owchar .35 .16
❑ 392 Jim Roberts .35 .16
❑ 393 Mike Veisor .50 .23
❑ 394 Bob Hess .35 .16
❑ 395 Curt Ridley .35 .16
❑ 396 Mike Lampman 1.00 .25

## 1977-78 O-Pee-Chee WHA

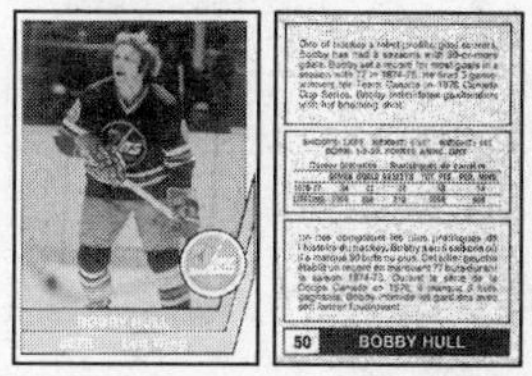


The 1977-78 O-Pee-Chee WHA set consists of 66 color standard-size cards. Printed in Canada, the cards were originally sold in 15-cent wax packs containing 12 cards and gum. Bilingual backs feature player statistics and a short biography. Card number 1 features Gordie Howe's 1000th career goal. There are no key Rookie Cards in this set. This was the final WHA set. The league disbanded following the 1978-79 season with the four surviving teams (Edmonton, New England/Hartford, Quebec and Winnipeg) merging with the NHL.

| | NRMT-MT | EXC |
|---|---|---|
| COMPLETE SET (66) | 70.00 | 32.00 |
| COMMON CARD (1-66) | .75 | .35 |

❑ 1 Gordie Howe 30.00 7.50
❑ 2 Jean Bernier .75 .35
❑ 3 Anders Hedberg 2.00 .90
❑ 4 Ken Broderick 1.50 .70
❑ 5 Joe Noris .75 .35
❑ 6 Blaine Stoughton 1.50 .70
❑ 7 Claude St.Sauveur .75 .35
❑ 8 Real Cloutier 1.50 .70
❑ 9 Joe Daley 1.50 .70
❑ 10 Ron Chipperfield .75 .35
❑ 11 Wayne Rutledge 1.50 .70
❑ 12 Mark Napier 1.50 .70
❑ 13 Rich Leduc .75 .35
❑ 14 Don McLeod 1.50 .70
❑ 15 Ulf Nilsson 2.00 .90
❑ 16 Blair MacDonald .75 .35
❑ 17 Mike Rogers 1.50 .70
❑ 18 Gary Inness 1.50 .70
❑ 19 Larry Lund .75 .35
❑ 20 Marc Tardif 1.50 .70

❑ 21 Lars-Erik Sjoberg 1.50 .70
❑ 22 Bryan Campbell .75 .35
❑ 23 John Garrett 1.50 .70
❑ 24 Ron Plumb .75 .35
❑ 25 Mark Howe 6.00 2.70
❑ 26 Garry Lariviere .75 .35
❑ 27 Peter Sullivan .75 .35
❑ 28 Dave Dryden 1.50 .70
❑ 29 Reg Thomas .75 .35
❑ 30 Andre Lacroix 1.50 .70
❑ 31 Paul Henderson 1.50 .70
❑ 32 Paulin Bordeleau .75 .35
❑ 33 Juha Widing 1.50 .70
❑ 34 Mike Antonovich .75 .35
❑ 35 Robbie Ftorek 1.50 .70
❑ 36 Rosaire Paiement .75 .35
❑ 37 Terry Ruskowski 1.50 .70
❑ 38 Richard Brodeur 3.00 1.35
❑ 39 Willy Lindstrom 2.50 1.10
❑ 40 Al Hamilton .75 .35
❑ 41 John McKenzie 1.50 .70
❑ 42 Wayne Wood 1.50 .70
❑ 43 Claude Larose .75 .35
❑ 44 J.C. Tremblay .75 .35
❑ 45 Gary Bromley 1.50 .70
❑ 46 Ken Baird .75 .35
❑ 47 Bobby Sheehan .75 .35
❑ 48 Don Larway .75 .35
❑ 49 Al Smith 1.50 .70
❑ 50 Bobby Hull 20.00 9.00
❑ 51 Peter Marrin .75 .35
❑ 52 Norm Ferguson .75 .35
❑ 53 Dennis Sobchuk .75 .35
❑ 54 Norm Dube .75 .35
❑ 55 Tom Webster .75 .35
❑ 56 Jim Park 1.50 .70
❑ 57 Dan Labraaten 2.00 .90
❑ 58 Checklist Card 10.00 2.50
❑ 59 Paul Shmyr .75 .35
❑ 60 Serge Bernier 1.50 .70
❑ 61 Frank Mahovlich 4.00 1.80
❑ 62 Michel Dion 1.50 .70
❑ 63 Poul Popiel .75 .35
❑ 64 Lyle Moffat .75 .35
❑ 65 Marty Howe 1.50 .70
❑ 66 Don Burgess 2.00 .50

## 1978-79 O-Pee-Chee

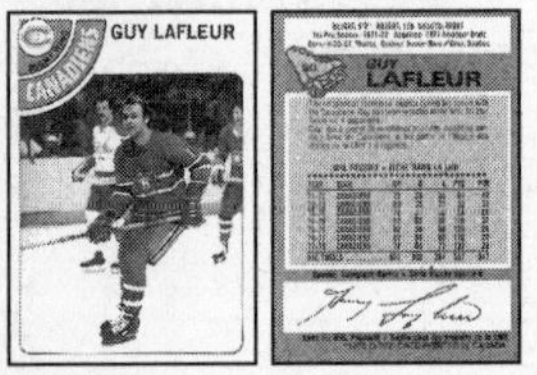


The 1978-79 O-Pee-Chee set consists of 396 standard-size cards. Bilingual backs feature the card number (pictured in a hockey skate), year-by-year player statistics, a short biography and a facsimile autograph. Unlike Topps, All-Star designations do not appear on the front of cards of those players named to the All-Star team. An All-Star subset (325-336) serves to recognize these players. Card number 300 honors Bobby Orr's retirement early in the season. Rookie Cards include Mike Bossy, Randy Carlyle, Ron Duguay, Bernie Federko, Brian Sutter, Dave Taylor and Doug Wilson.

| | NRMT-MT | EXC |
|---|---|---|
| COMPLETE SET (396) | 150.00 | 70.00 |
| COMMON CARD (1-396) | .25 | .11 |

❑ 1 Mike Bossy HL 8.00 2.00
Goals by Rookie
❑ 2 Phil Esposito HL 1.50 .70
29th Hat Trick
❑ 3 Guy Lafleur HL 1.50 .70
Scores against
Every Team
❑ 4 Darryl Sittler HL .75 .35
Goals In Nine
Straight Games
❑ 5 Garry Unger HL .40 .18
803 Consec. Games
❑ 6 Gary Edwards .40 .18
❑ 7 Rick Blight .25 .11
❑ 8 Larry Patey .25 .11
❑ 9 Craig Ramsay .25 .11
❑ 10 Bryan Trottier 10.00 4.50
❑ 11 Don Murdoch .25 .11
❑ 12 Phil Russell .25 .11
❑ 13 Doug Jarvis .40 .18
❑ 14 Gene Carr .25 .11
❑ 15 Bernie Parent 2.00 .90
❑ 16 Perry Miller .25 .11
❑ 17 Kent-Erik Andersson .25 .11
❑ 18 Gregg Sheppard .25 .11
❑ 19 Dennis Owchar .25 .11
❑ 20 Rogatien Vachon .75 .35
❑ 21 Dan Maloney .25 .11
❑ 22 Guy Charron .25 .11
❑ 23 Dick Redmond .25 .11
❑ 24 Checklist 1-132 5.00 1.25
❑ 25 Anders Hedberg .40 .18
❑ 26 Mel Bridgman .25 .11
❑ 27 Lee Fogolin .25 .11
❑ 28 Gilles Meloche .40 .18
❑ 29 Garry Howatt .25 .11
❑ 30 Darryl Sittler 2.50 1.10
❑ 31 Curt Bennett .25 .11
❑ 32 Andre St.Laurent .25 .11
❑ 33 Blair Chapman .25 .11
❑ 34 Keith Magnuson .25 .11
❑ 35 Pierre Larouche .40 .18
❑ 36 Michel Plasse .40 .18
❑ 37 Gary Sargent .25 .11
❑ 38 Mike Walton .25 .11
❑ 39 Robert Picard .25 .11
❑ 40 Terry O'Reilly .40 .18
❑ 41 Dave Farrish .25 .11
❑ 42 Gary McAdam .25 .11
❑ 43 Joe Watson .25 .11
❑ 44 Yves Belanger .40 .18
❑ 45 Steve Jensen .25 .11
❑ 46 Bob Stewart .25 .11
❑ 47 Darcy Rota .25 .11
❑ 48 Dennis Hextall .25 .11
❑ 49 Bert Marshall .25 .11
❑ 50 Ken Dryden 12.00 5.50
❑ 51 Peter Mahovlich .40 .18
❑ 52 Dennis Ververgaert .25 .11
❑ 53 Inge Hammarstrom .25 .11
❑ 54 Doug Favell .40 .18
❑ 55 Steve Vickers .25 .11
❑ 56 Syl Apps .25 .11
❑ 57 Errol Thompson .25 .11
❑ 58 Don Luce .25 .11
❑ 59 Mike Milbury .75 .35
❑ 60 Yvan Cournoyer .75 .35
❑ 61 Kirk Bowman .25 .11
❑ 62 Billy Smith 1.50 .70
❑ 63 Goal Leaders 3.00 1.35
Guy Lafleur
Mike Bossy
Steve Shutt
❑ 64 Assist Leaders 2.50 1.10
Bryan Trottier
Guy Lafleur
Darryl Sittler
❑ 65 Scoring Leaders 2.50 1.10
Guy Lafleur
Bryan Trottier
Darryl Sittler
❑ 66 Penalty Minutes .50 .23
Leaders
Dave Schultz
Dave(Tiger) Williams
Dennis Polonich
❑ 67 Power Play Goal 3.00 1.35
Leaders
Mike Bossy
Phil Esposito
Steve Shutt
❑ 68 Goals Against 4.00 1.80
Average Leaders
Ken Dryden
Bernie Parent
Gilles Gilbert
❑ 69 Game Winning 2.00 .90
Goal Leaders
Guy Lafleur
Bill Barber
Darryl Sittler
Bob Bourne
❑ 70 Shutout Leaders 5.00 2.20
Bernie Parent
Ken Dryden
Don Edwards
Tony Esposito
Mike Palmateer
❑ 71 Bob Kelly .25 .11
❑ 72 Ron Stackhouse .25 .11
❑ 73 Wayne Dillon .25 .11
❑ 74 Jim Rutherford .40 .18
❑ 75 Stan Mikita 2.50 1.10
❑ 76 Bob Gainey 1.50 .70
❑ 77 Gerry Hart .25 .11
❑ 78 Lanny McDonald 1.50 .70
❑ 79 Brad Park 1.50 .70
❑ 80 Richard Martin .40 .18
❑ 81 Bernie Wolfe .40 .18
❑ 82 Bob MacMillan .25 .11
❑ 83 Brad Maxwell .25 .11
❑ 84 Mike Fidler .25 .11
❑ 85 Carol Vadnais .25 .11
❑ 86 Don Lever .25 .11
❑ 87 Phil Myre .40 .18
❑ 88 Paul Gardner .25 .11
❑ 89 Bob Murray .25 .11
❑ 90 Guy Lafleur 7.00 3.10
❑ 91 Bob Murdoch .25 .11
❑ 92 Ron Ellis .40 .18
❑ 93 Jude Drouin .25 .11
❑ 94 Jocelyn Guevremont .25 .11
❑ 95 Gilles Gilbert .40 .18
❑ 96 Bob Sirois .25 .11
❑ 97 Tom Lysiak .40 .18
❑ 98 Andre Dupont .25 .11
❑ 99 Per-Olov Brasar .25 .11
❑ 100 Phil Esposito 3.00 1.35
❑ 101 J.P. Bordeleau .25 .11
❑ 102 Pierre Mondou .75 .35
❑ 103 Wayne Bianchin .25 .11
❑ 104 Dennis O'Brien .25 .11
❑ 105 Glenn Resch .75 .35
❑ 106 Dennis Polonich .25 .11
❑ 107 Kris Manery .25 .11
❑ 108 Bill Hajt .25 .11
❑ 109 Jere Gillis .25 .11
❑ 110 Garry Unger .40 .18
❑ 111 Nick Beverley .25 .11
❑ 112 Pat Hickey .25 .11
❑ 113 Rick Middleton .75 .35
❑ 114 Orest Kindrachuk .25 .11
❑ 115 Mike Bossy 50.00 22.00
❑ 116 Pierre Bouchard .25 .11
❑ 117 Alain Daigle .25 .11
❑ 118 Terry Martin .25 .11
❑ 119 Tom Edur .25 .11
❑ 120 Marcel Dionne 3.00 1.35
❑ 121 Barry Beck 2.00 .90
❑ 122 Billy Lochead .25 .11
❑ 123 Paul Harrison .40 .18
❑ 124 Wayne Cashman .40 .18
❑ 125 Rick MacLeish .40 .18
❑ 126 Bob Bourne .40 .18
❑ 127 Ian Turnbull .25 .11
❑ 128 Gerry Meehan .25 .11
❑ 129 Eric Vail .25 .11
❑ 130 Gilbert Perreault .75 .35
❑ 131 Bob Dailey .25 .11
❑ 132 Dale McCourt .40 .18
❑ 133 John Wensink .75 .35
❑ 134 Bill Nyrop .25 .11
❑ 135 Ivan Boldirev .25 .11
❑ 136 Lucien DeBlois .25 .11
❑ 137 Brian Spencer .25 .11
❑ 138 Tim Young .25 .11
❑ 139 Ron Sedlbauer .25 .11
❑ 140 Gerry Cheevers 1.50 .70
❑ 141 Dennis Maruk .40 .18
❑ 142 Barry Dean .25 .11
❑ 143 Bernie Federko 10.00 4.50
❑ 144 Stefan Persson .25 .11
❑ 145 Wilf Paiement .40 .18
❑ 146 Dale Tallon .25 .11
❑ 147 Yvon Lambert .25 .11
❑ 148 Greg Joly .25 .11
❑ 149 Dean Talafous .25 .11
❑ 150 Don Edwards .40 .18
❑ 151 Butch Goring .40 .18
❑ 152 Tom Bladon .25 .11
❑ 153 Bob Nystrom .25 .11
❑ 154 Ron Greschner .40 .18
❑ 155 Jean Ratelle .75 .35
❑ 156 Russ Anderson .25 .11
❑ 157 John Marks .25 .11
❑ 158 Michel Larocque .40 .18
❑ 159 Paul Woods .25 .11
❑ 160 Mike Palmateer .40 .18
❑ 161 Jim Lorentz .25 .11
❑ 162 Dave Lewis .25 .11
❑ 163 Harvey Bennett .25 .11
❑ 164 Rick Smith .25 .11
❑ 165 Reggie Leach .40 .18
❑ 166 Wayne Thomas .40 .18
❑ 167 Dave Forbes .25 .11
❑ 168 Doug Wilson 10.00 4.50
❑ 169 Dan Bouchard .40 .18
❑ 170 Steve Shutt .75 .35
❑ 171 Mike Kaszycki .25 .11
❑ 172 Denis Herron .40 .18
❑ 173 Rick Bowness .40 .18
❑ 174 Rick Hampton .25 .11
❑ 175 Glen Sharpley .25 .11
❑ 176 Bill Barber .75 .35
❑ 177 Ron Duguay 4.00 1.80
❑ 178 Jim Schoenfeld .40 .18
❑ 179 Pierre Plante .25 .11
❑ 180 Jacques Lemaire .75 .35
❑ 181 Stan Jonathan .25 .11
❑ 182 Billy Harris .25 .11
❑ 183 Chris Oddleifson .25 .11
❑ 184 Jean Pronovost .40 .18
❑ 185 Fred Barrett .25 .11
❑ 186 Ross Lonsberry .25 .11
❑ 187 Mike McEwen .25 .11
❑ 188 Rene Robert .40 .18
❑ 189 J. Bob Kelly .25 .11
❑ 190 Serge Savard .25 .11
❑ 191 Dennis Kearns .25 .11
❑ 192 Flames Team 1.00 .45
❑ 193 Bruins Team 1.00 .45
❑ 194 Sabres Team 1.00 .45
❑ 195 Blackhawks Team 1.00 .45
❑ 196 Rockies Team 1.00 .45
❑ 197 Red Wings Team 1.00 .45
❑ 198 Kings Team 1.00 .45
❑ 199 North Stars Team 1.00 .45
❑ 200 Canadiens Team 1.00 .45
❑ 201 Islanders Team 1.00 .45
❑ 202 Rangers Team 1.00 .45
❑ 203 Flyers Team 1.00 .45
❑ 204 Penguins Team 1.00 .45
❑ 205 Blues Team 1.00 .45
❑ 206 Maple Leafs Team 1.00 .45
❑ 207 Canucks Team 1.00 .45
❑ 208 Capitals Team 1.00 .45
❑ 209 Danny Gare .40 .18
❑ 210 Larry Robinson 2.50 1.10
❑ 211 John Davidson .75 .35
❑ 212 Peter McNab .40 .18
❑ 213 Rick Kehoe .40 .18
❑ 214 Terry Harper .25 .11
❑ 215 Bobby Clarke 3.00 1.35
❑ 216 Bryan Maxwell UER .25 .11
(Photo actually
Brad Maxwell)
❑ 217 Ted Bulley .25 .11
❑ 218 Red Berenson .40 .18
❑ 219 Ron Grahame .40 .18
❑ 220 Clark Gillies .40 .18
❑ 221 Dave Maloney .25 .11
❑ 222 Derek Smith .25 .11
❑ 223 Wayne Stephenson .40 .18
❑ 224 John Van Boxmeer .25 .11
❑ 225 Dave Schultz .40 .18
❑ 226 Reed Larson .75 .35
❑ 227 Rejean Houle .25 .11
❑ 228 Doug Hicks .25 .11
❑ 229 Mike Murphy .25 .11
❑ 230 Pete Lopresti .40 .18
❑ 231 Jerry Korab .25 .11
❑ 232 Ed Westfall .40 .18
❑ 233 Greg Malone .25 .11
❑ 234 Paul Holmgren .40 .18
❑ 235 Walt Tkaczuk .40 .18
❑ 236 Don Marcotte .25 .11
❑ 237 Ron Low .40 .18
❑ 238 Rick Chartraw .25 .11
❑ 239 Cliff Koroll .25 .11
❑ 240 Borje Salming 2.00 .90
❑ 241 Roland Eriksson .25 .11
❑ 242 Ric Seiling .25 .11
❑ 243 Jim Bedard .40 .18
❑ 244 Peter Lee .40 .18
❑ 245 Denis Potvin 2.50 1.10
❑ 246 Greg Polis .25 .11
❑ 247 Jim Watson .25 .11
❑ 248 Bobby Schmautz .25 .11
❑ 249 Doug Risebrough .40 .18
❑ 250 Tony Esposito 2.50 1.10
❑ 251 Nick Libett .25 .11
❑ 252 Ron Zanussi .25 .11
❑ 253 Andre Savard .25 .11
❑ 254 Dave Burrows .25 .11
❑ 255 Ulf Nilsson .75 .35
❑ 256 Richard Mulhern .25 .11
❑ 257 Don Saleski .25 .11
❑ 258 Wayne Merrick .25 .11
❑ 259 Checklist 133-264 5.00 1.25
❑ 260 Guy Lapointe .40 .18
❑ 261 Grant Mulvey .25 .11
❑ 262 Stanley Cup Semifinals .50 .23
Canadiens Sweep
Maple Leafs
❑ 263 Stanley Cup Semifinals .50 .23
Bruins Skate
Past Flyers
❑ 264 Stanley Cup Finals .75 .35
Canadiens Win Third
Straight Cup
❑ 265 Bob Sauve .40 .18
❑ 266 Randy Manery .25 .11
❑ 267 Bill Fairbairn .25 .11
❑ 268 Garry Monahan .25 .11
❑ 269 Colin Campbell .40 .18
❑ 270 Dan Newman .25 .11
❑ 271 Dwight Foster .25 .11
❑ 272 Larry Carriere .25 .11
❑ 273 Michel Bergeron .25 .11
❑ 274 Scott Garland .25 .11
❑ 275 Bill McKenzie .40 .18
❑ 276 Garnet Bailey .25 .11
❑ 277 Ed Kea .25 .11
❑ 278 Dave Gardner .25 .11
❑ 279 Bruce Affleck .25 .11
❑ 280 Bruce Boudreau .25 .11
❑ 281 Jean Hamel .25 .11
❑ 282 Kurt Walker .25 .11
❑ 283 Denis Dupere .25 .11
❑ 284 Gordie Lane .25 .11
❑ 285 Bobby Lalonde .25 .11
❑ 286 Pit Martin .25 .11
❑ 287 Jean Potvin .25 .11
❑ 288 Jimmy Jones .25 .11
❑ 289 Dave Hutchinson .25 .11
❑ 290 Pete Stemkowski .25 .11
❑ 291 Mike Christie .25 .11
❑ 292 Bill Riley .25 .11
❑ 293 Rey Comeau .25 .11
❑ 294 Jack McIlhargey .25 .11
❑ 295 Tom Younghans .25 .11
❑ 296 Mario Faubert .25 .11
❑ 297 Checklist 265-396 5.00 1.25
❑ 298 Rob Palmer .25 .11
❑ 299 Dave Hudson .25 .11
❑ 300 Bobby Orr 40.00 18.00
❑ 301 Lorne Stamler .25 .11
❑ 302 Curt Ridley .25 .11
❑ 303 Greg Smith .25 .11
❑ 304 Jerry Butler .25 .11
❑ 305 Gary Doak .25 .11
❑ 306 Danny Grant .40 .18
❑ 307 Mark Suzor .25 .11
❑ 308 Rick Bragnalo .25 .11
❑ 309 John Gould .25 .11
❑ 310 Sheldon Kannegiesser .25 .11
❑ 311 Bobby Sheehan .25 .11
❑ 312 Randy Carlyle 5.00 2.20
❑ 313 Lorne Henning .25 .11
❑ 314 Tom Williams .25 .11
❑ 315 Ron Andruff .25 .11
❑ 316 Bryan Watson .25 .11
❑ 317 Willi Plett .25 .11
❑ 318 John Grisdale .25 .11
❑ 319 Brian Sutter 8.00 3.60
❑ 320 Trevor Johansen .25 .11
❑ 321 Vic Venasky .25 .11
❑ 322 Rick Lapointe .25 .11
❑ 323 Ron Delorme .25 .11
❑ 324 Yvon Labre .25 .11
❑ 325 Bryan Trottier AS UER 4.00 1.80
(Misspelled Brian
on card front)
❑ 326 Guy Lafleur AS 2.50 1.10
❑ 327 Clark Gillies AS .40 .18
❑ 328 Borje Salming AS .40 .18
❑ 329 Larry Robinson AS .75 .35
❑ 330 Ken Dryden AS 5.00 2.20
❑ 331 Darryl Sittler AS .75 .35
❑ 332 Terry O'Reilly AS .25 .11
❑ 333 Steve Shutt AS .40 .18
❑ 334 Denis Potvin AS .75 .35
❑ 335 Serge Savard AS .25 .11
❑ 336 Don Edwards AS .25 .11
❑ 337 Glenn Goldup .25 .11
❑ 338 Mike Kitchen .25 .11
❑ 339 Bob Girard .25 .11
❑ 340 Guy Chouinard .40 .18
❑ 341 Randy Holt .25 .11
❑ 342 Jim Roberts .25 .11
❑ 343 Dave Logan .25 .11
❑ 344 Walt McKechnie .25 .11
❑ 345 Brian Glennie .25 .11
❑ 346 Ralph Klassen .25 .11
❑ 347 Gord Smith .25 .11
❑ 348 Ken Houston .25 .11
❑ 349 Bob Manno .25 .11
❑ 350 Jean-Paul Parise .25 .11
❑ 351 Don Ashby .25 .11
❑ 352 Fred Stanfield .25 .11
❑ 353 Dave Taylor 15.00 6.75
❑ 354 Nelson Pyatt .25 .11
❑ 355 Blair Stewart .25 .11
❑ 356 David Shand .25 .11
❑ 357 Hilliard Graves .25 .11
❑ 358 Bob Hess .25 .11
❑ 359 Dave(Tiger) Williams 1.50 .70
❑ 360 Larry Wright .25 .11
❑ 361 Larry Brown .25 .11
❑ 362 Gary Croteau .25 .11
❑ 363 Rick Green .40 .18
❑ 364 Bill Clement .40 .18
❑ 365 Gerry O'Flaherty .25 .11
❑ 366 John Baby .25 .11
❑ 367 Nick Fotiu .40 .18
❑ 368 Pat Price .25 .11
❑ 369 Bert Wilson .25 .11
❑ 370 Bryan Lefley .25 .11
❑ 371 Ron Lalonde .25 .11
❑ 372 Bobby Simpson .25 .11
❑ 373 Doug Grant .40 .18
❑ 374 Pat Boutette .25 .11
❑ 375 Bob Paradise .25 .11
❑ 376 Mario Tremblay .40 .18
❑ 377 Darryl Edestrand .25 .11
❑ 378 Andy Spruce .25 .11
❑ 379 Jack Brownschidle .25 .11
❑ 380 Harold Snepsts .75 .35
❑ 381 Al MacAdam .25 .11
❑ 382 Neil Komadoski .25 .11
❑ 383 Don Awrey .25 .11
❑ 384 Ron Schock .25 .11
❑ 385 Gary Simmons .40 .18
❑ 386 Fred Ahern .25 .11
❑ 387 Larry Bolonchuk .25 .11
❑ 388 Brad Gassoff .25 .11
❑ 389 Chuck Arnason .25 .11
❑ 390 Barry Gibbs .25 .11
❑ 391 Jack Valiquette .25 .11
❑ 392 Doug Halward .25 .11
❑ 393 Hartland Monahan .25 .11
❑ 394 Rod Seiling .25 .11
❑ 395 George Ferguson .25 .11
❑ 396 Al Cameron .75 .19

## 1979-80 O-Pee-Chee

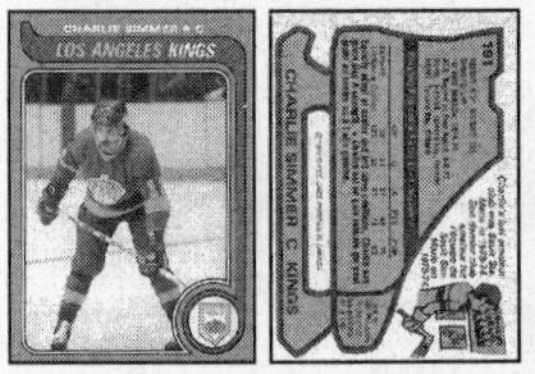


The 1979-80 O-Pee-Chee set consists of 396 standard-size cards. Cards 81, 82, 141, 163, and 263 differ from that of the corresponding Topps issue. Wax packs had 14 cards plus a bubble-gum piece. The fronts feature distinctive blue borders (that are prone to chipping), while bilingual backs feature 1978-79 and career stats, a short biography and a cartoon-illustrated fact about the player. Team cards (#244-261) have checklist backs. The Rookie Card of Wayne Gretzky (No. 18) has been illegally reprinted. Most of the reprints were discovered and then destroyed or clearly marked as reprints. However some still exist in the market. The reprint is difficult to distinguish from the real card, hence, collectors and dealers should be careful. The set also marks the last cards of Ken Dryden, Gordie Howe, Bobby Hull, and Stan Mikita. In addition to Gretzky, Rookie Cards include Barry Melrose, John Tonelli, Charlie Simmer, and Bobby Smith.

| | NRMT-MT | EXC |
|---|---|---|
| COMPLETE SET (396) | 1100.00 | 500.00 |
| COMMON CARD (1-396) | .60 | .25 |

❑ 1 Goal Leaders 4.00 1.80
Mike Bossy
Marcel Dionne
Guy Lafleur
❑ 2 Assist Leaders 3.00 1.35
Bryan Trottier
Guy Lafleur
Marcel Dionne
Bob MacMillan
❑ 3 Scoring Leaders 3.00 1.35
Bryan Trottier
Marcel Dionne
Guy Lafleur
❑ 4 Penalty Minute .75 .35

Leaders
Dave(Tiger) Williams
Randy Holt
Dave Schultz
❑ 5 Power Play ........................ 2.50 1.10
Goal Leaders
Mike Bossy
Marcel Dionne
Paul Gardner
Lanny McDonald
❑ 6 Goals Against ..................... 4.00 1.80
Average Leaders
Ken Dryden
Glenn Resch
Bernie Parent
❑ 7 Game Winning.................... 3.50 1.55
Goals Leaders
Guy Lafleur
Mike Bossy
Bryan Trottier
Jean Pronovost
Ted Bulley
❑ 8 Shutout Leaders ................ 5.00 2.20
Ken Dryden
Tony Esposito
Mario Lessard
Mike Palmateer
Bernie Parent
❑ 9 Greg Malone ............................. .60 .25
❑ 10 Rick Middleton .................. 1.50 .70
❑ 11 Greg Smith .............................. .60 .25
❑ 12 Rene Robert .................... 1.00 .45
❑ 13 Doug Risebrough ............ 1.00 .45
❑ 14 Bob Kelly ............................. .60 .25
❑ 15 Walt Tkaczuk .................... 1.00 .45
❑ 16 John Marks.............................. .60 .25
❑ 17 Willie Huber.............................. .60 .25
❑ 18 Wayne Gretzky............. 900.00 400.00
❑ 19 Ron Sedlbauer ......................... .60 .25
❑ 20 Glenn Resch AS2............. 1.50 .70
❑ 21 Blair Chapman ........................ .60 .25
❑ 22 Ron Zanussi ............................ .60 .25
❑ 23 Brad Park........................... 1.50 .70
❑ 24 Yvon Lambert .......................... .60 .25
❑ 25 Andre Savard ........................... .60 .25
❑ 26 Jim Watson .............................. .60 .25
❑ 27 Hal Philipoff .............................. .60 .25
❑ 28 Dan Bouchard.................... 1.00 .45
❑ 29 Bob Sirois.................................. .60 .25
❑ 30 Ulf Nilsson........................ 1.00 .45
❑ 31 Mike Murphy ............................ .60 .25
❑ 32 Stefan Persson ........................ .60 .25
❑ 33 Garry Unger...................... 1.00 .45
❑ 34 Rejean Houle ............................ .60 .25
❑ 35 Barry Beck......................... 1.00 .45
❑ 36 Tim Young................................ .60 .25
❑ 37 Rick Dudley .............................. .60 .25
❑ 38 Wayne Stephenson........... 1.00 .45
❑ 39 Peter McNab...................... 1.00 .45
❑ 40 Borje Salming AS2............ 1.50 .70
❑ 41 Tom Lysiak .............................. .60 .25
❑ 42 Don Maloney .................... 1.50 .70
❑ 43 Mike Rogers ...................... 1.00 .45
❑ 44 Dave Lewis .............................. .60 .25
❑ 45 Peter Lee ................................. .60 .25
❑ 46 Marty Howe ...................... 1.50 .70
❑ 47 Serge Bernier............................ .60 .25
❑ 48 Paul Woods .............................. .60 .25
❑ 49 Bob Sauve ........................ 1.00 .45
❑ 50 Larry Robinson AS1 ......... 2.50 1.10
❑ 51 Tom Gorence ............................ .60 .25
❑ 52 Gary Sargent............................. .60 .25
❑ 53 Thomas Gradin ................. 1.50 .70
❑ 54 Dean Talafous........................... .60 .25
❑ 55 Bob Murray................................ .60 .25
❑ 56 Bob Bourne....................... 1.00 .45
❑ 57 Larry Patey ............................... .60 .25
❑ 58 Ross Lonsberry ......................... .60 .25
❑ 59 Rick Smith UER ........................ .60 .25
(Born Kinston,
should be Kingston)
❑ 60 Guy Chouinard.................. 1.00 .45
❑ 61 Danny Gare........................ 1.00 .45
❑ 62 Jim Bedard ........................ 1.00 .45
❑ 63 Dale McCourt UER .............. .60 .25
(Pictured in Kings'
sweater, but he never
played for the Kings)
❑ 64 Steve Payne ............................. .60 .25
❑ 65 Pat Hughes ............................... .60 .25
❑ 66 Mike McEwen ............................ .60 .25
❑ 67 Reg Kerr .................................... .60 .25
❑ 68 Walt McKechnie......................... .60 .25
❑ 69 Michel Plasse .................... 1.00 .45
❑ 70 Denis Potvin AS1.............. 2.00 .90
❑ 71 Dave Dryden ..................... 1.50 .70
❑ 72 Gary McAdam............................ .60 .25
❑ 73 Andre St.Laurent ...................... .60 .25
❑ 74 Jerry Korab................................ .60 .25
❑ 75 Rick MacLeish .................. 1.50 .70
❑ 76 Dennis Kearns ........................... .60 .25
❑ 77 Jean Pronovost.................. 1.00 .45
❑ 78 Ron Greschner .................. 1.00 .45
❑ 79 Wayne Cashman................ 1.50 .70
❑ 80 Tony Esposito.................... 2.00 .90
❑ 81 Jets Emblem.................... 10.00 4.50
(checklist back)
❑ 82 Oilers Emblem ................ 12.00 5.50
(checklist back)
❑ 83 Stanley Cup Finals ............ 1.50 .70
Canadiens Make It
Four Straight Cups
❑ 84 Brian Sutter ...................... 2.50 1.10
❑ 85 Gerry Cheevers.................. 1.50 .70
❑ 86 Pat Hickey................................. .60 .25
❑ 87 Mike Kaszycki ........................... .60 .25
❑ 88 Grant Mulvey ........................... .60 .25
❑ 89 Derek Smith.............................. .60 .25
❑ 90 Steve Shutt........................ 1.50 .70
❑ 91 Robert Picard ............................ .60 .25
❑ 92 Dan Labraaten ........................... .60 .25
❑ 93 Glen Sharpley ............................ .60 .25
❑ 94 Denis Herron ..................... 1.00 .45
❑ 95 Reggie Leach..................... 1.50 .70
❑ 96 John Van Boxmeer ..................... .60 .25
❑ 97 Dave(Tiger) Williams ......... 1.50 .70
❑ 98 Butch Goring ..................... 1.00 .45
❑ 99 Don Marcotte ............................ .60 .25
❑ 100 Bryan Trottier AS1 ......... 4.00 1.80
❑ 101 Serge Savard AS2........... 1.50 .70
❑ 102 Cliff Koroll.............................. .60 .25
❑ 103 Gary Smith ....................... 1.00 .45
❑ 104 Al MacAdam ........................... .60 .25
❑ 105 Don Edwards .................... 1.00 .45
❑ 106 Errol Thompson....................... .60 .25
❑ 107 Andre Lacroix .................. 1.00 .45
❑ 108 Marc Tardif ...................... 1.00 .45
❑ 109 Rick Kehoe ...................... 1.00 .45
❑ 110 John Davidson.................. 1.50 .70
❑ 111 Behn Wilson ............................ .60 .25
❑ 112 Doug Jarvis ...................... 1.00 .45
❑ 113 Tom Rowe ............................... .60 .25
❑ 114 Mike Milbury.................... 1.50 .70
❑ 115 Billy Harris.............................. .60 .25
❑ 116 Greg Fox.................................. .60 .25
❑ 117 Curt Fraser.............................. .60 .25
❑ 118 Jean-Paul Parise...................... .60 .25
❑ 119 Ric Seiling .............................. .60 .25
❑ 120 Darryl Sittler ................... 1.50 .70
❑ 121 Rick Lapointe.......................... .60 .25
❑ 122 Jim Rutherford ................ 1.00 .45
❑ 123 Mario Tremblay ............... 1.50 .70
❑ 124 Randy Carlyle .................. 1.50 .70
❑ 125 Bobby Clarke ................... 2.50 1.10
❑ 126 Wayne Thomas................. 1.00 .45
❑ 127 Ivan Boldirev.......................... .60 .25
❑ 128 Ted Bulley............................... .60 .25
❑ 129 Dick Redmond ........................ .60 .25
❑ 130 Clark Gillies AS1 ............. 1.50 .70
❑ 131 Checklist 1-132............. 10.00 4.50
❑ 132 Vaclav Nedomansky ............... .60 .25
❑ 133 Richard Mulhern..................... .60 .25
❑ 134 Dave Schultz.................... 1.50 .70
❑ 135 Guy Lapointe .................. 1.00 .45
❑ 136 Gilles Meloche ................ 1.50 .70
❑ 137 Randy Pierce UER ................. .60 .25
(Photo actually
Ron Delorme)
❑ 138 Cam Connor ........................... .60 .25
❑ 139 George Ferguson .................... .60 .25
❑ 140 Bill Barber....................... 1.50 .70
❑ 141 Terry Ruskowski UER..... 1.00 .45
(Misspelled Ruskouski
on both sides)
❑ 142 Wayne Babych......................... .60 .25
❑ 143 Phil Russell............................. .60 .25
❑ 144 Bobby Schmautz...................... .60 .25
❑ 145 Carol Vadnais ......................... .60 .25
❑ 146 John Tonelli..................... 6.00 2.70
❑ 147 Peter Marsh............................ .60 .25
❑ 148 Thommie Bergman .................. .60 .25
❑ 149 Richard Martin................ 1.50 .70
❑ 150 Ken Dryden AS1 .......... 10.00 4.50
❑ 151 Kris Manery ............................ .60 .25
❑ 152 Guy Charron ........................... .60 .25
❑ 153 Lanny McDonald.............. 1.50 .70
❑ 154 Ron Stackhouse ...................... .60 .25
❑ 155 Stan Mikita ..................... 2.50 1.10
❑ 156 Paul Holmgren......................... .60 .25
❑ 157 Perry Miller............................. .60 .25
❑ 158 Gary Croteau........................... .60 .25
❑ 159 Dave Maloney ......................... .60 .25
❑ 160 Marcel Dionne AS2......... 3.00 1.35
❑ 161 Mike Bossy RB ............... 3.00 1.35
Most Goals,
RW Season
❑ 162 Don Maloney RB.................... .75 .35
Rookie, Most Points,
Playoff Series
❑ 163 Whalers Emblem .......... 10.00 4.50
(checklist back)
❑ 164 Brad Park RB ......................... .75 .35
Most Career Playoff
Goals, Defenseman
❑ 165 Bryan Trottier RB............ 1.50 .70
Most Points, Period
❑ 166 Al Hill...................................... .60 .25
❑ 167 Gary Bromley UER.......... 1.00 .45
(Photo actually
Glen Hanlon)
❑ 168 Don Murdoch .......................... .60 .25
❑ 169 Wayne Merrick ....................... .60 .25
❑ 170 Bob Gainey ..................... 1.50 .70
❑ 171 Jim Schoenfeld................ 1.50 .70
❑ 172 Gregg Sheppard ..................... .60 .25
❑ 173 Dan Bolduc.............................. .60 .25
❑ 174 Blake Dunlop .......................... .60 .25
❑ 175 Gordie Howe................. 30.00 13.50
❑ 176 Richard Brodeur ............. 1.50 .70
❑ 177 Tom Younghans ...................... .60 .25
❑ 178 Andre Dupont ......................... .60 .25
❑ 179 Ed Johnstone........................... .60 .25
❑ 180 Gilbert Perreault ............. 1.50 .70
❑ 181 Bob Lorimer ............................ .60 .25
❑ 182 John Wensink.......................... .60 .25
❑ 183 Lee Fogolin.............................. .60 .25
❑ 184 Greg Carroll ............................ .60 .25
❑ 185 Bobby Hull.................... 25.00 11.00
❑ 186 Harold Snepsts ....................... .60 .25
❑ 187 Peter Mahovlich.............. 1.00 .45
❑ 188 Eric Vail .................................. .60 .25
❑ 189 Phil Myre ........................ 1.00 .45
❑ 190 Wilf Paiement ................. 1.00 .45
❑ 191 Charlie Simmer............... 6.00 2.70
❑ 192 Per-Olov Brasar ...................... .60 .25
❑ 193 Lorne Henning ........................ .60 .25
❑ 194 Don Luce ................................. .60 .25
❑ 195 Steve Vickers........................... .60 .25
❑ 196 Bob Miller ....................... 1.00 .45
❑ 197 Mike Palmateer............... 1.00 .45
❑ 198 Nick Libett .............................. .60 .25
❑ 199 Pat Ribble ............................... .60 .25
❑ 200 Guy Lafleur AS1.............. 6.00 2.70
❑ 201 Mel Bridgman ................. 1.00 .45
❑ 202 Morris Lukowich...................... .60 .25
❑ 203 Don Lever ............................... .60 .25
❑ 204 Tom Bladon ............................ .60 .25
❑ 205 Garry Howatt .......................... .60 .25
❑ 206 Bobby Smith.................... 6.00 2.70
❑ 207 Craig Ramsay ................. 1.00 .45
❑ 208 Ron Duguay.................... 1.50 .70
❑ 209 Gilles Gilbert.................. 1.00 .45
❑ 210 Bob MacMillan........................ .60 .25
❑ 211 Pierre Mondou........................ .60 .25
❑ 212 J.P. Bordeleau ........................ .60 .25
❑ 213 Reed Larson ................... 1.00 .45
❑ 214 Dennis Ververgaert ................. .60 .25
❑ 215 Bernie Federko................ 5.00 2.20
❑ 216 Mark Howe ..................... 3.00 1.35
❑ 217 Bob Nystrom .......................... .60 .25
❑ 218 Orest Kindrachuk.................... .60 .25
❑ 219 Mike Fidler.............................. .60 .25
❑ 220 Phil Esposito.................. 1.50 .70
❑ 221 Bill Hajt.................................. .60 .25
❑ 222 Mark Napier.................... 1.00 .45
❑ 223 Dennis Maruk ................. 1.00 .45
❑ 224 Dennis Polonich ..................... .60 .25
❑ 225 Jean Ratelle.................... 1.50 .70
❑ 226 Bob Dailey ............................. .60 .25
❑ 227 Alain Daigle............................ .60 .25
❑ 228 Ian Turnbull ........................... .60 .25
❑ 229 Jack Valiquette ....................... .60 .25
❑ 230 Mike Bossy AS2........... 15.00 6.75
❑ 231 Brad Maxwell.......................... .60 .25
❑ 232 Dave Taylor..................... 5.00 2.20
❑ 233 Pierre Larouche .............. 1.50 .70
❑ 234 Rod Schutt ............................. .60 .25
❑ 235 Rogatien Vachon ............ 1.50 .70
❑ 236 Ryan Walter.................... 1.50 .70
❑ 237 Checklist 133-264 UER. 10.00 4.50
(245 Buins, should
be Bruins)
❑ 238 Terry O'Reilly................. 1.50 .70
❑ 239 Real Cloutier .................. 1.00 .45
❑ 240 Anders Hedberg.............. 1.00 .45
❑ 241 Ken Linseman................. 4.00 1.80
❑ 242 Billy Smith ..................... 1.50 .70
❑ 243 Rick Chartraw ......................... .60 .25
❑ 244 Flames Team .................. 2.50 1.10
❑ 245 Bruins Team ................... 2.50 1.10
❑ 246 Sabres Team................... 2.50 1.10
❑ 247 Blackhawks Team ........... 2.50 1.10
❑ 248 Rockies Team ................. 2.50 1.10
❑ 249 Red Wings Team ............. 2.50 1.10
❑ 250 Kings Team..................... 2.50 1.10
❑ 251 North Stars Team ........... 2.50 1.10
❑ 252 Canadiens Team ............. 2.50 1.10
❑ 253 Islanders Team ............... 2.50 1.10
❑ 254 Rangers Team ................. 2.50 1.10
❑ 255 Flyers Team .................... 2.50 1.10
❑ 256 Penguins Team................ 2.50 1.10
❑ 257 Blues Team..................... 2.50 1.10
❑ 258 Maple Leafs Team ........... 2.50 1.10
❑ 259 Canucks Team ................. 2.50 1.10
❑ 260 Capitals Team ................. 2.50 1.10
❑ 261 Nordiques Team .......... 10.00 4.50
❑ 262 Jean Hamel............................. .60 .25
❑ 263 Stan Jonathan......................... .60 .25
❑ 264 Russ Anderson ....................... .60 .25
❑ 265 Gordie Roberts ....................... .60 .25
❑ 266 Bill Flett.................................. .60 .25
❑ 267 Robbie Ftorek ................. 1.00 .45
❑ 268 Mike Amodeo .......................... .60 .25
❑ 269 Vic Venasky ............................ .60 .25
❑ 270 Bob Manno ............................. .60 .25
❑ 271 Dan Maloney........................... .60 .25
❑ 272 Al Sims .................................. .60 .25
❑ 273 Greg Polis............................... .60 .25
❑ 274 Doug Favell..................... 1.50 .70
❑ 275 Pierre Plante .......................... .60 .25
❑ 276 Bob Murdoch .......................... .60 .25
❑ 277 Lyle Moffat ............................. .60 .25
❑ 278 Jack Brownschidle.................. .60 .25
❑ 279 Dave Keon ...................... 1.50 .70
❑ 280 Darryl Edestrand..................... .60 .25
❑ 281 Greg Millen..................... 4.00 1.80
❑ 282 John Gould ............................. .60 .25
❑ 283 Rich Leduc ............................. .60 .25
❑ 284 Ron Delorme .......................... .60 .25
❑ 285 Gord Smith ............................. .60 .25
❑ 286 Nick Fotiu ....................... 1.00 .45
❑ 287 Kevin McCarthy ...................... .60 .25
❑ 288 Jimmy Jones ........................... .60 .25
❑ 289 Pierre Bouchard...................... .60 .25
❑ 290 Wayne Bianchin ...................... .60 .25
❑ 291 Garry Lariviere ....................... .60 .25
❑ 292 Steve Jensen .......................... .60 .25
❑ 293 John Garrett ................... 1.00 .45
❑ 294 Hilliard Graves ....................... .60 .25
❑ 295 Bill Clement ................... 1.00 .45
❑ 296 Michel Larocque.............. 1.50 .70
❑ 297 Bob Stewart............................ .60 .25
❑ 298 Doug Patey ............................ .60 .25
❑ 299 Dave Farrish .......................... .60 .25
❑ 300 Al Smith.......................... 1.00 .45
❑ 301 Billy Lochead ......................... .60 .25
❑ 302 Dave Hutchinson .................... .60 .25
❑ 303 Bill Riley ................................ .60 .25
❑ 304 Barry Gibbs............................. .60 .25
❑ 305 Chris Oddleifson ..................... .60 .25
❑ 306 J. Bob Kelly UER.................... .60 .25
(Photo actually
Bob Kelly)
❑ 307 Al Hangsleben......................... .60 .25
❑ 308 Curt Brackenbury.................... .60 .25
❑ 309 Rick Green...................... 1.00 .45
❑ 310 Ken Houston............................ .60 .25
❑ 311 Greg Joly ................................ .60 .25
❑ 312 Bill Lesuk................................ .60 .25
❑ 313 Bill Stewart ............................ .60 .25
❑ 314 Rick Ley.................................. .60 .25
❑ 315 Brett Callighen ....................... .60 .25
❑ 316 Michel Dion .................... 1.00 .45
❑ 317 Randy Manery ........................ .60 .25
❑ 318 Barry Dean.............................. .60 .25
❑ 319 Pat Boutette ........................... .60 .25
❑ 320 Mark Heaslip........................... .60 .25
❑ 321 Dave Inkpen............................ .60 .25
❑ 322 Jere Gillis................................ .60 .25
❑ 323 Larry Brown............................ .60 .25
❑ 324 Alain Cote .............................. .60 .25
❑ 325 Gordie Lane ............................ .60 .25
❑ 326 Bobby Lalonde........................ .60 .25
❑ 327 Ed Staniowski ......................... .60 .25
❑ 328 Ron Plumb .............................. .60 .25
❑ 329 Jude Drouin............................. .60 .25
❑ 330 Rick Hampton.......................... .60 .25
❑ 331 Stan Weir................................ .60 .25
❑ 332 Blair Stewart........................... .60 .25
❑ 333 Mike Polich............................. .60 .25
❑ 334 Jean Potvin............................. .60 .25
❑ 335 Jordy Douglas ......................... .60 .25
❑ 336 Joel Quenneville ..................... .60 .25
❑ 337 Glen Hanlon.................... 2.50 1.10
❑ 338 Dave Hoyda ............................ .60 .25
❑ 339 Colin Campbell ............... 1.00 .45
❑ 340 John Smrke............................. .60 .25
❑ 341 Brian Glennie.......................... .60 .25
❑ 342 Don Kozak .............................. .60 .25
❑ 343 Yvon Labre ............................. .60 .25
❑ 344 Curt Bennett ........................... .60 .25
❑ 345 Mike Christie.......................... .60 .25
❑ 346 Checklist 265-396......... 10.00 4.50
❑ 347 Pat Price ................................ .60 .25
❑ 348 Ron Low ......................... 1.00 .45
❑ 349 Mike Antonovich...................... .60 .25
❑ 350 Roland Eriksson ...................... .60 .25
❑ 351 Bob Murdoch........................... .60 .25
❑ 352 Rob Palmer............................. .60 .25
❑ 353 Brad Gassoff........................... .60 .25
❑ 354 Bruce Boudreau....................... .60 .25
❑ 355 Al Hamilton............................. .60 .25
❑ 356 Blaine Stoughton ............ 1.00 .45
❑ 357 John Baby............................... .60 .25
❑ 358 Gary Inness .................... 1.00 .45
❑ 359 Wayne Dillon .......................... .60 .25
❑ 360 Darcy Rota.............................. .60 .25
❑ 361 Brian Engblom ................ 1.00 .45
❑ 362 Bill Hogaboam ......................... .60 .25
❑ 363 Dave Debol ............................. .60 .25
❑ 364 Pete Lopresti .................. 1.00 .45
❑ 365 Gerry Hart............................... .60 .25
❑ 366 Syl Apps ................................. .60 .25
❑ 367 Jack McIlhargey ...................... .60 .25
❑ 368 Willy Lindstrom ...................... .60 .25
❑ 369 Don Laurence ......................... .60 .25
❑ 370 Chuck Luksa ........................... .60 .25
❑ 371 Dave Semenko................. 4.00 1.80
❑ 372 Paul Baxter ............................. .60 .25
❑ 373 Ron Ellis ......................... 1.00 .45
❑ 374 Leif Svensson.......................... .60 .25
❑ 375 Dennis O'Brien........................ .60 .25
❑ 376 Glenn Goldup.......................... .60 .25
❑ 377 Terry Richardson..................... .60 .25
❑ 378 Peter Sullivan ......................... .60 .25
❑ 379 Doug Hicks ............................. .60 .25
❑ 380 Jamie Hislop ........................... .60 .25
❑ 381 Jocelyn Guevremont................ .60 .25
❑ 382 Willi Plett ........................ 1.00 .45
❑ 383 Larry Goodenough................... .60 .25
❑ 384 Jim Warner............................. .60 .25
❑ 385 Rey Comeau ........................... .60 .25
❑ 386 Barry Melrose .................. 6.00 2.70
❑ 387 Dave Hunter............................ .60 .25
❑ 388 Wally Weir.............................. .60 .25
❑ 389 Mario Lessard.................. 1.00 .45
❑ 390 Ed Kea .................................... .60 .25
❑ 391 Bob Stephenson ...................... .60 .25
❑ 392 Dennis Hextall......................... .60 .25
❑ 393 Jerry Butler............................. .60 .25
❑ 394 David Shand ........................... .60 .25
❑ 395 Rick Blight ............................. .60 .25
❑ 396 Lars-Erik Sjoberg............ 3.00 1.35

## 1980-81 O-Pee-Chee

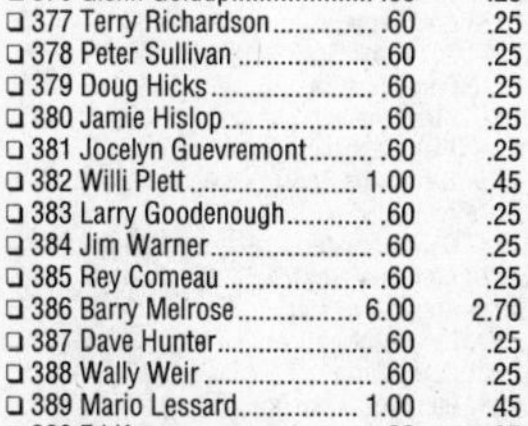

Card fronts of this 396-card standard-size set contain the player's name and position (bilingual text) in a hockey puck on the lower right of the front. Unlike the Topps set of this year, the puck was not issued with a black scratch-off covering. The team name is listed to the left of the puck. The cards were originally sold in 10-card 20-cent wax packs. Bilingual backs feature a short list of career milestones, 1979-80 season and career statistics along with short trivia comments. Members of the U.S. Olympic hockey team (USA in checklist below) are honored with the USA hockey emblem on the card front. A great crop of Rookie Cards includes Ray Bourque, Dave Christian, Mike Foligno, Mike Gartner, Michel Goulet, Rod Langway, Mike Liut, Brad Marsh, Mark Messier, Kent Nilsson, John Ogrodnick, Pete Peeters, Brian Propp, Rob Ramage, Mike Ramsey and Rick Vaive. Beware when purchasing the cards of Ray Bourque and Mark Messier as they have been counterfeited.

| | NRMT-MT | EXC |
|---|---|---|
| COMPLETE SET (396) | 500.00 | 220.00 |
| COMMON CARD (1-396) | .35 | .16 |

❑ 1 Flyers Streak to 35 RB ........ 1.25 .55
Longest in
Sports History
❑ 2 Ray Bourque RB ............... 10.00 4.50
65 Pts., Record for
Rookie Defenseman
❑ 3 Wayne Gretzky RB ........... 30.00 13.50
Youngest Ever
50-goal Scorer
❑ 4 Charlie Simmer RB .............. .50 .23
Scores 13th Straight
Game, NHL Record
❑ 5 Billy Smith RB ...................... .50 .23
First Goalie to
Score a Goal
❑ 6 Jean Ratelle ......................... .75 .35
❑ 7 Dave Maloney ....................... .35 .16
❑ 8 Phil Myre .............................. .75 .35
❑ 9 Ken Morrow USA............... 1.50 .70
❑ 10 Guy Lafleur ...................... 3.00 1.35
❑ 11 Bill Derlago........................... .35 .16
❑ 12 Doug Wilson..................... 1.00 .45
❑ 13 Craig Ramsay ....................... .35 .16
❑ 14 Pat Boutette .......................... .35 .16
❑ 15 Eric Vail ................................ .35 .16
❑ 16 Mike Foligno ......................... .60 .25
Red Wings Scoring Leaders
(checklist back)
❑ 17 Bobby Smith..................... 2.00 .90
❑ 18 Rick Kehoe ............................ .75 .35
❑ 19 Joel Quenneville .................... .35 .16
❑ 20 Marcel Dionne ................. 1.50 .70
❑ 21 Kevin McCarthy ..................... .35 .16
❑ 22 Jim Craig USA .................. 2.50 1.10
❑ 23 Steve Vickers......................... .35 .16
❑ 24 Ken Linseman.................. 1.00 .45
❑ 25 Mike Bossy....................... 7.00 3.10
❑ 26 Serge Savard ......................... .75 .35
❑ 27 Grant Mulvey ......................... .60 .25
Blackhawks Scoring Leaders
(checklist back)
❑ 28 Pat Hickey............................. .35 .16
❑ 29 Peter Sullivan ........................ .35 .16
❑ 30 Blaine Stoughton ................... .75 .35
❑ 31 Mike Liut.......................... 7.00 3.10
❑ 32 Blair MacDonald .................... .35 .16
❑ 33 Rick Green............................. .35 .16
❑ 34 Al MacAdam .......................... .35 .16
❑ 35 Robbie Ftorek ........................ .35 .16
❑ 36 Dick Redmond........................ .35 .16
❑ 37 Ron Duguay........................... .35 .16
❑ 38 Danny Gare........................... .60 .25
Sabres Scoring Leaders
(checklist back)
❑ 39 Brian Propp ...................... 7.00 3.10
❑ 40 Bryan Trottier ................... 2.50 1.10
❑ 41 Rich Preston.......................... .35 .16
❑ 42 Pierre Mondou....................... .35 .16
❑ 43 Reed Larson .......................... .35 .16
❑ 44 George Ferguson .................... .35 .16
❑ 45 Guy Chouinard....................... .75 .35
❑ 46 Billy Harris............................ .35 .16
❑ 47 Gilles Meloche ....................... .75 .35
❑ 48 Blair Chapman ....................... .35 .16
❑ 49 Mike Gartner .................... 6.00 2.70
Capitals Scoring Leaders
(checklist back)
❑ 50 Darryl Sittler .................... 1.00 .45
❑ 51 Richard Martin....................... .75 .35
❑ 52 Ivan Boldirev......................... .35 .16
❑ 53 Craig Norwich........................ .35 .16
❑ 54 Dennis Polonich .................... .35 .16
❑ 55 Bobby Clarke ................... 1.50 .70
❑ 56 Terry O'Reilly........................ .75 .35
❑ 57 Carol Vadnais ........................ .35 .16
❑ 58 Bob Gainey ...................... 1.00 .45
❑ 59 Blaine Stoughton ................... .60 .25
Whalers Scoring Leaders
(checklist back)
❑ 60 Billy Smith ............................ .75 .35
❑ 61 Mike O'Connell ..................... .75 .35
❑ 62 Lanny McDonald............... 1.00 .45
❑ 63 Lee Fogolin............................ .35 .16
❑ 64 Rocky Saganiuk...................... .35 .16
❑ 65 Rolf Edberg........................... .35 .16
❑ 66 Paul Shmyr........................... .35 .16
❑ 67 Michel Goulet ................. 15.00 6.75
❑ 68 Dan Bouchard ....................... .75 .35
❑ 69 Mark Johnson USA............... .75 .35
❑ 70 Reggie Leach......................... .75 .35
❑ 71 Bernie Federko...................... .60 .25
Blues Scoring Leaders
(checklist back)
❑ 72 Peter Mahovlich.................... .75 .35

❑ 73 Anders Hedberg .75 .35
❑ 74 Brad Park .75 .35
❑ 75 Clark Gillies .75 .35
❑ 76 Doug Jarvis .35 .16
❑ 77 John Garrett .75 .35
❑ 78 Dave Hutchinson .35 .16
❑ 79 John Anderson .35 .16
❑ 80 Gilbert Perreault 1.00 .45
❑ 81 Marcel Dionne ASI 1.00 .45
❑ 82 Guy Lafleur AS1 1.50 .70
❑ 83 Charlie Simmer AS1 .50 .23
❑ 84 Larry Robinson AS1 .50 .23
❑ 85 Borje Salming AS1 .50 .23
❑ 86 Tony Esposito AS1 1.00 .45
❑ 87 Wayne Gretzky AS2 50.00 22.00
❑ 88 Danny Gare AS2 .50 .23
❑ 89 Steve Shutt AS2 .50 .23
❑ 90 Barry Beck AS2 .50 .23
❑ 91 Mark Howe AS2 .50 .23
❑ 92 Don Edwards AS2 .50 .23
❑ 93 Tom McCarthy .35 .16
❑ 94 Peter McNab/Rick Middleton .60 .25
Bruins Scoring Leaders
(checklist back)
❑ 95 Mike Palmateer .75 .35
❑ 96 Jim Schoenfeld .75 .35
❑ 97 Jordy Douglas .35 .16
❑ 98 Keith Brown .35 .16
❑ 99 Dennis Ververgaert .35 .16
❑ 100 Phil Esposito 1.00 .45
❑ 101 Jack Brownschidle .35 .16
❑ 102 Bob Nystrom .35 .16
❑ 103 Steve Christoff USA .50 .23
❑ 104 Rob Palmer .35 .16
❑ 105 Dave(Tiger) Williams .75 .35
❑ 106 Kent Nilsson .60 .25
Flames Scoring Leaders
(checklist back)
❑ 107 Morris Lukowich .75 .35
❑ 108 Jack Valiquette .35 .16
❑ 109 Richie Dunn .35 .16
❑ 110 Rogatien Vachon .75 .35
❑ 111 Mark Napier .35 .16
❑ 112 Gordie Roberts .35 .16
❑ 113 Stan Jonathan .35 .16
❑ 114 Brett Callighen .35 .16
❑ 115 Rick MacLeish .75 .35
❑ 116 Ulf Nilsson .75 .35
❑ 117 Rick Kehoe .60 .25
Penguins Scoring Leaders
(checklist back)
❑ 118 Dan Maloney .35 .16
❑ 119 Terry Ruskowski .35 .16
❑ 120 Denis Potvin 1.50 .70
❑ 121 Wayne Stephenson .75 .35
❑ 122 Rich Leduc .35 .16
❑ 123 Checklist 1-132 6.00 2.70
❑ 124 Don Lever .35 .16
❑ 125 Jim Rutherford .75 .35
❑ 126 Ray Allison .35 .16
❑ 127 Mike Ramsey USA 3.00 1.35
❑ 128 Stan Smyl .60 .25
Canucks Scoring Leaders
(checklist back)
❑ 129 Al Secord 3.00 1.35
❑ 130 Denis Herron .75 .35
❑ 131 Bob Dailey .35 .16
❑ 132 Dean Talafous .35 .16
❑ 133 Ian Turnbull .35 .16
❑ 134 Ron Sedlbauer .35 .16
❑ 135 Tom Bladon .35 .16
❑ 136 Bernie Federko 2.50 1.10
❑ 137 Dave Taylor 3.00 1.35
❑ 138 Bob Lorimer .35 .16
❑ 139 Al MacAdam/Steve Payne .60 .25
North Stars Scoring Leaders
(checkist back)
❑ 140 Ray Bourque 110.00 50.00
❑ 141 Glen Hanlon .75 .35
❑ 142 Willy Lindstrom .35 .16
❑ 143 Mike Rogers .35 .16
❑ 144 Tony McKegney .35 .16
❑ 145 Behn Wilson .35 .16
❑ 146 Lucien DeBlois .35 .16
❑ 147 Dave Burrows .35 .16
❑ 148 Paul Woods .35 .16
❑ 149 Phil Esposito 1.00 .45
Rangers Scoring Leaders
(checklist back)
❑ 150 Tony Esposito 1.50 .70
❑ 151 Pierre Larouche .75 .35
❑ 152 Brad Maxwell .35 .16
❑ 153 Stan Weir .35 .16
❑ 154 Ryan Walter .35 .16
❑ 155 Dale Hoganson .35 .16
❑ 156 Anders Kallur .35 .16
❑ 157 Paul Reinhart 1.00 .45
❑ 158 Greg Millen .75 .35
❑ 159 Ric Seiling .35 .16
❑ 160 Mark Howe 1.50 .70
❑ 161 Goals Leaders .50 .23
Danny Gare (1)
Charlie Simmer (1)
B. Stoughton (1)
❑ 162 Assists Leaders 15.00 6.75
Wayne Gretzky (1)
Marcel Dionne (2)
Guy Lafleur (3)
❑ 163 Scoring Leaders 15.00 6.75
Marcel Dionne (1)
Wayne Gretzky (1)
Guy Lafleur (3)
❑ 164 Penalty Minutes .50 .23
Leaders
Jimmy Mann (1)
Dave(Tiger) Williams (2)
Paul Holmgren (3)
❑ 165 Power Play Goals 1.00 .45
Leaders
Charlie Simmer (1)
Marcel Dionne (2)
Danny Gare (2)
Steve Shutt (2)
Darryl Sittler (2)
❑ 166 Goals Against Avg. .50 .23
Leaders
Bob Sauve (1)
Denis Herron (2)
Don Edwards (3)
❑ 167 Game-Winning Goals .50 .23
Leaders
Danny Gare (1)
Peter McNab (2)
Blaine Stoughton (2)
❑ 168 Shutout Leaders 1.50 .70
Tony Esposito (1)
Gerry Cheevers (2)
Bob Sauve (2)
Rogatien Vachon (2)
❑ 169 Perry Turnbull .35 .16
❑ 170 Barry Beck .75 .35
❑ 171 Charlie Simmer .60 .25
Kings Scoring Leaders
(checklist back)
❑ 172 Paul Holmgren .75 .35
❑ 173 Willie Huber .35 .16
❑ 174 Tim Young .35 .16
❑ 175 Gilles Gilbert .75 .35
❑ 176 Dave Christian USA 3.00 1.35
❑ 177 Lars Lindgren .35 .16
❑ 178 Real Cloutier .35 .16
❑ 179 Laurie Boschman .35 .16
❑ 180 Steve Shutt .35 .16
❑ 181 Bob Murray .35 .16
❑ 182 Wayne Gretzky 20.00 9.00
Oilers Scoring Leaders
(checklist back)
❑ 183 John Van Boxmeer .35 .16
❑ 184 Nick Fotiu .75 .35
❑ 185 Mike McEwen .35 .16
❑ 186 Greg Malone .35 .16
❑ 187 Mike Foligno 4.00 1.80
❑ 188 Dave Langevin .35 .16
❑ 189 Mel Bridgman .35 .16
❑ 190 John Davidson .75 .35
❑ 191 Mike Milbury .75 .35
❑ 192 Ron Zanussi .35 .16
❑ 193 Darryl Sittler .75 .35
Maple Leafs Scoring Leaders
(checklist back)
❑ 194 John Marks .35 .16
❑ 195 Mike Gartner 50.00 22.00
❑ 196 Dave Lewis .35 .16
❑ 197 Kent Nilsson 5.00 2.20
❑ 198 Rick Ley .35 .16
❑ 199 Derek Smith .35 .16
❑ 200 Bill Barber .75 .35
❑ 201 Guy Lapointe .35 .16
❑ 202 Vaclav Nedomansky .35 .16
❑ 203 Don Murdoch .35 .16
❑ 204 Mike Bossy 1.50 .70
Islanders Scoring Leaders
(checklist back)
❑ 205 Pierre Hamel .75 .35
❑ 206 Mike Eaves .35 .16
❑ 207 Doug Halward .35 .16
❑ 208 Stan Smyl 1.00 .45
❑ 209 Mike Zuke .35 .16
❑ 210 Borje Salming .75 .35
❑ 211 Walt Tkaczuk .75 .35
❑ 212 Grant Mulvey .35 .16
❑ 213 Rob Ramage 3.00 1.35
❑ 214 Tom Rowe .35 .16
❑ 215 Don Edwards .35 .16
❑ 216 Guy Lafleur 1.00 .45
Pierre Larouche
Canadiens Scoring Leaders
(checklist back)
❑ 217 Dan Labraaten .35 .16
❑ 218 Glen Sharpley .35 .16
❑ 219 Stefan Persson .35 .16
❑ 220 Peter McNab .35 .16
❑ 221 Doug Hicks .35 .16
❑ 222 Bengt Gustafsson .35 .16
❑ 223 Michel Dion .75 .35
❑ 224 Jim Watson .35 .16
❑ 225 Wilf Paiement .35 .16
❑ 226 Phil Russell .35 .16
❑ 227 Morris Lukowich .50 .23
Jets Scoring Leaders
(checklist back)
❑ 228 Ron Stackhouse .35 .16
❑ 229 Ted Bulley .35 .16
❑ 230 Larry Robinson 1.00 .45
❑ 231 Don Maloney .35 .16
❑ 232 Rob McClanahan USA .50 .23
❑ 233 Al Sims .35 .16
❑ 234 Errol Thompson .35 .16
❑ 235 Glenn Resch .75 .35
❑ 236 Bob Miller .35 .16
❑ 237 Gary Sargent .35 .16
❑ 238 Real Cloutier .60 .25
Nordiques Scoring Leaders
(checklist back)
❑ 239 Rene Robert .75 .35
❑ 240 Charlie Simmer 2.00 .90
❑ 241 Thomas Gradin .35 .16
❑ 242 Rick Vaive 3.00 1.35
❑ 243 Ron Wilson .35 .16
❑ 244 Brian Sutter 1.00 .45
❑ 245 Dale McCourt .35 .16
❑ 246 Yvon Lambert .35 .16
❑ 247 Tom Lysiak .35 .16
❑ 248 Ron Greschner .35 .16
❑ 249 Reggie Leach .60 .25
Flyers Scoring Leaders
(checklist back)
❑ 250 Wayne Gretzky 150.00 70.00
❑ 251 Rick Middleton .75 .35
❑ 252 Al Smith .75 .35
❑ 253 Fred Barrett .35 .16
❑ 254 Butch Goring .75 .35
❑ 255 Robert Picard .35 .16
❑ 256 Marc Tardif .35 .16
❑ 257 Checklist 133-264 6.00 2.70
❑ 258 Barry Long .35 .16
❑ 259 Rene Robert .60 .25
Rockies Scoring Leaders
(checklist back)
❑ 260 Danny Gare .75 .35
❑ 261 Rejean Houle .35 .16
❑ 262 Stanley Cup Semifinals .50 .23
Islanders-Sabres
❑ 263 Stanley Cup Semifinals .50 .23
Flyers-North Stars
❑ 264 Stanley Cup Finals 1.00 .45
Islanders win 1st
❑ 265 Bobby Lalonde .35 .16
❑ 266 Bob Sauve .75 .35
❑ 267 Bob MacMillan .35 .16
❑ 268 Greg Fox .35 .16
❑ 269 Hardy Astrom .75 .35
❑ 270 Greg Joly .35 .16
❑ 271 Dave Lumley .35 .16
❑ 272 Dave Keon .75 .35
❑ 273 Garry Unger .75 .35
❑ 274 Steve Payne .35 .16
❑ 275 Doug Risebrough UER .35 .16
(Photo actually
Serge Savard)
❑ 276 Bob Bourne .35 .16
❑ 277 Ed Johnstone .35 .16
❑ 278 Peter Lee .35 .16
❑ 279 Pete Peeters 6.00 2.70
❑ 280 Ron Chipperfield .35 .16
❑ 281 Wayne Babych .75 .35
❑ 282 David Shand .35 .16
❑ 283 Jere Gillis .35 .16
❑ 284 Dennis Maruk .75 .35
❑ 285 Jude Drouin .35 .16
❑ 286 Mike Murphy .35 .16
❑ 287 Curt Fraser .35 .16
❑ 288 Gary McAdam .35 .16
❑ 289 Mark Messier UER 150.00 70.00
(Back says shoots right)
❑ 290 Vic Venasky .35 .16
❑ 291 Per-Olov Brasar .35 .16
❑ 292 Orest Kindrachuk .35 .16
❑ 293 Dave Hunter .35 .16
❑ 294 Steve Jensen .35 .16
❑ 295 Chris Oddleifson .35 .16
❑ 296 Larry Playfair .35 .16
❑ 297 Mario Tremblay .35 .16
❑ 298 Gilles Lupien .35 .16
❑ 299 Pat Price .35 .16
❑ 300 Jerry Korab .35 .16
❑ 301 Darcy Rota .35 .16
❑ 302 Don Luce .35 .16
❑ 303 Ken Houston .35 .16
❑ 304 Brian Engblom .35 .16
❑ 305 John Tonelli 2.00 .90
❑ 306 Doug Sulliman .35 .16
❑ 307 Rod Schutt .35 .16
❑ 308 Norm Barnes .35 .16
❑ 309 Serge Bernier .35 .16
❑ 310 Larry Patey .35 .16
❑ 311 Dave Farrish .35 .16
❑ 312 Harold Snepsts .75 .35
❑ 313 Bob Sirois .35 .16
❑ 314 Peter Marsh .35 .16
❑ 315 Risto Siltanen .35 .16
❑ 316 Andre St.Laurent .35 .16
❑ 317 Craig Hartsburg 3.00 1.35
❑ 318 Wayne Cashman .75 .35
❑ 319 Lindy Ruff .35 .16
❑ 320 Willi Plett .75 .35
❑ 321 Ron Delorme .35 .16
❑ 322 Gaston Gingras .35 .16
❑ 323 Gordie Lane .35 .16
❑ 324 Doug Soetaert .35 .16
❑ 325 Gregg Sheppard .35 .16
❑ 326 Mike Busniuk .35 .16
❑ 327 Jamie Hislop .35 .16
❑ 328 Ed Staniowski .35 .16
❑ 329 Ron Ellis .75 .35
❑ 330 Gary Bromley UER .75 .35
(Photo actually
Curt Ridley)
❑ 331 Mark Lofthouse .35 .16
❑ 332 Dave Hoyda .35 .16
❑ 333 Ron Low .35 .16
❑ 334 Barry Gibbs .35 .16
❑ 335 Gary Edwards .75 .35
❑ 336 Don Marcotte .35 .16
❑ 337 Bill Hajt .35 .16
❑ 338 Brad Marsh 4.00 1.80
❑ 339 J.P. Bordeleau .35 .16
❑ 340 Randy Pierce .35 .16
❑ 341 Eddie Mio .75 .35
❑ 342 Randy Manery .35 .16
❑ 343 Tom Younghans .35 .16
❑ 344 Rod Langway 6.00 2.70
❑ 345 Wayne Merrick .35 .16
❑ 346 Steve Baker .75 .35
❑ 347 Pat Hughes .35 .16
❑ 348 Al Hill .35 .16
❑ 349 Gerry Hart .35 .16
❑ 350 Richard Mulhern .35 .16
❑ 351 Jerry Butler .35 .16
❑ 352 Guy Charron .35 .16
❑ 353 Jimmy Mann .75 .35
❑ 354 Brad McCrimmon 2.00 .90
❑ 355 Rick Dudley .35 .16
❑ 356 Pekka Rautakallio .35 .16
❑ 357 Tim Trimper .35 .16
❑ 358 Mike Christie .35 .16
❑ 359 John Ogrodnick 3.00 1.35
❑ 360 Dave Semenko .75 .35
❑ 361 Mike Veisor .75 .35
❑ 362 Syl Apps .35 .16
❑ 363 Mike Polich .35 .16
❑ 364 Rick Chartraw .35 .16
❑ 365 Steve Tambellini .35 .16
❑ 366 Ed Hospodar .35 .16
❑ 367 Randy Carlyle .75 .35
❑ 368 Tom Gorence .35 .16
❑ 369 Pierre Plante .35 .16
❑ 370 Blake Dunlop .35 .16
❑ 371 Mike Kaszycki .35 .16
❑ 372 Rick Blight .35 .16
❑ 373 Pierre Bouchard .35 .16
❑ 374 Gary Doak .35 .16
❑ 375 Andre Savard .35 .16
❑ 376 Bill Clement .75 .35
❑ 377 Reg Kerr .35 .16
❑ 378 Walt McKechnie .35 .16
❑ 379 George Lyle .35 .16
❑ 380 Colin Campbell .35 .16
❑ 381 Dave Debol .35 .16
❑ 382 Glenn Goldup .35 .16
❑ 383 Kent-Erik Andersson .35 .16
❑ 384 Tony Currie .35 .16
❑ 385 Richard Sevigny .75 .35
❑ 386 Garry Howatt .35 .16
❑ 387 Cam Connor .35 .16
❑ 388 Ross Lonsberry .35 .16
❑ 389 Frank Bathe .35 .16
❑ 390 John Wensink .35 .16
❑ 391 Paul Harrison .75 .35
❑ 392 Dennis Kearns .35 .16
❑ 393 Pat Ribble .35 .16
❑ 394 Markus Mattsson .75 .35
❑ 395 Chuck Lefley .35 .16
❑ 396 Checklist 265-396 8.00 3.60

## 1980-81 O-Pee-Chee Super

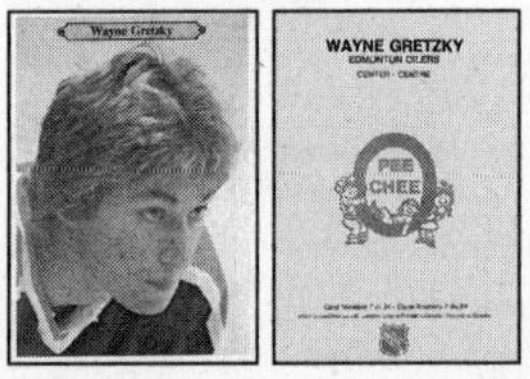

These large (approximately 5" by 7") full-color photos are numbered on the back. They are made of thicker cardboard stock. They were a separate issue rather than an insert. Player information on the card back is sparse.

| | NRMT-MT | EXC. |
|---|---|---|
| COMPLETE SET (24) | 40.00 | 18.00 |
| COMMON CARD (1-24) | .50 | .23 |

❑ 1 Brad Park 2.00 .90
❑ 2 Gilbert Perreault 1.50 .70
❑ 3 Kent Nilsson .75 .35
❑ 4 Tony Esposito 2.00 .90
❑ 5 Lanny McDonald 1.50 .70
❑ 6 Pete Mahovlich .75 .35
❑ 7 Wayne Gretzky 20.00 9.00
❑ 8 Marcel Dionne 2.50 1.10
❑ 9 Bob Gainey 1.50 .70
❑ 10 Guy Lafleur 4.00 1.80
❑ 11 Larry Robinson 2.00 .90
❑ 12 Mike Bossy 6.00 2.70
❑ 13 Denis Potvin 1.50 .70
❑ 14 Phil Esposito 3.00 1.35
❑ 15 Anders Hedberg .60 .25
❑ 16 Bobby Clarke 2.50 1.10
❑ 17 Marc Tardif .50 .23
❑ 18 Bernie Federko .75 .35
❑ 19 Borje Salming 1.00 .45
❑ 20 Darryl Sittler 2.00 .90
❑ 21 Ian Turnbull .50 .23
❑ 22 Glen Hanlon .60 .25
❑ 23 Mike Palmateer 1.00 .45
❑ 24 Morris Lukowich .50 .23

## 1981-82 O-Pee-Chee

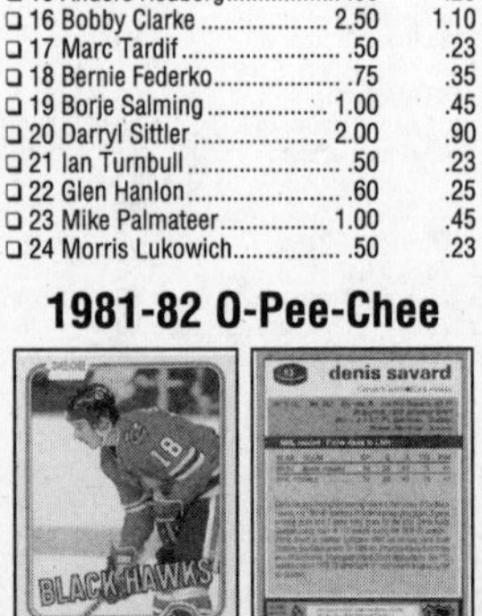

The 396 standard-size cards in this set features the player's name, position and team logo along the front bottom border. The team name appears in bold letters across the lower portion of the photo. Bilingual backs feature yearly and career statistics and biographical data. Super Action (SA) cards are designated in the list below. The set is essentially numbered in team order with the team leader (TL) card typically portraying the team's leading scorer. However, team names are updated to reflect off-season trades. Rookie Cards in this set include Glenn Anderson, Don Beaupre, Dino Ciccarelli, Paul Coffey, Dale Hunter, Tim Kerr, Jari Kurri, Rejean Lemelin, Kevin Lowe, Andy Moog, Larry Murphy, Denis Savard and Peter Stastny. Beware when purchasing the Rookie Card of Paul Coffey as it has been counterfeited.

| | NRMT-MT | EXC |
|---|---|---|
| COMPLETE SET (396) | 400.00 | 180.00 |
| COMMON CARD (1-396) | .35 | .16 |

❑ 1 Ray Bourque 30.00 13.50
❑ 2 Rick Middleton .60 .25
❑ 3 Dwight Foster .35 .16
❑ 4 Steve Kasper 1.50 .70
❑ 5 Peter McNab .35 .16
❑ 6 Mike O'Connell .60 .25
❑ 7 Terry O'Reilly .60 .25
❑ 8 Brad Park .60 .25
❑ 9 Dick Redmond .35 .16
❑ 10 Rogatien Vachon .60 .25
❑ 11 Wayne Cashman .60 .25
❑ 12 Mike Gillis .35 .16
❑ 13 Stan Jonathan .35 .16
❑ 14 Don Marcotte .35 .16
❑ 15 Brad McCrimmon .60 .25
❑ 16 Mike Milbury .60 .25
❑ 17 Ray Bourque SA 6.00 2.70
❑ 18 Rick Middleton SA .60 .25
❑ 19 Rick Middleton .40 .18
Bruins Leaders
❑ 20 Danny Gare .60 .25
❑ 21 Don Edwards .35 .16
❑ 22 Tony McKegney .35 .16
❑ 23 Bob Sauve .60 .25
❑ 24 Andre Savard .35 .16
❑ 25 Derek Smith .35 .16
❑ 26 John Van Boxmeer .35 .16
❑ 27 Danny Gare SA .60 .25
❑ 28 Danny Gare .40 .18
Sabres Leaders
❑ 29 Richie Dunn .35 .16
❑ 30 Gilbert Perreault .75 .35
❑ 31 Craig Ramsay .35 .16
❑ 32 Ric Seiling .35 .16
❑ 33 Guy Chouinard .60 .25
❑ 34 Kent Nilsson .60 .25
❑ 35 Willi Plett .35 .16
❑ 36 Paul Reinhart .35 .16
❑ 37 Pat Riggin .60 .25
❑ 38 Eric Vail .35 .16
❑ 39 Bill Clement .60 .25
❑ 40 Jamie Hislop .35 .16
❑ 41 Randy Holt .35 .16
❑ 42 Dan Labraaten .35 .16
❑ 43 Kevin Lavallee .35 .16
❑ 44 Rejean Lemelin 5.00 2.20
❑ 45 Don Lever .35 .16
❑ 46 Bob MacMillan .35 .16
❑ 47 Brad Marsh .75 .35
❑ 48 Bob Murdoch .35 .16
❑ 49 Jim Peplinski 2.00 .90
❑ 50 Pekka Rautakallio .35 .16
❑ 51 Phil Russell .35 .16
❑ 52 Kent Nilsson SA .60 .25
❑ 53 Kent Nilsson .40 .18
Flames Leaders
❑ 54 Tony Esposito .75 .35
❑ 55 Keith Brown .35 .16
❑ 56 Ted Bulley .35 .16
❑ 57 Tim Higgins .35 .16
❑ 58 Reg Kerr .35 .16
❑ 59 Tom Lysiak .35 .16
❑ 60 Grant Mulvey .35 .16
❑ 61 Bob Murray .35 .16
❑ 62 Terry Ruskowski .35 .16
❑ 63 Denis Savard 20.00 9.00
❑ 64 Glen Sharpley .35 .16
❑ 65 Darryl Sutter 1.50 .70
❑ 66 Doug Wilson .75 .35
❑ 67 Tony Esposito SA .60 .25
❑ 68 Murray Bannerman .60 .25
❑ 69 Greg Fox .35 .16
❑ 70 John Marks .35 .16
❑ 71 Peter Marsh .35 .16
❑ 72 Al Secord .75 .35
❑ 73 Tom Lysiak .40 .18
Blackhawks Leaders
❑ 74 Lucien DeBlois .35 .16
❑ 75 Paul Gagne .35 .16
❑ 76 Merlin Malinowski .35 .16
❑ 77 Lanny McDonald .60 .25
❑ 78 Joel Quenneville .35 .16
❑ 79 Rob Ramage .60 .25
❑ 80 Glenn Resch .60 .25
❑ 81 Steve Tambellini .35 .16
❑ 82 Ron Delorme .35 .16
❑ 83 Mike Kitchen .35 .16
❑ 84 Yvon Vautour .35 .16
❑ 85 Lanny McDonald .40 .18
Rockies Leaders
❑ 86 Dale McCourt .35 .16
❑ 87 Mike Foligno .60 .25
❑ 88 Gilles Gilbert .60 .25
❑ 89 Willie Huber .35 .16
❑ 90 Mark Kirton .35 .16
❑ 91 Jim Korn .35 .16
❑ 92 Reed Larson .35 .16

❑ 93 Gary McAdam .35 .16
❑ 94 Vaclav Nedomansky .35 .16
❑ 95 John Ogrodnick .35 .16
❑ 96 Dale McCourt SA .35 .16
❑ 97 Jean Hamel .35 .16
❑ 98 Glen Hicks .35 .16
❑ 99 Larry Lozinski .60 .25
❑ 100 George Lyle .35 .16
❑ 101 Perry Miller .35 .16
❑ 102 Brad Maxwell .35 .16
❑ 103 Brad Smith .35 .16
❑ 104 Paul Woods .35 .16
❑ 105 Dale McCourt .40 .18
Red Wings Leaders
❑ 106 Wayne Gretzky 60.00 27.00
❑ 107 Jari Kurri 35.00 16.00
❑ 108 Glenn Anderson 15.00 6.75
❑ 109 Curt Brackenbury .35 .16
❑ 110 Brett Callighen .35 .16
❑ 111 Paul Coffey 80.00 36.00
❑ 112 Lee Fogolin .35 .16
❑ 113 Matti Hagman .35 .16
❑ 114 Doug Hicks .35 .16
❑ 115 Dave Hunter .35 .16
❑ 116 Garry Lariviere .35 .16
❑ 117 Kevin Lowe 5.00 2.20
❑ 118 Mark Messier 50.00 22.00
❑ 119 Eddie Mio .60 .25
❑ 120 Andy Moog 25.00 11.00
❑ 121 Dave Semenko .60 .25
❑ 122 Risto Siltanen .35 .16
❑ 123 Garry Unger .60 .25
❑ 124 Stan Weir .35 .16
❑ 125 Wayne Gretzky SA 25.00 11.00
❑ 126 Wayne Gretzky 10.00 4.50
Oilers Leaders
❑ 127 Mike Rogers .35 .16
❑ 128 Mark Howe .75 .35
❑ 129 Dave Keon .60 .25
❑ 130 Warren Miller .35 .16
❑ 131 Al Sims .35 .16
❑ 132 Blaine Stoughton .60 .25
❑ 133 Rick MacLeish .60 .25
❑ 134 Greg Millen .60 .25
❑ 135 Mike Rogers SA .35 .16
❑ 136 Mike Fidler .35 .16
❑ 137 John Garrett .35 .16
❑ 138 Don Nachbaur .35 .16
❑ 139 Tom Rowe .35 .16
❑ 140 Mike Rogers .40 .18
Whalers Leaders
❑ 141 Marcel Dionne .75 .35
❑ 142 Charlie Simmer .75 .35
❑ 143 Dave Taylor 1.50 .70
❑ 144 Billy Harris .35 .16
❑ 145 Jerry Korab .35 .16
❑ 146 Mario Lessard .60 .25
❑ 147 Don Luce .35 .16
❑ 148 Larry Murphy 20.00 9.00
❑ 149 Mike Murphy .35 .16
❑ 150 Marcel Dionne SA .75 .35
❑ 151 Charlie Simmer SA .60 .25
❑ 152 Dave Taylor SA .60 .25
❑ 153 Jim Fox .35 .16
❑ 154 Steve Jensen .35 .16
❑ 155 Greg Terrion .35 .16
❑ 156 Marcel Dionne .60 .25
Kings Leaders
❑ 157 Bobby Smith .60 .25
❑ 158 Kent-Erik Andersson .35 .16
❑ 159 Don Beaupre 5.00 2.20
❑ 160 Steve Christoff .35 .16
❑ 161 Dino Ciccarelli 20.00 9.00
❑ 162 Craig Hartsburg .35 .16
❑ 163 Al MacAdam .35 .16
❑ 164 Tom McCarthy .35 .16
❑ 165 Gilles Meloche .60 .25
❑ 166 Steve Payne .35 .16
❑ 167 Gordie Roberts .35 .16
❑ 168 Greg Smith .35 .16
❑ 169 Tim Young .35 .16
❑ 170 Bobby Smith SA .60 .25
❑ 171 Mike Eaves .35 .16
❑ 172 Mike Polich .35 .16
❑ 173 Tom Younghans .35 .16
❑ 174 Bobby Smith .40 .18
North Stars Leaders
❑ 175 Brian Engblom .35 .16
❑ 176 Bob Gainey .75 .35
❑ 177 Guy Lafleur 2.50 1.10
❑ 178 Mark Napier .35 .16
❑ 179 Larry Robinson .75 .35
❑ 180 Steve Shutt .35 .16
❑ 181 Keith Acton .75 .35
❑ 182 Gaston Gingras .35 .16
❑ 183 Rejean Houle .35 .16
❑ 184 Doug Jarvis .35 .16
❑ 185 Yvon Lambert .35 .16
❑ 186 Rod Langway 1.50 .70
❑ 187 Pierre Larouche .60 .25
❑ 188 Pierre Mondou .35 .16
❑ 189 Robert Picard .35 .16
❑ 190 Doug Risebrough .35 .16
❑ 191 Richard Sevigny .60 .25
❑ 192 Mario Tremblay .35 .16
❑ 193 Doug Wickenheiser .35 .16
❑ 194 Bob Gainey SA .60 .25
❑ 195 Guy Lafleur SA .75 .35
❑ 196 Larry Robinson SA .35 .16
❑ 197 Steve Shutt .40 .18
Canadiens Leaders
❑ 198 Mike Bossy 4.00 1.80
❑ 199 Denis Potvin 1.00 .45
❑ 200 Bryan Trottier 1.50 .70
❑ 201 Bob Bourne .35 .16
❑ 202 Clark Gillies .60 .25
❑ 203 Butch Goring .60 .25
❑ 204 Anders Kallur .35 .16
❑ 205 Ken Morrow .60 .25
❑ 206 Stefan Persson .35 .16
❑ 207 Billy Smith .60 .25
❑ 208 Mike Bossy SA 1.50 .70
❑ 209 Denis Potvin SA .60 .25
❑ 210 Bryan Trottier SA .75 .35
❑ 211 Duane Sutter 1.00 .45
❑ 212 Gordie Lane .35 .16
❑ 213 Dave Langevin .35 .16
❑ 214 Bob Lorimer .35 .16
❑ 215 Mike McEwen .35 .16
❑ 216 Wayne Merrick .35 .16
❑ 217 Bob Nystrom .35 .16
❑ 218 John Tonelli .75 .35
❑ 219 Mike Bossy .75 .35
Islanders Leaders
❑ 220 Barry Beck .60 .25
❑ 221 Mike Allison .35 .16
❑ 222 John Davidson .60 .25
❑ 223 Ron Duguay .35 .16
❑ 224 Ron Greschner .35 .16
❑ 225 Anders Hedberg .60 .25
❑ 226 Ed Johnstone .35 .16
❑ 227 Dave Maloney .35 .16
❑ 228 Don Maloney .35 .16
❑ 229 Ulf Nilsson .60 .25
❑ 230 Barry Beck SA .60 .25
❑ 231 Steve Baker .60 .25
❑ 232 Jere Gillis .35 .16
❑ 233 Ed Hospodar .35 .16
❑ 234 Tom Laidlaw .35 .16
❑ 235 Dean Talafous .35 .16
❑ 236 Carol Vadnais .35 .16
❑ 237 Anders Hedberg .40 .18
Rangers Leaders
❑ 238 Bill Barber .60 .25
❑ 239 Behn Wilson .35 .16
❑ 240 Bobby Clarke .75 .35
❑ 241 Bob Dailey .35 .16
❑ 242 Paul Holmgren .60 .25
❑ 243 Reggie Leach .60 .25
❑ 244 Ken Linseman .60 .25
❑ 245 Pete Peeters 1.50 .70
❑ 246 Brian Propp 2.00 .90
❑ 247 Bill Barber SA .60 .25
❑ 248 Mel Bridgman .35 .16
❑ 249 Mike Busniuk .35 .16
❑ 250 Tom Gorence .35 .16
❑ 251 Tim Kerr 4.00 1.80
❑ 252 Rick St.Croix .60 .25
❑ 253 Bill Barber .40 .18
Flyers Leaders
❑ 254 Rick Kehoe .60 .25
❑ 255 Pat Boutette .35 .16
❑ 256 Randy Carlyle .60 .25
❑ 257 Paul Gardner .35 .16
❑ 258 Peter Lee .35 .16
❑ 259 Rod Schutt .35 .16
❑ 260 Rick Kehoe SA .60 .25
❑ 261 Mario Faubert .35 .16
❑ 262 George Ferguson .35 .16
❑ 263 Ross Lonsberry .35 .16
❑ 264 Greg Malone .35 .16
❑ 265 Pat Price .35 .16
❑ 266 Ron Stackhouse .35 .16
❑ 267 Rick Kehoe .40 .18
Penguins Leaders
❑ 268 Jacques Richard .35 .16
❑ 269 Peter Stastny 15.00 6.75
❑ 270 Dan Bouchard .60 .25
❑ 271 Kim Clackson .35 .16
❑ 272 Alain Cote .35 .16
❑ 273 Andre Dupont .35 .16
❑ 274 Robbie Ftorek .35 .16
❑ 275 Michel Goulet 3.00 1.35
❑ 276 Dale Hoganson .35 .16
❑ 277 Dale Hunter 8.00 3.60
❑ 278 Pierre Lacroix .35 .16
❑ 279 Mario Marois .35 .16
❑ 280 Dave Pichette .35 .16
❑ 281 Michel Plasse .60 .25
❑ 282 Anton Stastny .75 .35
❑ 283 Marc Tardif .35 .16
❑ 284 Wally Weir .35 .16
❑ 285 Jacques Richard SA .35 .16
❑ 286 Peter Stastny SA 5.00 2.20
❑ 287 Peter Stastny 3.00 1.35
Nordiques Leaders
❑ 288 Bernie Federko 1.50 .70
❑ 289 Mike Liut 1.50 .70
❑ 290 Wayne Babych .35 .16
❑ 291 Blair Chapman .35 .16
❑ 292 Tony Currie .35 .16
❑ 293 Blake Dunlop .35 .16
❑ 294 Ed Kea .35 .16
❑ 295 Rick Lapointe .35 .16
❑ 296 Jorgen Pettersson .35 .16
❑ 297 Brian Sutter .60 .25
❑ 298 Perry Turnbull .35 .16
❑ 299 Mike Zuke .35 .16
❑ 300 Bernie Federko SA .60 .25
❑ 301 Mike Liut SA .60 .25
❑ 302 Jack Brownschidle .35 .16
❑ 303 Larry Patey .35 .16
❑ 304 Bernie Federko .40 .18
Blues Leaders
❑ 305 Bill Derlago .35 .16
❑ 306 Wilf Paiement .35 .16
❑ 307 Borje Salming .60 .25
❑ 308 Darryl Sittler .75 .35
❑ 309 Ian Turnbull .35 .16
❑ 310 Rick Vaive .60 .25
❑ 311 Wilf Paiement SA .35 .16
❑ 312 Darryl Sittler SA .60 .25
❑ 313 John Anderson .35 .16
❑ 314 Laurie Boschman .60 .25
❑ 315 Jiri Crha .60 .25
❑ 316 Vitezslav Duris .35 .16
❑ 317 Dave Farrish .35 .16
❑ 318 Pat Hickey .35 .16
❑ 319 Michel Larocque .60 .25
❑ 320 Dan Maloney .35 .16
❑ 321 Terry Martin .35 .16
❑ 322 Rene Robert .60 .25
❑ 323 Rocky Saganiuk .35 .16
❑ 324 Ron Sedlbauer .35 .16
❑ 325 Ron Zanussi .35 .16
❑ 326 Wilf Paiement .40 .18
Maple Leafs Leaders
❑ 327 Thomas Gradin .60 .25
❑ 328 Stan Smyl .60 .25
❑ 329 Ivan Boldirev .35 .16
❑ 330 Per-Olov Brasar UER .35 .16
(Photo actually
Brent Ashton)
❑ 331 Richard Brodeur .60 .25
❑ 332 Jerry Butler .35 .16
❑ 333 Colin Campbell .35 .16
❑ 334 Curt Fraser .35 .16
❑ 335 Doug Halward .35 .16
❑ 336 Glen Hanlon .60 .25
❑ 337 Dennis Kearns .35 .16
❑ 338 Rick Lanz UER .35 .16
(Photo actually
Thomas Gradin)
❑ 339 Pat Ribble .35 .16
❑ 340 Blair MacDonald .35 .16
❑ 341 Kevin McCarthy .35 .16
❑ 342 Gerry Minor .35 .16
❑ 343 Darcy Rota .35 .16
❑ 344 Harold Snepsts .35 .16
❑ 345 Dave(Tiger) Williams .60 .25
❑ 346 Thomas Gradin .40 .18
Canucks Leaders
❑ 347 Mike Gartner 12.00 5.50
❑ 348 Rick Green .35 .16
❑ 349 Bob Kelly .35 .16
❑ 350 Dennis Maruk .60 .25
❑ 351 Mike Palmateer .60 .25
❑ 352 Ryan Walter .35 .16
❑ 353 Bengt Gustafsson .35 .16
❑ 354 Al Hangsleben .35 .16
❑ 355 Jean Pronovost .60 .25
❑ 356 Dennis Ververgaert .35 .16
❑ 357 Dennis Maruk .40 .18
Capitals Leaders
❑ 358 Dave Babych 1.50 .70
❑ 359 Dave Christian .60 .25
❑ 360 Dave Christian SA .60 .25
❑ 361 Rick Bowness .60 .25
❑ 362 Rick Dudley .35 .16
❑ 363 Norm Dupont .35 .16
❑ 364 Dan Geoffrion .35 .16
❑ 365 Pierre Hamel .60 .25
❑ 366 Dave Hoyda UER .35 .16
(Photo actually
Doug Lecuyer)
❑ 367 Doug Lecuyer .35 .16
❑ 368 Willy Lindstrom .35 .16
❑ 369 Barry Long .35 .16
❑ 370 Morris Lukowich .35 .16
❑ 371 Kris Manery .35 .16
❑ 372 Jimmy Mann .60 .25
❑ 373 Moe Mantha .35 .16
❑ 374 Markus Mattsson .60 .25
❑ 375 Don Spring .35 .16
❑ 376 Tim Trimper .35 .16
❑ 377 Ron Wilson .35 .16
❑ 378 Dave Christian .40 .18
Jets Leaders
❑ 379 Checklist 1-132 5.00 2.20
❑ 380 Checklist 133-264 5.00 2.20
❑ 381 Checklist 265-396 5.00 2.20
❑ 382 Mike Bossy .75 .35
Goals Leader
❑ 383 Wayne Gretzky 10.00 4.50
Assists Leader
❑ 384 Wayne Gretzky 10.00 4.50
Scoring Leader
❑ 385 Dave(Tiger) Williams .40 .18
Penalty Minutes Leader
❑ 386 Mike Bossy .75 .35
Power-play Goals Leader
❑ 387 Richard Sevigny .40 .18
Goals Against Ave. Leader
❑ 388 Mike Bossy .75 .35
Game Winning Goals Ldr.
❑ 389 Don Edward .40 .18
Glenn Resch
Shutout Leaders
❑ 390 Mike Bossy RB .75 .35
Eight hat tricks
in one season
❑ 391 Marcel Dionne 2.50 1.10
Charlie Simmer
Dave Taylor RB
100 points each
❑ 392 Wayne Gretzky RB 10.00 4.50
Season scoring record
❑ 393 Larry Murphy RB 3.00 1.35
Highest scoring
rookie defenseman
❑ 394 Mike Palmateer RB .40 .18
Seventh assist,
new goalie record
❑ 395 Peter Stastny RB 3.00 1.35
Rookie scoring record
❑ 396 Bob Manno .75 .35

## 1981-82 O-Pee-Chee Stickers

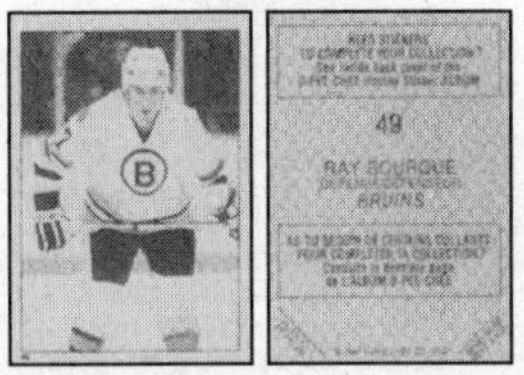

Similar in size and format to the baseball and football stickers of recent years, this 269-sticker set features foil cards of significant events and star players. Stickers measure approximately 1 15/16" by 2 9/16". The backs printed in both English and French contain the card number, the player's name and team, an advertisement for an O-Pee-Chee hockey sticker album, and a 1981 O-Pee-Chee copyright date. The sticker number also appears within the border at the lower left corner on the front. On the inside back cover of the sticker album the company offered (via direct mail-order) any ten different stickers (but no more than two foil) of your choice for one dollar; this is one reason why the values of the most popular players in these sticker sets are somewhat depressed compared to traditional card set prices.

| | NRMT-MT | EXC |
|---|---|---|
| COMPLETE SET (269) | 45.00 | 20.00 |
| COMMON STICKER (1-269) | .05 | .02 |

❑ 1 The Stanley Cup .25 .11
FOIL
❑ 2 The Stanley Cup .25 .11
FOIL
❑ 3 The Stanley Cup .25 .11
FOIL
❑ 4 The Stanley Cup .25 .11
FOIL
❑ 5 The Stanley Cup .25 .11
FOIL
❑ 6 The Stanley Cup .25 .11
FOIL
❑ 7 Oilers vs. Islanders .25 .11
❑ 8 Oilers vs. Islanders .25 .11
❑ 9 Oilers vs. Islanders .25 .11
❑ 10 Oilers vs. Islanders .25 .11
❑ 11 Jari Kurri 3.50 1.55
❑ 12 Pat Riggin .25 .11
❑ 13 Flames vs. Flyers .05 .02
❑ 14 Flames vs. Flyers .05 .02
❑ 15 Flames vs. Flyers .05 .02
❑ 16 Flames vs. Flyers .05 .02
❑ 17 Stanley Cup Winner .05 .02
1980-81
❑ 18 Stanley Cup Winner .05 .02
1980-81
❑ 19 Conn Smythe Trophy .25 .11
FOIL
❑ 20 Butch Goring .05 .02
❑ 21 North Stars vs. .05 .02
Islanders
❑ 22 Steve Payne .05 .02
❑ 23 North Stars vs. .05 .02
Islanders
❑ 24 North Stars vs. .05 .02
Islanders
❑ 25 North Stars vs. .05 .02
Islanders
❑ 26 North Stars vs. .05 .02
Islanders
❑ 27 Prince of Wales .25 .11
Trophy FOIL
❑ 28 Prince of Wales .25 .11
Trophy FOIL
❑ 29 Guy Lafleur .75 .35
❑ 30 Bob Gainey .25 .11
❑ 31 Larry Robinson .25 .11
❑ 32 Steve Shutt .25 .11
❑ 33 Brian Engblom .05 .02
❑ 34 Doug Jarvis .05 .02
❑ 35 Yvon Lambert .05 .02
❑ 36 Mark Napier .05 .02
❑ 37 Rejean Houle .05 .02
❑ 38 Pierre Larouche .25 .11
❑ 39 Rod Langway .25 .11
❑ 40 Richard Sevigny .25 .11
❑ 41 Guy Lafleur .75 .35
❑ 42 Larry Robinson .25 .11
❑ 43 Bob Gainey .25 .11
❑ 44 Steve Shutt .25 .11
❑ 45 Rick Middleton .25 .11
❑ 46 Peter McNab .05 .02
❑ 47 Rogatien Vachon .25 .11
❑ 48 Brad Park .25 .11
❑ 49 Ray Bourque 3.00 1.35
❑ 50 Terry O'Reilly .25 .11
❑ 51 Steve Kasper .05 .02
❑ 52 Dwight Foster .05 .02
❑ 53 Danny Gare .25 .11
❑ 54 Andre Savard .05 .02
❑ 55 Don Edwards .05 .02
❑ 56 Bob Sauve .25 .11
❑ 57 Tony McKegney .05 .02
❑ 58 John Van Boxmeer .05 .02
❑ 59 Derek Smith .05 .02
❑ 60 Gilbert Perreault .25 .11
❑ 61 Mike Rogers .05 .02
❑ 62 Mark Howe .25 .11
❑ 63 Blaine Stoughton .25 .11
❑ 64 Rick Ley .05 .02
❑ 65 Jordy Douglas .05 .02
❑ 66 Al Sims .05 .02
❑ 67 Norm Barnes .05 .02
❑ 68 John Garrett .25 .11
❑ 69 Peter Stastny 1.50 .70
❑ 70 Anton Stastny .25 .11
❑ 71 Jacques Richard .05 .02
❑ 72 Robbie Ftorek .05 .02
❑ 73 Dan Bouchard .25 .11
❑ 74 Real Cloutier .05 .02
❑ 75 Michel Goulet .75 .35
❑ 76 Marc Tardif .05 .02
❑ 77 Capitals vs. Maple .05 .02
Leafs
❑ 78 Capitals vs. Maple .05 .02
Leafs
❑ 79 Capitals vs. Maple .05 .02
Leafs
❑ 80 Capitals vs. Maple .05 .02
Leafs
❑ 81 Whalers vs. Capitals .05 .02
❑ 82 Whalers vs. Capitals .05 .02
❑ 83 Canadiens vs. Capitals .05 .02
❑ 84 Dan Bouchard .25 .11
❑ 85 North Stars vs. .05 .02
Capitals
❑ 86 North Stars vs. .05 .02
Capitals
❑ 87 Bruins vs. Capitals .05 .02
❑ 88 Bobby Smith .25 .11
❑ 89 Don Beaupre .50 .23
❑ 90 Al MacAdam .05 .02
❑ 91 Craig Hartsburg .25 .11
❑ 92 Steve Payne .05 .02
❑ 93 Gilles Meloche .25 .11
❑ 94 Tim Young .05 .02
❑ 95 Tom McCarthy .05 .02
❑ 96 Wilf Paiement .05 .02
❑ 97 Darryl Sittler .50 .23
❑ 98 Borje Salming .25 .11
❑ 99 Bill Derlago .05 .02
❑ 100 Ian Turnbull .05 .02
❑ 101 Rick Vaive .25 .11
❑ 102 Dan Maloney .05 .02
❑ 103 Laurie Boschman .05 .02
❑ 104 Pat Hickey .05 .02
❑ 105 Michel Larocque .25 .11
❑ 106 Jiri Crha .05 .02
❑ 107 John Anderson .05 .02
❑ 108 Bill Derlago .05 .02
❑ 109 Darryl Sittler .50 .23
❑ 110 Wilf Paiement .05 .02
❑ 111 Borje Salming .25 .11
❑ 112 Denis Savard 2.00 .90
❑ 113 Tony Esposito .50 .23
❑ 114 Tom Lysiak .25 .11
❑ 115 Keith Brown .05 .02
❑ 116 Glen Sharpley .05 .02
❑ 117 Terry Ruskowski .05 .02
❑ 118 Reg Kerr .05 .02
❑ 119 Bob Murray .05 .02
❑ 120 Dale McCourt .05 .02
❑ 121 John Ogrodnick .25 .11
❑ 122 Mike Foligno .25 .11
❑ 123 Gilles Gilbert .25 .11
❑ 124 Reed Larson .05 .02
❑ 125 Vaclav Nedomansky .05 .02
❑ 126 Willie Huber .05 .02
❑ 127 Jim Korn .05 .02
❑ 128 Bernie Federko .25 .11
❑ 129 Mike Liut .25 .11
❑ 130 Wayne Babych .05 .02
❑ 131 Blake Dunlop .05 .02
❑ 132 Mike Zuke .05 .02
❑ 133 Brian Sutter .25 .11
❑ 134 Rick Lapointe .05 .02
❑ 135 Jorgen Pettersson .05 .02
❑ 136 Dave Christian .25 .11
❑ 137 Dave Babych .05 .02
❑ 138 Morris Lukowich .05 .02
❑ 139 Norm Dupont .05 .02
❑ 140 Ron Wilson .05 .02
❑ 141 Dan Geoffrion .05 .02
❑ 142 Barry Long .05 .02
❑ 143 Pierre Hamel .05 .02
❑ 144 Charlie Simmer AS .25 .11
FOIL
❑ 145 Mark Howe AS FOIL .50 .23
❑ 146 Don Beaupre AS FOIL .50 .23
❑ 147 Marcel Dionne AS .75 .35
FOIL
❑ 148 Larry Robinson AS .75 .35
FOIL
❑ 149 Dave Taylor AS FOIL .50 .23
❑ 150 Mike Bossy AS FOIL 1.00 .45
❑ 151 Denis Potvin AS FOIL .70 .30
❑ 152 Bryan Trottier AS .75 .35
FOIL
❑ 153 Mike Liut AS FOIL .50 .23
❑ 154 Rob Ramage AS FOIL .50 .23
❑ 155 Bill Barber AS FOIL .50 .23
❑ 156 Campbell Bowl FOIL .25 .11
❑ 157 Campbell Bowl FOIL .25 .11
❑ 158 Mike Bossy .75 .35
❑ 159 Denis Potvin .50 .23
❑ 160 Bryan Trottier .50 .23
❑ 161 Billy Smith .25 .11
❑ 162 Anders Kallur .05 .02
❑ 163 Bob Bourne .05 .02
❑ 164 Clark Gillies .05 .02
❑ 165 Ken Morrow .25 .11
❑ 166 Anders Hedberg .25 .11

❑ 167 Ron Greschner .25 .11
❑ 168 Barry Beck .05 .02
❑ 169 Ed Johnstone .05 .02
❑ 170 Don Maloney .25 .11
❑ 171 Ron Duguay .25 .11
❑ 172 Ulf Nilsson .05 .02
❑ 173 Dave Maloney .05 .02
❑ 174 Bill Barber .25 .11
❑ 175 Behn Wilson .05 .02
❑ 176 Ken Linseman .25 .11
❑ 177 Pete Peeters .25 .11
❑ 178 Bobby Clarke .50 .23
❑ 179 Paul Holmgren .25 .11
❑ 180 Brian Propp .50 .23
❑ 181 Reggie Leach .25 .11
❑ 182 Rick Kehoe .05 .02
❑ 183 Randy Carlyle .05 .02
❑ 184 George Ferguson .05 .02
❑ 185 Peter Lee .05 .02
❑ 186 Rod Schutt .05 .02
❑ 187 Paul Gardner .05 .02
❑ 188 Ron Stackhouse .05 .02
❑ 189 Mario Faubert .05 .02
❑ 190 Mike Gartner 1.25 .55
❑ 191 Dennis Maruk .05 .02
❑ 192 Ryan Walter .25 .11
❑ 193 Rick Green .05 .02
❑ 194 Mike Palmateer .25 .11
❑ 195 Bob Kelly .05 .02
❑ 196 Jean Pronovost .05 .02
❑ 197 Al Hangsleben .05 .02
❑ 198 Flames vs. Capitals .05 .02
❑ 199 Oilers vs. Islanders .25 .11
❑ 200 Oilers vs. Islanders .25 .11
❑ 201 Oilers vs. Islanders .25 .11
❑ 202 Oilers vs. Islanders .25 .11
❑ 203 Rangers vs. Islanders .05 .02
❑ 204 Rangers vs. Islanders .05 .02
❑ 205 Flyers vs. Capitals .05 .02
❑ 206 Flyers vs. Capitals .05 .02
❑ 207 Rangers vs. Capitals .05 .02
❑ 208 Canadiens vs. Capitals .05 .02
❑ 209 Wayne Gretzky 10.00 4.50
❑ 210 Mark Messier 5.00 2.20
❑ 211 Jari Kurri 3.50 1.55
❑ 212 Brett Callighen .05 .02
❑ 213 Matti Hagman .05 .02
❑ 214 Risto Siltanen .25 .11
❑ 215 Lee Fogolin .05 .02
❑ 216 Eddie Mio .05 .02
❑ 217 Glenn Anderson 1.25 .55
❑ 218 Kent Nilsson .25 .11
❑ 219 Guy Chouinard .05 .02
❑ 220 Eric Vail .05 .02
❑ 221 Pat Riggin .25 .11
❑ 222 Willi Plett .05 .02
❑ 223 Pekka Rautakallio .05 .02
❑ 224 Paul Reinhart .25 .11
❑ 225 Brad Marsh .25 .11
❑ 226 Phil Russell .05 .02
❑ 227 Lanny McDonald .25 .11
❑ 228 Merlin Malinowski .05 .02
❑ 229 Rob Ramage .25 .11
❑ 230 Glenn Resch .25 .11
❑ 231 Ron Delorme .05 .02
❑ 232 Lucien DeBlois .05 .02
❑ 233 Paul Gagne .05 .02
❑ 234 Joel Quenneville .05 .02
❑ 235 Marcel Dionne .25 .11
❑ 236 Charlie Simmer .25 .11
❑ 237 Dave Taylor .25 .11
❑ 238 Mario Lessard .05 .02
❑ 239 Larry Murphy 1.25 .55
❑ 240 Jerry Korab .05 .02
❑ 241 Mike Murphy .05 .02
❑ 242 Billy Harris .05 .02
❑ 243 Thomas Gradin .25 .11
❑ 244 Per-Olov Brasar .05 .02
❑ 245 Glen Hanlon .25 .11
❑ 246 Chris Oddleifson .05 .02
❑ 247 Dave(Tiger) Williams .25 .11
❑ 248 Kevin McCarthy .05 .02
❑ 249 Dennis Kearns .05 .02
❑ 250 Harold Snepsts .25 .11
❑ 251 Art Ross Trophy FOIL .25 .11
❑ 252 Wayne Gretzky 10.00 4.50
❑ 253 Mike Bossy .75 .35
❑ 254 Norris Trophy FOIL .25 .11
❑ 255 Randy Carlyle .05 .02
❑ 256 Richard Sevigny .25 .11
❑ 257 Vezina Trophy FOIL .25 .11
❑ 258 Denis Herron .05 .02
❑ 259 Michel Larocque .25 .11
❑ 260 Lady Byng Trophy FOIL .25 .11
❑ 261 Rick Kehoe .05 .02
❑ 262 Calder Trophy FOIL .25 .11
❑ 263 Peter Stastny 1.50 .70
❑ 264 Wayne Gretzky 10.00 4.50
❑ 265 Hart Trophy FOIL .25 .11
❑ 266 Charlie Simmer .25 .11
❑ 267 Marcel Dionne .25 .11
❑ 268 Dave Taylor .25 .11
❑ 269 Bob Gainey .25 .11
❑ xx Sticker Album 5.00 2.20

## 1982-83 O-Pee-Chee

Because Topps did not issue a set for a two-year period, this 396-card set marks the first time since the pre-war era that O-Pee-Chee manufactured hockey cards without competition. Card fronts display the player's name, team and position at the top. The backs have yearly statistics, highlights and a section devoted to team records. A team logo appears

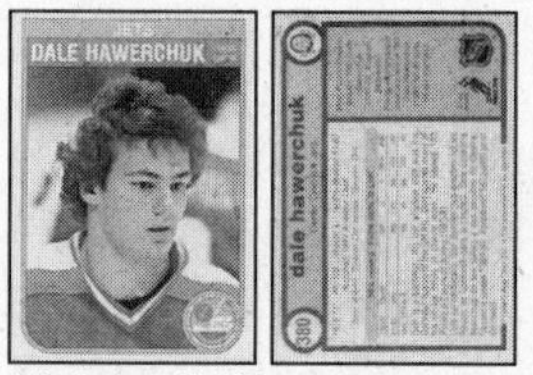


at the bottom. Highlight cards, team scoring leaders cards, league leaders cards and In-Action cards are contained within the set. The cards are essentially in team order. However, text on front is updated to reflect off-season trades. Rookie Cards in this set include Neal Broten, Ron Francis, Grant Fuhr, Dale Hawerchuk, Joe Mullen, Brent Sutter and Thomas Steen.

| | MINT | NRMT |
|---|---|---|
| COMPLETE SET (396) | 100.00 | 45.00 |
| COMMON CARD (1-396) | .20 | .09 |

❑ 1 Wayne Gretzky HL 10.00 4.50
More Records
❑ 2 Mike Bossy HL .75 .35
Record 147 Points
❑ 3 Dale Hawerchuk HL 4.00 1.80
Rookie Record
❑ 4 Mikko Leinonen HL .20 .09
Six Assists One Game
❑ 5 Bryan Trottier HL .75 .35
Sets Assist Mark
❑ 6 Rick Middleton .35 .16
❑ 7 Ray Bourque 10.00 4.50
❑ 8 Wayne Cashman .35 .16
❑ 9 Bruce Crowder .20 .09
❑ 10 Keith Crowder .20 .09
❑ 11 Tom Fergus .35 .16
❑ 12 Steve Kasper .20 .09
❑ 13 Normand Leveille .75 .35
❑ 14 Don Marcotte .20 .09
❑ 15 Rick Middleton .35 .16
❑ 16 Peter McNab .20 .09
❑ 17 Mike O'Connell .20 .09
❑ 18 Terry O'Reilly .35 .16
❑ 19 Brad Park .35 .16
❑ 20 Barry Pederson 1.00 .45
❑ 21 Brad Palmer .20 .09
❑ 22 Pete Peeters .75 .35
❑ 23 Rogatien Vachon .35 .16
❑ 24 Ray Bourque IA 3.00 1.35
❑ 25 Gilbert Perreault .35 .16
❑ 26 Mike Foligno .35 .16
❑ 27 Yvon Lambert .20 .09
❑ 28 Dale McCourt .20 .09
❑ 29 Tony McKegney .20 .09
❑ 30 Gilbert Perreault .75 .35
❑ 31 Lindy Ruff .20 .09
❑ 32 Mike Ramsey .20 .09
❑ 33 J.F. Sauve .20 .09
❑ 34 Bob Sauve .35 .16
❑ 35 Ric Seiling .20 .09
❑ 36 John Van Boxmeer .20 .09
❑ 37 John Van Boxmeer IA .20 .09
❑ 38 Lanny McDonald .35 .16
❑ 39 Mel Bridgman .20 .09
❑ 40 Mel Bridgman IA .20 .09
❑ 41 Guy Chouinard .20 .09
❑ 42 Steve Christoff .20 .09
❑ 43 Denis Cyr .20 .09
❑ 44 Bill Clement .35 .16
❑ 45 Richie Dunn .20 .09
❑ 46 Don Edwards .20 .09
❑ 47 Jamie Hislop .20 .09
❑ 48 Steve Konroyd .20 .09
❑ 49 Kevin Lavallee .20 .09
❑ 50 Rejean Lemelin 1.00 .45
❑ 51 Lanny McDonald .35 .16
❑ 52 Lanny McDonald IA .35 .16
❑ 53 Bob Murdoch .20 .09
❑ 54 Kent Nilsson .35 .16
❑ 55 Jim Peplinski .20 .09
❑ 56 Paul Reinhart .20 .09
❑ 57 Doug Risebrough .20 .09
❑ 58 Phil Russell .20 .09
❑ 59 Howard Walker .20 .09
❑ 60 Al Secord .35 .16
❑ 61 Murray Bannerman .35 .16
❑ 62 Keith Brown .20 .09
❑ 63 Doug Crossman .75 .35
❑ 64 Tony Esposito .75 .35
❑ 65 Greg Fox .20 .09
❑ 66 Tim Higgins .20 .09
❑ 67 Reg Kerr .20 .09
❑ 68 Tom Lysiak .20 .09
❑ 69 Grant Mulvey .20 .09
❑ 70 Bob Murray .20 .09
❑ 71 Rich Preston .20 .09
❑ 72 Terry Ruskowski .20 .09
❑ 73 Denis Savard 4.00 1.80
❑ 74 Al Secord .35 .16
❑ 75 Glen Sharpley .20 .09
❑ 76 Darryl Sutter .35 .16
❑ 77 Doug Wilson .75 .35
❑ 78 Doug Wilson IA .35 .16
❑ 79 John Ogrodnick .35 .16
❑ 80 John Barrett .20 .09
❑ 81 Mike Blaisdell .20 .09
❑ 82 Colin Campbell .20 .09
❑ 83 Danny Gare .35 .16
❑ 84 Gilles Gilbert .35 .16
❑ 85 Willie Huber .20 .09
❑ 86 Greg Joly .20 .09
❑ 87 Mark Kirton .20 .09
❑ 88 Reed Larson .20 .09
❑ 89 Reed Larson IA .20 .09
❑ 90 Reggie Leach .35 .16
❑ 91 Walt McKechnie .20 .09
❑ 92 John Ogrodnick .20 .09
❑ 93 Mark Osborne .35 .16
❑ 94 Jim Schoenfeld .35 .16
❑ 95 Derek Smith .20 .09
❑ 96 Greg Smith .20 .09
❑ 97 Eric Vail .20 .09
❑ 98 Paul Woods .20 .09
❑ 99 Wayne Gretzky 5.00 2.20
❑ 100 Glenn Anderson 3.00 1.35
❑ 101 Paul Coffey 15.00 6.75
❑ 102 Paul Coffey IA 5.00 2.20
❑ 103 Brett Callighen .20 .09
❑ 104 Lee Fogolin .20 .09
❑ 105 Grant Fuhr 30.00 13.50
❑ 106 Wayne Gretzky 40.00 18.00
❑ 107 Wayne Gretzky IA 15.00 6.75
❑ 108 Matti Hagman .20 .09
❑ 109 Pat Hughes .20 .09
❑ 110 Dave Hunter .20 .09
❑ 111 Jari Kurri 8.00 3.60
❑ 112 Ron Low .20 .09
❑ 113 Kevin Lowe 1.50 .70
❑ 114 Dave Lumley .20 .09
❑ 115 Ken Linseman .35 .16
❑ 116 Garry Lariviere .20 .09
❑ 117 Mark Messier 20.00 9.00
❑ 118 Tom Roulston .20 .09
❑ 119 Dave Semenko .35 .16
❑ 120 Garry Unger .35 .16
❑ 121 Checklist 1-132 2.50 1.10
❑ 122 Blaine Stoughton .35 .16
❑ 123 Ron Francis 20.00 9.00
❑ 124 Chris Kotsopoulos .20 .09
❑ 125 Pierre Larouche .35 .16
❑ 126 Greg Millen .35 .16
❑ 127 Warren Miller .20 .09
❑ 128 Merlin Malinowski .20 .09
❑ 129 Risto Siltanen .20 .09
❑ 130 Blaine Stoughton .35 .16
❑ 131 Blaine Stoughton IA .35 .16
❑ 132 Doug Sulliman .20 .09
❑ 133 Blake Wesley .20 .09
❑ 134 Steve Tambellini .20 .09
❑ 135 Brent Ashton .20 .09
❑ 136 Aaron Broten .20 .09
❑ 137 Joe Cirella .20 .09
❑ 138 Dwight Foster .20 .09
❑ 139 Paul Gagne .20 .09
❑ 140 Garry Howatt .20 .09
❑ 141 Don Lever .20 .09
❑ 142 Bob Lorimer .20 .09
❑ 143 Bob MacMillan .20 .09
❑ 144 Rick Meagher .20 .09
❑ 145 Glenn Resch .35 .16
❑ 146 Glenn Resch IA .35 .16
❑ 147 Steve Tambellini .20 .09
❑ 148 Carol Vadnais .20 .09
❑ 149 Marcel Dionne .35 .16
❑ 150 Dan Bonar .20 .09
❑ 151 Steve Bozek .20 .09
❑ 152 Marcel Dionne .75 .35
❑ 153 Marcel Dionne IA .35 .16
❑ 154 Jim Fox .20 .09
❑ 155 Mark Hardy .20 .09
❑ 156 Mario Lessard .20 .09
❑ 157 Dave Lewis .20 .09
❑ 158 Larry Murphy 3.00 1.35
❑ 159 Charlie Simmer .75 .35
❑ 160 Doug Smith .20 .09
❑ 161 Dave Taylor .75 .35
❑ 162 Dino Ciccarelli .75 .35
❑ 163 Don Beaupre 1.00 .45
❑ 164 Neal Broten 5.00 2.20
❑ 165 Dino Ciccarelli 4.00 1.80
❑ 166 Curt Giles .20 .09
❑ 167 Craig Hartsburg .20 .09
❑ 168 Brad Maxwell .20 .09
❑ 169 Tom McCarthy .20 .09
❑ 170 Gilles Meloche .35 .16
❑ 171 Al MacAdam .20 .09
❑ 172 Steve Payne .20 .09
❑ 173 Willi Plett .20 .09
❑ 174 Gordie Roberts .20 .09
❑ 175 Bobby Smith .35 .16
❑ 176 Bobby Smith IA .35 .16
❑ 177 Tim Young .20 .09
❑ 178 Mark Napier .20 .09
❑ 179 Keith Acton .20 .09
❑ 180 Keith Acton IA .20 .09
❑ 181 Bob Gainey .75 .35
❑ 182 Gaston Gingras .20 .09
❑ 183 Rick Green .20 .09
❑ 184 Rejean Houle .20 .09
❑ 185 Mark Hunter .20 .09
❑ 186 Guy Lafleur .75 .35
❑ 187 Guy Lafleur IA .75 .35
❑ 188 Pierre Mondou .20 .09
❑ 189 Mark Napier .20 .09
❑ 190 Robert Picard .20 .09
❑ 191 Larry Robinson .35 .16
❑ 192 Steve Shutt .35 .16
❑ 193 Mario Tremblay .20 .09
❑ 194 Ryan Walter .20 .09
❑ 195 Rick Wamsley 1.50 .70
❑ 196 Doug Wickenheiser .20 .09
❑ 197 Mike Bossy .75 .35
❑ 198 Bob Bourne .20 .09
❑ 199 Mike Bossy .75 .35
❑ 200 Butch Goring .35 .16
❑ 201 Clark Gillies .35 .16
❑ 202 Tomas Jonsson .20 .09
❑ 203 Anders Kallur .20 .09
❑ 204 Dave Langevin .20 .09
❑ 205 Wayne Merrick .20 .09
❑ 206 Ken Morrow .35 .16
❑ 207 Mike McEwen .20 .09
❑ 208 Bob Nystrom .20 .09
❑ 209 Stefan Persson .35 .16
❑ 210 Denis Potvin .75 .35
❑ 211 Billy Smith .35 .16
❑ 212 Duane Sutter .20 .09
❑ 213 John Tonelli .75 .35
❑ 214 Bryan Trottier .75 .35
❑ 215 Bryan Trottier IA .75 .35
❑ 216 Brent Sutter 2.50 1.10
❑ 217 Ron Duguay .20 .09
❑ 218 Kent-Erik Andersson .20 .09
❑ 219 Barry Beck .20 .09
❑ 220 Barry Beck IA .20 .09
❑ 221 Ron Duguay .20 .09
❑ 222 Nick Fotiu .35 .16
❑ 223 Robbie Ftorek .20 .09
❑ 224 Ron Greschner .20 .09
❑ 225 Anders Hedberg .35 .16
❑ 226 Ed Johnstone .20 .09
❑ 227 Tom Laidlaw .20 .09
❑ 228 Dave Maloney .20 .09
❑ 229 Don Maloney .20 .09
❑ 230 Eddie Mio .35 .16
❑ 231 Mark Pavelich .20 .09
❑ 232 Mike Rogers .20 .09
❑ 233 Reijo Ruotsalainen .20 .09
❑ 234 Steve Weeks .20 .09
❑ 235 Wayne Gretzky 5.00 2.20
(Goals Leader)
❑ 236 Paul Gardner .20 .09
(Power Play Goals Leader)
❑ 237 Wayne Gretzky 5.00 2.20
Michel Goulet
(Shorthanded Goals Leader)
❑ 238 Paul Baxter .20 .09
(Penalty Minutes Leader)
❑ 239 Denis Herron .35 .16
(Goals Against Average Leader)
❑ 240 Wayne Gretzky 5.00 2.20
(Assists Leader)
❑ 241 Denis Herron .35 .16
(Shutouts Leader)
❑ 242 Wayne Gretzky 5.00 2.20
(Game Winning Goals Leader)
❑ 243 Wayne Gretzky UER 5.00 2.20
Scoring Leader
(Ilsanders instead of Islanders
on back)
❑ 244 Bill Barber .35 .16
(Flyers Scoring Leaders)
❑ 245 Fred Arthur .20 .09
❑ 246 Bill Barber .35 .16
❑ 247 Bill Barber IA .35 .16
❑ 248 Bobby Clarke .75 .35
❑ 249 Ron Flockhart .20 .09
❑ 250 Tom Gorence .20 .09
❑ 251 Paul Holmgren .35 .16
❑ 252 Mark Howe .75 .35
❑ 253 Tim Kerr 1.00 .45
❑ 254 Brad Marsh .20 .09
❑ 255 Brad McCrimmon .35 .16
❑ 256 Brian Propp 1.00 .45
❑ 257 Darryl Sittler .75 .35
❑ 258 Rick St.Croix .20 .09
❑ 259 Jim Watson .20 .09
❑ 260 Behn Wilson .20 .09
❑ 261 Checklist 133-264 2.50 1.10
❑ 262 Mike Bullard .20 .09
❑ 263 Pat Boutette .20 .09
❑ 264 Mike Bullard 1.00 .45
❑ 265 Randy Carlyle .35 .16
❑ 266 Randy Carlyle IA .20 .09
❑ 267 Michel Dion .35 .16
❑ 268 George Ferguson .20 .09
❑ 269 Paul Gardner .20 .09
❑ 270 Denis Herron .35 .16
❑ 271 Rick Kehoe .35 .16
❑ 272 Greg Malone .20 .09
❑ 273 Rick MacLeish .35 .16
❑ 274 Pat Price .20 .09
❑ 275 Ron Stackhouse .20 .09
❑ 276 Peter Stastny .75 .35
❑ 277 Pierre Aubry .20 .09
❑ 278 Dan Bouchard .35 .16
❑ 279 Real Cloutier .20 .09
❑ 280 Real Cloutier IA .20 .09
❑ 281 Alain Cote .20 .09
❑ 282 Andre Dupont .20 .09
❑ 283 John Garrett .20 .09
❑ 284 Michel Goulet 2.00 .90
❑ 285 Dale Hunter 2.00 .90
❑ 286 Pierre Lacroix .20 .09
❑ 287 Mario Marois .20 .09
❑ 288 Wilf Paiement .20 .09
❑ 289 Dave Pichette .20 .09
❑ 290 Jacques Richard .20 .09
❑ 291 Normand Rochefort .20 .09
❑ 292 Peter Stastny 3.00 1.35
❑ 293 Peter Stastny IA 1.50 .70
❑ 294 Anton Stastny .35 .16
❑ 295 Marian Stastny .35 .16
❑ 296 Marc Tardif .20 .09
❑ 297 Wally Weir .20 .09
❑ 298 Brian Sutter .35 .16
❑ 299 Wayne Babych .20 .09
❑ 300 Jack Brownschidle .20 .09
❑ 301 Blake Dunlop .20 .09
❑ 302 Bernie Federko .75 .35
❑ 303 Bernie Federko IA .35 .16
❑ 304 Pat Hickey .20 .09
❑ 305 Guy Lapointe .20 .09
❑ 306 Mike Liut .75 .35
❑ 307 Joe Mullen 8.00 3.60
❑ 308 Larry Patey .20 .09
❑ 309 Jorgen Pettersson .20 .09
❑ 310 Rob Ramage .20 .09
❑ 311 Brian Sutter .35 .16
❑ 312 Perry Turnbull .20 .09
❑ 313 Mike Zuke .20 .09
❑ 314 Rick Vaive .20 .09
❑ 315 John Anderson .20 .09
❑ 316 Normand Aubin .20 .09
❑ 317 Jim Benning .20 .09
❑ 318 Fred Boimistruck .20 .09
❑ 319 Bill Derlago .20 .09
❑ 320 Bill Derlago IA .20 .09
❑ 321 Miroslav Frycer .20 .09
❑ 322 Billy Harris .20 .09
❑ 323 Jim Korn .20 .09
❑ 324 Michel Larocque .35 .16
❑ 325 Bob Manno .20 .09
❑ 326 Dan Maloney .20 .09
❑ 327 Bob McGill .20 .09
❑ 328 Barry Melrose .35 .16
❑ 329 Terry Martin .20 .09
❑ 330 Rene Robert .35 .16
❑ 331 Rocky Saganiuk .20 .09
❑ 332 Borje Salming .35 .16
❑ 333 Greg Terrion .20 .09
❑ 334 Vincent Tremblay .20 .09
❑ 335 Rick Vaive .20 .09
❑ 336 Rick Vaive IA .20 .09
❑ 337 Thomas Gradin .20 .09
❑ 338 Ivan Boldirev .20 .09
❑ 339 Richard Brodeur .35 .16
❑ 340 Richard Brodeur IA .35 .16
❑ 341 Tony Currie .20 .09
❑ 342 Marc Crawford 2.00 .90
❑ 343 Curt Fraser .20 .09
❑ 344 Thomas Gradin .20 .09
❑ 345 Thomas Gradin IA .20 .09
❑ 346 Ivan Hlinka UER .20 .09
(Photo actually
Jiri Bubla)
❑ 347 Ron Delorme .20 .09
❑ 348 Rick Lanz .20 .09
❑ 349 Lars Lindgren .20 .09
❑ 350 Blair MacDonald .20 .09
❑ 351 Kevin McCarthy .20 .09
❑ 352 Gerry Minor .20 .09
❑ 353 Lars Molin .20 .09
❑ 354 Gary Lupul .20 .09
❑ 355 Darcy Rota .20 .09
❑ 356 Stan Smyl .20 .09
❑ 357 Harold Snepsts .20 .09
❑ 358 Dave(Tiger) Williams .35 .16
❑ 359 Dennis Maruk .35 .16
❑ 360 Ted Bulley .20 .09
❑ 361 Bob Carpenter 1.00 .45
❑ 362 Brian Engblom .20 .09
❑ 363 Mike Gartner 5.00 2.20
❑ 364 Bengt Gustafsson .20 .09
❑ 365 Doug Hicks .20 .09
❑ 366 Ken Houston .20 .09
❑ 367 Doug Jarvis .20 .09
❑ 368 Rod Langway .75 .35
❑ 369 Dennis Maruk .35 .16
❑ 370 Dennis Maruk IA .35 .16
❑ 371 Dave Parro .35 .16
❑ 372 Pat Riggin .35 .16
❑ 373 Chris Valentine .20 .09
❑ 374 Dale Hawerchuk 3.00 1.35
❑ 375 Dave Babych .20 .09
❑ 376 Dave Babych IA .20 .09
❑ 377 Dave Christian .35 .16
❑ 378 Norm Dupont .20 .09
❑ 379 Lucien DeBlois .20 .09
❑ 380 Dale Hawerchuk 15.00 6.75
❑ 381 Dale Hawerchuk IA 4.00 1.80
❑ 382 Craig Levie .20 .09
❑ 383 Morris Lukowich .20 .09
❑ 384 Willy Lindstrom .20 .09
❑ 385 Bengt Lundholm .20 .09
❑ 386 Paul MacLean UER .75 .35
Photo of Larry Hopkins
❑ 387 Bryan Maxwell .20 .09
❑ 388 Doug Smail .20 .09
❑ 389 Doug Soetaert .20 .09
❑ 390 Serge Savard .35 .16
❑ 391 Thomas Steen 3.00 1.35
❑ 392 Don Spring .20 .09
❑ 393 Ed Staniowski .20 .09
❑ 394 Tim Trimper .20 .09
❑ 395 Tim Watters .20 .09
❑ 396 Checklist 265-396 2.50 1.10

## 1982-83 O-Pee-Chee Stickers

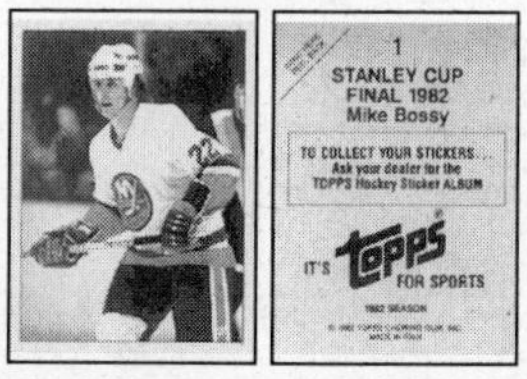


This set of 263 stickers is exactly the same as the Topps stickers issued this year except for minor back differences. Foil cards of players and trophies are contained within this set. The stickers in the set are 1 15/16" by 2 9/16". The

card numbers appear at the lower right within the border on the fronts of the cards as well as appearing on the back. The backs of the stickers contain an ad for an O-Pee-Chee hockey sticker album (in both English and French), the player's name and team, a 1982 Topps copyright date, and a statement to the fact that these cards were made in Italy. The checklist and prices below apply to both O-Pee-Chee and Topps stickers for this year. On the inside back cover of the sticker album the company offered (via direct mail-order) any ten different stickers (but no more than two foil) of your choice for one dollar; this is one reason why the values of the most popular players in these sticker sets are somewhat depressed compared to traditional card set prices.

| | MINT | NRMT |
|---|---|---|
| COMPLETE SET (263) | 45.00 | 20.00 |
| COMMON STICKER (1-263) | .05 | .02 |
| COMMON FOIL | .25 | .11 |

❑ 1 Mike Bossy .50 .23
❑ 2 Conn Smythe Trophy FOIL .25 .11
❑ 3 1981-82 Stanley Cup Winners .05 .02
❑ 4 1981-82 Stanley Cup Winners .05 .02
❑ 5 Stanley Cup Finals .25 .11
❑ 6 Stanley Cup Finals .25 .11
❑ 7 Richard Brodeur .25 .11
❑ 8 Victory/Victoire .05 .02
❑ 9 Stanley Cup Finals .25 .11
❑ 10 Stanley Cup Finals .25 .11
❑ 11 Canucks vs. Chicago .05 .02
❑ 12 Canucks vs. Chicago .05 .02
❑ 13 Canucks vs. Chicago .05 .02
❑ 14 Tom Lysiak .25 .11
❑ 15 Peter Stastny .75 .35
❑ 16 Islanders vs. Quebec .05 .02
❑ 17 Islanders vs. Quebec .05 .02
❑ 18 Islanders vs. Quebec .05 .02
❑ 19 Peter Stastny .75 .35
❑ 20 Marian Stastny .05 .02
❑ 21 Marc Tardif .25 .11
❑ 22 Wilf Paiement .05 .02
❑ 23 Real Cloutier .05 .02
❑ 24 Anton Stastny .25 .11
❑ 25 Michel Goulet .50 .23
❑ 26 Dale Hunter .25 .11
❑ 27 Dan Bouchard .25 .11
❑ 28 Guy Lafleur .50 .23
❑ 29 Guy Lafleur .50 .23
❑ 30 Mario Tremblay .25 .11
❑ 31 Larry Robinson .25 .11
❑ 32 Steve Shutt .25 .11
❑ 33 Steve Shutt .25 .11
❑ 34 Rod Langway .25 .11
❑ 35 Pierre Mondou .05 .02
❑ 36 Bob Gainey .25 .11
❑ 37 Rick Wamsley .25 .11
❑ 38 Mark Napier .25 .11
❑ 39 Mark Napier .25 .11
❑ 40 Doug Jarvis .25 .11
❑ 41 Denis Herron .25 .11
❑ 42 Keith Acton .05 .02
❑ 43 Keith Acton .05 .02
❑ 44 Prince of Wales Trophy FOIL .25 .11
❑ 45 Prince of Wales Trophy FOIL .25 .11
❑ 46 Denis Potvin .25 .11
❑ 47 Bryan Trottier .25 .11
❑ 48 Bryan Trottier .25 .11
❑ 49 John Tonelli .25 .11
❑ 50 Mike Bossy .50 .23
❑ 51 Mike Bossy .50 .23
❑ 52 Duane Sutter .25 .11
❑ 53 Bob Bourne .05 .02
❑ 54 Clark Gillies .25 .11
❑ 55 Clark Gillies .25 .11
❑ 56 Brent Sutter .25 .11
❑ 57 Anders Kallur .05 .02
❑ 58 Ken Morrow .25 .11
❑ 59 Bob Nystrom .25 .11
❑ 60 Billy Smith .25 .11
❑ 61 Billy Smith .25 .11
❑ 62 Rick Vaive .25 .11
❑ 63 Rick Vaive .25 .11
❑ 64 Jim Benning .05 .02
❑ 65 Miroslav Frycer .05 .02
❑ 66 Terry Martin .05 .02
❑ 67 Bill Derlago .05 .02
❑ 68 Bill Derlago .05 .02
❑ 69 Rocky Saganiuk .05 .02
❑ 70 Vincent Tremblay .05 .02
❑ 71 Bob Manno .05 .02
❑ 72 Dan Maloney .05 .02
❑ 73 John Anderson .05 .02
❑ 74 John Anderson .05 .02
❑ 75 Borje Salming .25 .11
❑ 76 Borje Salming .25 .11
❑ 77 Michel Larocque .25 .11
❑ 78 Rick Middleton .25 .11
❑ 79 Rick Middleton .25 .11
❑ 80 Keith Crowder .05 .02
❑ 81 Steve Kasper .25 .11
❑ 82 Brad Park .25 .11
❑ 83 Peter McNab .25 .11
❑ 84 Peter McNab .25 .11
❑ 85 Terry O'Reilly .25 .11
❑ 86 Ray Bourque 1.50 .70
❑ 87 Ray Bourque 1.50 .70
❑ 88 Tom Fergus .05 .02
❑ 89 Mike O'Connell .05 .02
❑ 90 Brad McCrimmon .25 .11
❑ 91 Don Marcotte .05 .02
❑ 92 Barry Pederson .25 .11
❑ 93 Barry Pederson .25 .11
❑ 94 Mark Messier 4.00 1.80
❑ 95 Grant Fuhr 2.00 .90
❑ 96 Kevin Lowe .50 .23
❑ 97 Wayne Gretzky 6.00 2.70
❑ 98 Wayne Gretzky 6.00 2.70
❑ 99 Glenn Anderson .50 .23
❑ 100 Glenn Anderson .50 .23
❑ 101 Dave Lumley .05 .02
❑ 102 Dave Hunter .05 .02
❑ 103 Matti Hagman .05 .02
❑ 104 Paul Coffey 2.00 .90
❑ 105 Paul Coffey 2.00 .90
❑ 106 Lee Fogolin .05 .02
❑ 107 Ron Low .25 .11
❑ 108 Jari Kurri 1.00 .45
❑ 109 Jari Kurri 1.00 .45
❑ 110 Bill Barber .25 .11
❑ 111 Brian Propp .25 .11
❑ 112 Ken Linseman .25 .11
❑ 113 Ron Flockhart .25 .11
❑ 114 Darryl Sittler .25 .11
❑ 115 Bobby Clarke .50 .23
❑ 116 Paul Holmgren .25 .11
❑ 117 Pete Peeters .25 .11
❑ 118 Gilbert Perreault .25 .11
❑ 119 Dale McCourt .05 .02
❑ 120 Mike Foligno .25 .11
❑ 121 John Van Boxmeer .05 .02
❑ 122 Tony McKegney .25 .11
❑ 123 Ric Seiling .05 .02
❑ 124 Don Edwards .25 .11
❑ 125 Yvon Lambert .05 .02
❑ 126 Blaine Stoughton .25 .11
❑ 127 Pierre Larouche .25 .11
❑ 128 Doug Sulliman .05 .02
❑ 129 Ron Francis 3.00 1.35
❑ 130 Greg Millen .25 .11
❑ 131 Mark Howe .25 .11
❑ 132 Chris Kotsopoulos .05 .02
❑ 133 Garry Howatt .05 .02
❑ 134 Ron Duguay .25 .11
❑ 135 Barry Beck .25 .11
❑ 136 Mike Rogers .05 .02
❑ 137 Don Maloney .25 .11
❑ 138 Mark Pavelich .25 .11
❑ 139 Ed Johnstone .05 .02
❑ 140 Dave Maloney .05 .02
❑ 141 Steve Weeks .25 .11
❑ 142 Eddie Mio .25 .11
❑ 143 Rick Kehoe .25 .11
❑ 144 Randy Carlyle .25 .11
❑ 145 Paul Gardner .05 .02
❑ 146 Michel Dion .25 .11
❑ 147 Rick MacLeish .25 .11
❑ 148 Pat Boutette .25 .11
❑ 149 Mike Bullard .25 .11
❑ 150 George Ferguson .05 .02
❑ 151 Dennis Maruk .25 .11
❑ 152 Ryan Walter .25 .11
❑ 153 Mike Gartner .50 .23
❑ 154 Bob Carpenter .50 .23
❑ 155 Chris Valentine .05 .02
❑ 156 Rick Green .25 .11
❑ 157 Bengt Gustafsson .05 .02
❑ 158 Dave Parro .05 .02
❑ 159 Mark Messier AS FOIL 4.00 1.80
❑ 160 Paul Coffey AS FOIL 3.00 1.35
❑ 161 Grant Fuhr AS FOIL 3.00 1.35
❑ 162 Wayne Gretzky AS FOIL 10.00 4.50
❑ 163 Doug Wilson AS FOIL .50 .23
❑ 164 Dave Taylor AS FOIL .50 .23
❑ 165 Mike Bossy AS FOIL 1.00 .45
❑ 166 Ray Bourque AS FOIL 2.50 1.10
❑ 167 Peter Stastny AS FOIL 1.00 .45
❑ 168 Michel Dion AS FOIL .25 .11
❑ 169 Larry Robinson AS FOIL .50 .23
❑ 170 Bill Barber AS FOIL .50 .23
❑ 171 Denis Savard .50 .23
❑ 172 Doug Wilson .25 .11
❑ 173 Grant Mulvey .25 .11
❑ 174 Tom Lysiak .25 .11
❑ 175 Al Secord .25 .11
❑ 176 Reg Kerr .05 .02
❑ 177 Tim Higgins .05 .02
❑ 178 Terry Ruskowski .25 .11
❑ 179 John Ogrodnick .25 .11
❑ 180 Reed Larson .05 .02
❑ 181 Bob Sauve .25 .11
❑ 182 Mark Osborne .05 .02
❑ 183 Jim Schoenfeld .25 .11
❑ 184 Danny Gare .25 .11
❑ 185 Willie Huber .05 .02
❑ 186 Walt McKechnie .05 .02
❑ 187 Paul Woods .25 .11
❑ 188 Bobby Smith .25 .11
❑ 189 Dino Ciccarelli .75 .35
❑ 190 Neal Broten .50 .23
❑ 191 Steve Payne .25 .11
❑ 192 Craig Hartsburg .25 .11
❑ 193 Don Beaupre .25 .11
❑ 194 Steve Christoff .25 .11
❑ 195 Gilles Meloche .25 .11
❑ 196 Mike Liut .25 .11
❑ 197 Bernie Federko .25 .11
❑ 198 Brian Sutter .25 .11
❑ 199 Blake Dunlop .05 .02
❑ 200 Joe Mullen 1.00 .45
❑ 201 Wayne Babych .05 .02
❑ 202 Jorgen Pettersson .05 .02
❑ 203 Perry Turnbull .05 .02
❑ 204 Dale Hawerchuk 2.50 1.10
❑ 205 Morris Lukowich .05 .02
❑ 206 Dave Christian .25 .11
❑ 207 Dave Babych .25 .11
❑ 208 Paul MacLean .25 .11
❑ 209 Willy Lindstrom .05 .02
❑ 210 Ed Staniowski .05 .02
❑ 211 Doug Soetaert .25 .11
❑ 212 Lucien DeBlois .05 .02
❑ 213 Mel Bridgman .25 .11
❑ 214 Lanny McDonald .25 .11
❑ 215 Guy Chouinard .25 .11
❑ 216 Jim Peplinski .25 .11
❑ 217 Kent Nilsson .25 .11
❑ 218 Pekka Rautakallio .25 .11
❑ 219 Paul Reinhart .25 .11
❑ 220 Kevin Lavallee .05 .02
❑ 221 Ken Houston .05 .02
❑ 222 Glenn Resch .25 .11
❑ 223 Rob Ramage .25 .11
❑ 224 Don Lever .05 .02
❑ 225 Bob MacMillan .05 .02
❑ 226 Steve Tambellini .05 .02
❑ 227 Brent Ashton .05 .02
❑ 228 Bob Lorimer .05 .02
❑ 229 Merlin Malinowski .05 .02
❑ 230 Marcel Dionne .25 .11
❑ 231 Dave Taylor .25 .11
❑ 232 Larry Murphy .50 .23
❑ 233 Steve Bozek .05 .02
❑ 234 Greg Terrion .05 .02
❑ 235 Jim Fox .05 .02
❑ 236 Mario Lessard .25 .11
❑ 237 Charlie Simmer .25 .11
❑ 238 Campbell Bowl FOIL .25 .11
❑ 239 Campbell Bowl FOIL .25 .11
❑ 240 Thomas Gradin .25 .11
❑ 241 Ivan Boldirev .05 .02
❑ 242 Stan Smyl .25 .11
❑ 243 Harold Snepsts .25 .11
❑ 244 Curt Fraser .05 .02
❑ 245 Lars Molin .05 .02
❑ 246 Kevin McCarthy .05 .02
❑ 247 Richard Brodeur .25 .11
❑ 248 Calder Trophy FOIL .25 .11
❑ 249 Dale Hawerchuk 2.50 1.10
❑ 250 Vezina Trophy FOIL .25 .11
❑ 251 Billy Smith .25 .11
❑ 252 Denis Herron and Rick Wamsley .25 .11
❑ 253 Steve Kasper .25 .11
❑ 254 Doug Wilson .25 .11
❑ 255 Norris Trophy FOIL .25 .11
❑ 256 Wayne Gretzky 6.00 2.70
❑ 257 Wayne Gretzky 6.00 2.70
❑ 258 Wayne Gretzky 6.00 2.70
❑ 259 Wayne Gretzky 6.00 2.70
❑ 260 Hart Trophy FOIL .25 .11
❑ 261 Art Ross Trophy FOIL .25 .11
❑ 262 Rick Middleton .25 .11
❑ 263 Lady Byng Trophy FOIL .25 .11
❑ xx Sticker Album 5.00 2.20

## 1983-84 O-Pee-Chee

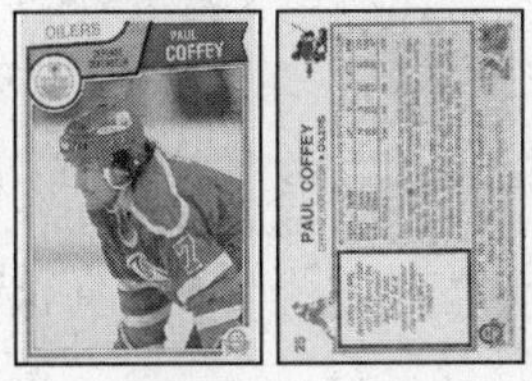


This 396-card standard-size set features card fronts that contain player name, position, team name and team logo at the top. The player's position appears within an area that resembles a hockey stick blade with the team logo fronting the blade as if to be a puck. Bilingual backs contain yearly, career statistics and a section devoted to team records. Each team has a Highlight (HL) and scoring leaders (SL) card. However, updated text on front reflects off-season trades. Rookie Cards include Brian Bellows, Guy Carbonneau, Phil Housley, Steve Larmer, Pelle Lindbergh, Brian Mullen, Mats Naslund, Bernie Nicholls and Scott Stevens. For the second straight year, Topps did not produce a set.

| | MINT | NRMT |
|---|---|---|
| COMPLETE SET (396) | 120.00 | 55.00 |
| COMMON CARD (1-396) | .20 | .09 |

❑ 1 Mike Bossy SL .75 .35
❑ 2 Denis Potvin HL .40 .18
❑ 3 Mike Bossy .75 .35
❑ 4 Bob Bourne .20 .09
❑ 5 Billy Carroll .20 .09
❑ 6 Clark Gillies .40 .18
❑ 7 Butch Goring .40 .18
❑ 8 Mats Hallin .20 .09
❑ 9 Tomas Jonsson .20 .09
❑ 10 Gordie Lane .20 .09
❑ 11 Dave Langevin .20 .09
❑ 12 Rollie Melanson .75 .35
❑ 13 Ken Morrow .20 .09
❑ 14 Bob Nystrom .20 .09
❑ 15 Stefan Persson .20 .09
❑ 16 Denis Potvin .75 .35
❑ 17 Billy Smith .40 .18
❑ 18 Brent Sutter .75 .35
❑ 19 Duane Sutter .20 .09
❑ 20 John Tonelli .40 .18
❑ 21 Bryan Trottier .75 .35
❑ 22 Wayne Gretzky SL 5.00 2.20
❑ 23 Mark Messier 40.00 18.00
Wayne Gretzky
(Oilers Highlights)
❑ 24 Glenn Anderson 1.50 .70
❑ 25 Paul Coffey 10.00 4.50
❑ 26 Lee Fogolin .20 .09
❑ 27 Grant Fuhr 7.00 3.10
❑ 28 Randy Gregg .75 .35
❑ 29 Wayne Gretzky 30.00 13.50
❑ 30 Charlie Huddy 1.00 .45
❑ 31 Pat Hughes .20 .09
❑ 32 Dave Hunter .20 .09
❑ 33 Don Jackson .20 .09
❑ 34 Jari Kurri 6.00 2.70
❑ 35 Willy Lindstrom .20 .09
❑ 36 Ken Linseman .40 .18
❑ 37 Kevin Lowe .75 .35
❑ 38 Dave Lumley .20 .09
❑ 39 Mark Messier 15.00 6.75
❑ 40 Andy Moog 6.00 2.70
❑ 41 Jaroslav Pouzar .20 .09
❑ 42 Tom Roulston .20 .09
❑ 43 Rick Middleton SL .40 .18
❑ 44 Pete Peeters HL .40 .18
❑ 45 Ray Bourque UER 8.00 3.60
(Text on back indicates Ray won the Calder in 1978-79; he won it in 1979-80)
❑ 46 Bruce Crowder .20 .09
❑ 47 Keith Crowder .20 .09
❑ 48 Luc Dufour .40 .18
❑ 49 Tom Fergus .20 .09
❑ 50 Steve Kasper .20 .09
❑ 51 Gord Kluzak .75 .35
❑ 52 Mike Krushelnyski .40 .18
❑ 53 Peter McNab .20 .09
❑ 54 Rick Middleton .40 .18
❑ 55 Mike Milbury .40 .18
❑ 56 Mike O'Connell .20 .09
❑ 57 Barry Pederson .20 .09
❑ 58 Pete Peeters .40 .18
❑ 59 Jim Schoenfeld .40 .18
❑ 60 Tony McKegney SL .20 .09
❑ 61 Bob Sauve HL .40 .18
❑ 62 Real Cloutier .20 .09
❑ 63 Mike Foligno .40 .18
❑ 64 Bill Hajt .20 .09
❑ 65 Phil Housley 4.00 1.80
❑ 66 Dale McCourt .20 .09
❑ 67 Gilbert Perreault .75 .35
❑ 68 Brent Peterson .20 .09
❑ 69 Craig Ramsay .20 .09
❑ 70 Mike Ramsey .20 .09
❑ 71 Bob Sauve .40 .18
❑ 72 Ric Seiling .20 .09
❑ 73 John Van Boxmeer .20 .09
❑ 74 Lanny McDonald SL .40 .18
❑ 75 Lanny McDonald HL .40 .18
❑ 76 Ed Beers .20 .09
❑ 77 Steve Bozek .20 .09
❑ 78 Guy Chouinard .20 .09
❑ 79 Mike Eaves .20 .09
❑ 80 Don Edwards .20 .09
❑ 81 Kari Eloranta .20 .09
❑ 82 Dave Hindmarch .20 .09
❑ 83 Jamie Hislop .20 .09
❑ 84 Jim Jackson .20 .09
❑ 85 Steve Konroyd .20 .09
❑ 86 Rejean Lemelin .75 .35
❑ 87 Lanny McDonald .40 .18
❑ 88 Greg Meredith .20 .09
❑ 89 Kent Nilsson .40 .18
❑ 90 Jim Peplinski .20 .09
❑ 91 Paul Reinhart .20 .09
❑ 92 Doug Risebrough .20 .09
❑ 93 Steve Tambellini .20 .09
❑ 94 Mickey Volcan .20 .09
❑ 95 Al Secord SL .40 .18
❑ 96 Denis Savard HL .40 .18
❑ 97 Murray Bannerman .40 .18
❑ 98 Keith Brown .20 .09
❑ 99 Tony Esposito .75 .35
❑ 100 Dave Feamster .20 .09
❑ 101 Greg Fox .20 .09
❑ 102 Curt Fraser .20 .09
❑ 103 Bill Gardner .20 .09
❑ 104 Tim Higgins .20 .09
❑ 105 Steve Larmer UER 10.00 4.50
(Photo actually Steve Ludzik)
❑ 106 Steve Ludzik UER 2.00 .90
(Photo actually Steve Larmer)
❑ 107 Tom Lysiak .20 .09
❑ 108 Bob Murray .20 .09
❑ 109 Rick Paterson .20 .09
❑ 110 Rich Preston .20 .09
❑ 111 Denis Savard 2.50 1.10
❑ 112 Al Secord .40 .18
❑ 113 Darryl Sutter .20 .09
❑ 114 Doug Wilson .75 .35
❑ 115 John Ogrodnick SL .20 .09
❑ 116 Corrado Micalef HL .20 .09
❑ 117 John Barrett .20 .09
❑ 118 Ivan Boldirev .20 .09
❑ 119 Colin Campbell .20 .09
❑ 120 Murray Craven .75 .35
❑ 121 Ron Duguay .20 .09
❑ 122 Dwight Foster .20 .09
❑ 123 Danny Gare .40 .18
❑ 124 Ed Johnstone .20 .09
❑ 125 Reed Larson .20 .09
❑ 126 Corrado Micalef .20 .09
❑ 127 Eddie Mio .40 .18
❑ 128 John Ogrodnick .20 .09
❑ 129 Brad Park .40 .18
❑ 130 Greg Smith .20 .09
❑ 131 Ken Solheim .20 .09
❑ 132 Bob Manno .20 .09
❑ 133 Paul Woods .20 .09
❑ 134 Checklist 1-132 2.50 1.10
❑ 135 Blaine Stoughton SL .40 .18
❑ 136 Blaine Stoughton HL .40 .18
❑ 137 Richie Dunn .20 .09
❑ 138 Ron Francis 6.00 2.70
❑ 139 Marty Howe .40 .18
❑ 140 Mark Johnson .20 .09
❑ 141 Paul Lawless .20 .09
❑ 142 Merlin Malinowski .20 .09
❑ 143 Greg Millen .40 .18
❑ 144 Ray Neufeld .20 .09
❑ 145 Joel Quenneville .20 .09
❑ 146 Risto Siltanen .20 .09
❑ 147 Blaine Stoughton .40 .18
❑ 148 Doug Sulliman .20 .09
❑ 149 Bob Sullivan .20 .09
❑ 150 Marcel Dionne SL .40 .18
❑ 151 Marcel Dionne HL .40 .18
❑ 152 Marcel Dionne .75 .35
❑ 153 Daryl Evans .20 .09
❑ 154 Jim Fox .20 .09
❑ 155 Mark Hardy .20 .09
❑ 156 Gary Laskoski .20 .09
❑ 157 Kevin Lavallee .20 .09
❑ 158 Dave Lewis .20 .09
❑ 159 Larry Murphy 1.50 .70
❑ 160 Bernie Nicholls 6.00 2.70
❑ 161 Terry Ruskowski .20 .09
❑ 162 Charlie Simmer .40 .18
❑ 163 Dave Taylor .75 .35
❑ 164 Dino Ciccarelli SL .40 .18
❑ 165 Brian Bellows HL .75 .35
❑ 166 Don Beaupre .75 .35
❑ 167 Brian Bellows 4.00 1.80
❑ 168 Neal Broten .75 .35
❑ 169 Steve Christoff .20 .09
❑ 170 Dino Ciccarelli 2.50 1.10
❑ 171 George Ferguson .20 .09
❑ 172 Craig Hartsburg .20 .09
❑ 173 Al MacAdam .20 .09
❑ 174 Dennis Maruk .40 .18
❑ 175 Brad Maxwell .20 .09
❑ 176 Tom McCarthy .20 .09
❑ 177 Gilles Meloche .40 .18
❑ 178 Steve Payne .20 .09
❑ 179 Willi Plett .20 .09
❑ 180 Gordie Roberts .20 .09
❑ 181 Bobby Smith .40 .18
❑ 182 Mark Napier SL .20 .09
❑ 183 Guy Lafleur HL .75 .35
❑ 184 Keith Acton .20 .09
❑ 185 Guy Carbonneau 5.00 2.20
❑ 186 Gilbert Delorme .20 .09
❑ 187 Bob Gainey .75 .35
❑ 188 Rick Green .20 .09
❑ 189 Guy Lafleur .75 .35
❑ 190 Craig Ludwig 1.00 .45
❑ 191 Pierre Mondou .20 .09
❑ 192 Mark Napier .20 .09
❑ 193 Mats Naslund 3.00 1.35
❑ 194 Chris Nilan 1.50 .70
❑ 195 Larry Robinson .40 .18
❑ 196 Bill Root .20 .09
❑ 197 Richard Sevigny .20 .09
❑ 198 Steve Shutt .20 .09
❑ 199 Mario Tremblay .20 .09
❑ 200 Ryan Walter .20 .09
❑ 201 Rick Wamsley .40 .18
❑ 202 Doug Wickenheiser .20 .09
❑ 203 Wayne Gretzky 5.00 2.20
(Hart Trophy)
❑ 204 Wayne Gretzky 5.00 2.20
(Ross Trophy)
❑ 205 Mike Bossy .75 .35
(Lady Byng Trophy)
❑ 206 Steve Larmer 3.00 1.35
(Calder Trophy)
❑ 207 Rod Langway .25 .11
(Norris Trophy)
❑ 208 Lanny McDonald .25 .11
(Masterton Trophy)
❑ 209 Pete Peeters .25 .11
(Vezina Trophy)
❑ 210 Mike Bossy RB .75 .35
Scores 50 goals, first six seasons
❑ 211 Marcel Dionne RB .40 .18
Scores 100 points in seven seasons
❑ 212 Wayne Gretzky RB 5.00 2.20
Scores in 30 consecutive games
❑ 213 Pat Hughes RB .20 .09
Two short-handed goals within 25 seconds
❑ 214 Rick Middleton RB .40 .18
19 points in one playoff series
❑ 215 Wayne Gretzky 5.00 2.20
(Goals Leaders)
❑ 216 Wayne Gretzky 5.00 2.20
(Assists Leaders)
❑ 217 Wayne Gretzky 5.00 2.20
(Scoring Leaders)
❑ 218 Brian Propp .20 .09

(Game Winning Goal Leaders)
❑ 219 Paul Gardner/Al Secord .20 .09
(Power Play Goal Leaders)
❑ 220 Randy Holt .20 .09
(Penalty Minute Leaders)
❑ 221 Pete Peeters .40 .18
(Goals Against Average Leaders)
❑ 222 Pete Peeters .40 .18
(Shutout Leaders)
❑ 223 Steve Tambellini .20 .09
(Devils Scoring Leaders)
❑ 224 Don Lever .20 .09
(Devils Highlights)
❑ 225 Brent Ashton .20 .09
❑ 226 Mel Bridgman .20 .09
❑ 227 Aaron Broten .20 .09
❑ 228 Murray Brumwell .20 .09
❑ 229 Garry Howatt .20 .09
❑ 230 Jeff Larmer .20 .09
❑ 231 Don Lever .20 .09
❑ 232 Bob Lorimer .20 .09
❑ 233 Ron Low .40 .18
❑ 234 Bob MacMillan .20 .09
❑ 235 Hector Marini .20 .09
❑ 236 Glenn Resch .40 .18
❑ 237 Phil Russell .20 .09
❑ 238 Mark Pavelich SL .20 .09
❑ 239 Mark Pavelich HL .20 .09
❑ 240 Bill Baker .40 .18
❑ 241 Barry Beck .20 .09
❑ 242 Mike Blaisdell .20 .09
❑ 243 Nick Fotiu .40 .18
❑ 244 Robbie Ftorek .20 .09
❑ 245 Anders Hedberg .40 .18
❑ 246 Willie Huber .20 .09
❑ 247 Tom Laidlaw .20 .09
❑ 248 Mikko Leinonen .20 .09
❑ 249 Dave Maloney .20 .09
❑ 250 Don Maloney .20 .09
❑ 251 Rob McClanahan .20 .09
❑ 252 Mark Osborne .20 .09
❑ 253 Mark Pavelich .20 .09
❑ 254 Mike Rogers .20 .09
❑ 255 Reijo Ruotsalainen .20 .09
❑ 256 Checklist 133-264 2.50 1.10
❑ 257 Darryl SittlerSL .40 .18
❑ 258 Darryl Sittler HL .40 .18
❑ 259 Ray Allison .20 .09
❑ 260 Bill Barber .40 .18
❑ 261 Lindsay Carson .20 .09
❑ 262 Bobby Clarke .75 .35
❑ 263 Doug Crossman .20 .09
❑ 264 Ron Flockhart .20 .09
❑ 265 Bob Froese .75 .35
❑ 266 Paul Holmgren .40 .18
❑ 267 Mark Howe .75 .35
❑ 268 Pelle Lindbergh 12.00 5.50
❑ 269 Brad Marsh .20 .09
❑ 270 Brad McCrimmon .40 .18
❑ 271 Brian Propp .75 .35
❑ 272 Darryl Sittler .75 .35
❑ 273 Mark Taylor .20 .09
❑ 274 Rick Kehoe SL .40 .18
❑ 275 Paul Gardner HL .20 .09
❑ 276 Pat Boutette .20 .09
❑ 277 Mike Bullard .20 .09
❑ 278 Randy Carlyle .20 .09
❑ 279 Michel Dion .20 .09
❑ 280 Paul Gardner .20 .09
❑ 281 Dave Hannan .40 .18
❑ 282 Rick Kehoe .40 .18
❑ 283 Randy Boyd .20 .09
❑ 284 Greg Malone .20 .09
❑ 285 Doug Shedden .20 .09
❑ 286 Andre St.Laurent .20 .09
❑ 287 Michel Goulet SL .75 .35
❑ 288 Michel Goulet HL .75 .35
❑ 289 Pierre Aubry .20 .09
❑ 290 Dan Bouchard .40 .18
❑ 291 Alain Cote .20 .09
❑ 292 Michel Goulet .75 .35
❑ 293 Dale Hunter .75 .35
❑ 294 Rick Lapointe .20 .09
❑ 295 Mario Marois .20 .09
❑ 296 Tony McKegney .20 .09
❑ 297 Randy Moller .20 .09
❑ 298 Wilf Paiement .20 .09
❑ 299 Dave Pichette .20 .09
❑ 300 Normand Rochefort .20 .09
❑ 301 Louis Sleigher .20 .09
❑ 302 Anton Stastny .40 .18
❑ 303 Marian Stastny .40 .18
❑ 304 Peter Stastny 1.50 .70
❑ 305 Marc Tardif .20 .09
❑ 306 Wally Weir .20 .09
❑ 307 Blake Wesley .20 .09
(Stat line on back has '82-38 instead of '83-84)
❑ 308 Brian Sutter SL .40 .18
❑ 309 Mike Liut HL .40 .18
❑ 310 Wayne Babych .20 .09
❑ 311 Jack Brownschidle .20 .09
❑ 312 Mike Crombeen .20 .09
❑ 313 Andre Dore .20 .09
❑ 314 Blake Dunlop .20 .09
❑ 315 Bernie Federko .75 .35
❑ 316 Mike Liut .75 .35
❑ 317 Joe Mullen 2.00 .90
❑ 318 Jorgen Pettersson .20 .09
❑ 319 Rob Ramage .20 .09
❑ 320 Brian Sutter .40 .18
❑ 321 Perry Turnbull .20 .09
❑ 322 Mike Zuke .20 .09
❑ 323 Rick Vaive SL .20 .09
❑ 324 Rick Vaive HL .20 .09
❑ 325 John Anderson .20 .09
❑ 326 Jim Benning .20 .09
❑ 327 Bill Derlago .20 .09
❑ 328 Dan Daoust .20 .09
❑ 329 Dave Farrish .20 .09
❑ 330 Miroslav Frycer .20 .09
❑ 331 Stewart Gavin .20 .09
❑ 332 Gaston Gingras .20 .09
❑ 333 Billy Harris .20 .09
❑ 334 Peter Ihnacak .20 .09
❑ 335 Jim Korn .20 .09
❑ 336 Terry Martin .20 .09
❑ 337 Frank Nigro .20 .09
❑ 338 Mike Palmateer .40 .18
❑ 339 Walt Poddubny .20 .09
❑ 340 Rick St.Croix .20 .09
❑ 341 Borje Salming .40 .18
❑ 342 Greg Terrion .20 .09
❑ 343 Rick Vaive .20 .09
❑ 344 Darcy Rota SL .20 .09
❑ 345 Darcy Rota HL .20 .09
❑ 346 Richard Brodeur .40 .18
❑ 347 Jiri Bubla .20 .09
❑ 348 Ron Delorme .20 .09
❑ 349 John Garrett .40 .18
❑ 350 Thomas Gradin .20 .09
❑ 351 Doug Halward .20 .09
❑ 352 Mark Kirton .20 .09
❑ 353 Rick Lanz .20 .09
❑ 354 Lars Lindgren .20 .09
❑ 355 Gary Lupul .20 .09
❑ 356 Kevin McCarthy .20 .09
❑ 357 Jim Nill .20 .09
❑ 358 Darcy Rota .20 .09
❑ 359 Stan Smyl .20 .09
❑ 360 Harold Snepsts .20 .09
❑ 361 Patrik Sundstrom .20 .09
❑ 362 Tony Tanti .75 .35
❑ 363 Dave(Tiger) Williams .40 .18
❑ 364 Mike Gartner SL .75 .35
❑ 365 Rod Langway HL .40 .18
❑ 366 Bob Carpenter .20 .09
❑ 367 Dave Christian .20 .09
❑ 368 Brian Engblom .20 .09
❑ 369 Mike Gartner 4.00 1.80
❑ 370 Bengt Gustafsson .20 .09
❑ 371 Ken Houston .20 .09
❑ 372 Doug Jarvis .20 .09
❑ 373 Al Jensen .40 .18
❑ 374 Rod Langway .40 .18
❑ 375 Craig Laughlin .20 .09
❑ 376 Scott Stevens 6.00 2.70
❑ 377 Dale Hawerchuk SL .75 .35
❑ 378 Lucien DeBlois HL .20 .09
❑ 379 Scott Arniel .20 .09
❑ 380 Dave Babych .20 .09
❑ 381 Laurie Boschman .20 .09
❑ 382 Wade Campbell .20 .09
❑ 383 Lucien DeBlois .20 .09
❑ 384 Murray Eaves .20 .09
❑ 385 Dale Hawerchuk 4.00 1.80
❑ 386 Morris Lukowich .20 .09
❑ 387 Bengt Lundholm .20 .09
❑ 388 Paul MacLean .20 .09
❑ 389 Brian Mullen .20 .09
❑ 390 Doug Smail .20 .09
❑ 391 Doug Soetaert .40 .18
❑ 392 Don Spring .20 .09
❑ 393 Thomas Steen .75 .35
❑ 394 Tim Watters .20 .09
❑ 395 Tim Young .20 .09
❑ 396 Checklist 265-396 2.50 1.10

## 1983-84 O-Pee-Chee Stickers

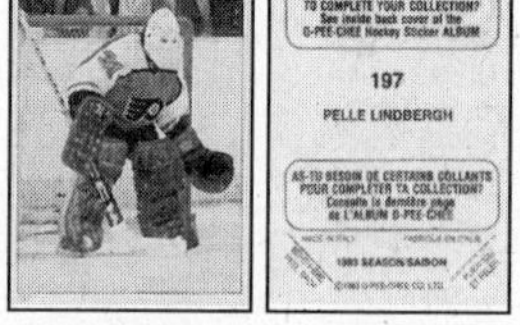


This sticker set consists of 330 stickers in full color and was put out by both O-Pee-Chee and Topps. The foil stickers are numbers 1-4, 15, 22-24, 299-300, 304-305, 308-311, 314-315, 319-330. Stickers measure 1 15/16" by 2 9/16". An album is available for these stickers. The Topps set is distinguishable only by minor back differences. The checklist and prices below apply to both O-Pee-Chee and Topps stickers for this year. On the inside back cover of the sticker album the company offered (via direct mail-order) any ten different stickers of your choice for one dollar; this is one reason why the values of the most popular players in these sticker sets are somewhat depressed compared to traditional card set prices.

| | MINT | NRMT |
|---|---|---|
| COMPLETE SET (330) | 40.00 | 18.00 |
| COMMON STICKER (1-330) | .05 | .02 |
| COMMON FOIL | .15 | .07 |

❑ 1 Marcel Dionne FOIL .50 .23
❑ 2 Guy Lafleur FOIL 1.00 .45
❑ 3 Darryl Sittler FOIL .50 .23
❑ 4 Gilbert Perreault FOIL .50 .23
❑ 5 Bill Barber .25 .11
❑ 6 Steve Shutt .25 .11
❑ 7 Wayne Gretzky 6.00 2.70
❑ 8 Lanny McDonald .25 .11
❑ 9 Reggie Leach .25 .11
❑ 10 Mike Bossy .50 .23
❑ 11 Rick Kehoe .25 .11
❑ 12 Bobby Clarke .25 .11
❑ 13 Butch Goring .25 .11
❑ 14 Rick Middleton .25 .11
❑ 15 Conn Smythe .15 .07
Trophy FOIL
❑ 16 Billy Smith .25 .11
❑ 17 Lee Fogolin .05 .02
❑ 18 Stanley Cup Finals .25 .11
❑ 19 Stanley Cup Finals .25 .11
❑ 20 Stanley Cup Finals .25 .11
❑ 21 Stanley Cup Finals .25 .11
❑ 22 Stanley Cup FOIL .25 .11
❑ 23 Stanley Cup FOIL .25 .11
❑ 24 Stanley Cup FOIL .25 .11
❑ 25 Rick Vaive .25 .11
❑ 26 Rick Vaive .25 .11
❑ 27 Billy Harris .05 .02
❑ 28 Dan Daoust .05 .02
❑ 29 Dan Daoust .05 .02
❑ 30 John Anderson .05 .02
❑ 31 John Anderson .05 .02
❑ 32 Peter Ihnacak .05 .02
❑ 33 Borje Salming .25 .11
❑ 34 Borje Salming .25 .11
❑ 35 Bill Derlago .05 .02
❑ 36 Rick St.Croix .25 .11
❑ 37 Greg Terrion .05 .02
❑ 38 Miroslav Frycer .05 .02
❑ 39 Mike Palmateer .25 .11
❑ 40 Gaston Gingras .05 .02
❑ 41 Pete Peeters .25 .11
❑ 42 Pete Peeters .25 .11
❑ 43 Mike Krushelnyski .25 .11
❑ 44 Rick Middleton .25 .11
❑ 45 Rick Middleton .25 .11
❑ 46 Ray Bourque 1.00 .45
❑ 47 Ray Bourque 1.00 .45
❑ 48 Brad Park .25 .11
❑ 49 Barry Pederson .25 .11
❑ 50 Barry Pederson .25 .11
❑ 51 Peter McNab .25 .11
❑ 52 Mike O'Connell .05 .02
❑ 53 Steve Kasper .25 .11
❑ 54 Marty Howe .25 .11
❑ 55 Tom Fergus .05 .02
❑ 56 Keith Crowder .05 .02
❑ 57 Steve Shutt .25 .11
❑ 58 Guy Lafleur .50 .23
❑ 59 Guy Lafleur .50 .23
❑ 60 Larry Robinson .25 .11
❑ 61 Larry Robinson .25 .11
❑ 62 Ryan Walter .25 .11
❑ 63 Ryan Walter .25 .11
❑ 64 Mark Napier .05 .02
❑ 65 Mark Napier .25 .11
❑ 66 Bob Gainey .25 .11
❑ 67 Doug Wickenheiser .05 .02
❑ 68 Pierre Mondou .05 .02
❑ 69 Mario Tremblay .25 .11
❑ 70 Gilbert Delorme .05 .02
❑ 71 Mats Naslund .25 .11
❑ 72 Rick Wamsley .25 .11
❑ 73 Ken Morrow .25 .11
❑ 74 John Tonelli .25 .11
❑ 75 John Tonelli .25 .11
❑ 76 Bryan Trottier .25 .11
❑ 77 Bryan Trottier .25 .11
❑ 78 Mike Bossy .50 .23
❑ 79 Mike Bossy .50 .23
❑ 80 Bob Bourne .05 .02
❑ 81 Denis Potvin .25 .11
❑ 82 Denis Potvin .25 .11
❑ 83 Dave Langevin .05 .02
❑ 84 Clark Gillies .25 .11
❑ 85 Bob Nystrom .25 .11
❑ 86 Billy Smith .25 .11
❑ 87 Tomas Jonsson .05 .02
❑ 88 Rollie Melanson .25 .11
❑ 89 Wayne Gretzky 6.00 2.70
❑ 90 Wayne Gretzky 6.00 2.70
❑ 91 Willy Lindstrom .05 .02
❑ 92 Glenn Anderson .50 .23
❑ 93 Glenn Anderson .50 .23
❑ 94 Paul Coffey 1.00 .45
❑ 95 Paul Coffey 1.00 .45
❑ 96 Charlie Huddy .25 .11
❑ 97 Mark Messier 2.00 .90
❑ 98 Mark Messier 2.00 .90
❑ 99 Andy Moog 1.00 .45
❑ 100 Lee Fogolin .05 .02
❑ 101 Kevin Lowe .25 .11
❑ 102 Ken Linseman .25 .11
❑ 103 Tom Roulston .05 .02
❑ 104 Jari Kurri 1.00 .45
❑ 105 Darryl Sutter .25 .11
❑ 106 Denis Savard .25 .11
❑ 107 Denis Savard .25 .11
❑ 108 Steve Larmer 2.00 .90
❑ 109 Bob Murray .05 .02
❑ 110 Tom Lysiak .25 .11
❑ 111 Al Secord .25 .11
❑ 112 Doug Wilson .25 .11
❑ 113 Murray Bannerman .25 .11
❑ 114 Gordie Roberts .05 .02
❑ 115 Tom McCarthy .05 .02
❑ 116 Bobby Smith .25 .11
❑ 117 Craig Hartsburg .25 .11
❑ 118 Dino Ciccarelli .50 .23
❑ 119 Dino Ciccarelli .50 .23
❑ 120 Neal Broten .25 .11
❑ 121 Steve Payne .05 .02
❑ 122 Don Beaupre .25 .11
❑ 123 Jorgen Pettersson .05 .02
❑ 124 Perry Turnbull .05 .02
❑ 125 Bernie Federko .25 .11
❑ 126 Mike Crombeen .05 .02
❑ 127 Brian Sutter .25 .11
❑ 128 Brian Sutter .25 .11
❑ 129 Mike Liut .25 .11
❑ 130 Rob Ramage .25 .11
❑ 131 Blake Dunlop .05 .02
❑ 132 Ivan Boldirev .05 .02
❑ 133 Dwight Foster .05 .02
❑ 134 Reed Larson .05 .02
❑ 135 Danny Gare .25 .11
❑ 136 Jim Schoenfeld .25 .11
❑ 137 John Ogrodnick .25 .11
❑ 138 John Ogrodnick .25 .11
❑ 139 Willie Huber .05 .02
❑ 140 Greg Smith .05 .02
❑ 141 Ed Beers .05 .02
❑ 142 Brian Bellows .50 .23
❑ 143 Jiri Bubla .05 .02
❑ 144 Daryl Evans .05 .02
❑ 145 Randy Gregg .05 .02
❑ 146 Jim Jackson .05 .02
❑ 147 Corrado Micalef .05 .02
❑ 148 Brian Mullen .25 .11
❑ 149 Frank Nigro .05 .02
❑ 150 Walt Poddubny .05 .02
❑ 151 Jaroslav Pouzar .05 .02
❑ 152 Patrik Sundstrom .25 .11
❑ 153 Denis Savard .50 .23
❑ 154 Dave Hunter .05 .02
❑ 155 Andy Moog 1.00 .45
❑ 156 Al Secord .25 .11
❑ 157 Mark Messier 2.00 .90
❑ 158 Glenn Anderson .50 .23
❑ 159 Jaroslav Pouzar .05 .02
❑ 160 Al Secord AS .05 .02
❑ 161 Wayne Gretzky AS 6.00 2.70
❑ 162 Lanny McDonald AS .25 .11
❑ 163 Dave Babych AS .05 .02
❑ 164 Murray Bannerman AS .25 .11
❑ 165 Doug Wilson AS .05 .02
❑ 166 Michel Goulet AS .25 .11
❑ 167 Peter Stastny AS .50 .23
❑ 168 Marian Stastny AS .25 .11
❑ 169 Denis Potvin AS .25 .11
❑ 170 Pete Peeters AS .25 .11
❑ 171 Mark Howe AS .25 .11
❑ 172 Luc Dufour .05 .02
❑ 173 Ray Bourque 1.00 .45
❑ 174 Bob Bourne .05 .02
❑ 175 Denis Potvin .25 .11
❑ 176 Mike Bossy .50 .23
❑ 177 Butch Goring .25 .11
❑ 178 Brad Park .25 .11
❑ 179 Murray Brumwell .05 .02
❑ 180 Guy Carbonneau 1.00 .45
❑ 181 Lindsay Carson .05 .02
❑ 182 Luc Dufour .05 .02
❑ 183 Bob Froese .25 .11
❑ 184 Mats Hallin .05 .02
❑ 185 Gord Kluzak .25 .11
❑ 186 Jeff Larmer .05 .02
❑ 187 Milan Novy .05 .02
❑ 188 Scott Stevens 2.00 .90
❑ 189 Bob Sullivan .05 .02
❑ 190 Mark Taylor .05 .02
❑ 191 Darryl Sittler .25 .11
❑ 192 Ron Flockhart .05 .02
❑ 193 Brad McCrimmon .25 .11
❑ 194 Bill Barber .25 .11
❑ 195 Mark Howe .25 .11
❑ 196 Mark Howe .25 .11
❑ 197 Pelle Lindbergh 4.00 1.80
❑ 198 Bobby Clarke .25 .11
❑ 199 Brian Propp .25 .11
❑ 200 Ken Houston .05 .02
❑ 201 Rod Langway .25 .11
❑ 202 Al Jensen .25 .11
❑ 203 Brian Engblom .05 .02
❑ 204 Dennis Maruk .25 .11
❑ 205 Dennis Maruk .25 .11
❑ 206 Bob Carpenter .25 .11
❑ 207 Mike Gartner .50 .23
❑ 208 Doug Jarvis .25 .11
❑ 209 Eddie Mio .25 .11
❑ 210 Barry Beck .25 .11
❑ 211 Dave Maloney .25 .11
❑ 212 Don Maloney .25 .11
❑ 213 Mark Pavelich .25 .11
❑ 214 Mark Pavelich .05 .02
❑ 215 Anders Hedberg .25 .11
❑ 216 Reijo Ruotsalainen .05 .02
❑ 217 Mike Rogers .05 .02
❑ 218 Don Lever .05 .02
❑ 219 Steve Tambellini .05 .02
❑ 220 Bob MacMillan .05 .02
❑ 221 Hector Marini .05 .02
❑ 222 Glenn Resch .25 .11
❑ 223 Glenn Resch .25 .11
❑ 224 Carol Vadnais .05 .02
❑ 225 Joel Quenneville .05 .02
❑ 226 Aaron Broten .05 .02
❑ 227 Randy Carlyle .25 .11
❑ 228 Doug Shedden .05 .02
❑ 229 Greg Malone .05 .02
❑ 230 Paul Gardner .05 .02
❑ 231 Rick Kehoe .25 .11
❑ 232 Rick Kehoe .25 .11
❑ 233 Pat Boutette .05 .02
❑ 234 Michel Dion .25 .11
❑ 235 Mike Bullard .25 .11
❑ 236 Dale McCourt .05 .02
❑ 237 Mike Foligno .25 .11
❑ 238 Phil Housley 1.00 .45
❑ 239 Tony McKegney .25 .11
❑ 240 Gilbert Perreault .25 .11
❑ 241 Gilbert Perreault .25 .11
❑ 242 Bob Sauve .25 .11
❑ 243 Mike Ramsey .25 .11
❑ 244 John Van Boxmeer .05 .02
❑ 245 Dan Bouchard .25 .11
❑ 246 Real Cloutier .05 .02
❑ 247 Marc Tardif .25 .11
❑ 248 Randy Moller .05 .02
❑ 249 Michel Goulet .25 .11
❑ 250 Michel Goulet .25 .11
❑ 251 Marian Stastny .25 .11
❑ 252 Anton Stastny .25 .11
❑ 253 Peter Stastny .50 .23
❑ 254 Mark Johnson .25 .11
❑ 255 Ron Francis 1.50 .70
❑ 256 Doug Sulliman .05 .02
❑ 257 Risto Siltanen .05 .02
❑ 258 Blaine Stoughton .25 .11
❑ 259 Blaine Stoughton .25 .11
❑ 260 Ray Neufeld .05 .02
❑ 261 Pierre Lacroix .05 .02
❑ 262 Greg Millen .25 .11
❑ 263 Lanny McDonald .25 .11
❑ 264 Paul Reinhart .25 .11
❑ 265 Mel Bridgman .25 .11
❑ 266 Rejean Lemelin .25 .11
❑ 267 Kent Nilsson .25 .11
❑ 268 Kent Nilsson .25 .11
❑ 269 Doug Risebrough .25 .11
❑ 270 Kari Eloranta .05 .02
❑ 271 Phil Russell .05 .02
❑ 272 Darcy Rota .05 .02
❑ 273 Thomas Gradin .25 .11
❑ 274 Stan Smyl .25 .11
❑ 275 John Garrett .25 .11
❑ 276 Richard Brodeur .25 .11
❑ 277 Richard Brodeur .25 .11
❑ 278 Doug Halward .05 .02
❑ 279 Kevin McCarthy .05 .02
❑ 280 Rick Lanz .05 .02
❑ 281 Morris Lukowich .05 .02
❑ 282 Dale Hawerchuk 1.00 .45
❑ 283 Paul MacLean .25 .11
❑ 284 Lucien DeBlois .05 .02
❑ 285 Dave Babych .25 .11
❑ 286 Dave Babych .05 .02
❑ 287 Doug Smail .05 .02
❑ 288 Doug Soetaert .05 .02
❑ 289 Thomas Steen .25 .11
❑ 290 Charlie Simmer .25 .11
❑ 291 Terry Ruskowski .25 .11
❑ 292 Bernie Nicholls 2.00 .90
❑ 293 Jim Fox .05 .02
❑ 294 Marcel Dionne .25 .11
❑ 295 Marcel Dionne .25 .11
❑ 296 Gary Laskoski .05 .02
❑ 297 Jerry Korab .05 .02
❑ 298 Larry Murphy .50 .23
❑ 299 Hart Trophy FOIL .15 .07
❑ 300 Hart Trophy FOIL .15 .07
❑ 301 Wayne Gretzky 6.00 2.70
❑ 302 Bobby Clarke .25 .11
❑ 303 Lanny McDonald .25 .11
❑ 304 Lady Byng .15 .07
Trophy FOIL
❑ 305 Lady Byng .15 .07
Trophy FOIL
❑ 306 Mike Bossy .50 .23
❑ 307 Wayne Gretzky 6.00 2.70
❑ 308 Art Ross .15 .07
Trophy FOIL
❑ 309 Art Ross .15 .07
Trophy FOIL
❑ 310 Calder Trophy FOIL .15 .07
❑ 311 Calder Trophy FOIL .15 .07
❑ 312 Steve Larmer 1.50 .70
❑ 313 Rod Langway .25 .11
❑ 314 Norris Trophy FOIL .15 .07
❑ 315 Norris Trophy FOIL .15 .07
❑ 316 Billy Smith .25 .11
❑ 317 Roland Melanson .25 .11
❑ 318 Pete Peeters .25 .11
❑ 319 Vezina Trophy FOIL .15 .07
❑ 320 Vezina Trophy FOIL .15 .07
❑ 321 Mike Bossy FOIL .50 .23
❑ 322 Mike Bossy FOIL .50 .23
❑ 323 Marcel Dionne FOIL .50 .23
❑ 324 Marcel Dionne FOIL .50 .23
❑ 325 Wayne Gretzky FOIL 8.00 3.60
❑ 326 Wayne Gretzky FOIL 8.00 3.60
❑ 327 Pat Hughes FOIL .15 .07
❑ 328 Pat Hughes FOIL .15 .07
❑ 329 Rick Middleton FOIL .15 .07
❑ 330 Rick Middleton FOIL .15 .07
❑ xx Sticker Album 4.00 1.80

## 1984-85 O-Pee-Chee

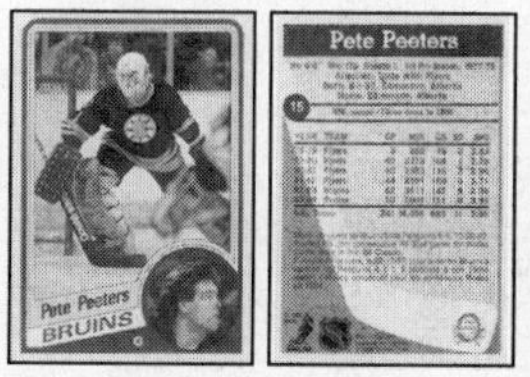


This 396-card standard-size set features two player photos on the front. A small head shot appears in a circle toward the bottom of the

card. Bilingual backs contain yearly and career statistics and career highlights. All-Stars are featured on cards 207-218. Cards 352-372 feature each team's leading goal scorer on the front and team individual scoring statistics on the back. The cards are essentially in team order. However, updated text on some card fronts reflects off-season trades. A healthy selection of Rookie Cards includes Dave Andreychuk, Tom Barrasso, Chris Chelios, Doug Gilmour, Pat LaFontaine, Cam Neely, Dave Poulin, Pat Verbeek, and Steve Yzerman. The Instant Winner card (one in 662 packs) could be redeemed for prizes including Stanley Cup Finals tickets, hockey equipment and sets of uncut card sheets from this year.

| | MINT | NRMT |
|---|---|---|
| COMPLETE SET (396) | 225.00 | 100.00 |
| COMMON CARD (1-396) | .20 | .09 |

❑ 1 Ray Bourque 6.00 2.70
❑ 2 Keith Crowder .20 .09
❑ 3 Luc Dufour .20 .09
❑ 4 Tom Fergus .20 .09
❑ 5 Doug Keans .20 .09
❑ 6 Gord Kluzak .20 .09
❑ 7 Ken Linseman .40 .18
❑ 8 Nevin Markwart .20 .09
❑ 9 Rick Middleton .40 .18
❑ 10 Mike Milbury .20 .09
❑ 11 Jim Nill .20 .09
❑ 12 Mike O'Connell .20 .09
❑ 13 Terry O'Reilly .40 .18
❑ 14 Barry Pederson .20 .09
❑ 15 Pete Peeters .40 .18
❑ 16 Dave Silk .20 .09
❑ 17 Dave Andreychuk 5.00 2.20
❑ 18 Tom Barrasso 5.00 2.20
❑ 19 Real Cloutier .20 .09
❑ 20 Mike Foligno .40 .18
❑ 21 Bill Hajt .20 .09
❑ 22 Gilles Hamel .20 .09
❑ 23 Phil Housley .75 .35
❑ 24 Gilbert Perreault .40 .18
❑ 25 Brent Peterson .20 .09
❑ 26 Larry Playfair .20 .09
❑ 27 Craig Ramsay .20 .09
❑ 28 Mike Ramsey .20 .09
❑ 29 Lindy Ruff .20 .09
❑ 30 Bob Sauve .40 .18
❑ 31 Ric Seiling .20 .09
❑ 32 Murray Bannerman .40 .18
❑ 33 Keith Brown .20 .09
❑ 34 Curt Fraser .20 .09
❑ 35 Bill Gardner .20 .09
❑ 36 Jeff Larmer .20 .09
❑ 37 Steve Larmer 2.50 1.10
❑ 38 Steve Ludzik .20 .09
❑ 39 Tom Lysiak .20 .09
❑ 40 Bob MacMillan .20 .09
❑ 41 Bob Murray .20 .09
❑ 42 Troy Murray .75 .35
❑ 43 Jack O'Callahan .20 .09
❑ 44 Rick Paterson .20 .09
❑ 45 Denis Savard 1.50 .70
❑ 46 Al Secord .40 .18
❑ 47 Darryl Sutter .40 .18
❑ 48 Doug Wilson .40 .18
❑ 49 John Barrett .20 .09
❑ 50 Ivan Boldirev .20 .09
❑ 51 Colin Campbell .20 .09
❑ 52 Ron Duguay .20 .09
❑ 53 Dwight Foster .20 .09
❑ 54 Danny Gare .20 .09
(Mike Gartner in photo)
❑ 55 Ed Johnstone .20 .09
❑ 56 Kelly Kisio .40 .18
❑ 57 Lane Lambert .20 .09
❑ 58 Reed Larson .20 .09
❑ 59 Bob Manno .20 .09
❑ 60 Randy Ladouceur .20 .09
❑ 61 Eddie Mio .40 .18
❑ 62 John Ogrodnick .20 .09
❑ 63 Brad Park .40 .18
❑ 64 Greg Smith .20 .09
❑ 65 Greg Stefan .40 .18
❑ 66 Paul Woods .20 .09
❑ 67 Steve Yzerman 80.00 36.00
❑ 68 Bob Crawford .20 .09
❑ 69 Richie Dunn .20 .09
❑ 70 Ron Francis 4.00 1.80
❑ 71 Marty Howe .20 .09
❑ 72 Mark Johnson .20 .09
❑ 73 Chris Kotsopoulos .20 .09
❑ 74 Greg Malone .20 .09
❑ 75 Greg Millen .40 .18
❑ 76 Ray Neufeld .20 .09
❑ 77 Joel Quenneville .20 .09
❑ 78 Risto Siltanen .20 .09
❑ 79 Sylvain Turgeon .40 .18
❑ 80 Mike Zuke .20 .09
❑ 81 Steve Christoff .20 .09
❑ 82 Marcel Dionne .75 .35
❑ 83 Brian Engblom .20 .09
❑ 84 Jim Fox .20 .09
❑ 85 Anders Hakansson .20 .09
❑ 86 Mark Hardy .20 .09
❑ 87 Brian MacLellan .20 .09
❑ 88 Bernie Nicholls 2.00 .90
❑ 89 Terry Ruskowski .20 .09
❑ 90 Charlie Simmer .40 .18
❑ 91 Doug Smith .20 .09
❑ 92 Dave Taylor .40 .18
❑ 93 Keith Acton .20 .09
❑ 94 Don Beaupre .40 .18
❑ 95 Brian Bellows .75 .35
❑ 96 Neal Broten .75 .35
❑ 97 Dino Ciccarelli .75 .35
❑ 98 Craig Hartsburg .20 .09
❑ 99 Tom Hirsch .20 .09
❑ 100 Paul Holmgren .40 .18
❑ 101 Dennis Maruk .40 .18
❑ 102 Brad Maxwell .20 .09
❑ 103 Tom McCarthy .20 .09
❑ 104 Gilles Meloche .40 .18
❑ 105 Mark Napier .20 .09
❑ 106 Steve Payne .20 .09
❑ 107 Gordie Roberts .20 .09
❑ 108 Harold Snepsts .20 .09
❑ 109 Mel Bridgman .20 .09
❑ 110 Joe Cirella .20 .09
❑ 111 Tim Higgins .20 .09
❑ 112 Don Lever .20 .09
❑ 113 Dave Lewis .20 .09
❑ 114 Bob Lorimer .20 .09
❑ 115 Ron Low .20 .09
❑ 116 Jan Ludvig .20 .09
❑ 117 Gary McAdam .20 .09
❑ 118 Rich Preston .20 .09
❑ 119 Glenn Resch .40 .18
❑ 120 Phil Russell .20 .09
❑ 121 Pat Verbeek 10.00 4.50
❑ 122 Mike Bossy .75 .35
❑ 123 Bob Bourne .20 .09
❑ 124 Pat Flatley .75 .35
❑ 125 Greg Gilbert .20 .09
❑ 126 Clark Gillies .40 .18
❑ 127 Butch Goring .40 .18
❑ 128 Tomas Jonsson .20 .09
❑ 129 Pat LaFontaine 15.00 6.75
❑ 130 Rollie Melanson .40 .18
❑ 131 Ken Morrow .20 .09
❑ 132 Bob Nystrom .20 .09
❑ 133 Stefan Persson .20 .09
❑ 134 Denis Potvin .75 .35
❑ 135 Billy Smith .40 .18
❑ 136 Brent Sutter .20 .09
❑ 137 Duane Sutter .20 .09
❑ 138 John Tonelli .40 .18
❑ 139 Bryan Trottier .75 .35
❑ 140 Barry Beck .20 .09
❑ 141 Ron Greschner .20 .09
❑ 142 Glen Hanlon .40 .18
❑ 143 Anders Hedberg .40 .18
❑ 144 Tom Laidlaw .20 .09
❑ 145 Pierre Larouche .40 .18
❑ 146 Dave Maloney .20 .09
❑ 147 Don Maloney .20 .09
❑ 148 Mark Osborne .20 .09
❑ 149 Larry Patey .20 .09
❑ 150 James Patrick .75 .35
❑ 151 Mark Pavelich .20 .09
❑ 152 Mike Rogers .20 .09
❑ 153 Reijo Ruotsalainen .20 .09
❑ 154 Blaine Stoughton .40 .18
❑ 155 Peter Sundstrom .20 .09
❑ 156 Bill Barber .40 .18
❑ 157 Doug Crossman .20 .09
❑ 158 Thomas Eriksson .20 .09
❑ 159 Bob Froese .40 .18
❑ 160 Paul Guay .20 .09
❑ 161 Mark Howe .40 .18
❑ 162 Tim Kerr .40 .18
❑ 163 Brad Marsh .20 .09
❑ 164 Brad McCrimmon .40 .18
❑ 165 Dave Poulin 2.00 .90
❑ 166 Brian Propp .40 .18
❑ 167 Ilkka Sinisalo .20 .09
❑ 168 Darryl Sittler .75 .35
❑ 169 Rich Sutter .40 .18
❑ 170 Ron Sutter .75 .35
❑ 171 Pat Boutette .20 .09
❑ 172 Mike Bullard .40 .18
❑ 173 Michel Dion .40 .18
❑ 174 Ron Flockhart .20 .09
❑ 175 Greg Fox .20 .09
❑ 176 Denis Herron .40 .18
❑ 177 Rick Kehoe .40 .18
❑ 178 Kevin McCarthy .20 .09
❑ 179 Tom Roulston .20 .09
❑ 180 Mark Taylor .20 .09
❑ 181 Wayne Babych .20 .09
❑ 182 Tim Bothwell .20 .09
❑ 183 Kevin Lavallee .20 .09
❑ 184 Bernie Federko .40 .18
❑ 185 Doug Gilmour 30.00 13.50
❑ 186 Terry Johnson .20 .09
❑ 187 Mike Liut .40 .18
❑ 188 Joe Mullen 1.25 .55
❑ 189 Jorgen Pettersson .20 .09
❑ 190 Rob Ramage .20 .09
❑ 191 Dwight Schofield .20 .09
❑ 192 Brian Sutter .40 .18
❑ 193 Doug Wickenheiser .20 .09
❑ 194 Bob Carpenter .20 .09
❑ 195 Dave Christian .20 .09
❑ 196 Bob Gould .20 .09
❑ 197 Mike Gartner 3.00 1.35
❑ 198 Bengt Gustafsson .20 .09
❑ 199 Alan Haworth .20 .09
❑ 200 Doug Jarvis .20 .09
❑ 201 Al Jensen .40 .18
❑ 202 Rod Langway .40 .18
❑ 203 Craig Laughlin .20 .09
❑ 204 Larry Murphy .75 .35
❑ 205 Pat Riggin .40 .18
❑ 206 Scott Stevens 2.50 1.10
❑ 207 Michel Goulet AS .40 .18
❑ 208 Wayne Gretzky AS 5.00 2.20
❑ 209 Mike Bossy AS .75 .35
❑ 210 Rod Langway AS .40 .18
❑ 211 Ray Bourque AS 1.50 .70
❑ 212 Tom Barrasso AS .75 .35
❑ 213 Mark Messier AS 2.50 1.10
❑ 214 Bryan Trottier AS .75 .35
❑ 215 Jari Kurri AS .75 .35
❑ 216 Denis Potvin AS .40 .18
❑ 217 Paul Coffey AS 1.50 .70
❑ 218 Pat Riggin AS .40 .18
❑ 219 Ed Beers .20 .09
❑ 220 Steve Bozek .20 .09
❑ 221 Mike Eaves .20 .09
❑ 222 Don Edwards .40 .18
❑ 223 Kari Eloranta .20 .09
❑ 224 Dave Hindmarch .20 .09
❑ 225 Jim Jackson .20 .09
❑ 226 Steve Konroyd .20 .09
❑ 227 Richard Kromm .20 .09
❑ 228 Rejean Lemelin .40 .18
❑ 229 Hakan Loob 2.50 1.10
❑ 230 Jamie Macoun .40 .18
❑ 231 Lanny McDonald .40 .18
❑ 232 Kent Nilsson .40 .18
❑ 233 Jim Peplinski .20 .09
❑ 234 Dan Quinn .75 .35
❑ 235 Paul Reinhart .20 .09
❑ 236 Doug Risebrough .20 .09
❑ 237 Steve Tambellini .20 .09
❑ 238 Glenn Anderson .75 .35
❑ 239 Paul Coffey 6.00 2.70
❑ 240 Lee Fogolin .20 .09
❑ 241 Grant Fuhr 5.00 2.20
❑ 242 Randy Gregg .20 .09
❑ 243 Wayne Gretzky 20.00 9.00
❑ 244 Charlie Huddy .40 .18
❑ 245 Pat Hughes .20 .09
❑ 246 Dave Hunter .20 .09
❑ 247 Don Jackson .20 .09
❑ 248 Mike Krushelnyski .20 .09
❑ 249 Jari Kurri 4.00 1.80
❑ 250 Willy Lindstrom .20 .09
❑ 251 Kevin Lowe .75 .35
❑ 252 Dave Lumley .20 .09
❑ 253 Kevin McClelland .20 .09
❑ 254 Mark Messier 10.00 4.50
❑ 255 Andy Moog 4.00 1.80
❑ 256 Jaroslav Pouzar .20 .09
❑ 257 Guy Carbonneau .75 .35
❑ 258 John Chabot .20 .09
❑ 259 Chris Chelios 30.00 13.50
❑ 260 Lucien DeBlois .20 .09
❑ 261 Bob Gainey .75 .35
❑ 262 Rick Green .20 .09
❑ 263 Jean Hamel .20 .09
❑ 264 Guy Lafleur .75 .35
❑ 265 Craig Ludwig .20 .09
❑ 266 Pierre Mondou .20 .09
❑ 267 Mats Naslund .75 .35
❑ 268 Chris Nilan .20 .09
❑ 269 Steve Penney .40 .18
❑ 270 Larry Robinson .40 .18
❑ 271 Bill Root .20 .09
❑ 272 Steve Shutt .20 .09
❑ 273 Bobby Smith .40 .18
❑ 274 Mario Tremblay .20 .09
❑ 275 Ryan Walter .20 .09
❑ 276 Bo Berglund .20 .09
❑ 277 Dan Bouchard .40 .18
❑ 278 Alain Cote .20 .09
❑ 279 Andre Dore .20 .09
❑ 280 Michel Goulet .75 .35
❑ 281 Dale Hunter .40 .18
❑ 282 Mario Marois .20 .09
❑ 283 Tony McKegney .20 .09
❑ 284 Randy Moller .20 .09
❑ 285 Wilf Paiement .20 .09
❑ 286 Pat Price .20 .09
❑ 287 Normand Rochefort .20 .09
❑ 288 Andre Savard .20 .09
❑ 289 Richard Sevigny .20 .09
❑ 290 Louis Sleigher .20 .09
❑ 291 Anton Stastny .40 .18
❑ 292 Marian Stastny .40 .18
❑ 293 Peter Stastny .75 .35
❑ 294 Blake Wesley .20 .09
❑ 295 John Anderson .20 .09
❑ 296 Jim Benning .20 .09
❑ 297 Allan Bester UER .40 .18
(Name misspelled Alan on both sides)
❑ 298 Rich Costello .20 .09
❑ 299 Dan Daoust .20 .09
❑ 300 Bill Derlago .20 .09
❑ 301 Dave Farrish .20 .09
❑ 302 Stewart Gavin .20 .09
❑ 303 Gaston Gingras .20 .09
❑ 304 Jim Korn .20 .09
❑ 305 Gary Leeman .20 .09
❑ 306 Terry Martin .20 .09
❑ 307 Gary Nylund .20 .09
❑ 308 Mike Palmateer .40 .18
❑ 309 Walt Poddubny .20 .09
❑ 310 Rick St.Croix .20 .09
❑ 311 Borje Salming .40 .18
❑ 312 Greg Terrion .20 .09
❑ 313 Rick Vaive .20 .09
❑ 314 Richard Brodeur .40 .18
❑ 315 Jiri Bubla .20 .09
❑ 316 Ron Delorme .40 .18
❑ 317 John Garrett .40 .18
❑ 318 Jere Gillis .20 .09
❑ 319 Thomas Gradin .20 .09
❑ 320 Doug Halward .20 .09
❑ 321 Rick Lanz .20 .09
❑ 322 Moe Lemay .20 .09
❑ 323 Gary Lupul .20 .09
❑ 324 Al MacAdam .20 .09
❑ 325 Rob McClanahan .20 .09
❑ 326 Peter McNab .20 .09
❑ 327 Cam Neely 20.00 9.00
❑ 328 Darcy Rota .20 .09
❑ 329 Andy Schliebener .20 .09
❑ 330 Stan Smyl .20 .09
❑ 331 Patrik Sundstrom .20 .09
❑ 332 Tony Tanti .20 .09
❑ 333 Scott Arniel .20 .09
❑ 334 Dave Babych .20 .09
❑ 335 Laurie Boschman .20 .09
❑ 336 Wade Campbell .20 .09
❑ 337 Randy Carlyle .20 .09
❑ 338 Jordy Douglas .20 .09
❑ 339 Dale Hawerchuk 3.00 1.35
❑ 340 Morris Lukowich .20 .09
❑ 341 Bengt Lundholm .20 .09
❑ 342 Paul MacLean .20 .09
❑ 343 Andrew McBain .20 .09
❑ 344 Brian Mullen .20 .09
❑ 345 Robert Picard .20 .09
❑ 346 Doug Smail .20 .09
❑ 347 Doug Soetaert .40 .18
❑ 348 Thomas Steen .20 .09
❑ 349 Perry Turnbull .20 .09
❑ 350 Tim Watters .20 .09
❑ 351 Tim Young .20 .09
❑ 352 Rick Middleton SL .40 .18
❑ 353 Dave Andreychuk SL 1.50 .70
❑ 354 Ed Beers SL .20 .09
❑ 355 Denis Savard SL .40 .18
❑ 356 John Ogrodnick SL .20 .09
❑ 357 Wayne Gretzky SL 5.00 2.20
❑ 358 Charlie Simmer SL .40 .18
❑ 359 Brian Bellows SL .40 .18
❑ 360 Guy Lafleur SL .75 .35
❑ 361 Mel Bridgman SL .20 .09
❑ 362 Mike Bossy SL .75 .35
❑ 363 Pierre Larouche SL .40 .18
❑ 364 Tim Kerr SL .40 .18
❑ 365 Mike Bullard SL .20 .09
❑ 366 Michel Goulet SL .40 .18
❑ 367 Bernie Federko .75 .35
Joe Mullen UER SL
❑ 368 Rick Vaive .20 .09
❑ 369 Tony Tanti .20 .09
❑ 370 Mike Gartner .75 .35
❑ 371 Paul MacLean SL .20 .09
❑ 372 Sylvain Turgeon SL .40 .18
❑ 373 Wayne Gretzky 5.00 2.20
(Art Ross Trophy)
❑ 374 Wayne Gretzky 5.00 2.20
(Hart Trophy)
❑ 375 Tom Barasso .75 .35
(Calder Trophy)
❑ 376 Mike Bossy .75 .35
(Lady Byng Trophy)
❑ 377 Rod Langway .20 .09
(Norris Trophy)
❑ 378 Brad Park .40 .18
(Masterton Trophy)
❑ 379 Tom Barrasso .75 .35
(Vezina Trophy)
❑ 380 Wayne Gretzky 5.00 2.20
(Scoring Leaders)
❑ 381 Wayne Gretzky 5.00 2.20
(Goals Leaders)
❑ 382 Wayne Gretzky 5.00 2.20
(Assists Leaders)
❑ 383 Wayne Gretzky 5.00 2.20
(Power Play Goal Leaders)
❑ 384 Michel Goulet .40 .18
(Game Winning Goal Leaders)
❑ 385 Steve Yzerman UER 10.00 4.50
(Rookie Scoring Leaders)
(Gilmour misspelled as Gilmore on reverse)
❑ 386 Pat Riggin .40 .18
(Goals Against Average Leaders)
❑ 387 Rollie Melanson .40 .18
(Save Percentage Leaders)
❑ 388 Wayne Gretzky RB 5.00 2.20
Scores in 51 Straight Games
❑ 389 Denis Potvin RB .40 .18
20 Goals, Eight Seasons, Defenseman
❑ 390 Brad Park RB .40 .18
Most Career Assists, Defenseman
❑ 391 Michel Goulet RB .40 .18
Most Points, Season, Left Wing
❑ 392 Pat LaFontaine RB 4.00 1.80
Rookie Scoring Mark
❑ 393 Dale Hawerchuk RB .75 .35
Five Assists, Period
❑ 394 Checklist 1-132 2.00 .90
❑ 395 Checklist 133-264 UER 2.00 .90
(185 Gilmore)
❑ 396 Checklist 265-396 2.00 .90
❑ NNO Instant Winner Card 100.00 45.00

## 1984-85 O-Pee-Chee Stickers

This sticker set consists of 292 stickers in full color and was put out by O-Pee-Chee. The foil stickers are listed in the checklist below explicitly. The stickers measure approximately 1 15/16" by 2 9/16". An album is available for these stickers. Those stickers which are pairs are indicated in the checklist below by noting parenthetically the other member of the pair.

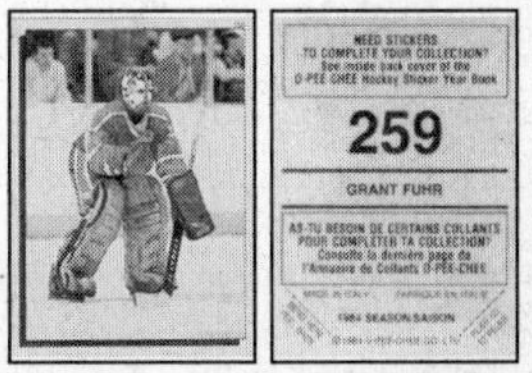


On the inside back cover of the sticker album the company offered (via direct mail-order) any ten different stickers of your choice for one dollar; this is one reason why the values of the most popular players in these sticker sets are somewhat depressed compared to traditional card set prices.

| | MINT | NRMT |
|---|---|---|
| COMPLETE SET (292) | 40.00 | 18.00 |
| COMMON STICKER (1-292) | .05 | .02 |
| COMMON FOILS | .20 | .09 |
| COMMON HALF FOILS | .15 | .07 |

❑ 1 Stanley Cup .25 .11
❑ 2 Stanley Cup .25 .11
❑ 3 Stanley Cup .25 .11
❑ 4 Stanley Cup .25 .11
❑ 5 Mark Messier 1.25 .55
❑ 6 Maple Leafs Logo (23) .15 .07
FOIL
❑ 7 Borje Salming .05 .02
❑ 8 Borje Salming .05 .02
❑ 9 Dan Daoust .05 .02
❑ 10 Dan Daoust .05 .02
❑ 11 Rick Vaive .05 .02
❑ 12 Rick Vaive .05 .02
❑ 13 Dale McCourt .05 .02
❑ 14 Bill Derlago .05 .02
❑ 15 Gary Nylund .05 .02
❑ 16 Gary Nylund .05 .02
❑ 17 Jim Korn .05 .02
❑ 18 John Anderson .05 .02
❑ 19 Greg Terrion .05 .02
❑ 20 Allan Bester .05 .02
❑ 21 Jim Benning .05 .02
❑ 22 Mike Palmateer .25 .11
❑ 23 Blackhawks Logo (6) .15 .07
FOIL
❑ 24 Denis Savard .50 .23
❑ 25 Denis Savard .50 .23
❑ 26 Bob Murray .05 .02
❑ 27 Doug Wilson .05 .02
❑ 28 Keith Brown .05 .02
❑ 29 Steve Larmer .50 .23
❑ 30 Darryl Sutter .05 .02
❑ 31 Tom Lysiak .05 .02
❑ 32 Murray Bannerman .25 .11
❑ 33 Red Wings Logo (43) .15 .07
FOIL
❑ 34 John Ogrodnick .05 .02
❑ 35 John Ogrodnick .05 .02
❑ 36 Reed Larson .05 .02
❑ 37 Steve Yzerman 12.00 5.50
❑ 38 Brad Park .25 .11
❑ 39 Ivan Boldirev .05 .02
❑ 40 Kelly Kisio .05 .02
❑ 41 Greg Stefan .05 .02
❑ 42 Ron Duguay .05 .02
❑ 43 North Stars Logo (33) .15 .07
FOIL
❑ 44 Brian Bellows .25 .11
❑ 45 Brian Bellows .25 .11
❑ 46 Neal Broten .25 .11
❑ 47 Dino Ciccarelli .50 .23
❑ 48 Dennis Maruk .05 .02
❑ 49 Steve Payne .05 .02
❑ 50 Brad Maxwell .05 .02
❑ 51 Gilles Meloche .25 .11
❑ 52 Tom McCarthy .05 .02
❑ 53 Blues Logo (67) .15 .07
FOIL
❑ 54 Bernie Federko .05 .02
❑ 55 Bernie Federko .05 .02
❑ 56 Brian Sutter .05 .02
❑ 57 Mike Liut .25 .11
❑ 58 Doug Wickenheiser .05 .02
❑ 59 Jorgen Pettersson .05 .02
❑ 60 Doug Gilmour 4.00 1.80
❑ 61 Joe Mullen .25 .11
❑ 62 Rob Ramage .05 .02
❑ 63 Wayne Gretzky (64) 6.00 2.70
FOIL
❑ 64 Michel Goulet (63) 6.00 2.70
FOIL
❑ 65 Pat Riggin (66) .15 .07
FOIL
❑ 66 Denis Potvin (65) .15 .07
FOIL
❑ 67 Devils Logo (53) .15 .07
FOIL
❑ 68 Glenn Resch .25 .11
❑ 69 Glenn Resch .25 .11
❑ 70 Don Lever .05 .02
❑ 71 Mel Bridgman .05 .02
❑ 72 Bob MacMillan .05 .02
❑ 73 Pat Verbeek .50 .23
❑ 74 Joe Cirella .05 .02
❑ 75 Phil Russell .05 .02
❑ 76 Jan Ludvig .05 .02
❑ 77 Islanders Logo (94) .15 .07
FOIL
❑ 78 Denis Potvin .25 .11
❑ 79 Denis Potvin .25 .11
❑ 80 John Tonelli .05 .02

□ 81 John Tonelli .05 .02
□ 82 Mike Bossy .50 .23
□ 83 Mike Bossy .50 .23
□ 84 Butch Goring .05 .02
□ 85 Bob Nystrom .05 .02
□ 86 Bryan Trottier .25 .11
□ 87 Bryan Trottier .25 .11
□ 88 Brent Sutter .05 .02
□ 89 Bob Bourne .05 .02
□ 90 Greg Gilbert .05 .02
□ 91 Billy Smith .05 .02
□ 92 Rollie Melanson .25 .11
□ 93 Ken Morrow .05 .02
□ 94 Rangers Logo (77) .15 .07
FOIL
□ 95 Don Maloney .05 .02
□ 96 Don Maloney .05 .02
□ 97 Mark Pavelich .05 .02
□ 98 Glen Hanlon .25 .11
□ 99 Mike Rogers .05 .02
□ 100 Barry Beck .05 .02
□ 101 Reijo Ruotsalainen .05 .02
□ 102 Anders Hedberg .05 .02
□ 103 Pierre Larouche .25 .11
□ 104 Flyers Logo (114) .15 .07
FOIL
□ 105 Tim Kerr .05 .02
□ 106 Tim Kerr .05 .02
□ 107 Ron Sutter .25 .11
□ 108 Darryl Sittler .25 .11
□ 109 Mark Howe .25 .11
□ 110 Dave Poulin .05 .02
□ 111 Rich Sutter .25 .11
□ 112 Brian Propp .05 .02
□ 113 Bob Froese .25 .11
□ 114 Penguins Logo (104) .15 .07
FOIL
□ 115 Ron Flockhart .05 .02
□ 116 Ron Flockhart .05 .02
□ 117 Rick Kehoe .05 .02
□ 118 Mike Bullard .05 .02
□ 119 Kevin McCarthy .05 .02
□ 120 Doug Shedden .05 .02
□ 121 Mark Taylor .05 .02
□ 122 Denis Herron .05 .02
□ 123 Tom Roulston .05 .02
□ 124 Capitals Logo (146) .15 .07
FOIL
□ 125 Rod Langway .05 .02
□ 126 Rod Langway .05 .02
□ 127 Larry Murphy .25 .11
□ 128 Al Jensen .05 .02
□ 129 Doug Jarvis .05 .02
□ 130 Bengt Gustafsson .05 .02
□ 131 Mike Gartner .50 .23
□ 132 Bob Carpenter .05 .02
□ 133 Dave Christian .05 .02
□ 134 Paul Coffey FOIL 1.00 .45
□ 135 Murray Bannerman .25 .11
FOIL
□ 136 Rob Ramage FOIL .25 .11
□ 137 John Ogrodnick .25 .11
FOIL
□ 138 Wayne Gretzky 6.00 2.70
FOIL
□ 139 Rick Vaive FOIL .25 .11
□ 140 Michel Goulet .50 .23
FOIL
□ 141 Peter Stastny FOIL .50 .23
□ 142 Rick Middleton .25 .11
FOIL
□ 143 Ray Bourque FOIL 1.00 .45
□ 144 Pete Peeters FOIL .25 .11
□ 145 Denis Potvin FOIL .50 .23
□ 146 Canadiens Logo (124) .15 .07
FOIL
□ 147 Larry Robinson .25 .11
□ 148 Larry Robinson .25 .11
□ 149 Guy Lafleur .50 .23
□ 150 Guy Lafleur .50 .23
□ 151 Bobby Smith .05 .02
□ 152 Bobby Smith .05 .02
□ 153 Bob Gainey .25 .11
□ 154 Craig Ludwig .05 .02
□ 155 Mats Naslund .25 .11
□ 156 Mats Naslund .25 .11
□ 157 Rick Wamsley .25 .11
□ 158 Jean Hamel .05 .02
□ 159 Ryan Walter .05 .02
□ 160 Guy Carbonneau .25 .11
□ 161 Mario Tremblay .05 .02
□ 162 Pierre Mondou .05 .02
□ 163 Nordiques Logo (180) .15 .07
FOIL
□ 164 Peter Stastny .50 .23
□ 165 Peter Stastny .50 .23
□ 166 Mario Marois .05 .02
□ 167 Mario Marois .05 .02
□ 168 Michel Goulet .25 .11
□ 169 Michel Goulet .25 .11
□ 170 Andre Savard .05 .02
□ 171 Tony McKegney .05 .02
□ 172 Dan Bouchard .25 .11
□ 173 Dan Bouchard .25 .11
□ 174 Randy Moller .05 .02
□ 175 Wilf Paiement .05 .02
□ 176 Normand Rochefort .05 .02
□ 177 Marian Stastny .05 .02
□ 178 Anton Stastny .05 .02
□ 179 Dale Hunter .25 .11
□ 180 Bruins Logo (163) .15 .07
FOIL
□ 181 Rick Middleton .25 .11
□ 182 Rick Middleton .25 .11
□ 183 Ray Bourque .75 .35
□ 184 Pete Peeters .25 .11
□ 185 Mike O'Connell .05 .02
□ 186 Gord Kluzak .05 .02
□ 187 Barry Pederson .05 .02
□ 188 Mike Krushelnyski .05 .02
□ 189 Tom Fergus .05 .02
□ 190 Whalers Logo (200) .15 .07
FOIL
□ 191 Sylvain Turgeon .05 .02
□ 192 Sylvain Turgeon .05 .02
□ 193 Mark Johnson .05 .02
□ 194 Greg Malone .05 .02
□ 195 Mike Zuke .05 .02
□ 196 Ron Francis 1.00 .45
□ 197 Bob Crawford .05 .02
□ 198 Greg Millen .25 .11
□ 199 Ray Neufeld .05 .02
□ 200 Sabres Logo (190) .15 .07
FOIL
□ 201 Gilbert Perreault .25 .11
□ 202 Gilbert Perreault .25 .11
□ 203 Phil Housley .50 .23
□ 204 Phil Housley .50 .23
□ 205 Tom Barrasso .75 .35
□ 206 Tom Barrasso .75 .35
□ 207 Larry Playfair .05 .02
□ 208 Bob Sauve .25 .11
□ 209 Dave Andreychuk 1.00 .45
□ 210 Dave Andreychuk 1.00 .45
□ 211 Mike Ramsey .05 .02
□ 212 Mike Foligno .05 .02
□ 213 Lindy Ruff .05 .02
□ 214 Bill Hajt .05 .02
□ 215 Craig Ramsay .05 .02
□ 216 Ric Seiling .05 .02
□ 217 Hart Trophy (224) .15 .07
FOIL
□ 218 Vezina Trophy (223) .15 .07
FOIL
□ 219 Jennings Trophy (221) .15 .07
FOIL
□ 220 Calder Trophy (225) .15 .07
FOIL
□ 221 Art Ross Trophy (219) .15 .07
FOIL
□ 222 Norris Trophy (283) .15 .07
FOIL
□ 223 Masterton Trophy .15 .07
(218) FOIL
□ 224 Selke Trophy (217) .15 .07
FOIL
□ 225 Lady Byng Trophy(220) .15 .07
FOIL
□ 226 Wayne Gretzky (227) 4.00 1.80
□ 227 Tom Barrasso (226) 4.00 1.80
□ 228 Tom Barrasso (229) 4.00 1.80
□ 229 Wayne Gretzky (228) 4.00 1.80
□ 230 Rod Langway (231) .25 .11
□ 231 Brad Park (230) .25 .11
□ 232 Al Jensen (233) .25 .11
□ 233 Pat Riggin (232) .25 .11
□ 234 Doug Jarvis (235) .25 .11
□ 235 Mike Bossy (234) .25 .11
□ 236 Flames Logo (246) .15 .07
FOIL
□ 237 Lanny McDonald .25 .11
□ 238 Lanny McDonald .25 .11
□ 239 Steve Tambellini .05 .02
□ 240 Rejean Lemelin .25 .11
□ 241 Doug Risebrough .05 .02
□ 242 Hakan Loob .25 .11
□ 243 Ed Beers .05 .02
□ 244 Mike Eaves .05 .02
□ 245 Kent Nilsson .05 .02
□ 246 Oilers Logo (236) .15 .07
FOIL
□ 247 Glenn Anderson .25 .11
□ 248 Glenn Anderson .25 .11
□ 249 Jari Kurri .50 .23
□ 250 Jari Kurri .50 .23
□ 251 Paul Coffey .75 .35
□ 252 Paul Coffey .75 .35
□ 253 Kevin Lowe .25 .11
□ 254 Lee Fogolin .05 .02
□ 255 Wayne Gretzky 4.00 1.80
□ 256 Wayne Gretzky 4.00 1.80
□ 257 Randy Gregg .05 .02
□ 258 Charlie Huddy .05 .02
□ 259 Grant Fuhr .50 .23
□ 260 Willy Lindstrom .05 .02
□ 261 Mark Messier 1.25 .55
□ 262 Andy Moog .50 .23
□ 263 Kings Logo (273) .15 .07
FOIL
□ 264 Marcel Dionne .25 .11
□ 265 Marcel Dionne .25 .11
□ 266 Charlie Simmer .05 .02
□ 267 Dave Taylor .05 .02
□ 268 Jim Fox .05 .02
□ 269 Bernie Nicholls .50 .23
□ 270 Terry Ruskowski .05 .02
□ 271 Brian Engblom .05 .02
□ 272 Mark Hardy .05 .02
□ 273 Canucks Logo (263) .15 .07
FOIL
□ 274 Tony Tanti .05 .02
□ 275 Tony Tanti .05 .02
□ 276 Rick Lanz .05 .02
□ 277 Richard Brodeur .25 .11
□ 278 Doug Halward .05 .02
□ 279 Patrik Sundstrom .25 .11
□ 280 Darcy Rota .05 .02
□ 281 Stan Smyl .05 .02
□ 282 Thomas Gradin .05 .02
□ 283 Jets Logo (222) .15 .07
FOIL
□ 284 Dale Hawerchuk .50 .23
□ 285 Dale Hawerchuk .50 .23
□ 286 Scott Arniel .05 .02
□ 287 Dave Babych .05 .02
□ 288 Laurie Boschman .05 .02
□ 289 Paul MacLean .05 .02
□ 290 Lucien DeBlois .05 .02
□ 291 Randy Carlyle .05 .02
□ 292 Thomas Steen .05 .02
□ xx Sticker Album 5.00 2.20

## 1985-86 O-Pee-Chee

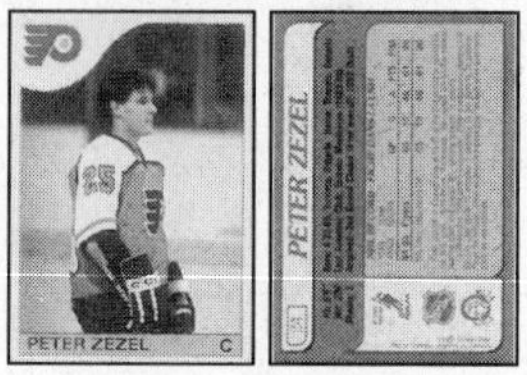

The 1985-86 O-Pee-Chee set contains 264 standard-size cards. The fronts have player name and position at the bottom with team logo at the top right or left. Bilingual backs contain yearly and career stats and highlights. The key Rookie Card in this set is Mario Lemieux. Other rookies include Kevin Dineen, Dave Ellett, Kelly Hrudey, Al Iafrate, Al MacInnis, Kirk Muller, Tomas Sandstrom and Peter Zezel. Printed later than Topps, O-Pee-Chee was able to issue a Memorial card of the late Pelle Lindbergh. Beware when purchasing the Rookie Card of Mario Lemieux as it has been counterfeited.

| | MINT | NRMT |
|---|---|---|
| COMPLETE SET (264) | 500.00 | 220.00 |
| COMMON CARD (1-264) | .40 | .18 |

□ 1 Lanny McDonald 1.50 .70
□ 2 Mike O'Connell .40 .18
□ 3 Curt Fraser .40 .18
□ 4 Steve Penney .40 .18
□ 5 Brian Engblom .40 .18
□ 6 Ron Sutter .40 .18
□ 7 Joe Mullen 1.50 .70
□ 8 Rod Langway .75 .35
□ 9 Mario Lemieux 300.00 135.00
□ 10 Dave Babych .40 .18
□ 11 Bob Nystrom .40 .18
□ 12 Andy Moog 4.00 1.80
□ 13 Dino Ciccarelli 1.50 .70
□ 14 Dwight Foster .40 .18
□ 15 James Patrick .40 .18
□ 16 Thomas Gradin .40 .18
□ 17 Mike Foligno .75 .35
□ 18 Mario Gosselin .40 .18
□ 19 Mike Zuke .40 .18
□ 20 John Anderson .40 .18
□ 21 Dave Pichette .40 .18
□ 22 Nick Fotiu .75 .35
□ 23 Tom Lysiak .40 .18
□ 24 Peter Zezel 1.50 .70
□ 25 Denis Potvin .75 .35
□ 26 Bob Carpenter .40 .18
□ 27 Murray Bannerman .75 .35
□ 28 Gordie Roberts .40 .18
□ 29 Steve Yzerman 40.00 18.00
□ 30 Phil Russell .40 .18
□ 31 Peter Stastny 1.50 .70
□ 32 Craig Ramsay .40 .18
□ 33 Terry Ruskowski .40 .18
□ 34 Kevin Dineen 4.00 1.80
□ 35 Mark Howe .75 .35
□ 36 Glenn Resch .75 .35
□ 37 Danny Gare .75 .35
□ 38 Doug Bodger .75 .35
□ 39 Mike Rogers .40 .18
□ 40 Ray Bourque 6.00 2.70
□ 41 John Tonelli .75 .35
□ 42 Mel Bridgman .40 .18
□ 43 Sylvain Turgeon .75 .35
□ 44 Mark Johnson .40 .18
□ 45 Doug Wilson .75 .35
□ 46 Mike Gartner 3.00 1.35
□ 47 Brent Peterson .40 .18
□ 48 Paul Reinhart .40 .18
□ 49 Mike Krushelnyski .75 .35
□ 50 Brian Bellows 1.50 .70
□ 51 Chris Chelios 8.00 3.60
□ 52 Barry Pederson .40 .18
□ 53 Murray Craven .40 .18
□ 54 Pierre Larouche .75 .35
□ 55 Reed Larson .40 .18
□ 56 Pat Verbeek 1.50 .70
□ 57 Randy Carlyle .40 .18
□ 58 Ray Neufeld .40 .18
□ 59 Keith Brown .40 .18
□ 60 Bryan Trottier 1.50 .70
□ 61 Jim Fox .40 .18
□ 62 Scott Stevens 2.50 1.10
□ 63 Phil Housley 1.50 .70
□ 64 Rick Middleton .75 .35
□ 65 Steve Payne .40 .18
□ 66 Dave Lewis .40 .18
□ 67 Mike Bullard .40 .18
□ 68 Stan Smyl .40 .18
□ 69 Mark Pavelich .40 .18
□ 70 John Ogrodnick .40 .18
□ 71 Bill Derlago .40 .18
□ 72 Brad Marsh .40 .18
□ 73 Denis Savard 1.50 .70
□ 74 Mark Fusco .40 .18
□ 75 Pete Peeters .75 .35
□ 76 Doug Gilmour 10.00 4.50
□ 77 Mike Ramsey .40 .18
□ 78 Anton Stastny .75 .35
□ 79 Steve Kasper .40 .18
□ 80 Bryan Erickson .40 .18
□ 81 Clark Gillies .75 .35
□ 82 Keith Acton .40 .18
□ 83 Pat Flatley .40 .18
□ 84 Kirk Muller 4.00 1.80
□ 85 Paul Coffey 6.00 2.70
□ 86 Ed Olczyk .75 .35
□ 87 Charlie Simmer .75 .35
□ 88 Mike Liut .75 .35
□ 89 Dave Maloney .40 .18
□ 90 Marcel Dionne .75 .35
□ 91 Tim Kerr .75 .35
□ 92 Ivan Boldirev .40 .18
□ 93 Ken Morrow .40 .18
□ 94 Don Maloney .40 .18
□ 95 Rejean Lemelin .75 .35
□ 96 Curt Giles .40 .18
□ 97 Bob Bourne .40 .18
□ 98 Joe Cirella .40 .18
□ 99 Dave Christian .40 .18
□ 100 Darryl Sutter .40 .18
□ 101 Kelly Kisio .75 .35
□ 102 Mats Naslund .75 .35
□ 103 Joel Quenneville .40 .18
□ 104 Bernie Federko .75 .35
□ 105 Tom Barrasso 1.50 .70
□ 106 Rick Vaive .40 .18
□ 107 Brent Sutter .40 .18
□ 108 Wayne Babych .40 .18
□ 109 Dale Hawerchuk 3.00 1.35
□ 110 Pelle Lindbergh 12.00 5.50
(Memorial)
□ 111 Dennis Maruk .75 .35
□ 112 Reijo Ruotsalainen .40 .18
□ 113 Tom Fergus .40 .18
□ 114 Bob Murray .40 .18
□ 115 Patrik Sundstrom .40 .18
□ 116 Ron Duguay .40 .18
□ 117 Alan Haworth .40 .18
□ 118 Greg Malone .40 .18
□ 119 Bill Hajt .40 .18
□ 120 Wayne Gretzky 30.00 13.50
□ 121 Craig Redmond .40 .18
□ 122 Kelly Hrudey 5.00 2.20
□ 123 Tomas Sandstrom 5.00 2.20
□ 124 Neal Broten .75 .35
□ 125 Moe Mantha .40 .18
□ 126 Greg Gilbert .40 .18
□ 127 Bruce Driver 1.50 .70
□ 128 Dave Poulin .40 .18
□ 129 Morris Lukowich .40 .18
□ 130 Mike Bossy 1.50 .70
□ 131 Larry Playfair .40 .18
□ 132 Steve Larmer 1.50 .70
□ 133 Doug Keans .40 .18
□ 134 Bob Manno .40 .18
□ 135 Brian Sutter .75 .35
□ 136 Pat Riggin .75 .35
□ 137 Pat LaFontaine 5.00 2.20
□ 138 Barry Beck .40 .18
□ 139 Rich Preston .40 .18
□ 140 Ron Francis 4.00 1.80
□ 141 Brian Propp .75 .35
□ 142 Don Beaupre .75 .35
□ 143 Dave Andreychuk 1.50 .70
□ 144 Ed Beers .40 .18
□ 145 Paul MacLean .40 .18
□ 146 Troy Murray .40 .18
□ 147 Larry Robinson .75 .35
□ 148 Bernie Nicholls 1.50 .70
□ 149 Glen Hanlon .75 .35
□ 150 Michel Goulet 1.50 .70
□ 151 Doug Jarvis .40 .18
□ 152 Warren Young .40 .18
□ 153 Tony Tanti .40 .18
□ 154 Tomas Jonsson .40 .18
□ 155 Jari Kurri 4.00 1.80
□ 156 Tony McKegney .40 .18
□ 157 Greg Stefan .75 .35
□ 158 Brad McCrimmon .75 .35
□ 159 Keith Crowder .40 .18
□ 160 Gilbert Perreault .75 .35
□ 161 Tim Bothwell .40 .18
□ 162 Bob Crawford .40 .18
□ 163 Paul Gagne .40 .18
□ 164 Dan Daoust .40 .18
□ 165 Checklist 1-132 4.00 1.80
□ 166 Tim Bernhardt .40 .18
□ 167 Gord Kluzak .40 .18
□ 168 Glenn Anderson 1.50 .70
□ 169 Bob Gainey 1.50 .70
□ 170 Brent Ashton .40 .18
□ 171 Ron Flockhart .40 .18
□ 172 Gary Nylund .40 .18
□ 173 Moe Lemay .40 .18
□ 174 Bob Sauve .75 .35
□ 175 Doug Smail .40 .18
□ 176 Dan Quinn .40 .18
□ 177 Mark Messier 10.00 4.50
□ 178 Jay Wells .75 .35
□ 179 Dale Hunter .75 .35
□ 180 Richard Brodeur .75 .35
□ 181 Bobby Smith .75 .35
□ 182 Ron Greschner .40 .18
□ 183 Don Edwards .40 .18
□ 184 Hakan Loob .75 .35
□ 185 Dave Ellett .75 .35
□ 186 Denis Herron .40 .18
□ 187 Charlie Huddy .75 .35
□ 188 Ilkka Sinisalo .40 .18
□ 189 Doug Halward .40 .18
□ 190 Craig Laughlin .40 .18
□ 191 Carey Wilson .40 .18
□ 192 Craig Ludwig .40 .18
□ 193 Bob MacMillan .40 .18
□ 194 Mario Marois .40 .18
□ 195 Brian Mullen .40 .18
□ 196 Rob Ramage .40 .18
□ 197 Rick Lanz .40 .18
□ 198 Miroslav Frycer .40 .18
□ 199 Randy Gregg .40 .18
□ 200 Corrado Micalef .40 .18
□ 201 Jamie Macoun .40 .18
□ 202 Bob Brooke .40 .18
□ 203 Billy Carroll .40 .18
□ 204 Brian MacLellan .40 .18
□ 205 Alain Cote .40 .18
□ 206 Thomas Steen .40 .18
□ 207 Grant Fuhr 4.00 1.80
□ 208 Rich Sutter .40 .18
□ 209 Al MacAdam .40 .18
□ 210 Al Iafrate 6.00 2.70
□ 211 Pierre Mondou .40 .18
□ 212 Randy Hillier .40 .18
□ 213 Mike Eaves .40 .18
□ 214 Dave Taylor .75 .35
□ 215 Robert Picard .40 .18
□ 216 Randy Ladouceur .40 .18
□ 217 Willy Lindstrom .40 .18
□ 218 Torrie Robertson .40 .18
□ 219 Tom Kurvers .75 .35
□ 220 John Garrett .40 .18
□ 221 Greg Millen .75 .35
□ 222 Richard Kromm .40 .18
□ 223 Bob Janecyk .75 .35
□ 224 Brad Maxwell .40 .18
□ 225 Mike McPhee 1.50 .70
□ 226 Brian Hayward 1.50 .70
□ 227 Duane Sutter .40 .18
□ 228 Cam Neely 10.00 4.50
□ 229 Doug Wickenheiser .40 .18
□ 230 Rollie Melanson .75 .35
□ 231 Bruce Bell .40 .18
□ 232 Harold Snepsts .40 .18
□ 233 Guy Carbonneau 1.50 .70
□ 234 Doug Sulliman .40 .18
□ 235 Lee Fogolin .40 .18
□ 236 Larry Murphy 1.50 .70
□ 237 Al MacInnis 25.00 11.00
□ 238 Don Lever .40 .18
□ 239 Kevin Lowe .75 .35
□ 240 Randy Moller .40 .18
□ 241 Doug Lidster .75 .35
□ 242 Craig Hartsburg .40 .18
□ 243 Doug Risebrough .40 .18
□ 244 John Chabot .40 .18
□ 245 Mario Tremblay .40 .18
□ 246 Dan Bouchard .75 .35
□ 247 Doug Shedden .40 .18
□ 248 Borje Salming .75 .35
□ 249 Aaron Broten .40 .18
□ 250 Jim Benning .40 .18
□ 251 Laurie Boschman .40 .18
□ 252 George McPhee .40 .18
□ 253 Mark Napier .40 .18
□ 254 Perry Turnbull .40 .18
□ 255 Warren Skorodenski .75 .35
□ 256 Checklist 133-264 4.00 1.80
□ 257 Wayne Gretzky 7.00 3.10
(Goals Leaders)
□ 258 Wayne Gretzky 7.00 3.10
(Assists Leaders)
□ 259 Wayne Gretzky 7.00 3.10
(Scoring Leaders)
□ 260 Tim Kerr .75 .35
(Power Play Goals Leaders)
□ 261 Jari Kurri 1.50 .70
(Game Winning Goals Leaders)
□ 262 Mario Lemieux 40.00 18.00
(Rookie Scoring Leaders)
□ 263 Tom Barrasso .75 .35
(Goals Against Average Leaders)
□ 264 Warren Skorodenski .75 .35
(Save Percentage Leaders)

## 1985-86 O-Pee-Chee Box Bottoms

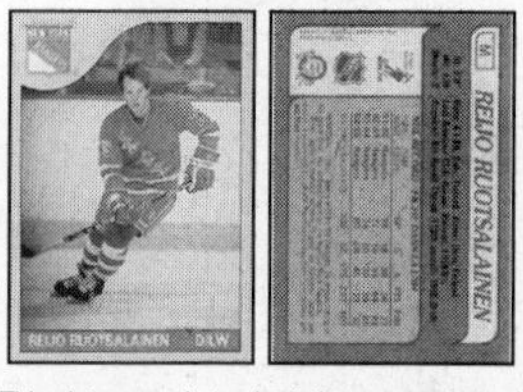

This sixteen-card standard-size set was issued in sets of four on the bottom of the 1985-86 O-Pee-Chee wax pack boxes. Complete box bottom panels are valued at a 25 percent premium above the prices listed below. The card back includes statistical information, is written in English and French. The cards are lettered rather than numbered. The key card in the set is obviously Mario Lemieux, pictured in his rookie year for cards.

| | MINT | NRMT |
|---|---|---|
| COMPLETE SET (16) | 100.00 | 45.00 |
| COMMON CARD (A-P) | .50 | .23 |

□ A Brian Bellows .75 .35

| | | |
|---|---|---|
| ❑ B Ray Bourque | 3.00 | 1.35 |
| ❑ C Bob Carpenter | .50 | .23 |
| ❑ D Chris Chelios | 5.00 | 2.20 |
| ❑ E Marcel Dionne | 2.00 | .90 |
| ❑ F Ron Francis | 3.00 | 1.35 |
| ❑ G Wayne Gretzky | 30.00 | 13.50 |
| ❑ H Tim Kerr | .50 | .23 |
| ❑ I Mario Lemieux | 75.00 | 34.00 |
| ❑ J John Ogrodnick | .50 | .23 |
| ❑ K Gilbert Perreault | 1.00 | .45 |
| ❑ L Glenn Resch | 1.00 | .45 |
| ❑ M Reijo Ruotsalainen | .50 | .23 |
| ❑ N Brian Sutter | .75 | .35 |
| ❑ O John Tonelli | .50 | .23 |
| ❑ P Doug Wilson | .75 | .35 |

## 1985-86 O-Pee-Chee Stickers

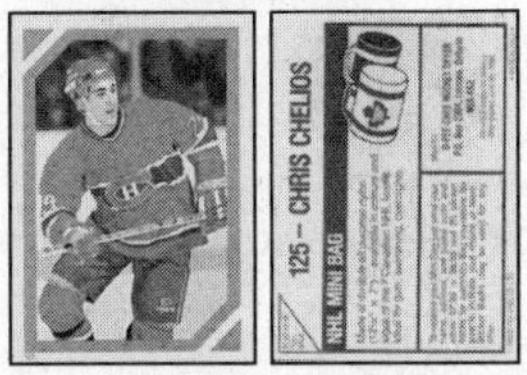


This sticker set consists of 255 stickers in full color and was put out by O-Pee-Chee. The foil stickers are listed in the checklist below explicitly. The stickers measure approximately 2 1/8" by 3". An album is available for these stickers. Those stickers which are pairs are indicated in the checklist below by noting parenthetically the other member of the pair. On the inside back cover of the sticker album the company offered (via direct mail-order) any ten different stickers of your choice for one dollar; this is one reason why the values of the most popular players in these sticker sets are somewhat depressed compared to traditional card set prices. For example, anyone wanting Mario Lemieux, Wayne Gretzky, and eight others could get them for one dollar directly through this offer.

| | MINT | NRMT |
|---|---|---|
| COMPLETE SET (255) | 40.00 | 18.00 |
| COMMON STICKER (1-255) | .10 | .05 |
| COMMON HALF CARD | .05 | .02 |
| COMMON FOILS | .15 | .07 |
| COMMON HALF FOILS | .10 | .05 |

| | | |
|---|---|---|
| ❑ 1 Stanley Cup Finals | .25 | .11 |
| ❑ 2 Stanley Cup Finals | .10 | .05 |
| ❑ 3 Stanley Cup Finals | .10 | .05 |
| ❑ 4 Stanley Cup Finals | .10 | .05 |
| ❑ 5 Wayne Gretzky | 5.00 | 2.20 |
| ❑ 6 Rick Vaive | .10 | .05 |
| ❑ 7 Bill Derlago | .10 | .05 |
| ❑ 8 Rick St. Croix (136) | .05 | .02 |
| ❑ 9 Tim Bernhardt (137) | .05 | .02 |
| ❑ 10 John Anderson (138) | .05 | .02 |
| ❑ 11 Dan Daoust (139) | .05 | .02 |
| ❑ 12 Borje Salming | .10 | .05 |
| ❑ 13 Al Iafrate (143) | .50 | .23 |
| ❑ 14 Gary Nylund (144) | .05 | .02 |
| ❑ 15 Bob McGill (145) | .05 | .02 |
| ❑ 16 Jim Benning (146) | .25 | .11 |
| ❑ 17 Stewart Gavin (148) | .05 | .02 |
| ❑ 18 Greg Terrion (149) | .05 | .02 |
| ❑ 19 Peter Ihnacak (150) | .05 | .02 |
| ❑ 20 Russ Courtnall (151) | .50 | .23 |
| ❑ 21 Miroslav Frycer | .10 | .05 |
| ❑ 22 Denis Savard | .25 | .11 |
| ❑ 23 Steve Yzerman (152) | 2.00 | .90 |
| ❑ 24 Curt Fraser (153) | .05 | .02 |
| ❑ 25 Doug Wilson | .10 | .05 |
| ❑ 26 Ed Olczyk (154) | .25 | .11 |
| ❑ 27 Murray Bannerman (155) | .05 | .02 |
| ❑ 28 Steve Larmer (158) | .25 | .11 |
| ❑ 29 Troy Murray (159) | .10 | .05 |
| ❑ 30 Steve Yzerman | 3.00 | 1.35 |
| ❑ 31 Greg Stefan (161) | .05 | .02 |
| ❑ 32 Ron Duguay (162) | .05 | .02 |
| ❑ 33 Reed Larson (163) | .05 | .02 |
| ❑ 34 Ivan Boldirev (164) | .05 | .02 |
| ❑ 35 Danny Gare (166) | .05 | .02 |
| ❑ 36 Darryl Sittler (167) | .10 | .05 |
| ❑ 37 John Ogrodnick | .10 | .05 |
| ❑ 38 Keith Acton | .10 | .05 |
| ❑ 39 Dino Ciccarelli (168) | .25 | .11 |
| ❑ 40 Neal Broten (169) | .25 | .11 |
| ❑ 41 Brian Bellows | .25 | .11 |
| ❑ 42 Steve Payne (170) | .05 | .02 |
| ❑ 43 Gordie Roberts (171) | .05 | .02 |
| ❑ 44 Harold Snepsts (175) | .10 | .05 |
| ❑ 45 Tony McKegney (176) | .05 | .02 |
| ❑ 46 Brian Sutter | .10 | .05 |
| ❑ 47 Joe Mullen (177) | .25 | .11 |
| ❑ 48 Doug Gilmour (178) | 1.00 | .45 |
| ❑ 49 Tim Bothwell (180) | .05 | .02 |
| ❑ 50 Mark Johnson (181) | .05 | .02 |
| ❑ 51 Greg Millen (182) | .05 | .02 |
| ❑ 52 Doug Wickenheiser (183) | .05 | .02 |
| ❑ 53 Bernie Federko | .10 | .05 |
| ❑ 54 Wayne Gretzky (197) FOIL | 4.00 | 1.80 |
| ❑ 55 Tom Barrasso (203) FOIL | .25 | .11 |
| ❑ 56 Paul Coffey (204) FOIL | .50 | .23 |
| ❑ 57 Mel Bridgman | .10 | .05 |
| ❑ 58 Phil Russell (184) | .05 | .02 |
| ❑ 59 Dave Lewis (185) | .05 | .02 |
| ❑ 60 Paul Gagne (186) | .05 | .02 |
| ❑ 61 Glenn Resch (187) | .25 | .11 |
| ❑ 62 Aaron Broten (189) | .25 | .11 |
| ❑ 63 Dave Pichette (190) | .05 | .02 |
| ❑ 64 Kirk Muller | 1.00 | .45 |
| ❑ 65 Bryan Trottier | .25 | .11 |
| ❑ 66 Mike Bossy | .25 | .11 |
| ❑ 67 Bob Bourne (191) | .25 | .11 |
| ❑ 68 Clark Gillies (192) | .10 | .05 |
| ❑ 69 Bob Nystrom (193) | 2.00 | .90 |
| ❑ 70 Denis Potvin (198) | 4.00 | 1.80 |
| ❑ 71 Brent Sutter | 7.50 | 3.40 |
| ❑ 72 Duane Sutter (199) | .10 | .05 |
| ❑ 73 Pat Flatley (200) | .10 | .05 |
| ❑ 74 Pat LaFontaine (201) | 1.00 | .45 |
| ❑ 75 Greg Gilbert (202) | 4.00 | 1.80 |
| ❑ 76 Billy Smith (209) | .25 | .11 |
| ❑ 77 Gordie Lane (210) | .05 | .02 |
| ❑ 78 Tomas Jonsson (211) | .05 | .02 |
| ❑ 79 Kelly Hrudey (212) | .75 | .35 |
| ❑ 80 John Tonelli | .10 | .05 |
| ❑ 81 Reijo Ruotsalainen | .10 | .05 |
| ❑ 82 Barry Beck (213) | .10 | .05 |
| ❑ 83 James Patrick (214) | .25 | .11 |
| ❑ 84 Mark Pavelich | .10 | .05 |
| ❑ 85 Pierre Larouche | .05 | .02 |
| ❑ 86 Mike Rogers (219) | .25 | .11 |
| ❑ 87 Glen Hanlon (220) | .25 | .11 |
| ❑ 88 John Vanbiesbrouck (221) | 3.00 | 1.35 |
| ❑ 89 Dave Poulin | .10 | .05 |
| ❑ 90 Brian Propp (223) | .10 | .05 |
| ❑ 91 Pelle Lindbergh (224) | 2.00 | .90 |
| ❑ 92 Brad McCrimmon (225) | .10 | .05 |
| ❑ 93 Mark Howe (226) | .25 | .11 |
| ❑ 94 Peter Zezel (227) | .25 | .11 |
| ❑ 95 Murray Craven (228) | .50 | .23 |
| ❑ 96 Tim Kerr | .10 | .05 |
| ❑ 97 Mario Lemieux | 15.00 | 6.75 |
| ❑ 98 Moe Mantha (229) | .05 | .02 |
| ❑ 99 Doug Bodger (230) | .05 | .02 |
| ❑ 100 Warren Young | .10 | .05 |
| ❑ 101 John Chabot (233) | .05 | .02 |
| ❑ 102 Doug Shedden (234) | .05 | .02 |
| ❑ 103 Wayne Babych (236) | .05 | .02 |
| ❑ 104 Mike Bullard (237) | .05 | .02 |
| ❑ 105 Rod Langway | .10 | .05 |
| ❑ 106 Pat Riggin (238) | .10 | .05 |
| ❑ 107 Scott Stevens (239) | .25 | .11 |
| ❑ 108 Alan Haworth (241) | .05 | .02 |
| ❑ 109 Doug Jarvis (242) | .05 | .02 |
| ❑ 110 Dave Christian (243) | .05 | .02 |
| ❑ 111 Mike Gartner (244) | .25 | .11 |
| ❑ 112 Bob Carpenter | .10 | .05 |
| ❑ 113 Rod Langway FOIL | .15 | .07 |
| ❑ 114 Tom Barrasso FOIL | .25 | .11 |
| ❑ 115 Ray Bourque FOIL | 1.00 | .45 |
| ❑ 116 John Tonelli FOIL | .15 | .07 |
| ❑ 117 Brent Sutter FOIL | .15 | .07 |
| ❑ 118 Mike Bossy FOIL | .50 | .23 |
| ❑ 119 John Ogrodnick FOIL | .15 | .07 |
| ❑ 120 Wayne Gretzky FOIL | 5.00 | 2.20 |
| ❑ 121 Jari Kurri FOIL | .75 | .35 |
| ❑ 122 Doug Wilson FOIL | .15 | .07 |
| ❑ 123 Andy Moog FOIL | .50 | .23 |
| ❑ 124 Paul Coffey FOIL | 1.00 | .45 |
| ❑ 125 Chris Chelios | 1.00 | .45 |
| ❑ 126 Steve Penney | .10 | .05 |
| ❑ 127 Chris Nilan (245) | .10 | .05 |
| ❑ 128 Ron Flockhart (246) | .05 | .02 |
| ❑ 129 Tom Kurvers (249) | .05 | .02 |
| ❑ 130 Craig Ludwig (250) | .05 | .02 |
| ❑ 131 Mats Naslund | .10 | .05 |
| ❑ 132 Bobby Smith (252) | .10 | .05 |
| ❑ 133 Pierre Mondou (253) | .05 | .02 |
| ❑ 134 Mario Tremblay (254) | .05 | .02 |
| ❑ 135 Guy Carbonneau (255) | .25 | .11 |
| ❑ 136 Doug Soetaert (8) | .05 | .02 |
| ❑ 137 Mark Hunter (9) | .05 | .02 |
| ❑ 138 Bob Gainey (10) | .05 | .02 |
| ❑ 139 Petr Svoboda (11) | .25 | .11 |
| ❑ 140 Larry Robinson | .25 | .11 |
| ❑ 141 Michel Goulet | .25 | .11 |
| ❑ 142 Bruce Bell | .10 | .05 |
| ❑ 143 Dan Bouchard (13) | .50 | .23 |
| ❑ 144 Mario Marois (14) | .05 | .02 |
| ❑ 145 Randy Moller (15) | .05 | .02 |
| ❑ 146 Mario Gosselin (16) | .25 | .11 |
| ❑ 147 Anton Stastny | .10 | .05 |
| ❑ 148 Normand Rochefort(17) | .05 | .02 |
| ❑ 149 Alain Cote (18) | .05 | .02 |
| ❑ 150 Paul Gillis (19) | .05 | .02 |
| ❑ 151 Dale Hunter (20) | .50 | .23 |
| ❑ 152 Wilf Paiement (23) | .05 | .02 |
| ❑ 153 Brent Ashton (24) | .05 | .02 |
| ❑ 154 Brad Maxwell (26) | .25 | .11 |
| ❑ 155 J.F. Sauve (27) | .05 | .02 |
| ❑ 156 Peter Stastny | .25 | .11 |
| ❑ 157 Ray Bourque | .50 | .23 |
| ❑ 158 Charlie Simmer (28) | .25 | .11 |
| ❑ 159 Rick Middleton (29) | .10 | .05 |
| ❑ 160 Pete Peeters | .10 | .05 |
| ❑ 161 Mike O'Connell (31) | .05 | .02 |
| ❑ 162 Terry O'Reilly (32) | .10 | .05 |
| ❑ 163 Keith Crowder (33) | .05 | .02 |
| ❑ 164 Tom Fergus (34) | .05 | .02 |
| ❑ 165 Sylvain Turgeon | .10 | .05 |
| ❑ 166 Greg Malone (35) | .05 | .02 |
| ❑ 167 Bob Crawford (36) | .05 | .02 |
| ❑ 168 Kevin Dineen (39) | .25 | .11 |
| ❑ 169 Mike Liut (40) | .25 | .11 |
| ❑ 170 Joel Quenneville (42) | .05 | .02 |
| ❑ 171 Ray Neufeld (43) | .05 | .02 |
| ❑ 172 Ron Francis | .50 | .23 |
| ❑ 173 Phil Housley | .25 | .11 |
| ❑ 174 Mike Foligno | .10 | .05 |
| ❑ 175 Craig Ramsay (44) | .05 | .02 |
| ❑ 176 Bill Hajt (45) | .05 | .02 |
| ❑ 177 Dave Maloney (47) | .25 | .11 |
| ❑ 178 Brent Peterson (48) | .05 | .02 |
| ❑ 179 Tom Barrasso | .25 | .11 |
| ❑ 180 Mike Ramsey (49) | .05 | .02 |
| ❑ 181 Bob Sauve (50) | .05 | .02 |
| ❑ 182 Ric Seiling (51) | .05 | .02 |
| ❑ 183 Paul Cyr (52) | .05 | .02 |
| ❑ 184 John Tucker (58) | .05 | .02 |
| ❑ 185 Gilles Hamel (59) | .05 | .02 |
| ❑ 186 Malcolm Davis (60) | .05 | .02 |
| ❑ 187 Dave Andreychuk (61) | .25 | .11 |
| ❑ 188 Gilbert Perreault | .25 | .11 |
| ❑ 189 Tom Barrasso (62) | .25 | .11 |
| ❑ 190 Bob Sauve (63) | .05 | .02 |
| ❑ 191 Paul Coffey (67) | .25 | .11 |
| ❑ 192 Craig Ramsay (68) | .05 | .02 |
| ❑ 193 Pelle Lindbergh (69) | 2.00 | .90 |
| ❑ 194 Jennings Trophy (205) FOIL | .10 | .05 |
| ❑ 195 Norris Trophy (206) FOIL | .10 | .05 |
| ❑ 196 Selke Trophy (207) FOIL | .10 | .05 |
| ❑ 197 Vezina Trophy (54) FOIL | 4.00 | 1.80 |
| ❑ 198 Wayne Gretzky (70) | 4.00 | 1.80 |
| ❑ 199 Mario Lemieux (72) | 7.50 | 3.40 |
| ❑ 200 Anders Hedberg (73) | .10 | .05 |
| ❑ 201 Jari Kurri (74) | 1.00 | .45 |
| ❑ 202 Wayne Gretzky (75) | 4.00 | 1.80 |
| ❑ 203 Hart Trophy (55) FOIL | .25 | .11 |
| ❑ 204 Calder Trophy (56) FOIL | .50 | .23 |
| ❑ 205 Masterton Trophy(194) FOIL | .10 | .05 |
| ❑ 206 Lady Byng Trophy(195) FOIL | .10 | .05 |
| ❑ 207 Art Ross Trophy (207) FOIL | .10 | .05 |
| ❑ 208 Kent Nilsson | 25.00 | 11.00 |
| ❑ 209 Paul Reinhart (76) | .25 | .11 |
| ❑ 210 Rejean Lemelin (77) | .10 | .05 |
| ❑ 211 Al MacInnis (78) | 2.00 | .90 |
| ❑ 212 Jamie Macoun (79) | .10 | .05 |
| ❑ 213 Carey Wilson (82) | .25 | .11 |
| ❑ 214 Ed Beers (83) | .25 | .11 |
| ❑ 215 Lanny McDonald | .25 | .11 |
| ❑ 216 Charlie Huddy | .10 | .05 |
| ❑ 217 Paul Coffey | .50 | .23 |
| ❑ 218 Lee Fogolin (85) | .05 | .02 |
| ❑ 219 Kevin Lowe (86) | .25 | .11 |
| ❑ 220 Andy Moog (87) | .25 | .11 |
| ❑ 221 Grant Fuhr (88) | .25 | .11 |
| ❑ 222 Wayne Gretzky | 5.00 | 2.20 |
| ❑ 223 Mike Krushelnyski(90) | .10 | .05 |
| ❑ 224 Billy Carroll (91) | .05 | .02 |
| ❑ 225 Randy Gregg (92) | .10 | .05 |
| ❑ 226 Willy Lindstrom (93) | .25 | .11 |
| ❑ 227 Glenn Anderson (94) | .25 | .11 |
| ❑ 228 Mark Messier (95) | .50 | .23 |
| ❑ 229 Pat Hughes (98) | .05 | .02 |
| ❑ 230 Kevin McClelland (99) | .05 | .02 |
| ❑ 231 Jari Kurri | .50 | .23 |
| ❑ 232 Bernie Nicholls | .25 | .11 |
| ❑ 233 Brian Engblom (101) | .05 | .02 |
| ❑ 234 Mark Hardy (102) | .05 | .02 |
| ❑ 235 Marcel Dionne | .25 | .11 |
| ❑ 236 Jim Fox (103) | .05 | .02 |
| ❑ 237 Terry Ruskowski (104) | .05 | .02 |
| ❑ 238 Dave Taylor (106) | .10 | .05 |
| ❑ 239 Bob Janecyk (107) | .25 | .11 |
| ❑ 240 Thomas Gradin | .10 | .05 |
| ❑ 241 Patrik Sundstrom(108) | .05 | .02 |
| ❑ 242 Al MacAdam (109) | .05 | .02 |
| ❑ 243 Doug Halward (110) | .05 | .02 |
| ❑ 244 Peter McNab (111) | .05 | .02 |
| ❑ 245 Tony Tanti (127) | .10 | .05 |
| ❑ 246 Moe Lemay (128) | .05 | .02 |
| ❑ 247 Stan Smyl | .10 | .05 |
| ❑ 248 Dale Hawerchuk | .50 | .23 |
| ❑ 249 Dave Babych (129) | .05 | .02 |
| ❑ 250 Paul MacLean (130) | .05 | .02 |
| ❑ 251 Randy Carlyle | .10 | .05 |
| ❑ 252 Robert Picard (132) | .05 | .02 |
| ❑ 253 Thomas Steen (133) | .05 | .02 |
| ❑ 254 Laurie Boschman (134) | .05 | .02 |
| ❑ 255 Doug Smail (135) | .25 | .11 |
| ❑ xx Sticker Album | 5.00 | 2.20 |

## 1986-87 O-Pee-Chee

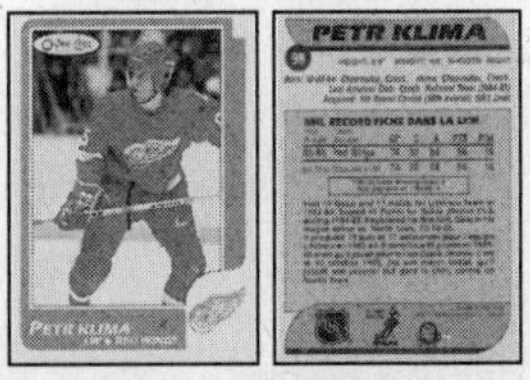


This 1986-87 O-Pee-Chee set consists of 264 standard-size cards. Card fronts feature player name, team, team logo and position at the bottom. Bilingual backs feature yearly and career statistics as well as the number of game-winning goals scored in 1985-86. The key Rookie Card in this set is Patrick Roy. Other Rookie Cards include Wendel Clark, Russ Courtnall, Ray Ferraro, Dirk Graham, John MacLean, Craig MacTavish, Mike Ridley, Gary Suter, Steve Thomas and John Vanbiesbrouck. Beware when purchasing the Wayne Gretzky card from this set as it has been counterfeited.

| | MINT | NRMT |
|---|---|---|
| COMPLETE SET (264) | 350.00 | 160.00 |
| COMMON CARD (1-264) | .25 | .11 |

| | | |
|---|---|---|
| ❑ 1 Ray Bourque | 4.00 | 1.80 |
| ❑ 2 Pat LaFontaine | 3.00 | 1.35 |
| ❑ 3 Wayne Gretzky | 25.00 | 11.00 |
| ❑ 4 Lindy Ruff | .25 | .11 |
| ❑ 5 Brad McCrimmon | .25 | .11 |
| ❑ 6 Dave(Tiger) Williams | .50 | .23 |
| ❑ 7 Denis Savard | 1.25 | .55 |
| ❑ 8 Lanny McDonald | .50 | .23 |
| ❑ 9 John Vanbiesbrouck | 40.00 | 18.00 |
| ❑ 10 Greg Adams | 2.00 | .90 |
| ❑ 11 Steve Yzerman | 20.00 | 9.00 |
| ❑ 12 Craig Hartsburg | .25 | .11 |
| ❑ 13 John Anderson | .25 | .11 |
| ❑ 14 Bob Bourne | .25 | .11 |
| ❑ 15 Kjell Dahlin | .25 | .11 |
| ❑ 16 Dave Andreychuk | 1.25 | .55 |
| ❑ 17 Rob Ramage | .25 | .11 |
| ❑ 18 Ron Greschner | .25 | .11 |
| ❑ 19 Bruce Driver | .50 | .23 |
| ❑ 20 Peter Stastny | .50 | .23 |
| ❑ 21 Dave Christian | .25 | .11 |
| ❑ 22 Doug Keans | .25 | .11 |
| ❑ 23 Scott Bjugstad | .25 | .11 |
| ❑ 24 Doug Bodger | .25 | .11 |
| ❑ 25 Troy Murray | .25 | .11 |
| ❑ 26 Al Iafrate | 1.25 | .55 |
| ❑ 27 Kelly Hrudey | 1.25 | .55 |
| ❑ 28 Doug Jarvis | .25 | .11 |
| ❑ 29 Rich Sutter | .25 | .11 |
| ❑ 30 Marcel Dionne | .50 | .23 |
| ❑ 31 Curt Fraser | .25 | .11 |
| ❑ 32 Doug Lidster | .25 | .11 |
| ❑ 33 Brian MacLellan | .25 | .11 |
| ❑ 34 Barry Pederson | .25 | .11 |
| ❑ 35 Craig Laughlin | .25 | .11 |
| ❑ 36 Ilkka Sinisalo | .25 | .11 |
| ❑ 37 John MacLean | 4.00 | 1.80 |
| ❑ 38 Brian Mullen | .25 | .11 |
| ❑ 39 Duane Sutter | .25 | .11 |
| ❑ 40 Brian Engblom | .25 | .11 |
| ❑ 41 Chris Cichocki | .25 | .11 |
| ❑ 42 Gordie Roberts | .25 | .11 |
| ❑ 43 Ron Francis | 2.50 | 1.10 |
| ❑ 44 Joe Mullen | 1.25 | .55 |
| ❑ 45 Moe Mantha | .25 | .11 |
| ❑ 46 Pat Verbeek | 1.25 | .55 |
| ❑ 47 Clint Malarchuk | 1.25 | .55 |
| ❑ 48 Bob Brooke | .25 | .11 |
| ❑ 49 Darryl Sutter | .25 | .11 |
| ❑ 50 Stan Smyl | .25 | .11 |
| ❑ 51 Greg Stefan | .50 | .23 |
| ❑ 52 Bill Hajt | .25 | .11 |
| ❑ 53 Patrick Roy | 200.00 | 90.00 |
| ❑ 54 Gord Kluzak | .25 | .11 |
| ❑ 55 Bob Froese | .50 | .23 |
| ❑ 56 Grant Fuhr | 2.50 | 1.10 |
| ❑ 57 Mark Hunter | .25 | .11 |
| ❑ 58 Dana Murzyn | .25 | .11 |
| ❑ 59 Mike Gartner | 1.25 | .55 |
| ❑ 60 Dennis Maruk | .25 | .11 |
| ❑ 61 Rich Preston | .25 | .11 |
| ❑ 62 Larry Robinson | .50 | .23 |
| ❑ 63 Dave Taylor | .50 | .23 |
| ❑ 64 Bob Murray | .25 | .11 |
| ❑ 65 Ken Morrow | .25 | .11 |
| ❑ 66 Mike Ridley | 1.25 | .55 |
| ❑ 67 John Tucker | .50 | .23 |
| ❑ 68 Miroslav Frycer | .25 | .11 |
| ❑ 69 Danny Gare | .50 | .23 |
| ❑ 70 Randy Burridge | 1.25 | .55 |
| ❑ 71 Dave Poulin | .25 | .11 |
| ❑ 72 Brian Sutter | .50 | .23 |
| ❑ 73 Dave Babych | .25 | .11 |
| ❑ 74 Dale Hawerchuk | 1.25 | .55 |
| ❑ 75 Brian Bellows | 1.25 | .55 |
| ❑ 76 Dave Pasin UER (Team name missing from stat box) | .25 | .11 |
| ❑ 77 Pete Peeters | .50 | .23 |
| ❑ 78 Tomas Jonsson | .25 | .11 |
| ❑ 79 Gilbert Perreault | .50 | .23 |
| ❑ 80 Glenn Anderson | 1.25 | .55 |
| ❑ 81 Don Maloney | .25 | .11 |
| ❑ 82 Ed Olczyk | .25 | .11 |
| ❑ 83 Mike Bullard | .25 | .11 |
| ❑ 84 Tom Fergus | .25 | .11 |
| ❑ 85 Dave Lewis | .25 | .11 |
| ❑ 86 Brian Propp | .50 | .23 |
| ❑ 87 John Ogrodnick | .25 | .11 |
| ❑ 88 Kevin Dineen | 1.25 | .55 |
| ❑ 89 Don Beaupre | .50 | .23 |
| ❑ 90 Mike Bossy | 1.25 | .55 |
| ❑ 91 Tom Barrasso | 1.25 | .55 |
| ❑ 92 Michel Goulet | .50 | .23 |
| ❑ 93 Doug Gilmour | 5.00 | 2.20 |
| ❑ 94 Kirk Muller | 1.25 | .55 |
| ❑ 95 Larry Melnyk | .25 | .11 |
| ❑ 96 Bob Gainey | 1.25 | .55 |
| ❑ 97 Steve Kasper | .25 | .11 |
| ❑ 98 Petr Klima | 1.25 | .55 |
| ❑ 99 Neal Broten | .50 | .23 |
| ❑ 100 Al Secord | .25 | .11 |
| ❑ 101 Bryan Erickson | .25 | .11 |
| ❑ 102 Rejean Lemelin | .50 | .23 |
| ❑ 103 Sylvain Turgeon | .25 | .11 |
| ❑ 104 Bob Nystrom | .25 | .11 |
| ❑ 105 Bernie Federko | .50 | .23 |
| ❑ 106 Doug Wilson | .50 | .23 |
| ❑ 107 Alan Haworth | .25 | .11 |
| ❑ 108 Jari Kurri | 2.50 | 1.10 |
| ❑ 109 Ron Sutter | .25 | .11 |
| ❑ 110 Reed Larson | .25 | .11 |
| ❑ 111 Terry Ruskowski | .25 | .11 |
| ❑ 112 Mark Johnson | .25 | .11 |
| ❑ 113 James Patrick | .25 | .11 |
| ❑ 114 Paul MacLean | .25 | .11 |
| ❑ 115 Mike Ramsey | .25 | .11 |
| ❑ 116 Kelly Kisio | .25 | .11 |
| ❑ 117 Brent Sutter | .25 | .11 |
| ❑ 118 Joel Quenneville | .25 | .11 |
| ❑ 119 Curt Giles | .25 | .11 |
| ❑ 120 Tony Tanti | .25 | .11 |
| ❑ 121 Doug Sulliman | .25 | .11 |
| ❑ 122 Mario Lemieux | 60.00 | 27.00 |
| ❑ 123 Mark Howe | .50 | .23 |
| ❑ 124 Bob Sauve | .50 | .23 |
| ❑ 125 Anton Stastny | .25 | .11 |
| ❑ 126 Scott Stevens | 1.25 | .55 |
| ❑ 127 Mike Foligno | .25 | .11 |
| ❑ 128 Reijo Ruotsalainen | .25 | .11 |
| ❑ 129 Denis Potvin | .50 | .23 |
| ❑ 130 Keith Crowder | .25 | .11 |
| ❑ 131 Bob Janecyk | .50 | .23 |
| ❑ 132 John Tonelli | .25 | .11 |
| ❑ 133 Mike Liut | .50 | .23 |
| ❑ 134 Tim Kerr | .50 | .23 |
| ❑ 135 Al Jensen | .50 | .23 |
| ❑ 136 Mel Bridgman | .25 | .11 |
| ❑ 137 Paul Coffey | 4.00 | 1.80 |
| ❑ 138 Dino Ciccarelli | 1.25 | .55 |
| ❑ 139 Steve Larmer | 1.25 | .55 |
| ❑ 140 Mike O'Connell | .25 | .11 |
| ❑ 141 Clark Gillies | .50 | .23 |
| ❑ 142 Phil Russell | .25 | .11 |
| ❑ 143 Dirk Graham | 2.00 | .90 |
| ❑ 144 Randy Carlyle | .25 | .11 |
| ❑ 145 Charlie Simmer | .50 | .23 |
| ❑ 146 Ron Flockhart | .25 | .11 |
| ❑ 147 Tom Laidlaw | .25 | .11 |
| ❑ 148 Dave Tippett | .25 | .11 |
| ❑ 149 Wendel Clark | 30.00 | 13.50 |
| ❑ 150 Bob Carpenter | .25 | .11 |
| ❑ 151 Bill Watson | .25 | .11 |
| ❑ 152 Roberto Romano | .25 | .11 |
| ❑ 153 Doug Shedden | .25 | .11 |
| ❑ 154 Phil Housley | 1.25 | .55 |
| ❑ 155 Bryan Trottier | 1.25 | .55 |
| ❑ 156 Patrik Sundstrom | .25 | .11 |
| ❑ 157 Rick Middleton | .50 | .23 |
| ❑ 158 Glenn Resch | .50 | .23 |
| ❑ 159 Bernie Nicholls | .50 | .23 |
| ❑ 160 Ray Ferraro | 4.00 | 1.80 |
| ❑ 161 Mats Naslund | .50 | .23 |
| ❑ 162 Pat Flatley | .25 | .11 |
| ❑ 163 Joe Cirella | .25 | .11 |
| ❑ 164 Rod Langway | .50 | .23 |
| ❑ 165 Checklist 1-132 | 3.00 | 1.35 |
| ❑ 166 Carey Wilson | .25 | .11 |
| ❑ 167 Murray Craven | .50 | .23 |
| ❑ 168 Paul Gillis | .25 | .11 |
| ❑ 169 Borje Salming | .25 | .11 |
| ❑ 170 Perry Turnbull | .25 | .11 |
| ❑ 171 Chris Chelios | 5.00 | 2.20 |
| ❑ 172 Keith Acton | .25 | .11 |
| ❑ 173 Al MacInnis | 8.00 | 3.60 |
| ❑ 174 Russ Courtnall | 4.00 | 1.80 |
| ❑ 175 Brad Marsh | .50 | .23 |
| ❑ 176 Guy Carbonneau | .50 | .23 |
| ❑ 177 Ray Neufeld | .25 | .11 |
| ❑ 178 Craig MacTavish | 2.00 | .90 |
| ❑ 179 Rick Lanz | .25 | .11 |
| ❑ 180 Murray Bannerman | .25 | .11 |
| ❑ 181 Brent Ashton | .25 | .11 |
| ❑ 182 Jim Peplinski | .25 | .11 |
| ❑ 183 Mark Napier | .25 | .11 |
| ❑ 184 Laurie Boschman | .25 | .11 |
| ❑ 185 Larry Murphy | 1.25 | .55 |
| ❑ 186 Mark Messier | 6.00 | 2.70 |
| ❑ 187 Risto Siltanen | .25 | .11 |
| ❑ 188 Bobby Smith | .50 | .23 |
| ❑ 189 Gary Suter | 3.00 | 1.35 |
| ❑ 190 Peter Zezel | .25 | .11 |
| ❑ 191 Rick Vaive | .25 | .11 |
| ❑ 192 Dale Hunter | .50 | .23 |
| ❑ 193 Mike Krushelnyski | .25 | .11 |
| ❑ 194 Scott Arniel | .25 | .11 |
| ❑ 195 Larry Playfair | .25 | .11 |
| ❑ 196 Doug Risebrough | .25 | .11 |
| ❑ 197 Kevin Lowe | .50 | .23 |
| ❑ 198 Checklist 133-264 | 3.00 | 1.35 |
| ❑ 199 Chris Nilan | .25 | .11 |
| ❑ 200 Paul Cyr | .25 | .11 |
| ❑ 201 Ric Seiling | .25 | .11 |
| ❑ 202 Doug Smith | .25 | .11 |
| ❑ 203 Jamie Macoun | .25 | .11 |
| ❑ 204 Dan Quinn | .25 | .11 |
| ❑ 205 Paul Reinhart | .25 | .11 |
| ❑ 206 Keith Brown | .25 | .11 |
| ❑ 207 Jack O'Callahan | .25 | .11 |
| ❑ 208 Steve Richmond | .25 | .11 |
| ❑ 209 Warren Young | .25 | .11 |
| ❑ 210 Lee Fogolin | .25 | .11 |
| ❑ 211 Charlie Huddy | .25 | .11 |
| ❑ 212 Andy Moog | 2.50 | 1.10 |
| ❑ 213 Wayne Babych | .25 | .11 |
| ❑ 214 Torrie Robertson | .25 | .11 |
| ❑ 215 Jim Fox | .25 | .11 |
| ❑ 216 Phil Sykes | .25 | .11 |

□ 217 Jay Wells .25 .11
□ 218 Dave Langevin .25 .11
□ 219 Steve Payne .25 .11
□ 220 Craig Ludwig .25 .11
□ 221 Mike McPhee .25 .11
□ 222 Steve Penney .50 .23
□ 223 Mario Tremblay .25 .11
□ 224 Ryan Walter .25 .11
□ 225 Alain Chevrier .50 .23
□ 226 Uli Hiemer .25 .11
□ 227 Tim Higgins .25 .11
□ 228 Billy Smith .50 .23
□ 229 Richard Kromm .25 .11
□ 230 Tomas Sandstrom 1.25 .55
□ 231 Jim Johnson .25 .11
□ 232 Willy Lindstrom .25 .11
□ 233 Alain Cote .25 .11
□ 234 Gilbert Delorme .25 .11
□ 235 Mario Gosselin .50 .23
□ 236 David Shaw .25 .11
□ 237 Dave Barr .25 .11
□ 238 Ed Beers .25 .11
□ 239 Charlie Bourgeois .25 .11
□ 240 Rick Wamsley .25 .11
□ 241 Dan Daoust .25 .11
□ 242 Brad Maxwell .25 .11
□ 243 Gary Nylund .25 .11
□ 244 Greg Terrion .25 .11
□ 245 Steve Thomas 2.50 1.10
□ 246 Richard Brodeur .50 .23
□ 247 Joel Otto UER 1.25 .55
(Photo actually
Moe Lemay)
□ 248 Doug Halward .25 .11
□ 249 Moe Lemay UER .25 .11
(Photo actually
Joel Otto)
□ 250 Cam Neely 5.00 2.20
□ 251 Brent Peterson .25 .11
□ 252 Petri Skriko .25 .11
□ 253 Greg C. Adams .25 .11
□ 254 Bill Derlago .25 .11
□ 255 Brian Hayward .50 .23
□ 256 Doug Smail .25 .11
□ 257 Thomas Steen .25 .11
□ 258 Jari Kurri 1.25 .55
(Goals Leaders)
□ 259 Wayne Gretzky 6.00 2.70
(Assists Leaders)
□ 260 Wayne Gretzky 6.00 2.70
(Points Leaders)
□ 261 Tim Kerr .25 .11
(Power Play Goal Leaders)
□ 262 Kjell Dahlin .25 .11
(Rookie Scoring Leaders)
□ 263 Bob Froese .50 .23
(Goals Against Average Leaders)
□ 264 Bob Froese .50 .23
(Save Percentage Leaders)

## 1986-87 O-Pee-Chee Box Bottoms

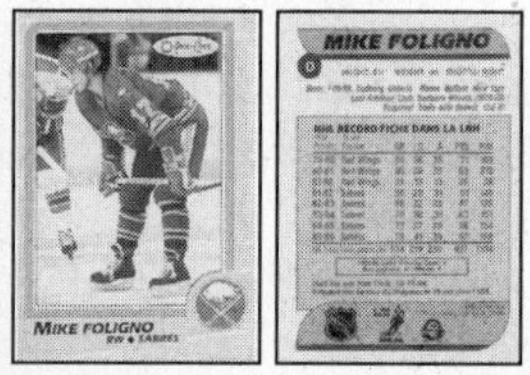

This sixteen-card standard-size set was issued in sets of four on the bottom of the 1986-87 O-Pee-Chee wax pack boxes. Complete box bottom panels are valued at a 25 percent premium above the prices listed below. This set features some of the leading NHL players including Mike Bossy, Wayne Gretzky, Mario Lemieux, and Bryan Trottier. The front presents a color action photo with various color borders, with the team's logo in the lower right hand corner. The back includes statistical information, is written in English and French, and is printed in blue with black ink. The cards are lettered rather than numbered.

| | MINT | NRMT |
|---|---|---|
| COMPLETE SET (16) | 40.00 | 18.00 |
| COMMON CARD (A-P) | .25 | .11 |

□ A Greg Adams .50 .23
□ B Mike Bossy 1.50 .70
□ C Dave Christian .25 .11
□ D Mike Foligno .50 .23
□ E Michel Goulet .75 .35
□ F Wayne Gretzky 20.00 9.00
□ G Tim Kerr .25 .11
□ H Jari Kurri 2.50 1.10
□ I Mario Lemieux 25.00 11.00
□ J Lanny McDonald .75 .35
□ K Bernie Nicholls .75 .35
□ L Mike Ridley .75 .35
□ M Larry Robinson .75 .35
□ N Denis Savard .75 .35
□ O Brian Sutter .25 .11
□ P Bryan Trottier 1.00 .45

## 1986-87 O-Pee-Chee Stickers

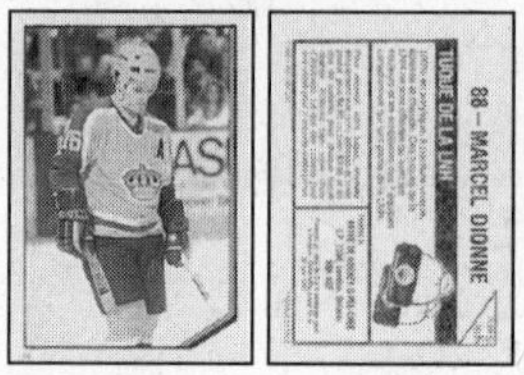

This sticker set consists of 255 stickers in full color and was put out by O-Pee-Chee. The foil stickers are listed in the checklist below explicitly. The stickers measure approximately 2 1/8" by 3". An album is available for these stickers. Those stickers which are pairs are indicated in the checklist below by noting parenthetically the other member of the pair. On the inside back cover of the sticker album the company offered (via direct mail-order) any ten different stickers of your choice for one dollar; this is one reason why the values of the most popular players in these sticker sets are somewhat depressed compared to traditional card set prices.

| | MINT | NRMT |
|---|---|---|
| COMPLETE SET (255) | 40.00 | 18.00 |
| COMMON STICKER (1-255) | .10 | .05 |
| COMMON HALF STICKER | .05 | .02 |
| COMMON FOILS | .20 | .09 |
| COMMON HALF FOILS | .15 | .07 |

□ 1 Stanley Cup Action .50 .23
□ 2 Stanley Cup Action .25 .11
□ 3 Stanley Cup Action .25 .11
□ 4 Stanley Cup Action .25 .11
□ 5 Patrick Roy FOIL 15.00 6.75
□ 6 Chris Chelios (151) .25 .11
□ 7 Guy Carbonneau (152) .05 .02
□ 8 Larry Robinson .10 .05
□ 9 Mario Tremblay (154) .05 .02
□ 10 Tom Kurvers (155) .05 .02
□ 11 Mats Naslund .10 .05
□ 12 Bob Gainey .75 .35
□ 13 Bobby Smith .10 .05
□ 14 Craig Ludwig (156) .05 .02
□ 15 Mike McPhee (157) .05 .02
□ 16 Doug Soetaert (159) .05 .02
□ 17 Petr Svoboda (160) .05 .02
□ 18 Kjell Dahlin .10 .05
□ 19 Patrick Roy 10.00 4.50
□ 20 Alain Cote (161) .05 .02
□ 21 Mario Gosselin (162) .05 .02
□ 22 Michel Goulet .25 .11
□ 23 J.F. Sauve (163) .05 .02
□ 24 Paul Gillis (164) .05 .02
□ 25 Brent Ashton .10 .05
□ 26 Peter Stastny .25 .11
□ 27 Anton Stastny .10 .05
□ 28 Gilbert Delorme (167) .05 .02
□ 29 Risto Siltanen (168) .05 .02
□ 30 Robert Picard (170) .05 .02
□ 31 David Shaw (171) .05 .02
□ 32 Dale Hunter .10 .05
□ 33 Clint Malarchuk .25 .11
□ 34 Ray Bourque .50 .23
□ 35 Rick Middleton (172) .05 .02
□ 36 Charlie Simmer (173) .05 .02
□ 37 Keith Crowder .10 .05
□ 38 Barry Pederson (175) .05 .02
□ 39 Reed Larson (176) .05 .02
□ 40 Steve Kasper (177) .05 .02
□ 41 Pat Riggin (178) .05 .02
□ 42 Mike Foligno .10 .05
□ 43 Gilbert Perreault .05 .02
(179)
□ 44 Mike Ramsey (180) .05 .02
□ 45 Tom Barrasso (186) .25 .11
□ 46 Brian Engblom (187) .05 .02
□ 47 Phil Housley (188) .25 .11
□ 48 John Tucker (189) .05 .02
□ 49 Dave Andreychuk .25 .11
□ 50 Dave Babych .10 .05
□ 51 Ron Francis (190) .25 .11
□ 52 Mike Liut (191) .25 .11
□ 53 Sylvain Turgeon .10 .05
□ 54 John Anderson (192) .05 .02
□ 55 Joel Quenneville (193) .05 .02
□ 56 Kevin Dineen (194) .25 .11
□ 57 Ray Ferraro (195) .05 .02
□ 58 Action Sticker .10 .05
□ 59 Action Sticker .10 .05
□ 60 Action Sticker .10 .05
□ 61 Action Sticker .10 .05
□ 62 Action Sticker .10 .05
□ 63 Action Sticker .10 .05
□ 64 Action Sticker .10 .05
□ 65 Action Sticker .10 .05
□ 66 Andy Moog (197) .25 .11
□ 67 Grant Fuhr (198) .25 .11
□ 68 Paul Coffey .50 .23
□ 69 Charlie Huddy (199) .05 .02
□ 70 Kevin Lowe (200) .25 .11
□ 71 Lee Fogolin .10 .05
□ 72 Wayne Gretzky 4.00 1.80
□ 73 Jari Kurri .25 .11
□ 74 Mike Krushelnyski .05 .02
(201)
□ 75 Mark Napier (202) .05 .02
□ 76 Craig MacTavish (204) .05 .02
□ 77 Kevin McClelland .05 .02
(205)
□ 78 Glenn Anderson .25 .11
□ 79 Mark Messier .75 .35
□ 80 Lanny McDonald .25 .11
□ 81 John Tonelli (207) .05 .02
□ 82 Joe Mullen (208) .25 .11
□ 83 Reggie Lemelin .25 .11
□ 84 Jim Peplinski (212) .05 .02
□ 85 Jamie Macoun (213) .05 .02
□ 86 Al MacInnis (214) .50 .23
□ 87 Dan Quinn (215) .05 .02
□ 88 Marcel Dionne .25 .11
□ 89 Jim Fox (219) .05 .02
□ 90 Dave Taylor (220) .05 .02
□ 91 Bob Janecyk (222) .05 .02
□ 92 Jay Wells (223) .05 .02
□ 93 Bryan Erickson (224) .05 .02
□ 94 Dave(Tiger) Williams .05 .02
(225)
□ 95 Bernie Nicholls .25 .11
□ 96 Stan Smyl .10 .05
□ 97 Doug Halward (227) .05 .02
□ 98 Richard Brodeur (228) .05 .02
□ 99 Tony Tanti .10 .05
□ 100 Brent Peterson (229) .05 .02
□ 101 Patrik Sundstrom .05 .02
(230)
□ 102 Doug Lidster (231) .05 .02
□ 103 Petri Skriko (232) .05 .02
□ 104 Dale Hawerchuk .25 .11
□ 105 Bill Derlago (234) .05 .02
□ 106 Ray Neufeld (235) .05 .02
□ 107 Randy Carlyle (237) .05 .02
□ 108 Paul MacLean (238) .05 .02
□ 109 Brian Mullen (242) .05 .02
□ 110 Thomas Steen (243) .05 .02
□ 111 Laurie Boschman .10 .05
□ 112 Paul Coffey (126) .50 .23
FOIL
□ 113 Michel Goulet (127) .15 .07
FOIL
□ 114 John Vanbiesbrouck 2.50 1.10
(128) FOIL
□ 115 Wayne Gretzky (129) 3.00 1.35
FOIL
□ 116 Mark Howe (130) .15 .07
FOIL
□ 117 Mike Bossy (131) .50 .23
FOIL
□ 118 Jari Kurri (132) .50 .23
FOIL
□ 119 Ray Bourque (133) .50 .23
FOIL
□ 120 Mario Lemieux (134) 3.00 1.35
FOIL
□ 121 Grant Fuhr (135) .15 .07
FOIL
□ 122 Mats Naslund (182) .15 .07
FOIL
□ 123 Larry Robinson (183) .15 .07
FOIL
□ 124 Chris Cichocki (184) .15 .07
FOIL
□ 125 Wendel Clark (185) 2.00 .90
FOIL
□ 126 Kjell Dahlin (112) .15 .07
FOIL
□ 127 Pelle Eklund (113) .15 .07
FOIL
□ 128 Jim Johnson (114) .15 .07
FOIL
□ 129 Petr Klima (115) .15 .07
FOIL
□ 130 Joel Otto (116) .15 .07
FOIL
□ 131 Mike Ridley (117) .50 .23
FOIL
□ 132 Patrick Roy (118) 8.00 3.60
FOIL
□ 133 David Shaw (119) .15 .07
FOIL
□ 134 Gary Suter (120) .15 .07
FOIL
□ 135 Steve Thomas (121) .15 .07
FOIL
□ 136 Borje Salming (244) .05 .02
□ 137 Gary Nylund (245) .05 .02
□ 138 Rick Vaive .10 .05
□ 139 Don Edwards (249) .05 .02
□ 140 Steve Thomas (250) .25 .11
□ 141 Wendel Clark 1.00 .45
□ 142 Miroslav Frycer .10 .05
□ 143 Tom Fergus .10 .05
□ 144 Marian Stastny (252) .05 .02
□ 145 Brad Maxwell (253) .05 .02
□ 146 Dan Daoust (254) .05 .02
□ 147 Greg Terrion (255) .05 .02
□ 148 Al Iafrate .25 .11
□ 149 Russ Courtnall .25 .11
□ 150 Denis Savard .25 .11
□ 151 Darryl Sutter (6) .05 .02
□ 152 Bob Sauve (7) .05 .02
□ 153 Doug Wilson .10 .05
□ 154 Troy Murray (9) .05 .02
□ 155 Al Secord (10) .05 .02
□ 156 Ed Olczyk (14) .05 .02
□ 157 Steve Larmer (15) .25 .11
□ 158 John Ogrodnick .10 .05
□ 159 Danny Gare (16) .05 .02
□ 160 Petr Svoboda (160) .05 .02
□ 161 Steve Yzerman (20) 2.00 .90
□ 162 Petr Klima (21) .05 .02
□ 163 Kelly Kisio (23) .05 .02
□ 164 Doug Shedden (24) .05 .02
□ 165 Greg Stefan .10 .05
□ 166 Neal Broten .25 .11
□ 167 Brian Bellows (28) .05 .02
□ 168 Scott Bjugstad (29) .05 .02
□ 169 Dino Ciccarelli .25 .11
□ 170 Dennis Maruk (30) .05 .02
□ 171 Dirk Graham (31) .25 .11
□ 172 Curt Giles (35) .05 .02
□ 173 Craig Hartsburg (36) .05 .02
□ 174 Bernie Federko .10 .05
□ 175 Brian Sutter (38) .05 .02
□ 176 Ron Flockhart (39) .05 .02
□ 177 Doug Gilmour (40) .50 .23
□ 178 Charlie Bourgeois .05 .02
(41)
□ 179 Rick Wamsley (43) .05 .02
□ 180 Rob Ramage (44) .05 .02
□ 181 Mark Hunter .10 .05
□ 182 Bob Froese (122) .15 .07
FOIL
□ 183 Wayne Gretzky (123) 3.00 1.35
FOIL
□ 184 Mark Howe (124) .15 .07
FOIL
□ 185 Jari Kurri (125) .50 .23
FOIL
□ 186 Bob Froese (45) .05 .02
□ 187 Darren Jensen (46) .05 .02
□ 188 Paul Coffey (47) .25 .11
□ 189 Troy Murray (48) .05 .02
□ 190 John Vanbiesbrouck 1.00 .45
(51)
□ 191 Wayne Gretzky (52) 3.00 1.35
□ 192 Gary Suter (54) .05 .02
□ 193 Bob Froese (55) .25 .11
□ 194 Mike Bossy (56) .05 .02
□ 195 Wayne Gretzky (57) 3.00 1.35
□ 196 Greg Adams .10 .05
□ 197 Dave Lewis (66) .05 .02
□ 198 Joe Cirella (67) .05 .02
□ 199 Rich Preston (69) .05 .02
□ 200 Mark Johnson (70) .05 .02
□ 201 Kirk Muller (74) .25 .11
□ 202 Pat Verbeek (75) .25 .11
□ 203 Mel Bridgman .10 .05
□ 204 Bob Nystrom (76) .05 .02
□ 205 Clark Gillies (77) .05 .02
□ 206 Pat LaFontaine .75 .35
□ 207 Pat Flatley (81) .05 .02
□ 208 Bob Bourne (82) .05 .02
□ 209 Denis Potvin .25 .11
□ 210 Duane Sutter .10 .05
□ 211 Brent Sutter .10 .05
□ 212 Kelly Hrudey (84) .50 .23
□ 213 Billy Smith (85) .25 .11
□ 214 Tomas Jonsson (86) .05 .02
□ 215 Ken Morrow (87) .05 .02
□ 216 Bryan Trottier .25 .11
□ 217 Mike Bossy .25 .11
□ 218 John Vanbiesbrouck 2.00 .90
□ 219 Bob Brooke (89) .05 .02
□ 220 James Patrick (90) .05 .02
□ 221 Mike Ridley .25 .11
□ 222 Ron Greschner (91) .05 .02
□ 223 Tom Laidlaw (92) .05 .02
□ 224 Larry Melnyk (93) .05 .02
□ 225 Reijo Ruotsalainen .05 .02
(94)
□ 226 Terry Ruskowski .10 .05
□ 227 Willy Lindstrom (97) .05 .02
□ 228 Mike Bullard (98) .05 .02
□ 229 Roberto Romano (100) .05 .02
□ 230 John Chabot (101) .05 .02
□ 231 Moe Mantha (102) .05 .02
□ 232 Doug Bodger (103) .05 .02
□ 233 Mario Lemieux 8.00 3.60
□ 234 Glenn Resch (105) .25 .11
□ 235 Brad Marsh (106) .05 .02
□ 236 Bob Froese .10 .05
□ 237 Doug Crossman (107) .05 .02
□ 238 Ilkka Sinisalo (108) .05 .02
□ 239 Brian Propp .10 .05
□ 240 Tim Kerr .10 .05
□ 241 Dave Poulin 1.00 .45
□ 242 Rich Sutter (109) .05 .02
□ 243 Ron Sutter (110) .05 .02
□ 244 Murray Craven (136) .05 .02
□ 245 Peter Zezel (137) .05 .02
□ 246 Mark Howe .10 .05
□ 247 Brad McCrimmon .10 .05
□ 248 Dave Christian .10 .05
□ 249 Rod Langway (139) .05 .02
□ 250 Bob Carpenter (140) .05 .02
□ 251 Mike Gartner .25 .11
□ 252 Al Jensen (144) .05 .02
□ 253 Craig Laughlin (145) .05 .02
□ 254 Scott Stevens (146) .25 .11
□ 255 Alan Haworth (147) .05 .02
□ xx Sticker Album 4.00 1.80

## 1987-88 O-Pee-Chee

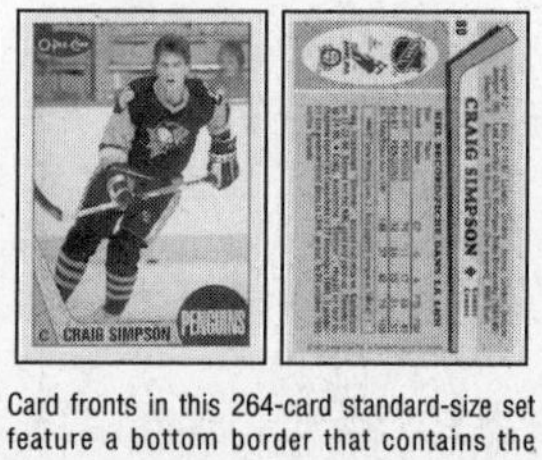

Card fronts in this 264-card standard-size set feature a bottom border that contains the design of a hockey stick with which the player's name appears. Also, the team name appears within a puck. Bilingual backs contain yearly and career statistics along with highlights. Rookie Cards in this set include Vincent Damphousse, Kevin Hatcher, Ron Hextall, Claude Lemieux, Marty McSorley, Adam Oates, Bill Ranford, Stephane Richer, Luc Robitaille, Ulf Samuelsson, Esa Tikkanen, Rick Tocchet, Mike Vernon and Ken Wregget. Beware when purchasing the cards of Wayne Gretzky, Adam Oates and Luc Robitaille from this set as they have been counterfeited.

| | MINT | NRMT |
|---|---|---|
| COMPLETE SET (264) | 175.00 | 80.00 |
| COMPLETE FACT.SET (264) | 175.00 | 80.00 |
| COMMON CARD (1-264) | .15 | .07 |

□ 1 Denis Potvin .40 .18
□ 2 Rick Tocchet 10.00 4.50
□ 3 Dave Andreychuk .75 .35
□ 4 Stan Smyl .15 .07
□ 5 Dave Babych .15 .07
□ 6 Pat Verbeek .75 .35
□ 7 Esa Tikkanen 8.00 3.60
□ 8 Mike Ridley .40 .18
□ 9 Randy Carlyle UER .15 .07
(Misspelled Calryle
on card front)
□ 10 Greg Paslawski .15 .07
□ 11 Neal Broten .40 .18
□ 12 Wendel Clark 5.00 2.20
□ 13 Bill Ranford UER 8.00 3.60
(Date of birth given is
12-12-66; should be 12-14-66)
□ 14 Doug Wilson .40 .18
□ 15 Mario Lemieux 25.00 11.00
□ 16 Mats Naslund .40 .18
□ 17 Mel Bridgman .15 .07
□ 18 James Patrick .15 .07
□ 19 Rollie Melanson .40 .18
□ 20 Lanny McDonald .40 .18
□ 21 Peter Stastny .40 .18
□ 22 Murray Craven .15 .07
□ 23 Ulf Samuelsson 5.00 2.20
□ 24 Michael Thelven .15 .07
□ 25 Scott Stevens .75 .35
□ 26 Petr Klima .15 .07
□ 27 Brent Sutter .15 .07
□ 28 Tomas Sandstrom .75 .35
□ 29 Tim Bothwell .15 .07
□ 30 Bob Carpenter .15 .07
□ 31 Brian MacLellan .15 .07
□ 32 John Chabot .15 .07
□ 33 Phil Housley .40 .18
□ 34 Patrik Sundstrom .15 .07
□ 35 Dave Ellett .40 .18
□ 36 John Vanbiesbrouck 15.00 6.75
□ 37 Dave Lewis .15 .07
□ 38 Tom McCarthy .15 .07
□ 39 Dave Poulin .15 .07
□ 40 Mike Foligno .15 .07
□ 41 Gordie Roberts .15 .07
□ 42 Luc Robitaille 20.00 9.00
□ 43 Duane Sutter .15 .07
□ 44 Pete Peeters .40 .18
□ 45 John Anderson .15 .07
□ 46 Aaron Broten .15 .07
□ 47 Keith Brown .15 .07
□ 48 Bobby Smith .40 .18
□ 49 Don Maloney .15 .07
□ 50 Mark Hunter .15 .07
□ 51 Moe Mantha .15 .07
□ 52 Charlie Simmer .40 .18
□ 53 Wayne Gretzky 20.00 9.00
□ 54 Mark Howe .40 .18
□ 55 Bob Gould .15 .07
□ 56 Steve Yzerman 10.00 4.50
□ 57 Larry Playfair .15 .07
□ 58 Alain Chevrier .40 .18
□ 59 Steve Larmer .75 .35
□ 60 Bryan Trottier .75 .35
□ 61 Stewart Gavin .15 .07
□ 62 Russ Courtnall .75 .35
□ 63 Mike Ramsey .15 .07
□ 64 Bob Brooke .15 .07
□ 65 Rick Wamsley .40 .18
□ 66 Ken Morrow .15 .07
□ 67 Gerard Gallant UER .15 .07
(Misspelled Gerald
on both sides)
□ 68 Kevin Hatcher 2.50 1.10
□ 69 Cam Neely 3.00 1.35
□ 70 Sylvain Turgeon .15 .07
□ 71 Peter Zezel .15 .07
□ 72 Al MacInnis 4.00 1.80
□ 73 Terry Ruskowski .15 .07
□ 74 Troy Murray .15 .07
□ 75 Jim Fox .15 .07
□ 76 Kelly Kisio .15 .07
□ 77 Michel Goulet .40 .18
□ 78 Tom Barrasso .75 .35
□ 79 Bruce Driver .15 .07
□ 80 Craig Simpson .40 .18
□ 81 Dino Ciccarelli .40 .18
□ 82 Gary Nylund .15 .07
□ 83 Bernie Federko .40 .18
□ 84 John Tonelli .15 .07
□ 85 Brad McCrimmon .15 .07
□ 86 Dave Tippett .15 .07
□ 87 Ray Bourque 3.00 1.35
□ 88 Dave Christian .15 .07
□ 89 Glen Hanlon .40 .18
□ 90 Brian Curran .15 .07
□ 91 Paul MacLean .15 .07

□ 92 Jimmy Carson .40 .18
□ 93 Willie Huber .15 .07
□ 94 Brian Bellows .40 .18
□ 95 Doug Jarvis .15 .07
□ 96 Clark Gillies .40 .18
□ 97 Tony Tanti .15 .07
□ 98 Pelle Eklund .40 .18
□ 99 Paul Coffey 3.00 1.35
□ 100 Brent Ashton .15 .07
□ 101 Mark Johnson .15 .07
□ 102 Greg Johnston .15 .07
□ 103 Ron Flockhart .15 .07
□ 104 Ed Olczyk .15 .07
□ 105 Mike Bossy .40 .18
□ 106 Chris Chelios 3.00 1.35
□ 107 Gilles Meloche .40 .18
□ 108 Rod Langway .15 .07
□ 109 Ray Ferraro .75 .35
□ 110 Ron Duguay .15 .07
□ 111 Al Secord .15 .07
□ 112 Mark Messier 4.00 1.80
□ 113 Ron Sutter .15 .07
□ 114 Darren Veitch .15 .07
□ 115 Rick Middleton .40 .18
□ 116 Doug Sulliman .15 .07
□ 117 Dennis Maruk .15 .07
□ 118 Dave Taylor .40 .18
□ 119 Kelly Hrudey .75 .35
□ 120 Tom Fergus .15 .07
□ 121 Christian Ruuttu .15 .07
□ 122 Brian Benning .15 .07
□ 123 Adam Oates 15.00 6.75
□ 124 Kevin Dineen .40 .18
□ 125 Doug Bodger .15 .07
□ 126 Joe Mullen .75 .35
□ 127 Denis Savard .40 .18
□ 128 Brad Marsh .40 .18
□ 129 Marcel Dionne .40 .18
□ 130 Bryan Erickson .15 .07
□ 131 Reed Larson .15 .07
□ 132 Don Beaupre .40 .18
□ 133 Larry Murphy .40 .18
□ 134 John Ogrodnick .40 .18
□ 135 Greg Adams .15 .07
□ 136 Pat Flatley .15 .07
□ 137 Scott Arniel .15 .07
□ 138 Dana Murzyn .15 .07
□ 139 Greg C. Adams .15 .07
□ 140 Bob Sauve .40 .18
□ 141 Mike O'Connell .15 .07
□ 142 Walt Poddubny .15 .07
□ 143 Paul Reinhart .15 .07
□ 144 Tim Kerr .40 .18
□ 145 Brian Lawton .15 .07
□ 146 Gino Cavallini .15 .07
□ 147 Doug Keans .15 .07
□ 148 Jari Kurri .75 .35
□ 149 Dale Hawerchuk .75 .35
□ 150 Randy Cunneyworth .15 .07
□ 151 Jay Wells .15 .07
□ 152 Mike Liut .40 .18
□ 153 Steve Konroyd .15 .07
□ 154 John Tucker .15 .07
□ 155 Rick Vaive .40 .18
□ 156 Bob Murray .15 .07
□ 157 Kirk Muller .75 .35
□ 158 Brian Propp .40 .18
□ 159 Ron Greschner .15 .07
□ 160 Rob Ramage .15 .07
□ 161 Craig Laughlin .15 .07
□ 162 Steve Kasper .15 .07
□ 163 Patrick Roy 50.00 22.00
□ 164 Shawn Burr .40 .18
□ 165 Craig Hartsburg .15 .07
□ 166 Dean Evason .40 .18
□ 167 Bob Bourne .40 .18
□ 168 Mike Gartner .75 .35
□ 169 Ron Hextall 10.00 4.50
□ 170 Joe Cirella .15 .07
□ 171 Dan Quinn .15 .07
□ 172 Tony McKegney .15 .07
□ 173 Pat LaFontaine .75 .35
□ 174 Allen Pedersen .15 .07
□ 175 Doug Gilmour 3.00 1.35
□ 176 Gary Suter .75 .35
□ 177 Barry Pederson .15 .07
□ 178 Grant Fuhr .75 .35
□ 179 Wayne Presley .15 .07
□ 180 Wilf Paiement .15 .07
□ 181 Doug Smail .15 .07
□ 182 Doug Crossman .15 .07
□ 183 Bernie Nicholls UER .40 .18
(Misspelled Nichols on both sides)
□ 184 Dirk Graham UER .40 .18
(Misspelled Dick)
□ 185 Anton Stastny .15 .07
□ 186 Greg Stefan .40 .18
□ 187 Ron Francis .75 .35
□ 188 Steve Thomas .40 .18
□ 189 Kelly Miller .40 .18
□ 190 Tomas Jonsson .15 .07
□ 191 John MacLean .75 .35
□ 192 Larry Robinson .40 .18
□ 193 Doug Wickenheiser .15 .07
□ 194 Keith Crowder .15 .07
□ 195 Bob Froese .40 .18
□ 196 Jim Johnson .15 .07
□ 197 Checklist 1-132 1.50 .70
□ 198 Checklist 133-264 1.50 .70
□ 199 Glenn Anderson .40 .18
□ 200 Kevin Lowe .40 .18
□ 201 Kevin McClelland .15 .07
□ 202 Mike Krushelnyski .15 .07
□ 203 Craig MacTavish .40 .18
□ 204 Andy Moog 1.50 .70
□ 205 Marty McSorley 6.00 2.70
□ 206 Craig Muni .15 .07
□ 207 Charlie Huddy .15 .07
□ 208 Hakan Loob .40 .18
□ 209 Jim Peplinski .15 .07
□ 210 Mike Bullard .15 .07
□ 211 Carey Wilson .15 .07
□ 212 Joel Otto .15 .07
□ 213 Neil Sheehy .15 .07
□ 214 Jamie Macoun .15 .07
□ 215 Mike Vernon 15.00 6.75
□ 216 Steve Bozek .15 .07
□ 217 Daniel Berthiaume .40 .18
□ 218 Gilles Hamel .15 .07
□ 219 Tim Watters .15 .07
□ 220 Mario Marois .15 .07
□ 221 Thomas Steen .15 .07
□ 222 Laurie Boschman .15 .07
□ 223 Steve Rooney .15 .07
□ 224 Ron Wilson .15 .07
□ 225 Fredrik Olausson .40 .18
□ 226 Jim Kyte .15 .07
□ 227 Claude Lemieux 15.00 6.75
□ 228 Bob Gainey .75 .35
□ 229 Gaston Gingras .15 .07
□ 230 Brian Hayward .40 .18
□ 231 Ryan Walter .15 .07
□ 232 Guy Carbonneau .40 .18
□ 233 Stephane Richer 5.00 2.20
□ 234 Rick Green .15 .07
□ 235 Brian Skrudland 1.50 .70
□ 236 Allan Bester .40 .18
□ 237 Borje Salming .40 .18
□ 238 Al Iafrate .75 .35
□ 239 Rick Lanz .15 .07
□ 240 Gary Leeman .15 .07
□ 241 Greg Terrion .15 .07
□ 242 Ken Wregget 4.00 1.80
□ 243 Vincent Damphousse 10.00 4.50
□ 244 Chris Kotsopoulos .15 .07
□ 245 Dale Hunter .40 .18
□ 246 Clint Malarchuk .40 .18
□ 247 Paul Gillis .15 .07
□ 248 Robert Picard .15 .07
□ 249 Doug Shedden .15 .07
□ 250 Mario Gosselin .40 .18
□ 251 Randy Moller .15 .07
□ 252 David Shaw .15 .07
□ 253 Mike Eagles .15 .07
□ 254 Alain Cote .15 .07
□ 255 Petri Skriko .15 .07
□ 256 Doug Lidster .15 .07
□ 257 Richard Brodeur UER .40 .18
(Photo actually Frank Caprice)
□ 258 Rich Sutter .15 .07
□ 259 Steve Tambellini .15 .07
□ 260 Jim Benning .15 .07
□ 261 Dave Richter .15 .07
□ 262 Michel Petit .15 .07
□ 263 Brent Peterson .15 .07
□ 264 Jim Sandlak .40 .18

## 1987-88 O-Pee-Chee Box Bottoms

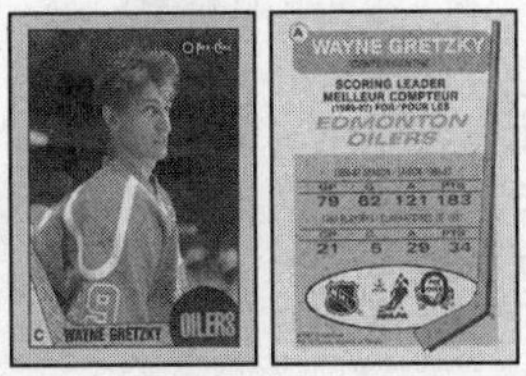


This sixteen-card set was issued in sets of four on the bottom of the 1987-88 O-Pee-Chee wax pack boxes. Complete box bottom panels are valued at a 25 percent premium above the prices listed below. The cards are in the same design as the 1987-88 O-Pee-Chee regular issues except they are bordered in yellow. The backs are printed in red and black ink and give statistical information. The cards are lettered rather than numbered.

| | MINT | NRMT |
|---|---|---|
| COMPLETE SET (16) | 35.00 | 16.00 |
| COMMON CARD (A-P) | .25 | .11 |

□ A Wayne Gretzky 15.00 6.75
□ B Tim Kerr .35 .16
□ C Steve Yzerman 7.00 3.10
□ D Luc Robitaille 8.00 3.60
□ E Doug Gilmour 2.00 .90
□ F Ray Bourque 2.00 .90
□ G Joe Mullen .75 .35
□ H Larry Murphy .75 .35
□ I Dale Hawerchuk 1.00 .45
□ J Ron Francis 2.00 .90
□ K Walt Poddubny .25 .11
□ L Mats Naslund .50 .23
□ M Michel Goulet .75 .35
□ N Denis Savard .75 .35
□ O Bryan Trottier 1.00 .45
□ P Russ Courtnall .75 .35

## 1987-88 O-Pee-Chee Minis

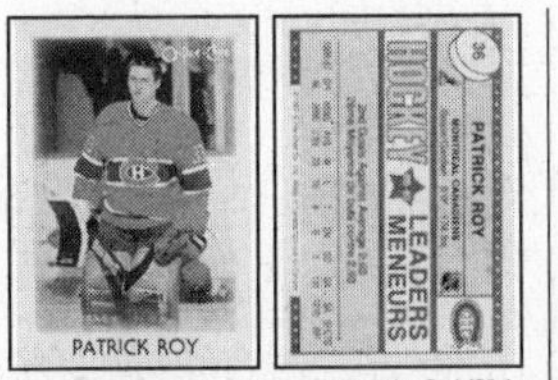


The 1987-88 O-Pee-Chee Minis set contains 42 cards measuring approximately 2 1/8" by 3". The fronts are white with vignette-style color photos and player names in navy blue. The backs are pale pink and blue, and show 1986-87 stats. The cards were distributed five per cello pack at a suggested retail price of 25 cents.

| | MINT | NRMT |
|---|---|---|
| COMPLETE SET (42) | 20.00 | 9.00 |
| COMMON CARD (1-42) | .10 | .05 |

□ 1 Glenn Anderson .25 .11
□ 2 Brian Benning .10 .05
□ 3 Daniel Berthiaume .15 .07
□ 4 Ray Bourque 1.00 .45
□ 5 Shawn Burr .10 .05
□ 6 Jimmy Carson .15 .07
□ 7 Dino Ciccarelli .25 .11
□ 8 Paul Coffey 1.00 .45
□ 9 Pelle Eklund .10 .05
□ 10 Ron Francis 1.00 .45
□ 11 Doug Gilmour 1.00 .45
□ 12 Michel Goulet .25 .11
□ 13 Wayne Gretzky 6.00 2.70
□ 14 Glen Hanlon .15 .07
□ 15 Brian Hayward .15 .07
□ 16 Ron Hextall 2.00 .90
□ 17 Phil Housley .25 .11
□ 18 Mark Howe .15 .07
□ 19 Doug Jarvis .10 .05
□ 20 Tim Kerr .15 .07
□ 21 Jari Kurri .50 .23
□ 22 Pat LaFontaine .50 .23
□ 23 Mario Lemieux 6.00 2.70
□ 24 Mike Liut .20 .09
□ 25 Kevin Lowe .15 .07
□ 26 Al MacInnis .35 .16
□ 27 Brad McCrimmon .10 .05
□ 28 Mark Messier 1.50 .70
□ 29 Joe Mullen .25 .11
□ 30 Craig Muni .10 .05
□ 31 Larry Murphy .25 .11
□ 32 Dave Poulin .15 .07
□ 33 Brian Propp .15 .07
□ 34 Paul Reinhart .15 .07
□ 35 Luc Robitaille 4.00 1.80
□ 36 Patrick Roy 10.00 4.50
□ 37 Christian Ruuttu .10 .05
□ 38 Tomas Sandstrom .25 .11
□ 39 Denis Savard .25 .11
□ 40 Petri Skriko .10 .05
□ 41 Bryan Trottier .50 .23
□ 42 Checklist 1-42 .10 .05

## 1987-88 O-Pee-Chee Stickers

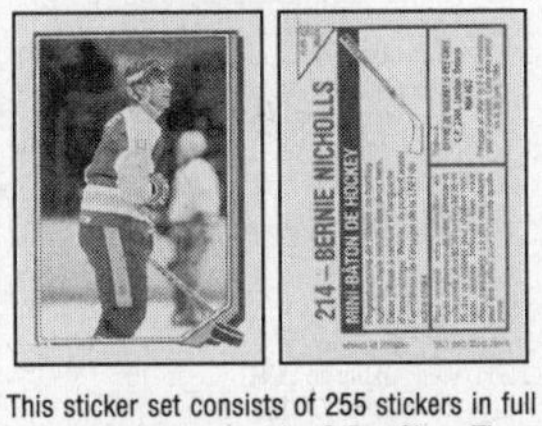


This sticker set consists of 255 stickers in full color and was put out by O-Pee-Chee. There are no foil stickers in this set. The stickers measure approximately 2 1/8" by 3". An album is available for these stickers. Those stickers which are pairs are indicated in the checklist below by noting parenthetically the other member of the pair. On the inside back cover of the sticker album the company offered (via direct mail-order) up to 25 different stickers of your choice for ten cents each; this is one reason why the values of the most popular players in these sticker sets are somewhat depressed compared to traditional card set prices.

| | MINT | NRMT |
|---|---|---|
| COMPLETE SET (255) | 30.00 | 13.50 |
| COMMON STICKER (1-255) | .10 | .05 |
| COMMON HALF STICKER | .05 | .02 |

□ 1 Ron Hextall MVP .25 .11
□ 2 Stanley Cup Action .25 .11
□ 3 Stanley Cup Action .25 .11
□ 4 Stanley Cup Action .25 .11
□ 5 Stanley Cup Action .25 .11
□ 6 Mats Naslund .25 .11
□ 7 Guy Carbonneau (146) .25 .11
□ 8 Gaston Gingras (147) .05 .02
□ 9 Chris Chelios .50 .23
□ 10 Bobby Smith .25 .11
□ 11 Rick Green (149) .05 .02
□ 12 Bob Gainey (150) .25 .11
□ 13 Patrick Roy 8.00 3.60
□ 14 Kjell Dahlin (153) .05 .02
□ 15 Chris Nilan (154) .05 .02
□ 16 Larry Robinson .25 .11
□ 17 Ryan Walter (157) .05 .02
□ 18 Petr Svoboda (158) .05 .02
□ 19 Claude Lemieux 1.50 .70
□ 20 Rob Ramage (160) .05 .02
□ 21 Mark Hunter (161) .05 .02
□ 22 Rick Wamsley (163) .05 .02
□ 23 Greg Paslawski (164) .05 .02
□ 24 Bernie Federko .25 .11
□ 25 Ron Flockhart (166) .05 .02
□ 26 Tim Bothwell (167) .05 .02
□ 27 Doug Gilmour .50 .23
□ 28 Kelly Kisio (168) .05 .02
□ 29 Don Maloney (169) .05 .02
□ 30 James Patrick (171) .05 .02
□ 31 Willie Huber (172) .05 .02
□ 32 Walt Poddubny .10 .05
□ 33 John Vanbiesbrouck .75 .35
(178)
□ 34 Marcel Dionne (179) .25 .11
□ 35 Tomas Sandstrom .25 .11
□ 36 Joe Mullen .25 .11
□ 37 Mike Bullard (180) .05 .02
□ 38 Neil Sheehy (181) .05 .02
□ 39 Paul Reinhart .10 .05
□ 40 Al MacInnis .25 .11
□ 41 Mike Vernon (182) .50 .23
□ 42 Joel Otto (183) .05 .02
□ 43 Lanny McDonald .25 .11
□ 44 Hakan Loob (184) .25 .11
□ 45 Carey Wilson (185) .05 .02
□ 46 Jim Peplinski .10 .05
□ 47 John Tonelli (186) .05 .02
□ 48 Jamie Macoun (187) .05 .02
□ 49 Gary Suter .25 .11
□ 50 Dennis Maruk (189) .05 .02
□ 51 Don Beaupre (190) .25 .11
□ 52 Neal Broten (193) .25 .11
□ 53 Brian Bellows (194) .25 .11
□ 54 Craig Hartsburg .05 .02
□ 55 Gordie Roberts (196) .05 .02
□ 56 Steve Payne (197) .05 .02
□ 57 Dino Ciccarelli .25 .11
□ 58 Pat Verbeek (199) .05 .02
□ 59 Doug Sulliman (200) .05 .02
□ 60 Bruce Driver (202) .05 .02
□ 61 Joe Cirella (203) .05 .02
□ 62 Aaron Broten .10 .05
□ 63 Alain Chevrier (204) .05 .02
□ 64 Mark Johnson (205) .05 .02
□ 65 Kirk Muller .25 .11
□ 66A Face-Off Action .10 .05
(Sandlak)
□ 66B Face-Off Action .10 .05
(Kasper)
□ 67 Action Sticker .10 .05
□ 68 Action Sticker .10 .05
□ 69 Murray Craven IA .10 .05
□ 70 Bruins Action .10 .05
□ 71 Islanders Action .10 .05
□ 72 Action Sticker .10 .05
□ 73 Action Sticker .10 .05
□ 74 Al Secord (207) .05 .02
□ 75 Bob Sauve (208) .05 .02
□ 76 Ed Olczyk (210) .05 .02
□ 77 Doug Wilson (211) .05 .02
□ 78 Denis Savard .25 .11
□ 79 Troy Murray (212) .05 .02
□ 80 Gary Nylund (213) .05 .02
□ 81 Steve Larmer .25 .11
□ 82 Jari Kurri .25 .11
□ 83 Esa Tikkanen (215) .75 .35
□ 84 Kevin Lowe (216) .05 .02
□ 85 Grant Fuhr .25 .11
□ 86 Wayne Gretzky 4.00 1.80
□ 87 Charlie Huddy (219) .05 .02
□ 88 Kent Nilsson (220) .05 .02
□ 89 Paul Coffey .50 .23
□ 90 Mike Krushelnyski .05 .02
(223)
□ 91 Craig MacTavish (224) .05 .02
□ 92 Mark Messier 1.00 .45
□ 93 Andy Moog (226) .25 .11
□ 94 Randy Gregg (227) .05 .02
□ 95 Glenn Anderson .25 .11
□ 96 Peter Zezel (229) .25 .11
□ 97 Brian Propp (230) .25 .11
□ 98 Dave Poulin (232) .05 .02
□ 99 Brad McCrimmon (233) .05 .02
□ 100 Mark Howe .25 .11
□ 101 Ron Hextall (234) .75 .35
□ 102 Ron Sutter (235) .05 .02
□ 103 Tim Kerr .10 .05
□ 104 Petr Klima (237) .25 .11
□ 105 Adam Oates (238) 1.50 .70
□ 106 Gerard Gallant (240) .05 .02
□ 107 Mike O'Connell (241) .05 .02
□ 108 Brent Ashton .10 .05
□ 109 Glen Hanlon (242) .05 .02
□ 110 Harold Snepsts (243) .05 .02
□ 111 Steve Yzerman 1.00 .45
□ 112 Mark Howe (124) .25 .11
□ 113 Michel Goulet (125) .25 .11
□ 114 Ron Hextall (126) .50 .23
□ 115 Wayne Gretzky (127) 3.00 1.35
□ 116 Ray Bourque (128) .25 .11
□ 117 Jari Kurri (129) .25 .11
□ 118 Dino Ciccarelli (130) .25 .11
□ 119 Larry Murphy (131) .25 .11
□ 120 Mario Lemieux (132) 2.00 .90
□ 121 Mike Liut (133) .25 .11
□ 122 Luc Robitaille (134) 1.00 .45
□ 123 Al MacInnis (135) .25 .11
□ 124 Brian Benning (112) .05 .02
□ 125 Shawn Burr (113) .05 .02
□ 126 Jimmy Carson (114) .25 .11
□ 127 Shayne Corson (115) .25 .11
□ 128 Vincent Damphousse .75 .35
(116)
□ 129 Ron Hextall (117) .50 .23
□ 130 Jason Lafreniere .05 .02
(118)
□ 131 Ken Leiter (119) .05 .02
□ 132 Allen Pedersen (120) .05 .02
□ 133 Luc Robitaille (121) 1.00 .45
□ 134 Christian Ruuttu .25 .11
(122)
□ 135 Jim Sandlak (123) .05 .02
□ 136 Keith Crowder (245) .05 .02
□ 137 Charlie Simmer (246) .05 .02
□ 138 Rick Middleton (248) .05 .02
□ 139 Doug Keans (249) .05 .02
□ 140 Ray Bourque .25 .11
□ 141 Tom McCarthy (250) .05 .02
□ 142 Reed Larson (251) .05 .02
□ 143 Cam Neely .50 .23
□ 144 Christian Ruuttu .05 .02
(253)
□ 145 John Tucker (254) .05 .02
□ 146 Steve Dykstra (7) .05 .02
□ 147 Dave Andreychuk (8) .25 .11
□ 148 Tom Barrasso .25 .11
□ 149 Mike Ramsey (11) .05 .02
□ 150 Mike Foligno (12) .05 .02
□ 151 Phil Housley .25 .11
□ 152 Wendel Clark .50 .23
□ 153 Greg Terrion (14) .05 .02
□ 154 Steve Thomas (15) .25 .11
□ 155 Rick Vaive .10 .05
□ 156 Russ Courtnall .25 .11
□ 157 Rick Lanz (17) .05 .02
□ 158 Miroslav Frycer (18) .05 .02
□ 159 Tom Fergus .10 .05
□ 160 Al Iafrate (20) .25 .11
□ 161 Gary Leeman (21) .05 .02
□ 162 Allan Bester .25 .11
□ 163 Todd Gill (22) .05 .02
□ 164 Ken Wregget (23) .50 .23
□ 165 Borje Salming .25 .11
□ 166 Craig Simpson (25) .25 .11
□ 167 Terry Ruskowski (26) .05 .02
□ 168 Gilles Meloche (28) .05 .02
□ 169 John Chabot (29) .05 .02
□ 170 Mario Lemieux 3.00 1.35
□ 171 Moe Mantha (30) .05 .02
□ 172 Jim Johnson (31) .05 .02
□ 173 Dan Quinn .10 .05
□ 174 Wayne Gretzky (176) 3.00 1.35
□ 175 Brian Hayward (177) .25 .11
□ 176 Mark Howe (174) .25 .11
□ 177 Luc Robitaille (175) 1.00 .45
□ 178 Ray Bourque (33) .25 .11
□ 179 Dave Poulin (34) .05 .02
□ 180 Wayne Gretzky (37) 3.00 1.35
Hart Trophy Winner
□ 181 Wayne Gretzky (38) 3.00 1.35
Ross Trophy Winner
□ 182 Ron Hextall (41) .75 .35
□ 183 Doug Jarvis (42) .05 .02
□ 184 Brian Hayward (44) .25 .11
□ 185 Patrick Roy (45) 3.50 1.55
□ 186 Joe Mullen (47) .25 .11
□ 187 Luc Robitaille (48) 1.00 .45
□ 188 Barry Pederson .10 .05
□ 189 Richard Brodeur (50) .05 .02
□ 190 Dave Richter (51) .05 .02
□ 191 Doug Lidster .10 .05
□ 192 Petri Skriko .10 .05
□ 193 Rich Sutter (52) .05 .02
□ 194 Jim Sandlak (53) .05 .02
□ 195 Tony Tanti .10 .05
□ 196 Michel Petit (55) .05 .02
□ 197 Jim Benning (56) .05 .02
□ 198 Stan Smyl .10 .05
□ 199 Brent Peterson (58) .05 .02
□ 200 Garth Butcher (59) .25 .11
□ 201 Patrik Sundstrom .10 .05
□ 202 Kevin Dineen (60) .05 .02
□ 203 Sylvain Turgeon (61) .05 .02
□ 204 John Anderson (63) .05 .02
□ 205 Ulf Samuelsson (64) .25 .11
□ 206 Ron Francis .50 .23
□ 207 Doug Jarvis (74) .05 .02
□ 208 Dave Babych (75) .05 .02
□ 209 Mike Liut .25 .11
□ 210 Jimmy Carson (76) .25 .11
□ 211 Larry Playfair (77) .05 .02
□ 212 Jay Wells (79) .05 .02
□ 213 Rollie Melanson (80) .05 .02
□ 214 Bernie Nicholls .25 .11
□ 215 Dave Taylor (83) .05 .02
□ 216 Jim Fox (84) .05 .02
□ 217 Luc Robitaille 3.00 1.35
□ 218 John Ogrodnick .10 .05
□ 219 Jason Lafreniere (87) .05 .02
□ 220 Mike Hough (88) .05 .02
□ 221 Paul Gillis .10 .05
□ 222 Peter Stastny .25 .11
□ 223 David Shaw (90) .05 .02
□ 224 Bill Derlago (91) .05 .02
□ 225 Michel Goulet .25 .11
□ 226 Doug Shedden (93) .05 .02
□ 227 Basil McRae (94) .05 .02
□ 228 Anton Stastny .10 .05
□ 229 Randy Moller (96) .05 .02
□ 230 Robert Picard (97) .05 .02
□ 231 Mario Gosselin .25 .11
□ 232 Larry Murphy (98) .25 .11
□ 233 Scott Stevens (99) .25 .11
□ 234 Mike Ridley (101) .25 .11

□ 235 Dave Christian (102) .05 .02
□ 236 Rod Langway .25 .11
□ 237 Bob Gould (104) .05 .02
□ 238 Bob Mason (105) .05 .02
□ 239 Mike Gartner .25 .11
□ 240 Bryan Trottier (106) .25 .11
□ 241 Brent Sutter (107) .05 .02
□ 242 Kelly Hrudey (109) .25 .11
□ 243 Pat LaFontaine (110) .50 .23
□ 244 Mike Bossy .25 .11
□ 245 Pat Flatley (136) .05 .02
□ 246 Ken Morrow (137) .05 .02
□ 247 Denis Potvin .25 .11
□ 248 Randy Carlyle (138) .05 .02
□ 249 Daniel Berthiaume .25 .11
(139)
□ 250 Mario Marois (141) .05 .02
□ 251 Dave Ellett (142) .05 .02
□ 252 Paul MacLean .10 .05
□ 253 Gilles Hamel (144) .05 .02
□ 254 Doug Smail (145) .05 .02
□ 255 Dale Hawerchuk .25 .11
□ xx Sticker Album 4.00 1.80

## 1988-89 O-Pee-Chee

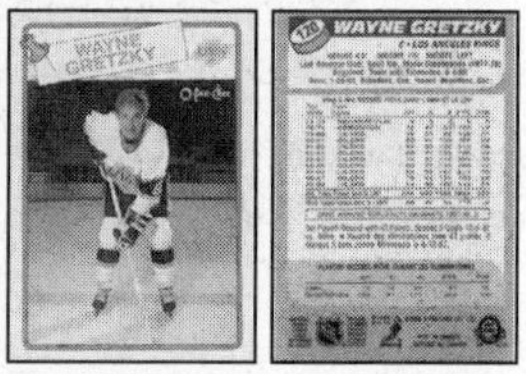

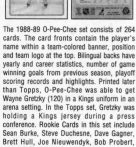

The 1988-89 O-Pee-Chee set consists of 264 cards. The card fronts contain the player's name within a team-colored banner, position and team logo at the top. Bilingual backs have yearly and career statistics, number of game winning goals from previous season, playoff scoring records and highlights. Printed later than Topps, O-Pee-Chee was able to get Wayne Gretzky (120) in a Kings uniform in an arena setting. In the Topps set, Gretzky was holding a Kings jersey during a press conference. Rookie Cards in this set include Sean Burke, Steve Duchesne, Dave Gagner, Brett Hull, Joe Nieuwendyk, Bob Probert, Brendan Shanahan, Ray Sheppard and Pierre Turgeon. Beware when purchasing the cards of Gretzky, Hull, Lemieux, Nieuwendyk, and Turgeon as they have been counterfeited.

| | MINT | NRMT |
|---|---|---|
| COMPLETE SET (264) | 140.00 | 65.00 |
| COMPLETE FACT.SET (264) | 150.00 | 70.00 |
| COMMON CARD (1-264) | .15 | .07 |

□ 1 Mario Lemieux 10.00 4.50
□ 2 Bob Joyce .15 .07
□ 3 Joel Quenneville .15 .07
□ 4 Tony McKegney .15 .07
□ 5 Stephane Richer .75 .35
□ 6 Mark Howe .15 .07
□ 7 Brent Sutter .15 .07
□ 8 Gilles Meloche .40 .18
□ 9 Jimmy Carson .15 .07
□ 10 John MacLean .40 .18
□ 11 Gary Leeman .15 .07
□ 12 Gerard Gallant .15 .07
□ 13 Marcel Dionne .40 .18
□ 14 Dave Christian .15 .07
□ 15 Gary Nylund .15 .07
□ 16 Joe Nieuwendyk 10.00 4.50
□ 17 Billy Smith .40 .18
□ 18 Christian Ruuttu .15 .07
□ 19 Randy Cunneyworth .15 .07
□ 20 Brian Lawton .15 .07
□ 21 Scott Mellanby 2.50 1.10
□ 22 Peter Stastny .40 .18
□ 23 Gord Kluzak .15 .07
□ 24 Sylvain Turgeon .15 .07
□ 25 Clint Malarchuk .40 .18
□ 26 Denis Savard .40 .18
□ 27 Craig Simpson .15 .07
□ 28 Petr Klima .15 .07
□ 29 Pat Verbeek .40 .18
□ 30 Moe Mantha .15 .07
□ 31 Chris Nilan .15 .07
□ 32 Barry Pederson .15 .07
□ 33 Randy Burridge .15 .07
□ 34 Ron Hextall 2.00 .90
□ 35 Gaston Gingras .15 .07
□ 36 Kevin Dineen .15 .07
□ 37 Tom Laidlaw .15 .07
□ 38 Paul MacLean .15 .07
□ 39 John Chabot .15 .07
□ 40 Lindy Ruff .15 .07
□ 41 Dan Quinn .15 .07
□ 42 Don Beaupre .40 .18
□ 43 Gary Suter .40 .18
□ 44 Mikko Makela .15 .07
□ 45 Mark Johnson .15 .07
□ 46 Dave Taylor .40 .18
□ 47 Ulf Dahlen .75 .35
□ 48 Jeff Sharples .15 .07
□ 49 Chris Chelios 2.00 .90
□ 50 Mike Gartner .40 .18
□ 51 Darren Pang .75 .35
□ 52 Ron Francis .75 .35
□ 53 Ken Morrow .15 .07
□ 54 Michel Goulet .40 .18
□ 55 Ray Sheppard 2.50 1.10
□ 56 Doug Gilmour 2.00 .90
□ 57 David Shaw .15 .07
□ 58 Cam Neely .75 .35
□ 59 Grant Fuhr .75 .35
□ 60 Scott Stevens .40 .18
□ 61 Bob Brooke .15 .07
□ 62 Dave Hunter .15 .07
□ 63 Alan Kerr .15 .07
□ 64 Brad Marsh .15 .07
□ 65 Dale Hawerchuk .40 .18
□ 66 Brett Hull 50.00 22.00
□ 67 Patrik Sundstrom .15 .07
□ 68 Greg Stefan .40 .18
□ 69 James Patrick .15 .07
□ 70 Dale Hunter .40 .18
□ 71 Al Iafrate .40 .18
□ 72 Bob Carpenter .15 .07
□ 73 Ray Bourque 2.00 .90
□ 74 John Tucker .15 .07
□ 75 Carey Wilson .15 .07
□ 76 Joe Mullen .40 .18
□ 77 Rick Vaive .15 .07
□ 78 Shawn Burr .15 .07
□ 79 Murray Craven .15 .07
□ 80 Clark Gillies .40 .18
□ 81 Bernie Federko .40 .18
□ 82 Tony Tanti .15 .07
□ 83 Greg Gilbert .15 .07
□ 84 Kirk Muller .40 .18
□ 85 Dave Tippett .15 .07
□ 86 Kevin Hatcher .40 .18
□ 87 Rick Middleton .40 .18
□ 88 Bobby Smith .40 .18
□ 89 Doug Wilson .40 .18
□ 90 Scott Arniel .15 .07
□ 91 Brian Mullen .15 .07
□ 92 Mike O'Connell .15 .07
□ 93 Mark Messier 3.00 1.35
□ 94 Sean Burke 2.50 1.10
□ 95 Brian Bellows .15 .07
□ 96 Doug Bodger .15 .07
□ 97 Bryan Trottier .75 .35
□ 98 Anton Stastny .15 .07
□ 99A Checklist 1-99 .75 .35
(found in vending cases)
□ 99B Checklist 1-132 .75 .35
(found in wax cases)
□ 100 Dave Poulin .15 .07
□ 101 Bob Bourne .15 .07
□ 102 John Vanbiesbrouck 10.00 4.50
□ 103 Allen Pedersen .15 .07
□ 104 Mike Ridley .15 .07
□ 105 Andrew McBain .15 .07
□ 106 Troy Murray .15 .07
□ 107 Tom Barrasso .40 .18
□ 108 Tomas Jonsson .15 .07
□ 109 Rob Brown .15 .07
□ 110 Hakan Loob .15 .07
□ 111 Ilkka Sinisalo .15 .07
□ 112 Dave Archibald .15 .07
□ 113 Doug Halward .15 .07
□ 114 Ray Ferraro .15 .07
□ 115 Doug Brown .40 .18
□ 116 Patrick Roy 15.00 6.75
□ 117 Greg Millen .40 .18
□ 118 Ken Linseman .15 .07
□ 119 Phil Housley .15 .07
□ 120 Wayne Gretzky UER 15.00 6.75
(No position on front)
□ 121 Tomas Sandstrom .40 .18
□ 122 Brendan Shanahan 50.00 22.00
□ 123 Pat LaFontaine .75 .35
□ 124 Luc Robitaille 4.00 1.80
□ 125 Ed Olczyk .15 .07
□ 126 Ron Sutter .15 .07
□ 127 Mike Liut .40 .18
□ 128 Brent Ashton .15 .07
□ 129 Tony Hrkac .15 .07
□ 130 Kelly Miller .15 .07
□ 131 Alan Haworth .15 .07
□ 132 Dave McLlwain .15 .07
□ 133 Mike Ramsey .15 .07
□ 134 Bob Sweeney .15 .07
□ 135 Dirk Graham .15 .07
□ 136 Ulf Samuelsson .75 .35
□ 137 Petri Skriko .15 .07
□ 138 Aaron Broten .15 .07
□ 139 Jim Fox .15 .07
□ 140 Randy Wood .15 .07
□ 141 Larry Murphy .40 .18
□ 142 Daniel Berthiaume .40 .18
□ 143 Kelly Kisio .15 .07
□ 144 Neal Broten .15 .07
□ 145 Reed Larson .15 .07
□ 146 Peter Zezel .15 .07
□ 147 Jari Kurri .75 .35
□ 148 Jim Johnson .15 .07
□ 149 Gino Cavallini .15 .07
□ 150 Glen Hanlon .40 .18
□ 151 Bengt Gustafsson .15 .07
□ 152 Mike Bullard .15 .07
□ 153 John Ogrodnick .15 .07
□ 154 Steve Larmer .40 .18
□ 155 Kelly Hrudey .40 .18
□ 156 Mats Naslund .15 .07
□ 157 Bruce Driver .15 .07
□ 158 Randy Hillier .15 .07
□ 159 Craig Hartsburg .15 .07
□ 160 Rollie Melanson .40 .18
□ 161 Adam Oates 4.00 1.80
□ 162 Greg Adams .15 .07
□ 163 Dave Andreychuk .40 .18
□ 164 Dave Babych .15 .07
□ 165 Brian Noonan .15 .07
□ 166 Glen Wesley .40 .18
□ 167 Dave Ellett .15 .07
□ 168 Brian Propp .15 .07
□ 169 Bernie Nicholls .40 .18
□ 170 Walt Poddubny .15 .07
□ 171 Steve Konroyd .15 .07
□ 172 Doug Sulliman .15 .07
□ 173 Mario Gosselin .40 .18
□ 174 Brian Benning .15 .07
□ 175 Dino Ciccarelli .40 .18
□ 176 Steve Kasper .15 .07
□ 177 Rick Tocchet 2.00 .90
□ 178 Brad McCrimmon .15 .07
□ 179 Paul Coffey 2.00 .90
□ 180 Pete Peeters .40 .18
□ 181 Bob Probert 4.00 1.80
□ 182 Steve Duchesne 3.00 1.35
□ 183 Russ Courtnall .40 .18
□ 184 Mike Foligno .15 .07
□ 185 Wayne Presley .15 .07
□ 186 Rejean Lemelin .40 .18
□ 187 Mark Hunter .15 .07
□ 188 Joe Cirella .15 .07
□ 189 Glenn Anderson .40 .18
□ 190 John Anderson .15 .07
□ 191 Pat Flatley .15 .07
□ 192 Rod Langway .15 .07
□ 193 Brian MacLellan .15 .07
□ 194 Pierre Turgeon 15.00 6.75
□ 195 Brian Hayward .40 .18
□ 196 Steve Yzerman 6.00 2.70
□ 197 Doug Crossman .15 .07
□ 198A Checklist 100-198 .75 .35
(Found in vending cases)
□ 198B Checklist 133-264 UER .75 .35
(Found in wax cases;
233 Mario Marios)
□ 199 Greg C. Adams .15 .07
□ 200 Laurie Boschman .15 .07
□ 201 Jeff Brown .75 .35
□ 202 Garth Butcher .15 .07
□ 203 Guy Carbonneau .40 .18
□ 204 Randy Carlyle .15 .07
□ 205 Alain Cote .15 .07
□ 206 Keith Crowder .15 .07
□ 207 Vincent Damphousse 2.00 .90
□ 208 Gaetan Duchesne .15 .07
□ 209 Iain Duncan .15 .07
□ 210 Tommy Albelin .15 .07
□ 211 Pelle Eklund .15 .07
□ 212 Jan Erixon .15 .07
□ 213 Paul Fenton .15 .07
□ 214 Tom Fergus .15 .07
□ 215 Dave Gagner 2.00 .90
□ 216 Bob Gainey .75 .35
□ 217 Stewart Gavin .15 .07
□ 218 Charlie Huddy .15 .07
□ 219 Jeff Jackson .15 .07
□ 220 Uwe Krupp 1.00 .45
□ 221 Mike Krushelnyski .15 .07
□ 222 Tom Kurvers .15 .07
□ 223 Jason Lafreniere .15 .07
□ 224 Lane Lambert .15 .07
□ 225 Rick Lanz .15 .07
□ 226 Brad Lauer .15 .07
□ 227 Claude Lemieux 3.00 1.35
□ 228 Doug Lidster .15 .07
□ 229 Kevin Lowe UER .40 .18
(Has Gretzky's stats)
□ 230 Craig Ludwig .15 .07
□ 231 Al MacInnis 1.50 .70
□ 232 Craig MacTavish .40 .18
□ 233 Mario Marois .15 .07
(misspelled Marios
on checklist 198b)
□ 234 Lanny McDonald .40 .18
□ 235 Rick Meagher .15 .07
□ 236 Craig Muni .15 .07
□ 237 Mike McPhee .15 .07
□ 238 Ric Nattress .15 .07
□ 239 Ray Neufeld .15 .07
□ 240 Lee Norwood .15 .07
□ 241 Mark Osborne UER .15 .07
(Misspelled Osbourne
on both sides)
□ 242 Joel Otto .15 .07
□ 243 Jim Peplinski .15 .07
□ 244 Rob Ramage .15 .07
□ 245 Luke Richardson .15 .07
□ 246 Larry Robinson .40 .18
□ 247 Borje Salming .15 .07
□ 248 David Saunders .15 .07
□ 249 Al Secord .15 .07
□ 250 Charlie Simmer .15 .07
□ 251 Doug Smail .15 .07
□ 252 Steve Smith UER .75 .35
(Card front states he
was traded to Sabres;
this never happened.)
□ 253 Stan Smyl .15 .07
□ 254 Thomas Steen .15 .07
□ 255 Rich Sutter .15 .07
□ 256 Petr Svoboda .40 .18
□ 257 Peter Taglianetti .15 .07
□ 258 Steve Tambellini .15 .07
□ 259 Steve Thomas .40 .18
□ 260 Esa Tikkanen 1.50 .70
□ 261 Mike Vernon 3.00 1.35
□ 262 Ryan Walter .15 .07
□ 263 Doug Wickenheiser .15 .07
□ 264 Ken Wregget .75 .35

## 1988-89 O-Pee-Chee Box Bottoms

This sixteen-card set was issued in sets of four on the bottom of the 1988-89 O-Pee-Chee wax pack boxes. Complete box bottom panels are valued at a 25 percent premium above the prices listed below. The cards are in the same design as the 1988-89 O-Pee-Chee regular issues. The backs are printed in purple on orange background and give statistical information. The cards are lettered rather than numbered.

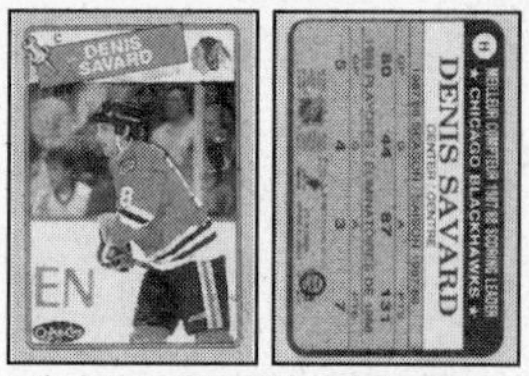

| | MINT | NRMT |
|---|---|---|
| COMPLETE SET (16) | 15.00 | 6.75 |
| COMMON CARD (A-P) | .25 | .11 |

□ A Ron Francis 1.00 .45
□ B Wayne Gretzky 8.00 3.60
□ C Pat LaFontaine 1.00 .45
□ D Bobby Smith .35 .16
□ E Bernie Federko .35 .16
□ F Kirk Muller .75 .35
□ G Ed Olczyk .25 .11
□ H Denis Savard .75 .35
□ I Ray Bourque 1.50 .70
□ J Murray Craven and .25 .11
Brian Propp
□ K Dale Hawerchuk .75 .35
□ L Steve Yzerman 4.00 1.80
□ M Dave Andreychuk .50 .23
□ N Mike Gartner .75 .35
□ O Hakan Loob .35 .16
□ P Luc Robitaille 1.50 .70

## 1988-89 O-Pee-Chee Minis

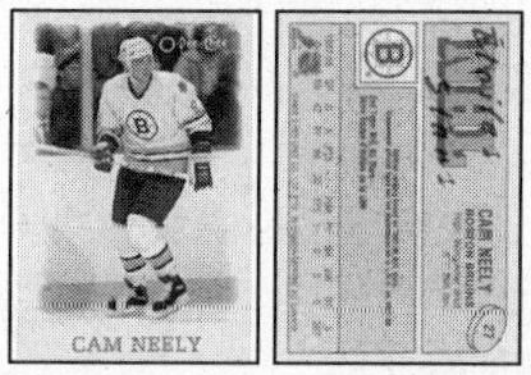

The 1988-89 O-Pee-Chee Minis set contains 46 numbered cards measuring approximately 2 1/8" by 3". The fronts are white with vignette-style color photos and player names in navy blue. The backs are pale pink and blue, and show 1987-88 stats. The key card in the set is Brett Hull, appearing in his Rookie Card year. The set numbering is alphabetical by player's name.

| | MINT | NRMT |
|---|---|---|
| COMPLETE SET (46) | 20.00 | 9.00 |
| COMMON CARD (1-46) | .05 | .02 |

□ 1 Tom Barrasso .25 .11
□ 2 Bob Bourne .05 .02
□ 3 Ray Bourque .75 .35
□ 4 Guy Carbonneau .15 .07
□ 5 Jimmy Carson .10 .05
□ 6 Paul Coffey .75 .35
□ 7 Ulf Dahlen .15 .07
□ 8 Marcel Dionne .35 .16
□ 9 Grant Fuhr .50 .23
□ 10 Michel Goulet .25 .11
□ 11 Wayne Gretzky 6.00 2.70
□ 12 Dale Hawerchuk .35 .16
□ 13 Brian Hayward .15 .07
□ 14 Ron Hextall .50 .23
□ 15 Tony Hrkac .05 .02
□ 16 Brett Hull 5.00 2.20
□ 17 Steve Larmer .25 .11
□ 18 Rejean Lemelin .15 .07
□ 19 Mario Lemieux 5.00 2.20
□ 20 Mike Liut .15 .07
□ 21 Hakan Loob .25 .11
□ 22 Al MacInnis .25 .11
□ 23 Paul MacLean .10 .05
□ 24 Brad McCrimmon .05 .02
□ 25 Mark Messier 1.50 .70
□ 26 Mats Naslund .25 .11
□ 27 Cam Neely .75 .35
□ 28 Bernie Nicholls .25 .11
□ 29 Joe Nieuwendyk 2.00 .90
□ 30 Pete Peeters .15 .07
□ 31 Stephane Richer .35 .16
□ 32 Luc Robitaille .75 .35
□ 33 Patrick Roy 5.00 2.20
□ 34 Denis Savard .35 .16
□ 35 Ray Sheppard .50 .23
□ 36 Craig Simpson .10 .05
□ 37 Peter Stastny .35 .16
□ 38 Greg Stefan .10 .05
□ 39 Scott Stevens .25 .11
□ 40 Gary Suter .15 .07
□ 41 Petr Svoboda .10 .05
□ 42 John Vanbiesbrouck 3.00 1.35
□ 43 Pat Verbeek .35 .16
□ 44 Mike Vernon .50 .23
□ 45 Carey Wilson .05 .02
□ 46 Checklist Card .05 .02

## 1988-89 O-Pee-Chee Stickers

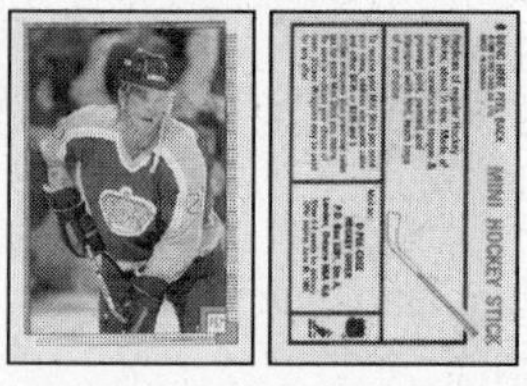

This set consists of 270 stickers in full color and was put out by O-Pee-Chee. There are no foil stickers in this set. The stickers measure approximately 2 1/8" by 3". An album is available for these stickers. Those stickers which are pairs are indicated in the checklist below by noting parenthetically the other member of the pair. The backs of the stickers are three types: trivia questions and answers (42 different red Level I and blue Level II), various souvenir offers, and the colorful Future Stars (which are considered a separate set in their own right). On the inside back cover of the sticker album the company offered (via direct mail-order) up to 20 different stickers of your choice for ten cents each; this is one reason why the values of the most popular players in these sticker sets are somewhat depressed compared to traditional card set prices.

| | MINT | NRMT |
|---|---|---|
| COMPLETE SET (270) | 20.00 | 9.00 |
| COMMON STICKER (1-270) | .10 | .05 |
| COMMON HALF STICKER | .05 | .02 |

□ 1 Wayne Gretzky MVP 4.00 1.80
□ 2 Oilers/Bruins Action .10 .05
□ 3 Oilers/Bruins Action .25 .11
□ 4 Oilers/Bruins Action .25 .11
□ 5 Oilers/Bruins Action .10 .05
□ 6 Doug Wilson (135) .25 .11
□ 7 Dirk Graham (136) .05 .02
□ 8 Darren Pang (137) .05 .02
□ 9 Rick Vaive (138) .05 .02
□ 10 Troy Murray (139) .05 .02
□ 11 Brian Noonan (140) 1.00 .45
Kirk McLean-Future Star
□ 12 Steve Larmer .25 .11
□ 13 Denis Savard .25 .11
□ 14 Mark Hunter (141) .05 .02
□ 15 Brian Sutter (142) .05 .02
□ 16 Brett Hull (145) 2.00 .90
□ 17 Tony McKegney (146) .05 .02
□ 18 Brian Benning (151) .05 .02
Darren Pang-Future Star
□ 19 Tony Hrkac (152) .05 .02
□ 20 Doug Gilmour .50 .23
□ 21 Bernie Federko .10 .05
□ 22 Cam Neely .50 .23
□ 23 Ray Bourque .50 .23
Doug Brown-Future Star
□ 24 Rejean Lemelin (153) .05 .02
□ 25 Gord Kluzak (154) .05 .02
□ 26 Rick Middleton (155) .25 .11
□ 27 Steve Kasper (156) .05 .02
□ 28 Bob Sweeney (168) .05 .02
□ 29 Randy Burridge (169) .05 .02
□ 30 Bruins/Whalers Action .10 .05
□ 31 Canadiens/Bruins .10 .05
Action
□ 32 Canadiens/Bruins .10 .05
Action
□ 33 Blues/Red Wings .10 .05
Action
□ 34 Canadiens/Bruins .10 .05
Action
□ 35 Canadiens/Bruins .10 .05
Action
□ 36 Canadiens/Bruins .10 .05
Action, Tony Hrkac-Future Star
□ 37 Canadiens/Bruins .10 .05
Action
□ 38 Canadiens/Bruins .10 .05
Action
□ 39 Larry Robinson (170) .25 .11
□ 40 Ryan Walter (171) .05 .02
□ 41 Guy Carbonneau (172) .05 .02
□ 42 Bob Gainey (173) .25 .11
□ 43 Claude Lemieux (176) .50 .23
□ 44 Petr Svoboda (177) .05 .02
□ 45 Patrick Roy 3.00 1.35
□ 46 Bobby Smith .25 .11
□ 47 Mike McPhee (182) .05 .02
□ 48 Craig Ludwig (183) .05 .02
□ 49 Stephane Richer .25 .11
□ 50 Mats Naslund .10 .05
□ 51 Chris Chelios .50 .23
□ 52 Brian Hayward .25 .11
□ 53 Larry Melnyk (184) .05 .02
David Archibald-Future Star
□ 54 Garth Butcher (185) .05 .02
□ 55 Kirk McLean (186) .25 .11
□ 56 Doug Wickenheiser .05 .02
(187)
□ 57 Rich Sutter (190) .05 .02
□ 58 Jim Benning (191) .05 .02

❑ 59 Tony Tanti .10 .05
❑ 60 Stan Smyl .10 .05
❑ 61 David Saunders (196) .05 .02
❑ 62 Steve Tambellini .05 .02
(197)
❑ 63 Doug Lidster .10 .05
Rob Brown-Future Star
❑ 64 Petri Skriko .10 .05
❑ 65 Barry Pederson .10 .05
❑ 66 Greg Adams .10 .05
❑ 67 Mike Gartner .25 .11
❑ 68 Scott Stevens .25 .11
Bob Sweeney-Future Star
❑ 69 Rod Langway (198) 2.50 1.10
Pierre Turgeon-Future Star
❑ 70 Dave Christian (199) .05 .02
❑ 71 Larry Murphy (200) .05 .02
❑ 72 Clint Malarchuk (201) .25 .11
❑ 73 Dale Hunter (204) .25 .11
❑ 74 Mike Ridley (205) .10 .05
Jeff Sharples-Future Star
❑ 75 Kirk Muller .25 .11
❑ 76 Aaron Broten .10 .05
❑ 77 Bruce Driver (206) .05 .02
❑ 78 John MacLean (207) .25 .11
❑ 79 Joe Cirella (208) .05 .02
❑ 80 Doug Brown (209) .05 .02
❑ 81 Pat Verbeek (210) 4.00 1.80
Brett Hull-Future Star
❑ 82 Sean Burke (211) .25 .11
❑ 83 Joel Otto (212) .05 .02
❑ 84 Rob Ramage (213) .05 .02
❑ 85 Lanny McDonald (215) .25 .11
Glen Wesley-Future Star
❑ 86 Mike Vernon (216) .25 .11
❑ 87 John Tonelli (217) .05 .02
❑ 88 Jim Peplinski (218) .05 .02
❑ 89 Gary Suter .25 .11
❑ 90 Joe Nieuwendyk 1.00 .45
Craig Janney-Future Star
❑ 91 Ric Nattress (219) .05 .02
❑ 92 Al MacInnis (220) .25 .11
❑ 93 Mike Bullard .10 .05
❑ 94 Hakan Loob .10 .05
❑ 95 Joe Mullen .25 .11
❑ 96 Brad McCrimmon .10 .05
❑ 97 Brian Propp (221) .05 .02
❑ 98 Murray Craven (222) .05 .02
❑ 99 Rick Tocchet (225) .50 .23
❑ 100 Doug Crossman (226) .05 .02
❑ 101 Brad Marsh (233) .05 .02
❑ 102 Peter Zezel (234) .05 .02
❑ 103 Ron Hextall .25 .11
❑ 104 Mark Howe .25 .11
❑ 105 Brent Sutter (235) .05 .02
❑ 106 Alan Kerr (236) .05 .02
❑ 107 Randy Wood (237) .05 .02
❑ 108 Mikko Makela (238) .05 .02
Iain Duncan-Future Star
❑ 109 Kelly Hrudey (241) .25 .11
❑ 110 Steve Konroyd (242) .05 .02
❑ 111 Pat LaFontaine .50 .23
❑ 112 Bryan Trottier .25 .11
❑ 113 Gary Suter (243) .05 .02
❑ 114 Luc Robitaille (244) .50 .23
❑ 115 Patrick Roy (245) 1.50 .70
❑ 116 Mario Lemieux (246) 1.50 .70
❑ 117 Ray Bourque (247) .25 .11
❑ 118 Hakan Loob (248) .05 .02
❑ 119 Mike Bullard (249) .05 .02
❑ 120 Brad McCrimmon (250) .05 .02
❑ 121 Wayne Gretzky (251) 2.00 .90
❑ 122 Grant Fuhr (252) .25 .11
❑ 123 Craig Simpson (255) .25 .11
Glenn Healy-Future Star
❑ 124 Mark Howe (256) .05 .02
❑ 125 Joe Nieuwendyk (257) .25 .11
❑ 126 Ray Sheppard (258) .25 .11
Ulf Dahlen-Future Star
❑ 127 Brett Hull (259) 2.00 .90
❑ 128 Ulf Dahlen (260) .25 .11
❑ 129 Tony Hrkac (265) .05 .02
❑ 130 Bob Sweeney (266) .05 .02
❑ 131 Rob Brown (267) .25 .11
❑ 132 Iain Duncan (268) .05 .02
❑ 133 Pierre Turgeon (269) 1.00 .45
❑ 134 Calle Johansson (270) 1.00 .45
Joe Nieuwendyk-Future Star
❑ 135 Darren Pang (6) .25 .11
❑ 136 Kirk McLean (7) .25 .11
❑ 137 Doug Smail (8) .05 .02
❑ 138 Thomas Steen (9) .05 .02
❑ 139 Laurie Boschman (10) .05 .02
❑ 140 Iain Duncan (11) 1.00 .45
Kirk McLean-Future Star
❑ 141 Ray Neufeld (14) .05 .02
❑ 142 Mario Marois (15) .05 .02
❑ 143 Dale Hawerchuk .25 .11
❑ 144 Paul MacLean .10 .05
❑ 145 Jim Kyte (16) .05 .02
❑ 146 Pokey Reddick (17) .05 .02
❑ 147 Andrew McBain .10 .05
Brian Noonan-Future Star
❑ 148 Randy Carlyle .10 .05
❑ 149 Daniel Berthiaume .25 .11
❑ 150 Dave Ellett .10 .05
❑ 151 Roland Melanson (18) .05 .02
Darren Pang-Future Star
❑ 152 Steve Duchesne (19) .25 .11
❑ 153 Bob Carpenter (24) .05 .02
❑ 154 Jim Fox (25) .05 .02
❑ 155 Dave Taylor (26) .05 .02
❑ 156 Bernie Nicholls (27) .25 .11
❑ 157 Luc Robitaille .75 .35
❑ 158 Jimmy Carson .50 .23
Sean Burke-Future Star
❑ 159 Canadiens/Bruins .10 .05
Action
❑ 160 Devils/Nordiques .10 .05
Action
❑ 161 Devils/Nordiques .50 .23
Action, Ray Sheppard-Future Star
❑ 162 Devils/North Stars .10 .05
Action
❑ 163 Oilers/Flames Action .10 .05
❑ 164 Oilers/Flames Action .10 .05
❑ 165 Oilers/Flames Action .10 .05
❑ 166 Oilers/Flames Action .10 .05
❑ 167 Canadiens/Bruins .10 .05
Action
❑ 168 Mark Osborne (28) .05 .02
❑ 169 Dan Daoust (29) .05 .02
❑ 170 Tom Fergus (39) .05 .02
❑ 171 Vincent Damphousse .25 .11
(40)
❑ 172 Wendel Clark (41) .25 .11
❑ 173 Luke Richardson (42) .05 .02
❑ 174 Borje Salming .25 .11
❑ 175 Russ Courtnall .25 .11
❑ 176 Rick Lanz (43) .05 .02
❑ 177 Ken Wregget (44) .25 .11
❑ 178 Gary Leeman .10 .05
❑ 179 Al Secord .10 .05
❑ 180 Al Iafrate .25 .11
❑ 181 Ed Olczyk .10 .05
❑ 182 Normand Rochefort .05 .02
(47)
❑ 183 Lane Lambert (48) .05 .02
❑ 184 Tommy Albelin (53) .05 .02
David Archibald-Future Star
❑ 185 Jason Lafreniere (54) .05 .02
❑ 186 Alain Cote (55) .05 .02
❑ 187 Gaetan Duchesne (56) .05 .02
❑ 188 Michel Goulet .25 .11
❑ 189 Peter Stastny 3.00 1.35
Brian Leetch-Future Star
❑ 190 Jeff Jackson (57) .05 .02
❑ 191 Mike Eagles (58) .05 .02
❑ 192 Jeff Brown .50 .23
❑ 193 Mario Gosselin .25 .11
❑ 194 Anton Stastny .10 .05
❑ 195 Alan Haworth .10 .05
❑ 196 Don Beaupre (61) .25 .11
❑ 197 Brian MacLellan (62) .05 .02
❑ 198 Brian Lawton (69) 2.50 1.10
Pierre Turgeon-Future Star
❑ 199 Craig Hartsburg (70) .05 .02
❑ 200 Moe Mantha (71) .05 .02
❑ 201 Neal Broten (72) .05 .02
❑ 202 Dino Ciccarelli .25 .11
Randy Wood-Future Star
❑ 203 Brian Bellows .10 .05
❑ 204 Mario Lemieux (73) 1.50 .70
❑ 205 Joe Nieuwendyk (74) .25 .11
Jeff Sharples-Future Star
❑ 206 Brad McCrimmon (77) .05 .02
❑ 207 Pete Peeters (78) .25 .11
❑ 208 Norris Trophy Winner .25 .11
Ray Bourque (79)
❑ 209 Frank J. Selke .10 .05
Trophy Winner
Guy Carbonneau (80)
❑ 210 Hart Trophy Winner 4.00 1.80
Mario Lemieux (81),
Brett Hull-Future Star
❑ 211 Art Ross 1.00 .45
Trophy Winner
Mario Lemieux (82)
❑ 212 Vezina Trophy Winner .25 .11
Grant Fuhr (83)
❑ 213 Bill Masterton .10 .05
Trophy Winner
Bob Bourne (84)
❑ 214 William Jennings 1.00 .45
Trophy Winners
Brian Hayward and
Patrick Roy
❑ 215 Lady Byng .25 .11
Trophy Winner
Mats Naslund (85),
Glen Wesley-Future Star
❑ 216 Calder Trophy Winner .50 .23
Joe Nieuwendyk (86)
❑ 217 Craig MacTavish (87) .05 .02
❑ 218 Chris Joseph (88) .05 .02
❑ 219 Kevin Lowe (91) .05 .02
❑ 220 Esa Tikkanen (92) .50 .23
❑ 221 Charlie Huddy (97) .05 .02
❑ 222 Geoff Courtnall (98) .25 .11
❑ 223 Grant Fuhr .25 .11
❑ 224 Wayne Gretzky 4.00 1.80
❑ 225 Steve Smith (99) .25 .11
❑ 226 Mike Krushelnyski .05 .02
(100)
❑ 227 Jari Kurri .25 .11
❑ 228 Craig Simpson .10 .05
❑ 229 Glenn Anderson .25 .11
❑ 230 Mark Messier .50 .23
❑ 231 Randy Cunneyworth .10 .05
❑ 232 Mario Lemieux 3.00 1.35
❑ 233 Paul Coffey (101) .25 .11
❑ 234 Doug Bodger (102) .05 .02
❑ 235 Dave Hunter (105) .05 .02
❑ 236 Dan Quinn (106) .05 .02
❑ 237 Rob Brown (107) .05 .02
❑ 238 Gilles Meloche (108) .05 .02
Iain Duncan-Future Star
❑ 239 Kelly Kisio .10 .05
❑ 240 Walt Poddubny .10 .05
❑ 241 John Vanbiesbrouck .50 .23
(109)
❑ 242 Tomas Sandstrom (110) .05 .02
❑ 243 David Shaw (113) .05 .02
❑ 244 Marcel Dionne (114) .25 .11
❑ 245 Chris Nilan (115) .05 .02
❑ 246 James Patrick (116) .05 .02
❑ 247 Bob Probert (117) .50 .23
❑ 248 Mike O'Connell (118) .05 .02
❑ 249 Jeff Sharples (119) .05 .02
❑ 250 Brent Ashton (120) .05 .02
❑ 251 Petr Klima (121) .05 .02
❑ 252 Greg Stefan (122) .05 .02
❑ 253 Steve Yzerman 1.00 .45
❑ 254 Gerard Gallant .25 .11
Calle Johansson-Future Star
❑ 255 Phil Housley (123) .25 .11
Glenn Healy-Future Star
❑ 256 Christian Ruuttu .05 .02
(124)
❑ 257 Mike Foligno (125) .05 .02
❑ 258 Scott Arniel (126) .25 .11
Ulf Dahlen-Future Star
❑ 259 Tom Barrasso (127) .25 .11
❑ 260 Mike Ramsey (128) .05 .02
❑ 261 Dave Andreychuk .25 .11
❑ 262 Ray Sheppard .25 .11
❑ 263 Mike Liut .25 .11
❑ 264 Ron Francis .50 .23
❑ 265 Ulf Samuelsson (129) .05 .02
❑ 266 Carey Wilson (130) .05 .02
❑ 267 Dave Babych (131) .05 .02
❑ 268 Ray Ferraro (132) .05 .02
❑ 269 Kevin Dineen (133) .05 .02
❑ 270 John Anderson (134) 1.00 .45
Joe Nieuwendyk-Future Star
❑ xx Sticker Album 3.00 1.35

## 1989-90 O-Pee-Chee

This 330-card standard-size set is O-Pee-Chee's largest issue since 1984-85. The fronts feature color action photos with "blue ice" borders and player name and team logo at the lower right-hand corner. Solid blue borders appear at the top and bottom on the card face. Bilingual backs are tinted red with black lettering and provide career and playoff statistics as well as highlights. The team cards in the set (298-318) are actually action scenes with no players explicitly identified. This set was produced in mass quantity as O-Pee-Chee gave dealers the option to order vending cases following the initial printing. A second printing allowed for these orders to be filled, saturating the market. Most dealers believe that this O-Pee-Chee set was produced in an amount much greater than the Topps production of this year. Rookie Cards in this set include Brian Bradley, Shayne Corson, Geoff Courtnall, Theoren Fleury, Benoit Hogue, Craig Janney, Brian Leetch, Trevor Linden, Kirk McLean, Daren Puppa, Gary Roberts, Cliff Ronning and Joe Sakic.

| | MINT | NRMT |
|---|---|---|
| COMPLETE SET (330) | 15.00 | 6.75 |
| COMP.FACT.SET (330) | 20.00 | 9.00 |
| COMMON CARD (1-330) | .05 | .02 |

❑ 1 Mario Lemieux 1.50 .70
❑ 2 Ulf Dahlen .05 .02
❑ 3 Terry Carkner .05 .02
❑ 4 Tony McKegney .05 .02
❑ 5 Denis Savard .15 .07
❑ 6 Derek King .30 .14
❑ 7 Lanny McDonald .15 .07
❑ 8 John Tonelli .05 .02
❑ 9 Tom Kurvers .05 .02
❑ 10 Dave Archibald .05 .02
❑ 11 Peter Sidorkiewicz .15 .07
❑ 12 Esa Tikkanen .15 .07
❑ 13 Dave Barr .05 .02
❑ 14 Brent Sutter .05 .02
❑ 15 Cam Neely .30 .14
❑ 16 Calle Johansson .15 .07
❑ 17 Patrick Roy 1.50 .70
❑ 18 Dale DeGray .05 .02
❑ 19 Phil Bourque .05 .02
❑ 20 Kevin Dineen .05 .02
❑ 21 Mike Bullard .05 .02
❑ 22 Gary Leeman .05 .02
❑ 23 Greg Stefan .15 .07
❑ 24 Brian Mullen .05 .02
❑ 25 Pierre Turgeon .50 .23
❑ 26 Bob Rouse .05 .02
❑ 27 Peter Zezel .05 .02
❑ 28 Jeff Brown .15 .07
❑ 29 Andy Brickley .05 .02
❑ 30 Mike Gartner .15 .07
❑ 31 Darren Pang .15 .07
❑ 32 Pat Verbeek .05 .02
❑ 33 Petri Skriko .05 .02
❑ 34 Tom Laidlaw .05 .02
❑ 35 Randy Wood .05 .02
❑ 36 Tom Barrasso .15 .07
❑ 37 John Tucker .05 .02
❑ 38 Andrew McBain .05 .02
❑ 39 David Shaw .05 .02
❑ 40 Rejean Lemelin .15 .07
❑ 41 Dino Ciccarelli .15 .07
❑ 42 Jeff Sharples .05 .02
❑ 43 Jari Kurri .15 .07
❑ 44 Murray Craven .05 .02
❑ 45 Cliff Ronning .30 .14
❑ 46 Dave Babych .05 .02
❑ 47 Bernie Nicholls .15 .07
❑ 48 Jon Casey .15 .07
❑ 49 Al MacInnis .15 .07
❑ 50 Bob Errey .05 .02
❑ 51 Glen Wesley .05 .02
❑ 52 Dirk Graham .05 .02
❑ 53 Guy Carbonneau .15 .07
❑ 54 Tomas Sandstrom .15 .07
❑ 55 Rod Langway .15 .07
❑ 56 Patrik Sundstrom .05 .02
❑ 57 Michel Goulet .15 .07
❑ 58 Dave Taylor .15 .07
❑ 59 Phil Housley .15 .07
❑ 60 Pat LaFontaine .15 .07
❑ 61 Kirk McLean 1.00 .45
❑ 62 Ken Linseman .05 .02
❑ 63 Randy Cunneyworth .05 .02
❑ 64 Tony Hrkac .05 .02
❑ 65 Mark Messier .50 .23
❑ 66 Carey Wilson .05 .02
❑ 67 Stephen Leach .05 .02
❑ 68 Christian Ruuttu .05 .02
❑ 69 Dave Ellett .05 .02
❑ 70 Ray Ferraro .05 .02
❑ 71 Colin Patterson .05 .02
❑ 72 Tim Kerr .05 .02
❑ 73 Bob Joyce .05 .02
❑ 74 Doug Gilmour .30 .14
❑ 75 Lee Norwood .05 .02
❑ 76 Dale Hunter .15 .07
❑ 77 Jim Johnson .05 .02
❑ 78 Mike Foligno .05 .02
❑ 79 Al Iafrate .15 .07
❑ 80 Rick Tocchet .30 .14
❑ 81 Greg Hawgood .05 .02
❑ 82 Steve Thomas .05 .02
❑ 83 Steve Yzerman 1.00 .45
❑ 84 Mike McPhee .05 .02
❑ 85 David Volek .05 .02
❑ 86 Brian Benning .05 .02
❑ 87 Neal Broten .05 .02
❑ 88 Luc Robitaille .30 .14
❑ 89 Trevor Linden 1.25 .55
❑ 90 James Patrick .05 .02
❑ 91 Brian Lawton .05 .02
❑ 92 Sean Burke .15 .07
❑ 93 Scott Stevens .15 .07
❑ 94 Pat Elynuik .05 .02
❑ 95 Paul Coffey .30 .14
❑ 96 Jan Erixon .05 .02
❑ 97 Mike Liut .15 .07
❑ 98 Wayne Presley .05 .02
❑ 99 Craig Simpson .05 .02
❑ 100 Kjell Samuelsson .05 .02
❑ 101 Shawn Burr .05 .02
❑ 102 John MacLean .15 .07
❑ 103 Tom Fergus .05 .02
❑ 104 Mike Krushelnyski .05 .02
❑ 105 Gary Nylund .05 .02
❑ 106 Dave Andreychuk .15 .07
❑ 107 Bernie Federko .15 .07
❑ 108 Gary Suter .05 .02
❑ 109 Dave Gagner .05 .02
❑ 110 Ray Bourque .30 .14
❑ 111 Geoff Courtnall .60 .25
❑ 112 Doug Wilson .15 .07
❑ 113 Joe Sakic 5.00 2.20
❑ 114 John Vanbiesbrouck .75 .35
❑ 115 Dave Poulin .05 .02
❑ 116 Rick Meagher .05 .02
❑ 117 Kirk Muller .15 .07
❑ 118 Mats Naslund .05 .02
❑ 119 Ray Sheppard .15 .07
❑ 120 Jeff Norton .05 .02
❑ 121 Randy Burridge .05 .02
❑ 122 Dale Hawerchuk .15 .07
❑ 123 Steve Duchesne .15 .07
❑ 124 John Anderson .05 .02
❑ 125 Rick Vaive .05 .02
❑ 126 Randy Hillier .05 .02
❑ 127 Jimmy Carson .05 .02
❑ 128 Larry Murphy .15 .07
❑ 129 Paul MacLean .05 .02
❑ 130 Joe Cirella .05 .02
❑ 131 Kelly Miller .05 .02
❑ 132 Alain Chevrier .15 .07
❑ 133 Ed Olczyk .05 .02
❑ 134 Dave Tippett .05 .02
❑ 135 Bob Sweeney .05 .02
❑ 136 Brian Leetch 3.00 1.35
❑ 137 Greg Millen .15 .07
❑ 138 Joe Nieuwendyk .15 .07
❑ 139 Brian Propp .05 .02
❑ 140 Mike Ramsey .05 .02
❑ 141 Mike Allison .05 .02
❑ 142 Shawn Chambers .05 .02
❑ 143 Peter Stastny .15 .07
❑ 144 Glen Hanlon .15 .07
❑ 145 John Cullen .15 .07
❑ 146 Kevin Hatcher .15 .07
❑ 147 Brendan Shanahan 2.00 .90
❑ 148 Paul Reinhart .05 .02
❑ 149 Bryan Trottier .30 .14
❑ 150 Dave Manson .15 .07
❑ 151 Marc Habscheid .05 .02
❑ 152 Dan Quinn .05 .02
❑ 153 Stephane Richer .15 .07
❑ 154 Doug Bodger .05 .02
❑ 155 Ron Hextall .30 .14
❑ 156 Wayne Gretzky 2.00 .90
❑ 157 Steve Tuttle .05 .02
❑ 158 Charlie Huddy .05 .02
❑ 159 Dave Christian .05 .02
❑ 160 Andy Moog .30 .14
❑ 161 Tony Granato .15 .07
❑ 162 Sylvain Cote .05 .02
❑ 163 Mike Vernon .15 .07
❑ 164 Steve Chiasson .15 .07
❑ 165 Mike Ridley .05 .02
❑ 166 Kelly Hrudey .15 .07
❑ 167 Bob Carpenter .05 .02
❑ 168 Zarley Zalapski .15 .07
❑ 169 Derek Laxdal .05 .02
❑ 170 Clint Malarchuk .15 .07
❑ 171 Kelly Kisio .05 .02
❑ 172 Gerard Gallant .05 .02
❑ 173 Ron Sutter .05 .02
❑ 174 Chris Chelios .30 .14
❑ 175 Ron Francis .15 .07
❑ 176 Gino Cavallini .05 .02
❑ 177 Brian Bellows .05 .02
❑ 178 Greg C. Adams .05 .02
❑ 179 Steve Larmer .15 .07
❑ 180 Aaron Broten .05 .02
❑ 181 Brent Ashton .05 .02
❑ 182 Gerald Diduck .05 .02
❑ 183 Paul MacDermid .05 .02
❑ 184 Walt Poddubny .05 .02
❑ 185 Adam Oates .30 .14
❑ 186 Brett Hull 1.50 .70
❑ 187 Scott Arniel .05 .02
❑ 188 Bobby Smith .15 .07
❑ 189 Guy Lafleur .15 .07
❑ 190 Craig Janney .50 .23
❑ 191 Mark Howe .05 .02
❑ 192 Grant Fuhr .30 .14
❑ 193 Rob Brown .05 .02
❑ 194 Steve Kasper .05 .02
❑ 195 Pete Peeters .15 .07
❑ 196 Joe Mullen .15 .07
❑ 197 Checklist 1-110 .10 .05
❑ 198 Checklist 111-220 .10 .05
❑ 199 Keith Crowder .05 .02
❑ 200 Daren Puppa .75 .35
❑ 201 Benoit Hogue .30 .14
❑ 202 Gary Roberts .50 .23
❑ 203 Brad McCrimmon .05 .02
❑ 204 Rick Wamsley .05 .02
❑ 205 Joel Otto .05 .02
❑ 206 Jim Peplinski .05 .02
❑ 207 Jamie Macoun .05 .02
❑ 208 Brian MacLellan .05 .02
❑ 209 Scott Young .30 .14
❑ 210 Ulf Samuelsson .05 .02
❑ 211 Joel Quenneville UER .05 .02
(Misspelled Quennville
on card back)
❑ 212 Tim Watters .05 .02
❑ 213 Curt Giles .05 .02
❑ 214 Stewart Gavin .05 .02
❑ 215 Bob Brooke .05 .02
❑ 216 Basil McRae .05 .02
❑ 217 Frank Musil .05 .02
❑ 218 Adam Creighton .15 .07
❑ 219 Troy Murray .05 .02
❑ 220 Steve Konroyd .15 .07
❑ 221 Duane Sutter .05 .02
❑ 222 Trent Yawney .05 .02
❑ 223 Mike O'Connell .05 .02
❑ 224 Jim Nill .05 .02
❑ 225 John Chabot .05 .02
❑ 226 Glenn Anderson .15 .07
❑ 227 Kevin Lowe .15 .07
❑ 228 Steve Smith .05 .02
❑ 229 Randy Gregg .05 .02
❑ 230 Craig MacTavish .15 .07
❑ 231 Craig Muni .05 .02
❑ 232 Theoren Fleury 5.00 2.20
❑ 233 Bill Ranford .30 .14
❑ 234 Claude Lemieux .30 .14
❑ 235 Larry Robinson .15 .07
❑ 236 Craig Ludwig .05 .02
❑ 237 Brian Hayward .15 .07
❑ 238 Petr Svoboda .05 .02
❑ 239 Russ Courtnall .15 .07
❑ 240 Ryan Walter .05 .02
❑ 241 Tommy Albelin .05 .02
❑ 242 Doug Brown .05 .02
❑ 243 Ken Daneyko .05 .02
❑ 244 Mark Johnson .05 .02
❑ 245 Randy Velischek .05 .02
❑ 246 Brad Dalgarno .05 .02
❑ 247 Mikko Makela .05 .02
❑ 248 Shayne Corson 1.00 .45
❑ 249 Marc Bergevin .05 .02
❑ 250 Pat Flatley .05 .02
❑ 251 Michel Petit .05 .02
❑ 252 Mark Hardy .05 .02
❑ 253 Scott Mellanby .15 .07
❑ 254 Keith Acton .05 .02
❑ 255 Ken Wregget .15 .07
❑ 256 Gord Dineen .05 .02
❑ 257 Dave Hannan .05 .02
❑ 258 Mario Gosselin .15 .07
❑ 259 Randy Moller .05 .02
❑ 260 Mario Marois .05 .02
❑ 261 Robert Picard .05 .02
❑ 262 Marc Fortier .05 .02
❑ 263 Ron Tugnutt 1.50 .70
❑ 264 Iiro Jarvi .05 .02
❑ 265 Paul Gillis .05 .02
❑ 266 Mike Hough .05 .02

❑ 267 Jim Sandlak .05 .02
❑ 268 Greg Paslawski .05 .02
❑ 269 Paul Cavallini .05 .02
❑ 270 Gaston Gingras .05 .02
❑ 271 Allan Bester .15 .07
❑ 272 Vincent Damphousse .15 .07
❑ 273 Daniel Marois .05 .02
❑ 274 Mark Osborne UER .05 .02
(Misspelled Osbourne on card front)
❑ 275 Craig Laughlin .05 .02
❑ 276 Brad Marsh .05 .02
❑ 277 Dan Daoust .05 .02
❑ 278 Borje Salming .05 .02
❑ 279 Chris Kotsopoulos .05 .02
❑ 280 Tony Tanti .05 .02
❑ 281 Barry Pederson .05 .02
❑ 282 Rich Sutter .05 .02
❑ 283 Stan Smyl .05 .02
❑ 284 Doug Lidster .05 .02
❑ 285 Steve Weeks .05 .02
❑ 286 Harold Snepsts .05 .02
❑ 287 Brian Bradley .50 .23
❑ 288 Larry Melnyk .05 .02
❑ 289 Bob Gould .05 .02
❑ 290 Thomas Steen .05 .02
❑ 291 Randy Carlyle .05 .02
❑ 292 Hannu Jarvenpaa UER .05 .02
(Misspelled Jaryenpaa on card front)
❑ 293 Iain Duncan .05 .02
❑ 294 Doug Smail .05 .02
❑ 295 Jim Kyte .05 .02
❑ 296 Daniel Berthiaume .15 .07
❑ 297 Peter Taglianetti .05 .02
❑ 298 Boston Bruins .05 .02
Action Scene
(Craig Janney)
❑ 299 Buffalo Sabres .05 .02
Action Scene
(Dave Andreychuk)
❑ 300 Calgary Flames .05 .02
Action Scene
(Mike Vernon)
❑ 301 Chicago Blackhawks .05 .02
Action Scene
(Dirk Graham)
❑ 302 Detroit Red Wings .05 .02
Action Scene
(Gerard Gallant)
❑ 303 Edmonton Oilers .05 .02
Action Scene
(Glenn Anderson)
❑ 304 Hartford Whalers .05 .02
Action Scene
(Kevin Dineen)
❑ 305 Los Angeles Kings .05 .02
Action Scene
(Kelly Hrudey)
❑ 306 Minnesota North Stars .05 .02
Action Scene
(Neal Broten)
❑ 307 Montreal Canadiens .15 .07
Action Scene
(Chris Chelios)
❑ 308 New Jersey Devils .05 .02
Action Scene
(Aaron Broten)
❑ 309 New York Islanders .05 .02
Action Scene
(David Volek)
❑ 310 New York Rangers .05 .02
Action Scene
(Tony Granato)
❑ 311 Philadelphia Flyers .05 .02
Action Scene
(Ron Hextall)
❑ 312 Pittsburgh Penguins .40 .18
Action Scene
(Mario Lemieux)
❑ 313 Quebec Nordiques .60 .25
Action Scene
(Joe Sakic)
❑ 314 St. Louis Blues .05 .02
Action Scene
(Greg Millen)
❑ 315 Toronto Maple Leafs .05 .02
Action Scene
(Brian Bradley)
❑ 316 Vancouver Canucks .05 .02
Action Scene
(Jim Sandlak,
Ray Bourque defending)
❑ 317 Washington Capitals .05 .02
Action Scene
(Mike Liut)
❑ 318 Winnipeg Jets .05 .02
Action Scene
(Andrew McBain)
❑ 319 Art Ross Trophy .75 .35
Mario Lemieux
❑ 320 Hart Trophy .75 .35
Wayne Gretzky
❑ 321 Calder Trophy .30 .14
Brian Leetch
❑ 322 Vezina Trophy .75 .35
Patrick Roy
❑ 323 Norris Trophy .15 .07
Chris Chelios
❑ 324 Lady Byng Trophy .05 .02
Joe Mullen
❑ 325 1988-89 Highlight .75 .35
Wayne Gretzky
❑ 326 1988-89 Highlight .30 .14
Brian Leetch UER
(Photo actually
David Shaw)
❑ 327 1988-89 Highlight .75 .35
Mario Lemieux
❑ 328 1988-89 Highlight .05 .02
Esa Tikkanen
❑ 329 Coupe Stanley Cup .05 .02
❑ 330 Checklist 221-330 .10 .05

## 1989-90 O-Pee-Chee Box Bottoms

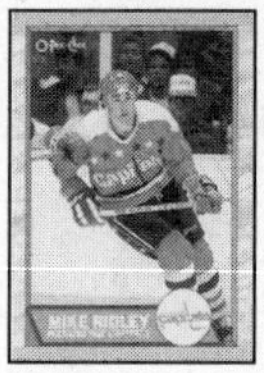

This sixteen-card set was issued in sets of four on the bottom of the 1989-90 O-Pee-Chee wax pack boxes. Complete box bottom panels are valued at a 25 percent premium above the prices listed below. The cards feature sixteen NHL star players who were scoring leaders on their teams. A color action photo appears on the front and the player's name, team, and team logo at the bottom of the picture. The back is printed in red and black ink and gives the player's position and statistical information. The cards are lettered rather than numbered.

| | MINT | NRMT |
|---|---|---|
| COMPLETE SET (16) | 10.00 | 4.50 |
| COMMON CARD (A-P) | .25 | .11 |

❑ A Mario Lemieux 4.00 1.80
❑ B Mike Ridley .25 .11
❑ C Tomas Sandstrom .25 .11
❑ D Petri Skriko .25 .11
❑ E Wayne Gretzky 4.00 1.80
❑ F Brett Hull 2.00 .90
❑ G Tim Kerr .25 .11
❑ H Mats Naslund .25 .11
❑ I Jari Kurri .50 .23
❑ J Steve Larmer .50 .23
❑ K Cam Neely .75 .35
❑ L Steve Yzerman 2.00 .90
❑ M Kevin Dineen .25 .11
❑ N Dave Gagner .35 .16
❑ O Joe Mullen .35 .16
❑ P Pierre Turgeon .75 .35

## 1989-90 O-Pee-Chee Stickers

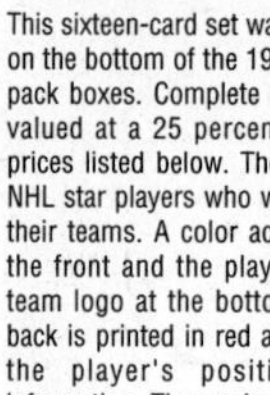

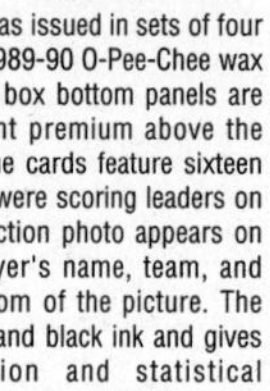

The 1989-90 O-Pee-Chee set contains 270 stickers. The standard size stickers measure 2 1/8" by 3"; some stickers consist of two half-size stickers. The fronts feature color action photos of players, teams, and trophies. The sticker backs are of four types: trivia questions and answers (green Level III), souvenir offers, Future Stars, and All-Stars. A full-color glossy album was issued with the set for holding the stickers. Some team action shots are a composite of two or four stickers; in the checklist below these stickers are denoted by L (left half) and R (right half), with the additional prefixes U (upper) and L (lower) for the four sticker pictures. The stickers are numbered on the front and are checklisted below accordingly. For those stickers that consist of two half-size stickers, we have noted the other number of the pair parenthetically after the player's name.

| | MINT | NRMT |
|---|---|---|
| COMPLETE SET (270) | 20.00 | 9.00 |
| COMMON STICKER (1-270) | .10 | .05 |
| COMMON HALF STICKER | .05 | .02 |

❑ 1 Flames/Canadiens .10 .05
action UL
❑ 2 Flames/Canadiens .25 .11
action UR, Zarley Zalapski-Future Star
❑ 3 Flames/Canadiens .10 .05
action LL
❑ 4 Flames/Canadiens .10 .05
action LR, Bob Joyce-Future Star
❑ 5 Al MacInnis .25 .11
Conn Smythe
Trophy Winner
❑ 6 Flames/Canadiens .10 .05
action UL
❑ 7 Flames/Canadiens .10 .05
action UR, Iiro Jarvi-Future Star
❑ 8 Flames/Canadiens .10 .05
action LL
❑ 9 Flames/Canadiens .10 .05
action LR
❑ 10 Darren Pang (150) .25 .11
Tony Granato-Future Star
❑ 11 Troy Murray (151) .05 .02
❑ 12 Dirk Graham (152) .05 .02
❑ 13 Dave Manson (153) .05 .02
❑ 14 Doug Wilson (156) 1.50 .70
Patrick Roy-All Star
❑ 15 Steve Thomas (157) .05 .02
❑ 16 Denis Savard .25 .11
❑ 17 Steve Larmer .25 .11
❑ 18 Paul MacLean (158) .05 .02
❑ 19 Paul Cavallini (159) .05 .02
❑ 20 Cliff Ronning (160) .25 .11
❑ 21 Gaston Gingras (161) .25 .11
Al MacInnis-All Star
❑ 22 Brett Hull 1.00 .45
❑ 23 Peter Zezel .10 .05
❑ 24 Brian Benning (162) .05 .02
❑ 25 Tony Hrkac (163) .05 .02
❑ 26 Ken Linseman (164) .05 .02
❑ 27 Glen Wesley (165) .05 .02
❑ 28 Randy Burridge (166) .05 .02
❑ 29 Craig Janney (167) .25 .11
❑ 30 Andy Moog (170) .25 .11
❑ 31 Bob Joyce (171) .05 .02
❑ 32 Ray Bourque .50 .23
Gerard Gallant-All Star
❑ 33 Cam Neely .50 .23
❑ 34 Sean Burke (174) .05 .02
❑ 35 Pat Elynuik (175) .50 .23
Craig Janney-Future Star
❑ 36 Tony Granato (176) .05 .02
❑ 37 Benoit Hogue (177) .25 .11
❑ 38 Craig Janney (180) .25 .11
❑ 39 Brian Leetch (181) .50 .23
❑ 40 Trevor Linden (184) .50 .23
❑ 41 Joe Sakic (185) 3.00 1.35
Joe Sakic-Future Star
❑ 42 Peter Sidorkiewicz .05 .02
(188)
❑ 43 Dave Volek (189) .05 .02
❑ 44 Scott Young (190) .05 .02
❑ 45 Zarley Zalapski (191) .05 .02
❑ 46 Mats Naslund .10 .05
❑ 47 Bobby Smith 3.00 1.35
Wayne Gretzky-All Star
❑ 48 Guy Carbonneau (194) .05 .02
❑ 49 Shayne Corson (195) .05 .02
❑ 50 Brian Hayward .10 .05
❑ 51 Stephane Richer .10 .05
❑ 52 Claude Lemieux (196) .50 .23
❑ 53 Russ Courtnall (197) .05 .02
❑ 54 Petr Svoboda (198) .50 .23
Chris Chelios-All Star
❑ 55 Larry Robinson (199) 3.00 1.35
Mario Lemieux-All Star
❑ 56 Chris Chelios .50 .23
❑ 57 Patrick Roy 1.50 .70
❑ 58 Bob Gainey (200) .05 .02
❑ 59 Mike McPhee (201) .05 .02
❑ 60 Barry Pederson .10 .05
Jiri Hrdina-Future Star
❑ 61 Trevor Linden .75 .35
Joe Mullen-All Star
❑ 62 Rich Sutter (204) .05 .02
❑ 63 Brian Bradley (205) .25 .11
Bob Essensa-Future Star
❑ 64 Kirk McLean .25 .11
John Cullen-Future Star
❑ 65 Paul Reinhart .25 .11
Steve Duchesne-All Star
❑ 66 Robert Nordmark (206) .05 .02
Pat Elynuik-Future Star
❑ 67 Steve Bozek (207) .05 .02
Greg Hawgood-Future Star
❑ 68 Stan Smyl (208) .05 .02
❑ 69 Doug Lidster (209) .05 .02
❑ 70 Petri Skriko .10 .05
❑ 71 Tony Tanti .10 .05
❑ 72 Garth Butcher (210) .50 .23
Ray Bourque-All Star
❑ 73 Larry Melnyk (212) .05 .02
❑ 74 Kelly Miller (213) .05 .02
❑ 75 Dino Ciccarelli (214) .05 .02
❑ 76 Scott Stevens (215) .25 .11
Mike Vernon-All Star
❑ 77 Rod Langway (216) .25 .11
Benoit Hogue-Future Star
❑ 78 Dave Christian (219) .05 .02
❑ 79 Stephen Leach (220) .05 .02
❑ 80 Geoff Courtnall .25 .11
❑ 81 Mike Ridley .10 .05
❑ 82 Patrik Sundstrom .05 .02
(223)
❑ 83 Kirk Muller (224) .05 .02
❑ 84 Tom Kurvers (225) .05 .02
❑ 85 Walt Poddubny (226) .05 .02
❑ 86 Sean Burke .25 .11
❑ 87 John MacLean .10 .05
❑ 88 Aaron Broten (229) .05 .02
Gordon Murphy-Future Star
❑ 89 Brendan Shanahan 1.00 .45
(230)
❑ 90 Joe Mullen .25 .11
❑ 91 Brad McCrimmon 1.50 .70
Brian Leetch-Future Star
❑ 92 Lanny McDonald (231) .05 .02
❑ 93 Rick Wamsley (232) .05 .02
❑ 94 Mike Vernon .25 .11
❑ 95 Al MacInnis .25 .11
❑ 96 Joel Otto (233) .05 .02
Scott Young-Future Star
❑ 97 Jiri Hrdina (234) .05 .02
❑ 98 Gary Roberts (235) .25 .11
❑ 99 Jim Peplinski (236) .05 .02
❑ 100 Gary Suter .10 .05
❑ 101 Joe Nieuwendyk .25 .11
❑ 102 Colin Patterson (239) .05 .02
Dan Marois-Future Star
❑ 103 Doug Gilmour (240) .25 .11
❑ 104 Mike Bullard (241) .05 .02
❑ 105 Pelle Eklund (242) .05 .02
❑ 106 Brian Propp (245) .05 .02
❑ 107 Ron Sutter (246) .25 .11
Geoff Courtnall-All Star
❑ 108 Rick Tocchet (247) .25 .11
❑ 109 Mark Howe (248) .05 .02
❑ 110 Tim Kerr .10 .05
❑ 111 Ron Hextall .25 .11
❑ 112 Mikko Makela (249) 1.00 .45
Trevor Linden-All Star
❑ 113 Dave Volek (250) .05 .02
❑ 114 Gary Nylund (251) .05 .02
❑ 115 Brent Sutter (252) .05 .02
❑ 116 Derek King (255) .25 .11
❑ 117 Gerald Diduck (256) .05 .02
Rob Brown-All Star
❑ 118 Bryan Trottier .25 .11
Peter Sidorkiewicz-Future Star
❑ 119 Pat LaFontaine .50 .23
❑ 120 Blues/Bruins action L .10 .05
❑ 121 Blues/Bruins action R .10 .05
❑ 122 Bruins/Rangers .10 .05
action L
❑ 123 Bruins/Rangers .10 .05
action R
❑ 124 Blackhawks action .10 .05
❑ 125 Bruins/Canadiens .25 .11
action (Ray Bourque)
❑ 126 Devils/Bruins action .10 .05
❑ 127 Flames/Devils action .10 .05
❑ 128 Canadiens/Flyers .10 .05
action
❑ 129 Flyers/Oilers action .10 .05
❑ 130 Canucks/Bruins .10 .05
action L
❑ 131 Canucks/Bruins .10 .05
action R
❑ 132 North Stars/Bruins .10 .05
action L
❑ 133 North Stars/Bruins .10 .05
action R
❑ 134 Dale Hawerchuk .25 .11
❑ 135 Andrew McBain .10 .05
❑ 136 Iain Duncan (257) .05 .02
❑ 137 Eldon Reddick (258) .05 .02
❑ 138 Brent Ashton .10 .05
❑ 139 Dave Ellett .10 .05
❑ 140 Jim Kyte (259) .05 .02
❑ 141 Doug Smail (260) .05 .02
❑ 142 Pat Elynuik (263) .05 .02
❑ 143 Randy Carlyle (264) .05 .02
❑ 144 Thomas Steen .10 .05
❑ 145 Hannu Jarvenpaa .10 .05
❑ 146 Peter Taglianetti .05 .02
(265)Vincent Riendeau, Future Star
❑ 147 Laurie Boschman (266) .05 .02
❑ 148 Luc Robitaille (267) .50 .23
❑ 149 Kelly Hrudey (268) .05 .02
❑ 150 Steve Duchesne (10) .05 .02
Tony Granato-Future Star
❑ 151 Dave Taylor (11) .05 .02
❑ 152 Steve Kasper (12) .05 .02
❑ 153 Mike Krushelnyski .05 .02
(13)
❑ 154 Wayne Gretzky 2.00 .90
❑ 155 Bernie Nicholls .10 .05
❑ 156 Chris Chelios (14) 1.50 .70
Patrick Roy-All Star
❑ 157 Gerard Gallant (15) .05 .02
❑ 158 Mario Lemieux (18) 1.00 .45
❑ 159 Al MacInnis (19) .05 .02
❑ 160 Joe Mullen (20) .05 .02
❑ 161 Patrick Roy (21) 1.00 .45
Al MacInnis-All Star
❑ 162 Ray Bourque (24) .25 .11
❑ 163 Rob Brown (25) .05 .02
❑ 164 Geoff Courtnall (26) .05 .02
❑ 165 Steve Duchesne (27) .05 .02
❑ 166 Wayne Gretzky (28) 1.50 .70
❑ 167 Mike Vernon (29) .25 .11
❑ 168 Gary Leeman .10 .05
❑ 169 Allan Bester .10 .05
❑ 170 David Reid (30) .05 .02
❑ 171 Craig Laughlin (31) .05 .02
❑ 172 Ed Olczyk .10 .05
❑ 173 Tom Fergus .10 .05
❑ 174 Mark Osborne (34) .05 .02
❑ 175 Brad Marsh (35) .50 .23
Craig Janney-Future Star
❑ 176 Daniel Marois (36) .05 .02
❑ 177 Dan Daoust (37) .05 .02
❑ 178 Al Iafrate .25 .11
❑ 179 Vincent Damphousse .25 .11
❑ 180 Chris Kotsopoulos .05 .02
(38)
❑ 181 Derek Laxdal (39) .05 .02
❑ 182 Peter Stastny .25 .11
❑ 183 Paul Gillis .10 .05
❑ 184 Jeff Jackson (40) .05 .02
❑ 185 Mario Marois (41) 3.00 1.35
Joe Sakic-Future Star
❑ 186 Michel Goulet .25 .11
❑ 187 Joe Sakic 4.00 1.80
Dave Volek-Future Star
❑ 188 Bob Mason (42) .05 .02
❑ 189 Marc Fortier (43) .05 .02
❑ 190 Robert Picard (44) .05 .02
❑ 191 Steven Finn (45) .05 .02
❑ 192 Iiro Jarvi .10 .05
❑ 193 Jeff Brown .25 .11
❑ 194 Gaetan Duchesne (48) .05 .02
❑ 195 Randy Moller (49) .05 .02
❑ 196 Mike Gartner (52) .25 .11
❑ 197 Jon Casey (53) .25 .11
❑ 198 Marc Habscheid (54) .50 .23
Chris Chelios-All Star
❑ 199 Larry Murphy (55) 3.00 1.35
Mario Lemieux-All Star
❑ 200 Brian Bellows (58) .05 .02
❑ 201 Dave Archibald (59) .05 .02
❑ 202 Neal Broten .10 .05
❑ 203 Dave Gagner .50 .23
Sean Burke-Future Star
❑ 204 Vezina Trophy (62) .05 .02
❑ 205 Jennings Trophy (63) .25 .11
Bob Essensa-Future Star
❑ 206 Selke Trophy (66) .05 .02
Pat Elynuik-Future Star
❑ 207 Masterton Trophy (67) .05 .02
Greg Hawgood-Future Star
❑ 208 Mario Lemieux (68) 1.00 .45
Ross Trophy Winner
❑ 209 Wayne Gretzky (69) 1.50 .70
Hart Trophy Winner
❑ 210 Patrick Roy (72) 1.00 .45
Vezina Trophy Winner,
Ray Bourque-All Star
❑ 211 Patrick Roy and .75 .35
Brian Hayward
Jennings Trophy Winners
❑ 212 Chris Chelios (73) .25 .11
Norris Trophy Winner
❑ 213 Guy Carbonneau (74) .05 .02
Selke Trophy Winner
❑ 214 Joe Mullen (75) .05 .02
Lady Byng Trophy Winner
❑ 215 Brian Leetch (76) .50 .23
Calder Trophy Winner, Mike Vernon-All Star
❑ 216 Tim Kerr (77) .25 .11
Masterton Trophy Winner,
Benoit Hogue-Future Star
❑ 217 Craig Simpson .10 .05
❑ 218 Glenn Anderson .10 .05
❑ 219 Esa Tikkanen (78) .25 .11
❑ 220 Charlie Huddy (79) .05 .02
❑ 221 Jari Kurri .25 .11
❑ 222 Jimmy Carson .10 .05
❑ 223 Steve Smith (82) .05 .02
❑ 224 Kevin Lowe (83) .05 .02
❑ 225 Chris Joseph (84) .05 .02
❑ 226 Craig MacTavish (85) .05 .02
❑ 227 Mark Messier .50 .23
❑ 228 Grant Fuhr .25 .11
❑ 229 Craig Muni (88) .05 .02
Gordon Murphy-Future Star
❑ 230 Bill Ranford (89) .50 .23
❑ 231 John Cullen (92) .25 .11
❑ 232 Zarley Zalapski (93) .05 .02
❑ 233 Bob Errey (96) .05 .02
Scott Young-Future Star
❑ 234 Dan Quinn (97) .05 .02
❑ 235 Tom Barrasso (98) .05 .02
❑ 236 Rob Brown (99) .05 .02
❑ 237 Paul Coffey .50 .23
❑ 238 Mario Lemieux 1.50 .70
❑ 239 Carey Wilson (102) .05 .02
Dan Marois-Future Star
❑ 240 Brian Leetch (103) .50 .23
❑ 241 Tony Granato (104) .05 .02
❑ 242 James Patrick (105) .05 .02
❑ 243 Brian Mullen .10 .05
❑ 244 Tomas Sandstrom .10 .05
❑ 245 Guy Lafleur (106) .25 .11
❑ 246 John Vanbiesbrouck .50 .23
(107)Geoff Courtnall-All Star
❑ 247 Bernie Federko (108) .05 .02
❑ 248 Greg Stefan (109) .05 .02
❑ 249 Mike O'Connell (112) 1.00 .45
Trevor Linden-All Star
❑ 250 Dave Barr (113) .25 .11
❑ 251 Lee Norwood (114) .05 .02
❑ 252 Shawn Burr (115) .05 .02
❑ 253 Gerard Gallant .10 .05
❑ 254 Steve Yzerman .75 .35
❑ 255 Christian Ruuttu .05 .02
(116)
❑ 256 Rick Vaive (117) .05 .02
Rob Brown-All Star
❑ 257 Doug Bodger (136) .05 .02
❑ 258 Dave Andreychuk (137) .05 .02
❑ 259 Ray Sheppard (140) .05 .02
❑ 260 Mike Foligno (141) .05 .02
❑ 261 Phil Housley .25 .11
❑ 262 Pierre Turgeon .50 .23
❑ 263 Ray Ferraro (142) .05 .02
❑ 264 Scott Young (143) .05 .02
❑ 265 Dave Babych (146) .05 .02
Vincent Riendeau, Future Star
❑ 266 Paul MacDermid (147) .05 .02
❑ 267 Mike Liut (148) .05 .02
❑ 268 Dave Tippett (149) .05 .02
❑ 269 Ron Francis .50 .23
❑ 270 Kevin Dineen .10 .05
❑ xx Sticker Album 2.00 .90

## 1990-91 O-Pee-Chee

At 528 cards, this is the largest set ever issued by O-Pee-Chee. Cards measure the standard 2 1/2" by 3 1/2". The fronts feature color photos bordered by team colors. A hockey stick is superimposed over the picture at the top

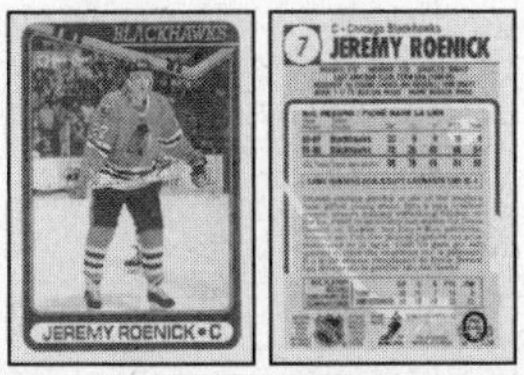


border. Bilingual backs have blue lettering on a pale green background and have biographical information and career statistics. Rookie Cards in this set include Rod Brind'Amour, Stephane Fiset, Adam Graves, Arturs Irbe, Curtis Joseph, Igor Larionov, Sergei Makarov, Mike Modano, Alexander Mogilny, Mark Recchi, and Jeremy Roenick, and Kevin Stevens.

| | MINT | NRMT |
|---|---|---|
| COMPLETE SET (528) | 15.00 | 6.75 |
| COMP.FACT.SET (528) | 20.00 | 9.00 |
| COMMON CARD (1-528) | .05 | .02 |

❑ 1 Gretzky Tribute .75 .35
Indianapolis Racers
❑ 2 Gretzky Tribute .75 .35
❑ 3 Gretzky Tribute .75 .35
❑ 4 Brett Hull HL .25 .11
❑ 5 Jari Kurri HL UER .10 .05
(Misspelled Jarri)
❑ 6 Bryan Trottier HL .10 .05
❑ 7 Jeremy Roenick 1.00 .45
❑ 8 Brian Propp .05 .02
❑ 9 Jim Hrivnak .10 .05
❑ 10 Mick Vukota .05 .02
❑ 11 Tom Kurvers .05 .02
❑ 12 Ulf Dahlen .05 .02
❑ 13 Bernie Nicholls .10 .05
❑ 14 Peter Sidorkiewicz .10 .05
❑ 15 Peter Zezel .05 .02
❑ 16 Mike Hartman .05 .02
❑ 17 Kings Team .05 .02
(Marty McSorley et al.)
❑ 18 Jim Sandlak .05 .02
❑ 19 Rob Brown .05 .02
❑ 20 Paul Ranheim .05 .02
❑ 21 Rick Zombo .05 .02
❑ 22 Paul Gillis .05 .02
❑ 23 Brian Hayward .10 .05
❑ 24 Brent Ashton .05 .02
❑ 25 Mark Lamb .05 .02
❑ 26 Rick Tocchet .10 .05
❑ 27 Slava Fetisov .05 .02
❑ 28 Denis Savard .10 .05
❑ 29 Chris Chelios .25 .11
❑ 30 Janne Ojanen .05 .02
❑ 31 Don Maloney .05 .02
❑ 32 Allan Bester .10 .05
❑ 33 Geoff Smith .05 .02
❑ 34 Daniel Shank .05 .02
❑ 35 Mikael Andersson .05 .02
❑ 36 Gino Cavallini .05 .02
❑ 37 Rob Murphy .05 .02
❑ 38 Flames Team .05 .02
(Goal celebration)
❑ 39 Laurie Boschman .05 .02
❑ 40 Craig Wolanin .05 .02
❑ 41 Phil Bourque .05 .02
❑ 42 Alexander Mogilny 1.00 .45
❑ 43 Ray Bourque .25 .11
❑ 44 Mike Liut .10 .05
❑ 45 Ron Sutter .05 .02
❑ 46 Bob Kudelski .05 .02
❑ 47 Larry Murphy .10 .05
❑ 48 Darren Turcotte .05 .02
❑ 49 Paul Ysebaert .05 .02
❑ 50 Alan Kerr .05 .02
❑ 51 Randy Carlyle .05 .02
❑ 52 Iiro Jarvi .05 .02
❑ 53 Don Barber .05 .02
❑ 54 Carey Wilson UER .05 .02
(Misspelled Cary
on both sides)
❑ 55 Joey Kocur .05 .02
❑ 56 Steve Larmer .10 .05
❑ 57 Paul Cavallini .05 .02
❑ 58 Shayne Corson .05 .02
❑ 59 Canucks Team .05 .02
(Brian Bradley)
❑ 60 Sergei Makarov .05 .02
❑ 61 Kjell Samuelsson .05 .02
❑ 62 Tony Granato .05 .02
❑ 63 Tom Fergus .05 .02
❑ 64 Martin Gelinas .40 .18
❑ 65 Tom Barrasso .10 .05
❑ 66 Pierre Turgeon .10 .05
❑ 67 Randy Cunneyworth .05 .02
❑ 68 Michal Pivonka .05 .02
❑ 69 Cam Neely .10 .05
❑ 70 Brian Bellows .05 .02
❑ 71 Pat Elynuik .05 .02
❑ 72 Doug Crossman .05 .02
❑ 73 Sylvain Turgeon .05 .02
❑ 74 Shawn Burr .05 .02
❑ 75 John Vanbiesbrouck .50 .23
❑ 76 Steve Bozek .05 .02
❑ 77 Brett Hull .60 .25
❑ 78 Zarley Zalapski .05 .02
❑ 79 Wendel Clark .10 .05
❑ 80 Flyers Team .05 .02
(Wendell Young/Kjell Samuelsson)
❑ 81 Kelly Miller .05 .02
❑ 82 Mark Pederson .05 .02
❑ 83 Adam Creighton .05 .02
❑ 84 Scott Young .05 .02
❑ 85 Petr Klima .05 .02
❑ 86 Steve Duchesne .05 .02
❑ 87 Joe Nieuwendyk .10 .05
❑ 88 Andy Brickley .05 .02
❑ 89 Phil Housley .10 .05
❑ 90 Neal Broten .10 .05
❑ 91 Al Iafrate .10 .05
❑ 92 Steve Thomas .05 .02
❑ 93 Guy Carbonneau .10 .05
❑ 94 Steve Chiasson .05 .02
❑ 95 Mike Tomlak .05 .02
❑ 96 Roger Johansson .05 .02
❑ 97 Randy Wood .05 .02
❑ 98 Jim Johnson .05 .02
❑ 99 Bob Sweeney .05 .02
❑ 100 Dino Ciccarelli .10 .05
❑ 101 Rangers Team .05 .02
(Goal celebration)
❑ 102 Mike Ramsey .05 .02
❑ 103 Kelly Hrudey .10 .05
❑ 104 Dave Ellett .05 .02
❑ 105 Bob Brooke .05 .02
❑ 106 Greg Adams .05 .02
❑ 107 Joe Cirella .05 .02
❑ 108 Jari Kurri .10 .05
❑ 109 Pete Peeters .10 .05
❑ 110 Paul MacLean .05 .02
❑ 111 Doug Wilson .10 .05
❑ 112 Pat Verbeek .05 .02
❑ 113 Bob Beers .05 .02
❑ 114 Mike O'Connell .05 .02
❑ 115 Brian Bradley .05 .02
❑ 116 Paul Coffey .25 .11
❑ 117 Doug Brown .05 .02
❑ 118 Aaron Broten .05 .02
❑ 119 Bob Essensa .10 .05
❑ 120 Wayne Gretzky UER 1.50 .70
(1302 career assists,
not 13102)
❑ 121 Vincent Damphousse .10 .05
❑ 122 Nordiques Team .05 .02
(Paul Gillis)
❑ 123 Mike Foligno .05 .02
❑ 124 Russ Courtnall .05 .02
❑ 125 Rick Meagher .05 .02
❑ 126 Craig Fisher .05 .02
❑ 127 Al MacInnis .10 .05
❑ 128 Derek King .05 .02
❑ 129 Dale Hunter .05 .02
❑ 130 Mark Messier UER .40 .18
(Position LW,
should be C)
❑ 131 James Patrick UER .05 .02
(Blue border,
should be orange)
❑ 132 Checklist 1-132 UER .05 .02
(132 Cary Wilson,
should be Carey)
❑ 133 Red Wings Team .25 .11
(Steve Yzerman)
❑ 134 Barry Pederson .05 .02
❑ 135 Gary Leeman .05 .02
❑ 136 Doug Gilmour .25 .11
❑ 137 Mike McPhee .05 .02
❑ 138 Bob Murray .05 .02
❑ 139 Bob Carpenter .05 .02
❑ 140 Sean Burke .10 .05
❑ 141 Dale Hawerchuk .10 .05
❑ 142 Guy Lafleur .25 .11
❑ 143 Lindy Ruff .05 .02
❑ 144 Whalers Team .05 .02
(Brad Shaw)
❑ 145 Glenn Anderson .10 .05
❑ 146 Dave Chyzowski .05 .02
❑ 147 Kevin Hatcher .05 .02
❑ 148 Rick Vaive .05 .02
❑ 149 Adam Oates .10 .05
❑ 150 Garth Butcher .05 .02
❑ 151 Basil McRae .05 .02
❑ 152 Ilkka Sinisalo .05 .02
❑ 153 Steve Kasper .05 .02
❑ 154 Greg Paslawski .05 .02
❑ 155 Brad Marsh .05 .02
❑ 156 Esa Tikkanen .05 .02
❑ 157 Tony Tanti .05 .02
❑ 158 Mario Marois UER .05 .02
(On front, "oi" in
Marois is out of line)
❑ 159 Sylvain Lefebvre .05 .02
❑ 160 Troy Murray .05 .02
❑ 161 Gary Roberts .05 .02
❑ 162 Randy Ladouceur .05 .02
❑ 163 John Chabot .05 .02
❑ 164 Calle Johansson .05 .02
❑ 165 Bruins Team .05 .02
(Goal celebration)
❑ 166 Jeff Norton .05 .02
❑ 167 Mike Krushelnyski .05 .02
❑ 168 Dave Gagner .10 .05
❑ 169 Dave Andreychuk .10 .05
❑ 170 Dave Capuano .05 .02
❑ 171 Curtis Joseph 1.00 .45
❑ 172 Bruce Driver .05 .02
❑ 173 Scott Mellanby .10 .05
❑ 174 John Ogrodnick .05 .02
❑ 175 Mario Lemieux 1.25 .55
❑ 176 Marc Fortier .05 .02
❑ 177 Vincent Riendeau .05 .02
❑ 178 Mark Johnson .05 .02
❑ 179 Dirk Graham .05 .02
❑ 180 Jets Team .05 .02
(Keith Acton breaking in on
Daniel Berthiaume)
❑ 181 Robb Stauber .10 .05
❑ 182 Christian Ruuttu .05 .02
❑ 183 Dave Tippett .05 .02
❑ 184 Pat LaFontaine .10 .05
❑ 185 Mark Howe .05 .02
❑ 186 Stephane Richer .10 .05
❑ 187 Jan Erixon .05 .02
❑ 188 Neil Sheehy .05 .02
❑ 189 Craig MacTavish .05 .02
❑ 190 Randy Burridge .05 .02
❑ 191 Bernie Federko .10 .05
❑ 192 Shawn Chambers .05 .02
❑ 193 Mark Messier AS1 .25 .11
❑ 194 Luc Robitaille AS1 .10 .05
❑ 195 Brett Hull AS1 .25 .11
❑ 196 Ray Bourque AS1 .25 .11
❑ 197 Al MacInnis AS1 .10 .05
❑ 198 Patrick Roy AS1 .50 .23
❑ 199 Wayne Gretzky AS2 .75 .35
❑ 200 Brian Bellows AS2 .05 .02
❑ 201 Cam Neely AS2 .10 .05
❑ 202 Paul Coffey AS2 .25 .11
❑ 203 Doug Wilson AS2 .10 .05
❑ 204 Daren Puppa AS2 UER .10 .05
(Misspelled Darren)
❑ 205 Gary Suter .05 .02
❑ 206 Ed Olczyk .05 .02
❑ 207 Doug Lidster .05 .02
❑ 208 John Cullen .05 .02
❑ 209 Luc Robitaille .10 .05
❑ 210 Tim Kerr .05 .02
❑ 211 Scott Stevens .10 .05
❑ 212 Craig Janney .10 .05
❑ 213 Kevin Dineen .05 .02
❑ 214 Jimmy Waite .10 .05
❑ 215 Benoit Hogue .05 .02
❑ 216 Curtis Leschyshyn .05 .02
❑ 217 Brad Lauer .05 .02
❑ 218 Joe Mullen .10 .05
❑ 219 Patrick Roy 1.25 .55
❑ 220 Blues Team .05 .02
(Gathering at bench)
❑ 221 Brian Leetch .40 .18
❑ 222 Steve Yzerman .75 .35
❑ 223 Stephane Beauregard .10 .05
❑ 224 John MacLean .10 .05
❑ 225 Trevor Linden .10 .05
❑ 226 Bill Ranford .10 .05
❑ 227 Mark Osborne .05 .02
❑ 228 Curt Giles .05 .02
❑ 229 Mikko Makela .05 .02
❑ 230 Bob Errey .05 .02
❑ 231 Jimmy Carson .05 .02
❑ 232 Kay Whitmore .10 .05
❑ 233 Gary Nylund .05 .02
❑ 234 Jiri Hrdina .05 .02
❑ 235 Stephen Leach .05 .02
❑ 236 Greg Hawgood UER .05 .02
(Photo actually
Don Sweeney)
❑ 237 Jocelyn Lemieux .05 .02
❑ 238 Daren Puppa .10 .05
❑ 239 Kelly Kisio .05 .02
❑ 240 Craig Simpson .05 .02
❑ 241 Maple Leafs Team .10 .05
(Vincent Damphousse)
❑ 242 Fredrik Olausson .05 .02
❑ 243 Ron Hextall .10 .05
❑ 244 Sergio Momesso .05 .02
❑ 245 Kirk Muller .05 .02
❑ 246 Petr Svoboda .05 .02
❑ 247 Daniel Berthiaume .10 .05
❑ 248 Andrew McBain .05 .02
❑ 249 Jeff Jackson UER .05 .02
('89-90 stats should
be 65, not 0)
❑ 250 Randy Gilhen .05 .02
❑ 251 Oilers Team .05 .02
(Adam Graves)
❑ 252 Rick Bennett .05 .02
❑ 253 Don Beaupre .10 .05
❑ 254 Pelle Eklund .05 .02
❑ 255 Greg Gilbert .05 .02
❑ 256 Gordie Roberts .05 .02
❑ 257 Kirk McLean .10 .05
❑ 258 Brent Sutter .05 .02
❑ 259 Brendan Shanahan .75 .35
❑ 260 Todd Krygier .05 .02
❑ 261 Larry Robinson UER .10 .05
('80-81 season stats
missing making career
totals wrong)
❑ 262 Sabres Team .05 .02
(Phil Housley celebrating goal)
❑ 263 Dave Christian .05 .02
❑ 264 Checklist 133-264 .05 .02
❑ 265 Jamie Macoun .05 .02
❑ 266 Glen Hanlon .10 .05
❑ 267 Daniel Marois .05 .02
❑ 268 Doug Smail .05 .02
❑ 269 Jon Casey .10 .05
❑ 270 Brian Skrudland .05 .02
❑ 271 Michel Petit .05 .02
❑ 272 Dan Quinn .05 .02
❑ 273 Geoff Courtnall .05 .02
❑ 274 Mike Bullard .05 .02
❑ 275 Randy Gregg .05 .02
❑ 276 Keith Brown .05 .02
❑ 277 Troy Mallette .05 .02
❑ 278 Steve Tuttle .05 .02
❑ 279 Brad Shaw .05 .02
❑ 280 Mark Recchi .50 .23
❑ 281 John Tonelli .05 .02
❑ 282 Doug Bodger .05 .02
❑ 283 Thomas Steen .05 .02
❑ 284 Devils Team .05 .02
(Terreri making save)
❑ 285 Lee Norwood .05 .02
❑ 286 Brian MacLellan .05 .02
❑ 287 Bobby Smith .10 .05
❑ 288 Rob Cimetta .05 .02
❑ 289 Rob Zettler .05 .02
❑ 290 David Reid .05 .02
❑ 291 Bryan Trottier .10 .05
❑ 292 Brian Mullen .05 .02
❑ 293 Paul Reinhart .05 .02
❑ 294 Andy Moog .10 .05
❑ 295 Jeff Brown .05 .02
❑ 296 Ryan Walter .05 .02
❑ 297 Trent Yawney .05 .02
❑ 298 John Druce .05 .02
❑ 299 Dave McLlwain .05 .02
❑ 300 David Volek .05 .02
❑ 301 Tomas Sandstrom .05 .02
❑ 302 Gord Murphy .05 .02
❑ 303 Lou Franceschetti .05 .02
❑ 304 Dana Murzyn .05 .02
❑ 305 North Stars Team .05 .02
❑ 306 Patrik Sundstrom .05 .02
❑ 307 Kevin Lowe .05 .02
❑ 308 Dave Barr .05 .02
❑ 309 Wendell Young .10 .05
❑ 310 Darrin Shannon .05 .02
❑ 311 Ron Francis .10 .05
❑ 312 Stephane Fiset .50 .23
❑ 313 Paul Fenton .05 .02
❑ 314 Dave Taylor .10 .05
❑ 315 Islanders Team .05 .02
(Pat LaFontaine)
❑ 316 Petri Skriko .05 .02
❑ 317 Rob Ramage .05 .02
❑ 318 Murray Craven .05 .02
❑ 319 Gaetan Duchesne .05 .02
❑ 320 Brad McCrimmon .05 .02
❑ 321 Grant Fuhr .10 .05
❑ 322 Gerard Gallant .05 .02
❑ 323 Tommy Albelin .05 .02
❑ 324 Scott Arniel .05 .02
❑ 325 Mike Keane .05 .02
❑ 326 Penguins Team .05 .02
❑ 327 Mike Ridley .05 .02
❑ 328 Dave Babych .05 .02
❑ 329 Michel Goulet .10 .05
❑ 330 Mike Richter 1.00 .45
❑ 331 Garry Galley .05 .02
❑ 332 Rod Brind'Amour .75 .35
❑ 333 Tony McKegney .05 .02
❑ 334 Peter Stastny .10 .05
❑ 335 Greg Millen .10 .05
❑ 336 Ray Ferraro .05 .02
❑ 337 Miloslav Horava .05 .02
❑ 338 Paul MacDermid .05 .02
❑ 339 Craig Coxe .05 .02
❑ 340 Dave Snuggerud .05 .02
❑ 341 Mike Lalor .05 .02
❑ 342 Marc Habscheid .05 .02
❑ 343 Rejean Lemelin .10 .05
❑ 344 Charlie Huddy .05 .02
❑ 345 Ken Linseman .05 .02
❑ 346 Canadiens Team .05 .02
(Goal celebration)
❑ 347 Troy Loney .05 .02
❑ 348 Mike Modano 1.25 .55
❑ 349 Jeff Reese .05 .02
❑ 350 Pat Flatley .05 .02
❑ 351 Mike Vernon .10 .05
❑ 352 Todd Elik .05 .02
❑ 353 Rod Langway .05 .02
❑ 354 Moe Mantha .05 .02
❑ 355 Keith Acton .05 .02
❑ 356 Scott Pearson .05 .02
❑ 357 Perry Berezan .05 .02
❑ 358 Alexei Kasatonov .05 .02
❑ 359 Igor Larionov .50 .23
❑ 360 Kevin Stevens .05 .02
❑ 361 Yves Racine .05 .02
❑ 362 Dave Poulin .05 .02
❑ 363 Blackhawks Team .05 .02
(Manson et al.)
❑ 364 Yvon Corriveau .05 .02
❑ 365 Brian Benning .05 .02
❑ 366 Hubie McDonough .05 .02
❑ 367 Ron Tugnutt .10 .05
❑ 368 Steve Smith .05 .02
❑ 369 Joel Otto .05 .02
❑ 370 Dave Lowry .05 .02
❑ 371 Clint Malarchuk .10 .05
❑ 372 Mathieu Schneider .05 .02
❑ 373 Mike Gartner .10 .05
❑ 374 John Tucker .05 .02
❑ 375 Chris Terreri .10 .05
❑ 376 Dean Evason .05 .02
❑ 377 Jamie Leach .05 .02
❑ 378 Jacques Cloutier .10 .05
❑ 379 Glen Wesley .05 .02
❑ 380 Vladimir Krutov .10 .05
❑ 381 Terry Carkner .05 .02
❑ 382 John McIntyre .05 .02
❑ 383 Ville Siren .05 .02
❑ 384 Joe Sakic .75 .35
❑ 385 Teppo Numminen .05 .02
❑ 386 Theoren Fleury .10 .05
❑ 387 Glen Featherstone .05 .02
❑ 388 Stephan Lebeau .05 .02
❑ 389 Kevin McClelland .05 .02
❑ 390 Uwe Krupp .05 .02
❑ 391 Mark Janssens .05 .02
❑ 392 Marty McSorley .05 .02
❑ 393 Vladimir Ruzicka .05 .02
❑ 394 Capitals Team .05 .02
(Scott Stevens/Kirk Muller)
❑ 395 Mark Fitzpatrick .10 .05
❑ 396 Checklist 265-396 .05 .02
❑ 397 Dave Manson .05 .02
❑ 398 Bob Gould .05 .02
❑ 399 Bill Houlder .05 .02
❑ 400 Glenn Healy .10 .05
❑ 401 John Kordic UER .05 .02
(Listed as Defence,
should be LW)
❑ 402 Stewart Gavin .05 .02
❑ 403 David Shaw .05 .02
❑ 404 Ed Kastelic .05 .02
❑ 405 Rich Sutter .05 .02
❑ 406 Grant Ledyard .05 .02
❑ 407 Steve Weeks .10 .05
❑ 408 Randy Hillier .05 .02
❑ 409 Rick Wamsley .10 .05
❑ 410 Doug Houda .05 .02
❑ 411 Ken McRae .05 .02
❑ 412 Craig Ludwig .05 .02
❑ 413 Doug Evans .05 .02
❑ 414 Ken Baumgartner .05 .02
❑ 415 Ken Wregget .10 .05
❑ 416 Eric Weinrich .05 .02
❑ 417 Mike Allison .05 .02
❑ 418 Joel Quenneville .05 .02
❑ 419 Larry Melnyk .05 .02
❑ 420 Colin Patterson .05 .02
❑ 421 Gerald Diduck .05 .02
❑ 422 Brent Gilchrist .05 .02
❑ 423 Craig Muni .05 .02
❑ 424 Mike Hudson .05 .02
❑ 425 Eric Desjardins .05 .02
❑ 426 Walt Poddubny .05 .02
❑ 427 Mike Hough .05 .02
❑ 428 Luke Richardson .05 .02
❑ 429 Joe Murphy .05 .02
❑ 430 Tim Cheveldae .10 .05
❑ 431 Adam Burt .05 .02
❑ 432 Kelly Chase .05 .02
❑ 433 Robert Nordmark .05 .02
❑ 434 Tim Hunter .05 .02
❑ 435 Peter Taglianetti .05 .02
❑ 436 Alain Chevrier .10 .05
❑ 437 Darin Kimble .05 .02
❑ 438 David Maley .05 .02
❑ 439 Jim Wiemer .05 .02
❑ 440 Nick Kypreos .05 .02
❑ 441 Lucien DeBlois .05 .02
❑ 442 Mario Gosselin .10 .05
❑ 443 Neil Wilkinson .05 .02
❑ 444 Mark Kumpel .05 .02
❑ 445 Sergei Mylnikov UER .05 .02
(Misspelled Sergi)
❑ 446 Ray Sheppard .10 .05
❑ 447 Ron Greschner .05 .02
❑ 448 Craig Berube .05 .02
❑ 449 Dave Hannan .05 .02
❑ 450 Jim Korn UER .05 .02
(Photo actually
Paul Ranheim)
❑ 451 Claude Lemieux .10 .05
❑ 452 Eldon Reddick .10 .05
❑ 453 Randy Velischek .05 .02
❑ 454 Chris Nilan .05 .02
❑ 455 Jim Benning .05 .02
❑ 456 Wayne Presley .05 .02
❑ 457 Jon Morris .05 .02
❑ 458 Clark Donatelli .05 .02
❑ 459 Ric Nattress .05 .02
❑ 460 Rob Murray .05 .02
❑ 461 Tim Watters .05 .02
❑ 462 Checklist 397-528 .05 .02
❑ 463 Derrick Smith .05 .02
❑ 464 Lyndon Byers .05 .02
❑ 465 Jeff Chychrun .05 .02
❑ 466 Duane Sutter .05 .02
❑ 467 Conn Smythe Trophy .10 .05
Bill Ranford
❑ 468 Anatoli Semenov .05 .02
❑ 469 Konstantin Kurashov .05 .02
❑ 470 Gord Dineen .05 .02
❑ 471 Jeff Beukeboom .05 .02
❑ 472 Andrei Lomakin .05 .02
❑ 473 Doug Sulliman .05 .02
❑ 474 Alexander Kerch .05 .02
❑ 475 Norris Trophy .10 .05
Ray Bourque
❑ 476 Keith Crowder .05 .02
❑ 477 Oleg Znarok .05 .02
❑ 478 Dimitri Zinovyev .05 .02
❑ 479 Igor Esmantovich .05 .02
❑ 480 Adam Graves .50 .23
❑ 481 Petr Prajsler .05 .02
❑ 482 Sergei Yashin .05 .02
❑ 483 Jeff Bloemberg .05 .02
❑ 484 Yuri Strakhov .05 .02
❑ 485 Sergei B. Makarov .05 .02
❑ 486 Jennings Trophy .10 .05
Rejean Lemelin,
Andy Moog
❑ 487 Sergei Zaltsev .05 .02
❑ 488 Selke Trophy .05 .02
Rick Meagher
❑ 489 Yuri Kusnetsov .05 .02
❑ 490 Tom Chorske .05 .02
❑ 491 Igor Akulinin .05 .02
❑ 492 Mikhail Panin .05 .02
❑ 493 Sergei Nemchinov .05 .02
❑ 494 Vladimir Yurzinov .05 .02
❑ 495 Gord Kluzak .05 .02
❑ 496 Sergei Skosyrev .05 .02
❑ 497 Jeff Parker .05 .02
❑ 498 Tom Tilley .05 .02
❑ 499 Alexander Smirnov .05 .02
❑ 500 Alexander Lysenko .05 .02
❑ 501 Arturs Irbe UER .75 .35
(Misspelled Artur;
played in 7 games of

Dynamo Riga's tour)
❑ 502 Alexei Frolikov .05 .02
❑ 503 Calder Trophy .05 .02
Sergei Makarov
❑ 504 Nikolai Varjanov .05 .02
❑ 505 Allen Pedersen .05 .02
❑ 506 Vladimir Shashov .05 .02
❑ 507 Tim Bergland .05 .02
❑ 508 Gennady Lebedev .05 .02
❑ 509 Rod Buskas .05 .02
❑ 510 Grant Jennings .05 .02
❑ 511 Ulf Samuelsson .05 .02
❑ 512 Vezina Trophy .50 .23
Patrick Roy
❑ 513 Lady Byng Trophy .25 .11
Brett Hull
❑ 514 Dimitri Mironov .05 .02
❑ 515 Randy Moller .05 .02
❑ 516 Kerry Huffman .05 .02
❑ 517 Gilbert Delorme .05 .02
❑ 518 Greg C. Adams .05 .02
❑ 519 Hart Trophy .25 .11
Mark Messier
❑ 520 Sheldon Kennedy .05 .02
❑ 521 Harijs Vitolins .05 .02
❑ 522 Art Ross Trophy .75 .35
Wayne Gretzky
❑ 523 Dmitri Frolov .05 .02
❑ 524 Tom Laidlaw .05 .02
❑ 525 Oleg Bratash UER .10 .05
(Played in 2 games of Wings' 1990 NHL tour)
❑ 526 Kris King .05 .02
❑ 527 Wayne Van Dorp .05 .02
❑ 528 Chris Dahlquist .05 .02

## 1990-91 O-Pee-Chee Box Bottoms

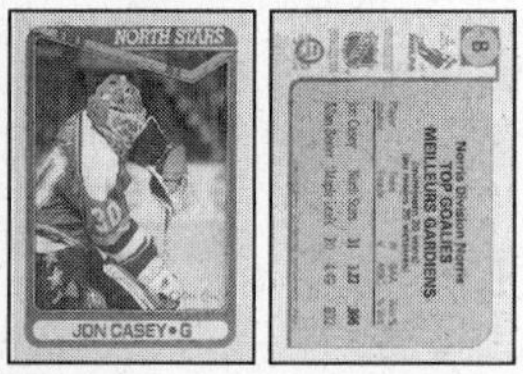

This sixteen-card set was issued in sets of four on the bottom of the 1990-91 O-Pee-Chee wax pack boxes. Complete box bottom panels are valued at a 25 percent premium above the prices listed below. The cards are lettered rather than numbered.

| | MINT | NRMT |
|---|---|---|
| COMPLETE SET (16) | 10.00 | 4.50 |
| COMMON CARD (A-P) | .25 | .11 |

❑ A Alexander Mogilny .75 .35
❑ B Jon Casey .35 .16
❑ C Paul Coffey .75 .35
❑ D Wayne Gretzky 3.00 1.35
❑ E Patrick Roy 2.00 .90
❑ F Mike Modano 1.00 .45
❑ G Mario Lemieux 2.00 .90
❑ H Al MacInnis .50 .23
❑ I Ray Bourque .75 .35
❑ J Steve Yzerman 1.50 .70
❑ K Darren Turcotte .25 .11
❑ L Mike Vernon .50 .23
❑ M Pierre Turgeon .50 .23
❑ N Doug Wilson .25 .11
❑ O Don Beaupre .35 .16
❑ P Sergei Makarov .50 .23

## 1990-91 O-Pee-Chee Red Army

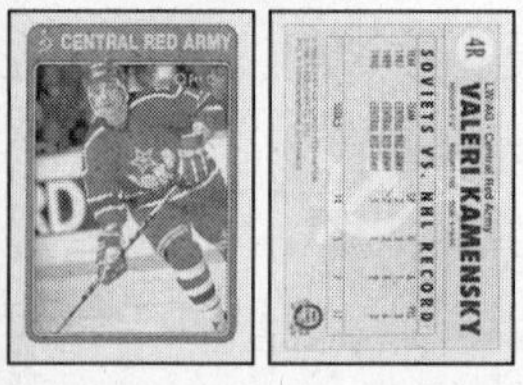

This 22-card standard-size set was distributed one card per 1990-91 O-Pee-Chee wax pack. The fronts feature color action photos surrounded by red borders. The words "Central Red Army" appear above the photos in the red border. The horizontally designed backs contain the player's statistics compiled from the Super Series tour against the NHL. The statistical information on the back is superimposed over a white Soviet star and a "hammer and sickle" insignia. The card number is followed by an R suffix. Parts of the first print run suffered from pin punctures and other quality control flaws. First cards of Sergei Fedorov, Arturs Irbe, and Valeri Kamensky are a part of this set. Because this is an insert set, these cards are not considered Rookie Cards.

| | MINT | NRMT |
|---|---|---|
| COMPLETE SET (22) | 8.00 | 3.60 |
| COMMON CARD (1R-22R) | .25 | .11 |

❑ 1R Ilya Byalsin .25 .11
❑ 2R Vladimir Malakhov .50 .23
❑ 3R Andrei Khomutov .25 .11
❑ 4R Valeri Kamensky 1.50 .70
❑ 5R Dimitri Motkov .25 .11
❑ 6R Evgeny Shastin .25 .11
❑ 7R Arturs Irbe UER 1.00 .45
(Misspelled Artur; played in 3 games in Red Army's NHL tour)
❑ 8R Igor Chibirev .25 .11
❑ 9R Maxim Mikhailovsky UER .25 .11
(Played one game not one minute on 1990 NHL tour)
❑ 10R Viacheslav Bykov .25 .11
❑ 11R Central Red Army Team .25 .11
(Igor Kravchuk)
❑ 12R Central Red Army Team .25 .11
❑ 13R Valeri Shirjaev .25 .11
❑ 14R Igor Maslennikov .25 .11
❑ 15R Igor Malykhin .25 .11
❑ 16R Dimitri Khristich .50 .23
❑ 17R Viktor Tikhonov CO .25 .11
❑ 18R Eugeny Davydov .25 .11
❑ 19R Sergei Fedorov 5.00 2.20
❑ 20R Pavel Kostichkin .25 .11
❑ 21R Vladimir Konstantinov 1.00 .45
❑ 22R Checklist Card .25 .11

## 1990-91 OPC Premier

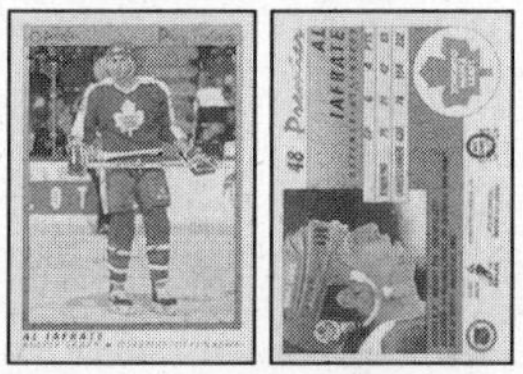

The 1990-91 O-Pee-Chee Premier hockey set contains 132 standard-size cards. The fronts feature color action photos of the players and have the words "O-Pee-Chee Premier" in a gold border above the picture. Border colors according to team frame the photo. Horizontal backs contain 1989-90 and career statistics. A player photo appears in the upper left hand corner. The checklist is numbered alphabetically. Rookie Cards include Rob Blake, Peter Bondra, Tie Domi, Sergei Fedorov, Jaromir Jagr, Curtis Joseph, Mike Modano, Alexander Mogilny, Petr Nedved, Owen Nolan, Keith Primeau, Mike Ricci, Robert Reichel, Jeremy Roenick, Kevin Stevens, and Mats Sundin.

| | MINT | NRMT |
|---|---|---|
| COMPLETE SET (132) | 80.00 | 36.00 |
| COMP.FACT.SET (132) | 100.00 | 45.00 |
| COMMON CARD (1-132) | .15 | .07 |

❑ 1 Scott Arniel .15 .07
❑ 2 Jergus Baca .15 .07
❑ 3 Brian Bellows .15 .07
❑ 4 Jean-Claude Bergeron .15 .07
❑ 5 Daniel Berthiaume .40 .18
❑ 6 Rob Blake 1.00 .45
❑ 7 Peter Bondra 4.00 1.80
❑ 8 Laurie Boschman .15 .07
❑ 9 Ray Bourque .75 .35
❑ 10 Aaron Broten .15 .07
❑ 11 Greg Brown .15 .07
❑ 12 Jimmy Carson .15 .07
❑ 13 Chris Chelios .75 .35
❑ 14 Dino Ciccarelli .40 .18
❑ 15 Zdeno Ciger .15 .07
❑ 16 Paul Coffey .75 .35
❑ 17 Danton Cole .15 .07
❑ 18 Geoff Courtnall .15 .07
❑ 19 Mike Craig UER .15 .07
(Played Juniors at Oshawa, not Minors)
❑ 20 John Cullen .15 .07
❑ 21 Vincent Damphousse .40 .18
❑ 22 Gerald Diduck .15 .07
❑ 23 Kevin Dineen .15 .07
❑ 24 Per-Olav Djoos UER .15 .07
(Photo shoots right, back says shoots left)
❑ 25 Tie Domi 1.50 .70
❑ 26 Peter Douris .15 .07
❑ 27 Rob DiMaio .15 .07
❑ 28 Pat Elynuik .15 .07
❑ 29 Bob Essensa .40 .18
❑ 30 Sergei Fedorov 15.00 6.75
❑ 31 Brent Fedyk .15 .07
❑ 32 Ron Francis .40 .18
❑ 33 Link Gaetz .15 .07
❑ 34 Troy Gamble .40 .18
❑ 35 Johan Garpenlov .15 .07
❑ 36 Mike Gartner .40 .18
❑ 37 Rick Green .15 .07
❑ 38 Wayne Gretzky 5.00 2.20
❑ 39 Jeff Hackett 1.50 .70
❑ 40 Dale Hawerchuk UER .40 .18
(Misspelled Hawerchuck)
❑ 41 Ron Hextall .40 .18
❑ 42 Bruce Hoffort .15 .07
❑ 43 Bobby Holik 1.25 .55
❑ 44 Martin Hostak .15 .07
❑ 45 Phil Housley .40 .18
❑ 46 Jody Hull .15 .07
❑ 47 Brett Hull 2.00 .90
❑ 48 Al Iafrate .40 .18
❑ 49 Peter Ing .40 .18
❑ 50 Jaromir Jagr 35.00 16.00
❑ 51 Curtis Joseph 5.00 2.20
❑ 52 Robert Kron .15 .07
❑ 53 Frantisek Kucera .15 .07
❑ 54 Dale Kushner .15 .07
❑ 55 Guy Lafleur .75 .35
❑ 56 Pat LaFontaine .40 .18
❑ 57 Mike Lalor .15 .07
❑ 58 Steve Larmer .40 .18
❑ 59 Jiri Latal .15 .07
❑ 60 Jamie Leach .15 .07
❑ 61 Brian Leetch 1.25 .55
❑ 62 Claude Lemieux .40 .18
❑ 63 Mario Lemieux 4.00 1.80
❑ 64 Craig Ludwig .15 .07
❑ 65 Al MacInnis .40 .18
❑ 66 Mikko Makela .15 .07
❑ 67 David Marcinyshyn .15 .07
❑ 68 Stephane Matteau .15 .07
❑ 69 Brad McCrimmon .15 .07
❑ 70 Kirk McLean .40 .18
❑ 71 Mark Messier 1.25 .55
❑ 72 Kelly Miller .15 .07
❑ 73 Kevin Miller .15 .07
❑ 74 Mike Modano 12.00 5.50
❑ 75 Alexander Mogilny 2.00 .90
❑ 76 Andy Moog .40 .18
❑ 77 Joe Mullen .40 .18
❑ 78 Kirk Muller .15 .07
❑ 79 Pat Murray .15 .07
❑ 80 Jarmo Myllys .15 .07
❑ 81 Petr Nedved 2.50 1.10
❑ 82 Cam Neely .40 .18
❑ 83 Bernie Nicholls .40 .18
❑ 84 Joe Nieuwendyk .40 .18
❑ 85 Chris Nilan .15 .07
❑ 86 Owen Nolan 2.00 .90
❑ 87 Brian Noonan UER .15 .07
(Photo actually Dan Vincelette)
❑ 88 Adam Oates .40 .18
❑ 89 Greg Parks UER .15 .07
(Back photo actually Scott Arniel)
❑ 90 Adrien Plavsic .15 .07
❑ 91 Keith Primeau 2.50 1.10
❑ 92 Brian Propp .15 .07
❑ 93 Dan Quinn .15 .07
❑ 94 Bill Ranford .40 .18
❑ 95 Robert Reichel 1.50 .70
❑ 96 Mike Ricci UER 1.00 .45
(Born 11/27/71, should be October)
❑ 97 Steven Rice UER .15 .07
(Played Juniors at Kitchener, not Minors)
❑ 98 Stephane Richer .40 .18
❑ 99 Luc Robitaille .40 .18
❑ 100 Jeremy Roenick 4.00 1.80
❑ 101 Patrick Roy 4.00 1.80
❑ 102 Joe Sakic 2.50 1.10
❑ 103 Denis Savard .40 .18
❑ 104 Anatoli Semenov .15 .07
❑ 105 Brendan Shanahan 2.50 1.10
❑ 106 Ray Sheppard .40 .18
❑ 107 Mike Sillinger UER .15 .07
(Played Juniors at Regina, not Minors)
❑ 108 Ilkka Sinisalo .15 .07
❑ 109 Bobby Smith .40 .18
❑ 110 Paul Stanton .15 .07
❑ 111 Kevin Stevens 1.00 .45
❑ 112 Scott Stevens .40 .18
❑ 113 Alan Stewart .15 .07
❑ 114 Mats Sundin 5.00 2.20
❑ 115 Brent Sutter .15 .07
❑ 116 Tim Sweeney .15 .07
❑ 117 Peter Taglianetti .15 .07
❑ 118 John Tanner .25 .11
❑ 119 Dave Tippett .15 .07
❑ 120 Rick Tocchet .40 .18
❑ 121 Bryan Trottier .40 .18
❑ 122 John Tucker .15 .07
❑ 123 Darren Turcotte 1.00 .45
❑ 124 Pierre Turgeon .40 .18
❑ 125 Randy Velischek .15 .07
❑ 126 Mike Vernon .40 .18
❑ 127 Wes Walz .15 .07
❑ 128 Carey Wilson .15 .07
❑ 129 Doug Wilson .40 .18
❑ 130 Steve Yzerman 2.50 1.10
❑ 131 Peter Zezel .15 .07
❑ 132 Checklist 1-132 .15 .07

## 1991-92 OPC/Topps

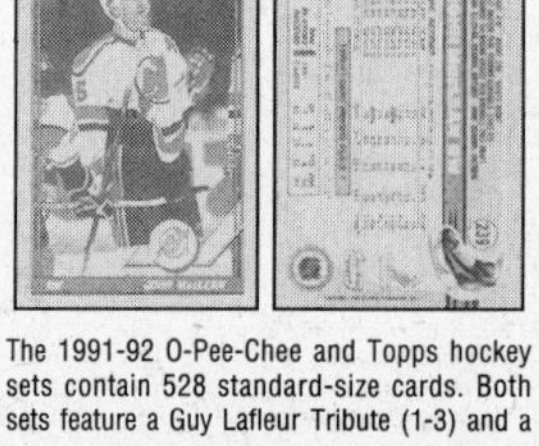

The 1991-92 O-Pee-Chee and Topps hockey sets contain 528 standard-size cards. Both sets feature a Guy Lafleur Tribute (1-3) and a Super Rookie (4-13) subset. Topps hockey cards were sold in 15-card packs that included a bonus team scoring leader card, whereas the O-Pee-Chee cards were sold in nine-card wax packs that included a stick of gum plus one insert card from a special 66-card insert set. The fronts have glossy color action player photos, with two different color border stripes and a white card face. In the lower right corner, the team logo appears as a hockey puck superimposed on a hockey stick. They present full player information, including biography, statistics, 1990-91 game-winning goals, and NHL playoff record (the OPC cards present player information in French as well as English). The card number appears next to a hockey skate in the upper right corner of the back. Rookie Cards in this set include Tony Amonte, Valeri Kamensky and John LeClair.

| | MINT | NRMT |
|---|---|---|
| COMPLETE SET (528) | 12.00 | 5.50 |
| COMP.FACT.SET (528) | 12.00 | 5.50 |
| COMMON CARD (1-528) | .05 | .02 |

❑ 1 Lafleur Tribute .10 .05
Goodbye Guy
❑ 2 Lafleur Tribute .10 .05
Gueeey's Last Hoorah
❑ 3 Lafleur Tribute .10 .05
Guy Bids Farewell
❑ 4 Ed Belfour SR .10 .05
❑ 5 Ken Hodge Jr. SR .05 .02
❑ 6 Rob Blake SR UER .10 .05
(Center on back, should say Defense)
❑ 7 Bobby Holik SR .05 .02
❑ 8 Sergei Fedorov SR UER .10 .05
(Name misspelled on front and in stats)
❑ 9 Jaromir Jagr SR .10 .05
❑ 10 Eric Weinrich SR .05 .02
❑ 11 Mike Richter SR .10 .05
❑ 12 Mats Sundin SR .10 .05
❑ 13 Mike Ricci SR .10 .05
❑ 14 Eric Desjardins .05 .02
❑ 15 Paul Ranheim .05 .02
❑ 16 Joe Sakic .40 .18
❑ 17 Curt Giles .05 .02
❑ 18 Mike Foligno .05 .02
❑ 19 Brad Marsh .05 .02
❑ 20 Ed Belfour .25 .11
❑ 21 Steve Smith .05 .02
❑ 22 Kirk Muller .05 .02
❑ 23 Kelly Chase .05 .02
❑ 24 Jim McKenzie .05 .02
❑ 25 Mick Vukota .05 .02
❑ 26 Tony Amonte .60 .25
❑ 27 Danton Cole .05 .02
❑ 28 Jay Mazur .05 .02
❑ 29 Pete Peeters .10 .05
❑ 30 Petri Skriko .05 .02
❑ 31 Steve Duchesne .05 .02
❑ 32 Sabres Team .05 .02
❑ 33 Phil Bourque UER .05 .02
(Born Chelmford, should be Chelmsford)
❑ 34 Tim Bergland .05 .02
❑ 35 Tim Cheveldae .10 .05
❑ 36 Bill Armstrong .05 .02
❑ 37 John McIntyre .05 .02
❑ 38 Dave Andreychuk .10 .05
❑ 39 Curtis Leschyshyn .05 .02
❑ 40 Jaromir Jagr .50 .23
❑ 41 Craig Janney .10 .05
❑ 42 Doug Brown .05 .02
❑ 43 Ken Sabourin .05 .02
❑ 44 North Stars Team .05 .02
❑ 45 Fredrik Olausson UER .05 .02
(Misspelled Clausson on card front)
❑ 46 Mike Gartner UER .10 .05
(No italics or diamond 81-82 GP)
❑ 47 Mark Fitzpatrick .10 .05
❑ 48 Joe Murphy .05 .02
❑ 49 Doug Wilson .10 .05
❑ 50 Brian MacLellan .05 .02
❑ 51 Bob Bassen .05 .02
❑ 52 Robert Kron .05 .02
❑ 53 Roger Johansson .05 .02
❑ 54 Guy Carbonneau UER .10 .05
(No italics or diamond 85-86 GP)
❑ 55 Rob Ramage .05 .02
❑ 56 Bobby Holik .05 .02
❑ 57 Alan May .05 .02
❑ 58 Rick Meagher .05 .02
❑ 59 Cliff Ronning .05 .02
❑ 60 Red Wings Team .05 .02
❑ 61 Bob Kudelski .05 .02
❑ 62 Wayne McBean .05 .02
❑ 63 Craig MacTavish .05 .02
❑ 64 Owen Nolan .10 .05
❑ 65 Dale Hawerchuk .10 .05
❑ 66 Ray Bourque .25 .11
❑ 67 Sean Burke .10 .05
❑ 68 Frank Musil .05 .02
❑ 69 Joe Mullen .10 .05
❑ 70 Drake Berehowsky .05 .02
❑ 71 Darren Turcotte .05 .02
❑ 72 Randy Carlyle .05 .02
❑ 73 Paul Cyr .05 .02
❑ 74 Dave Gagner .10 .05
❑ 75 Steve Larmer .10 .05
❑ 76 Petr Svoboda .05 .02
❑ 77 Keith Acton .05 .02
❑ 78 Dimitri Khristich .05 .02
❑ 79 Brad McCrimmon .05 .02
❑ 80 Pat LaFontaine UER .10 .05
(Should be lower case a in name, not d)
❑ 81 Jeff Reese .05 .02
❑ 82 Mario Marois .05 .02
❑ 83 Rob Brown .05 .02
❑ 84 Grant Fuhr .10 .05
❑ 85 Carey Wilson .05 .02
❑ 86 Garry Galley .05 .02
❑ 87 Troy Murray .05 .02
❑ 88 Tony Granato .05 .02
❑ 89 Gord Murphy UER .05 .02
(No italics or diamond 90-91 GP)
❑ 90 Brent Gilchrist .05 .02
❑ 91 Mike Richter .25 .11
❑ 92 Eric Weinrich .05 .02
❑ 93 Marc Bureau .05 .02
❑ 94 Bob Errey .05 .02
❑ 95 Dave McLlwain .05 .02
❑ 96 Nordiques Team .05 .02
❑ 97 Clint Malarchuk UER .10 .05
(Center on front)
❑ 98 Shawn Antoski UER .05 .02
(Admirals are in IHL, not AHL)
❑ 99 Bob Sweeney .05 .02
❑ 100 Stephen Leach .05 .02
❑ 101 Gary Nylund .05 .02
❑ 102 Lucien DeBlois .05 .02
❑ 103 Oilers Team .05 .02
❑ 104 Jimmy Carson .05 .02
❑ 105 Rod Langway .05 .02
❑ 106 Jeremy Roenick .25 .11
❑ 107 Mike Vernon .10 .05
❑ 108 Brian Leetch .25 .11
❑ 109 Mark Hunter .05 .02
❑ 110 Brian Bellows .05 .02
❑ 111 Pelle Eklund .05 .02
❑ 112 Rob Blake .10 .05
❑ 113 Mike Hough .05 .02
❑ 114 Frank Pietrangelo .10 .05
❑ 115 Christian Ruuttu .05 .02
❑ 116 Bryan Marchment .05 .02
❑ 117 Garry Valk .05 .02
❑ 118 Ken Daneyko UER .05 .02
(No italics or diamond 90-91 GP)
❑ 119 Russ Courtnall .05 .02
❑ 120 Ron Wilson .05 .02
❑ 121 Shayne Stevenson .05 .02
❑ 122 Bill Berg .05 .02
❑ 123 Maple Leafs Team .05 .02
❑ 124 Glenn Anderson .10 .05
❑ 125 Kevin Miller .05 .02
❑ 126 Calle Johansson .05 .02
❑ 127 Jimmy Waite .10 .05
❑ 128 Allen Pedersen .05 .02
❑ 129 Brian Mullen .05 .02
❑ 130 Ron Francis .10 .05
❑ 131 Jergus Baca .05 .02
❑ 132 Checklist 1-132 .05 .02
❑ 133 Tony Tanti .05 .02
❑ 134 Wes Walz .05 .02
❑ 135 Stephan Lebeau .05 .02
❑ 136 Ken Wregget .10 .05
❑ 137 Scott Arniel UER .05 .02
(No italics or diamond 85-86 GP)
❑ 138 Dave Taylor .05 .02
❑ 139 Steven Finn .05 .02
❑ 140 Brendan Shanahan .40 .18
❑ 141 Petr Nedved .10 .05
❑ 142 Chris Dahlquist .05 .02
❑ 143 Rich Sutter .05 .02
❑ 144 Joe Reekie .05 .02
❑ 145 Peter Ing .10 .05
❑ 146 Ken Linseman .05 .02
❑ 147 Dave Barr .05 .02
❑ 148 Al Iafrate .10 .05
❑ 149 Greg Gilbert .05 .02
❑ 150 Craig Ludwig .05 .02
❑ 151 Gary Suter .05 .02
❑ 152 Jan Erixon .05 .02
❑ 153 Mario Lemieux .75 .35
❑ 154 Mike Liut UER .10 .05
(In stats 84-85 repeats for 85-86 thru 89-90)
❑ 155 Uwe Krupp .05 .02
❑ 156 Darin Kimble .05 .02
❑ 157 Shayne Corson .05 .02
❑ 158 Jets Team .05 .02
❑ 159 Stephane Morin UER .05 .02
(Photo actually Jeff Jackson)
❑ 160 Rick Tocchet .10 .05
❑ 161 John Tonelli UER .05 .02
(No italics or diamond 81-82 GP)
❑ 162 Adrien Plavsic .05 .02
❑ 163 Jason Miller .05 .02
❑ 164 Tim Kerr .05 .02
❑ 165 Brent Sutter .05 .02
❑ 166 Michel Petit .05 .02
❑ 167 Adam Graves .10 .05
❑ 168 Jamie Macoun .05 .02
❑ 169 Terry Yake .05 .02
❑ 170 Bruins Team .05 .02
❑ 171 Alexander Mogilny .10 .05
❑ 172 Karl Dykhuis .05 .02
Top Prospect
❑ 173 Tomas Sandstrom .05 .02
❑ 174 Bernie Nicholls .10 .05

❑ 175 Slava Fetisov .05 .02
❑ 176 Andrew Cassels .05 .02
❑ 177 Ulf Dahlen .05 .02
❑ 178 Brian Hayward .10 .05
❑ 179 Doug Lidster .05 .02
❑ 180 Dave Lowry .05 .02
❑ 181 Ron Tugnutt UER .10 .05
(Birthplace and home should be Ontario, not Quebec)
❑ 182 Ed Olczyk .05 .02
❑ 183 Paul Coffey .25 .11
❑ 184 Shawn Burr UER .05 .02
(No italics or diamond 90-91 GP)
❑ 185 Whalers Team .05 .02
❑ 186 Mark Janssens .05 .02
❑ 187 Mike Craig .05 .02
❑ 188 Gary Leeman .05 .02
❑ 189 Phil Sykes .05 .02
❑ 190 Brett Hull LL .10 .05
❑ 191 Devils Team .05 .02
❑ 192 Cam Neely .10 .05
❑ 193 Petr Klima .05 .02
❑ 194 Mike Ricci .05 .02
❑ 195 Kelly Hrudey .10 .05
❑ 196 Mark Recchi .10 .05
❑ 197 Mikael Andersson .05 .02
❑ 198 Bob Probert .10 .05
❑ 199 Craig Wolanin .05 .02
❑ 200 Scott Mellanby .10 .05
❑ 201 Wayne Gretzky HL UER .50 .23
(Thomas Sandstrom mentioned on back)
❑ 202 Laurie Boschman .05 .02
❑ 203 Gino Odjick .05 .02
❑ 204 Garth Butcher .05 .02
❑ 205 Randy Wood .05 .02
❑ 206 John Druce .05 .02
❑ 207 Doug Bodger .05 .02
❑ 208 Doug Gilmour .25 .11
❑ 209 John LeClair 1.50 .70
❑ 210 Steve Thomas .05 .02
❑ 211 Kjell Samuelsson .05 .02
❑ 212 Daniel Marois .05 .02
❑ 213 Jiri Hrdina .05 .02
❑ 214 Darrin Shannon .05 .02
❑ 215 Rangers Team .05 .02
❑ 216 Bob McGill .05 .02
❑ 217 Dirk Graham UER .05 .02
(No italics or diamond 85-86 or 90-91 GP)
❑ 218 Thomas Steen .05 .02
❑ 219 Mats Sundin .10 .05
❑ 220 Kevin Lowe UER .05 .02
(No italics or diamond 81-82 GP)
❑ 221 Kirk McLean .10 .05
❑ 222 Jeff Brown .05 .02
❑ 223 Joe Nieuwendyk .10 .05
❑ 224 Wayne Gretzky LL .50 .23
❑ 225 Marty McSorley .05 .02
❑ 226 John Cullen .05 .02
❑ 227 Brian Propp UER .05 .02
(No italics or diamond 81-82 GP)
❑ 228 Yves Racine .05 .02
❑ 229 Dale Hunter .05 .02
❑ 230 Dennis Vaske .05 .02
❑ 231 Sylvain Turgeon .05 .02
❑ 232 Ron Sutter .05 .02
❑ 233 Chris Chelios .25 .11
❑ 234 Brian Bradley .05 .02
❑ 235 Scott Young .05 .02
❑ 236 Mike Ramsey UER .05 .02
(No italics or diamond 81-82 GP)
❑ 237 Jon Casey .10 .05
❑ 238 Nevin Markwart .05 .02
❑ 239 John MacLean .10 .05
❑ 240 Brent Ashton .05 .02
❑ 241 Tony Hrkac .05 .02
❑ 242 Canucks Team .05 .02
❑ 243 Jeff Norton .05 .02
❑ 244 Martin Gelinas .05 .02
❑ 245 Mike Ridley .05 .02
❑ 246 Pat Jablonski .10 .05
❑ 247 Flames Team .05 .02
❑ 248 Paul Ysebaert .05 .02
❑ 249 Sylvain Cote .05 .02
❑ 250 Marc Habscheid .05 .02
❑ 251 Todd Elik .05 .02
❑ 252 Mike McPhee .05 .02
❑ 253 James Patrick .05 .02
❑ 254 Murray Craven .05 .02
❑ 255 Trent Yawney .05 .02
❑ 256 Rob Cimetta .05 .02
❑ 257 Wayne Gretzky LL .50 .23
❑ 258 Wayne Gretzky AS .50 .23
❑ 259 Brett Hull AS .10 .05
❑ 260 Luc Robitaille AS .10 .05
❑ 261 Ray Bourque AS .10 .05
❑ 262 Al MacInnis AS .10 .05
❑ 263 Ed Belfour AS .10 .05
❑ 264 Checklist 133-264 .05 .02
❑ 265 Adam Oates AS .05 .02
❑ 266 Cam Neely AS .10 .05
❑ 267 Kevin Stevens AS .05 .02
❑ 268 Chris Chelios AS .10 .05
❑ 269 Brian Leetch AS .10 .05
❑ 270 Patrick Roy AS .40 .18
❑ 271 Ed Belfour LL .10 .05
❑ 272 Rob Zettler .05 .02
❑ 273 Donald Audette .10 .05
❑ 274 Teppo Numminen .05 .02
❑ 275 Peter Stastny UER .10 .05
(No italics or diamond 81-82 GP)
❑ 276 Dave Christian .05 .02
❑ 277 Larry Murphy .10 .05
❑ 278 Johan Garpenlov .05 .02
❑ 279 Tom Fitzgerald .05 .02
❑ 280 Gerald Diduck .05 .02
❑ 281 Gino Cavallini .05 .02
❑ 282 Theoren Fleury .10 .05
❑ 283 Kings Team .05 .02
❑ 284 Jeff Beukeboom .05 .02
❑ 285 Kevin Dineen .05 .02
❑ 286 Jacques Cloutier .10 .05
❑ 287 Tom Chorske .05 .02
❑ 288 Ed Belfour LL .10 .05
❑ 289 Ray Sheppard .10 .05
❑ 290 Olaf Kolzig .10 .05
❑ 291 Terry Carkner .05 .02
❑ 292 Benoit Hogue .05 .02
❑ 293 Mike Peluso .05 .02
❑ 294 Bruce Driver .05 .02
❑ 295 Jari Kurri .10 .05
❑ 296 Peter Sidorkiewicz .10 .05
❑ 297 Scott Pearson .05 .02
❑ 298 Canadiens Team .05 .02
❑ 299 Vincent Damphousse .10 .05
❑ 300 John Carter .05 .02
❑ 301 Geoff Smith .05 .02
❑ 302 Steve Kasper UER .05 .02
(No italics or diamond 85-86 GP)
❑ 303 Brett Hull .30 .14
❑ 304 Ray Ferraro .05 .02
❑ 305 Geoff Courtnall .05 .02
❑ 306 David Shaw .05 .02
❑ 307 Bob Essensa .10 .05
❑ 308 Mark Tinordi .05 .02
❑ 309 Keith Primeau .10 .05
❑ 310 Kevin Hatcher .05 .02
❑ 311 Chris Nilan .05 .02
❑ 312 Trevor Kidd .10 .05
Top Prospect
❑ 313 Daniel Berthiaume .10 .05
❑ 314 Adam Creighton .05 .02
❑ 315 Everett Sanipass .05 .02
❑ 316 Ken Baumgartner .05 .02
❑ 317 Sheldon Kennedy .05 .02
❑ 318 Dave Capuano .05 .02
❑ 319 Don Sweeney .05 .02
❑ 320 Gary Roberts .05 .02
❑ 321 Wayne Gretzky 1.25 .55
❑ 322 Theoren Fleury and .10 .05
Marty McSorley UER
(Name misspelled McSorely on both sides of card)
❑ 323 Ulf Samuelsson .05 .02
❑ 324 Mike Krushelnyski .05 .02
❑ 325 Dean Evason .05 .02
❑ 326 Pat Elynuik .05 .02
❑ 327 Michal Pivonka .05 .02
❑ 328 Paul Cavallini .05 .02
❑ 329 Flyers Team .05 .02
❑ 330 Denis Savard .10 .05
❑ 331 Paul Fenton .05 .02
❑ 332 Jon Morris .05 .02
❑ 333 Daren Puppa .10 .05
❑ 334 Doug Smail .05 .02
❑ 335 Kelly Kisio .05 .02
❑ 336 Michel Goulet UER .10 .05
(No italics or diamond 81-82 GP)
❑ 337 Mike Sillinger .05 .02
❑ 338 Andy Moog .10 .05
❑ 339 Paul Stanton .05 .02
❑ 340 Greg Adams .05 .02
❑ 341 Doug Crossman UER .05 .02
(No italics or diamond 85-86 GP)
❑ 342 Kelly Miller .05 .02
❑ 343 Pat Flatley .05 .02
❑ 344 Zarley Zalapski .05 .02
❑ 345 Mark Osborne UER .05 .02
(No italics or diamond 81-82 GP)
❑ 346 Mark Messier .25 .11
❑ 347 Blues Team .05 .02
❑ 348 Neil Wilkinson .05 .02
❑ 349 Brian Skrudland .05 .02
❑ 350 Lyle Odelein .05 .02
❑ 351 Luke Richardson .05 .02
❑ 352 Zdeno Ciger .05 .02
❑ 353 John Vanbiesbrouck .30 .14
❑ 354 Lou Franceschetti .05 .02
❑ 355 Alexei Gusarov .05 .02
❑ 356 Bill Ranford .10 .05
❑ 357 Normand Lacombe .05 .02
❑ 358 Randy Burridge .05 .02
❑ 359 Brian Benning .05 .02
❑ 360 Dave Hannan .05 .02
❑ 361 Todd Gill .05 .02
❑ 362 Peter Bondra .25 .11
❑ 363 Mike Hartman .05 .02
❑ 364 Trevor Linden .10 .05
❑ 365 John Ogrodnick .05 .02
❑ 366 Steve Konroyd .05 .02
❑ 367 Mike Modano .25 .11
❑ 368 Glenn Healy .10 .05
❑ 369 Stephane Richer .10 .05
❑ 370 Vincent Riendeau .10 .05
❑ 371 Randy Moller .05 .02
❑ 372 Penguins Team .05 .02
❑ 373 Murray Baron .05 .02
❑ 374 Troy Crowder .05 .02
❑ 375 Rick Tabaracci .10 .05
❑ 376 Brent Fedyk .05 .02
❑ 377 Randy Velischek .05 .02
❑ 378 Esa Tikkanen .05 .02
❑ 379 Richard Pilon .05 .02
❑ 380 Jeff Lazaro .05 .02
❑ 381 Dave Ellett .05 .02
❑ 382 Jeff Hackett .10 .05
❑ 383 Stephane Matteau .05 .02
❑ 384 Capitals Team .05 .02
❑ 385 Wayne Presley .05 .02
❑ 386 Grant Ledyard .05 .02
❑ 387 Kip Miller .05 .02
❑ 388 Dean Kennedy .05 .02
❑ 389 Hubie McDonough .05 .02
❑ 390 Anatoli Semenov .05 .02
❑ 391 Daryl Reaugh .05 .02
❑ 392 Mathieu Schneider .05 .02
❑ 393 Dan Quinn .05 .02
❑ 394 Claude Lemieux .10 .05
❑ 395 Phil Housley .10 .05
❑ 396 Checklist 265-396 .05 .02
❑ 397 Steve Bozek .05 .02
❑ 398 Bobby Smith .10 .05
❑ 399 Mark Pederson .05 .02
❑ 400 Kevin Todd .05 .02
❑ 401 Sergei Fedorov .50 .23
❑ 402 Tom Barrasso .10 .05
❑ 403 Brett Hull HL .10 .05
❑ 404 Bob Carpenter UER .05 .02
(No italics or diamond 85-86 or 90-91 GP)
❑ 405 Luc Robitaille .10 .05
❑ 406 Mark Hardy .05 .02
❑ 407 Neil Sheehy .05 .02
❑ 408 Mike McNeil .05 .02
❑ 409 Dave Manson .05 .02
❑ 410 Mike Tomlak .05 .02
❑ 411 Robert Reichel .05 .02
❑ 412 Islanders Team .05 .02
❑ 413 Patrick Roy .75 .35
❑ 414 Shaun Van Allen .05 .02
❑ 415 Dale Kushner .05 .02
❑ 416 Pierre Turgeon .10 .05
❑ 417 Curtis Joseph .25 .11
❑ 418 Randy Gilhen .05 .02
❑ 419 Jyrki Lumme .05 .02
❑ 420 Neal Broten .10 .05
❑ 421 Kevin Stevens .05 .02
❑ 422 Chris Terreri .10 .05
❑ 423 David Reid .05 .02
❑ 424 Steve Yzerman .50 .23
❑ 425 Ed Belfour LL .10 .05
❑ 426 Jim Johnson .05 .02
❑ 427 Joey Kocur .05 .02
❑ 428 Joel Otto .05 .02
❑ 429 Dino Ciccarelli .10 .05
❑ 430 Blackhawks Team .05 .02
❑ 431 Claude Lapointe .05 .02
❑ 432 Chris Joseph .05 .02
❑ 433 Gaetan Duchesne .05 .02
❑ 434 Mike Keane .05 .02
❑ 435 Dave Chyzowski .05 .02
❑ 436 Glen Featherstone .05 .02
❑ 437 Jim Paek .05 .02
❑ 438 Doug Evans .05 .02
❑ 439 Alexei Kasatonov UER .05 .02
(Misspelled Alexi on card back)
❑ 440 Ken Hodge Jr. .05 .02
❑ 441 Dave Snuggerud .05 .02
❑ 442 Brad Shaw .05 .02
❑ 443 Gerard Gallant .05 .02
❑ 444 Jiri Latal .05 .02
❑ 445 Peter Zezel .05 .02
❑ 446 Troy Gamble .10 .05
❑ 447 Craig Coxe .05 .02
❑ 448 Adam Oates .10 .05
❑ 449 Todd Krygier .05 .02
❑ 450 Andre Racicot .10 .05
❑ 451 Patrik Sundstrom .05 .02
❑ 452 Glen Wesley UER .05 .02
(No italics or diamond 90-91 GP)
❑ 453 Jocelyn Lemieux .05 .02
❑ 454 Rick Zombo .05 .02
❑ 455 Derek King .05 .02
❑ 456 J.J. Daigneault .05 .02
❑ 457 Rick Vaive .05 .02
❑ 458 Larry Robinson .10 .05
❑ 459 Rick Wamsley .10 .05
❑ 460 Craig Simpson .05 .02
❑ 461 Corey Millen .05 .02
❑ 462 Sergio Momesso .05 .02
❑ 463 Paul MacDermid .05 .02
❑ 464 Wendel Clark .10 .05
❑ 465 Mikhail Tatarinov .05 .02
❑ 466 Mark Howe .05 .02
❑ 467 Jay Miller .05 .02
❑ 468 Grant Jennings .05 .02
❑ 469 Paul Gillis .05 .02
❑ 470 Ron Hextall .10 .05
❑ 471 Alexander Godynyuk .05 .02
❑ 472 Bryan Trottier .10 .05
❑ 473 Kevin Haller .05 .02
❑ 474 Troy Mallette .05 .02
❑ 475 Jim Wiemer .05 .02
❑ 476 David Maley .05 .02
❑ 477 Moe Mantha UER .05 .02
(Photo actually Paul MacDermid)
❑ 478 Brad Jones .05 .02
❑ 479 Craig Muni .05 .02
❑ 480 Igor Larionov .05 .02
❑ 481 Scott Stevens .10 .05
❑ 482 Sergei Makarov .05 .02
❑ 483 Mike Lalor .05 .02
❑ 484 Tony McKegney .05 .02
❑ 485 Perry Berezan .05 .02
❑ 486 Derrick Smith .05 .02
❑ 487 Jim Hrivnak .10 .05
❑ 488 David Volek .05 .02
❑ 489 Sylvain Lefebvre .05 .02
❑ 490 Rod Brind'Amour .10 .05
❑ 491 Al MacInnis .10 .05
❑ 492 Jamie Leach .05 .02
❑ 493 Robert Dirk .05 .02
❑ 494 Gordie Roberts .05 .02
❑ 495 Mike Hudson .05 .02
❑ 496 Frank Breault .05 .02
❑ 497 Rejean Lemelin .10 .05
❑ 498 Kris King .05 .02
❑ 499 Pat Verbeek .05 .02
❑ 500 Bryan Fogarty .05 .02
❑ 501 Perry Anderson .05 .02
❑ 502 Joe Cirella .05 .02
❑ 503 Mikko Makela .05 .02
❑ 504 Paul Coffey HL UER .10 .05
(Misspelled Coffee and Dennis Potvin on card back; date 12/22/90 in English, but 12/23/90 in French)
❑ 505 Don Beaupre .10 .05
❑ 506 Brian Glynn .05 .02
❑ 507 Dave Poulin .05 .02
❑ 508 Steve Chiasson .05 .02
❑ 509 Myles O'Connor .05 .02
❑ 510 Ilkka Sinisalo .05 .02
❑ 511 Nick Kypreos .05 .02
❑ 512 Doug Houda UER .05 .02
(No position after name on back)
❑ 513 Valeri Kamensky .40 .18
❑ 514 Sergei Nemchinov .05 .02
❑ 515 Dimitri Mironov .05 .02
❑ 516 Brett Hull Hart .10 .05
❑ 517 Ray Bourque Norris .10 .05
❑ 518 Ed Belfour Calder .10 .05
❑ 519 Ed Belfour UER .10 .05
Vezina Trophy
(Georges misspelled as George)
❑ 520 Wayne Gretzky Byng .50 .23
❑ 521 Dirk Graham Selke .05 .02
❑ 522 Wayne Gretzky Ross .50 .23
❑ 523 Mario Lemieux Smythe .40 .18
❑ 524 Wayne Gretzky HL .50 .23
❑ 525 Sharks Logo .05 .02
❑ 526 Lightning Logo .05 .02
(Card back states team will play in Orlando for 1992-93 if arena is not complete. The Lightning played at Tampa Expo Hall.)
❑ 527 Senators Logo .25 .11
❑ 528 Checklist 397-528 .05 .02

## 1991-92 O-Pee-Chee Inserts

Inserted one per 1991-92 O-Pee-Chee nine-card wax pack, this 66-card standard-size set features ten cards of San Jose Sharks (1S-10S) and 56 Russian hockey players (11R-66R). Among the 56 Russian player cards are those from Central Red Army (11R-30R), Dynamo Moscow (31R-48R), and Khimik (49R-66R). The Sharks' cards have either posed or action player photos with gray and teal border stripes. The player's name appears in the bottom teal border stripe, while the team logo is superimposed over a hockey stick at the lower right corner. Card backs present biography and statistics. The Russian player cards have color action player photos enclosed by yellow and red borders. On a red and white background, the backs carry a blue hammer and sickle emblem, a blue Russian star, biography, and statistics versus NHL clubs while touring. The cards are numbered on the back. Sergei Zubov and Alexei Zhamnov are part of this set.

| | MINT | NRMT |
|---|---|---|
| COMPLETE SET (66) | 10.00 | 4.50 |
| COMMON CARD (1S-10S) | .10 | .05 |
| COMMON CARD (11R-66R) | .15 | .07 |

❑ 1S Link Gaetz .10 .05
❑ 2S Bengt Gustafsson .10 .05
❑ 3S Dan Keczmer .10 .05
❑ 4S Dean Kolstad .10 .05
❑ 5S Peter Lappin .10 .05
❑ 6S Jeff Madill .10 .05
❑ 7S Mike McHugh .10 .05
❑ 8S Jarmo Myllys UER .30 .14
(Stat line is for Offense/Defense)
❑ 9S Doug Zmolek .10 .05
❑ 10S Sharks Checklist .10 .05
❑ 11R Vadim Brezgunov .15 .07
❑ 12R Vyacheslav Butsayev .15 .07
❑ 13R Ilya Byakin .15 .07
❑ 14R Igor Chibirev .15 .07
❑ 15R Victor Gordiouk .30 .14
❑ 16R Yuri Khmylev .40 .18
❑ 17R Pavel Kostichkin .15 .07
❑ 18R Andrei Kovalenko .40 .18
❑ 19R Igor Kravchuk .30 .14
❑ 20R Igor Malykhin .15 .07
❑ 21R Igor Maslennikov .15 .07
❑ 22R Maxim Mikhailovsky .30 .14
❑ 23R Dimitri Mironov .40 .18
❑ 24R Sergei Nemchinov .40 .18
❑ 25R Alexander Prokopjev .15 .07
❑ 26R Igor Stelnov .15 .07
❑ 27R Sergei Vostrikov .15 .07
❑ 28R Sergei Zubov 1.25 .55
❑ 29R Central Red Army Team .15 .07
❑ 30R Central Red Army Team .40 .18
❑ 31R Alexander Andreivsky .15 .07
❑ 32R Igor Dorofeyev .15 .07
❑ 33R Alexander Galchenyuk .15 .07
❑ 34R Roman Ilyin .15 .07
❑ 35R Alexander Karpovtsev .30 .14
❑ 36R Ravil Khaidarov .15 .07
❑ 37R Igor Korolytov .40 .18
❑ 38R Andrei Kovalyov .15 .07
❑ 39R Yuri Leonov .15 .07
❑ 40R Andrei Lomakin UER .15 .07
(Misspelled Adrei on card front)
❑ 41R Evgeny Popikhin .15 .07
❑ 42R Alexander Semak .40 .18
❑ 43R Mikhail Shtalenkov .40 .18
❑ 44R Sergei Sorokin .15 .07
❑ 45R Andrei Trefilov .40 .18
❑ 46R Ravil Yakubov .30 .14
❑ 47R Alexander Yudin .15 .07
❑ 48R Alexei Zhamnov .75 .35
❑ 49R Andrei Basalgin .15 .07
❑ 50R Lev Berdichevsky .15 .07
❑ 51R Konstantin Kapkaikin .30 .14
❑ 52R Konstantin Kurashov .15 .07
❑ 53R Andrei Kvartalnov UER .15 .07
❑ 54R Albert Malgin .15 .07
❑ 55R Nikolai Maslov .15 .07
❑ 56R Anatoli Naida .15 .07
❑ 57R Roman Oksiuta .40 .18
❑ 58R Sergei Selyanin .15 .07
❑ 59R Valeri Shiryev .15 .07
❑ 60R Alexander Smirnov .15 .07
❑ 61R Leonid Trukhno .15 .07
❑ 62R Igor Ulanov UER .15 .07
(Misspelled Vlanov on card front)
❑ 63R Andrei Yakovenko .15 .07
❑ 64R Oleg Yashin .15 .07
❑ 65R Valeri Zelepukin .30 .14
❑ 66R Russian Checklist .15 .07

## 1991-92 OPC Premier

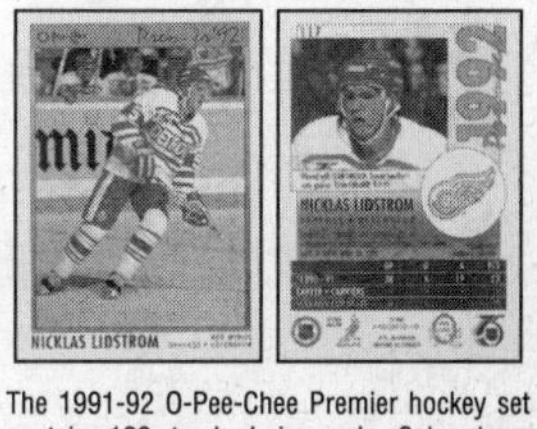

The 1991-92 O-Pee-Chee Premier hockey set contains 198 standard-size cards. Color player photos are bordered above and below in gold. Player name, team and position appear at the bottom. The backs have a small color player photo, biography, team logo and statistics. Rookie Cards in this set include Tony Amonte, Josef Beranek, Vladimir Konstantinov, Nicklas Lidstrom, and Doug Weight. A Konstantinov variation can be found with Lidstrom's photo on the back. Very few of these variations have been located. To commemorate the 75th Anniversary of the NHL, throwback sweaters were worn several times during the 1991-92 campaign by the original six teams. Cards portraying players in those sweaters are indicated by ORIG6.

| | MINT | NRMT |
|---|---|---|
| COMPLETE SET (198) | 10.00 | 4.50 |
| COMP.FACT.SET (198) | 12.00 | 5.50 |
| COMMON CARD (1-198) | .05 | .02 |

❑ 1 Dale Hawerchuk .10 .05
❑ 2 Ray Sheppard .10 .05
❑ 3 Wayne Gretzky UER 1.50 .70
(Canada Cup stats incorrect)
❑ 4 John MacLean .10 .05
❑ 5 Pat Verbeek .05 .02
❑ 6 Doug Wilson .10 .05
❑ 7 Adam Oates .10 .05
❑ 8 Bob McGill .05 .02
❑ 9 Mike Vernon .10 .05
❑ 10 Glenn Anderson .10 .05
❑ 11 Tony Amonte .75 .35
❑ 12 Stephen Leach .05 .02
❑ 13 Steve Duchesne .05 .02
❑ 14 Patrick Roy 1.25 .55
❑ 15 Jarmo Myllys .05 .02
❑ 16 Yanic Dupre .05 .02
❑ 17 Chris Chelios .25 .11

❑ 18 Bill Ranford .10 .05
❑ 19 Ed Belfour .25 .11
❑ 20 Michel Picard .05 .02
❑ 21 Rob Zettler .05 .02
❑ 22 Kevin Todd .05 .02
❑ 23 Mike Ricci .05 .02
❑ 24 Jaromir Jagr .75 .35
❑ 25 Sergei Nemchinov .05 .02
❑ 26 Kevin Stevens .05 .02
❑ 27 Dan Quinn .05 .02
❑ 28 Adam Graves .10 .05
❑ 29 Pat Jablonski .10 .05
❑ 30 Scott Mellanby .05 .02
❑ 31 Tomas Forslund .05 .02
❑ 32 Doug Weight .75 .35
❑ 33 Peter Ing .10 .05
❑ 34 Luc Robitaille .10 .05
❑ 35 Scott Niedermayer .10 .05
❑ 36 Dean Evason .05 .02
❑ 37 John Tonelli .05 .02
❑ 38 Ron Hextall .10 .05
❑ 39 Troy Mallette .05 .02
❑ 40 Tony Hrkac .05 .02
❑ 41 Ken Hodge Jr. .05 .02
❑ 42 Kip Miller .05 .02
❑ 43 Randy Burridge .05 .02
❑ 44 Rob Blake .10 .05
❑ 45 Sergei Makarov .05 .02
❑ 46 Luke Richardson .05 .02
❑ 47 Craig Berube .05 .02
❑ 48 Joe Nieuwendyk .10 .05
❑ 49 Brett Hull .50 .23
❑ 50 Phil Housley .10 .05
❑ 51 Mark Messier .35 .16
❑ 52 Jeremy Roenick .25 .11
❑ 53 Dave Christian .05 .02
❑ 54 Dave Barr .05 .02
❑ 55 Sergio Momesso .05 .02
❑ 56 Pat Falloon .05 .02
❑ 57 Brian Leetch .25 .11
❑ 58 Russ Courtnall .05 .02
❑ 59 Pierre Turgeon .10 .05
❑ 60 Steve Larmer .10 .05
❑ 61 Petr Klima .05 .02
❑ 62 Mikhail Tatarinov .05 .02
❑ 63 Rick Tocchet .10 .05
❑ 64 Pat LaFontaine .10 .05
❑ 65 Rob Pearson .05 .02
❑ 66 Glen Featherstone .05 .02
❑ 67 Pavel Bure .75 .35
❑ 68 Sergei Fedorov .75 .35
❑ 69 Kelly Kisio .05 .02
❑ 70 Joe Sakic .60 .25
❑ 71 Denis Savard .10 .05
❑ 72 Andrew Cassels .05 .02
❑ 73 Steve Yzerman .75 .35
❑ 74 Todd Elik .05 .02
❑ 75 Troy Murray .05 .02
❑ 76 Rob Ramage .05 .02
❑ 77 Trevor Linden .10 .05
❑ 78 Mike Richter .25 .11
❑ 79 Paul Coffey .25 .11
❑ 80 Craig Ludwig .05 .02
❑ 81 Al MacInnis .10 .05
❑ 82 Tomas Sandstrom .05 .02
❑ 83 Tim Kerr .05 .02
❑ 84 Scott Stevens .10 .05
❑ 85 Steve Kasper .05 .02
❑ 86 Kirk Muller .05 .02
❑ 87 Pat MacLeod .05 .02
❑ 88 Kevin Hatcher .05 .02
❑ 89 Wayne Presley .05 .02
❑ 90 Darryl Sydor .05 .02
❑ 91 Tom Chorske .05 .02
❑ 92 Theoren Fleury .10 .05
❑ 93 Craig Janney .10 .05
❑ 94 Rod Brind'Amour .10 .05
❑ 95 Ron Sutter .05 .02
❑ 96 Matt DelGuidice .05 .02
❑ 97 Rollie Melanson .10 .05
❑ 98 Tom Kurvers .05 .02
❑ 99 Bryan Marchment .05 .02
❑ 100 Grant Fuhr .10 .05
❑ 101 Geoff Courtnall .05 .02
❑ 102 Joel Otto .05 .02
❑ 103 Tom Barrasso .10 .05
❑ 104 Vincent Damphousse .10 .05
❑ 105 John LeClair 2.00 .90
❑ 106 Gary Leeman .05 .02
❑ 107 Cam Neely .10 .05
❑ 108 Jeff Hackett .10 .05
❑ 109 Stu Barnes .05 .02
❑ 110 Neil Wilkinson .05 .02
❑ 111 Jari Kurri .10 .05
❑ 112 Jon Casey .10 .05
❑ 113 Stephane Richer .10 .05
❑ 114 Mario Lemieux 1.25 .55
❑ 115 Brad Jones .05 .02
❑ 116 Wendel Clark .10 .05
❑ 117 Nicklas Lidstrom 1.00 .45
❑ 118A Vladimir Konstantinov 10.00 4.50
ERR
(Lidstrom photo on back)
❑ 118B Vladimir Konstantinov .25 .11
COR
❑ 119 Ray Bourque .25 .11
❑ 120 Ron Francis .10 .05
❑ 121 Esa Tikkanen .05 .02
❑ 122 Randy Hillier .05 .02
❑ 123 Randy Gilhen .05 .02
❑ 124 Barry Pederson .05 .02
❑ 125 Charlie Huddy .05 .02
(Bruce McNall in background)
❑ 126 Gary Roberts .05 .02
❑ 127 John Cullen .05 .02
❑ 128 Dave Gagner .10 .05
❑ 129 Bob Kudelski .05 .02
❑ 130 Brendan Shanahan .60 .25
❑ 131 Dirk Graham .05 .02
❑ 132 Checklist 1-99 .05 .02
❑ 133 Andy Moog .10 .05
❑ 134 Gary Leeman ORIG6 .05 .02
❑ 135 Steve Larmer ORIG6 .10 .05
❑ 136 Steve Smith .05 .02
❑ 137 Dave Manson .05 .02
❑ 138 Nelson Emerson .05 .02
❑ 139 Doug Weight ORIG6 .10 .05
❑ 140 Uwe Krupp .05 .02
❑ 141 Peter Douris ORIG6 .05 .02
❑ 142 Steve Yzerman ORIG6 .50 .23
❑ 143 Derian Hatcher .05 .02
❑ 144 Vladimir Ruzicka ORIG6 .05 .02
❑ 145 Kirk Muller ORIG6 .05 .02
❑ 146 Darrin Shannon .05 .02
❑ 147 Mike Gartner ORIG6 .10 .05
❑ 148 Bob Carpenter ORIG6 .05 .02
❑ 149 Josef Beranek .05 .02
❑ 150 Chris Chelios ORIG6 .25 .11
❑ 151 Bob Rouse ORIG6 .05 .02
❑ 152 Guy Carbonneau ORIG6 .10 .05
❑ 153 Joe Mullen .10 .05
❑ 154 Ken Hodge Jr. ORIG6 .05 .02
❑ 155 Vladimir Konstantinov .05 .02
ORIG6
❑ 156 Brent Sutter .05 .02
❑ 157 Eric Desjardins ORIG6 .05 .02
❑ 158 Kirk McLean UER .10 .05
(Photo on back actually Frank Caprice)
❑ 159 John Tonelli ORIG6 .05 .02
❑ 160 Rob Cimetta ORIG6 .05 .02
❑ 161 Shayne Corson .05 .02
❑ 162 Russ Romaniuk .05 .02
❑ 163 Nicklas Lidstrom ORIG6 .10 .05
❑ 164 Mike Gartner .10 .05
❑ 165 Curtis Joseph .25 .11
❑ 166 Brian Mullen .05 .02
❑ 167 Jimmy Carson .05 .02
❑ 168 Petr Svoboda ORIG6 .05 .02
❑ 169 Troy Crowder .05 .02
❑ 170 Patrick Roy ORIG6 .75 .35
❑ 171 Adam Creighton .05 .02
❑ 172 James Patrick ORIG6 .05 .02
❑ 173 Sergei Fedorov ORIG6 .50 .23
❑ 174 Jeremy Roenick ORIG6 .25 .11
❑ 175 Tim Cheveldae ORIG6 .10 .05
❑ 176 Dimitri Khristich .05 .02
❑ 177 Wendel Clark ORIG6 .10 .05
❑ 178 Andrei Lomakin .05 .02
❑ 179 Benoit Hogue .05 .02
❑ 180 Dave Ellett ORIG6 .05 .02
❑ 181 Mathieu Schneider ORIG6 .05 .02
❑ 182 Kay Whitmore .10 .05
❑ 183 Brian Leetch ORIG6 .25 .11
❑ 184 Sylvain Turgeon ORIG6 .05 .02
❑ 185 Brian Bradley ORIG6 .05 .02
❑ 186 John LeClair ORIG6 .50 .23
❑ 187 Paul Fenton .05 .02
❑ 188 Alain Cote ORIG6 .05 .02
❑ 189 Mike Krushelnyski .05 .02
ORIG6 UER
(Misspelled on back as Krushelnynski)
❑ 190 Brian Bradley .05 .02
❑ 191 Grant Fuhr ORIG6 .10 .05
❑ 192 Ray Bourque ORIG6 .25 .11
❑ 193 Owen Nolan .10 .05
❑ 194 Russ Courtnall ORIG6 .05 .02
❑ 195 Steve Thomas .05 .02
❑ 196 Ed Olczyk .05 .02
❑ 197 Chris Terreri .10 .05
❑ 198 Checklist 100-198 .05 .02

## 1992-93 O-Pee-Chee

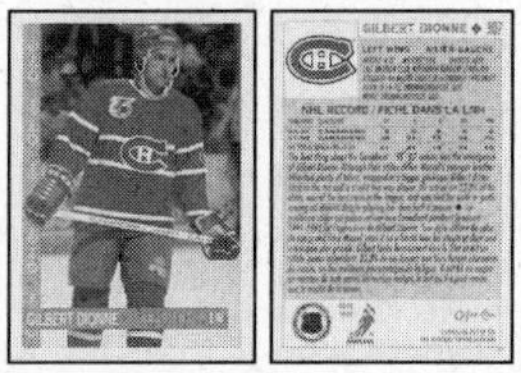

The 1992-93 set marks O-Pee-Chee's 25th consecutive year of manufacturing hockey cards. The set contains 396 standard-size cards. The set includes 25 special 25th Anniversary Tribute cards. The same 25 players are featured in a 25th Anniversary wax pack insert set. O-Pee-Chee produced 12,000 Special Anniversary Collector sets which included the complete 396-card set and the 26-card (including checklist) anniversary insert set. Also, 750 additional factory sets were allocated across Canada for confectionary customers and O-Pee-Chee employees to purchase. Card fronts feature color player photos bordered by a metallic blue stripe on the left and full-bleed on the other three sides. The player's name, team name, and position appear in a gray stripe toward the bottom of the card. The bilingual backs carry the team logo, biography, complete statistics, and player profile. Guy Hebert is the only Rookie Card of note.

| | MINT | NRMT |
|---|---|---|
| COMPLETE SET (396) | 20.00 | 9.00 |
| COMP.FACT.SET (396) | 25.00 | 11.00 |
| COMPLETE ANN.FACT.SET (422) | 70.00 | 32.00 |
| COMMON CARD (1-396) | .05 | .02 |

❑ 1 Kevin Todd .05 .02
❑ 2 Robert Kron .05 .02
❑ 3 David Volek .05 .02
❑ 4 Teppo Numminen .05 .02
❑ 5 Paul Coffey .25 .11
❑ 6 Luc Robitaille .10 .05
❑ 7 Steven Finn .05 .02
❑ 8 Gord Hynes .05 .02
❑ 9 Dave Ellett .05 .02
❑ 10 Alexander Godynyuk .05 .02
❑ 11 Darryl Sydor .05 .02
❑ 12 Randy Carlyle .05 .02
❑ 13 Chris Chelios .25 .11
❑ 14 Kent Manderville .05 .02
❑ 15 Wayne Gretzky 1.50 .70
❑ 16 Jon Casey .10 .05
❑ 17 Mark Tinordi .05 .02
❑ 18 Dale Hunter .05 .02
❑ 19 Martin Gelinas UER .05 .02
(Trade was 8-9-88, not 8-9-89)
❑ 20 Todd Elik .05 .02
❑ 21 Bob Sweeney .05 .02
❑ 22 Chris Dahlquist .05 .02
❑ 23 Joe Mullen .10 .05
❑ 24 Shawn Burr .05 .02
❑ 25 Pavel Bure .40 .18
❑ 26 Randy Gilhen .05 .02
❑ 27 Brian Bradley .05 .02
❑ 28 Don Beaupre .10 .05
❑ 29 Kevin Stevens .05 .02
❑ 30 Michal Pivonka .05 .02
❑ 31 Grant Fuhr .10 .05
❑ 32 Steve Larmer .10 .05
❑ 33 Gary Leeman .05 .02
❑ 34 Tony Tanti .05 .02
❑ 35 Denis Savard .10 .05
❑ 36 Paul Ranheim .05 .02
❑ 37 Andrei Lomakin .05 .02
❑ 38 Perry Anderson .05 .02
❑ 39 Stu Barnes .05 .02
❑ 40 Don Sweeney .05 .02
❑ 41 Jamie Baker .05 .02
❑ 42 Ray Ferraro .05 .02
❑ 43 Bobby Clarke 70-71 .10 .05
❑ 44 Kelly Hrudey .10 .05
❑ 45 Brian Skrudland .05 .02
❑ 46 Paul Ysebaert .05 .02
❑ 47 Pierre Turgeon .10 .05
❑ 48 Keith Brown .05 .02
❑ 49 Rod Brind'Amour .10 .05
❑ 50 Wayne McBean .05 .02
❑ 51 Doug Lidster .05 .02
❑ 52 Bernie Nicholls .10 .05
❑ 53 Daren Puppa .10 .05
❑ 54 Joe Sakic .40 .18
❑ 55 Joe Sakic 89-90 .40 .18
❑ 56 Dave Manson .05 .02
❑ 57 Denis Potvin 74-75 .05 .02
❑ 58 Daniel Marois .05 .02
❑ 59 Martin Brodeur .75 .35
❑ 60 Brent Sutter .05 .02
❑ 61 Steve Yzerman .60 .25
❑ 62 Neal Broten .10 .05
❑ 63 Darcy Wakaluk .10 .05
❑ 64 Troy Murray .05 .02
❑ 65 Tony Granato .05 .02
❑ 66 Frank Musil .05 .02
❑ 67 Claude Lemieux .10 .05
❑ 68 Brian Benning .05 .02
❑ 69 Stephane Matteau .05 .02
❑ 70 Tomas Forslund .05 .02
❑ 71 Dmitri Mironov .05 .02
❑ 72 Gary Roberts .05 .02
❑ 73 Felix Potvin .25 .11
❑ 74 Glen Murray UER .05 .02
(Misspelled Glenn on both sides)
❑ 75 Stephane Fiset .10 .05
❑ 76 Stephane Richer .10 .05
❑ 77 Jeff Reese .05 .02
❑ 78 Marc Bureau .05 .02
❑ 79 Derek King .05 .02
❑ 80 Dave Gagner .10 .05
❑ 81 Ed Belfour .25 .11
❑ 82 Joel Otto .05 .02
❑ 83 Anatoli Semenov .05 .02
❑ 84 Ron Hextall .10 .05
❑ 85 Adam Creighton .05 .02
❑ 86 Kris King .05 .02
❑ 87 Brett Hull .30 .14
❑ 88 Zdeno Ciger .05 .02
❑ 89 Petr Nedved .10 .05
❑ 90 Sergei Makarov .05 .02
❑ 91 Tomas Sandstrom .05 .02
❑ 92 Steve Heinze .05 .02
❑ 93 Robert Reichel .05 .02
❑ 94 Cliff Ronning .05 .02
❑ 95 Eric Weinrich .05 .02
❑ 96 Wendel Clark .10 .05
❑ 97 Rick Zombo .05 .02
❑ 98 Ric Nattress .05 .02
❑ 99 Theoren Fleury .10 .05
❑ 100 Joe Murphy .05 .02
❑ 101 Gord Murphy .05 .02
❑ 102 Jaromir Jagr .60 .25
❑ 103 Mike Craig .05 .02
❑ 104 John Cullen .05 .02
❑ 105 John Druce .05 .02
❑ 106 Peter Bondra .25 .11
❑ 107 Bryan Trottier 76-77 .10 .05
❑ 108 Steve Smith .05 .02
❑ 109 Petr Svoboda .05 .02
❑ 110 Mats Sundin .25 .11
❑ 111 Patrick Roy 86-87 2.50 1.10
❑ 112 Steve Leach .05 .02
❑ 113 Jacques Cloutier .10 .05
❑ 114 Doug Weight .10 .05
❑ 115 Frank Pietrangelo .10 .05
❑ 116 Guy Hebert .60 .25
❑ 117 Donald Audette .10 .05
❑ 118 Craig MacTavish .05 .02
❑ 119 Grant Fuhr 82-83 .10 .05
❑ 120 Trevor Linden .10 .05
❑ 121 Fredrik Olausson .05 .02
❑ 122 Geoff Sanderson .10 .05
❑ 123 Derian Hatcher .05 .02
❑ 124 Brett Hull 88-89 .50 .23
❑ 125 Kelly Buchberger .05 .02
❑ 126 Ray Bourque .25 .11
❑ 127 Murray Craven .05 .02
❑ 128 Tim Cheveldae .10 .05
❑ 129 Ulf Dahlen .05 .02
❑ 130 Bryan Trottier .10 .05
❑ 131 Bob Carpenter .05 .02
❑ 132 Benoit Hogue .05 .02
❑ 133 Claude Vilgrain .05 .02
❑ 134 Glenn Anderson .10 .05
❑ 135 Marty McInnis .05 .02
❑ 136 Rob Pearson .05 .02
❑ 137 Bill Ranford .10 .05
❑ 138 Mario Lemieux 1.00 .45
❑ 139 Bob Bassen .05 .02
❑ 140 Scott Mellanby .10 .05
❑ 141 Dave Andreychuk .10 .05
❑ 142 Kelly Miller .05 .02
❑ 143 Gaetan Duchesne .05 .02
❑ 144 Mike Sullivan .05 .02
❑ 145 Kevin Hatcher .05 .02
❑ 146 Doug Bodger .05 .02
❑ 147 Craig Berube .05 .02
❑ 148 Rick Tocchet .10 .05
❑ 149 Luciano Borsato .05 .02
❑ 150 Glen Wesley .05 .02
❑ 151 Mike Donnelly .05 .02
❑ 152 Jimmy Carson .05 .02
❑ 153 Jocelyn Lemieux .05 .02
❑ 154 Ray Sheppard .10 .05
❑ 155 Tony Amonte .10 .05
❑ 156 Adrien Plavsic .05 .02
❑ 157 Mark Pederson .05 .02
❑ 158 Adam Graves .10 .05
❑ 159 Igor Larionov .05 .02
❑ 160 Steve Chiasson .05 .02
❑ 161 Igor Kravchuk .05 .02
❑ 162 Slava Fetisov .05 .02
❑ 163 Gerard Gallant .05 .02
❑ 164 Patrick Roy 1.00 .45
❑ 165 Ken Sutton .05 .02
❑ 166 Mathieu Schneider .05 .02
❑ 167 Larry Robinson 73-74 .10 .05
❑ 168 Jim Sandlak .05 .02
❑ 169 Joey Kocur .05 .02
❑ 170 Rob Brown .05 .02
❑ 171 Luke Richardson .05 .02
❑ 172 Adam Oates 87-88 .10 .05
❑ 173 Uwe Krupp .05 .02
❑ 174 Cam Neely .10 .05
❑ 175 Peter Sidorkiewicz .10 .05
❑ 176 Geoff Courtnall .05 .02
❑ 177 Doug Gilmour .25 .11
❑ 178 Josef Beranek .05 .02
❑ 179 Michel Picard .05 .02
❑ 180 Terry Carkner .05 .02
❑ 181 Nelson Emerson .05 .02
❑ 182 Perry Berezan .05 .02
❑ 183 Checklist C .05 .02
❑ 184 Andy Moog .10 .05
❑ 185 Michel Petit .05 .02
❑ 186 Mark Greig .05 .02
❑ 187 Paul Coffey 81-82 .25 .11
❑ 188 Ron Francis .10 .05
❑ 189 Joe Juneau .10 .05
❑ 190 Jeff Odgers .05 .02
❑ 191 Darryl Sittler 75-76 .10 .05
❑ 192 Vincent Damphousse .10 .05
❑ 193 Greg Paslawski .05 .02
❑ 194 Tony Esposito 69-70 .10 .05
❑ 195 Sergei Fedorov .40 .18
❑ 196 Doug Small .05 .02
❑ 197 Pat Verbeek .05 .02
❑ 198 Dominic Roussel .10 .05
❑ 199 Mike McPhee .05 .02
❑ 200 Kevin Dineen .05 .02
❑ 201 Pat Elynuik .05 .02
❑ 202 Tom Kurvers .05 .02
❑ 203 Chris Joseph .05 .02
❑ 204 Mark Fitzpatrick .10 .05
❑ 205 Jari Kurri .10 .05
❑ 206 Guy Carbonneau .10 .05
❑ 207 Jan Erixon .05 .02
❑ 208 Mark Messier .30 .14
❑ 209 Larry Murphy .10 .05
❑ 210 Dirk Graham .05 .02
❑ 211 Ron Tugnutt .10 .05
❑ 212 Dale Hawerchuk .10 .05
❑ 213 Dave Babych .05 .02
❑ 214 Mikael Andersson .05 .02
❑ 215 James Patrick .05 .02
❑ 216 Peter Stastny .10 .05
❑ 217 Bernie Parent 68-69 .25 .11
❑ 218 Jeff Hackett .10 .05
❑ 219 Dave Lowry .05 .02
❑ 220 Wayne Gretzky 79-80 3.00 1.35
❑ 221 Brent Gilchrist .05 .02
❑ 222 Andrew Cassels .05 .02
❑ 223 Calle Johansson .05 .02
❑ 224 Joe Reekie .05 .02
❑ 225 Craig Simpson .05 .02
❑ 226 Bob Essensa .10 .05
❑ 227 Pat Falloon .05 .02
❑ 228 Vladimir Ruzicka .05 .02
❑ 229 Igor Ulanov .05 .02
❑ 230 Kjell Samuelsson .05 .02
❑ 231 Shayne Corson .05 .02
❑ 232 Kelly Kisio .05 .02
❑ 233 Gordie Roberts .05 .02
❑ 234 Brian Noonan .05 .02
❑ 235 Slava Kozlov UER .10 .05
❑ 236 Checklist B .05 .02
❑ 237 Jeff Beukeboom .05 .02
❑ 238 Steve Konroyd .05 .02
❑ 239 Patrice Brisebois .05 .02
❑ 240 Mario Lemieux .50 .23
Playoff MVP
❑ 241 Dana Murzyn .05 .02
❑ 242 Pelle Eklund .05 .02
❑ 243 Rob Blake .10 .05
❑ 244 Brendan Shanahan .40 .18
❑ 245 Mike Gartner HL .10 .05
❑ 246 David Bruce .05 .02
❑ 247 Mike Vernon .10 .05
❑ 248 Zarley Zalapski .05 .02
❑ 249 Dino Ciccarelli .10 .05
❑ 250 David Williams .05 .02
❑ 251 Scott Stevens 83-84 .10 .05
❑ 252 Bob Probert .10 .05
❑ 253 Mikhail Tatarinov .05 .02
❑ 254 Bobby Holik .05 .02
❑ 255 Tony Amonte 91-92 .10 .05
❑ 256 Brad May .10 .05
❑ 257 Philippe Bozon .05 .02
❑ 258 Mark Messier 80-81 .50 .23
❑ 259 Mike Richter .25 .11
❑ 260 Brian Mullen .05 .02
❑ 261 Marty McSorley .05 .02
❑ 262 Glenn Healy .10 .05
❑ 263 Russ Romaniuk .05 .02
❑ 264 Dan Quinn .05 .02
❑ 265 Jyrki Lumme .05 .02
❑ 266 Valeri Kamensky .10 .05
❑ 267 Vladimir Konstantinov .05 .02
❑ 268 Peter Ahola .05 .02
❑ 269 Guy Larose .05 .02
❑ 270 Ulf Samuelsson .05 .02
❑ 271 Dale Craigwell .05 .02
❑ 272 Adam Oates .10 .05
❑ 273 Pat MacLeod .05 .02
❑ 274 Mike Keane .05 .02
❑ 275 John Vanbiesbrouck .30 .14
❑ 276 Brian Lawton .05 .02
❑ 277 Sylvain Cote .05 .02
❑ 278 Gary Suter .05 .02
❑ 279 Alexander Mogilny .10 .05
❑ 280 Garth Butcher .05 .02
❑ 281 Doug Wilson .10 .05
❑ 282 Chris Terreri .10 .05
❑ 283 Phil Esposito 77-78 .10 .05
❑ 284 Russ Courtnall .05 .02
❑ 285 Pat LaFontaine .10 .05
❑ 286 Dimitri Khristich .05 .02
❑ 287 John LeBlanc .05 .02
❑ 288 Randy Velischek .05 .02
❑ 289 Dave Christian .05 .02
❑ 290 Kevin Haller .05 .02
❑ 291 Kevin Miller .05 .02
❑ 292 Mario Lemieux 85-86 2.50 1.10
❑ 293 Stephan Lebeau .05 .02
❑ 294 Marcel Dionne 71-72 .05 .02
❑ 295 Barry Pederson .05 .02
❑ 296 Steve Duchesne .05 .02
❑ 297 Yves Racine .05 .02
❑ 298 Phil Housley .10 .05
❑ 299 Randy Ladouceur .05 .02
❑ 300 Mike Gartner .10 .05
❑ 301 Dominik Hasek .75 .35
❑ 302 Kevin Lowe .05 .02
❑ 303 Sylvain Lefebvre .05 .02
❑ 304 J.J. Daigneault .05 .02
❑ 305 Mike Ridley .05 .02
❑ 306 Curtis Leschyshyn .05 .02
❑ 307 Gilbert Dionne .05 .02
❑ 308 Bill Guerin .05 .02
❑ 309 Gerald Diduck .05 .02
❑ 310 Rick Wamsley .10 .05
❑ 311 Pat Jablonski UER .10 .05
(Listed as Ottawa Senator on both sides, should be Tampa Bay Lightning)
❑ 312 Jay More .05 .02
❑ 313 Mike Modano .40 .18
❑ 314 Checklist A .05 .02
❑ 315 Slyvain Turgeon .05 .02
❑ 316 Sergei Nemchinov .05 .02
❑ 317 Garry Galley .05 .02
❑ 318 Paul Coffey HL .25 .11
❑ 319 Esa Tikkanen .05 .02
❑ 320 Claude LaPointe .05 .02
❑ 321 Steve Yzerman 84-85 .60 .25
❑ 322 Mark Lamb .05 .02
❑ 323 Bob Errey .05 .02
❑ 324 Pavel Bure 92-93 .50 .23
❑ 325 Craig Janney .10 .05
❑ 326 Bob Kudelski .05 .02
❑ 327 Kirk Muller .05 .02
❑ 328 Jim Paek .05 .02
❑ 329 Mike Ricci .05 .02
❑ 330 Al MacInnis .10 .05
❑ 331 Mike Hudson .05 .02
❑ 332 Darrin Shannon .05 .02
❑ 333 Doug Brown .05 .02
❑ 334 Corey Millen .05 .02
❑ 335 Mike Krushelnyski .05 .02
❑ 336 Scott Stevens .10 .05

| | | |
|---|---|---|
| ❑ 337 Peter Zezel | .05 | .02 |
| ❑ 338 Geoff Smith | .05 | .02 |
| ❑ 339 Curtis Joseph | .25 | .11 |
| ❑ 340 Tom Barrasso | .10 | .05 |
| ❑ 341 Al Iafrate | .10 | .05 |
| ❑ 342 Patrick Flatley | .10 | .05 |
| ❑ 343 Gerry Cheevers 72-73 Cleveland Crusaders | .10 | .05 |
| ❑ 344 Norm Maciver | .05 | .02 |
| ❑ 345 Jeremy Roenick | .25 | .11 |
| ❑ 346 Keith Tkachuk UER (Photo actually Petri Skriko) | .50 | .23 |
| ❑ 347 Rod Langway | .05 | .02 |
| ❑ 348 Ray Bourque HL | .10 | .05 |
| ❑ 349 Kirk McLean | .10 | .05 |
| ❑ 350 Brian Propp | .05 | .02 |
| ❑ 351 John Ogrodnick | .05 | .02 |
| ❑ 352 Benoit Brunet | .05 | .02 |
| ❑ 353 Alexei Kasatonov | .05 | .02 |
| ❑ 354 Joe Nieuwendyk | .10 | .05 |
| ❑ 355 Joe Sacco | .05 | .02 |
| ❑ 356 Tom Fergus | .05 | .02 |
| ❑ 357 Dan Lambert | .05 | .02 |
| ❑ 358 Michel Goulet | .10 | .05 |
| ❑ 359 Shawn McEachern | .05 | .02 |
| ❑ 360 Eric Desjardins | .05 | .02 |
| ❑ 361 Paul Stanton | .05 | .02 |
| ❑ 362 Ron Sutter | .05 | .02 |
| ❑ 363 Derrick Smith | .05 | .02 |
| ❑ 364 Paul Broten | .05 | .02 |
| ❑ 365 Greg Adams | .05 | .02 |
| ❑ 366 Rob Zettler | .05 | .02 |
| ❑ 367 Dave Poulin | .05 | .02 |
| ❑ 368 Keith Acton | .05 | .02 |
| ❑ 369 Nicklas Lidstrom | .10 | .05 |
| ❑ 370 Randy Burridge | .05 | .02 |
| ❑ 371 Jamie Macoun | .05 | .02 |
| ❑ 372 Craig Billington | .10 | .05 |
| ❑ 373 Mark Recchi | .10 | .05 |
| ❑ 374 Kris Draper | .05 | .02 |
| ❑ 375 Ed Olczyk | .05 | .02 |
| ❑ 376 Tom Draper | .10 | .05 |
| ❑ 377 Sergio Momesso | .05 | .02 |
| ❑ 378 Brian Leetch | .25 | .11 |
| ❑ 379 Paul Cavallini | .05 | .02 |
| ❑ 380 Paul Fenton | .05 | .02 |
| ❑ 381 Dean Evason | .05 | .02 |
| ❑ 382 Owen Nolan | .10 | .05 |
| ❑ 383 Jeremy Roenick 90-91 | .25 | .11 |
| ❑ 384 Brian Bellows | .05 | .02 |
| ❑ 385 Thomas Steen | .05 | .02 |
| ❑ 386 John LeClair | .50 | .23 |
| ❑ 387 Darren Turcotte | .05 | .02 |
| ❑ 388 James Black | .05 | .02 |
| ❑ 389 Alexei Gusarov | .05 | .02 |
| ❑ 390 Scott Lachance | .05 | .02 |
| ❑ 391 Mike Bossy 78-79 | .10 | .05 |
| ❑ 392 Mike Hough | .05 | .02 |
| ❑ 393 Grant Ledyard | .05 | .02 |
| ❑ 394 Tom Fitzgerald | .05 | .02 |
| ❑ 395 Steve Thomas | .05 | .02 |
| ❑ 396 Bobby Smith | .10 | .05 |

## 1992-93 O-Pee-Chee 25th Anniv. Inserts

This insert was included in 1992-93 O-Pee-Chee wax packs. The first 25 cards commemorate each of the past 25 years, beginning with the 1968-69 series. The cards measure the standard size and each one is a reproduction of the actual card design from each of the past 25 years; the front is bordered in silver metallic ink with a "watermark" mat varnish logo to commemorate the 25th Anniversary. The cards are numbered on the back as originally issued; however, the set has been renumbered on the front at the lower left and are checklisted below accordingly. Cards can be found with and without the 25th Anniversary emblem embossed on the front.

| | MINT | NRMT |
|---|---|---|
| COMPLETE SET (26) | 15.00 | 6.75 |
| COMMON CARD (1-25) | .20 | .09 |
| ❑ 1 Bernie Parent | .50 | .23 |
| ❑ 2 Tony Esposito | .50 | .23 |
| ❑ 3 Bobby Clarke | .20 | .09 |
| ❑ 4 Marcel Dionne | .20 | .09 |
| ❑ 5 Gerry Cheevers | .50 | .23 |
| ❑ 6 Larry Robinson | .20 | .09 |
| ❑ 7 Denis Potvin | .20 | .09 |
| ❑ 8 Darryl Sittler | .20 | .09 |
| ❑ 9 Bryan Trottier | .20 | .09 |
| ❑ 10 Phil Esposito | .50 | .23 |
| ❑ 11 Mike Bossy | .50 | .23 |
| ❑ 12 Wayne Gretzky | 4.00 | 1.80 |
| ❑ 13 Mark Messier | 1.00 | .45 |
| ❑ 14 Paul Coffey | .75 | .35 |
| ❑ 15 Grant Fuhr | .50 | .23 |
| ❑ 16 Scott Stevens | .20 | .09 |
| ❑ 17 Steve Yzerman | 2.00 | .90 |
| ❑ 18 Mario Lemieux | 3.00 | 1.35 |
| ❑ 19 Patrick Roy | 3.00 | 1.35 |
| ❑ 20 Adam Oates | .50 | .23 |
| ❑ 21 Brett Hull | .60 | .25 |
| ❑ 22 Joe Sakic | 1.50 | .70 |
| ❑ 23 Jeremy Roenick | .75 | .35 |
| ❑ 24 Tony Amonte | .20 | .09 |
| ❑ 25 Pavel Bure | 1.25 | .55 |
| ❑ NNO Checklist | .20 | .09 |

## 1992-93 O-Pee-Chee Trophy Winners

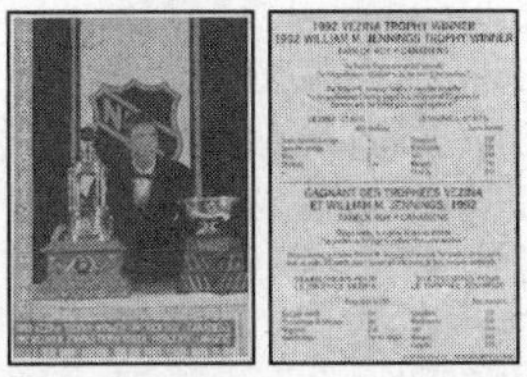

These four oversized cards measure approximately 4 7/8" by 6 3/4" and were bottoms from 1992-93 O-Pee-Chee pack boxes. Each features on its front a white-bordered color shot of the player in a tuxedo, holding his trophy and standing in front of an NHL backdrop. The player's name, team, and the trophy name appear in a dark gray stripe near the bottom. O-Pee-Chee appears vertically in a blue stripe along the left edge of the photo. In both French and English, the back has the trophy name, player name and team, and stats in blue lettering. The cards are unnumbered and checklisted below in alphabetical order.

| | MINT | NRMT |
|---|---|---|
| COMPLETE SET (4) | 5.00 | 2.20 |
| COMMON CARD (1-4) | .75 | .35 |
| ❑ 1 Pavel Bure | 2.00 | .90 |
| ❑ 2 Brian Leetch | .75 | .35 |
| ❑ 3 Mark Messier | 1.25 | .55 |
| ❑ 4 Patrick Roy | 2.50 | 1.10 |

## 1993 O-Pee-Chee Canadiens Hockey Fest

Sold initially only at Hockey Fest '93 (February 4-7, 1993) and the Montreal Forum, this 66-card standard-size set features tribute cards to the Stanley Cup, the Montreal Forum, and past and present stars of the Montreal Canadiens. The production run was 5,000 sets, and each set came in a puck-shaped display box that bore the set serial number. A portion of the proceeds went to the Montreal Canadiens Old Timers Association. Current players are shown in color action photos with white borders and a red stripe at the top. Cards showing former players and people associated with the team have either color or sepia-tone photos framed by red borders on a white card face. The backs of all cards display a variegated pale blue panel containing text or statistics. The current player cards also carry a close-up player photo on the back. Former player cards have a red border around the panel. All the cards have a royal blue outer border.

| | MINT | NRMT |
|---|---|---|
| COMPLETE SET (66) | 70.00 | 32.00 |
| COMMON CARD (1-66) | .25 | .11 |
| ❑ 1 Montreal Forum 1924 | 1.00 | .45 |
| ❑ 2 Emile Bouchard | .25 | .11 |
| ❑ 3 Henri Richard | 2.00 | .90 |
| ❑ 4 Serge Savard | .50 | .23 |
| ❑ 5 Toe Blake CO HL | 2.00 | .90 |
| ❑ 6 Maurice Richard HL | 3.00 | 1.35 |
| ❑ 7 Stephan Lebeau | .25 | .11 |
| ❑ 8 Kevin Haller | .25 | .11 |
| ❑ 9 Guy Carbonneau | .50 | .23 |
| ❑ 10 Jacques Demers CO | .35 | .16 |
| ❑ 11 Serge Savard | .50 | .23 |
| ❑ 12 Montreal Forum 1968 | 2.00 | .90 |
| ❑ 13 Howie Morenz | 5.00 | 2.20 |
| ❑ 14 Jean Beliveau | 3.00 | 1.35 |
| ❑ 15 Jacques Laperriere | .50 | .23 |
| ❑ 16 Bob Gainey | .75 | .35 |
| ❑ 17 Guy Lafleur HL | 2.00 | .90 |
| ❑ 18 Jacques Raymond | .25 | .11 |
| ❑ 19 Sean Hill | .25 | .11 |
| ❑ 20 Eric Desjardins | .35 | .16 |
| ❑ 21 Aurel Joliat | 2.00 | .90 |
| ❑ 22 Doug Harvey | 2.00 | .90 |
| ❑ 23 Yvan Cournoyer | .75 | .35 |
| ❑ 24 Frank Mahovlich HL | 1.00 | .45 |
| ❑ 25 J.J. Daigneault | .25 | .11 |
| ❑ 26 Kirk Muller | .35 | .16 |
| ❑ 27 Jean Beliveau | 4.00 | 1.80 |
| ❑ 28 Georges Vezina | 5.00 | 2.20 |
| ❑ 29 Maurice Richard | 5.00 | 2.20 |
| ❑ 30 Patrick Roy | 12.00 | 5.50 |
| ❑ 31 Benoit Brunet | .25 | .11 |
| ❑ 32 Jacques Plante HL | 3.00 | 1.35 |
| ❑ 33 Ralph Backstrom | .25 | .11 |
| ❑ 34 Elmer Lach | 1.00 | .45 |
| ❑ 35 Stanley Cup Champions | .50 | .23 |
| ❑ 36 Jacques Laperriere | .50 | .23 |
| ❑ 37 Montreal Individual Records--Playoffs | .25 | .11 |
| ❑ 38 Vincent Damphousse | .75 | .35 |
| ❑ 39 Frank Mahovlich | 2.00 | .90 |
| ❑ 40 Jacques Plante | 5.00 | 2.20 |
| ❑ 41 Stanley Cup Champions | .50 | .23 |
| ❑ 42 Kenny Reardon | .75 | .35 |
| ❑ 43 Claude Provost | .25 | .11 |
| ❑ 44 Jean Beliveau HL | 2.50 | 1.10 |
| ❑ 45 Edward Ronan | .25 | .11 |
| ❑ 46 Canadiens NHL Individual Records | .25 | .11 |
| ❑ 47 Bill Durnan | 2.00 | .90 |
| ❑ 48 Stanley Cup | .50 | .23 |
| ❑ 49 Patrice Brisebois | .35 | .16 |
| ❑ 50 Denis Savard | .75 | .35 |
| ❑ 51 Ken Dryden | 5.00 | 2.20 |
| ❑ 52 Lou Fontinato | .35 | .16 |
| ❑ 53 Jean-Guy Talbot | .50 | .23 |
| ❑ 54 BoomBoom Geoffrion | 2.00 | .90 |
| ❑ 55 Joe Malone | 2.00 | .90 |
| ❑ 56 Oleg Petrov | .25 | .11 |
| ❑ 57 Guy Lafleur | 2.50 | 1.10 |
| ❑ 58 Bert Olmstead | .50 | .23 |
| ❑ 59 The Dream Team<br>Jacques Plante<br>Larry Robinson<br>Toe Blake CO<br>Jean Beliveau<br>Dickie Moore<br>Doug Harvey<br>Maurice Richard<br>Aurel Joliat<br>Bob Gainey | 4.00 | 1.80 |
| ❑ 60 Brian Bellows | .35 | .16 |
| ❑ 61 Henri Richard HL | 1.00 | .45 |
| ❑ 62 Jacques Lemaire | .75 | .35 |
| ❑ 63 Dickie Moore | 1.50 | .70 |
| ❑ 64 Lorne Worsley | 1.50 | .70 |
| ❑ 65 Toe Blake | 2.50 | 1.10 |
| ❑ 66 Checklist Card | .25 | .11 |
| ❑ NNO Advertisement Card | .25 | .11 |

## 1993 O-Pee-Chee Canadiens Panel

This approximately 5" by 7" panel displays samples of the O-Pee-Chee Canadiens Hockey Fest cards. If the cards were cut, they would measure the standard size. The front features three cards with posed color player photos with red borders, and one sepia-tone action player photo with red borders. The cards are printed on a white card face. The back show variegated pale blue panels containing statistics. The panels are bordered in dark blue and set on a red background.

| | MINT | NRMT |
|---|---|---|
| COMPLETE SET (1) | 10.00 | 4.50 |
| COMMON PANEL | 10.00 | 4.50 |
| ❑ 1 Canadiens Panel<br>Henri Richard<br>Jean Beliveau<br>Yvan Cournoyer<br>Maurice Richard | 10.00 | 4.50 |

## 1992-93 OPC Premier

The 1992-93 O-Pee-Chee Premier hockey set consists of 132 cards, each measuring the standard size. The fronts feature action color player photos with white borders. A team color-coded stripe accents the top edge of each picture. The O-Pee-Chee logo overlaps the picture at the lower right corner. The player's name and position appear in the bottom border. The backs show a slightly offset, pale, team color-coded panel which carries a close-up photo and biographical data. A darker team color-coded bar with a speckled effect presents statistics and appears at the bottom. The team logo overlaps the picture panel at the lower left corner of the photo. Each pack contained an insert from either the Top Rookie set or the 22-card Star Performers set. According to O-Pee-Chee, every ninth pack contained a Top Rookie card as its insert with the other packs containing a Star Performers card. The production quantity reportedly was 7,500 20-box wax cases. Rookie Cards in the set include Roman Hamrlik, Guy Hebert, Andrei Kovalenko, and Martin Straka.

| | MINT | NRMT |
|---|---|---|
| COMPLETE SET (132) | 10.00 | 4.50 |
| COMMON CARD (1-132) | .05 | .02 |
| ❑ 1 Dave Christian | .05 | .02 |
| ❑ 2 Christian Ruuttu | .05 | .02 |
| ❑ 3 Vincent Damphousse | .10 | .05 |
| ❑ 4 Chris Lindberg | .05 | .02 |
| ❑ 5 Bill Lindsay | .05 | .02 |
| ❑ 6 Dmitri Kvartalnov | .05 | .02 |
| ❑ 7 Darcy Loewen | .05 | .02 |
| ❑ 8 Ed Courtenay | .05 | .02 |
| ❑ 9 Sergei Krivokrasov | .10 | .05 |
| ❑ 10 Shawn Antoski | .05 | .02 |
| ❑ 11 Andre Racicot | .10 | .05 |
| ❑ 12 Marty McInnis | .05 | .02 |
| ❑ 13 Alexei Zhamnov | .10 | .05 |
| ❑ 14 Keith Jones | .25 | .11 |
| ❑ 15 Steve Konowalchuk | .05 | .02 |
| ❑ 16 Darryl Sydor | .05 | .02 |
| ❑ 17 Janne Ojanen | .05 | .02 |
| ❑ 18 Doug Zmolek | .05 | .02 |
| ❑ 19 Michael Nylander | .05 | .02 |
| ❑ 20 Russ Courtnall | .05 | .02 |
| ❑ 21 Martin Straka | .75 | .35 |
| ❑ 22 Kevin Dahl | .05 | .02 |
| ❑ 23 Kent Manderville | .05 | .02 |
| ❑ 24 Steve Heinze | .05 | .02 |
| ❑ 25 Philippe Bozon | .05 | .02 |
| ❑ 26 Brent Fedyk | .05 | .02 |
| ❑ 27 Kris Draper | .05 | .02 |
| ❑ 28 Brad Schlegel | .05 | .02 |
| ❑ 29 Patric Kjellberg | .05 | .02 |
| ❑ 30 Ted Donato | .05 | .02 |
| ❑ 31 Vyatcheslav Butsayev | .05 | .02 |
| ❑ 32 Tyler Wright | .05 | .02 |
| ❑ 33 Tom Pederson | .05 | .02 |
| ❑ 34 Jim Hiller | .05 | .02 |
| ❑ 35 Chris Luongo | .05 | .02 |
| ❑ 36 Robert Petrovicky | .05 | .02 |
| ❑ 37 Jean-Francois Quintin | .05 | .02 |
| ❑ 38 Chris Dahlquist | .05 | .02 |
| ❑ 39 Daniel LaPerriere | .05 | .02 |
| ❑ 40 Guy Hebert | .75 | .35 |
| ❑ 41 Ed Ronan | .05 | .02 |
| ❑ 42 Shawn Cronin | .05 | .02 |
| ❑ 43 Keith Tkachuk | .60 | .25 |
| ❑ 44 Dino Ciccarelli | .10 | .05 |
| ❑ 45 Doug Evans | .05 | .02 |
| ❑ 46 Roman Hamrlik | .40 | .18 |
| ❑ 47 Robert Lang | .05 | .02 |
| ❑ 48 Kerry Huffman | .05 | .02 |
| ❑ 49 Pat Conacher | .05 | .02 |
| ❑ 50 Dominik Hasek | 1.00 | .45 |
| ❑ 51 Dominic Roussel | .10 | .05 |
| ❑ 52 Glen Murray | .05 | .02 |
| ❑ 53 Igor Korolev | .05 | .02 |
| ❑ 54 Jiri Slegr | .05 | .02 |
| ❑ 55 Mikael Andersson | .05 | .02 |
| ❑ 56 Bob Babcock | .05 | .02 |
| ❑ 57 Ron Hextall | .10 | .05 |
| ❑ 58 Jeff Daniels | .05 | .02 |
| ❑ 59 Doug Crossman | .05 | .02 |
| ❑ 60 Viktor Gordiouk | .05 | .02 |
| ❑ 61 Adam Creighton | .05 | .02 |
| ❑ 62 Rob DiMaio | .05 | .02 |
| ❑ 63 Eric Weinrich | .05 | .02 |
| ❑ 64 Vitali Prokhorov | .05 | .02 |
| ❑ 65 Dimitri Yushkevich | .05 | .02 |
| ❑ 66 Evgeny Davydov | .05 | .02 |
| ❑ 67 Dixon Ward | .05 | .02 |
| ❑ 68 Teemu Selanne | 1.25 | .55 |
| ❑ 69 Rob Zamuner | .05 | .02 |
| ❑ 70 Joe Reekie | .05 | .02 |
| ❑ 71 Slava Kozlov | .10 | .05 |
| ❑ 72 Philippe Boucher | .05 | .02 |
| ❑ 73 Phil Bourque | .05 | .02 |
| ❑ 74 Yvon Corriveau | .05 | .02 |
| ❑ 75 Brian Bellows | .05 | .02 |
| ❑ 76 Wendell Young | .10 | .05 |
| ❑ 77 Bobby Holik | .05 | .02 |
| ❑ 78 Bob Carpenter | .05 | .02 |
| ❑ 79 Scott Lachance | .05 | .02 |
| ❑ 80 John Druce | .05 | .02 |
| ❑ 81 Keith Carney | .05 | .02 |
| ❑ 82 Neil Brady | .05 | .02 |
| ❑ 83 Richard Matvichuk | .05 | .02 |
| ❑ 84 Sergei Bautin | .05 | .02 |
| ❑ 85 Patrick Poulin | .05 | .02 |
| ❑ 86 Gordie Roberts | .05 | .02 |
| ❑ 87 Kay Whitmore | .10 | .05 |
| ❑ 88 Steph Beauregard | .10 | .05 |
| ❑ 89 Vladimir Malakhov | .05 | .02 |
| ❑ 90 Richard Smehlik | .05 | .02 |
| ❑ 91 Mike Ricci | .05 | .02 |
| ❑ 92 Sean Burke | .10 | .05 |
| ❑ 93 Andrei Kovalenko | .05 | .02 |
| ❑ 94 Shawn McEachern | .05 | .02 |
| ❑ 95 Pat Jablonski | .10 | .05 |
| ❑ 96 Oleg Petrov | .05 | .02 |
| ❑ 97 Glenn Mulvenna | .05 | .02 |
| ❑ 98 Jason Woolley | .05 | .02 |
| ❑ 99 Mark Greig | .05 | .02 |
| ❑ 100 Nikolai Borschevsky | .05 | .02 |
| ❑ 101 Joe Juneau | .10 | .05 |
| ❑ 102 Eric Lindros | 2.00 | .90 |
| ❑ 103 Darius Kasparaitis | .05 | .02 |
| ❑ 104 Sandis Ozolinsh | .10 | .05 |
| ❑ 105 Stan Drulia | .05 | .02 |
| ❑ 106 Mike Needham | .05 | .02 |
| ❑ 107 Norm Maciver | .05 | .02 |
| ❑ 108 Sylvain Lefebvre | .05 | .02 |
| ❑ 109 Tommy Sjodin | .05 | .02 |
| ❑ 110 Bob Sweeney | .05 | .02 |
| ❑ 111 Brian Mullen | .05 | .02 |
| ❑ 112 Peter Sidorkiewicz | .10 | .05 |
| ❑ 113 Scott Niedermayer | .10 | .05 |
| ❑ 114 Felix Potvin | .25 | .11 |
| ❑ 115 Robb Stauber | .10 | .05 |
| ❑ 116 Sylvain Turgeon | .05 | .02 |
| ❑ 117 Mark Janssens | .05 | .02 |
| ❑ 118 Darren Banks | .05 | .02 |
| ❑ 119 Pat Elynuik | .05 | .02 |
| ❑ 120 Bill Guerin | .05 | .02 |
| ❑ 121 Reggie Savage | .05 | .02 |
| ❑ 122 Enrico Ciccone | .05 | .02 |
| ❑ 123 Chris Kontos | .05 | .02 |
| ❑ 124 Martin Rucinsky | .05 | .02 |
| ❑ 125 Alexei Zhitnik | .05 | .02 |
| ❑ 126 Alexei Kovalev | .10 | .05 |
| ❑ 127 Tim Kerr | .05 | .02 |
| ❑ 128 Guy Larose | .05 | .02 |
| ❑ 129 Brent Gilchrist | .05 | .02 |
| ❑ 130 Steve Duchesne | .05 | .02 |
| ❑ 131 Drake Berehowsky | .05 | .02 |
| ❑ 132 Checklist 1-132 | .05 | .02 |

## 1992-93 OPC Premier Star Performers

This 22-card standard-size set was randomly inserted in 1992-93 O-Pee-Chee Premier foil packs. According to O-Pee-Chee, the insertion rate was eight out of every nine packs. The other packs contained Top Rookie inserts. Card fronts are similar to the basic Premier issue. The difference being a red "Star Performers" stripe at the top. The backs are also like those of Premier with a small player photo and team logo included.

| | MINT | NRMT |
|---|---|---|
| COMPLETE SET (22) | 10.00 | 4.50 |
| COMMON CARD (1-22) | .15 | .07 |
| ❑ 1 Ray Ferraro | .15 | .07 |
| ❑ 2 Dale Hunter | .15 | .07 |
| ❑ 3 Murray Craven | .15 | .07 |
| ❑ 4 Paul Coffey | .50 | .23 |
| ❑ 5 Jeremy Roenick | .50 | .23 |
| ❑ 6 Denis Savard | .25 | .11 |
| ❑ 7 Jon Casey | .25 | .11 |
| ❑ 8 Doug Gilmour | .25 | .11 |
| ❑ 9 Rod Brind'Amour | .25 | .11 |
| ❑ 10 Pavel Bure | 1.00 | .45 |
| ❑ 11 Joe Sakic | 1.00 | .45 |
| ❑ 12 Pat Falloon | .15 | .07 |
| ❑ 13 Adam Oates | .25 | .11 |
| ❑ 14 Gary Roberts | .15 | .07 |
| ❑ 15 Mark Messier | .75 | .35 |
| ❑ 16 Phil Housley | .15 | .07 |
| ❑ 17 Pat LaFontaine | .25 | .11 |
| ❑ 18 Stephane Richer | .15 | .07 |
| ❑ 19 Bill Ranford | .25 | .11 |
| ❑ 20 Sergei Fedorov | 1.00 | .45 |
| ❑ 21 Brett Hull | .75 | .35 |
| ❑ 22 Mario Lemieux | 2.50 | 1.10 |

## 1992-93 OPC Premier Top Rookies

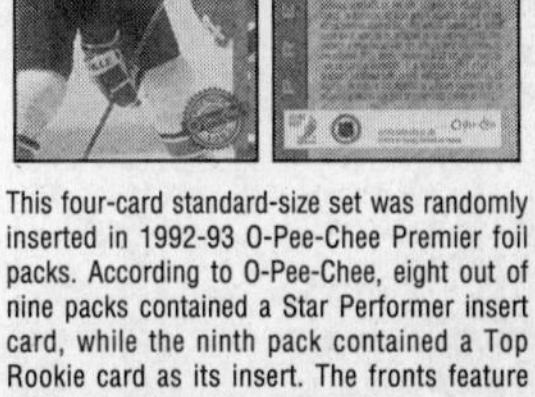

This four-card standard-size set was randomly inserted in 1992-93 O-Pee-Chee Premier foil packs. According to O-Pee-Chee, eight out of nine packs contained a Star Performer insert card, while the ninth pack contained a Top Rookie card as its insert. The fronts feature full-bleed color action player photos. A color bar carrying the player's name runs down the right side and intersects the 1993 O-Pee-Chee Premier logo at the lower right corner. Inside red border stripes on the top and left, the backs present a close-up photo, team logo, and player profile (in French and English) on a gradated rose panel. The cards are numbered on the back at the upper left corner.

| | MINT | NRMT |
|---|---|---|
| COMPLETE SET (4) | 6.00 | 2.70 |

| | MINT | NRMT |
|---|---|---|
| COMMON CARD (1-4) | .50 | .23 |
| ❑ 1 Eric Lindros | 4.00 | 1.80 |
| ❑ 2 Roman Hamrlik | 1.00 | .45 |
| ❑ 3 Dominic Roussel | .50 | .23 |
| ❑ 4 Felix Potvin | 1.00 | .45 |

## 1993-94 OPC Premier Black Gold

These 24 standard-size Black Gold cards were randomly inserted in O-Pee-Chee packs. The white-bordered fronts feature color player action shots with darkened backgrounds. Gold-foil stripes above and below the photo carry multiple-set logos. The player's name appears in white lettering within a black stripe through the lower gold-foil stripe. The white-bordered and horizontal back carries a color player cutout on one side, and career highlights in French and English within a purple rectangle on the other.

| | MINT | NRMT |
|---|---|---|
| COMPLETE SET (24) | 120.00 | 55.00 |
| COMPLETE SERIES 1 (12) | 60.00 | 27.00 |
| COMPLETE SERIES 2 (12) | 60.00 | 27.00 |
| COMMON CARD (1-24) | 1.50 | .70 |
| ❑ 1 Wayne Gretzky | 20.00 | 9.00 |
| ❑ 2 Vincent Damphousse | 2.00 | .90 |
| ❑ 3 Adam Oates | 2.00 | .90 |
| ❑ 4 Phil Housley | 1.50 | .70 |
| ❑ 5 Mike Vernon | 2.00 | .90 |
| ❑ 6 Mats Sundin | 2.00 | .90 |
| ❑ 7 Pavel Bure | 6.00 | 2.70 |
| ❑ 8 Patrick Roy | 15.00 | 6.75 |
| ❑ 9 Tom Barrasso | 2.00 | .90 |
| ❑ 10 Alexander Mogilny | 2.00 | .90 |
| ❑ 11 Doug Gilmour | 2.00 | .90 |
| ❑ 12 Eric Lindros | 15.00 | 6.75 |
| ❑ 13 Theoren Fleury | 2.00 | .90 |
| ❑ 14 Pat LaFontaine | 2.00 | .90 |
| ❑ 15 Joe Sakic | 8.00 | 3.60 |
| ❑ 16 Ed Belfour | 3.00 | 1.35 |
| ❑ 17 Felix Potvin | 3.00 | 1.35 |
| ❑ 18 Mario Lemieux | 15.00 | 6.75 |
| ❑ 19 Jaromir Jagr | 10.00 | 4.50 |
| ❑ 20 Teemu Selanne | 6.00 | 2.70 |
| ❑ 21 Ray Bourque | 3.00 | 1.35 |
| ❑ 22 Brett Hull | 4.00 | 1.80 |
| ❑ 23 Steve Yzerman | 10.00 | 4.50 |
| ❑ 24 Kirk Muller | 1.50 | .70 |

## 1993-94 OPC Premier Team Canada

Randomly inserted in second-series OPC Premier packs, these 19 standard-size cards feature borderless color player action shots on their fronts. The player's name and the Hockey Canada logo appear at the bottom. The red back carries the player's name and position at the top, followed below by biography, player photo, career highlights in English and French, and statistics. The cards are numbered on the back as "X of 19."

| | MINT | NRMT |
|---|---|---|
| COMPLETE SET (19) | 40.00 | 18.00 |
| COMMON CARD (1-19) | 1.50 | .70 |
| ❑ 1 Brett Lindros | 3.00 | 1.35 |
| ❑ 2 Manny Legace | 3.00 | 1.35 |
| ❑ 3 Adrian Aucoin | 1.50 | .70 |
| ❑ 4 Ken Lovsin | 1.50 | .70 |
| ❑ 5 Craig Woodcroft | 1.50 | .70 |
| ❑ 6 Derek Mayer | 1.50 | .70 |
| ❑ 7 Fabian Joseph | 1.50 | .70 |
| ❑ 8 Todd Brost | 1.50 | .70 |
| ❑ 9 Chris Therien | 3.00 | 1.35 |
| ❑ 10 Brad Turner | 1.50 | .70 |
| ❑ 11 Trevor Sim | 1.50 | .70 |
| ❑ 12 Todd Hlushko | 1.50 | .70 |
| ❑ 13 Dwayne Norris | 1.50 | .70 |
| ❑ 14 Chris Kontos | 1.50 | .70 |
| ❑ 15 Petr Nedved | 7.00 | 3.10 |
| ❑ 16 Brian Savage | 3.00 | 1.35 |
| ❑ 17 Paul Kariya | 25.00 | 11.00 |
| ❑ 18 Corey Hirsch | 5.00 | 2.20 |
| ❑ 19 Todd Warriner | 3.00 | 1.35 |

## 1994-95 O-Pee-Chee Finest Inserts

The 23 cards in this set were randomly inserted at a rate of 1:36 OPC Premier series 1 packs. The set includes top rookies of 1993-94. Cards feature an isolated player photo over a textured rainbow background. A reflective rainbow border is broken up by the player name. Premier Finest is written across the top of the card. Backs have a small player photo with brief personal information, and statistical breakdown. Cards are numbered "X of 23".

| | MINT | NRMT |
|---|---|---|
| COMPLETE SET (23) | 125.00 | 55.00 |
| COMMON CARD (1-23) | 1.50 | .70 |
| ❑ 1 Patrik Carnback | 1.50 | .70 |
| ❑ 2 Bryan Smolinski | 1.50 | .70 |
| ❑ 3 Derek Plante | 1.50 | .70 |
| ❑ 4 Alexander Karpovtsev | 1.50 | .70 |
| ❑ 5 Trevor Kidd | 6.00 | 2.70 |
| ❑ 6 Iain Fraser | 1.50 | .70 |
| ❑ 7 Alexandre Daigle | 6.00 | 2.70 |
| ❑ 8 Chris Osgood | 20.00 | 9.00 |
| ❑ 9 Rob Niedermayer | 6.00 | 2.70 |
| ❑ 10 Jason Arnott | 15.00 | 6.75 |
| ❑ 11 Chris Pronger | 6.00 | 2.70 |
| ❑ 12 Jesse Belanger | 1.50 | .70 |
| ❑ 13 Oleg Petrov | 1.50 | .70 |
| ❑ 14 Martin Brodeur | 30.00 | 13.50 |
| ❑ 15 Alexei Yashin | 6.00 | 2.70 |
| ❑ 16 Mikael Renberg | 6.00 | 2.70 |
| ❑ 17 Boris Mironov | 1.50 | .70 |
| ❑ 18 Damian Rhodes | 6.00 | 2.70 |
| ❑ 19 Darren McCarty | 6.00 | 2.70 |
| ❑ 20 Chris Gratton | 6.00 | 2.70 |
| ❑ 21 Jamie McLennan | 1.50 | .70 |
| ❑ 22 Nathan Lafayette | 1.50 | .70 |
| ❑ 23 Jeff Shantz | 1.50 | .70 |

## 1998-99 OPC Chrome

The 1998-99 OPC Chrome set was issue in one series by Topps totalling 242 cards and was distributed in four card packs with a suggested retail price of $3. The fronts feature color action photos of veteran players, 1998 NHL Draft Picks, and CHL All-Stars. The backs carry player information and career statistics.

| | MINT | NRMT |
|---|---|---|
| COMPLETE SET (242) | 175.00 | 80.00 |
| COMMON CARD (1-242) | .40 | .18 |
| ❑ 1 Peter Forsberg | 5.00 | 2.20 |
| ❑ 2 Petr Sykora | .40 | .18 |
| ❑ 3 Byron Dafoe | 1.25 | .55 |
| ❑ 4 Ron Francis | 1.25 | .55 |
| ❑ 5 Alexei Yashin | 1.25 | .55 |
| ❑ 6 Dave Ellett | .40 | .18 |
| ❑ 7 Jamie Langenbrunner | .40 | .18 |
| ❑ 8 Doug Weight | 1.25 | .55 |
| ❑ 9 Jason Woolley | .40 | .18 |
| ❑ 10 Paul Coffey | 1.50 | .70 |
| ❑ 11 Uwe Krupp | .40 | .18 |
| ❑ 12 Tomas Sandstrom | .40 | .18 |
| ❑ 13 Scott Mellanby | .40 | .18 |
| ❑ 14 Vladimir Tsyplakov | .40 | .18 |
| ❑ 15 Martin Rucinsky | .40 | .18 |
| ❑ 16 Mikael Renberg | 1.25 | .55 |
| ❑ 17 Marco Sturm | .40 | .18 |
| ❑ 18 Eric Lindros | 5.00 | 2.20 |
| ❑ 19 Sean Burke | 1.25 | .55 |
| ❑ 20 Martin Brodeur | 4.00 | 1.80 |
| ❑ 21 Boyd Devereaux | .40 | .18 |
| ❑ 22 Kelly Buchberger | .40 | .18 |
| ❑ 23 Scott Stevens | .40 | .18 |
| ❑ 24 Jamie Storr | 1.25 | .55 |
| ❑ 25 Anders Eriksson | .40 | .18 |
| ❑ 26 Gary Suter | .40 | .18 |
| ❑ 27 Theoren Fleury | 1.50 | .70 |
| ❑ 28 Steve Leach | .40 | .18 |
| ❑ 29 Felix Potvin | 1.50 | .70 |
| ❑ 30 Brett Hull | 2.00 | .90 |
| ❑ 31 Mike Grier | .40 | .18 |
| ❑ 32 Cale Hulse | .40 | .18 |
| ❑ 33 Larry Murphy | 1.25 | .55 |
| ❑ 34 Rick Tocchet | 1.25 | .55 |
| ❑ 35 Eric Desjardins | .40 | .18 |
| ❑ 36 Igor Kravchuk | .40 | .18 |
| ❑ 37 Rob Niedermayer | .40 | .18 |
| ❑ 38 Bryan Smolinski | .40 | .18 |
| ❑ 39 Valeri Kamensky | .40 | .18 |
| ❑ 40 Ryan Smyth | 1.25 | .55 |
| ❑ 41 Bruce Driver | .40 | .18 |
| ❑ 42 Mike Johnson | .40 | .18 |
| ❑ 43 Rob Zamuner | .40 | .18 |
| ❑ 44 Steve Duchesne | .40 | .18 |
| ❑ 45 Martin Straka | .40 | .18 |
| ❑ 46 Bill Houlder | .40 | .18 |
| ❑ 47 Craig Conroy | .40 | .18 |
| ❑ 48 Guy Hebert | 1.25 | .55 |
| ❑ 49 Colin Forbes | .40 | .18 |
| ❑ 50 Mike Modano | 2.00 | .90 |
| ❑ 51 Jamie Pushor | .40 | .18 |
| ❑ 52 Jarome Iginla | .40 | .18 |
| ❑ 53 Paul Kariya | 6.00 | 2.70 |
| ❑ 54 Mattias Ohlund | 1.25 | .55 |
| ❑ 55 Sergei Berezin | 1.25 | .55 |
| ❑ 56 Peter Zezel | .40 | .18 |
| ❑ 57 Teppo Numminen | .40 | .18 |
| ❑ 58 Dale Hunter | .40 | .18 |
| ❑ 59 Sandy Moger | .40 | .18 |
| ❑ 60 John LeClair | 2.50 | 1.10 |
| ❑ 61 Wade Redden | .40 | .18 |
| ❑ 62 Patrik Elias | 1.25 | .55 |
| ❑ 63 Rob Blake | 1.25 | .55 |
| ❑ 64 Todd Marchant | .40 | .18 |
| ❑ 65 Claude Lemieux | 1.25 | .55 |
| ❑ 66 Trevor Kidd | 1.25 | .55 |
| ❑ 67 Sergei Fedorov | 3.00 | 1.35 |
| ❑ 68 Joe Sakic | 3.00 | 1.35 |
| ❑ 69 Derek Morris | .40 | .18 |
| ❑ 70 Alexei Morozov | .40 | .18 |
| ❑ 71 Mats Sundin | 1.50 | .70 |
| ❑ 72 Daymond Langkow | .40 | .18 |
| ❑ 73 Kevin Hatcher | .40 | .18 |
| ❑ 74 Damian Rhodes | 1.25 | .55 |
| ❑ 75 Brian Leetch | 1.50 | .70 |
| ❑ 76 Saku Koivu | 2.50 | 1.10 |
| ❑ 77 Rick Tabaracci | 1.25 | .55 |
| ❑ 78 Bernie Nicholls | 1.25 | .55 |
| ❑ 79 Alyn McCauley | 1.25 | .55 |
| ❑ 80 Patrice Brisebois | .40 | .18 |
| ❑ 81 Bret Hedican | .40 | .18 |
| ❑ 82 Sandy McCarthy | .40 | .18 |
| ❑ 83 Viktor Kozlov | .40 | .18 |
| ❑ 84 Derek King | .40 | .18 |
| ❑ 85 Alexander Selivanov | .40 | .18 |
| ❑ 86 Mike Vernon | 1.25 | .55 |
| ❑ 87 Jeff Beukeboom | .40 | .18 |
| ❑ 88 Tommy Salo | 1.25 | .55 |
| ❑ 89 Adam Graves | 1.25 | .55 |
| ❑ 90 Randy McKay | .40 | .18 |
| ❑ 91 Rich Pilon | .40 | .18 |
| ❑ 92 Richard Zednik | .40 | .18 |
| ❑ 93 Jeff Hackett | 1.25 | .55 |
| ❑ 94 Michael Peca | .40 | .18 |
| ❑ 95 Brent Gilchrist | .40 | .18 |
| ❑ 96 Stu Grimson | .40 | .18 |
| ❑ 97 Bob Probert | .40 | .18 |
| ❑ 98 Stu Barnes | .40 | .18 |
| ❑ 99 Ruslan Salei | .40 | .18 |
| ❑ 100 Al MacInnis | 1.25 | .55 |
| ❑ 101 Ken Daneyko | .40 | .18 |
| ❑ 102 Paul Ranheim | .40 | .18 |
| ❑ 103 Marty McInnis | .40 | .18 |
| ❑ 104 Marian Hossa | 1.25 | .55 |
| ❑ 105 Darren McCarty | 1.25 | .55 |
| ❑ 106 Guy Carbonneau | .40 | .18 |
| ❑ 107 Dallas Drake | .40 | .18 |
| ❑ 108 Sergei Samsonov | 2.50 | 1.10 |
| ❑ 109 Teemu Selanne | 3.00 | 1.35 |
| ❑ 110 Checklist | .40 | .18 |
| ❑ 111 Jaromir Jagr | 5.00 | 2.20 |
| ❑ 112 Joe Thornton | 1.50 | .70 |
| ❑ 113 Jon Klemm | .40 | .18 |
| ❑ 114 Grant Fuhr | 1.25 | .55 |
| ❑ 115 Nikolai Khabibulin | 1.25 | .55 |
| ❑ 116 Rod Brind'Amour | 1.25 | .55 |
| ❑ 117 Trevor Linden | 1.25 | .55 |
| ❑ 118 Vincent Damphousse | 1.25 | .55 |
| ❑ 119 Dino Ciccarelli | 1.25 | .55 |
| ❑ 120 Pat Verbeek | .40 | .18 |
| ❑ 121 Sandis Ozolinsh | 1.25 | .55 |
| ❑ 122 Garth Snow | 1.25 | .55 |
| ❑ 123 Ed Belfour | 1.50 | .70 |
| ❑ 124 Keith Primeau | 1.25 | .55 |
| ❑ 125 Jason Allison | 1.25 | .55 |
| ❑ 126 Peter Bondra | 1.50 | .70 |
| ❑ 127 Ulf Samuelsson | .40 | .18 |
| ❑ 128 Jeff Friesen | 1.25 | .55 |
| ❑ 129 Jason Bonsignore | .40 | .18 |
| ❑ 130 Daniel Alfredsson | 1.25 | .55 |
| ❑ 131 Bobby Holik | .40 | .18 |
| ❑ 132 Jozef Stumpel | 1.25 | .55 |
| ❑ 133 Brian Bellows | .40 | .18 |
| ❑ 134 Chris Osgood | 1.50 | .70 |
| ❑ 135 Alexei Zhamnov | .40 | .18 |
| ❑ 136 Mattias Norstrom | .40 | .18 |
| ❑ 137 Drake Berehowsky | .40 | .18 |
| ❑ 138 Mark Messier | 2.00 | .90 |
| ❑ 139 Geoff Courtnall | .40 | .18 |
| ❑ 140 Marc Bureau | .40 | .18 |
| ❑ 141 Don Sweeney | .40 | .18 |
| ❑ 142 Wendel Clark | 1.25 | .55 |
| ❑ 143 Scott Niedermayer | .40 | .18 |
| ❑ 144 Chris Therien | .40 | .18 |
| ❑ 145 Kirk Muller | .40 | .18 |
| ❑ 146 Wayne Primeau | .40 | .18 |
| ❑ 147 Tony Granato | .40 | .18 |
| ❑ 148 Derian Hatcher | .40 | .18 |
| ❑ 149 Daniel Briere | .40 | .18 |
| ❑ 150 Fredrik Olausson | .40 | .18 |
| ❑ 151 Joe Juneau | 1.25 | .55 |
| ❑ 152 Michal Grosek | .40 | .18 |
| ❑ 153 Janne Laukkanen | .40 | .18 |
| ❑ 154 Keith Tkachuk | 2.00 | .90 |
| ❑ 155 Marty McSorley | .40 | .18 |
| ❑ 156 Owen Nolan | 1.25 | .55 |
| ❑ 157 Mark Tinordi | .40 | .18 |
| ❑ 158 Steve Washburn | .40 | .18 |
| ❑ 159 Luke Richardson | .40 | .18 |
| ❑ 160 Kris King | .40 | .18 |
| ❑ 161 Joe Nieuwendyk | 1.25 | .55 |
| ❑ 162 Travis Green | .40 | .18 |
| ❑ 163 Dominik Hasek | 3.00 | 1.35 |
| ❑ 164 Dimitri Khristich | .40 | .18 |
| ❑ 165 Dave Manson | .40 | .18 |
| ❑ 166 Chris Chelios | 1.50 | .70 |
| ❑ 167 Claude LaPointe | .40 | .18 |
| ❑ 168 Kris Draper | .40 | .18 |
| ❑ 169 Brad Isbister | .40 | .18 |
| ❑ 170 Patrick Marleau | .40 | .18 |
| ❑ 171 Jeremy Roenick | 1.50 | .70 |
| ❑ 172 Darren Langdon | .40 | .18 |
| ❑ 173 Kevin Dineen | .40 | .18 |
| ❑ 174 Luc Robitaille | 1.25 | .55 |
| ❑ 175 Steve Yzerman | 5.00 | 2.20 |
| ❑ 176 Sergei Zubov | .40 | .18 |
| ❑ 177 Ed Jovanovski | .40 | .18 |
| ❑ 178 Sami Kapanen | 1.25 | .55 |
| ❑ 179 Adam Oates | 1.25 | .55 |
| ❑ 180 Pavel Bure | 3.00 | 1.35 |
| ❑ 181 Chris Pronger | 1.25 | .55 |
| ❑ 182 Pat Falloon | .40 | .18 |
| ❑ 183 Darcy Tucker | .40 | .18 |
| ❑ 184 Zigmund Palffy | 1.50 | .70 |
| ❑ 185 Curtis Brown | .40 | .18 |
| ❑ 186 Curtis Joseph | 1.50 | .70 |
| ❑ 187 Valeri Zelepukin | .40 | .18 |
| ❑ 188 Russ Courtnall | .40 | .18 |
| ❑ 189 Adam Foote | .40 | .18 |
| ❑ 190 Patrick Roy | 8.00 | 3.60 |
| ❑ 191 Cory Stillman | .40 | .18 |
| ❑ 192 Alexei Zhitnik | .40 | .18 |
| ❑ 193 Olaf Kolzig | 1.25 | .55 |
| ❑ 194 Mark Fitzpatrick | .40 | .18 |
| ❑ 195 Eric Daze | .40 | .18 |
| ❑ 196 Zarley Zalapski | .40 | .18 |
| ❑ 197 Niklas Sundstrom | .40 | .18 |
| ❑ 198 Bryan Berard | 1.25 | .55 |
| ❑ 199 Jason Arnott | 1.25 | .55 |
| ❑ 200 Mike Richter | 1.50 | .70 |
| ❑ 201 Ken Baumgartner | .40 | .18 |
| ❑ 202 Jason Dawe | .40 | .18 |
| ❑ 203 Nicklas Lidstrom | 1.25 | .55 |
| ❑ 204 Tony Amonte | 1.25 | .55 |
| ❑ 205 Kjell Samuelsson | .40 | .18 |
| ❑ 206 Ray Bourque | 1.50 | .70 |
| ❑ 207 Alexander Mogilny | 1.25 | .55 |
| ❑ 208 Pierre Turgeon | 1.25 | .55 |
| ❑ 209 Tom Barrasso | 1.25 | .55 |
| ❑ 210 Richard Matvichuk | .40 | .18 |
| ❑ 211 Sergei Krivokrasov | .40 | .18 |
| ❑ 212 Ted Drury | .40 | .18 |
| ❑ 213 Matthew Barnaby | .40 | .18 |
| ❑ 214 Denis Pederson | .40 | .18 |
| ❑ 215 John Vanbiesbrouck | 2.50 | 1.10 |
| ❑ 216 Brendan Shanahan | 3.00 | 1.35 |
| ❑ 217 Jocelyn Thibault | 1.25 | .55 |
| ❑ 218 Nelson Emerson | .40 | .18 |
| ❑ 219 Wayne Gretzky | 10.00 | 4.50 |
| ❑ 220 Checklist | .40 | .18 |
| ❑ 221 Ramzi Abid | 8.00 | 3.60 |
| ❑ 222 Mark Bell | 8.00 | 3.60 |
| ❑ 223 Michael Henrich | 8.00 | 3.60 |
| ❑ 224 Vincent LeCavalier | 12.00 | 5.50 |
| ❑ 225 Rico Fata | 6.00 | 2.70 |
| ❑ 226 Bryan Allen | 2.00 | .90 |
| ❑ 227 Daniel Tkaczuk | 2.00 | .90 |
| ❑ 228 Brad Stuart | 2.00 | .90 |
| ❑ 229 Derrick Walser | 2.00 | .90 |
| ❑ 230 Jonathan Cheechoo | 8.00 | 3.60 |
| ❑ 231 Sergei Varlamov | 6.00 | 2.70 |
| ❑ 232 Scott Gomez | 6.00 | 2.70 |
| ❑ 233 Jeff Heerema | 5.00 | 2.20 |
| ❑ 234 David Legwand | 8.00 | 3.60 |
| ❑ 235 Manny Malhotra | 8.00 | 3.60 |
| ❑ 236 Michael Rupp | 6.00 | 2.70 |
| ❑ 237 Alex Tanguay | 8.00 | 3.60 |
| ❑ 238 Mathieu Biron | 5.00 | 2.20 |
| ❑ 239 Bujar Amidovski | 6.00 | 2.70 |
| ❑ 240 Brian Finley | 8.00 | 3.60 |
| ❑ 241 Philippe Sauve | 2.00 | .90 |
| ❑ 242 Jiri Fischer | 2.00 | .90 |

## 1998-99 OPC Chrome Refractors

Randomly inserted in packs at the rate of one in 12, this 242-card set is a refractive parallel version of the base set.

| | MINT | NRMT |
|---|---|---|
| COMPLETE SET (242) | 1600.00 | 700.00 |
| COMMON CARD (1-242) | 4.00 | 1.80 |

*STARS: 5X TO 10X BASIC CARDS
*YOUNG STARS: 4X TO 8X
*RC's: 2X TO 4X

## 1998-99 OPC Chrome Blast From the Past

Randomly inserted into packs at the rate of one in 28, this 10-card set features reprints of the rookie cards of selected great retired as well as current stars. A refractor parallel version of this set was also produced with an insertion rate of 1:112.

| | MINT | NRMT |
|---|---|---|
| COMPLETE SET (10) | 100.00 | 45.00 |
| COMMON CARD (1-10) | 8.00 | 3.60 |
| ❑ 1 Wayne Gretzky | 20.00 | 9.00 |
| ❑ 2 Mark Messier | 8.00 | 3.60 |
| ❑ 3 Ray Bourque | 8.00 | 3.60 |
| ❑ 4 Patrick Roy | 15.00 | 6.75 |
| ❑ 5 Grant Fuhr | 8.00 | 3.60 |
| ❑ 6 Brett Hull | 8.00 | 3.60 |
| ❑ 7 Gordie Howe | 20.00 | 9.00 |
| ❑ 8 Stan Mikita | 10.00 | 4.50 |
| ❑ 9 Bobby Hull | 12.00 | 5.50 |
| ❑ 10 Phil Esposito | 10.00 | 4.50 |

## 1998-99 OPC Chrome Board Members

Randomly inserted into packs at the rate of one in 12, this 15-card set features color action photos of some of the great defensive superstars of the NHL. A refractor parallel version of this set was also produced with an insertion rate of 1:36.

| | MINT | NRMT |
|---|---|---|
| COMPLETE SET (15) | 70.00 | 32.00 |
| COMMON CARD (B1-B15) | 3.00 | 1.35 |
| ❑ B1 Chris Pronger | 5.00 | 2.20 |
| ❑ B2 Chris Chelios | 8.00 | 3.60 |
| ❑ B3 Brian Leetch | 8.00 | 3.60 |
| ❑ B4 Ray Bourque | 8.00 | 3.60 |
| ❑ B5 Mattias Ohlund | 5.00 | 2.20 |
| ❑ B6 Nicklas Lidstrom | 5.00 | 2.20 |
| ❑ B7 Sergei Zubov | 5.00 | 2.20 |
| ❑ B8 Scott Niedermayer | 5.00 | 2.20 |
| ❑ B9 Larry Murphy | 5.00 | 2.20 |
| ❑ B10 Sandis Ozolinsh | 5.00 | 2.20 |
| ❑ B11 Rob Blake | 5.00 | 2.20 |
| ❑ B12 Scott Stevens | 3.00 | 1.35 |
| ❑ B13 Derian Hatcher | 3.00 | 1.35 |
| ❑ B14 Kevin Hatcher | 3.00 | 1.35 |
| ❑ B15 Wade Redden | 3.00 | 1.35 |

## 1998-99 OPC Chrome Season's Best

Randomly inserted into packs at the rate of one in eight, this 30-card set features color action photos of top players in five distinct categories: Net Minders, the league's top goalies; Sharpshooters, the top scoring leaders; Puck Providers, assist leaders; Performers Plus, leaders in ice time by plus/minus ratio; and Ice Hot, powerful rookies. A refractor parellel version of this set was also produced with an insertion rate of 1:24.

| | MINT | NRMT |
|---|---|---|
| COMPLETE SET (30) | 100.00 | 45.00 |
| COMMON CARD (SB1-SB30) | 1.00 | .45 |
| ❑ SB1 Dominik Hasek | 5.00 | 2.20 |
| ❑ SB2 Martin Brodeur | 6.00 | 2.70 |
| ❑ SB3 Ed Belfour | 2.50 | 1.10 |
| ❑ SB4 Curtis Joseph | 2.50 | 1.10 |
| ❑ SB5 Jeff Hackett | 2.00 | .90 |
| ❑ SB6 Tom Barrasso | 2.00 | .90 |
| ❑ SB7 Mike Johnson | 2.00 | .90 |
| ❑ SB8 Sergei Samsonov | 4.00 | 1.80 |
| ❑ SB9 Patrik Elias | 2.00 | .90 |
| ❑ SB10 Patrick Marleau | 1.00 | .45 |
| ❑ SB11 Mattias Ohlund | 2.00 | .90 |
| ❑ SB12 Marco Sturm | 2.00 | .90 |
| ❑ SB13 Teemu Selanne | 5.00 | 2.20 |
| ❑ SB14 Peter Bondra | 2.50 | 1.10 |
| ❑ SB15 Pavel Bure | 6.00 | 2.70 |

| | | |
|---|---|---|
| ❑ SB16 John LeClair | 4.00 | 1.80 |
| ❑ SB17 Zigmund Palffy | 2.50 | 1.10 |
| ❑ SB18 Keith Tkachuk | 3.00 | 1.35 |
| ❑ SB19 Jaromir Jagr | 8.00 | 3.60 |
| ❑ SB20 Wayne Gretzky | 15.00 | 6.75 |
| ❑ SB21 Peter Forsberg | 8.00 | 3.60 |
| ❑ SB22 Ron Francis | 1.00 | .45 |
| ❑ SB23 Adam Oates | 1.00 | .45 |
| ❑ SB24 Jozef Stumpel | 1.00 | .45 |
| ❑ SB25 Chris Pronger | 1.00 | .45 |
| ❑ SB26 Larry Murphy | 1.00 | .45 |
| ❑ SB27 Jason Allison | 1.00 | .45 |
| ❑ SB28 John LeClair | 4.00 | 1.80 |
| ❑ SB29 Randy McKay | 1.00 | .45 |
| ❑ SB30 Dainius Zubrus | 1.00 | .45 |

## 1976 Old Timers

This 18-card set of indeterminate origin measures approximately 2 1/2" by 3 5/8" and features black-and-white player photos in a white border. Members of the Red Wings, Maple Leafs and Blackhawks are pictured.The backs are blank. The cards are unnumbered and checklisted below in alphabetical order.

| | MINT | NRMT |
|---|---|---|
| COMPLETE SET (18) | 60.00 | 27.00 |
| COMMON CARD (1-18) | 2.50 | 1.10 |

| | | |
|---|---|---|
| ❑ 1 Gerry Abel | 2.50 | 1.10 |
| ❑ 2 Sid Abel | 8.00 | 3.60 |
| ❑ 3 Doug Barkley | 2.50 | 1.10 |
| ❑ 4 Joe Carveth | 2.50 | 1.10 |
| ❑ 5 Billy Dea | 4.00 | 1.80 |
| ❑ 6 Alex Delvecchio | 15.00 | 6.75 |
| ❑ 7 Bill Gadsby | 5.00 | 2.20 |
| ❑ 8 Hal Jackson | 2.50 | 1.10 |
| ❑ 9 Joe Klukay | 2.50 | 1.10 |
| ❑ 10 Ted Lindsay | 15.00 | 6.75 |
| ❑ 11 Jim Orlando | 2.50 | 1.10 |
| ❑ 12 Marty Pavlich | 2.50 | 1.10 |
| ❑ 13 Jim Peters | 2.50 | 1.10 |
| ❑ 14 Marcel Pronovost | 5.00 | 2.20 |
| ❑ 15 Marc Reaume | 2.50 | 1.10 |
| ❑ 16 Leo Reise | 2.50 | 1.10 |
| ❑ 17 Glen Skov | 2.50 | 1.10 |
| ❑ 18 Jack Stewart | 4.00 | 1.80 |

## 1997-98 Pacific

The 1997-98 inaugural issue of the Pacific Crown Collection NHL Hockey cards was issued in one series totaling 350 cards and was distributed in eight-card packs. The fronts feature color action player photos with gold foil highlights. The backs carry player information. Pacific chose not to print a card #66, as a tribute to Mario Lemieux

| | MINT | NRMT |
|---|---|---|
| COMPLETE SET (350) | 40.00 | 18.00 |
| COMMON CARD (1-351) | .15 | .07 |

| | | |
|---|---|---|
| ❑ 1 Ray Bourque | .50 | .23 |
| ❑ 2 Brian Leetch | .50 | .23 |
| ❑ 3 Claude Lemieux | .40 | .18 |
| ❑ 4 Mike Modano | .60 | .25 |
| ❑ 5 Zigmund Palffy | .50 | .23 |
| ❑ 6 Nikolai Khabibulin | .40 | .18 |
| ❑ 7 Chris Chelios | .50 | .23 |
| ❑ 8 Teemu Selanne | 1.00 | .45 |
| ❑ 9 Paul Kariya | 2.00 | .90 |
| ❑ 10 John LeClair | .75 | .35 |
| ❑ 11 Mark Messier | .60 | .25 |
| ❑ 12 Jarome Iginla | .40 | .18 |
| ❑ 13 Petr Nedved | .40 | .18 |
| ❑ 14 Brendan Shanahan | 1.00 | .45 |
| ❑ 15 Dino Ciccarelli | .15 | .07 |
| ❑ 16 Brett Hull | .60 | .25 |
| ❑ 17 Wendel Clark | .40 | .18 |
| ❑ 18 Peter Bondra | .50 | .23 |
| ❑ 19 Steve Yzerman | 1.50 | .70 |
| ❑ 20 Ed Belfour | .50 | .23 |
| ❑ 21 Peter Forsberg | 1.50 | .70 |
| ❑ 22 Mike Gartner | .40 | .18 |
| ❑ 23 Jim Carey | .40 | .18 |
| ❑ 24 Mike Vernon | .40 | .18 |
| ❑ 25 Vincent Damphousse | .40 | .18 |
| ❑ 26 Adam Graves | .40 | .18 |
| ❑ 27 Ron Hextall | .40 | .18 |
| ❑ 28 Keith Tkachuk | .60 | .25 |
| ❑ 29 Felix Potvin | .50 | .23 |
| ❑ 30 Martin Brodeur | 1.25 | .55 |
| ❑ 31 Rod Brind'Amour | .40 | .18 |
| ❑ 32 Pierre Turgeon | .40 | .18 |
| ❑ 33 Patrick Roy | 2.50 | 1.10 |
| ❑ 34 John Vanbiesbrouck | .75 | .35 |
| ❑ 35 Andy Moog | .40 | .18 |
| ❑ 36 Sergei Berezin | .15 | .07 |
| ❑ 37 Adam Oates | .40 | .18 |
| ❑ 38 Joe Sakic | 1.00 | .45 |
| ❑ 39 Dominik Hasek | 1.00 | .45 |
| ❑ 40 Patrick Lalime | .40 | .18 |
| ❑ 41 Bobby Dollas | .15 | .07 |
| ❑ 42 Kyle McLaren | .15 | .07 |
| ❑ 43 Wayne Primeau | .15 | .07 |
| ❑ 44 Stephane Richer | .15 | .07 |
| ❑ 45 Theoren Fleury | .40 | .18 |
| ❑ 46 Kevin Miller | .15 | .07 |
| ❑ 47 Adam Deadmarsh | .40 | .18 |
| ❑ 48 Darryl Sydor | .15 | .07 |
| ❑ 49 Igor Larionov | .15 | .07 |
| ❑ 50 Radek Dvorak | .15 | .07 |
| ❑ 51 Andrei Kovalenko | .15 | .07 |
| ❑ 52 Keith Primeau | .15 | .07 |
| ❑ 53 Ray Ferraro | .15 | .07 |
| ❑ 54 David Wilkie | .15 | .07 |
| ❑ 55 Bobby Holik | .15 | .07 |
| ❑ 56 Tommy Salo | .40 | .18 |
| ❑ 57 Jeff Beukeboom | .15 | .07 |
| ❑ 58 Daniel Alfredsson | .40 | .18 |
| ❑ 59 Mikael Renberg | .40 | .18 |
| ❑ 60 Norm Maciver | .15 | .07 |
| ❑ 61 Darius Kasparaitis | .15 | .07 |
| ❑ 62 Geoff Courtnall | .15 | .07 |
| ❑ 63 Jeff Friesen | .40 | .18 |
| ❑ 64 Brian Bradley | .15 | .07 |
| ❑ 65 Tie Domi | .15 | .07 |
| ❑ 67 Martin Gelinas | .15 | .07 |
| ❑ 68 Jaromir Jagr | 1.50 | .70 |
| ❑ 69 Steve Konowalchuk | .15 | .07 |
| ❑ 70 Brian Bellows | .15 | .07 |
| ❑ 71 Jozef Stumpel | .40 | .18 |
| ❑ 72 Darryl Shannon | .15 | .07 |
| ❑ 73 Todd Simpson | .15 | .07 |
| ❑ 74 Ulf Dahlen | .15 | .07 |
| ❑ 75 Sandis Ozolinsh | .40 | .18 |
| ❑ 76 Sergei Zubov | .15 | .07 |
| ❑ 77 Paul Coffey | .50 | .23 |
| ❑ 78 Nicklas Lidstrom | .40 | .18 |
| ❑ 79 Jason Arnott | .40 | .18 |
| ❑ 80 Ray Sheppard | .15 | .07 |
| ❑ 81 Sean Burke | .40 | .18 |
| ❑ 82 Vladimir Tsyplakov | .15 | .07 |
| ❑ 83 Darcy Tucker | .15 | .07 |
| ❑ 84 Dave Andreychuk | .15 | .07 |
| ❑ 85 Scott Lachance | .15 | .07 |
| ❑ 86 Niklas Sundstrom | .15 | .07 |
| ❑ 87 Ron Tugnutt | .40 | .18 |
| ❑ 88 Eric Lindros | 1.50 | .70 |
| ❑ 89 Alexander Mogilny | .40 | .18 |
| ❑ 90 Kris King | .15 | .07 |
| ❑ 91 Sergei Fedorov | 1.00 | .45 |
| ❑ 92 Ed Olczyk | .15 | .07 |
| ❑ 93 Doug Gilmour | .50 | .23 |
| ❑ 94 Ryan Smyth | .40 | .18 |
| ❑ 95 Scott Pellerin | .15 | .07 |
| ❑ 96 Pavel Bure | 1.00 | .45 |
| ❑ 97 Jeremy Roenick | .50 | .23 |
| ❑ 98 Todd Gill | .15 | .07 |
| ❑ 99 Wayne Gretzky | 3.00 | 1.35 |
| ❑ 100 Roman Hamrlik | .15 | .07 |
| ❑ 101 Rob Zettler | .15 | .07 |
| ❑ 102 Sergei Nemchinov | .15 | .07 |
| ❑ 103 Sergei Gonchar | .15 | .07 |
| ❑ 104 Steve Rucchin | .15 | .07 |
| ❑ 105 Landon Wilson | .15 | .07 |
| ❑ 106 Anatoli Semenov | .15 | .07 |
| ❑ 107 Corey Millen | .40 | .18 |
| ❑ 108 Eric Daze | .40 | .18 |
| ❑ 109 Mike Ricci | .15 | .07 |
| ❑ 110 Jamie Langenbrunner | .15 | .07 |
| ❑ 111 Viacheslav Fetisov | .15 | .07 |
| ❑ 112 Rem Murray | .15 | .07 |
| ❑ 113 Tom Fitzgerald | .15 | .07 |
| ❑ 114 Robert Kron | .15 | .07 |
| ❑ 115 Kevin Stevens | .40 | .18 |
| ❑ 116 Valeri Bure | .15 | .07 |
| ❑ 117 Bill Guerin | .40 | .18 |
| ❑ 118 Bryan McCabe | .15 | .07 |
| ❑ 119 Alexei Kovalev | .15 | .07 |
| ❑ 120 Alexei Yashin | .40 | .18 |
| ❑ 121 Eric Desjardins | .15 | .07 |
| ❑ 122 Teppo Numminen | .15 | .07 |
| ❑ 123 Ron Francis | .40 | .18 |
| ❑ 124 Chris Pronger | .40 | .18 |
| ❑ 125 Viktor Kozlov | .15 | .07 |
| ❑ 126 Corey Schwab | .40 | .18 |
| ❑ 127 Fredrik Modin | .15 | .07 |
| ❑ 128 Markus Naslund | .15 | .07 |
| ❑ 129 Dale Hunter | .15 | .07 |
| ❑ 130 Warren Rychel | .15 | .07 |
| ❑ 131 Anson Carter | .15 | .07 |
| ❑ 132 Miroslav Satan | .15 | .07 |
| ❑ 133 Trevor Kidd | .40 | .18 |
| ❑ 134 Sergei Krivokrasov | .15 | .07 |
| ❑ 135 Adam Foote | .15 | .07 |
| ❑ 136 Brent Gilchrist | .15 | .07 |
| ❑ 137 Chris Osgood | .50 | .23 |
| ❑ 138 Doug Weight | .40 | .18 |
| ❑ 139 Martin Straka | .15 | .07 |
| ❑ 140 Jeff O'Neill | .15 | .07 |
| ❑ 141 Byron Dafoe | .40 | .18 |
| ❑ 142 Brian Savage | .15 | .07 |
| ❑ 143 Lyle Odelein | .15 | .07 |
| ❑ 144 Niklas Andersson | .15 | .07 |
| ❑ 145 Luc Robitaille | .40 | .18 |
| ❑ 146 Damian Rhodes | .40 | .18 |
| ❑ 147 Garth Snow | .40 | .18 |
| ❑ 148 Craig Janney | .15 | .07 |
| ❑ 149 Fredrik Olausson | .15 | .07 |
| ❑ 150 Joe Murphy | .15 | .07 |
| ❑ 151 Owen Nolan | .40 | .18 |
| ❑ 152 Shawn Burr | .15 | .07 |
| ❑ 153 Dimitri Yushkevich | .15 | .07 |
| ❑ 154 Trevor Linden | .40 | .18 |
| ❑ 155 Joe Juneau | .40 | .18 |
| ❑ 156 Sean Pronger | .15 | .07 |
| ❑ 157 Jeff Odgers | .15 | .07 |
| ❑ 158 Brian Holzinger | .15 | .07 |
| ❑ 159 Dave Gagner | .15 | .07 |
| ❑ 160 Jeff Hackett | .40 | .18 |
| ❑ 161 Eric Lacroix | .15 | .07 |
| ❑ 162 Pat Verbeek | .15 | .07 |
| ❑ 163 Darren McCarty | .15 | .07 |
| ❑ 164 Mike Grier | .15 | .07 |
| ❑ 165 Per Gustafsson | .40 | .18 |
| ❑ 166 Andrew Cassels | .15 | .07 |
| ❑ 167 Vitali Yachmenev | .15 | .07 |
| ❑ 168 Jocelyn Thibault | .40 | .18 |
| ❑ 169 John MacLean | .15 | .07 |
| ❑ 170 Travis Green | .15 | .07 |
| ❑ 171 Ulf Samuelsson | .15 | .07 |
| ❑ 172 Bruce Gardiner | .15 | .07 |
| ❑ 173 Janne Niinimaa | .40 | .18 |
| ❑ 174 Jim Johnson | .15 | .07 |
| ❑ 175 Stu Barnes | .15 | .07 |
| ❑ 176 Harry York | .15 | .07 |
| ❑ 177 Al Iafrate | .15 | .07 |
| ❑ 178 Paul Ysebaert | .15 | .07 |
| ❑ 179 Mathieu Schneider | .15 | .07 |
| ❑ 180 Corey Hirsch | .40 | .18 |
| ❑ 181 Mark Tinordi | .15 | .07 |
| ❑ 182 Kevin Todd | .15 | .07 |
| ❑ 183 Tim Sweeney | .15 | .07 |
| ❑ 184 Donald Audette | .15 | .07 |
| ❑ 185 Jonas Hoglund | .15 | .07 |
| ❑ 186 Brent Sutter | .15 | .07 |
| ❑ 187 Scott Young | .15 | .07 |
| ❑ 188 Arturs Irbe | .40 | .18 |
| ❑ 189 Vladimir Konstantinov | .15 | .07 |
| ❑ 190 Mats Lindgren | .15 | .07 |
| ❑ 191 David Nemirovsky | .15 | .07 |
| ❑ 192 Sami Kapanen | .40 | .18 |
| ❑ 193 Rob Blake | .15 | .07 |
| ❑ 194 Sebastien Bordeleau | .15 | .07 |
| ❑ 195 Steve Thomas | .15 | .07 |
| ❑ 196 Bryan Smolinski | .15 | .07 |
| ❑ 197 Mike Richter | .50 | .23 |
| ❑ 198 Randy Cunneyworth | .15 | .07 |
| ❑ 199 Pat Falloon | .15 | .07 |
| ❑ 200 Cliff Ronning | .15 | .07 |
| ❑ 201 Ken Wregget | .40 | .18 |
| ❑ 202 Al MacInnis | .40 | .18 |
| ❑ 203 Tony Granato | .15 | .07 |
| ❑ 204 Rob Zamuner | .15 | .07 |
| ❑ 205 Mats Sundin | .50 | .23 |
| ❑ 206 Mike Ridley | .15 | .07 |
| ❑ 207 Sylvain Cote | .15 | .07 |
| ❑ 208 Joe Sacco | .15 | .07 |
| ❑ 209 Ted Donato | .15 | .07 |
| ❑ 210 Matthew Barnaby | .15 | .07 |
| ❑ 211 Cory Stillman | .15 | .07 |
| ❑ 212 Gary Suter | .15 | .07 |
| ❑ 213 Valeri Kamensky | .40 | .18 |
| ❑ 214 Derian Hatcher | .15 | .07 |
| ❑ 215 Jamie Pushor | .15 | .07 |
| ❑ 216 Mariusz Czerkawski | .15 | .07 |
| ❑ 217 Kirk Muller | .15 | .07 |
| ❑ 218 Kevin Dineen | .15 | .07 |
| ❑ 219 Dimitri Khristich | .15 | .07 |
| ❑ 220 Martin Rucinsky | .15 | .07 |
| ❑ 221 Denis Pederson | .15 | .07 |
| ❑ 222 Bryan Berard | .40 | .18 |
| ❑ 223 Alexander Karpovtsev | .15 | .07 |
| ❑ 224 Shawn McEachern | .15 | .07 |
| ❑ 225 Dale Hawerchuk | .40 | .18 |
| ❑ 226 Bob Corkum | .15 | .07 |
| ❑ 227 Kevin Hatcher | .15 | .07 |
| ❑ 228 Grant Fuhr | .40 | .18 |
| ❑ 229 Darren Turcotte | .15 | .07 |
| ❑ 230 Patrick Poulin | .15 | .07 |
| ❑ 231 Jamie Macoun | .15 | .07 |
| ❑ 232 Jyrki Lumme | .15 | .07 |
| ❑ 233 Bill Ranford | .40 | .18 |
| ❑ 234 Dmitri Mironov | .15 | .07 |
| ❑ 235 Mattias Timander | .15 | .07 |
| ❑ 236 Alexei Zhitnik | .15 | .07 |
| ❑ 237 Hnat Domenichelli | .15 | .07 |
| ❑ 238 Murray Craven | .15 | .07 |
| ❑ 239 Mike Keane | .15 | .07 |
| ❑ 240 Benoit Hogue | .15 | .07 |
| ❑ 241 Martin Lapointe | .15 | .07 |
| ❑ 242 Curtis Joseph | .50 | .23 |
| ❑ 243 Robert Svehla | .15 | .07 |
| ❑ 244 Glen Wesley | .15 | .07 |
| ❑ 245 Stephane Fiset | .40 | .18 |
| ❑ 246 Shayne Corson | .15 | .07 |
| ❑ 247 Scott Niedermayer | .15 | .07 |
| ❑ 248 Steve Webb | .15 | .07 |
| ❑ 249 Esa Tikkanen | .15 | .07 |
| ❑ 250 Alexandre Daigle | .40 | .18 |
| ❑ 251 Trent Klatt | .15 | .07 |
| ❑ 252 Oleg Tverdovsky | .15 | .07 |
| ❑ 253 Dave Roche | .15 | .07 |
| ❑ 254 Tony Twist | .15 | .07 |
| ❑ 255 Bernie Nicholls | .15 | .07 |
| ❑ 256 Rick Tabaracci | .40 | .18 |
| ❑ 257 Todd Warriner | .15 | .07 |
| ❑ 258 Kirk McLean | .40 | .18 |
| ❑ 259 Phil Housley | .15 | .07 |
| ❑ 260 Guy Hebert | .40 | .18 |
| ❑ 261 Steve Heinze | .15 | .07 |
| ❑ 262 Derek Plante | .15 | .07 |
| ❑ 263 German Titov | .15 | .07 |
| ❑ 264 Tony Amonte | .40 | .18 |
| ❑ 265 Uwe Krupp | .15 | .07 |
| ❑ 266 Joe Nieuwendyk | .40 | .18 |
| ❑ 267 Vyacheslav Kozlov | .15 | .07 |
| ❑ 268 Kelly Buchberger | .15 | .07 |
| ❑ 269 Rob Niedermayer | .15 | .07 |
| ❑ 270 Geoff Sanderson | .40 | .18 |
| ❑ 271 Jan Vopat | .15 | .07 |
| ❑ 272 Saku Koivu | .75 | .35 |
| ❑ 273 Scott Stevens | .15 | .07 |
| ❑ 274 Eric Fichaud | .40 | .18 |
| ❑ 275 Russ Courtnall | .15 | .07 |
| ❑ 276 Wade Redden | .15 | .07 |
| ❑ 277 Petr Svoboda | .15 | .07 |
| ❑ 278 Andreas Dackell | .15 | .07 |
| ❑ 279 Jason Woolley | .15 | .07 |
| ❑ 280 Stephane Matteau | .15 | .07 |
| ❑ 281 Stephen Guolla | .15 | .07 |
| ❑ 282 John Cullen | .15 | .07 |
| ❑ 283 Steve Sullivan | .15 | .07 |
| ❑ 284 Bret Hedican | .15 | .07 |
| ❑ 285 Michal Pivonka | .15 | .07 |
| ❑ 286 Darren Van Impe | .15 | .07 |
| ❑ 287 Rob DiMaio | .15 | .07 |
| ❑ 288 Garry Galley | .15 | .07 |
| ❑ 289 Kent Manderville | .15 | .07 |
| ❑ 290 Bob Probert | .15 | .07 |
| ❑ 291 Keith Jones | .15 | .07 |
| ❑ 292 Guy Carbonneau | .15 | .07 |
| ❑ 293 Tomas Sandstrom | .15 | .07 |
| ❑ 294 Daniel McGillis | .15 | .07 |
| ❑ 295 Brian Skrudland | .15 | .07 |
| ❑ 296 Stu Grimson | .15 | .07 |
| ❑ 297 Doug Zmolek | .15 | .07 |
| ❑ 298 Mark Recchi | .40 | .18 |
| ❑ 299 Valeri Zelepukin | .15 | .07 |
| ❑ 300 Derek Armstrong | .15 | .07 |
| ❑ 301 Eric Cairns | .15 | .07 |
| ❑ 302 Steve Duchesne | .15 | .07 |
| ❑ 303 Dainius Zubrus | .50 | .23 |
| ❑ 304 Deron Quint | .15 | .07 |
| ❑ 305 Joe Dziedzic | .15 | .07 |
| ❑ 306 Mike Peluso | .15 | .07 |
| ❑ 307 Andrei Nazarov | .15 | .07 |
| ❑ 308 Chris Gratton | .40 | .18 |
| ❑ 309 Mike Craig | .15 | .07 |
| ❑ 310 Lonny Bohonos | .15 | .07 |
| ❑ 311 Rick Tocchet | .40 | .18 |
| ❑ 312 Ted Drury | .15 | .07 |
| ❑ 313 Jean-Yves Roy | .15 | .07 |
| ❑ 314 Jason Dawe | .15 | .07 |
| ❑ 315 Jamie Allison | .15 | .07 |
| ❑ 316 Alexei Zhamnov | .15 | .07 |
| ❑ 317 Aaron Miller | .15 | .07 |
| ❑ 318 Todd Krygier | .15 | .07 |
| ❑ 319 Tomas Holmstrom | .15 | .07 |
| ❑ 320 Todd Marchant | .15 | .07 |
| ❑ 321 Scott Mellanby | .15 | .07 |
| ❑ 322 Marek Malik | .15 | .07 |
| ❑ 323 Dan Rylsma | .15 | .07 |
| ❑ 324 Stephane Quintal | .15 | .07 |
| ❑ 325 Ken Daneyko | .15 | .07 |
| ❑ 326 Robert Reichel | .15 | .07 |
| ❑ 327 Daniel Goneau | .15 | .07 |
| ❑ 328 Sergei Zholtok | .15 | .07 |
| ❑ 329 Kjell Samuelsson | .15 | .07 |
| ❑ 330 Shane Doan | .15 | .07 |
| ❑ 331 Radek Bonk | .15 | .07 |
| ❑ 332 Jim Campbell | .15 | .07 |
| ❑ 333 Marty McSorley | .15 | .07 |
| ❑ 334 Brantt Myhres | .15 | .07 |
| ❑ 335 Mike Johnson | .60 | .25 |
| ❑ 336 Mike Sillinger | .15 | .07 |
| ❑ 337 Kelly Hrudey | .40 | .18 |
| ❑ 338 Joel Bouchard | .15 | .07 |
| ❑ 339 Brian Noonan | .15 | .07 |
| ❑ 340 Dean Chynoweth | .15 | .07 |
| ❑ 341 Michael Peca | .15 | .07 |
| ❑ 342 Jeff Toms | .15 | .07 |
| ❑ 343 Denis Savard | .15 | .07 |
| ❑ 344 Stephane Yelle | .15 | .07 |
| ❑ 345 Grant Ledyard | .15 | .07 |
| ❑ 346 Ronnie Stern | .15 | .07 |
| ❑ 347 Petr Klima | .15 | .07 |
| ❑ 348 Johan Garpenlov | .15 | .07 |
| ❑ 349 Nelson Emerson | .15 | .07 |
| ❑ 350 Matt Johnson | .15 | .07 |
| ❑ 351 Ken Belanger | .15 | .07 |
| ❑ CM1 Mark Messier | 5.00 | 2.20 |

## 1997-98 Pacific Card-Supials

Randomly inserted one in every 37 packs, this 20-card set features color action player photos of some of the great players in Hockey. A smaller card is made to pair with the regular size card of the same player. The backs carry a slot for insertion of the small card.

| | MINT | NRMT |
|---|---|---|
| COMPLETE SET (40) | 300.00 | 135.00 |
| COMP.LARGE SET (20) | 200.00 | 90.00 |
| COMMON LARGE (1-20) | 3.00 | 1.35 |

| | | |
|---|---|---|
| ❑ 1 Paul Kariya | 15.00 | 6.75 |
| ❑ 2 Teemu Selanne | 8.00 | 3.60 |
| ❑ 3 Jarome Iginla | 4.00 | 1.80 |
| ❑ 4 Peter Forsberg | 12.00 | 5.50 |
| ❑ 5 Mike Modano | 5.00 | 2.20 |
| ❑ 6 Sergei Fedorov | 8.00 | 3.60 |
| ❑ 7 Vladimir Konstantinov | 3.00 | 1.35 |
| ❑ 8 Steve Yzerman | 12.00 | 5.50 |
| ❑ 9 John Vanbiesbrouck | 6.00 | 2.70 |
| ❑ 10 Martin Brodeur | 10.00 | 4.50 |
| ❑ 11 Doug Gilmour | 4.00 | 1.80 |
| ❑ 12 Wayne Gretzky | 25.00 | 11.00 |
| ❑ 13 Mark Messier | 5.00 | 2.20 |
| ❑ 14 John LeClair | 6.00 | 2.70 |
| ❑ 15 Eric Lindros | 12.00 | 5.50 |
| ❑ 16 Jeremy Roenick | 4.00 | 1.80 |
| ❑ 17 Keith Tkachuk | 5.00 | 2.20 |
| ❑ 18 Brett Hull | 5.00 | 2.20 |
| ❑ 19 Felix Potvin | 4.00 | 1.80 |
| ❑ 20 Pavel Bure | 8.00 | 3.60 |

## 1997-98 Pacific Card-Supials Minis

These 20 cards were intended to fit into the larger Card-Supial issue. The cards, with a different design from the regular issue, fit into the pouch of the regular cards. They are valued slightly less than the regular issue Card-Supials.

| | MINT | NRMT |
|---|---|---|
| COMPLETE SET (20) | 100.00 | 45.00 |
| COMMON CARD (1-20) | 2.00 | .90 |

*MINIS: .3X TO .6X BASIC CARD-SUPIALS

## 1997-98 Pacific Cramer's Choice Awards

Randomly inserted in packs at the rate of one in 721, this 10-card set features top NHL Hockey players as chosen by Pacific President and CEO, Michael Cramer. The fronts display a color action player cut-out on a pyramid die-cut shaped background.

| | MINT | NRMT |
|---|---|---|
| COMPLETE SET (10) | 1200.00 | 550.00 |
| COMMON CARD (1-10) | 50.00 | 22.00 |

| | | |
|---|---|---|
| ❑ 1 Paul Kariya | 150.00 | 70.00 |
| ❑ 2 Dominik Hasek | 80.00 | 36.00 |
| ❑ 3 Jarome Iginla | 50.00 | 22.00 |
| ❑ 4 Peter Forsberg | 120.00 | 55.00 |
| ❑ 5 Patrick Roy | 200.00 | 90.00 |
| ❑ 6 Steve Yzerman | 120.00 | 55.00 |
| ❑ 7 Wayne Gretzky | 250.00 | 110.00 |
| ❑ 8 Mark Messier | 60.00 | 27.00 |
| ❑ 9 Eric Lindros | 120.00 | 55.00 |
| ❑ 10 Jaromir Jagr | 120.00 | 55.00 |

## 1997-98 Pacific Gold Crown Die-Cuts

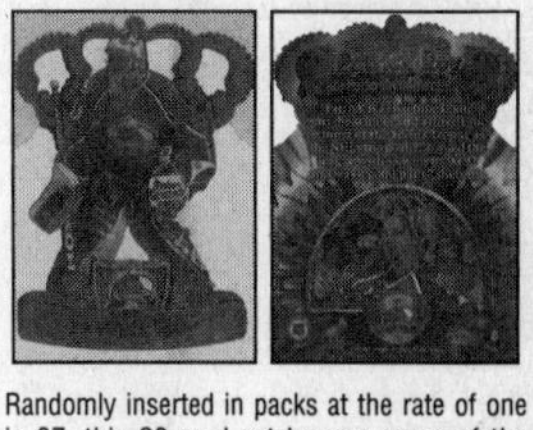

Randomly inserted in packs at the rate of one in 37, this 20-card set honors some of the NHL top current stars. The fronts feature color action player photos with a die-cut gold crown at the top and gold foil printing. The backs carry player information.

| | MINT | NRMT |
|---|---|---|
| COMPLETE SET (20) | 300.00 | 135.00 |
| COMMON CARD (1-20) | 4.00 | 1.80 |

| | | |
|---|---|---|
| ❑ 1 Paul Kariya | 25.00 | 11.00 |
| ❑ 2 Teemu Selanne | 12.00 | 5.50 |
| ❑ 3 Dominik Hasek | 12.00 | 5.50 |
| ❑ 4 Michael Peca | 4.00 | 1.80 |
| ❑ 5 Jarome Iginla | 5.00 | 2.20 |
| ❑ 6 Chris Chelios | 6.00 | 2.70 |
| ❑ 7 Peter Forsberg | 20.00 | 9.00 |
| ❑ 8 Patrick Roy | 30.00 | 13.50 |
| ❑ 9 Joe Sakic | 12.00 | 5.50 |
| ❑ 10 Brendan Shanahan | 12.00 | 5.50 |
| ❑ 11 Steve Yzerman | 20.00 | 9.00 |
| ❑ 12 Ryan Smyth | 5.00 | 2.20 |
| ❑ 13 John Vanbiesbrouck | 10.00 | 4.50 |
| ❑ 14 Martin Brodeur | 15.00 | 6.75 |

| | | |
|---|---|---|
| ❑ 15 Wayne Gretzky | 40.00 | 18.00 |
| ❑ 16 Mark Messier | 8.00 | 3.60 |
| ❑ 17 Eric Lindros | 20.00 | 9.00 |
| ❑ 18 Jaromir Jagr | 20.00 | 9.00 |
| ❑ 19 Brett Hull | 8.00 | 3.60 |
| ❑ 20 Pavel Bure | 12.00 | 5.50 |

## 1997-98 Pacific In The Cage Laser Cuts

Randomly inserted in packs at the rate of one in 145, this 20-card set honors top goalies of the NHL. The laser-cut fronts feature color player photos with the net as the background. The backs carry player information.

| | MINT | NRMT |
|---|---|---|
| COMPLETE SET (20) | 600.00 | 275.00 |
| COMMON CARD (1-20) | 20.00 | 9.00 |
| ❑ 1 Guy Hebert | 20.00 | 9.00 |
| ❑ 2 Dominik Hasek | 50.00 | 22.00 |
| ❑ 3 Trevor Kidd | 20.00 | 9.00 |
| ❑ 4 Jeff Hackett | 20.00 | 9.00 |
| ❑ 5 Patrick Roy | 100.00 | 45.00 |
| ❑ 6 Andy Moog | 20.00 | 9.00 |
| ❑ 7 Chris Osgood | 25.00 | 11.00 |
| ❑ 8 Mike Vernon | 20.00 | 9.00 |
| ❑ 9 Curtis Joseph | 25.00 | 11.00 |
| ❑ 10 John Vanbiesbrouck | 40.00 | 18.00 |
| ❑ 11 Jocelyn Thibault | 25.00 | 11.00 |
| ❑ 12 Martin Brodeur | 60.00 | 27.00 |
| ❑ 13 Mike Richter | 25.00 | 11.00 |
| ❑ 14 Ron Hextall | 20.00 | 9.00 |
| ❑ 15 Garth Snow | 20.00 | 9.00 |
| ❑ 16 Nikolai Khabibulin | 20.00 | 9.00 |
| ❑ 17 Patrick Lalime | 25.00 | 11.00 |
| ❑ 18 Grant Fuhr | 20.00 | 9.00 |
| ❑ 19 Ed Belfour | 25.00 | 11.00 |
| ❑ 20 Felix Potvin | 20.00 | 9.00 |

## 1997-98 Pacific Ice Blue

Randomly inserted in packs at the rate of one in 73, this 350-card set is a parallel version of the regular Pacific set with platinum blue foil highlights.

| | MINT | NRMT |
|---|---|---|
| COMMON CARD (1-351) | 15.00 | 6.75 |

*STARS: 75X TO 150X BASIC CARDS
*YOUNG STARS: 60X TO 120X BASIC CARDS

## 1997-98 Pacific Slap Shots Die-Cuts

Randomly inserted in packs at the rate of one in 73, this 36-card set features color player photos of top NHL players. Three cards of players from the same team were made to fit on top of each other to form a hockey stick on the cards' right sides with the words, "Pacific Trading Cards," printed on the middle section of the stick. The cards that go together have the same number with the letters, "A, B, or C" after the number to indicate where the cards should be placed to form the giant hockey stick.

| | MINT | NRMT |
|---|---|---|
| COMPLETE SET (36) | 700.00 | 325.00 |
| COMMON CARD (1A-12C) | 10.00 | 4.50 |
| CONDITION SENSITIVE SET | | |
| ❑ 1A Paul Kariya | 50.00 | 22.00 |
| ❑ 1B Jari Kurri | 10.00 | 4.50 |
| ❑ 1C Teemu Selanne | 25.00 | 11.00 |
| ❑ 2A Peter Forsberg | 40.00 | 18.00 |
| ❑ 2B Joe Sakic | 25.00 | 11.00 |
| ❑ 2C Claude Lemieux | 10.00 | 4.50 |
| ❑ 3A Brendan Shanahan | 25.00 | 11.00 |
| ❑ 3B Sergei Fedorov | 25.00 | 11.00 |
| ❑ 3C Steve Yzerman | 40.00 | 18.00 |
| ❑ 4A Mark Recchi | 10.00 | 4.50 |
| ❑ 4B Vincent Damphousse | 10.00 | 4.50 |
| ❑ 4C Stephane Richer | 10.00 | 4.50 |
| ❑ 5A Wayne Gretzky | 80.00 | 36.00 |
| ❑ 5B Mark Messier | 15.00 | 6.75 |
| ❑ 5C Brian Leetch | 12.00 | 5.50 |
| ❑ 6A Rod Brind'Amour | 10.00 | 4.50 |
| ❑ 6B Eric Lindros | 40.00 | 18.00 |
| ❑ 6C John LeClair | 20.00 | 9.00 |
| ❑ 7A Keith Tkachuk | 15.00 | 6.75 |
| ❑ 7B Jeremy Roenick | 12.00 | 5.50 |
| ❑ 7C Mike Gartner | 10.00 | 4.50 |
| ❑ 8A Petr Nedved | 10.00 | 4.50 |
| ❑ 8B Ron Francis | 10.00 | 4.50 |
| ❑ 8C Jaromir Jagr | 40.00 | 18.00 |
| ❑ 9A Geoff Courtnall | 10.00 | 4.50 |
| ❑ 9B Pierre Turgeon | 10.00 | 4.50 |
| ❑ 9C Brett Hull | 15.00 | 6.75 |
| ❑ 10A Wendel Clark | 10.00 | 4.50 |
| ❑ 10B Mats Sundin | 12.00 | 5.50 |
| ❑ 10C Sergei Berezin | 15.00 | 6.75 |
| ❑ 11A Pavel Bure | 25.00 | 11.00 |
| ❑ 11B Trevor Linden | 10.00 | 4.50 |
| ❑ 11C Alexander Mogilny | 10.00 | 4.50 |
| ❑ 12A Joe Juneau | 10.00 | 4.50 |
| ❑ 12B Adam Oates | 10.00 | 4.50 |
| ❑ 12C Peter Bondra | 12.00 | 5.50 |

## 1997-98 Pacific Team Checklist Cel Cards

Randomly inserted in packs at the rate of one in 73, this 26-card set features color player photos with the player's team logo in a circle next to the player's image. The backs carry the checklist of the team the player plays on.

| | MINT | NRMT |
|---|---|---|
| COMPLETE SET (26) | 400.00 | 180.00 |
| COMMON CARD (1-26) | 6.00 | 2.70 |
| ❑ 1 Teemu Selanne | 20.00 | 9.00 |
| ❑ 2 Ray Bourque | 10.00 | 4.50 |
| ❑ 3 Dominik Hasek | 20.00 | 9.00 |
| ❑ 4 Jarome Iginla | 8.00 | 3.60 |
| ❑ 5 Keith Primeau | 8.00 | 3.60 |
| ❑ 6 Chris Chelios | 10.00 | 4.50 |
| ❑ 7 Patrick Roy | 50.00 | 22.00 |
| ❑ 8 Mike Modano | 12.00 | 5.50 |
| ❑ 9 Steve Yzerman | 30.00 | 13.50 |
| ❑ 10 Curtis Joseph | 10.00 | 4.50 |
| ❑ 11 John Vanbiesbrouck | 15.00 | 6.75 |
| ❑ 12 Rob Blake | 6.00 | 2.70 |
| ❑ 13 Stephane Richer | 8.00 | 3.60 |
| ❑ 14 Martin Brodeur | 25.00 | 11.00 |
| ❑ 15 Zigmund Palffy | 10.00 | 4.50 |
| ❑ 16 Wayne Gretzky | 60.00 | 27.00 |
| ❑ 17 Alexandre Daigle | 8.00 | 3.60 |
| ❑ 18 Eric Lindros | 40.00 | 18.00 |
| ❑ 19 Jeremy Roenick | 10.00 | 4.50 |
| ❑ 20 Jaromir Jagr | 30.00 | 13.50 |
| ❑ 21 Brett Hull | 12.00 | 5.50 |
| ❑ 22 Owen Nolan | 8.00 | 3.60 |
| ❑ 23 Dino Ciccarelli | 8.00 | 3.60 |
| ❑ 24 Felix Potvin | 10.00 | 4.50 |
| ❑ 25 Pavel Bure | 20.00 | 9.00 |
| ❑ 26 Peter Bondra | 10.00 | 4.50 |

## 1998-99 Pacific

The 1998-99 Pacific set was issued in one series totalling 450 cards and was distributed in 10-card packs. The fronts features borderless action color player photos. The backs carry player information and career statistics.

| | MINT | NRMT |
|---|---|---|
| COMPLETE SET (450) | 40.00 | 18.00 |
| COMMON CARD (1-450) | .15 | .07 |
| ❑ 1 Damian Rhodes | .40 | .18 |
| ❑ 2 Mattias Ohlund | .40 | .18 |
| ❑ 3 Craig Ludwig | .15 | .07 |
| ❑ 4 Rob Blake | .40 | .18 |
| ❑ 5 Nicklas Lidstrom | .40 | .18 |
| ❑ 6 Calle Johansson | .15 | .07 |
| ❑ 7 Chris Chelios | .50 | .23 |
| ❑ 8 Teemu Selanne | 1.00 | .45 |
| ❑ 9 Paul Kariya | 2.00 | .90 |
| ❑ 10 Pavel Bure | 1.00 | .45 |
| ❑ 11 Mark Messier | .60 | .25 |
| ❑ 12 Peter Bondra | .50 | .23 |
| ❑ 13 Mats Sundin | .50 | .23 |
| ❑ 14 Brendan Shanahan | 1.00 | .45 |
| ❑ 15 Jamie Langenbrunner | .15 | .07 |
| ❑ 16 Brett Hull | .60 | .25 |
| ❑ 17 Rod Brind'Amour | .40 | .18 |
| ❑ 18 Adam Deadmarsh | .40 | .18 |
| ❑ 19 Steve Yzerman | 1.50 | .70 |
| ❑ 20 Ed Belfour | .50 | .23 |
| ❑ 21 Peter Forsberg | 1.50 | .70 |
| ❑ 22 Dino Ciccarelli | .40 | .18 |
| ❑ 23 Brian Bellows | .15 | .07 |
| ❑ 24 Janne Niinimaa | .15 | .07 |
| ❑ 25 Joe Nieuwendyk | .40 | .18 |
| ❑ 26 Patrik Elias | .40 | .18 |
| ❑ 27 Michael Peca | .15 | .07 |
| ❑ 28 Tie Domi | .15 | .07 |
| ❑ 29 Felix Potvin | .50 | .23 |
| ❑ 30 Martin Brodeur | 1.25 | .55 |
| ❑ 31 Grant Fuhr | .40 | .18 |
| ❑ 32 Trevor Linden | .15 | .07 |
| ❑ 33 Patrick Roy | 2.50 | 1.10 |
| ❑ 34 John Vanbiesbrouck | .75 | .35 |
| ❑ 35 Tom Barrasso | .40 | .18 |
| ❑ 36 Matthew Barnaby | .15 | .07 |
| ❑ 37 Olaf Kolzig | .40 | .18 |
| ❑ 38 Pavol Demitra | .40 | .18 |
| ❑ 39 Dominik Hasek | 1.00 | .45 |
| ❑ 40 Chris Terreri | .40 | .18 |
| ❑ 41 Jason Allison | .40 | .18 |
| ❑ 42 Richard Smehlik | .15 | .07 |
| ❑ 43 Frank Banham | .15 | .07 |
| ❑ 44 Chris Pronger | .40 | .18 |
| ❑ 45 Matt Cullen | .15 | .07 |
| ❑ 46 Mike Rucinski | .15 | .07 |
| ❑ 47 Mike Crowley | .40 | .18 |
| ❑ 48 Scott Young | .15 | .07 |
| ❑ 49 Brian Savage | .15 | .07 |
| ❑ 50 Travis Green | .15 | .07 |
| ❑ 51 John LeClair | .75 | .35 |
| ❑ 52 Adam Foote | .15 | .07 |
| ❑ 53 Derek Morris | .15 | .07 |
| ❑ 54 Guy Hebert | .40 | .18 |
| ❑ 55 Chris Gratton | .40 | .18 |
| ❑ 56 Sergei Zubov | .15 | .07 |
| ❑ 57 Dave Karpa | .15 | .07 |
| ❑ 58 Sergei Varlamov | .15 | .07 |
| ❑ 59 Josef Marha | .15 | .07 |
| ❑ 60 Jason Marshall | .15 | .07 |
| ❑ 61 Jeff Nielsen | .15 | .07 |
| ❑ 62 Steve Rucchin | .15 | .07 |
| ❑ 63 Tomas Sandstrom | .15 | .07 |
| ❑ 64 Jason Bonsignore | .15 | .07 |
| ❑ 65 Mikhail Shtalenkov | .15 | .07 |
| ❑ 67 Tom Askey RC | .15 | .07 |
| ❑ 68 Jaromir Jagr | 1.50 | .70 |
| ❑ 69 Per Axelsson | .15 | .07 |
| ❑ 70 Ken Baumgartner | .15 | .07 |
| ❑ 71 Jiri Slegr | .15 | .07 |
| ❑ 72 Mathieu Schneider | .15 | .07 |
| ❑ 73 Anson Carter | .15 | .07 |
| ❑ 74 Byron Dafoe | .40 | .18 |
| ❑ 75 Rob DiMaio | .15 | .07 |
| ❑ 76 Ted Donato | .15 | .07 |
| ❑ 77 Ray Bourque | .50 | .23 |
| ❑ 78 Dave Ellett | .15 | .07 |
| ❑ 79 Steve Heinze | .15 | .07 |
| ❑ 80 Geoff Sanderson | .40 | .18 |
| ❑ 81 Miroslav Satan | .15 | .07 |
| ❑ 82 Martin Straka | .15 | .07 |
| ❑ 83 Dimitri Khristich | .15 | .07 |
| ❑ 84 Grant Ledyard | .15 | .07 |
| ❑ 85 Cameron Mann | .40 | .18 |
| ❑ 86 Kyle McLaren | .15 | .07 |
| ❑ 87 Sergei Samsonov | .75 | .35 |
| ❑ 88 Eric Lindros | 1.50 | .70 |
| ❑ 89 Alexander Mogilny | .40 | .18 |
| ❑ 90 Joe Juneau | .40 | .18 |
| ❑ 91 Sergei Fedorov | 1.00 | .45 |
| ❑ 92 Rick Tocchet | .40 | .18 |
| ❑ 93 Doug Gilmour | .40 | .18 |
| ❑ 94 Ryan Smyth | .40 | .18 |
| ❑ 95 Alexei Morozov | .15 | .07 |
| ❑ 96 Phil Housley | .40 | .18 |
| ❑ 97 Jeremy Roenick | .50 | .23 |
| ❑ 98 Jay More | .15 | .07 |
| ❑ 99 Wayne Gretzky | 3.00 | 1.35 |
| ❑ 100 Robbie Tallas | .40 | .18 |
| ❑ 101 Tim Taylor | .15 | .07 |
| ❑ 102 Joe Thornton | .50 | .23 |
| ❑ 103 Donald Audette | .15 | .07 |
| ❑ 104 Curtis Brown | .15 | .07 |
| ❑ 105 Michal Grosek | .15 | .07 |
| ❑ 106 Brian Holzinger | .15 | .07 |
| ❑ 107 Derek Plante | .15 | .07 |
| ❑ 108 Rob Ray | .15 | .07 |
| ❑ 109 Darryl Shannon | .15 | .07 |
| ❑ 110 Steve Shields | .40 | .18 |
| ❑ 111 Vaclav Varada | .15 | .07 |
| ❑ 112 Dixon Ward | .15 | .07 |
| ❑ 113 Jason Woolley | .15 | .07 |
| ❑ 114 Alexei Zhitnik | .15 | .07 |
| ❑ 115 Andrew Cassels | .15 | .07 |
| ❑ 116 Hnat Domenichelli | .15 | .07 |
| ❑ 117 Theoren Fleury | .50 | .23 |
| ❑ 118 Denis Gauthier | .15 | .07 |
| ❑ 119 Cale Hulse | .15 | .07 |
| ❑ 120 Jarome Iginla | .15 | .07 |
| ❑ 121 Marty McInnis | .15 | .07 |
| ❑ 122 Tyler Moss | .15 | .07 |
| ❑ 123 Michael Nylander | .15 | .07 |
| ❑ 124 Dwayne Roloson | .40 | .18 |
| ❑ 125 Cory Stillman | .15 | .07 |
| ❑ 126 Rick Tabaracci | .40 | .18 |
| ❑ 127 German Titov | .15 | .07 |
| ❑ 128 Jason Wiemer | .15 | .07 |
| ❑ 129 Steve Chiasson | .15 | .07 |
| ❑ 130 Kevin Dineen | .15 | .07 |
| ❑ 131 Nelson Emerson | .15 | .07 |
| ❑ 132 Martin Gelinas | .15 | .07 |
| ❑ 133 Stu Grimson | .15 | .07 |
| ❑ 134 Sami Kapanen | .40 | .18 |
| ❑ 135 Trevor Kidd | .40 | .18 |
| ❑ 136 Robert Kron | .15 | .07 |
| ❑ 137 Jeff O'Neill | .15 | .07 |
| ❑ 138 Keith Primeau | .40 | .18 |
| ❑ 139 Paul Ranheim | .15 | .07 |
| ❑ 140 Gary Roberts | .15 | .07 |
| ❑ 141 Glen Wesley | .15 | .07 |
| ❑ 142 Tony Amonte | .40 | .18 |
| ❑ 143 Eric Daze | .15 | .07 |
| ❑ 144 Jeff Hackett | .40 | .18 |
| ❑ 145 Greg Johnson | .15 | .07 |
| ❑ 146 Chad Kilger | .15 | .07 |
| ❑ 147 Sergei Krivokrasov | .15 | .07 |
| ❑ 148 Christian LaFlamme | .15 | .07 |
| ❑ 149 Jean-Yves Leroux | .15 | .07 |
| ❑ 150 Dmitri Nabakov | .15 | .07 |
| ❑ 151 Jeff Shantz | .15 | .07 |
| ❑ 152 Gary Suter | .15 | .07 |
| ❑ 153 Eric Weinrich | .15 | .07 |
| ❑ 154 Todd White | .15 | .07 |
| ❑ 155 Alexei Zhamnov | .15 | .07 |
| ❑ 156 Wade Belak | .15 | .07 |
| ❑ 157 Craig Billington | .40 | .18 |
| ❑ 158 Rene Corbet | .15 | .07 |
| ❑ 159 Shean Donovan | .15 | .07 |
| ❑ 160 Valeri Kamensky | .15 | .07 |
| ❑ 161 Uwe Krupp | .15 | .07 |
| ❑ 162 Jari Kurri | .40 | .18 |
| ❑ 163 Eric Lacroix | .15 | .07 |
| ❑ 164 Claude Lemieux | .40 | .18 |
| ❑ 165 Eric Messier | .15 | .07 |
| ❑ 166 Jeff Odgers | .15 | .07 |
| ❑ 167 Sandis Ozolinsh | .40 | .18 |
| ❑ 168 Warren Rychel | .15 | .07 |
| ❑ 169 Joe Sakic | 1.00 | .45 |
| ❑ 170 Stephane Yelle | .15 | .07 |
| ❑ 171 Greg Adams | .15 | .07 |
| ❑ 172 Jason Botterill | .15 | .07 |
| ❑ 173 Guy Carbonneau | .15 | .07 |
| ❑ 174 Shawn Chambers | .15 | .07 |
| ❑ 175 Manny Fernandez | .15 | .07 |
| ❑ 176 Derian Hatcher | .15 | .07 |
| ❑ 177 Benoit Hogue | .15 | .07 |
| ❑ 178 Mike Keane | .15 | .07 |
| ❑ 179 Jere Lehtinen | .15 | .07 |
| ❑ 180 Juha Lind | .15 | .07 |
| ❑ 181 Mike Modano | .60 | .25 |
| ❑ 182 Brian Skrudland | .15 | .07 |
| ❑ 183 Darryl Sydor | .15 | .07 |
| ❑ 184 Roman Turek | .40 | .18 |
| ❑ 185 Pat Verbeek | .15 | .07 |
| ❑ 186 Jamie Wright | .15 | .07 |
| ❑ 187 Doug Brown | .15 | .07 |
| ❑ 188 Kris Draper | .15 | .07 |
| ❑ 189 Anders Eriksson | .15 | .07 |
| ❑ 190 Viacheslav Fetisov | .15 | .07 |
| ❑ 191 Brent Gilchrist | .15 | .07 |
| ❑ 192 Kevin Hodson | .40 | .18 |
| ❑ 193 Tomas Holmstrom | .15 | .07 |
| ❑ 194 Michael Knuble | .40 | .18 |
| ❑ 195 Joey Kocur | .15 | .07 |
| ❑ 196 Vyacheslav Kozlov | .40 | .18 |
| ❑ 197 Martin Lapointe | .15 | .07 |
| ❑ 198 Igor Larionov | .15 | .07 |
| ❑ 199 Kirk Maltby | .15 | .07 |
| ❑ 200 Norm Maracle | .75 | .35 |
| ❑ 201 Darren McCarty | .40 | .18 |
| ❑ 202 Dmitri Mironov | .15 | .07 |
| ❑ 203 Larry Murphy | .40 | .18 |
| ❑ 204 Chris Osgood | .50 | .23 |
| ❑ 205 Kelly Buchberger | .15 | .07 |
| ❑ 206 Bob Essensa | .40 | .18 |
| ❑ 207 Scott Fraser | .15 | .07 |
| ❑ 208 Mike Grier | .40 | .18 |
| ❑ 209 Bill Guerin | .40 | .18 |
| ❑ 210 Tony Hrkac | .15 | .07 |
| ❑ 211 Curtis Joseph | .50 | .23 |
| ❑ 212 Mats Lindgren | .15 | .07 |
| ❑ 213 Todd Marchant | .15 | .07 |
| ❑ 214 Dean McAmmond | .15 | .07 |
| ❑ 215 Craig Millar | .15 | .07 |
| ❑ 216 Boris Mironov | .15 | .07 |
| ❑ 217 Doug Weight | .40 | .18 |
| ❑ 218 Valeri Zelepukin | .15 | .07 |
| ❑ 219 Roman Hamrlik | .15 | .07 |
| ❑ 220 Radek Dvorak | .15 | .07 |
| ❑ 221 Dave Gagner | .15 | .07 |
| ❑ 222 Ed Jovanovski | .15 | .07 |
| ❑ 223 Viktor Kozlov | .15 | .07 |
| ❑ 224 Paul Laus | .15 | .07 |
| ❑ 225 Kirk McLean | .40 | .18 |
| ❑ 226 Scott Mellanby | .15 | .07 |
| ❑ 227 Kirk Muller | .15 | .07 |
| ❑ 228 Robert Svehla | .15 | .07 |
| ❑ 229 Steve Washburn | .15 | .07 |
| ❑ 230 Kevin Weekes | .40 | .18 |
| ❑ 231 Ray Whitney | .15 | .07 |
| ❑ 232 Peter Worrell | .15 | .07 |
| ❑ 233 Russ Courtnall | .40 | .18 |
| ❑ 234 Stephane Fiset | .40 | .18 |
| ❑ 235 Garry Galley | .15 | .07 |
| ❑ 236 Craig Johnson | .15 | .07 |
| ❑ 237 Ian Laperriere | .15 | .07 |
| ❑ 238 Donald MacLean | .15 | .07 |
| ❑ 239 Steve McKenna | .15 | .07 |
| ❑ 240 Sandy Moger | .15 | .07 |
| ❑ 241 Glen Murray | .15 | .07 |
| ❑ 242 Sean O'Donnell | .15 | .07 |
| ❑ 243 Yanic Perreault | .15 | .07 |
| ❑ 244 Luc Robitaille | .40 | .18 |
| ❑ 245 Jamie Storr | .40 | .18 |
| ❑ 246 Jozef Stumpel | .40 | .18 |
| ❑ 247 Vladimir Tsyplakov | .15 | .07 |
| ❑ 248 Benoit Brunet | .15 | .07 |
| ❑ 249 Shayne Corson | .15 | .07 |
| ❑ 250 Vincent Damphousse | .15 | .07 |
| ❑ 251 Eric Houde | .15 | .07 |
| ❑ 252 Saku Koivu | .75 | .35 |
| ❑ 253 Vladimir Malakhov | .15 | .07 |
| ❑ 254 Dave Manson | .15 | .07 |
| ❑ 255 Andy Moog | .40 | .18 |
| ❑ 256 Mark Recchi | .40 | .18 |
| ❑ 257 Martin Rucinsky | .15 | .07 |
| ❑ 258 Jocelyn Thibault | .40 | .18 |
| ❑ 259 Mick Vukota | .15 | .07 |
| ❑ 260 Dave Andreychuk | .40 | .18 |
| ❑ 261 Jason Arnott | .40 | .18 |
| ❑ 262 Mike Dunham | .40 | .18 |
| ❑ 263 Bobby Holik | .15 | .07 |
| ❑ 264 Randy McKay | .15 | .07 |
| ❑ 265 Brendan Morrison | .40 | .18 |
| ❑ 266 Scott Niedermayer | .15 | .07 |
| ❑ 267 Lyle Odelein | .15 | .07 |
| ❑ 268 Krzysztof Oliwa | .15 | .07 |
| ❑ 269 Denis Pederson | .15 | .07 |
| ❑ 270 Brian Rolston | .15 | .07 |
| ❑ 271 Sheldon Souray | .15 | .07 |
| ❑ 272 Scott Stevens | .15 | .07 |
| ❑ 273 Petr Sykora | .15 | .07 |
| ❑ 274 Steve Thomas | .15 | .07 |
| ❑ 275 Bryan Berard | .40 | .18 |
| ❑ 276 Zdeno Chara | .15 | .07 |
| ❑ 277 Vladimir Chebaturkin | .15 | .07 |
| ❑ 278 Tom Chorske | .15 | .07 |
| ❑ 279 Mariusz Czerkawski | .15 | .07 |
| ❑ 280 Jason Dawe | .15 | .07 |
| ❑ 281 Wade Flaherty | .40 | .18 |
| ❑ 282 Kenny Jonsson | .15 | .07 |
| ❑ 283 Sergei Nemchinov | .15 | .07 |
| ❑ 284 Zigmund Palffy | .50 | .23 |
| ❑ 285 Richard Pilon | .15 | .07 |
| ❑ 286 Robert Reichel | .15 | .07 |
| ❑ 287 Joe Sacco | .15 | .07 |
| ❑ 288 Tommy Salo | .40 | .18 |
| ❑ 289 Bryan Smolinski | .15 | .07 |
| ❑ 290 Jeff Beukeboom | .15 | .07 |
| ❑ 291 Dan Cloutier | .15 | .07 |
| ❑ 292 Bruce Driver | .15 | .07 |
| ❑ 293 Adam Graves | .40 | .18 |
| ❑ 294 Alexei Kovalev | .15 | .07 |
| ❑ 295 Pat LaFontaine | .40 | .18 |
| ❑ 296 Darren Langdon | .15 | .07 |
| ❑ 297 Brian Leetch | .50 | .23 |
| ❑ 298 Mike Richter | .50 | .23 |
| ❑ 299 Ulf Samuelsson | .15 | .07 |
| ❑ 300 Marc Savard | .15 | .07 |
| ❑ 301 Kevin Stevens | .40 | .18 |
| ❑ 302 Niklas Sundstrom | .15 | .07 |
| ❑ 303 Tim Sweeney | .15 | .07 |
| ❑ 304 Vladimir Vorobiev | .15 | .07 |
| ❑ 305 Daniel Alfredsson | .40 | .18 |
| ❑ 306 Magnus Arvedson | .15 | .07 |
| ❑ 307 Radek Bonk | .15 | .07 |
| ❑ 308 Andreas Dackell | .15 | .07 |
| ❑ 309 Bruce Gardiner | .15 | .07 |
| ❑ 310 Igor Kravchuk | .15 | .07 |
| ❑ 311 Denny Lambert | .15 | .07 |
| ❑ 312 Janne Laukkanen | .15 | .07 |
| ❑ 313 Shawn McEachern | .15 | .07 |
| ❑ 314 Chris Phillips | .15 | .07 |
| ❑ 315 Wade Redden | .15 | .07 |
| ❑ 316 Ron Tugnutt | .40 | .18 |
| ❑ 317 Shaun Van Allen | .15 | .07 |
| ❑ 318 Alexei Yashin | .40 | .18 |
| ❑ 319 Jason York | .15 | .07 |
| ❑ 320 Sergei Zholtok | .15 | .07 |
| ❑ 321 Sean Burke | .15 | .07 |
| ❑ 322 Paul Coffey | .50 | .23 |
| ❑ 323 Alexandre Daigle | .15 | .07 |
| ❑ 324 Eric Desjardins | .15 | .07 |
| ❑ 325 Colin Forbes | .15 | .07 |
| ❑ 326 Ron Hextall | .40 | .18 |
| ❑ 327 Trent Klatt | .15 | .07 |
| ❑ 328 Dan McGillis | .15 | .07 |
| ❑ 329 Joel Otto | .15 | .07 |
| ❑ 330 Shjon Podein | .15 | .07 |
| ❑ 331 Mike Sillinger | .15 | .07 |
| ❑ 332 Chris Therien | .15 | .07 |
| ❑ 333 Dainius Zubrus | .15 | .07 |
| ❑ 334 Bob Corkum | .15 | .07 |
| ❑ 335 Jim Cummins | .15 | .07 |
| ❑ 336 Jason Doig | .15 | .07 |
| ❑ 337 Dallas Drake | .15 | .07 |
| ❑ 338 Mike Gartner | .40 | .18 |
| ❑ 339 Brad Isbister | .15 | .07 |
| ❑ 340 Craig Janney | .15 | .07 |
| ❑ 341 Nikolai Khabibulin | .40 | .18 |
| ❑ 342 Teppo Numminen | .15 | .07 |
| ❑ 343 Cliff Ronning | .15 | .07 |
| ❑ 344 Keith Tkachuk | .60 | .25 |
| ❑ 345 Oleg Tverdovsky | .15 | .07 |
| ❑ 346 Jim Waite | .40 | .18 |
| ❑ 347 Juha Ylonen | .15 | .07 |
| ❑ 348 Stu Barnes | .15 | .07 |
| ❑ 349 Rob Brown | .15 | .07 |
| ❑ 350 Robert Dome | .15 | .07 |
| ❑ 351 Ron Francis | .40 | .18 |
| ❑ 352 Kevin Hatcher | .15 | .07 |
| ❑ 353 Alex Hicks | .15 | .07 |
| ❑ 354 Darius Kasparaitis | .15 | .07 |
| ❑ 355 Robert Lang | .15 | .07 |
| ❑ 356 Fredrik Olausson | .15 | .07 |
| ❑ 357 Ed Olczyk | .15 | .07 |
| ❑ 358 Peter Skudra | .15 | .07 |
| ❑ 359 Chris Tamer | .15 | .07 |
| ❑ 360 Ken Wregget | .40 | .18 |
| ❑ 361 Blair Atcheynum | .15 | .07 |
| ❑ 362 Jim Campbell | .15 | .07 |
| ❑ 363 Kelly Chase | .15 | .07 |
| ❑ 364 Craig Conroy | .15 | .07 |
| ❑ 365 Geoff Courtnall | .15 | .07 |
| ❑ 366 Steve Duchesne | .40 | .18 |
| ❑ 367 Todd Gill | .15 | .07 |
| ❑ 368 Al MacInnis | .40 | .18 |
| ❑ 369 Jamie McLennan | .15 | .07 |
| ❑ 370 Scott Pellerin | .15 | .07 |
| ❑ 371 Pascal Rheaume | .15 | .07 |
| ❑ 372 Jamie Rivers | .40 | .18 |
| ❑ 373 Darren Turcotte | .15 | .07 |
| ❑ 374 Pierre Turgeon | .40 | .18 |
| ❑ 375 Tony Twist | .15 | .07 |
| ❑ 376 Terry Yake | .15 | .07 |
| ❑ 377 Richard Brennan | .15 | .07 |
| ❑ 378 Murray Craven | .15 | .07 |
| ❑ 379 Jeff Friesen | .40 | .18 |
| ❑ 380 Tony Granato | .15 | .07 |
| ❑ 381 Bill Houlder | .15 | .07 |
| ❑ 382 Kelly Hrudey | .40 | .18 |

❑ 383 Alexander Korolyuk .40 .18
❑ 384 John MacLean .15 .07
❑ 385 Bryan Marchment .15 .07
❑ 386 Patrick Marleau .15 .07
❑ 387 Stephane Matteau .15 .07
❑ 388 Marty McSorley .15 .07
❑ 389 Bernie Nicholls .15 .07
❑ 390 Owen Nolan .40 .18
❑ 391 Mike Ricci .40 .18
❑ 392 Marco Sturm .15 .07
❑ 393 Mike Vernon .40 .18
❑ 394 Andrei Zyuzin .15 .07
❑ 395 Mikael Andersson .15 .07
❑ 396 Zac Bierk .15 .07
❑ 397 Enrico Ciccone .15 .07
❑ 398 Louie DeBrusk .15 .07
❑ 399 Karl Dykhuis .15 .07
❑ 400 Daymond Langkow .15 .07
❑ 401 Mike McBain .15 .07
❑ 402 Sandy McCarthy .15 .07
❑ 403 Daren Puppa .40 .18
❑ 404 Mikael Renberg .40 .18
❑ 405 Stephane Richer .40 .18
❑ 406 Alexander Selivanov .15 .07
❑ 407 Darcy Tucker .15 .07
❑ 408 Paul Ysebaert .15 .07
❑ 409 Rob Zamuner .15 .07
❑ 410 Sergei Berezin .40 .18
❑ 411 Wendel Clark .40 .18
❑ 412 Sylvain Cote .15 .07
❑ 413 Mike Johnson .15 .07
❑ 414 Derek King .15 .07
❑ 415 Kris King .15 .07
❑ 416 Igor Korolev .15 .07
❑ 417 Daniil Markov .15 .07
❑ 418 Alyn McCauley .15 .07
❑ 419 Fredrik Modin .15 .07
❑ 420 Martin Prochazka .15 .07
❑ 421 Jason Smith .15 .07
❑ 422 Steve Sullivan .15 .07
❑ 423 Yannick Tremblay .15 .07
❑ 424 Todd Bertuzzi .15 .07
❑ 425 Donald Brashear .15 .07
❑ 426 Bret Hedican .15 .07
❑ 427 Arturs Irbe .40 .18
❑ 428 Jyrki Lumme .15 .07
❑ 429 Brad May .15 .07
❑ 430 Bryan McCabe .15 .07
❑ 431 Markus Naslund .15 .07
❑ 432 Brian Noonan .15 .07
❑ 433 Dave Scatchard .15 .07
❑ 434 Garth Snow .40 .18
❑ 435 Scott Walker .15 .07
❑ 436 Peter Zezel .15 .07
❑ 437 Craig Berube .15 .07
❑ 438 Jeff Brown .15 .07
❑ 439 Andrew Brunette .15 .07
❑ 440 Jan Bulis .15 .07
❑ 441 Sergei Gonchar .15 .07
❑ 442 Dale Hunter .40 .18
❑ 443 Steve Konowalchuk .15 .07
❑ 444 Kelly Miller .15 .07
❑ 445 Adam Oates .40 .18
❑ 446 Bill Ranford .40 .18
❑ 447 Jaroslav Svejkovsky .15 .07
❑ 448 Esa Tikkanen .15 .07
❑ 449 Mark Tinordi .15 .07
❑ 450 Brendan Witt .15 .07
❑ 451 Richard Zednik .15 .07
❑ S181 Mike Modano SAMPLE. 2.00 .90

## 1998-99 Pacific Ice Blue

Randomly inserted in packs at the rate of one in 73, this 450-card set is a blue foil parallel version of the base set.

| | MINT | NRMT |
|---|---|---|
| COMMON CARD (1-450) | 20.00 | 9.00 |
| SEMISTARS/GOALIES | 60.00 | 27.00 |
| UNLISTED STARS | 80.00 | 36.00 |

*STARS: 75X TO 150X BASIC CARD
*YOUNG STARS: 60X TO 120X BASIC CARD
*RC's: 50X TO 100X BASIC CARD

## 1998-99 Pacific Red

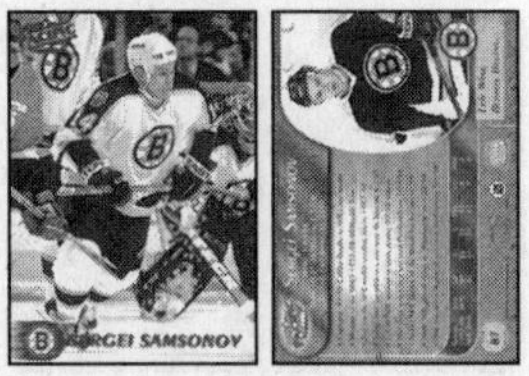

Inserted one per special pack, this 450-card set is a Treat only parallel version of the regular Pacific set with red foil highlights.

| | MINT | NRMT |
|---|---|---|
| COMPLETE SET (450) | 300.00 | 135.00 |
| COMMON CARD (1-450) | 1.00 | .45 |

*STARS: 4X TO 8X BASIC CARD
*YOUNG STARS: 3X TO 6X BASIC CARD
*RC's: 2X TO 4X BASIC CARD

## 1998-99 Pacific Cramer's Choice Awards

Randomly inserted in packs at the rate of one in 721, this 10-card set features action color photos of players picked by President/CEO

Michael Cramer and printed on die-cut trophy cards.

| | MINT | NRMT |
|---|---|---|
| COMPLETE SET (10) | 1200.00 | 550.00 |
| COMMON CARD (1-10) | 50.00 | 22.00 |

❑ 1 Sergei Samsonov 60.00 27.00
❑ 2 Dominik Hasek 80.00 36.00
❑ 3 Peter Forsberg 120.00 55.00
❑ 4 Patrick Roy 200.00 90.00
❑ 5 Mike Modano 50.00 22.00
❑ 6 Martin Brodeur 100.00 45.00
❑ 7 Wayne Gretzky 250.00 110.00
❑ 8 Eric Lindros 120.00 55.00
❑ 9 Jaromir Jagr 120.00 55.00
❑ 10 Pavel Bure 80.00 36.00

## 1998-99 Pacific Dynagon Ice Inserts

Randomly inserted in packs at the rate of four in 37, this 20-card set features color photos of some of the NHL's most exciting players printed on mirror-patterned full-foil cards.

| | MINT | NRMT |
|---|---|---|
| COMPLETE SET (20) | 100.00 | 45.00 |
| COMMON CARD (1-20) | 1.50 | .70 |

❑ 1 Paul Kariya 8.00 3.60
❑ 2 Teemu Selanne 4.00 1.80
❑ 3 Sergei Samsonov 3.00 1.35
❑ 4 Dominik Hasek 4.00 1.80
❑ 5 Peter Forsberg 6.00 2.70
❑ 6 Patrick Roy 10.00 4.50
❑ 7 Joe Sakic 4.00 1.80
❑ 8 Mike Modano 2.50 1.10
❑ 9 Sergei Fedorov 4.00 1.80
❑ 10 Steve Yzerman 6.00 2.70
❑ 11 Saku Koivu 3.00 1.35
❑ 12 Martin Brodeur 5.00 2.20
❑ 13 Wayne Gretzky 12.00 5.50
❑ 14 John LeClair 3.00 1.35
❑ 15 Eric Lindros 6.00 2.70
❑ 16 Jaromir Jagr 6.00 2.70
❑ 17 Pavel Bure 4.00 1.80
❑ 18 Mark Messier 2.50 1.10
❑ 19 Peter Bondra 2.00 .90
❑ 20 Olaf Kolzig 1.50 .70

## 1998-99 Pacific Titanium Ice

Randomly inserted into packs, this 20-card set is an insert to the Pacific base set. Only 99 serially numbered sets were made.

| | MINT | NRMT |
|---|---|---|
| COMPLETE SET (20) | 3000.00 | 1350.00 |
| COMMON CARD (1-20) | 50.00 | 22.00 |

❑ 1 Paul Kariya 250.00 110.00
❑ 2 Teemu Selanne 120.00 55.00
❑ 3 Sergei Samsonov 100.00 45.00
❑ 4 Dominik Hasek 120.00 55.00
❑ 5 Peter Forsberg 200.00 90.00
❑ 6 Patrick Roy 300.00 135.00
❑ 7 Joe Sakic 120.00 55.00
❑ 8 Mike Modano 80.00 36.00
❑ 9 Sergei Fedorov 120.00 55.00
❑ 10 Steve Yzerman 200.00 90.00
❑ 11 Saku Koivu 100.00 45.00
❑ 12 Martin Brodeur 150.00 70.00
❑ 13 Wayne Gretzky 400.00 180.00
❑ 14 John LeClair 100.00 45.00
❑ 15 Eric Lindros 200.00 90.00
❑ 16 Jaromir Jagr 200.00 90.00
❑ 17 Pavel Bure 120.00 55.00
❑ 18 Mark Messier 80.00 36.00
❑ 19 Peter Bondra 60.00 27.00
❑ 20 Olaf Kolzig 50.00 22.00

## 1998-99 Pacific Gold Crown Die-Cuts

Randomly inserted in packs at the rate of one in 37, this 36-card set features color photos of top NHL stars printed on die-cut crown design 24-point card stock with laser cutting and dual foil.

| | MINT | NRMT |
|---|---|---|
| COMPLETE SET (36) | 400.00 | 180.00 |
| COMMON CARD (1-36) | 5.00 | 2.20 |

❑ 1 Paul Kariya 25.00 11.00
❑ 2 Teemu Selanne 12.00 5.50
❑ 3 Sergei Samsonov 10.00 4.50
❑ 4 Dominik Hasek 12.00 5.50
❑ 5 Michael Peca 5.00 2.20
❑ 6 Theoren Fleury 6.00 2.70
❑ 7 Chris Chelios 6.00 2.70
❑ 8 Peter Forsberg 20.00 9.00
❑ 9 Patrick Roy 30.00 13.50
❑ 10 Joe Sakic 12.00 5.50
❑ 11 Ed Belfour 6.00 2.70
❑ 12 Mike Modano 8.00 3.60
❑ 13 Sergei Fedorov 12.00 5.50
❑ 14 Chris Osgood 6.00 2.70
❑ 15 Brendan Shanahan 12.00 5.50
❑ 16 Steve Yzerman 20.00 9.00
❑ 17 Saku Koivu 10.00 4.50
❑ 18 Martin Brodeur 15.00 6.75
❑ 19 Patrik Elias 5.00 2.20
❑ 20 Doug Gilmour 6.00 2.70
❑ 21 Trevor Linden 5.00 2.20
❑ 22 Zigmund Palffy 6.00 2.70
❑ 23 Wayne Gretzky 40.00 18.00
❑ 24 John LeClair 10.00 4.50
❑ 25 Eric Lindros 20.00 9.00
❑ 26 Dainius Zubrus 5.00 2.20
❑ 27 Keith Tkachuk 8.00 3.60
❑ 28 Tom Barrasso 5.00 2.20
❑ 29 Jaromir Jagr 20.00 9.00
❑ 30 Brett Hull 8.00 3.60
❑ 31 Felix Potvin 6.00 2.70
❑ 32 Mats Sundin 6.00 2.70
❑ 33 Pavel Bure 12.00 5.50
❑ 34 Mark Messier 8.00 3.60
❑ 35 Peter Bondra 6.00 2.70
❑ 36 Olaf Kolzig 5.00 2.20

## 1998-99 Pacific Team Checklists

Randomly inserted in packs at the rate of two in 37, this 30-card set features color photos of a superstar player from each team printed on embossed full holographic silver foil cards with the team logo in the background.. The backs carry the complete checklist of the pictured player's team.

| | MINT | NRMT |
|---|---|---|
| COMPLETE SET (30) | 150.00 | 70.00 |
| COMMON CARD (1-30) | 2.00 | .90 |

❑ 1 Paul Kariya 15.00 6.75
❑ 2 Sergei Samsonov 6.00 2.70
❑ 3 Dominik Hasek 8.00 3.60
❑ 4 Theoren Fleury 4.00 1.80
❑ 5 Keith Primeau 3.00 1.35
❑ 6 Chris Chelios 4.00 1.80
❑ 7 Patrick Roy 20.00 9.00
❑ 8 Mike Modano 5.00 2.20
❑ 9 Steve Yzerman 12.00 5.50
❑ 10 Ryan Smyth 3.00 1.35
❑ 11 John Vanbiesbrouck 6.00 2.70
❑ 12 Jozef Stumpel 3.00 1.35
❑ 13 Saku Koivu 6.00 2.70
❑ 14 Mike Dunham 3.00 1.35
❑ 15 Martin Brodeur 10.00 4.50
❑ 16 Zigmund Palffy 4.00 1.80
❑ 17 Wayne Gretzky 25.00 11.00
❑ 18 Alexei Yashin 3.00 1.35
❑ 19 Eric Lindros 12.00 5.50
❑ 20 Keith Tkachuk 5.00 2.20
❑ 21 Jaromir Jagr 12.00 5.50
❑ 22 Brett Hull 5.00 2.20
❑ 23 Patrick Marleau 2.00 .90
❑ 24 Rob Zamuner 2.00 .90
❑ 25 Mats Sundin 4.00 1.80
❑ 26 Pavel Bure 8.00 3.60
❑ 27 Olaf Kolzig 3.00 1.35
❑ 28 Atlanta Thrashers 4.00 1.80
❑ 29 Minnesota Wild 4.00 1.80
❑ 30 Columbus Blue Jackets 4.00 1.80

## 1998-99 Pacific Timelines

Randomly inserted into packs at the rate of

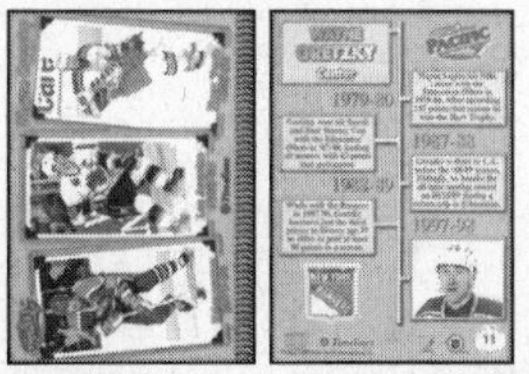

one in 181, this 10-card set is an insert to the Pacific base set.

| | MINT | NRMT |
|---|---|---|
| COMPLETE SET (20) | 1200.00 | 550.00 |
| COMMON CARD (1-20) | 25.00 | 11.00 |

❑ 1 Teemu Selanne 60.00 27.00
❑ 2 Dominik Hasek 60.00 27.00
❑ 3 Peter Forsberg 100.00 45.00
❑ 4 Patrick Roy 150.00 70.00
❑ 5 Joe Sakic 60.00 27.00
❑ 6 Ed Belfour 30.00 13.50
❑ 7 Brendan Shanahan 60.00 27.00
❑ 8 Steve Yzerman 100.00 45.00
❑ 9 Mike Modano 40.00 18.00
❑ 10 Doug Gilmour 25.00 11.00
❑ 11 Wayne Gretzky 200.00 90.00
❑ 12 Pat LaFontaine 25.00 11.00
❑ 13 John LeClair 50.00 22.00
❑ 14 Eric Lindros 100.00 45.00
❑ 15 Keith Tkachuk 40.00 18.00
❑ 16 Jaromir Jagr 100.00 45.00
❑ 17 Brett Hull 40.00 18.00
❑ 18 Mats Sundin 30.00 13.50
❑ 19 Pavel Bure 60.00 27.00
❑ 20 Mark Messier 40.00 18.00

## 1998-99 Pacific Trophy Winners

Randomly inserted into Canadian packs only at the rate of one in 37, this 10-card set is a Canadian insert to the Pacific base set.

| | MINT | NRMT |
|---|---|---|
| COMPLETE SET (10) | 120.00 | 55.00 |
| COMMON CARD (1-10) | 4.00 | 1.80 |

❑ 1 Martin Brodeur 20.00 9.00
❑ 2 Dominik Hasek 15.00 6.75
❑ 3 Jaromir Jagr 25.00 11.00
❑ 4 Sergei Samsonov 12.00 5.50
❑ 5 Sergei Fedorov 15.00 6.75
❑ 6 Nicklas Lidstrom 5.00 2.20
❑ 7 Darren McCarty 4.00 1.80
❑ 8 Chris Osgood 8.00 3.60
❑ 9 Brendan Shanahan 15.00 6.75
❑ 10 Steve Yzerman 25.00 11.00

## 1999-00 Pacific

| | MINT | NRMT |
|---|---|---|
| COMPLETE SET (450) | 40.00 | 18.00 |
| COMMON CARD (1-450) | .15 | .07 |

❑ 1 Matt Cullen .15 .07
❑ 2 Johan Davidsson .15 .07
❑ 3 Scott Ferguson .15 .07
❑ 4 Travis Green .15 .07
❑ 5 Stu Grimson .15 .07
❑ 6 Kevin Haller .15 .07
❑ 7 Guy Hebert .15 .07
❑ 8 Paul Kariya 2.00 .90
❑ 9 Marty McInnis .15 .07
❑ 10 Jim McKenzie .15 .07
❑ 11 Fredrik Olausson .15 .07
❑ 12 Dominic Roussel .15 .07
❑ 13 Steve Rucchin .15 .07
❑ 14 Ruslan Salei .15 .07
❑ 15 Tomas Sandstrom .15 .07
❑ 16 Teemu Selanne 1.00 .45
❑ 17 Jason Allison .40 .18
❑ 18 P.J. Axelsson .15 .07
❑ 19 Shawn Bates .15 .07
❑ 20 Ray Bourque .50 .23
❑ 21 Anson Carter .15 .07
❑ 22 Byron Dafoe .15 .07
❑ 23 Hal Gill .15 .07
❑ 24 Steve Heinze .15 .07
❑ 25 Dimitri Khristich .15 .07
❑ 26 Cameron Mann .15 .07
❑ 27 Kyle McLaren .15 .07
❑ 28 Sergei Samsonov .75 .35
❑ 29 Robbie Tallas .40 .18
❑ 30 Joe Thornton .50 .23
❑ 31 Landon Wilson .15 .07
❑ 32 Jonathan Girard .15 .07
Andre Savage
❑ 33 Stu Barnes .15 .07
❑ 34 Martin Biron .15 .07
❑ 35 Curtis Brown .15 .07
❑ 36 Michal Grosek .15 .07
❑ 37 Dominik Hasek 1.00 .45
❑ 38 Brian Holzinger .40 .18
❑ 39 Joe Juneau .40 .18
❑ 40 Jay McKee .15 .07
❑ 41 Michael Peca .40 .18
❑ 42 Erik Rasmussen .15 .07
❑ 43 Rob Ray .15 .07
❑ 44 Geoff Sanderson .40 .18
❑ 45 Miroslav Satan .40 .18
❑ 46 Darryl Shannon .15 .07
❑ 47 Vaclav Varada .15 .07
❑ 48 Dixon Ward .15 .07
❑ 49 Jason Woolley .15 .07
❑ 50 Alexei Zhitnik .15 .07
❑ 51 Fred Brathwaite .40 .18
❑ 52 Valeri Bure .15 .07
❑ 53 Andrew Cassels .15 .07
❑ 54 Rene Corbet .15 .07
❑ 55 J.S. Giguere .40 .18
❑ 56 Phil Housley .15 .07
❑ 57 Jarome Iginla .15 .07
❑ 58 Derek Morris .15 .07
❑ 59 Andrei Nazarov .15 .07
❑ 60 Jeff Shantz .15 .07
❑ 61 Todd Simpson .15 .07
❑ 62 Cory Stillman .15 .07
❑ 63 Jason Wiemer .15 .07
❑ 64 Clarke Wilm .15 .07
❑ 65 Ken Wregget .40 .18
❑ 66 Rico Fata .40 .18
Tyrone Garner
❑ 67 Bates Battaglia .15 .07
❑ 68 Paul Coffey .50 .23
❑ 69 Kevin Dineen .15 .07
❑ 70 Ron Francis .15 .07
❑ 71 Martin Gelinas .15 .07
❑ 72 Arturs Irbe .40 .18
❑ 73 Sami Kapanen .40 .18
❑ 74 Trevor Kidd .40 .18
❑ 75 Andrei Kovalenko .15 .07
❑ 76 Robert Kron .15 .07
❑ 77 Kent Manderville .15 .07
❑ 78 Jeff O'Neill .15 .07
❑ 79 Keith Primeau .40 .18
❑ 80 Gary Roberts .15 .07
❑ 81 Ray Sheppard .40 .18
❑ 82 Glen Wesley .15 .07
❑ 83 Byron Ritchie .40 .18
Craig MacDonald
❑ 84 Tony Amonte .40 .18
❑ 85 Eric Daze .15 .07
❑ 86 J.P. Dumont .15 .07
❑ 87 Anders Eriksson .15 .07
❑ 88 Mark Fitzpatrick .15 .07
❑ 89 Doug Gilmour .50 .23
❑ 90 J.Y. Leroux .15 .07
❑ 91 Dave Manson .15 .07
❑ 92 Josef Marha .15 .07
❑ 93 Dean McAmmond .15 .07
❑ 94 Boris Mironov .15 .07
❑ 95 Ed Olczyk .15 .07
❑ 96 Bob Probert .15 .07
❑ 97 Jocelyn Thibault .40 .18
❑ 98 Alexei Zhamnov .15 .07
❑ 99 Remi Royer .15 .07
Ty Jones
❑ 100 Craig Billington .40 .18
❑ 101 Adam Deadmarsh .40 .18
❑ 102 Chris Drury .40 .18
❑ 103 Theoren Fleury .50 .23
❑ 104 Adam Foote .15 .07
❑ 105 Peter Forsberg 1.50 .70
❑ 106 Milan Hejduk .40 .18
❑ 107 Dale Hunter .15 .07
❑ 108 Valeri Kamensky .40 .18
❑ 109 Sylvain Lefebvre .15 .07
❑ 110 Claude Lemieux .15 .07
❑ 111 Aaron Miller .15 .07
❑ 112 Jeff Odgers .15 .07
❑ 113 Sandis Ozolinsh .40 .18
❑ 114 Patrick Roy 2.50 1.10
❑ 115 Joe Sakic 1.25 .55
❑ 116 Stephane Yelle .15 .07
❑ 117 Ed Belfour .50 .23
❑ 118 Derian Hatcher .15 .07
❑ 119 Benoit Hogue .15 .07
❑ 120 Brett Hull .60 .25
❑ 121 Mike Keane .15 .07
❑ 122 Jamie Langenbrunner .15 .07
❑ 123 Jere Lehtinen .40 .18
❑ 124 Brad Lukowich .15 .07
❑ 125 Grant Marshall .15 .07
❑ 126 Mike Modano .60 .25
❑ 127 Joe Nieuwendyk .40 .18
❑ 128 Derek Plante .15 .07
❑ 129 Darryl Sydor .15 .07
❑ 130 Roman Turek .40 .18
❑ 131 Pat Verbeek .15 .07
❑ 132 Sergei Zubov .15 .07
❑ 133 Jonathan Sim .15 .07
Blake Sloan
❑ 134 Doug Brown .15 .07
❑ 135 Chris Chelios .50 .23
❑ 136 Wendel Clark .40 .18
❑ 137 Kris Draper .15 .07

❑ 138 Sergei Fedorov 1.00 .45
❑ 139 Tomas Holmstrom .15 .07
❑ 140 Vyacheslav Kozlov .40 .18
❑ 141 Martin Lapointe .15 .07
❑ 142 Igor Larionov .15 .07
❑ 143 Nicklas Lidstrom .40 .18
❑ 144 Darren McCarty .15 .07
❑ 145 Larry Murphy .40 .18
❑ 146 Chris Osgood .50 .23
❑ 147 Bill Ranford .40 .18
❑ 148 Ulf Samuelsson .15 .07
❑ 149 Brendan Shanahan 1.00 .45
❑ 150 Aaron Ward .15 .07
❑ 151 Steve Yzerman 1.50 .70
❑ 152 Josef Beranek .15 .07
❑ 153 Pat Falloon .15 .07
❑ 154 Mike Grier .15 .07
❑ 155 Bill Guerin .40 .18
❑ 156 Roman Hamrlik .15 .07
❑ 157 Chad Kilger .15 .07
❑ 158 Georges Laraque .15 .07
❑ 159 Todd Marchant .15 .07
❑ 160 Ethan Moreau .15 .07
❑ 161 Rem Murray .15 .07
❑ 162 Janne Niinimaa .15 .07
❑ 163 Tom Poti .15 .07
❑ 164 Tommy Salo .40 .18
❑ 165 Alexander Selivanov .15 .07
❑ 166 Ryan Smyth .40 .18
❑ 167 Doug Weight .40 .18
❑ 168 Steve Passmore .15 .07
❑ 169 Pavel Bure 1.00 .45
❑ 170 Sean Burke .15 .07
❑ 171 Dino Ciccarelli .40 .18
❑ 172 Radek Dvorak .15 .07
❑ 173 Viktor Kozlov .15 .07
❑ 174 Oleg Kvasha .15 .07
❑ 175 Paul Laus .15 .07
❑ 176 Bill Lindsay .15 .07
❑ 177 Kirk McLean .40 .18
❑ 178 Scott Mellanby .15 .07
❑ 179 Rob Niedermayer .15 .07
❑ 180 Mark Parrish .40 .18
❑ 181 Jaroslav Spacek .15 .07
❑ 182 Robert Svehla .15 .07
❑ 183 Ray Whitney .15 .07
❑ 184 Peter Worrell .15 .07
❑ 185 D.Boyle .40 .18
M.Nilson
❑ 186 Donald Audette .15 .07
❑ 187 Rob Blake .15 .07
❑ 188 Russ Courtnall .15 .07
❑ 189 Ray Ferraro .15 .07
❑ 190 Stephane Fiset .40 .18
❑ 191 Craig Johnson .15 .07
❑ 192 Olli Jokinen .15 .07
❑ 193 Glen Murray .15 .07
❑ 194 Mattias Norstrom .15 .07
❑ 195 Sean O'Donnell .15 .07
❑ 196 Luc Robitaille .40 .18
❑ 197 Pavel Rosa .40 .18
❑ 198 Jamie Storr .40 .18
❑ 199 Jozef Stumpel .40 .18
❑ 200 Vladimir Tsyplakov .15 .07
❑ 201 Benoit Brunet .15 .07
❑ 202 Shayne Corson .15 .07
❑ 203 Jeff Hackett .40 .18
❑ 204 Matt Higgins .15 .07
❑ 205 Saku Koivu .75 .35
❑ 206 Vladimir Malakhov .15 .07
❑ 207 Patrick Poulin .15 .07
❑ 208 Stephane Quintal .15 .07
❑ 209 Martin Rucinsky .15 .07
❑ 210 Brian Savage .15 .07
❑ 211 Turner Stevenson .15 .07
❑ 212 Jose Theodore .40 .18
❑ 213 Eric Weinrich .15 .07
❑ 214 Sergei Zholtok .15 .07
❑ 215 Dainius Zubrus .40 .18
❑ 216 Terry Ryan .15 .07
Miloslav Guren
❑ 217 Drake Berehowsky .15 .07
❑ 218 Sebastien Bordeleau .15 .07
❑ 219 Bob Boughner .15 .07
❑ 220 Andrew Brunette .15 .07
❑ 221 Patrick Cote .15 .07
❑ 222 Mike Dunham .40 .18
❑ 223 Tom Fitzgerald .15 .07
❑ 224 Jamie Heward .15 .07
❑ 225 Greg Johnson .15 .07
❑ 226 Patric Kjellberg .15 .07
❑ 227 Sergei Krivokrasov .15 .07
❑ 228 Denny Lambert .15 .07
❑ 229 David Legwand .50 .23
❑ 230 Mark Mowers .15 .07
❑ 231 Cliff Ronning .15 .07
❑ 232 Tomas Vokoun .15 .07
❑ 233 Scott Walker .15 .07
❑ 234 Jason Arnott .40 .18
❑ 235 Martin Brodeur 1.25 .55
❑ 236 Ken Daneyko .15 .07
❑ 237 Patrik Elias .40 .18
❑ 238 Bobby Holik .40 .18
❑ 239 John Madden .15 .07
❑ 240 Randy McKay .15 .07
❑ 241 Brendan Morrison .40 .18
❑ 242 Scott Niedermayer .15 .07
❑ 243 Lyle Odelein .15 .07
❑ 244 Krzysztof Oliwa .15 .07
❑ 245 Jay Pandolfo .15 .07
❑ 246 Brian Rolston .15 .07
❑ 247 Vadim Sharifijanov .15 .07
❑ 248 Petr Sykora .15 .07
❑ 249 Chris Terreri .40 .18
❑ 250 Scott Stevens .15 .07
❑ 251 Eric Brewer .40 .18
❑ 252 Zdeno Chara .15 .07
❑ 253 Mariusz Czerkawski .15 .07
❑ 254 Wade Flaherty .15 .07
❑ 255 Kenny Jonsson .15 .07
❑ 256 Claude Lapointe .15 .07
❑ 257 Mark Lawrence .15 .07
❑ 258 Trevor Linden .15 .07
❑ 259 Mats Lindgren .15 .07
❑ 260 Warren Luhning .15 .07
❑ 261 Zigmund Palffy .50 .23
❑ 262 Richard Pilon .15 .07
❑ 263 Felix Potvin .50 .23
❑ 264 Barry Richter .15 .07
❑ 265 Bryan Smolinski .15 .07
❑ 266 Mike Watt .15 .07
❑ 267 Dan Cloutier .15 .07
❑ 268 Brent Fedyk .15 .07
❑ 269 Adam Graves .40 .18
❑ 270 Todd Harvey .15 .07
❑ 271 Mike Knuble .15 .07
❑ 272 Brian Leetch .50 .23
❑ 273 John MacLean .15 .07
❑ 274 Manny Malhotra .40 .18
❑ 275 Rumun Ndur .15 .07
❑ 276 Petr Nedved .40 .18
❑ 277 Peter Popovic .15 .07
❑ 278 Mike Richter .50 .23
❑ 279 Marc Savard .15 .07
❑ 280 Mathieu Schneider .15 .07
❑ 281 Kevin Stevens .40 .18
❑ 282 Niklas Sundstrom .40 .18
❑ 283 Daniel Alfredsson .40 .18
❑ 284 Magnus Arvedson .15 .07
❑ 285 Radek Bonk .15 .07
❑ 286 Andreas Dackell .15 .07
❑ 287 Bruce Gardiner .15 .07
❑ 288 Marian Hossa .15 .07
❑ 289 Andreas Johansson .15 .07
❑ 290 Igor Kravchuk .15 .07
❑ 291 Shawn McEachern .15 .07
❑ 292 Vaclav Prospal .15 .07
❑ 293 Wade Redden .15 .07
❑ 294 Damian Rhodes .40 .18
❑ 295 Sami Salo .15 .07
❑ 296 Ron Tugnutt .40 .18
❑ 297 Alexei Yashin .40 .18
❑ 298 Jason York .15 .07
❑ 299 Rod Brind'Amour .40 .18
❑ 300 Adam Burt .15 .07
❑ 301 Eric Desjardins .15 .07
❑ 302 Ron Hextall .40 .18
❑ 303 Jody Hull .15 .07
❑ 304 Keith Jones .15 .07
❑ 305 Daymond Langkow .15 .07
❑ 306 John LeClair .75 .35
❑ 307 Eric Lindros 2.00 .90
❑ 308 Sandy McCarthy .15 .07
❑ 309 Dan McGillis .15 .07
❑ 310 Mark Recchi .40 .18
❑ 311 Mikael Renberg .40 .18
❑ 312 Chris Therien .15 .07
❑ 313 John Vanbiesbrouck .75 .35
❑ 314 Valeri Zelepukin .15 .07
❑ 315 Greg Adams .15 .07
❑ 316 Keith Carney .15 .07
❑ 317 Bob Corkum .15 .07
❑ 318 Jim Cummins .15 .07
❑ 319 Shane Doan .15 .07
❑ 320 Dallas Drake .15 .07
❑ 321 Nikolai Khabibulin .40 .18
❑ 322 Jyrki Lumme .15 .07
❑ 323 Teppo Numminen .15 .07
❑ 324 Robert Reichel .15 .07
❑ 325 Jeremy Roenick .50 .23
❑ 326 Mikhail Shtalenkov .15 .07
❑ 327 Mike Stapleton .15 .07
❑ 328 Keith Tkachuk .60 .25
❑ 329 Rick Tocchet .40 .18
❑ 330 Oleg Tverdovsky .15 .07
❑ 331 Juha Ylonen .15 .07
❑ 332 Robert Esche .15 .07
Scott Langkow
❑ 333 Matthew Barnaby .40 .18
❑ 334 Tom Barrasso .40 .18
❑ 335 Rob Brown .15 .07
❑ 336 Kevin Hatcher .15 .07
❑ 337 Jan Hrdina .15 .07
❑ 338 Jaromir Jagr 1.50 .70
❑ 339 Darius Kasparaitis .15 .07
❑ 340 Dan Kesa .15 .07
❑ 341 Alexei Kovalev .15 .07
❑ 342 Robert Lang .15 .07
❑ 343 Kip Miller .15 .07
❑ 344 Alexei Morozov .40 .18
❑ 345 Peter Skudra .15 .07
❑ 346 Jiri Slegr .15 .07
❑ 347 Martin Straka .40 .18
❑ 348 German Titov .15 .07
❑ 349 Brad Werenka .15 .07
❑ 350 J.S. Aubin .40 .18
Brian Bonin
❑ 351 Blair Atcheynum .15 .07
❑ 352 Lubos Bartecko .15 .07
❑ 353 Craig Conroy .15 .07
❑ 354 Geoff Courtnall .40 .18
❑ 355 Pavol Demitra .40 .18
❑ 356 Grant Fuhr .40 .18
❑ 357 Michal Handzus .40 .18
❑ 358 Al MacInnis .40 .18
❑ 359 Jamal Mayers .15 .07
❑ 360 Jamie McLennan .40 .18
❑ 361 Scott Pellerin .15 .07
❑ 362 Chris Pronger .40 .18
❑ 363 Pascal Rheaume .15 .07
❑ 364 Pierre Turgeon .40 .18
❑ 365 Tony Twist .40 .18
❑ 366 Scott Young .15 .07
❑ 367 Jochen Hecht .15 .07
Brent Johnson
❑ 368 Tyson Nash .15 .07
Marty Reasoner
❑ 369 Vincent Damphousse .40 .18
❑ 370 Jeff Friesen .15 .07
❑ 371 Tony Granato .15 .07
❑ 372 Bill Houlder .15 .07
❑ 373 Alexander Korolyuk .15 .07
❑ 374 Bryan Marchment .15 .07
❑ 375 Patrick Marleau .40 .18
❑ 376 Stephane Matteau .15 .07
❑ 377 Joe Murphy .15 .07
❑ 378 Owen Nolan .40 .18
❑ 379 Mike Rathje .15 .07
❑ 380 Mike Ricci .15 .07
❑ 381 Steve Shields .40 .18
❑ 382 Ronnie Stern .15 .07
❑ 383 Marco Sturm .15 .07
❑ 384 Mike Vernon .40 .18
❑ 385 Scott Hannan .40 .18
Shawn Heins
❑ 386 Cory Cross .15 .07
❑ 387 Alexandre Daigle .15 .07
❑ 388 Colin Forbes .15 .07
❑ 389 Chris Gratton .15 .07
❑ 390 Kevin Hodson .40 .18
❑ 391 Pavel Kubina .15 .07
❑ 392 Vincent Lecavalier .60 .25
❑ 393 Michael Nylander .15 .07
❑ 394 Stephane Richer .15 .07
❑ 395 Corey Schwab .15 .07
❑ 396 Mike Sillinger .15 .07
❑ 397 Petr Svoboda .15 .07
❑ 398 Darcy Tucker .15 .07
❑ 399 Rob Zamuner .15 .07
❑ 400 Paul Mara .40 .18
Mario Larocque
❑ 401 Bryan Berard .40 .18
❑ 402 Sergei Berezin .40 .18
❑ 403 Lonny Bohonos .15 .07
❑ 404 Sylvain Cote .15 .07
❑ 405 Tie Domi .15 .07
❑ 406 Mike Johnson .15 .07
❑ 407 Curtis Joseph .50 .23
❑ 408 Tomas Kaberle .15 .07
❑ 409 Alexander Karpovtsev .15 .07
❑ 410 Derek King .15 .07
❑ 411 Igor Korolev .15 .07
❑ 412 Adam Mair .15 .07
❑ 413 Alyn McCauley .40 .18
❑ 414 Yanic Perreault .15 .07
❑ 415 Steve Sullivan .15 .07
❑ 416 Mats Sundin .50 .23
❑ 417 Steve Thomas .15 .07
❑ 418 Garry Valk .15 .07
❑ 419 Adrian Aucion .15 .07
❑ 420 Todd Bertuzzi .15 .07
❑ 421 Donald Brashear .15 .07
❑ 422 Dave Gagner .15 .07
❑ 423 Josh Holden .15 .07
❑ 424 Ed Jovanovski .15 .07
❑ 425 Bryan McCabe .40 .18
❑ 426 Mark Messier .60 .25
❑ 427 Alexander Mogilny .40 .18
❑ 428 Bill Muckalt .40 .18
❑ 429 Markus Naslund .15 .07
❑ 430 Mattias Ohlund .40 .18
❑ 431 Dave Scatchard .15 .07
❑ 432 Peter Schaefer .15 .07
❑ 433 Garth Snow .40 .18
❑ 434 Kevin Weekes .15 .07
❑ 435 Brian Bellows .15 .07
❑ 436 James Black .15 .07
❑ 437 Peter Bondra .50 .23
❑ 438 Jan Bulis .15 .07
❑ 439 Sergei Gonchar .15 .07
❑ 440 Benoit Gratton .15 .07
❑ 441 Calle Johansson .15 .07
❑ 442 Ken Klee .15 .07
❑ 443 Olaf Kolzig .40 .18
❑ 444 Steve Konowalchuk .15 .07
❑ 445 Andrei Nikolishin .15 .07
❑ 446 Adam Oates .40 .18
❑ 447 Jaroslav Svejkovsky .15 .07
❑ 448 Rick Tabaracci .40 .18
❑ 449 Richard Zednik .15 .07
❑ 450 Nolan Baumgartner .15 .07
Alexei Tezikov

## 1999-00 Pacific Copper

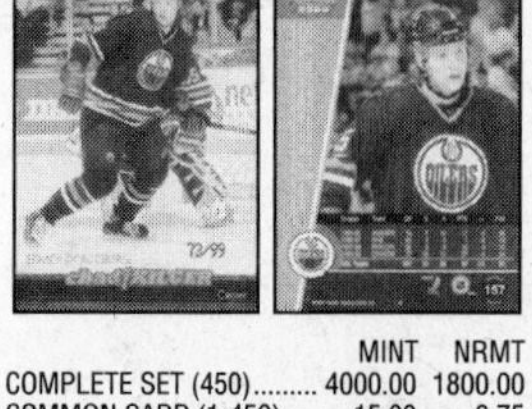

| | MINT | NRMT |
|---|---|---|
| COMPLETE SET (450) | 4000.00 | 1800.00 |
| COMMON CARD (1-450) | 15.00 | 6.75 |

*STARS: 40X TO 100X BASIC CARDS

## 1999-00 Pacific Gold

| | MINT | NRMT |
|---|---|---|
| COMPLETE SET (450) | 1500.00 | 700.00 |
| COMMON CARD (1-450) | 6.00 | 2.70 |

*STARS: 15X TO 40X BASIC CARDS

## 1999-00 Pacific Ice Blue

| | MINT | NRMT |
|---|---|---|
| COMPLETE SET (450) | 5000.00 | 2200.00 |
| COMMON CARD (1-450) | 20.00 | 9.00 |

*STARS: 50X TO 125X BASIC CARDS

## 1999-00 Pacific Premiere Date

| | MINT | NRMT |
|---|---|---|
| COMPLETE SET (450) | 6000.00 | 2700.00 |
| COMMON CARD (1-450) | 25.00 | 11.00 |

*STARS: 60X TO 150X BASIC CARDS

## 1999-00 Pacific Cramer's Choice Awards

| | MINT | NRMT |
|---|---|---|
| COMPLETE SET (10) | 1000.00 | 450.00 |
| COMMON CARD (1-10) | 40.00 | 18.00 |

STATED PRINT RUN 299 SERIAL #'d SETS
RANDOM INSERTS IN PACKS

❑ 1 Paul Kariya 150.00 70.00
❑ 2 Dominik Hasek 80.00 36.00
❑ 3 Peter Forsberg 120.00 55.00
❑ 4 Patrick Roy 200.00 90.00
❑ 5 Joe Sakic 80.00 36.00
❑ 6 Mike Modano 50.00 22.00
❑ 7 Steve Yzerman 120.00 55.00
❑ 8 Eric Lindros 120.00 55.00
❑ 9 Jaromir Jagr 120.00 55.00
❑ 10 Curtis Joseph 40.00 18.00

## 1999-00 Pacific Gold Crown Die-Cuts

| | MINT | NRMT |
|---|---|---|
| COMPLETE SET (36) | 250.00 | 110.00 |
| COMMON CARD (1-36) | 3.00 | 1.35 |

❑ 1 Paul Kariya 20.00 9.00
❑ 2 Teemu Selanne 10.00 4.50
❑ 3 Ray Bourque 5.00 2.20
❑ 4 Byron Dafoe 4.00 1.80
❑ 5 Dominik Hasek 10.00 4.50
❑ 6 Michael Peca 3.00 1.35
❑ 7 Chris Drury 4.00 1.80
❑ 8 Theoren Fleury 5.00 2.20
❑ 9 Peter Forsberg 15.00 6.75
❑ 10 Milan Hejduk 4.00 1.80
❑ 11 Patrick Roy 25.00 11.00
❑ 12 Joe Sakic 10.00 4.50
❑ 13 Ed Belfour 5.00 2.20
❑ 14 Brett Hull 6.00 2.70
❑ 15 Mike Modano 6.00 2.70
❑ 16 Chris Chelios 5.00 2.20
❑ 17 Brendan Shanahan 10.00 4.50
❑ 18 Steve Yzerman 15.00 6.75
❑ 19 Pavel Bure 10.00 4.50
❑ 20 David Legwand 4.00 1.80
❑ 21 Martin Brodeur 12.00 5.50
❑ 22 Felix Potvin 5.00 2.20
❑ 23 Mike Richter 5.00 2.20
❑ 24 Alexei Yashin 5.00 2.20
❑ 25 John LeClair 8.00 3.60
❑ 26 Eric Lindros 15.00 6.75
❑ 27 Mark Recchi 4.00 1.80
❑ 28 John Vanbiesbrouck 8.00 3.60
❑ 29 Jeremy Roenick 5.00 2.20
❑ 30 Keith Tkachuk 6.00 2.70
❑ 31 Jaromir Jagr 15.00 6.75
❑ 32 Vincent Lecavalier 6.00 2.70
❑ 33 Sergei Berezin 3.00 1.35
❑ 34 Curtis Joseph 5.00 2.20
❑ 35 Mats Sundin 5.00 2.20
❑ 36 Mark Messier 6.00 2.70

## 1999-00 Pacific Home and Away

| | MINT | NRMT |
|---|---|---|
| COMPLETE SET (20) | | |
| COMMON CARD (1-20) | | |

11-20 STATED ODDS 2:25 HOBBY

❑ 1 Paul Kariya
❑ 2 Teemu Selanne
❑ 3 Dominik Hasek
❑ 4 Peter Forsberg
❑ 5 Patrick Roy
❑ 6 Mike Modano
❑ 7 Steve Yzerman
❑ 8 John LeClair
❑ 9 Eric Lindros
❑ 10 Jaromir Jagr
❑ 11 Paul Kariya 10.00 4.50
❑ 12 Teemu Selanne 5.00 2.20
❑ 13 Dominik Hasek 5.00 2.20
❑ 14 Peter Forsberg 8.00 3.60
❑ 15 Patrick Roy 12.00 5.50
❑ 16 Mike Modano 3.00 1.35
❑ 17 Steve Yzerman 8.00 3.60
❑ 18 John LeClair 4.00 1.80
❑ 19 Eric Lindros 8.00 3.60
❑ 20 Jaromir Jagr 8.00 3.60

## 1999-00 Pacific In the Cage Net-Fusions

| | MINT | NRMT |
|---|---|---|
| COMPLETE SET (20) | 450.00 | 200.00 |
| COMMON CARD (1-20) | 15.00 | 6.75 |

❑ 1 Guy Hebert 15.00 6.75
❑ 2 Byron Dafoe 15.00 6.75
❑ 3 Dominik Hasek 40.00 18.00
❑ 4 Arturs Irbe 15.00 6.75
❑ 5 Patrick Roy 100.00 45.00
❑ 6 Ed Belfour 20.00 9.00
❑ 7 Chris Osgood 20.00 9.00
❑ 8 Tommy Salo 15.00 6.75
❑ 9 Jeff Hackett 15.00 6.75
❑ 10 Martin Brodeur 50.00 22.00
❑ 11 Felix Potvin 20.00 9.00
❑ 12 Mike Richter 20.00 9.00
❑ 13 Ron Tugnutt 15.00 6.75
❑ 14 John Vanbiesbrouck 30.00 13.50
❑ 15 Nikolai Khabibulin 15.00 6.75
❑ 16 Tom Barrasso 15.00 6.75
❑ 17 Grant Fuhr 15.00 6.75
❑ 18 Mike Vernon 15.00 6.75
❑ 19 Curtis Joseph 20.00 9.00
❑ 20 Olaf Kolzig 15.00 6.75

## 1999-00 Pacific Past and Present

| | MINT | NRMT |
|---|---|---|
| COMPLETE SET (20) | 300.00 | 135.00 |
| COMMON CARD (1-20) | 8.00 | 3.60 |

❑ 1 Paul Kariya 30.00 13.50
❑ 2 Teemu Selanne 15.00 6.75
❑ 3 Ray Bourque 8.00 3.60
❑ 4 Dominik Hasek 15.00 6.75
❑ 5 Theo Fleury 8.00 3.60
❑ 6 Peter Forsberg 25.00 11.00
❑ 7 Patrick Roy 40.00 18.00
❑ 8 Joe Sakic 15.00 6.75
❑ 9 Ed Belfour 8.00 3.60
❑ 10 Brett Hull 10.00 4.50
❑ 11 Mike Modano 10.00 4.50
❑ 12 Brendan Shanahan 15.00 6.75
❑ 13 Steve Yzerman 25.00 11.00
❑ 14 Pavel Bure 15.00 6.75

| | | |
|---|---|---|
| 15 Martin Brodeur | 20.00 | 9.00 |
| 16 John LeClair | 12.00 | 5.50 |
| 17 Eric Lindros | 25.00 | 11.00 |
| 18 John Vanbiesbrouck | 12.00 | 5.50 |
| 19 Jaromir Jagr | 25.00 | 11.00 |
| 20 Curtis Joseph | 8.00 | 3.60 |

## 1999-00 Pacific Team Leaders

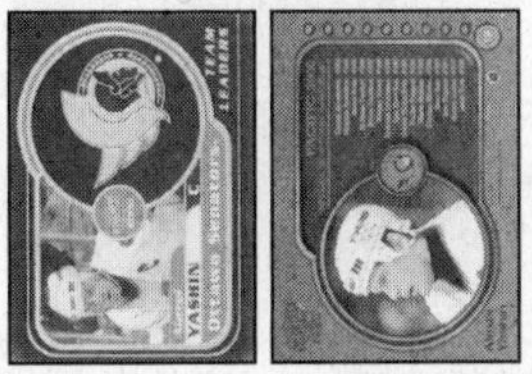

| | MINT | NRMT |
|---|---|---|
| COMPLETE SET (28) | 100.00 | 45.00 |
| COMMON CARD (1-28) | 1.50 | .70 |
| 1 Paul Kariya | 10.00 | 4.50 |
| 2 Atlanta Thrashers | 5.00 | 2.20 |
| 3 Ray Bourque | 2.50 | 1.10 |
| 4 Dominik Hasek | 5.00 | 2.20 |
| 5 Jarome Iginla | 1.50 | .70 |
| 6 Arturs Irbe | 2.00 | .90 |
| 7 Doug Gilmour | 2.50 | 1.10 |
| 8 Patrick Roy | 12.00 | 5.50 |
| 9 Mike Modano | 3.00 | 1.35 |
| 10 Steve Yzerman | 8.00 | 3.60 |
| 11 Bill Guerin | 1.50 | .70 |
| 12 Pavel Bure | 5.00 | 2.20 |
| 13 Luc Robitaille | 2.00 | .90 |
| 14 Saku Koivu | 4.00 | 1.80 |
| 15 Mike Dunham | 2.00 | .90 |
| 16 Martin Brodeur | 6.00 | 2.70 |
| 17 Zigmund Palffy | 2.50 | 1.10 |
| 18 Mike Richter | 2.50 | 1.10 |
| 19 Alexei Yashin | 2.50 | 1.10 |
| 20 Eric Lindros | 8.00 | 3.60 |
| 21 Keith Tkachuk | 3.00 | 1.35 |
| 22 Jaromir Jagr | 8.00 | 3.60 |
| 23 Grant Fuhr | 2.00 | .90 |
| 24 Mike Vernon | 2.00 | .90 |
| 25 Vincent Lecavalier | 3.00 | 1.35 |
| 26 Curtis Joseph | 2.50 | 1.10 |
| 27 Mark Messier | 3.00 | 1.35 |
| 28 Peter Bondra | 2.50 | 1.10 |

## 1998-99 Pacific Aurora

The 1998-99 Pacific Aurora set was issued in one series with a total of 200 standard size cards. The six-card packs retail for $2.99 each. The fronts feature color game-action photos with a smaller head-shot of the featured player in the upper right hand corner. The super-thick card also offers a challenging trivia question on the back.

| | MINT | NRMT |
|---|---|---|
| COMPLETE SET (200) | 40.00 | 18.00 |
| COMMON CARD (1-200) | .20 | .09 |
| 1 Travis Green | .20 | .09 |
| 2 Guy Hebert | .50 | .23 |
| 3 Paul Kariya | 2.50 | 1.10 |
| 4 Steve Rucchin | .20 | .09 |
| 5 Tomas Sandstrom | .20 | .09 |
| 6 Teemu Selanne | 1.25 | .55 |
| 7 Jason Allison | .50 | .23 |
| 8 Ray Bourque | .60 | .25 |
| 9 Anson Carter | .20 | .09 |
| 10 Byron Dafoe | .50 | .23 |
| 11 Ted Donato | .20 | .09 |
| 12 Dave Ellett | .20 | .09 |
| 13 Dimitri Khristich | .20 | .09 |
| 14 Sergei Samsonov | 1.00 | .45 |
| 15 Matthew Barnaby | .20 | .09 |
| 16 Michal Grosek | .20 | .09 |
| 17 Dominik Hasek | 1.25 | .55 |
| 18 Brian Holzinger | .20 | .09 |
| 19 Michael Peca | .20 | .09 |
| 20 Miroslav Satan | .50 | .23 |
| 21 Dixon Ward | .20 | .09 |
| 22 Alexei Zhitnik | .20 | .09 |
| 23 Andrew Cassels | .20 | .09 |
| 24 Theoren Fleury | .60 | .25 |
| 25 Jarome Iginla | .20 | .09 |
| 26 Marty McInnis | .20 | .09 |
| 27 Derek Morris | .20 | .09 |
| 28 Michael Nylander | .20 | .09 |
| 29 Cory Stillman | .20 | .09 |
| 30 Kevin Dineen | .20 | .09 |
| 31 Nelson Emerson | .20 | .09 |
| 32 Martin Gelinas | .20 | .09 |
| 33 Sami Kapanen | .50 | .23 |
| 34 Trevor Kidd | .50 | .23 |
| 35 Robert Kron | .20 | .09 |
| 36 Jeff O'Neill | .20 | .09 |
| 37 Keith Primeau | .50 | .23 |
| 38 Tony Amonte | .50 | .23 |
| 39 Chris Chelios | .60 | .25 |
| 40 Eric Daze | .20 | .09 |
| 41 Jeff Hackett | .50 | .23 |
| 42 Jean-Yves Leroux | .20 | .09 |
| 43 Jeff Shantz | .20 | .09 |
| 44 Alexei Zhamnov | .20 | .09 |
| 45 Adam Deadmarsh | .50 | .23 |
| 46 Peter Forsberg | 2.00 | .90 |
| 47 Valeri Kamensky | .20 | .09 |
| 48 Claude Lemieux | .50 | .23 |
| 49 Eric Messier | .20 | .09 |
| 50 Sandis Ozolinsh | .50 | .23 |
| 51 Patrick Roy | 3.00 | 1.35 |
| 52 Joe Sakic | 1.25 | .55 |
| 53 Ed Belfour | .60 | .25 |
| 54 Derian Hatcher | .20 | .09 |
| 55 Brett Hull | .75 | .35 |
| 56 Jamie Langenbrunner | .20 | .09 |
| 57 Jere Lehtinen | .20 | .09 |
| 58 Mike Modano | .75 | .35 |
| 59 Joe Nieuwendyk | .50 | .23 |
| 60 Darryl Sydor | .20 | .09 |
| 61 Sergei Zubov | .20 | .09 |
| 62 Sergei Fedorov | 1.25 | .55 |
| 63 Vyacheslav Kozlov | .50 | .23 |
| 64 Igor Larionov | .20 | .09 |
| 65 Nicklas Lidstrom | .50 | .23 |
| 66 Darren McCarty | .20 | .09 |
| 67 Chris Osgood | .60 | .25 |
| 68 Brendan Shanahan | 1.25 | .55 |
| 69 Steve Yzerman | 2.00 | .90 |
| 70 Kelly Buchberger | .20 | .09 |
| 71 Mike Grier | .20 | .09 |
| 72 Bill Guerin | .50 | .23 |
| 73 Roman Hamrlik | .20 | .09 |
| 74 Boris Mironov | .20 | .09 |
| 75 Janne Niinimaa | .20 | .09 |
| 76 Ryan Smyth | .50 | .23 |
| 77 Doug Weight | .50 | .23 |
| 78 Dino Ciccarelli | .50 | .23 |
| 79 Dave Gagner | .20 | .09 |
| 80 Ed Jovanovski | .20 | .09 |
| 81 Viktor Kozlov | .20 | .09 |
| 82 Paul Laus | .20 | .09 |
| 83 Scott Mellanby | .20 | .09 |
| 84 Ray Whitney | .20 | .09 |
| 85 Rob Blake | .50 | .23 |
| 86 Stephane Fiset | .50 | .23 |
| 87 Yanic Perreault | .20 | .09 |
| 88 Luc Robitaille | .50 | .23 |
| 89 Jamie Storr | .50 | .23 |
| 90 Jozef Stumpel | .50 | .23 |
| 91 Vladimir Tsyplakov | .20 | .09 |
| 92 Shayne Corson | .20 | .09 |
| 93 Vincent Damphousse | .20 | .09 |
| 94 Saku Koivu | 1.00 | .45 |
| 95 Mark Recchi | .50 | .23 |
| 96 Martin Rucinsky | .20 | .09 |
| 97 Brian Savage | .20 | .09 |
| 98 Jocelyn Thibault | .50 | .23 |
| 99 Andrew Brunette | .20 | .09 |
| 100 Mike Dunham | .50 | .23 |
| 101 Tom Fitzgerald | .20 | .09 |
| 102 Sergei Krivokrasov | .20 | .09 |
| 103 Denny Lambert | .20 | .09 |
| 104 Mikhail Shtalenkov | .20 | .09 |
| 105 Darren Turcotte | .20 | .09 |
| 106 Dave Andreychuk | .50 | .23 |
| 107 Jason Arnott | .50 | .23 |
| 108 Martin Brodeur | 1.50 | .70 |
| 109 Patrik Elias | .50 | .23 |
| 110 Bobby Holik | .20 | .09 |
| 111 Randy McKay | .20 | .09 |
| 112 Scott Niedermayer | .20 | .09 |
| 113 Scott Stevens | .20 | .09 |
| 114 Bryan Berard | .50 | .23 |
| 115 Jason Dawe | .20 | .09 |
| 116 Trevor Linden | .50 | .23 |
| 117 Zigmund Palffy | .60 | .25 |
| 118 Robert Reichel | .20 | .09 |
| 119 Tommy Salo | .50 | .23 |
| 120 Bryan Smolinski | .20 | .09 |
| 121 Adam Graves | .50 | .23 |
| 122 Wayne Gretzky | 4.00 | 1.80 |
| 123 Alexei Kovalev | .20 | .09 |
| 124 Brian Leetch | .60 | .25 |
| 125 Mike Richter | .60 | .25 |
| 126 Ulf Samuelsson | .20 | .09 |
| 127 Kevin Stevens | .50 | .23 |
| 128 Daniel Alfredsson | .50 | .23 |
| 129 Andreas Dackell | .20 | .09 |
| 130 Igor Kravchuk | .20 | .09 |
| 131 Shawn McEachern | .20 | .09 |
| 132 Chris Phillips | .20 | .09 |
| 133 Damian Rhodes | .50 | .23 |
| 134 Alexei Yashin | .50 | .23 |
| 135 Rod Brind'Amour | .50 | .23 |
| 136 Alexandre Daigle | .20 | .09 |
| 137 Eric Desjardins | .20 | .09 |
| 138 Chris Gratton | .50 | .23 |
| 139 Ron Hextall | .50 | .23 |
| 140 John LeClair | 1.00 | .45 |
| 141 Eric Lindros | 2.00 | .90 |
| 142 John Vanbiesbrouck | 1.00 | .45 |
| 143 Dainius Zubrus | .20 | .09 |
| 144 Brad Isbister | .20 | .09 |
| 145 Nikolai Khabibulin | .50 | .23 |
| 146 Jeremy Roenick | .60 | .25 |
| 147 Cliff Ronning | .20 | .09 |
| 148 Keith Tkachuk | .75 | .35 |
| 149 Rick Tocchet | .50 | .23 |
| 150 Oleg Tverdovsky | .20 | .09 |
| 151 Stu Barnes | .20 | .09 |
| 152 Tom Barrasso | .50 | .23 |
| 153 Kevin Hatcher | .20 | .09 |
| 154 Jaromir Jagr | 2.00 | .90 |
| 155 Darius Kasparaitis | .20 | .09 |
| 156 Alexei Morozov | .20 | .09 |
| 157 Martin Straka | .20 | .09 |
| 158 Jim Campbell | .20 | .09 |
| 159 Geoff Courtnall | .20 | .09 |
| 160 Grant Fuhr | .50 | .23 |
| 161 Al MacInnis | .50 | .23 |
| 162 Jamie McLennan | .20 | .09 |
| 163 Chris Pronger | .50 | .23 |
| 164 Pierre Turgeon | .50 | .23 |
| 165 Tony Twist | .20 | .09 |
| 166 Jeff Friesen | .50 | .23 |
| 167 Tony Granato | .20 | .09 |
| 168 Patrick Marleau | .20 | .09 |
| 169 Marty McSorley | .20 | .09 |
| 170 Owen Nolan | .50 | .23 |
| 171 Marco Sturm | .20 | .09 |
| 172 Mike Vernon | .50 | .23 |
| 173 Karl Dykhuis | .20 | .09 |
| 174 Mikael Renberg | .50 | .23 |
| 175 Stephane Richer | .50 | .23 |
| 176 Alexander Selivanov | .20 | .09 |
| 177 Paul Ysebaert | .20 | .09 |
| 178 Rob Zamuner | .20 | .09 |
| 179 Sergei Berezin | .50 | .23 |
| 180 Tie Domi | .20 | .09 |
| 181 Mike Johnson | .50 | .23 |
| 182 Curtis Joseph | .60 | .25 |
| 183 Igor Korolev | .20 | .09 |
| 184 Mathieu Schneider | .20 | .09 |
| 185 Mats Sundin | .60 | .25 |
| 186 Todd Bertuzzi | .20 | .09 |
| 187 Donald Brashear | .20 | .09 |
| 188 Pavel Bure | 1.25 | .55 |
| 189 Mark Messier | .75 | .35 |
| 190 Alexander Mogilny | .50 | .23 |
| 191 Mattias Ohlund | .50 | .23 |
| 192 Garth Snow | .50 | .23 |
| 193 Brian Bellows | .20 | .09 |
| 194 Peter Bondra | .60 | .25 |
| 195 Sergei Gonchar | .20 | .09 |
| 196 Calle Johansson | .20 | .09 |
| 197 Joe Juneau | .50 | .23 |
| 198 Olaf Kolzig | .50 | .23 |
| 199 Adam Oates | .50 | .23 |
| 200 Richard Zednik | .20 | .09 |

## 1998-99 Pacific Aurora Atomic Laser Cuts

Randomly inserted in hobby packs only at a rate of one in 4:37, this 20-card set is an insert to the Pacific Aurora base set.

| | MINT | NRMT |
|---|---|---|
| COMPLETE SET (20) | 100.00 | 45.00 |
| COMMON CARD (1-20) | 2.00 | .90 |
| 1 Paul Kariya | 8.00 | 3.60 |
| 2 Teemu Selanne | 4.00 | 1.80 |
| 3 Sergei Samsonov | 3.00 | 1.35 |
| 4 Dominik Hasek | 4.00 | 1.80 |
| 5 Peter Forsberg | 6.00 | 2.70 |
| 6 Patrick Roy | 10.00 | 4.50 |
| 7 Joe Sakic | 4.00 | 1.80 |
| 8 Mike Modano | 2.50 | 1.10 |
| 9 Sergei Fedorov | 4.00 | 1.80 |
| 10 Brendan Shanahan | 4.00 | 1.80 |
| 11 Steve Yzerman | 6.00 | 2.70 |
| 12 Martin Brodeur | 5.00 | 2.20 |
| 13 Wayne Gretzky | 12.00 | 5.50 |
| 14 John LeClair | 3.00 | 1.35 |
| 15 Eric Lindros | 6.00 | 2.70 |
| 16 Jaromir Jagr | 6.00 | 2.70 |
| 17 Mats Sundin | 2.00 | .90 |
| 18 Pavel Bure | 4.00 | 1.80 |
| 19 Mark Messier | 2.50 | 1.10 |
| 20 Peter Bondra | 2.00 | .90 |

## 1998-99 Pacific Aurora Championship Fever

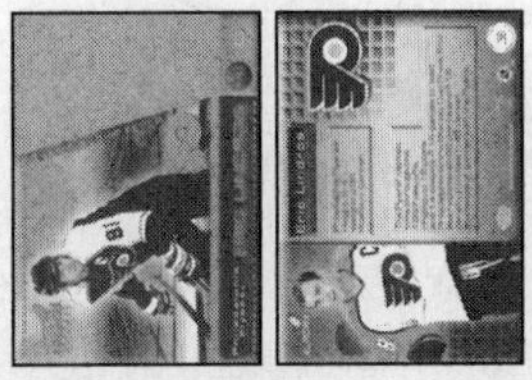

Inserted one in every pack, this 50-card features color action photos of top NHL superstars printed on fully foiled and etched cards. An Ice Blue Parallel set was also produced and serially numbered to 100. A retail only Silver Parallel version of this set was made and serially numbered to 250. Only 20 serial-numbered hobby only Copper Parallel sets were made. All-Star goaltender Martin Brodeur autographed 97 of his regular Championship Fever cards and one each in the parallel versions. A special Red Parallel version was made for Treat Entertainment with an insertion rate of 1:4 in its packs.

| | MINT | NRMT |
|---|---|---|
| COMPLETE SET (50) | 100.00 | 45.00 |
| COMMON CARD (1-50) | .60 | .25 |
| COMP.COPPER SET (50) | | |
| COMMON COPPER (1-50) | 150.00 | 70.00 |
| *COPPER STARS: 150X TO 250X BASIC CARDS | | |
| COPPER RANDOM INS.IN PACKS | | |
| COPPER PRINT RUN 20 SETS | | |
| COMP.ICE BLUE SET (50) | | |
| COMMON ICE BLUE (1-50) | 50.00 | 22.00 |
| *ICE BLUE STARS: 40X TO 80X BASIC CARDS | | |
| ICE BLUE RANDOM INS.IN PACKS | | |
| ICE BLUE PRINT RUN 100 SETS | | |
| COMP.RED SET (50) | | |
| COMMON RED (1-50) | 2.50 | 1.10 |
| *RED STARS: 2X TO 4X BASIC CARDS | | |
| COMP.SILVER SET (50) | | |
| COMMON SILVER (1-50) | 20.00 | 9.00 |
| *SILVER STARS: 15X TO 30X BASIC CARDS | | |
| SILVER RANDOM INS.IN PACKS | | |
| SILVER STATED PRINT RUN 250 SETS | | |
| M.BRODEUR ICE BLUE AU 1/1 EXISTS | | |
| M.BRODEUR COPPER AU 1/1 EXISTS | | |
| M.BRODEUR RED AU 1/1 EXISTS | | |
| 1 Paul Kariya | 3.00 | 1.35 |
| 2 Teemu Selanne | 1.50 | .70 |
| 3 Ray Bourque | .75 | .35 |
| 4 Byron Dafoe | .60 | .25 |
| 5 Sergei Samsonov | 1.25 | .55 |
| 6 Dominik Hasek | 1.50 | .70 |
| 7 Michael Peca | .60 | .25 |
| 8 Theoren Fleury | .75 | .35 |
| 9 Keith Primeau | .60 | .25 |
| 10 Chris Chelios | .75 | .35 |
| 11 Peter Forsberg | 2.50 | 1.10 |
| 12 Patrick Roy | 4.00 | 1.80 |
| 13 Joe Sakic | 1.50 | .70 |
| 14 Ed Belfour | .75 | .35 |
| 15 Mike Modano | 1.00 | .45 |
| 16 Sergei Fedorov | 1.50 | .70 |
| 17 Nicklas Lidstrom | .60 | .25 |
| 18 Chris Osgood | .75 | .35 |
| 19 Brendan Shanahan | 1.50 | .70 |
| 20 Steve Yzerman | 2.50 | 1.10 |
| 21 Doug Weight | .60 | .25 |
| 22 Dino Ciccarelli | .60 | .25 |
| 23 Rob Blake | .60 | .25 |
| 24 Saku Koivu | 1.25 | .55 |
| 25 Mark Recchi | .60 | .25 |
| 26 Martin Brodeur | 2.00 | .90 |
| 27 Patrik Elias | .60 | .25 |
| 28 Trevor Linden | .60 | .25 |
| 29 Zigmund Palffy | .60 | .25 |
| 30 Wayne Gretzky | 5.00 | 2.20 |
| 31 Mike Richter | .75 | .35 |
| 32 Daniel Alfredsson | .60 | .25 |
| 33 Damian Rhodes | .60 | .25 |
| 34 Alexei Yashin | .60 | .25 |
| 35 John LeClair | 1.25 | .55 |
| 36 Eric Lindros | 2.50 | 1.10 |
| 37 Dainius Zubrus | .60 | .25 |
| 38 Keith Tkachuk | 1.00 | .45 |
| 39 Tom Barrasso | .60 | .25 |
| 40 Jaromir Jagr | 2.50 | 1.10 |
| 41 Grant Fuhr | .60 | .25 |
| 42 Pierre Turgeon | .60 | .25 |
| 43 Patrick Marleau | .60 | .25 |
| 44 Mike Vernon | .60 | .25 |
| 45 Rob Zamuner | .60 | .25 |
| 46 Mats Sundin | .75 | .35 |
| 47 Pavel Bure | 1.50 | .70 |
| 48 Mark Messier | 1.00 | .45 |
| 49 Peter Bondra | .75 | .35 |
| 50 Olaf Kolzig | .60 | .25 |
| NNO M.Brodeur Gold AU/97 | 150.00 | 70.00 |

## 1998-99 Pacific Aurora Cubes

These cubes, inserted one per hobby box, feature 20 of the leading players in Hockey in an innovative cube design.

| | MINT | NRMT |
|---|---|---|
| COMPLETE SET (20) | 175.00 | 80.00 |
| COMMON CARD (1-20) | 3.00 | 1.35 |
| 1 Paul Kariya | 15.00 | 6.75 |
| 2 Teemu Selanne | 8.00 | 3.60 |
| 3 Dominik Hasek | 8.00 | 3.60 |
| 4 Peter Forsberg | 12.00 | 5.50 |
| 5 Patrick Roy | 20.00 | 9.00 |
| 6 Joe Sakic | 8.00 | 3.60 |
| 7 Mike Modano | 5.00 | 2.20 |
| 8 Sergei Fedorov | 8.00 | 3.60 |
| 9 Brendan Shanahan | 8.00 | 3.60 |
| 10 Steve Yzerman | 12.00 | 5.50 |
| 11 Martin Brodeur | 10.00 | 4.50 |
| 12 Wayne Gretzky | 25.00 | 11.00 |
| 13 John LeClair | 6.00 | 2.70 |
| 14 Eric Lindros | 12.00 | 5.50 |
| 15 Jaromir Jagr | 12.00 | 5.50 |
| 16 Mats Sundin | 4.00 | 1.80 |
| 17 Pavel Bure | 8.00 | 3.60 |
| 18 Mark Messier | 5.00 | 2.20 |
| 19 Peter Bondra | 4.00 | 1.80 |
| 20 Olaf Kolzig | 3.00 | 1.35 |

## 1998-99 Pacific Aurora Front Line Copper

Randomly inserted in Canadian packs only at the rate of one in 97, this 10-card set features action color player photos with copper foil highlights. Only 80 sets were made. A limited Ice Blue Parallel version of this set was also produced with a print run of 15 and inserted in Canadian packs. Only five very limited numbered Red Parallel versions of this set were made.

| | MINT | NRMT |
|---|---|---|
| COMPLETE SET (10) | 1800.00 | 800.00 |
| COMMON CARD (1-10) | 40.00 | 18.00 |
| RED PARALLEL #'d/5 EXISTS | | |
| 1 Dominik Hasek | 120.00 | 55.00 |
| 2 Peter Forsberg | 200.00 | 90.00 |
| 3 Patrick Roy | 300.00 | 135.00 |
| 4 Joe Sakic | 120.00 | 55.00 |
| 5 Steve Yzerman | 200.00 | 90.00 |
| 6 Daniel Alfredsson | 40.00 | 18.00 |
| 7 Eric Lindros | 200.00 | 90.00 |
| 8 Jaromir Jagr | 200.00 | 90.00 |
| 9 Wayne Gretzky | 400.00 | 180.00 |
| 10 Tie Domi | 40.00 | 18.00 |

## 1998-99 Pacific Aurora Man Advantage Cel-Fusions

Randomly inserted in packs at a rate of one in 73, this 20-card set is an insert to the Pacific Aurora base set. The distinctive fronts feature color action photos on a full-foil, die-cut card that resembles a hockey puck.

| | MINT | NRMT |
|---|---|---|
| COMPLETE SET (20) | 400.00 | 180.00 |
| COMMON CARD (1-20) | 8.00 | 3.60 |
| 1 Paul Kariya | 40.00 | 18.00 |
| 2 Teemu Selanne | 20.00 | 9.00 |
| 3 Ray Bourque | 10.00 | 4.50 |
| 4 Michael Peca | 8.00 | 3.60 |
| 5 Peter Forsberg | 30.00 | 13.50 |
| 6 Joe Sakic | 20.00 | 9.00 |
| 7 Mike Modano | 12.00 | 5.50 |
| 8 Joe Nieuwendyk | 8.00 | 3.60 |
| 9 Brendan Shanahan | 20.00 | 9.00 |
| 10 Steve Yzerman | 30.00 | 13.50 |
| 11 Shayne Corson | 8.00 | 3.60 |
| 12 Zigmund Palffy | 10.00 | 4.50 |
| 13 Wayne Gretzky | 60.00 | 27.00 |
| 14 John LeClair | 15.00 | 6.75 |
| 15 Eric Lindros | 30.00 | 13.50 |
| 16 Jaromir Jagr | 30.00 | 13.50 |
| 17 Mats Sundin | 10.00 | 4.50 |
| 18 Pavel Bure | 20.00 | 9.00 |
| 19 Mark Messier | 12.00 | 5.50 |
| 20 Peter Bondra | 10.00 | 4.50 |

## 1998-99 Pacific Aurora NHL Command

Randomly inserted in packs at a rate of one in 361, this 10-card set is an insert to the Pacific Aurora base set. The horizontal fronts feature color action photography with the featured player's name, team name, and team number in the upper right hand corner.

| | MINT | NRMT |
|---|---|---|
| COMPLETE SET (10) | 1000.00 | 450.00 |
| COMMON CARD (1-10) | 40.00 | 18.00 |
| 1 Teemu Selanne | 60.00 | 27.00 |
| 2 Dominik Hasek | 60.00 | 27.00 |
| 3 Peter Forsberg | 100.00 | 45.00 |
| 4 Patrick Roy | 150.00 | 70.00 |
| 5 Mike Modano | 40.00 | 18.00 |
| 6 Steve Yzerman | 100.00 | 45.00 |
| 7 Martin Brodeur | 80.00 | 36.00 |
| 8 Wayne Gretzky | 200.00 | 90.00 |
| 9 Eric Lindros | 100.00 | 45.00 |
| 10 Jaromir Jagr | 100.00 | 45.00 |

## 1997-98 Pacific Dynagon

The 1997-98 Pacific Dynagon set was issued in one series totalling 156 cards and was distributed in three-card packs with a suggested retail price of $2.49. The fronts feature color action player photos printed on fully foiled and double etched cards. The backs carry a small circular player head photo and player information.

| | MINT | NRMT |
|---|---|---|
| COMPLETE SET (156) | 150.00 | 70.00 |
| COMMON CARD (1-144/NNO) | .60 | .25 |
| COMP.COPPER SET (156) | 1400.00 | 650.00 |
| COMMON COPPER (1-144/NNO) | 6.00 | 2.70 |

*COPPER STARS: 4X TO 8X BASIC CARDS
*COPPER YNG.STARS: 3X TO 6X BASIC CARDS
*COPPER RC's: 2.5X TO 5X BASIC CARDS

| | | |
|---|---|---|
| COMP.EMERALD SET (156) | 1400.00 | 650.00 |
| COMMON EMRLD.(1-144/NNO) | 6.00 | 2.70 |

*EME.GREEN STARS: 4X TO 8X BASIC CARDS
*EMERALD YNG.STARS: 3X TO 6X BASIC CARDS
*EMERALD RC's: 2.5X TO 5X BASIC CARDS

| | | |
|---|---|---|
| COMP.RED SET (156) | 3000.00 | 1350.00 |
| COMMON RED (1-144/NNO) | 12.00 | 5.50 |

*RED STARS: 10X TO 20X BASIC CARDS
*RED YNG.STARS: 7.5X TO 15X BASIC CARDS
*RED RC's: 6X TO 12X BASIC CARDS

| | | |
|---|---|---|
| COMP.SILVER SET (156) | 1600.00 | 700.00 |
| COMMON SILVER (1-144/NNO) | 8.00 | 3.60 |

*SILVER STARS: 5X TO 10X BASIC CARD
*SILVER YNG.STARS: 4X TO 8X
*SILVER RC's: 3X TO 6X BASIC CARDS

| | | |
|---|---|---|
| ❑ 1 Brian Bellows | .60 | .25 |
| ❑ 2 Guy Hebert | 1.25 | .55 |
| ❑ 3 Paul Kariya | 6.00 | 2.70 |
| ❑ 4 Steve Rucchin | .60 | .25 |
| ❑ 5 Teemu Selanne | 3.00 | 1.35 |
| ❑ 6 Jason Allison | 1.25 | .55 |
| ❑ 7 Ray Bourque | 1.50 | .70 |
| ❑ 8 Jim Carey | 1.25 | .55 |
| ❑ 9 Jozef Stumpel | 1.25 | .55 |
| ❑ 10 Dominik Hasek | 3.00 | 1.35 |
| ❑ 11 Brian Holzinger | .60 | .25 |
| ❑ 12 Michael Peca | .60 | .25 |
| ❑ 13 Derek Plante | .60 | .25 |
| ❑ 14 Miroslav Satan | .60 | .25 |
| ❑ 15 Theoren Fleury | 1.25 | .55 |
| ❑ 16 Jonas Hoglund | .60 | .25 |
| ❑ 17 Jarome Iginla | 1.25 | .55 |
| ❑ 18 Trevor Kidd | 1.25 | .55 |
| ❑ 19 German Titov | .60 | .25 |
| ❑ 20 Sean Burke | 1.25 | .55 |
| ❑ 21 Andrew Cassels | .60 | .25 |
| ❑ 22 Keith Primeau | .60 | .25 |
| ❑ 23 Geoff Sanderson | 1.25 | .55 |
| ❑ 24 Tony Amonte | 1.25 | .55 |
| ❑ 25 Chris Chelios | 1.50 | .70 |
| ❑ 26 Eric Daze | 1.25 | .55 |
| ❑ 27 Jeff Hackett | 1.25 | .55 |
| ❑ 28 Ethan Moreau | .60 | .25 |
| ❑ 29 Peter Forsberg | 5.00 | 2.20 |
| ❑ 30 Valeri Kamensky | 1.25 | .55 |
| ❑ 31 Claude Lemieux | 1.25 | .55 |
| ❑ 32 Sandis Ozolinsh | 1.25 | .55 |
| ❑ 33 Patrick Roy | 8.00 | 3.60 |
| ❑ 34 Joe Sakic | 3.00 | 1.35 |
| ❑ 35 Derian Hatcher | .60 | .25 |
| ❑ 36 Jamie Langenbrunner | .60 | .25 |
| ❑ 37 Mike Modano | 2.00 | .90 |
| ❑ 38 Joe Nieuwendyk | 1.25 | .55 |
| ❑ 39 Darryl Sydor | .60 | .25 |
| ❑ 40 Sergei Zubov | .60 | .25 |
| ❑ 41 Sergei Fedorov | 3.00 | 1.35 |
| ❑ 42 Vladimir Konstantinov | .60 | .25 |
| ❑ 43 Chris Osgood | 1.50 | .70 |
| ❑ 44 Brendan Shanahan | 3.00 | 1.35 |
| ❑ 45 Mike Vernon | 1.25 | .55 |
| ❑ 46 Steve Yzerman | 5.00 | 2.20 |
| ❑ 47 Kelly Buchberger | .60 | .25 |
| ❑ 48 Mike Grier | .60 | .25 |
| ❑ 49 Curtis Joseph | 1.50 | .70 |
| ❑ 50 Rem Murray | .60 | .25 |
| ❑ 51 Ryan Smyth | 1.25 | .55 |
| ❑ 52 Doug Weight | 1.25 | .55 |
| ❑ 53 Ed Jovanovski | 1.25 | .55 |
| ❑ 54 Scott Mellanby | .60 | .25 |
| ❑ 55 Ray Sheppard | .60 | .25 |
| ❑ 56 Robert Svehla | .60 | .25 |
| ❑ 57 John Vanbiesbrouck | 2.50 | 1.10 |
| ❑ 58 Rob Blake | .60 | .25 |
| ❑ 59 Ray Ferraro | .60 | .25 |
| ❑ 60 Dimitri Khristich | .60 | .25 |
| ❑ 61 Vladimir Tsyplakov | .60 | .25 |
| ❑ 62 Vincent Damphousse | 1.25 | .55 |
| ❑ 63 Saku Koivu | 2.50 | 1.10 |
| ❑ 64 Mark Recchi | 1.25 | .55 |
| ❑ 65 Stephane Richer | .60 | .25 |
| ❑ 66 Jocelyn Thibault | 1.25 | .55 |
| ❑ 67 Dave Andreychuk | .60 | .25 |
| ❑ 68 Martin Brodeur | 4.00 | 1.80 |
| ❑ 69 Doug Gilmour | 1.50 | .70 |
| ❑ 70 Bobby Holik | .60 | .25 |
| ❑ 71 John MacLean | .60 | .25 |
| ❑ 72 Bryan Berard | 1.25 | .55 |
| ❑ 73 Travis Green | .60 | .25 |
| ❑ 74 Zigmund Palffy | 1.50 | .70 |
| ❑ 75 Tommy Salo | 1.25 | .55 |
| ❑ 76 Bryan Smolinski | .60 | .25 |
| ❑ 77 Adam Graves | 1.25 | .55 |
| ❑ 78 Wayne Gretzky | 10.00 | 4.50 |
| ❑ 79 Alexei Kovalev | .60 | .25 |
| ❑ 80 Brian Leetch | 1.50 | .70 |
| ❑ 81 Mark Messier | 2.00 | .90 |
| ❑ 82 Mike Richter | 1.50 | .70 |
| ❑ 83 Daniel Alfredsson | 1.25 | .55 |
| ❑ 84 Alexandre Daigle | 1.25 | .55 |
| ❑ 85 Wade Redden | .60 | .25 |
| ❑ 86 Damian Rhodes | 1.25 | .55 |
| ❑ 87 Alexei Yashin | 1.25 | .55 |
| ❑ 88 Rod Brind'Amour | 1.25 | .55 |
| ❑ 89 Ron Hextall | 1.25 | .55 |
| ❑ 90 John LeClair | 2.50 | 1.10 |
| ❑ 91 Eric Lindros | 5.00 | 2.20 |
| ❑ 92 Janne Niinimaa | 1.25 | .55 |
| ❑ 93 Garth Snow | 1.25 | .55 |
| ❑ 94 Dainius Zubrus | 1.50 | .70 |
| ❑ 95 Mike Gartner | 1.25 | .55 |
| ❑ 96 Nikolai Khabibulin | 1.25 | .55 |
| ❑ 97 Jeremy Roenick | 1.50 | .70 |
| ❑ 98 Keith Tkachuk | 2.00 | .90 |
| ❑ 99 Oleg Tverdovsky | .60 | .25 |
| ❑ 100 Ron Francis | 1.25 | .55 |
| ❑ 101 Kevin Hatcher | .60 | .25 |
| ❑ 102 Jaromir Jagr | 5.00 | 2.20 |
| ❑ 103 Patrick Lalime | 1.25 | .55 |
| ❑ 104 Petr Nedved | 1.25 | .55 |
| ❑ 105 Jim Campbell | .60 | .25 |
| ❑ 106 Grant Fuhr | 1.25 | .55 |
| ❑ 107 Brett Hull | 2.00 | .90 |
| ❑ 108 Pierre Turgeon | 1.25 | .55 |
| ❑ 109 Harry York | .60 | .25 |
| ❑ 110 Jeff Friesen | 1.25 | .55 |
| ❑ 111 Tony Granato | .60 | .25 |
| ❑ 112 Stephen Guolla | .60 | .25 |
| ❑ 113 Viktor Kozlov | .60 | .25 |
| ❑ 114 Owen Nolan | 1.25 | .55 |
| ❑ 115 Dino Ciccarelli | .60 | .25 |
| ❑ 116 John Cullen | .60 | .25 |
| ❑ 117 Chris Gratton | 1.25 | .55 |
| ❑ 118 Roman Hamrlik | .60 | .25 |
| ❑ 119 Daymond Langkow | .60 | .25 |
| ❑ 120 Sergei Berezin | .60 | .25 |
| ❑ 121 Wendel Clark | 1.25 | .55 |
| ❑ 122 Felix Potvin | 1.50 | .70 |
| ❑ 123 Steve Sullivan | .60 | .25 |
| ❑ 124 Mats Sundin | 1.50 | .70 |
| ❑ 125 Pavel Bure | 3.00 | 1.35 |
| ❑ 126 Martin Gelinas | .60 | .25 |
| ❑ 127 Trevor Linden | 1.25 | .55 |
| ❑ 128 Kirk McLean | 1.25 | .55 |
| ❑ 129 Alexander Mogilny | 1.25 | .55 |
| ❑ 130 Peter Bondra | 1.50 | .70 |
| ❑ 131 Joe Juneau | 1.25 | .55 |
| ❑ 132 Steve Konowalchuk | .60 | .25 |
| ❑ 133 Adam Oates | 1.25 | .55 |
| ❑ 134 Bill Ranford | 1.25 | .55 |
| ❑ 135 P.Kariya/T.Selanne | 4.00 | 1.80 |
| ❑ 136 D.Hasek/M.Peca | 1.25 | .55 |
| ❑ 137 T.Fleury/J.Iginla | 1.25 | .55 |
| ❑ 138 P.Forsberg/P.Roy | 5.00 | 2.20 |
| ❑ 139 B.Shanahan/S.Yzerman | 3.00 | 1.35 |
| ❑ 140 W.Gretzky/M.Messier | 5.00 | 2.20 |
| ❑ 141 J.LeClair/E.Lindros | 4.00 | 1.80 |
| ❑ 142 J.Jagr/P.Lalime | 2.50 | 1.10 |
| ❑ 143 J.Campbell/B.Hull | 1.25 | .55 |
| ❑ 144 S.Berezin/M.Sundin | 1.25 | .55 |
| ❑ NNO Shawn Bates | 1.00 | .45 |
| ❑ NNO Daniel Cleary | 1.50 | .70 |
| ❑ NNO Marian Hossa | 12.00 | 5.50 |
| ❑ NNO Olli Jokinen | 2.50 | 1.10 |
| ❑ NNO Espen Knutsen | 1.00 | .45 |
| ❑ NNO Patrick Marleau | 3.00 | 1.35 |
| ❑ NNO Alyn McCauley | 1.25 | .55 |
| ❑ NNO Mattias Ohlund | 1.50 | .70 |
| ❑ NNO Chris Phillips | .60 | .25 |
| ❑ NNO Erik Rasmussen | .75 | .35 |
| ❑ NNO Sergei Samsonov | 4.00 | 1.80 |
| ❑ NNO Joe Thornton | 3.00 | 1.35 |

## 1997-98 Pacific Dynagon Ice Blue

Randomly inserted in packs at the rate of one in 73, this 156-card set is a parallel version of the base set and is distinguished by the blue foil enhancements.

| | MINT | NRMT |
|---|---|---|
| COMMON CARD (1-144) | 15.00 | 6.75 |
| SEMISTARS/GOALIES | 40.00 | 18.00 |
| UNLISTED STARS | 50.00 | 22.00 |

*STARS: 15X TO 30X BASIC CARDS
*YOUNG STARS: 12.5X TO 25X HI

## 1997-98 Pacific Dynagon Best Kept Secrets

Randomly inserted one per pack, this 110-card set features color action player photos of the top NHL players made to resemble a picture paper clipped to a file. A small slide-look version of the player's picture appears at the top. The backs carry player information and career statistics.

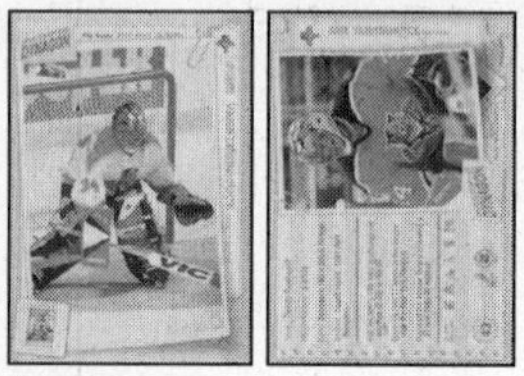

| | MINT | NRMT |
|---|---|---|
| COMPLETE SET (110) | 25.00 | 11.00 |
| COMMON CARD (1-110) | .10 | .05 |
| ❑ 1 J.J. Daigneault | .10 | .05 |
| ❑ 2 Paul Kariya | 1.50 | .70 |
| ❑ 3 Dave Karpa | .10 | .05 |
| ❑ 4 Teemu Selanne | .75 | .35 |
| ❑ 5 Ray Bourque | .40 | .18 |
| ❑ 6 Jim Carey | .25 | .11 |
| ❑ 7 Davis Payne | .10 | .05 |
| ❑ 8 Paxton Schafer | .10 | .05 |
| ❑ 9 Bob Boughner | .10 | .05 |
| ❑ 10 Dominik Hasek | .75 | .35 |
| ❑ 11 Brad May | .10 | .05 |
| ❑ 12 Cale Hulse | .10 | .05 |
| ❑ 13 Jarome Iginla | .25 | .11 |
| ❑ 14 James Patrick | .10 | .05 |
| ❑ 15 Zarley Zalapski | .10 | .05 |
| ❑ 16 Jeff Brown | .10 | .05 |
| ❑ 17 Keith Primeau | .25 | .11 |
| ❑ 18 Steven Rice | .10 | .05 |
| ❑ 19 James Black | .10 | .05 |
| ❑ 20 Chris Chelios | .40 | .18 |
| ❑ 21 Steve Dubinsky | .10 | .05 |
| ❑ 22 Steve Smith | .10 | .05 |
| ❑ 23 Craig Billington | .25 | .11 |
| ❑ 24 Peter Forsberg | 1.25 | .55 |
| ❑ 25 Jon Klemm | .10 | .05 |
| ❑ 26 Patrick Roy | 2.00 | .90 |
| ❑ 27 Joe Sakic | .75 | .35 |
| ❑ 28 Neal Broten | .10 | .05 |
| ❑ 29 Richard Matvichuk | .10 | .05 |
| ❑ 30 Mike Modano | .50 | .23 |
| ❑ 31 Andy Moog | .25 | .11 |
| ❑ 32 Sergei Fedorov | .75 | .35 |
| ❑ 33 Kirk Maltby | .10 | .05 |
| ❑ 34 Brendan Shanahan | .75 | .35 |
| ❑ 35 Tim Taylor | .10 | .05 |
| ❑ 36 Steve Yzerman | 1.25 | .55 |
| ❑ 37 Louie DeBrusk | .10 | .05 |
| ❑ 38 Joe Hulbig | .10 | .05 |
| ❑ 39 Ryan Smyth | .25 | .11 |
| ❑ 40 Mike Hough | .10 | .05 |
| ❑ 41 Jody Hull | .10 | .05 |
| ❑ 42 Paul Laus | .25 | .11 |
| ❑ 43 John Vanbiesbrouck | .60 | .25 |
| ❑ 44 Aki Berg | .10 | .05 |
| ❑ 45 Ray Ferraro | .10 | .05 |
| ❑ 46 Craig Johnson | .10 | .05 |
| ❑ 47 Ian Laperriere | .10 | .05 |
| ❑ 48 Vincent Damphousse | .25 | .11 |
| ❑ 49 Dave Manson | .10 | .05 |
| ❑ 50 Stephane Richer | .25 | .11 |
| ❑ 51 Craig Rivet | .10 | .05 |
| ❑ 52 Martin Brodeur | 1.00 | .45 |
| ❑ 53 Jay Pandolfo | .10 | .05 |
| ❑ 54 Brian Rolston | .10 | .05 |
| ❑ 55 Doug Houda | .10 | .05 |
| ❑ 56 Brent Hughes | .10 | .05 |
| ❑ 57 Zigmund Palffy | .40 | .18 |
| ❑ 58 Adam Graves | .25 | .11 |
| ❑ 59 Wayne Gretzky | 2.50 | 1.10 |
| ❑ 60 Chris Ferraro | .10 | .05 |
| ❑ 61 Glenn Healy | .25 | .11 |
| ❑ 62 Brian Leetch | .40 | .18 |
| ❑ 63 Mark Messier | .50 | .23 |
| ❑ 64 Radim Bicanek | .10 | .05 |
| ❑ 65 Philip Crowe | .10 | .05 |
| ❑ 66 Christer Olsson | .10 | .05 |
| ❑ 67 Jason York | .10 | .05 |
| ❑ 68 Rod Brind'Amour | .25 | .11 |
| ❑ 69 John Druce | .10 | .05 |
| ❑ 70 Daniel Lacroix | .10 | .05 |
| ❑ 71 John LeClair | .60 | .25 |
| ❑ 72 Eric Lindros | 1.25 | .55 |
| ❑ 73 Murray Baron | .10 | .05 |
| ❑ 74 Mike Gartner | .25 | .11 |
| ❑ 75 Brad McCrimmon | .10 | .05 |
| ❑ 76 Keith Tkachuk | .50 | .23 |
| ❑ 77 Jaromir Jagr | 1.25 | .55 |
| ❑ 78 Patrick Lalime | .25 | .11 |
| ❑ 79 Ian Moran | .10 | .05 |
| ❑ 80 Petr Nedved | .25 | .11 |
| ❑ 81 Brett Hull | .50 | .23 |
| ❑ 82 Robert Petrovicky | .10 | .05 |
| ❑ 83 Pierre Turgeon | .25 | .11 |
| ❑ 84 Trent Yawney | .10 | .05 |
| ❑ 85 Tim Hunter | .10 | .05 |
| ❑ 86 Marcus Ragnarsson | .10 | .05 |
| ❑ 87 Dody Wood | .10 | .05 |
| ❑ 88 Dino Ciccarelli | .10 | .05 |
| ❑ 89 Alexander Selivanov | .10 | .05 |
| ❑ 90 Jason Wiemer | .10 | .05 |
| ❑ 91 Sergei Berezin | .25 | .11 |
| ❑ 92 Felix Potvin | .40 | .18 |
| ❑ 93 Mats Sundin | .40 | .18 |
| ❑ 94 Craig Wolanin | .10 | .05 |
| ❑ 95 Pavel Bure | .75 | .35 |
| ❑ 96 Troy Crowder | .10 | .05 |
| ❑ 97 Dana Murzyn | .10 | .05 |
| ❑ 98 Gino Odjick | .25 | .11 |
| ❑ 99 Craig Berube | .10 | .05 |
| ❑ 100 Peter Bondra | .40 | .18 |
| ❑ 101 Mike Eagles | .10 | .05 |
| ❑ 102 Andrei Nikolishin | .10 | .05 |
| ❑ 103 Paul Kariya | 1.50 | .70 |
| ❑ 104 Dominik Hasek | .75 | .35 |
| ❑ 105 Michael Peca | .10 | .05 |
| ❑ 106 M.Brodeur/M.Dunham | .50 | .23 |
| ❑ 107 Bryan Berard | .25 | .11 |
| ❑ 108 Brian Leetch | .40 | .18 |
| ❑ 109 Tony Granato | .10 | .05 |
| ❑ 110 Trevor Linden | .25 | .11 |

## 1997-98 Pacific Dynagon Dynamic Duos

Randomly inserted in packs at the rate of one in 37, this 30-card set features color action images of the NHL's top teammates printed on a die-cut gold foil card and framed with a textured hockey puck border. When placed side by side, the matching cards are joined together by their team logo.

| | MINT | NRMT |
|---|---|---|
| COMPLETE SET (30) | 400.00 | 180.00 |
| COMMON CARD (1A-15B) | 3.00 | 1.35 |
| ❑ 1A Paul Kariya | 30.00 | 13.50 |
| ❑ 1B Teemu Selanne | 15.00 | 6.75 |
| ❑ 2A Ray Bourque | 8.00 | 3.60 |
| ❑ 2B Jim Carey | 6.00 | 2.70 |
| ❑ 3A Dominik Hasek | 15.00 | 6.75 |
| ❑ 3B Michael Peca | 6.00 | 2.70 |
| ❑ 4A Theoren Fleury | 6.00 | 2.70 |
| ❑ 4B Jarome Iginla | 6.00 | 2.70 |
| ❑ 5A Peter Forsberg | 25.00 | 11.00 |
| ❑ 5B Claude Lemieux | 6.00 | 2.70 |
| ❑ 6A Patrick Roy | 40.00 | 18.00 |
| ❑ 6B Joe Sakic | 15.00 | 6.75 |
| ❑ 7A Sergei Fedorov | 15.00 | 6.75 |
| ❑ 7B Vladimir Konstantinov | 6.00 | 2.70 |
| ❑ 8A Brendan Shanahan | 15.00 | 6.75 |
| ❑ 8B Steve Yzerman | 25.00 | 11.00 |
| ❑ 9A Bryan Berard | 6.00 | 2.70 |
| ❑ 9B Zigmund Palffy | 8.00 | 3.60 |
| ❑ 10A Wayne Gretzky | 50.00 | 22.00 |
| ❑ 10B Mark Messier | 10.00 | 4.50 |
| ❑ 11A Eric Lindros | 25.00 | 11.00 |
| ❑ 11B Dainius Zubrus | 6.00 | 2.70 |
| ❑ 12A Jeremy Roenick | 8.00 | 3.60 |
| ❑ 12B Keith Tkachuk | 10.00 | 4.50 |
| ❑ 13A Jaromir Jagr | 25.00 | 11.00 |
| ❑ 13B Patrick Lalime | 6.00 | 2.70 |
| ❑ 14A Jim Campbell | 3.00 | 1.35 |
| ❑ 14B Brett Hull | 10.00 | 4.50 |
| ❑ 15A Pavel Bure | 15.00 | 6.75 |
| ❑ 15B Alexander Mogilny | 6.00 | 2.70 |

## 1997-98 Pacific Dynagon Kings of the NHL

Randomly inserted in packs at the rate of one in 361, this 10-card set features color images of top NHL players on foiled cards with the words, "Kings of the NHL" printed in a circular pattern in the background.

| | MINT | NRMT |
|---|---|---|
| COMPLETE SET (10) | 1000.00 | 450.00 |
| COMMON CARD (1-10) | 40.00 | 18.00 |
| ❑ 1 Paul Kariya | 120.00 | 55.00 |
| ❑ 2 Peter Forsberg | 100.00 | 45.00 |
| ❑ 3 Patrick Roy | 150.00 | 70.00 |
| ❑ 4 Joe Sakic | 60.00 | 27.00 |
| ❑ 5 John Vanbiesbrouck | 50.00 | 22.00 |
| ❑ 6 Wayne Gretzky | 200.00 | 90.00 |
| ❑ 7 Mark Messier | 40.00 | 18.00 |
| ❑ 8 Eric Lindros | 100.00 | 45.00 |
| ❑ 9 Jaromir Jagr | 100.00 | 45.00 |
| ❑ 10 Pavel Bure | 60.00 | 27.00 |

## 1997-98 Pacific Dynagon Stonewallers

Randomly inserted in packs at the rate of one in 73, this 20-card set features color photos of the best NHL goalies printed on a dual-foiled die-cut card with a combination of holographic silver and red foil enhancements.

| | MINT | NRMT |
|---|---|---|
| COMPLETE SET (20) | 400.00 | 180.00 |
| COMMON CARD (1-20) | 12.00 | 5.50 |
| ❑ 1 Guy Hebert | 12.00 | 5.50 |
| ❑ 2 Jim Carey | 12.00 | 5.50 |
| ❑ 3 Dominik Hasek | 30.00 | 13.50 |
| ❑ 4 Trevor Kidd | 12.00 | 5.50 |
| ❑ 5 Jeff Hackett | 12.00 | 5.50 |
| ❑ 6 Patrick Roy | 80.00 | 36.00 |
| ❑ 7 Chris Osgood | 15.00 | 6.75 |
| ❑ 8 Mike Vernon | 12.00 | 5.50 |
| ❑ 9 Curtis Joseph | 15.00 | 6.75 |
| ❑ 10 John Vanbiesbrouck | 25.00 | 11.00 |
| ❑ 11 Jocelyn Thibault | 15.00 | 6.75 |
| ❑ 12 Martin Brodeur | 40.00 | 18.00 |
| ❑ 13 Tommy Salo | 12.00 | 5.50 |
| ❑ 14 Mike Richter | 15.00 | 6.75 |
| ❑ 15 Ron Hextall | 12.00 | 5.50 |
| ❑ 16 Garth Snow | 12.00 | 5.50 |
| ❑ 17 Nikolai Khabibulin | 12.00 | 5.50 |
| ❑ 18 Patrick Lalime | 12.00 | 5.50 |
| ❑ 19 Grant Fuhr | 12.00 | 5.50 |
| ❑ 20 Felix Potvin | 12.00 | 5.50 |

## 1997-98 Pacific Dynagon Tandems

Randomly inserted in packs at the rate of one in 37, this 72-card set features color player images printed on double front, holographic fully foiled, double etched cards.

| | MINT | NRMT |
|---|---|---|
| COMPLETE SET (72) | 1800.00 | 800.00 |
| COMMON CARD (1-72) | 10.00 | 4.50 |
| ❑ 1 Wayne Gretzky<br>Eric Lindros | 120.00 | 55.00 |
| ❑ 2 Joe Sakic<br>Paul Kariya | 100.00 | 45.00 |
| ❑ 3 Jarome Iginla<br>Mark Messier | 25.00 | 11.00 |
| ❑ 4 Patrick Roy<br>Dominik Hasek | 80.00 | 36.00 |
| ❑ 5 Peter Forsberg<br>Jaromir Jagr | 80.00 | 36.00 |
| ❑ 6 Brendan Shanahan<br>Keith Tkachuk | 40.00 | 18.00 |
| ❑ 7 Steve Yzerman<br>Teemu Selanne | 60.00 | 27.00 |
| ❑ 8 Sergei Fedorov<br>Brett Hull | 40.00 | 18.00 |
| ❑ 9 Danius Zubrus<br>Patrick Lalime | 15.00 | 6.75 |
| ❑ 10 Sergei Berezin<br>Mike Grier | 15.00 | 6.75 |
| ❑ 11 Zigmund Palffy<br>Curtis Joseph | 10.00 | 4.50 |
| ❑ 12 Chris Osgood<br>Martin Brodeur | 40.00 | 18.00 |
| ❑ 13 John Vanbiesbrouck<br>Jocelyn Thibault | 20.00 | 9.00 |
| ❑ 14 Saku Koivu<br>Pavel Bure | 40.00 | 18.00 |
| ❑ 15 John LeClair<br>Peter Bondra | 30.00 | 13.50 |
| ❑ 16 Mats Sundin<br>Janne Niinimaa | 10.00 | 4.50 |
| ❑ 17 Felix Potvin<br>Jim Carey | 15.00 | 6.75 |
| ❑ 18 Grant Fuhr<br>Brett Hull<br>Jim Campbell | 30.00 | 13.50 |
| ❑ 19 Wayne Gretzky<br>Mark Messier<br>Brian Leetch | 100.00 | 45.00 |
| ❑ 20 Eric Lindros<br>John LeClair<br>Rod Brind'Amour | 60.00 | 27.00 |
| ❑ 21 Dominik Hasek<br>Michael Peca<br>Miroslav Satan | 40.00 | 18.00 |
| ❑ 22 Jaromir Jagr<br>Patrick Lalime<br>Petr Nedved | 50.00 | 22.00 |
| ❑ 23 Jarome Iginla<br>Theo Fleury<br>Trevor Kidd | 15.00 | 6.75 |
| ❑ 24 Paul Kariya<br>Teemu Selanne<br>Guy Hebert | 80.00 | 36.00 |
| ❑ 25 Peter Forsberg<br>Patrick Roy<br>Claude Lemieux | 100.00 | 45.00 |
| ❑ 26 Steve Yzerman<br>Brendand Shanahan<br>Vladimir Konstantinov | 80.00 | 36.00 |
| ❑ 27 Mats Sundin<br>Sergei Berezin<br>Wendel Clark | 20.00 | 9.00 |
| ❑ 28 Ray Bourque<br>Derek Plante | 20.00 | 9.00 |
| ❑ 29 Brian Bellows | 15.00 | 6.75 |

Jason Allison
❑ 30 Steve Rucchin 15.00 6.75
Keith Primeau
❑ 31 Jozef Stumpel 15.00 6.75
Eric Daze
❑ 32 Brian Holzinger 15.00 6.75
Jamie Langenbrunner
❑ 33 Michael Peca 15.00 6.75
Tony Amonte
❑ 34 German Titov 10.00 4.50
Darryl Sydor
❑ 35 Theo Fleury 25.00 11.00
Chris Chelios
❑ 36 Jonas Hoglund 10.00 4.50
Dimitri Khristich
❑ 37 Sean Burke 15.00 6.75
Dave Andreychuk
❑ 38 Geoff Sanderson 15.00 6.75
Derian Hatcher
❑ 39 Andrew Cassels 15.00 6.75
Jeff Hackett
❑ 40 Ethan Moreau 10.00 4.50
Ray Ferraro
❑ 41 Sandis Ozolinsh 20.00 9.00
Doug Gilmour
❑ 42 Valeri Kamensky 25.00 11.00
Mike Modano
❑ 43 Joe Nieuwendyk 15.00 6.75
Vladimir Tsyplakov
❑ 44 Sergei Zubov 15.00 6.75
Mike Vernon
❑ 45 Rob Blake 10.00 4.50
Bobby Holik
❑ 46 Vincent Damphousse 15.00 6.75
Doug Weight
❑ 47 Mark Recchi 15.00 6.75
Ryan Smyth
❑ 48 Stephane Richer 15.00 6.75
John MacLean
❑ 49 Kelly Buchberger 10.00 4.50
Ed Jovanovski
❑ 50 Rem Murray 15.00 6.75
Owen Nolan
❑ 51 Robert Svehla 15.00 6.75
Bill Ranford
❑ 52 Ray Sheppard 15.00 6.75
Steve Sullivan
❑ 53 Scott Mellanby 10.00 4.50
John Cullen
❑ 54 Garth Snow 15.00 6.75
Alexandre Daigle
❑ 55 Ron Hextall 15.00 6.75
Alexander Mogilny
❑ 56 Kirk McLean 15.00 6.75
Adam Oates
❑ 57 Joe Juneau 15.00 6.75
Dino Ciccarelli
❑ 58 Steve Konowalchuk 10.00 4.50
Jim Campbell
❑ 59 Trevor Linden 15.00 6.75
Pierre Turgeon
❑ 60 Martin Gelinas 15.00 6.75
Jeff Friesen
❑ 61 Roman Hamrlik 10.00 4.50
Harry York
❑ 62 Kevin Hatcher 15.00 6.75
Chris Gratton
❑ 63 Ron Francis 15.00 6.75
Jeremy Roenick
❑ 64 Nikolai Khabibulin 15.00 6.75
Viktor Kozlov
❑ 65 Daymond Langkow 15.00 6.75
Mike Gartner
❑ 66 Oleg Tverdovsky 10.00 4.50
Steve Guolla
❑ 67 Tony Granato 15.00 6.75
Tommy Salo
❑ 68 Bryan Smolinski 15.00 6.75
Wade Redden
❑ 69 Adam Graves 15.00 6.75
Damian Rhodes
❑ 70 Mike Richter 20.00 9.00
Alexei Yashin
❑ 71 Daniel Alfredsson 20.00 9.00
Bryan Berard
❑ 72 Travis Green 10.00 4.50
Alexei Kovalev

## 1998-99 Pacific Dynagon Ice

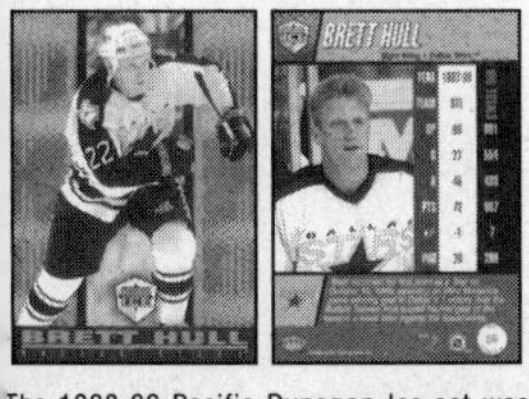

The 1998-99 Pacific Dynagon Ice set was issued in one series totalling 200 cards and was distributed in five-card packs with a suggested retail price of $2.49. The set features color action player photos printed on gold foil cards with player highlights and statistics displayed on the backs.

| | MINT | NRMT |
|---|---|---|
| COMPLETE SET (200) | 60.00 | 27.00 |
| COMMON CARD (1-200) | .25 | .11 |

❑ 1 Travis Green .25 .11
❑ 2 Guy Hebert .60 .25
❑ 3 Paul Kariya 3.00 1.35
❑ 4 Steve Rucchin .25 .11
❑ 5 Tomas Sandstrom .25 .11
❑ 6 Teemu Selanne 1.50 .70
❑ 7 Jason Allison .60 .25
❑ 8 Ray Bourque .75 .35
❑ 9 Byron Dafoe .60 .25
❑ 10 Anson Carter .25 .11
❑ 11 Dimitri Khristich .25 .11
❑ 12 Antti Laaksonen .25 .11
❑ 13 Peter Nordstrom .25 .11
❑ 14 Sergei Samsonov 1.25 .55
❑ 15 Joe Thornton .75 .35
❑ 16 Matthew Barnaby .25 .11
❑ 17 Michal Grosek .25 .11
❑ 18 Dominik Hasek 1.50 .70
❑ 19 Brian Holzinger .25 .11
❑ 20 Michael Peca .25 .11
❑ 21 Miroslav Satan .60 .25
❑ 22 Vaclav Varada .25 .11
❑ 23 Andrew Cassels .25 .11
❑ 24 Rico Fata .60 .25
❑ 25 Theoren Fleury .75 .35
❑ 26 Phil Housley .25 .11
❑ 27 Jarome Iginla .25 .11
❑ 28 Martin St. Louis .60 .25
❑ 29 Ken Wregget .60 .25
❑ 30 Kevin Dineen .25 .11
❑ 31 Ron Francis .60 .25
❑ 32 Martin Gelinas .25 .11
❑ 33 Arturs Irbe .60 .25
❑ 34 Sami Kapanen .60 .25
❑ 35 Trevor Kidd .60 .25
❑ 36 Robert Kron .25 .11
❑ 37 Keith Primeau .60 .25
❑ 38 Tony Amonte .60 .25
❑ 39 Chris Chelios .75 .35
❑ 40 Eric Daze .25 .11
❑ 41 Doug Gilmour .60 .25
❑ 42 Jeff Hackett .60 .25
❑ 43 Ty Jones .60 .25
❑ 44 Bob Probert .25 .11
❑ 45 Adam Deadmarsh .60 .25
❑ 46 Chris Drury 1.00 .45
❑ 47 Peter Forsberg 2.50 1.10
❑ 48 Milan Hejduk 1.25 .55
❑ 49 Valeri Kamensky .25 .11
❑ 50 Claude Lemieux .60 .25
❑ 51 Patrick Roy 4.00 1.80
❑ 52 Joe Sakic 1.50 .70
❑ 53 Ed Belfour .75 .35
❑ 54 Sergey Gusev .25 .11
❑ 55 Derian Hatcher .25 .11
❑ 56 Brett Hull 1.00 .45
❑ 57 Jamie Langenbrunner .25 .11
❑ 58 Jere Lehtinen .25 .11
❑ 59 Mike Modano 1.00 .45
❑ 60 Joe Nieuwendyk .60 .25
❑ 61 Sergei Zubov .25 .11
❑ 62 Sergei Fedorov 1.50 .70
❑ 63 Vyacheslav Kozlov .60 .25
❑ 64 Uwe Krupp .25 .11
❑ 65 Nicklas Lidstrom .60 .25
❑ 66 Darren McCarty .25 .11
❑ 67 Chris Osgood .75 .35
❑ 68 Brendan Shanahan 1.50 .70
❑ 69 Steve Yzerman 2.50 1.10
❑ 70 Bob Essensa .60 .25
❑ 71 Mike Grier .25 .11
❑ 72 Bill Guerin .60 .25
❑ 73 Roman Hamrlik .25 .11
❑ 74 Janne Niinimaa .25 .11
❑ 75 Tom Poti .25 .11
❑ 76 Ryan Smyth .60 .25
❑ 77 Doug Weight .60 .25
❑ 78 Sean Burke .25 .11
❑ 79 Dino Ciccarelli .60 .25
❑ 80 Dave Gagner .25 .11
❑ 81 Ed Jovanovski .25 .11
❑ 82 Viktor Kozlov .25 .11
❑ 83 Oleg Kvasha .75 .35
❑ 84 Paul Laus .25 .11
❑ 85 Mark Parrish 1.25 .55
❑ 86 Rob Blake .25 .11
❑ 87 Stephane Fiset .60 .25
❑ 88 Josh Green .25 .11
❑ 89 Yanic Perreault .25 .11
❑ 90 Luc Robitaille .60 .25
❑ 91 Jozef Stumpel .60 .25
❑ 92 Vladimir Tsyplakov .25 .11
❑ 93 Brad Brown .25 .11
❑ 94 Shayne Corson .60 .25
❑ 95 Vincent Damphousse .60 .25
❑ 96 Saku Koivu 1.25 .55
❑ 97 Mark Recchi .60 .25
❑ 98 Jocelyn Thibault .60 .25
❑ 99 Sergei Zholtok .25 .11
❑ 100 Andrew Brunette .25 .11
❑ 101 Mike Dunham .60 .25
❑ 102 Tom Fitzgerald .25 .11
❑ 103 Patrik Kjellberg .25 .11
❑ 104 Sergei Krivokrasov .25 .11
❑ 105 Darren Turcotte .25 .11
❑ 106 Dave Andreychuk .60 .25
❑ 107 Jason Arnott .60 .25
❑ 108 Martin Brodeur 2.00 .90
❑ 109 Patrik Elias .60 .25
❑ 110 Bobby Holik .25 .11
❑ 111 Brendan Morrison .60 .25
❑ 112 Scott Stevens .25 .11
❑ 113 Bryan Berard .60 .25
❑ 114 Eric Brewer .25 .11
❑ 115 Trevor Linden .60 .25
❑ 116 Zigmund Palffy .75 .35
❑ 117 Robert Reichel .25 .11
❑ 118 Tommy Salo .60 .25
❑ 119 Bryan Smolinski .25 .11
❑ 120 Adam Graves .60 .25
❑ 121 Wayne Gretzky 5.00 2.20
❑ 122 Alexei Kovalev .25 .11
❑ 123 Brian Leetch .75 .35
❑ 124 Manny Malhotra .25 .11
❑ 125 Mike Richter .75 .35
❑ 126 Daniel Alfredsson .60 .25
❑ 127 Igor Kravchuk .25 .11
❑ 128 Shawn McEachern .25 .11
❑ 129 Vaclav Prospal .60 .25
❑ 130 Damian Rhodes .60 .25
❑ 131 Sami Salo .60 .25
❑ 132 Alexei Yashin .60 .25
❑ 133 Rod Brind'Amour .60 .25
❑ 134 Alexandre Daigle .25 .11
❑ 135 Chris Gratton .60 .25
❑ 136 Ron Hextall .60 .25
❑ 137 John LeClair 1.25 .55
❑ 138 Eric Lindros 2.50 1.10
❑ 139 Mike Maneluk 1.00 .45
❑ 140 John Vanbiesbrouck 1.00 .45
❑ 141 Dainius Zubrus .25 .11
❑ 142 Brad Isbister .25 .11
❑ 143 Nikolai Khabibulin .60 .25
❑ 144 Jeremy Roenick .75 .35
❑ 145 Keith Tkachuk 1.00 .45
❑ 146 Rick Tocchet .60 .25
❑ 147 Oleg Tverdovsky .25 .11
❑ 148 Tom Barrasso .60 .25
❑ 149 Kevin Hatcher .25 .11
❑ 150 Jan Hrdina 1.00 .45
❑ 151 Jaromir Jagr 2.50 1.10
❑ 152 Alexei Morozov .25 .11
❑ 153 Jiri Slegr .25 .11
❑ 154 Martin Straka .25 .11
❑ 155 Jim Campbell .25 .11
❑ 156 Geoff Courtnall .25 .11
❑ 157 Grant Fuhr .60 .25
❑ 158 Michal Handzus .75 .35
❑ 159 Al MacInnis .60 .25
❑ 160 Jamie McLennan .60 .25
❑ 161 Chris Pronger .60 .25
❑ 162 Marty Reasoner .25 .11
❑ 163 Pierre Turgeon .60 .25
❑ 164 Jeff Friesen .60 .25
❑ 165 Tony Granato .25 .11
❑ 166 Scott Hannan .60 .25
❑ 167 Patrick Marleau .25 .11
❑ 168 Owen Nolan .60 .25
❑ 169 Marco Sturm .25 .11
❑ 170 Mike Vernon .60 .25
❑ 171 Wendel Clark .60 .25
❑ 172 John Cullen .25 .11
❑ 173 Vincent Lecavalier 2.50 1.10
❑ 174 Stephane Richer .60 .25
❑ 175 Paul Ysebaert .25 .11
❑ 176 Rob Zamuner .25 .11
❑ 177 Sergei Berezin .60 .25
❑ 178 Tie Domi .25 .11
❑ 179 Mike Johnson .25 .11
❑ 180 Curtis Joseph .75 .35
❑ 181 Tomas Kaberle .25 .11
❑ 182 Igor Korolev .25 .11
❑ 183 Alyn McCauley .25 .11
❑ 184 Mats Sundin .75 .35
❑ 185 Todd Bertuzzi .25 .11
❑ 186 Donald Brashear .25 .11
❑ 187 Pavel Bure 1.50 .70
❑ 188 Matt Cooke .25 .11
❑ 189 Mark Messier 1.00 .45
❑ 190 Alexander Mogilny .60 .25
❑ 191 Mattias Ohlund .25 .11
❑ 192 Garth Snow .60 .25
❑ 193 Peter Bondra .75 .35
❑ 194 Matthew Herr .25 .11
❑ 195 Calle Johansson .25 .11
❑ 196 Joe Juneau .60 .25
❑ 197 Olaf Kolzig .60 .25
❑ 198 Adam Oates .60 .25
❑ 199 Jaroslav Svejkovsky .25 .11
❑ 200 Richard Zednik .25 .11

## 1998-99 Pacific Dynagon Ice Blue

Randomly inserted into packs, this 200-card set is a blue foil parallel version of the base set. Only 67 serially numbered sets were made.

| | MINT | NRMT |
|---|---|---|
| COMMON CARD (1-200) | 20.00 | 9.00 |
| SEMISTARS/GOALIES | 50.00 | 22.00 |
| UNLISTED STARS | 60.00 | 27.00 |

*STARS: 40X to 80X BASIC CARDS

## 1998-99 Pacific Dynagon Ice Adrenaline Rush

Randomly inserted into Canadian retail packs only at the rate of one in 37, this 10-card set is a Canadian insert to the Pacific Dynagon Ice base set. Four limited edition parallel sets were also made and inserted into packs: Bronze with only 180 sets made, Ice Blue with 10 sets made, Red with 79 sets made, and Silver with 120 sets made.

| | MINT | NRMT |
|---|---|---|
| COMPLETE SET (10) | 400.00 | 180.00 |
| COMMON CARD (1-10) | 25.00 | 11.00 |

❑ 1 Paul Kariya 50.00 22.00
❑ 2 Teemu Selanne 25.00 11.00
❑ 3 Dominik Hasek 25.00 11.00
❑ 4 Peter Forsberg 40.00 18.00
❑ 5 Patrick Roy 60.00 27.00
❑ 6 Joe Sakic 25.00 11.00
❑ 7 Steve Yzerman 40.00 18.00
❑ 8 Wayne Gretzky 80.00 36.00
❑ 9 Eric Lindros 40.00 18.00
❑ 10 Jaromir Jagr 40.00 18.00

## 1998-99 Pacific Dynagon Ice Forward Thinking

Randomly inserted into packs at the rate of one in 37, this 20-card set features color action photos of the NHL's finest front-line players printed on full foil cards. The backs carry insightful information about the player.

| | MINT | NRMT |
|---|---|---|
| COMPLETE SET (20) | 200.00 | 90.00 |
| COMMON CARD (1-20) | 4.00 | 1.80 |

❑ 1 Paul Kariya 20.00 9.00
❑ 2 Teemu Selanne 10.00 4.50
❑ 3 Michael Peca 4.00 1.80
❑ 4 Doug Gilmour 5.00 2.20
❑ 5 Peter Forsberg 15.00 6.75
❑ 6 Joe Sakic 10.00 4.50
❑ 7 Brett Hull 6.00 2.70
❑ 8 Mike Modano 6.00 2.70
❑ 9 Sergei Fedorov 10.00 4.50
❑ 10 Brendan Shanahan 10.00 4.50
❑ 11 Steve Yzerman 15.00 6.75
❑ 12 Saku Koivu 8.00 3.60
❑ 13 Wayne Gretzky 30.00 13.50
❑ 14 John LeClair 8.00 3.60
❑ 15 Eric Lindros 15.00 6.75
❑ 16 Jaromir Jagr 15.00 6.75
❑ 17 Vincent Lecavalier 10.00 4.50
❑ 18 Mats Sundin 5.00 2.20
❑ 19 Mark Messier 6.00 2.70
❑ 20 Peter Bondra 5.00 2.20

## 1998-99 Pacific Dynagon Ice Watchmen

Randomly inserted into packs at the rate of one in 73, this 10-card set features color close-up photos of top NHL goaltenders printed on full foil cards. The backs carry puck-stopping action photos of the featured goalies.

| | MINT | NRMT |
|---|---|---|
| COMPLETE SET (10) | 175.00 | 80.00 |
| COMMON CARD (1-10) | 10.00 | 4.50 |

❑ 1 Dominik Hasek 25.00 11.00
❑ 2 Patrick Roy 60.00 27.00
❑ 3 Ed Belfour 12.00 5.50
❑ 4 Chris Osgood 12.00 5.50
❑ 5 Martin Brodeur 30.00 13.50
❑ 6 Mike Richter 12.00 5.50
❑ 7 John Vanbiesbrouck 15.00 6.75
❑ 8 Grant Fuhr 10.00 4.50
❑ 9 Curtis Joseph 12.00 5.50
❑ 10 Olaf Kolzig 10.00 4.50

## 1998-99 Pacific Dynagon Ice Preeminent Players

Randomly inserted into packs at the rate of one in 181, this 10-card set features color action photos of some of the NHL's most sensational players printed on full foil cards. The backs carry informative hockey facts.

| | MINT | NRMT |
|---|---|---|
| COMPLETE SET (10) | 600.00 | 275.00 |
| COMMON CARD (1-10) | 25.00 | 11.00 |

❑ 1 Paul Kariya 80.00 36.00
❑ 2 Dominik Hasek 40.00 18.00
❑ 3 Peter Forsberg 60.00 27.00
❑ 4 Patrick Roy 100.00 45.00
❑ 5 Mike Modano 25.00 11.00
❑ 6 Steve Yzerman 60.00 27.00
❑ 7 Martin Brodeur 50.00 22.00
❑ 8 Wayne Gretzky 120.00 55.00
❑ 9 Eric Lindros 60.00 27.00
❑ 10 Jaromir Jagr 60.00 27.00

## 1998-99 Pacific Dynagon Ice Rookies

Randomly inserted into hobby packs only at the rate of one in 73, this 10-card hobby insert set features color action photos of top current NHL rookies with their team logos. The backs carry information about the player.

| | MINT | NRMT |
|---|---|---|
| COMPLETE SET (10) | 150.00 | 70.00 |
| COMMON CARD (1-10) | 12.00 | 5.50 |

❑ 1 Chris Drury 20.00 9.00
❑ 2 Milan Hejduk 20.00 9.00
❑ 3 Mark Parrish 20.00 9.00
❑ 4 Brendan Morrison 15.00 6.75
❑ 5 Mike Maneluk 15.00 6.75
❑ 6 Jan Hrdina 12.00 5.50
❑ 7 Marty Reasoner 12.00 5.50
❑ 8 Vincent Lecavalier 40.00 18.00
❑ 9 Tomas Kaberle 12.00 5.50
❑ 10 Bill Muckalt 15.00 6.75

## 1998-99 Pacific Dynagon Ice Team Checklists

Randomly inserted into packs at the rate of two in 37, this 27-card set features color photos of a top star from each of the 27 NHL teams with the team logo in the background. The backs carry the team checklist.

| | MINT | NRMT |
|---|---|---|
| COMPLETE SET (27) | 150.00 | 70.00 |
| COMMON CARD (1-27) | 2.50 | 1.10 |

❑ 1 Paul Kariya 12.00 5.50
❑ 2 Ray Bourque 3.00 1.35
❑ 3 Dominik Hasek 6.00 2.70
❑ 4 Theoren Fleury 3.00 1.35
❑ 5 Keith Primeau 2.50 1.10
❑ 6 Chris Chelios 3.00 1.35
❑ 7 Patrick Roy 15.00 6.75
❑ 8 Mike Modano 4.00 1.80
❑ 9 Steve Yzerman 10.00 4.50
❑ 10 Ryan Smyth 2.50 1.10
❑ 11 Dino Ciccarelli 2.50 1.10
❑ 12 Rob Blake 2.50 1.10
❑ 13 Saku Koivu 5.00 2.20
❑ 14 Mike Dunham 2.50 1.10
❑ 15 Martin Brodeur 8.00 3.60
❑ 16 Trevor Linden 2.50 1.10
❑ 17 Wayne Gretzky 20.00 9.00
❑ 18 Alexei Yashin 2.50 1.10
❑ 19 Eric Lindros 10.00 4.50
❑ 20 Keith Tkachuk 4.00 1.80
❑ 21 Jaromir Jagr 10.00 4.50
❑ 22 Grant Fuhr 2.50 1.10
❑ 23 Mike Vernon 2.50 1.10
❑ 24 Vincent Lecavalier 6.00 2.70
❑ 25 Mats Sundin 3.00 1.35
❑ 26 Mark Messier 4.00 1.80
❑ 27 Peter Bondra 3.00 1.35

## 1997-98 Pacific Invincible

The 1997-98 Pacific Invincible set was issued in one series totalling 150 cards and distributed in three-card packs. The fronts feature color action player images with gold foil background enhancements and a small player head photo in a clear, circular "window" at the bottom. The backs carry player information.

| | MINT | NRMT |
|---|---|---|
| COMPLETE SET (150) | 160.00 | 70.00 |
| COMMON CARD (1-150) | .75 | .35 |
| COMP.COPPER SET (150) | 1400.00 | 650.00 |
| COMMON COPPER (1-150) | 6.00 | 2.70 |

*COPPER STARS: 4X TO 8X BASIC CARDS
*COPPER YNG.STARS: 3X TO 6X BASIC CARDS

| | | |
|---|---|---|
| COMP.EMERALD SET (150) | 1600.00 | 700.00 |
| COMMON EMERALD (1-150) | 8.00 | 3.60 |

*EME.GREEN STARS: 5X TO 10X BASIC CARDS
*EMERALD YNG.STARS: 4X TO 8X BASIC CARDS

| | | |
|---|---|---|
| COMP.RED SET (150) | 3000.00 | 1350.00 |
| COMMON RED (1-150) | 12.00 | 5.50 |

*RED STARS: 10X TO 20X BASIC CARDS
*RED YNG.STARS: 7.5X TO 15X BASIC CARDS

| | | |
|---|---|---|
| COMP.SILVER SET (150) | 1600.00 | 700.00 |
| COMMON SILVER (1-150) | 8.00 | 3.60 |

*SILVER STARS: 5X TO 10X BASIC CARDS
*SILVER YNG.STARS: 4X TO 8X BASIC CARDS

| | | |
|---|---|---|
| ❑ 1 Brian Bellows | .75 | .35 |
| ❑ 2 Guy Hebert | 1.50 | .70 |
| ❑ 3 Paul Kariya | 8.00 | 3.60 |
| ❑ 4 Teemu Selanne | 4.00 | 1.80 |
| ❑ 5 Darren Van Impe | .75 | .35 |
| ❑ 6 Jason Allison | 1.50 | .70 |
| ❑ 7 Ray Bourque | 2.00 | .90 |
| ❑ 8 Jim Carey | 1.50 | .70 |
| ❑ 9 Ted Donato | .75 | .35 |
| ❑ 10 Jozef Stumpel | 1.50 | .70 |
| ❑ 11 Jason Dawe | .75 | .35 |
| ❑ 12 Dominik Hasek | 4.00 | 1.80 |
| ❑ 13 Michael Peca | .75 | .35 |
| ❑ 14 Derek Plante | .75 | .35 |
| ❑ 15 Miroslav Satan | .75 | .35 |
| ❑ 16 Theoren Fleury | 1.50 | .70 |
| ❑ 17 Dave Gagner | .75 | .35 |
| ❑ 18 Jonas Hoglund | .75 | .35 |
| ❑ 19 Jarome Iginla | 1.50 | .70 |
| ❑ 20 Trevor Kidd | 1.50 | .70 |
| ❑ 21 German Titov | .75 | .35 |
| ❑ 22 Sean Burke | 1.50 | .70 |
| ❑ 23 Andrew Cassels | .75 | .35 |
| ❑ 24 Derek King | .75 | .35 |
| ❑ 25 Keith Primeau | .75 | .35 |
| ❑ 26 Geoff Sanderson | 1.50 | .70 |
| ❑ 27 Tony Amonte | 1.50 | .70 |
| ❑ 28 Chris Chelios | 2.00 | .90 |
| ❑ 29 Eric Daze | 1.50 | .70 |
| ❑ 30 Jeff Hackett | 1.50 | .70 |
| ❑ 31 Ethan Moreau | .75 | .35 |
| ❑ 32 Alexei Zhamnov | .75 | .35 |
| ❑ 33 Adam Deadmarsh | 1.50 | .70 |
| ❑ 34 Peter Forsberg | 6.00 | 2.70 |
| ❑ 35 Valeri Kamensky | 1.50 | .70 |
| ❑ 36 Claude Lemieux | 1.50 | .70 |
| ❑ 37 Sandis Ozolinsh | 1.50 | .70 |
| ❑ 38 Patrick Roy | 10.00 | 4.50 |
| ❑ 39 Joe Sakic | 4.00 | 1.80 |
| ❑ 40 Jamie Langenbrunner | .75 | .35 |
| ❑ 41 Mike Modano | 2.50 | 1.10 |
| ❑ 42 Andy Moog | 1.50 | .70 |
| ❑ 43 Joe Nieuwendyk | 1.50 | .70 |
| ❑ 44 Pat Verbeek | .75 | .35 |
| ❑ 45 Sergei Zubov | .75 | .35 |
| ❑ 46 Sergei Fedorov | 4.00 | 1.80 |
| ❑ 47 Vladimir Konstantinov | .75 | .35 |
| ❑ 48 Vyacheslav Kozlov | .75 | .35 |
| ❑ 49 Nicklas Lidstrom | 1.50 | .70 |
| ❑ 50 Chris Osgood | 2.00 | .90 |
| ❑ 51 Brendan Shanahan | 4.00 | 1.80 |
| ❑ 52 Mike Vernon | 1.50 | .70 |
| ❑ 53 Steve Yzerman | 6.00 | 2.70 |
| ❑ 54 Jason Arnott | 1.50 | .70 |
| ❑ 55 Mike Grier | .75 | .35 |
| ❑ 56 Curtis Joseph | 2.00 | .90 |
| ❑ 57 Rem Murray | .75 | .35 |
| ❑ 58 Ryan Smyth | 1.50 | .70 |
| ❑ 59 Doug Weight | 1.50 | .70 |
| ❑ 60 Ed Jovanovski | 1.50 | .70 |
| ❑ 61 Scott Mellanby | .75 | .35 |
| ❑ 62 Kirk Muller | .75 | .35 |
| ❑ 63 Ray Sheppard | .75 | .35 |
| ❑ 64 John Vanbiesbrouck | 3.00 | 1.35 |
| ❑ 65 Rob Blake | .75 | .35 |
| ❑ 66 Ray Ferraro | .75 | .35 |
| ❑ 67 Stephane Fiset | 1.50 | .70 |
| ❑ 68 Dimitri Khristich | .75 | .35 |
| ❑ 69 Vladimir Tsyplakov | .75 | .35 |
| ❑ 70 Vincent Damphousse | 1.50 | .70 |
| ❑ 71 Saku Koivu | 3.00 | 1.35 |
| ❑ 72 Mark Recchi | 1.50 | .70 |
| ❑ 73 Stephane Richer | .75 | .35 |
| ❑ 74 Jocelyn Thibault | 1.50 | .70 |
| ❑ 75 Dave Andreychuk | .75 | .35 |
| ❑ 76 Martin Brodeur | 5.00 | 2.20 |
| ❑ 77 Doug Gilmour | 2.00 | .90 |
| ❑ 78 Bobby Holik | .75 | .35 |
| ❑ 79 Denis Pederson | .75 | .35 |
| ❑ 80 Bryan Berard | 1.50 | .70 |
| ❑ 81 Travis Green | .75 | .35 |
| ❑ 82 Zigmund Palffy | 2.00 | .90 |
| ❑ 83 Tommy Salo | 1.50 | .70 |
| ❑ 84 Bryan Smolinski | .75 | .35 |
| ❑ 85 Adam Graves | 1.50 | .70 |
| ❑ 86 Wayne Gretzky | 12.00 | 5.50 |
| ❑ 87 Alexei Kovalev | .75 | .35 |
| ❑ 88 Brian Leetch | 2.00 | .90 |
| ❑ 89 Mark Messier | 2.50 | 1.10 |
| ❑ 90 Mike Richter | 2.00 | .90 |
| ❑ 91 Luc Robitaille | 1.50 | .70 |
| ❑ 92 Daniel Alfredsson | 1.50 | .70 |
| ❑ 93 Alexandre Daigle | 1.50 | .70 |
| ❑ 94 Steve Duchesne | .75 | .35 |
| ❑ 95 Wade Redden | .75 | .35 |
| ❑ 96 Ron Tugnutt | 1.50 | .70 |
| ❑ 97 Alexei Yashin | 1.50 | .70 |
| ❑ 98 Rod Brind'Amour | 1.50 | .70 |
| ❑ 99 Paul Coffey | 2.00 | .90 |
| ❑ 100 Ron Hextall | 1.50 | .70 |
| ❑ 101 John LeClair | 3.00 | 1.35 |
| ❑ 102 Eric Lindros | 6.00 | 2.70 |
| ❑ 103 Janne Niinimaa | 1.50 | .70 |
| ❑ 104 Mikael Renberg | 1.50 | .70 |
| ❑ 105 Dainius Zubrus | 2.00 | .90 |
| ❑ 106 Mike Gartner | 1.50 | .70 |
| ❑ 107 Nikolai Khabibulin | 1.50 | .70 |
| ❑ 108 Jeremy Roenick | 2.00 | .90 |
| ❑ 109 Keith Tkachuk | 2.50 | 1.10 |
| ❑ 110 Oleg Tverdovsky | .75 | .35 |
| ❑ 111 Ron Francis | 1.50 | .70 |
| ❑ 112 Kevin Hatcher | .75 | .35 |
| ❑ 113 Jaromir Jagr | 6.00 | 2.70 |
| ❑ 114 Patrick Lalime | 1.50 | .70 |
| ❑ 115 Petr Nedved | 1.50 | .70 |
| ❑ 116 Ed Olczyk | .75 | .35 |
| ❑ 117 Jim Campbell | .75 | .35 |
| ❑ 118 Geoff Courtnall | .75 | .35 |
| ❑ 119 Grant Fuhr | 1.50 | .70 |
| ❑ 120 Brett Hull | 2.50 | 1.10 |
| ❑ 121 Sergio Momesso | .75 | .35 |
| ❑ 122 Pierre Turgeon | 1.50 | .70 |
| ❑ 123 Ed Belfour | 2.00 | .90 |
| ❑ 124 Jeff Friesen | 1.50 | .70 |
| ❑ 125 Tony Granato | .75 | .35 |
| ❑ 126 Stephen Guolla | .75 | .35 |
| ❑ 127 Bernie Nicholls | .75 | .35 |
| ❑ 128 Owen Nolan | 1.50 | .70 |
| ❑ 129 Dino Ciccarelli | .75 | .35 |
| ❑ 130 John Cullen | .75 | .35 |
| ❑ 131 Chris Gratton | 1.50 | .70 |
| ❑ 132 Roman Hamrlik | .75 | .35 |
| ❑ 133 Daymond Langkow | .75 | .35 |
| ❑ 134 Paul Ysebaert | .75 | .35 |
| ❑ 135 Sergei Berezin | .75 | .35 |
| ❑ 136 Wendel Clark | 1.50 | .70 |
| ❑ 137 Felix Potvin | 2.00 | .90 |
| ❑ 138 Steve Sullivan | .75 | .35 |
| ❑ 139 Mats Sundin | 2.00 | .90 |
| ❑ 140 Pavel Bure | 4.00 | 1.80 |
| ❑ 141 Martin Gelinas | .75 | .35 |
| ❑ 142 Trevor Linden | 1.50 | .70 |
| ❑ 143 Kirk McLean | 1.50 | .70 |
| ❑ 144 Alexander Mogilny | 1.50 | .70 |
| ❑ 145 Peter Bondra | 2.00 | .90 |
| ❑ 146 Dale Hunter | .75 | .35 |
| ❑ 147 Joe Juneau | 1.50 | .70 |
| ❑ 148 Steve Konowalchuk | .75 | .35 |
| ❑ 149 Adam Oates | 1.50 | .70 |
| ❑ 150 Bill Ranford | 1.50 | .70 |

## 1997-98 Pacific Invincible Ice Blue

Randomly inserted in packs at the rate of one in 73, this 150-card set is parallel to the regular gold foil base set only with blue foil enhancements.

| | MINT | NRMT |
|---|---|---|
| COMMON CARD (1-150) | 20.00 | 9.00 |

*STARS: 15X TO 30X BASIC CARDS
*YOUNG STARS: 12.5X TO 25X

## 1997-98 Pacific Invincible Attack Zone

Randomly inserted in packs at the rate of one in 37, this 24-card set features color action player images on a bright, colorful background. The backs carry player information.

| | MINT | NRMT |
|---|---|---|
| COMPLETE SET (24) | 300.00 | 135.00 |
| COMMON CARD (1-24) | 3.00 | 1.35 |
| ❑ 1 Paul Kariya | 25.00 | 11.00 |
| ❑ 2 Teemu Selanne | 12.00 | 5.50 |
| ❑ 3 Michael Peca | 5.00 | 2.20 |
| ❑ 4 Jarome Iginla | 5.00 | 2.20 |
| ❑ 5 Peter Forsberg | 20.00 | 9.00 |
| ❑ 6 Claude Lemieux | 5.00 | 2.20 |
| ❑ 7 Joe Sakic | 12.00 | 5.50 |
| ❑ 8 Mike Modano | 8.00 | 3.60 |
| ❑ 9 Sergei Federov | 12.00 | 5.50 |
| ❑ 10 Brendan Shanahan | 12.00 | 5.50 |
| ❑ 11 Steve Yzerman | 20.00 | 9.00 |
| ❑ 12 Bryan Berard | 5.00 | 2.20 |
| ❑ 13 Zigmund Palffy | 6.00 | 2.70 |
| ❑ 14 Wayne Gretzky | 40.00 | 18.00 |
| ❑ 15 Brian Leetch | 6.00 | 2.70 |
| ❑ 16 Mark Messier | 8.00 | 3.60 |
| ❑ 17 John LeClair | 10.00 | 4.50 |
| ❑ 18 Eric Lindros | 20.00 | 9.00 |
| ❑ 19 Ron Francis | 5.00 | 2.20 |
| ❑ 20 Jaromir Jagr | 20.00 | 9.00 |
| ❑ 21 Brett Hull | 8.00 | 3.60 |
| ❑ 22 Dino Ciccarelli | 3.00 | 1.35 |
| ❑ 23 Pavel Bure | 12.00 | 5.50 |
| ❑ 24 Alexander Mogilny | 5.00 | 2.20 |

## 1997-98 Pacific Invincible Feature Performers

Randomly inserted in packs at the rate of two in 37, this 36-card set features color action player made to look as if they are breaking through the ice.

| | MINT | NRMT |
|---|---|---|
| COMPLETE SET (36) | 300.00 | 135.00 |
| COMMON CARD (1-36) | 3.00 | 1.35 |
| ❑ 1 Paul Kariya | 20.00 | 9.00 |
| ❑ 2 Teemu Selanne | 10.00 | 4.50 |
| ❑ 3 Ray Bourque | 5.00 | 2.20 |
| ❑ 4 Dominik Hasek | 10.00 | 4.50 |
| ❑ 5 Jarome Iginla | 4.00 | 1.80 |
| ❑ 6 Chris Chelios | 5.00 | 2.20 |
| ❑ 7 Peter Forsberg | 15.00 | 6.75 |
| ❑ 8 Claude Lemieux | 4.00 | 1.80 |
| ❑ 9 Patrick Roy | 25.00 | 11.00 |
| ❑ 10 Joe Sakic | 10.00 | 4.50 |
| ❑ 11 Mike Modano | 6.00 | 2.70 |
| ❑ 12 Sergei Fedorov | 10.00 | 4.50 |
| ❑ 13 Vladimir Konstantinov | 3.00 | 1.35 |
| ❑ 14 Brendan Shanahan | 10.00 | 4.50 |
| ❑ 15 Mike Vernon | 4.00 | 1.80 |
| ❑ 16 Steve Yzerman | 15.00 | 6.75 |
| ❑ 17 John Vanbiesbrouck | 8.00 | 3.60 |
| ❑ 18 Saku Koivu | 8.00 | 3.60 |
| ❑ 19 Martin Brodeur | 12.00 | 5.50 |
| ❑ 20 Zigmund Palffy | 5.00 | 2.20 |
| ❑ 21 Wayne Gretzky | 30.00 | 13.50 |
| ❑ 22 Mark Messier | 6.00 | 2.70 |
| ❑ 23 Alexandre Daigle | 4.00 | 1.80 |
| ❑ 24 John LeClair | 8.00 | 3.60 |
| ❑ 25 Eric Lindros | 15.00 | 6.75 |
| ❑ 26 Janne Niinimaa | 4.00 | 1.80 |
| ❑ 27 Jeremy Roenick | 5.00 | 2.20 |
| ❑ 28 Jaromir Jagr | 15.00 | 6.75 |
| ❑ 29 Patrick Lalime | 4.00 | 1.80 |
| ❑ 30 Jim Campbell | 3.00 | 1.35 |
| ❑ 31 Brett Hull | 6.00 | 2.70 |
| ❑ 32 Sergei Berezin | 4.00 | 1.80 |
| ❑ 33 Felix Potvin | 5.00 | 2.20 |
| ❑ 34 Mats Sundin | 5.00 | 2.20 |
| ❑ 35 Alexander Mogilny | 4.00 | 1.80 |
| ❑ 36 Peter Bondra | 5.00 | 2.20 |

## 1997-98 Pacific Invincible NHL Regime Bonus

Randomly inserted one in every pack, this 220-card set features color action player photos with a faint lavender border. The backs carry player information.

| | MINT | NRMT |
|---|---|---|
| COMPLETE SET (220) | 25.00 | 11.00 |
| COMMON CARD (1-220) | .15 | .07 |
| ❑ 1 Ken Baumgartner | .15 | .07 |
| ❑ 2 Mark Janssens | .15 | .07 |
| ❑ 3 Jean-Francois Jomphe | .15 | .07 |
| ❑ 4 Paul Kariya | 1.25 | .55 |
| ❑ 5 Jason Marshall | .15 | .07 |
| ❑ 6 Richard Park | .15 | .07 |
| ❑ 7 Teemu Selanne | .60 | .25 |
| ❑ 8 Mikhail Shtalenkov | .15 | .07 |
| ❑ 9 Bob Beers | .15 | .07 |
| ❑ 10 Ray Bourque | .30 | .14 |
| ❑ 11 Jim Carey | .25 | .11 |
| ❑ 12 Brett Harkins | .15 | .07 |
| ❑ 13 Sheldon Kennedy | .15 | .07 |
| ❑ 14 Troy Mallette | .15 | .07 |
| ❑ 15 Sandy Moger | .15 | .07 |
| ❑ 16 Jon Rohloff | .15 | .07 |
| ❑ 17 Don Sweeney | .15 | .07 |
| ❑ 18 Randy Burridge | .15 | .07 |
| ❑ 19 Michal Grosek | .15 | .07 |
| ❑ 20 Dominik Hasek | .60 | .25 |
| ❑ 21 Rob Ray | .15 | .07 |
| ❑ 22 Steve Shields | .25 | .11 |
| ❑ 23 Richard Smehlik | .15 | .07 |
| ❑ 24 Dixon Ward | .15 | .07 |
| ❑ 25 Mike Wilson | .15 | .07 |
| ❑ 26 Tommy Albelin | .15 | .07 |
| ❑ 27 Aaron Gavey | .15 | .07 |
| ❑ 28 Todd Hlushko | .15 | .07 |
| ❑ 29 Jarome Iginla | .25 | .11 |
| ❑ 30 Yves Racine | .15 | .07 |
| ❑ 31 Dwayne Roloson | .15 | .07 |
| ❑ 32 Mike Sullivan | .15 | .07 |
| ❑ 33 Ed Ward | .15 | .07 |
| ❑ 34 Adam Burt | .15 | .07 |
| ❑ 35 Nelson Emerson | .15 | .07 |
| ❑ 36 Kevin Haller | .15 | .07 |
| ❑ 37 Derek King | .15 | .07 |
| ❑ 38 Curtis Leschyshyn | .15 | .07 |
| ❑ 39 Chris Murray | .15 | .07 |
| ❑ 40 Jason Muzzatti | .15 | .07 |
| ❑ 41 Keith Carney | .15 | .07 |
| ❑ 42 Chris Chelios | .30 | .14 |
| ❑ 43 Enrico Ciccone | .15 | .07 |
| ❑ 44 Jim Cummins | .15 | .07 |
| ❑ 45 Cam Russell | .15 | .07 |
| ❑ 46 Jeff Shantz | .15 | .07 |
| ❑ 47 Michal Sykora | .15 | .07 |
| ❑ 48 Chris Terreri | .25 | .11 |
| ❑ 49 Eric Weinrich | .15 | .07 |
| ❑ 50 Rene Corbet | .15 | .07 |
| ❑ 51 Peter Forsberg | 1.00 | .45 |
| ❑ 52 Alexei Gusarov | .15 | .07 |
| ❑ 53 Uwe Krupp | .15 | .07 |
| ❑ 54 Sylvain Lefebvre | .15 | .07 |
| ❑ 55 Eric Messier | .25 | .11 |
| ❑ 56 Patrick Roy | 1.50 | .70 |
| ❑ 57 Joe Sakic | .60 | .25 |
| ❑ 58 Brent Severyn | .15 | .07 |
| ❑ 59 Greg Adams | .15 | .07 |
| ❑ 60 Todd Harvey | .15 | .07 |
| ❑ 61 Jere Lehtinen | .15 | .07 |
| ❑ 62 Craig Ludwig | .15 | .07 |
| ❑ 63 Mike Modano | .40 | .18 |
| ❑ 64 Andy Moog | .25 | .11 |
| ❑ 65 Dave Reid | .15 | .07 |
| ❑ 66 Roman Turek | .15 | .07 |
| ❑ 67 Doug Brown | .15 | .07 |
| ❑ 68 Kris Draper | .15 | .07 |
| ❑ 69 Sergei Fedorov | .60 | .25 |
| ❑ 70 Joey Kocur | .15 | .07 |
| ❑ 71 Kirk Maltby | .15 | .07 |
| ❑ 72 Bob Rouse | .15 | .07 |
| ❑ 73 Brendan Shanahan | .60 | .25 |
| ❑ 74 Aaron Ward | .15 | .07 |
| ❑ 75 Steve Yzerman | 1.00 | .45 |
| ❑ 76 Greg DeVries | .15 | .07 |
| ❑ 77 Bob Essensa | .25 | .11 |
| ❑ 78 Kevin Lowe | .15 | .07 |
| ❑ 79 Bryan Marchment | .15 | .07 |
| ❑ 80 Dean McAmmond | .15 | .07 |
| ❑ 81 Boris Mironov | .15 | .07 |
| ❑ 82 Luke Richardson | .15 | .07 |
| ❑ 83 Ryan Smyth | .25 | .11 |
| ❑ 84 Terry Carkner | .15 | .07 |
| ❑ 85 Ed Jovanovski | .15 | .07 |
| ❑ 86 Bill Lindsay | .15 | .07 |
| ❑ 87 Dave Lowry | .15 | .07 |
| ❑ 88 Gord Murphy | .15 | .07 |
| ❑ 89 John Vanbiesbrouck | .50 | .23 |
| ❑ 90 Steve Washburn | .15 | .07 |
| ❑ 91 Chris Wells | .15 | .07 |
| ❑ 92 Philippe Boucher | .15 | .07 |
| ❑ 93 Steven Finn | .15 | .07 |
| ❑ 94 Mattias Norstrom | .15 | .07 |
| ❑ 95 Kai Nurminen | .15 | .07 |
| ❑ 96 Sean O'Donnell | .15 | .07 |
| ❑ 97 Yanic Perreault | .15 | .07 |
| ❑ 98 Jeff Shevalier | .15 | .07 |
| ❑ 99 Brad Smyth | .15 | .07 |
| ❑ 100 Brad Brown | .15 | .07 |
| ❑ 101 Jassen Cullimore | .15 | .07 |
| ❑ 102 Vincent Damphousse | .25 | .11 |
| ❑ 103 Vladimir Malakhov | .15 | .07 |
| ❑ 104 Peter Popovic | .15 | .07 |
| ❑ 105 Stephane Richer | .25 | .11 |
| ❑ 106 Turner Stevenson | .15 | .07 |
| ❑ 107 Jose Theodore | .25 | .11 |
| ❑ 108 Martin Brodeur | .75 | .35 |
| ❑ 109 Bob Carpenter | .15 | .07 |
| ❑ 110 Mike Dunham | .25 | .11 |
| ❑ 111 Patrik Elias | .30 | .14 |
| ❑ 112 Dave Ellett | .15 | .07 |
| ❑ 113 Doug Gilmour | .25 | .11 |
| ❑ 114 Randy McKay | .15 | .07 |
| ❑ 115 Todd Bertuzzi | .15 | .07 |
| ❑ 116 Kenny Jonsson | .15 | .07 |
| ❑ 117 Paul Kruse | .15 | .07 |
| ❑ 118 Claude Lapointe | .15 | .07 |
| ❑ 119 Zigmund Palffy | .30 | .14 |
| ❑ 120 Richard Pilon | .15 | .07 |
| ❑ 121 Dan Plante | .15 | .07 |
| ❑ 122 Dennis Vaske | .15 | .07 |
| ❑ 123 Shane Churla | .15 | .07 |
| ❑ 124 Bruce Driver | .15 | .07 |
| ❑ 125 Mike Eastwood | .15 | .07 |
| ❑ 126 Patrick Flatley | .15 | .07 |
| ❑ 127 Adam Graves | .25 | .11 |
| ❑ 128 Wayne Gretzky | 2.00 | .90 |
| ❑ 129 Brian Leetch | .30 | .14 |
| ❑ 130 Doug Lidster | .15 | .07 |
| ❑ 131 Mark Messier | .40 | .18 |
| ❑ 132 Tom Chorske | .15 | .07 |
| ❑ 133 Sean Hill | .15 | .07 |
| ❑ 134 Denny Lambert | .15 | .07 |
| ❑ 135 Janne Laukkanen | .15 | .07 |
| ❑ 136 Frank Musil | .15 | .07 |
| ❑ 137 Lance Pitlick | .15 | .07 |
| ❑ 138 Shaun Van Allen | .15 | .07 |
| ❑ 139 Rod Brind'Amour | .25 | .11 |
| ❑ 140 Paul Coffey | .30 | .14 |
| ❑ 141 Karl Dykhuis | .15 | .07 |
| ❑ 142 Dan Kordic | .15 | .07 |
| ❑ 143 Daniel Lacroix | .15 | .07 |
| ❑ 144 John LeClair | .50 | .23 |
| ❑ 145 Eric Lindros | 1.00 | .45 |
| ❑ 146 Joel Otto | .15 | .07 |
| ❑ 147 Shjon Podein | .15 | .07 |
| ❑ 148 Chris Therien | .15 | .07 |
| ❑ 149 Shane Doan | .15 | .07 |
| ❑ 150 Dallas Drake | .15 | .07 |
| ❑ 151 Jeff Finley | .15 | .07 |
| ❑ 152 Mike Gartner | .15 | .07 |
| ❑ 153 Nikolai Khabibulin | .25 | .11 |
| ❑ 154 Darrin Shannon | .15 | .07 |
| ❑ 155 Mike Stapleton | .15 | .07 |
| ❑ 156 Keith Tkachuk | .50 | .23 |
| ❑ 157 Tom Barrasso | .25 | .11 |
| ❑ 158 Josef Beranek | .15 | .07 |
| ❑ 159 Alex Hicks | .15 | .07 |
| ❑ 160 Jaromir Jagr | 1.00 | .45 |
| ❑ 161 Patrick Lalime | .25 | .11 |
| ❑ 162 Francois Leroux | .15 | .07 |
| ❑ 163 Petr Nedved | .25 | .11 |
| ❑ 164 Roman Oksiuta | .15 | .07 |
| ❑ 165 Chris Tamer | .15 | .07 |
| ❑ 166 Marc Bergevin | .15 | .07 |
| ❑ 167 Jon Casey | .25 | .11 |
| ❑ 168 Craig Conroy | .15 | .07 |
| ❑ 169 Brett Hull | .40 | .18 |
| ❑ 170 Igor Kravchuk | .15 | .07 |
| ❑ 171 Stephen Leach | .15 | .07 |
| ❑ 172 Ricard Persson | .15 | .07 |
| ❑ 173 Pierre Turgeon | .25 | .11 |
| ❑ 174 Ed Belfour | .30 | .14 |
| ❑ 175 Doug Bodger | .15 | .07 |
| ❑ 176 Shean Donovan | .15 | .07 |
| ❑ 177 Bob Errey | .15 | .07 |
| ❑ 178 Todd Ewen | .15 | .07 |
| ❑ 179 Wade Flaherty | .15 | .07 |
| ❑ 180 Mike Rathje | .15 | .07 |
| ❑ 181 Ron Sutter | .15 | .07 |
| ❑ 182 Mikael Andersson | .15 | .07 |
| ❑ 183 Dino Ciccarelli | .15 | .07 |
| ❑ 184 Cory Cross | .15 | .07 |
| ❑ 185 Jamie Huscroft | .15 | .07 |
| ❑ 186 Rudy Poeschek | .15 | .07 |
| ❑ 187 Daren Puppa | .25 | .11 |
| ❑ 188 David Shaw | .15 | .07 |
| ❑ 189 Jay Wells | .15 | .07 |
| ❑ 190 Jamie Baker | .15 | .07 |
| ❑ 191 Sergei Berezin | .25 | .11 |
| ❑ 192 Brandon Convery | .15 | .07 |
| ❑ 193 Darby Hendrickson | .15 | .07 |
| ❑ 194 Matt Martin | .15 | .07 |
| ❑ 195 Felix Potvin | .30 | .14 |
| ❑ 196 Jason Smith | .15 | .07 |
| ❑ 197 Craig Wolanin | .15 | .07 |
| ❑ 198 Adrian Aucoin | .15 | .07 |
| ❑ 199 Dave Babych | .15 | .07 |
| ❑ 200 Donald Brashear | .15 | .07 |
| ❑ 201 Pavel Bure | .60 | .25 |
| ❑ 202 Chris Joseph | .15 | .07 |
| ❑ 203 Alexander Mogilny | .25 | .11 |
| ❑ 204 David Roberts | .15 | .07 |
| ❑ 205 Scott Walker | .15 | .07 |
| ❑ 206 Peter Bondra | .30 | .14 |
| ❑ 207 Andrew Brunette | .15 | .07 |
| ❑ 208 Calle Johansson | .15 | .07 |
| ❑ 209 Ken Klee | .15 | .07 |
| ❑ 210 Olaf Kolzig | .25 | .11 |
| ❑ 211 Kelly Miller | .15 | .07 |
| ❑ 212 Joe Reekie | .15 | .07 |
| ❑ 213 Chris Simon | .15 | .07 |
| ❑ 214 Brendan Witt | .15 | .07 |
| ❑ 215 Paul Kariya TL | .60 | .25 |
| ❑ 216 Peter Forsberg TL | .50 | .23 |
| ❑ 217 Patrick Roy TL | .75 | .35 |
| ❑ 218 Wayne Gretzky TL | 1.00 | .45 |
| ❑ 219 Eric Lindros TL | .50 | .23 |
| ❑ 220 Jaromir Jagr TL | .50 | .23 |

## 1997-98 Pacific Invincible Off The Glass

Randomly inserted in packs at the rate of one in 73, this 20-card set features borderless color action photos of top hockey players with gold foil highlights.

| | MINT | NRMT |
|---|---|---|
| COMPLETE SET (20) | 500.00 | 220.00 |
| COMMON CARD (1-20) | 6.00 | 2.70 |
| ❑ 1 Paul Kariya | 50.00 | 22.00 |
| ❑ 2 Teemu Selanne | 25.00 | 11.00 |
| ❑ 3 Michael Peca | 8.00 | 3.60 |
| ❑ 4 Jarome Iginla | 8.00 | 3.60 |
| ❑ 5 Peter Forsberg | 40.00 | 18.00 |
| ❑ 6 Joe Sakic | 25.00 | 11.00 |
| ❑ 7 Sergei Fedorov | 25.00 | 11.00 |
| ❑ 8 Brendan Shanahan | 25.00 | 11.00 |
| ❑ 9 Steve Yzerman | 40.00 | 18.00 |
| ❑ 10 Mike Grier | 6.00 | 2.70 |
| ❑ 11 Saku Koivu | 20.00 | 9.00 |
| ❑ 12 Wayne Gretzky | 80.00 | 36.00 |
| ❑ 13 Mark Messier | 15.00 | 6.75 |
| ❑ 14 Eric Lindros | 40.00 | 18.00 |
| ❑ 15 Dainius Zubrus | 8.00 | 3.60 |
| ❑ 16 Keith Tkachuk | 15.00 | 6.75 |
| ❑ 17 Jaromir Jagr | 40.00 | 18.00 |
| ❑ 18 Brett Hull | 15.00 | 6.75 |
| ❑ 19 Sergei Berezin | 8.00 | 3.60 |
| ❑ 20 Pavel Bure | 25.00 | 11.00 |

## 1997-98 Pacific Omega

The 1997-98 Pacific Omega set was issued in one series totalling 250 cards and was distributed in six-card packs with a suggested retail price of $1.99. The fronts feature color action photos etched in foil of players who are popular with fans. The backs carry another photo and the player's accomplishments.

| | MINT | NRMT |
|---|---|---|
| COMPLETE SET (250) | 40.00 | 18.00 |
| COMMON CARD (1-250) | .15 | .07 |

| | | |
|---|---|---|
| ❑ 1 Matt Cullen | .15 | .07 |
| ❑ 2 Guy Hebert | .30 | .14 |
| ❑ 3 Paul Kariya | 1.50 | .70 |
| ❑ 4 Dmitri Mironov | .15 | .07 |
| ❑ 5 Steve Rucchin | .15 | .07 |
| ❑ 6 Tomas Sandstrom | .15 | .07 |
| ❑ 7 Dimitri Khristich | .15 | .07 |
| ❑ 8 Mikhail Shtalenkov | .15 | .07 |
| ❑ 9 Pavel Trnka | .15 | .07 |
| ❑ 10 Jason Allison | .30 | .14 |
| ❑ 11 Per Axelsson | .15 | .07 |
| ❑ 12 Ray Bourque | .40 | .18 |
| ❑ 13 Anson Carter | .15 | .07 |
| ❑ 14 Byron Dafoe | .30 | .14 |
| ❑ 15 Ted Donato | .15 | .07 |
| ❑ 16 Hal Gill | .15 | .07 |
| ❑ 17 Dmitri Khristich | .15 | .07 |
| ❑ 18 Sergei Samsonov | 1.00 | .45 |
| ❑ 19 Joe Thornton | .75 | .35 |
| ❑ 20 Jason Dawe | .15 | .07 |
| ❑ 21 Michal Grosek | .15 | .07 |
| ❑ 22 Dominik Hasek | .75 | .35 |
| ❑ 23 Brian Holzinger | .15 | .07 |
| ❑ 24 Michael Peca | .15 | .07 |
| ❑ 25 Derek Plante | .15 | .07 |
| ❑ 26 Miroslav Satan | .15 | .07 |
| ❑ 27 Steve Shields | .30 | .14 |
| ❑ 28 Andrew Cassels | .15 | .07 |
| ❑ 29 Theoren Fleury | .30 | .14 |
| ❑ 30 Jarome Iginla | .30 | .14 |
| ❑ 31 Derek Morris | .15 | .07 |
| ❑ 32 Tyler Moss | .15 | .07 |
| ❑ 33 Michael Nylander | .15 | .07 |
| ❑ 34 Dwayne Roloson | .30 | .14 |
| ❑ 35 Cory Stillman | .15 | .07 |
| ❑ 36 Rick Tabaracci | .30 | .14 |
| ❑ 37 German Titov | .15 | .07 |
| ❑ 38 Jon Battaglia | .15 | .07 |
| ❑ 39 Nelson Emerson | .15 | .07 |
| ❑ 40 Martin Gelinas | .15 | .07 |
| ❑ 41 Sami Kapanen | .30 | .14 |
| ❑ 42 Trevor Kidd | .30 | .14 |
| ❑ 43 Kevin Dineen | .15 | .07 |
| ❑ 44 Keith Primeau | .15 | .07 |
| ❑ 45 Gary Roberts | .15 | .07 |
| ❑ 46 Tony Amonte | .30 | .14 |
| ❑ 47 Keith Carney | .15 | .07 |
| ❑ 48 Chris Chelios | .40 | .18 |
| ❑ 49 Eric Daze | .30 | .14 |
| ❑ 50 Brian Felsner | .15 | .07 |
| ❑ 51 Jeff Hackett | .30 | .14 |
| ❑ 52 Christian LaFlamme | .15 | .07 |
| ❑ 53 Alexei Zhamnov | .15 | .07 |
| ❑ 54 Craig Billington | .30 | .14 |
| ❑ 55 Adam Deadmarsh | .30 | .14 |
| ❑ 56 Peter Forsberg | 1.25 | .55 |
| ❑ 57 Valeri Kamensky | .30 | .14 |
| ❑ 58 Uwe Krupp | .15 | .07 |
| ❑ 59 Jari Kurri | .30 | .14 |
| ❑ 60 Claude Lemieux | .30 | .14 |
| ❑ 61 Eric Messier | .30 | .14 |
| ❑ 62 Jeff Odgers | .15 | .07 |
| ❑ 63 Sandis Ozolinsh | .30 | .14 |
| ❑ 64 Patrick Roy | 2.00 | .90 |
| ❑ 65 Joe Sakic | .75 | .35 |
| ❑ 66 Greg Adams | .15 | .07 |
| ❑ 67 Ed Belfour | .40 | .18 |
| ❑ 68 Manny Fernandez | .15 | .07 |
| ❑ 69 Derian Hatcher | .15 | .07 |
| ❑ 70 Jamie Langenbrunner | .15 | .07 |
| ❑ 71 Jere Lehtinen | .15 | .07 |
| ❑ 72 Juha Lind | .15 | .07 |
| ❑ 73 Mike Modano | .50 | .23 |
| ❑ 74 Joe Nieuwendyk | .30 | .14 |
| ❑ 75 Darryl Sydor | .15 | .07 |
| ❑ 76 Pat Verbeek | .15 | .07 |
| ❑ 77 Sergei Zubov | .15 | .07 |
| ❑ 78 Viacheslav Fetisov | .15 | .07 |
| ❑ 79 Brent Gilchrist | .15 | .07 |
| ❑ 80 Kevin Hodson | .30 | .14 |
| ❑ 81 Vyacheslav Kozlov | .15 | .07 |
| ❑ 82 Igor Larionov | .15 | .07 |
| ❑ 83 Nicklas Lidstrom | .30 | .14 |
| ❑ 84 Darren McCarty | .15 | .07 |
| ❑ 85 Larry Murphy | .15 | .07 |
| ❑ 86 Chris Osgood | .40 | .18 |
| ❑ 87 Brendan Shanahan | .75 | .35 |
| ❑ 88 Steve Yzerman | 1.25 | .55 |
| ❑ 89 Kelly Buchberger | .15 | .07 |
| ❑ 90 Mike Grier | .15 | .07 |
| ❑ 91 Bill Guerin | .30 | .14 |
| ❑ 92 Roman Hamrlik | .15 | .07 |
| ❑ 93 Curtis Joseph | .40 | .18 |
| ❑ 94 Boris Mironov | .15 | .07 |
| ❑ 95 Ryan Smyth | .30 | .14 |
| ❑ 96 Doug Weight | .30 | .14 |
| ❑ 97 Dino Ciccarelli | .15 | .07 |
| ❑ 98 Dave Gagner | .15 | .07 |
| ❑ 99 Ed Jovanovski | .30 | .14 |
| ❑ 100 Scott Mellanby | .15 | .07 |
| ❑ 101 Robert Svehla | .15 | .07 |
| ❑ 102 John Vanbiesbrouck | .60 | .25 |
| ❑ 103 Steve Washburn | .15 | .07 |
| ❑ 104 Kevin Weekes | .15 | .07 |
| ❑ 105 Ray Whitney | .15 | .07 |
| ❑ 106 Rob Blake | .15 | .07 |
| ❑ 107 Stephane Fiset | .30 | .14 |
| ❑ 108 Garry Galley | .15 | .07 |
| ❑ 109 Steve McKenna | .15 | .07 |
| ❑ 110 Glen Murray | .15 | .07 |
| ❑ 111 Yanic Perreault | .15 | .07 |
| ❑ 112 Luc Robitaille | .30 | .14 |
| ❑ 113 Jamie Storr | .30 | .14 |
| ❑ 114 Jozef Stumpel | .30 | .14 |
| ❑ 115 Vladimir Tsyplakov | .15 | .07 |
| ❑ 116 Shayne Corson | .15 | .07 |
| ❑ 117 Vincent Damphousse | .30 | .14 |
| ❑ 118 Saku Koivu | .60 | .25 |
| ❑ 119 Vladimir Malakhov | .15 | .07 |
| ❑ 120 Andy Moog | .30 | .14 |
| ❑ 121 Mark Recchi | .30 | .14 |
| ❑ 122 Martin Rucinsky | .15 | .07 |
| ❑ 123 Brian Savage | .15 | .07 |
| ❑ 124 Jocelyn Thibault | .30 | .14 |
| ❑ 125 Jason Arnott | .30 | .14 |
| ❑ 126 Brad Bombardir | .15 | .07 |
| ❑ 127 Martin Brodeur | 1.00 | .45 |
| ❑ 128 Patrik Elias | .50 | .23 |
| ❑ 129 Doug Gilmour | .40 | .18 |
| ❑ 130 Bobby Holik | .15 | .07 |
| ❑ 131 Randy McKay | .15 | .07 |
| ❑ 132 Scott Niedermayer | .15 | .07 |
| ❑ 133 Krzysztof Oliwa | .15 | .07 |
| ❑ 134 Scott Stevens | .15 | .07 |
| ❑ 135 Petr Sykora | .15 | .07 |
| ❑ 136 Bryan Berard | .15 | .07 |
| ❑ 137 Travis Green | .15 | .07 |
| ❑ 138 Bryan McCabe | .15 | .07 |
| ❑ 139 Sergei Nemchinov | .15 | .07 |
| ❑ 140 Zigmund Palffy | .40 | .18 |
| ❑ 141 Robert Reichel | .15 | .07 |
| ❑ 142 Tommy Salo | .30 | .14 |
| ❑ 143 Bryan Smolinski | .15 | .07 |
| ❑ 144 Adam Graves | .30 | .14 |
| ❑ 145 Wayne Gretzky | 2.50 | 1.10 |
| ❑ 146 Pat LaFontaine | .30 | .14 |
| ❑ 147 Brian Leetch | .40 | .18 |
| ❑ 148 Mike Richter | .40 | .18 |
| ❑ 149 Kevin Stevens | .30 | .14 |
| ❑ 150 Niklas Sundstrom | .15 | .07 |
| ❑ 151 Tim Sweeney | .15 | .07 |
| ❑ 152 Daniel Alfredsson | .30 | .14 |
| ❑ 153 Magnus Arvedson | .15 | .07 |
| ❑ 154 Andreas Dackell | .15 | .07 |
| ❑ 155 Igor Kravchuk | .15 | .07 |
| ❑ 156 Shawn McEachern | .15 | .07 |
| ❑ 157 Damian Rhodes | .30 | .14 |
| ❑ 158 Ron Tugnutt | .30 | .14 |
| ❑ 159 Alexei Yashin | .30 | .14 |
| ❑ 160 Rod Brind'Amour | .30 | .14 |
| ❑ 161 Paul Coffey | .40 | .18 |
| ❑ 162 Eric Desjardins | .15 | .07 |
| ❑ 163 Colin Forbes | .15 | .07 |
| ❑ 164 Chris Gratton | .30 | .14 |
| ❑ 165 Ron Hextall | .30 | .14 |
| ❑ 166 Trent Klatt | .15 | .07 |
| ❑ 167 John LeClair | .60 | .25 |
| ❑ 168 Eric Lindros | 1.25 | .55 |
| ❑ 169 Joel Otto | .15 | .07 |
| ❑ 170 Garth Snow | .30 | .14 |
| ❑ 171 Dainius Zubrus | .40 | .18 |
| ❑ 172 Dallas Drake | .15 | .07 |
| ❑ 173 Mike Gartner | .30 | .14 |
| ❑ 174 Nikolai Khabibulin | .30 | .14 |
| ❑ 175 Teppo Numminen | .15 | .07 |
| ❑ 176 Jeremy Roenick | .40 | .18 |
| ❑ 177 Keith Tkachuk | .50 | .23 |
| ❑ 178 Rick Tocchet | .30 | .14 |
| ❑ 179 Oleg Tverdovsky | .15 | .07 |
| ❑ 180 Juha Ylonen | .15 | .07 |
| ❑ 181 Stu Barnes | .15 | .07 |
| ❑ 182 Tom Barrasso | .30 | .14 |
| ❑ 183 Rob Brown | .15 | .07 |
| ❑ 184 Ron Francis | .30 | .14 |
| ❑ 185 Kevin Hatcher | .15 | .07 |
| ❑ 186 Jaromir Jagr | 1.25 | .55 |
| ❑ 187 Alexei Morozov | .30 | .14 |
| ❑ 188 Ed Olczyk | .15 | .07 |
| ❑ 189 Jim Campbell | .15 | .07 |
| ❑ 190 Geoff Courtnall | .15 | .07 |
| ❑ 191 Pavol Demitra | .15 | .07 |
| ❑ 192 Steve Duchesne | .15 | .07 |
| ❑ 193 Grant Fuhr | .30 | .14 |
| ❑ 194 Brett Hull | .50 | .23 |
| ❑ 195 Al MacInnis | .30 | .14 |
| ❑ 196 Chris Pronger | .30 | .14 |
| ❑ 197 Pascal Rheaume | .15 | .07 |
| ❑ 198 Jamie Rivers | .15 | .07 |
| ❑ 199 Pierre Turgeon | .30 | .14 |
| ❑ 200 Jeff Friesen | .30 | .14 |
| ❑ 201 Tony Granato | .15 | .07 |
| ❑ 202 John MacLean | .15 | .07 |
| ❑ 203 Patrick Marleau | .75 | .35 |
| ❑ 204 Marty McSorley | .15 | .07 |
| ❑ 205 Owen Nolan | .30 | .14 |
| ❑ 206 Marco Sturm | .60 | .25 |
| ❑ 207 Mike Vernon | .30 | .14 |
| ❑ 208 Andrei Zyuzin | .15 | .07 |
| ❑ 209 Karl Dykhuis | .15 | .07 |
| ❑ 210 Daymond Langkow | .15 | .07 |
| ❑ 211 Louie DeBrusk | .15 | .07 |
| ❑ 212 Daren Puppa | .30 | .14 |
| ❑ 213 Mikael Renberg | .30 | .14 |
| ❑ 214 Alexander Selivanov | .15 | .07 |
| ❑ 215 Paul Ysebaert | .15 | .07 |
| ❑ 216 Rob Zamuner | .15 | .07 |
| ❑ 217 Sergei Berezin | .15 | .07 |
| ❑ 218 Wendel Clark | .30 | .14 |
| ❑ 219 Marcel Cousineau | .30 | .14 |
| ❑ 220 Tie Domi | .15 | .07 |
| ❑ 221 Mike Johnson | .40 | .18 |
| ❑ 222 Igor Korolev | .15 | .07 |
| ❑ 223 Felix Potvin | .40 | .18 |
| ❑ 224 Mathieu Schneider | .15 | .07 |
| ❑ 225 Mats Sundin | .40 | .18 |
| ❑ 226 Yannick Tremblay | .15 | .07 |
| ❑ 227 Donald Brashear | .15 | .07 |
| ❑ 228 Pavel Bure | .75 | .35 |
| ❑ 229 Sean Burke | .30 | .14 |
| ❑ 230 Trevor Linden | .30 | .14 |
| ❑ 231 Mark Messier | .50 | .23 |
| ❑ 232 Alexander Mogilny | .30 | .14 |
| ❑ 233 Markus Naslund | .15 | .07 |
| ❑ 234 Mattias Ohlund | .30 | .14 |
| ❑ 235 Dave Scatchard | .15 | .07 |
| ❑ 236 Peter Bondra | .40 | .18 |
| ❑ 237 Andrew Brunette | .15 | .07 |
| ❑ 238 Phil Housley | .15 | .07 |
| ❑ 239 Dale Hunter | .15 | .07 |
| ❑ 240 Calle Johansson | .15 | .07 |
| ❑ 241 Joe Juneau | .30 | .14 |
| ❑ 242 Olaf Kolzig | .30 | .14 |
| ❑ 243 Adam Oates | .30 | .14 |
| ❑ 244 Richard Zednik | .15 | .07 |
| ❑ 245 Chris Chelios<br>Keith Tkachuk | .30 | .14 |
| ❑ 246 Mike Modano<br>Ed Belfour | .15 | .07 |
| ❑ 247 Teemu Selanne<br>Saku Koivu | .40 | .18 |
| ❑ 248 Eric Lindros<br>Shayne Corson | .60 | .25 |
| ❑ 249 Patrick Roy<br>Martin Brodeur | 1.00 | .45 |
| ❑ 250 Wayne Gretzky<br>Mark Messier | 1.50 | .70 |
| ❑ S73 Mike Modano SAMPLE | 1.00 | .45 |

## 1997-98 Pacific Omega Ice Blue

Randomly inserted in both Canadian and U.S. hobby and retail packs at the rate of one in 73, this 250-card set is parallel to the base set with blue foil highlights.

| | MINT | NRMT |
|---|---|---|
| COMMON CARD (1-250) | 15.00 | 6.75 |
| SEMISTARS/GOALIES | 40.00 | 18.00 |
| UNLISTED STARS | 50.00 | 22.00 |

*STARS: 60X TO 120X BASIC CARDS
*YNG.STARS: 50X TO 100X
*RC's: 40X TO 80X

## 1997-98 Pacific Omega Game Face Die-Cut Cel-Fusions

Randomly inserted in hobby and retail packs at the rate of one in 37, this 20-card set features color photos of top goalies printed on die-cut helment-shaped cards with a cel facemask. The backs carry player information and describe his talents as a goalie.

| | MINT | NRMT |
|---|---|---|
| COMPLETE SET (20) | 200.00 | 90.00 |
| COMMON CARD (1-20) | 4.00 | 1.80 |

| | | |
|---|---|---|
| ❑ 1 Paul Kariya | 20.00 | 9.00 |
| ❑ 2 Teemu Selanne | 10.00 | 4.50 |
| ❑ 3 Peter Forsberg | 15.00 | 6.75 |
| ❑ 4 Joe Sakic | 10.00 | 4.50 |
| ❑ 5 Mike Modano | 6.00 | 2.70 |
| ❑ 6 Nicklas Lidstrom | 4.00 | 1.80 |
| ❑ 7 Brendan Shanahan | 10.00 | 4.50 |
| ❑ 8 Steve Yzerman | 15.00 | 6.75 |
| ❑ 9 Ryan Smyth | 4.00 | 1.80 |
| ❑ 10 Saku Koivu | 8.00 | 3.60 |
| ❑ 11 Wayne Gretzky | 30.00 | 13.50 |
| ❑ 12 John LeClair | 8.00 | 3.60 |
| ❑ 13 Eric Lindros | 15.00 | 6.75 |
| ❑ 14 Dainius Zubrus | 4.00 | 1.80 |
| ❑ 15 Keith Tkachuk | 6.00 | 2.70 |
| ❑ 16 Jaromir Jagr | 15.00 | 6.75 |
| ❑ 17 Brett Hull | 6.00 | 2.70 |
| ❑ 18 Pavel Bure | 10.00 | 4.50 |
| ❑ 19 Mark Messier | 6.00 | 2.70 |
| ❑ 20 Peter Bondra | 5.00 | 2.20 |

## 1997-98 Pacific Omega No Scoring Zone

Randomly inserted in hobby and retail packs at the rate of two in 37, this 10-card set features color photos of the most popular goalies printed on full foil cards with foil highlights.

| | MINT | NRMT |
|---|---|---|
| COMPLETE SET (10) | 80.00 | 36.00 |
| COMMON CARD (1-10) | 4.00 | 1.80 |

| | | |
|---|---|---|
| ❑ 1 Dominik Hasek | 10.00 | 4.50 |
| ❑ 2 Patrick Roy | 25.00 | 11.00 |
| ❑ 3 Ed Belfour | 5.00 | 2.20 |
| ❑ 4 Chris Osgood | 5.00 | 2.20 |
| ❑ 5 John Vanbiesbrouck | 8.00 | 3.60 |
| ❑ 6 Andy Moog | 4.00 | 1.80 |
| ❑ 7 Martin Brodeur | 12.00 | 5.50 |
| ❑ 8 Mike Richter | 5.00 | 2.20 |
| ❑ 9 Ron Hextall | 4.00 | 1.80 |
| ❑ 10 Felix Potvin | 5.00 | 2.20 |

## 1997-98 Pacific Omega Silks

Randomly inserted in hobby and retail packs at the rate of one in 73, this 12-card set features color photos of top players printed on a silk-like fabric card stock.

| | MINT | NRMT |
|---|---|---|
| COMPLETE SET (12) | 300.00 | 135.00 |
| COMMON CARD (1-12) | 12.00 | 5.50 |

| | | |
|---|---|---|
| ❑ 1 Paul Kariya | 40.00 | 18.00 |
| ❑ 2 Teemu Selanne | 20.00 | 9.00 |
| ❑ 3 Peter Forsberg | 30.00 | 13.50 |
| ❑ 4 Patrick Roy | 50.00 | 22.00 |
| ❑ 5 Joe Sakic | 20.00 | 9.00 |
| ❑ 6 Steve Yzerman | 30.00 | 13.50 |
| ❑ 7 Martin Brodeur | 25.00 | 11.00 |
| ❑ 8 Wayne Gretzky | 60.00 | 27.00 |
| ❑ 9 Eric Lindros | 30.00 | 13.50 |
| ❑ 10 Jaromir Jagr | 30.00 | 13.50 |
| ❑ 11 Pavel Bure | 20.00 | 9.00 |
| ❑ 12 Mark Messier | 12.00 | 5.50 |

## 1997-98 Pacific Omega Stick Handle Laser Cuts

Randomly inserted in hobby and retail packs at the rate of one in 145, this 20-card set features color photos of popular players printed on full foil card stock with laser-cut hockey sticks crossing in the background. The backs carry a description of the player's accomplishments on ice.

| | MINT | NRMT |
|---|---|---|
| COMPLETE SET (20) | 600.00 | 275.00 |
| COMMON CARD (1-20) | 12.00 | 5.50 |

| | | |
|---|---|---|
| ❑ 1 Paul Kariya | 60.00 | 27.00 |
| ❑ 2 Teemu Selanne | 30.00 | 13.50 |
| ❑ 3 Theoren Fleury | 12.00 | 5.50 |
| ❑ 4 Chris Chelios | 15.00 | 6.75 |
| ❑ 5 Peter Forsberg | 50.00 | 22.00 |
| ❑ 6 Joe Sakic | 30.00 | 13.50 |
| ❑ 7 Mike Modano | 20.00 | 9.00 |
| ❑ 8 Brendan Shanahan | 30.00 | 13.50 |
| ❑ 9 Steve Yzerman | 50.00 | 22.00 |
| ❑ 10 Saku Koivu | 25.00 | 11.00 |
| ❑ 11 Doug Gilmour | 15.00 | 6.75 |
| ❑ 12 Zigmund Palffy | 15.00 | 6.75 |
| ❑ 13 Wayne Gretzky | 100.00 | 45.00 |
| ❑ 14 Pat LaFontaine | 12.00 | 5.50 |
| ❑ 15 John LeClair | 25.00 | 11.00 |
| ❑ 16 Eric Lindros | 50.00 | 22.00 |
| ❑ 17 Jaromir Jagr | 50.00 | 22.00 |
| ❑ 18 Mats Sundin | 15.00 | 6.75 |
| ❑ 19 Pavel Bure | 30.00 | 13.50 |
| ❑ 20 Mark Messier | 20.00 | 9.00 |

## 1997-98 Pacific Omega Team Leaders

Randomly inserted in Canadian retail packs only at the rate of two in 48, this 20-card set features color photos of top favorite players printed on fully foiled cards. The backs carry a description of their accomplishments on ice.

| | MINT | NRMT |
|---|---|---|
| COMPLETE SET (20) | 250.00 | 110.00 |
| COMMON CARD (1-20) | 4.00 | 1.80 |

| | | |
|---|---|---|
| ❑ 1 Paul Kariya | 25.00 | 11.00 |
| ❑ 2 Ray Bourque | 6.00 | 2.70 |
| ❑ 3 Theoren Fleury | 5.00 | 2.20 |
| ❑ 4 Patrick Roy | 30.00 | 13.50 |
| ❑ 5 Joe Sakic | 12.00 | 5.50 |
| ❑ 6 Ed Belfour | 6.00 | 2.70 |
| ❑ 7 Joe Nieuwendyk | 5.00 | 2.20 |
| ❑ 8 Brendan Shanahan | 12.00 | 5.50 |
| ❑ 9 Steve Yzerman | 20.00 | 9.00 |
| ❑ 10 Ryan Smyth | 5.00 | 2.20 |
| ❑ 11 Shayne Corson | 4.00 | 1.80 |
| ❑ 12 Mark Recchi | 5.00 | 2.20 |
| ❑ 13 Martin Brodeur | 15.00 | 6.75 |
| ❑ 14 Wayne Gretzky | 40.00 | 18.00 |
| ❑ 15 Rod Brind'Amour | 5.00 | 2.20 |
| ❑ 16 Eric Lindros | 20.00 | 9.00 |
| ❑ 17 Chris Pronger | 5.00 | 2.20 |
| ❑ 18 Felix Potvin | 6.00 | 2.70 |
| ❑ 19 Pavel Bure | 12.00 | 5.50 |
| ❑ 20 Mark Messier | 8.00 | 3.60 |

## 1998-99 Pacific Omega

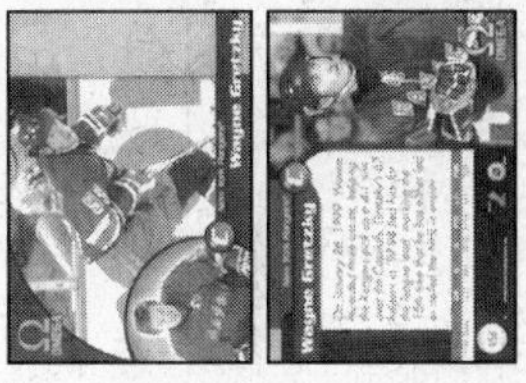

The 1998-99 Pacific Omega set was issued in one series totalling 250 cards and was distributed in six-card packs with a suggested retail price of $1.99. The fronts feature color action photos of the NHL's greatest stars and most exciting rookies printed on etched silver foil cards. The backs carry player information and career statistics.

| | MINT | NRMT |
|---|---|---|
| COMPLETE SET (252) | 80.00 | 36.00 |
| COMP.SET w/o SP's (1-250) | 40.00 | 18.00 |
| COMMON CARD (1-252) | .15 | .07 |

| | | |
|---|---|---|
| ❑ 1 Travis Green | .15 | .07 |
| ❑ 2 Stu Grimson | .15 | .07 |
| ❑ 3 Guy Hebert | .30 | .14 |
| ❑ 4 Paul Kariya | 1.50 | .70 |
| ❑ 5 Marty McInnis | .15 | .07 |
| ❑ 6 Fredrik Olausson | .15 | .07 |
| ❑ 7 Steve Rucchin | .15 | .07 |
| ❑ 8 Teemu Selanne | .75 | .35 |
| ❑ 9 Johan Davidsson<br>Antti Aalto | .40 | .18 |
| ❑ 10 Jason Allison | .30 | .14 |
| ❑ 11 Ken Belanger | .15 | .07 |
| ❑ 12 Ray Bourque | .40 | .18 |
| ❑ 13 Anson Carter | .15 | .07 |
| ❑ 14 Byron Dafoe | .30 | .14 |
| ❑ 15 Steve Heinze | .15 | .07 |
| ❑ 16 Dimitri Khristich | .15 | .07 |
| ❑ 17 Sergei Samsonov | .50 | .23 |
| ❑ 18 Robbie Tallas | .30 | .14 |
| ❑ 19 Joe Thornton | .15 | .07 |
| ❑ 20 Matthew Barnaby | .30 | .14 |
| ❑ 21 Curtis Brown | .15 | .07 |
| ❑ 22 Michal Grosek | .15 | .07 |
| ❑ 23 Dominik Hasek | .75 | .35 |
| ❑ 24 Brian Holzinger | .30 | .14 |
| ❑ 25 Micael Peca | .30 | .14 |
| ❑ 26 Rob Ray | .15 | .07 |
| ❑ 27 Geoff Sanderson | .30 | .14 |
| ❑ 28 Miroslav Satan | .30 | .14 |
| ❑ 29 Dixon Ward | .15 | .07 |
| ❑ 30 Valeri Bure | .15 | .07 |
| ❑ 31 Theoren Fleury | .40 | .18 |
| ❑ 32 Jean-Sebastien Giguere | .30 | .14 |
| ❑ 33 Jarome Iginla | .30 | .14 |
| ❑ 34 Tyler Moss | .15 | .07 |

| | | |
|---|---|---|
| ❑ 35 Cory Stillman | .15 | .07 |
| ❑ 36 Jason Wiemer | .15 | .07 |
| ❑ 37 Clarke Wilm | .15 | .07 |
| ❑ 38 Martin St.Louis<br>Rico Fata | .30 | .14 |
| ❑ 39 Paul Coffey | .40 | .18 |
| ❑ 40 Ron Francis | .30 | .14 |
| ❑ 41 Martin Gelinas | .15 | .07 |
| ❑ 42 Arturs Irbe | .30 | .14 |
| ❑ 43 Sami Kapanen | .30 | .14 |
| ❑ 44 Trevor Kidd | .30 | .14 |
| ❑ 45 Keith Primeau | .30 | .14 |
| ❑ 46 Gary Roberts | .15 | .07 |
| ❑ 47 Ray Sheppard | .30 | .14 |
| ❑ 48 Tony Amonte | .30 | .14 |
| ❑ 49 Chris Chelios | .40 | .18 |
| ❑ 50 Eric Daze | .15 | .07 |
| ❑ 51 Nelson Emerson | .15 | .07 |
| ❑ 52 Doug Gilmour | .40 | .18 |
| ❑ 53 Mike Maneluk | .50 | .23 |
| ❑ 54 Bob Probert | .15 | .07 |
| ❑ 55 Jocelyn Thibault | .30 | .14 |
| ❑ 56 Alexei Zhamnov | .15 | .07 |
| ❑ 57 Todd White<br>Brad Brown | .15 | .07 |
| ❑ 58 Adam Deadmarsh | .30 | .14 |
| ❑ 59 Marc Denis | .30 | .14 |
| ❑ 60 Peter Forsberg | 1.25 | .55 |
| ❑ 61 Claude Lemieux | .30 | .14 |
| ❑ 62 Jeff Odgers | .15 | .07 |
| ❑ 63 Sandis Ozolinsh | .30 | .14 |
| ❑ 64 Patrick Roy | 2.00 | .90 |
| ❑ 65 Joe Sakic | .75 | .35 |
| ❑ 66 Wade Belak<br>Scott Parker | .30 | .14 |
| ❑ 67 Chris Drury<br>Milan Hejduk | 3.00 | 1.35 |
| ❑ 68 Ed Belfour | .40 | .18 |
| ❑ 69 Derian Hatcher | .15 | .07 |
| ❑ 70 Brett Hull | .50 | .23 |
| ❑ 71 Jamie Langenbrunner | .15 | .07 |
| ❑ 72 Jere Lehtinen | .30 | .14 |
| ❑ 73 Mike Modano | .50 | .23 |
| ❑ 74 Joe Nieuwendyk | .30 | .14 |
| ❑ 75 Darryl Sydor | .15 | .07 |
| ❑ 76 Roman Turek | .30 | .14 |
| ❑ 77 Sergei Zubov | .15 | .07 |
| ❑ 78 Sergei Gusev<br>Jamie Wright | .15 | .07 |
| ❑ 79 Sergei Fedorov | .75 | .35 |
| ❑ 80 Joey Kocur | .15 | .07 |
| ❑ 81 Martin LaPointe | .15 | .07 |
| ❑ 82 Igor Larionov | .15 | .07 |
| ❑ 83 Nicklas Lidstrom | .30 | .14 |
| ❑ 84 Darren McCarty | .15 | .07 |
| ❑ 85 Larry Murphy | .30 | .14 |
| ❑ 86 Chris Osgood | .40 | .18 |
| ❑ 87 Brendan Shanahan | .75 | .35 |
| ❑ 88 Steve Yzerman | 1.25 | .55 |
| ❑ 89 Norm Maracle<br>Stacy Roest | .60 | .25 |
| ❑ 90 Josef Beranek | .15 | .07 |
| ❑ 91 Sean Brown | .15 | .07 |
| ❑ 92 Bill Guerin | .30 | .14 |
| ❑ 93 Roman Hamrlik | .15 | .07 |
| ❑ 94 Janne Niinimaa | .15 | .07 |
| ❑ 95 Mikhail Shtalenkov | .15 | .07 |
| ❑ 96 Ryan Smyth | .30 | .14 |
| ❑ 97 Doug Weight | .30 | .14 |
| ❑ 98 Tom Poti<br>Craig Millar | .30 | .14 |
| ❑ 99 Pavel Bure | .75 | .35 |
| ❑ 100 Sean Burke | .30 | .14 |
| ❑ 101 Dino Ciccarelli | .30 | .14 |
| ❑ 102 Bret Hedican | .15 | .07 |
| ❑ 103 Viktor Kozlov | .15 | .07 |
| ❑ 104 Paul Laus | .15 | .07 |
| ❑ 105 Rob Niedermayer | .15 | .07 |
| ❑ 106 Mark Parrish | .60 | .25 |
| ❑ 107 Ray Whitney | .15 | .07 |
| ❑ 108 Oleg Kvasha<br>Peter Worrell | .40 | .18 |
| ❑ 109 Rob Blake | .30 | .14 |
| ❑ 110 Stephane Fiset | .30 | .14 |
| ❑ 111 Glen Murray | .15 | .07 |
| ❑ 112 Luc Robitaille | .30 | .14 |
| ❑ 113 Jamie Storr | .30 | .14 |
| ❑ 114 Jozef Stumpel | .30 | .14 |
| ❑ 115 Vladimir Tsyplakov | .15 | .07 |
| ❑ 116 Mark Visheau<br>Josh Green | .15 | .07 |
| ❑ 117 Olli Jokinen<br>Pavel Rosa | .30 | .14 |
| ❑ 118 Benoit Brunet | .15 | .07 |
| ❑ 119 Shayne Corson | .30 | .14 |
| ❑ 120 Vincent Damphousse | .30 | .14 |
| ❑ 121 Jeff Hackett | .30 | .14 |
| ❑ 122 Matt Higgins | .15 | .07 |
| ❑ 123 Saku Koivu | .60 | .25 |
| ❑ 124 Mark Recchi | .30 | .14 |
| ❑ 125 Martin Rucinsky | .15 | .07 |
| ❑ 126 Brian Savage | .15 | .07 |
| ❑ 127 Andrew Brunette | .15 | .07 |
| ❑ 128 Mike Dunham | .30 | .14 |
| ❑ 129 Greg Johnson | .15 | .07 |
| ❑ 130 Sergei Krivokrasov | .15 | .07 |
| ❑ 131 Denny Lambert | .15 | .07 |
| ❑ 132 Cliff Ronning | .15 | .07 |
| ❑ 133 Tomas Vokoun | .15 | .07 |
| ❑ 134 Patrick Cote<br>Kimmo Timonen | .30 | .14 |
| ❑ 135 Jason Arnott | .30 | .14 |
| ❑ 136 Martin Brodeur | 1.00 | .45 |
| ❑ 137 Patrik Elias | .30 | .14 |
| ❑ 138 Bobby Holik | .15 | .07 |
| ❑ 139 Brendan Morrison | .30 | .14 |
| ❑ 140 Krzysztof Oliwa | .15 | .07 |
| ❑ 141 Brian Rolston | .15 | .07 |
| ❑ 142 Vadim Sharifijanov | .15 | .07 |
| ❑ 143 Scott Stevens | .15 | .07 |
| ❑ 144 Petr Sykora | .15 | .07 |
| ❑ 145 Ted Donato | .15 | .07 |
| ❑ 146 Kenny Jonsson | .15 | .07 |
| ❑ 147 Trevor Linden | .30 | .14 |
| ❑ 148 Gino Odjick | .15 | .07 |
| ❑ 149 Zigmund Palffy | .40 | .18 |
| ❑ 150 Felix Potvin | .40 | .18 |
| ❑ 151 Robert Reichel | .15 | .07 |
| ❑ 152 Tommy Salo | .30 | .14 |
| ❑ 153 Mike Watt<br>Eric Brewer | .30 | .14 |
| ❑ 154 Dan Cloutier | .30 | .14 |
| ❑ 155 Adam Graves | .30 | .14 |
| ❑ 156 Wayne Gretzky | 2.50 | 1.10 |
| ❑ 157 Todd Harvey | .15 | .07 |
| ❑ 158 Brian Leetch | .40 | .18 |
| ❑ 159 Manny Malhotra | .30 | .14 |
| ❑ 160 Petr Nedved | .30 | .14 |
| ❑ 161 Mike Richter | .40 | .18 |
| ❑ 162 Esa Tikkanen | .15 | .07 |
| ❑ 163 Daniel Alfredsson | .30 | .14 |
| ❑ 164 Marian Hossa | .30 | .14 |
| ❑ 165 Andreas Johansson | .15 | .07 |
| ❑ 166 Shawn McEachern | .15 | .07 |
| ❑ 167 Wade Redden | .15 | .07 |
| ❑ 168 Damian Rhodes | .30 | .14 |
| ❑ 169 Ron Tugnutt | .30 | .14 |
| ❑ 170 Alexei Yashin | .40 | .18 |
| ❑ 171 Patrick Traverse<br>Sami Salo | .15 | .07 |
| ❑ 172 Rod Brind'Amour | .30 | .14 |
| ❑ 173 Eric Desjardins | .15 | .07 |
| ❑ 174 Ron Hextall | .30 | .14 |
| ❑ 175 Keith Jones | .30 | .14 |
| ❑ 176 John LeClair | .60 | .25 |
| ❑ 177 Eric Lindros | 1.25 | .55 |
| ❑ 178 Mikael Renberg | .30 | .14 |
| ❑ 179 Dimitri Tertyshny | .15 | .07 |
| ❑ 180 John Vanbiesbrouck | .60 | .25 |
| ❑ 181 Dainius Zubrus | .15 | .07 |
| ❑ 182 Daniel Briere | .15 | .07 |
| ❑ 183 Dallas Drake | .15 | .07 |
| ❑ 184 Nikolai Khabibulin | .30 | .14 |
| ❑ 185 Jyrki Lumme | .15 | .07 |
| ❑ 186 Teppo Numminen | .15 | .07 |
| ❑ 187 Jeremy Roenick | .40 | .18 |
| ❑ 188 Keith Tkachuk | .50 | .23 |
| ❑ 189 Rick Tocchet | .30 | .14 |
| ❑ 190 Oleg Tverdovsky | .15 | .07 |
| ❑ 191 Jim Waite | .30 | .14 |
| ❑ 192 Jean-Sebastien Aubin | .30 | .14 |
| ❑ 193 Stu Barnes | .15 | .07 |
| ❑ 194 Tom Barrasso | .30 | .14 |
| ❑ 195 Jaromir Jagr | 1.25 | .55 |
| ❑ 196 Alexei Kovalev | .15 | .07 |
| ❑ 197 Robert Lang | .15 | .07 |
| ❑ 198 Alexei Morozov | .15 | .07 |
| ❑ 199 Martin Straka | .15 | .07 |
| ❑ 200 Jan Hrdina<br>Maxim Galanov | .15 | .07 |
| ❑ 201 Pavol Demitra | .30 | .14 |
| ❑ 202 Grant Fuhr | .30 | .14 |
| ❑ 203 Al MacInnis | .30 | .14 |
| ❑ 204 Jamie McLennan | .15 | .07 |
| ❑ 205 Chris Pronger | .30 | .14 |
| ❑ 206 Pierre Turgeon | .30 | .14 |
| ❑ 207 Tony Twist | .15 | .07 |
| ❑ 208 Marty Reasoner<br>Lubos Bartecko | .15 | .07 |
| ❑ 209 Jeff Friesen | .15 | .07 |
| ❑ 210 Bryan Marchment | .15 | .07 |
| ❑ 211 Patrick Marleau | .30 | .14 |
| ❑ 212 Owen Nolan | .30 | .14 |
| ❑ 213 Mike Ricci | .30 | .14 |
| ❑ 214 Steve Shields | .30 | .14 |
| ❑ 215 Marco Sturm | .30 | .14 |
| ❑ 216 Mike Vernon | .30 | .14 |
| ❑ 217 Wendel Clark | .30 | .14 |
| ❑ 218 Chris Gratton | .30 | .14 |
| ❑ 219 Vincent Lecavalier | 1.25 | .55 |
| ❑ 220 Sandy McCarthy | .15 | .07 |
| ❑ 221 Stephane Richer | .30 | .14 |
| ❑ 222 Darcy Tucker | .15 | .07 |
| ❑ 223 Rob Zamuner | .15 | .07 |
| ❑ 224 Pavel Kubina<br>Zac Bierk | .15 | .07 |
| ❑ 225 Bryan Berard | .15 | .07 |
| ❑ 226 Tie Domi | .15 | .07 |
| ❑ 227 Mike Johnson | .30 | .14 |
| ❑ 228 Curtis Joseph | .40 | .18 |
| ❑ 229 Igor Korolev | .15 | .07 |
| ❑ 230 Alyn McCauley | .15 | .07 |
| ❑ 231 Mats Sundin | .40 | .18 |
| ❑ 232 Steve Thomas | .15 | .07 |
| ❑ 233 Tomas Kaberle<br>Daniil Markov | .30 | .14 |
| ❑ 234 Adrian Aucoin | .15 | .07 |
| ❑ 235 Corey Hirsch | .15 | .07 |
| ❑ 236 Mark Messier | .50 | .23 |
| ❑ 237 Alexander Mogilny | .30 | .14 |
| ❑ 238 Bill Muckalt | .50 | .23 |
| ❑ 239 Markus Naslund | .15 | .07 |
| ❑ 240 Mattias Ohlund | .30 | .14 |
| ❑ 241 Garth Snow | .30 | .14 |
| ❑ 242 Matt Cooke<br>Peter Schaefer | .15 | .07 |
| ❑ 243 Brian Bellows | .15 | .07 |
| ❑ 244 Craig Berube | .15 | .07 |
| ❑ 245 Peter Bondra | .40 | .18 |
| ❑ 246 Matt Herr | .15 | .07 |
| ❑ 247 Joe Juneau | .30 | .14 |
| ❑ 248 Olaf Kolzig | .30 | .14 |
| ❑ 249 Adam Oates | .30 | .14 |
| ❑ 250 Richard Zednik | .15 | .07 |
| ❑ 251 Last Game at MLG SP | 20.00 | 9.00 |
| ❑ 252 First Game at ACC SP | 20.00 | 9.00 |

## 1998-99 Pacific Omega Opening Day Issue

Randomly inserted into packs, this 250-card set is parallel to the base set. Only 56 serially numbered sets were made.

| | MINT | NRMT |
|---|---|---|
| COMPLETE SET (250) | 8000.00 | 3600.00 |
| COMMON CARD (1-250) | 20.00 | 9.00 |

*STARS: 100X TO 200X BASIC CARDS
*YOUNG STARS: 75X TO 150X
*RC's: 40X TO 80X

## 1998-99 Pacific Omega Championship Spotlight

Randomly inserted in special packs at the rate of one in 49, this 10-card set features color action photos of top NHL players with player information on the backs. Three limited edition parallel sets were also produced to be inserted into Treat packs. Only 50 serially numbered Green parallel versions were made, 10 serially numbered Red parallel versions, and one Gold parallel version.

| | MINT | NRMT |
|---|---|---|
| COMPLETE SET (10) | 400.00 | 180.00 |
| COMMON CARD (1-10) | 12.00 | 5.50 |

STATED ODDS 1:49 TREAT

| | | |
|---|---|---|
| COMP.GREEN SET (10) | 4000.00 | 1800.00 |
| COMMON GREEN (1-10) | 120.00 | 55.00 |

*GREEN STARS: 5X TO 10X HI COLUMN
STATED PRINT RUN 50 SERIAL #'d SETS
RANDOM INSERT IN TREAT PACKS

| | | |
|---|---|---|
| COMP.RED SET (10) | 10000.00 | 4500.00 |
| COMMON RED (1-10) | 300.00 | 135.00 |

*RED STARS: 12.5X TO 25X HI
STATED PRINT RUN 10 SERIAL #'d SETS
RANDOM INSERT IN TREAT PACKS
GOLD 1/1 PARALLEL EXISTS

| | | |
|---|---|---|
| ❑ 1 Paul Kariya | 50.00 | 22.00 |
| ❑ 2 Dominik Hasek | 25.00 | 11.00 |
| ❑ 3 Patrick Roy | 60.00 | 27.00 |
| ❑ 4 Steve Yzerman | 40.00 | 18.00 |
| ❑ 5 Pavel Bure | 25.00 | 11.00 |
| ❑ 6 Martin Brodeur | 30.00 | 13.50 |
| ❑ 7 Wayne Gretzky | 80.00 | 36.00 |
| ❑ 8 Eric Lindros | 40.00 | 18.00 |
| ❑ 9 Jaromir Jagr | 40.00 | 18.00 |
| ❑ 10 Curtis Joseph | 12.00 | 5.50 |

## 1998-99 Pacific Omega EO Portraits

Randomly inserted into packs at the rate of one in 73, this 20-card set features color player images of some of hockey's biggest superstars printed using Electro-Optical technology to laser-cut the player image into every card. A special one of a kind Hobby only parallel set was also produced with "1/1" laser-cut into each card.

| | MINT | NRMT |
|---|---|---|
| COMPLETE SET (20) | 500.00 | 220.00 |
| COMMON CARD (1-20) | 10.00 | 4.50 |

| | | |
|---|---|---|
| ❑ 1 Paul Kariya | 40.00 | 18.00 |
| ❑ 2 Teemu Selanne | 20.00 | 9.00 |
| ❑ 3 Dominik Hasek | 20.00 | 9.00 |
| ❑ 4 Peter Forsberg | 30.00 | 13.50 |
| ❑ 5 Patrick Roy | 50.00 | 22.00 |
| ❑ 6 Joe Sakic | 20.00 | 9.00 |
| ❑ 7 Brett Hull | 12.00 | 5.50 |
| ❑ 8 Mike Modano | 12.00 | 5.50 |
| ❑ 9 Sergei Fedorov | 20.00 | 9.00 |
| ❑ 10 Brendan Shanahan | 20.00 | 9.00 |
| ❑ 11 Steve Yzerman | 30.00 | 13.50 |
| ❑ 12 Pavel Bure | 20.00 | 9.00 |
| ❑ 13 Martin Brodeur | 25.00 | 11.00 |
| ❑ 14 Wayne Gretzky | 60.00 | 27.00 |
| ❑ 15 John LeClair | 15.00 | 6.75 |
| ❑ 16 Eric Lindros | 30.00 | 13.50 |
| ❑ 17 Keith Tkachuk | 12.00 | 5.50 |
| ❑ 18 Jaromir Jagr | 30.00 | 13.50 |
| ❑ 19 Mats Sundin | 10.00 | 4.50 |
| ❑ 20 Mark Messier | 12.00 | 5.50 |

## 1998-99 Pacific Omega Face to Face

Randomly inserted into packs at the rate of one in 145, this 10-card set features color portraits of top NHL players printed on silver-foiled and etched cards. Two players are matched on every card creating an all-star faceoff effect.

| | MINT | NRMT |
|---|---|---|
| COMPLETE SET (10) | 500.00 | 220.00 |
| COMMON CARD (1-10) | 30.00 | 13.50 |

| | | |
|---|---|---|
| ❑ 1 Patrick Roy<br>Martin Brodeur | 100.00 | 45.00 |
| ❑ 2 Wayne Gretzky<br>Paul Kariya | 120.00 | 55.00 |
| ❑ 3 Dominik Hasek<br>Jaromir Jagr | 60.00 | 27.00 |
| ❑ 4 Sergei Fedorov<br>Pavel Bure | 50.00 | 22.00 |
| ❑ 5 Keith Tkachuk<br>Brendan Shanahan | 40.00 | 18.00 |
| ❑ 6 Steve Yzerman<br>Joe Sakic | 60.00 | 27.00 |
| ❑ 7 Teemu Selanne<br>Saku Koivu | 40.00 | 18.00 |
| ❑ 8 Peter Forsberg<br>Mats Sundin | 50.00 | 22.00 |
| ❑ 9 Mike Modano<br>John LeClair | 30.00 | 13.50 |
| ❑ 10 Eric Lindros<br>Mark Messier | 40.00 | 18.00 |

## 1998-99 Pacific Omega Online

Randomly inserted into packs at the rate of four in 37, this 36-card set features color photos of NHL stars with interesting player facts on the backs. Each card invites fans to learn more about each player and team by logging on to their respective internet sites at www.nhlpa.com and www.nhl.com.

| | MINT | NRMT |
|---|---|---|
| COMPLETE SET (36) | 120.00 | 55.00 |
| COMMON CARD (1-36) | 1.50 | .70 |

| | | |
|---|---|---|
| ❑ 1 Paul Kariya | 8.00 | 3.60 |
| ❑ 2 Teemu Selanne | 4.00 | 1.80 |
| ❑ 3 Ray Bourque | 2.00 | .90 |
| ❑ 4 Dominik Hasek | 4.00 | 1.80 |
| ❑ 5 Theoren Fleury | 2.00 | .90 |
| ❑ 6 Chris Chelios | 2.00 | .90 |
| ❑ 7 Doug Gilmour | 2.00 | .90 |
| ❑ 8 Patrick Roy | 10.00 | 4.50 |
| ❑ 10 Joe Sakic | 4.00 | 1.80 |
| ❑ 11 Ed Belfour | 2.00 | .90 |
| ❑ 12 Brett Hull | 2.50 | 1.10 |
| ❑ 13 Mike Modano | 2.50 | 1.10 |
| ❑ 14 Sergei Fedorov | 4.00 | 1.80 |
| ❑ 15 Brendan Shanahan | 4.00 | 1.80 |
| ❑ 16 Steve Yzerman | 6.00 | 2.70 |
| ❑ 17 Pavel Bure | 4.00 | 1.80 |
| ❑ 18 Saku Koivu | 3.00 | 1.35 |
| ❑ 19 Martin Brodeur | 5.00 | 2.20 |
| ❑ 20 Brendan Morrison | 1.50 | .70 |
| ❑ 21 Zigmund Palffy | 2.00 | .90 |
| ❑ 22 Felix Potvin | 2.00 | .90 |
| ❑ 23 Wayne Gretzky | 12.00 | 5.50 |
| ❑ 24 Alexei Yashin | 2.00 | .90 |
| ❑ 25 John LeClair | 3.00 | 1.35 |
| ❑ 26 Eric Lindros | 6.00 | 2.70 |
| ❑ 27 John Vanbiesbrouck | 3.00 | 1.35 |
| ❑ 28 Nikolai Khabibulin | 1.50 | .70 |
| ❑ 29 Keith Tkachuk | 2.50 | 1.10 |
| ❑ 30 Jaromir Jagr | 6.00 | 2.70 |
| ❑ 31 Vincent Lecavalier | 4.00 | 1.80 |
| ❑ 32 Curtis Joseph | 2.00 | .90 |
| ❑ 33 Mats Sundin | 2.00 | .90 |
| ❑ 34 Mark Messier | 2.50 | 1.10 |
| ❑ 35 Bill Muckalt | 2.50 | 1.10 |
| ❑ 36 Peter Bondra | 2.00 | .90 |

## 1998-99 Pacific Omega Planet Ice

Randomly inserted into hobby packs only with an insertion rate of four in 37, this 30-card set features action color photos of top NHL players. The backs carry player information.

| | MINT | NRMT |
|---|---|---|
| COMPLETE SET (30) | 120.00 | 55.00 |
| COMMON CARD (1-30) | 2.00 | .90 |

| | | |
|---|---|---|
| ❑ 1 Ray Bourque | 2.00 | .90 |
| ❑ 2 Chris Chelios | 2.00 | .90 |
| ❑ 3 Vincent Lecavalier | 4.00 | 1.80 |
| ❑ 4 Mark Parrish | 5.00 | 2.20 |
| ❑ 5 Felix Potvin | 2.00 | .90 |
| ❑ 6 Alexei Yashin | 2.00 | .90 |
| ❑ 7 Ed Belfour | 2.00 | .90 |
| ❑ 8 Peter Bondra | 2.00 | .90 |
| ❑ 9 Brett Hull | 2.50 | 1.10 |
| ❑ 10 Mark Messier | 2.50 | 1.10 |
| ❑ 11 Mats Sundin | 2.00 | .90 |
| ❑ 12 John Vanbiesbrouck | 3.00 | 1.35 |
| ❑ 13 Sergei Fedorov | 4.00 | 1.80 |
| ❑ 14 Curtis Joseph | 2.00 | .90 |
| ❑ 15 John LeClair | 3.00 | 1.35 |
| ❑ 16 Mike Modano | 2.50 | 1.10 |
| ❑ 17 Brendan Shanahan | 4.00 | 1.80 |
| ❑ 18 Keith Tkachuk | 2.50 | 1.10 |
| ❑ 19 Martin Brodeur | 5.00 | 2.20 |
| ❑ 20 Pavel Bure | 4.00 | 1.80 |
| ❑ 21 Dominik Hasek | 4.00 | 1.80 |
| ❑ 22 Joe Sakic | 4.00 | 1.80 |
| ❑ 23 Teemu Selanne | 4.00 | 1.80 |
| ❑ 24 Steve Yzerman | 6.00 | 2.70 |
| ❑ 25 Peter Forsberg | 6.00 | 2.70 |
| ❑ 26 Wayne Gretzky | 12.00 | 5.50 |
| ❑ 27 Jaromir Jagr | 6.00 | 2.70 |
| ❑ 28 Paul Kariya | 8.00 | 3.60 |
| ❑ 29 Eric Lindros | 6.00 | 2.70 |
| ❑ 30 Patrick Roy | 10.00 | 4.50 |

## 1998-99 Pacific Omega Planet Ice Parallel

Randomly inserted into hobby packs only, this 30-card set is a parallel version of the regular Pacific Omega Planet Ice insert set. The set is spun off into five different tiers of six cards each. Each serially numbered tier is foiled in its own unique color with varying amounts of each tier produced. Tier 1 (1-6) is printed with blue foil and serially numbered to 100. Tier 2 (7-12) is a red foil set and serially numbered to 75. Tier 3 (13-18) has green foil highlights and only 50 sets were made. Tier 4 (19-24) is printed in purple foil with a print run of 25 serially numbered sets. Tier 5 (25-30) is a gold foil set with only 1 of each card produced.

| | MINT | NRMT |
|---|---|---|
| COMMON CARD (1-30) | 60.00 | 27.00 |

*TIER 1 (1-6): 15X TO 30X HI COLUMN
*TIER 2 (7-12): 20X TO 40X HI
*TIER 3 (13-18): 30X TO 60X HI
*TIER 4 (19-24): 50X TO 100X HI
TIER 1 STATED PRINT RUN 100 SETS
TIER 2 STATED PRINT RUN 75 SETS
TIER 3 STATED PRINT RUN 50 SETS
TIER 4 STATED PRINT RUN 25 SETS
TIER 5 STATED PRINT RUN 1 SET

## 1998-99 Pacific Omega Prism

Randomly inserted into packs at the rate of one in 37, this 20-card set features color action player photos printed on prismatic foil cards. The backs carry player information.

| | MINT | NRMT |
|---|---|---|
| COMPLETE SET (20) | 250.00 | 110.00 |
| COMMON CARD (1-20) | 5.00 | 2.20 |

| | | |
|---|---|---|
| ❑ 1 Paul Kariya | 20.00 | 9.00 |
| ❑ 2 Teemu Selanne | 10.00 | 4.50 |
| ❑ 3 Dominik Hasek | 10.00 | 4.50 |
| ❑ 4 Peter Forsberg | 15.00 | 6.75 |
| ❑ 5 Patrick Roy | 25.00 | 11.00 |
| ❑ 6 Joe Sakic | 10.00 | 4.50 |

❑ 7 Mike Modano 6.00 2.70
❑ 8 Sergei Fedorov 10.00 4.50
❑ 9 Brendan Shanahan 10.00 4.50
❑ 10 Steve Yzerman 15.00 6.75
❑ 11 Pavel Bure 10.00 4.50
❑ 12 Martin Brodeur 12.00 5.50
❑ 13 Wayne Gretzky 30.00 13.50
❑ 14 Alexei Yashin 5.00 2.20
❑ 15 John LeClair 8.00 3.60
❑ 16 Eric Lindros 15.00 6.75
❑ 17 Keith Tkachuk 6.00 2.70
❑ 18 Jaromir Jagr 15.00 6.75
❑ 19 Mats Sundin 5.00 2.20
❑ 20 Mark Messier 6.00 2.70

## 1997-98 Pacific Paramount

The 1997-98 Pacific Paramount set was issued in one series totalling 200 cards and distributed in five-card packs. The fronts feature color action player photos with holographic gold foil highlights. The backs carry another action player photo and player information.

MINT NRMT
COMPLETE SET (200) 30.00 13.50
COMMON CARD (1-200) .10 .05
COMP.COPPER SET (200) 250.00 110.00
COMMON COPPER (1-200) .60 .25
*STARS: 3X TO 6X BASIC CARDS
*YOUNG STARS: 2.5X TO 5X BASIC CARDS
COMP.DARK GREY SET (200) 250.00 110.00
COMMON DARK GREY (1-200) .60 .25
*DARK GREY STARS: 3X TO 6X BASIC CARDS
*DARK GREY YNG.STARS: 2.5X TO 5X BASIC CARDS
COMP.EMERALD SET (200) 250.00 110.00
COMMON EMERALD (1-200) .60 .25
*STARS: 3X TO 6X BASIC CARDS
*EMERALD YNG.STARS: 2.5X TO 5X BASIC CARDS
COMP.RED SET (200) 500.00 220.00
COMMON RED (1-200) 1.25 .55
*RED STARS: 6X TO 12X BASIC CARDS
*RED YNG.STARS: 5X TO 10X BASIC CARDS
COMP.SILVER SET (200) 250.00 110.00
COMMON SILVER (1-200) .60 .25
*STARS: 3X TO 6X BASIC CARDS
*YOUNG STARS: 2.5X TO 5X BASIC CARDS

❑ 1 Guy Hebert .25 .11
❑ 2 Paul Kariya 1.25 .55
❑ 3 Espen Knutsen .10 .05
❑ 4 Dmitri Mironov .10 .05
❑ 5 Steve Rucchin .10 .05
❑ 6 Tomas Sandstrom .10 .05
❑ 7 Teemu Selanne .60 .25
❑ 8 Scott Young .10 .05
❑ 9 Ray Bourque .30 .14
❑ 10 Jim Carey .25 .11
❑ 11 Anson Carter .10 .05
❑ 12 Ted Donato .10 .05
❑ 13 Dave Ellett .10 .05
❑ 14 Dimitri Khristich .10 .05
❑ 15 Sergei Samsonov .75 .35
❑ 16 Joe Thornton .60 .25
❑ 17 Matthew Barnaby .10 .05
❑ 18 Jason Dawe .10 .05
❑ 19 Dominik Hasek .60 .25
❑ 20 Brian Holzinger .10 .05
❑ 21 Michael Peca .10 .05
❑ 22 Derek Plante .10 .05
❑ 23 Erik Rasmussen .10 .05
❑ 24 Miroslav Satan .10 .05
❑ 25 Steve Begin .10 .05
❑ 26 Andrew Cassels .10 .05
❑ 27 Chris Dingman .10 .05
❑ 28 Theoren Fleury .25 .11
❑ 29 Jonas Hoglund .10 .05
❑ 30 Jarome Iginla .25 .11
❑ 31 Rick Tabaracci .25 .11
❑ 32 German Titov .10 .05
❑ 33 Kevin Dineen .10 .05
❑ 34 Nelson Emerson .10 .05
❑ 35 Trevor Kidd .25 .11
❑ 36 Stephen Leach .10 .05
❑ 37 Keith Primeau .10 .05
❑ 38 Steven Rice .10 .05
❑ 39 Gary Roberts .10 .05
❑ 40 Tony Amonte .25 .11
❑ 41 Chris Chelios .30 .14
❑ 42 Daniel Cleary .25 .11
❑ 43 Eric Daze .25 .11
❑ 44 Jeff Hackett .25 .11
❑ 45 Sergei Krivokrasov .10 .05
❑ 46 Ethan Moreau .10 .05
❑ 47 Alexei Zhamnov .10 .05
❑ 48 Adam Deadmarsh .25 .11
❑ 49 Peter Forsberg 1.00 .45
❑ 50 Valeri Kamensky .25 .11
❑ 51 Jari Kurri .25 .11
❑ 52 Claude Lemieux .25 .11
❑ 53 Sandis Ozolinsh .25 .11
❑ 54 Patrick Roy 1.50 .70
❑ 55 Joe Sakic .60 .25
❑ 56 Ed Belfour .30 .14
❑ 57 Derian Hatcher .10 .05
❑ 58 Jamie Langenbrunner .10 .05
❑ 59 Jere Lehtinen .10 .05
❑ 60 Mike Modano .40 .18
❑ 61 Joe Nieuwendyk .25 .11
❑ 62 Darryl Sydor .10 .05
❑ 63 Pat Verbeek .10 .05
❑ 64 Anders Eriksson .10 .05
❑ 65 Sergei Fedorov .60 .25
❑ 66 Vyacheslav Kozlov .10 .05
❑ 67 Nicklas Lidstrom .25 .11
❑ 68 Darren McCarty .10 .05
❑ 69 Chris Osgood .30 .14
❑ 70 Brendan Shanahan .60 .25
❑ 71 Steve Yzerman 1.00 .45
❑ 72 Jason Arnott .25 .11
❑ 73 Boyd Devereaux .10 .05
❑ 74 Mike Grier .10 .05
❑ 75 Curtis Joseph .30 .14
❑ 76 Andrei Kovalenko .10 .05
❑ 77 Ryan Smyth .25 .11
❑ 78 Doug Weight .25 .11
❑ 79 Dave Gagner .10 .05
❑ 80 Ed Jovanovski .25 .11
❑ 81 Scott Mellanby .10 .05
❑ 82 Kirk Muller .10 .05
❑ 83 Rob Niedermayer .10 .05
❑ 84 Ray Sheppard .10 .05
❑ 85 Esa Tikkanen .10 .05
❑ 86 John Vanbiesbrouck .50 .23
❑ 87 Rob Blake .10 .05
❑ 88 Stephane Fiset .25 .11
❑ 89 Garry Galley .10 .05
❑ 90 Olli Jokinen .50 .23
❑ 91 Luc Robitaille .25 .11
❑ 92 Jozef Stumpel .25 .11
❑ 93 Shayne Corson .10 .05
❑ 94 Vincent Damphousse .25 .11
❑ 95 Saku Koivu .50 .23
❑ 96 Andy Moog .25 .11
❑ 97 Mark Recchi .25 .11
❑ 98 Stephane Richer .10 .05
❑ 99 Brian Savage .10 .05
❑ 100 Dave Andreychuk .10 .05
❑ 101 Martin Brodeur .75 .35
❑ 102 Doug Gilmour .30 .14
❑ 103 Bobby Holik .10 .05
❑ 104 John MacLean .10 .05
❑ 105 Brian Rolston .10 .05
❑ 106 Bryan Berard .25 .11
❑ 107 Todd Bertuzzi .10 .05
❑ 108 Travis Green .10 .05
❑ 109 Zigmund Palffy .30 .14
❑ 110 Robert Reichel .10 .05
❑ 111 Tommy Salo .25 .11
❑ 112 Bryan Smolinski .10 .05
❑ 113 Christian Dube .10 .05
❑ 114 Adam Graves .25 .11
❑ 115 Wayne Gretzky 2.00 .90
❑ 116 Alexei Kovalev .10 .05
❑ 117 Pat LaFontaine .25 .11
❑ 118 Brian Leetch .30 .14
❑ 119 Mike Richter .30 .14
❑ 120 Brian Skrudland .10 .05
❑ 121 Kevin Stevens .25 .11
❑ 122 Daniel Alfredsson .25 .11
❑ 123 Radek Bonk .25 .11
❑ 124 Alexandre Daigle .25 .11
❑ 125 Marian Hossa 1.50 .70
❑ 126 Igor Kravchuk .10 .05
❑ 127 Chris Phillips .10 .05
❑ 128 Damian Rhodes .25 .11
❑ 129 Alexei Yashin .25 .11
❑ 130 Rod Brind'Amour .25 .11
❑ 131 Chris Gratton .25 .11
❑ 132 Ron Hextall .25 .11
❑ 133 John LeClair .50 .23
❑ 134 Eric Lindros 1.00 .45
❑ 135 Janne Niinimaa .25 .11
❑ 136 Vaclav Prospal .50 .23
❑ 137 Garth Snow .25 .11
❑ 138 Dainius Zubrus .30 .14
❑ 139 Mike Gartner .25 .11
❑ 140 Brad Isbister .10 .05
❑ 141 Nikolai Khabibulin .25 .11
❑ 142 Jeremy Roenick .30 .14
❑ 143 Cliff Ronning .10 .05
❑ 144 Keith Tkachuk .40 .18
❑ 145 Rick Tocchet .25 .11
❑ 146 Oleg Tverdovsky .10 .05
❑ 147 Tom Barrasso .25 .11
❑ 148 Ron Francis .25 .11
❑ 149 Kevin Hatcher .10 .05
❑ 150 Jaromir Jagr 1.00 .45
❑ 151 Darius Kasparaitis .10 .05
❑ 152 Alexei Morozov .25 .11
❑ 153 Petr Nedved .25 .11
❑ 154 Ed Olczyk .10 .05
❑ 155 Jim Campbell .10 .05
❑ 156 Kelly Chase .10 .05
❑ 157 Geoff Courtnall .10 .05
❑ 158 Grant Fuhr .25 .11
❑ 159 Brett Hull .40 .18
❑ 160 Joe Murphy .10 .05
❑ 161 Pierre Turgeon .25 .11
❑ 162 Tony Twist .25 .11
❑ 163 Shawn Burr .10 .05
❑ 164 Jeff Friesen .25 .11
❑ 165 Tony Granato .10 .05
❑ 166 Viktor Kozlov .10 .05
❑ 167 Patrick Marleau .60 .25
❑ 168 Stephane Matteau .10 .05
❑ 169 Owen Nolan .25 .11
❑ 170 Mike Vernon .25 .11
❑ 171 Dino Ciccarelli .10 .05
❑ 172 Karl Dykhuis .10 .05
❑ 173 Roman Hamrlik .10 .05
❑ 174 Daymond Langkow .10 .05
❑ 175 Mikael Renberg .25 .11
❑ 176 Alexander Selivanov .10 .05
❑ 177 Paul Ysebaert .10 .05
❑ 178 Sergei Berezin .10 .05
❑ 179 Wendel Clark .25 .11
❑ 180 Glenn Healy .25 .11
❑ 181 Derek King .10 .05
❑ 182 Alyn McCauley .25 .11
❑ 183 Felix Potvin .30 .14
❑ 184 Martin Prochazka .10 .05
❑ 185 Mats Sundin .30 .14
❑ 186 Pavel Bure .60 .25
❑ 187 Martin Gelinas .10 .05
❑ 188 Trevor Linden .25 .11
❑ 189 Kirk McLean .25 .11
❑ 190 Mark Messier .40 .18
❑ 191 Markus Naslund .10 .05
❑ 192 Mattias Ohlund .25 .11
❑ 193 Peter Bondra .30 .14
❑ 194 Dale Hunter .10 .05
❑ 195 Joe Juneau .25 .11
❑ 196 Olaf Kolzig .25 .11
❑ 197 Steve Konowalchuk .10 .05
❑ 198 Adam Oates .25 .11
❑ 199 Bill Ranford .25 .11
❑ 200 Jaroslav Svejkovsky .25 .11
❑ P60 Mike Modano PROMO 1.00 .45

## 1997-98 Pacific Paramount Ice Blue

Randomly inserted in hobby and retail packs at the rate of one in 73, this 200-card set is parallel to the base set with holographic blue foil highlights.

MINT NRMT
COMMON CARD (1-200) 10.00 4.50
SEMISTARS/GOALIES 25.00 11.00
UNLISTED STARS 30.00 13.50
*STARS: 50X TO 100X BASIC CARDS
*YOUNG STARS: 40X TO 80X BASIC CARDS

## 1997-98 Pacific Paramount Big Numbers Die-Cuts

Randomly inserted in packs at the rate of one in 37, this 20-card set features die-cut textured cards in the shape of the players jersey number. The backs carry a small player head photo and player information in a newspaper story design.

MINT NRMT
COMPLETE SET (20) 250.00 110.00
COMMON CARD (1-20) 5.00 2.20

❑ 1 Paul Kariya 20.00 9.00
❑ 2 Teemu Selanne 10.00 4.50
❑ 3 Joe Thornton 10.00 4.50
❑ 4 Dominik Hasek 10.00 4.50
❑ 5 Peter Forsberg 15.00 6.75
❑ 6 Patrick Roy 25.00 11.00
❑ 7 Joe Sakic 10.00 4.50
❑ 8 Sergei Fedorov 10.00 4.50
❑ 9 Brendan Shanahan 10.00 4.50
❑ 10 Steve Yzerman 15.00 6.75
❑ 11 John Vanbiesbrouck 8.00 3.60
❑ 12 Martin Brodeur 12.00 5.50
❑ 13 Doug Gilmour 6.00 2.70
❑ 14 Wayne Gretzky 30.00 13.50
❑ 15 Eric Lindros 15.00 6.75
❑ 16 Keith Tkachuk 6.00 2.70
❑ 17 Jaromir Jagr 15.00 6.75
❑ 18 Brett Hull 6.00 2.70
❑ 19 Pavel Bure 10.00 4.50
❑ 20 Mark Messier 6.00 2.70

## 1997-98 Pacific Paramount Canadian Greats

Randomly inserted two in every 48 Canadian retail packs only, this 12-card set features color photos of star players. The backs carry player information.

MINT NRMT
COMPLETE SET (12) 150.00 70.00
COMMON CARD (1-12) 4.00 1.80

❑ 1 Paul Kariya 20.00 9.00
❑ 2 Joe Thornton 10.00 4.50
❑ 3 Jarome Iginla 4.00 1.80
❑ 4 Patrick Roy 25.00 11.00
❑ 5 Joe Sakic 10.00 4.50
❑ 6 Brendan Shanahan 10.00 4.50
❑ 7 Steve Yzerman 15.00 6.75
❑ 8 Ryan Smyth 4.00 1.80
❑ 9 Martin Brodeur 12.00 5.50
❑ 10 Wayne Gretzky 30.00 13.50
❑ 11 Eric Lindros 15.00 6.75
❑ 12 Mark Messier 6.00 2.70

## 1997-98 Pacific Paramount Glove Side Laser Cuts

Randomly inserted in packs at the rate of one in 73, this 20-card set features color photos of top goalies printed on a die-cut card in the shape of the goalie's glove.

MINT NRMT
COMPLETE SET (20) 400.00 180.00
COMMON CARD (1-20) 12.00 5.50
CONDITION SENSITIVE SET

❑ 1 Guy Hebert 12.00 5.50
❑ 2 Dominik Hasek 30.00 13.50
❑ 3 Trevor Kidd 12.00 5.50
❑ 4 Jeff Hackett 12.00 5.50
❑ 5 Patrick Roy 80.00 36.00
❑ 6 Ed Belfour 20.00 9.00
❑ 7 Chris Osgood 20.00 9.00
❑ 8 Curtis Joseph 20.00 9.00
❑ 9 John Vanbiesbrouck 25.00 11.00
❑ 10 Andy Moog 12.00 5.50
❑ 11 Martin Brodeur 40.00 18.00
❑ 12 Tommy Salo 12.00 5.50
❑ 13 Mike Richter 20.00 9.00
❑ 14 Ron Hextall 12.00 5.50
❑ 15 Garth Snow 12.00 5.50
❑ 16 Nikolai Khabibulin 12.00 5.50
❑ 17 Tom Barrasso 12.00 5.50
❑ 18 Grant Fuhr 12.00 5.50
❑ 19 Mike Vernon 12.00 5.50
❑ 20 Felix Potvin 20.00 9.00

## 1997-98 Pacific Paramount Photoengravings

Randomly inserted in packs at the rate of two in 37, this 20-card set features color images of top stars using photoengraving technology and printed with a textured paper stock finish.

MINT NRMT
COMPLETE SET (20) 200.00 90.00
COMMON CARD (1-20) 5.00 2.20

❑ 1 Paul Kariya 15.00 6.75
❑ 2 Teemu Selanne 8.00 3.60
❑ 3 Joe Thornton 6.00 2.70
❑ 4 Dominik Hasek 8.00 3.60
❑ 5 Peter Forsberg 12.00 5.50
❑ 6 Patrick Roy 20.00 9.00
❑ 7 Joe Sakic 8.00 3.60
❑ 8 Mike Modano 5.00 2.20
❑ 9 Brendan Shanahan 8.00 3.60
❑ 10 Steve Yzerman 12.00 5.50
❑ 11 John Vanbiesbrouck 6.00 2.70
❑ 12 Saku Koivu 6.00 2.70
❑ 13 Wayne Gretzky 25.00 11.00
❑ 14 John LeClair 6.00 2.70
❑ 15 Eric Lindros 12.00 5.50
❑ 16 Keith Tkachuk 5.00 2.20
❑ 17 Jaromir Jagr 12.00 5.50
❑ 18 Brett Hull 5.00 2.20
❑ 19 Pavel Bure 8.00 3.60
❑ 20 Mark Messier 5.00 2.20

## 1998-99 Pacific Paramount

The 1998-99 Pacific Paramount set consists of 250 standard-size cards. The fronts feature full bleed action photos with the player's name and team logo on holographic gold foil. The flipside offers the player's statistics. Each pack contains six cards. The cards were released around October, 1998.

MINT NRMT
COMPLETE SET (250) 30.00 13.50
COMMON CARD (1-250) .10 .05

❑ 1 Travis Green .10 .05
❑ 2 Guy Hebert .25 .11
❑ 3 Paul Kariya 1.25 .55
❑ 4 Josef Marha .10 .05
❑ 5 Steve Rucchin .10 .05
❑ 6 Tomas Sandstrom .10 .05
❑ 7 Teemu Selanne .60 .25
❑ 8 Jason Allison .25 .11
❑ 9 Per Axelsson .10 .05
❑ 10 Ray Bourque .30 .14
❑ 11 Anson Carter .10 .05
❑ 12 Byron Dafoe .25 .11
❑ 13 Ted Donato .10 .05
❑ 14 Dave Ellett .10 .05
❑ 15 Dimitri Khristich .10 .05
❑ 16 Sergei Samsonov .50 .23
❑ 17 Matthew Barnaby .10 .05
❑ 18 Michal Grosek .10 .05
❑ 19 Dominik Hasek .60 .25
❑ 20 Brian Holzinger .10 .05
❑ 21 Michael Peca .10 .05
❑ 22 Miroslav Satan .25 .11
❑ 23 Vaclav Varada .10 .05
❑ 24 Dixon Ward .10 .05
❑ 25 Alexei Zhitnik .10 .05
❑ 26 Andrew Cassels .10 .05
❑ 27 Theoren Fleury .30 .14
❑ 28 Jarome Iginla .10 .05
❑ 29 Marty McInnis .10 .05
❑ 30 Derek Morris .10 .05
❑ 31 Michael Nylander .10 .05
❑ 32 Cory Stillman .10 .05
❑ 33 Rick Tabaracci .10 .05
❑ 34 Kevin Dineen .10 .05
❑ 35 Nelson Emerson .10 .05
❑ 36 Martin Gelinas .10 .05
❑ 37 Sami Kapanen .25 .11
❑ 38 Trevor Kidd .25 .11
❑ 39 Robert Kron .10 .05
❑ 40 Jeff O'Neill .10 .05
❑ 41 Keith Primeau .25 .11
❑ 42 Gary Roberts .10 .05
❑ 43 Tony Amonte .25 .11
❑ 44 Chris Chelios .30 .14
❑ 45 Paul Coffey .30 .14
❑ 46 Eric Daze .10 .05
❑ 47 Doug Gilmour .25 .11
❑ 48 Jeff Hackett .25 .11
❑ 49 Jean-Yves Leroux .10 .05
❑ 50 Eric Weinrich .10 .05
❑ 51 Alexei Zhamnov .10 .05
❑ 52 Craig Billington .25 .11
❑ 53 Adam Deadmarsh .25 .11
❑ 54 Adam Foote .10 .05
❑ 55 Peter Forsberg 1.00 .45
❑ 56 Valeri Kamensky .10 .05
❑ 57 Claude Lemieux .25 .11
❑ 58 Eric Messier .10 .05
❑ 59 Sandis Ozolinsh .25 .11
❑ 60 Patrick Roy 1.50 .70
❑ 61 Joe Sakic .60 .25
❑ 62 Ed Belfour .30 .14
❑ 63 Derian Hatcher .10 .05
❑ 64 Brett Hull .40 .18
❑ 65 Jamie Langenbrunner .10 .05
❑ 66 Jere Lehtinen .10 .05
❑ 67 Juha Lind .10 .05
❑ 68 Mike Modano .40 .18
❑ 69 Joe Nieuwendyk .25 .11
❑ 70 Darryl Sydor .10 .05
❑ 71 Roman Turek .25 .11
❑ 72 Sergei Zubov .10 .05
❑ 73 Anders Eriksson .10 .05
❑ 74 Sergei Fedorov .60 .25
❑ 75 Kevin Hodson .25 .11
❑ 76 Vyacheslav Kozlov .25 .11
❑ 77 Igor Larionov .10 .05
❑ 78 Nicklas Lidstrom .25 .11
❑ 79 Darren McCarty .10 .05
❑ 80 Larry Murphy .25 .11
❑ 81 Chris Osgood .30 .14
❑ 82 Brendan Shanahan .60 .25
❑ 83 Steve Yzerman 1.00 .45
❑ 84 Kelly Buchberger .10 .05
❑ 85 Mike Grier .10 .05
❑ 86 Bill Guerin .25 .11
❑ 87 Roman Hamrlik .10 .05
❑ 88 Todd Marchant .10 .05
❑ 89 Dean McAmmond .10 .05
❑ 90 Boris Mironov .10 .05
❑ 91 Janne Niinimaa .25 .11
❑ 92 Ryan Smyth .25 .11
❑ 93 Doug Weight .25 .11
❑ 94 Dino Ciccarelli .25 .11
❑ 95 Dave Gagner .10 .05
❑ 96 Ed Jovanovski .10 .05
❑ 97 Viktor Kozlov .10 .05
❑ 98 Paul Laus .10 .05
❑ 99 Scott Mellanby .10 .05
❑ 100 Robert Svehla .10 .05

| | | |
|---|---|---|
| ❑ 101 Ray Whitney | .10 | .05 |
| ❑ 102 Rob Blake | .25 | .11 |
| ❑ 103 Russ Courtnall | .10 | .05 |
| ❑ 104 Stephane Fiset | .25 | .11 |
| ❑ 105 Glen Murray | .10 | .05 |
| ❑ 106 Yanic Perreault | .10 | .05 |
| ❑ 107 Luc Robitaille | .25 | .11 |
| ❑ 108 Jamie Storr | .25 | .11 |
| ❑ 109 Jozef Stumpel | .25 | .11 |
| ❑ 110 Vladimir Tsyplakov | .10 | .05 |
| ❑ 111 Shayne Corson | .10 | .05 |
| ❑ 112 Vincent Damphousse | .25 | .11 |
| ❑ 113 Saku Koivu | .50 | .23 |
| ❑ 114 Vladimir Malakhov | .10 | .05 |
| ❑ 115 Dave Manson | .10 | .05 |
| ❑ 116 Mark Recchi | .25 | .11 |
| ❑ 117 Martin Rucinsky | .10 | .05 |
| ❑ 118 Brian Savage | .10 | .05 |
| ❑ 119 Jocelyn Thibault | .25 | .11 |
| ❑ 120 Blair Atcheynum | .10 | .05 |
| ❑ 121 Andrew Brunette | .10 | .05 |
| ❑ 122 Mike Dunham | .25 | .11 |
| ❑ 123 Tom Fitzgerald | .10 | .05 |
| ❑ 124 Sergei Krivokrasov | .10 | .05 |
| ❑ 125 Denny Lambert | .10 | .05 |
| ❑ 126 Jay More | .10 | .05 |
| ❑ 127 Mikhail Shtalenkov | .10 | .05 |
| ❑ 128 Darren Turcotte | .10 | .05 |
| ❑ 129 Scott Walker | .10 | .05 |
| ❑ 130 Dave Andreychuk | .25 | .11 |
| ❑ 131 Jason Arnott | .25 | .11 |
| ❑ 132 Martin Brodeur | .75 | .35 |
| ❑ 133 Patrik Elias | .25 | .11 |
| ❑ 134 Bobby Holik | .10 | .05 |
| ❑ 135 Randy McKay | .10 | .05 |
| ❑ 136 Scott Niedermayer | .10 | .05 |
| ❑ 137 Krzysztof Oliwa | .10 | .05 |
| ❑ 138 Sheldon Souray | .25 | .11 |
| ❑ 139 Scott Stevens | .10 | .05 |
| ❑ 140 Bryan Berard | .25 | .11 |
| ❑ 141 Mariusz Czerkawski | .10 | .05 |
| ❑ 142 Jason Dawe | .10 | .05 |
| ❑ 143 Kenny Jonsson | .10 | .05 |
| ❑ 144 Trevor Linden | .25 | .11 |
| ❑ 145 Zigmund Palffy | .30 | .14 |
| ❑ 146 Richard Pilon | .10 | .05 |
| ❑ 147 Robert Reichel | .10 | .05 |
| ❑ 148 Tommy Salo | .25 | .11 |
| ❑ 149 Bryan Smolinski | .10 | .05 |
| ❑ 150 Dan Cloutier | .10 | .05 |
| ❑ 151 Adam Graves | .25 | .11 |
| ❑ 152 Wayne Gretzky | 2.00 | .90 |
| ❑ 153 Alexei Kovalev | .10 | .05 |
| ❑ 154 Pat LaFontaine | .25 | .11 |
| ❑ 155 Brian Leetch | .30 | .14 |
| ❑ 156 Mike Richter | .30 | .14 |
| ❑ 157 Ulf Samuelsson | .10 | .05 |
| ❑ 158 Kevin Stevens | .10 | .05 |
| ❑ 159 Niklas Sundstrom | .10 | .05 |
| ❑ 160 Daniel Alfredsson | .25 | .11 |
| ❑ 161 Magnus Arvedson | .10 | .05 |
| ❑ 162 Andreas Dackell | .10 | .05 |
| ❑ 163 Igor Kravchuk | .10 | .05 |
| ❑ 164 Shawn McEachern | .10 | .05 |
| ❑ 165 Chris Phillips | .10 | .05 |
| ❑ 166 Damian Rhodes | .25 | .11 |
| ❑ 167 Ron Tugnutt | .25 | .11 |
| ❑ 168 Alexei Yashin | .25 | .11 |
| ❑ 169 Rod Brind'Amour | .25 | .11 |
| ❑ 170 Alexandre Daigle | .10 | .05 |
| ❑ 171 Eric Desjardins | .10 | .05 |
| ❑ 172 Colin Forbes | .10 | .05 |
| ❑ 173 Chris Gratton | .25 | .11 |
| ❑ 174 Ron Hextall | .25 | .11 |
| ❑ 175 Trent Klatt | .10 | .05 |
| ❑ 176 John LeClair | .50 | .23 |
| ❑ 177 Eric Lindros | 1.00 | .45 |
| ❑ 178 John Vanbiesbrouck | .50 | .23 |
| ❑ 179 Dainius Zubrus | .10 | .05 |
| ❑ 180 Dallas Drake | .10 | .05 |
| ❑ 181 Brad Isbister | .10 | .05 |
| ❑ 182 Nikolai Khabibulin | .25 | .11 |
| ❑ 183 Teppo Numminen | .10 | .05 |
| ❑ 184 Jeremy Roenick | .30 | .14 |
| ❑ 185 Cliff Ronning | .10 | .05 |
| ❑ 186 Keith Tkachuk | .40 | .18 |
| ❑ 187 Rick Tocchet | .25 | .11 |
| ❑ 188 Oleg Tverdovsky | .10 | .05 |
| ❑ 189 Stu Barnes | .10 | .05 |
| ❑ 190 Tom Barrasso | .25 | .11 |
| ❑ 191 Kevin Hatcher | .10 | .05 |
| ❑ 192 Jaromir Jagr | 1.00 | .45 |
| ❑ 193 Darius Kasparaitis | .10 | .05 |
| ❑ 194 Alexei Morozov | .10 | .05 |
| ❑ 195 Fredrik Olausson | .10 | .05 |
| ❑ 196 Jiri Slegr | .10 | .05 |
| ❑ 197 Martin Straka | .10 | .05 |
| ❑ 198 Jim Campbell | .10 | .05 |
| ❑ 199 Kelly Chase | .10 | .05 |
| ❑ 200 Craig Conroy | .10 | .05 |
| ❑ 201 Geoff Courtnall | .10 | .05 |
| ❑ 202 Pavol Demitra | .25 | .11 |
| ❑ 203 Grant Fuhr | .25 | .11 |
| ❑ 204 Al MacInnis | .25 | .11 |
| ❑ 205 Jamie McLennan | .10 | .05 |
| ❑ 206 Chris Pronger | .25 | .11 |
| ❑ 207 Pierre Turgeon | .25 | .11 |
| ❑ 208 Tony Twist | .10 | .05 |
| ❑ 209 Jeff Friesen | .25 | .11 |
| ❑ 210 Tony Granato | .10 | .05 |
| ❑ 211 Patrick Marleau | .10 | .05 |
| ❑ 212 Stephane Matteau | .10 | .05 |
| ❑ 213 Marty McSorley | .10 | .05 |
| ❑ 214 Owen Nolan | .25 | .11 |
| ❑ 215 Marco Sturm | .25 | .11 |
| ❑ 216 Mike Vernon | .25 | .11 |
| ❑ 217 Karl Dykhuis | .10 | .05 |
| ❑ 218 Sandy McCarty | .10 | .05 |
| ❑ 219 Mikael Renberg | .25 | .11 |
| ❑ 220 Stephane Richer | .25 | .11 |
| ❑ 221 Alexander Selivanov | .10 | .05 |
| ❑ 222 Paul Ysebaert | .10 | .05 |
| ❑ 223 Rob Zamuner | .10 | .05 |
| ❑ 224 Sergei Berezin | .25 | .11 |
| ❑ 225 Tie Domi | .10 | .05 |
| ❑ 226 Mike Johnson | .10 | .05 |
| ❑ 227 Curtis Joseph | .30 | .14 |
| ❑ 228 Derek King | .10 | .05 |
| ❑ 229 Igor Korolev | .10 | .05 |
| ❑ 230 Mathieu Schneider | .10 | .05 |
| ❑ 231 Mats Sundin | .30 | .14 |
| ❑ 232 Todd Bertuzzi | .10 | .05 |
| ❑ 233 Donald Brashear | .10 | .05 |
| ❑ 234 Pavel Bure | .60 | .25 |
| ❑ 235 Arturs Irbe | .25 | .11 |
| ❑ 236 Mark Messier | .40 | .18 |
| ❑ 237 Alexander Mogilny | .25 | .11 |
| ❑ 238 Mattias Ohlund | .25 | .11 |
| ❑ 239 Dave Scatchard | .10 | .05 |
| ❑ 240 Garth Snow | .25 | .11 |
| ❑ 241 Brian Bellows | .10 | .05 |
| ❑ 242 Peter Bondra | .30 | .14 |
| ❑ 243 Jeff Brown | .10 | .05 |
| ❑ 244 Sergei Gonchar | .10 | .05 |
| ❑ 245 Calle Johansson | .10 | .05 |
| ❑ 246 Joe Juneau | .25 | .11 |
| ❑ 247 Olaf Kolzig | .25 | .11 |
| ❑ 248 Steve Konowalchuk | .10 | .05 |
| ❑ 249 Adam Oates | .25 | .11 |
| ❑ 250 Richard Zednik | .10 | .05 |
| ❑ NNO Martin Brodeur SAMPLE | 2.00 | .90 |

## 1998-99 Pacific Paramount Copper

The 1998-99 Pacific Paramount Copper set consists of 250 cards and is a parallel of the regular Pacific Paramount base set. The set is a U.S. Hobby set only and the cards are randomly inserted in packs at a rate of one in one.

| | MINT | NRMT |
|---|---|---|
| COMPLETE SET (250) | 200.00 | 90.00 |
| COMMON CARD (1-250) | .60 | .25 |

*STARS: 3X TO 6X BASIC CARD
*YOUNG STARS: 2X TO 4X

## 1998-99 Pacific Paramount Emerald Green

The 1998-99 Pacific Paramount Emerald Green set consists of 250 cards and is a parallel of the regular Pacific Paramount base set. The set is a Canadian Hobby set only and the cards are randomly inserted in packs at a rate of one in one.

| | MINT | NRMT |
|---|---|---|
| COMPLETE SET (250) | 200.00 | 90.00 |
| COMMON CARD (1-250) | .60 | .25 |

*STARS: 3X TO 6X BASIC CARD
*YOUNG STARS: 2.5X TO 5X

## 1998-99 Pacific Paramount Holo-Electric

Randomly inserted in hobby packs only, this 250-card set is a hobby parallel version of the base set and features holographic silver soil along with a special gold foil impression. Only 99 serial-numbered sets were made.

| | MINT | NRMT |
|---|---|---|
| COMPLETE SET (250) | 6000.00 | 2700.00 |
| COMMON CARD (1-250) | 20.00 | 9.00 |
| SEMISTARS/GOALIES | 50.00 | 22.00 |
| UNLISTED STARS | 60.00 | 27.00 |

*STARS: 100X TO 200X BASIC CARDS
*YOUNG STARS: 75X TO 150X

| | | |
|---|---|---|
| ❑ 3 Paul Kariya | 20.00 | 9.00 |
| ❑ 7 Teemu Selanne | 20.00 | 9.00 |
| ❑ 19 Dominik Hasek | 20.00 | 9.00 |
| ❑ 55 Peter Forsberg | 20.00 | 9.00 |
| ❑ 60 Patrick Roy | 20.00 | 9.00 |
| ❑ 61 Joe Sakic | 20.00 | 9.00 |
| ❑ 74 Sergei Fedorov | 20.00 | 9.00 |
| ❑ 82 Brendan Shanahan | 20.00 | 9.00 |
| ❑ 83 Steve Yzerman | 20.00 | 9.00 |
| ❑ 113 Saku Koivu | 20.00 | 9.00 |
| ❑ 132 Martin Brodeur | 20.00 | 9.00 |
| ❑ 152 Wayne Gretzky | 20.00 | 9.00 |
| ❑ 176 John LeClair | 20.00 | 9.00 |
| ❑ 177 Eric Lindros | 20.00 | 9.00 |
| ❑ 178 John Vanbiesbrouck | 20.00 | 9.00 |
| ❑ 192 Jaromir Jagr | 20.00 | 9.00 |
| ❑ 234 Pavel Bure | 20.00 | 9.00 |

## 1998-99 Pacific Paramount Ice Blue

The 1998-99 Pacific Paramount Ice Blue set consists of 250 cards and is a parallel of the regular Pacific Paramount base set. The cards are randomly inserted in packs at rate of one in 73.

| | MINT | NRMT |
|---|---|---|
| COMPLETE SET (250) | 5000.00 | 2200.00 |
| COMMON CARD (1-250) | 15.00 | 6.75 |
| SEMISTARS/GOALIES | 40.00 | 18.00 |
| UNLISTED STARS | 50.00 | 22.00 |

*STARS: 75X TO 150X BASIC CARD
*YOUNG STARS: 50X TO 100X BASIC CARD

## 1998-99 Pacific Paramount Silver

The 1998-99 Pacific Paramount Silver set consists of 250 cards and is a parallel of the regular Pacific Paramount baser set. The set is a retail set only and the cards are randomly inserted in packs at a rate of one in one.

| | MINT | NRMT |
|---|---|---|
| COMPLETE SET (250) | 250.00 | 110.00 |
| COMMON CARD (1-250) | .75 | .35 |

*STARS: 4X TO 8X BASIC CARD
*YOUNG STARS: 3X TO 6X BASIC CARD

## 1998-99 Pacific Paramount Glove Side Laser Cuts

The 1998-99 Pacific Paramount Glove Side Laser Cuts set consists of 20 cards and is an insert of the regular Pacific Paramount base set. The cards are randomly inserted in packs at a rate of one in 73. The cards feature 20 superstar goalies delivered on one of the most unique designs.

| | MINT | NRMT |
|---|---|---|
| COMPLETE SET (20) | 350.00 | 160.00 |
| COMMON CARD (1-20) | 12.00 | 5.50 |

| | | |
|---|---|---|
| ❑ 1 Guy Hebert | 12.00 | 5.50 |
| ❑ 2 Byron Dafoe | 12.00 | 5.50 |
| ❑ 3 Dominik Hasek | 30.00 | 13.50 |
| ❑ 4 Trevor Kidd | 12.00 | 5.50 |
| ❑ 5 Jeff Hackett | 12.00 | 5.50 |
| ❑ 6 Patrick Roy | 80.00 | 36.00 |
| ❑ 7 Ed Belfour | 20.00 | 9.00 |
| ❑ 8 Chris Osgood | 20.00 | 9.00 |
| ❑ 9 Mike Dunham | 12.00 | 5.50 |
| ❑ 10 Martin Brodeur | 40.00 | 18.00 |
| ❑ 11 Tommy Salo | 12.00 | 5.50 |
| ❑ 12 Mike Richter | 20.00 | 9.00 |
| ❑ 13 Damian Rhodes | 12.00 | 5.50 |
| ❑ 14 Ron Hextall | 12.00 | 5.50 |
| ❑ 15 Nikolai Khabibulin | 12.00 | 5.50 |
| ❑ 16 Tom Barrasso | 12.00 | 5.50 |
| ❑ 17 Grant Fuhr | 12.00 | 5.50 |
| ❑ 18 Mike Vernon | 12.00 | 5.50 |
| ❑ 19 Curtis Joseph | 20.00 | 9.00 |
| ❑ 20 Olaf Kolzig | 12.00 | 5.50 |

## 1998-99 Pacific Paramount Hall of Fame Bound

The 1998-99 Pacific Paramount Hall of Fame Bound set consists of 10 cards and is an insert of the regular Pacific Paramount base set. The cards are randomly inserted in packs at a rate of one in 361. The cards honor 10 NHL superstars on a fully foiled and etched card.

| | MINT | NRMT |
|---|---|---|
| COMPLETE SET (10) | 1000.00 | 450.00 |
| COMMON CARD (1-10) | 40.00 | 18.00 |

| | | |
|---|---|---|
| ❑ 1 Teemu Selanne | 60.00 | 27.00 |
| ❑ 2 Dominik Hasek | 60.00 | 27.00 |
| ❑ 3 Peter Forsberg | 100.00 | 45.00 |
| ❑ 4 Patrick Roy | 150.00 | 70.00 |
| ❑ 5 Steve Yzerman | 100.00 | 45.00 |
| ❑ 6 Martin Brodeur | 80.00 | 36.00 |
| ❑ 7 Wayne Gretzky | 200.00 | 90.00 |
| ❑ 8 Eric Lindros | 100.00 | 45.00 |
| ❑ 9 Jaromir Jagr | 100.00 | 45.00 |
| ❑ 10 Mark Messier | 40.00 | 18.00 |

## 1998-99 Pacific Paramount Hall of Fame Bound Pacific Proofs

Randomly inserted into packs, this 10-card set is a parallel version of the regular Pacific Paramount Hall of Fame Bound insert set.

| | MINT | NRMT |
|---|---|---|
| COMPLETE SET (10) | 2500.00 | 1100.00 |
| COMMON CARD (1-10) | 100.00 | 45.00 |

*STARS: 3X TO 6X BASIC CARDS

## 1998-99 Pacific Paramount Ice Galaxy

Randomly inserted into Canadian retail packs only, this 10-card set features action color player photos with bronze foil highlights. Only 140 sets were made. A silver foil parallel set was also produced. Only 50 of these sets were made. A very limited gold foil parallel set was produced with a print run of only 10 sets.

| | MINT | NRMT |
|---|---|---|
| COMPLETE SET (10) | 1500.00 | 700.00 |
| COMMON CARD (1-10) | 40.00 | 18.00 |

BRONZE PRINT RUN 140 SETS

| | | |
|---|---|---|
| COMP.SILVER SET (10) | 3500.00 | 1600.00 |
| COMMON SILVER (1-10) | 100.00 | 45.00 |

*SILVER STARS: 1.25X TO 2.5X BASIC CARDS
SILVER PRINT RUN 50 SETS

| | | |
|---|---|---|
| COMP.GOLD SET (10) | | |
| COMMON GOLD (1-10) | 300.00 | 135.00 |

*GOLD STARS: 3.5X TO 7X BASIC CARDS
GOLD PRINT RUN 10 SETS

| | | |
|---|---|---|
| ❑ 1 Paul Kariya | 200.00 | 90.00 |
| ❑ 2 Peter Forsberg | 150.00 | 70.00 |
| ❑ 3 Patrick Roy | 250.00 | 110.00 |
| ❑ 4 Joe Sakic | 100.00 | 45.00 |
| ❑ 5 Steve Yzerman | 150.00 | 70.00 |
| ❑ 6 Martin Brodeur | 120.00 | 55.00 |
| ❑ 7 Wayne Gretzky | 300.00 | 135.00 |
| ❑ 8 Alexei Yashin | 40.00 | 18.00 |
| ❑ 9 Eric Lindros | 150.00 | 70.00 |
| ❑ 10 Curtis Joseph | 50.00 | 22.00 |

## 1998-99 Pacific Paramount Special Delivery Die-Cuts

The 1998-99 Pacific Paramount Special Delivery Die Cuts set consists of 20 cards and is an insert of the regular Pacific Paramount base set. The cards are randomly inserted in packs at a rate of one in 37. The set features 20 of the most exciting offensive talents in the NHL on high-tech fully foiled cards.

| | MINT | NRMT |
|---|---|---|
| COMPLETE SET (20) | 200.00 | 90.00 |
| COMMON CARD (1-20) | 5.00 | 2.20 |

| | | |
|---|---|---|
| ❑ 1 Paul Kariya | 20.00 | 9.00 |
| ❑ 2 Teemu Selanne | 10.00 | 4.50 |
| ❑ 3 Sergei Samsonov | 8.00 | 3.60 |
| ❑ 4 Peter Forsberg | 15.00 | 6.75 |
| ❑ 5 Joe Sakic | 10.00 | 4.50 |
| ❑ 6 Mike Modano | 6.00 | 2.70 |
| ❑ 7 Sergei Fedorov | 10.00 | 4.50 |
| ❑ 8 Brendan Shanahan | 10.00 | 4.50 |
| ❑ 9 Steve Yzerman | 15.00 | 6.75 |
| ❑ 10 Saku Koivu | 8.00 | 3.60 |
| ❑ 11 Zigmund Palffy | 6.00 | 2.70 |
| ❑ 12 Wayne Gretzky | 30.00 | 13.50 |
| ❑ 13 John LeClair | 8.00 | 3.60 |
| ❑ 14 Eric Lindros | 15.00 | 6.75 |
| ❑ 15 Keith Tkachuk | 6.00 | 2.70 |
| ❑ 16 Jaromir Jagr | 15.00 | 6.75 |
| ❑ 17 Mats Sundin | 5.00 | 2.20 |
| ❑ 18 Pavel Bure | 10.00 | 4.50 |
| ❑ 19 Mark Messier | 6.00 | 2.70 |
| ❑ 20 Peter Bondra | 5.00 | 2.20 |

## 1998-99 Pacific Paramount Team Checklists Die-Cuts

The 1998-99 Pacific Paramount Team Checklists Die-Cuts set consists of 27 cards and is an insert of the regular Pacific Paramount base set. The cards are randomly inserted in packs at a rate of two in 37. The set is fully foiled and features all 27 NHL teams, including the league's 1998-99 expansion franchise, the Nashville Predators. The front features an NHL superstar and the back features the team's complete main set checklist.

| | MINT | NRMT |
|---|---|---|
| COMPLETE SET (27) | 175.00 | 80.00 |
| COMMON CARD (1-27) | 1.25 | .55 |

| | | |
|---|---|---|
| ❑ 1 Teemu Selanne | 8.00 | 3.60 |
| ❑ 2 Sergei Samsonov | 6.00 | 2.70 |
| ❑ 3 Dominik Hasek | 8.00 | 3.60 |
| ❑ 4 Theoren Fleury | 1.25 | .55 |
| ❑ 5 Keith Primeau | 1.25 | .55 |
| ❑ 6 Chris Chelios | 1.25 | .55 |
| ❑ 7 Patrick Roy | 20.00 | 9.00 |
| ❑ 8 Mike Modano | 5.00 | 2.20 |
| ❑ 9 Steve Yzerman | 12.00 | 5.50 |
| ❑ 10 Ryan Smyth | 1.25 | .55 |
| ❑ 11 Dino Ciccarelli | 1.25 | .55 |
| ❑ 12 Rob Blake | 1.25 | .55 |
| ❑ 13 Saku Koivu | 6.00 | 2.70 |
| ❑ 14 Tom Fitzgerald | 1.25 | .55 |
| ❑ 15 Martin Brodeur | 10.00 | 4.50 |
| ❑ 16 Zigmund Palffy | 1.25 | .55 |
| ❑ 17 Wayne Gretzky | 25.00 | 11.00 |
| ❑ 18 Alexei Yashin | 1.25 | .55 |
| ❑ 19 Eric Lindros | 12.00 | 5.50 |
| ❑ 20 Keith Tkachuk | 5.00 | 2.20 |
| ❑ 21 Jaromir Jagr | 12.00 | 5.50 |
| ❑ 22 Grant Fuhr | 1.25 | .55 |
| ❑ 23 Patrick Marleau | 1.25 | .55 |
| ❑ 24 Rob Zamuner | 1.25 | .55 |
| ❑ 25 Mats Sundin | 1.25 | .55 |
| ❑ 26 Mark Messier | 5.00 | 2.20 |
| ❑ 27 Peter Bondra | 1.25 | .55 |

## 1987-88 Panini Stickers

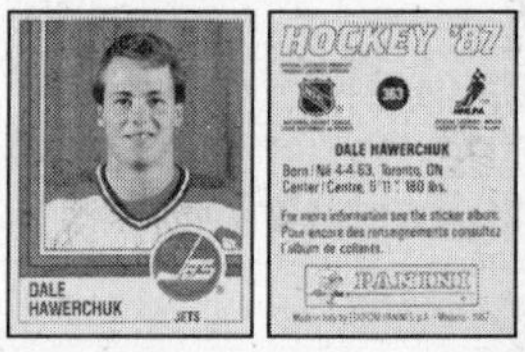

This set of 396 hockey stickers was produced and distributed by Panini. The sticker number is only on the backing of the sticker. The stickers measure approximately 2 1/8" by 2 11/16". The team logos are foil stickers. On the inside back cover of the sticker album the company offered (via direct mail-order) up to 30 different stickers of your choice for either ten cents each or in trade one-for-one for your unwanted extra stickers plus 1.00 for postage and handling; this is one reason why the values of the most popular players in these sticker sets are somewhat depressed compared to traditional card prices.

| | MINT | NRMT |
|---|---|---|
| COMPLETE SET (396) | 35.00 | 16.00 |
| COMMON STICKER (1-396) | .05 | .02 |

| | | |
|---|---|---|
| ❑ 1 Stanley Cup | .10 | .05 |
| ❑ 2 Bruins Action | .05 | .02 |
| ❑ 3 Bruins Emblem | .05 | .02 |
| ❑ 4 Doug Keans | .05 | .02 |
| ❑ 5 Bill Ranford | 1.50 | .70 |
| ❑ 6 Ray Bourque | .50 | .23 |
| ❑ 7 Reed Larson | .05 | .02 |
| ❑ 8 Mike Milbury | .05 | .02 |
| ❑ 9 Michael Thelven | .05 | .02 |
| ❑ 10 Cam Neely | .50 | .23 |
| ❑ 11 Charlie Simmer | .05 | .02 |
| ❑ 12 Rick Middleton | .05 | .02 |
| ❑ 13 Tom McCarthy | .05 | .02 |
| ❑ 14 Keith Crowder | .05 | .02 |
| ❑ 15 Steve Kasper | .05 | .02 |
| ❑ 16 Ken Linseman | .05 | .02 |
| ❑ 17 Dwight Foster | .05 | .02 |
| ❑ 18 Jay Miller | .05 | .02 |
| ❑ 19 Sabres Action | .05 | .02 |
| ❑ 20 Sabres Emblem | .05 | .02 |
| ❑ 21 Jacques Cloutier | .10 | .05 |
| ❑ 22 Tom Barrasso | .10 | .05 |
| ❑ 23 Daren Puppa | .10 | .05 |
| ❑ 24 Phil Housley | .05 | .02 |
| ❑ 25 Mike Ramsey | .05 | .02 |
| ❑ 26 Bill Hajt | .05 | .02 |
| ❑ 27 Dave Andreychuk | .10 | .05 |
| ❑ 28 Christian Ruuttu | .05 | .02 |
| ❑ 29 Mike Foligno | .05 | .02 |
| ❑ 30 John Tucker | .05 | .02 |

❑ 31 Adam Creighton .05 .02
❑ 32 Wilf Paiement .05 .02
❑ 33 Paul Cyr .05 .02
❑ 34 Clark Gillies .05 .02
❑ 35 Lindy Ruff .05 .02
❑ 36 Whalers Action .05 .02
❑ 37 Whalers Emblem .05 .02
❑ 38 Mike Liut .10 .05
❑ 39 Steve Weeks .05 .02
❑ 40 Dave Babych .05 .02
❑ 41 Ulf Samuelsson .50 .23
❑ 42 Dana Murzyn .05 .02
❑ 43 Ron Francis .10 .05
❑ 44 Kevin Dineen .05 .02
❑ 45 John Anderson .05 .02
❑ 46 Ray Ferraro .05 .02
❑ 47 Dean Evason .05 .02
❑ 48 Paul Lawless .05 .02
❑ 49 Stewart Gavin .05 .02
❑ 50 Sylvain Turgeon .05 .02
❑ 51 Dave Tippett .05 .02
❑ 52 Doug Jarvis .05 .02
❑ 53 Canadiens Action .05 .02
❑ 54 Canadiens Emblem .05 .02
❑ 55 Brian Hayward .10 .05
❑ 56 Patrick Roy 3.00 1.35
❑ 57 Larry Robinson .10 .05
❑ 58 Chris Chelios .60 .25
❑ 59 Craig Ludwig .05 .02
❑ 60 Rick Green .05 .02
❑ 61 Mats Naslund .05 .02
❑ 62 Bobby Smith .05 .02
❑ 63 Claude Lemieux 1.50 .70
❑ 64 Guy Carbonneau .10 .05
❑ 65 Stephane Richer .75 .35
❑ 66 Mike McPhee .10 .05
❑ 67 Brian Skrudland .05 .02
❑ 68 Chris Nilan .05 .02
❑ 69 Bob Gainey .10 .05
❑ 70 Devils Action .05 .02
❑ 71 Devils Emblem .05 .02
❑ 72 Craig Billington .10 .05
❑ 73 Alain Chevrier .05 .02
❑ 74 Bruce Driver .05 .02
❑ 75 Joe Cirella .05 .02
❑ 76 Ken Daneyko .05 .02
❑ 77 Craig Wolanin .05 .02
❑ 78 Aaron Broten .05 .02
❑ 79 Kirk Muller .10 .05
❑ 80 John MacLean .05 .02
❑ 81 Pat Verbeek .05 .02
❑ 82 Doug Sulliman .05 .02
❑ 83 Mark Johnson .05 .02
❑ 84 Greg Adams .05 .02
❑ 85 Claude Loiselle .05 .02
❑ 86 Andy Brickley .05 .02
❑ 87 Islanders Action .05 .02
❑ 88 Islanders Emblem .05 .02
❑ 89 Billy Smith .10 .05
❑ 90 Kelly Hrudey .10 .05
❑ 91 Denis Potvin .05 .02
❑ 92 Tomas Jonsson .05 .02
❑ 93 Ken Leiter .05 .02
❑ 94 Ken Morrow .05 .02
❑ 95 Brian Curran .05 .02
❑ 96 Bryan Trottier .10 .05
❑ 97 Mike Bossy .50 .23
❑ 98 Pat LaFontaine .50 .23
❑ 99 Brent Sutter .05 .02
❑ 100 Mikko Makela .05 .02
❑ 101 Pat Flatley .05 .02
❑ 102 Duane Sutter .05 .02
❑ 103 Rich Kromm .05 .02
❑ 104 Rangers Action .05 .02
❑ 105 Rangers Emblem .05 .02
❑ 106 John Vanbiesbrouck 2.00 .90
❑ 107 James Patrick .05 .02
❑ 108 Ron Greschner .05 .02
❑ 109 Willie Huber .05 .02
❑ 110 Curt Giles .05 .02
❑ 111 Larry Melnyk .05 .02
❑ 112 Walt Poddubny .05 .02
❑ 113 Marcel Dionne .50 .23
❑ 114 Tomas Sandstrom .05 .02
❑ 115 Kelly Kisio .05 .02
❑ 116 Pierre Larouche .05 .02
❑ 117 Don Maloney .05 .02
❑ 118 Tony McKegney .05 .02
❑ 119 Ron Duguay .05 .02
❑ 120 Jan Erixon .05 .02
❑ 121 Flyers Action .05 .02
❑ 122 Flyers Emblem .05 .02
❑ 123 Ron Hextall 1.00 .45
❑ 124 Mark Howe .05 .02
❑ 125 Doug Crossman .05 .02
❑ 126 Brad McCrimmon .05 .02
❑ 127 Brad Marsh .05 .02
❑ 128 Tim Kerr .05 .02
❑ 129 Peter Zezel .05 .02
❑ 130 Dave Poulin .05 .02
❑ 131 Brian Propp .05 .02
❑ 132 Pelle Eklund .05 .02
❑ 133 Murray Craven .05 .02
❑ 134 Rick Tocchet 1.00 .45
❑ 135 Derrick Smith .05 .02
❑ 136 Ilkka Sinisalo .05 .02
❑ 137 Ron Sutter .05 .02
❑ 138 Penguins Action .05 .02
❑ 139 Penguins Emblem .05 .02
❑ 140 Gilles Meloche .10 .05
❑ 141 Doug Bodger .05 .02
❑ 142 Moe Mantha .05 .02
❑ 143 Jim Johnson .05 .02
❑ 144 Rod Buskas .05 .02
❑ 145 Randy Hillier .05 .02
❑ 146 Mario Lemieux 3.00 1.35
❑ 147 Dan Quinn .05 .02
❑ 148 Randy Cunneyworth .05 .02
❑ 149 Craig Simpson .05 .02
❑ 150 Terry Ruskowski .05 .02
❑ 151 John Chabot .05 .02
❑ 152 Bob Errey .05 .02
❑ 153 Dan Frawley .05 .02
❑ 154 Dave Hannan .05 .02
❑ 155 Nordiques Action .05 .02
❑ 156 Nordiques Emblem .05 .02
❑ 157 Mario Gosselin .10 .05
❑ 158 Clint Malarchuk .10 .05
❑ 159 Risto Siltanen .05 .02
❑ 160 Robert Picard .05 .02
❑ 161 Normand Rochefort .05 .02
❑ 162 Randy Moller .05 .02
❑ 163 Michel Goulet .10 .05
❑ 164 Peter Stastny .10 .05
❑ 165 John Ogrodnick .05 .02
❑ 166 Anton Stastny .05 .02
❑ 167 Paul Gillis .05 .02
❑ 168 Dale Hunter .05 .02
❑ 169 Alain Cote .05 .02
❑ 170 Mike Eagles .05 .02
❑ 171 Jason Lafreniere .05 .02
❑ 172 Capitals Action .05 .02
❑ 173 Capitals Emblem .05 .02
❑ 174 Pete Peeters .10 .05
❑ 175 Bob Mason .10 .05
❑ 176 Larry Murphy .50 .23
❑ 177 Scott Stevens .10 .05
❑ 178 Rod Langway .05 .02
❑ 179 Kevin Hatcher .50 .23
❑ 180 Mike Gartner .50 .23
❑ 181 Mike Ridley .05 .02
❑ 182 Craig Laughlin .05 .02
❑ 183 Gaetan Duchesne .05 .02
❑ 184 Dave Christian .05 .02
❑ 185 Greg Adams .05 .02
❑ 186 Kelly Miller .05 .02
❑ 187 Alan Haworth .05 .02
❑ 188 Lou Franceschetti .05 .02
❑ 189 Stanley Cup .10 .05
(top half)
❑ 190 Stanley Cup .10 .05
(bottom half)
❑ 191 Ron Hextall 1.50 .70
❑ 192 Wayne Gretzky 4.00 1.80
❑ 193 Brian Propp .05 .02
❑ 194 Mark Messier 1.00 .45
❑ 195 Flyers/Oilers Action .05 .02
❑ 196 Flyers/Oilers Action .05 .02
❑ 197 Gretzky Holding Cup 1.00 .45
(upper left)
❑ 198 Gretzky Holding Cup 1.00 .45
(upper right)
❑ 199 Gretzky Holding Cup 1.00 .45
(lower left)
❑ 200 Gretzky Holding Cup 1.00 .45
(lower right)
❑ 201 Flames Action .05 .02
❑ 202 Flames Emblem .05 .02
❑ 203 Mike Vernon 1.50 .70
❑ 204 Rejean Lemelin .10 .05
❑ 205 Al MacInnis .40 .18
❑ 206 Paul Reinhart .05 .02
❑ 207 Gary Suter .10 .05
❑ 208 Jamie Macoun .05 .02
❑ 209 Neil Sheehy .05 .02
❑ 210 Joe Mullen .10 .05
❑ 211 Carey Wilson .05 .02
❑ 212 Joel Otto .05 .02
❑ 213 Jim Peplinski .05 .02
❑ 214 Hakan Loob .05 .02
❑ 215 Lanny McDonald .05 .02
❑ 216 Tim Hunter .05 .02
❑ 217 Gary Roberts .10 .05
❑ 218 Blackhawks Action .05 .02
❑ 219 Blackhawks Emblem .05 .02
❑ 220 Bob Sauve .10 .05
❑ 221 Murray Bannerman .05 .02
❑ 222 Doug Wilson .05 .02
❑ 223 Bob Murray .05 .02
❑ 224 Gary Nylund .05 .02
❑ 225 Denis Savard .10 .05
❑ 226 Steve Larmer .10 .05
❑ 227 Troy Murray .05 .02
❑ 228 Wayne Presley .05 .02
❑ 229 Al Secord .05 .02
❑ 230 Ed Olczyk .05 .02
❑ 231 Curt Fraser .05 .02
❑ 232 Bill Watson .05 .02
❑ 233 Keith Brown .05 .02
❑ 234 Darryl Sutter .05 .02
❑ 235 Red Wings Action .05 .02
❑ 236 Red Wings Emblem .05 .02
❑ 237 Greg Stefan .05 .02
❑ 238 Glen Hanlon .10 .05
❑ 239 Darren Veitch .05 .02
❑ 240 Mike O'Connell .05 .02
❑ 241 Harold Snepsts .05 .02
❑ 242 Dave Lewis .05 .02
❑ 243 Steve Yzerman 2.00 .90
❑ 244 Brent Ashton .05 .02
❑ 245 Gerard Gallant .05 .02
❑ 246 Petr Klima .05 .02
❑ 247 Shawn Burr .05 .02
❑ 248 Adam Oates 2.00 .90
❑ 249 Mel Bridgman .05 .02
❑ 250 Tim Higgins .05 .02
❑ 251 Joey Kocur .05 .02
❑ 252 Oilers Action .05 .02
❑ 253 Oilers Emblem .05 .02
❑ 254 Grant Fuhr .50 .23
❑ 255 Andy Moog .10 .05
❑ 256 Paul Coffey .50 .23
❑ 257 Kevin Lowe .10 .05
❑ 258 Craig Muni .05 .02
❑ 259 Steve Smith .05 .02
❑ 260 Charlie Huddy .05 .02
❑ 261 Wayne Gretzky 4.00 1.80
❑ 262 Jari Kurri .50 .23
❑ 263 Mark Messier 1.00 .45
❑ 264 Esa Tikkanen 1.00 .45
❑ 265 Glenn Anderson .10 .05
❑ 266 Mike Krushelnyski .05 .02
❑ 267 Craig MacTavish .05 .02
❑ 268 Dave Hunter .05 .02
❑ 269 Kings Action .05 .02
❑ 270 Kings Emblem .05 .02
❑ 271 Roland Melanson .10 .05
❑ 272 Darren Eliot .05 .02
❑ 273 Grant Ledyard .05 .02
❑ 274 Jay Wells .05 .02
❑ 275 Mark Hardy .05 .02
❑ 276 Dean Kennedy .05 .02
❑ 277 Luc Robitaille 2.50 1.10
❑ 278 Bernie Nicholls .10 .05
❑ 279 Jimmy Carson .05 .02
❑ 280 Dave Taylor .05 .02
❑ 281 Jim Fox .05 .02
❑ 282 Bryan Erickson .05 .02
❑ 283 Dave(Tiger) Williams .05 .02
❑ 284 Sean McKenna .05 .02
❑ 285 Phil Sykes .05 .02
❑ 286 North Stars Action .05 .02
❑ 287 North Stars Emblem .05 .02
❑ 288 Kari Takko .10 .05
❑ 289 Don Beaupre .10 .05
❑ 290 Craig Hartsburg .05 .02
❑ 291 Ron Wilson .05 .02
❑ 292 Frantisek Musil .05 .02
❑ 293 Dino Ciccarelli .10 .05
❑ 294 Brian MacLellan .05 .02
❑ 295 Dirk Graham .05 .02
❑ 296 Brian Bellows .05 .02
❑ 297 Neal Broten .05 .02
❑ 298 Dennis Maruk .05 .02
❑ 299 Keith Acton .05 .02
❑ 300 Brian Lawton .05 .02
❑ 301 Bob Brooke .05 .02
❑ 302 Willi Plett .05 .02
❑ 303 Blues Action .05 .02
❑ 304 Blues Emblem .05 .02
❑ 305 Rick Wamsley .10 .05
❑ 306 Rob Ramage .05 .02
❑ 307 Ric Nattress .05 .02
❑ 308 Bruce Bell .05 .02
❑ 309 Charlie Bourgeois .05 .02
❑ 310 Jim Pavese .05 .02
❑ 311 Doug Gilmour .50 .23
❑ 312 Bernie Federko .05 .02
❑ 313 Mark Hunter .05 .02
❑ 314 Greg Paslawski .05 .02
❑ 315 Gino Cavallini .05 .02
❑ 316 Rick Meagher .05 .02
❑ 317 Ron Flockhart .05 .02
❑ 318 Doug Wickenheiser .05 .02
❑ 319 Jocelyn Lemieux .05 .02
❑ 320 Maple Leafs Action .05 .02
❑ 321 Maple Leafs Emblem .05 .02
❑ 322 Ken Wregget .10 .05
❑ 323 Allan Bester .10 .05
❑ 324 Todd Gill .05 .02
❑ 325 Al Iafrate .05 .02
❑ 326 Borje Salming .05 .02
❑ 327 Russ Courtnall .05 .02
❑ 328 Rick Vaive .05 .02
❑ 329 Steve Thomas .05 .02
❑ 330 Wendel Clark .75 .35
❑ 331 Gary Leeman .05 .02
❑ 332 Tom Fergus .05 .02
❑ 333 Vincent Damphousse 1.00 .45
❑ 334 Peter Ihnacak .05 .02
❑ 335 Brad Smith .05 .02
❑ 336 Miroslav Ihnacak .05 .02
❑ 337 Canucks Action .05 .02
❑ 338 Canucks Emblem .05 .02
❑ 339 Frank Caprice .05 .02
❑ 340 Richard Brodeur .05 .02
❑ 341 Doug Lidster .05 .02
❑ 342 Michel Petit .05 .02
❑ 343 Garth Butcher .05 .02
❑ 344 Dave Richter .05 .02
❑ 345 Tony Tanti .05 .02
❑ 346 Barry Pederson .05 .02
❑ 347 Petri Skriko .05 .02
❑ 348 Patrik Sundstrom .05 .02
❑ 349 Stan Smyl .05 .02
❑ 350 Rich Sutter .05 .02
❑ 351 Steve Tambellini .05 .02
❑ 352 Jim Sandlak .05 .02
❑ 353 Dave Lowry .05 .02
❑ 354 Jets Action .05 .02
❑ 355 Jets Emblem .05 .02
❑ 356 Daniel Berthiaume .10 .05
❑ 357 Pokey Reddick .05 .02
❑ 358 Dave Ellett .05 .02
❑ 359 Mario Marois .05 .02
❑ 360 Randy Carlyle .05 .02
❑ 361 Fredrick Olausson .05 .02
❑ 362 Jim Kyte .05 .02
❑ 363 Dale Hawerchuk .10 .05
❑ 364 Paul MacLean .05 .02
❑ 365 Thomas Steen .05 .02
❑ 366 Gilles Hamel .05 .02
❑ 367 Doug Smail .05 .02
❑ 368 Laurie Boschman .05 .02
❑ 369 Ray Neufeld .05 .02
❑ 370 Andrew McBain .05 .02
❑ 371 Wayne Gretzky 4.00 1.80
❑ 372 Hart Trophy .05 .02
❑ 373 Wayne Gretzky 4.00 1.80
❑ 374 Art Ross Trophy .05 .02
❑ 375 Jennings Trophy .05 .02
❑ 376A Brian Hayward .10 .05
❑ 376B Patrick Roy 3.00 1.35
❑ 377 Vezina Trophy .05 .02
❑ 378 Ron Hextall .50 .23
❑ 379 Luc Robitaille 2.50 1.10
❑ 380 Calder Trophy .05 .02
❑ 381 Ray Bourque .50 .23
❑ 382 Norris Trophy .05 .02
❑ 383 Lady Byng Trophy .05 .02
❑ 384 Joe Mullen .10 .05
❑ 385 Frank Selke Trophy .05 .02
❑ 386 Dave Poulin .05 .02
❑ 387 Doug Jarvis .05 .02
❑ 388 Masterton Trophy .05 .02
❑ 389 Wayne Gretzky 4.00 1.80
❑ 390 Emery Edge Award .05 .02
❑ 391 Flyers Team Photo .05 .02
(left half)
❑ 392 Flyers Team Photo .05 .02
(right half)
❑ 393 Prince of Wales .05 .02
Trophy
❑ 394 Clarence S. Campbell .05 .02
Bowl
❑ 395 Oilers Team Photo .05 .02
(left half)
❑ 396 Oilers Team Photo .05 .02
(right half)
❑ xx Sticker Album 5.00 2.20

## 1988-89 Panini Stickers

This set of 408 hockey stickers was produced and distributed by Panini. The sticker number is only on the backing of the sticker. The stickers measure approximately 2 1/8" by 2 11/16". The team picture cards are double stickers with each sticker showing half of the photo; in the checklist below these halves are denoted by LH (left half) and RH (right half). There was an album issued with the set for holding the stickers. On the inside back cover of the sticker album the company offered (via direct mail-order) up to 30 different stickers of your choice for either ten cents each or in trade one-for-one for your unwanted extra stickers plus 1.00 for postage and handling; this is one reason why the values of the most popular players in these sticker sets are somewhat depressed compared to traditional card prices.

| | MINT | NRMT |
|---|---|---|
| COMPLETE SET (408) | 30.00 | 13.50 |
| COMMON STICKER (1-408) | .05 | .02 |

❑ 1 Road to the Cup .05 .02
Stanley Cup Draw
❑ 2 Flames Emblem .05 .02
❑ 3 Flames Uniform .05 .02
❑ 4 Mike Vernon .10 .05
❑ 5 Al MacInnis .10 .05
❑ 6 Brad McCrimmon .05 .02
❑ 7 Gary Suter .10 .05
❑ 8 Mike Bullard .05 .02
❑ 9 Hakan Loob .05 .02
❑ 10 Lanny McDonald .05 .02
❑ 11 Joe Mullen .10 .05
❑ 12 Joe Nieuwendyk 1.25 .55
❑ 13 Joel Otto .05 .02
❑ 14 Jim Peplinski .05 .02
❑ 15 Gary Roberts .10 .05
❑ 16 Flames Team LH .05 .02
❑ 17 Flames Team RH .05 .02
❑ 18 Blackhawks Emblem .05 .02
❑ 19 Blackhawks Uniform .05 .02
❑ 20 Bob Mason .10 .05
❑ 21 Darren Pang .10 .05
❑ 22 Bob Murray .05 .02
❑ 23 Gary Nylund .05 .02
❑ 24 Doug Wilson .05 .02
❑ 25 Dirk Graham .05 .02
❑ 26 Steve Larmer .10 .05
❑ 27 Troy Murray .05 .02
❑ 28 Brian Noonan .05 .02
❑ 29 Denis Savard .10 .05
❑ 30 Steve Thomas .05 .02
❑ 31 Rick Vaive .05 .02
❑ 32 Blackhawks Team LH .05 .02
❑ 33 Blackhawks Team RH .05 .02
❑ 34 Red Wings Emblem .05 .02
❑ 35 Red Wings Uniform .05 .02
❑ 36 Glen Hanlon .10 .05
❑ 37 Greg Stefan .10 .05
❑ 38 Jeff Sharples .05 .02
❑ 39 Darren Veitch .05 .02
❑ 40 Brent Ashton .05 .02
❑ 41 Shawn Burr .05 .02
❑ 42 John Chabot .05 .02
❑ 43 Gerard Gallant .05 .02
❑ 44 Petr Klima .05 .02
❑ 45 Adam Oates .10 .05
❑ 46 Bob Probert .75 .35
❑ 47 Steve Yzerman 1.50 .70
❑ 48 Red Wings Team LH .05 .02
❑ 49 Red Wings Team RH .05 .02
❑ 50 Oilers Emblem .05 .02
❑ 51 Oilers Uniform .05 .02
❑ 52 Grant Fuhr .50 .23
❑ 53 Charlie Huddy .05 .02
❑ 54 Kevin Lowe .10 .05
❑ 55 Steve Smith .05 .02
❑ 56 Jeff Beukeboom .05 .02
❑ 57 Glenn Anderson .10 .05
❑ 58 Wayne Gretzky 2.50 1.10
❑ 59 Jari Kurri .50 .23
❑ 60 Craig MacTavish .05 .02
❑ 61 Mark Messier .75 .35
❑ 62 Craig Simpson .05 .02
❑ 63 Esa Tikkanen .10 .05
❑ 64 Oilers Team LH .05 .02
❑ 65 Oilers Team RH .05 .02
❑ 66 Kings Emblem .05 .02
❑ 67 Kings Uniform .05 .02
❑ 68 Glenn Healy .50 .23
❑ 69 Roland Melanson .10 .05
❑ 70 Steve Duchesne .50 .23
❑ 71 Tom Laidlaw .05 .02
❑ 72 Jay Wells .05 .02
❑ 73 Mike Allison .05 .02
❑ 74 Bob Carpenter .05 .02
❑ 75 Jimmy Carson .05 .02
❑ 76 Jim Fox .05 .02
❑ 77 Bernie Nicholls .10 .05
❑ 78 Luc Robitaille .50 .23
❑ 79 Dave Taylor .05 .02
❑ 80 Kings Team LH .05 .02
❑ 81 Kings Team RH .05 .02
❑ 82 North Stars Emblem .05 .02
❑ 83 North Stars Uniform .05 .02
❑ 84 Don Beaupre .10 .05
❑ 85 Kari Takko .10 .05
❑ 86 Craig Hartsburg .05 .02
❑ 87 Frantisek Musil .05 .02
❑ 88 Dave Archibald .05 .02
❑ 89 Brian Bellows .05 .02
❑ 90 Scott Bjugstad .05 .02
❑ 91 Bob Brooke .05 .02
❑ 92 Neal Broten .05 .02
❑ 93 Dino Ciccarelli .10 .05
❑ 94 Brian Lawton .05 .02
❑ 95 Brian MacLellan .05 .02
❑ 96 North Stars Team LH .05 .02
❑ 97 North Stars Team RH .05 .02
❑ 98 Blues Emblem .05 .02
❑ 99 Blues Uniform .05 .02
❑ 100 Greg Millen .10 .05
❑ 101 Brian Benning .05 .02
❑ 102 Gordie Roberts .05 .02
❑ 103 Gino Cavallini .05 .02
❑ 104 Bernie Federko .05 .02
❑ 105 Doug Gilmour .50 .23
❑ 106 Tony Hrkac .05 .02
❑ 107 Brett Hull 3.00 1.35
❑ 108 Mark Hunter .05 .02
❑ 109 Tony McKegney .05 .02
❑ 110 Rick Meagher .05 .02
❑ 111 Brian Sutter .05 .02
❑ 112 Blues Team LH .05 .02
❑ 113 Blues Team RH .05 .02
❑ 114 Maple Leafs Emblem .05 .02
❑ 115 Maple Leafs Uniform .05 .02
❑ 116 Allan Bester .10 .05
❑ 117 Ken Wregget .10 .05
❑ 118 Al Iafrate .05 .02
❑ 119 Luke Richardson .05 .02
❑ 120 Borje Salming .05 .02
❑ 121 Wendel Clark .10 .05
❑ 122 Russ Courtnall .05 .02
❑ 123 Vincent Damphousse .10 .05
❑ 124 Dan Daoust .05 .02
❑ 125 Gary Leeman .05 .02
❑ 126 Ed Olczyk .05 .02
❑ 127 Mark Osborne .05 .02
❑ 128 Maple Leafs Team LH .05 .02
❑ 129 Maple Leafs Team RH .05 .02
❑ 130 Canucks Emblem .05 .02
❑ 131 Canucks Uniform .05 .02
❑ 132 Kirk McLean .10 .05
❑ 133 Jim Benning .05 .02
❑ 134 Garth Butcher .05 .02
❑ 135 Doug Lidster .05 .02
❑ 136 Greg Adams .05 .02
❑ 137 David Bruce .05 .02
❑ 138 Barry Pederson .05 .02
❑ 139 Jim Sandlak .05 .02
❑ 140 Petri Skriko .05 .02
❑ 141 Stan Smyl .05 .02
❑ 142 Rich Sutter .05 .02
❑ 143 Tony Tanti .05 .02
❑ 144 Canucks Team LH .05 .02
❑ 145 Canucks Team RH .05 .02
❑ 146 Jets Emblem .05 .02
❑ 147 Jets Uniform .05 .02
❑ 148 Daniel Berthiaume .10 .05
❑ 149 Randy Carlyle .05 .02
❑ 150 Dave Ellett .05 .02
❑ 151 Mario Marois .05 .02
❑ 152 Peter Taglianetti .05 .02
❑ 153 Laurie Boschman .05 .02
❑ 154 Iain Duncan .05 .02
❑ 155 Dale Hawerchuk .10 .05
❑ 156 Paul MacLean .05 .02
❑ 157 Andrew McBain .05 .02
❑ 158 Doug Smail .05 .02
❑ 159 Thomas Steen .05 .02
❑ 160 Jets Team LH .05 .02
❑ 161 Jets Team RH .05 .02

❑ 162 Prince of Wales Trophy .05 .02
❑ 163 Caps/Flyers Action .05 .02
❑ 164 Bruins/Canadiens Action .05 .02
❑ 165 Caps/Devils Action .05 .02
❑ 166 Bruins/Devils Action LH .05 .02
❑ 167 Bruins/Devils Action RH .05 .02
❑ 168 Flames/Kings Action .05 .02
❑ 169 Clarence S. Campbell Bowl .05 .02
❑ 170 Oilers/Flames Action .05 .02
❑ 171 Blues/Red Wings Action .05 .02
❑ 172 Oilers/Red Wings Action LH .05 .02
❑ 173 Oilers/Red Wings Action RH .05 .02
❑ 174 Oilers Celebrate .05 .02
❑ 175 Oilers/Bruins Action .05 .02
❑ 176 Stanley Cup (top half) .10 .05
❑ 177 Stanley Cup (bottom half) .10 .05
❑ 178 Wayne Gretzky 2.50 1.10
❑ 179 Oilers/Bruins Action RH .05 .02
❑ 180 Oilers/Bruins Action .05 .02
❑ 181 Wayne Gretzky 2.50 1.10
❑ 182 Conn Smythe Trophy .05 .02
❑ 183 Oilers Celebrate UL .05 .02
❑ 184 Oilers Celebrate UR .05 .02
❑ 185 Oilers Celebrate LL .05 .02
❑ 186 Oilers Celebrate LR .05 .02
❑ 187 Flames Action .05 .02
❑ 188 Grant Fuhr .50 .23
❑ 189 Devils Action .05 .02
❑ 190 Marcel Dionne .50 .23
❑ 191 Bruins Action .05 .02
❑ 192 Capitals Action .05 .02
❑ 193 Wayne Gretzky 2.50 1.10
❑ 194 Oilers Action .05 .02
❑ 195 Bruins/Canadiens Action .05 .02
❑ 196 Blues Action .05 .02
❑ 197 Caps/Flyers Action .05 .02
❑ 198 Islanders Action .05 .02
❑ 199 Flames Action .05 .02
❑ 200 Penguins Action .05 .02
❑ 201 Bruins Emblem .05 .02
❑ 202 Bruins Uniform .05 .02
❑ 203 Rejean Lemelin .10 .05
❑ 204 Ray Bourque .50 .23
❑ 205 Gord Kluzak .05 .02
❑ 206 Michael Thelven .05 .02
❑ 207 Glen Wesley .05 .02
❑ 208 Randy Burridge .05 .02
❑ 209 Keith Crowder .05 .02
❑ 210 Steve Kasper .05 .02
❑ 211 Ken Linseman .05 .02
❑ 212 Jay Miller .05 .02
❑ 213 Cam Neely .50 .23
❑ 214 Bob Sweeney .05 .02
❑ 215 Bruins Team LH .05 .02
❑ 216 Bruins Team RH .05 .02
❑ 217 Sabres Emblem .05 .02
❑ 218 Sabres Uniform .05 .02
❑ 219 Tom Barrasso .10 .05
❑ 220 Phil Housley .05 .02
❑ 221 Calle Johansson .05 .02
❑ 222 Mike Ramsey .05 .02
❑ 223 Dave Andreychuk .10 .05
❑ 224 Scott Arniel .05 .02
❑ 225 Adam Creighton .05 .02
❑ 226 Mike Foligno .05 .02
❑ 227 Christian Ruuttu .05 .02
❑ 228 Ray Sheppard .50 .23
❑ 229 John Tucker .05 .02
❑ 230 Pierre Turgeon 1.50 .70
❑ 231 Sabres Team LH .05 .02
❑ 232 Sabres Team RH .05 .02
❑ 233 Whalers Emblem .05 .02
❑ 234 Whalers Uniform .05 .02
❑ 235 Mike Liut .10 .05
❑ 236 Dave Babych .05 .02
❑ 237 Sylvain Cote .05 .02
❑ 238 Ulf Samuelsson .05 .02
❑ 239 John Anderson .05 .02
❑ 240 Kevin Dineen .05 .02
❑ 241 Ray Ferraro .05 .02
❑ 242 Ron Francis .10 .05
❑ 243 Paul MacDermid .05 .02
❑ 244 Dave Tippett .05 .02
❑ 245 Sylvain Turgeon .05 .02
❑ 246 Carey Wilson .05 .02
❑ 247 Whalers Team LH .05 .02
❑ 248 Whalers Team RH .05 .02
❑ 249 Canadiens Emblem .05 .02
❑ 250 Canadiens Uniform .05 .02
❑ 251 Brian Hayward .10 .05
❑ 252 Patrick Roy 2.00 .90
❑ 253 Chris Chelios .50 .23
❑ 254 Craig Ludwig .05 .02
❑ 255 Petr Svoboda .05 .02
❑ 256 Guy Carbonneau .10 .05
❑ 257 Claude Lemieux .50 .23
❑ 258 Mike McPhee .05 .02
❑ 259 Mats Naslund .05 .02
❑ 260 Stephane Richer .10 .05
❑ 261 Bobby Smith .05 .02
❑ 262 Ryan Walter .05 .02
❑ 263 Canadiens Team LH .05 .02
❑ 264 Canadiens Team RH .05 .02
❑ 265 Devils Emblem .05 .02
❑ 266 Devils Uniform .05 .02
❑ 267 Sean Burke .50 .23
❑ 268 Joe Cirella .05 .02
❑ 269 Bruce Driver .05 .02
❑ 270 Craig Wolanin .05 .02
❑ 271 Aaron Broten .05 .02
❑ 272 Doug Brown .05 .02
❑ 273 Claude Loiselle .05 .02
❑ 274 John MacLean .05 .02
❑ 275 Kirk Muller .10 .05
❑ 276 Brendan Shanahan 3.00 1.35
❑ 277 Patrik Sundstrom .05 .02
❑ 278 Pat Verbeek .05 .02
❑ 279 Devils Team LH .05 .02
❑ 280 Devils Team RH .05 .02
❑ 281 Islanders Emblem .05 .02
❑ 282 Islanders Uniform .05 .02
❑ 283 Kelly Hrudey .10 .05
❑ 284 Steve Konroyd .05 .02
❑ 285 Ken Morrow .05 .02
❑ 286 Pat Flatley .05 .02
❑ 287 Greg Gilbert .05 .02
❑ 288 Alan Kerr .05 .02
❑ 289 Derek King .05 .02
❑ 290 Pat LaFontaine .50 .23
❑ 291 Mikko Makela .05 .02
❑ 292 Brent Sutter .05 .02
❑ 293 Bryan Trottier .10 .05
❑ 294 Randy Wood .05 .02
❑ 295 Islanders Team .05 .02
❑ 296 Islanders Team .05 .02
❑ 297 Rangers Emblem .05 .02
❑ 298 Rangers Uniform .05 .02
❑ 299 Bob Froese .10 .05
❑ 300 John Vanbiesbrouck 1.00 .45
❑ 301 Brian Leetch 2.00 .90
❑ 302 Norm Maciver .05 .02
❑ 303 James Patrick .05 .02
❑ 304 Michel Petit .05 .02
❑ 305 Ulf Dahlen .05 .02
❑ 306 Jan Erixon .05 .02
❑ 307 Kelly Kisio .05 .02
❑ 308 Don Maloney .05 .02
❑ 309 Walt Poddubny .05 .02
❑ 310 Tomas Sandstrom .05 .02
❑ 311 Rangers Team LH .05 .02
❑ 312 Rangers Team RH .05 .02
❑ 313 Flyers Emblem .05 .02
❑ 314 Flyers Uniform .05 .02
❑ 315 Ron Hextall .10 .05
❑ 316 Mark Howe .05 .02
❑ 317 Kerry Huffman .05 .02
❑ 318 Kjell Samuelsson .05 .02
❑ 319 Dave Brown .05 .02
❑ 320 Murray Craven .05 .02
❑ 321 Tim Kerr .05 .02
❑ 322 Scott Mellanby .10 .05
❑ 323 Dave Poulin .05 .02
❑ 324 Brian Propp .05 .02
❑ 325 Ilkka Sinisalo .05 .02
❑ 326 Rick Tocchet .10 .05
❑ 327 Flyers Team LH .05 .02
❑ 328 Flyers Team RH .05 .02
❑ 329 Penguins Emblem .05 .02
❑ 330 Penguins Uniform .05 .02
❑ 331 Frank Pietrangelo .10 .05
❑ 332 Doug Bodger .05 .02
❑ 333 Paul Coffey .50 .23
❑ 334 Jim Johnson .05 .02
❑ 335 Ville Siren .05 .02
❑ 336 Rob Brown .05 .02
❑ 337 Randy Cunneyworth .05 .02
❑ 338 Dan Frawley .05 .02
❑ 339 Dave Hunter .05 .02
❑ 340 Mario Lemieux 2.00 .90
❑ 341 Troy Loney .05 .02
❑ 342 Dan Quinn .05 .02
❑ 343 Penguins Team LH .05 .02
❑ 344 Penguins Team RH .05 .02
❑ 345 Nordiques Emblem .05 .02
❑ 346 Nordiques Uniform .05 .02
❑ 347 Mario Gosselin .10 .05
❑ 348 Tommy Albelin .05 .02
❑ 349 Jeff Brown .05 .02
❑ 350 Steven Finn .05 .02
❑ 351 Randy Moller .05 .02
❑ 352 Alain Cote .05 .02
❑ 353 Gaetan Duchesne .05 .02
❑ 354 Mike Eagles .05 .02
❑ 355 Michel Goulet .10 .05
❑ 356 Lane Lambert .05 .02
❑ 357 Anton Stastny .05 .02
❑ 358 Peter Stastny .10 .05
❑ 359 Nordiques Team LH .05 .02
❑ 360 Nordiques Team RH .05 .02
❑ 361 Capitals Emblem .05 .02
❑ 362 Capitals Uniform .05 .02
❑ 363 Clint Malarchuk .10 .05
❑ 364 Pete Peeters .10 .05
❑ 365 Kevin Hatcher .10 .05
❑ 366 Rod Langway .05 .02
❑ 367 Larry Murphy .10 .05
❑ 368 Scott Stevens .10 .05
❑ 369 Dave Christian .05 .02
❑ 370 Mike Gartner .50 .23
❑ 371 Bengt Gustafsson .05 .02
❑ 372 Dale Hunter .05 .02
❑ 373 Kelly Miller .05 .02
❑ 374 Mike Ridley .05 .02
❑ 375 Capitals Team LH .05 .02
❑ 376 Capitals Team RH .05 .02
❑ 377 Hockey Rink Schematic .05 .02
❑ 378 Hockey Rink Schematic .05 .02
❑ 379 Cross-checking .05 .02
❑ 380 Elbowing .05 .02
❑ 381 High-sticking .05 .02
❑ 382 Holding .05 .02
❑ 383 Hooking .05 .02
❑ 384 Interference .05 .02
❑ 385 Spearing .05 .02
❑ 386 Tripping .05 .02
❑ 387 Boarding .05 .02
❑ 388 Charging .05 .02
❑ 389 Delayed Calling of Penalty .05 .02
❑ 390 Kneeing .05 .02
❑ 391 Misconduct .05 .02
❑ 392 Roughing .05 .02
❑ 393 Slashing .05 .02
❑ 394 Unsportsmanlike Conduct .05 .02
❑ 395 Wash-out .05 .02
❑ 396 Icing .05 .02
❑ 397 Off-side .05 .02
❑ 398 Wash-out .05 .02
❑ 399 Bill Masterton Memorial Trophy Bob Bourne .05 .02
❑ 400 Hart Memorial Trophy Mario Lemieux 1.00 .45
❑ 401 Art Ross Trophy Mario Lemieux 1.00 .45
❑ 402 William M. Jennings Trophy Brian Hayward and Patrick Roy 1.00 .45
❑ 403 Vezina Trophy Grant Fuhr .10 .05
❑ 404 Calder Memorial Trophy Joe Nieuwendyk .10 .05
❑ 405 James Norris Memorial Trophy Ray Bourque .50 .23
❑ 406 Lady Byng Trophy Mats Naslund .10 .05
❑ 407 Frank J. Selke Trophy Guy Carbonneau .10 .05
❑ 408 Emery Edge Award Brad McCrimmon .10 .05
❑ xx Sticker Album 5.00 2.20

## 1989-90 Panini Stickers

This set of 384 hockey stickers was produced and distributed by Panini. The stickers are numbered on the back and measure 1 7/8" by 3". The stickers display color action shots of players, teams, arenas, and logos. Some team pictures consist of two stickers, each showing half of the photo; in the checklist below these halves are denoted by LH (left half) and RH (right half), and in the case of a four sticker picture, note the additional prefixes U (upper) and L (lower). A 52-page, full-color glossy album was issued with the set for holding the stickers. The album includes player information and statistics in English and French.

| | MINT | NRMT |
|---|---|---|
| COMPLETE SET (384) | 25.00 | 11.00 |
| COMMON STICKER (1-384) | .05 | .02 |

❑ 1 NHL Logo .05 .02
❑ 2 Playoff schedule .05 .02
❑ 3 Flames/Blackhawks action .05 .02
❑ 4 Flames/Canucks action .05 .02
❑ 5 Kings/Oilers action .05 .02
❑ 6 Vernon goal LH .05 .02
❑ 7 Vernon goal RH .05 .02
❑ 8 Bruins/Sabres action .05 .02
❑ 9 Canadiens/Bruins action .05 .02
❑ 10 Flyers score .05 .02
❑ 11 Canadiens/Flyers action LH .05 .02
❑ 12 Canadiens/Flyers action RH .05 .02
❑ 13 Canadiens/Flames action .05 .02
❑ 14 Canadiens celebration .05 .02
❑ 15 Canadiens/Flames action .05 .02
❑ 16 Canadiens/Flames action .05 .02
❑ 17 Flames celebration .05 .02
❑ 18 Flames/Canadiens action LH .05 .02
❑ 19 Flames/Canadiens action RH .05 .02
❑ 20 Al MacInnis Conn Smythe Trophy .10 .05
❑ 21 Stanley Cup/Flames UL .10 .05
❑ 22 Stanley Cup/Flames UR .10 .05
❑ 23 Stanley Cup/Flames LL .10 .05
❑ 24 Stanley Cup/Flames LR .10 .05
❑ 25 Stanley Cup .10 .05
❑ 26 Calgary Flames logo .05 .02
❑ 27 Joe Mullen .10 .05
❑ 28 Doug Gilmour .50 .23
❑ 29 Joe Nieuwendyk .10 .05
❑ 30 Gary Suter .10 .05
❑ 31 Flames team .05 .02
❑ 32 Al MacInnis .10 .05
❑ 33 Brad McCrimmon .05 .02
❑ 34 Mike Vernon .10 .05
❑ 35 Gary Roberts .10 .05
❑ 36 Colin Patterson .05 .02
❑ 37 Jim Peplinski .05 .02
❑ 38 Jamie Macoun .05 .02
❑ 39 Lanny McDonald .10 .05
❑ 40 Saddledome .05 .02
❑ 41 Chicago Blackhawks logo .05 .02
❑ 42 Darren Pang .10 .05
❑ 43 Steve Larmer .10 .05
❑ 44 Dirk Graham .05 .02
❑ 45 Doug Wilson .05 .02
❑ 46 Blackhawks/Oilers action (Ed Belfour shown) .05 .02
❑ 47 Dave Manson .05 .02
❑ 48 Troy Murray .05 .02
❑ 49 Denis Savard .10 .05
❑ 50 Steve Thomas .05 .02
❑ 51 Adam Creighton .05 .02
❑ 52 Wayne Presley .05 .02
❑ 53 Trent Yawney .05 .02
❑ 54 Alain Chevrier .05 .02
❑ 55 Chicago Stadium .05 .02
❑ 56 Detroit Red Wings logo .05 .02
❑ 57 Steve Yzerman 1.25 .55
❑ 58 Gerard Gallant .05 .02
❑ 59 Greg Stefan .10 .05
❑ 60 Dave Barr .05 .02
❑ 61 Red Wings team .05 .02
❑ 62 Steve Chiasson .05 .02
❑ 63 Shawn Burr .05 .02
❑ 64 Rick Zombo .05 .02
❑ 65 Glen Hanlon .10 .05
❑ 66 Jeff Sharples .05 .02
❑ 67 Joey Kocur .05 .02
❑ 68 Lee Norwood .05 .02
❑ 69 Mike O'Connell .05 .02
❑ 70 Joe Louis Arena .05 .02
❑ 71 Edmonton Oilers logo .05 .02
❑ 72 Jimmy Carson .05 .02
❑ 73 Jari Kurri .50 .23
❑ 74 Mark Messier .50 .23
❑ 75 Craig Simpson .05 .02
❑ 76 Oilers/Flyers action .05 .02
❑ 77 Glenn Anderson .10 .05
❑ 78 Craig MacTavish .05 .02
❑ 79 Kevin Lowe .10 .05
❑ 80 Craig Muni .05 .02
❑ 81 Bill Ranford .10 .05
❑ 82 Charlie Huddy .05 .02
❑ 83 Steve Smith .05 .02
❑ 84 Normand Lacombe .05 .02
❑ 85 Northlands Coliseum .05 .02
❑ 86 L.A. Kings logo .05 .02
❑ 87 Wayne Gretzky 2.50 1.10
❑ 88 Bernie Nicholls .10 .05
❑ 89 Kelly Hrudey .10 .05
❑ 90 John Tonelli .05 .02
❑ 91 Oilers/Kings action .05 .02
❑ 92 Steve Kasper .05 .02
❑ 93 Steve Duchesne .05 .02
❑ 94 Mike Krushelnyski .05 .02
❑ 95 Luc Robitaille .50 .23
❑ 96 Ron Duguay .05 .02
❑ 97 Glenn Healy .10 .05
❑ 98 Dave Taylor .05 .02
❑ 99 Marty McSorley .05 .02
❑ 100 The Great Western Forum .05 .02
❑ 101 Minnesota North Stars logo .05 .02
❑ 102 Kari Takko .10 .05
❑ 103 Dave Gagner .05 .02
❑ 104 Mike Gartner .50 .23
❑ 105 Brian Bellows .05 .02
❑ 106 North Stars team .05 .02
❑ 107 Neal Broten .05 .02
❑ 108 Larry Murphy .10 .05
❑ 109 Basil McRae .05 .02
❑ 110 Perry Berezan .05 .02
❑ 111 Shawn Chambers .05 .02
❑ 112 Curt Giles .05 .02
❑ 113 Stewart Gavin .05 .02
❑ 114 Jon Casey .10 .05
❑ 115 Metropolitan Sports Center .05 .02
❑ 116 St. Louis Blues logo .05 .02
❑ 117 Brett Hull 1.00 .45
❑ 118 Peter Zezel .05 .02
❑ 119 Tony Hrkac .05 .02
❑ 120 Vincent Riendeau .10 .05
❑ 121 Blues/Islanders action .05 .02
❑ 122 Cliff Ronning .05 .02
❑ 123 Gino Cavallini .05 .02
❑ 124 Brian Benning .05 .02
❑ 125 Rick Meagher .05 .02
❑ 126 Steve Tuttle .05 .02
❑ 127 Paul Cavallini .05 .02
❑ 128 Tom Tilley .05 .02
❑ 129 Greg Millen .10 .05
❑ 130 St. Louis Arena .05 .02
❑ 131 Toronto Maple Leafs logo .05 .02
❑ 132 Ed Olczyk .05 .02
❑ 133 Gary Leeman .05 .02
❑ 134 Vincent Damphousse .10 .05
❑ 135 Tom Fergus .05 .02
❑ 136 Maple Leafs action .05 .02
❑ 137 Daniel Marois .05 .02
❑ 138 Mark Osborne .05 .02
❑ 139 Allan Bester .10 .05
❑ 140 Al Iafrate .05 .02
❑ 141 Brad Marsh .05 .02
❑ 142 Luke Richardson .05 .02
❑ 143 Todd Gill .05 .02
❑ 144 Wendel Clark .10 .05
❑ 145 Maple Leafs Gardens .05 .02
❑ 146 Vancouver Canucks logo .05 .02
❑ 147 Petri Skriko .05 .02
❑ 148 Trevor Linden .50 .23
❑ 149 Tony Tanti .05 .02
❑ 150 Steve Weeks .05 .02
❑ 151 Canucks/Islanders action .05 .02
❑ 152 Brian Bradley .05 .02
❑ 153 Barry Pederson .05 .02
❑ 154 Greg Adams .05 .02
❑ 155 Kirk McLean .10 .05
❑ 156 Jim Sandlak .05 .02
❑ 157 Rich Sutter .05 .02
❑ 158 Garth Butcher .05 .02
❑ 159 Stan Smyl .05 .02
❑ 160 Pacific Coliseum .05 .02
❑ 161 Winnipeg Jets logo .05 .02
❑ 162 Dale Hawerchuk .10 .05
❑ 163 Thomas Steen .05 .02
❑ 164 Brent Ashton .05 .02
❑ 165 Pat Elynuik .05 .02
❑ 166 Jets/Islanders action .05 .02
❑ 167 Dave Ellett .05 .02
❑ 168 Randy Carlyle .05 .02
❑ 169 Laurie Boschman .05 .02
❑ 170 Iain Duncan .05 .02
❑ 171 Doug Smail .05 .02
❑ 172 Teppo Numminen .05 .02
❑ 173 Bob Essensa .10 .05
❑ 174 Peter Taglianetti .05 .02
❑ 175 Winnipeg Arena .05 .02
❑ 176 Steve Duchesne AS .05 .02
❑ 177 Luc Robitaille AS .10 .05
❑ 178 Mike Vernon AS .10 .05
❑ 179 Wayne Gretzky AS 1.25 .55
❑ 180 Kevin Lowe AS .10 .05
❑ 181 Jari Kurri AS .50 .23
❑ 182 Cam Neely AS .50 .23
❑ 183 Paul Coffey AS .50 .23
❑ 184 Mario Lemieux AS 1.00 .45
❑ 185 Sean Burke AS .10 .05
❑ 186 Rob Brown AS .05 .02
❑ 187 Ray Bourque AS .50 .23
❑ 188 Boston Bruins logo .05 .02
❑ 189 Greg Hawgood .05 .02
❑ 190 Ken Linseman .05 .02
❑ 191 Andy Moog .10 .05
❑ 192 Cam Neely .50 .23
❑ 193 Bruins/Flyers action .05 .02
❑ 194 Andy Brickley .05 .02
❑ 195 Rejean Lemelin .10 .05
❑ 196 Bob Carpenter .05 .02
❑ 197 Randy Burridge .05 .02
❑ 198 Craig Janney .05 .02
❑ 199 Bob Joyce .05 .02
❑ 200 Glen Wesley .05 .02
❑ 201 Ray Bourque .50 .23
❑ 202 Boston Garden .05 .02
❑ 203 Buffalo Sabres logo .05 .02
❑ 204 Pierre Turgeon .10 .05
❑ 205 Phil Housley .05 .02
❑ 206 Rick Vaive .05 .02
❑ 207 Christian Ruuttu .05 .02
❑ 208 Flyers/Sabres action .05 .02
❑ 209 Doug Bodger .05 .02
❑ 210 Mike Foligno .05 .02
❑ 211 Ray Sheppard .05 .02
❑ 212 John Tucker .05 .02
❑ 213 Scott Arniel .05 .02
❑ 214 Daren Puppa .10 .05
❑ 215 Dave Andreychuk .10 .05
❑ 216 Uwe Krupp .05 .02
❑ 217 Memorial Auditorium .05 .02
❑ 218 Hartford Whalers logo .05 .02
❑ 219 Kevin Dineen .05 .02
❑ 220 Peter Sidorkiewicz .10 .05
❑ 221 Ron Francis .10 .05
❑ 222 Ray Ferraro .05 .02
❑ 223 Islanders/Whalers action .05 .02
❑ 224 Scott Young .05 .02
❑ 225 Dave Babych .05 .02
❑ 226 Dave Tippett .05 .02
❑ 227 Paul MacDermid .05 .02
❑ 228 Ulf Samuelsson .05 .02
❑ 229 Sylvain Cote .05 .02
❑ 230 Jody Hull .05 .02
❑ 231 Don Maloney .05 .02
❑ 232 Hartford Civic Center .05 .02
❑ 233 Montreal Canadiens logo .05 .02
❑ 234 Mats Naslund .05 .02
❑ 235 Patrick Roy 2.00 .90
❑ 236 Bobby Smith .05 .02
❑ 237 Chris Chelios .50 .23
❑ 238 Flames/Canadiens action .05 .02
❑ 239 Stephane Richer .10 .05

❑ 240 Claude Lemieux .10 .05
❑ 241 Guy Carbonneau .10 .05
❑ 242 Shayne Corson .05 .02
❑ 243 Mike McPhee .05 .02
❑ 244 Petr Svoboda .05 .02
❑ 245 Larry Robinson .10 .05
❑ 246 Brian Hayward .10 .05
❑ 247 Montreal Forum .05 .02
❑ 248 New Jersey Devils logo .05 .02
❑ 249 John MacLean .05 .02
❑ 250 Patrik Sundstrom .05 .02
❑ 251 Kirk Muller .10 .05
❑ 252 Tom Kurvers .05 .02
❑ 253 Bruins/Devils action .05 .02
❑ 254 Aaron Broten .05 .02
❑ 255 Brendan Shanahan 1.00 .45
❑ 256 Sean Burke .10 .05
❑ 257 Tommy Albelin .05 .02
❑ 258 Ken Daneyko .05 .02
❑ 259 Randy Velischek .05 .02
❑ 260 Mark Johnson .05 .02
❑ 261 Jim Korn .05 .02
❑ 262 Brendan Byrne Arena .05 .02
❑ 263 New York Islanders logo .05 .02
❑ 264 Pat LaFontaine .10 .05
❑ 265 Mark Fitzpatrick .10 .05
❑ 266 Brent Sutter .05 .02
❑ 267 David Volek .05 .02
❑ 268 Islanders/Rangers action .05 .02
❑ 269 Bryan Trottier .10 .05
❑ 270 Mikko Makela .05 .02
❑ 271 Derek King .05 .02
❑ 272 Pat Flatley .05 .02
❑ 273 Jeff Norton .05 .02
❑ 274 Gerald Diduck .05 .02
❑ 275 Alan Kerr .05 .02
❑ 276 Jeff Hackett .10 .05
❑ 277 Nassau Veterans Memorial Coliseum .05 .02
❑ 278 New York Rangers logo .05 .02
❑ 279 Brian Leetch .50 .23
❑ 280 Carey Wilson .05 .02
❑ 281 Tomas Sandstrom .05 .02
❑ 282 John Vanbiesbrouck 1.00 .45
❑ 283 Oilers/Rangers action .05 .02
❑ 284 Bob Froese .10 .05
❑ 285 Tony Granato .05 .02
❑ 286 Brian Mullen .05 .02
❑ 287 Kelly Kisio .05 .02
❑ 288 Ulf Dahlen .05 .02
❑ 289 James Patrick .05 .02
❑ 290 John Ogrodnick .05 .02
❑ 291 Michel Petit .05 .02
❑ 292 Madison Square Garden .05 .02
❑ 293 Philadelphia Flyers logo .05 .02
❑ 294 Tim Kerr .05 .02
❑ 295 Rick Tocchet .10 .05
❑ 296 Pelle Eklund .05 .02
❑ 297 Terry Carkner .05 .02
❑ 298 Flyers/Canadiens action .05 .02
❑ 299 Ron Sutter .05 .02
❑ 300 Mark Howe .05 .02
❑ 301 Keith Acton .05 .02
❑ 302 Ron Hextall .10 .05
❑ 303 Gord Murphy .05 .02
❑ 304 Derrick Smith .05 .02
❑ 305 Dave Poulin .05 .02
❑ 306 Brian Propp .05 .02
❑ 307 The Spectrum .05 .02
❑ 308 Pittsburgh Penguins logo .05 .02
❑ 309 Mario Lemieux 2.00 .90
❑ 310 Rob Brown .05 .02
❑ 311 Paul Coffey .50 .23
❑ 312 Tom Barrasso .10 .05
❑ 313 Penguins/Flyers action .05 .02
❑ 314 Dan Quinn .05 .02
❑ 315 Bob Errey .05 .02
❑ 316 John Cullen .05 .02
❑ 317 Phil Bourque .05 .02
❑ 318 Zarley Zalapski .05 .02
❑ 319 Troy Loney .05 .02
❑ 320 Jim Johnson .05 .02
❑ 321 Kevin Stevens .75 .35
❑ 322 Civic Arena .05 .02
❑ 323 Quebec Nordiques logo .05 .02
❑ 324 Peter Stastny .10 .05
❑ 325 Jeff Brown .05 .02
❑ 326 Michel Goulet .10 .05
❑ 327 Joe Sakic 4.00 1.80
❑ 328 Flyers/Nordiques action .05 .02
❑ 329 Iiro Jarvi .05 .02
❑ 330 Paul Gillis .05 .02
❑ 331 Randy Moller .05 .02
❑ 332 Ron Tugnutt .50 .23
❑ 333 Robert Picard .05 .02
❑ 334 Curtis Leschyshyn .05 .02
❑ 335 Marc Fortier .05 .02
❑ 336 Mario Marois .05 .02
❑ 337 Le Colisee .05 .02
❑ 338 Washington Capitals logo .05 .02
❑ 339 Mike Ridley .05 .02
❑ 340 Geoff Courtnall .05 .02
❑ 341 Scott Stevens .10 .05
❑ 342 Dino Ciccarelli .10 .05
❑ 343 Capitals/Flames action .05 .02
❑ 344 Bob Mason .10 .05
❑ 345 Dave Christian .05 .02
❑ 346 Dale Hunter .05 .02
❑ 347 Kevin Hatcher .10 .05
❑ 348 Kelly Miller .05 .02
❑ 349 Stephen Leach .05 .02
❑ 350 Rod Langway .05 .02
❑ 351 Bob Rouse .05 .02
❑ 352 Capital Centre .05 .02
❑ 353 Calgary Flames logo .05 .02
❑ 354 Edmonton Oilers logo .05 .02
❑ 355 Winnipeg Jets logo .05 .02
❑ 356 Toronto Maple Leafs logo .05 .02
❑ 357 Buffalo Sabres logo .05 .02
❑ 358 Montreal Canadiens logo .05 .02
❑ 359 Quebec Nordiques logo .05 .02
❑ 360 New Jersey Devils logo .05 .02
❑ 361 Boston Bruins logo .05 .02
❑ 362 Hartford Whalers logo .05 .02
❑ 363 Vancouver Canucks logo .05 .02
❑ 364 Minnesota North Stars logo .05 .02
❑ 365 Los Angeles Kings logo .05 .02
❑ 366 St. Louis Blues logo .05 .02
❑ 367 Chicago Blackhawks logo .05 .02
❑ 368 Detroit Red Wings logo .05 .02
❑ 369 Pittsburgh Penguins logo .05 .02
❑ 370 Washington Capitals logo .05 .02
❑ 371 Philadelphia Flyers logo .05 .02
❑ 372 New York Rangers logo .05 .02
❑ 373 New York Islanders logo .05 .02
❑ 374 Wayne Gretzky 2.50 1.10
❑ 375 Mario Lemieux 2.00 .90
❑ 376 Patrick Roy and Brian Hayward .75 .35
❑ 377 Tim Kerr .05 .02
❑ 378 Brian Leetch .75 .35
❑ 379 Chris Chelios .50 .23
❑ 380 Joe Mullen .10 .05
❑ 381 Guy Carbonneau .10 .05
❑ 382 Bryan Trottier .10 .05
❑ 383 Patrick Roy 2.00 .90
❑ 384 Joe Mullen .10 .05
❑ xx Sticker Album 2.50 1.10

## 1990-91 Panini Stickers

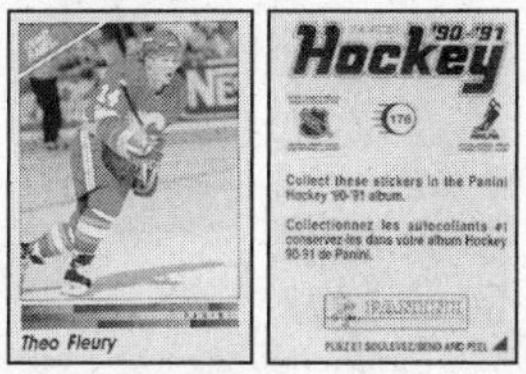


This set of 351 hockey stickers was produced and distributed by Panini. The stickers are numbered on the back and measure approximately 2 1/16" by 2 15/16". The fronts feature full color action photos of the players. Different color triangles (in one of the team's colors) overlay the upper left corner of the pictures, with the team name in white lettering. A variegated stripe appears below the player photos, with the player's name below. The team logo and conference stickers are in foil. The stickers are arranged according to alphabetical team order.

| | MINT | NRMT |
|---|---|---|
| COMPLETE SET (351) | 20.00 | 9.00 |
| COMMON STICKER (1-351) | .05 | .02 |

❑ 1 Prince of Wales Conference .05 .02
❑ 2 Clarence Campbell Conference .05 .02
❑ 3 Stanley Cup .10 .05
❑ 4 Dave Poulin .05 .02
❑ 5 Brian Propp .05 .02
❑ 6 Glen Wesley .05 .02
❑ 7 Bob Carpenter .05 .02
❑ 8 John Carter .05 .02
❑ 9 Cam Neely .50 .23
❑ 10 Greg Hawgood .05 .02
❑ 11 Andy Moog .10 .05
❑ 12 Boston Bruins logo .05 .02
❑ 13 Rejean Lemelin .10 .05
❑ 14 Craig Janney .05 .02
❑ 15 Bob Sweeney .05 .02
❑ 16 Andy Brickley .05 .02
❑ 17 Ray Bourque .50 .23
❑ 18 Dave Christian .05 .02
❑ 19 Dave Snuggerud .05 .02
❑ 20 Christian Ruuttu .05 .02
❑ 21 Phil Housley .05 .02
❑ 22 Uwe Krupp .05 .02
❑ 23 Rick Vaive .05 .02
❑ 24 Mike Ramsey .05 .02
❑ 25 Mike Foligno .05 .02
❑ 26 Clint Malarchuk .10 .05
❑ 27 Buffalo Sabres logo .05 .02
❑ 28 Pierre Turgeon .10 .05
❑ 29 Dave Andreychuk .10 .05
❑ 30 Scott Arniel .05 .02
❑ 31 Daren Puppa .10 .05
❑ 32 Mike Hartman .05 .02
❑ 33 Doug Bodger .05 .02
❑ 34 Scott Young .05 .02
❑ 35 Todd Krygier .05 .02
❑ 36 Pat Verbeek .05 .02
❑ 37 Dave Tippett .05 .02
❑ 38 Peter Sidorkiewicz .10 .05
❑ 39 Ron Francis .10 .05
❑ 40 Dave Babych .05 .02
❑ 41 Randy Ladouceur .05 .02
❑ 42 Hartford Whalers logo .05 .02
❑ 43 Kevin Dineen .05 .02
❑ 44 Dean Evason .05 .02
❑ 45 Ray Ferraro .05 .02
❑ 46 Mike Tomlak .05 .02
❑ 47 Mikael Andersson .05 .02
❑ 48 Brad Shaw .05 .02
❑ 49 Chris Chelios .50 .23
❑ 50 Petr Svoboda .05 .02
❑ 51 Patrick Roy 1.50 .70
❑ 52 Bobby Smith .05 .02
❑ 53 Stephane Richer .10 .05
❑ 54 Shayne Corson .05 .02
❑ 55 Brian Skrudland .05 .02
❑ 56 Russ Courtnall .05 .02
❑ 57 Montreal Canadiens logo .05 .02
❑ 58 Guy Carbonneau .10 .05
❑ 59 Sylvain Lefebvre .05 .02
❑ 60 Mathieu Schneider .05 .02
❑ 61 Brian Hayward .10 .05
❑ 62 Mats Naslund .05 .02
❑ 63 Mike McPhee .05 .02
❑ 64 Brendan Shanahan .50 .23
❑ 65 Patrik Sundstrom .05 .02
❑ 66 Mark Johnson .05 .02
❑ 67 Doug Brown .05 .02
❑ 68 Chris Terreri .10 .05
❑ 69 Bruce Driver .05 .02
❑ 70 Peter Stastny .10 .05
❑ 71 Sylvain Turgeon .05 .02
❑ 72 New Jersey Devils logo .05 .02
❑ 73 Kirk Muller .10 .05
❑ 74 John MacLean .05 .02
❑ 75 Viacheslav Fetisov .05 .02
❑ 76 Tommy Albelin .05 .02
❑ 77 Sean Burke .10 .05
❑ 78 Janne Ojanen .05 .02
❑ 79 Randy Wood .05 .02
❑ 80 Gary Nylund .05 .02
❑ 81 Pat LaFontaine .10 .05
❑ 82 Pat Flatley .05 .02
❑ 83 Bryan Trottier .10 .05
❑ 84 Don Maloney .05 .02
❑ 85 Gerald Diduck .05 .02
❑ 86 Mark Fitzpatrick .10 .05
❑ 87 New York Islanders logo .05 .02
❑ 88 Glenn Healy .10 .05
❑ 89 Alan Kerr .05 .02
❑ 90 Brent Sutter .05 .02
❑ 91 Doug Crossman .05 .02
❑ 92 Hubie McDonough .05 .02
❑ 93 Jeff Norton .05 .02
❑ 94 Kelly Kisio .05 .02
❑ 95 Brian Leetch .50 .23
❑ 96 Brian Mullen .05 .02
❑ 97 James Patrick .05 .02
❑ 98 Mike Richter .10 .05
❑ 99 John Ogrodnick .05 .02
❑ 100 Troy Mallette .05 .02
❑ 101 Mark Janssens .05 .02
❑ 102 New York Rangers logo .05 .02
❑ 103 Mike Gartner .50 .23
❑ 104 Jan Erixon .05 .02
❑ 105 Carey Wilson .05 .02
❑ 106 Bernie Nicholls .10 .05
❑ 107 Darren Turcotte .10 .05
❑ 108 John Vanbiesbrouck 1.00 .45
❑ 109 Ron Sutter .05 .02
❑ 110 Kjell Samuelsson .05 .02
❑ 111 Ken Linseman .05 .02
❑ 112 Ken Wregget .10 .05
❑ 113 Pelle Eklund .05 .02
❑ 114 Terry Carkner .05 .02
❑ 115 Gord Murphy .05 .02
❑ 116 Murray Craven .05 .02
❑ 117 Philadelphia Flyers logo .05 .02
❑ 118 Ron Hextall .10 .05
❑ 119 Mike Bullard .05 .02
❑ 120 Tim Kerr .05 .02
❑ 121 Rick Tocchet .10 .05
❑ 122 Mark Howe .05 .02
❑ 123 Ilkka Sinisalo .05 .02
❑ 124 Tony Tanti .05 .02
❑ 125 John Cullen .05 .02
❑ 126 Zarley Zalapski .05 .02
❑ 127 Wendell Young .10 .05
❑ 128 Rob Brown .05 .02
❑ 129 Phil Bourque .05 .02
❑ 130 Mark Recchi .50 .23
❑ 131 Kevin Stevens .05 .02
❑ 132 Pittsburgh Penguins logo .05 .02
❑ 133 Bob Errey .05 .02
❑ 134 Tom Barrasso .10 .05
❑ 135 Paul Coffey .50 .23
❑ 136 Mario Lemieux 1.50 .70
❑ 137 Randy Hillier .05 .02
❑ 138 Troy Loney .05 .02
❑ 139 Joe Sakic 2.00 .90
❑ 140 Lucien DeBlois .05 .02
❑ 141 Joe Cirella .05 .02
❑ 142 Ron Tugnutt .10 .05
❑ 143 Paul Gillis .05 .02
❑ 144 Bryan Fogarty .05 .02
❑ 145 Guy Lafleur .10 .05
❑ 146 Tony Hrkac .05 .02
❑ 147 Quebec Nordiques logo .05 .02
❑ 148 Michel Petit .05 .02
❑ 149 Tony McKegney .05 .02
❑ 150 Curtis Leschyshyn .05 .02
❑ 151 Claude Loiselle .05 .02
❑ 152 Mario Brunetta .05 .02
❑ 153 Marc Fortier .05 .02
❑ 154 Michal Pivonka .05 .02
❑ 155 Scott Stevens .10 .05
❑ 156 Kelly Miller .05 .02
❑ 157 John Tucker .05 .02
❑ 158 Don Beaupre .10 .05
❑ 159 Geoff Courtnall .05 .02
❑ 160 Alan May .05 .02
❑ 161 Dino Ciccarelli .10 .05
❑ 162 Washington Capitals logo .05 .02
❑ 163 Mike Ridley .05 .02
❑ 164 Bob Rouse .05 .02
❑ 165 Mike Liut .10 .05
❑ 166 Stephen Leach .05 .02
❑ 167 Kevin Hatcher .10 .05
❑ 168 Dale Hunter .05 .02
❑ 169 Prince of Wales Trophy .05 .02
❑ 170 Clarence Campbell Trophy .05 .02
❑ 171 Stanley Cup Championship .10 .05
❑ 172 Doug Gilmour .50 .23
❑ 173 Brad McCrimmon .05 .02
❑ 174 Joe Nieuwendyk .10 .05
❑ 175 Mike Vernon .05 .02
❑ 176 Theoren Fleury .50 .23
❑ 177 Gary Suter .10 .05
❑ 178 Jamie Macoun .05 .02
❑ 179 Gary Roberts .10 .05
❑ 180 Calgary Flames logo .05 .02
❑ 181 Paul Ranheim .05 .02
❑ 182 Jiri Hrdina .05 .02
❑ 183 Joe Mullen .10 .05
❑ 184 Sergei Makarov .05 .02
❑ 185 Al MacInnis .10 .05
❑ 186 Rick Wamsley .10 .05
❑ 187 Trent Yawney .05 .02
❑ 188 Greg Millen .10 .05
❑ 189 Doug Wilson .10 .05
❑ 190 Jocelyn Lemieux .05 .02
❑ 191 Dirk Graham .05 .02
❑ 192 Keith Brown .05 .02
❑ 193 Adam Creighton .05 .02
❑ 194 Steve Larmer .10 .05
❑ 195 Chicago Blackhawks logo .05 .02
❑ 196 Greg Gilbert .05 .02
❑ 197 Jacques Cloutier .10 .05
❑ 198 Denis Savard .10 .05
❑ 199 Dave Manson .05 .02
❑ 200 Troy Murray .05 .02
❑ 201 Jeremy Roenick 1.00 .45
❑ 202 Lee Norwood .05 .02
❑ 203 Glen Hanlon .10 .05
❑ 204 Marc Habscheid .05 .02
❑ 205 Gerard Gallant .05 .02
❑ 206 Rick Zombo .05 .02
❑ 207 Steve Chiasson .05 .02
❑ 208 Steve Yzerman 1.00 .45
❑ 209 Bernie Federko .05 .02
❑ 210 Detroit Red Wings logo .05 .02
❑ 211 Joey Kocur .05 .02
❑ 212 Tim Cheveldae .10 .05
❑ 213 Shawn Burr .05 .02
❑ 214 Jimmy Carson .05 .02
❑ 215 Mike O'Connell .05 .02
❑ 216 John Chabot .05 .02
❑ 217 Craig Muni .05 .02
❑ 218 Bill Ranford .10 .05
❑ 219 Mark Messier .50 .23
❑ 220 Craig MacTavish .05 .02
❑ 221 Charlie Huddy .05 .02
❑ 222 Jari Kurri .50 .23
❑ 223 Esa Tikkanen .05 .02
❑ 224 Kevin Lowe .10 .05
❑ 225 Edmonton Oilers logo .05 .02
❑ 226 Steve Smith .05 .02
❑ 227 Glenn Anderson .10 .05
❑ 228 Petr Klima .05 .02
❑ 229 Craig Simpson .05 .02
❑ 230 Grant Fuhr .50 .23
❑ 231 Randy Gregg .05 .02
❑ 232 Bob Kudelski .05 .02
❑ 233 Luc Robitaille .10 .05
❑ 234 Marty McSorley .05 .02
❑ 235 John Tonelli .05 .02
❑ 236 Dave Taylor .05 .02
❑ 237 Mikko Makela .05 .02
❑ 238 Steve Kasper .05 .02
❑ 239 Tony Granato .05 .02
❑ 240 Los Angeles Kings logo .05 .02
❑ 241 Steve Duchesne .05 .02
❑ 242 Wayne Gretzky 2.00 .90
❑ 243 Tomas Sandstrom .05 .02
❑ 244 Larry Robinson .10 .05
❑ 245 Mike Krushelnyski .05 .02
❑ 246 Kelly Hrudey .10 .05
❑ 247 Aaron Broten .05 .02
❑ 248 Dave Gagner .05 .02
❑ 249 Basil McRae .05 .02
❑ 250 Curt Giles .05 .02
❑ 251 Larry Murphy .10 .05
❑ 252 Shawn Chambers .05 .02
❑ 253 Mike Modano 1.00 .45
❑ 254 Jon Casey .10 .05
❑ 255 Minnesota North Stars logo .05 .02
❑ 256 Gaetan Duchesne .05 .02
❑ 257 Brian Bellows .05 .02
❑ 258 Frantisek Musil .05 .02
❑ 259 Don Barber .05 .02
❑ 260 Stewart Gavin .05 .02
❑ 261 Neal Broten .05 .02
❑ 262 Brett Hull .50 .23
❑ 263 Sergio Momesso .05 .02
❑ 264 Peter Zezel .05 .02
❑ 265 Gino Cavallini .05 .02
❑ 266 Rod Brind'Amour .50 .23
❑ 267 Mike Lalor .05 .02
❑ 268 Vincent Riendeau .10 .05
❑ 269 Gordie Roberts .05 .02
❑ 270 St. Louis Blues logo .05 .02
❑ 271 Paul MacLean .05 .02
❑ 272 Curtis Joseph 1.00 .45
❑ 273 Rick Meagher .05 .02
❑ 274 Jeff Brown .05 .02
❑ 275 Adam Oates .10 .05
❑ 276 Paul Cavallini .05 .02
❑ 277 Brad Marsh .05 .02
❑ 278 Mark Osborne .05 .02
❑ 279 Gary Leeman .05 .02
❑ 280 Rob Ramage .05 .02
❑ 281 Jeff Reese .10 .05
❑ 282 Tom Fergus .05 .02
❑ 283 Ed Olczyk .05 .02
❑ 284 Daniel Marois .05 .02
❑ 285 Toronto Maple Leafs logo .05 .02
❑ 286 Wendel Clark .10 .05
❑ 287 Tom Kurvers .05 .02
❑ 288 Gilles Thibaudeau .05 .02
❑ 289 Lou Franceschetti .05 .02
❑ 290 Al Iafrate .05 .02
❑ 291 Vincent Damphousse .10 .05
❑ 292 Stan Smyl .05 .02
❑ 293 Paul Reinhart .05 .02
❑ 294 Igor Larionov .10 .05
❑ 295 Doug Lidster .05 .02
❑ 296 Kirk McLean .10 .05
❑ 297 Andrew McBain .05 .02
❑ 298 Petri Skriko .05 .02
❑ 299 Trevor Linden .10 .05
❑ 300 Vancouver Canucks logo .05 .02
❑ 301 Steve Bozek .05 .02
❑ 302 Brian Bradley .05 .02
❑ 303 Greg Adams .05 .02
❑ 304 Vladimir Krutov .05 .02
❑ 305 Dan Quinn .05 .02
❑ 306 Jim Sandlak .05 .02
❑ 307 Teppo Numminen .05 .02
❑ 308 Doug Smail .05 .02
❑ 309 Greg Paslawski .05 .02
❑ 310 Dave Ellett .05 .02
❑ 311 Bob Essensa .10 .05
❑ 312 Pat Elynuik .05 .02
❑ 313 Paul Fenton .05 .02
❑ 314 Randy Carlyle .05 .02
❑ 315 Winnipeg Jets logo .05 .02
❑ 316 Thomas Steen .05 .02
❑ 317 Dale Hawerchuk .10 .05
❑ 318 Fredrik Olausson .05 .02
❑ 319 Dave McLlwain .05 .02
❑ 320 Laurie Boschman .05 .02
❑ 321 Brent Ashton .05 .02
❑ 322 Ray Bourque .50 .23
❑ 323 Patrick Roy 1.50 .70
❑ 324 Paul Coffey .50 .23
❑ 325 Brian Propp .05 .02
❑ 326 Mario Lemieux 1.50 .70
❑ 327 Cam Neely .50 .23
❑ 328 Al MacInnis .10 .05
❑ 329 Mike Vernon .10 .05
❑ 330 Kevin Lowe .10 .05
❑ 331 Luc Robitaille .10 .05
❑ 332 Wayne Gretzky 2.00 .90
❑ 333 Brett Hull .50 .23
❑ 334 Sergei Makarov .05 .02
❑ 335 Alexei Kasatonov .05 .02
❑ 336 Igor Larionov .05 .02
❑ 337 Vladimir Krutov .05 .02
❑ 338 Alexander Mogilny 1.00 .45
❑ 339 Viacheslav Fetisov .05 .02
❑ 340 Mike Modano .50 .23
❑ 341 Mark Recchi .50 .23
❑ 342 Paul Ranheim .05 .02
❑ 343 Rod Brind'Amour .10 .05
❑ 344 Brad Shaw .05 .02
❑ 345 Mike Richter .10 .05
❑ 346 Hart Trophy .05 .02
❑ 347 Art Ross Trophy .05 .02
❑ 348 Calder Memorial Trophy .05 .02
❑ 349 Lady Byng Trophy .05 .02
❑ 350 Norris Trophy .05 .02
❑ 351 Vezina Trophy .05 .02
❑ xx Sticker Album 2.50 1.10

## 1991-92 Panini Stickers

This set of 344 stickers was produced by Panini. They measure approximately 1 7/8" by 2 7/8" and were to be pasted in a 8 1/4" by 10 1/2" bilingual sticker album. The fronts feature

color action shots of the players. Pages 2-5 of the album picture highlights of the 1991 Stanley Cup playoffs and finals. Team pages have team colors that highlight player stickers. The NHL 75th Anniversary logo (3-4) and the circular-shaped team logos (148-169) are foil. The stickers are numbered on the back and checklist below alphabetically according to team.

| | MINT | NRMT |
|---|---|---|
| COMPLETE SET (344) | 20.00 | 9.00 |
| COMMON STICKER (1-344) | .05 | .02 |

❑ 1 NHL Logo .05 .02
❑ 2 NHLPA Logo .05 .02
❑ 3 NHL Logo 75th .05 .02
Anniversary (Left)
❑ 4 NHL Logo 75th .05 .02
Anniversary (Right)
❑ 5 Clarence Campbell .05 .02
Conference Logo
❑ 6 Prince of Wales .05 .02
Conference Logo
❑ 7 Stanley Cup .10 .05
Championship Logo
❑ 8 Steve Larmer .10 .05
❑ 9 Ed Belfour .50 .23
❑ 10 Chris Chelios .50 .23
❑ 11 Michel Goulet .10 .05
❑ 12 Jeremy Roenick .50 .23
❑ 13 Adam Creighton .05 .02
❑ 14 Steve Thomas .05 .02
❑ 15 Dave Manson .05 .02
❑ 16 Dirk Graham .05 .02
❑ 17 Troy Murray .05 .02
❑ 18 Doug Wilson .05 .02
❑ 19 Wayne Presley .05 .02
❑ 20 Jocelyn Lemieux .05 .02
❑ 21 Keith Brown .05 .02
❑ 22 Curtis Joseph .50 .23
❑ 23 Jeff Brown .05 .02
❑ 24 Gino Cavallini .05 .02
❑ 25 Brett Hull .50 .23
❑ 26 Scott Stevens .10 .05
❑ 27 Dan Quinn .05 .02
❑ 28 Garth Butcher .05 .02
❑ 29 Bob Bassen .05 .02
❑ 30 Rod Brind'Amour .05 .02
❑ 31 Adam Oates .10 .05
❑ 32 Dave Lowry .05 .02
❑ 33 Rich Sutter .05 .02
❑ 34 Ron Wilson .05 .02
❑ 35 Paul Cavallini .05 .02
❑ 36 Trevor Linden .10 .05
❑ 37 Troy Gamble .05 .02
❑ 38 Geoff Courtnall .05 .02
❑ 39 Greg Adams .05 .02
❑ 40 Doug Lidster .05 .02
❑ 41 Dave Capuano .05 .02
❑ 42 Igor Larionov .05 .02
❑ 43 Tom Kurvers .05 .02
❑ 44 Sergio Momesso .05 .02
❑ 45 Kirk McLean .10 .05
❑ 46 Cliff Ronning .05 .02
❑ 47 Robert Kron .05 .02
❑ 48 Steve Bozek .05 .02
❑ 49 Petr Nedved .10 .05
❑ 50 Al MacInnis .10 .05
❑ 51 Theoren Fleury .50 .23
❑ 52 Gary Roberts .10 .05
❑ 53 Joe Nieuwendyk .10 .05
❑ 54 Paul Ranheim .05 .02
❑ 55 Mike Vernon .10 .05
❑ 56 Carey Wilson .05 .02
❑ 57 Gary Suter .10 .05
❑ 58 Sergei Makarov .05 .02
❑ 59 Doug Gilmour .50 .23
❑ 60 Joel Otto .05 .02
❑ 61 Jamie Macoun .05 .02
❑ 62 Stephane Matteau .05 .02
❑ 63 Robert Reichel .05 .02
❑ 64 Ed Olczyk .05 .02
❑ 65 Phil Housley .05 .02
❑ 66 Pat Elynuik .05 .02
❑ 67 Fredrik Olausson .05 .02
❑ 68 Thomas Steen .05 .02
❑ 69 Paul MacDermid .05 .02
❑ 70 Brent Ashton .05 .02
❑ 71 Teppo Numminen .05 .02
❑ 72 Danton Cole .05 .02
❑ 73 Dave McLlwain .05 .02
❑ 74 Scott Arniel .05 .02
❑ 75 Bob Essensa .10 .05
❑ 76 Randy Carlyle .05 .02
❑ 77 Mark Osborne .05 .02
❑ 78 Wayne Gretzky 3.00 1.35
❑ 79 Tomas Sandstrom .05 .02
❑ 80 Steve Duchesne .05 .02
❑ 81 Kelly Hrudey .10 .05
❑ 82 Larry Robinson .10 .05
❑ 83 Tony Granato .05 .02
❑ 84 Marty McSorley .05 .02
❑ 85 Todd Elik .05 .02
❑ 86 Rob Blake .10 .05
❑ 87 Bob Kudelski .05 .02
❑ 88 Steve Kasper .05 .02
❑ 89 Dave Taylor .05 .02
❑ 90 John Tonelli .05 .02
❑ 91 Luc Robitaille .10 .05
❑ 92 Vincent Damphousse .10 .05
❑ 93 Brian Bradley .05 .02
❑ 94 Dave Ellett .05 .02
❑ 95 Daniel Marois .05 .02
❑ 96 Rob Ramage .05 .02
❑ 97 Mike Krushelnyski .05 .02
❑ 98 Michel Petit .05 .02
❑ 99 Peter Ing .05 .02
❑ 100 Lucien DeBlois .05 .02
❑ 101 Bob Rouse .05 .02
❑ 102 Wendel Clark .10 .05
❑ 103 Peter Zezel .05 .02
❑ 104 David Reid .05 .02
❑ 105 Aaron Broten .05 .02
❑ 106 Brian Hayward .10 .05
❑ 107 Neal Broten .05 .02
❑ 108 Brian Bellows .05 .02
❑ 109 Mark Tinordi .05 .02
❑ 110 Ulf Dahlen .05 .02
❑ 111 Doug Smail .05 .02
❑ 112 Dave Gagner .05 .02
❑ 113 Bobby Smith .05 .02
❑ 114 Brian Glynn .05 .02
❑ 115 Brian Propp .05 .02
❑ 116 Mike Modano .50 .23
❑ 117 Gaetan Duchesne .05 .02
❑ 118 Jon Casey .10 .05
❑ 119 Basil McRae .05 .02
❑ 120 Glenn Anderson .10 .05
❑ 121 Steve Smith .05 .02
❑ 122 Adam Graves .10 .05
❑ 123 Esa Tikkanen .10 .05
❑ 124 Mark Messier .50 .23
❑ 125 Bill Ranford .10 .05
❑ 126 Petr Klima .05 .02
❑ 127 Anatoli Semenov .05 .02
❑ 128 Martin Gelinas .05 .02
❑ 129 Charlie Huddy .05 .02
❑ 130 Craig Simpson .05 .02
❑ 131 Kevin Lowe .10 .05
❑ 132 Craig MacTavish .05 .02
❑ 133 Craig Muni .05 .02
❑ 134 Steve Yzerman 1.50 .70
❑ 135 Shawn Burr .05 .02
❑ 136 Tim Cheveldae .10 .05
❑ 137 Rick Zombo .05 .02
❑ 138 Marc Habscheid .05 .02
❑ 139 Jimmy Carson .05 .02
❑ 140 Brent Fedyk .05 .02
❑ 141 Yves Racine .05 .02
❑ 142 Gerard Gallant .05 .02
❑ 143 Steve Chiasson .05 .02
❑ 144 Johan Garpenlov .05 .02
❑ 145 Sergei Fedorov 1.25 .55
❑ 146 Bob Probert .10 .05
❑ 147 Rick Green .05 .02
❑ 148 Chicago Blackhawks .05 .02
Logo
❑ 149 Detroit Red Wings .05 .02
Logo
❑ 150 Minnesota North Stars .05 .02
Logo
❑ 151 St. Louis Blues .05 .02
Logo
❑ 152 Toronto Maple Leafs .05 .02
Logo
❑ 153 Calgary Flames .05 .02
Logo
❑ 154 Edmonton Oilers .05 .02
Logo
❑ 155 Los Angeles Kings .05 .02
Logo
❑ 156 San Jose Sharks .05 .02
Logo
❑ 157 Vancouver Canucks .05 .02
Logo
❑ 158 Winnipeg Jets .05 .02
Logo
❑ 159 Boston Bruins .05 .02
Logo
❑ 160 Buffalo Sabres .05 .02
Logo
❑ 161 Hartford Whalers .05 .02
Logo
❑ 162 Montreal Canadiens .05 .02
Logo
❑ 163 Quebec Nordiques .05 .02
Logo
❑ 164 New Jersey Devils .05 .02
Logo
❑ 165 New York Islanders .05 .02
Logo
❑ 166 New York Rangers .05 .02
Logo
❑ 167 Philadelphia Flyers .05 .02
Logo
❑ 168 Pittsburgh Penguins .05 .02
Logo
❑ 169 Washington Capitals .05 .02
Logo
❑ 170 Craig Janney .05 .02
❑ 171 Ray Bourque .50 .23
❑ 172 Rejean Lemelin .10 .05
❑ 173 Dave Christian .05 .02
❑ 174 Randy Burridge .05 .02
❑ 175 Garry Galley .05 .02
❑ 176 Cam Neely .50 .23
❑ 177 Bob Sweeney .05 .02
❑ 178 Ken Hodge Jr. .05 .02
❑ 179 Andy Moog .10 .05
❑ 180 Don Sweeney .05 .02
❑ 181 Bob Carpenter .05 .02
❑ 182 Glen Wesley .05 .02
❑ 183 Chris Nilan .05 .02
❑ 184 Patrick Roy 2.50 1.10
❑ 185 Petr Svoboda .05 .02
❑ 186 Russ Courtnall .05 .02
❑ 187 Denis Savard .10 .05
❑ 188 Mike McPhee .05 .02
❑ 189 Eric Desjardins .05 .02
❑ 190 Mike Keane .05 .02
❑ 191 Stephan Lebeau .05 .02
❑ 192 J.J. Daigneault .05 .02
❑ 193 Stephane Richer .10 .05
❑ 194 Brian Skrudland .05 .02
❑ 195 Mathieu Schneider .05 .02
❑ 196 Shayne Corson .05 .02
❑ 197 Guy Carbonneau .10 .05
❑ 198 Kevin Hatcher .10 .05
❑ 199 Mike Ridley .05 .02
❑ 200 John Druce .05 .02
❑ 201 Don Beaupre .10 .05
❑ 202 Kelly Miller .05 .02
❑ 203 Dale Hunter .05 .02
❑ 204 Nick Kypreos .05 .02
❑ 205 Calle Johansson .05 .02
❑ 206 Michal Pivonka .05 .02
❑ 207 Dino Ciccarelli .10 .05
❑ 208 Al Iafrate .05 .02
❑ 209 Rod Langway .05 .02
❑ 210 Mikhail Tatarinov .05 .02
❑ 211 Stephen Leach .05 .02
❑ 212 Sean Burke .10 .05
❑ 213 John MacLean .05 .02
❑ 214 Lee Norwood .05 .02
❑ 215 Laurie Boschman .05 .02
❑ 216 Alexei Kasatonov .05 .02
❑ 217 Patrik Sundstrom .05 .02
❑ 218 Ken Daneyko .05 .02
❑ 219 Kirk Muller .10 .05
❑ 220 Peter Stastny .10 .05
❑ 221 Chris Terreri .10 .05
❑ 222 Brendan Shanahan .50 .23
❑ 223 Eric Weinrich .05 .02
❑ 224 Claude Lemieux .10 .05
❑ 225 Bruce Driver .05 .02
❑ 226 Tim Kerr .05 .02
❑ 227 Ron Hextall .10 .05
❑ 228 Pelle Eklund .05 .02
❑ 229 Rick Tocchet .10 .05
❑ 230 Gord Murphy .05 .02
❑ 231 Mike Ricci .05 .02
❑ 232 Derrick Smith .05 .02
❑ 233 Ron Sutter .05 .02
❑ 234 Murray Craven .05 .02
❑ 235 Terry Carkner .05 .02
❑ 236 Ken Wregget .10 .05
❑ 237 Keith Acton .05 .02
❑ 238 Scott Mellanby .10 .05
❑ 239 Kjell Samuelsson .05 .02
❑ 240 Jeff Hackett .10 .05
❑ 241 David Volek .05 .02
❑ 242 Craig Ludwig .05 .02
❑ 243 Pat LaFontaine .10 .05
❑ 244 Randy Wood .05 .02
❑ 245 Pat Flatley .05 .02
❑ 246 Brent Sutter .05 .02
❑ 247 Derek King .05 .02
❑ 248 Jeff Norton .05 .02
❑ 249 Glenn Healy .10 .05
❑ 250 Ray Ferraro .05 .02
❑ 251 Gary Nylund .05 .02
❑ 252 Joe Reekie .05 .02
❑ 253 Dave Chyzowski .05 .02
❑ 254 Mike Hough .05 .02
❑ 255 Mats Sundin .10 .05
❑ 256 Curtis Leschyshyn .05 .02
❑ 257 Joe Sakic 1.50 .70
❑ 258 Stephane Fiset .10 .05
❑ 259 Bryan Fogarty .05 .02
❑ 260 Alexei Gusarov .05 .02
❑ 261 Steven Finn .05 .02
❑ 262 Everett Sanipass .05 .02
❑ 263 Stephane Morin .05 .02
❑ 264 Craig Wolanin .05 .02
❑ 265 Randy Velischek .05 .02
❑ 266 Owen Nolan .10 .05
❑ 267 Ron Tugnutt .10 .05
❑ 268 Mario Lemieux 2.50 1.10
❑ 269 Kevin Stevens .05 .02
❑ 270 Larry Murphy .10 .05
❑ 271 Tom Barrasso .10 .05
❑ 272 Phil Bourque .05 .02
❑ 273 Scott Young .05 .02
❑ 274 Paul Stanton .05 .02
❑ 275 Jaromir Jagr 2.00 .90
❑ 276 Paul Coffey .50 .23
❑ 277 Ulf Samuelsson .05 .02
❑ 278 Joe Mullen .10 .05
❑ 279 Bob Errey .05 .02
❑ 280 Mark Recchi .10 .05
❑ 281 Ron Francis .10 .05
❑ 282 John Vanbiesbrouck 1.00 .45
❑ 283 Jan Erixon .05 .02
❑ 284 Brian Leetch .50 .23
❑ 285 Darren Turcotte .10 .05
❑ 286 Ray Sheppard .05 .02
❑ 287 James Patrick .05 .02
❑ 288 Bernie Nicholls .10 .05
❑ 289 Brian Mullen .05 .02
❑ 290 Mike Richter .10 .05
❑ 291 Kelly Kisio .05 .02
❑ 292 Mike Gartner .50 .23
❑ 293 John Ogrodnick .05 .02
❑ 294 David Shaw .05 .02
❑ 295 Troy Mallette .05 .02
❑ 296 Dale Hawerchuk .10 .05
❑ 297 Rick Vaive .05 .02
❑ 298 Daren Puppa .10 .05
❑ 299 Mike Ramsey .05 .02
❑ 300 Benoit Hogue .05 .02
❑ 301 Clint Malarchuk .10 .05
❑ 302 Mikko Makela .05 .02
❑ 303 Pierre Turgeon .10 .05
❑ 304 Alexander Mogilny .10 .05
❑ 305 Uwe Krupp .05 .02
❑ 306 Christian Ruuttu .05 .02
❑ 307 Doug Bodger .05 .02
❑ 308 Dave Snuggerud .05 .02
❑ 309 Dave Andreychuk .10 .05
❑ 310 Peter Sidorkiewicz .10 .05
❑ 311 Brad Shaw .05 .02
❑ 312 Dean Evason .05 .02
❑ 313 Pat Verbeek .05 .02
❑ 314 John Cullen .05 .02
❑ 315 Rob Brown .05 .02
❑ 316 Bobby Holik .05 .02
❑ 317 Todd Krygier .05 .02
❑ 318 Adam Burt .05 .02
❑ 319 Mike Tomlak .05 .02
❑ 320 Randy Cunneyworth .05 .02
❑ 321 Paul Cyr .05 .02
❑ 322 Zarley Zalapski .05 .02
❑ 323 Kevin Dineen .05 .02
❑ 324 Luc Robitaille .10 .05
❑ 325 Brett Hull .50 .23
❑ 326 All-Star Game Logo .05 .02
❑ 327 Wayne Gretzky 3.00 1.35
❑ 328 Mike Vernon .10 .05
❑ 329 Chris Chelios .50 .23
❑ 330 Al MacInnis .10 .05
❑ 331 Rick Tocchet .10 .05
❑ 332 Cam Neely .50 .23
❑ 333 Patrick Roy 2.50 1.10
❑ 334 Joe Sakic 1.50 .70
❑ 335 Ray Bourque .50 .23
❑ 336 Paul Coffey .50 .23
❑ 337 Ed Belfour .50 .23
❑ 338 Mike Ricci .05 .02
❑ 339 Rob Blake .10 .05
❑ 340 Sergei Fedorov 1.25 .55
❑ 341 Ken Hodge Jr. .05 .02
❑ 342 Bobby Holik .05 .02
❑ 343 Robert Reichel .05 .02
❑ 344 Jaromir Jagr 2.00 .90
❑ xx Sticker Album 1.50 .70

## 1992-93 Panini Stickers

This set of 330 stickers was produced by Panini. They measure approximately 2 3/8" by 3 3/8" and were to be pasted in a 9" by 11" album. The fronts have action color player photos with statistics running down the right side in a colored bar. The player's name appears at the top. The team logo is superimposed on the photo at the lower left corner. The backs feature questions and answers that go with the Slap-shot game that is included in the album. The team logos scattered throughout the set are foil. The stickers are numbered on the front on a puck icon at the lower right corner. They are checklisted below alphabetically according to teams in the Campbell and Wales Conferences. Also included are subsets of the 1992 NHL's Top Rookies (270-275), the 1992 All-Star Game (276-289), the European Invasion (290-302), and The Trophies (303-308). Randomly inserted throughout the packs were 22 lettered "Ice-Breaker" stickers, each featuring a star player from each of the 22 NHL teams (minus the new expansion teams, the Tampa Bay Lightning and the Ottawa Senators.

| | MINT | NRMT |
|---|---|---|
| COMPLETE SET (330) | 35.00 | 16.00 |
| COMMON STICKER (1-308) | .05 | .02 |
| COMMON STICKER (A-V) | .35 | .16 |

*FRENCH: SAME VALUE

❑ 1 Stanley Cup .10 .05
❑ 2 Blackhawks logo .05 .02
❑ 3 Ed Belfour .50 .23
❑ 4 Jeremy Roenick .50 .23
❑ 5 Steve Larmer .10 .05
❑ 6 Michel Goulet .10 .05
❑ 7 Dirk Graham .05 .02
❑ 8 Jocelyn Lemieux .05 .02
❑ 9 Brian Noonan .05 .02
❑ 10 Rob Brown .05 .02
❑ 11 Chris Chelios .50 .23
❑ 12 Steve Smith .05 .02
❑ 13 Keith Brown .05 .02
❑ 14 St. Louis Blues .05 .02
❑ 15 Curtis Joseph .10 .05
❑ 16 Brett Hull .50 .23
❑ 17 Brendan Shanahan .50 .23
❑ 18 Ron Wilson .05 .02
❑ 19 Rich Sutter .05 .02
❑ 20 Ron Sutter .05 .02
❑ 21 Dave Lowry .05 .02
❑ 22 Craig Janney .05 .02
❑ 23 Paul Cavallini .05 .02
❑ 24 Garth Butcher .05 .02
❑ 25 Jeff Brown .05 .02
❑ 26 Canucks Logo .05 .02
❑ 27 Kirk McLean .10 .05
❑ 28 Trevor Linden .10 .05
❑ 29 Geoff Courtnall .05 .02
❑ 30 Cliff Ronning .05 .02
❑ 31 Petr Nedved .10 .05
❑ 32 Igor Larionov .05 .02
❑ 33 Robert Kron .05 .02
❑ 34 Jim Sandlak .05 .02
❑ 35 Dave Babych .05 .02
❑ 36 Jyrki Lumme .05 .02
❑ 37 Doug Lidster .05 .02
❑ 38 Flames Logo .05 .02
❑ 39 Mike Vernon .10 .05
❑ 40 Joe Nieuwendyk .10 .05
❑ 41 Gary Leeman .05 .02
❑ 42 Robert Reichel .05 .02
❑ 43 Joel Otto .05 .02
❑ 44 Paul Ranheim .05 .02
❑ 45 Gary Roberts .10 .05
❑ 46 Theo Fleury .35 .16
❑ 47 Sergei Makarov .05 .02
❑ 48 Gary Suter .10 .05
❑ 49 Al MacInnis .10 .05
❑ 50 Jets Logo .05 .02
❑ 51 Bob Essensa .10 .05
❑ 52 Teppo Numminen .05 .02
❑ 53 Thomas Steen .05 .02
❑ 54 Pat Elynuik .05 .02
❑ 55 Ed Olczyk .05 .02
❑ 56 Danton Cole .05 .02
❑ 57 Troy Murray .05 .02
❑ 58 Darrin Shannon .05 .02
❑ 59 Russ Romaniuk .05 .02
❑ 60 Fredrik Olausson .05 .02
❑ 61 Phil Housley .05 .02
❑ 62 Kings Logo .05 .02
❑ 63 Kelly Hrudey .10 .05
❑ 64 Wayne Gretzky 1.50 .70
❑ 65 Luc Robitaille .10 .05
❑ 66 Jari Kurri .50 .23
❑ 67 Tomas Sandstrom .05 .02
❑ 68 Tony Granato .05 .02
❑ 69 Bob Kudelski .05 .02
❑ 70 Corey Millen .05 .02
❑ 71 Rob Blake .10 .05
❑ 72 Paul Coffey .50 .23
❑ 73 Marty McSorley .05 .02
❑ 74 Maple Leafs Logo .05 .02
❑ 75 Grant Fuhr .50 .23
❑ 76 Glenn Anderson .10 .05
❑ 77 Doug Gilmour .50 .23
❑ 78 Mike Krushelnyski .05 .02
❑ 79 Wendel Clark .10 .05
❑ 80 Rob Pearson .05 .02
❑ 81 Peter Zezel .05 .02
❑ 82 Todd Gill .05 .02
❑ 83 Dave Ellett .05 .02
❑ 84 Mike Foligno .05 .02
❑ 85 Ken Baumgartner .05 .02
❑ 86 North Stars Logo .05 .02
❑ 87 Jon Casey .10 .05
❑ 88 Brian Bellows .05 .02
❑ 89 Neal Broten .05 .02
❑ 90 Dave Gagner .05 .02
❑ 91 Mike Modano .50 .23
❑ 92 Ulf Dahlen .05 .02
❑ 93 Brian Propp .05 .02
❑ 94 Jim Johnson .05 .02
❑ 95 Mike Craig .05 .02
❑ 96 Bobby Smith .05 .02
❑ 97 Mark Tinordi .05 .02
❑ 98 Oilers Logo .05 .02
❑ 99 Bill Ranford .10 .05
❑ 100 Joe Murphy .10 .05
❑ 101 Craig MacTavish .05 .02
❑ 102 Craig Simpson .05 .02
❑ 103 Esa Tikkanen .10 .05
❑ 104 Vincent Damphousse .10 .05
❑ 105 Petr Klima .05 .02
❑ 106 Martin Gelinas .05 .02
❑ 107 Kevin Lowe .10 .05
❑ 108 Dave Manson .05 .02
❑ 109 Bernie Nicholls .10 .05
❑ 110 Red Wings Logo .05 .02
❑ 111 Tim Cheveldae .10 .05
❑ 112 Steve Yzerman 1.00 .45
❑ 113 Sergei Fedorov .75 .35
❑ 114 Jimmy Carson .05 .02
❑ 115 Kevin Miller .05 .02
❑ 116 Gerard Gallant .05 .02
❑ 117 Keith Primeau .05 .02
❑ 118 Paul Ysebaert .05 .02
❑ 119 Yves Racine .05 .02
❑ 120 Steve Chiasson .05 .02
❑ 121 Ray Sheppard .05 .02
❑ 122 Sharks Logo .05 .02
❑ 123 Jeff Hackett .10 .05
❑ 124 Kelly Kisio .05 .02
❑ 125 Brian Mullen .05 .02
❑ 126 David Bruce .05 .02
❑ 127 Rob Zettler .05 .02
❑ 128 Neil Wilkinson .05 .02
❑ 129 Doug Wilson .05 .02
❑ 130 Jeff Odgers .05 .02
❑ 131 Dean Evason .05 .02
❑ 132 Brian Lawton .05 .02
❑ 133 Dale Craigwell .05 .02
❑ 134 Bruins Logo .05 .02
❑ 135 Andy Moog .10 .05

❑ 136 Adam Oates .10 .05
❑ 137 Dave Poulin .05 .02
❑ 138 Vladimir Ruzicka .05 .02
❑ 139 Jeff Lazaro .05 .02
❑ 140 Bob Carpenter .05 .02
❑ 141 Peter Douris .05 .02
❑ 142 Glen Murray .05 .02
❑ 143 Cam Neely .50 .23
❑ 144 Ray Bourque .50 .23
❑ 145 Glen Wesley .05 .02
❑ 146 Canadiens Logo .05 .02
❑ 147 Patrick Roy 1.25 .55
❑ 148 Kirk Muller .10 .05
❑ 149 Guy Carbonneau .10 .05
❑ 150 Shayne Corson .05 .02
❑ 151 Stephan Lebeau .05 .02
❑ 152 Denis Savard .10 .05
❑ 153 Brent Gilchrist .05 .02
❑ 154 Russ Courtnall .05 .02
❑ 155 Patrice Brisebois .05 .02
❑ 156 Eric Desjardins .05 .02
❑ 157 Matt Schneider .05 .02
❑ 158 Capitals Logo .05 .02
❑ 159 Don Beaupre .10 .05
❑ 160 Dino Ciccarelli .10 .05
❑ 161 Michal Pivonka .05 .02
❑ 162 Mike Ridley .05 .02
❑ 163 Randy Burridge .05 .02
❑ 164 Peter Bondra .10 .05
❑ 165 Dale Hunter .05 .02
❑ 166 Kelly Miller .05 .02
❑ 167 Kevin Hatcher .10 .05
❑ 168 Al Iafrate .05 .02
❑ 169 Rod Langway .05 .02
❑ 170 Devils Logo .05 .02
❑ 171 Chris Terreri .10 .05
❑ 172 Claude Lemieux .10 .05
❑ 173 Stephane Richer .10 .05
❑ 174 Peter Stastny .10 .05
❑ 175 Zdeno Ciger .05 .02
❑ 176 Alexander Semak .05 .02
❑ 177 Valeri Zelepukin .05 .02
❑ 178 Bruce Driver .05 .02
❑ 179 Scott Niedermayer .05 .02
❑ 180 Alexei Kasatonov .05 .02
❑ 181 Scott Stevens .10 .05
❑ 182 Flyers Logo .05 .02
❑ 183 Dominic Roussel .10 .05
❑ 184 Mike Ricci .05 .02
❑ 185 Mark Recchi .10 .05
❑ 186 Kevin Dineen .05 .02
❑ 187 Rod Brind'Amour .05 .02
❑ 188 Mark Pederson .05 .02
❑ 189 Pelle Eklund .05 .02
❑ 190 Terry Carkner .05 .02
❑ 191 Mark Howe .05 .02
❑ 192 Steve Duchesne .05 .02
❑ 193 Andrei Lomakin .05 .02
❑ 194 Islanders Logo .05 .02
❑ 195 Mark Fitzpatrick .10 .05
❑ 196 Pierre Turgeon .10 .05
❑ 197 Benoit Hogue .05 .02
❑ 198 Ray Ferraro .05 .02
❑ 199 Derek King .05 .02
❑ 200 David Volek .05 .02
❑ 201 Patrick Flatley .05 .02
❑ 202 Uwe Krupp .05 .02
❑ 203 Steve Thomas .05 .02
❑ 204 Adam Creighton .05 .02
❑ 205 Jeff Norton .05 .02
❑ 206 Nordiques Logo .05 .02
❑ 207 Stephane Fiset .10 .05
❑ 208 Mikhail Tatarinov .05 .02
❑ 209 Joe Sakic .75 .35
❑ 210 Owen Nolan .10 .05
❑ 211 Mike Hough .05 .02
❑ 212 Mats Sundin .10 .05
❑ 213 Claude Lapointe .05 .02
❑ 214 Stephane Morin .05 .02
❑ 215 Alexei Gusarov .05 .02
❑ 216 Steven Finn .05 .02
❑ 217 Curtis Leschyshyn .05 .02
❑ 218 Penguins Logo .05 .02
❑ 219 Tom Barrasso .10 .05
❑ 220 Mario Lemieux 1.25 .55
❑ 221 Kevin Stevens .05 .02
❑ 222 Shawn McEachern .05 .02
❑ 223 Joe Mullen .10 .05
❑ 224 Ron Francis .10 .05
❑ 225 Phil Bourque .05 .02
❑ 226 Rick Tocchet .10 .05
❑ 227 Bryan Trottier .10 .05
❑ 228 Larry Murphy .10 .05
❑ 229 Ulf Samuelsson .05 .02
❑ 230 Rangers Logo .05 .02
❑ 231 Mike Richter .10 .05
❑ 232 John Vanbiesbrouck .50 .23
❑ 233 Mark Messier .50 .23
❑ 234 Sergei Nemchinov .05 .02
❑ 235 Darren Turcotte .10 .05
❑ 236 Doug Weight .10 .05
❑ 237 Mike Gartner .50 .23
❑ 238 Adam Graves .10 .05
❑ 239 Brian Leetch .50 .23
❑ 240 James Patrick .05 .02
❑ 241 Jan Erixon .05 .02
❑ 242 Sabres Logo .05 .02
❑ 243 Tom Draper .05 .02
❑ 244 Grant Ledyard .05 .02
❑ 245 Doug Bodger .05 .02
❑ 246 Pat LaFontaine .10 .05
❑ 247 Dale Hawerchuk .10 .05
❑ 248 Alexander Mogilny .10 .05
❑ 249 Dave Andreychuk .10 .05
❑ 250 Christian Ruuttu .05 .02
❑ 251 Randy Wood .05 .02
❑ 252 Brad May .10 .05
❑ 253 Mike Ramsey .05 .02
❑ 254 Whalers Logo .05 .02
❑ 255 Kay Whitmore .10 .05
❑ 256 Pat Verbeek .05 .02
❑ 257 John Cullen .05 .02
❑ 258 Mikael Andersson .05 .02
❑ 259 Yvon Corriveau .05 .02
❑ 260 Randy Cunneyworth .05 .02
❑ 261 Robert Holik .05 .02
❑ 262 Murray Craven .05 .02
❑ 263 Zarley Zalapski .05 .02
❑ 264 Adam Burt .05 .02
❑ 265 Brad Shaw .05 .02
❑ 266 Lightning Logo .05 .02
❑ 267 Lightning Jersey .05 .02
❑ 268 Senators Logo .05 .02
❑ 269 Senators Jersey .05 .02
❑ 270 Tony Amonte .35 .16
❑ 271 Pavel Bure .75 .35
❑ 272 Gilbert Dionne .05 .02
❑ 273 Pat Falloon .05 .02
❑ 274 Nicklas Lidstrom .10 .05
❑ 275 Kevin Todd .05 .02
❑ 276 Prince of Wales Conference Logo .05 .02
❑ 277 Patrick Roy AS .75 .35
❑ 278 Paul Coffey AS .50 .23
❑ 279 Ray Bourque AS .50 .23
❑ 280 Mario Lemieux AS .75 .35
❑ 281 Kevin Stevens AS .05 .02
❑ 282 Jaromir Jagr AS .50 .23
❑ 283 Clarence Campbell Conference Logo .05 .02
❑ 284 Ed Belfour AS .50 .23
❑ 285 Al MacInnis AS .10 .05
❑ 286 Chris Chelios AS .50 .23
❑ 287 Wayne Gretzky AS 1.50 .70
❑ 288 Luc Robitaille AS .10 .05
❑ 289 Brett Hull AS .50 .23
❑ 290 Pavel Bure .75 .35
❑ 291 Sergei Fedorov .75 .35
❑ 292 Dominik Hasek .50 .23
❑ 293 Robert Holik .05 .02
❑ 294 Jaromir Jagr 1.00 .45
❑ 295 Valeri Kamensky .05 .02
❑ 296 Alexander Semak .05 .02
❑ 297 Igor Kravchuk .05 .02
❑ 298 Nicklas Lidstrom .10 .05
❑ 299 Alexander Mogilny .10 .05
❑ 300 Petr Nedved .10 .05
❑ 301 Robert Reichel .05 .02
❑ 302 Mats Sundin .10 .05
❑ 303 Calder Trophy .05 .02
❑ 304 Hart Trophy .05 .02
❑ 305 Lady Byng Trophy .05 .02
❑ 306 Norris Trophy .05 .02
❑ 307 Selke Trophy .05 .02
❑ 308 Vezina Trophy .05 .02
❑ A Igor Kravchuk .35 .16
❑ B Nelson Emerson .35 .16
❑ C Pavel Bure 3.00 1.35
❑ D Tomas Forslund .35 .16
❑ E Luciano Borsato .35 .16
❑ F Darryl Sydor .35 .16
❑ G Felix Potvin 2.00 .90
❑ H Derian Hatcher .35 .16
❑ I Joseph Beranek .35 .16
❑ J Nicklas Lidstrom 1.00 .45
❑ K Pat Falloon .35 .16
❑ L Joe Juneau .35 .16
❑ M Gilbert Dionne .35 .16
❑ N Dimitri Khristich .35 .16
❑ O Kevin Todd .35 .16
❑ P Eric Lindros 6.00 2.70
❑ Q Scott Lachance .35 .16
❑ R Valeri Kamensky .50 .23
❑ S Jaromir Jagr 5.00 2.20
❑ T Tony Amonte .50 .23
❑ U Donald Audette .35 .16
❑ V Geoff Sanderson .35 .16
❑ xx Sticker Album 1.50 .70

## 1993-94 Panini Stickers

This set of 300 stickers was produced by Panini. They measure approximately 2 3/8" by 3 3/8" and were to be pasted in a 9" by 11" sticker album. The fronts have action color player photos with the player's name and the team name printed to the left side of the photo. The backs promote collecting Panini stickers. Also included are a subset Best of the Best (133-144), and a subset of 24 glitter stickers of Panini's superstars (A-X), one per team. The stickers are numbered on the back. The album also includes players' statistics and and a Stanley Cup final review.

| | MINT | NRMT |
|---|---|---|
| COMPLETE SET (300) | 25.00 | 11.00 |
| COMMON CARD (1-276) | .05 | .02 |
| COMMON GLITTER (A-X) | .35 | .16 |

❑ 1 Bruins Logo .05 .02
❑ 2 Adam Oates .10 .05
❑ 3 Cam Neely .50 .23
❑ 4 Dave Poulin .05 .02
❑ 5 Steve Leach .05 .02
❑ 6 Glen Wesley .05 .02
❑ 7 Dmitri Kvartalnov .05 .02
❑ 8 Ted Donato .05 .02
❑ 9 Andy Moog .10 .05
❑ 10 Ray Bourque .50 .23
❑ 11 Don Sweeney .05 .02
❑ 12 Canadiens Logo .05 .02
❑ 13 Vincent Damphousse .10 .05
❑ 14 Kirk Muller .10 .05
❑ 15 Brian Bellows .05 .02
❑ 16 Stephan Lebeau .05 .02
❑ 17 Denis Savard .10 .05
❑ 18 Gilbert Dionne .05 .02
❑ 19 Guy Carbonneau .10 .05
❑ 20 Benoit Brunet .05 .02
❑ 21 Eric Desjardins .05 .02
❑ 22 Mathieu Schneider .05 .02
❑ 23 Capitals Logo .05 .02
❑ 24 Peter Bondra .10 .05
❑ 25 Mike Ridley .05 .02
❑ 26 Dale Hunter .05 .02
❑ 27 Michal Pivonka .05 .02
❑ 28 Dimitri Khristich .10 .05
❑ 29 Pat Elynuik .05 .02
❑ 30 Kelly Miller .05 .02
❑ 31 Calle Johansson .05 .02
❑ 32 Al Iafrate .05 .02
❑ 33 Don Beaupre .10 .05
❑ 34 Devils Logo .05 .02
❑ 35 Claude Lemieux .10 .05
❑ 36 Alexander Semak .05 .02
❑ 37 Stephane Richer .10 .05
❑ 38 Valeri Zelepukin .05 .02
❑ 39 Bernie Nicholls .10 .05
❑ 40 John MacLean .05 .02
❑ 41 Peter Stastny .10 .05
❑ 42 Scott Niedermayer .05 .02
❑ 43 Scott Stevens .10 .05
❑ 44 Bruce Driver .05 .02
❑ 45 Flyers Logo .05 .02
❑ 46 Mark Recchi .10 .05
❑ 47 Rod Brind'Amour .05 .02
❑ 48 Brent Fedyk .05 .02
❑ 49 Kevin Dineen .05 .02
❑ 50 Keith Acton .05 .02
❑ 51 Pelle Eklund .05 .02
❑ 52 Andrei Lomakin .05 .02
❑ 53 Garry Galley .05 .02
❑ 54 Terry Carkner .05 .02
❑ 55 Tommy Soderstrom .05 .02
❑ 56 Islanders Logo .05 .02
❑ 57 Steve Thomas .05 .02
❑ 58 Derek King .05 .02
❑ 59 Benoit Hogue .05 .02
❑ 60 Patrick Flatley .05 .02
❑ 61 Brian Mullen .05 .02
❑ 62 Marty McInnis .05 .02
❑ 63 Scott Lachance .05 .02
❑ 64 Jeff Norton .05 .02
❑ 65 Glenn Healy .10 .05
❑ 66 Mark Fitzpatrick .10 .05
❑ 67 Nordiques Logo .05 .02
❑ 68 Mats Sundin .10 .05
❑ 69 Mike Ricci .05 .02
❑ 70 Owen Nolan .10 .05
❑ 71 Andrei Kovalenko .05 .02
❑ 72 Valeri Kamensky .05 .02
❑ 73 Scott Young .05 .02
❑ 74 Martin Rucinsky .05 .02
❑ 75 Steven Finn .05 .02
❑ 76 Steve Duchesne .05 .02
❑ 77 Ron Hextall .10 .05
❑ 78 Penguins Logo .05 .02
❑ 79 Kevin Stevens .05 .02
❑ 80 Rick Tocchet .10 .05
❑ 81 Ron Francis .10 .05
❑ 82 Jaromir Jagr 2.00 .90
❑ 83 Joe Mullen .10 .05
❑ 84 Shawn McEachern .05 .02
❑ 85 Dave Tippett .05 .02
❑ 86 Larry Murphy .10 .05
❑ 87 Ulf Samuelsson .05 .02
❑ 88 Tom Barrasso .10 .05
❑ 89 Rangers Logo .05 .02
❑ 90 Tony Amonte .10 .05
❑ 91 Mike Gartner .50 .23
❑ 92 Adam Graves .10 .05
❑ 93 Sergei Nemchinov .05 .02
❑ 94 Darren Turcotte .05 .02
❑ 95 Esa Tikkanen .10 .05
❑ 96 Brian Leetch .50 .23
❑ 97 Kevin Lowe .10 .05
❑ 98 John Vanbiesbrouck .75 .35
❑ 99 Mike Richter .10 .05
❑ 100 Sabres Logo .05 .02
❑ 101 Pat LaFontaine .10 .05
❑ 102 Dale Hawerchuk .10 .05
❑ 103 Donald Audette .10 .05
❑ 104 Bob Sweeney .05 .02
❑ 105 Randy Wood .05 .02
❑ 106 Yuri Khmylev .05 .02
❑ 107 Wayne Presley .05 .02
❑ 108 Grant Fuhr .50 .23
❑ 109 Doug Bodger .05 .02
❑ 110 Richard Smehlik .05 .02
❑ 111 Senators Logo .05 .02
❑ 112 Norm Maciver .05 .02
❑ 113 Jamie Baker .05 .02
❑ 114 Bob Kudelski .05 .02
❑ 115 Jody Hull .05 .02
❑ 116 Mike Peluso .05 .02
❑ 117 Mark Lamb .05 .02
❑ 118 Mark Freer .05 .02
❑ 119 Neil Brady .05 .02
❑ 120 Brad Shaw .05 .02
❑ 121 Peter Sidorkiewicz .10 .05
❑ 122 Whalers Logo .05 .02
❑ 123 Andrew Cassels .05 .02
❑ 124 Pat Verbeek .05 .02
❑ 125 Terry Yake .05 .02
❑ 126 Patrick Poulin .05 .02
❑ 127 Mark Janssens .05 .02
❑ 128 Michael Nylander .05 .02
❑ 129 Zarley Zalapski .05 .02
❑ 130 Eric Weinrich .05 .02
❑ 131 Sean Burke .10 .05
❑ 132 Frank Pietrangelo .10 .05
❑ 133 Phil Housley .05 .02
❑ 134 Paul Coffey .50 .23
❑ 135 Larry Murphy .10 .05
❑ 136 Mario Lemieux 1.50 .70
❑ 137 Pat LaFontaine .10 .05
❑ 138 Adam Oates .10 .05
❑ 139 Felix Potvin .50 .23
❑ 140 Ed Belfour .50 .23
❑ 141 Tom Barrasso .10 .05
❑ 142 Teemu Selanne .75 .35
❑ 143 Joe Juneau .05 .02
❑ 144 Eric Lindros 1.50 .70
❑ 145 Blackhawks Logo .05 .02
❑ 146 Steve Larmer .10 .05
❑ 147 Dirk Graham .05 .02
❑ 148 Michel Goulet .10 .05
❑ 149 Brian Noonan .05 .02
❑ 150 Stephane Matteau .05 .02
❑ 151 Brent Sutter .05 .02
❑ 152 Jocelyn Lemieux .05 .02
❑ 153 Chris Chelios .50 .23
❑ 154 Steve Smith .05 .02
❑ 155 Ed Belfour .50 .23
❑ 156 Blues Logo .05 .02
❑ 157 Craig Janney .05 .02
❑ 158 Brendan Shanahan .50 .23
❑ 159 Nelson Emerson .10 .05
❑ 160 Rich Sutter .05 .02
❑ 161 Ron Sutter .05 .02
❑ 162 Ron Wilson .05 .02
❑ 163 Bob Bassen .05 .02
❑ 164 Garth Butcher .05 .02
❑ 165 Jeff Brown .05 .02
❑ 166 Curtis Joseph .10 .05
❑ 167 Canucks Logo .05 .02
❑ 168 Cliff Ronning .05 .02
❑ 169 Murray Craven .05 .02
❑ 170 Geoff Courtnall .05 .02
❑ 171 Petr Nedved .10 .05
❑ 172 Trevor Linden .10 .05
❑ 173 Greg Adams .05 .02
❑ 174 Anatoli Semenov .05 .02
❑ 175 Jyrki Lumme .05 .02
❑ 176 Doug Lidster .05 .02
❑ 177 Kirk McLean .10 .05
❑ 178 Flames Logo .05 .02
❑ 179 Theoren Fleury .35 .16
❑ 180 Robert Reichel .05 .02
❑ 181 Gary Roberts .10 .05
❑ 182 Joe Nieuwendyk .10 .05
❑ 183 Sergei Makarov .05 .02
❑ 184 Paul Ranheim .05 .02
❑ 185 Joel Otto .05 .02
❑ 186 Gary Suter .10 .05
❑ 187 Jeff Reese .05 .02
❑ 188 Mike Vernon .10 .05
❑ 189 Jets Logo .05 .02
❑ 190 Alexei Zhamnov .05 .02
❑ 191 Thomas Steen .05 .02
❑ 192 Darrin Shannon .05 .02
❑ 193 Keith Tkachuk .50 .23
❑ 194 Evgeny Davydov .05 .02
❑ 195 Luciano Borsato .05 .02
❑ 196 Phil Housley .05 .02
❑ 197 Teppo Numminen .05 .02
❑ 198 Fredrik Olausson .05 .02
❑ 199 Bob Essensa .10 .05
❑ 200 Kings Logo .05 .02
❑ 201 Luc Robitaille .10 .05
❑ 202 Jari Kurri .50 .23
❑ 203 Tony Granato .05 .02
❑ 204 Jimmy Carson .05 .02
❑ 205 Tomas Sandstrom .05 .02
❑ 206 Dave Taylor .05 .02
❑ 207 Corey Millen .05 .02
❑ 208 Marty McSorley .05 .02
❑ 209 Rob Blake .10 .05
❑ 210 Kelly Hrudey .10 .05
❑ 211 Lightning Logo .05 .02
❑ 212 John Tucker .05 .02
❑ 213 Chris Kontos .05 .02
❑ 214 Rob Zamuner .05 .02
❑ 215 Adam Creighton .05 .02
❑ 216 Mikael Andersson .05 .02
❑ 217 Bob Beers .05 .02
❑ 218 Rob DiMaio .05 .02
❑ 219 Shawn Chambers .05 .02
❑ 220 J.C. Bergeron .05 .02
❑ 221 Wendell Young .10 .05
❑ 222 Maple Leafs Logo .05 .02
❑ 223 Dave Andreychuk .10 .05
❑ 224 Nikolai Borschevsky .05 .02
❑ 225 Glenn Anderson .10 .05
❑ 226 John Cullen .05 .02
❑ 227 Wendel Clark .10 .05
❑ 228 Mike Foligno .05 .02
❑ 229 Mike Krushelnyski .05 .02
❑ 230 James Macoun .05 .02
❑ 231 Dave Ellett .05 .02
❑ 232 Felix Potvin .50 .23
❑ 233 Oilers Logo .05 .02
❑ 234 Petr Klima .05 .02
❑ 235 Doug Weight .10 .05
❑ 236 Shayne Corson .05 .02
❑ 237 Craig Simpson .05 .02
❑ 238 Todd Elik .05 .02
❑ 239 Zdeno Ciger .05 .02
❑ 240 Craig MacTavish .05 .02
❑ 241 Kelly Buchberger .05 .02
❑ 242 Dave Manson .05 .02
❑ 243 Scott Mellanby .10 .05
❑ 244 Red Wings Logo .05 .02
❑ 245 Dino Ciccarelli .10 .05
❑ 246 Sergei Fedorov .50 .23
❑ 247 Ray Sheppard .05 .02
❑ 248 Paul Ysebaert .05 .02
❑ 249 Bob Probert .10 .05
❑ 250 Keith Primeau .05 .02
❑ 251 Steve Chiasson .05 .02
❑ 252 Paul Coffey .50 .23
❑ 253 Nicklas Lidstrom .05 .02
❑ 254 Tim Cheveldae .10 .05
❑ 255 Sharks Logo .05 .02
❑ 256 Kelly Kisio .05 .02
❑ 257 Johan Garpenlov .05 .02
❑ 258 Robert Gaudreau .05 .02
❑ 259 Dean Evason .05 .02
❑ 260 Jeff Odgers .05 .02
❑ 261 Ed Courtenay .05 .02
❑ 262 Mike Sullivan .05 .02
❑ 263 Doug Zmolek .05 .02
❑ 264 Doug Wilson .05 .02
❑ 265 Brian Hayward .10 .05
❑ 266 Stars Logo .05 .02
❑ 267 Brian Propp .05 .02
❑ 268 Russ Courtnall .05 .02
❑ 269 Dave Gagner .05 .02
❑ 270 Ulf Dahlen .05 .02
❑ 271 Mike Craig .05 .02
❑ 272 Neal Broten .05 .02
❑ 273 Gaetan Duchesne .05 .02
❑ 274 Derian Hatcher .05 .02
❑ 275 Mark Tinordi .05 .02
❑ 276 Jon Casey .10 .05
❑ A Joe Juneau .35 .16
❑ B Patrick Roy 3.00 1.35
❑ C Kevin Hatcher .35 .16
❑ D Chris Terreri .50 .23
❑ E Eric Lindros 2.00 .90
❑ F Pierre Turgeon .50 .23
❑ G Joe Sakic 2.00 .90
❑ H Mario Lemieux 3.00 1.35
❑ I Mark Messier .75 .35
❑ J Alexander Mogilny .50 .23
❑ K Sylvain Turgeon .35 .16
❑ L Geoff Sanderson .35 .16
❑ M Jeremy Roenick .50 .23
❑ N Brett Hull .50 .23
❑ O Pavel Bure 1.25 .55
❑ P Al MacInnis .35 .16
❑ Q Teemu Selanne 1.50 .70
❑ R Wayne Gretzky 4.00 1.80
❑ S Brian Bradley .35 .16
❑ T Doug Gilmour .50 .23
❑ U Bill Ranford .50 .23
❑ V Steve Yzerman 2.00 .90
❑ W Pat Falloon .35 .16
❑ X Mike Modano 1.00 .45

## 1993-94 Panthers Team Issue

These eight blank-backed cards were printed on thin stock and measure approximately 3 3/4" by 7". They feature on their white-bordered fronts black-and-white action shots framed by a thin red line. The player's uniform number (in large red characters), his name and position, and the Panthers' logo are printed across the top. The cards are unnumbered and checklisted below in alphabetical order.

| | MINT | NRMT |
|---|---|---|
| COMPLETE SET (8) | 12.00 | 5.50 |
| COMMON CARD (1-8) | 1.50 | .70 |

❑ 1 Joe Cirella 1.50 .70
❑ 2 Tom Fitzgerald 1.50 .70
❑ 3 Mike Foligno 1.50 .70
❑ 4 Paul Laus 1.75 .80
❑ 5 Bill Lindsay 1.50 .70
❑ 6 Andrei Lomakin 1.50 .70
❑ 7 Scott Mellanby 3.00 1.35
❑ 8 Brent Severyn 1.50 .70

## 1994-95 Panthers Pop-ups

Issued by Health Plan of Florida, these cards measure 4" x 10". They were given away at five different home games throughout the season.

Back has biographical information.

| | MINT | NRMT |
|---|---|---|
| COMPLETE SET (5) | 10.00 | 4.50 |
| COMMON CARD (1-5) | 1.50 | .70 |

❑ 1 Brian Skrudland 1.50 .70
❑ 2 John Vanbiesbrouck 4.00 1.80
❑ 3 Scott Mellanby 1.50 .70
❑ 4 Stu Barnes 1.50 .70
❑ 5 Jesse Belanger 1.50 .70

## 1951-52 Parkhurst

The 1951-52 Parkhurst set contains 105 small cards in crude color. Cards are 1 3/4" by 2 1/2". The player's name, team, card number, and 1950-51 statistics all appear on the front of the card. The backs of the cards are blank. Unopened wax packs, though rarely seen, consist of five cards. The cards feature players from each of the six NHL teams. The set numbering is basically according to teams, i.e., Montreal Canadiens (1-18), Boston Bruins (19-35), Chicago Blackhawks (36-51 and 53), Detroit Red Wings (54-69), Toronto Maple Leafs (70-88), and New York Rangers (89-105). Card #52 features a photo of one of the most famous goals in hockey history as Bill Barilko scored the Stanley Cup winning goal and then went flying into the air. The set features the first cards of hockey greats Gordie Howe and Maurice Richard. Other notable Rookie Cards in this set are Alex Delvecchio, Boom Boom Geoffrion, Doug Harvey, Red Kelly, Ted Lindsay, Gerry McNeil and Terry Sawchuk. Please be alert when purchasing cards of Maurice Richard, Gordie Howe and Terry Sawchuk as counterfeits are known to exist of these players.

| | NRMT | VG-E |
|---|---|---|
| COMPLETE SET (105) | 12000.00 | 5400.00 |
| COMMON CARD (1-105) | 50.00 | 22.00 |

❑ 1 Elmer Lach 400.00 100.00
❑ 2 Paul Meger 50.00 22.00
❑ 3 Butch Bouchard 100.00 45.00
❑ 4 Maurice Richard 1600.00 700.00
❑ 5 Bert Olmstead 100.00 45.00
❑ 6 Bud MacPherson 50.00 22.00
❑ 7 Tom Johnson 80.00 36.00
❑ 8 Paul Masnick 50.00 22.00
❑ 9 Calum Mackay 50.00 22.00
❑ 10 Doug Harvey 600.00 275.00
❑ 11 Ken Mosdell 60.00 27.00
❑ 12 Floyd(Busher) Curry 60.00 27.00
❑ 13 Billy Reay 60.00 27.00
❑ 14 Bernie Geoffrion 600.00 275.00
❑ 15 Gerry McNeil 250.00 110.00
❑ 16 Dick Gamble 50.00 22.00
❑ 17 Gerry Couture 50.00 22.00
❑ 18 Ross Robert Lowe 50.00 22.00
❑ 19 Jim Henry 125.00 55.00
❑ 20 Victor Ivan Lynn 50.00 22.00
❑ 21 Walter(Gus) Kyle 50.00 22.00
❑ 22 Ed Sandford 50.00 22.00
❑ 23 John Henderson 50.00 22.00
❑ 24 Dunc Fisher 50.00 22.00
❑ 25 Hal Laycoe 50.00 22.00
❑ 26 Bill Quackenbush 125.00 55.00
❑ 27 George Sullivan 50.00 22.00
❑ 28 Woody Dumart 80.00 36.00
❑ 29 Milt Schmidt 125.00 55.00
❑ 30 Adam Brown 50.00 22.00
❑ 31 Pentti Lund 50.00 22.00
❑ 32 Ray Barry 50.00 22.00
❑ 33 Ed Kryznowski UER 50.00 22.00
(Misspelled Kryzanowski on card)
❑ 34 Johnny Peirson 50.00 22.00
❑ 35 Lorne Ferguson 50.00 22.00
❑ 36 Clare(Rags) Raglan 50.00 22.00
❑ 37 Bill Gadsby 100.00 45.00
❑ 38 Al Dewsbury 50.00 22.00
❑ 39 George Clare Martin 50.00 22.00
❑ 40 Gus Bodnar 50.00 22.00
❑ 41 Jim Peters 50.00 22.00
❑ 42 Bep Guidolin 50.00 22.00
❑ 43 George Gee 50.00 22.00
❑ 44 Jim McFadden 50.00 22.00
❑ 45 Fred Hucul 50.00 22.00
❑ 46 John Lee Fogolin 50.00 22.00
❑ 47 Harry Lumley 150.00 70.00
❑ 48 Doug Bentley 100.00 45.00
❑ 49 Bill Mosienko 100.00 45.00
❑ 50 Roy Conacher 60.00 27.00
❑ 51 Pete Babando 50.00 22.00
❑ 52 The Winning Goal 450.00 200.00
(Bill Barilko against Gerry McNeil)
❑ 53 Jack Stewart 60.00 27.00
❑ 54 Marty Pavelich 50.00 22.00
❑ 55 Red Kelly 300.00 135.00
❑ 56 Ted Lindsay 300.00 135.00
❑ 57 Glen Skov 50.00 22.00
❑ 58 Benny Woit 50.00 22.00
❑ 59 Tony Leswick 50.00 22.00
❑ 60 Fred Glover 50.00 22.00
❑ 61 Terry Sawchuk 1200.00 550.00
❑ 62 Vic Stasiuk 60.00 27.00
❑ 63 Alex Delvecchio 350.00 160.00
❑ 64 Sid Abel 80.00 36.00
❑ 65 Metro Prystai 50.00 22.00
❑ 66 Gordie Howe 3000.00 1350.00
❑ 67 Bob Goldham 50.00 22.00
❑ 68 Marcel Pronovost 80.00 36.00
❑ 69 Leo Reise 50.00 22.00
❑ 70 Harry Watson 80.00 36.00
❑ 71 Danny Lewicki 50.00 22.00
❑ 72 Howie Meeker 150.00 70.00
❑ 73 Gus Mortson 50.00 22.00
❑ 74 Joe Klukay 50.00 22.00
❑ 75 Turk Broda 200.00 90.00
❑ 76 Al Rollins 100.00 45.00
❑ 77 Bill Juzda 50.00 22.00
❑ 78 Ray Timgren 50.00 22.00
❑ 79 Hugh Bolton 50.00 22.00
❑ 80 Fern Flaman 80.00 36.00
❑ 81 Max Bentley 80.00 36.00
❑ 82 Jim Thomson 50.00 22.00
❑ 83 Fleming Mackell 50.00 22.00
❑ 84 Sid Smith 50.00 22.00
❑ 85 Cal Gardner 50.00 22.00
❑ 86 Teeder Kennedy 200.00 90.00
❑ 87 Tod Sloan 50.00 22.00
❑ 88 Bob Solinger 50.00 22.00
❑ 89 Frank Eddolls 50.00 22.00
❑ 90 Jack Evans 50.00 22.00
❑ 91 Hy Buller 50.00 22.00
❑ 92 Steve Kraftcheck 50.00 22.00
❑ 93 Don(Bones) Raleigh 50.00 22.00
❑ 94 Allan Stanley 150.00 70.00
❑ 95 Paul Ronty 50.00 22.00
❑ 96 Edgar Laprade 80.00 36.00
❑ 97 Nick Mickoski 50.00 22.00
❑ 98 Jack McLeod 50.00 22.00
❑ 99 Gaye Stewart 50.00 22.00
❑ 100 Wally Hergesheimer 50.00 22.00
❑ 101 Ed Kullman 50.00 22.00
❑ 102 Ed Slowinski 50.00 22.00
❑ 103 Reg Sinclair 50.00 22.00
❑ 104 Chuck Rayner 125.00 55.00
❑ 105 Jim Conacher 200.00 50.00

## 1952-53 Parkhurst

The 1952-53 Parkhurst set contains 105 color, line-drawing cards. Cards are approximately 1 15/16" by 2 15/16". The obverse contains a facsimile autograph of the player pictured while the backs contain a short biography in English and 1951-52 statistics. The backs also contain the card number and a special album (for holding a set of cards) offer. The cards feature players from each of the Original Six NHL teams. The set numbering is roughly according to teams, i.e., Montreal Canadiens (1-15, 52, 93), Boston Bruins (68-85), Chicago Blackhawks (16-17, 26-27, 29-33, 35-41, 55-56), Detroit Red Wings (53, 60-67, 86-92, 104), Toronto Maple Leafs (28, 34, 42-48, 50-51, 54, 58-59, 94-96, 105), and New York Rangers (18-25, 49, 57, 97-103). The key Rookie Cards in this set are George Armstrong, Tim Horton, and Dickie Moore.

| | NRMT | VG-E |
|---|---|---|
| COMPLETE SET (105) | 7000.00 | 3200.00 |
| COMMON CARD (1-105) | 30.00 | 13.50 |

❑ 1 Maurice Richard 1200.00 300.00
❑ 2 Billy Reay 35.00 16.00
❑ 3 Bernie Geoffrion 250.00 110.00
UER (Misspelled Gioffrion on back)
❑ 4 Paul Meger 30.00 13.50
❑ 5 Dick Gamble 35.00 16.00
❑ 6 Elmer Lach 80.00 36.00
❑ 7 Floyd(Busher) Curry 35.00 16.00
❑ 8 Ken Mosdell 35.00 16.00
❑ 9 Tom Johnson 50.00 22.00
❑ 10 Dickie Moore 250.00 110.00
❑ 11 Bud MacPherson 30.00 13.50
❑ 12 Gerry McNeil 100.00 45.00
❑ 13 Butch Bouchard 50.00 22.00
❑ 14 Doug Harvey 250.00 110.00
❑ 15 John McCormack 30.00 13.50
❑ 16 Pete Babando 30.00 13.50
❑ 17 Al Dewsbury 30.00 13.50
❑ 18 Ed Kullman 30.00 13.50
❑ 19 Ed Slowinski 30.00 13.50
❑ 20 Wally Hergesheimer 35.00 16.00
❑ 21 Allan Stanley 80.00 36.00
❑ 22 Chuck Rayner 60.00 27.00
❑ 23 Steve Kraftcheck 30.00 13.50
❑ 24 Paul Ronty 30.00 13.50
❑ 25 Gaye Stewart 30.00 13.50
❑ 26 Fred Hucul 30.00 13.50
❑ 27 Bill Mosienko 50.00 22.00
❑ 28 Jim Morrison 30.00 13.50
❑ 29 Ed Kryznowski 30.00 13.50
❑ 30 Cal Gardner 35.00 16.00
❑ 31 Al Rollins 60.00 27.00
❑ 32 Enio Sclisizzi 30.00 13.50
❑ 33 Pete Conacher 35.00 16.00
❑ 34 Leo Boivin 60.00 27.00
❑ 35 Jim Peters 30.00 13.50
❑ 36 George Gee 30.00 13.50
❑ 37 Gus Bodnar 35.00 16.00
❑ 38 Jim McFadden 30.00 13.50
❑ 39 Gus Mortson 35.00 16.00
❑ 40 Fred Glover 30.00 13.50
❑ 41 Gerry Couture 30.00 13.50
❑ 42 Howie Meeker 80.00 36.00
❑ 43 Jim Thomson 30.00 13.50
❑ 44 Teeder Kennedy 100.00 45.00
❑ 45 Sid Smith 35.00 16.00
❑ 46 Harry Watson 40.00 18.00
❑ 47 Fern Flaman 40.00 18.00
❑ 48 Tod Sloan 35.00 16.00
❑ 49 Leo Reise 30.00 13.50
❑ 50 Bob Solinger 30.00 13.50
❑ 51 George Armstrong 200.00 90.00
❑ 52 Dollard St.Laurent 40.00 18.00
❑ 53 Alex Delvecchio 150.00 70.00
❑ 54 Gord Hannigan 30.00 13.50
❑ 55 Lee Fogolin 30.00 13.50
❑ 56 Bill Gadsby 50.00 22.00
❑ 57 Herb Dickenson 30.00 13.50
❑ 58 Tim Horton 600.00 275.00
❑ 59 Harry Lumley 100.00 45.00
❑ 60 Metro Prystai 30.00 13.50
❑ 61 Marcel Pronovost 40.00 18.00
❑ 62 Benny Woit 30.00 13.50
❑ 63 Glen Skov 30.00 13.50
❑ 64 Bob Goldham 30.00 13.50
❑ 65 Tony Leswick 30.00 13.50
❑ 66 Marty Pavelich 30.00 13.50
❑ 67 Red Kelly 150.00 70.00
❑ 68 Bill Quackenbush 40.00 18.00
❑ 69 Ed Sandford 30.00 13.50
❑ 70 Milt Schmidt 60.00 27.00
❑ 71 Hal Laycoe 35.00 16.00
❑ 72 Woody Dumart 40.00 18.00
❑ 73 Zellio Toppazzini 30.00 13.50
❑ 74 Jim Henry 60.00 27.00
❑ 75 Joe Klukay 30.00 13.50
❑ 76 Dave Creighton 40.00 18.00
❑ 77 Jack McIntyre 30.00 13.50
❑ 78 Johnny Peirson 30.00 13.50
❑ 79 George Sullivan 35.00 16.00
❑ 80 Real Chevrefils 40.00 18.00
❑ 81 Leo Labine 35.00 16.00
❑ 82 Fleming Mackell 35.00 16.00
❑ 83 Pentti Lund 30.00 13.50
❑ 84 Bob Armstrong 30.00 13.50
❑ 85 Warren Godfrey 30.00 13.50
❑ 86 Terry Sawchuk 500.00 220.00
❑ 87 Ted Lindsay 150.00 70.00
❑ 88 Gordie Howe 1200.00 550.00
❑ 89 Johnny Wilson 30.00 13.50
❑ 90 Vic Stasiuk 35.00 16.00
❑ 91 Larry Zeidel 30.00 13.50
❑ 92 Larry Wilson 30.00 13.50
❑ 93 Bert Olmstead 50.00 22.00
❑ 94 Ron Stewart 40.00 18.00
❑ 95 Max Bentley 50.00 22.00
❑ 96 Rudy Migay 30.00 13.50
❑ 97 Jack Stoddard 30.00 13.50
❑ 98 Hy Buller 30.00 13.50
❑ 99 Don(Bones) Raleigh 30.00 13.50
UER (James on back)
❑ 100 Edgar Laprade 35.00 16.00
❑ 101 Nick Mickoski 30.00 13.50
❑ 102 Jack McLeod UER 30.00 13.50
(Robert on back)
❑ 103 Jim Conacher 35.00 16.00
❑ 104 Reg Sinclair 30.00 13.50
❑ 105 Bob Hassard 100.00 25.00

## 1953-54 Parkhurst

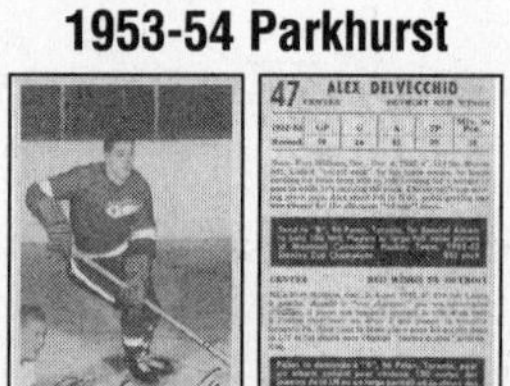

The 1953-54 Parkhurst set contains 100 cards in full color. Cards measure approximately 2 1/2" by 3 5/8". The cards were sold in five-cent wax packs each containing four cards and gum. The size of the card increased from the previous year, and the picture and color show marked improvement. A facsimile autograph of the player is found on the front. The backs contain the card number, 1952-53 statistics, a short biography, and an album offer. The back data is presented in both English and French. The cards feature players from each of the six NHL teams. The set numbering is basically according to teams, i.e., Toronto Maple Leafs (1-17), Montreal Canadiens (18-35), Detroit Red Wings (36-52), New York Rangers (53-68), Chicago Blackhawks (69-84), and Boston Bruins (85-100). The key Rookie Cards in this set are Al Arbour, Andy Bathgate, Jean Beliveau, Harry Howell, and Gump Worsley.

| | NRMT | VG-E |
|---|---|---|
| COMPLETE SET (100) | 4500.00 | 2000.00 |
| COMMON CARD (1-100) | 30.00 | 13.50 |

❑ 1 Harry Lumley 250.00 60.00
❑ 2 Sid Smith 30.00 13.50
❑ 3 Gord Hannigan 30.00 13.50
❑ 4 Bob Hassard 30.00 13.50
❑ 5 Tod Sloan 30.00 13.50
❑ 6 Leo Boivin 30.00 13.50
❑ 7 Teeder Kennedy 60.00 27.00
❑ 8 Jim Thomson 30.00 13.50
❑ 9 Ron Stewart 30.00 13.50
❑ 10 Eric Nesterenko 60.00 27.00
❑ 11 George Armstrong 100.00 45.00
❑ 12 Harry Watson 30.00 13.50
❑ 13 Tim Horton 300.00 135.00
❑ 14 Fern Flaman 40.00 18.00
❑ 15 Jim Morrison 30.00 13.50
❑ 16 Bob Solinger 30.00 13.50
❑ 17 Rudy Migay 30.00 13.50
❑ 18 Dick Gamble 30.00 13.50
❑ 19 Bert Olmstead 40.00 18.00
❑ 20 Eddie Mazur 30.00 13.50
❑ 21 Paul Meger 30.00 13.50
❑ 22 Bud MacPherson 30.00 13.50
❑ 23 Dollard St.Laurent 30.00 13.50
❑ 24 Maurice Richard 500.00 220.00
❑ 25 Gerry McNeil 80.00 36.00
❑ 26 Doug Harvey 200.00 90.00
❑ 27 Jean Beliveau 600.00 275.00
❑ 28 Dickie Moore UER 125.00 55.00
(Photo actually Jean Beliveau)
❑ 29 Bernie Geoffrion 200.00 90.00
❑ 30 Lach/Richard 200.00 90.00
Elmer Lach and Maurice Richard
❑ 31 Elmer Lach 60.00 27.00
❑ 32 Butch Bouchard 40.00 18.00
❑ 33 Ken Mosdell 30.00 13.50
❑ 34 John McCormack 30.00 13.50
❑ 35 Floyd (Busher) Curry 30.00 13.50
❑ 36 Earl Reibel 30.00 13.50
❑ 37 Bill Dineen UER 60.00 27.00
(Photo actually Al Arbour)
❑ 38 Al Arbour UER 100.00 45.00
(Photo actually Bill Dineen)
❑ 39 Vic Stasiuk 30.00 13.50
❑ 40 Red Kelly 100.00 45.00
❑ 41 Marcel Pronovost 40.00 18.00
❑ 42 Metro Prystai 30.00 13.50
❑ 43 Tony Leswick 30.00 13.50
❑ 44 Marty Pavelich 30.00 13.50
❑ 45 Benny Woit 30.00 13.50
❑ 46 Terry Sawchuk 350.00 160.00
❑ 47 Alex Delvecchio 100.00 45.00
❑ 48 Glen Skov 30.00 13.50
❑ 49 Bob Goldham 30.00 13.50
❑ 50 Gordie Howe 800.00 350.00
❑ 51 Johnny Wilson 30.00 13.50
❑ 52 Ted Lindsay 100.00 45.00
❑ 53 Gump Worsley 400.00 180.00
❑ 54 Jack Evans 30.00 13.50
❑ 55 Max Bentley 40.00 18.00
❑ 56 Andy Bathgate 150.00 70.00
❑ 57 Harry Howell 150.00 70.00
❑ 58 Hy Buller 30.00 13.50
❑ 59 Chuck Rayner 40.00 18.00
❑ 60 Jack Stoddard 30.00 13.50
❑ 61 Ed Kullman 30.00 13.50
❑ 62 Nick Mickoski 30.00 13.50
❑ 63 Paul Ronty 30.00 13.50
❑ 64 Allan Stanley 60.00 27.00
❑ 65 Leo Reise 30.00 13.50
❑ 66 Aldo Guidolin 30.00 13.50
❑ 67 Wally Hergesheimer 30.00 13.50
❑ 68 Don Raleigh 30.00 13.50
❑ 69 Jim Peters 30.00 13.50
❑ 70 Pete Conacher 30.00 13.50
❑ 71 Fred Hucul 30.00 13.50
❑ 72 Lee Fogolin 30.00 13.50
❑ 73 Larry Zeidel 30.00 13.50
❑ 74 Larry Wilson 30.00 13.50
❑ 75 Gus Bodnar 30.00 13.50
❑ 76 Bill Gadsby 40.00 18.00
❑ 77 Jim McFadden 30.00 13.50
❑ 78 Al Dewsbury 30.00 13.50
❑ 79 Clare Raglan 30.00 13.50
❑ 80 Bill Mosienko 40.00 18.00
❑ 81 Gus Mortson 30.00 13.50
❑ 82 Al Rollins 40.00 18.00
❑ 83 George Gee 30.00 13.50
❑ 84 Gerry Couture 30.00 13.50
❑ 85 Dave Creighton 30.00 13.50
❑ 86 Jim Henry 40.00 18.00
❑ 87 Hal Laycoe 30.00 13.50
❑ 88 Johnny Peirson UER 30.00 13.50
(Misspelled Pierson on card back)
❑ 89 Real Chevrefils 30.00 13.50
❑ 90 Ed Sandford 30.00 13.50
❑ 91A Fleming Mackell ERR 40.00 18.00
(No bio)
❑ 91B Fleming Mackell COR 40.00 18.00
❑ 92 Milt Schmidt 60.00 27.00
❑ 93 Leo Labine 30.00 13.50
❑ 94 Joe Klukay 30.00 13.50
❑ 95 Warren Godfrey 30.00 13.50
❑ 96 Woody Dumart 30.00 13.50
❑ 97 Frank Martin 30.00 13.50
❑ 98 Jerry Toppazzini 30.00 13.50
❑ 99 Cal Gardner 30.00 13.50
❑ 100 Bill Quackenbush 80.00 20.00

## 1954-55 Parkhurst

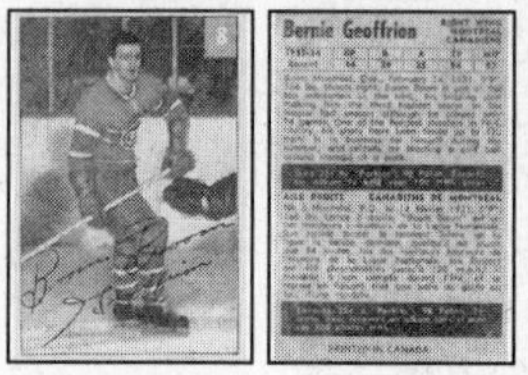

The 1954-55 Parkhurst set contains 100 cards in full color with both the card number and a facsimile autograph on the fronts. Cards in the set measure approximately 2 1/2" by 3 5/8". Unopened wax packs consisted of four cards. The backs, in both English and French, contain 1953-54 statistics, a short player biography, and an album offer (contained only on cards 1-88). Cards 1-88 feature players from each of the six NHL teams and the remaining cards are action scenes. Cards 1-88 were available with either a stat or a premium back. The cards with the statistics on the back are more desirable but there is currently no price differential. The player/set numbering is basically according to teams, i.e., Montreal Canadiens (1-15), Toronto Maple Leafs (16-32), Detroit Red Wings (33-48), Boston Bruins (49-64), New York Rangers (65-76), and Chicago Blackhawks (77-88), and All-Star selections from the previous season are noted discreetly on the card front by a red star (first team selection) or blue star (second team). The key Rookie Card in this set is Johnny Bower, although there are several Action Scene cards featuring Jacques Plante in the year before his regular Rookie Card.

| | NRMT | VG-E |
|---|---|---|
| COMPLETE SET (100) | 4000.00 | 1800.00 |
| COMMON CARD (1-100) | 25.00 | 11.00 |

❑ 1 Gerry McNeil 100.00 25.00
❑ 2 Dickie Moore 80.00 36.00
❑ 3 Jean Beliveau 300.00 135.00
❑ 4 Eddie Mazur 25.00 11.00
❑ 5 Bert Olmstead 30.00 13.50
❑ 6 Butch Bouchard 30.00 13.50
❑ 7 Maurice Richard 400.00 180.00
❑ 8 Bernie Geoffrion 125.00 55.00
❑ 9 John McCormack 25.00 11.00
❑ 10 Tom Johnson 30.00 13.50
❑ 11 Calum Mackay 25.00 11.00
❑ 12 Ken Mosdell 25.00 11.00
❑ 13 Paul Masnick 25.00 11.00
❑ 14 Doug Harvey 125.00 55.00
❑ 15 Floyd(Busher) Curry 25.00 11.00
❑ 16 Harry Lumley 40.00 18.00
❑ 17 Harry Watson 25.00 11.00
❑ 18 Jim Morrison 25.00 11.00
❑ 19 Eric Nesterenko 25.00 11.00
❑ 20 Fern Flaman 30.00 13.50
❑ 21 Rudy Migay 25.00 11.00
❑ 22 Sid Smith 25.00 11.00
❑ 23 Ron Stewart 25.00 11.00
❑ 24 George Armstrong 80.00 36.00
❑ 25 Earl Balfour 25.00 11.00
❑ 26 Leo Boivin 25.00 11.00
❑ 27 Gord Hannigan 25.00 11.00
❑ 28 Bob Bailey 25.00 11.00
❑ 29 Teeder Kennedy 50.00 22.00
❑ 30 Tod Sloan 25.00 11.00
❑ 31 Tim Horton 250.00 110.00
❑ 32 Jim Thomson 25.00 11.00
❑ 33 Terry Sawchuk 250.00 110.00
❑ 34 Marcel Pronovost 30.00 13.50
❑ 35 Metro Prystai 25.00 11.00
❑ 36 Alex Delvecchio 80.00 36.00
❑ 37 Earl Reibel 25.00 11.00
❑ 38 Benny Woit 25.00 11.00
❑ 39 Bob Goldham 25.00 11.00
❑ 40 Glen Skov 25.00 11.00
❑ 41 Gordie Howe 600.00 275.00
❑ 42 Red Kelly 80.00 36.00
❑ 43 Marty Pavelich 25.00 11.00
❑ 44 Johnny Wilson 25.00 11.00
❑ 45 Tony Leswick 25.00 11.00
❑ 46 Ted Lindsay 80.00 36.00
❑ 47 Keith Allen 30.00 13.50
❑ 48 Bill Dineen 25.00 11.00
❑ 49 Jim Henry 40.00 18.00
❑ 50 Fleming Mackell 25.00 11.00
❑ 51 Bill Quackenbush 25.00 11.00
❑ 52 Hal Laycoe 25.00 11.00
❑ 53 Cal Gardner 25.00 11.00
❑ 54 Joe Klukay 25.00 11.00
❑ 55 Bob Armstrong 25.00 11.00
❑ 56 Warren Godfrey 25.00 11.00
❑ 57 Doug Mohns 40.00 18.00
❑ 58 Dave Creighton 25.00 11.00
❑ 59 Milt Schmidt 30.00 13.50
❑ 60 Johnny Peirson 25.00 11.00
❑ 61 Leo Labine 25.00 11.00
❑ 62 Gus Bodnar 25.00 11.00
❑ 63 Real Chevrefils 25.00 11.00
❑ 64 Ed Sandford 25.00 11.00
❑ 65 Johnny Bower UER 400.00 180.00
(Misspelled Bowers)

❑ 66 Paul Ronty 25.00 11.00
❑ 67 Leo Reise 25.00 11.00
❑ 68 Don Raleigh 25.00 11.00
❑ 69 Bob Chrystal 25.00 11.00
❑ 70 Harry Howell 60.00 27.00
❑ 71 Wally Hergesheimer 25.00 11.00
❑ 72 Jack Evans 25.00 11.00
❑ 73 Camille Henry 30.00 13.50
❑ 74 Dean Prentice 40.00 18.00
❑ 75 Nick Mickoski 25.00 11.00
❑ 76 Ron Murphy 25.00 11.00
❑ 77 Al Rollins 40.00 18.00
❑ 78 Al Dewsbury 25.00 11.00
❑ 79 Lou Jankowski 25.00 11.00
❑ 80 George Gee 25.00 11.00
❑ 81 Gus Mortson 25.00 11.00
❑ 82 Fred Saskamoose UER 50.00 22.00
(born on Dec. 25 on Whitefish Reserve)
❑ 83 Ike Hildebrand 25.00 11.00
❑ 84 Lee Fogolin 25.00 11.00
❑ 85 Larry Wilson 25.00 11.00
❑ 86 Pete Conacher 25.00 11.00
❑ 87 Bill Gadsby 30.00 13.50
❑ 88 Jack McIntyre 25.00 11.00
❑ 89 Busher Curry goes 25.00 11.00
up and over
❑ 90 Delvecchio finds 30.00 13.50
Leaf defense
hard to crack
(Tim Horton)
❑ 91 Battle of All-Stars 40.00 18.00
(Red Kelly and
Harry Lumley)
❑ 92 Lum stops Howe 100.00 45.00
With help of
Stewart's stick
❑ 93 Net-minders nightmare 25.00 11.00
(Harry Lumley
and others)
❑ 94 Meger goes down 25.00 11.00
and under
(Jim Morrison)
❑ 95 Harvey takes nosedive 50.00 22.00
(Eric Nesterenko)
❑ 96 Terry boots out 80.00 36.00
Teeder's blast
(Terry Sawchuk and
Teeder Kennedy)
❑ 97 Reibel tests Habs 100.00 45.00
Rookie %%Mr. Zero~
(Jacques Plante and
Butch Bouchard)
❑ 98 Plante protects 100.00 45.00
against slippery
Sloan
(Doug Harvey)
❑ 99 Placid Plante foils 100.00 45.00
tireless Teeder
❑ 100 Sawchuck stops 150.00 38.00
Boom Boom

## 1955-56 Parkhurst

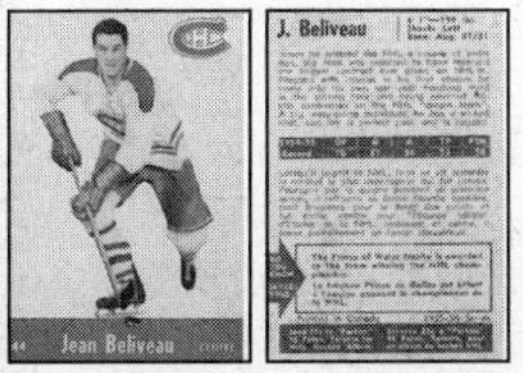

The 1955-56 Parkhurst set contains 79 cards in full color with the number and team insignia on the fronts. Cards in the set measure approximately 2 1/2" by 3 9/16". The set features players from Montreal and Toronto as well as Old-Time Greats. The Old-Time Great selections are numbers 21-32 and 55-66. The backs, printed in red ink, in both English and French, contain 1954-55 statistics, a short biography, a "Do You Know" information section, and an album offer. The key Rookie Card in this set is Jacques Plante. The same 79 cards can also be found with Quaker Oats backs, i.e., green printing on back. The Quaker Oats version is much tougher to locate. Using regular Parkhurst card values as a base, multipliers can be found in the header below to determine value for these. Reportedly, cards #1, 33 and 37 are extremely difficult to acquire in the Quaker Oats version, and can sell for much more than the suggested multipliers.

NRMT VG-E
COMPLETE SET (79) 4000.00 1800.00
COMMON CARD (1-79) 20.00 9.00
*QUAKER OATS: 2X TO 3X BASIC CARDS

❑ 1 Harry Lumley 300.00 75.00
❑ 2 Sid Smith 25.00 11.00
❑ 3 Tim Horton 250.00 110.00
❑ 4 George Armstrong 80.00 36.00
❑ 5 Ron Stewart 25.00 11.00
❑ 6 Joe Klukay 20.00 9.00
❑ 7 Marc Reaume 20.00 9.00
❑ 8 Jim Morrison 20.00 9.00
❑ 9 Parker MacDonald 20.00 9.00
❑ 10 Tod Sloan 20.00 9.00
❑ 11 Jim Thomson 20.00 9.00
❑ 12 Rudy Migay 20.00 9.00
❑ 13 Brian Cullen 30.00 13.50
❑ 14 Hugh Bolton 20.00 9.00
❑ 15 Eric Nesterenko 25.00 11.00
❑ 16 Larry Cahan 20.00 9.00
❑ 17 Willie Marshall 20.00 9.00
❑ 18 Dick Duff 80.00 36.00
❑ 19 Jack Caffery 20.00 9.00
❑ 20 Billy Harris 30.00 13.50
❑ 21 Lorne Chabot OTG 25.00 11.00
❑ 22 Harvey(Busher) Jackson. 50.00 22.00
OTG
❑ 23 Turk Broda OTG 100.00 45.00
❑ 24 Joe Primeau OTG 40.00 18.00
❑ 25 Gordie Drillon OTG 25.00 11.00
❑ 26 Chuck Conacher OTG 40.00 18.00
❑ 27 Sweeney Schriner OTG 25.00 11.00
❑ 28 Syl Apps OTG 40.00 18.00
❑ 29 Teeder Kennedy OTG 50.00 22.00
❑ 30 Ace Bailey OTG 60.00 27.00
❑ 31 Babe Pratt OTG 25.00 11.00
❑ 32 Harold Cotton OTG 25.00 11.00
❑ 33 King Clancy 100.00 45.00
❑ 34 Hap Day 25.00 11.00
❑ 35 Don Marshall 40.00 18.00
❑ 36 Jackie LeClair 25.00 11.00
❑ 37 Maurice Richard 400.00 180.00
❑ 38 Dickie Moore 80.00 36.00
❑ 39 Ken Mosdell 25.00 11.00
❑ 40 Floyd(Busher) Curry 20.00 9.00
❑ 41 Calum Mackay 20.00 9.00
❑ 42 Bert Olmstead 30.00 13.50
❑ 43 Bernie Geoffrion 125.00 55.00
❑ 44 Jean Beliveau 300.00 135.00
❑ 45 Doug Harvey 125.00 55.00
❑ 46 Butch Bouchard 30.00 13.50
❑ 47 Bud MacPherson 20.00 9.00
❑ 48 Dollard St.Laurent 20.00 9.00
❑ 49 Tom Johnson 30.00 13.50
❑ 50 Jacques Plante 800.00 350.00
❑ 51 Paul Meger 20.00 9.00
❑ 52 Gerry McNeil 40.00 18.00
❑ 53 Jean-Guy Talbot 30.00 13.50
❑ 54 Bob Turner 20.00 9.00
❑ 55 Newsy Lalonde OTG 60.00 27.00
❑ 56 Georges Vezina OTG 125.00 55.00
❑ 57 Howie Morenz OTG 100.00 45.00
❑ 58 Aurel Joliat OTG 60.00 27.00
❑ 59 Geo. Hainsworth OTG 100.00 45.00
❑ 60 Sylvio Mantha OTG 25.00 11.00
❑ 61 Battleship Leduc OTG 25.00 11.00
❑ 62 Babe Siebert OTG UER 30.00 13.50
(Misspelled Seibert
on both sides)
❑ 63 Bill Durnan OTG 60.00 27.00
❑ 64 Ken Reardon OTG 50.00 22.00
❑ 65 Johnny Gagnon OTG 25.00 11.00
❑ 66 Billy Reay OTG 25.00 11.00
❑ 67 Toe Blake CO 50.00 22.00
❑ 68 Frank Selke MG 30.00 13.50
❑ 69 Hugh beats Hodge 30.00 13.50
(Hugh Bolton and
Charlie Hodge)
❑ 70 Lum stops Boom Boom 60.00 27.00
(Harry Lumley)
❑ 71 Plante is protected 75.00 34.00
(Butch Bouchard
and Tom Johnson)
❑ 72 Rocket roars through 75.00 34.00
(Maurice Richard)
❑ 73 Richard tests Lumley 75.00 34.00
(Maurice Richard)
❑ 74 Beliveau bats puck 60.00 27.00
(Harry Lumley)
❑ 75 Leaf speedsters attack 75.00 34.00
(Eric Nesterenko,
Sid Smith, and
Jacques Plante)
❑ 76 Curry scores again 25.00 11.00
(Harry Lumley and
Jim Morrison)
❑ 77 Jammed on the boards 75.00 34.00
(Tod Sloan,
Parker MacDonald,
Doug Harvey, and
Jean Beliveau)
❑ 78 The Montreal Forum 300.00 135.00
❑ 79 Maple Leaf Gardens 300.00 75.00

## 1957-58 Parkhurst

The 1957-58 Parkhurst set contains 50 color cards featuring Montreal and Toronto players. Cards are approximately 2 7/16" by 3 5/8". There are card numbers 1 to 25 for Montreal (M prefix in checklist) and card numbers 1 to 25 for Toronto (T prefix in checklist). The cards are numbered on the fronts and the backs feature resumes in both French and English. The card number, the player's name, and his position appear in a red rectangle on the front. The backs are printed in blue ink. The key Rookie Cards in this set are Frank Mahovlich and Henri Richard. There was no Parkhurst hockey set in 1956-57 reportedly due to market re-evaluation.

NRMT VG-E
COMPLETE SET (50) 2500.00 1100.00
COMMON MONTREAL (M1-M20) 20.00 9.00
COMMON TORONTO (T1-T25) 20.00 9.00

❑ M1 Doug Harvey 250.00 110.00
❑ M2 Bernie Geoffrion 125.00 55.00
❑ M3 Jean Beliveau 300.00 135.00
❑ M4 Henri Richard 600.00 275.00
❑ M5 Maurice Richard 400.00 180.00
❑ M6 Tom Johnson 25.00 11.00
❑ M7 Andre Pronovost 40.00 18.00
❑ M8 Don Marshall 20.00 9.00
❑ M9 Jean-Guy Talbot 20.00 9.00
❑ M10 Dollard St.Laurent 20.00 9.00
❑ M11 Phil Goyette 40.00 18.00
❑ M12 Claude Provost 40.00 18.00
❑ M13 Bob Turner 20.00 9.00
❑ M14 Dickie Moore 60.00 27.00
❑ M15 Jacques Plante 400.00 180.00
❑ M16 Toe Blake CO 40.00 18.00
❑ M17 Charlie Hodge 80.00 36.00
❑ M18 Marcel Bonin 20.00 9.00
❑ M19 Bert Olmstead 25.00 11.00
❑ M20 Floyd (Busher) Curry 25.00 11.00
❑ M21 Canadiens on guard 40.00 18.00
(Len Broderick)
❑ M22 Brian Cullen scores 20.00 9.00
❑ M23 Puck and sticks high 40.00 18.00
(Len Broderick and
Doug Harvey)
❑ M24 Geoffrion side- 50.00 22.00
steps Chadwick
❑ M25 Olmstead beats 30.00 13.50
Chadwick
❑ T1 George Armstrong 80.00 36.00
❑ T2 Ed Chadwick 100.00 45.00
❑ T3 Dick Duff 50.00 22.00
❑ T4 Bob Pulford 100.00 45.00
❑ T5 Tod Sloan 25.00 11.00
❑ T6 Rudy Migay 20.00 9.00
❑ T7 Ron Stewart 20.00 9.00
❑ T8 Gerry James 25.00 11.00
❑ T9 Brian Cullen 20.00 9.00
❑ T10 Sid Smith 20.00 9.00
❑ T11 Jim Morrison 20.00 9.00
❑ T12 Marc Reaume 20.00 9.00
❑ T13 Hugh Bolton 20.00 9.00
❑ T14 Pete Conacher 25.00 11.00
❑ T15 Billy Harris 20.00 9.00
❑ T16 Mike Nykoluk 20.00 9.00
❑ T17 Frank Mahovlich 500.00 220.00
❑ T18 Ken Girard 20.00 9.00
❑ T19 Al MacNeil 20.00 9.00
❑ T20 Bob Baun 100.00 45.00
❑ T21 Barry Cullen 20.00 9.00
❑ T22 Tim Horton 175.00 80.00
❑ T23 Gary Collins 20.00 9.00
❑ T24 Gary Aldcorn 20.00 9.00
❑ T25 Billy Reay CO 30.00 13.50

## 1958-59 Parkhurst

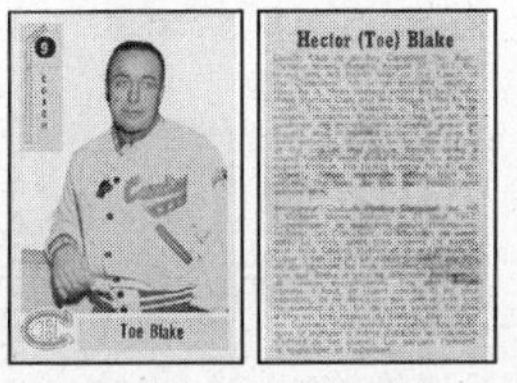

The 1958-59 Parkhurst set contains 50 color cards of Montreal and Toronto players. Cards are approximately 2 7/16" by 3 5/8". In contrast to the 1957-58 Parkhurst set, the cards, numbered on the fronts, are numbered continuously from 1 to 50. Resumes on the backs of the cards are in both French and English. The player's name and the team logo appears in a yellow rectangle at the bottom on the front. The number, position, and (usually) a hockey stick appear on the front at the upper left. The backs are printed in black ink. The key Rookie Card in this set is Ralph Backstrom.

NRMT VG-E
COMPLETE SET (50) 1800.00 800.00
COMMON CARD (1-50) 15.00 6.75

❑ 1 Pulford Comes Close 50.00 12.50
❑ 2 Henri Richard 200.00 90.00
❑ 3 Andre Pronovost 15.00 6.75
❑ 4 Billy Harris 20.00 9.00
❑ 5 Albert Langlois 15.00 6.75
❑ 6 Noel Price 15.00 6.75
❑ 7 Armstrong Breaks 25.00 11.00
Through
(Tom Johnson)
❑ 8 Dickie Moore 40.00 18.00
❑ 9 Toe Blake CO 25.00 11.00
❑ 10 Tom Johnson 25.00 11.00
❑ 11 An Object of Interest 50.00 22.00
(Jacques Plante and
George Armstrong)
❑ 12 Ed Chadwick 40.00 18.00
❑ 13 Bob Nevin 25.00 11.00
❑ 14 Ron Stewart 20.00 9.00
❑ 15 Bob Baun 40.00 18.00
❑ 16 Ralph Backstrom 50.00 22.00
❑ 17 Charlie Hodge 40.00 18.00
❑ 18 Gary Aldcorn 15.00 6.75
❑ 19 Willie Marshall 15.00 6.75
❑ 20 Marc Reaume 15.00 6.75
❑ 21 All Eyes on Puck 60.00 27.00
(Jacques Plante
and others)
❑ 22 Jacques Plante 300.00 135.00
❑ 23 Allan Stanley 25.00 11.00
❑ 24 Ian Cushenan 15.00 6.75
❑ 25 Billy Reay CO 20.00 9.00
❑ 26 Plante Catches a Shot 60.00 27.00
❑ 27 Bert Olmstead 25.00 11.00
❑ 28 Bernie Geoffrion 80.00 36.00
❑ 29 Dick Duff 25.00 11.00
❑ 30 Ab McDonald 15.00 6.75
❑ 31 Barry Cullen 15.00 6.75
❑ 32 Marcel Bonin 15.00 6.75
❑ 33 Frank Mahovlich 200.00 90.00
❑ 34 Jean Beliveau 200.00 90.00
❑ 35 Canadiens on Guard 60.00 27.00
(Jacques Plante
and others)
❑ 36 Brian Cullen Shoots 20.00 9.00
❑ 37 Steve Kraftcheck 15.00 6.75
❑ 38 Maurice Richard 300.00 135.00
❑ 39 Action Around the Net 60.00 27.00
(Jacques Plante
and others)
❑ 40 Bob Turner 15.00 6.75
❑ 41 Jean-Guy Talbot 20.00 9.00
❑ 42 Tim Horton 125.00 55.00
❑ 43 Claude Provost 20.00 9.00
❑ 44 Don Marshall 20.00 9.00
❑ 45 Bob Pulford 30.00 13.50
❑ 46 Johnny Bower UER 150.00 70.00
(Misspelled Bowers
on card front)
❑ 47 Phil Goyette 20.00 9.00
❑ 48 George Armstrong 40.00 18.00
❑ 49 Doug Harvey 80.00 36.00
❑ 50 Brian Cullen 30.00 7.50

## 1959-60 Parkhurst

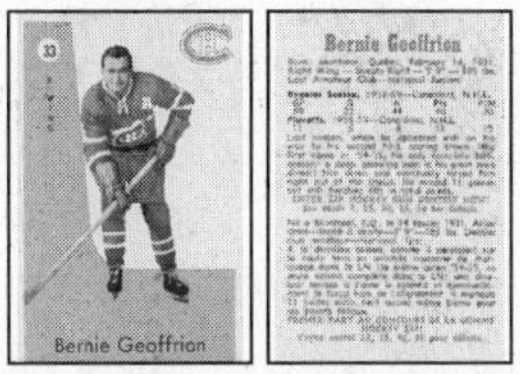

The 1959-60 Parkhurst set contains 50 color cards of Montreal and Toronto players. Cards are approximately 2 7/16" by 3 5/8". The cards are numbered on the fronts. The backs, which contain 1958-59 statistics, a short biography, and a Hockey Gum contest ad, are written in both French and English. The key Rookie Cards in this set are Carl Brewer and Punch Imlach.

NRMT VG-E
COMPLETE SET (50) 1400.00 650.00
COMMON CARD (1-50) 15.00 6.75

❑ 1 Canadiens on Guard 125.00 31.00
(Versus Maple Leafs)
❑ 2 Maurice Richard 250.00 110.00
❑ 3 Carl Brewer 50.00 22.00
❑ 4 Phil Goyette 20.00 9.00
❑ 5 Ed Chadwick 30.00 13.50
❑ 6 Jean Beliveau 125.00 55.00
❑ 7 George Armstrong 25.00 11.00
❑ 8 Doug Harvey 60.00 27.00
❑ 9 Billy Harris 15.00 6.75
❑ 10 Tom Johnson 20.00 9.00
❑ 11 Marc Reaume 15.00 6.75
❑ 12 Marcel Bonin 15.00 6.75
❑ 13 Johnny Wilson 15.00 6.75
❑ 14 Dickie Moore 30.00 13.50
❑ 15 Punch Imlach CO/MG 40.00 18.00
❑ 16 Charlie Hodge 30.00 13.50
❑ 17 Larry Regan 15.00 6.75
❑ 18 Claude Provost 20.00 9.00
❑ 19 Gerry Ehman 15.00 6.75
❑ 20 Ab McDonald 15.00 6.75
❑ 21 Bob Baun 25.00 11.00
❑ 22 Ken Reardon VP 20.00 9.00
❑ 23 Tim Horton 100.00 45.00
❑ 24 Frank Mahovlich 125.00 55.00
❑ 25 Johnny Bower IA 40.00 18.00
❑ 26 Ron Stewart 15.00 6.75
❑ 27 Toe Blake CO 20.00 9.00
❑ 28 Bob Pulford 20.00 9.00
❑ 29 Ralph Backstrom 20.00 9.00
❑ 30 Action Around the Net 18.00 8.00
❑ 31 Bill Hicke 20.00 9.00
❑ 32 Johnny Bower 100.00 45.00
❑ 33 Bernie Geoffrion 60.00 27.00
❑ 34 Ted Hampson 15.00 6.75
❑ 35 Andre Pronovost 15.00 6.75
❑ 36 Stafford Smythe CHC 20.00 9.00
❑ 37 Don Marshall 20.00 9.00
❑ 38 Dick Duff 20.00 9.00
❑ 39 Henri Richard 125.00 55.00
❑ 40 Bert Olmstead 15.00 6.75
❑ 41 Jacques Plante 250.00 110.00
❑ 42 Noel Price 15.00 6.75
❑ 43 Bob Turner 15.00 6.75
❑ 44 Allan Stanley 20.00 9.00
❑ 45 Albert Langlois 15.00 6.75
❑ 46 Officials Intervene 18.00 8.00
❑ 47 Frank Selke MD 20.00 9.00
❑ 48 Gary Edmundson 15.00 6.75
❑ 49 Jean-Guy Talbot 20.00 9.00
❑ 50 King Clancy AGM 80.00 20.00

## 1960-61 Parkhurst

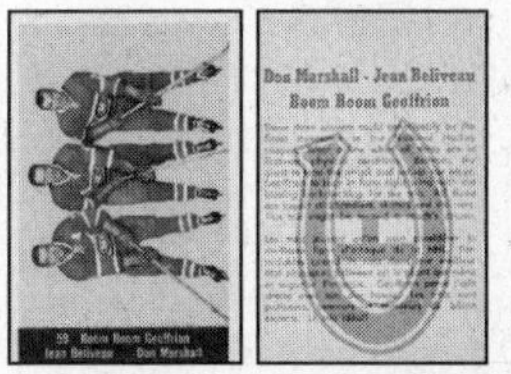

The 1960-61 Parkhurst set of 61 color cards, numbered on the fronts, contains players from Montreal, Toronto, and Detroit. The numbering of the players in the set is basically by teams, i.e., Toronto Maple Leafs (1-19), Detroit Red Wings (20-37), and Montreal Canadiens (38-55). Cards in the set are 2 7/16" by 3 5/8". The backs, in both French and English, are printed in blue ink and contain NHL lifetime records, vital statistics, and biographical data of the player. This set contains the last card of Maurice "Rocket" Richard. The key Rookie Card in this set is John McKenzie.

NRMT VG-E
COMPLETE SET (61) 1700.00 750.00
COMMON CARD (1-61) 15.00 6.75

❑ 1 Tim Horton 150.00 38.00
❑ 2 Frank Mahovlich 100.00 45.00
❑ 3 Johnny Bower 80.00 36.00
❑ 4 Bert Olmstead 20.00 9.00
❑ 5 Gary Edmundson 15.00 6.75
❑ 6 Ron Stewart 20.00 9.00
❑ 7 Gerry James 20.00 9.00
❑ 8 Gerry Ehman 15.00 6.75
❑ 9 Red Kelly 30.00 13.50
❑ 10 Dave Creighton 15.00 6.75
❑ 11 Bob Baun 20.00 9.00
❑ 12 Dick Duff 20.00 9.00
❑ 13 Larry Regan 15.00 6.75
❑ 14 Johnny Wilson 15.00 6.75
❑ 15 Billy Harris 15.00 6.75
❑ 16 Allan Stanley 20.00 9.00
❑ 17 George Armstrong 20.00 9.00
❑ 18 Carl Brewer 20.00 9.00
❑ 19 Bob Pulford 20.00 9.00
❑ 20 Gordie Howe 350.00 160.00
❑ 21 Val Fonteyne 20.00 9.00
❑ 22 Murray Oliver 20.00 9.00
❑ 23 Sid Abel CO 20.00 9.00
❑ 24 Jack McIntyre 15.00 6.75
❑ 25 Marc Reaume 15.00 6.75
❑ 26 Norm Ullman 50.00 22.00
❑ 27 Brian Smith 15.00 6.75
❑ 28 Gerry Melnyk UER 15.00 6.75
(Misspelled Jerry
on both sides)
❑ 29 Marcel Pronovost 20.00 9.00
❑ 30 Warren Godfrey 15.00 6.75
❑ 31 Terry Sawchuk 150.00 70.00
❑ 32 Barry Cullen 15.00 6.75
❑ 33 Gary Aldcorn 15.00 6.75
❑ 34 Pete Goegan 15.00 6.75
❑ 35 Len Lunde 15.00 6.75
❑ 36 Alex Delvecchio 30.00 13.50
❑ 37 John McKenzie 25.00 11.00
❑ 38 Dickie Moore 25.00 11.00
❑ 39 Albert Langlois 15.00 6.75
❑ 40 Bill Hicke 15.00 6.75
❑ 41 Ralph Backstrom 20.00 9.00
❑ 42 Don Marshall 20.00 9.00
❑ 43 Bob Turner 15.00 6.75
❑ 44 Tom Johnson 20.00 9.00
❑ 45 Maurice Richard 225.00 100.00
❑ 46 Bernie Geoffrion 50.00 22.00
❑ 47 Henri Richard 100.00 45.00
❑ 48 Doug Harvey 50.00 22.00
❑ 49 Jean Beliveau 100.00 45.00
❑ 50 Phil Goyette 20.00 9.00
❑ 51 Marcel Bonin 15.00 6.75
❑ 52 Jean-Guy Talbot 20.00 9.00
❑ 53 Jacques Plante 200.00 90.00
❑ 54 Claude Provost 20.00 9.00
❑ 55 Andre Pronovost 15.00 6.75
❑ 56 Bill Hicke 20.00 9.00
Ab McDonald
Ralph Backstrom
❑ 57 Don Marshall 50.00 22.00
Dickie Moore
Henri Richard
❑ 58 Claude Provost 20.00 9.00
Jean Pronovost
Phil Goyette
❑ 59 Boom Boom Geoffrion 80.00 36.00
Don Marshall
Jean Beliveau
❑ 60 Ab McDonald 15.00 6.75
❑ 61 Jim Morrison 100.00 25.00

## 1961-62 Parkhurst

The 1961-62 Parkhurst set contains 51 cards in full color, numbered on the fronts. Cards are 2 7/16" by 3 5/8". The backs contain 1960-61 statistics and a cartoon; the punch line for which could be seen by rubbing the card with a coin. The cards contain players from Montreal, Toronto, and Detroit. The numbering

of the players in the set is basically by teams, i.e., Toronto Maple Leafs (1-18), Detroit Red Wings (19-34), and Montreal Canadiens (35-51). The backs are in both French and English. The key Rookie Card in this set is Dave Keon.

| | NRMT | VG-E |
|---|---|---|
| COMPLETE SET (51) | 1400.00 | 650.00 |
| COMMON CARD (1-51) | 15.00 | 6.75 |
| ❑ 1 Tim Horton | 150.00 | 38.00 |
| ❑ 2 Frank Mahovlich | 80.00 | 36.00 |
| ❑ 3 Johnny Bower | 60.00 | 27.00 |
| ❑ 4 Bert Olmstead | 15.00 | 6.75 |
| ❑ 5 Dave Keon | 200.00 | 90.00 |
| ❑ 6 Ron Stewart | 15.00 | 6.75 |
| ❑ 7 Eddie Shack | 100.00 | 45.00 |
| ❑ 8 Bob Pulford | 20.00 | 9.00 |
| ❑ 9 Red Kelly | 25.00 | 11.00 |
| ❑ 10 Bob Nevin | 15.00 | 6.75 |
| ❑ 11 Bob Baun | 20.00 | 9.00 |
| ❑ 12 Dick Duff | 15.00 | 6.75 |
| ❑ 13 Larry Keenan | 15.00 | 6.75 |
| ❑ 14 Larry Hillman | 15.00 | 6.75 |
| ❑ 15 Billy Harris | 15.00 | 6.75 |
| ❑ 16 Allan Stanley | 20.00 | 9.00 |
| ❑ 17 George Armstrong | 20.00 | 9.00 |
| ❑ 18 Carl Brewer | 15.00 | 6.75 |
| ❑ 19 Howie Glover | 15.00 | 6.75 |
| ❑ 20 Gordie Howe | 300.00 | 135.00 |
| ❑ 21 Val Fonteyne | 15.00 | 6.75 |
| ❑ 22 Al Johnson | 15.00 | 6.75 |
| ❑ 23 Pete Goegan | 15.00 | 6.75 |
| ❑ 24 Len Lunde | 15.00 | 6.75 |
| ❑ 25 Alex Delvecchio | 25.00 | 11.00 |
| ❑ 26 Norm Ullman | 40.00 | 18.00 |
| ❑ 27 Bill Gadsby | 15.00 | 6.75 |
| ❑ 28 Ed Litzenberger | 15.00 | 6.75 |
| ❑ 29 Marcel Pronovost | 15.00 | 6.75 |
| ❑ 30 Warren Godfrey | 15.00 | 6.75 |
| ❑ 31 Terry Sawchuk | 125.00 | 55.00 |
| ❑ 32 Vic Stasiuk | 15.00 | 6.75 |
| ❑ 33 Leo Labine | 15.00 | 6.75 |
| ❑ 34 John McKenzie | 20.00 | 9.00 |
| ❑ 35 Bernie Geoffrion | 50.00 | 22.00 |
| ❑ 36 Dickie Moore | 20.00 | 9.00 |
| ❑ 37 Albert Langlois | 15.00 | 6.75 |
| ❑ 38 Bill Hicke | 15.00 | 6.75 |
| ❑ 39 Ralph Backstrom | 15.00 | 6.75 |
| ❑ 40 Don Marshall | 15.00 | 6.75 |
| ❑ 41 Bob Turner | 15.00 | 6.75 |
| ❑ 42 Tom Johnson | 15.00 | 6.75 |
| ❑ 43 Henri Richard | 80.00 | 36.00 |
| ❑ 44 Wayne Connelly UER (Misspelled Conolly on both sides) | 20.00 | 9.00 |
| ❑ 45 Jean Beliveau | 80.00 | 36.00 |
| ❑ 46 Phil Goyette | 15.00 | 6.75 |
| ❑ 47 Marcel Bonin | 15.00 | 6.75 |
| ❑ 48 Jean-Guy Talbot | 15.00 | 6.75 |
| ❑ 49 Jacques Plante | 175.00 | 80.00 |
| ❑ 50 Claude Provost | 15.00 | 6.75 |
| ❑ 51 Andre Pronovost UER (Shown as Montreal, should be Boston) | 40.00 | 10.00 |

## 1962-63 Parkhurst

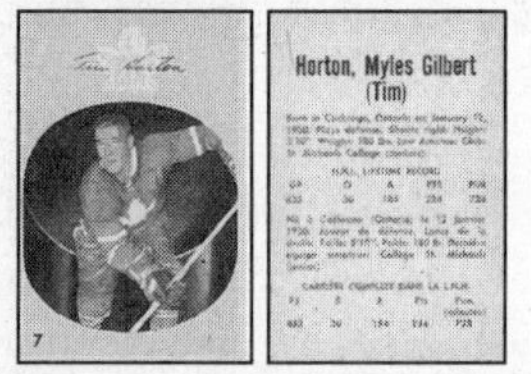


The 1962-63 Parkhurst set contains 55 cards in full color, with the card number and, on some cards, a facsimile autograph on the front. There is also one unnumbered checklist which is part of the complete set price. An unnumbered game or tally card, which is also referred to as the "Zip" card, is not part of the set. Both of these are considered rather difficult to obtain. Cards are approximately 2 7/16" by 3 5/8". The backs, in both French and English, contain player lifetime statistics and player vital statistics in paragraph form. There are several different styles or designs within this set depending on card number, e.g., some cards have a giant puck as background for their photo on the front. Other cards have the player's team logo as background. The numbering of the players in the set is basically by teams, i.e., Toronto Maple Leafs (1-18), Detroit Red Wings (19-36), and Montreal Canadiens (37-54). The notable Rookie Cards in this set are Bobby Rousseau, Gilles Tremblay, and J.C.Tremblay.

| | NRMT | VG-E |
|---|---|---|
| COMPLETE SET (55) | 1600.00 | 700.00 |
| COMMON CARD (1-54) | 12.00 | 5.50 |
| ❑ 1 Billy Harris | 40.00 | 10.00 |
| ❑ 2 Dick Duff | 15.00 | 6.75 |
| ❑ 3 Bob Baun | 15.00 | 6.75 |
| ❑ 4 Frank Mahovlich | 70.00 | 32.00 |
| ❑ 5 Red Kelly | 25.00 | 11.00 |
| ❑ 6 Ron Stewart | 12.00 | 5.50 |
| ❑ 7 Tim Horton | 100.00 | 45.00 |
| ❑ 8 Carl Brewer | 15.00 | 6.75 |
| ❑ 9 Allan Stanley | 15.00 | 6.75 |
| ❑ 10 Bob Nevin | 15.00 | 6.75 |
| ❑ 11 Bob Pulford | 15.00 | 6.75 |
| ❑ 12 Ed Litzenberger | 12.00 | 5.50 |
| ❑ 13 George Armstrong | 15.00 | 6.75 |
| ❑ 14 Eddie Shack | 60.00 | 27.00 |
| ❑ 15 Dave Keon | 100.00 | 45.00 |
| ❑ 16 Johnny Bower | 50.00 | 22.00 |
| ❑ 17 Larry Hillman | 15.00 | 6.75 |
| ❑ 18 Frank Mahovlich | 70.00 | 32.00 |
| ❑ 19 Hank Bassen | 15.00 | 6.75 |
| ❑ 20 Gerry Odrowski | 12.00 | 5.50 |
| ❑ 21 Norm Ullman | 30.00 | 13.50 |
| ❑ 22 Vic Stasiuk | 12.00 | 5.50 |
| ❑ 23 Bruce MacGregor | 12.00 | 5.50 |
| ❑ 24 Claude Laforge | 12.00 | 5.50 |
| ❑ 25 Bill Gadsby | 12.00 | 5.50 |
| ❑ 26 Leo Labine | 12.00 | 5.50 |
| ❑ 27 Val Fonteyne | 12.00 | 5.50 |
| ❑ 28 Howie Glover | 12.00 | 5.50 |
| ❑ 29 Marc Boileau | 12.00 | 5.50 |
| ❑ 30 Gordie Howe | 250.00 | 110.00 |
| ❑ 31 Gordie Howe | 250.00 | 110.00 |
| ❑ 32 Alex Delvecchio | 25.00 | 11.00 |
| ❑ 33 Marcel Pronovost | 15.00 | 6.75 |
| ❑ 34 Sid Abel CO | 15.00 | 6.75 |
| ❑ 35 Len Lunde | 12.00 | 5.50 |
| ❑ 36 Warren Godfrey | 12.00 | 5.50 |
| ❑ 37 Phil Goyette | 12.00 | 5.50 |
| ❑ 38 Henri Richard | 75.00 | 34.00 |
| ❑ 39 Jean Beliveau | 75.00 | 34.00 |
| ❑ 40 Bill Hicke | 12.00 | 5.50 |
| ❑ 41 Claude Provost | 12.00 | 5.50 |
| ❑ 42 Dickie Moore | 15.00 | 6.75 |
| ❑ 43 Don Marshall | 15.00 | 6.75 |
| ❑ 44 Ralph Backstrom | 15.00 | 6.75 |
| ❑ 45 Marcel Bonin | 12.00 | 5.50 |
| ❑ 46 Gilles Tremblay | 25.00 | 11.00 |
| ❑ 47 Bobby Rousseau | 25.00 | 11.00 |
| ❑ 48 Bernie Geoffrion | 40.00 | 18.00 |
| ❑ 49 Jacques Plante | 125.00 | 55.00 |
| ❑ 50 Tom Johnson | 15.00 | 6.75 |
| ❑ 51 Jean-Guy Talbot | 15.00 | 6.75 |
| ❑ 52 Lou Fontinato | 15.00 | 6.75 |
| ❑ 53 Bernie Geoffrion | 40.00 | 18.00 |
| ❑ 54 J.C. Tremblay | 60.00 | 27.00 |
| ❑ NNO1 Tally Game Card | 150.00 | 70.00 |
| ❑ NNO2 Checklist Card | 350.00 | 90.00 |

## 1963-64 Parkhurst

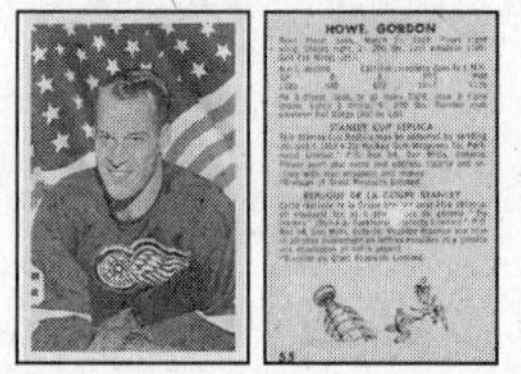


The 1963-64 Parkhurst set contains 99 color cards. Cards measure approximately 2 7/16" by 3 5/8". The fronts of the cards feature the player with a varying background depending upon whether the player is on Detroit (American flag), Toronto (Canadian Red Ensign), or Montreal (multi-color striped background). The numbering of the players in the set is basically by teams, i.e., Toronto Maple Leafs (1-20 and 61-79), Detroit Red Wings (41-60), and Montreal Canadiens (21-40 and 80-99). The backs, in both French and English, contain the card number, player lifetime NHL statistics, player biography, and a Stanley Cup replica offer. The set includes two different cards of each Montreal and Toronto player and only one of each Detroit player (with the following exceptions, numbers 15, 20, and 75 (single card Maple Leafs). Each Toronto player's double is obtained by adding 60, e.g., 1 and 61, 2 and 62, 3 and 63, etc., are the same player. Each Montreal player's double is obtained by adding 59, e.g., 21 and 80, 22 and 81, 23 and 82, etc., are the same player. The key Rookie Cards in the set are Red Berenson, Alex Faulkner, John Ferguson, Jacques Laperriere, and Cesare Maniago. Maniago is the last card in the set and is not often found in top condition.

| | NRMT | VG-E |
|---|---|---|
| COMPLETE SET (99) | 2200.00 | 1000.00 |
| COMMON CARD (1-99) | 12.00 | 5.50 |
| ❑ 1 Allan Stanley | 40.00 | 10.00 |
| ❑ 2 Don Simmons | 15.00 | 6.75 |
| ❑ 3 Red Kelly | 20.00 | 9.00 |
| ❑ 4 Dick Duff | 15.00 | 6.75 |
| ❑ 5 Johnny Bower | 50.00 | 22.00 |
| ❑ 6 Ed Litzenberger | 12.00 | 5.50 |
| ❑ 7 Kent Douglas | 12.00 | 5.50 |
| ❑ 8 Carl Brewer | 15.00 | 6.75 |
| ❑ 9 Eddie Shack | 50.00 | 22.00 |
| ❑ 10 Bob Nevin | 15.00 | 6.75 |
| ❑ 11 Billy Harris | 12.00 | 5.50 |
| ❑ 12 Bob Pulford | 15.00 | 6.75 |
| ❑ 13 George Armstrong | 15.00 | 6.75 |
| ❑ 14 Ron Stewart | 12.00 | 5.50 |
| ❑ 15 John McMillan | 12.00 | 5.50 |
| ❑ 16 Tim Horton | 80.00 | 36.00 |
| ❑ 17 Frank Mahovlich | 70.00 | 32.00 |
| ❑ 18 Bob Baun | 15.00 | 6.75 |
| ❑ 19 Punch Imlach ACO/GM | 20.00 | 9.00 |
| ❑ 20 King Clancy ACO | 30.00 | 13.50 |
| ❑ 21 Gilles Tremblay | 15.00 | 6.75 |
| ❑ 22 Jean-Guy Talbot | 15.00 | 6.75 |
| ❑ 23 Henri Richard | 70.00 | 32.00 |
| ❑ 24 Ralph Backstrom | 15.00 | 6.75 |
| ❑ 25 Bill Hicke | 12.00 | 5.50 |
| ❑ 26 Red Berenson | 40.00 | 18.00 |
| ❑ 27 Jacques Laperriere | 50.00 | 22.00 |
| ❑ 28 Jean Gauthier | 12.00 | 5.50 |
| ❑ 29 Bernie Geoffrion | 40.00 | 18.00 |
| ❑ 30 Jean Beliveau | 75.00 | 34.00 |
| ❑ 31 J.C. Tremblay | 15.00 | 6.75 |
| ❑ 32 Terry Harper | 30.00 | 13.50 |
| ❑ 33 John Ferguson | 80.00 | 36.00 |
| ❑ 34 Toe Blake CO | 15.00 | 6.75 |
| ❑ 35 Bobby Rousseau | 15.00 | 6.75 |
| ❑ 36 Claude Provost | 12.00 | 5.50 |
| ❑ 37 Marc Reaume | 12.00 | 5.50 |
| ❑ 38 Dave Balon | 12.00 | 5.50 |
| ❑ 39 Gump Worsley | 40.00 | 18.00 |
| ❑ 40 Cesare Maniago | 50.00 | 22.00 |
| ❑ 41 Bruce MacGregor | 12.00 | 5.50 |
| ❑ 42 Alex Faulkner | 80.00 | 36.00 |
| ❑ 43 Pete Goegan | 12.00 | 5.50 |
| ❑ 44 Parker MacDonald | 12.00 | 5.50 |
| ❑ 45 Andre Pronovost | 12.00 | 5.50 |
| ❑ 46 Marcel Pronovost | 15.00 | 6.75 |
| ❑ 47 Bob Dillabough | 12.00 | 5.50 |
| ❑ 48 Larry Jeffrey | 12.00 | 5.50 |
| ❑ 49 Ian Cushenan | 12.00 | 5.50 |
| ❑ 50 Alex Delvecchio | 20.00 | 9.00 |
| ❑ 51 Hank Ciesla | 12.00 | 5.50 |
| ❑ 52 Norm Ullman | 30.00 | 13.50 |
| ❑ 53 Terry Sawchuk | 110.00 | 50.00 |
| ❑ 54 Ron Ingram | 12.00 | 5.50 |
| ❑ 55 Gordie Howe | 450.00 | 200.00 |
| ❑ 56 Billy McNeil | 12.00 | 5.50 |
| ❑ 57 Floyd Smith | 12.00 | 5.50 |
| ❑ 58 Vic Stasiuk | 12.00 | 5.50 |
| ❑ 59 Bill Gadsby | 12.00 | 5.50 |
| ❑ 60 Doug Barkley | 12.00 | 5.50 |
| ❑ 61 Allan Stanley | 15.00 | 6.75 |
| ❑ 62 Don Simmons | 15.00 | 6.75 |
| ❑ 63 Red Kelly | 20.00 | 9.00 |
| ❑ 64 Dick Duff | 15.00 | 6.75 |
| ❑ 65 Johnny Bower | 50.00 | 22.00 |
| ❑ 66 Ed Litzenberger | 12.00 | 5.50 |
| ❑ 67 Kent Douglas | 12.00 | 5.50 |
| ❑ 68 Carl Brewer | 15.00 | 6.75 |
| ❑ 69 Eddie Shack | 50.00 | 22.00 |
| ❑ 70 Bob Nevin | 15.00 | 6.75 |
| ❑ 71 Billy Harris | 12.00 | 5.50 |
| ❑ 72 Bob Pulford | 15.00 | 6.75 |
| ❑ 73 George Armstrong | 15.00 | 6.75 |
| ❑ 74 Ron Stewart | 12.00 | 5.50 |
| ❑ 75 Dave Keon | 80.00 | 36.00 |
| ❑ 76 Tim Horton | 80.00 | 36.00 |
| ❑ 77 Frank Mahovlich | 70.00 | 32.00 |
| ❑ 78 Bob Baun | 15.00 | 6.75 |
| ❑ 79 Punch Imlach ACO/GM | 20.00 | 9.00 |
| ❑ 80 Gilles Tremblay | 15.00 | 6.75 |
| ❑ 81 Jean-Guy Talbot | 12.00 | 5.50 |
| ❑ 82 Henri Richard | 70.00 | 32.00 |
| ❑ 83 Ralph Backstrom | 15.00 | 6.75 |
| ❑ 84 Bill Hicke | 12.00 | 5.50 |
| ❑ 85 Red Berenson | 40.00 | 18.00 |
| ❑ 86 Jacques Laperriere | 40.00 | 18.00 |
| ❑ 87 Jean Gauthier | 12.00 | 5.50 |
| ❑ 88 Bernie Geoffrion | 40.00 | 18.00 |
| ❑ 89 Jean Beliveau | 75.00 | 34.00 |
| ❑ 90 J.C. Tremblay | 15.00 | 6.75 |
| ❑ 91 Terry Harper | 30.00 | 13.50 |
| ❑ 92 John Ferguson | 70.00 | 32.00 |
| ❑ 93 Toe Blake CO | 15.00 | 6.75 |
| ❑ 94 Bobby Rousseau | 15.00 | 6.75 |
| ❑ 95 Claude Provost | 12.00 | 5.50 |
| ❑ 96 Marc Reaume | 12.00 | 5.50 |
| ❑ 97 Dave Balon | 12.00 | 5.50 |
| ❑ 98 Gump Worsley | 40.00 | 18.00 |
| ❑ 99 Cesare Maniago | 150.00 | 38.00 |

## 1991-92 Parkhurst

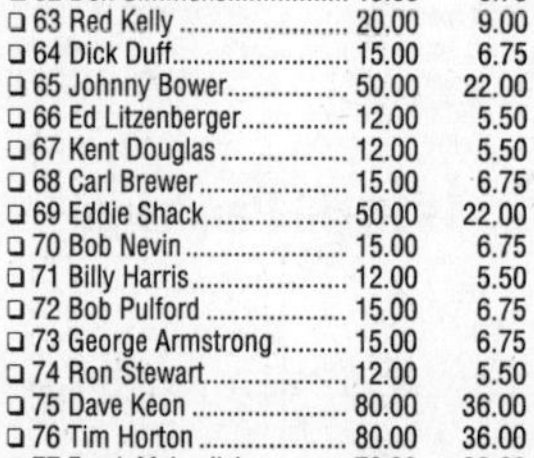


The 1991-92 Parkhurst hockey set marks Pro Set's resurrection of this venerable hockey card brand. The set was primarily released in two series. Both series contain 225 standard-size cards and five (four in the second series) special PHC collectible cards randomly inserted into foil packs. First and second series production quantities were each reported to be 15,000 numbered ten-box foil cases, including 2,500 cases that were translated into French and distributed predominantely to Quebec. The fronts feature full-bleed glossy color photos, bordered on the left by a dark brown marbled border stripe. The player's name appears in the stripe; Parkhurst's teal oval-shaped logo in the lower left corner rounds out the card face. The backs carry a color head shot, with biography, career statistics, and player profile all on a bronze background. The NNO Santa Claus card was randomly inserted in first series packs. The key Rookie Cards in the set are Tony Amonte, Dominik Hasek, Joe Juneau, Valeri Kamensky, Vladimir Konstantinov, Slava Kozlov, Nicklas Lidstrom, Geoff Sanderson, Keith Tkachuk, and Doug Weight. A special promotion offer for a 25-card Final Update set was included on Parkhurst Series II packs. It is estimated that less than 15,000 of these sets exist.

| | MINT | NRMT |
|---|---|---|
| COMPLETE SET (450) | 20.00 | 9.00 |
| COMPLETE SERIES 1 (225) | 10.00 | 4.50 |
| COMPLETE SERIES 2 (225) | 10.00 | 4.50 |
| COMMON CARD (1-450) | .05 | .02 |
| COMP.FINAL UPD.SET (25) | 60.00 | 27.00 |
| COMMON UPDATE (451-475) | .75 | .35 |
| *FRENCH: SAME VALUE | | |
| ❑ 1 Matt DelGuidice | .10 | .05 |
| ❑ 2 Ken Hodge Jr. | .05 | .02 |
| ❑ 3 Vladimir Ruzicka UER (Misspelled Vladimar Ruzika on card front) | .05 | .02 |
| ❑ 4 Craig Janney | .10 | .05 |
| ❑ 5 Glen Wesley | .05 | .02 |
| ❑ 6 Stephen Leach | .05 | .02 |
| ❑ 7 Garry Galley | .05 | .02 |
| ❑ 8 Andy Moog | .10 | .05 |
| ❑ 9 Ray Bourque | .25 | .11 |
| ❑ 10 Brad May | .10 | .05 |
| ❑ 11 Donald Audette | .10 | .05 |
| ❑ 12 Alexander Mogilny | .10 | .05 |
| ❑ 13 Randy Wood | .05 | .02 |
| ❑ 14 Daren Puppa | .10 | .05 |
| ❑ 15 Doug Bodger | .05 | .02 |
| ❑ 16 Pat LaFontaine | .10 | .05 |
| ❑ 17 Dave Andreychuk | .10 | .05 |
| ❑ 18 Dale Hawerchuk | .10 | .05 |
| ❑ 19 Mike Ramsey | .05 | .02 |
| ❑ 20 Tomas Forslund UER (Misspelled Thomas on card back) | .05 | .02 |
| ❑ 21 Robert Reichel | .05 | .02 |
| ❑ 22 Theoren Fleury | .10 | .05 |
| ❑ 23 Joe Nieuwendyk | .10 | .05 |
| ❑ 24 Gary Roberts | .05 | .02 |
| ❑ 25 Gary Suter | .05 | .02 |
| ❑ 26 Doug Gilmour | .25 | .11 |
| ❑ 27 Mike Vernon | .10 | .05 |
| ❑ 28 Al MacInnis | .10 | .05 |
| ❑ 29 Jeremy Roenick | .25 | .11 |
| ❑ 30 Ed Belfour | .25 | .11 |
| ❑ 31 Steve Smith | .05 | .02 |
| ❑ 32 Chris Chelios | .25 | .11 |
| ❑ 33 Dirk Graham | .05 | .02 |
| ❑ 34 Steve Larmer | .10 | .05 |
| ❑ 35 Brent Sutter | .05 | .02 |
| ❑ 36 Michel Goulet | .10 | .05 |
| ❑ 37 Nicklas Lidstrom UER (Misspelled Niklas on card front) | 1.25 | .55 |
| ❑ 38 Sergei Fedorov | .75 | .35 |
| ❑ 39 Tim Cheveldae | .10 | .05 |
| ❑ 40 Kevin Miller | .05 | .02 |
| ❑ 41 Ray Sheppard | .10 | .05 |
| ❑ 42 Paul Ysebaert | .05 | .02 |
| ❑ 43 Jimmy Carson | .05 | .02 |
| ❑ 44 Steve Yzerman | .75 | .35 |
| ❑ 45 Shawn Burr | .05 | .02 |
| ❑ 46 Vladimir Konstantinov | .40 | .18 |
| ❑ 47 Josef Beranek | .05 | .02 |
| ❑ 48 Vincent Damphousse | .10 | .05 |
| ❑ 49 Dave Manson | .05 | .02 |
| ❑ 50 Scott Mellanby | .10 | .05 |
| ❑ 51 Kevin Lowe | .05 | .02 |
| ❑ 52 Joe Murphy | .05 | .02 |
| ❑ 53 Bill Ranford | .10 | .05 |
| ❑ 54 Craig Simpson | .05 | .02 |
| ❑ 55 Esa Tikkanen | .05 | .02 |
| ❑ 56 Michel Picard | .05 | .02 |
| ❑ 57 Geoff Sanderson | .50 | .23 |
| ❑ 58 Kay Whitmore | .10 | .05 |
| ❑ 59 John Cullen | .05 | .02 |
| ❑ 60 Rob Brown | .05 | .02 |
| ❑ 61 Zarley Zalapski | .05 | .02 |
| ❑ 62 Brad Shaw | .05 | .02 |
| ❑ 63 Mikael Andersson | .05 | .02 |
| ❑ 64 Pat Verbeek | .05 | .02 |
| ❑ 65 Peter Ahola | .05 | .02 |
| ❑ 66 Tony Granato | .05 | .02 |
| ❑ 67 Dave Taylor | .10 | .05 |
| ❑ 68 Luc Robitaille | .10 | .05 |
| ❑ 69 Marty McSorley | .05 | .02 |
| ❑ 70 Tomas Sandstrom | .05 | .02 |
| ❑ 71 Kelly Hrudey | .10 | .05 |
| ❑ 72 Jari Kurri | .10 | .05 |
| ❑ 73 Wayne Gretzky | 1.50 | .70 |
| ❑ 74 Larry Robinson | .10 | .05 |
| ❑ 75 Derian Hatcher | .05 | .02 |
| ❑ 76 Ulf Dahlen | .05 | .02 |
| ❑ 77 Jon Casey | .10 | .05 |
| ❑ 78 Dave Gagner | .10 | .05 |
| ❑ 79 Brian Bellows | .05 | .02 |
| ❑ 80 Neal Broten | .10 | .05 |
| ❑ 81 Mike Modano | .30 | .14 |
| ❑ 82 Brian Propp | .05 | .02 |
| ❑ 83 Bobby Smith | .10 | .05 |
| ❑ 84 John LeClair | 3.00 | 1.35 |
| ❑ 85 Eric Desjardins | .05 | .02 |
| ❑ 86 Shayne Corson | .05 | .02 |
| ❑ 87 Stephan Lebeau | .05 | .02 |
| ❑ 88 Mathieu Schneider | .05 | .02 |
| ❑ 89 Kirk Muller | .05 | .02 |
| ❑ 90 Patrick Roy | 1.25 | .55 |
| ❑ 91 Sylvain Turgeon | .05 | .02 |
| ❑ 92 Guy Carbonneau | .10 | .05 |
| ❑ 93 Denis Savard | .10 | .05 |
| ❑ 94 Scott Niedermayer | .10 | .05 |
| ❑ 95 Tom Chorske | .05 | .02 |
| ❑ 96 Slava Fetisov | .05 | .02 |
| ❑ 97 Kevin Todd | .05 | .02 |
| ❑ 98 Chris Terreri | .10 | .05 |
| ❑ 99 David Maley | .05 | .02 |
| ❑ 100 Stephane Richer | .10 | .05 |
| ❑ 101 Claude Lemieux | .10 | .05 |
| ❑ 102 Scott Stevens | .05 | .02 |
| ❑ 103 Peter Stastny | .10 | .05 |
| ❑ 104 David Volek | .05 | .02 |
| ❑ 105 Steve Thomas | .05 | .02 |
| ❑ 106 Pierre Turgeon | .10 | .05 |
| ❑ 107 Glenn Healy UER (Misspelled Healey on card back) | .10 | .05 |
| ❑ 108 Derek King | .05 | .02 |
| ❑ 109 Uwe Krupp | .05 | .02 |
| ❑ 110 Ray Ferraro | .05 | .02 |
| ❑ 111 Pat Flatley | .05 | .02 |
| ❑ 112 Tom Kurvers | .05 | .02 |
| ❑ 113 Adam Creighton | .05 | .02 |
| ❑ 114 Tony Amonte UER (Back says shoots right) | 1.00 | .45 |
| ❑ 115 John Ogrodnick | .05 | .02 |
| ❑ 116 Doug Weight | 1.00 | .45 |
| ❑ 117 Mike Richter | .25 | .11 |
| ❑ 118 Darren Turcotte | .10 | .05 |
| ❑ 119 Brian Leetch | .25 | .11 |
| ❑ 120 James Patrick | .05 | .02 |
| ❑ 121 Mark Messier | .50 | .23 |
| ❑ 122 Mike Gartner | .10 | .05 |
| ❑ 123 Mike Ricci | .05 | .02 |
| ❑ 124 Rod Brind'Amour | .10 | .05 |
| ❑ 125 Steve Duchesne | .05 | .02 |
| ❑ 126 Ron Hextall | .10 | .05 |
| ❑ 127 Brad Jones | .05 | .02 |
| ❑ 128 Pelle Eklund | .05 | .02 |
| ❑ 129 Rick Tocchet | .10 | .05 |
| ❑ 130 Mark Howe | .05 | .02 |
| ❑ 131 Andrei Lomakin | .05 | .02 |
| ❑ 132 Jaromir Jagr | .75 | .35 |
| ❑ 133 Jim Paek | .05 | .02 |
| ❑ 134 Mark Recchi | .10 | .05 |
| ❑ 135 Kevin Stevens | .05 | .02 |
| ❑ 136 Phil Bourque | .05 | .02 |
| ❑ 137 Mario Lemieux | 1.25 | .55 |
| ❑ 138 Bob Errey | .05 | .02 |
| ❑ 139 Tom Barrasso | .10 | .05 |
| ❑ 140 Paul Coffey | .25 | .11 |
| ❑ 141 Joe Mullen | .10 | .05 |
| ❑ 142 Kip Miller | .05 | .02 |
| ❑ 143 Owen Nolan | .10 | .05 |
| ❑ 144 Mats Sundin | .25 | .11 |
| ❑ 145 Mikhail Tatarinov | .05 | .02 |
| ❑ 146 Bryan Fogarty | .05 | .02 |
| ❑ 147 Stephane Morin | .05 | .02 |
| ❑ 148 Joe Sakic | .60 | .25 |
| ❑ 149 Ron Tugnutt | .10 | .05 |
| ❑ 150 Mike Hough | .05 | .02 |
| ❑ 151 Nelson Emerson | .05 | .02 |
| ❑ 152 Curtis Joseph | .25 | .11 |
| ❑ 153 Brendan Shanahan | .60 | .25 |
| ❑ 154 Paul Cavallini | .05 | .02 |
| ❑ 155 Adam Oates | .10 | .05 |
| ❑ 156 Jeff Brown | .05 | .02 |
| ❑ 157 Brett Hull | .50 | .23 |
| ❑ 158 Ron Sutter | .05 | .02 |
| ❑ 159 Dave Christian | .05 | .02 |
| ❑ 160 Pat Falloon | .05 | .02 |
| ❑ 161 Pat MacLeod | .05 | .02 |
| ❑ 162 Jarmo Myllys | .05 | .02 |
| ❑ 163 Wayne Presley | .05 | .02 |
| ❑ 164 Perry Anderson | .05 | .02 |
| ❑ 165 Kelly Kisio | .05 | .02 |
| ❑ 166 Brian Mullen | .05 | .02 |
| ❑ 167 Brian Lawton | .05 | .02 |
| ❑ 168 Doug Wilson | .10 | .05 |
| ❑ 169 Rob Pearson | .05 | .02 |
| ❑ 170 Wendel Clark | .10 | .05 |
| ❑ 171 Brian Bradley | .05 | .02 |
| ❑ 172 Dave Ellett | .05 | .02 |
| ❑ 173 Gary Leeman | .05 | .02 |
| ❑ 174 Peter Zezel | .05 | .02 |
| ❑ 175 Grant Fuhr | .10 | .05 |
| ❑ 176 Bob Rouse | .05 | .02 |
| ❑ 177 Glenn Anderson | .10 | .05 |
| ❑ 178 Petr Nedved | .10 | .05 |
| ❑ 179 Trevor Linden | .10 | .05 |
| ❑ 180 Jyrki Lumme | .05 | .02 |
| ❑ 181 Kirk McLean | .10 | .05 |
| ❑ 182 Cliff Ronning | .05 | .02 |
| ❑ 183 Greg Adams | .05 | .02 |
| ❑ 184 Doug Lidster | .05 | .02 |
| ❑ 185 Sergio Momesso | .05 | .02 |
| ❑ 186 Geoff Courtnall | .05 | .02 |
| ❑ 187 Dave Babych | .05 | .02 |
| ❑ 188 Peter Bondra | .25 | .11 |
| ❑ 189 Dimitri Khristich | .05 | .02 |
| ❑ 190 Randy Burridge | .05 | .02 |
| ❑ 191 Kevin Hatcher | .05 | .02 |
| ❑ 192 Mike Ridley | .05 | .02 |
| ❑ 193 Dino Ciccarelli | .10 | .05 |

❑ 194 Al Iafrate .10 .05
❑ 195 Dale Hunter .10 .05
❑ 196 Mike Liut .10 .05
❑ 197 Rod Langway .05 .02
❑ 198 Russell Romaniuk .05 .02
❑ 199 Bob Essensa .10 .05
❑ 200 Teppo Numminen .05 .02
❑ 201 Darrin Shannon .05 .02
❑ 202 Pat Elynuik .05 .02
❑ 203 Fredrik Olausson .05 .02
❑ 204 Ed Olczyk .05 .02
❑ 205 Phil Housley .10 .05
❑ 206 Troy Murray .05 .02
❑ 207 Wayne Gretzky 1000 1.00 .45
❑ 208 Bryan Trottier 1000 .10 .05
❑ 209 Peter Stastny 1000 .10 .05
❑ 210 Jari Kurri 1000 .10 .05
❑ 211 Denis Savard 1000 .10 .05
❑ 212 Paul Coffey 1000 .25 .11
❑ 213 Mark Messier 1000 .25 .11
❑ 214 Dave Taylor 1000 .10 .05
❑ 215 Michel Goulet 1000 .10 .05
❑ 216 Dale Hawerchuk 1000 .10 .05
❑ 217 Bobby Smith 1000 .10 .05
❑ 218 Ed Belfour LL .10 .05
❑ 219 Brett Hull LL .10 .05
❑ 220 Patrick Roy AS .50 .23
❑ 221 Ray Bourque AS .10 .05
❑ 222 Wayne Gretzky AS 1.00 .45
❑ 223 Jari Kurri AS .05 .02
❑ 224 Luc Robitaille AS .05 .02
❑ 225 Paul Coffey AS .10 .05
❑ 226 Bob Carpenter .05 .02
❑ 227 Gord Murphy .05 .02
❑ 228 Don Sweeney .05 .02
❑ 229 Glen Murray .05 .02
❑ 230 Ted Donato .05 .02
❑ 231 Jozef Stumpel .75 .35
❑ 232 Stephen Heinze .05 .02
❑ 233 Adam Oates .10 .05
❑ 234 Joe Juneau .75 .35
❑ 235 Gord Hynes .05 .02
❑ 236 Tony Tanti .05 .02
❑ 237 Petr Svoboda .05 .02
❑ 238 Bob Corkum .05 .02
❑ 239 Ken Sutton .05 .02
❑ 240 Tom Draper .10 .05
❑ 241 Grant Ledyard .05 .02
❑ 242 Christian Ruuttu .05 .02
❑ 243 Brad Miller .05 .02
❑ 244 Clint Malarchuk .10 .05
❑ 245 Trent Yawney .05 .02
❑ 246 Craig Berube .05 .02
❑ 247 Sergei Makarov .05 .02
❑ 248 Alexander Godynyuk .10 .05
❑ 249 Paul Ranheim .05 .02
❑ 250 Jeff Reese .05 .02
❑ 251 Chris Lindberg .05 .02
❑ 252 Michel Petit .05 .02
❑ 253 Joel Otto .05 .02
❑ 254 Gary Leeman .05 .02
❑ 255 Ray LeBlanc .10 .05
❑ 256 Jocelyn Lemieux .05 .02
❑ 257 Igor Kravchuk .05 .02
❑ 258 Rob Brown .05 .02
❑ 259 Stephane Matteau .05 .02
❑ 260 Mike Hudson .05 .02
❑ 261 Keith Brown .05 .02
❑ 262 Karl Dykhuis .05 .02
❑ 263 Dominik Hasek 4.00 1.80
❑ 264 Brian Noonan .05 .02
❑ 265 Yves Racine .05 .02
❑ 266 Slava Kozlov .75 .35
❑ 267 Martin Lapointe .05 .02
❑ 268 Steve Chiasson .05 .02
❑ 269 Gerard Gallant .05 .02
❑ 270 Brent Fedyk .05 .02
❑ 271 Brad McCrimmon .05 .02
❑ 272 Bob Probert .10 .05
❑ 273 Alan Kerr .05 .02
❑ 274 Luke Richardson .05 .02
❑ 275 Kelly Buchberger .05 .02
❑ 276 Craig MacTavish .05 .02
❑ 277 Ron Tugnutt .10 .05
❑ 278 Bernie Nicholls .10 .05
❑ 279 Anatoli Semenov .05 .02
❑ 280 Petr Klima .05 .02
❑ 281 Louie DeBrusk .05 .02
❑ 282 Norm Maciver .05 .02
❑ 283 Martin Gelinas .05 .02
❑ 284 Randy Cunneyworth .05 .02
❑ 285 Andrew Cassels .05 .02
❑ 286 Peter Sidorkiewicz .10 .05
❑ 287 Steve Konroyd .05 .02
❑ 288 Murray Craven .05 .02
❑ 289 Randy Ladouceur .05 .02
❑ 290 Bobby Holik .05 .02
❑ 291 Adam Burt .05 .02
❑ 292 Corey Millen .05 .02
❑ 293 Rob Blake .10 .05
❑ 294 Mike Donnelly .05 .02
❑ 295 Kyosti Karjalainen .10 .05
❑ 296 John McIntyre .05 .02
❑ 297 Paul Coffey .25 .11
❑ 298 Charlie Huddy .05 .02
❑ 299 Bob Kudelski .05 .02
❑ 300 Todd Elik .05 .02
❑ 301 Mike Craig .05 .02
❑ 302 Marc Bureau .05 .02
❑ 303 Jim Johnson .05 .02
❑ 304 Mark Tinordi .05 .02
❑ 305 Gaetan Duchesne .05 .02
❑ 306 Darcy Wakaluk .10 .05
❑ 307 Sylvain Lefebvre .05 .02
❑ 308 Russ Courtnall .05 .02
❑ 309 Patrice Brisebois .05 .02
❑ 310 Mike McPhee .05 .02
❑ 311 Mike Keane .05 .02
❑ 312 J.J. Daigneault .05 .02
❑ 313 Gilbert Dionne .05 .02
❑ 314 Brian Skrudland .05 .02
❑ 315 Brent Gilchrist .05 .02
❑ 316 Laurie Boschman .05 .02
❑ 317 Ken Daneyko .05 .02
❑ 318 Eric Weinrich .05 .02
❑ 319 Alexei Kasatonov .05 .02
❑ 320 Craig Billington .10 .05
❑ 321 Claude Vilgrain .05 .02
❑ 322 Bruce Driver .05 .02
❑ 323 Alexander Semak .05 .02
❑ 324 Valeri Zelepukin .05 .02
❑ 325 Rob DiMaio .05 .02
❑ 326 Scott Lachance .05 .02
❑ 327 Marty McInnis .05 .02
❑ 328 Joe Reekie .05 .02
❑ 329 Daniel Marois .05 .02
❑ 330 Wayne McBean .05 .02
❑ 331 Jeff Norton .05 .02
❑ 332 Benoit Hogue .05 .02
❑ 333 Tie Domi .10 .05
❑ 334 Sergei Nemchinov .05 .02
❑ 335 Randy Gilhen .05 .02
❑ 336 Paul Broten .05 .02
❑ 337 Kris King .05 .02
❑ 338 John Vanbiesbrouck .50 .23
❑ 339 Adam Graves .10 .05
❑ 340 Joe Cirella .05 .02
❑ 341 Jeff Beukeboom .05 .02
❑ 342 Terry Carkner .05 .02
❑ 343 Mark Freer .05 .02
❑ 344 Corey Foster .05 .02
❑ 345 Mark Pederson .05 .02
❑ 346 Kimbi Daniels .05 .02
❑ 347 Mark Recchi .10 .05
❑ 348 Kevin Dineen .05 .02
❑ 349 Kerry Huffman .05 .02
❑ 350 Garry Galley .05 .02
❑ 351 Dan Quinn .05 .02
❑ 352 Troy Loney .05 .02
❑ 353 Ron Francis .10 .05
❑ 354 Rick Tocchet .10 .05
❑ 355 Shawn McEachern .50 .23
❑ 356 Kjell Samuelsson .05 .02
❑ 357 Ken Wreggett .10 .05
❑ 358 Larry Murphy .10 .05
❑ 359 Ken Priestlay .05 .02
❑ 360 Bryan Trottier .10 .05
❑ 361 Ulf Samuelsson .05 .02
❑ 362 Valeri Kamensky .75 .35
❑ 363 Stephane Fiset .10 .05
❑ 364 Alexei Gusarov .05 .02
❑ 365 Greg Paslawski .05 .02
❑ 366 Martin Rucinsky .40 .18
❑ 367 Curtis Leschyshyn .05 .02
❑ 368 Jacques Cloutier .10 .05
❑ 369 Craig Wolanin .05 .02
❑ 370 Claude Lapointe .05 .02
❑ 371 Adam Foote .25 .11
❑ 372 Rich Sutter .05 .02
❑ 373 Lee Norwood .05 .02
❑ 374 Garth Butcher .05 .02
❑ 375 Philippe Bozon .05 .02
❑ 376 Dave Lowry .05 .02
❑ 377 Darin Kimble .05 .02
❑ 378 Craig Janney .10 .05
❑ 379 Bob Bassen .05 .02
❑ 380 Rick Zombo .05 .02
❑ 381 Perry Berezan .05 .02
❑ 382 Neil Wilkinson .05 .02
❑ 383 Mike Sullivan .05 .02
❑ 384 David Bruce .05 .02
❑ 385 Johan Garpenlov .05 .02
❑ 386 Jeff Odgers .05 .02
❑ 387 Jay More .05 .02
❑ 388 Dean Evason .05 .02
❑ 389 Dale Craigwell .05 .02
❑ 390 Darryl Shannon .05 .02
❑ 391 Dimitri Mironov .05 .02
❑ 392 Kent Manderville .05 .02
❑ 393 Todd Gill .05 .02
❑ 394 Rick Wamsley .10 .05
❑ 395 Joe Sacco .05 .02
❑ 396 Doug Gilmour .25 .11
❑ 397 Mike Bullard .05 .02
❑ 398 Felix Potvin .75 .35
❑ 399 Guy Larose .05 .02
❑ 400 Tom Fergus .05 .02
❑ 401 Ryan Walter .05 .02
❑ 402 Troy Gamble .10 .05
❑ 403 Robert Dirk .05 .02
❑ 404 Pavel Bure .75 .35
❑ 405 Jim Sandlak .05 .02
❑ 406 Igor Larionov .05 .02
❑ 407 Gerald Diduck .05 .02
❑ 408 Todd Krygier .05 .02
❑ 409 Tim Bergland .05 .02
❑ 410 Calle Johansson .05 .02
❑ 411 Nick Kypreos .05 .02
❑ 412 Michal Pivonka .05 .02
❑ 413 Brad Schlegel .05 .02
❑ 414 Kelly Miller .05 .02
❑ 415 John Druce .05 .02
❑ 416 Don Beaupre .10 .05
❑ 417 Alan May .05 .02
❑ 418 Randy Carlyle .05 .02
❑ 419 Stu Barnes .05 .02
❑ 420 Mike Eagles .05 .02
❑ 421 Igor Ulanov .05 .02
❑ 422 Evgeny Davydov .05 .02
❑ 423 Shawn Cronin .05 .02
❑ 424 Keith Tkachuk 2.50 1.10
❑ 425 Luciano Borsato .05 .02
❑ 426 Stephane Beauregard .10 .05
❑ 427 Mike Lalor .05 .02
❑ 428 Michel Goulet 500 .05 .02
❑ 429 Wayne Gretzky 500 1.00 .45
❑ 430 Mike Gartner 500 .05 .02
❑ 431 Bryan Trottier 500 .05 .02
❑ 432 Brett Hull LL .10 .05
❑ 433 Wayne Gretzky LL 1.00 .45
❑ 434 Steve Yzerman LL .40 .18
❑ 435 Paul Ysebaert LL .05 .02
❑ 436 Gary Roberts LL .05 .02
❑ 437 Dave Andreychuk LL .05 .02
❑ 438 Brian Leetch LL .10 .05
❑ 439 Jeremy Roenick LL .10 .05
❑ 440 Kirk McLean LL .05 .02
❑ 441 Tim Cheveldae LL .05 .02
❑ 442 Patrick Roy LL .25 .11
❑ 443 Tony Amonte RL .10 .05
❑ 444 Kevin Todd RL .05 .02
❑ 445 Nicklas Lidstrom RL .10 .05
❑ 446 Pavel Bure RL .75 .35
❑ 447 Gilbert Dionne RL .05 .02
❑ 448 Tom Draper RL .10 .05
❑ 449 Dominik Hasek RL 1.00 .45
❑ 450 Dominic Roussel RL .10 .05
❑ 451 Header/Checklist .25 .11
❑ 452 Trent Klatt .05 .02
❑ 453 Bill Guerin 2.50 1.10
❑ 454 Ray Whitney .05 .02
❑ 455 Boston Bruins .25 .11
Adams Winner
(Paul DiPietro/Chris Winnes)
❑ 456 Pittsburgh Penguins 1.50 .70
Patrick Winner
(Larry Murphy et al.)
❑ 457 Chicago Blackhawks .05 .02
Norris Winner
(Pile up in front of net)
❑ 458 Edmonton Oilers .05 .02
Smythe Winner
(Oiler celebrate win;
Joe Murphy/Petr Klima et al.)
❑ 459 Pittsburgh Penguins 2.00 .90
Wales Winner
(Andy Moog with glove save;
Mario Lemieux in background)
❑ 460 Chicago Blackhawks .05 .02
Campbell Winner
(Brent Sutter and Craig Muni
in front of Bill Ranford)
❑ 461 Pittsburgh Penguins 1.50 .70
Stanley Cup Winner
(Igor Kravchuk checking Bryan Trottier)
❑ 462 Pavel Bure 8.00 3.60
Calder Winner
❑ 463 Patrick Roy 12.00 5.50
Vezina Winner
❑ 464 Brian Leetch 3.00 1.35
Norris Winner
❑ 465 Wayne Gretzky 15.00 6.75
Lady Byng Winner
❑ 466 Guy Carbonneau .10 .05
Selke Winner
❑ 467 Mario Lemieux 12.00 5.50
Smythe Winner
❑ 468 Mark Messier 4.00 1.80
Pearson Winner
❑ 469 Ray Bourque 3.00 1.35
Clancy Winner
❑ 470 Patrick Roy AS 12.00 5.50
❑ 471 Brian Leetch AS 3.00 1.35
❑ 472 Ray Bourque AS 3.00 1.35
❑ 473 Kevin Stevens AS .05 .02
❑ 474 Brett Hull AS 5.00 2.20
❑ 475 Mark Messier AS 4.00 1.80
❑ NNO Santa Claus 1.00 .45
❑ NNO Robert Reichel PROMO 4.00 1.80
❑ NNO Doug Gilmour PROMO 4.00 1.80

## 1991-92 Parkhurst PHC

This nine card standard-size set was randomly inserted in packs of 1991-92 Parkhurst hockey cards with cards 1-5 being in the first series and 6-9 in the second series, which featured award winners. PHC stands for Parkhurst Collectibles. The cards are numbered with a "PHC" prefix. A French version of these cards exist. Multipliers can be found in the header below to determine values for these.

MINT NRMT
COMPLETE SET (9) 15.00 6.75
COMMON CARD (PHC1-PHC9) .75 .35
*FRENCH: SAME VALUE

❑ PHC1 Gordie Howe 3.00 1.35
❑ PHC2 Alex Delvecchio 1.00 .45
❑ PHC3 Ken Hodge Jr. .75 .35
❑ PHC4 Robert Kron .75 .35
❑ PHC5 Sergei Fedorov 3.00 1.35
❑ PHC6 Brett Hull 2.00 .90
❑ PHC7 Mario Lemieux 6.00 2.70
❑ PHC8 New York Rangers 1.50 .70
(Brian Leetch/Mark Messier/
Mike Gartner/John Ziegler)
❑ PHC9 Terry Sawchuk 1.50 .70

## 1992-93 Parkhurst Previews

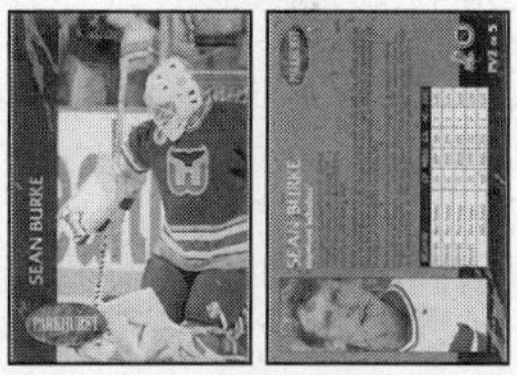

Randomly inserted in 1992-93 Pro Set foil packs, these five preview standard-size cards were issued to show the design of the 1992-93 Parkhurst issue. The fronts feature color action player photos that are full-bleed except for one edge that is bordered by a dark blue-green marbleized stripe. The player's name is printed vertically in this stripe. The Parkhurst logo overlays the stripe. The backs have a bluish-green background and carry small close-up shots, biography, statistics, and career highlights in French and English. The cards are numbered on the back with a "PV" prefix.

MINT NRMT
COMPLETE SET (5) 5.00 2.20
COMMON CARD (PV1-PV5) 1.00 .45

❑ PV1 Paul Ysebaert 1.00 .45
❑ PV2 Sean Burke 1.50 .70
❑ PV3 Gilbert Dionne 1.00 .45
❑ PV4 Ken Hammond 1.00 .45
❑ PV5 Grant Fuhr 2.00 .90

## 1992-93 Parkhurst

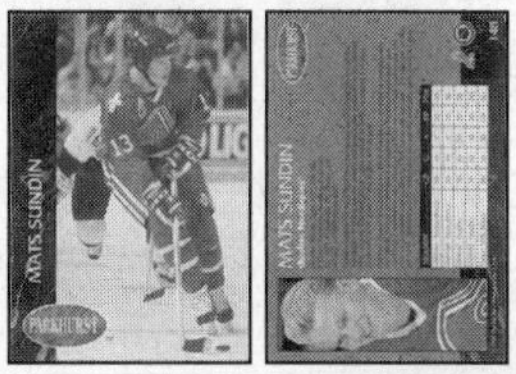

The 1992-93 Parkhurst set consists of 480 standard-size cards plus a 30-card update set. The set was released in two series of 240. The final 30 cards were issued in set form only and are slightly more difficult to obtain. The fronts feature color action player photos that are full-bleed except for one edge that is bordered by a dark blue-green marbleized stripe. The Parkhurst logo overlays the stripe. The backs have a bluish green background and carry small close-up shots, biographies, statistics, and career highlights in French and English. The second series featured traded players in their new uniforms as well as 35 Calder Candidates. The cards are checklisted alphabetically according to teams. Rookie Cards in the set include Roman Hamrlik, Guy Hebert, Andrei Kovalenko, Bryan Smolinski, Tommy Soderstrom and Sergei Zubov.

MINT NRMT
COMPLETE SET (480) 30.00 13.50
COMPLETE SERIES 1 (240) 18.00 8.00
COMPLETE SERIES 2 (240) 12.00 5.50
COMMON CARD (1-480) .05 .02
COMPLETE FINAL UPD. (30) 10.00 4.50
COMMON UPDATE (481-510) .15 .07

❑ 1 Ray Bourque .25 .11
❑ 2 Joe Juneau .10 .05
❑ 3 Andy Moog .10 .05
❑ 4 Adam Oates .10 .05
❑ 5 Vladimir Ruzicka .05 .02
❑ 6 Glen Wesley .05 .02
❑ 7 Dmitri Kvartalnov .05 .02
❑ 8 Ted Donato .05 .02
❑ 9 Glen Murray .05 .02
❑ 10 Dave Andreychuk .10 .05
❑ 11 Dale Hawerchuk .10 .05
❑ 12 Pat LaFontaine .10 .05
❑ 13 Alexander Mogilny .10 .05
❑ 14 Richard Smehlik .05 .02
❑ 15 Keith Carney .05 .02
❑ 16 Philippe Boucher .05 .02
❑ 17 Viktor Gordiouk .05 .02
❑ 18 Donald Audette .10 .05
❑ 19 Theoren Fleury .10 .05
❑ 20 Al MacInnis .10 .05
❑ 21 Joe Nieuwendyk .10 .05
❑ 22 Gary Roberts .05 .02
❑ 23 Gary Suter .05 .02
❑ 24 Mike Vernon .10 .05
❑ 25 Sergei Makarov .05 .02
❑ 26 Robert Reichel .05 .02
❑ 27 Chris Lindberg .05 .02
❑ 28 Ed Belfour .25 .11
❑ 29 Chris Chelios .25 .11
❑ 30 Steve Larmer .10 .05
❑ 31 Jeremy Roenick .25 .11
❑ 32 Steve Smith .05 .02
❑ 33 Brent Sutter .05 .02
❑ 34 Christian Ruuttu .05 .02
❑ 35 Igor Kravchuk .05 .02
❑ 36 Sergei Krivokasov .05 .02
❑ 37 Tim Cheveldae .10 .05
❑ 38 Mike Sillinger .05 .02
❑ 39 Sergei Fedorov .50 .23
❑ 40 Viacheslav Kozlov .10 .05
❑ 41 Bob Probert .10 .05
❑ 42 Nicklas Lidstrom .10 .05
❑ 43 Paul Ysebaert .05 .02
❑ 44 Steve Yzerman .75 .35
❑ 45 Dino Ciccarelli .10 .05
❑ 46 Esa Tikkanen .05 .02
❑ 47 Dave Manson .05 .02
❑ 48 Craig MacTavish .05 .02
❑ 49 Bernie Nicholls .10 .05
❑ 50 Bill Ranford .10 .05
❑ 51 Craig Simpson .05 .02
❑ 52 Scott Mellanby .10 .05
❑ 53 Shayne Corson .05 .02
❑ 54 Petr Klima .05 .02
❑ 55 Murray Craven .05 .02
❑ 56 Eric Weinrich .05 .02
❑ 57 Sean Burke .10 .05
❑ 58 Pat Verbeek .05 .02
❑ 59 Zarley Zalapski .05 .02
❑ 60 Patrick Poulin .05 .02
❑ 61 Robert Petrovicky UER .05 .02
(Assists total for 1990-91
reads 114)
❑ 62 Geoff Sanderson .10 .05
❑ 63 Paul Coffey .25 .11
❑ 64 Robert Lang .05 .02
❑ 65 Wayne Gretzky 1.50 .70
❑ 66 Kelly Hrudey .10 .05
❑ 67 Jari Kurri .10 .05
❑ 68 Luc Robitaille .10 .05
❑ 69 Darryl Sydor .05 .02
❑ 70 Jim Hiller .05 .02
❑ 71 Alexei Zhitnik .05 .02
❑ 72 Derian Hatcher .05 .02
❑ 73 Jon Casey .10 .05
❑ 74 Richard Matvichuk .05 .02
❑ 75 Mike Modano .40 .18
❑ 76 Mark Tinordi .05 .02
❑ 77 Todd Elik .05 .02
❑ 78 Russ Courtnall .05 .02
❑ 79 Tommy Sjodin .05 .02
❑ 80 Eric Desjardins .05 .02
❑ 81 Gilbert Dionne .05 .02
❑ 82 Stephan Lebeau .05 .02
❑ 83 Kirk Muller .05 .02
❑ 84 Patrick Roy 1.25 .55
❑ 85 Denis Savard .10 .05
❑ 86 Vincent Damphousse .10 .05
❑ 87 Brian Bellows .05 .02
❑ 88 Ed Ronan .05 .02
❑ 89 Claude Lemieux .10 .05
❑ 90 John MacLean .10 .05
❑ 91 Stephane Richer .10 .05
❑ 92 Scott Stevens .10 .05
❑ 93 Chris Terreri .10 .05
❑ 94 Kevin Todd .05 .02
❑ 95 Scott Niedermayer .10 .05
❑ 96 Bobby Holik .05 .02
❑ 97 Bill Guerin .05 .02
❑ 98 Ray Ferraro .05 .02
❑ 99 Mark Fitzpatrick .10 .05
❑ 100 Derek King .05 .02
❑ 101 Uwe Krupp .05 .02
❑ 102 Darius Kasparaitis .05 .02
❑ 103 Pierre Turgeon .10 .05
❑ 104 Benoit Hogue .05 .02
❑ 105 Scott Lachance .05 .02
❑ 106 Marty McInnis .05 .02
❑ 107 Tony Amonte .10 .05
❑ 108 Mike Gartner .10 .05
❑ 109 Alexei Kovalev .10 .05
❑ 110 Brian Leetch .25 .11
❑ 111 Mark Messier .40 .18
❑ 112 Mike Richter .25 .11
❑ 113 James Patrick .05 .02
❑ 114 Sergei Nemchinov .05 .02
❑ 115 Doug Weight .10 .05
❑ 116 Mark Lamb .05 .02
❑ 117 Norm Maciver .05 .02
❑ 118 Mike Peluso .05 .02
❑ 119 Jody Hull .05 .02
❑ 120 Peter Sidorkiewicz .10 .05
❑ 121 Sylvain Turgeon .05 .02
❑ 122 Laurie Boschman .05 .02
❑ 123 Brad Marsh .05 .02
❑ 124 Neil Brady .05 .02
❑ 125 Brian Benning .05 .02
❑ 126 Rod BrindAmour .10 .05
❑ 127 Kevin Dineen .05 .02
❑ 128 Eric Lindros 2.00 .90
❑ 129 Dominic Roussel .10 .05
❑ 130 Mark Recchi .10 .05
❑ 131 Brent Fedyk .05 .02
❑ 132 Greg Paslawski .05 .02
❑ 133 Dimitri Yushkevich .05 .02
❑ 134 Tom Barrasso .10 .05
❑ 135 Jaromir Jagr .75 .35
❑ 136 Mario Lemieux 1.25 .55
❑ 137 Larry Murphy .10 .05
❑ 138 Kevin Stevens .10 .05
❑ 139 Rick Tocchet .10 .05
❑ 140 Martin Straka .75 .35
❑ 141 Ron Francis .10 .05
❑ 142 Shawn McEachern .05 .02
❑ 143 Steve Duchesne .05 .02
❑ 144 Ron Hextall .10 .05
❑ 145 Owen Nolan .10 .05

❑ 146 Mike Ricci .05 .02
❑ 147 Joe Sakic .50 .23
❑ 148 Mats Sundin .25 .11
❑ 149 Martin Rucinsky .05 .02
❑ 150 Andrei Kovalenko .05 .02
❑ 151 Dave Karpa .05 .02
❑ 152 Nelson Emerson .05 .02
❑ 153 Brett Hull .40 .18
❑ 154 Craig Janney .10 .05
❑ 155 Curtis Joseph .25 .11
❑ 156 Brendan Shanahan .50 .23
❑ 157 Vitali Prokhorov .05 .02
❑ 158 Igor Korolev .05 .02
❑ 159 Philippe Bozon .05 .02
❑ 160 Ray Whitney .05 .02
❑ 161 Pat Falloon .05 .02
❑ 162 Jeff Hackett .10 .05
❑ 163 Brian Lawton .05 .02
❑ 164 Sandis Ozolinsh .10 .05
❑ 165 Neil Wilkinson .05 .02
❑ 166 Kelly Kisio .05 .02
❑ 167 Doug Wilson .10 .05
❑ 168 Dale Craigwell .05 .02
❑ 169 Mikael Andersson .05 .02
❑ 170 Wendell Young .10 .05
❑ 171 Rob Zamuner .05 .02
❑ 172 Adam Creighton .05 .02
❑ 173 Roman Hamrlik .40 .18
❑ 174 Brian Bradley .05 .02
❑ 175 Rob Ramage .05 .02
❑ 176 Chris Kontos .05 .02
❑ 177 Stan Drulia .05 .02
❑ 178 Glenn Anderson .10 .05
❑ 179 Wendel Clark .10 .05
❑ 180 John Cullen .05 .02
❑ 181 Dave Ellett .05 .02
❑ 182 Grant Fuhr .10 .05
❑ 183 Doug Gilmour .25 .11
❑ 184 Kent Manderville .05 .02
❑ 185 Joe Sacco .05 .02
❑ 186 Nikolai Borschevsky .05 .02
❑ 187 Felix Potvin .25 .11
❑ 188 Pavel Bure .50 .23
❑ 189 Geoff Courtnall .05 .02
❑ 190 Trevor Linden .10 .05
❑ 191 Jyrki Lumme .05 .02
❑ 192 Kirk McLean .10 .05
❑ 193 Cliff Ronning .05 .02
❑ 194 Dixon Ward .05 .02
❑ 195 Greg Adams .05 .02
❑ 196 Jiri Slegr .05 .02
❑ 197 Don Beaupre .10 .05
❑ 198 Kevin Hatcher .05 .02
❑ 199 Brad Schlegel .05 .02
❑ 200 Mike Ridley .05 .02
❑ 201 Calle Johansson .05 .02
❑ 202 Steve Konowalchuk .05 .02
❑ 203 Al Iafrate .10 .05
❑ 204 Peter Bondra .25 .11
❑ 205 Pat Elynuik .05 .02
❑ 206 Keith Tkachuk .60 .25
❑ 207 Bob Essensa .10 .05
❑ 208 Phil Housley .10 .05
❑ 209 Teemu Selanne 1.25 .55
❑ 210 Alexei Zhamnov .10 .05
❑ 211 Evgeny Davydov .05 .02
❑ 212 Fredrik Olausson .05 .02
❑ 213 Ed Olczyk .05 .02
❑ 214 Thomas Steen .05 .02
❑ 215 Darius Kasparaitis .05 .02
❑ 216 Nikolai Borschevsky .05 .02
❑ 217 Teemu Selanne .60 .25
❑ 218 Alexander Mogilny .10 .05
❑ 219 Sergei Fedorov .25 .11
❑ 220 Jaromir Jagr .40 .18
❑ 221 Mats Sundin .25 .11
❑ 222 Dimitri Kvartalnov .05 .02
❑ 223 Andrei Kovalenko .05 .02
❑ 224 Tommy Sjodin .05 .02
❑ 225 Alexei Kovalev .10 .05
❑ 226 Evgeny Davydov .05 .02
❑ 227 Robert Lang .05 .02
❑ 228 Valeri Zelepukin .05 .02
❑ 229 Doug Weight .10 .05
❑ 230 Valeri Kamensky .10 .05
❑ 231 Donald Audette .10 .05
❑ 232 Nelson Emerson .05 .02
❑ 233 Pat Falloon .05 .02
❑ 234 Pavel Bure .25 .11
❑ 235 Tony Amonte .05 .02
❑ 236 Sergei Nemchinov .05 .02
❑ 237 Gilbert Dionne .05 .02
❑ 238 Kevin Todd .05 .02
❑ 239 Nicklas Lidstrom .10 .05
❑ 240 Brad May .10 .05
❑ 241 Stephen Leach .05 .02
❑ 242 Dave Poulin .05 .02
❑ 243 Grigori Panteleyev .05 .02
❑ 244 Don Sweeney .05 .02
❑ 245 John Blue .10 .05
❑ 246 C.J. Young .05 .02
❑ 247 Stephen Heinze .05 .02
❑ 248 Cam Neely .10 .05
❑ 249 David Reid .05 .02
❑ 250 Grant Fuhr .10 .05
❑ 251 Bob Sweeney .05 .02
❑ 252 Rob Ray .05 .02
❑ 253 Doug Bodger .05 .02
❑ 254 Ken Sutton .05 .02
❑ 255 Yuri Khmylev .05 .02
❑ 256 Mike Ramsey .05 .02
❑ 257 Brad May .10 .05
❑ 258 Brent Ashton .05 .02
❑ 259 Joel Otto .05 .02
❑ 260 Paul Ranheim .05 .02
❑ 261 Kevin Dahl .05 .02
❑ 262 Trent Yawney .05 .02
❑ 263 Roger Johansson .05 .02
❑ 264 Jeff Reese .05 .02
❑ 265 Ron Stern .05 .02
❑ 266 Brian Skrudland .05 .02
❑ 267 Bryan Marchment .05 .02
❑ 268 Stephane Matteau .05 .02
❑ 269 Frantisek Kucera .05 .02
❑ 270 Jim Waite .10 .05
❑ 271 Dirk Graham .05 .02
❑ 272 Michel Goulet .10 .05
❑ 273 Joe Murphy .05 .02
❑ 274 Keith Brown .05 .02
❑ 275 Jocelyn Lemieux .05 .02
❑ 276 Paul Coffey .25 .11
❑ 277 Keith Primeau .10 .05
❑ 278 Vincent Riendeau .10 .05
❑ 279 Mark Howe .05 .02
❑ 280 Ray Sheppard .10 .05
❑ 281 Jim Hiller .05 .02
❑ 282 Steve Chiasson .05 .02
❑ 283 Vladimir Konstantinov .05 .02
❑ 284 Brian Benning .05 .02
❑ 285 Kevin Todd .05 .02
❑ 286 Zdeno Ciger .05 .02
❑ 287 Brian Glynn .05 .02
❑ 288 Shaun Van Allen .05 .02
❑ 289 Brad Werenka .05 .02
❑ 290 Ron Tugnutt .10 .05
❑ 291 Igor Kravchuk .05 .02
❑ 292 Todd Elik .05 .02
❑ 293 Terry Yake .05 .02
❑ 294 Michael Nylander .05 .02
❑ 295 Yvon Corriveau .05 .02
❑ 296 Frank Pietrangelo .10 .05
❑ 297 Nick Kypreos .05 .02
❑ 298 Andrew Cassels .05 .02
❑ 299 Steve Konroyd .05 .02
❑ 300 Allen Pedersen .05 .02
❑ 301 Tony Granato .05 .02
❑ 302 Rob Blake .10 .05
❑ 303 Robb Stauber .10 .05
❑ 304 Marty McSorley .05 .02
❑ 305 Lonnie Loach .05 .02
❑ 306 Corey Millen .05 .02
❑ 307 Dave Taylor .10 .05
❑ 308 Jimmy Carson .05 .02
❑ 309 Warren Rychel .05 .02
❑ 310 Ulf Dahlen .05 .02
❑ 311 Dave Gagner .10 .05
❑ 312 Brad Berry .05 .02
❑ 313 Neal Broten .10 .05
❑ 314 Mike Craig .05 .02
❑ 315 Darcy Wakaluk .10 .05
❑ 316 Shane Churla .05 .02
❑ 317 Trent Klatt .05 .02
❑ 318 Mike Keane .05 .02
❑ 319 Mathieu Schneider .05 .02
❑ 320 Patrice Brisebois .05 .02
❑ 321 Andre Racicot .10 .05
❑ 322 Mario Roberge .05 .02
❑ 323 Gary Leeman .05 .02
❑ 324 Jean-Jacques Daigneault .05 .02
❑ 325 Lyle Odelein .05 .02
❑ 326 John LeClair .60 .25
❑ 327 Valeri Zelepukin .05 .02
❑ 328 Bernie Nicholls .10 .05
❑ 329 Alexander Semak .05 .02
❑ 330 Craig Billington .10 .05
❑ 331 Randy McKay .05 .02
❑ 332 Ken Daneyko .05 .02
❑ 333 Bruce Driver .05 .02
❑ 334 Slava Fetisov .05 .02
❑ 335 Dennis Vaske .05 .02
❑ 336 Brad Dalgarno .05 .02
❑ 337 Jeff Norton .05 .02
❑ 338 Steve Thomas .05 .02
❑ 339 Vladimir Malakhov .05 .02
❑ 340 David Volek .05 .02
❑ 341 Glenn Healy .10 .05
❑ 342 Patrick Flatley .05 .02
❑ 343 Travis Green .05 .02
❑ 344 Corey Hirsch .50 .23
❑ 345 Darren Turcotte .05 .02
❑ 346 Adam Graves .10 .05
❑ 347 Steve King .05 .02
❑ 348 Kevin Lowe .05 .02
❑ 349 John Vanbiesbrouck .40 .18
❑ 350 Ed Olczyk .05 .02
❑ 351 Sergei Zubov .60 .25
❑ 352 Brad Shaw .05 .02
❑ 353 Jamie Baker .05 .02
❑ 354 Mark Freer .05 .02
❑ 355 Darcy Loewen .05 .02
❑ 356 Darren Rumble .05 .02
❑ 357 Bob Kudelski .05 .02
❑ 358 Ken Hammond .05 .02
❑ 359 Daniel Berthiaume .10 .05
❑ 360 Josef Beranek .05 .02
❑ 361 Greg Hawgood .05 .02
❑ 362 Terry Carkner .05 .02
❑ 363 Vyatcheslav Butsayev .05 .02
❑ 364 Garry Galley .05 .02
❑ 365 Andre Faust .05 .02
❑ 366 Ryan McGill .05 .02
❑ 367 Tommy Soderstrom .10 .05
❑ 368 Joe Mullen .10 .05
❑ 369 Ulf Samuelsson .05 .02
❑ 370 Mike Needham .05 .02
❑ 371 Ken Wregget .10 .05
❑ 372 Dave Tippett .05 .02
❑ 373 Kjell Samuelsson .05 .02
❑ 374 Bob Errey .05 .02
❑ 375 Jim Paek .05 .02
❑ 376 Bill Lindsay .05 .02
❑ 377 Valeri Kamensky .10 .05
❑ 378 Stephane Fiset .10 .05
❑ 379 Steven Finn .05 .02
❑ 380 Mike Hough .05 .02
❑ 381 Scott Pearson .05 .02
❑ 382 Kerry Huffman .05 .02
❑ 383 Scott Young .05 .02
❑ 384 Stephane Quintal .05 .02
❑ 385 Bret Hedican .05 .02
❑ 386 Guy Hebert .75 .35
❑ 387 Vitali Karamnov .05 .02
❑ 388 Doug Crossman .05 .02
❑ 389 Ron Sutter .05 .02
❑ 390 Garth Butcher .05 .02
❑ 391 Basil McRae .05 .02
❑ 392 Dean Evason .05 .02
❑ 393 Doug Zmolek .05 .02
❑ 394 Jay More .05 .02
❑ 395 Mike Sullivan .05 .02
❑ 396 Arturs Irbe .10 .05
❑ 397 Johan Garpenlov .05 .02
❑ 398 Jeff Odgers .05 .02
❑ 399 Jaroslav Otevrel .05 .02
❑ 400 Marc Bureau .05 .02
❑ 401 Bob Beers .05 .02
❑ 402 Rob DiMaio .05 .02
❑ 403 Steve Kasper .05 .02
❑ 404 Pat Jablonski .10 .05
❑ 405 John Tucker .05 .02
❑ 406 Shawn Chambers .05 .02
❑ 407 Mike Hartman .05 .02
❑ 408 Danton Cole .05 .02
❑ 409 Dave Andreychuk .10 .05
❑ 410 Peter Zezel .05 .02
❑ 411 Mike Krushelnyski .05 .02
❑ 412 Daren Puppa .10 .05
❑ 413 Ken Baumgartner .05 .02
❑ 414 Rob Pearson .05 .02
❑ 415 Mike Foligno .05 .02
❑ 416 Sylvain Lefebvre .05 .02
❑ 417 Dimitri Mironov .05 .02
❑ 418 Petr Nedved .10 .05
❑ 419 Gerald Diduck .05 .02
❑ 420 Anatoli Semenov .05 .02
❑ 421 Sergio Momesso .05 .02
❑ 422 Gino Odjick .05 .02
❑ 423 Kay Whitmore .10 .05
❑ 424 Dave Babych .05 .02
❑ 425 Robert Dirk .05 .02
❑ 426 Reggie Savage .05 .02
❑ 427 Keith Jones .25 .11
❑ 428 Dimitri Khristich .10 .05
❑ 429 Jason Woolley .05 .02
❑ 430 Jim Hrivnak .10 .05
❑ 431 Sylvain Cote .05 .02
❑ 432 Michal Pivonka .05 .02
❑ 433 Rod Langway .05 .02
❑ 434 Tie Domi .10 .05
❑ 435 Sergei Bautin .05 .02
❑ 436 Darrin Shannon .05 .02
❑ 437 John Druce .05 .02
❑ 438 Teppo Numminen .05 .02
❑ 439 Luciano Borsato .05 .02
❑ 440 Igor Ulanov .05 .02
❑ 441 Mike O'Neill .05 .02
❑ 442 Kris King .05 .02
❑ 443 Roman Hamrlik .10 .05
❑ 444 Steve Smith .05 .02
❑ 445 Jari Kurri .10 .05
❑ 446 Ulf Samuelsson .05 .02
❑ 447 Sergei Nemchinov .05 .02
❑ 448 Tommy Soderstrom .10 .05
❑ 449 Petr Nedved .10 .05
❑ 450 Peter Sidorkiewicz .10 .05
❑ 451 Nicklas Lidstrom .10 .05
❑ 452 Philippe Bozon .05 .02
❑ 453 Uwe Krupp .05 .02
❑ 454 Steve Thomas .05 .02
❑ 455 Owen Nolan .10 .05
❑ 456 Steve Yzerman .40 .18
❑ 457 Chris Chelios .25 .11
❑ 458 Paul Coffey .25 .11
❑ 459 Brett Hull .25 .11
❑ 460 Pavel Bure .25 .11
❑ 461 Ed Belfour .25 .11
❑ 462 Mario Lemieux .60 .25
❑ 463 Patrick Roy .60 .25
❑ 464 Ray Bourque .25 .11
❑ 465 Jaromir Jagr .40 .18
❑ 466 Kevin Stevens .05 .02
❑ 467 Brian Leetch .25 .11
❑ 468 Bobby Clarke .10 .05
❑ 469 Bill Barber .05 .02
❑ 470 Bernie Parent .10 .05
❑ 471 Reggie Leach .05 .02
❑ 472 Rick MacLeish .05 .02
❑ 473 Dave Schultz .05 .02
❑ 474 Joe Watson .05 .02
❑ 475 Bobby Taylor .05 .02
❑ 476 Orest Kindrachuk .05 .02
❑ 477 Bob Kelly .05 .02
❑ 478 Bill Clement .10 .05
❑ 479 Ed Van Impe .05 .02
❑ 480 Fred Shero .10 .05
❑ 481 Bryan Smolinski .50 .23
❑ 482 Sergei Zholtok .10 .05
❑ 483 Matthew Barnaby .25 .11
❑ 484 Gary Shuchuk .10 .05
❑ 485 Guy Carbonneau .25 .11
❑ 486 Oleg Petrov .10 .05
❑ 487 Sean Hill .10 .05
❑ 488 Jesse Belanger .10 .05
❑ 489 Paul DiPietro .10 .05
❑ 490 Rich Pilon .10 .05
❑ 491 Greg Parks .10 .05
❑ 492 Jeff Daniels .10 .05
❑ 493 Denny Felsner .10 .05
❑ 494 Mike Eastwood .10 .05
❑ 495 Murray Craven .10 .05
❑ 496 Vincent Damphousse .25 .11
❑ 497 Grant Fuhr .10 .05
❑ 498 Mario Lemieux 3.00 1.35
❑ 499 Ray Ferraro .05 .02
❑ 500 Teemu Selanne 2.00 .90
❑ 501 Luc Robitaille .10 .05
❑ 502 Doug Gilmour .25 .11
❑ 503 Curtis Joseph .25 .11
❑ 504 Kirk Muller .05 .02
❑ 505 Glenn Healy .10 .05
❑ 506 Pavel Bure 1.50 .70
❑ 507 Felix Potvin .25 .11
❑ 508 Guy Carbonneau .05 .02
❑ 509 Wayne Gretzky 4.00 1.80
❑ 510 Patrick Roy 3.00 1.35

## 1992-93 Parkhurst Emerald Ice

The '92-93 Parkhurst Emerald Ice set consists of 480 cards and a 30 card update set. This parallel set version can be differentiated from its basic set counterpart by the company's use of an "emerald green" embossed-foil Parkhurst logo on the lower left of the card. Cards 1-240 were inserted one per foil pack, two per jumbo pack in series one product; likewise for cards 241-480 in series two product. Cards 481-510 were available in set form only, and are slightly more difficult to obtain.

| | MINT | NRMT |
|---|---|---|
| COMPLETE SET (480) | 180.00 | 80.00 |
| COMPLETE SERIES 1 (240) | 100.00 | 45.00 |
| COMPLETE SERIES 2 (240) | 80.00 | 36.00 |
| COMPLETE FIN.UPDATE (30) | 25.00 | 11.00 |

*STARS: 2X TO 5X BASIC CARDS
*YOUNG STARS: 2X TO 4X BASIC CARDS

## 1992-93 Parkhurst Cherry Picks

Randomly inserted in second series Parkhurst foil packs, this 21-card standard-size set features Don Cherry's "Cherry Picks" as selected by the ex-coach and host of "Coach's Corner" on Hockey Night in Canada. The cards feature full-bleed, color action player photos. The player's name is printed in gold foil near the bottom of the card along with the Cherry Picks logo. The backs have a dark blue-gray and black stripe background. Set at an angle on this background is a hockey arena graphic design that carries comments from Don Cherry in French and English. Overlapping the arena design is a small, action player photo. The cards are numbered on the backs with a "CP" prefix. The cover card carries a message from Don Cherry. The Doug Gilmour card (CP 1993) was randomly inserted in Final Update sets.

| | MINT | NRMT |
|---|---|---|
| COMPLETE SET (21) | 60.00 | 27.00 |
| COMMON CARD (CP1-CP20) | 2.50 | 1.10 |

❑ CP1 Doug Gilmour 4.00 1.80
❑ CP2 Jeremy Roenick 5.00 2.20
❑ CP3 Brent Sutter 2.50 1.10
❑ CP4 Mark Messier 8.00 3.60
❑ CP5 Kirk Muller 2.50 1.10
❑ CP6 Eric Lindros 20.00 9.00
❑ CP7 Dale Hunter 2.50 1.10
❑ CP8 Gary Roberts 2.50 1.10
❑ CP9 Bob Probert 2.50 1.10
❑ CP10 Brendan Shanahan 10.00 4.50
❑ CP11 Wendel Clark 4.00 1.80
❑ CP12 Rick Tocchet 4.00 1.80
❑ CP13 Owen Nolan 4.00 1.80
❑ CP14 Cam Neely 4.00 1.80
❑ CP15 Dave Manson 2.50 1.10
❑ CP16 Chris Chelios 5.00 2.20
❑ CP17 Marty McSorley 2.50 1.10
❑ CP18 Scott Stevens 2.50 1.10
❑ CP19 John Blue 4.00 1.80
❑ CP20 Ron Hextall 4.00 1.80
❑ CP1993 Doug Gilmour 15.00 6.75

Cherry Pick of the Year
❑ NNO Don Cherry AU 150.00 70.00
❑ NNO Don Cherry 20.00 9.00
Checklist back
❑ NNO Don Cherry 10.00 4.50
Redemption

## 1992-93 Parkhurst Cherry Picks Sheet

This approximately 11" by 8 1/2" sheet displays the cards of the 1992-93 Parkhurst Cherry Picks insert set. The sheet could be obtained by collectors in exchange for four Don Cherry redemption cards, which were randomly inserted in 1992-93 Parkhurst series II packs. The sheet pictures the fronts of the cards from the 1992-93 Cherry Picks set with Don Cherry's card in the middle. The words "1993 Cherry Picks Promo" are printed in a pink to purple shaded bar at the top of the sheet. The back is blank and the sheet is unnumbered.

| | MINT | NRMT |
|---|---|---|
| COMPLETE SET (1) | 50.00 | 22.00 |
| COMMON SHEET | 50.00 | 22.00 |

❑ 1 Dale Hunter 50.00 22.00
Dave Manson
Doug Gilmour
Gary Roberts
Chris Chelios
Jeremy Roenick
Bob Probert
Marty McSorley
Brent Sutter
Brendan Shanahan
Don Cherry
Mark Messier
Wendel Clark
Kirk Muller
Rick Tocchet
Scott Stevens
Eric Lindros
Owen Nolan
John Blue
Ron Hextall

## 1992-93 Parkhurst Parkie Reprints

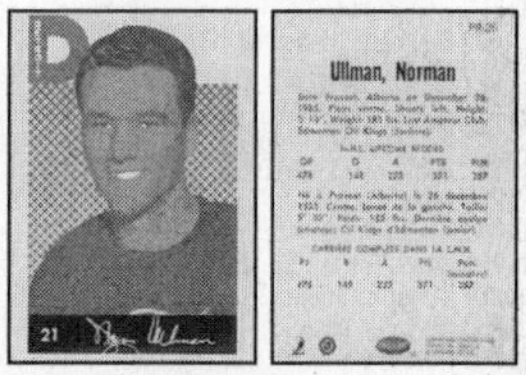

This set of 36 cards was issued in four separate series. The cards are reprints of cards from the 1950s. Capturing eight goalies from the 1950's Parkhurst collections, the first set was undercollated into first series 12-card foil packs. The second eight cards showcase defensemen; these cards were randomly inserted in series 1 jumbo packs. Forwards (17-24) were inserted in second series foil with the remaining forwards (25-32) inserted in second series jumbo packs. The cover cards, which reproduce Parkhurst wrappers on their fronts (1953-54 and 1955-56), have a checklist on their backs. The fronts vary in design but all carry a color shot of the featured player. The players' names are on the fronts, some in print, some in signature form. The backs carry the information from the original card. The print varies from red to black to a combination. The Turk Broda and Terry Sawchuk cards are blank on the back as the originals are. The cards are numbered on the back with a "PR" prefix. Only Canadian cases included a newly created 1954-55 Don Cherry Parkie 101 card. The Parkie Reprints set is considered complete without it.

| | MINT | NRMT |
|---|---|---|
| COMPLETE SET (36) | 225.00 | 100.00 |
| COMP.SER.1 (PR1-PR8/CL1) | 75.00 | 34.00 |
| COMP.SER.2 (PR9-PR16/CL2) | 50.00 | 22.00 |
| COMP.SER.3 (PR17-PR24/CL3) | 60.00 | 27.00 |
| COMP.SER.4 (PR25-PR32/CL4) | 60.00 | 27.00 |
| COMMON CARD (PR1-PR32) | 5.00 | 2.20 |
| COMMON CL (CL1-CL4) | 10.00 | 4.50 |

❑ PR1 Jacques Plante 15.00 6.75
❑ PR2 Terry Sawchuk 15.00 6.75
❑ PR3 Johnny Bower 5.00 2.20

❑ PR4 Gump Worsley............ 10.00 4.50
❑ PR5 Harry Lumley.............. 5.00 2.20
❑ PR6 Turk Broda.................. 5.00 2.20
❑ PR7 Jim Henry...................... 5.00 2.20
❑ PR8 Al Rollins....................... 5.00 2.20
❑ PR9 Bill Gadsby.................... 5.00 2.20
❑ PR10 Red Kelly...................... 5.00 2.20
❑ PR11 Allan Stanley.............. 5.00 2.20
❑ PR12 Bob Baun...................... 5.00 2.20
❑ PR13 Carl Brewer................... 5.00 2.20
❑ PR14 Doug Harvey.............. 10.00 4.50
❑ PR15 Harry Howell................ 5.00 2.20
❑ PR16 Tim Horton................ 12.00 5.50
❑ PR17 George Armstrong...... 5.00 2.20
❑ PR18 Ralph Backstrom........ 5.00 2.20
❑ PR19 Alex Delvecchio.......... 5.00 2.20
❑ PR20 Bill Mosienko.............. 5.00 2.20
❑ PR21 Dave Keon.................. 5.00 2.20
❑ PR22 Andy Bathgate............. 5.00 2.20
❑ PR23 Milt Schmidt................ 5.00 2.20
❑ PR24 Dick Duff..................... 5.00 2.20
❑ PR25 Norm Ullman............... 5.00 2.20
❑ PR26 Dickie Moore............... 5.00 2.20
❑ PR27 Jerry Toppazzini........... 5.00 2.20
❑ PR28 Henri Richard............... 5.00 2.20
❑ PR29 Frank Mahovlich.......... 5.00 2.20
❑ PR30 Jean Beliveau........... 12.00 5.50
❑ PR31 Ted Lindsay................. 5.00 2.20
❑ PR32 Bernie Geoffrion......... 10.00 4.50
❑ CL1 Parkies Checklist 1....... 10.00 4.50
(Repro of 1955-56
Parkie Wrapper)
❑ CL2 Parkies Checklist 2....... 10.00 4.50
(Repro of 1953-54
Parkie Wrapper)
❑ CL3 Parkies Checklist 3....... 10.00 4.50
(Repro of 1958-59
Parkie Wrapper)
❑ CL4 Parkies Checklist 4....... 10.00 4.50
(Repro of 1954-55
Parkie Wrapper)
❑ AU Don Cherry Parkie AU.. 150.00 70.00
❑ NNO D.Cherry Parkie 101.... 40.00 18.00

## 1992-93 Parkhurst Arena Tour Sheets

Each sheet in this set of eight measures approximately 11" by 8 1/2" and commemorates a stop on the Canadian Arena Tour. The fronts feature color photos of 1992-93 Parkhurst hockey cards against a blue-green background that shades from dark to light. A thin metallic gold line frames the cards, and the word "Commemorative" is printed in large white letters on this line at the top of the sheet. Near the center are the words "Canadian Arena Tour" and a specific arena name along with the date the sheet was distributed. The team logo is printed above this text. Each sheet carries a serial number and the production run. The backs are blank. The sheets are unnumbered and checklisted below in chronological order. The Montreal sheet was not distributed at the Forum; reportedly because the sheet was not bilingual.

| | MINT | NRMT |
|---|---|---|
| COMPLETE SET (8) | 90.00 | 40.00 |
| COMMON SHEET (1-8) | 10.00 | 4.50 |

❑ 1 Calgary Flames................ 10.00 4.50
Olympic Saddledome
April 1, 1993 (22,000)
Mike Vernon
Theoren Fleury
Trent Yawney
Brian Skrudland
Joel Otto
Al MacInnis
❑ 2 Edmonton Oilers.............. 10.00 4.50
Northlands Coliseum
April 3, 1993 (22,000)
Zdeno Ciger
Bill Ranford
Todd Elik
Igor Kravchuk
Craig MacTavish
Shayne Corson
❑ 3 Quebec Nordiques........... 10.00 4.50
Colisee de Quebec
April 6, 1993 (22,000)
Bill Lindsay
Ron Hextall
Valeri Kamensky
Kerry Huffman
Mats Sundin
Joe Sakic
❑ 4 Vancouver Canucks.......... 15.00 6.75
Pacific Coliseum
April 11, 1993 (22,000)
Dave Babych
Pavel Bure
Petr Nedved
Anatoli Semenov
Kirk McLean
Trevor Linden
❑ 5 Montreal Canadiens......... 25.00 11.00
The Forum
April 12, 1993 (22,000)
Denis Savard
Kirk Muller
J.J. Daigneault
Patrice Brisebois
Mathieu Schneider
Patrick Roy
❑ 6 Toronto Maple Leafs......... 20.00 9.00
Maple Leaf Gardens
April 13, 1993 (22,000)
Felix Potvin
Dave Andreychuk
Wendel Clark
Peter Zezel
Doug Gilmour
Sylvain Lefebvre
❑ 7 Ottawa Senators............... 10.00 4.50
Ottawa Civic Centre
April 14, 1993 (22,000)
Brad Marsh
Ken Hammond
Bob Kudelski
Peter Sidorkiewicz
Sylvain Turgeon
Mark Freer
❑ 8 Winnipeg Jets.................. 10.00 4.50
Winnipeg Arena
April 15, 1993 (22,000)
Phil Housley
John Druce
Sergei Bautin
Tie Domi
Evgeny Davydov
Teemu Selanne

## 1992-93 Parkhurst Parkie Sheets

These five commemorative sheets measure approximately 8 1/2" by 11". The sheets are individually numbered; the production quantities are listed in the checklist below. The sheets were distributed one per case as an insert with the various series of 1992-93 Parkhurst hockey cards. The players pictured are the players in that respective Parkie reprint series. The Stanley Cup Commemorative Update sheet was issued one per case of Final Update. These unnumbered sheets are numbered chronologically below for convenience in reference.

| | MINT | NRMT |
|---|---|---|
| COMPLETE SET (5) | 110.00 | 50.00 |
| COMMON SHEET (1-5) | 20.00 | 9.00 |

❑ 1 Goalies.............................. 20.00 9.00
(7000 sheets issued)
❑ 2 Defensemen..................... 25.00 11.00
(3000 sheets issued)
❑ 3 Forwards/Wingers............ 20.00 9.00
(7000 sheets issued)
❑ 4 Forwards/Centers............ 30.00 13.50
(3000 sheets issued)
❑ 5 Stanley Cup Update.......... 40.00 18.00
(1000 sheets issued)

## 1992-93 Parkhurst Promo Sheets

These 11" by 8 1/2" sheets were promos of the 1992-93 Parkhurst Limited Edition Commemorative Sheets. The fronts feature color photos of actual Parkhurst Parkies. The cards are set against a dark green marbleized background. A thin metallic gold line frames the cards. The words "Commemorative Sheet" are printed in white over the gold line near the top of the sheet. Above this, are the words "1992-93 Parkhurst Limited Edition" printed in metallic gold. A gold or white oval at the bottom right corner carries the word "Promo." The backs are blank. The sheets are unnumbered.

| | MINT | NRMT |
|---|---|---|
| COMPLETE SET (2) | 40.00 | 18.00 |
| COMMON CARD (1-2) | 15.00 | 6.75 |

❑ 1 Toronto Maple Leafs......... 25.00 11.00
vs. Montreal Canadiens
Alumni Game
April 4, 1993
Maple Leaf Gardens
Johnny Bower
Harry Lumley
Jacques Plante
Dave Keon
Doug Harvey
Tim Horton
Ralph Backstrom
Frank Mahovlich
❑ 2 Dave Keon........................ 15.00 6.75
Milt Schmidt
Dick Duff
Bill Mosienko
Alex Delvecchio
Ralph Backstrom
George Armstrong
Andy Bathgate

## 1993-94 Parkhurst

Issued in two series, these 540 standard-size cards feature color player action shots on their fronts. They are borderless, except on the right, where black and green stripes set off by a silver-foil line carry the player's name in white lettering; and at the lower left, where a black and green corner backs up the silver-foil-stamped Parkhurst logo. The player's team name appears near the right edge in vertical silver-foil lettering. The horizontal back carries another color player action shot on the right. On the left are the player's team name, position, biography, career highlights, and statistics. Card numbers 398 and 498 were not issued. Rookie Cards include Jason Arnott, Valeri Bure, Jeff Friesen, Chris Osgood, Jamie Storr, Jocelyn Thibault, German Titov and Oleg Tverdovksy.

| | MINT | NRMT |
|---|---|---|
| COMPLETE SET (540) | 30.00 | 13.50 |
| COMPLETE SERIES 1 (270) | 15.00 | 6.75 |
| COMPLETE SERIES 2 (270) | 15.00 | 6.75 |
| COMMON CARD (1-540) | .10 | .05 |

❑ 1 Steven King.......................... .10 .05
❑ 2 Sean Hill.............................. .10 .05
❑ 3 Anatoli Semenov.................. .10 .05
❑ 4 Garry Valk............................ .10 .05
❑ 5 Todd Ewen........................... .10 .05
❑ 6 Bob Corkum......................... .10 .05
❑ 7 Tim Sweeney....................... .10 .05
❑ 8 Patrick Carnback.................. .10 .05
❑ 9 Troy Loney.......................... .10 .05
❑ 10 Cam Neely.......................... .15 .07
❑ 11 Adam Oates........................ .15 .07
❑ 12 Jon Casey.......................... .15 .07
❑ 13 Don Sweeney..................... .10 .05
❑ 14 Ray Bourque...................... .25 .11
❑ 15 Jozef Stumpel.................... .10 .05
❑ 16 Glen Murray....................... .10 .05
❑ 17 Glen Wesley....................... .10 .05
❑ 18 Fred Knipscheer................. .10 .05
❑ 19 Craig Simpson.................... .10 .05
❑ 20 Richard Smehlik................. .10 .05
❑ 21 Alexander Mogilny.............. .15 .07
❑ 22 Grant Fuhr......................... .15 .07
❑ 23 Dale Hawerchuk.................. .15 .07
❑ 24 Philippe Boucher................ .10 .05
❑ 25 Scott Thomas..................... .10 .05
❑ 26 Donald Audette................... .15 .07
❑ 27 Brad May............................ .15 .07
❑ 28 Theoren Fleury................... .15 .07
❑ 29 Andrei Trefilov.................... .10 .05
❑ 30 Sandy McCarthy.................. .10 .05
❑ 31 Joe Nieuwendyk................. .15 .07
❑ 32 Paul Ranheim...................... .10 .05
❑ 33 Kelly Kisio........................... .10 .05
❑ 34 Joel Otto............................ .10 .05
❑ 35 Ted Drury........................... .10 .05
❑ 36 Al MacInnis......................... .15 .07
❑ 37 Kevin Todd.......................... .10 .05
❑ 38 Joe Murphy......................... .10 .05
❑ 39 Christian Ruuttu.................. .10 .05
❑ 40 Steve Dubinsky................... .10 .05
❑ 41 Stephane Matteau............... .10 .05
❑ 42 Ivan Droppa........................ .10 .05
❑ 43 Jocelyn Lemieux................. .10 .05
❑ 44 Ed Belfour........................... .25 .11
❑ 45 Chris Chelios...................... .25 .11
❑ 46 Derian Hatcher.................... .10 .05
❑ 47 Andy Moog.......................... .15 .07
❑ 48 Trent Klatt........................... .10 .05
❑ 49 Mike Modano....................... .30 .14
❑ 50 Paul Cavallini...................... .10 .05
❑ 51 Mike McPhee....................... .10 .05
❑ 52 Brent Gilchrist..................... .10 .05
❑ 53 Russ Courtnall..................... .10 .05
❑ 54 Neal Broten.......................... .15 .07
❑ 55 Steve Chiasson.................... .10 .05
❑ 56 Paul Coffey.......................... .25 .11
❑ 57 Slava Kozlov......................... .15 .07
❑ 58 Sergei Fedorov..................... .50 .23
❑ 59 Tim Cheveldae...................... .15 .07
❑ 60 Dino Ciccarelli....................... .15 .07
❑ 61 Dallas Drake.......................... .10 .05
❑ 62 Nicklas Lidstrom.................... .15 .07
❑ 63 Martin Lapointe..................... .10 .05
❑ 64 Dean McAmmond.................. .10 .05
❑ 65 Igor Kravchuk........................ .10 .05
❑ 66 Shjon Podein.......................... .10 .05
❑ 67 Bill Ranford............................ .15 .07
❑ 68 Brad Werenka......................... .10 .05
❑ 69 Doug Weight........................... .15 .07
❑ 70 Ian Herbers............................ .10 .05
❑ 71 Todd Elik................................ .10 .05
❑ 72 Steven Rice............................ .10 .05
❑ 73 John Vanbiesbrouck............... .40 .18
❑ 74 Alexander Godynyuk............... .10 .05
❑ 75 Brian Skrudland...................... .10 .05
❑ 76 Jody Hull................................ .10 .05
❑ 77 Brent Severyn......................... .10 .05
❑ 78 Evegny Davydov..................... .10 .05
❑ 79 Dave Lowry............................. .10 .05
❑ 80 Scott Levins............................ .10 .05
❑ 81 Scott Mellanby........................ .15 .07
❑ 82 Dan Keczmer.......................... .10 .05
❑ 83 Michael Nylander.................... .10 .05
❑ 84 Jim Sandlak............................ .10 .05
❑ 85 Brian Propp............................ .10 .05
❑ 86 Geoff Sanderson..................... .15 .07
❑ 87 Mike Lenarduzzi...................... .10 .05
❑ 88 Zarley Zalapski....................... .10 .05
❑ 89 Robert Petrovicky.................... .10 .05
❑ 90 Robert Kron............................ .10 .05
❑ 91 Luc Robitaille.......................... .15 .07
❑ 92 Alexei Zhitnik.......................... .10 .05
❑ 93 Tony Granato.......................... .10 .05
❑ 94 Rob Blake................................ .10 .05
❑ 95 Gary Shuchuk.......................... .10 .05
❑ 96 Darryl Sydor............................ .10 .05
❑ 97 Kelly Hrudey............................ .15 .07
❑ 98 Warren Rychel......................... .10 .05
❑ 99 Wayne Gretzky..................... 1.50 .70
❑ 100 Patrick Roy........................ 1.25 .55
❑ 101 Gilbert Dionne........................ .10 .05
❑ 102 Eric Desjardins....................... .10 .05
❑ 103 Peter Popovic......................... .10 .05
❑ 104 Vincent Damphousse.............. .15 .07
❑ 105 Patrice Brisebois.................... .10 .05
❑ 106 Pierre Sevigny........................ .10 .05
❑ 107 John LeClair........................... .40 .18
❑ 108 Paul DiPietro........................... .10 .05
❑ 109 Alexander Semak.................... .10 .05
❑ 110 Claude Lemieux...................... .15 .07
❑ 111 Scott Niedermayer.................. .10 .05
❑ 112 Chris Terreri........................... .15 .07
❑ 113 Stephane Richer..................... .15 .07
❑ 114 Scott Stevens......................... .15 .07
❑ 115 John MacLean........................ .15 .07
❑ 116 Scott Pellerin.......................... .10 .05
❑ 117 Bernie Nicholls....................... .10 .05
❑ 118 Ron Hextall............................. .15 .07
❑ 119 Derek King.............................. .10 .05
❑ 120 Scott Lachance........................ .10 .05
❑ 121 Scott Scissons......................... .10 .05
❑ 122 Darius Kasparaitis................... .10 .05
❑ 123 Ray Ferraro............................. .10 .05
❑ 124 Steve Thomas......................... .10 .05
❑ 125 Vladimir Malakhov................... .10 .05
❑ 126 Travis Green........................... .15 .07
❑ 127 Mark Messier........................... .30 .14
❑ 128 Sergei Nemchinov................... .10 .05
❑ 129 Mike Richter............................ .25 .11
❑ 130 Alexei Kovalev........................ .15 .07
❑ 131 Brian Leetch............................ .25 .11
❑ 132 Tony Amonte........................... .15 .07
❑ 133 Sergei Zubov.......................... .10 .05
❑ 134 Adam Graves.......................... .15 .07
❑ 135 Esa Tikkanen.......................... .10 .05
❑ 136 Sylvain Turgeon...................... .10 .05
❑ 137 Norm Maciver.......................... .10 .05
❑ 138 Craig Billington........................ .15 .07
❑ 139 Dmitri Filiminov....................... .10 .05
❑ 140 Pavel Demitra......................... .10 .05
❑ 141 Brian Glynn............................. .10 .05
❑ 142 Darrin Madeley........................ .10 .05
❑ 143 Radek Hamr............................ .10 .05
❑ 144 Robert Burakovsky.................. .10 .05
❑ 145 Dimitri Yushkevich.................. .10 .05
❑ 146 Claude Boivin.......................... .10 .05
❑ 147 Pelle Eklund............................ .10 .05
❑ 148 Brent Fedyk............................ .10 .05
❑ 149 Mark Recchi............................ .15 .07
❑ 150 Tommy Soderstrom................. .15 .07
❑ 151 Vyacheslav Butsayev.............. .10 .05
❑ 152 Rod Brind'Amour..................... .15 .07
❑ 153 Josef Beranek......................... .10 .05
❑ 154 Jaromir Jagr............................ .75 .35
❑ 155 Ulf Samuelsson....................... .10 .05
❑ 156 Martin Straka.......................... .10 .05
❑ 157 Tom Barrasso.......................... .15 .07
❑ 158 Kevin Stevens.......................... .10 .05
❑ 159 Joe Mullen............................... .15 .07
❑ 160 Ron Francis............................. .15 .07
❑ 161 Marty McSorley........................ .10 .05
❑ 162 Larry Murphy........................... .15 .07
❑ 163 Owen Nolan............................. .15 .07
❑ 164 Stephane Fiset........................ .15 .07
❑ 165 Dave Karpa.............................. .10 .05
❑ 166 Martin Gelinas......................... .10 .05
❑ 167 Andrei Kovalenko..................... .10 .05
❑ 168 Steve Duchesne....................... .10 .05
❑ 169 Joe Sakic................................. .50 .23
❑ 170 Martin Rucinsky........................ .10 .05
❑ 171 Chris Simon............................. .10 .05
❑ 172 Brendan Shanahan.................. .50 .23
❑ 173 Jeff Brown............................... .10 .05
❑ 174 Phil Housley............................ .15 .07
❑ 175 Curtis Joseph.......................... .25 .11
❑ 176 Jim Montgomery...................... .10 .05
❑ 177 Bret Hedican............................ .10 .05
❑ 178 Kevin Miller.............................. .10 .05
❑ 179 Philippe Bozon......................... .10 .05
❑ 180 Brett Hull.................................. .30 .14
❑ 181 Jimmy Waite............................. .15 .07
❑ 182 Ray Whitney............................. .10 .05
❑ 183 Pat Falloon............................... .10 .05
❑ 184 Tom Pederson.......................... .10 .05
❑ 185 Igor Larionov............................ .10 .05
❑ 186 Dody Wood............................... .10 .05
❑ 187 Sandis Ozolinsh....................... .15 .07
❑ 188 Sergei Makarov......................... .10 .05
❑ 189 Rob Gaudreau........................... .10 .05
❑ 190 Roman Hamrlik.......................... .15 .07
❑ 191 Stan Drulia................................ .10 .05
❑ 192 Pat Jablonski............................. .15 .07
❑ 193 Denis Savard............................. .15 .07
❑ 194 Rob Zamuner............................. .10 .05
❑ 195 Petr Klima.................................. .10 .05
❑ 196 Rob Dimiao................................ .10 .05
❑ 197 Chris Kontos.............................. .10 .05
❑ 198 Mikael Andersson....................... .10 .05
❑ 199 Drake Berehowsky..................... .10 .05
❑ 200 Dave Andreychuk....................... .15 .07
❑ 201 Glenn Anderson.......................... .15 .07
❑ 202 Felix Potvin................................ .25 .11
❑ 203 Nikolai Borschevsky.................. .10 .05
❑ 204 Kent Manderville........................ .10 .05
❑ 205 Dave Ellett................................. .10 .05
❑ 206 Peter Zezel................................. .10 .05
❑ 207 Ken Baumgartner........................ .10 .05
❑ 208 Murray Craven............................ .10 .05
❑ 209 Dixon Ward................................. .10 .05
❑ 210 Cliff Ronning............................... .10 .05
❑ 211 Pavel Bure.................................. .50 .23
❑ 212 Sergio Momesso......................... .10 .05
❑ 213 Kirk McLean................................ .15 .07
❑ 214 Jiri Slegr...................................... .10 .05
❑ 215 Trevor Linden.............................. .15 .07
❑ 216 Geoff Courtnall............................ .10 .05
❑ 217 Al Iafrate..................................... .10 .05
❑ 218 Mike Ridley.................................. .10 .05
❑ 219 Enrico Ciccone............................. .10 .05
❑ 220 Dimitri Khristich........................... .10 .05
❑ 221 Kevin Hatcher.............................. .15 .07
❑ 222 Peter Bondra................................ .25 .11
❑ 223 Steve Konowalchuk...................... .10 .05
❑ 224 Pat Elynuik................................... .10 .05
❑ 225 Don Beaupre................................. .15 .07
❑ 226 Stu Barnes..................................... .10 .05
❑ 227 Fredrik Olausson............................ .10 .05
❑ 228 Keith Thachuk................................ .30 .14
❑ 229 Mike Eagles................................... .10 .05
❑ 230 Tie Domi........................................ .15 .07
❑ 231 Teppo Numminen........................... .10 .05
❑ 232 Arto Blomsten................................ .10 .05
❑ 233 Teemu Selanne.............................. .60 .25
❑ 234 Bob Essensa.................................. .15 .07
❑ 235 Teemu Selanne SPH...................... .30 .14
❑ 236 Eric Lindros SPH............................ .50 .23
❑ 237 Felix Potvin SPH............................ .25 .11
❑ 238 Alexei Kovalev SPH........................ .15 .07
❑ 239 Vladimir Malakhov SPH.................. .10 .05
❑ 240 Scott Niedermayer SPH.................. .10 .05
❑ 241 Joe Juneau SPH............................. .15 .07
❑ 242 Shawn McEachern SPH.................. .10 .05
❑ 243 Alexei Zhamnov SPH...................... .15 .07
❑ 244 Alexandre Daigle PKP.................... .10 .05
❑ 245 Markus Naslund PKP...................... .10 .05
❑ 246 Rob Niedermayer PKP.................... .15 .07
❑ 247 Jocelyn Thibault PKP.................. 1.00 .45
❑ 248 Brent Gretzky PKP.......................... .10 .05
❑ 249 Chris Pronger PKP........................... .15 .07
❑ 250 Chris Gratton PKP............................ .15 .07
❑ 251 Mikael Renberg PKP........................ .25 .11
❑ 252 Jarkko Varvio PKP............................ .10 .05
❑ 253 Micah Aivazoff PKP.......................... .10 .05
❑ 254 Alexei Yashin PKP........................... .15 .07
❑ 255 German Titov PKP............................ .10 .05
❑ 256 Mattias Norstrom PKP...................... .10 .05
❑ 257 Michal Sykora PKP........................... .10 .05
❑ 258 Roman Oksiuta PKP......................... .10 .05
❑ 259 Bryan Smolinski PKP........................ .10 .05
❑ 260 Alexei Kudashov PKP....................... .10 .05
❑ 261 Jason Arnott PKP............................. .75 .35
❑ 262 Aaron Ward PKP............................... .10 .05
❑ 263 Vesa Vitakoski PKP.......................... .10 .05
❑ 264 Boris Mironov PKP............................ .10 .05
❑ 265 Darren McCarty PKP......................... .30 .14
❑ 266 Vlastimil Kroupa PKP........................ .10 .05
❑ 267 Denny Felsner PKP........................... .10 .05
❑ 268 Milos Holan PKP............................... .10 .05
❑ 269 Alex. Karpovtsev PKP....................... .10 .05
❑ 270 Greg Johnson PKP............................ .10 .05
❑ 271 Terry Yake.......................................... .10 .05
❑ 272 Bill Houlder......................................... .10 .05
❑ 273 Joe Sacco........................................... .10 .05
❑ 274 Myles O'Connor.................................. .10 .05
❑ 275 Mark Ferner........................................ .10 .05
❑ 276 Alexei Kasatanov................................ .10 .05
❑ 277 Stu Grimson........................................ .10 .05
❑ 278 Shaun Van Allen................................. .10 .05
❑ 279 Guy Hebert.......................................... .15 .07
❑ 280 Joe Juneau.......................................... .15 .07
❑ 281 Sergei Zholtok..................................... .10 .05
❑ 282 Daniel Marois...................................... .10 .05
❑ 283 Ted Donato.......................................... .10 .05
❑ 284 Cam Stewart........................................ .10 .05
❑ 285 Stephen Leach.................................... .15 .07
❑ 286 Darren Banks....................................... .10 .05
❑ 287 Dmitri Kvartalnov................................. .10 .05

| | | |
|---|---|---|
| 288 Paul Stanton | .10 | .05 |
| 289 Pat LaFontaine | .15 | .07 |
| 290 Bob Sweeney | .10 | .05 |
| 291 Craig Muni | .10 | .05 |
| 292 Sergei Petrenko | .10 | .05 |
| 293 Derek Plante | .10 | .05 |
| 294 Wayne Presley | .10 | .05 |
| 295 Mark Astley | .10 | .05 |
| 296 Matthew Barnaby | .15 | .07 |
| 297 Randy Wood | .10 | .05 |
| 298 Kevin Dahl | .10 | .05 |
| 299 Gary Suter | .10 | .05 |
| 300 Robert Reichel | .10 | .05 |
| 301 Mike Vernon | .15 | .07 |
| 302 Gary Roberts | .10 | .05 |
| 303 Ronnie Stern | .10 | .05 |
| 304 Michel Petit | .10 | .05 |
| 305 Wes Walz | .10 | .05 |
| 306 Brad Miller | .10 | .05 |
| 307 Patrick Poulin | .10 | .05 |
| 308 Brent Sutter | .10 | .05 |
| 309 Jeremy Roenick | .25 | .11 |
| 310 Steve Smith | .10 | .05 |
| 311 Eric Weinrich | .10 | .05 |
| 312 Jeff Hackett | .15 | .07 |
| 313 Michel Goulet | .15 | .07 |
| 314 Jeff Shantz | .10 | .05 |
| 315 Neil Wilkinson | .10 | .05 |
| 316 Shane Churla | .10 | .05 |
| 317 Dave Gagner | .15 | .07 |
| 318 Chris Tancill | .10 | .05 |
| 319 Dean Evason | .10 | .05 |
| 320 Mark Tinordi | .10 | .05 |
| 321 Grant Ledyard | .10 | .05 |
| 322 Ulf Dahlen | .10 | .05 |
| 323 Mike Craig | .10 | .05 |
| 324 Paul Broten | .10 | .05 |
| 325 Vladimir Konstantinov | .10 | .05 |
| 326 Steve Yzerman | .75 | .35 |
| 327 Keith Primeau | .15 | .07 |
| 328 Shawn Burr | .10 | .05 |
| 329 Chris Osgood | 1.50 | .70 |
| 330 Ray Sheppard | .10 | .05 |
| 331 Mike Sillinger | .10 | .05 |
| 332 Terry Carkner | .10 | .05 |
| 333 Bob Probert | .15 | .07 |
| 334 Adam Bennett | .10 | .05 |
| 335 Dave Manson | .10 | .05 |
| 336 Zdeno Ciger | .10 | .05 |
| 337 Louie DeBrusk | .10 | .05 |
| 338 Shayne Corson | .10 | .05 |
| 339 Vladimir Vujtek | .10 | .05 |
| 340 Tyler Wright | .10 | .05 |
| 341 Ilya Byakin | .10 | .05 |
| 342 Craig MacTavish | .10 | .05 |
| 343 Brian Benning | .10 | .05 |
| 344 Mark Fitzpatrick | .15 | .07 |
| 345 Gord Murphy | .10 | .05 |
| 346 Jesse Belanger | .10 | .05 |
| 347 Joe Cirella | .10 | .05 |
| 348 Tom Fitzgerald | .10 | .05 |
| 349 Andrei Lomakin | .10 | .05 |
| 350 Bill Lindsay | .10 | .05 |
| 351 Len Barrie | .10 | .05 |
| 352 Frank Pietrangelo | .15 | .07 |
| 353 Pat Verbeek | .10 | .05 |
| 354 Jim Storm | .10 | .05 |
| 355 Mark Janssens | .10 | .05 |
| 356 Darren Turcotte | .10 | .05 |
| 357 Jim McKenzie | .10 | .05 |
| 358 Brad McCrimmon | .10 | .05 |
| 359 Andrew Cassels | .10 | .05 |
| 360 James Patrick | .10 | .05 |
| 361 Bob Jay | .10 | .05 |
| 362 Tomas Sandstrom | .10 | .05 |
| 363 Pat Conacher | .10 | .05 |
| 364 Shawn McEachern | .10 | .05 |
| 365 Jari Kurri | .15 | .07 |
| 366 Dominic Lavoie | .10 | .05 |
| 367 Dave Taylor | .15 | .07 |
| 368 Jimmy Carson | .10 | .05 |
| 369 Mike Donnelly | .10 | .05 |
| 370 Lyle Odelein | .10 | .05 |
| 371 Brian Bellows | .10 | .05 |
| 372 Guy Carbonneau | .10 | .05 |
| 373 Mathieu Schneider | .10 | .05 |
| 374 Stephan Lebeau | .10 | .05 |
| 375 Benoit Brunet | .10 | .05 |
| 376 Kevin Haller | .10 | .05 |
| 377 J.J. Daigneault | .10 | .05 |
| 378 Kirk Muller | .10 | .05 |
| 379 Jason Smith | .10 | .05 |
| 380 Martin Brodeur | .75 | .35 |
| 381 Corey Millen | .10 | .05 |
| 382 Bill Guerin | .10 | .05 |
| 383 Valeri Zelepukin | .10 | .05 |
| 384 Tom Chorske | .10 | .05 |
| 385 Bobby Holik | .10 | .05 |
| 386 Jaroslav Modry | .10 | .05 |
| 387 Ken Daneyko | .10 | .05 |
| 388 Uwe Krupp | .10 | .05 |
| 389 Pierre Turgeon | .15 | .07 |
| 390 Marty McInnis | .10 | .05 |
| 391 Patrick Flatley | .10 | .05 |
| 392 Tom Kurvers | .10 | .05 |
| 393 Brad Dalgarno | .10 | .05 |
| 394 Steve Junker | .10 | .05 |
| 395 David Volek | .10 | .05 |
| 396 Benoit Hogue | .10 | .05 |
| 397 Zigmund Palffy | .25 | .11 |
| 399 Joby Messier | .10 | .05 |
| 400 Mike Gartner | .15 | .07 |
| 401 Joey Kocur | .10 | .05 |
| 402 Ed Olczyk | .10 | .05 |
| 403 Doug Lidster | .10 | .05 |
| 404A Greg Gilbert | .10 | .05 |

| | | |
|---|---|---|
| 404B Steve Larmer UER | .15 | .07 |
| (Should be 398) | | |
| 405 Glenn Healy | .15 | .07 |
| 406 Dennis Vial | .10 | .05 |
| 407 Darcy Loewen | .10 | .05 |
| 408 Bob Kudelski | .10 | .05 |
| 409 Hank Lammens | .10 | .05 |
| 410 Jarmo Kekalainen | .10 | .05 |
| 411 Darren Rumble | .10 | .05 |
| 412 Francois Leroux | .10 | .05 |
| 413 Troy Mallette | .10 | .05 |
| 414 Bill Huard | .10 | .05 |
| 415 Ryan McGill | .10 | .05 |
| 416 Eric Lindros | 1.00 | .45 |
| 417 Dominic Roussel | .15 | .07 |
| 418 Jason Bowen | .10 | .05 |
| 419 Andre Faust | .10 | .05 |
| 420 Stewart Malgunas | .10 | .05 |
| 421 Kevin Dineen | .10 | .05 |
| 422 Yves Racine | .10 | .05 |
| 423 Garry Galley | .10 | .05 |
| 424 Doug Brown | .10 | .05 |
| 425 Mario Lemieux | 1.25 | .55 |
| 426 Ladislav Karabin | .10 | .05 |
| 427 Grant Jennings | .10 | .05 |
| 428 Rick Tocchet | .15 | .07 |
| 429 Jeff Daniels | .10 | .05 |
| 430 Peter Taglianetti | .10 | .05 |
| 431 Bryan Trottier | .15 | .07 |
| 432 Kjell Samuelsson | .10 | .05 |
| 433 Rene Corbet | .10 | .05 |
| 434 Iain Fraser | .10 | .05 |
| 435 Mats Sundin | .15 | .07 |
| 436 Curtis Leschyshyn | .10 | .05 |
| 437 Claude LaPointe | .10 | .05 |
| 438 Valeri Kamensky | .15 | .07 |
| 439 Mike Ricci | .10 | .05 |
| 440 Chris Lindberg | .10 | .05 |
| 441 Alexei Gusarov | .10 | .05 |
| 442 Tom Tilley | .10 | .05 |
| 443 Craig Janney | .15 | .07 |
| 444 Vitali Karamnov | .10 | .05 |
| 445 Bob Bassen | .10 | .05 |
| 446 Igor Korolev | .10 | .05 |
| 447 Kevin Miehm | .10 | .05 |
| 448 Tony Hrkac | .10 | .05 |
| 449 Garth Butcher | .10 | .05 |
| 450 Vitali Prokhorov | .10 | .05 |
| 451 Arturs Irbe | .15 | .07 |
| 452 Jay More | .10 | .05 |
| 453 Bob Errey | .10 | .05 |
| 454 Mike Sullivan | .10 | .05 |
| 455 Jeff Norton | .10 | .05 |
| 456 Gaeten Duchesne | .10 | .05 |
| 457 Doug Zmolek | .10 | .05 |
| 458 Mike Rathje | .10 | .05 |
| 459 Jamie Baker | .10 | .05 |
| 460 Joe Reekie | .10 | .05 |
| 461 Mark Bureau | .10 | .05 |
| 462 John Tucker | .10 | .05 |
| 463 Bill McDougall | .10 | .05 |
| 464 Danton Cole | .10 | .05 |
| 465 Brian Bradley | .10 | .05 |
| 466 Jason Lafreniere | .10 | .05 |
| 467 Donald Dufresne | .10 | .05 |
| 468 Daren Puppa | .15 | .07 |
| 469 Doug Gilmour | .25 | .11 |
| 470 Damian Rhodes | .15 | .07 |
| 471 Matt Martin | .10 | .05 |
| 472 Bill Berg | .10 | .05 |
| 473 John Cullen | .10 | .05 |
| 474 Rob Pearson | .10 | .05 |
| 475 Wendel Clark | .15 | .07 |
| 476 Mark Osborne | .10 | .05 |
| 477 Dmitri Mironov | .10 | .05 |
| 478A Kay Whitmore | .15 | .07 |
| 478B Kris King UER | .10 | .05 |
| (Should be 498) | | |
| 479 Shawn Antoski | .10 | .05 |
| 480 Greg Adams | .10 | .05 |
| 481 Dave Babych | .10 | .05 |
| 482 John McIntyre | .10 | .05 |
| 483 Jyrki Lumme | .10 | .05 |
| 484 Jose Charbonneau | .10 | .05 |
| 485 Gino Odjick | .10 | .05 |
| 486 Dana Murzyn | .10 | .05 |
| 487 Michal Pivonka | .10 | .05 |
| 488 Dave Poulin | .10 | .05 |
| 489 Sylvain Cote | .10 | .05 |
| 490 Jason Woolley | .10 | .05 |
| 491 Kelly Miller | .10 | .05 |
| 492 Randy Burridge | .10 | .05 |
| 493 Kevin Kaminski | .10 | .05 |
| 494 John Slaney | .10 | .05 |
| 495 Keith Jones | .10 | .05 |
| 496 Harijs Vitolinsh | .10 | .05 |
| 497 Nelson Emerson | .10 | .05 |
| 499 Darrin Shannon | .10 | .05 |
| 500 Stephane Quintal | .10 | .05 |
| 501 Luciano Borsato | .10 | .05 |
| 502 Thomas Steen | .10 | .05 |
| 503 Alexei Zhamnov | .15 | .07 |
| 504 Paul Ysebaert | .10 | .05 |
| 505 Jeff Friesen | .60 | .25 |
| 506 Niklas Sundstrom | .10 | .05 |
| 507 Nick Stajduhar | .10 | .05 |
| 508 Jamie Storr | .40 | .18 |
| 509 Valeri Varvio | .10 | .05 |
| 510 Jason Bonsignore | .10 | .05 |
| 511 Mats Lindgren | .10 | .05 |
| 512 Yannick Dube | .10 | .05 |
| 513 Todd Harvey | .10 | .05 |
| 514 Ladislav Prokupek | .10 | .05 |
| 515 Tomas Vlasak | .10 | .05 |
| 516 Josef Marha | .10 | .05 |
| 517 Tomas Blazek | .10 | .05 |

| | | |
|---|---|---|
| 518 Zdenek Nedved | .10 | .05 |
| 519 Jaroslav Miklenda | .15 | .07 |
| 520 Janne Niinimaa | 2.00 | .90 |
| 521 Saku Koivu | 1.25 | .55 |
| 522 Tommi Miettinen | .15 | .07 |
| 523 Tuomas Gronman | .10 | .05 |
| 524 Jani Nikko | .10 | .05 |
| 525 Jouni Vauhkonen | .10 | .05 |
| 526 Nikolai Tsulygin | .10 | .05 |
| 527 Vadim Sharifjanov | .15 | .07 |
| 528 Valeri Bure | .15 | .07 |
| 529 Alexander Kharlamov | .10 | .05 |
| 530 Nikolai Zavarukhin | .10 | .05 |
| 531 Oleg-Tverdovsky | .50 | .23 |
| 532 Sergei Kondrashkin | .10 | .05 |
| 533 Evgeni Ryabchikov | .10 | .05 |
| 534 Mats Lindgren | .10 | .05 |
| 535 Kenny Jonsson | .10 | .05 |
| 536 Edvin Frylen | .10 | .05 |
| 537 Mathias Johansson | .10 | .05 |
| 538 Johan Davidsson | .10 | .05 |
| 539 Mikael Hakansson | .10 | .05 |
| 540 Anders Eriksson | .10 | .05 |

## 1993-94 Parkhurst Emerald Ice

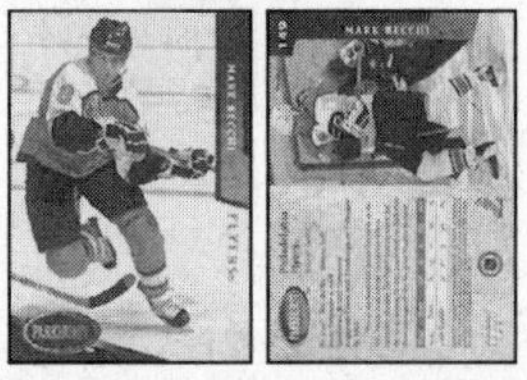

The 540 cards in this parallel set can be found one per foil pack and two per jumbo pack. The Parkhurst logo, team name, and vertical strip near the right edge of the card are adorned with green foil, as opposed to the silver foil used for the basic card set.

| | MINT | NRMT |
|---|---|---|
| COMPLETE SET (540) | 250.00 | 110.00 |
| COMPLETE SERIES 1 (270) | 125.00 | 55.00 |
| COMPLETE SERIES 2 (270) | 125.00 | 55.00 |
| COMMON CARD (1-540) | .25 | .11 |

*STARS: 3X TO 6X BASIC CARDS
*YOUNG STARS: 2.5X TO 5X BASIC CARDS

## 1993-94 Parkhurst Calder Candidates

Randomly inserted in U.S. second-series retail foil packs, these 20 cards feature color player action shots of some of the NHL's top rookies on their fronts. The cards are numbered on the back with a "C" prefix. The silver trade card randomly inserted in '93-94 Parkhurst packs was redeemable for this Calder Candidates insert set; the gold trade card was redeemable for a gold foil-enhanced edition; multipliers can be found below to determine values for these. The expiration date for both trade cards was July 31st, 1994.

| | MINT | NRMT |
|---|---|---|
| COMPLETE SET (20) | 50.00 | 22.00 |
| COMMON CARD (C1-C20) | 1.00 | .45 |
| COMP.GOLD SET (20) | 80.00 | 36.00 |

*GOLD REDEEMED CARDS: 1X TO 1.5X SILVER VERSION

| | | |
|---|---|---|
| C1 Alexandre Daigle | 3.00 | 1.35 |
| C2 Chris Pronger | 3.00 | 1.35 |
| C3 Chris Gratton | 3.00 | 1.35 |
| C4 Rob Niedermayer | 3.00 | 1.35 |
| C5 Markus Naslund | 1.00 | .45 |
| C6 Jason Arnott | 6.00 | 2.70 |
| C7 Pierre Sevigny | 1.00 | .45 |
| C8 Jarkko Varvio | 1.00 | .45 |
| C9 Dean McAmmond | 1.00 | .45 |
| C10 Alexei Yashin | 3.00 | 1.35 |
| C11 Philippe Boucher | 1.00 | .45 |
| C12 Mikael Renberg | 3.00 | 1.35 |
| C13 Chris Simon | 1.00 | .45 |
| C14 Brent Gretzky | 1.00 | .45 |
| C15 Jesse Belanger | 1.00 | .45 |
| C16 Jocelyn Thibault | 8.00 | 3.60 |
| C17 Chris Osgood | 12.00 | 5.50 |
| C18 Derek Plante | 4.00 | 1.80 |
| C19 Iain Fraser | 1.00 | .45 |
| C20 Vesa Viitakoski | 1.00 | .45 |
| NNO Gold Trade Card | 6.00 | 2.70 |
| NNO Silver Trade Card | 4.00 | 1.80 |

## 1993-94 Parkhurst Cherry's Playoff Heroes

Randomly inserted in Canadian second-series foil packs, these twenty different cards feature color player action shots on their fronts and a photo of Machiavellian TV personality Don Cherry -- who chose the players to be featured in this set based on his unique set of standards -- on the back. The cards are numbered with a "D" prefix.

| | MINT | NRMT |
|---|---|---|
| COMPLETE SET (20) | 300.00 | 135.00 |
| COMMON CARD (D1-D20) | 4.00 | 1.80 |

| | | |
|---|---|---|
| D1 Wayne Gretzky | 50.00 | 22.00 |
| D2 Mario Lemieux | 40.00 | 18.00 |
| D3 Al MacInnis | 4.00 | 1.80 |
| D4 Mark Messier | 10.00 | 4.50 |
| D5 Dino Ciccarelli | 4.00 | 1.80 |
| D6 Dale Hunter | 4.00 | 1.80 |
| D7 Grant Fuhr | 6.00 | 2.70 |
| D8 Paul Coffey | 8.00 | 3.60 |
| D9 Doug Gilmour | 6.00 | 2.70 |
| D10 Patrick Roy | 40.00 | 18.00 |
| D11 Alexandre Daigle | 6.00 | 2.70 |
| D12 Chris Gratton | 4.00 | 1.80 |
| D13 Chris Pronger | 6.00 | 2.70 |
| D14 Felix Potvin | 8.00 | 3.60 |
| D15 Eric Lindros | 30.00 | 13.50 |
| D16 Maurice Richard | 12.00 | 5.50 |
| D17 Gordie Howe | 20.00 | 9.00 |
| D18 Henri Richard | 6.00 | 2.70 |
| D19 Reggie Leach | 4.00 | 1.80 |
| D20 Checklist | 15.00 | 6.75 |
| Don Cherry and Blue | | |

## 1993-94 Parkhurst East/West Stars

Randomly inserted in U.S. second-series hobby packs, these cards feature color player action shots on their fronts. They are borderless, except on the right, where a blue stripe carries the player's name in vertical white lettering highlighted by white stars. The set's gold-foil logo appears at the upper right; the gold foil-stamped Parkhurst logo rests at the lower left. The first ten cards feature Eastern Conference stars, numbered with an "E" prefix, while the last ten cards present Western Conference stars, numbered with a "W" prefix.

| | MINT | NRMT |
|---|---|---|
| COMPLETE SET (20) | 120.00 | 55.00 |
| COMPLETE EAST SERIES (10) | 60.00 | 27.00 |
| COMPLETE WEST SET (10) | 60.00 | 27.00 |
| COMMON EAST (E1-E10) | 2.50 | 1.10 |
| COMMON WEST (W1-W10) | 2.50 | 1.10 |

| | | |
|---|---|---|
| E1 Eric Lindros | 12.00 | 5.50 |
| E2 Mario Lemieux | 15.00 | 6.75 |
| E3 Alexandre Daigle | 2.50 | 1.10 |
| E4 Patrick Roy | 15.00 | 6.75 |
| E5 Rob Niedermayer | 2.50 | 1.10 |
| E6 Chris Gratton | 2.50 | 1.10 |
| E7 Alexei Yashin | 2.50 | 1.10 |
| E8 Pat LaFontaine | 2.50 | 1.10 |
| E9 Joe Sakic | 6.00 | 2.70 |
| E10 Pierre Turgeon | 5.00 | 2.20 |
| W1 Wayne Gretzky | 20.00 | 9.00 |
| W2 Pavel Bure | 6.00 | 2.70 |
| W3 Teemu Selanne | 10.00 | 4.50 |
| W4 Doug Gilmour | 5.00 | 2.20 |
| W5 Steve Yzerman | 10.00 | 4.50 |
| W6 Jeremy Roenick | 6.00 | 2.70 |
| W7 Brett Hull | 5.00 | 2.20 |
| W8 Jason Arnott | 5.00 | 2.20 |
| W9 Felix Potvin | 2.50 | 1.10 |
| W10 Sergei Fedorov | 6.00 | 2.70 |

## 1993-94 Parkhurst First Overall

Randomly inserted in Canadian first-series retail foil packs, these ten standard-size cards feature on their fronts color action shots of players drafted first overall in the annual NHL

Entry Draft over the past decade. They are borderless, except on the left, where a copper-foil stripe carries the Parkhurst name, and a bar that shades from green to black carries the player's name in vertical white lettering. The copper-foil set logo at the lower right carries the year that the player was "First Overall" in the NHL draft. The horizontal back carries a color player action cutout on the right. On the left are the player's team name, position, career highlights, and chart showing the Top-10 NHL draft picks the year the featured player was the first. The cards are numbered on the back with an "F" prefix.

| | MINT | NRMT |
|---|---|---|
| COMPLETE SET (10) | 60.00 | 27.00 |
| COMMON CARD (F1-F10) | 2.50 | 1.10 |

| | | |
|---|---|---|
| F1 Alexandre Daigle | 6.00 | 2.70 |
| F2 Roman Hamrlik | 6.00 | 2.70 |
| F3 Eric Lindros | 20.00 | 9.00 |
| F4 Owen Nolan | 6.00 | 2.70 |
| F5 Mats Sundin | 6.00 | 2.70 |
| F6 Mike Modano | 6.00 | 2.70 |
| F7 Pierre Turgeon | 5.00 | 2.20 |
| F8 Joe Murphy | 2.50 | 1.10 |
| F9 Wendel Clark | 6.00 | 2.70 |
| F10 Mario Lemieux | 25.00 | 11.00 |

## 1993-94 Parkhurst Parkie Reprints

A continuation of the '92-93 Parkie Reprints set, these 40 (numbered 33-68, plus four checklists) cards measure the standard-size. The first ten cards (33-41, plus checklist (5) were randomly inserted in '93-94 Parkhurst series I foil packs. The second series (42-50, plus checklist (6) were random inserts in Parkhurst series one jumbo packs only. The third series (51-59, plus checklist (7) were random inserts in all series two Parkhurst packs. The fourth Parkie Reprints series (60-68, plus checklist (8) were random inserts in Parkhurst series two jumbo packs. The fronts are that of 1951-64 Parkhurst styles, but all carry a color player photo. The backs carry the information from the original card. The print varies from red to black to a combination. The cards are numbered on the back with a "PR" prefix. A hobby exclusive Parkie Reprints bonus pack was included in every series one and series two case.

| | MINT | NRMT |
|---|---|---|
| COMPLETE SET (40) | 300.00 | 135.00 |
| COMP.SER.1 (PR33-PR41/CL5) | 80.00 | 36.00 |
| COMP.SER.2 (PR42-PR50/CL6) | 90.00 | 40.00 |
| COMP.SER.3 (PR51-PR59/CL7) | 70.00 | 32.00 |
| COMP.SER.4 (PR60-PR68/CL8) | 70.00 | 32.00 |
| COMMON CARD (PR33-PR68) | 5.00 | 2.20 |

| | | |
|---|---|---|
| PR33 Gordie Howe | 20.00 | 9.00 |
| PR34 Tim Horton | 10.00 | 4.50 |
| PR35 Bill Barilko | 10.00 | 4.50 |
| PR36 Elmer Lach | 5.00 | 2.20 |
| Maurice Richard | | |
| PR37 Terry Sawchuk | 12.00 | 5.50 |
| PR38 George Armstrong | 5.00 | 2.20 |
| PR39 William Harris | 5.00 | 2.20 |
| PR40 Doug Harvey | 5.00 | 2.20 |
| PR41 Gump Worsley | 5.00 | 2.20 |
| PR42 Gordie Howe | 20.00 | 9.00 |
| PR43 Jacques Plante | 12.00 | 5.50 |
| PR44 Frank Mahovlich | 5.00 | 2.20 |
| PR45 Fern Flaman | 5.00 | 2.20 |
| PR46 Bernie Geoffrion | 10.00 | 4.50 |
| PR47 Toe Blake CO | 5.00 | 2.20 |
| PR48 Maurice Richard | 15.00 | 6.75 |
| PR49 Ted Lindsay | 5.00 | 2.20 |
| PR50 Camille Henry | 5.00 | 2.20 |
| PR51 Gordie Howe | 20.00 | 9.00 |
| PR52 Jean-Guy Talbot | 5.00 | 2.20 |
| PR53 Terry Sawchuk | 5.00 | 2.20 |
| PR54 Warren Godfrey | 5.00 | 2.20 |
| PR55 Tom Johnson | 5.00 | 2.20 |
| PR56 Bert Olmstead | 5.00 | 2.20 |
| PR57 Cal Gardner | 5.00 | 2.20 |
| PR58 Red Kelly | 5.00 | 2.20 |
| PR59 Phil Goyette | 5.00 | 2.20 |

❑ PR60 Gordie Howe 20.00 9.00
❑ PR61 Lou Fontinato 5.00 2.20
❑ PR62 Bill Dineen 5.00 2.20
❑ PR63 Maurice Richard 15.00 6.75
❑ PR64 Vic Stasiuk 5.00 2.20
❑ PR65 Marcel Pronovost 5.00 2.20
❑ PR66 Ed Litzenberger 5.00 2.20
❑ PR67 Dave Keon 5.00 2.20
❑ PR68 Dollard St. Laurent 5.00 2.20
❑ CL5 Parkies Checklist 5 10.00 4.50
❑ CL6 Parkies Checklist 6 10.00 4.50
❑ CL7 Parkies Checklist 7 10.00 4.50
❑ CL8 Parkies Checklist 8 10.00 4.50

## 1993-94 Parkhurst Parkie Reprints Case Inserts

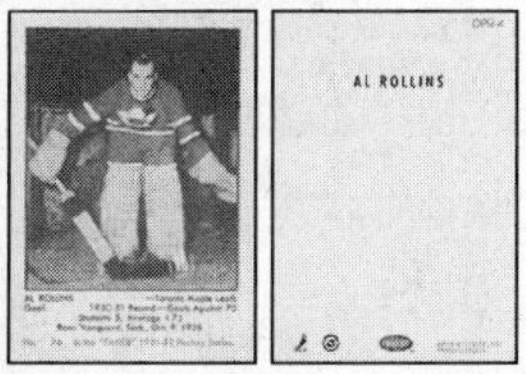

These sets were inserted one per hobby case. Cards 1-6 were found in series I cases, while 7-12 were inserted in series II cases. Parkhurst selected vintage cards from its past to reprint in this 12-card standard-size set. The cards are coated on both sides and are easily recognizable as reprints. The cards are numbered on the back with the prefix "DPR".

| | MINT | NRMT |
|---|---|---|
| COMP.SERIES 1 SET (6) | 30.00 | 13.50 |
| COMP.SERIES 2 SET (6) | 25.00 | 11.00 |
| COMMON CARD (1-12) | 6.00 | 2.70 |

❑ 1 Gordie Howe 15.00 6.75
❑ 2 Milt Schmidt 6.00 2.70
❑ 3 Tim Horton 8.00 3.60
❑ 4 Al Rollins 6.00 2.70
❑ 5 Maurice Richard 10.00 4.50
❑ 6 Harry Howell 6.00 2.70
❑ 7 Gordie Howe 15.00 6.75
❑ 8 Johnny Bower 10.00 4.50
❑ 9 Dean Prentice 6.00 2.70
❑ 10 Leo Labine 6.00 2.70
❑ 11 Harry Watson 7.00 3.10
❑ 12 Dickie Moore 7.00 3.10

## 1993-94 Parkhurst USA/Canada Gold

Randomly inserted at the rate of 1:30 U.S. first-series foil packs, Upper Deck selected the top five players from NHL teams based in the United States and the top five players from NHL teams based in Canada for this 10-card standard-size set. Accordingly, cards 1-5 are USA Gold while cards 6-10 are Canadian Gold. The fronts of the USA cards feature full-bleed colour action player photos with a gold and blue vertical stripe on the left featuring a gold star, the word "USA" and the player's name. The Canadian version is the same except that the stripe is gold and red and features a maple leaf instead of a star and the word "Canada". A gold-foil Parkhurst logo appears in the lower right corner. The horizontal backs feature a color action cutout on a gold blended background using the same stripe as the front but on the right side. The player profile is to the left of the cutout. The cards are numbered on the back with a "G" prefix.

| | MINT | NRMT |
|---|---|---|
| COMPLETE SET (10) | 70.00 | 32.00 |
| COMMON CARD (G1-G10) | 3.00 | 1.35 |

❑ G1 Wayne Gretzky 15.00 6.75
❑ G2 Mario Lemieux 12.00 5.50
❑ G3 Eric Lindros 12.00 5.50
❑ G4 Brett Hull 4.00 1.80
❑ G5 Rob Niedermayer 3.00 1.35
❑ G6 Alexandre Daigle 3.00 1.35
❑ G7 Pavel Bure 5.00 2.20
❑ G8 Teemu Selanne 5.00 2.20
❑ G9 Patrick Roy 12.00 5.50
❑ G10 Doug Gilmour 4.00 1.80

## 1994 Parkhurst Missing Link

This 180-card set attempts to capture what a Parkhurst set might have looked like had one been produced for the 1956-57 NHL campaign. Although the inclusion of all six original teams may seem somewhat anachronistic (keeping in mind that Parkhurst, at that time, issued cards featuring Canadian-based players only) the set does capture the old-time flavor. The simple design includes an isolated player photo (taken during the 1955-56 season) over a cream colored background. A black bar runs along the left side of the card front, and contains the player name and team logo. Card backs include stats for the 1955-56 season and biographical information in both French and English. Subsets include All-Stars (135-146), Trophy Winners (147-152), Action Shots (153-168), Team Leaders (169-174) and Playoffs (175-178). The set was issued in 10-card wax packs and production was limited to 1956 numbered cases for each of the Canadian and American markets.

| | MINT | NRMT |
|---|---|---|
| COMPLETE SET (180) | 35.00 | 16.00 |
| COMMON CARD (1-180) | .10 | .05 |

❑ 1 Jerry Toppazzini .10 .05
❑ 2 Fern Flaman .35 .16
❑ 3 Fleming MacKell .10 .05
❑ 4 Leo Labine .20 .09
❑ 5 John Peirson .15 .07
❑ 6 Don McKenney .15 .07
❑ 7 Bob Armstrong .10 .05
❑ 8 Real Chevrefils .10 .05
❑ 9 Vic Stasiuk .15 .07
❑ 10 Cal Gardner .10 .05
❑ 11 Leo Boivin .35 .16
❑ 12 Jack Caffery .10 .05
❑ 13 Bob Beckett .10 .05
❑ 14 Jack Bionda .10 .05
❑ 15 Claude Pronovost .35 .16
❑ 16 Larry Regan .10 .05
❑ 17 Terry Sawchuk 2.50 1.10
❑ 18 Doug Mohns .20 .09
❑ 19 Marcel Bonin .15 .07
❑ 20 Allan Stanley .50 .23
❑ 21 Milt Schmidt CO .50 .23
❑ 22 Al Dewsbury .10 .05
❑ 23 Glen Skov .15 .07
❑ 24 Ed Litzenberger .15 .07
❑ 25 Nick Mickoski .10 .05
❑ 26 Wally Hergesheimer .10 .05
❑ 27 Jack McIntyre .10 .05
❑ 28 Al Rollins .50 .23
❑ 29 Hank Ciesla .10 .05
❑ 30 Gus Mortson .10 .05
❑ 31 Elmer Vasko .15 .07
❑ 32 Pierre Pilote .50 .23
❑ 33 Ron Ingram .10 .05
❑ 34 Frank Martin .10 .05
❑ 35 Forbes Kennedy .20 .09
❑ 36 Harry Watson .15 .07
❑ 37 Eddie Kachur .10 .05
❑ 38 Hec Lalande .10 .05
❑ 39 Eric Nesterenko .20 .09
❑ 40 Ben Woit .10 .05
❑ 41 Ken Mosdell .15 .07
❑ 42 Tommy Ivan CO .35 .16
❑ 43 Gordie Howe 4.00 1.80
❑ 44 Ted Lindsay .50 .23
❑ 45 Norm Ullman .50 .23
❑ 46 Glenn Hall 1.00 .45
❑ 47 Billy Dea .10 .05
❑ 48 Bill McNeill .10 .05
❑ 49 Earl Reibel .15 .07
❑ 50 Bill Dineen .20 .09
❑ 51 Warren Godfrey .15 .07
❑ 52 Red Kelly .50 .23
❑ 53 Marty Pavelich .10 .05
❑ 54 Lorne Ferguson .10 .05
❑ 55 Larry Hillman .15 .07
❑ 56 John Bucyk .50 .23
❑ 57 Metro Prystai .10 .05
❑ 58 Marcel Pronovost .50 .23
❑ 59 Alex Delvecchio .50 .23
❑ 60 Murray Costello .10 .05
❑ 61 Al Arbour .50 .23
❑ 62 Bucky Hollingworth .10 .05
❑ 63 Jim Skinner CO .10 .05
❑ 64 Jean Beliveau 2.00 .90
❑ 65 Maurice Richard 2.50 1.10
❑ 66 Henri Richard .50 .23
❑ 67 Doug Harvey .50 .23
❑ 68 Bernie Geoffrion .75 .35
❑ 69 Dollard St. Laurent .25 .11
❑ 70 Dickie Moore .50 .23
❑ 71 Bert Olmstead .35 .16
❑ 72 Jacques Plante 2.50 1.10
❑ 73 Claude Provost .35 .16
❑ 74 Phil Goyette .15 .07
❑ 75 Andre Pronovost .15 .07
❑ 76 Don Marshall .25 .11
❑ 77 Ralph Backstrom .20 .09
❑ 78 Floyd Curry .20 .09
❑ 79 Tom Johnson .50 .23
❑ 80 Jean Guy Talbot .20 .09
❑ 81 Bob Turner .10 .05
❑ 82 Connie Broden .10 .05
❑ 83 Jackie Leclair .10 .05
❑ 84 Toe Blake CO .75 .35
❑ 85 Frank Selke MD .50 .23
❑ 86 George Sullivan .10 .05
❑ 87 Larry Cahan .10 .05
❑ 88 Jean Guy Gendron .10 .05
❑ 89 Bill Gadsby .50 .23
❑ 90 Andy Bathgate .50 .23
❑ 91 Dean Prentice .10 .05
❑ 92 Gump Worsley 1.00 .45
❑ 93 Lou Fontinato .15 .07
❑ 94 Gerry Foley .10 .05
❑ 95 Larry Popein .15 .07
❑ 96 Harry Howell .50 .23
❑ 97 Andy Hebenton .10 .05
❑ 98 Danny Lewicki .10 .05
❑ 99 Dave Creighton .10 .05
❑ 100 Camille Henry .10 .05
❑ 101 Jack Evans .10 .05
❑ 102 Ron Murphy .10 .05
❑ 103 Johnny Bower .75 .35
❑ 104 Parker MacDonald .10 .05
❑ 105 Bronco Horvath .20 .09
❑ 106 Bruce Cline .10 .05
❑ 107 Ivan Irwin .10 .05
❑ 108 Phil Watson CO .10 .05
❑ 109 Sid Smith .10 .05
❑ 110 Ron Stewart .10 .05
❑ 111 Rudy Migay .10 .05
❑ 112 Tod Sloan .15 .07
❑ 113 Bob Pulford .50 .23
❑ 114 Marc Reaume .15 .07
❑ 115 Jim Morrison .15 .07
❑ 116 Ted Kennedy .50 .23
❑ 117 Gerry James .20 .09
❑ 118 Brian Cullen .25 .11
❑ 119 Jim Thomson .10 .05
❑ 120 Barry Cullen .10 .05
❑ 121 Al MacNeil .15 .07
❑ 122 Gary Aldcorn .10 .05
❑ 123 Bob Baun .50 .23
❑ 124 Hugh Bolton .10 .05
❑ 125 George Armstrong .50 .23
❑ 126 Dick Duff .50 .23
❑ 127 Tim Horton 2.00 .90
❑ 128 Ed Chadwick .50 .23
❑ 129 Billy Harris .35 .16
❑ 130 Mike Nykoluk .10 .05
❑ 131 Noel Price .10 .05
❑ 132 Ken Girard .10 .05
❑ 133 Howie Meeker .50 .23
❑ 134 Hap Day CO .25 .11
❑ 135 Jacques Plante AS 1.00 .45
❑ 136 Doug Harvey AS .50 .23
❑ 137 Bill Gadsby AS .50 .23
❑ 138 Jean Beliveau AS .75 .35
❑ 139 Maurice Richard AS 1.00 .45
❑ 140 Ted Lindsay AS .35 .16
❑ 141 Glenn Hall AS .50 .23
❑ 142 Red Kelly AS .50 .23
❑ 143 Tom Johnson AS .50 .23
❑ 144 Tod Sloan AS .15 .07
❑ 145 Gordie Howe AS 1.50 .70
❑ 146 Bert Olmstead AS .25 .11
❑ 147 Earl Reibel AW Lady Byng .10 .05
❑ 148 Doug Harvey AW Norris .50 .23
❑ 149 Jean Beliveau AW Hart .75 .35
❑ 150 Jean Beliveau AW Art Ross .75 .35
❑ 151 Jacques Plante AW Vezina 1.00 .45
❑ 152 Glenn Hall AW Calder .50 .23
❑ 153 Terry Sawchuk IA 1.00 .45
❑ 154 Action Shot .25 .11
❑ 155 Action Shot .25 .11
❑ 156 Jean Beliveau IA .75 .35
❑ 157 Jean Beliveau IA .75 .35
❑ 158 Action Shot .25 .11
❑ 159 Action Shot .25 .11
❑ 160 Gordie Howe IA 1.50 .70
❑ 161 Jacques Plante IA 1.00 .45
❑ 162 Gordie Howe IA 1.50 .70
❑ 163 Jacques Plante IA 1.00 .45
❑ 164 Action Shot .25 .11
❑ 165 Action Shot .25 .11
❑ 166 Action Shot .25 .11
❑ 167 Terry Sawchuk IA 1.00 .45
❑ 168 Terry Sawchuk IA 1.00 .45
❑ 169 Vic Stasiuk SL .15 .07
❑ 170 George Sullivan SL .15 .07
❑ 171 Gordie Howe SL 1.50 .70
❑ 172 Jean Beliveau SL .75 .35
❑ 173 Andy Bathgate SL .50 .23
❑ 174 Tod Sloan SL .15 .07
❑ 175 Stanley Cup .25 .11
❑ 176 Stanley Cup .25 .11
❑ 177 Stanley Cup .25 .11
❑ 178 Stanley Cup .25 .11
❑ 179 Checklist 1 .10 .05
❑ 180 Checklist 2 .10 .05

## 1994 Parkhurst Missing Link Autographs

The 1994 Parkhurst Missing Link Autograph set is comprised of six Hall of Famers. Randomly inserted in Missing Link packs, the cards are autographed on the front and numbered "X of 956" on the back. The cards are also numbered for set purposes A1-A6. The design is different from those found in the Missing Link issue. Card fronts are color, but do not contain the player's name (except for autograph) or team name. The backs provide a congratulatory note to the collector.

| | MINT | NRMT |
|---|---|---|
| COMPLETE SET (6) | 750.00 | 350.00 |
| COMMON CARD (1-6) | 100.00 | 45.00 |

❑ 1 Gordie Howe 200.00 90.00
❑ 2 Maurice Richard 175.00 80.00
❑ 3 Bernie Geoffrion 100.00 45.00
❑ 4 Gump Worsley 100.00 45.00
❑ 5 Jean Beliveau 150.00 70.00
❑ 6 Frank Mahovlich 100.00 45.00

## 1994 Parkhurst Missing Link Future Stars

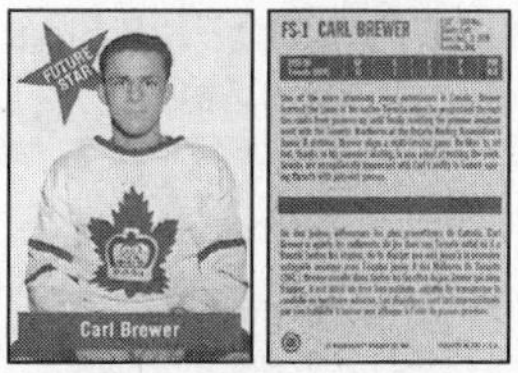

The six cards in this set were randomly inserted in both US and Canadian product and feature well-known players who had yet to make their mark in the league by the 1956-57 season, the year which is represented in this set. Card fronts feature an isolated player photo (depicting the player in his junior sweater) over a cream colored background. The set logo appears in the top left corner, while the player's name is found in a blue bar along the bottom. Card backs include 1955-56 amateur stats, a report on the player's prospects in both French and English, and a merchandise offer. Cards are numbered with an "FS" prefix.

| | MINT | NRMT |
|---|---|---|
| COMPLETE SET (6) | 70.00 | 32.00 |
| COMMON CARD (FS1-FS6) | 8.00 | 3.60 |

❑ FS1 Carl Brewer 8.00 3.60
❑ FS2 Dave Keon 12.00 5.50
❑ FS3 Stan Mikita 18.00 8.00
❑ FS4 Eddie Shack 12.00 5.50
❑ FS5 Frank Mahovlich 18.00 8.00
❑ FS6 Charlie Hodge 12.00 5.50

## 1994 Parkhurst Missing Link Pop-Ups

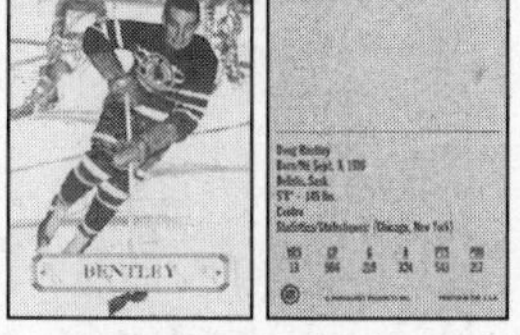

These 12 die-cut cards were randomly inserted over two distribution channels: cards 1-6 in Canadian cases and 7-12 in American product. The cards feature the heroes of hockey's past in a design which approximates the style made famous by the 1936-37 O-Pee-Chee V304D set. The cards are created in such a way that they may be popped open for a 3-D effect; collectors are strongly urged not to follow this course of action unless you're not concerned about the card's value. Card backs contain brief personal information, as well as a wrap-up of career statistics. The cards are numbered with a P prefix in the top left corner. Only 1,000 of each card were circulated.

| | MINT | NRMT |
|---|---|---|
| COMPLETE SET (12) | 350.00 | 160.00 |
| COMPLETE CDN SERIES (6) | 200.00 | 90.00 |
| COMPLETE US SERIES (6) | 150.00 | 70.00 |
| COMMON CARD (P1-P6) | 30.00 | 13.50 |
| COMMON CARD (P7-P12) | 25.00 | 11.00 |

❑ P1 Howie Morenz 50.00 22.00
❑ P2 George Hainsworth 35.00 16.00
❑ P3 Georges Vezina 50.00 22.00
❑ P4 King Clancy 35.00 16.00
❑ P5 Syl Apps 30.00 13.50
❑ P6 Turk Broda 35.00 16.00
❑ P7 Eddie Shore 50.00 22.00
❑ P8 Bill Cook 25.00 11.00
❑ P9 Woody Dumart 25.00 11.00
❑ P10 Lester Patrick 30.00 13.50
❑ P11 Doug Bentley 25.00 11.00
❑ P12 Earl Seibert 25.00 11.00

## 1994 Parkhurst Tall Boys

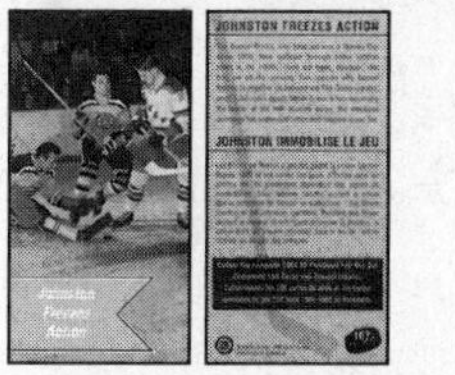

This 180-card set recreates what might have been had the Parkhurst company issued a set of NHL player cards for the 1964-65 season. As the title suggests, the card size matches that of the 1964-65 Topps Tall Boys set (2 1/2" by 4 11/16"). Announced production was 1,964 cases for each of the US and Canadian hobby markets.

| | MINT | NRMT |
|---|---|---|
| COMPLETE SET (180) | 12.00 | 5.50 |
| COMMON CARD (1-180) | .10 | .05 |

❑ 1 John Bucyk .35 .16
❑ 2 Murray Oliver .10 .05
❑ 3 Ted Green .15 .07
❑ 4 Tom Williams .10 .05
❑ 5 Dean Prentice .10 .05
❑ 6 Ed Westfall .10 .05
❑ 7 Orland Kurtenbach .10 .05
❑ 8 Reg Fleming .10 .05
❑ 9 Leo Boivin .15 .07
❑ 10 Bob McCord .10 .05
❑ 11 Bob Leiter .10 .05
❑ 12 Tom Johnson .25 .11
❑ 13 Bob Woytowich .10 .05
❑ 14 Ab McDonald .10 .05
❑ 15 Ed Johnston .25 .11
❑ 16 Forbes Kennedy .15 .07
❑ 17 Murray Balfour .10 .05
❑ 18 Wayne Cashman .15 .07
❑ 19 Don Awrey .10 .05
❑ 20 Gary Dornhoefer .15 .07
❑ 21 Ron Schock .10 .05
❑ 22 Milt Schmidt .50 .23
❑ 23 Ken Wharram .15 .07
❑ 24 Chico Maki .10 .05
❑ 25 Bobby Hull 2.00 .90
❑ 26 Stan Mikita .75 .35
❑ 27 Doug Mohns .15 .07
❑ 28 Denis DeJordy .20 .09
❑ 29 Phil Esposito .50 .23
❑ 30 Elmer Vasko .10 .05
❑ 31 Pierre Pilote .25 .11
❑ 32 Glenn Hall .75 .35
❑ 33 Eric Nesterenko .10 .05
❑ 34 Doug Robinson .10 .05
❑ 35 Matt Ravlich .10 .05
❑ 36 John McKenzie .15 .07
❑ 37 Fred Stanfield .10 .05
❑ 38 Doug Jarrett .10 .05
❑ 39 Dennis Hull .20 .09
❑ 40 Al MacNeil .10 .05
❑ 41 Wayne Hillman .10 .05
❑ 42 Bill Hay .10 .05
❑ 43 Billy Reay .10 .05
❑ 44 Parker MacDonald .10 .05
❑ 45 Floyd Smith .10 .05
❑ 46 Gordie Howe 2.50 1.10
❑ 47 Bruce MacGregor .10 .05
❑ 48 Ron Murphy .10 .05
❑ 49 Doug Barkley .10 .05
❑ 50 Paul Henderson .15 .07
❑ 51 Pit Martin .15 .07
❑ 52 Al Langlois .10 .05
❑ 53 Roger Crozier .25 .11
❑ 54 Bill Gadsby .25 .11
❑ 55 Marcel Pronovost .35 .16
❑ 56 Alex Delvecchio .35 .16
❑ 57 Gary Bergman .10 .05
❑ 58 Norm Ullman .35 .16
❑ 59 Larry Jeffrey .10 .05
❑ 60 Lowell MacDonald .10 .05
❑ 61 Pete Goegan .10 .05
❑ 62 Andre Pronovost .15 .07
❑ 63 Warren Godfrey .15 .07
❑ 64 Ted Lindsay .35 .16
❑ 65 Sid Abel .35 .16
❑ 66 John Ferguson .15 .07
❑ 67 Henri Richard .50 .23
❑ 68 Dave Balon .10 .05
❑ 69 Noel Picard .10 .05
❑ 70 Claude Provost .15 .07
❑ 71 Claude Larose .10 .05
❑ 72 Jacques Laperriere .25 .11

❑ 73 Ralph Backstrom .15 .07
❑ 74 J.C. Tremblay .15 .07
❑ 75 Yvan Cournoyer .35 .16
❑ 76 Jean-Guy Talbot .15 .07
❑ 77 Gilles Tremblay .10 .05
❑ 78 Ted Harris .10 .05
❑ 79 Jim Roberts .10 .05
❑ 80 Red Berenson .15 .07
❑ 81 Gump Worsley .75 .35
❑ 82 Charlie Hodge .25 .11
❑ 83 Terry Harper .10 .05
❑ 84 Bobby Rousseau .10 .05
❑ 85 Jean Beliveau 1.50 .70
❑ 86 Bill Hicke .10 .05
❑ 87 Toe Blake .50 .23
❑ 88 Don Marshall .15 .07
❑ 89 Jean Ratelle .35 .16
❑ 90 Vic Hadfield .10 .05
❑ 91 Earl Ingarfield .10 .05
❑ 92 Harry Howell .35 .16
❑ 93 Rod Seiling .10 .05
❑ 94 Dave Richardson .10 .05
❑ 95 Val Fonteyne .10 .05
❑ 96 Lou Angotti .10 .05
❑ 97 Arnie Brown .10 .05
❑ 98 Don Johns .10 .05
❑ 99 Jim Mikol .10 .05
❑ 100 Jacques Plante 2.00 .90
❑ 101 Marcel Paille .15 .07
❑ 102 Jim Neilson .10 .05
❑ 103 Bob Nevin .10 .05
❑ 104 Rod Gilbert .35 .16
❑ 105 Phil Goyette .10 .05
❑ 106 Dick Duff .25 .11
❑ 107 Camille Henry .10 .05
❑ 108 Red Sullivan .10 .05
❑ 109 Kent Douglas .10 .05
❑ 110 Bob Pulford .15 .07
❑ 111 Dave Keon .50 .23
❑ 112 Don McKenney .10 .05
❑ 113 Pete Stemkowski .10 .05
❑ 114 Carl Brewer .15 .07
❑ 115 Allan Stanley .25 .11
❑ 116 Dickie Moore .35 .16
❑ 117 Ed Shack .50 .23
❑ 118 Larry Hillman .10 .05
❑ 119 Terry Sawchuk 2.00 .90
❑ 120 Bob Baun .25 .11
❑ 121 Brit Selby .10 .05
❑ 122 George Armstrong .50 .23
❑ 123 Jim Pappin .10 .05
❑ 124 Andy Bathgate .35 .16
❑ 125 Ron Ellis .10 .05
❑ 126 Billy Harris .10 .05
❑ 127 Red Kelly .20 .09
❑ 128 Ron Stewart .10 .05
❑ 129 Johnny Bower .50 .23
❑ 130 Frank Mahovlich .50 .23
❑ 131 Tim Horton 1.50 .70
❑ 132 King Clancy .35 .16
❑ 133 Glenn Hall AS .50 .23
❑ 134 Pierre Pilote AS .25 .11
❑ 135 Tim Horton AS .75 .35
❑ 136 Bobby Hull AS 1.00 .45
❑ 137 Ken Wharram AS .15 .07
❑ 138 Stan Mikita AS .50 .23
❑ 139 Charlie Hodge AS .15 .07
❑ 140 Jacques Laperriere AS .15 .07
❑ 141 Elmer Vasko AS .10 .05
❑ 142 Jean Beliveau AS .75 .35
❑ 143 Frank Mahovlich AS .35 .16
❑ 144 Gordie Howe AS 1.50 .70
❑ 145 Pierre Pilote .25 .11
❑ 146 Jean Beliveau .75 .35
❑ 147 Stan Mikita .40 .18
❑ 148 Charlie Hodge .25 .11
❑ 149 Jacques Laperriere .25 .11
❑ 150 Ken Wharram .15 .07
❑ 151 1964 All Star Game .15 .07
❑ 152 Ratelle Invades Crease .25 .11
❑ 153 Center Ice Action .15 .07
❑ 154 Old Teammates Duel 1.50 .70
❑ 155 All Eyes on the Puck .15 .07
❑ 156 Detroit Defense Stands Tall 1.00 .45
❑ 157 Crozier Makes The Stretch .15 .07
❑ 158 Crozier Plays Center Field .25 .11
❑ 159 Hawks Eye Beliveau .75 .35
❑ 160 Montreal's Speedy Rookie .15 .07
❑ 161 Laperriere Wins Race .15 .07
❑ 162 Ellis Robbed by Habs .15 .07
❑ 163 Sawchuk Eyes Bouncing Disc 1.00 .45
❑ 164 Shack Entertains .35 .16
❑ 165 ~Mr. Goalie~ In Action .50 .23
❑ 166 Hall Holds His Ground .35 .16
❑ 167 Johnston Freezes Action .15 .07
❑ 168 Ellis Robbed By Johnston .15 .07
❑ 169 Murray Oliver LL .10 .05
❑ 170 Stan Mikita LL .50 .23
❑ 171 Gordie Howe LL 1.50 .70
❑ 172 Jean Beliveau LL .75 .35
❑ 173 Phil Goyette LL .10 .05
❑ 174 Andy Bathgate LL .25 .11
❑ 175 Stanley Cup Semi-Finals .10 .05
❑ 176 Stanley Cup Semi-Finals .10 .05
❑ 177 Stanley Cup Finals 1.50 .70
❑ 178 Stanley Cup .25 .11
❑ 179 Checklist 1 .10 .05
❑ 180 Checklist 2 .10 .05

## 1994 Parkhurst Tall Boys Autographs

964 of each of these six cards were randomly inserted throughout the production run of 1994 Parkhurst Tall Boys. The cards featured an isolated player photo over a team color-coded background. The player's autograph appears in a white, oblong box along the bottom. A congratulatory note, which serves to authenticate the signature, appears on the back along with a whimsical caricature of company mascot, Mr. Parkie. The cards are serially numbered out of 964 on the back.

| | MINT | NRMT |
|---|---|---|
| COMPLETE SET (6) | 500.00 | 220.00 |
| COMMON CARD (A1-A6) | 50.00 | 22.00 |

❑ A1 Rod Gilbert 50.00 22.00
❑ A2 Yvan Cournoyer 60.00 27.00
❑ A3 Bobby Hull 125.00 55.00
❑ A4 Phil Esposito 100.00 45.00
❑ A5 Gordie Howe 150.00 70.00
❑ A6 Dave Keon 80.00 36.00

## 1994 Parkhurst Tall Boys Future Stars

The six cards in this set were randomly inserted in both US and Canadian product and feature well-known players who had yet to make their mark in the league by the 1964-65 season, the year which is represented in this set. Card fronts feature and isolated player photo (depicting the player in his junior sweater) displayed over a large half-star design and a team color-coded background. Set logo and player name appear in white lettering along the right-hand side. Card backs include 1963-64 amateur stats, a report on the player's prospects in both French and English, and a merchandise offer. Cards are numbered with an "FS" prefix.

| | MINT | NRMT |
|---|---|---|
| COMPLETE SET (6) | 80.00 | 36.00 |
| COMMON CARD (FS1-FS6) | 10.00 | 4.50 |

❑ FS1 Jacques Lemaire 15.00 6.75
❑ FS2 Gerry Cheevers 25.00 11.00
❑ FS3 Ken Hodge 10.00 4.50
❑ FS4 Bernie Parent 18.00 8.00
❑ FS5 Rogatien Vachon 15.00 6.75
❑ FS6 Derek Sanderson 20.00 9.00

## 1994 Parkhurst Tall Boys Greats

The 12 cards in this set were split over two distribution channels: cards 1-6 were randomly inserted in Canadian wax, while 7-12 were inserted in American. The cards feature legendary greats from the game's past. These oddly designed cards were the same size as the regular Tall Boys if maintained intact. A large, beige border surrounded the "real card", which approximates the appearance and size of the smaller 1951-52 Parkhurst issue. Although the cards are scored so that they may be punched out from the larger background, collectors are strongly advised against doing this. Card backs are blank. 1,000 copies of each of these cards were circulated.

| | MINT | NRMT |
|---|---|---|
| COMPLETE SET (12) | 250.00 | 110.00 |
| COMMON CARD (1-12) | 15.00 | 6.75 |

❑ 1 Ace Bailey 30.00 13.50
❑ 2 Alex Levinsky 15.00 6.75
❑ 3 Babe Pratt 15.00 6.75
❑ 4 Elmer Lach 15.00 6.75
❑ 5 Maurice Richard 40.00 18.00
❑ 6 Bill Durnan 30.00 13.50
❑ 7 Frank Brimsek 30.00 13.50
❑ 8 Dit Clapper 20.00 9.00
❑ 9 Tiny Thompson 30.00 13.50
❑ 10 Bun Cook 15.00 6.75
❑ 11 Ching Johnson 20.00 9.00
❑ 12 Lionel Conacher 30.00 13.50

## 1994 Parkhurst Tall Boys Mail-Ins

Available through a mail-in offer, the cards in these three six-card sets measure 2 1/2" by 4 3/4". To obtain one of the sets, the collector sent in 10 "Tall Boy" wrappers and a check or money order for 12.95. The fronts feature color action cutouts on team color-coded backgrounds. The information on the beige backs varies depending on the particular series. At the bottom, each card carries its serial number out of a total of 1,964. The cards are arranged below as follows: All-Stars, Scoring Leaders, and Trophy Winners.

| | MINT | NRMT |
|---|---|---|
| COMPLETE SET (18) | 60.00 | 27.00 |
| COMPLETE ALL-STAR (6) | 18.00 | 8.00 |
| COMPLETE SC. LEADER (6) | 12.00 | 5.50 |
| COMPLETE TR. WINNER (6) | 30.00 | 13.50 |
| COMMON ALL-STAR (AS1-AS6) | 1.00 | .45 |
| COMMON SC. LEADER (SL1-SL6) | 1.00 | .45 |
| COMMON TR. WINNER (TW1-TW6) | 2.00 | .90 |

❑ AS1 Roger Crozier 2.50 1.10
❑ AS2 Pierre Pilote 2.00 .90
❑ AS3 Jacques Laperriere 2.00 .90
❑ AS4 Norm Ullman 2.50 1.10
❑ AS5 Bobby Hull 10.00 4.50
❑ AS6 Claude Provost 1.00 .45
❑ SL1 John Bucyk 2.50 1.10
❑ SL2 Stan Mikita 4.00 1.80
❑ SL3 Norm Ullman 2.50 1.10
❑ SL4 Claude Provost 1.00 .45
❑ SL5 Rod Gilbert 2.50 1.10
❑ SL6 Frank Mahovlich 4.00 1.80
❑ TW1 Pierre Pilote 2.00 .90
❑ TW2 Bobby Hull 10.00 4.50
❑ TW3 Stan Mikita 4.00 1.80
❑ TW4 Terry Sawchuk Johnny Bower 6.00 2.70
❑ TW5 Roger Crozier 2.50 1.10
❑ TW6 Bobby Hull 10.00 4.50

## 1994-95 Parkhurst

This 315-card set was issued in one series. Due to the NHL lockout, series two was not released; therefore, this set does not have a comprehensive player selection. Ten card packs retailed for 99 cents in 36 pack boxes. Sixteen-card jumbo packs also were produced. The design features a nearly full-bleed front, broken only in the lower right corner where a small gray bar features a silver foil hockey player icon. The green Parkhurst logo appears in an upper corner with player name running down either side. Card backs are unique in that they have full career stats and a player photo. Subsets included Rookie Standouts (270-294) and Parkie's Best (295-315). Rookie cards in this set include Mariusz Czerkawski and Mikhail Shtalenkov. This set is noteworthy for being the last product domestically released by Upper Deck using the Parkhurst name. Although no second series was domestically released, a European-only product - Parkhurst SE - appears to have been the remnants of that planned issue. Prices for that set appear elsewhere.

| | MINT | NRMT |
|---|---|---|
| COMPLETE SET (315) | 18.00 | 8.00 |
| COMMON CARD (1-315) | .05 | .02 |

❑ 1 Anatoli Semenov .05 .02
❑ 2 Stephan Lebeau .05 .02
❑ 3 Stu Grimson .05 .02
❑ 4 Mikhail Shtalenkov .05 .02
❑ 5 Troy Loney .05 .02
❑ 6 Sean Hill UER .05 .02 ('92-93 points total is 54 instead of 8 and career total is 81 instead of 35)
❑ 7 Patrik Carnback .05 .02
❑ 8 John Lilley .05 .02
❑ 9 Tim Sweeney .05 .02
❑ 10 Maxim Bets .05 .02
❑ 11 Cam Neely .10 .05
❑ 12 Bryan Smolinski .05 .02
❑ 13 Ray Bourque .20 .09
❑ 14 Vincent Riendeau .10 .05
❑ 15 Al Iafrate .05 .02
❑ 16 Andrew McKim .05 .02
❑ 17 Glen Wesley .05 .02
❑ 18 Daniel Marois .05 .02
❑ 19 Josef Stumpel .05 .02
❑ 20 Mariusz Czerkawski .05 .02
❑ 21 Alexander Mogilny .10 .05
❑ 22 Yuri Khmylev .05 .02
❑ 23 Donald Audette .10 .05
❑ 24 Dominik Hasek .50 .23
❑ 25 Randy Wood .05 .02
❑ 26 Brad May .10 .05
❑ 27 Wayne Presley .05 .02
❑ 28 Richard Smehlik .05 .02
❑ 29 Dale Hawerchuk .10 .05
❑ 30 Rob Ray .05 .02
❑ 31 Zarley Zalapski .05 .02
❑ 32 Michael Nylander .05 .02
❑ 33 Joe Nieuwendyk .10 .05
❑ 34 Robert Reichel .05 .02
❑ 35 Al MacInnis .10 .05
❑ 36 Andrei Trefilov .05 .02
❑ 37 Leonard Esau .05 .02
❑ 38 Wes Walz .05 .02
❑ 39 Michel Petit .05 .02
❑ 40 James Patrick .05 .02
❑ 41 Ed Belfour .20 .09
❑ 42 Christian Ruuttu .05 .02
❑ 43 Eric Weinrich .05 .02
❑ 44 Joe Murphy .05 .02
❑ 45 Chris Chelios .20 .09
❑ 46 Jeff Shantz .05 .02
❑ 47 Gary Suter .05 .02
❑ 48 Paul Ysebaert .05 .02
❑ 49 Ivan Droppa .05 .02
❑ 50 Keith Carney .05 .02
❑ 51 Andy Moog .10 .05
❑ 52 Russ Courtnall .05 .02
❑ 53 Neal Broten .10 .05
❑ 54 Mike Craig .05 .02
❑ 55 Brent Gilchrist .05 .02
❑ 56 Pelle Eklund .05 .02
❑ 57 Richard Matvichuk .05 .02
❑ 58 Dave Gagner .10 .05
❑ 59 Mark Tinordi .05 .02
❑ 60 Paul Broten .05 .02
❑ 61 Nicklas Lidstrom .10 .05
❑ 62 Shawn Burr .05 .02
❑ 63 Paul Coffey .20 .09
❑ 64 Bob Essensa .10 .05
❑ 65 Dino Ciccarelli .10 .05
❑ 66 Slava Kozlov .10 .05
❑ 67 Keith Primeau .10 .05
❑ 68 Steve Chiasson .05 .02
❑ 69 Terry Carkner .05 .02
❑ 70 Martin Lapointe .05 .02
❑ 71 Bob Probert .10 .05
❑ 72 Bill Ranford .10 .05
❑ 73 Scott Thornton .05 .02
❑ 74 Doug Weight .10 .05
❑ 75 Shayne Corson .05 .02
❑ 76 Zdeno Ciger .05 .02
❑ 77 Adam Bennett .05 .02
❑ 78 Scott Pearson .05 .02
❑ 79 Brent Grieve .05 .02
❑ 80 Gordon Mark .05 .02
❑ 81 Shjon Podein .05 .02
❑ 82 Geoff Smith .05 .02
❑ 83 Bob Kudelski .05 .02
❑ 84 Andrei Lomakin .05 .02
❑ 85 Scott Mellanby .10 .05
❑ 86 Jesse Belanger .05 .02
❑ 87 Mark Fitzpatrick .10 .05
❑ 88 Peter Andersson .05 .02
❑ 89 Jody Hull .05 .02
❑ 90 Brent Severyn .05 .02
❑ 91 Jim Sandlak .05 .02
❑ 92 Pat Verbeek .05 .02
❑ 93 Ted Crowley .05 .02
❑ 94 Robert Petrovicky .05 .02
❑ 95 Geoff Sanderson .10 .05
❑ 96 Ted Drury .05 .02
❑ 97 Andrew Cassels .05 .02
❑ 98 Igor Chibirev .05 .02
❑ 99 Kevin Smyth .05 .02
❑ 100 Alexander Godynyuk .05 .02
❑ 101 Alexei Zhitnik .05 .02
❑ 102 Dixon Ward .05 .02
❑ 103 Wayne Gretzky 1.50 .70
❑ 104 Jari Kurri .10 .05
❑ 105 Rob Blake .05 .02
❑ 106 Marty McSorley .05 .02
❑ 107 Pat Conacher .05 .02
❑ 108 Kevin Todd .05 .02
❑ 109 Robb Stauber .10 .05
❑ 110 Keith Redmond .05 .02
❑ 111 John LeClair .30 .14
❑ 112 Brian Bellows .05 .02
❑ 113 Patrick Roy 1.00 .45
❑ 114 Les Kuntar .05 .02
❑ 115 Vincent Damphousse .10 .05
❑ 116 Patrice Brisebois .05 .02
❑ 117 Pierre Sevigny .05 .02
❑ 118 Eric Desjardins .05 .02
❑ 119 Oleg Petrov .05 .02
❑ 120 Kevin Haller .05 .02
❑ 121 Christian Proulx .05 .02
❑ 122 Corey Millen .05 .02
❑ 123 Jaroslav Modry .05 .02
❑ 124 Valeri Zelepukin .05 .02
❑ 125 John MacLean .10 .05
❑ 126 Martin Brodeur .50 .23
❑ 127 Bill Guerin .05 .02
❑ 128 Bobby Holik .05 .02
❑ 129 Claude Lemieux .10 .05
❑ 130 Jason Smith .05 .02
❑ 131 Ken Daneyko .05 .02
❑ 132 Derek King .05 .02
❑ 133 Darius Kasparaitis .05 .02
❑ 134 Ray Ferraro .05 .02
❑ 135 Pierre Turgeon .10 .05
❑ 136 Ron Hextall .10 .05
❑ 137 Travis Green .10 .05
❑ 138 Joe Day .05 .02
❑ 139 David Volek .05 .02
❑ 140 Scott Lachance .05 .02
❑ 141 Dennis Vaske .05 .02
❑ 142 Alexei Kovalev .10 .05
❑ 143 Brian Noonan .05 .02
❑ 144 Sergei Zubov .05 .02
❑ 145 Craig MacTavish .05 .02
❑ 146 Steve Larmer .10 .05
❑ 147 Adam Graves .10 .05
❑ 148 Jeff Beukeboom .05 .02
❑ 149 Corey Hirsch .10 .05
❑ 150 Stephane Matteau .05 .02
❑ 151 Brian Leetch .20 .09
❑ 152 Mattias Norstrom .10 .05
❑ 153 Sylvain Turgeon .05 .02
❑ 154 Norm Maciver .05 .02
❑ 155 Scott Levins .05 .02
❑ 156 Derek Mayer .05 .02
❑ 157 Dave McLlwain .05 .02
❑ 158 Craig Billington .10 .05
❑ 159 Claude Boivin .05 .02
❑ 160 Troy Mallette .05 .02
❑ 161 Evgeny Davydov .05 .02
❑ 162 Dmitri Filimonov .05 .02
❑ 163 Dimitri Yushkevich .05 .02
❑ 164 Rob Zettler .05 .02
❑ 165 Mark Recchi .10 .05
❑ 166 Josef Beranek .05 .02
❑ 167 Rod Brind'Amour .10 .05
❑ 168 Yves Racine .05 .02
❑ 169 Dominic Roussel .10 .05
❑ 170 Brent Fedyk .05 .02
❑ 171 Bob Wilkie .05 .02
❑ 172 Kevin Dineen .05 .02
❑ 173 Shawn McEachern .05 .02
❑ 174 Jaromir Jagr .60 .25
❑ 175 Tomas Sandstrom .05 .02
❑ 176 Ron Francis .10 .05
❑ 177 Kevin Stevens .05 .02
❑ 178 Jim McKenzie .05 .02
❑ 179 Larry Murphy .10 .05
❑ 180 Joe Mullen .10 .05
❑ 181 Greg Hawgood .05 .02
❑ 182 Tom Barrasso .10 .05
❑ 183 Ulf Samuelsson .05 .02
❑ 184 Bob Bassen .05 .02
❑ 185 Mats Sundin .10 .05
❑ 186 Mike Ricci .05 .02
❑ 187 Iain Fraser .05 .02
❑ 188 Garth Butcher .05 .02
❑ 189 Jocelyn Thibault .20 .09
❑ 190 Valeri Kamensky .10 .05
❑ 191 Martin Rucinsky .05 .02
❑ 192 Ron Sutter .05 .02
❑ 193 Rene Corbet .05 .02
❑ 194 Reggie Savage .05 .02
❑ 195 Alexei Kasatonov .05 .02
❑ 196 Brendan Shanahan .40 .18
❑ 197 Phil Housley .10 .05
❑ 198 Jim Montgomery .05 .02
❑ 199 Curtis Joseph .20 .09
❑ 200 Craig Janney .10 .05
❑ 201 David Roberts .05 .02
❑ 202 Dave Mackey .05 .02
❑ 203 Peter Stastny .10 .05
❑ 204 Terry Hollinger .05 .02
❑ 205 Steve Duchesne .05 .02
❑ 206 Vitali Prokhorov .05 .02
❑ 207 Rob Gaudreau .05 .02
❑ 208 Sandis Ozolinsh .10 .05
❑ 209 Johan Garpenlov .05 .02
❑ 210 Todd Elik .05 .02
❑ 211 Sergei Makarov .05 .02
❑ 212 Jean-Francois Quintin .05 .02
❑ 213 Vyacheslav Butsayev .05 .02
❑ 214 Jimmy Waite .10 .05
❑ 215 Ulf Dahlen .05 .02
❑ 216 Andrei Nazarov .05 .02
❑ 217 Denis Savard .10 .05
❑ 218 Brent Gretzky .05 .02
❑ 219 Petr Klima .05 .02
❑ 220 Chris Gratton .10 .05
❑ 221 Brian Bradley .05 .02
❑ 222 Adam Creighton .05 .02
❑ 223 Shawn Chambers .05 .02
❑ 224 Rob Zamuner .05 .02
❑ 225 Daren Puppa .10 .05

| | | |
|---|---|---|
| ❑ 226 Mikael Andersson | .05 | .02 |
| ❑ 227 Dave Ellett | .05 | .02 |
| ❑ 228 Mike Gartner | .10 | .05 |
| ❑ 229 Felix Potvin | .20 | .09 |
| ❑ 230 Yanic Perreault | .05 | .02 |
| ❑ 231 Nikolai Borschevsky | .05 | .02 |
| ❑ 232 Dmitri Mironov | .05 | .02 |
| ❑ 233 Todd Gill | .05 | .02 |
| ❑ 234 Eric Lacroix | .05 | .02 |
| ❑ 235 Kent Manderville | .05 | .02 |
| ❑ 236 Chris Govedaris | .05 | .02 |
| ❑ 237 Frank Bialowas | .05 | .02 |
| ❑ 238 Kirk McLean | .10 | .05 |
| ❑ 239 Jimmy Carson | .05 | .02 |
| ❑ 240 Geoff Courtnall | .05 | .02 |
| ❑ 241 Trevor Linden | .10 | .05 |
| ❑ 242 Murray Craven | .05 | .02 |
| ❑ 243 Bret Hedican | .05 | .02 |
| ❑ 244 Jeff Brown | .05 | .02 |
| ❑ 245 Mike Peca | .05 | .02 |
| ❑ 246 Yevgeny Namestnikov | .05 | .02 |
| ❑ 247 Nathan Lafayette | .05 | .02 |
| ❑ 248 Shawn Antoski | .05 | .02 |
| ❑ 249 Sergio Momesso | .05 | .02 |
| ❑ 250 Mike Ridley | .05 | .02 |
| ❑ 251 Peter Bondra | .20 | .09 |
| ❑ 252 Dimitri Khristich | .05 | .02 |
| ❑ 253 Dave Poulin | .05 | .02 |
| ❑ 254 Dale Hunter | .05 | .02 |
| ❑ 255 Rick Tabaracci | .10 | .05 |
| ❑ 256 Kelly Miller | .05 | .02 |
| ❑ 257 John Slaney | .05 | .02 |
| ❑ 258 Todd Krygier | .05 | .02 |
| ❑ 259 Kevin Hatcher | .05 | .02 |
| ❑ 260 Alexei Zhamnov | .10 | .05 |
| ❑ 261 Dallas Drake | .05 | .02 |
| ❑ 262 Dave Manson | .05 | .02 |
| ❑ 263 Thomas Steen | .05 | .02 |
| ❑ 264 Keith Tkachuk | .25 | .11 |
| ❑ 265 Russ Romaniuk | .05 | .02 |
| ❑ 266 Michal Grosek | .05 | .02 |
| ❑ 267 Nelson Emerson | .05 | .02 |
| ❑ 268 Michael O'Neill | .05 | .02 |
| ❑ 269 Kris King | .05 | .02 |
| ❑ 270 Teppo Numminen | .05 | .02 |
| ❑ 271 Jason Arnott | .10 | .05 |
| ❑ 272 Mikael Renberg | .10 | .05 |
| ❑ 273 Alexei Yashin | .10 | .05 |
| ❑ 274 Chris Pronger | .10 | .05 |
| ❑ 275 Jocelyn Thibault | .20 | .09 |
| ❑ 276 Bryan Smolinski | .05 | .02 |
| ❑ 277 Derek Plante | .05 | .02 |
| ❑ 278 Martin Brodeur | .20 | .09 |
| ❑ 279 Jim Dowd | .05 | .02 |
| ❑ 280 Iain Fraser | .05 | .02 |
| ❑ 281 Pat Peake | .05 | .02 |
| ❑ 282 Chris Gratton | .10 | .05 |
| ❑ 283 Chris Osgood | .20 | .09 |
| ❑ 284 Jesse Belanger | .05 | .02 |
| ❑ 285 Alexandre Daigle | .05 | .02 |
| ❑ 286 Robert Lang | .05 | .02 |
| ❑ 287 Markus Naslund | .05 | .02 |
| ❑ 288 Trevor Kidd | .10 | .05 |
| ❑ 289 Jeff Shantz | .05 | .02 |
| ❑ 290 Jaroslav Modry | .05 | .02 |
| ❑ 291 Oleg Petrov | .05 | .02 |
| ❑ 292 Scott Levins | .05 | .02 |
| ❑ 293 Josef Stumpel | .05 | .02 |
| ❑ 294 Rob Niedermayer | .10 | .05 |
| ❑ 295 Brent Gretzky | .05 | .02 |
| ❑ 296 Mario Lemieux | .75 | .35 |
| ❑ 297 Pavel Bure | .20 | .09 |
| ❑ 298 Brendan Shanahan | .20 | .09 |
| ❑ 299 Steve Yzerman | .20 | .09 |
| ❑ 300 Teemu Selanne | .20 | .09 |
| ❑ 301 Eric Lindros | .60 | .25 |
| ❑ 302 Jeremy Roenick | .20 | .09 |
| ❑ 303 Dave Andreychuk | .10 | .05 |
| ❑ 304 Ray Bourque | .20 | .09 |
| ❑ 305 Sergei Fedorov | .20 | .09 |
| ❑ 306 Wayne Gretzky | 1.00 | .45 |
| ❑ 307 Adam Graves | .10 | .05 |
| ❑ 308 Mike Modano | .30 | .14 |
| ❑ 309 Brett Hull | .20 | .09 |
| ❑ 310 Pat LaFontaine | .10 | .05 |
| ❑ 311 Adam Oates | .10 | .05 |
| ❑ 312 Patrick Roy | .75 | .35 |
| ❑ 313 Doug Gilmour | .20 | .09 |
| ❑ 314 Jaromir Jagr | .20 | .09 |
| ❑ 315 Mark Recchi | .10 | .05 |

## 1994-95 Parkhurst Gold

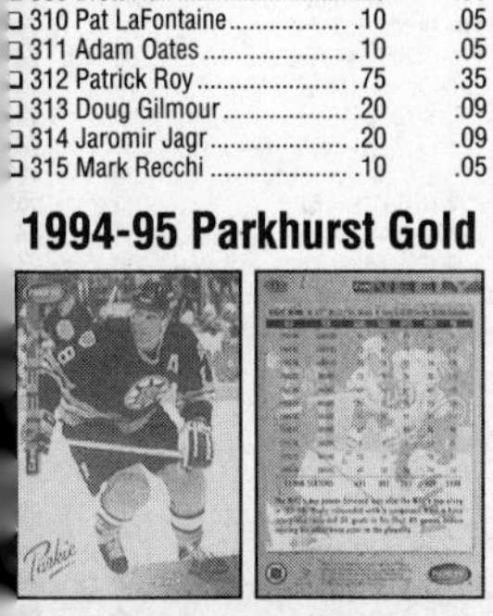

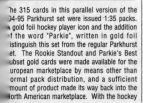

'he 315 cards in this parallel version of the 94-95 Parkhurst set were issued 1:35 packs. gold foil hockey player icon and the addition f the word "Parkie", written in gold foil istinguish this set from the regular Parkhurst et. The Rookie Standout and Parkie's Best ubset gold cards were made available for the uropean marketplace by means other than ormal pack distribution, and a sufficient mount of product made its way back into the orth American marketplace. With the hockey card market not having absorbed the saturation, multipliers for these subset cards are lower than other cards from this set.

| | MINT | NRMT |
|---|---|---|
| COMPLETE SET (315) | 900.00 | 400.00 |
| COMMON CARD (1-315) | 2.00 | .90 |

*STARS: 20X TO 50X BASIC CARDS
*YOUNG STARS: 12X TO 30X BASIC CARDS
*RC'S: 8X TO 20X BASIC CARDS

## 1994-95 Parkhurst Crash The Game

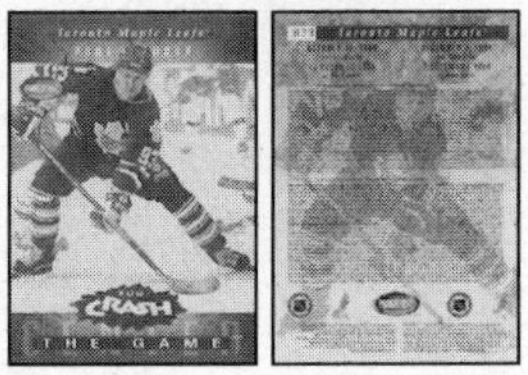

The 28 cards in this set were randomly inserted into Parkhurst product at a rate of 1:23 packs. The cards feature a cutout player photo on a black and white background. A black color bar runs across the top and bottom of the card. Player name and team are printed across the top. The words "You Crash The Game" are printed in colored foil on the bottom of the card. There are three variations of each card in this set. Each of the three foil logo colors reflects the different distribution method. Red foil indicates Canadian packaging, blue foil U.S. retail and green foil U.S. hobby. The cards are numbered on the back with a corresponding prefix of C, R, or H. Since the cards were created to be used as an interactive game, the backs contain the rules in extremely fine-print legalese in both English and French, as well as two game dates. If the team featured on the front won on one or both of those dates, the card could be redeemed for a specially foiled set. Unfortunately, the NHL lockout of 1994 prevented the games from being played. As a result, Upper Deck declared all cards winners, enabling each to be redeemed for a 28-card gold-foil version of the set by mail. Because these gold foil versions are so plentiful, they are worth considerably less than their inserted counterparts. Furthermore, the gold version is more commonly seen in complete set form than the other versions, further dampening demand for this product. The prices below reflect green, red and blue versions. The expiration date for the exchange was June 30th, 1995.

| | MINT | NRMT |
|---|---|---|
| COMPLETE SET (28) | 100.00 | 45.00 |
| COMMON CARD (1-28) | .50 | .23 |
| *BLUE/GREEN/RED FOIL: ALL EQUAL VALUE | | |
| COMP.GOLD SET (28) | 15.00 | 6.75 |
| COMMON GOLD (G1-G28) | .25 | .11 |
| *GOLD: .25X BASIC CRASH CARDS | | |

| | | |
|---|---|---|
| ❑ 1 Stephan Lebeau | .50 | .23 |
| ❑ 2 Ray Bourque | 2.00 | .90 |
| ❑ 3 Pat LaFontaine | 1.50 | .70 |
| ❑ 4 Joe Nieuwendyk | .50 | .23 |
| ❑ 5 Jeremy Roenick | 2.00 | .90 |
| ❑ 6 Mike Modano | 1.50 | .70 |
| ❑ 7 Sergei Fedorov | 4.00 | 1.80 |
| ❑ 8 Jason Arnott | 1.50 | .70 |
| ❑ 9 John Vanbiesbrouck | 4.00 | 1.80 |
| ❑ 10 Geoff Sanderson | .50 | .23 |
| ❑ 11 Wayne Gretzky | 12.00 | 5.50 |
| ❑ 12 Patrick Roy | 8.00 | 3.60 |
| ❑ 13 Scott Stevens | .50 | .23 |
| ❑ 14 Pierre Turgeon | .50 | .23 |
| ❑ 15 Adam Graves | .50 | .23 |
| ❑ 16 Alexei Yashin | .50 | .23 |
| ❑ 17 Eric Lindros | 8.00 | 3.60 |
| ❑ 18 Mario Lemieux | 10.00 | 4.50 |
| ❑ 19 Joe Sakic | 5.00 | 2.20 |
| ❑ 20 Brett Hull | 3.00 | 1.35 |
| ❑ 21 Sandis Ozolinsh | .50 | .23 |
| ❑ 22 Chris Gratton | .50 | .23 |
| ❑ 23 Doug Gilmour | 1.50 | .70 |
| ❑ 24 Pavel Bure | 4.00 | 1.80 |
| ❑ 25 Joe Juneau | .50 | .23 |
| ❑ 26 Teemu Selanne | 4.00 | 1.80 |
| ❑ 27 Mark Messier<br>Eastern Conference | 4.00 | 1.80 |
| ❑ 28 Wayne Gretzky<br>Western Conference | 12.00 | 5.50 |

## 1994-95 Parkhurst Vintage

The 90 cards in this set were included one per Parkhurst pack. They are printed on heavy white card stock with a design that hearkens back to the style of Parkhurst issues of the '50s and '60s. The player photo is cut out and placed on a white and tan background. The player's name appears in a black bar on the lower portion of the card, alongside the set logo. The card backs are an unfinished

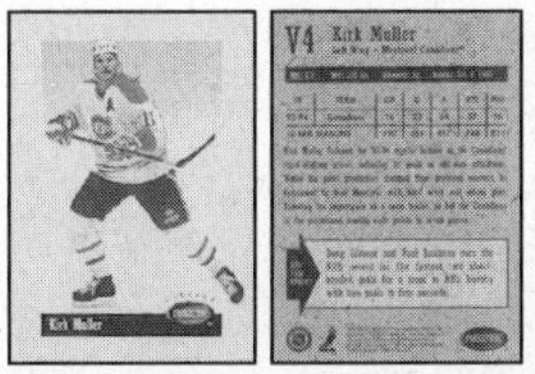

cardboard and feature professional statistics, biography and a "Did You Know" section containing interesting trivia. This trivia did not apply to the player pictured. The cards were numbered with a "V" prefix.

| | MINT | NRMT |
|---|---|---|
| COMPLETE SET (90) | 30.00 | 13.50 |
| COMMON CARD (V1-V90) | .15 | .07 |

| | | |
|---|---|---|
| ❑ V1 Dominik Hasek | 2.00 | .90 |
| ❑ V2 Mike Modano | 1.25 | .55 |
| ❑ V3 Shayne Corson | .15 | .07 |
| ❑ V4 Kirk Muller | .15 | .07 |
| ❑ V5 Mike Richter | .75 | .35 |
| ❑ V6 Mario Lemieux | 5.00 | 2.20 |
| ❑ V7 Sandis Ozolinsh | .15 | .07 |
| ❑ V8 Dave Ellett | .15 | .07 |
| ❑ V9 Dave Manson | .15 | .07 |
| ❑ V10 Terry Yake | .15 | .07 |
| ❑ V11 Craig Simpson | .15 | .07 |
| ❑ V12 Paul Cavallini | .15 | .07 |
| ❑ V13 John Vanbiesbrouck | 1.50 | .70 |
| ❑ V14 Gilbert Dionne | .15 | .07 |
| ❑ V15 Brian Leetch | .75 | .35 |
| ❑ V16 Martin Straka | .15 | .07 |
| ❑ V17 Curtis Joseph | .75 | .35 |
| ❑ V18 Pavel Bure | 2.00 | .90 |
| ❑ V19 Garry Valk | .15 | .07 |
| ❑ V20 Theoren Fleury | .25 | .11 |
| ❑ V21 Brent Gilchrist | .15 | .07 |
| ❑ V22 Rob Niedermayer | .15 | .07 |
| ❑ V23 Vincent Damphousse | .25 | .11 |
| ❑ V24 Alexei Kovalev | .15 | .07 |
| ❑ V25 Rick Tocchet | .15 | .07 |
| ❑ V26 Steve Duchesne | .15 | .07 |
| ❑ V27 Jiri Slegr | .15 | .07 |
| ❑ V28 Patrick Carnback | .15 | .07 |
| ❑ V29 Gary Roberts | .15 | .07 |
| ❑ V30 Derian Hatcher | .15 | .07 |
| ❑ V31 Jesse Belanger | .15 | .07 |
| ❑ V32 Mathieu Schneider | .15 | .07 |
| ❑ V33 Mark Messier | 1.25 | .55 |
| ❑ V34 Joe Sakic | 2.00 | .90 |
| ❑ V35 Brett Hull | 1.25 | .55 |
| ❑ V36 Martin Gelinas | .15 | .07 |
| ❑ V37 Maxim Bets | .15 | .07 |
| ❑ V38 Joel Otto | .15 | .07 |
| ❑ V39 Sergei Fedorov | 2.00 | .90 |
| ❑ V40 Chris Pronger | .25 | .11 |
| ❑ V41 Scott Stevens | .15 | .07 |
| ❑ V42 Alexandre Daigle | .25 | .11 |
| ❑ V43 Owen Nolan | .25 | .11 |
| ❑ V44 Petr Nedved | .15 | .07 |
| ❑ V45 Jeff Brown | .15 | .07 |
| ❑ V46 Adam Oates | .25 | .11 |
| ❑ V47 Robert Reichel | .15 | .07 |
| ❑ V48 Slava Kozlov | .25 | .11 |
| ❑ V49 Geoff Sanderson | .25 | .11 |
| ❑ V50 Stephane Richer | .15 | .07 |
| ❑ V51 Sylvain Turgeon | .15 | .07 |
| ❑ V52 Mats Sundin | .25 | .11 |
| ❑ V53 Roman Hamrlik | .25 | .11 |
| ❑ V54 Kevin Hatcher | .15 | .07 |
| ❑ V55 Mariusz Czerkawski | .15 | .07 |
| ❑ V56 Tony Amonte | .25 | .11 |
| ❑ V57 Steve Yzerman | 3.00 | 1.35 |
| ❑ V58 Andrew Cassels | .15 | .07 |
| ❑ V59 Claude Lemieux | .15 | .07 |
| ❑ V60 Derek Mayer | .15 | .07 |
| ❑ V61 Jocelyn Thibault | .75 | .35 |
| ❑ V62 Brent Gretzky | .15 | .07 |
| ❑ V63 Pat Peake | .15 | .07 |
| ❑ V64 Cam Neely | .25 | .11 |
| ❑ V65 Jeremy Roenick | .75 | .35 |
| ❑ V66 Keith Primeau | .25 | .11 |
| ❑ V67 Luc Robitaille | .25 | .11 |
| ❑ V68 Steve Thomas | .15 | .07 |
| ❑ V69 Eric Lindros | 3.00 | 1.35 |
| ❑ V70 Pat Falloon | .15 | .07 |
| ❑ V71 Brian Bradley | .15 | .07 |
| ❑ V72 Mike Ridley | .15 | .07 |
| ❑ V73 Pat LaFontaine | .25 | .11 |
| ❑ V74 Gary Suter | .15 | .07 |
| ❑ V75 Bill Ranford | .25 | .11 |
| ❑ V76 Tony Granato | .15 | .07 |
| ❑ V77 Vladimir Malakhov | .15 | .07 |
| ❑ V78 Mikael Renberg | .25 | .11 |
| ❑ V79 Arturs Irbe | .25 | .11 |
| ❑ V80 Doug Gilmour | .25 | .11 |
| ❑ V81 Teemu Selanne | 2.00 | .90 |
| ❑ V82 Derek Plante | .15 | .07 |
| ❑ V83 Eric Weinrich | .15 | .07 |
| ❑ V84 Jason Arnott | .25 | .11 |
| ❑ V85 Rob Blake | .15 | .07 |
| ❑ V86 Ray Ferraro | .15 | .07 |
| ❑ V87 Garry Galley | .15 | .07 |
| ❑ V88 Igor Larionov | .15 | .07 |
| ❑ V89 Dave Andreychuk | .15 | .07 |
| ❑ V90 Dallas Drake | .15 | .07 |

## 1994-95 Parkhurst SE

This 270-card set apparently was designed to serve as the second series to the 1994-95

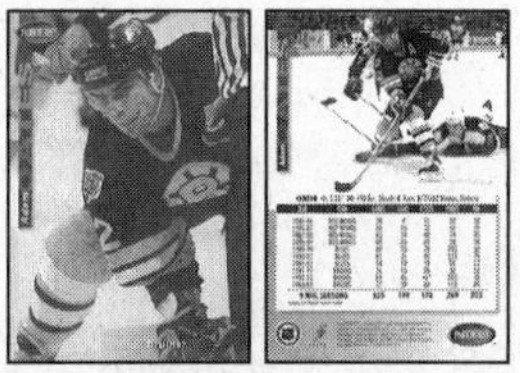

Parkhurst product. In the wake of the NHL lockout of that year, licensing regulations were relaxed, and Upper Deck chose to release the SP line instead. This product subsequently was issued in eleven European countries. However, large quantities eventually made their way to North America. The basic cards have the same design as Parkhurst. Although essentially a companion issue to Parkhurst, this set is numbered from 1-270, with an SE prefix. Subsets include World Junior Championships (206-250) and CAHA Program of Excellence (251-270). Although this set contains the first year cards of many players, they are not recognized as Rookie Cards because of the European-only distribution. A 4" X 6" blowup version of 1994-95 Upper Deck #226, which commemorates Wayne Gretzky's 802 career goals, is inserted at the top of each box.

| | MINT | NRMT |
|---|---|---|
| COMPLETE SET (270) | 20.00 | 9.00 |
| COMMON CARD (SE1-SE270) | .10 | .05 |

| | | |
|---|---|---|
| ❑ SE1 Guy Hebert | .15 | .07 |
| ❑ SE2 Bob Corkum | .10 | .05 |
| ❑ SE3 Randy Ladouceur | .10 | .05 |
| ❑ SE4 Tom Kurvers | .10 | .05 |
| ❑ SE5 Joe Sacco | .10 | .05 |
| ❑ SE6 Valeri Karpov | .10 | .05 |
| ❑ SE7 Garry Valk | .10 | .05 |
| ❑ SE8 Paul Kariya | 1.50 | .70 |
| ❑ SE9 Alexei Kasatonov | .10 | .05 |
| ❑ SE10 Sergei Zholtok | .10 | .05 |
| ❑ SE11 Glen Murray | .10 | .05 |
| ❑ SE12 David Reid | .10 | .05 |
| ❑ SE13 Adam Oates | .15 | .07 |
| ❑ SE14 Ted Donato | .10 | .05 |
| ❑ SE15 Don Sweeney | .10 | .05 |
| ❑ SE16 Philippe Boucher | .10 | .05 |
| ❑ SE17 Bob Sweeney | .10 | .05 |
| ❑ SE18 Pat LaFontaine | .15 | .07 |
| ❑ SE19 Derek Plante | .15 | .07 |
| ❑ SE20 Jason Dawe | .10 | .05 |
| ❑ SE21 Petr Svoboda | .10 | .05 |
| ❑ SE22 Craig Simpson | .10 | .05 |
| ❑ SE23 Viktor Gordiouk | .10 | .05 |
| ❑ SE24 Trevor Kidd | .15 | .07 |
| ❑ SE25 Todd Hlushko | .10 | .05 |
| ❑ SE26 German Titov | .15 | .07 |
| ❑ SE27 Gary Roberts | .10 | .05 |
| ❑ SE28 Theoren Fleury | .15 | .07 |
| ❑ SE29 Cory Stillman | .15 | .07 |
| ❑ SE30 Phil Housley | .15 | .07 |
| ❑ SE31 Joel Otto | .10 | .05 |
| ❑ SE32 Patrick Poulin | .10 | .05 |
| ❑ SE33 Christian Soucy | .15 | .07 |
| ❑ SE34 Karl Dykhuis | .10 | .05 |
| ❑ SE35 Jeremy Roenick | .30 | .14 |
| ❑ SE36 Tony Amonte | .15 | .07 |
| ❑ SE37 Sergei Krivokrasov | .10 | .05 |
| ❑ SE38 Bernie Nicholls | .10 | .05 |
| ❑ SE39 Todd Harvey | .15 | .07 |
| ❑ SE40 Jarkko Varvio | .10 | .05 |
| ❑ SE41 Shane Churla | .10 | .05 |
| ❑ SE42 Paul Cavallini | .10 | .05 |
| ❑ SE43 Trent Klatt | .10 | .05 |
| ❑ SE44 Darcy Wakaluk | .10 | .05 |
| ❑ SE45 Derian Hatcher | .10 | .05 |
| ❑ SE46 Dean Evason | .10 | .05 |
| ❑ SE47 Mike Modano | .40 | .18 |
| ❑ SE48 Greg Johnson | .10 | .05 |
| ❑ SE49 Ray Sheppard | .15 | .07 |
| ❑ SE50 Sergei Fedorov | .60 | .25 |
| ❑ SE51 Bob Rouse | .10 | .05 |
| ❑ SE52 Mike Vernon | .15 | .07 |
| ❑ SE53 Vladimir Konstantinov | .10 | .05 |
| ❑ SE54 Chris Osgood | .50 | .23 |
| ❑ SE55 Steve Yzerman | 1.00 | .45 |
| ❑ SE56 Jason York | .15 | .07 |
| ❑ SE57 Boris Mironov | .10 | .05 |
| ❑ SE58 Igor Kravchuk | .10 | .05 |
| ❑ SE59 Jason Arnott | .15 | .07 |
| ❑ SE60 David Oliver | .15 | .07 |
| ❑ SE61 Todd Marchant | .10 | .05 |
| ❑ SE62 Dean McAmmond | .10 | .05 |
| ❑ SE63 Brian Skrudland | .10 | .05 |
| ❑ SE64 Tom Fitzgerald | .10 | .05 |
| ❑ SE65 Brian Benning | .10 | .05 |
| ❑ SE66 Stu Barnes | .10 | .05 |
| ❑ SE67 John Vanbiesbrouck | .50 | .23 |
| ❑ SE68 Rob Niedermayer | .15 | .07 |
| ❑ SE69 Jimmy Carson | .10 | .05 |
| ❑ SE70 Mark Janssens | .10 | .05 |
| ❑ SE71 Sean Burke | .15 | .07 |
| ❑ SE72 Andrei Nikolishin | .10 | .05 |
| ❑ SE73 Chris Pronger | .15 | .07 |
| ❑ SE74 Jeff Reese | .15 | .07 |
| ❑ SE75 Darren Turcotte | .10 | .05 |
| ❑ SE76 Robert Kron | .10 | .05 |
| ❑ SE77 Kevin Brown | .10 | .05 |
| ❑ SE78 Robert Lang | .10 | .05 |
| ❑ SE79 Rick Tocchet | .15 | .07 |
| ❑ SE80 Jamie Storr | .15 | .07 |
| ❑ SE81 Kelly Hrudey | .15 | .07 |
| ❑ SE82 Darryl Sydor | .10 | .05 |
| ❑ SE83 Tony Granato | .10 | .05 |
| ❑ SE84 Warren Rychel | .10 | .05 |
| ❑ SE85 Gary Shuchuk | .10 | .05 |
| ❑ SE86 Peter Popovic | .10 | .05 |
| ❑ SE87 Valeri Bure | .15 | .07 |
| ❑ SE88 Kirk Muller | .15 | .07 |
| ❑ SE89 Lyle Odelein | .10 | .05 |
| ❑ SE90 Brian Savage | .10 | .05 |
| ❑ SE91 Gilbert Dionne | .10 | .05 |
| ❑ SE92 Mathieu Schneider | .10 | .05 |
| ❑ SE93 Jim Montgomery | .10 | .05 |
| ❑ SE94 Chris Terreri | .15 | .07 |
| ❑ SE95 Scott Niedermayer | .15 | .07 |
| ❑ SE96 Bob Carpenter | .10 | .05 |
| ❑ SE97 Scott Stevens | .15 | .07 |
| ❑ SE98 Jim Dowd | .10 | .05 |
| ❑ SE99 Brian Rolston | .10 | .05 |
| ❑ SE100 Stephane Richer | .15 | .07 |
| ❑ SE101 Mick Vukota | .10 | .05 |
| ❑ SE102 Steve Thomas | .10 | .05 |
| ❑ SE103 Patrick Flatley | .10 | .05 |
| ❑ SE104 Marty McInnis | .10 | .05 |
| ❑ SE105 Rich Pilon | .10 | .05 |
| ❑ SE106 Benoit Hogue | .10 | .05 |
| ❑ SE107 Zigmund Palffy | .15 | .07 |
| ❑ SE108 Vladimir Malakhov | .10 | .05 |
| ❑ SE109 Brett Lindros | .10 | .05 |
| ❑ SE110 Mike Richter | .30 | .14 |
| ❑ SE111 Greg Gilbert | .10 | .05 |
| ❑ SE112 Kevin Lowe | .10 | .05 |
| ❑ SE113 Mark Messier | .40 | .18 |
| ❑ SE114 Alexander Karpovtsev | .10 | .05 |
| ❑ SE115 Sergei Nemchinov | .10 | .05 |
| ❑ SE116 Petr Nedved | .15 | .07 |
| ❑ SE117 Glenn Healy | .15 | .07 |
| ❑ SE118 Dave Archibald | .10 | .05 |
| ❑ SE119 Alexandre Daigle | .15 | .07 |
| ❑ SE120 Darrin Madeley | .10 | .05 |
| ❑ SE121 Pavol Demitra | .10 | .05 |
| ❑ SE122 Brad Shaw | .10 | .05 |
| ❑ SE123 Alexei Yashin | .15 | .07 |
| ❑ SE124 Sean Hill | .10 | .05 |
| ❑ SE125 Vladislav Boulin | .10 | .05 |
| ❑ SE126 Kevin Haller | .10 | .05 |
| ❑ SE127 Chris Therien | .10 | .05 |
| ❑ SE128 Garry Galley | .10 | .05 |
| ❑ SE129 Mikael Renberg | .15 | .07 |
| ❑ SE130 Ron Hextall | .15 | .07 |
| ❑ SE131 Eric Lindros | 1.25 | .55 |
| ❑ SE132 Craig MacTavish | .10 | .05 |
| ❑ SE133 Patrik Juhlin | .15 | .07 |
| ❑ SE134 Martin Straka | .10 | .05 |
| ❑ SE135 Doug Brown | .10 | .05 |
| ❑ SE136 Markus Naslund | .10 | .05 |
| ❑ SE137 Luc Robitaille | .15 | .07 |
| ❑ SE138 Kjell Samuelsson | .10 | .05 |
| ❑ SE139 Ken Wregget | .15 | .07 |
| ❑ SE140 John Cullen | .10 | .05 |
| ❑ SE141 Peter Taglianetti | .10 | .05 |
| ❑ SE142 Janne Laukkanen | .10 | .05 |
| ❑ SE143 Owen Nolan | .15 | .07 |
| ❑ SE144 Adam Deadmarsh | .15 | .07 |
| ❑ SE145 Dave Karpa | .10 | .05 |
| ❑ SE146 Wendel Clark | .15 | .07 |
| ❑ SE147 Joe Sakic | .60 | .25 |
| ❑ SE148 Alexei Gusarov | .10 | .05 |
| ❑ SE149 Peter Forsberg | 1.50 | .70 |
| ❑ SE150 Kevin Miller | .10 | .05 |
| ❑ SE151 Denny Felsner | .10 | .05 |
| ❑ SE152 Al MacInnis | .15 | .07 |
| ❑ SE153 Philippe Bozon | .10 | .05 |
| ❑ SE154 Brett Hull | .40 | .18 |
| ❑ SE155 Guy Carbonneau | .10 | .05 |
| ❑ SE156 Igor Korolev | .10 | .05 |
| ❑ SE157 Esa Tikkanen | .15 | .07 |
| ❑ SE158 Jon Casey | .15 | .07 |
| ❑ SE159 Viktor Kozlov | .15 | .07 |
| ❑ SE160 Mike Rathje | .10 | .05 |
| ❑ SE161 Bob Errey | .10 | .05 |
| ❑ SE162 Arturs Irbe | .15 | .07 |
| ❑ SE163 Ray Whitney | .10 | .05 |
| ❑ SE164 Igor Larionov | .10 | .05 |
| ❑ SE165 Pat Falloon | .10 | .05 |
| ❑ SE166 Jeff Friesen | .15 | .07 |
| ❑ SE167 Vlastimil Kroupa | .10 | .05 |
| ❑ SE168 Chris Joseph | .10 | .05 |
| ❑ SE169 Danton Cole | .10 | .05 |
| ❑ SE170 John Tucker | .10 | .05 |
| ❑ SE171 Roman Hamrlik | .15 | .07 |
| ❑ SE172 Jason Wiemer | .10 | .05 |
| ❑ SE173 Kenny Jonsson | .10 | .05 |
| ❑ SE174 Eric Fichaud | .75 | .35 |
| ❑ SE175 Mats Sundin | .15 | .07 |
| ❑ SE176 Doug Gilmour | .30 | .14 |
| ❑ SE177 Drake Berehowsky | .10 | .05 |
| ❑ SE178 Mike Ridley | .10 | .05 |
| ❑ SE179 Jamie Macoun | .10 | .05 |
| ❑ SE180 Alexei Kudashov | .10 | .05 |
| ❑ SE181 Bill Berg | .10 | .05 |
| ❑ SE182 Dave Andreychuk | .15 | .07 |
| ❑ SE183 Mike Eastwood | .10 | .05 |
| ❑ SE184 Martin Gelinas | .10 | .05 |
| ❑ SE185 Greg Adams | .10 | .05 |
| ❑ SE186 Gino Odjick | .10 | .05 |
| ❑ SE187 Pavel Bure | .60 | .25 |
| ❑ SE188 Cliff Ronning | .10 | .05 |
| ❑ SE189 Jiri Slegr | .10 | .05 |
| ❑ SE190 Jyrki Lumme | .10 | .05 |
| ❑ SE191 Jassen Cullimore | .10 | .05 |
| ❑ SE192 Steve Konowalchuk | .10 | .05 |
| ❑ SE193 Sylvain Cote | .10 | .05 |
| ❑ SE194 Jason Allison | .15 | .07 |
| ❑ SE195 Sergei Gonchar | .10 | .05 |

❑ SE196 Pat Peake .10 .05
❑ SE197 Calle Johansson .10 .05
❑ SE198 Joe Juneau .15 .07
❑ SE199 Jeff Nelson .10 .05
❑ SE200 Luciano Borsato .10 .05
❑ SE201 Teemu Selanne .60 .25
❑ SE202 Tie Domi .15 .07
❑ SE203 Tim Cheveldae .15 .07
❑ SE204 Darrin Shannon .10 .05
❑ SE205 Ravil Gusmanov .10 .05
❑ SE206 Todd Harvey .10 .05
❑ SE207 Ed Jovanovski .30 .14
❑ SE208 Jason Allison .10 .05
❑ SE209 Bryan McCabe .15 .07
❑ SE210 Dan Cloutier .30 .14
❑ SE211 Ladislav Kohn .15 .07
❑ SE212 Marek Malik .15 .07
❑ SE213 Jan Hlavac .15 .07
❑ SE214 Petr Cajanek .15 .07
❑ SE215 Jussi Markkanen .15 .07
❑ SE216 Jere Karalahti .15 .07
❑ SE217 Janne Niinimaa .50 .23
❑ SE218 Kimmo Timonen .15 .07
❑ SE219 Mikko Helisten .15 .07
❑ SE220 Niko Halttunen .15 .07
❑ SE221 Tommi Miettinen .15 .07
❑ SE222 Veli-Pekka Nutikka .15 .07
❑ SE223 Timo Salonen .15 .07
❑ SE224 Tommi Sova .15 .07
❑ SE225 Jussi Tarvainen .15 .07
❑ SE226 Tommi Rajamaki .15 .07
❑ SE227 Antti Alto .15 .07
❑ SE228 Alexandre Koroliouk .15 .07
❑ SE229 Vitali Yachmenev .15 .07
❑ SE230 Nikolai Zavaroukhine .15 .07
❑ SE231 Vadim Epantchinsev .15 .07
❑ SE232 Dmitri Klevakin .15 .07
❑ SE233 Anders Eriksson .15 .07
❑ SE234 Anders Soderberg .15 .07
❑ SE235 Per Svartvadet .15 .07
❑ SE236 Johan Davidsson .10 .05
❑ SE237 Niklas Sundstrom .15 .07
❑ SE238 J. Andersson-Junkka .15 .07
❑ SE239 Dick Tarnstrom .15 .07
❑ SE240 Per-Johan Axelsson .15 .07
❑ SE241 Frederik Johansson .15 .07
❑ SE242 Peter Strom .15 .07
❑ SE243 Mattias Ohlund .15 .07
❑ SE244 Jesper Mattsson .15 .07
❑ SE245 Jonas Forsberg .15 .07
❑ SE246 Adam Deadmarsh .15 .07
❑ SE247 Deron Quint .15 .07
❑ SE248 Jamie Langenbrunner .10 .05
❑ SE249 Richard Park .10 .05
❑ SE250 Bryan Berard 1.50 .70
❑ SE251 David Belitski .15 .07
❑ SE252 Mike McBain .15 .07
❑ SE253 Hugh Hamilton .15 .07
❑ SE254 Jason Doig .15 .07
❑ SE255 Xavier Delisle .15 .07
❑ SE256 Wade Redden .50 .23
❑ SE257 Jeffrey Ware .15 .07
❑ SE258 Christian Dube .50 .23
❑ SE259 L.-Phillipe Sevigny .15 .07
❑ SE260 Jarome Iginla 1.50 .70
❑ SE261 Daniel Briere 1.00 .45
❑ SE262 Justin Kurtz .15 .07
❑ SE263 Marc Savard .10 .05
❑ SE264 Alyn McCauley 1.00 .45
❑ SE265 Brad Mehalko .15 .07
❑ SE266 Jeffrey Ambrosio .15 .07
❑ SE267 Todd Norman .15 .07
❑ SE268 Brian Scott .15 .07
❑ SE269 Brad Larsen .15 .07
❑ SE270 Jean Sebastien Giguere .50 .23
❑ NNO Wayne Gretzky Large 4.00 1.80

## 1994-95 Parkhurst SE Gold

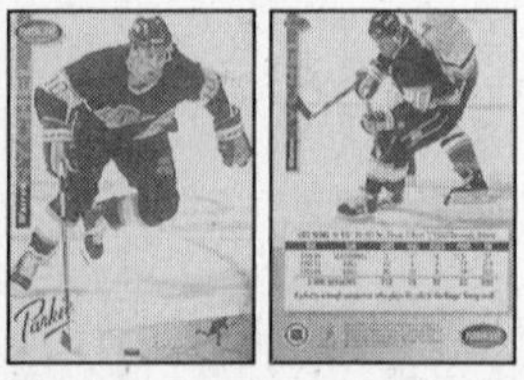

This 270-card set parallels the regular Parkhurst SE issue. The distinguishing feature between the two is that the normally silver player icon on the card front is now gold with the word "Parkie" printed alongside it in gold foil. Interestingly, these cards, which were inserted at a rate of one per pack, are significantly easier to find than the gold cards which paralleled the regular Parkhurst set which were inserted 1:35 packs. The cards are grouped alphabetically within teams and checklisted as in the regular set.

| | MINT | NRMT |
|---|---|---|
| COMPLETE SET (270) | 200.00 | 90.00 |
| COMMON CARD (1-270) | .25 | .11 |

*STARS: 4X TO 8X BASIC CARDS
*YOUNG STARS: 2X TO 5X BASIC CARDS

## 1994-95 Parkhurst SE Euro-Stars

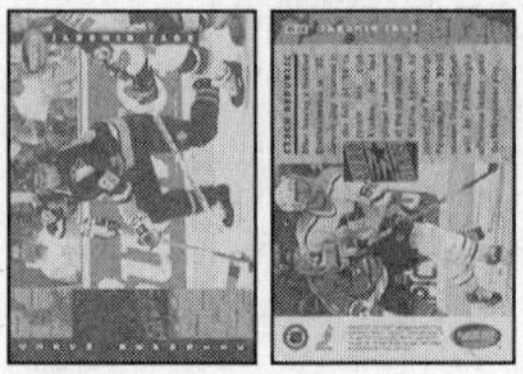

The 20 cards in this set were randomly inserted in Parkhurst SE product at an approximate rate of 1:8 packs. The set has some of the top European-born talent in the NHL. The cards feature a horizontal design with an action photo on the right and set logo and European map elements on the left. Card numbers have an "ES" prefix.

| | MINT | NRMT |
|---|---|---|
| COMPLETE SET (20) | 25.00 | 11.00 |
| COMMON CARD (ES1-ES20) | .40 | .18 |

❑ ES1 Peter Forsberg 8.00 3.60
❑ ES2 Mats Sundin .75 .35
❑ ES3 Mikael Renberg .75 .35
❑ ES4 Nicklas Lidstrom .75 .35
❑ ES5 Mariusz Czerkawski .40 .18
❑ ES6 Ulf Dahlen .40 .18
❑ ES7 Kjell Samuelsson .40 .18
❑ ES8 Jyrki Lumme .40 .18
❑ ES9 Jari Kurri .75 .35
❑ ES10 Teppo Numminen .40 .18
❑ ES11 Esa Tikkanen .40 .18
❑ ES12 Christian Ruuttu .40 .18
❑ ES13 Teemu Selanne 3.00 1.35
❑ ES14 Alexander Mogilny .75 .35
❑ ES15 Pavel Bure 3.00 1.35
❑ ES16 Sergei Fedorov 3.00 1.35
❑ ES17 Arturs Irbe .75 .35
❑ ES18 Alexei Kovalev .75 .35
❑ ES19 Dominik Hasek 3.00 1.35
❑ ES20 Jaromir Jagr 5.00 2.20

## 1994-95 Parkhurst SE Vintage

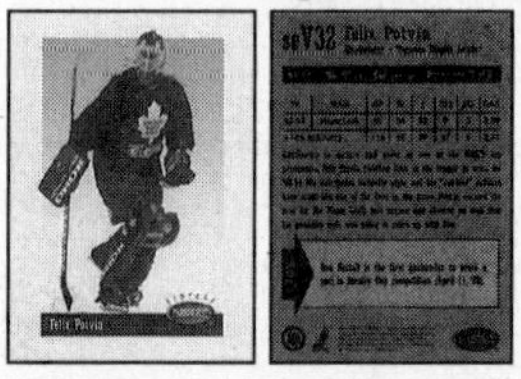

This 45-card standard-size was inserted in Parkhurst SE packs at approximately the rate of 1:6. They are printed on heavy white card stock with a design that hearkens back to the style of Parkhurst issues of the 1950s and 1960s. The player photo is cut out and placed on a white-and-tan background. The player's name appears in a black bar on the lower portion of the card, alongside the set logo. The card backs are an unfinished cardboard and feature professional statistics, biography and a "Did You Know" section containing interesting trivia, which did not apply to the player pictured. The cards were numbered with a "seV" prefix.

| | MINT | NRMT |
|---|---|---|
| COMPLETE SET (45) | 40.00 | 18.00 |
| COMMON CARD (seV1-seV45) | .25 | .11 |

❑ 1 Paul Kariya 6.00 2.70
❑ 2 Dino Ciccarelli .25 .11
❑ 3 Patrick Roy 8.00 3.60
❑ 4 Markus Naslund .25 .11
❑ 5 Trevor Linden 1.25 .55
❑ 6 Valeri Karpov .25 .11
❑ 7 Pat Verbeek .25 .11
❑ 8 Martin Brodeur 4.00 1.80
❑ 9 Kevin Stevens .25 .11
❑ 10 Kirk McLean 1.25 .55
❑ 11 Stephan Lebeau .25 .11
❑ 12 Scott Niedermayer .25 .11
❑ 13 Peter Bondra 1.25 .55
❑ 14 Ed Belfour 1.50 .70
❑ 15 Paul Coffey 1.50 .70
❑ 16 Chris Gratton 1.25 .55
❑ 17 Joe Juneau 1.25 .55
❑ 18 Ray Bourque 1.50 .70
❑ 19 Sergei Krivokrasov .25 .11
❑ 20 Wayne Gretzky 10.00 4.50
❑ 21 Alexei Yashin 1.25 .55
❑ 22 Al Iafrate .25 .11
❑ 23 Doug Weight 1.25 .55
❑ 24 Jari Kurri .25 .11
❑ 25 Rod Brind'Amour 1.25 .55
❑ 26 Bryan Smolinski .25 .11
❑ 27 Darius Kasparaitis .25 .11
❑ 28 Mark Recchi .25 .11
❑ 29 Mike Gartner 1.25 .55
❑ 30 Russ Courtnall .25 .11
❑ 31 Pierre Turgeon 1.25 .55
❑ 32 Felix Potvin 1.50 .70
❑ 33 Nelson Emerson .25 .11
❑ 34 Alexander Mogilny 1.25 .55
❑ 35 Bob Kudelski .25 .11
❑ 36 Brett Lindros .25 .11
❑ 37 Mats Sundin 1.50 .70
❑ 38 Keith Tkachuk 2.00 .90
❑ 39 Derek Plante .25 .11
❑ 40 Oleg Petrov .25 .11
❑ 41 Adam Graves 1.25 .55
❑ 42 Jaromir Jagr 5.00 2.20
❑ 43 Viktor Kozlov .25 .11
❑ 44 Nathan Lafayette .25 .11
❑ 45 Alexei Zhamnov 1.25 .55

## 1995-96 Parkhurst '66-67 Promos

This five-card set was issued to promote the third installment of the Missing Link trilogy. The cards mirror the corresponding regular versions, save for the word PROMO stamped on the back, and a statement which reveals these cards were limited to 1966 copies.

| | MINT | NRMT |
|---|---|---|
| COMPLETE SET (5) | 15.00 | 6.75 |
| COMMON CARD (1-5) | .75 | .35 |

❑ 1 Gerry Cheevers 3.00 1.35
Boston Bruins
❑ 2 Bob Nevin .75 .35
New York Rangers
❑ 3 Jacques Laperriere .75 .35
Norris Trophy Winner
❑ 4 Jean Beliveau 4.00 1.80
Stan Mikita AS
❑ 5 Gordie Howe 10.00 4.50
Detroit Red Wings

## 1995-96 Parkhurst '66-67

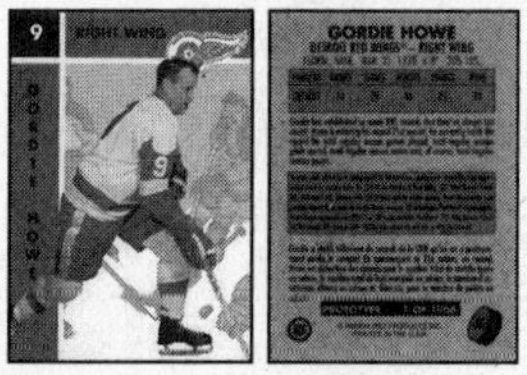

This 150-card set lovingly speculates on what might have been had Parkhurst, the venerable Canadian card manufacturer, been active during Bobby Orr's rookie card season. 2500 numbered 16-box cases were produced of the eight-card packs. The cards utilized period photos and a design element consistent with the time. There were two five-card insert sets honoring "Super Rookie" Orr and "Mr. Hockey" Gordie Howe. Orr and Howe autographed 500 of each card in their respective sets. The five promo cards were issued in set form. They are identical to the regular versions of the cards, save for the bold notation on the back which proclaims them to be prototypes limited to 1966 copies.

| | MINT | NRMT |
|---|---|---|
| COMPLETE SET (150) | 25.00 | 11.00 |
| COMMON CARD (1-150) | .10 | .05 |

❑ 1 Pit Martin .15 .07
❑ 2 Ron Stewart .15 .07
❑ 3 Joe Watson .10 .05
❑ 4 Ed Westfall .10 .05
❑ 5 John Bucyk .25 .11
❑ 6 Ted Green .15 .07
❑ 7 Bobby Orr 5.00 2.20
❑ 8 Bob Woytowich .10 .05
❑ 9 Murray Oliver .10 .05
❑ 10 John McKenzie .15 .07
❑ 11 Tom Williams .10 .05
❑ 12 Don Awrey .10 .05
❑ 13 Ron Schock .10 .05
❑ 14 Bernie Parent 1.00 .45
❑ 15 Ron Murphy .10 .05
❑ 16 Gerry Cheevers 1.00 .45
❑ 17 Gilles Marotte .10 .05
❑ 18 Ed Johnston .15 .07
❑ 19 Derek Sanderson 1.00 .45
❑ 20 Wayne Connelly .10 .05
❑ 21 Bobby Hull 3.00 1.35
❑ 22 Matt Ravlich .10 .05
❑ 23 Ken Hodge .15 .07
❑ 24 Stan Mikita 1.50 .70
❑ 25 Fred Stanfield .10 .05
❑ 26 Eric Nesterenko .15 .07
❑ 27 Doug Jarrett .10 .05
❑ 28 Lou Angotti .10 .05
❑ 29 Ken Wharram .10 .05
❑ 30 Bill Hay .10 .05
❑ 31 Glenn Hall 1.50 .70
❑ 32 Chico Maki .10 .05
❑ 33 Phil Esposito 1.50 .70
❑ 34 Pierre Pilote .25 .11
❑ 35 Doug Mohns .10 .05
❑ 36 Ed Van Impe .10 .05
❑ 37 Dennis Hull .15 .07
❑ 38 Pat Stapleton .10 .05
❑ 39 Denis DeJordy .10 .05
❑ 40 Paul Henderson .15 .07
❑ 41 Gary Bergman .10 .05
❑ 42 Gordie Howe 4.00 1.80
❑ 43 Bob McCord .10 .05
❑ 44 Andy Bathgate .25 .11
❑ 45 Norm Ullman .25 .11
❑ 46 Peter Mahovlich .15 .07
❑ 47 Ted Hampson .10 .05
❑ 48 Leo Boivin .25 .11
❑ 49 Bruce MacGregor .10 .05
❑ 50 Ab McDonald .15 .07
❑ 51 Dean Prentice .10 .05
❑ 52 Floyd Smith .10 .05
❑ 53 Alex Delvecchio .25 .11
❑ 54 Pete Goegan .10 .05
❑ 55 Parker MacDonald .10 .05
❑ 56 Roger Crozier .15 .07
❑ 57 Val Fonteyne .10 .05
❑ 58 Henri Richard 1.00 .45
❑ 59 John Ferguson .15 .07
❑ 60 Yvan Cournoyer .25 .11
❑ 61 Claude Provost .15 .07
❑ 62 Dave Balon .10 .05
❑ 63 Ted Harris .10 .05
❑ 64 Ralph Backstrom .15 .07
❑ 65 Jacques Laperriere .25 .11
❑ 66 Terry Harper .15 .07
❑ 67 J.C. Tremblay .15 .07
❑ 68 Jean Guy Talbot .15 .07
❑ 69 Claude Larose .15 .07
❑ 70 Charlie Hodge .15 .07
❑ 71 Gilles Tremblay .10 .05
❑ 72 Jim Roberts .10 .05
❑ 73 Jean Beliveau 1.50 .70
❑ 74 Serge Savard .25 .11
❑ 75 Rogatien Vachon .75 .35
❑ 76 Lorne Worsley 1.50 .70
❑ 77 Bobby Rousseau .15 .07
❑ 78 Dick Duff .15 .07
❑ 79 Rod Gilbert .25 .11
❑ 80 Harry Howell .25 .11
❑ 81 Jim Neilson .10 .05
❑ 82 Don Marshall .10 .05
❑ 83 Reg Fleming .10 .05
❑ 84 Wayne Hillman .10 .05
❑ 85 Bob Nevin .10 .05
❑ 86 Arnie Brown .10 .05
❑ 87 Earl Ingarfield .10 .05
❑ 88 Jean Ratelle .25 .11
❑ 89 Bernie Geoffrion 1.00 .45
❑ 90 Orland Kurtenbach .10 .05
❑ 91 Bill Hicke .10 .05
❑ 92 Red Berenson .15 .07
❑ 93 Ed Giacomin .25 .11
❑ 94 Al MacNeil .10 .05
❑ 95 Rod Seiling .10 .05
❑ 96 Doug Robinson .10 .05
❑ 97 Cesare Maniago .15 .07
❑ 98 Vic Hadfield .10 .05
❑ 99 Phil Goyette .10 .05
❑ 100 Dave Keon .25 .11
❑ 101 Mike Walton .10 .05
❑ 102 Frank Mahovlich 1.50 .70
❑ 103 Tim Horton 1.50 .70
❑ 104 Larry Hillman .10 .05
❑ 105 Kent Douglas .10 .05
❑ 106 Ron Ellis .10 .05
❑ 107 Jim Pappin .10 .05
❑ 108 Marcel Pronovost .25 .11
❑ 109 Red Kelly .25 .11
❑ 110 Allan Stanley .25 .11
❑ 111 Brit Selby .10 .05
❑ 112 Pete Stemkowski .10 .05
❑ 113 Eddie Shack 1.00 .45
❑ 114 Bob Pulford .25 .11
❑ 115 Larry Jeffrey .10 .05
❑ 116 George Armstrong .25 .11
❑ 117 Bob Baun .15 .07
❑ 118 Bruce Gamble .10 .05
❑ 119 Johnny Bower 1.50 .70
❑ 120 Terry Sawchuk 2.00 .90
❑ 121 Hall/Worsley AS .75 .35
❑ 122 Laperriere/Stanley AS .15 .07
❑ 123 Pilote/Stapleton AS .15 .07
❑ 124 Hull/Mahovlich AS 1.00 .45
❑ 125 Mikita/Beliveau AS .75 .35
❑ 126 Howe/Rousseau AS 1.50 .70
❑ 127 Alex Delvecchio .15 .07
Lady Byng
❑ 128 Jacques Laperriere .15 .07
Norris
❑ 129 Bobby Hull 1.50 .70
Hart
❑ 130 Bobby Hull 1.50 .70
Art Ross
❑ 131 Worsley/Hodge .50 .23
Vezina
❑ 132 Brit Selby .10 .05
Calder
❑ 133 Action Card .15 .07
All-Star Game
❑ 134 Action Card .15 .07
❑ 135 Action Card .15 .07
❑ 136 Action Card .15 .07
❑ 137 Action Card .15 .07
❑ 138 Action Card .15 .07
❑ 139 Action Card .15 .07
❑ 140 Murray Oliver L .10 .05
❑ 141 Bobby Hull L 1.50 .70
❑ 142 Gordie Howe L 2.00 .90
❑ 143 Bobby Rousseau L .10 .05
❑ 144 Bob Nevin L .10 .05
❑ 145 Mahovlich/Pulford L .25 .11
❑ 146 Stanley Cup Playoffs .15 .07
Semifinals
❑ 147 Stanley Cup Playoffs .15 .07
Semifinals
❑ 148 Stanley Cup Playoffs Finals .15 .07
❑ 149 Checklist .10 .05
❑ 150 Checklist .10 .05
❑ PR16 Gerry Cheevers promo 5.00 2.20
❑ PR42 Gordie Howe promo 20.00 9.00
❑ PR125 Stan Mikita/Jean Beliveau 5.00 2.20
AS promo
❑ PR128 Jacques Laperriere .75 .35
TW promo
❑ PR144 Bob Nevin SL promo .50 .23
❑ SR1 Bobby Orr 15.00 6.75
❑ SR2 Bobby Orr 15.00 6.75
❑ SR3 Bobby Orr 15.00 6.75
❑ SR4 Bobby Orr 15.00 6.75
❑ SR5 Bobby Orr 15.00 6.75
❑ MHA1 Gordie Howe AU 125.00 55.00
❑ MHA2 Gordie Howe AU 125.00 55.00
❑ MHA3 Gordie Howe AU 125.00 55.00
❑ MHA4 Gordie Howe AU 125.00 55.00
❑ MHA5 Gordie Howe AU 125.00 55.00
❑ MRH1 Gordie Howe 12.00 5.50
❑ MRH2 Gordie Howe 12.00 5.50
❑ MRH3 Gordie Howe 12.00 5.50
❑ MRH4 Gordie Howe 12.00 5.50
❑ MRH5 Gordie Howe 12.00 5.50
❑ SRA1 Bobby Orr AU 200.00 90.00
❑ SRA2 Bobby Orr AU 200.00 90.00
❑ SRA3 Bobby Orr AU 200.00 90.00
❑ SRA4 Bobby Orr AU 200.00 90.00
❑ SRA5 Bobby Orr AU 200.00 90.00

## 1995-96 Parkhurst '66-67 Coins

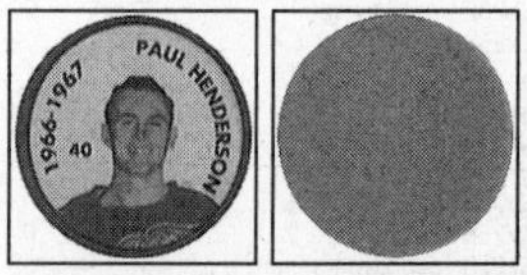


In tip of the hat fashion, this 120-coin insert set recreates the popular Shirriff coins of the 1960s. The plastic coins were team color coded, and were inserted one per pack. The coins measure about 1 3/8" in diameter. They are numbered in identical fashion to the card set as the same players are featured. Several collectors and dealers have reported the Paul Henderson coin (#40) as being difficult to locate. Parkhurst officials, however, say no coin was printed in shorter quantity than any other. There also were five black coins randomly inserted honoring Bobby Orr and Gordie Howe.

| | MINT | NRMT |
|---|---|---|
| COMPLETE SET (120) | 175.00 | 80.00 |
| COMMON COIN (1-120) | .60 | .25 |

❑ 1 Pit Martin 1.00 .45
❑ 2 Ron Stewart 1.00 .45
❑ 3 Joe Watson .60 .25
❑ 4 Ed Westfall .60 .25
❑ 5 John Bucyk 1.50 .70
❑ 6 Ted Green 1.00 .45
❑ 7 Bobby Orr 10.00 4.50
❑ 8 Bob Woytowich .60 .25
❑ 9 Murray Oliver .60 .25
❑ 10 John McKenzie 1.00 .45
❑ 11 Tom Williams .60 .25
❑ 12 Don Awrey .60 .25
❑ 13 Ron Schock .60 .25
❑ 14 Bernie Parent 3.00 1.35
❑ 15 Ron Murphy .60 .25
❑ 16 Gerry Cheevers 3.00 1.35
❑ 17 Gilles Marotte .60 .25
❑ 18 Ed Johnston 1.00 .45
❑ 19 Derek Sanderson 3.00 1.35
❑ 20 Wayne Connelly .60 .25
❑ 21 Bobby Hull 6.00 2.70
❑ 22 Matt Ravlich .60 .25
❑ 23 Ken Hodge 1.00 .45
❑ 24 Stan Mikita 4.00 1.80
❑ 25 Fred Stanfield .60 .25
❑ 26 Eric Nesterenko 1.00 .45
❑ 27 Doug Jarrett .60 .25
❑ 28 Lou Angotti .60 .25
❑ 29 Ken Wharram .60 .25
❑ 30 Bill Hay .60 .25
❑ 31 Glenn Hall 4.00 1.80
❑ 32 Chico Maki .60 .25
❑ 33 Phil Esposito 4.00 1.80
❑ 34 Pierre Pilote 1.50 .70
❑ 35 Doug Mohns .60 .25
❑ 36 Ed Van Impe .60 .25
❑ 37 Dennis Hull 1.00 .45
❑ 38 Pat Stapleton .60 .25
❑ 39 Denis DeJordy .60 .25
❑ 40 Paul Henderson 10.00 4.50
❑ 41 Gary Bergman .60 .25
❑ 42 Gordie Howe 8.00 3.60
❑ 43 Bob McCord .60 .25
❑ 44 Andy Bathgate 1.50 .70
❑ 45 Norm Ullman 1.50 .70
❑ 46 Peter Mahovlich 1.00 .45
❑ 47 Ted Hampson .60 .25
❑ 48 Leo Boivin 1.50 .70
❑ 49 Bruce MacGregor .60 .25
❑ 50 Ab McDonald 1.00 .45
❑ 51 Dean Prentice .60 .25
❑ 52 Floyd Smith .60 .25

| | | |
|---|---|---|
| ❑ 53 Alex Delvecchio | 1.50 | .70 |
| ❑ 54 Pete Goegan | .60 | .25 |
| ❑ 55 Parker MacDonald | .60 | .25 |
| ❑ 56 Roger Crozier | 1.00 | .45 |
| ❑ 57 Val Fonteyne | .60 | .25 |
| ❑ 58 Henri Richard | 3.00 | 1.35 |
| ❑ 59 John Ferguson | 1.00 | .45 |
| ❑ 60 Yvan Cournoyer | 1.50 | .70 |
| ❑ 61 Claude Provost | 1.00 | .45 |
| ❑ 62 Dave Balon | .60 | .25 |
| ❑ 63 Ted Harris | .60 | .25 |
| ❑ 64 Ralph Backstrom | 1.00 | .45 |
| ❑ 65 Jacques Laperriere | 1.50 | .70 |
| ❑ 66 Terry Harper | 1.00 | .45 |
| ❑ 67 J.C. Tremblay | 1.00 | .45 |
| ❑ 68 Jean Guy Talbot | 1.00 | .45 |
| ❑ 69 Claude Larose | 1.00 | .45 |
| ❑ 70 Charlie Hodge | 1.00 | .45 |
| ❑ 71 Gilles Tremblay | .60 | .25 |
| ❑ 72 Jim Roberts | .60 | .25 |
| ❑ 73 Jean Beliveau | 4.00 | 1.80 |
| ❑ 74 Serge Savard | 1.50 | .70 |
| ❑ 75 Rogatien Vachon | 3.00 | 1.35 |
| ❑ 76 Lorne Worsley | 4.00 | 1.80 |
| ❑ 77 Bobby Rousseau | 1.00 | .45 |
| ❑ 78 Dick Duff | 1.00 | .45 |
| ❑ 79 Rod Gilbert | 1.50 | .70 |
| ❑ 80 Harry Howell | 1.50 | .70 |
| ❑ 81 Jim Neilson | .60 | .25 |
| ❑ 82 Don Marshall | .60 | .25 |
| ❑ 83 Reg Fleming | .60 | .25 |
| ❑ 84 Wayne Hillman | .60 | .25 |
| ❑ 85 Bob Nevin | .60 | .25 |
| ❑ 86 Arnie Brown | .60 | .25 |
| ❑ 87 Earl Ingarfield | .60 | .25 |
| ❑ 88 Jean Ratelle | 1.50 | .70 |
| ❑ 89 Bernie Geoffrion | 3.00 | 1.35 |
| ❑ 90 Orland Kurtenbach | .60 | .25 |
| ❑ 91 Bill Hicke | .60 | .25 |
| ❑ 92 Red Berenson | 1.00 | .45 |
| ❑ 93 Ed Giacomin | 1.50 | .70 |
| ❑ 94 Al MacNeil | .60 | .25 |
| ❑ 95 Rod Seiling | .60 | .25 |
| ❑ 96 Doug Robinson | .60 | .25 |
| ❑ 97 Cesare Maniago | 1.00 | .45 |
| ❑ 98 Vic Hadfield | .60 | .25 |
| ❑ 99 Phil Goyette | .60 | .25 |
| ❑ 100 Dave Keon | 1.50 | .70 |
| ❑ 101 Mike Walton | .60 | .25 |
| ❑ 102 Frank Mahovlich | 4.00 | 1.80 |
| ❑ 103 Tim Horton | 4.00 | 1.80 |
| ❑ 104 Larry Hillman | .60 | .25 |
| ❑ 105 Kent Douglas | .60 | .25 |
| ❑ 106 Ron Ellis | .60 | .25 |
| ❑ 107 Jim Pappin | .60 | .25 |
| ❑ 108 Marcel Pronovost | 1.50 | .70 |
| ❑ 109 Red Kelly | 1.50 | .70 |
| ❑ 110 Allan Stanley | 1.50 | .70 |
| ❑ 111 Brit Selby | .60 | .25 |
| ❑ 112 Pete Stemkowski | .60 | .25 |
| ❑ 113 Eddie Shack | 3.00 | 1.35 |
| ❑ 114 Bob Pulford | 1.50 | .70 |
| ❑ 115 Larry Jeffrey | .60 | .25 |
| ❑ 116 George Armstrong | 1.50 | .70 |
| ❑ 117 Bob Baun | 1.00 | .45 |
| ❑ 118 Bruce Gamble | .60 | .25 |
| ❑ 119 Johnny Bower | 4.00 | 1.80 |
| ❑ 120 Terry Sawchuk | 5.00 | 2.20 |
| ❑ BO1 Bobby Orr Black Coin | 10.00 | 4.50 |
| ❑ BO2 Bobby Orr Black Coin | 10.00 | 4.50 |
| ❑ BO3 Bobby Orr Black Coin | 10.00 | 4.50 |
| ❑ BO4 Bobby Orr Black Coin | 10.00 | 4.50 |
| ❑ BO5 Bobby Orr Black Coin | 10.00 | 4.50 |
| ❑ GH1 Gordie Howe Black Coin | 8.00 | 3.60 |
| ❑ GH2 Gordie Howe Black Coin | 8.00 | 3.60 |
| ❑ GH3 Gordie Howe Black Coin | 8.00 | 3.60 |
| ❑ GH4 Gordie Howe Black Coin | 8.00 | 3.60 |
| ❑ GH5 Gordie Howe Black Coin | 8.00 | 3.60 |

## 1995-96 Parkhurst International

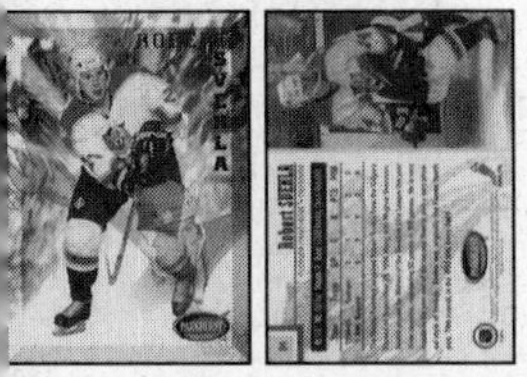

his two-series issue was produced by arkhurst in Canada for release in eleven uropean countries. Interest in the cards, which featured NHL players and were licensed y both the NHL and NHLPA, was such that ey became widely available throughout North merica. The first series was produced in rger quantities than the second series, which y some estimates was limited to around 900 ases. Each box included 48 14-card packs. e second series is notable for including the st card of Wayne Gretzky in a St. Louis Blues niform. Two different players autographed rds for insertion in each series: Teemu elanne and Mikael Renberg each signed 500 cards for series 1, while Martin Brodeur d Saku Koivu inked up 2,500 each for series One jumbo Saku Koivu card was inserted in ch series 2 box; autographed copies of this mbo card were randomly inserted as well.

| | MINT | NRMT |
|---|---|---|
| COMPLETE SET (540) | 45.00 | 20.00 |
| COMPLETE SERIES 1 (270) | 20.00 | 9.00 |
| COMPLETE SERIES 2 (270) | 25.00 | 11.00 |
| COMMON CARD (1-540) | .10 | .05 |
| ❑ 1 Patrik Carnback | .10 | .05 |
| ❑ 2 Milos Holan | .10 | .05 |
| ❑ 3 Paul Kariya | 1.00 | .45 |
| ❑ 4 Guy Hebert | .15 | .07 |
| ❑ 5 Garry Valk | .10 | .05 |
| ❑ 6 Mikhail Shtalenkov | .10 | .05 |
| ❑ 7 Randy Ladouceur | .10 | .05 |
| ❑ 8 Shaun Van Allen | .10 | .05 |
| ❑ 9 Oleg Tverdovsky | .15 | .07 |
| ❑ 10 Kevin Stevens | .10 | .05 |
| ❑ 11 Ray Bourque | .25 | .11 |
| ❑ 12 Cam Neely | .15 | .07 |
| ❑ 13 Jozef Stumpel | .10 | .05 |
| ❑ 14 Blaine Lacher | .15 | .07 |
| ❑ 15 Alexei Kasatonov | .10 | .05 |
| ❑ 16 Adam Oates | .15 | .07 |
| ❑ 17 Ted Donato | .10 | .05 |
| ❑ 18 Mariusz Czerkawski | .10 | .05 |
| ❑ 19 Alexei Zhitnik | .10 | .05 |
| ❑ 20 Pat LaFontaine | .15 | .07 |
| ❑ 21 Garry Galley | .10 | .05 |
| ❑ 22 Scott Pearson | .10 | .05 |
| ❑ 23 Yuri Khmylev | .10 | .05 |
| ❑ 24 Jason Dawe | .10 | .05 |
| ❑ 25 Robb Stauber | .15 | .07 |
| ❑ 26 Wayne Primeau | .10 | .05 |
| ❑ 27 Brian Holzinger | .25 | .11 |
| ❑ 28 German Titov | .10 | .05 |
| ❑ 29 Theoren Fleury | .15 | .07 |
| ❑ 30 Phil Housley | .15 | .07 |
| ❑ 31 Zarley Zalapski | .10 | .05 |
| ❑ 32 Rick Tabaracci | .15 | .07 |
| ❑ 33 Joe Nieuwendyk | .15 | .07 |
| ❑ 34 Michael Nylander | .10 | .05 |
| ❑ 35 Trevor Kidd | .15 | .07 |
| ❑ 36 Dean Evason | .10 | .05 |
| ❑ 37 Bernie Nicholls | .10 | .05 |
| ❑ 38 Chris Chelios | .25 | .11 |
| ❑ 39 Gary Suter | .10 | .05 |
| ❑ 40 Denis Savard | .15 | .07 |
| ❑ 41 Ed Belfour | .25 | .11 |
| ❑ 42 Patrick Poulin | .10 | .05 |
| ❑ 43 Steve Smith | .10 | .05 |
| ❑ 44 Jeff Hackett | .15 | .07 |
| ❑ 45 Eric Daze | .25 | .11 |
| ❑ 46 Joe Sakic | .50 | .23 |
| ❑ 47 John Slaney | .10 | .05 |
| ❑ 48 Valeri Kamensky | .15 | .07 |
| ❑ 49 Owen Nolan | .15 | .07 |
| ❑ 50 Uwe Krupp | .10 | .05 |
| ❑ 51 Andrei Kovalenko | .10 | .05 |
| ❑ 52 Janne Laukkanen | .10 | .05 |
| ❑ 53 Jocelyn Thibault | .25 | .11 |
| ❑ 54 Adam Deadmarsh | .15 | .07 |
| ❑ 55 Mike Modano | .40 | .18 |
| ❑ 56 Kevin Hatcher | .10 | .05 |
| ❑ 57 Mike Donnelly | .10 | .05 |
| ❑ 58 Derian Hatcher | .10 | .05 |
| ❑ 59 Andy Moog | .15 | .07 |
| ❑ 60 Jamie Langenbrunner | .10 | .05 |
| ❑ 61 Shane Churla | .10 | .05 |
| ❑ 62 Todd Harvey | .10 | .05 |
| ❑ 63 Manny Fernandez | .10 | .05 |
| ❑ 64 Nicklas Lidstrom | .15 | .07 |
| ❑ 65 Vyacheslav Kozlov | .10 | .05 |
| ❑ 66 Paul Coffey | .25 | .11 |
| ❑ 67 Chris Osgood | .25 | .11 |
| ❑ 68 Viacheslav Fetisov | .10 | .05 |
| ❑ 69 Vladimir Konstantinov | .10 | .05 |
| ❑ 70 Steve Yzerman | .75 | .35 |
| ❑ 71 Aaron Ward | .10 | .05 |
| ❑ 72 Keith Primeau | .15 | .07 |
| ❑ 73 Jason Arnott | .15 | .07 |
| ❑ 74 Igor Kravchuk | .10 | .05 |
| ❑ 75 Boris Mironov | .10 | .05 |
| ❑ 76 David Oliver | .10 | .05 |
| ❑ 77 Kelly Buchberger | .10 | .05 |
| ❑ 78 Bill Ranford | .15 | .07 |
| ❑ 79 Zdeno Ciger | .10 | .05 |
| ❑ 80 Jason Bonsignore | .10 | .05 |
| ❑ 81 Louie DeBrusk | .10 | .05 |
| ❑ 82 Rob Niedermayer | .15 | .07 |
| ❑ 83 Magnus Svensson | .10 | .05 |
| ❑ 84 Robert Svehla | .10 | .05 |
| ❑ 85 John Vanbiesbrouck | .40 | .18 |
| ❑ 86 Stu Barnes | .10 | .05 |
| ❑ 87 Jesse Belanger | .10 | .05 |
| ❑ 88 Mark Fitzpatrick | .15 | .07 |
| ❑ 89 Jason Woolley | .10 | .05 |
| ❑ 90 Johan Garpenlov | .10 | .05 |
| ❑ 91 Geoff Sanderson | .15 | .07 |
| ❑ 92 Robert Kron | .10 | .05 |
| ❑ 93 Darren Turcotte | .10 | .05 |
| ❑ 94 Andrei Nikolishin | .10 | .05 |
| ❑ 95 Steven Rice | .10 | .05 |
| ❑ 96 Sean Burke | .15 | .07 |
| ❑ 97 Brendan Shanahan | .50 | .23 |
| ❑ 98 Glen Wesley | .10 | .05 |
| ❑ 99 Marek Malik | .10 | .05 |
| ❑ 100 Wayne Gretzky | 2.00 | .90 |
| ❑ 101 Robert Lang | .10 | .05 |
| ❑ 102 Jari Kurri | .15 | .07 |
| ❑ 103 Kelly Hrudey | .15 | .07 |
| ❑ 104 Jamie Storr | .15 | .07 |
| ❑ 105 Marty McSorley | .10 | .05 |
| ❑ 106 Rob Blake | .10 | .05 |
| ❑ 107 Eric LaCroix | .10 | .05 |
| ❑ 108 Dimitri Khristich | .10 | .05 |
| ❑ 109 Pierre Turgeon | .15 | .07 |
| ❑ 110 Vincent Damphousse | .15 | .07 |
| ❑ 111 Peter Popovic | .10 | .05 |
| ❑ 112 Brian Savage | .10 | .05 |
| ❑ 113 Patrick Roy | 1.25 | .55 |
| ❑ 114 Valeri Bure | .15 | .07 |
| ❑ 115 Vladimir Malakhov | .10 | .05 |
| ❑ 116 Benoit Brunet | .10 | .05 |
| ❑ 117 Stephane Quintal | .10 | .05 |
| ❑ 118 Stephane Richer | .15 | .07 |
| ❑ 119 Sergei Brylin | .10 | .05 |
| ❑ 120 Neal Broten | .15 | .07 |
| ❑ 121 Scott Stevens | .15 | .07 |
| ❑ 122 Martin Brodeur | .60 | .25 |
| ❑ 123 John MacLean | .15 | .07 |
| ❑ 124 Bill Guerin | .10 | .05 |
| ❑ 125 Bobby Holik | .10 | .05 |
| ❑ 126 Tommy Albelin | .10 | .05 |
| ❑ 127 Tommy Soderstrom | .15 | .07 |
| ❑ 128 Tommy Salo | .15 | .07 |
| ❑ 129 Kirk Muller | .10 | .05 |
| ❑ 130 Mathieu Schneider | .10 | .05 |
| ❑ 131 Zigmund Palffy | .15 | .07 |
| ❑ 132 Derek King | .10 | .05 |
| ❑ 133 Brett Lindros | .10 | .05 |
| ❑ 134 Marty McInnis | .10 | .05 |
| ❑ 135 Alexander Semak | .10 | .05 |
| ❑ 136 Mark Messier | .40 | .18 |
| ❑ 137 Adam Graves | .15 | .07 |
| ❑ 138 Mike Richter | .25 | .11 |
| ❑ 139 Alexei Kovalev | .10 | .05 |
| ❑ 140 Luc Robitaille | .15 | .07 |
| ❑ 141 Sergei Nemchinov | .10 | .05 |
| ❑ 142 Alexander Karpovtsev | .10 | .05 |
| ❑ 143 Mattias Norstrom | .10 | .05 |
| ❑ 144 Brian Leetch | .25 | .11 |
| ❑ 145 Martin Straka | .10 | .05 |
| ❑ 146 Sylvain Turgeon | .10 | .05 |
| ❑ 147 Radek Bonk | .10 | .05 |
| ❑ 148 Stanislav Neckar | .10 | .05 |
| ❑ 149 Pavol Demitra | .10 | .05 |
| ❑ 150 Alexandre Daigle | .10 | .05 |
| ❑ 151 Alexei Yashin | .15 | .07 |
| ❑ 152 Don Beaupre | .15 | .07 |
| ❑ 153 Steve Duchesne | .10 | .05 |
| ❑ 154 Eric Lindros | .75 | .35 |
| ❑ 155 Kjell Samuelsson | .10 | .05 |
| ❑ 156 Chris Therien | .10 | .05 |
| ❑ 157 John LeClair | .40 | .18 |
| ❑ 158 Rod Brind'Amour | .15 | .07 |
| ❑ 159 Ron Hextall | .15 | .07 |
| ❑ 160 Patrik Juhlin | .10 | .05 |
| ❑ 161 Mikael Renberg | .15 | .07 |
| ❑ 162 Joel Otto | .10 | .05 |
| ❑ 163 Markus Naslund | .10 | .05 |
| ❑ 164 Ron Francis | .15 | .07 |
| ❑ 165 Jaromir Jagr | .75 | .35 |
| ❑ 166 Tomas Sandstrom | .10 | .05 |
| ❑ 167 Ken Wregget | .15 | .07 |
| ❑ 168 Bryan Smolinski | .10 | .05 |
| ❑ 169 Richard Park | .10 | .05 |
| ❑ 170 Mario Lemieux | 1.25 | .55 |
| ❑ 171 Norm Maciver | .10 | .05 |
| ❑ 172 Brett Hull | .40 | .18 |
| ❑ 173 Esa Tikkanen | .10 | .05 |
| ❑ 174 Shayne Corson | .10 | .05 |
| ❑ 175 Chris Pronger | .15 | .07 |
| ❑ 176 Ian Laperriere | .10 | .05 |
| ❑ 177 Jon Casey | .15 | .07 |
| ❑ 178 Al MacInnis | .15 | .07 |
| ❑ 179 David Roberts | .10 | .05 |
| ❑ 180 Dale Hawerchuk | .15 | .07 |
| ❑ 181 Michal Sykora | .10 | .05 |
| ❑ 182 Jeff Friesen | .15 | .07 |
| ❑ 183 Ray Whitney | .10 | .05 |
| ❑ 184 Igor Larionov | .10 | .05 |
| ❑ 185 Sandis Ozolinsh | .15 | .07 |
| ❑ 186 Andrei Nazarov | .10 | .05 |
| ❑ 187 Viktor Kozlov | .10 | .05 |
| ❑ 188 Arturs Irbe | .15 | .07 |
| ❑ 189 Wade Flaherty | .15 | .07 |
| ❑ 190 Brian Bradley | .10 | .05 |
| ❑ 191 Paul Ysebaert | .10 | .05 |
| ❑ 192 John Tucker | .10 | .05 |
| ❑ 193 Jason Wiemer | .10 | .05 |
| ❑ 194 Alexander Selivanov | .10 | .05 |
| ❑ 195 Daren Puppa | .15 | .07 |
| ❑ 196 Mikael Andersson | .10 | .05 |
| ❑ 197 Petr Klima | .10 | .05 |
| ❑ 198 Roman Hamrlik | .15 | .07 |
| ❑ 199 Doug Gilmour | .25 | .11 |
| ❑ 200 Damian Rhodes | .15 | .07 |
| ❑ 201 Mats Sundin | .15 | .07 |
| ❑ 202 Todd Gill | .10 | .05 |
| ❑ 203 Kenny Jonsson | .10 | .05 |
| ❑ 204 Felix Potvin | .25 | .11 |
| ❑ 205 Tie Domi | .10 | .05 |
| ❑ 206 Mike Gartner | .15 | .07 |
| ❑ 207 Larry Murphy | .15 | .07 |
| ❑ 208 Josef Beranek | .10 | .05 |
| ❑ 209 Trevor Linden | .15 | .07 |
| ❑ 210 Russ Courtnall | .10 | .05 |
| ❑ 211 Roman Oksiuta | .10 | .05 |
| ❑ 212 Alexander Mogilny | .15 | .07 |
| ❑ 213 Kirk McLean | .15 | .07 |
| ❑ 214 Mike Ridley | .10 | .05 |
| ❑ 215 Jyrki Lumme | .10 | .05 |
| ❑ 216 Bret Hedican | .10 | .05 |
| ❑ 217 Keith Jones | .10 | .05 |
| ❑ 218 Calle Johansson | .10 | .05 |
| ❑ 219 Kelly Miller | .10 | .05 |
| ❑ 220 Olaf Kolzig | .15 | .07 |
| ❑ 221 Joe Juneau | .10 | .05 |
| ❑ 222 Sylvain Cote | .10 | .05 |
| ❑ 223 Dale Hunter | .10 | .05 |
| ❑ 224 Mark Tinordi | .10 | .05 |
| ❑ 225 Sergei Gonchar | .10 | .05 |
| ❑ 226 Alexei Zhamnov | .15 | .07 |
| ❑ 227 Igor Korolev | .10 | .05 |
| ❑ 228 Teppo Numminen | .10 | .05 |
| ❑ 229 Craig Martin | .10 | .05 |
| ❑ 230 Nikolai Khabibulin | .15 | .07 |
| ❑ 231 Michal Grosek | .10 | .05 |
| ❑ 232 Teemu Selanne | .50 | .23 |
| ❑ 233 Dave Manson | .10 | .05 |
| ❑ 234 Tim Cheveldae | .15 | .07 |
| ❑ 235 Esa Tikkanen | .10 | .05 |
| ❑ 236 Dominik Hasek | .25 | .11 |
| ❑ 237 Peter Forsberg | .40 | .18 |
| ❑ 238 Sergei Fedorov | .25 | .11 |
| ❑ 239 Jari Kurri | .15 | .07 |
| ❑ 240 Tommy Soderstrom | .15 | .07 |
| ❑ 241 Alexei Zhamnov | .15 | .07 |
| ❑ 242 Alexei Yashin | .15 | .07 |
| ❑ 243 Mikael Renberg | .15 | .07 |
| ❑ 244 Jaromir Jagr | .40 | .18 |
| ❑ 245 Ulf Dahlen | .10 | .05 |
| ❑ 246 Alexander Mogilny | .15 | .07 |
| ❑ 247 Mats Sundin | .15 | .07 |
| ❑ 248 Pavel Bure | .25 | .11 |
| ❑ 249 Viacheslav Fetisov | .10 | .05 |
| ❑ 250 Teemu Selanne | .25 | .11 |
| ❑ 251 Arturs Irbe | .15 | .07 |
| ❑ 252 Nicklas Lidstrom | .15 | .07 |
| ❑ 253 Aki-Petteri Berg | .10 | .05 |
| ❑ 254 Zdenek Nedved | .10 | .05 |
| ❑ 255 Chad Kilger | .10 | .05 |
| ❑ 256 Bryan McCabe | .10 | .05 |
| ❑ 257 Daniel Alfredsson | .60 | .25 |
| ❑ 258 Brendan Witt | .10 | .05 |
| ❑ 259 Jeff O'Neill | .10 | .05 |
| ❑ 260 Radek Dvorak | .10 | .05 |
| ❑ 261 Niklas Sundstrom | .10 | .05 |
| ❑ 262 Kyle McLaren | .10 | .05 |
| ❑ 263 Saku Koivu | .40 | .18 |
| ❑ 264 Todd Bertuzzi | .10 | .05 |
| ❑ 265 Jere Lehtinen | .10 | .05 |
| ❑ 266 Vitali Yachmenev | .10 | .05 |
| ❑ 267 Shane Doan | .10 | .05 |
| ❑ 268 Marko Kiprusoff | .10 | .05 |
| ❑ 269 Deron Quint | .10 | .05 |
| ❑ 270 Daymond Langkow | .25 | .11 |
| ❑ 271 Alex Hicks | .10 | .05 |
| ❑ 272 Steve Rucchin | .10 | .05 |
| ❑ 273 David Karpa | .10 | .05 |
| ❑ 274 Mike Sillinger | .10 | .05 |
| ❑ 275 Teemu Selanne | .50 | .23 |
| ❑ 276 Todd Krygier | .10 | .05 |
| ❑ 277 Valeri Karpov | .10 | .05 |
| ❑ 278 Peter Douris | .10 | .05 |
| ❑ 279 Team Checklist | .10 | .05 |
| ❑ 280 Shawn McEachern | .10 | .05 |
| ❑ 281 Dave Ried | .10 | .05 |
| ❑ 282 Bill Ranford | .15 | .07 |
| ❑ 283 Don Sweeney | .10 | .05 |
| ❑ 284 Stephen Leach | .10 | .05 |
| ❑ 285 Craig Billington | .15 | .07 |
| ❑ 286 Clayton Beddoes | .10 | .05 |
| ❑ 287 Rick Tocchet | .15 | .07 |
| ❑ 288 Team Checklist | .10 | .05 |
| ❑ 289 Brad May | .15 | .07 |
| ❑ 290 Mike Peca | .10 | .05 |
| ❑ 291 Dominik Hasek | .50 | .23 |
| ❑ 292 Donald Audette | .15 | .07 |
| ❑ 293 Randy Burridge | .10 | .05 |
| ❑ 294 Derek Plante | .10 | .05 |
| ❑ 295 Martin Biron | .15 | .07 |
| ❑ 296 Andrei Trefilov | .10 | .05 |
| ❑ 297 Team Checklist | .10 | .05 |
| ❑ 298 Steve Chiasson | .10 | .05 |
| ❑ 299 Cory Stillman | .10 | .05 |
| ❑ 300 Mike Sullivan | .10 | .05 |
| ❑ 301 Gary Roberts | .15 | .07 |
| ❑ 302 Pavel Torgajev | .10 | .05 |
| ❑ 303 James Patrick | .10 | .05 |
| ❑ 304 Corey Millen | .10 | .05 |
| ❑ 305 Ed Ward | .15 | .07 |
| ❑ 306 Team Checklist | .10 | .05 |
| ❑ 307 Jeremy Roenick | .25 | .11 |
| ❑ 308 Mike Prokopec | .10 | .05 |
| ❑ 309 Joe Murphy | .10 | .05 |
| ❑ 310 Eric Weinrich | .10 | .05 |
| ❑ 311 Tony Amonte | .15 | .07 |
| ❑ 312 Bob Probert | .15 | .07 |
| ❑ 313 Murray Craven | .10 | .05 |
| ❑ 314 Sergei Krivokrasov | .10 | .05 |
| ❑ 315 Team Checklist | .10 | .05 |
| ❑ 316 Peter Forsberg | .75 | .35 |
| ❑ 317 Stephane Fiset | .15 | .07 |
| ❑ 318 Mike Ricci | .10 | .05 |
| ❑ 319 Claude Lemieux | .15 | .07 |
| ❑ 320 Sandis Ozolinsh | .15 | .07 |
| ❑ 321 Sylvain Lefebvre | .10 | .05 |
| ❑ 322 Scott Young | .10 | .05 |
| ❑ 323 Patrick Roy | 1.25 | .55 |
| ❑ 324 Team Checklist | .10 | .05 |
| ❑ 325 Brent Fedyk | .10 | .05 |
| ❑ 326 Brent Gilchrist | .10 | .05 |
| ❑ 327 Greg Adams | .10 | .05 |
| ❑ 328 Richard Matvichuk | .10 | .05 |
| ❑ 329 Joe Nieuwendyk | .15 | .07 |
| ❑ 330 Benoit Hogue | .10 | .05 |
| ❑ 331 Darcy Wakaluk | .15 | .07 |
| ❑ 332 Guy Carbonneau | .10 | .05 |
| ❑ 333 Team Checklist | .10 | .05 |
| ❑ 334 Mike Vernon | .15 | .07 |
| ❑ 335 Mathieu Dandenault | .10 | .05 |
| ❑ 336 Igor Larionov | .10 | .05 |
| ❑ 337 Sergei Fedorov | .50 | .23 |
| ❑ 338 Greg Johnson | .10 | .05 |
| ❑ 339 Dino Ciccarelli | .15 | .07 |
| ❑ 340 Martin Lapointe | .10 | .05 |
| ❑ 341 Darren McCarty | .10 | .05 |
| ❑ 342 Team Checklist | .10 | .05 |
| ❑ 343 Joaquin Gage | .10 | .05 |
| ❑ 344 Jiri Slegr | .10 | .05 |
| ❑ 345 Mariusz Czerkawski | .10 | .05 |
| ❑ 346 Doug Weight | .15 | .07 |
| ❑ 347 Todd Marchant | .10 | .05 |
| ❑ 348 Miroslav Satan | .10 | .05 |
| ❑ 349 Jeff Norton | .10 | .05 |
| ❑ 350 Curtis Joseph | .25 | .11 |
| ❑ 351 Team Checklist | .10 | .05 |
| ❑ 352 Tom Fitzgerald | .10 | .05 |
| ❑ 353 Jody Hull | .10 | .05 |
| ❑ 354 Terry Carkner | .10 | .05 |
| ❑ 355 Scott Mellanby | .15 | .07 |
| ❑ 356 Bill Lindsay | .10 | .05 |
| ❑ 357 Gord Murphy | .10 | .05 |
| ❑ 358 Brian Skrudland | .10 | .05 |
| ❑ 359 David Nemirovsky | .10 | .05 |
| ❑ 360 Team Checklist | .10 | .05 |
| ❑ 361 Paul Ranheim | .10 | .05 |
| ❑ 362 Jason Muzzatti | .15 | .07 |
| ❑ 363 Glen Featherstone | .10 | .05 |
| ❑ 364 Andrew Cassels | .10 | .05 |
| ❑ 365 Jeff Brown | .10 | .05 |
| ❑ 366 Kevin Dineen | .10 | .05 |
| ❑ 367 Nelson Emerson | .10 | .05 |
| ❑ 368 Gerald Diduck | .10 | .05 |
| ❑ 369 Team Checklist | .10 | .05 |
| ❑ 370 Kevin Stevens | .10 | .05 |
| ❑ 371 Darryl Sydor | .10 | .05 |
| ❑ 372 Yanic Perreault | .10 | .05 |
| ❑ 373 Arto Blomsten | .10 | .05 |
| ❑ 374 Kevin Todd | .10 | .05 |
| ❑ 375 Byron Dafoe | .15 | .07 |
| ❑ 376 Tony Granato | .10 | .05 |
| ❑ 377 Vladimir Tsyplakov | .10 | .05 |
| ❑ 378 Team Checklist | .10 | .05 |
| ❑ 379 Martin Rucinsky | .10 | .05 |
| ❑ 380 Patrice Brisebois | .10 | .05 |
| ❑ 381 Lyle Odelein | .10 | .05 |
| ❑ 382 Andrei Kovalenko | .10 | .05 |
| ❑ 383 Mark Recchi | .15 | .07 |
| ❑ 384 Jocelyn Thibault | .25 | .11 |
| ❑ 385 Turner Stevenson | .10 | .05 |
| ❑ 386 Pat Jablonski | .15 | .07 |
| ❑ 387 Team Checklist | .10 | .05 |
| ❑ 388 Scott Niedermayer | .10 | .05 |
| ❑ 389 Corey Schwab | .15 | .07 |
| ❑ 390 Steve Thomas | .10 | .05 |
| ❑ 391 Valeri Zelepukin | .10 | .05 |
| ❑ 392 Shawn Chambers | .10 | .05 |
| ❑ 393 Jocelyn Lemieux | .10 | .05 |
| ❑ 394 Brian Rolston | .10 | .05 |
| ❑ 395 Denis Pederson | .10 | .05 |
| ❑ 396 Team Checklist | .10 | .05 |
| ❑ 397 Martin Straka | .10 | .05 |
| ❑ 398 Niclas Andersson | .10 | .05 |
| ❑ 399 Wendel Clark | .15 | .07 |
| ❑ 400 Travis Green | .15 | .07 |
| ❑ 401 Chris Marinucci | .10 | .05 |
| ❑ 402 Darius Kasparaitis | .10 | .05 |
| ❑ 403 Patrick Flatley | .10 | .05 |
| ❑ 404 Jamie McLennan | .10 | .05 |
| ❑ 405 Team Checklist | .10 | .05 |
| ❑ 406 Glenn Healy | .15 | .07 |
| ❑ 407 Pat Verbeek | .10 | .05 |
| ❑ 408 Ian Laperriere | .10 | .05 |
| ❑ 409 Ray Ferraro | .10 | .05 |
| ❑ 410 Jeff Beukeboom | .10 | .05 |
| ❑ 411 Ulf Samuelsson | .10 | .05 |
| ❑ 412 Doug Lidster | .10 | .05 |
| ❑ 413 Bruce Driver | .10 | .05 |
| ❑ 414 Team Checklist | .10 | .05 |
| ❑ 415 Antti Tormanen | .10 | .05 |
| ❑ 416 Sean Hill | .10 | .05 |
| ❑ 417 Damian Rhodes | .15 | .07 |
| ❑ 418 Jaroslav Modry | .10 | .05 |
| ❑ 419 Mike Bales | .10 | .05 |
| ❑ 420 Trent McCleary | .10 | .05 |
| ❑ 421 Randy Cunneyworth | .10 | .05 |
| ❑ 422 Ted Drury | .10 | .05 |
| ❑ 423 Team Checklist | .10 | .05 |
| ❑ 424 Pat Falloon | .10 | .05 |
| ❑ 425 Garth Snow | .15 | .07 |
| ❑ 426 Shjon Podein | .10 | .05 |
| ❑ 427 Petr Svoboda | .10 | .05 |
| ❑ 428 Eric Desjardins | .10 | .05 |
| ❑ 429 Anatoli Semenov | .10 | .05 |
| ❑ 430 Kevin Haller | .10 | .05 |
| ❑ 431 Rob Dimaio | .10 | .05 |
| ❑ 432 Team Checklist | .10 | .05 |
| ❑ 433 Chris Joseph | .10 | .05 |
| ❑ 434 Sergei Zubov | .10 | .05 |
| ❑ 435 Tom Barrasso | .15 | .07 |
| ❑ 436 Chris Tamer | .10 | .05 |
| ❑ 437 Dmitri Mironov | .10 | .05 |
| ❑ 438 Petr Nedved | .15 | .07 |
| ❑ 439 Neil Wilkinson | .10 | .05 |
| ❑ 440 Glen Murray | .10 | .05 |
| ❑ 441 Team Checklist | .10 | .05 |
| ❑ 442 J.J. Daigneault | .10 | .05 |
| ❑ 443 Grant Fuhr | .15 | .07 |
| ❑ 444 Adam Creighton | .10 | .05 |
| ❑ 445 Brian Noonan | .10 | .05 |
| ❑ 446 Stephane Matteau | .10 | .05 |
| ❑ 447 Roman Vopat | .10 | .05 |
| ❑ 448 Geoff Courtnall | .10 | .05 |
| ❑ 449 Wayne Gretzky | 2.00 | .90 |
| ❑ 450 Team Checklist | .10 | .05 |
| ❑ 451 Chris Terreri | .15 | .07 |
| ❑ 452 Ulf Dahlen | .10 | .05 |
| ❑ 453 Owen Nolan | .15 | .07 |
| ❑ 454 Doug Bodger | .10 | .05 |
| ❑ 455 Craig Janney | .15 | .07 |
| ❑ 456 Ville Peltonen | .10 | .05 |
| ❑ 457 Ray Sheppard | .15 | .07 |
| ❑ 458 Shean Donovan | .10 | .05 |

❑ 459 Team Checklist .10 .05
❑ 460 Jeff Reese .10 .05
❑ 461 Shawn Burr .10 .05
❑ 462 Chris Gratton .15 .07
❑ 463 John Cullen .10 .05
❑ 464 Bill Houlder .10 .05
❑ 465 J.C. Bergeron .10 .05
❑ 466 Brian Bellows .10 .05
❑ 467 Drew Bannister .10 .05
❑ 468 Team Checklist .10 .05
❑ 469 Dimitri Yushkevich .10 .05
❑ 470 Dave Andreychuk .15 .07
❑ 471 Dave Gagner .15 .07
❑ 472 Todd Warriner .10 .05
❑ 473 Sergio Momesso .10 .05
❑ 474 Kirk Muller .10 .05
❑ 475 Dave Ellett .10 .05
❑ 476 Ken Baumgartner .10 .05
❑ 477 Team Checklist .10 .05
❑ 478 Esa Tikkanen .10 .05
❑ 479 Cliff Ronning .10 .05
❑ 480 Martin Gelinas .10 .05
❑ 481 Brian Loney .10 .05
❑ 482 Pavel Bure .50 .23
❑ 483 Corey Hirsch .15 .07
❑ 484 Scott Walker .10 .05
❑ 485 Jim Dowd .10 .05
❑ 486 Team Checklist .10 .05
❑ 487 Michal Pivonka .10 .05
❑ 488 Pat Peake .10 .05
❑ 489 Martin Gendron .10 .05
❑ 490 Peter Bondra .25 .11
❑ 491 Nolan Baumgartner .10 .05
❑ 492 Jim Carey .25 .11
❑ 493 Steve Konowalchuk .10 .05
❑ 494 Jason Allison .10 .05
❑ 495 Team Checklist .10 .05
❑ 496 Oleg Tverdovsky .15 .07
❑ 497 Craig Mills .10 .05
❑ 498 Darren Turcotte .10 .05
❑ 499 Norm Maciver .10 .05
❑ 500 Chad Kilger .10 .05
❑ 501 Keith Tkachuk .30 .14
❑ 502 Kris King .10 .05
❑ 503 Dallas Drake .10 .05
❑ 504 Team Checklist .10 .05
❑ 505 Saku Koivu .25 .11
❑ 506 Vitali Yachmenev .10 .05
❑ 507 Daniel Alfredsson .15 .07
❑ 508 Radek Dvorak .10 .05
❑ 509 Miroslav Satan .10 .05
❑ 510 Aki Berg .10 .05
❑ 511 Valeri Dure .15 .07
❑ 512 Petr Sykora .10 .05
❑ 513 Andrei Vasiliev .10 .05
❑ 514 Niklas Sundstrom .10 .05
❑ 515 Viktor Kozlov .10 .05
❑ 516 Sami Kapanen .15 .07
❑ 517 Anders Myrvold .10 .05
❑ 518 Jere Lehtinen .10 .05
❑ 519 Marcus Ragnarsson .10 .05
❑ 520 Stefan Ustorf .10 .05
❑ 521 Ville Peltonen .10 .05
❑ 522 Antti Tormanen .10 .05
❑ 523 Petr Sykora .10 .05
❑ 524 Scott Bailey .10 .05
❑ 525 Kevin Hodson .50 .23
❑ 526 Landon Wilson .10 .05
❑ 527 Aaron Gavey .10 .05
❑ 528 Darren Langdon .10 .05
❑ 529 Jason Doig .10 .05
❑ 530 Marty Murray .10 .05
❑ 531 Marcus Ragnarsson .10 .05
❑ 532 Peter Ferraro .10 .05
❑ 533 Grant Marshall .10 .05
❑ 534 Mike Wilson .10 .05
❑ 535 Rory Fitzpatrick .10 .05
❑ 536 Ed Jovanovski .25 .11
❑ 537 Eric Fichaud .15 .07
❑ 538 Stefan Ustorf .10 .05
❑ 539 Stephane Yelle .10 .05
❑ 540 Ethan Moreau .25 .11
❑ NNO1 M.Renberg AU2500 20.00 9.00
❑ NNO2 T.Selanne AU2500 60.00 27.00
❑ NNO3 M.Brodeur AU1500 80.00 36.00
❑ NNO4 S.Koivu AU1500 50.00 22.00
❑ NNO5 Saku Koivu Jumbo 2.50 1.10
❑ NNO6 Saku Koivu Jumbo AU 40.00 18.00

## 1995-96 Parkhurst International Emerald Ice

This 540-card set was issued as a parallel to the regular Parkhurst International series. The cards feature the standard card player photo superimposed on brilliant emerald green foil. The cards were inserted at a rate of 1:3 packs.

| | MINT | NRMT |
|---|---|---|
| COMPLETE SET (540) | 750.00 | 350.00 |
| COMPLETE SERIES 1 (270) | 300.00 | 135.00 |
| COMPLETE SERIES 2 (270) | 450.00 | 200.00 |
| COMMON CARD (1-270) | .50 | .23 |
| COMMON CARD (271-540) | .75 | .35 |

*SER.1 STARS: 7.5X TO 15X BASIC CARDS
*SER.1 YOUNG STARS: 5X TO 10X BASIC CARDS
*SER.2 STARS: 10X TO 20X BASIC CARDS
*SER.2 YOUNG STARS: 6X TO 12X BASIC CARDS

## 1995-96 Parkhurst International All-Stars

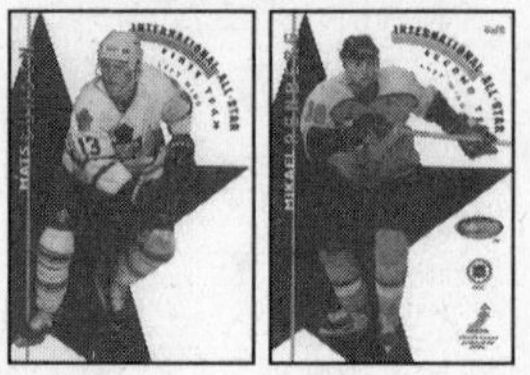

These six two-sided cards feature the best foreign-born stars in the NHL at each position. The cards were randomly inserted at a rate of 1:96 first series packs.

| | MINT | NRMT |
|---|---|---|
| COMPLETE SET (6) | 75.00 | 34.00 |
| COMMON CARD (1-6) | 5.00 | 2.20 |

❑ 1 Dominik Hasek 10.00 4.50
Arturs Irbe
❑ 2 Nicklas Lidstrom 5.00 2.20
Sandis Ozolinsh
❑ 3 Sergei Zubov 5.00 2.20
Alexei Zhitnik
❑ 4 Sergei Fedorov 25.00 11.00
Peter Forsberg
❑ 5 Jaromir Jagr 25.00 11.00
Teemu Selanne
❑ 6 Mats Sundin 5.00 2.20
Mikael Renberg

## 1995-96 Parkhurst International Crown Collection Silver Series 1

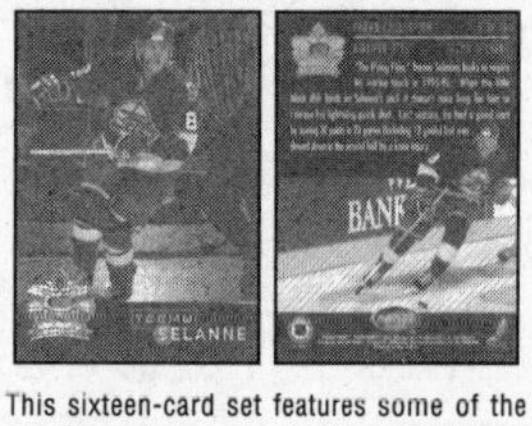

This sixteen-card set features some of the most popular players in the game on an attractive silver etched foil background. The cards were inserted 1:16 series 1 packs. A gold parallel version of this set exists as well. These cards were significantly tougher, coming out of 1:96 series 1 packs.

| | MINT | NRMT |
|---|---|---|
| COMPLETE SET (16) | 100.00 | 45.00 |
| COMMON CARD (1-16) | 1.50 | .70 |

*GOLD VERSION: 1.5X to 3X SILVER CARDS

❑ 1 Eric Lindros 15.00 6.75
❑ 2 Felix Potvin 3.00 1.35
❑ 3 Mario Lemieux 20.00 9.00
❑ 4 Paul Kariya 15.00 6.75
❑ 5 Pavel Bure 8.00 3.60
❑ 6 Wayne Gretzky 25.00 11.00
❑ 7 Mikael Renberg 1.50 .70
❑ 8 Paul Coffey 3.00 1.35
❑ 9 Teemu Selanne 8.00 3.60
❑ 10 Brett Hull 5.00 2.20
❑ 11 Martin Brodeur 10.00 4.50
❑ 12 Doug Gilmour 1.50 .70
❑ 13 Peter Forsberg 12.00 5.50
❑ 14 Sergei Fedorov 8.00 3.60
❑ 15 Saku Koivu 8.00 3.60
❑ 16 Jim Carey 1.50 .70

## 1995-96 Parkhurst International Crown Collection Silver Series 2

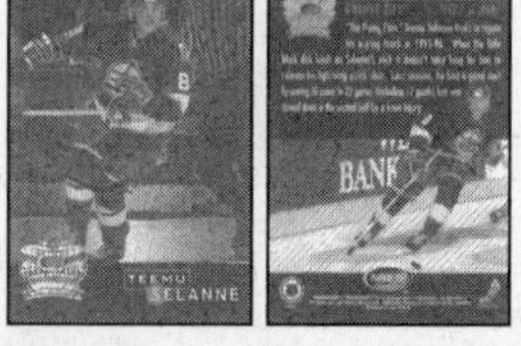

This 16-card set of the NHL's top stars was randomly inserted in series 2 packs. Although this set echoes the theme of the series 1 Crown Collection, the numbering again is 1-16. There also are several players who make return appearances in this set. As with series one, the silver version come 1:16 packs, while the gold are found 1:96 packs.

| | MINT | NRMT |
|---|---|---|
| COMPLETE SET (16) | 80.00 | 36.00 |
| COMMON CARD (1-16) | 1.50 | .70 |

*GOLD VERSION: 1.5X to 3X SILVER CARDS

❑ 1 Jaromir Jagr 12.00 5.50
❑ 2 Patrick Roy 20.00 9.00
❑ 3 Alexander Mogilny 1.50 .70
❑ 4 Paul Kariya 15.00 6.75
❑ 5 Dominik Hasek 8.00 3.60
❑ 6 Peter Forsberg 12.00 5.50
❑ 7 Mark Messier 5.00 2.20
❑ 8 Mats Sundin 3.00 1.35
❑ 9 Ray Bourque 3.00 1.35
❑ 10 Wayne Gretzky 25.00 11.00
❑ 11 Eric Lindros 15.00 6.75
❑ 12 John Vanbiesbrouck 6.00 2.70
❑ 13 Chris Chelios 3.00 1.35
❑ 14 Brian Leetch 3.00 1.35
❑ 15 Daniel Alfredsson 1.50 .70
❑ 16 Eric Daze 1.50 .70

## 1995-96 Parkhurst International Goal Patrol

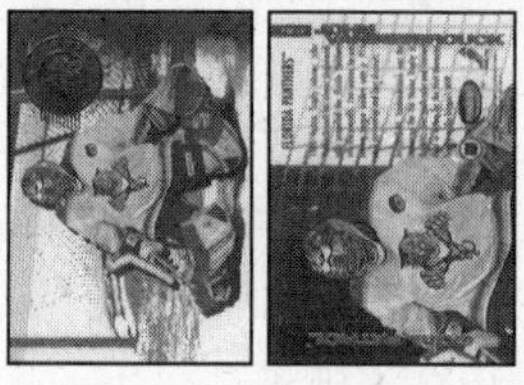

This 12-card, horizontally-oriented set salutes the top netminders in the NHL. The cards feature an embossed photo in the Action Packed style, and were inserted 1:24 series 1 packs.

| | MINT | NRMT |
|---|---|---|
| COMPLETE SET (12) | 60.00 | 27.00 |
| COMMON CARD (1-12) | 3.00 | 1.35 |

❑ 1 Martin Brodeur 8.00 3.60
❑ 2 Felix Potvin 4.00 1.80
❑ 3 Patrick Roy 15.00 6.75
❑ 4 Dominik Hasek 6.00 2.70
❑ 5 Jim Carey 3.00 1.35
❑ 6 Ed Belfour 4.00 1.80
❑ 7 John Vanbiesbrouck 5.00 2.20
❑ 8 Trevor Kidd 3.00 1.35
❑ 9 Bill Ranford 3.00 1.35
❑ 10 Arturs Irbe 3.00 1.35
❑ 11 Kirk McLean 3.00 1.35
❑ 12 Mike Richter 4.00 1.80

## 1995-96 Parkhurst International NHL All-Stars

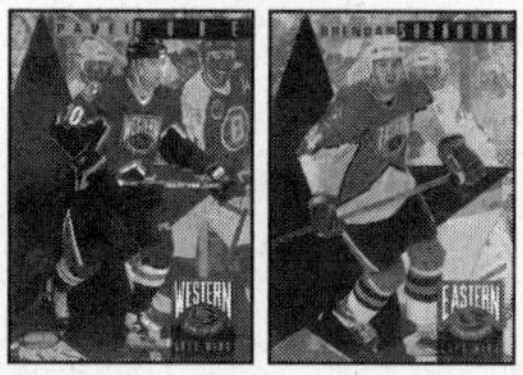

These six, two-sided cards feature the NHL's top players by position. The cards were randomly inserted in series 2 packs at a rate of 1:96.

| | MINT | NRMT |
|---|---|---|
| COMPLETE SET (6) | 125.00 | 55.00 |
| COMMON CARD (1-6) | 5.00 | 2.20 |

❑ 1 Mario Lemieux 60.00 27.00
Wayne Gretzky
❑ 2 Jaromir Jagr 20.00 9.00
Brett Hull
❑ 3 Brendan Shanahan 15.00 6.75
Pavel Bure
❑ 4 Scott Stevens 5.00 2.20
Chris Chelios
❑ 5 Ray Bourque 7.00 3.10
Paul Coffey
❑ 6 Martin Brodeur 15.00 6.75
Ed Belfour

## 1995-96 Parkhurst International Parkie's Trophy Picks

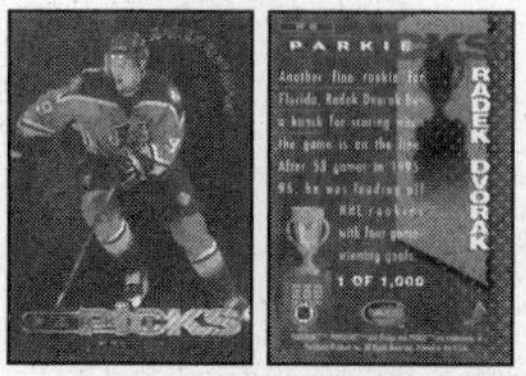

This 54-card set illustrates Parkhurst's choices for the key individual awards for the 1995-96 NHL season. The cards were noted as being one of 1,000 produced, but were not individually numbered. The odds of pulling one from a second series pack were 1:48.

| | MINT | NRMT |
|---|---|---|
| COMPLETE SET (54) | 500.00 | 220.00 |
| COMMON CARD (PP1-PP54) | 2.00 | .90 |

❑ PP1 Eric Lindros 20.00 9.00
❑ PP2 Mario Lemieux 30.00 13.50
❑ PP3 Sergei Fedorov 12.00 5.50
❑ PP4 Peter Forsberg 20.00 9.00
❑ PP5 John Vanbiesbrouck 10.00 4.50
❑ PP6 Mark Messier 8.00 3.60
❑ PP7 Jaromir Jagr 20.00 9.00
❑ PP8 Joe Sakic 12.00 5.50
❑ PP9 Grant Fuhr 4.00 1.80
❑ PP10 Eric Lindros 20.00 9.00
❑ PP11 Mario Lemieux 30.00 13.50
❑ PP12 Mark Messier 8.00 3.60
❑ PP13 Peter Forsberg 20.00 9.00
❑ PP14 Jaromir Jagr 20.00 9.00
❑ PP15 Paul Kariya 25.00 11.00
❑ PP16 Joe Sakic 12.00 5.50
❑ PP17 Teemu Selanne 12.00 5.50
❑ PP18 Alexander Mogilny 4.00 1.80
❑ PP19 Paul Coffey 6.00 2.70
❑ PP20 Chris Chelios 6.00 2.70
❑ PP21 Brian Leetch 6.00 2.70
❑ PP22 Ray Bourque 6.00 2.70
❑ PP23 Larry Murphy 2.00 .90
❑ PP24 Nicklas Lidstrom 2.00 .90
❑ PP25 Roman Hamrlik 4.00 1.80
❑ PP26 Gary Suter 2.00 .90
❑ PP27 Sergei Zubov 2.00 .90
❑ PP28 Dominik Hasek 12.00 5.50
❑ PP29 John Vanbiesbrouck 10.00 4.50
❑ PP30 Chris Osgood 6.00 2.70
❑ PP31 Mike Richter 6.00 2.70
❑ PP32 Martin Brodeur 15.00 6.75
❑ PP33 Ron Hextall 4.00 1.80
❑ PP34 Grant Fuhr 4.00 1.80
❑ PP35 Patrick Roy 30.00 13.50
❑ PP36 Jim Carey 6.00 2.70
❑ PP37 Vitali Yachmenev 2.00 .90
❑ PP38 Daniel Alfredsson 4.00 1.80
❑ PP39 Saku Koivu 10.00 4.50
❑ PP40 Eric Daze 4.00 1.80
❑ PP41 Marcus Ragnarsson 2.00 .90
❑ PP42 Ed Jovanovski 4.00 1.80
❑ PP43 Petr Sykora 2.00 .90
❑ PP44 Todd Bertuzzi 2.00 .90
❑ PP45 Radek Dvorak 2.00 .90
❑ PP46 Paul Kariya 25.00 11.00
❑ PP47 Ron Francis 4.00 1.80
❑ PP48 Alexander Mogilny 4.00 1.80
❑ PP49 Pat LaFontaine 4.00 1.80
❑ PP50 Pierre Turgeon 4.00 1.80
❑ PP51 Teemu Selanne 12.00 5.50
❑ PP52 Sergei Fedorov 12.00 5.50
❑ PP53 Adam Oates 4.00 1.80
❑ PP54 Brett Hull 8.00 3.60

## 1995-96 Parkhurst International Trophy Winners

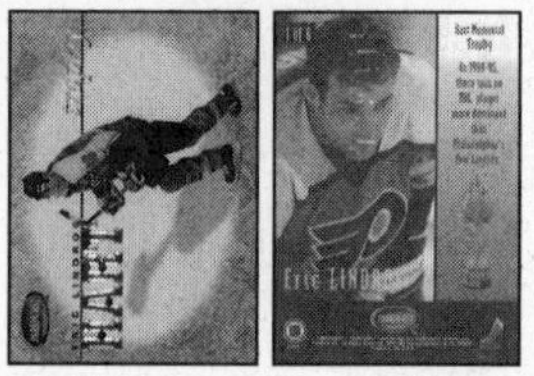

This six-card set recognizes the winners of the key individual trophies from the 1994-95 season. The cards were inserted at a rate of 1:24 series one packs.

| | MINT | NRMT |
|---|---|---|
| COMPLETE SET (6) | 40.00 | 18.00 |
| COMMON CARD (1-6) | 2.50 | 1.10 |

❑ 1 Eric Lindros-Hart 12.00 5.50
❑ 2 Jaromir Jagr-Art Ross 10.00 4.50
❑ 3 Peter Forsberg-Calder 10.00 4.50
❑ 4 Paul Coffey-Norris 5.00 2.20
❑ 5 Dominik Hasek-Vezina 6.00 2.70
❑ 6 Ron Francis-Lady Byng 2.50 1.10

## 1996 Parkhurst Beehive Promos

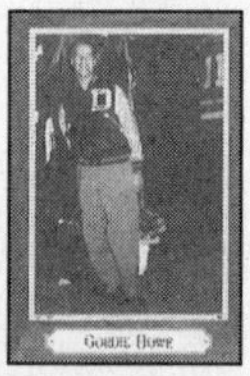

These cards were available as part of a card show wrapper redemption offer. The five Howe cards were available at the 1996 National in Anaheim in exchange for Parkhurst '66-67 wrappers. The Orr promos were available at several major shows.

| | MINT | NRMT |
|---|---|---|
| COMPLETE SET (10) | 75.00 | 34.00 |
| COMMON CARD | 7.50 | 3.40 |

❑ NNO Bobby Orr 10.00 4.50
❑ NNO Bobby Orr 10.00 4.50
❑ NNO Bobby Orr 10.00 4.50
❑ NNO Bobby Orr 10.00 4.50
❑ NNO Bobby Orr 10.00 4.50
❑ NNO Gordie Howe 7.50 3.40
❑ NNO Gordie Howe 7.50 3.40
❑ NNO Gordie Howe 7.50 3.40
❑ NNO Gordie Howe 7.50 3.40
❑ NNO Gordie Howe 7.50 3.40

## 1971-72 Penguins Postcards

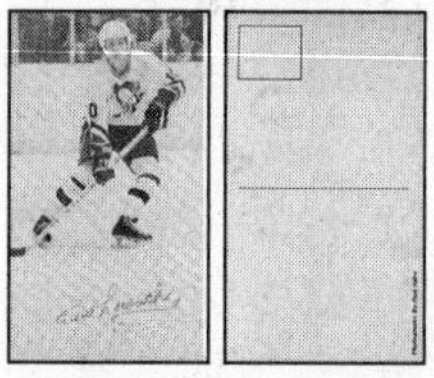

This 22-card set (measuring approximately 3 1/2" by 5 1/2") features full-bleed posed action color player photos. The top edges of the card show signs of perforation. The backs carry the player's name and biography in blue print on a white background. Only the Red Kelly card has a career summary on its back. The cards are unnumbered and checklisted below in alphabetical order. The set is dated by the inclusion of Roy Edwards, whose only season with the Penguins was 1971-72.

| | NRMT-MT | EXC |
|---|---|---|
| COMPLETE SET (22) | 40.00 | 18.00 |
| COMMON CARD (1-22) | 1.50 | .70 |

❑ 1 Syl Apps 2.50 1.10
❑ 2 Les Binkley 2.50 1.10
❑ 3 Dave Burrows 2.00 .90
❑ 4 Darryl Edestrand 1.50 .70
❑ 5 Roy Edwards 2.00 .90
❑ 6 Val Fonteyne 1.50 .70
❑ 7 Nick Harbaruk 1.50 .70
❑ 8 Bryan Hextall 4.00 1.80
❑ 9 Sheldon Kannegiesser 1.50 .70
❑ 10 Red Kelly CO 4.00 1.80
❑ 11 Bob Leiter 1.50 .70
❑ 12 Keith McCreary 1.50 .70
❑ 13 Joe Noris 1.50 .70
❑ 14 Greg Polis 1.50 .70
❑ 15 Jean Pronovost 4.00 1.80
❑ 16 Rene Robert 2.50 1.10
❑ 17 Jim Rutherford 2.50 1.10
❑ 18 Ken Schinkel 1.50 .70
❑ 19 Ron Schock 2.00 .90
❑ 20 Bryan Watson 2.00 .90
❑ 21 Bob Woytowich 1.50 .70
❑ 22 Title Card 1.50 .70

## 1974-75 Penguins Postcards

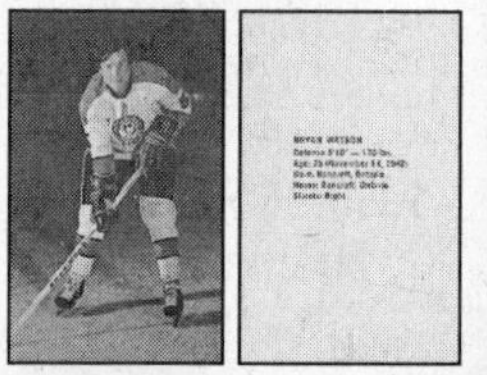

This 22-card set features full-bleed black and white action pictures by photographer Paul Salva. The player's autograph is inscribed across the bottom of the picture. The cards are in the postcard format and measure approximately 3 1/2" by 5 1/2". The horizontal backs are blank. The cards are unnumbered and checklisted below in alphabetical order. The set is dated by the fact that Nelson Debenedet was only with the Penguins during the 1974-75 season. Pierre Larouche appears in this set prior to his Rookie Card appearance.

| | NRMT-MT | EXC |
|---|---|---|
| COMPLETE SET (22) | 30.00 | 13.50 |
| COMMON CARD (1-22) | 1.50 | .70 |

❑ 1 Syl Apps 2.50 1.10
❑ 2 Chuck Arnason 1.50 .7
❑ 3 Dave Burrows 2.00 .90
❑ 4 Colin Campbell 2.50 1.10
❑ 5 Nelson Debenedet 1.50 .7
❑ 6 Steve Durbano 1.50 .7
❑ 7 Vic Hadfield 2.00 .9
❑ 8 Gary Inness 2.00 .9
❑ 9 Bob(B.J.) Johnson 1.50 .7
❑ 10 Rick Kehoe 2.50 1.1
❑ 11 Bob Kelly 1.50 .7
❑ 12 Jean-Guy Lagace 1.50 .7
❑ 13 Ron Lalonde 1.50 .7
❑ 14 Pierre Larouche 5.00 2.2

❑ 15 Lowell MacDonald 2.00 .90
❑ 16 Dennis Owchar 1.50 .70
❑ 17 Bob Paradise 1.50 .70
❑ 18 Kelly Pratt 1.50 .70
❑ 19 Jean Pronovost 2.00 .90
❑ 20 Ron Schock 2.00 .90
❑ 21 Ron Stackhouse 2.00 .90
❑ 22 Barry Williams 1.50 .70

## 1977-78 Penguins Puck Bucks

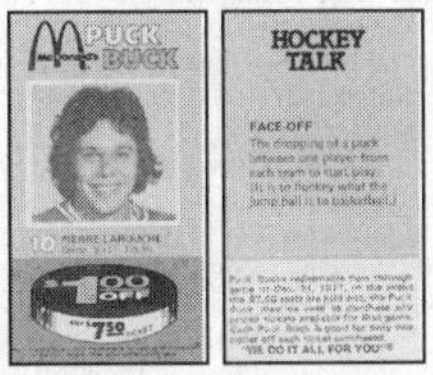


This 18-card set of Pittsburgh Penguins was sponsored by McDonald's restaurants, whose company logo appears at the top of the card face. The cards measure approximately 1 15/16" by 3 1/2" and are perforated so that the bottom tab (measuring 1 15/16" by 1") may be removed. The front of the top portion features a color head shot of the player, with a white border on a mustard-colored background. The back of the top portion has "Hockey Talk," in which a hockey term is explained. The front side of the tab portion shows a hockey puck on an orange background. Its back states that the "puck bucks" are coupons worth 1.00 toward the purchase of any 7.50 Penguins game ticket. These coupons had to be redeemed no later than December 31, 1977.

| | NRMT-MT | EXC |
|---|---|---|
| COMPLETE SET (18) | 25.00 | 11.00 |
| COMMON CARD | 1.00 | .45 |

❑ 1 Denis Herron 3.00 1.35
❑ 3 Ron Stackhouse 2.00 .90
❑ 4 Dave Burrows 1.50 .70
❑ 6 Colin Campbell 2.50 1.10
❑ 7 Russ Anderson 1.50 .70
❑ 9 Blair Chapman 1.50 .70
❑ 10 Pierre Larouche 3.00 1.35
❑ 12 Greg Malone 2.00 .90
❑ 14 Wayne Bianchin 1.50 .70
❑ 17 Rick Kehoe 3.00 1.35
❑ 18 Lowell MacDonald 2.00 .90
❑ 19 Jean Pronovost 2.50 1.10
❑ 23 Jim Hamilton 1.50 .70
❑ 25 Dennis Owchar 1.50 .70
❑ 26 Syl Apps 2.00 .90
❑ 27 Mike Corrigan 1.50 .70
❑ 29 Dunc Wilson 2.00 .90
❑ NNO Johnny Wilson CO 1.00 .45

## 1983-84 Penguins Coke

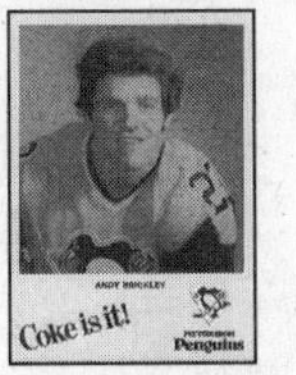


This 19-card set of the Pittsburgh Penguins measures approximately 5" by 7". The fronts feature black-and-white player portraits framed in white with the player's name, team name, team logo, and the words "Coke is it!" printed in black in the wide white bottom border. The backs are blank. The cards are unnumbered and checklisted below in alphabetical order. The card of Marty McSorley appears four years before his rookie card.

| | MINT | NRMT |
|---|---|---|
| COMPLETE SET (19) | 25.00 | 11.00 |
| COMMON CARD (1-19) | 1.00 | .45 |

❑ 1 Pat Boutette 1.50 .70
❑ 2 Andy Brickley 1.00 .45
❑ 3 Mike Bullard 2.00 .90
❑ 4 Ted Bulley 1.00 .45
❑ 5 Rod Buskas 1.00 .45
❑ 6 Randy Carlyle 2.00 .90
❑ 7 Michel Dion 2.00 .90
❑ 8 Bob Errey 2.00 .90
❑ 9 Ron Flockhart 1.50 .70
❑ 10 Steve Gatzos 1.00 .45
❑ 11 Jim Hamilton 1.00 .45
❑ 12 Dave Hannan 1.00 .45
❑ 13 Denis Herron 2.50 1.10
❑ 14 Troy Loney 1.00 .45
❑ 15 Bryan Maxwell 1.00 .45
❑ 16 Marty McSorley 5.00 2.20
❑ 17 Norm Schmidt 1.00 .45
❑ 18 Mark Taylor 1.00 .45
❑ 19 Greg Tebbutt 1.00 .45

## 1983-84 Penguins Heinz Photos

This Pittsburgh Penguins "Photo Pak" was sponsored by Heinz. The cards are unnumbered and checklisted below in alphabetical order. They were giveaways at Pittsburgh Penguins home games. Each photo measures approximately 6" by 9" and they were produced on one large folded sheet.

| | MINT | NRMT |
|---|---|---|
| COMPLETE SET (22) | 25.00 | 11.00 |
| COMMON CARD (1-22) | 1.00 | .45 |

❑ 1 Paul Baxter 1.50 .70
❑ 2 Pat Boutette 1.50 .70
❑ 3 Randy Boyd 1.00 .45
❑ 4 Mike Bullard 2.00 .90
❑ 5 Randy Carlyle 2.00 .90
❑ 6 Marc Chorney 1.00 .45
❑ 7 Michel Dion 2.00 .90
❑ 8 Bill Gardner 1.00 .45
❑ 9 Pat Graham 1.00 .45
❑ 10 Anders Hakansson 1.00 .45
❑ 11 Dave Hannan 1.00 .45
❑ 12 Denis Herron 2.50 1.10
❑ 13 Greg Hotham 1.00 .45
❑ 14 Stan Jonathan 1.50 .70
❑ 15 Rick Kehoe 2.50 1.10
❑ 16 Peter Lee 2.00 .90
❑ 17 Greg Malone 1.50 .70
❑ 18 Kevin McClelland 1.00 .45
❑ 19 Ron Meighan 1.00 .45
❑ 20 Doug Shedden 1.00 .45
❑ 21 Andre St. Laurent 1.00 .45
❑ 22 Rich Sutter 1.50 .70

## 1983-84 Penguins Team Issue Photos

| | MINT | NRMT |
|---|---|---|
| COMPLETE SET (32) | 30.00 | 13.50 |
| COMMON CARD (1-32) | 1.00 | .45 |

❑ 1 Phil Bourque 1.50 .70
❑ 2 Pat Boutette 1.00 .45
❑ 3 Randy Boyd 1.00 .45
❑ 4 Mike Bullard 2.00 .90
❑ 5 Ted Bulley 1.00 .45
❑ 6 Rod Buskas 1.00 .45
❑ 7 Randy Carlyle 2.00 .90
❑ 8 Marc Chorney 1.00 .45
❑ 9 Michel Dion 2.00 .90
❑ 10 Bob Errey 1.00 .45
❑ 11 Paul Gardner 1.00 .45
❑ 12 Steve Gatzos 1.00 .45
❑ 13 Jim Hamilton 1.00 .45
❑ 14 Dave Hannan 1.00 .45
❑ 15 Denis Herron 2.50 1.10
❑ 16 Greg Hotham 1.00 .45
❑ 17 Tim Hrynewich 1.00 .45
❑ 18 Eddie Johnston 1.50 .70
❑ 19 Rick Kehoe 2.50 1.10
❑ 20 Mitch Lamoureux 1.00 .45
❑ 21 Troy Loney 1.00 .45
❑ 22 Kevin McClelland 1.00 .45
❑ 23 Marty McSorley 2.00 .90
❑ 24 Ron Meighan 1.00 .45
❑ 25 Gary Rissling 1.00 .45
❑ 26 Roberto Romano 1.00 .45
❑ 27 Rocky Saganiuk 1.00 .45
❑ 28 Norm Schmidt 1.00 .45
❑ 29 Rod Schutt 1.00 .45
❑ 30 Doug Shedden 1.00 .45
❑ 31 Andre St. Laurent 1.00 .45
❑ 32 Vincent Tremblay 1.00 .45

## 1984-85 Penguins Heinz Photos

This Pittsburgh Penguins "Photo Pak" was sponsored by Heinz. The cards are unnumbered and checklisted below in alphabetical order. They were giveaways at Pittsburgh Penguins home games. Each photo measures approximately 6" by 9" and they were produced on one large folded sheet.

| | MINT | NRMT |
|---|---|---|
| COMPLETE SET (22) | 25.00 | 11.00 |
| COMMON CARD (1-22) | 1.00 | .45 |

❑ 1 Pat Boutette 1.50 .70
❑ 2 Andy Brickley 1.00 .45
❑ 3 Mike Bullard 2.00 .90
❑ 4 Rod Buskas 1.00 .45
❑ 5 Randy Carlyle 2.00 .90
❑ 6 Michel Dion 2.00 .90
❑ 7 Bob Errey 1.50 .70
❑ 8 Ron Flockhart 1.00 .45
❑ 9 Greg Fox 1.00 .45
❑ 10 Steve Gatzos 1.00 .45
❑ 11 Denis Herron 2.50 1.10
❑ 12 Greg Hotham 1.00 .45
❑ 13 Rick Kehoe 2.00 .90
❑ 14 Bryan Maxwell 1.50 .70
❑ 15 Marty McSorley 5.00 2.20
❑ 16 Tom O'Regan 1.00 .45
❑ 17 Gary Rissling 1.00 .45
❑ 18 Roberto Romano 1.50 .70
❑ 19 Tom Roulston 1.00 .45
❑ 20 Rocky Saganiuk 1.00 .45
❑ 21 Doug Shedden 1.50 .70
❑ 22 Mark Taylor 1.00 .45

## 1986-87 Penguins Kodak

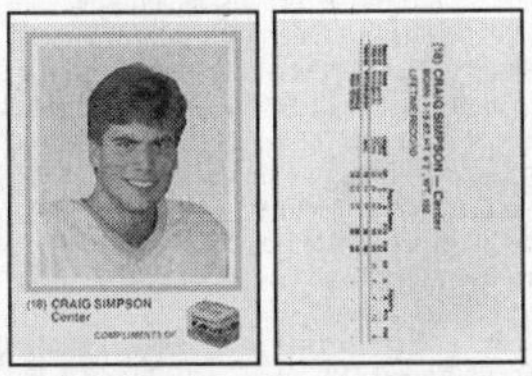

The 1986-87 Pittsburgh Penguins Team Photo Album was sponsored by Kodak and commemorates the team's 20 years in the NHL. It consists of three large sheets, each measuring approximately 11" by 8 1/4", joined together to form one continuous sheet. The first panel has a team photo of the 1967 Pittsburgh Penguins. The second panel presents three rows of five cards each. The third panel presents two rows of five cards, with five Kodak coupons completing the left over portion of the panel. After perforation, the cards measure approximately 2 3/16" by 2 1/2". They feature color posed photos bordered in yellow, with player information below the picture. A Kodak film box serving as a logo completes the card face. The back has biographical and statistical information in a horizontal format. We have checklisted the names below in alphabetical order, with the uniform number to the right of the name.

| | MINT | NRMT |
|---|---|---|
| COMPLETE SET (26) | 40.00 | 18.00 |
| COMMON CARD (1-25) | .50 | .23 |

❑ 1 Bob Berry CO .50 .23
❑ 2 Mike Blaisdell 26 1.00 .45
❑ 3 Doug Bodger 3 1.00 .45
❑ 4 Rod Buskas 7 .75 .35
❑ 5 John Chabot 9 .75 .35
❑ 6 Randy Cunneyworth 15 .75 .35
❑ 7 Ron Duguay 10 1.00 .45
❑ 8 Bob Errey 12 1.00 .45
❑ 9 Dan Frawley 28 .75 .35
❑ 10 Dave Hannan 32 .75 .35
❑ 11 Randy Hillier 23 .75 .35
❑ 12 Jim Johnson 6 .75 .35
❑ 13 Kevin Lavallee 16 .75 .35
❑ 14 Mario Lemieux 66 25.00 11.00
❑ 15 Willy Lindstrom 19 .75 .35
❑ 16 Moe Mantha 20 .75 .35
❑ 17 Gilles Meloche 27 1.00 .45
❑ 18 Dan Quinn 14 1.00 .45
❑ 19 Jim Roberts CO .50 .23
❑ 20 Roberto Romano 30 1.00 .45
❑ 21 Terry Ruskowski 8 1.00 .45
❑ 22 Norm Schmidt 25 .75 .35
❑ 23 Craig Simpson 18 1.50 .70
❑ 24 Ville Siren 5 .75 .35
❑ 25 Warren Young 35 1.00 .45
❑ NNO '67 Team Photo 2.00 .90

## 1987-88 Penguins Masks

These masks were issued by KDKA and Eagle Food Stores. Mask fronts show top of players head, and backs feature name, stats, and sponsors logos. These masks are unnumbered and checklisted below in alphabetical order.

| | MINT | NRMT |
|---|---|---|
| COMPLETE SET (10) | 20.00 | 9.00 |
| COMMON MASK (1-10) | 1.00 | .45 |

❑ 1 Doug Bodger 1.00 .45
❑ 2 Randy Cunneyworth 1.00 .45
❑ 3 Bob Errey 1.00 .45
❑ 4 Dan Frawley 1.00 .45
❑ 5 Jim Johnson 1.00 .45
❑ 6 Mario Lemieux 10.00 4.50
❑ 7 Gilles Meloche 2.00 .90
❑ 8 Dan Quinn 1.00 .45
❑ 9 Craig Simpson 2.00 .90
❑ 10 Ville Siren 1.00 .45

## 1987-88 Penguins Kodak

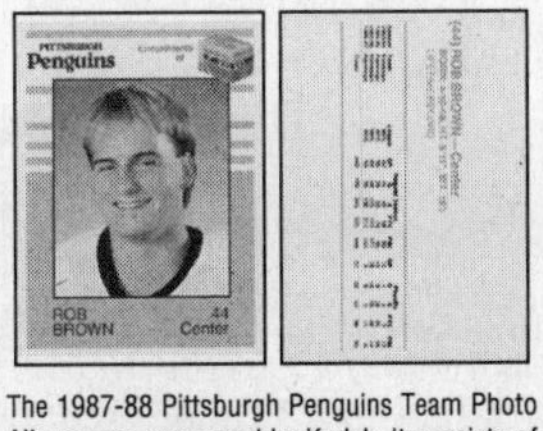

The 1987-88 Pittsburgh Penguins Team Photo Album was sponsored by Kodak. It consists of three large sheets, each measuring approximately 11" by 8 1/4", joined together to form one continuous sheet. The first panel has a team photo, with the players' names listed according to rows below the picture. The second panel presents three rows of five cards each. The third panel presents two rows of five cards, with five Kodak coupons completing the left over portion of the panel. After perforation, the cards measure approximately 2 3/16" by 2 1/2". A Kodak film box serves as a logo in the upper right hand corner of the card face. The front features a color head shot inside a thin black border. The picture is set on a Kodak %%yellow~ background, with white stripes traversing the top of the card. The player's name, number, and position are printed in black lettering below the picture. The back has biographical information and career statistics in a horizontal format. We have checklisted the cards below in alphabetical order, with the player's number to the right of his name.

| | MINT | NRMT |
|---|---|---|
| COMPLETE SET (26) | 30.00 | 13.50 |
| COMMON CARD (1-25) | .75 | .35 |

❑ 1 Doug Bodger 3 .75 .35
❑ 2 Rob Brown 44 1.00 .45
❑ 3 Rod Buskas 7 .75 .35
❑ 4 Jock Callander 36 .75 .35
❑ 5 Paul Coffey 77 2.00 .90
❑ 6 Randy Cunneyworth 15 .75 .35
❑ 7 Chris Dahlquist 4 .75 .35
❑ 8 Bob Errey 12 .75 .35
❑ 9 Dan Frawley 28 .75 .35
❑ 10 Steve Guenette 30 1.00 .45
❑ 11 Randy Hillier 23 .75 .35
❑ 12 Dave Hunter 20 .75 .35
❑ 13 Jim Johnson 6 .75 .35
❑ 14 Mark Kachowski 26 .75 .35
❑ 15 Chris Kontos 14 .75 .35
❑ 16 Mario Lemieux 66 15.00 6.75
❑ 17 Troy Loney 24 .75 .35
❑ 18 Dwight Mathiasen 34 .75 .35
❑ 19 Dave McLlwain 19 .75 .35
❑ 20 Gilles Meloche 27 1.00 .45
❑ 21 Dan Quinn 10 1.00 .45
❑ 22 Pat Riggin 1 1.00 .45
❑ 23 Charlie Simmer 16 1.00 .45
❑ 24 Ville Siren 5 .75 .35
❑ 25 Wayne Van Dorp .75 .35
❑ NNO Large Team Photo 4.00 1.80

## 1989-90 Penguins Coke/Elby's

This set measures approximately 4" by 6" and features color action player photos bordered in white with player information at the top and sponsor logos in the bottom margin. The backs are blank except for a coupon for free burger and fries at participating Elby's Big Boy restaurants. The cards are unnumbered and checklisted below in alphabetical order.

| | MINT | NRMT |
|---|---|---|
| COMPLETE SET (5) | 12.00 | 5.50 |
| COMMON CARD (1-5) | .50 | .23 |

❑ 1 Phil Bourque .50 .23
❑ 2 Rob Brown .75 .35
❑ 3 Mario Lemieux 10.00 4.50
❑ 4 Kevin Stevens 2.00 .90
❑ 5 Zarley Zalapski .75 .35

## 1989-90 Penguins Foodland

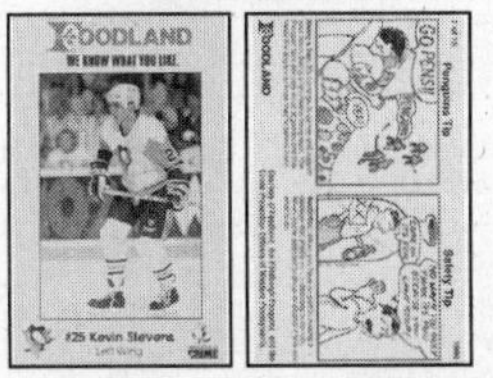


This 15-card set was sponsored by Foodland in conjunction with the Pittsburgh Penguins and the Crime Prevention Officers of Western Pennsylvania. The Foodland company logo appears on the top and back of each card. The cards measure approximately 2 9/16" by 4 1/8" and could be collected from police officers. The front features a color action photo with a thin black border on white card stock. The player information below the picture is sandwiched between the Penguin and the Crime Dog McGruff logos. The back is dated and presents a Penguins tip and a safety tip (both illustrated with cartoons) in a horizontal format. There were two late issue cards distributed after trades. They are rather scarce and not typically considered part of the complete set.

| | MINT | NRMT |
|---|---|---|
| COMPLETE SET (15) | 20.00 | 9.00 |
| COMMON CARD (1-15) | .50 | .23 |

❑ 1 Rob Brown .75 .35
❑ 2 Jim Johnson .50 .23
❑ 3 Zarley Zalapski .75 .35
❑ 4 Paul Coffey 2.00 .90
❑ 5 Phil Bourque .50 .23
❑ 6A Dan Quinn .75 .35
❑ 6B Gilbert Delorme SP 2.00 .90
❑ 7 Kevin Stevens 2.00 .90
❑ 8 Bob Errey .50 .23
❑ 9 John Cullen .75 .35
❑ 10 Mario Lemieux 10.00 4.50
❑ 11 Randy Hillier .50 .23
❑ 12 Jay Caufield .50 .23
❑ 13A Andrew McBain .50 .23
❑ 13B Troy Loney SP 2.00 .90
❑ 14 Wendell Young .75 .35
❑ 15 Tom Barrasso 1.00 .45

## 1990-91 Penguins Foodland

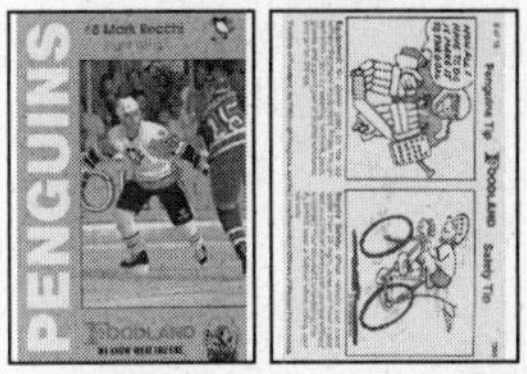


This 15-card set was sponsored by Foodland in conjunction with the Pittsburgh Penguins and the Crime Prevention Officers of Western Pennsylvania. The Foodland company logo appears at the bottom of the card front and the top of the horizontally oriented back. The cards measure approximately 2 11/16" by 4 1/8" and could be collected from police officers. The front features a color action photo with a thin black border surrounded by wide yellow margins on three sides. The team name is printed in white block lettering, running the length of the card on the left side of the picture. The back presents a Penguins tip and a safety tip (both illustrated with cartoons). The set features the appearance of three Penguins, Jaromir Jagr, Mark Recchi, and Kevin Stevens, in their Rookie Card year.

| | MINT | NRMT |
|---|---|---|
| COMPLETE SET (15) | 20.00 | 9.00 |
| COMMON CARD (1-15) | .25 | .11 |

❑ 1 Phil Bourque 29 .25 .11
❑ 2 Paul Coffey 77 1.00 .45
❑ 3 Randy Hillier 23 .25 .11
❑ 4 Barry Pederson 10 .35 .16
❑ 5 Tom Barrasso 35 .75 .35
❑ 6 Mark Recchi 8 2.00 .90
❑ 7 Bob Johnson CO 2.00 .90
❑ 8 Joe Mullen 7 .75 .35
❑ 9 Kevin Stevens 25 1.50 .70
❑ 10 John Cullen 11 .35 .16
❑ 11 Jaromir Jagr 68 10.00 4.50
❑ 12 Zarley Zalapski 33 .35 .16
❑ 13 Mario Lemieux 66 8.00 3.60
❑ 14 Tony Tanti 9 .25 .11
❑ 15 Bryan Trottier 19 .75 .35

## 1991-92 Penguins Coke/Elby's

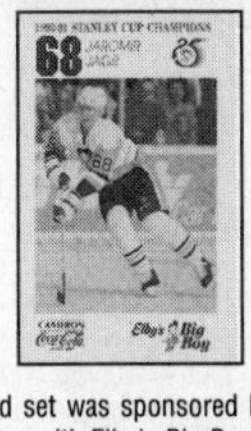

This 24-card set was sponsored by Cola-Cola in conjunction with Elby's Big Boy restaurants. The cards measure approximately 4" by 6" and are printed on thin card stock. The headline "1990-91 Stanley Cup Champions" adorns the top of each front. Immediately below appears the uniform number, player's name, and a twenty-fifth anniversary team logo. The color action player photos are bordered in white, with the two sponsor logos appearing in the bottom white border. The backs are blank. The cards are skip-numbered by uniform number and checklisted below accordingly.

| | MINT | NRMT |
|---|---|---|
| COMPLETE SET (24) | 25.00 | 11.00 |
| COMMON CARD | .50 | .23 |

❑ 1 Wendell Young .75 .35
❑ 2 Jim Paek .50 .23
❑ 3 Grant Jennings .50 .23
❑ 5 Ulf Samuelsson 1.00 .45
❑ 7 Joe Mullen 1.00 .45
❑ 8 Mark Recchi 2.00 .90
❑ 10 Ron Francis 2.50 1.10
❑ 16 Jay Caufield .50 .23
❑ 18 Ken Priestlay .50 .23
❑ 19 Bryan Trottier 1.00 .45
❑ 20 Jamie Leach .50 .23
❑ 22 Paul Stanton .50 .23
❑ 24 Troy Loney .50 .23
❑ 25 Kevin Stevens 1.00 .45

| | MINT | NRMT |
|---|---|---|
| ❑ 28 Gord Roberts | .50 | .23 |
| ❑ 29 Phil Bourque | .50 | .23 |
| ❑ 32 Peter Taglianetti | .50 | .23 |
| ❑ 40 Frank Pietrangelo | .75 | .35 |
| ❑ 43 Jeff Daniels | .50 | .23 |
| ❑ 55 Larry Murphy | 1.00 | .45 |
| ❑ 66 Mario Lemieux | 6.00 | 2.70 |
| ❑ 68 Jaromir Jagr | 6.00 | 2.70 |
| ❑ NNO Scotty Bowman CO | 1.00 | .45 |

## 1991-92 Penguins Foodland

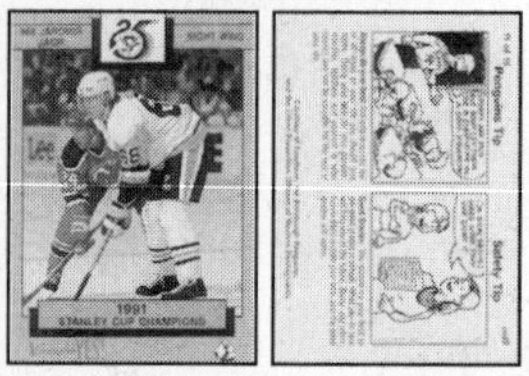

This 15-card standard-size set was sponsored by Foodland in conjunction with the Pittsburgh Penguins and the Crime Prevention Officers of Western Pennsylvania. The Foodland logo and McGruff the Crime Dog appear at the bottom of the card face, while a 25th year anniversary emblem appears at the top center. The fronts feature color action player photos on an orangish-yellow card face. The player's name, uniform number, and his position appear in the top silver stripe; the words "1991 Stanley Cup Champions" appears in another silver stripe beneath the picture. The horizontally oriented backs have a "Penguins Tip" and a "Safety Tip," each of which is illustrated by a cartoon.

| | MINT | NRMT |
|---|---|---|
| COMPLETE SET (15) | 15.00 | 6.75 |
| COMMON CARD (1-15) | .50 | .23 |
| ❑ 1 Jim Paek | .50 | .23 |
| ❑ 2 Ulf Samuelsson | .75 | .35 |
| ❑ 3 Ron Francis | 1.50 | .70 |
| ❑ 4 Mario Lemieux | 6.00 | 2.70 |
| ❑ 5 Rick Tocchet | .75 | .35 |
| ❑ 6 Joe Mullen | .75 | .35 |
| ❑ 7 Troy Loney | .50 | .23 |
| ❑ 8 Kevin Stevens | .75 | .35 |
| ❑ 9 Tom Barrasso | 1.00 | .45 |
| ❑ 10 Larry Murphy | .75 | .35 |
| ❑ 11 Jaromir Jagr | 6.00 | 2.70 |
| ❑ 12 Bryan Trottier | .75 | .35 |
| ❑ 13 Paul Stanton | .50 | .23 |
| ❑ 14 Peter Taglianetti | .50 | .23 |
| ❑ 15 Phil Bourque | .50 | .23 |

## 1991-92 Penguins Foodland Coupon Stickers

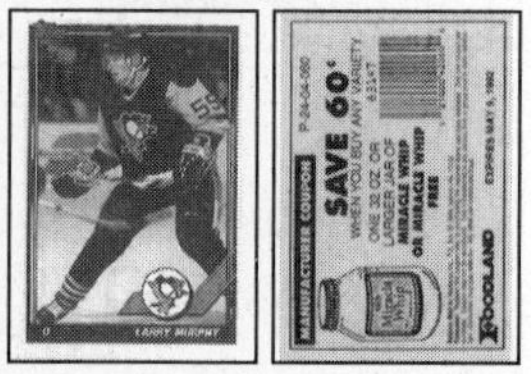

This set of twelve stickers is the result of a unique cross-promotion with Topps and the Foodland stores of Pittsburgh. The stickers, issued in a 3-sticker sheet over a four week period, mimic the 1991-92 Topps card of a Penguin player on the front, with a coupon for Foodland on the peel-off backs. Most feature the player's regular card front; exceptions are Jaromir Jagr (Super Rookie), Mario Lemieux (Award Winner) and Kevin Stevens (All-Star). The stickers are unnumbered, but are listed below in issue of order, top to bottom, per week.

| | MINT | NRMT |
|---|---|---|
| COMPLETE SET (12) | 15.00 | 6.75 |
| COMMON CARD (1-12) | .75 | .35 |
| ❑ 1 Bryan Trottier | .75 | .35 |
| ❑ 2 Joe Mullen | .75 | .35 |
| ❑ 3 Larry Murphy | .75 | .35 |
| ❑ 4 Tom Barrasso | .75 | .35 |
| ❑ 5 Ron Francis | 1.50 | .70 |
| ❑ 6 Ulf Samuelsson | .75 | .35 |
| ❑ 7 Jaromir Jagr | 6.00 | 2.70 |
| ❑ 8 Mario Lemieux | 6.00 | 2.70 |
| ❑ 9 Kevin Stevens | .75 | .35 |
| ❑ 10 Mark Recchi | 1.00 | .45 |
| ❑ 11 Paul Coffey | 1.50 | .70 |
| ❑ 12 Frank Pietrangelo | .75 | .35 |

## 1992-93 Penguins Coke/Clark

This 26-card set was sponsored by Cola-Cola and Clark. These cards followed the same concept as Coke/Elby's sets of the previous years, i.e., large autograph cards issued to the players for use in personal appearances. The cards measure approximately 4" by 6" and were printed on thin card stock. The backs are blank. The cards are unnumbered and checklisted below in alphabetical order.

| | MINT | NRMT |
|---|---|---|
| COMPLETE SET (26) | 25.00 | 11.00 |
| COMMON CARD (1-26) | .25 | .11 |
| ❑ 1 Tom Barrasso | 1.00 | .45 |
| ❑ 2 Scotty Bowman CO | 1.25 | .55 |
| ❑ 3 Jay Caufield | .50 | .23 |
| ❑ 4 Jeff Daniels | .50 | .23 |
| ❑ 5 Bob Errey | .50 | .23 |
| ❑ 6 Bryan Fogarty | .50 | .23 |
| ❑ 7 Ron Francis | 2.00 | .90 |
| ❑ 8 Jaromir Jagr | 5.00 | 2.20 |
| ❑ 9 Grant Jennings | .50 | .23 |
| ❑ 10 Mario Lemieux | 5.00 | 2.20 |
| ❑ 11 Troy Loney | .50 | .23 |
| ❑ 12 Shawn McEachern | 1.00 | .45 |
| ❑ 13 Joe Mullen | 1.00 | .45 |
| ❑ 14 Larry Murphy | 1.00 | .45 |
| ❑ 15 Mike Needham | .50 | .23 |
| ❑ 16 Jim Paek | .50 | .23 |
| ❑ 17 Kjell Samuelsson | .50 | .23 |
| ❑ 18 Ulf Samuelsson | .75 | .35 |
| ❑ 19 Paul Stanton | .50 | .23 |
| ❑ 20 Mike Stapleton | .50 | .23 |
| ❑ 21 Kevin Stevens | .75 | .35 |
| ❑ 22 Martin Straka | 1.00 | .45 |
| ❑ 23 Dave Tippett | .50 | .23 |
| ❑ 24 Rick Tocchet | 1.25 | .55 |
| ❑ 25 Ken Wregget | 1.25 | .55 |
| ❑ 26 Penguins Mascot | .25 | .11 |

## 1992-93 Penguins Foodland

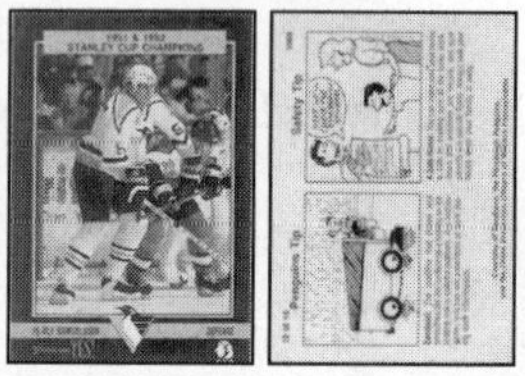

This 18-card standard-size set was sponsored by Foodland in conjunction with the Pittsburgh Penguins and the Crime Prevention Officers of Western Pennsylvania. The cards feature color action player photos with orange-yellow borders on a black card face. The player's name is printed in an orange-yellow stripe below the photo. The words "1991 and 1992 Stanley Cup Champions" are on an orange-yellow bar that overlaps the top of the picture. The Foodland logo and McGruff the Crime Dog appear at the bottom. The horizontal backs have a "Penguins Tip" and a "Safety Tip," each illustrated with a cartoon.

| | MINT | NRMT |
|---|---|---|
| COMPLETE SET (18) | 15.00 | 6.75 |
| COMMON CARD (1-18) | .25 | .11 |
| ❑ 1 Mario Lemieux | 5.00 | 2.20 |
| ❑ 2 Bob Errey | .50 | .23 |
| ❑ 3 Jaromir Jagr | 5.00 | 2.20 |
| ❑ 4 Rick Tocchet | 1.25 | .55 |
| ❑ 5 Tom Barrasso | 1.00 | .45 |
| ❑ 6 Joe Mullen | 1.00 | .45 |
| ❑ 7 Ron Francis | 2.00 | .90 |
| ❑ 8 Troy Loney | .50 | .23 |
| ❑ 9 Shawn McEachern | 1.00 | .45 |
| ❑ 10 Larry Murphy | 1.00 | .45 |
| ❑ 11 Jim Paek | .50 | .23 |
| ❑ 12 Ulf Samuelsson | .75 | .35 |
| ❑ 13 Paul Stanton | .50 | .23 |
| ❑ 14 Kjell Samuelsson | .50 | .23 |
| ❑ 15 Kevin Stevens | .75 | .35 |
| ❑ 16 Dave Tippett | .50 | .23 |
| ❑ 17 Martin Straka | 1.00 | .45 |
| ❑ 18 Penguins Mascot | .25 | .11 |

## 1992-93 Penguins Stickers

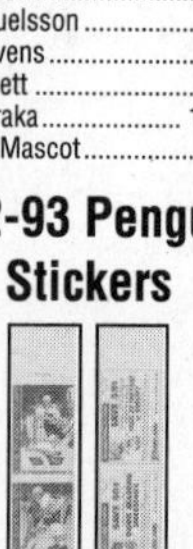

Sponsored by Foodland and issued in four three-sticker vertical strips, this 12-sticker set features white-bordered color player action photos, with the peel-away backs doubling as manufacturer coupons for different products. Each sticker measures the standard size. The player's name and uniform number appear in a yellow bar under the photo and the words "Back to Back Champs" are printed in a bar alongside the left. The team logo also appears on the front. The strips are numbered as Week 1-4; the stickers themselves are unnumbered. The players are listed below in alphabetical order; W1 to W4 indicates the week the stickers were issued.

| | MINT | NRMT |
|---|---|---|
| COMPLETE SET (12) | 15.00 | 6.75 |
| COMMON CARD (1-12) | .50 | .23 |
| ❑ 1 Tom Barrasso W2 | 1.00 | .45 |
| ❑ 2 Ron Francis W1 | 1.50 | .70 |
| ❑ 3 Jaromir Jagr W4 | 5.00 | 2.20 |
| ❑ 4 Mario Lemieux W2 | 5.00 | 2.20 |
| ❑ 5 Troy Loney W2 | .50 | .23 |
| ❑ 6 Shawn McEachern W4 | 1.00 | .45 |
| ❑ 7 Joe Mullen W3 | .75 | .35 |
| ❑ 8 Larry Murphy W4 | .75 | .35 |
| ❑ 9 Jim Paek W1 | .50 | .23 |
| ❑ 10 Ulf Samuelsson W3 | .75 | .35 |
| ❑ 11 Kevin Stevens W1 | .75 | .35 |
| ❑ 12 Rick Tocchet W3 | 1.00 | .45 |

## 1993-94 Penguins Foodland

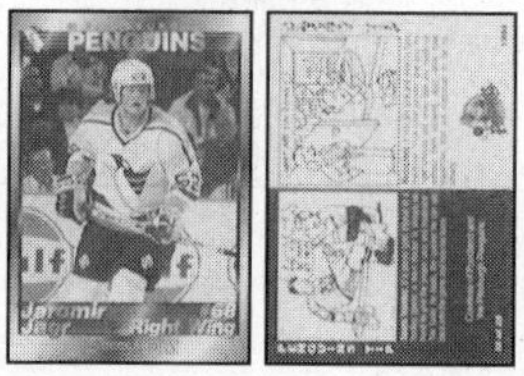

Sponsored by Foodland, this 25-card standard-size set features the 1993-94 Pittsburgh Penguins. The fronts have color action player photos with black borders on gray backgrounds. The team name appears in the top part of the card, while the player's name, number and position are printed under the photo. The sponsor's logo on the bottom rounds out the front. The horizontal backs have a "Penguin Tip" and a "Safety Tip," each illustrated with a cartoon.

| | MINT | NRMT |
|---|---|---|
| COMPLETE SET (25) | 14.00 | 6.25 |
| COMMON CARD (1-25) | .25 | .11 |
| ❑ 1 Mario Lemieux | 4.00 | 1.80 |
| ❑ 2 Grant Jennings | .35 | .16 |
| ❑ 3 Ulf Samuelsson | .50 | .23 |
| ❑ 4 Rick Tocchet | .75 | .35 |
| ❑ 5 Marty McSorley | .75 | .35 |
| ❑ 6 Rick Kehoe ACO | .25 | .11 |
| ❑ 7 Doug Brown | .35 | .16 |
| ❑ 8 Martin Straka | .75 | .35 |
| ❑ 9 Jim Paek | .35 | .16 |
| ❑ 10 Ken Wregget | .75 | .35 |
| ❑ 11 Jeff Daniels | .35 | .16 |
| ❑ 12 Bryan Trottier | .50 | .23 |
| ❑ 13 Larry Murphy | .50 | .23 |
| ❑ 14 Ron Francis | 1.00 | .45 |
| ❑ 15 Mike Needham | .35 | .16 |
| ❑ 16 Mike Ramsey | .35 | .16 |
| ❑ 17 Kevin Stevens | .50 | .23 |
| ❑ 18 Kjell Samuelsson | .35 | .16 |
| ❑ 19 Ed Johnston CO | .25 | .11 |
| ❑ 20 Markus Naslund | .50 | .23 |
| ❑ 21 Mike Stapleton | .35 | .16 |
| ❑ 22 Peter Taglianetti | .35 | .16 |
| ❑ 23 Jaromir Jagr | 3.00 | 1.35 |
| ❑ 24 Tom Barrasso | .50 | .23 |
| ❑ 25 Joe Mullen | .50 | .23 |

## 1994-95 Penguins Foodland

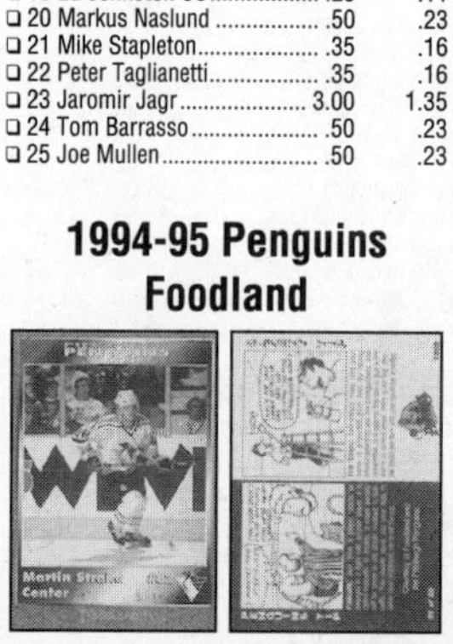

Sponsored by Foodland, this 25-card standard-size set features the 1994-1995 Pittsburgh Penguins. The fronts have color action player photos with gray borders on marbleized gray backgrounds. The team name across the top part of the card, while the player's name, number, position, and the team logo are printed under the picture. The horizontal backs carry a "Penguin Tip" and a "Safety Tip", each illustrated with a cartoon.

| | MINT | NRMT |
|---|---|---|
| COMPLETE SET (25) | 12.00 | 5.50 |
| COMMON CARD (1-25) | .25 | .11 |
| ❑ 1 Grant Jennings | .35 | .16 |
| ❑ 2 Greg Hawgood | .35 | .16 |
| ❑ 3 Shawn McEachern | .50 | .23 |
| ❑ 4 Len Barrie | .35 | .16 |
| ❑ 5 Ulf Samuelsson | .50 | .23 |
| ❑ 6 Joe Mullen | .50 | .23 |
| ❑ 7 John Cullen | .35 | .16 |
| ❑ 8 Mike Hudson | .35 | .16 |
| ❑ 9 Ron Francis | 1.00 | .45 |
| ❑ 10 Tomas Sandstrom | .50 | .23 |
| ❑ 11 Eddie Johnston CO | .25 | .11 |
| ❑ 12 Chris Tamer | .35 | .16 |
| ❑ 13 Francois Leroux | .35 | .16 |
| ❑ 14 Luc Robitaille | 1.00 | .45 |
| ❑ 15 Markus Naslund | .50 | .23 |
| ❑ 16 Ken Wregget | .50 | .23 |
| ❑ 17 Chris Joseph | .35 | .16 |
| ❑ 18 Peter Taglianetti | .35 | .16 |
| ❑ 19 Kevin Stevens | .50 | .23 |
| ❑ 20 Jim McKenzie | .35 | .16 |
| ❑ 21 Kjell Samuelsson | .35 | .16 |
| ❑ 22 Tom Barrasso | .50 | .23 |
| ❑ 23 Jaromir Jagr | 4.00 | 1.80 |
| ❑ 24 Larry Murphy | .50 | .23 |
| ❑ 25 Martin Straka | .35 | .16 |

## 1995-96 Penguins Foodland

This 25-card set maintains the string of issues released by Foodland, a Pittsburgh-area grocery chain, to honor the hometown Penguins. The cards feature action player photos surrounded by an icy blue border on the front. The backs have two Penguin tips, and the card number. Card number 24 erroneously pictures Ian Moran instead of Bryan Smolinski. The error is not believed to have been corrected.

| | MINT | NRMT |
|---|---|---|
| COMPLETE SET (25) | 10.00 | 4.50 |
| COMMON CARD (1-25) | .10 | .05 |
| ❑ 1 Ron Francis | 1.00 | .45 |
| ❑ 2 Glen Murray | .25 | .11 |
| ❑ 3 Chris Wells | .25 | .11 |
| ❑ 4 Markus Naslund | .35 | .16 |
| ❑ 5 Jaromir Jagr | 3.00 | 1.35 |
| ❑ 6 Francois Leroux | .25 | .11 |
| ❑ 7 Richard Park | .25 | .11 |
| ❑ 8 Norm Maciver | .25 | .11 |
| ❑ 9 Ken Wregget | .50 | .23 |
| ❑ 10 Tom Barrasso | .50 | .23 |
| ❑ 11 Rick Kehoe ACO | .25 | .11 |
| ❑ 12 Sergei Zubov | .50 | .23 |
| ❑ 13 Joe Dziedzic | .25 | .11 |
| ❑ 14 Ed Patterson | .25 | .11 |
| ❑ 15 Tomas Sandstrom | .35 | .16 |
| ❑ 16 Dave Roche | .25 | .11 |
| ❑ 17 Petr Nedved | .50 | .23 |
| ❑ 18 Chris Tamer | .25 | .11 |
| ❑ 19 Chris Joseph | .25 | .11 |
| ❑ 20 Ian Moran | .25 | .11 |
| ❑ 21 Iceburgh (Mascot) | .10 | .05 |
| ❑ 22 Ed Johnston CO | .25 | .11 |
| ❑ 23 Mario Lemieux | 4.00 | 1.80 |
| ❑ 24 Bryan Smolinski UER photo shown Ian Moran | .35 | .16 |
| ❑ 25 Dmitri Mironov | .35 | .16 |

## 1996-97 Penguins Tribune-Review

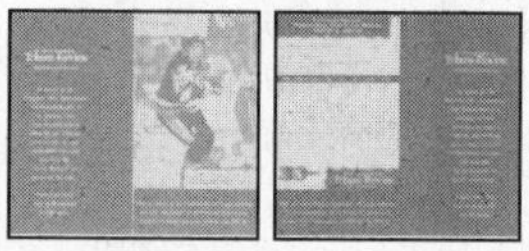

These oversized 5" x 7" thick stock cards were distributed as inserts in the Penguins game programs to honor the club's two Cup championships of the early '90s. As issued, the cards were folded in half, with the first two "pages" explaining the promotion,the third page actually containing the card/photo, and the fourth page offering biographical info and stats from one of the two seasons.

| | MINT | NRMT |
|---|---|---|
| COMPLETE SET (8) | 30.00 | 13.50 |
| COMMON CARD (1-8) | 2.00 | .90 |
| ❑ 1 Ron Francis | 4.00 | 1.80 |
| ❑ 2 Joe Mullen | 2.00 | .90 |
| ❑ 3 Ulf Samuelsson | 2.00 | .90 |
| ❑ 4 Bryan Trottier | 3.00 | 1.35 |
| ❑ 5 Tom Barrasso | 2.00 | .90 |
| ❑ 6 Kevin Stevens | 3.00 | 1.35 |
| ❑ 7 Jaromir Jagr | 8.00 | 3.60 |
| ❑ 8 Mario Lemieux | 10.00 | 4.50 |

## 1980-81 Pepsi-Cola Caps

This set of 140 bottle caps features 20 players

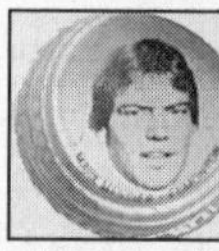

from each of the seven Canadian hockey teams. The bottle caps are written in French and English. There are two sizes of caps depending on whether the cap was from a small or large bottle. The top of the cap displays the Pepsi logo in the familiar red, white, and blue. The sides of the cap were done in blue and white lettering on a pink background. On the inside of the cap is a "black and aluminum" head shot of the player, with his name and the city (from which the team hails) below. We have checklisted the caps in alphabetical order of the teams as follows: Calgary Flames (1-20), Edmonton Oilers (21-40), Montreal Canadiens (41-60), Quebec Nordiques (61-80), Toronto Maple Leafs (81-100), Vancouver Canucks (101-120), and Winnipeg Jets (121-140). Also the players' names have been alphabetized within their teams. Also available through a mail-in offer -- in either English or French -- was a white plastic circular display plaque (approximately 24" by 24") for the caps. The French version sometimes sells for a slight premium. There also are reports that two different size variations exist: a 10 ounce and a 26 ounce size. There does not appear to be a premium on either size cap at this time.

| | NRMT-MT | EXC |
|---|---|---|
| COMPLETE SET (140) | 200.00 | 90.00 |
| COMMON CARD (1-140) | 1.50 | .70 |
| ❑ 1 Dan Bouchard | 2.00 | .90 |
| ❑ 2 Guy Chouinard | 2.00 | .90 |
| ❑ 3 Bill Clement | 2.00 | .90 |
| ❑ 4 Randy Holt | 1.50 | .70 |
| ❑ 5 Ken Houston | 1.50 | .70 |
| ❑ 6 Kevin Lavallee | 1.50 | .70 |
| ❑ 7 Don Lever | 1.50 | .70 |
| ❑ 8 Bob MacMillan | 1.50 | .70 |
| ❑ 9 Brad Marsh | 2.50 | 1.10 |
| ❑ 10 Bob Murdoch | 1.50 | .70 |
| ❑ 11 Kent Nilsson | 2.00 | .90 |
| ❑ 12 Willi Plott | 2.00 | .90 |
| ❑ 13 Jim Peplinski | 2.00 | .90 |
| ❑ 14 Pekka Rautakillio | 1.50 | .70 |
| ❑ 15 Paul Reinhart | 2.00 | .90 |
| ❑ 16 Pat Riggin | 2.00 | .90 |
| ❑ 17 Phil Russell | 1.50 | .70 |
| ❑ 18 Brad Smith | 1.50 | .70 |
| ❑ 19 Eric Vail | 1.50 | .70 |
| ❑ 20 Bert Wilson | 1.50 | .70 |
| ❑ 21 Glenn Anderson | 4.00 | 1.80 |
| ❑ 22 Curt Brackenbury | 1.50 | .70 |
| ❑ 23 Brett Callighen | 1.50 | .70 |
| ❑ 24 Paul Coffey | 15.00 | 6.75 |
| ❑ 25 Lee Fogolin | 1.50 | .70 |
| ❑ 26 Matti Hagman | 1.50 | .70 |
| ❑ 27 John Hughes | 1.50 | .70 |
| ❑ 28 Dave Hunter | 1.50 | .70 |
| ❑ 29 Jari Kurri | 8.00 | 3.60 |
| ❑ 30 Ron Low | 2.00 | .90 |
| ❑ 31 Kevin Lowe | 2.50 | 1.10 |
| ❑ 32 Dave Lumley | 1.50 | .70 |
| ❑ 33 Blair MacDonald | 1.50 | .70 |
| ❑ 34 Mark Messier | 25.00 | 11.00 |
| ❑ 35 Ed Mio | 2.00 | .90 |
| ❑ 36 Don Murdoch | 1.50 | .70 |
| ❑ 37 Pat Price | 1.50 | .70 |
| ❑ 38 Dave Semenko | 2.00 | .90 |
| ❑ 39 Risto Siltanen | 1.50 | .70 |
| ❑ 40 Stan Weir | 1.50 | .70 |
| ❑ 41 Keith Acton | 1.50 | .70 |
| ❑ 42 Brian Engblom | 1.50 | .70 |
| ❑ 43 Bob Gainey | 3.00 | 1.35 |
| ❑ 44 Gaston Gingras | 1.50 | .70 |
| ❑ 45 Denis Herron | 2.00 | .90 |
| ❑ 46 Rejean Houle | 1.50 | .70 |
| ❑ 47 Doug Jarvis | 1.50 | .70 |
| ❑ 48 Yvon Lambert | 1.50 | .70 |
| ❑ 49 Rod Langway | 3.00 | 1.35 |
| ❑ 50 Guy Lapointe | 2.00 | .90 |
| ❑ 51 Pierre Larouche | 2.50 | 1.10 |
| ❑ 52 Pierre Mondou | 1.50 | .70 |
| ❑ 53 Mark Napier | 2.00 | .90 |
| ❑ 54 Chris Nilan | 2.50 | 1.10 |
| ❑ 55 Doug Risebrough | 1.50 | .70 |
| ❑ 56 Larry Robinson | 4.00 | 1.80 |
| ❑ 57 Serge Savard | 2.00 | .90 |
| ❑ 58 Steve Shutt | 3.00 | 1.35 |
| ❑ 59 Mario Tremblay | 2.00 | .90 |
| ❑ 60 Doug Wickenheiser | 1.50 | .70 |
| ❑ 61 Serge Bernier | 1.50 | .70 |
| ❑ 62 Kim Clackson | 1.75 | .80 |
| ❑ 63 Real Cloutier | 1.50 | .70 |
| ❑ 64 Andre Dupont | 1.50 | .70 |
| ❑ 65 Robbie Ftorek | 2.00 | .90 |
| ❑ 66 Michel Goulet | 5.00 | 2.20 |
| ❑ 67 Jamie Hislop | 1.50 | .70 |
| ❑ 68 Dale Hoganson | 1.50 | .70 |
| ❑ 69 Dale Hunter | 4.00 | 1.80 |
| ❑ 70 Pierre Lacroix | 1.50 | .70 |
| ❑ 71 Garry Lariviere | 1.50 | .70 |
| ❑ 72 Rich Leduc | 1.50 | .70 |
| ❑ 73 John Paddock | 2.00 | .90 |
| ❑ 74 Michel Plasse | 2.00 | .90 |

❑ 75 Jacques Richard ........ 1.50 .70
❑ 76 Anton Stastny ........ 2.00 .90
❑ 77 Peter Stastny ........ 6.00 2.70
❑ 78 Mark Tardif ........ 2.00 .90
❑ 79 Wally Weir ........ 1.50 .70
❑ 80 John Wensink ........ 2.00 .90
❑ 81 John Anderson ........ 1.50 .70
❑ 82 Laurie Boschman ........ 1.50 .70
❑ 83 Jiri Crha ........ 2.00 .90
❑ 84 Bill Derlago ........ 1.50 .70
❑ 85 Vitezslav Duris ........ 1.50 .70
❑ 86 Ron Ellis ........ 2.00 .90
❑ 87 Dave Farrish ........ 1.50 .70
❑ 88 Stewart Gavin ........ 2.00 .90
❑ 89 Pat Hickey ........ 1.50 .70
❑ 90 Dan Maloney ........ 2.00 .90
❑ 91 Terry Martin ........ 1.50 .70
❑ 92 Barry Melrose ........ 2.00 .90
❑ 93 Wilf Paiement ........ 2.00 .90
❑ 94 Robert Picard ........ 1.50 .70
❑ 95 Jim Rutherford ........ 2.50 1.10
❑ 96 Rocky Saganiuk ........ 1.50 .70
❑ 97 Borje Salming ........ 3.00 1.35
❑ 98 David Shand ........ 1.50 .70
❑ 99 Ian Turnbull ........ 2.00 .90
❑ 100 Rick Vaive ........ 2.50 1.10
❑ 101 Brent Ashton ........ 1.50 .70
❑ 102 Ivan Boldirev ........ 1.50 .70
❑ 103 Per-Olov Brasar ........ 1.50 .70
❑ 104 Richard Brodeur ........ 2.50 1.10
❑ 105 Jerry Butler ........ 1.50 .70
❑ 106 Colin Campbell ........ 2.00 .90
❑ 107 Curt Fraser ........ 1.50 .70
❑ 108 Thomas Gradin ........ 2.00 .90
❑ 109 Dennis Kearns ........ 1.50 .70
❑ 110 Rick Lanz ........ 1.50 .70
❑ 111 Lars Lindgren ........ 1.50 .70
❑ 112 Dave Logan ........ 1.50 .70
❑ 113 Mario Marois ........ 1.50 .70
❑ 114 Kevin McCarthy ........ 1.50 .70
❑ 115 Gerald Minor ........ 1.50 .70
❑ 116 Darcy Rota ........ 1.50 .70
❑ 117 Bobby Schmautz ........ 1.50 .70
❑ 118 Stan Smyl ........ 2.00 .90
❑ 119 Harold Snepsts ........ 2.50 1.10
❑ 120 Dave(Tiger) Williams ........ 2.50 1.10
❑ 121 Dave Babych ........ 2.00 .90
❑ 122 Al Cameron ........ 1.50 .70
❑ 123 Scott Campbell ........ 1.50 .70
❑ 124 Dave Christian ........ 2.00 .90
❑ 125 Jude Drouin ........ 1.50 .70
❑ 126 Norm Dupont ........ 1.50 .70
❑ 127 Dan Geoffrion ........ 1.50 .70
❑ 128 Pierre Hamel ........ 1.50 .70
❑ 129 Barry Legge ........ 1.50 .70
❑ 130 Willy Lindstrom ........ 1.50 .70
❑ 131 Barry Long ........ 1.50 .70
❑ 132 Kris Manery ........ 1.50 .70
❑ 133 Jimmy Mann ........ 1.75 .80
❑ 134 Moe Mantha ........ 1.50 .70
❑ 135 Markus Mattsson ........ 2.00 .90
❑ 136 Doug Smail ........ 2.00 .90
❑ 137 Don Spring ........ 1.50 .70
❑ 138 Anders Steen ........ 1.50 .70
❑ 139 Peter Sullivan ........ 1.50 .70
❑ 140 Ron Wilson ........ 1.50 .70
❑ NNO Plastic Circular Display 80.00 36.00

## 1974-75 Phoenix Roadrunners WHA Pins

These pins feature color head shots and measure 3 1/2" in diameter. Player name and team name are featured in a black rectangle at the bottom of the pin. Pins are checklisted below in alphabetical order.

| | MINT | NRMT |
|---|---|---|
| COMPLETE SET (9) | 40.00 | 18.00 |
| COMMON PIN (1-9) | 4.00 | 1.80 |

❑ 1 Bob Barlow ........ 4.00 1.80
❑ 2 Cam Connor ........ 4.00 1.80
❑ 3 Michel Cormier ........ 4.00 1.80
❑ 4 Robbie Ftorek ........ 12.00 5.50
❑ 5 Dave Gorman ........ 4.00 1.80
❑ 6 John Hughes ........ 4.00 1.80
❑ 7 Murray Koegan ........ 4.00 1.80
❑ 8 Dennis Sobchuk ........ 4.00 1.80
❑ 9 Howie Young ........ 4.00 1.80

## 1991-92 Pinnacle

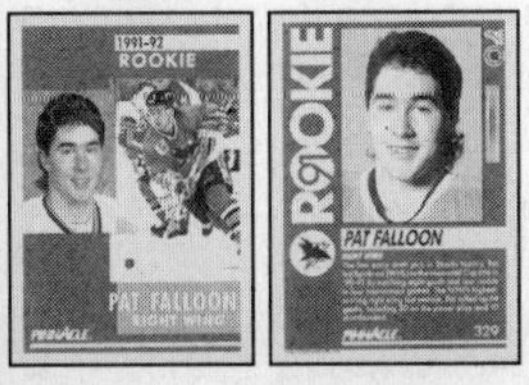


The 1991-92 (Score) Pinnacle Hockey set was issued in English and French editions; each set consists of 420 standard-size cards. The front design of the veteran player cards features two color photos, an action photo and a head shot, on a black background with white borders. The card backs have a color action shot silhouetted against a black background. The rookie cards have the same design, except with green background on the front, and black-and-white head shots rather than action shots on the back. The backs of the veteran player cards include biography, player profile, and statistics, while those of the rookie cards only have a player profile. Rookie Cards include Tony Amonte, Valeri Kamensky, John LeClair, Nicklas Lidstrom, Geoff Sanderson and Doug Weight.

| | MINT | NRMT |
|---|---|---|
| COMPLETE SET (420) | 35.00 | 16.00 |
| COMMON CARD (1-420) | .10 | .05 |
| *FRENCH: SAME VALUE | | |

❑ 1 Mario Lemieux ........ 2.00 .90
❑ 2 Trevor Linden ........ .25 .11
❑ 3 Kirk Muller ........ .10 .05
❑ 4 Phil Housley ........ .25 .11
❑ 5 Mike Modano ........ .50 .23
❑ 6 Adam Oates ........ .25 .11
❑ 7 Tom Kurvers ........ .10 .05
❑ 8 Doug Bodger ........ .10 .05
❑ 9 Rod Brind'Amour ........ .25 .11
❑ 10 Mats Sundin ........ .50 .23
❑ 11 Gary Suter ........ .10 .05
❑ 12 Glenn Anderson ........ .25 .11
❑ 13 Doug Wilson ........ .25 .11
❑ 14 Stephane Richer ........ .25 .11
❑ 15 Ray Bourque ........ .40 .18
❑ 16 Adam Graves ........ .25 .11
❑ 17 Luc Robitaille ........ .25 .11
❑ 18 Steve Smith ........ .10 .05
❑ 19 Uwe Krupp ........ .10 .05
❑ 20 Rick Tocchet ........ .25 .11
❑ 21 Tim Cheveldae ........ .25 .11
❑ 22 Kay Whitmore ........ .25 .11
❑ 23 Kelly Miller ........ .10 .05
❑ 24 Esa Tikkanen ........ .10 .05
❑ 25 Pat LaFontaine ........ .25 .11
❑ 26 James Patrick ........ .10 .05
❑ 27 Daniel Marois ........ .10 .05
❑ 28 Denis Savard ........ .25 .11
❑ 29 Steve Larmer ........ .25 .11
❑ 30 Pierre Turgeon ........ .25 .11
❑ 31 Gary Leeman ........ .10 .05
❑ 32 Mike Ricci ........ .10 .05
❑ 33 Troy Murray ........ .10 .05
❑ 34 Sergio Momesso ........ .10 .05
❑ 35 Marty McSorley ........ .10 .05
❑ 36 Paul Ysebaert ........ .10 .05
❑ 37 Gary Roberts ........ .10 .05
❑ 38 Mike Hudson ........ .10 .05
❑ 39 Kelly Hrudey ........ .25 .11
❑ 40 Dale Hunter ........ .10 .05
❑ 41 Brendan Shanahan ........ 1.00 .45
❑ 42 Steve Duchesne ........ .10 .05
❑ 43 Pat Verbeek ........ .10 .05
❑ 44 Tom Barrasso ........ .25 .11
❑ 45 Scott Mellanby ........ .25 .11
❑ 46 Stephen Leach ........ .10 .05
❑ 47 Darren Turcotte ........ .10 .05
❑ 48 Jari Kurri ........ .25 .11
❑ 49 Michel Petit ........ .10 .05
❑ 50 Mark Messier ........ .60 .25
❑ 51 Terry Carkner ........ .10 .05
❑ 52 Tim Kerr ........ .10 .05
❑ 53 Jaromir Jagr ........ 1.25 .55
❑ 54 Joe Nieuwendyk ........ .25 .11
❑ 55 Randy Burridge ........ .10 .05
❑ 56 Robert Reichel ........ .10 .05
❑ 57 Craig Janney ........ .25 .11
❑ 58 Chris Chelios ........ .40 .18
❑ 59 Bryan Fogarty ........ .10 .05
❑ 60 Christian Ruuttu ........ .10 .05
❑ 61 Steve Bozek ........ .10 .05
❑ 62 Dave Manson ........ .10 .05
❑ 63 Bruce Driver ........ .10 .05
❑ 64 Mike Ramsey ........ .10 .05
❑ 65 Bobby Holik ........ .10 .05
❑ 66 Bob Essensa ........ .25 .11
❑ 67 Pat Flatley ........ .10 .05
❑ 68 Wayne Presley ........ .10 .05
❑ 69 Mike Bullard ........ .10 .05
❑ 70 Claude Lemieux ........ .25 .11
❑ 71 Dave Gagner ........ .25 .11
❑ 72 Jeff Brown ........ .10 .05
❑ 73 Eric Desjardins ........ .10 .05
❑ 74 Fredrik Olausson ........ .10 .05
❑ 75 Steve Yzerman ........ 1.00 .45
❑ 76 Tony Granato ........ .10 .05
❑ 77 Adam Burt ........ .10 .05
❑ 78 Cam Neely ........ .25 .11
❑ 79 Brent Sutter ........ .10 .05
❑ 80 Dale Hawerchuk ........ .25 .11
❑ 81 Scott Stevens ........ .25 .11
❑ 82 Adam Creighton ........ .10 .05
❑ 83 Brian Hayward ........ .25 .11
❑ 84 Dan Quinn ........ .10 .05
❑ 85 Garth Butcher ........ .10 .05
❑ 86 Shawn Burr ........ .10 .05
❑ 87 Peter Bondra ........ .40 .18
❑ 88 Brad Shaw ........ .10 .05
❑ 89 Eric Weinrich ........ .10 .05
❑ 90 Brian Bradley ........ .10 .05
❑ 91 Vincent Damphousse ........ .25 .11
❑ 92 Doug Gilmour ........ .40 .18
❑ 93 Martin Gelinas ........ .10 .05
❑ 94 Mike Ridley ........ .10 .05
❑ 95 Ron Sutter ........ .10 .05
❑ 96 Mark Osborne ........ .10 .05
❑ 97 Mikhail Tatarinov ........ .10 .05
❑ 98 Bob McGill ........ .10 .05
❑ 99 Bob Carpenter ........ .10 .05
❑ 100 Wayne Gretzky ........ 2.50 1.10
❑ 101 Slava Fetisov ........ .10 .05
❑ 102 Shayne Corson ........ .10 .05
❑ 103 Clint Malarchuk ........ .25 .11
❑ 104 Randy Wood ........ .10 .05
❑ 105 Curtis Joseph ........ .50 .23
❑ 106 Cliff Ronning ........ .10 .05
❑ 107 Derek King ........ .10 .05
❑ 108 Neil Wilkinson ........ .10 .05
❑ 109 Michel Goulet ........ .25 .11
❑ 110 Zarley Zalapski ........ .10 .05
❑ 111 Dave Ellett ........ .10 .05
❑ 112 Glen Wesley ........ .10 .05
❑ 113 Bob Kudelski ........ .10 .05
❑ 114 Jamie Macoun ........ .10 .05
❑ 115 John MacLean ........ .25 .11
❑ 116 Steve Thomas ........ .10 .05
❑ 117 Pat Elynuik ........ .10 .05
❑ 118 Ron Hextall ........ .25 .11
❑ 119 Jeff Hackett ........ .25 .11
❑ 120 Jeremy Roenick ........ .50 .23
❑ 121 John Vanbiesbrouck ........ .60 .25
❑ 122 Dave Andreychuk ........ .25 .11
❑ 123 Ray Ferraro ........ .10 .05
❑ 124 Ron Tugnutt ........ .25 .11
❑ 125 John Cullen ........ .10 .05
❑ 126 Andy Moog ........ .25 .11
❑ 127 Ed Belfour ........ .40 .18
❑ 128 Dino Ciccarelli ........ .25 .11
❑ 129 Brian Bellows ........ .10 .05
❑ 130 Guy Carbonneau ........ .25 .11
❑ 131 Kevin Hatcher ........ .10 .05
❑ 132 Mike Vernon ........ .25 .11
❑ 133 Kevin Miller ........ .10 .05
❑ 134 Pelle Eklund ........ .10 .05
❑ 135 Brian Mullen ........ .10 .05
❑ 136 Brian Leetch ........ .40 .18
❑ 137 Daren Puppa ........ .25 .11
❑ 138 Steven Finn ........ .10 .05
❑ 139 Stephan Lebeau ........ .10 .05
❑ 140 Gord Murphy ........ .10 .05
❑ 141 Rob Brown ........ .10 .05
❑ 142 Ken Daneyko ........ .10 .05
❑ 143 Larry Murphy ........ .25 .11
❑ 144 Jon Casey ........ .25 .11
❑ 145 John Ogrodnick ........ .10 .05
❑ 146 Benoit Hogue ........ .10 .05
❑ 147 Mike McPhee ........ .10 .05
❑ 148 Don Beaupre ........ .25 .11
❑ 149 Kjell Samuelsson ........ .10 .05
❑ 150 Joe Sakic ........ .75 .35
❑ 151 Mark Recchi ........ .25 .11
❑ 152 Ulf Dahlen ........ .10 .05
❑ 153 Dean Evason ........ .10 .05
❑ 154 Keith Brown ........ .10 .05
❑ 155 Ray Sheppard ........ .25 .11
❑ 156 Owen Nolan ........ .25 .11
❑ 157 Sergei Fedorov ........ 1.00 .45
❑ 158 Kirk McLean ........ .25 .11
❑ 159 Petr Klima ........ .10 .05
❑ 160 Brian Skrudland ........ .10 .05
❑ 161 Neal Broten ........ .25 .11
❑ 162 Dimitri Khristich ........ .10 .05
❑ 163 Alexander Mogilny ........ .40 .18
❑ 164 Mike Richter ........ .50 .23
❑ 165 Daniel Berthiaume ........ .25 .11
❑ 166 Teppo Numminen ........ .10 .05
❑ 167 Ron Francis ........ .25 .11
❑ 168 Grant Fuhr ........ .25 .11
❑ 169 Mike Liut ........ .25 .11
❑ 170 Bill Ranford ........ .25 .11
❑ 171 Garry Galley ........ .10 .05
❑ 172 Jeff Norton ........ .10 .05
❑ 173 Jimmy Carson ........ .10 .05
❑ 174 Peter Zezel ........ .10 .05
❑ 175 Patrick Roy ........ 2.00 .90
❑ 176 Joe Mullen ........ .25 .11
❑ 177 Murray Craven ........ .10 .05
❑ 178 Tomas Sandstrom ........ .10 .05
❑ 179 Joel Otto ........ .10 .05
❑ 180 Steve Konroyd ........ .10 .05
❑ 181 Vladimir Ruzicka ........ .10 .05
❑ 182 Paul Cavallini ........ .10 .05
❑ 183 Bob Probert ........ .25 .11
❑ 184 Brian Propp ........ .10 .05
❑ 185 Glenn Healy ........ .25 .11
❑ 186 Paul Coffey ........ .40 .18
❑ 187 Jan Erixon ........ .10 .05
❑ 188 Kevin Lowe ........ .10 .05
❑ 189 Doug Lidster ........ .10 .05
❑ 190 Theoren Fleury ........ .25 .11
❑ 191 Kevin Stevens ........ .10 .05
❑ 192 Petr Nedved ........ .25 .11
❑ 193 Ed Olczyk ........ .10 .05
❑ 194 Mike Hough ........ .10 .05
❑ 195 Rod Langway ........ .10 .05
❑ 196 Craig Simpson ........ .10 .05
❑ 197 Petr Svoboda ........ .10 .05
❑ 198 David Volek ........ .10 .05
❑ 199 Mark Tinordi ........ .10 .05
❑ 200 Brett Hull ........ .75 .35
❑ 201 Rob Blake ........ .25 .11
❑ 202 Mike Gartner ........ .25 .11
❑ 203 Ken Hodge Jr. ........ .10 .05
❑ 204 Murray Baron ........ .10 .05
❑ 205 Gerard Gallant ........ .10 .05
❑ 206 Joe Murphy ........ .10 .05
❑ 207 Al Iafrate ........ .25 .11
❑ 208 Larry Robinson ........ .25 .11
❑ 209 Mathieu Schneider ........ .10 .05
❑ 210 Bobby Smith ........ .25 .11
❑ 211 Gerald Diduck ........ .10 .05
❑ 212 Luke Richardson ........ .10 .05
❑ 213 Rob Zettler ........ .10 .05
❑ 214 Brad McCrimmon ........ .10 .05
❑ 215 Craig MacTavish ........ .10 .05
❑ 216 Gino Cavallini ........ .10 .05
❑ 217 Craig Wolanin ........ .10 .05
❑ 218 Greg Adams ........ .10 .05
❑ 219 Mike Craig ........ .10 .05
❑ 220 Al MacInnis ........ .25 .11
❑ 221 Sylvain Cote ........ .10 .05
❑ 222 Bob Sweeney ........ .10 .05
❑ 223 Dave Snuggerud ........ .10 .05
❑ 224 Randy Ladouceur ........ .10 .05
❑ 225 Charlie Huddy ........ .10 .05
❑ 226 Sylvain Turgeon ........ .10 .05
❑ 227 Phil Bourque ........ .10 .05
❑ 228 Rob Ramage ........ .10 .05
❑ 229 Jeff Beukeboom ........ .10 .05
❑ 230 Alexei Gusarov ........ .10 .05
❑ 231 Kelly Kisio ........ .10 .05
❑ 232 Calle Johansson ........ .10 .05
❑ 233 Yves Racine ........ .10 .05
❑ 234 Peter Sidorkiewicz ........ .25 .11
❑ 235 Jim Johnson ........ .10 .05
❑ 236 Brent Gilchrist ........ .10 .05
❑ 237 Jyrki Lumme ........ .10 .05
❑ 238 Randy Gilhen ........ .10 .05
❑ 239 Ken Baumgartner ........ .10 .05
❑ 240 Joey Kocur ........ .10 .05
❑ 241 Bryan Trottier ........ .25 .11
❑ 242 Todd Krygier ........ .10 .05
❑ 243 Darrin Shannon ........ .10 .05
❑ 244 Dave Christian ........ .10 .05
❑ 245 Stephane Morin ........ .10 .05
❑ 246 Kevin Dineen ........ .10 .05
❑ 247 Chris Terreri ........ .25 .11
❑ 248 Craig Ludwig ........ .10 .05
❑ 249 Dave Taylor ........ .25 .11
❑ 250 Wendel Clark ........ .25 .11
❑ 251 David Shaw ........ .10 .05
❑ 252 Paul Ranheim ........ .10 .05
❑ 253 Mark Hunter ........ .10 .05
❑ 254 Russ Courtnall ........ .10 .05
❑ 255 Alexei Kasatonov ........ .10 .05
❑ 256 Randy Moller ........ .10 .05
❑ 257 Bob Errey ........ .10 .05
❑ 258 Curtis Leschyshyn ........ .10 .05
❑ 259 Rick Zombo ........ .10 .05
❑ 260 Dana Murzyn ........ .10 .05
❑ 261 Dirk Graham ........ .10 .05
❑ 262 Craig Muni ........ .10 .05
❑ 263 Geoff Courtnall ........ .10 .05
❑ 264 Todd Elik ........ .10 .05
❑ 265 Mike Keane ........ .10 .05
❑ 266 Peter Stastny ........ .25 .11
❑ 267 Ulf Samuelsson ........ .10 .05
❑ 268 Rich Sutter ........ .10 .05
❑ 269 Mike Krushelnyski ........ .10 .05
❑ 270 Dave Babych ........ .10 .05
❑ 271 Sergei Makarov ........ .10 .05
❑ 272 David Maley ........ .10 .05
❑ 273 Normand Rochefort ........ .10 .05
❑ 274 Gordie Roberts ........ .10 .05
❑ 275 Thomas Steen ........ .10 .05
❑ 276 Dave Lowry ........ .10 .05
❑ 277 Michal Pivonka ........ .10 .05
❑ 278 Todd Gill ........ .10 .05
❑ 279 Paul MacDermid ........ .10 .05
❑ 280 Brent Ashton ........ .10 .05
❑ 281 Randy Hillier ........ .10 .05
❑ 282 Frank Musil ........ .10 .05
❑ 283 Geoff Smith ........ .10 .05
❑ 284 John Tonelli ........ .10 .05
❑ 285 Joe Reekie ........ .10 .05
❑ 286 Greg Paslawski ........ .10 .05
❑ 287 Perry Berezan ........ .10 .05
❑ 288 Randy Carlyle ........ .10 .05
❑ 289 Chris Nilan ........ .10 .05
❑ 290 Patrik Sundstrom ........ .10 .05
❑ 291 Garry Valk ........ .10 .05
❑ 292 Mike Foligno ........ .10 .05
❑ 293 Igor Larionov ........ .10 .05
❑ 294 Jim Sandlak ........ .10 .05
❑ 295 Tom Chorske ........ .10 .05
❑ 296 Claude Loiselle ........ .10 .05
❑ 297 Mark Howe ........ .10 .05
❑ 298 Steve Chiasson ........ .10 .05
❑ 299 Mike Donnelly ........ .10 .05
❑ 300 Bernie Nicholls ........ .25 .11
❑ 301 Tony Amonte ........ 1.50 .70
❑ 302 Brad May ........ .25 .11
❑ 303 Josef Beranek ........ .10 .05
❑ 304 Rob Pearson ........ .10 .05
❑ 305 Andrei Lomakin ........ .10 .05
❑ 306 Kip Miller ........ .10 .05
❑ 307 Kevin Haller ........ .10 .05
❑ 308 Kevin Todd ........ .10 .05
❑ 309 Geoff Sanderson ........ .75 .35
❑ 310 Doug Weight ........ 1.50 .70
❑ 311 Vladimir Konstantinov ........ .50 .23
❑ 312 Peter Ahola ........ .10 .05
❑ 313 Claude Lapointe ........ .10 .05
❑ 314 Nelson Emerson ........ .10 .05
❑ 315 Pavel Bure ........ 1.25 .55
❑ 316 Jimmy Waite ........ .25 .11
❑ 317 Sergei Nemchinov ........ .10 .05
❑ 318 Alexander Godynyuk ........ .10 .05
❑ 319 Stu Barnes ........ .10 .05
❑ 320 Nicklas Lidstrom ........ 1.50 .70
❑ 321 Daryl Sydor ........ .10 .05
❑ 322 John LeClair ........ 4.00 1.80
❑ 323 Arturs Irbe ........ .25 .11
❑ 324 Ross Romaniuk ........ .10 .05
❑ 325 Ken Sutton ........ .10 .05
❑ 326 Bob Beers ........ .10 .05
❑ 327 Michel Picard ........ .10 .05
❑ 328 Derian Hatcher ........ .10 .05
❑ 329 Pat Falloon ........ .10 .05
❑ 330 Donald Audette ........ .25 .11
❑ 331 Pat Jablonski ........ .25 .11
❑ 332 Corey Foster ........ .10 .05
❑ 333 Tomas Forslund ........ .10 .05
❑ 334 Steven Rice ........ .10 .05
❑ 335 Marc Bureau ........ .10 .05
❑ 336 Kimbi Daniels ........ .10 .05
❑ 337 Adam Foote ........ .40 .18
❑ 338 Dan Kordic ........ .10 .05
❑ 339 Link Gaetz ........ .10 .05
❑ 340 Valeri Kamensky ........ 1.00 .45
❑ 341 Tom Draper ........ .25 .11
❑ 342 Jay More ........ .10 .05
❑ 343 Dominic Roussel ........ .25 .11
❑ 344 Jim Paek ........ .10 .05
❑ 345 Felix Potvin ........ 1.00 .45
❑ 346 Dan Lambert ........ .10 .05
❑ 347 Louie DeBrusk ........ .10 .05
❑ 348 Jamie Baker ........ .10 .05
❑ 349 Scott Niedermayer ........ .25 .11
❑ 350 Paul DiPietro ........ .10 .05
❑ 351 Chris Winnes ........ .10 .05
❑ 352 Mark Greig ........ .10 .05
❑ 353 Luciano Borsato ........ .10 .05
❑ 354 Valeri Zelepukin ........ .10 .05
❑ 355 Martin Lapointe ........ .10 .05
❑ 356 Brett Hull GW ........ .40 .18
❑ 357 Steve Larmer GW ........ .25 .11
❑ 358 Theoren Fleury GW ........ .25 .11
❑ 359 Jeremy Roenick GW ........ .40 .18
❑ 360 Mark Recchi GW ........ .25 .11
❑ 361 Brad Marsh ........ .10 .05
❑ 362 Kris King ........ .10 .05
❑ 363 Doug Brown ........ .10 .05
❑ 364 Carey Wilson ........ .10 .05
❑ 365 Eric Lindros ........ 3.00 1.35
❑ 366 Kevin Dineen GG ........ .10 .05
❑ 367 John Vanbiesbrouck GG ........ .30 .14
❑ 368 Ray Bourque GG ........ .40 .18
❑ 369 Doug Wilson GG ........ .25 .11
❑ 370 Keith Brown GG ........ .10 .05
❑ 371 Kevin Lowe GG ........ .10 .05
❑ 372 Kelly Miller GG ........ .10 .05
❑ 373 Dave Taylor GG ........ .25 .11
❑ 374 Guy Carbonneau GG ........ .25 .11
❑ 375 Tim Hunter GG ........ .10 .05
❑ 376 Brett Hull TECH ........ .40 .18
❑ 377 Paul Coffey TECH ........ .40 .18
❑ 378 Adam Oates TECH ........ .25 .11
❑ 379 Andy Moog TECH ........ .25 .11
❑ 380 Mario Lemieux TECH ........ .75 .35
❑ 381 Joe Sakic IDOL ........ 1.00 .45
(Wayne Gretzky)
❑ 382 Rob Blake IDOL ........ .25 .11
(Larry Robinson)
❑ 383 Doug Weight IDOL ........ .50 .23
(Steve Yzerman)
❑ 384 Mike Richter IDOL ........ .40 .18
(Bernie Parent)
❑ 385 Luc Robitaille IDOL ........ .25 .11
(Marcel Dionne)
❑ 386 Ed Olczyk IDOL ........ .10 .05
(Bobby Clarke)
❑ 387 Patrick Roy IDOL ........ .75 .35
(Rogatien Vachon)
❑ 388 Ed Belfour IDOL ........ .40 .18
(Tony Esposito)
❑ 389 Mats Sundin IDOL ........ .25 .11
(Mats Naslund)
❑ 390 Tony Amonte IDOL ........ .40 .18
(Mark Messier)
❑ 391 John Cullen IDOL ........ .10 .05
(Ray Cullen)
❑ 392 Gary Suter IDOL ........ .50 .23
(Bobby Orr)
❑ 393 Rick Zombo IDOL ........ .10 .05
(Glenn Resch)
❑ 394 Todd Krygier IDOL ........ .25 .11
(Gilbert Perreault)
❑ 395 John Druce IDOL ........ .10 .05
(Bob Gainey)
❑ 396 Bob Carpenter SL ........ .10 .05
❑ 397 Clint Malarchuk SL ........ .25 .11
❑ 398 Jim Kyte SL ........ .10 .05
❑ 399 Al MacInnis SL ........ .25 .11
❑ 400 Ed Belfour SL ........ .40 .18
❑ 401 Brad Marsh SL ........ .10 .05
❑ 402 Brian Benning SL ........ .10 .05
❑ 403 Larry Robinson SL ........ .25 .11
❑ 404 Craig Ludwig SL ........ .10 .05
❑ 405 Pat Flatley SL ........ .10 .05
❑ 406 Gary Nylund SL ........ .10 .05
❑ 407 Kjell Samuelsson SL ........ .10 .05
❑ 408 Dan Quinn SL ........ .10 .05
❑ 409 Garth Butcher SL ........ .10 .05
❑ 410 Rick Zombo SL ........ .10 .05
❑ 411 Paul Cavallini SL ........ .10 .05
❑ 412 Link Gaetz SL ........ .10 .05
❑ 413 Dave Hannan SL ........ .10 .05
❑ 414 Peter Zezel SL ........ .10 .05
❑ 415 Randy Gregg SL ........ .10 .05
❑ 416 Pat Elynuik SL ........ .10 .05
❑ 417 Rod Buskas SL ........ .10 .05
❑ 418 Mark Howe SL ........ .10 .05
❑ 419 Don Sweeney ........ .10 .05
❑ 420 Mark Hardy ........ .10 .05

## 1991-92 Pinnacle B

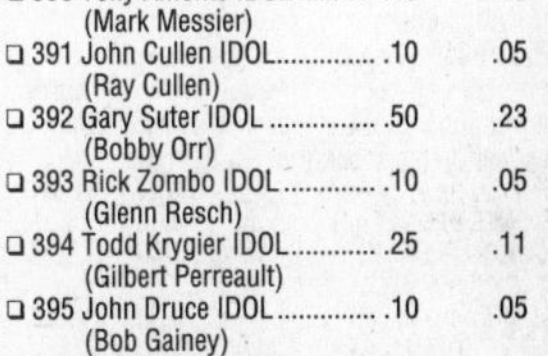


This 12-card standard-size set presents the

starting lineup from the 1991 All-Star Game. It features six players each from the Wales Conference (B1-B6) and the Campbell Conference (B7-B12). The cards were inserted into Pinnacle French and English foil packs. The French version has a red name plate, while the English version has a blue name plate. The fronts feature black-and-white head shots, with black borders on three sides and a thicker white border at the bottom. The words "Team Pinnacle" appear in the top black border, while the player's name and team affiliation are listed in the bottom white border. The border design on the back is similar and frames a player profile. The cards are numbered on the back with a "B" prefix.

| | MINT | NRMT |
|---|---|---|
| COMPLETE SET (12) | 300.00 | 135.00 |
| COMMON CARD (B1-B12) | 15.00 | 6.75 |
| *FRENCH: SAME VALUE | | |
| ❑ B1 Patrick Roy | 60.00 | 27.00 |
| ❑ B2 Ray Bourque | 20.00 | 9.00 |
| ❑ B3 Brian Leetch | 20.00 | 9.00 |
| ❑ B4 Kevin Stevens | 15.00 | 6.75 |
| ❑ B5 Mario Lemieux | 60.00 | 27.00 |
| ❑ B6 Cam Neely | 25.00 | 11.00 |
| ❑ B7 Bill Ranford | 25.00 | 11.00 |
| ❑ B8 Al MacInnis | 25.00 | 11.00 |
| ❑ B9 Chris Chelios | 20.00 | 9.00 |
| ❑ B10 Luc Robitaille | 25.00 | 11.00 |
| ❑ B11 Wayne Gretzky | 80.00 | 36.00 |
| ❑ B12 Brett Hull | 15.00 | 6.75 |

## 1992-93 Pinnacle American Promo Panel

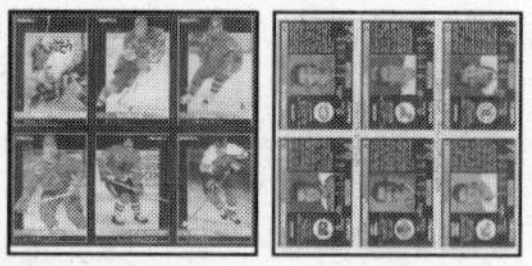

This promo sheet features six standard-size cards and was issued to promote the U.S. edition of Pinnacle hockey cards. The cards feature color action photos with the players extending beyond the picture background. The card face is black and a thin white line forms a frame around the picture. The player's name appears in a gradated bar at the bottom that matches the team colors. The horizontal backs feature the player's name in a gradated turquoise bar at the top. Close-up player photos are surrounded by biography, statistics, and career highlights on a black background. The backs have white borders. This sheet was intended to remain uncut and the disclaimers "Not For Resale" and "For Promotional Use Only" are printed in the white borders between the rows of cards. The cards are numbered on the back and listed as they appear on the sheet from left to right.

| | MINT | NRMT |
|---|---|---|
| COMPLETE SET (1) | 3.00 | 1.35 |
| COMMON PANEL | 3.00 | 1.35 |
| ❑ 1 Promo Sheet<br>91 Andy Moog<br>36 Nelson Emerson<br>61 Denis Savard<br>6 Owen Nolan<br>22 Michel Goulet<br>88 Eric Lindros | 3.00 | 1.35 |

## 1992-93 Pinnacle Canadian Promo Panels

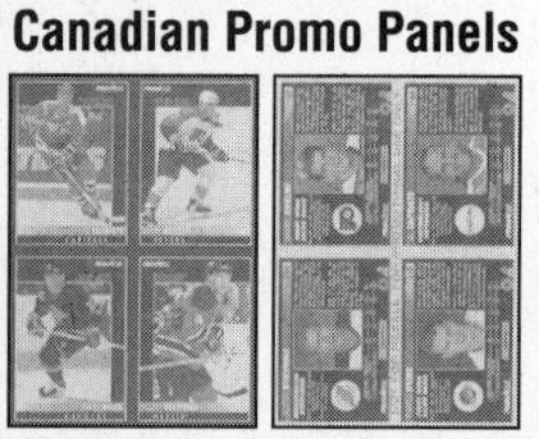

These three promo panels were issued to preview the design of the Canadian version of the 1992-93 Pinnacle hockey series. Measuring approximately 5" by 7", each panel consists of four standard-size cards. The fronts display glossy color action photos framed by black borders. The horizontal backs feature the player's name in a gradated burgundy bar at the top. Closeup photos are surrounded by biography, statistics, and career highlights on a black background. The sheet was intended to remain uncut and the disclaimers "Not For Resale" and "For Promotional Use Only" are printed in the white borders between the rows of cards. The cards on the panels are listed below alphabetically according to player's last name.

| | MINT | NRMT |
|---|---|---|
| COMPLETE SET (3) | 6.00 | 2.70 |
| COMMON PANEL (1-3) | 2.00 | .90 |
| ❑ 1 Promo Panel<br>Pavel Bure<br>Al Iafrate<br>Mark Recchi<br>Scott Stevens | 3.00 | 1.35 |
| ❑ 2 Promo Panel<br>Brian Bradley<br>Kirk Muller<br>Kevin Stevens<br>Pierre Turgeon | 2.00 | .90 |
| ❑ 3 Promo Panel<br>Doug Gilmour<br>Alexander Mogilny<br>Luc Robitaille<br>Teemu Selanne | 2.00 | .90 |

## 1992-93 Pinnacle

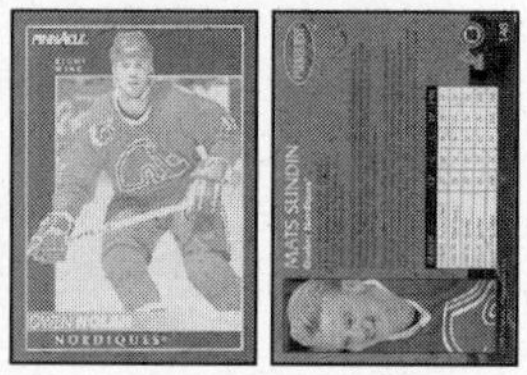

The 1992-93 Pinnacle Hockey set was issued in U.S. and Canadian bilingual editions; each set consists of 420 cards. While card numbers 1-220 and 271-390 have different front photography in the U.S. and Canadian versions, the subset cards (221-270) depict the same photos. Rookie Cards in the set include Roman Hamrlik, Andrei Kovalenko, and Martin Straka.

| | MINT | NRMT |
|---|---|---|
| COMPLETE SET (420) | 30.00 | 13.50 |
| COMMON CARD (1-420) | .10 | .05 |
| *FRENCH: 1X TO 1.25X BASIC CARDS | | |
| ❑ 1 Mark Messier | .50 | .23 |
| ❑ 2 Ray Bourque | .30 | .14 |
| ❑ 3 Gary Roberts | .10 | .05 |
| ❑ 4 Bill Ranford | .20 | .09 |
| ❑ 5 Gilbert Dionne | .10 | .05 |
| ❑ 6 Owen Nolan | .20 | .09 |
| ❑ 7 Pat LaFontaine | .20 | .09 |
| ❑ 8 Nicklas Lidstrom | .20 | .09 |
| ❑ 9 Pat Falloon | .10 | .05 |
| ❑ 10 Jeremy Roenick | .30 | .14 |
| ❑ 11 Kevin Hatcher | .10 | .05 |
| ❑ 12 Cliff Ronning | .10 | .05 |
| ❑ 13 Jeff Brown | .10 | .05 |
| ❑ 14 Kevin Dineen | .10 | .05 |
| ❑ 15 Brian Leetch | .30 | .14 |
| ❑ 16 Eric Desjardins | .10 | .05 |
| ❑ 17 Derek King | .10 | .05 |
| ❑ 18 Mark Tinordi | .10 | .05 |
| ❑ 19 Kelly Hrudey | .20 | .09 |
| ❑ 20 Sergei Fedorov | .60 | .25 |
| ❑ 21 Mike Ramsey | .10 | .05 |
| ❑ 22 Michel Goulet | .20 | .09 |
| ❑ 23 Joe Murphy | .10 | .05 |
| ❑ 24 Mark Fitzpatrick | .20 | .09 |
| ❑ 25 Cam Neely | .20 | .09 |
| ❑ 26 Rod Brind'Amour | .20 | .09 |
| ❑ 27 Neil Wilkinson | .10 | .05 |
| ❑ 28 Greg Adams | .10 | .05 |
| ❑ 29 Thomas Steen | .10 | .05 |
| ❑ 30 Calle Johansson | .10 | .05 |
| ❑ 31 Joe Nieuwendyk | .20 | .09 |
| ❑ 32 Rob Blake | .20 | .09 |
| ❑ 33 Darren Turcotte | .10 | .05 |
| ❑ 34 Derian Hatcher | .10 | .05 |
| ❑ 35 Mikhail Tatarinov | .10 | .05 |
| ❑ 36 Nelson Emerson | .10 | .05 |
| ❑ 37 Tim Cheveldae | .20 | .09 |
| ❑ 38 Donald Audette | .20 | .09 |
| ❑ 39 Brent Sutter | .10 | .05 |
| ❑ 40 Adam Oates | .20 | .09 |
| ❑ 41 Luke Richardson | .10 | .05 |
| ❑ 42 Jon Casey | .20 | .09 |
| ❑ 43 Guy Carbonneau | .20 | .09 |
| ❑ 44 Patrick Flatley | .10 | .05 |
| ❑ 45 Brian Benning | .10 | .05 |
| ❑ 46 Curtis Leschyshyn | .10 | .05 |
| ❑ 47 Trevor Linden | .20 | .09 |
| ❑ 48 Don Beaupre | .20 | .09 |
| ❑ 49 Troy Murray | .10 | .05 |
| ❑ 50 Paul Coffey | .30 | .14 |
| ❑ 51 Frank Musil | .10 | .05 |
| ❑ 52 Doug Wilson | .20 | .09 |
| ❑ 53 Pat Elynuik | .10 | .05 |
| ❑ 54 Curtis Joseph | .30 | .14 |
| ❑ 55 Tony Amonte | .20 | .09 |
| ❑ 56 Bob Probert | .20 | .09 |
| ❑ 57 Steve Smith | .10 | .05 |
| ❑ 58 Dave Andreychuk | .20 | .09 |
| ❑ 59 Vladimir Ruzicka | .10 | .05 |
| ❑ 60 Jari Kurri | .20 | .09 |
| ❑ 61 Denis Savard | .20 | .09 |
| ❑ 62 Benoit Hogue | .10 | .05 |
| ❑ 63 Terry Carkner | .10 | .05 |
| ❑ 64 Valeri Kamensky | .20 | .09 |
| ❑ 65 Jyrki Lumme | .10 | .05 |
| ❑ 66 Al Iafrate | .20 | .09 |
| ❑ 67 Paul Ranheim | .10 | .05 |
| ❑ 68 Ulf Dahlen | .10 | .05 |
| ❑ 69 Tony Granato | .10 | .05 |
| ❑ 70 Phil Housley | .20 | .09 |
| ❑ 71 Brian Lawton | .10 | .05 |
| ❑ 72 Garth Butcher | .10 | .05 |
| ❑ 73 Steve Leach | .10 | .05 |
| ❑ 74 Steve Larmer | .20 | .09 |
| ❑ 75 Mike Richter | .30 | .14 |
| ❑ 76 Vladimir Konstantinov | .10 | .05 |
| ❑ 77 Alexander Mogilny | .20 | .09 |
| ❑ 78 Craig MacTavish | .10 | .05 |
| ❑ 79 Mathieu Schneider | .10 | .05 |
| ❑ 80 Mark Recchi | .20 | .09 |
| ❑ 81 Gerald Diduck | .10 | .05 |
| ❑ 82 Peter Bondra | .30 | .14 |
| ❑ 83 Al MacInnis | .20 | .09 |
| ❑ 84 Bob Kudelski | .10 | .05 |
| ❑ 85 Dave Gagner | .20 | .09 |
| ❑ 86 Uwe Krupp | .10 | .05 |
| ❑ 87 Randy Carlyle | .10 | .05 |
| ❑ 88 Eric Lindros | 2.50 | 1.10 |
| ❑ 89 Rob Zettler | .10 | .05 |
| ❑ 90 Mats Sundin | .30 | .14 |
| ❑ 91 Andy Moog | .20 | .09 |
| ❑ 92 Keith Brown | .10 | .05 |
| ❑ 93 Paul Ysebaert | .10 | .05 |
| ❑ 94 Mike Gartner | .20 | .09 |
| ❑ 95 Kelly Buchberger | .10 | .05 |
| ❑ 96 Dominic Roussel | .20 | .09 |
| ❑ 97 Doug Bodger | .10 | .05 |
| ❑ 98 Mike Donnelly | .10 | .05 |
| ❑ 99 Mike Craig | .10 | .05 |
| ❑ 100 Brett Hull | .50 | .23 |
| ❑ 101 Robert Reichel | .10 | .05 |
| ❑ 102 Jeff Norton | .10 | .05 |
| ❑ 103 Garry Galley | .10 | .05 |
| ❑ 104 Dale Hunter | .10 | .05 |
| ❑ 105 Jeff Hackett | .20 | .09 |
| ❑ 106 Darrin Shannon | .10 | .05 |
| ❑ 107 Craig Wolanin | .10 | .05 |
| ❑ 108 Adam Graves | .20 | .09 |
| ❑ 109 Chris Chelios | .30 | .14 |
| ❑ 110 Pavel Bure | .60 | .25 |
| ❑ 111 Kirk Muller | .10 | .05 |
| ❑ 112 Jeff Beukeboom | .10 | .05 |
| ❑ 113 Mike Hough | .10 | .05 |
| ❑ 114 Brendan Shanahan | .60 | .25 |
| ❑ 115 Randy Burridge | .10 | .05 |
| ❑ 116 Dave Poulin | .10 | .05 |
| ❑ 117 Petr Svoboda | .10 | .05 |
| ❑ 118 Ed Belfour | .30 | .14 |
| ❑ 119 Ray Sheppard | .20 | .09 |
| ❑ 120 Bernie Nicholls | .10 | .05 |
| ❑ 121 Glenn Healy | .20 | .09 |
| ❑ 122 Johan Garpenlov | .10 | .05 |
| ❑ 123 Mike Lalor | .10 | .05 |
| ❑ 124 Brad McCrimmon | .10 | .05 |
| ❑ 125 Theoren Fleury | .20 | .09 |
| ❑ 126 Randy Gilhen | .10 | .05 |
| ❑ 127 Petr Nedved | .20 | .09 |
| ❑ 128 Steve Thomas | .10 | .05 |
| ❑ 129 Rick Zombo | .10 | .05 |
| ❑ 130 Patrick Roy | 1.50 | .70 |
| ❑ 131 Rod Langway | .10 | .05 |
| ❑ 132 Gord Murphy | .10 | .05 |
| ❑ 133 Randy Wood | .10 | .05 |
| ❑ 134 Mike Hudson | .10 | .05 |
| ❑ 135 Gerard Gallant | .10 | .05 |
| ❑ 136 Brian Glynn | .10 | .05 |
| ❑ 137 Jim Johnson | .10 | .05 |
| ❑ 138 Corey Millen | .10 | .05 |
| ❑ 139 Daniel Marois | .10 | .05 |
| ❑ 140 James Patrick | .10 | .05 |
| ❑ 141 Claude Lapointe | .10 | .05 |
| ❑ 142 Bobby Smith | .20 | .09 |
| ❑ 143 Charlie Huddy | .10 | .05 |
| ❑ 144 Murray Baron | .10 | .05 |
| ❑ 145 Ed Olczyk | .10 | .05 |
| ❑ 146 Dimitri Khristich | .10 | .05 |
| ❑ 147 Doug Lidster | .10 | .05 |
| ❑ 148 Perry Berezan | .10 | .05 |
| ❑ 149 Pelle Eklund | .10 | .05 |
| ❑ 150 Joe Sakic | .60 | .25 |
| ❑ 151 Michal Pivonka | .10 | .05 |
| ❑ 152 Joe Kocur | .20 | .09 |
| ❑ 153 Patrice Brisebois | .10 | .05 |
| ❑ 154 Ray Ferraro | .10 | .05 |
| ❑ 155 Mike Modano | .40 | .18 |
| ❑ 156 Marty McSorley | .10 | .05 |
| ❑ 157 Norm Maciver | .10 | .05 |
| ❑ 158 Sergei Nemchinov | .10 | .05 |
| ❑ 159 David Bruce | .10 | .05 |
| ❑ 160 Kelly Miller | .10 | .05 |
| ❑ 161 Alexei Gusarov | .10 | .05 |
| ❑ 162 Andrei Lomakin | .10 | .05 |
| ❑ 163 Sergio Momesso | .10 | .05 |
| ❑ 164 Mike Keane | .10 | .05 |
| ❑ 165 Pierre Turgeon | .20 | .09 |
| ❑ 166 Martin Gelinas | .10 | .05 |
| ❑ 167 Chris Dahlquist | .10 | .05 |
| ❑ 168 Kris King | .10 | .05 |
| ❑ 169 Dean Evason | .10 | .05 |
| ❑ 170 Mike Ridley | .10 | .05 |
| ❑ 171 Shawn Burr | .10 | .05 |
| ❑ 172 Dana Murzyn | .10 | .05 |
| ❑ 173 Dirk Graham | .10 | .05 |
| ❑ 174 Trent Yawney | .10 | .05 |
| ❑ 175 Luc Robitaille | .20 | .09 |
| ❑ 176 Randy Moller | .10 | .05 |
| ❑ 177 Vincent Riendeau | .20 | .09 |
| ❑ 178 Brian Propp | .10 | .05 |
| ❑ 179 Don Sweeney | .10 | .05 |
| ❑ 180 Stephane Matteau | .10 | .05 |
| ❑ 181 Garry Valk | .10 | .05 |
| ❑ 182 Sylvain Cote | .10 | .05 |
| ❑ 183 Dave Snuggerud | .10 | .05 |
| ❑ 184 Gary Leeman | .10 | .05 |
| ❑ 185 John Druce | .10 | .05 |
| ❑ 186 John Vanbiesbrouck | .50 | .23 |
| ❑ 187 Geoff Courtnall | .10 | .05 |
| ❑ 188 David Volek | .10 | .05 |
| ❑ 189 Doug Weight | .20 | .09 |
| ❑ 190 Bob Essensa | .20 | .09 |
| ❑ 191 Jan Erixon | .10 | .05 |
| ❑ 192 Geoff Smith | .10 | .05 |
| ❑ 193 Dave Christian | .10 | .05 |
| ❑ 194 Brian Noonan | .10 | .05 |
| ❑ 195 Gary Suter | .10 | .05 |
| ❑ 196 Craig Janney | .20 | .09 |
| ❑ 197 Brad May | .20 | .09 |
| ❑ 198 Gaetan Duchesne | .10 | .05 |
| ❑ 199 Adam Creighton | .10 | .05 |
| ❑ 200 Wayne Gretzky | 2.00 | .90 |
| ❑ 201 Dave Babych | .10 | .05 |
| ❑ 202 Fredrik Olausson | .10 | .05 |
| ❑ 203 Bob Bassen | .10 | .05 |
| ❑ 204 Todd Krygier | .10 | .05 |
| ❑ 205 Grant Ledyard | .10 | .05 |
| ❑ 206 Michel Petit | .10 | .05 |
| ❑ 207 Todd Elik | .10 | .05 |
| ❑ 208 Josef Beranek | .10 | .05 |
| ❑ 209 Neal Broten | .20 | .09 |
| ❑ 210 Jim Sandlak | .10 | .05 |
| ❑ 211 Kevin Haller | .10 | .05 |
| ❑ 212 Paul Broten | .10 | .05 |
| ❑ 213 Mark Pederson | .10 | .05 |
| ❑ 214 John McIntyre | .10 | .05 |
| ❑ 215 Teppo Numminen | .10 | .05 |
| ❑ 216 Ken Sutton | .10 | .05 |
| ❑ 217 Ronnie Stern | .10 | .05 |
| ❑ 218 Luciano Borsato | .10 | .05 |
| ❑ 219 Claude Loiselle | .10 | .05 |
| ❑ 220 Mark Hardy | .10 | .05 |
| ❑ 221 Joe Juneau RK | .20 | .09 |
| ❑ 222 Keith Tkachuk RK | .75 | .35 |
| ❑ 223 Scott Lachance RK | .10 | .05 |
| ❑ 224 Glen Murray RK | .10 | .05 |
| ❑ 225 Igor Kravchuk RK | .10 | .05 |
| ❑ 226 Evgeny Davydov RK | .10 | .05 |
| ❑ 227 Ray Whitney RK | .10 | .05 |
| ❑ 228 Bret Hedican RK | .10 | .05 |
| ❑ 229 Keith Carney RK | .10 | .05 |
| ❑ 230 Slava Kozlov RK | .20 | .09 |
| ❑ 231 Drake Berehowsky RK | .10 | .05 |
| ❑ 232 Cam Neely SL | .20 | .09 |
| ❑ 233 Al Iafrate SL | .10 | .05 |
| ❑ 234 Randy Wood SL | .10 | .05 |
| ❑ 235 Luke Richardson SL | .10 | .05 |
| ❑ 236 Eric Lindros SL | .75 | .35 |
| ❑ 237 Dale Hunter SL | .10 | .05 |
| ❑ 238 Pat Falloon SL | .10 | .05 |
| ❑ 239 Dean Kennedy SL | .10 | .05 |
| ❑ 240 Uwe Krupp SL | .20 | .09 |
| ❑ 241 Scott Niedermayer IDOL (Steve Yzerman) | .50 | .23 |
| ❑ 242 Gary Roberts IDOL (Lanny McDonald) | .10 | .05 |
| ❑ 243 Peter Ahola IDOL (Jari Kurri) | .10 | .05 |
| ❑ 244 Scott Lachance IDOL (Mark Howe) | .10 | .05 |
| ❑ 245 Rob Pearson IDOL (Mike Bossy) | .10 | .05 |
| ❑ 246 Kirk McLean IDOL (Bernie Parent) | .20 | .09 |
| ❑ 247 Dmitri Mironov IDOL (Viacheslav Fetisov) | .10 | .05 |
| ❑ 248 Brendan Shanahan IDOL (Darryl Sittler) | .20 | .09 |
| ❑ 249 Petr Nedved IDOL (Wayne Gretzky) | 1.00 | .45 |
| ❑ 250 Todd Ewen IDOL (Clark Gillies) | .10 | .05 |
| ❑ 251 Luc Robitaille GG | .20 | .09 |
| ❑ 252 Mark Tinordi GG | .10 | .05 |
| ❑ 253 Kris King GG | .10 | .05 |
| ❑ 254 Pat LaFontaine GG | .20 | .09 |
| ❑ 255 Ryan Walter GG | .10 | .05 |
| ❑ 256 Jeremy Roenick GW | .30 | .14 |
| ❑ 257 Brett Hull GW | .30 | .14 |
| ❑ 258 Steve Yzerman GW | .50 | .23 |
| ❑ 259 Claude Lemieux GW | .20 | .09 |
| ❑ 260 Mike Modano GW | .20 | .09 |
| ❑ 261 Vincent Damphousse GW | .20 | .09 |
| ❑ 262 Tony Granato GW | .10 | .05 |
| ❑ 263 Andy Moog MASK | .30 | .14 |
| ❑ 264 Curtis Joseph MASK | 3.00 | 1.35 |
| ❑ 265 Ed Belfour MASK | 3.00 | 1.35 |
| ❑ 266 Brian Hayward MASK | .30 | .14 |
| ❑ 267 Grant Fuhr MASK | 2.00 | .90 |
| ❑ 268 Don Beaupre MASK | 2.00 | .90 |
| ❑ 269 Tim Cheveldae MASK | 2.00 | .90 |
| ❑ 270 Mike Richter MASK | 3.00 | 1.35 |
| ❑ 271 Zarley Zalapski | .10 | .05 |
| ❑ 272 Kevin Todd | .10 | .05 |
| ❑ 273 Dave Ellett | .10 | .05 |
| ❑ 274 Chris Terreri | .20 | .09 |
| ❑ 275 Jaromir Jagr | 1.00 | .45 |
| ❑ 276 Wendel Clark | .20 | .09 |
| ❑ 277 Bobby Holik | .10 | .05 |
| ❑ 278 Bruce Driver | .10 | .05 |
| ❑ 279 Doug Gilmour | .30 | .14 |
| ❑ 280 Scott Stevens | .20 | .09 |
| ❑ 281 Murray Craven | .10 | .05 |
| ❑ 282 Rick Tocchet | .20 | .09 |
| ❑ 283 Peter Zezel | .10 | .05 |
| ❑ 284 Claude Lemieux | .20 | .09 |
| ❑ 285 John Cullen | .10 | .05 |
| ❑ 286 Valeri Zelepukin | .10 | .05 |
| ❑ 287 Rob Pearson | .10 | .05 |
| ❑ 288 Kevin Stevens | .10 | .05 |
| ❑ 289 Alexei Kasatonov | .10 | .05 |
| ❑ 290 Todd Gill | .10 | .05 |
| ❑ 291 Randy Ladouceur | .10 | .05 |
| ❑ 292 Larry Murphy | .20 | .09 |
| ❑ 293 Tom Chorske | .10 | .05 |
| ❑ 294 Jamie Macoun | .10 | .05 |
| ❑ 295 Sean Burke | .20 | .09 |
| ❑ 296 Ulf Samuelsson | .10 | .05 |
| ❑ 297 Eric Weinrich | .10 | .05 |
| ❑ 298 Tom Barrasso | .20 | .09 |
| ❑ 299 Slava Fetisov | .10 | .05 |
| ❑ 300 Mario Lemieux | 1.50 | .70 |
| ❑ 301 Grant Fuhr | .20 | .09 |
| ❑ 302 Zdeno Ciger | .10 | .05 |
| ❑ 303 Ron Francis | .20 | .09 |
| ❑ 304 Scott Niedermayer | .20 | .09 |
| ❑ 305 Mark Osborne | .10 | .05 |
| ❑ 306 Kjell Samuelsson | .10 | .05 |
| ❑ 307 Geoff Sanderson | .20 | .09 |
| ❑ 308 Paul Stanton | .10 | .05 |
| ❑ 309 Frank Pietrangelo | .20 | .09 |
| ❑ 310 Bob Errey | .10 | .05 |
| ❑ 311 Dino Ciccarelli | .20 | .09 |
| ❑ 312 Gordie Roberts | .10 | .05 |
| ❑ 313 Kevin Miller | .10 | .05 |
| ❑ 314 Mike Ricci | .10 | .05 |
| ❑ 315 Bob Carpenter | .10 | .05 |
| ❑ 316 Dale Hawerchuk | .20 | .09 |
| ❑ 317 Christian Ruuttu | .10 | .05 |
| ❑ 318 Mike Vernon | .20 | .09 |
| ❑ 319 Paul Cavallini | .10 | .05 |
| ❑ 320 Steve Duchesne | .10 | .05 |
| ❑ 321 Craig Simpson | .10 | .05 |
| ❑ 322 Mark Howe | .10 | .05 |
| ❑ 323 Shayne Corson | .10 | .05 |
| ❑ 324 Tom Kurvers | .10 | .05 |
| ❑ 325 Brian Bellows | .10 | .05 |
| ❑ 326 Glen Wesley | .10 | .05 |
| ❑ 327 Daren Puppa | .20 | .09 |
| ❑ 328 Joel Otto | .10 | .05 |
| ❑ 329 Jimmy Carson | .10 | .05 |
| ❑ 330 Kirk McLean | .20 | .09 |
| ❑ 331 Rob Brown | .10 | .05 |
| ❑ 332 Yves Racine | .10 | .05 |
| ❑ 333 Brian Mullen | .10 | .05 |
| ❑ 334 Dave Manson | .10 | .05 |
| ❑ 335 Sergei Makarov | .10 | .05 |
| ❑ 336 Esa Tikkanen | .10 | .05 |
| ❑ 337 Russ Courtnall | .10 | .05 |
| ❑ 338 Kevin Lowe | .10 | .05 |
| ❑ 339 Steve Chiasson | .10 | .05 |
| ❑ 340 Ron Hextall | .20 | .09 |
| ❑ 341 Stephen Lebeau | .10 | .05 |
| ❑ 342 Mike McPhee | .10 | .05 |
| ❑ 343 David Shaw | .10 | .05 |
| ❑ 344 Petr Klima | .10 | .05 |
| ❑ 345 Tomas Sandstrom | .10 | .05 |
| ❑ 346 Scott Mellanby | .20 | .09 |
| ❑ 347 Brian Skrudland | .10 | .05 |
| ❑ 348 Pat Verbeek | .10 | .05 |
| ❑ 349 Vincent Damphousse | .20 | .09 |
| ❑ 350 Steve Yzerman | 1.00 | .45 |
| ❑ 351 John MacLean | .20 | .09 |
| ❑ 352 Steve Konroyd | .10 | .05 |
| ❑ 353 Phil Bourque | .10 | .05 |
| ❑ 354 Ken Daneyko | .10 | .05 |
| ❑ 355 Glenn Anderson | .20 | .09 |
| ❑ 356 Ken Wregget | .20 | .09 |
| ❑ 357 Brent Gilchrist | .10 | .05 |
| ❑ 358 Bob Rouse | .10 | .05 |
| ❑ 359 Peter Stastny | .20 | .09 |
| ❑ 360 Joe Mullen | .20 | .09 |
| ❑ 361 Stephane Richer | .20 | .09 |
| ❑ 362 Kelly Kisio | .10 | .05 |
| ❑ 363 Keith Acton | .10 | .05 |
| ❑ 364 Felix Potvin | .30 | .14 |
| ❑ 365 Martin Lapointe | .10 | .05 |
| ❑ 366 Ron Tugnutt | .20 | .09 |
| ❑ 367 Dave Taylor | .20 | .09 |
| ❑ 368 Tim Kerr | .10 | .05 |
| ❑ 369 Carey Wilson | .10 | .05 |
| ❑ 370 Greg Paslawski | .10 | .05 |
| ❑ 371 Peter Sidorkiewicz | .20 | .09 |
| ❑ 372 Brad Shaw | .10 | .05 |
| ❑ 373 Sylvain Turgeon | .10 | .05 |
| ❑ 374 Mark Lamb | .10 | .05 |
| ❑ 375 Laurie Boschman | .10 | .05 |
| ❑ 376 Mark Osiecki | .10 | .05 |
| ❑ 377 Doug Smail | .10 | .05 |
| ❑ 378 Brad Marsh | .10 | .05 |
| ❑ 379 Mike Peluso | .10 | .05 |
| ❑ 380 Steve Weeks | .20 | .09 |
| ❑ 381 Wendell Young | .20 | .09 |
| ❑ 382 Joe Reekie | .10 | .05 |
| ❑ 383 Peter Taglianetti | .10 | .05 |
| ❑ 384 Mikael Andersson | .10 | .05 |
| ❑ 385 Marc Bergevin | .10 | .05 |
| ❑ 386 Anatoli Semenov | .10 | .05 |
| ❑ 387 Brian Bradley | .10 | .05 |
| ❑ 388 Michel Mongeau | .10 | .05 |
| ❑ 389 Rob Ramage | .10 | .05 |
| ❑ 390 Ken Hodge Jr. | .10 | .05 |
| ❑ 391 Richard Matvichuk | .10 | .05 |
| ❑ 392 Alexei Zhitnik UER (Drafted in fourth round, not third as bio indicates) | .10 | .05 |
| ❑ 393 Dallas Drake | .10 | .05 |
| ❑ 394 Dimitri Yushkevich | .10 | .05 |
| ❑ 395 Andrei Kovalenko | .10 | .05 |
| ❑ 396 Vladimir Vujtek | .10 | .05 |
| ❑ 397 Nikolai Borschevsky | .10 | .05 |
| ❑ 398 Vitali Karamnov | .10 | .05 |
| ❑ 399 Jim Hiller | .10 | .05 |
| ❑ 400 Michael Nylander | .10 | .05 |
| ❑ 401 Tommy Sjodin | .10 | .05 |
| ❑ 402 Martin Straka | .10 | .05 |
| ❑ 403 Alexei Kovalev | .20 | .09 |
| ❑ 404 Vitali Prokhorov | .10 | .05 |

❑ 405 Dmitri Kvartalnov .10 .05
❑ 406 Teemu Selanne 1.50 .70
❑ 407 Darius Kasparaitis .10 .05
❑ 408 Roman Hamrlik .50 .23
❑ 409 Vladimir Malakhov .10 .05
❑ 410 Sergei Krivokrasov .10 .05
❑ 411 Robert Lang .10 .05
❑ 412 Jozef Stumpel .10 .05
❑ 413 Denny Felsner .10 .05
❑ 414 Rob Zamuner .10 .05
❑ 415 Jason Woolley .10 .05
❑ 416 Alexei Zhamnov .20 .09
❑ 417 Igor Korolev .10 .05
❑ 418 Patrick Poulin .10 .05
❑ 419 Dmitri Mironov .10 .05
❑ 420 Shawn McEachern .10 .05

## 1992-93 Pinnacle Team 2000

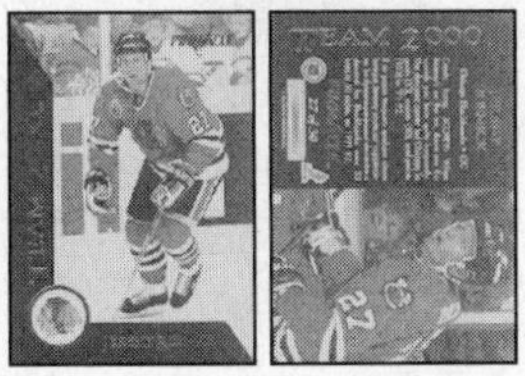

Inserted two per 27-card super pack, these 30 standard-size cards feature players who Pinnacle predicts will be stars in the NHL in the year 2000. The U.S. version features glossy color action photos that are full-bleed on the top and right and edged by black wedged-shaped borders on the left and bottom. In a gold-foil edged circle, the team logo appears in the lower left corner at the intersection of these two stripes. In gold-foil lettering, the words "Team 2000" are printed vertically in the left stripe while the player's name appears in the bottom stripe. The Canadian version offers different player photos and has a maple leaf following the Team 2000 insignia.The horizontal backs have a black panel with bilingual player profile on the left half and a full-bleed color close-up photo on the right.

| | MINT | NRMT |
|---|---|---|
| COMPLETE SET (30) | 30.00 | 13.50 |
| COMMON CARD (1-30) | .40 | .18 |

*FRENCH: 1X TO 1.25X BASIC CARDS

❑ 1 Eric Lindros 3.00 1.35
❑ 2 Mike Modano 1.50 .70
❑ 3 Nicklas Lidstrom .75 .35
❑ 4 Tony Amonte .75 .35
❑ 5 Felix Potvin 1.50 .70
❑ 6 Scott Lachance .40 .18
❑ 7 Mats Sundin 1.50 .70
❑ 8 Pavel Bure 2.50 1.10
❑ 9 Eric Desjardins .40 .18
❑ 10 Owen Nolan .75 .35
❑ 11 Dominic Roussel .75 .35
❑ 12 Scott Niedermayer .75 .35
❑ 13 Slava Kozlov .75 .35
❑ 14 Patrick Poulin .40 .18
❑ 15 Jaromir Jagr 4.00 1.80
❑ 16 Rob Blake .40 .18
❑ 17 Pierre Turgeon .75 .35
❑ 18 Rod Brind'Amour .75 .35
❑ 19 Joe Juneau .40 .18
❑ 20 Tim Cheveldae .75 .35
❑ 21 Joe Sakic 2.50 1.10
❑ 22 Kevin Todd .40 .18
❑ 23 Rob Pearson .40 .18
❑ 24 Trevor Linden .75 .35
❑ 25 Dimitri Khristich .40 .18
❑ 26 Pat Falloon .40 .18
❑ 27 Jeremy Roenick 1.50 .70
❑ 28 Alexander Mogilny .75 .35
❑ 29 Gilbert Dionne .40 .18
❑ 30 Sergei Fedorov 2.50 1.10

## 1992-93 Pinnacle Team Pinnacle

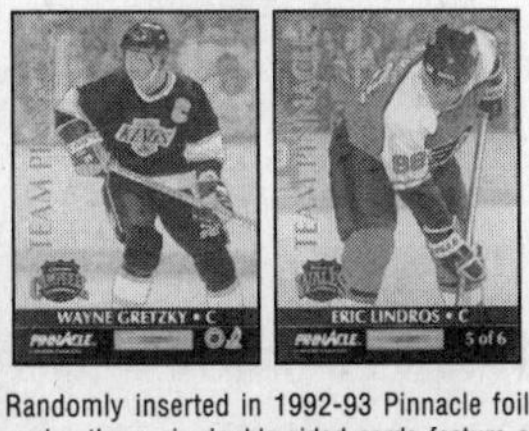

Randomly inserted in 1992-93 Pinnacle foil packs, these six double-sided cards feature a top player from the Campbell Conference with his Wales Conference counterpart on the other side. According to Score, the odds of finding a card are not less than 1:125 packs. Painted by Score artist Christopher Greco, the pictures are full-bleed on three sides but edged on the bottom by a gold-foil stripe that features the player's name and position. A black stripe immediately below completes the card face. The words "Team Pinnacle" are printed in turquoise (pink in the Canadian version) vertically near the left edge of both sides of the card, and the conference logo appears below it. The backs of these cards may be distinguished from the fronts by the card number in the lower right corner.

| | MINT | NRMT |
|---|---|---|
| COMPLETE SET (6) | 50.00 | 22.00 |
| COMMON CARD (1-6) | 5.00 | 2.20 |

*FRENCH: 1X TO 1.25X BASIC CARDS

❑ 1 Mike Richter 8.00 3.60
Ed Belfour
❑ 2 Ray Bourque 5.00 2.20
Chris Chelios
❑ 3 Brian Leetch 5.00 2.20
Paul Coffey
❑ 4 Kevin Stevens 6.00 2.70
Pavel Bure
❑ 5 Eric Lindros 20.00 9.00
Wayne Gretzky
❑ 6 Jaromir Jagr 10.00 4.50
Brett Hull

## 1992-93 Pinnacle Eric Lindros

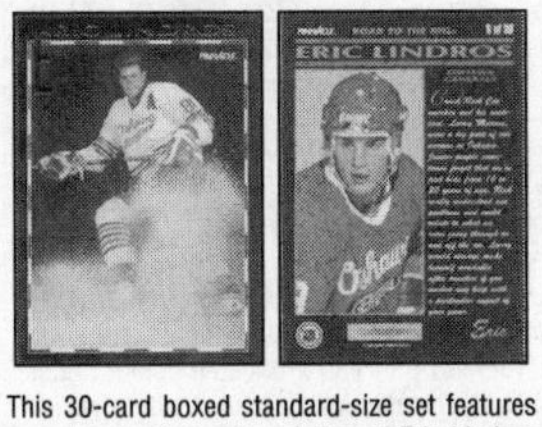

This 30-card boxed standard-size set features posed and action color photos of Eric Lindros as he has progressed from the junior leagues to the NHL. The set begins when Eric Lindros first received attention as a 14-year-old with the St. Michael's Buzzers and ends with his playing for the Philadelphia Flyers. According to Pinnacle, 3,750 numbered cases were produced. The cards have black borders, and his name is printed in gold foil at the top. The backs display a vertical, color photo and Eric's comments about a particular phase of his career.

| | MINT | NRMT |
|---|---|---|
| COMPLETE SET (30) | 12.00 | 5.50 |
| COMMON CARD (1-30) | .50 | .23 |

❑ 1 St. Michael's Buzzers .75 .35
❑ 2 Detroit Compuware .50 .23
❑ 3 Oshawa Generals .50 .23
❑ 4 Oshawa Generals .50 .23
❑ 5 Oshawa Generals .50 .23
❑ 6 Oshawa Generals .50 .23
❑ 7 Memorial Cup .50 .23
❑ 8 World Junior .50 .23
Championship
❑ 9 World Junior .50 .23
Championship
❑ 10 World Junior 1.00 .45
Championship
❑ 11 Canada Cup 1.00 .45
❑ 12 Canada Cup .50 .23
❑ 13 Canadian National 1.00 .45
❑ 14 Canadian National 1.00 .45
❑ 15 Canadian National .50 .23
❑ 16 Canadian National .50 .23
❑ 17 First-Round Draft Pick .50 .23
❑ 18 Trade To Philadelphia .50 .23
❑ 19 Happy Flyer .50 .23
❑ 20 Preseason Action .50 .23
❑ 21 Preseason Action .50 .23
❑ 22 Regular Season Debut .50 .23
❑ 23 First NHL Goal .50 .23
❑ 24 Winning Home Debut .50 .23
❑ 25 First NHL Hat Trick .50 .23
❑ 26 Playing Golf .50 .23
❑ 27 Backyard Fun .50 .23
❑ 28 Fan Favorite .50 .23
❑ 29 Welcome To Philly .50 .23
❑ 30 Philly Hero 1.00 .45

## 1993-94 Pinnacle I Samples

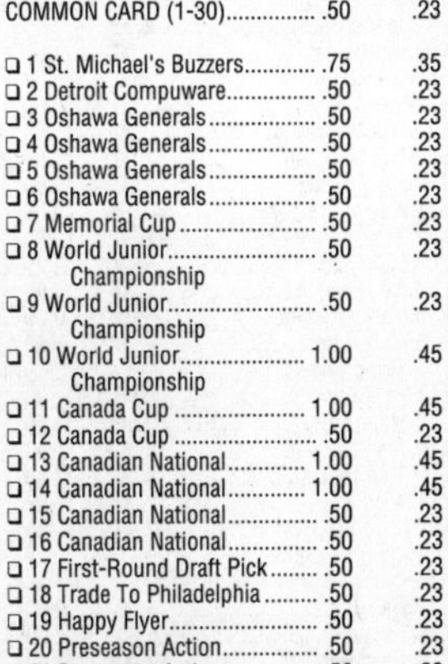

These six cards were distributed to dealers and media during the summer of 1993 to show the style of the upcoming Pinnacle hockey cards for the 1993-94 season. The cards can be differentiated from regular issues by the presence of dashes rather than stats in the tables on the reverse.

| | MINT | NRMT |
|---|---|---|
| COMPLETE SET (6) | 4.00 | 1.80 |
| COMMON CARD (1-6) | .10 | .05 |

❑ 1 Tony Amonte .30 .14
❑ 2 Tom Barrasso .10 .05
❑ 3 Joe Juneau .25 .11
❑ 4 Eric Lindros 2.00 .90
❑ 5 Teemu Selanne 1.50 .70
❑ 6 Mats Sundin .50 .23

## 1993-94 Pinnacle II Hobby Samples

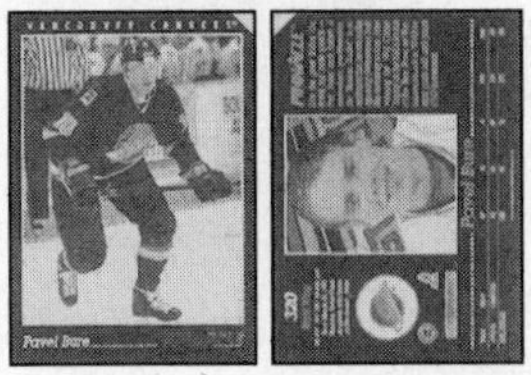

This 11-card hobby sample set was enclosed in a cello pack. With the exception of the Mogilny "Nifty 50" card, the top right corners of each card have been cut off, apparently to indicate that these are promo cards. The disclaimer "SAMPLE" is stamped across the photo on the back of the Mogilny, WJC card, and the Lindros redemption card.

| | MINT | NRMT |
|---|---|---|
| COMPLETE SEALED SET (11) | 10.00 | 4.50 |
| COMMON CARD | .01 | .01 |

❑ 275 Brian Leetch .05 .02
❑ 280 Guy Carbonneau .05 .02
❑ 300 Pat LaFontaine .05 .02
❑ 320 Pavel Bure .25 .11
❑ 340 Terry Yake .01 .01
❑ 341 Brian Benning .01 .01
❑ 0 Player Unnamed .75 .35
(World Jr. Championships)
❑ NF9 Alexander Mogilny 3.00 1.35
Nifty 50
❑ SR1 Alexandre Daigle .50 .23
Super Rookie
❑ NNO Ad Card .50 .23
❑ NNO You're A Winner 15.00 6.75
(Lindros Instant
Winner Game)

## 1993-94 Pinnacle

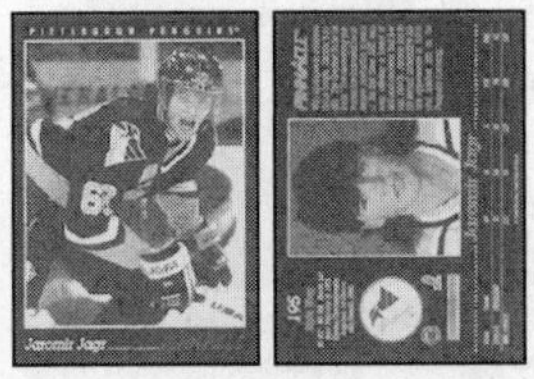

Issued in two series of 236 and 275 cards, respectively, the 1993-94 Pinnacle hockey set consists of 511 standard-size cards. On a black background with a thin white border, the fronts feature color action player photos. The team's name in white letters appears above the photo, while the player's name, also in white letters, and Pinnacle's logo in gold foil are printed at the bottom. On a black background, the horizontal backs carry a color head shot in the center with the player's biography and the team logo on the left, while his profile is on the right. The player's name and stats appear at the bottom. Both series were offered in both a U.S. version as well as a Canadian, bilingual version. Former prospect Brett Lindros is featured on a pair of cards with his talented brother Eric. Inserted at a rate of 1:100 packs, the cards are similar, but feature different photos for the U.S. and Canadian versions; the Canadian card also features bilingual text. A card honoring Wayne Gretzky's 802nd career goal was included in second series jumbo packs. Because of its distribution, the card (No. 512) is not considered part of the set. Rookie Cards include Jason Arnott, Jeff Friesen, Todd Harvey, Chris Osgood, Jamie Storr, Jocelyn Thibault and Oleg Tverdovsky.

| | MINT | NRMT |
|---|---|---|
| COMPLETE SET (511) | 35.00 | 16.00 |
| COMPLETE SERIES 1 (236) | 15.00 | 6.75 |
| COMPLETE SERIES 2 (275) | 20.00 | 9.00 |
| COMMON CARD (1-511) | .10 | .05 |

*US AND CDN: SAME VALUE

❑ 1 Eric Lindros 1.25 .55
❑ 2 Mats Sundin .15 .07
❑ 3 Tom Barrasso .15 .07
❑ 4 Teemu Selanne .75 .35
❑ 5 Joe Juneau .15 .07
❑ 6 Tony Amonte .15 .07
❑ 7 Bob Probert .15 .07
❑ 8 Chris Kontos .10 .05
❑ 9 Geoff Sanderson .15 .07
❑ 10 Alexander Mogilny .15 .07
❑ 11 Kevin Lowe .10 .05
❑ 12 Nikolai Borschevsky .10 .05
❑ 13 Dale Hunter .10 .05
❑ 14 Gary Suter .10 .05
❑ 15 Curtis Joseph .30 .14
❑ 16 Mark Tinordi .10 .05
❑ 17 Doug Weight .15 .07
❑ 18 Benoit Hogue .10 .05
❑ 19 Tommy Soderstrom .15 .07
❑ 20 Pat Falloon .10 .05
❑ 21 Jyrki Lumme .10 .05
❑ 22 Brian Bellows .10 .05
❑ 23 Alexei Zhitnik .10 .05
❑ 24 Dirk Graham .10 .05
❑ 25 Scott Stevens .15 .07
❑ 26 Adam Foote .10 .05
❑ 27 Mike Gartner .15 .07
❑ 28 Dallas Drake .10 .05
❑ 29 Ulf Samuelsson .10 .05
❑ 30 Cam Neely .15 .07
❑ 31 Sean Burke .15 .07
❑ 32 Petr Svoboda .10 .05
❑ 33 Keith Tkachuk .40 .18
❑ 34 Roman Hamrlik .15 .07
❑ 35 Robert Reichel .10 .05
❑ 36 Igor Kravchuk .10 .05
❑ 37 Mathieu Schneider .10 .05
❑ 38 Bob Kudelski .10 .05
❑ 39 Jeff Brown .10 .05
❑ 40 Mike Modano .40 .18
❑ 41 Rob Gaudreau .10 .05
❑ 42 Dave Andreychuk .15 .07
❑ 43 Trevor Linden .15 .07
❑ 44 Dimitri Khristich .10 .05
❑ 45 Joe Murphy .10 .05
❑ 46 Rob Blake .10 .05
❑ 47 Alexander Semak .10 .05
❑ 48 Ray Ferraro .10 .05
❑ 49 Curtis Leschyshyn .10 .05
❑ 50 Mark Recchi .15 .07
❑ 51 Sergei Nemchinov .10 .05
❑ 52 Larry Murphy .15 .07
❑ 53 Steve Heinze .10 .05
❑ 54 Sergei Fedorov .60 .25
❑ 55 Gary Roberts .10 .05
❑ 56 Alexei Zhamnov .15 .07
❑ 57 Derian Hatcher .10 .05
❑ 58 Kelly Buchberger .10 .05
❑ 59 Eric Desjardins .10 .05
❑ 60 Brian Bradley .10 .05
❑ 61 Patrick Poulin .10 .05
❑ 62 Scott Lachance .10 .05
❑ 63 Johan Garpenlov .10 .05
❑ 64 Sylvain Turgeon .10 .05
❑ 65 Grant Fuhr .15 .07
❑ 66 Garth Butcher .10 .05
❑ 67 Michal Pivonka .10 .05
❑ 68 Todd Gill .10 .05
❑ 69 Cliff Ronning .10 .05
❑ 70 Steve Smith .10 .05
❑ 71 Bobby Holik .10 .05
❑ 72 Garry Galley .10 .05
❑ 73 Steve Leach .10 .05
❑ 74 Ron Francis .15 .07
❑ 75 Jari Kurri .15 .07
❑ 76 Alexei Kovalev .15 .07
❑ 77 Dave Gagner .15 .07
❑ 78 Steve Duchesne .10 .05
❑ 79 Theoren Fleury .15 .07
❑ 80 Paul Coffey .30 .14
❑ 81 Bill Ranford .15 .07
❑ 82 Doug Bodger .10 .05
❑ 83 Nick Kypreos .10 .05
❑ 84 Darius Kasparaitis .10 .05
❑ 85 Vincent Damphousse .15 .07
❑ 86 Arturs Irbe .15 .07
❑ 87 Shawn Chambers .10 .05
❑ 88 Murray Craven .10 .05
❑ 89 Rob Pearson .10 .05
❑ 90 Kevin Hatcher .10 .05
❑ 91 Brent Sutter .10 .05
❑ 92 Teppo Numminen .10 .05
❑ 93 Shawn Burr .10 .05
❑ 94 Valeri Zelepukin .10 .05
❑ 95 Ron Sutter .10 .05
❑ 96 Craig MacTavish .10 .05
❑ 97 Dominic Roussel .15 .07
❑ 98 Nicklas Lidstrom .10 .05
❑ 99 Adam Graves .15 .07
❑ 100 Doug Gilmour .30 .14
❑ 101 Frank Musil .10 .05
❑ 102 Ted Donato .10 .05
❑ 103 Andrew Cassels .10 .05
❑ 104 Vladimir Malakhov .10 .05
❑ 105 Shawn McEachern .10 .05
❑ 106 Petr Nedved .15 .07
❑ 107 Calle Johansson .10 .05
❑ 108 Rich Sutter .10 .05
❑ 109 Evgeny Davydov .10 .05
❑ 110 Mike Ricci .10 .05
❑ 111 Scott Niedermayer .10 .05
❑ 112 John LeClair .50 .23
❑ 113 Darryl Sydor .10 .05
❑ 114 Paul DiPietro .10 .05
❑ 115 Stephane Fiset .15 .07
❑ 116 Christian Ruuttu .10 .05
❑ 117 Doug Zmolek .10 .05
❑ 118 Bob Sweeney .10 .05
❑ 119 Brent Fedyk .10 .05
❑ 120 Norm Maciver .10 .05
❑ 121 Rob Zamuner .10 .05
❑ 122 Brian Mullen .10 .05
❑ 123 Trent Yawney .10 .05
❑ 124 David Shaw .10 .05
❑ 125 Mark Messier .40 .18
❑ 126 Kevin Miller .10 .05
❑ 127 Dino Ciccarelli .15 .07
❑ 128 Derek King .10 .05
❑ 129 Scott Young .10 .05
❑ 130 Craig Janney .15 .07
❑ 131 Jamie Macoun .10 .05
❑ 132 Geoff Courtnall .10 .05
❑ 133 Bob Essensa .15 .07
❑ 134 Ken Daneyko .10 .05
❑ 135 Mike Ridley .10 .05
❑ 136 Stephan Lebeau .10 .05
❑ 137 Tony Granato .10 .05
❑ 138 Kay Whitmore .15 .07
❑ 139 Luke Richardson .10 .05
❑ 140 Jeremy Roenick .30 .14
❑ 141 Brad May .15 .07
❑ 142 Sandis Ozolinsh .15 .07
❑ 143 Stephane Richer .15 .07
❑ 144 John Tucker .10 .05
❑ 145 Luc Robitaille .15 .07
❑ 146 Dimitri Yushkevich .10 .05
❑ 147 Sean Hill .10 .05
❑ 148 John Vanbiesbrouck .50 .23
❑ 149 Kevin Stevens .10 .05
❑ 150 Patrick Roy 1.50 .70
❑ 151 Owen Nolan .15 .07
❑ 152 Richard Smehlik .10 .05
❑ 153 Ray Sheppard .15 .07
❑ 154 Ed Olczyk .10 .05
❑ 155 Al MacInnis .15 .07
❑ 156 Sergei Zubov .10 .05
❑ 157 Wendel Clark .15 .07
❑ 158 Kirk McLean .15 .07
❑ 159 Thomas Steen .10 .05
❑ 160 Pierre Turgeon .15 .07
❑ 161 Dmitri Kvartalnov .10 .05
❑ 162 Brian Noonan .10 .05
❑ 163 Mike McPhee .10 .05
❑ 164 Peter Bondra .30 .14
❑ 165 Bernie Nicholls .10 .05
❑ 166 Michael Nylander .10 .05
❑ 167 Guy Hebert .15 .07
❑ 168 Scott Mellanby .15 .07
❑ 169 Bob Bassen .10 .05
❑ 170 Rod Brind'Amour .15 .07
❑ 171 Andrei Kovalenko .10 .05
❑ 172 Mike Donnelly .10 .05
❑ 173 Steve Thomas .10 .05
❑ 174 Rick Tocchet .15 .07
❑ 175 Steve Yzerman 1.00 .45
❑ 176 Dixon Ward .10 .05
❑ 177 Randy Wood .10 .05
❑ 178 Dean Kennedy .10 .05
❑ 179 Joel Otto .10 .05
❑ 180 Kirk Muller .10 .05
❑ 181 Chris Chelios .30 .14
❑ 182 Richard Matvichuk .10 .05
❑ 183 John MacLean .15 .07
❑ 184 Joe Kocur .15 .07
❑ 185 Adam Oates .15 .07
❑ 186 Bob Beers .10 .05
❑ 187 Ron Tugnutt .15 .07
❑ 188 Brian Skrudland .10 .05
❑ 189 Al Iafrate .10 .05
❑ 190 Felix Potvin .30 .14
❑ 191 David Reid .10 .05
❑ 192 Jim Johnson .10 .05
❑ 193 Kevin Haller .10 .05
❑ 194 Steve Chiasson .10 .05
❑ 195 Jaromir Jagr 1.00 .45
❑ 196 Martin Rucinsky .10 .05
❑ 197 Sergei Bautin .10 .05
❑ 198 Joe Nieuwendyk .15 .07
❑ 199 Gilbert Dionne .10 .05
❑ 200 Brett Hull .40 .18
❑ 201 Yuri Khmylev .10 .05
❑ 202 Todd Elik .10 .05
❑ 203 Patrick Flatley .10 .05
❑ 204 Martin Straka .10 .05
❑ 205 Brendan Shanahan .60 .25
❑ 206 Mark Beaufait .10 .05
❑ 207 Mike Lenarduzzi .10 .05
❑ 208 Chris LiPuma .10 .05
❑ 209 Andre Faust .10 .05
❑ 210 Ben Hankinson .10 .05
❑ 211 Darrin Madeley .10 .05
❑ 212 Oleg Petrov .10 .05
❑ 213 Philippe Boucher .10 .05
❑ 214 Tyler Wright .10 .05
❑ 215 Jason Bowen .10 .05
❑ 216 Matthew Barnaby .15 .07
❑ 217 Bryan Smolinski .10 .05
❑ 218 Dan Keczmer .10 .05
❑ 219 Chris Simon .10 .05
❑ 220 Corey Hirsch AW .15 .07
❑ 221 Mario Lemieux AW .75 .35
❑ 222 Teemu Selanne AW .40 .18
❑ 223 Chris Chelios AW .15 .07
❑ 224 Ed Belfour AW .15 .07
❑ 225 Pierre Turgeon AW .15 .07
❑ 226 Doug Gilmour AW .15 .07
❑ 227 Ed Belfour AW .30 .14
❑ 228 Patrick Roy AW .75 .35
❑ 229 Dave Poulin AW .10 .05
❑ 230 Mario Lemieux AW .75 .35
❑ 231 Mike Vernon HH .15 .07
❑ 232 Vincent Damphousse HH .15 .07
❑ 233 Chris Chelios HH .15 .07
❑ 234 Cliff Ronning HH .10 .05
❑ 235 Mark Howe HH .10 .05
❑ 236 Alexandre Daigle .10 .05
❑ 237 Wayne Gretzky HH 1.50 .70
❑ 238 Mark Messier .30 .14
❑ 239 Dino Ciccarelli .15 .07
❑ 240 Joe Mullen .15 .07

❑ 241 Mike Gartner .15 .07
❑ 242 Mike Richter .30 .14
❑ 243 Pat Verbeek .10 .05
❑ 244 Valeri Kamensky .15 .07
❑ 245 Nelson Emerson .10 .05
❑ 246 James Patrick .10 .05
❑ 247 Greg Adams .10 .05
❑ 248 Ulf Dahlen .10 .05
❑ 249 Shayne Corson .10 .05
❑ 250 Ray Bourque .30 .14
❑ 251 Claude Lemieux .15 .07
❑ 252 Kelly Hrudey .15 .07
❑ 253 Patrice Brisebois .10 .05
❑ 254 Mark Howe .10 .05
❑ 255 Ed Belfour .30 .14
❑ 256 Pelle Eklund .10 .05
❑ 257 Zarley Zalapski .10 .05
❑ 258 Sylvain Cote .10 .05
❑ 259 Uwe Krupp .10 .05
❑ 260 Dale Hawerchuk .15 .07
❑ 261 Alexei Gusarov .10 .05
❑ 262 Dave Ellett .10 .05
❑ 263 Tomas Sandstrom .10 .05
❑ 264 Vladimir Konstantinov .10 .05
❑ 265 Paul Ranheim .10 .05
❑ 266 Darrin Shannon .10 .05
❑ 267 Chris Terreri .15 .07
❑ 268 Russ Courtnall .10 .05
❑ 269 Don Sweeney .10 .05
❑ 270 Kevin Todd .10 .05
❑ 271 Brad Shaw .10 .05
❑ 272 Adam Creighton .10 .05
❑ 273 Dana Murzyn .10 .05
❑ 274 Donald Audette .15 .07
❑ 275 Brian Leetch .30 .14
❑ 276 Kevin Dineen .10 .05
❑ 277 Bruce Driver .10 .05
❑ 278 Jim Paek .10 .05
❑ 279 Esa Tikkanen .10 .05
❑ 280 Guy Carbonneau .10 .05
❑ 281 Eric Weinrich .10 .05
❑ 282 Tim Cheveldae .15 .07
❑ 283 Bryan Marchment .10 .05
❑ 284 Kelly Miller .10 .05
❑ 285 Jimmy Carson .10 .05
❑ 286 Terry Carkner .10 .05
❑ 287 Mike Sullivan .10 .05
❑ 288 Joe Reekie .10 .05
❑ 289 Bob Rouse .10 .05
❑ 290 Joe Sakic .60 .25
❑ 291 Gerald Diduck .10 .05
❑ 292 Don Beaupre .15 .07
❑ 293 Kjell Samuelsson .10 .05
❑ 294 Claude Lapointe .10 .05
❑ 295 Tie Domi .15 .07
❑ 296 Charlie Huddy .10 .05
❑ 297 Peter Zezel .10 .05
❑ 298 Craig Muni .10 .05
❑ 299 Rick Tabaracci .15 .07
❑ 300 Pat LaFontaine .15 .07
❑ 301 Lyle Odelein .10 .05
❑ 302 Jocelyn Lemieux .10 .05
❑ 303 Craig Ludwig .10 .05
❑ 304 Marc Bergevin .10 .05
❑ 305 Bill Guerin .10 .05
❑ 306 Rick Zombo .10 .05
❑ 307 Steven Finn .10 .05
❑ 308 Gino Odjick .10 .05
❑ 309 Jeff Beukeboom .10 .05
❑ 310 Mario Lemieux 1.50 .70
❑ 311 J.J. Daigneault .10 .05
❑ 312 Vincent Riendeau .15 .07
❑ 313 Adam Burt .10 .05
❑ 314 Mike Craig .10 .05
❑ 315 Bret Hedican .10 .05
❑ 316 Kris King .10 .05
❑ 317 Sylvain Lefebvre .10 .05
❑ 318 Troy Murray .10 .05
❑ 319 Gordie Roberts .10 .05
❑ 320 Pavel Bure .60 .25
❑ 321 Marc Bureau .10 .05
❑ 322 Randy McKay .10 .05
❑ 323 Mark Lamb .10 .05
❑ 324 Brian Mullen .10 .05
❑ 325 Ken Wregget .15 .07
❑ 326 Stephane Quintal .10 .05
❑ 327 Robert Dirk .10 .05
❑ 328 Mike Krushelnyski .10 .05
❑ 329 Mikael Andersson .10 .05
❑ 330 Paul Stanton .10 .05
❑ 331 Phil Bourque .10 .05
❑ 332 Andre Racicot .15 .07
❑ 333 Brad Dalgarno .10 .05
❑ 334 Neal Broten .15 .07
❑ 335 John Blue .15 .07
❑ 336 Ken Sutton .10 .05
❑ 337 Greg Paslawski .10 .05
❑ 338 Robb Stauber .15 .07
❑ 339 Mike Keane .10 .05
❑ 340 Terry Yake .10 .05
❑ 341 Brian Benning .10 .05
❑ 342 Brian Propp .10 .05
❑ 343 Frank Pietrangelo .15 .07
❑ 344 Stephane Matteau .10 .05
❑ 345 Steven King .10 .05
❑ 346 Joe Cirella .10 .05
❑ 347 Andy Moog .15 .07
❑ 348 Paul Ysebaert .10 .05
❑ 349 Petr Klima .10 .05
❑ 350 Corey Millen .10 .05
❑ 351 Phil Housley .15 .07
❑ 352 Craig Billington .15 .07
❑ 353 Jeff Norton .10 .05
❑ 354 Neil Wilkinson .10 .05
❑ 355 Doug Lidster .10 .05
❑ 356 Steve Larmer .15 .07
❑ 357 Jon Casey .15 .07
❑ 358 Brad McCrimmon .10 .05
❑ 359 Alexei Kasatonov .10 .05
❑ 360 Andrei Lomakin .10 .05
❑ 361 Daren Puppa .15 .07
❑ 362 Sergei Makarov .10 .05
❑ 363 Dave Manson .10 .05
❑ 364 Jim Sandlak .10 .05
❑ 365 Glenn Healy .15 .07
❑ 366 Martin Gelinas .10 .05
❑ 367 Igor Larionov .10 .05
❑ 368 Anatoli Semenov .10 .05
❑ 369 Mark Fitzpatrick .15 .07
❑ 370 Paul Cavallini .10 .05
❑ 371 Jimmy Waite .15 .07
❑ 372 Yves Racine .10 .05
❑ 373 Jeff Hackett .15 .07
❑ 374 Marty McSorley .10 .05
❑ 375 Scott Pearson .10 .05
❑ 376 Ron Hextall .15 .07
❑ 377 Gaetan Duchesne .10 .05
❑ 378 Jamie Baker .10 .05
❑ 379 Troy Loney .10 .05
❑ 380 Gord Murphy .10 .05
❑ 381 Peter Sidorkiewicz .15 .07
❑ 382 Pat Elynuik .10 .05
❑ 383 Glen Wesley .10 .05
❑ 384 Dean Evason .10 .05
❑ 385 Mike Peluso .10 .05
❑ 386 Darren Turcotte .10 .05
❑ 387 Dave Poulin .10 .05
❑ 388 John Cullen .10 .05
❑ 389 Randy Ladouceur .10 .05
❑ 390 Tom Fitzgerald .10 .05
❑ 391 Denis Savard .15 .07
❑ 392 Fredrik Olausson .10 .05
❑ 393 Sergio Momesso .10 .05
❑ 394 Mike Ramsey .10 .05
❑ 395 Kelly Kisio .10 .05
❑ 396 Craig Simpson .10 .05
❑ 397 Slava Fetisov .10 .05
❑ 398 Glenn Anderson .15 .07
❑ 399 Michel Goulet .15 .07
❑ 400 Wayne Gretzky 2.00 .90
❑ 401 Stu Grimson .10 .05
❑ 402 Mike Hough .10 .05
❑ 403 Dominik Hasek 1.00 .45
❑ 404 Gerard Gallant .10 .05
❑ 405 Greg Gilbert .10 .05
❑ 406 Vladimir Ruzicka .10 .05
❑ 407 Jim Hrivnak .15 .07
❑ 408 Dave Lowry .10 .05
❑ 409 Todd Ewen .10 .05
❑ 410 Bob Errey .10 .05
❑ 411 Bryan Trottier .15 .07
❑ 412 Dave Taylor .15 .07
❑ 413 Grant Ledyard .10 .05
❑ 414 Chris Dahlquist .10 .05
❑ 415 Brent Gilchrist .10 .05
❑ 416 Geoff Smith .10 .05
❑ 417 Jiri Slegr .10 .05
❑ 418 Randy Burridge .10 .05
❑ 419 Sergei Krivokrasov .10 .05
❑ 420 Keith Primeau .15 .07
❑ 421 Robert Kron .10 .05
❑ 422 Keith Brown .10 .05
❑ 423 David Volek .10 .05
❑ 424 Josef Beranek .10 .05
❑ 425 Wayne Presley .10 .05
❑ 426 Stu Barnes .10 .05
❑ 427 Milos Holan .10 .05
❑ 428 Jeff Shantz .10 .05
❑ 429 Brent Gretzky .10 .05
❑ 430 Jarkko Varvio .10 .05
❑ 431 Chris Osgood 2.00 .90
❑ 432 Aaron Ward .10 .05
❑ 433 Jason Smith .10 .05
❑ 434 Cam Stewart .10 .05
❑ 435 Derek Plante .10 .05
❑ 436 Pat Peake .10 .05
❑ 437 Alexander Karpovtsev .10 .05
❑ 438 Jim Montgomery .10 .05
❑ 439 Rob Niedermayer .15 .07
❑ 440 Jocelyn Thibault 1.25 .55
❑ 441 Jason Arnott 1.00 .45
❑ 442 Mike Rathje .10 .05
❑ 443 Chris Gratton .15 .07
❑ 444 Vesa Vitakoski .10 .05
❑ 445 Alexei Kudashov .10 .05
❑ 446 Pavol Demitra .10 .05
❑ 447 Ted Drury .10 .05
❑ 448 Rene Corbet .15 .07
❑ 449 Markus Naslund .10 .05
❑ 450 Dmitri Filimonov .10 .05
❑ 451 Roman Oksiuta .10 .05
❑ 452 Michal Sykora .10 .05
❑ 453 Greg Johnson .10 .05
❑ 454 Mikael Renberg .30 .14
❑ 455 Alexei Yashin .15 .07
❑ 456 Chris Pronger .15 .07
❑ 457 Emmanuel Fernandez .15 .07
❑ 458 Jamie Storr .50 .23
❑ 459 Chris Armstrong .10 .05
❑ 460 Drew Bannister .10 .05
❑ 461 Joel Bouchard .10 .05
❑ 462 Bryan McCabe .40 .18
❑ 463 Nick Stajduhar .10 .05
❑ 464 Brent Tully .10 .05
❑ 465 Brendan Witt .10 .05
❑ 466 Jason Allison .60 .25
❑ 467 Jason Botterill .10 .05
❑ 468 Curtis Bowen .10 .05
❑ 469 Anson Carter .30 .14
❑ 470 Brandon Convery .10 .05
❑ 471 Yanick Dube .10 .05
❑ 472 Jeff Friesen .75 .35
❑ 473 Aaron Gavey .10 .05
❑ 474 Martin Gendron .10 .05
❑ 475 Rick Girard .10 .05
❑ 476 Todd Harvey .25 .11
❑ 477 Marty Murray .10 .05
❑ 478 Mike Peca 1.00 .45
❑ 479 Aaron Ellis .10 .05
❑ 480 Toby Kvalevog .15 .07
❑ 481 Jon Coleman .10 .05
❑ 482 Ashlin Halfnight .10 .05
❑ 483 Jason McBain .10 .05
❑ 484 Chris O'Sullivan .10 .05
❑ 485 Deron Quint .30 .14
❑ 486 Blake Sloan .10 .05
❑ 487 David Wilkie .10 .05
❑ 488 Kevyn Adams .10 .05
❑ 489 Jason Bonsignore .10 .05
❑ 490 Andy Brink .10 .05
❑ 491 Adam Deadmarsh .15 .07
❑ 492 John Emmons .10 .05
❑ 493 Kevin Hilton .10 .05
❑ 494 Jason Karmanos .10 .05
❑ 495 Bob Lachance .10 .05
❑ 496 Jamie Langenbrunner 1.00 .45
❑ 497 Jay Pandolfo .10 .05
❑ 498 Richard Park .10 .05
❑ 499 Ryan Sittler .10 .05
❑ 500 John Varga .10 .05
❑ 501 Valeri Bure .15 .07
❑ 502 Maxim Bets .10 .05
❑ 503 Vadim Sharifjanov .15 .07
❑ 504 Alexander Kharlamov .10 .05
❑ 505 Pavel Desyatkov .10 .05
❑ 506 Oleg Tverdovsky .60 .25
❑ 507 Nikolai Tsulygin .10 .05
❑ 508 Evgeni Ryabchikov .15 .07
❑ 509 Sergei Brylin .10 .05
❑ 510 Maxim Sushinski .10 .05
❑ 511 Sergei Kondrashkin .10 .05
❑ 512 Wayne Gretzky HL SP 8.00 3.60
❑ AU1 Alexandre Daigle 40.00 18.00
Autographed card
❑ AU2 Eric Lindros 150.00 70.00
Autographed card
❑ NNO Eric Lindros 15.00 6.75
Brett Lindros
Canadian version
❑ NNO Eric Lindros 15.00 6.75
Brett Lindros
U.S. version
❑ NNO Eric Lindros 40.00 18.00
Expired Redemption

## 1993-94 Pinnacle All-Stars

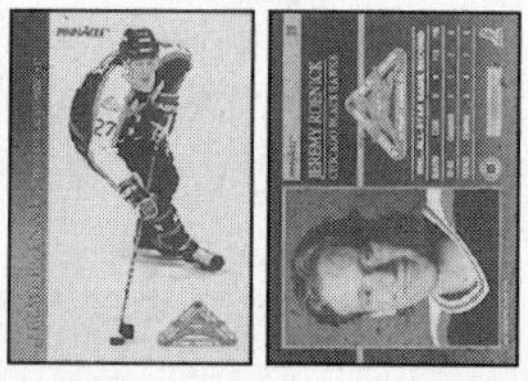

One bonus Pinnacle All-Star card was inserted in every U.S. and Canadian pack of '93-94 Score series 1 hockey cards. The wrappers from those packs carried a mail-away offer for cards 46-50. These cards feature on their fronts color action shots of players in their All-Star uniforms. The photos of Canadian and U.S. cards differ, but there is no way of discerning the two.

| | MINT | NRMT |
|---|---|---|
| COMPLETE INSERT SET (45) | 10.00 | 4.50 |
| COMMON CARD (1-45) | .15 | .07 |
| *US AND CDN: SAME VALUE | | |
| COMPLETE MAIL-IN SET (5) | 25.00 | 11.00 |
| COMMON MAIL-IN (46-50) | 4.00 | 1.80 |

❑ 1 Craig Billington .20 .09
❑ 2 Zarley Zalapski .15 .07
❑ 3 Kevin Lowe .15 .07
❑ 4 Scott Stevens .15 .07
❑ 5 Pierre Turgeon .20 .09
❑ 6 Mark Recchi .20 .09
❑ 7 Kirk Muller .15 .07
❑ 8 Mike Gartner .20 .09
❑ 9 Adam Oates .20 .09
❑ 10 Brad Marsh .15 .07
❑ 11 Pat LaFontaine .20 .09
❑ 12 Peter Bondra .20 .09
❑ 13 Joe Sakic .50 .23
❑ 14 Rick Tocchet .20 .09
❑ 15 Kevin Stevens .20 .09
❑ 16 Steve Duchesne .15 .07
❑ 17 Peter Sidorkiewicz .20 .09
❑ 18 Patrick Roy 1.25 .55
❑ 19 Al Iafrate .15 .07
❑ 20 Jaromir Jagr .75 .35
❑ 21 Ray Bourque .25 .11
❑ 22 Alexander Mogilny .20 .09
❑ 23 Steve Chiasson .15 .07
❑ 24 Garth Butcher .15 .07
❑ 25 Phil Housley .15 .07
❑ 26 Chris Chelios .25 .11
❑ 27 Randy Carlyle .15 .07
❑ 28 Mike Modano .30 .14
❑ 29 Gary Roberts .15 .07
❑ 30 Kelly Kisio .15 .07
❑ 31 Pavel Bure .50 .23
❑ 32 Teemu Selanne .60 .25
❑ 33 Brian Bradley .15 .07
❑ 34 Brett Hull .30 .14
❑ 35 Jari Kurri .20 .09
❑ 36 Steve Yzerman .75 .35
❑ 37 Luc Robitaille .20 .09
❑ 38 Dave Manson .15 .07
❑ 39 Jeremy Roenick .25 .11
❑ 40 Mike Vernon .20 .09
❑ 41 Jon Casey .20 .09
❑ 42 Ed Belfour .25 .11
❑ 43 Paul Coffey .25 .11
❑ 44 Doug Gilmour .20 .09
❑ 45 Wayne Gretzky 1.50 .70
❑ 46 Mike Gartner EXCH 4.00 1.80
❑ 47 Al Iafrate EXCH 4.00 1.80
❑ 48 Ray Bourque EXCH 8.00 3.60
❑ 49 Jon Casey EXCH 4.00 1.80
❑ 50 Campbell Conf. EXCH 5.00 2.20

## 1993-94 Pinnacle Captains

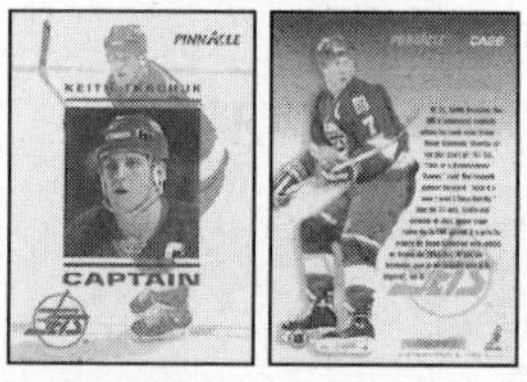

Randomly inserted in second-series jumbo packs at a rate of 1:4, these 27 standard-size cards feature on their fronts two photos of each NHL team captain. The photos of the Canadian and U.S. versions differ. The large borderless photo is a ghosted colour action shot; the smaller image in the center overlays the larger and is a full-contrast color head shot. The player's name in gold-foil lettering appears above the smaller photo. The grayish back carries a color action cutout on the left and a player profile in English (bilingual for the Canadian version) on the right. The cards are numbered on the back with a "CA" prefix.

| | MINT | NRMT |
|---|---|---|
| COMPLETE SET (27) | 150.00 | 70.00 |
| COMMON CARD (1-27) | 2.00 | .90 |
| *U.S. AND CDN: SAME VALUE | | |

❑ 1 Troy Loney 2.00 .90
❑ 2 Ray Bourque 6.00 2.70
❑ 3 Pat LaFontaine 5.00 2.20
❑ 4 Joe Nieuwendyk 2.00 .90
❑ 5 Dirk Graham 2.00 .90
❑ 6 Mark Tinordi 2.00 .90
❑ 7 Steve Yzerman 20.00 9.00
❑ 8 Craig MacTavish 2.00 .90
❑ 9 Brian Skrudland 2.00 .90
❑ 10 Pat Verbeek 2.00 .90
❑ 11 Wayne Gretzky 40.00 18.00
❑ 12 Guy Carbonneau 2.00 .90
❑ 13 Scott Stevens 5.00 2.20
❑ 14 Pat Flatley 2.00 .90
❑ 15 Mark Messier 8.00 3.60
❑ 16 Mark Lamb 2.00 .90
Brad Shaw
❑ 17 Kevin Dineen 2.00 .90
❑ 18 Mario Lemieux 30.00 13.50
❑ 19 Joe Sakic 12.00 5.50
❑ 20 Brett Hull 8.00 3.60
❑ 21 Bob Errey 2.00 .90
❑ 22 Marc Bergevin 2.00 .90
Denis Savard
John Tucker
❑ 23 Wendel Clark 5.00 2.20
❑ 24 Trevor Linden 5.00 2.20
❑ 25 Kevin Hatcher 2.00 .90
❑ 26 Keith Tkachuk 8.00 3.60
❑ 27 Checklist 15.00 6.75

## 1993-94 Pinnacle Expansion

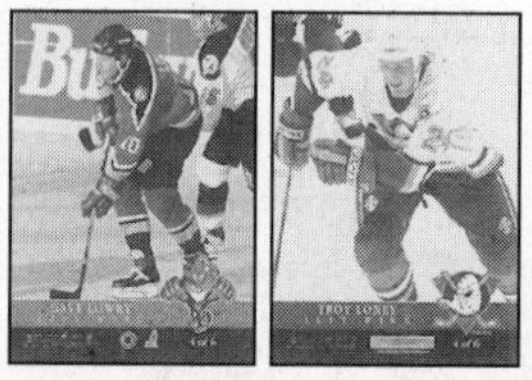

Inserted one per series 1 hobby box, this six-card set measures the standard size. One side features a color action shot of a player from the Anaheim Mighty Ducks; the other, his counterpart at that position from the Florida Panthers. Each player's name and position, along with his team's logo, appear in a team color-coded bar below the photo. The cards are numbered on both sides as "X of 6."

| | MINT | NRMT |
|---|---|---|
| COMPLETE SET (6) | 15.00 | 6.75 |
| COMMON CARD (1-6) | 2.00 | .90 |

❑ 1 John Vanbiesbrouck 6.00 2.70
Guy Hebert
❑ 2 Gord Murphy 2.00 .90
Randy Ladouceur
❑ 3 Joe Cirella 2.00 .90
Sean Hill
❑ 4 Dave Lowry 2.00 .90
Troy Loney
❑ 5 Brian Skrudland 2.00 .90
Terry Yake
❑ 6 Scott Mellanby 3.00 1.35
Steven King

## 1993-94 Pinnacle Masks

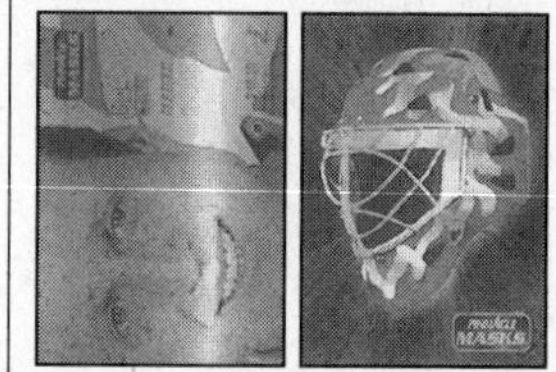

Randomly inserted in first-series packs at a rate of 1:24 packs, this 10-card standard-size set showcases some of the elaborate masks NHL goalies wear. Each metallic front features a colorful rendering of a goalie mask on a dark background highlighted by radial lines. The metallic, borderless, and horizontal backs carry a color player head shot on the left with his name and team name appearing alongside on the right. The cards are numbered on the back as "X of 10."

| | MINT | NRMT |
|---|---|---|
| COMPLETE SET (10) | 150.00 | 70.00 |
| COMMON CARD (1-10) | 15.00 | 6.75 |

❑ 1 Grant Fuhr 30.00 13.50
❑ 2 Mike Vernon 20.00 9.00
❑ 3 Robb Stauber 15.00 6.75
❑ 4 Dominic Roussel 15.00 6.75
❑ 5 Pat Jablonski 15.00 6.75
❑ 6 Stephane Fiset 20.00 9.00
❑ 7 Wendell Young 15.00 6.75
❑ 8 Ron Hextall 30.00 13.50
❑ 9 John Vanbiesbrouck 25.00 11.00
❑ 10 Peter Sidorkiewicz 15.00 6.75

## 1993-94 Pinnacle Nifty Fifty

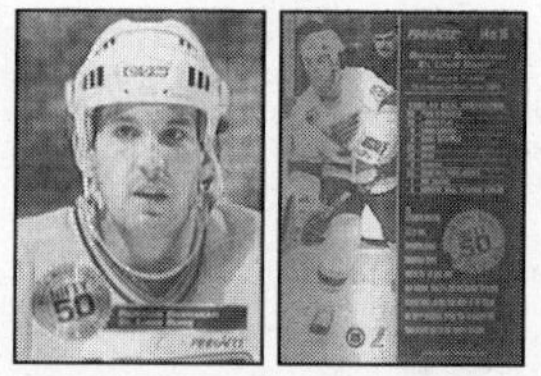

Randomly inserted in second-series foil packs at a rate of 1:36 and featuring Pinnacle's Dufex process, this 15-card standard-size set spotlights players who scored 50 or more goals. The borderless fronts feature metallic color head shots with a gold-foil Nifty Fifty logo at the lower left. The player's name and team name appear in a black bar next to the logo. The metallic backs carry a color action shot on the left side, with statistics and player profile appearing on a black background to the right. The cards are numbered on the back as "X of 15."

| | MINT | NRMT |
|---|---|---|
| COMPLETE SET (15) | 200.00 | 90.00 |
| COMMON CARD (1-15) | 6.00 | 2.70 |

❑ 1 Introductory CL Card 40.00 18.00
❑ 2 Alexander Mogilny 15.00 6.75
❑ 3 Teemu Selanne 20.00 9.00
❑ 4 Mario Lemieux 40.00 18.00
❑ 5 Luc Robitaille 15.00 6.75
❑ 6 Pavel Bure 15.00 6.75
❑ 7 Pierre Turgeon 15.00 6.75
❑ 8 Steve Yzerman 25.00 11.00
❑ 9 Kevin Stevens 6.00 2.70
❑ 10 Brett Hull 12.00 5.50
❑ 11 Dave Andreychuk 6.00 2.70
❑ 12 Pat LaFontaine 15.00 6.75
❑ 13 Mark Recchi 6.00 2.70
❑ 14 Brendan Shanahan 15.00 6.75
❑ 15 Jeremy Roenick 8.00 3.60

## 1993-94 Pinnacle Super Rookies

Randomly inserted in second-series hobby foil packs at a rate of 1:36, this nine-card standard-size set spotlights players who were rookies in 1993-94. The fronts feature color action player shots on darkened backgrounds. The player's name in gold-foil lettering appears at the lower right. On a dark red background, the horizontal backs carry a color player cutout

on the left, with career highlights to the right. The set was issued in Canadian and U.S. versions. Each version carries its own front photos and the backs of the Canadian cards are bilingual. The cards are numbered on the back with an "SR" prefix.

|  | MINT | NRMT |
|---|---|---|
| COMPLETE SET (9) | 10.00 | 4.50 |
| COMMON CARD (1-9) | .50 | .23 |

*U.S. AND CDN: SAME VALUE

| □ 1 Alexandre Daigle | 1.00 | .45 |
| □ 2 Chris Pronger | 1.00 | .45 |
| □ 3 Chris Gratton | 1.00 | .45 |
| □ 4 Rob Niedermayer | 1.00 | .45 |
| □ 5 Alexei Yashin | 1.00 | .45 |
| □ 6 Mikael Renberg | 1.00 | .45 |
| □ 7 Jason Arnott | 4.00 | 1.80 |
| □ 8 Markus Naslund | .50 | .23 |
| □ 9 Pat Peake | .50 | .23 |

## 1993-94 Pinnacle Team Pinnacle

Randomly inserted in packs at a rate of 1:90, this 12-card set measures the standard size. On the U.S. version, one side features a black-bordered color drawing of a player from the Eastern Conference, the other, one of a player from the Western Conference. The player's name and position appear below. The Canadian version carries color photos instead of color drawings. The cards are numbered on both sides as "X of 12."

|  | MINT | NRMT |
|---|---|---|
| COMPLETE SET (12) | 320.00 | 145.00 |
| COMPLETE SERIES 1 (6) | 200.00 | 90.00 |
| COMPLETE SERIES 2 (6) | 120.00 | 55.00 |
| COMMON CARD (1-12) | 15.00 | 6.75 |

*CDN VERSION: 1X TO 1.25X HI COLUMN

| □ 1 Patrick Roy | 50.00 | 22.00 |
| Ed Belfour | | |
| □ 2 Brian Leetch | 20.00 | 9.00 |
| Chris Chelios | | |
| □ 3 Scott Stevens | 15.00 | 6.75 |
| Al MacInnis | | |
| □ 4 Kevin Stevens | 15.00 | 6.75 |
| Luc Robitaille | | |
| □ 5 Mario Lemieux | 100.00 | 45.00 |
| Wayne Gretzky | | |
| □ 6 Jaromir Jagr | 50.00 | 22.00 |
| Brett Hull | | |
| □ 7 Tom Barrasso | 15.00 | 6.75 |
| Kirk McLean | | |
| □ 8 Ray Bourque | 20.00 | 9.00 |
| Paul Coffey | | |
| □ 9 Al Iafrate | 15.00 | 6.75 |
| Phil Housley | | |
| □ 10 Vincent Damphousse | 25.00 | 11.00 |
| Pavel Bure | | |
| □ 11 Eric Lindros | 40.00 | 18.00 |
| Jeremy Roenick | | |
| □ 12 Alexander Mogilny | 30.00 | 13.50 |
| Teemu Selanne | | |

## 1993-94 Pinnacle Team 2001

Inserted one per first-series jumbo pack, this 30-card set measures the standard size. The fronts feature color action player photos. The words "Team 2001" are printed in gold foil inside a black bar on the left, while the player's name in gold foil appears in a black bar on the bottom, along with the team logo. The horizontal backs carry a color head shot on the

right. On a black background to the left of the photo are the player's name in gold foil and career highlights to the right. The Canadian version carries color player drawings instead of photos. The cards are numbered on the back as "X of 30."

|  | MINT | NRMT |
|---|---|---|
| COMPLETE SET (30) | 50.00 | 22.00 |
| COMMON CARD (1-30) | 1.00 | .45 |

*CDN VERSION: 6X TO 12X U.S. VERSION

| □ 1 Eric Lindros | 12.00 | 5.50 |
| □ 2 Alexander Mogilny | 1.25 | .55 |
| □ 3 Pavel Bure | 5.00 | 2.20 |
| □ 4 Joe Juneau | 1.25 | .55 |
| □ 5 Felix Potvin | 2.50 | 1.10 |
| □ 6 Nicklas Lidstrom | 1.25 | .55 |
| □ 7 Alexei Kovalev | 1.25 | .55 |
| □ 8 Patrick Poulin | 1.00 | .45 |
| □ 9 Shawn McEachern | 1.00 | .45 |
| □ 10 Teemu Selanne | 5.00 | 2.20 |
| □ 11 Rod Brind'Amour | 1.25 | .55 |
| □ 12 Jaromir Jagr | 8.00 | 3.60 |
| □ 13 Pierre Turgeon | 1.25 | .55 |
| □ 14 Scott Niedermayer | 1.25 | .55 |
| □ 15 Mats Sundin | 1.25 | .55 |
| □ 16 Trevor Linden | 1.25 | .55 |
| □ 17 Mike Modano | 3.00 | 1.35 |
| □ 18 Roman Hamrlik | 1.25 | .55 |
| □ 19 Tony Amonte | 1.25 | .55 |
| □ 20 Jeremy Roenick | 2.50 | 1.10 |
| □ 21 Scott Lachance | 1.00 | .45 |
| □ 22 Mike Ricci | 1.00 | .45 |
| □ 23 Dimitri Khristich | 1.00 | .45 |
| □ 24 Sergei Fedorov | 5.00 | 2.20 |
| □ 25 Joe Sakic | 6.00 | 2.70 |
| □ 26 Pat Falloon | 1.00 | .45 |
| □ 27 Mathieu Schneider | 1.00 | .45 |
| □ 28 Owen Nolan | 1.25 | .55 |
| □ 29 Brendan Shanahan | 5.00 | 2.20 |
| □ 30 Mark Recchi | 1.25 | .55 |

## 1993-94 Pinnacle Daigle Entry Draft

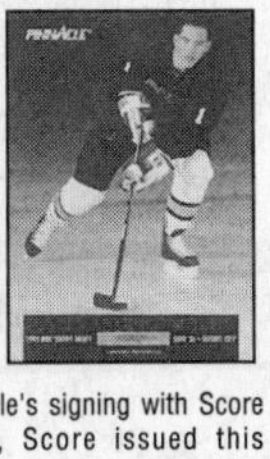

To commemorate Daigle's signing with Score as a spokesperson, Score issued this standard-size card and distributed it to the news media and others who attended the 1993 NHL Draft in Quebec on June 26. The card was also distributed to media at the 1993 National Sports Collectors Convention in Chicago. The front features a color close-up photo with white borders. Daigle is pictured wearing a jersey with "Score" emblazoned across it. The back has a full-bleed action shot with Daigle wearing a "Pinnacle" jersey. A black stripe at the bottom carries the player's name and the anti-counterfeiting device. The card is unnumbered.

|  | MINT | NRMT |
|---|---|---|
| COMPLETE SET (1) | 10.00 | 4.50 |
| COMMON CARD | 10.00 | 4.50 |

| □ 1 Alexandre Daigle | 10.00 | 4.50 |

## 1994-95 Pinnacle I Hobby Samples

These standard-size cards were issued in a sealed ten-card pack to preview the 1994-95 Pinnacle I regular series. They are identical to the regular issue counterparts, except that the upper right corner has been cut off, and the printing of the names on fronts is done in the style of Rink Collection, rather than regular, cards. The cards are numbered on the

|  | MINT | NRMT |
|---|---|---|
| COMPLETE SEALED SET (10) | 2.50 | 1.10 |
| COMMON CARD (1-10) | .05 | .02 |

| □ 1 Eric Lindros | 1.00 | .45 |
| □ 2 Alexandre Daigle | .20 | .09 |
| □ 3 Mike Modano | .50 | .23 |
| □ 4 Vincent Damphousse | .10 | .05 |
| □ 5 Dave Andreychuk | .10 | .05 |
| □ 6 Curtis Joseph | .30 | .14 |
| □ 7 Joe Juneau | .10 | .05 |
| □ 246 Mariusz Czerkawski | .05 | .02 |

| □ BR1 Al Iafrate | .25 | .11 |
| (Boomers insert set) | | |
| □ NNO Title Card | .50 | .23 |

## 1994-95 Pinnacle

This 540-card standard-size set was issued in two series of 270 cards. Cards were distributed in 14-card U.S. and Canadian packs, and 17-card jumbo packs. Series 1 packs had exclusive Canadian and U.S. inserts, series 2 did not. Members of the St. Louis Blues and Calgary Flames are posed in front of a locker which displays their newly designed sweaters. Rookie Cards include Mariusz Czerkawski, Eric Daze, Eric Fichaud, Ed Jovanovski, Jeff O'Neill and Wade Redden. A one-per-case (360 packs) insert card was produced for Canadian, and U.S. series 1 packs. Pavel Bure is numbered MVPC, while Dominik Hasek is MVPU. Both cards have MVP printed at top front and utilize a silver Dufex design. The backs feature dual photos over a silver reflective background.

|  | MINT | NRMT |
|---|---|---|
| COMPLETE SET (540) | 25.00 | 11.00 |
| COMPLETE SERIES 1 (270) | 15.00 | 6.75 |
| COMPLETE SERIES 2 (270) | 10.00 | 4.50 |
| COMMON CARD (1-540) | .10 | .05 |

| □ 1 Eric Lindros | 1.00 | .45 |
| □ 2 Alexandre Daigle | .10 | .05 |
| □ 3 Mike Modano | .40 | .18 |
| □ 4 Vincent Damphousse | .15 | .07 |
| □ 5 Dave Andreychuk | .15 | .07 |
| □ 6 Curtis Joseph | .30 | .14 |
| □ 7 Joe Juneau | .15 | .07 |
| □ 8 Trevor Linden | .15 | .07 |
| □ 9 Rob Blake | .10 | .05 |
| □ 10 Mike Richter | .30 | .14 |
| □ 11 Chris Pronger | .15 | .07 |
| □ 12 Robert Reichel | .10 | .05 |
| □ 13 Bryan Smolinski | .10 | .05 |
| □ 14 Ray Sheppard | .15 | .07 |
| □ 15 Guy Hebert | .15 | .07 |
| □ 16 Tony Amonte | .15 | .07 |
| □ 17 Richard Smehlik | .10 | .05 |
| □ 18 Doug Weight | .15 | .07 |
| □ 19 Chris Gratton | .15 | .07 |
| □ 20 Tom Barrasso | .15 | .07 |
| □ 21 Brian Skrudland | .10 | .05 |
| □ 22 Sandis Ozolinsh | .15 | .07 |
| □ 23 Bill Guerin | .10 | .05 |
| □ 24 Curtis Leschyshyn | .10 | .05 |
| □ 25 Teemu Selanne | .60 | .25 |
| □ 26 Darius Kasparaitis | .10 | .05 |
| □ 27 Garry Galley | .10 | .05 |
| □ 28 Alexei Yashin | .15 | .07 |
| □ 29 Mark Tinordi | .10 | .05 |
| □ 30 Patrick Roy | 1.50 | .70 |
| □ 31 Mike Gartner | .15 | .07 |
| □ 32 Brendan Shanahan | .60 | .25 |
| □ 33 Sylvain Cote | .10 | .05 |
| □ 34 Jeff Brown | .10 | .05 |
| □ 35 Jari Kurri | .15 | .07 |
| □ 36 Sergei Zubov | .15 | .07 |
| □ 37 Pat Verbeek | .10 | .05 |
| □ 38 Theoren Fleury | .15 | .07 |
| □ 39 Al Iafrate | .10 | .05 |
| □ 40 Keith Primeau | .15 | .07 |
| □ 41 Bobby Dollas | .10 | .05 |
| □ 42 Ed Belfour | .30 | .14 |
| □ 43 Dale Hawerchuk | .15 | .07 |
| □ 44 Shayne Corson | .10 | .05 |
| □ 45 Danton Cole | .10 | .05 |
| □ 46 Ulf Samuelsson | .10 | .05 |
| □ 47 Stu Barnes | .10 | .05 |
| □ 48 Ulf Dahlen | .10 | .05 |
| □ 49 Valeri Zelepukin | .10 | .05 |
| □ 50 Joe Sakic | .60 | .25 |
| □ 51 Dave Manson | .10 | .05 |
| □ 52 Steve Thomas | .10 | .05 |
| □ 53 Mark Recchi | .15 | .07 |
| □ 54 Dave McLlwain | .10 | .05 |
| □ 55 Derian Hatcher | .10 | .05 |
| □ 56 Mathieu Schneider | .10 | .05 |
| □ 57 Bill Berg | .10 | .05 |
| □ 58 Petr Nedved | .15 | .07 |
| □ 59 Dimitri Khristich | .10 | .05 |
| □ 60 Kirk McLean | .15 | .07 |
| □ 61 Marty McSorley | .10 | .05 |
| □ 62 Adam Graves | .15 | .07 |
| □ 63 Geoff Sanderson | .15 | .07 |
| □ 64 Frank Musil | .10 | .05 |
| □ 65 Cam Neely | .15 | .07 |
| □ 66 Nicklas Lidstrom | .15 | .07 |
| □ 67 Stephan Lebeau | .10 | .05 |
| □ 68 Joe Murphy | .10 | .05 |
| □ 69 Yuri Khmylev | .10 | .05 |
| □ 70 Zdeno Ciger | .10 | .05 |
| □ 71 Daren Puppa | .10 | .05 |
| □ 72 Ron Francis | .15 | .07 |
| □ 73 Scott Mellanby | .15 | .07 |

| □ 74 Igor Larionov | .10 | .05 |
| □ 75 Scott Niedermayer | .10 | .05 |
| □ 76 Owen Nolan | .15 | .07 |
| □ 77 Teppo Numminen | .10 | .05 |
| □ 78 Pierre Turgeon | .15 | .07 |
| □ 79 Mikael Renberg | .15 | .07 |
| □ 80 Norm Maciver | .10 | .05 |
| □ 81 Paul Cavallini | .10 | .05 |
| □ 82 Kirk Muller | .10 | .05 |
| □ 83 Felix Potvin | .30 | .14 |
| □ 84 Craig Janney | .10 | .05 |
| □ 85 Dale Hunter | .10 | .05 |
| □ 86 Jyrki Lumme | .10 | .05 |
| □ 87 Alexei Zhitnik | .10 | .05 |
| □ 88 Steve Larmer | .15 | .07 |
| □ 89 Jocelyn Lemieux | .10 | .05 |
| □ 90 Joe Nieuwendyk | .15 | .07 |
| □ 91 Don Sweeney | .10 | .05 |
| □ 92 Slava Kozlov | .15 | .07 |
| □ 93 Tim Sweeney | .10 | .05 |
| □ 94 Chris Chelios | .30 | .14 |
| □ 95 Derek Plante | .15 | .07 |
| □ 96 Igor Kravchuk | .10 | .05 |
| □ 97 Shawn Chambers | .10 | .05 |
| □ 98 Jaromir Jagr | 1.00 | .45 |
| □ 99 Jeff Norton | .10 | .05 |
| □ 100 John Vanbiesbrouck | .50 | .23 |
| □ 101 John MacLean | .15 | .07 |
| □ 102 Stephane Fiset | .15 | .07 |
| □ 103 Keith Tkachuk | .40 | .18 |
| □ 104 Vladimir Malakhov | .10 | .05 |
| □ 105 Mike McPhee | .10 | .05 |
| □ 106 Eric Desjardins | .15 | .07 |
| □ 107 Alexei Kovalev | .15 | .07 |
| □ 108 Steve Duchesne | .10 | .05 |
| □ 109 Peter Zezel | .10 | .05 |
| □ 110 Randy Burridge | .10 | .05 |
| □ 111 Jason Bowen | .10 | .05 |
| □ 112 Phil Bourque | .10 | .05 |
| □ 113 Cliff Ronning | .15 | .07 |
| □ 114 Sean Burke | .15 | .07 |
| □ 115 Gary Roberts | .15 | .07 |
| □ 116 Vladimir Konstantinov | .15 | .07 |
| □ 117 Brent Sutter | .10 | .05 |
| □ 118 Tony Granato | .10 | .05 |
| □ 119 Garry Valk | .10 | .05 |
| □ 120 Adam Oates | .15 | .07 |
| □ 121 Arturs Irbe | .15 | .07 |
| □ 122 Jesse Belanger | .10 | .05 |
| □ 123 Roman Hamrlik | .15 | .07 |
| □ 124 Jason Arnott | .15 | .07 |
| □ 125 Alexander Mogilny | .15 | .07 |
| □ 126 Bruce Driver | .10 | .05 |
| □ 127 Shawn McEachern | .10 | .05 |
| □ 128 Andrei Kovalenko | .10 | .05 |
| □ 129 Benoit Hogue | .10 | .05 |
| □ 130 Tim Cheveldae | .15 | .07 |
| □ 131 Brian Noonan | .10 | .05 |
| □ 132 Lyle Odelein | .10 | .05 |
| □ 133 Russ Courtnall | .10 | .05 |
| □ 134 Peter Stastny | .15 | .07 |
| □ 135 Doug Gilmour | .30 | .14 |
| □ 136 Pat Peake | .10 | .05 |
| □ 137 Gary Suter | .10 | .05 |
| □ 138 Paul Ranheim | .10 | .05 |
| □ 139 Troy Murray | .10 | .05 |
| □ 140 Pavel Bure | .60 | .25 |
| □ 141 Gord Murphy | .10 | .05 |
| □ 142 Michael Nylander | .10 | .05 |
| □ 143 Craig Muni | .10 | .05 |
| □ 144 Bob Corkum | .10 | .05 |
| □ 145 Martin Brodeur | .75 | .35 |
| □ 146 Ted Donato | .10 | .05 |
| □ 147 Alexei Zhamnov | .15 | .07 |
| □ 148 Josef Beranek | .10 | .05 |
| □ 149 Joe Mullen | .15 | .07 |
| □ 150 Sergei Fedorov | .60 | .25 |
| □ 151 Mike Keane | .10 | .05 |
| □ 152 Sergei Makarov | .10 | .05 |
| □ 153 Marty McInnis | .10 | .05 |
| □ 154 Steven Rice | .10 | .05 |
| □ 155 Brian Leetch | .30 | .14 |
| □ 156 Chris Joseph | .10 | .05 |
| □ 157 Darcy Wakaluk | .15 | .07 |
| □ 158 Kelly Miller | .10 | .05 |
| □ 159 Jim Montgomery | .10 | .05 |
| □ 160 Nikolai Borschevsky | .10 | .05 |
| □ 161 Darren Turcotte | .10 | .05 |
| □ 162 Brad Shaw | .10 | .05 |
| □ 163 Mark Lamb | .10 | .05 |
| □ 164 Alexei Gusarov | .10 | .05 |
| □ 165 Jeremy Roenick | .30 | .14 |
| □ 166 Stephane Richer | .15 | .07 |
| □ 167 German Titov | .10 | .05 |
| □ 168 Rob Niedermayer | .15 | .07 |
| □ 169 Glen Murray | .10 | .05 |
| □ 170 Mario Lemieux | 1.50 | .70 |
| □ 171 Thomas Steen | .10 | .05 |
| □ 172 Ron Tugnutt | .10 | .05 |
| □ 173 Pat Falloon | .10 | .05 |
| □ 174 Esa Tikkanen | .10 | .05 |
| □ 175 Dominik Hasek | .75 | .35 |
| □ 176 Patrick Flatley | .10 | .05 |
| □ 177 Gino Odjick | .10 | .05 |
| □ 178 Charlie Huddy | .10 | .05 |
| □ 179 Dave Poulin | .10 | .05 |
| □ 180 Darren McCarty | .10 | .05 |
| □ 181 Todd Gill | .10 | .05 |
| □ 182 Tom Chorske | .10 | .05 |
| □ 183 Marc Bergevin | .10 | .05 |
| □ 184 Dave Lowry | .10 | .05 |
| □ 185 Brent Gilchrist | .10 | .05 |
| □ 186 Eric Weinrich | .10 | .05 |
| □ 187 Ted Drury | .10 | .05 |
| □ 188 Boris Mironov | .10 | .05 |
| □ 189 Patrik Carnback | .10 | .05 |

| □ 190 Ray Bourque | .30 | .14 |
| □ 191 Patrice Brisebois | .10 | .05 |
| □ 192 Bob Errey | .10 | .05 |
| □ 193 Scott Lachance | .10 | .05 |
| □ 194 Brad May | .15 | .07 |
| □ 195 Jeff Beukeboom | .10 | .05 |
| □ 196 James Patrick | .10 | .05 |
| □ 197 Doug Brown | .10 | .05 |
| □ 198 Dana Murzyn | .10 | .05 |
| □ 199 Chris Osgood | .50 | .23 |
| □ 200 Wayne Gretzky | 2.00 | .90 |
| □ 201 Bob Carpenter | .10 | .05 |
| □ 202 Evgeny Davydov | .10 | .05 |
| □ 203 Oleg Petrov | .10 | .05 |
| □ 204 Grant Ledyard | .10 | .05 |
| □ 205 Jocelyn Thibault | .30 | .14 |
| □ 206 Bill Houlder | .10 | .05 |
| □ 207 Tom Fitzgerald | .10 | .05 |
| □ 208 Dominic Roussel | .15 | .07 |
| □ 209 Dave Ellett | .10 | .05 |
| □ 210 Frank Kucera | .10 | .05 |
| □ 211 Steve Smith | .10 | .05 |
| □ 212 Vincent Riendeau | .15 | .07 |
| □ 213 Scott Pearson | .10 | .05 |
| □ 214 John Slaney | .10 | .05 |
| □ 215 Larry Murphy | .15 | .07 |
| □ 216 Travis Green | .15 | .07 |
| □ 217 Joel Otto | .10 | .05 |
| □ 218 Randy Wood | .10 | .05 |
| □ 219 Gaetan Duchesne | .10 | .05 |
| □ 220 Sergei Nemchinov | .10 | .05 |
| □ 221 Terry Carkner | .10 | .05 |
| □ 222 Randy McKay | .10 | .05 |
| □ 223 Mike Donnelly | .10 | .05 |
| □ 224 J.J. Daigneault | .10 | .05 |
| □ 225 Dallas Drake | .10 | .05 |
| □ 226 John Tucker | .10 | .05 |
| □ 227 Dimitri Yushkevich | .10 | .05 |
| □ 228 Mike Stapleton | .10 | .05 |
| □ 229 Dmitri Mironov | .10 | .05 |
| □ 230 Ken Wregget | .15 | .07 |
| □ 231 Claude Lapointe | .10 | .05 |
| □ 232 Joe Sacco | .10 | .05 |
| □ 233 Craig Ludwig | .10 | .05 |
| □ 234 David Reid | .10 | .05 |
| □ 235 Rich Sutter | .10 | .05 |
| □ 236 Mark Fitzpatrick | .15 | .07 |
| □ 237 Jim Storm | .10 | .05 |
| □ 238 Brad Dalgarno | .10 | .05 |
| □ 239 Dixon Ward | .10 | .05 |
| □ 240 Greg Adams | .10 | .05 |
| □ 241 Dino Ciccarelli | .15 | .07 |
| □ 242 Vlastimil Kroupa | .10 | .05 |
| □ 243 Joe Kocur | .10 | .05 |
| □ 244 Donald Audette | .10 | .05 |
| □ 245 Trent Yawney | .10 | .05 |
| □ 246 Mariusz Czerkawski | .10 | .05 |
| □ 247 Jason Allison | .15 | .07 |
| □ 248 Brian Savage | .10 | .05 |
| □ 249 Fred Knipscheer | .10 | .05 |
| □ 250 Jamie McLennan | .10 | .05 |
| □ 251 Aaron Gavey | .10 | .05 |
| □ 252 Jeff Friesen | .15 | .07 |
| □ 253 Adam Deadmarsh | .15 | .07 |
| □ 254 Jamie Storr | .15 | .07 |
| □ 255 Brian Rolston | .10 | .05 |
| □ 256 Zigmund Palffy | .30 | .14 |
| □ 257 Brett Lindros | .10 | .05 |
| □ 258 Denis Tsygurov | .10 | .05 |
| □ 259 Chris Tamer | .10 | .05 |
| □ 260 Mike Peca | .15 | .07 |
| □ 261 Oleg Tverdovsky | .15 | .07 |
| □ 262 Todd Harvey | .10 | .05 |
| □ 263 Yan Kaminsky | .10 | .05 |
| □ 264 Kenny Jonsson | .10 | .05 |
| □ 265 Paul Kariya | 1.50 | .70 |
| □ 266 Peter Forsberg | 1.25 | .55 |
| □ 267 Atlantic Division | .10 | .05 |
| Checklist | | |
| □ 268 Northeast Division | .10 | .05 |
| Checklist | | |
| □ 269 Central Division | .10 | .05 |
| Checklist | | |
| □ 270 Pacific Division | .10 | .05 |
| Checklist | | |
| □ 271 Steve Yzerman | 1.00 | .45 |
| □ 272 John LeClair | .50 | .23 |
| □ 273 Rod Brind'Amour | .15 | .07 |
| □ 274 Ron Hextall | .15 | .07 |
| □ 275 Todd Elik | .10 | .05 |
| □ 276 Geoff Courtnall | .10 | .05 |
| □ 277 Kjell Samuelsson | .10 | .05 |
| □ 278 Brian Bradley | .10 | .05 |
| □ 279 Darrin Shannon | .10 | .05 |
| □ 280 Mike Ricci | .10 | .05 |
| □ 281 Peter Bondra | .30 | .14 |
| □ 282 Terry Yake | .10 | .05 |
| □ 283 Patrick Poulin | .10 | .05 |
| □ 284 Bob Kudelski | .10 | .05 |
| □ 285 Bill Ranford | .15 | .07 |
| □ 286 Alexander Godynyuk | .10 | .05 |
| □ 287 Claude Lemieux | .15 | .07 |
| □ 288 Sylvain Turgeon | .10 | .05 |
| □ 289 Kevin Miller | .10 | .05 |
| □ 290 Brian Bellows | .10 | .05 |
| □ 291 Murray Craven | .10 | .05 |
| □ 292 Kelly Hrudey | .15 | .07 |
| □ 293 Neal Broten | .10 | .05 |
| □ 294 Craig Simpson | .10 | .05 |
| □ 295 Mark Howe | .10 | .05 |
| □ 296 Johan Garpenlov | .10 | .05 |
| □ 297 Jamie Macoun | .10 | .05 |
| □ 298 Steve Leach | .10 | .05 |
| □ 299 Kevin Stevens | .15 | .07 |
| □ 300 Mark Messier | .40 | .18 |
| □ 301 Paul Ysebaert | .10 | .05 |

□ 302 Derek King .10 .05
□ 303 Fredrik Olausson .10 .05
□ 304 John Druce .10 .05
□ 305 Calle Johansson .10 .05
□ 306 Kelly Kisio .10 .05
□ 307 Sergio Momesso .10 .05
□ 308 Joe Cirella .10 .05
□ 309 Tommy Soderstrom .15 .07
□ 310 Scott Stevens .15 .07
□ 311 Petr Klima .10 .05
□ 312 Steven Finn .10 .05
□ 313 Tomas Sandstrom .10 .05
□ 314 Ray Ferraro .10 .05
□ 315 Andy Moog .15 .07
□ 316 Ray Whitney .10 .05
□ 317 Dirk Graham .10 .05
□ 318 Shawn Burr .10 .05
□ 319 Andrew Cassels .10 .05
□ 320 Craig Billington .15 .07
□ 321 Wayne Presley .10 .05
□ 322 Anatoli Semenov .10 .05
□ 323 Michal Pivonka .10 .05
□ 324 Martin Gelinas .10 .05
□ 325 Nelson Emerson .10 .05
□ 326 Brent Fedyk .10 .05
□ 327 Bob Bassen .10 .05
□ 328 Darryl Sydor .10 .05
□ 329 Stephane Matteau .10 .05
□ 330 Ken Daneyko .10 .05
□ 331 Mikhail Shtalenkov .10 .05
□ 332 Kelly Buchberger .10 .05
□ 333 Mike Hough .10 .05
□ 334 Dave Gagner .15 .07
□ 335 Chris Terreri .15 .07
□ 336 Robert Kron .10 .05
□ 337 Andrei Lomakin .10 .05
□ 338 Kevin Lowe .10 .05
□ 339 Steve Konroyd .10 .05
□ 340 Denis Savard .15 .07
□ 341 Steve Heinze .10 .05
□ 342 Zarley Zalapski .10 .05
□ 343 Valeri Kamensky .15 .07
□ 344 Tie Domi .15 .07
□ 345 Kevin Hatcher .10 .05
□ 346 Dean Evason .10 .05
□ 347 Bobby Holik .10 .05
□ 348 Steve Konowalchuk .10 .05
□ 349 Rob Gaudreau .10 .05
□ 350 Pat LaFontaine .15 .07
□ 351 Joe Reekie .10 .05
□ 352 Martin Straka .10 .05
□ 353 Dave Babych .10 .05
□ 354 Geoff Smith .10 .05
□ 355 Don Beaupre .15 .07
□ 356 Adam Burt .10 .05
□ 357 Doug Bodger .10 .05
□ 358 Dean McAmmond .10 .05
□ 359 Gerald Diduck .10 .05
□ 360 Rob DiMaio .10 .05
□ 361 Scott Young .10 .05
□ 362 Alexander Semak .10 .05
□ 363 Mike Rathje .10 .05
□ 364 Alexander Karpovtsev .10 .05
□ 365 Trevor Kidd .15 .07
□ 366 Jason Dawe .10 .05
□ 367 Vitali Prokhorov .10 .05
□ 368 Keith Brown .10 .05
□ 369 Bret Hedican .10 .05
□ 370 Markus Naslund .10 .05
□ 371 Rick Tocchet .15 .07
□ 372 Guy Carbonneau .10 .05
□ 373 Kevin Haller .10 .05
□ 374 Bob Rouse .10 .05
□ 375 Rob Pearson .10 .05
□ 376 Steve Chiasson .10 .05
□ 377 Mike Vernon .15 .07
□ 378 Keith Jones .10 .05
□ 379 Sylvain Lefebvre .10 .05
□ 380 Tom Kurvers .10 .05
□ 381 Pat Elynuik .10 .05
□ 382 Uwe Krupp .10 .05
□ 383 Ron Sutter .10 .05
□ 384 Mike Ridley .10 .05
□ 385 Wendel Clark .15 .07
□ 386 Mats Sundin .15 .07
□ 387 Al MacInnis .15 .07
□ 388 Glen Wesley .10 .05
□ 389 Jim Paek .10 .05
□ 390 Rudy Poeschek .10 .05
□ 391 Yves Racine .10 .05
□ 392 Craig MacTavish .10 .05
□ 393 Jon Casey .15 .07
□ 394 Garth Butcher .10 .05
□ 395 Sean Hill .10 .05
□ 396 Troy Loney .10 .05
□ 397 John Cullen .10 .05
□ 398 Alexei Kasatonov .10 .05
□ 399 Mike Craig .10 .05
□ 400 Luc Robitaille .15 .07
□ 401 Randy Moller .10 .05
□ 402 Chris Dahlquist .10 .05
□ 403 Pat Conacher .10 .05
□ 404 Bob Probert .15 .07
□ 405 Robert Dirk .10 .05
□ 406 Randy Cunneyworth .10 .05
□ 407 Bryan Marchment .10 .05
□ 408 Nick Kypreos .10 .05
□ 409 Doug Lidster .10 .05
□ 410 Phil Housley .15 .07
□ 411 Bob Sweeney .10 .05
□ 412 Mike Ramsey .10 .05
□ 413 Robert Lang .10 .05
□ 414 Brian Benning .10 .05
□ 415 Greg Gilbert .10 .05
□ 416 Martin Rucinsky .10 .05
□ 417 Jason Smith .10 .05
□ 418 Jozef Stumpel .10 .05
□ 419 Bob Beers .10 .05
□ 420 Ed Olczyk .10 .05
□ 421 Grant Fuhr .15 .07
□ 422 Gilbert Dionne .10 .05
□ 423 Mike Peluso .10 .05
□ 424 Petr Svoboda .10 .05
□ 425 Corey Millen .10 .05
□ 426 Kevin Dineen .10 .05
□ 427 Brad McCrimmon .10 .05
□ 428 Bob Essensa .15 .07
□ 429 Paul Coffey .30 .14
□ 430 Glenn Healy .15 .07
□ 431 Luke Richardson .10 .05
□ 432 Adam Foote .10 .05
□ 433 Paul Broten .10 .05
□ 434 Christian Ruuttu .10 .05
□ 435 David Shaw .10 .05
□ 436 Jimmy Carson .10 .05
□ 437 Ken Sutton .10 .05
□ 438 Kay Whitmore .15 .07
□ 439 Jim Dowd .10 .05
□ 440 Jim Johnson .10 .05
□ 441 Kirk Maltby .10 .05
□ 442 Trent Klatt .10 .05
□ 443 Paul DiPietro .10 .05
□ 444 Rick Tabaracci .15 .07
□ 445 Craig Wolanin .10 .05
□ 446 Dave Hannan .10 .05
□ 447 Rick Zombo .10 .05
□ 448 Tom Pederson .10 .05
□ 449 Martin Lapointe .10 .05
□ 450 Brett Hull .40 .18
□ 451 Mikael Andersson .10 .05
□ 452 Benoit Brunet .10 .05
□ 453 Nathan Lafayette .10 .05
□ 454 Kent Manderville .10 .05
□ 455 Todd Krygier .10 .05
□ 456 Dennis Vaske .10 .05
□ 457 Peter Popovic .10 .05
□ 458 Jeff Shantz .10 .05
□ 459 Darrin Madeley .10 .05
□ 460 Rene Corbet .10 .05
□ 461 Alexander Daigle IB .10 .05
□ 462 Martin Brodeur IB .75 .35
□ 463 Jason Arnott IB .15 .07
□ 464 Mikael Renberg IB .15 .07
□ 465 Alexei Yashin IB .15 .07
□ 466 Chris Pronger IB .15 .07
□ 467 Mariusz Czerkawski IB .10 .05
□ 468 Chris Gratton IB .15 .07
□ 469 Rob Niedermayer IB .15 .07
□ 470 Bryan Smolinski IB .10 .05
□ 471 Chris Osgood IB .50 .23
□ 472 Derek Plante IB .10 .05
□ 473 Brian Rolston IB .10 .05
□ 474 Jason Allison IB .10 .05
□ 475 Jamie Storr IB .15 .07
□ 476 Kenny Jonsson IB .10 .05
□ 477 Viktor Kozlov IB .10 .05
□ 478 Brett Lindros IB .10 .05
□ 479 Peter Forsberg IB 1.25 .55
□ 480 Paul Kariya IB 1.50 .70
□ 481 Viktor Kozlov .10 .05
□ 482 Michal Grosek .10 .05
□ 483 Maxim Bets .10 .05
□ 484 Jason Wiemer .10 .05
□ 485 Janne Laukkanen .10 .05
□ 486 Valeri Karpov .10 .05
□ 487 Andrei Nikolishhin .10 .05
□ 488 Dan Plante .10 .05
□ 489 Mattias Norstrom .10 .05
□ 490 David Oliver .10 .05
□ 491 Todd Simon .10 .05
□ 492 Valeri Bure .15 .07
□ 493 Eric Fichaud .75 .35
□ 494 Cory Stillman .10 .05
□ 495 Chris Therien .10 .05
□ 496 Matt Johnson .10 .05
□ 497 Joby Messier .10 .05
□ 498 Slava Butsayev .10 .05
□ 499 Bernie Nicholls .10 .05
□ 500 Mark Osborne .10 .05
□ 501 Stephane Quintal .10 .05
□ 502 Jamie Baker .10 .05
□ 503 Todd Ewen .10 .05
□ 504 Dan Quinn .10 .05
□ 505 Peter Taglianetti .10 .05
□ 506 Chris Simon .10 .05
□ 507 Jay Wells .10 .05
□ 508 Tommy Albelin .10 .05
□ 509 Warren Rychel .10 .05
□ 510 Brent Hughes .10 .05
□ 511 Greg Johnson .10 .05
□ 512 Stu Grimson .10 .05
□ 513 Iain Fraser .10 .05
□ 514 Rob Ray .10 .05
□ 515 Craig Berube .10 .05
□ 516 Shane Churla .10 .05
□ 517 Checklist .10 .05
□ 518 Checklist .10 .05
□ 519 Checklist .10 .05
□ 520 Checklist .10 .05
□ 521 Jamie Storr .15 .07
□ 522 Dan Cloutier .40 .18
□ 523 Bryan McCabe .10 .05
□ 524 Ed Jovanovski .50 .23
□ 525 Nolan Baumgartner .10 .05
□ 526 Jamie Rivers .10 .05
□ 527 Wade Redden .50 .23
□ 528 Lee Sorochan .10 .05
□ 529 Eric Daze 1.25 .55
□ 530 Jason Allison .10 .05
□ 531 Alexandre Daigle .10 .05
□ 532 Jeff Friesen .15 .07
□ 533 Todd Harvey .10 .05
□ 534 Jeff O'Neill .40 .18
□ 535 Ryan Smyth 1.50 .70
□ 536 Marty Murray .10 .05
□ 537 Darcy Tucker .10 .05
□ 538 Denis Pederson .25 .11
□ 539 Shean Donovan .10 .05
□ 540 Larry Courville .10 .05
□ MVPC Pavel Bure 30.00 13.50
□ MVPU Dominik Hasek 30.00 13.50

## 1994-95 Pinnacle Artist's Proofs

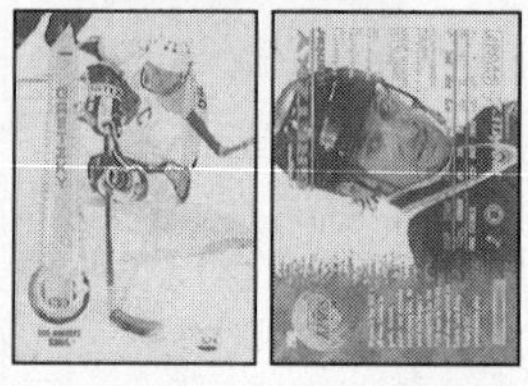

This set is a parallel version of the standard set. The difference is a reflective gold foil Artist's Proof logo on the front. Series 1 cards also featured an Artist's Proof logo on the back; this logo did not appear on series 2 card backs. The Pinnacle and player name bearing icon, which is gold on normal cards, is printed with a more reflective gold foil on these inserts. Series two production made this feature more bold than in series 1. Cards were inserted at a rate of 1:36 packs in both series 1 and 2 14 card packs. There are no Artist's Proof versions of the first series checklists, however, there is an Artist's Proof version of the second series checklists. Estimated production of these cards varies; one press release suggests "less than 700 sets", while wrappers state "less than 500".

| | MINT | NRMT |
|---|---|---|
| COMPLETE SET (536) | 4500.00 | 2000.00 |
| COMPLETE SERIES 1 (266) | 2500.00 | 1100.00 |
| COMPLETE SERIES 2 (270) | 2000.00 | 900.00 |
| COMMON CARD (1-540) | 4.00 | 1.80 |

*STARS: 50X TO 100X BASIC CARDS
*YOUNG STARS: 30X TO 60X BASIC CARDS
*RCs: 15X TO 30X BASIC CARDS

□ 1 Eric Lindros 120.00 55.00
□ 25 Teemu Selanne 60.00 27.00
□ 30 Patrick Roy 150.00 70.00
□ 32 Brendan Shanahan 60.00 27.00
□ 50 Joe Sakic 80.00 36.00
□ 98 Jaromir Jagr 120.00 55.00
□ 100 John Vanbiesbrouck 80.00 36.00
□ 140 Pavel Bure 60.00 27.00
□ 145 Martin Brodeur 60.00 27.00
□ 150 Sergei Fedorov 60.00 27.00
□ 170 Mario Lemieux 150.00 70.00
□ 175 Dominik Hasek 60.00 27.00
□ 200 Wayne Gretzky 400.00 180.00
□ 265 Paul Kariya 150.00 70.00
□ 266 Peter Forsberg 120.00 55.00
□ 271 Steve Yzerman 100.00 45.00
□ 479 Peter Forsberg IB 120.00 55.00
□ 480 Paul Kariya IB 150.00 70.00
□ 535 Ryan Smyth WJC 60.00 27.00

## 1994-95 Pinnacle Rink Collection

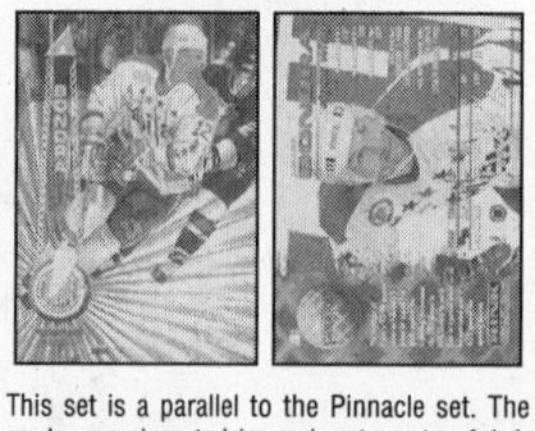

This set is a parallel to the Pinnacle set. The cards were inserted in packs at a rate of 1:4. The fronts have a full-color action photo with the player's last name on the left surrounded by the chain for a gold medallion at the bottom. The background consists of silver-foil sunrays. The backs have a color photo with player information and statistics. The bottom has the words "Rink Collection" and the Pinnacle emblem.

| | MINT | NRMT |
|---|---|---|
| COMPLETE SET (540) | 1300.00 | 575.00 |
| COMPLETE SERIES 1 (270) | 700.00 | 325.00 |
| COMPLETE SERIES 2 (270) | 600.00 | 275.00 |
| COMMON CARD (1-540) | 1.50 | .70 |

*STARS: 10X TO 25X BASIC CARDS
*YOUNG STARS: 6X TO 15X BASIC CARDS
*RCs: 4X TO 10X BASIC CARDS

## 1994-95 Pinnacle Boomers

This 18-card set could be found randomly

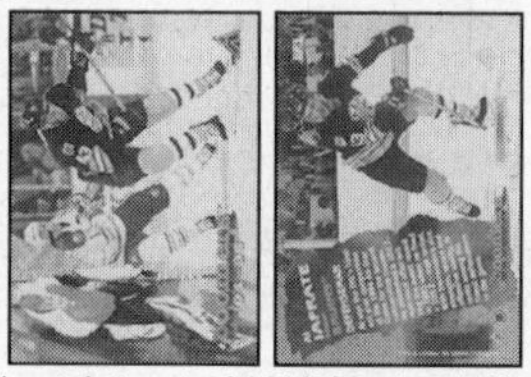

inserted at a rate of 1:24 U.S. series 1 hobby packs. These horizontally-oriented cards are notable for their design, which utilizes two-thirds of the space for an action shot of the featured player shooting the puck. The remaining third featured a ghosted goalie image. The player's last name is printed in gold foil down the left side of the card. "Boomers" is written in blue and red on the bottom left portion. The backs are occupied mostly with a player photo, while text assumes the remaining third. Cards are numbered with a "BR" prefix.

| | MINT | NRMT |
|---|---|---|
| COMPLETE SET (18) | 80.00 | 36.00 |
| COMMON CARD (BR1-BR18) | 2.00 | .90 |

□ BR1 Al Iafrate 2.00 .90
□ BR2 Vladimir Malakhov 2.00 .90
□ BR3 Al MacInnis 2.00 .90
□ BR4 Chris Chelios 4.00 1.80
□ BR5 Mike Modano 6.00 2.70
□ BR6 Brendan Shanahan 8.00 3.60
□ BR7 Ray Bourque 4.00 1.80
□ BR8 Geoff Sanderson 3.00 1.35
□ BR9 Brett Hull 6.00 2.70
□ BR10 Rob Blake 2.00 .90
□ BR11 Steve Thomas 2.00 .90
□ BR12 Cam Neely 3.00 1.35
□ BR13 Pavel Bure 8.00 3.60
□ BR14 Stephane Richer 2.00 .90
□ BR15 Teemu Selanne 8.00 3.60
□ BR16 Eric Lindros 15.00 6.75
□ BR17 Alexander Mogilny 3.00 1.35
□ BR18 Rick Tocchet 2.00 .90

## 1994-95 Pinnacle Gamers

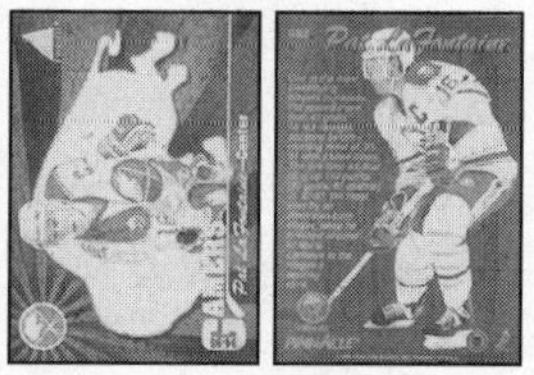

This 18-card set was randomly inserted 1:18 packs of all Pinnacle series 2 product. The cards are enhanced by the Dufex printing technology. Each card is color-coded to the team colors of the player. The player is pictured inside a shape which approximates the design of his team's emblem. The backs are reflective colored, with a photo and paragraph of information. Cards are numbered with a "GR" prefix.

| | MINT | NRMT |
|---|---|---|
| COMPLETE SET (18) | 120.00 | 55.00 |
| COMMON CARD (GR1-GR18) | 2.50 | 1.10 |

□ GR1 Teemu Selanne 12.00 5.50
□ GR2 Pat LaFontaine 4.00 1.80
□ GR3 Sergei Fedorov 12.00 5.50
□ GR4 Pavel Bure 12.00 5.50
□ GR5 Jaromir Jagr 20.00 9.00
□ GR6 Alexandre Daigle 4.00 1.80
□ GR7 Kirk Muller 2.50 1.10
□ GR8 Mike Modano 8.00 3.60
□ GR9 Mark Messier 8.00 3.60
□ GR10 Brendan Shanahan 12.00 5.50
□ GR11 Doug Gilmour 4.00 1.80
□ GR12 Rick Tocchet 2.50 1.10
□ GR13 Wendel Clark 2.50 1.10
□ GR14 Jeremy Roenick 6.00 2.70
□ GR15 Adam Graves 4.00 1.80
□ GR16 Eric Lindros 25.00 11.00
□ GR17 Cam Neely 4.00 1.80
□ GR18 Keith Tkachuk 8.00 3.60

## 1994-95 Pinnacle Goaltending Greats

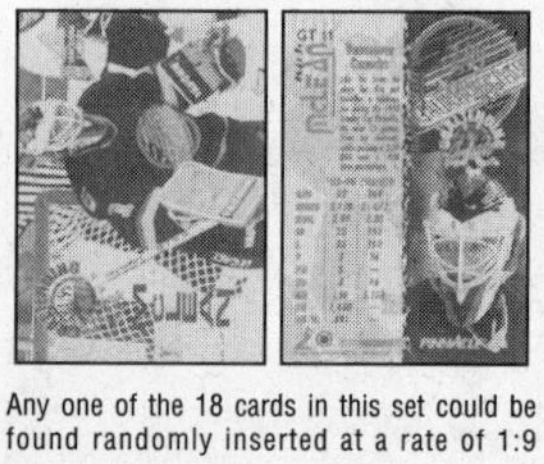

Any one of the 18 cards in this set could be found randomly inserted at a rate of 1:9 Pinnacle series 2 jumbo packs. This horizontal set has a full-bleed photo design, with the set logo and player name in gold foil on the left side of the card. Vertical backs have a crowded design, with a small player photo on the lower left, personal information and statistics. Cards are numbered with a "GT" prefix.

| | MINT | NRMT |
|---|---|---|
| COMPLETE SET (18) | 150.00 | 70.00 |
| COMMON CARD (GT1-GT18) | 5.00 | 2.20 |

□ GT1 Dominik Hasek 15.00 6.75
□ GT2 Mike Richter 10.00 4.50
□ GT3 John Vanbiesbrouck 12.00 5.50
□ GT4 Ed Belfour 10.00 4.50
□ GT5 Patrick Roy 40.00 18.00
□ GT6 Bill Ranford 8.00 3.60
□ GT7 Martin Brodeur 20.00 9.00
□ GT8 Felix Potvin 10.00 4.50
□ GT9 Arturs Irbe 5.00 2.20
□ GT10 Mike Vernon 5.00 2.20
□ GT11 Kirk McLean 5.00 2.20
□ GT12 Sean Burke 5.00 2.20
□ GT13 Curtis Joseph 10.00 4.50
□ GT14 Andy Moog 5.00 2.20
□ GT15 Daren Puppa 5.00 2.20
□ GT16 Chris Osgood 12.00 5.50
□ GT17 Tom Barrasso 5.00 2.20
□ GT18 Jocelyn Thibault 10.00 4.50

## 1994-95 Pinnacle Masks

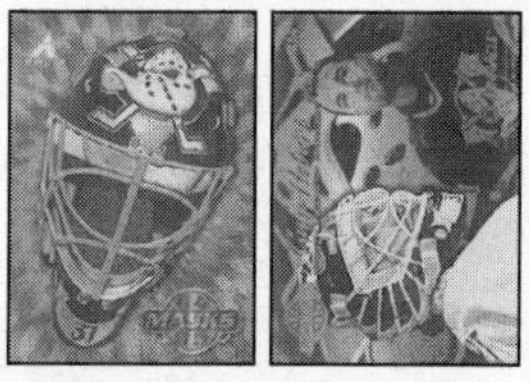

This popular ten-card insert set was inserted in Canadian series 1 product at the rate of 1:90 packs. The cards feature a photo of a goaltender's mask over a metallic blue Dufex background. No team or player name appears on the front. Backs feature dual photos on a mirror finish and the player and team names. Cards are numbered with an "MA" prefix.

| | MINT | NRMT |
|---|---|---|
| COMPLETE SET (10) | 300.00 | 135.00 |
| COMMON CARD (MA1-MA10) | 30.00 | 13.50 |

□ MA1 Patrick Roy 120.00 55.00
□ MA2 John Vanbiesbrouck 40.00 18.00
□ MA3 Kelly Hrudey 30.00 13.50
□ MA4 Guy Hebert 30.00 13.50
□ MA5 Rick Tabaracci 30.00 13.50
□ MA6 Ron Hextall 30.00 13.50
□ MA7 Trevor Kidd 30.00 13.50
□ MA8 Andy Moog 30.00 13.50
□ MA9 Jimmy Waite 30.00 13.50
□ MA10 Curtis Joseph 60.00 27.00

## 1994-95 Pinnacle Northern Lights

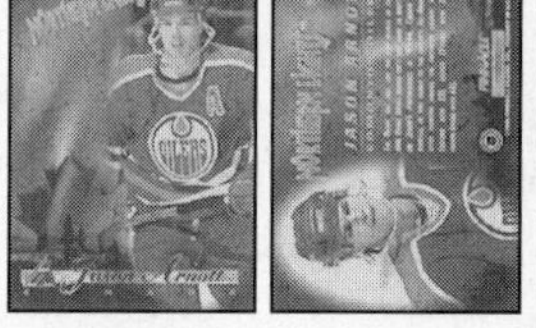

This 18-card insert set was randomly inserted 1:24 Canadian series 1 hobby packs. The series highlights the top players from Canadian-based teams. The fronts have a player photo which fades into a sky design with a northern lights image on the left side. The player name is stamped in gold foil above the word "Canada", written in yellow. The horizontal backs have a photo on the left, with some personal information printed over another interpretation of the famous northern lights. Cards are numbered with an "NL" prefix in a red maple leaf.

| | MINT | NRMT |
|---|---|---|
| COMPLETE SET (18) | 125.00 | 55.00 |
| COMMON CARD (NL1-NL18) | 2.50 | 1.10 |

□ NL1 Patrick Roy 30.00 13.50
□ NL2 Kirk Muller 2.50 1.10
□ NL3 Vincent Damphousse 4.00 1.80
□ NL4 Joe Sakic 12.00 5.50
□ NL5 Wendel Clark 2.50 1.10
□ NL6 Alexandre Daigle 4.00 1.80
□ NL7 Alexei Yashin 4.00 1.80
□ NL8 Doug Gilmour 6.00 2.70
□ NL9 Felix Potvin 6.00 2.70
□ NL10 Mats Sundin 4.00 1.80
□ NL11 Teemu Selanne 12.00 5.50
□ NL12 Keith Tkachuk 8.00 3.60
□ NL13 Bill Ranford 4.00 1.80
□ NL14 Jason Arnott 4.00 1.80

| | MINT | NRMT |
|---|---|---|
| ❑ NL15 Theoren Fleury | 4.00 | 1.80 |
| ❑ NL16 Gary Roberts | 2.50 | 1.10 |
| ❑ NL17 Pavel Bure | 12.00 | 5.50 |
| ❑ NL18 Trevor Linden | 4.00 | 1.80 |

## 1994-95 Pinnacle Rookie Team Pinnacle

The 12 cards in this set, featuring a player from each conference on either side, were inserted in Pinnacle series 2 product at the rate of 1:90 packs. The set focuses on 24 top rookies in the league. Cards are printed using the Gold-line foil technology; either side could be found with the Gold-line foil finish. The cards feature a cutout player photo on a striped background of reds and yellows. The player name is printed on a black border on the top of the card. One side has the card number with an "RTP" prefix and the Pinnacle anti-counterfeiting device.

| | MINT | NRMT |
|---|---|---|
| COMPLETE SET (12) | 150.00 | 70.00 |
| COMMON CARD (1-12) | 10.00 | 4.50 |
| ❑ 1 Corey Hirsch | 15.00 | 6.75 |
| Jamie Storr | | |
| ❑ 2 Mattias Norstrom | 12.00 | 5.50 |
| Oleg Tverdovsky | | |
| ❑ 3 Denis Tsygurov | 10.00 | 4.50 |
| Janne Laukkanen | | |
| ❑ 4 Chris Tamer | 10.00 | 4.50 |
| Kenny Jonsson | | |
| ❑ 5 Zigmund Palffy | | |
| Viktor Kozlov | | |
| ❑ 6 Rene Corbet | 10.00 | 4.50 |
| Maxim Bets | | |
| ❑ 7 Jason Allison | 10.00 | 4.50 |
| Jeff Friesen | | |
| ❑ 8 Brian Rolston | 12.00 | 5.50 |
| Michael Peca | | |
| ❑ 9 Peter Forsberg | 80.00 | 36.00 |
| Paul Kariya | | |
| ❑ 10 Brian Savage | 10.00 | 4.50 |
| Todd Harvey | | |
| ❑ 11 Brett Lindros | 10.00 | 4.50 |
| Valeri Karpov | | |
| ❑ 12 Mariusz Czerkawski | 10.00 | 4.50 |
| Sergei Krivokrasov | | |

## 1994-95 Pinnacle Team Pinnacle

This 12-card set features 24 top players in the league, 12 per conference (one player on either side of the card). These were inserted in series 1 U.S. product at the rate of 1:90 packs. Cards have full-bleed photos on each side. Either side could be found with the Dufex technology, while the other has a mirror finish. The Dufexing of one particular side could have an effect on the value, depending upon the player and regional premium demands. The words "Team Pinnacle '94-95" are printed in gold on both sides. The player's last name is printed in an ovoid sphere along the bottom. Cards are numbered on one side with a "TP" prefix.

| | MINT | NRMT |
|---|---|---|
| COMPLETE SET (12) | 400.00 | 180.00 |
| COMMON CARD (TP1-TP12) | 15.00 | 6.75 |
| ❑ TP1 Felix Potvin | 60.00 | 27.00 |
| Patrick Roy | | |
| ❑ TP2 Curtis Joseph | 25.00 | 11.00 |
| Mike Richter | | |
| ❑ TP3 Ray Bourque | 25.00 | 11.00 |
| Chris Chelios | | |
| ❑ TP4 Brian Leetch | 20.00 | 9.00 |
| Rob Blake | | |
| ❑ TP5 Scott Stevens | 20.00 | 9.00 |
| Paul Coffey | | |
| ❑ TP6 Adam Graves | 20.00 | 9.00 |
| Brendan Shanahan | | |
| ❑ TP7 Kevin Stevens | 15.00 | 6.75 |
| Luc Robitaille | | |
| ❑ TP8 Eric Lindros | 50.00 | 22.00 |
| Sergei Fedorov | | |

| | MINT | NRMT |
|---|---|---|
| ❑ TP9 Wayne Gretzky | 100.00 | 45.00 |
| Mark Messier | | |
| ❑ TP10 Doug Gilmour | 60.00 | 27.00 |
| Mario Lemieux | | |
| ❑ TP11 Jaromir Jagr | 40.00 | 18.00 |
| Brett Hull | | |
| ❑ TP12 Pavel Bure | 30.00 | 13.50 |
| Cam Neely | | |

## 1994-95 Pinnacle World Edition

The 18 cards in this set were randomly inserted at a rate of 1:18 Pinnacle series 2 hobby packs. The cards feature a player photo with his native country's flag as a background. The World Edition logo is stamped in gold foil on the upper left corner. Horizontal backs have a small player photo on the left and a paragraph of information. The cards are numbered with a "WE" prefix. The Pinnacle anti-counterfeiting device also appears on the back.

| | MINT | NRMT |
|---|---|---|
| COMPLETE SET (18) | 60.00 | 27.00 |
| COMMON CARD (WE1-WE18) | 1.00 | .45 |
| ❑ WE1 Teemu Selanne | 6.00 | 2.70 |
| ❑ WE2 Doug Gilmour | 2.00 | .90 |
| ❑ WE3 Jeremy Roenick | 3.00 | 1.35 |
| ❑ WE4 Ulf Dahlen | 1.00 | .45 |
| ❑ WE5 Sergei Fedorov | 6.00 | 2.70 |
| ❑ WE6 Dominik Hasek | 6.00 | 2.70 |
| ❑ WE7 Jari Kurri | 2.00 | .90 |
| ❑ WE8 Mario Lemieux | 15.00 | 6.75 |
| ❑ WE9 Mike Modano | 4.00 | 1.80 |
| ❑ WE10 Mikael Renberg | 2.00 | .90 |
| ❑ WE11 Sandis Ozolinsh | 2.00 | .90 |
| ❑ WE12 Alexei Kovalev | 1.00 | .45 |
| ❑ WE13 Robert Reichel | 1.00 | .45 |
| ❑ WE14 Eric Lindros | 15.00 | 6.75 |
| ❑ WE15 Brian Leetch | 3.00 | 1.35 |
| ❑ WE16 Nicklas Lidstrom | 2.00 | .90 |
| ❑ WE17 Alexei Yashin | 2.00 | .90 |
| ❑ WE18 Petr Nedved | 2.00 | .90 |

## 1995-96 Pinnacle

This single-series issue of 225 cards was left incomplete when Pinnacle decided to release the Summit brand in the place of Pinnacle series 2. Nevertheless, most major stars are included. The highlight of the set is a large rookies subset, extending from card #201-220. However, there are no key Rookie Cards in this set.

| | MINT | NRMT |
|---|---|---|
| COMPLETE SET (225) | 12.00 | 5.50 |
| COMMON CARD (1-225) | .10 | .05 |
| ❑ 1 Pavel Bure | .60 | .25 |
| ❑ 2 Paul Kariya | 1.25 | .55 |
| ❑ 3 Adam Oates | .15 | .07 |
| ❑ 4 Garry Galley | .10 | .05 |
| ❑ 5 Mark Messier | .40 | .18 |
| ❑ 6 Theoren Fleury | .15 | .07 |
| ❑ 7 Alexandre Daigle | .10 | .05 |
| ❑ 8 Joe Murphy | .10 | .05 |
| ❑ 9 Eric Lindros | 1.00 | .45 |
| ❑ 10 Kevin Hatcher | .10 | .05 |
| ❑ 11 Jaromir Jagr | 1.00 | .45 |
| ❑ 12 Owen Nolan | .15 | .05 |
| ❑ 13 Ulf Dahlen | .10 | .05 |
| ❑ 14 Paul Coffey | .30 | .14 |
| ❑ 15 Brett Hull | .40 | .18 |
| ❑ 16 Jason Arnott | .15 | .07 |
| ❑ 17 Paul Ysebaert | .10 | .05 |
| ❑ 18 Jesse Belanger | .10 | .05 |
| ❑ 19 Mats Sundin | .15 | .07 |
| ❑ 20 Darren Turcotte | .10 | .05 |
| ❑ 21 Dale Hunter | .10 | .05 |
| ❑ 22 Jari Kurri | .15 | .05 |
| ❑ 23 Alexei Zhamnov | .10 | .05 |
| ❑ 24 Mark Recchi | .15 | .05 |
| ❑ 25 Dallas Drake | .10 | .05 |
| ❑ 26 John MacLean | .15 | .05 |
| ❑ 27 Keith Jones | .10 | .05 |
| ❑ 28 Mathieu Schneider | .10 | .05 |
| ❑ 29 Jeff Brown | .10 | .05 |
| ❑ 30 Patrick Flatley | .10 | .05 |

| | MINT | NRMT |
|---|---|---|
| ❑ 31 Dave Andreychuk | .15 | .07 |
| ❑ 32 Bill Guerin | .10 | .05 |
| ❑ 33 Chris Gratton | .15 | .07 |
| ❑ 34 Pierre Turgeon | .15 | .07 |
| ❑ 35 Stephane Richer | .15 | .07 |
| ❑ 36 Marty McSorley | .10 | .05 |
| ❑ 37 Craig Janney | .15 | .07 |
| ❑ 38 Geoff Sanderson | .15 | .07 |
| ❑ 39 Ron Francis | .15 | .07 |
| ❑ 40 Stu Barnes | .10 | .05 |
| ❑ 41 Mikael Renberg | .15 | .07 |
| ❑ 42 David Oliver | .10 | .05 |
| ❑ 43 Radek Bonk | .10 | .05 |
| ❑ 44 Sergei Fedorov | .50 | .23 |
| ❑ 45 Adam Graves | .15 | .07 |
| ❑ 46 Uwe Krupp | .10 | .05 |
| ❑ 47 Mike Richter | .30 | .14 |
| ❑ 48 Todd Harvey | .10 | .05 |
| ❑ 49 Stanislav Neckar | .10 | .05 |
| ❑ 50 Chris Chelios | .30 | .14 |
| ❑ 51 John LeClair | .50 | .23 |
| ❑ 52 German Titov | .10 | .05 |
| ❑ 53 Garth Butcher | .10 | .05 |
| ❑ 54 Pat LaFontaine | .15 | .07 |
| ❑ 55 Jeff Friesen | .15 | .07 |
| ❑ 56 Ray Bourque | .30 | .14 |
| ❑ 57 Esa Tikkanen | .10 | .05 |
| ❑ 58 Steve Rucchin | .15 | .07 |
| ❑ 59 Roman Hamrlik | .15 | .07 |
| ❑ 60 Oleg Tverdovsky | .15 | .07 |
| ❑ 61 Doug Gilmour | .30 | .14 |
| ❑ 62 Jocelyn Lemieux | .10 | .05 |
| ❑ 63 Roman Oksiuta | .10 | .05 |
| ❑ 64 Alexei Zhitnik | .10 | .05 |
| ❑ 65 Sylvain Cote | .10 | .05 |
| ❑ 66 Paul Kruse | .10 | .05 |
| ❑ 67 Teppo Numminen | .10 | .05 |
| ❑ 68 Gary Suter | .10 | .05 |
| ❑ 69 Darrin Shannon | .10 | .05 |
| ❑ 70 Derian Hatcher | .10 | .05 |
| ❑ 71 Sergei Gonchar | .15 | .05 |
| ❑ 72 Adam Deadmarsh | .15 | .07 |
| ❑ 73 Jyrki Lumme | .10 | .05 |
| ❑ 74 Dino Ciccarelli | .15 | .07 |
| ❑ 75 Mike Gartner | .15 | .07 |
| ❑ 76 Todd Marchant | .10 | .05 |
| ❑ 77 Jason Wiemer | .10 | .05 |
| ❑ 78 Scott Mellanby | .10 | .05 |
| ❑ 79 Al MacInnis | .15 | .07 |
| ❑ 80 Glen Wesley | .10 | .05 |
| ❑ 81 Igor Larionov | .10 | .05 |
| ❑ 82 Eric Lacroix | .10 | .05 |
| ❑ 83 Mike Keane | .10 | .05 |
| ❑ 84 Vincent Damphousse | .15 | .07 |
| ❑ 85 Robert Kron | .10 | .05 |
| ❑ 86 Scott Stevens | .15 | .07 |
| ❑ 87 Don Beaupre | .10 | .05 |
| ❑ 88 Zigmund Palffy | .15 | .07 |
| ❑ 89 Kevin Lowe | .10 | .05 |
| ❑ 90 Tommy Soderstrom | .10 | .05 |
| ❑ 91 Glenn Healy | .15 | .07 |
| ❑ 92 Randy McKay | .10 | .05 |
| ❑ 93 Sean Hill | .10 | .05 |
| ❑ 94 Brian Savage | .15 | .07 |
| ❑ 95 Ron Hextall | .15 | .07 |
| ❑ 96 Darryl Sydor | .10 | .05 |
| ❑ 97 Tom Barrasso | .15 | .07 |
| ❑ 98 Andrei Nikolishin | .10 | .05 |
| ❑ 99 Viktor Kozlov | .10 | .05 |
| ❑ 100 Rob Niedermayer | .15 | .07 |
| ❑ 101 Wayne Gretzky | 2.00 | .90 |
| ❑ 102 Shaun Van Allen | .10 | .05 |
| ❑ 103 Dave Manson | .10 | .05 |
| ❑ 104 Donald Audette | .15 | .05 |
| ❑ 105 Daren Puppa | .15 | .05 |
| ❑ 106 Jeremy Roenick | .30 | .14 |
| ❑ 107 Ken Wregget | .15 | .05 |
| ❑ 108 Mike Modano | .40 | .18 |
| ❑ 109 Rod Brind'Amour | .15 | .07 |
| ❑ 110 Eric Desjardins | .10 | .05 |
| ❑ 111 Pat Verbeek | .15 | .07 |
| ❑ 112 Jeff Beukeboom | .10 | .05 |
| ❑ 113 John Druce | .10 | .05 |
| ❑ 114 Andy Moog | .15 | .07 |
| ❑ 115 Turner Stevenson | .10 | .05 |
| ❑ 116 Alexander Selivanov | .10 | .05 |
| ❑ 117 Neal Broten | .15 | .07 |
| ❑ 118 Nikolai Khabibulin | .15 | .07 |
| ❑ 119 Claude Lemieux | .15 | .07 |
| ❑ 120 Sergei Brylin | .10 | .05 |
| ❑ 121 Bob Corkum | .10 | .05 |
| ❑ 122 Kelly Hrudey | .15 | .07 |
| ❑ 123 Jason Dawe | .10 | .05 |
| ❑ 124 Sean Burke | .15 | .07 |
| ❑ 125 Dave Gagner | .15 | .07 |
| ❑ 126 Kirk Maltby | .10 | .05 |
| ❑ 127 Ian Laperriere | .10 | .05 |
| ❑ 128 Slava Kozlov | .15 | .07 |
| ❑ 129 Vladimir Konstantinov | .10 | .05 |
| ❑ 130 Kenny Jonsson | .10 | .05 |
| ❑ 131 Sylvain Lefebvre | .10 | .05 |
| ❑ 132 Kirk McLean | .15 | .07 |
| ❑ 133 Brian Leetch | .30 | .14 |
| ❑ 134 Olaf Kolzig | .15 | .07 |
| ❑ 135 Patrick Poulin | .10 | .05 |
| ❑ 136 Tim Cheveldae | .15 | .07 |
| ❑ 137 Gary Roberts | .15 | .07 |
| ❑ 138 Jim Carey | .30 | .14 |
| ❑ 139 Dominik Hasek | .60 | .25 |
| ❑ 140 Josef Beranek | .10 | .05 |
| ❑ 141 Don Sweeney | .10 | .05 |
| ❑ 142 Felix Potvin | .30 | .14 |
| ❑ 143 Guy Hebert | .15 | .07 |
| ❑ 144 Guy Carbonneau | .10 | .05 |
| ❑ 145 Mikhail Shtalenkov | .10 | .05 |
| ❑ 146 Kevin Miller | .10 | .05 |

| | MINT | NRMT |
|---|---|---|
| ❑ 147 Blaine Lacher | .15 | .07 |
| ❑ 148 Craig MacTavish | .10 | .05 |
| ❑ 149 Derek Plante | .10 | .05 |
| ❑ 150 Kevin Dineen | .10 | .05 |
| ❑ 151 Trevor Kidd | .15 | .07 |
| ❑ 152 Sergei Nemchinov | .10 | .05 |
| ❑ 153 Ed Belfour | .30 | .14 |
| ❑ 154 Sergei Krivokrasov | .10 | .05 |
| ❑ 155 Mike Rathje | .10 | .05 |
| ❑ 156 Mike Donnelly | .10 | .05 |
| ❑ 157 David Roberts | .10 | .05 |
| ❑ 158 Jocelyn Thibault | .30 | .14 |
| ❑ 159 Tie Domi | .15 | .07 |
| ❑ 160 Chris Osgood | .30 | .14 |
| ❑ 161 Martin Gelinas | .10 | .05 |
| ❑ 162 Scott Thornton | .10 | .05 |
| ❑ 163 Bob Rouse | .10 | .05 |
| ❑ 164 Randy Wood | .10 | .05 |
| ❑ 165 Chris Therien | .10 | .05 |
| ❑ 166 Steven Rice | .10 | .05 |
| ❑ 167 Scott Lachance | .10 | .05 |
| ❑ 168 Petr Svoboda | .10 | .05 |
| ❑ 169 Patrick Roy | 1.50 | .70 |
| ❑ 170 Norm Maciver | .10 | .05 |
| ❑ 171 Todd Gill | .10 | .05 |
| ❑ 172 Brian Rolston | .15 | .07 |
| ❑ 173 Wade Flaherty | .15 | .07 |
| ❑ 174 Valeri Bure | .15 | .07 |
| ❑ 175 Mark Fitzpatrick | .10 | .05 |
| ❑ 176 Darren McCarty | .15 | .07 |
| ❑ 177 Ken Daneyko | .10 | .05 |
| ❑ 178 Yves Racine | .10 | .05 |
| ❑ 179 Murray Craven | .10 | .05 |
| ❑ 180 Nicklas Lidstrom | .15 | .05 |
| ❑ 181 Gord Murphy | .10 | .05 |
| ❑ 182 Eric Weinrich | .10 | .05 |
| ❑ 183 Todd Krygier | .10 | .05 |
| ❑ 184 Cliff Ronning | .15 | .05 |
| ❑ 185 Mariusz Czerkawski | .10 | .05 |
| ❑ 186 Benoit Hogue | .10 | .05 |
| ❑ 187 Richard Smehlik | .10 | .05 |
| ❑ 188 Jeff Norton | .10 | .05 |
| ❑ 189 Steve Chiasson | .10 | .05 |
| ❑ 190 Andrei Nazarov | .10 | .05 |
| ❑ 191 Steve Smith | .10 | .05 |
| ❑ 192 Mario Lemieux | 1.50 | .70 |
| ❑ 193 Trent Klatt | .10 | .05 |
| ❑ 194 Valeri Zelepukin | .10 | .05 |
| ❑ 195 Adam Foote | .10 | .05 |
| ❑ 196 Lyle Odelein | .10 | .05 |
| ❑ 197 Keith Primeau | .15 | .07 |
| ❑ 198 Rob Blake | .15 | .07 |
| ❑ 199 Dave Lowry | .10 | .05 |
| ❑ 200 Adam Burt | .10 | .05 |
| ❑ 201 Martin Gendron | .10 | .05 |
| ❑ 202 Tommy Salo | .40 | .18 |
| ❑ 203 Eric Daze | .30 | .14 |
| ❑ 204 Ryan Smyth | .30 | .14 |
| ❑ 205 Brian Holzinger | .30 | .14 |
| ❑ 206 Chris Marinucci | .10 | .05 |
| ❑ 207 Jason Bonsignore | .10 | .05 |
| ❑ 208 Craig Johnson | .10 | .05 |
| ❑ 209 Steve Larouche | .10 | .05 |
| ❑ 210 Chris McAlpine | .10 | .05 |
| ❑ 211 Shean Donovan | .10 | .05 |
| ❑ 212 Cory Stillman | .10 | .05 |
| ❑ 213 Craig Darby | .10 | .05 |
| ❑ 214 Philippe DeRouville | .10 | .05 |
| ❑ 215 Kevin Brown | .10 | .05 |
| ❑ 216 Manny Fernandez | .15 | .07 |
| ❑ 217 Radim Bicanek | .10 | .05 |
| ❑ 218 Craig Conroy | .10 | .05 |
| ❑ 219 Todd Warriner | .10 | .05 |
| ❑ 220 Richard Park | .10 | .05 |
| ❑ 221 Checklist | .10 | .05 |
| ❑ 222 Checklist | .10 | .05 |
| ❑ 223 Checklist | .10 | .05 |
| ❑ 224 Checklist | .10 | .05 |
| ❑ 225 Checklist | .10 | .05 |

## 1995-96 Pinnacle Artist's Proofs

This 225-card set is a high-end parallel of the standard Pinnacle issue. The cards utilize the same Dufex technology as the Rink Collection cards, but have the Artist's Proof logo embossed on, typically in the lower right corner. On some cards, this can be very difficult to detect: collectors should double check all dufexed cards before buying or selling to ensure which type they are. These cards were inserted at a rate of 1:48 packs.

| | MINT | NRMT |
|---|---|---|
| COMPLETE SET (225) | 2000.00 | 900.00 |
| COMMON CARD (1-225) | 4.00 | 1.80 |
| *STARS: 40X TO 100X BASIC CARDS | | |
| *YOUNG STARS: 25X TO 60X BASIC CARDS | | |

## 1995-96 Pinnacle Rink Collection

These 225 cards form a low-end parallel version of the Pinnacle set. The cards, which utilize the Dufex process, are difficult to distinguish from the very similar, but much more expensive Artist's Proof cards. Collectors are advised to carefully look for the embossed AP symbol in the lower right corner before buying or selling the 1995-96 Dufexed cards. The Rink Collection cards were inserted at a rate of 1:4 packs.

| | MINT | NRMT |
|---|---|---|
| COMPLETE SET (225) | 300.00 | 135.00 |
| COMMON CARD (1-225) | 1.00 | .45 |
| *STARS: 8X TO 20X BASIC CARDS | | |
| *YOUNG STARS: 5X TO 12X BASIC CARDS | | |

## 1995-96 Pinnacle Clear Shots

Fifteen veteran superstars are recognized in this set which is distinguished by its use of a clear plastic rainbow holographic printing technology. The cards were inserted at a rate of 1:60 hobby and retail packs.

| | MINT | NRMT |
|---|---|---|
| COMPLETE SET (15) | 200.00 | 90.00 |
| COMMON CARD (1-15) | 5.00 | 2.20 |
| ❑ 1 Martin Brodeur | 12.00 | 5.50 |
| ❑ 2 Brett Hull | 8.00 | 3.60 |
| ❑ 3 Paul Kariya | 20.00 | 9.00 |
| ❑ 4 Eric Lindros | 15.00 | 6.75 |
| ❑ 5 Cam Neely | 5.00 | 2.20 |
| ❑ 6 Doug Gilmour | 5.00 | 2.20 |
| ❑ 7 Sergei Fedorov | 10.00 | 4.50 |
| ❑ 8 Peter Forsberg | 15.00 | 6.75 |
| ❑ 9 Wayne Gretzky | 30.00 | 13.50 |
| ❑ 10 Patrick Roy | 25.00 | 11.00 |
| ❑ 11 Jaromir Jagr | 15.00 | 6.75 |
| ❑ 12 Pavel Bure | 10.00 | 4.50 |
| ❑ 13 Mario Lemieux | 25.00 | 11.00 |
| ❑ 14 Pierre Turgeon | 5.00 | 2.20 |
| ❑ 15 Dominik Hasek | 10.00 | 4.50 |

## 1995-96 Pinnacle First Strike

This 15-card set focusing on gamebreaking players is enhanced by the use of spot micro-etch technology. The cards were randomly inserted at a rate of 1:24 retail packs only.

| | MINT | NRMT |
|---|---|---|
| COMPLETE SET (15) | 150.00 | 70.00 |
| COMMON CARD (1-15) | 2.50 | 1.10 |
| ❑ 1 Mark Messier | 4.00 | 1.80 |
| ❑ 2 Wayne Gretzky | 20.00 | 9.00 |
| ❑ 3 Doug Gilmour | 3.00 | 1.35 |
| ❑ 4 Patrick Roy | 15.00 | 6.75 |
| ❑ 5 Cam Neely | 3.00 | 1.35 |
| ❑ 6 Brian Leetch | 3.00 | 1.35 |
| ❑ 7 Ed Belfour | 3.00 | 1.35 |
| ❑ 8 Wendel Clark | 2.50 | 1.10 |
| ❑ 9 Chris Chelios | 3.00 | 1.35 |
| ❑ 10 Claude Lemieux | 3.00 | 1.35 |
| ❑ 11 Peter Forsberg | 10.00 | 4.50 |
| ❑ 12 Brett Hull | 4.00 | 1.80 |
| ❑ 13 Mario Lemieux | 15.00 | 6.75 |
| ❑ 14 Dominik Hasek | 6.00 | 2.70 |
| ❑ 15 Theoren Fleury | 3.00 | 1.35 |

## 1995-96 Pinnacle Full Contact

This 12-card set used the spot micro-etch technology to bring out the best of the NHL's top bangers and bruisers. The cards were randomly inserted 1:9 retail jumbo packs.

| | MINT | NRMT |
|---|---|---|
| COMPLETE SET (12) | 50.00 | 22.00 |
| COMMON CARD (1-12) | 2.00 | .90 |
| ❑ 1 Cam Neely | 4.00 | 1.80 |
| ❑ 2 Scott Stevens | 2.00 | .90 |
| ❑ 3 Owen Nolan | 4.00 | 1.80 |
| ❑ 4 Jeremy Roenick | 6.00 | 2.70 |
| ❑ 5 Brendan Shanahan | 12.00 | 5.50 |

| | MINT | NRMT |
|---|---|---|
| ❑ 6 Chris Chelios | 6.00 | 2.70 |
| ❑ 7 Brett Lindros | 2.00 | .90 |
| ❑ 8 Jason Arnott | 4.00 | 1.80 |
| ❑ 9 Tie Domi | 2.00 | .90 |
| ❑ 10 Mark Tinordi | 2.00 | .90 |
| ❑ 11 Keith Tkachuk | 8.00 | 3.60 |
| ❑ 12 Mark Messier | 8.00 | 3.60 |

## 1995-96 Pinnacle Global Gold

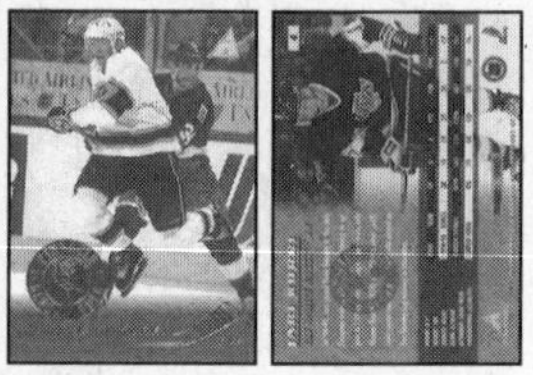

These 25 cards set were randomly inserted into Pinnacle International boxes at a rate of 1:6 packs. These cards are identical to the ones found in the Pinnacle U.S. basic set, save for the circular gold-foil stamp on the front that reads, "Global Gold", and the numbering on the back reading "X of 25" instead of the regular card number.

| | MINT | NRMT |
|---|---|---|
| COMPLETE SET (25) | 25.00 | 11.00 |
| COMMON CARD (1-25) | .50 | .23 |
| ❑ 1 Pavel Bure | 4.00 | 1.80 |
| ❑ 2 Jaromir Jagr | 8.00 | 3.60 |
| ❑ 3 Mats Sundin | 1.50 | .70 |
| ❑ 4 Jari Kurri | 1.00 | .45 |
| ❑ 5 Mikael Renberg | 1.00 | .45 |
| ❑ 6 Radek Bonk | .50 | .23 |
| ❑ 7 Sergei Fedorov | 5.00 | 2.20 |
| ❑ 8 Uwe Krupp | .50 | .23 |
| ❑ 9 German Titov | .50 | .23 |
| ❑ 10 Esa Tikkanen | .75 | .35 |
| ❑ 11 Oleg Tverdovsky | .75 | .35 |
| ❑ 12 Teppo Numminen | .50 | .23 |
| ❑ 13 Jyrki Lumme | .50 | .23 |
| ❑ 14 Zigmund Palffy | 1.50 | .70 |
| ❑ 15 Tommy Soderstrom | .75 | .35 |
| ❑ 16 Viktor Kozlov | .50 | .23 |
| ❑ 17 Alexander Selivanov | .75 | .35 |
| ❑ 18 Sergei Brylin | .50 | .23 |
| ❑ 19 Dominik Hasek | 4.00 | 1.80 |
| ❑ 20 Sergei Nemchinov | .50 | .23 |
| ❑ 21 Petr Svoboda | .50 | .23 |
| ❑ 22 Valeri Bure | .50 | .23 |
| ❑ 23 Nicklas Lidstrom | .75 | .35 |
| ❑ 24 Mariusz Czerkawski | .50 | .23 |
| ❑ 25 Valeri Zelepukin | .50 | .23 |

## 1995-96 Pinnacle Masks

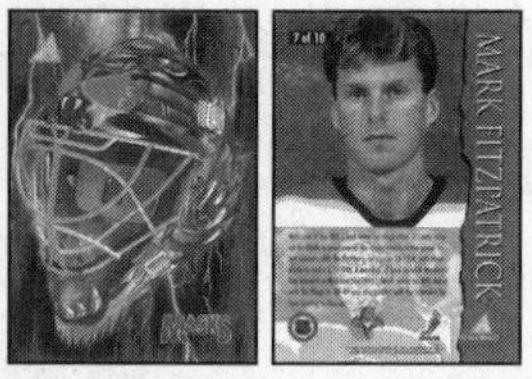


This popular Dufex set returns for the third year to spotlight the unique and colorful world of protection NHL style. No team or player names appear on the front. The cards were randomly inserted at the rate of 1:90 retail and hobby packs.

| | MINT | NRMT |
|---|---|---|
| COMPLETE SET (10) | 300.00 | 135.00 |
| COMMON CARD (1-10) | 25.00 | 11.00 |
| ❑ 1 Blaine Lacher | 25.00 | 11.00 |
| ❑ 2 Martin Brodeur | 100.00 | 45.00 |
| ❑ 3 Jim Carey | 25.00 | 11.00 |
| ❑ 4 Felix Potvin | 25.00 | 11.00 |
| ❑ 5 Andy Moog | 25.00 | 11.00 |
| ❑ 6 Mike Vernon | 25.00 | 11.00 |
| ❑ 7 Mark Fitzpatrick | 25.00 | 11.00 |
| ❑ 8 Ron Hextall | 25.00 | 11.00 |
| ❑ 9 Sean Burke | 25.00 | 11.00 |
| ❑ 10 Jocelyn Thibault | 25.00 | 11.00 |

## 1995-96 Pinnacle Roaring 20s

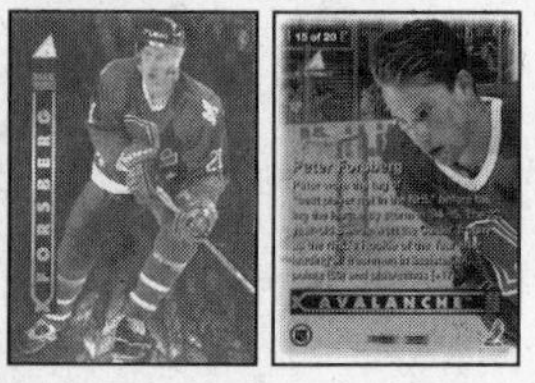


This 20-card set highlights the young guns of the NHL. The cards benefit from the use of the spot micro-etch technology and were randomly inserted in 1:19 hobby packs.

| | MINT | NRMT |
|---|---|---|
| COMPLETE SET (20) | 100.00 | 45.00 |
| COMMON CARD (1-20) | 2.50 | 1.10 |
| ❑ 1 Eric Lindros | 10.00 | 4.50 |
| ❑ 2 Paul Kariya | 12.00 | 5.50 |
| ❑ 3 Martin Brodeur | 8.00 | 3.60 |
| ❑ 4 Jeremy Roenick | 3.00 | 1.35 |
| ❑ 5 Mike Modano | 4.00 | 1.80 |
| ❑ 6 Sergei Fedorov | 6.00 | 2.70 |
| ❑ 7 Mats Sundin | 2.50 | 1.10 |
| ❑ 8 Pavel Bure | 6.00 | 2.70 |
| ❑ 9 Jim Carey | 3.00 | 1.35 |
| ❑ 10 Felix Potvin | 3.00 | 1.35 |
| ❑ 11 Alexei Zhamnov | 2.50 | 1.10 |
| ❑ 12 Mikael Renberg | 2.50 | 1.10 |
| ❑ 13 Jaromir Jagr | 10.00 | 4.50 |
| ❑ 14 Peter Bondra | 2.50 | 1.10 |
| ❑ 15 Peter Forsberg | 10.00 | 4.50 |
| ❑ 16 John LeClair | 5.00 | 2.20 |
| ❑ 17 Joe Sakic | 6.00 | 2.70 |
| ❑ 18 Brendan Shanahan | 6.00 | 2.70 |
| ❑ 19 Teemu Selanne | 6.00 | 2.70 |
| ❑ 20 Pierre Turgeon | 2.50 | 1.10 |

## 1995-96 Pinnacle Fantasy

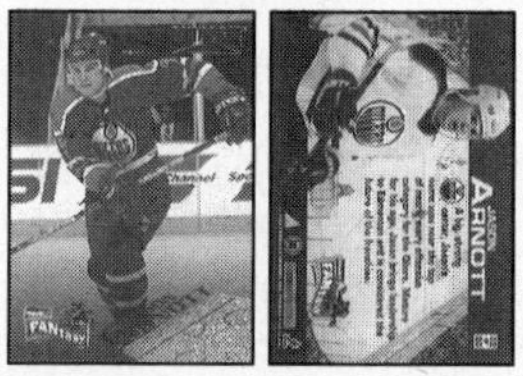


This 30-card set was distributed as a promotional item at the 1996 All-Star FanFest in Boston and features players from that game as well as four extra Boston Bruins. The cards were available in 2-card packs, free for the asking. Pinnacle later handed out remaining packs at several large sportscard conventions in Canada and the U.S. Card #31 features Bobby Orr and injured collegiate player Travis Roy. This tribute card was shortprinted, and the set is considered complete without it.

| | MINT | NRMT |
|---|---|---|
| COMPLETE SET (30) | 45.00 | 20.00 |
| COMMON CARD (1-30) | .35 | .16 |
| ❑ 1 Cam Neely | .75 | .35 |
| ❑ 2 Ray Bourque | 1.00 | .45 |
| ❑ 3 Alexandre Daigle | .35 | .16 |
| ❑ 4 Mariusz Czerkawski | .35 | .16 |
| ❑ 5 Adam Oates | .50 | .23 |
| ❑ 6 Brendan Shanahan | 3.00 | 1.35 |
| ❑ 7 Arturs Irbe | .50 | .23 |
| ❑ 8 Mario Lemieux | 8.00 | 3.60 |
| ❑ 9 Theoren Fleury | .50 | .23 |
| ❑ 10 Patrick Roy | 8.00 | 3.60 |
| ❑ 11 Roman Hamrlik | .50 | .23 |
| ❑ 12 Pavel Bure | 3.00 | 1.35 |
| ❑ 13 Wayne Gretzky | 10.00 | 4.50 |
| ❑ 14 Mike Modano | .50 | .23 |
| ❑ 15 Teemu Selanne | 3.00 | 1.35 |
| ❑ 16 John Vanbiesbrouck | 4.00 | 1.80 |
| ❑ 17 Dominik Hasek | 3.00 | 1.35 |
| ❑ 18 Mark Messier | 2.50 | 1.10 |
| ❑ 19 Martin Brodeur | 3.00 | 1.35 |
| ❑ 20 Jim Carey | 2.00 | .90 |
| ❑ 21 Wendel Clark | .35 | .16 |
| ❑ 22 Jason Arnott | .75 | .35 |
| ❑ 23 Jeremy Roenick | 1.50 | .70 |
| ❑ 24 Brett Hull | 2.50 | 1.10 |
| ❑ 25 Peter Forsberg | 6.00 | 2.70 |
| ❑ 26 Paul Kariya | 6.00 | 2.70 |
| ❑ 27 Eric Lindros | 6.00 | 2.70 |
| ❑ 28 Kevin Stevens | .35 | .16 |
| ❑ 29 Felix Potvin | 2.50 | 1.10 |
| ❑ 30 Sergei Fedorov | 3.00 | 1.35 |
| ❑ 31 Travis Roy Bobby Orr SP | 20.00 | 9.00 |

## 1996-97 Pinnacle

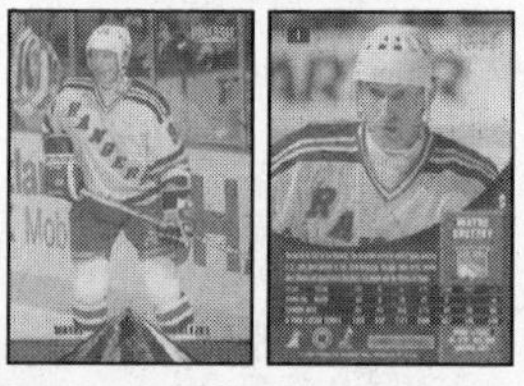

This 250-card set was distributed in 10-card packs with a suggested retail price of $2.49. The set featured color action player photos with player statistics and included a rookie subset plus three numerical checklist cards. Rookies of note include Ethan Moreau and Kevin Hodson.

| | MINT | NRMT |
|---|---|---|
| COMPLETE SET (250) | 20.00 | 9.00 |
| COMMON CARD (1-250) | .10 | .05 |
| COMP.FOIL SET (250) | 30.00 | 13.50 |
| COMMON FOIL (1-250) | .15 | .07 |
| *FOIL STARS: 1.5X BASIC CARDS | | |
| COMP.PRM.STOCK SET (250) | 60.00 | 27.00 |
| COMMON PRM.STOCK (1-250) | .25 | .11 |
| *PRM.STOCK: 1.5X TO 3X BASIC CARDS | | |
| ❑ 1 Wayne Gretzky | 3.00 | 1.35 |
| ❑ 2 Mark Messier | .50 | .23 |
| ❑ 3 Kevin Hatcher | .10 | .05 |
| ❑ 4 Scott Stevens | .25 | .11 |
| ❑ 5 Derek Plante | .10 | .05 |
| ❑ 6 Theoren Fleury | .25 | .11 |
| ❑ 7 Brian Rolston | .10 | .05 |
| ❑ 8 Teppo Numminen | .10 | .05 |
| ❑ 9 Adam Graves | .25 | .11 |
| ❑ 10 Jason Dawe | .10 | .05 |
| ❑ 11 Sergei Nemchinov | .10 | .05 |
| ❑ 12 Jeff Brown | .10 | .05 |
| ❑ 13 Alexei Zhamnov | .25 | .11 |
| ❑ 14 Paul Coffey | .40 | .18 |
| ❑ 15 Kevin Miller | .10 | .05 |
| ❑ 16 Mike Vernon | .25 | .11 |
| ❑ 17 Brian Bradley | .10 | .05 |
| ❑ 18 Jeff Friesen | .25 | .11 |
| ❑ 19 Phil Housley | .25 | .11 |
| ❑ 20 Ray Whitney | .10 | .05 |
| ❑ 21 Sergei Fedorov | .60 | .25 |
| ❑ 22 Pierre Turgeon | .25 | .11 |
| ❑ 23 Rick Tocchet | .25 | .11 |
| ❑ 24 Uwe Krupp | .10 | .05 |
| ❑ 25 Steve Yzerman | 1.25 | .55 |
| ❑ 26 Tom Chorske | .10 | .05 |
| ❑ 27 Pat LaFontaine | .25 | .11 |
| ❑ 28 Nicklas Lidstrom | .25 | .11 |
| ❑ 29 Ray Ferraro | .10 | .05 |
| ❑ 30 Brian Noonan | .10 | .05 |
| ❑ 31 Dino Ciccarelli | .25 | .11 |
| ❑ 32 Rob Niedermayer | .25 | .11 |
| ❑ 33 Stephane Richer | .25 | .11 |
| ❑ 34 Chris Chelios | .40 | .18 |
| ❑ 35 Mike Gartner | .25 | .11 |
| ❑ 36 German Titov | .10 | .05 |
| ❑ 37 Sean Burke | .25 | .11 |
| ❑ 38 Robert Svehla | .10 | .05 |
| ❑ 39 Dave Gagner | .25 | .11 |
| ❑ 40 Sergei Gonchar | .10 | .05 |
| ❑ 41 Bernie Nicholls | .10 | .05 |
| ❑ 42 Yanic Perreault | .10 | .05 |
| ❑ 43 Adam Deadmarsh | .25 | .11 |
| ❑ 44 Dale Hawerchuk | .25 | .11 |
| ❑ 45 Alexei Kovalev | .10 | .05 |
| ❑ 46 Esa Tikkanen | .10 | .05 |
| ❑ 47 Valeri Kamensky | .25 | .11 |
| ❑ 48 Craig Janney | .25 | .11 |
| ❑ 49 John LeClair | .60 | .25 |
| ❑ 50 Radek Bonk | .10 | .05 |
| ❑ 51 David Oliver | .10 | .05 |
| ❑ 52 Todd Harvey | .10 | .05 |
| ❑ 53 Steve Thomas | .10 | .05 |
| ❑ 54 Tony Amonte | .25 | .11 |
| ❑ 55 Mikael Renberg | .25 | .11 |
| ❑ 56 Brendan Shanahan | .75 | .35 |
| ❑ 57 Tom Fitzgerald | .10 | .05 |
| ❑ 58 Chris Pronger | .25 | .11 |
| ❑ 59 Donald Audette | .25 | .11 |
| ❑ 60 Nelson Emerson | .10 | .05 |
| ❑ 61 Joe Mullen | .25 | .11 |
| ❑ 62 Marty McInnis | .10 | .05 |
| ❑ 63 Martin Rucinsky | .10 | .05 |
| ❑ 64 Mark Recchi | .25 | .11 |
| ❑ 65 Vladimir Konstantinov | .10 | .05 |
| ❑ 66 Rick Tabaracci | .25 | .11 |
| ❑ 67 Marty McSorley | .10 | .05 |
| ❑ 68 Pat Verbeek | .10 | .05 |
| ❑ 69 Garry Galley | .10 | .05 |
| ❑ 70 Travis Green | .25 | .11 |
| ❑ 71 Chris Tancill | .10 | .05 |
| ❑ 72 Vincent Damphousse | .25 | .11 |
| ❑ 73 Benoit Hogue | .10 | .05 |
| ❑ 74 Igor Larionov | .10 | .05 |
| ❑ 75 Russ Courtnall | .10 | .05 |
| ❑ 76 Mike Hough | .10 | .05 |
| ❑ 77 Alexander Selivanov | .10 | .05 |
| ❑ 78 Peter Forsberg | 1.25 | .55 |
| ❑ 79 Petr Klima | .10 | .05 |
| ❑ 80 Adam Creighton | .10 | .05 |
| ❑ 81 Dave Lowry | .10 | .05 |
| ❑ 82 Andrew Cassels | .10 | .05 |
| ❑ 83 Martin Gelinas | .10 | .05 |
| ❑ 84 Bob Probert | .25 | .11 |
| ❑ 85 Calle Johansson | .10 | .05 |
| ❑ 86 Mario Lemieux | 2.00 | .90 |
| ❑ 87 Alexander Mogilny | .25 | .11 |
| ❑ 88 Guy Hebert | .25 | .11 |
| ❑ 89 Bill Ranford | .25 | .11 |
| ❑ 90 Kirk McLean | .25 | .11 |
| ❑ 91 Kenny Jonsson | .10 | .05 |
| ❑ 92 Martin Brodeur | 1.00 | .45 |
| ❑ 93 Keith Jones | .10 | .05 |
| ❑ 94 Ed Belfour | .40 | .18 |
| ❑ 95 Tom Barrasso | .25 | .11 |
| ❑ 96 Felix Potvin | .40 | .18 |
| ❑ 97 Daren Puppa | .25 | .11 |
| ❑ 98 Jeremy Roenick | .40 | .18 |
| ❑ 99 Chris Osgood UER Kevin Hodson pictured on back | .40 | .18 |
| ❑ 100 Zigmund Palffy | .40 | .18 |
| ❑ 101 Ron Hextall | .25 | .11 |
| ❑ 102 Jaromir Jagr | 1.25 | .55 |
| ❑ 103 Chris Terreri | .25 | .11 |
| ❑ 104 Shayne Corson | .10 | .05 |
| ❑ 105 Jim Carey | .40 | .18 |
| ❑ 106 Dominik Hasek | .75 | .35 |
| ❑ 107 Eric Lindros | 1.25 | .55 |
| ❑ 108 Petr Nedved | .25 | .11 |
| ❑ 109 Peter Bondra | .40 | .18 |
| ❑ 110 Jeff Hackett | .25 | .11 |
| ❑ 111 Trevor Linden | .25 | .11 |
| ❑ 112 Mike Richter | .40 | .18 |
| ❑ 113 Claude Lemieux | .25 | .11 |
| ❑ 114 Keith Tkachuk | .50 | .23 |
| ❑ 115 Pat Falloon | .10 | .05 |
| ❑ 116 Brent Fedyk | .10 | .05 |
| ❑ 117 Todd Marchant | .10 | .05 |
| ❑ 118 Jason Arnott | .25 | .11 |
| ❑ 119 Zarley Zalapski | .10 | .05 |
| ❑ 120 Kelly Hrudey | .25 | .11 |
| ❑ 121 Alexei Yashin | .25 | .11 |
| ❑ 122 Sergei Zubov | .10 | .05 |
| ❑ 123 Rod Brind'Amour | .25 | .11 |
| ❑ 124 Mathieu Schneider | .10 | .05 |
| ❑ 125 Bryan Smolinski | .10 | .05 |
| ❑ 126 Scott Mellanby | .25 | .11 |
| ❑ 127 Doug Gilmour | .40 | .18 |
| ❑ 128 Brett Hull | .50 | .23 |
| ❑ 129 Vyacheslav Kozlov | .10 | .05 |
| ❑ 130 Adam Oates | .25 | .11 |
| ❑ 131 Steve Konowalchuk | .10 | .05 |
| ❑ 132 Robert Kron | .10 | .05 |
| ❑ 133 Alexandre Daigle | .10 | .05 |
| ❑ 134 Brian Savage | .10 | .05 |
| ❑ 135 Stu Barnes | .10 | .05 |
| ❑ 136 Cam Neely | .25 | .11 |
| ❑ 137 Steve Rucchin | .10 | .05 |
| ❑ 138 Patrick Roy | 2.00 | .90 |
| ❑ 139 Roman Oksiuta | .10 | .05 |
| ❑ 140 Greg Johnson | .10 | .05 |
| ❑ 141 Chris Gratton | .25 | .11 |
| ❑ 142 Jocelyn Thibault | .40 | .18 |
| ❑ 143 Ron Francis | .25 | .11 |
| ❑ 144 Mats Sundin | .25 | .11 |
| ❑ 145 Oleg Tverdovsky | .25 | .11 |
| ❑ 146 Geoff Courtnall | .10 | .05 |
| ❑ 147 Kirk Muller | .10 | .05 |
| ❑ 148 Zdeno Ciger | .10 | .05 |
| ❑ 149 John MacLean | .25 | .11 |
| ❑ 150 Damian Rhodes | .25 | .11 |
| ❑ 151 Michael Nylander | .10 | .05 |
| ❑ 152 Andrei Kovalenko | .10 | .05 |
| ❑ 153 Al MacInnis | .25 | .11 |
| ❑ 154 Mike Modano | .50 | .23 |
| ❑ 155 Teemu Selanne | .75 | .35 |
| ❑ 156 Tomas Sandstrom | .10 | .05 |
| ❑ 157 Bobby Dollas | .10 | .05 |
| ❑ 158 Doug Weight | .25 | .11 |
| ❑ 159 Sandis Ozolinsh | .25 | .11 |
| ❑ 160 Joe Juneau | .10 | .05 |
| ❑ 161 Nikolai Khabibulin | .25 | .11 |
| ❑ 162 Murray Craven | .10 | .05 |
| ❑ 163 Cliff Ronning | .10 | .05 |
| ❑ 164 Curtis Joseph | .40 | .18 |
| ❑ 165 Darren Turcotte | .10 | .05 |
| ❑ 166 Andy Moog | .25 | .11 |
| ❑ 167 Mariusz Czerkawski | .10 | .05 |
| ❑ 168 Keith Primeau | .25 | .11 |
| ❑ 169 Eric Desjardins | .25 | .11 |
| ❑ 170 Bill Guerin | .10 | .05 |
| ❑ 171 Glenn Anderson | .25 | .11 |
| ❑ 172 Mike Ridley | .10 | .05 |
| ❑ 173 Michal Pivonka | .10 | .05 |
| ❑ 174 Trevor Kidd | .25 | .11 |
| ❑ 175 Pavel Bure | .75 | .35 |
| ❑ 176 Todd Gill | .10 | .05 |
| ❑ 177 Dave Andreychuk | .25 | .11 |
| ❑ 178 Roman Hamrlik | .25 | .11 |
| ❑ 179 Andrei Nikolishin | .10 | .05 |
| ❑ 180 Alexei Zhitnik | .10 | .05 |
| ❑ 181 Grant Fuhr | .25 | .11 |
| ❑ 182 Dave Reid | .10 | .05 |
| ❑ 183 Joe Nieuwendyk | .25 | .11 |
| ❑ 184 Paul Kariya | 1.50 | .70 |
| ❑ 185 Jyrki Lumme | .10 | .05 |
| ❑ 186 Owen Nolan | .25 | .11 |
| ❑ 187 Geoff Sanderson | .25 | .11 |
| ❑ 188 Alexander Semak | .10 | .05 |
| ❑ 189 Larry Murphy | .25 | .11 |
| ❑ 190 Dimitri Khristich | .10 | .05 |
| ❑ 191 Shane Churla | .10 | .05 |
| ❑ 192 Bill Lindsay | .10 | .05 |
| ❑ 193 Brian Leetch | .40 | .18 |
| ❑ 194 Greg Adams | .10 | .05 |
| ❑ 195 Gary Suter | .10 | .05 |
| ❑ 196 Wendel Clark | .25 | .11 |
| ❑ 197 Scott Young | .10 | .05 |
| ❑ 198 Randy Burridge | .10 | .05 |
| ❑ 199 Ray Bourque | .40 | .18 |
| ❑ 200 Joe Murphy | .10 | .05 |
| ❑ 201 Joe Sakic | .75 | .35 |
| ❑ 202 Saku Koivu | .60 | .25 |
| ❑ 203 John Vanbiesbrouck | .60 | .25 |
| ❑ 204 Ed Jovanovski | .25 | .11 |
| ❑ 205 Daniel Alfredsson | .25 | .11 |
| ❑ 206 Vitali Yachmenev | .10 | .05 |
| ❑ 207 Marcus Ragnarsson | .10 | .05 |
| ❑ 208 Todd Bertuzzi | .10 | .05 |
| ❑ 209 Valeri Bure | .25 | .11 |
| ❑ 210 Jeff O'Neill | .10 | .05 |
| ❑ 211 Corey Hirsch | .25 | .11 |
| ❑ 212 Eric Daze | .25 | .11 |
| ❑ 213 David Sacco | .10 | .05 |
| ❑ 214 Jan Vopat | .10 | .05 |
| ❑ 215 Scott Bailey | .10 | .05 |
| ❑ 216 Jamie Rivers | .10 | .05 |
| ❑ 217 Jose Theodore | .25 | .11 |
| ❑ 218 Peter Ferraro | .10 | .05 |
| ❑ 219 Anders Eriksson | .10 | .05 |
| ❑ 220 Wayne Primeau | .10 | .05 |
| ❑ 221 Denis Pederson | .10 | .05 |
| ❑ 222 Jay McKee | .10 | .05 |
| ❑ 223 Sean Pronger | .10 | .05 |
| ❑ 224 Martin Biron | .25 | .11 |
| ❑ 225 Marek Malik | .10 | .05 |
| ❑ 226 Steve Sullivan | .10 | .05 |
| ❑ 227 Curtis Brown | .10 | .05 |
| ❑ 228 Eric Fichaud | .25 | .11 |
| ❑ 229 Jan Caloun | .10 | .05 |
| ❑ 230 Niklas Sundblad | .10 | .05 |
| ❑ 231 Steve Staios | .10 | .05 |
| ❑ 232 Steve Washburn | .10 | .05 |
| ❑ 233 Chris Ferraro | .10 | .05 |
| ❑ 234 Marko Kiprusoff | .10 | .05 |
| ❑ 235 Larry Courville | .10 | .05 |
| ❑ 236 David Nemirovsky | .10 | .05 |
| ❑ 237 Ralph Intranuovo | .10 | .05 |
| ❑ 238 Kevin Hodson | .40 | .18 |
| ❑ 239 Ethan Moreau RC | .40 | .18 |
| ❑ 240 Daymond Langkow | .10 | .05 |
| ❑ 241 Brandon Convery | .10 | .05 |
| ❑ 242 Cale Hulse | .10 | .05 |
| ❑ 243 Zdenek Nedved | .10 | .05 |
| ❑ 244 Tommy Salo | .25 | .11 |
| ❑ 245 Nolan Baumgartner | .10 | .05 |
| ❑ 246 Patrick Labrecque | .10 | .05 |
| ❑ 247 Jamie Langenbrunner | .10 | .05 |
| ❑ 248 Pavel Bure CL (1-126) | .40 | .18 |
| ❑ 249 Peter Forsberg CL (127-250) | .40 | .18 |
| ❑ 250 Teemu Selanne CL (inserts) | .40 | .18 |

## 1996-97 Pinnacle Artist's Proofs

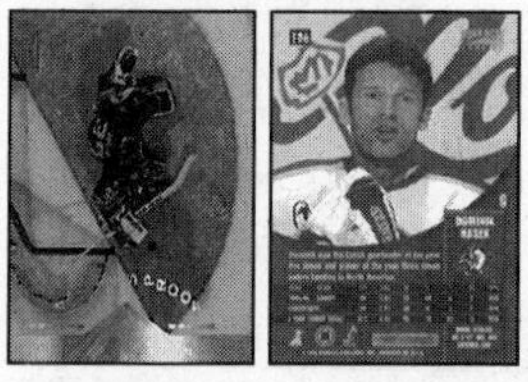

Randomly inserted in packs at a rate of one in 47, this 250-card parallel set was distinguishable from the regular set by the inclusion of a special holographic foil-stamped Artist's Proof logo.

| | MINT | NRMT |
|---|---|---|
| COMPLETE SET (250) | 2000.00 | 900.00 |
| COMMON CARD (1-250) | 4.00 | 1.80 |
| *STARS: 40X TO 80X BASIC CARDS | | |
| *YOUNG STARS: 25X TO 50X BASIC CARDS | | |

## 1996-97 Pinnacle Rink Collection

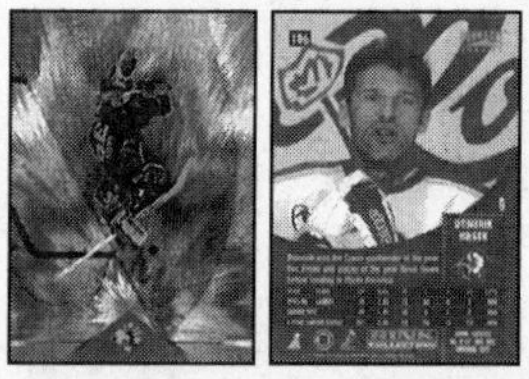

Randomly inserted in packs at a rate of one in seven, this 250-card parallel set was distinguished from the regular set through the use of the all-foil Dufex print technology. A Rink Collection logo is also found on the back of each card.

| | MINT | NRMT |
|---|---|---|
| COMPLETE SET (250) | 400.00 | 180.00 |
| COMMON CARD (1-250) | 1.50 | .70 |
| *STARS: 8X TO 20X BASIC CARDS | | |
| *YOUNG STARS: 7X TO 12X | | |

## 1996-97 Pinnacle By The Numbers

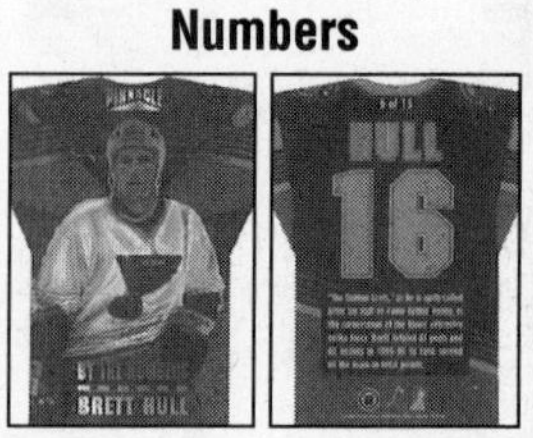


Randomly inserted in packs at a rate of one in 23, this 15-card, die-cut set honored the league's top statistical standouts. The etched metal, Dufex insert pictured the player with a likeness of his jersey serving as the background. The backs carried the reason for his selection to this insert set. The Brett Hull promo was not die-cut like the rest of the set. This design mirrored that which would later be used in the Premium Stock parallel version of this issue. The Hull is notable for the word PROMO written on the back.

| | MINT | NRMT |
|---|---|---|
| COMPLETE SET (15) | 120.00 | 55.00 |
| COMMON CARD (1-15) | 3.00 | 1.35 |
| ❑ 1 Teemu Selanne | 8.00 | 3.60 |
| ❑ 2 Brendan Shanahan | 8.00 | 3.60 |

| Card | MINT | NRMT |
|---|---|---|
| ❑ 3 Sergei Fedorov | 8.00 | 3.60 |
| ❑ 4 Ed Jovanovski | 4.00 | 1.80 |
| ❑ 5 Doug Weight | 4.00 | 1.80 |
| ❑ 6 Brett Hull | 5.00 | 2.20 |
| ❑ 7 Doug Gilmour | 4.00 | 1.80 |
| ❑ 8 Jaromir Jagr | 12.00 | 5.50 |
| ❑ 9 Wayne Gretzky | 25.00 | 11.00 |
| ❑ 10 Daniel Alfredsson | 4.00 | 1.80 |
| ❑ 11 Eric Daze | 4.00 | 1.80 |
| ❑ 12 Mark Messier | 5.00 | 2.20 |
| ❑ 13 Jocelyn Thibault | 4.00 | 1.80 |
| ❑ 14 Eric Lindros | 12.00 | 5.50 |
| ❑ 15 Pavel Bure | 8.00 | 3.60 |
| ❑ P1 Teemu Selanne promo | 5.00 | 2.20 |
| ❑ P16 Brett Hull promo | 3.00 | 1.35 |

## 1996-97 Pinnacle Masks

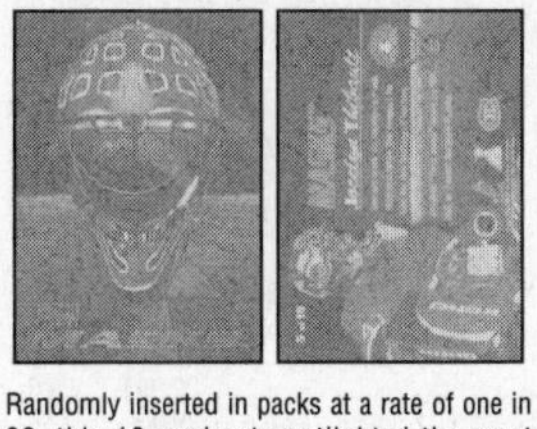

Randomly inserted in packs at a rate of one in 90, this 10-card set spotlighted the most colorful protective headgear worn in the NHL.

| | MINT | NRMT |
|---|---|---|
| COMPLETE SET (10) | 300.00 | 135.00 |
| COMMON CARD (1-10) | 15.00 | 6.75 |
| ❑ 1 Patrick Roy | 120.00 | 55.00 |
| ❑ 2 Jim Carey | 30.00 | 13.50 |
| ❑ 3 John Vanbiesbrouck | 40.00 | 18.00 |
| ❑ 4 Martin Brodeur | 60.00 | 27.00 |
| ❑ 5 Jocelyn Thibault | 25.00 | 11.00 |
| ❑ 6 Ron Hextall | 15.00 | 6.75 |
| ❑ 7 Nikolai Khabibulin | 15.00 | 6.75 |
| ❑ 8 Stephane Fiset | 15.00 | 6.75 |
| ❑ 9 Mike Richter | 25.00 | 11.00 |
| ❑ 10 Kelly Hrudey | 15.00 | 6.75 |

## 1996-97 Pinnacle Masks Die Cuts

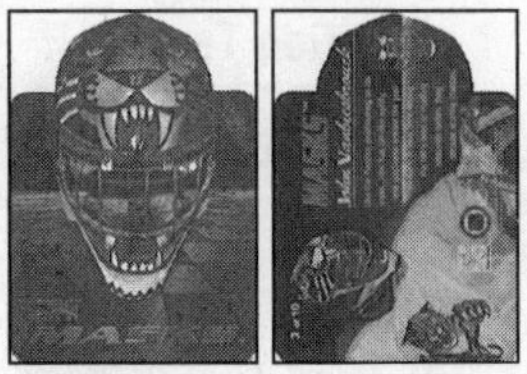

Randomly inserted in hobby packs only at a rate of one in 300, this very scarce 10-card parallel set was a die-cut version of the regular Masks insert set.

| | MINT | NRMT |
|---|---|---|
| COMPLETE SET (10) | 500.00 | 220.00 |
| COMMON CARD (1-10) | 25.00 | 11.00 |

*DIE CUT STARS: .75X TO 1.5X BASIC CARDS

## 1996-97 Pinnacle Team Pinnacle

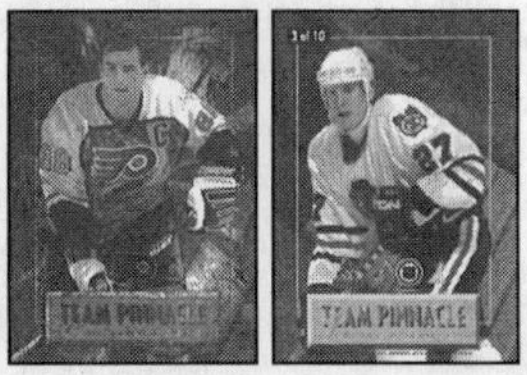

Randomly inserted in packs at a rate of one in 90, this 10-card set featured a double-front card design which showcased top players by position from both the Eastern and Western Conferences, back to back. One player from each conference was displayed on opposite sides of the cards, with one side also being enhanced with Dufex technology. Although a small premium might be attached to the card depending upon which side was Dufexed, this premium was not universally applied.

| | MINT | NRMT |
|---|---|---|
| COMPLETE SET (10) | 300.00 | 135.00 |
| COMMON CARD (1-10) | 15.00 | 6.75 |
| ❑ 1 Wayne Gretzky<br>Joe Sakic | 60.00 | 27.00 |
| ❑ 2 Mario Lemieux<br>Peter Forsberg | 50.00 | 22.00 |
| ❑ 3 Eric Lindros<br>Jeremy Roenick | 25.00 | 11.00 |
| ❑ 4 Mark Messier<br>Doug Weight | 15.00 | 6.75 |
| ❑ 5 Brendan Shanahan<br>Paul Kariya | 40.00 | 18.00 |
| ❑ 6 Jaromir Jagr<br>Brett Hull | 30.00 | 13.50 |
| ❑ 7 Ed Jovanovski<br>Paul Coffey | 15.00 | 6.75 |
| ❑ 8 John Vanbiesbrouck<br>Patrick Roy | 50.00 | 22.00 |
| ❑ 9 Martin Brodeur<br>Chris Osgood | 30.00 | 13.50 |
| ❑ 10 Saku Koivu<br>Eric Daze | 20.00 | 9.00 |

## 1996-97 Pinnacle Trophies

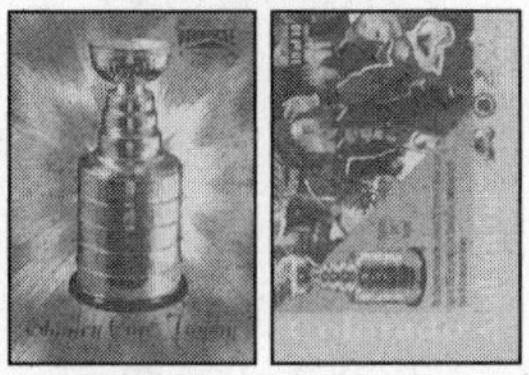

Randomly inserted only in prepriced magazine packs at a rate of one in 33, this 10-card set featured NHL trophies with the previous season's winners on the card backs. Card fronts were printed with Dufex technology and featured the trophy itself. The card backs featured the recipients.

| | MINT | NRMT |
|---|---|---|
| COMPLETE SET (10) | 300.00 | 135.00 |
| COMMON CARD (1-10) | 8.00 | 3.60 |
| ❑ 1 Mario Lemieux | 80.00 | 36.00 |
| ❑ 2 Paul Kariya | 60.00 | 27.00 |
| ❑ 3 Sergei Fedorov | 30.00 | 13.50 |
| ❑ 4 Daniel Alfredsson | 10.00 | 4.50 |
| ❑ 5 Jim Carey | 15.00 | 6.75 |
| ❑ 6 Chris Osgood<br>Mike Vernon | 30.00 | 13.50 |
| ❑ 7 Kris King | 8.00 | 3.60 |
| ❑ 8 Chris Chelios | 15.00 | 6.75 |
| ❑ 9 Joe Sakic | 30.00 | 13.50 |
| ❑ 10 Colorado Avalanche | 30.00 | 13.50 |

## 1997-98 Pinnacle

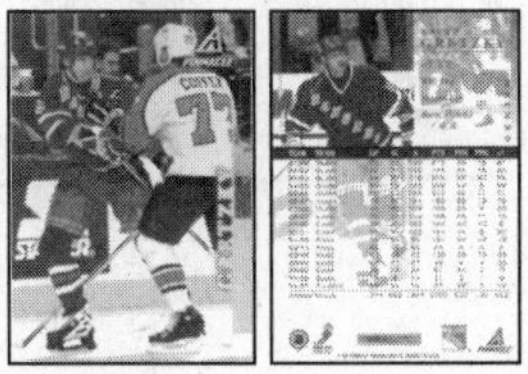

The 1997-98 Pinnacle set was issued in one series totalling 200 cards and was distributed in packs and collectible Mask tins. The fronts feature color action player photos. The backs carry player information.

| | MINT | NRMT |
|---|---|---|
| COMPLETE SET (200) | 25.00 | 11.00 |
| COMMON CARD (1-200) | .10 | .05 |
| ❑ 1 Espen Knutsen | .10 | .05 |
| ❑ 2 Juha Lind | .10 | .05 |
| ❑ 3 Erik Rasmussen | .10 | .05 |
| ❑ 4 Olli Jokinen | .60 | .25 |
| ❑ 5 Chris Phillips | .10 | .05 |
| ❑ 6 Alexei Morozov | .30 | .14 |
| ❑ 7 Chris Dingman | .10 | .05 |
| ❑ 8 Mattias Ohlund | .30 | .14 |
| ❑ 9 Sergei Samsonov | 1.00 | .45 |
| ❑ 10 Daniel Cleary | .30 | .14 |
| ❑ 11 Terry Ryan | .10 | .05 |
| ❑ 12 Patrick Marleau | .75 | .35 |
| ❑ 13 Boyd Devereaux | .10 | .05 |
| ❑ 14 Donald MacLean | .10 | .05 |
| ❑ 15 Marc Savard | .10 | .05 |
| ❑ 16 Magnus Arvedson | .10 | .05 |
| ❑ 17 Marian Hossa | 2.00 | .90 |
| ❑ 18 Alyn McCauley | .30 | .14 |
| ❑ 19 Vaclav Prospal | .50 | .23 |
| ❑ 20 Brad Isbister | .10 | .05 |
| ❑ 21 Robert Dome | .10 | .05 |
| ❑ 22 Kevyn Adams | .10 | .05 |
| ❑ 23 Joe Thornton | .75 | .35 |
| ❑ 24 Jan Bulis | .10 | .05 |
| ❑ 25 Jaroslav Svejkovsky | .30 | .14 |
| ❑ 26 Saku Koivu | .60 | .25 |
| ❑ 27 Mark Messier | .50 | .23 |
| ❑ 28 Dominik Hasek | .75 | .35 |
| ❑ 29 Patrick Roy | 2.00 | .90 |
| ❑ 30 Jaromir Jagr | 1.25 | .55 |
| ❑ 31 Jarome Iginla | .30 | .14 |
| ❑ 32 Joe Sakic | .75 | .35 |
| ❑ 33 Jeremy Roenick | .40 | .18 |
| ❑ 34 Chris Osgood | .40 | .18 |
| ❑ 35 Brett Hull | .50 | .23 |
| ❑ 36 Mike Vernon | .30 | .14 |
| ❑ 37 John Vanbiesbrouck | .60 | .25 |
| ❑ 38 Ray Bourque | .40 | .18 |
| ❑ 39 Doug Gilmour | .40 | .18 |
| ❑ 40 Keith Tkachuk | .50 | .23 |
| ❑ 41 Pavel Bure | .75 | .35 |
| ❑ 42 Sean Burke | .30 | .14 |
| ❑ 43 Martin Brodeur | 1.00 | .45 |
| ❑ 44 Damian Rhodes | .30 | .14 |
| ❑ 45 Geoff Sanderson | .30 | .14 |
| ❑ 46 Bill Ranford | .30 | .14 |
| ❑ 47 Kevin Hodson | .30 | .14 |
| ❑ 48 Eric Lindros | 1.25 | .55 |
| ❑ 49 Owen Nolan | .30 | .14 |
| ❑ 50 Mats Sundin | .40 | .18 |
| ❑ 51 Ed Belfour | .40 | .18 |
| ❑ 52 Stephane Fiset | .30 | .14 |
| ❑ 53 Paul Kariya | 1.50 | .70 |
| ❑ 54 Doug Weight | .30 | .14 |
| ❑ 55 Mike Richter | .40 | .18 |
| ❑ 56 Zigmund Palffy | .40 | .18 |
| ❑ 57 John LeClair | .60 | .25 |
| ❑ 58 Alexander Mogilny | .30 | .14 |
| ❑ 59 Tommy Salo | .30 | .14 |
| ❑ 60 Trevor Kidd | .30 | .14 |
| ❑ 61 Jason Arnott | .30 | .14 |
| ❑ 62 Adam Oates | .30 | .14 |
| ❑ 63 Garth Snow | .30 | .14 |
| ❑ 64 Rob Blake | .10 | .05 |
| ❑ 65 Chris Chelios | .40 | .18 |
| ❑ 66 Eric Fichaud | .30 | .14 |
| ❑ 67 Wayne Gretzky | 2.50 | 1.10 |
| ❑ 68 Dino Ciccarelli | .10 | .05 |
| ❑ 69 Pat LaFontaine | .30 | .14 |
| ❑ 70 Andy Moog | .30 | .14 |
| ❑ 71 Steve Yzerman | 1.25 | .55 |
| ❑ 72 Jeff Hackett | .30 | .14 |
| ❑ 73 Peter Forsberg | 1.25 | .55 |
| ❑ 74 Arturs Irbe | .30 | .14 |
| ❑ 75 Pierre Turgeon | .30 | .14 |
| ❑ 76 Tom Barrasso | .30 | .14 |
| ❑ 77 Sergei Fedorov | .75 | .35 |
| ❑ 78 Ron Francis | .30 | .14 |
| ❑ 79 Mike Dunham | .30 | .14 |
| ❑ 80 Brendan Shanahan | .75 | .35 |
| ❑ 81 Grant Fuhr | .30 | .14 |
| ❑ 82 Jamie Storr | .30 | .14 |
| ❑ 83 Jim Carey | .30 | .14 |
| ❑ 84 Daren Puppa | .30 | .14 |
| ❑ 85 Vincent Damphousse | .30 | .14 |
| ❑ 86 Teemu Selanne | .75 | .35 |
| ❑ 87 Dwayne Roloson | .30 | .14 |
| ❑ 88 Kirk McLean | .30 | .14 |
| ❑ 89 Olaf Kolzig | .30 | .14 |
| ❑ 90 Guy Hebert | .30 | .14 |
| ❑ 91 Mike Modano | .50 | .23 |
| ❑ 92 Brian Leetch | .40 | .18 |
| ❑ 93 Curtis Joseph | .40 | .18 |
| ❑ 94 Nikolai Khabibulin | .30 | .14 |
| ❑ 95 Felix Potvin | .40 | .18 |
| ❑ 96 Ken Wregget | .30 | .14 |
| ❑ 97 Steve Shields | .30 | .14 |
| ❑ 98 Jocelyn Thibault | .30 | .14 |
| ❑ 99 Ron Tugnutt | .30 | .14 |
| ❑ 100 Ron Hextall | .30 | .14 |
| ❑ 101 Mike Peca | .10 | .05 |
| ❑ 102 Donald Audette | .10 | .05 |
| ❑ 103 Theoren Fleury | .30 | .14 |
| ❑ 104 Mark Recchi | .30 | .14 |
| ❑ 105 Dainius Zubrus | .40 | .18 |
| ❑ 106 Trevor Linden | .30 | .14 |
| ❑ 107 Joe Juneau | .30 | .14 |
| ❑ 108 Matthew Barnaby | .10 | .05 |
| ❑ 109 Keith Primeau | .10 | .05 |
| ❑ 110 Joe Nieuwendyk | .30 | .14 |
| ❑ 111 Rod Brind'Amour | .30 | .14 |
| ❑ 112 Daymond Langkow | .10 | .05 |
| ❑ 113 Ed Jovanovski | .30 | .14 |
| ❑ 114 Adam Deadmarsh | .30 | .14 |
| ❑ 115 Scott Niedermayer | .10 | .05 |
| ❑ 116 Al MacInnis | .30 | .14 |
| ❑ 117 Slava Kozlov | .30 | .14 |
| ❑ 118 Jere Lehtinen | .10 | .05 |
| ❑ 119 Jeff Friesen | .30 | .14 |
| ❑ 120 Alexei Kovalev | .10 | .05 |
| ❑ 121 Eric Daze | .30 | .14 |
| ❑ 122 Mariusz Czerkawski | .10 | .05 |
| ❑ 123 Alexei Zhamnov | .10 | .05 |
| ❑ 124 Petr Nedved | .30 | .14 |
| ❑ 125 Dimitri Mironov | .10 | .05 |
| ❑ 126 Alexei Yashin | .30 | .14 |
| ❑ 127 Todd Marchant | .10 | .05 |
| ❑ 128 Sandis Ozolinsh | .30 | .14 |
| ❑ 129 Igor Larionov | .10 | .05 |
| ❑ 130 Jim Campbell | .10 | .05 |
| ❑ 131 Dave Andreychuk | .10 | .05 |
| ❑ 132 Glen Wesley | .10 | .05 |
| ❑ 133 Rem Murray | .10 | .05 |
| ❑ 134 Steve Sullivan | .10 | .05 |
| ❑ 135 Miroslav Satan | .10 | .05 |
| ❑ 136 Bill Guerin | .30 | .14 |
| ❑ 137 Mike Gartner | .30 | .14 |
| ❑ 138 Jozef Stumpel | .30 | .14 |
| ❑ 139 Darryl Sydor | .10 | .05 |
| ❑ 140 Darcy Tucker | .10 | .05 |
| ❑ 141 Robert Svehla | .10 | .05 |
| ❑ 142 Steve Duchesne | .10 | .05 |
| ❑ 143 Kevin Stevens | .30 | .14 |
| ❑ 144 Mikael Renberg | .30 | .14 |
| ❑ 145 Bryan Berard | .30 | .14 |
| ❑ 146 Ray Ferraro | .10 | .05 |
| ❑ 147 Jason Allison | .30 | .14 |
| ❑ 148 Tony Amonte | .30 | .14 |
| ❑ 149 Luc Robitaille | .30 | .14 |
| ❑ 150 Mathieu Schneider | .10 | .05 |
| ❑ 151 Steve Rucchin | .10 | .05 |
| ❑ 152 Brian Savage | .10 | .05 |
| ❑ 153 Paul Coffey | .40 | .18 |
| ❑ 154 Jeff O'Neill | .10 | .05 |
| ❑ 155 Daniel Alfredsson | .30 | .14 |
| ❑ 156 Dave Gagner | .10 | .05 |
| ❑ 157 Rob Niedermayer | .10 | .05 |
| ❑ 158 Scott Stevens | .10 | .05 |
| ❑ 159 Alexandre Daigle | .30 | .14 |
| ❑ 160 Stephane Richer | .10 | .05 |
| ❑ 161 Harry York | .10 | .05 |
| ❑ 162 Sergei Berezin | .10 | .05 |
| ❑ 163 Claude Lemieux | .30 | .14 |
| ❑ 164 Ray Sheppard | .10 | .05 |
| ❑ 165 Bernie Nicholls | .10 | .05 |
| ❑ 166 Oleg Tverdovsky | .10 | .05 |
| ❑ 167 Travis Green | .10 | .05 |
| ❑ 168 Martin Gelinas | .10 | .05 |
| ❑ 169 Derek Plante | .10 | .05 |
| ❑ 170 Gary Roberts | .10 | .05 |
| ❑ 171 Kevin Hatcher | .10 | .05 |
| ❑ 172 Martin Rucinsky | .10 | .05 |
| ❑ 173 Pat Verbeek | .10 | .05 |
| ❑ 174 Adam Graves | .30 | .14 |
| ❑ 175 Roman Hamrlik | .10 | .05 |
| ❑ 176 Darren McCarty | .10 | .05 |
| ❑ 177 Mike Grier | .10 | .05 |
| ❑ 178 Andrew Cassels | .10 | .05 |
| ❑ 179 Dimitri Khristich | .10 | .05 |
| ❑ 180 Tomas Sandstrom | .10 | .05 |
| ❑ 181 Peter Bondra | .40 | .18 |
| ❑ 182 Derian Hatcher | .10 | .05 |
| ❑ 183 Chris Gratton | .30 | .14 |
| ❑ 184 John MacLean | .10 | .05 |
| ❑ 185 Wendel Clark | .30 | .14 |
| ❑ 186 Valeri Kamensky | .30 | .14 |
| ❑ 187 Tony Granato | .10 | .05 |
| ❑ 188 Vladimir Vorobiev | .10 | .05 |
| ❑ 189 Ethan Moreau | .10 | .05 |
| ❑ 190 Kirk Muller | .10 | .05 |
| ❑ 191 Peter Forsberg SM | .40 | .18 |
| ❑ 192 Wayne Gretzky SM | .40 | .18 |
| ❑ 193 Jaromir Jagr SM | .40 | .18 |
| ❑ 194 Mark Messier SM | .40 | .18 |
| ❑ 195 Brian Leetch SM | .40 | .18 |
| ❑ 196 John LeClair SM | .30 | .14 |
| ❑ 197 Jeremy Roenick SM | .30 | .14 |
| ❑ 198 Checklist | .10 | .05 |
| ❑ 199 Checklist | .10 | .05 |
| ❑ 200 Checklist | .10 | .05 |
| ❑ NNO Paul Kariya 3x5 PROMO | 5.00 | 2.20 |
| ❑ NNO Vanbiesbrouck 3x5 PROMO | 2.00 | .90 |

## 1997-98 Pinnacle Artist's Proofs

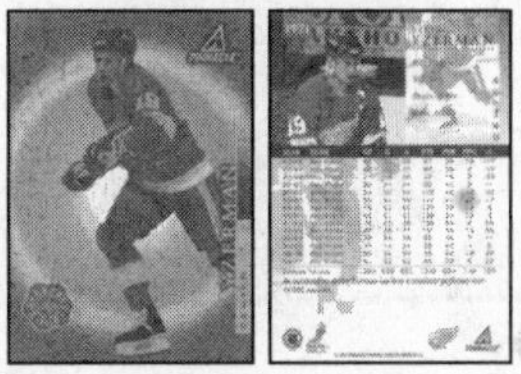

Randomly inserted in packs at the rate of one in 39 and in tins at the rate of one in 13, this 100-card set is a partial parallel version of the base set. The fronts display the "Artist's Proof" seal.

| | MINT | NRMT |
|---|---|---|
| COMPLETE SET (100) | 2000.00 | 900.00 |
| COMMON CARD (1-100) | 4.00 | 1.80 |

*STARS: 20X TO 50X BASIC CARDS
*YOUNG STARS: 15X TO 40X BASIC CARDS

## 1997-98 Pinnacle Epix Game Orange

Randomly inserted in packs at the rate of one in 19, this 24-card set displays the most memorable game for each player printed on "dot matrix hologram" cards with orange foil highlights. The set was printed in progressively-scarce three color versions: orange, purple, and emerald.

| | MINT | NRMT |
|---|---|---|
| COMMON CARD (1-24) | 5.00 | 2.20 |

*PURPLE CARDS: .75X TO 1.5X ORANGE
*EMERALD CARDS: 1.5X TO 3X ORANGE
LESS THAN 50 SEASON EMERALD EXIST
LESS THAN 30 MOMENT EMERALD EXIST
ONLY ORANGE CARDS LISTED BELOW
CARDS 1-6 FOUND IN SCORE PACKS
CARDS 7-12 FOUND IN PIN.CERT.PACKS
CARDS 13-18 FOUND IN ZENITH PACKS
CARDS 19-24 FOUND IN PINNACLE PACKS

| Card | MINT | NRMT |
|---|---|---|
| ❑ 1 Wayne Gretzky | 40.00 | 18.00 |
| ❑ 2 John Vanbiesbrouck | 10.00 | 4.50 |
| ❑ 3 Joe Sakic | 12.00 | 5.50 |
| ❑ 4 Alexei Yashin | 5.00 | 2.20 |
| ❑ 5 Sergei Fedorov | 12.00 | 5.50 |
| ❑ 6 Keith Tkachuk | 8.00 | 3.60 |
| ❑ 7 Patrick Roy | 30.00 | 13.50 |
| ❑ 8 Martin Brodeur | 15.00 | 6.75 |
| ❑ 9 Steve Yzerman | 20.00 | 9.00 |
| ❑ 10 Saku Koivu | 10.00 | 4.50 |
| ❑ 11 Felix Potvin | 6.00 | 2.70 |
| ❑ 12 Mark Messier | 10.00 | 4.50 |
| ❑ 13 Eric Lindros | 20.00 | 9.00 |
| ❑ 14 Peter Forsberg | 20.00 | 9.00 |
| ❑ 15 Teemu Selanne | 12.00 | 5.50 |
| ❑ 16 Brendan Shanahan | 12.00 | 5.50 |
| ❑ 17 Curtis Joseph | 6.00 | 2.70 |
| ❑ 18 Brett Hull | 8.00 | 3.60 |
| ❑ 19 Paul Kariya | 25.00 | 11.00 |
| ❑ 20 Jaromir Jagr | 20.00 | 9.00 |
| ❑ 21 Pavel Bure | 12.00 | 5.50 |
| ❑ 22 Dominik Hasek | 12.00 | 5.50 |
| ❑ 23 John LeClair | 10.00 | 4.50 |
| ❑ 24 Doug Gilmour | 6.00 | 2.70 |

## 1997-98 Pinnacle Epix Moment Orange

Randomly inserted in packs at the rate of one in 19, this 24-card set displays the most memorable moment for each player printed on "dot matrix hologram" cards with orange foil highlights. The set was printed in progressively-scarce three color versions: orange, purple, and emerald.

| | MINT | NRMT |
|---|---|---|
| COMMON CARD (1-24) | 20.00 | 9.00 |

*PURPLE CARDS: .75X TO 1.5X ORANGE
*EMERALD CARDS: 1.5X TO 3X ORANGE
LESS THAN 50 SEASON EMERALD EXIST
LESS THAN 30 MOMENT EMERALD EXIST
ONLY ORANGE CARDS LISTED BELOW
CARDS 1-6 FOUND IN ZENITH PACKS
CARDS 7-12 FOUND IN PINNACLE PACKS
CARDS 13-18 FOUND IN SCORE PACKS
CARDS 19-24 FOUND IN PIN.CERT.PACKS

| Card | MINT | NRMT |
|---|---|---|
| ❑ 1 Wayne Gretzky | 250.00 | 110.00 |
| ❑ 2 John Vanbiesbrouck | 40.00 | 18.00 |
| ❑ 3 Joe Sakic | 50.00 | 22.00 |
| ❑ 4 Alexei Yashin | 20.00 | 9.00 |
| ❑ 5 Sergei Fedorov | 50.00 | 22.00 |
| ❑ 6 Keith Tkachuk | 30.00 | 13.50 |
| ❑ 7 Patrick Roy | 120.00 | 55.00 |
| ❑ 8 Martin Brodeur | 60.00 | 27.00 |
| ❑ 9 Steve Yzerman | 80.00 | 36.00 |
| ❑ 10 Saku Koivu | 40.00 | 18.00 |
| ❑ 11 Felix Potvin | 25.00 | 11.00 |
| ❑ 12 Mark Messier | 40.00 | 18.00 |
| ❑ 13 Eric Lindros | 80.00 | 36.00 |
| ❑ 14 Peter Forsberg | 80.00 | 36.00 |
| ❑ 15 Teemu Selanne | 50.00 | 22.00 |
| ❑ 16 Brendan Shanahan | 50.00 | 22.00 |
| ❑ 17 Curtis Joseph | 25.00 | 11.00 |
| ❑ 18 Brett Hull | 30.00 | 13.50 |
| ❑ 19 Paul Kariya | 100.00 | 45.00 |
| ❑ 20 Jaromir Jagr | 80.00 | 36.00 |
| ❑ 21 Pavel Bure | 50.00 | 22.00 |
| ❑ 22 Dominik Hasek | 50.00 | 22.00 |
| ❑ 23 John LeClair | 40.00 | 18.00 |
| ❑ 24 Doug Gilmour | 25.00 | 11.00 |

## 1997-98 Pinnacle Epix Play Orange

Randomly inserted in packs at the rate of one in 19, this 24-card set displays the most memorable play for each player printed on "dot matrix hologram" cards with orange foil highlights. The set was printed in progressively-scarce three color versions: orange, purple, and emerald.

| | MINT | NRMT |
|---|---|---|
| COMMON CARD (1-24) | 3.00 | 1.35 |

*PURPLE CARDS: .75X TO 1.5X ORANGE
*EMERALD CARDS: 1.5X TO 3X ORANGE

| Card | MINT | NRMT |
|---|---|---|
| ❑ 1 Wayne Gretzky | 25.00 | 11.00 |
| ❑ 2 John Vanbiesbrouck | 6.00 | 2.70 |
| ❑ 3 Joe Sakic | 8.00 | 3.60 |
| ❑ 4 Alexei Yashin | 3.00 | 1.35 |
| ❑ 5 Sergei Fedorov | 8.00 | 3.60 |
| ❑ 6 Keith Tkachuk | 5.00 | 2.20 |
| ❑ 7 Patrick Roy | 20.00 | 9.00 |
| ❑ 8 Martin Brodeur | 10.00 | 4.50 |
| ❑ 9 Steve Yzerman | 12.00 | 5.50 |
| ❑ 10 Saku Koivu | 6.00 | 2.70 |
| ❑ 11 Felix Potvin | 4.00 | 1.80 |
| ❑ 12 Mark Messier | 6.00 | 2.70 |
| ❑ 13 Eric Lindros | 15.00 | 6.75 |
| ❑ 14 Peter Forsberg | 15.00 | 6.75 |
| ❑ 15 Teemu Selanne | 10.00 | 4.50 |
| ❑ 16 Brendan Shanahan | 10.00 | 4.50 |
| ❑ 17 Curtis Joseph | 5.00 | 2.20 |
| ❑ 18 Brett Hull | 6.00 | 2.70 |
| ❑ 19 Paul Kariya | 20.00 | 9.00 |
| ❑ 20 Jaromir Jagr | 15.00 | 6.75 |
| ❑ 21 Pavel Bure | 10.00 | 4.50 |
| ❑ 22 Dominik Hasek | 10.00 | 4.50 |
| ❑ 23 John LeClair | 8.00 | 3.60 |
| ❑ 24 Doug Gilmour | 5.00 | 2.20 |

## 1997-98 Pinnacle Epix Season Orange

Randomly inserted in packs at the rate of one in 19, this 24-card set displays the most memorable season for each player printed on "dot matrix hologram" cards with orange foil highlights. The set was printed in progressively-scarce three color versions: orange, purple, and emerald.

| | MINT | NRMT |
|---|---|---|
| COMMON CARD (1-24) | 10.00 | 4.50 |
| ❑ 1 Wayne Gretzky | 80.00 | 36.00 |
| ❑ 2 John Vanbiesbrouck | 20.00 | 9.00 |
| ❑ 3 Joe Sakic | 25.00 | 11.00 |
| ❑ 4 Alexei Yashin | 10.00 | 4.50 |
| ❑ 5 Sergei Fedorov | 25.00 | 11.00 |
| ❑ 6 Keith Tkachuk | 15.00 | 6.75 |
| ❑ 7 Patrick Roy | 60.00 | 27.00 |
| ❑ 8 Martin Brodeur | 30.00 | 13.50 |
| ❑ 9 Steve Yzerman | 40.00 | 18.00 |
| ❑ 10 Saku Koivu | 20.00 | 9.00 |

❑ 11 Felix Potvin 12.00 5.50
❑ 12 Mark Messier 20.00 9.00
❑ 13 Eric Lindros 40.00 18.00
❑ 14 Peter Forsberg 40.00 18.00
❑ 15 Teemu Selanne 25.00 11.00
❑ 16 Brendan Shanahan 25.00 11.00
❑ 17 Curtis Joseph 12.00 5.50
❑ 18 Brett Hull 15.00 6.75
❑ 19 Paul Kariya 50.00 22.00
❑ 20 Jaromir Jagr 40.00 18.00
❑ 21 Pavel Bure 25.00 11.00
❑ 22 Dominik Hasek 25.00 11.00
❑ 23 John LeClair 20.00 9.00
❑ 24 Doug Gilmour 12.00 5.50

## 1997-98 Pinnacle Rink Collection

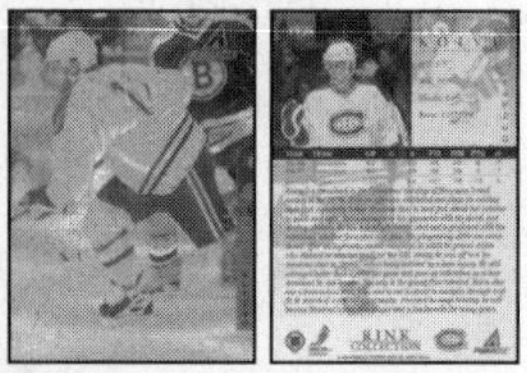

Randomly inserted in packs at the rate of one in seven, this 100-card set is a partial parallel version of the 1997-98 Pinnacle base set printed using Dufex Technology.

| | MINT | NRMT |
|---|---|---|
| COMPLETE SET (100) | 500.00 | 220.00 |
| COMMON CARD (1-100) | 1.50 | .70 |

*STARS: 6X TO 12X BASIC CARDS
*YOUNG STARS: 5X TO 10X BASIC CARDS
*RC'S 4X TO 8X BASIC CARDS

## 1997-98 Pinnacle Masks

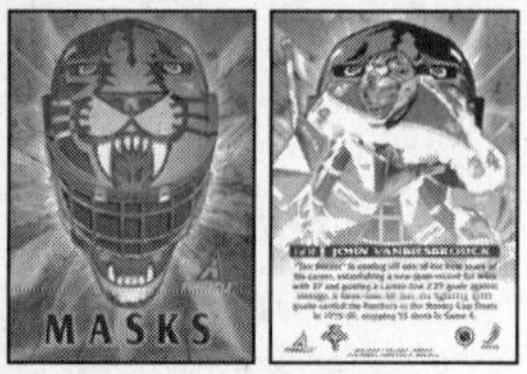

Randomly inserted in packs at the rate of one in 89 and in tins at the rate of one in 30, this ten-card set features color photos of masks worn by the NHL's elite goalies printed on Dufex technology.

| | MINT | NRMT |
|---|---|---|
| COMPLETE SET (10) | 275.00 | 125.00 |
| COMMON CARD (1-10) | 12.00 | 5.50 |

❑ 1 John Vanbiesbrouck 30.00 13.50
❑ 2 Mike Richter 20.00 9.00
❑ 3 Martin Brodeur 50.00 22.00
❑ 4 Curtis Joseph 20.00 9.00
❑ 5 Patrick Roy 100.00 45.00
❑ 6 Guy Hebert 12.00 5.50
❑ 7 Jeff Hackett 12.00 5.50
❑ 8 Garth Snow 12.00 5.50
❑ 9 Nikolai Khabibulin 12.00 5.50
❑ 10 Grant Fuhr 12.00 5.50

## 1997-98 Pinnacle Masks Die Cuts

Randomly inserted into hobby packs only at a rate of one in 299 packs and one in 100 tins, this ten-card set is a parallel version of the Pinnacle Masks regular set and features a die-cut design, with all other features being the same as their regular counterparts.

| | MINT | NRMT |
|---|---|---|
| COMPLETE SET (10) | 500.00 | 220.00 |
| COMMON CARD (1-10) | 25.00 | 11.00 |

*DIE CUT STARS: .75X TO 1.5X

## 1997-98 Pinnacle Masks Jumbos

These cards featured the same design as the Pinnacle Masks insert set and were issued one per large pack.

| | MINT | NRMT |
|---|---|---|
| COMPLETE SET (10) | 150.00 | 70.00 |
| COMMON CARD (1-10) | 15.00 | 6.75 |

❑ 1 John Vanbiesbrouck 20.00 9.00
❑ 2 Mike Richter 20.00 9.00
❑ 3 Martin Brodeur 20.00 9.00
❑ 4 Curtis Joseph 20.00 9.00
❑ 5 Patrick Roy 30.00 13.50
❑ 6 Guy Hebert 15.00 6.75
❑ 7 Jeff Hackett 15.00 6.75
❑ 8 Garth Snow 15.00 6.75
❑ 9 Nikolai Khabibulin 15.00 6.75
❑ 10 Grant Fuhr 15.00 6.75

## 1997-98 Pinnacle Masks Promos

| | MINT | NRMT |
|---|---|---|
| COMPLETE SET (10) | 40.00 | 18.00 |
| COMMON CARD (1-10) | 3.00 | 1.35 |

❑ 1 John Vanbiesbrouck 5.00 2.20
❑ 2 Mike Richter 5.00 2.20
❑ 3 Martin Brodeur 5.00 2.20
❑ 4 Curtis Joseph 5.00 2.20
❑ 5 Patrick Roy 8.00 3.60
❑ 6 Guy Hebert 3.00 1.35
❑ 7 Jeff Hackett 3.00 1.35
❑ 8 Garth Snow 3.00 1.35
❑ 9 Nikolai Khabibulin 3.00 1.35

## 1997-98 Pinnacle Team Pinnacle

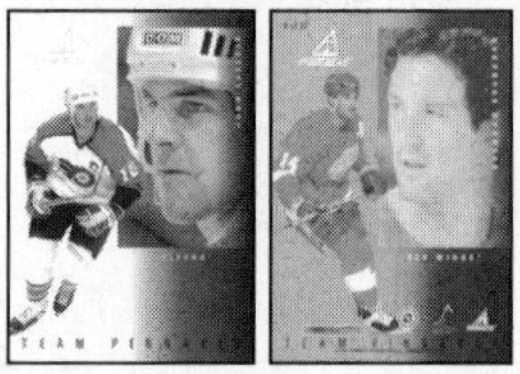

Randomly inserted in packs at the rate of one in 99 and in tins at the rate of one in 33, this 10-card set features color action photos of the game's biggest stars as voted by Hockey fans and printed on double-sided cards with mirror-mylar technology.

| | MINT | NRMT |
|---|---|---|
| COMPLETE SET (10) | 400.00 | 180.00 |
| COMMON CARD (1-10) | 15.00 | 6.75 |

*MIRRORS: 10X TO 20X BASIC CARDS
MIRRORS RANDOM INSERTS IN PACKS
WHITE/SILVER FRONT: SAME VALUE

❑ 1 Martin Brodeur/Patrick Roy 60.00 27.00
❑ 2 Dominik Hasek/Curtis Joseph 25.00 11.00
❑ 3 Brian Leetch/Chris Chelios 15.00 6.75
❑ 4 Wayne Gretzky/Paul Kariya 80.00 36.00
❑ 5 Eric Lindros/Mark Messier 40.00 18.00
❑ 6 Jaromir Jagr/Keith Tkachuk 40.00 18.00
❑ 7 Saku Koivu/Peter Forsberg 40.00 18.00
❑ 8 John LeClair/Brendan Shanahan 30.00 13.50
❑ 9 Doug Gilmour/Steve Yzerman 30.00 13.50
❑ 10 John Vanbiesbrouck/Chris Osgood 25.00 11.00

## 1997-98 Pinnacle Tins

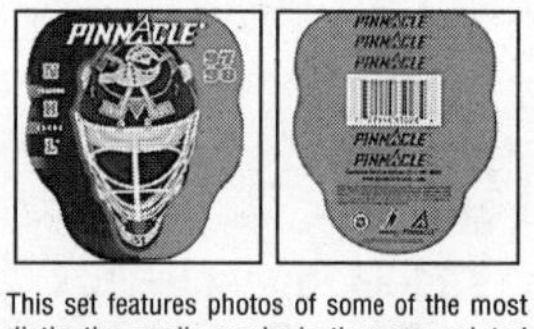

This set features photos of some of the most distinctive goalie masks in the game printed on collectible tins. Each tin contains 30 cards from the 1997-98 Pinnacle Hockey base set as well as insert sets. The tins are unnumbered and checklisted below in alphabetical order.

| | MINT | NRMT |
|---|---|---|
| COMPLETE SET (10) | 15.00 | 6.75 |
| COMMON TIN (1-10) | 1.00 | .45 |

❑ 1 Martin Brodeur 3.00 1.35
❑ 2 Grant Fuhr 1.00 .45
❑ 3 Jeff Hackett 1.00 .45
❑ 4 Guy Hebert 1.00 .45
❑ 5 Curtis Joseph 1.25 .55
❑ 6 Nikolai Khabibulin 1.00 .45
❑ 7 Mike Richter 1.25 .55
❑ 8 Patrick Roy 5.00 2.20
❑ 9 Garth Snow 1.00 .45
❑ 10 John Vanbiesbrouck 2.00 .90

## 1997-98 Pinnacle Certified

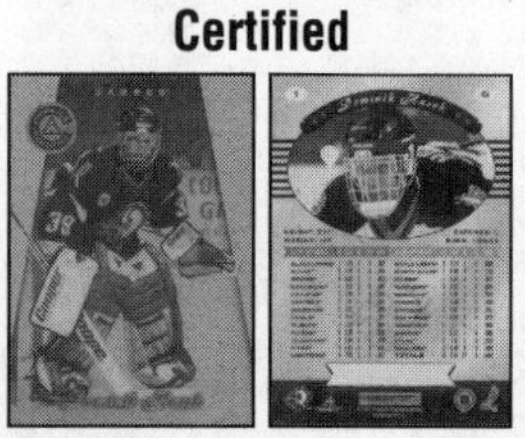

The 1997-98 Pinnacle Certified set was issued in one series totalling 130 cards and was distributed in five-card hobby packs only with a suggested retail price of $4.99. The fronts feature borderless color action player photos. The backs carry player information.

| | MINT | NRMT |
|---|---|---|
| COMPLETE SET (130) | 40.00 | 18.00 |
| COMMON CARD (1-130) | .20 | .09 |
| EPIX REDEMPT.PLAY | 6.00 | 2.70 |
| EPIX REDEMPT.GAME | 8.00 | 3.60 |
| EPIX REDEMPT.SEASON | 12.00 | 5.50 |
| EPIX REDEMPT.MOMENT | 20.00 | 9.00 |

❑ 1 Dominik Hasek 1.50 .70
❑ 2 Patrick Roy 4.00 1.80
❑ 3 Martin Brodeur 2.00 .90
❑ 4 Chris Osgood .75 .35
❑ 5 Andy Moog .50 .23
❑ 6 John Vanbiesbrouck 1.25 .55
❑ 7 Steve Shields .50 .23
❑ 8 Mike Vernon .50 .23
❑ 9 Ed Belfour .75 .35
❑ 10 Grant Fuhr .50 .23
❑ 11 Felix Potvin .75 .35
❑ 12 Bill Ranford .50 .23
❑ 13 Mike Richter .75 .35
❑ 14 Stephane Fiset .50 .23
❑ 15 Jim Carey .50 .23
❑ 16 Nikolai Khabibulin .50 .23
❑ 17 Ken Wregget .50 .23
❑ 18 Curtis Joseph .75 .35
❑ 19 Guy Hebert .50 .23
❑ 20 Damian Rhodes .50 .23
❑ 21 Trevor Kidd .50 .23
❑ 22 Daren Puppa .50 .23
❑ 23 Patrick Lalime .50 .23
❑ 24 Tommy Salo .50 .23
❑ 25 Sean Burke .50 .23
❑ 26 Jocelyn Thibault .50 .23
❑ 27 Kirk McLean .50 .23
❑ 28 Garth Snow .50 .23
❑ 29 Ron Tugnutt .50 .23
❑ 30 Jeff Hackett .50 .23
❑ 31 Eric Lindros 2.50 1.10
❑ 32 Peter Forsberg 2.50 1.10
❑ 33 Mike Modano 1.00 .45
❑ 34 Paul Kariya 3.00 1.35
❑ 35 Jaromir Jagr 2.50 1.10
❑ 36 Brian Leetch .75 .35
❑ 37 Keith Tkachuk 1.00 .45
❑ 38 Steve Yzerman 2.50 1.10
❑ 39 Teemu Selanne 1.50 .70
❑ 40 Bryan Berard .50 .23
❑ 41 Ray Bourque .75 .35
❑ 42 Theoren Fleury .50 .23
❑ 43 Mark Messier 1.00 .45
❑ 44 Saku Koivu 1.25 .55
❑ 45 Pavel Bure 1.50 .70
❑ 46 Peter Bondra .75 .35
❑ 47 Dave Gagner .20 .09
❑ 48 Ed Jovanovski .50 .23
❑ 49 Adam Oates .50 .23
❑ 50 Joe Sakic 1.50 .70
❑ 51 Doug Gilmour .75 .35
❑ 52 Jim Campbell .20 .09
❑ 53 Mats Sundin .75 .35
❑ 54 Darien Hatcher .20 .09
❑ 55 Jarome Iginla .50 .23
❑ 56 Sergei Fedorov 1.50 .70
❑ 57 Keith Primeau .20 .09
❑ 58 Mark Recchi .50 .23
❑ 59 Owen Nolan .50 .23
❑ 60 Alexander Mogilny .50 .23
❑ 61 Brendan Shanahan 1.50 .70
❑ 62 Pierre Turgeon .50 .23
❑ 63 Joe Juneau .50 .23
❑ 64 Steve Rucchin .20 .09
❑ 65 Jeremy Roenick .75 .35
❑ 66 Doug Weight .50 .23
❑ 67 Valeri Kamensky .50 .23
❑ 68 Tony Amonte .50 .23
❑ 69 Dave Andreychuk .20 .09
❑ 70 Brett Hull 1.00 .45
❑ 71 Wendel Clark .50 .23
❑ 72 Vincent Damphousse .50 .23
❑ 73 Mike Grier .20 .09
❑ 74 Chris Chelios .75 .35
❑ 75 Nicklas Lidstrom .50 .23
❑ 76 Joe Nieuwendyk .50 .23
❑ 77 Rob Blake .20 .09
❑ 78 Alexei Yashin .50 .23
❑ 79 Ryan Smyth .50 .23
❑ 80 Pat LaFontaine .50 .23
❑ 81 Jeff Friesen .50 .23
❑ 82 Ray Ferraro .20 .09
❑ 83 Steve Sullivan .20 .09
❑ 84 Chris Gratton .50 .23
❑ 85 Mike Gartner .50 .23
❑ 86 Kevin Hatcher .20 .09
❑ 87 Ted Donato .20 .09
❑ 88 German Titov .20 .09
❑ 89 Sandis Ozolinsh .50 .23
❑ 90 Ray Sheppard .20 .09
❑ 91 John MacLean .50 .23
❑ 92 Luc Robitaille .50 .23
❑ 93 Rod Brind'Amour .50 .23
❑ 94 Zigmund Palffy .75 .35
❑ 95 Petr Nedved .50 .23
❑ 96 Adam Graves .50 .23
❑ 97 Jozef Stumpel .50 .23
❑ 98 Alexandre Daigle .50 .23
❑ 99 Mike Peca .20 .09
❑ 100 Wayne Gretzky 5.00 2.20
❑ 101 Alexei Zhamnov .20 .09
❑ 102 Paul Coffey .75 .35
❑ 103 Oleg Tverdovsky .20 .09
❑ 104 Trevor Linden .50 .23
❑ 105 Dino Ciccarelli .20 .09
❑ 106 Andrei Kovalenko .20 .09
❑ 107 Scott Mellanby .20 .09
❑ 108 Bryan Smolinski .20 .09
❑ 109 Bernie Nicholls .20 .09
❑ 110 Derek Plante .20 .09
❑ 111 Pat Verbeek .20 .09
❑ 112 Adam Deadmarsh .50 .23
❑ 113 Martin Gelinas .20 .09
❑ 114 Daniel Alfredsson .50 .23
❑ 115 Scott Stevens .20 .09
❑ 116 Dainius Zubrus .75 .35
❑ 117 Kirk Muller .20 .09
❑ 118 Brian Holzinger .20 .09
❑ 119 John LeClair 1.25 .55
❑ 120 Al MacInnis .50 .23
❑ 121 Ron Francis .50 .23
❑ 122 Eric Daze .50 .23
❑ 123 Travis Green .20 .09
❑ 124 Jason Arnott .50 .23
❑ 125 Geoff Sanderson .50 .23
❑ 126 Dimitri Khristich .20 .09
❑ 127 Sergei Berezin .20 .09
❑ 128 Jeff O'Neill .20 .09
❑ 129 Claude Lemieux .50 .23
❑ 130 Andrew Cassels .20 .09

## 1997-98 Pinnacle Certified Red

Randomly inserted in packs at the rate of one in five, this 130-card set is parallel to the Pinnacle Certified base set and is distinguished by the red treatment of the mirror mylar regular cards.

| | MINT | NRMT |
|---|---|---|
| COMPLETE SET (130) | 600.00 | 275.00 |
| COMMON CARD (1-130) | 2.00 | .90 |

*RED STARS: 4X TO 8X BASIC CARD
*RED YOUNG STARS: 3X TO 6X
*RED RC'S: 2X TO X BASIC CARDS

## 1997-98 Pinnacle Certified Mirror Blue

Randomly inserted in packs at the rate of one in 199, this 130-card set is parallel to the Pinnacle Certified base set. The difference is found in the blue design element on holographic foil.

| | MINT | NRMT |
|---|---|---|
| COMMON CARD (1-130) | 40.00 | 18.00 |
| SEMISTARS/GOALIES | 80.00 | 36.00 |
| UNLISTED STARS | 100.00 | 45.00 |

*STARS: 60X TO 150X BASIC CARDS
*GOALIES: 40X TO 100X
*YOUNG STARS: 40X TO 100X

❑ 1 Dominik Hasek 40.00 18.00
❑ 2 Patrick Roy 40.00 18.00
❑ 3 Martin Brodeur 40.00 18.00
❑ 6 John Vanbiesbrouck 40.00 18.00
❑ 31 Eric Lindros 40.00 18.00
❑ 32 Peter Forsberg 40.00 18.00
❑ 33 Mike Modano 40.00 18.00
❑ 34 Paul Kariya 40.00 18.00
❑ 35 Jaromir Jagr 40.00 18.00
❑ 37 Keith Tkachuk 40.00 18.00
❑ 38 Steve Yzerman 40.00 18.00
❑ 39 Teemu Selanne 40.00 18.00
❑ 43 Mark Messier 40.00 18.00
❑ 44 Saku Koivu 40.00 18.00
❑ 45 Pavel Bure 40.00 18.00
❑ 50 Joe Sakic 40.00 18.00
❑ 56 Sergei Fedorov 40.00 18.00
❑ 61 Brendan Shanahan 40.00 18.00
❑ 70 Brett Hull 40.00 18.00
❑ 94 Zigmund Palffy 40.00 18.00
❑ 100 Wayne Gretzky 40.00 18.00
❑ 119 John LeClair 40.00 18.00

## 1997-98 Pinnacle Certified Mirror Gold

Randomly inserted in packs at the rate of one in 299, this 130-card set is parallel to the Pinnacle Certified base set. The difference is found in the golden holographic mirror mylar highlights of the set.

| | MINT | NRMT |
|---|---|---|
| COMMON CARD (1-130) | 100.00 | 45.00 |
| SEMISTARS/GOALIES | 150.00 | 70.00 |

❑ 1 Dominik Hasek 400.00 180.00
❑ 2 Patrick Roy 800.00 350.00
❑ 3 Martin Brodeur 500.00 220.00
❑ 4 Chris Osgood 150.00 70.00
❑ 6 John Vanbiesbrouck 300.00 135.00
❑ 9 Ed Belfour 150.00 70.00
❑ 13 Mike Richter 150.00 70.00
❑ 18 Curtis Joseph 150.00 70.00
❑ 26 Jocelyn Thibault 100.00 45.00
❑ 31 Eric Lindros 1200.00 550.00
❑ 32 Peter Forsberg 1000.00 450.00
❑ 33 Mike Modano 300.00 135.00
❑ 34 Paul Kariya 1200.00 550.00
❑ 35 Jaromir Jagr 1000.00 450.00
❑ 36 Brian Leetch 250.00 110.00
❑ 37 Keith Tkachuk 300.00 135.00
❑ 38 Steve Yzerman 800.00 350.00
❑ 39 Teemu Selanne 500.00 220.00
❑ 41 Ray Bourque 250.00 110.00
❑ 43 Mark Messier 300.00 135.00
❑ 44 Saku Koivu 500.00 220.00
❑ 45 Pavel Bure 500.00 220.00
❑ 50 Joe Sakic 500.00 220.00
❑ 53 Mats Sundin 250.00 110.00
❑ 56 Sergei Fedorov 500.00 220.00
❑ 61 Brendan Shanahan 500.00 220.00
❑ 65 Jeremy Roenick 200.00 90.00
❑ 70 Brett Hull 300.00 135.00
❑ 74 Chris Chelios 250.00 110.00
❑ 94 Zigmund Palffy 250.00 110.00
❑ 100 Wayne Gretzky 2500.00 1100.00
❑ 102 Paul Coffey 250.00 110.00
❑ 119 John LeClair 500.00 220.00

## 1997-98 Pinnacle Certified Mirror Red

Randomly inserted in packs at the rate of one in 99, this 130-card set is parallel to the Pinnacle Certified base set. The difference is found in the holographic red foil design of the set.

| | MINT | NRMT |
|---|---|---|
| COMMON CARD (1-130) | 20.00 | 9.00 |
| SEMISTARS/GOALIES | 40.00 | 18.00 |
| UNLISTED STARS | 60.00 | 27.00 |

*STARS: 30X TO 80X BASIC CARDS
*GOALIES: 25X TO 60X
*YOUNG STARS: 30X TO 60X

❑ 1 Dominik Hasek 20.00 9.00
❑ 2 Patrick Roy 20.00 9.00
❑ 3 Martin Brodeur 20.00 9.00
❑ 6 John Vanbiesbrouck 20.00 9.00
❑ 31 Eric Lindros 20.00 9.00
❑ 32 Peter Forsberg 20.00 9.00
❑ 33 Mike Modano 20.00 9.00
❑ 34 Paul Kariya 20.00 9.00
❑ 35 Jaromir Jagr 20.00 9.00
❑ 37 Keith Tkachuk 20.00 9.00
❑ 38 Steve Yzerman 20.00 9.00
❑ 39 Teemu Selanne 20.00 9.00
❑ 43 Mark Messier 20.00 9.00
❑ 44 Saku Koivu 20.00 9.00
❑ 45 Pavel Bure 20.00 9.00
❑ 50 Joe Sakic 20.00 9.00
❑ 56 Sergei Fedorov 20.00 9.00
❑ 61 Brendan Shanahan 20.00 9.00
❑ 70 Brett Hull 20.00 9.00
❑ 100 Wayne Gretzky 20.00 9.00
❑ 119 John LeClair 20.00 9.00

## 1997-98 Pinnacle Certified Team

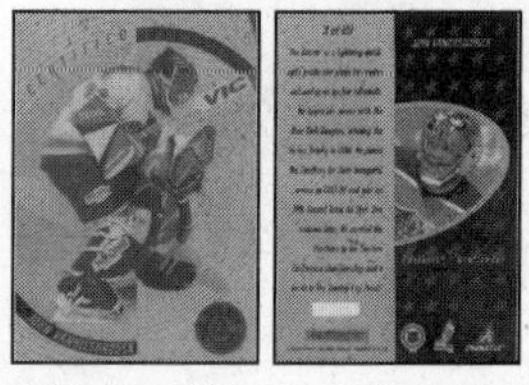

Randomly inserted in packs at the rate of one in 19, this 20-card set features color action photos of 10 Eastern Conference megastars matched with 10 Western Conference superstar counterparts and printed on mirror mylar all-foil card stock.

| | MINT | NRMT |
|---|---|---|
| COMPLETE SET (20) | 250.00 | 110.00 |
| COMMON CARD (1-20) | 4.00 | 1.80 |

❑ 1 Martin Brodeur 12.00 5.50
❑ 2 Patrick Roy 25.00 11.00
❑ 3 John Vanbiesbrouck 8.00 3.60
❑ 4 Dominik Hasek 10.00 4.50
❑ 5 Chris Chelios 4.00 1.80
❑ 6 Brian Leetch 4.00 1.80
❑ 7 Wayne Gretzky 30.00 13.50
❑ 8 Eric Lindros 15.00 6.75
❑ 9 Paul Kariya 20.00 9.00
❑ 10 Peter Forsberg 15.00 6.75
❑ 11 Keith Tkachuk 6.00 2.70
❑ 12 Mark Messier 6.00 2.70
❑ 13 Steve Yzerman 15.00 6.75
❑ 14 Jaromir Jagr 15.00 6.75
❑ 15 Mats Sundin 4.00 1.80
❑ 16 Teemu Selanne 10.00 4.50
❑ 17 Brendan Shanahan 10.00 4.50
❑ 18 Saku Koivu 8.00 3.60
❑ 19 Brett Hull 6.00 2.70
❑ 20 John LeClair 8.00 3.60

## 1997-98 Pinnacle Certified Gold Team

Randomly inserted in packs, this 20-card set is parallel to the Pinnacle Certified Gold Team insert set and is printed on full micro-etched, mirror mylar foil card stock with gold accents and foil stamping. Only 300 of this set were produced and are sequentially numbered.

| | MINT | NRMT |
|---|---|---|
| COMPLETE SET (20) | 1500.00 | 700.00 |
| COMMON CARD (1-20) | 25.00 | 11.00 |

*GOLD STARS: 3X TO 6X BASIC CARDS

## 1997-98 Pinnacle Certified Rookie Redemption

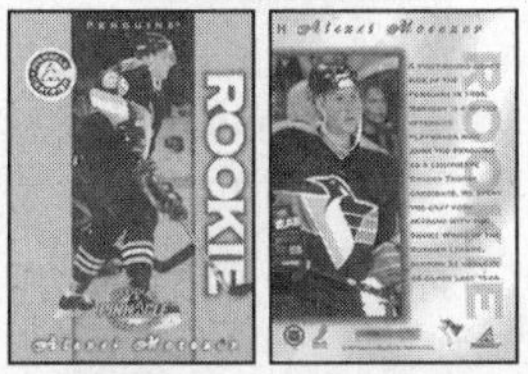

Randomly inserted in packs at the rate of one in 19, this 12-card set was obtained through the mail with the redemption card and features color action player photos printed on super-premium 24-point card stock with an exclusive authenticator bar to protect the set from counterfeiting. Gold and Mirror Gold versions of these cards were also available via redemption.

| | MINT | NRMT |
|---|---|---|
| COMPLETE SET (12) | 100.00 | 45.00 |
| COMMON CARD (1-12) | 4.00 | 1.80 |
| COMP.GOLD SET (12) | 500.00 | 220.00 |
| COMMON GOLD (1-12) | 20.00 | 9.00 |

*GOLD CARDS: 2.5X TO 5X BASIC CARDS
GOLD PRINT RUN 250 SETS

COMMON MIRROR GOLD (1-12) 60.00 27.00
*MIRROR GOLD: 10X TO 20X BASIC CARDS

❑ A Joe Thornton ........ 10.00 4.50
❑ B Chris Phillips ........ 4.00 1.80
❑ C Patrick Marleau ........ 10.00 4.50
❑ D Sergei Samsonov ........ 15.00 6.75
❑ E Daniel Cleary ........ 4.00 1.80
❑ F Olli Jokinen ........ 12.00 5.50
❑ G Alyn McCauley ........ 4.00 1.80
❑ H Alexei Morozov ........ 6.00 2.70
❑ I Brad Isbister ........ 4.00 1.80
❑ J Boyd Devereaux ........ 4.00 1.80
❑ K Espen Knutsen ........ 4.00 1.80
❑ L Marc Savard ........ 4.00 1.80

## 1997-98 Pinnacle Certified Summit Silver

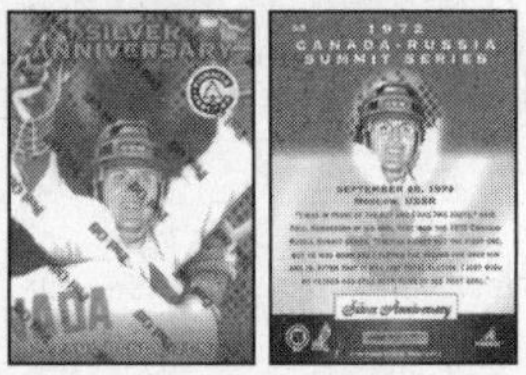

Randomly inserted in packs at the rate of one in 29, this five card set features color action redentions of Paul Henderson by artist Daniel Parry printed on mirror mylar and commemorates Paul Henderson's winning goal at the 1972 Canada-Russia Summit Series. Only 1,000 of each card were produced and are sequentially numbered.

| | MINT | NRMT |
|---|---|---|
| COMMON CARD (1-5) | 10.00 | 4.50 |
| HENDERSON BLACK AU/700 | 60.00 | 27.00 |
| HENDERSON SILVER AU/200 | 120.00 | 55.00 |
| HENDERSON GOLD AU/100 | 250.00 | 110.00 |

## 1996-97 Pinnacle Fantasy

This 20-card set was made available to attendees of the All-Star FanFest held in San Jose in January, 1997. The cards were distributed in three-card packs, and featured an action photo with a blue foil sharkbite design along the top. A 21st card featuring Sharks netminder Kelly Hrudey was available through a redemption card which was randomly inserted in packs. The card had to be redeemed at a San Jose-area card shop. There were, in fact, two variations of the Hrudey card, the more difficult of which featured a refractor-like gloss. Collectors may also run across what appears to be a non-gloss parallel version of this set. The cards are smaller and are in playing card form, with black along the top and a uniform black back with a Pinnacle logo. These were used for a promotion at the show and were not licensed by the NHL or NHLPA. Therefore, these cards will not be listed in the annual.

| | MINT | NRMT |
|---|---|---|
| COMPLETE SET (20) | 50.00 | 22.00 |
| COMMON CARD (FC1-FC20) | .50 | .23 |

❑ FC1 Ray Bourque ........ 1.50 .70
❑ FC2 Paul Coffey ........ 1.50 .70
❑ FC3 Eric Lindros ........ 6.00 2.70
❑ FC4 Mario Lemieux ........ 8.00 3.60
❑ FC5 Wayne Gretzky ........ 10.00 4.50
❑ FC6 Mark Messier ........ 2.50 1.10
❑ FC7 Jaromir Jagr ........ 6.00 2.70
❑ FC8 Brendan Shanahan ........ 4.00 1.80
❑ FC9 John Vanbiesbrouck ........ 3.00 1.35
❑ FC10 Mike Richter ........ 1.50 .70
❑ FC11 Chris Chelios ........ 1.50 .70
❑ FC12 Nicklas Lidstrom ........ .60 .25
❑ FC13 Sergei Fedorov ........ 4.00 1.80
❑ FC14 Pavel Bure ........ 4.00 1.80
❑ FC15 Peter Forsberg ........ 6.00 2.70
❑ FC16 Brett Hull ........ 2.50 1.10
❑ FC17 Joe Sakic ........ 4.00 1.80
❑ FC18 Owen Nolan ........ .50 .23
❑ FC19 Patrick Roy ........ 8.00 3.60
❑ FC20 Ed Belfour ........ 1.50 .70
❑ NNO1 Kelly Hrudey ........ 25.00 11.00
❑ NNO2 Kelly Hrudey holofoil . 35.00 16.00
❑ NNO3 Kelly Hrudey offer card 10.00 4.50

## 1997-98 Pinnacle Inside

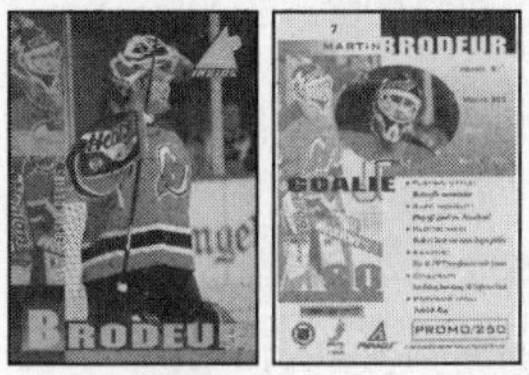

The 1997-98 Pinnacle Inside set was issued in one series totalling 190 cards and was distributed inside 24 different collectible player cans with ten cards to a can. The fronts feature color action player photos printed on 20 pt. card stock. The backs carry player information.

| | MINT | NRMT |
|---|---|---|
| COMPLETE SET (190) | 40.00 | 18.00 |
| COMMON CARD (1-190) | .20 | .09 |

❑ 1 Brendan Shanahan ........ 1.25 .55
❑ 2 Dominik Hasek ........ 1.25 .55
❑ 3 Wayne Gretzky ........ 4.00 1.80
❑ 4 Eric Lindros ........ 2.00 .90
❑ 5 Keith Tkachuk ........ .75 .35
❑ 6 Jaromir Jagr ........ 2.00 .90
❑ 7 Martin Brodeur ........ 1.50 .70
❑ 8 Peter Forsberg ........ 2.00 .90
❑ 9 Chris Osgood ........ .60 .25
❑ 10 Paul Kariya ........ 2.50 1.10
❑ 11 Pavel Bure ........ 1.25 .55
❑ 12 Brett Hull ........ .75 .35
❑ 13 Saku Koivu ........ 1.00 .45
❑ 14 Zigmund Palffy ........ .60 .25
❑ 15 Mike Modano ........ .75 .35
❑ 16 Ray Bourque ........ .60 .25
❑ 17 Jarome Iginla ........ .50 .23
❑ 18 Chris Chelios ........ .60 .25
❑ 19 John Vanbiesbrouck ........ 1.00 .45
❑ 20 Brian Leetch ........ .60 .25
❑ 21 Mats Sundin ........ .60 .25
❑ 22 Ron Hextall ........ .50 .23
❑ 23 Stephane Fiset ........ .50 .23
❑ 24 Steve Yzerman ........ 2.00 .90
❑ 25 Curtis Joseph ........ .60 .25
❑ 26 Daniel Alfredsson ........ .50 .23
❑ 27 Owen Nolan ........ .50 .23
❑ 28 Adam Oates ........ .50 .23
❑ 29 Corey Hirsch ........ .50 .23
❑ 30 Sean Burke ........ .50 .23
❑ 31 Eric Fichaud ........ .50 .23
❑ 32 Ken Wregget ........ .50 .23
❑ 33 Dainius Zubrus ........ .60 .25
❑ 34 Alexander Mogilny ........ .50 .23
❑ 35 Bill Ranford ........ .50 .23
❑ 36 Vincent Damphousse ........ .50 .23
❑ 37 Patrick Roy ........ 3.00 1.35
❑ 38 Teemu Selanne ........ 1.25 .55
❑ 39 Pat LaFontaine ........ .50 .23
❑ 40 Theoren Fleury ........ .50 .23
❑ 41 Jeff Hackett ........ .50 .23
❑ 42 Sergei Fedorov ........ 1.25 .55
❑ 43 Jocelyn Thibault ........ .50 .23
❑ 44 Nikolai Khabibulin ........ .50 .23
❑ 45 Daren Puppa ........ .50 .23
❑ 46 Felix Potvin ........ .60 .25
❑ 47 Andy Moog ........ .50 .23
❑ 48 Doug Weight ........ .50 .23
❑ 49 Tommy Salo ........ .50 .23
❑ 50 Mark Messier ........ .75 .35
❑ 51 Grant Fuhr ........ .50 .23
❑ 52 Ron Francis ........ .50 .23
❑ 53 Tony Amonte ........ .50 .23
❑ 54 Joe Sakic ........ 1.25 .55
❑ 55 Jason Arnott ........ .50 .23
❑ 56 Jose Theodore ........ .50 .23
❑ 57 Alexei Yashin ........ .50 .23
❑ 58 John LeClair ........ 1.00 .45
❑ 59 Jeremy Roenick ........ .60 .25
❑ 60 Kirk McLean ........ .50 .23
❑ 61 Arturs Irbe ........ .50 .23
❑ 62 Jim Carey ........ .50 .23
❑ 63 J.S. Giguere ........ .50 .23
❑ 64 Marc Denis ........ .50 .23
❑ 65 Damian Rhodes ........ .50 .23
❑ 66 Jim Campbell ........ .20 .09
❑ 67 Patrick Lalime ........ .50 .23
❑ 68 Garth Snow ........ .50 .23
❑ 69 Marcel Cousineau ........ .50 .23
❑ 70 Guy Hebert ........ .50 .23
❑ 71 Rob Blake ........ .20 .09
❑ 72 Tomas Vokoun ........ .20 .09
❑ 73 Doug Gilmour ........ .60 .25
❑ 74 Ed Belfour ........ .60 .25
❑ 75 Parris Duffus ........ .20 .09
❑ 76 Mike Fountain ........ .20 .09
❑ 77 Steve Shields ........ .50 .23
❑ 78 Geoff Sanderson ........ .50 .23
❑ 79 Roman Turek ........ .50 .23
❑ 80 Bryan Berard ........ .50 .23
❑ 81 Mike Richter ........ .60 .25
❑ 82 Ron Tugnutt ........ .50 .23
❑ 83 Peter Bondra ........ .60 .25
❑ 84 Mike Vernon ........ .50 .23
❑ 85 Mike Grier ........ .20 .09
❑ 86 Ed Jovanovski ........ .50 .23
❑ 87 Trevor Kidd ........ .50 .23
❑ 88 Eric Daze ........ .50 .23
❑ 89 Wendel Clark ........ .50 .23
❑ 90 Checklist (1-190) ........ .20 .09
❑ 91 Nicklas Lidstrom ........ .50 .23
❑ 92 Rod Brind'Amour ........ .50 .23
❑ 93 Hnat Domenichelli ........ .20 .09
❑ 94 Rem Murray ........ .20 .09
❑ 95 Scott Niedermayer ........ .20 .09
❑ 96 Martin Rucinsky ........ .20 .09
❑ 97 Mike Gartner ........ .50 .23
❑ 98 Kevin Hatcher ........ .20 .09
❑ 99 Daymond Langkow ........ .20 .09
❑ 100 Jamie Langenbrunner ........ .20 .09
❑ 101 Ted Donato ........ .20 .09
❑ 102 Steve Sullivan ........ .20 .09
❑ 103 Martin Gelinas ........ .20 .09
❑ 104 Adam Graves ........ .50 .23
❑ 105 Donald Audette ........ .20 .09
❑ 106 Andrew Cassels ........ .20 .09
❑ 107 Alexei Zhamnov ........ .20 .09
❑ 108 Kirk Muller ........ .20 .09
❑ 109 Alexandre Daigle ........ .50 .23
❑ 110 Chris Gratton ........ .50 .23
❑ 111 Andrew Brunette ........ .20 .09
❑ 112 Mark Recchi ........ .50 .23
❑ 113 Jari Kurri ........ .50 .23
❑ 114 Valeri Kamensky ........ .50 .23
❑ 115 Joe Nieuwendyk ........ .50 .23
❑ 116 Slava Kozlov ........ .20 .09
❑ 117 Steve Kelly ........ .20 .09
❑ 118 Dave Andreychuk ........ .20 .09
❑ 119 Mikael Renberg ........ .50 .23
❑ 120 Sergei Berezin ........ .20 .09
❑ 121 Jeff Friesen ........ .50 .23
❑ 122 Pierre Turgeon ........ .50 .23
❑ 123 Vladimir Vorobiev ........ .20 .09
❑ 124 Dimitri Khristich ........ .20 .09
❑ 125 Jaroslav Svejkovsky ........ .50 .23
❑ 126 Vladimir Konstantinov ........ .20 .09
❑ 127 Jozef Stumpel ........ .50 .23
❑ 128 Mike Peca ........ .20 .09
❑ 129 Jonas Hoglund ........ .20 .09
❑ 130 Travis Green ........ .20 .09
❑ 131 Bill Guerin ........ .50 .23
❑ 132 Oleg Tverdovsky ........ .20 .09
❑ 133 Petr Nedved ........ .50 .23
❑ 134 Dino Ciccarelli ........ .20 .09
❑ 135 Brian Savage ........ .20 .09
❑ 136 Steve Duchesne ........ .20 .09
❑ 137 Sandis Ozolinsh ........ .50 .23
❑ 138 Derian Hatcher ........ .20 .09
❑ 139 Ray Sheppard ........ .20 .09
❑ 140 Brian Bellows ........ .20 .09
❑ 141 Paul Brousseau ........ .20 .09
❑ 142 Tony Granato ........ .20 .09
❑ 143 Vaclav Prospal ........ 1.00 .45
❑ 144 Vitali Yachmenev ........ .20 .09
❑ 145 John MacLean ........ .20 .09
❑ 146 Igor Larionov ........ .20 .09
❑ 147 Jason Allison ........ .50 .23
❑ 148 Derek Plante ........ .20 .09
❑ 149 Jeff O'Neill ........ .20 .09
❑ 150 Trevor Linden ........ .50 .23
❑ 151 Joe Juneau ........ .50 .23
❑ 152 Brandon Convery ........ .20 .09
❑ 153 Kevin Stevens ........ .20 .09
❑ 154 Scott Stevens ........ .20 .09
❑ 155 Niklas Sundstrom ........ .20 .09
❑ 156 Claude Lemieux ........ .50 .23
❑ 157 Pat Verbeek ........ .20 .09
❑ 158 Mariusz Czerkawski ........ .20 .09
❑ 159 Robert Svehla ........ .20 .09
❑ 160 Paul Coffey ........ .60 .25
❑ 161 Al MacInnis ........ .50 .23
❑ 162 Roman Hamrlik ........ .20 .09
❑ 163 Brian Holzinger ........ .20 .09
❑ 164 Cory Stillman ........ .20 .09
❑ 165 Scott Mellanby ........ .20 .09
❑ 166 Todd Warriner ........ .20 .09
❑ 167 Terry Ryan ........ .20 .09
❑ 168 Luc Robitaille ........ .50 .23
❑ 169 Ed Olczyk ........ .20 .09
❑ 170 Adam Deadmarsh ........ .50 .23
❑ 171 Anson Carter ........ .20 .09
❑ 172 Mike Knuble ........ .20 .09
❑ 173 Cliff Ronning ........ .20 .09
❑ 174 Rick Tocchet ........ .50 .23
❑ 175 Chris Pronger ........ .50 .23
❑ 176 Matthew Barnaby ........ .20 .09
❑ 177 Andrei Kovalenko ........ .20 .09
❑ 178 Bryan Smolinski ........ .20 .09
❑ 179 Janne Niinimaa ........ .50 .23
❑ 180 Ray Ferraro ........ .20 .09
❑ 181 Dave Gagner ........ .20 .09
❑ 182 Rob Niedermayer ........ .20 .09
❑ 183 Vadim Sharifijanov ........ .20 .09
❑ 184 Ethan Moreau ........ .20 .09
❑ 185 Bernie Nicholls ........ .20 .09
❑ 186 Jean-Yves Leroux ........ .20 .09
❑ 187 Jere Lehtinen ........ .20 .09
❑ 188 Steve Rucchin ........ .20 .09
❑ 189 Keith Primeau ........ .20 .09
❑ 190 Red Wings Stanley Cup Champs CL (inserts) ........ .50 .23
❑ P1 Brendan Shanahan PROMO 2.00 .90
❑ P8 Peter Forsberg PROMO ........ .60 .25
❑ P70 Guy Hebert PROMO ........ 1.00 .45
❑ P84 Mike Vernon PROMO ........ .50 .23

## 1997-98 Pinnacle Inside Coach's Collection

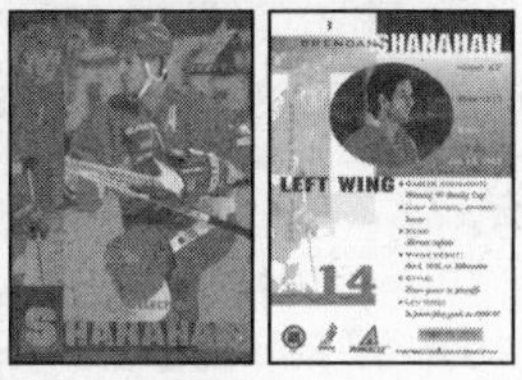

Randomly inserted in cans at the rate of one in seven, this 90-card set is a partial parallel version of the base set and highlights some of the NHL's top impact players. The cards are printed entirely on silver foil with bronze foil stamped accents.

| | MINT | NRMT |
|---|---|---|
| COMPLETE SET (90) | 500.00 | 220.00 |
| COMMON CARD (1-90) | .75 | .35 |

*STARS: 6X TO 12X BASIC CARDS
*YOUNG STARS: 5X TO 10X

## 1997-98 Pinnacle Inside Executive Collection

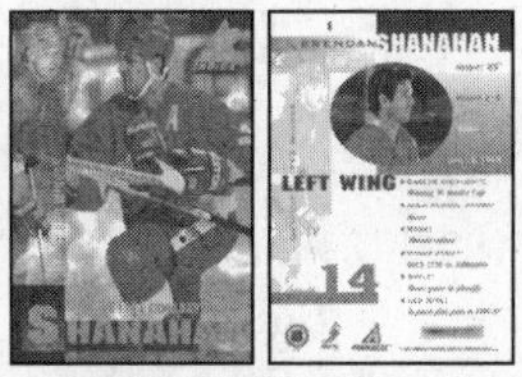

Randomly inserted in cans at the rate of one in 57, this 90-card set is a partial parallel version of the base set printed on full prismatic foil with foil stamped treatments and an external die-cut card design.

| | MINT | NRMT |
|---|---|---|
| COMMON CARD (1-90) | 20.00 | 9.00 |

*STARS: 50X TO 100X BASIC CARDS
*YOUNG STARS: 40X TO 80X

## 1997-98 Pinnacle Inside Stand Up Guys

Inserted one per mask can, this 20-card set features color action photos of top goalies on one side with close-up photos of their masks on the flipsides.

| | MINT | NRMT |
|---|---|---|
| COMPLETE SET (20) | 50.00 | 22.00 |
| COMMON CARD (1A/B-10C/D) | 1.50 | .70 |

C/D CARDS EQUAL VALUE TO A/B CARDS

❑ 1A/B Mike Vernon ........ 1.50 .70
Tom Barasso
❑ 2A/B John Vanbiesbrouck ........ 5.00 2.20
Martin Brodeur
❑ 3A/B Jocelyn Thibault ........ 1.50 .70
Jim Carey
❑ 4A/B Garth Snow ........ 1.50 .70
Marcel Cousineau
❑ 5A/B Patrick Roy ........ 10.00 4.50
Eric Fichaud
❑ 6A/B Patrick Lalime ........ 1.50 .70
Grant Fuhr
❑ 7A/B Olaf Kolzig ........ 1.50 .70
Jeff Hackett
❑ 8A/B Trevor Kidd ........ 1.50 .70
Guy Hebert
❑ 9A/B Nikolai Khabibulin ........ 1.50 .70
Corey Hirsch
❑ 10A/B Curtis Joesph ........ 2.00 .90
Kelly Hrudey

## 1997-98 Pinnacle Inside Stoppers

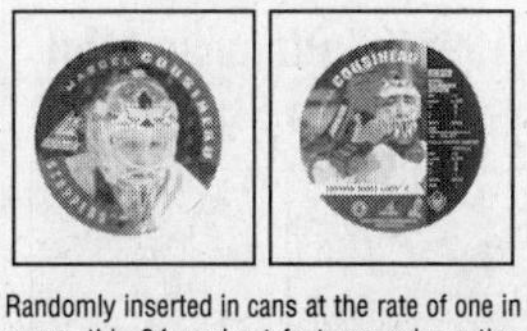

Randomly inserted in cans at the rate of one in seven, this 24-card set features color action photos of the NHL's top goal tenders printed on circular die-cut card stock in 3-D.

| | MINT | NRMT |
|---|---|---|
| COMPLETE SET (24) | 100.00 | 45.00 |
| COMMON CARD (1-24) | 2.50 | 1.10 |

❑ 1 Patrick Roy ........ 20.00 9.00
❑ 2 John Vanbiesbrouck ........ 6.00 2.70
❑ 3 Dominik Hasek ........ 8.00 3.60
❑ 4 Martin Brodeur ........ 10.00 4.50
❑ 5 Mike Richter ........ 4.00 1.80
❑ 6 Guy Hebert ........ 2.50 1.10
❑ 7 Jim Carey ........ 2.50 1.10
❑ 8 Jeff Hackett ........ 2.50 1.10
❑ 9 Roman Turek ........ 2.50 1.10
❑ 10 Kevin Hodson ........ 2.50 1.10
❑ 11 Mike Vernon ........ 2.50 1.10
❑ 12 Curtis Joseph ........ 4.00 1.80
❑ 13 J.S. Giguere ........ 2.50 1.10
❑ 14 Jose Theodore ........ 2.50 1.10
❑ 15 Jocelyn Thibault ........ 2.50 1.10
❑ 16 Nikolai Khabibulin ........ 2.50 1.10
❑ 17 Garth Snow ........ 2.50 1.10
❑ 18 Ron Hextall ........ 2.50 1.10
❑ 19 Steve Shields ........ 2.50 1.10
❑ 20 Grant Fuhr ........ 2.50 1.10
❑ 21 Felix Potvin ........ 4.00 1.80
❑ 22 Marcel Cousineau ........ 2.50 1.10
❑ 23 Bill Ranford ........ 2.50 1.10
❑ 24 Ed Belfour ........ 4.00 1.80

## 1997-98 Pinnacle Inside Track

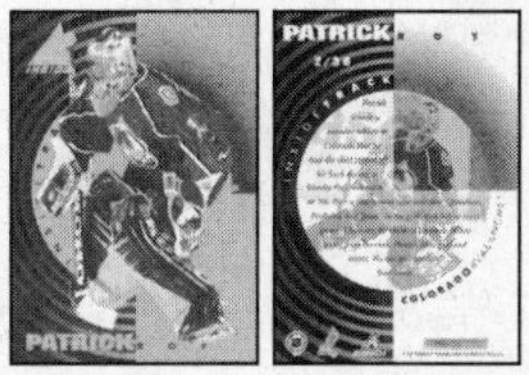

Randomly inserted in cans at the rate of one in 19, this 30-card set features color action photos of some of the game's elite stars with information as to how they became the best players in the NHL.

| | MINT | NRMT |
|---|---|---|
| COMPLETE SET (30) | 600.00 | 275.00 |
| COMMON CARD (1-30) | 8.00 | 3.60 |

❑ 1 Wayne Gretzky ........ 60.00 27.00
❑ 2 Patrick Roy ........ 50.00 22.00
❑ 3 Eric Lindros ........ 30.00 13.50
❑ 4 Paul Kariya ........ 40.00 18.00
❑ 5 Peter Forsberg ........ 30.00 13.50
❑ 6 Martin Brodeur ........ 25.00 11.00
❑ 7 John Vanbiesbrouck ........ 15.00 6.75
❑ 8 Joe Sakic ........ 20.00 9.00
❑ 9 Steve Yzerman ........ 30.00 13.50
❑ 10 Jaromir Jagr ........ 30.00 13.50
❑ 11 Teemu Selanne ........ 20.00 9.00
❑ 12 Pavel Bure ........ 20.00 9.00
❑ 13 Sergei Fedorov ........ 20.00 9.00
❑ 14 Brendan Shanahan ........ 20.00 9.00
❑ 15 Dominik Hasek ........ 20.00 9.00
❑ 16 Saku Koivu ........ 15.00 6.75
❑ 17 Jocelyn Thibault ........ 10.00 4.50
❑ 18 Mark Messier ........ 12.00 5.50
❑ 19 Brett Hull ........ 12.00 5.50
❑ 20 Felix Potvin ........ 10.00 4.50
❑ 21 Curtis Joseph ........ 10.00 4.50
❑ 22 Zigmund Palffy ........ 10.00 4.50
❑ 23 Mats Sundin ........ 10.00 4.50
❑ 24 Keith Tkachuk ........ 12.00 5.50
❑ 25 John LeClair ........ 15.00 6.75
❑ 26 Mike Richter ........ 10.00 4.50
❑ 27 Alexander Mogilny ........ 10.00 4.50
❑ 28 Jarome Iginla ........ 10.00 4.50
❑ 29 Mike Grier ........ 8.00 3.60
❑ 30 Dainius Zubrus ........ 10.00 4.50

## 1997-98 Pinnacle Inside Cans

This 24-can set features eight of the most distinctive goalie masks in the game and photos of 16 of the hottest superstars reproduced on the can labels and painted directly on the metal.

| | MINT | NRMT |
|---|---|---|
| COMPLETE SET (24) | 20.00 | 9.00 |
| COMMON CAN (1-24) | .40 | .18 |
| COMMON SEALED CAN | 3.00 | 1.35 |

*SEALED: 1.25X TO 2.5X HI ON 1.50+CANS
*OPENED GOLD CANS: 3X TO 6X HI
*SEALED GOLD: 7X TO 15X HI ON 1.50+CANS

❑ 1 Brendan Shanahan ........ .75 .35
❑ 2 Jaromir Jagr ........ 1.25 .55
❑ 3 Saku Koivu ........ .60 .25
❑ 4 Mats Sundin ........ .50 .23
❑ 5 Mike Vernon ........ .40 .18
❑ 6 John LeClair ........ .60 .25
❑ 7 Keith Tkachuk ........ .50 .23
❑ 8 Joe Sakic ........ .75 .35
❑ 9 Steve Yzerman ........ 1.25 .55
❑ 10 Eric Lindros ........ 1.25 .55
❑ 11 Guy Hebert ........ .40 .18
❑ 12 Patrick Roy ........ 2.00 .90
❑ 13 Pavel Bure ........ .75 .35
❑ 14 Jocelyn Thibault ........ .40 .18
❑ 15 Paul Kariya ........ 1.50 .70
❑ 16 Peter Forsberg ........ 1.25 .55

❑ 17 Martin Brodeur 1.00 .45
❑ 18 Wayne Gretzky 2.50 1.10
❑ 19 Teemu Selanne .75 .35
❑ 20 John Vanbiesbrouck .60 .25
❑ 21 Mark Messier .50 .23
❑ 22 Mike Richter .40 .18
❑ 23 Brett Hull .50 .23
❑ 24 Curtis Joseph .40 .18

## 1997 Pinnacle Mario's Moments

The Pinnacle Mario Lemieux "Moments" set was issued in one series totalling 18 cards. The set was a Pittsburgh area regional set and was sold over a period of six weeks in three-card packs at Giant Eagle grocery stores. A folder to hold the set, which pictured Lemieux, was available for 99 cents during the first week of the promotion. A parallel version of the set also can be found. These cards, issued at a rate of one per ten packs, featured gold foil lettering of Lemieux's name. Authentic autographed cards also were randomly inserted into packs. Reports from the manufacturer suggest approximately 700 of these were available.

MINT NRMT
COMPLETE SET (18) 25.00 11.00
COMMON CARD (1-18) 1.50 .70

❑ 1 Mario Lemieux 1.50 .70
1984-85 NHL ROY
❑ 2 Mario Lemieux 1.50 .70
1991-92 MVP
❑ 3 Mario Lemieux 1.50 .70
2nd Consecutive Stanley Cup
❑ 4 Mario Lemieux 1.50 .70
Mark Messier
❑ 5 Mario Lemieux 1.50 .70
Art Ross Trophy
❑ 6 Mario Lemieux 1.50 .70
Loses his cool
❑ 7 Mario Lemieux 1.50 .70
All-Star Game MVP
❑ 8 Mario Lemieux 1.50 .70
Pre-game warm-up
❑ 9 Mario Lemieux 1.50 .70
500th NHL Goal
❑ 10 Mario Lemieux 2.00 .90
Jaromir Jagr
❑ 11 Mario Lemieux 1.50 .70
Another great goal
❑ 12 Mario Lemieux 1.50 .70
Final Season?
❑ 13 Mario Lemieux 1.50 .70
1987 Canada Cup
❑ 14 Mario Lemieux 1.50 .70
Regardless of Injuries
❑ 15 Mario Lemieux 1.50 .70
Determined Competitor
❑ 16 Mario Lemieux 3.00 1.35
Wayne Gretzky
❑ 17 Mario Lemieux 1.50 .70
Leads NHL in Goals Per Game
❑ 18 Mario Lemieux 1.50 .70
Leader, Champion , Family Man
❑ XXX Mario Lemieux AUTO. 250.00 110.00

## 1996-97 Pinnacle Mint

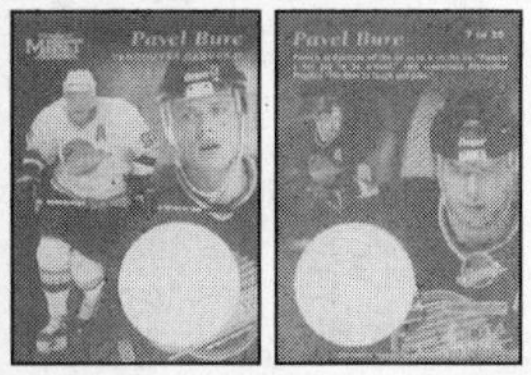

The 1996-97 Pinnacle Mint set was issued in one series totalling 30 cards and was distributed in packs of three cards and two coins for a suggested retail price of $3.99. The challenge was to fit the coins with the die-cut cards that pictured the same player on the minted coin. The fronts feature color action player images on a sepia player portrait background with a cut-out area for the matching coin. Eric Lindros was featured on two promo cards, issued to dealers along with their ordering forms. The cards are identical to the regular die-cut and bronze cards except for the word "promo" written on the right hand side of the card back.

MINT NRMT
COMP.DIE CUT SET (30) 20.00 9.00
COMMON DIE CUT (1-30) .30 .14

❑ 1 Mario Lemieux 2.00 .90
❑ 2 Dominik Hasek 1.00 .45
❑ 3 Eric Lindros 1.50 .70
❑ 4 Jaromir Jagr 1.50 .70
❑ 5 Paul Kariya 1.75 .80
❑ 6 Peter Forsberg 1.50 .70
❑ 7 Pavel Bure 1.00 .45
❑ 8 Sergei Fedorov 1.00 .45
❑ 9 Saku Koivu .75 .35
❑ 10 Daniel Alfredsson .40 .18
❑ 11 Joe Sakic 1.00 .45
❑ 12 Steve Yzerman 1.50 .70
❑ 13 Teemu Selanne 1.00 .45
❑ 14 Brett Hull .60 .25
❑ 15 Jeremy Roenick .50 .23
❑ 16 Mark Messier .60 .25
❑ 17 Mats Sundin .50 .23
❑ 18 Brendan Shanahan 1.00 .45
❑ 19 Keith Tkachuk .60 .25
❑ 20 Paul Coffey .50 .23
❑ 21 Patrick Roy 2.00 .90
❑ 22 Chris Chelios .50 .23
❑ 23 Martin Brodeur 1.25 .55
❑ 24 Felix Potvin .50 .23
❑ 25 Chris Osgood .50 .23
❑ 26 John Vanbiesbrouck .75 .35
❑ 27 Jocelyn Thibault .40 .18
❑ 28 Jim Carey .30 .14
❑ 29 Jarome Iginla .40 .18
❑ 30 Jim Campbell .30 .14
❑ P3A Eric Lindros Bronze Promo 5.00 2.20
❑ P3B Eric Lindros Die-Cut Promo 1.00 .45

## 1996-97 Pinnacle Mint Bronze

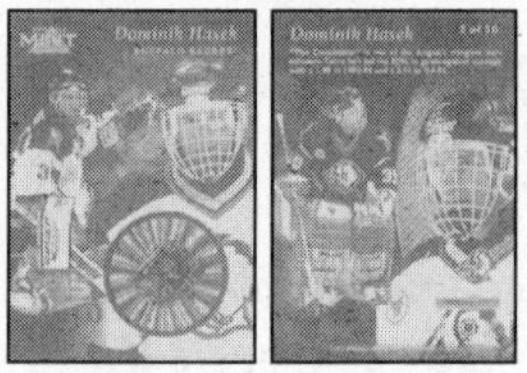

This 30-card version of the 1996-97 Pinnacle Mint set features color action player images on a sepia player portrait background with a bronze foil stamp instead of the die-cut area.

MINT NRMT
COMPLETE SET (30) 40.00 18.00
COMMON CARD (1-30) .60 .25
*BRONZE: 1X TO 2X BASIC CARDS

## 1996-97 Pinnacle Mint Gold

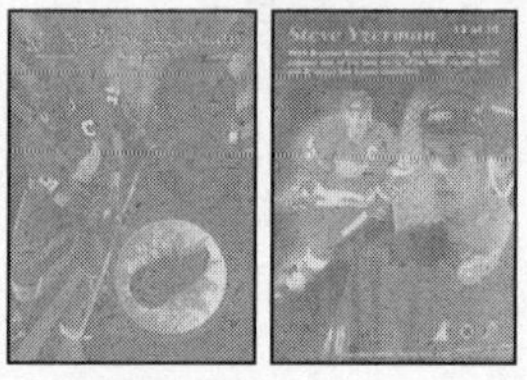

Randomly inserted in packs at a rate of one in 48 (and one in 72 magazine packs), this 30-card set parallels the regular issue version and is distinguished by the use of full Gold-foil dufex print technologies.

MINT NRMT
COMPLETE SET (30) 500.00 220.00
COMMON CARD (1-30) 8.00 3.60
*GOLD: 12.5X TO 25X BASIC CARDS

## 1996-97 Pinnacle Mint Silver

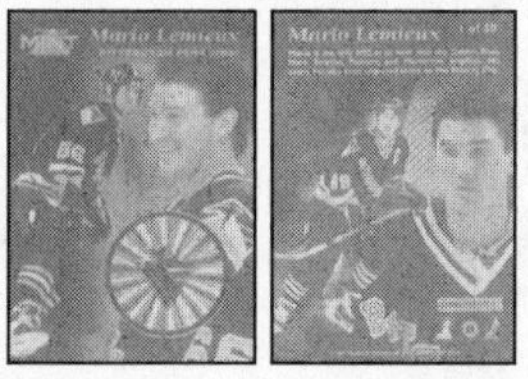

Randomly inserted in packs at a rate of one in 15 (and one in 23 magazine packs), this 30-card set is a parallel to the 1996-97 Pinnacle Mint set and features color action player images on a sepia player portrait background with a silver foil stamp instead of the die-cut area.

MINT NRMT
COMPLETE SET (30) 250.00 110.00
COMMON CARD (1-30) 4.00 1.80
*SILVER: 6X TO X BASIC CARDS

## 1996-97 Pinnacle Mint Coins Brass

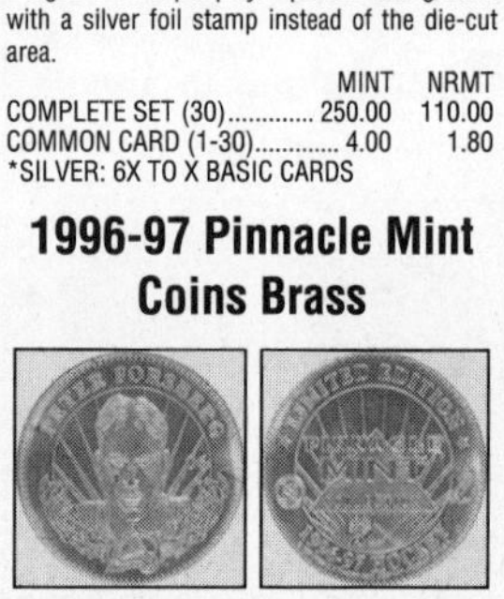

This 30-coin set features embossed brass coins designed to be inserted into a die-cut card of the player who is pictured on the coin. Additional quantities the Eric Lindros coin were mailed out to dealers with their order forms.

MINT NRMT
COMP.BRASS SET (30) 60.00 27.00
COMMON BRASS (1-30) 1.00 .45

❑ 1 Mario Lemieux 6.00 2.70
❑ 2 Dominik Hasek 2.50 1.10
❑ 3 Eric Lindros 4.00 1.80
❑ 4 Jaromir Jagr 4.00 1.80
❑ 5 Paul Kariya 5.00 2.20
❑ 6 Peter Forsberg 4.00 1.80
❑ 7 Pavel Bure 2.50 1.10
❑ 8 Sergei Fedorov 2.50 1.10
❑ 9 Saku Koivu 2.00 .90
❑ 10 Daniel Alfredsson 1.00 .45
❑ 11 Joe Sakic 2.50 1.10
❑ 12 Steve Yzerman 4.00 1.80
❑ 13 Teemu Selanne 2.50 1.10
❑ 14 Brett Hull 1.50 .70
❑ 15 Jeremy Roenick 1.25 .55
❑ 16 Mark Messier 1.50 .70
❑ 17 Mats Sundin 1.25 .55
❑ 18 Brendan Shanahan 2.50 1.10
❑ 19 Keith Tkachuk 1.50 .70
❑ 20 Paul Coffey 1.25 .55
❑ 21 Patrick Roy 6.00 2.70
❑ 22 Chris Chelios 1.25 .55
❑ 23 Martin Brodeur 3.00 1.35
❑ 24 Felix Potvin 1.25 .55
❑ 25 Chris Osgood 1.25 .55
❑ 26 John Vanbiesbrouck 2.00 .90
❑ 27 Jocelyn Thibault 1.00 .45
❑ 28 Jim Carey 1.00 .45
❑ 29 Jarome Iginla 1.00 .45
❑ 30 Jim Campbell 1.00 .45

## 1996-97 Pinnacle Mint Coins Gold Plated

Randomly inserted in retail packs only at a rate of one in 72, this set is parallel to the regular brass coin set and features 24kt. Gold plated coins with embossed player heads.

MINT NRMT
COMPLETE SET (30) 750.00 350.00
COMMON CARD (1-30) 12.00 5.50
*GOLD PLATED: 6X TO 12X BRASS COINS

## 1996-97 Pinnacle Mint Coins Nickel

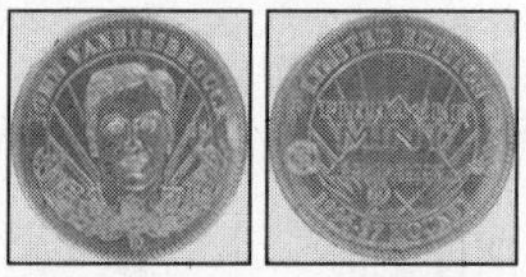

Randomly inserted in retail packs only at a rate of one in 30, this set is parallel to the regular brass coin set and features minted Nickel-Silver coins with embossed player heads.

MINT NRMT
COMPLETE SET (30) 300.00 135.00
COMMON CARD (1-30) 5.00 2.20
*NICKEL: 2.5X TO 5X BRASS COINS 5.00 2.20

## 1997-98 Pinnacle Mint

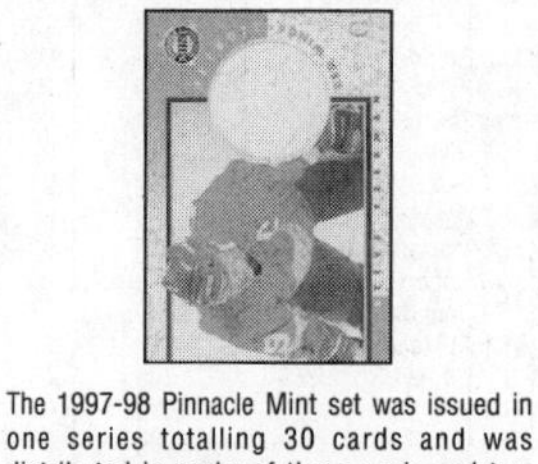

The 1997-98 Pinnacle Mint set was issued in one series totalling 30 cards and was distributed in packs of three cards and two coins with a suggested retail price of $3.99. The challenge was to fit the coins with the die-cut cards that pictured the same player on the minted coin. The fronts feature color player photos with a cut-out area for the matching coin.

MINT NRMT
COMP.DIE CUT SET (30) 20.00 9.00
COMMON DIE CUT (1-30) .20 .09

❑ 1 Eric Lindros 1.25 .55
❑ 2 Paul Kariya 1.50 .70
❑ 3 Peter Forsberg 1.25 .55
❑ 4 John Vanbiesbrouck .60 .25
❑ 5 Steve Yzerman 1.25 .55
❑ 6 Brendan Shanahan .75 .35
❑ 7 Teemu Selanne .75 .35
❑ 8 Dominik Hasek .75 .35
❑ 9 Jarome Iginla .30 .14
❑ 10 Mats Sundin .40 .18
❑ 11 Patrick Roy 2.00 .90
❑ 12 Joe Sakic .75 .35
❑ 13 Mark Messier .50 .23
❑ 14 Sergei Fedorov .75 .35
❑ 15 Saku Koivu .60 .25
❑ 16 Martin Brodeur 1.00 .45
❑ 17 Pavel Bure .75 .35
❑ 18 Wayne Gretzky 3.00 1.35
❑ 19 Brian Leetch .40 .18
❑ 20 John LeClair .60 .25
❑ 21 Keith Tkachuk .50 .23
❑ 22 Jaromir Jagr 1.25 .55
❑ 23 Brett Hull .50 .23
❑ 24 Curtis Joseph .40 .18
❑ 25 Jaroslav Svejkovsky .30 .14
❑ 26 Sergei Samsonov 1.00 .45
❑ 27 Alexei Morozov .30 .14
❑ 28 Alyn McCauley .30 .14
❑ 29 Joe Thornton 1.00 .45
❑ 30 Vaclav Prospal .50 .23

## 1997-98 Pinnacle Mint Coins Brass

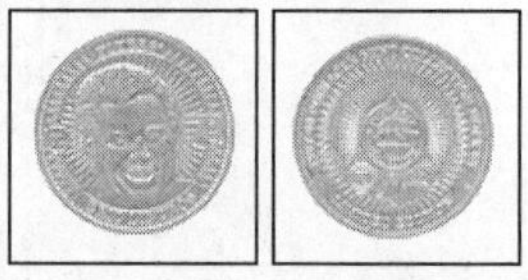

Randomly inserted in packs, this 30-coin set features embossed brass coins designed to be inserted into a die-cut card of the player who is pictured on the coin.

MINT NRMT
COMP.BRASS SET (30) 60.00 27.00
COMMON BRASS (1-30) .60 .25
COMP.BRASS AP SET (30) 900.00 400.00
*BRASS AP's: 7.5X TO 15X BASIC COINS
BRASS AP PRINT RUN 500 SETS
COMP.NICKEL SET (30) 300.00 135.00
COMMON NICKEL (1-30) 3.00 1.35
*NICKEL STARS: 2.5X TO 5X BASIC COINS
NICKEL STATED ODDS 1:41 HOB, RET
COMP.NICKEL AP SET (30) 1500.00 700.00
*NICKEL AP's: 12.5X TO 25X BASIC COINS
NICKEL AP RANDOM INSERTS IN PACKS
NICKEL AP PRINT RUN 250 SETS
COMP.GLD.PLTD.SET (30) 1400.00 650.00
COMON GOLD PLTD. (1-30) 15.00 6.75
*GOLD PLTD.STARS: 12.5X TO 25X BASIC COINS
GOLD PLTD. STATED ODDS 1:199 HOB, RET
COMP.GOLD PLTD.AP SET (30) 3500.00 1600.00
*GOLD PLTD.AP's: 30X TO 60X BASIC COINS
G.PLTD.PRINT RUN 100 SETS
BRASS COINS LISTED BELOW

❑ 1 Eric Lindros 3.00 1.35
❑ 2 Paul Kariya 4.00 1.80
❑ 3 Peter Forsberg 3.00 1.35
❑ 4 John Vanbiesbrouck 1.50 .70
❑ 5 Steve Yzerman 3.00 1.35
❑ 6 Brendan Shanahan 2.00 .90
❑ 7 Teemu Selanne 2.00 .90
❑ 8 Dominik Hasek 2.00 .90
❑ 9 Jarome Iginla .60 .25
❑ 10 Mats Sundin 1.00 .45
❑ 11 Patrick Roy 5.00 2.20
❑ 12 Joe Sakic 2.00 .90
❑ 13 Mark Messier 1.25 .55
❑ 14 Sergei Fedorov 2.00 .90
❑ 15 Saku Koivu 1.50 .70
❑ 16 Martin Brodeur 2.50 1.10
❑ 17 Pavel Bure 2.00 .90
❑ 18 Wayne Gretzky 6.00 2.70
❑ 19 Brian Leetch 1.00 .45
❑ 20 John LeClair 1.50 .70
❑ 21 Keith Tkachuk 1.25 .55
❑ 22 Jaromir Jagr 3.00 1.35
❑ 23 Brett Hull 1.25 .55
❑ 24 Curtis Joseph 1.00 .45
❑ 25 Jaroslav Svejkovsky .75 .35
❑ 26 Sergei Samsonov 2.00 .90
❑ 27 Alexei Morozov .75 .35
❑ 28 Alyn McCauley .75 .35
❑ 29 Joe Thornton 2.00 .90
❑ 30 Vaclav Prospal 1.00 .45

## 1997-98 Pinnacle Mint Minternational

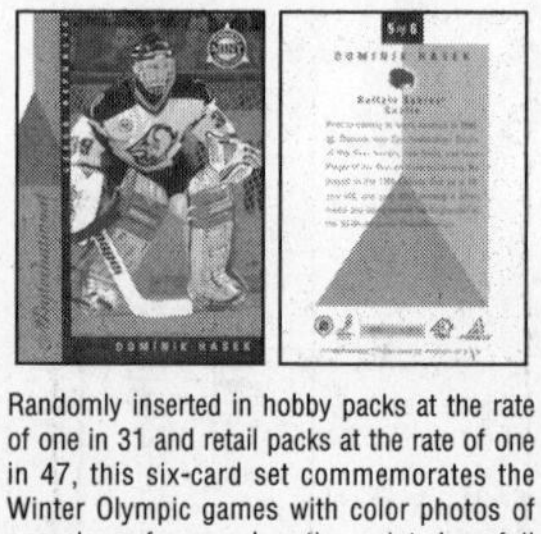

Randomly inserted in hobby packs at the rate of one in 31 and retail packs at the rate of one in 47, this six-card set commemorates the Winter Olympic games with color photos of one player from each nation printed on full silver foil card stock.

MINT NRMT
COMPLETE SET (6) 70.00 32.00
COMMON CARD (1-6) 6.00 2.70

❑ 1 Eric Lindros 15.00 6.75
❑ 2 Peter Forsberg 15.00 6.75
❑ 3 Brett Hull 6.00 2.70
❑ 4 Teemu Selanne 10.00 4.50
❑ 5 Dominik Hasek 10.00 4.50
❑ 6 Pavel Bure 10.00 4.50

## 1997-98 Pinnacle Mint Minternational Coins

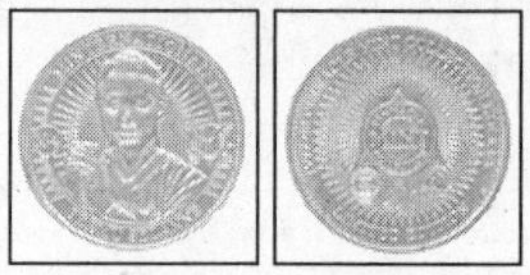

Randomly inserted in hobby packs only at the rate of one in 31, this six-coin set is parallel to the 1997-98 Pinnacle Mint Minternational set and features the six players on double-sized embossed coins.

MINT NRMT
COMPLETE SET (6) 80.00 36.00
COMMON COINS (1-6) 8.00 3.60

❑ 1 Eric Lindros 20.00 9.00
❑ 2 Peter Forsberg 20.00 9.00
❑ 3 Brett Hull 8.00 3.60
❑ 4 Teemu Selanne 12.00 5.50
❑ 5 Dominik Hasek 12.00 5.50
❑ 6 Pavel Bure 12.00 5.50

## 1997-98 Pinnacle Power Pack

Randomly inserted in packs, this 24-card set features color action photos of some of the hottest players in the NHL printed on 3" by 5" cards.

MINT NRMT
COMPLETE SET (24) 40.00 18.00
COMMON CARD (1-24) .60 .25

❑ 1 Eric Lindros 3.00 1.35
❑ 2 Paul Kariya 3.00 1.35
❑ 3 Joe Thornton 2.00 .90
❑ 4 Dominik Hasek 1.50 .70
❑ 5 Patrick Roy 4.00 1.80
❑ 6 Keith Tkachuk 1.00 .45
❑ 7 Martin Brodeur 2.00 .90
❑ 8 Brett Hull 1.00 .45
❑ 9 Mark Messier 1.00 .45
❑ 10 Saku Koivu 1.50 .70
❑ 11 Jaromir Jagr 2.50 1.10
❑ 12 Joe Sakic 2.00 .90
❑ 13 John Vanbiesbrouck 1.25 .55
❑ 14 Pavel Bure 1.50 .70
❑ 15 Jarome Iginla .60 .25
❑ 16 Mats Sundin .75 .35
❑ 17 Wayne Gretzky 5.00 2.20
❑ 18 Steve Yzerman 2.50 1.10
❑ 19 Peter Forsberg 2.50 1.10
❑ 20 Brendan Shanahan 1.50 .70
❑ 21 Sergei Fedorov 1.50 .70
❑ 22 Curtis Joseph .75 .35
❑ 23 John LeClair 1.25 .55
❑ 24 Teemu Selanne 1.50 .70
❑ P2 Paul Kariya PROMO .75 .35
❑ P13 John Vanbiesbrouck PROMO .60 .25

## 1997-98 Pinnacle Totally Certified Platinum Gold

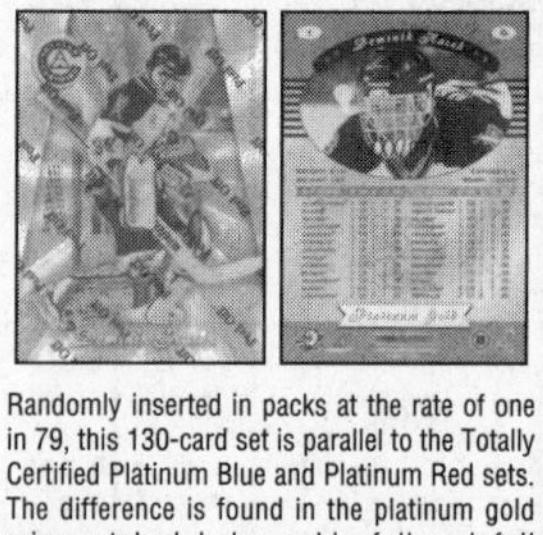

Randomly inserted in packs at the rate of one in 79, this 130-card set is parallel to the Totally Certified Platinum Blue and Platinum Red sets. The difference is found in the platinum gold micro-etched holographic foil and foil stamping. Only 59 serially numbered goalie cards and 69 serially numbered skater cards were printed.

MINT NRMT
COMMON CARD 40.00 18.00
GOLD STATED ODDS 1:79
SKATER PRINT RUN 69 SERIAL #'d SETS
GOALIE PRINT RUN 59 SERIAL #'d SETS
*MIRROR PLAT.GOLD STARS: 1.5X TO 2.5X HI COLUMN

❑ 1 Dominik Hasek 250.00 110.00
❑ 2 Patrick Roy 750.00 350.00
❑ 3 Martin Brodeur 300.00 135.00
❑ 4 Chris Osgood 120.00 55.00
❑ 5 Andy Moog 80.00 36.00
❑ 6 John Vanbiesbrouck 200.00 90.00
❑ 7 Steve Shields 80.00 36.00
❑ 8 Mike Vernon 80.00 36.00

❑ 9 Ed Belfour 120.00 55.00
❑ 10 Grant Fuhr 80.00 36.00
❑ 11 Felix Potvin 120.00 55.00
❑ 12 Bill Ranford 80.00 36.00
❑ 13 Mike Richter 120.00 55.00
❑ 14 Stephane Fiset 80.00 36.00
❑ 15 Jim Carey 80.00 36.00
❑ 16 Nikolai Khabibulin 80.00 36.00
❑ 17 Ken Wregget 80.00 36.00
❑ 18 Curtis Joseph 120.00 55.00
❑ 19 Guy Hebert 80.00 36.00
❑ 20 Damian Rhodes 80.00 36.00
❑ 21 Trevor Kidd 80.00 36.00
❑ 22 Daren Puppa 80.00 36.00
❑ 23 Patrick Lalime 80.00 36.00
❑ 24 Tommy Salo 80.00 36.00
❑ 25 Sean Burke 80.00 36.00
❑ 26 Jocelyn Thibault 80.00 36.00
❑ 27 Kirk McLean 80.00 36.00
❑ 28 Garth Snow 80.00 36.00
❑ 29 Ron Tugnutt 80.00 36.00
❑ 30 Jeff Hackett 80.00 36.00
❑ 31 Eric Lindros 400.00 180.00
❑ 32 Peter Forsberg 400.00 180.00
❑ 33 Mike Modano 150.00 70.00
❑ 34 Paul Kariya 500.00 220.00
❑ 35 Jaromir Jagr 400.00 180.00
❑ 36 Brian Leetch 120.00 55.00
❑ 37 Keith Tkachuk 150.00 70.00
❑ 38 Steve Yzerman 400.00 180.00
❑ 39 Teemu Selanne 250.00 110.00
❑ 40 Bryan Berard 80.00 36.00
❑ 41 Ray Bourque 120.00 55.00
❑ 42 Theoren Fleury 80.00 36.00
❑ 43 Mark Messier 150.00 70.00
❑ 44 Saku Koivu 200.00 90.00
❑ 45 Pavel Bure 250.00 110.00
❑ 46 Peter Bondra 120.00 55.00
❑ 47 Dave Gagner 40.00 18.00
❑ 48 Ed Jovanovski 40.00 18.00
❑ 49 Adam Oates 80.00 36.00
❑ 50 Joe Sakic 300.00 135.00
❑ 51 Doug Gilmour 80.00 36.00
❑ 52 Jim Campbell 40.00 18.00
❑ 53 Mats Sundin 120.00 55.00
❑ 54 Derian Hatcher 40.00 18.00
❑ 55 Jarome Iginla 80.00 36.00
❑ 56 Sergei Fedorov 250.00 110.00
❑ 57 Keith Primeau 80.00 36.00
❑ 58 Mark Recchi 80.00 36.00
❑ 59 Owen Nolan 80.00 36.00
❑ 60 Alexander Mogilny 80.00 36.00
❑ 61 Brendan Shanahan 250.00 110.00
❑ 62 Pierre Turgeon 80.00 36.00
❑ 63 Joe Juneau 80.00 36.00
❑ 64 Steve Rucchin 40.00 18.00
❑ 65 Jeremy Roenick 120.00 55.00
❑ 66 Doug Weight 80.00 36.00
❑ 67 Valeri Kamensky 40.00 18.00
❑ 68 Tony Amonte 80.00 36.00
❑ 69 Dave Andreychuk 40.00 18.00
❑ 70 Brett Hull 150.00 70.00
❑ 71 Wendel Clark 40.00 18.00
❑ 72 Vincent Damphousse 80.00 36.00
❑ 73 Mike Grier 40.00 18.00
❑ 74 Chris Chelios 120.00 55.00
❑ 75 Nicklas Lidstrom 80.00 36.00
❑ 76 Joe Nieuwendyk 80.00 36.00
❑ 77 Rob Blake 40.00 18.00
❑ 78 Alexei Yashin 80.00 36.00
❑ 79 Ryan Smyth 40.00 18.00
❑ 80 Pat Lafontaine 80.00 36.00
❑ 81 Jeff Friesen 80.00 36.00
❑ 82 Ray Ferraro 40.00 18.00
❑ 83 Steve Sullivan 40.00 18.00
❑ 84 Chris Gratton 40.00 18.00
❑ 85 Mike Gartner 80.00 36.00
❑ 86 Kevin Hatcher 40.00 18.00
❑ 87 Ted Donato 40.00 18.00
❑ 88 German Titov 40.00 18.00
❑ 89 Sandis Ozolinsh 80.00 36.00
❑ 90 Ray Sheppard 80.00 36.00
❑ 91 John MacLean 40.00 18.00
❑ 92 Luc Robitaille 80.00 36.00
❑ 93 Rod Brind'Amour 80.00 36.00
❑ 94 Zigmund Palffy 120.00 55.00
❑ 95 Petr Nedved 80.00 36.00
❑ 96 Adam Graves 80.00 36.00
❑ 97 Jozef Stumpel 40.00 18.00
❑ 98 Alexandre Daigle 40.00 18.00
❑ 99 Mike Peca 40.00 18.00
❑ 100 Wayne Gretzky 1000.00 450.00
❑ 101 Alexei Zhamnov 40.00 18.00
❑ 102 Paul Coffey 120.00 55.00
❑ 103 Oleg Tverdovsky 40.00 18.00
❑ 104 Trevor Linden 80.00 36.00
❑ 105 Dino Ciccarelli 40.00 18.00
❑ 106 Andrei Kovalenko 40.00 18.00
❑ 107 Scott Mellanby 40.00 18.00
❑ 108 Bryan Smolinski 40.00 18.00
❑ 109 Bernie Nicholls 40.00 18.00
❑ 110 Derek Plante 40.00 18.00
❑ 111 Pat Verbeek 40.00 18.00
❑ 112 Adam Deadmarsh 80.00 36.00
❑ 113 Martin Gelinas 40.00 18.00
❑ 114 Daniel Alfredsson 80.00 36.00
❑ 115 Scott Stevens 40.00 18.00
❑ 116 Dainius Zubrus 40.00 18.00
❑ 117 Kirk Muller 40.00 18.00
❑ 118 Brian Holzinger 40.00 18.00
❑ 119 John LeClair 200.00 90.00
❑ 120 Al MacInnis 40.00 18.00
❑ 121 Ron Francis 80.00 36.00
❑ 122 Eric Daze 40.00 18.00
❑ 123 Travis Green 40.00 18.00
❑ 124 Jason Arnott 80.00 36.00
❑ 125 Geoff Sanderson 40.00 18.00
❑ 126 Dimitri Khristich 40.00 18.00
❑ 127 Sergei Berezin 40.00 18.00
❑ 128 Jeff O'Neill 40.00 18.00
❑ 129 Claude Lemieux 40.00 18.00
❑ 130 Andrew Cassels 40.00 18.00

## 1997-98 Pinnacle Totally Certified Platinum Red

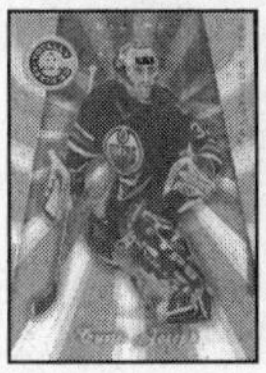
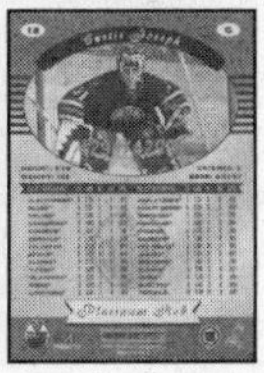

Randomly inserted in packs at the rate of two to a pack, this 130-card set was distributed in three card packs with a suggested retail price of $7.99 and featured color player photos printed on 24 pt. card stock with micro-etched holographic foil and platinum red foil stamping. Only 4299 goalie cards and 6199 skater cards were printed and serially numbered.

| | MINT | NRMT |
|---|---|---|
| COMPLETE SET (130) | 250.00 | 110.00 |
| COMMON SKATER | 2.00 | .90 |
| COMMON GOALIE | 2.50 | 1.10 |
| COMP.BLUE SET (130) | 500.00 | 220.00 |
| COMMON BLUE SKATER | 4.00 | 1.80 |
| COMMON BLUE GOALIE | 5.00 | 2.20 |

*BLUE CARDS: .75X TO 2X RED
BLUE GOALIES: .75X TO 2X RED
BLUE STATED ODDS: ONE PER PACK
BLUE SKAT.PRINT RUN 3099 SERIAL #'d SETS
BLUE GOAL.PRINT RUN 2599 SERIAL #'d SETS

❑ 1 Dominik Hasek 10.00 4.50
❑ 2 Patrick Roy 25.00 11.00
❑ 3 Martin Brodeur 12.00 5.50
❑ 6 John Vanbiesbrouck 8.00 3.60
❑ 31 Eric Lindros 12.00 5.50
❑ 32 Peter Forsberg 12.00 5.50
❑ 33 Mike Modano 5.00 2.20
❑ 34 Paul Kariya 15.00 6.75
❑ 35 Jaromir Jagr 12.00 5.50
❑ 37 Keith Tkachuk 5.00 2.20
❑ 38 Steve Yzerman 12.00 5.50
❑ 39 Teemu Selanne 8.00 3.60
❑ 43 Mark Messier 5.00 2.20
❑ 44 Saku Koivu 6.00 2.70
❑ 45 Pavel Bure 8.00 3.60
❑ 50 Joe Sakic 8.00 3.60
❑ 56 Sergei Fedorov 8.00 3.60
❑ 61 Brendan Shanahan 8.00 3.60
❑ 70 Brett Hull 5.00 2.20
❑ 94 Zigmund Palffy 2.00 .90
❑ 100 Wayne Gretzky 25.00 11.00
❑ 119 John LeClair 6.00 2.70

## 1995-96 Playoff One on One

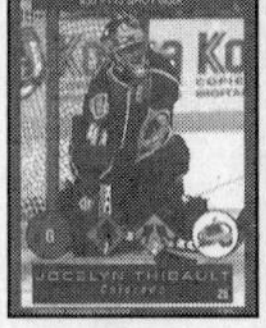
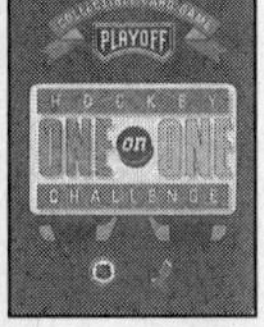

The 1995-96 Playoff One on One Hockey Challenge is a set of 330 cards which can be used to play a fantasy game. The cards could be found in four different card types: Common (1-110), Uncommon (111-220), Rare, Ultra Rare (found in Booster Packs) and Ultra Rare (found in Starter Packs). The scarcer the card, the higher the point values that can be used during the game. Fifty-card starter decks, including three dice and a rule book, were available for $9.95 ea. Game players could add to the power of their decks by purchasing booster packs for $2.50 ea. Ultra rare cards are designated with suffixes below. URS cards were found in starter packs, while URB were hidden in booster packs.

| | MINT | NRMT |
|---|---|---|
| COMPLETE SET (330) | 1200.00 | 550.00 |
| COMMON GREEN CARD (1-110) | .10 | .05 |
| COMMON VIOLET CARD (UNCOMMON 111-220) | .15 | .07 |
| COMMON RARE-SILVER CARD | .40 | .18 |

❑ 1 Guy Hebert .20 .09
❑ 2 Paul Kariya 2.00 .90
❑ 3 Mike Sillinger .10 .05
❑ 4 Oleg Tverdovsky .10 .05
❑ 5 Ray Bourque .30 .14
❑ 6 Alexei Kasatonov .10 .05
❑ 7 Blaine Lacher .10 .05
❑ 8 Cam Neely .20 .09
❑ 9 Adam Oates .20 .09
❑ 10 Kevin Stevens .10 .05
❑ 11 Donald Audette .10 .05
❑ 12 Dominik Hasek 1.00 .45
❑ 13 Pat LaFontaine .20 .09
❑ 14 Alexei Zhitnik .10 .05
❑ 15 Steve Chiasson .10 .05
❑ 16 Theoren Fleury .30 .14
❑ 17 Phil Housley .10 .05
❑ 18 Joe Nieuwendyk .20 .09
❑ 19 Gary Roberts .10 .05
❑ 20 German Titov .10 .05
❑ 21 Ed Belfour .30 .14
❑ 22 Chris Chelios .30 .14
❑ 23 Bernie Nicholls .10 .05
❑ 24 Jeremy Roenick .30 .14
❑ 25 Peter Forsberg 1.50 .70
❑ 26 Sylvain Lefebvre .10 .05
❑ 27 Owen Nolan .20 .09
❑ 28 Joe Sakic 1.00 .45
❑ 29 Jocelyn Thibault .25 .11
❑ 30 Dave Gagner .10 .05
❑ 31 Mike Modano .75 .35
❑ 32 Andy Moog .20 .09
❑ 33 Paul Coffey .30 .14
❑ 34 Sergei Fedorov 1.00 .45
❑ 35 Keith Primeau .15 .07
❑ 36 Ray Sheppard .10 .05
❑ 37 Jason Arnott .15 .07
❑ 38 David Oliver .10 .05
❑ 39 Mike Stapleton .10 .05
❑ 40 Jesse Belanger .10 .05
❑ 41 Paul Laus .10 .05
❑ 42 Rob Niedermayer .20 .09
❑ 43 Brian Skrudland .10 .05
❑ 44 John Vanbiesbrouck 1.00 .45
❑ 45 Sean Burke .10 .05
❑ 46 Andrew Cassels .10 .05
❑ 47 Brendan Shanahan 1.00 .45
❑ 48 Rob Blake .10 .05
❑ 49 Tony Granato .10 .05
❑ 50 Wayne Gretzky 3.00 1.35
❑ 51 Marty McSorley .10 .05
❑ 52 Jamie Storr .40 .18
❑ 53 Vincent Damphousse .20 .09
❑ 54 Mark Recchi .20 .09
❑ 55 Patrick Roy 2.00 .90
❑ 56 Pierre Turgeon .20 .09
❑ 57 Martin Brodeur 1.25 .55
❑ 58 Bill Guerin .10 .05
❑ 59 Scott Niedermayer .10 .05
❑ 60 Stephane Richer .10 .05
❑ 61 Scott Stevens .10 .05
❑ 62 Patrick Flatley .10 .05
❑ 63 Brett Lindros .10 .05
❑ 64 Mathieu Schneider .10 .05
❑ 65 Kirk Muller .10 .05
❑ 66 Adam Graves .10 .05
❑ 67 Alexei Kovalev .10 .05
❑ 68 Brian Leetch .30 .14
❑ 69 Mike Richter .30 .14
❑ 70 Pat Verbeek .10 .05
❑ 71 Luc Robitaille .20 .09
❑ 72 Radek Bonk .10 .05
❑ 73 Alexandre Daigle .10 .05
❑ 74 Alexei Yashin .30 .14
❑ 75 Eric Desjardins .10 .05
❑ 76 Eric Lindros 1.50 .70
❑ 77 Ron Francis .20 .09
❑ 78 Jaromir Jagr 1.50 .70
❑ 79 Mario Lemieux 2.00 .90
❑ 80 Ken Wregget .10 .05
❑ 81 Francois Leroux .10 .05
❑ 82 Pat Falloon .10 .05
❑ 83 Jeff Friesen .10 .05
❑ 84 Arturs Irbe .20 .09
❑ 85 Igor Larionov .10 .05
❑ 86 Shayne Corson .10 .05
❑ 87 Geoff Courtnall .10 .05
❑ 88 Steve Duchesne .10 .05
❑ 89 Brett Hull .75 .35
❑ 90 Al MacInnis .10 .05
❑ 91 Brian Bellows .10 .05
❑ 92 Chris Gratton .10 .05
❑ 93 Dave Andreychuk .20 .09
❑ 94 Tie Domi .10 .05
❑ 95 Mike Gartner .15 .07
❑ 96 Doug Gilmour .30 .14
❑ 97 Larry Murphy .15 .07
❑ 98 Felix Potvin .30 .14
❑ 99 Mats Sundin .30 .14
❑ 100 Pavel Bure 1.00 .45
❑ 101 Kirk McLean .10 .05
❑ 102 Alexander Mogilny .25 .11
❑ 103 Christian Ruuttu .10 .05
❑ 104 Jim Carey .25 .11
❑ 105 Joe Juneau .15 .07
❑ 106 Jason Allison .10 .05
❑ 107 Teppo Numminen .10 .05
❑ 108 Teemu Selanne 1.00 .45
❑ 109 Keith Tkachuk .75 .35
❑ 110 Alexei Zhamnov .10 .05
❑ 111 Patrik Carnback .15 .07
❑ 112 Bobby Dollas .15 .07
❑ 113 Guy Hebert .40 .18
❑ 114 Paul Kariya 4.00 1.80
❑ 115 Shaun Van Allen .15 .07
❑ 116 Ray Bourque .60 .25
❑ 117 Mariusz Czerkawski .15 .07
❑ 118 Todd Elik .15 .07
❑ 119 Blaine Lacher .40 .18
❑ 120 Cam Neely .40 .18
❑ 121 Adam Oates .40 .18
❑ 122 Dave Reid .15 .07
❑ 123 Kevin Stevens .20 .09
❑ 124 Garry Galley .15 .07
❑ 125 Dominik Hasek 2.00 .90
❑ 126 Brian Holzinger .25 .11
❑ 127 Pat LaFontaine .40 .18
❑ 128 Mike Peca .50 .23
❑ 129 Phil Housley .25 .11
❑ 130 Paul Kruse .15 .07
❑ 131 Ronnie Stern .15 .07
❑ 132 Zarley Zalapski .15 .07
❑ 133 Patrick Poulin .15 .07
❑ 134 Bob Probert .25 .11
❑ 135 Jeremy Roenick .60 .25
❑ 136 Adam Deadmarsh .40 .18
❑ 137 Peter Forsberg 3.00 1.35
❑ 138 Andrei Kovalenko .15 .07
❑ 139 Joe Sakic 2.00 .90
❑ 140 Derian Hatcher .15 .07
❑ 141 Grant Ledyard .15 .07
❑ 142 Mike Modano 1.00 .45
❑ 143 Paul Coffey .60 .25
❑ 144 Sergei Fedorov 2.00 .90
❑ 145 Vladimir Konstantinov .40 .18
❑ 146 Nicklas Lidstrom .40 .18
❑ 147 Steve Yzerman 3.00 1.35
❑ 148 Igor Kravchuk .15 .07
❑ 149 Kirk Maltby .15 .07
❑ 150 Boris Mironov .15 .07
❑ 151 Bill Ranford .40 .18
❑ 152 Stu Barnes .20 .09
❑ 153 Jesse Belanger .15 .07
❑ 154 Scott Mellanby .20 .09
❑ 155 Adam Burt .15 .07
❑ 156 Steven Rice .15 .07
❑ 157 Brendan Shanahan 2.00 .90
❑ 158 Glen Wesley .15 .07
❑ 159 Wayne Gretzky 6.00 2.70
❑ 160 Darryl Sydor .15 .07
❑ 161 Rick Tocchet .25 .11
❑ 162 Benoit Brunet .15 .07
❑ 163 J.J. Daigneault .15 .07
❑ 164 Saku Koivu 1.00 .45
❑ 165 Lyle Odelein .15 .07
❑ 166 Patrick Roy 5.00 2.20
❑ 167 Scott Stevens .25 .11
❑ 168 Valeri Zelepukin .15 .07
❑ 169 Steve Thomas .20 .09
❑ 170 Dennis Vaske .15 .07
❑ 171 Brett Lindros .15 .07
❑ 172 Zigmund Palffy .60 .25
❑ 173 Ray Ferraro .20 .09
❑ 174 Brian Leetch .60 .25
❑ 175 Mark Messier 1.00 .45
❑ 176 Ulf Samuelsson .15 .07
❑ 177 Don Beaupre .25 .11
❑ 178 Alexandre Daigle .25 .11
❑ 179 Steve Larouche .15 .07
❑ 180 Scott Levins .15 .07
❑ 181 Ron Hextall .40 .18
❑ 182 Eric Lindros 3.00 1.35
❑ 183 Mikael Renberg .40 .18
❑ 184 Kjell Samuelsson .15 .07
❑ 185 Jaromir Jagr 3.00 1.35
❑ 186 Mario Lemieux 5.00 2.20
❑ 187 Sergei Zubov .25 .11
❑ 188 Bryan Smolinski .15 .07
❑ 189 Dmitri Mironov .15 .07
❑ 190 Ulf Dahlen .15 .07
❑ 191 Arturs Irbe .25 .11
❑ 192 Craig Janney .20 .09
❑ 193 Sandis Ozolinsh .25 .11
❑ 194 Jon Casey .20 .09
❑ 195 Brett Hull 1.00 .45
❑ 196 Esa Tikkanen .25 .11
❑ 197 Brian Bradley .15 .07
❑ 198 Daren Puppa .25 .11
❑ 199 Alexander Selivanov .15 .07
❑ 200 Rob Zamuner .15 .07
❑ 201 Ken Baumgartner .15 .07
❑ 202 Doug Gilmour .60 .25
❑ 203 Kenny Jonsson .25 .11
❑ 204 Felix Potvin .60 .25
❑ 205 Randy Wood .15 .07
❑ 206 Jeff Brown .25 .11
❑ 207 Pavel Bure 2.00 .90
❑ 208 Trevor Linden .25 .11
❑ 209 Alexander Mogilny .40 .18
❑ 210 Roman Oksiuta .15 .07
❑ 211 Cliff Ronning .15 .07
❑ 212 Peter Bondra .60 .25
❑ 213 Jim Carey .40 .18
❑ 214 Pat Peake .15 .07
❑ 215 Mark Tinordi .15 .07
❑ 216 Mike Eastwood .15 .07
❑ 217 Nelson Emerson .25 .11
❑ 218 Dave Manson .15 .07
❑ 219 Teemu Selanne 2.00 .90
❑ 220 Keith Tkachuk 1.00 .45
❑ 221 Bob Corkum R .40 .18
❑ 222 Peter Douris R .40 .18
❑ 223 Paul Kariya URB 100.00 45.00
❑ 224 Todd Krygier URS 8.00 3.60
❑ 225 Mike Sillinger R .40 .18
❑ 226 Ray Bourque URB 15.00 6.75
❑ 227 Fred Knipscheer R .40 .18
❑ 228 Cam Neely URB 15.00 6.75
❑ 229 Adam Oates URB 12.00 5.50
❑ 230 Jason Dawe R .40 .18
❑ 231 Yuri Khmylev R .40 .18
❑ 232 Bob Sweeney URS 8.00 3.60
❑ 233 Trevor Kidd R .75 .35
❑ 234 Eric Daze R 3.00 1.35
❑ 235 Tony Amonte R 1.00 .45
❑ 236 Jeremy Roenick URB 20.00 9.00
❑ 237 Denis Savard R .75 .35
❑ 238 Gary Suter R .40 .18
❑ 239 Peter Forsberg URS 80.00 36.00
❑ 240 Curtis Leschyshyn R .40 .18
❑ 241 Owen Nolan URB 12.00 5.50
❑ 242 Joe Sakic URS 60.00 27.00
❑ 243 Valeri Kamensky R .75 .35
❑ 244 Claude Lemieux R 1.00 .45
❑ 245 Bob Bassen R .40 .18
❑ 246 Shane Churla R .40 .18
❑ 247 Todd Harvey R .50 .23
❑ 248 Kevin Hatcher URS 8.00 3.60
❑ 249 Richard Matvichuk R .50 .23
❑ 250 Mike Modano URB 12.00 5.50
❑ 251 Dino Ciccarelli R .60 .25
❑ 252 Paul Coffey URS 15.00 6.75
❑ 253 Sergei Fedorov URS 40.00 18.00
❑ 254 Vyacheslav Kozlov R .60 .25
❑ 255 Mike Vernon R 1.00 .45
❑ 256 Jason Bonsignore R .40 .18
❑ 257 Dean McAmmond R .40 .18
❑ 258 Bill Ranford R .60 .25
❑ 259 Doug Weight URB 12.00 5.50
❑ 260 Bob Kudelski R .40 .18
❑ 261 Dave Lowry R .40 .18
❑ 262 Gord Murphy R .40 .18
❑ 263 Rob Niedermayer URS 12.00 5.50
❑ 264 Frantisek Kucera R .40 .18
❑ 265 Paul Ranheim R .40 .18
❑ 266 Geoff Sanderson URS 12.00 5.50
❑ 267 Darren Turcotte R .40 .18
❑ 268 Pat Conacher R .40 .18
❑ 269 Wayne Gretzky URB 200.00 90.00
❑ 270 Kelly Hrudey R .60 .25
❑ 271 Jari Kurri R .75 .35
❑ 272 Patrice Brisebois R .40 .18
❑ 273 Vladimir Malakhov R .40 .18
❑ 274 Patrick Roy URB 125.00 55.00
❑ 275 Martin Brodeur URB 40.00 18.00
❑ 276 Neal Broten R .60 .25
❑ 277 Sergei Brylin R .40 .18
❑ 278 John MacLean R .40 .18
❑ 279 Wendel Clark R .75 .35
❑ 280 Travis Green R .40 .18
❑ 281 Scott Lachance URS 8.00 3.60
❑ 282 Tommy Salo R .75 .35
❑ 283 Brian Leetch URB 15.00 6.75
❑ 284 Mark Messier URB 30.00 13.50
❑ 285 Sergei Nemchinov R .40 .18
❑ 286 Luc Robitaille URS 15.00 6.75
❑ 287 Sean Hill R .40 .18
❑ 288 Jim Paek URS 8.00 3.60
❑ 289 Martin Straka R .75 .35
❑ 290 Sylvain Turgeon R .40 .18
❑ 291 Rod Brind'Amour URS 12.00 5.50
❑ 292 Kevin Haller R .40 .18
❑ 293 John LeClair R 3.00 1.35
❑ 294 Eric Lindros URB 80.00 36.00
❑ 295 Joel Otto R .40 .18
❑ 296 Chris Therien R .60 .25
❑ 297 Jaromir Jagr URS 80.00 36.00
❑ 298 Mario Lemieux URB 125.00 55.00
❑ 299 Glen Murray R .40 .18
❑ 300 Petr Nedved R .60 .25
❑ 301 Jamie Baker R .40 .18
❑ 302 Arturs Irbe URB 8.00 3.60
❑ 303 Jayson More R .40 .18
❑ 304 Ray Whitney R .40 .18
❑ 305 Geoff Courtnall URS 8.00 3.60
❑ 306 Dale Hawerchuk R .75 .35
❑ 307 Brett Hull URB 30.00 13.50
❑ 308 Ian Laperriere R .40 .18
❑ 309 Chris Pronger R .75 .35
❑ 310 Roman Hamrlik R .75 .35
❑ 311 Petr Klima URS 8.00 3.60
❑ 312 John Tucker R .40 .18
❑ 313 Paul Ysebaert URB 8.00 3.60
❑ 314 Ken Baumgartner R .40 .18
❑ 315 Doug Gilmour URB 15.00 6.75
❑ 316 Pavel Bure URB 60.00 27.00
❑ 317 Bret Hedican R .40 .18
❑ 318 Alexander Mogilny URS 15.00 6.75
❑ 319 Mike Ridley R .40 .18
❑ 320 Peter Bondra R 1.50 .70
❑ 321 Sylvain Cote R .40 .18
❑ 322 Dale Hunter R .60 .25
❑ 323 Keith Jones URS 8.00 3.60
❑ 324 Kelly Miller R .40 .18
❑ 325 Tim Cheveldae R .60 .25
❑ 326 Dallas Drake R .40 .18
❑ 327 Igor Korolev R .40 .18
❑ 328 Teppo Numminen R .40 .18
❑ 329 Teemu Selanne URB 40.00 18.00
❑ 330 Alexei Zhamnov URS 8.00 3.60

## 1996-97 Playoff One on One

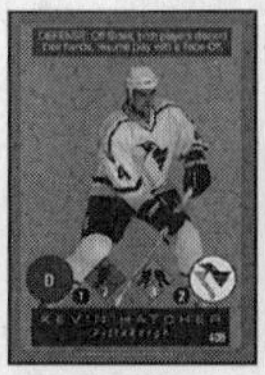
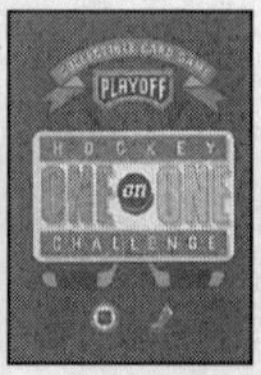

This 110-card set serves as a follow-up to the '95-96 game set of the same name, allowing collectors/players to expand their playing experience. As with the previous set, the cards were available in varying degrees of difficulty. The suffixes below indicate how difficult each is to obtain: C is common, UC is uncommon,

R is rare and UR is ultra rare. The cards can also be differentiated quickly be referring to the background color: commons are green, uncommons are violet, rares are silver and ultra rares are gold.

| | MINT | NRMT |
|---|---|---|
| COMPLETE SET (110) | 800.00 | 350.00 |
| COMMON CARD (331-440) | .10 | .05 |
| COMMON CARD (368-404) | .10 | .05 |
| COMMON CARD (405-427) | .10 | .05 |
| COMMON CARD (428-440) | .10 | .05 |

| | | |
|---|---|---|
| ❑ 331 Mike Sillinger C | .10 | .05 |
| ❑ 332 Oleg Tverdovsky C | .25 | .11 |
| ❑ 333 Kevin Stevens C | .15 | .07 |
| ❑ 334 Joe Nieuwendyk C | .20 | .09 |
| ❑ 335 Owen Nolan C | .25 | .11 |
| ❑ 336 Jocelyn Thibault C | .40 | .18 |
| ❑ 337 Dave Gagner C | .10 | .05 |
| ❑ 338 Ray Sheppard C | .15 | .07 |
| ❑ 339 Jesse Belanger C | .10 | .05 |
| ❑ 340 Tony Granato C | .10 | .05 |
| ❑ 341 Daniel Alfredsson C | .30 | .14 |
| ❑ 342 Stephane Richer C | .15 | .07 |
| ❑ 343 Mathieu Schneider C | .15 | .07 |
| ❑ 344 Kirk Muller C | .15 | .07 |
| ❑ 345 Arturs Irbe C | .20 | .09 |
| ❑ 346 Igor Larionov C | .15 | .07 |
| ❑ 347 Steve Duchesne C | .10 | .05 |
| ❑ 348 Dave Andreychuk C | .10 | .05 |
| ❑ 349 Mike Gartner C | .20 | .09 |
| ❑ 350 Teppo Numminen C | .10 | .05 |
| ❑ 351 Keith Tkachuk C | .75 | .35 |
| ❑ 352 Mike Modano C | .75 | .35 |
| ❑ 353 Paul Kariya C | 1.50 | .70 |
| ❑ 354 German Titov C | .10 | .05 |
| ❑ 355 Bernie Nicholls C | .10 | .05 |
| ❑ 356 Doug Gilmour C | .50 | .23 |
| ❑ 357 Peter Forsberg C | 1.00 | .45 |
| ❑ 358 David Oliver C | .10 | .05 |
| ❑ 359 Pat Verbeek C | .15 | .07 |
| ❑ 360 Ron Francis C | .20 | .09 |
| ❑ 361 Pat Falloon C | .10 | .05 |
| ❑ 362 Jeff Friesen C | .15 | .07 |
| ❑ 363 Todd Krygier C | .10 | .05 |
| ❑ 364 Felix Potvin C | .50 | .23 |
| ❑ 365 Shane Churla C | .15 | .07 |
| ❑ 366 Steve Yzerman C | 1.00 | .45 |
| ❑ 367 Kelly Hrudey C | .15 | .07 |
| ❑ 368 Mariusz Czerkawski U | .20 | .09 |
| ❑ 369 Patrick Poulin U | .20 | .09 |
| ❑ 370 Chris Chelios U | .75 | .35 |
| ❑ 371 Ray Bourque U | .75 | .35 |
| ❑ 372 Igor Kravchuk U | .20 | .09 |
| ❑ 373 Kirk Maltby U | .20 | .09 |
| ❑ 374 Bill Ranford U | .30 | .14 |
| ❑ 375 Darryl Sydor U | .20 | .09 |
| ❑ 376 Rick Tocchet U | .30 | .14 |
| ❑ 377 J.J. Daigneault U | .20 | .09 |
| ❑ 378 Chris Osgood U | 2.00 | .90 |
| ❑ 379 Zigmund Palffy U | .75 | .35 |
| ❑ 380 Ray Ferraro U | .20 | .09 |
| ❑ 381 Don Beaupre U | .30 | .14 |
| ❑ 382 Andy Moog U | .50 | .23 |
| ❑ 383 Sergei Zubov U | .25 | .11 |
| ❑ 384 Craig Janney U | .20 | .09 |
| ❑ 385 Sandis Ozolinsh U | .50 | .23 |
| ❑ 386 Dave Reid U | .20 | .09 |
| ❑ 387 Scott Mellanby U | .30 | .14 |
| ❑ 388 Saku Koivu U | 2.00 | .90 |
| ❑ 389 Bryan Smolinski U | .30 | .14 |
| ❑ 390 Alexander Selivanov U | .20 | .09 |
| ❑ 391 Peter Bondra U | .75 | .35 |
| ❑ 392 Esa Tikkanen U | .30 | .14 |
| ❑ 393 Ken Baumgartner U | .20 | .09 |
| ❑ 394 Ed Belfour U | .75 | .35 |
| ❑ 395 Randy Wood U | .20 | .09 |
| ❑ 396 Jeff Brown U | .20 | .09 |
| ❑ 397 Roman Oksiuta U | .20 | .09 |
| ❑ 398 Cliff Ronning U | .20 | .09 |
| ❑ 399 Mike Eastwood U | .20 | .09 |
| ❑ 400 Nelson Emerson U | .20 | .09 |
| ❑ 401 Dave Manson U | .20 | .09 |
| ❑ 402 Jamie Baker U | .20 | .09 |
| ❑ 403 Ian Laperriere U | .20 | .09 |
| ❑ 404 Petr Klima U | .20 | .09 |
| ❑ 405 Dallas Drake R | 1.00 | .45 |
| ❑ 406 Tim Cheveldae R | 1.50 | .70 |
| ❑ 407 Igor Korolev R | 1.00 | .45 |
| ❑ 408 Kevin Hatcher R | 1.00 | .45 |
| ❑ 409 Dale Hawerchuk R | 2.00 | .90 |
| ❑ 410 Martin Straka R | 2.00 | .90 |
| ❑ 411 Wendel Clark R | 3.00 | 1.35 |
| ❑ 412 Jari Kurri R | 3.00 | 1.35 |
| ❑ 413 Darren Turcotte R | 1.00 | .45 |
| ❑ 414 Yuri Khmylev R | 1.00 | .45 |
| ❑ 415 Bob Corkum R | 1.00 | .45 |
| ❑ 416 Roman Hamrlik R | 2.00 | .90 |
| ❑ 417 Jayson More R | 1.00 | .45 |
| ❑ 418 Travis Green R | 1.50 | .70 |
| ❑ 419 Dean McAmmond R | 1.00 | .45 |
| ❑ 420 Valeri Kamensky R | 1.50 | .70 |
| ❑ 421 Jason Dawe R | 1.00 | .45 |
| ❑ 422 Alexander Mogilny R | 3.00 | 1.35 |
| ❑ 423 Keith Jones R | 1.00 | .45 |
| ❑ 424 Mark Messier R | 10.00 | 4.50 |
| ❑ 425 John Vanbiesbrouck R | 15.00 | 6.75 |
| ❑ 426 Jim Carey R | 6.00 | 2.70 |
| ❑ 427 Brett Hull R | 10.00 | 4.50 |
| ❑ 428 Teemu Selanne UR | 60.00 | 27.00 |
| ❑ 429 Phil Housley UR | 15.00 | 6.75 |
| ❑ 430 Wayne Gretzky UR | 200.00 | 90.00 |
| ❑ 431 Patrick Roy UR | 150.00 | 70.00 |
| ❑ 432 Joe Sakic UR | 60.00 | 27.00 |
| ❑ 433 Jaromir Jagr UR | 125.00 | 55.00 |
| ❑ 434 Doug Weight UR | 15.00 | 6.75 |
| ❑ 435 Rob Niedermayer UR | 15.00 | 6.75 |
| ❑ 436 Mario Lemieux UR | 150.00 | 70.00 |
| ❑ 437 Sergei Fedorov UR | 60.00 | 27.00 |
| ❑ 438 Pavel Bure UR | 60.00 | 27.00 |
| ❑ 439 Eric Lindros UR | 125.00 | 55.00 |
| ❑ 440 Martin Brodeur UR | 80.00 | 36.00 |

## 1975-76 Popsicle

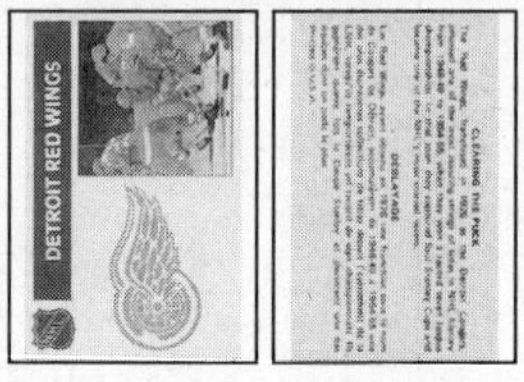

This 18-card set presents the teams of the NHL. The cards measure approximately 3 3/8" by 2 1/8" and are printed in the "credit card format", only slightly thinner than an actual credit card. The front has the NHL logo in the upper left hand corner, and the city and team names in the black bar across the top. A colorful team logo appears on the left side of the card face, while a color action shot of the teams' players appears on the right side. The back provides a brief history of the team. The set was issued in two versions (English and bilingual). We have checklisted the cards below in alphabetical order of the team nicknames.

| | NRMT-MT | EXC |
|---|---|---|
| COMPLETE SET (18) | 30.00 | 13.50 |
| COMMON TEAM (1-18) | 2.00 | .90 |

| | | |
|---|---|---|
| ❑ 1 Chicago Blackhawks | 3.00 | 1.35 |
| ❑ 2 St. Louis Blues | 2.00 | .90 |
| ❑ 3 Boston Bruins | 3.00 | 1.35 |
| ❑ 4 Montreal Canadiens | 3.00 | 1.35 |
| ❑ 5 Vancouver Canucks | 2.00 | .90 |
| ❑ 6 Washington Capitals | 2.00 | .90 |
| ❑ 7 Atlanta Flames | 3.00 | 1.35 |
| ❑ 8 Philadelphia Flyers | 2.00 | .90 |
| ❑ 9 California Golden Seals | 3.00 | 1.35 |
| ❑ 10 New York Islanders | 2.00 | .90 |
| ❑ 11 Los Angeles Kings | 2.00 | .90 |
| ❑ 12 Toronto Maple Leafs | 3.00 | 1.35 |
| ❑ 13 Minnesota North Stars | 2.00 | .90 |
| ❑ 14 Pittsburgh Penguins | 2.00 | .90 |
| ❑ 15 New York Rangers | 3.00 | 1.35 |
| ❑ 16 Detroit Red Wings | 3.00 | 1.35 |
| ❑ 17 Buffalo Sabres | 2.00 | .90 |
| ❑ 18 Kansas City Scouts | 3.00 | 1.35 |

## 1976-77 Popsicle

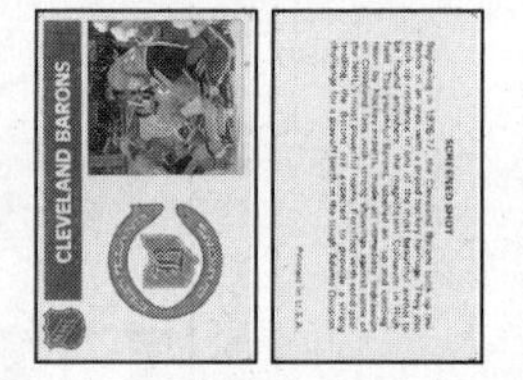

This 18-card set presents the teams of the NHL. The cards measure approximately 3 3/8" by 2 1/8" and are printed in the "credit card format", only slightly thinner than an actual credit card. The front has the NHL logo in the upper left hand corner, and the city and team names in the black bar across the top. A colorful team logo appears on the left side of the card face, while a color action shot of the teams' players appears on the right side. The back provides a brief history of the team. The set was issued in two versions (English and bilingual); a bilingual membership card is known to exist. We have checklisted the cards below in alphabetical order of the team nicknames.

| | NRMT-MT | EXC |
|---|---|---|
| COMPLETE SET (19) | 40.00 | 18.00 |
| COMMON TEAM (1-18) | 2.00 | .90 |

| | | |
|---|---|---|
| ❑ 1 Cleveland Barons | 3.00 | 1.35 |
| ❑ 2 Chicago Blackhawks | 3.00 | 1.35 |
| ❑ 3 St. Louis Blues | 2.00 | .90 |
| ❑ 4 Boston Bruins | 3.00 | 1.35 |
| ❑ 5 Montreal Canadiens | 3.00 | 1.35 |
| ❑ 6 Vancouver Canucks | 2.00 | .90 |
| ❑ 7 Washington Capitals | 2.00 | .90 |
| ❑ 8 Atlanta Flames | 3.00 | 1.35 |
| ❑ 9 Philadelphia Flyers | 2.00 | .90 |
| ❑ 10 New York Islanders | 2.00 | .90 |
| ❑ 11 Los Angeles Kings | 2.00 | .90 |
| ❑ 12 Toronto Maple Leafs | 3.00 | 1.35 |
| ❑ 13 Minnesota North Stars | 2.00 | .90 |
| ❑ 14 Pittsburgh Penguins | 2.00 | .90 |
| ❑ 15 New York Rangers | 3.00 | 1.35 |
| ❑ 16 Detroit Red Wings | 3.00 | 1.35 |
| ❑ 17 Colorado Rockies | 3.00 | 1.35 |
| ❑ 18 Buffalo Sabres | 2.00 | .90 |
| ❑ 19 Membership Card | 3.00 | 1.35 |

## 1967-68 Post Flip Books

This 1967-68 Post set consists of 12 flip books. They display a Montreal player on one side of the page and a Toronto player on the other side. In the listing below, the Montreal player is listed first.

| | NRMT-MT | EXC |
|---|---|---|
| COMPLETE SET (12) | 200.00 | 90.00 |
| COMMON CARD (1-12) | 10.00 | 4.50 |

| | | |
|---|---|---|
| ❑ 1 Gump Worsley<br>Johnny Bower | 25.00 | 11.00 |
| ❑ 2 Rogatien Vachon<br>Johnny Bower | 30.00 | 13.50 |
| ❑ 3 J.C. Tremblay<br>Tim Horton | 25.00 | 11.00 |
| ❑ 4 Jacques Laperriere<br>Marcel Pronovost | 15.00 | 6.75 |
| ❑ 5 Henri Richard<br>Frank Mahovlich | 25.00 | 11.00 |
| ❑ 6 Dick Duff<br>Dave Keon | 20.00 | 9.00 |
| ❑ 7 Jean Beliveau<br>Jim Pappin | 30.00 | 13.50 |
| ❑ 8 Jean Beliveau<br>Ron Ellis | 30.00 | 13.50 |
| ❑ 9 Gilles Tremblay<br>George Armstrong | 20.00 | 9.00 |
| ❑ 10 J.C. Tremblay<br>Pete Stemkowski | 10.00 | 4.50 |
| ❑ 11 Ralph Backstrom<br>Bob Pulford | 15.00 | 6.75 |
| ❑ 12 Bobby Rousseau<br>Wayne Hillman | 10.00 | 4.50 |

## 1968-69 Post Cereal Marbles

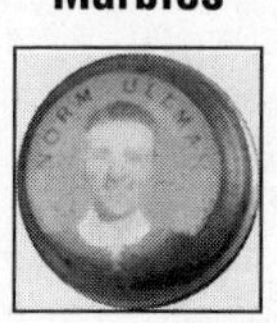

This set of 30 marbles was issued by Post Cereal in Canada and features players of the Montreal Canadiens (MC) and the Toronto Maple Leafs (TML). Also produced was an attractive game board which is rather difficult to find and not included in the complete set price below.

| | NRMT-MT | EXC |
|---|---|---|
| COMPLETE SET (30) | 400.00 | 180.00 |
| COMMON CARD (1-30) | 6.00 | 2.70 |

| | | |
|---|---|---|
| ❑ 1 Ralph Backstrom MC | 6.00 | 2.70 |
| ❑ 2 Jean Beliveau MC | 30.00 | 13.50 |
| ❑ 3 Johnny Bower TML | 12.00 | 5.50 |
| ❑ 4 Wayne Carleton TML | 6.00 | 2.70 |
| ❑ 5 Yvan Cournoyer MC | 15.00 | 6.75 |
| ❑ 6 Ron Ellis TML | 6.00 | 2.70 |
| ❑ 7 John Ferguson MC | 6.00 | 2.70 |
| ❑ 8 Bruce Gamble TML | 6.00 | 2.70 |
| ❑ 9 Terry Harper MC | 6.00 | 2.70 |
| ❑ 10 Ted Harris MC | 6.00 | 2.70 |
| ❑ 11 Paul Henderson TML | 8.00 | 3.60 |
| ❑ 12 Tim Horton TML | 30.00 | 13.50 |
| ❑ 13 Dave Keon TML | 20.00 | 9.00 |
| ❑ 14 Jacques Laperriere MC | 8.00 | 3.60 |
| ❑ 15 Jacques Lemaire MC | 20.00 | 9.00 |
| ❑ 16 Murray Oliver TML | 6.00 | 2.70 |
| ❑ 17 Mike Pelyk TML | 6.00 | 2.70 |
| ❑ 18 Pierre Pilote TML | 8.00 | 3.60 |
| ❑ 19 Marcel Pronovost TML | 8.00 | 3.60 |
| ❑ 20 Bob Pulford TML | 8.00 | 3.60 |
| ❑ 21 Henri Richard MC | 15.00 | 6.75 |
| ❑ 22 Bobby Rousseau MC | 6.00 | 2.70 |
| ❑ 23 Serge Savard MC | 8.00 | 3.60 |
| ❑ 24 Floyd Smith TML | 6.00 | 2.70 |
| ❑ 25 Gilles Tremblay MC | 6.00 | 2.70 |
| ❑ 26 J.C. Tremblay MC | 6.00 | 2.70 |
| ❑ 27 Norm Ullman TML | 8.00 | 3.60 |
| ❑ 28 Rogatien Vachon MC | 25.00 | 11.00 |
| ❑ 29 Mike Walton TML | 6.00 | 2.70 |
| ❑ 30 Gump Worsley MC | 15.00 | 6.75 |
| ❑ xx Game Board | 175.00 | 80.00 |

## 1970-71 Post Cereal Shooters

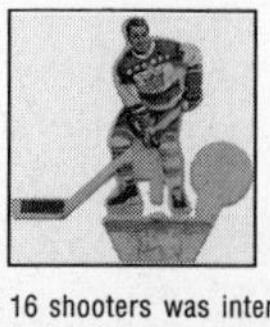

This set of 16 shooters was intended to be used with the hockey game that Post had advertised as a premium. The shooter consists of a plastic figure with a colorful adhesive decal sheet, with stickers that could be applied to the shooter for identification. All players come with home and away, i.e., red or blue shoulders. The figures measure approximately 3 1/2" by 4 1/2". Players are featured in their NHLPA uniform. They are unnumbered and hence are listed below in alphabetical order.

| | NRMT-MT | EXC |
|---|---|---|
| COMPLETE SET (16) | 300.00 | 135.00 |
| COMMON CARD (1-16) | 10.00 | 4.50 |

| | | |
|---|---|---|
| ❑ 1 Johnny Bucyk | 15.00 | 6.75 |
| ❑ 2 Ron Ellis | 10.00 | 4.50 |
| ❑ 3 Ed Giacomin | 20.00 | 9.00 |
| ❑ 4 Paul Henderson | 15.00 | 6.75 |
| ❑ 5 Ken Hodge | 12.50 | 5.50 |
| ❑ 6 Dennis Hull | 12.50 | 5.50 |
| ❑ 7 Orland Kurtenbach | 10.00 | 4.50 |
| ❑ 8 Jacques Laperriere | 12.50 | 5.50 |
| ❑ 9 Jacques Lemaire | 15.00 | 6.75 |
| ❑ 10 Frank Mahovlich | 15.00 | 6.75 |
| ❑ 11 Peter Mahovlich | 12.50 | 5.50 |
| ❑ 12 Bobby Orr | 100.00 | 45.00 |
| ❑ 13 Jacques Plante | 40.00 | 18.00 |
| ❑ 14 Jean Ratelle | 15.00 | 6.75 |
| ❑ 15 Dale Tallon | 10.00 | 4.50 |
| ❑ 16 J.C. Tremblay | 12.50 | 5.50 |

## 1972-73 Post Action Transfers

These 12 cards feature two players on each transfer. Each card depicts an important facet of the game. We are listing the players first and then the English title of the card afterwards.

| | MINT | NRMT |
|---|---|---|
| COMPLETE SET (12) | 250.00 | 110.00 |
| COMMON CARD (1-12) | 15.00 | 6.75 |

| | | |
|---|---|---|
| ❑ 1 Garry Unger<br>Bobby Orr<br>Defense | 60.00 | 27.00 |
| ❑ 2 Red Berenson<br>Dale Tallon<br>In the Corner | 15.00 | 6.75 |
| ❑ 3 Gary Dornhoeffer<br>Wayne Cashman<br>Face Off | 15.00 | 6.75 |
| ❑ 4 Jim McKenny<br>Ed Giacomin<br>Power Save | 20.00 | 9.00 |
| ❑ 5 Pat Quinn<br>Keith Magnuson<br>Power Play Goal | 15.00 | 6.75 |
| ❑ 6 Paul Shmyr<br>Rod Seiling<br>Break Away | 15.00 | 6.75 |
| ❑ 7 Danny Grant<br>Jacques Plante<br>Slap Shot | 20.00 | 9.00 |
| ❑ 8 Syl Apps Jr.<br>Serge Savard<br>Rebound | 20.00 | 9.00 |
| ❑ 9 Gump Worsley<br>Gary Bergman<br>Wrist Shot | 25.00 | 11.00 |
| ❑ 10 Roger Crozier<br>Ed Westfall<br>Last Minute | 20.00 | 9.00 |
| ❑ 11 Dennis Hull<br>Orland Kurtenbach<br>Goalmouth Scramble | 15.00 | 6.75 |
| ❑ 12 Rogatien Vachon<br>Yvan Cournoyer<br>Chest Save | 30.00 | 13.50 |

## 1981-82 Post Standups

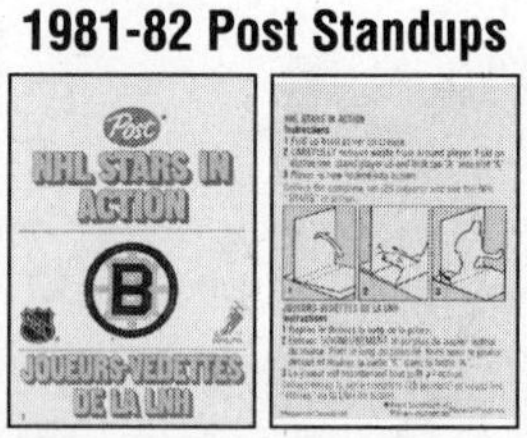

Each thick card in this 28-card set measures approximately 2 13/16" by 3 3/4" and consists of three panels joined together at one end. The front of the first panel has the logos of Post, the NHL, the NHLPA, and a NHL team, with the title NHL Stars in Action in English and French. The back of the first panel has a full color action photo of a player from the NHL team featured on the card. The second panel is blank backed and features a standup of the player, with his signature at the bottom of the standup. The front of the third panel has the player's name and statistics (from the 1980-81 regular season) in English and French for that player as well as for his entire team, with instructions on the card back in both languages for creating the standup. These three dimensional cards were issued in cellophane packs with one card per specially marked box of Post Sugar-Crisp, Honeycomb, or Alpha-Bits. The set is composed of two players from each Canadian team and one player from each American NHL team. The promotion included a mail-in offer for an official NHL fact chart, which featured the new NHL divisional alignment. Also available, but hard to find, is a two-piece display box; the cover has logos of all NHL teams with two slots inside for cards and space to display one "opened" card.

| | NRMT-MT | EXC |
|---|---|---|
| COMPLETE SET (28) | 50.00 | 22.00 |
| COMMON CARD (1-28) | 1.00 | .45 |

| | | |
|---|---|---|
| ❑ 1 Ray Bourque | 8.00 | 3.60 |
| ❑ 2 Gilbert Perreault | 2.50 | 1.10 |
| ❑ 3 Denis Savard | 4.00 | 1.80 |
| ❑ 4 Dale McCourt | 1.00 | .45 |
| ❑ 5 Bobby Smith | 1.50 | .70 |
| ❑ 6 Mike Bossy | 6.00 | 2.70 |
| ❑ 7 Bobby Clarke | 4.00 | 1.80 |
| ❑ 8 Randy Carlyle | 1.00 | .45 |
| ❑ 9 Mike Palmateer | 2.00 | .90 |
| ❑ 10 Dave(Tiger) Williams | 1.50 | .70 |
| ❑ 11 Mark Howe | 2.00 | .90 |
| ❑ 12 Marcel Dionne | 3.00 | 1.35 |
| ❑ 13 Mike Liut | 1.50 | .70 |
| ❑ 14 Barry Beck | 1.00 | .45 |
| ❑ 15 Mark Messier | 12.00 | 5.50 |
| ❑ 16 Larry Robinson | 3.00 | 1.35 |
| ❑ 17 Real Cloutier | 1.00 | .45 |
| ❑ 18 Borje Salming | 2.00 | .90 |
| ❑ 19 Morris Lukowich | 1.00 | .45 |
| ❑ 20 Brett Callighen | 1.00 | .45 |
| ❑ 21 Rob Ramage | 1.50 | .70 |
| ❑ 22 Wilf Paiement | 1.00 | .45 |
| ❑ 23 Mario Tremblay | 1.50 | .70 |
| ❑ 24 Robbie Ftorek | 1.00 | .45 |
| ❑ 25 Stan Smyl | 1.50 | .70 |
| ❑ 26 Dave Babych | 1.00 | .45 |
| ❑ 27 Willi Plett | 1.00 | .45 |
| ❑ 28 Kent Nilsson | 2.00 | .90 |
| ❑ xx Display Box | 20.00 | 9.00 |

## 1982-83 Post Cereal

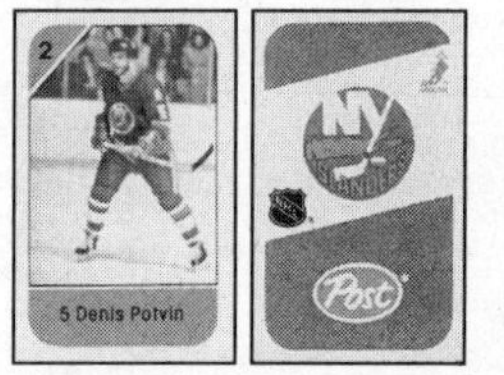

This set is composed of panels of 16 mini playing cards, each measuring approximately 1 1/4" by 2" after perforation. The cards were issued in panel form in a cellophane wrapper inside specially marked packages of Post Cereal. The front of each individual card has an action color photo of the player, with uniform number in the upper left-hand corner, and the player's name and uniform number beneath the picture. The back is done in the team's colors and includes the logos of the team, the sponsor (Post), the NHL, and the NHLPA. There were 21 panels produced, one for each NHL team. Game instructions were included in each box so that one could play Shut-out, Face Off, or Hockey Match with the set of 16 hockey playing cards. By mailing in the UPC code or a reasonable hand drawn facsimile, one could enter the sweepstakes for the grand prize of a trip for two to a Stanley Cup Final playoff game. The complete set was available for a limited time through a mail-in offer. Apparently, a salesman's promo kit was produced in conjunction with this offer, which included six oversized sample cards (Dale Hawerchuk, Real Cloutier, Kent Nilsson, Glenn Anderson, Bob Gainey and Rick Vaive). Not enough is known about this kit at this time to assign a value to it or the singles.

| | MINT | NRMT |
|---|---|---|
| COMPLETE SET (21) | 75.00 | 34.00 |
| COMMON PANEL (1-21) | 2.50 | 1.10 |

| | | |
|---|---|---|
| ❑ 1 Boston Bruins<br>1 Rogie Vachon<br>7 Ray Bourque<br>8 Peter McNab<br>11 Steve Kasper<br>12 Wayne Cashman<br>14 Mike Gillis<br>16 Rick Middleton<br>17 Stan Jonathan<br>20 Mike O'Connell<br>22 Brad Park<br>24 Terry O'Reilly<br>26 Mike Milbury<br>28 Tom Fergus<br>29 Brad McCrimmon<br>32 Bruce Crowder<br>33 Larry Melynk | 5.00 | 2.20 |
| ❑ 2 Buffalo Sabres<br>1 Don Edwards<br>3 Richie Dunn<br>4 John Van Boxmeer<br>5 Mike Ramsey<br>7 Dale McCourt<br>8 Tony McKegney<br>10 Craig Ramsay<br>11 Gilbert Perreault<br>12 Andre Savard<br>15 Yvon Lambert<br>16 Ric Seiling<br>17 Mike Foligno | 3.50 | 1.55 |

21 J. Francois Sauve
22 Lindy Ruff
24 Bill Hait
27 Larry Playfair

❑ 3 Calgary Flames .................. 3.50 1.55
1 Pat Riggin
4 Pekka Rautakallio
5 Phil Russell
6 Ken Houston
9 Lanny McDonald
12 Dennis Cyr
14 Kent Nilsson
15 Kevin Lavalle
16 Guy Chouinard
17 Jamie Hislop
20 Bob Murdoch
23 Paul Reinhart
24 Jim Peplinski
25 Willi Plett
26 Mel Bridgeman
28 Gary McAdam

❑ 4 Chicago Blackhawks .......... 5.00 2.20
2 Greg Fox
5 Dave Hutchison
8 Terry Ruskowski
10 Reg Kerr
12 Tom Lysiak
14 Bill Gardner
15 Tim Higgins
16 Rich Preston
18 Denis Savard
20 Al Secord
22 Grant Mulvey
23 Doug Crossman
24 Doug Wilson
26 Rick Paterson
29 Ted Bulley
35 Tony Esposito

❑ 5 Detroit Red Wings ............. 2.50 1.10
2 Jim Schoenfeld
3 John Barrett
5 Greg Smith
7 Willie Huber
11 Walt McKechnie
15 Paul Woods
16 Mark Kirton
18 Danny Gare
20 Vaclav Nedomansky
21 Mike Blaisdell
22 Greg Joly
23 Mark Osborne
24 Derrek Smith
25 John Ogrodnick
Reed Larson
31 Bob Sauve

❑ 6 Edmonton Oilers .............. 20.00 9.00
1 Grant Fuhr
2 Lee Fogolin
4 Kevin Lowe
6 Garry Lariviere
7 Paul Coffey
8 Risto Siltanen
9 Glenn Anderson
10 Matti Hagman
11 Mark Messier
12 Dave Hunter
16 Pat Hughes
17 Jari Kurri
18 Brett Callighen
20 Dave Lumley
27 Dave Semenko
99 Wayne Gretzky

❑ 7 Hartford Whalers ............... 3.50 1.55
3 Paul Shmyr
4 Ron Francis
5 Mark Howe
6 Blake Wesley
8 Garry Howatt
11 Jordy Douglas
14 Dave Keon
16 George Lyle
21 Blaine Stoughton
22 Doug Sulliman
24 Chris Kotsopoulos
26 Don Nachbaur
27 Warren Miller
28 Pierre Larouche
30 Greg Millen

❑ 8 Los Angeles Kings ............. 3.50 1.55
1 Mario Lessard
2 Rick Chartraw
4 Jerry Korab
5 Larry Murphy
11 Charlie Simmer
12 Dean Hopkins
16 Marcel Dionne
17 John P. Kelly
18 Dave Taylor
19 Jim Fox
20 Mark Hardy
22 Steve Jensen
23 Doug Smith
24 Jay Wells
25 Dave Lewis
26 Steve Bozek

❑ 9 Minnesota North Stars....... 2.50 1.10
2 Curt Giles
3 Fred Barrett
4 Craig Hartsburg
5 Brad Maxwell
8 K.E. Anderson
10 Gord Roberts
11 Tom McCarthy
14 Brad Palmer
15 Bobby Smith
17 Tim Young
20 Dino Ciccarelli
22 Gary Sargent
25 Al MacAdam
26 Steve Payne
27 Gilles Meloche
28 Steve Christoff

❑ 10 Montreal Canadiens .......... 7.50 3.40
3 Brian Engblom
6 Pierre Mondou
8 Doug Risebrough
10 Guy Lafleur
12 Keith Acton
14 Mario Tremblay
17 Rod Langway
19 Larry Robinson
20 Mark Hunter
21 Doug Jarvis
22 Steve Shutt
23 Bob Gainey
24 Robert Picard
26 Craig Laughlin
31 Mark Napier
33 Richard Sevigny

❑ 11 New Jersey Devils ........... 2.50 1.10
(Colorado Rockies)
1 Glenn Resch
2 Joe Cirella
4 Bob Lorimer
5 Rob Ramage
6 Joe Micheletti
9 Don Lever
10 Dave Cameron
12 Bob MacMillan
14 Steve Tambellini
15 Brent Ashton
16 Merlin Malinowski
18 Bobby Miller
20 Dwight Fostet
21 Kevin Maxwell
26 Mike Kitchen
27 John Wensink

❑ 12 New York Islanders .......... 7.50 3.40
2 Mike McEwen
3 Tomas Jonsson
5 Denis Potvin
6 Ken Morrow
7 Stefan Persson
9 Clark Gillies
11 Wayne Merrick
14 Bob Bourne
19 Bryan Trottier
22 Mike Bossy
23 Bob Nystrom
26 Dave Langevin
27 John Tonelli
28 Anders Kallur
31 Billy Smith
91 Butch Goring

❑ 13 New York Rangers ........... 2.50 1.10
2 Tom Laidlaw
3 Barry Beck
4 Ron Greschner
8 Steve Vickers
10 Ron Duguay
12 Don Maloney
14 Mike Allison
17 Ed Johnstone
22 Nick Fotiu
26 Dave Maloney
27 Mike Rogers
29 Reijo Ruotsalainen
31 Steve Weeks
33 Andre Dore
38 Robbie Ftorek
40 Mark Pavelich

❑ 14 Philadelphia Flyers........... 5.00 2.20
3 Behn Wilson
6 Fred Arthur
7 Bill Barber
8 Brad Marsh
9 Reid Bailey
9 Darryl Sittler
12 Tim Kerr
14 Kenny Linseman
16 Bobby Clarke
17 Paul Holmgren
20 Jimmy Watson
23 Ilkka Sinisalo
26 Brian Propp
27 Reggie Leach
29 Glen Cochrane
33 Pete Peeters

❑ 15 Pittsburgh Penguins ......... 2.50 1.10
2 Pat Price
3 Ron Stackhouse
4 Paul Baxter
10 Peter Lee
11 George Ferguson
12 Greg Malone
14 Doug Shedden
15 Pat Boutette
16 Marc Chorney
17 Rick Kehoe
19 Gregg Sheppard
20 Paul Gardner
22 Mike Bullard
24 Pat Graham
25 Randy Cartyle
29 Michel Dion

❑ 16 Quebec Nordiques ............ 3.50 1.55
1 John Garrett
2 Wally Weir
5 Normand Rochefort
8 Marc Tardif
9 Real Cloutier
12 Jere Gillis
16 Michel Goulet
18 Marion Stastny
19 Alain Cote
20 Anton Stastny
22 Mario Marois
23 Jacques Richard
26 Peter Stastny
27 Wilf Paiement
28 Andre Dupont
32 Dale Hunter

❑ 17 St. Louis Blues ................. 2.50 1.10
1 Mike Liut
5 Guy Lapointe
6 Larry Patey
9 Perry Turnbull
10 Wayne Babych
11 Brian Sutter
16 Jack Brownschidle
17 Ed Kea
18 Rick Lapointe
19 Blake Dunlop
21 Mike Zuke
22 Jorgen Pettersson
24 Bernie Federko
25 Bill Baker
26 Mike Crombeen
35 Jim Payese

❑ 18 Toronto Maple Leafs......... 3.50 1.55
1 Michel Larocque
3 Bob Manno
4 Bob McGill
7 Rocky Saganiuk
10 John Anderson
11 Fred Boimistruck
12 Walt Poddubny
14 Miroslav Frycer
15 Jim Benning
17 Stewart Gavin
19 Bill Derlago
21 Borje Salming
22 Rick Vaive
24 Normand Aubin
25 Terry Martin
26 Barry Melrose

❑ 19 Vancouver Canucks .......... 2.50 1.10
2 Doug Halward
7 Gary Lupul
9 Ivan Boldirev
12 Stan Smyl
13 Lars Lindgren
18 Darcy Rota
19 Ron Delorme
21 Ivan Hlinka
22 Dave(Tiger) Williams
23 Thomas Gradin
24 Curt Fraser
25 Kevin McCarthy
26 Lars Molin
27 Harold Snepsts
28 Marc Crawford
35 Richard Brodeur

❑ 20 Washington Capitals......... 3.50 1.55
2 Doug Hicks
4 Randy Holt
5 Rick Green
6 Darren Veitch
9 Ryan Walter
10 Bob Carpenter
11 Mike Gartner
12 Glen Currie
14 Gaetan Duchesne
16 Bengt Gustafsson
20 Greg Theberge
21 Dennis Maruk
23 Bob Gould
25 Terry Murray
28 Chris Valentine
35 Al Jensen

❑ 21 Winnipeg Jets................... 3.50 1.55
3 Bryan Maxwell
7 Tim Watters
10 Dale Hawerchuk
11 Scott Arniel
12 Morris Lukowich
13 Dave Christian
14 Tim Trimper
15 Paul MacLean
18 Serge Savard
20 Willy Lindstrom
22 Bengt Lundholm
23 Lucien DeBlois
27 Don Spring
28 Norm Dupont
31 Ed Staniowski
44 Dave Babych

## 1994-95 Post Cereal Box Backs

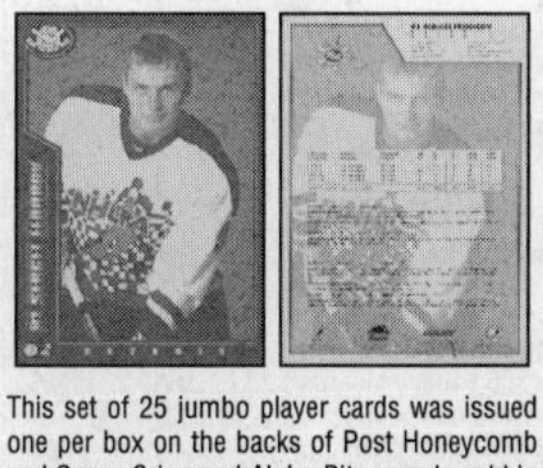

This set of 25 jumbo player cards was issued one per box on the backs of Post Honeycomb and Sugar-Crisp qnd Alpha-Bits cereals sold in Canada. Each jumbo card measures 8 3/4" by 12 1/4". Inside the box was information on a mail-in offer whereby the collector could receive a complete set by mailing in 4 UPC symbols and 8.00. The offer was valid while supplies lasted, and in no event extended beyond September 30, 1995. The fronts feature posed color photos framed by a black-and-red border design. The player's name and his number are printed vertically along the lower left edge, while the team's city is printed beneath the picture. On a ghosted version of the front photo, the bilingual backs present biography, statistics, and player profile. The prices below are for cut backs; complete, unopened cereal boxes sell for a premium of about two times the prices listed below. The box backs are unnumbered and checklisted below in alphabetical order.

| | MINT | NRMT |
|---|---|---|
| COMPLETE SET (25) | 70.00 | 32.00 |
| COMMON CARD (1-25) | 1.50 | .70 |
| ❑ 1 Tony Amonte | 1.50 | .70 |
| ❑ 2 Jason Arnott | 1.50 | .70 |
| ❑ 3 Raymond Bourque | 3.00 | 1.35 |
| ❑ 4 Martin Brodeur | 5.00 | 2.20 |
| ❑ 5 Pavel Bure | 4.00 | 1.80 |
| ❑ 6 Chris Chelios | 3.00 | 1.35 |
| ❑ 7 Geoff Courtnall | 1.50 | .70 |
| ❑ 8 Russ Courtnall | 1.50 | .70 |
| ❑ 9 Steve Duchesne | 1.50 | .70 |
| ❑ 10 Sergei Fedorov | 4.00 | 1.80 |
| ❑ 11 Theoren Fleury | 1.50 | .70 |
| ❑ 12 Doug Gilmour | 1.50 | .70 |
| ❑ 13 Wayne Gretzky | 12.00 | 5.50 |
| ❑ 14 Jari Kurri | 1.50 | .70 |
| ❑ 15 Eric Lindros | 9.00 | 4.00 |
| ❑ 16 Marty McSorley | 1.50 | .70 |
| ❑ 17 Alexander Mogilny | 1.50 | .70 |
| ❑ 18 Kirk Muller | 1.50 | .70 |
| ❑ 19 Rob Niedermayer | 1.50 | .70 |
| ❑ 20 Felix Potvin | 2.00 | .90 |
| ❑ 21 Luc Robitaille | 1.50 | .70 |
| ❑ 22 Joe Sakic | 5.00 | 2.20 |
| ❑ 23 Teemu Selanne | 4.00 | 1.80 |
| ❑ 24 Alexei Yashin | 1.50 | .70 |
| ❑ 25 Title Card | 1.50 | .70 |

## 1995-96 Post Upper Deck

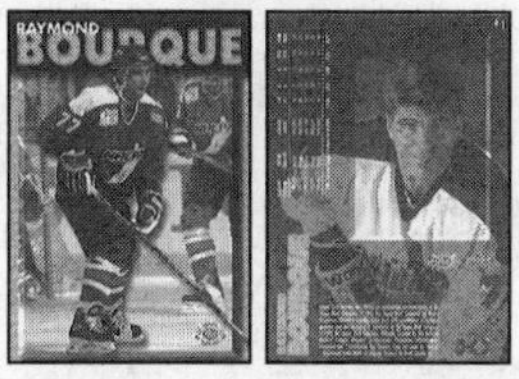

This 24-card set features color action photos on the front with the player's name in a black bar at the top. The backs carry a color player portrait, biographical information, and statistics. The cards were inserted one per specially marked box of Post cereals in Canada. Collectors also could get the cards through the mail in complete set form with proofs of purchase and a small charge. These factory sets included the NNO title and checklist cards. Cards still in the original cellophane wrapper from the cereal boxes are somewhat more desirable and can carry a slight premium of up to 1.5X the basic card. There were only 500 copies of the Wayne Gretzky autographed cards randomly inserted into Post cereal boxes. Lucky collectors who found this card could call a toll-free number to have their find certified by Upper Deck. The set is considered complete without the signed card.

| | MINT | NRMT |
|---|---|---|
| COMPLETE FACTORY SET (26) | 35.00 | 16.00 |
| COMPLETE CELLO. BOX SET (24) | 50.00 | 22.00 |
| COMMON CARD (1-24) | .25 | .11 |
| ❑ 1 Ray Bourque | 1.50 | .70 |
| ❑ 2 Martin Brodeur | 4.00 | 1.80 |
| ❑ 3 Steve Duchesne | .25 | .11 |
| ❑ 4 Vincent Damphousse | .35 | .16 |
| ❑ 5 Eric Desjardins | .25 | .11 |
| ❑ 6 Eric Lindros | 5.00 | 2.20 |
| ❑ 7 Joe Juneau | .35 | .16 |
| ❑ 8 Luc Robitaille | .35 | .16 |
| ❑ 9 Mark Recchi | .35 | .16 |
| ❑ 10 Patrick Roy | 8.00 | 3.60 |
| ❑ 11 Brendan Shanahan | 3.00 | 1.35 |
| ❑ 12 Scott Stevens | .25 | .11 |
| ❑ 13 Jason Arnott | .50 | .23 |
| ❑ 14 Trevor Linden | .25 | .11 |
| ❑ 15 Chris Chelios | 1.50 | .70 |
| ❑ 16 Paul Coffey | 1.50 | .70 |
| ❑ 17 Wayne Gretzky | 10.00 | 4.50 |
| ❑ 18 Doug Gilmour | 1.50 | .70 |
| ❑ 19 Kelly Hrudey | .25 | .11 |
| ❑ 20 Paul Kariya | 6.00 | 2.70 |
| ❑ 21 Larry Murphy | .25 | .11 |
| ❑ 22 Felix Potvin | 1.50 | .70 |
| ❑ 23 Keith Tkachuk | 2.00 | .90 |
| ❑ 24 Rob Blake | .25 | .11 |
| ❑ AU17 W.Gretzky AU (500) | 1200.00 | 550.00 |
| ❑ NNO Title card | .25 | .11 |
| ❑ NNO Checklist | .25 | .11 |

## 1996-97 Post Upper Deck

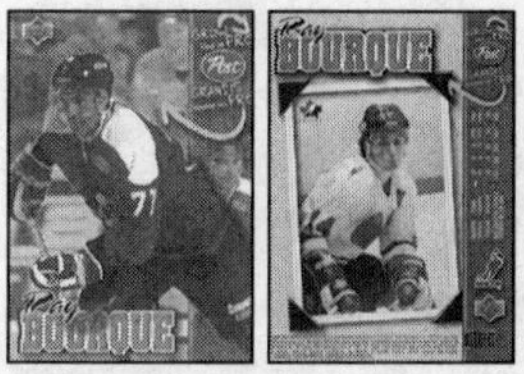

This 24-card set marks the third consecutive season for Post's collaboration with the NHLPA, and second with Upper Deck. The cards feature action photography on the fronts, with all players pictured in NHLPA togs. The cards were issued one per specially marked box of Post Cereals during the mid-part of the '96-97 season. Unlike the '95-96 product, these cards were actually inserted into the cereal bag itself, making theft from stores more difficult. Because this factor was negated, fewer complete sets hit the market, hence the slightly higher values. The player's name and the logos of Upper Deck and Post also are prominently featured, the latter in the blue or purple border which defines the right side of the card. The backs are noteworthy for including a childhood photo of the player, as well as '95-96 and career totals. The cards are unnumbered, and are listed below in alphabetical order.

| | MINT | NRMT |
|---|---|---|
| COMPLETE SET (24) | 45.00 | 20.00 |
| COMMON CARD (1-24) | .35 | .16 |
| ❑ 1 Ray Bourque | 1.50 | .70 |
| ❑ 2 Chris Chelios | 1.50 | .70 |
| ❑ 3 Paul Coffey | 1.50 | .70 |
| ❑ 4 Vincent Damphousse | .50 | .23 |
| ❑ 5 Steve Duchesne | .35 | .16 |
| ❑ 6 Theoren Fleury | 1.50 | .70 |
| ❑ 7 Doug Gilmour | 1.50 | .70 |
| ❑ 8 Wayne Gretzky | 10.00 | 4.50 |
| ❑ 9 Curtis Joseph | 1.50 | .70 |
| ❑ 10 Ed Jovanovski | .50 | .23 |
| ❑ 11 Paul Kariya | 6.00 | 2.70 |
| ❑ 12 Eric Lindros | 5.00 | 2.20 |
| ❑ 13 Al MacInnis | .50 | .23 |
| ❑ 14 Felix Potvin | 1.50 | .70 |
| ❑ 15 Mark Recchi | .50 | .23 |
| ❑ 16 Luc Robitaille | .50 | .23 |
| ❑ 17 Jeremy Roenick | 1.50 | .70 |
| ❑ 18 Patrick Roy | 8.00 | 3.60 |
| ❑ 19 Joe Sakic | 3.00 | 1.35 |
| ❑ 20 Mathieu Schneider | .50 | .23 |
| ❑ 21 Brendan Shanahan | 3.00 | 1.35 |
| ❑ 22 Scott Stevens | .35 | .16 |
| ❑ 23 John Vanbiesbrouck | 2.50 | 1.10 |
| ❑ 24 Alexei Yashin | 1.50 | .70 |

## 1997 Post Pinnacle

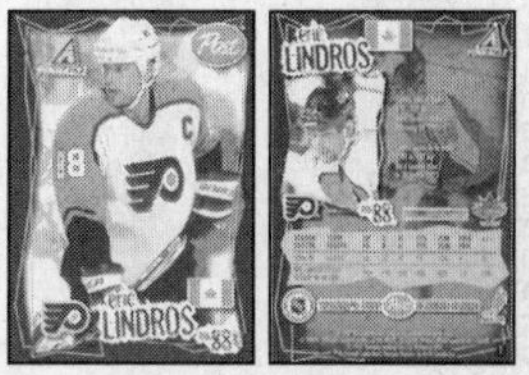

Card fronts feature full color photos on the front with jersey number and a Canadian flag also prominently displayed. Backs feature biographical information and 96-97 season stats.

| | MINT | NRMT |
|---|---|---|
| COMPLETE SET (24) | 30.00 | 13.50 |
| COMMON CARD (1-24) | .40 | .18 |
| ❑ 1 Eric Lindros | 2.50 | 1.10 |
| ❑ 2 Patrick Roy | 4.00 | 1.80 |
| ❑ 3 Joe Sakic | 1.50 | .70 |
| ❑ 4 Brian Leetch | .75 | .35 |
| ❑ 5 Mark Messier | 1.00 | .45 |
| ❑ 6 Jason Arnott | .60 | .25 |
| ❑ 7 Paul Kariya | 3.00 | 1.35 |
| ❑ 8 Martin Brodeur | 2.00 | .90 |
| ❑ 9 Vincent Damphousse | .60 | .25 |
| ❑ 10 Steve Yzerman | 2.50 | 1.10 |
| ❑ 11 Brett Hull | 1.00 | .45 |
| ❑ 12 Chris Chelios | .75 | .35 |
| ❑ 13 Sergei Fedorov | 1.50 | .70 |
| ❑ 14 Nicklas Lidstrom | .60 | .25 |
| ❑ 15 Sergei Berezin | .40 | .18 |
| ❑ 16 Dominik Hasek | 1.50 | .70 |
| ❑ 17 Pavel Bure | 1.50 | .70 |
| ❑ 18 Saku Koivu | 1.25 | .55 |
| ❑ 19 Teemu Selanne | 1.50 | .70 |
| ❑ 20 Peter Forsberg | 2.50 | 1.10 |
| ❑ 21 Jaromir Jagr | 2.50 | 1.10 |

❑ 22 Peter Bondra .75 .35
❑ 23 Alexei Yashin .60 .25
❑ 24 Viacheslav Fetisov .40 .18

## 1993-94 PowerPlay

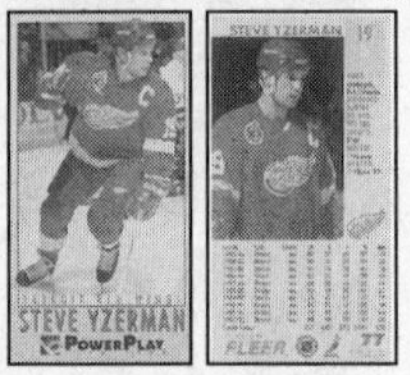

This 520-card set measures 2 1/2" by 4 3/4". The fronts feature color action shots set within a blended team-colored border. The team name and the player's name appear in team-colored lettering below the photo. The backs carry color player photos at the upper left. The player's name appears above; his number, position, and a short biography are displayed alongside. Statistics are shown below. The cards are checklisted alphabetically according to teams. Rookie Cards include Jason Arnott, Chris Osgood, Damian Rhodes, and Jocelyn Thibault.

| | MINT | NRMT |
|---|---|---|
| COMPLETE SET (520) | 60.00 | 27.00 |
| COMPLETE SERIES 1 (280) | 30.00 | 13.50 |
| COMPLETE SERIES 2 (240) | 30.00 | 13.50 |
| COMMON CARD (1-520) | .10 | .05 |

❑ 1 Stu Grimson .10 .05
❑ 2 Guy Hebert .25 .11
❑ 3 Sean Hill .10 .05
❑ 4 Bill Houlder .10 .05
❑ 5 Alexei Kasatonov .10 .05
❑ 6 Steven King .10 .05
❑ 7 Lonnie Loach .10 .05
❑ 8 Troy Loney .10 .05
❑ 9 Joe Sacco .10 .05
❑ 10 Anatoli Semenov .10 .05
❑ 11 Jarrod Skalde .10 .05
❑ 12 Tim Sweeney .10 .05
❑ 13 Ron Tugnutt .25 .11
❑ 14 Terry Yake .10 .05
❑ 15 Shaun Van Allen .10 .05
❑ 16 Ray Bourque .50 .23
❑ 17 Jon Casey .25 .11
❑ 18 Ted Donato .10 .05
❑ 19 Joe Juneau .25 .11
❑ 20 Dmitri Kvartalnov .10 .05
❑ 21 Steve Leach .10 .05
❑ 22 Cam Neely .25 .11
❑ 23 Adam Oates .25 .11
❑ 24 Don Sweeney .10 .05
❑ 25 Glen Wesley .10 .05
❑ 26 Doug Bodger .10 .05
❑ 27 Grant Fuhr .25 .11
❑ 28 Viktor Gordiouk .10 .05
❑ 29 Dale Hawerchuk .25 .11
❑ 30 Yuri Khmylev .10 .05
❑ 31 Pat LaFontaine .25 .11
❑ 32 Alexander Mogilny .25 .11
❑ 33 Richard Smehlik .10 .05
❑ 34 Bob Sweeney .10 .05
❑ 35 Randy Wood .10 .05
❑ 36 Theoren Fleury .25 .11
❑ 37 Kelly Kisio .10 .05
❑ 38 Al MacInnis .25 .11
❑ 39 Joe Nieuwendyk .25 .11
❑ 40 Joel Otto .10 .05
❑ 41 Robert Reichel .10 .05
❑ 42 Gary Roberts .10 .05
❑ 43 Ronnie Stern .10 .05
❑ 44 Gary Suter .10 .05
❑ 45 Mike Vernon .25 .11
❑ 46 Ed Belfour .50 .23
❑ 47 Chris Chelios .50 .23
❑ 48 Karl Dykhuis .10 .05
❑ 49 Michel Goulet .25 .11
❑ 50 Dirk Graham .10 .05
❑ 51 Sergei Krivokrasov .10 .05
❑ 52 Steve Larmer .25 .11
❑ 53 Joe Murphy .10 .05
❑ 54 Jeremy Roenick .50 .23
❑ 55 Steve Smith .10 .05
❑ 56 Brent Sutter .10 .05
❑ 57 Neal Broten .25 .11
❑ 58 Russ Courtnall .10 .05
❑ 59 Ulf Dahlen .10 .05
❑ 60 Dave Gagner .25 .11
❑ 61 Derian Hatcher .10 .05
❑ 62 Trent Klatt .10 .05
❑ 63 Mike Modano .60 .25
❑ 64 Andy Moog .25 .11
❑ 65 Tommy Sjodin .10 .05
❑ 66 Mark Tinordi .10 .05
❑ 67 Tim Cheveldae .25 .11
❑ 68 Steve Chiasson .10 .05
❑ 69 Dino Ciccarelli .25 .11
❑ 70 Paul Coffey .50 .23
❑ 71 Dallas Drake .10 .05
❑ 72 Sergei Fedorov 1.00 .45
❑ 73 Vladimir Konstantinov .10 .05
❑ 74 Nicklas Lidstrom .25 .11
❑ 75 Keith Primeau .25 .11
❑ 76 Ray Sheppard .25 .11
❑ 77 Steve Yzerman 1.50 .70
❑ 78 Zdeno Ciger .10 .05
❑ 79 Shayne Corson .10 .05
❑ 80 Todd Elik .10 .05
❑ 81 Igor Kravchuk .10 .05
❑ 82 Craig MacTavish .10 .05
❑ 83 Dave Manson .10 .05
❑ 84 Shjon Podein .10 .05
❑ 85 Bill Ranford .25 .11
❑ 86 Steven Rice .10 .05
❑ 87 Doug Weight .25 .11
❑ 88 Doug Barrault .10 .05
❑ 89 Jesse Belanger .10 .05
❑ 90 Brian Benning .10 .05
❑ 91 Joe Cirella .10 .05
❑ 92 Mark Fitzpatrick .25 .11
❑ 93 Randy Gilhen .10 .05
❑ 94 Mike Hough .10 .05
❑ 95 Bill Lindsay .10 .05
❑ 96 Andrei Lomakin .10 .05
❑ 97 Dave Lowry .10 .05
❑ 98 Scott Mellanby .25 .11
❑ 99 Gord Murphy .10 .05
❑ 100 Brian Skrudland .10 .05
❑ 101 Milan Tichy .10 .05
❑ 102 John Vanbiesbrouck .75 .35
❑ 103 Sean Burke .25 .11
❑ 104 Andrew Cassels .10 .05
❑ 105 Nick Kypreos .10 .05
❑ 106 Michael Nylander .10 .05
❑ 107 Robert Petrovicky .10 .05
❑ 108 Patrick Poulin .10 .05
❑ 109 Geoff Sanderson .25 .11
❑ 110 Pat Verbeek .10 .05
❑ 111 Eric Weinrich .10 .05
❑ 112 Zarley Zalapski .10 .05
❑ 113 Rob Blake .10 .05
❑ 114 Jimmy Carson .10 .05
❑ 115 Tony Granato .10 .05
❑ 116 Wayne Gretzky 3.00 1.35
❑ 117 Kelly Hrudey .25 .11
❑ 118 Jari Kurri .25 .11
❑ 119 Shawn McEachern .10 .05
❑ 120 Luc Robitaille .25 .11
❑ 121 Tomas Sandstrom .10 .05
❑ 122 Darryl Sydor .10 .05
❑ 123 Alexei Zhitnik .10 .05
❑ 124 Brian Bellows .10 .05
❑ 125 Patrice Brisebois .10 .05
❑ 126 Guy Carbonneau .10 .05
❑ 127 Vincent Damphousse .25 .11
❑ 128 Eric Desjardins .10 .05
❑ 129 Mike Keane .10 .05
❑ 130 Stephan Lebeau .10 .05
❑ 131 Kirk Muller .10 .05
❑ 132 Lyle Odelein .10 .05
❑ 133 Patrick Roy 2.50 1.10
❑ 134 Mathieu Schneider .10 .05
❑ 135 Bruce Driver .10 .05
❑ 136 Slava Fetisov .10 .05
❑ 137 Claude Lemieux .25 .11
❑ 138 John MacLean .25 .11
❑ 139 Bernie Nicholls .10 .05
❑ 140 Scott Niedermayer .10 .05
❑ 141 Stephane Richer .25 .11
❑ 142 Alexander Semak .10 .05
❑ 143 Scott Stevens .25 .11
❑ 144 Chris Terreri .25 .11
❑ 145 Valeri Zelepukin .10 .05
❑ 146 Patrick Flatley .10 .05
❑ 147 Ron Hextall .25 .11
❑ 148 Benoit Hogue .10 .05
❑ 149 Darius Kasparaitis .10 .05
❑ 150 Derek King .10 .05
❑ 151 Uwe Krupp .10 .05
❑ 152 Scott Lachance .10 .05
❑ 153 Vladimir Malakhov .10 .05
❑ 154 Steve Thomas .10 .05
❑ 155 Pierre Turgeon .25 .11
❑ 156 Tony Amonte .25 .11
❑ 157 Mike Gartner .25 .11
❑ 158 Adam Graves .25 .11
❑ 159 Alexei Kovalev .25 .11
❑ 160 Brian Leetch .50 .23
❑ 161 Joby Messier .10 .05
❑ 162 Mark Messier .60 .25
❑ 163 Sergei Nemchinov .10 .05
❑ 164 James Patrick .10 .05
❑ 165 Mike Richter .50 .23
❑ 166 Darren Turcotte .10 .05
❑ 167 Sergei Zubov .10 .05
❑ 168 Dave Archibald .10 .05
❑ 169 Craig Billington .25 .11
❑ 170 Bob Kudelski .10 .05
❑ 171 Mark Lamb .10 .05
❑ 172 Norm Maciver .10 .05
❑ 173 Darren Rumble .10 .05
❑ 174 Vladimir Ruzicka .10 .05
❑ 175 Brad Shaw .10 .05
❑ 176 Sylvain Turgeon .10 .05
❑ 177 Josef Beranek .10 .05
❑ 178 Rod Brind'Amour .25 .11
❑ 179 Kevin Dineen .10 .05
❑ 180 Pelle Eklund .10 .05
❑ 181 Brent Fedyk .10 .05
❑ 182 Garry Galley .10 .05
❑ 183 Eric Lindros 2.00 .90
❑ 184 Mark Recchi .25 .11
❑ 185 Tommy Soderstrom .25 .11
❑ 186 Dimitri Yushkevich .10 .05
❑ 187 Tom Barrasso .25 .11
❑ 188 Ron Francis .25 .11
❑ 189 Jaromir Jagr 1.50 .70
❑ 190 Mario Lemieux 2.50 1.10
❑ 191 Marty McSorley .10 .05
❑ 192 Joe Mullen .25 .11
❑ 193 Larry Murphy .25 .11
❑ 194 Ulf Samuelsson .10 .05
❑ 195 Kevin Stevens .10 .05
❑ 196 Rick Tocchet .25 .11
❑ 197 Steve Duchesne .10 .05
❑ 198 Stephane Fiset .25 .11
❑ 199 Valeri Kamensky .25 .11
❑ 200 Andrei Kovalenko .10 .05
❑ 201 Owen Nolan .25 .11
❑ 202 Mike Ricci .10 .05
❑ 203 Martin Rucinsky .10 .05
❑ 204 Joe Sakic 1.00 .45
❑ 205 Mats Sundin .25 .11
❑ 206 Scott Young .10 .05
❑ 207 Jeff Brown .10 .05
❑ 208 Garth Butcher .10 .05
❑ 209 Nelson Emerson .10 .05
❑ 210 Bret Hedican .10 .05
❑ 211 Brett Hull .60 .25
❑ 212 Craig Janney .25 .11
❑ 213 Curtis Joseph .50 .23
❑ 214 Igor Korolev .10 .05
❑ 215 Kevin Miller .10 .05
❑ 216 Brendan Shanahan 1.00 .45
❑ 217 Ed Courtenay .10 .05
❑ 218 Pat Falloon .10 .05
❑ 219 Johan Garpenlov .10 .05
❑ 220 Rob Gaudreau .10 .05
❑ 221 Artus Irbe .25 .11
❑ 222 Sergei Makarov .10 .05
❑ 223 Jeff Norton .10 .05
❑ 224 Jeff Odgers .10 .05
❑ 225 Sandis Ozolinsh .25 .11
❑ 226 Tom Pederson .10 .05
❑ 227 Bob Beers .10 .05
❑ 228 Brian Bradley .10 .05
❑ 229 Shawn Chambers .10 .05
❑ 230 Gerard Gallant .10 .05
❑ 231 Roman Hamrlik .25 .11
❑ 232 Petr Klima .10 .05
❑ 233 Chris Kontos .10 .05
❑ 234 Daren Puppa .25 .11
❑ 235 John Tucker .10 .05
❑ 236 Rob Zamuner .10 .05
❑ 237 Glenn Anderson .25 .11
❑ 238 Dave Andreychuk .25 .11
❑ 239 Drake Berehowsky .10 .05
❑ 240 Nikolai Borschevsky .10 .05
❑ 241 Wendel Clark .25 .11
❑ 242 John Cullen .10 .05
❑ 243 Dave Ellett .10 .05
❑ 244 Doug Gilmour .50 .23
❑ 245 Dimitri Mironov .10 .05
❑ 246 Felix Potvin .50 .23
❑ 247 Greg Adams .10 .05
❑ 248 Pavel Bure 1.00 .45
❑ 249 Geoff Courtnall .10 .05
❑ 250 Gerald Diduck .10 .05
❑ 251 Trevor Linden .25 .11
❑ 252 Jyrki Lumme .10 .05
❑ 253 Kirk McLean .25 .11
❑ 254 Petr Nedved .25 .11
❑ 255 Cliff Ronning .10 .05
❑ 256 Jiri Slegr .10 .05
❑ 257 Dixon Ward .10 .05
❑ 258 Peter Bondra .50 .23
❑ 259 Sylvain Cote .10 .05
❑ 260 Pat Elynuik .10 .05
❑ 261 Kevin Hatcher .10 .05
❑ 262 Dale Hunter .10 .05
❑ 263 Al Iafrate .10 .05
❑ 264 Dimitri Khristich .10 .05
❑ 265 Michal Pivonka .10 .05
❑ 266 Mike Ridley .10 .05
❑ 267 Rick Tabaracci .25 .11
❑ 268 Sergei Bautin .10 .05
❑ 269 Evgeny Davydov .10 .05
❑ 270 Bob Essensa .25 .11
❑ 271 Phil Housley .25 .11
❑ 272 Teppo Numminen .10 .05
❑ 273 Fredrik Olausson .10 .05
❑ 274 Teemu Selanne 1.00 .45
❑ 275 Thomas Steen .10 .05
❑ 276 Keith Tkachuk .60 .25
❑ 277 Paul Ysebaert .10 .05
❑ 278 Alexei Zhamnov .25 .11
❑ 279 Checklist .10 .05
❑ 280 Checklist .10 .05
❑ 281 Patrick Carnback .10 .05
❑ 282 Bob Corkum .10 .05
❑ 283 Bobby Dollas .10 .05
❑ 284 Peter Douris .10 .05
❑ 285 Todd Ewen .10 .05
❑ 286 Garry Valk .10 .05
❑ 287 John Blue .25 .11
❑ 288 Glen Featherstone .10 .05
❑ 289 Steve Heinze .10 .05
❑ 290 David Reid .10 .05
❑ 291 Bryan Smolinski .10 .05
❑ 292 Cam Stewart .10 .05
❑ 293 Jozef Stumpel .10 .05
❑ 294 Sergei Zholtok .10 .05
❑ 295 Donald Audette .25 .11
❑ 296 Philippe Boucher .10 .05
❑ 297 Dominik Hasek 1.00 .45
❑ 298 Brad May .25 .11
❑ 299 Craig Muni .10 .05
❑ 300 Derek Plante .10 .05
❑ 301 Craig Simpson .10 .05
❑ 302 Scott Thomas .10 .05
❑ 303 Ted Drury .10 .05
❑ 304 Dan Keczmer .10 .05
❑ 305 Trevor Kidd .25 .11
❑ 306 Sandy McCarthy .10 .05
❑ 307 Frank Musil .10 .05
❑ 308 Michel Petit .10 .05
❑ 309 Paul Ranheim .10 .05
❑ 310 German Titov .10 .05
❑ 311 Andrei Trefilov .10 .05
❑ 312 Jeff Hackett .25 .11
❑ 313 Stephane Matteau .10 .05
❑ 314 Brian Noonan .10 .05
❑ 315 Patrick Poulin .10 .05
❑ 316 Jeff Shantz .10 .05
❑ 317 Rich Sutter .10 .05
❑ 318 Kevin Todd .10 .05
❑ 319 Eric Weinrich .10 .05
❑ 320 Dave Barr .10 .05
❑ 321 Paul Cavallini .10 .05
❑ 322 Mike Craig .10 .05
❑ 323 Dean Evason .10 .05
❑ 324 Brent Gilchrist .10 .05
❑ 325 Grant Ledyard .10 .05
❑ 326 Mike McPhee .10 .05
❑ 327 Darcy Wakaluk .25 .11
❑ 328 Terry Carkner .10 .05
❑ 329 Mark Howe .10 .05
❑ 330 Greg Johnson .10 .05
❑ 331 Slava Kozlov .25 .11
❑ 332 Martin Lapointe .10 .05
❑ 333 Darren McCarty .60 .25
❑ 334 Chris Osgood 2.50 1.10
❑ 335 Bob Probert .25 .11
❑ 336 Mike Sillinger .10 .05
❑ 337 Jason Arnott 1.25 .55
❑ 338 Bob Beers .10 .05
❑ 339 Fred Brathwaite .25 .11
❑ 340 Kelly Buchberger .10 .05
❑ 341 Ilya Byakin .10 .05
❑ 342 Fredrik Olausson .10 .05
❑ 343 Vladimir Vujtek .10 .05
❑ 344 Peter White .10 .05
❑ 345 Stu Barnes .10 .05
❑ 346 Mike Foligno .10 .05
❑ 347 Greg Hawgood .10 .05
❑ 348 Bob Kudelski .10 .05
❑ 349 Rob Niedermayer .25 .11
❑ 350 Igor Chibirev .10 .05
❑ 351 Robert Kron .10 .05
❑ 352 Bryan Marchment .10 .05
❑ 353 James Patrick .10 .05
❑ 354 Chris Pronger .25 .11
❑ 355 Jeff Reese .10 .05
❑ 356 Jim Storm .10 .05
❑ 357 Darren Turcotte .10 .05
❑ 358 Pat Conacher .10 .05
❑ 359 Mike Donnelly .10 .05
❑ 360 John Druce .10 .05
❑ 361 Charlie Huddy .10 .05
❑ 362 Warren Rychel .10 .05
❑ 363 Robb Stauber .25 .11
❑ 364 Dave Taylor .25 .11
❑ 365 Dixon Ward .10 .05
❑ 366 Benoit Brunet .10 .05
❑ 367 J.J. Daigneault .10 .05
❑ 368 Gilbert Dionne .10 .05
❑ 369 Paul DiPietro .10 .05
❑ 370 Kevin Haller .10 .05
❑ 371 Oleg Petrov .10 .05
❑ 372 Peter Popovic .10 .05
❑ 373 Ron Wilson .10 .05
❑ 374 Martin Brodeur 1.00 .45
❑ 375 Tom Chorske .10 .05
❑ 376 Jim Dowd .10 .05
❑ 377 David Emma .10 .05
❑ 378 Bobby Holik .10 .05
❑ 379 Corey Millen .10 .05
❑ 380 Jaroslav Modry .10 .05
❑ 381 Jason Smith .10 .05
❑ 382 Ray Ferraro .10 .05
❑ 383 Travis Green .25 .11
❑ 384 Tom Kurvers .10 .05
❑ 385 Marty McInnis .10 .05
❑ 386 Jamie McLennan .30 .14
❑ 387 Dennis Vaske .10 .05
❑ 388 Dave Volek .10 .05
❑ 389 Jeff Beukeboom .10 .05
❑ 390 Glenn Healy .25 .11
❑ 391 Alexander Karpovtsev .10 .05
❑ 392 Steve Larmer .25 .11
❑ 393 Kevin Lowe .10 .05
❑ 394 Ed Olczyk .10 .05
❑ 395 Esa Tikkanen .10 .05
❑ 396 Alexandre Daigle .10 .05
❑ 397 Evgeny Davydov .10 .05
❑ 398 Dmitri Filimonov .10 .05
❑ 399 Brian Glynn .10 .05
❑ 400 Darrin Madeley .10 .05
❑ 401 Troy Mallette .10 .05
❑ 402 Dave McLlwain .10 .05
❑ 403 Alexei Yashin .25 .11
❑ 404 Jason Bowen .10 .05
❑ 405 Jeff Finley .10 .05
❑ 406 Yves Racine .10 .05
❑ 407 Rob Ramage .10 .05
❑ 408 Mikael Renberg .50 .23
❑ 409 Dominic Roussel .25 .11
❑ 410 Dave Tippett .10 .05
❑ 411 Doug Brown .10 .05
❑ 412 Markus Naslund .10 .05
❑ 413 Pat Neaton .10 .05
❑ 414 Kjell Samuelsson .10 .05
❑ 415 Martin Straka .10 .05
❑ 416 Bryan Trottier .25 .11
❑ 417 Ken Wregget .25 .11
❑ 418 Adam Foote .10 .05
❑ 419 Iain Fraser .10 .05
❑ 420 Alexei Gusarov .10 .05
❑ 421 Dave Karpa .10 .05
❑ 422 Claude Lapointe .10 .05
❑ 423 Curtis Leschyshyn .10 .05
❑ 424 Mike McKee .10 .05
❑ 425 Garth Snow .40 .18
❑ 426 Jocelyn Thibault 1.50 .70
❑ 427 Phil Housley .25 .11
❑ 428 Jim Hrivnak .25 .11
❑ 429 Vitali Karamnov .10 .05
❑ 430 Basil McRae .10 .05
❑ 431 Jim Montgomery .10 .05
❑ 432 Vitali Prokhorov .10 .05
❑ 433 Gaetan Duchesne .10 .05
❑ 434 Todd Elik .10 .05
❑ 435 Bob Errey .10 .05
❑ 436 Igor Larionov .10 .05
❑ 437 Mike Rathje .10 .05
❑ 438 Jim Waite .25 .11
❑ 439 Ray Whitney .10 .05
❑ 440 Mikael Anderson .10 .05
❑ 441 Danton Cole .10 .05
❑ 442 Pat Elynuik .10 .05
❑ 443 Chris Gratton .25 .11
❑ 444 Pat Jablonski .25 .11
❑ 445 Chris Joseph .10 .05
❑ 446 Chris LiPuma .10 .05
❑ 447 Denis Savard .25 .11
❑ 448 Ken Baumgartner .10 .05
❑ 449 Todd Gill .10 .05
❑ 450 Sylvain Lefebvre .10 .05
❑ 451 Jamie Macoun .10 .05
❑ 452 Mark Osborne .10 .05
❑ 453 Rob Pearson .10 .05
❑ 454 Damian Rhodes .25 .11
❑ 455 Peter Zezel .10 .05
❑ 456 Dave Babych .10 .05
❑ 457 Jose Charbonneau .10 .05
❑ 458 Murray Craven .10 .05
❑ 459 Neil Eisenhut .10 .05
❑ 460 Dan Kesa .10 .05
❑ 461 Gino Odjick .10 .05
❑ 462 Kay Whitmore .25 .11
❑ 463 Don Beaupre .25 .11
❑ 464 Randy Burridge .10 .05
❑ 465 Calle Johansson .10 .05
❑ 466 Keith Jones .10 .05
❑ 467 Todd Krygier .10 .05
❑ 468 Kelly Miller .10 .05
❑ 469 Pat Peake .10 .05
❑ 470 Dave Poulin .10 .05
❑ 471 Luciano Borsato .10 .05
❑ 472 Nelson Emerson .10 .05
❑ 473 Randy Gilhen .10 .05
❑ 474 Boris Mironov .10 .05
❑ 475 Stephane Quintal .10 .05
❑ 476 Thomas Steen .10 .05
❑ 477 Igor Ulanov .10 .05
❑ 478 Adrian Aucoin .10 .05
❑ 479 Todd Brost .10 .05
❑ 480 Martin Gendron .10 .05
❑ 481 David Harlock .10 .05
❑ 482 Corey Hirsch .25 .11
❑ 483 Todd Hlushko .10 .05
❑ 484 Fabian Joseph .10 .05
❑ 485 Paul Kariya 8.00 3.60
❑ 486 Brett Lindros .10 .05
❑ 487 Ken Lovsin .10 .05
❑ 488 Jason Marshall .10 .05
❑ 489 Derek Mayer .10 .05
❑ 490 Petr Nedved .25 .11
❑ 491 Dwayne Norris .10 .05
❑ 492 Russ Romaniuk .10 .05
❑ 493 Brian Savage .50 .23
❑ 494 Trevor Sim .10 .05
❑ 495 Chris Therien .10 .05
❑ 496 Todd Warriner .10 .05
❑ 497 Craig Woodcroft .10 .05
❑ 498 Mark Beaufait .10 .05
❑ 499 Jim Campbell .10 .05
❑ 500 Ted Crowley .10 .05
❑ 501 Mike Dunham .25 .11
❑ 502 Chris Ferraro .10 .05
❑ 503 Peter Ferraro .10 .05
❑ 504 Brett Hauer .10 .05
❑ 505 Darby Hendrickson .10 .05
❑ 506 Chris Imes .10 .05
❑ 507 Craig Johnson .10 .05
❑ 508 Peter Laviolette .10 .05
❑ 509 Jeff Lazaro .10 .05
❑ 510 John Lilley .10 .05
❑ 511 Todd Marchant .10 .05
❑ 512 Ian Moran .10 .05
❑ 513 Travis Richards .25 .11
❑ 514 Barry Richter .10 .05
❑ 515 David Roberts .10 .05
❑ 516 Brian Rolston .10 .05
❑ 517 David Sacco .10 .05
❑ 518 Checklist .10 .05
❑ 519 Checklist .10 .05
❑ 520 Checklist .10 .05

## 1993-94 PowerPlay Gamebreakers

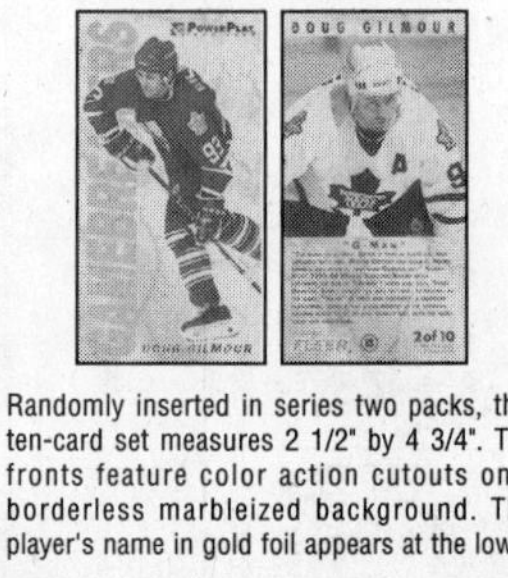

Randomly inserted in series two packs, this ten-card set measures 2 1/2" by 4 3/4". The fronts feature color action cutouts on a borderless marbleized background. The player's name in gold foil appears at the lower

right, while the word "Gamebreakers" is printed vertically in pastel-colored lettering on the left side. On the same marbleized background, the backs carry another color photo, with the player's name displayed above and career highlights shown below. The cards are numbered on the back as "X of 10."

| | MINT | NRMT |
|---|---|---|
| COMPLETE SET (10) | 30.00 | 13.50 |
| COMMON CARD (1-10) | 1.00 | .45 |
| ❑ 1 Sergei Fedorov | 2.00 | .90 |
| ❑ 2 Doug Gilmour | 1.00 | .45 |
| ❑ 3 Wayne Gretzky | 6.00 | 2.70 |
| ❑ 4 Curtis Joseph | 1.00 | .45 |
| ❑ 5 Mario Lemieux | 5.00 | 2.20 |
| ❑ 6 Eric Lindros | 4.00 | 1.80 |
| ❑ 7 Felix Potvin | 1.00 | .45 |
| ❑ 8 Jeremy Roenick | 1.00 | .45 |
| ❑ 9 Patrick Roy | 5.00 | 2.20 |
| ❑ 10 Steve Yzerman | 3.00 | 1.35 |

## 1993-94 PowerPlay Global Greats

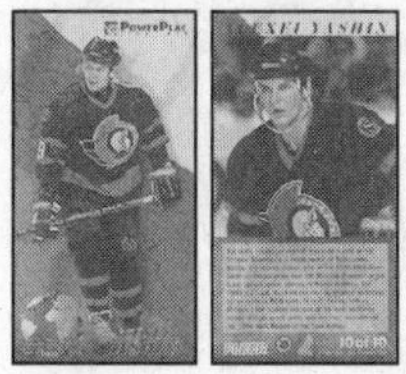

Randomly inserted in series two packs, this 10-card set measures 2 1/2" by 4 3/4". The borderless fronts feature color action cutouts superimposed on the player's national flag. The player's name and the Global Greats logo in gold foil appear at the bottom. On the same national flag background, the backs carry another color photo with the player's name above and career highlights below. The cards are numbered on the back as "X of 10."

| | MINT | NRMT |
|---|---|---|
| COMPLETE SET (10) | 18.00 | 8.00 |
| COMMON CARD (1-10) | .50 | .23 |
| ❑ 1 Pavel Bure | 2.50 | 1.10 |
| ❑ 2 Sergei Fedorov | 2.50 | 1.10 |
| ❑ 3 Jaromir Jagr | 4.00 | 1.80 |
| ❑ 4 Jari Kurri | .75 | .35 |
| ❑ 5 Alexander Mogilny | .75 | .35 |
| ❑ 6 Mikael Renberg | .75 | .35 |
| ❑ 7 Teemu Selanne | 2.50 | 1.10 |
| ❑ 8 Mats Sundin | .75 | .35 |
| ❑ 9 Esa Tikkanen | .50 | .23 |
| ❑ 10 Alexei Yashin | 1.00 | .45 |

## 1993-94 PowerPlay Netminders

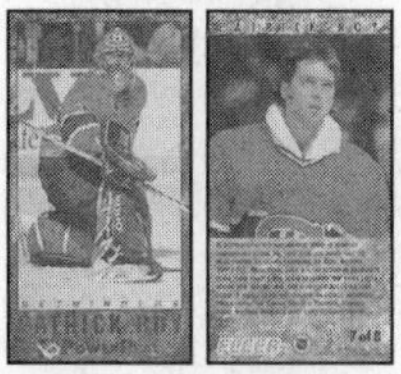

Randomly inserted at a rate of 1:8 series one packs, this eight-card set measures 2 1/2" by 4 3/4". On a blue marbleized background, the fronts feature color action photos with the goalie's name in blue-foil lettering under the photo. On a lighter blue marbleized background, the backs carry another color photo, with the player's name displayed above and career highlights shown below. The cards are numbered on the back as "X of 8."

| | MINT | NRMT |
|---|---|---|
| COMPLETE SET (8) | 45.00 | 20.00 |
| COMMON CARD (1-8) | 3.00 | 1.35 |
| ❑ 1 Tom Barrasso | 3.00 | 1.35 |
| ❑ 2 Ed Belfour | 5.00 | 2.20 |
| ❑ 3 Grant Fuhr | 4.00 | 1.80 |
| ❑ 4 Curtis Joseph | 5.00 | 2.20 |
| ❑ 5 Felix Potvin | 5.00 | 2.20 |
| ❑ 6 Bill Ranford | 3.00 | 1.35 |
| ❑ 7 Patrick Roy | 20.00 | 9.00 |
| ❑ 8 Tommy Soderstrom | 3.00 | 1.35 |

## 1993-94 PowerPlay Point Leaders

Randomly inserted at a rate of 1:2 series one packs, this 20-card set measures 2 1/2" by 4 3/4". The yellow-bordered fronts feature color action cutouts against a yellow-tinted background. The player's name in silver foil appears under the photo. On a yellow background, the backs carry another color photo with the player's name in silver foil

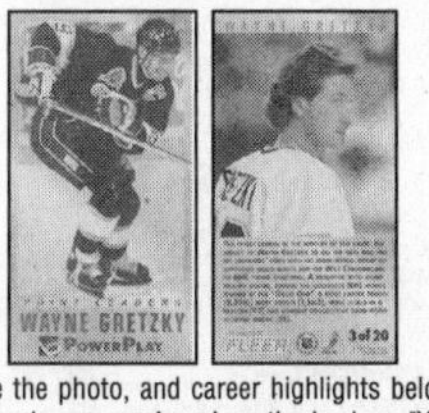

above the photo, and career highlights below. The cards are numbered on the back as "X of 20."

| | MINT | NRMT |
|---|---|---|
| COMPLETE SET (20) | 30.00 | 13.50 |
| COMMON CARD (1-20) | .50 | .23 |
| ❑ 1 Pavel Bure | 2.00 | .90 |
| ❑ 2 Doug Gilmour | .75 | .35 |
| ❑ 3 Wayne Gretzky | 6.00 | 2.70 |
| ❑ 4 Brett Hull | 1.25 | .55 |
| ❑ 5 Jaromir Jagr | 3.00 | 1.35 |
| ❑ 6 Joe Juneau | .75 | .35 |
| ❑ 7 Pat LaFontaine | .75 | .35 |
| ❑ 8 Mario Lemieux | 5.00 | 2.20 |
| ❑ 9 Mark Messier | 1.25 | .55 |
| ❑ 10 Alexander Mogilny | .75 | .35 |
| ❑ 11 Adam Oates | .75 | .35 |
| ❑ 12 Mark Recchi | .50 | .23 |
| ❑ 13 Luc Robitaille | .50 | .23 |
| ❑ 14 Jeremy Roenick | 1.00 | .45 |
| ❑ 15 Joe Sakic | 2.00 | .90 |
| ❑ 16 Teemu Selanne | 2.00 | .90 |
| ❑ 17 Kevin Stevens | .50 | .23 |
| ❑ 18 Mats Sundin | 1.00 | .45 |
| ❑ 19 Pierre Turgeon | .75 | .35 |
| ❑ 20 Steve Yzerman | 3.00 | 1.35 |

## 1993-94 PowerPlay Rising Stars

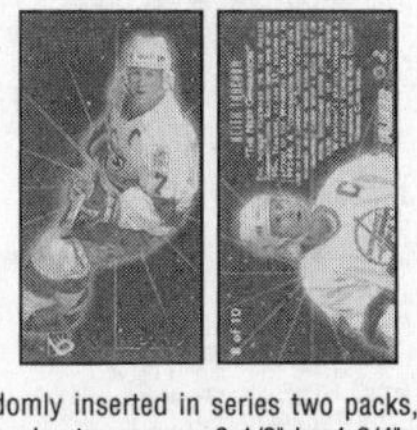

Randomly inserted in series two packs, this ten-card set measures 2 1/2" by 4 3/4". Each borderless front features a color action cutout, highlighted with a yellow "aura" and yellow radial lines, set on a stellar background. The player's name and the words "Rising Star" in silver foil appear in a top corner. On a similar background, the borderless horizontal back carries another color cutout on the left, with the player's name and career highlights to the right. The cards are numbered on the back as "X of 10."

| | MINT | NRMT |
|---|---|---|
| COMPLETE SET (10) | 40.00 | 18.00 |
| COMMON CARD (1-10) | 2.50 | 1.10 |
| ❑ 1 Arturs Irbe | 3.00 | 1.35 |
| ❑ 2 Slava Kozlov | 3.00 | 1.35 |
| ❑ 3 Felix Potvin | 4.00 | 1.80 |
| ❑ 4 Keith Primeau | 3.00 | 1.35 |
| ❑ 5 Robert Reichel | 2.50 | 1.10 |
| ❑ 6 Geoff Sanderson | 2.50 | 1.10 |
| ❑ 7 Martin Straka | 3.00 | 1.35 |
| ❑ 8 Keith Tkachuk | 8.00 | 3.60 |
| ❑ 9 Alexei Zhamnov | 2.50 | 1.10 |
| ❑ 10 Sergei Zubov | 2.50 | 1.10 |

## 1993-94 PowerPlay Rookie Standouts

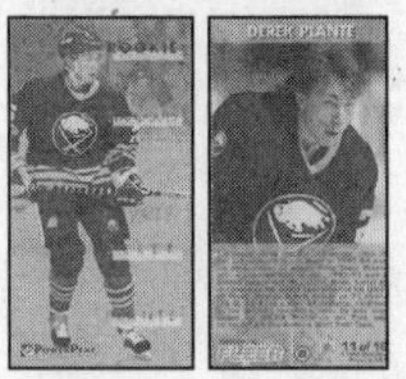

Randomly inserted in series two packs, this 16-card set measures 2 1/2" by 4 3/4". The borderless fronts feature color player action shots on grainy and ghosted backgrounds. The player's name and the words "Rookie Standouts" in gold foil are printed atop ghosted bars to the right of the player. The backs carry a color player close-up, with the player's name above and career highlights below. The cards are numbered on the back as "X of 16."

| | MINT | NRMT |
|---|---|---|
| COMPLETE SET (16) | 25.00 | 11.00 |
| COMMON CARD (1-16) | .50 | .23 |
| ❑ 1 Jason Arnott | 4.00 | 1.80 |
| ❑ 2 Jesse Belanger | .50 | .23 |
| ❑ 3 Alexandre Daigle | 1.50 | .70 |
| ❑ 4 Iain Fraser | .50 | .23 |
| ❑ 5 Chris Gratton | .50 | .23 |
| ❑ 6 Boris Mironov | .50 | .23 |
| ❑ 7 Jaroslav Modry | .50 | .23 |
| ❑ 8 Rob Niedermayer | 2.00 | .90 |
| ❑ 9 Chris Osgood | 8.00 | 3.60 |
| ❑ 10 Pat Peake | .50 | .23 |
| ❑ 11 Derek Plante | .50 | .23 |
| ❑ 12 Chris Pronger | 1.50 | .70 |
| ❑ 13 Mikael Renberg | 2.00 | .90 |
| ❑ 14 Bryan Smolinski | 1.50 | .70 |
| ❑ 15 Jocelyn Thibault | 5.00 | 2.20 |
| ❑ 16 Alexei Yashin | 2.00 | .90 |

## 1993-94 PowerPlay Second Year Stars

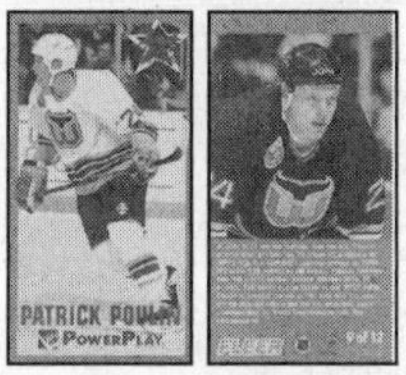

Randomly inserted at a rate of 1:3 series one packs, this 12-card set measures 2 1/2" by 4 3/4". The fronts feature color action photos with light blue metallic borders. The player's name in gold foil appears on the bottom, while the words "2nd Year Stars" are printed in gold foil in an upper corner. On the same light blue metallic background, the backs carry another color player photo with the player's name above and career highlights below. The cards are numbered on the back as "X of 12."

| | MINT | NRMT |
|---|---|---|
| COMPLETE SET (12) | 10.00 | 4.50 |
| COMMON CARD (1-12) | .50 | .23 |
| ❑ 1 Rob Gaudreau | .50 | .23 |
| ❑ 2 Joe Juneau | .60 | .25 |
| ❑ 3 Darius Kasparaitis | .50 | .23 |
| ❑ 4 Dmitri Kvartalnov | .50 | .23 |
| ❑ 5 Eric Lindros | 4.00 | 1.80 |
| ❑ 6 Vladimir Malakhov | .50 | .23 |
| ❑ 7 Shawn McEachern | .60 | .25 |
| ❑ 8 Felix Potvin | 1.00 | .45 |
| ❑ 9 Patrick Poulin | .50 | .23 |
| ❑ 10 Teemu Selanne | 2.00 | .90 |
| ❑ 11 Tommy Soderstrom | .50 | .23 |
| ❑ 12 Alexei Zhamnov | .50 | .23 |

## 1993-94 PowerPlay Slapshot Artists

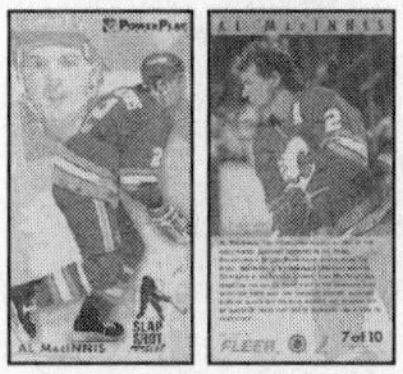

Randomly inserted in series two packs, this ten-card set measures 2 1/2" by 4 3/4". On a team-colored tinted background, the fronts feature color action cutouts with a smaller tinted head shot in an upper corner. The player's name and the Slapshot Artist logo in gold foil appear at the bottom. The bottom portion of the back's color player action photo is ghosted and team color-screened, and carries the player's career highlights. His name appears in black lettering in the team-colored margin above the photo. The cards are numbered on the back as "X of 10."

| | MINT | NRMT |
|---|---|---|
| COMPLETE SET (10) | 30.00 | 13.50 |
| COMMON CARD (1-10) | 1.00 | .45 |
| ❑ 1 Dave Andreychuk | 1.00 | .45 |
| ❑ 2 Ray Bourque | 3.00 | 1.35 |
| ❑ 3 Sergei Fedorov | 6.00 | 2.70 |
| ❑ 4 Brett Hull | 4.00 | 1.80 |
| ❑ 5 Al Iafrate | 1.00 | .45 |
| ❑ 6 Brian Leetch | 3.00 | 1.35 |
| ❑ 7 Al MacInnis | 1.00 | .45 |
| ❑ 8 Mike Modano | 4.00 | 1.80 |
| ❑ 9 Teemu Selanne | 8.00 | 3.60 |
| ❑ 10 Brendan Shanahan | 6.00 | 2.70 |

## 1995-96 Pro Magnets

This set of 130 magnets was produced by Chris Martin Enterprises. Each magnet featured a color photo of the player on front, along with his name and team. The backs were simply a black magnetic surface. The checklist to this set mirrors that of the NHL Pro Stamps.

| | MINT | NRMT |
|---|---|---|
| COMPLETE SET (130) | 75.00 | 34.00 |
| COMMON MAGNET (1-130) | .50 | .23 |
| ❑ 1 Stephane Fiset | .75 | .35 |
| ❑ 2 Peter Forsberg | 3.00 | 1.35 |
| ❑ 3 Claude Lemieux | .50 | .23 |
| ❑ 4 Mike Ricci | .50 | .23 |
| ❑ 5 Joe Sakic | 2.50 | 1.10 |
| ❑ 6 Ed Belfour | .75 | .35 |
| ❑ 7 Chris Chelios | .75 | .35 |
| ❑ 8 Joe Murphy | .50 | .23 |
| ❑ 9 Bernie Nicholls | .50 | .23 |
| ❑ 10 Jeremy Roenick | .75 | .35 |
| ❑ 11 Geoff Courtnall | .50 | .23 |
| ❑ 12 Brett Hull | 1.00 | .45 |
| ❑ 13 Al MacInnis | .50 | .23 |
| ❑ 14 Chris Pronger | .50 | .23 |
| ❑ 15 Esa Tikkanen | .50 | .23 |
| ❑ 16 Ray Bourque | .75 | .35 |
| ❑ 17 Blaine Lacher | .75 | .35 |
| ❑ 18 Cam Neely | .75 | .35 |
| ❑ 19 Adam Oates | .50 | .23 |
| ❑ 20 Kevin Stevens | .50 | .23 |
| ❑ 21 Valeri Bure | .50 | .23 |
| ❑ 22 Vincent Damphousse | .75 | .35 |
| ❑ 23 Mark Recchi | .50 | .23 |
| ❑ 24 Patrick Roy | 4.00 | 1.80 |
| ❑ 25 Pierre Turgeon | .75 | .35 |
| ❑ 26 Pavel Bure | 1.50 | .70 |
| ❑ 27 Trevor Linden | .75 | .35 |
| ❑ 28 Kirk McLean | .75 | .35 |
| ❑ 29 Alexander Mogilny | .75 | .35 |
| ❑ 30 Cliff Ronning | .50 | .23 |
| ❑ 31 Jason Allison | .50 | .23 |
| ❑ 32 Jim Carey | 1.00 | .45 |
| ❑ 33 Dale Hunter | .50 | .23 |
| ❑ 34 Joe Juneau | .50 | .23 |
| ❑ 35 Brendan Witt | .50 | .23 |
| ❑ 36 Martin Brodeur | 1.50 | .70 |
| ❑ 37 John MacLean | .50 | .23 |
| ❑ 38 Scott Niedermayer | .50 | .23 |
| ❑ 39 Stephane Richer | .50 | .23 |
| ❑ 40 Scott Stevens | .50 | .23 |
| ❑ 41 Patrik Carnback | .50 | .23 |
| ❑ 42 Guy Hebert | .75 | .35 |
| ❑ 43 Paul Kariya | 3.50 | 1.55 |
| ❑ 44 Oleg Tverdovsky | .50 | .23 |
| ❑ 45 Garry Valk | .50 | .23 |
| ❑ 46 Theoren Fleury | .75 | .35 |
| ❑ 47 Trevor Kidd | .75 | .35 |
| ❑ 48 Joe Nieuwendyk | .50 | .23 |
| ❑ 49 Gary Roberts | .50 | .23 |
| ❑ 50 German Titov | .50 | .23 |
| ❑ 51 Rod Brind'Amour | .50 | .23 |
| ❑ 52 Ron Hextall | .50 | .23 |
| ❑ 53 John LeClair | 1.00 | .45 |
| ❑ 54 Eric Lindros | 3.50 | 1.55 |
| ❑ 55 Mikael Renberg | .75 | .35 |
| ❑ 56 Brett Lindros | .50 | .23 |
| ❑ 57 Wendel Clark | .50 | .23 |
| ❑ 58 Patrick Flatley | .50 | .23 |
| ❑ 59 Kirk Muller | .50 | .23 |
| ❑ 60 Mathieu Schneider | .50 | .23 |
| ❑ 61 Tim Cheveldae | .75 | .35 |
| ❑ 62 Dallas Drake | .50 | .23 |
| ❑ 63 Teemu Selanne | 1.50 | .70 |
| ❑ 64 Keith Tkachuk | 1.00 | .45 |
| ❑ 65 Alexei Zhamnov | .50 | .23 |
| ❑ 66 Rob Blake | .50 | .23 |
| ❑ 67 Wayne Gretzky | 5.00 | 2.20 |
| ❑ 68 Jari Kurri | .50 | .23 |
| ❑ 69 Jamie Storr | .75 | .35 |
| ❑ 70 Rick Tocchet | .50 | .23 |
| ❑ 71 Brian Bradley | .50 | .23 |
| ❑ 72 Chris Gratton | .50 | .23 |
| ❑ 73 Roman Hamrlik | .50 | .23 |
| ❑ 74 Paul Ysebaert | .50 | .23 |
| ❑ 75 Rob Zamuner | .50 | .23 |
| ❑ 76 Dave Andreychuk | .50 | .23 |
| ❑ 77 Doug Gilmour | .75 | .35 |
| ❑ 78 Kenny Jonsson | .50 | .23 |
| ❑ 79 Felix Potvin | 1.00 | .45 |
| ❑ 80 Mats Sundin | 1.00 | .45 |
| ❑ 81 Jason Arnott | .75 | .35 |
| ❑ 82 Jason Bonsignore | .50 | .23 |
| ❑ 83 Todd Marchant | .50 | .23 |
| ❑ 84 Bill Ranford | .75 | .35 |
| ❑ 85 Doug Weight | .75 | .35 |
| ❑ 86 Jody Hull | .50 | .23 |
| ❑ 87 Bob Kudelski | .50 | .23 |
| ❑ 88 Scott Mellanby | .50 | .23 |
| ❑ 89 Rob Niedermayer | .50 | .23 |
| ❑ 90 John Vanbiesbrouck | 2.50 | 1.10 |
| ❑ 91 Ron Francis | .75 | .35 |
| ❑ 92 Jaromir Jagr | 3.50 | 1.55 |
| ❑ 93 Mario Lemieux | 4.00 | 1.80 |
| ❑ 94 Bryan Smolinski | .50 | .23 |
| ❑ 95 Sergei Zubov | .50 | .23 |
| ❑ 96 Adam Graves | .50 | .23 |
| ❑ 97 Brian Leetch | .75 | .35 |
| ❑ 98 Mark Messier | 1.00 | .45 |
| ❑ 99 Mike Richter | 1.00 | .45 |
| ❑ 100 Luc Robitaille | .75 | .35 |
| ❑ 101 Paul Coffey | .50 | .23 |
| ❑ 102 Sergei Fedorov | 1.50 | .70 |
| ❑ 103 Nicklas Lidstrom | .50 | .23 |
| ❑ 104 Ray Sheppard | .50 | .23 |
| ❑ 105 Steve Yzerman | 2.50 | 1.10 |
| ❑ 106 Donald Audette | .50 | .23 |
| ❑ 107 Dominik Hasek | 1.00 | .45 |
| ❑ 108 Yuri Khmylev | .50 | .23 |
| ❑ 109 Pat LaFontaine | .50 | .23 |
| ❑ 110 Alexei Zhitnik | .50 | .23 |
| ❑ 111 Radek Bonk | .50 | .23 |
| ❑ 112 Randy Cunneyworth | .50 | .23 |
| ❑ 113 Alexandre Daigle | .50 | .23 |
| ❑ 114 Steve Larouche | .50 | .23 |
| ❑ 115 Martin Straka | .50 | .23 |
| ❑ 116 Ulf Dahlen | .50 | .23 |
| ❑ 117 Pat Falloon | .50 | .23 |
| ❑ 118 Jeff Friesen | .50 | .23 |
| ❑ 119 Arturs Irbe | .75 | .35 |
| ❑ 120 Craig Janney | .50 | .23 |
| ❑ 121 Shane Churla | .50 | .23 |
| ❑ 122 Todd Harvey | .50 | .23 |
| ❑ 123 Derian Hatcher | .50 | .23 |
| ❑ 124 Mike Modano | .75 | .35 |
| ❑ 125 Andy Moog | .75 | .35 |
| ❑ 126 Sean Burke | .75 | .35 |
| ❑ 127 Andrew Cassels | .50 | .23 |
| ❑ 128 Geoff Sanderson | .50 | .23 |
| ❑ 129 Brendan Shanahan | 1.00 | .45 |
| ❑ 130 Darren Turcotte | .50 | .23 |

## 1990-91 Pro Set

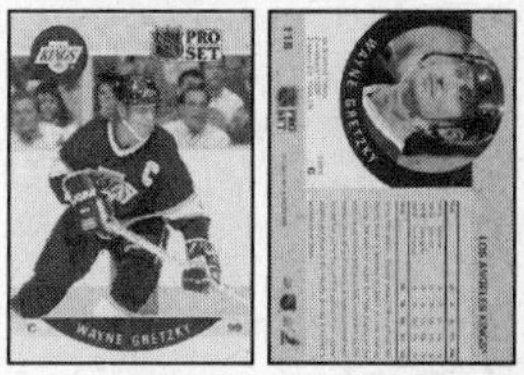

The inaugural Pro Set issue contains 705 cards measuring the standard size, with the first series containing 405 cards followed by a 300 card second series. The fronts feature a color action photo, banded above and below in the team's colors. The horizontally oriented backs have a head shot of each player and player information sandwiched between color stripes in the team's colors. Many grammatical, statistical and factual errors punctuated this issue. The key Rookie Cards in the set are Ed Belfour, Sergei Fedorov, Jaromir Jagr, Curtis Joseph, Mike Modano, Alexander Mogilny, Petr Nedved, Owen Nolan, Keith Primeau, Mike Richter, Jeremy Roenick, Kevin Stevens and Mats Sundin.

| | MINT | NRMT |
|---|---|---|
| COMPLETE SET (705) | 15.00 | 6.75 |
| COMPLETE SERIES 1 (405) | 8.00 | 3.60 |
| COMPLETE SERIES 2 (300) | 8.00 | 3.60 |
| COMMON CARD (1-705) | .05 | .02 |
| ❑ 1A Brett Hull Promo UER (Born 9/9/64, 85 games in '87-88, height 6-0, TM under Pro Set logos, aqua blue team color) | 2.00 | .90 |
| ❑ 1B Ray Bourque ERR (Misspelled Borque on card front) | .25 | .11 |
| ❑ 1C Ray Bourque COR | .15 | .07 |
| ❑ 2 Randy Burridge | .05 | .02 |
| ❑ 3 Lyndon Byers | .05 | .02 |
| ❑ 4 Bob Carpenter UER (Front LW, back C) | .05 | .02 |
| ❑ 5 John Carter | .05 | .02 |
| ❑ 6 Dave Christian UER (28 games with Washington, 50 with Boston) | .05 | .02 |
| ❑ 7A Garry Galley ERR (Misspelled Gary on card back) | .10 | .05 |
| ❑ 7B Garry Galley COR | .10 | .05 |
| ❑ 8 Craig Janney | .10 | .05 |
| ❑ 9 Rejean Lemelin UER (Wrong headings, not for goalie; '89-90 stats are Andy Moog's) | .10 | .05 |
| ❑ 10 Andy Moog UER ('89-90 stats are Reggie Lemelin's; he was 3rd, not 2nd in Vezina voting) | .10 | .05 |
| ❑ 11 Cam Neely UER (Bruins not capitalized in text) | .10 | .05 |
| ❑ 12 Allen Pedersen | .05 | .02 |
| ❑ 13 Dave Poulin UER (Flyers' stats missing from '89-90) | .05 | .02 |
| ❑ 14 Brian Propp UER (No Flyer stats, only Boston) | .05 | .02 |
| ❑ 15 Bob Sweeney | .05 | .02 |
| ❑ 16 Glen Wesley | .05 | .02 |
| ❑ 17A Dave Andreychuk ERR (Photo actually Scott Arniel on back) | .10 | .05 |
| ❑ 17B Dave Andreychuk COR | .10 | .05 |
| ❑ 18A Scott Arniel ERR (Photo actually Dave Andreychuk on back) | .05 | .02 |
| ❑ 18B Scott Arniel COR | .05 | .02 |
| ❑ 19 Doug Bodger | .05 | .02 |
| ❑ 20 Mike Foligno | .05 | .02 |
| ❑ 21A Phil Housley ERR (No traded stripe) | .10 | .05 |
| ❑ 21B Phil Housley COR (Traded stripe on card front) | .10 | .05 |
| ❑ 22 Dean Kennedy UER (Born Redvers, not Redver) | .05 | .02 |
| ❑ 23 Uwe Krupp | .05 | .02 |
| ❑ 24 Grant Ledyard | .05 | .02 |

☐ 25 Clint Malarchuk UER .......... .10 .05
(Back in action 11 days
after hurt, not 2 as
said on card)
☐ 26 Alexander Mogilny .............. .40 .18
☐ 27 Daren Puppa UER ............... .10 .05
(Born 3/23/65,
not 3/23/63)
☐ 28 Mike Ramsey ...................... .05 .02
☐ 29 Christian Ruuttu UER .......... .05 .02
(Misspelled Ruutu)
☐ 30 Dave Snuggerud .................. .05 .02
☐ 31 Pierre Turgeon ..................... .10 .05
☐ 32 Rick Vaive UER ..................... .05 .02
(Sweater 22, not 12)
☐ 33 Theoren Fleury ...................... .10 .05
☐ 34 Doug Gilmour ........................ .15 .07
☐ 35 Al MacInnis UER ................... .10 .05
(Misspelled Allan
on card back)
☐ 36 Brian MacLellan ...................... .05 .02
☐ 37 Jamie Macoun UER ................ .05 .02
(Born 8/17/61,
not 8/7/61)
☐ 38 Sergei Makarov ....................... .20 .09
☐ 39A Brad McCrimmon ................ .05 .02
(No traded stripe,
39 on front)
☐ 39B Brad McCrimmon ................ .05 .02
(Traded stripe,
4 on front)
☐ 40A Joe Mullen ........................... .10 .05
(No traded stripe)
☐ 40B Joe Mullen ........................... .10 .05
(Traded stripe on
card front)
☐ 41 Dana Murzyn ........................ .05 .02
☐ 42A Joe Nieuwendyk ERR ......... .50 .23
(Misspelled Niewendyk
on card front)
☐ 42B Joe Nieuwendyk COR ......... .10 .05
☐ 43 Joel Otto ............................... .05 .02
☐ 44 Paul Ranheim UER ............... .05 .02
(Front LW, Back C)
☐ 45 Gary Roberts ........................ .05 .02
☐ 46 Gary Suter UER .................... .05 .02
(No space between
sentences)
☐ 47 Mike Vernon ......................... .10 .05
☐ 48 Rick Wamsley ....................... .10 .05
(Misspelled Rich in
bio on card back)
☐ 49 Keith Brown .......................... .05 .02
☐ 50 Adam Creighton .................... .05 .02
☐ 51 Dirk Graham UER ................. .05 .02
(Sparking, should
be sparkling; season was
'88-89, not '89-90)
☐ 52 Steve Konroyd UER ............. .05 .02
(Front D, back LW)
☐ 53A Steve Larmer ERR ............. .10 .05
(Position and sweater
number in white,
should be black)
☐ 53B Steve Larmer COR ............. .10 .05
☐ 54A Dave Manson ERR .............. .05 .02
(Both photos actually
Steve Konroyd)
☐ 54B Dave Manson COR ............. .05 .02
☐ 55A Bob McGill ERR ................. .05 .02
(No PIM totals on back)
☐ 55B Bob McGill COR ................. .05 .02
☐ 56 Greg Millen ........................... .10 .05
☐ 57A Troy Murray ...................... .05 .02
(Position and sweater
number are white)
☐ 57B Troy Murray ...................... .05 .02
(Position and sweater
number are black)
☐ 58 Jeremy Roenick .................... .50 .23
☐ 59A Denis Savard ..................... .10 .05
(No traded stripe;
played 70 games
in '86-87)
☐ 59B Denis Savard ..................... .10 .05
(Traded stripe;
played 70 games
in '86-87)
☐ 60A Al Secord ........................... .05 .02
(Called Alan on back)
☐ 60B Al Secord ........................... .05 .02
(Called Al on back)
☐ 61A Duane Sutter ..................... .05 .02
(No retired stripe)
☐ 61B Duane Sutter ..................... .05 .02
(Retired stripe on front)
☐ 62 Steve Thomas ...................... .05 .02
☐ 63A Doug Wilson ....................... .10 .05
(Position and sweater
number are white)
☐ 63B Doug Wilson ....................... .10 .05
(Position and sweater
number are black)
☐ 64 Trent Yawney ........................ .05 .02
☐ 65 Dave Barr .............................. .05 .02
☐ 66 Shawn Burr ........................... .05 .02
☐ 67 Jimmy Carson ....................... .05 .02
☐ 68 John Chabot ......................... .05 .02
☐ 69 Steve Chiasson ..................... .05 .02
☐ 70 Bernie Federko UER ............. .10 .05
(Says only player from
Foam Lake, but
Elynuik was too)
☐ 71 Gerard Gallant ....................... .05 .02
☐ 72 Glen Hanlon ........................... .10 .05
☐ 73 Joey Kocur ............................ .05 .02
☐ 74 Lee Norwood ......................... .05 .02
☐ 75 Mike O'Connell ..................... .05 .02
(No retired stripe)
☐ 76 Bob Probert ........................... .10 .05
☐ 77 Torrie Robertson ................... .05 .02
☐ 78 Daniel Shank ......................... .05 .02
☐ 79 Steve Yzerman ...................... .40 .18
☐ 80 Rick Zombo ........................... .05 .02
☐ 81 Glenn Anderson ..................... .10 .05
☐ 82 Grant Fuhr ............................. .10 .05
☐ 83 Martin Gelinas UER ............... .05 .02
(Back photo actually
Joe Murphy)
☐ 84 Adam Graves UER ................. .25 .11
(Stats missing '89-90
Detroit info)
☐ 85 Charlie Huddy UER ................ .05 .02
(No accent in 1st e
in Defenseur)
☐ 86 Petr Klima UER ..................... .05 .02
(Born Chomulov, should
be Chaomutov)
☐ 87A Jari Kurri ............................ .10 .05
(No signed stripe)
☐ 87B Jari Kurri ............................ .10 .05
(Signed with Milan)
☐ 88 Mark Lamb ............................. .05 .02
☐ 89 Kevin Lowe UER .................... .05 .02
(No accent in 1st e
in Defenseur)
☐ 90 Craig MacTavish ..................... .05 .02
☐ 91 Mark Messier .......................... .20 .09
☐ 92 Craig Muni .............................. .05 .02
☐ 93 Joe Murphy ............................ .05 .02
☐ 94 Bill Ranford ............................ .10 .05
☐ 95 Craig Simpson UER ............... .05 .02
(Should be LW, not C)
☐ 96 Steve Smith UER .................... .05 .02
(No accent in 1st e
in Defenseur)
☐ 97 Esa Tikkanen .......................... .05 .02
☐ 98 Mikael Andersson ................... .05 .02
☐ 99 Dave Babych UER .................. .05 .02
(Extra space included
after Forum)
☐ 100 Yvon Corriveau UER ............ .05 .02
(Washington and Hartford
games not separate)
☐ 101 Randy Cunneyworth UER .. .05 .02
(Front LW, back C)
☐ 102 Kevin Dineen ....................... .05 .02
☐ 103 Dean Evason ....................... .05 .02
☐ 104 Ray Ferraro ......................... .05 .02
☐ 105 Ron Francis .......................... .10 .05
☐ 106 Grant Jennings .................... .05 .02
☐ 107 Todd Krygier ........................ .05 .02
☐ 108 Randy Ladouceur ................. .05 .02
☐ 109 Ulf Samuelsson .................... .05 .02
☐ 110 Brad Shaw ........................... .05 .02
☐ 111 Dave Tippett UER ................. .05 .02
(Front LW, back C)
☐ 112 Pat Verbeek ......................... .05 .02
☐ 113 Scott Young ......................... .05 .02
☐ 114 Brian Benning UER .............. .05 .02
(St.Louis and Los Angeles
stats not separate)
☐ 115 Steve Duchesne UER ........... .05 .02
(Kings, should be Kings')
☐ 116 Todd Elik .............................. .05 .02
☐ 117 Tony Granato UER ............... .05 .02
(Plays RW, not C)
☐ 118 Wayne Gretzky ..................... .75 .35
☐ 119 Kelly Hrudey ......................... .10 .05
☐ 120 Steve Kasper ........................ .05 .02
☐ 121A Mike Kushelnyski ERR .... .05 .02
(No position and number
on card front)
☐ 121B Mike Kushelnyski COR ... .05 .02
☐ 122 Bob Kudelski UER ................ .05 .02
(Born Springfield, not
Feeding Hills)
☐ 123 Tom Laidlaw ......................... .05 .02
☐ 124 Marty McSorley ..................... .05 .02
☐ 125 Larry Robinson ...................... .10 .05
☐ 126 Luc Robitaille UER ................ .10 .05
(Kings, should be Kings')
☐ 127 Tomas Sandstrom UER ....... .05 .02
('89-90 Rangers stats
not printed)
☐ 128 Dave Taylor ........................... .10 .05
☐ 129A John Tonelli ERR .............. .05 .02
(Misspelled Tonnelli
on card front)
☐ 129B John Tonelli COR ............. .25 .11
☐ 130A Brian Bellows ERR ............ .05 .02
(Back photo actually Dave
Gagner; front LW, back RW)
☐ 130B Brian Bellows COR/ERR .. .05 .02
(Back photo correct,
facing forward;
front LW, back RW)
☐ 131 Aaron Broten UER ................ .05 .02
(New Jersey and Minnesota
stats not separate)
☐ 132 Neal Broten .......................... .10 .05
☐ 133 Jon Casey UER ..................... .10 .05
(GAA 3.22, not 3122)
☐ 134 Shawn Chambers UER ......... .05 .02
(Back photo reversed)
☐ 135 Shane Churla ........................ .05 .02
☐ 136 Ulf Dahlen UER .................... .05 .02
(Rangers and Minnesota
stats not separate)
☐ 137 Gaetan Duchesne ................. .05 .02
☐ 138 Dave Gagner ......................... .10 .05
☐ 139 Stewart Gavin ....................... .05 .02
☐ 140 Curt Giles .............................. .05 .02
☐ 141 Basil McRae .......................... .05 .02
☐ 142 Mike Modano ......................... .60 .25
☐ 143 Larry Murphy ......................... .10 .05
☐ 144 Ville Siren .............................. .05 .02
☐ 145 Mark Tinordi ........................... .05 .02
☐ 146 Guy Carbonneau UER ........... .10 .05
(Sep Iles should be
Sept-Iles)
☐ 147A Chris Chelios ...................... .15 .07
(No traded stripe)
☐ 147B Chris Chelios ...................... .15 .07
(Traded stripe)
☐ 148 Shayne Corson ...................... .05 .02
☐ 149 Russ Courtnall UER ............... .05 .02
(Front RW, back C)
☐ 150 Brian Hayward ....................... .10 .05
☐ 151 Mike Keane ............................ .05 .02
☐ 152 Stephan Lebeau ..................... .05 .02
☐ 153 Claude Lemieux UER ............ .10 .05
(Reason is misspelled
as reson)
☐ 154 Craig Ludwig .......................... .05 .02
☐ 155 Mike McPhee ......................... .05 .02
☐ 156 Stephane Richer .................... .10 .05
☐ 157 Patrick Roy ............................ .60 .25
☐ 158 Mathieu Schneider ................. .05 .02
☐ 159 Brian Skrudland ...................... .05 .02
☐ 160 Bobby Smith UER .................. .10 .05
(No mention of trade from
Montreal to Minnesota)
☐ 161 Petr Svoboda ......................... .05 .02
☐ 162 Tommy Albelin ....................... .05 .02
☐ 163 Doug Brown UER ................... .05 .02
(Born 6/12/64,
not 7/12/64)
☐ 164 Sean Burke ............................ .10 .05
☐ 165 Ken Daneyko .......................... .05 .02
☐ 166 Bruce Driver ........................... .05 .02
☐ 167A Slava Fetisov ...................... .05 .02
ERR (Misspelled
Vlacheslav on front)
☐ 167B Slava Fetisov ...................... .05 .02
COR
☐ 168 Mark Johnson ........................ .05 .02
☐ 169 Alexei Kasatonov UER .......... .05 .02
(Stats should indicate
either Soviet or NHL)
☐ 170 John MacLean UER ............... .10 .05
(Should have apostrophe
after Devils)
☐ 171A David Maley ERR ............... .05 .02
(Front LW, back C)
☐ 171B David Maley COR .............. .05 .02
(LW on both sides)
☐ 172 Kirk Muller .............................. .05 .02
☐ 173 Janne Ojanen ......................... .05 .02
☐ 174 Brendan Shanahan ................ .40 .18
☐ 175A Peter Stastny ERR .............. .10 .05
(Front photo actually
Patrik Sundstrom)
☐ 175B Peter Stastny COR ............. .10 .05
☐ 176A Patrik Sundstrom ERR ....... .05 .02
(Front photo actually
Peter Stastny)
☐ 176B Patrik Sundstrom COR ....... .05 .02
☐ 177 Sylvain Turgeon ..................... .05 .02
☐ 178 Ken Baumgartner .................... .05 .02
☐ 179 Doug Crossman UER ............. .05 .02
(Born 6/30/60,
not 5/30/60)
☐ 180 Gerald Diduck ........................ .05 .02
☐ 181 Mark Fitzpatrick ...................... .10 .05
☐ 182 Pat Flatley UER ...................... .05 .02
(Front C, back RW)
☐ 183 Glen Healy UER ..................... .10 .05
(Misspelled Glenn
on card back)
☐ 184 Alan Kerr ................................. .05 .02
☐ 185 Derek King .............................. .05 .02
☐ 186 Pat LaFontaine ........................ .10 .05
☐ 187 Don Maloney ........................... .05 .02
☐ 188 Hubie McDonough UER ........ .05 .02
(Kings and Islanders
stats not separate)
☐ 189 Jeff Norton UER ...................... .05 .02
(Born Cambridge, Mass.,
not Acton)
☐ 190 Gary Nylund ............................ .05 .02
☐ 191 Brent Sutter ............................ .05 .02
☐ 192 Bryan Trottier UER ................. .10 .05
(Finish the season,
not finished)
☐ 193 David Volek UER .................... .05 .02
(Front LW, back RW)
☐ 194 Randy Wood ........................... .05 .02
☐ 195 Jan Erixon ............................... .05 .02
☐ 196 Mike Gartner UER .................. .10 .05
(Minnesota and Rangers
stats not separate)
☐ 197 Ron Greschner ........................ .05 .02
☐ 198A Miloslav Horava ERR .......... .05 .02
(Mispelled Miroslav)
☐ 198B Miloslav Horava COR ......... .05 .02
☐ 199 Mark Janssens ........................ .05 .02
☐ 200 Kelly Kisio .............................. .05 .02
☐ 201 Brian Leetch ............................ .15 .07
☐ 202 Randy Moller ........................... .05 .02
☐ 203 Brian Mullen ............................ .05 .02
☐ 204 Bernie Nicholls UER .............. .10 .05
(Kings and Rangers
stats not separate)
☐ 205A Chris Nilan .......................... .05 .02
(No traded stripe)
☐ 205B Chris Nilan .......................... .05 .02
(Traded stripe on front)
☐ 206 John Ogrodnick ....................... .05 .02
☐ 207 James Patrick .......................... .05 .02
☐ 208 Darren Turcotte UER .............. .05 .02
(GP total says 97,
should be 96)
☐ 209 John Vanbiesbrouck UER . .25 .11
(Front C, back G)
☐ 210 Carey Wilson ........................... .05 .02
☐ 211 Mike Bullard ............................ .05 .02
☐ 212 Terry Carkner .......................... .05 .02
☐ 213 Jeff Chychrun .......................... .05 .02
☐ 214 Murray Craven ......................... .05 .02
☐ 215 Pelle Eklund UER .................... .05 .02
(Centre and previous, not
Center and previously)
☐ 216 Ron Hextall UER ..................... .10 .05
(Born 5/3/64,
not 3/3/64)
☐ 217 Mark Howe .............................. .05 .02
☐ 218 Tim Kerr .................................. .05 .02
☐ 219 Ken Linseman UER ................. .05 .02
(Bruins and Flyers
stats not separate)
☐ 220 Scott Mellanby ........................ .10 .05
☐ 221 Gord Murphy ........................... .05 .02
☐ 222 Kjell Samuelsson UER ........... .05 .02
(Born 10/18/58,
not 10/18/56)
☐ 223 Ilkka Sinisalo ........................... .05 .02
☐ 224 Ron Sutter ............................... .05 .02
☐ 225 Rick Tocchet ............................ .10 .05
☐ 226 Ken Wregget ............................ .10 .05
☐ 227 Tom Barrasso ........................... .10 .05
☐ 228A Phil Bourque ERR ................ .05 .02
(Misspelled Borque
on both sides)
☐ 228B Phil Bourque COR ............... .05 .02
☐ 229 Rob Brown UER ...................... .05 .02
(Front RW, back C;
actual position is LW)
☐ 230 Alain Chevrier UER ................ .10 .05
(Chicago and Pittsburgh
stats not separate)
☐ 231 Paul Coffey ............................. .15 .07
☐ 232 John Cullen ............................. .05 .02
☐ 233 Gord Dineen UER ................... .05 .02
(Born Toronto,
not Quebec City)
☐ 234 Bob Errey ................................ .05 .02
☐ 235 Jim Johnson UER .................... .05 .02
(Born Minnesota,
not Michigan)
☐ 236 Mario Lemieux UER ............... .60 .25
(Missed 21 games,
not 11)
☐ 237 Troy Loney .............................. .05 .02
☐ 238 Barry Pederson UER .............. .05 .02
(No Vancouver stats
included)
☐ 239 Mark Recchi ............................ .25 .11
☐ 240 Kevin Stevens UER ................ .05 .02
(Front LW, back C)
☐ 241 Tony Tanti UER ...................... .05 .02
(No Vancouver stats
included)
☐ 242 Zarley Zalapski UER .............. .05 .02
(Pittsburgh misspelled
as Pittsburg)
☐ 243 Joe Cirella ............................... .05 .02
☐ 244 Lucien DeBlois UER ............... .05 .02
(Front C, back RW;
misspelled Deblois in
bio on card back)
☐ 245A Marc Fortier ERR ................. .05 .02
(Misspelled Mark
on both sides)
☐ 245B Marc Fortier COR ................. .05 .02
☐ 246 Paul Gillis ................................ .05 .02
☐ 247 Mike Hough ............................. .05 .02
☐ 248 Tony Hrkac UER ..................... .05 .02
(Blues and Nordiques
stats not separate)
☐ 249 Jeff Jackson ............................. .05 .02
☐ 250 Guy Lafleur ............................... .15 .07
☐ 251 Curtis Leschyshyn ................... .05 .02
☐ 252 Claude Loiselle ........................ .05 .02
☐ 253 Mario Marois ............................ .05 .02
☐ 254 Tony McKegney UER .............. .05 .02
(Red Wings and Nordiques
stats not separate)
☐ 255 Ken McRae ............................... .05 .02
☐ 256A Michel Petit ERR ................... .05 .02
(Front 21, back 24)
☐ 256B Michel Petit COR .................. .05 .02
☐ 257 Joe Sakic UER .......................... .40 .18
(Front 88, back 19)
☐ 258 Ron Tugnutt ............................. .10 .05
☐ 259 Rod Brind'Amour UER ............ .40 .18
(Misspelled Rob
on card back)
☐ 260 Jeff Brown UER ....................... .05 .02
(Nordiques and Blues
stats not separate)
☐ 261 Gino Cavallini UER .................. .05 .02
(On back Meagher is mis-
spelled as Meager)
☐ 262 Paul Cavallini ............................ .05 .02
☐ 263 Brett Hull ................................... .30 .14
☐ 264 Mike Lalor UER ......................... .05 .02
(No mention of trade
to Washington)
☐ 265 Dave Lowry ................................ .05 .02
☐ 266 Paul MacLean ............................ .05 .02
☐ 267 Rick Meagher ............................. .05 .02
☐ 268 Sergio Momesso UER .............. .05 .02
(Text has 55 pts. in
'89-90, stats 56)
☐ 269 Adam Oates ............................... .10 .05
☐ 270 Vincent Riendeau ....................... .10 .05
☐ 271 Gordie Roberts ........................... .05 .02
☐ 272 Rich Sutter UER .......................... .05 .02
(Canucks and Blues
stats not separate)
☐ 273 Steve Tuttle ................................. .05 .02
☐ 274 Peter Zezel UER .......................... .05 .02
(No traded stripe)
☐ 275A Allan Bester ERR ..................... .10 .05
(Misspelled Alan
on card front)
☐ 275B Allan Bester COR ..................... .10 .05
☐ 276 Wendel Clark ................................ .10 .05
☐ 277 Brian Curran UER ........................ .05 .02
(Plays, not played)
☐ 278 Vincent Damphousse .................. .10 .05
(Name not listed on
one line)
☐ 279A Tom Fergus ERR ...................... .05 .02
(Fourth line in bio has
Tl, should be that)
☐ 279B Tom Fergus COR ...................... .05 .02
☐ 280 Lou Franceschetti ......................... .05 .02
☐ 281 Al Iafrate ........................................ .10 .05
☐ 282 Tom Kurvers UER ......................... .05 .02
(Played for Toronto
in 71, not 70)
☐ 283 Gary Leeman ................................. .05 .02
☐ 284 Daniel Marois ................................ .05 .02
☐ 285 Brad Marsh .................................... .05 .02
☐ 286 Ed Olczyk UER ............................... .05 .02
(Front C, back RW)
☐ 287 Mark Osborne ................................ .05 .02
☐ 288 Rob Ramage .................................. .05 .02
☐ 289 Luke Richardson ............................ .05 .02
☐ 290 Gilles Thibaudeau UER ................. .05 .02
(Islanders and Leafs
stats not separate)
☐ 291 Greg Adams UER ........................... .05 .02
(Front LW, back C)
☐ 292 Jim Benning ..................................... .05 .02
☐ 293 Steve Bozek ..................................... .05 .02
☐ 294 Brian Bradley .................................... .05 .02
☐ 295 Garth Butcher ................................... .05 .02
☐ 296 Vladimir Krutov ................................. .10 .05
☐ 297 Igor Larionov UER ............................ .05 .02
(Stats should indicate
either Soviet or NHL)
☐ 298 Doug Lidster ...................................... .05 .02
☐ 299 Trevor Linden .................................... .10 .05
☐ 300 Jyrki Lumme UER .............................. .05 .02
('89-90 Canadiens and
Canucks stats
not separate)
☐ 301A Andrew McBain ERR ...................... .05 .02
(Back photo actually
Jim Sandlak)
☐ 301B Andrew McBain COR ...................... .05 .02
☐ 302 Kirk McLean UER ................................ .10 .05
(Career GAA should
be 3.46, not 6.50)
☐ 303 Dan Quinn UER ................................... .05 .02
(Penguins and Canucks
stats not separate)
☐ 304 Paul Reinhart UER ............................... .05 .02
(Born 1/8/60, not 1/6/60)
☐ 305 Jim Sandlak .......................................... .05 .02
☐ 306 Petri Skriko ........................................... .05 .02
☐ 307 Don Beaupre .......................................... .10 .05
☐ 308 Dino Ciccarelli ........................................ .10 .05
☐ 309 Geoff Courtnall UER .............................. .05 .02
(Trade stripe missing)
☐ 310 John Druce ............................................ .05 .02
☐ 311 Kevin Hatcher ......................................... .05 .02
☐ 312 Dale Hunter UER ................................... .05 .02
(Text has rougish,
should be roguish)
☐ 313 Calle Johansson UER ............................ .05 .02
(No accent in first e
in Defenseur)
☐ 314 Rod Langway ......................................... .05 .02
☐ 315 Stephen Leach ........................................ .05 .02
☐ 316 Mike Liut UER ......................................... .10 .05
(Capitals and Whalers
stats not separate)
☐ 317 Alan May .................................................. .05 .02
☐ 318 Kelly Miller UER ....................................... .05 .02
(Front LW, back C)
☐ 319 Michal Pivonka UER ................................. .05 .02
(1988-89 Goals should
be 8, not 38)
☐ 320A Mike Ridley ERR ..................................... .05 .02
(Errant text reads
points.s)
☐ 320B Mike Ridley COR ..................................... .05 .02
☐ 321 Scott Stevens UER ..................................... .10 .05
(No accent in first e
in Defenseur;
1987-886)
☐ 322 John Tucker UER ......................................... .05 .02
(1989-90 Buffalo Sabres
team affiliation and
stats missing 8 games;
Ottawa misspelled Ottowa)
☐ 323 Brent Ashton ................................................ .05 .02
☐ 324 Laurie Boschman ......................................... .05 .02
☐ 325 Randy Carlyle ............................................... .05 .02
☐ 326 Dave Ellett .................................................... .05 .02
☐ 327 Pat Elynuik .................................................... .05 .02
☐ 328 Bob Essensa ................................................. .10 .05
☐ 329 Paul Fenton UER .......................................... .05 .02
(Front LW, back C)
☐ 330A Dale Hawerchuk ......................................... .10 .05
(No traded stripe;

19089-90; Center
should be Centre)
❑ 330B Dale Hawerchuk ............. .10 .05
(Traded stripe on
front; 19089-90; Center
should be Centre)
❑ 331 Paul MacDermid ............... .05 .02
❑ 332 Moe Mantha ..................... .05 .02
❑ 333 Dave McLlwain UER ......... .05 .02
(Born 1/9/67, not 6/9/67)
❑ 334 Teppo Numminen ............. .05 .02
❑ 335A Fredrik Olausson ERR ..... .05 .02
(Misspelled Frederik
on both sides)
❑ 335B Fredrik Olausson COR ..... .05 .02
❑ 336 Greg Paslawski ................. .05 .02
(TM after Jets is larger
than other TM symbols)
❑ 337 Al MacInnis AS ................. .10 .05
❑ 338 Mike Vernon AS ................ .10 .05
❑ 339 Kevin Lowe AS .................. .05 .02
❑ 340 Wayne Gretzky AS ............ .40 .18
❑ 341 Luc Robitaille AS UER ...... .10 .05
(Fewest shots by Eastern
AS's, not Boston)
❑ 342 Brett Hull AS ..................... .20 .09
❑ 343 Joe Mullen AS ................... .10 .05
❑ 344 Joe Nieuwendyk AS UER .. .10 .05
(Front 26, should be 25)
❑ 345 Steve Larmer AS ............... .10 .05
❑ 346 Doug Wilson AS UER ........ .10 .05
(Premier is spelled
premiere)
❑ 347 Steve Yzerman AS ............ .20 .09
❑ 348A Jari Kurri AS .................... .10 .05
(No signed stripe)
❑ 348B Jari Kurri AS .................... .10 .05
(Signed stripe on front)
❑ 349 Mark Messier AS ............... .20 .09
❑ 350 Steve Duchesne AS UER... .05 .02
(Shot record held by
Boston, not East)
❑ 351 Mike Gartner AS UER ....... .10 .05
(Front 12, should be 11)
❑ 352 Bernie Nicholls AS ............ .10 .05
❑ 353 Paul Cavallini AS ............... .05 .02
❑ 354 Al Iafrate AS ...................... .10 .05
❑ 355 Kirk McLean AS ................. .10 .05
❑ 356 Thomas Steen AS UER ..... .05 .02
(Should be Doug Smail)
❑ 357 Ray Bourque AS ................ .15 .07
❑ 358 Cam Neely AS .................... .10 .05
❑ 359 Patrick Roy AS ................... .30 .14
❑ 360 Brian Propp AS UER ......... .05 .02
(Games misspelled
as gamies)
❑ 361 Paul Coffey AS UER .......... .15 .07
(Front 7, should be 77)
❑ 362 Mario Lemieux AS ............ .30 .14
❑ 363 Dave Andreychuk AS ........ .10 .05
❑ 364 Phil Housley AS ................ .10 .05
❑ 365 Daren Puppa AS ................ .10 .05
❑ 366 Pierre Turgeon AS ............ .10 .05
❑ 367 Ron Francis AS .................. .10 .05
❑ 368 Chris Chelios AS ............... .15 .07
❑ 369A Shayne Corson AS ERR.. .05 .02
(Misspelled Shane)
❑ 369B Shayne Corson AS COR . .05 .02
❑ 370 Stephane Richer AS .......... .10 .05
❑ 371 Kirk Muller AS ................... .05 .02
❑ 372 Pat LaFontaine AS ............ .10 .05
❑ 373 Brian Leetch AS ................ .15 .07
❑ 374 Rick Tocchet AS ................ .10 .05
❑ 375 Joe Sakic AS ..................... .20 .09
❑ 376 Kevin Hatcher AS .............. .05 .02
❑ 377 Bob Murdoch Adams UER .05 .02
(One tie in 1989-90,
should be 11 ties)
❑ 378 Brett Hull Byng UER ......... .15 .07
(Should be Lady Byng
Memorial Trophy)
❑ 379 Sergei Makarov Calder ...... .05 .02
❑ 380 Kevin Lowe Clancy ............ .05 .02
❑ 381 Mark Messier Hart ............. .15 .07
❑ 382 Moog/Lemelin Jennings ... .05 .02
❑ 383 Gord Kluzak Mast UER ..... .05 .02
(Should be Bill Masterton
Memorial Trophy)
❑ 384 Ray Bourque Norris .......... .15 .07
❑ 385A Len Ceglarski Patrick ...... .05 .02
ERR (No number on back)
❑ 385B Len Ceglarski Patrick ...... .05 .02
COR
❑ 386 Mark Messier Pearson ...... .15 .07
❑ 387 Boston Bruins .................... .05 .02
❑ 388 Wayne Gretzky Ross UER. .40 .18
(Gretzky has won eight
Art Ross Trophies)
❑ 389 Rick Meagher Selke .......... .05 .02
❑ 390 Bill Ranford Smythe .......... .10 .05
❑ 391 Patrick Roy Vezina ............ .30 .14
❑ 392 Edmonton Oilers UER ....... .05 .02
(Should be Clarence
S. Campbell Bowl)
❑ 393 Boston Bruins .................... .05 .02
❑ 394 Wayne Gretzky LL UER ..... .40 .18
(Lemieux and Dionne,
should read Lemieux only)
❑ 395 Brett Hull LL UER ............. .15 .07
(Born 8/9/64,
not 9/9/64)
❑ 396 Sergei Makarov ROY ........ .05 .02
❑ 397 Mark Messier MVP ............ .15 .07
❑ 398 Mike Richter RLL UER ....... .15 .07
(Plays, not lays)
❑ 399 Patrick Roy LL ................... .30 .14
❑ 400 Darren Turcotte RLL ......... .05 .02
UER (Front RW, back C)
❑ 401 Owen Nolan FDP ............... .30 .14
❑ 402 Petr Nedved FDP ............... .30 .14
❑ 403 Phil Esposito HOF ............. .10 .05
❑ 404 Darryl Sittler HOF UER ...... .10 .05
(Career: 15 seasons,
not stats)
❑ 405 Stan Mikita HOF ................ .10 .05
❑ 406 Andy Brickley UER ............ .05 .02
(Front LW, back C/LW)
❑ 407 Peter Douris ...................... .05 .02
❑ 408 Nevin Markwart ................. .05 .02
❑ 409 Chris Nilan ........................ .05 .02
❑ 410 Stephane Quintal .............. .05 .02
❑ 411 Bruce Shoebottom ............ .05 .02
❑ 412 Don Sweeney .................... .05 .02
❑ 413 Jim Wiemer ....................... .05 .02
❑ 414 Mike Hartman .................... .05 .02
❑ 415 Dale Hawerchuk ................ .10 .05
❑ 416 Benoit Hogue .................... .05 .02
❑ 417 Bill Houlder ....................... .05 .02
❑ 418 Mikko Makela ..................... .05 .02
❑ 419 Robert Ray ........................ .05 .02
❑ 420 John Tucker ....................... .05 .02
❑ 421 Jiri Hrdina UER .................. .05 .02
(Calgary logo on front,
should be Pittsburgh)
❑ 422 Mark Hunter ....................... .05 .02
❑ 423 Tim Hunter ......................... .05 .02
❑ 424 Roger Johansson ............... .05 .02
❑ 425 Frank Musil ........................ .05 .02
❑ 426 Ric Nattress ....................... .05 .02
❑ 427 Chris Chelios ..................... .15 .07
❑ 428 Jacques Cloutier ............... .10 .05
(White position and num-
ber on front, not black)
❑ 429 Greg Gilbert ....................... .05 .02
❑ 430 Michel Goulet .................... .10 .05
(White position and num-
ber on front, not black)
❑ 431 Mike Hudson ...................... .05 .02
❑ 432 Jocelyn Lemieux ................ .05 .02
❑ 433 Brian Noonan ..................... .05 .02
❑ 434 Wayne Presley ................... .05 .02
❑ 435 Brent Fedyk ........................ .05 .02
❑ 436 Rick Green .......................... .05 .02
❑ 437 Marc Habscheid ................. .05 .02
❑ 438 Brad McCrimmon ............... .05 .02
❑ 439 Jeff Beukeboom .................. .05 .02
❑ 440 Dave Brown ........................ .05 .02
❑ 441 Kelly Buchberger ................ .05 .02
❑ 442 Greg Hawgood .................... .05 .02
❑ 443 Chris Joseph ....................... .05 .02
❑ 444 Ken Linseman ..................... .05 .02
❑ 445 Eldon Reddick .................... .10 .05
(G on back in
smaller type)
❑ 446 Geoff Smith ......................... .05 .02
❑ 447 Adam Burt ........................... .05 .02
❑ 448 Sylvain Cote ........................ .05 .02
❑ 449 Paul Cyr .............................. .05 .02
❑ 450 Ed Kastelic .......................... .05 .02
❑ 451 Peter Sidorkiewicz .............. .10 .05
❑ 452 Mike Tomlak ........................ .05 .02
❑ 453 Carey Wilson ....................... .05 .02
❑ 454 Daniel Berthiaume .............. .10 .05
❑ 455 Scott Bjugstad ..................... .05 .02
❑ 456 Rod Buskas ......................... .05 .02
❑ 457 John McIntyre ...................... .05 .02
❑ 458 Tim Watters .......................... .05 .02
❑ 459 Perry Berezan ...................... .05 .02
❑ 460 Brian Propp .......................... .05 .02
❑ 461 Ilkka Sinisalo ........................ .05 .02
❑ 462 Doug Smail ........................... .05 .02
❑ 463 Bobby Smith ......................... .10 .05
❑ 464 Chris Dahlquist ..................... .05 .02
❑ 465 Neil Wilkinson UER ............... .05 .02
Uniform number on front
is 5; should be 35)
❑ 466 J.J. Daigneault UER ............. .05 .02
(Front Jean Jacques,
back J.J.)
❑ 467 Eric Desjardins ..................... .05 .02
❑ 468 Gerald Diduck ....................... .05 .02
❑ 469 Donald Dufresne ................... .05 .02
❑ 470A Todd Ewen ERR .................. .05 .02
(Photo on back act-
ually Eric Desjardins)
❑ 470B Todd Ewen COR .................. .05 .02
(Photo on back facing
forward)
❑ 471 Brent Gilchrist ...................... .05 .02
❑ 472 Sylvain Lefebvre ................... .05 .02
❑ 473 Denis Savard ........................ .10 .05
❑ 474 Sylvain Turgeon .................... .05 .02
❑ 475 Ryan Walter UER ................... .05 .02
(Front C, back C/LW)
❑ 476 Laurie Boschman ................... .05 .02
❑ 477 Pat Conacher ......................... .05 .02
❑ 478 Claude Lemieux ...................... .10 .05
❑ 479 Walt Poddubny ....................... .05 .02
❑ 480 Alan Stewart ........................... .05 .02
❑ 481 Chris Terreri ............................ .10 .05
❑ 482 Brad Dalgarno ......................... .05 .02
❑ 483 Dave Chyzowski ...................... .05 .02
❑ 484 Craig Ludwig ........................... .05 .02
❑ 485 Wayne McBean ....................... .05 .02
❑ 486 Richard Pilon ........................... .05 .02
❑ 487 Joe Reekie ............................... .05 .02
❑ 488 Mick Vukota ............................. .05 .02
❑ 489 Mark Hardy ............................... .05 .02
❑ 490 Jody Hull .................................. .05 .02
❑ 491 Kris King ................................... .05 .02
❑ 492 Troy Mallette ............................ .05 .02
❑ 493 Kevin Miller ............................... .05 .02
❑ 494 Normand Rochefort .......... .05 .02
❑ 495 David Shaw ........................ .05 .02
❑ 496 Ray Sheppard ..................... .10 .05
❑ 497 Keith Acton ......................... .05 .02
❑ 498 Craig Berube ...................... .05 .02
❑ 499 Tony Horacek ..................... .05 .02
❑ 500 Normand Lacombe ............ .05 .02
❑ 501 Jiri Latal .............................. .05 .02
❑ 502 Pete Peeters ....................... .10 .05
❑ 503 Derrick Smith ...................... .05 .02
❑ 504 Jay Caufield ........................ .05 .02
❑ 505 Peter Taglianetti UER ......... .05 .02
(Front Pete, back Peter)
❑ 506 Randy Gilhen ...................... .05 .02
❑ 507 Randy Hillier ....................... .05 .02
❑ 508 Joe Mullen .......................... .10 .05
❑ 509 Frank Pietrangelo ............... .10 .05
❑ 510 Gordie Roberts ................... .05 .02
❑ 511 Bryan Trottier ..................... .10 .05
❑ 512 Wendell Young .................... .10 .05
❑ 513 Shawn Anderson ................. .05 .02
❑ 514 Steven Finn ......................... .05 .02
❑ 515 Bryan Fogarty ...................... .05 .02
❑ 516 Mike Hough UER ................. .05 .02
(Front RW, back LW)
❑ 517 Darin Kimble ........................ .05 .02
❑ 518 Randy Velischek .................. .05 .02
❑ 519 Craig Wolanin ...................... .05 .02
❑ 520 Bob Bassen .......................... .05 .02
❑ 521 Geoff Courtnall .................... .05 .02
❑ 522 Robert Dirk .......................... .05 .02
❑ 523 Glen Featherstone ............... .05 .02
❑ 524 Mario Marois ........................ .05 .02
❑ 525 Herb Raglan ......................... .05 .02
❑ 526 Cliff Ronning ........................ .05 .02
❑ 527 Harold Snepsts .................... .05 .02
❑ 528 Scott Stevens ...................... .10 .05
❑ 529 Ron Wilson ........................... .05 .02
❑ 530 Aaron Broten ........................ .05 .02
❑ 531 Lucien DeBlois ..................... .05 .02
❑ 532 Dave Ellett ............................ .05 .02
❑ 533A Paul Fenton ERR ............... .05 .02
(Trademark on front
next to name)
❑ 533B Paul Fenton COR ............... .05 .02
❑ 534 Todd Gill ................................ .05 .02
❑ 535 Dave Hannan ........................ .05 .02
❑ 536 John Kordic ........................... .05 .02
❑ 537 Mike Krushelnyski ................. .05 .02
❑ 538 Kevin Maguire ........................ .05 .02
❑ 539 Michel Petit ............................ .05 .02
❑ 540 Jeff Reese .............................. .05 .02
❑ 541 David Reid ............................. .05 .02
❑ 542 Doug Shedden ....................... .05 .02
❑ 543 Dave Capuano ....................... .05 .02
❑ 544 Craig Coxe ............................. .05 .02
❑ 545 Kevan Guy ............................. .05 .02
❑ 546 Rob Murphy ........................... .05 .02
❑ 547 Robert Nordmark ................... .05 .02
❑ 548 Stan Smyl ............................... .05 .02
❑ 549 Ronnie Stern .......................... .05 .02
❑ 550 Tim Bergland .......................... .05 .02
❑ 551 Nick Kypreos .......................... .05 .02
❑ 552 Mike Lalor ............................... .05 .02
❑ 553 Rob Murray ............................. .05 .02
❑ 554 Bob Rouse ............................... .05 .02
❑ 555 Dave Tippett ........................... .05 .02
❑ 556 Peter Zezel UER ..................... .05 .02
(Card says number 25,
sweater shows 9)
❑ 557 Scott Arniel ............................. .05 .02
❑ 558 Don Barber .............................. .05 .02
❑ 559 Shawn Cronin .......................... .05 .02
❑ 560 Gord Donnelly .......................... .05 .02
❑ 561 Doug Evans .............................. .05 .02
❑ 562 Phil Housley ............................. .10 .05
❑ 563 Ed Olczyk .................................. .05 .02
❑ 564 Mark Osborne ........................... .05 .02
❑ 565 Thomas Steen ........................... .05 .02
❑ 566 Boston Bruins Logo .................. .05 .02
❑ 567 Buffalo Sabres Logo ................. .05 .02
❑ 568 Calgary Flames Logo ............... .05 .02
❑ 569 Chicago Blackhawks ................. .05 .02
Logo
❑ 570 Detroit Red Wings .................... .05 .02
Logo
❑ 571 Edmonton Oilers Logo .............. .05 .02
❑ 572 Hartford Whalers Logo ............. .05 .02
❑ 573A Los Angeles Kings ................. .05 .02
Logo ERR
(Registration mark
missing from Kings
on card front)
❑ 573B Los Angeles Kings .................. .05 .02
Logo COR
❑ 574 Minn. North Stars ...................... .05 .02
Logo
❑ 575 Montreal Canadiens .................. .05 .02
Logo
❑ 576 New Jersey Devils ..................... .05 .02
Logo
❑ 577 New York Islanders ................... .05 .02
Logo
❑ 578 New York Rangers Logo .......... .05 .02
❑ 579 Philadelphia Flyers .................... .05 .02
Logo
❑ 580 Pittsburgh Penguins .................. .05 .02
Logo
❑ 581 Quebec Nordiques Logo ........... .05 .02
❑ 582 St. Louis Blues Logo ................. .05 .02
❑ 583 Toronto Maple Leafs .................. .05 .02
Logo
❑ 584 Vancouver Canucks .................... .05 .02
Logo
❑ 585 Washington Capitals ................... .05 .02
Logo
❑ 586 Winnipeg Jets Logo .......... .05 .02
❑ 587 Ken Hodge Jr. ..................... .05 .02
❑ 588 Vladimir Ruzicka ................ .05 .02
❑ 589 Wes Walz ............................ .05 .02
❑ 590 Greg Brown ......................... .05 .02
❑ 591 Brad Miller ........................... .05 .02
❑ 592 Darrin Shannon ................... .05 .02
❑ 593 Stephane Matteau UER ...... .05 .02
(Front RW, back LW)
❑ 594 Sergei Priakin ...................... .05 .02
❑ 595 Robert Reichel ..................... .20 .09
❑ 596 Ken Sabourin UER ............... .05 .02
(Front LW, back D;
actual position is C)
❑ 597 Tim Sweeney ........................ .05 .02
❑ 598 Ed Belfour UER .................... .60 .25
(Born Carmen,
should be Carman)
❑ 599 Frantisek Kucera .................. .05 .02
❑ 600 Mike McNeil UER .................. .05 .02
(Front C, back LW)
❑ 601 Mike Peluso .......................... .05 .02
❑ 602 Tim Cheveldae ..................... .10 .05
❑ 603 Per Djoos ............................. .05 .02
❑ 604 Sergei Fedorov ................... 1.00 .45
❑ 605 Johan Garpenlov .................. .05 .02
❑ 606 Keith Primeau ...................... .25 .11
❑ 607 Paul Ysebaert ...................... .05 .02
❑ 608 Anatoli Semenov .................. .05 .02
❑ 609 Bobby Holik .......................... .05 .02
❑ 610 Kay Whitmore ....................... .10 .05
❑ 611 Rob Blake ............................. .30 .14
❑ 612 Francois Breault ................... .05 .02
❑ 613 Mike Craig UER .................... .05 .02
(Wearing 50,
card says 20)
❑ 614 J.C. Bergeron UER ............... .05 .02
(Front J.C.,
back Jean Claude)
❑ 615 Andrew Cassels .................... .05 .02
❑ 616 Tom Chorske ........................ .05 .02
❑ 617 Lyle Odelein .......................... .05 .02
❑ 618 Mark Pederson ...................... .05 .02
❑ 619 Zdeno Ciger .......................... .05 .02
❑ 620 Troy Crowder ......................... .05 .02
❑ 621 Jon Morris .............................. .05 .02
❑ 622 Eric Weinrich ......................... .05 .02
❑ 623 David Marcinyshyn ................ .05 .02
(Card number smaller
than other cards in set)
❑ 624 Jeff Hackett ............................ .10 .05
❑ 625 Rob DiMaio ............................ .05 .02
❑ 626 Steven Rice ............................ .05 .02
❑ 627 Mike Richter .......................... .50 .23
❑ 628 Dennis Vial ............................. .05 .02
❑ 629 Martin Hostak ........................ .05 .02
❑ 630 Pat Murray .............................. .05 .02
❑ 631 Mike Ricci UER ...................... .25 .11
(Born October,
not November)
❑ 632 Jaromir Jagr ERR ................. 2.00 .90
(Stat header not lined
up with stats on back)
❑ 632B Jaromir Jagr COR ............ 1.00 .45
(Stat header lined
up with stats on back)
❑ 633 Paul Stanton .......................... .05 .02
❑ 634 Scott Gordon .......................... .05 .02
❑ 635 Owen Nolan ............................ .25 .11
❑ 636 Mats Sundin ........................... .50 .23
❑ 637 John Tanner ............................ .05 .02
❑ 638 Curtis Joseph .......................... .50 .23
❑ 639 Peter Ing .................................. .10 .05
❑ 640 Scott Thornton ......................... .05 .02
❑ 641 Troy Gamble ............................ .10 .05
❑ 642 Robert Kron ............................. .05 .02
❑ 643 Petr Nedved ............................. .30 .14
❑ 644 Adrien Plavsic .......................... .05 .02
❑ 645 Peter Bondra ............................ .40 .18
❑ 646 Jim Hrivnak .............................. .10 .05
❑ 647 Mikhail Tatarinov ..................... .05 .02
❑ 648 Stephane Beauregard ............. .10 .05
❑ 649 Rick Tabaracci ......................... .10 .05
❑ 650 Mike Bossy CPL ..................... .10 .05
❑ 651 Bobby Clarke CPL .................. .10 .05
❑ 652 Alex Delvecchio CPL ............... .10 .05
❑ 653 Marcel Dionne CPL ................. .10 .05
❑ 654 Gordie Howe CPL ................... .25 .11
❑ 655 Stan Mikita CPL ...................... .10 .05
❑ 656 Denis Potvin CPL ..................... .10 .05
❑ 657 Bobby Clarke HOF .................. .10 .05
❑ 658 Alex Delvecchio HOF ............... .10 .05
❑ 659 Tony Esposito HOF .................. .10 .05
❑ 660 Gordie Howe HOF .................... .25 .11
❑ 661 Mike Milbury CO ...................... .05 .02
❑ 662 Rick Dudley CO ........................ .05 .02
❑ 663 Doug Risebrough CO ............... .05 .02
❑ 664 Bryan Murray CO ..................... .05 .02
❑ 665 John Muckler CO ..................... .05 .02
❑ 666 Rick Ley CO ............................. .05 .02
❑ 667 Tom Webster CO ..................... .05 .02
❑ 668 Bob Gainey CO UER ................ .05 .02
(Stats and bio are
Bob McCammon's)
❑ 669 Pat Burns CO ........................... .05 .02
❑ 670 John Cunniff CO ...................... .05 .02
❑ 671 Al Arbour CO ............................ .05 .02
❑ 672 Roger Neilson CO .................... .05 .02
❑ 673 Paul Holmgren CO ................... .05 .02
❑ 674 Bob Johnson CO ...................... .05 .02
❑ 675 Dave Chambers CO ................. .05 .02
❑ 676 Brian Sutter CO UER ................ .05 .02
(Coaching totals say
0-69-21, should
be 70-69-21)
❑ 677 Tom Watt CO ............................ .05 .02
❑ 678 Bob McCammon CO UER .. .05 .02
(Stats and bio are
Bob Gainey's)
❑ 679 Terry Murray CO .............. .05 .02
❑ 680 Bob Murdoch CO .............. .05 .02
❑ 681 Ron Asselstine REF .......... .05 .02
❑ 682 Wayne Bonney REF .......... .05 .02
❑ 683 Kevin Collins REF .............. .05 .02
❑ 684 Pat Dapuzzo REF .............. .05 .02
❑ 685 Ron Finn REF ..................... .05 .02
❑ 686 Kerry Fraser REF ............... .05 .02
❑ 687 Gerard Gauthier REF ......... .05 .02
❑ 688 Terry Gregson REF ............ .05 .02
❑ 689 Bob Hodges REF ............... .05 .02
❑ 690 Ron Hoggarth REF ............. .05 .02
❑ 691 Don Koharski REF ............. .05 .02
❑ 692 Dan Marouelli REF ............. .05 .02
❑ 693 Danny McCourt REF UER .. .05 .02
(Front Dan, back Danny)
❑ 694 Bill McCreary REF .............. .05 .02
❑ 695 Denis Morel REF ................. .05 .02
❑ 696 Jerry Pateman REF ............ .05 .02
❑ 697 Ray Scapinello REF ............ .05 .02
❑ 698 Rob Shick REF .................... .05 .02
❑ 699 Paul Stewart REF ............... .05 .02
❑ 700 Leon Stickle REF ................ .05 .02
❑ 701 Andy van Hellemond REF .. .05 .02
❑ 702 Mark Vines REF .................. .05 .02
❑ 703 Wayne Gretzky 2000th ....... .40 .18
(2.33 goals per game,
should be points) UER
❑ 704 Stanley Cup Champs ......... .05 .02
❑ 705 The Puck-La Rondelle ........ .05 .02
❑ NNO Stanley Cup Hologram 80.00 36.00

## 1990-91 Pro Set Player of the Month

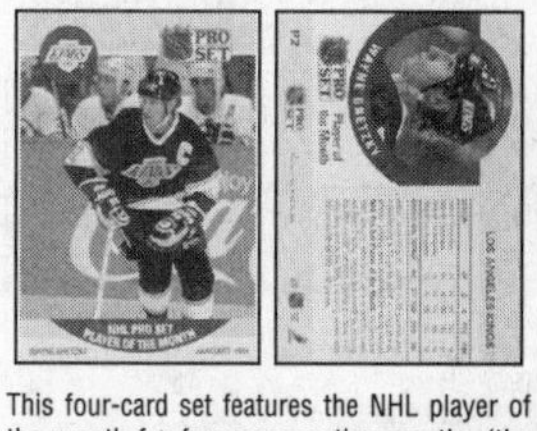

This four-card set features the NHL player of the month for four consecutive months (the month for which the player won the award is listed below his name). All cards feature the basic 1990-91 Pro Set design, and say NHL Pro Set Player of the Month and the date at the bottom of each obverse. The cards are numbered on the back; note that the Peeters card has no number. The cards were issued in the home rink of the winner each month after announcement of the winner. Pro Set sponsored the Player of the Week/Month/Year Awards for the NHL. Reportedly less than 25,000 of each POM card were produced.

| | MINT | NRMT |
|---|---|---|
| COMPLETE SET (4) | 20.00 | 9.00 |
| COMMON CARD | 4.00 | 1.80 |

❑ P1 Tom Barrasso ................ 4.00 1.80
POM December 1990
❑ P2 Wayne Gretzky ............. 10.00 4.50
POM January 1991
❑ P3 Brett Hull ....................... 6.00 2.70
POM February 1991
❑ NNO Pete Peeters ............. 4.00 1.80
POM November 1990

## 1991-92 Pro Set Preview

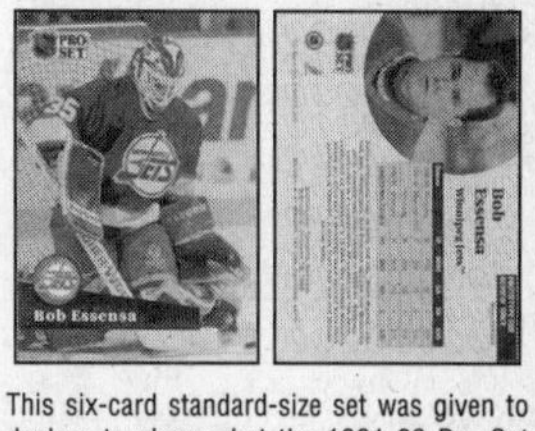

This six-card standard-size set was given to dealers to show what the 1991-92 Pro Set hockey set would look like. There is really not that much interest in the set due to the egregiously poor player selection, i.e., no superstars in the set. The setup of the text on the card backs of these preview cards is different from the regular issue cards; cards are labelled "Promo" on the back where the card number is in the regular issue cards. The David Reid card has an entirely different photo. Even though the cards are unnumbered, they are assigned reference numbers below according to their numbers in the 1991-92 Pro Set regular issue.

| | MINT | NRMT |
|---|---|---|
| COMPLETE SET (6) | 1.50 | .70 |
| COMMON CARD | .10 | .05 |

❑ 151 Randy Wood NNO .............. .25 .11
❑ 171 Gord Murphy NNO ............ .25 .11
❑ 203 Craig Wolanin NNO ........... .25 .11

❑ 229 David Reid NNO .25 .11
❑ 266 Bob Essensa NNO .25 .11
❑ NNO Title Card .10 .05

## 1991-92 Pro Set

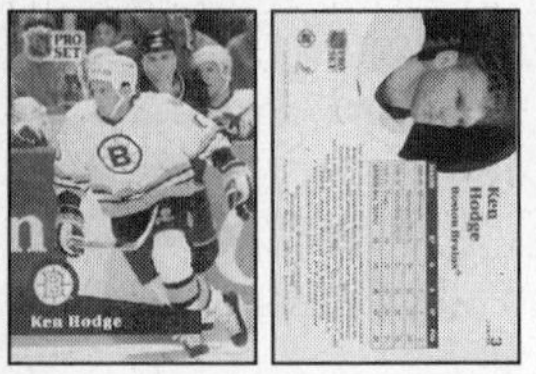

The Pro Set hockey issue contains 615 numbered cards. The set was released in two series of 345 and 270 cards, respectively. The fronts feature a borderless color action photo, with the team logo in the lower left corner, and the player's name in a black wedge below the logo. The backs have a color head and shoulders shot of the player (circular format) in the upper left corner, as well as biographical and statistical information on a white and gray hockey puck background. Pro Set also issued a French version which carries the same value. French wax boxes contained randomly inserted Patrick Roy personally autographed cards signed and numbered on the back; 1,000 of card number 125 (first series) and 1,000 of card number 599 numbered 1001 to 2000 (second series). Roy also signed 500 cards for distribution in Canadian collector's kits. These Canadian collector kit cards are valued at $200-$300. Randomly inserted in U.S. packs were a limited quantity of Kirk McLean autographed cards. Ten thousand hand-numbered 3-D hologram cards were inserted in second series foil packs to commemorate the NHL's Diamond Anniversary. Rookie Cards include Tony Amonte, Dominik Hasek, John LeClair, Nicklas Lidstrom, Geoff Sanderson, and Doug Weight.

| | MINT | NRMT |
|---|---|---|
| COMPLETE SET (615) | 15.00 | 6.75 |
| COMPLETE SERIES 1 (345) | 8.00 | 3.60 |
| COMPLETE SERIES 2 (270) | 8.00 | 3.60 |
| COMMON CARD (1-615) | .05 | .02 |

*FRENCH VERSION: SAME VALUE

❑ 1 Glen Wesley .05 .02
❑ 2 Craig Janney .10 .05
❑ 3 Ken Hodge Jr. .05 .02
❑ 4 Randy Burridge .05 .02
❑ 5 Cam Neely .10 .05
❑ 6 Bob Sweeney .05 .02
❑ 7 Garry Galley .05 .02
❑ 8 Petri Skriko .05 .02
❑ 9 Ray Bourque .15 .07
❑ 10 Andy Moog UER .10 .05
(4.0 record, should be 4-0)
❑ 11 Dave Christian .05 .02
❑ 12 Dave Poulin .05 .02
❑ 13 Jeff Lazaro .05 .02
❑ 14 Darrin Shannon .05 .02
❑ 15 Pierre Turgeon UER .10 .05
(Born 8/29, not 8/28)
❑ 16 Alexander Mogilny .30 .14
❑ 17 Benoit Hogue UER .05 .02
(Stats show two seasons with Winnipeg, should say Buffalo)
❑ 18 Dave Snuggerud .05 .02
❑ 19 Doug Bodger UER .05 .02
(Second highest offensive total of his career, should say third highest)
❑ 20 Uwe Krupp .05 .02
❑ 21 Daren Puppa .10 .05
❑ 22 Christian Ruuttu .05 .02
❑ 23 Dave Andreychuk .10 .05
❑ 24 Dale Hawerchuk .10 .05
❑ 25 Mike Ramsey .05 .02
❑ 26 Rick Vaive .05 .02
❑ 27 Stephane Matteau .05 .02
❑ 28 Theoren Fleury .10 .05
❑ 29 Joe Nieuwendyk .10 .05
❑ 30 Gary Roberts .05 .02
❑ 31 Paul Ranheim .05 .02
❑ 32 Gary Suter .05 .02
❑ 33 Al MacInnis .10 .05
❑ 34 Doug Gilmour .15 .07
❑ 35 Mike Vernon .10 .05
❑ 36 Carey Wilson .05 .02
❑ 37 Joel Otto .05 .02
❑ 38 Jamie Macoun .05 .02
❑ 39 Sergei Makarov .05 .02
❑ 40 Jeremy Roenick .15 .07
❑ 41 Dave Manson .05 .02
❑ 42 Adam Creighton .05 .02
❑ 43 Ed Belfour .15 .07
❑ 44 Wayne Presley .05 .02
❑ 45 Steve Thomas .05 .02
❑ 46 Troy Murray .05 .02
❑ 47 Bob McGill .05 .02
❑ 48 Chris Chelios .15 .07
❑ 49 Steve Larmer .10 .05
❑ 50 Michel Goulet .10 .05
❑ 51 Dirk Graham .05 .02
❑ 52 Doug Wilson .10 .05
❑ 53 Sergei Fedorov .30 .14
❑ 54 Yves Racine .05 .02
❑ 55 Jimmy Carson .05 .02
❑ 56 Johan Garpenlov .05 .02
❑ 57 Tim Cheveldae .10 .05
❑ 58 Shawn Burr .05 .02
❑ 59 Paul Ysebaert .05 .02
❑ 60 Kevin Miller .05 .02
❑ 61 Bob Probert .10 .05
❑ 62 Steve Yzerman .40 .18
❑ 63 Gerard Gallant .05 .02
❑ 64 Rick Zombo .05 .02
❑ 65 Dave Barr .05 .02
❑ 66 Martin Gelinas .05 .02
❑ 67 Adam Graves UER .10 .05
(Kid Line included Gelinas, not Simpson)
❑ 68 Joe Murphy .05 .02
❑ 69 Craig Simpson .05 .02
❑ 70 Bill Ranford .10 .05
❑ 71 Esa Tikkanen .05 .02
❑ 72 Petr Klima .05 .02
❑ 73 Steve Smith .05 .02
❑ 74 Mark Messier .25 .11
❑ 75 Glenn Anderson .10 .05
❑ 76 Kevin Lowe .05 .02
❑ 77 Craig MacTavish .05 .02
❑ 78 Grant Fuhr .10 .05
❑ 79 Bobby Holik .05 .02
❑ 80 Rob Brown .05 .02
❑ 81 Doug Houda .05 .02
❑ 82 Sylvain Cote .05 .02
❑ 83 Todd Krygier .05 .02
❑ 84 Dean Evason .05 .02
❑ 85 John Cullen .05 .02
❑ 86 Pat Verbeek .05 .02
❑ 87 Brad Shaw .05 .02
❑ 88 Paul Cyr UER .05 .02
(Stats show New York, should say NY Rangers)
❑ 89 Kevin Dineen .05 .02
❑ 90 Peter Sidorkiewicz .10 .05
❑ 91 Zarley Zalapski .05 .02
❑ 92 Rob Blake .10 .05
❑ 93 Jari Kurri UER .10 .05
(No transaction line on front, although back says Kings)
❑ 94 Todd Elik .05 .02
❑ 95 Luc Robitaille .10 .05
❑ 96 Steve Duchesne .05 .02
❑ 97 Tomas Sandstrom .05 .02
❑ 98 Tony Granato .05 .02
❑ 99 Bob Kudelski .05 .02
❑ 100 Marty McSorley .05 .02
❑ 101 Wayne Gretzky .75 .35
❑ 102 Kelly Hrudey .10 .05
❑ 103 Dave Taylor .10 .05
❑ 104 Larry Robinson .10 .05
❑ 105 Mike Modano .20 .09
❑ 106 Ulf Dahlen .05 .02
❑ 107 Mark Tinordi .05 .02
❑ 108 Dave Gagner .10 .05
❑ 109 Brian Bellows .05 .02
❑ 110 Gaetan Duchesne .05 .02
❑ 111 Jon Casey .10 .05
❑ 112 Neal Broten .10 .05
❑ 113 Brian Propp .05 .02
❑ 114 Curt Giles .05 .02
❑ 115 Bobby Smith .10 .05
❑ 116 Jim Johnson .05 .02
❑ 117 Doug Smail .05 .02
❑ 118 Eric Desjardins .05 .02
❑ 119 Mathieu Schneider .05 .02
❑ 120 Stephan Lebeau .05 .02
❑ 121 Mike Keane .05 .02
❑ 122 Stephane Richer .10 .05
❑ 123 Petr Svoboda .05 .02
❑ 124 J.J. Daigneault .05 .02
❑ 125 Patrick Roy .60 .25
❑ 126 Russ Courtnall .05 .02
❑ 127 Brian Skrudland .05 .02
❑ 128 Denis Savard .10 .05
❑ 129 Mike McPhee .05 .02
❑ 130 Guy Carbonneau .10 .05
❑ 131 Brendan Shanahan .30 .14
❑ 132 Sean Burke .10 .05
❑ 133 Eric Weinrich .05 .02
❑ 134 Kirk Muller .05 .02
❑ 135 Claude Lemieux .10 .05
❑ 136 John MacLean .10 .05
❑ 137 Chris Terreri .10 .05
❑ 138 Doug Brown .05 .02
❑ 139 Ken Daneyko .05 .02
❑ 140 Bruce Driver .05 .02
❑ 141 Patrik Sundstrom .05 .02
❑ 142 Slava Fetisov .05 .02
❑ 143 Peter Stastny .10 .05
❑ 144 Wayne McBean .05 .02
❑ 145 Bill Berg .05 .02
❑ 146 Derek King .05 .02
❑ 147 David Volek .05 .02
❑ 148 Jeff Norton .05 .02
❑ 149 Pat LaFontaine .10 .05
❑ 150 Gary Nylund .05 .02
❑ 151 Randy Wood .05 .02
❑ 152 Pat Flatley .05 .02
❑ 153 Glenn Healy .10 .05
❑ 154 Brent Sutter .05 .02
❑ 155 Craig Ludwig .05 .02
❑ 156 Ray Ferraro .05 .02
❑ 157 Troy Mallette .05 .02
❑ 158 Mark Janssens .05 .02
❑ 159 Brian Leetch UER .15 .07
(Career points total 329, should be 229)
❑ 160 Darren Turcotte .05 .02
❑ 161 Mike Richter .15 .07
❑ 162 Ray Sheppard .10 .05
❑ 163 Randy Moller .05 .02
❑ 164 James Patrick .05 .02
❑ 165 Brian Mullen UER .05 .02
(Transaction says drafted by San Jose, was actually traded)
❑ 166 Bernie Nicholls .10 .05
❑ 167 Mike Gartner .10 .05
❑ 168 Kelly Kisio UER .05 .02
(Transaction says drafted by Minnesota, was actually traded to San Jose)
❑ 169 John Ogrodnick .05 .02
❑ 170 Mike Ricci .05 .02
❑ 171 Gord Murphy .05 .02
❑ 172 Scott Mellanby .10 .05
❑ 173 Terry Carkner .05 .02
❑ 174 Derrick Smith .05 .02
❑ 175 Murray Craven .05 .02
❑ 176 Ron Hextall .10 .05
❑ 177 Rick Tocchet .10 .05
❑ 178 Ron Sutter .05 .02
❑ 179 Pelle Eklund .05 .02
❑ 180 Tim Kerr UER .05 .02
(Only transaction line to show a date)
❑ 181 Kjell Samuelsson .05 .02
❑ 182 Mark Howe .05 .02
❑ 183 Jaromir Jagr .40 .18
❑ 184 Mark Recchi .10 .05
❑ 185 Kevin Stevens .05 .02
❑ 186 Tom Barrasso .10 .05
❑ 187 Bob Errey .05 .02
❑ 188 Ron Francis .10 .05
❑ 189 Phil Bourque .05 .02
❑ 190 Paul Coffey .15 .07
❑ 191 Joe Mullen .10 .05
❑ 192 Bryan Trottier .10 .05
❑ 193 Larry Murphy .10 .05
❑ 194 Mario Lemieux .60 .25
❑ 195 Scott Young .05 .02
❑ 196 Owen Nolan .10 .05
❑ 197 Mats Sundin .10 .05
❑ 198 Curtis Leschyshyn .05 .02
❑ 199 Joe Sakic .30 .14
❑ 200 Bryan Fogarty .05 .02
❑ 201 Stephane Morin .05 .02
❑ 202 Ron Tugnutt .10 .05
❑ 203 Craig Wolanin .05 .02
❑ 204 Steven Finn .05 .02
❑ 205 Tony Hrkac .05 .02
❑ 206 Randy Velischek .05 .02
❑ 207 Alexei Gusarov .05 .02
❑ 208 Scott Pearson .05 .02
❑ 209 Dan Quinn .05 .02
❑ 210 Garth Butcher .05 .02
❑ 211 Rod Brind'Amour UER .10 .05
(Type in stat box is smaller than others)
❑ 212 Jeff Brown .05 .02
❑ 213 Vincent Riendeau .10 .05
❑ 214 Paul Cavallini .05 .02
❑ 215 Brett Hull .25 .11
❑ 216 Scott Stevens .10 .05
❑ 217 Rich Sutter .05 .02
❑ 218 Gino Cavallini .05 .02
❑ 219 Adam Oates UER .10 .05
(Stats are off-line from top to bottom)
❑ 220 Ron Wilson .05 .02
❑ 221 Bob Bassen .05 .02
❑ 222 Peter Ing .10 .05
❑ 223 Daniel Marois .05 .02
❑ 224 Vincent Damphousse .10 .05
❑ 225 Wendel Clark UER .10 .05
(Connecticut not capitalized in last line)
❑ 226 Todd Gill .05 .02
❑ 227 Peter Zezel .05 .02
❑ 228 Bob Rouse .05 .02
❑ 229 David Reid .05 .02
❑ 230 Dave Ellett .05 .02
❑ 231 Gary Leeman .05 .02
❑ 232 Rob Ramage .05 .02
❑ 233 Mike Krushelnyski .05 .02
❑ 234 Tom Fergus .05 .02
❑ 235 Petr Nedved .10 .05
❑ 236 Trevor Linden .10 .05
❑ 237 Dave Capuano .05 .02
❑ 238 Troy Gamble .10 .05
❑ 239 Robert Kron UER .05 .02
(Type in stat box is smaller than others)
❑ 240 Jyrki Lumme .05 .02
❑ 241 Cliff Ronning .05 .02
❑ 242 Sergio Momesso .05 .02
❑ 243 Greg Adams .05 .02
❑ 244 Tom Kurvers .05 .02
❑ 245 Geoff Courtnall .05 .02
❑ 246 Igor Larionov .05 .02
❑ 247 Doug Lidster UER .05 .02
(No space between 51 and assist in last line of text)
❑ 248 Calle Johansson .05 .02
❑ 249 Kevin Hatcher .05 .02
❑ 250 Al Iafrate .10 .05
❑ 251 John Druce .05 .02
❑ 252 Michal Pivonka .05 .02
❑ 253 Stephen Leach .05 .02
❑ 254 Mike Ridley .05 .02
❑ 255 Mike Lalor .05 .02
❑ 256 Kelly Miller .05 .02
❑ 257 Don Beaupre .10 .05
❑ 258 Dino Ciccarelli .10 .05
❑ 259 Rod Langway .05 .02
❑ 260 Dimitri Khristich .05 .02
❑ 261 Teppo Numminen .05 .02
❑ 262 Pat Elynuik .05 .02
❑ 263 Danton Cole .05 .02
❑ 264 Fredrik Olausson UER .05 .02
(Fifth line of text, the word the is missing between in and 10th)
❑ 265 Ed Olczyk .05 .02
❑ 266 Bob Essensa .10 .05
❑ 267 Phil Housley .10 .05
❑ 268 Shawn Cronin .05 .02
❑ 269 Paul MacDermid .05 .02
❑ 270 Mark Osborne .05 .02
❑ 271 Thomas Steen .05 .02
❑ 272 Brent Ashton .05 .02
❑ 273 Randy Carlyle .05 .02
❑ 274 Theoren Fleury AS .10 .05
❑ 275 Al MacInnis AS .10 .05
❑ 276 Gary Suter AS .05 .02
❑ 277 Mike Vernon AS .10 .05
❑ 278 Chris Chelios AS .15 .07
❑ 279 Steve Larmer AS .10 .05
❑ 280 Jeremy Roenick AS .15 .07
❑ 281 Steve Yzerman AS .20 .09
❑ 282 Mark Messier AS .15 .07
❑ 283 Bill Ranford AS .10 .05
❑ 284 Steve Smith AS .05 .02
❑ 285 Wayne Gretzky AS .40 .18
❑ 286 Luc Robitaille AS .10 .05
❑ 287 Tomas Sandstrom AS .05 .02
❑ 288 Dave Gagner AS .05 .02
❑ 289 Bobby Smith AS .05 .02
❑ 290 Brett Hull AS .15 .07
❑ 291 Adam Oates AS .10 .05
❑ 292 Scott Stevens AS .10 .05
❑ 293 Vincent Damphousse AS .10 .05
❑ 294 Trevor Linden AS .10 .05
❑ 295 Phil Housley AS .10 .05
❑ 296 Ray Bourque AS .15 .07
❑ 297 Dave Christian AS .05 .02
❑ 298 Garry Galley AS .05 .02
❑ 299 Andy Moog AS .10 .05
❑ 300 Cam Neely AS .10 .05
❑ 301 Uwe Krupp AS .05 .02
❑ 302 John Cullen AS .05 .02
❑ 303 Pat Verbeek AS .05 .02
❑ 304 Patrick Roy AS .30 .14
❑ 305 Denis Savard AS .10 .05
❑ 306 Brian Skrudland AS .05 .02
❑ 307 John MacLean AS .05 .02
❑ 308 Pat LaFontaine AS .10 .05
❑ 309 Brian Leetch AS .15 .07
❑ 310 Darren Turcotte AS .05 .02
❑ 311 Rick Tocchet AS .10 .05
❑ 312 Paul Coffey AS .15 .07
❑ 313 Mark Recchi AS .10 .05
❑ 314 Kevin Stevens AS .05 .02
❑ 315 Joe Sakic AS .15 .07
❑ 316 Kevin Hatcher AS .05 .02
❑ 317 Guy Lafleur AS .15 .07
❑ 318 Mario Lemieux .30 .14
Conn Smythe
❑ 319 Pittsburgh Penguins .05 .02
Stanley Cup Champs UER
(On fourth line, says won in 5 games, should say 6 games)
❑ 320 Brett Hull .15 .07
Hart Trophy
❑ 321 Ed Belfour .15 .07
Vezina/Jennings
❑ 322 Ray Bourque .15 .07
Norris
❑ 323 Dirk Graham .05 .02
Selke
❑ 324 Wayne Gretzky .40 .18
Ross/Lady Byng
❑ 325 Dave Taylor .10 .05
King Clancy Trophy
❑ 326 Brett Hull .15 .07
PS Player of the Year
❑ 327 Brian Hayward .10 .05
❑ 328 Neil Wilkinson UER .05 .02
(Born Manitoba, not Minnesota)
❑ 329 Craig Coxe .05 .02
❑ 330 Rob Zettler .05 .02
❑ 331 Jeff Hackett .10 .05
❑ 332 Joe Malone .05 .02
❑ 333 Georges Vezina .05 .02
❑ 334 The Modern Arena .05 .02
❑ 335 Ace Bailey Benefit .15 .07
❑ 336 Howie Morenz .10 .05
❑ 337 The Punch Line .05 .02
❑ 338 The Kid Line .05 .02
❑ 339 Before the Zamboni .15 .07
❑ 340 Bill Barilko .05 .02
❑ 341 Jacques Plante .10 .05
❑ 342 Arena Designs .05 .02
❑ 343 Terry Sawchuk .10 .05
❑ 344 Gordie Howe .25 .11
❑ 345 Guy Carbonneau .10 .05
Play Smart
❑ 346 Stephen Leach .05 .02
❑ 347 Peter Douris .05 .02
❑ 348 David Reid .05 .02
❑ 349 Bob Carpenter .05 .02
❑ 350 Stephane Quintal .05 .02
❑ 351 Barry Pederson .05 .02
❑ 352 Brent Ashton .05 .02
❑ 353 Vladimir Ruzicka .05 .02
❑ 354 Brad Miller .05 .02
❑ 355 Robert Ray .05 .02
❑ 356 Colin Patterson .05 .02
❑ 357 Gord Donnelly .05 .02
❑ 358 Pat LaFontaine .10 .05
❑ 359 Randy Wood .05 .02
❑ 360 Randy Hillier .05 .02
❑ 361 Robert Reichel .05 .02
❑ 362 Ronnie Stern .05 .02
❑ 363 Ric Nattress .05 .02
❑ 364 Tim Sweeney .05 .02
❑ 365 Marc Habscheid .05 .02
❑ 366 Tim Hunter .05 .02
❑ 367 Rick Wamsley .10 .05
❑ 368 Frank Musil .05 .02
❑ 369 Mike Hudson .05 .02
❑ 370 Steve Smith .05 .02
❑ 371 Keith Brown .05 .02
❑ 372 Greg Gilbert .05 .02
❑ 373 John Tonelli .05 .02
❑ 374 Brent Sutter .05 .02
❑ 375 Brad Lauer .05 .02
❑ 376 Alan Kerr .05 .02
❑ 377 Brad McCrimmon .05 .02
❑ 378 Brad Marsh .05 .02
❑ 379 Brent Fedyk .05 .02
❑ 380 Ray Sheppard .10 .05
❑ 381 Vincent Damphousse .10 .05
❑ 382 Craig Muni .05 .02
❑ 383 Scott Mellanby .10 .05
❑ 384 Geoff Smith .05 .02
❑ 385 Kelly Buchberger .05 .02
❑ 386 Bernie Nicholls .10 .05
❑ 387 Luke Richardson .05 .02
❑ 388 Peter Ing .10 .05
❑ 389 Dave Manson .05 .02
❑ 390 Mark Hunter .05 .02
❑ 391 Jim McKenzie .05 .02
❑ 392 Randy Cunneyworth .05 .02
❑ 393 Murray Craven .05 .02
❑ 394 Mikael Andersson .05 .02
❑ 395 Andrew Cassels .05 .02
❑ 396 Randy Ladouceur .05 .02
❑ 397 Marc Bergevin .05 .02
❑ 398 Brian Benning .05 .02
❑ 399 Mike Donnelly .05 .02
❑ 400 Charlie Huddy .05 .02
❑ 401 John McIntyre .05 .02
❑ 402 Jay Miller .05 .02
❑ 403 Randy Gilhen .05 .02
❑ 404 Stewart Gavin .05 .02
❑ 405 Mike Craig .05 .02
❑ 406 Brian Glynn .05 .02
❑ 407 Rob Ramage .05 .02
❑ 408 Chris Dahlquist .05 .02
❑ 409 Basil McRae .05 .02
❑ 410 Todd Elik .05 .02
❑ 411 Craig Ludwig .05 .02
❑ 412 Kirk Muller .05 .02
❑ 413 Shayne Corson .05 .02
❑ 414 Brent Gilchrist .05 .02
❑ 415 Mario Roberge .05 .02
❑ 416 Sylvain Turgeon .05 .02
❑ 417 Alain Cote .05 .02
❑ 418 Donald Dufresne .05 .02
❑ 419 Todd Ewen .05 .02
❑ 420 Stephane Richer .10 .05
❑ 421 David Maley .05 .02
❑ 422 Randy McKay .05 .02
❑ 423 Scott Stevens .10 .05
❑ 424 Jon Morris .05 .02
❑ 425 Claude Vilgrain .05 .02
❑ 426 Laurie Boschman .05 .02
❑ 427 Pat Conacher .05 .02
❑ 428 Tom Kurvers .05 .02
❑ 429 Joe Reekie .05 .02
❑ 430 Rob DiMaio .05 .02
❑ 431 Tom Fitzgerald .05 .02
❑ 432 Ken Baumgartner .05 .02
❑ 433 Pierre Turgeon .10 .05
❑ 434 Dave McLlwain .05 .02
❑ 435 Benoit Hogue .05 .02
❑ 436 Uwe Krupp .05 .02
❑ 437 Adam Creighton .05 .02
❑ 438 Steve Thomas .05 .02
❑ 439 Mark Messier .25 .11
❑ 440 Tie Domi .10 .05
❑ 441 Sergei Nemchinov .05 .02
❑ 442 Mark Hardy .05 .02
❑ 443 Adam Graves .10 .05
❑ 444 Jeff Beukeboom .05 .02
❑ 445 Kris King .05 .02
❑ 446 Tim Kerr .05 .02
❑ 447 John Vanbiesbrouck .20 .09
❑ 448 Steve Duchesne .05 .02
❑ 449 Steve Kasper .05 .02
❑ 450 Ken Wregget .10 .05
❑ 451 Kevin Dineen .05 .02
❑ 452 Dave Brown .05 .02
❑ 453 Rod Brind'Amour .10 .05
❑ 454 Jiri Latal .05 .02
❑ 455 Tony Horacek .05 .02
❑ 456 Brad Jones .05 .02
❑ 457 Paul Stanton .05 .02
❑ 458 Gordie Roberts .05 .02
❑ 459 Ulf Samuelsson .05 .02
❑ 460 Ken Priestlay .05 .02
❑ 461 Jiri Hrdina .05 .02
❑ 462 Mikhail Tatarinov .05 .02
❑ 463 Mike Hough .05 .02
❑ 464 Don Barber .05 .02
❑ 465 Greg Smyth .05 .02
❑ 466 Doug Smail .05 .02
❑ 467 Mike McNeill .05 .02
❑ 468 John Kordic .05 .02

❑ 469 Greg Paslawski .05 .02
❑ 470 Herb Raglan .05 .02
❑ 471 Dave Christian .05 .02
❑ 472 Murray Baron .05 .02
❑ 473 Curtis Joseph .15 .07
❑ 474 Rick Zombo .05 .02
❑ 475 Brendan Shanahan .30 .14
❑ 476 Ron Sutter .05 .02
❑ 477 Mario Marois .05 .02
❑ 478 Doug Wilson .10 .05
❑ 479 Kelly Kisio .05 .02
❑ 480 Bob McGill .05 .02
❑ 481 Perry Anderson .05 .02
❑ 482 Brian Lawton .05 .02
❑ 483 Neil Wilkinson .05 .02
❑ 484 Ken Hammond .05 .02
❑ 485 David Bruce .05 .02
❑ 486 Steve Bozek .05 .02
❑ 487 Perry Berezan .05 .02
❑ 488 Wayne Presley .05 .02
❑ 489 Brian Bradley .05 .02
❑ 490 Darryl Shannon .05 .02
❑ 491 Lucien DeBlois .05 .02
❑ 492 Michel Petit .05 .02
❑ 493 Claude Loiselle .05 .02
❑ 494 Grant Fuhr .10 .05
❑ 495 Craig Berube .05 .02
❑ 496 Mike Bullard .05 .02
❑ 497 Jim Sandlak .05 .02
❑ 498 Dana Murzyn .05 .02
❑ 499 Garry Valk .05 .02
❑ 500 Andrew McBain .05 .02
❑ 501 Kirk McLean .10 .05
❑ 502 Gerald Diduck .05 .02
❑ 503 Dave Babych .05 .02
❑ 504 Ryan Walter .05 .02
❑ 505 Gino Odjick .05 .02
❑ 506 Dale Hunter .05 .02
❑ 507 Tim Bergland .05 .02
❑ 508 Alan May .05 .02
❑ 509 Jim Hrivnak .10 .05
❑ 510 Randy Burridge .05 .02
❑ 511 Peter Bondra .15 .07
❑ 512 Sylvain Cote .05 .02
❑ 513 Nick Kypreos .05 .02
❑ 514 Troy Murray .05 .02
❑ 515 Darrin Shannon .05 .02
❑ 516 Bryan Erickson .05 .02
❑ 517 Petri Skriko .05 .02
❑ 518 Mike Eagles .05 .02
❑ 519 Mike Hartman .05 .02
❑ 520 Bob Beers .05 .02
❑ 521 Matt DelGuidice .05 .02
❑ 522 Chris Winnes .05 .02
❑ 523 Brad May .10 .05
❑ 524 Donald Audette .10 .05
❑ 525 Kevin Haller .05 .02
❑ 526 Martin Simard .05 .02
❑ 527 Tomas Forslund .05 .02
❑ 528 Mark Osiecki .05 .02
❑ 529 Dominik Hasek 1.50 .70
❑ 530 Jimmy Waite .10 .05
❑ 531 Nicklas Lidstrom UER .50 .23
(Misspelled Niklas on card front)
❑ 532 Martin Lapointe .05 .02
❑ 533 Vladimir Konstantinov .20 .09
❑ 534 Josef Beranek .05 .02
❑ 535 Louie DeBrusk .05 .02
❑ 536 Geoff Sanderson .25 .11
❑ 537 Mark Greig .05 .02
❑ 538 Michel Picard .05 .02
❑ 539 Chris Tancill .05 .02
❑ 540 Peter Ahola .05 .02
❑ 541 Francois Breault .05 .02
❑ 542 Darryl Sydor .05 .02
❑ 543 Derian Hatcher .05 .02
❑ 544 Marc Bureau .05 .02
❑ 545 John LeClair 1.25 .55
❑ 546 Paul DiPietro .05 .02
❑ 547 Scott Niedermayer UER .10 .05
(Misspelled on front as Neidermayer)
❑ 548 Kevin Todd .05 .02
❑ 549 Doug Weight .50 .23
❑ 550 Tony Amonte .50 .23
❑ 551 Corey Foster .05 .02
❑ 552 Dominic Roussel .10 .05
❑ 553 Dan Kordic .05 .02
❑ 554 Jim Paek .05 .02
❑ 555 Kip Miller .05 .02
❑ 556 Claude Lapointe .05 .02
❑ 557 Nelson Emerson .05 .02
❑ 558 Pat Falloon .05 .02
❑ 559 Pat MacLeod .05 .02
❑ 560 Rick Lessard .05 .02
❑ 561 Link Gaetz .05 .02
❑ 562 Rob Pearson .05 .02
❑ 563 Alexander Godynyuk .05 .02
❑ 564 Pavel Bure .40 .18
❑ 565 Russell Romaniuk .05 .02
❑ 566 Stu Barnes .05 .02
❑ 567 Ray Bourque CAP .15 .07
❑ 568 Mike Ramsey CAP .05 .02
❑ 569 Joe Nieuwendyk CAP .10 .05
❑ 570 Dirk Graham CAP .05 .02
❑ 571 Steve Yzerman CAP .20 .09
❑ 572 Kevin Lowe CAP .05 .02
❑ 573 Randy Ladouceur CAP .05 .02
❑ 574 Wayne Gretzky CAP .40 .18
❑ 575 Mark Tinordi CAP .05 .02
❑ 576 Guy Carbonneau CAP .10 .05
❑ 577 Bruce Driver CAP .05 .02
❑ 578 Pat Flatley CAP .05 .02
❑ 579 Mark Messier CAP .15 .07
❑ 580 Rick Tocchet CAP .10 .05
❑ 581 Mario Lemieux CAP .30 .14
❑ 582 Mike Hough CAP .05 .02
❑ 583 Garth Butcher CAP .05 .02
❑ 584 Doug Wilson CAP .10 .05
❑ 585 Wendel Clark CAP .10 .05
❑ 586 Trevor Linden CAP .10 .05
❑ 587 Rod Langway CAP .05 .02
❑ 588 Troy Murray CAP .05 .02
❑ 589 Practicing Outdoors .05 .02
❑ 590 Shape Up .05 .02
❑ 591 Boston Bruins Cartoon .05 .02
❑ 592 Opening Night .05 .02
❑ 593 Rod Gilbert .05 .02
❑ 594 Phil Esposito .10 .05
❑ 595 Dale Tallon .05 .02
❑ 596 Gilbert Perreault .10 .05
❑ 597 Bernie Federko .10 .05
❑ 598 All-Star Game .10 .05
❑ 599 Patrick Roy LL .30 .14
❑ 600 Ed Belfour LL .15 .07
❑ 601 Don Beaupre LL .10 .05
❑ 602 Bob Essensa LL .10 .05
❑ 603 Kirk McLean UER LL .10 .05
(Leader logo shows PPG, should be GAA)
❑ 604 Mike Gartner LL .10 .05
❑ 605 Jeremy Roenick LL .15 .07
❑ 606 Rob Brown LL .05 .02
❑ 607 Ulf Dahlen LL .05 .02
❑ 608 Paul Ysebaert LL .05 .02
❑ 609 Brad McCrimmon LL .05 .02
❑ 610 Nicklas Lidstrom LL .10 .05
❑ 611 Kelly Miller LL .05 .02
❑ 612 Jim Kyte SMART .05 .02
❑ 613 Patrick Roy SMART .30 .14
❑ 614 Alan May SMART .05 .02
❑ 615 Kelly Miller SMART .05 .02
❑ AU125 Patrick Roy AU 200.00 90.00
(Certified autograph)
❑ AU501 Kirk McLean AU 40.00 18.00
(Certified autograph)
❑ AU599 Patrick Roy AU 200.00 90.00
(Certified autograph)
❑ NNO 75th Anniversary 80.00 36.00
Hologram

## 1991-92 Pro Set CC

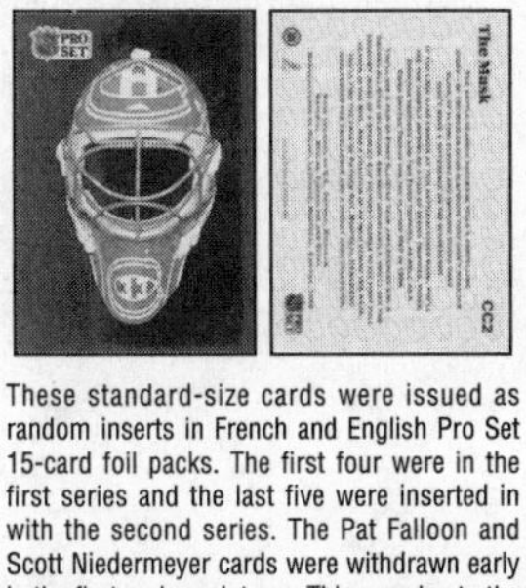


These standard-size cards were issued as random inserts in French and English Pro Set 15-card foil packs. The first four were in the first series and the last five were inserted in with the second series. The Pat Falloon and Scott Niedermeyer cards were withdrawn early in the first series print run. This was due to the cards being released prior to the players having appeared in an NHL game; a contravention of licensing regulations. The cards are numbered on the back with a "CC" prefix.

| | MINT | NRMT |
|---|---|---|
| COMPLETE SET (9) | 20.00 | 9.00 |
| COMMON CARD (CC1-CC9) | 1.00 | .45 |

*FRENCH VERSION: 1X TO X BASIC CC

❑ CC1 Entry Draft 1.00 .45
❑ CC2 The Mask 4.00 1.80
❑ CC3 Pat Falloon UER SP 4.00 1.80
(Born Birtle, not Foxwarren)
❑ CC4 Scott Niedermeyer SP 6.00 2.70
❑ CC5 Wayne Gretzky 5.00 2.20
❑ CC6 Brett Hull 1.50 .70
❑ CC7 Adam Oates 1.25 .55
❑ CC8 Mark Recchi 1.25 .55
❑ CC9 John Cullen 1.00 .45

## 1991-92 Pro Set Gazette

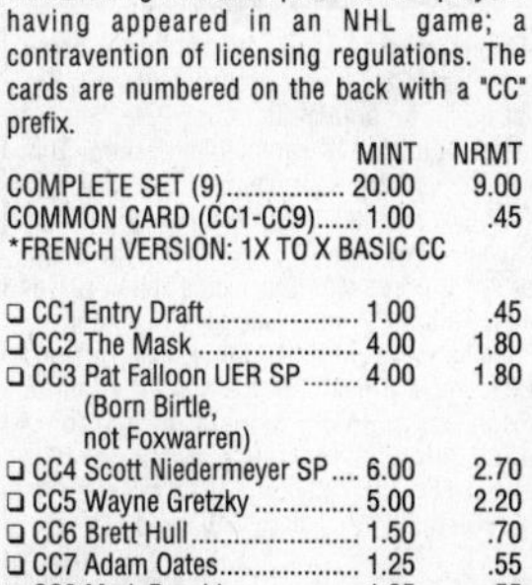


These standard-size cards were issued in a cello pack which The front of the Patrick Roy card (number 2) features a full-bleed color player photo, with the words "Pro Set Gazette" in the upper left corner and the player's name in a blue stripe near the bottom of the card. To the left of the number of the Roy card, it reads "Pro Set Gazette Collectible". The horizontally oriented back has a color close-up photo and summarizes some of Roy's activities off the ice. The SC1 Roy card has his name appearing in a red stripe at the bottom with the words "Goalie of the Year" in a blue stripe. The back shows a red stripe across the top with the player's name. A close-up color player photo and career highlights appear below the red stripe on a white background. The card is numbered "Special Collectible 1" on the back.

| | MINT | NRMT |
|---|---|---|
| COMPLETE SET (2) | 5.00 | 2.20 |
| COMMON CARD | 3.00 | 1.35 |

❑ 2 Patrick Roy 3.00 1.35
(Gazette Collectible)
❑ SC1 Patrick Roy 3.00 1.35
(Special Collectible 1)

## 1991-92 Pro Set HOF Induction

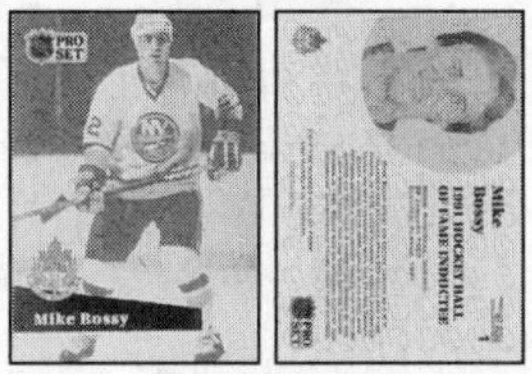


This 14-card set was issued by Pro Set to commemorate the 1991 Hockey Hall of Fame Induction Dinner and Ceremonies in September, 1991 held in Ottawa. The standard-size cards feature borderless glossy sepia-toned player or team photos on the fronts. A colorful insignia with the words "Hockey Hall of Fame and Museum" appears on the front of each card. The horizontally oriented backs have a facial drawing of the player (circular format) and career summary; the team cards have no drawings on the back. The team cards represent the past Ottawa Stanley Cup winning teams.

| | MINT | NRMT |
|---|---|---|
| COMPLETE SET (14) | 75.00 | 34.00 |
| COMMON CARD (1-14) | 4.00 | 1.80 |

❑ 1 Mike Bossy 15.00 6.75
1991 HOF Inductee
❑ 2 Denis Potvin 12.00 5.50
1991 HOF Inductee
❑ 3 Bob Pulford 8.00 3.60
1991 HOF Inductee
❑ 4 William Scott Bowman 12.00 5.50
1991 HOF Inductee
❑ 5 Neil P. Armstrong 6.00 2.70
1991 HOF Inductee
❑ 6 Clint Smith 6.00 2.70
1991 HOF Inductee
❑ 7 1903-04 Ottawa Silver 4.00 1.80
Seven
❑ 8 1905 Ottawa Silver 4.00 1.80
Seven
❑ 9 1909 Ottawa Senators 4.00 1.80
❑ 10 1911 Ottawa Senators 4.00 1.80
❑ 11 1920-21 Ottawa 4.00 1.80
Senators
❑ 12 1923 Ottawa Senators 4.00 1.80
❑ 13 1927 Ottawa Senators 4.00 1.80
❑ 14 Title Card 4.00 1.80
1991 Hockey Hall of Fame Dinner and Ceremonies

## 1991-92 Pro Set NHL Awards Special

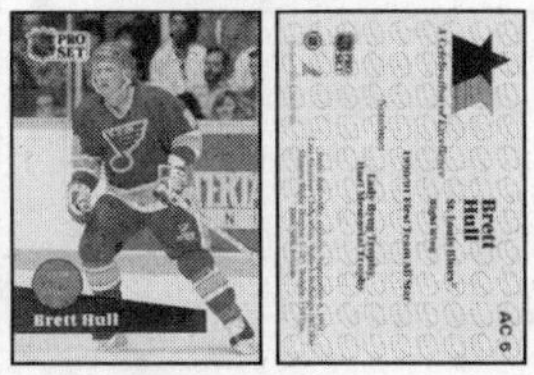


This 17-card standard-size set features NHL players who were All-Stars, nominees, or winners of prestigious trophies. The fronts feature a borderless color action photo, with the team logo in the lower left corner, and the player's name in the black wedge below the logo. The backs present player information and the award which the player won or was nominated for, on a white and gray hockey puck background. The cards are numbered on the back and also have a star logo with the words "A Celebration of Excellence". The cards have the 1991-92 Pro Set style of design.

| | MINT | NRMT |
|---|---|---|
| COMPLETE SET (17) | 600.00 | 275.00 |
| COMMON CARD (AC1-AC16) | 5.00 | 2.20 |

❑ AC1 Ed Belfour 30.00 13.50
❑ AC2 Mike Richter 30.00 13.50
❑ AC3 Patrick Roy 150.00 70.00
❑ AC4 Wayne Gretzky 250.00 110.00
❑ AC5 Joe Sakic 80.00 36.00
❑ AC6 Brett Hull 40.00 18.00
❑ AC7 Ray Bourque 30.00 13.50
❑ AC8 Al MacInnis 10.00 4.50
❑ AC9 Luc Robitaille 15.00 6.75
❑ AC10 Sergei Fedorov 80.00 36.00
❑ AC11 Ken Hodge Jr. 4.00 1.80
❑ AC12 Dirk Graham 4.00 1.80
❑ AC13 Steve Larmer 6.00 2.70
❑ AC14 Esa Tikkanen 6.00 2.70
❑ AC15 Chris Chelios 30.00 13.50
❑ AC16 Dave Taylor 4.00 1.80
❑ NNO Title Card 2.00 .90

## 1991-92 Pro Set NHL Sponsor Awards

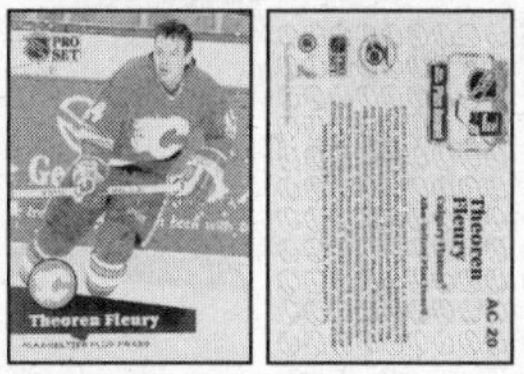


This eight-card standard-size set is numbered as an extension of the 1991-92 Pro Set NHL Awards Special. The cards feature the same glossy color player photos as does the regular issue. The fronts differ in having the name of the award inscribed across the bottom of the card face. Also the backs differ in that they omit the head and shoulders photo and have only a player profile. The cards were distributed at The Hockey News Sponsor Awards luncheon in Toronto on June 6, 1991.

| | MINT | NRMT |
|---|---|---|
| COMPLETE SET (8) | 80.00 | 36.00 |
| COMMON CARD (AC17-AC23) | 4.00 | 1.80 |

❑ AC17 Kevin Dineen 6.00 2.70
Bud Light/NHL Man of the Year Award
❑ AC18 Brett Hull 40.00 18.00
NHL Pro Set Player of the Year Award
❑ AC19 Ed Belfour 20.00 9.00
Trico Goaltender Award
❑ AC20 Theoren Fleury 20.00 9.00
Alka-Seltzer Plus Award
❑ AC21 Marty McSorley 6.00 2.70
Alka-Seltzer Plus Award
❑ AC22 Mike Ilitch 4.00 1.80
Detroit Red Wings OWN Lester Patrick Award
❑ AC23 Rod Gilbert 6.00 2.70
Lester Patrick Award
❑ NNO Title Card 1.00 .45
1990-91 NHL Sponsor Awards

## 1991-92 Pro Set Opening Night

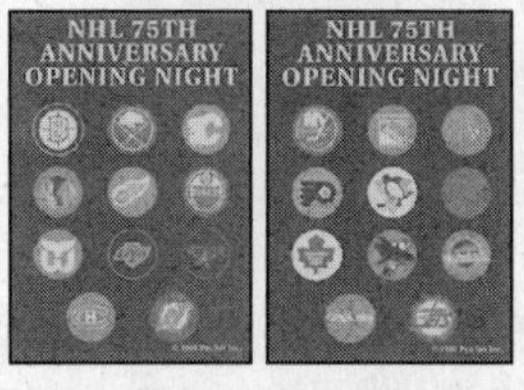


This six-card promo set was issued by Pro Set to commemorate the opening night of the 1991-92 NHL season. The standard-size player cards are the same as the regular issue, with borderless glossy color player photos on the fronts, and a color headshot and player information on the backs. Four (different each time) regular issue cards were included in each promo pack.

| | MINT | NRMT |
|---|---|---|
| COMPLETE SET (2) | 8.00 | 3.60 |
| COMMON CARD | 4.00 | 1.80 |

❑ NNO NHL 75th Anniversary 4.00 1.80
Opening Night
❑ NNO 1991-92 Opening Night. 4.00 1.80

## 1991-92 Pro Set Platinum

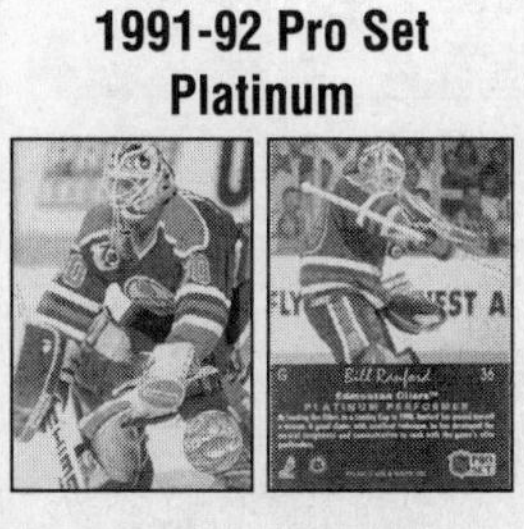

The 1991-92 Pro Set Platinum hockey set was released in two series of 150 standard-size cards. The front design features full-bleed glossy color action player photos, with the Pro Set Platinum icon superimposed at the lower right corner. Player names do not appear on the front.The key Rookie Cards in the set are Tony Amonte, Dominik Hasek, John LeClair, Nicklas Lidstrom, Geoff Sanderson and Doug Weight.

| | MINT | NRMT |
|---|---|---|
| COMPLETE SET (300) | 8.00 | 3.60 |
| COMPLETE SERIES 1 (150) | 4.00 | 1.80 |
| COMPLETE SERIES 2 (150) | 4.00 | 1.80 |
| COMMON CARD (1-300) | .05 | .02 |

❑ 1 Cam Neely .10 .05
❑ 2 Ray Bourque .20 .09
❑ 3 Craig Janney .10 .05
❑ 4 Andy Moog .10 .05
❑ 5 Dave Poulin .05 .02
❑ 6 Ken Hodge Jr. .05 .02
❑ 7 Glen Wesley .05 .02
❑ 8 Dave Andreychuk .10 .05
❑ 9 Daren Puppa .10 .05
❑ 10 Pierre Turgeon .10 .05
❑ 11 Dale Hawerchuk .10 .05
❑ 12 Doug Bodger .05 .02
❑ 13 Mike Ramsey .05 .02
❑ 14 Alexander Mogilny .40 .18
❑ 15 Sergei Makarov .05 .02
❑ 16 Theoren Fleury .10 .05
❑ 17 Joel Otto .05 .02
❑ 18 Joe Nieuwendyk .05 .02
❑ 19 Al MacInnis .10 .05
❑ 20 Gary Suter .05 .02
❑ 21 Mike Vernon .10 .05
❑ 22 John Tonelli .05 .02
❑ 23 Dirk Graham .05 .02
❑ 24 Jeremy Roenick .30 .14
❑ 25 Chris Chelios .20 .09
❑ 26 Ed Belfour .30 .14
❑ 27 Steve Smith .05 .02
❑ 28 Steve Larmer .05 .02
❑ 29 Johan Garpenlov .05 .02
❑ 30 Sergei Fedorov .50 .23
❑ 31 Tim Cheveldae .10 .05
❑ 32 Steve Yzerman .60 .25
❑ 33 Jimmy Carson .05 .02
❑ 34 Bob Probert .10 .05
❑ 35 Vincent Damphousse .10 .05
❑ 36 Bill Ranford .10 .05
❑ 37 Petr Klima .05 .02
❑ 38 Kevin Lowe .05 .02
❑ 39 Esa Tikkanen .10 .05
❑ 40 Craig Simpson .05 .02
❑ 41 Peter Ing .05 .02
❑ 42 Rob Brown .05 .02
❑ 43 Bobby Holik .05 .02
❑ 44 Pat Verbeek .05 .02
❑ 45 Brad Shaw .05 .02
❑ 46 Kevin Dineen .05 .02
❑ 47 Zarley Zalapski .05 .02
❑ 48 Jari Kurri .10 .05
❑ 49 Tony Granato .05 .02
❑ 50 Luc Robitaille .10 .05
❑ 51 Rob Blake .05 .02
❑ 52 Wayne Gretzky 1.25 .55
❑ 53 Tomas Sandstrom .05 .02
❑ 54 Kelly Hrudey .10 .05
❑ 55 Mike Modano .25 .11
❑ 56 Jon Casey .10 .05
❑ 57 Todd Elik .05 .02
❑ 58 Mark Tinordi .05 .02
❑ 59 Brian Bellows .05 .02
❑ 60 Dave Gagner .05 .02
❑ 61 Patrick Roy 1.00 .45
❑ 62 Russ Courtnall .05 .02
❑ 63 Guy Carbonneau .10 .05
❑ 64 Denis Savard .10 .05
❑ 65 Petr Svoboda .05 .02
❑ 66 Kirk Muller .05 .02
❑ 67 Stephane Richer .05 .02
❑ 68 Chris Terreri .10 .05
❑ 69 Bruce Driver .05 .02
❑ 70 John MacLean .05 .02
❑ 71 Patrik Sundstrom .05 .02
❑ 72 Scott Stevens .05 .02
❑ 73 Glenn Healy .10 .05
❑ 74 Brent Sutter .05 .02
❑ 75 David Volek .05 .02
❑ 76 Ray Ferraro .05 .02
❑ 77 Pat Flatley .05 .02
❑ 78 Jeff Norton .05 .02
❑ 79 Brian Leetch .20 .09
❑ 80 Tim Kerr .05 .02
❑ 81 Mark Messier .30 .14
❑ 82 James Patrick .05 .02
❑ 83 Mike Richter .20 .09
❑ 84 Mike Gartner .10 .05
❑ 85 Mike Ricci .10 .05
❑ 86 Steve Duchesne .10 .05
❑ 87 Ron Hextall .10 .05
❑ 88 Rick Tocchet .10 .05
❑ 89 Pelle Eklund .05 .02
❑ 90 Rod Brind'Amour .10 .05
❑ 91 Mario Lemieux 1.00 .45
❑ 92 Jaromir Jagr .60 .25
❑ 93 Kevin Stevens .10 .05
❑ 94 Paul Coffey .20 .09
❑ 95 Ulf Samuelsson .05 .02
❑ 96 Tom Barrasso .10 .05
❑ 97 Mark Recchi .10 .05
❑ 98 Ron Tugnutt .10 .05
❑ 99 Mats Sundin .30 .14
❑ 100 Stephane Morin .05 .02

❑ 101 Owen Nolan .10 .05
❑ 102 Joe Sakic .50 .23
❑ 103 Bryan Fogarty .05 .02
❑ 104 Kelly Kisio .05 .02
❑ 105 Tony Hrkac .05 .02
❑ 106 Brian Mullen .05 .02
❑ 107 Doug Wilson .10 .05
❑ 108 Rich Sutter .05 .02
❑ 109 Brett Hull .40 .18
❑ 110 Dave Christian .05 .02
❑ 111 Brendan Shanahan .50 .23
❑ 112 Vincent Riendeau .10 .05
❑ 113 Adam Oates .10 .05
❑ 114 Jeff Brown .05 .02
❑ 115 Gary Leeman .05 .02
❑ 116 Dave Ellett .05 .02
❑ 117 Grant Fuhr .10 .05
❑ 118 Daniel Marois .05 .02
❑ 119 Mike Krushelnyski .05 .02
❑ 120 Wendel Clark .10 .05
❑ 121 Troy Gamble .10 .05
❑ 122 Robert Kron .05 .02
❑ 123 Geoff Courtnall .05 .02
❑ 124 Trevor Linden .10 .05
❑ 125 Greg Adams .05 .02
❑ 126 Igor Larionov .05 .02
❑ 127 Kevin Hatcher .05 .02
❑ 128 Mike Ridley .05 .02
❑ 129 John Druce .05 .02
❑ 130 Al Iafrate .10 .05
❑ 131 Dino Ciccarelli .05 .02
❑ 132 Michal Pivonka .05 .02
❑ 133 Fredrik Olausson .05 .02
❑ 134 Ed Olczyk .05 .02
❑ 135 Bob Essensa .10 .05
❑ 136 Pat Elynuik .05 .02
❑ 137 Phil Housley .10 .05
❑ 138 Thomas Steen .05 .02
❑ 139 Don Beaupre .10 .05
❑ 140 Boston Bruins .05 .02
❑ 141 Chicago Blackhawks .10 .05
❑ 142 Los Angeles Kings .05 .02
❑ 143 Minnesota North Stars .05 .02
❑ 144 Pittsburgh Penguins .05 .02
❑ 145 Boston Bruins .05 .02
❑ 146 Chicago Blackhawks .05 .02
❑ 147 Detroit Red Wings .05 .02
❑ 148 Montreal Canadiens .05 .02
❑ 149 New York Rangers .05 .02
❑ 150 Toronto Maple Leafs .05 .02
❑ 151 Stephen Leach .05 .02
❑ 152 Vladimir Ruzicka .05 .02
❑ 153 Don Sweeney .05 .02
❑ 154 Bob Carpenter .05 .02
❑ 155 Brent Ashton .05 .02
❑ 156 Gord Murphy .05 .02
❑ 157 Pat LaFontaine .10 .05
❑ 158 Randy Hillier .05 .02
❑ 159 Clint Malarchuk .10 .05
❑ 160 Randy Wood .05 .02
❑ 161 Gary Roberts .05 .02
❑ 162 Gary Leeman .05 .02
❑ 163 Robert Reichel .10 .05
❑ 164 Brent Sutter .05 .02
❑ 165 Brian Noonan .05 .02
❑ 166 Michel Goulet UER .10 .05
(Prospect on front)
❑ 167 Paul Ysebaert .05 .02
❑ 168 Kevin Miller .05 .02
❑ 169 Ray Sheppard .05 .02
❑ 170 Brad McCrimmon .05 .02
❑ 171 Joe Murphy .10 .05
❑ 172 Dave Manson .05 .02
❑ 173 Scott Mellanby .10 .05
❑ 174 Bernie Nicholls .10 .05
❑ 175 John Cullen .05 .02
❑ 176 Marc Bergevin .05 .02
❑ 177 Steve Konroyd .05 .02
❑ 178 Kay Whitmore .10 .05
❑ 179 Murray Craven .05 .02
❑ 180 Mikael Andersson .05 .02
❑ 181 Bob Kudelski .05 .02
❑ 182 Brian Benning .05 .02
❑ 183 Mike Donnelly .05 .02
❑ 184 Marty McSorley .05 .02
❑ 185 Corey Millen .05 .02
❑ 186 Ulf Dahlen .05 .02
❑ 187 Brian Propp .05 .02
❑ 188 Neal Broten .05 .02
❑ 189 Mike Craig .05 .02
❑ 190 Stephan Lebeau .05 .02
❑ 191 Mike Keane .05 .02
❑ 192 Brent Gilchrist .05 .02
❑ 193 Eric Desjardins .05 .02
❑ 194 Peter Stastny .10 .05
❑ 195 Claude Vilgrain .05 .02
❑ 196 Claude Lemieux .10 .05
❑ 197 Craig Billington UER .10 .05
(Front photo actually Chris Terreri)
❑ 198 Alexei Kasatonov .05 .02
❑ 199 Slava Fetisov .05 .02
❑ 200 Benoit Hogue .05 .02
❑ 201 Derek King .05 .02
❑ 202 Uwe Krupp .05 .02
❑ 203 Steve Thomas .05 .02
❑ 204 John Ogrodnick .05 .02
❑ 205 Sergei Nemchinov .05 .02
❑ 206 Jeff Beukeboom .05 .02
❑ 207 Adam Graves .10 .05
❑ 208 Andrei Lomakin .05 .02
❑ 209 Dan Quinn .05 .02
❑ 210 Ken Wreggett .10 .05
❑ 211 Garry Galley .05 .02
❑ 212 Terry Carkner .05 .02
❑ 213 Larry Murphy .10 .05
❑ 214 Ron Francis .10 .05
❑ 215 Bob Errey .05 .02
❑ 216 Bryan Trottier .10 .05
❑ 217 Mike Hough .05 .02
❑ 218 Mikhail Tatarinov .05 .02
❑ 219 Jacques Cloutier .10 .05
❑ 220 Greg Paslawski .05 .02
❑ 221 Alexei Gusarov .05 .02
❑ 222 Ron Sutter .05 .02
❑ 223 Garth Butcher .05 .02
❑ 224 Paul Cavallini .05 .02
❑ 225 Curtis Joseph .30 .14
❑ 226 Jeff Hackett .10 .05
❑ 227 David Bruce .05 .02
❑ 228 Wayne Presley .05 .02
❑ 229 Neil Wilkinson .05 .02
❑ 230 Dean Evason .05 .02
❑ 231 Brian Bradley .05 .02
❑ 232 Peter Zezel .05 .02
❑ 233 Mike Bullard .05 .02
❑ 234 Doug Gilmour .20 .09
❑ 235 Jamie Macoun .05 .02
❑ 236 Cliff Ronning .05 .02
❑ 237 Jyrki Lumme .05 .02
❑ 238 Tom Fergus .05 .02
❑ 239 Kirk McLean .10 .05
❑ 240 Sergio Momesso .05 .02
❑ 241 Randy Burridge .05 .02
❑ 242 Dimitri Khristich .10 .05
❑ 243 Calle Johansson .05 .02
❑ 244 Peter Bondra .10 .05
❑ 245 Dale Hunter .05 .02
❑ 246 Darrin Shannon .05 .02
❑ 247 Troy Murray .05 .02
❑ 248 Teppo Numminen .05 .02
❑ 249 Donald Audette .10 .05
❑ 250 Kevin Haller .05 .02
❑ 251 Alexander Godynyuk .05 .02
❑ 252 Dominik Hasek 2.50 1.10
❑ 253 Nicklas Lidstrom .75 .35
❑ 254 Vladimir Konstantinov .25 .11
❑ 255 Josef Beranek .05 .02
❑ 256 Geoff Sanderson .30 .14
❑ 257 Peter Ahola .05 .02
❑ 258 Derian Hatcher .05 .02
❑ 259 John LeClair 2.00 .90
❑ 260 Kevin Todd .05 .02
❑ 261 Valeri Zelepukin .05 .02
❑ 262 Tony Amonte .75 .35
❑ 263 Doug Weight .75 .35
❑ 264 Claude Boivin .05 .02
❑ 265 Corey Foster .05 .02
❑ 266 Jim Paek .05 .02
❑ 267 Claude Lapointe .05 .02
❑ 268 Adam Foote .25 .11
❑ 269 Nelson Emerson .05 .02
❑ 270 Arturs Irbe .25 .11
❑ 271 Pat Falloon .05 .02
❑ 272 Pavel Bure .60 .25
❑ 273 Stu Barnes .05 .02
❑ 274 Russ Romaniuk .05 .02
❑ 275 Luciano Borsato .05 .02
❑ 276 Al MacInnis AS .10 .05
❑ 277 Sergei Fedorov AS .20 .09
❑ 278 Ray Bourque AS .20 .09
❑ 279 Mike Richter AS .20 .09
❑ 280 Campbell Conference .05 .02
❑ 281 Wales Conference .05 .02
❑ 282 Brett Hull PP .20 .09
❑ 283 Alexander Mogilny PP .10 .05
❑ 284 Brian Leetch PP .10 .05
❑ 285 Bob Essensa PP .10 .05
❑ 286 Derek King PP .05 .02
❑ 287 Steve Larmer PP .10 .05
❑ 288 Chris Terreri PP .10 .05
❑ 289 Terry O'Reilly CAP .05 .02
❑ 290 Burton Cummings CAP .05 .02
❑ 291 Marv Albert CAP .05 .02
❑ 292 Larry King CAP .05 .02
❑ 293 Jim Kelly CAP .05 .02
❑ 294 David Wheaton CAP .05 .02
❑ 295 Ralph Macchio CAP .05 .02
❑ 296 Rick Hansen CAP .05 .02
❑ 297 Fred Rogers CAP .05 .02
❑ 298 Gaetan Boucher CAP .05 .02
❑ 299 Susan Saint James CAP .05 .02
❑ 300 James Belushi CAP .05 .02

## 1991-92 Pro Set Platinum PC

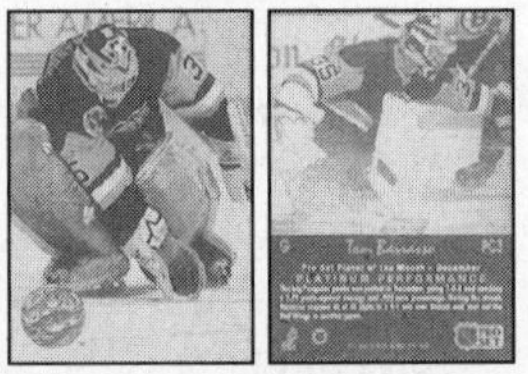

The 1991-92 Pro Set Platinum PC set consists of 20 standard size cards randomly inserted in Platinum foil packs. The first series inserts were a ten-card Platinum Collectibles subset featuring Players of the Month (PC1-PC6) and Sensational Sophomores (PC7-PC10). The second series inserts were subtitled Platinum Milestones (PC11-PC20).

| | MINT | NRMT |
|---|---|---|
| COMPLETE SET (20) | 25.00 | 11.00 |
| COMMON CARD (PC1-PC20) | .50 | .23 |

❑ PC1 John Vanbiesbrouck 2.00 .90
❑ PC2 Pete Peeters .75 .35
❑ PC3 Tom Barrasso .75 .35
❑ PC4 Wayne Gretzky 6.00 2.70
❑ PC5 Brett Hull 2.00 .90
❑ PC6 Kelly Hrudey .75 .35
❑ PC7 Sergei Fedorov 2.50 1.10
❑ PC8 Rob Blake .75 .35
❑ PC9 Ken Hodge Jr. .50 .23
❑ PC10 Eric Weinrich .50 .23
❑ PC11 Mike Gartner .75 .35
❑ PC12 Paul Coffey 1.00 .45
❑ PC13 Bobby Smith .50 .23
❑ PC14 Wayne Gretzky 6.00 2.70
❑ PC15 Michel Goulet .75 .35
❑ PC16 Mike Liut .75 .35
❑ PC17 Brian Propp .50 .23
❑ PC18 Denis Savard .75 .35
❑ PC19 Bryan Trottier .75 .35
❑ PC20 Mark Messier 2.00 .90

## 1991-92 Pro Set Platinum HOF 75th

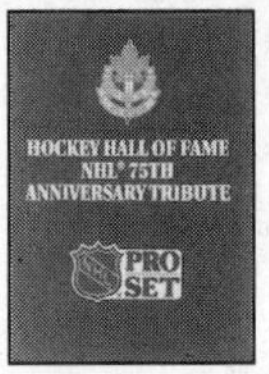


This eight-card standard-size set was issued in a cello pack to pay tribute to the NHL's 75th Anniversary. The set includes the Original Six team cards (indistinguishable from cards 145-150 in the regular set) from the 1991-92 Pro Set Platinum hockey set and two special cards. The Hockey Hall of Fame Collectible features on the front a full-bleed sepia-toned picture of Exhibition Place, where the Hockey Hall of Fame has been located since 1961. In addition to commentary, the back features a small color picture of BCE Place, its new location beginning in the fall of 1992. On a black background, the title card features the Hockey Hall of Fame and Museum logo at the top as well as the NHL and Pro Set logos at the bottom. The title card has a blank back. The actual numbering of the cards is reflected in the listing below.

| | MINT | NRMT |
|---|---|---|
| COMPLETE SET (8) | 8.00 | 3.60 |
| COMMON CARD | .10 | .05 |

❑ 145 Boston Bruins .10 .05
❑ 146 Chicago Blackhawks .10 .05
❑ 147 Detroit Red Wings .10 .05
❑ 148 Montreal Canadiens .10 .05
❑ 149 New York Rangers .10 .05
❑ 150 Toronto Maple Leafs .10 .05
❑ NNO Title Card 3.00 1.35
(Blank back)
❑ HHOF1 Hockey Hall of Fame .. 5.00 2.20
Collectible; Excellence, Education, Entertainment
(Pictures the opening of the Hall of Fame in 1961 in Toronto)

## 1991-92 Pro Set Player of the Month

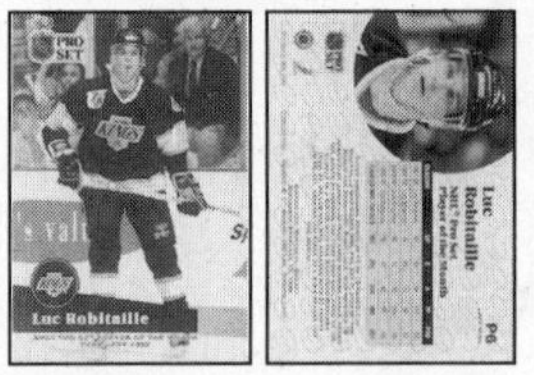


This six-card set was issued by Pro Set to honor hockey players for their outstanding performances during the season. The cards were distributed to all ticket holders at home games the evening of the presentation. Another feature of the presentation was a $1200 donation on behalf of the winning player to the youth hockey organization of his choice. Measuring the standard 2 1/2" by 3 1/2", card fronts feature borderless four-color action photographs. The player's team emblem appears in the lower left corner while the player's name is reversed-out white in a black wedge. On a screened hockey puck design, the horizontally oriented backs have a head shot in a circular format, biography, career statistics, and a summary of the outstanding achievement. The card number and team position appears in the upper right corner.

| | MINT | NRMT |
|---|---|---|
| COMPLETE SET (6) | 50.00 | 22.00 |
| COMMON CARD (P1-P6) | 4.00 | 1.80 |

❑ P1 Kirk McLean 4.00 1.80
POM October 1991
(Issued 11/19/91)
❑ P2 Kevin Stevens 4.00 1.80
POM November 1991
(Issued 12/26/91)
❑ P3 Mario Lemieux 25.00 11.00
POM December 1991
(Issued 1/28/92)
❑ P4 Andy Moog 8.00 3.60
POM January 1991
❑ P5 Pat LaFontaine 8.00 3.60
POM January 1991
❑ P6 Luc Robitaille 8.00 3.60
POM February 1991

## 1991-92 Pro Set Puck Candy Promos

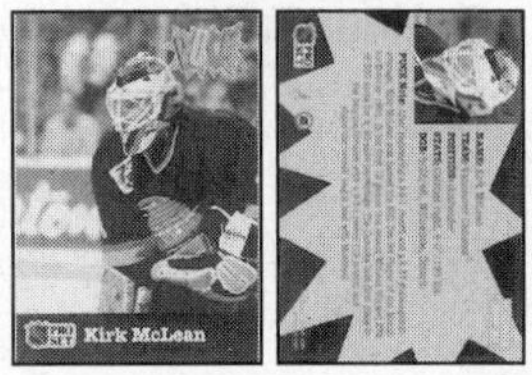


This set of three standard-size hockey cards was distributed in a cello pack to show the design of the upcoming Puck cards. The fronts of the promos are identical to the regular issue. Their backs differ in two respects: 1) instead of a card number, the promos have the words "Prototype For Review Only" in an aqua box; and 2) The "Puck Note" on the promos differs from that found on the regular cards. The cards are unnumbered and checklisted below in alphabetical order.

| | MINT | NRMT |
|---|---|---|
| COMPLETE SET (3) | 4.00 | 1.80 |
| COMMON CARD (1-3) | 1.00 | .45 |

❑ 1 Kirk McLean 1.00 .45
❑ 2 Andy Moog 2.00 .90
❑ 3 Pat Verbeek 1.00 .45

## 1991-92 Pro Set Puck Candy

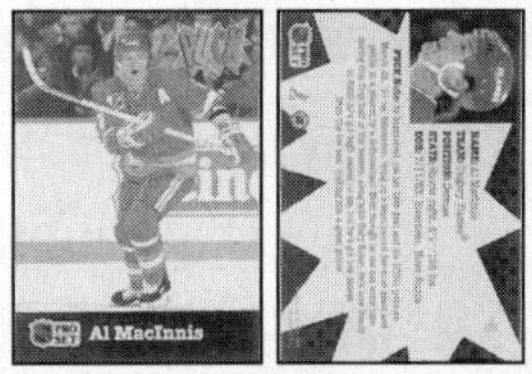


This set of thirty standard-size hockey cards was created for a new product, the NHL Pro Set Puck, a combination chocolate, peanut vanilla nougat, and caramel confection. This test product was available in all U.S. NHL and Northeast markets, and each candy package contained three Puck hockey cards. The fronts feature a borderless four-color action player photo with the Pro Set logo and player's name in the bottom border. The horizontally oriented backs have a head shot, biography, and a "Puck Note" that consists of personal information about the player. Pro Set advertised this 30-card set as Series 1; however no Series 2 was ever issued.

| | MINT | NRMT |
|---|---|---|
| COMPLETE SET (30) | 25.00 | 11.00 |
| COMMON CARD (1-30) | .40 | .18 |

❑ 1 Ray Bourque 1.50 .70
❑ 2 Andy Moog .75 .35
❑ 3 Doug Bodger .40 .18
❑ 4 Theoren Fleury .75 .35
❑ 5 Al MacInnis .75 .35
❑ 6 Jeremy Roenick 1.50 .70
❑ 7 Tim Cheveldae .40 .18
❑ 8 Steve Yzerman 5.00 2.20
❑ 9 Craig Simpson .40 .18
❑ 10 Pat Verbeek .40 .18
❑ 11 Wayne Gretzky 15.00 6.75
❑ 12 Luc Robitaille .75 .35
❑ 13 Brian Bellows .40 .18
❑ 14 Patrick Roy 8.00 3.60
❑ 15 Guy Carbonneau .40 .18
❑ 16 Peter Stastny .75 .35
❑ 17 Adam Creighton .40 .18
❑ 18 Glenn Healy .75 .35
❑ 19 Mark Messier 2.00 .90
❑ 20 Rod Brind'Amour .75 .35
❑ 21 Paul Coffey 1.50 .70
❑ 22 Tom Barrasso .75 .35
❑ 23 Joe Sakic 4.00 1.80
❑ 24 Brett Hull 2.00 .90
❑ 25 Adam Oates .75 .35
❑ 26 Kelly Kisio .40 .18
❑ 27 Grant Fuhr .75 .35
❑ 28 Kirk McLean .75 .35
❑ 29 Kevin Hatcher .40 .18
❑ 30 Phil Housley .40 .18

## 1991-92 Pro Set Rink Rat

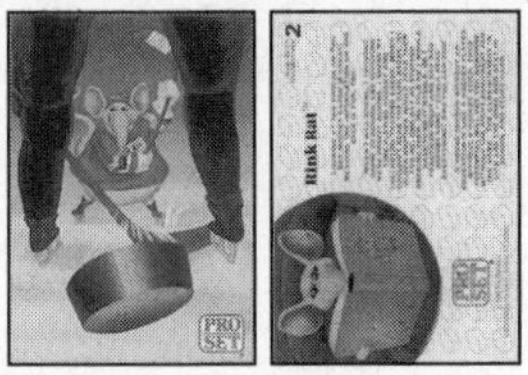


These standard-size cards were produced by Pro Set to promote education. On card number 2 the front cartoon portrays the Rink Rat shooting the puck through a defenseman's legs right toward the viewer of the card; on a screen design with miniature hockey pucks, the horizontally oriented back has another circular-shaped cartoon picture of the Rink Rat reading and a "stay in school/study hard" message.

| | MINT | NRMT |
|---|---|---|
| COMPLETE SET (2) | 8.00 | 3.60 |
| COMMON CARD (RR1-RR2) | 4.00 | 1.80 |

❑ RR1 Rink Rat 4.00 1.80
(Holding stick over head; copyright 1991)
❑ RR2 Rink Rat 4.00 1.80
(Shooting puck)

## 1991-92 Pro Set St. Louis Midwest

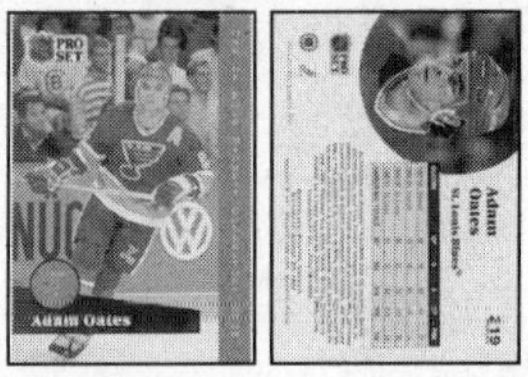


This four-card standard-size set was available at the Midwest Sports Collectors Show in St. Louis in November 1991. The cards were a special issue for the card show; in fact, Pro Set did not even issue a Meagher card in its regular set. All four cards show explicitly on the front that they were a special issue from this show. The fronts of these cards differ from the regular issue in two respects: 1) a royal blue border stripe runs the length of the card on the right side; and 2) the cards are numbered in the stripe "X of Four Midwest Collectors Show". The card backs are the same as the regular issue cards.

| | MINT | NRMT |
|---|---|---|
| COMPLETE SET (4) | 10.00 | 4.50 |
| COMMON CARD (1-4) | 1.00 | .45 |

❑ 1 Adam Oates 3.00 1.35
❑ 2 Paul Cavallini 1.00 .45
❑ 3 Rick Meagher 1.00 .45
❑ 4 Brett Hull 8.00 3.60

## 1992-93 Pro Set

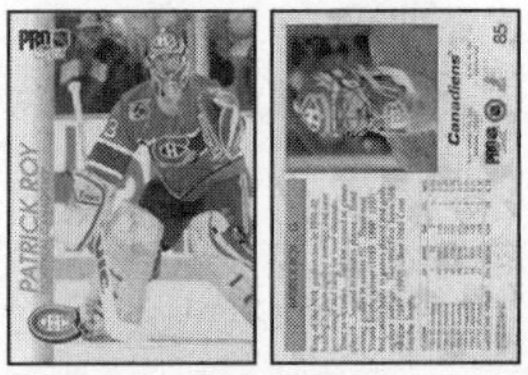


The 1992-93 Pro Set hockey set consists of 270 cards. The production run was 8,000 numbered 20-box foil cases and 2,000 20-box jumbo cases. One thousand Kirk McLean autographed cards were randomly inserted. The McLean cards have No. 239 on the back; his regular card is #193. The most noteworthy Rookie Card in the set is Bill Guerin.

| | MINT | NRMT |
|---|---|---|
| COMPLETE SET (270) | 15.00 | 6.75 |
| COMMON CARD (1-270) | .05 | .02 |

❑ 1 Mario Lemieux .50 .23
Pro Set POY
❑ 2 Patrick Roy .50 .23
Hockey News POY
❑ 3 Adam Oates .10 .05
❑ 4 Ray Bourque .25 .11
❑ 5 Vladimir Ruzicka .05 .02
❑ 6 Stephen Leach .05 .02
❑ 7 Andy Moog .10 .05

□ 8 Cam Neely .10 .05
□ 9 Dave Poulin .05 .02
□ 10 Glen Wesley .05 .02
□ 11 Gord Murphy .05 .02
□ 12 Dale Hawerchuk .10 .05
□ 13 Pat LaFontaine .10 .05
□ 14 Tom Draper .05 .02
□ 15 Dave Andreychuk .10 .05
□ 16 Petr Svoboda .05 .02
□ 17 Doug Bodger .05 .02
□ 18 Donald Audette .10 .05
□ 19 Alexander Mogilny .10 .05
□ 20 Randy Wood .05 .02
□ 21 Gary Roberts .05 .02
□ 22 Al MacInnis .10 .05
□ 23 Theoren Fleury .10 .05
□ 24 Sergei Makarov .05 .02
□ 25 Mike Vernon .10 .05
□ 26 Joe Nieuwendyk .10 .05
□ 27 Gary Suter .05 .02
□ 28 Joel Otto .05 .02
□ 29 Paul Ranheim .05 .02
□ 30 Jeremy Roenick .25 .11
□ 31 Steve Larmer .10 .05
□ 32 Michel Goulet .10 .05
□ 33 Ed Belfour .25 .11
□ 34 Chris Chelios .25 .11
□ 35 Igor Kravchuk .05 .02
□ 36 Brent Sutter .05 .02
□ 37 Steve Smith .05 .02
□ 38 Dirk Graham .05 .02
□ 39 Steve Yzerman .60 .25
□ 40 Sergei Fedorov .40 .18
□ 41 Paul Ysebaert .05 .02
□ 42 Nicklas Lidstrom .10 .05
□ 43 Tim Cheveldae .10 .05
□ 44 Vladimir Konstantinov .05 .02
□ 45 Shawn Burr .05 .02
□ 46 Bob Probert .10 .05
□ 47 Ray Sheppard .10 .05
□ 48 Kelly Buchberger .05 .02
□ 49 Joe Murphy .05 .02
□ 50 Norm Maciver .05 .02
□ 51 Bill Ranford .10 .05
□ 52 Bernie Nicholls .10 .05
□ 53 Esa Tikkanen .05 .02
□ 54 Scott Mellanby .10 .05
□ 55 Dave Manson .05 .02
□ 56 Craig Simpson .05 .02
□ 57 John Cullen .05 .02
□ 58 Pat Verbeek .05 .02
□ 59 Zarley Zalapski .05 .02
□ 60 Murray Craven .05 .02
□ 61 Bobby Holik .05 .02
□ 62 Steve Konroyd .05 .02
□ 63 Geoff Sanderson .10 .05
□ 64 Frank Pietrangelo .10 .05
□ 65 Mikael Andersson UER .05 .02
(Front notes traded, actually he was signed as free agent)
□ 66 Wayne Gretzky 1.25 .55
□ 67 Rob Blake .10 .05
□ 68 Jari Kurri .10 .05
□ 69 Marty McSorley .05 .02
□ 70 Kelly Hrudey .10 .05
□ 71 Paul Coffey .25 .11
□ 72 Luc Robitaille .10 .05
□ 73 Peter Ahola .05 .02
□ 74 Tony Granato .05 .02
□ 75 Derian Hatcher .05 .02
□ 76 Mike Modano .25 .11
□ 77 Dave Gagner .10 .05
□ 78 Mark Tinordi .05 .02
□ 79 Craig Ludwig .05 .02
□ 80 Ulf Dahlen .05 .02
□ 81 Bobby Smith .10 .05
□ 82 Jon Casey .10 .05
□ 83 Jim Johnson .05 .02
□ 84 Denis Savard .10 .05
□ 85 Patrick Roy 1.00 .45
□ 86 Eric Desjardins .05 .02
□ 87 Kirk Muller .05 .02
□ 88 Guy Carbonneau .10 .05
□ 89 Shayne Corson .05 .02
□ 90 Brent Gilchrist .05 .02
□ 91 Mathieu Schneider UER .05 .02
(Back photo actually Stephan Lebeau)
□ 92 Gilbert Dionne .05 .02
□ 93 Stephane Richer .10 .05
□ 94 Kevin Todd .10 .05
□ 95 Scott Stevens .10 .05
□ 96 Slava Fetisov .05 .02
□ 97 Chris Terreri .10 .05
□ 98 Claude Lemieux .10 .05
□ 99 Bruce Driver .05 .02
□ 100 Peter Stastny .10 .05
□ 101 Alexei Kasatonov .05 .02
□ 102 Patrick Flatley .05 .02
□ 103 Adam Creighton UER .05 .02
(Front notes traded, actually he was claimed via waivers)
□ 104 Pierre Turgeon .10 .05
□ 105 Ray Ferraro .05 .02
□ 106 Steve Thomas .05 .02
□ 107 Mark Fitzpatrick .10 .05
□ 108 Benoit Hogue .05 .02
□ 109 Uwe Krupp .05 .02
□ 110 Derek King .05 .02
□ 111 Mark Messier .30 .14
□ 112 Brian Leetch .25 .11
□ 113 Mike Gartner .10 .05
□ 114 Darren Turcotte .05 .02
□ 115 Adam Graves .10 .05
□ 116 Mike Richter .25 .11
□ 117 Sergei Nemchinov .05 .02
□ 118 Tony Amonte .10 .05
□ 119 James Patrick .05 .02
□ 120 Andrew McBain .05 .02
□ 121 Rob Murphy .05 .02
□ 122 Mike Peluso .05 .02
□ 123 Sylvain Turgeon .05 .02
□ 124 Brad Shaw .05 .02
□ 125 Peter Sidorkiewicz .10 .05
□ 126 Brad Marsh .05 .02
□ 127 Mark Freer .05 .02
□ 128 Marc Fortier .05 .02
□ 129 Ron Hextall .10 .05
□ 130 Claude Boivin .05 .02
□ 131 Mark Recchi .10 .05
□ 132 Rod Brind'Amour .10 .05
□ 133 Mike Ricci .05 .02
□ 134 Kevin Dineen .05 .02
□ 135 Brian Benning .05 .02
□ 136 Kerry Huffman .05 .02
□ 137 Steve Duchesne .05 .02
□ 138 Rick Tocchet .10 .05
□ 139 Mario Lemieux 1.00 .45
□ 140 Kevin Stevens .05 .02
□ 141 Jaromir Jagr .60 .25
□ 142 Joe Mullen .10 .05
□ 143 Ulf Samuelsson .05 .02
□ 144 Ron Francis .10 .05
□ 145 Tom Barrasso .10 .05
□ 146 Larry Murphy .10 .05
□ 147 Alexei Gusarov .05 .02
□ 148 Valeri Kamensky .10 .05
□ 149 Mats Sundin .25 .11
□ 150 Joe Sakic .40 .18
□ 151 Claude Lapointe .05 .02
□ 152 Stephane Fiset .10 .05
□ 153 Owen Nolan .10 .05
□ 154 Mike Hough .05 .02
□ 155 Greg Paslawski .05 .02
□ 156 Brett Hull .30 .14
□ 157 Craig Janney .10 .05
□ 158 Jeff Brown .05 .02
□ 159 Paul Cavallini .05 .02
□ 160 Garth Butcher .05 .02
□ 161 Nelson Emerson .05 .02
□ 162 Ron Sutter .05 .02
□ 163 Brendan Shanahan .40 .18
□ 164 Curtis Joseph .25 .11
□ 165 Doug Wilson .10 .05
□ 166 Pat Falloon .05 .02
□ 167 Kelly Kisio .05 .02
□ 168 Neil Wilkinson .05 .02
□ 169 Jay More .05 .02
□ 170 David Bruce .05 .02
□ 171 Jeff Hackett .10 .05
□ 172 David Williams .05 .02
□ 173 Brian Lawton .05 .02
□ 174 Brian Bradley .05 .02
□ 175 Jock Callander .05 .02
□ 176 Basil McRae .05 .02
□ 177 Rob Ramage .05 .02
□ 178 Pat Jablonski .10 .05
□ 179 Joe Reekie .05 .02
□ 180 Doug Crossman .05 .02
□ 181 Jim Benning .05 .02
□ 182 Ken Hodge Jr. .10 .05
□ 183 Grant Fuhr .10 .05
□ 184 Doug Gilmour .25 .11
□ 185 Glenn Anderson .10 .05
□ 186 Dave Ellett .05 .02
□ 187 Peter Zezel .05 .02
□ 188 Jamie Macoun .05 .02
□ 189 Wendel Clark .10 .05
□ 190 Bob Halkidis .05 .02
□ 191 Rob Pearson .05 .02
□ 192 Pavel Bure .40 .18
□ 193 Kirk McLean .10 .05
□ 194 Sergio Momesso .05 .02
□ 195 Cliff Ronning .05 .02
□ 196 Jyrki Lumme .05 .02
□ 197 Trevor Linden .10 .05
□ 198 Geoff Courtnall .05 .02
□ 199 Doug Lidster .05 .02
□ 200 Dave Babych .05 .02
□ 201 Michal Pivonka .05 .02
□ 202 Dale Hunter .05 .02
□ 203 Calle Johansson .05 .02
□ 204 Kevin Hatcher .05 .02
□ 205 Al Iafrate .10 .05
□ 206 Don Beaupre .10 .05
□ 207 Randy Burridge .05 .02
□ 208 Dimitri Khristich .05 .02
□ 209 Peter Bondra .25 .11
□ 210 Teppo Numminen .05 .02
□ 211 Bob Essensa .10 .05
□ 212 Phil Housley .10 .05
□ 213 Ed Olczyk .05 .02
□ 214 Pat Elynuik .05 .02
□ 215 Troy Murray .05 .02
□ 216 Igor Ulanov .05 .02
□ 217 Thomas Steen .05 .02
□ 218 Darrin Shannon .05 .02
□ 219 Joe Juneau UER .10 .05
(Back says shoots right, should be left)
□ 220 Stephen Heinze .05 .02
□ 221 Ted Donato .05 .02
□ 222 Glen Murray .05 .02
□ 223 Keith Carney .05 .02
□ 224 Dean McAmmond .05 .02
□ 225 Slava Kozlov .10 .05
□ 226 Martin Lapointe .05 .02
□ 227 Patrick Poulin .05 .02
□ 228 Darryl Sydor .05 .02
□ 229 Trent Klatt .05 .02
□ 230 Bill Guerin .05 .02
□ 231 Jarrod Skalde .05 .02
□ 232 Scott Niedermayer .10 .05
□ 233 Marty McInnis .05 .02
□ 234 Scott LaChance .05 .02
□ 235 Dominic Roussel .10 .05
□ 236 Eric Lindros 1.50 .70
□ 237 Shawn McEachern .05 .02
□ 238 Martin Rucinsky .05 .02
□ 239 Bill Lindsay .05 .02
□ 240 Bret Hedican .05 .02
□ 241 Ray Whitney .05 .02
□ 242 Felix Potvin .25 .11
□ 243 Keith Tkachuk .50 .23
□ 244 Evgeny Davydov .05 .02
□ 245 Brett Hull SL .10 .05
□ 246 Wayne Gretzky SL .60 .25
□ 247 Steve Yzerman SL .10 .05
□ 248 Paul Ysebaert SL .05 .02
□ 249 Dave Andreychuk SL .10 .05
□ 250 Kirk McLean SL .10 .05
□ 251 Tim Cheveldae SL .10 .05
□ 252 Jeremy Roenick SL .10 .05
□ 253 NHL Pro Set NR .05 .02
Youth Parade
□ 254 NHL Pro Set NR .05 .02
Youth Clinics
□ 255 NHL Pro Set NR .05 .02
All-Time Team
□ 256 Mike Gartner MS .10 .05
□ 257 Brian Propp MS .05 .02
□ 258 Dave Taylor MS .10 .05
□ 259 Bobby Smith MS .10 .05
□ 260 Denis Savard MS .10 .05
□ 261 Ray Bourque MS .10 .05
□ 262 Joe Mullen MS .10 .05
□ 263 John Tonelli MS .05 .02
□ 264 Brad Marsh MS .05 .02
□ 265 Randy Carlyle MS .05 .02
□ 266 Mike Hough PS .05 .02
Power
□ 267 Bob Essensa PS .10 .05
Achieve
□ 268 Mike Lalor PS .05 .02
Motivate
□ 269 Terry Carkner PS .05 .02
Attitude
□ 270 Todd Krygier PS .05 .02
Responsibility
□ AU239 Kirk McLean AUTO 40.00 18.00

## 1992-93 Pro Set Award Winners

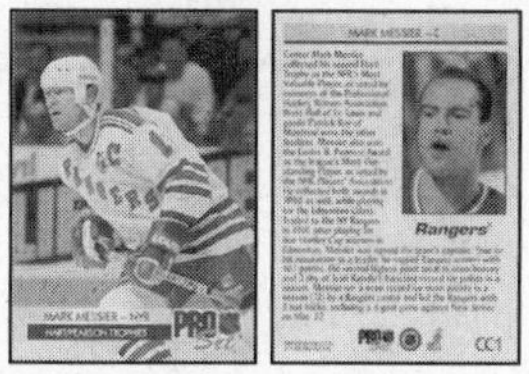

Randomly inserted in 1992-93 Pro Set packs, these five standard-size cards capture five NHL players who were honored with trophies for their outstanding play. The fronts feature full-bleed color action player photos. A gold-foil stamped "Award Winner" emblem is superimposed at the upper right corner. The player's name, team name, and trophy awarded appear in two bars toward the bottom of the picture. The backs carry a color headshot and a career summary.

| | MINT | NRMT |
|---|---|---|
| COMPLETE SET (5) | 25.00 | 11.00 |
| COMMON CARD (CC1-CC5) | 2.00 | .90 |

□ CC1 Mark Messier 3.00 1.35
Hart/Pearson Trophies
□ CC2 Patrick Roy 10.00 4.50
Vezina/Jennings Trophies
□ CC3 Pavel Bure 4.00 1.80
Calder Trophy
□ CC4 Brian Leetch 4.00 1.80
Norris Trophy
□ CC5 Guy Carbonneau 2.00 .90
Selke Trophy

## 1992-93 Pro Set Gold Team Leaders

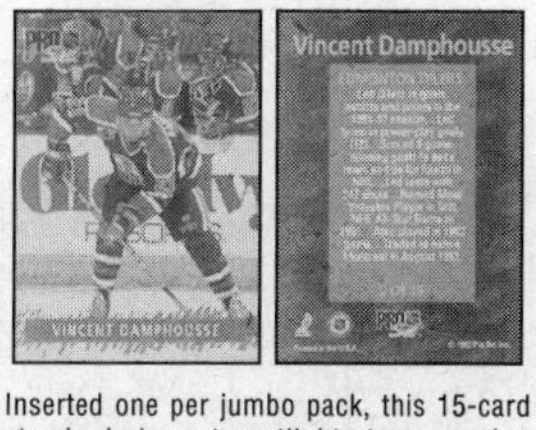

Inserted one per jumbo pack, this 15-card standard-size set spotlights team scoring leaders from the Campbell Conference. The color action player photos on the fronts are full-bleed with "1991-92 Team Leader" gold foil stamped on the picture at the upper right corner. Toward the bottom of the picture the player's name appears on a rust-colored bar that overlays a jagged design. Bordered by a dark brown screened background with Campbell Conference logos, the back carries career summary on a rust-colored panel. The cards are numbered on the back "X of 15."

| | MINT | NRMT |
|---|---|---|
| COMPLETE SET (15) | 30.00 | 13.50 |
| COMMON CARD (1-15) | .50 | .23 |

□ 1 Gary Roberts .50 .23
□ 2 Jeremy Roenick 2.00 .90
□ 3 Steve Yzerman 5.00 2.20
□ 4 Nicklas Lidstrom 1.50 .70
□ 5 Vincent Damphousse 1.50 .70
□ 6 Wayne Gretzky 12.00 5.50
□ 7 Mike Modano 2.50 1.10
□ 8 Brett Hull 2.50 1.10
□ 9 Nelson Emerson .50 .23
□ 10 Pat Falloon .50 .23
□ 11 Doug Gilmour 1.50 .70
□ 12 Trevor Linden 1.50 .70
□ 13 Pavel Bure 3.00 1.35
□ 14 Phil Housley .50 .23
□ 15 Luciano Borsato .50 .23

## 1992-93 Pro Set Rookie Goal Leaders

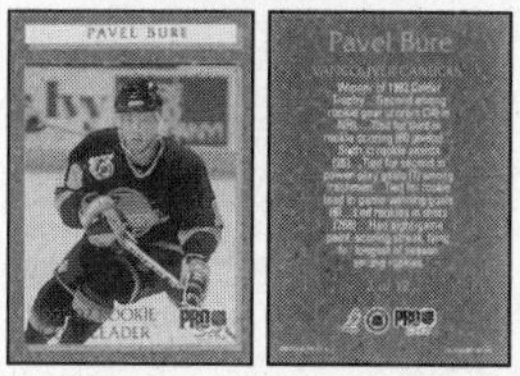

This 12-card Rookie Goal Leader standard-size set features the top rookie goal scorers from the 1991-92 season. The cards were randomly inserted in 1992-93 Pro Set packs. On a variegated purple card face, the fronts display color action player photos that are accented by gold drop borders. The player's name appears in a white bar above the picture, while the words "1991-92 Rookie Goal Leader" are gold foil-stamped across the bottom of the picture. On the same variegated purple background as the fronts, the backs present career summary.

| | MINT | NRMT |
|---|---|---|
| COMPLETE SET (12) | 20.00 | 9.00 |
| COMMON CARD (1-12) | 1.50 | .70 |

□ 1 Tony Amonte 3.00 1.35
□ 2 Pavel Bure 5.00 2.20
□ 3 Donald Audette 2.00 .90
□ 4 Pat Falloon 1.50 .70
□ 5 Nelson Emerson 1.50 .70
□ 6 Gilbert Dionne 1.50 .70
□ 7 Kevin Todd 1.50 .70
□ 8 Luciano Borsato 1.50 .70
□ 9 Rob Pearson 1.50 .70
□ 10 Valeri Zelepukin 1.50 .70
□ 11 Geoff Sanderson 2.50 1.10
□ 12 Claude Lapointe 1.50 .70

## 1987 Pro-Sport All-Stars

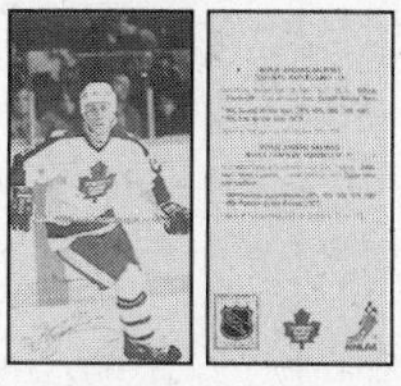

Issued in Canadian retail packs that included an LCD quartz watch, each of these red, white, and blue oversized cards measures approximately 11 3/4" by 10 1/2" when unfolded and features a color player action shot at the lower right. The player's name, along with his career highlights in English and French, are shown at the lower left. A middle section is cut away to accommodate the watch. The cards are numbered on the front with a "CW" prefix. These cards are priced below without the watches. Number 4 was apparently not issued.

| | MINT | NRMT |
|---|---|---|
| COMPLETE SET (17) | 50.00 | 22.00 |
| COMMON CARD (1-18) | 2.00 | .90 |

□ 1 Larry Robinson 3.00 1.35
□ 2 Guy Carbonneau 2.00 .90
□ 3 Chris Chelios 5.00 2.20
□ 5 Mario Lemieux 15.00 6.75
□ 6 Mike Bossy 4.00 1.80
□ 7 Dale Hawerchuk 3.00 1.35
□ 8 Joe Mullen 3.00 1.35
□ 9 Rick Vaive 2.00 .90
□ 10 Wendel Clark 4.00 1.80
□ 11 Michel Goulet 3.00 1.35
□ 12 Peter Stastny 3.00 1.35
□ 13 Mark Messier 6.00 2.70
□ 14 Paul Coffey 5.00 2.20
□ 15 Tony Tanti 2.00 .90
□ 16 Borje Salming 3.00 1.35
□ 17 Chris Nilan 2.00 .90
□ 18 Mats Naslund 3.00 1.35

## 1983-84 Puffy Stickers

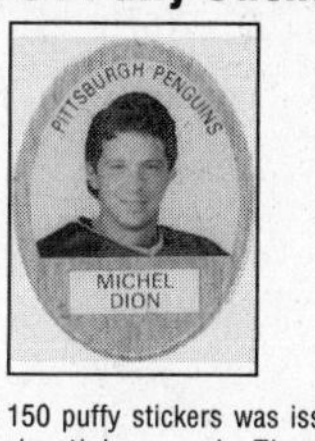


This set of 150 puffy stickers was issued in panels of six stickers each. The panels measure approximately 3 1/2" by 6". There are 21 player panels and four logo panels. The NHL and NHLPA logos appear in the center of each panel. The stickers are oval-shaped and measure approximately 1 1/4" by 1 3/4". In the top portion of the oval they feature a color head shot of the player, with the team name above the head and the player name below the picture in a white box. The sticker background is wood-grain in design. The 21 player panels are numbered and we have checklisted them below accordingly. The logo panels are unnumbered and they are listed after the player panels. The backs are blank. There was also an album produced for this set; the album is not included in the complete set price below.

| | MINT | NRMT |
|---|---|---|
| COMPLETE SET (25) | 75.00 | 34.00 |
| COMMON PANEL (1-21) | 1.50 | .70 |
| COMMON PANEL (22-25) | 5.00 | 2.20 |

□ 1 Doug Risebrough 15.00 6.75
Wayne Gretzky
Mats Naslund
Bill Derlago
Richard Brodeur
Dave Babych
□ 2 Glenn Anderson 3.50 1.55
Larry Robinson
Rick Vaive
Stan Smyl
Scott Arniel
Don Edwards
□ 3 Ryan Walter 2.50 1.10
Peter Ihnacak
Thomas Gradin
Morris Lukowich
Kent Nilsson
Paul Coffey
□ 4 John Anderson 6.00 2.70
Dave(Tiger) Williams
Brian Mullen
Steve Tambellini
Mark Messier
Guy Lafleur
□ 5 Darcy Rota 2.50 1.10
Dale Hawerchuk
Paul Reinhart
Jari Kurri
Mario Tremblay
Mike Palmateer
□ 6 Paul MacLean 3.50 1.55
Lanny McDonald
Ken Linseman
Steve Shutt
Borje Salming
Kevin McCarthy
□ 7 Barry Pederson 2.50 1.10
Mike Foligno
Jim Fox
Don Lever
Bobby Clarke
Greg Malone
□ 8 Gilbert Perreault 2.50 1.10
Charlie Simmer
Hector Marini
Mark Howe
Rick Kehoe
Jim Schoenfeld
□ 9 Larry Murphy 2.50 1.10
Phil Russell
Bill Barber
Mike Bullard
Pete Peeters
John Van Boxmeer
□ 10 Tapio Levo 3.50 1.55
Darryl Sittler
Paul Gardner
Rick Middleton
Real Cloutier
Bernie Nicholls
□ 11 Brian Propp 3.50 1.55
Michel Dion
Ray Bourque
Dale McCourt
Marcel Dionne
Bob MacMillan
□ 12 Randy Carlyle 2.50 1.10
Terry O'Reilly
Phil Housley
Dave Taylor

Glenn Resch
Behn Wilson
❑ 13 Tony Esposito 3.50 1.55
Ron Duguay
Pierre Larouche
Neal Broten
Peter Stastny
Blake Dunlop
❑ 14 Walt McKechnie 1.50 .70
Risto Siltanen
Bobby Smith
Anton Stastny
Mike Liut
Doug Wilson
❑ 15 Blaine Stoughton 2.50 1.10
Dino Ciccarelli
Michel Goulet
Jorgen Pettersson
Tom Lysiak
Brad Park
❑ 16 Craig Hartsburg 1.50 .70
Marian Stastny
Rob Ramage
Al Secord
John Ogrodnick
Greg Millen
❑ 17 Tony McKegney 1.50 .70
Brian Sutter
Steve Larmer
Danny Gare
Mark Johnson
Brian Bellows
❑ 18 Bernie Federko 2.50 1.10
Denis Savard
Reed Larson
Ron Francis
Dennis Maruk
Dan Bouchard
❑ 19 Mike Bossy 3.50 1.55
Anders Hedberg
Rod Langway
Billy Smith
Reijo Ruotsalainen
Milan Novy
❑ 20 Barry Beck 2.50 1.10
Bob Carpenter
Clark Gillies
Rob McClanahan
Brian Engblom
Denis Potvin
❑ 21 Mike Gartner 3.50 1.55
John Tonelli
Willie Huber
Pat Riggin
Bryan Trottier
Don Maloney
❑ 22 Norris Division 5.00 2.20
Blackhawks logo
Red Wings logo
North Stars logo
Blues logo
Maple Leafs logo
NHL logo
❑ 23 Patrick Division 5.00 2.20
Devils logo
Islanders logo
Rangers logo
Flyers logo
Penguins logo
Capitals logo
❑ 24 Adams Division 5.00 2.20
Bruins logo
Sabres logo
Whalers logo
Canadiens logo
Nordiques logo
NHL logo
❑ 25 Smythe Division 5.00 2.20
Flames logo
Oilers logo
Kings logo
Canucks logo
Jets logo
NHL logo
❑ xx Album 25.00 11.00

## 1938-39 Quaker Oats Photos

This 30-card set of Toronto Maple Leafs and Montreal Canadiens was sponsored by Quaker Oats. The photos were obtainable by mail with the redemption of proofs of purchase. These oversized cards (approximately 6 1/4" by 7 3/8") are unnumbered and hence are listed below alphabetically. Facsimile autographs are printed in white on the fronts of these blank-backed cards.

EX-MT VG-E
COMPLETE SET (30) 1500.00 750.00
COMMON CARD (1-30) 40.00 20.00

❑ 1 Syl Apps 100.00 50.00
❑ 2 Toe Blake 200.00 100.00
❑ 3 Buzz Boll 40.00 20.00
❑ 4 Turk Broda 150.00 75.00
❑ 5 Walter Buswell 40.00 20.00
❑ 6 Herb Cain 50.00 25.00
❑ 7 Murph Chamberlain 40.00 20.00
❑ 8 Wilf Cude 50.00 25.00
❑ 9 Bob Davidson 40.00 20.00
❑ 10 Gordie Drillon 80.00 40.00
❑ 11 Paul Drouin 40.00 20.00
❑ 12 Stew Evans 40.00 20.00
❑ 13 James Fowler 40.00 20.00
❑ 14 Johnny Gagnon 40.00 20.00
❑ 15 Robert Gracie 40.00 20.00
❑ 16 Reg Hamilton 40.00 20.00
❑ 17 Paul Haynes 40.00 20.00
❑ 18 Foster Hewitt 80.00 40.00
❑ 19 Red Horner 80.00 40.00
❑ 20 Harvey(Busher) Jackson 100.00 50.00
❑ 21 Bingo Kampman 40.00 20.00
❑ 22 Pep Kelly 40.00 20.00
❑ 23 Rod Lorrain 40.00 20.00
❑ 24 Georges Mantha 40.00 20.00
❑ 25 Nick Metz 40.00 20.00
❑ 26 George Parsons 40.00 20.00
❑ 27 Babe Siebert 80.00 40.00
❑ 28 Bill Thoms 40.00 20.00
❑ 29 James Ward 40.00 20.00
❑ 30 Cy Wentworth 50.00 25.00

## 1945-54 Quaker Oats Photos

Quaker Oats of Canada continued its tradition of redeeming proofs of purchase for photos of Montreal Canadiens and Toronto Maple Leafs in this nine-year series. Many players are featured in multiple versions, as their photos were updated over the years. The photos themselves are black and white with a thin white border and measure 8" X 10". Because of the numerous variations and the potential for more to be unearthed, no complete set price is listed below. Currently, 113 players are featured on 200 different photos. Anyone with information regarding other photos or variations is encouraged to contact Beckett Publications. The photos are blank-backed and unnumbered and are listed below in alphabetical order within their team (Toronto first, then Montreal).

EX-MT VG-E
COMMON CARD 10.00 5.00

❑ 1A Syl Apps 25.00 12.50
Home Still, CJS Apps auto.
❑ 1B Syl Apps 20.00 10.00
Home Still, Syl Apps auto.
❑ 1C Syl Apps 125.00 60.00
Away With Stanley Cup
❑ 2 George Armstrong 20.00 10.00
Home Action
❑ 3 Doug Baldwin 80.00 40.00
Home Still
❑ 4A Bill Barilko 20.00 10.00
Home Action
auto. 1/4" from border
❑ 4B Bill Barilko 20.00 10.00
Home Action
auto. 3/4" from border
❑ 4C Bill Barilko 20.00 10.00
Away Action
❑ 5 Baz Bastien 100.00 50.00
Home Still
❑ 6 Gordon Bell 100.00 50.00
Home Still
❑ 7A Max Bentley 15.00 7.50
Home Still
❑ 7B Max Bentley 125.00 60.00
Home Dressing Room
❑ 7C Max Bentley 15.00 7.50
Away Action
❑ 8 Gus Bodnar 30.00 15.00
Home Still
❑ 9A Garth Boesch 12.00 6.00
Home Still, closed B in auto.
❑ 9B Garth Boesch 12.00 6.00
Home Still, open B in auto.
❑ 9C Garth Boesch 80.00 40.00
Away Action
❑ 10 Hugh Bolton 10.00 5.00
Home Action
❑ 11 Leo Boivin 25.00 12.50
Home Action
❑ 12A Turk Broda 40.00 20.00
Away Splits, W.E. auto.
❑ 12B Turk Broda 30.00 15.00
Away Splits, Turk auto.
❑ 12C Turk Broda 30.00 15.00
Away Action
❑ 13 Lorne Carr 25.00 12.50
Home Still
❑ 14 Les Costello 25.00 12.50
Home Still
❑ 15 Bob Davidson 20.00 10.00
Home Still
❑ 16A Bill Ezinicki 15.00 7.50
cropped William auto., blue tint
❑ 16B Bill Ezinicki 10.00 5.00
entire William auto.
❑ 16C Bill Ezinicki 10.00 5.00
Home Still, Bill auto.
❑ 16D Bill Ezinicki 10.00 5.00
Away Action
❑ 17 Fernie Flaman 12.00 6.00
Home Action
❑ 18A Cal Gardner 10.00 5.00
Home Still
❑ 18B Cal Gardner 10.00 5.00
Away Action
❑ 19A Bob Goldham 10.00 5.00
sweeping G in auto.
❑ 19B Bob Goldham 10.00 5.00
normal G, entire blade
❑ 19C Bob Goldham 125.00 60.00
normal G, blade cropped
❑ 20 Gord Hannigan 25.00 12.50
Home Action
❑ 21 Bob Hassard 40.00 20.00
Away Action
❑ 22 Mel Hill 60.00 30.00
Home Still
❑ 23 Tim Horton 80.00 40.00
Home Action
❑ 24A Bill Judza 10.00 5.00
Home Still
❑ 24B Bill Judza 10.00 5.00
Away Action
❑ 25A Ted Kennedy 40.00 20.00
Home Still, blade in corner
❑ 25B Ted Kennedy 40.00 20.00
Home Still, large image
blade cropped, b,w tint
❑ 25C Ted Kennedy 80.00 40.00
Home Still, large image
blade cropped, blue tint
❑ 25D Ted Kennedy 15.00 7.50
Home Still, C on jersey
❑ 25E Ted Kennedy 150.00 75.00
Home With Stanley Cup
❑ 25F Ted Kennedy 15.00 7.50
Away Action
❑ 26A Joe Klukay 10.00 5.00
Home Still
❑ 26B Joe Klukay 10.00 5.00
Away Action
❑ 27 Danny Lewicki 12.00 6.00
Home Action
❑ 28 Harry Lumley 50.00 25.00
Home Action
❑ 29A Vic Lynn 10.00 5.00
Home Still
head 3/8" from border
❑ 29B Vic Lynn 25.00 12.50
Home Still
head 1/8" from border
❑ 29C Vic Lynn 10.00 5.00
Away Action
❑ 30A Fleming Mackell 10.00 5.00
Home Still
❑ 30B Fleming Mackell 12.00 6.00
Away Action
❑ 31 Phil Maloney 60.00 30.00
Home Action
❑ 32 Frank Mathers 30.00 15.00
Home Still
❑ 33 Frank McCool 100.00 50.00
Home Still
❑ 34 John McCormick 25.00 12.50
Away Action
❑ 35A Howie Meeker 15.00 7.50
Home Still, large image
❑ 35B Howie Meeker 15.00 7.50
Home Still, small image
❑ 35C Howie Meeker 15.00 7.50
Away Action
❑ 36A Don Metz 10.00 5.00
Home, posed to right
❑ 36B Don Metz 20.00 10.00
Home, center pose, b,w tint
❑ 36C Don Metz 60.00 30.00
Home, center pose, blue tint
❑ 37A Nick Metz 10.00 5.00
Home Still, original stick
❑ 37B Nick Metz 20.00 10.00
Home Still, stick retouched
3/8" from border
❑ 37C Nick Metz 40.00 20.00
Home Still, stick retouched
1/8" from border
❑ 38 Rudy Migay 50.00 25.00
Home Action
❑ 39 Elwyn Morris 60.00 30.00
Home Still
❑ 40 Jim Morrison 10.00 5.00
Home Action
❑ 41A Gus Mortson 10.00 5.00
Home Still
❑ 41B Gus Mortson 10.00 5.00
Away Action
❑ 42 Eric Nesterenko 60.00 30.00
Home Action
❑ 43 Bud Poile 25.00 12.50
Home Still
❑ 44 Babe Pratt 80.00 40.00
Home Still
❑ 45 Al Rollins 20.00 10.00
Home Action
❑ 46 Dave Schriner 50.00 25.00
Home Still
❑ 47A Tod Sloan 20.00 10.00
Home Still
❑ 47B Tod Sloan 10.00 5.00
Home Action
❑ 48A Sid Smith 20.00 10.00
Home Still
❑ 48B Sid Smith 10.00 5.00
Away Action
❑ 49 Bob Solinger 25.00 12.50
❑ 50A Wally Stanowski 20.00 10.00
Home Still, entire blade
❑ 50B Wally Stanowski 10.00 5.00
Home Still, blade cropped
❑ 51A Gaye Stewart 80.00 40.00
Home Still
❑ 51B Gaye Stewart 10.00 5.00
Home Still, blue tint
❑ 52 Ron Stewart 80.00 40.00
Home Action
❑ 53 Harry Taylor 12.00 6.00
Home Still
❑ 54 Billy Taylor 40.00 20.00
Home Still
❑ 55 Cy Thomas 40.00 20.00
Home Still
❑ 56A Jim Thomson 50.00 25.00
Home Still, stick cropped
❑ 56B Jim Thomson 10.00 5.00
Home Still
stick touching border
❑ 56C Jim Thomson 50.00 25.00
Home Still
stick away from border
❑ 56D Jim Thomson 10.00 5.00
Away Action
❑ 57A Ray Timgren 12.00 6.00
Home Still
❑ 57B Ray Timgren 10.00 5.00
Away Action
❑ 58A Harry Watson 10.00 5.00
Home Still, tape on stick
❑ 58B Harry Watson 10.00 5.00
Home Still, no tape visible
❑ 58C Harry Watson 10.00 5.00
Away Action
❑ 59 1947-9 Toronto Maple Leafs 50.00 25.00
❑ 60A Leafs Attack McNeil 150.00 75.00
❑ 60B Gardner attacks Harvey 150.00 75.00
❑ 60C Rollins, Judza stop Curry 150.00 75.00
❑ 60D McNeil Saves on Gardner 150.00 75.00
❑ 61 George Allen 10.00 5.00
Home Still
❑ 62 Jean Beliveau 150.00 75.00
Home Action
❑ 63 Joe Benoit 15.00 7.50
Home Still
❑ 64A Toe Blake 125.00 60.00
Hector Toe Blake auto.
❑ 64B Toe Blake 15.00 7.50
Toe Blake auto. above skates
❑ 64C Toe Blake 15.00 7.50
Toe Blake auto. below skate
❑ 65A Butch Bouchard 10.00 5.00
Home Still, entire skate
❑ 65B Butch Bouchard 10.00 5.00
Home Still, skate cropped
❑ 65C Butch Bouchard 12.00 6.00
Home Action
❑ 66 Todd Campeau 10.00 5.00
Home Still
❑ 67 Bob Carse 10.00 5.00
Home Still
❑ 68 Joe Carveth 10.00 5.00
Home Portrait
❑ 69A Murph Chamberlain 15.00 7.50
facing sideways, entire skates
❑ 69B Murph Chamberlain 15.00 7.50
facing sideways, skates cropped
❑ 69C Murph Chamberlain 25.00 12.50
Home Still, facing forward
❑ 70 Gerry Couture 10.00 5.00
Home Action
❑ 71A Floyd Curry 100.00 50.00
Home Still
❑ 71B Floyd Curry 10.00 5.00
Home Action
❑ 72 Ed Dorohoy 10.00 5.00
Home Action
❑ 73A Bill Durnan 20.00 10.00
Home Still
stick handle cropped
❑ 73B Bill Durnan 40.00 20.00
Home Still
stick handle touching border
❑ 73C Bill Durnan 150.00 75.00
Home Still
stick handle away from border
❑ 73D Bill Durnan 25.00 12.50
Home Action
❑ 74A Norm Dussault 10.00 5.00
Home Portrait
❑ 74B Norm Dussault 25.00 12.50
Home Action
❑ 75 Frank Eddolls 15.00 7.50
Home Still
❑ 76A Bob Fillion 40.00 20.00
Home Still
small image
❑ 76B Bob Fillion 10.00 5.00
Home Still
large image, screen background
❑ 76C Bob Fillion 20.00 10.00
Home Still
large image
air brushed background
❑ 76D Bob Fillion 10.00 5.00
Home Action
❑ 77 Dick Gamble 15.00 7.50
Away Action
❑ 78 Bernie Geoffrion 25.00 12.50
Home Action
❑ 79A Leo Gravelle 10.00 5.00
Home Still
❑ 79B Leo Gravelle 40.00 20.00
Away Still
❑ 79C Leo Gravelle 10.00 5.00
Home Action
❑ 80A Glen Harmon 10.00 5.00
Home Still, entire puck
❑ 80B Glen Harmon 10.00 5.00
Home Still, no puck
❑ 80C Glen Harmon 20.00 10.00
Home Action
❑ 81A Doug Harvey 20.00 10.00
Home Still
❑ 81B Doug Harvey 15.00 7.50
Home Action
❑ 82 Dutch Hiller 15.00 7.50
Home Still
❑ 83 Bert Hirschfeld 15.00 7.50
Home Action
❑ 84 Tom Johnson 15.00 7.50
Home Action
❑ 85 Vern Kaiser 15.00 7.50
Home Action
❑ 86A Elmer Lach 15.00 7.50
Home Still, stick in corner
❑ 86B Elmer Lach 15.00 7.50
Home Still, stick cropped
❑ 86C Elmer Lach 60.00 30.00
Home Still
stick 1/2" up from corner
❑ 86D Elmer Lach 15.00 7.50
Home Action
❑ 87A Leo Lamoureaux 20.00 10.00
Home Still, entire blade
❑ 87B Leo Lamoureaux 15.00 7.50
Home Still, blade cropped
❑ 88A Hal Laycoe 80.00 40.00
Home Portrait
❑ 88B Hal Laycoe 10.00 5.00
Home Action
❑ 89A Roger Leger 10.00 5.00
Home Still
light background
❑ 89B Roger Leger 10.00 5.00
Home Still
dark background
❑ 89C Roger Leger 40.00 20.00
Home Action
❑ 90 Jacques Locas 15.00 7.50
Home Still
❑ 91 Ross Lowe 15.00 7.50
Away Action
❑ 92 Calum MacKay 10.00 5.00
Home Action
❑ 93 Murdo MacKay 10.00 5.00
Home Portrait
❑ 94 James MacPherson 10.00 5.00
Home Action
❑ 95 Paul Masnick 10.00 5.00
Home Action
❑ 96A John McCormick 80.00 40.00
Home Action, vertical
❑ 96B John McCormick 50.00 25.00
Home Action, horizontal
❑ 97 Mike McMahon 80.00 40.00
Home Still
❑ 98 Gerry McNeil 15.00 7.50
Home Action
❑ 99 Paul Meger 12.00 6.00
Home Action
❑ 100 Dickie Moore 25.00 12.50
Home Action
❑ 101A Ken Mosdell 10.00 5.00
Home Still, small image
❑ 101B Ken Mosdell 40.00 20.00
Home Still, large image
auto. cropped
❑ 101C Ken Mosdell 40.00 20.00
Home Still, large image
auto. not cropped
❑ 101D Ken Mosdell 10.00 5.00
Home Action
❑ 102A Buddy O'Connor 30.00 15.00
Home Still, entire blade
❑ 102B Buddy O'Connor 15.00 7.50
Home Still, blade cropped
❑ 103 Bert Olmstead 20.00 10.00
Home Action
❑ 104A Jim Peters 10.00 5.00
Home Still, large image
❑ 104B Jim Peters 10.00 5.00
Home Still, small image
❑ 105 Gerry Plamondon 12.00 6.00
Home Action
❑ 106 Johnny Quilty 12.00 6.00
Home Portrait
❑ 107A Ken Reardon 15.00 7.50
Home Still, large image
❑ 107B Ken Reardon 25.00 12.50
Home Still, small image
❑ 107C Kenny Reardon 15.00 7.50
Home Action
❑ 108A Billy Reay 10.00 5.00
Home Still, large image
stick touching border
❑ 108B Billy Reay 10.00 5.00
Home Still, large image
stick away from border
❑ 108C Billy Reay 100.00 50.00
Home Still, small image
❑ 108D Billy Reay 10.00 5.00
Home Action
❑ 109A Maurice Richard 250.00 125.00
Home, screen background
❑ 109B Maurice Richard 25.00 12.50
Home, large image
auto. cropped
❑ 109C Maurice Richard 25.00 12.50
Home, large image
entire auto.
❑ 109D Maurice Richard 50.00 25.00
Home Action
❑ 110A Howie Riopelle 15.00 7.50
Home Still
❑ 110B Howie Riopelle 15.00 7.50
Home Action
❑ 111 George Robertson 30.00 15.00
Home Action
❑ 112 Dollard St. Laurent 50.00 25.00
Home Action
❑ 113 Grant Warwick 60.00 30.00
Home Action

## 1973-74 Quaker Oats WHA

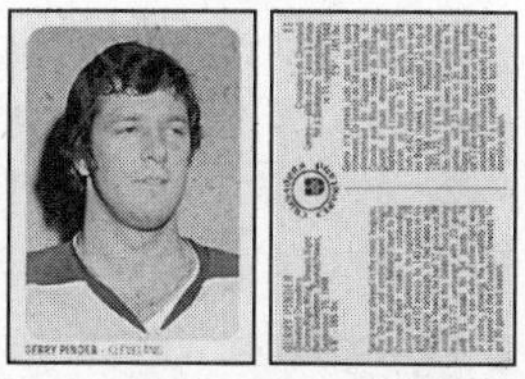

This set of 50 cards features players of the World Hockey Association. The cards were issued in strips (panels) of five in Quaker Oats products. The cards measure approximately 2 1/4" by 3 1/4" and are numbered on the back. The information on the card backs is written in English and French. The value of unseparated panels would be approximately 20 percent greater than the sum of the individual values listed below.

| | NRMT-MT | EXC |
|---|---|---|
| COMPLETE SET (50) | 250.00 | 110.00 |
| COMMON CARD (1-50) | 4.00 | 1.80 |
| ❑ 1 Jim Wiste | 5.00 | 2.20 |
| ❑ 2 Al Smith | 6.00 | 2.70 |
| ❑ 3 Rosaire Paiement | 5.00 | 2.20 |
| ❑ 4 Ted Hampson | 4.00 | 1.80 |
| ❑ 5 Gavin Kirk | 4.00 | 1.80 |
| ❑ 6 Andre Lacroix | 6.00 | 2.70 |
| ❑ 7 John Schella | 4.00 | 1.80 |
| ❑ 8 Gerry Cheevers | 20.00 | 9.00 |
| ❑ 9 Norm Beaudin | 4.00 | 1.80 |
| ❑ 10 Jim Harrison | 4.00 | 1.80 |
| ❑ 11 Gerry Pinder | 5.00 | 2.20 |
| ❑ 12 Bob Sicinski | 4.00 | 1.80 |
| ❑ 13 Bryan Campbell | 4.00 | 1.80 |
| ❑ 14 Murray Hall | 4.00 | 1.80 |
| ❑ 15 Chris Bordeleau | 5.00 | 2.20 |
| ❑ 16 Al Hamilton | 6.00 | 2.70 |
| ❑ 17 Jimmy McLeod | 4.00 | 1.80 |
| ❑ 18 Larry Pleau | 5.00 | 2.20 |
| ❑ 19 Larry Lund | 4.00 | 1.80 |
| ❑ 20 Bobby Sheehan | 5.00 | 2.20 |
| ❑ 21 Jan Popiel | 4.00 | 1.80 |
| ❑ 22 Andre Guadette | 4.00 | 1.80 |
| ❑ 23 Bob Charlebois | 4.00 | 1.80 |
| ❑ 24 Gene Peacosh | 4.00 | 1.80 |
| ❑ 25 Rick Ley | 5.00 | 2.20 |
| ❑ 26 Larry Hornung | 4.00 | 1.80 |
| ❑ 27 Gary Jarrett | 4.00 | 1.80 |
| ❑ 28 Ted Taylor | 4.00 | 1.80 |
| ❑ 29 Pete Donnelly | 4.00 | 1.80 |
| ❑ 30 J.C. Tremblay | 6.00 | 2.70 |
| ❑ 31 Jim Cardiff | 4.00 | 1.80 |
| ❑ 32 Gary Veneruzzo | 4.00 | 1.80 |
| ❑ 33 John French | 4.00 | 1.80 |
| ❑ 34 Ron Ward | 5.00 | 2.20 |
| ❑ 35 Wayne Connelly | 5.00 | 2.20 |
| ❑ 36 Ron Buchanan | 4.00 | 1.80 |
| ❑ 37 Ken Block | 4.00 | 1.80 |
| ❑ 38 Alain Caron | 4.00 | 1.80 |
| ❑ 39 Brit Selby | 5.00 | 2.20 |
| ❑ 40 Guy Trottier | 4.00 | 1.80 |
| ❑ 41 Ernie Wakely | 6.00 | 2.70 |
| ❑ 42 J.P. LeBlanc | 4.00 | 1.80 |
| ❑ 43 Michel Parizeau | 4.00 | 1.80 |
| ❑ 44 Wayne Rivers | 4.00 | 1.80 |
| ❑ 45 Reg Fleming | 5.00 | 2.20 |
| ❑ 46 Don Herriman | 4.00 | 1.80 |
| ❑ 47 Jim Dorey | 4.00 | 1.80 |
| ❑ 48 Danny Lawson | 6.00 | 2.70 |
| ❑ 49 Dick Paradise | 4.00 | 1.80 |
| ❑ 50 Bobby Hull | 60.00 | 27.00 |

## 1989-90 Rangers Marine Midland Bank

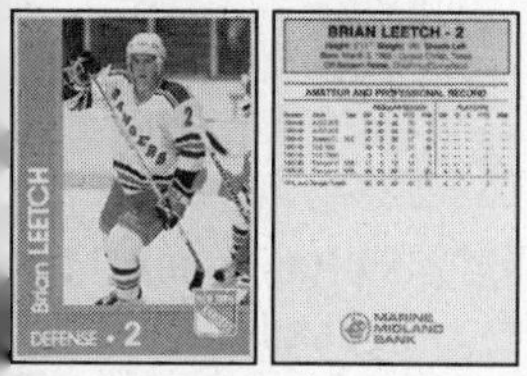

This 30-card set of New York Rangers was sponsored by Marine Midland Bank; the card backs have the bank's logo and name at the bottom. The cards measure approximately 2 5/8" by 3 5/8". The fronts feature color action photos of the players, with a thin red border on the left and bottom of the picture. Outside the red border appears a blue margin, with the player's name, position, and jersey number printed at right angles to one another. The Rangers' logo in the lower right hand corner completes the face of the card. The back has biographical information and career statistics. The cards have been listed below according to sweater number. The key cards in the set are early cards of Brian Leetch and Mike Richter.

| | MINT | NRMT |
|---|---|---|
| COMPLETE SET (30) | 25.00 | 11.00 |
| COMMON CARD | .25 | .11 |
| ❑ 2 Brian Leetch | 5.00 | 2.20 |
| ❑ 3 James Patrick | .75 | .35 |
| ❑ 4 Ron Greschner | 1.00 | .45 |
| ❑ 5 Normand Rochefort | .50 | .23 |
| ❑ 6 Miloslav Horava | .50 | .23 |
| ❑ 8 Darren Turcotte | .75 | .35 |
| ❑ 9 Bernie Nicholls | 1.50 | .70 |
| ❑ 11 Kelly Kisio | .75 | .35 |
| ❑ 12 Kris King | 1.00 | .45 |
| ❑ 14 Mark Hardy | .50 | .23 |
| ❑ 15 Mark Janssens | .50 | .23 |
| ❑ 16 Ulf Dahlen | .75 | .35 |
| ❑ 17 Carey Wilson | .50 | .23 |
| ❑ 19 Brian Mullen | .75 | .35 |
| ❑ 20 Jan Erixon | .50 | .23 |
| ❑ 21 David Shaw | .50 | .23 |
| ❑ 23 Corey Millen | .50 | .23 |
| ❑ 24 Randy Moller | .50 | .23 |
| ❑ 25 John Ogrodnick | 1.00 | .45 |
| ❑ 26 Troy Mallette | .50 | .23 |
| ❑ 29 Rudy Poeschek | .75 | .35 |
| ❑ 30 Chris Nilan | 1.00 | .45 |
| ❑ 33 Bob Froese | .75 | .35 |
| ❑ 34 John Vanbiesbrouck | 4.00 | 1.80 |
| ❑ 35 Mike Richter | 5.00 | 2.20 |
| ❑ 37 Paul Broten | .50 | .23 |
| ❑ 38 Jeff Bloemberg | .50 | .23 |
| ❑ 44 Lindy Ruff | .50 | .23 |
| ❑ NNO Roger Neilson CO | .50 | .23 |
| ❑ NNO Rangers MasterCard | .25 | .11 |

## 1998-99 Rangers Power Play

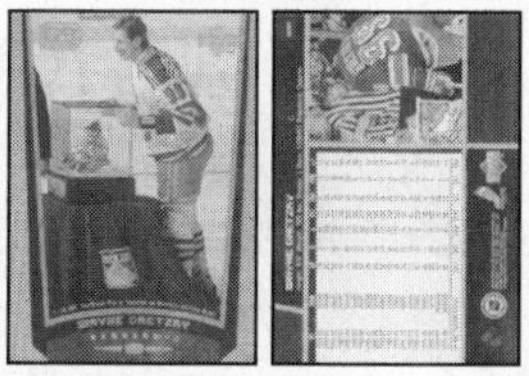

Cards were distributed in a sealed pack and were made available through give-aways at various arenas, in conjunction with Power Play magazine. Each packet contains 4-cards, similar in design to the base set from each manufacturer, but featuring a different card number on the back.

| | MINT | NRMT |
|---|---|---|
| COMPLETE SET (4) | 5.00 | 2.20 |
| COMMON CARD (1-4) | .30 | .14 |
| ❑ NYR1 Wayne Gretzky | 4.00 | 1.80 |
| ❑ NYR2 Todd Harvey | .30 | .14 |
| ❑ NYR3 Brian Leetch | .50 | .23 |
| ❑ NYR4 Mike Richter | .50 | .23 |

## 1970-71 Red Wings Marathon

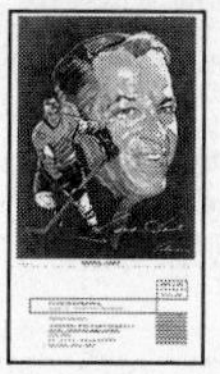

This 11-card (artistic) portrait set of Detroit Red Wings was part of a (Pro Star Portraits) promotion by Marathon Oil. The cards measure approximately 7 1/2" by 14"; the bottom portion, which measures 7 1/2" by 4 1/16", was a tear-off postcard in the form of a credit card application. The front features a full color portrait by Nicholas Volpe, with a facsimile autograph of the player inscribed across the bottom of the painting. The back included an offer for other sports memorabilia on the upper portion.

| | NRMT-MT | EXC |
|---|---|---|
| COMPLETE SET (11) | 80.00 | 36.00 |
| COMMON CARD (1-11) | 3.50 | 1.55 |
| ❑ 1 Gary Bergman | 5.00 | 2.20 |
| ❑ 2 Wayne Connelly | 3.50 | 1.55 |
| ❑ 3 Alex Delvecchio | 10.00 | 4.50 |
| ❑ 4 Roy Edwards | 5.00 | 2.20 |
| ❑ 5 Gordie Howe | 50.00 | 22.00 |
| ❑ 6 Bruce MacGregor | 3.50 | 1.55 |
| ❑ 7 Frank Mahovlich | 12.00 | 5.50 |
| ❑ 8 Dale Rolfe | 3.50 | 1.55 |
| ❑ 9 Jim Rutherford | 6.00 | 2.70 |
| ❑ 10 Garry Unger | 5.00 | 2.20 |
| ❑ 11 Tom Webster | 5.00 | 2.20 |

## 1971 Red Wings Citgo Tumblers

These tumblers were available at Citgo gas stations and measure approximately 8" high. Tumblers feature color head shots,a facsimile autograph, and a color artwork action shot. They are made by Cinemac Inc, and feature a copyright of 1971.

| | MINT | NRMT |
|---|---|---|
| COMPLETE SET | 200.00 | 90.00 |
| COMMON TUMBLER | 20.00 | 9.00 |
| ❑ 1 Wayne Connelly | 25.00 | 11.00 |
| ❑ 2 Alex Delvecchio | 40.00 | 18.00 |
| ❑ 3 Don Edwards | 20.00 | 9.00 |
| ❑ 4 Garry Unger | 20.00 | 9.00 |
| ❑ 5 Gordie Howe | 75.00 | 34.00 |
| ❑ 6 Frank Mahovlich | 30.00 | 13.50 |

## 1973-74 Red Wings Team Issue

Cards measure 8 3/4" x 10 3/4". Fronts feature color photos, and backs are blank. Cards are unnumbered and checklisted below in alphabetical order.

| | MINT | NRMT |
|---|---|---|
| COMPLETE SET (18) | 100.00 | 45.00 |
| COMMON CARD (1-18) | 5.00 | 2.20 |
| ❑ 1 Ace Bailey | 5.00 | 2.20 |
| ❑ 2 Red Berenson | 8.00 | 3.60 |
| ❑ 3 Gary Bergman | 5.00 | 2.20 |
| ❑ 4 Thommie Bergman | 8.00 | 3.60 |
| ❑ 5 Guy Charron | 5.00 | 2.20 |
| ❑ 6 Bill Collins | 5.00 | 2.20 |
| ❑ 7 Denis Dejordy | 8.00 | 3.60 |
| ❑ 8 Alex Delvecchio | 15.00 | 6.75 |
| ❑ 9 Marcel Dionne | 15.00 | 6.75 |
| ❑ 10 Gary Doak | 5.00 | 2.20 |
| ❑ 11 Tim Ecclestone | 5.00 | 2.20 |
| ❑ 12 Larry Johnston | 5.00 | 2.20 |
| ❑ 13 Al Karlander | 5.00 | 2.20 |
| ❑ 14 Brian Lavender | 5.00 | 2.20 |
| ❑ 15 Nick Libett | 5.00 | 2.20 |
| ❑ 16 Ken Murphy | 5.00 | 2.20 |
| ❑ 17 Mickey Redmond | 15.00 | 6.75 |
| ❑ 18 Ron Stackhouse | 5.00 | 2.20 |

## 1973-75 Red Wings McCarthy Postcards

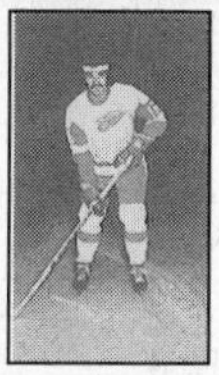

Measuring approximately 3 1/4" by 5 1/2", these postcards display color posed action shots on their fronts. The backs are blank. Since there is no Marcel Dionne or Alex Delvecchio (the latter played 11 games in 1973-74 before coaching), it is doubtful that this is a complete set. The date is established by two players: Brent Hughes (1973-74 was his only season with the Red Wings) and Tom Mellor (1974-75). The cards are unnumbered and checklisted below in alphabetical order. The photos and cards were produced by noted photographer J.D. McCarthy.

| | NRMT-MT | EXC |
|---|---|---|
| COMPLETE SET (15) | 25.00 | 11.00 |
| COMMON CARD (1-15) | 2.00 | .90 |
| ❑ 1 Garnet Bailey | 2.00 | .90 |
| ❑ 2 Thommie Bergman | 2.00 | .90 |
| ❑ 3 Henry Boucha | 2.50 | 1.10 |
| ❑ 4 Guy Charron | 2.00 | .90 |
| ❑ 5 Bill Collins | 2.00 | .90 |
| ❑ 6 Doug Grant | 2.00 | .90 |
| ❑ 7 Ted Harris | 2.00 | .90 |
| ❑ 8 Bill Hogaboam | 2.00 | .90 |
| ❑ 9 Brent Hughes | 2.00 | .90 |
| ❑ 10 Pierre Jarry | 2.00 | .90 |
| ❑ 11 Larry Johnston | 2.00 | .90 |
| ❑ 12 Nick Libett | 2.00 | .90 |
| ❑ 13 Tom Mellor | 2.00 | .90 |
| ❑ 14 Doug Roberts | 2.00 | .90 |
| ❑ 15 Ron Stackhouse | 2.00 | .90 |

## 1979 Red Wings Postcards

This set features borderless color fronts and was issued by the Red Wings during the 1979 season.

| | MINT | NRMT |
|---|---|---|
| COMPLETE SET (18) | 15.00 | 6.75 |
| COMMON CARD (1-18) | .75 | .35 |
| ❑ 1 Thommie Bergman | .75 | .35 |
| ❑ 2 Dan Bolduc | .75 | .35 |
| ❑ 3 Mike Foligno | 2.50 | 1.10 |
| ❑ 4 Jean Hamel | .75 | .35 |
| ❑ 5 Glen Hicks | .75 | .35 |
| ❑ 6 Greg Joly | .75 | .35 |
| ❑ 7 Willie Huber | .75 | .35 |
| ❑ 8 Jim Korn | .75 | .35 |
| ❑ 9 Dan Labraaten | .75 | .35 |
| ❑ 10 Barry Long | .75 | .35 |
| ❑ 11 Reed Larson | .75 | .35 |
| ❑ 12 Dale McCourt | 1.00 | .45 |
| ❑ 13 Vaclav Nedomansky | .75 | .35 |
| ❑ 14 Jim Rutherford | 1.50 | .70 |
| ❑ 15 Dennis Polonich | .75 | .35 |
| ❑ 16 Errol Thompson | .75 | .35 |
| ❑ 17 Rogie Vachon | 2.50 | 1.10 |
| ❑ 18 Paul Woods | .75 | .35 |

## 1987-88 Red Wings Little Caesars

This 30-card set was sponsored by Little Caesars Pizza and measures approximately 3 3/4" by 6". The fronts have color action player photos with white borders. The player's name appears below the photo, along with the team and sponsor logos. The backs are blank. The cards are unnumbered and checklisted below in alphabetical order.

| | MINT | NRMT |
|---|---|---|
| COMPLETE SET (30) | 45.00 | 20.00 |
| COMMON CARD (1-30) | 1.00 | .45 |
| ❑ 1 Brent Ashton | 1.00 | .45 |
| ❑ 2 Dave Barr | 1.00 | .45 |
| ❑ 3 Mel Bridgman | 1.00 | .45 |
| ❑ 4 Shawn Burr | 2.00 | .90 |
| ❑ 5 John Chabot | 1.00 | .45 |
| ❑ 6 Steve Chiasson | 1.50 | .70 |
| ❑ 7 Gilbert Delorme | 1.00 | .45 |
| ❑ 8 Jacques Demers CO | 2.00 | .90 |
| ❑ 9 Ron Duguay | 1.50 | .70 |
| ❑ 10 Dwight Foster | 1.00 | .45 |
| ❑ 11 Gerard Gallant | 1.00 | .45 |
| ❑ 12 Adam Graves | 4.00 | 1.80 |
| ❑ 13 Doug Halward | 1.00 | .45 |
| ❑ 14 Glen Hanlon | 1.50 | .70 |
| ❑ 15 Tim Higgins | 1.00 | .45 |
| ❑ 16 Petr Klima | 1.50 | .70 |
| ❑ 17 Joe Kocur | 2.00 | .90 |
| ❑ 18 Lane Lambert | 1.00 | .45 |
| ❑ 19 Joe Murphy | 2.50 | 1.10 |
| ❑ 20 Lee Norwood | 1.00 | .45 |
| ❑ 21 Adam Oates | 10.00 | 4.50 |
| ❑ 22 Mike O'Connell | 1.00 | .45 |
| ❑ 23 John Ogrodnick | 1.50 | .70 |
| ❑ 24 Bob Probert | 4.00 | 1.80 |
| ❑ 25 Jeff Sharples | 1.00 | .45 |
| ❑ 26 Greg Smith | 1.00 | .45 |
| ❑ 27 Greg Stefan | 1.50 | .70 |
| ❑ 28 Darren Veitch | 1.00 | .45 |
| ❑ 29 Steve Yzerman | 10.00 | 4.50 |
| ❑ 30 Rick Zombo | 1.00 | .45 |

## 1988-89 Red Wings Little Caesars

Set features color action photos with a white border. Players name and team logo are also visible on the front. Cards are blank backed and checklisted below in alphabetical order.

| | MINT | NRMT |
|---|---|---|
| COMPLETE SET (24) | 25.00 | 11.00 |
| COMMON CARD (1-24) | 1.00 | .45 |
| ❑ 1 David Barr | 1.00 | .45 |
| ❑ 2 Shawn Burr | 1.00 | .45 |
| ❑ 3 John Chabot | 1.00 | .45 |
| ❑ 4 Steve Chiasson | 2.00 | .90 |
| ❑ 5 Gilbert Delorme | 1.00 | .45 |
| ❑ 6 Jacques Demers | 1.00 | .45 |
| ❑ 7 Gerard Gallant | 1.00 | .45 |
| ❑ 8 Adam Graves | 2.00 | .90 |
| ❑ 9 Doug Houda | 1.00 | .45 |
| ❑ 10 Glen Hanlon | 1.50 | .70 |
| ❑ 11 Kris King | 1.00 | .45 |
| ❑ 12 Petr Klima | 1.00 | .45 |
| ❑ 13 Joe Kocur | 1.50 | .70 |
| ❑ 14 Paul Maclean | 1.00 | .45 |
| ❑ 15 Jim Nill | 1.00 | .45 |
| ❑ 16 Lee Norwood | 1.00 | .45 |
| ❑ 17 Adam Oates | 3.00 | 1.35 |
| ❑ 18 Mike O'Connell | 1.00 | .45 |
| ❑ 19 Jim Pavese | 1.00 | .45 |
| ❑ 20 Bob Probert | 2.00 | .90 |
| ❑ 21 Jeff Sharples | 1.00 | .45 |
| ❑ 22 Greg Stefan | 1.50 | .70 |
| ❑ 23 Steve Yzerman | 6.00 | 2.70 |
| ❑ 24 Rick Zombo | 1.00 | .45 |

## 1989-90 Red Wings Little Caesars

Set features color action photos with a white border. Players name and team logo are also visible on the front. Cards are blank backed and checklisted below in alphabetical order.

| | MINT | NRMT |
|---|---|---|
| COMPLETE SET (20) | 25.00 | 11.00 |
| COMMON CARD (1-20) | 1.00 | .45 |
| ❑ 1 Dave Barr | 1.00 | .45 |
| ❑ 2 Shawn Burr | 1.00 | .45 |
| ❑ 3 Jim Carson | 2.50 | 1.10 |
| ❑ 4 John Chabot | 1.00 | .45 |
| ❑ 5 Steve Chiasson | 1.50 | .70 |
| ❑ 6 Bernie Federko | 2.00 | .90 |
| ❑ 7 Gerard Gallant | 1.00 | .45 |
| ❑ 8 Marc Habscheid | 1.00 | .45 |
| ❑ 9 Glen Hanlon | 1.50 | .70 |
| ❑ 10 Doug Houda | 1.00 | .45 |
| ❑ 11 Joey Kocur | 1.50 | .70 |
| ❑ 12 Kevin McLelland | 1.00 | .45 |
| ❑ 13 Lee Norwood | 1.00 | .45 |
| ❑ 14 Mike O'Connell | 1.00 | .45 |
| ❑ 15 Borje Salming | 1.00 | .45 |
| ❑ 16 Greg Stefan | 1.50 | .70 |
| ❑ 17 Steve Yzerman | 6.00 | 2.70 |
| ❑ 18 Rick Zombo | 1.00 | .45 |
| ❑ 19 Jacques Demers CO | 1.00 | .45 |
| ❑ 20 Team Photo | 2.00 | .90 |

## 1990-91 Red Wings Little Caesars

Set features color action photos with a white border. Players name and team logo are also visible on the front. Cards are blank backed and checklisted below in alphabetical order.

| | MINT | NRMT |
|---|---|---|
| COMPLETE SET (20) | 40.00 | 18.00 |
| COMMON CARD (1-20) | 1.00 | .45 |
| ❑ 1 Dave Barr | 1.00 | .45 |
| ❑ 2 Shawn Burr | 1.00 | .45 |
| ❑ 3 John Chabot | 1.00 | .45 |
| ❑ 4 Tim Cheveldae | 1.50 | .70 |
| ❑ 5 Per Djoos | 1.00 | .45 |
| ❑ 6 Bobby Dollas | 1.00 | .45 |
| ❑ 7 Sergei Fedorov | 10.00 | 4.50 |
| ❑ 8 Brent Fedyk | 1.00 | .45 |
| ❑ 9 Johan Garpenlov | 1.00 | .45 |
| ❑ 10 Rick Green | 1.00 | .45 |
| ❑ 11 Sheldon Kennedy | 2.00 | .90 |
| ❑ 12 Kevin McClelland | 1.00 | .45 |
| ❑ 13 Brad McCrimmon | 1.00 | .45 |
| ❑ 14 Randy McKay | 1.00 | .45 |
| ❑ 15 Keith Primeau | 4.00 | 1.80 |
| ❑ 16 Bob Probert | 3.00 | 1.35 |
| ❑ 17 Steve Yzerman | 5.00 | 2.20 |
| ❑ 18 Rick Zombo | 1.00 | .45 |
| ❑ 19 Bryan Murray CO | 1.00 | .45 |
| ❑ 20 Team Photo | 2.00 | .90 |

## 1991-92 Red Wings Little Caesars

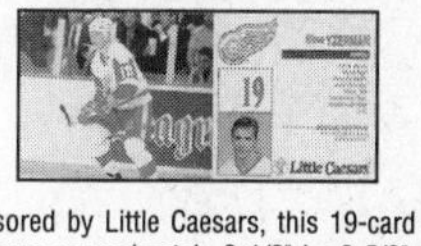

Sponsored by Little Caesars, this 19-card set measures approximately 8 1/2" by 3 5/8" and features a color, action player photo on the left half of the card. The right half displays the player's name, position, biographical information, early career history, and jersey number, along with a close-up player photo. The backs are blank. The cards are unnumbered and checklisted below in alphabetical order.

| | MINT | NRMT |
|---|---|---|
| COMPLETE SET (19) | 40.00 | 18.00 |
| COMMON CARD (1-19) | .50 | .23 |
| ❑ 1 Shawn Burr | 1.00 | .45 |
| ❑ 2 Jimmy Carson | 1.00 | .45 |
| ❑ 3 Steve Chiasson | 1.00 | .45 |
| ❑ 4 Sergei Fedorov | 8.00 | 3.60 |
| ❑ 5 Gerard Gallant | 1.00 | .45 |
| ❑ 6 Johan Garpenlov | 1.00 | .45 |
| ❑ 7 Rick Green | 1.00 | .45 |
| ❑ 8 Marc Habscheid | 1.00 | .45 |
| ❑ 9 Sheldon Kennedy | 1.00 | .45 |
| ❑ 10 Martin Lapointe | 1.50 | .70 |
| ❑ 11 Nicklas Lidstrom | 2.50 | 1.10 |
| ❑ 12 Brad McCrimmon | 1.00 | .45 |
| ❑ 13 Bryan Murray CO/MG | .50 | .23 |
| ❑ 14 Keith Primeau | 1.50 | .70 |
| ❑ 15 Bob Probert | 2.00 | .90 |
| ❑ 16 Dennis Vial | 1.00 | .45 |
| ❑ 17 Paul Ysebaert | 1.00 | .45 |
| ❑ 18 Steve Yzerman | 10.00 | 4.50 |
| ❑ 19 Team Card | 4.00 | 1.80 |

## 1996-97 Red Wings Detroit News/Free Press

These five posters were issued one per week in the Sunday editions of the Detroit News/Free Press. They measure approximately 12 by 18 inches and feature a full color photo on the front. The backs feature an ad for the issuing paper.

| | MINT | NRMT |
|---|---|---|
| COMPLETE SET (5) | 20.00 | 9.00 |
| COMMON CARD (1-5) | 5.00 | 2.20 |
| ❑ 1 Darren McCarty<br>Kris Draper<br>Kirk Maltby<br>Joe Kocur | 5.00 | 2.20 |

❑ 2 Sergei Fedorov 5.00 2.20
❑ 3 Mike Vernon 5.00 2.20
❑ 4 Mike Vernon 5.00 2.20
❑ 5 Sergei Fedorov 5.00 2.20

## 1997-98 Revolution

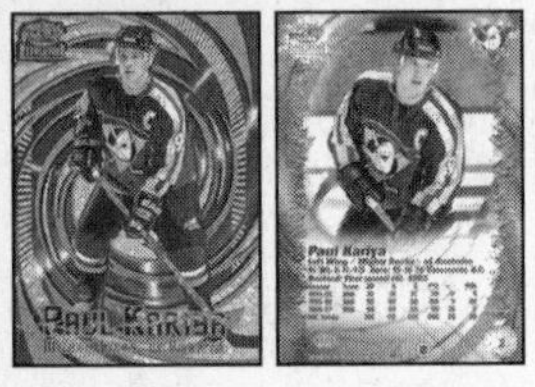

The 1997-98 Pacific Revolution set was issued in one series totalling 150 cards and distributed in three-card packs. The fronts feature color player images printed with etched gold and holographic silver foils on the circular design background. The backs carry another player photo and career statistics.

| | MINT | NRMT |
|---|---|---|
| COMPLETE SET (150) | 150.00 | 70.00 |
| COMMON CARD (1-150) | .60 | .25 |

❑ 1 Guy Hebert 1.25 .55
❑ 2 Paul Kariya 6.00 2.70
❑ 3 Dmitri Mironov .60 .25
❑ 4 Ruslan Salei .60 .25
❑ 5 Teemu Selanne 3.00 1.35
❑ 6 Jason Allison 1.25 .55
❑ 7 Ray Bourque 1.50 .70
❑ 8 Byron Dafoe 1.25 .55
❑ 9 Ted Donato .60 .25
❑ 10 Dimitri Khristich .60 .25
❑ 11 Joe Thornton 3.00 1.35
❑ 12 Matthew Barnaby .60 .25
❑ 13 Jason Dawe .60 .25
❑ 14 Dominik Hasek 3.00 1.35
❑ 15 Michael Peca .60 .25
❑ 16 Miroslav Satan .60 .25
❑ 17 Theoren Fleury 1.25 .55
❑ 18 Jarome Iginla 1.25 .55
❑ 19 Marty McInnis .60 .25
❑ 20 Cory Stillman .60 .25
❑ 21 Rick Tabaracci 1.25 .55
❑ 22 Martin Gelinas .60 .25
❑ 23 Sami Kapanen 1.25 .55
❑ 24 Trevor Kidd 1.25 .55
❑ 25 Keith Primeau .60 .25
❑ 26 Gary Roberts .60 .25
❑ 27 Tony Amonte 1.25 .55
❑ 28 Chris Chelios 1.50 .70
❑ 29 Eric Daze 1.25 .55
❑ 30 Jeff Hackett 1.25 .55
❑ 31 Dmitri Nabokov .60 .25
❑ 32 Peter Forsberg 5.00 2.20
❑ 33 Valeri Kamensky 1.25 .55
❑ 34 Jari Kurri 1.25 .55
❑ 35 Claude Lemieux 1.25 .55
❑ 36 Eric Messier 1.25 .55
❑ 37 Sandis Ozolinsh 1.25 .55
❑ 38 Patrick Roy 8.00 3.60
❑ 39 Joe Sakic 3.00 1.35
❑ 40 Ed Belfour 1.50 .70
❑ 41 Jamie Langenbrunner .60 .25
❑ 42 Jere Lehtinen .60 .25
❑ 43 Mike Modano 2.00 .90
❑ 44 Joe Nieuwendyk 1.25 .55
❑ 45 Sergei Zubov .60 .25
❑ 46 Viacheslav Fetisov .60 .25
❑ 47 Nicklas Lidstrom 1.25 .55
❑ 48 Darren McCarty .60 .25
❑ 49 Larry Murphy .60 .25
❑ 50 Chris Osgood 1.50 .70
❑ 51 Brendan Shanahan 3.00 1.35
❑ 52 Steve Yzerman 5.00 2.20
❑ 53 Roman Hamrlik .60 .25
❑ 54 Bill Guerin 1.25 .55
❑ 55 Curtis Joseph 1.50 .70
❑ 56 Ryan Smyth 1.25 .55
❑ 57 Doug Weight 1.25 .55
❑ 58 Dino Ciccarelli .60 .25
❑ 59 Dave Gagner .60 .25
❑ 60 Ed Jovanovski 1.25 .55
❑ 61 Paul Laus .60 .25
❑ 62 John Vanbiesbrouck 2.50 1.10
❑ 63 Ray Whitney .60 .25
❑ 64 Russ Courtnall .60 .25
❑ 65 Yanic Perreault .60 .25
❑ 66 Luc Robitaille 1.25 .55
❑ 67 Jozef Stumpel 1.25 .55
❑ 68 Vladimir Tsyplakov .60 .25
❑ 69 Shayne Corson .60 .25
❑ 70 Vincent Damphousse 1.25 .55
❑ 71 Saku Koivu 2.50 1.10
❑ 72 Andy Moog 1.25 .55
❑ 73 Mark Recchi 1.25 .55
❑ 74 Jocelyn Thibault 1.25 .55
❑ 75 Martin Brodeur 4.00 1.80
❑ 76 Patrik Elias 2.00 .90
❑ 77 Doug Gilmour 1.50 .70
❑ 78 Bobby Holik .60 .25
❑ 79 Scott Niedermayer .60 .25
❑ 80 Bryan Berard 1.25 .55
❑ 81 Travis Green .60 .25
❑ 82 Zigmund Palffy 1.50 .70
❑ 83 Robert Reichel .60 .25
❑ 84 Tommy Salo 1.25 .55
❑ 85 Dan Cloutier .60 .25
❑ 86 Adam Graves 1.25 .55
❑ 87 Wayne Gretzky 10.00 4.50
❑ 88 Pat LaFontaine 1.25 .55
❑ 89 Brian Leetch 1.50 .70
❑ 90 Mike Richter 1.50 .70
❑ 91 Kevin Stevens 1.25 .55
❑ 92 Daniel Alfredsson 1.25 .55
❑ 93 Shawn McEachern .60 .25
❑ 94 Damian Rhodes 1.25 .55
❑ 95 Ron Tugnutt 1.25 .55
❑ 96 Alexei Yashin 1.25 .55
❑ 97 Rod Brind'Amour 1.25 .55
❑ 98 Paul Coffey 1.50 .70
❑ 99 Alexandre Daigle 1.25 .55
❑ 100 Chris Gratton 1.25 .55
❑ 101 Ron Hextall 1.25 .55
❑ 102 John LeClair 2.50 1.10
❑ 103 Eric Lindros 5.00 2.20
❑ 104 Dainius Zubrus 1.50 .70
❑ 105 Mike Gartner 1.25 .55
❑ 106 Craig Janney .60 .25
❑ 107 Nikolai Khabibulin 1.25 .55
❑ 108 Jeremy Roenick 1.50 .70
❑ 109 Keith Tkachuk 2.00 .90
❑ 110 Stu Barnes .60 .25
❑ 111 Tom Barrasso 1.25 .55
❑ 112 Ron Francis 1.25 .55
❑ 113 Jaromir Jagr 5.00 2.20
❑ 114 Peter Skudra .60 .25
❑ 115 Martin Straka .60 .25
❑ 116 Blair Atcheynum .60 .25
❑ 117 Jim Campbell .60 .25
❑ 118 Geoff Courtnall .60 .25
❑ 119 Steve Duchesne .60 .25
❑ 120 Grant Fuhr 1.25 .55
❑ 121 Brett Hull 2.00 .90
❑ 122 Pierre Turgeon 1.25 .55
❑ 123 Jeff Friesen 1.25 .55
❑ 124 John MacLean .60 .25
❑ 125 Patrick Marleau 3.00 1.35
❑ 126 Owen Nolan 1.25 .55
❑ 127 Marco Sturm 2.50 1.10
❑ 128 Mike Vernon 1.25 .55
❑ 129 Daren Puppa 1.25 .55
❑ 130 Mikael Renberg 1.25 .55
❑ 131 Paul Ysebaert .60 .25
❑ 132 Rob Zamuner .60 .25
❑ 133 Wendel Clark 1.25 .55
❑ 134 Tie Domi .60 .25
❑ 135 Igor Korolev .60 .25
❑ 136 Felix Potvin 1.50 .70
❑ 137 Mats Sundin 1.50 .70
❑ 138 Donald Brashear .60 .25
❑ 139 Pavel Bure 3.00 1.35
❑ 140 Sean Burke 1.25 .55
❑ 141 Trevor Linden 1.25 .55
❑ 142 Mark Messier 2.00 .90
❑ 143 Alexander Mogilny 1.25 .55
❑ 144 Mattias Ohlund 1.25 .55
❑ 145 Peter Bondra 1.50 .70
❑ 146 Phil Housley .60 .25
❑ 147 Dale Hunter .60 .25
❑ 148 Joe Juneau 1.25 .55
❑ 149 Olaf Kolzig 1.25 .55
❑ 150 Adam Oates 1.25 .55

## 1997-98 Revolution Ice Blue

Randomly inserted in packs at the rate of one in 49, this 150-card set is parallel to the base set and is similar in design. The difference is seen in the blue foil design element.

| | MINT | NRMT |
|---|---|---|
| COMMON CARD (1-150) | 15.00 | 6.75 |
| SEMISTARS/GOALIES | 40.00 | 18.00 |
| UNLISTED STARS | 50.00 | 22.00 |

*STARS: 15X TO 30X BASIC CARDS
*YOUNG STARS: 12.5X TO 25X BASIC CARDS

## 1997-98 Revolution 1998 All-Star Game Die-Cuts

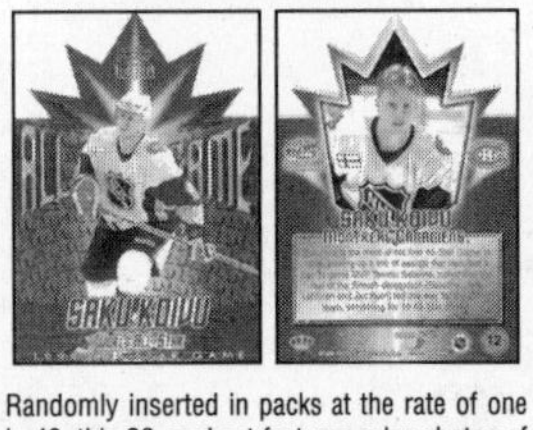

Randomly inserted in packs at the rate of one in 49, this 20-card set features color photos of the hottest players named to the 1998 NHL All-Star game printed on a die-cut star-background card and appearing in their All-Star uniform from the game in Vancouver.

| | MINT | NRMT |
|---|---|---|
| COMPLETE SET (20) | 400.00 | 180.00 |
| COMMON CARD (1-20) | 10.00 | 4.50 |

❑ 1 Teemu Selanne 20.00 9.00
❑ 2 Ray Bourque 10.00 4.50
❑ 3 Dominik Hasek 20.00 9.00
❑ 4 Theoren Fleury 10.00 4.50
❑ 5 Chris Chelios 10.00 4.50
❑ 6 Peter Forsberg 30.00 13.50
❑ 7 Patrick Roy 50.00 22.00
❑ 8 Joe Sakic 20.00 9.00
❑ 9 Ed Belfour 10.00 4.50
❑ 10 Mike Modano 12.00 5.50
❑ 11 Brendan Shanahan 20.00 9.00
❑ 12 Saku Koivu 15.00 6.75
❑ 13 Martin Brodeur 25.00 11.00
❑ 14 Wayne Gretzky 60.00 27.00
❑ 15 John LeClair 15.00 6.75
❑ 16 Eric Lindros 30.00 13.50
❑ 17 Jaromir Jagr 30.00 13.50
❑ 18 Pavel Bure 20.00 9.00
❑ 19 Mark Messier 12.00 5.50
❑ 20 Peter Bondra 10.00 4.50

## 1997-98 Revolution NHL Icons Die-Cuts

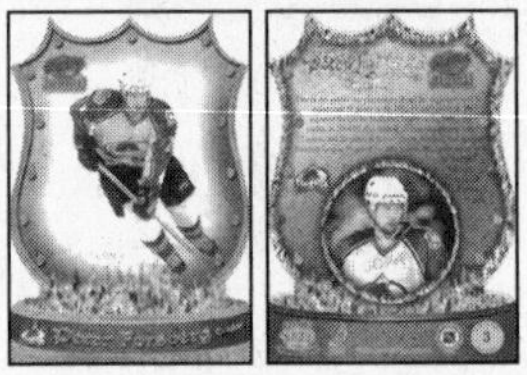

Randomly inserted in packs at the rate of one in 121, this 10-card set features color photos of today's living legends of hockey printed on a die-cut card.

| | MINT | NRMT |
|---|---|---|
| COMPLETE SET (10) | 500.00 | 220.00 |
| COMMON CARD (1-10) | 30.00 | 13.50 |

❑ 1 Paul Kariya 60.00 27.00
❑ 2 Teemu Selanne 30.00 13.50
❑ 3 Peter Forsberg 50.00 22.00
❑ 4 Patrick Roy 80.00 36.00
❑ 5 Steve Yzerman 50.00 22.00
❑ 6 Martin Brodeur 40.00 18.00
❑ 7 Wayne Gretzky 100.00 45.00
❑ 8 Eric Lindros 50.00 22.00
❑ 9 Jaromir Jagr 50.00 22.00
❑ 10 Pavel Bure 30.00 13.50

## 1997-98 Revolution Return to Sender Die-Cuts

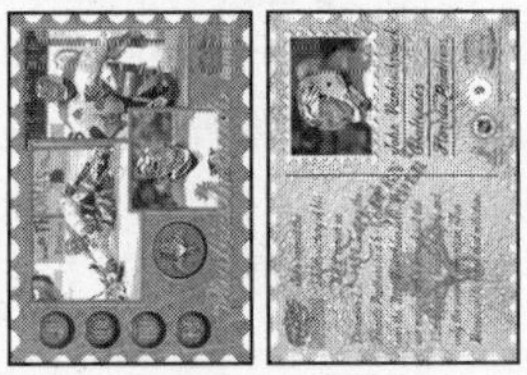

Randomly inserted in packs at the rate of one in 25, this 20-card set features color photos of the top goalies printed on a postage stamp shaped die-cut card.

| | MINT | NRMT |
|---|---|---|
| COMPLETE SET (20) | 200.00 | 90.00 |
| COMMON CARD (1-20) | 8.00 | 3.60 |

❑ 1 Guy Hebert 10.00 4.50
❑ 2 Byron Dafoe 10.00 4.50
❑ 3 Dominik Hasek 20.00 9.00
❑ 4 Jeff Hackett 10.00 4.50
❑ 5 Patrick Roy 50.00 22.00
❑ 6 Ed Belfour 12.00 5.50
❑ 7 Chris Osgood 12.00 5.50
❑ 8 Curtis Joseph 12.00 5.50
❑ 9 John Vanbiesbrouck 15.00 6.75
❑ 10 Andy Moog 10.00 4.50
❑ 11 Martin Brodeur 25.00 11.00
❑ 12 Tommy Salo 10.00 4.50
❑ 13 Mike Richter 12.00 5.50
❑ 14 Ron Hextall 10.00 4.50
❑ 15 Nikolai Khabibulin 10.00 4.50
❑ 16 Tom Barrasso 10.00 4.50
❑ 17 Grant Fuhr 10.00 4.50
❑ 18 Mike Vernon 10.00 4.50
❑ 19 Felix Potvin 10.00 4.50
❑ 20 Olaf Kolzig 10.00 4.50

## 1997-98 Revolution Team Checklist Laser Cuts

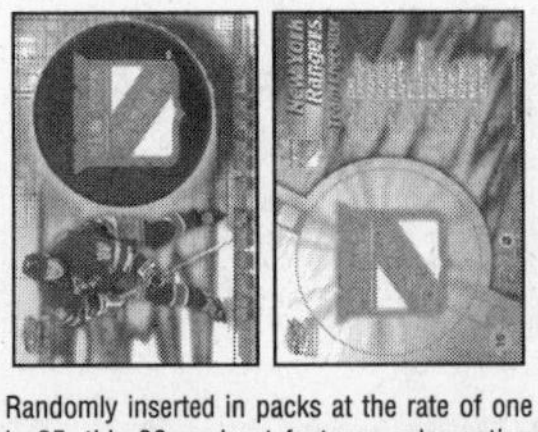

Randomly inserted in packs at the rate of one in 25, this 26-card set features color action photos of top players with his laser-cut team logo beside the player image. The backs carry a Revolution main set checklist.

| | MINT | NRMT |
|---|---|---|
| COMPLETE SET (26) | 300.00 | 135.00 |
| COMMON CARD (1-26) | 2.50 | 1.10 |

❑ 1 Paul Kariya 30.00 13.50
❑ 2 Joe Thornton 12.00 5.50
❑ 3 Michael Peca 6.00 2.70
❑ 4 Theoren Fleury 6.00 2.70
❑ 5 Keith Primeau 6.00 2.70
❑ 6 Chris Chelios 8.00 3.60
❑ 7 Patrick Roy 40.00 18.00
❑ 8 Mike Modano 10.00 4.50
❑ 9 Steve Yzerman 25.00 11.00
❑ 10 Ryan Smyth 6.00 2.70
❑ 11 John Vanbiesbrouck 12.00 5.50
❑ 12 Jozef Stumpel 6.00 2.70
❑ 13 Saku Koivu 12.00 5.50
❑ 14 Martin Brodeur 20.00 9.00
❑ 15 Zigmund Palffy 8.00 3.60
❑ 16 Wayne Gretzky 50.00 22.00
❑ 17 Daniel Alfredsson 6.00 2.70
❑ 18 Eric Lindros 25.00 11.00
❑ 19 Keith Tkachuk 10.00 4.50
❑ 20 Jaromir Jagr 25.00 11.00
❑ 21 Brett Hull 10.00 4.50
❑ 22 Mike Vernon 6.00 2.70
❑ 23 Rob Zamuner 2.50 1.10
❑ 24 Mats Sundin 8.00 3.60
❑ 25 Pavel Bure 15.00 6.75
❑ 26 Peter Bondra 8.00 3.60

## 1998-99 Revolution

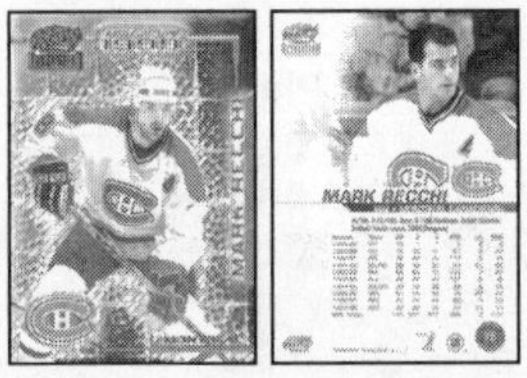

The 1998-99 Pacific Revolution set was issued in one series totalling 150 cards and distributed in three-card packs with a suggested retail price of $3.99. The set features color action player photos on dual-foiled, etched and embossed cards. The backs carry another player photos, biographical information, and career statistics.

| | MINT | NRMT |
|---|---|---|
| COMPLETE SET (150) | 150.00 | 70.00 |
| COMMON CARD (1-150) | .60 | .25 |

❑ 1 Guy Hebert 1.25 .55
❑ 2 Paul Kariya 6.00 2.70
❑ 3 Marty McInnis .60 .25
❑ 4 Steve Rucchin .60 .25
❑ 5 Teemu Selanne 3.00 1.35
❑ 6 Jason Allison 1.25 .55
❑ 7 Ray Bourque 1.50 .70
❑ 8 Anson Carter .60 .25
❑ 9 Byron Dafoe 1.25 .55
❑ 10 Dimitri Khristich .60 .25
❑ 11 Sergei Samsonov 2.50 1.10
❑ 12 Matthew Barnaby .60 .25
❑ 13 Michal Grosek .60 .25
❑ 14 Dominik Hasek 3.00 1.35
❑ 15 Michael Peca .60 .25
❑ 16 Miroslav Satan 1.25 .55
❑ 17 Dixon Ward .60 .25
❑ 18 Theoren Fleury 1.50 .70
❑ 19 Jean-Sebastien Giguere 1.25 .55
❑ 20 Jarome Iginla .60 .25
❑ 21 Tyler Moss .60 .25
❑ 22 Cory Stillman .60 .25
❑ 23 Ron Francis 1.25 .55
❑ 24 Arturs Irbe 1.25 .55
❑ 25 Trevor Kidd 1.25 .55
❑ 26 Keith Primeau 1.25 .55
❑ 27 Ray Sheppard .60 .25
❑ 28 Tony Amonte 1.25 .55
❑ 29 Chris Chelios 1.50 .70
❑ 30 Eric Daze .60 .25
❑ 31 Doug Gilmour 1.25 .55
❑ 32 Jocelyn Thibault 1.25 .55
❑ 33 Adam Deadmarsh 1.25 .55
❑ 34 Chris Drury 2.00 .90
❑ 35 Peter Forsberg 5.00 2.20
❑ 36 Milan Hejduk 5.00 2.20
❑ 37 Claude Lemieux 1.25 .55
❑ 38 Patrick Roy 8.00 3.60
❑ 39 Joe Sakic 3.00 1.35
❑ 40 Ed Belfour 1.50 .70
❑ 41 Brett Hull 2.00 .90
❑ 42 Jamie Langenbrunner .60 .25
❑ 43 Jere Lehtinen .60 .25
❑ 44 Mike Modano 2.00 .90
❑ 45 Joe Nieuwendyk 1.25 .55
❑ 46 Darryl Sydor .60 .25
❑ 47 Sergei Fedorov 3.00 1.35
❑ 48 Nicklas Lidstrom 1.25 .55
❑ 49 Norm Maracle 2.00 .90
❑ 50 Darren McCarty .60 .25
❑ 51 Chris Osgood 1.50 .70
❑ 52 Brendan Shanahan 3.00 1.35
❑ 53 Steve Yzerman 5.00 2.20
❑ 54 Bill Guerin 1.25 .55
❑ 55 Andrei Kovalenko .60 .25
❑ 56 Mikhail Shtalenkov .60 .25
❑ 57 Ryan Smyth 1.25 .55
❑ 58 Doug Weight 1.25 .55
❑ 59 Pavel Bure 3.00 1.35
❑ 60 Sean Burke .60 .25
❑ 61 Dino Ciccarelli 1.25 .55
❑ 62 Viktor Kozlov .60 .25
❑ 63 Rob Niedermayer .60 .25
❑ 64 Mark Parrish 5.00 2.20
❑ 65 Rob Blake 1.25 .55
❑ 66 Stephane Fiset 1.25 .55
❑ 67 Olli Jokinen .60 .25
❑ 68 Luc Robitaille 1.25 .55
❑ 69 Pavel Rosa .60 .25
❑ 70 Jozef Stumpel 1.25 .55
❑ 71 Shayne Corson .60 .25
❑ 72 Vincent Damphousse 1.25 .55
❑ 73 Jeff Hackett 1.25 .55
❑ 74 Saku Koivu 2.50 1.10
❑ 75 Mark Recchi 1.25 .55
❑ 76 Brian Savage .60 .25
❑ 77 Andrew Brunette .60 .25
❑ 78 Mike Dunham 1.25 .55
❑ 79 Sergei Krivokrasov .60 .25
❑ 80 Cliff Ronning .60 .25
❑ 81 Tomas Vokoun .60 .25
❑ 82 Jason Arnott 1.25 .55
❑ 83 Martin Brodeur 4.00 1.80
❑ 84 Patrik Elias 1.25 .55
❑ 85 Bobby Holik .60 .25
❑ 86 Brendan Morrison .60 .25
❑ 87 Kenny Jonsson .60 .25
❑ 88 Trevor Linden 1.25 .55
❑ 89 Zigmund Palffy 1.50 .70
❑ 90 Tommy Salo 1.25 .55
❑ 91 Mike Watt .60 .25
❑ 92 Wayne Gretzky 10.00 4.50
❑ 93 Todd Harvey .60 .25
❑ 94 Brian Leetch 1.50 .70
❑ 95 Manny Malhotra .60 .25
❑ 96 Petr Nedved 1.25 .55
❑ 97 Mike Richter 1.50 .70
❑ 98 Daniel Alfredsson 1.25 .55
❑ 99 Marian Hossa 1.25 .55
❑ 100 Shawn McEachern .60 .25
❑ 101 Damian Rhodes 1.25 .55
❑ 102 Alexei Yashin 1.25 .55
❑ 103 Rod Brind'Amour 1.25 .55
❑ 104 Ron Hextall 1.25 .55
❑ 105 John LeClair 2.50 1.10
❑ 106 Eric Lindros 5.00 2.20
❑ 107 John Vanbiesbrouck 2.50 1.10
❑ 108 Dainius Zubrus .60 .25
❑ 109 Daniel Briere .60 .25
❑ 110 Nikolai Khabibulin 1.25 .55
❑ 111 Jeremy Roenick 1.50 .70
❑ 112 Keith Tkachuk 2.00 .90
❑ 113 Rick Tocchet 1.25 .55
❑ 114 Jim Waite 1.25 .55
❑ 115 Jean-Sebastien Aubin .60 .25
❑ 116 Stu Barnes .60 .25
❑ 117 Tom Barrasso 1.25 .55
❑ 118 Jaromir Jagr 5.00 2.20
❑ 119 Alexei Kovalev .60 .25
❑ 120 Martin Straka .60 .25
❑ 121 Pavol Demitra 1.25 .55
❑ 122 Grant Fuhr 1.25 .55
❑ 123 Al MacInnis 1.25 .55
❑ 124 Chris Pronger 1.25 .55
❑ 125 Pierre Turgeon 1.25 .55
❑ 126 Jeff Friesen 1.25 .55
❑ 127 Patrick Marleau .60 .25
❑ 128 Owen Nolan 1.25 .55
❑ 129 Marco Sturm .60 .25
❑ 130 Mike Vernon 1.25 .55
❑ 131 Wendel Clark 1.25 .55
❑ 132 Daren Puppa 1.25 .55
❑ 133 Vincent Lecavalier 4.00 1.80
❑ 134 Stephane Richer 1.25 .55
❑ 135 Rob Zamuner .60 .25
❑ 136 Tie Domi .60 .25
❑ 137 Mike Johnson .60 .25
❑ 138 Curtis Joseph 1.50 .70
❑ 139 Tomas Kaberle .60 .25
❑ 140 Mats Sundin 1.50 .70
❑ 141 Mark Messier 2.00 .90
❑ 142 Alexander Mogilny 1.25 .55
❑ 143 Bill Muckalt 4.00 1.80
❑ 144 Mattias Ohlund 1.25 .55
❑ 145 Garth Snow 1.25 .55
❑ 146 Peter Bondra 1.50 .70
❑ 147 Joe Juneau 1.25 .55
❑ 148 Olaf Kolzig 1.25 .55
❑ 149 Adam Oates 1.25 .55
❑ 150 Richard Zednik .60 .25

## 1998-99 Revolution Ice Shadow

Randomly inserted into hobby packs only, this 150-card set is a limited blue foil hobby parallel version of the base set. Only 99 serial-numbered sets were made.

| | MINT | NRMT |
|---|---|---|
| COMMON CARD (1-150) | 20.00 | 9.00 |

*STARS: 15X TO 40X BASIC CARDS
*YOUNG STARS: 12.5X TO 30X
*RC's: 8X TO 20X

## 1998-99 Revolution Red

Randomly inserted into retail packs only, this 150-card set is a red foil retail parallel version of the base set. Only 299 serial-numbered sets were made.

| | MINT | NRMT |
|---|---|---|
| COMPLETE SET (150) | 1000.00 | 450.00 |

| | | |
|---|---|---|
| COMMON CARD (1-150) | 4.00 | 1.80 |

*STARS: 3X TO 6X BASIC CARDS
*YOUNG STARS: 2X TO 4X
*RC's: 1.5X TO 3X

## 1998-99 Revolution All-Star Die Cuts

Randomly inserted in packs at the rate of one in 25, this 30-card set features color images of players from the 1999 World and North America All-Star teams printed on full-foil die-cut cards with a jagged star design at the top.

| | MINT | NRMT |
|---|---|---|
| COMPLETE SET (30) | 350.00 | 160.00 |
| COMMON CARD (1-30) | 3.00 | 1.35 |
| ❑ 1 Tony Amonte | 6.00 | 2.70 |
| ❑ 2 Ed Belfour | 8.00 | 3.60 |
| ❑ 3 Peter Bondra | 8.00 | 3.60 |
| ❑ 4 Ray Bourque | 8.00 | 3.60 |
| ❑ 5 Martin Brodeur | 20.00 | 9.00 |
| ❑ 6 Theoren Fleury | 8.00 | 3.60 |
| ❑ 7 Peter Forsberg | 25.00 | 11.00 |
| ❑ 8 Wayne Gretzky | 50.00 | 22.00 |
| ❑ 9 Dominik Hasek | 15.00 | 6.75 |
| ❑ 10 Bobby Holik | 3.00 | 1.35 |
| ❑ 11 Arturs Irbe | 6.00 | 2.70 |
| ❑ 12 Jaromir Jagr | 25.00 | 11.00 |
| ❑ 13 Paul Kariya | 30.00 | 13.50 |
| ❑ 14 Nikolai Khabibulin | 6.00 | 2.70 |
| ❑ 15 Sergei Krivokrasov | 3.00 | 1.35 |
| ❑ 16 John LeClair | 12.00 | 5.50 |
| ❑ 17 Nicklas Lidstrom | 6.00 | 2.70 |
| ❑ 18 Eric Lindros | 25.00 | 11.00 |
| ❑ 19 Al MacInnis | 6.00 | 2.70 |
| ❑ 20 Mike Modano | 10.00 | 4.50 |
| ❑ 21 Mattias Ohlund | 6.00 | 2.70 |
| ❑ 22 Keith Primeau | 6.00 | 2.70 |
| ❑ 23 Chris Pronger | 6.00 | 2.70 |
| ❑ 24 Mark Recchi | 6.00 | 2.70 |
| ❑ 25 Jeremy Roenick | 8.00 | 3.60 |
| ❑ 26 Teemu Selanne | 15.00 | 6.75 |
| ❑ 27 Brendan Shanahan | 15.00 | 6.75 |
| ❑ 28 Mats Sundin | 8.00 | 3.60 |
| ❑ 29 Keith Tkachuk | 10.00 | 4.50 |
| ❑ 30 Steve Yzerman | 25.00 | 11.00 |

## 1998-99 Revolution Chalk Talk Laser-Cuts

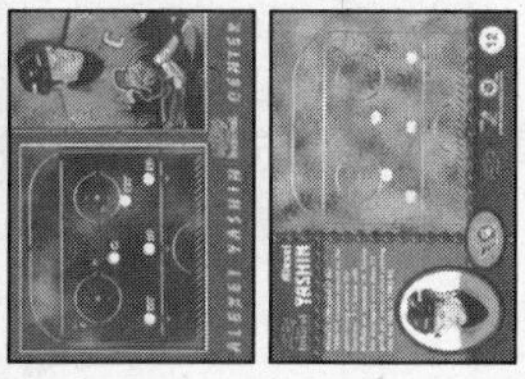

Randomly inserted into packs at the rate of one in 49, this 20-card set features color action player photos printed on full-foil horizontal cards alongside plays diagramed on a laser cut chalkboard.

| | MINT | NRMT |
|---|---|---|
| COMPLETE SET (20) | 250.00 | 110.00 |
| COMMON CARD (1-20) | 5.00 | 2.20 |
| ❑ 1 Paul Kariya | 25.00 | 11.00 |
| ❑ 2 Teemu Selanne | 12.00 | 5.50 |
| ❑ 3 Theoren Fleury | 6.00 | 2.70 |
| ❑ 4 Peter Forsberg | 20.00 | 9.00 |
| ❑ 5 Joe Sakic | 12.00 | 5.50 |
| ❑ 6 Brett Hull | 8.00 | 3.60 |
| ❑ 7 Mike Modano | 8.00 | 3.60 |
| ❑ 8 Sergei Fedorov | 12.00 | 5.50 |
| ❑ 9 Brendan Shanahan | 12.00 | 5.50 |
| ❑ 10 Steve Yzerman | 20.00 | 9.00 |
| ❑ 11 Wayne Gretzky | 40.00 | 18.00 |
| ❑ 12 Alexei Yashin | | |
| ❑ 13 John LeClair | 10.00 | 4.50 |
| ❑ 14 Eric Lindros | 20.00 | 9.00 |
| ❑ 15 Keith Tkachuk | 8.00 | 3.60 |
| ❑ 16 Jaromir Jagr | 20.00 | 9.00 |
| ❑ 17 Vincent Lecavalier | 15.00 | 6.75 |
| ❑ 18 Mats Sundin | 6.00 | 2.70 |
| ❑ 19 Mark Messier | 8.00 | 3.60 |
| ❑ 20 Peter Bondra | 6.00 | 2.70 |

## 1998-99 Revolution NHL Icons

Randomly inserted into packs at the rate of one in 121, this 10-card set features color images of some of the most renown players in hockey printed on die-cut silver foil cards.

| | MINT | NRMT |
|---|---|---|
| COMPLETE SET (10) | 500.00 | 220.00 |
| COMMON CARD (1-10) | 20.00 | 9.00 |
| ❑ 1 Paul Kariya | 60.00 | 27.00 |
| ❑ 2 Dominik Hasek | 30.00 | 13.50 |
| ❑ 3 Peter Forsberg | 50.00 | 22.00 |
| ❑ 4 Patrick Roy | 80.00 | 36.00 |
| ❑ 5 Mike Modano | 20.00 | 9.00 |
| ❑ 6 Steve Yzerman | 50.00 | 22.00 |
| ❑ 7 Martin Brodeur | 40.00 | 18.00 |
| ❑ 8 Wayne Gretzky | 100.00 | 45.00 |
| ❑ 9 Eric Lindros | 50.00 | 22.00 |
| ❑ 10 Jaromir Jagr | 50.00 | 22.00 |

## 1998-99 Revolution Showstoppers

Randomly inserted into packs at the rate of two in 25, this 36-card set features color action photos of players known for their game-winning heroics printed on holographic silver foil cards.

| | MINT | NRMT |
|---|---|---|
| COMPLETE SET (36) | 250.00 | 110.00 |
| COMMON CARD (1-36) | 3.00 | 1.35 |
| ❑ 1 Paul Kariya | 15.00 | 6.75 |
| ❑ 2 Teemu Selanne | 8.00 | 3.60 |
| ❑ 3 Ray Bourque | 4.00 | 1.80 |
| ❑ 4 Dominik Hasek | 8.00 | 3.60 |
| ❑ 5 Michael Peca | 3.00 | 1.35 |
| ❑ 6 Theoren Fleury | 4.00 | 1.80 |
| ❑ 7 Tony Amonte | 3.00 | 1.35 |
| ❑ 8 Chris Chelios | 4.00 | 1.80 |
| ❑ 9 Doug Gilmour | 4.00 | 1.80 |
| ❑ 10 Peter Forsberg | 12.00 | 5.50 |
| ❑ 11 Patrick Roy | 20.00 | 9.00 |
| ❑ 12 Joe Sakic | 8.00 | 3.60 |
| ❑ 13 Ed Belfour | 4.00 | 1.80 |
| ❑ 14 Brett Hull | 5.00 | 2.20 |
| ❑ 15 Mike Modano | 5.00 | 2.20 |
| ❑ 16 Sergei Fedorov | 8.00 | 3.60 |
| ❑ 17 Brendan Shanahan | 8.00 | 3.60 |
| ❑ 18 Steve Yzerman | 12.00 | 5.50 |
| ❑ 19 Mark Parrish | 10.00 | 4.50 |
| ❑ 20 Saku Koivu | 6.00 | 2.70 |
| ❑ 21 Martin Brodeur | 10.00 | 4.50 |
| ❑ 22 Zigmund Palffy | 4.00 | 1.80 |
| ❑ 23 Wayne Gretzky | 25.00 | 11.00 |
| ❑ 24 Alexei Yashin | 3.00 | 1.35 |
| ❑ 25 John LeClair | 6.00 | 2.70 |
| ❑ 26 Eric Lindros | 12.00 | 5.50 |
| ❑ 27 John Vanbiesbrouck | 6.00 | 2.70 |
| ❑ 28 Nikolai Khabibulin | 3.00 | 1.35 |
| ❑ 29 Jeremy Roenick | 4.00 | 1.80 |
| ❑ 30 Keith Tkachuk | 5.00 | 2.20 |
| ❑ 31 Jaromir Jagr | 12.00 | 5.50 |
| ❑ 32 Vincent Lecavalier | 10.00 | 4.50 |
| ❑ 33 Curtis Joseph | 4.00 | 1.80 |
| ❑ 34 Mats Sundin | 4.00 | 1.80 |
| ❑ 35 Mark Messier | 5.00 | 2.20 |
| ❑ 36 Peter Bondra | 4.00 | 1.80 |

## 1998-99 Revolution Three Pronged Attack

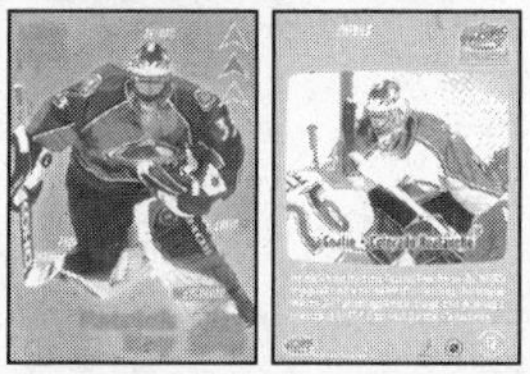

Randomly inserted into hobby packs only at the rate of four in 25, this 30-card set features color action photos of some of the NHL's top players. A parallel version of this set was also produced and inserted only in hobby packs. The parallel consists of three separate tiers of 10 cards each with each tier serially numbered in varying amounts. Only 99 serial-numbered Tier 1 (cards #1-10) sets were made; 199 Tier 2 (11-20) serial-numbered sets were made; and 299 serial-numbered Tier 3 (21-30) sets were produced.

| | MINT | NRMT |
|---|---|---|
| COMPLETE SET (30) | 120.00 | 55.00 |
| COMMON CARD (1-30) | 1.50 | .70 |

*TIER 1 STARS: 12.5X TO 25X HI COLUMN
*TIER 2 STARS: 6X TO 12X HI
*TIER 3 STARS: 4X TO 8X HI
TIER 1 (1-10), 99 SERIAL #'d SETS
TIER 2 (11-20), 199 SERIAL #'d SETS
TIER 3 (21-30), 299 SERIAL #'d SETS
TIER 1,2,3 RANDOM INSERTS IN PACKS

| | | |
|---|---|---|
| ❑ 1 Matthew Barnaby | 1.50 | .70 |
| ❑ 2 Theo Fleury | 2.50 | 1.10 |
| ❑ 3 Chris Chelios | 2.50 | 1.10 |
| ❑ 4 Darren McCarty | 1.50 | .70 |
| ❑ 5 Brendan Shanahan | 5.00 | 2.20 |
| ❑ 6 Eric Lindros | 8.00 | 3.60 |
| ❑ 7 Keith Tkachuk | 3.00 | 1.35 |
| ❑ 8 Tony Twist | 1.50 | .70 |
| ❑ 9 Tie Domi | 1.50 | .70 |
| ❑ 10 Donald Brashear | 1.50 | .70 |
| ❑ 11 Dominik Hasek | 5.00 | 2.20 |
| ❑ 12 Patrick Roy | 12.00 | 5.50 |
| ❑ 13 Ed Belfour | 2.50 | 1.10 |
| ❑ 14 Chris Osgood | 2.50 | 1.10 |
| ❑ 15 Martin Brodeur | 6.00 | 2.70 |
| ❑ 16 Mike Richter | 2.50 | 1.10 |
| ❑ 17 John Vanbiesbrouck | 4.00 | 1.80 |
| ❑ 18 Nikolai Khabibulin | 2.00 | .90 |
| ❑ 19 Curtis Joseph | 2.50 | 1.10 |
| ❑ 20 Olaf Kolzig | 2.00 | .90 |
| ❑ 21 Paul Kariya | 10.00 | 4.50 |
| ❑ 22 Teemu Selanne | 5.00 | 2.20 |
| ❑ 23 Peter Forsberg | 8.00 | 3.60 |
| ❑ 24 Joe Sakic | 5.00 | 2.20 |
| ❑ 25 Mike Modano | 1.50 | .70 |
| ❑ 26 Steve Yzerman | 8.00 | 3.60 |
| ❑ 27 Wayne Gretzky | 15.00 | 6.75 |
| ❑ 28 John LeClair | 4.00 | 1.80 |
| ❑ 29 Jaromir Jagr | 8.00 | 3.60 |
| ❑ 30 Pavel Bure | 5.00 | 2.20 |

## 1975-76 Roadrunners Phoenix WHA

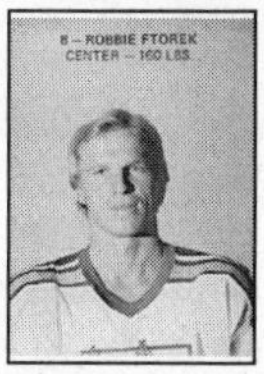

This 22-card set features players of the WHA Phoenix Roadrunners. The cards measure approximately 3" by 4" and the backs are blank. The front features a poor quality black and white head-and-shoulders shot of the player with a white border. The cards are numbered by the uniform number on the front and we have checklisted them below accordingly. The player's position and weight are also given.

| | NRMT-MT | EXC |
|---|---|---|
| COMPLETE SET (22) | 20.00 | 9.00 |
| COMMON CARD | 1.00 | .45 |
| ❑ 1 Gary Kurt | 1.50 | .70 |
| ❑ 2 Jim Niekamp | 1.00 | .45 |
| ❑ 3 Al McLeod | 1.50 | .70 |
| ❑ 4 Garry Lariviere | 1.50 | .70 |
| ❑ 5 Serge Beaudoin | 1.00 | .45 |
| ❑ 6 Ron Serafini | 1.00 | .45 |
| ❑ 7 Peter McNamee | 1.00 | .45 |
| ❑ 8 Robbie Ftorek | 3.00 | 1.35 |
| ❑ 9 Del Hall | 1.00 | .45 |
| ❑ 10 Dave Gorman | 1.00 | .45 |
| ❑ 11 Murray Keogan | 1.00 | .45 |
| ❑ 12 Ron Huston | 1.00 | .45 |
| ❑ 14 Jim Boyd | 1.00 | .45 |
| ❑ 15 John Gray | 1.00 | .45 |
| ❑ 16 Michel Cormier | 1.00 | .45 |
| ❑ 17 Cam Connor | 1.50 | .70 |
| ❑ 18 John Migneault | 1.00 | .45 |
| ❑ 19 Pekka Rautakallio | 1.50 | .70 |
| ❑ 21 Barry Dean | 1.00 | .45 |
| ❑ 24 Lauri Mononen | 1.00 | .45 |
| ❑ 26 Jim Clarke | 1.00 | .45 |
| ❑ 30 Jack Norris | 1.50 | .70 |

## 1976-77 Roadrunners Phoenix WHA

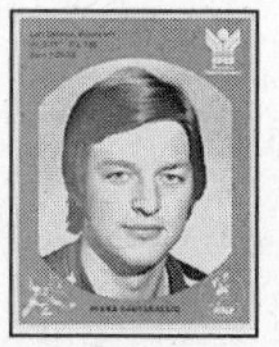

This 18-card set features players of the WHA Phoenix Roadrunners. Each card measures approximately 3 3/8" by 4 5/16". The front features a black and white head shot of the player, enframed by an aqua blue border on white card stock. The top and bottom inner borders are curved, creating space for the basic biographical information as well as the team and league logos that surround the picture. The backs are blank. The cards are unnumbered and we have checklisted them below in alphabetical order.

| | NRMT-MT | EXC |
|---|---|---|
| COMPLETE SET (18) | 18.00 | 8.00 |
| COMMON CARD (1-18) | 1.00 | .45 |
| ❑ 1 Serge Beaudoin | 1.00 | .45 |
| ❑ 2 Michel Cormier | 1.00 | .45 |
| ❑ 3 Robbie Ftorek | 3.00 | 1.35 |
| ❑ 4 Del Hall | 1.00 | .45 |
| ❑ 5 Clay Hebenton | 1.00 | .45 |
| ❑ 6 Andre Hinse | 1.00 | .45 |
| ❑ 7 Mike Hobin | 1.00 | .45 |
| ❑ 8 Frank Hughes | 1.00 | .45 |
| ❑ 9 Ron Huston | 1.00 | .45 |
| ❑ 10 Gary Kurt | 1.50 | .70 |
| ❑ 11 Garry Lariviere | 1.50 | .70 |
| ❑ 12 Bob Liddington | 1.00 | .45 |
| ❑ 13 Lauri Mononen | 1.00 | .45 |
| ❑ 14 Jim Niekamp | 1.00 | .45 |
| ❑ 15 Pekka Rautakallio | 1.50 | .70 |
| ❑ 16 Seppo Repo | 1.00 | .45 |
| ❑ 17 Jerry Rollins | 1.00 | .45 |
| ❑ 18 Juhani Tamminen | 1.50 | .70 |

## 1976-77 Rockies Puck Bucks

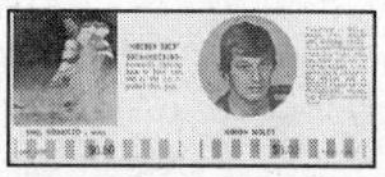

This 20-card set measures approximately 2 9/16" by 2 1/8" (after perforation) and features members of the then-expansion Colorado Rockies team. The set was issued in the Greater Denver area as part of a regional promotion for the Rockies. The cards feature a horizontal format on the front which has the player's photo. The cards were issued two to a panel (they could be separated, but then one couldn't compete in contest). Left side and right side in the rules refers to the two different cards that were joined: an action scene on the left side and a posed head shot in a circle on the right side). If the same player appeared in the action scene and in the circle, and if the ticket values and the color bars below both pictures matched, the contestant became an instant winner of two Colorado Rockies' hockey tickets, whose value is shown in the color bar. One could also save all player pictures until one had the same player appearing in the action scene and in the circle both with matching ticket values and matching color bars. The color bars at the bottom appeared in four different colors (yellow, blue, green, or orange). The cards feature either a "Play Puck Bucks" logo on the back, which also features a skeletal-like picture of a player, or a rules definition. Winners had to claim prizes by February 20, 1977. Since there is no numerical designation for the cards, they are checklisted alphabetically below.

| | NRMT-MT | EXC |
|---|---|---|
| COMPLETE SET (20) | 60.00 | 27.00 |
| COMMON CARD (1-20) | 3.00 | 1.35 |
| ❑ 1 Ron Andruff | 3.00 | 1.35 |
| ❑ 2 Chuck Arnason | 3.00 | 1.35 |
| ❑ 3 Henry Boucha | 4.00 | 1.80 |
| ❑ 4 Colin Campbell | 5.00 | 2.20 |
| ❑ 5 Gary Croteau | 3.00 | 1.35 |
| ❑ 6 Guy Delparte | 3.00 | 1.35 |
| ❑ 7 Steve Durbano | 4.00 | 1.80 |
| ❑ 8 Tom Edur | 3.00 | 1.35 |
| ❑ 9 Doug Favell | 5.00 | 2.20 |
| ❑ 10 Dave Hudson | 3.00 | 1.35 |
| ❑ 11 Bryan Lefley | 3.00 | 1.35 |
| ❑ 12 Roger Lemelin | 3.00 | 1.35 |
| ❑ 13 Simon Nolet | 3.00 | 1.35 |
| ❑ 14 Wilf Paiement | 4.00 | 1.80 |
| ❑ 15 Michel Plasse | 5.00 | 2.20 |
| ❑ 16 Tracy Pratt | 3.00 | 1.35 |
| ❑ 17 Nelson Pyatt | 3.00 | 1.35 |
| ❑ 18 Phil Roberto | 3.00 | 1.35 |
| ❑ 19 Sean Shanahan | 3.00 | 1.35 |
| ❑ 20 Larry Skinner | 3.00 | 1.35 |

## 1979-80 Rockies

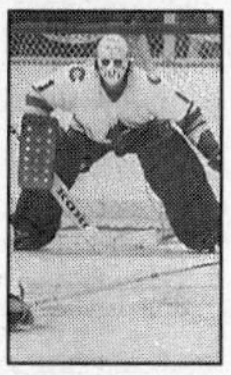

This 23-card set of the Colorado Rockies measures approximately 4" by 6". The fronts feature black-and-white action player phots. The backs are blank. The cards are unnumbered and checklisted below in alphabetical order.

| | NRMT-MT | EXC |
|---|---|---|
| COMPLETE SET (23) | 40.00 | 18.00 |
| COMMON CARD (1-23) | 1.50 | .70 |
| ❑ 1 Hardy Astrom | 3.00 | 1.35 |
| ❑ 2 Doug Berry | 1.50 | .70 |
| ❑ 3 Nick Beverley | 2.00 | .90 |
| ❑ 4 Mike Christie | 1.50 | .70 |
| ❑ 5 Gary Croteau | 2.00 | .90 |
| ❑ 6 Lucien Deblois | 2.00 | .90 |
| ❑ 7 Ron Delorme | 1.50 | .70 |
| ❑ 8 Mike Gillis | 1.50 | .70 |
| ❑ 9 Trevor Johansen | 1.50 | .70 |
| ❑ 10 Mike Kitchen | 1.50 | .70 |
| ❑ 11 Lanny McDonald | 5.00 | 2.20 |
| ❑ 12 Mike McEwen | 1.50 | .70 |
| ❑ 13 Bill McKenzie | 1.50 | .70 |
| ❑ 14 Kevin Morrison | 1.50 | .70 |
| ❑ 15 Bill Olesehuk | 1.50 | .70 |
| ❑ 16 Randy Pierce | 1.50 | .70 |
| ❑ 17 Michel Plasse | 3.00 | 1.35 |
| ❑ 18 Joel Quenneville | 2.00 | .90 |
| ❑ 19 Rob Ramage | 5.00 | 2.20 |
| ❑ 20 Rene Robert | 2.00 | .90 |
| ❑ 21 Don Saleski | 2.00 | .90 |
| ❑ 22 Barry Smith | 2.00 | .90 |
| ❑ 23 Jack Valiquette | 1.50 | .70 |

## 1981-82 Rockies Postcards

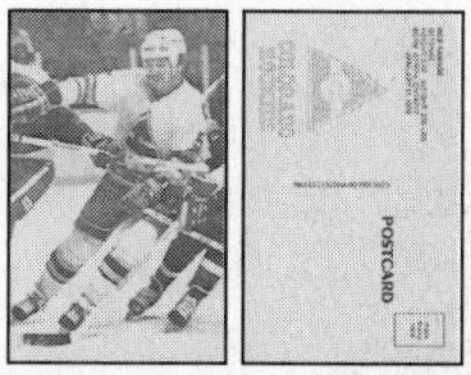

This 30-card postcard set measures 3 1/2" by 5 1/2" and features borderless black-and-white action player photos of the Colorado Rockies. The backs have the standard white postcard design with the player's name and biographical information in the upper left corner. The team emblem is printed in light gray on the left side. The cards are unnumbered and checklisted below in alphabetical order.

| | NRMT-MT | EXC |
|---|---|---|
| COMPLETE SET (30) | 35.00 | 16.00 |
| COMMON CARD (1-30) | 1.00 | .45 |
| ❑ 1 Brent Ashton | 2.00 | .90 |
| ❑ 2 Aaron Broten | 1.00 | .45 |
| ❑ 3 Dave Cameron | 1.00 | .45 |
| ❑ 4 Joe Cirella | 2.00 | .90 |
| ❑ 5 Dwight Foster | 1.00 | .45 |
| ❑ 6 Paul Gagne | 1.00 | .45 |
| ❑ 7 Marshall Johnston CO | 1.00 | .45 |
| ❑ 8 Veli-Pekka Ketola | 1.50 | .70 |
| ❑ 9 Mike Kitchen | 1.00 | .45 |
| ❑ 10 Rick Laferriere | 1.00 | .45 |
| ❑ 11 Don Lever | 1.50 | .70 |
| ❑ 12 Tapio Levo | 1.00 | .45 |
| ❑ 13 Bob Lorimer | 1.00 | .45 |
| ❑ 14 Bill MacMillan | 1.00 | .45 |
| ❑ 15 Bob MacMillan VP | 1.50 | .70 |
| ❑ 16 Merlin Malinowski | 1.50 | .70 |
| ❑ 17 Bert Marshall GM | 1.00 | .45 |
| ❑ 18 Kevin Maxwell | 1.00 | .45 |
| ❑ 19 Joe Micheletti | 2.00 | .90 |
| ❑ 20 Bobby Miller | 1.00 | .45 |
| ❑ 21 Phil Myre | 2.00 | .90 |
| ❑ 22 Graeme Nicolson | 1.00 | .45 |
| ❑ 23 Jukka Porvari | 1.00 | .45 |
| ❑ 24 Joel Quenneville | 1.50 | .70 |
| ❑ 25 Rob Ramage | 3.00 | 1.35 |
| ❑ 26 Glenn Resch | 3.00 | 1.35 |
| ❑ 27 Steve Tambellini | 1.50 | .70 |
| ❑ 28 Yvon Vautour | 1.00 | .45 |
| ❑ 29 John Wensink | 1.50 | .70 |
| ❑ 30 Title Card (Team logo) | 2.00 | .90 |

## 1952 Royal Desserts Hockey

The 1952 Royal Desserts Hockey set contains eight cards. The cards measure approximately 2 5/8" by 3 1/4". The set is cataloged as F219-2. The cards formed the backs of Royal Desserts packages of the period; consequently many cards are found with uneven edges stemming from the method of cutting the cards off the box. Each card has its number and the statement "Royal Stars of Hockey" in a red rectangle at the top. The blue tinted picture also features a facsimile autograph of the player. An album was presumably available as it is advertised on the card. The exact year (or years) of issue of these cards is not verified at this time.

| | EX-MT | VG-E |
|---|---|---|
| COMPLETE SET (8) | 12000.00 | 5400.00 |
| COMMON CARD (1-8) | 500.00 | 220.00 |
| ❑ 1 Tony Leswick | 500.00 | 220.00 |
| ❑ 2 Chuck Rayner | 750.00 | 350.00 |
| ❑ 3 Edgar Laprade | 600.00 | 275.00 |
| ❑ 4 Sid Abel | 1000.00 | 450.00 |
| ❑ 5 Ted Lindsay | 1000.00 | 450.00 |
| ❑ 6 Leo Reise | 500.00 | 220.00 |
| ❑ 7 Red Kelly | 1000.00 | 450.00 |
| ❑ 8 Gordie Howe | 7500.00 | 3400.00 |

## 1971-72 Sabres Postcards

These standard sized postcards feature borderless color photos. Backs feature players name, position, uniform number, and biographical information. These postcards were issued in a binder with perforated top edges so as to be torn out of the binder. Checklist below may be incomplete. Please forward any information pertaining to this set to Beckett Publications. The postcards are unnumbered and checklisted below in alphabetical order.

| | MINT | NRMT |
|---|---|---|
| COMPLETE SET (21) | 30.00 | 13.50 |
| COMMON CARD | 1.00 | .45 |

| | | |
|---|---|---|
| ❑ 1 Ron Anderson | 1.00 | .45 |
| ❑ 2 Steve Atkinson | 1.00 | .45 |
| ❑ 3 Doug Barrie | 1.00 | .45 |
| ❑ 4 Roger Crozier | 1.00 | .45 |
| ❑ 5 Dave Dryden | 1.50 | .70 |
| ❑ 6 Dick Duff | 1.00 | .45 |
| ❑ 7 Phil Goyette | 1.00 | .45 |
| ❑ 8 Punch Imlach CO | 2.00 | .90 |
| ❑ 9 Danny Lawson | 1.00 | .45 |
| ❑ 10 Jim Lorentz | 1.00 | .45 |
| ❑ 11 Richard Martin | 3.00 | 1.35 |
| ❑ 12 Randy McKay | 1.00 | .45 |
| ❑ 13 Gerry Meehan | 1.00 | .45 |
| ❑ 14 Kevin O'Shea | 1.00 | .45 |
| ❑ 15 Gil Perreault | 8.00 | 3.60 |
| ❑ 16 Tracy Pratt | 1.00 | .45 |
| ❑ 17 Mike Robitaille | 1.00 | .45 |
| ❑ 18 Eddie Shack | 2.00 | .90 |
| ❑ 19 Floyd Smith | 1.00 | .45 |
| ❑ 20 Jim Watson | 1.00 | .45 |
| ❑ 21 Rod Zaine | 1.00 | .45 |

## 1972-73 Sabres Pepsi Pinback Buttons

| | MINT | NRMT |
|---|---|---|
| COMPLETE SET (9) | 40.00 | 18.00 |
| COMMON PIN | 4.00 | 1.80 |
| ❑ 1 Roger Crozier | 4.00 | 1.80 |
| ❑ 2 Don Luce | 4.00 | 1.80 |
| ❑ 3 Rick Martin (action) | 4.00 | 1.80 |
| ❑ 4 Rick Martin (head) | 4.00 | 1.80 |
| ❑ 5 Gilbert Perreault (action) | 6.00 | 2.70 |
| ❑ 6 Gilbert Perreault (head) | 6.00 | 2.70 |
| ❑ 7 Rene Robert | 4.00 | 1.80 |
| ❑ 8 Jim Schoenfeld | 4.00 | 1.80 |
| ❑ 9 French Connection | 4.00 | 1.80 |

## 1973-74 Sabres Bells

This set of four photos of Buffalo Sabres players was sponsored by Bells Markets. The photos measure approximately 3 15/16" by 5 1/2". The front has a color action photo. These blank-backed cards are unnumbered and listed alphabetically in the checklist below.

| | NRMT-MT | EXC |
|---|---|---|
| COMPLETE SET (4) | 25.00 | 11.00 |
| COMMON CARD (1-4) | 5.00 | 2.20 |
| ❑ 1 Roger Crozier | 8.00 | 3.60 |
| ❑ 2 Jim Lorentz | 5.00 | 2.20 |
| ❑ 3 Richard Martin | 8.00 | 3.60 |
| ❑ 4 Gilbert Perreault | 12.00 | 5.50 |

## 1973-74 Sabres Postcards

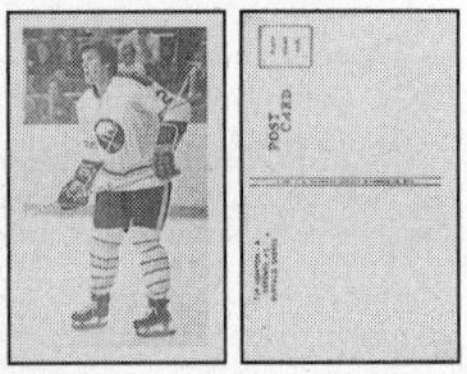

This 13-card set was published by Robert B. Shaver of Kenmore, New York. The cards are in the postcard format and measure approximately 3 1/2" by 5 1/2". The fronts feature a black-and-white action shot with white borders. The backs carry the player's name, position, and team name at the upper left and are divided in the middle. The set is dated by the inclusion of Joe Noris, who played with the Sabres only during the 1973-74 season. The cards are unnumbered and checklisted below in alphabetical order.

| | NRMT-MT | EXC |
|---|---|---|
| COMPLETE SET (13) | 40.00 | 18.00 |
| COMMON CARD (1-13) | 2.00 | .90 |
| ❑ 1 Roger Crozier | 4.00 | 1.80 |
| ❑ 2 Dave Dryden | 4.00 | 1.80 |
| ❑ 3 Tim Horton | 8.00 | 3.60 |
| ❑ 4 Jim Lorentz | 2.00 | .90 |
| ❑ 5 Don Luce | 2.50 | 1.10 |
| ❑ 6 Rick Martin | 4.00 | 1.80 |
| ❑ 7 Gerry Meehan | 3.00 | 1.35 |
| ❑ 8 Larry Mickey | 2.00 | .90 |
| ❑ 9 Joe Noris | 2.00 | .90 |
| ❑ 10 Gilbert Perreault | 8.00 | 3.60 |
| ❑ 11 Mike Robitaille | 2.00 | .90 |
| ❑ 12 Jim Schoenfeld | 4.00 | 1.80 |
| ❑ 13 Paul Terbenche | 2.00 | .90 |

## 1976-77 Sabres Glasses

Glasses feature a black and white portrait of the player. Glasses were available at Your Host restaurants.

| | MINT | NRMT |
|---|---|---|
| COMPLETE SET (4) | 25.00 | 11.00 |
| COMMON GLASS | 6.00 | 2.70 |
| ❑ 1 Jerry Korab | 6.00 | 2.70 |
| ❑ 2 Rick Martin | 6.00 | 2.70 |
| ❑ 3 Gilbert Perreault | 8.00 | 3.60 |
| ❑ 4 Jim Schoenfeld | 6.00 | 2.70 |

## 1979-80 Sabres Bells

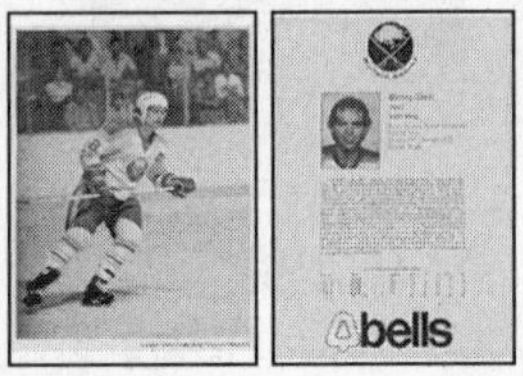

This set of nine photos of Buffalo Sabres players was sponsored by Bells Markets. The photos measure approximately 7 5/8" by 10". The front has a color action photo, with the player's name and team name in the white border at the lower right hand corner. The back is printed in blue and has the Sabres' logo, a head shot of the player, biographical information, and career statistics.

| | NRMT-MT | EXC |
|---|---|---|
| COMPLETE SET (9) | 20.00 | 9.00 |
| COMMON CARD (1-9) | 2.00 | .90 |
| ❑ 1 Don Edwards | 4.00 | 1.80 |
| ❑ 2 Danny Gare | 2.50 | 1.10 |
| ❑ 3 Jerry Korab | 2.00 | .90 |
| ❑ 4 Richard Martin | 4.00 | 1.80 |
| ❑ 5 Tony McKegney | 2.50 | 1.10 |
| ❑ 6 Craig Ramsay | 2.00 | .90 |
| ❑ 7 Bob Sauve | 4.00 | 1.80 |
| ❑ 8 Jim Schoenfeld | 3.00 | 1.35 |
| ❑ 9 John Van Boxmeer | 2.00 | .90 |

## 1979-80 Sabres Milk Panels

| | MINT | NRMT |
|---|---|---|
| COMPLETE SET (4) | 6.00 | 2.70 |
| COMMON CARD (1-4) | 1.00 | .45 |
| ❑ 1 Don Edwards | 1.00 | .45 |
| ❑ 2 Ric Seiling | 1.00 | .45 |
| ❑ 3 Jerry Korab | 1.50 | .70 |
| ❑ 4 Gil Perreault | 2.50 | 1.10 |

## 1980-81 Sabres Milk Panels

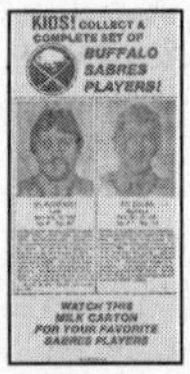

This set of Buffalo Sabres was issued on the side of half gallon milk cartons. After cutting, the panels measure approximately 3 3/4" by 7 1/2", with two players per panel. The picture and text of the player panels are printed in red; the set can also be found in blue print. The top of the panel reads "Kids, Collect a Complete Set of Buffalo Sabres Players". Arranged alongside each other, the panel features for each player a head shot, biographical information, and player profile. The panels are subtly dated and numbered below the photo area in the following way, Perreault/Seiling is M325-80-4H (M325 is the product code, the number 80 gives the last two digits of the year, and 4 is the card number perhaps also indicating release week).

| | NRMT-MT | EXC |
|---|---|---|
| COMPLETE SET (2) | 30.00 | 13.50 |
| COMMON PANEL | 12.00 | 5.50 |
| ❑ 4 Gilbert Perreault and Ric Seiling | 20.00 | 9.00 |
| ❑ 8 Bob Sauve and Richard Martin | 12.00 | 5.50 |

## 1981-82 Sabres Milk Panels

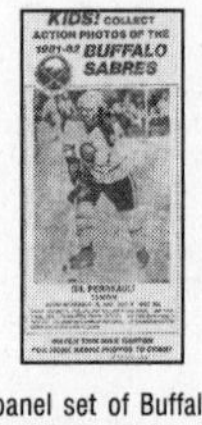

This sixteen-panel set of Buffalo Sabres was issued by Wilson Farms Dairy on the side of 2 percent milkfat and homogenized Vitamin D half gallon milk cartons. After cutting, the panels measure approximately 3 3/4" by 7 1/2". Although the 2 percent milk fat cartons have some lime green lettering and a lime green stripe, the picture and text of the player panels are printed in red on both cartons. The top of the panel reads "Kids, Collect Action Photos of the 1981-82 Buffalo Sabres." Inside a red broken border, the panel has a action player photo, with player information and career summary beneath the picture. The panels are subtly dated and numbered below the photo area in the following way, Gilbert Perreault is M325-81-4H (M325 is the product code, the number 81 gives the last two digits of year, and 4 is the card number perhaps also indicating release week). The set can also be found in blue print.

| | NRMT-MT | EXC |
|---|---|---|
| COMPLETE SET (16) | 150.00 | 70.00 |
| COMMON CARD (1-17) | 10.00 | 4.50 |
| ❑ 1 Craig Ramsay | 10.00 | 4.50 |
| ❑ 2 John Van Boxmeer | 10.00 | 4.50 |
| ❑ 3 Don Edwards | 12.00 | 5.50 |
| ❑ 4 Gilbert Perreault | 20.00 | 9.00 |
| ❑ 5 Alan Haworth | 10.00 | 4.50 |
| ❑ 6 Jim Schoenfeld | 15.00 | 6.75 |
| ❑ 7 Richie Dunn | 10.00 | 4.50 |
| ❑ 8 Bob Sauve | 12.00 | 5.50 |
| ❑ 9 Bill Hajt | 10.00 | 4.50 |
| ❑ 10 Larry Playfair | 10.00 | 4.50 |
| ❑ 11 Tony McKegney | 12.00 | 5.50 |
| ❑ 12 Mike Ramsey | 12.00 | 5.50 |
| ❑ 13 Andre Savard | 10.00 | 4.50 |
| ❑ 15 Ric Seiling | 10.00 | 4.50 |
| ❑ 16 Yvon Lambert | 10.00 | 4.50 |
| ❑ 17 Dale McCourt | 10.00 | 4.50 |

## 1982-83 Sabres Milk Panels

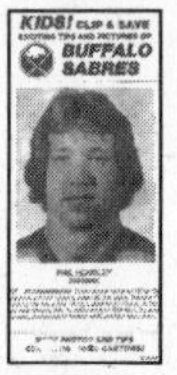

This seventeen-panel set of Buffalo Sabres was issued on the side of half gallon milk cartons. After cutting, the panels measure approximately 3 3/4" by 7 1/2". The picture and text of the player panels are printed in blue. The top of the panel reads "Kids, Clip and Save Exciting Tips and Pictures of Buffalo Sabres." Inside a blue broken border, the panel has a posed head and shoulders shot, with the player's name, position, and a hockey tip beneath the picture. The panels are subtly dated and numbered below the photo area in the following way, Gilbert Perreault is M325-82-7H. Phil Housley's card predates his Rookie Card.

| | MINT | NRMT |
|---|---|---|
| COMPLETE SET (17) | 150.00 | 70.00 |
| COMMON CARD (2-18) | 10.00 | 4.50 |
| ❑ 2 1982-83 Home Schedule | 15.00 | 6.75 |
| ❑ 3 Craig Ramsay | 10.00 | 4.50 |
| ❑ 4 John Van Boxmeer | 10.00 | 4.50 |
| ❑ 5 Lindy Ruff | 10.00 | 4.50 |
| ❑ 6 Bob Sauve | 12.00 | 5.50 |
| ❑ 7 Gilbert Perreault | 20.00 | 9.00 |
| ❑ 8 Ric Seiling | 10.00 | 4.50 |
| ❑ 9 Jacques Cloutier | 12.00 | 5.50 |
| ❑ 10 Larry Playfair | 10.00 | 4.50 |
| ❑ 11 Phil Housley | 20.00 | 9.00 |
| ❑ 12 Mike Foligno | 12.00 | 5.50 |
| ❑ 13 Tony McKegney | 12.00 | 5.50 |
| ❑ 14 Dale McCourt | 10.00 | 4.50 |
| ❑ 15 Mike Ramsey | 10.00 | 4.50 |
| ❑ 16 Hannu Virta | 10.00 | 4.50 |
| ❑ 17 Brent Peterson | 10.00 | 4.50 |
| ❑ 18 Scott Bowman GM | 20.00 | 9.00 |

## 1984-85 Sabres Blue Shield

This 21-card set was issued by the Buffalo Sabres in conjunction with Blue Shield of Western New York. The cards measure approximately 2 1/2" by 3 3/4". It has been reported that only 500 sets were printed as a test for future issues. The fronts feature a head and shoulders color photo with player information below the picture. The card backs have the Blue Shield logo and the words "The Caring Card -- The Blue Shield of Western New York, Inc." We have checklisted the cards below in alphabetical order. Dave Andreychuk and Tom Barrasso appear in their Rookie Card year.

| | MINT | NRMT |
|---|---|---|
| COMPLETE SET (21) | 100.00 | 45.00 |
| COMMON CARD (1-21) | 3.00 | 1.35 |
| ❑ 1 Dave Andreychuk | 20.00 | 9.00 |
| ❑ 2 Tom Barrasso | 20.00 | 9.00 |
| ❑ 3 Adam Creighton | 5.00 | 2.20 |
| ❑ 4 Paul Cyr | 3.00 | 1.35 |
| ❑ 5 Malcolm Davis | 3.00 | 1.35 |
| ❑ 6 Mike Foligno | 5.00 | 2.20 |
| ❑ 7 Bill Hajt | 3.00 | 1.35 |
| ❑ 8 Gilles Hamel | 3.00 | 1.35 |
| ❑ 9 Phil Housley | 10.00 | 4.50 |
| ❑ 10 Sean McKenna | 3.00 | 1.35 |
| ❑ 11 Mike Moller | 3.00 | 1.35 |
| ❑ 12 Gilbert Perreault | 15.00 | 6.75 |
| ❑ 13 Brent Peterson | 3.00 | 1.35 |
| ❑ 14 Larry Playfair | 3.00 | 1.35 |
| ❑ 15 Craig Ramsay | 5.00 | 2.20 |
| ❑ 16 Mike Ramsey | 5.00 | 2.20 |
| ❑ 17 Lindy Ruff | 5.00 | 2.20 |
| ❑ 18 Bob Sauve | 5.00 | 2.20 |
| ❑ 19 Ric Seiling | 3.00 | 1.35 |
| ❑ 20 John Tucker | 5.00 | 2.20 |
| ❑ 21 Hannu Virta | 3.00 | 1.35 |

## 1985-86 Sabres Blue Shield

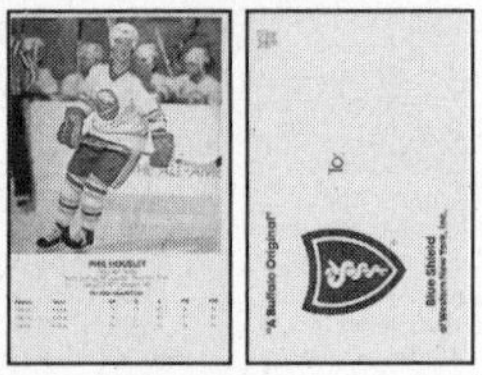

This 28-card set was issued by the Buffalo Sabres in conjunction with Blue Shield of Western New York. The cards were printed in two different sizes: large (4" by 6" with postcard backs) and small (2 1/2" by 3 1/2"). Both sizes have the Blue Shield logo on the backs. Though both sizes are scarce, the small cards are considered harder to obtain. The front of the large card features a color action photo of the player, with his name as well as biographical and statistical information below the picture. The front of the small card is identical except for the omission of the statistical information. The firing of Sabres' coach Jim Schoenfeld at the time the cards were issued makes his card rare as he was removed from the set. The set is priced below as complete without the Schoenfeld card. Daren Puppa's card predates his Rookie Card by three years.

| | MINT | NRMT |
|---|---|---|
| COMPLETE SET (27) | 40.00 | 18.00 |
| COMMON CARD (1-28) | 1.00 | .45 |
| ❑ 1 Mikael Andersson | 1.00 | .45 |
| ❑ 2 Dave Andreychuk | 5.00 | 2.20 |
| ❑ 3 Tom Barrasso | 4.00 | 1.80 |
| ❑ 4 Adam Creighton | 1.50 | .70 |
| ❑ 5 Paul Cyr | 1.00 | .45 |
| ❑ 6 Malcolm Davis | 1.00 | .45 |
| ❑ 7 Steve Dykstra | 1.00 | .45 |
| ❑ 8 Dave Fenyves | 1.00 | .45 |
| ❑ 9 Mike Foligno | 1.50 | .70 |
| ❑ 10 Bill Hajt | 1.00 | .45 |
| ❑ 11 Bob Halkidis | 1.00 | .45 |
| ❑ 12 Gilles Hamel | 1.00 | .45 |
| ❑ 13 Phil Housley | 4.00 | 1.80 |
| ❑ 14 Pat Hughes | 1.00 | .45 |
| ❑ 15 Normand Lacombe | 1.00 | .45 |
| ❑ 16 Chris Langevin | 1.00 | .45 |
| ❑ 17 Sean McKenna | 1.00 | .45 |
| ❑ 18 Gates Orlando | 1.00 | .45 |
| ❑ 19 Gilbert Perreault | 5.00 | 2.20 |
| ❑ 20 Larry Playfair | 1.00 | .45 |
| ❑ 21 Daren Puppa | 7.50 | 3.40 |
| ❑ 22 Craig Ramsay ACO | 1.00 | .45 |
| ❑ 23 Mike Ramsey | 1.50 | .70 |
| ❑ 24 Lindy Ruff | 1.00 | .45 |
| ❑ 25 Jim Schoenfeld CO SP | 15.00 | 6.75 |
| ❑ 26 Ric Seiling | 1.00 | .45 |
| ❑ 27 John Tucker | 1.25 | .55 |
| ❑ 28 Hannu Virta | 1.00 | .45 |

## 1986-87 Sabres Blue Shield

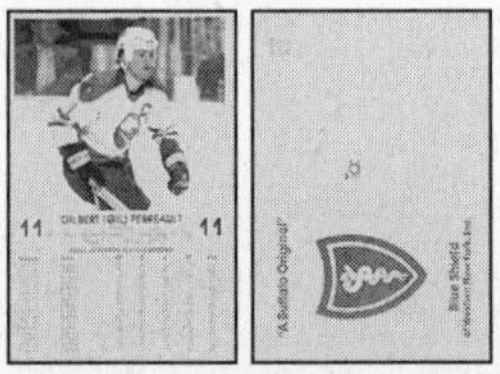

This 28-card set was issued by the Buffalo Sabres in conjunction with Blue Shield of Western New York. In contrast to the previous year's issue, the cards were printed only in one size, the approximately 4" by 6" postcard type with the Blue Shield logo on the backs. The front of the cards can be distinguished from the previous year's issue by the addition of the player's uniform number (inadvertently omitted on the Creighton and Fenyves cards) and updated statistics.

| | MINT | NRMT |
|---|---|---|
| COMPLETE SET (28) | 30.00 | 13.50 |
| COMMON CARD (1-28) | .75 | .35 |
| ❑ 1 Shawn Anderson | .75 | .35 |
| ❑ 2 Dave Andreychuk | 6.00 | 2.70 |
| ❑ 3 Scott Arniel | .75 | .35 |
| ❑ 4 Tom Barrasso | 3.00 | 1.35 |
| ❑ 5 Jacques Cloutier | 1.00 | .45 |
| ❑ 6 Adam Creighton | 1.00 | .45 |
| ❑ 7 Paul Cyr | .75 | .35 |
| ❑ 8 Steve Dykstra | .75 | .35 |
| ❑ 9 Dave Fenyves | .75 | .35 |
| ❑ 10 Mike Foligno | 1.50 | .70 |
| ❑ 11 Clark Gillies | 2.00 | .90 |
| ❑ 12 Bill Hajt | .75 | .35 |
| ❑ 13 Bob Halkidis | .75 | .35 |
| ❑ 14 Jim Hofford | .75 | .35 |
| ❑ 15 Phil Housley | 2.50 | 1.10 |
| ❑ 16 Jim Korn | .75 | .35 |
| ❑ 17 Uwe Krupp | 1.50 | .70 |
| ❑ 18 Tom Kurvers | .75 | .35 |
| ❑ 19 Norm Lacombe | .75 | .35 |
| ❑ 20 Gates Orlando | .75 | .35 |
| ❑ 21 Wilf Paiement | 1.00 | .45 |
| ❑ 22 Gilbert Perreault | 5.00 | 2.20 |
| ❑ 23 Daren Puppa | 3.00 | 1.35 |
| ❑ 24 Mike Ramsey | 1.00 | .45 |
| ❑ 25 Lindy Ruff | .75 | .35 |
| ❑ 26 Christian Ruuttu | .75 | .35 |
| ❑ 27 Doug Smith | .75 | .35 |
| ❑ 28 John Tucker | 1.00 | .45 |

## 1986-87 Sabres Blue Shield Small

Same as the regular Sabres Shield set only in a smaller format.

| | MINT | NRMT |
|---|---|---|
| COMPLETE SET (28) | 35.00 | 16.00 |
| COMMON CARD (1-28) | .75 | .35 |
| ❑ 1 Shawn Anderson | .75 | .35 |
| ❑ 2 Dave Andreychuk | 6.00 | 2.70 |
| ❑ 3 Scott Arniel | .75 | .35 |
| ❑ 4 Tom Barrasso | 3.00 | 1.35 |
| ❑ 5 Jacques Cloutier | 1.00 | .45 |
| ❑ 6 Adam Creighton | 1.00 | .45 |
| ❑ 7 Paul Cyr | .75 | .35 |
| ❑ 8 Steve Dykstra | .75 | .35 |
| ❑ 9 Dave Fenyves | .75 | .35 |
| ❑ 10 Mike Foligno | 1.50 | .70 |
| ❑ 11 Clark Gillies | 2.00 | .90 |
| ❑ 12 Bill Hajt | .75 | .35 |
| ❑ 13 Bob Halkidis | .75 | .35 |
| ❑ 14 Jim Hofford | .75 | .35 |
| ❑ 15 Phil Housley | 3.00 | 1.35 |
| ❑ 16 Jim Korn | .75 | .35 |
| ❑ 17 Uwe Krupp | 1.50 | .70 |
| ❑ 18 Tom Kurvers | .75 | .35 |
| ❑ 19 Norm Lacombe | .75 | .35 |
| ❑ 20 Gates Orlando | .75 | .35 |
| ❑ 21 Wilf Paiement | 1.00 | .45 |
| ❑ 22 Gilbert Perreault | 5.00 | 2.20 |
| ❑ 23 Daren Puppa | 3.00 | 1.35 |
| ❑ 24 Mike Ramsey | 1.00 | .45 |
| ❑ 25 Lindy Ruff | .75 | .35 |
| ❑ 26 Christian Ruuttu | .75 | .35 |
| ❑ 27 Doug Smith | .75 | .35 |
| ❑ 28 John Tucker | 1.00 | .45 |

## 1987-88 Sabres Blue Shield

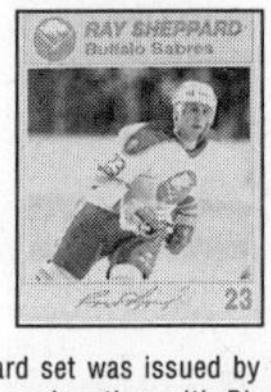

This 28-card set was issued by the Buffalo Sabres in conjunction with Blue Shield of Western New York. In contrast to the previous year's issue, the cards are a different size, approximately 4" by 5", again in the postcard format with the Blue Shield logo on the backs. The front of the cards feature a color action photo of the player, with the player's name, team name, and team logo in a yellow stripe at the top. The player's number and a facsimile autograph appear in blue at the bottom on the front. Supposedly there exists a rare variation on the Phil Housley card which has his last name misspelled "Housely". The card of Pierre Turgeon predates his Rookie Card by one year.

| | MINT | NRMT |
|---|---|---|
| COMPLETE SET (28) | 25.00 | 11.00 |
| COMMON CARD (1-28) | .75 | .35 |
| ❑ 1 Mikael Andersson 14 | .75 | .35 |
| ❑ 2 Dave Andreychuk 25 | 3.00 | 1.35 |
| ❑ 3 Scott Arniel 9 | .75 | .35 |
| ❑ 4 Tom Barrasso 30 | 1.50 | .70 |
| ❑ 5 Jacques Cloutier 1 | 1.00 | .45 |

| | MINT | NRMT |
|---|---|---|
| ❑ 6 Adam Creighton 38 | 1.00 | .45 |
| ❑ 7 Mike Donnelly 16 | .75 | .35 |
| ❑ 8 Mike Foligno 17 | 1.00 | .45 |
| ❑ 9 Clark Gillies 90 | 1.00 | .45 |
| ❑ 10 Bob Halkidis 18 | .75 | .35 |
| ❑ 11 Mike Hartman 20 | .75 | .35 |
| ❑ 12 Ed Hospodar 24 | .75 | .35 |
| ❑ 13 Phil Housley 6 | 1.50 | .70 |
| ❑ 14 Calle Johansson 3 | 1.00 | .45 |
| ❑ 15 Uwe Krupp 40 | 1.00 | .45 |
| ❑ 16 Jan Ludvig 36 | .75 | .35 |
| ❑ 17 Kevin Maguire 19 | .75 | .35 |
| ❑ 18 Mark Napier 65 | .75 | .35 |
| ❑ 19 Ken Priestlay 12 | .75 | .35 |
| ❑ 20 Daren Puppa 35 | 1.50 | .70 |
| ❑ 21 Mike Ramsey 5 | 1.00 | .45 |
| ❑ 22 Joe Reekie 27 | .75 | .35 |
| ❑ 23 Lindy Ruff 22 | .75 | .35 |
| ❑ 24 Christian Ruuttu 21 | 1.00 | .45 |
| ❑ 25 Ray Sheppard 23 | 3.00 | 1.35 |
| ❑ 26 Doug Smith 15 | .75 | .35 |
| ❑ 27 John Tucker 7 | 1.00 | .45 |
| ❑ 28 Pierre Turgeon 77 | 10.00 | 4.50 |

## 1987-88 Sabres Wonder Bread/Hostess

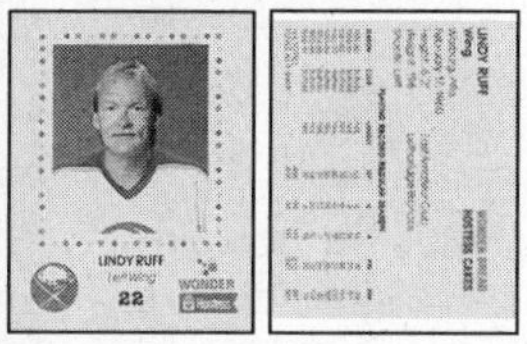

The 1987-88 Buffalo Sabres Team Photo Album was sponsored by Wonder Bread and Hostess Cakes. It consists of three large sheets, each measuring approximately 13 1/2" by 10 1/4" and joined together to form one continuous sheet. The first panel has a team photo of the Buffalo Sabres. The second and third panels present three rows of five cards each. After perforation, the cards measure approximately 2 5/8" by 3 3/8". They feature color posed photos bordered in various color dots, with player information below the picture sandwiched between the Sabres' and sponsors' logos. The back has biographical and statistical information in a horizontal format. We have checklisted the names below in alphabetical order, with the uniform number to the right of the name. The set features an early card of Pierre Turgeon pre-dating his Rookie Cards by one year.

| | MINT | NRMT |
|---|---|---|
| COMPLETE SET (31) | 20.00 | 9.00 |
| COMMON CARD (1-30) | .50 | .23 |
| ❑ 1 Mikael Andersson 14 | .50 | .23 |
| ❑ 2 Shawn Anderson 37 | .50 | .23 |
| ❑ 3 Dave Andreychuk 25 | 2.50 | 1.10 |
| ❑ 4 Scott Arniel 9 | .50 | .23 |
| ❑ 5 Tom Barrasso 30 | 2.00 | .90 |
| ❑ 6 Jacques Cloutier 1 | .75 | .35 |
| ❑ 7 Adam Creighton 38 | .75 | .35 |
| ❑ 8 Steve Dykstra 4 | .50 | .23 |
| ❑ 9 Mike Foligno 17 | .75 | .35 |
| ❑ 10 Clark Gillies 90 | .75 | .35 |
| ❑ 11 Ed Hospodar 24 | .50 | .23 |
| ❑ 12 Phil Housley 6 | 1.25 | .55 |
| ❑ 13 Calle Johansson 3 | .75 | .35 |
| ❑ 14 Uwe Krupp 40 | .75 | .35 |
| ❑ 15 Don Lever CO | .50 | .23 |
| ❑ 16 Bob Logan 26 | .50 | .23 |
| ❑ 17 Jan Ludvig 36 | .50 | .23 |
| ❑ 18 Kevin Maguire 19 | .50 | .23 |
| ❑ 19 Mark Napier 65 | .75 | .35 |
| ❑ 20 Daren Puppa 31 | 1.50 | .70 |
| ❑ 21 Mike Ramsey 5 | .75 | .35 |
| ❑ 22 Joe Reekie 27 | .75 | .35 |
| ❑ 23 Lindy Ruff 22 | .50 | .23 |
| ❑ 24 Christian Ruuttu 21 | .75 | .35 |
| ❑ 25 Ted Sator CO | .50 | .23 |
| ❑ 26 Ray Sheppard 23 | 2.00 | .90 |
| ❑ 27 Barry Smith CO | .50 | .23 |
| ❑ 28 Doug Smith 15 | .50 | .23 |
| ❑ 29 John Tucker 7 | .75 | .35 |
| ❑ 30 Pierre Turgeon 77 | 8.00 | 3.60 |
| ❑ NNO Large Team Photo | 3.00 | 1.35 |

## 1988-89 Sabres Blue Shield

This 28-card set was issued by the Buffalo Sabres in conjunction with Blue Shield of Western New York. The cards measure approximately 4" by 6" and are in the postcard format, with the Blue Shield logo on the backs. The fronts feature a color action photo of the player. The picture is sandwiched between yellow stripes, with team logo and player's name above, and player information below. The cards are unnumbered and we have checklisted them below in alphabetical order, with the uniform number next to the player's name. The cards of Benoit Hogue, Jan Ludvig, Mark Napier, and Joe Reekie were apparently late additions to the set; they are marked as SP in the checklist below.

| | MINT | NRMT |
|---|---|---|
| COMPLETE SET (28) | 25.00 | 11.00 |
| COMMON CARD (1-28) | .25 | .11 |
| ❑ 1 Mikael Andersson 14 | .50 | .23 |
| ❑ 2 Dave Andreychuk 25 | 1.50 | .70 |
| ❑ 3 Scott Arniel 9 | .25 | .11 |
| ❑ 4 Doug Bodger 8 | .75 | .35 |
| ❑ 5 Jacques Cloutier 1 | .75 | .35 |
| ❑ 6 Mike Donnelly 16 | .50 | .23 |
| ❑ 7 Mike Foligno 17 | .75 | .35 |
| ❑ 8 Bob Halkidis 18 | .25 | .11 |
| ❑ 9 Mike Hartman 20 | .25 | .11 |
| ❑ 10 Benoit Hogue 33 SP | 3.00 | 1.35 |
| ❑ 11 Phil Housley 6 | 1.00 | .45 |
| ❑ 12 Calle Johansson 3 | .75 | .35 |
| ❑ 13 Uwe Krupp 4 | .75 | .35 |
| ❑ 14 Jan Ludvig 36 SP | 2.00 | .90 |
| ❑ 15 Kevin Maguire 19 | .25 | .11 |
| ❑ 16 Mark Napier 65 SP | 2.00 | .90 |
| ❑ 17 Jeff Parker 29 | .25 | .11 |
| ❑ 18 Larry Playfair 27 | .25 | .11 |
| ❑ 19 Daren Puppa 31 | 2.00 | .90 |
| ❑ 20 Mike Ramsey 5 | .50 | .23 |
| ❑ 21 Joe Reekie 55 SP | 2.00 | .90 |
| ❑ 22 Lindy Ruff 22 | .25 | .11 |
| ❑ 23 Christian Ruuttu 21 | .50 | .23 |
| ❑ 24 Sabretooth Mascot | .25 | .11 |
| ❑ 25 Ray Sheppard 23 | 1.50 | .70 |
| ❑ 26 John Tucker 7 | .50 | .23 |
| ❑ 27 Pierre Turgeon 77 | 6.00 | 2.70 |
| ❑ 28 Rick Vaive 12 | .75 | .35 |

## 1988-89 Sabres Wonder Bread/Hostess

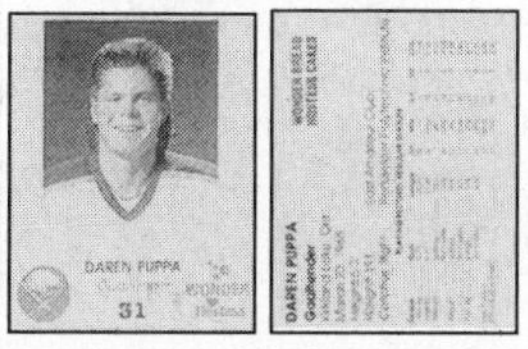

The 1988-89 Buffalo Sabres Team Photo Album was sponsored by Wonder Bread and Hostess Cakes. It consists of three large sheets, each measuring approximately 13 1/2" by 10 1/4" and joined together to form one continuous sheet. The first panel has a team photo of the Sabres in civilian clothing. The second and third panels present three rows of five cards each. After perforation, the cards measure approximately 2 5/8" by 3 3/8". They feature color posed photos on white card stock. The top half has thin diagonal blue lines traversing the white background. Player information appears below the picture, between the Sabres' and sponsors' logos. The back has biographical and statistical information in a horizontal format. The cards are unnumbered and we have checklisted them below in alphabetical order, with the uniform number to the right of the player's name.

| | MINT | NRMT |
|---|---|---|
| COMPLETE SET (31) | 20.00 | 9.00 |
| COMMON CARD (1-30) | .50 | .23 |
| ❑ 1 Mikael Andersson 14 | .50 | .23 |
| ❑ 2 Dave Andreychuk 25 | 1.50 | .70 |
| ❑ 3 Scott Arniel 9 | .50 | .23 |
| ❑ 4 Doug Bodger 8 | .75 | .35 |
| ❑ 5 Jacques Cloutier 1 | .75 | .35 |
| ❑ 6 Adam Creighton 38 | .60 | .25 |
| ❑ 7 Mike Foligno 17 | .75 | .35 |
| ❑ 8 Bob Halkidis 18 | .50 | .23 |
| ❑ 9 Mike Hartman 20 | .50 | .23 |
| ❑ 10 Benoit Hogue 33 | 1.00 | .45 |
| ❑ 11 Phil Housley 6 | 1.00 | .45 |
| ❑ 12 Calle Johansson 3 | .75 | .35 |
| ❑ 13 Uwe Krupp 4 | .75 | .35 |
| ❑ 14 Don Lever CO | .50 | .23 |
| ❑ 15 Jan Ludvig 36 | .50 | .23 |
| ❑ 16 Kevin Maguire 19 | .50 | .23 |
| ❑ 17 Brad Miller 44 | .50 | .23 |
| ❑ 18 Mark Napier 65 | .50 | .23 |
| ❑ 19 Jeff Parker 29 | .50 | .23 |
| ❑ 20 Larry Playfair 27 | .50 | .23 |
| ❑ 21 Daren Puppa 31 | 2.00 | .90 |
| ❑ 22 Mike Ramsey 5 | .50 | .23 |
| ❑ 23 Joe Reekie 55 | .50 | .23 |
| ❑ 24 Lindy Ruff 22 | .50 | .23 |
| ❑ 25 Christian Ruuttu 21 | .50 | .23 |
| ❑ 26 Ted Sator CO | .50 | .23 |
| ❑ 27 Ray Sheppard 23 | 1.50 | .70 |
| ❑ 28 Barry Smith CO | .50 | .23 |
| ❑ 29 John Tucker 7 | .50 | .23 |
| ❑ 30 Pierre Turgeon 77 | 6.00 | 2.70 |
| ❑ xx Large Team Photo | 1.00 | .45 |

## 1989-90 Sabres Blue Shield

This 24-card set was issued by the Buffalo Sabres in conjunction with Blue Shield of Western New York. The cards measure approximately 4" by 6" and are in the postcard

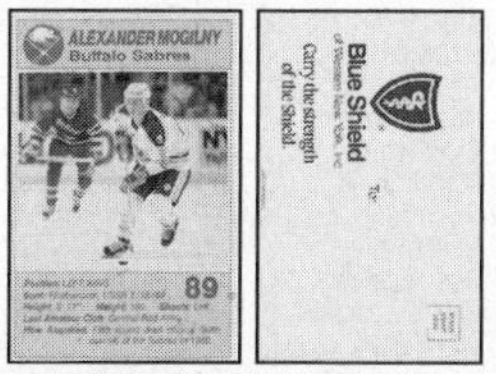

format, with the Blue Shield logo on the backs. The fronts feature a color action photo of the player. The picture is sandwiched between yellow stripes, with team logo and player's name above, and player information below. The cards are unnumbered and we have checklisted them below in alphabetical order, with the uniform number next to the player's name. The card of Alexander Mogilny predates his Rookie Card by one year.

| | MINT | NRMT |
|---|---|---|
| COMPLETE SET (24) | 18.00 | 8.00 |
| COMMON CARD (1-24) | .25 | .11 |
| ❑ 1 Dave Andreychuk 25 | 1.50 | .70 |
| ❑ 2 Scott Arniel 9 | .50 | .23 |
| ❑ 3 Doug Bodger 8 | .50 | .23 |
| ❑ 4 Mike Foligno 17 | .75 | .35 |
| ❑ 5 Mike Hartman 20 | .50 | .23 |
| ❑ 6 Benoit Hogue 33 | 1.00 | .45 |
| ❑ 7 Phil Housley 6 | 1.00 | .45 |
| ❑ 8 Dean Kennedy 26 | .50 | .23 |
| ❑ 9 Uwe Krupp 4 | .75 | .35 |
| ❑ 10 Grant Ledyard 3 | .50 | .23 |
| ❑ 11 Kevin Maguire 19 | .50 | .23 |
| ❑ 12 Clint Malarchuk 30 | .75 | .35 |
| ❑ 13 Alexander Mogilny 89 | 5.00 | 2.20 |
| ❑ 14 Jeff Parker 29 | .50 | .23 |
| ❑ 15 Larry Playfair 27 | .50 | .23 |
| ❑ 16 Ken Priestlay 56 | .50 | .23 |
| ❑ 17 Daren Puppa 31 | 1.50 | .70 |
| ❑ 18 Mike Ramsey 5 | .50 | .23 |
| ❑ 19 Christian Ruuttu 21 | .50 | .23 |
| ❑ 20 Ray Sheppard 23 | 1.00 | .45 |
| ❑ 21 Dave Snuggerud 18 | .50 | .23 |
| ❑ 22 Sabretooth Mascot | .25 | .11 |
| ❑ 23 Pierre Turgeon 77 | 3.00 | 1.35 |
| ❑ 24 Rick Vaive 22 | .75 | .35 |

## 1989-90 Sabres Campbell's

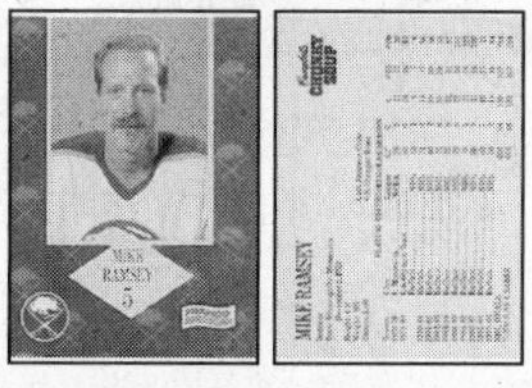

The 1989-90 Buffalo Sabres Team Photo Album was sponsored by Campbell's and commemorates 20 years in the NHL. It consists of three large sheets (the first two measuring approximately 10" by 13 1/2" and the third smaller), all joined together to form one continuous sheet. The first panel has three color action shots superimposed on a large black and white picture of the Sabres. While the second panel presents four rows of four cards each (16 player cards), the third panel presents four rows of three cards each (11 player cards and a 20th year card). After perforation, the cards measure approximately 2 1/2" by 3 3/8". They feature color posed photos bordered in yellow (on three sides), on a dark blue background interspersed with Sabres' logos in light blue. Player information appears below the picture in a yellow diamond, sandwiched between the Sabres' and the Franco-American logos. The back has biographical and statistical information in a horizontal format. We have checklisted the names below in alphabetical order, with the uniform number to the right of the name. The card of Alexander Mogilny predates his Rookie Card by one year.

| | MINT | NRMT |
|---|---|---|
| COMPLETE SET (28) | 18.00 | 8.00 |
| COMMON CARD (1-27) | .50 | .23 |
| ❑ 1 Shawn Anderson 37 | .50 | .23 |
| ❑ 2 Dave Andreychuk 25 | 1.50 | .70 |
| ❑ 3 Scott Arniel 9 | .50 | .23 |
| ❑ 4 Doug Bodger 8 | .50 | .23 |
| ❑ 5 Rick Dudley CO | .75 | .35 |
| ❑ 6 Mike Foligno 17 | .75 | .35 |
| ❑ 7 Mike Hartman 20 | .50 | .23 |
| ❑ 8 Benoit Hogue 33 | 1.00 | .45 |
| ❑ 9 Phil Housley 6 | 1.00 | .45 |
| ❑ 10 Dean Kennedy 26 | .50 | .23 |
| ❑ 11 Uwe Krupp 4 | .75 | .35 |
| ❑ 12 Grant Ledyard 3 | .50 | .23 |
| ❑ 13 Kevin Maguire 19 | .50 | .23 |
| ❑ 14 Clint Malarchuk 30 | .75 | .35 |
| ❑ 15 Alexander Mogilny 89 | 5.00 | 2.20 |
| ❑ 16 Mark Napier 65 | .50 | .23 |
| ❑ 17 Jeff Parker 29 | .50 | .23 |
| ❑ 18 Larry Playfair 27 | .50 | .23 |
| ❑ 19 Daren Puppa 31 | 1.50 | .70 |
| ❑ 20 Mike Ramsey 5 | .50 | .23 |
| ❑ 21 Robert Ray 32 | 1.00 | .45 |
| ❑ 22 Christian Ruuttu 21 | .50 | .23 |
| ❑ 23 Ray Sheppard 23 | 1.00 | .45 |
| ❑ 24 Dave Snuggerud 18 | .50 | .23 |
| ❑ 25 John Tortorella CO | .50 | .23 |
| ❑ 26 Pierre Turgeon 77 | 3.00 | 1.35 |
| ❑ 27 Rick Vaive 22 | .75 | .35 |
| ❑ xx Large Team Photo | 1.00 | .45 |

## 1990-91 Sabres Blue Shield

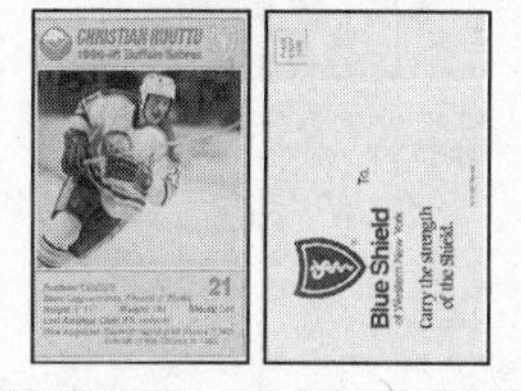

This 26-card set was issued by the Buffalo Sabres in conjunction with Blue Shield of Western New York. The cards measure approximately 4" by 6" and are in the postcard format, with the Blue Shield logo on the backs. The fronts feature a color action photo of the player. The picture is sandwiched between yellow stripes, with team logo and player's name above, and player information below. These cards may be distinguished from the previous year's issue by the "medical shield logo" in the upper right corner. The cards are unnumbered and we have checklisted them below in alphabetical order, with the uniform number next to the player's name.

| | MINT | NRMT |
|---|---|---|
| COMPLETE SET (26) | 15.00 | 6.75 |
| COMMON CARD (1-26) | .25 | .11 |
| ❑ 1 Dave Andreychuk 25 | .75 | .35 |
| ❑ 2 Donald Audette 28 | 1.00 | .45 |
| ❑ 3 Doug Bodger 8 | .50 | .23 |
| ❑ 4 Greg Brown 9 | .50 | .23 |
| ❑ 5 Brian Curran 39 | .50 | .23 |
| ❑ 6 Lou Franceschetti 15 | .50 | .23 |
| ❑ 7 Mike Hartman 20 | .50 | .23 |
| ❑ 8 Dale Hawerchuk 10 | 1.00 | .45 |
| ❑ 9 Benoit Hogue 33 | .60 | .25 |
| ❑ 10 Dean Kennedy 26 | .50 | .23 |
| ❑ 11 Uwe Krupp 4 | .75 | .35 |
| ❑ 12 Grant Ledyard 3 | .50 | .23 |
| ❑ 13 Mikko Makela 42 | .50 | .23 |
| ❑ 14 Clint Malarchuk 30 | .75 | .35 |
| ❑ 15 Alexander Mogilny 89 | 3.00 | 1.35 |
| ❑ 16 Daren Puppa 31 | 1.00 | .45 |
| ❑ 17 Mike Ramsey 5 | .50 | .23 |
| ❑ 18 Robert Ray 32 | .75 | .35 |
| ❑ 19 Christian Ruuttu 21 | .50 | .23 |
| ❑ 20 Sabretooth Mascot | .25 | .11 |
| ❑ 21 Jiri Sejba 23 | .50 | .23 |
| ❑ 22 Dave Snuggerud 18 | .50 | .23 |
| ❑ 23 John Tucker 7 | .50 | .23 |
| ❑ 24 Pierre Turgeon 77 | 1.50 | .70 |
| ❑ 25 Rick Vaive 22 | .50 | .23 |
| ❑ 26 Jay Wells 24 | .50 | .23 |

## 1990-91 Sabres Campbell's

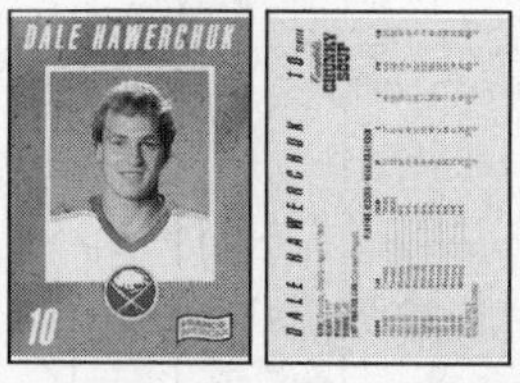

The 1990-91 Buffalo Sabres Team Photo Album was sponsored by Campbell's. It consists of three large sheets, each measuring approximately 10" by 13 1/2" and joined together to form one continuous sheet. The first panel has a team photo of the Sabres in street clothing. The second and third panels present four rows of four cards each (31 player cards plus a Sabres' logo card). After perforation, the cards measure approximately 2 1/2" by 3 3/8". They feature color posed photos bordered in white, on a dark blue background. The player's name is given above the picture, with the Sabres' logo, uniform number, and Franco-American logo below the picture. The back has biographical and statistical information in a horizontal format. We have checklisted the names below in alphabetical order, with the uniform number to the right of the name.

| | MINT | NRMT |
|---|---|---|
| COMPLETE SET (32) | 15.00 | 6.75 |
| COMMON CARD (1-31) | .25 | .11 |
| ❑ 1 Dave Andreychuk 25 | .75 | .35 |
| ❑ 2 Donald Audette 28 | 1.00 | .45 |
| ❑ 3 Doug Bodger 8 | .50 | .23 |
| ❑ 4 Greg Brown 9 | .50 | .23 |
| ❑ 5 Bob Corkum 19 | .50 | .23 |
| ❑ 6 Rick Dudley CO | .25 | .11 |
| ❑ 7 Mike Foligno 17 | .75 | .35 |
| ❑ 8 Mike Hartman 20 | .50 | .23 |
| ❑ 9 Dale Hawerchuk 10 | 1.00 | .45 |
| ❑ 10 Benoit Hogue 33 | .60 | .25 |
| ❑ 11 Dean Kennedy 26 | .50 | .23 |
| ❑ 12 Uwe Krupp 4 | .75 | .35 |
| ❑ 13 Grant Ledyard 3 | .50 | .23 |
| ❑ 14 Darcy Loewen 36 | .50 | .23 |
| ❑ 15 Mikko Makela 42 | .50 | .23 |
| ❑ 16 Clint Malarchuk 30 | .75 | .35 |
| ❑ 17 Brad Miller 44 | .50 | .23 |
| ❑ 18 Alexander Mogilny 89 | 3.00 | 1.35 |
| ❑ 19 Daren Puppa 31 | 1.00 | .45 |
| ❑ 20 Mike Ramsey 5 | .50 | .23 |
| ❑ 21 Robert Ray 32 | .75 | .35 |
| ❑ 22 Christian Ruuttu 21 | .50 | .23 |
| ❑ 23 Jiri Sejba 23 | .50 | .23 |
| ❑ 24 Darrin Shannon 16 | .50 | .23 |
| ❑ 25 Dave Snuggerud 18 | .50 | .23 |
| ❑ 26 John Tortorella CO | .25 | .11 |
| ❑ 27 John Tucker 7 | .50 | .23 |
| ❑ 28 Pierre Turgeon 77 | 1.50 | .70 |
| ❑ 29 Rick Vaive 22 | .50 | .23 |
| ❑ 30 John Van Boxmeer CO | .25 | .11 |
| ❑ 31 Jay Wells 24 | .50 | .23 |
| ❑ xx Large Team Photo (In street clothes) | 1.00 | .45 |

## 1991-92 Sabres Blue Shield

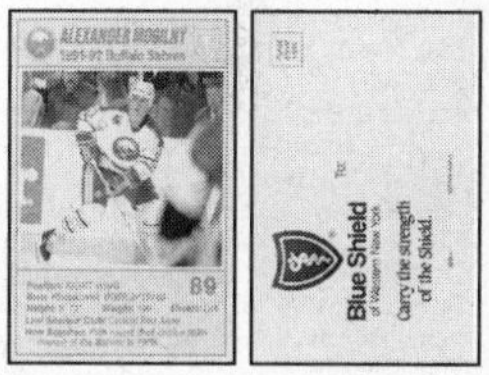

This 26-card postcard set of Buffalo Sabres measuring approximately 4" by 6" features an action photograph enclosed in white and blue borders. The player's name, date, and team name appear in blue lettering on a gold background and are flanked on the right and left by the team logo and Blue Shield of Western New York's logo. Biographical information and the player's jersey number appear in blue over gold within a blue border at the bottom. Card backs carry a large Blue Shield logo and motto on the left side. The cards are unnumbered and checklisted below in alphabetical order, with the jersey number to the right of the name.

| | MINT | NRMT |
|---|---|---|
| COMPLETE SET (26) | 15.00 | 6.75 |
| COMMON CARD (1-26) | .25 | .11 |
| ❑ 1 Dave Andreychuk 25 | 1.00 | .45 |
| ❑ 2 Donald Audette 28 | .75 | .35 |
| ❑ 3 Doug Bodger 8 | .60 | .25 |
| ❑ 4 Gord Donnelly 34 | .50 | .23 |
| ❑ 5 Tom Draper 35 | .60 | .25 |
| ❑ 6 Kevin Haller 7 | .50 | .23 |
| ❑ 7 Dale Hawerchuk 10 | 1.50 | .70 |
| ❑ 8 Randy Hillier 23 | .50 | .23 |
| ❑ 9 Pat LaFontaine 16 | 2.00 | .90 |
| ❑ 10 Grant Ledyard 3 | .50 | .23 |
| ❑ 11 Clint Malarchuk 30 | .75 | .35 |
| ❑ 12 Brad May 27 | 1.00 | .45 |
| ❑ 13 Brad Miller 44 | .50 | .23 |
| ❑ 14 Alexander Mogilny 89 | 3.00 | 1.35 |
| ❑ 15 Colin Patterson 17 | .50 | .23 |
| ❑ 16 Daren Puppa 31 | 1.00 | .45 |
| ❑ 17 Mike Ramsey 5 | .50 | .23 |
| ❑ 18 Robert Ray 32 | .75 | .35 |
| ❑ 19 Christian Ruuttu 21 | .50 | .23 |
| ❑ 20 Dave Snuggerud 18 | .50 | .23 |
| ❑ 21 Ken Sutton 41 | .50 | .23 |
| ❑ 22 Tony Tanti 19 | .50 | .23 |
| ❑ 23 Rick Vaive 22 | .60 | .25 |
| ❑ 24 Jay Wells 24 | .50 | .23 |
| ❑ 25 Randy Wood 15 | .50 | .23 |
| ❑ 26 Sabretooth (Mascot) | .25 | .11 |

## 1991-92 Sabres Pepsi/Campbell's

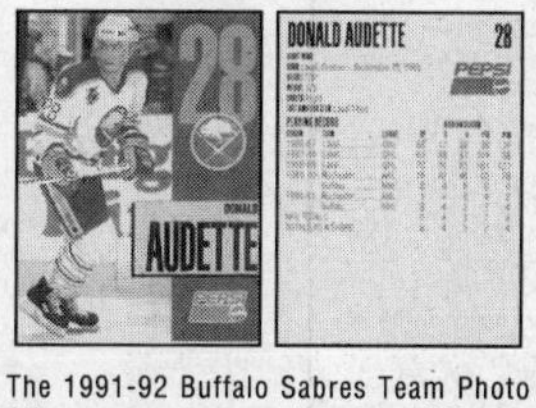

The 1991-92 Buffalo Sabres Team Photo Album was sponsored in two different varieties. One version was sponsored by Pepsi

in conjunction with the Sheriff's Office of Erie County. The Pepsi logo appears on both sides of each card. A second version was sponsored by Campbell's; the card fronts have the Campbell's Chunky soup logo and the flipside carries the Franco-American emblem. The set consists of three large sheets, joined together to form one continuous sheet. The first panel has a team photo of the Sabres in street clothing, superimposed over lightning streaks on the left side. The second (10" by 13") and third (7 1/2" by 13") panels present 28 cards; after perforation, the cards measure 2 1/2" by 3 1/4". The color action photos are full-bleed on three sides; the blue border running down their right side carries the jersey number, team logo, player's name (on a gold band which jets out into the photo), and the Pepsi logo. The backs list biographical and statistical information. The cards are unnumbered and checklisted below in alphabetical order, with the jersey number to the right of the name.

| | MINT | NRMT |
|---|---|---|
| COMPLETE SET (29) | 15.00 | 6.75 |
| COMMON CARD (1-28) | .25 | .11 |
| ❑ 1 Dave Andreychuk 25 | 1.00 | .45 |
| ❑ 2 Donald Audette 28 | .75 | .35 |
| ❑ 3 Doug Bodger 8 | .60 | .25 |
| ❑ 4 Gord Donnelly 34 | .50 | .23 |
| ❑ 5 Tom Draper 35 | .60 | .25 |
| ❑ 6 Kevin Haller 7 | .50 | .23 |
| ❑ 7 Dale Hawerchuk 10 | 1.50 | .70 |
| ❑ 8 Randy Hillier 23 | .50 | .23 |
| ❑ 9 Pat LaFontaine 16 | 2.00 | .90 |
| ❑ 10 Grant Ledyard 3 | .50 | .23 |
| ❑ 11 Clint Malarchuk 30 | .75 | .35 |
| ❑ 12 Brad May 27 | 1.00 | .45 |
| ❑ 13 Brad Miller 44 | .50 | .23 |
| ❑ 14 Alexander Mogilny 89 | 3.00 | 1.35 |
| ❑ 15 Colin Patterson 17 | .50 | .23 |
| ❑ 16 Daren Puppa 31 | 1.00 | .45 |
| ❑ 17 Mike Ramsey 5 | .50 | .23 |
| ❑ 18 Robert Ray 32 | .75 | .35 |
| ❑ 19 Christian Ruuttu 21 | .50 | .23 |
| ❑ 20 Dave Snuggerud 18 | .50 | .23 |
| ❑ 21 Ken Sutton 41 | .50 | .23 |
| ❑ 22 Tony Tanti 19 | .50 | .23 |
| ❑ 23 Rick Vaive 22 | .50 | .23 |
| ❑ 24 Jay Wells 24 | .50 | .23 |
| ❑ 25 Randy Wood 15 | .50 | .23 |
| ❑ 26 Sabretooth (Mascot) | .25 | .11 |
| ❑ 27 Team Logo | .25 | .11 |
| ❑ 28 NHL Logo | .25 | .11 |
| ❑ xx Large Team Photo (In street clothes) | 1.00 | .45 |

## 1992-93 Sabres Blue Shield

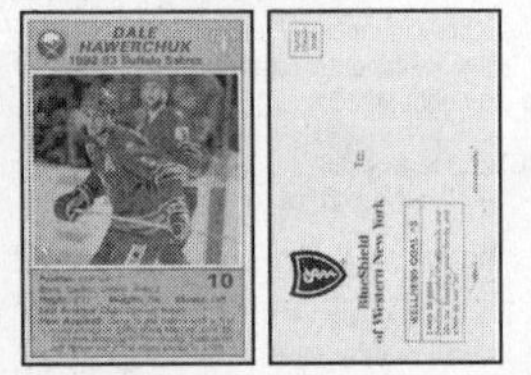


Sponsored by Blue Shield of Western New York, this 26-card postcard set measures approximately 4" by 6" and features color action player photos. In a mustard-colored box at the top are printed the player's name, the year and team name, and the team and sponsor logos. In a mustard-colored box at the bottom is biographical information. These boxes and the photo are outlined by a thin royal blue line. The horizontal backs have a light blue postcard design with the sponsor logo and a "Wellness Goal." The cards are unnumbered and checklisted below in alphabetical order.

| | MINT | NRMT |
|---|---|---|
| COMPLETE SET (26) | 15.00 | 6.75 |
| COMMON CARD (1-26) | .25 | .11 |
| ❑ 1 Dave Andreychuk | .75 | .35 |
| ❑ 2 Donald Audette | 1.00 | .45 |
| ❑ 3 Doug Bodger | .35 | .16 |
| ❑ 4 Bob Corkum | .35 | .16 |
| ❑ 5 Gord Donnelly | .35 | .16 |
| ❑ 6 Dave Hannan | .35 | .16 |
| ❑ 7 Dominik Hasek | 6.00 | 2.70 |
| ❑ 8 Dale Hawerchuk | 1.00 | .45 |
| ❑ 9 Yuri Khmylev | .35 | .16 |
| ❑ 10 Pat LaFontaine | 1.50 | .70 |
| ❑ 11 Grant Ledyard | .35 | .16 |
| ❑ 12 Brad May | .75 | .35 |
| ❑ 13 Alexander Mogilny | 2.50 | 1.10 |
| ❑ 14 Randy Moller | .35 | .16 |
| ❑ 15 John Muckler CO | .35 | .16 |
| ❑ 16 Colin Patterson | .35 | .16 |
| ❑ 17 Wayne Presley | .35 | .16 |
| ❑ 18 Daren Puppa | 1.00 | .45 |
| ❑ 19 Mike Ramsey | .35 | .16 |
| ❑ 20 Rob Ray | .40 | .18 |
| ❑ 21 Richard Smehlik | .35 | .16 |
| ❑ 22 Ken Sutton | .35 | .16 |
| ❑ 23 Petr Svoboda | .50 | .23 |
| ❑ 24 Bob Sweeney | .35 | .16 |
| ❑ 25 Randy Wood | .35 | .16 |
| ❑ 26 Sabretooth (Mascot) | .25 | .11 |

## 1992-93 Sabres Jubilee Foods

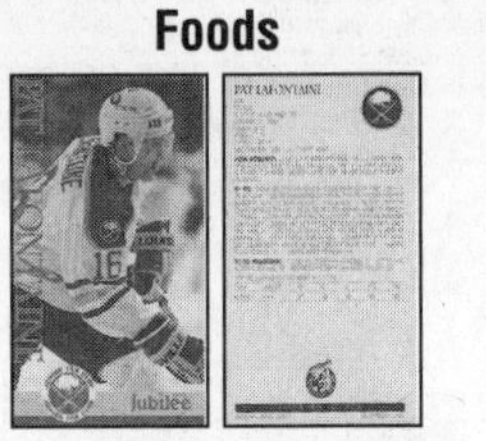

Printed on thin white stock, the cards of this set, which are subtitled "Junior Fan Club," measure approximately 4" by 7" and feature color action shots of Sabres players on their fronts. These photos are borderless, except across the bottom, where a half-inch wide, mustard-colored stripe carries the sponsor's name. A thin blue stripe edges the card at the very bottom. The player's name appears vertically in blue lettering down one side. The Junior Fan Club logo in the lower left straddles the bottom of the photo and the two stripes. The backs have the player's name and biography in the upper left and the Sabres logo in the upper right. Beneath are highlights and stats from the 1991-92 season. The Stanley Cup logo at the bottom rounds out the card. The cards are unnumbered and checklisted below in alphabetical order.

| | MINT | NRMT |
|---|---|---|
| COMPLETE SET (16) | 12.00 | 5.50 |
| COMMON CARD (1-16) | .35 | .16 |
| ❑ 1 Dave Andreychuk | .75 | .35 |
| ❑ 2 Doug Bodger | .35 | .16 |
| ❑ 3 Gord Donnelly<br>Rob Ray | .60 | .25 |
| ❑ 4 Dominik Hasek<br>Daren Puppa | 6.00 | 2.70 |
| ❑ 5 Dale Hawerchuk | 1.00 | .45 |
| ❑ 6 Yuri Khmylev<br>Viktor Gordijuk | .35 | .16 |
| ❑ 7 Pat LaFontaine | 1.50 | .70 |
| ❑ 8 Brad May | .75 | .35 |
| ❑ 9 Alexander Mogilny | 2.50 | 1.10 |
| ❑ 10 Randy Moller<br>Ken Sutton | .35 | .16 |
| ❑ 11 Wayne Presley<br>Donald Audette | .75 | .35 |
| ❑ 12 Mike Ramsey | .35 | .16 |
| ❑ 13 Richard Smehlik<br>Bob Corkum | .35 | .16 |
| ❑ 14 Petr Svoboda | .50 | .23 |
| ❑ 15 Bob Sweeney | .35 | .16 |
| ❑ 16 Randy Wood | .35 | .16 |

## 1993-94 Sabres Limited Edition Team Issue

Given out one per fan at a Sabres home game during the 93-94 season, these blank back cards with color action photos on the front are limited to 5,000 sets. There is a yellow stripe at the bottom of the card with the players name, and Sabres logo. Cards are unnumbered and checklisted below in alphabetical order.

| | MINT | NRMT |
|---|---|---|
| COMPLETE SET (4) | 10.00 | 4.50 |
| COMMON CARD (1-4) | 1.00 | .45 |
| ❑ 1 Doug Bodger | 1.00 | .45 |
| ❑ 2 Dominik Hasek | 5.00 | 2.20 |
| ❑ 3 Dale Hawerchuk | 2.00 | .90 |
| ❑ 4 Alexander Mogilny | 2.00 | .90 |

## 1993-94 Sabres Noco

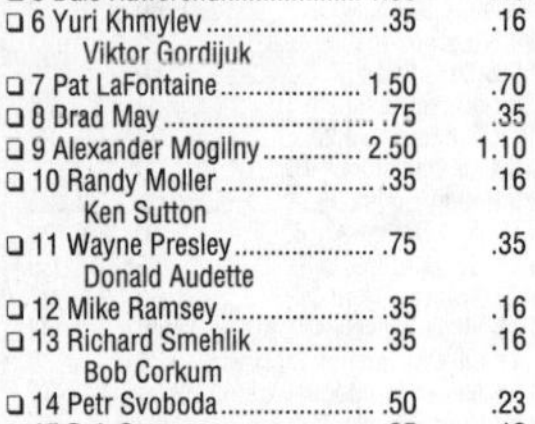


Subtitled Sabres Stars and issued in five-card perforated strips, these 20 standard-size cards feature on their fronts white-bordered color player action shots framed by a yellow line. The player's name and the team logo appear in the white margin below the photo. The white back carries the player's name and number at the top, followed below by statistics and career highlights. The logo for the set's sponsor, Noco Express Shop, rounds out the card at the bottom. The cards are unnumbered and checklisted below in alphabetical order.

| | MINT | NRMT |
|---|---|---|
| COMPLETE SET (20) | 12.00 | 5.50 |
| COMMON CARD (1-20) | .35 | .16 |
| ❑ 1 Roger Crozier | .60 | .25 |
| ❑ 2 Rick Dudley | .50 | .23 |
| ❑ 3 Mike Foligno | .50 | .23 |
| ❑ 4 Grant Fuhr | 1.00 | .45 |
| ❑ 5 Danny Gare | .50 | .23 |
| ❑ 6 Dominik Hasek | 5.00 | 2.20 |
| ❑ 7 Dale Hawerchuk | .75 | .35 |
| ❑ 8 Tim Horton | 2.00 | .90 |
| ❑ 9 Pat LaFontaine | 1.25 | .55 |
| ❑ 10 Don Luce | .50 | .23 |
| ❑ 11 Rick Martin | .75 | .35 |
| ❑ 12 Brad May | .60 | .25 |
| ❑ 13 Alexander Mogilny | 1.25 | .55 |
| ❑ 14 Gilbert Perreault | 1.00 | .45 |
| ❑ 15 Craig Ramsay | .50 | .23 |
| ❑ 16 Mike Ramsey | .50 | .23 |
| ❑ 17 Rene Robert | .60 | .25 |
| ❑ 18 Sabretooth Mascot | .35 | .16 |
| ❑ 19 Jim Schoenfeld | .75 | .35 |
| ❑ 20 Knoxes Unveil<br>Sabres Uniform<br>Northrup Knox<br>Punch Imlach<br>Seymour Knox | .35 | .16 |

## 1976-77 San Diego Mariners WHA

These cards measure 5" x 8" and were issued in two sheets of seven players each. Card fronts feature black and white photos with a white border. Backs feature player statistics. Cards are unnumbered and checklisted below alpabetically. Prices below are for individual cards.

| | MINT | NRMT |
|---|---|---|
| COMPLETE SET (14) | 12.00 | 5.50 |
| COMMON CARD | 1.00 | .45 |
| ❑ 1 Kevin Devine | 1.00 | .45 |
| ❑ 2 Bob Dobek | 1.00 | .45 |
| ❑ 3 Norm Ferguson | 1.50 | .70 |
| ❑ 4 Brent Hughes | 1.00 | .45 |
| ❑ 5 Randy Legge | 1.00 | .45 |
| ❑ 6 Ken Lockett | 1.00 | .45 |
| ❑ 7 Kevin Morrison | 1.00 | .45 |
| ❑ 8 Joe Norris | 1.00 | .45 |
| ❑ 9 Gerry Pinder | 1.00 | .45 |
| ❑ 10 Brad Rhiness | 1.00 | .45 |
| ❑ 11 Wayne Rivers | 1.00 | .45 |
| ❑ 12 Paul Shmyr | 1.00 | .45 |
| ❑ 13 Gary Veneruzzo | 1.00 | .45 |
| ❑ 14 Ernie Wakely | 1.50 | .70 |

## 1970-71 Sargent Promotions Stamps

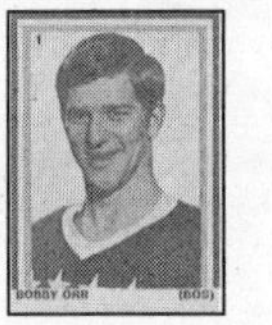


This set consists of 224 total stamps, 16 for each NHL team. Individual stamps measure approximately 2" by 2 1/2". The set could be put into a album featuring Bobby Orr on the cover. Stamp fronts feature a full-color head shot of the player, player's name, and team. The stamp number is located in the upper left corner. The 1970-71 set features one-time appearances in Eddie Sargent Promotions sets by Hall of Famers Gordie Howe, Jean Beliveau, Andy Bathgate. The set also features first appearances of Gil Perreault, Brad Park, and Bobby Clarke. The three have Rookie Cards in both Topps and O-Pee-Chee for the same year.

| | NRMT-MT | EXC |
|---|---|---|
| COMPLETE SET (224) | 650.00 | 300.00 |
| COMMON STAMP (1-224) | 1.00 | .45 |
| ❑ 1 Bobby Orr | 125.00 | 55.00 |
| ❑ 2 Don Awrey | 1.00 | .45 |
| ❑ 3 Derek Sanderson | 10.00 | 4.50 |
| ❑ 4 Ted Green | 1.25 | .55 |
| ❑ 5 Eddie Johnston | 2.50 | 1.10 |
| ❑ 6 Wayne Carleton | 1.00 | .45 |
| ❑ 7 Ed Westfall | 1.50 | .70 |
| ❑ 8 Johnny Bucyk | 5.00 | 2.20 |
| ❑ 9 John McKenzie | 1.00 | .45 |
| ❑ 10 Ken Hodge | 2.00 | .90 |
| ❑ 11 Rick Smith | 1.00 | .45 |
| ❑ 12 Fred Stanfield | 1.00 | .45 |
| ❑ 13 Garnet Bailey | 1.00 | .45 |
| ❑ 14 Phil Esposito | 20.00 | 9.00 |
| ❑ 15 Gerry Cheevers | 10.00 | 4.50 |
| ❑ 16 Dallas Smith | 1.00 | .45 |
| ❑ 17 Joe Daley | 2.00 | .90 |
| ❑ 18 Ron Anderson | 1.00 | .45 |
| ❑ 19 Tracy Pratt | 1.00 | .45 |
| ❑ 20 Gerry Meehan | 1.50 | .70 |
| ❑ 21 Reg Fleming | 1.00 | .45 |
| ❑ 22 Al Hamilton | 1.25 | .55 |
| ❑ 23 Gil Perreault | 25.00 | 11.00 |
| ❑ 24 Skip Krake | 1.00 | .45 |
| ❑ 25 Kevin O'Shea | 1.00 | .45 |
| ❑ 26 Roger Crozier | 3.00 | 1.35 |
| ❑ 27 Bill Inglis | 1.00 | .45 |
| ❑ 28 Mike McMahon | 1.00 | .45 |
| ❑ 29 Cliff Schmautz | 1.00 | .45 |
| ❑ 30 Floyd Smith | 1.00 | .45 |
| ❑ 31 Randy Wyrozub | 1.00 | .45 |
| ❑ 32 Jim Watson | 1.00 | .45 |
| ❑ 33 Tony Esposito | 30.00 | 13.50 |
| ❑ 34 Doug Jarrett | 1.00 | .45 |
| ❑ 35 Keith Magnuson | 1.25 | .55 |
| ❑ 36 Dennis Hull | 2.00 | .90 |
| ❑ 37 Cliff Koroll | 1.00 | .45 |
| ❑ 38 Eric Nesterenko | 1.50 | .70 |
| ❑ 39 Pit Martin | 1.25 | .55 |
| ❑ 40 Lou Angotti | 1.00 | .45 |
| ❑ 41 Jim Pappin | 1.25 | .55 |
| ❑ 42 Gerry Pinder | 1.25 | .55 |
| ❑ 43 Bobby Hull | 50.00 | 22.00 |
| ❑ 44 Pat Stapleton | 1.25 | .55 |
| ❑ 45 Gerry Desjardins | 2.00 | .90 |
| ❑ 46 Chico Maki | 1.25 | .55 |
| ❑ 47 Doug Mohns | 1.25 | .55 |
| ❑ 48 Stan Mikita | 20.00 | 9.00 |
| ❑ 49 Gary Bergman | 1.25 | .55 |
| ❑ 50 Pete Stemkowski | 1.25 | .55 |
| ❑ 51 Bruce MacGregor | 1.00 | .45 |
| ❑ 52 Ron Harris | 1.00 | .45 |
| ❑ 53 Billy Dea | 1.00 | .45 |
| ❑ 54 Wayne Connelly | 1.00 | .45 |
| ❑ 55 Dale Rolfe | 1.00 | .45 |
| ❑ 56 Gordie Howe | 80.00 | 36.00 |
| ❑ 57 Tom Webster | 1.25 | .55 |
| ❑ 58 Al Karlander | 1.00 | .45 |
| ❑ 59 Alex Delvecchio | 5.00 | 2.20 |
| ❑ 60 Nick Libett | 1.25 | .55 |
| ❑ 61 Garry Unger | 2.00 | .90 |
| ❑ 62 Roy Edwards | 2.00 | .90 |
| ❑ 63 Frank Mahovlich | 10.00 | 4.50 |
| ❑ 64 Bob Baun | 2.50 | 1.10 |
| ❑ 65 Dick Duff | 2.00 | .90 |
| ❑ 66 Ross Lonsberry | 1.00 | .45 |
| ❑ 67 Ed Joyal | 1.00 | .45 |
| ❑ 68 Dale Hoganson | 1.00 | .45 |
| ❑ 69 Eddie Shack | 5.00 | 2.20 |
| ❑ 70 Real Lemieux | 1.00 | .45 |
| ❑ 71 Matt Ravlich | 1.00 | .45 |
| ❑ 72 Bob Pulford | 3.00 | 1.35 |
| ❑ 73 Denis DeJordy | 2.50 | 1.10 |
| ❑ 74 Larry Mickey | 1.00 | .45 |
| ❑ 75 Bill Flett | 1.00 | .45 |
| ❑ 76 Juha Widing | 1.50 | .70 |
| ❑ 77 Jim Peters | 1.25 | .55 |
| ❑ 78 Gilles Marotte | 1.25 | .55 |
| ❑ 79 Larry Cahan | 1.00 | .45 |
| ❑ 80 Howie Hughes | 1.00 | .45 |
| ❑ 81 Cesare Maniago | 2.50 | 1.10 |
| ❑ 82 Ted Harris | 1.00 | .45 |
| ❑ 83 Tom Williams | 1.00 | .45 |
| ❑ 84 Gump Worsley | 10.00 | 4.50 |
| ❑ 85 Tom Reid | 1.00 | .45 |
| ❑ 86 Murray Oliver | 1.00 | .45 |
| ❑ 87 Charlie Burns | 1.00 | .45 |
| ❑ 88 Jude Drouin | 1.00 | .45 |
| ❑ 89 Walt McKechnie | 1.00 | .45 |
| ❑ 90 Danny O'Shea | 1.00 | .45 |
| ❑ 91 Barry Gibbs | 1.00 | .45 |
| ❑ 92 Danny Grant | 1.25 | .55 |
| ❑ 93 Bob Barlow | 1.00 | .45 |
| ❑ 94 J.P. Parise | 1.25 | .55 |
| ❑ 95 Bill Goldsworthy | 1.50 | .70 |
| ❑ 96 Bobby Rousseau | 1.25 | .55 |
| ❑ 97 Jacques Laperriere | 2.00 | .90 |
| ❑ 98 Henri Richard | 10.00 | 4.50 |
| ❑ 99 J.C. Tremblay | 1.50 | .70 |
| ❑ 100 Rogie Vachon | 8.00 | 3.60 |
| ❑ 101 Claude Larose | 1.00 | .45 |
| ❑ 102 Pete Mahovlich | 1.50 | .70 |
| ❑ 103 Jacques Lemaire | 8.00 | 3.60 |
| ❑ 104 Bill Collins | 1.00 | .45 |
| ❑ 105 Guy Lapointe | 3.00 | 1.35 |
| ❑ 106 Mickey Redmond | 5.00 | 2.20 |
| ❑ 107 Larry Pleau | 1.25 | .55 |
| ❑ 108 Jean Beliveau | 25.00 | 11.00 |
| ❑ 109 Yvan Cournoyer | 8.00 | 3.60 |
| ❑ 110 Serge Savard | 8.00 | 3.60 |
| ❑ 111 Terry Harper | 1.25 | .55 |
| ❑ 112 Phil Myre | 2.00 | .90 |
| ❑ 113 Syl Apps | 1.25 | .55 |
| ❑ 114 Ted Irvine | 1.00 | .45 |
| ❑ 115 Ed Giacomin | 10.00 | 4.50 |
| ❑ 116 Arnie Brown | 1.00 | .45 |
| ❑ 117 Walt Tkaczuk | 1.25 | .55 |
| ❑ 118 Jean Ratelle | 5.00 | 2.20 |
| ❑ 119 Dave Balon | 1.00 | .45 |
| ❑ 120 Ron Stewart | 1.00 | .45 |
| ❑ 121 Jim Neilson | 1.00 | .45 |
| ❑ 122 Rod Gilbert | 5.00 | 2.20 |
| ❑ 123 Bill Fairbairn | 1.00 | .45 |
| ❑ 124 Brad Park | 20.00 | 9.00 |
| ❑ 125 Tim Horton | 15.00 | 6.75 |
| ❑ 126 Vic Hadfield | 1.50 | .70 |
| ❑ 127 Bob Nevin | 1.00 | .45 |
| ❑ 128 Rod Seiling | 1.00 | .45 |
| ❑ 129 Gary Smith | 2.50 | 1.10 |
| ❑ 130 Carol Vadnais | 1.00 | .45 |
| ❑ 131 Bert Marshall | 1.00 | .45 |
| ❑ 132 Earl Ingarfield | 1.00 | .45 |
| ❑ 133 Dennis Hextall | 1.25 | .55 |
| ❑ 134 Harry Howell | 3.00 | 1.35 |
| ❑ 135 Wayne Muloin | 1.00 | .45 |
| ❑ 136 Mike Laughton | 1.00 | .45 |
| ❑ 137 Ted Hampson | 1.00 | .45 |
| ❑ 138 Doug Roberts | 1.00 | .45 |
| ❑ 139 Dick Mattiussi | 1.00 | .45 |
| ❑ 140 Gary Jarrett | 1.00 | .45 |
| ❑ 141 Gary Croteau | 1.00 | .45 |
| ❑ 142 Norm Ferguson | 1.00 | .45 |
| ❑ 143 Bill Hicke | 1.00 | .45 |
| ❑ 144 Gerry Ehman | 1.00 | .45 |
| ❑ 145 Ralph McSweyn | 1.00 | .45 |
| ❑ 146 Bernie Parent | 15.00 | 6.75 |
| ❑ 147 Brent Hughes | 1.00 | .45 |
| ❑ 148 Bobby Clarke | 40.00 | 18.00 |
| ❑ 149 Gary Dornhoefer | 1.25 | .55 |
| ❑ 150 Simon Nolet | 1.00 | .45 |
| ❑ 151 Garry Peters | 1.00 | .45 |
| ❑ 152 Doug Favell | 2.50 | 1.10 |
| ❑ 153 Jim Johnson | 1.00 | .45 |
| ❑ 154 Andre Lacroix | 1.50 | .70 |
| ❑ 155 Larry Hale | 1.00 | .45 |
| ❑ 156 Joe Watson | 1.00 | .45 |
| ❑ 157 Jean-Guy Gendron | 1.00 | .45 |
| ❑ 158 Larry Hillman | 1.00 | .45 |
| ❑ 159 Ed Van Impe | 1.00 | .45 |
| ❑ 160 Wayne Hillman | 1.00 | .45 |
| ❑ 161 Al Smith | 2.00 | .90 |
| ❑ 162 Jean Pronovost | 1.25 | .55 |
| ❑ 163 Bob Woytowich | 1.00 | .45 |
| ❑ 164 Bryan Watson | 1.25 | .55 |
| ❑ 165 Dean Prentice | 1.50 | .70 |
| ❑ 166 Duane Rupp | 1.00 | .45 |
| ❑ 167 Glen Sather | 2.00 | .90 |
| ❑ 168 Keith McCreary | 1.00 | .45 |
| ❑ 169 Jim Morrison | 1.00 | .45 |
| ❑ 170 Ron Schock | 1.00 | .45 |
| ❑ 171 Wally Boyer | 1.00 | .45 |
| ❑ 172 Nick Harbaruk | 1.00 | .45 |
| ❑ 173 Andy Bathgate | 5.00 | 2.20 |
| ❑ 174 Ken Schinkel | 1.00 | .45 |
| ❑ 175 Les Binkley | 2.00 | .90 |
| ❑ 176 Val Fonteyne | 1.00 | .45 |
| ❑ 177 Red Berenson | 1.50 | .70 |
| ❑ 178 Ab McDonald | 1.00 | .45 |
| ❑ 179 Jim Roberts | 1.00 | .45 |
| ❑ 180 Frank St. Marseille | 1.00 | .45 |
| ❑ 181 Ernie Wakely | 2.50 | 1.10 |
| ❑ 182 Terry Crisp | 1.25 | .55 |
| ❑ 183 Bob Plager | 1.50 | .70 |
| ❑ 184 Barclay Plager | 1.50 | .70 |
| ❑ 185 Chris Bordeleau | 1.00 | .45 |
| ❑ 186 Gary Sabourin | 1.00 | .45 |
| ❑ 187 Bill Plager | 1.25 | .55 |
| ❑ 188 Tim Ecclestone | 1.00 | .45 |
| ❑ 189 Jean-Guy Talbot | 1.50 | .70 |
| ❑ 190 Noel Picard | 1.00 | .45 |
| ❑ 191 Bob Wall | 1.00 | .45 |
| ❑ 192 Jim Lorentz | 1.00 | .45 |
| ❑ 193 Bruce Gamble | 3.00 | 1.35 |
| ❑ 194 Jim Harrison | 1.00 | .45 |
| ❑ 195 Paul Henderson | 3.00 | 1.35 |
| ❑ 196 Brian Glennie | 1.00 | .45 |
| ❑ 197 Jim Dorey | 1.00 | .45 |
| ❑ 198 Rick Ley | 1.25 | .55 |
| ❑ 199 Jacques Plante | 25.00 | 11.00 |
| ❑ 200 Ron Ellis | 1.50 | .70 |
| ❑ 201 Jim McKenny | 1.00 | .45 |
| ❑ 202 Brit Selby | 1.00 | .45 |
| ❑ 203 Mike Pelyk | 1.00 | .45 |
| ❑ 204 Norm Ullman | 5.00 | 2.20 |
| ❑ 205 Bill MacMillan | 1.00 | .45 |
| ❑ 206 Mike Walton | 1.25 | .55 |
| ❑ 207 Garry Monahan | 1.00 | .45 |
| ❑ 208 Dave Keon | 5.00 | 2.20 |
| ❑ 209 Pat Quinn | 2.00 | .90 |
| ❑ 210 Wayne Maki | 1.00 | .45 |
| ❑ 212 Orland Kurtenbach | 1.25 | .55 |
| ❑ 213 Paul Popiel | 1.25 | .55 |
| ❑ 214 Dan Johnson | 1.00 | .45 |
| ❑ 215 Dale Tallon | 1.25 | .55 |
| ❑ 216 Ray Cullen | 1.25 | .55 |
| ❑ 217 Bob Dillabough | 1.00 | .45 |
| ❑ 218 Gary Doak | 1.00 | .45 |
| ❑ 219 Andre Boudrias | 1.50 | .70 |
| ❑ 220 Rosaire Paiement | 1.25 | .55 |
| ❑ 221 Darryl Sly | 1.00 | .45 |
| ❑ 222 George Gardner | 1.00 | .45 |
| ❑ 223 Jim Wiste | 1.00 | .45 |
| ❑ 224 Murray Hall | 1.00 | .45 |
| ❑ xx Stamp Album (Bobby Orr on cover) | 35.00 | 16.00 |

## 1971-72 Sargent Promotions Stamps

Issued by Eddie Sargent Promotions in a series of 16 ten-cent sheets of 14 NHL players each, this 224-stamp set featured posed color photos of players in their NHLPA jerseys. The pictures are framed on their tops and sides in different color borders with the players' names and teams appearing along the bottom. Each sheet measured approximately 7 7/8" by 10" and was divided into four rows, with four 2" by 2 1/2" stamps per row. Two of these 16 sections gave the series number (e.g., Series 1), resulting in a total of 14 players per sheet. The sections are perforated and the backs are blank. There was a stamp album (approximately 9 1/2" by 13") which featured information on the team history and individual players. The stamps are numbered in the upper left corner and they are grouped into 14 teams of 16 players each as follows: Boston Bruins (1-16), Buffalo Sabres (17-32), Chicago Blackhawks (33-48), Detroit Red Wings (49-64), Los Angeles Kings (65-80), Minnesota North Stars (81-96), Montreal Canadiens (97-112), New York Rangers (113-128), California

Golden Seals (129-144), Philadelphia Flyers (145-160), Pittsburgh Penguins (161-176), St. Louis Blues (177-192), Toronto Maple Leafs (193-208), and Vancouver Canucks (209-224).

| | NRMT-MT | EXC |
|---|---|---|
| COMPLETE SET (224) | 450.00 | 200.00 |
| COMMON STAMP (1-224) | 1.00 | .45 |
| ❑ 1 Fred Stanfield | 1.00 | .45 |
| ❑ 2 Ed Westfall | 1.50 | .70 |
| ❑ 3 John McKenzie | 1.00 | .45 |
| ❑ 4 Derek Sanderson | 8.00 | 3.60 |
| ❑ 5 Rick Smith | 1.00 | .45 |
| ❑ 6 Teddy Green | 1.25 | .55 |
| ❑ 7 Phil Esposito | 15.00 | 6.75 |
| ❑ 8 Ken Hodge | 2.00 | .90 |
| ❑ 9 Johnny Bucyk | 8.00 | 3.60 |
| ❑ 10 Bobby Orr | 100.00 | 45.00 |
| ❑ 11 Dallas Smith | 1.00 | .45 |
| ❑ 12 Mike Walton | 1.25 | .55 |
| ❑ 13 Don Awrey | 1.00 | .45 |
| ❑ 14 Unknown | 1.00 | .45 |
| ❑ 15 Eddie Johnston | 2.00 | .90 |
| ❑ 16 Gerry Cheevers | 8.00 | 3.60 |
| ❑ 17 Gerry Meehan | 1.50 | .70 |
| ❑ 18 Ron Anderson | 1.00 | .45 |
| ❑ 19 Gilbert Perreault | 12.00 | 5.50 |
| ❑ 20 Eddie Shack | 4.00 | 1.80 |
| ❑ 21 Jim Watson | 1.00 | .45 |
| ❑ 22 Kevin O'Shea | 1.00 | .45 |
| ❑ 23 Al Hamilton | 1.00 | .45 |
| ❑ 24 Dick Duff | 1.50 | .70 |
| ❑ 25 Tracy Pratt | 1.00 | .45 |
| ❑ 26 Don Luce | 1.00 | .45 |
| ❑ 27 Roger Crozier | 2.00 | .90 |
| ❑ 28 Doug Barrie | 1.00 | .45 |
| ❑ 29 Mike Robitaille | 1.00 | .45 |
| ❑ 30 Phil Goyette | 1.00 | .45 |
| ❑ 31 Larry Keenan | 1.00 | .45 |
| ❑ 32 Dave Dryden | 2.00 | .90 |
| ❑ 33 Stan Mikita | 12.00 | 5.50 |
| ❑ 34 Bobby Hull | 40.00 | 18.00 |
| ❑ 35 Cliff Koroll | 1.00 | .45 |
| ❑ 36 Chico Maki | 1.25 | .55 |
| ❑ 37 Danny O'Shea | 1.00 | .45 |
| ❑ 38 Lou Angotti | 1.00 | .45 |
| ❑ 39 Andre Lacroix | 1.25 | .55 |
| ❑ 40 Jim Pappin | 1.00 | .45 |
| ❑ 41 Doug Jarrett | 1.00 | .45 |
| ❑ 42 Pit Martin | 1.25 | .55 |
| ❑ 43 Gary Smith | 2.00 | .90 |
| ❑ 44 Tony Esposito | 15.00 | 6.75 |
| ❑ 45 Pat Stapleton | 1.00 | .45 |
| ❑ 46 Dennis Hull | 2.00 | .90 |
| ❑ 47 Bill White | 1.00 | .45 |
| ❑ 48 Keith Magnuson | 1.25 | .55 |
| ❑ 49 Bill Collins | 1.00 | .45 |
| ❑ 50 Bob Wall | 1.00 | .45 |
| ❑ 51 Red Berenson | 1.50 | .70 |
| ❑ 52 Mickey Redmond | 3.00 | 1.35 |
| ❑ 53 Nick Libett | 1.00 | .45 |
| ❑ 54 Gary Bergman | 1.25 | .55 |
| ❑ 55 Alex Delvecchio | 5.00 | 2.20 |
| ❑ 56 Tim Ecclestone | 1.00 | .45 |
| ❑ 57 Arnie Brown | 1.00 | .45 |
| ❑ 58 Ron Harris | 1.00 | .45 |
| ❑ 59 Ab McDonald | 1.00 | .45 |
| ❑ 60 Guy Charron | 1.25 | .55 |
| ❑ 61 Al Smith | 2.00 | .90 |
| ❑ 62 Joe Daley | 2.00 | .90 |
| ❑ 63 Leon Rochefort | 1.00 | .45 |
| ❑ 64 Ron Stackhouse | 1.00 | .45 |
| ❑ 65A Larry Johnston | 1.50 | .70 |
| ❑ 65B Juha Widing | 1.00 | .45 |
| ❑ 66 Bob Pulford | 2.00 | .90 |
| ❑ 67 Bill Flett | 1.00 | .45 |
| ❑ 68 Rogie Vachon | 5.00 | 2.20 |
| ❑ 69 Ross Lonsberry | 1.00 | .45 |
| ❑ 70 Gilles Marotte | 1.00 | .45 |
| ❑ 71 Harry Howell | 2.00 | .90 |
| ❑ 72 Real Lemieux | 1.00 | .45 |
| ❑ 73 Butch Goring | 1.00 | .45 |
| ❑ 74 Ed Joyal | 1.00 | .45 |
| ❑ 75 Larry Hillman | 1.00 | .45 |
| ❑ 76 Lucien Grenier | 1.00 | .45 |
| ❑ 77 Paul Curtis | 1.00 | .45 |
| ❑ 78 Unknown | 1.00 | .45 |
| ❑ 79 Unknown | 1.00 | .45 |
| ❑ 80 Unknown | 1.00 | .45 |
| ❑ 81 Jude Drouin | 1.00 | .45 |
| ❑ 82 Tom Reid | 1.00 | .45 |
| ❑ 83 J.P. Parise | 1.25 | .55 |
| ❑ 84 Doug Mohns | 1.25 | .55 |
| ❑ 85 Danny Grant | 1.25 | .55 |
| ❑ 86 Bill Goldsworthy | 1.50 | .70 |
| ❑ 87 Charlie Burns | 1.00 | .45 |
| ❑ 88 Murray Oliver | 1.00 | .45 |
| ❑ 89 Dean Prentice | 1.50 | .70 |
| ❑ 90 Bob Nevin | 1.25 | .55 |
| ❑ 91 Ted Harris | 1.25 | .55 |
| ❑ 92 Cesare Maniago | 2.00 | .90 |
| ❑ 93 Lou Nanne | 1.25 | .55 |
| ❑ 94 Ted Hampton | 1.00 | .45 |
| ❑ 95 Barry Gibbs | 1.00 | .45 |
| ❑ 96 Gump Worsley | 8.00 | 3.60 |
| ❑ 97 J.C. Tremblay | 1.50 | .70 |
| ❑ 98 Guy Lapointe | 2.00 | .90 |
| ❑ 99 Pete Mahovlich | 1.50 | .70 |
| ❑ 100 Larry Pleau | 1.25 | .55 |
| ❑ 101 Phil Myre | 2.00 | .90 |
| ❑ 102 Yvan Cournoyer | 5.00 | 2.20 |
| ❑ 103 Henri Richard | 10.00 | 4.50 |
| ❑ 104 Frank Mahovlich | 10.00 | 4.50 |
| ❑ 105 Jacques Lemaire | 4.00 | 1.80 |
| ❑ 106 Claude Larose | 1.00 | .45 |
| ❑ 107 Terry Harper | 1.25 | .55 |
| ❑ 108 Jacques Laperriere | 2.00 | .90 |
| ❑ 109 Phil Roberto | 1.00 | .45 |
| ❑ 110 Serge Savard | 4.00 | 1.80 |
| ❑ 111 Marc Tardif | 1.25 | .55 |
| ❑ 112 Pierre Bouchard | 1.25 | .55 |
| ❑ 113 Rod Gilbert | 5.00 | 2.20 |
| ❑ 114 Jean Ratelle | 5.00 | 2.20 |
| ❑ 115 Pete Stemkowski | 1.00 | .45 |
| ❑ 116 Brad Park | 8.00 | 3.60 |
| ❑ 117 Bobby Rousseau | 1.00 | .45 |
| ❑ 118 Dale Rolfe | 1.00 | .45 |
| ❑ 119 Rod Seiling | 1.00 | .45 |
| ❑ 120 Walt Tkaczuk | 1.00 | .45 |
| ❑ 121 Vic Hadfield | 1.25 | .55 |
| ❑ 122 Jim Neilson | 1.00 | .45 |
| ❑ 123 Bill Fairbairn | 1.00 | .45 |
| ❑ 124 Bruce MacGregor | 1.00 | .45 |
| ❑ 125 Dave Balon | 1.00 | .45 |
| ❑ 126 Ted Irvine | 1.00 | .45 |
| ❑ 127 Gilles Villemure | 2.00 | .90 |
| ❑ 128 Ed Giacomin | 8.00 | 3.60 |
| ❑ 129 Walt McKechnie | 1.00 | .45 |
| ❑ 130 Tom Williams | 1.00 | .45 |
| ❑ 131 Wayne Carleton | 1.25 | .55 |
| ❑ 132 Gerry Pinder | 1.00 | .45 |
| ❑ 133 Gary Croteau | 1.00 | .45 |
| ❑ 134 Bert Marshall | 1.00 | .45 |
| ❑ 135 Tom Webster | 1.00 | .45 |
| ❑ 136 Norm Ferguson | 1.00 | .45 |
| ❑ 137 Carol Vadnais | 1.00 | .45 |
| ❑ 138 Gary Jarrett | 1.00 | .45 |
| ❑ 139 Ernie Hicke | 1.00 | .45 |
| ❑ 140 Paul Shmyr | 1.00 | .45 |
| ❑ 141 Marshall Johnston | 1.00 | .45 |
| ❑ 142 Don O'Donoghue | 1.00 | .45 |
| ❑ 143 Joey Johnston | 1.00 | .45 |
| ❑ 144 Dick Redmond | 1.00 | .45 |
| ❑ 145 Simon Nolet | 1.00 | .45 |
| ❑ 146 Wayne Hillman | 1.00 | .45 |
| ❑ 147 Brent Hughes | 1.00 | .45 |
| ❑ 148 Jim Johnson | 1.00 | .45 |
| ❑ 149 Larry Mickey | 1.00 | .45 |
| ❑ 150 Ed Van Impe | 1.00 | .45 |
| ❑ 151 Gary Dornhoefer | 1.25 | .55 |
| ❑ 152 Bobby Clarke | 25.00 | 11.00 |
| ❑ 153 Jean-Guy Gendron | 1.00 | .45 |
| ❑ 154 Larry Hale | 1.00 | .45 |
| ❑ 155 Serge Bernier | 1.00 | .45 |
| ❑ 156 Doug Favell | 2.00 | .90 |
| ❑ 157 Bob Kelly | 1.00 | .45 |
| ❑ 158 Joe Watson | 1.00 | .45 |
| ❑ 159 Larry Brown | 1.00 | .45 |
| ❑ 160 Bruce Gamble | 2.00 | .90 |
| ❑ 161 Syl Apps | 1.25 | .55 |
| ❑ 162 Ken Schinkel | 1.00 | .45 |
| ❑ 163 Val Fonteyne | 1.00 | .45 |
| ❑ 164 Bryan Watson | 1.50 | .70 |
| ❑ 165 Bob Woytowich | 1.00 | .45 |
| ❑ 166 Les Binkley | 2.00 | .90 |
| ❑ 167 Roy Edwards | 2.00 | .90 |
| ❑ 168 Jean Pronovost | 1.25 | .55 |
| ❑ 169 Tim Horton | 12.00 | 5.50 |
| ❑ 170 Ron Schock | 1.00 | .45 |
| ❑ 171 Nick Harbaruk | 1.00 | .45 |
| ❑ 172 Greg Polis | 1.00 | .45 |
| ❑ 173 Bryan Hextall | 1.25 | .55 |
| ❑ 174 Keith McCreary | 1.00 | .45 |
| ❑ 175 Bill Hicke | 1.00 | .45 |
| ❑ 176 Jim Rutherford | 2.00 | .90 |
| ❑ 177 Gary Sabourin | 1.00 | .45 |
| ❑ 178 Garry Unger | 2.00 | .90 |
| ❑ 179 Terry Crisp | 1.25 | .55 |
| ❑ 180 Noel Picard | 1.00 | .45 |
| ❑ 181 Jim Roberts | 1.00 | .45 |
| ❑ 182 Barclay Plager | 1.50 | .70 |
| ❑ 183 Brit Selby | 1.00 | .45 |
| ❑ 184 Frank St. Marseille | 1.00 | .45 |
| ❑ 185 Ernie Wakely | 2.00 | .90 |
| ❑ 186 Wayne Connelly | 1.00 | .45 |
| ❑ 187 Chris Bordeleau | 1.00 | .45 |
| ❑ 188 Bill Sutherland | 1.00 | .45 |
| ❑ 189 Bob Plager | 1.50 | .70 |
| ❑ 190 Bill Plager | 1.25 | .55 |
| ❑ 191 George Morrison | 1.00 | .45 |
| ❑ 192 Jim Lorentz | 1.00 | .45 |
| ❑ 193 Norm Ullman | 5.00 | 2.20 |
| ❑ 194 Jim McKenny | 1.00 | .45 |
| ❑ 195 Rick Ley | 1.00 | .45 |
| ❑ 196 Bob Baun | 2.00 | .90 |
| ❑ 197 Mike Pelyk | 1.00 | .45 |
| ❑ 198 Bill MacMillan | 1.00 | .45 |
| ❑ 199 Garry Monahan | 1.00 | .45 |
| ❑ 200 Paul Henderson | 3.00 | 1.35 |
| ❑ 201 Jim Dorey | 1.00 | .45 |
| ❑ 202 Jim Harrison | 1.00 | .45 |
| ❑ 203 Ron Ellis | 1.50 | .70 |
| ❑ 204 Darryl Sittler | 6.00 | 2.70 |
| ❑ 205 Bernie Parent | 5.00 | 2.20 |
| ❑ 206 Dave Keon | 5.00 | 2.20 |
| ❑ 207 Brad Selwood | 1.00 | .45 |
| ❑ 208 Don Marshall | 1.00 | .45 |
| ❑ 209 Dale Tallon | 1.25 | .55 |
| ❑ 210 Dan Johnson | 1.00 | .45 |
| ❑ 211 Murray Hall | 1.00 | .45 |
| ❑ 212 Paul Popiel | 1.25 | .55 |
| ❑ 213 George Gardner | 1.00 | .45 |
| ❑ 214 Gary Doak | 1.00 | .45 |
| ❑ 215 Andre Boudrias | 1.25 | .55 |
| ❑ 216 Orland Kurtenbach | 1.25 | .55 |
| ❑ 217 Wayne Maki | 1.00 | .45 |
| ❑ 218 Rosaire Paiement | 1.25 | .55 |
| ❑ 219 Pat Quinn | 2.00 | .90 |
| ❑ 220 Fred Speck | 1.00 | .45 |
| ❑ 221 Barry Wilkins | 1.00 | .45 |
| ❑ 222 Dunc Wilson | 2.00 | .90 |
| ❑ 223 Ted Taylor | 1.00 | .45 |
| ❑ 224 Mike Corrigan | 1.00 | .45 |
| ❑ xx Stamp Album (Bobby Orr on cover) | 25.00 | 11.00 |

## 1972-73 Sargent Promotions Stamps

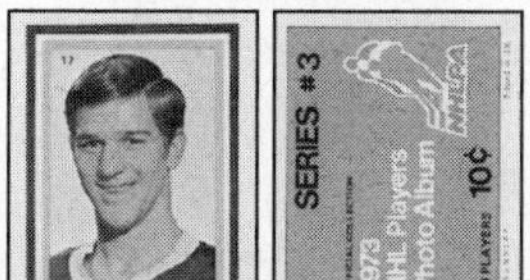


During the 1972-73 hockey season, Eddie Sargent Promotions produced a set of 224 stamps. They were issued in cello packages in a series of 16 sheets and, at that time, sold for ten cents per sheet with one sheet being available each week of the promotion. Each sheet measures approximately 7 7/8" by 10" and was divided into four rows, with four 2" by 2 1/2" sections per row. Since two of the 16 sections gave the series number (e.g., Series 1), color photos of fourteen NHL players were featured in each series. The set features 224 players from sixteen NHL teams. The pictures were numbered in the upper left hand corner and are checklisted below accordingly. The pictures are framed on their top and sides in different color borders, with the player's name and the team's city name given below. There are two sticker albums (approximately 11 1/4" by 12") available for the set, both of which are bilingual. After a general introduction, the album is divided into team sections, with two pages devoted to each team. A brief history of each team is presented, followed by 14 numbered sticker slots. Biographical information and career summary appear below each stamp slot on the page itself. The typically found album has Bobby Orr on the cover. Another album is the more difficult Paul Henderson Team Canada cover. The toughest of the three is the Richard Martin cover. The stamps are numbered on the front and checklisted below alphabetically according to teams as follows: Atlanta Flames (1-14), Boston Bruins (15-28), Buffalo Sabres (29-42), California Seals (43-56), Chicago Blackhawks (57-70), Detroit Red Wings (71-84), Los Angeles Kings (85-98), Minnesota North Stars (99-112), Montreal Canadiens (113-126), New York Islanders (127-140), New York Rangers (141-154), Philadelphia Flyers (155-168), Pittsburgh Penguins (169-182), St. Louis Blues (183-196), Toronto Maple Leafs (197-210), and Vancouver Canucks (211-224).

| | NRMT-MT | EXC |
|---|---|---|
| COMPLETE SET (224) | 200.00 | 90.00 |
| COMMON STAMP (1-224) | .50 | .23 |
| ❑ 1 Lucien Grenier | .50 | .23 |
| ❑ 2 Phil Myre | 1.00 | .45 |
| ❑ 3 Ernie Hicke | .50 | .23 |
| ❑ 4 Keith McCreary | .50 | .23 |
| ❑ 5 Bill MacMillan | .50 | .23 |
| ❑ 6 Pat Quinn | 1.00 | .45 |
| ❑ 7 Bill Plager | .75 | .35 |
| ❑ 8 Noel Price | .50 | .23 |
| ❑ 9 Bob Leiter | .50 | .23 |
| ❑ 10 Randy Manery | .50 | .23 |
| ❑ 11 Bob Paradise | .50 | .23 |
| ❑ 12 Larry Romanchych | .50 | .23 |
| ❑ 13 Lew Morrison | .50 | .23 |
| ❑ 14 Dan Bouchard | 1.00 | .45 |
| ❑ 15 Fred Stanfield | .50 | .23 |
| ❑ 16 Johnny Bucyk | 3.00 | 1.35 |
| ❑ 17 Bobby Orr | 40.00 | 18.00 |
| ❑ 18 Wayne Cashman | .75 | .35 |
| ❑ 19 Dallas Smith | .50 | .23 |
| ❑ 20 Ed Johnston | 1.50 | .70 |
| ❑ 21 Phil Esposito | 10.00 | 4.50 |
| ❑ 22 Ken Hodge | 1.00 | .45 |
| ❑ 23 Don Awrey | .50 | .23 |
| ❑ 24 Mike Walton | .50 | .23 |
| ❑ 25 Carol Vadnais | .50 | .23 |
| ❑ 26 Doug Roberts | .50 | .23 |
| ❑ 27 Don Marcotte | .50 | .23 |
| ❑ 28 Garnet Bailey | .50 | .23 |
| ❑ 29 Gerry Meehan | .50 | .23 |
| ❑ 30 Tracy Pratt | .50 | .23 |
| ❑ 31 Gilbert Perreault | 4.00 | 1.80 |
| ❑ 32 Roger Crozier | 2.00 | .90 |
| ❑ 33 Don Luce | .50 | .23 |
| ❑ 34 Dave Dryden | 1.00 | .45 |
| ❑ 35 Richard Martin | 1.00 | .45 |
| ❑ 36 Jim Lorentz | .50 | .23 |
| ❑ 37 Tim Horton | 8.00 | 3.60 |
| ❑ 38 Craig Ramsay | .50 | .23 |
| ❑ 39 Larry Hillman | .50 | .23 |
| ❑ 40 Steve Atkinson | .50 | .23 |
| ❑ 41 Jim Schoenfeld | .75 | .35 |
| ❑ 42 Rene Robert | .75 | .35 |
| ❑ 43 Walt McKechnie | .50 | .23 |
| ❑ 44 Marshall Johnston | .50 | .23 |
| ❑ 45 Joey Johnston | .50 | .23 |
| ❑ 46 Dick Redmond | .50 | .23 |
| ❑ 47 Bert Marshall | .50 | .23 |
| ❑ 48 Gary Croteau | .50 | .23 |
| ❑ 49 Marv Edwards | 1.00 | .45 |
| ❑ 50 Gilles Meloche | 1.00 | .45 |
| ❑ 51 Ivan Boldirev | .50 | .23 |
| ❑ 52 Stan Gilbertson | .50 | .23 |
| ❑ 53 Peter Laframboise | .50 | .23 |
| ❑ 54 Reggie Leach | 1.00 | .45 |
| ❑ 55 Craig Patrick | 1.00 | .45 |
| ❑ 56 Bob Stewart | .50 | .23 |
| ❑ 57 Keith Magnuson | .75 | .35 |
| ❑ 58 Doug Jarrett | .50 | .23 |
| ❑ 59 Cliff Koroll | .50 | .23 |
| ❑ 60 Chico Maki | .50 | .23 |
| ❑ 61 Gary Smith | 1.00 | .45 |
| ❑ 62 Bill White | .50 | .23 |
| ❑ 63 Stan Mikita | 6.00 | 2.70 |
| ❑ 64 Jim Pappin | .50 | .23 |
| ❑ 65 Lou Angotti | .50 | .23 |
| ❑ 66 Tony Esposito | 8.00 | 3.60 |
| ❑ 67 Dennis Hull | 1.00 | .45 |
| ❑ 68 Pit Martin | .50 | .23 |
| ❑ 69 Pat Stapleton | .50 | .23 |
| ❑ 70 Dan Maloney | .50 | .23 |
| ❑ 71 Bill Collins | .50 | .23 |
| ❑ 72 Arnie Brown | .50 | .23 |
| ❑ 73 Red Berenson | .75 | .35 |
| ❑ 74 Mickey Redmond | 2.00 | .90 |
| ❑ 75 Nick Libett | .50 | .23 |
| ❑ 76 Alex Delvecchio | 2.50 | 1.10 |
| ❑ 77 Ron Stackhouse | .50 | .23 |
| ❑ 78 Tim Ecclestone | .50 | .23 |
| ❑ 79 Gary Bergman | .50 | .23 |
| ❑ 80 Guy Charron | .50 | .23 |
| ❑ 81 Leon Rochefort | .50 | .23 |
| ❑ 82 Larry Johnston | .50 | .23 |
| ❑ 83 Andy Brown | .50 | .23 |
| ❑ 84 Henry Boucha | .75 | .35 |
| ❑ 85 Paul Curtis | .50 | .23 |
| ❑ 86 Jim Stanfield | .50 | .23 |
| ❑ 87 Rogatien Vachon | 3.00 | 1.35 |
| ❑ 88 Ralph Backstrom | .75 | .35 |
| ❑ 89 Gilles Marotte | .50 | .23 |
| ❑ 90 Harry Howell | 1.50 | .70 |
| ❑ 91 Real Lemieux | .50 | .23 |
| ❑ 92 Butch Goring | .75 | .35 |
| ❑ 93 Juha Widing | .50 | .23 |
| ❑ 94 Mike Corrigan | .50 | .23 |
| ❑ 95 Larry Brown | .50 | .23 |
| ❑ 96 Terry Harper | .75 | .35 |
| ❑ 97 Serge Bernier | .50 | .23 |
| ❑ 98 Bob Berry | .50 | .23 |
| ❑ 99 Tom Reid | .50 | .23 |
| ❑ 100 Jude Drouin | .50 | .23 |
| ❑ 101 Jean-Paul Parise | .75 | .35 |
| ❑ 102 Doug Mohns | .75 | .35 |
| ❑ 103 Danny Grant | .75 | .35 |
| ❑ 104 Bill Goldsworthy | 1.00 | .45 |
| ❑ 105 Gump Worsley | 5.00 | 2.20 |
| ❑ 106 Charlie Burns | .50 | .23 |
| ❑ 107 Murray Oliver | .50 | .23 |
| ❑ 108 Barry Gibbs | .50 | .23 |
| ❑ 109 Ted Harris | .50 | .23 |
| ❑ 110 Cesare Maniago | 2.00 | .90 |
| ❑ 111 Lou Nanne | .75 | .35 |
| ❑ 112 Bob Nevin | .50 | .23 |
| ❑ 113 Guy Lapointe | 1.50 | .70 |
| ❑ 114 Peter Mahovlich | .75 | .35 |
| ❑ 115 Jacques Lemaire | 2.00 | .90 |
| ❑ 116 Pierre Bouchard | .50 | .23 |
| ❑ 117 Yvan Cournoyer | 2.50 | 1.10 |
| ❑ 118 Marc Tardif | .50 | .23 |
| ❑ 119 Henri Richard | 5.00 | 2.20 |
| ❑ 120 Frank Mahovlich | 5.00 | 2.20 |
| ❑ 121 Jacques Laperriere | 1.50 | .70 |
| ❑ 122 Claude Larose | .50 | .23 |
| ❑ 123 Serge Savard | 2.00 | .90 |
| ❑ 124 Ken Dryden | 20.00 | 9.00 |
| ❑ 125 Rejean Houle | .75 | .35 |
| ❑ 126 Jim Roberts | .50 | .23 |
| ❑ 127 Ed Westfall | .75 | .35 |
| ❑ 128 Terry Crisp | .75 | .35 |
| ❑ 129 Gerry Desjardins | 1.00 | .45 |
| ❑ 130 Denis DeJordy | 1.50 | .70 |
| ❑ 131 Billy Harris | .50 | .23 |
| ❑ 132 Brian Spencer | 1.00 | .45 |
| ❑ 133 Germaine Gagnon UER | .50 | .23 |
| ❑ 134 David Hedson | .50 | .23 |
| ❑ 135 Lorne Henning | .50 | .23 |
| ❑ 136 Brian Marchinko | .50 | .23 |
| ❑ 137 Tom Miller | .50 | .23 |
| ❑ 138 Gerry Hart | .50 | .23 |
| ❑ 139 Bryan Lefley | .50 | .23 |
| ❑ 140 James Mair | .50 | .23 |
| ❑ 141 Rod Gilbert | 2.50 | 1.10 |
| ❑ 142 Jean Ratelle | 2.50 | 1.10 |
| ❑ 143 Pete Stemkowski | .50 | .23 |
| ❑ 144 Brad Park | 3.00 | 1.35 |
| ❑ 145 Bobby Rousseau | .50 | .23 |
| ❑ 146 Dale Rolfe | .50 | .23 |
| ❑ 147 Ed Giacomin | 3.00 | 1.35 |
| ❑ 148 Rod Seiling | .50 | .23 |
| ❑ 149 Walt Tkaczuk | .50 | .23 |
| ❑ 150 Bill Fairbairn | .50 | .23 |
| ❑ 151 Vic Hadfield | .75 | .35 |
| ❑ 152 Ted Irvine | .50 | .23 |
| ❑ 153 Bruce MacGregor | .50 | .23 |
| ❑ 154 Jim Neilson | .50 | .23 |
| ❑ 155 Brent Hughes | .50 | .23 |
| ❑ 156 Wayne Hillman | .50 | .23 |
| ❑ 157 Doug Favell | 1.50 | .70 |
| ❑ 158 Simon Nolet | .50 | .23 |
| ❑ 159 Joe Watson | .50 | .23 |
| ❑ 160 Ed Van Impe | .50 | .23 |
| ❑ 161 Gary Dornhoefer | .75 | .35 |
| ❑ 162 Bobby Clarke | 10.00 | 4.50 |
| ❑ 163 Bob Kelly | .50 | .23 |
| ❑ 164 Bill Flett | .50 | .23 |
| ❑ 165 Rick Foley | .50 | .23 |
| ❑ 166 Ross Lonsberry | .50 | .23 |
| ❑ 167 Rick MacLeish | 1.00 | .45 |
| ❑ 168 Bill Clement | 1.00 | .45 |
| ❑ 169 Syl Apps | .75 | .35 |
| ❑ 170 Ken Schinkel | .50 | .23 |
| ❑ 171 Nick Harbaruk | .50 | .23 |
| ❑ 172 Bryan Watson | .75 | .35 |
| ❑ 173 Bryan Hextall | .75 | .35 |
| ❑ 174 Roy Edwards | 1.00 | .45 |
| ❑ 175 Jim Rutherford | 1.50 | .70 |
| ❑ 176 Jean Pronovost | .75 | .35 |
| ❑ 177 Rick Kessell | .50 | .23 |
| ❑ 178 Greg Polis | .50 | .23 |
| ❑ 179 Ron Schock | .50 | .23 |
| ❑ 180 Duane Rupp | .50 | .23 |
| ❑ 181 Darryl Edestrand | .50 | .23 |
| ❑ 182 Dave Burrows | .50 | .23 |
| ❑ 183 Gary Sabourin | .50 | .23 |
| ❑ 184 Garry Unger | 1.00 | .45 |
| ❑ 185 Noel Picard | .50 | .23 |
| ❑ 186 Bob Plager | .75 | .35 |
| ❑ 187 Barclay Plager | .75 | .35 |
| ❑ 188 Frank St. Marseille | .50 | .23 |
| ❑ 189 Danny O'Shea | .50 | .23 |
| ❑ 190 Kevin O'Shea | .50 | .23 |
| ❑ 191 Wayne Stephenson | 1.00 | .45 |
| ❑ 192 Chris Evans | .50 | .23 |
| ❑ 193 Jacques Caron | .50 | .23 |
| ❑ 194 Andre Dupont | .50 | .23 |
| ❑ 195 Mike Murphy | .50 | .23 |
| ❑ 196 Jack Egers | .50 | .23 |
| ❑ 197 Norm Ullman | 2.50 | 1.10 |
| ❑ 198 Jim McKenny | .50 | .23 |
| ❑ 199 Bob Baun | 1.00 | .45 |
| ❑ 200 Mike Pelyk | .50 | .23 |
| ❑ 201 Ron Ellis | .75 | .35 |
| ❑ 202 Garry Monahan | .50 | .23 |
| ❑ 203 Paul Henderson | 2.00 | .90 |
| ❑ 204 Darryl Sittler | 3.50 | 1.55 |
| ❑ 205 Brian Glennie | .50 | .23 |
| ❑ 206 Dave Keon | 2.50 | 1.10 |
| ❑ 207 Jacques Plante | 10.00 | 4.50 |
| ❑ 208 Pierre Jarry | .50 | .23 |
| ❑ 209 Rick Kehoe | .75 | .35 |
| ❑ 210 Denis Dupere | .50 | .23 |
| ❑ 211 Dale Tallon | .75 | .35 |
| ❑ 212 Murray Hall | .50 | .23 |
| ❑ 213 Dunc Wilson | 1.00 | .45 |
| ❑ 214 Andre Boudrias | .75 | .35 |
| ❑ 215 Orland Kurtenbach | .75 | .35 |
| ❑ 216 Wayne Maki | .50 | .23 |
| ❑ 217 Barry Wilkins | .50 | .23 |
| ❑ 218 Richard Lemieux | .50 | .23 |
| ❑ 219 Bobby Schmautz | .50 | .23 |
| ❑ 220 Dave Balon | .50 | .23 |
| ❑ 221 Robert Lalonde | .50 | .23 |
| ❑ 222 Jocelyn Guevremont | .50 | .23 |
| ❑ 223 Gregg Boddy | .50 | .23 |
| ❑ 224 Dennis Kearns | .50 | .23 |
| ❑ xx Stamp Album (Bobby Orr on cover) | 20.00 | 9.00 |
| ❑ XX Stamp Album Richard Martin | 50.00 | 22.00 |
| ❑ xx Stamp Album (Paul Henderson on cover) | 35.00 | 16.00 |

## 1990-91 Score Promos

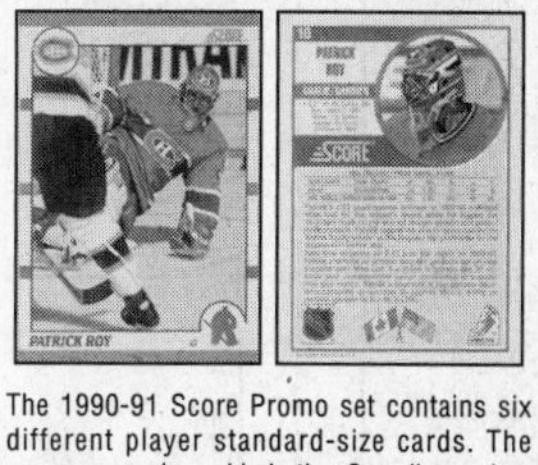


The 1990-91 Score Promo set contains six different player standard-size cards. The promos were issued in both a Canadian and an American version. Three (10 Patrick Roy, 40 Gary Leeman, and 100 Mark Messier) were distributed as Canadian promos and the other three were given to U.S. card dealer accounts. Though all these promo versions have the same numbering as the regular issues, several of them are easily distinguished from their regular issue counterparts. The Roy and Messier promos have different player photos on their fronts (Roy promo also has a different photo on its back). The photo on the front of the Roenick promo is cropped differently, and the blurb on its back is also slightly different. Even for those promos that appear to be otherwise identical with the regular cards, close inspection reveals the following distinguishing marks: 1) on the backs, the promos have the registered mark (circle R) by the Score logo, whereas the regular issues have instead the trademark (TM); and 2) on the back, the NHL logo is slightly larger on the promos and the text around it is only in English (the regular issues also have a French translation).

| | MINT | NRMT |
|---|---|---|
| COMPLETE SET (8) | 135.00 | 60.00 |
| COMMON CARD | 1.00 | .45 |

❑ 1A Wayne Gretzky ERR 75.00 34.00
(Catches Left)
❑ 1B Wayne Gretzky COR 30.00 13.50
(Shoots Left)
❑ 10 Patrick Roy 25.00 11.00
❑ 40 Gary Leeman .75 .35
❑ 100A Mark Messier ERR 25.00 11.00
(Won Smythe in 1990)
❑ 100B Mark Messier COR 10.00 4.50
(Won Smythe in 1984)
❑ 179 Jeremy Roenick 8.00 3.60
❑ 200 Ray Bourque 6.00 2.70

## 1990-91 Score

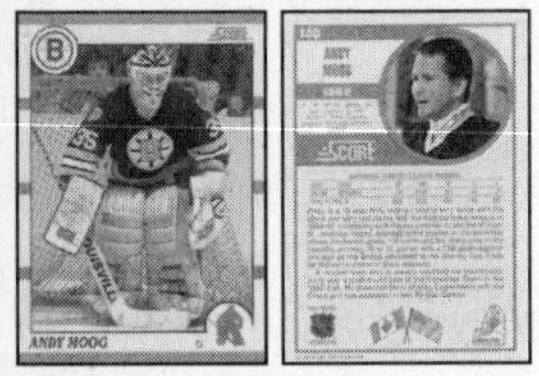

The 1990-91 Score hockey set contains 440 standard-size cards. The fronts feature a color action photo, superimposed over blue and red stripes on a white background. The team logo appears in the upper left hand corner, while an image of a hockey player (in various colors) appears in the lower right hand corner. The backs are outlined in a blue border and show a head shot of the player on the upper half. The career statistics and highlights on the lower half are printed on a pale yellow background. The complete factory set price includes the five Eric Lindros bonus cards (B1-B5) that were only available in the factory sets sold to hobby dealers. The few card numbers that are different in the Canadian and U.S. versions are labeled with an A (American) or C (Canadian) suffix after the card number. Rookie Cards include Rob Brind'Amour, Martin Brodeur, Nelson Emerson, Stephane Fiset, Adam Graves, Jaromir Jagr, Curtis Joseph, Trevor Kidd, Eric Lindros, Mike Modano, Alexander Mogilny, Owen Nolan, Keith Primeau, Mike Recchi, Mike Richter, Jeremy Roenick, Kevin Stevens, and Mats Sundin.

| | MINT | NRMT |
|---|---|---|
| COMPLETE SET (440) | 14.00 | 6.25 |
| COMP.FACT.SET (445) | 18.00 | 8.00 |
| COMMON CARD (1-440) | .05 | .02 |

❑ 1 Wayne Gretzky 1.25 .55
❑ 2 Mario Lemieux 1.00 .45
❑ 3 Steve Yzerman .60 .25
❑ 4 Cam Neely .10 .05
❑ 5 Al MacInnis .10 .05
❑ 6 Paul Coffey .25 .11
❑ 7 Brian Bellows .05 .02
❑ 8 Joe Sakic .60 .25
❑ 9 Bernie Nicholls .10 .05
❑ 10 Patrick Roy 1.00 .45
❑ 11 Doug Houda .05 .02
❑ 12 David Volek .05 .02
❑ 13 Esa Tikkanen .05 .02
❑ 14 Thomas Steen .05 .02
❑ 15 Chris Chelios .25 .11
❑ 16 Bob Carpenter .05 .02
❑ 17 Dirk Graham .05 .02
❑ 18 Garth Butcher .05 .02
❑ 19 Patrik Sundstrom .05 .02
❑ 20 Rod Langway .05 .02
❑ 21 Scott Young .05 .02
❑ 22 Ulf Dahlen .05 .02
❑ 23 Mike Ramsey .05 .02
❑ 24 Peter Zezel .05 .02
❑ 25 Ron Hextall .10 .05
❑ 26 Steve Duchesne .05 .02
❑ 27 Allan Bester .10 .05
❑ 28 Everett Sanipass .05 .02
❑ 29 Steve Konroyd .05 .02
❑ 30A Joe Nieuwendyk ERR .10 .05
(Text says, now I fell, should say feel)
❑ 30B Joe Nieuwendyk COR .10 .05
❑ 31A Brent Ashton ERR .05 .02
(No position on card front)
❑ 31B Brent Ashton COR .05 .02
(LW on card front)
❑ 32 Trevor Linden .10 .05
❑ 33 Mike Ridley .05 .02
❑ 34 Sean Burke .10 .05
❑ 35 Pat Verbeek .05 .02
❑ 36 Rob Ramage .05 .02
❑ 37 Kelly Kisio .05 .02
❑ 38A Craig Muni ERR .05 .02
(Back photo actually Craig Simpson)
❑ 38B Craig Muni COR .05 .02
❑ 39 Brent Sutter .05 .02
❑ 40 Gary Leeman .05 .02
❑ 41 Jeff Brown .05 .02
❑ 42 Greg Millen .10 .05
❑ 43 Alexander Mogilny .60 .25
❑ 44 Dale Hunter .05 .02
❑ 45 Randy Moller .05 .02
❑ 46 Peter Sidorkiewicz .10 .05
❑ 47 Terry Carkner .05 .02
❑ 48 Tony Granato .05 .02
❑ 49 Shawn Burr .05 .02
❑ 50 Dale Hawerchuk .10 .05
❑ 51A Don Sweeney ERR .05 .02
(Two black boxes at bottom of card)
❑ 51B Don Sweeney COR .05 .02
(Three black boxes at bottom of card)
❑ 52 Mike Vernon UER .10 .05
(Text says won WHL MVP twice, should be once)
❑ 53 Kevin Stevens .05 .02
❑ 54 Bryan Fogarty .05 .02
❑ 55 Dan Quinn .05 .02
❑ 56 Murray Craven .05 .02
❑ 57 Shawn Chambers .05 .02
❑ 58 Craig Simpson .05 .02
❑ 59 Doug Crossman .05 .02
❑ 60 Daren Puppa .10 .05
❑ 61 Bobby Smith .10 .05
❑ 62 Slava Fetisov .05 .02
❑ 63 Gino Cavallini .05 .02
❑ 64 Jimmy Carson .05 .02
❑ 65 Dave Ellett .05 .02
❑ 66 Steve Thomas .05 .02
❑ 67 Mike Lalor .05 .02
❑ 68 Mike Liut .10 .05
❑ 69 Tom Laidlaw .05 .02
❑ 70 Ron Francis .10 .05
❑ 71 Sergei Makarov .05 .02
❑ 72 Randy Burridge .05 .02
❑ 73 Doug Lidster .05 .02
❑ 74 Mike Richter .75 .35
❑ 75 Stephane Richer .10 .05
❑ 76 Randy Hillier .05 .02
❑ 77 Christian Ruuttu .05 .02
❑ 78 Marc Fortier .05 .02
❑ 79 Bill Ranford .10 .05
❑ 80 Rick Tocchet .10 .05
❑ 81 Fredrik Olausson .05 .02
❑ 82 Adam Creighton .05 .02
❑ 83 Sylvain Cote .05 .02
❑ 84 Brian Mullen .05 .02
❑ 85 Adam Oates .10 .05
❑ 86 Gary Nylund .05 .02
❑ 87 Tim Cheveldae .10 .05
❑ 88 Gary Suter .05 .02
❑ 89 John Tonelli .05 .02
❑ 90 Kevin Hatcher .05 .02
❑ 91 Guy Carbonneau .10 .05
❑ 92 Curtis Leschyshyn .05 .02
❑ 93 Kirk McLean .10 .05
❑ 94 Curt Giles .05 .02
❑ 95 Vincent Damphousse .10 .05
❑ 96 Peter Stastny .10 .05
❑ 97 Glen Wesley .05 .02
❑ 98 David Shaw .05 .02
❑ 99 Brad Shaw .05 .02
❑ 100 Mark Messier .30 .14
❑ 101 Rick Zombo .05 .02
❑ 102A Mark Fitzpatrick ERR .10 .05
(Catches right)
❑ 102B Mark Fitzpatrick COR .10 .05
(Catches left)
❑ 103 Rick Vaive .05 .02
❑ 104 Mark Osborne .05 .02
❑ 105 Rob Brown .05 .02
❑ 106 Gary Roberts .05 .02
❑ 107 Vincent Riendeau .10 .05
❑ 108 Dave Gagner .10 .05
❑ 109 Bruce Driver .05 .02
❑ 110 Pierre Turgeon .10 .05
❑ 111 Claude Lemieux .10 .05
❑ 112 Bob Essensa .10 .05
❑ 113 John Ogrodnick .05 .02
❑ 114 Glenn Anderson .10 .05
❑ 115 Kelly Hrudey .10 .05
❑ 116 Sylvain Turgeon .05 .02
❑ 117 Gord Murphy .05 .02
❑ 118 Craig Janney .10 .05
❑ 119 Randy Wood .05 .02
❑ 120 Mike Modano 1.00 .45
❑ 121 Tom Barrasso .10 .05
❑ 122 Daniel Marois .05 .02
❑ 123 Igor Larionov .40 .18
❑ 124 Geoff Courtnall .05 .02
❑ 125 Denis Savard .10 .05
❑ 126 Ron Tugnutt .10 .05
❑ 127 Mathieu Schneider .05 .02
❑ 128 Joel Otto .05 .02
❑ 129 Steve Smith .05 .02
❑ 130 Mike Gartner .10 .05
❑ 131 Rod Brind'Amour .60 .25
❑ 132 Jyrki Lumme .05 .02
❑ 133 Mike Foligno .05 .02
❑ 134 Ray Ferraro .05 .02
❑ 135 Steve Larmer .10 .05
❑ 136 Randy Carlyle .05 .02
❑ 137 Tony Tanti .05 .02
❑ 138 Jeff Chychrun .05 .02
❑ 139 Gerald Diduck .05 .02
❑ 140 Andy Moog .10 .05
❑ 141 Paul Gillis .05 .02
❑ 142 Tom Kurvers .05 .02
❑ 143 Bob Probert .10 .05
❑ 144 Neal Broten .10 .05
❑ 145 Phil Housley .10 .05
❑ 146 Brendan Shanahan .60 .25
❑ 147 Bob Rouse .05 .02
❑ 148 Russ Courtnall .05 .02
❑ 149 Normand Rochefort UER .05 .02
(RW, should be D)
❑ 150 Luc Robitaille .10 .05
❑ 151 Curtis Joseph .75 .35
❑ 152 Ulf Samuelsson .05 .02
❑ 153 Ron Sutter .05 .02
❑ 154 Petri Skriko .05 .02
❑ 155 Doug Gilmour .25 .11
❑ 156 Paul Fenton .05 .02
❑ 157 Jeff Norton .05 .02
❑ 158 Jari Kurri .10 .05
❑ 159 Rejean Lemelin .10 .05
❑ 160 Kirk Muller .05 .02
❑ 161 Keith Brown .05 .02
❑ 162 Aaron Broten UER .05 .02
(Photo actually Dave Archibald)
❑ 163 Adam Graves .40 .18
❑ 164 John Cullen UER .05 .02
(Birthdate 1/6/6, should be 1/9/64)
❑ 165 Craig Ludwig .05 .02
❑ 166 Dave Taylor .10 .05
❑ 167 Craig Wolanin .05 .02
❑ 168 Kelly Miller .05 .02
❑ 169 Uwe Krupp .05 .02
❑ 170 Kevin Lowe .05 .02
❑ 171 Wendel Clark .10 .05
❑ 172 Dave Babych .05 .02
❑ 173 Paul Reinhart .05 .02
❑ 174 Pat Flatley .05 .02
❑ 175 John Vanbiesbrouck .50 .23
❑ 176 Teppo Numminen .05 .02
❑ 177 Tim Kerr .05 .02
❑ 178 Ken Daneyko .05 .02
❑ 179 Jeremy Roenick .75 .35
❑ 180 Gerard Gallant .05 .02
❑ 181 Allen Pederson .05 .02
❑ 182 Jon Casey .10 .05
❑ 183 Tomas Sandstrom .05 .02
❑ 184 Brad McCrimmon .05 .02
❑ 185 Paul Cavallini .05 .02
❑ 186 Mark Recchi .40 .18
❑ 187 Michel Petit .05 .02
❑ 188 Scott Stevens .10 .05
❑ 189 Dave Andreychuk .10 .05
❑ 190 John MacLean .10 .05
❑ 191 Petr Svoboda .05 .02
❑ 192 Dave Tippett .05 .02
❑ 193 Dave Manson .05 .02
❑ 194 James Patrick .05 .02
❑ 195 Al Iafrate .10 .05
❑ 196 Doug Smail .05 .02
❑ 197 Kjell Samuelsson .05 .02
❑ 198 Brian Bradley .05 .02
❑ 199 Charlie Huddy .05 .02
❑ 200 Ray Bourque .25 .11
❑ 201 Joey Kocur .05 .02
❑ 202 Jim Johnson UER .05 .02
(Born Michigan, not Minnesota)
❑ 203 Paul MacLean .05 .02
❑ 204 Tim Watters .05 .02
❑ 205 Pat Elynuik .05 .02
❑ 206 Larry Murphy .10 .05
❑ 207 Claude Loiselle .05 .02
❑ 208 Joe Mullen .10 .05
❑ 209 Alexei Kasatonov .05 .02
❑ 210 Ed Olczyk .05 .02
❑ 211 Doug Bodger .05 .02
❑ 212 Kevin Dineen .05 .02
❑ 213 Shayne Corson .05 .02
❑ 214 Steve Chiasson .05 .02
❑ 215 Don Beaupre .10 .05
❑ 216 Jamie Macoun .05 .02
❑ 217 Dave Poulin .05 .02
❑ 218 Zarley Zalapski .05 .02
❑ 219 Brad Marsh .05 .02
❑ 220 Mark Howe .05 .02
❑ 221 Michel Goulet .10 .05
❑ 222 Hubie McDonough .05 .02
❑ 223 Frank Musil .05 .02
❑ 224 Sergio Momesso .05 .02
❑ 225 Brian Leetch .35 .16
❑ 226 Theoren Fleury .10 .05
❑ 227 Mike Krushelnyski .05 .02
❑ 228 Glen Hanlon .10 .05
❑ 229 Mario Marois .05 .02
❑ 230 Dino Ciccarelli .10 .05
❑ 231A Dave McLlwain ERR .05 .02
(Shoots right)
❑ 231B Dave McLlwain COR .05 .02
(Shoots left)
❑ 232 Petr Klima .05 .02
❑ 233 Grant Ledyard .05 .02
❑ 234 Phil Bourque .05 .02
❑ 235 Rob Sweeney .05 .02
❑ 236 Luke Richardson .05 .02
❑ 237 Todd Krygier .05 .02
❑ 238 Brian Skrudland .05 .02
❑ 239 Chris Terreri .10 .05
❑ 240 Greg Adams .05 .02
❑ 241 Darren Turcotte .05 .02
❑ 242 Scott Mellanby .10 .05
❑ 243 Troy Murray .05 .02
❑ 244 Stewart Gavin .05 .02
❑ 245 Gordie Roberts .05 .02
❑ 246 John Druce .05 .02
❑ 247 Steve Kasper .05 .02
❑ 248 Paul Ranheim .05 .02
❑ 249 Greg Paslawski .05 .02
❑ 250 Pat LaFontaine .10 .05
❑ 251 Scott Arniel .05 .02
❑ 252 Bernie Federko .10 .05
❑ 253 Garry Galley .05 .02
❑ 254 Carey Wilson .05 .02
❑ 255 Bob Errey .05 .02
❑ 256 Tony Hrkac .05 .02
❑ 257 Andrew McBain .05 .02
❑ 258 Craig MacTavish .05 .02
❑ 259A Dean Evason ERR .05 .02
(Reversed negative)
❑ 259B Dean Evason COR .05 .02
❑ 260 Larry Robinson .10 .05
❑ 261 Basil McRae .05 .02
❑ 262 Stephan Lebeau .05 .02
❑ 263 Ken Wregget .10 .05
❑ 264 Greg Gilbert .05 .02
❑ 265 Ken Baumgartner .05 .02
❑ 266 Lou Franceschetti .05 .02
❑ 267 Rick Meagher .05 .02
❑ 268 Michal Pivonka .05 .02
❑ 269 Brian Propp .05 .02
❑ 270 Bryan Trottier .10 .05
❑ 271 Marty McSorley .05 .02
❑ 272 Jan Erixon .05 .02
❑ 273 Vladimir Krutov .10 .05
❑ 274 Dana Murzyn .05 .02
❑ 275 Grant Fuhr .10 .05
❑ 276 Randy Cunneyworth .05 .02
❑ 277 John Chabot .05 .02
❑ 278 Walt Poddubny .05 .02
❑ 279 Stephen Leach .05 .02
❑ 280 Doug Wilson .10 .05
❑ 281 Rich Sutter .05 .02
❑ 282 Stephane Beauregard .10 .05
(Played at Ft. Wayne, not Ft. Worth) UER
❑ 283 John Carter .05 .02
❑ 284 Don Barber .05 .02
❑ 285 Tom Fergus .05 .02
❑ 286 Ilkka Sinisalo .05 .02
❑ 287 Kevin McClelland UER .05 .02
(Back has shoots, but no side indicated)
❑ 288 Troy Mallette .05 .02
❑ 289 Clint Malarchuk UER .10 .05
(Photo actually Tom Barrasso)
❑ 290 Guy Lafleur .25 .11
❑ 291 Bob Joyce .05 .02
❑ 292 Trent Yawney .05 .02
❑ 293 Joe Murphy .05 .02
❑ 294 Glenn Healy .10 .05
❑ 295 Dave Christian .05 .02
❑ 296 Paul MacDermid .05 .02
❑ 297 Todd Elik .05 .02
❑ 298 Wendell Young .10 .05
❑ 299 Dean Kennedy .05 .02
❑ 300 Brett Hull .50 .23
❑ 301A Keith Acton .05 .02
❑ 301C Martin Gelinas .25 .11
❑ 302A Yvon Corriveau .05 .02
❑ 302C Ric Nattress .05 .02
❑ 303A Don Maloney .05 .02
❑ 303C Jim Sandlak .05 .02
❑ 304A Mark Tinordi .05 .02
❑ 304C Brian Hayward .10 .05
❑ 305A Bob Kudelski .05 .02
❑ 305C Joe Cirella .05 .02
❑ 306A Brian Benning .05 .02
❑ 306C Randy Gregg .05 .02
❑ 307A Alan Kerr .05 .02
❑ 307C Sylvain Lefebvre .05 .02
❑ 308A Pelle Eklund .05 .02
❑ 308C Mark Lamb .05 .02
❑ 309A Calle Johansson .05 .02
❑ 309C Rick Wamsley .10 .05
❑ 310A David Maley .05 .02
❑ 310C Moe Mantha .05 .02
❑ 311A Chris Nilan .05 .02
❑ 311C Tony McKegney .05 .02
❑ 312 Patrick Roy AS1 .30 .14
❑ 313 Ray Bourque AS1 .25 .11
❑ 314 Al MacInnis AS1 .10 .05
❑ 315 Mark Messier AS1 .25 .11
❑ 316 Luc Robitaille AS1 .10 .05
❑ 317 Brett Hull AS1 .25 .11
❑ 318 Daren Puppa AS2 .10 .05
❑ 319 Paul Coffey AS2 .25 .11
❑ 320 Doug Wilson AS2 .10 .05
❑ 321 Wayne Gretzky AS2 .40 .18
❑ 322 Brian Bellows AS2 .05 .02
❑ 323 Cam Neely AS2 .10 .05
❑ 324 Bob Essensa ART .10 .05
❑ 325 Brad Shaw ART .05 .02
❑ 326 Geoff Smith ART .05 .02
❑ 327 Mike Modano ART .10 .05
❑ 328 Rod Brind'Amour ART .10 .05
❑ 329 Sergei Makarov ART .05 .02
❑ 330A Kip Miller Hobey ERR .05 .02
(No Score logo on card front)
❑ 330B Kip Miller Hobey COR .05 .02
❑ 330C Memorial Cup .50 .23
❑ 331 Edmonton Oilers Champs .05 .02
❑ 332 Paul Coffey Speed .25 .11
❑ 333 Mike Gartner Speed .10 .05
❑ 334 Al Iafrate Blaster .10 .05
❑ 335 Al MacInnis Blaster .10 .05
❑ 336 Wayne Gretzky Sniper .40 .18
❑ 337 Mario Lemieux Sniper .30 .14
❑ 338 Wayne Gretzky Magic .40 .18
❑ 339 Steve Yzerman Magic .25 .11
❑ 340 Cam Neely Banger .10 .05
❑ 341 Scott Stevens Banger .10 .05
❑ 342 Esa Tikkanen Shadow .05 .02
❑ 343 Jan Erixon Shadow .05 .02
❑ 344 Patrick Roy Stopper .30 .14
❑ 345 Bill Ranford Stopper .10 .05
❑ 346 Brett Hull RB .25 .11
❑ 347 Wayne Gretzky RB .40 .18
❑ 348 Jari Kurri LL .10 .05
❑ 349 Paul Cavallini LL .05 .02
❑ 350 Sergei Makarov RLL .05 .02
❑ 351 Brett Hull LL .25 .11
❑ 352 Wayne Gretzky LL .40 .18
❑ 353 Wayne Gretzky LL .40 .18
❑ 354 P.Roy/Liut LL .30 .14
❑ 355 Gilbert Perreault HOF .05 .02
❑ 356 Bill Barber HOF .05 .02
❑ 357 Fern Flaman HOF .05 .02
❑ 358 Bill Ranford Smythe .10 .05
❑ 359 Rick Meagher Selke .05 .02
❑ 360 Mark Messier Hart .25 .11
❑ 361 Wayne Gretzky Ross .40 .18
❑ 362 Sergei Makarov Calder .05 .02
❑ 363 Ray Bourque Norris .25 .11
❑ 364 Patrick Roy Vezina .30 .14
❑ 365 Moog/Lemelin Jennings .05 .02
❑ 366 Brett Hull Byng .25 .11
❑ 367 Gord Kluzak Mast .05 .02
❑ 368 Boston/Washington UER .05 .02
(Janney misspelled Janny on back)
❑ 369 Edmonton/Chicago .05 .02
❑ 370 Adam Burt .05 .02
❑ 371 Troy Loney .05 .02
❑ 372 Dave Chyzowski .05 .02
❑ 373 Geoff Smith .05 .02
❑ 374 Stan Smyl .05 .02
❑ 375 Gaetan Duchesne .05 .02
❑ 376 Bob Murray .05 .02
❑ 377 Daniel Shank .05 .02
❑ 378 Tommy Albelin .05 .02
❑ 379 Perry Berezan .05 .02
❑ 380 Ken Linseman .05 .02
❑ 381 Stephane Matteau .05 .02
❑ 382 Mario Thyer .05 .02
❑ 383 Nelson Emerson .05 .02
❑ 384 Kory Kocur .05 .02
❑ 385 Bob Beers .05 .02
❑ 386 Jim Hrivnak .10 .05
❑ 387 Mark Pederson .05 .02
❑ 388 Jeff Hackett .25 .11
❑ 389 Eric Weinrich .05 .02
❑ 390 Steven Rice .05 .02
❑ 391 Stu Barnes .05 .02
❑ 392 Olaf Kolzig .75 .35
❑ 393 Francois Leroux .05 .02
❑ 394 Adrien Plavsic .05 .02
❑ 395 Michel Mongeau .05 .02
❑ 396 Rick Corriveau .05 .02
❑ 397 Wayne Doucet .05 .02
❑ 398 Mats Sundin .75 .35
❑ 399 Murray Baron .05 .02
❑ 400 Rick Bennett .05 .02
❑ 401 Jon Morris .05 .02
❑ 402 Kay Whitmore .10 .05
❑ 403 Peter Lappin .05 .02
❑ 404 Kris Draper .25 .11
❑ 405 Shayne Stevenson .05 .02
❑ 406 Paul Ysebaert .05 .02
❑ 407A Jimmy Waite ERR .10 .05
(Catches right)
❑ 407B Jimmy Waite COR .10 .05
(Catches left)
❑ 408 Cam Russell .05 .02
❑ 409 Kim Issel UER .05 .02
(Photo shoots left, text has right)
❑ 410 Darrin Shannon .05 .02
❑ 411 Link Gaetz .05 .02
❑ 412 Craig Fisher .05 .02
❑ 413 Bruce Hoffort .05 .02
❑ 414 Peter Ing .10 .05
❑ 415 Stephane Fiset .40 .18
❑ 416 Dominic Lavoie .05 .02
❑ 417 Steve Maltais .05 .02
❑ 418 Wes Walz .05 .02
❑ 419 Terry Yake .05 .02
❑ 420 Jamie Leach .05 .02
❑ 421 Rob Blake .30 .14
❑ 422 Andrew Cassels .05 .02
❑ 423 Marc Bureau .05 .02
❑ 424 Scott Allison .05 .02
❑ 425 Darryl Sydor .40 .18
❑ 426 Turner Stevenson .05 .02
❑ 427 Brad May .10 .05
❑ 428 Jaromir Jagr 2.50 1.10
❑ 429 Shawn Antoski .05 .02
❑ 430 Derian Hatcher .05 .02
❑ 431 Mark Greig UER .05 .02
(No indication of how he shoots on card back)
❑ 432 Scott Scissons .05 .02
❑ 433 Mike Ricci UER .10 .05
(Born October, not November)
❑ 434 Drake Berehowsky .05 .02
❑ 435 Owen Nolan .50 .23
❑ 436 Keith Primeau .25 .11
❑ 437 Karl Dykhuis .05 .02
❑ 438 Trevor Kidd .25 .11
❑ 439 Martin Brodeur 4.00 1.80
❑ 440A Eric Lindros 5.00 2.20
❑ 440C Eric Lindros 8.00 3.60
❑ B1 Eric Lindros 2.00 .90
Junior B Team
❑ B2 Eric Lindros 2.00 .90
Regular Junior OHL
❑ B3 Eric Lindros 2.00 .90
OHL All-Star
❑ B4 Eric Lindros 2.00 .90
Oshawa Generals
(Non-action pose; head shot with his gloves over his mouth)
❑ B5 Eric Lindros 2.00 .90
Oshawa Generals
(Non-action pose; shot from waist up, arms draped over hockey stick across his back)

## 1990-91 Score Hottest/Rising Stars

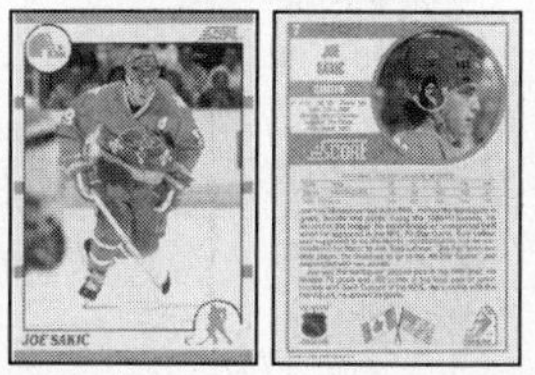

This 100-card standard-size set was released along with a special book. The book provided further information about the players. The fronts of the cards have the same photos as the regular Score issue but the numbers are different on the back.

| | MINT | NRMT |
|---|---|---|
| COMPLETE SET (100) | 15.00 | 6.75 |
| COMMON CARD (1-100) | .10 | .05 |
| ❑ 1 Wayne Gretzky | 5.00 | 2.20 |
| ❑ 2 Craig Simpson | .10 | .05 |
| ❑ 3 Brian Bellows | .10 | .05 |
| ❑ 4 Steve Yzerman | 2.50 | 1.10 |
| ❑ 5 Bernie Nicholls | .15 | .07 |
| ❑ 6 Esa Tikkanen | .15 | .07 |
| ❑ 7 Joe Sakic | 1.75 | .80 |
| ❑ 8 Thomas Steen | .10 | .05 |
| ❑ 9 Chris Chelios | .75 | .35 |
| ❑ 10 Patrik Sundstrom | .10 | .05 |
| ❑ 11 Rod Langway | .10 | .05 |
| ❑ 12 Scott Young | .10 | .05 |
| ❑ 13 Mike Ramsey | .10 | .05 |
| ❑ 14 Ron Hextall | .50 | .23 |
| ❑ 15 Steve Duchesne | .25 | .11 |
| ❑ 16 Trevor Linden | .50 | .23 |
| ❑ 17 Sean Burke | .50 | .23 |
| ❑ 18 Pat Verbeek | .25 | .11 |
| ❑ 19 Brent Sutter | .10 | .05 |
| ❑ 20 Gary Leeman | .10 | .05 |
| ❑ 21 Shawn Burr | .10 | .05 |
| ❑ 22 Dale Hawerchuk | .25 | .11 |
| ❑ 23 Mike Vernon | .25 | .11 |
| ❑ 24 Dan Quinn | .10 | .05 |
| ❑ 25 Patrick Roy | 4.00 | 1.80 |
| ❑ 26 Daren Puppa | .50 | .23 |
| ❑ 27 Gino Cavallini | .10 | .05 |
| ❑ 28 Jimmy Carson | .10 | .05 |
| ❑ 29 Dave Ellett | .10 | .05 |
| ❑ 30 Steve Thomas | .10 | .05 |
| ❑ 31 Jeremy Roenick | 1.50 | .70 |
| ❑ 32 Mike Liut | .15 | .07 |
| ❑ 33 Mark Messier | 1.25 | .55 |
| ❑ 34 Mario Lemieux | 4.00 | 1.80 |
| ❑ 35 Ray Bourque | .75 | .35 |
| ❑ 36 Al MacInnis | .50 | .23 |
| ❑ 37 Ron Francis | .50 | .23 |
| ❑ 38 Stephane Richer | .50 | .23 |
| ❑ 39 Bill Ranford | .50 | .23 |
| ❑ 40 Rick Tocchet | .20 | .09 |
| ❑ 41 Adam Oates | .50 | .23 |
| ❑ 42 Kevin Hatcher | .15 | .07 |
| ❑ 43 Guy Carbonneau | .15 | .07 |
| ❑ 44 Curtis Leschyshyn | .10 | .05 |
| ❑ 45 Joe Nieuwendyk | .50 | .23 |
| ❑ 46 Kirk McLean | .50 | .23 |
| ❑ 47 Vincent Damphousse | .50 | .23 |
| ❑ 48 Peter Stastny | .20 | .09 |
| ❑ 49 Rick Zombo | .10 | .05 |
| ❑ 50 Mark Fitzpatrick | .40 | .18 |
| ❑ 51 Rob Brown | .10 | .05 |
| ❑ 52 Dave Gagner | .10 | .05 |
| ❑ 53 Pierre Turgeon | .50 | .23 |
| ❑ 54 Glenn Anderson | .10 | .05 |
| ❑ 55 Kelly Hrudey | .50 | .23 |
| ❑ 56 Gord Murphy | .10 | .05 |
| ❑ 57 Glen Wesley | .10 | .05 |
| ❑ 58 Craig Janney | .25 | .11 |
| ❑ 59 Denis Savard | .25 | .11 |
| ❑ 60 Mike Gartner | .50 | .23 |
| ❑ 61 Steve Larmer | .20 | .09 |
| ❑ 62 Andy Moog | .50 | .23 |
| ❑ 63 Phil Housley | .20 | .09 |
| ❑ 64 Ulf Samuelsson | .15 | .07 |
| ❑ 65 Paul Coffey | .75 | .35 |
| ❑ 66 Luc Robitaille | .50 | .23 |
| ❑ 67 Cam Neely | .50 | .23 |
| ❑ 68 Doug Wilson | .10 | .05 |
| ❑ 69 Doug Gilmour | .50 | .23 |
| ❑ 70 Jeff Norton | .10 | .05 |
| ❑ 71 Kirk Muller | .10 | .05 |
| ❑ 72 Aaron Broten | .10 | .05 |
| ❑ 73 John Cullen | .10 | .05 |
| ❑ 74 Craig Ludwig | .10 | .05 |
| ❑ 75 Kevin Lowe | .15 | .07 |
| ❑ 76 John Vanbiesbrouck | 1.25 | .55 |
| ❑ 77 Tim Kerr | .10 | .05 |
| ❑ 78 Gerard Gallant | .10 | .05 |
| ❑ 79 Tomas Sandstrom | .15 | .07 |
| ❑ 80 Jon Casey | .50 | .23 |
| ❑ 81 Mark Recchi | .25 | .11 |
| ❑ 82 Scott Stevens | .20 | .09 |
| ❑ 83 John MacLean | .10 | .05 |
| ❑ 84 James Patrick | .10 | .05 |
| ❑ 85 Al Iafrate | .15 | .07 |
| ❑ 86 Pat Elyniuk | .10 | .05 |
| ❑ 87 Dave Andreychuk | .10 | .05 |
| ❑ 88 Joe Mullen | .15 | .07 |
| ❑ 89 Ed Olczyk | .10 | .05 |
| 90 Kevin Dineen | .15 | .07 |
| ❑ 91 Shayne Corson | .25 | .11 |
| ❑ 92 Mark Howe | .15 | .07 |
| ❑ 93 Brian Leetch | .75 | .35 |
| ❑ 94 Dino Ciccarelli | .20 | .09 |
| ❑ 95 Pat LaFontaine | .50 | .23 |
| ❑ 96 Guy Lafleur | .50 | .23 |
| ❑ 97 Mike Modano | 1.75 | .80 |
| ❑ 98 Rod Brind'Amour | .75 | .35 |
| ❑ 99 Sergei Makarov | .25 | .11 |
| ❑ 100 Brett Hull | 1.25 | .55 |

## 1990-91 Score Rookie/Traded

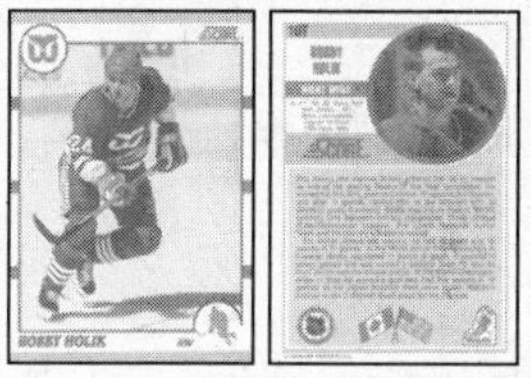

The 1990-91 Score Rookie and Traded hockey set contains 110 standard-size cards. The cards were issued as a complete set in a factory box. The fronts feature a color action photo, superimposed over blue and red stripes on a white background. The team logo appears in the upper left hand corner, while an image of a hockey player (in various colors) appears in the lower right hand corner. Yellow strips appear at the top and bottom of the card front. The backs are outlined in a yellow border and show a head shot of the player on the upper half. The career statistics and highlights on the lower half are printed on a pale blue background. Rookie Cards include Ed Belfour, Peter Bondra, Sergei Fedorov, Petr Nedved and Robert Reichel. The back of the set's custom box contains the set checklist. The cards are numbered with a "T" suffix.

| | MINT | NRMT |
|---|---|---|
| COMPLETE SET (110) | 10.00 | 4.50 |
| COMMON CARD (1T-110T) | .05 | .02 |
| ❑ 1T Denis Savard | .15 | .07 |
| ❑ 2T Dale Hawerchuk | .15 | .07 |
| ❑ 3T Phil Housley | .05 | .02 |
| ❑ 4T Chris Chelios | .40 | .18 |
| ❑ 5T Geoff Courtnall | .05 | .02 |
| ❑ 6T Peter Zezel | .05 | .02 |
| ❑ 7T Joe Mullen | .15 | .07 |
| ❑ 8T Craig Ludwig | .05 | .02 |
| ❑ 9T Claude Lemieux | .40 | .18 |
| ❑ 10T Bobby Holik | .15 | .07 |
| ❑ 11T Peter Ing | .15 | .07 |
| ❑ 12T Rod Buskas | .05 | .02 |
| ❑ 13T Tim Sweeney | .05 | .02 |
| ❑ 14T Don Barber | .05 | .02 |
| ❑ 15T Ray Ferraro | .05 | .02 |
| ❑ 16T Peter Taglianetti | .05 | .02 |
| ❑ 17T Johan Garpenlov | .05 | .02 |
| ❑ 18T Kevin Miller | .05 | .02 |
| ❑ 19T Frank Musil | .05 | .02 |
| ❑ 20T Sergei Fedorov | 2.00 | .90 |
| ❑ 21T Aaron Broten | .05 | .02 |
| ❑ 22T Chris Nilan | .05 | .02 |
| ❑ 23T Gerald Diduck | .05 | .02 |
| ❑ 24T Marc Habscheid | .05 | .02 |
| ❑ 25T Glen Featherstone | .05 | .02 |
| ❑ 26T Mikko Makela | .05 | .02 |
| ❑ 27T Paul Stanton | .05 | .02 |
| ❑ 28T Mark Osborne | .05 | .02 |
| ❑ 29T Dave Tippett | .05 | .02 |
| ❑ 30T Robert Reichel | .15 | .07 |
| ❑ 31T Grant Jennings | .05 | .02 |
| ❑ 32T Troy Gamble | .15 | .07 |
| ❑ 33T Mark Janssens | .05 | .02 |
| ❑ 34T Brian Propp | .05 | .02 |
| ❑ 35T Donald Dufresne | .05 | .02 |
| ❑ 36T Martin Hostak | .05 | .02 |
| ❑ 37T Brad McCrimmon | .05 | .02 |
| ❑ 38T Dave Lowry | .05 | .02 |
| ❑ 39T Anatoli Semenov | .05 | .02 |
| ❑ 40T Scott Stevens | .15 | .07 |
| ❑ 41T Paul Broten | .05 | .02 |
| ❑ 42T Carey Wilson | .05 | .02 |
| ❑ 43T Troy Crowder | .05 | .02 |
| ❑ 44T Vladimir Ruzicka | .05 | .02 |
| ❑ 45T Richard Pilon | .05 | .02 |
| ❑ 46T John McIntyre | .05 | .02 |
| ❑ 47T Mike Krushelnyski | .05 | .02 |
| ❑ 48T Dave Snuggerud | .05 | .02 |
| ❑ 49T Bob McGill | .05 | .02 |
| ❑ 50T Petr Nedved | .60 | .25 |
| ❑ 51T Ed Olczyk | .05 | .02 |
| ❑ 52T Doug Crossman | .05 | .02 |
| ❑ 53T Mikhail Tatarinov | .05 | .02 |
| ❑ 54T Michel Petit | .05 | .02 |
| ❑ 55T Frank Pietrangelo | .15 | .07 |
| ❑ 56T Brian MacLellan | .05 | .02 |
| ❑ 57T Paul Fenton | .05 | .02 |
| ❑ 58T Eric Desjardins | .15 | .07 |
| ❑ 59T Mike Craig | .05 | .02 |
| ❑ 60T Mike Ricci | .15 | .07 |
| ❑ 61T Harold Snepsts | .05 | .02 |
| ❑ 62T John Byce | .05 | .02 |
| ❑ 63T Laurie Boschman | .05 | .02 |
| ❑ 64T Randy Velischek | .05 | .02 |
| ❑ 65T Robert Kron | .05 | .02 |
| ❑ 66T Jocelyn Lemieux | .05 | .02 |
| ❑ 67T Dave Ellett | .05 | .02 |
| ❑ 68T Scott Arniel | .05 | .02 |
| ❑ 69T Doug Smail | .05 | .02 |
| ❑ 70T Jaromir Jagr | 3.00 | 1.35 |
| ❑ 71T Peter Bondra | .75 | .35 |
| ❑ 72T Paul Cyr | .05 | .02 |
| ❑ 73T Daniel Berthiaume | .15 | .07 |
| ❑ 74T Lee Norwood | .05 | .02 |
| ❑ 75T Bobby Smith | .15 | .07 |
| ❑ 76T Kris King | .05 | .02 |
| ❑ 77T Mark Hunter | .05 | .02 |
| ❑ 78T Brian Hayward | .15 | .07 |
| ❑ 79T Greg Hawgood | .05 | .02 |
| ❑ 80T Owen Nolan | .60 | .25 |
| ❑ 81T Cliff Ronning | .15 | .07 |
| ❑ 82T Zdeno Ciger | .05 | .02 |
| ❑ 83T Gordie Roberts | .05 | .02 |
| ❑ 84T Rick Green | .05 | .02 |
| ❑ 85T Ken Hodge Jr. | .05 | .02 |
| ❑ 86T Derek King | .05 | .02 |
| ❑ 87T Brent Gilchrist | .05 | .02 |
| ❑ 88T Eric Lindros | 3.00 | 1.35 |
| ❑ 89T Steve Bozek | .05 | .02 |
| ❑ 90T Keith Primeau | .40 | .18 |
| ❑ 91T Roger Johansson | .05 | .02 |
| ❑ 92T Wayne Presley | .05 | .02 |
| ❑ 93T Ilkka Sinisalo | .05 | .02 |
| ❑ 94T Mario Marois | .05 | .02 |
| ❑ 95T Ken Linseman | .05 | .02 |
| ❑ 96T Greg Brown | .05 | .02 |
| ❑ 97T Ray Sheppard | .15 | .07 |
| ❑ 98T Mike Lalor | .05 | .02 |
| ❑ 99T Normand Lacombe | .05 | .02 |
| ❑ 100T Mats Sundin | 1.00 | .45 |
| ❑ 101T Jergus Baca | .05 | .02 |
| ❑ 102T Mike Keane | .05 | .02 |
| ❑ 103T Ed Belfour | 1.50 | .70 |
| ❑ 104T Mark Hardy | .05 | .02 |
| ❑ 105T Dave Capuano | .05 | .02 |
| ❑ 106T Bryan Trottier | .15 | .07 |
| ❑ 107T Per Djoos | .05 | .02 |
| ❑ 108T Sylvain Turgeon | .05 | .02 |
| ❑ 109T David Reid | .05 | .02 |
| ❑ 110T Gretzky's 2000th Point | 1.00 | .45 |

## 1990-91 Score Young Superstars

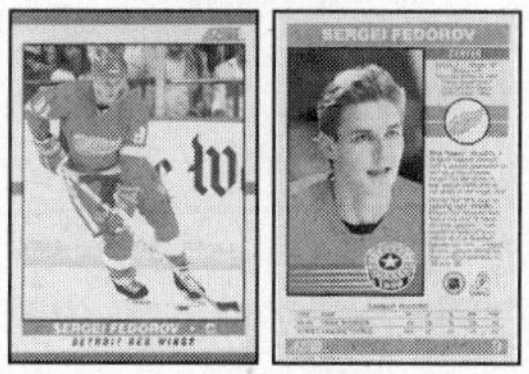

This 40-card standard-size set was issued by Score to honor some of the leading young players active in hockey. The set has a glossy sheen to it with an action shot of the player, while the back of the card has a portrait color shot on the back along with biographical and statistical information. The set was available only in this special box format. The set was also available direct to collectors through an offer detailed on certain wax wrappers.

| | MINT | NRMT |
|---|---|---|
| COMPLETE SET (40) | 15.00 | 6.75 |
| COMMON CARD (1-40) | .10 | .05 |
| ❑ 1 Pierre Turgeon | .50 | .23 |
| ❑ 2 Brian Leetch | .60 | .25 |
| ❑ 3 Daniel Marois | .10 | .05 |
| ❑ 4 Peter Sidorkiewicz | .50 | .23 |
| ❑ 5 Rob Brown | .10 | .05 |
| ❑ 6 Theoren Fleury | .75 | .35 |
| ❑ 7 Mats Sundin | .75 | .35 |
| ❑ 8 Glen Wesley | .10 | .05 |
| ❑ 9 Sergei Fedorov | 2.50 | 1.10 |
| ❑ 10 Joe Sakic | 1.25 | .55 |
| ❑ 11 Sean Burke | .50 | .23 |
| ❑ 12 Dave Chyzowski | .10 | .05 |
| ❑ 13 Gord Murphy | .10 | .05 |
| ❑ 14 Scott Young | .10 | .05 |
| ❑ 15 Curtis Joseph | 1.00 | .45 |
| ❑ 16 Darren Turcotte | .50 | .23 |
| ❑ 17 Kevin Stevens | .50 | .23 |
| ❑ 18 Mathieu Schneider | .10 | .05 |
| ❑ 19 Trevor Linden | .50 | .23 |
| ❑ 20 Mike Modano | 1.50 | .70 |
| ❑ 21 Martin Gelinas | .10 | .05 |
| ❑ 22 Stephane Fiset | .50 | .23 |
| ❑ 23 Brendan Shanahan | 1.25 | .55 |
| ❑ 24 Jeremy Roenick | .75 | .35 |
| ❑ 25 John Druce | .10 | .05 |
| ❑ 26 Alexander Mogilny | .50 | .23 |
| ❑ 27 Mike Richter | 1.00 | .45 |
| ❑ 28 Pat Elyniuk | .10 | .05 |
| ❑ 29 Robert Reichel | .10 | .05 |
| ❑ 30 Craig Janney | .10 | .05 |
| ❑ 31 Rod Brind'Amour | .50 | .23 |
| ❑ 32 Mark Fitzpatrick | .50 | .23 |
| ❑ 33 Tony Granato | .10 | .05 |
| ❑ 34 Bobby Holik | .10 | .05 |
| ❑ 35 Mark Recchi | .25 | .11 |
| ❑ 36 Owen Nolan | .50 | .23 |
| ❑ 37 Petr Nedved | .50 | .23 |
| ❑ 38 Keith Primeau | .50 | .23 |
| ❑ 39 Mike Ricci | .50 | .23 |
| ❑ 40 Eric Lindros | 5.00 | 2.20 |

## 1991 Score National

This ten-card standard-size set features outstanding hockey players. The cards were given out as a cello-wrapped complete set by Score at the National Sports Collectors Convention in Anaheim, at the Fanfest in Toronto, and at the National Candy Wholesalers Convention in St. Louis. Some dealers have reported selling the cards with the NCWA imprint and no imprint (FanFest) for a premium above the prices listed below. The front has an action photo of the player, bounded by diagonal green borders above and below the picture. The player's name and team name appear in the top green border. The light blue background shows through above and below the green borders, and it is decorated with hockey pucks and player icons. The back presents player information and career summary in a diagonal format similar to the design of the front. Some dealers have reported getting premiums of 2-3 times the values below for the Toronto FanFest versions.

| | MINT | NRMT |
|---|---|---|
| COMPLETE SET (10) | 30.00 | 13.50 |
| COMMON CARD (1-10) | 1.00 | .45 |
| ❑ 1 Wayne Gretzky | 10.00 | 4.50 |
| ❑ 2 Brett Hull | 2.00 | .90 |
| ❑ 3 Ray Bourque | 1.50 | .70 |
| ❑ 4 Al MacInnis | 1.00 | .45 |
| ❑ 5 Luc Robitaille | 1.00 | .45 |
| ❑ 6 Ed Belfour | 1.50 | .70 |
| ❑ 7 Steve Yzerman | 5.00 | 2.20 |
| ❑ 8 Cam Neely | 1.00 | .45 |
| ❑ 9 Paul Coffey | 1.50 | .70 |
| ❑ 10 Patrick Roy | 8.00 | 3.60 |

## 1991-92 Score American

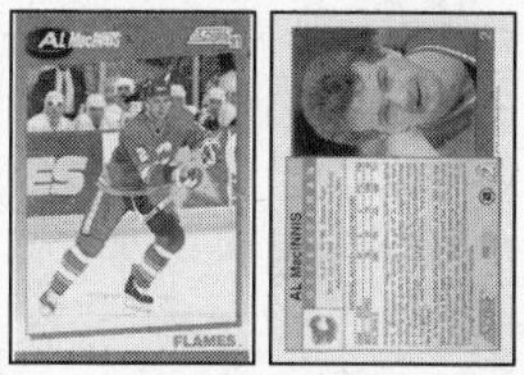

The 1991-92 Score American hockey set features 440 standard-size cards. As one moves down the card face, the fronts shade from purple to white. The color action player photo is enclosed by an thin red border, with a shadow border on the right and below. At the card top, the player's name is written over a hockey puck, and the team name is printed below the picture in the lower right corner. A purple border stripe at the bottom completes the front. In a horizontal format, the backs have biography, statistics, player profile, and a color close-up photo. The key Rookie Cards in this set are Tony Amonte, Dominik Hasek, John LeClair, Geoff Sanderson, and Doug Weight.

| | MINT | NRMT |
|---|---|---|
| COMPLETE SET (440) | 10.00 | 4.50 |
| COMP.FACT.SET (440) | 10.00 | 4.50 |
| COMMON CARD (1-440) | .05 | .02 |
| ❑ 1 Brett Hull | .30 | .14 |
| ❑ 2 Al MacInnis | .10 | .05 |
| ❑ 3 Luc Robitaille | .10 | .05 |
| ❑ 4 Pierre Turgeon | .10 | .05 |
| ❑ 5 Brian Leetch | .25 | .11 |
| ❑ 6 Cam Neely | .10 | .05 |
| ❑ 7 John Cullen | .05 | .02 |
| ❑ 8 Trevor Linden | .10 | .05 |
| ❑ 9 Rick Tocchet | .10 | .05 |
| ❑ 10 John Vanbiesbrouck | .30 | .14 |
| ❑ 11 Steve Smith | .05 | .02 |
| ❑ 12 Doug Smail | .05 | .02 |
| ❑ 13 Craig Ludwig | .05 | .02 |
| ❑ 14 Paul Fenton | .05 | .02 |
| ❑ 15 Dirk Graham | .05 | .02 |
| ❑ 16 Brad McCrimmon | .05 | .02 |
| ❑ 17 Dean Evason | .05 | .02 |
| ❑ 18 Fredrik Olausson | .05 | .02 |
| ❑ 19 Guy Carbonneau | .10 | .05 |
| ❑ 20 Kevin Hatcher | .05 | .02 |
| ❑ 21 Paul Ranheim | .05 | .02 |
| ❑ 22 Claude Lemieux | .10 | .05 |
| ❑ 23 Vincent Riendeau | .10 | .05 |
| ❑ 24 Garth Butcher | .05 | .02 |
| ❑ 25 Joe Sakic | .40 | .18 |
| ❑ 26 Rick Vaive | .05 | .02 |
| ❑ 27 Rob Blake | .05 | .02 |
| ❑ 28 Mike Ricci | .05 | .02 |
| ❑ 29 Pat Flatley | .05 | .02 |
| ❑ 30 Bill Ranford | .10 | .05 |
| ❑ 31 Larry Murphy | .10 | .05 |
| ❑ 32 Bobby Smith | .10 | .05 |
| ❑ 33 Mike Krushelnyski | .05 | .02 |
| ❑ 34 Gerard Gallant | .05 | .02 |
| ❑ 35 Doug Wilson | .10 | .05 |
| ❑ 36 John Ogrodnick | .05 | .02 |
| ❑ 37 Mikhail Tatarinov | .05 | .02 |
| ❑ 38 Doug Crossman | .05 | .02 |
| ❑ 39 Mark Osborne | .05 | .02 |
| ❑ 40 Scott Stevens | .10 | .05 |
| ❑ 41 Ron Tugnutt | .10 | .05 |
| ❑ 42 Russ Courtnall | .05 | .02 |
| ❑ 43 Gord Murphy | .05 | .02 |
| ❑ 44 Greg Adams | .05 | .02 |
| ❑ 45 Christian Ruuttu | .05 | .02 |
| ❑ 46 Ken Daneyko | .05 | .02 |
| ❑ 47 Glenn Anderson | .10 | .05 |
| ❑ 48 Ray Ferraro | .05 | .02 |
| ❑ 49 Tony Tanti | .05 | .02 |
| ❑ 50 Ray Bourque | .25 | .11 |
| ❑ 51 Sergei Makarov | .05 | .02 |
| ❑ 52 Jim Johnson | .05 | .02 |
| ❑ 53 Troy Murray | .05 | .02 |
| ❑ 54 Shawn Burr | .05 | .02 |
| ❑ 55 Peter Ing | .10 | .05 |
| ❑ 56 Dale Hunter | .05 | .02 |
| ❑ 57 Tony Granato | .05 | .02 |
| ❑ 58 Curtis Leschyshyn | .05 | .02 |
| ❑ 59 Brian Mullen | .05 | .02 |
| ❑ 60 Ed Olczyk | .05 | .02 |
| ❑ 61 Mike Ramsey | .05 | .02 |
| ❑ 62 Dan Quinn | .05 | .02 |
| ❑ 63 Rich Sutter | .05 | .02 |
| ❑ 64 Terry Carkner | .05 | .02 |
| ❑ 65 Shayne Corson | .05 | .02 |
| ❑ 66 Peter Stastny | .10 | .05 |
| ❑ 67 Craig Muni | .05 | .02 |
| ❑ 68 Glenn Healy | .10 | .05 |
| ❑ 69 Phil Bourque | .05 | .02 |
| ❑ 70 Pat Verbeek | .05 | .02 |
| ❑ 71 Garry Galley | .05 | .02 |
| ❑ 72 Dave Gagner | .10 | .05 |
| ❑ 73 Bob Probert | .10 | .05 |
| ❑ 74 Craig Wolanin | .05 | .02 |
| ❑ 75 Patrick Roy | .75 | .35 |
| ❑ 76 Keith Brown | .05 | .02 |
| ❑ 77 Gary Leeman | .05 | .02 |
| ❑ 78 Brent Ashton | .05 | .02 |
| ❑ 79 Randy Moller | .05 | .02 |
| ❑ 80 Mike Vernon | .10 | .05 |
| ❑ 81 Kelly Miller | .05 | .02 |
| ❑ 82 Ulf Samuelsson | .05 | .02 |
| ❑ 83 Todd Elik | .05 | .02 |
| ❑ 84 Uwe Krupp | .05 | .02 |
| ❑ 85 Rod Brind'Amour | .10 | .05 |
| ❑ 86 Dave Capuano | .05 | .02 |
| ❑ 87 Geoff Smith | .05 | .02 |
| ❑ 88 David Volek | .05 | .02 |
| ❑ 89 Bruce Driver | .05 | .02 |
| ❑ 90 Andy Moog | .10 | .05 |
| ❑ 91 Pelle Eklund | .05 | .02 |
| ❑ 92 Joey Kocur | .05 | .02 |
| ❑ 93 Mark Tinordi | .05 | .02 |
| ❑ 94 Steve Thomas | .05 | .02 |
| ❑ 95 Petr Svoboda | .05 | .02 |
| ❑ 96 Joel Otto | .05 | .02 |
| ❑ 97 Todd Krygier | .05 | .02 |
| ❑ 98 Jaromir Jagr | .50 | .23 |
| ❑ 99 Mike Liut | .10 | .05 |
| ❑ 100 Wayne Gretzky | 1.00 | .45 |
| ❑ 101 Teppo Numminen | .05 | .02 |
| ❑ 102 Randy Burridge | .05 | .02 |
| ❑ 103 Michel Petit | .05 | .02 |
| ❑ 104 Tony McKegney | .05 | .02 |
| ❑ 105 Mathieu Schneider | .05 | .02 |
| ❑ 106 Daren Puppa | .10 | .05 |
| ❑ 107 Paul Cavallini | .05 | .02 |
| ❑ 108 Tim Kerr | .05 | .02 |
| ❑ 109 Kevin Lowe | .05 | .02 |
| ❑ 110 Kirk Muller | .05 | .02 |
| ❑ 111 Zarley Zalapski | .05 | .02 |
| ❑ 112 Mike Hough | .05 | .02 |
| ❑ 113 Ken Hodge Jr. | .05 | .02 |
| ❑ 114 Grant Fuhr | .10 | .05 |
| ❑ 115 Paul Coffey | .25 | .11 |
| ❑ 116 Wendel Clark | .10 | .05 |
| ❑ 117 Patrik Sundstrom | .05 | .02 |
| ❑ 118 Kevin Dineen | .05 | .02 |
| ❑ 119 Eric Desjardins | .05 | .02 |
| ❑ 120 Mike Richter | .25 | .11 |
| ❑ 121 Sergio Momesso | .05 | .02 |
| ❑ 122 Tony Hrkac | .05 | .02 |
| ❑ 123 Joe Reekie | .05 | .02 |
| ❑ 124 Petr Nedved | .10 | .05 |
| ❑ 125 Randy Carlyle | .05 | .02 |
| ❑ 126 Kevin Miller | .05 | .02 |
| ❑ 127 Rejean Lemelin | .10 | .05 |
| ❑ 128 Dino Ciccarelli | .10 | .05 |
| ❑ 129 Sylvain Cote | .05 | .02 |
| ❑ 130 Mats Sundin | .25 | .11 |
| ❑ 131 Eric Weinrich | .05 | .02 |
| ❑ 132 Daniel Berthiaume | .10 | .05 |
| ❑ 133 Keith Acton | .05 | .02 |
| ❑ 134 Benoit Hogue | .05 | .02 |
| ❑ 135 Mike Gartner | .10 | .05 |
| ❑ 136 Petr Klima | .05 | .02 |
| ❑ 137 Curt Giles | .05 | .02 |
| ❑ 138 Scott Pearson | .05 | .02 |
| ❑ 139 Luke Richardson | .05 | .02 |
| ❑ 140 Steve Larmer | .10 | .05 |
| ❑ 141 Ken Wregget | .10 | .05 |
| ❑ 142 Frank Musil | .05 | .02 |
| ❑ 143 Owen Nolan | .10 | .05 |
| ❑ 144 Keith Primeau | .10 | .05 |
| ❑ 145 Mark Recchi | .10 | .05 |
| ❑ 146 Don Sweeney | .05 | .02 |
| ❑ 147 Mike McPhee | .05 | .02 |
| ❑ 148 Ken Baumgartner | .05 | .02 |
| ❑ 149 Dave Lowry | .05 | .02 |
| ❑ 150 Geoff Courtnall | .05 | .02 |
| ❑ 151 Chris Terreri | .10 | .05 |
| ❑ 152 Dave Manson | .05 | .02 |
| ❑ 153 Bobby Holik | .05 | .02 |
| ❑ 154 Bob Kudelski | .05 | .02 |
| ❑ 155 Calle Johansson | .05 | .02 |

❑ 156 Mark Hunter .05 .02
❑ 157 Randy Gilhen .05 .02
❑ 158 Yves Racine .05 .02
❑ 159 Martin Gelinas .05 .02
❑ 160 Brian Bellows .05 .02
❑ 161 David Shaw .05 .02
❑ 162 Bob Carpenter .05 .02
❑ 163 Doug Brown .05 .02
❑ 164 Ulf Dahlen .05 .02
❑ 165 Denis Savard .10 .05
❑ 166 Paul Ysebaert .05 .02
❑ 167 Derek King .05 .02
❑ 168 Igor Larionov .05 .02
❑ 169 Bob Errey .05 .02
❑ 170 Joe Nieuwendyk .10 .05
❑ 171 Normand Rochefort .05 .02
❑ 172 John Tonelli .05 .02
❑ 173 David Reid .05 .02
❑ 174 Tom Kurvers .05 .02
❑ 175 Dimitri Khristich .05 .02
❑ 176 Bob Sweeney .05 .02
❑ 177 Rick Zombo .05 .02
❑ 178 Troy Mallette .05 .02
❑ 179 Bob Bassen .05 .02
❑ 180 John Druce .05 .02
❑ 181 Mike Craig .05 .02
❑ 182 John McIntyre .05 .02
❑ 183 Murray Baron .05 .02
❑ 184 Slava Fetisov .05 .02
❑ 185 Don Beaupre .10 .05
❑ 186 Brian Benning .05 .02
❑ 187 Dave Barr .05 .02
❑ 188 Petri Skriko .05 .02
❑ 189 Steve Konroyd .05 .02
❑ 190 Steve Yzerman .50 .23
❑ 191 Jon Casey .10 .05
❑ 192 Gary Nylund .05 .02
❑ 193 Michal Pivonka .05 .02
❑ 194 Alexei Kasatonov .05 .02
❑ 195 Garry Valk .05 .02
❑ 196 Darren Turcotte .05 .02
❑ 197 Chris Nilan .05 .02
❑ 198 Thomas Steen .05 .02
❑ 199 Gary Roberts .05 .02
❑ 200 Mario Lemieux .75 .35
❑ 201 Michel Goulet .10 .05
❑ 202 Craig MacTavish .05 .02
❑ 203 Peter Sidorkiewicz .10 .05
❑ 204 Johan Garpenlov .05 .02
❑ 205 Steve Duchesne .05 .02
❑ 206 Dave Snuggerud .05 .02
❑ 207 Kjell Samuelsson .05 .02
❑ 208 Sylvain Turgeon .05 .02
❑ 209 Al Iafrate .10 .05
❑ 210 John MacLean .10 .05
❑ 211 Brian Hayward .10 .05
❑ 212 Cliff Ronning .05 .02
❑ 213 Ray Sheppard .10 .05
❑ 214 Dave Taylor .10 .05
❑ 215 Doug Lidster .05 .02
❑ 216 Peter Bondra .25 .11
❑ 217 Marty McSorley .05 .02
❑ 218 Doug Gilmour .25 .11
❑ 219 Paul MacDermid .05 .02
❑ 220 Jeremy Roenick .25 .11
❑ 221 Wayne Presley .05 .02
❑ 222 Jeff Norton .05 .02
❑ 223 Brian Propp .05 .02
❑ 224 Jimmy Carson .05 .02
❑ 225 Tom Barrasso .10 .05
❑ 226 Theoren Fleury .10 .05
❑ 227 Carey Wilson .05 .02
❑ 228 Rod Langway .05 .02
❑ 229 Bryan Trottier .10 .05
❑ 230 James Patrick .05 .02
❑ 231 Kelly Hrudey .10 .05
❑ 232 Dave Poulin .05 .02
❑ 233 Rob Ramage .05 .02
❑ 234 Stephane Richer .10 .05
❑ 235 Chris Chelios .25 .11
❑ 236 Alexander Mogilny .10 .05
❑ 237 Bryan Fogarty .05 .02
❑ 238 Adam Oates .10 .05
❑ 239 Ron Hextall .10 .05
❑ 240 Bernie Nicholls .10 .05
❑ 241 Esa Tikkanen .05 .02
❑ 242 Jyrki Lumme .05 .02
❑ 243 Brent Sutter .05 .02
❑ 244 Gary Suter .05 .02
❑ 245 Sean Burke .10 .05
❑ 246 Rob Brown .05 .02
❑ 247 Mike Modano .30 .14
❑ 248 Kevin Stevens .05 .02
❑ 249 Mike Lalor .05 .02
❑ 250 Sergei Fedorov .40 .18
❑ 251 Bob Essensa .10 .05
❑ 252 Mark Howe .05 .02
❑ 253 Craig Janney .10 .05
❑ 254 Daniel Marois .05 .02
❑ 255 Craig Simpson .05 .02
❑ 256 Steve Kasper .05 .02
❑ 257 Randy Velischek .05 .02
❑ 258 Gino Cavallini .05 .02
❑ 259 Dale Hawerchuk .10 .05
❑ 260 Pat LaFontaine .10 .05
❑ 261 Kirk McLean .10 .05
❑ 262 Murray Craven .05 .02
❑ 263 Robert Reichel .05 .02
❑ 264 Jan Erixon .05 .02
❑ 265 Adam Creighton .05 .02
❑ 266 Mark Fitzpatrick .10 .05
❑ 267 Ron Francis .10 .05
❑ 268 Joe Mullen .10 .05
❑ 269 Peter Zezel .05 .02
❑ 270 Tomas Sandstrom .05 .02
❑ 271 Phil Housley .10 .05
❑ 272 Tim Cheveldae .10 .05
❑ 273 Glen Wesley .05 .02
❑ 274 Stephan Lebeau .05 .02
❑ 275 Dave Ellett .05 .02
❑ 276 Jeff Brown .05 .02
❑ 277 Dave Andreychuk .10 .05
❑ 278 Steven Finn .05 .02
❑ 279 Scott Mellanby .10 .05
❑ 280 Neal Broten .10 .05
❑ 281 Randy Wood .05 .02
❑ 282 Troy Gamble .10 .05
❑ 283 Mike Ridley .05 .02
❑ 284 Jamie Macoun .05 .02
❑ 285 Mark Messier .25 .11
❑ 286 Brendan Shanahan .40 .18
❑ 287 Scott Young .05 .02
❑ 288 Kelly Kisio .05 .02
❑ 289 Brad Shaw .05 .02
❑ 290 Ed Belfour .25 .11
❑ 291 Larry Robinson .10 .05
❑ 292 Dave Christian .05 .02
❑ 293 Steve Chiasson .05 .02
❑ 294 Brian Skrudland .05 .02
❑ 295 Pat Elynuik .05 .02
❑ 296 Curtis Joseph .25 .11
❑ 297 Doug Bodger .05 .02
❑ 298 Ron Sutter .05 .02
❑ 299 Joe Murphy .05 .02
❑ 300 Vincent Damphousse .10 .05
❑ 301 Cam Neely CC .10 .05
❑ 302 Rick Tocchet CC .10 .05
❑ 303 Scott Stevens CC .10 .05
❑ 304 Ulf Samuelsson CC .05 .02
❑ 305 Jeremy Roenick CC .10 .05
❑ 306 The Hunter Brothers .05 .02
Dale Hunter
Mark Hunter
❑ 307 The Broten Brothers .05 .02
Aaron Broten
Neal Broten
❑ 308 The Cavallini Brothers .05 .02
Gino Cavallini
Paul Cavallini
❑ 309 The Miller Brothers .05 .02
Kelly Miller
Kevin Miller
❑ 310 Dennis Vaske TP .05 .02
❑ 311 Rob Pearson TP .05 .02
❑ 312 Jason Miller TP .05 .02
❑ 313 John LeClair TP 1.50 .70
❑ 314 Bryan Marchment TP .05 .02
❑ 315 Gary Shuchuk TP .05 .02
❑ 316 Dominik Hasek TP UER .. 2.00 .90
(Misspelled Dominic
on both sides)
❑ 317 Michel Picard TP .05 .02
❑ 318 Corey Millen TP .05 .02
❑ 319 Joe Sacco TP .05 .02
❑ 320 Reggie Savage TP .05 .02
❑ 321 Pat Murray TP .05 .02
❑ 322 Myles O'Connor TP .05 .02
❑ 323 Shawn Antoski TP .05 .02
❑ 324 Geoff Sanderson TP .30 .14
❑ 325 Chris Govedaris TP .05 .02
❑ 326 Alexei Gusarov TP .05 .02
❑ 327 Mike Sillinger TP .05 .02
❑ 328 Bob Wilkie TP .05 .02
❑ 329 Pat Jablonski TP .10 .05
❑ 330 David Emma .05 .02
Hobey Baker Award
❑ 331 Kirk Muller FP .05 .02
❑ 332 Pat LaFontaine FP .10 .05
❑ 333 Brian Leetch FP .10 .05
❑ 334 Rick Tocchet FP .10 .05
❑ 335 Mario Lemieux FP .40 .18
❑ 336 Joe Sakic FP .25 .11
❑ 337 Brett Hull FP .10 .05
❑ 338 Vincent Damphousse FP .10 .05
❑ 339 Trevor Linden FP .10 .05
❑ 340 Kevin Hatcher FP .05 .02
❑ 341 Pat Elynuik FP .05 .02
❑ 342 Patrick Roy DT .40 .18
❑ 343 Brian Leetch DT .10 .05
❑ 344 Ray Bourque DT .10 .05
❑ 345 Luc Robitaille DT .10 .05
❑ 346 Wayne Gretzky DT .50 .23
❑ 347 Brett Hull DT .10 .05
❑ 348 Ed Belfour ART .10 .05
❑ 349 Rob Blake ART .10 .05
❑ 350 Eric Weinrich ART .05 .02
❑ 351 Jaromir Jagr ART .25 .11
❑ 352 Sergei Fedorov ART .25 .11
❑ 353 Ken Hodge Jr. ART .05 .02
❑ 354 Eric Lindros Art .75 .35
❑ 355 Eric Lindros .75 .35
Awards and Honors
❑ 356 Eric Lindros .75 .35
'91 1st Rd Draft Choice
❑ 357 Dana Murzyn .05 .02
❑ 358 Adam Graves .10 .05
❑ 359 Ken Linseman .05 .02
❑ 360 Mike Keane .05 .02
❑ 361 Stephane Morin .05 .02
❑ 362 Grant Ledyard .05 .02
❑ 363 Kris King .05 .02
❑ 364 Paul Gillis .05 .02
❑ 365 Chris Dahlquist .05 .02
❑ 366 Paul Stanton .05 .02
❑ 367 Jeff Hackett .10 .05
❑ 368 Bob McGill .05 .02
❑ 369 Neil Wilkinson .05 .02
❑ 370 Rob Zettler .05 .02
❑ 371 Brett Hull MOY .10 .05
❑ 372 Paul Coffey 1000 .10 .05
❑ 373 Mark Messier 1000 .10 .05
❑ 374 Dave Taylor 1000 .10 .05
❑ 375 Michel Goulet 1000 .10 .05
❑ 376 Dale Hawerchuk 1000 .10 .05
❑ 377 The Turgeon Brothers .05 .02
Pierre Turgeon
Sylvain Turgeon
❑ 378 The Sutter Brothers .05 .02
Rich Sutter
Brian Sutter
Ron Sutter
❑ 379 The Mullen Brothers .05 .02
Brian Mullen
Joe Mullen
❑ 380 The Courtnall Brothers .05 .02
Geoff Courtnall
Russ Courtnall
❑ 381 Trevor Kidd TP .10 .05
❑ 382 Patrice Brisebois TP .05 .02
❑ 383 Mark Greig TP .05 .02
❑ 384 Kip Miller TP .05 .02
❑ 385 Drake Berehowsky TP .05 .02
❑ 386 Kevin Haller TP .05 .02
❑ 387 Dave Gagnon TP .05 .02
❑ 388 Jason Marshall TP .05 .02
❑ 389 Donald Audette TP .10 .05
❑ 390 Patrick Lebeau TP .05 .02
❑ 391 Alexander Godynyuk TP .05 .02
❑ 392 Jarrod Skalde TP .05 .02
❑ 393 Ken Sutton TP .05 .02
❑ 394 Sergei Kharin TP .05 .02
❑ 395 Andre Racicot TP .10 .05
❑ 396 Doug Weight TP .60 .25
❑ 397 Kevin Todd TP .05 .02
❑ 398 Tony Amonte TP .60 .25
❑ 399 Kimbi Daniels TP .05 .02
❑ 400 Jeff Daniels TP .05 .02
❑ 401 Guy Lafleur .10 .05
Speed and Grace
❑ 402 Guy Lafleur .10 .05
Awards and Achievements
❑ 403 Guy Lafleur .10 .05
A Hall of Famer
❑ 404 Brett Hull SL .10 .05
❑ 405 Wayne Gretzky SL .50 .23
❑ 406 Wayne Gretzky SL .50 .23
❑ 407 Theoren Fleury SL and .10 .05
Marty McSorley SL
❑ 408 Sergei Fedorov SL .25 .11
❑ 409 Al MacInnis SL .10 .05
❑ 410 Ed Belfour SL .10 .05
❑ 411 Ed Belfour SL .10 .05
❑ 412 Brett Hull HL .25 .11
(50 goals in 50 games)
❑ 413 Wayne Gretzky HL .50 .23
(700th goal)
❑ 414 San Jose Sharks .05 .02
❑ 415 Ray Bourque FP .10 .05
❑ 416 Pierre Turgeon FP .10 .05
❑ 417 Al MacInnis FP .10 .05
❑ 418 Jeremy Roenick FP .10 .05
❑ 419 Steve Yzerman FP .25 .11
❑ 420 Mark Messier FP .10 .05
❑ 421 John Cullen FP .05 .02
❑ 422 Wayne Gretzky FP .50 .23
❑ 423 Mike Modano FP .10 .05
❑ 424 Patrick Roy FP .40 .18
❑ 425 Stanley Cup Champs .05 .02
❑ 426 Mario Lemieux .40 .18
Conn Smythe Trophy
❑ 427 Wayne Gretzky .50 .23
Art Ross Trophy
❑ 428 Brett Hull .10 .05
Hart Memorial Trophy
❑ 429 Ray Bourque .10 .05
Norris Trophy
❑ 430 Ed Belfour .10 .05
Calder Trophy
❑ 431 Ed Belfour .10 .05
Vezina Trophy
❑ 432 Dirk Graham .05 .02
Frank J. Selke Trophy
❑ 433 Ed Belfour .10 .05
Jennings Trophy
❑ 434 Wayne Gretzky .50 .23
Lady Byng Trophy
❑ 435 Dave Taylor .10 .05
Bill Masterton Trophy
❑ 436 Randy Ladouceur .05 .02
❑ 437 Dave Tippett .05 .02
❑ 438 Clint Malarchuk .05 .02
❑ 439 Gordie Roberts .05 .02
❑ 440 Frank Pietrangelo .10 .05

## 1991-92 Score Canadian

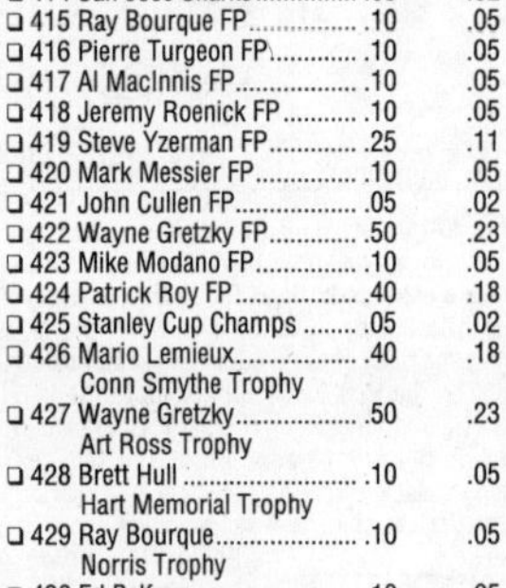

The 1991-92 Score Canadian hockey set features 660 standard-size cards. The set was released in two series of 330 cards each. The borders on the front of first series cards shade from red to white, top to bottom. The fronts of the second series cards shade from bright blue to white. The two series also differ in that first series cards have the player enclosed by a thin purple border and second series cards have a red border. At the top, the player's name is written over a hockey puck and the team name is printed below the picture in the lower right corner. A red border stripe at the bottom completes the front. In a horizontal format, the bilingual backs have biography, statistics, player profile, and a color close-up photo. An identical version (Score Canadian-English) to this set exists, with the difference being that the text on each card is strictly in English. There is no difference in card values for this version. Rookie Cards include Tony Amonte, Dominik Hasek, John LeClair, Nicklas Lidstrom, Geoff Sanderson and Doug Weight.

| | MINT | NRMT |
|---|---|---|
| COMPLETE SET (660) | 12.00 | 5.50 |
| COMP.FACT.SET (660) | 12.00 | 5.50 |
| COMPLETE SERIES 1 (330) | 6.00 | 2.70 |
| COMPLETE SERIES 2 (330) | 6.00 | 2.70 |
| COMMON CARD (1-660) | .05 | .02 |

❑ 1 Brett Hull .30 .14
❑ 2 Al MacInnis .10 .05
❑ 3 Luc Robitaille .10 .05
❑ 4 Pierre Turgeon .10 .05
❑ 5 Brian Leetch .25 .11
❑ 6 Cam Neely .10 .05
❑ 7 John Cullen .05 .02
❑ 8 Trevor Linden .10 .05
❑ 9 Rick Tocchet .10 .05
❑ 10 John Vanbiesbrouck .30 .14
❑ 11 Steve Smith .05 .02
❑ 12 Doug Smail .05 .02
❑ 13 Craig Ludwig .05 .02
❑ 14 Paul Fenton .05 .02
❑ 15 Dirk Graham .05 .02
❑ 16 Brad McCrimmon .05 .02
❑ 17 Dean Evason .05 .02
❑ 18 Fredrik Olausson .05 .02
❑ 19 Guy Carbonneau .10 .05
❑ 20 Kevin Hatcher .05 .02
❑ 21 Paul Ranheim .05 .02
❑ 22 Claude Lemieux .10 .05
❑ 23 Vincent Riendeau .10 .05
❑ 24 Garth Butcher .05 .02
❑ 25 Joe Sakic .40 .18
❑ 26 Rick Vaive .05 .02
❑ 27 Rob Blake .10 .05
❑ 28 Mike Ricci .05 .02
❑ 29 Pat Flatley .05 .02
❑ 30 Bill Ranford .10 .05
❑ 31 Larry Murphy .10 .05
❑ 32 Bobby Smith .10 .05
❑ 33 Mike Krushelnyski .05 .02
❑ 34 Gerard Gallant .05 .02
❑ 35 Doug Wilson .10 .05
❑ 36 John Ogrodnick .05 .02
❑ 37 Mikhail Tatarinov .05 .02
❑ 38 Doug Crossman .05 .02
❑ 39 Mark Osborne .05 .02
❑ 40 Scott Stevens .10 .05
❑ 41 Ron Tugnutt .10 .05
❑ 42 Russ Courtnall .05 .02
❑ 43 Gord Murphy .05 .02
❑ 44 Greg Adams .05 .02
❑ 45 Christian Ruuttu .05 .02
❑ 46 Ken Daneyko .05 .02
❑ 47 Glenn Anderson .10 .05
❑ 48 Ray Ferraro .05 .02
❑ 49 Tony Tanti .05 .02
❑ 50 Ray Bourque .25 .11
❑ 51 Sergei Makarov .05 .02
❑ 52 Jim Johnson .05 .02
❑ 53 Troy Murray .05 .02
❑ 54 Shawn Burr .05 .02
❑ 55 Peter Ing .10 .05
❑ 56 Dale Hunter .05 .02
❑ 57 Tony Granato .05 .02
❑ 58 Curtis Leschyshyn .05 .02
❑ 59 Brian Mullen .05 .02
❑ 60 Ed Olczyk .05 .02
❑ 61 Mike Ramsey .05 .02
❑ 62 Dan Quinn .05 .02
❑ 63 Rich Sutter .05 .02
❑ 64 Terry Carkner .05 .02
❑ 65 Shayne Corson .05 .02
❑ 66 Peter Stastny .10 .05
❑ 67 Craig Muni .05 .02
❑ 68 Glenn Healy .10 .05
❑ 69 Phil Bourque .05 .02
❑ 70 Pat Verbeek .05 .02
❑ 71 Garry Galley .05 .02
❑ 72 Dave Gagner .10 .05
❑ 73 Bob Probert .10 .05
❑ 74 Craig Wolanin .05 .02
❑ 75 Patrick Roy .75 .35
❑ 76 Keith Brown .05 .02
❑ 77 Gary Leeman .05 .02
❑ 78 Brent Ashton .05 .02
❑ 79 Randy Moller .05 .02
❑ 80 Mike Vernon .10 .05
❑ 81 Kelly Miller .05 .02
❑ 82 Ulf Samuelsson .05 .02
❑ 83 Todd Elik .05 .02
❑ 84 Uwe Krupp .05 .02
❑ 85 Rod Brind'Amour .10 .05
❑ 86 Dave Capuano .05 .02
❑ 87 Geoff Smith .05 .02
❑ 88 David Volek .05 .02
❑ 89 Bruce Driver .05 .02
❑ 90 Andy Moog .10 .05
❑ 91 Pelle Eklund .05 .02
❑ 92 Joey Kocur .05 .02
❑ 93 Mark Tinordi .05 .02
❑ 94 Steve Thomas .05 .02
❑ 95 Petr Svoboda .05 .02
❑ 96 Joel Otto .05 .02
❑ 97 Todd Krygier .05 .02
❑ 98 Jaromir Jagr .50 .23
❑ 99 Mike Liut .10 .05
❑ 100 Wayne Gretzky 1.00 .45
❑ 101 Teppo Numminen .05 .02
❑ 102 Randy Burridge .05 .02
❑ 103 Michel Petit .05 .02
❑ 104 Tony McKegney .05 .02
❑ 105 Mathieu Schneider .05 .02
❑ 106 Daren Puppa .10 .05
❑ 107 Paul Cavallini .05 .02
❑ 108 Tim Kerr .05 .02
❑ 109 Kevin Lowe .05 .02
❑ 110 Kirk Muller .05 .02
❑ 111 Zarley Zalapski .05 .02
❑ 112 Mike Hough .05 .02
❑ 113 Ken Hodge Jr. .05 .02
❑ 114 Grant Fuhr .10 .05
❑ 115 Paul Coffey .25 .11
❑ 116 Wendel Clark .10 .05
❑ 117 Patrik Sundstrom .05 .02
❑ 118 Kevin Dineen .05 .02
❑ 119 Eric Desjardins .05 .02
❑ 120 Mike Richter .25 .11
❑ 121 Sergio Momesso .05 .02
❑ 122 Tony Hrkac .05 .02
❑ 123 Joe Reekie .05 .02
❑ 124 Petr Nedved .10 .05
❑ 125 Randy Carlyle .05 .02
❑ 126 Kevin Miller .05 .02
❑ 127 Rejean Lemelin .10 .05
❑ 128 Dino Ciccarelli .10 .05
❑ 129 Sylvain Cote .05 .02
❑ 130 Mats Sundin .25 .11
❑ 131 Eric Weinrich .05 .02
❑ 132 Daniel Berthiaume .10 .05
❑ 133 Keith Acton .05 .02
❑ 134 Benoit Hogue .05 .02
❑ 135 Mike Gartner .10 .05
❑ 136 Petr Klima .05 .02
❑ 137 Curt Giles .05 .02
❑ 138 Scott Pearson .05 .02
❑ 139 Luke Richardson .05 .02
❑ 140 Steve Larmer .10 .05
❑ 141 Ken Wregget .10 .05
❑ 142 Frank Musil .05 .02
❑ 143 Owen Nolan .10 .05
❑ 144 Keith Primeau .10 .05
❑ 145 Mark Recchi .10 .05
❑ 146 Don Sweeney .05 .02
❑ 147 Mike McPhee .05 .02
❑ 148 Ken Baumgartner .05 .02
❑ 149 Dave Lowry .05 .02
❑ 150 Geoff Courtnall .05 .02
❑ 151 Chris Terreri .10 .05
❑ 152 Dave Manson .05 .02
❑ 153 Bobby Holik .05 .02
❑ 154 Bob Kudelski .05 .02
❑ 155 Calle Johansson .05 .02
❑ 156 Mark Hunter .05 .02
❑ 157 Randy Gilhen .05 .02
❑ 158 Yves Racine .05 .02
❑ 159 Martin Gelinas .05 .02
❑ 160 Brian Bellows .05 .02
❑ 161 David Shaw .05 .02
❑ 162 Bob Carpenter .05 .02
❑ 163 Doug Brown .05 .02
❑ 164 Ulf Dahlen .05 .02
❑ 165 Denis Savard .10 .05
❑ 166 Paul Ysebaert .05 .02
❑ 167 Derek King .05 .02
❑ 168 Igor Larionov .05 .02
❑ 169 Bob Errey .05 .02
❑ 170 Joe Nieuwendyk .10 .05
❑ 171 Normand Rochefort .05 .02
❑ 172 John Tonelli .05 .02
❑ 173 David Reid .05 .02
❑ 174 Tom Kurvers .05 .02
❑ 175 Dimitri Khristich .05 .02
❑ 176 Bob Sweeney .05 .02
❑ 177 Rick Zombo .05 .02
❑ 178 Troy Mallette .05 .02
❑ 179 Bob Bassen .05 .02
❑ 180 John Druce .05 .02
❑ 181 Mike Craig .05 .02
❑ 182 John McIntyre .05 .02
❑ 183 Murray Baron .05 .02
❑ 184 Slava Fetisov .05 .02
❑ 185 Don Beaupre .10 .05
❑ 186 Brian Benning .05 .02
❑ 187 Dave Barr .05 .02
❑ 188 Petri Skriko .05 .02
❑ 189 Steve Konroyd .05 .02
❑ 190 Steve Yzerman .50 .23
❑ 191 Jon Casey .10 .05
❑ 192 Gary Nylund .05 .02
❑ 193 Michal Pivonka .05 .02
❑ 194 Alexei Kasatonov .05 .02
❑ 195 Garry Valk .05 .02
❑ 196 Darren Turcotte .05 .02
❑ 197 Chris Nilan .05 .02
❑ 198 Thomas Steen .05 .02
❑ 199 Gary Roberts .05 .02
❑ 200 Mario Lemieux .75 .35
❑ 201 Michel Goulet .10 .05
❑ 202 Craig MacTavish .05 .02
❑ 203 Peter Sidorkiewicz .10 .05
❑ 204 Johan Garpenlov .05 .02
❑ 205 Steve Duchesne .05 .02
❑ 206 Dave Snuggerud .05 .02
❑ 207 Kjell Samuelsson .05 .02
❑ 208 Sylvain Turgeon .05 .02
❑ 209 Al Iafrate .10 .05
❑ 210 John MacLean .10 .05
❑ 211 Brian Hayward .10 .05

❑ 212 Cliff Ronning .05 .02
❑ 213 Ray Sheppard .10 .05
❑ 214 Dave Taylor .10 .05
❑ 215 Doug Lidster .05 .02
❑ 216 Peter Bondra .25 .11
❑ 217 Marty McSorley .05 .02
❑ 218 Doug Gilmour .25 .11
❑ 219 Paul MacDermid .05 .02
❑ 220 Jeremy Roenick .25 .11
❑ 221 Wayne Presley .05 .02
❑ 222 Jeff Norton .05 .02
❑ 223 Brian Propp .05 .02
❑ 224 Jimmy Carson .05 .02
❑ 225 Tom Barrasso .10 .05
❑ 226 Theoren Fleury .10 .05
❑ 227 Carey Wilson .05 .02
❑ 228 Rod Langway .05 .02
❑ 229 Bryan Trottier .10 .05
❑ 230 James Patrick .05 .02
❑ 231 Dana Murzyn .05 .02
❑ 232 Rick Wamsley .10 .05
❑ 233 Dave McLlwain .05 .02
❑ 234 Tom Fergus .05 .02
❑ 235 Adam Graves .10 .05
❑ 236 Jacques Cloutier .10 .05
❑ 237 Gino Odjick .05 .02
❑ 238 Andrew Cassels .05 .02
❑ 239 Ken Linseman .05 .02
❑ 240 Danton Cole .05 .02
❑ 241 Dave Hannan .05 .02
❑ 242 Stephane Matteau .05 .02
❑ 243 Gerald Diduck .05 .02
❑ 244 Rick Tabaracci .10 .05
❑ 245 Sylvain Lefebvre .05 .02
❑ 246 Bob Rouse .05 .02
❑ 247 Charlie Huddy .05 .02
❑ 248 Mike Foligno .05 .02
❑ 249 Ric Nattress .05 .02
❑ 250 Aaron Broten .05 .02
❑ 251 Mike Keane .05 .02
❑ 252 Steve Bozek .05 .02
❑ 253 Jeff Beukeboom .05 .02
❑ 254 Stephane Morin .05 .02
❑ 255 Brian Bradley .05 .02
❑ 256 Scott Arniel .05 .02
❑ 257 Robert Kron .05 .02
❑ 258 Anatoli Semenov .05 .02
❑ 259 Brent Gilchrist .05 .02
❑ 260 Jim Sandlak .05 .02
❑ 261 Brett Hull (Man of Year) .10 .05
❑ 262 Paul Coffey 1000 PTS .10 .05
❑ 263 Mark Messier 1000 PTS .10 .05
❑ 264 Dave Taylor 1000 PTS .10 .05
❑ 265 Michel Goulet 1000 PTS .10 .05
❑ 266 Dale Hawerchuk 1000 PTS .10 .05
❑ 267 The Turgeon Brothers .05 .02
Pierre Turgeon
Sylvain Turgeon
❑ 268 The Sutter Brothers .05 .02
Rich Sutter
Brian Sutter
Ron Sutter
❑ 269 The Mullen Brothers .05 .02
Brian Mullen
Joe Mullen
❑ 270 The Courtnall Brothers .05 .02
Geoff Courtnall
Russ Courtnall
❑ 271 Trevor Kidd TP .10 .05
❑ 272 Patrice Brisebois TP .05 .02
❑ 273 Mark Greig TP .05 .02
❑ 274 Kip Miller TP .05 .02
❑ 275 Drake Berehowsky TP .05 .02
❑ 276 Kevin Haller TP .05 .02
❑ 277 Dave Gagnon TP .05 .02
❑ 278 Jason Marshall TP .05 .02
❑ 279 Donald Audette TP .10 .05
❑ 280 Patrick Lebeau TP .05 .02
❑ 281 Alexander Godynyuk TP .05 .02
❑ 282 Jarrod Skalde TP .05 .02
❑ 283 Ken Sutton TP .05 .02
❑ 284 Sergei Kharin TP .05 .02
❑ 285 Andre Racicot TP .10 .05
❑ 286 Doug Weight TP .60 .25
❑ 287 Kevin Todd TP .05 .02
❑ 288 Tony Amonte TP .60 .25
❑ 289 Kimbi Daniels TP .05 .02
❑ 290 Jeff Daniels TP .05 .02
291 Guy Lafleur .10 .05
Speed and Grace
292 Guy Lafleur .10 .05
Awards and Achievements
293 Guy Lafleur .10 .05
A Hall of Famer
294 Brett Hull SL .10 .05
295 Wayne Gretzky SL .50 .23
296 Wayne Gretzky SL .50 .23
297 Theoren Fleury and .10 .05
Marty McSorley SL
298 Sergei Fedorov SL .25 .11
299 Al MacInnis SL .10 .05
300 Ed Belfour SL .10 .05
301 Ed Belfour SL .10 .05
302 Brett Hull 50/50 .25 .11
303 Wayne Gretzky .50 .23
700th Career Goal
304 San Jose Sharks Logo .05 .02
305 Cam Neely Crunch .10 .05
306 Rick Tocchet Crunch .10 .05
307 Scott Stevens Crunch .10 .05
308 Ulf Samuelsson Crunch .05 .02
309 Jeremy Roenick Crunch .10 .05
310 Mark Messier FRAN .10 .05
311 John Cullen FRAN .05 .02
312 Wayne Gretzky FRAN .50 .23
313 Mike Modano FRAN .10 .05

❑ 314 Patrick Roy FRAN .40 .18
❑ 315 Stanley Cup Champs .05 .02
❑ 316 Mario Lemieux .40 .18
Conn Smythe Trophy
❑ 317 Wayne Gretzky .50 .23
Art Ross Trophy
❑ 318 Brett Hull .10 .05
Hart Memorial Trophy
❑ 319 Ray Bourque .10 .05
Norris Trophy
❑ 320 Ed Belfour .10 .05
Calder Trophy
❑ 321 Ed Belfour .10 .05
Vezina Trophy
❑ 322 Dirk Graham .05 .02
Frank J. Selke Trophy
❑ 323 Ed Belfour .10 .05
Jennings Trophy
❑ 324 Wayne Gretzky .50 .23
Lady Byng Trophy
❑ 325 Dave Taylor .10 .05
Bill Masterton Trophy
❑ 326 Jeff Hackett .10 .05
❑ 327 Bob McGill .05 .02
❑ 328 Neil Wilkinson .05 .02
❑ 329 Eric Lindros .75 .35
1st Rd Draft Choice
❑ 330 Eric Lindros .75 .35
Awards and Honors
❑ 331 Ray Bourque FP .10 .05
❑ 332 Pierre Turgeon FP .10 .05
❑ 333 Al MacInnis FP .10 .05
❑ 334 Jeremy Roenick FP .10 .05
❑ 335 Steve Yzerman FP .25 .11
❑ 336 The Hunter Brothers .05 .02
Dale Hunter
Mark Hunter
❑ 337 The Broten Brothers .05 .02
Neal Broten
Aaron Broten
❑ 338 The Cavallini Brothers .05 .02
Gino Cavallini
Paul Cavallini
❑ 339 The Miller Brothers .05 .02
Kelly Miller
Kevin Miller
❑ 340 Dennis Vaske TP .05 .02
❑ 341 Rob Pearson TP .05 .02
❑ 342 Jason Miller TP .05 .02
❑ 343 John LeClair TP 1.50 .70
❑ 344 Bryan Marchment TP .05 .02
❑ 345 Gary Shuchuk TP .05 .02
❑ 346 Dominik Hasek TP 2.00 .90
❑ 347 Michel Picard TP .05 .02
❑ 348 Corey Millen TP .05 .02
❑ 349 Joe Sacco TP .05 .02
❑ 350 Reggie Savage TP .05 .02
❑ 351 Pat Murray TP .05 .02
❑ 352 Myles O'Connor TP .05 .02
❑ 353 Shawn Antoski TP .05 .02
❑ 354 Geoff Sanderson TP .30 .14
❑ 355 Chris Govedaris TP .05 .02
❑ 356 Alexei Gusarov TP .05 .02
❑ 357 Mike Sillinger TP .05 .02
❑ 358 Bob Wilkie TP .05 .02
❑ 359 Pat Jablonski TP .10 .05
❑ 360 Memorial Cup .05 .02
Spokane Chiefs
❑ 361 Kirk Muller FP .05 .02
❑ 362 Pat LaFontaine FP .10 .05
❑ 363 Brian Leetch FP .10 .05
❑ 364 Rick Tocchet FP .10 .05
❑ 365 Mario Lemieux FP .40 .18
❑ 366 Joe Sakic FP .25 .11
❑ 367 Brett Hull FP .10 .05
❑ 368 Vincent Damphousse FP .10 .05
❑ 369 Trevor Linden FP .10 .05
❑ 370 Kevin Hatcher FP .05 .02
❑ 371 Pat Elynuik FP .05 .02
❑ 372 Patrick Roy DT .40 .18
❑ 373 Brian Leetch DT .10 .05
❑ 374 Ray Bourque DT .10 .05
❑ 375 Luc Robitaille DT .10 .05
❑ 376 Wayne Gretzky DT .50 .23
❑ 377 Brett Hull DT .10 .05
❑ 378 Ed Belfour ART .10 .05
❑ 379 Rob Blake ART .10 .05
❑ 380 Eric Weinrich ART .05 .02
❑ 381 Jaromir Jagr ART .25 .11
❑ 382 Sergei Fedorov ART .25 .11
❑ 383 Ken Hodge Jr. ART .05 .02
❑ 384 Eric Lindros Art .75 .35
❑ 385 Eric Lindros .75 .35
with Rob Pearson
❑ 386 Ottawa/Tampa Bay .25 .11
Logo Card
❑ 387 Mick Vukota .05 .02
❑ 388 Lou Franceschetti .05 .02
❑ 389 Mike Hudson .05 .02
❑ 390 Frantisek Kucera .05 .02
❑ 391 Basil McRae .05 .02
❑ 392 Donald Dufresne .05 .02
❑ 393 Tommy Albelin .05 .02
❑ 394 Normand Lacombe .05 .02
❑ 395 Lucien DeBlois .05 .02
❑ 396 Tony Twist .05 .02
❑ 397 Rob Murphy .05 .02
❑ 398 Ken Sabourin .05 .02
❑ 399 Doug Evans .05 .02
❑ 400 Walt Poddubny .05 .02
❑ 401 Grant Ledyard .05 .02
❑ 402 Kris King .05 .02
❑ 403 Paul Gillis .05 .02
❑ 404 Chris Dahlquist .05 .02
❑ 405 Zdeno Ciger .05 .02
❑ 406 Paul Stanton .05 .02

❑ 407 Randy Ladouceur .05 .02
❑ 408 Ronnie Stern .05 .02
❑ 409 Dave Tippett .05 .02
❑ 410 Jeff Reese .05 .02
❑ 411 Vladimir Ruzicka .05 .02
❑ 412 Brent Fedyk .05 .02
❑ 413 Paul Cyr .05 .02
❑ 414 Mike Eagles .05 .02
❑ 415 Chris Joseph .05 .02
❑ 416 Brad Marsh .05 .02
❑ 417 Richard Pilon .05 .02
❑ 418 Jiri Hrdina .05 .02
❑ 419 Clint Malarchuk .10 .05
❑ 420 Steven Rice .05 .02
❑ 421 Mark Janssens .05 .02
❑ 422 Gordie Roberts .05 .02
❑ 423 Shawn Cronin .05 .02
❑ 424 Randy Cunneyworth .05 .02
❑ 425 Frank Pietrangelo .10 .05
❑ 426 David Maley .05 .02
❑ 427 Rod Buskas .05 .02
❑ 428 Dennis Vial .05 .02
❑ 429 Kelly Buchberger .05 .02
❑ 430 Wes Walz .05 .02
❑ 431 Dean Kennedy .05 .02
❑ 432 Nick Kypreos .05 .02
❑ 433 Stewart Gavin .05 .02
❑ 434 Norm Maciver .05 .02
❑ 435 Mark Pederson .05 .02
❑ 436 Laurie Boschman .05 .02
❑ 437 Stephane Quintal .05 .02
❑ 438 Darrin Shannon .05 .02
❑ 439 Trent Yawney .05 .02
❑ 440 Gaetan Duchesne .05 .02
❑ 441 Joe Cirella .05 .02
❑ 442 Doug Houda .05 .02
❑ 443 Dave Chyzowski .05 .02
❑ 444 Derrick Smith .05 .02
❑ 445 Jeff Lazaro .05 .02
❑ 446 Brian Glynn .05 .02
❑ 447 Jocelyn Lemieux .05 .02
❑ 448 Peter Taglianetti .05 .02
❑ 449 Adam Burt .05 .02
❑ 450 Hubie McDonough .05 .02
❑ 451 Kelly Hrudey .10 .05
❑ 452 Dave Poulin .05 .02
❑ 453 Mark Hardy .05 .02
❑ 454 Mike Hartman .05 .02
❑ 455 Chris Chelios .25 .11
❑ 456 Alexander Mogilny .10 .05
❑ 457 Bryan Fogarty .05 .02
❑ 458 Adam Oates .10 .05
❑ 459 Ron Hextall .10 .05
❑ 460 Bernie Nicholls .05 .02
❑ 461 Esa Tikkanen .05 .02
❑ 462 Jyrki Lumme .05 .02
❑ 463 Brent Sutter .05 .02
❑ 464 Gary Suter .05 .02
❑ 465 Sean Burke .10 .05
❑ 466 Rob Brown .05 .02
❑ 467 Mike Modano .25 .11
❑ 468 Kevin Stevens .05 .02
❑ 469 Mike Lalor .05 .02
❑ 470 Sergei Fedorov .40 .18
❑ 471 Bob Essensa .10 .05
❑ 472 Mark Howe .05 .02
❑ 473 Craig Janney .10 .05
❑ 474 Daniel Marois .05 .02
❑ 475 Craig Simpson .05 .02
❑ 476 Marc Bureau .05 .02
❑ 477 Randy Velischek .05 .02
❑ 478 Gino Cavallini .05 .02
❑ 479 Dale Hawerchuk .10 .05
❑ 480 Pat LaFontaine .10 .05
❑ 481 Kirk McLean .10 .05
❑ 482 Murray Craven .05 .02
❑ 483 Robert Reichel .05 .02
❑ 484 Jan Erixon .05 .02
❑ 485 Adam Creighton .05 .02
❑ 486 Mark Fitzpatrick .10 .05
❑ 487 Ron Francis .10 .05
❑ 488 Joe Mullen .10 .05
❑ 489 Peter Zezel .05 .02
❑ 490 Tomas Sandstrom .05 .02
❑ 491 Phil Housley .10 .05
❑ 492 Tim Cheveldae .10 .05
❑ 493 Glen Wesley .05 .02
❑ 494 Stephan Lebeau .05 .02
❑ 495 Dave Ellett .05 .02
❑ 496 Jeff Brown .05 .02
❑ 497 Dave Andreychuk .10 .05
❑ 498 Steven Finn .05 .02
❑ 499 Mike Donnelly .05 .02
❑ 500 Neal Broten .10 .05
❑ 501 Randy Wood .05 .02
❑ 502 Troy Gamble .10 .05
❑ 503 Mike Ridley .05 .02
❑ 504 Jamie Macoun .05 .02
❑ 505 Mark Messier .25 .11
❑ 506 Moe Mantha .05 .02
❑ 507 Scott Young .05 .02
❑ 508 Robert Dirk .05 .02
❑ 509 Brad Shaw .05 .02
❑ 510 Ed Belfour .25 .11
❑ 511 Larry Robinson .10 .05
❑ 512 Dale Kushner .05 .02
❑ 513 Steve Chiasson .05 .02
❑ 514 Brian Skrudland .05 .02
❑ 515 Pat Elynuik .05 .02
❑ 516 Curtis Joseph .25 .11
❑ 517 Doug Bodger .05 .02
❑ 518 Greg Brown .05 .02
❑ 519 Joe Murphy .05 .02
❑ 520 J.J. Daigneault .05 .02
❑ 521 Todd Gill .05 .02
❑ 522 Troy Loney .05 .02

❑ 523 Tim Watters .05 .02
❑ 524 Jody Hull .05 .02
❑ 525 Colin Patterson .05 .02
❑ 526 Darin Kimble .05 .02
❑ 527 Perry Berezan .05 .02
❑ 528 Lee Norwood .05 .02
❑ 529 Mike Peluso .05 .02
❑ 530 Wayne McBean .05 .02
❑ 531 Grant Jennings .05 .02
❑ 532 Claude Loiselle .05 .02
❑ 533 Ron Wilson .05 .02
❑ 534 Phil Sykes .05 .02
❑ 535 Jim Wiemer .05 .02
❑ 536 Herb Raglan .05 .02
❑ 537 Tim Hunter .05 .02
❑ 538 Mike Tomlak .05 .02
❑ 539 Greg Gilbert .05 .02
❑ 540 Jiri Latal .05 .02
❑ 541 Bill Berg .05 .02
❑ 542 Shane Churla .05 .02
❑ 543 Jay Miller .05 .02
❑ 544 Pete Peeters .10 .05
❑ 545 Alan May .05 .02
❑ 546 Mario Marois .05 .02
❑ 547 Jim Kyte .05 .02
❑ 548 Jon Morris .05 .02
❑ 549 Mikko Makela .05 .02
❑ 550 Nelson Emerson .05 .02
❑ 551 Doug Wilson .10 .05
❑ 552 Brian Mullen .05 .02
❑ 553 Kelly Kisio .05 .02
❑ 554 Brian Hayward .10 .05
❑ 555 Tony Hrkac .05 .02
❑ 556 Steve Bozek .05 .02
❑ 557 John Carter .05 .02
❑ 558 Neil Wilkinson .05 .02
❑ 559 Wayne Presley .05 .02
❑ 560 Bob McGill .05 .02
❑ 561 Craig Ludwig .05 .02
❑ 562 Mikhail Tatarinov .05 .02
❑ 563 Todd Elik .05 .02
❑ 564 Randy Burridge .05 .02
❑ 565 Tim Kerr .05 .02
❑ 566 Randy Gilhen .05 .02
❑ 567 John Tonelli .05 .02
❑ 568 Tom Kurvers .05 .02
❑ 569 Steve Duchesne .05 .02
❑ 570 Charlie Huddy .05 .02
❑ 571 Alan Kerr .05 .02
❑ 572 Shawn Chambers .05 .02
❑ 573 Rob Ramage .05 .02
❑ 574 Steve Kasper .05 .02
❑ 575 Scott Mellanby .10 .05
❑ 576 Stephen Leach .05 .02
❑ 577 Scott Niedermayer .10 .05
❑ 578 Craig Berube .05 .02
❑ 579 Greg Paslawski .05 .02
❑ 580 Randy Hillier .05 .02
❑ 581 Stephane Richer .10 .05
❑ 582 Brian MacLellan .05 .02
❑ 583 Marc Habscheid .05 .02
❑ 584 Dave Babych .05 .02
❑ 585 Troy Murray .05 .02
❑ 586 Ray Sheppard .10 .05
❑ 587 Glen Featherstone .05 .02
❑ 588 Brendan Shanahan .40 .18
❑ 589 Dave Christian .05 .02
❑ 590 Mike Bullard .05 .02
❑ 591 Ryan Walter .05 .02
❑ 592 Doug Smail .05 .02
❑ 593 Paul Fenton .05 .02
❑ 594 Adam Graves .10 .05
❑ 595 Scott Stevens .10 .05
❑ 596 Sylvain Cote .05 .02
❑ 597 Dave Barr .05 .02
❑ 598 Randy Gregg .05 .02
❑ 599 Allen Pedersen .05 .02
❑ 600 Jari Kurri .10 .05
❑ 601 Troy Mallette .05 .02
❑ 602 Troy Crowder .05 .02
❑ 603 Brad Jones .05 .02
❑ 604 Randy McKay .05 .02
❑ 605 Scott Thornton .05 .02
❑ 606 Bryan Marchment .05 .02
❑ 607 Andrew Cassels .05 .02
❑ 608 Grant Fuhr .10 .05
❑ 609 Vincent Damphousse .10 .05
❑ 610 Robert Ray .05 .02
❑ 611 Glenn Anderson .05 .02
❑ 612 Peter Ing .10 .05
❑ 613 Tom Chorske .05 .02
❑ 614 Kirk Muller .05 .02
❑ 615 Dan Quinn .05 .02
❑ 616 Murray Baron .05 .02
❑ 617 Sergei Nemchinov .05 .02
❑ 618 Rod Brind'Amour .10 .05
❑ 619 Ron Sutter .05 .02
❑ 620 Luke Richardson .05 .02
❑ 621 Nicklas Lidstrom .60 .25
❑ 622 Ken Linseman .05 .02
❑ 623 Steve Smith .05 .02
❑ 624 Dave Manson .05 .02
❑ 625 Kay Whitmore .10 .05
❑ 626 Jeff Chychrun .05 .02
❑ 627 Russ Romaniuk .05 .02
❑ 628 Brad May .10 .05
❑ 629 Tomas Forslund .05 .02
❑ 630 Stu Barnes .05 .02
❑ 631 Darryl Sydor .05 .02
❑ 632 Jimmy Waite .10 .05
❑ 633 Peter Douris .05 .02
❑ 634 Dave Brown .05 .02
❑ 635 Mark Messier .25 .11
❑ 636 Neil Sheehy .05 .02
❑ 637 Todd Krygier .05 .02
❑ 638 Stephane Beauregard .10 .05

❑ 639 Barry Pederson .05 .02
❑ 640 Pat Falloon .05 .02
❑ 641 Dean Evason .05 .02
❑ 642 Jeff Hackett .10 .05
❑ 643 Rob Zettler .05 .02
❑ 644 David Bruce .05 .02
❑ 645 Pat MacLeod .05 .02
❑ 646 Craig Coxe .05 .02
❑ 647 Ken Hammond .05 .02
❑ 648 Brian Lawton .05 .02
❑ 649 Perry Anderson .05 .02
❑ 650 Kevin Evans .05 .02
❑ 651 Mike McHugh .05 .02
❑ 652 Mark Lamb .05 .02
❑ 653 Darcy Wakaluk .10 .05
❑ 654 Pat Conacher .05 .02
❑ 655 Martin Lapointe .05 .02
❑ 656 Derian Hatcher .05 .02
❑ 657 Bryan Erickson .05 .02
❑ 658 Ken Priestlay .05 .02
❑ 659 Vladimir Konstantinov .05 .02
❑ 660 Andrei Lomakin .05 .02

## 1991-92 Score Bobby Orr

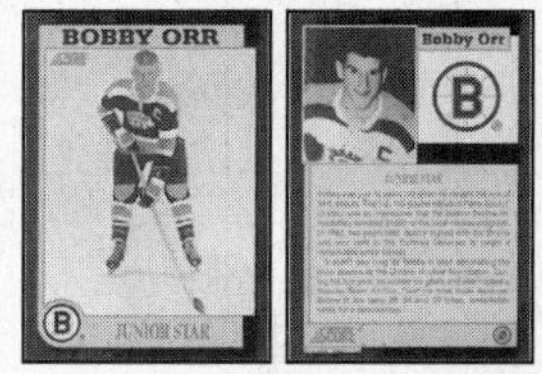


This six-card standard-size set highlights the career of Bobby Orr, one of hockey's all-time greats. The cards were inserted in 1991-92 Score hockey poly packs. Cards 1 and 2 were inserted in both American and Canadian editions. Cards 3 and 4 were inserted in Canadian packs, while cards 5 and 6 were inserted in American packs. On a black card face, the fronts feature color player photos enclosed by a thin red border and accented by yellow borders on three sides. The backs carry a close-up color photo and biographical comments on Orr's career. The cards are not numbered on the back. It is claimed that 270,000 of these Orr cards were produced, and that Orr personally signed 2,500 of each of these cards. The personally autographed cards are autographed on the card back and not individually numbered or certified. They are slightly different in design.

| | MINT | NRMT |
|---|---|---|
| COMPLETE SET (6) | 40.00 | 18.00 |
| COMMON ORR (1-6) | 8.00 | 3.60 |

❑ 1 Bobby Orr 8.00 3.60
Junior Star
❑ 2 Bobby Orr 8.00 3.60
Scoring Leader
❑ 3 Bobby Orr 8.00 3.60
Hall of Famer
(Issued in Canadian Bilingual packs)
❑ 4 Bobby Orr 8.00 3.60
Hall of Famer
(Issued in Canadian Bilingual packs)
❑ 5 Bobby Orr 8.00 3.60
The Rookie
(Found only in American English packs)
❑ 6 Bobby Orr 8.00 3.60
Award Winner
(Found only in American English packs)
❑ AU Bobby Orr AU 300.00 135.00
(Autographed card)

## 1991-92 Score Eric Lindros

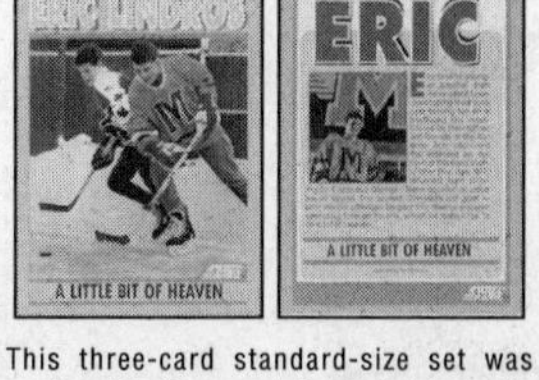


This three-card standard-size set was produced by Score and distributed in a cello pack with the first printing of Eric Lindros' autobiography "Fire on Ice". The cards feature on the fronts color photos that capture three different moments in Lindros' life (childhood, adolescence, and NHL Entry Draft). The pictures are bordered on all sides by light blue, with the player's name in block lettering between two red stripes at the card top. A red stripe at the bottom separates the picture from its title line. The backs have relevant

biographical comments as well as a second color photo. The cards are unnumbered and checklisted below in chronological order.

| | MINT | NRMT |
|---|---|---|
| COMPLETE SET (3) | 15.00 | 6.75 |
| COMMON LINDROS (1-3) | 5.00 | 2.20 |

| | | |
|---|---|---|
| ❑ 1 Eric Lindros<br>A Real Corker<br>(Baby on skates) | 5.00 | 2.20 |
| ❑ 2 Eric Lindros<br>A Little Bit of Heaven<br>(With brother Brett<br>in minor hockey sweaters) | 5.00 | 2.20 |
| ❑ 3 Eric Lindros<br>Graduation Day<br>(Nordiques sweater<br>in background) | 5.00 | 2.20 |

## 1991-92 Score Hot Cards

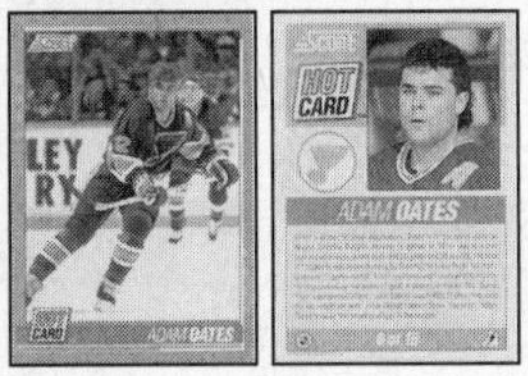

The 1991-92 Score Hot cards were inserted in American and Canadian English 100-card blister packs at a rate of one per pack. The standard size cards feature on the fronts color action player photos bordered in bright red. Thin yellow stripes accent the photos, and the player's name appears beneath the picture in a purple stripe. The back design reflects the same three colors as the front and features a color head shot, team logo, and player profile. The cards are numbered on the back. Hot Cards differ in design, photos, and text from the regular issues.

| | MINT | NRMT |
|---|---|---|
| COMPLETE SET (10) | 25.00 | 11.00 |
| COMMON CARD (1-10) | 1.25 | .55 |

| | | |
|---|---|---|
| ❑ 1 Eric Lindros | 6.00 | 2.70 |
| ❑ 2 Wayne Gretzky | 10.00 | 4.50 |
| ❑ 3 Brett Hull | 2.50 | 1.10 |
| ❑ 4 Sergei Fedorov | 3.00 | 1.35 |
| ❑ 5 Mario Lemieux | 8.00 | 3.60 |
| ❑ 6 Adam Oates | 1.25 | .55 |
| ❑ 7 Theoren Fleury | 1.25 | .55 |
| ❑ 8 Jaromir Jagr | 5.00 | 2.20 |
| ❑ 9 Ed Belfour | 2.00 | .90 |
| ❑ 10 Jeremy Roenick | 2.00 | .90 |

## 1991-92 Score Rookie/Traded

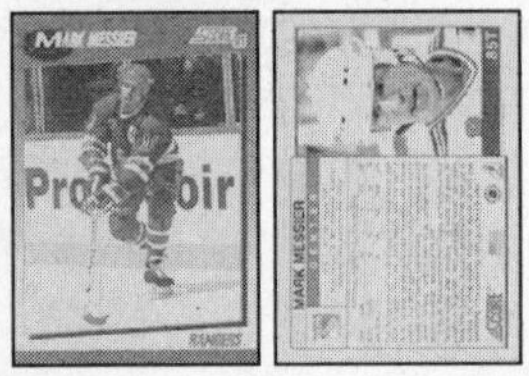

The 1991-92 Score Rookie and Traded hockey set contains 110 standard-size cards. It was issued only as a factory set. As one moves down the card face, the fronts shade from dark green to white. The color action player photo is enclosed by an thin red border, with a shadow border on the right and below. At the card top, the player's name is written over a hockey puck, and the team name is printed below the picture in the lower right corner. A dark green border stripe at the bottom rounds out the front. In a horizontal format, the backs present biography, statistics, player profile, and a color close-up photo. The cards are numbered on the back with a "T" suffix. The set includes Eric Lindros pictured in his World Junior uniform. The back of the set's custom box contains the set checklist. The key Rookie Cards in this set are Valeri Kamensky and Nicklas Lidstrom.

| | MINT | NRMT |
|---|---|---|
| COMPLETE SET (110) | 4.00 | 1.80 |
| COMMON CARD (1T-110T) | .05 | .02 |

| | | |
|---|---|---|
| ❑ 1T Doug Wilson | .05 | .02 |
| ❑ 2T Brian Mullen | .05 | .02 |
| ❑ 3T Kelly Kisio | .05 | .02 |
| ❑ 4T Brian Hayward | .10 | .05 |
| ❑ 5T Tony Hrkac | .05 | .02 |
| ❑ 6T Steve Bozek | .05 | .02 |
| ❑ 7T John Carter | .05 | .02 |
| ❑ 8T Neil Wilkinson | .05 | .02 |
| ❑ 9T Wayne Presley | .05 | .02 |
| ❑ 10T Bob McGill | .05 | .02 |
| ❑ 11T Craig Ludwig | .05 | .02 |
| ❑ 12T Mikhail Tatarinov | .05 | .02 |
| ❑ 13T Todd Elik | .05 | .02 |
| ❑ 14T Randy Burridge | .05 | .02 |
| ❑ 15T Tim Kerr | .05 | .02 |
| ❑ 16T Randy Gilhen | .05 | .02 |
| ❑ 17T John Tonelli | .05 | .02 |
| ❑ 18T Tom Kurvers | .05 | .02 |
| ❑ 19T Steve Duchesne | .10 | .05 |
| ❑ 20T Charlie Huddy | .05 | .02 |
| ❑ 21T Adam Creighton | .05 | .02 |
| ❑ 22T Brent Ashton | .05 | .02 |
| ❑ 23T Rob Ramage | .05 | .02 |
| ❑ 24T Steve Kasper | .05 | .02 |
| ❑ 25T Scott Mellanby | .10 | .05 |
| ❑ 26T Stephen Leach | .05 | .02 |
| ❑ 27T Scott Niedermayer | .10 | .05 |
| ❑ 28T Craig Berube | .05 | .02 |
| ❑ 29T Greg Paslawski | .05 | .02 |
| ❑ 30T Randy Hillier | .05 | .02 |
| ❑ 31T Stephane Richer | .05 | .02 |
| ❑ 32T Brian MacLellan | .05 | .02 |
| ❑ 33T Marc Habscheid | .05 | .02 |
| ❑ 34T Dave Babych | .05 | .02 |
| ❑ 35T Troy Murray | .05 | .02 |
| ❑ 36T Ray Sheppard | .10 | .05 |
| ❑ 37T Glen Featherstone | .05 | .02 |
| ❑ 38T Brendan Shanahan | .60 | .25 |
| ❑ 39T Dave Christian | .05 | .02 |
| ❑ 40T Mike Bullard | .05 | .02 |
| ❑ 41T Ryan Walter | .05 | .02 |
| ❑ 42T Randy Wood | .05 | .02 |
| ❑ 43T Vincent Riendeau | .10 | .05 |
| ❑ 44T Adam Graves | .10 | .05 |
| ❑ 45T Scott Stevens | .10 | .05 |
| ❑ 46T Sylvain Cote | .05 | .02 |
| ❑ 47T Dave Barr | .05 | .02 |
| ❑ 48T Randy Gregg | .05 | .02 |
| ❑ 49T Pavel Bure | 1.00 | .45 |
| ❑ 50T Jari Kurri | .10 | .05 |
| ❑ 51T Steve Thomas | .05 | .02 |
| ❑ 52T Troy Crowder | .05 | .02 |
| ❑ 53T Brad Jones | .05 | .02 |
| ❑ 54T Randy McKay | .05 | .02 |
| ❑ 55T Scott Thornton | .05 | .02 |
| ❑ 56T Bryan Marchment | .05 | .02 |
| ❑ 57T Andrew Cassels | .10 | .05 |
| ❑ 58T Grant Fuhr | .10 | .05 |
| ❑ 59T Vincent Damphousse | .10 | .05 |
| ❑ 60T Rick Zombo | .05 | .02 |
| ❑ 61T Glenn Anderson | .10 | .05 |
| ❑ 62T Peter Ing | .10 | .05 |
| ❑ 63T Tom Chorske | .05 | .02 |
| ❑ 64T Kirk Muller | .05 | .02 |
| ❑ 65T Dan Quinn | .05 | .02 |
| ❑ 66T Murray Baron | .05 | .02 |
| ❑ 67T Sergei Nemchinov | .05 | .02 |
| ❑ 68T Rod Brind'Amour | .10 | .05 |
| ❑ 69T Ron Sutter | .05 | .02 |
| ❑ 70T Luke Richardson | .05 | .02 |
| ❑ 71T Nicklas Lidstrom | .50 | .23 |
| ❑ 72T Petri Skriko | .05 | .02 |
| ❑ 73T Steve Smith | .05 | .02 |
| ❑ 74T Dave Manson | .05 | .02 |
| ❑ 75T Kay Whitmore | .10 | .05 |
| ❑ 76T Valeri Kamensky | .40 | .18 |
| ❑ 77T Russ Romaniuk | .05 | .02 |
| ❑ 78T Brad May | .05 | .02 |
| ❑ 79T Tomas Forslund | .05 | .02 |
| ❑ 80T Stu Barnes | .05 | .02 |
| ❑ 81T Darryl Sydor | .05 | .02 |
| ❑ 82T Jimmy Waite | .10 | .05 |
| ❑ 83T Vladimir Ruzicka | .05 | .02 |
| ❑ 84T Dave Brown | .05 | .02 |
| ❑ 85T Mark Messier | .50 | .23 |
| ❑ 86T Neil Sheehy | .05 | .02 |
| ❑ 87T Todd Krygier | .05 | .02 |
| ❑ 88T Eric Lindros | 2.50 | 1.10 |
| ❑ 89T Nelson Emerson | .05 | .02 |
| ❑ 90T Pat Falloon | .05 | .02 |
| ❑ 91T Dean Evason | .05 | .02 |
| ❑ 92T Jeff Hackett | .10 | .05 |
| ❑ 93T Rob Zettler | .05 | .02 |
| ❑ 94T Perry Berezan | .05 | .02 |
| ❑ 95T Pat MacLeod | .05 | .02 |
| ❑ 96T Craig Coxe | .05 | .02 |
| ❑ 97T Ken Hammond | .05 | .02 |
| ❑ 98T Brian Lawton | .05 | .02 |
| ❑ 99T Perry Anderson | .05 | .02 |
| ❑ 100T Pat LaFontaine | .10 | .05 |
| ❑ 101T Pierre Turgeon | .10 | .05 |
| ❑ 102T Dave McLlwain | .05 | .02 |
| ❑ 103T Brent Sutter | .05 | .02 |
| ❑ 104T Uwe Krupp | .05 | .02 |
| ❑ 105T Martin Lapointe | .05 | .02 |
| ❑ 106T Derian Hatcher | .05 | .02 |
| ❑ 107T Darrin Shannon | .05 | .02 |
| ❑ 108T Benoit Hogue | .05 | .02 |
| ❑ 109T Vladimir Konstantinov | .05 | .02 |
| ❑ 110T Andrei Lomakin | .05 | .02 |

## 1991-92 Score Kellogg's

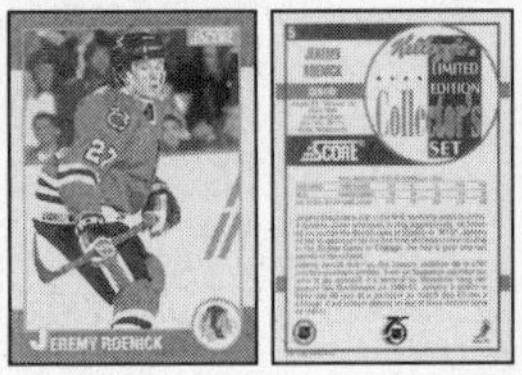

This 24-card standard-size set was produced by Score as a promotion for Kellogg's Canada. Two-card foil packs were inserted in specially marked 675-gram Kellogg's Corn Flakes cereals. The side panel of the cereal boxes presented a mail-in offer for the complete set and a card binder for 5.99 plus three proof of purchase tokens (one token featured per side panel). Card fronts have player action photos enclosed in a small red border, player's name in white reverse-out lettering, and team logo in bottom portion of the purple border. Card backs, also in purple, red, and white, carry the card number, Kellogg's Limited Edition Collector's Set logo, biography, statistics, and player profile in English and French.

| | MINT | NRMT |
|---|---|---|
| COMPLETE SET (24) | 35.00 | 16.00 |
| COMMON CARD (1-24) | .50 | .23 |

| | | |
|---|---|---|
| ❑ 1 Patrick Roy | 8.00 | 3.60 |
| ❑ 2 Rick Tocchet | 1.25 | .55 |
| ❑ 3 Wendel Clark | 1.25 | .55 |
| ❑ 4 Mike Modano | 2.00 | .90 |
| ❑ 5 Jeremy Roenick | 1.50 | .70 |
| ❑ 6 Pierre Turgeon | 1.25 | .55 |
| ❑ 7 Kevin Hatcher | .50 | .23 |
| ❑ 8 Brian Leetch | 1.50 | .70 |
| ❑ 9 Mark Recchi | 1.25 | .55 |
| ❑ 10 Andy Moog | 1.25 | .55 |
| ❑ 11 Kevin Dineen | .50 | .23 |
| ❑ 12 Joe Sakic | 3.00 | 1.35 |
| ❑ 13 John MacLean | .50 | .23 |
| ❑ 14 Steve Yzerman | 5.00 | 2.20 |
| ❑ 15 Pat LaFontaine | 1.25 | .55 |
| ❑ 16 Al MacInnis | 1.25 | .55 |
| ❑ 17 Petr Klima | .50 | .23 |
| ❑ 18 Ed Olczyk | .50 | .23 |
| ❑ 19 Doug Wilson | .50 | .23 |
| ❑ 20 Trevor Linden | 1.00 | .45 |
| ❑ 21 Brett Hull | 2.00 | .90 |
| ❑ 22 Rob Blake | .50 | .23 |
| ❑ 23 Dave Ellett | .50 | .23 |
| ❑ 24 Cornelius Rooster SP<br>Kellogg's mascot | 5.00 | 2.20 |
| ❑ NNO Card Binder | 5.00 | 2.20 |

## 1991-92 Score Young Superstars

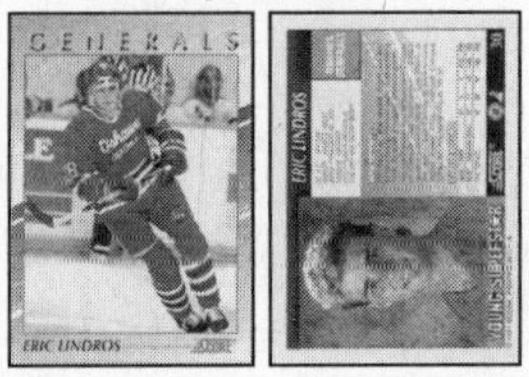

This 40-card standard-size set was issued by Score to showcase some of the leading young hockey players. The color action player photos on the fronts are framed in green on a card face consisting of blended diagonal taupe stripes. In a horizontal format, the backs have a color head shot on the left half while the right half carries biography, "Rink Report," and career statistics.

| | MINT | NRMT |
|---|---|---|
| COMPLETE SET (40) | 8.00 | 3.60 |
| COMMON CARD (1-40) | .15 | .07 |

| | | |
|---|---|---|
| ❑ 1 Sergei Fedorov | .75 | .35 |
| ❑ 2 Mike Richter | .50 | .23 |
| ❑ 3 Mats Sundin | .50 | .23 |
| ❑ 4 Theoren Fleury | .50 | .23 |
| ❑ 5 John Cullen | .15 | .07 |
| ❑ 6 Dimitri Khristich | .15 | .07 |
| ❑ 7 Stephan Lebeau | .15 | .07 |
| ❑ 8 Rob Blake | .40 | .18 |
| ❑ 9 Ken Hodge Jr. | .15 | .07 |
| ❑ 10 Mike Ricci | .40 | .18 |
| ❑ 11 Trevor Linden | .40 | .18 |
| ❑ 12 Peter Ing | .40 | .18 |
| ❑ 13 Alexander Mogilny | .40 | .18 |
| ❑ 14 Martin Gelinas | .15 | .07 |
| ❑ 15 Chris Terreri | .40 | .18 |
| ❑ 16 Jeff Norton | .15 | .07 |
| ❑ 17 Bob Essensa | .40 | .18 |
| ❑ 18 Mark Tinordi | .15 | .07 |
| ❑ 19 Curtis Joseph | .50 | .23 |
| ❑ 20 Joe Sakic | 1.00 | .45 |
| ❑ 21 Jeremy Roenick | .50 | .23 |
| ❑ 22 Mark Recchi | .40 | .18 |
| ❑ 23 Eric Desjardins | .15 | .07 |
| ❑ 24 Robert Reichel | .15 | .07 |
| ❑ 25 Tim Cheveldae | .40 | .18 |
| ❑ 26 Eric Weinrich | .15 | .07 |
| ❑ 27 Murray Baron | .15 | .07 |
| ❑ 28 Darren Turcotte | .15 | .07 |
| ❑ 29 Troy Gamble | .40 | .18 |
| ❑ 30 Eric Lindros | 3.00 | 1.35 |
| ❑ 31 Benoit Hogue | .15 | .07 |
| ❑ 32 Ed Belfour | .50 | .23 |
| ❑ 33 Ron Tugnutt | .40 | .18 |
| ❑ 34 Pat Elynuik | .15 | .07 |
| ❑ 35 Mike Modano | .50 | .23 |
| ❑ 36 Bobby Holik | .40 | .18 |
| ❑ 37 Yves Racine | .15 | .07 |
| ❑ 38 Jaromir Jagr | 1.50 | .70 |
| ❑ 39 Stephane Morin | .15 | .07 |
| ❑ 40 Kevin Miller | .15 | .07 |

## 1992-93 Score Canadian Promo Sheets

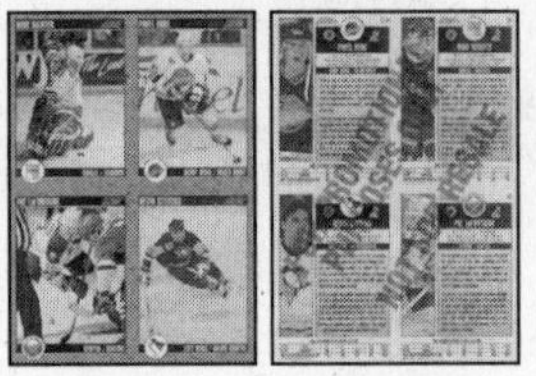

These two 5" by 7" promotional sheets each feature four uncut cards. If the cards were cut, they would measure the standard size. The fronts feature color action player photos bordered at the top and bottom by black stripes containing the player's name and position. The outer borders are metallic-blue with diagonal stripes formed by an alternating matte and glossy finish. The backs have the disclaimers "For Promotional Purposes Only" and "Not For Resale" overprinted in magenta. They show a white background with a narrow color player photo running along the left edge. Biography and career highlights are contained in a graded blue panel with black borders. Statistical information appears at the bottom. The cards are numbered on the back and are listed below as the appear on the sheets from left to right starting with the top row.

| | MINT | NRMT |
|---|---|---|
| COMPLETE SET (2) | 7.50 | 3.40 |
| COMMON PANEL (1-2) | 2.50 | 1.10 |

| | | |
|---|---|---|
| ❑ 1 Promo Sheet 1<br>6 Pat LaFontaine<br>25 Kevin Stevens<br>2 Chris Chelios<br>16 Esa Tikkanen | 2.50 | 1.10 |
| ❑ 2 Promo Sheet 2<br>5 Mike Richter<br>14 Pavel Bure<br>6 Pat LaFontaine<br>25 Kevin Stevens | 5.00 | 2.20 |

## 1992-93 Score

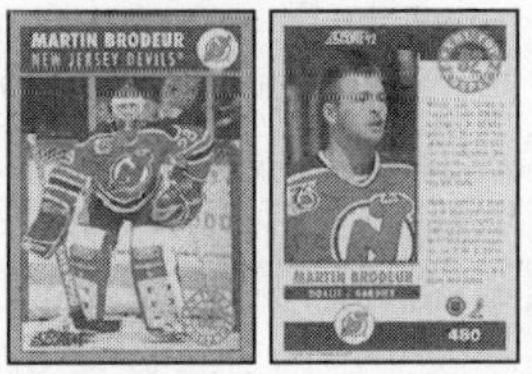

The 1992-93 Score hockey set contains 550 standard-size cards. The American and Canadian sets are identical in terms of player selection (except for card numbers 548-549) but feature different insert subsets (USA Greats in the American and Canadian Olympic Heroes in the Canadian). Moreover, the player photos and card design differ in each set. In the American set, the color action photos on the fronts have two-toned borders on three sides (icy gray diagonal stripes accented by either red, blue, or black); in the Canadian, the front borders are metallic blue with diagonally varnished stripes. The American backs are horizontally oriented and include biography, statistics, career summary, and a close-up photo; the Canadian backs are vertically oriented, bilingual, and have the same features in a different layout. A special Eric Lindros card, unnumbered and featuring his first photo in a Philadelphia Flyers uniform, was randomly inserted into packs. Reportedly more than 500 of these special Lindros "Press Conference" cards were given away to news media, members of the Flyers organization, and other guests attending the July 15 news conference which marked Lindros' signing with the Flyers. It is claimed that the odds of finding one of these cards are no less than one in 500 packs. Rookie Cards include Guy Hebert and Yanic Perrault.

| | MINT | NRMT |
|---|---|---|
| COMPLETE SET (550) | 15.00 | 6.75 |
| COMMON CARD (1-550) | .05 | .02 |
| *US AND CDN: SAME VALUE | | |

| | | |
|---|---|---|
| ❑ 1 Wayne Gretzky | 1.25 | .55 |
| ❑ 2 Chris Chelios | .25 | .11 |
| ❑ 3 Joe Mullen | .10 | .05 |
| ❑ 4 Russ Courtnall | .05 | .02 |
| ❑ 5 Mike Richter | .25 | .11 |
| ❑ 6 Pat LaFontaine | .10 | .05 |
| ❑ 7 Mark Tinordi | .05 | .02 |
| ❑ 8 Claude Lemieux | .10 | .05 |
| ❑ 9 Jimmy Carson | .05 | .02 |
| ❑ 10 Cam Neely | .10 | .05 |
| ❑ 11 Al Iafrate | .10 | .05 |
| ❑ 12 Steve Thomas | .05 | .02 |
| ❑ 13 Fredrik Olausson | .05 | .02 |
| ❑ 14 Pavel Bure | .40 | .18 |
| ❑ 15 Doug Wilson | .10 | .05 |
| ❑ 16 Esa Tikkanen | .05 | .02 |
| ❑ 17 Gary Suter | .05 | .02 |
| ❑ 18 Murray Craven | .05 | .02 |
| ❑ 19 Garry Galley | .05 | .02 |
| ❑ 20 Grant Fuhr | .10 | .05 |
| ❑ 21 Craig Wolanin | .05 | .02 |
| ❑ 22 Paul Cavallini | .05 | .02 |
| ❑ 23 Eric Desjardins | .05 | .02 |
| ❑ 24 Joe Kocur | .10 | .05 |
| ❑ 25 Kevin Stevens | .05 | .02 |
| ❑ 26 Marty McSorley | .05 | .02 |
| ❑ 27 Dirk Graham | .05 | .02 |
| ❑ 28 Mike Ramsey | .05 | .02 |
| ❑ 29 Gord Murphy | .05 | .02 |
| ❑ 30 John MacLean | .10 | .05 |
| ❑ 31 Vladimir Konstantinov | .05 | .02 |
| ❑ 32 Neal Broten | .10 | .05 |
| ❑ 33 Dimitri Khristich | .05 | .02 |
| ❑ 34 Gerald Diduck | .05 | .02 |
| ❑ 35 Ken Baumgartner | .05 | .02 |
| ❑ 36 Darrin Shannon | .05 | .02 |
| ❑ 37 Steve Bozek | .05 | .02 |
| ❑ 38 Michel Petit | .05 | .02 |
| ❑ 39 Kevin Lowe | .05 | .02 |
| ❑ 40 Doug Gilmour | .25 | .11 |
| ❑ 41 Peter Sidorkiewicz | .10 | .05 |
| ❑ 42 Gino Cavallini | .05 | .02 |
| ❑ 43 Dan Quinn | .05 | .02 |
| ❑ 44 Steven Finn | .05 | .02 |
| ❑ 45 Larry Murphy | .10 | .05 |
| ❑ 46 Brent Gilchrist | .05 | .02 |
| ❑ 47 Daren Puppa | .10 | .05 |
| ❑ 48 Steve Smith | .05 | .02 |
| ❑ 49 Dave Taylor | .10 | .05 |
| ❑ 50 Mike Gartner | .10 | .05 |
| ❑ 51 Derian Hatcher | .05 | .02 |
| ❑ 52 Bob Probert | .10 | .05 |
| ❑ 53 Ken Daneyko | .05 | .02 |
| ❑ 54 Steve Leach | .05 | .02 |
| ❑ 55 Kelly Miller | .05 | .02 |
| ❑ 56 Jeff Norton | .05 | .02 |
| ❑ 57 Kelly Kisio | .05 | .02 |
| ❑ 58 Igor Larionov | .05 | .02 |
| ❑ 59 Paul MacDermid | .05 | .02 |
| ❑ 60 Mike Vernon | .10 | .05 |
| ❑ 61 Randy Ladouceur | .05 | .02 |
| ❑ 62 Luke Richardson | .05 | .02 |
| ❑ 63 Daniel Marois | .05 | .02 |
| ❑ 64 Mike Hough | .05 | .02 |
| ❑ 65 Garth Butcher | .05 | .02 |
| ❑ 66 Terry Carkner | .05 | .02 |
| ❑ 67 Mike Donnelly | .05 | .02 |
| ❑ 68 Keith Brown | .05 | .02 |
| ❑ 69 Mathieu Schneider | .05 | .02 |
| ❑ 70 Tom Barrasso | .10 | .05 |
| ❑ 71 Adam Graves | .10 | .05 |
| ❑ 72 Brian Propp | .05 | .02 |
| ❑ 73 Randy Wood | .05 | .02 |
| ❑ 74 Yves Racine | .05 | .02 |
| ❑ 75 Scott Stevens | .10 | .05 |
| ❑ 76 Chris Nilan | .05 | .02 |
| ❑ 77 Uwe Krupp | .05 | .02 |
| ❑ 78 Sylvain Cote | .05 | .02 |
| ❑ 79 Sergio Momesso | .05 | .02 |
| ❑ 80 Thomas Steen | .05 | .02 |
| ❑ 81 Craig Muni | .05 | .02 |
| ❑ 82 Jeff Hackett | .10 | .05 |
| ❑ 83 Frank Musil | .05 | .02 |
| ❑ 84 Mike Ricci | .05 | .02 |
| ❑ 85 Brad Shaw | .05 | .02 |
| ❑ 86 Ron Sutter | .05 | .02 |
| ❑ 87 Curtis Leschyshyn | .05 | .02 |
| ❑ 88 Jamie Macoun | .05 | .02 |
| ❑ 89 Brian Noonan | .05 | .02 |
| ❑ 90 Ulf Samuelsson | .05 | .02 |
| ❑ 91 Mike McPhee | .05 | .02 |
| ❑ 92 Charlie Huddy | .05 | .02 |
| ❑ 93 Tim Kerr | .05 | .02 |
| ❑ 94 Craig Ludwig | .05 | .02 |
| ❑ 95 Paul Ysebaert | .05 | .02 |
| ❑ 96 Brad May | .10 | .05 |
| ❑ 97 Slava Fetisov | .05 | .02 |
| ❑ 98 Todd Krygier | .05 | .02 |
| ❑ 99 Patrick Flatley | .05 | .02 |
| ❑ 100 Ray Bourque | .25 | .11 |
| ❑ 101 Petr Nedved | .10 | .05 |
| ❑ 102 Teppo Numminen | .05 | .02 |
| ❑ 103 Dean Evason | .05 | .02 |
| ❑ 104 Ron Hextall | .10 | .05 |
| ❑ 105 Josef Beranek | .05 | .02 |
| ❑ 106 Robert Reichel | .05 | .02 |
| ❑ 107 Mikhail Tatarinov | .05 | .02 |
| ❑ 108 Geoff Sanderson | .10 | .05 |
| ❑ 109 Dave Lowry | .05 | .02 |
| ❑ 110 Wendel Clark | .10 | .05 |
| ❑ 111 Corey Millen UER<br>(Mike Donnelly pictured on front) | .05 | .02 |
| ❑ 112 Brent Sutter | .05 | .02 |
| ❑ 113 Jaromir Jagr | .60 | .25 |
| ❑ 114 Petr Svoboda | .05 | .02 |
| ❑ 115 Sergei Nemchinov | .05 | .02 |
| ❑ 116 Tony Tanti | .05 | .02 |
| ❑ 117 Stewart Gavin | .05 | .02 |
| ❑ 118 Doug Brown | .05 | .02 |
| ❑ 119 Gerard Gallant | .05 | .02 |
| ❑ 120 Andy Moog | .10 | .05 |
| ❑ 121 John Druce | .05 | .02 |
| ❑ 122 Dave McLlwain | .05 | .02 |
| ❑ 123 Bob Essensa | .10 | .05 |
| ❑ 124 Doug Lidster | .05 | .02 |
| ❑ 125 Pat Falloon | .05 | .02 |
| ❑ 126 Kelly Buchberger | .05 | .02 |
| ❑ 127 Carey Wilson | .05 | .02 |

❑ 128 Bobby Holik .05 .02
❑ 129 Andrei Lomakin .05 .02
❑ 130 Bob Rouse .05 .02
❑ 131 Adam Foote .05 .02
❑ 132 Bob Bassen .05 .02
❑ 133 Brian Benning .05 .02
❑ 134 Greg Gilbert .05 .02
❑ 135 Paul Stanton .05 .02
❑ 136 Brian Skrudland .05 .02
❑ 137 Jeff Beukeboom .05 .02
❑ 138 Clint Malarchuk .10 .05
❑ 139 Mike Modano .25 .11
❑ 140 Stephane Richer .10 .05
❑ 141 Brad McCrimmon .05 .02
❑ 142 Bob Carpenter .05 .02
❑ 143 Rod Langway .05 .02
❑ 144 Adam Creighton .05 .02
❑ 145 Ed Olczyk .05 .02
❑ 146 Greg Adams .05 .02
❑ 147 Jay More .05 .02
❑ 148 Scott Mellanby .10 .05
❑ 149 Paul Ranheim .05 .02
❑ 150 John Cullen .05 .02
❑ 151 Steve Duchesne .05 .02
❑ 152 Dave Ellett .05 .02
❑ 153 Mats Sundin .25 .11
❑ 154 Rick Zombo .05 .02
❑ 155 Kelly Hrudey .10 .05
❑ 156 Mike Hudson .05 .02
❑ 157 Bryan Trottier .10 .05
❑ 158 Shayne Corson .05 .02
❑ 159 Kevin Haller .05 .02
❑ 160 John Vanbiesbrouck .30 .14
❑ 161 Jim Johnson .05 .02
❑ 162 Kevin Todd .05 .02
❑ 163 Ray Sheppard .10 .05
❑ 164 Brent Ashton .05 .02
❑ 165 Peter Bondra .25 .11
❑ 166 David Volek .05 .02
❑ 167 Randy Carlyle .05 .02
❑ 168 Dana Murzyn .05 .02
❑ 169 Perry Berezan .05 .02
❑ 170 Vincent Damphousse .10 .05
❑ 171 Gary Leeman .05 .02
❑ 172 Steve Konroyd .05 .02
❑ 173 Pelle Eklund .05 .02
❑ 174 Peter Zezel .05 .02
❑ 175 Greg Paslawski .05 .02
❑ 176 Murray Baron .05 .02
❑ 177 Rob Blake .10 .05
❑ 178 Ed Belfour .25 .11
❑ 179 Mike Keane .05 .02
❑ 180 Mark Recchi .10 .05
❑ 181 Kris King .05 .02
❑ 182 Dave Snuggerud .05 .02
❑ 183 David Shaw .05 .02
❑ 184 Tom Chorske .05 .02
❑ 185 Steve Chiasson .05 .02
❑ 186 Don Sweeney .05 .02
❑ 187 Mike Ridley .05 .02
❑ 188 Glenn Healy .10 .05
❑ 189 Troy Murray .05 .02
❑ 190 Tom Fergus .05 .02
❑ 191 Rob Zettler .05 .02
❑ 192 Geoff Smith .05 .02
❑ 193 Joe Nieuwendyk .10 .05
❑ 194 Mark Hunter .05 .02
❑ 195 Kjell Samuelsson .05 .02
❑ 196 Todd Gill .05 .02
❑ 197 Doug Smail .05 .02
❑ 198 Dave Christian .05 .02
❑ 199 Tomas Sandstrom .05 .02
❑ 200 Jeremy Roenick .25 .11
❑ 201 Gordie Roberts .05 .02
❑ 202 Denis Savard .10 .05
❑ 203 James Patrick .05 .02
❑ 204 Dave Andreychuk .10 .05
❑ 205 Bobby Smith .10 .05
❑ 206 Valeri Zelepukin .05 .02
❑ 207 Shawn Burr .05 .02
❑ 208 Vladimir Ruzicka .05 .02
❑ 209 Calle Johansson .05 .02
❑ 210 Mark Fitzpatrick .10 .05
❑ 211 Dean Kennedy .05 .02
❑ 212 Dave Babych .05 .02
❑ 213 Wayne Presley .05 .02
❑ 214 Dave Manson .05 .02
❑ 215 Mikael Andersson .05 .02
❑ 216 Trent Yawney .05 .02
❑ 217 Mark Howe .05 .02
❑ 218 Mike Bullard .05 .02
❑ 219 Claude Lapointe .05 .02
❑ 220 Jeff Brown .05 .02
❑ 221 Bob Kudelski .05 .02
❑ 222 Michel Goulet .10 .05
❑ 223 Phil Bourque .05 .02
❑ 224 Darren Turcotte .05 .02
❑ 225 Kirk Muller .05 .02
❑ 226 Doug Bodger .05 .02
❑ 227 Dave Gagner .10 .05
❑ 228 Craig Billington .10 .05
❑ 229 Kevin Miller .05 .02
❑ 230 Glen Wesley .05 .02
❑ 231 Dale Hunter .05 .02
❑ 232 Tom Kurvers .05 .02
❑ 233 Pat Elynuik .05 .02
❑ 234 Geoff Courtnall .05 .02
❑ 235 Neil Wilkinson .05 .02
❑ 236 Bill Ranford .10 .05
❑ 237 Ronnie Stern .05 .02
238 Zarley Zalapski .05 .02
239 Kerry Huffman .05 .02
240 Joe Sakic .40 .18
241 Glenn Anderson .10 .05
242 Stephane Quintal .05 .02
243 Tony Granato .05 .02
❑ 244 Rob Brown .05 .02
❑ 245 Rick Tocchet .10 .05
❑ 246 Stephan Lebeau .05 .02
❑ 247 Mark Hardy .05 .02
❑ 248 Alexander Mogilny .10 .05
❑ 249 Jon Casey .10 .05
❑ 250 Adam Oates .10 .05
❑ 251 Bruce Driver .05 .02
❑ 252 Sergei Fedorov .40 .18
❑ 253 Michal Pivonka .05 .02
❑ 254 Cliff Ronning .05 .02
❑ 255 Derek King .05 .02
❑ 256 Luciano Borsato .05 .02
❑ 257 Paul Fenton .05 .02
❑ 258 Craig Berube .05 .02
❑ 259 Brian Bradley .05 .02
❑ 260 Craig Simpson .05 .02
❑ 261 Adam Burt .05 .02
❑ 262 Curtis Joseph .25 .11
❑ 263 Mark Pederson .05 .02
❑ 264 Alexei Gusarov .05 .02
❑ 265 Paul Coffey .25 .11
❑ 266 Steve Larmer .10 .05
❑ 267 Ron Francis .10 .05
❑ 268 Randy Gilhen .05 .02
❑ 269 Guy Carbonneau .10 .05
❑ 270 Chris Terreri .10 .05
❑ 271 Mike Craig .05 .02
❑ 272 Dale Hawerchuk .10 .05
❑ 273 Kevin Hatcher .05 .02
❑ 274 Ken Hodge Jr. .05 .02
❑ 275 Tim Cheveldae .10 .05
❑ 276 Benoit Hogue .05 .02
❑ 277 Mark Osborne .05 .02
❑ 278 Brian Mullen .05 .02
❑ 279 Robert Dirk .05 .02
❑ 280 Theoren Fleury .10 .05
❑ 281 Martin Gelinas .05 .02
❑ 282 Pat Verbeek .05 .02
❑ 283 Mike Krushelnyski .05 .02
❑ 284 Kevin Dineen .05 .02
❑ 285 Craig Janney .10 .05
❑ 286 Owen Nolan .10 .05
❑ 287 Bob Errey .05 .02
❑ 288 Bryan Marchment .05 .02
❑ 289 Randy Moller .05 .02
❑ 290 Luc Robitaille .10 .05
❑ 291 Peter Stastny .10 .05
❑ 292 Ken Sutton .05 .02
❑ 293 Brad Marsh .05 .02
❑ 294 Chris Dahlquist .05 .02
❑ 295 Patrick Roy 1.00 .45
❑ 296 Andy Brickley .05 .02
❑ 297 Randy Burridge .05 .02
❑ 298 Ray Ferraro .05 .02
❑ 299 Phil Housley .10 .05
❑ 300 Mark Messier .30 .14
❑ 301 David Bruce .05 .02
❑ 302 Al MacInnis .10 .05
❑ 303 Craig MacTavish .05 .02
❑ 304 Kay Whitmore .10 .05
❑ 305 Trevor Linden .10 .05
❑ 306 Steve Kasper .05 .02
❑ 307 Todd Elik .05 .02
❑ 308 Eric Weinrich .05 .02
❑ 309 Jocelyn Lemieux .05 .02
❑ 310 Peter Ahola .05 .02
❑ 311 J.J. Daigneault .05 .02
❑ 312 Colin Patterson .05 .02
❑ 313 Darcy Wakaluk .10 .05
❑ 314 Doug Weight .10 .05
❑ 315 Dave Barr .05 .02
❑ 316 Keith Primeau .10 .05
❑ 317 Bob Sweeney .05 .02
❑ 318 Jyrki Lumme .05 .02
❑ 319 Stu Barnes .05 .02
❑ 320 Don Beaupre .10 .05
❑ 321 Joe Murphy .05 .02
❑ 322 Gary Roberts .05 .02
❑ 323 Andrew Cassels .05 .02
❑ 324 Rod Brind'Amour .10 .05
❑ 325 Pierre Turgeon .10 .05
❑ 326 Claude Vilgrain .05 .02
❑ 327 Rich Sutter .05 .02
❑ 328 Claude Loiselle .05 .02
❑ 329 John Ogrodnick .05 .02
❑ 330 Ulf Dahlen .05 .02
❑ 331 Gilbert Dionne .05 .02
❑ 332 Joel Otto .05 .02
❑ 333 Rob Pearson .05 .02
❑ 334 Christian Ruuttu .05 .02
❑ 335 Brian Bellows .05 .02
❑ 336 Anatoli Semenov .05 .02
❑ 337 Brent Fedyk .05 .02
❑ 338 Gaetan Duchesne .05 .02
❑ 339 Randy McKay .05 .02
❑ 340 Bernie Nicholls .10 .05
❑ 341 Keith Acton .05 .02
❑ 342 John Tonelli .05 .02
❑ 343 Brian Lawton .05 .02
❑ 344 Ric Nattress .05 .02
❑ 345 Mike Eagles .05 .02
❑ 346 Frantisek Kucera .05 .02
❑ 347 John McIntyre .05 .02
❑ 348 Troy Loney .05 .02
❑ 349 Norm Maciver .05 .02
❑ 350 Brett Hull .30 .14
❑ 351 Rob Ramage .05 .02
❑ 352 Claude Boivin .05 .02
❑ 353 Paul Broten .05 .02
❑ 354 Stephane Fiset .10 .05
❑ 355 Garry Valk .05 .02
❑ 356 Basil McRae .05 .02
❑ 357 Alan May .05 .02
❑ 358 Grant Ledyard .05 .02
❑ 359 Dave Poulin .05 .02
❑ 360 Valeri Kamensky .10 .05
❑ 361 Brian Glynn .05 .02
❑ 362 Jan Erixon .05 .02
❑ 363 Mike Lalor .05 .02
❑ 364 Jeff Chychrun .05 .02
❑ 365 Ron Wilson .05 .02
❑ 366 Shawn Cronin .05 .02
❑ 367 Sylvain Turgeon .05 .02
❑ 368 Mike Liut .10 .05
❑ 369 Joe Cirella .05 .02
❑ 370 David Maley .05 .02
❑ 371 Lucien Deblois .05 .02
❑ 372 Per Djoos .05 .02
❑ 373 Dominik Hasek .75 .35
❑ 374 Laurie Boschman .05 .02
❑ 375 Brian Leetch .25 .11
❑ 376 Nelson Emerson .05 .02
❑ 377 Normand Rochefort .05 .02
❑ 378 Jacques Cloutier .10 .05
❑ 379 Jim Sandlak .05 .02
❑ 380 David Reid .05 .02
❑ 381 Gary Nylund .05 .02
❑ 382 Sergei Makarov .05 .02
❑ 383 Petr Klima .05 .02
❑ 384 Peter Douris .05 .02
❑ 385 Kirk McLean .10 .05
❑ 386 Bob McGill .05 .02
❑ 387 Ron Tugnutt .10 .05
❑ 388 Patrice Brisebois .05 .02
❑ 389 Tony Amonte .10 .05
❑ 390 Mario Lemieux 1.00 .45
❑ 391 Nicklas Lidstrom .10 .05
❑ 392 Brendan Shanahan .40 .18
❑ 393 Donald Audette .10 .05
❑ 394 Alexei Kasatonov .05 .02
❑ 395 Dino Ciccarelli .10 .05
❑ 396 Vincent Riendeau .10 .05
❑ 397 Joe Reekie .05 .02
❑ 398 Jari Kurri .10 .05
❑ 399 Ken Wregget .10 .05
❑ 400 Steve Yzerman .60 .25
❑ 401 Scott Niedermayer .10 .05
❑ 402 Stephane Beauregard .10 .05
❑ 403 Tim Hunter .05 .02
❑ 404 Marc Bergevin .05 .02
❑ 405 Sylvain Lefebvre .05 .02
❑ 406 Johan Garpenlov .05 .02
❑ 407 Tony Hrkac .05 .02
❑ 408 Tie Domi .10 .05
❑ 409 Martin Lapointe .05 .02
❑ 410 Darryl Sydor .05 .02
❑ 411 Brett Hull SL .25 .11
❑ 412 Wayne Gretzky SL .60 .25
❑ 413 Mario Lemieux SL .50 .23
❑ 414 Paul Ysebaert SL .05 .02
❑ 415 Tony Amonte SL .10 .05
❑ 416 Brian Leetch SL .25 .11
❑ 417 Tim Cheveldae SL .10 .05
Kirk McLean SL
❑ 418 Patrick Roy SL .50 .23
❑ 419 Ray Bourque FP .10 .05
❑ 420 Pat LaFontaine FP .10 .05
❑ 421 Al MacInnis FP .10 .05
❑ 422 Jeremy Roenick FP .25 .11
❑ 423 Steve Yzerman FP .25 .11
❑ 424 Bill Ranford FP .10 .05
❑ 425 John Cullen FP .05 .02
❑ 426 Wayne Gretzky FP .60 .25
❑ 427 Mike Modano FP .10 .05
❑ 428 Patrick Roy FP .50 .23
❑ 429 Scott Stevens FP .10 .05
❑ 430 Pierre Turgeon FP .10 .05
❑ 431 Mark Messier FP .25 .11
❑ 432 Eric Lindros FP 1.00 .45
❑ 433 Mario Lemieux FP .50 .23
❑ 434 Joe Sakic FP .10 .05
❑ 435 Brett Hull FP .10 .05
❑ 436 Pat Falloon FP .05 .02
❑ 437 Grant Fuhr FP .05 .02
❑ 438 Trevor Linden FP .10 .05
❑ 439 Kevin Hatcher FP .05 .02
❑ 440 Phil Housley FP .10 .05
❑ 441 Paul Coffey SH .25 .11
❑ 442 Brett Hull SH .25 .11
❑ 443 Mike Gartner SH .10 .05
❑ 444 Michel Goulet SH .10 .05
❑ 445 Mike Gartner SH .10 .05
❑ 446 Bobby Smith SH .10 .05
❑ 447 Ray Bourque SH .10 .05
❑ 448 Mario Lemieux SH .50 .23
❑ 449 Scott Lachance TP .05 .02
❑ 450 Keith Tkaczuk TP .50 .23
❑ 451 Alexander Semak TP .05 .02
❑ 452 John Tanner TP .05 .02
❑ 453 Joe Juneau TP .10 .05
❑ 454 Igor Kravchuk TP .05 .02
❑ 455 Brent Thompson TP .05 .02
❑ 456 Evgeny Davydov TP .05 .02
❑ 457 Arturs Irbe TP .10 .05
❑ 458 Kent Manderville TP .05 .02
❑ 459 Shawn McEachern TP .05 .02
❑ 460 Guy Hebert TP .60 .25
❑ 461 Keith Carney TP .05 .02
❑ 462 Karl Dykhuis TP .05 .02
❑ 463 Bill Lindsay TP .05 .02
❑ 464 Dominic Roussel TP .10 .05
❑ 465 Marty McInnis TP .05 .02
❑ 466 Dale Craigwell TP .05 .02
❑ 467 Igor Ulanov TP .05 .02
❑ 468 Dmitri Mironov TP .05 .02
❑ 469 Dean McAmmond TP .05 .02
❑ 470 Bill Guerin TP .05 .02
❑ 471 Bret Hedican TP .05 .02
❑ 472 Felix Potvin TP .25 .11
❑ 473 Slava Kozlov TP .10 .05
❑ 474 Martin Rucinsky TP .05 .02
❑ 475 Ray Whitney TP .05 .02
❑ 476 Stephen Heinze TP .05 .02
❑ 477 Brad Schlegel TP .05 .02
❑ 478 Patrick Poulin TP .05 .02
❑ 479 Ted Donato TP .05 .02
❑ 480 Martin Brodeur TP .75 .35
❑ 481 Denny Felsner TP .05 .02
❑ 482 Trent Klatt TP .05 .02
❑ 483 Gord Hynes TP .05 .02
❑ 484 Glen Murray TP .05 .02
❑ 485 Chris Lindberg TP .05 .02
❑ 486 Ray LeBlanc TP .10 .05
❑ 487 Yanic Perreault TP .05 .02
❑ 488 J.F. Quintin TP .05 .02
❑ 489 Patrick Roy DT .50 .23
❑ 490 Ray Bourque DT .10 .05
❑ 491 Brian Leetch DT .25 .11
❑ 492 Kevin Stevens DT .05 .02
❑ 493 Mark Messier DT .25 .11
❑ 494 Jaromir Jagr DT .25 .11
❑ 495 Bill Ranford DT .10 .05
❑ 496 Al MacInnis DT .10 .05
❑ 497 Chris Chelios DT .25 .11
❑ 498 Luc Robitaille DT .10 .05
❑ 499 Jeremy Roenick DT .25 .11
❑ 500 Brett Hull DT .25 .11
❑ 501 Felix Potvin RDT .25 .11
❑ 502 Nicklas Lidstrom RDT .10 .05
❑ 503 Vladimir Konstantinov .05 .02
RDT
❑ 504 Pavel Bure RDT .25 .11
❑ 505 Nelson Emerson RDT .05 .02
❑ 506 Tony Amonte RDT .10 .05
❑ 507 Tampa Bay Lightning .05 .02
Logo
❑ 508 Shawn Chambers .05 .02
❑ 509 Basil McRae .05 .02
❑ 510 Joe Reekie .05 .02
❑ 511 Wendell Young .10 .05
❑ 512 Ottawa Senators Logo .25 .11
❑ 513 Laurie Boschman .05 .02
❑ 514 Mark Lamb .05 .02
❑ 515 Peter Sidorkiewicz .10 .05
❑ 516 Sylvain Turgeon .05 .02
❑ 517 Bill Dineen .05 .02
Kevin Dineen
❑ 518 Stanley Cup .10 .05
Champions
❑ 519 Mario Lemieux AW .50 .23
Conn Smythe
❑ 520 Ray Bourque AW .10 .05
King Clancy
❑ 521 Mark Messier AW .25 .11
Hart Trophy
❑ 522 Brian Leetch AW .25 .11
Norris Trophy
❑ 523 Pavel Bure AW .25 .11
Calder Trophy
❑ 524 Guy Carbonneau AW .10 .05
Selke Trophy
❑ 525 Wayne Gretzky AW .60 .25
Lady Byng Trophy
❑ 526 Mark Fitzpatrick AW .10 .05
Masterton Trophy
❑ 527 Patrick Roy AW .50 .23
Vezina Trophy
❑ 528 Memorial Cup .05 .02
Kamloops Blazers
❑ 529 Rick Tabaracci .10 .05
❑ 530 Tom Draper .10 .05
❑ 531 Adrien Plavsic .05 .02
❑ 532 Joe Sacco .05 .02
❑ 533 Mike Sullivan .05 .02
❑ 534 Zdeno Ciger .05 .02
❑ 535 Frank Pietrangelo .10 .05
❑ 536 Mike Peluso .05 .02
❑ 537 Jim Paek .05 .02
❑ 538 Dave Hannan .05 .02
❑ 539 David Williams .05 .02
❑ 540 Gino Odjick .05 .02
❑ 541 Yvon Corriveau .05 .02
❑ 542 Grant Jennings .05 .02
❑ 543 Stephane Matteau .05 .02
❑ 544 Pat Conacher .05 .02
❑ 545 Steven Rice .05 .02
❑ 546 Marc Habscheid .05 .02
❑ 547 Steve Weeks .10 .05
❑ 548A Jay Wells USA .05 .02
❑ 548C Maurice Richard CAN .25 .11
❑ 549A Mick Vukota USA .05 .02
❑ 549C Maurice Richard CAN .25 .11
❑ 550 Eric Lindros UER 2.00 .90
(Acquired 6-30-92,
not 6-20-92)
❑ NNO Eric Lindros 25.00 11.00
Press Conference Card

## 1992-93 Score Canadian Olympians

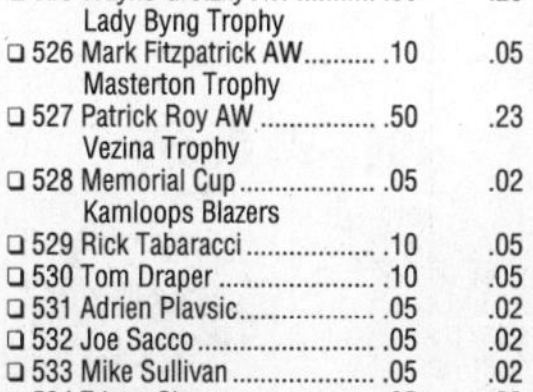

This 13-card standard-size set showcases Canadian hockey players who participated in the '92 Olympics in Albertville, France. The cards were randomly inserted at the rate of 1:24 '92-93 Score Canadian hockey packs. The color action photos on the fronts are highlighted by a red border with a diagonal white stripe. The year appears in a maple leaf at the upper left. The player's name and position are printed in the borders above and below the picture respectively. The backs feature the same red border design as the front with a player profile printed on a ghosted photo of the Canadian flag. The cards are numbered on the back. Not part of the set, but inserted in Canadian foil packs are two Maurice Richard cards and one autographed card of The Rocket.

| | MINT | NRMT |
|---|---|---|
| COMPLETE SET (13) | 60.00 | 27.00 |
| COMMON CARD (1-13) | 3.00 | 1.35 |

❑ 1 Eric Lindros 30.00 13.50
❑ 2 Joe Juneau 6.00 2.70
❑ 3 Dave Archibald 3.00 1.35
❑ 4 Randy Smith 3.00 1.35
❑ 5 Gord Hynes 3.00 1.35
❑ 6 Chris Lindberg 3.00 1.35
❑ 7 Jason Woolley 3.00 1.35
❑ 8 Fabian Joseph 3.00 1.35
❑ 9 Brad Schlegel 3.00 1.35
❑ 10 Kent Manderville 3.00 1.35
❑ 11 Adrien Plavsic 3.00 1.35
❑ 12 Trevor Kidd 4.00 1.80
❑ 13 Sean Burke 4.00 1.80
❑ NNO1 Maurice Richard 15.00 6.75
The Rocket
❑ NNO2 Maurice Richard 15.00 6.75
Stanley Cup Hero
❑ AU Maurice Richard AU 200.00 90.00
(Certified autograph)

## 1992-93 Score Sharpshooters

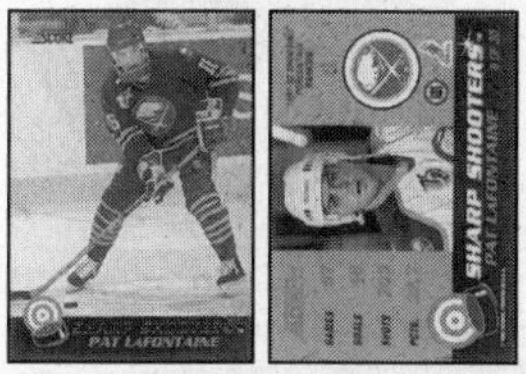

This 30-card standard-size set showcases the most accurate shooters during the 1991-92 season. Two cards were inserted in each 1992-93 Score jumbo pack. The cards feature full-bleed color action photos. A black border at the bottom contains the player's name in red and the words "Sharp Shooters" in gold foil lettering. A puck and target icon fills out the card front at the lower left corner. The horizontal backs carry close-up player photos with statistics and the team logo on either side against a gray background. A black border, nearly identical to the front, runs across the bottom. The cards are numbered on the back and arranged in descending order of 1991-92 shooting percentage ranking.

| | MINT | NRMT |
|---|---|---|
| COMPLETE SET (30) | 12.00 | 5.50 |
| COMMON CARD (1-30) | .25 | .11 |

*US AND CDN: SAME VALUE

❑ 1 Gary Roberts .25 .11
❑ 2 Sergei Makarov .25 .11
❑ 3 Ray Ferraro .25 .11
❑ 4 Dale Hunter .25 .11
❑ 5 Sergei Nemchinov .25 .11
❑ 6 Mike Ridley .25 .11
❑ 7 Gilbert Dionne .25 .11
❑ 8 Pat LaFontaine 1.00 .45
❑ 9 Jimmy Carson .25 .11
❑ 10 Jeremy Roenick 1.50 .70
❑ 11 Kelly Buchberger .25 .11
❑ 12 Owen Nolan 1.00 .45
❑ 13 Igor Larionov .25 .11
❑ 14 Claude Vilgrain .25 .11
❑ 15 Derek King .25 .11
❑ 16 Greg Paslawski .25 .11
❑ 17 Bob Probert .25 .11
❑ 18 Mark Recchi 1.00 .45
❑ 19 Donald Audette .25 .11
❑ 20 Ray Sheppard 1.00 .45
❑ 21 Benoit Hogue .25 .11
❑ 22 Rob Brown .25 .11
❑ 23 Pat Elyniuk .25 .11
❑ 24 Petr Klima .25 .11
❑ 25 Pierre Turgeon 1.00 .45
❑ 26 Corey Millen .25 .11
❑ 27 Dimitri Khristich .25 .11
❑ 28 Anatoli Semenov .25 .11
❑ 29 Kirk Muller .25 .11
❑ 30 Craig Simpson .25 .11

## 1992-93 Score USA Greats

This 15-card set showcases outstanding United States-born players. The standard-size cards were randomly inserted at the rate of

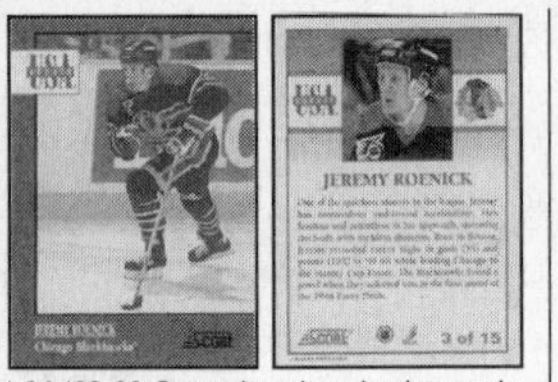

1:24 '92-93 Score American hockey packs. The color action photos on the fronts are full-bleed on the right side only and framed on the other three sides by a red foil stripe and a blue outer border. The backs feature a close-up photo and a player profile.

| | MINT | NRMT |
|---|---|---|
| COMPLETE SET (15) | 50.00 | 22.00 |
| COMMON CARD (1-15) | 2.50 | 1.10 |

| | | |
|---|---|---|
| ❑ 1 Pat LaFontaine | 5.00 | 2.20 |
| ❑ 2 Chris Chelios | 6.00 | 2.70 |
| ❑ 3 Jeremy Roenick | 6.00 | 2.70 |
| ❑ 4 Tony Granato | 2.50 | 1.10 |
| ❑ 5 Mike Modano | 6.00 | 2.70 |
| ❑ 6 Mike Richter | 6.00 | 2.70 |
| ❑ 7 John Vanbiesbrouck | 8.00 | 3.60 |
| ❑ 8 Brian Leetch | 6.00 | 2.70 |
| ❑ 9 Joe Mullen | 2.50 | 1.10 |
| ❑ 10 Kevin Stevens | 5.00 | 2.20 |
| ❑ 11 Craig Janney | 2.50 | 1.10 |
| ❑ 12 Brian Mullen | 2.50 | 1.10 |
| ❑ 13 Kevin Hatcher | 2.50 | 1.10 |
| ❑ 14 Kelly Miller | 2.50 | 1.10 |
| ❑ 15 Ed Olczyk | 2.50 | 1.10 |

## 1992-93 Score Young Superstars

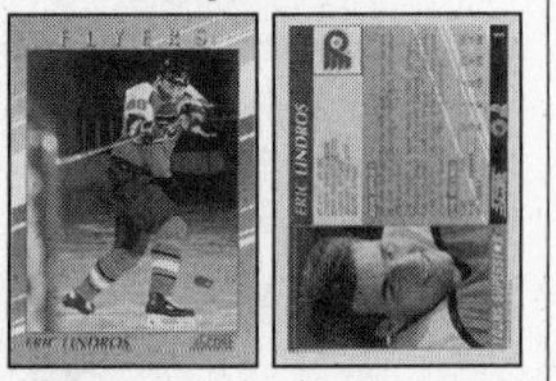

This 40-card, boxed standard-size set was issued to showcase some of the leading young hockey players. The fronts feature glossy color player photos with white and bluish-gray streaked borders. The player's team name is printed in the top border, while the player's name is printed in the bottom border. The horizontal backs carry a close-up color photo, biography, "Rink Report," and statistics.

| | MINT | NRMT |
|---|---|---|
| COMPLETE SET (40) | 8.00 | 3.60 |
| COMMON CARD (1-40) | .10 | .05 |

| | | |
|---|---|---|
| ❑ 1 Eric Lindros | 2.50 | 1.10 |
| ❑ 2 Tony Amonte | .30 | .14 |
| ❑ 3 Mats Sundin | .50 | .23 |
| ❑ 4 Jaromir Jagr | 2.00 | .90 |
| ❑ 5 Sergei Fedorov | 1.00 | .45 |
| ❑ 6 Gilbert Dionne | .10 | .05 |
| ❑ 7 Mark Recchi | .30 | .14 |
| ❑ 8 Alexander Mogilny | .30 | .14 |
| ❑ 9 Mike Richter | .50 | .23 |
| ❑ 10 Jeremy Roenick | .50 | .23 |
| ❑ 11 Nicklas Lidstrom | .30 | .14 |
| ❑ 12 Scott Lachance | .10 | .05 |
| ❑ 13 Nelson Emerson | .10 | .05 |
| ❑ 14 Pat Falloon | .10 | .05 |
| ❑ 15 Dimitri Khristich | .10 | .05 |
| ❑ 16 Trevor Linden | .30 | .14 |
| ❑ 17 Curtis Joseph | .50 | .23 |
| ❑ 18 Rob Pearson | .10 | .05 |
| ❑ 19 Kevin Todd | .10 | .05 |
| ❑ 20 Joe Sakic | 1.25 | .55 |
| ❑ 21 Tim Cheveldae | .30 | .14 |
| ❑ 22 Joe Juneau | .30 | .14 |
| ❑ 23 Vladimir Konstantinov | .10 | .05 |
| ❑ 24 Valeri Kamensky | .30 | .14 |
| ❑ 25 Ed Belfour | .50 | .23 |
| ❑ 26 Rod Brind'Amour | .30 | .14 |
| ❑ 27 Pierre Turgeon | .30 | .14 |
| ❑ 28 Eric Desjardins | .10 | .05 |
| ❑ 29 Keith Tkachuk | .60 | .25 |
| ❑ 30 Pavel Bure | 1.00 | .45 |
| ❑ 31 Patrick Poulin | .10 | .05 |
| ❑ 32 Viacheslav Kozlov | .30 | .14 |
| ❑ 33 Scott Niedermayer | .30 | .14 |
| ❑ 34 Jyrki Lumme | .10 | .05 |
| ❑ 35 Paul Ysebaert | .10 | .05 |
| ❑ 36 Dominic Roussel | .30 | .14 |
| ❑ 37 Owen Nolan | .30 | .14 |
| ❑ 38 Rob Blake | .10 | .05 |
| ❑ 39 Felix Potvin | .50 | .23 |
| ❑ 40 Mike Modano | .50 | .23 |

## 1993-94 Score Promo Panel

This promo panel was issued to promote the second series of the 1993-94 Score hockey series. Measuring approximately 5" by 2 1/2",

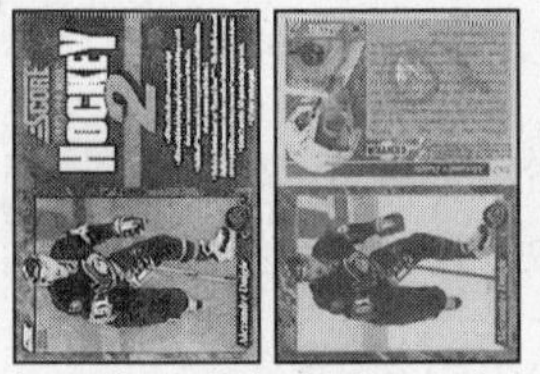

the panel is actually the size of two standard-size cards. The left front features a Gold Rush version of the Alexandre Daigle card. On a purple foil background, the right front presents an advertisement for the second series. The reverse of the left front is the expected card back as with a regular card; the reverse of the right front is the front of the regular issue Daigle card.

| | MINT | NRMT |
|---|---|---|
| COMPLETE SET (1) | 2.00 | .90 |
| COMMON PANEL | 2.00 | .90 |

| | | |
|---|---|---|
| ❑ 587 Alexandre Daigle | 2.00 | .90 |

## 1993-94 Score Samples

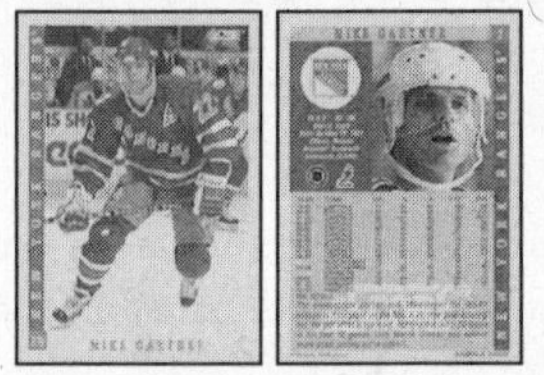

This six-card standard-size set was issued by Score as a preview of the design of the 1993-94 Score hockey set. The fronts display color action shots within a white border. The team name is printed on a team color-coded stripe along the left side. The player's position and name is printed across the bottom of the picture. The backs have team color-coded backgrounds with a head shot on the upper half and biography, statistics, and player profile. The words "sample card" are printed in the lower right corner.

| | MINT | NRMT |
|---|---|---|
| COMPLETE SET (6) | 7.00 | 3.10 |
| COMMON CARD (1-6) | .25 | .11 |

| | | |
|---|---|---|
| ❑ 1 Eric Lindros | 5.00 | 2.20 |
| ❑ 2 Mike Gartner | .50 | .23 |
| ❑ 3 Steve Larmer | .25 | .11 |
| ❑ 4 Brian Bellows | .25 | .11 |
| ❑ 5 Felix Potvin | 1.50 | .70 |
| ❑ 6 Pierre Turgeon | .75 | .35 |

## 1993-94 Score

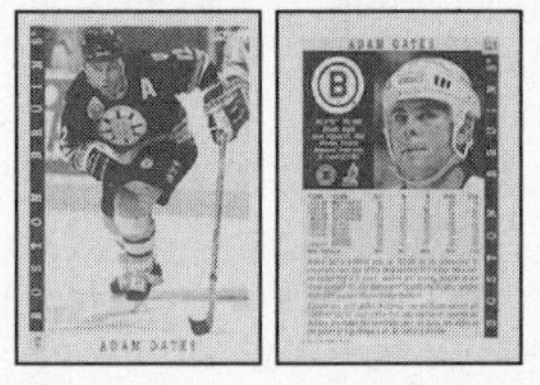

The 1993-94 Score hockey set consists of 661 standard-size cards. The first series contains 495 cards and the second series 166. The fronts of the first series feature white-bordered color player action shots. The player's name and position appear at the bottom, with his team name displayed vertically on the left within a team color-coded stripe. The back carries the player's name in team color-coded lettering at the top, with a head shot beneath and to the right. The player's biography and team logo appear alongside within a team color-coded rectangle. The team name appears vertically in a team color-coded stripe, this time on the right. The player's stat table in the middle portion of the card and his career highlights at the bottom round out the card. The second series was redesigned and consists of traded players in new uniforms, rookies and individual highlights. Blue borders surround the card with player name and team logo at the bottom. In addition to highlights and statistics, the backs contain another photo. The cards are numbered on the back. Several subsets grace the checklist: Little Big Men (441-445), Highlights (446-452), Top Rookies (453-476), and Season Leaders (477-485). Card 496, Alexandre Daigle, is the card received after mailing in the unnumbered Daigle redemption card. The set is considered complete without it. The redemption card was randomly inserted in first series packs. An Eric Lindros All-Star card was the SP insert in series two, at a rate of 1:360 packs. Rookie Cards include Jason Arnott, Chris Osgood, Jocelyn Thibault and Damian Rhodes.

| | MINT | NRMT |
|---|---|---|
| COMPLETE SET (661) | 20.00 | 9.00 |
| COMPLETE SERIES 1 (495) | 15.00 | 6.75 |
| COMPLETE SERIES 2 (166) | 5.00 | 2.20 |
| COMMON CARD (1-662) | .05 | .02 |

| | | |
|---|---|---|
| ❑ 1 Eric Lindros | .75 | .35 |
| ❑ 2 Mike Gartner | .10 | .05 |
| ❑ 3 Steve Larmer | .10 | .05 |
| ❑ 4 Brian Bellows | .05 | .02 |
| ❑ 5 Felix Potvin | .20 | .09 |
| ❑ 6 Pierre Turgeon | .10 | .05 |
| ❑ 7 Joe Mullen | .10 | .05 |
| ❑ 8 Craig MacTavish | .05 | .02 |
| ❑ 9 Mats Sundin | .10 | .05 |
| ❑ 10 Pat Verbeek | .05 | .02 |
| ❑ 11 Andy Moog | .10 | .05 |
| ❑ 12 Dirk Graham | .05 | .02 |
| ❑ 13 Gary Suter | .05 | .02 |
| ❑ 14 Brent Fedyk | .05 | .02 |
| ❑ 15 Brad Shaw | .05 | .02 |
| ❑ 16 Benoit Hogue | .05 | .02 |
| ❑ 17 Cliff Ronning | .05 | .02 |
| ❑ 18 Mathieu Schneider | .05 | .02 |
| ❑ 19 Bernie Nicholls | .05 | .02 |
| ❑ 20 Vladimir Konstantinov | .05 | .02 |
| ❑ 21 Doug Bodger | .05 | .02 |
| ❑ 22 Peter Stastny | .10 | .05 |
| ❑ 23 Larry Murphy | .10 | .05 |
| ❑ 24 Darren Turcotte | .05 | .02 |
| ❑ 25 Doug Crossman | .05 | .02 |
| ❑ 26 Bob Essensa | .10 | .05 |
| ❑ 27 Kelly Kisio | .05 | .02 |
| ❑ 28 Nelson Emerson | .05 | .02 |
| ❑ 29 Ray Bourque | .20 | .09 |
| ❑ 30 Kelly Miller | .05 | .02 |
| ❑ 31 Peter Zezel | .05 | .02 |
| ❑ 32 Owen Nolan | .10 | .05 |
| ❑ 33 Sergei Makarov | .05 | .02 |
| ❑ 34 Stephane Richer | .10 | .05 |
| ❑ 35 Adam Graves | .10 | .05 |
| ❑ 36 Rob Ramage | .05 | .02 |
| ❑ 37 Ed Olczyk | .05 | .02 |
| ❑ 38 Jeff Hackett | .10 | .05 |
| ❑ 39 Ron Sutter | .05 | .02 |
| ❑ 40 Dale Hunter | .05 | .02 |
| ❑ 41 Nikolai Borschevsky | .05 | .02 |
| ❑ 42 Curtis Leschyshyn | .05 | .02 |
| ❑ 43 Mike Vernon | .10 | .05 |
| ❑ 44 Brent Sutter | .05 | .02 |
| ❑ 45 Rod Brind'Amour | .10 | .05 |
| ❑ 46 Sylvain Turgeon | .05 | .02 |
| ❑ 47 Kirk McLean | .10 | .05 |
| ❑ 48 Derek King | .05 | .02 |
| ❑ 49 Murray Craven | .05 | .02 |
| ❑ 50 Jaromir Jagr | .60 | .25 |
| ❑ 51 Guy Carbonneau | .05 | .02 |
| ❑ 52 Tony Granato | .05 | .02 |
| ❑ 53 Mark Tinordi | .05 | .02 |
| ❑ 54 Brad McCrimmon | .05 | .02 |
| ❑ 55 Randy Wood | .05 | .02 |
| ❑ 56 Scott Young | .05 | .02 |
| ❑ 57 Jamie Baker | .05 | .02 |
| ❑ 58 Don Beaupre | .10 | .05 |
| ❑ 59 Bob Probert | .10 | .05 |
| ❑ 60 Ray Ferraro | .05 | .02 |
| ❑ 61 Alexei Kasatonov | .05 | .02 |
| ❑ 62 Corey Millen | .05 | .02 |
| ❑ 63 Scott Mellanby | .10 | .05 |
| ❑ 64 Brian Benning | .05 | .02 |
| ❑ 65 Doug Lidster | .05 | .02 |
| ❑ 66 Doug Gilmour | .20 | .09 |
| ❑ 67 Shawn McEachern | .05 | .02 |
| ❑ 68 Tim Cheveldae | .10 | .05 |
| ❑ 69 Jeff Norton | .05 | .02 |
| ❑ 70 Ed Belfour | .20 | .09 |
| ❑ 71 Thomas Steen | .05 | .02 |
| ❑ 72 Stephan Lebeau | .05 | .02 |
| ❑ 73 James Patrick | .05 | .02 |
| ❑ 74 Joel Otto | .05 | .02 |
| ❑ 75 Grant Fuhr | .10 | .05 |
| ❑ 76 Calle Johansson | .05 | .02 |
| ❑ 77 Donald Audette | .10 | .05 |
| ❑ 78 Geoff Courtnall | .05 | .02 |
| ❑ 79 Fredrik Olausson | .05 | .02 |
| ❑ 80 Dimitri Khristich | .05 | .02 |
| ❑ 81 John MacLean | .10 | .05 |
| ❑ 82 Dominic Roussel | .10 | .05 |
| ❑ 83 Ray Sheppard | .10 | .05 |
| ❑ 84 Christian Ruuttu | .05 | .02 |
| ❑ 85 Mike McPhee | .05 | .02 |
| ❑ 86 Adam Creighton | .05 | .02 |
| ❑ 87 Uwe Krupp | .05 | .02 |
| ❑ 88 Steve Leach | .05 | .02 |
| ❑ 89 Kevin Miller | .05 | .02 |
| ❑ 90 Charlie Huddy | .05 | .02 |
| ❑ 91 Mark Howe | .05 | .02 |
| ❑ 92 Sylvain Cote | .05 | .02 |
| ❑ 93 Anatoli Semenov | .05 | .02 |
| ❑ 94 Jeff Beukeboom | .05 | .02 |
| ❑ 95 Gord Murphy | .05 | .02 |
| ❑ 96 Rob Pearson | .05 | .02 |
| ❑ 97 Esa Tikkanen | .05 | .02 |
| ❑ 98 Dave Gagner | .10 | .05 |
| ❑ 99 Mike Richter | .20 | .09 |
| ❑ 100 Jari Kurri | .10 | .05 |
| ❑ 101 Chris Chelios | .20 | .09 |
| ❑ 102 Peter Sidorkiewicz | .10 | .05 |
| ❑ 103 Scott Lachance | .05 | .02 |
| ❑ 104 Zarley Zalapski | .05 | .02 |
| ❑ 105 Denis Savard | .10 | .05 |
| ❑ 106 Paul Coffey | .20 | .09 |
| ❑ 107 Ulf Dahlen | .05 | .02 |
| ❑ 108 Shayne Corson | .05 | .02 |
| ❑ 109 Jimmy Carson | .05 | .02 |
| ❑ 110 Petr Svoboda | .05 | .02 |
| ❑ 111 Scott Stevens | .10 | .05 |
| ❑ 112 Kevin Lowe | .05 | .02 |
| ❑ 113 Chris Kontos | .05 | .02 |
| ❑ 114 Evgeny Davydov | .05 | .02 |
| ❑ 115 Doug Wilson | .10 | .05 |
| ❑ 116 Curtis Joseph | .20 | .09 |
| ❑ 117 Trevor Linden | .10 | .05 |
| ❑ 118 Michal Pivonka | .05 | .02 |
| ❑ 119 Dave Ellett | .05 | .02 |
| ❑ 120 Mike Ricci | .05 | .02 |
| ❑ 121 Al MacInnis | .10 | .05 |
| ❑ 122 Kevin Dineen | .05 | .02 |
| ❑ 123 Norm Maciver | .05 | .02 |
| ❑ 124 Darius Kasparaitis | .05 | .02 |
| ❑ 125 Adam Oates | .10 | .05 |
| ❑ 126 Sean Burke | .10 | .05 |
| ❑ 127 Dave Manson | .05 | .02 |
| ❑ 128 Eric Desjardins | .05 | .02 |
| ❑ 129 Tomas Sandstrom | .05 | .02 |
| ❑ 130 Russ Courtnall | .05 | .02 |
| ❑ 131 Roman Hamrlik | .10 | .05 |
| ❑ 132 Teppo Numminen | .05 | .02 |
| ❑ 133 Pat Falloon | .05 | .02 |
| ❑ 134 Jyrki Lumme | .05 | .02 |
| ❑ 135 Joe Sakic | .40 | .18 |
| ❑ 136 Kevin Hatcher | .05 | .02 |
| ❑ 137 Wendel Clark | .10 | .05 |
| ❑ 138 Neil Wilkinson | .05 | .02 |
| ❑ 139 Craig Simpson | .05 | .02 |
| ❑ 140 Kelly Hrudey | .10 | .05 |
| ❑ 141 Steve Thomas | .05 | .02 |
| ❑ 142 Mike Modano | .25 | .11 |
| ❑ 143 Garry Galley | .05 | .02 |
| ❑ 144 Jim Johnson | .05 | .02 |
| ❑ 145 Rod Langway | .05 | .02 |
| ❑ 146 Bob Sweeney | .05 | .02 |
| ❑ 147 Gary Leeman | .05 | .02 |
| ❑ 148 Alexei Zhitnik | .05 | .02 |
| ❑ 149 Adam Foote | .05 | .02 |
| ❑ 150 Mark Recchi | .10 | .05 |
| ❑ 151 Ron Francis | .10 | .05 |
| ❑ 152 Ron Hextall | .10 | .05 |
| ❑ 153 Michel Goulet | .10 | .05 |
| ❑ 154 Vladimir Ruzicka | .05 | .02 |
| ❑ 155 Bill Ranford | .10 | .05 |
| ❑ 156 Mike Craig | .05 | .02 |
| ❑ 157 Vladimir Malakhov | .05 | .02 |
| ❑ 158 Nicklas Lidstrom | .10 | .05 |
| ❑ 159 Dale Hawerchuk | .10 | .05 |
| ❑ 160 Claude Lemieux | .10 | .05 |
| ❑ 161 Ulf Samuelsson | .05 | .02 |
| ❑ 162 John Vanbiesbrouck | .30 | .14 |
| ❑ 163 Patrice Brisebois | .05 | .02 |
| ❑ 164 Andrew Cassels | .05 | .02 |
| ❑ 165 Paul Ranheim | .05 | .02 |
| ❑ 166 Neal Broten | .10 | .05 |
| ❑ 167 Joe Reekie | .05 | .02 |
| ❑ 168 Adrian Hatcher | .05 | .02 |
| ❑ 169 Don Sweeney | .05 | .02 |
| ❑ 170 Mike Keane | .05 | .02 |
| ❑ 171 Mark Fitzpatrick | .10 | .05 |
| ❑ 172 Paul Cavallini | .05 | .02 |
| ❑ 173 Garth Butcher | .05 | .02 |
| ❑ 174 Andrei Kovalenko | .05 | .02 |
| ❑ 175 Shawn Burr | .05 | .02 |
| ❑ 176 Mike Donnelly | .05 | .02 |
| ❑ 177 Glenn Healy | .10 | .05 |
| ❑ 178 Gilbert Dionne | .05 | .02 |
| ❑ 179 Mike Ramsey | .05 | .02 |
| ❑ 180 Glenn Anderson | .10 | .05 |
| ❑ 181 Pelle Eklund | .05 | .02 |
| ❑ 182 Kerry Huffman | .05 | .02 |
| ❑ 183 Johan Garpenlov | .05 | .02 |
| ❑ 184 Kjell Samuelsson | .05 | .02 |
| ❑ 185 Todd Elik | .05 | .02 |
| ❑ 186 Craig Janney | .10 | .05 |
| ❑ 187 Dmitri Kvartalnov | .05 | .02 |
| ❑ 188 Al Iafrate | .05 | .02 |
| ❑ 189 John Cullen | .05 | .02 |
| ❑ 190 Steve Duchesne | .05 | .02 |
| ❑ 191 Theoren Fleury | .10 | .05 |
| ❑ 192 Steve Smith | .05 | .02 |
| ❑ 193 Jon Casey | .10 | .05 |
| ❑ 194 Jeff Brown | .05 | .02 |
| ❑ 195 Keith Tkachuk | .25 | .11 |
| ❑ 196 Greg Adams | .05 | .02 |
| ❑ 197 Mike Ridley | .05 | .02 |
| ❑ 198 Bobby Holik | .05 | .02 |
| ❑ 199 Joe Nieuwendyk | .10 | .05 |
| ❑ 200 Mark Messier | .25 | .11 |
| ❑ 201 Jim Hrivnak | .10 | .05 |
| ❑ 202 Patrick Poulin | .05 | .02 |
| ❑ 203 Alexei Kovalev | .10 | .05 |
| ❑ 204 Robert Reichel | .05 | .02 |
| ❑ 205 David Shaw | .05 | .02 |
| ❑ 206 Brent Gilchrist | .05 | .02 |
| ❑ 207 Craig Billington | .10 | .05 |
| ❑ 208 Bob Errey | .05 | .02 |
| ❑ 209 Dmitri Mironov | .05 | .02 |
| ❑ 210 Dixon Ward | .05 | .02 |
| ❑ 211 Rick Zombo | .05 | .02 |
| ❑ 212 Marty McSorley | .05 | .02 |
| ❑ 213 Geoff Sanderson | .10 | .05 |
| ❑ 214 Dino Ciccarelli | .10 | .05 |
| ❑ 215 Tony Amonte | .10 | .05 |
| ❑ 216 Dimitri Yushkevich | .05 | .02 |
| ❑ 217 Scott Niedermayer | .05 | .02 |
| ❑ 218 Sergei Nemchinov | .05 | .02 |
| ❑ 219 Steve Konroyd | .05 | .02 |
| ❑ 220 Patrick Flatley | .05 | .02 |
| ❑ 221 Steve Chiasson | .05 | .02 |
| ❑ 222 Alexander Mogilny | .10 | .05 |
| ❑ 223 Pat Elynuik | .05 | .02 |
| ❑ 224 Jamie Macoun | .05 | .02 |
| ❑ 225 Tom Barrasso | .10 | .05 |
| ❑ 226 Gaetan Duchesne | .05 | .02 |
| ❑ 227 Eric Weinrich | .05 | .02 |
| ❑ 228 Dave Poulin | .05 | .02 |
| ❑ 229 Slava Fetisov | .05 | .02 |
| ❑ 230 Brian Bradley | .05 | .02 |
| ❑ 231 Petr Nedved | .10 | .05 |
| ❑ 232 Phil Housley | .10 | .05 |
| ❑ 233 Terry Carkner | .05 | .02 |
| ❑ 234 Kirk Muller | .05 | .02 |
| ❑ 235 Brian Leetch | .20 | .09 |
| ❑ 236 Rob Blake | .05 | .02 |
| ❑ 237 Chris Terreri | .10 | .05 |
| ❑ 238 Brendan Shanahan | .40 | .18 |
| ❑ 239 Paul Ysebaert | .05 | .02 |
| ❑ 240 Jeremy Roenick | .20 | .09 |
| ❑ 241 Gary Roberts | .05 | .02 |
| ❑ 242 Petr Klima | .05 | .02 |
| ❑ 243 Glen Wesley | .05 | .02 |
| ❑ 244 Vincent Damphousse | .10 | .05 |
| ❑ 245 Luc Robitaille | .10 | .05 |
| ❑ 246 Dallas Drake | .05 | .02 |
| ❑ 247 Rob Gaudreau | .05 | .02 |
| ❑ 248 Tommy Sjodin | .05 | .02 |
| ❑ 249 Richard Smehlik | .05 | .02 |
| ❑ 250 Sergei Fedorov | .40 | .18 |
| ❑ 251 Steve Heinze | .05 | .02 |
| ❑ 252 Luke Richardson | .05 | .02 |
| ❑ 253 Doug Weight | .10 | .05 |
| ❑ 254 Martin Rucinsky | .05 | .02 |
| ❑ 255 Sergio Momesso | .05 | .02 |
| ❑ 256 Alexei Zhamnov | .10 | .05 |
| ❑ 257 Bob Kudelski | .05 | .02 |
| ❑ 258 Brian Skrudland | .05 | .02 |
| ❑ 259 Terry Yake | .05 | .02 |
| ❑ 260 Alexei Gusarov | .05 | .02 |
| ❑ 261 Sandis Ozolinsh | .10 | .05 |
| ❑ 262 Ted Donato | .05 | .02 |
| ❑ 263 Bruce Driver | .05 | .02 |
| ❑ 264 Yves Racine | .05 | .02 |
| ❑ 265 Mike Peluso | .05 | .02 |
| ❑ 266 Craig Muni | .05 | .02 |
| ❑ 267 Bob Carpenter | .05 | .02 |
| ❑ 268 Kevin Haller | .05 | .02 |
| ❑ 269 Brad May | .10 | .05 |
| ❑ 270 Joe Kocur | .10 | .05 |
| ❑ 271 Igor Korolev | .05 | .02 |
| ❑ 272 Troy Murray | .05 | .02 |
| ❑ 273 Daren Puppa | .10 | .05 |
| ❑ 274 Gordie Roberts | .05 | .02 |
| ❑ 275 Michel Petit | .05 | .02 |
| ❑ 276 Vincent Riendeau | .10 | .05 |
| ❑ 277 Robert Petrovicky | .05 | .02 |
| ❑ 278 Valeri Zelepukin | .05 | .02 |
| ❑ 279 Bob Bassen | .05 | .02 |
| ❑ 280 Darrin Shannon | .05 | .02 |
| ❑ 281 Dominik Hasek | .50 | .23 |
| ❑ 282 Craig Ludwig | .05 | .02 |
| ❑ 283 Lyle Odelein | .05 | .02 |
| ❑ 284 Alexander Semak | .05 | .02 |
| ❑ 285 Richard Matvichuk | .05 | .02 |
| ❑ 286 Ken Daneyko | .05 | .02 |
| ❑ 287 Jan Erixon | .05 | .02 |
| ❑ 288 Robert Dirk | .05 | .02 |
| ❑ 289 Laurie Boschman | .05 | .02 |
| ❑ 290 Greg Paslawski | .05 | .02 |
| ❑ 291 Rob Zamuner | .05 | .02 |
| ❑ 292 Todd Gill | .05 | .02 |
| ❑ 293 Neil Brady | .05 | .02 |
| ❑ 294 Murray Baron | .05 | .02 |
| ❑ 295 Peter Taglianetti | .05 | .02 |
| ❑ 296 Wayne Presley | .05 | .02 |
| ❑ 297 Paul Broten | .05 | .02 |
| ❑ 298 Dana Murzyn | .05 | .02 |
| ❑ 299 J.J. Daigneault | .05 | .02 |
| ❑ 300 Wayne Gretzky | 1.25 | .55 |
| ❑ 301 Keith Acton | .05 | .02 |
| ❑ 302 Yuri Khmylev | .05 | .02 |
| ❑ 303 Frank Musil | .05 | .02 |
| ❑ 304 Bob Rouse | .05 | .02 |
| ❑ 305 Greg Gilbert | .05 | .02 |
| ❑ 306 Geoff Smith | .05 | .02 |
| ❑ 307 Adam Burt | .05 | .02 |
| ❑ 308 Phil Bourque | .05 | .02 |
| ❑ 309 Igor Kravchuk | .05 | .02 |
| ❑ 310 Steve Yzerman | .60 | .25 |
| ❑ 311 Darryl Sydor | .05 | .02 |
| ❑ 312 Tie Domi | .10 | .05 |
| ❑ 313 Sergei Zubov | .05 | .02 |
| ❑ 314 Chris Dahlquist | .05 | .02 |
| ❑ 315 Patrick Roy | 1.00 | .45 |
| ❑ 316 Mark Osborne | .05 | .02 |
| ❑ 317 Kelly Buchberger | .05 | .02 |
| ❑ 318 John LeClair | .30 | .14 |
| ❑ 319 Randy McKay | .05 | .02 |
| ❑ 320 Jody Hull | .05 | .02 |
| ❑ 321 Paul Stanton | .05 | .02 |
| ❑ 322 Steven Finn | .05 | .02 |
| ❑ 323 Rich Sutter | .05 | .02 |
| ❑ 324 Ray Whitney | .05 | .02 |
| ❑ 325 Kevin Stevens | .05 | .02 |
| ❑ 326 Valeri Kamensky | .10 | .05 |
| ❑ 327 Doug Zmolek | .05 | .02 |
| ❑ 328 Mikhail Tatarinov | .05 | .02 |
| ❑ 329 Ken Wregget | .10 | .05 |
| ❑ 330 Joe Juneau | .10 | .05 |
| ❑ 331 Teemu Selanne | .50 | .23 |
| ❑ 332 Trent Yawney | .05 | .02 |
| ❑ 333 Pavel Bure | .40 | .18 |
| ❑ 334 Jim Paek | .05 | .02 |
| ❑ 335 Brett Hull | .25 | .11 |
| ❑ 336 Tommy Soderstrom | .10 | .05 |
| ❑ 337 Grigori Panteleyev | .05 | .02 |
| ❑ 338 Kevin Todd | .05 | .02 |
| ❑ 339 Mark Janssens | .05 | .02 |
| ❑ 340 Rick Tocchet | .10 | .05 |
| ❑ 341 Wendell Young | .05 | .05 |

❑ 342 Cam Neely .10 .05
❑ 343 Dave Andreychuk .10 .05
❑ 344 Peter Bondra .20 .09
❑ 345 Pat LaFontaine .10 .05
❑ 346 Robb Stauber .10 .05
❑ 347 Brian Mullen .05 .02
❑ 348 Joe Murphy .05 .02
❑ 349 Pat Jablonski .10 .05
❑ 350 Mario Lemieux 1.00 .45
❑ 351 Sergei Bautin .05 .02
❑ 352 Claude Lapointe .05 .02
❑ 353 Dean Evason .05 .02
❑ 354 John Tucker .05 .02
❑ 355 Drake Berehowsky .05 .02
❑ 356 Gerald Diduck .05 .02
❑ 357 Todd Krygier .05 .02
❑ 358 Adrien Plavsic .05 .02
❑ 359 Sylvain Lefebvre .05 .02
❑ 360 Kay Whitmore .10 .05
❑ 361 Sheldon Kennedy .05 .02
❑ 362 Kris King .05 .02
❑ 363 Marc Bergevin .05 .02
❑ 364 Keith Primeau .10 .05
❑ 365 Jimmy Waite .10 .05
❑ 366 Dean Kennedy .05 .02
❑ 367 Mike Krushelnyski .05 .02
❑ 368 Ron Tugnutt .10 .05
❑ 369 Bob Beers .05 .02
❑ 370 Randy Burridge .05 .02
❑ 371 David Reid .05 .02
❑ 372 Frantisek Kucera .05 .02
❑ 373 Scott Pellerin .05 .02
❑ 374 Brad Dalgarno .05 .02
❑ 375 Martin Straka .05 .02
❑ 376 Scott Pearson .05 .02
❑ 377 Arturs Irbe .10 .05
❑ 378 Jiri Slegr .05 .02
❑ 379 Stephane Fiset .10 .05
❑ 380 Stu Barnes .05 .02
❑ 381 Ric Nattress .05 .02
❑ 382 Steven King .05 .02
❑ 383 Michael Nylander .05 .02
❑ 384 Keith Brown .05 .02
❑ 385 Gino Odjick .05 .02
❑ 386 Bryan Marchment .05 .02
❑ 387 Mike Foligno .05 .02
❑ 388 Zdeno Ciger .05 .02
❑ 389 Dave Taylor .10 .05
❑ 390 Mike Sullivan .05 .02
❑ 391 Shawn Chambers .05 .02
❑ 392 Brad Marsh .05 .02
❑ 393 Mike Hough .05 .02
❑ 394 Jeff Reese .05 .02
❑ 395 Bill Guerin .05 .02
❑ 396 Greg Hawgood .05 .02
❑ 397 Jim Sandlak .05 .02
❑ 398 Stephane Matteau .05 .02
❑ 399 John Blue .10 .05
❑ 400 Tony Twist .05 .02
❑ 401 Luciano Borsato .05 .02
❑ 402 Gerard Gallant .05 .02
❑ 403 Rick Tabaracci .10 .05
❑ 404 Nick Kypreos .05 .02
❑ 405 Marty McInnis .05 .02
❑ 406 Craig Wolanin .05 .02
❑ 407 Mark Lamb .05 .02
❑ 408 Martin Gelinas .05 .02
❑ 409 Ronnie Stern .05 .02
❑ 410 Ken Sutton .05 .02
❑ 411 Brian Noonan .05 .02
❑ 412 Stephane Quintal .05 .02
❑ 413 Rob Zettler .05 .02
❑ 414 Gino Cavallini .05 .02
❑ 415 Mark Hardy .05 .02
❑ 416 Jay Wells .05 .02
❑ 417 Keith Jones .05 .02
❑ 418 Dave McLlwain .05 .02
❑ 419 Frank Pietrangelo .10 .05
❑ 420 Jocelyn Lemieux .05 .02
❑ 421 Slava Kozlov .10 .05
❑ 422 Randy Moller .05 .02
❑ 423 Kevin Dahl .05 .02
❑ 424 Shjon Podein .05 .02
❑ 425 Shane Churla .05 .02
❑ 426 Guy Hebert .10 .05
❑ 427 Mikael Andersson .05 .02
❑ 428 Robert Kron .05 .02
❑ 429 Mike Eagles .05 .02
❑ 430 Alan May .05 .02
❑ 431 Ron Wilson .05 .02
❑ 432 Darcy Wakaluk .10 .05
❑ 433 Rob Ray .05 .02
❑ 434 Brent Ashton .05 .02
❑ 435 Jason Woolley .05 .02
❑ 436 Basil McRae .05 .02
❑ 437 Andre Racicot .10 .05
❑ 438 Brad Werenka .05 .02
❑ 439 Josef Beranek .05 .02
❑ 440 Dave Christian .05 .02
❑ 441 Theoren Fleury LBM .10 .05
❑ 442 Mark Recchi LBM .10 .05
❑ 443 Cliff Ronning LBM .05 .02
❑ 444 Tony Granato LBM .05 .02
❑ 445 John Vanbiesbrouck LBM .20 .09
❑ 446 Jari Kurri HL .10 .05
500th goal
❑ 447 Mike Gartner HL .10 .05
14th Straight
30-goal season
❑ 448 Steve Yzerman HL .20 .09
1,000th Point
❑ 449 Glenn Anderson HL .10 .05
1,000th Point
❑ 450 Washington Caps HL .05 .02
Al Iafrate
Sylvain Cote
Kevin Hatcher
Highest Scoring Defense
in NHL History
❑ 451 Luc Robitaille HL .10 .05
Most Goals by
left winger
❑ 452 Pittsburgh Penguins HL .05 .02
17-Game Winning Streak
❑ 453 Corey Hirsch .10 .05
❑ 454 Jesse Belanger .05 .02
❑ 455 Philippe Boucher .05 .02
❑ 456 Robert Lang .05 .02
❑ 457 Doug Barrault .05 .02
❑ 458 Steve Konowalchuk .05 .02
❑ 459 Oleg Petrov .05 .02
❑ 460 Niclas Andersson .05 .02
❑ 461 Milan Tichy .05 .02
❑ 462 Darrin Madeley .05 .02
❑ 463 Tyler Wright .05 .02
❑ 464 Sergei Krivokrasov .05 .02
❑ 465 Vladimir Vujtek .05 .02
❑ 466 Rick Knickle .10 .05
❑ 467 Gord Kruppke .05 .02
❑ 468 David Emma .05 .02
❑ 469 Scott Thomas .05 .02
❑ 470 Shawn Rivers .05 .02
❑ 471 Jason Bowen .05 .02
❑ 472 Bryan Smolinski .05 .02
❑ 473 Chris Simon .05 .02
❑ 474 Peter Ciavaglia .05 .02
❑ 475 Sergei Zholtok .05 .02
❑ 476 Radek Hamr .05 .02
❑ 477 Teemu Selanne .25 .11
Alexander Mogilny
SL Goals
❑ 478 Adam Oates SL .10 .05
Assists
❑ 479 Mario Lemieux SL .50 .23
Points
❑ 480 Mario Lemieux SL .50 .23
Plus/Minus
❑ 481 Dave Andreychuk SL .10 .05
Power-Play Goals
❑ 482 Phil Housley SL .10 .05
Defenseman Scoring
❑ 483 Tom Barrasso SL .10 .05
Wins
❑ 484 Felix Potvin SL .20 .09
GAA
❑ 485 Ed Belfour SL .20 .09
❑ 486 Sault Ste. Marie .10 .05
Greyhounds
Memorial Cup Champions
❑ 487 Montreal Canadiens .10 .05
Stanley Cup Champions
❑ 488 Anaheim Mighty Ducks .50 .23
Logo
❑ 489 Guy Hebert .10 .05
❑ 490 Sean Hill .05 .02
❑ 491 Florida Panthers Logo .50 .23
❑ 492 John Vanbiesbrouck .20 .09
❑ 493 Tom Fitzgerald .05 .02
❑ 494 Paul DiPietro .05 .02
❑ 495 David Volek .05 .02
❑ 496 Alexander Daigle 4.00 1.80
(Mail-in)
❑ 497 Shawn McEachern .05 .02
❑ 498 Rich Sutter .05 .02
❑ 499 Evgeny Davydov .05 .02
❑ 500 Sean Hill .05 .02
❑ 501 John Vanbiesbrouck .20 .09
❑ 502 Guy Hebert .10 .05
❑ 503 Scott Mellanby .10 .05
❑ 504 Ron Tugnutt .10 .05
❑ 505 Brian Skrudland .05 .02
❑ 506 Nelson Emerson .05 .02
❑ 507 Kevin Todd .05 .02
❑ 508 Terry Carkner .05 .02
❑ 509 Stephane Quintal .05 .02
❑ 510 Paul Stanton .05 .02
❑ 511 Terry Yake .05 .02
❑ 512 Brian Benning .05 .02
❑ 513 Brian Propp .05 .02
❑ 514 Steven King .05 .02
❑ 515 Joe Cirella .05 .02
❑ 516 Andy Moog .10 .05
❑ 517 Paul Ysebaert .05 .02
❑ 518 Petr Klima .05 .02
❑ 519 Corey Millen .05 .02
❑ 520 Phil Housley .10 .05
❑ 521 Craig Billington .10 .05
❑ 522 Jeff Norton .05 .02
❑ 523 Neil Wilkinson .05 .02
❑ 524 Doug Lidster .05 .02
❑ 525 Steve Larmer .10 .05
❑ 526 Jon Casey .10 .05
❑ 527 Brad McCrimmon .05 .02
❑ 528 Alexei Kasatonov .05 .02
❑ 529 Andrei Lomakin .05 .02
❑ 530 Daren Puppa .10 .05
❑ 531 Sergei Makarov .05 .02
❑ 532 Jim Sandlak .05 .02
❑ 533 Glenn Healy .10 .05
❑ 534 Martin Gelinas .05 .02
❑ 535 Igor Larionov .05 .02
❑ 536 Anatoli Semenov .05 .02
❑ 537 Mark Fitzpatrick .10 .05
❑ 538 Paul Cavallini .05 .02
❑ 539 Jimmy Waite .10 .05
❑ 540 Yves Racine .05 .02
❑ 541 Jeff Hackett .10 .05
❑ 542 Marty McSorley .05 .02
❑ 543 Scott Pearson .05 .02
❑ 544 Ron Hextall .10 .05
❑ 545 Gaetan Duchesne .05 .02
❑ 546 Jamie Baker .05 .02
❑ 547 Troy Loney .05 .02
❑ 548 Gord Murphy .05 .02
❑ 549 Bob Kudelski .05 .02
❑ 550 Dean Evason .05 .02
❑ 551 Mike Peluso .05 .02
❑ 552 Dave Poulin .05 .02
❑ 553 Randy Ladouceur .05 .02
❑ 554 Tom Fitzgerald .05 .02
❑ 555 Denis Savard .10 .05
❑ 556 Kelly Kisio .05 .02
❑ 557 Craig Simpson .05 .02
❑ 558 Stu Grimson .05 .02
❑ 559 Mike Hough .05 .02
❑ 560 Gerard Gallant .05 .02
❑ 561 Greg Gilbert .05 .02
❑ 562 Vladimir Ruzicka .05 .02
❑ 563 Jim Hrivnak .10 .05
❑ 564 Dave Lowry .05 .02
❑ 565 Todd Ewen .05 .02
❑ 566 Bob Errey .05 .02
❑ 567 Bryan Trottier .10 .05
❑ 568 Grant Ledyard .05 .02
❑ 569 Keith Brown .05 .02
❑ 570 Darren Turcotte .05 .02
❑ 571 Patrick Poulin .05 .02
❑ 572 Jimmy Carson .05 .02
❑ 573 Eric Weinrich .05 .02
❑ 574 James Patrick .05 .02
❑ 575 Bob Beers .05 .02
❑ 576 Chris Joseph .05 .02
❑ 577 Bryan Marchment .05 .02
❑ 578 Bob Carpenter .05 .02
❑ 579 Craig Muni .05 .02
❑ 580 Pat Elynuik .05 .02
❑ 581 Todd Elik .05 .02
❑ 582 Doug Brown .05 .02
❑ 583 Dave McLlwain .05 .02
❑ 584 Dave Tippett .05 .02
❑ 585 Jesse Belanger .05 .02
❑ 586 Chris Pronger .10 .05
❑ 587 Alexandre Daigle .05 .02
❑ 588 Cam Stewart .05 .02
❑ 589 Derek Plante .05 .02
❑ 590 Pat Peake .05 .02
❑ 591 Alexander Karpovtsev .05 .02
❑ 592 Rob Niedermayer .10 .05
❑ 593 Jocelyn Thibault .75 .35
❑ 594 Jason Arnott .60 .25
❑ 595 Mike Rathje .05 .02
❑ 596 Chris Gratton .10 .05
❑ 597 Markus Naslund .05 .02
❑ 598 Dmitri Filimonov .05 .02
❑ 599 Andrei Trefilov .05 .02
❑ 600 Michal Sykora .05 .02
❑ 601 Greg Johnson .05 .02
❑ 602 Mikael Renberg .20 .09
❑ 603 Alexei Yashin .10 .05
❑ 604 Damian Rhodes .10 .05
❑ 605 Jeff Shantz .05 .02
❑ 606 Brent Gretzky .05 .02
❑ 607 Boris Mironov .05 .02
❑ 608 Ted Drury .05 .02
❑ 609 Chris Osgood 1.25 .55
❑ 610 Jim Storm .05 .02
❑ 611 Dave Karpa .05 .02
❑ 612 Stewart Malgunas .05 .02
❑ 613 Jason Smith .05 .02
❑ 614 German Titov .05 .02
❑ 615 Patrick Carnback .05 .02
❑ 616 Jaroslav Modry .05 .02
❑ 617 Scott Levins .05 .02
❑ 618 Fred Brathwaite .10 .05
❑ 619 Ilya Byakin .05 .02
❑ 620 Jarkko Varvio .05 .02
❑ 621 Jim Montgomery .05 .02
❑ 622 Vesa Viitakoski .05 .02
❑ 623 Alexei Kudashov .05 .02
❑ 624 Pavol Demitra .05 .02
❑ 625 Iain Fraser .05 .02
❑ 626 Peter Popovic .05 .02
❑ 627 Kirk Maltby .05 .02
❑ 628 Garth Snow .10 .05
❑ 629 Peter White .05 .02
❑ 630 Mike McKee .05 .02
❑ 631 Darren McCarty .25 .11
❑ 632 Pat Neaton .05 .02
❑ 633 Sandy McCarthy .05 .02
❑ 634 Pierre Sevigny .05 .02
❑ 635 Matt Martin .05 .02
❑ 636 John Slaney .05 .02
❑ 637 Bob Corkum .05 .02
❑ 638 Jose Charbonneau .05 .02
❑ 639 Bill Houlder .05 .02
❑ 640 Warren Rychel .05 .02
❑ 641 Garry Valk .05 .02
❑ 642 Greg Hawgood .05 .02
❑ 643 Randy Gilhen .05 .02
❑ 644 Stu Barnes .05 .02
❑ 645 Fredrik Olausson .05 .02
❑ 646 Geoff Smith .05 .02
❑ 647 Mike Foligno .05 .02
❑ 648 Martin Brodeur .50 .23
❑ 649 Ryan McGill .05 .02
❑ 650 Jeff Reese .05 .02
❑ 651 Mike Sillinger .05 .02
❑ 652 Brent Severyn .05 .02
❑ 653 Rob Ramage .10 .05
❑ 654 Dixon Ward .05 .02
❑ 655 Danton Cole .05 .02
❑ 656 Viacheslav Butsayev .05 .02
❑ 657 Ron Wilson .05 .02
❑ 658 Paul Broten .05 .02
❑ 659 Mike Hudson .05 .02
❑ 660 Trevor Kidd .10 .05
❑ 661 Travis Green .10 .05
❑ 662 Wayne Gretzky 2.50 1.10
❑ NNO Alexandre Daigle .50 .23
Redemption card
❑ NNO Eric Lindros AS SP 30.00 13.50

## 1993-94 Score Gold

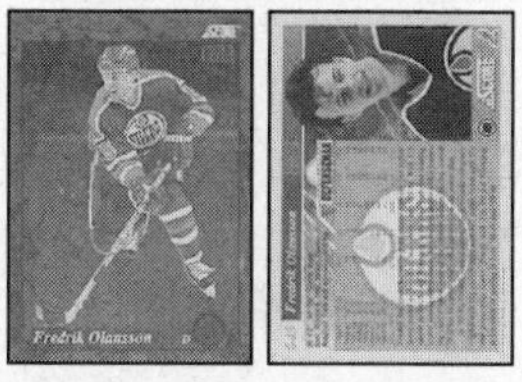

The 1993-94 Score Gold Rush set consists of 166 standard-size cards. The fronts are identical in design with the regular second-series Score cards, except for the metallic finish and gold marbleized borders. The backs are nearly identical to the regular issue cards, the Gold Rush logo at the top being the only difference. No Gold Rush parallels were produced for first series cards.

| | MINT | NRMT |
|---|---|---|
| COMPLETE SET (166) | 40.00 | 18.00 |
| COMMON CARD (497-662) | .15 | .07 |

*STARS: 3X TO 6X BASIC CARDS
*YOUNG STARS: 2X TO 4X BASIC CARDS

## 1993-94 Score Dream Team

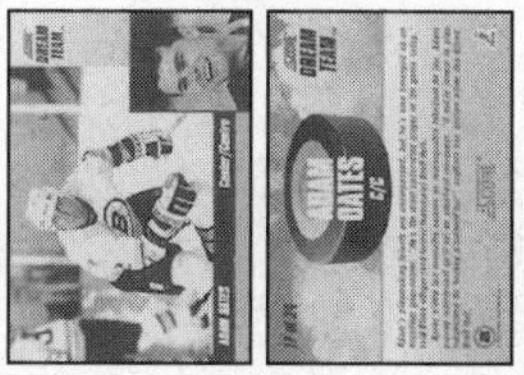

Randomly inserted at the rate of 1:24 first series Canadian packs, this 24 card standard-size set features Score's Dream Team selections. Horizontal fronts feature an action photo and a head shot at lower right. The player's name and position appear in beneath the large photo. The backs contain career highlights and are numbered "X of 24".

| | MINT | NRMT |
|---|---|---|
| COMPLETE SET (24) | 200.00 | 90.00 |
| COMMON CARD (1-24) | 2.50 | 1.10 |

❑ 1 Tom Barrasso 3.00 1.35
❑ 2 Patrick Roy 20.00 9.00
❑ 3 Chris Chelios 6.00 2.70
❑ 4 Al MacInnis 2.50 1.10
❑ 5 Scott Stevens 2.50 1.10
❑ 6 Brian Leetch 6.00 2.70
❑ 7 Ray Bourque 6.00 2.70
❑ 8 Paul Coffey 6.00 2.70
❑ 9 Al Iafrate 2.50 1.10
❑ 10 Mario Lemieux 20.00 9.00
❑ 11 Wayne Gretzky 25.00 11.00
❑ 12 Eric Lindros 20.00 9.00
❑ 13 Pat LaFontaine 3.00 1.35
❑ 14 Joe Sakic 10.00 4.50
❑ 15 Pierre Turgeon 3.00 1.35
❑ 16 Steve Yzerman 12.00 5.50
❑ 17 Adam Oates 3.00 1.35
❑ 18 Brett Hull 5.00 2.20
❑ 19 Pavel Bure 8.00 3.60
❑ 20 Alexander Mogilny 3.00 1.35
❑ 21 Teemu Selanne 8.00 3.60
❑ 22 Steve Larmer 2.50 1.10
❑ 23 Kevin Stevens 3.00 1.35
❑ 24 Luc Robitaille 3.00 1.35

## 1993-94 Score Dynamic Duos Canadian

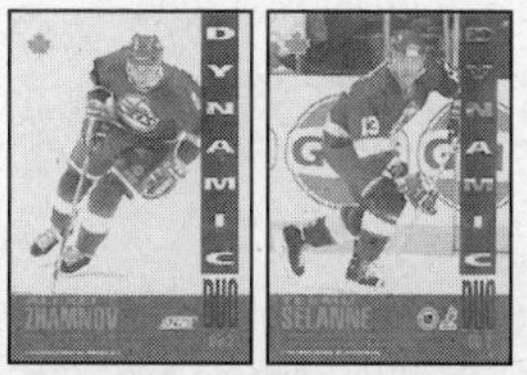

Randomly inserted at a rate of 1:48 Canadian second-series packs, this nine-card standard-size set highlights two team members on each card. Both the front and back of each card features a color player action shot. The player's name appears in red lettering within the team-colored bottom margin. The words "Dynamic Duos" appears in gold foil along the right side. A red maple leaf is placed at the upper left. A statement in English and French about the players begins on one side and is completed on the other. The cards are numbered on both the front and back with a "DD" prefix.

| | MINT | NRMT |
|---|---|---|
| COMPLETE SET (9) | 100.00 | 45.00 |
| COMMON CARD (1-9) | 4.00 | 1.80 |

❑ 1 Doug Gilmour 6.00 2.70
Dave Andreychuk
❑ 2 Teemu Selanne 15.00 6.75
Alexei Zhamnov
❑ 3 Alexandre Daigle 6.00 2.70
Alexei Yashin
❑ 4 Gary Roberts 4.00 1.80
Joe Nieuwendyk
❑ 5 Joe Sakic 15.00 6.75
Mats Sundin
❑ 6 Brian Bellows 4.00 1.80
Kirk Muller
❑ 7 Shayne Corson 10.00 4.50
Jason Arnott
❑ 8 Mario Lemieux 40.00 18.00
Kevin Stevens
❑ 9 Pierre Turgeon 6.00 2.70
Derek King

## 1993-94 Score Dynamic Duos U.S.

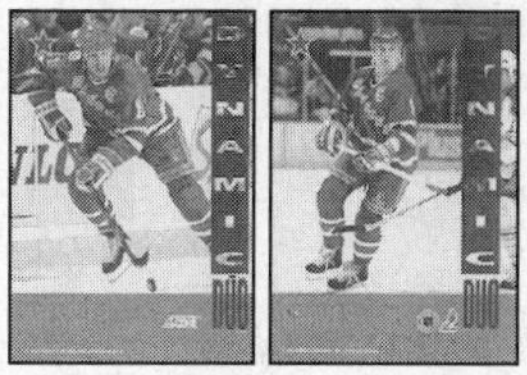

Randomly inserted at a rate of 1:48 U.S. second series packs, this nine-card standard-size set highlights two team members on each card. Both the front and back of each card features a color player action shot. The player's name appears in red lettering within the team-colored bottom margin. The words "Dynamic Duos" appear in gold foil along the right side. A blue star is placed at the upper left. A statement about the players begins on one side and is completed on the other. The cards are numbered on both the front and back with a "DD" prefix.

| | MINT | NRMT |
|---|---|---|
| COMPLETE SET (9) | 150.00 | 70.00 |
| COMMON CARD (1-9) | 4.00 | 1.80 |

❑ 1 Mark Recchi 30.00 13.50
Eric Lindros
❑ 2 Pat LaFontaine 6.00 2.70
Alexander Mogilny
❑ 3 Adam Oates 6.00 2.70
Joe Juneau
❑ 4 Brett Hull 12.00 5.50
Craig Janney
❑ 5 Mark Messier 12.00 5.50
Adam Graves
❑ 6 Jeremy Roenick 8.00 3.60
Joe Murphy
❑ 7 Jari Kurri 60.00 27.00
Wayne Gretzky
❑ 8 Sergei Makarov 4.00 1.80
Igor Larionov
❑ 9 Steve Yzerman 40.00 18.00
Sergei Fedorov

## 1993-94 Score Franchise

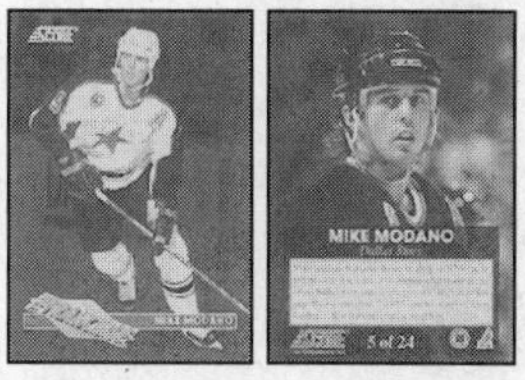

Randomly inserted at a rate of 1:24 U.S. first series packs, this 24 card standard-size set features borderless color player action shots on the fronts, the backgrounds of which are ghosted and darkened. The player's name appears in a team color-coded stripe near the bottom. The Franchise logo is displayed in the lower left. The back sports another full-bleed color player shot, with his name and team shown within a darkened and ghosted rectangle near the bottom. Within this rectangle, a smaller white rectangle carries the player's career highlights. The cards are numbered "X of 24" on the back.

| | MINT | NRMT |
|---|---|---|
| COMPLETE SET (24) | 225.00 | 100.00 |
| COMMON CARD (1-24) | 2.50 | 1.10 |

❑ 1 Ray Bourque 6.00 2.70
❑ 2 Pat LaFontaine 3.00 1.35
❑ 3 Al MacInnis 3.00 1.35
❑ 4 Jeremy Roenick 6.00 2.70
❑ 5 Mike Modano 5.00 2.20

❑ 6 Steve Yzerman 12.00 5.50
❑ 7 Bill Ranford 3.00 1.35
❑ 8 Sean Burke 3.00 1.35
❑ 9 Wayne Gretzky 25.00 11.00
❑ 10 Patrick Roy 20.00 9.00
❑ 11 Scott Stevens 2.50 1.10
❑ 12 Pierre Turgeon 3.00 1.35
❑ 13 Brian Leetch 6.00 2.70
❑ 14 Peter Sidorkiewicz 3.00 1.35
❑ 15 Eric Lindros 20.00 9.00
❑ 16 Mario Lemieux 20.00 9.00
❑ 17 Joe Sakic 10.00 4.50
❑ 18 Brett Hull 5.00 2.20
❑ 19 Pat Falloon 2.50 1.10
❑ 20 Brian Bradley 2.50 1.10
❑ 21 Doug Gilmour 3.00 1.35
❑ 22 Pavel Bure 8.00 3.60
❑ 23 Kevin Hatcher 2.50 1.10
❑ 24 Teemu Selanne 8.00 3.60

## 1993-94 Score International Stars

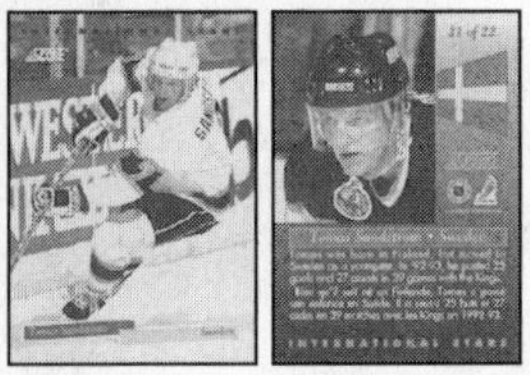

Inserted one per series one jumbo pack, this 22-card standard-size set highlights some of the NHL's hottest international stars. The fronts feature full-bleed color action shots, with the player's name and nationality appearing in a banner at the bottom that bears the colors of his national flag. The words "International Stars" in gold foil are printed at the top. On purplish backgrounds, the backs carry a color headshot at the upper left, with the player's national flag to the right and his name and country in his flag's colors below. Career highlights at the bottom round out the card. The cards are numbered on the back as "X of 22." Multipliers to determine values for the French version can be found in the header below.

| | MINT | NRMT |
|---|---|---|
| COMPLETE SET (22) | 40.00 | 18.00 |
| COMMON CARD (1-22) | 1.00 | .45 |

*CDN VERSION:1X TO 1.25X U.S. VERSION

❑ 1 Pavel Bure 2.00 .90
❑ 2 Teemu Selanne 2.00 .90
❑ 3 Sergei Fedorov 2.00 .90
❑ 4 Peter Bondra 2.00 .90
❑ 5 Tommy Soderstrom 1.50 .70
❑ 6 Robert Reichel 1.00 .45
❑ 7 Jari Kurri 1.50 .70
❑ 8 Alexander Mogilny 1.50 .70
❑ 9 Jaromir Jagr 2.00 .90
❑ 10 Mats Sundin 1.50 .70
❑ 11 Uwe Krupp 1.00 .45
❑ 12 Nikolai Borschevsky 1.00 .45
❑ 13 Ulf Dahlen 1.00 .45
❑ 14 Alexander Semak 1.00 .45
❑ 15 Michal Pivonka 1.00 .45
❑ 16 Sergei Nemchinov 1.00 .45
❑ 17 Darius Kasparaitis 1.00 .45
❑ 18 Sandis Ozolinsh 1.50 .70
❑ 19 Alexei Kovalev 1.50 .70
❑ 20 Dimitri Khristich 1.50 .70
❑ 21 Tomas Sandstrom 1.00 .45
❑ 22 Petr Nedved 1.50 .70

## 1994-95 Score Hobby Samples

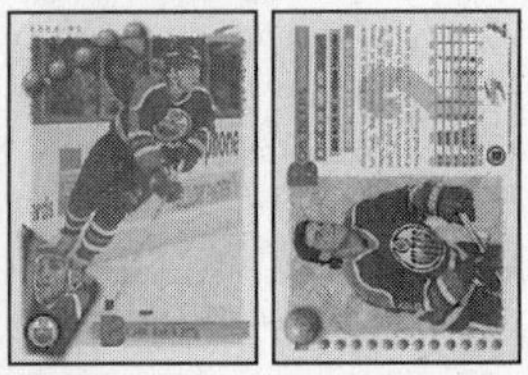

Issued in packs of 12, the 1994 Score hockey Hobby Sample cards measure the standard-size and preview the 1994 Score hockey issue. The top right and left corners have been cut off of some cards. The fronts feature color action player photos with white borders, and a small headshot in the left bottom corner. The player's name appears in colorful letters at the bottom of the picture. The horizontal backs carry another player photo on the left, along with the player's name, biography, career highlights and stats on the right.

| | MINT | NRMT |
|---|---|---|
| COMPLETE SEALED SET (12) | 7.00 | 3.10 |
| COMMON CARD | .05 | .02 |

❑ 1 Eric Lindros .35 .16
❑ 2 Pat LaFontaine .05 .02
❑ 3 Wendel Clark .05 .02
❑ 4 Cam Neely .05 .02
❑ 5 Larry Murphy .05 .02
❑ 6 Patrick Poulin .05 .02
❑ 7 Bob Beers .05 .02
❑ 254 Jason Arnott .10 .05
❑ C13 Darius Kasparaitis 4.00 1.80
Check-It
❑ TF16 Alexandre Daigle 3.00 1.35
The Franchise
❑ NNO Pro Debut Rookie 1.00 .45
Redemption Card
❑ NNO Title Card 1.00 .45

## 1994-95 Score

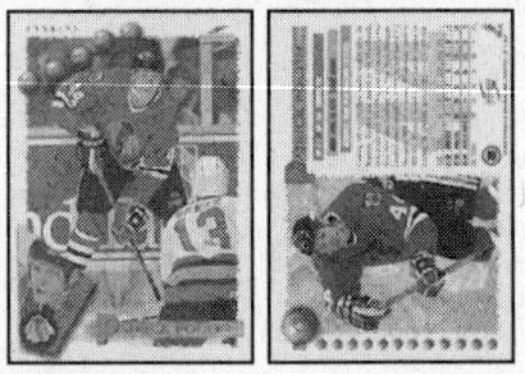

This 275-card standard-size set was issued in one series and does not have a comprehensive player selection. Due to the NHL lock-out, series two was replaced on the production schedule by Select; therefore many stars such as Patrick Roy and Wayne Gretzky were not featured in this set. The unique design features a full color player photo, surrounded by a white border. The Score logo appears in the top right corner, while a player head shot and team logo dominate the lower left. The upper right corner displays five globes; player name appears in a multi-hued strip along the card bottom. Cards were issued in 14-card U.S. and Canadian packs that included one Gold Line parallel card. Retail jumbo packs contained 30 cards and two Gold Line cards for $1.79. Subsets include World Junior Championships (201-215), Season Highlights (241-247), Young Stars (248-262), and Team Checklists (263-275). The only Rookie Card in the set features Mariusz Czerkawski.

| | MINT | NRMT |
|---|---|---|
| COMPLETE SET (275) | 12.00 | 5.50 |
| COMMON CARD (1-275) | .05 | .02 |

❑ 1 Eric Lindros .75 .35
❑ 2 Pat LaFontaine .10 .05
❑ 3 Wendel Clark .10 .05
❑ 4 Cam Neely .10 .05
❑ 5 Larry Murphy .10 .05
❑ 6 Patrick Poulin .05 .02
❑ 7 Bob Beers .05 .02
❑ 8 James Patrick .05 .02
❑ 9 Gino Odjick .05 .02
❑ 10 Arturs Irbe .10 .05
❑ 11 Darius Kasparaitis .05 .02
❑ 12 Peter Bondra .20 .09
❑ 13 Garth Butcher .05 .02
❑ 14 Sergei Nemchinov .05 .02
❑ 15 Doug Brown .05 .02
❑ 16 Anatoli Semenov .05 .02
❑ 17 Mike McPhee .05 .02
❑ 18 Joel Otto .05 .02
❑ 19 Dino Ciccarelli .10 .05
❑ 20 Marty McSorley .05 .02
❑ 21 Ron Tugnutt .10 .05
❑ 22 Scott Niedermayer .05 .02
❑ 23 John Tucker .05 .02
❑ 24 Norm Maciver .05 .02
❑ 25 Kevin Miller .05 .02
❑ 26 Garry Galley .05 .02
❑ 27 Ted Donato .05 .02
❑ 28 Bob Kudelski .05 .02
❑ 29 Craig Muni .05 .02
❑ 30 Nikolai Borschevsky .05 .02
❑ 31 Tom Barrasso .10 .05
❑ 32 Brent Sutter .05 .02
❑ 33 Igor Kravchuk .05 .02
❑ 34 Andrew Cassels .05 .02
❑ 35 Jyrki Lumme .05 .02
❑ 36 Sandis Ozolinsh .10 .05
❑ 37 Steve Thomas .05 .02
❑ 38 Dave Poulin .05 .02
❑ 39 Andrei Kovalenko .05 .02
❑ 40 Steve Larmer .10 .05
❑ 41 Nelson Emerson .05 .02
❑ 42 Guy Hebert .10 .05
❑ 43 Russ Courtnall .05 .02
❑ 44 Gary Suter .05 .02
❑ 45 Steve Chiasson .05 .02
❑ 46 Guy Carbonneau .05 .02
❑ 47 Rob Blake .05 .02
❑ 48 Roman Hamrlik .10 .05
❑ 49 Valeri Zelepukin .05 .02
❑ 50 Mark Recchi .10 .05
❑ 51 Darrin Madeley .05 .02
❑ 52 Steve Duchesne .05 .02
❑ 53 Brian Skrudland .05 .02
❑ 54 Craig Simpson .05 .02
❑ 55 Todd Gill .05 .02
❑ 56 Dirk Graham .05 .02
❑ 57 Joe Mullen .10 .05
❑ 58 Doug Weight .10 .05
❑ 59 Michael Nylander .05 .02
❑ 60 Kirk McLean .10 .05
❑ 61 Igor Larionov .05 .02
❑ 62 Vladimir Malakhov .05 .02
❑ 63 Kelly Miller .05 .02
❑ 64 Curtis Leschyshyn .05 .02
❑ 65 Thomas Steen .05 .02
❑ 66 Jeff Beukeboom .05 .02
❑ 67 Troy Loney .05 .02
❑ 68 Mark Tinordi .05 .02
❑ 69 Theoren Fleury .10 .05
❑ 70 Slava Kozlov .10 .05
❑ 71 Tony Granato .05 .02
❑ 72 Daren Puppa .10 .05
❑ 73 Brian Bellows .05 .02
❑ 74 Bernie Nicholls .05 .02
❑ 75 Rick Zombo .05 .02
❑ 76 Brad Shaw .05 .02
❑ 77 Josef Beranek .05 .02
❑ 78 Dominik Hasek .40 .18
❑ 79 Steve Leach .05 .02
❑ 80 David Reid .05 .02
❑ 81 Dave Lowry .05 .02
❑ 82 Martin Straka .05 .02
❑ 83 Dave Ellett .05 .02
❑ 84 Sean Burke .10 .05
❑ 85 Craig MacTavish .05 .02
❑ 86 Cliff Ronning .05 .02
❑ 87 Bob Errey .05 .02
❑ 88 Marty McInnis .05 .02
❑ 89 Mats Sundin .10 .05
❑ 90 Randy Burridge .05 .02
❑ 91 Teppo Numminen .05 .02
❑ 92 Tony Amonte .10 .05
❑ 93 Terry Yake .05 .02
❑ 94 Paul Cavallini .05 .02
❑ 95 German Titov .05 .02
❑ 96 Vladimir Konstantinov .05 .02
❑ 97 Darryl Sydor .05 .02
❑ 98 Chris Joseph .05 .02
❑ 99 Corey Millen .05 .02
❑ 100 Brett Hull .30 .14
❑ 101 Don Sweeney .05 .02
❑ 102 Scott Mellanby .10 .05
❑ 103 Mathieu Schneider .05 .02
❑ 104 Brad May .10 .05
❑ 105 Dominic Roussel .10 .05
❑ 106 Jamie Macoun .05 .02
❑ 107 Bryan Marchment .05 .02
❑ 108 Shawn McEachern .05 .02
❑ 109 Murray Craven .05 .02
❑ 110 Eric Desjardins .05 .02
❑ 111 Jon Casey .10 .05
❑ 112 Mike Gartner .10 .05
❑ 113 Neal Broten .10 .05
❑ 114 Jari Kurri .10 .05
❑ 115 Bruce Driver .05 .02
❑ 116 Patrick Flatley .05 .02
❑ 117 Gord Murphy .05 .02
❑ 118 Dimitri Khristich .05 .02
❑ 119 Nicklas Lidstrom .10 .05
❑ 120 Al MacInnis .10 .05
❑ 121 Steve Smith .05 .02
❑ 122 Zdeno Ciger .05 .02
❑ 123 Tie Domi .10 .05
❑ 124 Joe Juneau .10 .05
❑ 125 Todd Elik .05 .02
❑ 126 Stephane Fiset .10 .05
❑ 127 Craig Janney .10 .05
❑ 128 Stephan Lebeau .05 .02
❑ 129 Richard Smehlik .05 .02
❑ 130 Mike Richter .20 .09
❑ 131 Danton Cole .05 .02
❑ 132 Rod Brind'Amour .10 .05
❑ 133 Dave Archibald .05 .02
❑ 134 Dana Murzyn .05 .02
❑ 135 Jaromir Jagr .60 .25
❑ 136 Esa Tikkanen .05 .02
❑ 137 Rob Pearson .05 .02
❑ 138 Stu Barnes .05 .02
❑ 139 Frank Musil .05 .02
❑ 140 Ron Hextall .10 .05
❑ 141 Adam Oates .10 .05
❑ 142 Ken Daneyko .05 .02
❑ 143 Dale Hunter .05 .02
❑ 144 Geoff Sanderson .10 .05
❑ 145 Kelly Hrudey .10 .05
❑ 146 Kirk Muller .05 .02
❑ 147 Fredrik Olausson .05 .02
❑ 148 Derian Hatcher .05 .02
❑ 149 Ed Belfour .20 .09
❑ 150 Steve Yzerman .60 .25
❑ 151 Adam Foote .05 .02
❑ 152 Pat Falloon .05 .02
❑ 153 Shawn Chambers .05 .02
❑ 154 Alexei Zhamnov .10 .05
❑ 155 Brendan Shanahan .40 .18
❑ 156 Ulf Samuelsson .05 .02
❑ 157 Donald Audette .10 .05
❑ 158 Bob Corkum .05 .02
❑ 159 Joe Nieuwendyk .10 .05
❑ 160 Felix Potvin .20 .09
❑ 161 Geoff Courtnall .05 .02
❑ 162 Yves Racine .05 .02
❑ 163 Tom Fitzgerald .05 .02
❑ 164 Adam Graves .10 .05
❑ 165 Vincent Damphousse .10 .05
❑ 166 Pierre Turgeon .10 .05
❑ 167 Craig Billington .10 .05
❑ 168 Al Iafrate .05 .02
❑ 169 Darren Turcotte .05 .02
❑ 170 Joe Murphy .05 .02
❑ 171 Alexei Zhitnik .05 .02
❑ 172 John MacLean .10 .05
❑ 173 Andy Moog .10 .05
❑ 174 Shayne Corson .10 .05
❑ 175 Ray Sheppard .10 .05
❑ 176 Johan Garpenlov .05 .02
❑ 177 Ron Sutter .05 .02
❑ 178 Teemu Selanne .40 .18
❑ 179 Brian Bradley .05 .02
❑ 180 Ray Bourque .20 .09
❑ 181 Curtis Joseph .20 .09
❑ 182 Kevin Stevens .05 .02
❑ 183 Alexei Kasatonov .05 .02
❑ 184 Brian Leetch .20 .09
❑ 185 Doug Gilmour .20 .09
❑ 186 Gary Roberts .05 .02
❑ 187 Mike Keane .05 .02
❑ 188 Mike Modano .30 .14
❑ 189 Chris Chelios .20 .09
❑ 190 Pavel Bure .40 .18
❑ 191 Bob Essensa .10 .05
❑ 192 Dale Hawerchuk .10 .05
❑ 193 Scott Stevens .10 .05
❑ 194 Claude Lapointe .05 .02
❑ 195 Scott Lachance .05 .02
❑ 196 Gaetan Duchesne .05 .02
❑ 197 Kevin Dineen .05 .02
❑ 198 Doug Bodger .05 .02
❑ 199 Mike Ridley .05 .02
❑ 200 Alexander Mogilny .10 .05
❑ 201 Jamie Storr .10 .05
❑ 202 Jason Botterill .05 .02
❑ 203 Jeff Friesen .10 .05
❑ 204 Todd Harvey .05 .02
❑ 205 Brendan Witt .05 .02
❑ 206 Jason Allison .05 .02
❑ 207 Aaron Gavey .05 .02
❑ 208 Deron Quint .05 .02
❑ 209 Jason Bonsignore .05 .02
❑ 210 Richard Park .05 .02
❑ 211 Jamie Langenbrunner .05 .02
❑ 212 Vadim Sharifjanov .10 .05
❑ 213 Alexander Kharlamov .05 .02
❑ 214 Oleg Tverdovsky .10 .05
❑ 215 Valeri Bure .10 .05
❑ 216 Dane Jackson .05 .02
❑ 217 Josef Cierny .05 .02
❑ 218 Yevgeny Namestnikov .05 .02
❑ 219 Dan Laperriere .05 .02
❑ 220 Fred Knipscheer .05 .02
❑ 221 Yan Kaminsky .05 .02
❑ 222 David Roberts .05 .02
❑ 223 Derek Mayer .05 .02
❑ 224 Jamie McLennan .05 .02
❑ 225 Kevin Smyth .05 .02
❑ 226 Todd Marchant .05 .02
❑ 227 Mariusz Czerkawski .05 .02
❑ 228 John Lilley .05 .02
❑ 229 Aaron Ward .05 .02
❑ 230 Brian Savage .05 .02
❑ 231 Jason Allison .05 .02
❑ 232 Maxim Bets .05 .02
❑ 233 Ted Crowley .05 .02
❑ 234 Todd Simon .05 .02
❑ 235 Zigmund Palffy .10 .05
❑ 236 Rene Corbet .05 .02
❑ 237 Mike Peca .05 .02
❑ 238 Dwayne Norris .05 .02
❑ 239 Andrei Nazarov .05 .02
❑ 240 David Sacco .05 .02
❑ 241 Wayne Gretzky 1.00 .45
❑ 242 Mike Gartner .10 .05
❑ 243 Dino Ciccarelli .10 .05
❑ 244 Ron Francis .10 .05
❑ 245 Bernie Nicholls .05 .02
❑ 246 Dino Ciccarelli .10 .05
❑ 247 Brian Propp .05 .02
❑ 248 Alexandre Daigle .05 .02
❑ 249 Mikael Renberg .10 .05
❑ 250 Jocelyn Thibault .20 .09
❑ 251 Derek Plante .05 .02
❑ 252 Chris Pronger .10 .05
❑ 253 Alexei Yashin .10 .05
❑ 254 Jason Arnott .10 .05
❑ 255 Boris Mironov .05 .02
❑ 256 Chris Osgood .30 .14
❑ 257 Jesse Belanger .05 .02
❑ 258 Darren McCarty .05 .02
❑ 259 Trevor Kidd .10 .05
❑ 260 Oleg Petrov .05 .02
❑ 261 Mike Rathje .05 .02
❑ 262 John Slaney .05 .02
❑ 263 Anaheim Mighty Ducks .05 .02
Boston Bruins CL
❑ 264 Buffalo Sabres .05 .02
Calgary Flames CL
❑ 265 Chicago Blackhawks .05 .02
Dallas Stars CL
❑ 266 Detroit Red Wings .05 .02
Edmonton Oilers CL
❑ 267 Florida Panthers .05 .02
Hartford Whalers CL
❑ 268 Los Angeles Kings .05 .02
Montreal Canadiens CL
❑ 269 New Jersey Devils .05 .02
New York Islanders CL
❑ 270 New York Rangers .05 .02
Ottawa Senators CL
❑ 271 Philadelphia Flyers .05 .02
Pittsburgh Penguins CL
❑ 272 Quebec Nordiques .05 .02
St.Louis Blues CL
❑ 273 San Jose Sharks .05 .02
Tampa Bay Lightning CL
❑ 274 Toronto Maple Leafs .05 .02
Vancouver Canucks CL
❑ 275 Washington Capitals .05 .02
Winnipeg Jets CL

## 1994-95 Score Gold

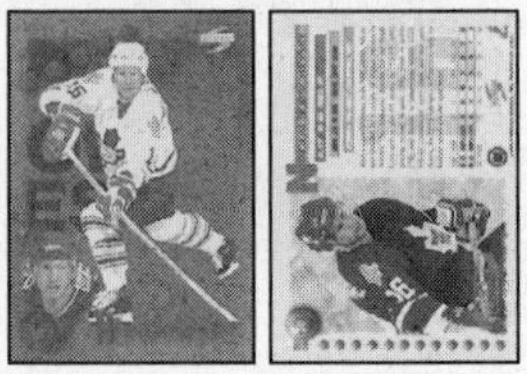

These parallel cards were issued one per regular or jumbo pack. These differ from the basic cards through the usage of a gold foil coating. In a unique offer designed to promote set building, Score offered collectors who submitted complete team sets a limited Platinum foil team set in return. Redeemed gold cards were returned with a Pinnacle brand logo hole-punched through them. Hole-punched gold cards have a value of roughly 2X to 3X that of the basic cards.

| | MINT | NRMT |
|---|---|---|
| COMPLETE SET (275) | 90.00 | 40.00 |
| COMMON CARD (1-275) | .25 | .11 |

*STARS: 5X TO 10X BASIC CARDS
*YOUNG STARS: 3X TO 7X BASIC CARDS

## 1994-95 Score Platinum Team Sets

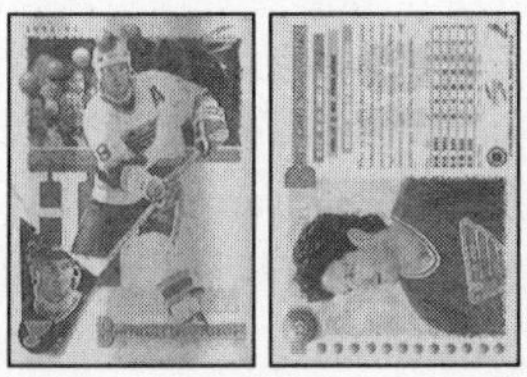

This set was a partial parallel set to Score. Platinum cards could only be obtained through a mail-in offer via the trading of complete Score Gold Line team sets. The cards from the World Junior subset (201-215) and Team Checklists (263-275) were not available through this offer. The cards feature a platinum reflective mirror finish. Because the cards are almost invariably traded in complete team set form, that is how they are listed below. Score reportedly made 1,994 of each team set available for redemption. Pinnacle officials report very few sets were redeemed.

| | MINT | NRMT |
|---|---|---|
| COMPLETE SET (247) | 400.00 | 180.00 |
| COMMON CARD (1-200/216-262) | 2.00 | .90 |

*STARS: 20X TO 40X BASIC CARDS
*YOUNG STARS: 12.5X TO 25X BASIC CARDS

| | MINT | NRMT |
|---|---|---|
| COMPLETE BLACKHAWKS (9) | 30.00 | 13.50 |
| COMPLETE BLUES (10) | 30.00 | 13.50 |
| COMPLETE BRUINS (11) | 25.00 | 11.00 |
| COMPLETE CANADIENS (10) | 25.00 | 11.00 |
| COMPLETE CANUCKS (11) | 40.00 | 18.00 |
| COMPLETE CAPITALS (10) | 15.00 | 6.75 |
| COMPLETE DEVILS (9) | 15.00 | 6.75 |
| COMPLETE FLAMES (10) | 25.00 | 11.00 |
| COMPLETE FLYERS (9) | 60.00 | 27.00 |
| COMPLETE ISLANDERS (11) | 15.00 | 6.75 |
| COMPLETE JETS (6) | 25.00 | 11.00 |
| COMPLETE KINGS (8) | 80.00 | 36.00 |
| COMPLETE LIGHTNING (7) | 15.00 | 6.75 |
| COMPLETE MAPLE LEAFS (11) | 30.00 | 13.50 |
| COMPLETE MIGHTY DUCKS (8) | 15.00 | 6.75 |
| COMPLETE NORDIQUES (11) | 30.00 | 13.50 |
| COMPLETE OILERS (10) | 25.00 | 11.00 |
| COMPLETE PANTHERS (8) | 15.00 | 6.75 |
| COMPLETE PENGUINS (10) | 35.00 | 16.00 |
| COMPLETE RANGERS (8) | 30.00 | 13.50 |
| COMPLETE RED WINGS (13) | 40.00 | 18.00 |
| COMPLETE SABRES (12) | 20.00 | 9.00 |
| COMPLETE SENATORS (8) | 15.00 | 6.75 |
| COMPLETE SHARKS (10) | 20.00 | 9.00 |
| COMPLETE STARS (8) | 15.00 | 6.75 |
| COMPLETE WHALERS (9) | 15.00 | 6.75 |

## 1994-95 Score Check It

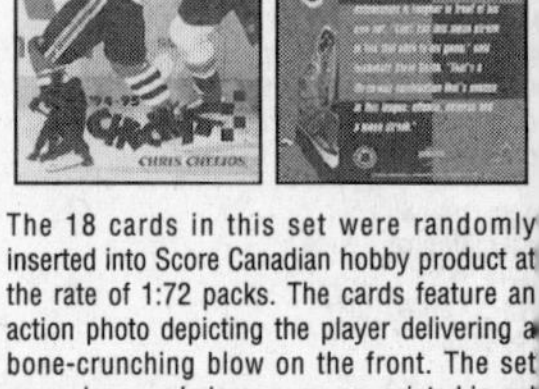

The 18 cards in this set were randomly inserted into Score Canadian hobby product at the rate of 1:72 packs. The cards feature an action photo depicting the player delivering a bone-crunching blow on the front. The set name, logo, and player name are printed in red foil along the bottom. Card backs are numbered with a CI prefix. The card back has a

small color photo on the left border. The rest of the card back has a black and red checkerboard design, over-written with player information.

| | MINT | NRMT |
|---|---|---|
| COMPLETE SET (18) | 400.00 | 180.00 |
| COMMON CARD (CI1-CI18) | 12.00 | 5.50 |
| ❑ CI1 Eric Lindros | 150.00 | 70.00 |
| ❑ CI2 Scott Stevens | 12.00 | 5.50 |
| ❑ CI3 Darius Kasparaitis | 12.00 | 5.50 |
| ❑ CI4 Kevin Stevens | 12.00 | 5.50 |
| ❑ CI5 Brendan Shanahan | 60.00 | 27.00 |
| ❑ CI6 Jeremy Roenick | 25.00 | 11.00 |
| ❑ CI7 Ulf Samuelsson | 12.00 | 5.50 |
| ❑ CI8 Cam Neely | 20.00 | 9.00 |
| ❑ CI9 Adam Graves | 20.00 | 9.00 |
| ❑ CI10 Kirk Muller | 12.00 | 5.50 |
| ❑ CI11 Rick Tocchet | 20.00 | 9.00 |
| ❑ CI12 Gary Roberts | 12.00 | 5.50 |
| ❑ CI13 Wendel Clark | 20.00 | 9.00 |
| ❑ CI14 Keith Tkachuk | 40.00 | 18.00 |
| ❑ CI15 Theoren Fleury | 20.00 | 9.00 |
| ❑ CI16 Claude Lemieux | 20.00 | 9.00 |
| ❑ CI17 Chris Chelios | 25.00 | 11.00 |
| ❑ CI18 Pat Verbeek | 12.00 | 5.50 |

## 1994-95 Score Dream Team

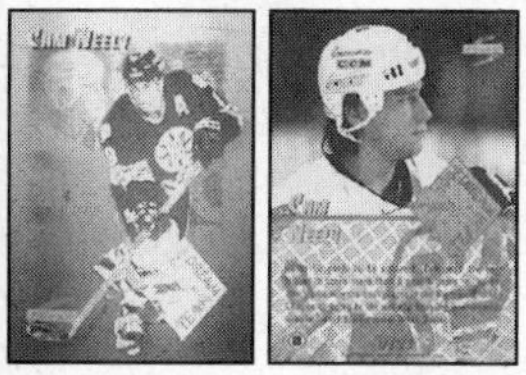

The 24 cards in this set were randomly inserted into all Score U.S. product at the rate of 1:36 packs. The cards feature a holographic mage on the front which must be angled oroperly in the light, along with player name and the 1994 Dream Team logo. A full color ohoto and player information appear on the oack. The cards are numbered with an "DT" orefix.

| | MINT | NRMT |
|---|---|---|
| COMPLETE SET (24) | 150.00 | 70.00 |
| COMMON CARD (DT1-DT24) | 2.50 | 1.10 |
| DT1 Patrick Roy | 20.00 | 9.00 |
| DT2 Felix Potvin | 5.00 | 2.20 |
| DT3 Ray Bourque | 5.00 | 2.20 |
| DT4 Brian Leetch | 5.00 | 2.20 |
| DT5 Scott Stevens | 2.50 | 1.10 |
| DT6 Paul Coffey | 5.00 | 2.20 |
| DT7 Al MacInnis | 2.50 | 1.10 |
| DT8 Chris Chelios | 5.00 | 2.20 |
| DT9 Adam Graves | 2.50 | 1.10 |
| DT10 Luc Robitaille | 2.50 | 1.10 |
| DT11 Dave Andreychuk | 2.50 | 1.10 |
| DT12 Sergei Fedorov | 10.00 | 4.50 |
| DT13 Doug Gilmour | 4.00 | 1.80 |
| DT14 Wayne Gretzky | 30.00 | 13.50 |
| DT15 Mario Lemieux | 25.00 | 11.00 |
| DT16 Mark Messier | 6.00 | 2.70 |
| DT17 Mike Modano | 6.00 | 2.70 |
| DT18 Jeremy Roenick | 5.00 | 2.20 |
| DT19 Eric Lindros | 15.00 | 6.75 |
| DT20 Steve Yzerman | 15.00 | 6.75 |
| DT21 Alexandre Daigle | 4.00 | 1.80 |
| DT22 Brett Hull | 6.00 | 2.70 |
| DT23 Cam Neely | 4.00 | 1.80 |
| DT24 Pavel Bure | 10.00 | 4.50 |

## 994-95 Score Franchise

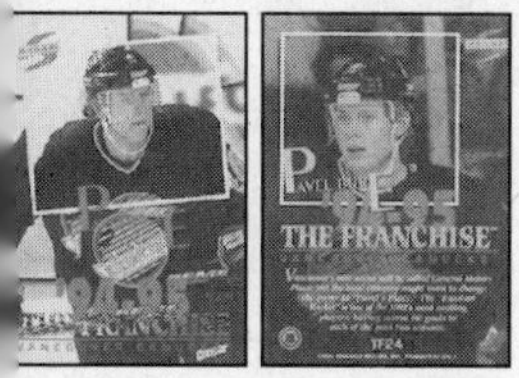

e 26 cards in this set were randomly serted into Score U.S. hobby product at the e of 1:72 packs. The cards feature red nting and gold foil on the card face. A rgely black and white action shot, with the ayer's head and torso punched out in full lor, dominates the card front. Cards are mbered with a TF prefix on the back. The cks also feature a color photo with text ormation.

| | MINT | NRMT |
|---|---|---|
| MPLETE SET (26) | 550.00 | 250.00 |
| MMON CARD (TF1-TF26) | 5.00 | 2.20 |
| TF1 Guy Hebert | 10.00 | 4.50 |
| TF2 Cam Neely | 10.00 | 4.50 |
| TF3 Pat LaFontaine | 10.00 | 4.50 |
| TF4 Theoren Fleury | 10.00 | 4.50 |
| TF5 Jeremy Roenick | 15.00 | 6.75 |
| TF6 Mike Modano | 20.00 | 9.00 |
| ❑ TF7 Sergei Fedorov | 30.00 | 13.50 |
| ❑ TF8 Jason Arnott | 10.00 | 4.50 |
| ❑ TF9 John Vanbiesbrouck | 25.00 | 11.00 |
| ❑ TF10 Geoff Sanderson | 10.00 | 4.50 |
| ❑ TF11 Wayne Gretzky | 100.00 | 45.00 |
| ❑ TF12 Patrick Roy | 75.00 | 34.00 |
| ❑ TF13 Scott Stevens | 5.00 | 2.20 |
| ❑ TF14 Pierre Turgeon | 10.00 | 4.50 |
| ❑ TF15 Mark Messier | 20.00 | 9.00 |
| ❑ TF16 Alexandre Daigle | 10.00 | 4.50 |
| ❑ TF17 Eric Lindros | 60.00 | 27.00 |
| ❑ TF18 Mario Lemieux | 75.00 | 34.00 |
| ❑ TF19 Joe Sakic | 30.00 | 13.50 |
| ❑ TF20 Brett Hull | 20.00 | 9.00 |
| ❑ TF21 Arturs Irbe | 10.00 | 4.50 |
| ❑ TF22 Daren Puppa | 10.00 | 4.50 |
| ❑ TF23 Doug Gilmour | 10.00 | 4.50 |
| ❑ TF24 Pavel Bure | 30.00 | 13.50 |
| ❑ TF25 Joe Juneau | 10.00 | 4.50 |
| ❑ TF26 Teemu Selanne | 30.00 | 13.50 |

## 1994-95 Score 90 Plus Club

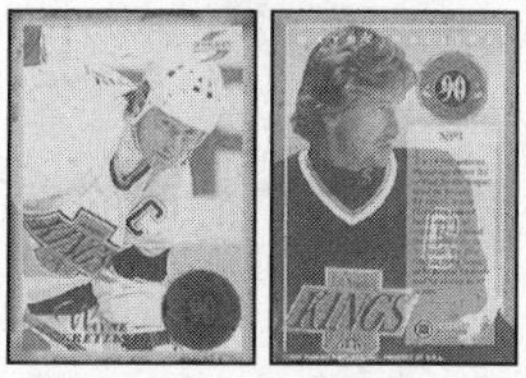

The 21 cards in this set were randomly inserted into Score retail jumbo packs at the rate of 1:4. The set features all players who tallied more than 90 points in the previous season. The cards have a full tan border. A simple round set logo is on the lower portion of the card. The player name is in gold foil. The backs are team color coordinated, with a player photo, and short text information. The cards are numbered with an "NP" prefix.

| | MINT | NRMT |
|---|---|---|
| COMPLETE SET (21) | 140.00 | 65.00 |
| COMMON CARD (1-21) | 1.00 | .45 |
| ❑ 1 Wayne Gretzky | 30.00 | 13.50 |
| ❑ 2 Sergei Fedorov | 10.00 | 4.50 |
| ❑ 3 Adam Oates | 2.50 | 1.10 |
| ❑ 4 Doug Gilmour | 2.50 | 1.10 |
| ❑ 5 Pavel Bure | 10.00 | 4.50 |
| ❑ 6 Jeremy Roenick | 5.00 | 2.20 |
| ❑ 7 Mark Recchi | 2.50 | 1.10 |
| ❑ 8 Brendan Shanahan | 10.00 | 4.50 |
| ❑ 9 Jaromir Jagr | 15.00 | 6.75 |
| ❑ 10 Dave Andreychuk | 1.00 | .45 |
| ❑ 11 Brett Hull | 6.00 | 2.70 |
| ❑ 12 Eric Lindros | 15.00 | 6.75 |
| ❑ 13 Rod Brind'Amour | 2.50 | 1.10 |
| ❑ 14 Pierre Turgeon | 2.50 | 1.10 |
| ❑ 15 Ray Sheppard | 2.50 | 1.10 |
| ❑ 16 Mike Modano | 6.00 | 2.70 |
| ❑ 17 Robert Reichel | 1.00 | .45 |
| ❑ 18 Ron Francis | 2.50 | 1.10 |
| ❑ 19 Joe Sakic | 10.00 | 4.50 |
| ❑ 20 Vincent Damphousse | 2.50 | 1.10 |
| ❑ 21 Ray Bourque | 5.00 | 2.20 |

## 1994-95 Score Team Canada

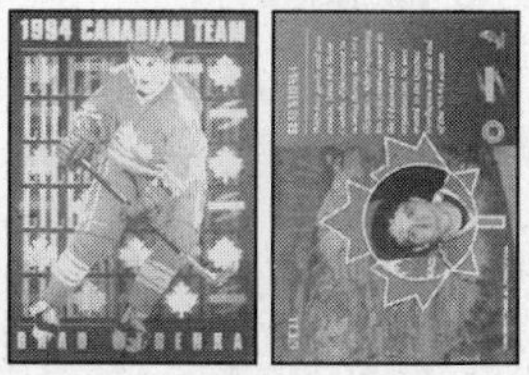

The 24 cards in this set were randomly inserted into Score Canadian retail and hobby product at the rate of 1:36 packs. The cards feature a holographic player photo front with a background that reads Lillehammer. The set highlights players from the Canadian Olympic team which took home the silver in the 1994 Games. Although included in this set, Brett Lindros actually did not play in Norway due to an injury. The backs have a full color player portrait over a maple leaf background. The cards are numbered with a CT prefix.

| | MINT | NRMT |
|---|---|---|
| COMPLETE SET (24) | 100.00 | 45.00 |
| COMMON CARD (CT1-CT24) | 4.00 | 1.80 |
| ❑ CT1 Paul Kariya | 20.00 | 9.00 |
| ❑ CT2 Petr Nedved | 6.00 | 2.70 |
| ❑ CT3 Todd Warriner | 4.00 | 1.80 |
| ❑ CT4 Corey Hirsch | 6.00 | 2.70 |
| ❑ CT5 Greg Johnson | 4.00 | 1.80 |
| ❑ CT6 Chris Kontos | 4.00 | 1.80 |
| ❑ CT7 Dwayne Norris | 4.00 | 1.80 |
| ❑ CT8 Brian Savage | 6.00 | 2.70 |
| ❑ CT9 Todd Hlushko | 4.00 | 1.80 |
| ❑ CT10 Fabian Joseph | 4.00 | 1.80 |
| ❑ CT11 Greg Parks | 4.00 | 1.80 |
| ❑ CT12 Jean-Yves Roy | 4.00 | 1.80 |
| ❑ CT13 Mark Astley | 4.00 | 1.80 |
| ❑ CT14 Adrian Aucoin | 4.00 | 1.80 |
| ❑ CT15 David Harlock | 4.00 | 1.80 |
| ❑ CT16 Ken Lovsin | 4.00 | 1.80 |
| ❑ CT17 Derek Mayer | 4.00 | 1.80 |
| ❑ CT18 Brad Schlegel | 4.00 | 1.80 |
| ❑ CT19 Chris Therien | 6.00 | 2.70 |
| ❑ CT20 Manny Legace | 6.00 | 2.70 |
| ❑ CT21 Brad Werenka | 4.00 | 1.80 |
| ❑ CT22 Wally Schreiber | 4.00 | 1.80 |
| ❑ CT23 Allain Roy | 4.00 | 1.80 |
| ❑ CT24 Brett Lindros | 4.00 | 1.80 |

## 1994-95 Score Top Rookie Redemption

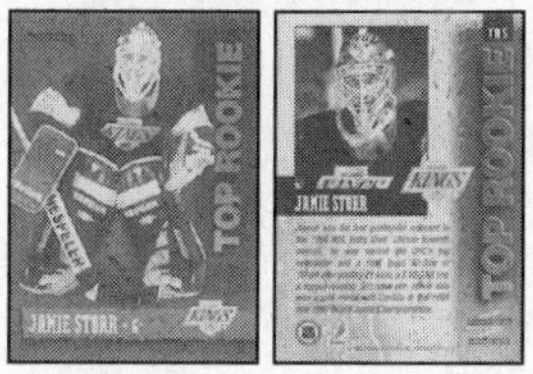

The 10 cards in this set were available only through a redemption card offer. Redemption cards were inserted at the rate of 1:48 Score packs. The redemption cards were individually numbered 1-10, but do not mention the player for whom they are redeemable. The mail-in offer expired April 1, 1995. These redemption cards are priced in the header below. Top Rookie redeemed cards have a cut-out photo of the player over a silver foil background. The Top Rookie logo runs down the right side of the card; the player name, position and team logo are on the bottom of the card. The back has a color photo with text information and is numbered with a "TR" prefix.

| | MINT | NRMT |
|---|---|---|
| COMPLETE SET (10) | 100.00 | 45.00 |
| COMMON CARD (1-10) | 2.50 | 1.10 |
| ❑ 1 Paul Kariya | 50.00 | 22.00 |
| ❑ 2 Peter Forsberg | 35.00 | 16.00 |
| ❑ 3 Brett Lindros | 2.50 | 1.10 |
| ❑ 4 Oleg Tverdovsky | 2.50 | 1.10 |
| ❑ 5 Jamie Storr | 5.00 | 2.20 |
| ❑ 6 Kenny Jonsson | 2.50 | 1.10 |
| ❑ 7 Brian Rolston | 2.50 | 1.10 |
| ❑ 8 Jeff Friesen | 10.00 | 4.50 |
| ❑ 9 Todd Harvey | 2.50 | 1.10 |
| ❑ 10 Victor Kozlov | 2.50 | 1.10 |

## 1995-96 Score Promos

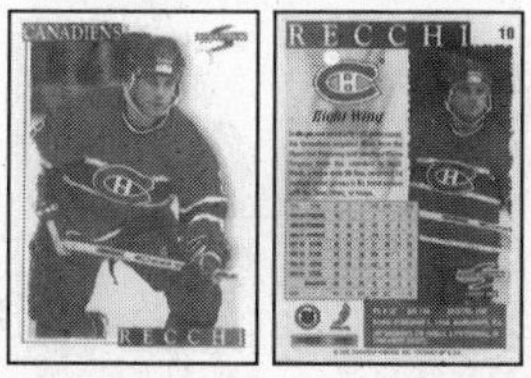

Enclosed in a cello pack, this nine-card standard-size set was issued to preview the 1995-96 Score hockey series. The cards are identical in design to their regular issue counterparts, save for the way the player's name is presented on the back and the hole punched into the upper right corner. On the promos, it is last name only, while the regular cards include Christian name as well.

| | MINT | NRMT |
|---|---|---|
| COMPLETE SEALED SET (9) | 2.00 | .90 |
| COMMON CARD | .05 | .02 |
| ❑ 3 Chris Chelios | .25 | .11 |
| ❑ 8 Jason Arnott | .10 | .05 |
| ❑ 10 Mark Recchi | .15 | .07 |
| ❑ 19 Trevor Kidd | .15 | .07 |
| ❑ 25 Martin Brodeur | .50 | .23 |
| ❑ 33 Keith Tkachuk | .35 | .16 |
| ❑ 313 Jamie Linden | .05 | .02 |
| ❑ 3 Cam Neely Border Battle | 1.00 | .45 |
| ❑ NNO Ad Card | 1.00 | .45 |

## 1995-96 Score

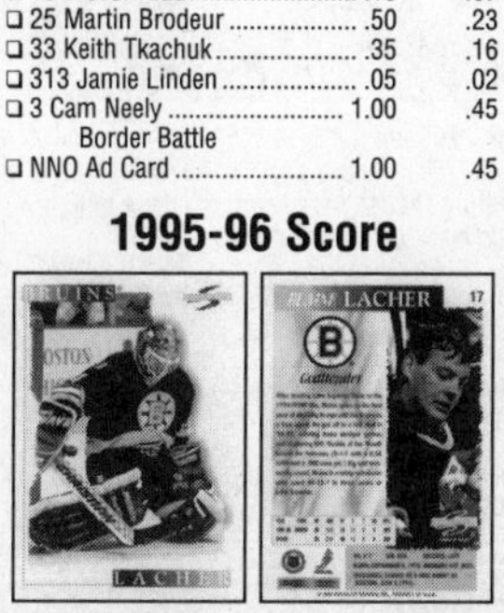

This 330-card standard-size set was issued in one series in packs of 12-card hobby, 12-card retail and 24-card retail jumbo. Canadian packs of 5-cards each also were available. These packs also held chase cards, but because of the pack size, the odds were considerably more difficult. The fronts feature a full-color action photo on a white background with the player's last name at the bottom and the team name at the top both in team colors. The backs have a color photo with the player's name at the top. Player information, statistics and the team emblem are also on the back of the card. Subsets are Rookies (291-315) and Stoppers (316-325). Top rookies in this set include Todd Warriner, Brian Holzinger and Tommy Salo. The Ron Hextall Contest Winner card (#AD4) was awarded to collectors who correctly spotted four errors in a photograph in a contest sponsored by Score. The card back approximates the standard Score issue, but the front uses a silver prismatic foil background.

| | MINT | NRMT |
|---|---|---|
| COMPLETE SET (330) | 15.00 | 6.75 |
| COMMON CARD (1-330) | .05 | .02 |
| ❑ 1 Jaromir Jagr | .60 | .25 |
| ❑ 2 Adam Graves | .10 | .05 |
| ❑ 3 Chris Chelios | .20 | .09 |
| ❑ 4 Felix Potvin | .20 | .09 |
| ❑ 5 Joe Sakic | .40 | .18 |
| ❑ 6 Chris Pronger | .10 | .05 |
| ❑ 7 Teemu Selanne | .40 | .18 |
| ❑ 8 Jason Arnott | .10 | .05 |
| ❑ 9 John LeClair | .30 | .14 |
| ❑ 10 Mark Recchi | .10 | .05 |
| ❑ 11 Rob Blake | .05 | .02 |
| ❑ 12 Kevin Hatcher | .05 | .02 |
| ❑ 13 Shawn Burr | .05 | .02 |
| ❑ 14 Brett Lindros | .05 | .02 |
| ❑ 15 Craig Janney | .10 | .05 |
| ❑ 16 Oleg Tverdovsky | .10 | .05 |
| ❑ 17 Blaine Lacher | .10 | .05 |
| ❑ 18 Alexandre Daigle | .05 | .02 |
| ❑ 19 Trevor Kidd | .10 | .05 |
| ❑ 20 Brendan Shanahan | .40 | .18 |
| ❑ 21 Alexander Mogilny | .10 | .05 |
| ❑ 22 Stu Barnes | .05 | .02 |
| ❑ 23 Jeff Brown | .05 | .02 |
| ❑ 24 Paul Coffey | .20 | .09 |
| ❑ 25 Martin Brodeur | .50 | .23 |
| ❑ 26 Darryl Sydor | .05 | .02 |
| ❑ 27 Steve Smith | .05 | .02 |
| ❑ 28 Ted Donato | .05 | .02 |
| ❑ 29 Bernie Nicholls | .05 | .02 |
| ❑ 30 Kenny Jonsson | .05 | .02 |
| ❑ 31 Peter Forsberg | .60 | .25 |
| ❑ 32 Sean Burke | .10 | .05 |
| ❑ 33 Keith Tkachuk | .25 | .11 |
| ❑ 34 Todd Marchant | .05 | .02 |
| ❑ 35 Mikael Renberg | .10 | .05 |
| ❑ 36 Vincent Damphousse | .10 | .05 |
| ❑ 37 Rick Tocchet | .10 | .05 |
| ❑ 38 Todd Harvey | .05 | .02 |
| ❑ 39 Chris Gratton | .10 | .05 |
| ❑ 40 Darius Kasparaitis | .05 | .02 |
| ❑ 41 Sergei Nemchinov | .05 | .02 |
| ❑ 42 Bob Corkum | .05 | .02 |
| ❑ 43 Bryan Smolinski | .05 | .02 |
| ❑ 44 Kevin Stevens | .05 | .02 |
| ❑ 45 Phil Housley | .10 | .05 |
| ❑ 46 Al MacInnis | .10 | .05 |
| ❑ 47 Alexei Zhitnik | .05 | .02 |
| ❑ 48 Rob Niedermayer | .10 | .05 |
| ❑ 49 Kirk McLean | .10 | .05 |
| ❑ 50 Mark Messier | .25 | .11 |
| ❑ 51 Nicklas Lidstrom | .10 | .05 |
| ❑ 52 Scott Niedermayer | .05 | .02 |
| ❑ 53 Peter Bondra | .20 | .09 |
| ❑ 54 Luc Robitaille | .10 | .05 |
| ❑ 55 Jeremy Roenick | .20 | .09 |
| ❑ 56 Mats Sundin | .10 | .05 |
| ❑ 57 Wendel Clark | .10 | .05 |
| ❑ 58 Todd Elik | .05 | .02 |
| ❑ 59 Dave Manson | .05 | .02 |
| ❑ 60 David Oliver | .05 | .02 |
| ❑ 61 Yuri Khmylev | .05 | .02 |
| ❑ 62 Sergei Krivokrasov | .05 | .02 |
| ❑ 63 Randy Wood | .05 | .02 |
| ❑ 64 Andy Moog | .10 | .05 |
| ❑ 65 Petr Klima | .05 | .02 |
| ❑ 66 Ray Ferraro | .05 | .02 |
| ❑ 67 Sandis Ozolinsh | .10 | .05 |
| ❑ 68 Joe Sacco | .05 | .02 |
| ❑ 69 Zarley Zalapski | .05 | .02 |
| ❑ 70 Ron Tugnutt | .10 | .05 |
| ❑ 71 German Titov | .05 | .02 |
| ❑ 72 Ian Laperriere | .05 | .02 |
| ❑ 73 Doug Gilmour | .20 | .09 |
| ❑ 74 Brian Skrudland | .05 | .02 |
| ❑ 75 Cliff Ronning | .05 | .02 |
| ❑ 76 Brian Savage | .05 | .02 |
| ❑ 77 John MacLean | .10 | .05 |
| ❑ 78 Jim Carey | .20 | .09 |
| ❑ 79 Alexei Kovalev | .05 | .02 |
| ❑ 80 Brian Rolston | .05 | .02 |
| ❑ 81 Shawn McEachern | .05 | .02 |
| ❑ 82 Gary Suter | .05 | .02 |
| ❑ 83 Owen Nolan | .10 | .05 |
| ❑ 84 Ray Whitney | .05 | .02 |
| ❑ 85 Alexei Zhamnov | .10 | .05 |
| ❑ 86 Shawn Chambers | .05 | .02 |
| ❑ 87 Ed Belfour | .20 | .09 |
| ❑ 88 Patrice Tardif | .05 | .02 |
| ❑ 89 Greg Adams | .05 | .02 |
| ❑ 90 Pierre Turgeon | .10 | .05 |
| ❑ 91 Jeff Friesen | .10 | .05 |
| ❑ 92 Marty McSorley | .05 | .02 |
| ❑ 93 Dave Gagner | .10 | .05 |
| ❑ 94 Guy Hebert | .10 | .05 |
| ❑ 95 Keith Jones | .05 | .02 |
| ❑ 96 Kirk Muller | .05 | .02 |
| ❑ 97 Gary Roberts | .05 | .02 |
| ❑ 98 Chris Therien | .05 | .02 |
| ❑ 99 Steve Duchesne | .05 | .02 |
| ❑ 100 Sergei Fedorov | .40 | .18 |
| ❑ 101 Donald Audette | .10 | .05 |
| ❑ 102 Jyrki Lumme | .05 | .02 |
| ❑ 103 Darrin Shannon | .05 | .02 |
| ❑ 104 Gord Murphy | .05 | .02 |
| ❑ 105 John Cullen | .05 | .02 |
| ❑ 106 Bill Guerin | .05 | .02 |
| ❑ 107 Dale Hunter | .05 | .02 |
| ❑ 108 Uwe Krupp | .05 | .02 |
| ❑ 109 Dave Andreychuk | .10 | .05 |
| ❑ 110 Joe Murphy | .05 | .02 |
| ❑ 111 Geoff Sanderson | .10 | .05 |
| ❑ 112 Garry Galley | .05 | .02 |
| ❑ 113 Ron Sutter | .05 | .02 |
| ❑ 114 Viktor Kozlov | .05 | .02 |
| ❑ 115 Jari Kurri | .10 | .05 |
| ❑ 116 Paul Ysebaert | .05 | .02 |
| ❑ 117 Vladimir Malakhov | .05 | .02 |
| ❑ 118 Josef Beranek | .05 | .02 |
| ❑ 119 Adam Oates | .10 | .05 |
| ❑ 120 Mike Modano | .25 | .11 |
| ❑ 121 Theoren Fleury | .10 | .05 |
| ❑ 122 Pat Verbeek | .05 | .02 |
| ❑ 123 Esa Tikkanen | .05 | .02 |
| ❑ 124 Brian Leetch | .20 | .09 |
| ❑ 125 Paul Kariya | .75 | .35 |
| ❑ 126 Ken Wregget | .10 | .05 |
| ❑ 127 Ray Sheppard | .10 | .05 |
| ❑ 128 Jason Allison | .05 | .02 |
| ❑ 129 Dave Ellett | .05 | .02 |
| ❑ 130 Stephane Richer | .10 | .05 |
| ❑ 131 Jocelyn Thibault | .20 | .09 |
| ❑ 132 Martin Straka | .05 | .02 |
| ❑ 133 Tony Amonte | .10 | .05 |
| ❑ 134 Scott Mellanby | .10 | .05 |
| ❑ 135 Pavel Bure | .40 | .18 |
| ❑ 136 Andrew Cassels | .05 | .02 |
| ❑ 137 Ulf Dahlen | .05 | .02 |
| ❑ 138 Valeri Bure | .10 | .05 |
| ❑ 139 Teppo Numminen | .05 | .02 |
| ❑ 140 Mike Richter | .20 | .09 |
| ❑ 141 Rob Gaudreau | .05 | .02 |
| ❑ 142 Nikolai Khabibulin | .10 | .05 |
| ❑ 143 Mariusz Czerkawski | .05 | .02 |
| ❑ 144 Mark Tinordi | .05 | .02 |
| ❑ 145 Patrick Roy | 1.00 | .45 |
| ❑ 146 Steve Chiasson | .05 | .02 |
| ❑ 147 Mike Donnelly | .05 | .02 |
| ❑ 148 Patrice Brisebois | .05 | .02 |
| ❑ 149 Jason Wiemer | .05 | .02 |
| ❑ 150 Eric Lindros | .60 | .25 |
| ❑ 151 Dimitri Khristich | .05 | .02 |
| ❑ 152 Tom Barrasso | .10 | .05 |
| ❑ 153 Curtis Leschyshyn | .05 | .02 |
| ❑ 154 Robert Kron | .05 | .02 |
| ❑ 155 Jesse Belanger | .05 | .02 |
| ❑ 156 Brian Noonan | .05 | .02 |
| ❑ 157 Mike Peca | .05 | .02 |
| ❑ 158 Patrick Poulin | .05 | .02 |
| ❑ 159 Sergei Makarov | .05 | .02 |
| ❑ 160 Scott Stevens | .10 | .05 |
| ❑ 161 Sergio Momesso | .05 | .02 |
| ❑ 162 Todd Gill | .05 | .02 |
| ❑ 163 Don Sweeney | .05 | .02 |
| ❑ 164 Randy Burridge | .05 | .02 |
| ❑ 165 Slava Kozlov | .10 | .05 |
| ❑ 166 Shaun Van Allen | .05 | .02 |
| ❑ 167 Steven Rice | .05 | .02 |
| ❑ 168 Adam Deadmarsh | .10 | .05 |
| ❑ 169 Andrei Nikolishin | .05 | .02 |
| ❑ 170 Valeri Karpov | .05 | .02 |
| ❑ 171 Doug Bodger | .05 | .02 |
| ❑ 172 Corey Millen | .05 | .02 |
| ❑ 173 Mark Fitzpatrick | .10 | .05 |
| ❑ 174 Bob Errey | .05 | .02 |
| ❑ 175 Dan Quinn | .05 | .02 |
| ❑ 176 Vladimir Konstantinov | .05 | .02 |
| ❑ 177 Scott Lachance | .05 | .02 |
| ❑ 178 Jeff Norton | .05 | .02 |
| ❑ 179 Valeri Zelepukin | .05 | .02 |
| ❑ 180 Dmitri Mironov | .05 | .02 |
| ❑ 181 Pat Peake | .05 | .02 |
| ❑ 182 Dominic Roussel | .10 | .05 |
| ❑ 183 Sylvain Cote | .05 | .02 |
| ❑ 184 Pat Falloon | .05 | .02 |
| ❑ 185 Roman Hamrlik | .10 | .05 |
| ❑ 186 Joel Otto | .05 | .02 |
| ❑ 187 Ron Francis | .10 | .05 |
| ❑ 188 Sergei Zubov | .05 | .02 |
| ❑ 189 Arturs Irbe | .10 | .05 |
| ❑ 190 Radek Bonk | .05 | .02 |
| ❑ 191 John Tucker | .05 | .02 |
| ❑ 192 Sylvain Lefebvre | .05 | .02 |
| ❑ 193 Doug Brown | .05 | .02 |
| ❑ 194 Glen Wesley | .05 | .02 |
| ❑ 195 Ron Hextall | .10 | .05 |
| ❑ 196 Patrick Flatley | .05 | .02 |
| ❑ 197 Darcy Wakaluk | .10 | .05 |
| ❑ 198 Kelly Hrudey | .10 | .05 |
| ❑ 199 Ray Bourque | .20 | .09 |
| ❑ 200 Dominik Hasek | .40 | .18 |
| ❑ 201 Pat LaFontaine | .10 | .05 |
| ❑ 202 Chris Osgood | .25 | .11 |
| ❑ 203 Ulf Samuelsson | .05 | .02 |
| ❑ 204 Mike Gartner | .10 | .05 |
| ❑ 205 Stephane Fiset | .10 | .05 |
| ❑ 206 Mathieu Schneider | .05 | .02 |

❑ 207 Eric Desjardins .05 .02
❑ 208 Trevor Linden .10 .05
❑ 209 Cam Neely .10 .05
❑ 210 Daren Puppa .10 .05
❑ 211 Steve Larmer .10 .05
❑ 212 Tim Cheveldae .10 .05
❑ 213 Derek Plante .05 .02
❑ 214 Murray Craven .05 .02
❑ 215 Tommy Soderstrom .10 .05
❑ 216 Bob Bassen .05 .02
❑ 217 Marty McInnis .05 .02
❑ 218 Dave Lowry .05 .02
❑ 219 Mike Vernon .10 .05
❑ 220 Petr Nedved .10 .05
❑ 221 Yves Racine .05 .02
❑ 222 Dale Hawerchuk .10 .05
❑ 223 Wayne Presley .05 .02
❑ 224 Darren Turcotte .05 .02
❑ 225 Derian Hatcher .05 .02
❑ 226 Steve Thomas .05 .02
❑ 227 Stephane Matteau .05 .02
❑ 228 Grant Fuhr .10 .05
❑ 229 Joe Nieuwendyk .10 .05
❑ 230 Alexei Yashin .10 .05
❑ 231 Brian Bellows .05 .02
❑ 232 Brian Bradley .05 .02
❑ 233 Tony Granato .05 .02
❑ 234 Mike Ricci .05 .02
❑ 235 Brett Hull .25 .11
❑ 236 Mike Ridley .05 .02
❑ 237 Al Iafrate .05 .02
❑ 238 Derek King .05 .02
❑ 239 Bill Ranford .10 .05
❑ 240 Steve Yzerman .60 .25
❑ 241 John Vanbiesbrouck .30 .14
❑ 242 Russ Courtnall .05 .02
❑ 243 Chris Terreri .10 .05
❑ 244 Rod Brind'Amour .10 .05
❑ 245 Shayne Corson .05 .02
❑ 246 Don Beaupre .10 .05
❑ 247 Dino Ciccarelli .10 .05
❑ 248 Kevin Lowe .05 .02
❑ 249 Craig MacTavish .05 .02
❑ 250 Wayne Gretzky 1.25 .55
❑ 251 Curtis Joseph .20 .09
❑ 252 Joe Mullen .10 .05
❑ 253 Andrei Kovalenko .05 .02
❑ 254 Igor Larionov .05 .02
❑ 255 Geoff Courtnall .05 .02
❑ 256 Joe Juneau .05 .02
❑ 257 Bruce Driver .05 .02
❑ 258 Michal Pivonka .05 .02
❑ 259 Nelson Emerson .05 .02
❑ 260 Larry Murphy .10 .05
❑ 261 Brent Gilchrist .05 .02
❑ 262 Benoit Hogue .05 .02
❑ 263 Doug Weight .10 .05
❑ 264 Keith Primeau .10 .05
❑ 265 Neal Broten .10 .05
❑ 266 Mike Keane .05 .02
❑ 267 Zigmund Palffy .10 .05
❑ 268 Valeri Kamensky .10 .05
❑ 269 Claude Lemieux .10 .05
❑ 270 Bryan Marchment .05 .02
❑ 271 Kelly Miller .05 .02
❑ 272 Brent Sutter .05 .02
❑ 273 Glenn Healy .10 .05
❑ 274 Sergei Brylin .05 .02
❑ 275 Tie Domi .10 .05
❑ 276 Norm Maciver .05 .02
❑ 277 Kevin Dineen .05 .02
❑ 278 Scott Young .05 .02
❑ 279 Tomas Sandstrom .05 .02
❑ 280 Guy Carbonneau .05 .02
❑ 281 Denis Savard .10 .05
❑ 282 Ed Olczyk .05 .02
❑ 283 Adam Creighton .05 .02
❑ 284 Tom Chorske .05 .02
❑ 285 Roman Oksiuta .05 .02
❑ 286 David Roberts .05 .02
❑ 287 Petr Svoboda .05 .02
❑ 288 Brad May .10 .05
❑ 289 Michael Nylander .05 .02
❑ 290 Jon Casey UER .10 .05
(back photo depicts Curtis Joseph)
❑ 291 Philippe DeRouville .05 .02
❑ 292 Craig Johnson .05 .02
❑ 293 Chris McAlpine .05 .02
❑ 294 Ralph Intranuovo .05 .02
❑ 295 Richard Park .05 .02
❑ 296 Todd Warriner .05 .02
❑ 297 Craig Conroy .05 .02
❑ 298 Marek Malik .05 .02
❑ 299 Manny Fernandez .10 .05
❑ 300 Cory Stillman .05 .02
❑ 301 Kevin Brown .05 .02
❑ 302 Steve Larouche .05 .02
❑ 303 Chris Taylor .05 .02
❑ 304 Ryan Smyth .05 .02
❑ 305 Craig Darby .05 .02
❑ 306 Radim Bicanek .05 .02
❑ 307 Shean Donovan .05 .02
❑ 308 Jason Bonsignore .05 .02
❑ 309 Chris Marinucci .05 .02
❑ 310 Brian Holzinger .20 .09
❑ 311 Mike Torchia .10 .05
❑ 312 Eric Daze .20 .09
❑ 313 Jamie Linden .05 .02
❑ 314 Tommy Salo .10 .05
❑ 315 Martin Gendron .05 .02
❑ 316 Felix Potvin ST .20 .09
❑ 317 Jim Carey ST .20 .09
❑ 318 Ed Belfour ST .20 .09
❑ 319 Mike Vernon ST .10 .05
❑ 320 Sean Burke ST .10 .05
❑ 321 Mike Richter ST .20 .09
❑ 322 John Vanbiesbrouck ST .20 .09
❑ 323 Martin Brodeur ST .20 .09
❑ 324 Patrick Roy ST .50 .23
❑ 325 Dominik Hasek ST .20 .09
❑ 326 Checklist .05 .02
Pacific Division
❑ 327 Checklist .05 .02
Central Division
❑ 328 Checklist .05 .02
Atlantic Division
❑ 329 Checklist .05 .02
Northeast Division
❑ 330 Checklist - Chase .05 .02
❑ AD4 Ron Hextall Contest Winner 5.00 2.20

## 1995-96 Score Black Ice Artist's Proofs

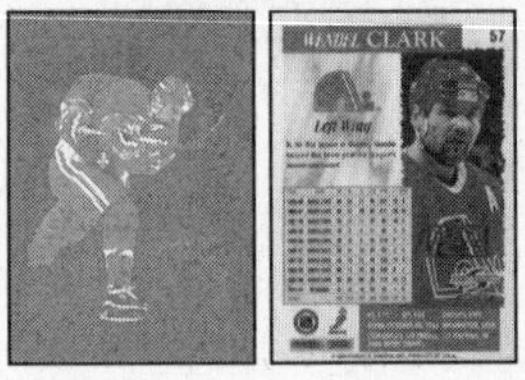

This 330-card set is a high-end parallel of the basic Score issue. The cards can be differentiated from the standard issue by a black foil background with the words "Artist's Proof" written throughout. The cards were randomly inserted 1:36 packs.

| | MINT | NRMT |
|---|---|---|
| COMPLETE SET (330) | 1500.00 | 700.00 |
| COMMON CARD (1-330) | 3.00 | 1.35 |

*STARS: 50X TO 100X BASIC CARDS
*YOUNG STARS: 30X TO 60X BASIC CARDS

## 1995-96 Score Black Ice

This 330-card set is a parallel version of the basic set. Card fronts differ in that they feature a silver, metallic background surrounded by a grayish border. The words "Black Ice" are stamped on the back in a gray block. They were inserted one in every three packs.

| | MINT | NRMT |
|---|---|---|
| COMPLETE SET (330) | 200.00 | 90.00 |
| COMMON CARD (1-330) | .25 | .11 |

*STARS: 5X TO 10X BASIC CARDS
*YOUNG STARS: 2.5X TO 5X BASIC CARDS

## 1995-96 Score Border Battle

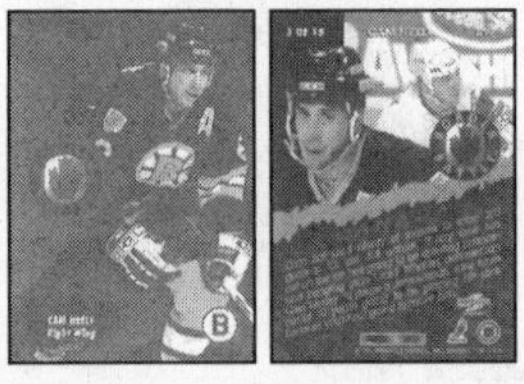

This 15-card standard-size set was inserted in 12-card hobby and retail packs at a rate of one in 12 and retail jumbos at a rate of one in 9. The set features the top players from different countries. The fronts have a color action photo with the background in the color of the player's home country. The left side of the card has a gold foil triangle jutting out with a red circle in it that has the words "Border Battle" and the country's flag. The backs have a color head shot and an action photo tinted in the color of the player's country. The backs also state the player's home country and have information on him. The cards are numbered "X of 15" at the bottom.

| | MINT | NRMT |
|---|---|---|
| COMPLETE SET (15) | 25.00 | 11.00 |
| COMMON CARD (1-15) | .60 | .25 |

❑ 1 Pierre Turgeon 1.25 .55
❑ 2 Wayne Gretzky 10.00 4.50
❑ 3 Cam Neely 1.25 .55
❑ 4 Joe Sakic 4.00 1.80
❑ 5 Doug Gilmour 1.25 .55
❑ 6 Brett Hull 2.00 .90
❑ 7 Pat LaFontaine 1.25 .55
❑ 8 Joe Mullen .60 .25
❑ 9 Mike Modano 2.00 .90
❑ 10 Jeremy Roenick 1.50 .70
❑ 11 Pavel Bure 3.00 1.35
❑ 12 Alexei Zhamnov 1.25 .55
❑ 13 Sergei Fedorov UER 3.00 1.35
❑ 14 Jaromir Jagr 5.00 2.20
❑ 15 Mats Sundin 1.50 .70

## 1995-96 Score Check It

This 12-card standard-size set was inserted in 12-card retail packs at a rate of 1:36, and in 1:86 Canadian packs. The set features many of the hardest hitters. The fronts have a full-color

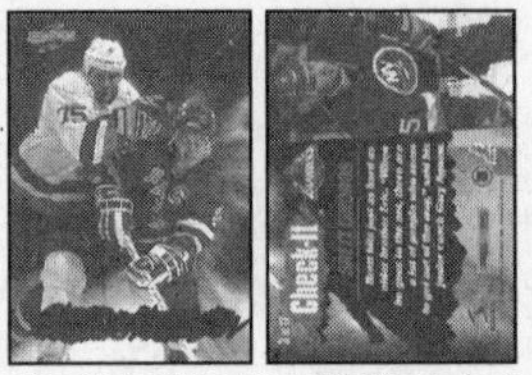

action photo of the player delivering a check. The bottom has the phrase "Check-It" and the player's name in black and red foil. The backs have a color photo on the right side and the left has his name and information. The phrase "Check-It" is also on the back alongside the card number "X of 12" at the top.

| | MINT | NRMT |
|---|---|---|
| COMPLETE SET (12) | 100.00 | 45.00 |
| COMMON CARD (1-12) | 3.00 | 1.35 |

❑ 1 Eric Lindros 40.00 18.00
❑ 2 Owen Nolan 8.00 3.60
❑ 3 Brett Lindros 3.00 1.35
❑ 4 Chris Gratton 3.00 1.35
❑ 5 Chris Pronger 3.00 1.35
❑ 6 Adam Deadmarsh 10.00 4.50
❑ 7 Peter Forsberg 40.00 18.00
❑ 8 Derian Hatcher 3.00 1.35
❑ 9 Rob Blake 3.00 1.35
❑ 10 Jeff Friesen 3.00 1.35
❑ 11 Keith Tkachuk 15.00 6.75
❑ 12 Mike Ricci 3.00 1.35

## 1995-96 Score Dream Team

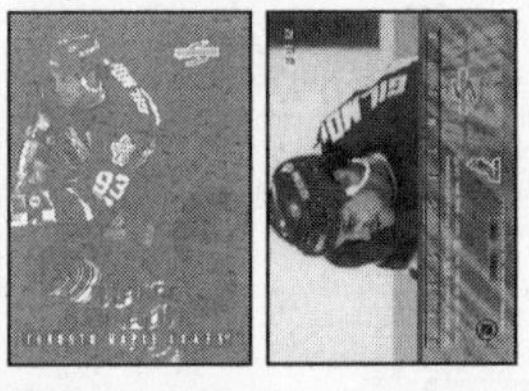

This 12-card standard-size set was inserted in 12-card hobby and retail packs at a rate of 1:72. The set features 12 of the best players in hockey. The fronts have a color action photo and a head shot at the bottom in the background. The words "Dream Team" are at the top and the player's name and team are at the bottom. The background is red and orange. The back has a color player photo at the top with his name and information at the bottom. The cards are numbered "X of 12" at the top.

| | MINT | NRMT |
|---|---|---|
| COMPLETE SET (12) | 150.00 | 70.00 |
| COMMON CARD (1-12) | 5.00 | 2.20 |

❑ 1 Wayne Gretzky 30.00 13.50
❑ 2 Sergei Fedorov 10.00 4.50
❑ 3 Eric Lindros 20.00 9.00
❑ 4 Mark Messier 6.00 2.70
❑ 5 Peter Forsberg 15.00 6.75
❑ 6 Doug Gilmour 5.00 2.20
❑ 7 Paul Kariya 20.00 9.00
❑ 8 Jaromir Jagr 15.00 6.75
❑ 9 Brett Hull 6.00 2.70
❑ 10 Pavel Bure 10.00 4.50
❑ 11 Patrick Roy 25.00 11.00
❑ 12 Jim Carey 5.00 2.20

## 1995-96 Score Golden Blades

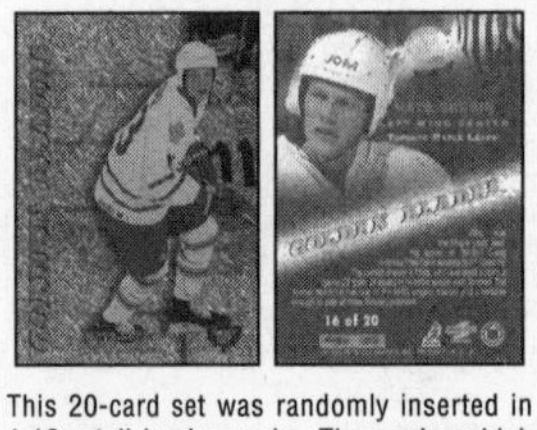

This 20-card set was randomly inserted in 1:18 retail jumbo packs. The cards, which feature the fastest skaters in the game, are printed on gold prismatic foil.

| | MINT | NRMT |
|---|---|---|
| COMPLETE SET (20) | 250.00 | 110.00 |
| COMMON CARD (1-20) | 4.00 | 1.80 |

❑ 1 Joe Sakic 20.00 9.00
❑ 2 Teemu Selanne 20.00 9.00
❑ 3 Alexander Mogilny 6.00 2.70
❑ 4 Peter Bondra 6.00 2.70
❑ 5 Paul Coffey 10.00 4.50
❑ 6 Mike Modano 12.00 5.50
❑ 7 Alexei Yashin 6.00 2.70
❑ 8 Pat LaFontaine 6.00 2.70
❑ 9 Paul Kariya 40.00 18.00
❑ 10 Peter Forsberg 30.00 13.50
❑ 11 Jeff Friesen 4.00 1.80
❑ 12 Steve Yzerman 30.00 13.50
❑ 13 Theoren Fleury 6.00 2.70
❑ 14 Stephane Richer 4.00 1.80
❑ 15 Mark Messier 12.00 5.50
❑ 16 Mats Sundin 6.00 2.70
❑ 17 Brendan Shanahan 15.00 6.75
❑ 18 Mark Recchi 4.00 1.80
❑ 19 Jeremy Roenick 10.00 4.50
❑ 20 Jason Arnott 6.00 2.70

## 1995-96 Score Lamplighters

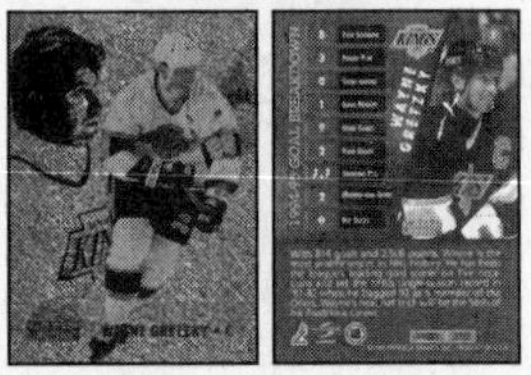

This 15-card standard-size set was inserted in 12-card hobby packs at a rate of 1:36. The cards, which feature the top goal scorers in the game, are printed on a silver prismatic foil card stock.

| | MINT | NRMT |
|---|---|---|
| COMPLETE SET (15) | 150.00 | 70.00 |
| COMMON CARD (1-15) | 2.00 | .90 |

❑ 1 Wayne Gretzky 40.00 18.00
❑ 2 Pavel Bure 12.00 5.50
❑ 3 Cam Neely 4.00 1.80
❑ 4 Owen Nolan 4.00 1.80
❑ 5 Sergei Fedorov 15.00 6.75
❑ 6 Pierre Turgeon 2.00 .90
❑ 7 Peter Bondra 8.00 3.60
❑ 8 Mikael Renberg 4.00 1.80
❑ 9 Luc Robitaille 2.00 .90
❑ 10 Alexei Zhamnov 4.00 1.80
❑ 11 Brett Hull 10.00 4.50
❑ 12 Jaromir Jagr 20.00 9.00
❑ 13 Theoren Fleury 4.00 1.80
❑ 14 Teemu Selanne 12.00 5.50
❑ 15 Eric Lindros 20.00 9.00

## 1996-97 Score Samples

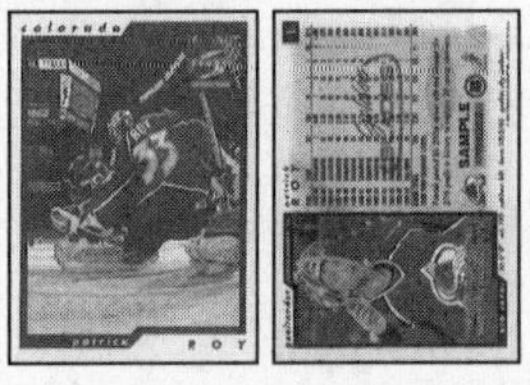

This eight-card set features samples of the 1996-97 Score hockey issue. Interestingly, all samples mirror the linen-stock Golden Blades parallel set rather than the basic issue. The cards are identical in design to their regular counterparts with the exception of the word "sample" printed on the backs at the bottom. The cards are listed below according to their regular issue numbers.

| | MINT | NRMT |
|---|---|---|
| COMPLETE SET (8) | 7.00 | 3.10 |
| COMMON CARD | .50 | .23 |

❑ 1 Patrick Roy 2.50 1.10
❑ 10 Martin Brodeur 1.25 .55
❑ 16 Alexander Mogilny .50 .23
❑ 19 Brett Hull .60 .25
❑ 63 John Vanbiesbrouck .75 .35
❑ 77 Sergei Fedorov 1.00 .45
❑ 236 Eric Daze .75 .35
❑ 238 Saku Koivu .75 .35

## 1996-97 Score

The 1996-97 Score set -- the first release of that season -- was issued in one series totalling 275 cards. The 10-card packs retailed for $.99 each. The cards featured action photography on the front complemented by simple white borders, while the backs were highlighted by another photograph and complete career stats. The only rookie of note is Ethan Moreau.

| | MINT | NRMT |
|---|---|---|
| COMPLETE SET (275) | 10.00 | 4.50 |
| COMMON CARD (1-275) | .05 | .02 |

❑ 1 Patrick Roy 1.25 .55
❑ 2 Brendan Shanahan .50 .23
❑ 3 Rob Niedermayer .10 .05
❑ 4 Jeff Friesen .05 .02
❑ 5 Teppo Numminen .05 .02
❑ 6 Mario Lemieux 1.25 .55
❑ 7 Eric Lindros .75 .35
❑ 8 Paul Kariya 1.00 .45
❑ 9 Joe Sakic .50 .23
❑ 10 Martin Brodeur .60 .25
❑ 11 Mark Tinordi .05 .02
❑ 12 Theoren Fleury .10 .05
❑ 13 Guy Hebert .10 .05
❑ 14 Dave Gagner .10 .05
❑ 15 Travis Green .10 .05
❑ 16 Alexander Mogilny .10 .05
❑ 17 Stephane Fiset .10 .05
❑ 18 Dominik Hasek .50 .23
❑ 19 Brett Hull .30 .14
❑ 20 Zdeno Ciger .05 .02
❑ 21 Pat Falloon .05 .02
❑ 22 Jyrki Lumme .05 .02
❑ 23 Rick Tabaracci .10 .05
❑ 24 Mark Messier .30 .14
❑ 25 Yanic Perreault .05 .02
❑ 26 Mark Recchi .10 .05
❑ 27 Alexander Selivanov .05 .02
❑ 28 Chris Terreri .10 .05
❑ 29 Jaromir Jagr .75 .35
❑ 30 Ted Donato .05 .02
❑ 31 Scott Mellanby .10 .05
❑ 32 Geoff Courtnall .05 .02
❑ 33 Michal Pivonka .05 .02
❑ 34 Glenn Healy .10 .05
❑ 35 Pavel Bure .50 .23
❑ 36 Chris Chelios .25 .11
❑ 37 Nelson Emerson .05 .02
❑ 38 Petr Nedved .10 .05
❑ 39 Greg Adams .05 .02
❑ 40 Bill Ranford .10 .05
❑ 41 Wayne Gretzky 1.50 .70
❑ 42 Wendel Clark .10 .05
❑ 43 Sandis Ozolinsh .10 .05
❑ 44 Dave Andreychuk .10 .05
❑ 45 Brian Bradley .05 .02
❑ 46 Sean Burke .10 .05
❑ 47 Keith Tkachuk .30 .14
❑ 48 Brad May .10 .05
❑ 49 Brent Gilchrist .05 .02
❑ 50 Vincent Damphousse .10 .05
❑ 51 Dale Hawerchuk .10 .05
❑ 52 Randy Burridge .05 .02
❑ 53 Ray Bourque .25 .11
❑ 54 Keith Primeau .10 .05
❑ 55 Jason Arnott .10 .05
❑ 56 Ron Francis .10 .05
❑ 57 Craig Janney .10 .05
❑ 58 Trevor Kidd .10 .05
❑ 59 Jason Dawe .05 .02
❑ 60 Steve Yzerman .75 .35
❑ 61 Alexei Kovalev .05 .02
❑ 62 Steve Duchesne .05 .02
❑ 63 John Vanbiesbrouck .40 .18
❑ 64 Steve Thomas .05 .02
❑ 65 Bernie Nicholls .05 .02
❑ 66 Alexandre Daigle .05 .02
❑ 67 Pat Peake .05 .02
❑ 68 Kelly Hrudey .10 .05
❑ 69 Owen Nolan .10 .05
❑ 70 Alexei Zhitnik .05 .02
❑ 71 Pierre Turgeon .10 .05
❑ 72 Mike Modano .30 .14
❑ 73 Viacheslav Fetisov .05 .02
❑ 74 Jim Carey .25 .11
❑ 75 Larry Murphy .10 .05
❑ 76 Roman Oksiuta .05 .02
❑ 77 Sergei Fedorov .40 .18
❑ 78 Shayne Corson .05 .02
❑ 79 Michael Nylander .05 .02
❑ 80 Ron Hextall .10 .05
❑ 81 Adam Graves .10 .05
❑ 82 Tommy Soderstrom .10 .05
❑ 83 Robert Svehla .05 .02
❑ 84 Vladimir Konstantinov .05 .02
❑ 85 Jeff Hackett .10 .05
❑ 86 Todd Harvey .05 .02
❑ 87 Jeff Brown .05 .02
❑ 88 Bryan Smolinski .05 .02
❑ 89 Oleg Tverdovsky .10 .05
❑ 90 Curtis Joseph .25 .11
❑ 91 Grant Fuhr .10 .05
❑ 92 Rick Tocchet .10 .05
❑ 93 Adam Deadmarsh .10 .05
❑ 94 Pat Verbeek .05 .02
❑ 95 Doug Gilmour .25 .11
❑ 96 Jocelyn Thibault .25 .11
❑ 97 Radek Bonk .05 .02
❑ 98 Martin Gelinas .05 .02
❑ 99 Peter Forsberg .75 .35
❑ 100 Joe Murphy .05 .02
❑ 101 Dino Ciccarelli .10 .05
❑ 102 Rod Brind'Amour .10 .05
❑ 103 Kirk Muller .05 .02
❑ 104 Andy Moog .10 .05
❑ 105 Nikolai Khabibulin .10 .05
❑ 106 Mike Ricci .05 .02
❑ 107 Ray Ferraro .05 .02
❑ 108 Scott Niedermayer .05 .02
❑ 109 Russ Courtnall .05 .02
❑ 110 Dale Hunter .05 .02
❑ 111 Cam Neely .10 .05
❑ 112 Ray Sheppard .10 .05
❑ 113 Luc Robitaille .10 .05
❑ 114 Al MacInnis .10 .05
❑ 115 Mathieu Schneider .05 .02
❑ 116 Claude Lemieux .10 .05

| | | |
|---|---|---|
| ❑ 117 Kevin Hatcher | .05 | .02 |
| ❑ 118 Daren Puppa | .10 | .05 |
| ❑ 119 Geoff Sanderson | .05 | .02 |
| ❑ 120 Zigmund Palffy | .05 | .02 |
| ❑ 121 Denis Savard | .10 | .05 |
| ❑ 122 Dimitri Khristich | .05 | .02 |
| ❑ 123 Ed Belfour | .25 | .11 |
| ❑ 124 Tom Barrasso | .10 | .05 |
| ❑ 125 Bob Rouse | .05 | .02 |
| ❑ 126 Tomas Sandstrom | .05 | .02 |
| ❑ 127 Roman Hamrlik | .10 | .05 |
| ❑ 128 Alexei Zhamnov | .05 | .02 |
| ❑ 129 Chris Osgood | .25 | .11 |
| ❑ 130 Rob Blake | .05 | .02 |
| ❑ 131 Garry Galley | .05 | .02 |
| ❑ 132 Greg Johnson | .05 | .02 |
| ❑ 133 Brian Skrudland | .05 | .02 |
| ❑ 134 Martin Rucinsky | .05 | .02 |
| ❑ 135 Steve Konowalchuk | .05 | .02 |
| ❑ 136 Damian Rhodes | .10 | .05 |
| ❑ 137 Jeremy Roenick | .25 | .11 |
| ❑ 138 Scott Stevens | .10 | .05 |
| ❑ 139 Pat LaFontaine | .10 | .05 |
| ❑ 140 Scott Young | .05 | .02 |
| ❑ 141 Benoit Hogue | .05 | .02 |
| ❑ 142 Paul Coffey | .25 | .11 |
| ❑ 143 John MacLean | .05 | .02 |
| ❑ 144 Joe Juneau | .05 | .02 |
| ❑ 145 Teemu Selanne | .50 | .23 |
| ❑ 146 Andrew Cassels | .05 | .02 |
| ❑ 147 Brian Savage | .05 | .02 |
| ❑ 148 Chris Gratton | .10 | .05 |
| ❑ 149 Corey Hirsch | .05 | .02 |
| ❑ 150 Mike Richter | .25 | .11 |
| ❑ 151 Shawn McEachern | .05 | .02 |
| ❑ 152 Joe Nieuwendyk | .05 | .02 |
| ❑ 153 Phil Housley | .10 | .05 |
| ❑ 154 Mike Gartner | .10 | .05 |
| ❑ 155 Kirk McLean | .10 | .05 |
| ❑ 156 Bob Probert | .10 | .05 |
| ❑ 157 Valeri Kamensky | .10 | .05 |
| ❑ 158 Vyacheslav Kozlov | .05 | .02 |
| ❑ 159 Eric Desjardins | .05 | .02 |
| ❑ 160 Mats Sundin | .10 | .05 |
| ❑ 161 John LeClair | .40 | .18 |
| ❑ 162 Adam Oates | .10 | .05 |
| ❑ 163 Cliff Ronning | .05 | .02 |
| ❑ 164 Mike Vernon | .10 | .05 |
| ❑ 165 German Titov | .05 | .02 |
| ❑ 166 Chris Pronger | .10 | .05 |
| ❑ 167 Norm MacIver | .05 | .02 |
| ❑ 168 Kenny Jonsson | .05 | .02 |
| ❑ 169 Tony Amonte | .10 | .05 |
| ❑ 170 Doug Weight | .10 | .05 |
| ❑ 171 Sergei Zubov | .05 | .02 |
| ❑ 172 Felix Potvin | .25 | .11 |
| ❑ 173 Trevor Linden | .10 | .05 |
| ❑ 174 Derek Plante | .05 | .02 |
| ❑ 175 Uwe Krupp | .05 | .02 |
| ❑ 176 Nicklas Lidstrom | .10 | .05 |
| ❑ 177 Mikael Renberg | .05 | .02 |
| ❑ 178 Igor Larionov | .05 | .02 |
| ❑ 179 Brian Leetch | .25 | .11 |
| ❑ 180 Stu Barnes | .05 | .02 |
| ❑ 181 Alexei Yashin | .05 | .02 |
| ❑ 182 Gary Suter | .05 | .02 |
| ❑ 183 Ken Wregget | .10 | .05 |
| ❑ 184 Mike Ridley | .05 | .02 |
| ❑ 185 Peter Bondra | .25 | .11 |
| ❑ 186 Steve Rucchin | .05 | .02 |
| ❑ 187 Jozef Stumpel | .05 | .02 |
| ❑ 188 Matthew Barnaby | .10 | .05 |
| ❑ 189 James Patrick | .05 | .02 |
| ❑ 190 Chris Simon | .05 | .02 |
| ❑ 191 Brent Fedyk | .05 | .02 |
| ❑ 192 Kris Draper | .05 | .02 |
| ❑ 193 David Oliver | .05 | .02 |
| ❑ 194 Dave Lowry | .05 | .02 |
| ❑ 195 Robert Kron | .05 | .02 |
| ❑ 196 Andrei Kovalenko | .05 | .02 |
| ❑ 197 Bill Guerin | .05 | .02 |
| ❑ 198 Ed Olczyk | .05 | .02 |
| ❑ 199 Yuri Khmylev | .05 | .02 |
| ❑ 200 Rob Ray | .05 | .02 |
| ❑ 201 Joe Mullen | .10 | .05 |
| ❑ 202 Petr Klima | .05 | .02 |
| ❑ 203 Todd Krygier | .05 | .02 |
| ❑ 204 Garth Snow | .10 | .05 |
| ❑ 205 Zarley Zalapski | .05 | .02 |
| ❑ 206 Ken Baumgartner | .05 | .02 |
| ❑ 207 Tony Twist | .05 | .02 |
| ❑ 208 Todd Gill | .05 | .02 |
| ❑ 209 Mike Peca | .05 | .02 |
| ❑ 210 Darcy Wakaluk | .10 | .05 |
| ❑ 211 Milos Holan | .05 | .02 |
| ❑ 212 Alexander Semak | .05 | .02 |
| ❑ 213 Jeff Reese | .05 | .02 |
| ❑ 214 Jon Casey | .10 | .05 |
| ❑ 215 Sandy McCarthy | .05 | .02 |
| ❑ 216 Curtis Leschyshyn | .05 | .02 |
| ❑ 217 Todd Marchant | .05 | .02 |
| ❑ 218 Bob Bassen | .05 | .02 |
| ❑ 219 Darren Turcotte | .05 | .02 |
| ❑ 220 David Reid | .05 | .02 |
| ❑ 221 Brian Bellows | .05 | .02 |
| ❑ 222 Jesse Belanger | .05 | .02 |
| ❑ 223 Bill Lindsay | .05 | .02 |
| ❑ 224 Lyle Odelein | .05 | .02 |
| ❑ 225 Keith Jones | .05 | .02 |
| ❑ 226 Sylvain Lefebvre | .05 | .02 |
| ❑ 227 Shaun Van Allen | .05 | .02 |
| ❑ 228 Dan Quinn | .05 | .02 |
| ❑ 229 Richard Matvichuk | .05 | .02 |
| ❑ 230 Craig MacTavish | .05 | .02 |
| ❑ 231 Craig Billington | .10 | .05 |
| ❑ 232 Stephane Richer | .10 | .05 |

| | | |
|---|---|---|
| ❑ 233 Donald Audette | .10 | .05 |
| ❑ 234 Ulf Dahlen | .05 | .02 |
| ❑ 235 Steve Chiasson | .05 | .02 |
| ❑ 236 Eric Daze | .10 | .05 |
| ❑ 237 Petr Sykora | .05 | .02 |
| ❑ 238 Saku Koivu | .40 | .18 |
| ❑ 239 Ed Jovanovski | .10 | .05 |
| ❑ 240 Daniel Alfredsson | .10 | .05 |
| ❑ 241 Vitali Yachmenev | .05 | .02 |
| ❑ 242 Marcus Ragnarsson | .05 | .02 |
| ❑ 243 Cory Stillman | .05 | .02 |
| ❑ 244 Todd Bertuzzi | .10 | .05 |
| ❑ 245 Valeri Bure | .10 | .05 |
| ❑ 246 Jere Lehtinen | .05 | .02 |
| ❑ 247 Radek Dvorak | .05 | .02 |
| ❑ 248 Niclas Andersson | .05 | .02 |
| ❑ 249 Miroslav Satan | .05 | .02 |
| ❑ 250 Jeff O'Neill | .05 | .02 |
| ❑ 251 Nolan Baumgartner | .05 | .02 |
| ❑ 252 Roman Vopat | .05 | .02 |
| ❑ 253 Bryan McCabe | .05 | .02 |
| ❑ 254 Jamie Langenbrunner | .05 | .02 |
| ❑ 255 Chad Kilger | .10 | .05 |
| ❑ 256 Eric Fichaud | .10 | .05 |
| ❑ 257 Landon Wilson | .05 | .02 |
| ❑ 258 Kyle McLaren | .05 | .02 |
| ❑ 259 Aaron Gavey | .05 | .02 |
| ❑ 260 Byron Dafoe | .05 | .02 |
| ❑ 261 Grant Marshall | .05 | .02 |
| ❑ 262 Shane Doan | .05 | .02 |
| ❑ 263 Ralph Intranuovo | .05 | .02 |
| ❑ 264 Aki-Petteri Berg | .05 | .02 |
| ❑ 265 Antti Tormanen | .05 | .02 |
| ❑ 266 Brian Holzinger | .10 | .05 |
| ❑ 267 Jose Theodore | .10 | .05 |
| ❑ 268 Ethan Moreau | .25 | .11 |
| ❑ 269 Niklas Sundstrom | .05 | .02 |
| ❑ 270 Brendan Witt | .05 | .02 |
| ❑ 271 Checklist (1-70) | .05 | .02 |
| ❑ 272 Checklist (71-140) | .05 | .02 |
| ❑ 273 Checklist (141-210) | .05 | .02 |
| ❑ 274 Checklist (211-275) | .05 | .02 |
| ❑ 275 Checklist (Chase Program) | .05 | .02 |

## 1996-97 Score Artist's Proofs

This 275-card parallel of the 1996-97 Score set could be differentiated from the regular cards by the bronze foil circular Artist's Proof logo on the card front. These chase cards were inserted 1:55 hobby and retail packs, and 1:27 magazine packs.

| | MINT | NRMT |
|---|---|---|
| COMPLETE SET (275) | 1500.00 | 700.00 |
| COMMON CARD (1-275) | 4.00 | 1.80 |
| *STARS: 30X TO 80X BASIC CARDS | | |
| *YOUNG STARS: 20X TO 50X | | |

## 1996-97 Score Dealer's Choice Artist's Proofs

Another parallel to the Score set, these cards were sent to dealers whose customers pulled winning Golden Blades cards. The dealer mailed in the winning card and was given two cards in exchange. The customer received the Special Artist Proof while the dealer received this version. Identical to regular Artist Proofs, only the words 'Dealers Choice' were added around the circular AP logo.

| | MINT | NRMT |
|---|---|---|
| COMPLETE SET (275) | 3000.00 | 1350.00 |
| COMMON CARD (1-275) | 10.00 | 4.50 |
| *STARS: 75X TO 150X BASIC CARDS | | |
| *YOUNG STARS: 40X TO 80X BASIC CARDS | | |

## 1996-97 Score Special Artist's Proofs

A parallel to the Score set, these cards were redemptions of winning Golden Blades cards, which had blacked out boxes readable only with a special lens available at hobby shops. Customers received a Special Artist Proof while the dealers who sent in the cards for the customers received similar versions called Dealer's Choice Artist Proofs. The only difference is on the Artist Proof logo, which adds the word 'Special' on these versions.

| | MINT | NRMT |
|---|---|---|
| COMPLETE SET (275) | 2500.00 | 1100.00 |
| COMMON CARD (1-275) | 8.00 | 3.60 |
| *STARS: 60X TO 120X BASIC CARDS | | |
| *YOUNG STARS: 30X TO 60X BASIC CARDS | | |

## 1996-97 Score Check It

Randomly inserted in magazine packs at a rate

of 1:35, this 16-card set features some of the toughest hitters in the game.

| | MINT | NRMT |
|---|---|---|
| COMPLETE SET (16) | 250.00 | 110.00 |
| COMMON CARD (1-16) | 6.00 | 2.70 |
| ❑ 1 Eric Lindros | 50.00 | 22.00 |
| ❑ 2 Peter Forsberg | 50.00 | 22.00 |
| ❑ 3 Keith Tkachuk | 20.00 | 9.00 |
| ❑ 4 Cam Neely | 12.00 | 5.50 |
| ❑ 5 Jeremy Roenick | 15.00 | 6.75 |
| ❑ 6 Brendan Shanahan | 30.00 | 13.50 |
| ❑ 7 Wendel Clark | 6.00 | 2.70 |
| ❑ 8 Owen Nolan | 12.00 | 5.50 |
| ❑ 9 Doug Gilmour | 12.00 | 5.50 |
| ❑ 10 Trevor Linden | 6.00 | 2.70 |
| ❑ 11 Saku Koivu | 25.00 | 11.00 |
| ❑ 12 Ed Jovanovski | 15.00 | 6.75 |
| ❑ 13 Theoren Fleury | 12.00 | 5.50 |
| ❑ 14 Doug Weight | 12.00 | 5.50 |
| ❑ 15 Chris Chelios | 15.00 | 6.75 |
| ❑ 16 Eric Daze | 12.00 | 5.50 |

## 1996-97 Score Golden Blades

This 275-card set was a parallel to the basic issue. The cards were inserted at rates of 1:7 hobby and retail packs, and 1:3 magazine packs. The cards were printed on linen stock and featured the Golden Blades logo superimposed over the stat package on the card backs. Each Golden Blades card has a rectangular box within the player's picture on the back which to the naked eye, resembles television snow. But placing a special Pinnacle device over the rectangle revealed (for one out of every eight Golden Blades) the words "Special Artist's Proof". These cards were eligible to be redeemed for two more parallel cards: a Special Artist's Proof for the collector and a Dealer's Choice Artist Proof for the redeeming hobby store owner. These SAP winner cards were inserted at appoximately the same rate as standard Artist Proof cards, but because of the limited redemption period, are in somewhat shorter supply.

| | MINT | NRMT |
|---|---|---|
| COMPLETE SET (275) | 250.00 | 110.00 |
| COMMON CARD (1-275) | .50 | .23 |
| *STARS: 6X TO 15X BASIC CARDS | | |
| *YOUNG STARS: 4X TO 8X | | |

## 1996-97 Score Dream Team

Randomly inserted in packs at a rate of 1:71 hobby and retail packs, this 12-card set features the top players at each position in the NHL today on an all-rainbow holographic foil card stock.

| | MINT | NRMT |
|---|---|---|
| COMPLETE SET (12) | 120.00 | 55.00 |
| COMMON CARD (1-12) | 4.00 | 1.80 |
| ❑ 1 Eric Lindros | 10.00 | 4.50 |
| ❑ 2 Paul Kariya | 12.00 | 5.50 |
| ❑ 3 Joe Sakic | 6.00 | 2.70 |
| ❑ 4 Peter Forsberg | 10.00 | 4.50 |
| ❑ 5 Mark Messier | 5.00 | 2.20 |
| ❑ 6 Mario Lemieux | 15.00 | 6.75 |
| ❑ 7 Jaromir Jagr | 10.00 | 4.50 |
| ❑ 8 Wayne Gretzky | 25.00 | 11.00 |
| ❑ 9 Alexander Mogilny | 4.00 | 1.80 |
| ❑ 10 Pavel Bure | 6.00 | 2.70 |
| ❑ 11 Sergei Fedorov | 6.00 | 2.70 |
| ❑ 12 Patrick Roy | 15.00 | 6.75 |

## 1996-97 Score Net Worth

Inserted exclusively into retail packs at a rate of 1:35, these cards feature the top netminders in the NHL today. Two photos grace the front of each card, with one being a black and silver metallic image.

| | MINT | NRMT |
|---|---|---|
| COMPLETE SET (18) | 150.00 | 70.00 |
| COMMON CARD (1-18) | 4.00 | 1.80 |
| ❑ 1 Patrick Roy | 50.00 | 22.00 |
| ❑ 2 Martin Brodeur | 25.00 | 11.00 |
| ❑ 3 Jim Carey | 12.00 | 5.50 |
| ❑ 4 Dominik Hasek | 20.00 | 9.00 |
| ❑ 5 Ed Belfour | 10.00 | 4.50 |
| ❑ 6 Chris Osgood | 10.00 | 4.50 |
| ❑ 7 Curtis Joseph | 10.00 | 4.50 |
| ❑ 8 John Vanbiesbrouck | 15.00 | 6.75 |
| ❑ 9 Jocelyn Thibault | 10.00 | 4.50 |
| ❑ 10 Stephane Fiset | 4.00 | 1.80 |
| ❑ 11 Ron Hextall | 4.00 | 1.80 |
| ❑ 12 Tom Barrasso | 4.00 | 1.80 |
| ❑ 13 Daren Puppa | 4.00 | 1.80 |
| ❑ 14 Mike Vernon | 4.00 | 1.80 |
| ❑ 15 Bill Ranford | 4.00 | 1.80 |
| ❑ 16 Corey Hirsch | 4.00 | 1.80 |
| ❑ 17 Damian Rhodes | 4.00 | 1.80 |
| ❑ 18 Nikolai Khabibulin | 10.00 | 4.50 |

## 1996-97 Score Sudden Death

Randomly inserted in hobby packs only at a rate of 1:35, this 15-card holofoil set features two action photos simulating matchups of some of the deadliest snipers against the stingiest netminders.

| | MINT | NRMT |
|---|---|---|
| COMPLETE SET (15) | 200.00 | 90.00 |
| COMMON CARD (1-15) | 6.00 | 2.70 |
| ❑ 1 Martin Brodeur / Pierre Turgeon | 6.00 | 2.70 |
| ❑ 2 Jim Carey / Steve Yzerman | 15.00 | 6.75 |
| ❑ 3 Dominik Hasek / Brendan Shanahan | 15.00 | 6.75 |
| ❑ 4 Ed Belfour / Brett Hull | 6.00 | 2.70 |
| ❑ 5 Chris Osgood / Jeremy Roenick | 8.00 | 3.60 |
| ❑ 6 Curtis Joseph / Pavel Bure | 10.00 | 4.50 |
| ❑ 7 John Vanbiesbrouck / Mario Lemieux | 25.00 | 11.00 |
| ❑ 8 Jocelyn Thibault / Alexander Mogilny | 6.00 | 2.70 |
| ❑ 9 Mike Richter / Jaromir Jagr | 15.00 | 6.75 |
| ❑ 10 Tom Barrasso / Mark Messier | 6.00 | 2.70 |
| ❑ 11 Darren Puppa / Joe Sakic | 10.00 | 4.50 |
| ❑ 12 Felix Potvin / Wayne Gretzky | 6.00 | 2.70 |
| ❑ 13 Corey Hirsch / Paul Kariya | 15.00 | 6.75 |
| ❑ 14 Ron Hextall / Sergei Fedorov | 10.00 | 4.50 |
| ❑ 15 Nikolai Khabibulin / Teemu Selanne | 10.00 | 4.50 |

## 1996-97 Score Superstitions

The 13-cards in this set (note the foolhardy use of this unlucky number!) highlight some of the unusual pre-game rituals and neuroses of some of the NHL's most successful players. The cards were randomly inserted 1:19 hobby and retail packs and 1:10 magazine packs.

| | MINT | NRMT |
|---|---|---|
| COMPLETE SET (13) | 25.00 | 11.00 |
| COMMON CARD (1-13) | 1.50 | .70 |
| ❑ 1 Teemu Selanne | 5.00 | 2.20 |
| ❑ 2 Doug Weight | 2.00 | .90 |
| ❑ 3 Mats Sundin | 2.00 | .90 |
| ❑ 4 Mike Modano | 4.00 | 1.80 |
| ❑ 5 Felix Potvin | 2.50 | 1.10 |
| ❑ 6 Paul Coffey | 2.50 | 1.10 |
| ❑ 7 Ray Bourque | 2.50 | 1.10 |
| ❑ 8 Chris Chelios | 2.50 | 1.10 |
| ❑ 9 Ron Hextall | 1.50 | .70 |
| ❑ 10 Alexander Selivanov | 1.50 | .70 |
| ❑ 11 Brett Hull | 4.00 | 1.80 |
| ❑ 12 Mike Richter | 2.50 | 1.10 |
| ❑ 13 Scott Mellanby | 2.00 | .90 |

## 1997-98 Score

The 1997-98 Score set was issued in one series totalling 270 cards and was distributed in packs with a suggested retail price of $.99. The fronts feature color player photos in white borders. The backs carry player information.

| | MINT | NRMT |
|---|---|---|
| COMPLETE SET (270) | 15.00 | 6.75 |
| COMMON CARD (1-270) | .05 | .02 |
| ❑ 1 Sean Burke | .15 | .07 |
| ❑ 2 Chris Osgood | .25 | .11 |
| ❑ 3 Garth Snow | .15 | .07 |
| ❑ 4 Mike Vernon | .15 | .07 |
| ❑ 5 Grant Fuhr | .15 | .07 |
| ❑ 6 Guy Hebert | .15 | .07 |
| ❑ 7 Arturs Irbe | .15 | .07 |
| ❑ 8 Andy Moog | .15 | .07 |
| ❑ 9 Tommy Salo | .15 | .07 |
| ❑ 10 Nikolai Khabibulin | .15 | .07 |
| ❑ 11 Mike Richter | .25 | .11 |
| ❑ 12 Corey Hirsch | .15 | .07 |
| ❑ 13 Bill Ranford | .15 | .07 |
| ❑ 14 Jim Carey | .15 | .07 |
| ❑ 15 Jeff Hackett | .15 | .07 |
| ❑ 16 Damian Rhodes | .15 | .07 |
| ❑ 17 Tom Barrasso | .15 | .07 |
| ❑ 18 Daren Puppa | .15 | .07 |
| ❑ 19 Craig Billington | .15 | .07 |
| ❑ 20 Ed Belfour | .25 | .11 |
| ❑ 21 Mikhail Shtalenkov | .05 | .02 |
| ❑ 22 Glenn Healy | .15 | .07 |
| ❑ 23 Marcel Cousineau | .15 | .07 |
| ❑ 24 Kevin Hodson | .15 | .07 |
| ❑ 25 Olaf Kolzig | .15 | .07 |
| ❑ 26 Eric Fichaud | .15 | .07 |
| ❑ 27 Ron Hextall | .15 | .07 |
| ❑ 28 Rick Tabaracci | .15 | .07 |
| ❑ 29 Felix Potvin | .25 | .11 |
| ❑ 30 Martin Brodeur | .60 | .25 |
| ❑ 31 Curtis Joseph | .25 | .11 |
| ❑ 32 Ken Wregget | .15 | .07 |
| ❑ 33 Patrick Roy | 1.25 | .55 |
| ❑ 34 John Vanbiesbrouck | .40 | .18 |
| ❑ 35 Stephane Fiset | .15 | .07 |
| ❑ 36 Roman Turek | .15 | .07 |
| ❑ 37 Trevor Kidd | .15 | .07 |
| ❑ 38 Dwayne Roloson | .05 | .02 |
| ❑ 39 Dominik Hasek | .50 | .23 |
| ❑ 40 Patrick Lalime | .15 | .07 |
| ❑ 41 Jocelyn Thibault | .15 | .07 |
| ❑ 42 Jose Theodore | .15 | .07 |
| ❑ 43 Kirk McLean | .15 | .07 |
| ❑ 44 Steve Shields | .15 | .07 |
| ❑ 45 Mike Dunham | .15 | .07 |
| ❑ 46 Jamie Storr | .15 | .07 |
| ❑ 47 Chris Terreri | .15 | .07 |
| ❑ 48 Byron Dafoe | .15 | .07 |
| ❑ 49 Ron Tugnutt | .15 | .07 |
| ❑ 50 Kelly Hrudey | .15 | .07 |
| ❑ 51 Vaclav Prospal | .40 | .18 |
| ❑ 52 Alyn McCauley | .15 | .07 |
| ❑ 53 Jaroslav Svejkovsky | .15 | .07 |
| ❑ 54 Steve Shields | .50 | .23 |
| ❑ 55 Chris Dingman | .05 | .02 |
| ❑ 56 Vadim Sharifijanov | .05 | .02 |
| ❑ 57 Larry Courville | .05 | .02 |
| ❑ 58 Erik Rasmussen | .05 | .02 |
| ❑ 59 Sergei Samsonov | .60 | .25 |
| ❑ 60 Kevyn Adams | .05 | .02 |
| ❑ 61 Daniel Cleary | .15 | .07 |
| ❑ 62 Martin Prochazka | .05 | .02 |
| ❑ 63 Mattias Ohlund | .15 | .07 |
| ❑ 64 Juha Lind | .05 | .02 |
| ❑ 65 Olli Jokinen | .40 | .18 |
| ❑ 66 Espen Knutsen | .05 | .02 |
| ❑ 67 Marc Savard | .15 | .07 |
| ❑ 68 Hnat Domenichelli | .05 | .02 |
| ❑ 69 Warren Luhning | .05 | .02 |

□ 70 Magnus Arvedson .05 .02
□ 71 Chris Phillips .05 .02
□ 72 Brad Isbister .05 .02
□ 73 Boyd Devereaux .05 .02
□ 74 Alexei Morozov .15 .07
□ 75 Vladimir Vorobiev .05 .02
□ 76 Steven Rice .05 .02
□ 77 Tony Granato .05 .02
□ 78 Lonny Bohonos .05 .02
□ 79 Dave Gagner .05 .02
□ 80 Brendan Shanahan .50 .23
□ 81 Brett Hull .30 .14
□ 82 Jaromir Jagr .75 .35
□ 83 Peter Forsberg .75 .35
□ 84 Paul Kariya 1.00 .45
□ 85 Mark Messier .30 .14
□ 86 Steve Yzerman .75 .35
□ 87 Keith Tkachuk .30 .14
□ 88 Eric Lindros .75 .35
□ 89 Ray Bourque .25 .11
□ 90 Chris Chelios .25 .11
□ 91 Sergei Fedorov .50 .23
□ 92 Mike Modano .30 .14
□ 93 Doug Gilmour .25 .11
□ 94 Saku Koivu .40 .18
□ 95 Mats Sundin .25 .11
□ 96 Pavel Bure .50 .23
□ 97 Theoren Fleury .15 .07
□ 98 Keith Primeau .05 .02
□ 99 Wayne Gretzky 1.50 .70
□ 100 Doug Weight .15 .07
□ 101 Alexandre Daigle .15 .07
□ 102 Owen Nolan .15 .07
□ 103 Peter Bondra .25 .11
□ 104 Pat LaFontaine .15 .07
□ 105 Kirk Muller .05 .02
□ 106 Zigmund Palffy .25 .11
□ 107 Jeremy Roenick .25 .11
□ 108 John LeClair .40 .18
□ 109 Derek Plante .05 .02
□ 110 Geoff Sanderson .15 .07
□ 111 Dimitri Khristich .05 .02
□ 112 Vincent Damphousse .15 .07
□ 113 Teemu Selanne .50 .23
□ 114 Tony Amonte .15 .07
□ 115 Dave Andreychuk .05 .02
□ 116 Alexei Yashin .15 .07
□ 117 Adam Oates .15 .07
□ 118 Pierre Turgeon .15 .07
□ 119 Dino Ciccarelli .05 .02
□ 120 Ryan Smyth .15 .07
□ 121 Ray Sheppard .05 .02
□ 122 Jozef Stumpel .15 .07
□ 123 Jarome Iginla .15 .07
□ 124 Pat Verbeek .05 .02
□ 125 Joe Sakic .50 .23
□ 126 Brian Leetch .25 .11
□ 127 Rod Brind'Amour .15 .07
□ 128 Wendel Clark .15 .07
□ 129 Alexander Mogilny .15 .07
□ 130 Mark Recchi .15 .07
□ 131 Daniel Alfredsson .15 .07
□ 132 Ron Francis .15 .07
□ 133 Martin Gelinas .05 .02
□ 134 Andrew Cassels .05 .02
□ 135 Joe Nieuwendyk .15 .07
□ 136 Jason Arnott .15 .07
□ 137 Bryan Berard .15 .07
□ 138 Mikael Renberg .15 .07
□ 139 Mike Gartner .15 .07
□ 140 Joe Juneau .15 .07
□ 141 John MacLean .05 .02
□ 142 Adam Graves .15 .07
□ 143 Petr Nedved .15 .07
□ 144 Trevor Linden .15 .07
□ 145 Sergei Berezin .05 .02
□ 146 Adam Deadmarsh .15 .07
□ 147 Jeff O'Neill .05 .02
□ 148 Rob Blake .05 .02
□ 149 Luc Robitaille .15 .07
□ 150 Markus Naslund .05 .02
□ 151 Ethan Moreau .05 .02
□ 152 Martin Rucinsky .05 .02
UER front Ruckinski
□ 153 Mike Grier .05 .02
□ 154 Craig Janney .05 .02
□ 155 John Cullen .05 .02
□ 156 Alexei Kovalev .05 .02
□ 157 Tony Twist .15 .07
□ 158 Claude Lemieux .15 .07
□ 159 Kevin Stevens .15 .07
□ 160 Mathieu Schneider .05 .02
□ 161 Randy Cunneyworth .05 .02
□ 162 Darius Kasparaitis .05 .02
□ 163 Joe Murphy .05 .02
□ 164 Brandon Convery .05 .02
□ 165 Janne Niinimaa .15 .07
□ 166 Paul Coffey .25 .11
□ 167 Daymond Langkow .05 .02
□ 168 Chris Gratton .15 .07
□ 169 Ray Ferraro .05 .02
□ 170 Jeff Friesen .15 .07
□ 171 Ted Donato .05 .02
□ 172 Brian Holzinger .05 .02
□ 173 Travis Green .05 .02
□ 174 Sandis Ozolinsh .15 .07
□ 175 Alexei Zhamnov .05 .02
□ 176 Steve Rucchin .05 .02
□ 177 Scott Mellanby .05 .02
□ 178 Andrei Kovalenko .05 .02
□ 179 Donald Audette .05 .02
□ 180 Bernie Nicholls .05 .02
□ 181 Jonas Hoglund .05 .02
□ 182 Nicklas Lidstrom .15 .07
□ 183 Bobby Holik .05 .02
□ 184 Geoff Courtnall .05 .02
□ 185 Steve Sullivan .05 .02
□ 186 Valeri Kamensky .15 .07
□ 187 Mike Peca .05 .02
□ 188 Jere Lehtinen .05 .02
□ 189 Robert Svehla .05 .02
□ 190 Darren McCarty .05 .02
□ 191 Brian Savage .05 .02
□ 192 Harry York .05 .02
□ 193 Eric Daze .15 .07
□ 194 Niklas Sundstrom .05 .02
□ 195 Oleg Tverdovsky .05 .02
□ 196 Eric Desjardins .05 .02
□ 197 German Titov .05 .02
□ 198 Derian Hatcher .05 .02
□ 199 Bill Guerin .15 .07
□ 200 Rob Zamuner .05 .02
□ 201 Dale Hunter .05 .02
□ 202 Darcy Tucker .05 .02
□ 203 Andreas Dackell .05 .02
□ 204 Jason Dawe .05 .02
□ 205 Brian Rolston .05 .02
□ 206 Ed Olczyk .05 .02
□ 207 Todd Warriner .05 .02
□ 208 Mariusz Czerkawski .05 .02
□ 209 Slava Kozlov .05 .02
□ 210 Marty McInnis .05 .02
□ 211 Jamie Langenbrunner .05 .02
□ 212 Vitali Yachmenev .05 .02
□ 213 Stephane Richer .05 .02
□ 214 Roman Hamrlik .05 .02
□ 215 Jim Campbell .05 .02
□ 216 Matthew Barnaby .05 .02
□ 217 Benoit Hogue .05 .02
□ 218 Robert Reichel .05 .02
□ 219 Tie Domi .05 .02
□ 220 Steve Konowalchuk .05 .02
□ 221 Radek Dvorak .05 .02
□ 222 Kevin Hatcher .05 .02
□ 223 Viktor Kozlov .05 .02
□ 224 Scott Stevens .05 .02
□ 225 Cory Stillman .05 .02
□ 226 Anson Carter .05 .02
□ 227 Rem Murray .05 .02
□ 228 Vladimir Konstantinov .05 .02
□ 229 Scott Niedermayer .05 .02
□ 230 Steve Duchesne .05 .02
□ 231 Valeri Bure .05 .02
□ 232 Miroslav Satan .05 .02
□ 233 Jason Allison .15 .07
□ 234 Mark Fitzpatrick .15 .07
□ 235 Ed Jovanovski .15 .07
□ 236 Esa Tikkanen .05 .02
□ 237 Stu Barnes .05 .02
□ 238 Darryl Sydor .05 .02
□ 239 Ulf Samuelsson .05 .02
□ 240 Dmitri Mironov .05 .02
□ 241 Bryan Smolinski .05 .02
□ 242 Rob Ray .05 .02
□ 243 Todd Marchant .05 .02
□ 244 Cliff Ronning .05 .02
□ 245 Alexander Selivanov .05 .02
□ 246 Rick Tocchet .15 .07
□ 247 Vladimir Malakhov .05 .02
□ 248 Al MacInnis .15 .07
□ 249 Dainius Zubrus .25 .11
□ 250 Keith Jones .05 .02
□ 251 Darren Turcotte .05 .02
□ 252 Ulf Dahlen .05 .02
□ 253 Rob Niedermayer .05 .02
□ 254 J.J. Daigneault .05 .02
□ 255 Michal Grosek .05 .02
□ 256 Chris Therien .05 .02
□ 257 Adam Foote .05 .02
□ 258 Tomas Sandstrom .05 .02
□ 259 Scott Lachance .05 .02
□ 260 Paul Kariya SM .25 .11
□ 261 Pavel Bure SM .25 .11
□ 262 Mike Modano SM .25 .11
□ 263 Steve Yzerman SM .25 .11
□ 264 Sergei Fedorov SM .25 .11
□ 265 Eric Lindros SM .25 .11
□ 266 Dominik Hasek CL (1-66) .15 .07
□ 267 Bryan Berard CL (67-132) .05 .02
□ 268 Mike Peca CL (133-201) .05 .02
□ 269 Martin Brodeur .05 .02
Mike Dunham CL (202-270)
□ 270 Paul Kariya CL (inserts) .25 .11
□ PR82 Jaromir Jagr PROMO 3.00 1.35
□ PR83 Peter Forsberg PROMO 3.00 1.35
□ PR84 Paul Kariya PROMO 4.00 1.80
□ PR86 Steve Yzerman PROMO 3.00 1.35

## 1997-98 Score Artist's Proofs

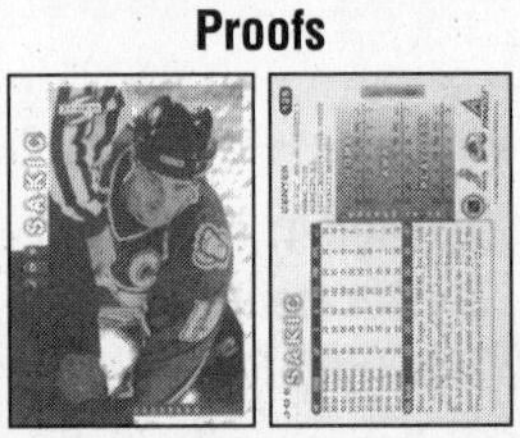

Randomly inserted in packs at the rate of one in 35, this 160-card set is a partial parallel version of the base set and is printed on prismatic foil board with the "Artist's Proof" seal on the front.

| | MINT | NRMT |
|---|---|---|
| COMPLETE SET (165) | 1500.00 | 700.00 |
| COMMON CARD (1-165) | 4.00 | 1.80 |

*STARS: 30X TO 60X BASIC CARDS
*YOUNG STARS: 25X TO 50X BASIC CARDS

## 1997-98 Score Golden Blades

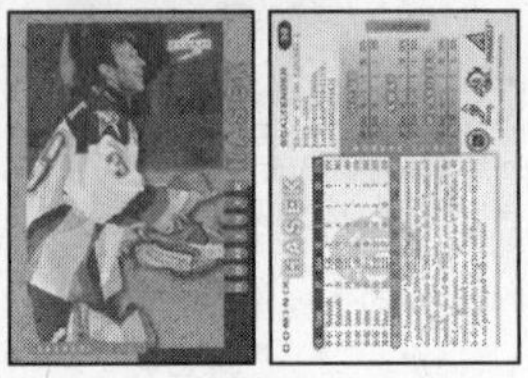

Randomly inserted in packs at the rate of one in seven, this 160-card set is a partial parallel version of the base set printed on silver gloss foil board.

| | MINT | NRMT |
|---|---|---|
| COMPLETE SET (165) | 200.00 | 90.00 |
| COMMON CARD (1-165) | .75 | .35 |

*STARS: 5X TO 10X BASIC CARDS
*YOUNG STARS: 4X TO 8X

## 1997-98 Score Check It

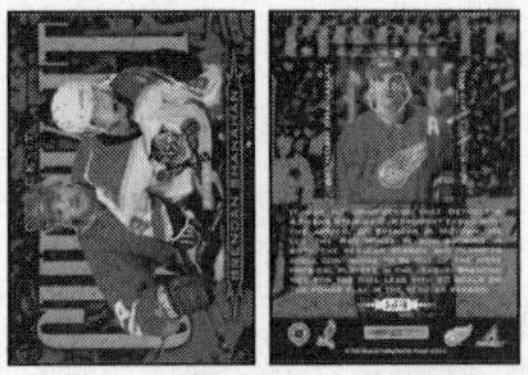

Randomly inserted in packs at the rate of one in 19, this 18-card set features action color photos of some of the toughest hitters in the game.

| | MINT | NRMT |
|---|---|---|
| COMPLETE SET (18) | 150.00 | 70.00 |
| COMMON CARD (1-18) | 4.00 | 1.80 |

□ 1 Eric Lindros 25.00 11.00
□ 2 Mark Recchi 6.00 2.70
□ 3 Brendan Shanahan 15.00 6.75
□ 4 Keith Tkachuk 10.00 4.50
□ 5 John LeClair 12.00 5.50
□ 6 Doug Gilmour 6.00 2.70
□ 7 Jarome Iginla 6.00 2.70
□ 8 Ryan Smyth 6.00 2.70
□ 9 Chris Chelios 8.00 3.60
□ 10 Mike Grier 4.00 1.80
□ 11 Vincent Damphousse 6.00 2.70
□ 12 Bryan Berard 6.00 2.70
□ 13 Jaromir Jagr 25.00 11.00
□ 14 Mike Peca 6.00 2.70
□ 15 Dino Ciccarelli 6.00 2.70
□ 16 Rod Brind'Amour 6.00 2.70
□ 17 Owen Nolan 6.00 2.70
□ 18 Pat Verbeek 4.00 1.80

## 1997-98 Score Net Worth

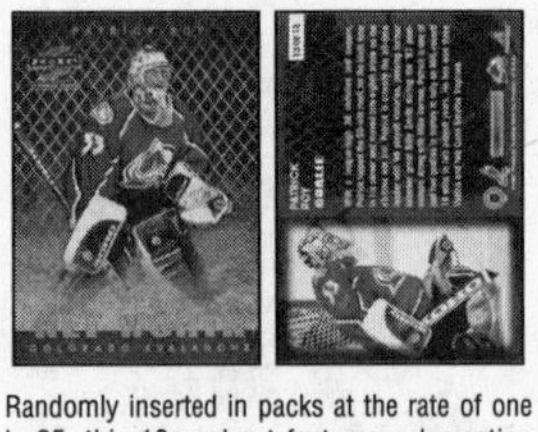

Randomly inserted in packs at the rate of one in 35, this 18-card set features color action photos of the NHL's best goalies.

| | MINT | NRMT |
|---|---|---|
| COMPLETE SET (18) | 200.00 | 90.00 |
| COMMON CARD (1-18) | 8.00 | 3.60 |

□ 1 Guy Hebert 8.00 3.60
□ 2 Jim Carey 8.00 3.60
□ 3 Trevor Kidd 8.00 3.60
□ 4 Chris Osgood 10.00 4.50
□ 5 Curtis Joseph 10.00 4.50
□ 6 Mike Richter 10.00 4.50
□ 7 Damian Rhodes 8.00 3.60
□ 8 Garth Snow 8.00 3.60
□ 9 Nikolai Khabibulin 8.00 3.60
□ 10 Grant Fuhr 8.00 3.60
□ 11 Jocelyn Thibault 10.00 4.50
□ 12 Tommy Salo 8.00 3.60
□ 13 Patrick Roy 50.00 22.00
□ 14 Martin Brodeur 25.00 11.00
□ 15 John Vanbiesbrouck 15.00 6.75
□ 16 Felix Potvin 10.00 4.50
□ 17 Dominik Hasek 20.00 9.00
□ 18 Ed Belfour 10.00 4.50

## 1997-98 Score Avalanche

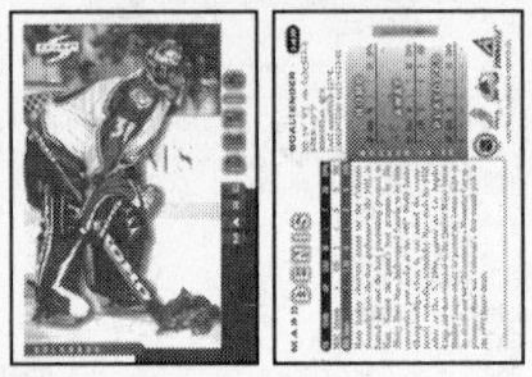

This 20-card team set of the Colorado Avalanche was produced by Pinnacle and features bordered color action player photos. The backs carry player information.

| | MINT | NRMT |
|---|---|---|
| COMPLETE SET (20) | 10.00 | 4.50 |
| COMMON CARD (1-20) | .25 | .11 |

*PLATINUM: 8X BASIC CARDS
*PREMIER: 3X BASIC CARDS

□ 1 Patrick Roy 4.00 1.80
□ 2 Craig Billington .60 .25
□ 3 Marc Denis .60 .25
□ 4 Peter Forsberg 2.50 1.10
□ 5 Jari Kurri .60 .25
□ 6 Sandis Ozolinsh .60 .25
□ 7 Valeri Kamensky .60 .25
□ 8 Adam Deadmarsh .60 .25
□ 9 Keith Jones .30 .14
□ 10 Josef Marha .25 .11
□ 11 Claude Lemieux .60 .25
□ 12 Adam Foote .30 .14
□ 13 Eric Lacroix .25 .11
□ 14 Rene Corbet .25 .11
□ 15 Uwe Krupp .25 .11
□ 16 Sylvain Lefebvre .25 .11
□ 17 Mike Ricci .60 .25
□ 18 Joe Sakic 2.00 .90
□ 19 Stephane Yelle .25 .11
□ 20 Yves Sarault .25 .11

## 1997-98 Score Blues

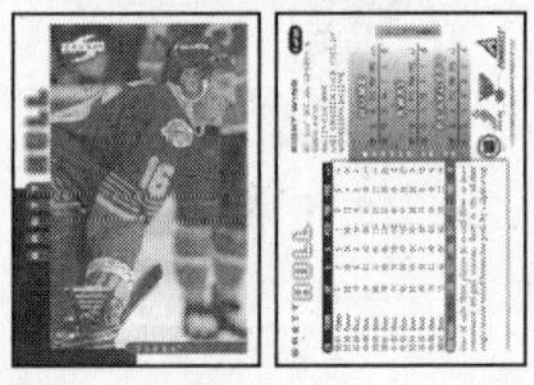

This 20-card team set of the St. Louis Blues was produced by Pinnacle and features bordered color action player photos. The backs carry player information.

| | MINT | NRMT |
|---|---|---|
| COMPLETE SET (20) | 8.00 | 3.60 |
| COMMON CARD (1-20) | .25 | .11 |

*PLATINUM: 8X BASIC CARDS
*PREMIER: 3X BASIC CARDS

□ 1 Brett Hull 1.00 .45
□ 2 Pierre Turgeon .60 .25
□ 3 Joe Murphy .25 .11
□ 4 Jim Campbell .25 .11
□ 5 Harry York .25 .11
□ 6 Al MacInnis .60 .25
□ 7 Chris Pronger .60 .25
□ 8 Darren Turcotte .25 .11
□ 9 Robert Petrovicky .25 .11
□ 10 Tony Twist .75 .35
□ 11 Grant Fuhr .60 .25
□ 12 Scott Pellerin .25 .11
□ 13 Jamie Rivers .25 .11
□ 14 Chris McAlpine .25 .11
□ 15 Geoff Courtnall .60 .25
□ 16 Steve Duchesne .50 .23
□ 17 Libor Zabransky .25 .11
□ 18 Pavol Demitra .60 .25
□ 19 Marc Bergevin .25 .11
□ 20 Jamie McLennan .25 .11

## 1997-98 Score Bruins

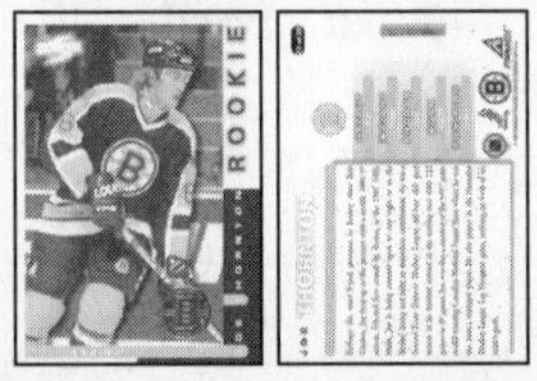

This 20-card team set of the Boston Bruins was produced by Pinnacle and features bordered color action player photos. The backs carry player information.

| | MINT | NRMT |
|---|---|---|
| COMPLETE SET (20) | 6.00 | 2.70 |
| COMMON CARD (1-20) | .25 | .11 |

*PLATINUM: 8X BASIC CARDS
*PREMIER: 3X BASIC CARDS

□ 1 Shawn Bates .25 .11
□ 2 Jim Carey .40 .18
□ 3 Rob Tallas .25 .11
□ 4 Ray Bourque .75 .35
□ 5 Dimitri Khristich .25 .11
□ 6 Ted Donato .25 .11
□ 7 Jason Allison .60 .25
□ 8 Anson Carter .40 .18
□ 9 Rob Dimaio .25 .11
□ 10 Steve Heinze .25 .11
□ 11 Jean Yves Roy .25 .11
□ 12 Randy Robitaille .25 .11
□ 13 Byron Dafoe .75 .35
□ 14 Sergei Samsonov 2.00 .90
□ 15 Ken Baumgartner .25 .11
□ 16 Dave Ellett .25 .11
□ 17 Joe Thornton 2.00 .90
□ 18 Jeff Odgers .25 .11
□ 19 Kyle McLaren .25 .11
□ 20 Don Sweeney .25 .11

## 1997-98 Score Canadiens

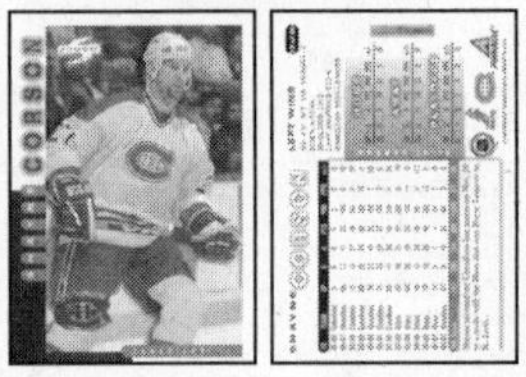

This 20-card team set of the Montreal Canadiens was produced by Pinnacle and features bordered color action player photos. The backs carry player information.

| | MINT | NRMT |
|---|---|---|
| COMPLETE SET (20) | 8.00 | 3.60 |
| COMMON CARD (1-20) | .25 | .11 |

*PLATINUM: 8X BASIC CARDS
*PREMIER: 3X BASIC CARDS

□ 1 Andy Moog .60 .25
□ 2 Jocelyn Thibault .60 .25
□ 3 Jose Theodore .60 .25
□ 4 Vincent Damphousse .60 .25
□ 5 Mark Recchi .60 .25
□ 6 Brian Savage .25 .11
□ 7 Saku Koivu 1.50 .70
□ 8 Stephane Richer .60 .25
□ 9 Martin Rucinsky .25 .11
□ 10 Valeri Bure .25 .11
□ 11 Vladimir Malakhov .25 .11
□ 12 Shayne Corson .60 .25
□ 13 Darcy Tucker .25 .11
□ 14 Sebastien Bordeleau .25 .11
□ 15 Terry Ryan .25 .11
□ 16 David Ling .25 .11
□ 17 Dave Manson .25 .11
□ 18 Benoit Brunet .25 .11
□ 19 Marc Bureau .25 .11
□ 20 Patrice Brisebois .25 .11

## 1997-98 Score Canucks

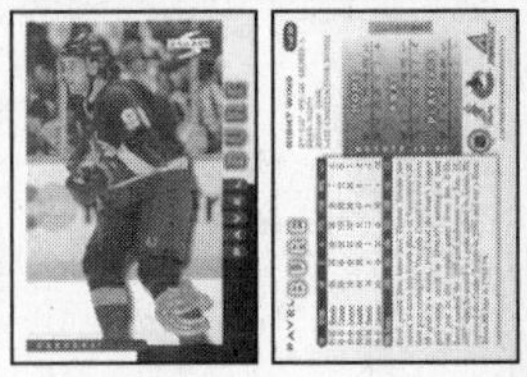

This 20-card team set of the Vancouver Canucks was produced by Pinnacle and features bordered color action player photos. The backs carry player information.

| | MINT | NRMT |
|---|---|---|
| COMPLETE SET (20) | 8.00 | 3.60 |
| COMMON CARD (1-20) | .25 | .11 |

*PLATINUM: 8X BASIC CARDS
*PREMIER: 3X BASIC CARDS

□ 1 Pavel Bure 1.50 .70
□ 2 Alexander Mogilny .60 .25
□ 3 Mark Messier 1.00 .45
□ 4 Trevor Linden .60 .25
□ 5 Martin Gelinas .25 .11
□ 6 Mattias Ohlund .40 .18
□ 7 Markus Naslund .25 .11
□ 8 Jyrki Lumme .25 .11
□ 9 Lonny Bohonos .25 .11
□ 10 Kirk McLean .60 .25
□ 11 Corey Hirsch .60 .25
□ 12 Arturs Irbe .60 .25
□ 13 Larry Courville .25 .11
□ 14 Adrian Aucoin .25 .11
□ 15 Grant Ledyard .25 .11
□ 16 Gino Odjick .25 .11
□ 17 Donald Brashear .25 .11
□ 18 Brian Noonan .25 .11
□ 19 David Roberts .25 .11
□ 20 Dave Babych .25 .11

## 1997-98 Score Devils

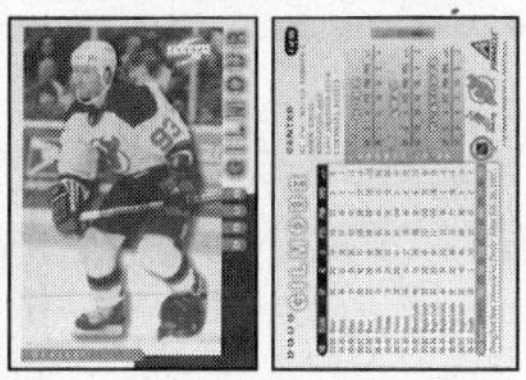

This 20-card team set of the New Jersey Devils was produced by Pinnacle and features bordered color action player photos. The backs carry player information.

| | MINT | NRMT |
|---|---|---|
| COMPLETE SET (20) | 7.00 | 3.10 |
| COMMON CARD (1-20) | .25 | .11 |

*PLATINUM: 8X BASIC CARDS
*PREMIER: 3X BASIC CARDS

| | | |
|---|---|---|
| □ 1 Doug Gilmour | .75 | .35 |
| □ 2 Bobby Holik | .25 | .11 |
| □ 3 Dave Andreychuk | .60 | .25 |
| □ 4 John MacLean | .25 | .11 |
| □ 5 Bill Guerin | .25 | .11 |
| □ 6 Brian Rolston | .25 | .11 |
| □ 7 Scott Niedermayer | .25 | .11 |
| □ 8 Scott Stevens | .25 | .11 |
| □ 9 Valeri Zelepukin | .25 | .11 |
| □ 10 Steve Thomas | .25 | .11 |
| □ 11 Denis Pederson | .25 | .11 |
| □ 12 Randy McKay | .25 | .11 |
| □ 13 Mike Dunham | .60 | .25 |
| □ 14 Petr Sykora | .40 | .18 |
| □ 15 Lyle Odelein | .25 | .11 |
| □ 16 Martin Brodeur | 2.00 | .90 |
| □ 17 Vadim Sharifijanov | .25 | .11 |
| □ 18 Bob Carpenter | .25 | .11 |
| □ 19 Sergei Brylin | .25 | .11 |
| □ 20 Ken Daneyko | .25 | .11 |

## 1997-98 Score Flyers

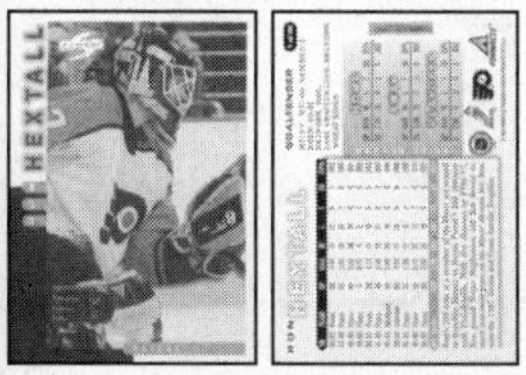

This 20-card team set of the Philadelphia Flyers was produced by Pinnacle and features bordered color action player photos. The backs carry player information.

| | MINT | NRMT |
|---|---|---|
| COMPLETE SET (20) | 10.00 | 4.50 |
| COMMON CARD (1-20) | .25 | .11 |

*PLATINUM: 8X BASIC CARDS
*PREMIER: 3X BASIC CARDS

| | | |
|---|---|---|
| □ 1 Ron Hextall | .60 | .25 |
| □ 2 Garth Snow | .60 | .25 |
| □ 3 Eric Lindros | 3.00 | 1.35 |
| □ 4 John LeClair | 1.50 | .70 |
| □ 5 Rod Brind'Amour | .60 | .25 |
| □ 6 Chris Gratton | .40 | .18 |
| □ 7 Eric Desjardins | .25 | .11 |
| □ 8 Trent Klatt | .25 | .11 |
| □ 9 Janne Niinimaa | .60 | .25 |
| □ 10 Luke Richardson | .25 | .11 |
| □ 11 Paul Coffey | .75 | .35 |
| □ 12 Dainius Zubrus | .75 | .35 |
| □ 13 Shjon Podein | .25 | .11 |
| □ 14 Joel Otto | .25 | .11 |
| □ 15 Chris Therien | .25 | .11 |
| □ 16 Pat Falloon | .25 | .11 |
| □ 17 Petr Svoboda | .25 | .11 |
| □ 18 Vaclav Prospal | .75 | .35 |
| □ 19 John Druce | .25 | .11 |
| □ 20 Daniel Lacroix | .25 | .11 |

## 1997-98 Score Maple Leafs

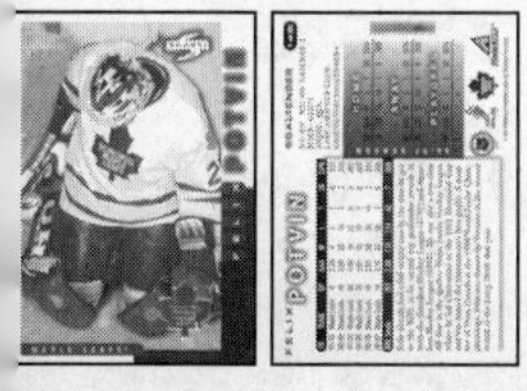

his 20-card team set of the Toronto Maple eafs was produced by Pinnacle and features ordered color action player photos. The backs rry player information.

| | MINT | NRMT |
|---|---|---|
| MPLETE SET (20) | 7.00 | 3.10 |
| MMON CARD (1-20) | .25 | .11 |

LATINUM: 8X BASIC CARDS
REMIER: 3X BASIC CARDS

| | | |
|---|---|---|
| □ 1 Felix Potvin | .75 | .35 |
| □ 2 Glenn Healy | .60 | .25 |
| □ 3 Marcel Cousineau | .60 | .25 |
| □ 4 Mats Sundin | .75 | .35 |
| □ 5 Wendel Clark | .60 | .25 |
| □ 6 Sergei Berezin | .60 | .25 |
| □ 7 Steve Sullivan | .25 | .11 |
| □ 8 Tie Domi | .30 | .14 |
| □ 9 Todd Warriner | .25 | .11 |
| □ 10 Mathieu Schneider | .25 | .11 |
| □ 11 Mike Craig | .25 | .11 |
| □ 12 Darby Hendrickson | .25 | .11 |
| □ 13 Fredrik Modin | .25 | .11 |
| □ 14 Brandon Convery | .25 | .11 |
| □ 15 Kevyn Adams | .25 | .11 |
| □ 16 Dimitri Yushkevich | .25 | .11 |
| □ 17 Alyn McCauley | .25 | .11 |
| □ 18 Derek King | .25 | .11 |
| □ 19 Jamie Baker | .25 | .11 |
| □ 20 Martin Prochazka | .25 | .11 |

## 1997-98 Score Mighty Ducks

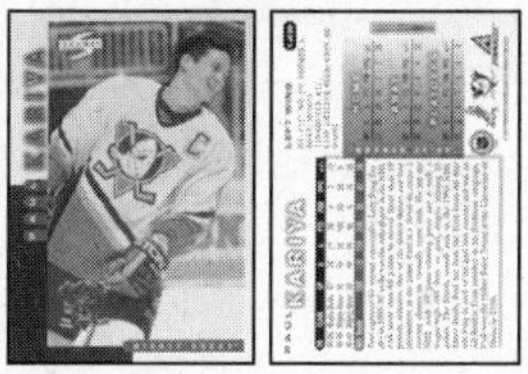

This 20-card team set of the Mighty Ducks of Anaheim was produced by Pinnacle and features bordered color action player photos. The backs carry player information.

| | MINT | NRMT |
|---|---|---|
| COMPLETE SET (20) | 10.00 | 4.50 |
| COMMON CARD (1-20) | .25 | .11 |

*PLATINUM: 8X BASIC CARDS
*PREMIER: 3X BASIC CARDS

| | | |
|---|---|---|
| □ 1 Paul Kariya | 3.00 | 1.35 |
| □ 2 Teemu Selanne | 1.75 | .80 |
| □ 3 Steve Rucchin | .25 | .11 |
| □ 4 Dmitri Mironov | .25 | .11 |
| □ 5 Matt Cullen | .25 | .11 |
| □ 6 Kevin Todd | .25 | .11 |
| □ 7 Joe Sacco | .25 | .11 |
| □ 8 J.J. Daigneault | .25 | .11 |
| □ 9 Darren Van Impe | .25 | .11 |
| □ 10 Scott Young | .25 | .11 |
| □ 11 Ted Drury | .25 | .11 |
| □ 12 Tomas Sandstrom | .25 | .11 |
| □ 13 Warren Rychel | .25 | .11 |
| □ 14 Guy Hebert | .60 | .25 |
| □ 15 Shawn Antoski | .25 | .11 |
| □ 16 Mikhail Shtalenkov | .60 | .25 |
| □ 17 Peter Leboutillier | .25 | .11 |
| □ 18 Sean Pronger | .25 | .11 |
| □ 19 Dave Karpa | .25 | .11 |
| □ 20 Espen Knutsen | .50 | .23 |

## 1997-98 Score Penguins

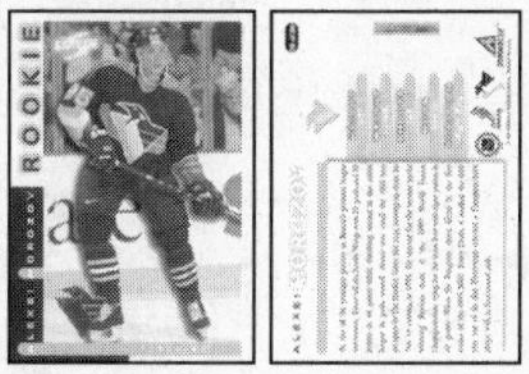

This 20-card team set of the Pittsburgh Penguins was produced by Pinnacle and features bordered color action player photos. The backs carry player information.

| | MINT | NRMT |
|---|---|---|
| COMPLETE SET (20) | 9.00 | 4.00 |
| COMMON CARD (1-20) | .25 | .11 |

*PLATINUM: 8X BASIC CARDS
*PREMIER: 3X BASIC CARDS

| | | |
|---|---|---|
| □ 1 Tom Barrasso | .25 | .11 |
| □ 2 Ken Wregget | .60 | .25 |
| □ 3 Patrick Lalime | .60 | .25 |
| □ 4 Jaromir Jagr | 2.50 | 1.10 |
| □ 5 Ron Francis | .60 | .25 |
| □ 6 Petr Nedved | .60 | .25 |
| □ 7 Ed Olczyk | .25 | .11 |
| □ 8 Kevin Hatcher | .25 | .11 |
| □ 9 Stu Barnes | .25 | .11 |
| □ 10 Darius Kasparaitis | .25 | .11 |
| □ 11 Greg Johnson | .25 | .11 |
| □ 12 Garry Valk | .25 | .11 |
| □ 13 Roman Oksiuta | .25 | .11 |
| □ 14 Dan Quinn | .25 | .11 |
| □ 15 Alex Hicks | .25 | .11 |
| □ 16 Robert Dome | .25 | .11 |
| □ 17 Dave Roche | .25 | .11 |
| □ 18 Alexei Morozov | .60 | .25 |
| □ 19 Rob Brown | .25 | .11 |
| □ 20 Domenic Pittis | .25 | .11 |

## 1997-98 Score Rangers

This 20-card team set of the New York

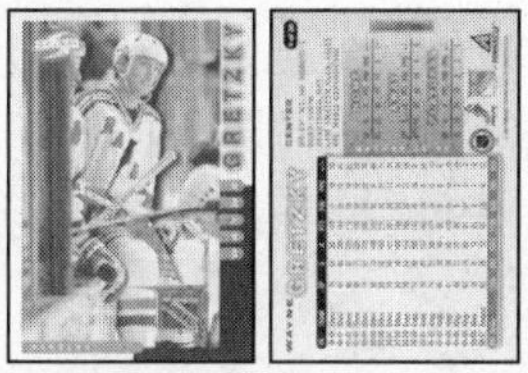

Rangers was produced by Pinnacle and features bordered color action player photos. The backs carry player information.

| | MINT | NRMT |
|---|---|---|
| COMPLETE SET (20) | 10.00 | 4.50 |
| COMMON CARD (1-20) | .25 | .11 |

*PLATINUM: 8X BASIC CARDS
*PREMIER: 3X BASIC CARDS

| | | |
|---|---|---|
| □ 1 Wayne Gretzky | 5.00 | 2.20 |
| □ 2 Brian Leetch | .75 | .35 |
| □ 3 Mike Keane | .25 | .11 |
| □ 4 Adam Graves | .60 | .25 |
| □ 5 Niklas Sundstrom | .25 | .11 |
| □ 6 Kevin Stevens | .25 | .11 |
| □ 7 Alexei Kovalev | .25 | .11 |
| □ 8 Alexander Karpovtsev | .25 | .11 |
| □ 9 Bill berg | .25 | .11 |
| □ 10 Pat Lafontaine | .60 | .25 |
| □ 11 Bruce Driver | .25 | .11 |
| □ 12 Pat Flatley | .25 | .11 |
| □ 13 Vladimir Vorobiev | .25 | .11 |
| □ 14 Christian Dube | .25 | .11 |
| □ 15 Ulf Samuelsson | .25 | .11 |
| □ 16 Mike Richter | .75 | .35 |
| □ 17 Jason Muzzatti | .25 | .11 |
| □ 18 Daniel Goneau | .25 | .11 |
| □ 19 Marc Savard | .25 | .11 |
| □ 20 Jeff Beukeboom | .25 | .11 |

## 1997-98 Score Red Wings

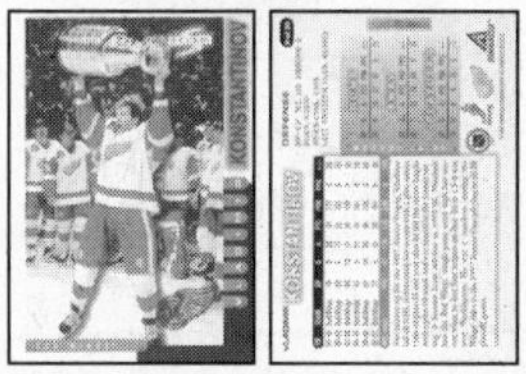

This 20-card team set of the Detroit Red Wings was produced by Pinnacle and features bordered color action player photos. The backs carry player information.

| | MINT | NRMT |
|---|---|---|
| COMPLETE SET (20) | 10.00 | 4.50 |
| COMMON CARD (1-20) | .25 | .11 |

*PLATINUM: 8X BASIC CARDS
*PREMIER: 3X BASIC CARDS

| | | |
|---|---|---|
| □ 1 Brendan Shanahan | 1.50 | .70 |
| □ 2 Steve Yzerman | 2.50 | 1.10 |
| □ 3 Sergei Fedorov | 1.50 | .70 |
| □ 4 Nicklas Lidstrom | .60 | .25 |
| □ 5 Igor Larionov | .40 | .18 |
| □ 6 Darren McCarty | .60 | .25 |
| □ 7 Slava Kozlov | .60 | .25 |
| □ 8 Larry Murphy | .60 | .25 |
| □ 9 Vladimir Konstantinov | .60 | .25 |
| □ 10 Martin Lapointe | .30 | .14 |
| □ 11 Slava Fetisov | .30 | .14 |
| □ 12 Kris Draper | .30 | .14 |
| □ 13 Doug Brown | .25 | .11 |
| □ 14 Brent Gilchrist | .25 | .11 |
| □ 15 Kirk Maltby | .25 | .11 |
| □ 16 Tomas Holmstrom | .25 | .11 |
| □ 17 Chris Osgood | .75 | .35 |
| □ 18 Kevin Hodson | .75 | .35 |
| □ 19 Jamie Pushor | .25 | .11 |
| □ 20 Mike Knuble | .60 | .25 |

## 1997-98 Score Sabres

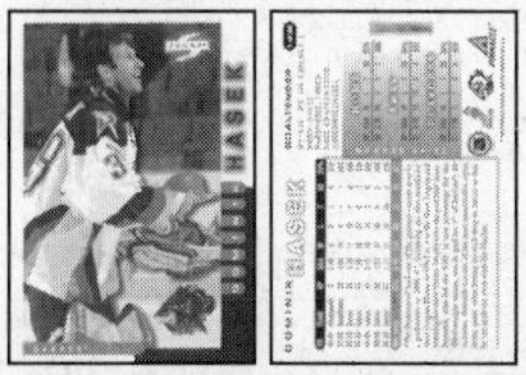

This 20-card team set of the Buffalo Sabres was produced by Pinnacle and features bordered color action player photos. The backs carry player information.

| | MINT | NRMT |
|---|---|---|
| COMPLETE SET (20) | 7.00 | 3.10 |
| COMMON CARD (1-20) | .25 | .11 |

*PLATINUM: 8X BASIC CARDS
*PREMIER: 3X BASIC CARDS

| | | |
|---|---|---|
| □ 1 Dominik Hasek | 1.75 | .80 |
| □ 2 Steve Shields | .60 | .25 |
| □ 3 Dixon Ward | .25 | .11 |
| □ 4 Donald Audette | .25 | .11 |
| □ 5 Matthew Barnaby | .25 | .11 |
| □ 6 Randy Burridge | .25 | .11 |
| □ 7 Jason Dawe | .25 | .11 |
| □ 8 Michael Grosek | .25 | .11 |
| □ 9 Brian Holzinger | .60 | .25 |
| □ 10 Brad May | .25 | .11 |
| □ 11 Mike Peca | .75 | .35 |
| □ 12 Derek Plante | .25 | .11 |
| □ 13 Wayne Primeau | .25 | .11 |
| □ 14 Rob Ray | .60 | .25 |
| □ 15 Miroslav Satan | .60 | .25 |
| □ 16 Erik Rasmussen | .25 | .11 |
| □ 17 Jason Wooley | .25 | .11 |
| □ 18 Alexei Zhitnik | .25 | .11 |
| □ 19 Darryl Shannon | .25 | .11 |
| □ 20 Mike Wilson | .25 | .11 |

## 1992-93 Seasons Patches

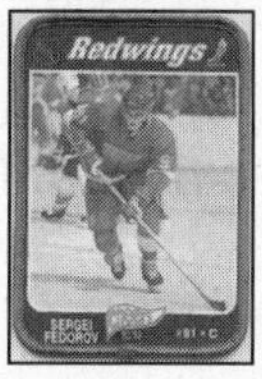

Each measuring approximately 3 1/8" by 4 1/4", these 70 patches were licensed by the NHL/NHLPA and feature color action player photos on black fabric. The player's team appears above the photo and his name, position, and sweater number are below. An embroidered border in the team color edges the patch. The patches come in a poly-wrap sleeve attached to a teal cardboard rack display. These displays were pegged on team customized counter display easels, showcasing four different players (six patches per player), for a total of 24 patches per team display. Two versions are available. The bilingual version has both French and English printed on the package. The other version is printed in English only. A checklist of 71 patches is printed on the back of the display. In the checklist, patch 22, an unnamed prototype, features ex-NHL star and Seasons President Grant Mulvey. Mulvey's patch was only available through him as a handout and could not be purchased by the public; it is not considered part of the complete set.

| | MINT | NRMT |
|---|---|---|
| COMPLETE SET (70) | 150.00 | 70.00 |
| COMMON PATCH (1-71) | 1.00 | .45 |

| | | |
|---|---|---|
| □ 1 Jeremy Roenick | 3.00 | 1.35 |
| □ 2 Steve Larmer | 2.00 | .90 |
| □ 3 Ed Belfour | 3.00 | 1.35 |
| □ 4 Chris Chelios | 3.00 | 1.35 |
| □ 5 Sergei Fedorov | 4.00 | 1.80 |
| □ 6 Steve Yzerman | 6.00 | 2.70 |
| □ 7 Tim Cheveldae | 1.50 | .70 |
| □ 8 Bob Probert | 2.00 | .90 |
| □ 9 Wayne Gretzky | 10.00 | 4.50 |
| □ 10 Luc Robitaille | 2.00 | .90 |
| □ 11 Tony Granato | 1.50 | .70 |
| □ 12 Kelly Hrudey | 2.00 | .90 |
| □ 13 Brett Hull | 3.50 | 1.55 |
| □ 14 Curtis Joseph | 3.00 | 1.35 |
| □ 15 Brendan Shanahan | 4.00 | 1.80 |
| □ 16 Nelson Emerson | 1.00 | .45 |
| □ 17 Ray Bourque | 3.00 | 1.35 |
| □ 18 Joe Juneau | 2.00 | .90 |
| □ 19 Andy Moog | 2.00 | .90 |
| □ 20 Adam Oates | 2.50 | 1.10 |
| □ 21 Patrick Roy | 8.00 | 3.60 |
| □ 22 Grant Mulvey (Prototype) | 20.00 | 9.00 |
| □ 23 Denis Savard | 2.00 | .90 |
| □ 24 Gilbert Dionne | 1.00 | .45 |
| □ 25 Kirk Muller | 2.00 | .90 |
| □ 26 Mark Messier | 3.50 | 1.55 |
| □ 27 Tony Amonte | 2.00 | .90 |
| □ 28 Brian Leetch | 3.00 | 1.35 |
| □ 29 Mike Richter | 3.00 | 1.35 |
| □ 30 Trevor Linden | 2.00 | .90 |
| □ 31 Pavel Bure | 4.00 | 1.80 |
| □ 32 Cliff Ronning | 1.00 | .45 |
| □ 33 Russ Courtnall | 1.50 | .70 |
| □ 34 Mario Lemieux | 8.00 | 3.60 |
| □ 35 Jaromir Jagr | 6.00 | 2.70 |
| □ 36 Tom Barrasso | 2.00 | .90 |
| □ 37 Rick Tocchet | 2.00 | .90 |
| □ 38 Eric Lindros | 6.00 | 2.70 |
| □ 39 Rod Brind'Amour | 2.00 | .90 |
| □ 40 Dominic Roussel | 1.50 | .70 |
| □ 41 Mark Recchi | 2.00 | .90 |
| □ 42 Pat LaFontaine | 2.00 | .90 |
| □ 43 Donald Audette | 1.50 | .70 |
| □ 44 Pat Verbeek | 2.00 | .90 |
| □ 45 John Cullen | 1.00 | .45 |
| □ 46 Owen Nolan | 2.00 | .90 |
| □ 47 Joe Sakic | 4.00 | 1.80 |
| □ 48 Kevin Hatcher | 1.00 | .45 |
| □ 49 Don Beaupre | 1.50 | .70 |
| □ 50 Scott Stevens | 2.00 | .90 |
| □ 51 Chris Terreri | 1.50 | .70 |
| □ 52 Scott Lachance | 1.00 | .45 |
| □ 53 Pierre Turgeon | 2.50 | 1.10 |
| □ 54 Grant Fuhr | 2.50 | 1.10 |
| □ 55 Doug Gilmour | 3.00 | 1.35 |
| □ 56 Dave Manson | 1.00 | .45 |
| □ 57 Bill Ranford | 2.00 | .90 |
| □ 58 Troy Murray | 1.00 | .45 |
| □ 59 Phil Housley | 1.50 | .70 |
| □ 60 Al MacInnis | 2.00 | .90 |
| □ 61 Mike Vernon | 2.00 | .90 |
| □ 62 Pat Falloon | 1.00 | .45 |
| □ 63 Doug Wilson | 2.00 | .90 |
| □ 64 Jon Casey | 1.50 | .70 |
| □ 65 Mike Modano | 3.50 | 1.55 |
| □ 66 Kevin Stevens | 1.50 | .70 |
| □ 67 Al Iafrate | 1.00 | .45 |
| □ 68 Dale Hawerchuk | 2.00 | .90 |
| □ 69 Igor Kravchuk | 1.00 | .45 |
| □ 70 Wendel Clark | 2.50 | 1.10 |
| □ 71 Kirk McLean | 2.00 | .90 |

## 1993-94 Seasons Patches

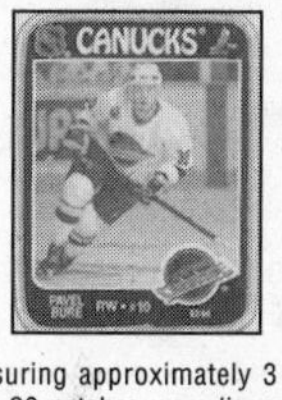

Each measuring approximately 3 1/8" by 4 1/4", these 20 patches were licensed by the NHL/NHLPA and feature color action player photos on black fabric. The player's team appears above the photo and his name, position, and jersey number are below. An embroidered border in the team color edges the patch. The team logo and year of issue in the lower right corner round out the front. The patches were encased in a hard plastic sleeve attached to a black cardboard rack display. A checklist was printed on the back of the display. The patches are unnumbered but are checklisted below according to the numbering of the checklist card.

| | MINT | NRMT |
|---|---|---|
| COMPLETE SET (20) | 60.00 | 27.00 |
| COMMON PATCH (1-20) | 1.00 | .45 |

| | | |
|---|---|---|
| □ 1 Ed Belfour | 1.50 | .70 |
| □ 2 Pavel Bure | 3.00 | 1.35 |
| □ 3 Paul Coffey | 1.50 | .70 |
| □ 4 Doug Gilmour | 1.50 | .70 |
| □ 5 Wayne Gretzky | 10.00 | 4.50 |
| □ 6 Brett Hull | 2.00 | .90 |
| □ 7 Jaromir Jagr | 5.00 | 2.20 |
| □ 8 Joe Juneau | 1.00 | .45 |
| □ 9 Mario Lemieux | 8.00 | 3.60 |
| □ 10 Eric Lindros | 5.00 | 2.20 |
| □ 11 Shawn McEachern | 1.00 | .45 |
| □ 12 Alexander Mogilny | 1.25 | .55 |
| □ 13 Adam Oates | 1.25 | .55 |
| □ 14 Felix Potvin | 1.50 | .70 |
| □ 15 Jeremy Roenick | 1.50 | .70 |
| □ 16 Patrick Roy | 8.00 | 3.60 |
| □ 17 Joe Sakic | 3.00 | 1.35 |
| □ 18 Teemu Selanne | 3.00 | 1.35 |
| □ 19 Kevin Stevens | 1.00 | .45 |
| □ 20 Steve Yzerman | 5.00 | 2.20 |

## 1994-95 Select Promos

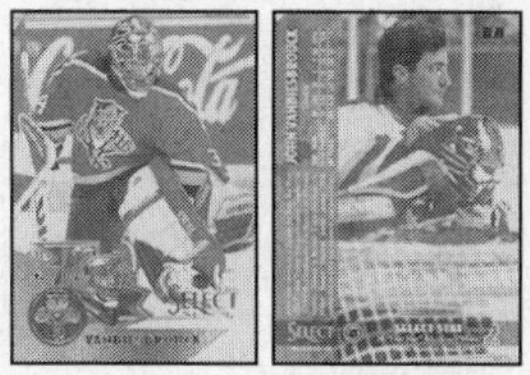

These nine standard-size cards were issued to herald the release of the 1994-95 Select hockey series. The fronts feature borderless color action player photos. The player's last name and position, the team logo and a small, sepia-toned player portrait appear on gold-foil background in the lower left corner. The backs carry another color action player photo with player biography, profile and stats next to it. The top right corner of these cards has been cut off to mark them as sample cards. The Jamie Storr YE1 card is a sample of the Youth Explosion insert set.

| | MINT | NRMT |
|---|---|---|
| COMPLETE SEALED SET (9) | 2.50 | 1.10 |
| COMMON CARD (1-9) | .05 | .02 |

| | | |
|---|---|---|
| □ 7 John Vanbiesbrouck | .15 | .07 |
| □ 90 Felix Potvin | .15 | .07 |
| □ 108 Stephane Richer | .05 | .02 |
| □ 118 Dino Ciccarelli | .05 | .02 |
| □ 128 Sylvain Cote | .05 | .02 |
| □ 142 Kevin Dineen | .05 | .02 |
| □ 194 Mattias Norstrom | .05 | .02 |

☐ YE1 Jamie Storr 2.00 .90
☐ NNO Title Card .50 .23

## 1994-95 Select

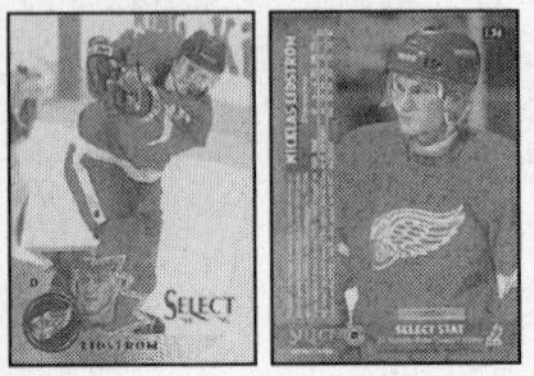

This 200-card set had an announced print run of 3,950, 24-box hobby-only cases. The design resembled a modernized version of the 1984-85 OPC set with a main action shot complemented by a corner head shot. The set is notable for the inclusion of 20 cards of players who competed in the 1994 Mexico Cup for 17-year-olds. One 4" by 6" bonus Mike Modano card featuring Sportflics technology was included in every box. Rookie cards include Bryan Berard, Marty Reasoner, Eric Rasmussen, Jarome Iginla, Wade Redden, Radek Bonk, Eric Fichaud and Mariusz Czerkawski.

MINT NRMT
COMPLETE SET (200) 15.00 6.75
COMMON CARD (1-200) .10 .05

☐ 1 Mark Messier .40 .18
☐ 2 Rick Tocchet .15 .07
☐ 3 Alexandre Daigle .10 .05
☐ 4 Owen Nolan .15 .07
☐ 5 Bill Ranford .15 .07
☐ 6 Dave Gagner .15 .07
☐ 7 John Vanbiesbrouck .50 .23
☐ 8 Sergei Makarov .10 .05
☐ 9 Derek King .10 .05
☐ 10 Sergei Fedorov .60 .25
☐ 11 Trevor Linden .15 .07
☐ 12 Don Beaupre .15 .07
☐ 13 Dave Manson .10 .05
☐ 14 Sergei Zubov .10 .05
☐ 15 Keith Primeau .15 .07
☐ 16 Joe Mullen .15 .07
☐ 17 Bernie Nicholls .10 .05
☐ 18 Ray Bourque .25 .11
☐ 19 Mike Ridley .10 .05
☐ 20 Wendel Clark .15 .07
☐ 21 Mats Sundin .15 .07
☐ 22 Alexander Mogilny .15 .07
☐ 23 Mathieu Schneider .10 .05
☐ 24 Brian Leetch .25 .11
☐ 25 Rob Niedermayer .15 .07
☐ 26 Donald Audette .15 .07
☐ 27 Doug Weight .15 .07
☐ 28 Al MacInnis .15 .07
☐ 29 Jeremy Roenick .25 .11
☐ 30 Mark Recchi .15 .07
☐ 31 Chris Chelios .25 .11
☐ 32 Luc Robitaille .15 .07
☐ 33 Dale Hunter .10 .05
☐ 34 Kelly Hrudey .15 .07
☐ 35 Steve Yzerman .75 .35
☐ 36 Martin Straka .10 .05
☐ 37 Arturs Irbe .15 .07
☐ 38 Mike Modano .40 .18
☐ 39 Cam Neely .15 .07
☐ 40 Igor Larionov .10 .05
☐ 41 Ray Ferraro .10 .05
☐ 42 Dale Hawerchuk .15 .07
☐ 43 Brian Bradley .10 .05
☐ 44 Joe Murphy .10 .05
☐ 45 Daren Puppa .15 .07
☐ 46 Pierre Turgeon .15 .07
☐ 47 Shayne Corson .10 .05
☐ 48 Adam Graves .15 .07
☐ 49 Craig Billington .15 .07
☐ 50 Derian Hatcher .10 .05
☐ 51 Alexei Zhamnov .15 .07
☐ 52 Dominik Hasek .60 .25
☐ 53 Ed Belfour .25 .11
☐ 54 Mike Vernon .15 .07
☐ 55 Bob Kudelski .10 .05
☐ 56 Ray Sheppard .15 .07
☐ 57 Pat LaFontaine .15 .07
☐ 58 Adam Oates .15 .07
☐ 59 Vincent Damphousse .15 .07
☐ 60 Jaromir Jagr 1.00 .45
☐ 61 Mikael Renberg .15 .07
☐ 62 Joe Sakic .60 .25
☐ 63 Sandis Ozolinsh .15 .07
☐ 64 Kirk McLean .15 .07
☐ 65 Stephan Lebeau .10 .05
☐ 66 Alexei Kovalev .15 .07
☐ 67 Ron Hextall .15 .07
☐ 68 Geoff Sanderson .15 .07
☐ 69 Doug Gilmour .25 .11
☐ 70 Russ Courtnall .10 .05
☐ 71 Jari Kurri .15 .07
☐ 72 Paul Coffey .25 .11
☐ 73 Claude Lemieux .15 .07
☐ 74 Teemu Selanne .60 .25
☐ 75 Keith Tkachuk .40 .18
☐ 76 Pat Verbeek .10 .05
☐ 77 Chris Gratton .15 .07
☐ 78 Martin Brodeur .75 .35
☐ 79 Guy Hebert .15 .07
☐ 80 Al Iafrate .10 .05
☐ 81 Glen Wesley .10 .05
☐ 82 Scott Stevens .15 .07
☐ 83 Wayne Gretzky 2.00 .90
☐ 84 Ron Francis .15 .07
☐ 85 Scott Mellanby .15 .07
☐ 86 Joe Juneau .15 .07
☐ 87 Jason Arnott .15 .07
☐ 88 Tom Barrasso .15 .07
☐ 89 Peter Bondra .25 .11
☐ 90 Felix Potvin .25 .11
☐ 91 Brian Bellows .10 .05
☐ 92 Pavel Bure .60 .25
☐ 93 Grant Fuhr .15 .07
☐ 94 Andy Moog .15 .07
☐ 95 Mike Gartner .15 .07
☐ 96 Patrick Roy 1.50 .70
☐ 97 Brett Hull .40 .18
☐ 98 Rob Blake .10 .05
☐ 99 Dave Andreychuk .15 .07
☐ 100 Eric Lindros 1.25 .55
☐ 101 Scott Niedermayer .10 .05
☐ 102 Tim Cheveldae .15 .07
☐ 103 Slava Kozlov .15 .07
☐ 104 Dimitri Khristich .10 .05
☐ 105 Steve Thomas .10 .05
☐ 106 Kevin Stevens .10 .05
☐ 107 Kirk Muller .10 .05
☐ 108 Stephane Richer .15 .07
☐ 109 Theoren Fleury .15 .07
☐ 110 Jeff Brown .10 .05
☐ 111 Chris Pronger .15 .07
☐ 112 Steve Larmer .15 .07
☐ 113 Eric Desjardins .10 .05
☐ 114 Mike Ricci .10 .05
☐ 115 Tony Amonte .15 .07
☐ 116 Pat Falloon .15 .07
☐ 117 Garry Galley .10 .05
☐ 118 Dino Ciccarelli .15 .07
☐ 119 Rod Brind'Amour .15 .07
☐ 120 Petr Nedved .15 .07
☐ 121 Curtis Joseph .25 .11
☐ 122 Cliff Ronning .10 .05
☐ 123 Ulf Dahlen .10 .05
☐ 124 Marty McSorley .10 .05
☐ 125 Nelson Emerson .10 .05
☐ 126 Brian Skrudland .10 .05
☐ 127 Sean Burke .15 .07
☐ 128 Sylvain Cote .10 .05
☐ 129 Brendan Shanahan .60 .25
☐ 130 Benoit Hogue .10 .05
☐ 131 Joe Nieuwendyk .15 .07
☐ 132 Bryan Smolinski .10 .05
☐ 133 Mike Richter .25 .11
☐ 134 Nicklas Lidstrom .15 .07
☐ 135 Alexei Yashin .15 .07
☐ 136 John MacLean .15 .07
☐ 137 Geoff Courtnall .10 .05
☐ 138 Robert Reichel .10 .05
☐ 139 Craig Janney .15 .07
☐ 140 Zarley Zalapski .10 .05
☐ 141 Andrew Cassels .10 .05
☐ 142 Kevin Dineen .10 .05
☐ 143 Larry Murphy .15 .07
☐ 144 Valeri Kamensky .15 .07
☐ 145 Steve Duchesne .10 .05
☐ 146 Phil Housley .10 .05
☐ 147 Gary Roberts .10 .05
☐ 148 Kevin Hatcher .10 .05
☐ 149 Bryan Berard 2.00 .90
☐ 150 Marty Reasoner 1.00 .45
☐ 151 Andrew Berenzweig .10 .05
☐ 152 Erik Rasmussen .60 .25
☐ 153 Luke Curtin .10 .05
☐ 154 Dan Lacouture .10 .05
☐ 155 Brian Boucher 1.50 .70
☐ 156 Wyatt Smith .10 .05
☐ 157 Maxim Kuznetsov .15 .07
☐ 158 Alexei Morozov 6.00 2.70
☐ 159 Dmitri Nabokov .75 .35
☐ 160 Wade Redden .40 .18
☐ 161 Jason Doig .10 .05
☐ 162 Alyn McCauley 2.00 .90
☐ 163 Jeff Ware .15 .07
☐ 164 Brad Larsen .10 .05
☐ 165 Jarome Iginla 1.00 .45
☐ 166 Christian Dube .40 .18
☐ 167 Mike McBain .10 .05
☐ 168 Todd Norman .10 .05
☐ 169 Oleg Tverdovsky .15 .07
☐ 170 Jamie Storr .15 .07
☐ 171 Jason Wiemer .15 .07
☐ 172 Kenny Jonsson .10 .05
☐ 173 Paul Kariya 1.75 .80
☐ 174 Viktor Kozlov .10 .05
☐ 175 Peter Forsberg 1.50 .70
☐ 176 Jeff Friesen .15 .07
☐ 177 Brian Rolston .10 .05
☐ 178 Brett Lindros .10 .05
☐ 179 Adam Deadmarsh .15 .07
☐ 180 Aaron Gavey .10 .05
☐ 181 Janne Laukkanen .10 .05
☐ 182 Todd Harvey .10 .05
☐ 183 Valeri Karpov .10 .05
☐ 184 Andrei Nikolishin .10 .05
☐ 185 Pavol Demitra .10 .05
☐ 186 Radek Bonk .40 .18
☐ 187 Valeri Bure .15 .07
☐ 188 Eric Fichaud .75 .35
☐ 189 Jamie McLennan .10 .05
☐ 190 Mariusz Czerkawski .10 .05
☐ 191 John Lilley .10 .05
☐ 192 Brian Savage .10 .05
☐ 193 Jason Allison .10 .05
☐ 194 Mattias Norstrom .10 .05
☐ 195 Todd Simon .10 .05
☐ 196 Zigmund Palffy .15 .07
☐ 197 Rene Corbet .10 .05
☐ 198 Mike Peca .10 .05
☐ 199 Checklist (1-100) .10 .05
☐ 200 Checklist (101-198) .10 .05
☐ NNO Mike Modano Large 2.00 .90

## 1994-95 Select Gold

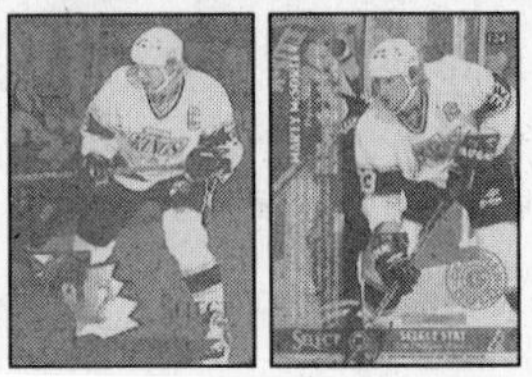

This 200-card set is a parallel version of the regular Select issue. These cards feature a gold foil printing process on the front, as well as a Certified Gold logo printed on the back. These were inserted at a rate of 1:3 packs.

MINT NRMT
COMPLETE SET (200) 300.00 135.00
COMMON CARD (1-200) .50 .23
*STARS: 10X TO 20X BASIC CARDS
*YOUNG STARS: 6X TO 12X BASIC CARDS
*RCs: 4X TO 8X BASIC CARDS

## 1994-95 Select First Line

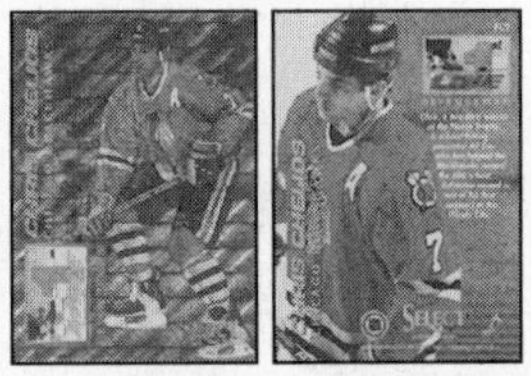

The 12 cards in this set utilize the Dufex printing technology and were inserted at a rate of 1:48 packs. The player's name, team affiliation and "1st Line" logo appear along the left card front. Cards are numbered with an "FL" prefix.

MINT NRMT
COMPLETE SET (12) 150.00 70.00
COMMON CARD (1-12) 4.00 1.80

☐ 1 Patrick Roy 30.00 13.50
☐ 2 Ray Bourque 6.00 2.70
☐ 3 Brian Leetch 6.00 2.70
☐ 4 Brendan Shanahan 12.00 5.50
☐ 5 Eric Lindros 25.00 11.00
☐ 6 Pavel Bure 12.00 5.50
☐ 7 Mike Richter 6.00 2.70
☐ 8 Scott Stevens 4.00 1.80
☐ 9 Chris Chelios 6.00 2.70
☐ 10 Luc Robitaille 4.00 1.80
☐ 11 Wayne Gretzky 40.00 18.00
☐ 12 Brett Hull 10.00 4.50

## 1994-95 Select Youth Explosion

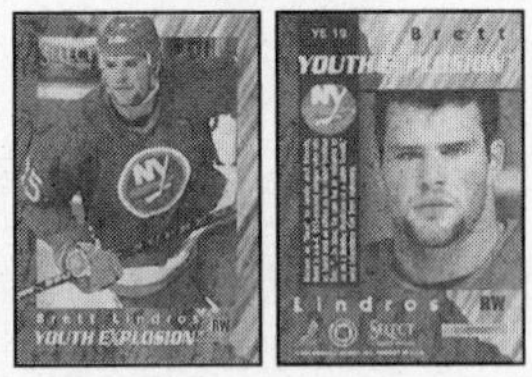

The 12 cards in this set were randomly inserted in Select product at the rate of 1:24 packs. The striking design benefits from the use of a special holographic silver foil printing. The borders are blue and silver with player name and position above the set title located near the bottom. The cards are numbered with a "YE" prefix.

MINT NRMT
COMPLETE SET (12) 75.00 34.00
COMMON CARD (YE1-YE12) 4.00 1.80

☐ YE1 Jamie Storr 5.00 2.20
☐ YE2 Oleg Tverdovsky 4.00 1.80
☐ YE3 Janne Laukkanen 4.00 1.80
☐ YE4 Kenny Jonsson 4.00 1.80
☐ YE5 Paul Kariya 20.00 9.00
☐ YE6 Viktor Kozlov 5.00 2.20
☐ YE7 Peter Forsberg 20.00 9.00
☐ YE8 Jason Allison 4.00 1.80
☐ YE9 Jeff Friesen 6.00 2.70
☐ YE10 Brian Rolston 4.00 1.80
☐ YE11 Mariusz Czerkawski 4.00 1.80
☐ YE12 Brett Lindros 4.00 1.80

## 1995-96 Select Certified Promos

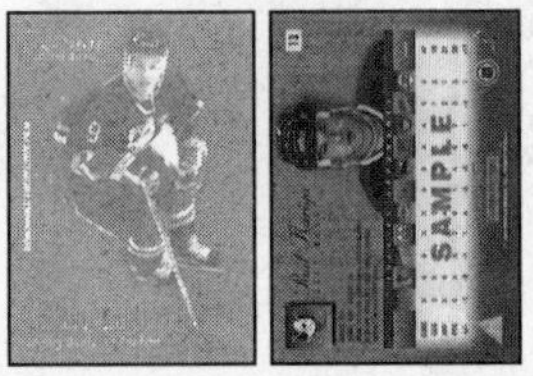

These cards are samples of the 1995-96 Select Certified series. Their description is the same as the regular series with the exception of the word "Sample" printed on the back of each one. The cards are listed below according to their number in their regular series. The Pavel Bure card is from the Gold Team insert series. It is identical to the expensive insert save for the word "sample" written on the card back.

MINT NRMT
COMPLETE SET (9) 30.00 13.50
COMMON CARD .25 .11

☐ 5 Pavel Bure Gold Team 15.00 6.75
☐ 12 Jim Carey 1.00 .45
☐ 13 Paul Kariya 10.00 4.50
☐ 17 Mike Modano 2.00 .90
☐ 19 Owen Nolan .75 .35
☐ 43 Alexander Mogilny 1.00 .45
☐ 68 Peter Forsberg 10.00 4.50
☐ 69 Felix Potvin 1.50 .70
☐ NNO Title Card .25 .11

## 1995-96 Select Certified

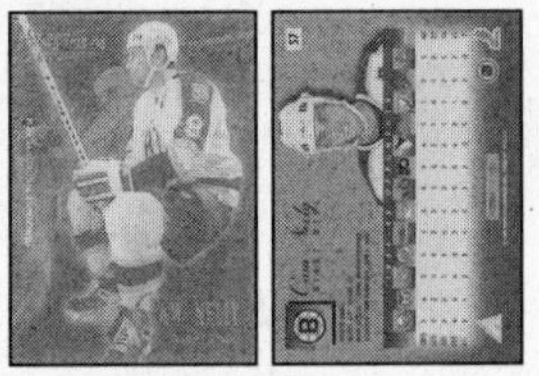

The 1995-96 Select Certified set was issued in one series totalling 144 cards. The 6-card packs retail for $4.99. The cards featured a smart, silver mirror finish, which was protected from routine scratching by a "Pinnacle Peel", which collectors could remove if they so wished. Although collectors are free to do so, cards without the foil may be slightly harder to resell, although they will be more sightly. The card stock was 24-point, double that of a normal card. Rookie Cards in this set include Daniel Alfredsson and Petr Sykora.

MINT NRMT
COMPLETE SET (144) 50.00 22.00
COMMON CARD (1-144) .25 .11

☐ 1 Mario Lemieux 6.00 2.70
☐ 2 Chris Chelios 1.00 .45
☐ 3 Scott Mellanby .50 .23
☐ 4 Brett Hull 1.50 .70
☐ 5 Theoren Fleury .50 .23
☐ 6 Alexei Zhamnov .50 .23
☐ 7 Mats Sundin .50 .23
☐ 8 Mathieu Schneider .25 .11
☐ 9 Jason Arnott .50 .23
☐ 10 Mark Recchi .50 .23
☐ 11 Adam Oates .50 .23
☐ 12 Jim Carey 1.00 .45
☐ 13 Paul Kariya 5.00 2.20
☐ 14 Mark Messier 1.50 .70
☐ 15 Eric Lindros 4.00 1.80
☐ 16 Pavel Bure 2.50 1.10
☐ 17 Mike Modano 1.50 .70
☐ 18 Pat LaFontaine .50 .23
☐ 19 Owen Nolan .50 .23
☐ 20 Roman Hamrlik .50 .23
☐ 21 Paul Coffey 1.00 .45
☐ 22 Alexandre Daigle .25 .11
☐ 23 Wayne Gretzky 8.00 3.60
☐ 24 Martin Brodeur 3.00 1.35
☐ 25 Ulf Dahlen .25 .11
☐ 26 Geoff Sanderson .50 .23
☐ 27 Brian Leetch 1.00 .45
☐ 28 Dave Andreychuk .50 .23
☐ 29 Sergei Fedorov 2.00 .90
☐ 30 Jocelyn Thibault 1.00 .45
☐ 31 Mikael Renberg .50 .23
☐ 32 Joe Nieuwendyk .50 .23
☐ 33 Craig Janney .50 .23
☐ 34 Ray Bourque 1.00 .45
☐ 35 Jari Kurri .50 .23
☐ 36 Alexei Yashin .50 .23
☐ 37 Keith Tkachuk 1.50 .70
☐ 38 Jaromir Jagr 4.00 1.80
☐ 39 Stephane Richer .50 .23
☐ 40 Trevor Kidd .50 .23
☐ 41 Kevin Hatcher .25 .11
☐ 42 Mike Vernon .50 .23
☐ 43 Alexander Mogilny .50 .23
☐ 44 John LeClair 2.00 .90
☐ 45 Joe Sakic 2.50 1.10
☐ 46 Kevin Stevens .25 .11
☐ 47 Adam Graves .50 .23
☐ 48 Doug Gilmour 1.00 .45
☐ 49 Pierre Turgeon .50 .23
☐ 50 Joe Murphy .25 .11
☐ 51 Peter Bondra 1.00 .45
☐ 52 Ron Francis .50 .23
☐ 53 Luc Robitaille .50 .23
☐ 54 Mike Gartner .50 .23
☐ 55 Bill Ranford .50 .23
☐ 56 Jeff Friesen .50 .23
☐ 57 Cam Neely .50 .23
☐ 58 Daren Puppa .50 .23
☐ 59 Rod Brind'Amour .50 .23
☐ 60 Jeremy Roenick 1.00 .45
☐ 61 Brett Lindros .25 .11
☐ 62 Todd Harvey .25 .11
☐ 63 Kirk McLean .50 .23
☐ 64 Brendan Shanahan 2.00 .90
☐ 65 Kelly Hrudey .50 .23
☐ 66 Scott Stevens .50 .23
☐ 67 Sergei Zubov .25 .11
☐ 68 Peter Forsberg 4.00 1.80
☐ 69 Felix Potvin 1.00 .45
☐ 70 Scott Niedermayer .25 .11
☐ 71 Keith Primeau .50 .23
☐ 72 Al MacInnis .50 .23
☐ 73 Mike Richter 1.00 .45
☐ 74 Rob Blake .25 .11
☐ 75 Vincent Damphousse .50 .23
☐ 76 Teemu Selanne 2.50 1.10
☐ 77 Andy Moog .50 .23
☐ 78 Ron Hextall .50 .23
☐ 79 Oleg Tverdovsky .50 .23
☐ 80 Joe Juneau .50 .23
☐ 81 Patrick Roy 6.00 2.70
☐ 82 Wendel Clark .50 .23
☐ 83 Brian Bradley .25 .11
☐ 84 Curtis Joseph 1.00 .45
☐ 85 John Vanbiesbrouck 2.00 .90
☐ 86 Phil Housley .50 .23
☐ 87 Trevor Linden .50 .23
☐ 88 Alexei Kovalev .25 .11
☐ 89 Dominik Hasek 2.50 1.10
☐ 90 Larry Murphy .50 .23
☐ 91 Arturs Irbe .50 .23
☐ 92 John MacLean .50 .23
☐ 93 Ed Belfour 1.00 .45
☐ 94 Steve Yzerman 4.00 1.80
☐ 95 Tom Barrasso .50 .23
☐ 96 Rob Niedermayer .50 .23
☐ 97 Dale Hawerchuk .50 .23
☐ 98 Rick Tocchet .50 .23
☐ 99 Claude Lemieux .50 .23
☐ 100 Sean Burke .50 .23
☐ 101 Shayne Corson .25 .11
☐ 102 Dino Ciccarelli .50 .23
☐ 103 Kirk Muller .25 .11
☐ 104 Don Beaupre .50 .23
☐ 105 Valeri Kamensky .50 .23
☐ 106 Markus Naslund .25 .11
☐ 107 Tomas Sandstrom .25 .11
☐ 108 Pat Verbeek .25 .11
☐ 109 Doug Weight .50 .23
☐ 110 Brian Holzinger 1.00 .45
☐ 111 Antti Tormanen .25 .11
☐ 112 Tommy Salo 1.50 .70
☐ 113 Jason Bonsignore .25 .11
☐ 114 Shane Doan .25 .11
☐ 115 Robert Svehla .25 .11
☐ 116 Chad Kilger .25 .11
☐ 117 Saku Koivu 2.00 .90
☐ 118 Jeff O'Neill .25 .11
☐ 119 Brendan Witt .25 .11
☐ 120 Byron Dafoe .50 .23
☐ 121 Ryan Smyth .25 .11
☐ 122 Daniel Alfredsson 2.00 .90
☐ 123 Todd Bertuzzi .50 .23
☐ 124 Daymond Langkow 1.00 .45
☐ 125 Miroslav Satan 4.00 1.80
☐ 126 Bryan McCabe .25 .11
☐ 127 Aki-Petteri Berg .25 .11
☐ 128 Cory Stillman .25 .11
☐ 129 Deron Quint .25 .11
☐ 130 Vitali Yachmenev .25 .11
☐ 131 Valeri Bure .50 .23
☐ 132 Eric Daze 1.00 .45
☐ 133 Radek Dvorak .25 .11
☐ 134 Landon Wilson .25 .11
☐ 135 Niklas Sundstrom .25 .11
☐ 136 Jamie Storr .50 .23
☐ 137 Ed Jovanovski 1.00 .45
☐ 138 Marcus Ragnarsson .25 .11
☐ 139 Kyle McLaren .25 .11
☐ 140 Sandy Moger .25 .11
☐ 141 Marty Murray .25 .11
☐ 142 Darby Hendrickson .25 .11
☐ 143 Corey Hirsch .50 .23
☐ 144 Petr Sykora .75 .35

## 1995-96 Select Certified Mirror Gold

The cards from this high-end parallel set of the base Select Certified issue were randomly inserted 1:5 packs. Instead of the typical silver finish, these, as the title suggests, had a golden background.

MINT NRMT
COMPLETE SET (144) 1200.00 550.00
COMMON CARD (1-144) 4.00 1.80
*STARS: 6X TO 12X BASIC CARDS
*YOUNG STARS: 5X TO 10X BASIC CARDS

## 1995-96 Select Certified Double Strike

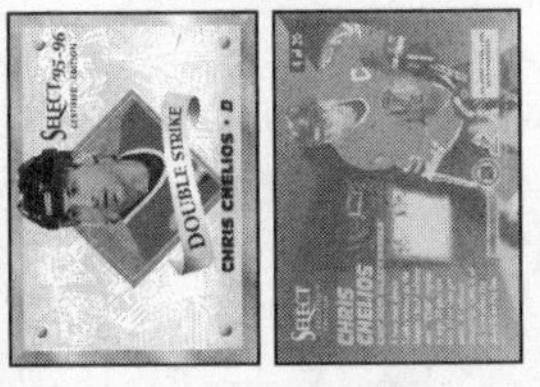

Randomly inserted in packs at a rate of 1:32, this 20-card set shines the spotlight on players whose abilities make them an imposing threat both offensively and defensively. The cards feature a rainbow silver foil background on the front, while the backs contain a note stating that no more than 1,975 complete sets were produced. There also was a Gold version of this set, with singles issued in black packs as inserts in roughly every 3.5 boxes. The fronts are essentially the same, save for the use of a gold foil background. The backs contain a small box reading "Case Chase" and "No more than 903 sets produced."

| | MINT | NRMT |
|---|---|---|
| COMPLETE SET (20) | 150.00 | 70.00 |
| COMMON CARD (1-20) | 5.00 | 2.20 |
| COMP.GOLD SET (20) | 350.00 | 160.00 |

*GOLD CARDS: 1.5X TO 2.5X SILVER VERSION

| | MINT | NRMT |
|---|---|---|
| ❑ 1 Doug Gilmour | 10.00 | 4.50 |
| ❑ 2 Ron Francis | 8.00 | 3.60 |
| ❑ 3 Ray Bourque | 10.00 | 4.50 |
| ❑ 4 Chris Chelios | 10.00 | 4.50 |
| ❑ 5 Adam Oates | 5.00 | 2.20 |
| ❑ 6 Mike Ricci | 5.00 | 2.20 |
| ❑ 7 Jeremy Roenick | 10.00 | 4.50 |
| ❑ 8 Jason Arnott | 8.00 | 3.60 |
| ❑ 9 Brendan Shanahan | 20.00 | 9.00 |
| ❑ 10 Joe Nieuwendyk | 5.00 | 2.20 |
| ❑ 11 Trevor Linden | 5.00 | 2.20 |
| ❑ 12 Mikael Renberg | 8.00 | 3.60 |
| ❑ 13 Theoren Fleury | 8.00 | 3.60 |
| ❑ 14 Sergei Fedorov | 20.00 | 9.00 |
| ❑ 15 Mark Messier | 12.00 | 5.50 |
| ❑ 16 Keith Primeau | 5.00 | 2.20 |
| ❑ 17 Keith Tkachuk | 12.00 | 5.50 |
| ❑ 18 Scott Stevens | 5.00 | 2.20 |
| ❑ 19 Claude Lemieux | 8.00 | 3.60 |
| ❑ 20 Alexei Zhamnov | 8.00 | 3.60 |

## 1995-96 Select Certified Future

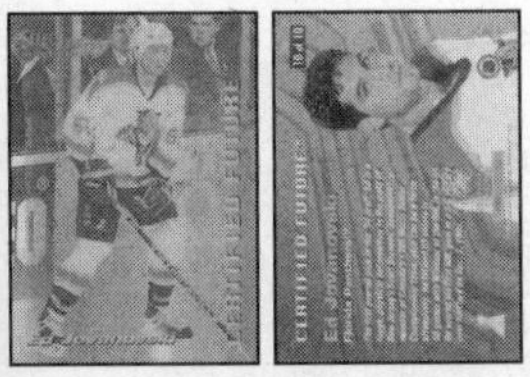

Randomly inserted in packs at a rate of one in 19, this 10-card set features some of the league's brightest future stars in silver rainbow holographic foil print technology.

| | MINT | NRMT |
|---|---|---|
| COMPLETE SET (10) | 100.00 | 45.00 |
| COMMON CARD (1-10) | 5.00 | 2.20 |
| ❑ 1 Peter Forsberg | 30.00 | 13.50 |
| ❑ 2 Jim Carey | 10.00 | 4.50 |
| ❑ 3 Paul Kariya | 40.00 | 18.00 |
| ❑ 4 Jocelyn Thibault | 10.00 | 4.50 |
| ❑ 5 Saku Koivu | 15.00 | 6.75 |
| ❑ 6 Brian Holzinger | 8.00 | 3.60 |
| ❑ 7 Todd Harvey | 5.00 | 2.20 |
| ❑ 8 Jeff O'Neill | 5.00 | 2.20 |
| ❑ 9 Oleg Tverdovsky | 5.00 | 2.20 |
| ❑ 10 Ed Jovanovski | 10.00 | 4.50 |

## 1995-96 Select Certified Gold Team

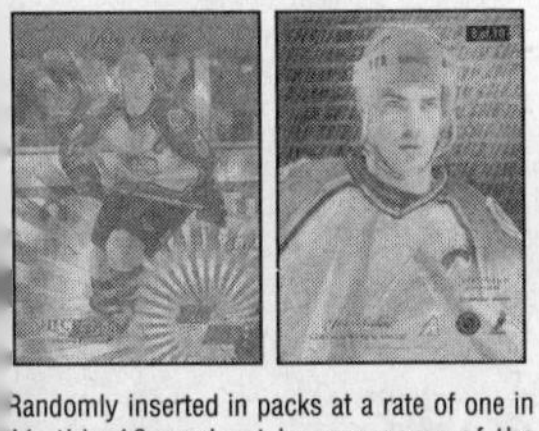

Randomly inserted in packs at a rate of one in 41, this 10-card set honors some of the league's top players, bestowing best-of-the-best honors with a Dufexed gold-foil design element. The presence of a Pavel Bure Gold Team sample card in the Promo set led to some softening of demand for the insert version of the card found in this set.

| | MINT | NRMT |
|---|---|---|
| COMPLETE SET (10) | 400.00 | 180.00 |
| COMMON CARD (1-10) | 15.00 | 6.75 |
| ❑ 1 Eric Lindros | 50.00 | 22.00 |
| ❑ 2 Wayne Gretzky | 100.00 | 45.00 |
| ❑ 3 Mario Lemieux | 80.00 | 36.00 |
| ❑ 4 Jaromir Jagr | 50.00 | 22.00 |
| ❑ 5 Pavel Bure | 30.00 | 13.50 |
| ❑ 6 Brett Hull | 25.00 | 11.00 |
| ❑ 7 Cam Neely | 15.00 | 6.75 |
| ❑ 8 Joe Sakic | 30.00 | 13.50 |
| ❑ 9 Martin Brodeur | 40.00 | 18.00 |
| ❑ 10 Patrick Roy | 80.00 | 36.00 |

## 1996-97 Select Certified

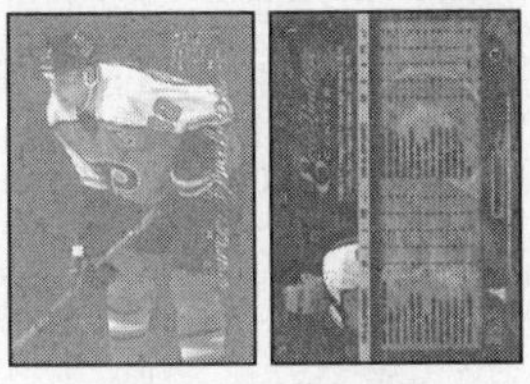

The 1996-97 Select Certified set was issued in one series totalling 120 cards. The cards featured a silver mirror-like background with player names scripted horizontally in gold foil on the front and complete stats on the reverse against each opposing team.

| | MINT | NRMT |
|---|---|---|
| COMPLETE SET (120) | 40.00 | 18.00 |
| COMMON CARD (1-120) | .20 | .09 |
| ❑ 1 Eric Lindros | 2.50 | 1.10 |
| ❑ 2 Mike Modano | 1.00 | .45 |
| ❑ 3 Jocelyn Thibault | .20 | .09 |
| ❑ 4 Wayne Gretzky | 5.00 | 2.20 |
| ❑ 5 Ray Bourque | .75 | .35 |
| ❑ 6 Martin Brodeur | 2.00 | .90 |
| ❑ 7 Rob Niedermayer | .40 | .18 |
| ❑ 8 Stephane Fiset | .40 | .18 |
| ❑ 9 Pat LaFontaine | .40 | .18 |
| ❑ 10 Mario Lemieux | 4.00 | 1.80 |
| ❑ 11 Ed Belfour | .75 | .35 |
| ❑ 12 Ron Francis | .40 | .18 |
| ❑ 13 Luc Robitaille | .40 | .18 |
| ❑ 14 Paul Kariya | 3.00 | 1.35 |
| ❑ 15 Doug Gilmour | .20 | .09 |
| ❑ 16 Joe Sakic | 1.50 | .70 |
| ❑ 17 Nikolai Khabibulin | .40 | .18 |
| ❑ 18 Valeri Bure | .40 | .18 |
| ❑ 19 Brett Hull | 1.00 | .45 |
| ❑ 20 Chris Osgood | .75 | .35 |
| ❑ 21 Trevor Kidd | .40 | .18 |
| ❑ 22 Kirk McLean | .40 | .18 |
| ❑ 23 Zigmund Palffy | .20 | .09 |
| ❑ 24 Keith Tkachuk | 1.00 | .45 |
| ❑ 25 Andy Moog | .40 | .18 |
| ❑ 26 Bill Guerin | .20 | .09 |
| ❑ 27 Chris Chelios | .75 | .35 |
| ❑ 28 Damian Rhodes | .40 | .18 |
| ❑ 29 Jim Carey | .20 | .09 |
| ❑ 30 Ed Jovanovski | .40 | .18 |
| ❑ 31 Felix Potvin | .20 | .09 |
| ❑ 32 Teemu Selanne | 1.50 | .70 |
| ❑ 33 John LeClair | 1.25 | .55 |
| ❑ 34 Pavel Bure | 1.50 | .70 |
| ❑ 35 Grant Fuhr | .40 | .18 |
| ❑ 36 Mark Messier | 1.00 | .45 |
| ❑ 37 Vincent Damphousse | .40 | .18 |
| ❑ 38 Jason Arnott | .40 | .18 |
| ❑ 39 Mike Richter | .75 | .35 |
| ❑ 40 Keith Primeau | .40 | .18 |
| ❑ 41 Steve Yzerman | 2.50 | 1.10 |
| ❑ 42 Trevor Linden | .40 | .18 |
| ❑ 43 Jaromir Jagr | 2.50 | 1.10 |
| ❑ 44 Sean Burke | .40 | .18 |
| ❑ 45 Alexei Zhitnik | .20 | .09 |
| ❑ 46 Dimitri Khristich | .20 | .09 |
| ❑ 47 Daniel Alfredsson | .40 | .18 |
| ❑ 48 Roman Hamrlik | .40 | .18 |
| ❑ 49 Pat Verbeek | .20 | .09 |
| ❑ 50 Doug Weight | .40 | .18 |
| ❑ 51 Adam Graves | .40 | .18 |
| ❑ 52 Michal Pivonka | .20 | .09 |
| ❑ 53 Claude Lemieux | .40 | .18 |
| ❑ 54 Scott Stevens | .40 | .18 |
| ❑ 55 Sergei Fedorov | 1.50 | .70 |
| ❑ 56 Owen Nolan | .40 | .18 |
| ❑ 57 Niklas Andersson | .20 | .09 |
| ❑ 58 Cory Stillman | .20 | .09 |
| ❑ 59 John Vanbiesbrouck | 1.25 | .55 |
| ❑ 60 Craig Janney | .40 | .18 |
| ❑ 61 Jeff Friesen | .40 | .18 |
| ❑ 62 Igor Larionov | .20 | .09 |
| ❑ 63 Ron Hextall | .40 | .18 |
| ❑ 64 Saku Koivu | 1.25 | .55 |
| ❑ 65 Wendel Clark | .40 | .18 |
| ❑ 66 Curtis Joseph | .20 | .09 |
| ❑ 67 Valeri Kamensky | .40 | .18 |
| ❑ 68 Adam Oates | .40 | .18 |
| ❑ 69 Daren Puppa | .40 | .18 |
| ❑ 70 Alexander Mogilny | .40 | .18 |
| ❑ 71 Corey Hirsch | .40 | .18 |
| ❑ 72 Brendan Shanahan | 1.50 | .70 |
| ❑ 73 Shayne Corson | .20 | .09 |
| ❑ 74 Dominik Hasek | 1.50 | .70 |
| ❑ 75 Theoren Fleury | .40 | .18 |
| ❑ 76 Brian Leetch | .75 | .35 |
| ❑ 77 Jeremy Roenick | .75 | .35 |
| ❑ 78 Peter Bondra | .20 | .09 |
| ❑ 79 Eric Daze | .40 | .18 |
| ❑ 80 Todd Bertuzzi | .20 | .09 |
| ❑ 81 Patrick Roy | 4.00 | 1.80 |
| ❑ 82 Pierre Turgeon | .40 | .18 |
| ❑ 83 Alexei Yashin | .40 | .18 |
| ❑ 84 Scott Mellanby | .40 | .18 |
| ❑ 85 Mats Sundin | .75 | .35 |
| ❑ 86 Jari Kurri | .40 | .18 |
| ❑ 87 Kelly Hrudey | .40 | .18 |
| ❑ 88 Joe Nieuwendyk | .40 | .18 |
| ❑ 89 Paul Coffey | .75 | .35 |
| ❑ 90 Jeff O'Neill | .20 | .09 |
| ❑ 91 Kai Nurminen | .20 | .09 |
| ❑ 92 Anders Eriksson | .20 | .09 |
| ❑ 93 Jarome Iginla | .20 | .09 |
| ❑ 94 Anson Carter | .20 | .09 |
| ❑ 95 Christian Dube | .20 | .09 |
| ❑ 96 Harry York | .20 | .09 |
| ❑ 97 Tomas Holmstrom | .40 | .18 |
| ❑ 98 Sergei Berezin | 1.25 | .55 |
| ❑ 99 Mattias Timander | .20 | .09 |
| ❑ 100 Wade Redden | .20 | .09 |
| ❑ 101 Mike Grier | 1.50 | .70 |
| ❑ 102 Jonas Hoglund | .20 | .09 |
| ❑ 103 Eric Fichaud | .40 | .18 |
| ❑ 104 Janne Niinimaa | .20 | .09 |
| ❑ 105 Tuomas Gronman | .20 | .09 |
| ❑ 106 Jim Campbell | .20 | .09 |
| ❑ 107 Daniel Goneau | .40 | .18 |
| ❑ 108 Patrick Lalime | .20 | .09 |
| ❑ 109 Ruslan Salei | .20 | .09 |
| ❑ 110 Richard Zednik | .40 | .18 |
| ❑ 111 Chris O'Sullivan | .20 | .09 |
| ❑ 112 Fredrik Modin | .40 | .18 |
| ❑ 113 Brad Smyth | .20 | .09 |
| ❑ 114 Bryan Berard | .75 | .35 |
| ❑ 115 Jamie Langenbrunner | .20 | .09 |
| ❑ 116 Ethan Moreau | .20 | .09 |
| ❑ 117 Daymond Langkow | .20 | .09 |
| ❑ 118 Andreas Dackell | .20 | .09 |
| ❑ 119 Rem Murray | .40 | .18 |
| ❑ 120 Dainius Zubrus | 1.50 | .70 |
| ❑ P60 Craig Janney PROMO | .50 | .23 |
| ❑ P65 Wendel Clark PROMO | .50 | .23 |

## 1996-97 Select Certified Artist's Proofs

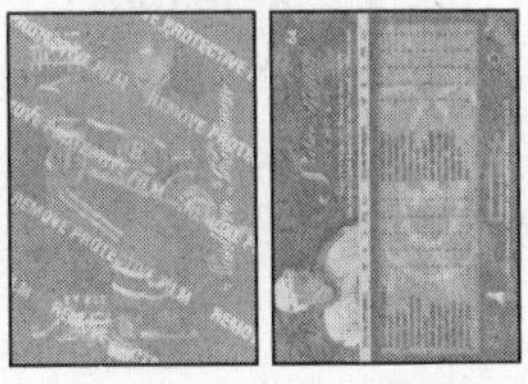

Inserted 1:48 packs, this insert parallels the base set. The cards can be distinguished by an Artist Proof logo stamped on the front of the card. Although the cards suggest that 500 were printed, there were, in fact, just 150 of each card made.

| | MINT | NRMT |
|---|---|---|
| COMPLETE SET (120) | 3500.00 | 1600.00 |
| COMMON CARD (1-120) | 8.00 | 3.60 |

*STARS: 25X TO 50X BASIC CARDS
*YOUNG STARS: 15X TO 30X

## 1996-97 Select Certified Blue

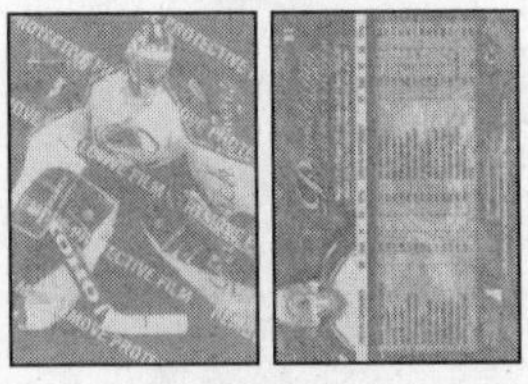

A one per 50 pack parallel insert, these cards can be differentiated from the base cards by the blue foil background on the front of the card.

| | MINT | NRMT |
|---|---|---|
| COMPLETE SET (120) | 3500.00 | 1600.00 |
| COMMON CARD (1-120) | 8.00 | 3.60 |

*STARS: 25X TO 50X BASIC CARDS
*YOUNG STARS: 15X TO 30X

## 1996-97 Select Certified Mirror Blue

A one per 200 pack parallel insert, these cards are differentiated by a blue holographic foil background on the front of the card and the words 'Mirror Blue' on the reverse. Though the actual number of cards printed is not known, sources estimate that only 36 copies of each Mirror Blue card exists.

| | MINT | NRMT |
|---|---|---|
| COMMON CARD (1-120) | 50.00 | 22.00 |

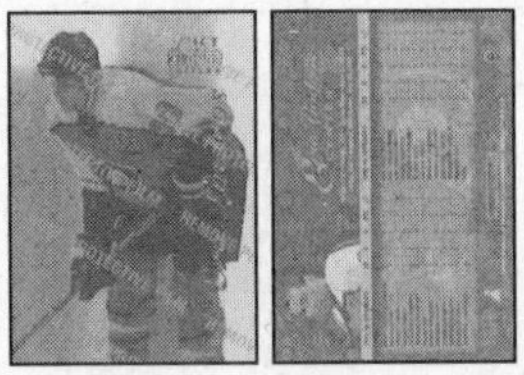

*STARS: 75X TO 200X BASIC CARDS
*YOUNG STARS: 60X TO 150X BASIC CARDS
*RC's: 30X TO 80X BASIC CARDS

| | MINT | NRMT |
|---|---|---|
| ❑ 1 Eric Lindros | 600.00 | 275.00 |
| ❑ 2 Mike Modano | 200.00 | 90.00 |
| ❑ 4 Wayne Gretzky | 1200.00 | 550.00 |
| ❑ 6 Martin Brodeur | 400.00 | 180.00 |
| ❑ 10 Mario Lemieux | 800.00 | 350.00 |
| ❑ 14 Paul Kariya | 600.00 | 275.00 |
| ❑ 16 Joe Sakic | 400.00 | 180.00 |
| ❑ 19 Brett Hull | 200.00 | 90.00 |
| ❑ 24 Keith Tkachuk | 200.00 | 90.00 |
| ❑ 32 Teemu Selanne | 300.00 | 135.00 |
| ❑ 33 John LeClair | 250.00 | 110.00 |
| ❑ 34 Pavel Bure | 300.00 | 135.00 |
| ❑ 36 Mark Messier | 200.00 | 90.00 |
| ❑ 41 Steve Yzerman | 500.00 | 220.00 |
| ❑ 43 Jaromir Jagr | 500.00 | 220.00 |
| ❑ 55 Sergei Fedorov | 300.00 | 135.00 |
| ❑ 59 John Vanbiesbrouck | 250.00 | 110.00 |
| ❑ 64 Saku Koivu | 300.00 | 135.00 |
| ❑ 72 Brendan Shanahan | 300.00 | 135.00 |
| ❑ 74 Dominik Hasek | 300.00 | 135.00 |
| ❑ 81 Patrick Roy | 800.00 | 350.00 |
| ❑ 120 Dainius Zubrus | 250.00 | 110.00 |

## 1996-97 Select Certified Mirror Gold

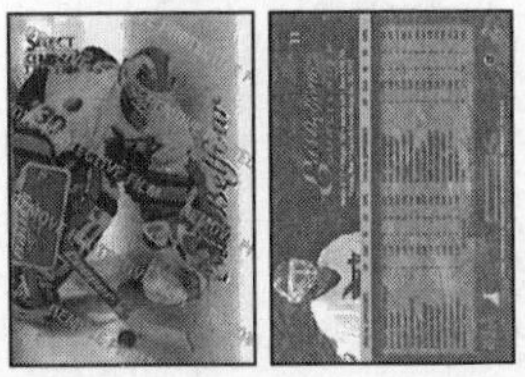

The scarcest modern hockey set, this is a one per 300 pack parallel insert. It can be differentiated from the base set by a gold holographic foil background on the front of the card and the words 'Mirror Gold' on the reverse. Though the actual number of cards printed is not known, sources estimate that only 24 copies of each Mirror Gold card exists.

| | MINT | NRMT |
|---|---|---|
| COMMON CARD (1-120) | 100.00 | 45.00 |

*STARS: 250X TO 400X BASIC CARDS
*YOUNG STARS: 175X TO 300X BASIC CARDS
*RC's: 60X TO 120X BASIC CARDS

| | MINT | NRMT |
|---|---|---|
| ❑ 1 Eric Lindros | 1500.00 | 700.00 |
| ❑ 2 Mike Modano | 400.00 | 180.00 |
| ❑ 4 Wayne Gretzky | 3000.00 | 1350.00 |
| ❑ 6 Martin Brodeur | 800.00 | 350.00 |
| ❑ 10 Mario Lemieux | 2000.00 | 900.00 |
| ❑ 14 Paul Kariya | 1500.00 | 700.00 |
| ❑ 16 Joe Sakic | 600.00 | 275.00 |
| ❑ 19 Brett Hull | 500.00 | 220.00 |
| ❑ 24 Keith Tkachuk | 400.00 | 180.00 |
| ❑ 32 Teemu Selanne | 800.00 | 350.00 |
| ❑ 33 John LeClair | 600.00 | 275.00 |
| ❑ 34 Pavel Bure | 800.00 | 350.00 |
| ❑ 36 Mark Messier | 500.00 | 220.00 |
| ❑ 41 Steve Yzerman | 1000.00 | 450.00 |
| ❑ 43 Jaromir Jagr | 1000.00 | 450.00 |
| ❑ 55 Sergei Fedorov | 600.00 | 275.00 |
| ❑ 59 John Vanbiesbrouck | 400.00 | 180.00 |
| ❑ 64 Saku Koivu | 500.00 | 220.00 |
| ❑ 66 Curtis Joseph | 300.00 | 135.00 |
| ❑ 72 Brendan Shanahan | 600.00 | 275.00 |
| ❑ 74 Dominik Hasek | 600.00 | 275.00 |
| ❑ 81 Patrick Roy | 2000.00 | 900.00 |

## 1996-97 Select Certified Mirror Red

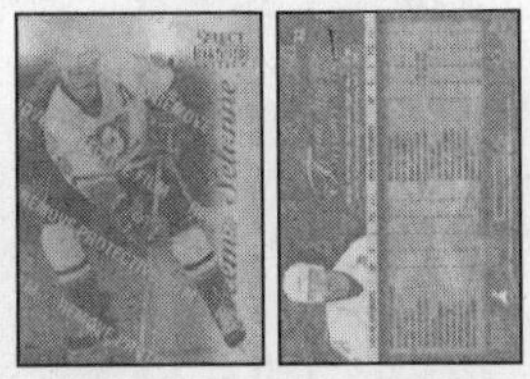

A one per 100 pack parallel insert, these cards can be differentiated from the base set by a red holographic foil background on the front of the card and the words 'Mirror Red' on the reverse.Though the actual number of cards printed is not known, sources estimate that just 72 copies of each Mirror Red card exists.

| | MINT | NRMT |
|---|---|---|
| COMMON CARD (1-120) | 25.00 | 11.00 |

*STARS: 40X TO 100X BASIC CARDS
*YOUNG STARS: 30X TO 80X BASIC CARDS
*RC's: 15X TO 40X BASIC CARDS

## 1996-97 Select Certified Red

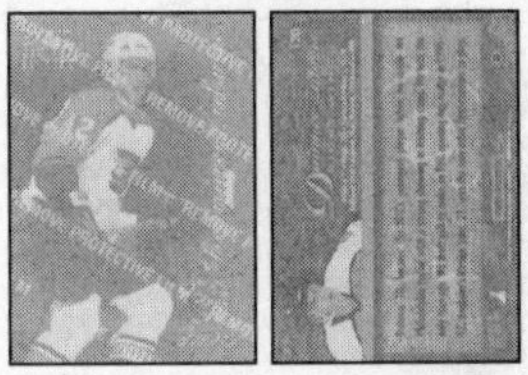

A one per 8 pack parallel insert, these cards are differentiated from those in the base set by a red foil background on the front of the card.

| | MINT | NRMT |
|---|---|---|
| COMPLETE SET (120) | 600.00 | 275.00 |
| COMMON CARD (1-120) | 2.00 | .90 |

*STARS: 4X TO 8X BASIC CARDS
*YOUNG STARS: 3X TO 6X

## 1996-97 Select Certified Cornerstones

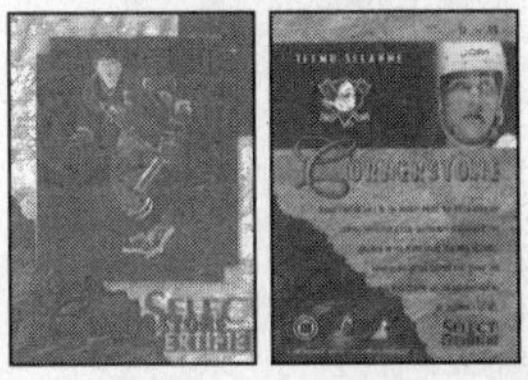

Randomly inserted in packs at a rate of one in 38, these cards feature a player photo framed in silver and black etched metal Dufex foil. The text on the card backs describe why each of the 15 players is considered his team's cornerstone player.

| | MINT | NRMT |
|---|---|---|
| COMPLETE SET (15) | 200.00 | 90.00 |
| COMMON CARD (1-15) | 6.00 | 2.70 |
| ❑ 1 Eric Lindros | 15.00 | 6.75 |
| ❑ 2 Mario Lemieux | 25.00 | 11.00 |
| ❑ 3 Jaromir Jagr | 15.00 | 6.75 |
| ❑ 4 Wayne Gretzky | 30.00 | 13.50 |
| ❑ 5 Mark Messier | 6.00 | 2.70 |
| ❑ 6 Brett Hull | 6.00 | 2.70 |
| ❑ 7 Pavel Bure | 10.00 | 4.50 |
| ❑ 8 Saku Koivu | 8.00 | 3.60 |
| ❑ 9 Joe Sakic | 10.00 | 4.50 |
| ❑ 10 Keith Tkachuk | 6.00 | 2.70 |
| ❑ 11 Paul Kariya | 20.00 | 9.00 |
| ❑ 12 Teemu Selanne | 10.00 | 4.50 |
| ❑ 13 Sergei Fedorov | 10.00 | 4.50 |
| ❑ 14 Steve Yzerman | 15.00 | 6.75 |
| ❑ 15 Peter Forsberg | 15.00 | 6.75 |

## 1996-97 Select Certified Freezers

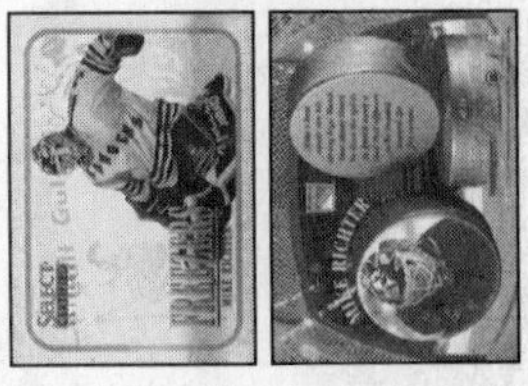

Randomly inserted in packs at a rate of one in 41, this set features silver holofoil cards of 15 highly regarded NHL goaltenders.

| | MINT | NRMT |
|---|---|---|
| COMPLETE SET (15) | 120.00 | 55.00 |
| COMMON CARD (1-15) | 6.00 | 2.70 |
| ❑ 1 Martin Brodeur | 15.00 | 6.75 |
| ❑ 2 Patrick Roy | 30.00 | 13.50 |
| ❑ 3 Jim Carey | 12.00 | 5.50 |
| ❑ 4 John Vanbiesbrouck | 10.00 | 4.50 |
| ❑ 5 Dominik Hasek | 15.00 | 6.75 |
| ❑ 6 Ed Belfour | 8.00 | 3.60 |
| ❑ 7 Curtis Joseph | 8.00 | 3.60 |
| ❑ 8 Felix Potvin | 20.00 | 9.00 |
| ❑ 9 Daren Puppa | 6.00 | 2.70 |
| ❑ 10 Chris Osgood | 8.00 | 3.60 |
| ❑ 11 Mike Richter | 8.00 | 3.60 |
| ❑ 12 Jocelyn Thibault | 8.00 | 3.60 |
| ❑ 13 Ron Hextall | 6.00 | 2.70 |
| ❑ 14 Nikolai Khabibulin | 6.00 | 2.70 |
| ❑ 15 Damian Rhodes | 6.00 | 2.70 |

## 1992-93 Senators

This 15-postcard set commemorates the inaugural season of the Ottawa Senators. The

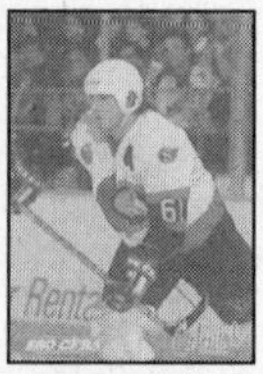

postcards feature full-bleed action photography, along with the logos of the set's two sponsors, CFRA Radio and Colonial Furniture. There is no indication of the player's identity anywhere on the card, so knowledge of obscure expansion draft-calibre players is a must to truly appreciate this set. The backs are blank. The cards are unnumbered, and are listed below alphabetically.

| | MINT | NRMT |
|---|---|---|
| COMPLETE SET (15) | 15.00 | 6.75 |
| COMMON CARD | 1.00 | .45 |
| ❑ 1 Jamie Baker | 1.00 | .45 |
| ❑ 2 Daniel Berthiaume | 1.50 | .70 |
| ❑ 3 Neil Brady | 1.00 | .45 |
| ❑ 4 Ken Hammond | 1.00 | .45 |
| ❑ 5 Dave Hannan | 1.00 | .45 |
| ❑ 6 Jody Hull | 1.00 | .45 |
| ❑ 7 Mark Lamb | 1.00 | .45 |
| ❑ 8 Darcy Loewen | 1.00 | .45 |
| ❑ 9 Norm Maciver | 1.00 | .45 |
| ❑ 10 Brad Marsh | 1.50 | .70 |
| ❑ 11 Andrew McBain | 1.00 | .45 |
| ❑ 12 Mike Peluso | 1.25 | .55 |
| ❑ 13 Darren Rumble | 1.00 | .45 |
| ❑ 14 Brad Shaw | 1.00 | .45 |
| ❑ 15 Sylvain Turgeon | 1.00 | .45 |

## 1993-94 Senators Kraft Sheets

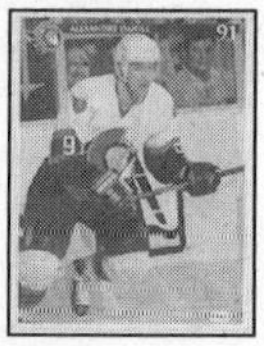

These 27 blank-backed photo sheets of the 1993-94 Ottawa Senators measure approximately 8 1/2" by 11" and feature color player action shots bordered in team colors (red, white, and gold). The player's name and uniform number, along with the Senators' logo, appear near the top. The logo for Kraft appears at the lower right; the logo for Loeb appears at the lower left. The production number out of the total produced for each sheet is shown within the white rectangle immediately above the Kraft logo. The sheets were produced in differing quantities. These production figures are shown in the checklist below. A special storage album was also available for the sheets. The sheets are unnumbered and checklisted below in alphabetical order.

| | MINT | NRMT |
|---|---|---|
| COMPLETE SET (27) | 150.00 | 70.00 |
| COMMON CARD (1-27) | 5.00 | 2.20 |
| ❑ 1 Dave Archibald 3,500 | 5.00 | 2.20 |
| ❑ 2 Craig Billington 6,500 | 6.00 | 2.70 |
| ❑ 3 Rick Bowness CO 6,500 | 5.00 | 2.20 |
| ❑ 4 Robert Burakovsky 1,500 | 7.00 | 3.10 |
| ❑ 5 Alexandre Daigle 6,500 | 7.00 | 3.10 |
| ❑ 6 Pavol Demitra 1,500 | 10.00 | 4.50 |
| ❑ 7 Gord Dineen 3,500 | 5.00 | 2.20 |
| ❑ 8 Dmitri Filimonov 1,500 | 7.00 | 3.10 |
| ❑ 9 Brian Glynn 1,500 | 7.00 | 3.10 |
| ❑ 10 Bill Huard 1,500 | 7.00 | 3.10 |
| ❑ 11 Jarmo Kekalainen 1,500 | 7.00 | 3.10 |
| ❑ 12 Bob Kudelski 1,500 | 7.00 | 3.10 |
| ❑ 13 Mark Lamb 1,500 | 7.00 | 3.10 |
| ❑ 14 Darcy Loewen 3,500 | 5.00 | 2.20 |
| ❑ 15 Norm Maciver 3,500 | 5.00 | 2.20 |
| ❑ 16 Darrin Madeley 1,500 | 7.00 | 3.10 |
| ❑ 17 Troy Mallette 3,500 | 5.00 | 2.20 |
| ❑ 18 Brad Marsh 6,500 | 7.00 | 3.10 |
| ❑ 19 Dave McLlwain 3,500 | 5.00 | 2.20 |
| ❑ 20 Darren Rumble 1,500 | 7.00 | 3.10 |
| ❑ 21 Vladimir Ruzicka 1,500 | 7.00 | 3.10 |
| ❑ 22 Brad Shaw 6,500 | 5.00 | 2.20 |
| ❑ 23 Graeme Townshend 1,500 | 7.00 | 3.10 |
| ❑ 24 Sylvain Turgeon 6,500 | 6.00 | 2.70 |
| ❑ 25 Dennis Vial 1,500 | 7.00 | 3.10 |
| ❑ 26 Alexei Yashin 6,500 | 10.00 | 4.50 |
| ❑ 27 Team Photo 12,500 | 5.00 | 2.20 |
| ❑ xx Album | 15.00 | 6.75 |
| ❑ NNO Team Photo | 5.00 | 2.20 |

## 1994-95 Senators Bell Mobility

Sponsored by Bell Mobility, this 28-card sets measures approximately 4" by 6" and features

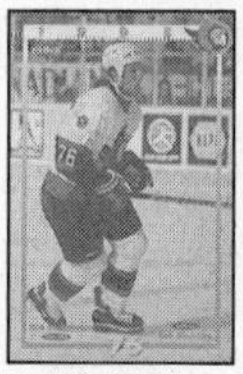

members of the 1994-95 Ottawa Senators. The fronts have full-bleed color action player photos with a fading team color-coded inside border. The player's name appears alongside the left, while his uniform number is on the bottom. The team logo in the upper right corner and sponsor logos in English and French on the bottom round out the card face. The backs are blank. The cards are unnumbered and checklisted below in alphabetical order.

| | MINT | NRMT |
|---|---|---|
| COMPLETE SET (28) | 15.00 | 6.75 |
| COMMON CARD (1-28) | .50 | .23 |
| ❑ 1 Dave Archibald | .50 | .23 |
| ❑ 2 Don Beaupre | .75 | .35 |
| ❑ 3 Radim Bicanek | .50 | .23 |
| ❑ 4 Craig Billington | .75 | .35 |
| ❑ 5 Claude Boivin | .50 | .23 |
| ❑ 6 Radek Bonk | 1.00 | .45 |
| ❑ 7 Phil Bourque | .50 | .23 |
| ❑ 8 Rick Bowness CO | .50 | .23 |
| ❑ 9 Randy Cunneyworth | .50 | .23 |
| ❑ 10 Chris Dahlquist | .50 | .23 |
| ❑ 11 Alexandre Daigle | 1.00 | .45 |
| ❑ 12 Pat Elynuik | .50 | .23 |
| ❑ 13 Rob Gaudreau | .50 | .23 |
| ❑ 14 Sean Hill | .50 | .23 |
| ❑ 15 Bill Huard | .50 | .23 |
| ❑ 16 Kerry Huffman | .50 | .23 |
| ❑ 17 Scott Levins | .50 | .23 |
| ❑ 18 Norm Maciver | .50 | .23 |
| ❑ 19 Darrin Madeley | .75 | .35 |
| ❑ 20 Troy Mallette | .50 | .23 |
| ❑ 21 Brad Marsh CO | .75 | .35 |
| ❑ 22 Dave McLlwain | .50 | .23 |
| ❑ 23 Troy Murray | .50 | .23 |
| ❑ 24 Stanislav Neckar | .60 | .25 |
| ❑ 25 Jim Paek | .50 | .23 |
| ❑ 26 Sylvain Turgeon | .50 | .23 |
| ❑ 27 Dennis Vial | .50 | .23 |
| ❑ 28 Alexei Yashin | 2.00 | .90 |

## 1995-96 Senators

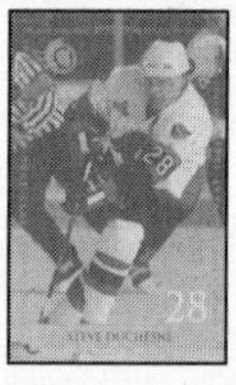

This 22-postcard set was produced by the Senators as a promotional giveaway. The cards feature full-bleed action photography with the club's name in both English and French inscribed along three borders. The fourth border displays the player's name. The backs are blank. As the cards are unnumbered, they are listed below in alphabetical order.

| | MINT | NRMT |
|---|---|---|
| COMPLETE SET (22) | 15.00 | 6.75 |
| COMMON CARD (1-22) | .50 | .23 |
| ❑ 1 Daniel Alfredsson | 3.00 | 1.35 |
| ❑ 2 Dave Archibald | .50 | .23 |
| ❑ 3 Mike Bales | .60 | .25 |
| ❑ 4 Radek Bonk | .60 | .25 |
| ❑ 5 Tom Chorske | .50 | .23 |
| ❑ 6 Randy Cunneyworth | .50 | .23 |
| ❑ 7 Alexandre Daigle | 1.50 | .70 |
| ❑ 8 Ted Drury | .50 | .23 |
| ❑ 9 Steve Duchesne | .75 | .35 |
| ❑ 10 Rob Gaudreau | .50 | .23 |
| ❑ 11 Sean Hill | .50 | .23 |
| ❑ 12 Kerry Huffman | .50 | .23 |
| ❑ 13 Scott Levins | .50 | .23 |
| ❑ 14 Troy Mallette | .50 | .23 |
| ❑ 15 Brad Marsh | .75 | .35 |
| ❑ 16 Trent McCleary | .50 | .23 |
| ❑ 17 Jaroslav Modry | .50 | .23 |
| ❑ 18 Frank Musil | .50 | .23 |
| ❑ 19 Stan Neckar | .60 | .25 |
| ❑ 20 Antti Tormanen | .50 | .23 |
| ❑ 21 Dennis Vial | .50 | .23 |
| ❑ 22 Alexei Yashin | 2.00 | .90 |

## 1996-97 Senators Pizza Hut

This 30-card set of the Ottawa Senators was produced in conjunction with Pizza Hut as a promotional giveaway. This standard postcard size set features glossy fronts and full-bleed action photography, with the player's name on the right side, and the Pizza Hut Canada logo

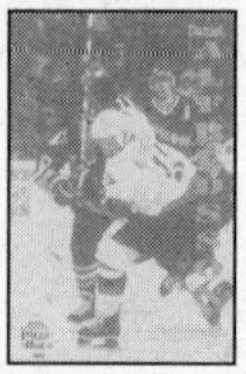

in the bottom left corner. The backs are blank. As the cards are unnumbered, they are listed below in alphabetical order.

| | MINT | NRMT |
|---|---|---|
| COMPLETE SET (32) | 20.00 | 9.00 |
| COMMON CARD | .50 | .23 |
| ❑ 1 Daniel Alfredsson | 2.00 | .90 |
| ❑ 2 Radek Bonk | .75 | .35 |
| ❑ 3 Tom Chorske | .50 | .23 |
| ❑ 4 Randy Cunneyworth | .50 | .23 |
| ❑ 5 Andreas Dackell | .75 | .35 |
| ❑ 6 Alexandre Daigle | 1.25 | .55 |
| ❑ 7 Steve Duchesne | .75 | .35 |
| ❑ 8 Bruce Gardiner | .60 | .25 |
| ❑ 9 Dave Hannan | .50 | .23 |
| ❑ 10 Sean Hill | .50 | .23 |
| ❑ 11 Denny Lambert | .50 | .23 |
| ❑ 12 Janne Laukkanen | .75 | .35 |
| ❑ 13 Jacques Martin CO | .50 | .23 |
| ❑ 14 Shawn Mceachern | .75 | .35 |
| ❑ 15 Frank Musil | .50 | .23 |
| ❑ 16 Phil Myre CO | .50 | .23 |
| ❑ 17 Stan Neckar | .60 | .25 |
| ❑ 18 Christer Olsson | .50 | .23 |
| ❑ 19 Perry Pearn CO | .50 | .23 |
| ❑ 20 Lance Pitlick | .50 | .23 |
| ❑ 21 Craig Ramsay | .50 | .23 |
| ❑ 22 Wade Redden | 1.00 | .45 |
| ❑ 23 Damian Rhodes | 1.00 | .45 |
| ❑ 24 Ron Tugnutt | 1.00 | .45 |
| ❑ 25 Shaun Van Allen | .50 | .23 |
| ❑ 26 Dennis Vial | .50 | .23 |
| ❑ 27 Alexei Yashin | 2.00 | .90 |
| ❑ 28 Jason York | .50 | .23 |
| ❑ 29 Jason Zent | .50 | .23 |
| ❑ 30 Sergei Zholtok | .50 | .23 |

## 1972-73 7-Eleven Slurpee Cups WHA

This 20-cup set features a color head shot and and facsimile autograph on the front, and a 7-11 logo, team logo, players name, and biographical information on the back. Cups are unnumbered and checklisted below alphabetically.

| | MINT | NRMT |
|---|---|---|
| COMPLETE SET (20) | 250.00 | 110.00 |
| COMMON CUP | 10.00 | 4.50 |
| ❑ 1 Norm Beaudin | 10.00 | 4.50 |
| ❑ 2 Chris Bordeleau | 10.00 | 4.50 |
| ❑ 3 Carl Brewer | 10.00 | 4.50 |
| ❑ 4 Wayne Carleton | 12.00 | 5.50 |
| ❑ 5 Gerry Cheevers | 25.00 | 11.00 |
| ❑ 6 Wayne Connelly | 15.00 | 6.75 |
| ❑ 7 Jean-Guy Gendron | 10.00 | 4.50 |
| ❑ 8 Ted Green | 10.00 | 4.50 |
| ❑ 9 Al Hamilton | 10.00 | 4.50 |
| ❑ 10 Jim Harrison | 10.00 | 4.50 |
| ❑ 11 Bobby Hull | 50.00 | 22.00 |
| ❑ 12 Andre Lacroix | 12.00 | 5.50 |
| ❑ 13 Danny Lawson | 10.00 | 4.50 |
| ❑ 14 John McKenzie | 10.00 | 4.50 |
| ❑ 15 Jim Mcleod | 10.00 | 4.50 |
| ❑ 16 Jack Norris | 10.00 | 4.50 |
| ❑ 17 John Schella | 10.00 | 4.50 |
| ❑ 18 J.C. Tremblay | 15.00 | 6.75 |
| ❑ 19 Ron Ward | 10.00 | 4.50 |
| ❑ 20 Jim Watson | 10.00 | 4.50 |

## 1984-85 7-Eleven Discs

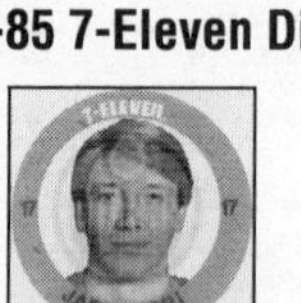


This set of 60 discs was sponsored by 7-Eleven. Each disc or coin measures approximately 2" in diameter and features an alternating portrait of the player and the team's logo. The coins are quite colorful and have adhesive backing. We have checklisted the coins below in alphabetical order of team name. Also the player's names have been alphabetized within their teams, and their uniform numbers placed to the right of their names. In addition, 7-Eleven also issued a large 4 1/2" diameter Wayne Gretzky disc which is not considered an essential part of the complete set. There is also a paper checklist sheet produced which pictured (in red, white, and blue) some of the coins and listed the players in the set.

| | MINT | NRMT |
|---|---|---|
| COMPLETE SET (60) | 125.00 | 55.00 |
| COMMON CARD (1-60) | 1.00 | .45 |
| ❑ 1 Ray Bourque 7 | 5.00 | 2.20 |
| ❑ 2 Rick Middleton 16 | 1.50 | .70 |
| ❑ 3 Tom Barrasso 30 | 2.50 | 1.10 |
| ❑ 4 Gilbert Perreault 11 | 2.00 | .90 |
| ❑ 5 Rejean Lemelin 31 | 1.50 | .70 |
| ❑ 6 Lanny McDonald 9 | 2.50 | 1.10 |
| ❑ 7 Paul Reinhart 23 | 1.00 | .45 |
| ❑ 8 Doug Risebrough 8 | 1.00 | .45 |
| ❑ 9 Denis Savard 18 | 2.50 | 1.10 |
| ❑ 10 Al Secord 20 | 1.00 | .45 |
| ❑ 11 Steve Yzerman 19 | 15.00 | 6.75 |
| ❑ 12 Dave(Tiger) Williams 55 | 1.50 | .70 |
| ❑ 13 Glenn Anderson 9 | 2.00 | .90 |
| ❑ 14 Paul Coffey 7 | 5.00 | 2.20 |
| ❑ 15 Michel Goulet 16 | 2.00 | .90 |
| ❑ 16 Wayne Gretzky 99 | 20.00 | 9.00 |
| ❑ 17 Charlie Huddy 22 | 1.00 | .45 |
| ❑ 18 Pat Hughes 16 | 1.00 | .45 |
| ❑ 19 Jari Kurri 17 | 3.00 | 1.35 |
| ❑ 20 Kevin Lowe 4 | 1.00 | .45 |
| ❑ 21 Mark Messier 11 | 8.00 | 3.60 |
| ❑ 22 Ron Francis 10 | 4.00 | 1.80 |
| ❑ 23 Sylvain Turgeon 16 | 1.00 | .45 |
| ❑ 24 Marcel Dionne 16 | 2.00 | .90 |
| ❑ 25 Dave Taylor 18 | 1.50 | .70 |
| ❑ 26 Brian Bellows 23 | 1.00 | .45 |
| ❑ 27 Dino Ciccarelli 20 | 1.50 | .70 |
| ❑ 28 Harold Snepsts 28 | 1.50 | .70 |
| ❑ 29 Bob Gainey 23 | 2.00 | .90 |
| ❑ 30 Larry Robinson 19 | 2.50 | 1.10 |
| ❑ 31 Mel Bridgman 18 | 1.00 | .45 |
| ❑ 32 Chico Resch 1 | 1.50 | .70 |
| ❑ 33 Mike Bossy 22 | 3.00 | 1.35 |
| ❑ 34 Bryan Trottier 19 | 2.50 | 1.10 |
| ❑ 35 Barry Beck 5 | 1.00 | .45 |
| ❑ 36 Don Maloney 12 | 1.00 | .45 |
| ❑ 37 Tim Kerr 12 | 1.50 | .70 |
| ❑ 38 Darryl Sittler 27 | 2.50 | 1.10 |
| ❑ 39 Mike Bullard 22 | 1.00 | .45 |
| ❑ 40 Rick Kehoe 17 | 1.50 | .70 |
| ❑ 41 Peter Stastny 26 | 3.00 | 1.35 |
| ❑ 42 Bernie Federko 24 | 1.50 | .70 |
| ❑ 43 Rob Ramage 5 | 1.00 | .45 |
| ❑ 44 John Anderson 10 | 1.00 | .45 |
| ❑ 45 Bill Derlago 19 | 1.00 | .45 |
| ❑ 46 Gary Nylund 2 | 1.00 | .45 |
| ❑ 47 Rick Vaive 22 | 1.00 | .45 |
| ❑ 48 Richard Brodeur 35 | 1.50 | .70 |
| ❑ 49 Gary Lupul 7 | 1.00 | .45 |
| ❑ 50 Darcy Rota 18 | 1.00 | .45 |
| ❑ 51 Stan Smyl 12 | 1.50 | .70 |
| ❑ 52 Tony Tanti 9 | 1.00 | .45 |
| ❑ 53 Mike Gartner 11 | 3.00 | 1.35 |
| ❑ 54 Rod Langway 5 | 1.00 | .45 |
| ❑ 55 Scott Arniel 11 | 1.00 | .45 |
| ❑ 56 Dave Babych 44 | 1.00 | .45 |
| ❑ 57 Laurie Boschman 16 | 1.00 | .45 |
| ❑ 58 Dale Hawerchuk 10 | 2.50 | 1.10 |
| ❑ 59 Paul MacLean 15 | 1.00 | .45 |
| ❑ 60 Brian Mullen 19 | 1.00 | .45 |
| ❑ NNO Wayne Gretzky Large | 25.00 | 11.00 |
| ❑ NNO Paper Checklist Sheet | 5.00 | 2.20 |

## 1985-86 7-Eleven Credit Cards

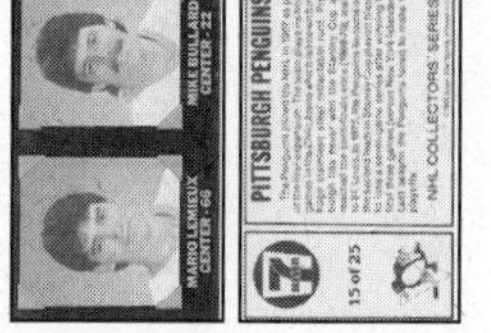


This 25-card set was sponsored by 7-Eleven. The cards measure approximately 3 3/8" by 2 1/8" and were issued in the "credit card" format. The front features color head and shoulder shots of two players from the same NHL team. These pictures are enframed by a black background, with the player's name, position, and uniform number in blue lettering below the photo. The information on the card back is framed in red boxes. In the smaller box on the left appears the 7-Eleven logo, card number, and the team logo. The right-hand box gives a brief history of the team. The key card in the set is Mario Lemieux, shown during his Rookie Card year.

| | MINT | NRMT |
|---|---|---|
| COMPLETE SET (25) | 35.00 | 16.00 |
| COMMON CARD (1-25) | .25 | .11 |
| ❑ 1 Ray Bourque and Rick Middleton | 2.00 | .90 |
| ❑ 2 Tom Barrasso and Gilbert Perreault | 1.50 | .70 |
| ❑ 3 Paul Reinhart and Lanny McDonald | 1.00 | .45 |
| ❑ 4 Denis Savard and Doug Wilson | 1.50 | .70 |
| ❑ 5 Ron Duguay and Steve Yzerman | 8.00 | 3.60 |
| ❑ 6 Paul Coffey and Jari Kurri | 2.50 | 1.10 |
| ❑ 7 Ron Francis and Mike Liut | 2.00 | .90 |
| ❑ 8 Marcel Dionne and Dave Taylor | 1.25 | .55 |
| ❑ 9 Brian Bellows and Dino Ciccarelli | 1.50 | .70 |
| ❑ 10 Larry Robinson and Guy Carbonneau | 1.50 | .70 |
| ❑ 11 Mel Bridgman and Chico Resch | .75 | .35 |
| ❑ 12 Mike Bossy and Bryan Trottier | 2.50 | 1.10 |
| ❑ 13 Reijo Ruotsalainen and Barry Beck | .75 | .35 |
| ❑ 14 Tim Kerr and Mark Howe | .75 | .35 |
| ❑ 15 Mario Lemieux and Mike Bullard | 20.00 | 9.00 |
| ❑ 16 Peter Stastny and Michel Goulet | 2.50 | 1.10 |
| ❑ 17 Rob Ramage and Brian Sutter | .75 | .35 |
| ❑ 18 Rick Vaive and Borje Salming | 1.00 | .45 |
| ❑ 19 Patrik Sundstrom and Stan Smyl | .75 | .35 |
| ❑ 20 Rod Langway and Mike Gartner | 1.25 | .55 |
| ❑ 21 Dale Hawerchuk and Paul MacLean | 1.00 | .45 |
| ❑ 22 Stanley Cup Winners | .75 | .35 |
| ❑ 23 Prince of Wales Trophy Winners | .75 | .35 |
| ❑ 24 Clarence S. Campbell Bowl Winners | .75 | .35 |
| ❑ 25 Title Card | .25 | .11 |

## 1972-73 Sharks Los Angeles WHA

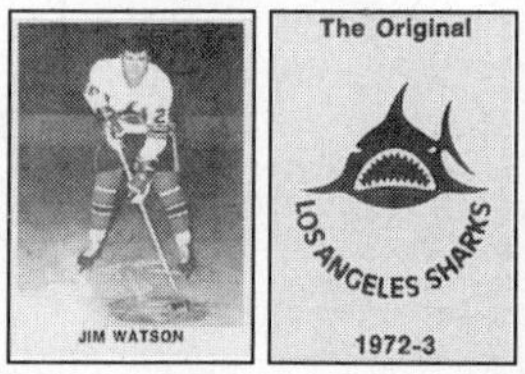


This 19-card standard-size set features on the front black and white posed player photos, surrounded by a white border. The player's name is given in black lettering below the picture. The backs read "The Original Los Angeles Sharks, 1972-73" and have the Sharks' logo in the center.

| | NRMT-MT | EXC |
|---|---|---|
| COMPLETE SET (19) | 40.00 | 18.00 |
| COMMON CARD (1-19) | 2.50 | 1.10 |
| ❑ 1 Mike Byers | 2.50 | 1.10 |
| ❑ 2 Bart Crashley | 4.00 | 1.80 |
| ❑ 3 George Gardner | 2.50 | 1.10 |
| ❑ 4 Russ Gillow | 2.50 | 1.10 |
| ❑ 5 Tom Gilmore | 2.50 | 1.10 |
| ❑ 6 Earl Heiskala | 2.50 | 1.10 |
| ❑ 7 J.P. LeBlanc | 3.00 | 1.35 |
| ❑ 8 Ralph McSweyn | 2.50 | 1.10 |
| ❑ 9 Ted McCaskill | 2.50 | 1.10 |
| ❑ 10 Jim Niekamp | 2.50 | 1.10 |
| ❑ 11 Gerry Odrowski | 3.00 | 1.35 |
| ❑ 12 Tom Serviss | 2.50 | 1.10 |
| ❑ 13 Peter Slater | 2.50 | 1.10 |
| ❑ 14 Steve Sutherland | 2.50 | 1.10 |
| ❑ 15 Joe Szura | 3.00 | 1.35 |
| ❑ 16 Gary Veneruzzo | 2.50 | 1.10 |
| ❑ 17 Jim Watson | 2.50 | 1.10 |
| ❑ 18 Alton White | 2.50 | 1.10 |
| ❑ 19 Bill Young | 2.50 | 1.10 |

## 1991-92 Sharks San Jose Sports Action

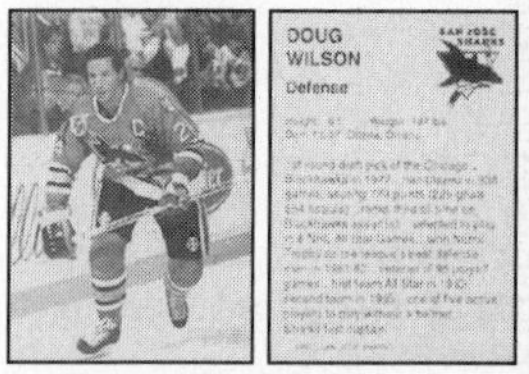


This 22-card standard-size set was issued by Sports Action and features members of the 1991-92 San Jose Sharks. The cards are printed on thin card stock. The fronts feature full-bleed glossy color action photos. The backs carry brief biography, career summary, and the team logo. The cards are unnumbered and checklisted below in alphabetical order.

| | MINT | NRMT |
|---|---|---|
| COMPLETE SET (22) | 10.00 | 4.50 |
| COMMON CARD (1-22) | .50 | .23 |
| ❑ 1 Perry Anderson | .50 | .23 |
| ❑ 2 Perry Berezan | .50 | .23 |
| ❑ 3 Steve Bozek | .50 | .23 |
| ❑ 4 Dean Evason | .50 | .23 |
| ❑ 5 Pat Falloon | .75 | .35 |
| ❑ 6 Paul Fenton | .50 | .23 |

| | | |
|---|---|---|
| ❑ 7 Link Gaetz | .50 | .23 |
| ❑ 8 Jeff Hackett | 1.00 | .45 |
| ❑ 9 Ken Hammond | .50 | .23 |
| ❑ 10 Brian Hayward | .75 | .35 |
| ❑ 11 Tony Hrkac | .50 | .23 |
| ❑ 12 Kelly Kisio | .60 | .25 |
| ❑ 13 Brian Lawton | .50 | .23 |
| ❑ 14 Pat MacLeod | .50 | .23 |
| ❑ 15 Bob McGill | .50 | .23 |
| ❑ 16 Brian Mullen | .50 | .23 |
| ❑ 17 Jarmo Myllys | .60 | .25 |
| ❑ 18 Wayne Presley | .50 | .23 |
| ❑ 19 Neil Wilkinson | .60 | .25 |
| ❑ 20 Doug Wilson | 1.00 | .45 |
| ❑ 21 Rob Zettler | .50 | .23 |
| ❑ 22 San Jose Sharks Game action | .75 | .35 |

## 1997 Sharks Fleer All-Star Sheet

This odd-sized sheet was handed out to attendees of the '97 NHL All-Star Game to promote the '96-97 line of Fleer hockey products. The sheet also was available at the All-Star Fanfest card show. It features eight members of the hometown San Jose Sharks on three different types of Fleer cards; the brand pictured is listed after each player's name.

| | MINT | NRMT |
|---|---|---|
| COMMON SHEET | 5.00 | 2.20 |
| ❑ 1 Sharks Sheet | 5.00 | 2.20 |

Doug Bodger Fleer Picks
Kelly Hrudey Metal Universe
Al Iafrate Metal Universe
Bernie Nicholls Metal Universe
Owen Nolan Fleer
Marcus Ragnarsson Fleer
Chris Terreri Fleer
Alexei Yegorov Fleer Picks

## 1960-61 Shirriff Coins

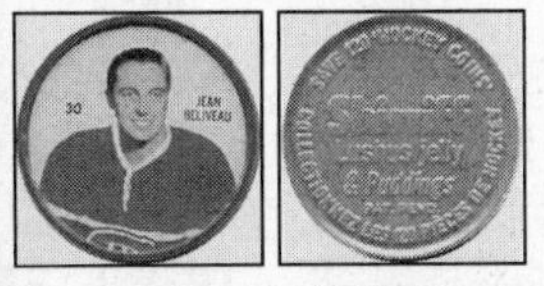

This set of 120 coins (each measuring approximately 1 3/8" in diameter) features players from all six NHL teams. These plastic coins are in color and numbered on the front. The coins are checklisted below according to teams as follows: Toronto Maple Leafs (1-20), Montreal Canadiens (21-40), Detroit Red Wings (41-60), Chicago Blackhawks (61-80), New York Rangers (81-100), and Boston Bruins (101-120). The set was also issued on a limited basis as a factory set in a black presentation box.

| | NRMT | VG-E |
|---|---|---|
| COMPLETE SET (120) | 500.00 | 220.00 |
| COMMON COIN (1-120) | 3.00 | 1.35 |
| ❑ 1 Johnny Bower | 10.00 | 4.50 |
| ❑ 2 Dick Duff | 4.00 | 1.80 |
| ❑ 3 Carl Brewer | 4.00 | 1.80 |
| ❑ 4 Red Kelly | 8.00 | 3.60 |
| ❑ 5 Tim Horton | 15.00 | 6.75 |
| ❑ 6 Allan Stanley | 5.00 | 2.20 |
| ❑ 7 Bob Baun | 4.00 | 1.80 |
| ❑ 8 Billy Harris | 3.00 | 1.35 |
| ❑ 9 George Armstrong | 6.00 | 2.70 |
| ❑ 10 Ron Stewart | 3.00 | 1.35 |
| ❑ 11 Bert Olmstead | 5.00 | 2.20 |
| ❑ 12 Frank Mahovlich | 15.00 | 6.75 |
| ❑ 13 Bob Pulford | 5.00 | 2.20 |
| ❑ 14 Gary Edmundson | 3.00 | 1.35 |
| ❑ 15 Johnny Wilson | 3.00 | 1.35 |
| ❑ 16 Larry Regan | 3.00 | 1.35 |
| ❑ 17 Gerry James | 4.00 | 1.80 |
| ❑ 18 Rudy Migay | 3.00 | 1.35 |
| ❑ 19 Gerry Ehman | 3.00 | 1.35 |
| ❑ 20 Punch Imlach CO | 4.00 | 1.80 |
| ❑ 21 Jacques Plante | 25.00 | 11.00 |
| ❑ 22 Dickie Moore | 6.00 | 2.70 |
| ❑ 23 Don Marshall | 3.00 | 1.35 |
| ❑ 24 Albert Langlois | 3.00 | 1.35 |
| ❑ 25 Tom Johnson | 5.00 | 2.20 |
| ❑ 26 Doug Harvey | 10.00 | 4.50 |
| ❑ 27 Phil Goyette | 3.00 | 1.35 |
| ❑ 28 Boom Boom Geoffrion | 12.00 | 5.50 |
| ❑ 29 Marcel Bonin | 3.00 | 1.35 |
| ❑ 30 Jean Beliveau | 20.00 | 9.00 |
| ❑ 31 Ralph Backstrom | 4.00 | 1.80 |
| ❑ 32 Andre Pronovost | 3.00 | 1.35 |
| ❑ 33 Claude Provost | 4.00 | 1.80 |
| ❑ 34 Henri Richard | 15.00 | 6.75 |
| ❑ 35 Jean-Guy Talbot | 4.00 | 1.80 |
| ❑ 36 J.C. Tremblay | 4.00 | 1.80 |
| ❑ 37 Bob Turner | 3.00 | 1.35 |
| ❑ 38 Bill Hicke | 3.00 | 1.35 |
| ❑ 39 Charlie Hodge | 5.00 | 2.20 |
| ❑ 40 Toe Blake CO | 5.00 | 2.20 |
| ❑ 41 Terry Sawchuk | 20.00 | 9.00 |
| ❑ 42 Gordie Howe | 50.00 | 22.00 |
| ❑ 43 John McKenzie | 3.00 | 1.35 |
| ❑ 44 Alex Delvecchio | 8.00 | 3.60 |
| ❑ 45 Norm Ullman | 6.00 | 2.70 |
| ❑ 46 Jack McIntyre | 3.00 | 1.35 |
| ❑ 47 Barry Cullen | 4.00 | 1.80 |
| ❑ 48 Val Fonteyne | 3.00 | 1.35 |
| ❑ 49 Warren Godfrey | 3.00 | 1.35 |
| ❑ 50 Pete Goegan | 3.00 | 1.35 |
| ❑ 51 Gerry Melnyk | 3.00 | 1.35 |
| ❑ 52 Marc Reaume | 3.00 | 1.35 |
| ❑ 53 Gary Aldcorn | 3.00 | 1.35 |
| ❑ 54 Len Lunde | 3.00 | 1.35 |
| ❑ 55 Murray Oliver | 3.00 | 1.35 |
| ❑ 56 Marcel Pronovost | 5.00 | 2.20 |
| ❑ 57 Howie Glover | 3.00 | 1.35 |
| ❑ 58 Gerry Odrowski | 3.00 | 1.35 |
| ❑ 59 Parker MacDonald | 3.00 | 1.35 |
| ❑ 60 Sid Abel CO | 5.00 | 2.20 |
| ❑ 61 Glenn Hall | 12.00 | 5.50 |
| ❑ 62 Ed Litzenberger | 3.00 | 1.35 |
| ❑ 63 Bobby Hull | 40.00 | 18.00 |
| ❑ 64 Tod Sloan | 3.00 | 1.35 |
| ❑ 65 Murray Balfour | 3.00 | 1.35 |
| ❑ 66 Pierre Pilote | 5.00 | 2.20 |
| ❑ 67 Al Arbour | 5.00 | 2.20 |
| ❑ 68 Earl Balfour | 3.00 | 1.35 |
| ❑ 69 Eric Nesterenko | 4.00 | 1.80 |
| ❑ 70 Ken Wharram | 4.00 | 1.80 |
| ❑ 71 Stan Mikita | 25.00 | 11.00 |
| ❑ 72 Ab McDonald | 3.00 | 1.35 |
| ❑ 73 Elmer Vasko | 3.00 | 1.35 |
| ❑ 74 Dollard St.Laurent | 4.00 | 1.80 |
| ❑ 75 Ron Murphy | 3.00 | 1.35 |
| ❑ 76 Jack Evans | 3.00 | 1.35 |
| ❑ 77 Bill(Red) Hay | 3.00 | 1.35 |
| ❑ 78 Reg Fleming | 3.00 | 1.35 |
| ❑ 79 Cecil Hoekstra | 3.00 | 1.35 |
| ❑ 80 Tommy Ivan CO | 4.00 | 1.80 |
| ❑ 81 Jack McCartan | 5.00 | 2.20 |
| ❑ 82 Red Sullivan | 3.00 | 1.35 |
| ❑ 83 Camille Henry | 4.00 | 1.80 |
| ❑ 84 Larry Popein | 3.00 | 1.35 |
| ❑ 85 John Hanna | 3.00 | 1.35 |
| ❑ 86 Harry Howell | 5.00 | 2.20 |
| ❑ 87 Eddie Shack | 10.00 | 4.50 |
| ❑ 88 Irv Spencer | 3.00 | 1.35 |
| ❑ 89 Andy Bathgate | 6.00 | 2.70 |
| ❑ 90 Bill Gadsby | 5.00 | 2.20 |
| ❑ 91 Andy Hebenton | 3.00 | 1.35 |
| ❑ 92 Earl Ingarfield | 3.00 | 1.35 |
| ❑ 93 Don Johns | 3.00 | 1.35 |
| ❑ 94 Dave Balon | 3.00 | 1.35 |
| ❑ 95 Jim Morrison | 3.00 | 1.35 |
| ❑ 96 Ken Schinkel | 3.00 | 1.35 |
| ❑ 97 Lou Fontinato | 3.00 | 1.35 |
| ❑ 98 Ted Hampson | 3.00 | 1.35 |
| ❑ 99 Brian Cullen | 4.00 | 1.80 |
| ❑ 100 Alf Pike CO | 3.00 | 1.35 |
| ❑ 101 Don Simmons | 5.00 | 2.20 |
| ❑ 102 Fern Flaman | 5.00 | 2.20 |
| ❑ 103 Vic Stasiuk | 4.00 | 1.80 |
| ❑ 104 Johnny Bucyk | 8.00 | 3.60 |
| ❑ 105 Bronco Horvath | 4.00 | 1.80 |
| ❑ 106 Doug Mohns | 8.00 | 3.60 |
| ❑ 107 Leo Boivin | 5.00 | 2.20 |
| ❑ 108 Don McKenney | 3.00 | 1.35 |
| ❑ 109 Jean-Guy Gendron | 3.00 | 1.35 |
| ❑ 110 Jerry Toppazzini | 3.00 | 1.35 |
| ❑ 111 Dick Meissner | 3.00 | 1.35 |
| ❑ 112 Autry Erickson | 3.00 | 1.35 |
| ❑ 113 Jim Bartlett | 3.00 | 1.35 |
| ❑ 114 Orval Tessier | 4.00 | 1.80 |
| ❑ 115 Billy Carter | 3.00 | 1.35 |
| ❑ 116 Dallas Smith | 4.00 | 1.80 |
| ❑ 117 Leo Labine | 3.00 | 1.35 |
| ❑ 118 Bob Armstrong | 3.00 | 1.35 |
| ❑ 119 Bruce Gamble | 5.00 | 2.20 |
| ❑ 120 Milt Schmidt CO | 6.00 | 2.70 |

## 1961-62 Shirriff/Salada Coins

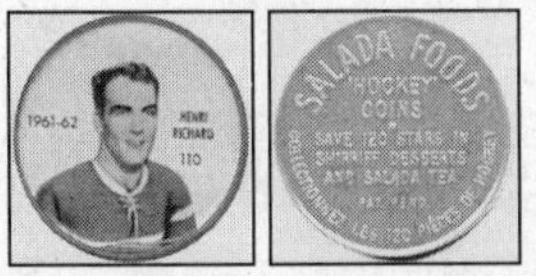

This set of 120 coins (each measuring approximately 1 3/8" in diameter) features players of the NHL, all six teams. These plastic coins are in color and numbered on the front. The coins are numbered according to teams as follows: Boston Bruins (1-20), Chicago Blackhawks (21-40), Toronto Maple Leafs (41-60), Detroit Red Wings (61-80), New York Rangers (81-100), and Montreal Canadiens (101-120). The coins were also produced in identical fashion for Salada with a Salada imprint; the Salada version has the same values as listed below. This was the only year of Shirriff coins where collectors could obtain plastic shields for displaying their collection. These shields are not considered part of the complete set.

| | NRMT | VG-E |
|---|---|---|
| COMPLETE SET (120) | 400.00 | 180.00 |
| COMMON COIN (1-120) | 2.50 | 1.10 |
| ❑ 1 Cliff Pennington | 2.50 | 1.10 |
| ❑ 2 Dallas Smith | 4.00 | 1.80 |
| ❑ 3 Andre Pronovost | 2.50 | 1.10 |
| ❑ 4 Charlie Burns | 2.50 | 1.10 |
| ❑ 5 Leo Boivin | 5.00 | 2.20 |
| ❑ 6 Don McKenney | 2.50 | 1.10 |
| ❑ 7 Johnny Bucyk | 8.00 | 3.60 |
| ❑ 8 Murray Oliver | 2.50 | 1.10 |
| ❑ 9 Jerry Toppazzini | 2.50 | 1.10 |
| ❑ 10 Doug Mohns | 4.00 | 1.80 |
| ❑ 11 Don Head | 4.00 | 1.80 |
| ❑ 12 Bob Armstrong | 2.50 | 1.10 |
| ❑ 13 Pat Stapleton | 4.00 | 1.80 |
| ❑ 14 Orland Kurtenbach | 4.00 | 1.80 |
| ❑ 15 Dick Meissner | 2.50 | 1.10 |
| ❑ 16 Ted Green | 4.00 | 1.80 |
| ❑ 17 Tom Williams | 2.50 | 1.10 |
| ❑ 18 Autry Erickson | 2.50 | 1.10 |
| ❑ 19 Phil Watson CO | 5.00 | 2.20 |
| ❑ 20 Ed Chadwick | 5.00 | 2.20 |
| ❑ 21 Wayne Hillman | 10.00 | 4.50 |
| ❑ 22 Stan Mikita | 12.00 | 5.50 |
| ❑ 23 Eric Nesterenko | 4.00 | 1.80 |
| ❑ 24 Reg Fleming | 2.50 | 1.10 |
| ❑ 25 Bobby Hull | 25.00 | 11.00 |
| ❑ 26 Elmer Vasko | 2.50 | 1.10 |
| ❑ 27 Pierre Pilote | 5.00 | 2.20 |
| ❑ 28 Chico Maki | 4.00 | 1.80 |
| ❑ 29 Glenn Hall | 10.00 | 4.50 |
| ❑ 30 Murray Balfour | 2.50 | 1.10 |
| ❑ 31 Bronco Horvath | 3.00 | 1.35 |
| ❑ 32 Ken Wharram | 4.00 | 1.80 |
| ❑ 33 Ab McDonald | 2.50 | 1.10 |
| ❑ 34 Bill(Red) Hay | 2.50 | 1.10 |
| ❑ 35 Dollard St.Laurent | 4.00 | 1.80 |
| ❑ 36 Ron Murphy | 2.50 | 1.10 |
| ❑ 37 Bob Turner | 2.50 | 1.10 |
| ❑ 38 Gerry Melnyk | 2.50 | 1.10 |
| ❑ 39 Jack Evans | 2.50 | 1.10 |
| ❑ 40 Rudy Pilous CO | 5.00 | 2.20 |
| ❑ 41 Johnny Bower | 10.00 | 4.50 |
| ❑ 42 Allan Stanley | 6.00 | 2.70 |
| ❑ 43 Frank Mahovlich | 10.00 | 4.50 |
| ❑ 44 Tim Horton | 15.00 | 6.75 |
| ❑ 45 Carl Brewer | 4.00 | 1.80 |
| ❑ 46 Bob Pulford | 5.00 | 2.20 |
| ❑ 47 Bob Nevin | 4.00 | 1.80 |
| ❑ 48 Eddie Shack | 8.00 | 3.60 |
| ❑ 49 Red Kelly | 8.00 | 3.60 |
| ❑ 50 Bob Baun | 4.00 | 1.80 |
| ❑ 51 George Armstrong | 6.00 | 2.70 |
| ❑ 52 Bert Olmstead | 5.00 | 2.20 |
| ❑ 53 Dick Duff | 4.00 | 1.80 |
| ❑ 54 Billy Harris | 4.00 | 1.80 |
| ❑ 55 Larry Keenan | 2.50 | 1.10 |
| ❑ 56 Johnny MacMillan | 2.50 | 1.10 |
| ❑ 57 Punch Imlach CO | 4.00 | 1.80 |
| ❑ 58 Dave Keon | 15.00 | 6.75 |
| ❑ 59 Larry Hillman | 2.50 | 1.10 |
| ❑ 60 Al Arbour | 5.00 | 2.20 |
| ❑ 61 Sid Abel CO | 5.00 | 2.20 |
| ❑ 62 Warren Godfrey | 2.50 | 1.10 |
| ❑ 63 Vic Stasiuk | 2.50 | 1.10 |
| ❑ 64 Leo Labine | 2.50 | 1.10 |
| ❑ 65 Howie Glover | 2.50 | 1.10 |
| ❑ 66 Gordie Howe | 40.00 | 18.00 |
| ❑ 67 Val Fonteyne | 2.50 | 1.10 |
| ❑ 68 Marcel Pronovost | 5.00 | 2.20 |
| ❑ 69 Parker MacDonald | 2.50 | 1.10 |
| ❑ 70 Alex Delvecchio | 8.00 | 3.60 |
| ❑ 71 Ed Litzenberger | 2.50 | 1.10 |
| ❑ 72 Al Johnson | 2.50 | 1.10 |
| ❑ 73 Bruce MacGregor | 2.50 | 1.10 |
| ❑ 74 Howie Young | 2.50 | 1.10 |
| ❑ 75 Pete Goegan | 2.50 | 1.10 |
| ❑ 76 Norm Ullman | 6.00 | 2.70 |
| ❑ 77 Terry Sawchuk | 25.00 | 11.00 |
| ❑ 78 Gerry Odrowski | 2.50 | 1.10 |
| ❑ 79 Bill Gadsby | 5.00 | 2.20 |
| ❑ 80 Hank Bassen | 4.00 | 1.80 |
| ❑ 81 Doug Harvey | 8.00 | 3.60 |
| ❑ 82 Earl Ingarfield | 2.50 | 1.10 |
| ❑ 83 Pat Hannigan | 2.50 | 1.10 |
| ❑ 84 Dean Prentice | 4.00 | 1.80 |
| ❑ 85 Gump Worsley | 10.00 | 4.50 |
| ❑ 86 Irv Spencer | 2.50 | 1.10 |
| ❑ 87 Camille Henry | 4.00 | 1.80 |
| ❑ 88 Andy Bathgate | 6.00 | 2.70 |
| ❑ 89 Harry Howell | 5.00 | 2.20 |
| ❑ 90 Andy Hebenton | 2.50 | 1.10 |
| ❑ 91 Red Sullivan | 2.50 | 1.10 |
| ❑ 92 Ted Hampson | 2.50 | 1.10 |
| ❑ 93 Jean-Guy Gendron | 2.50 | 1.10 |
| ❑ 94 Albert Langlois | 2.50 | 1.10 |
| ❑ 95 Larry Cahan | 2.50 | 1.10 |
| ❑ 96 Bob Cunningham | 2.50 | 1.10 |
| ❑ 97 Vic Hadfield | 4.00 | 1.80 |
| ❑ 98 Jean Ratelle | 10.00 | 4.50 |
| ❑ 99 Ken Schinkel | 2.50 | 1.10 |
| ❑ 100 Johnny Wilson | 2.50 | 1.10 |
| ❑ 101 Toe Blake CO | 5.00 | 2.20 |
| ❑ 102 Jean Beliveau | 20.00 | 9.00 |
| ❑ 103 Don Marshall | 2.50 | 1.10 |
| ❑ 104 Boom Boom Geoffrion | 12.00 | 5.50 |
| ❑ 105 Claude Provost | 4.00 | 1.80 |
| ❑ 106 Tom Johnson | 5.00 | 2.20 |
| ❑ 107 Dickie Moore | 8.00 | 3.60 |
| ❑ 108 Bill Hicke | 2.50 | 1.10 |
| ❑ 109 Jean-Guy Talbot | 4.00 | 1.80 |
| ❑ 110 Henri Richard | 10.00 | 4.50 |
| ❑ 111 Lou Fontinato | 3.00 | 1.35 |
| ❑ 112 Gilles Tremblay | 2.50 | 1.10 |
| ❑ 113 Jacques Plante | 20.00 | 9.00 |
| ❑ 114 Ralph Backstrom | 4.00 | 1.80 |
| ❑ 115 Marcel Bonin | 2.50 | 1.10 |
| ❑ 116 Phil Goyette | 2.50 | 1.10 |
| ❑ 117 Bobby Rousseau | 4.00 | 1.80 |
| ❑ 118 J.C. Tremblay | 4.00 | 1.80 |
| ❑ 119 Al MacNeil | 2.50 | 1.10 |
| ❑ 120 Jean Gauthier | 2.50 | 1.10 |
| ❑ S1 Boston Bruins Shield | 50.00 | 22.00 |
| ❑ S2 Chicago Blackhawks Shield | 50.00 | 22.00 |
| ❑ S3 Detroit Red Wings Shield | 50.00 | 22.00 |
| ❑ S4 Montreal Canadiens Shield | 50.00 | 22.00 |
| ❑ S5 New York Rangers Shield | 50.00 | 22.00 |
| ❑ S6 Toronto Maple Leafs Shield | 50.00 | 22.00 |

## 1962-63 Shirriff Metal Coins

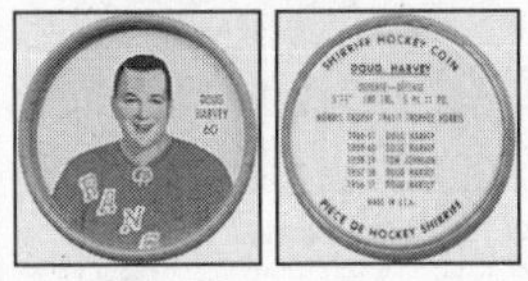

This set of 60 coins (each measuring approximately 1 1/2" in diameter) features 12 All-Stars, six Trophy winners, and players from Montreal (20) and Toronto (22). The four American teams in the NHL were not included in this set except where they appeared as All-Stars or Trophy winners. These metal coins are in color and numbered on the front. The backs are written in French and English.

| | NRMT | VG-E |
|---|---|---|
| COMPLETE SET (60) | 400.00 | 180.00 |
| COMMON COIN (1-60) | 4.00 | 1.80 |
| ❑ 1 Johnny Bower | 10.00 | 4.50 |
| ❑ 2 Allan Stanley | 8.00 | 3.60 |
| ❑ 3 Frank Mahovlich | 20.00 | 9.00 |
| ❑ 4 Tim Horton | 20.00 | 9.00 |
| ❑ 5 Carl Brewer | 5.00 | 2.20 |
| ❑ 6 Bob Pulford | 8.00 | 3.60 |
| ❑ 7 Bob Nevin | 5.00 | 2.20 |
| ❑ 8 Eddie Shack | 8.00 | 3.60 |
| ❑ 9 Red Kelly | 8.00 | 3.60 |
| ❑ 10 George Armstrong | 8.00 | 3.60 |
| ❑ 11 Bert Olmstead | 6.00 | 2.70 |
| ❑ 12 Dick Duff | 5.00 | 2.20 |
| ❑ 13 Billy Harris | 4.00 | 1.80 |
| ❑ 14 Johnny MacMillan | 4.00 | 1.80 |
| ❑ 15 Punch Imlach CO | 5.00 | 2.20 |
| ❑ 16 Dave Keon | 15.00 | 6.75 |
| ❑ 17 Larry Hillman | 4.00 | 1.80 |
| ❑ 18 Ed Litzenberger | 4.00 | 1.80 |
| ❑ 19 Bob Baun | 6.00 | 2.70 |
| ❑ 20 Al Arbour | 8.00 | 3.60 |
| ❑ 21 Ron Stewart | 4.00 | 1.80 |
| ❑ 22 Don Simmons | 6.00 | 2.70 |
| ❑ 23 Lou Fontinato | 4.00 | 1.80 |
| ❑ 24 Gilles Tremblay | 4.00 | 1.80 |
| ❑ 25 Jacques Plante | 25.00 | 11.00 |
| ❑ 26 Ralph Backstrom | 5.00 | 2.20 |
| ❑ 27 Marcel Bonin | 4.00 | 1.80 |
| ❑ 28 Phil Goyette | 4.00 | 1.80 |
| ❑ 29 Bobby Rousseau | 5.00 | 2.20 |
| ❑ 30 J.C. Tremblay | 5.00 | 2.20 |
| ❑ 31 Toe Blake CO | 8.00 | 3.60 |
| ❑ 32 Jean Beliveau | 20.00 | 9.00 |
| ❑ 33 Don Marshall | 4.00 | 1.80 |
| ❑ 34 Boom Boom Geoffrion | 12.00 | 5.50 |
| ❑ 35 Claude Provost | 5.00 | 2.20 |
| ❑ 36 Tom Johnson | 6.00 | 2.70 |
| ❑ 37 Dickie Moore | 10.00 | 4.50 |
| ❑ 38 Bill Hicke | 4.00 | 1.80 |
| ❑ 39 Jean-Guy Talbot | 5.00 | 2.20 |
| ❑ 40 Al MacNeil | 5.00 | 2.20 |
| ❑ 41 Henri Richard | 15.00 | 6.75 |
| ❑ 42 Red Berenson | 5.00 | 2.20 |
| ❑ 43 Jacques Plante AS | 25.00 | 11.00 |
| ❑ 44 Jean-Guy Talbot AS | 5.00 | 2.20 |
| ❑ 45 Doug Harvey AS | 10.00 | 4.50 |
| ❑ 46 Stan Mikita AS | 10.00 | 4.50 |
| ❑ 47 Bobby Hull AS | 25.00 | 11.00 |
| ❑ 48 Andy Bathgate AS | 8.00 | 3.60 |
| ❑ 49 Glenn Hall AS | 10.00 | 4.50 |
| ❑ 50 Pierre Pilote AS | 8.00 | 3.60 |
| ❑ 51 Carl Brewer AS | 5.00 | 2.20 |
| ❑ 52 Dave Keon AS | 15.00 | 6.75 |
| ❑ 53 Frank Mahovlich AS | 15.00 | 6.75 |
| ❑ 54 Gordie Howe AS | 40.00 | 18.00 |
| ❑ 55 Dave Keon Byng | 15.00 | 6.75 |
| ❑ 56 Bobby Rousseau Calder | 5.00 | 2.20 |
| ❑ 57 Bobby Hull Ross | 25.00 | 11.00 |
| ❑ 58 Jacques Plante Vezina | 25.00 | 11.00 |
| ❑ 59 Jacques Plante Hart | 25.00 | 11.00 |
| ❑ 60 Doug Harvey Norris | 10.00 | 4.50 |

## 1968-69 Shirriff Coins

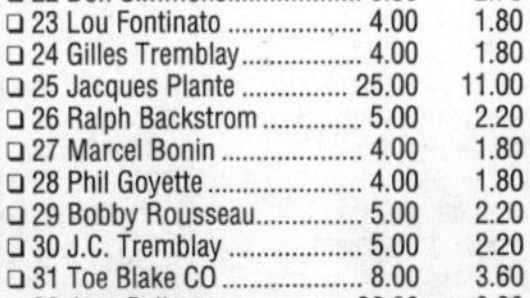

This set of 176 coins (each measuring approximately 1 3/8" in diameter) features players from all of the teams in the NHL. These plastic coins are in color and numbered on the front. However the coins are numbered by Shirriff within each team and not for the whole set. The correspondence between the actual coin numbers and the numbers assigned below should be apparent. For those few situations where two coins from the same team have the same number, that number is listed in the checklist below next to the name. The coins are checklisted below according to teams as follows: Boston Bruins (1-16), Chicago Blackhawks (17-33), Detroit Red Wings (34-49), Los Angeles Kings (50-61), Minnesota North Stars (62-74), Montreal Canadiens (75-92), New York Rangers (93-108), Oakland Seals (109-121), Philadelphia Flyers (122-134), Pittsburgh Penguins (135-146), St. Louis Blues (147-158), and Toronto Maple Leafs (159-176). Some of the coins are quite challenging to find. It seems the higher numbers within each team and the coins from the players on the expansion teams are more difficult to find; these are marked by SP in the list below.

| | NRMT-MT | EXC |
|---|---|---|
| COMPLETE SET (176) | 6000.00 | 2700.00 |
| COMMON COIN (1-176) | 4.00 | 1.80 |
| ❑ 1 Eddie Shack | 10.00 | 4.50 |
| ❑ 2 Ed Westfall | 5.00 | 2.20 |
| ❑ 3 Don Awrey | 4.00 | 1.80 |
| ❑ 4 Gerry Cheevers | 12.00 | 5.50 |
| ❑ 5 Bobby Orr | 100.00 | 45.00 |
| ❑ 6 Johnny Bucyk | 10.00 | 4.50 |
| ❑ 7 Derek Sanderson | 20.00 | 9.00 |
| ❑ 8 Phil Esposito | 20.00 | 9.00 |
| ❑ 9 Fred Stanfield | 4.00 | 1.80 |
| ❑ 10 Ken Hodge | 6.00 | 2.70 |
| ❑ 11 John McKenzie | 4.00 | 1.80 |
| ❑ 12 Ted Green | 5.00 | 2.20 |
| ❑ 13 Dallas Smith SP | 100.00 | 45.00 |
| ❑ 14 Gary Doak SP | 100.00 | 45.00 |
| ❑ 15 Glen Sather SP | 100.00 | 45.00 |
| ❑ 16 Tom Williams SP | 75.00 | 34.00 |
| ❑ 17 Bobby Hull | 50.00 | 22.00 |
| ❑ 18 Pat Stapleton | 4.00 | 1.80 |
| ❑ 19 Wayne Maki | 4.00 | 1.80 |
| ❑ 20 Denis DeJordy | 8.00 | 3.60 |
| ❑ 21 Ken Wharram | 5.00 | 2.20 |
| ❑ 22 Pit Martin | 4.00 | 1.80 |
| ❑ 23 Chico Maki | 4.00 | 1.80 |
| ❑ 24 Doug Mohns | 5.00 | 2.20 |
| ❑ 25 Stan Mikita | 15.00 | 6.75 |
| ❑ 26 Doug Jarrett | 4.00 | 1.80 |
| ❑ 27 Dennis Hull 11 SP (small portrait) | 100.00 | 45.00 |
| ❑ 28 Dennis Hull 11 (large portrait) | 25.00 | 11.00 |
| ❑ 29 Matt Ravlich | 4.00 | 1.80 |
| ❑ 30 Dave Dryden SP | 80.00 | 36.00 |
| ❑ 31 Eric Nesterenko SP | 80.00 | 36.00 |
| ❑ 32 Gilles Marotte SP | 80.00 | 36.00 |
| ❑ 33 Jim Pappin SP | 80.00 | 36.00 |
| ❑ 34 Gary Bergman | 4.00 | 1.80 |
| ❑ 35 Roger Crozier | 8.00 | 3.60 |
| ❑ 36 Peter Mahovlich | 6.00 | 2.70 |
| ❑ 37 Alex Delvecchio | 8.00 | 3.60 |
| ❑ 38 Dean Prentice | 5.00 | 2.20 |
| ❑ 39 Kent Douglas | 4.00 | 1.80 |
| ❑ 40 Roy Edwards | 6.00 | 2.70 |
| ❑ 41 Bruce MacGregor | 4.00 | 1.80 |
| ❑ 42 Garry Unger | 6.00 | 2.70 |
| ❑ 43 Pete Stemkowski | 4.00 | 1.80 |
| ❑ 44 Gordie Howe | 80.00 | 36.00 |
| ❑ 45 Frank Mahovlich | 12.00 | 5.50 |
| ❑ 46 Bob Baun SP | 80.00 | 36.00 |
| ❑ 47 Brian Conacher SP | 80.00 | 36.00 |
| ❑ 48 Jim Watson SP | 80.00 | 36.00 |
| ❑ 49 Nick Libett SP | 80.00 | 36.00 |
| ❑ 50 Real Lemieux | 5.00 | 2.20 |
| ❑ 51 Ted Irvine | 5.00 | 2.20 |
| ❑ 52 Bob Wall | 5.00 | 2.20 |
| ❑ 53 Bill White | 5.00 | 2.20 |
| ❑ 54 Gord Labossiere | 5.00 | 2.20 |
| ❑ 55 Eddie Joyal | 4.00 | 1.80 |
| ❑ 56 Lowell MacDonald | 5.00 | 2.20 |
| ❑ 57 Bill Flett | 5.00 | 2.20 |
| ❑ 58 Wayne Rutledge | 6.00 | 2.70 |
| ❑ 59 Dave Amadio | 4.00 | 1.80 |
| ❑ 60 Skip Krake SP | 50.00 | 22.00 |
| ❑ 61 Doug Robinson SP | 50.00 | 22.00 |
| ❑ 62 Wayne Connelly | 5.00 | 2.20 |
| ❑ 63 Bob Woytowich | 5.00 | 2.20 |
| ❑ 64 Andre Boudrias | 5.00 | 2.20 |
| ❑ 65 Bill Goldsworthy | 6.00 | 2.70 |
| ❑ 66 Cesare Maniago | 8.00 | 3.60 |
| ❑ 67 Milan Marcetta | 5.00 | 2.20 |
| ❑ 68 Bill Collins SP 7 | 50.00 | 22.00 |
| ❑ 69 Claude Larose SP 7 | 100.00 | 45.00 |
| ❑ 70 Parker MacDonald | 5.00 | 2.20 |
| ❑ 71 Ray Cullen | 5.00 | 2.20 |
| ❑ 72 Mike McMahon | 5.00 | 2.20 |
| ❑ 73 Bob McCord SP | 50.00 | 22.00 |
| ❑ 74 Larry Hillman SP | 50.00 | 22.00 |
| ❑ 75 Gump Worsley | 10.00 | 4.50 |
| ❑ 76 Rogatien Vachon | 15.00 | 6.75 |
| ❑ 77 Ted Harris | 4.00 | 1.80 |
| ❑ 78 Jacques Laperriere | 6.00 | 2.70 |
| ❑ 79 J.C. Tremblay | 5.00 | 2.20 |
| ❑ 80 Jean Beliveau | 30.00 | 13.50 |
| ❑ 81 Gilles Tremblay | 4.00 | 1.80 |
| ❑ 82 Ralph Backstrom | 5.00 | 2.20 |
| ❑ 83 Bobby Rousseau | 4.00 | 1.80 |
| ❑ 84 John Ferguson | 6.00 | 2.70 |

| | | |
|---|---|---|
| ☐ 85 Dick Duff | 6.00 | 2.70 |
| ☐ 86 Terry Harper | 6.00 | 2.70 |
| ☐ 87 Yvan Cournoyer | 8.00 | 3.60 |
| ☐ 88 Jacques Lemaire | 12.00 | 5.50 |
| ☐ 89 Henri Richard | 12.00 | 5.50 |
| ☐ 90 Claude Provost SP | 100.00 | 45.00 |
| ☐ 91 Serge Savard SP | 150.00 | 70.00 |
| ☐ 92 Mickey Redmond SP | 150.00 | 70.00 |
| ☐ 93 Rod Seiling | 4.00 | 1.80 |
| ☐ 94 Jean Ratelle | 8.00 | 3.60 |
| ☐ 95 Ed Giacomin | 15.00 | 6.75 |
| ☐ 96 Reg Fleming | 4.00 | 1.80 |
| ☐ 97 Phil Goyette | 4.00 | 1.80 |
| ☐ 98 Arnie Brown | 4.00 | 1.80 |
| ☐ 99 Don Marshall | 4.00 | 1.80 |
| ☐ 100 Orland Kurtenbach | 6.00 | 2.70 |
| ☐ 101 Bob Nevin | 4.00 | 1.80 |
| ☐ 102 Rod Gilbert | 8.00 | 3.60 |
| ☐ 103 Harry Howell | 6.00 | 2.70 |
| ☐ 104 Jim Neilson | 4.00 | 1.80 |
| ☐ 105 Vic Hadfield SP | 150.00 | 70.00 |
| ☐ 106 Larry Jeffrey SP | 250.00 | 110.00 |
| ☐ 107 Dave Balon SP | 150.00 | 70.00 |
| ☐ 108 Ron Stewart SP | 150.00 | 70.00 |
| ☐ 109 Gerry Ehman | 4.00 | 1.80 |
| ☐ 110 John Brenneman | 5.00 | 2.20 |
| ☐ 111 Ted Hampson | 5.00 | 2.20 |
| ☐ 112 Billy Harris | 5.00 | 2.20 |
| ☐ 113 George Swarbrick SP 5 | 100.00 | 45.00 |
| ☐ 114 Carol Vadnais SP 5 | 500.00 | 220.00 |
| ☐ 115 Gary Smith | 8.00 | 3.60 |
| ☐ 116 Charlie Hodge | 8.00 | 3.60 |
| ☐ 117 Bert Marshall | 5.00 | 2.20 |
| ☐ 118 Bill Hicke | 5.00 | 2.20 |
| ☐ 119 Tracy Pratt | 5.00 | 2.20 |
| ☐ 120 Gary Jarrett SP | 500.00 | 220.00 |
| ☐ 121 Howie Young SP | 500.00 | 220.00 |
| ☐ 122 Bernie Parent | 40.00 | 18.00 |
| ☐ 123 John Miszuk | 5.00 | 2.20 |
| ☐ 124 Ed Hoekstra SP 3 | 100.00 | 45.00 |
| ☐ 125 Allan Stanley SP 3 | 100.00 | 45.00 |
| ☐ 126 Gary Dornhoefer | 6.00 | 2.70 |
| ☐ 127 Doug Favell | 8.00 | 3.60 |
| ☐ 128 Andre Lacroix | 5.00 | 2.20 |
| ☐ 129 Brit Selby | 5.00 | 2.20 |
| ☐ 130 Don Blackburn | 5.00 | 2.20 |
| ☐ 131 Leon Rochefort | 5.00 | 2.20 |
| ☐ 132 Forbes Kennedy | 5.00 | 2.20 |
| ☐ 133 Claude Laforge SP | 80.00 | 36.00 |
| ☐ 134 Pat Hannigan SP | 80.00 | 36.00 |
| ☐ 135 Ken Schinkel | 5.00 | 2.20 |
| ☐ 136 Earl Ingarfield | 5.00 | 2.20 |
| ☐ 137 Val Fonteyne | 4.00 | 1.80 |
| ☐ 138 Noel Price | 4.00 | 1.80 |
| ☐ 139 Andy Bathgate | 8.00 | 3.60 |
| ☐ 140 Les Binkley | 8.00 | 3.60 |
| ☐ 141 Leo Boivin | 5.00 | 2.20 |
| ☐ 142 Paul Andrea | 4.00 | 1.80 |
| ☐ 143 Dunc McCallum | 6.00 | 2.70 |
| ☐ 144 Keith McCreary | 5.00 | 2.20 |
| ☐ 145 Lou Angotti SP | 80.00 | 36.00 |
| ☐ 146 Wally Boyer SP | 80.00 | 36.00 |
| ☐ 147 Ron Schock | 5.00 | 2.20 |
| ☐ 148 Bob Plager | 6.00 | 2.70 |
| ☐ 149 Al Arbour | 8.00 | 3.60 |
| ☐ 150 Red Berenson | 6.00 | 2.70 |
| ☐ 151 Glenn Hall | 15.00 | 6.75 |
| ☐ 152 Jim Roberts | 5.00 | 2.20 |
| ☐ 153 Noel Picard | 5.00 | 2.20 |
| ☐ 154 Barclay Plager | 6.00 | 2.70 |
| ☐ 155 Larry Keenan | 5.00 | 2.20 |
| ☐ 156 Terry Crisp | 6.00 | 2.70 |
| ☐ 157 Gary Sabourin SP | 80.00 | 36.00 |
| ☐ 158 Ab McDonald SP | 80.00 | 36.00 |
| ☐ 159 George Armstrong | 8.00 | 3.60 |
| ☐ 160 Wayne Carleton | 4.00 | 1.80 |
| ☐ 161 Paul Henderson | 6.00 | 2.70 |
| ☐ 162 Bob Pulford | 6.00 | 2.70 |
| ☐ 163 Mike Walton | 5.00 | 2.20 |
| ☐ 164 Johnny Bower | 8.00 | 3.60 |
| ☐ 165 Ron Ellis | 5.00 | 2.20 |
| ☐ 166 Mike Pelyk | 4.00 | 1.80 |
| ☐ 167 Murray Oliver | 4.00 | 1.80 |
| ☐ 168 Norm Ullman | 8.00 | 3.60 |
| ☐ 169 Dave Keon | 8.00 | 3.60 |
| ☐ 170 Floyd Smith | 4.00 | 1.80 |
| ☐ 171 Marcel Pronovost | 6.00 | 2.70 |
| ☐ 172 Tim Horton | 15.00 | 6.75 |
| ☐ 173 Bruce Gamble | 6.00 | 2.70 |
| ☐ 174 Jim McKenny SP | 100.00 | 45.00 |
| ☐ 175 Mike Byers SP | 100.00 | 45.00 |
| ☐ 176 Pierre Pilote SP | 150.00 | 70.00 |

## 1995-96 SkyBox Impact Promo Panel

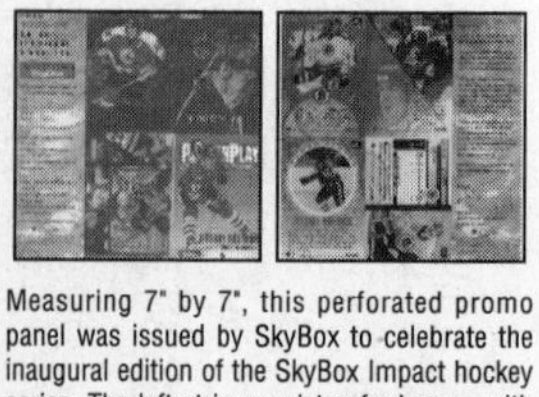

Measuring 7" by 7", this perforated promo panel was issued by SkyBox to celebrate the inaugural edition of the SkyBox Impact hockey series. The left strip consists of ad copy, with four standard-size player cards filling out the rest of the panel. As indicated in the listing below, Blaine Lacher is featured on two cards: a regular card as well as a Deflector insert card. The only difference from their regular issue counterparts is that these cards have the word "SAMPLE" on a black rectangle in place of card number.

| | MINT | NRMT |
|---|---|---|
| COMPLETE SET | 1.00 | .45 |
| COMMON CARD | 1.00 | .45 |
| ☐ 1 Theo Fleury<br>Blaine Lacher<br>Blaine Lacher<br>Jeremy Roenick | 1.00 | .45 |

## 1995-96 SkyBox Impact

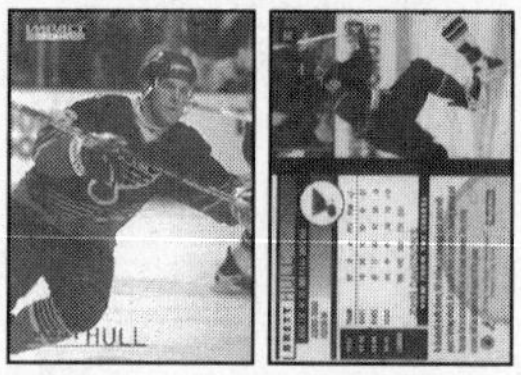

The 1996 Skybox Impact set was issued in one series totalling 250 cards. The 10-card packs retailed for $1.29. Each pack included an NHL on Fox Slapshot Instant Win Game Card, offering a chance at more than 20,000 prizes. The unused game cards sell for about ten cents. The Blaine Lacher SkyMotion exchange card was randomly inserted at a rate of 1:360 packs. The exchange deadline for the Lacher SkyMotion card was December 31st, 1996. Prices for the expired card and the redeemed card are listed below.

| | MINT | NRMT |
|---|---|---|
| COMPLETE SET (250) | 15.00 | 6.75 |
| COMMON CARD (1-250) | .05 | .02 |
| ☐ 1 Bobby Dollas | .05 | .02 |
| ☐ 2 Guy Hebert | .10 | .05 |
| ☐ 3 Paul Kariya | .75 | .35 |
| ☐ 4 Todd Krygier | .05 | .02 |
| ☐ 5 Oleg Tverdovsky | .10 | .05 |
| ☐ 6 Shaun Van Allen | .05 | .02 |
| ☐ 7 Ray Bourque | .20 | .09 |
| ☐ 8 Al Iafrate | .05 | .02 |
| ☐ 9 Blaine Lacher | .10 | .05 |
| ☐ 10 Joe Mullen | .10 | .05 |
| ☐ 11 Cam Neely | .10 | .05 |
| ☐ 12 Adam Oates | .10 | .05 |
| ☐ 13 Kevin Stevens | .05 | .02 |
| ☐ 14 Donald Audette | .10 | .05 |
| ☐ 15 Garry Galley | .05 | .02 |
| ☐ 16 Dominik Hasek | .40 | .18 |
| ☐ 17 Pat LaFontaine | .10 | .05 |
| ☐ 18 Derek Plante | .05 | .02 |
| ☐ 19 Alexei Zhitnik | .05 | .02 |
| ☐ 20 Steve Chiasson | .05 | .02 |
| ☐ 21 Theoren Fleury | .10 | .05 |
| ☐ 22 Phil Housley | .10 | .05 |
| ☐ 23 Trevor Kidd | .10 | .05 |
| ☐ 24 Joe Nieuwendyk | .10 | .05 |
| ☐ 25 German Titov | .05 | .02 |
| ☐ 26 Zarley Zalapski | .05 | .02 |
| ☐ 27 Ed Belfour | .20 | .09 |
| ☐ 28 Chris Chelios | .20 | .09 |
| ☐ 29 Sergei Krivokrasov | .05 | .02 |
| ☐ 30 Joe Murphy | .05 | .02 |
| ☐ 31 Bernie Nicholls | .05 | .02 |
| ☐ 32 Patrick Poulin | .05 | .02 |
| ☐ 33 Jeremy Roenick | .20 | .09 |
| ☐ 34 Gary Suter | .05 | .02 |
| ☐ 35 Peter Forsberg | .60 | .25 |
| ☐ 36 Valeri Kamensky | .10 | .05 |
| ☐ 37 Claude Lemieux | .10 | .05 |
| ☐ 38 Curtis Leschyshyn | .05 | .02 |
| ☐ 39 Sandis Ozolinsh | .10 | .05 |
| ☐ 40 Mike Ricci | .05 | .02 |
| ☐ 41 Joe Sakic | .40 | .18 |
| ☐ 42 Jocelyn Thibault | .20 | .09 |
| ☐ 43 Bob Bassen | .05 | .02 |
| ☐ 44 Dave Gagner | .10 | .05 |
| ☐ 45 Todd Harvey | .05 | .02 |
| ☐ 46 Derian Hatcher | .05 | .02 |
| ☐ 47 Kevin Hatcher | .05 | .02 |
| ☐ 48 Mike Modano | .30 | .14 |
| ☐ 49 Andy Moog | .10 | .05 |
| ☐ 50 Dino Ciccarelli | .10 | .05 |
| ☐ 51 Paul Coffey | .20 | .09 |
| ☐ 52 Sergei Fedorov | .40 | .18 |
| ☐ 53 Vladimir Konstantinov | .05 | .02 |
| ☐ 54 Slava Kozlov | .10 | .05 |
| ☐ 55 Nicklas Lidstrom | .10 | .05 |
| ☐ 56 Chris Osgood | .20 | .09 |
| ☐ 57 Keith Primeau | .10 | .05 |
| ☐ 58 Steve Yzerman | .60 | .25 |
| ☐ 59 Jason Arnott | .10 | .05 |
| ☐ 60 Curtis Joseph | .20 | .09 |
| ☐ 61 Igor Kravchuk | .05 | .02 |
| ☐ 62 Todd Marchant | .05 | .02 |
| ☐ 63 David Oliver | .05 | .02 |
| ☐ 64 Bill Ranford | .10 | .05 |
| ☐ 65 Doug Weight | .10 | .05 |
| ☐ 66 Stu Barnes | .05 | .02 |
| ☐ 67 Jesse Belanger | .05 | .02 |
| ☐ 68 Gord Murphy | .05 | .02 |
| ☐ 69 Magnus Svensson | .05 | .02 |
| ☐ 70 John Vanbiesbrouck | .30 | .14 |
| ☐ 71 Sean Burke | .10 | .05 |
| ☐ 72 Andrew Cassels | .05 | .02 |
| ☐ 73 Nelson Emerson | .05 | .02 |
| ☐ 74 Andrei Nikolishin | .05 | .02 |
| ☐ 75 Geoff Sanderson | .10 | .05 |
| ☐ 76 Brendan Shanahan | .40 | .18 |
| ☐ 77 Glen Wesley | .05 | .02 |
| ☐ 78 Rob Blake | .05 | .02 |
| ☐ 79 Wayne Gretzky | 1.50 | .70 |
| ☐ 80 Dimitri Khristich | .05 | .02 |
| ☐ 81 Jari Kurri | .10 | .05 |
| ☐ 82 Darryl Sydor | .05 | .02 |
| ☐ 83 Rick Tocchet | .10 | .05 |
| ☐ 84 Vincent Damphousse | .10 | .05 |
| ☐ 85 Vladimir Malakhov | .05 | .02 |
| ☐ 86 Mark Recchi | .10 | .05 |
| ☐ 87 Patrick Roy | 1.00 | .45 |
| ☐ 88 Brian Savage | .05 | .02 |
| ☐ 89 Pierre Turgeon | .10 | .05 |
| ☐ 90 Martin Brodeur | .50 | .23 |
| ☐ 91 Neal Broten | .10 | .05 |
| ☐ 92 Shawn Chambers | .05 | .02 |
| ☐ 93 John MacLean | .10 | .05 |
| ☐ 94 Randy McKay | .05 | .02 |
| ☐ 95 Scott Niedermayer | .05 | .02 |
| ☐ 96 Stephane Richer | .10 | .05 |
| ☐ 97 Scott Stevens | .10 | .05 |
| ☐ 98 Steve Thomas | .05 | .02 |
| ☐ 99 Wendel Clark | .10 | .05 |
| ☐ 100 Patrick Flatley | .05 | .02 |
| ☐ 101 Scott Lachance | .05 | .02 |
| ☐ 102 Brett Lindros | .05 | .02 |
| ☐ 103 Kirk Muller | .05 | .02 |
| ☐ 104 Tommy Salo | .30 | .14 |
| ☐ 105 Mathieu Schneider | .05 | .02 |
| ☐ 106 Dennis Vaske | .05 | .02 |
| ☐ 107 Ray Ferraro | .05 | .02 |
| ☐ 108 Adam Graves | .10 | .05 |
| ☐ 109 Alexei Kovalev | .05 | .02 |
| ☐ 110 Brian Leetch | .20 | .09 |
| ☐ 111 Mark Messier | .30 | .14 |
| ☐ 112 Mike Richter | .20 | .09 |
| ☐ 113 Luc Robitaille | .10 | .05 |
| ☐ 114 Ulf Samuelsson | .05 | .02 |
| ☐ 115 Pat Verbeek | .05 | .02 |
| ☐ 116 Don Beaupre | .10 | .05 |
| ☐ 117 Radek Bonk | .05 | .02 |
| ☐ 118 Alexandre Daigle | .05 | .02 |
| ☐ 119 Steve Duchesne | .05 | .02 |
| ☐ 120 Dan Quinn | .05 | .02 |
| ☐ 121 Martin Straka | .05 | .02 |
| ☐ 122 Alexei Yashin | .10 | .05 |
| ☐ 123 Rod Brind'Amour | .10 | .05 |
| ☐ 124 Eric Desjardins | .05 | .02 |
| ☐ 125 Ron Hextall | .10 | .05 |
| ☐ 126 John LeClair | .30 | .14 |
| ☐ 127 Eric Lindros | .60 | .25 |
| ☐ 128 Mikael Renberg | .10 | .05 |
| ☐ 129 Chris Therien | .05 | .02 |
| ☐ 130 Ron Francis | .10 | .05 |
| ☐ 131 Jaromir Jagr | .60 | .25 |
| ☐ 132 Mario Lemieux | 1.00 | .45 |
| ☐ 133 Petr Nedved | .10 | .05 |
| ☐ 134 Tomas Sandstrom | .05 | .02 |
| ☐ 135 Bryan Smolinski | .05 | .02 |
| ☐ 136 Ken Wregget | .10 | .05 |
| ☐ 137 Sergei Zubov | .05 | .02 |
| ☐ 138 Shayne Corson | .05 | .02 |
| ☐ 139 Geoff Courtnall | .05 | .02 |
| ☐ 140 Dale Hawerchuk | .10 | .05 |
| ☐ 141 Brett Hull | .30 | .14 |
| ☐ 142 Ian Laperriere | .05 | .02 |
| ☐ 143 Al MacInnis | .10 | .05 |
| ☐ 144 Chris Pronger | .10 | .05 |
| ☐ 145 Esa Tikkanen | .05 | .02 |
| ☐ 146 Ulf Dahlen | .05 | .02 |
| ☐ 147 Jeff Friesen | .10 | .05 |
| ☐ 148 Arturs Irbe | .10 | .05 |
| ☐ 149 Craig Janney | .10 | .05 |
| ☐ 150 Owen Nolan | .10 | .05 |
| ☐ 151 Mike Rathje | .05 | .02 |
| ☐ 152 Ray Sheppard | .10 | .05 |
| ☐ 153 Brian Bradley | .05 | .02 |
| ☐ 154 Chris Gratton | .10 | .05 |
| ☐ 155 Roman Hamrlik | .10 | .05 |
| ☐ 156 Petr Klima | .05 | .02 |
| ☐ 157 Daren Puppa | .10 | .05 |
| ☐ 158 Dave Andreychuk | .10 | .05 |
| ☐ 159 Mike Gartner | .10 | .05 |
| ☐ 160 Todd Gill | .05 | .02 |
| ☐ 161 Doug Gilmour | .20 | .09 |
| ☐ 162 Kenny Jonsson | .05 | .02 |
| ☐ 163 Larry Murphy | .10 | .05 |
| ☐ 164 Felix Potvin | .20 | .09 |
| ☐ 165 Mats Sundin | .10 | .05 |
| ☐ 166 Jeff Brown | .05 | .02 |
| ☐ 167 Pavel Bure | .40 | .18 |
| ☐ 168 Russ Courtnall | .05 | .02 |
| ☐ 169 Trevor Linden | .10 | .05 |
| ☐ 170 Kirk McLean | .10 | .05 |
| ☐ 171 Alexander Mogilny | .10 | .05 |
| ☐ 172 Roman Oksiuta | .05 | .02 |
| ☐ 173 Mike Ridley | .05 | .02 |
| ☐ 174 Peter Bondra | .20 | .09 |
| ☐ 175 Jim Carey | .20 | .09 |
| ☐ 176 Sergei Gonchar | .05 | .02 |
| ☐ 177 Dale Hunter | .05 | .02 |
| ☐ 178 Calle Johansson | .05 | .02 |
| ☐ 179 Joe Juneau | .05 | .02 |
| ☐ 180 Michal Pivonka | .05 | .02 |
| ☐ 181 Nikolai Khabibulin | .10 | .05 |
| ☐ 182 Dave Manson | .05 | .02 |
| ☐ 183 Teppo Numminen | .05 | .02 |
| ☐ 184 Teemu Selanne | .40 | .18 |
| ☐ 185 Keith Tkachuk | .25 | .11 |
| ☐ 186 Darren Turcotte | .05 | .02 |
| ☐ 187 Alexei Zhamnov | .10 | .05 |
| ☐ 188 Chad Kilger | .05 | .02 |
| ☐ 189 Kyle McLaren | .05 | .02 |
| ☐ 190 Brian Holzinger | .20 | .09 |
| ☐ 191 Wayne Primeau | .05 | .02 |
| ☐ 192 Marty Murray | .05 | .02 |
| ☐ 193 Eric Daze | .20 | .09 |
| ☐ 194 Jon Klemm | .05 | .02 |
| ☐ 195 Jere Lehtinen | .05 | .02 |
| ☐ 196 Jason Bonsignore | .05 | .02 |
| ☐ 197 Miroslav Satan | 1.00 | .45 |
| ☐ 198 Ryan Smyth | .05 | .02 |
| ☐ 199 Tyler Wright | .05 | .02 |
| ☐ 200 Radek Dvorak | .05 | .02 |
| ☐ 201 Ed Jovanovski | .20 | .09 |
| ☐ 202 Jeff O'Neill | .05 | .02 |
| ☐ 203 Aki-Petteri Berg | .05 | .02 |
| ☐ 204 Jamie Storr | .10 | .05 |
| ☐ 205 Vitali Yachmenov | .05 | .02 |
| ☐ 206 Saku Koivu | .40 | .18 |
| ☐ 207 Denis Pederson | .05 | .02 |
| ☐ 208 Todd Bertuzzi | .10 | .05 |
| ☐ 209 Bryan McCabe | .05 | .02 |
| ☐ 210 Shane Doan | .05 | .02 |
| ☐ 211 Peter Ferraro | .05 | .02 |
| ☐ 212 Darren Langdon | .05 | .02 |
| ☐ 213 Niklas Sundstrom | .05 | .02 |
| ☐ 214 Daniel Alfredsson | .60 | .25 |
| ☐ 215 Garth Snow | .10 | .05 |
| ☐ 216 Ian Moran | .05 | .02 |
| ☐ 217 Richard Park | .05 | .02 |
| ☐ 218 Jamie Rivers | .05 | .02 |
| ☐ 219 Roman Vopat | .05 | .02 |
| ☐ 220 Marcus Ragnarsson | .05 | .02 |
| ☐ 221 Aaron Gavey | .05 | .02 |
| ☐ 222 Daymond Langkow | .20 | .09 |
| ☐ 223 Darby Hendrickson | .05 | .02 |
| ☐ 224 Martin Gendron | .05 | .02 |
| ☐ 225 Brendan Witt | .05 | .02 |
| ☐ 226 Shane Doan | .05 | .02 |
| ☐ 227 Deron Quint | .05 | .02 |
| ☐ 228 Jim Carey HH | .20 | .09 |
| ☐ 229 Peter Forsberg HH | .40 | .18 |
| ☐ 230 Paul Kariya HH | .50 | .23 |
| ☐ 231 David Oliver HH | .05 | .02 |
| ☐ 232 Blaine Lacher HH | .10 | .05 |
| ☐ 233 Todd Harvey HH | .05 | .02 |
| ☐ 234 Todd Marchant HH | .05 | .02 |
| ☐ 235 Jeff Friesen HH | .10 | .05 |
| ☐ 236 Oleg Tverdovsky HH | .10 | .05 |
| ☐ 237 Jason Arnott HH | .10 | .05 |
| ☐ 238 Cam Neely PP | .10 | .05 |
| ☐ 239 Keith Tkachuk PP | .20 | .09 |
| ☐ 240 Owen Nolan PP | .10 | .05 |
| ☐ 241 Keith Primeau PP | .10 | .05 |
| ☐ 242 Peter Bondra PP | .20 | .09 |
| ☐ 243 Jeremy Roenick PP | .20 | .09 |
| ☐ 244 John LeClair PP | .20 | .09 |
| ☐ 245 Mikael Renberg PP | .10 | .05 |
| ☐ 246 Dave Andreychuk PP | .10 | .05 |
| ☐ 247 Rick Tocchet PP | .10 | .05 |
| ☐ NNO Blaine Lacher<br>Exchange card | .05 | .02 |
| ☐ NNO Blaine Lacher<br>SkyMotion card | 15.00 | 6.75 |

## 1995-96 SkyBox Impact Deflectors

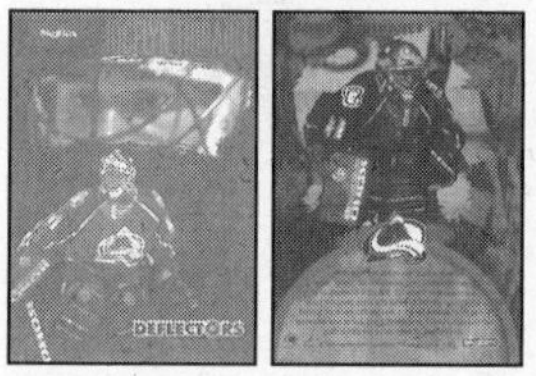


Randomly inserted in packs at a rate of 1:10, this 12-card set features top NHL goalies.

| | MINT | NRMT |
|---|---|---|
| COMPLETE SET (12) | 20.00 | 9.00 |
| COMMON CARD (1-12) | 1.00 | .45 |
| ☐ 1 Dominik Hasek | 1.25 | .55 |
| ☐ 2 Jim Carey | 1.00 | .45 |
| ☐ 3 Felix Potvin | 1.00 | .45 |
| ☐ 4 Sean Burke | 1.00 | .45 |
| ☐ 5 Blaine Lacher | 1.00 | .45 |
| ☐ 6 John Vanbiesbrouck | 1.50 | .70 |
| ☐ 7 Jocelyn Thibault | 1.00 | .45 |
| ☐ 8 Patrick Roy | 3.00 | 1.35 |
| ☐ 9 Ed Belfour | 1.25 | .55 |
| ☐ 10 Trevor Kidd | 1.00 | .45 |
| ☐ 11 Martin Brodeur | 2.00 | .90 |
| ☐ 12 Kirk McLean | 1.00 | .45 |

## 1995-96 SkyBox Impact Countdown to Impact

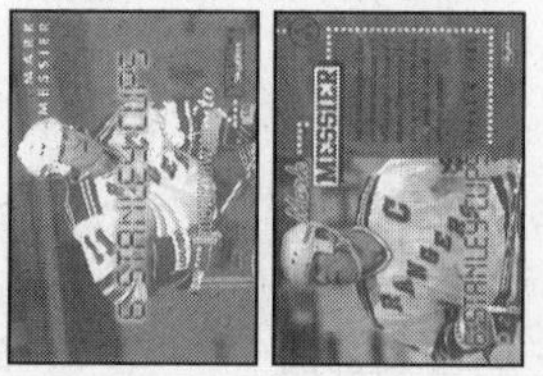

Randomly inserted in hobby packs only at a rate of 1:60, this set features nine explosive stars whose names can be found on the backs of many fans jerseys at NHL arenas across North America. The card fronts also point to statistical milestones that are within range for that player.

| | MINT | NRMT |
|---|---|---|
| COMPLETE SET (9) | 120.00 | 55.00 |
| COMMON CARD (1-9) | 5.00 | 2.20 |
| ☐ 1 Eric Lindros | 15.00 | 6.75 |
| ☐ 2 Jaromir Jagr | 15.00 | 6.75 |
| ☐ 3 Mario Lemieux | 25.00 | 11.00 |
| ☐ 4 Wayne Gretzky | 40.00 | 18.00 |
| ☐ 5 Mark Messier | 8.00 | 3.60 |
| ☐ 6 Sergei Fedorov | 10.00 | 4.50 |
| ☐ 7 Paul Kariya | 20.00 | 9.00 |
| ☐ 8 Doug Gilmour | 5.00 | 2.20 |
| ☐ 9 Pavel Bure | 10.00 | 4.50 |

## 1995-96 SkyBox Impact Ice Quake

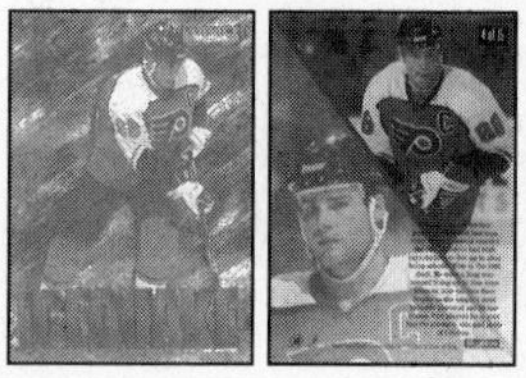

Randomly inserted in packs at a rate of 1:20, this 15-card set delivers the rumble that goalies feel when the NHL's best forwards have the puck on their sticks and start skating towards the net.

| | MINT | NRMT |
|---|---|---|
| COMPLETE SET (15) | 100.00 | 45.00 |
| COMMON CARD (1-15) | 2.00 | .90 |
| ☐ 1 Jaromir Jagr | 15.00 | 6.75 |
| ☐ 2 Brett Hull | 6.00 | 2.70 |
| ☐ 3 Pavel Bure | 10.00 | 4.50 |
| ☐ 4 Eric Lindros | 20.00 | 9.00 |
| ☐ 5 Mark Messier | 6.00 | 2.70 |
| ☐ 6 Wayne Gretzky | 30.00 | 13.50 |
| ☐ 7 Mario Lemieux | 25.00 | 11.00 |
| ☐ 8 Peter Forsberg | 15.00 | 6.75 |
| ☐ 9 Sergei Fedorov | 10.00 | 4.50 |
| ☐ 10 Cam Neely | 2.00 | .90 |
| ☐ 11 Owen Nolan | 2.00 | .90 |
| ☐ 12 Alexei Zhamnov | 2.00 | .90 |
| ☐ 13 Theoren Fleury | 2.00 | .90 |
| ☐ 14 Luc Robitaille | 2.00 | .90 |
| ☐ 15 Teemu Selanne | 10.00 | 4.50 |

## 1995-96 SkyBox Impact NHL On Fox

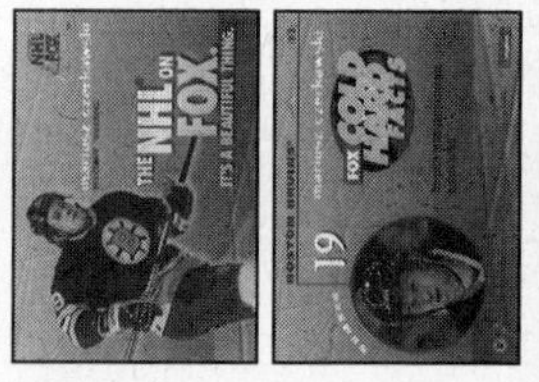


Randomly inserted in packs at a rate of 1:3, this 18-card set showcases both bright young stars and the company's strong affiliation with the NHL broadcasts on the Fox television network in the States.

| | MINT | NRMT |
|---|---|---|
| COMPLETE SET (18) | 8.00 | 3.60 |
| COMMON CARD (1-18) | .40 | .18 |
| ☐ 1 Mariusz Czerkawski | .40 | .18 |
| ☐ 2 Roman Oksiuta | .40 | .18 |
| ☐ 3 David Oliver | .40 | .18 |
| ☐ 4 Adam Deadmarsh | .75 | .35 |
| ☐ 5 Denis Chasse | .40 | .18 |
| ☐ 6 Sergei Krivokrasov | .40 | .18 |
| ☐ 7 Ian Laperriere | .40 | .18 |
| ☐ 8 Chris Therien | .40 | .18 |
| ☐ 9 Brian Savage | .40 | .18 |
| ☐ 10 Todd Marchant | .75 | .35 |
| ☐ 11 Jeff O'Neill | .75 | .35 |
| ☐ 12 Brett Lindros | .40 | .18 |
| ☐ 13 Kenny Jonsson | .75 | .35 |
| ☐ 14 Manny Fernandez | .40 | .18 |
| ☐ 15 Brian Holzinger | .75 | .35 |
| ☐ 16 Niklas Sundstrom | .75 | .35 |
| ☐ 17 Eric Daze | .75 | .35 |
| ☐ 18 Chad Kilger | .40 | .18 |

## 1996-97 SkyBox Impact

This 175-card set featured color action player photos of 118 seasoned stars plus a 20-card Rookies subset (#119-#138) and a 10-card Power Play subset (#139-#148). These ten Power Play cards had front designs that actually looked like minature magazine covers. A special Stanley Cup logo appeared on all Colorado Avalanche player cards. The backs carried player stats, bio information, and a statement about the player as written by

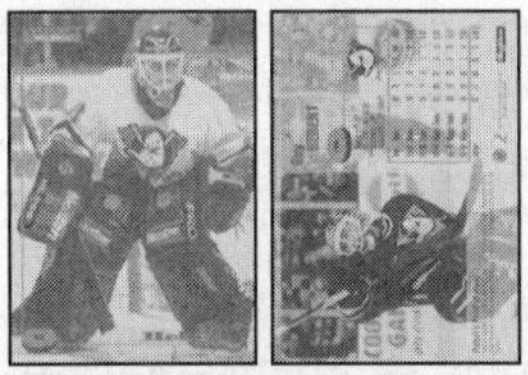

hockey HOF and Fox broadcaster Denis Potvin. A "John LeClair SkyPin Exchange" card, inserted at the rate of one in every 180 packs, entitled the collector to send for a John LeClair "preview card" from the proposed -- but never materialized -- SkyPin trading card line. One "SkyBox/Fox Game" card was inserted in every pack which enabled the holder to win big prizes from SkyBox, Fox, and the NHL.

| | MINT | NRMT |
|---|---|---|
| COMPLETE SET (175) | 12.00 | 5.50 |
| COMMON CARD (1-175) | .10 | .05 |
| ❑ 1 Guy Hebert | .15 | .07 |
| ❑ 2 Paul Kariya | 1.00 | .45 |
| ❑ 3 Roman Oksiuta | .10 | .05 |
| ❑ 4 Teemu Selanne | .50 | .23 |
| ❑ 5 Ray Bourque | .25 | .11 |
| ❑ 6 Kyle McLaren | .10 | .05 |
| ❑ 7 Adam Oates | .15 | .07 |
| ❑ 8 Bill Ranford | .15 | .07 |
| ❑ 9 Rick Tocchet | .15 | .07 |
| ❑ 10 Dominik Hasek | .50 | .23 |
| ❑ 11 Pat LaFontaine | .15 | .07 |
| ❑ 12 Mike Peca | .10 | .05 |
| ❑ 13 Theoren Fleury | .15 | .07 |
| ❑ 14 Trevor Kidd | .15 | .07 |
| ❑ 15 German Titov | .10 | .05 |
| ❑ 16 Tony Amonte | .15 | .07 |
| ❑ 17 Ed Belfour | .25 | .11 |
| ❑ 18 Chris Chelios | .25 | .11 |
| ❑ 19 Eric Daze | .15 | .07 |
| ❑ 20 Gary Suter | .10 | .05 |
| ❑ 21 Alexei Zhamnov | .15 | .07 |
| ❑ 22 Peter Forsberg | .75 | .35 |
| ❑ 23 Valeri Kamensky | .15 | .07 |
| ❑ 24 Uwe Krupp | .10 | .05 |
| ❑ 25 Claude Lemieux | .15 | .07 |
| ❑ 26 Sandis Ozolinsh | .15 | .07 |
| ❑ 27 Patrick Roy | 1.25 | .55 |
| ❑ 28 Joe Sakic | .50 | .23 |
| ❑ 29 Derian Hatcher | .10 | .05 |
| ❑ 30 Mike Modano | .30 | .14 |
| ❑ 31 Joe Nieuwendyk | .15 | .07 |
| ❑ 32 Sergei Zubov | .10 | .05 |
| ❑ 33 Paul Coffey | .25 | .11 |
| ❑ 34 Sergei Fedorov | .50 | .23 |
| ❑ 35 Vladimir Konstantinov | .10 | .05 |
| ❑ 36 Slava Kozlov | .15 | .07 |
| ❑ 37 Nicklas Lidstrom | .15 | .07 |
| ❑ 38 Chris Osgood | .25 | .11 |
| ❑ 39 Keith Primeau | .15 | .07 |
| ❑ 40 Steve Yzerman | .75 | .35 |
| ❑ 41 Jason Arnott | .15 | .07 |
| ❑ 42 Curtis Joseph | .25 | .11 |
| ❑ 43 Doug Weight | .15 | .07 |
| ❑ 44 Radek Dvorak | .10 | .05 |
| ❑ 45 Ed Jovanovski | .15 | .07 |
| ❑ 46 Scott Mellanby | .15 | .07 |
| ❑ 47 Rob Niedermayer | .15 | .07 |
| ❑ 48 Ray Sheppard | .15 | .07 |
| ❑ 49 Robert Svehla | .10 | .05 |
| ❑ 50 John Vanbiesbrouck | .40 | .18 |
| ❑ 51 Jeff Brown | .10 | .05 |
| ❑ 52 Sean Burke | .15 | .07 |
| ❑ 53 Andrew Cassels | .10 | .05 |
| ❑ 54 Geoff Sanderson | .15 | .07 |
| ❑ 55 Brendan Shanahan | .60 | .25 |
| ❑ 56 Byron Dafoe | .15 | .07 |
| ❑ 57 Ray Ferraro | .10 | .05 |
| ❑ 58 Dimitri Khristich | .10 | .05 |
| ❑ 59 Vitali Yachmenev | .10 | .05 |
| ❑ 60 Valeri Bure | .15 | .07 |
| ❑ 61 Vincent Damphousse | .15 | .07 |
| ❑ 62 Saku Koivu | .40 | .18 |
| ❑ 63 Mark Recchi | .15 | .07 |
| ❑ 64 Martin Rucinsky | .10 | .05 |
| ❑ 65 Jocelyn Thibault | .25 | .11 |
| ❑ 66 Pierre Turgeon | .15 | .07 |
| ❑ 67 Dave Andreychuk | .15 | .07 |
| ❑ 68 Martin Brodeur | .60 | .25 |
| ❑ 69 Bill Guerin | .10 | .05 |
| ❑ 70 Scott Niedermayer | .10 | .05 |
| ❑ 71 Scott Stevens | .15 | .07 |
| ❑ 72 Petr Sykora | .10 | .05 |
| ❑ 73 Steve Thomas | .10 | .05 |
| ❑ 74 Todd Bertuzzi | .10 | .05 |
| ❑ 75 Travis Green | .15 | .07 |
| ❑ 76 Kenny Jonsson | .10 | .05 |
| ❑ 77 Zigmund Palffy | .25 | .11 |
| ❑ 78 Adam Graves | .15 | .07 |
| ❑ 79 Wayne Gretzky | 2.50 | 1.10 |
| ❑ 80 Alexei Kovalev | .10 | .05 |
| ❑ 81 Brian Leetch | .25 | .11 |
| ❑ 82 Mark Messier | .30 | .14 |
| ❑ 83 Mike Richter | .25 | .11 |
| ❑ 84 Ulf Samuelsson | .10 | .05 |
| ❑ 85 Niklas Sundstrom | .10 | .05 |
| ❑ 86 Daniel Alfredsson | .15 | .07 |
| ❑ 87 Radek Bonk | .10 | .05 |
| ❑ 88 Alexandre Daigle | .10 | .05 |
| ❑ 89 Steve Duchesne | .10 | .05 |
| ❑ 90 Damian Rhodes | .15 | .07 |
| ❑ 91 Alexei Yashin | .15 | .07 |
| ❑ 92 Rod Brind'Amour | .15 | .07 |
| ❑ 93 Eric Desjardins | .10 | .05 |
| ❑ 94 Dale Hawerchuk | .15 | .07 |
| ❑ 95 Ron Hextall | .15 | .07 |
| ❑ 96 John LeClair | .40 | .18 |
| ❑ 97 Eric Lindros | .75 | .35 |
| ❑ 98 Mikael Renberg | .15 | .07 |
| ❑ 99 Tom Barrasso | .15 | .07 |
| ❑ 100 Ron Francis | .15 | .07 |
| ❑ 101 Jaromir Jagr | .75 | .35 |
| ❑ 102 Mario Lemieux | 1.25 | .55 |
| ❑ 103 Petr Nedved | .15 | .07 |
| ❑ 104 Bryan Smolinski | .10 | .05 |
| ❑ 105 Nikolai Khabibulin | .15 | .07 |
| ❑ 106 Teppo Numminen | .10 | .05 |
| ❑ 107 Keith Tkachuk | .30 | .14 |
| ❑ 108 Jeremy Roenick | .25 | .11 |
| ❑ 109 Oleg Tverdovsky | .15 | .07 |
| ❑ 110 Shayne Corson | .10 | .05 |
| ❑ 111 Geoff Courtnall | .10 | .05 |
| ❑ 112 Grant Fuhr | .15 | .07 |
| ❑ 113 Brett Hull | .30 | .14 |
| ❑ 114 Al MacInnis | .15 | .07 |
| ❑ 115 Chris Pronger | .15 | .07 |
| ❑ 116 Jeff Friesen | .15 | .07 |
| ❑ 117 Owen Nolan | .15 | .07 |
| ❑ 118 Marcus Ragnarsson | .10 | .05 |
| ❑ 119 Chris Terreri | .15 | .07 |
| ❑ 120 Brian Bradley | .10 | .05 |
| ❑ 121 Chris Gratton | .15 | .07 |
| ❑ 122 Roman Hamrlik | .15 | .07 |
| ❑ 123 Daren Puppa | .15 | .07 |
| ❑ 124 Alexander Selivanov | .10 | .05 |
| ❑ 125 Wendel Clark | .15 | .07 |
| ❑ 126 Doug Gilmour | .25 | .11 |
| ❑ 127 Kirk Muller | .10 | .05 |
| ❑ 128 Larry Murphy | .15 | .07 |
| ❑ 129 Felix Potvin | .25 | .11 |
| ❑ 130 Mats Sundin | .15 | .07 |
| ❑ 131 Pavel Bure | .50 | .23 |
| ❑ 132 Russ Courtnall | .10 | .05 |
| ❑ 133 Trevor Linden | .15 | .07 |
| ❑ 134 Kirk McLean | .15 | .07 |
| ❑ 135 Alexander Mogilny | .15 | .07 |
| ❑ 136 Peter Bondra | .25 | .11 |
| ❑ 137 Jim Carey | .25 | .11 |
| ❑ 138 Sylvain Cote | .10 | .05 |
| ❑ 139 Sergei Gonchar | .10 | .05 |
| ❑ 140 Phil Housley | .15 | .07 |
| ❑ 141 Joe Juneau | .10 | .05 |
| ❑ 142 Michal Pivonka | .10 | .05 |
| ❑ 143 Brendan Witt | .10 | .05 |
| ❑ 144 Nolan Baumgartner | .10 | .05 |
| ❑ 145 Martin Biron | .15 | .07 |
| ❑ 146 Jason Bonsignore | .10 | .05 |
| ❑ 147 Andrew Brunette | .10 | .05 |
| ❑ 148 Jason Doig | .10 | .05 |
| ❑ 149 Peter Ferraro | .10 | .05 |
| ❑ 150 Eric Fichaud | .15 | .07 |
| ❑ 151 Ladislav Kohn | .10 | .05 |
| ❑ 152 Jamie Langenbrunner | .10 | .05 |
| ❑ 153 Daymond Langkow | .10 | .05 |
| ❑ 154 Jay McKee | .10 | .05 |
| ❑ 155 Marty Murray | .10 | .05 |
| ❑ 156 Wayne Primeau | .10 | .05 |
| ❑ 157 Jamie Pushor | .10 | .05 |
| ❑ 158 Jamie Rivers | .10 | .05 |
| ❑ 159 Jamie Storr | .15 | .07 |
| ❑ 160 Steve Sullivan | .10 | .05 |
| ❑ 161 Jose Theodore | .15 | .07 |
| ❑ 162 Roman Vopat | .10 | .05 |
| ❑ 163 Alexei Yegorov | .10 | .05 |
| ❑ 164 Daniel Alfredsson PP | .15 | .07 |
| ❑ 165 Niklas Andersson PP | .10 | .05 |
| ❑ 166 Todd Bertuzzi PP | .10 | .05 |
| ❑ 167 Valeri Bure PP | .15 | .07 |
| ❑ 168 Eric Daze PP | .15 | .07 |
| ❑ 169 Saku Koivu PP | .25 | .11 |
| ❑ 170 Miroslav Satan PP | .10 | .05 |
| ❑ 171 Petr Sykora PP | .10 | .05 |
| ❑ 172 Cory Stillman PP | .10 | .05 |
| ❑ 173 Vitali Yachmenev PP | .10 | .05 |
| ❑ 174 Checklist 1 | .10 | .05 |
| ❑ 175 Checklist 2 UER<br>Pavel Bure misidentified as Paul<br>Palffy misspelled with one F<br>Lafontaine, not Lafontanine<br>Selanne, not Selanna | .10 | .05 |
| ❑ S1 John LeClair PROMO | 1.00 | .45 |
| ❑ NNO SkyPin exchange card | 1.00 | .45 |
| ❑ NNO John Leclair SkyPin | 25.00 | 11.00 |

## 1996-97 SkyBox Impact BladeRunners

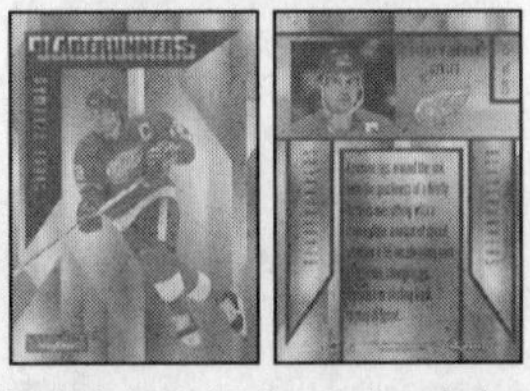

Randomly inserted at the rate of one in three packs, this 25-card set featured some of the fastest hockey players on ice. The fronts carried a color action player photo while the backs displayed player information.

| | MINT | NRMT |
|---|---|---|
| COMPLETE SET (25) | 40.00 | 18.00 |
| COMMON CARD (1-25) | .75 | .35 |
| ❑ 1 Brian Bradley | .75 | .35 |
| ❑ 2 Chris Chelios | 2.00 | .90 |
| ❑ 3 Peter Forsberg | 6.00 | 2.70 |
| ❑ 4 Ron Francis | 2.00 | .90 |
| ❑ 5 Mike Gartner | 2.00 | .90 |
| ❑ 6 Doug Gilmour | 2.00 | .90 |
| ❑ 7 Phil Housley | .75 | .35 |
| ❑ 8 Brett Hull | 2.50 | 1.10 |
| ❑ 9 Valeri Kamensky | 2.00 | .90 |
| ❑ 10 Pat LaFontaine | .75 | .35 |
| ❑ 11 John LeClair | 2.00 | .90 |
| ❑ 12 Claude Lemieux | 2.00 | .90 |
| ❑ 13 Nicklas Lidstrom | 2.00 | .90 |
| ❑ 14 Mark Messier | 2.50 | 1.10 |
| ❑ 15 Alexander Mogilny | 2.00 | .90 |
| ❑ 16 Petr Nedved | .75 | .35 |
| ❑ 17 Adam Oates | 2.00 | .90 |
| ❑ 18 Zigmund Palffy | 2.00 | .90 |
| ❑ 19 Jeremy Roenick | 2.00 | .90 |
| ❑ 20 Teemu Selanne | 4.00 | 1.80 |
| ❑ 21 Brendan Shanahan | 4.00 | 1.80 |
| ❑ 22 Keith Tkachuk | 2.50 | 1.10 |
| ❑ 23 Pierre Turgeon | 2.00 | .90 |
| ❑ 24 Doug Weight | 2.00 | .90 |
| ❑ 25 Steve Yzerman | 6.00 | 2.70 |

## 1996-97 SkyBox Impact Countdown to Impact

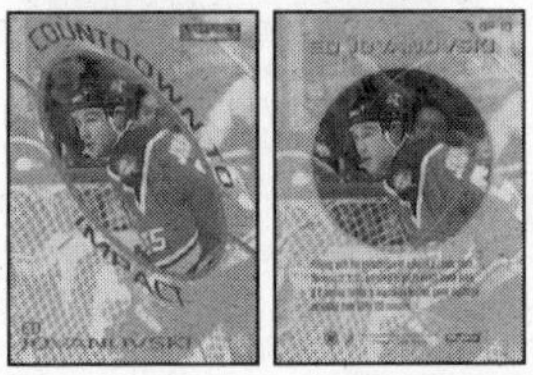

Randomly inserted in hobby packs only at the rate of one in 30, this 10-card insert set focused on the true superstars of the game. The fronts displayed color player photos while the backs carried player information.

| | MINT | NRMT |
|---|---|---|
| COMPLETE SET (10) | 250.00 | 110.00 |
| COMMON CARD (1-10) | 10.00 | 4.50 |
| ❑ 1 Pavel Bure | 15.00 | 6.75 |
| ❑ 2 Sergei Fedorov | 15.00 | 6.75 |
| ❑ 3 Wayne Gretzky | 50.00 | 22.00 |
| ❑ 4 Jaromir Jagr | 25.00 | 11.00 |
| ❑ 5 Ed Jovanovski | 10.00 | 4.50 |
| ❑ 6 Paul Kariya | 30.00 | 13.50 |
| ❑ 7 Mario Lemieux | 40.00 | 18.00 |
| ❑ 8 Eric Lindros | 25.00 | 11.00 |
| ❑ 9 Patrick Roy | 40.00 | 18.00 |
| ❑ 10 Joe Sakic | 15.00 | 6.75 |

## 1996-97 SkyBox Impact NHL on Fox

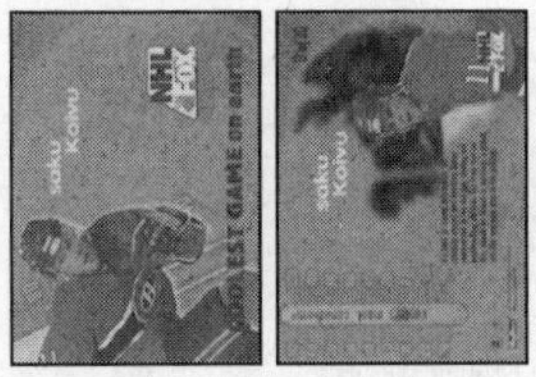

Randomly inserted at the rate of one in ten packs, this 20-card set was a joint venture with Fox TV. The cards featured color action player photos with cool graphics. The backs carried player information.

| | MINT | NRMT |
|---|---|---|
| COMPLETE SET (20) | 50.00 | 22.00 |
| COMMON CARD (1-20) | 1.00 | .45 |
| ❑ 1 Daniel Alfredsson | 4.00 | 1.80 |
| ❑ 2 Todd Bertuzzi | 1.00 | .45 |
| ❑ 3 Ray Bourque | 8.00 | 3.60 |
| ❑ 4 Valeri Bure | 1.00 | .45 |
| ❑ 5 Chris Chelios | 8.00 | 3.60 |
| ❑ 6 Paul Coffey | 8.00 | 3.60 |
| ❑ 7 Eric Daze | 4.00 | 1.80 |
| ❑ 8 Eric Desjardins | 1.00 | .45 |
| ❑ 9 Sergei Gonchar | 1.00 | .45 |
| ❑ 10 Phil Housley | 1.00 | .45 |
| ❑ 11 Ed Jovanovski | 4.00 | 1.80 |
| ❑ 12 Vladimir Konstantinov | 1.00 | .45 |
| ❑ 13 Saku Koivu | 12.00 | 5.50 |
| ❑ 14 Brian Leetch | 8.00 | 3.60 |
| ❑ 15 Larry Murphy | 1.00 | .45 |
| ❑ 16 Teppo Numminen | 1.00 | .45 |
| ❑ 17 Sandis Ozolinsh | 1.00 | .45 |
| ❑ 18 Marcus Ragnarsson | 1.00 | .45 |
| ❑ 19 Petr Sykora | 1.00 | .45 |
| ❑ 20 Vitali Yachmenev | 1.00 | .45 |

## 1996-97 SkyBox Impact VersaTeam

Randomly inserted at the rate of one in 120 packs, this 10-card set featured the NHL's best multi-skilled players. The fronts displayed

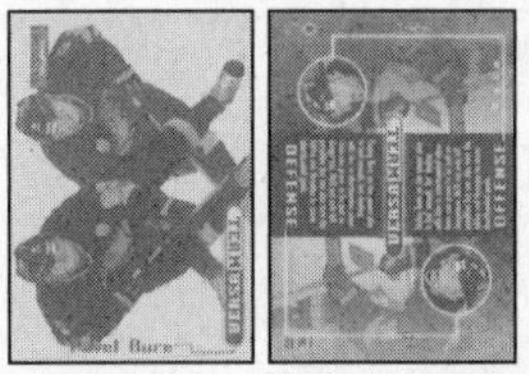

color player photos while the backs carried player information.

| | MINT | NRMT |
|---|---|---|
| COMPLETE SET (10) | 400.00 | 180.00 |
| COMMON CARD (1-10) | 25.00 | 11.00 |
| ❑ 1 Pavel Bure | 25.00 | 11.00 |
| ❑ 2 Sergei Fedorov | 25.00 | 11.00 |
| ❑ 3 Peter Forsberg | 40.00 | 18.00 |
| ❑ 4 Wayne Gretzky | 80.00 | 36.00 |
| ❑ 5 Jaromir Jagr | 40.00 | 18.00 |
| ❑ 6 Paul Kariya | 50.00 | 22.00 |
| ❑ 7 Mario Lemieux | 60.00 | 27.00 |
| ❑ 8 Eric Lindros | 40.00 | 18.00 |
| ❑ 9 Joe Sakic | 25.00 | 11.00 |
| ❑ 10 Teemu Selanne | 25.00 | 11.00 |

## 1996-97 SkyBox Impact Zero Heroes

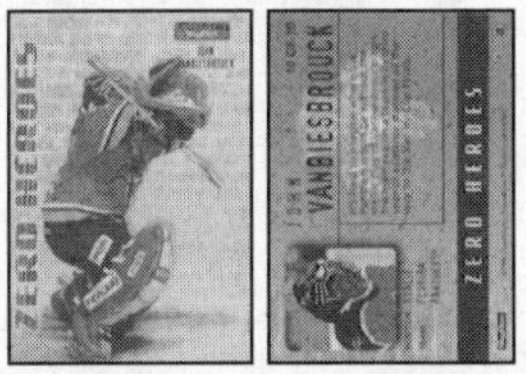

Randomly inserted in retail packs only at the rate of one in 30, this 10-card set featured the stingiest goaltenders in the league. The fronts displayed color player photos while the backs carried player information.

| | MINT | NRMT |
|---|---|---|
| COMPLETE SET (10) | 175.00 | 80.00 |
| COMMON CARD (1-10) | 4.00 | 1.80 |
| ❑ 1 Ed Belfour | 12.00 | 5.50 |
| ❑ 2 Sean Burke | 4.00 | 1.80 |
| ❑ 3 Jim Carey | 15.00 | 6.75 |
| ❑ 4 Dominik Hasek | 25.00 | 11.00 |
| ❑ 5 Ron Hextall | 4.00 | 1.80 |
| ❑ 6 Chris Osgood | 12.00 | 5.50 |
| ❑ 7 Felix Potvin | 25.00 | 11.00 |
| ❑ 8 Daren Puppa | 4.00 | 1.80 |
| ❑ 9 Patrick Roy | 60.00 | 27.00 |
| ❑ 10 John Vanbiesbrouck | 20.00 | 9.00 |

## 1994-95 SP

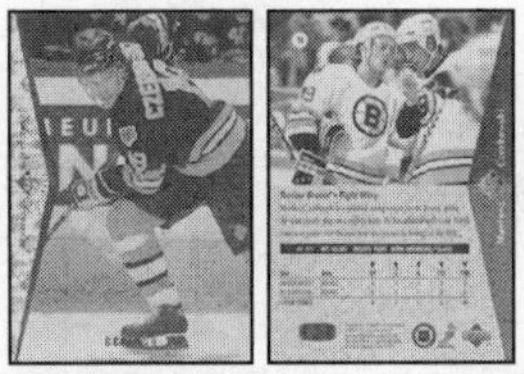

This super premium set of 195 cards was released following the 1995 season. This hobby-only product was issued in boxes of 32 packs, each containing eight cards. Cards 1-135 feature a gold foil border on the left side that includes the player's name and brand logo. The team name is stamped in gold near the bottom border. The cards are grouped alphabetically within teams. The set closes with the World Junior Championships subset which is organized according to countries. All card backs feature limited stats, a photo, and a gold rectangular hologram. Wayne Gretzky's card number 54 was released as a promo. The only discernible difference between the two versions is that the foil on the promo is a brighter gold than the regular issue card. A special Wayne Gretzky 2500 point card was inserted one per case. This card is designed horizontally with die-cutting of the top corners. Wayne appears on a gold background with "2500" in block numbers on the front of the card. Rookie cards in the set include Bryan Berard, Radek Bonk, Jim Carey, Mariusz Czerkawski, Jarome Iginla, Ed Jovanovski, Alyn McAuley, Janne Niinimaa, Jeff O'Neill, Sergei Samsonov and Vitali Yachmenev.

| | MINT | NRMT |
|---|---|---|
| COMPLETE SET (195) | 50.00 | 22.00 |
| COMMON CARD (1-195) | .15 | .07 |
| ❑ 1 Paul Kariya | 3.50 | 1.55 |
| ❑ 2 Oleg Tverdovsky | .30 | .14 |
| ❑ 3 Stephan Lebeau | .15 | .07 |
| ❑ 4 Bob Corkum | .15 | .07 |
| ❑ 5 Guy Hebert | .30 | .14 |
| ❑ 6 Ray Bourque | .60 | .25 |
| ❑ 7 Blaine Lacher | .30 | .14 |
| ❑ 8 Adam Oates | .30 | .14 |
| ❑ 9 Cam Neely | .30 | .14 |
| ❑ 10 Mariusz Czerkawski | .15 | .07 |
| ❑ 11 Bryan Smolinski | .15 | .07 |
| ❑ 12 Pat LaFontaine | .30 | .14 |
| ❑ 13 Alexander Mogilny | .30 | .14 |
| ❑ 14 Dominik Hasek | 1.25 | .55 |
| ❑ 15 Dale Hawerchuk | .30 | .14 |
| ❑ 16 Alexei Zhitnik | .15 | .07 |
| ❑ 17 Theoren Fleury | .30 | .14 |
| ❑ 18 German Titov | .15 | .07 |
| ❑ 19 Phil Housley | .30 | .14 |
| ❑ 20 Joe Nieuwendyk | .30 | .14 |
| ❑ 21 Trevor Kidd | .30 | .14 |
| ❑ 22 Jeremy Roenick | .60 | .25 |
| ❑ 23 Chris Chelios | .60 | .25 |
| ❑ 24 Ed Belfour | .60 | .25 |
| ❑ 25 Bernie Nicholls | .15 | .07 |
| ❑ 26 Tony Amonte | .30 | .14 |
| ❑ 27 Joe Murphy | .15 | .07 |
| ❑ 28 Mike Modano | .75 | .35 |
| ❑ 29 Trent Klatt | .15 | .07 |
| ❑ 30 Dave Gagner | .30 | .14 |
| ❑ 31 Kevin Hatcher | .15 | .07 |
| ❑ 32 Andy Moog | .30 | .14 |
| ❑ 33 Sergei Fedorov | 1.25 | .55 |
| ❑ 34 Steve Yzerman | 2.00 | .90 |
| ❑ 35 Slava Kozlov | .30 | .14 |
| ❑ 36 Paul Coffey | .60 | .25 |
| ❑ 37 Keith Primeau | .30 | .14 |
| ❑ 38 Ray Sheppard | .30 | .14 |
| ❑ 39 Doug Weight | .30 | .14 |
| ❑ 40 Jason Arnott | .30 | .14 |
| ❑ 41 Bill Ranford | .30 | .14 |
| ❑ 42 Shayne Corson | .15 | .07 |
| ❑ 43 Stu Barnes | .15 | .07 |
| ❑ 44 John Vanbiesbrouck | 1.00 | .45 |
| ❑ 45 Johan Garpenlov | .15 | .07 |
| ❑ 46 Bob Kudelski | .15 | .07 |
| ❑ 47 Scott Mellanby | .30 | .14 |
| ❑ 48 Chris Pronger | .30 | .14 |
| ❑ 49 Darren Turcotte | .15 | .07 |
| ❑ 50 Andrew Cassels | .15 | .07 |
| ❑ 51 Sean Burke | .30 | .14 |
| ❑ 52 Geoff Sanderson | .30 | .14 |
| ❑ 53 Rob Blake | .15 | .07 |
| ❑ 54A Wayne Gretzky | 4.00 | 1.80 |
| ❑ 54B Wayne Gretzky PROMO | 10.00 | 4.50 |
| ❑ 55 Rick Tocchet | .30 | .14 |
| ❑ 56 Tony Granato | .15 | .07 |
| ❑ 57 Jari Kurri | .30 | .14 |
| ❑ 58 Vincent Damphousse | .30 | .14 |
| ❑ 59 Patrick Roy | 3.00 | 1.35 |
| ❑ 60 Vladimir Malakhov | .15 | .07 |
| ❑ 61 Pierre Turgeon | .30 | .14 |
| ❑ 62 Mark Recchi | .30 | .14 |
| ❑ 63 Martin Brodeur | 1.50 | .70 |
| ❑ 64 Stephane Richer | .30 | .14 |
| ❑ 65 John MacLean | .30 | .14 |
| ❑ 66 Scott Stevens | .30 | .14 |
| ❑ 67 Scott Niedermayer | .15 | .07 |
| ❑ 68 Kirk Muller | .15 | .07 |
| ❑ 69 Ray Ferraro | .15 | .07 |
| ❑ 70 Brett Lindros | .15 | .07 |
| ❑ 71 Steve Thomas | .15 | .07 |
| ❑ 72 Pat Verbeek | .15 | .07 |
| ❑ 73 Mark Messier | .75 | .35 |
| ❑ 74 Brian Leetch | .60 | .25 |
| ❑ 75 Mike Richter | .60 | .25 |
| ❑ 76 Alexei Kovalev | .30 | .14 |
| ❑ 77 Adam Graves | .30 | .14 |
| ❑ 78 Sergei Zubov | .15 | .07 |
| ❑ 79 Alexei Yashin | .30 | .14 |
| ❑ 80 Radek Bonk | .40 | .18 |
| ❑ 81 Alexandre Daigle | .15 | .07 |
| ❑ 82 Don Beaupre | .30 | .14 |
| ❑ 83 Mikael Renberg | .30 | .14 |
| ❑ 84 Eric Lindros | 2.50 | 1.10 |
| ❑ 85 John LeClair | 1.00 | .45 |
| ❑ 86 Rod Brind'Amour | .30 | .14 |
| ❑ 87 Ron Hextall | .30 | .14 |
| ❑ 88 Ken Wregget | .30 | .14 |
| ❑ 89 Jaromir Jagr | 2.00 | .90 |
| ❑ 90 Tomas Sandstrom | .15 | .07 |
| ❑ 91 John Cullen | .15 | .07 |
| ❑ 92 Ron Francis | .30 | .14 |
| ❑ 93 Luc Robitaille | .30 | .14 |
| ❑ 94 Joe Sakic | 1.25 | .55 |
| ❑ 95 Owen Nolan | .30 | .14 |
| ❑ 96 Peter Forsberg | 3.00 | 1.35 |
| ❑ 97 Wendel Clark | .30 | .14 |
| ❑ 98 Mike Ricci | .15 | .07 |
| ❑ 99 Stephane Fiset | .30 | .14 |
| ❑ 100 Brett Hull | .75 | .35 |
| ❑ 101 Brendan Shanahan | 1.25 | .55 |
| ❑ 102 Curtis Joseph | .60 | .25 |
| ❑ 103 Esa Tikkanen | .15 | .07 |
| ❑ 104 Al MacInnis | .30 | .14 |
| ❑ 105 Arturs Irbe | .30 | .14 |
| ❑ 106 Ray Whitney | .15 | .07 |
| ❑ 107 Sergei Makarov | .15 | .07 |
| ❑ 108 Sandis Ozolinsh | .30 | .14 |
| ❑ 109 Craig Janney | .30 | .14 |
| ❑ 110 Petr Klima | .15 | .07 |
| ❑ 111 Chris Gratton | .30 | .14 |
| ❑ 112 Roman Hamrlik | .30 | .14 |
| ❑ 113 Alexander Selivanov | .15 | .07 |
| ❑ 114 Brian Bradley | .15 | .07 |
| ❑ 115 Doug Gilmour | .60 | .25 |
| ❑ 116 Mats Sundin | .30 | .14 |
| ❑ 117 Felix Potvin | .60 | .25 |
| ❑ 118 Mike Ridley | .15 | .07 |
| ❑ 119 Dave Andreychuk | .30 | .14 |
| ❑ 120 Dmitri Mironov | .15 | .07 |

❑ 121 Pavel Bure 1.25 .55
❑ 122 Trevor Linden .30 .14
❑ 123 Jeff Brown .15 .07
❑ 124 Kirk McLean .30 .14
❑ 125 Geoff Courtnall .15 .07
❑ 126 Joe Juneau .30 .14
❑ 127 Dale Hunter .15 .07
❑ 128 Jim Carey 1.00 .45
❑ 129 Peter Bondra .60 .25
❑ 130 Dimitri Khristich .15 .07
❑ 131 Teemu Selanne 1.25 .55
❑ 132 Keith Tkachuk .75 .35
❑ 133 Alexei Zhamnov .30 .14
❑ 134 Dave Manson .15 .07
❑ 135 Nelson Emerson .15 .07
❑ 136 Alexandre Daigle .15 .07
❑ 137 Jamie Storr .30 .14
❑ 138 Todd Harvey .15 .07
❑ 139 Wade Redden .75 .35
❑ 140 Ed Jovanovski .75 .35
❑ 141 Jamie Rivers .15 .07
❑ 142 Ryan Smyth 2.50 1.10
❑ 143 Jason Botterill .15 .07
❑ 144 Denis Pederson .50 .23
❑ 145 Jeff Friesen .30 .14
❑ 146 Dan Cloutier .60 .25
❑ 147 Lee Sorochan .15 .07
❑ 148 Marty Murray .15 .07
❑ 149 Shean Donovan .15 .07
❑ 150 Larry Courville .15 .07
❑ 151 Jason Allison .15 .07
❑ 152 Jeff O'Neill .50 .23
❑ 153 Bryan McCabe .15 .07
❑ 154 Miloslav Guren .30 .14
❑ 155 Petr Buzek .30 .14
❑ 156 Tomas Blazek .25 .11
❑ 157 Josef Marha .15 .07
❑ 158 Jan Hlavac .30 .14
❑ 159 Veli-Pekka Nutikka .30 .14
❑ 160 Kimmo Timonen .30 .14
❑ 161 Antti Aalto .30 .14
❑ 162 Janne Niinimaa 1.00 .45
❑ 163 Nikolai Zavaroukhine .15 .07
❑ 164 Vadim Epantchinsev .30 .14
❑ 165 Alexandre Koroliouk .15 .07
❑ 166 Dmitri Klevakin .30 .14
❑ 167 Vitali Yachmenev .15 .07
❑ 168 Niklas Sundstrom .15 .07
❑ 169 Anders Soderberg .30 .14
❑ 170 Anders Eriksson .15 .07
❑ 171 Jesper Mattsson .30 .14
❑ 172 Mattias Ohlund 2.00 .90
❑ 173 Jason Bonsignore .15 .07
❑ 174 Bryan Berard 4.00 1.80
❑ 175 Richard Park .15 .07
❑ 176 Mike McBain .15 .07
❑ 177 Jason Doig .15 .07
❑ 178 Xavier Delisle .30 .14
❑ 179 Christian Dube .75 .35
❑ 180 Louis-Philippe Sevigny .15 .07
❑ 181 Jarome Iginla 2.50 1.10
❑ 182 Marc Savard .15 .07
❑ 183 Alyn McCauley 4.00 1.80
❑ 184 Brad Mehalko .30 .14
❑ 185 Todd Norman .15 .07
❑ 186 Brian Scott .15 .07
❑ 187 Brad Larsen .15 .07
❑ 188 Jeffrey Ware .60 .25
❑ 189 Sergei Samsonov 15.00 6.75
❑ 190 Andrei Petrunin .60 .25
❑ 191 Sean Haggerty .30 .14
❑ 192 Rory Fitzpatrick .15 .07
❑ 193 Deron Quint .15 .07
❑ 194 Jamie Langenbrunner .15 .07
❑ 195 Jeff Mitchell .15 .07
❑ SP1 Wayne Gretzky 2500 80.00 36.00

## 1994-95 SP Die Cuts

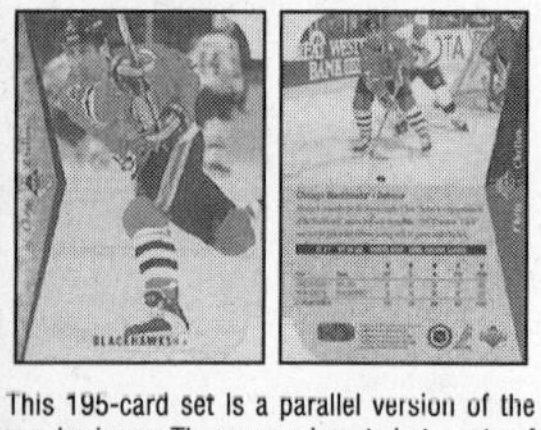

This 195-card set is a parallel version of the regular issue. These were inserted at a rate of one per pack. They are distinguished by the die-cutting of the top and bottom right corners of the card, and the use of a silver instead of gold hologram. The numbering of the cards is consistent with the regular issue.

| | MINT | NRMT |
|---|---|---|
| COMPLETE SET (195) | 125.00 | 55.00 |
| COMMON CARD (1-195) | .25 | .11 |

*STARS: 1.5X TO 3X BASIC CARDS
*YOUNG STARS: 1X TO 2.5X BASIC CARDS

## 1994-95 SP Premier

The 30 cards in this set were randomly inserted in SP at the rate of 1:9 packs. The cards are printed on white paper stock and have a full white border. The action photo has a ghosted background, making the picture look slightly out of focus. The set name is embossed on the lower card front. Player name and position are printed above and below the set name. Player photo and limited

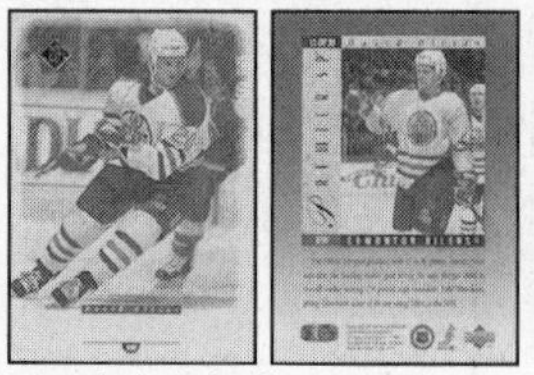

text are the back. A gold rectangular hologram is used on this version.

| | MINT | NRMT |
|---|---|---|
| COMPLETE SET (30) | 150.00 | 70.00 |
| COMMON CARD (1-30) | 2.00 | .90 |

❑ 1 Paul Kariya 12.00 5.50
❑ 2 Peter Forsberg 12.00 5.50
❑ 3 Viktor Kozlov 2.00 .90
❑ 4 Todd Marchant 2.00 .90
❑ 5 Oleg Tverdovsky 2.00 .90
❑ 6 Todd Harvey 2.00 .90
❑ 7 Kenny Jonsson 2.00 .90
❑ 8 Blaine Lacher 3.00 1.35
❑ 9 Radek Bonk 2.00 .90
❑ 10 Brett Lindros 2.00 .90
❑ 11 Valeri Bure 3.00 1.35
❑ 12 Brian Rolston 2.00 .90
❑ 13 David Oliver 2.00 .90
❑ 14 Ian Laperriere 2.00 .90
❑ 15 Adam Deadmarsh 4.00 1.80
❑ 16 Pavel Bure 6.00 2.70
❑ 17 Wayne Gretzky 20.00 9.00
❑ 18 Jeremy Roenick 4.00 1.80
❑ 19 Dominik Hasek 8.00 3.60
❑ 20 Ray Bourque 4.00 1.80
❑ 21 Doug Gilmour 3.00 1.35
❑ 22 Teemu Selanne 6.00 2.70
❑ 23 Cam Neely 3.00 1.35
❑ 24 Sergei Fedorov 6.00 2.70
❑ 25 Bernie Nicholls 2.00 .90
❑ 26 Jaromir Jagr 10.00 4.50
❑ 27 Joe Sakic 6.00 2.70
❑ 28 Mark Messier 4.00 1.80
❑ 29 Brett Hull 4.00 1.80
❑ 30 Eric Lindros 12.00 5.50

## 1994-95 SP Premier Die-Cuts

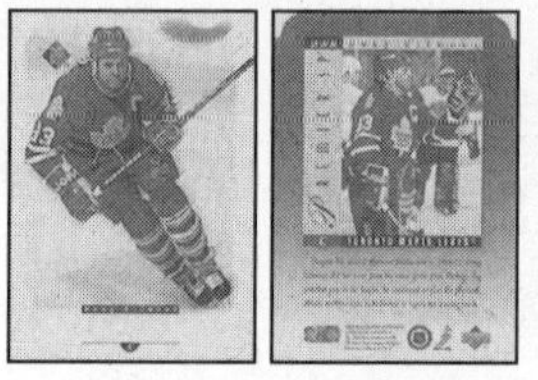

This 30-card set is a parallel of the SP Premier set. They are inserted at a rate of 1:75 SP packs. The cards are identical to the regular SP Premier inserts save for the die-cutting of all four corners, and a silver instead of gold hologram on the back.

| | MINT | NRMT |
|---|---|---|
| COMPLETE SET (30) | 700.00 | 325.00 |
| COMMON CARD (1-30) | 8.00 | 3.60 |

*STARS: 2.5X TO 6X BASIC CARDS

## 1995-96 SP

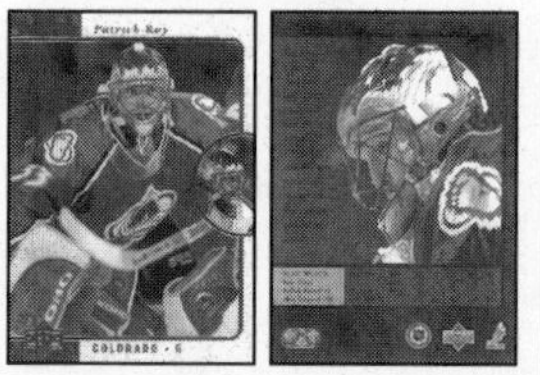

The 1995-96 Upper Deck SP set was issued in one series totaling 188 cards. The 8-card packs had a suggested retail of $4.39 each. The Great Connections inserts -- Wayne Gretzky (GC1) and Sergei Samsonov (GC2) -- were randomly inserted at the rate of 1:381 packs. The set includes several key Rookie Cards featuring players from the 1996 World Junior Championships, including Chris Phillips, Marcus Nilsson and Alexei Kolkunov. Other rookies include Chad Kilger, Daymond Langkow, Daniel Alfredsson and Petr Sykora. There are two versions of card number 66. The first features Wayne Gretzky in an All-Star sweater. This was used as a promotional card and was issued with the dealer solicitation. The second is the regular number 66 found in packs and features Craig Johnson, a player acquired by the Kings in the Gretzky trade.

| | MINT | NRMT |
|---|---|---|
| COMPLETE SET (188) | 40.00 | 18.00 |
| COMMON CARD (1-188) | .15 | .07 |

❑ 1 Paul Kariya 2.50 1.10
❑ 2 Teemu Selanne 1.25 .55
❑ 3 Guy Hebert .30 .14
❑ 4 Steve Rucchin .15 .07
❑ 5 Ray Bourque .60 .25
❑ 6 Cam Neely .30 .14
❑ 7 Adam Oates .30 .14
❑ 8 Kyle McLaren .60 .25
❑ 9 Bill Ranford .30 .14
❑ 10 Shawn McEachern .15 .07
❑ 11 Don Sweeney .15 .07
❑ 12 Pat LaFontaine .30 .14
❑ 13 Dominik Hasek 1.50 .70
❑ 14 Brian Holzinger .60 .25
❑ 15 Alexei Zhitnik .15 .07
❑ 16 Theoren Fleury .30 .14
❑ 17 Cory Stillman .15 .07
❑ 18 German Titov .15 .07
❑ 19 Phil Housley .30 .14
❑ 20 Michael Nylander .15 .07
❑ 21 Trevor Kidd .30 .14
❑ 22 Eric Daze .60 .25
❑ 23 Chris Chelios .60 .25
❑ 24 Jeremy Roenick .60 .25
❑ 25 Gary Suter .15 .07
❑ 26 Bernie Nicholls .15 .07
❑ 27 Ed Belfour .60 .25
❑ 28 Tony Amonte .30 .14
❑ 29 Peter Forsberg 2.00 .90
❑ 30 Patrick Roy 3.00 1.35
❑ 31 Joe Sakic 1.25 .55
❑ 32 Sandis Ozolinsh .30 .14
❑ 33 Adam Deadmarsh .30 .14
❑ 34 Stephane Fiset .30 .14
❑ 35 Claude Lemieux .30 .14
❑ 36 Mike Modano .75 .35
❑ 37 Kevin Hatcher .15 .07
❑ 38 Joe Nieuwendyk .30 .14
❑ 39 Todd Harvey .15 .07
❑ 40 Derian Hatcher .15 .07
❑ 41 Jere Lehtinen .15 .07
❑ 42 Nicklas Lidstrom .30 .14
❑ 43 Mathieu Dandenault .15 .07
❑ 44 Sergei Fedorov 1.25 .55
❑ 45 Paul Coffey .60 .25
❑ 46 Steve Yzerman 2.00 .90
❑ 47 Keith Primeau .30 .14
❑ 48 Chris Osgood .60 .25
❑ 49 Vyacheslav Kozlov .15 .07
❑ 50 Doug Weight .30 .14
❑ 51 Jason Arnott .30 .14
❑ 52 Miroslav Satan 2.00 .90
❑ 53 Zdeno Ciger .15 .07
❑ 54 Curtis Joseph .60 .25
❑ 55 Scott Mellanby .30 .14
❑ 56 John Vanbiesbrouck 1.00 .45
❑ 57 Jody Hull .15 .07
❑ 58 Ed Jovanovski .60 .25
❑ 59 Radek Dvorak .15 .07
❑ 60 Rob Niedermayer .30 .14
❑ 61 Andrew Cassels .15 .07
❑ 62 Brendan Shanahan 1.25 .55
❑ 63 Nelson Emerson .15 .07
❑ 64 Jeff O'Neill .15 .07
❑ 65 Sean Burke .30 .14
❑ 66A Wayne Gretzky 10.00 4.50
promo card
❑ 66B Craig Johnson .15 .07
❑ 67 Dimitri Khristich .15 .07
❑ 68 Vitali Yachmenev .15 .07
❑ 69 Aki Berg .15 .07
❑ 70 Byron Dafoe .30 .14
❑ 71 Pierre Turgeon .30 .14
❑ 72 Mark Recchi .30 .14
❑ 73 Saku Koivu 1.25 .55
❑ 74 Valeri Bure .30 .14
❑ 75 Vincent Damphousse .30 .14
❑ 76 Jocelyn Thibault .60 .25
❑ 77 Patrice Brisebois .15 .07
❑ 78 John MacLean .30 .14
❑ 79 Martin Brodeur 1.50 .70
❑ 80 Steve Thomas .15 .07
❑ 81 Scott Stevens .30 .14
❑ 82 Bill Guerin .15 .07
❑ 83 Petr Sykora .60 .25
❑ 84 Scott Niedermayer .15 .07
❑ 85 Stephane Richer .30 .14
❑ 86 Zigmund Palffy .60 .25
❑ 87 Travis Green .30 .14
❑ 88 Todd Bertuzzi .30 .14
❑ 89 Mathieu Schneider .15 .07
❑ 90 Eric Fichaud .30 .14
❑ 91 Bryan McCabe .15 .07
❑ 92 Mark Messier .75 .35
❑ 93 Pat Verbeek .15 .07
❑ 94 Brian Leetch .60 .25
❑ 95 Mike Richter .60 .25
❑ 96 Niklas Sundstrom .15 .07
❑ 97 Luc Robitaille .30 .14
❑ 98 Adam Graves .30 .14
❑ 99 Alexei Kovalev .15 .07
❑ 100 Daniel Alfredsson 1.50 .70
❑ 101 Alexei Yashin .30 .14
❑ 102 Radek Bonk .15 .07
❑ 103 Alexandre Daigle .15 .07
❑ 104 Damian Rhodes .30 .14
❑ 105 Antti Tormanen .15 .07
❑ 106 Eric Lindros 2.50 1.10
❑ 107 Mikael Renberg .30 .14
❑ 108 John LeClair 1.00 .45
❑ 109 Ron Hextall .30 .14
❑ 110 Rod Brind'Amour .30 .14
❑ 111 Joel Otto .15 .07
❑ 112 Eric Desjardins .15 .07
❑ 113 Mario Lemieux 3.00 1.35
❑ 114 Jaromir Jagr 2.00 .90
❑ 115 Ron Francis .30 .14
❑ 116 Markus Naslund .15 .07
❑ 117 Sergei Zubov .15 .07
❑ 118 Tomas Sandstrom .15 .07
❑ 119 Tom Barrasso .30 .14
❑ 120 Richard Park .15 .07
❑ 121 Brett Hull .75 .35
❑ 122 Shayne Corson .15 .07
❑ 123 Dale Hawerchuk .30 .14
❑ 124 Chris Pronger .30 .14
❑ 125 Al MacInnis .30 .14
❑ 126 Grant Fuhr .30 .14
❑ 127 Wayne Gretzky 4.00 1.80
❑ 128 Geoff Courtnall .15 .07
❑ 129 Owen Nolan .30 .14
❑ 130 Ray Sheppard .30 .14
❑ 131 Chris Terreri .30 .14
❑ 132 Marcus Ragnarsson .15 .07
❑ 133 Jeff Friesen .30 .14
❑ 134 Doug Bodger .15 .07
❑ 135 Roman Hamrlik .30 .14
❑ 136 Petr Klima .15 .07
❑ 137 Daren Puppa .30 .14
❑ 138 Aaron Gavey .15 .07
❑ 139 Daymond Langkow .75 .35
❑ 140 Alexander Selivanov .15 .07
❑ 141 Mats Sundin .30 .14
❑ 142 Kirk Muller .15 .07
❑ 143 Larry Murphy .30 .14
❑ 144 Doug Gilmour .60 .25
❑ 145 Darby Hendrickson .15 .07
❑ 146 Felix Potvin .60 .25
❑ 147 Kenny Jonsson .15 .07
❑ 148 Alexander Mogilny .30 .14
❑ 149 Pavel Bure 1.25 .55
❑ 150 Trevor Linden .30 .14
❑ 151 Corey Hirsch .30 .14
❑ 152 Kirk McLean .30 .14
❑ 153 Esa Tikkanen .15 .07
❑ 154 Cliff Ronning .15 .07
❑ 155 Peter Bondra .60 .25
❑ 156 Jim Carey .60 .25
❑ 157 Michal Pivonka .15 .07
❑ 158 Joe Juneau .15 .07
❑ 159 Dale Hunter .15 .07
❑ 160 Steve Konowalchuk .15 .07
❑ 161 Stefan Ustorf .15 .07
❑ 162 Brendan Witt .15 .07
❑ 163 Chad Kilger .15 .07
❑ 164 Keith Tkachuk .75 .35
❑ 165 Deron Quint .15 .07
❑ 166 Oleg Tverdovsky .30 .14
❑ 167 Alexei Zhamnov .30 .14
❑ 168 Igor Korolev .15 .07
❑ 169 Wade Redden .30 .14
❑ 170 Jarome Iginla 1.00 .45
❑ 171 Christian Dube .15 .07
❑ 172 Jason Podollan .15 .07
❑ 173 Alyn McCauley .75 .35
❑ 174 Nolan Baumgartner .15 .07
❑ 175 Jason Botterill .15 .07
❑ 176 Chris Phillips 1.00 .45
❑ 177 Dmitri Nabokov .30 .14
❑ 178 Andrei Petrunin .15 .07
❑ 179 Alexander Korolyuk .15 .07
❑ 180 Sergei Samsonov 2.50 1.10
❑ 181 Ilja Gorokhov .30 .14
❑ 182 Alexei Kolkunov .50 .23
❑ 183 Samuel Pahlsson .15 .07
❑ 184 Mattias Ohlund .15 .07
❑ 185 Marcus Nilsson .75 .35
❑ 186 Daniel Tjarnqvist .15 .07
❑ 187 Per Anton Lundstrom .15 .07
❑ 188 Fredrik Loven .15 .07
❑ GC1 Wayne Gretzky 100.00 45.00
❑ GC2 Sergei Samsonov 60.00 27.00

## 1995-96 SP Holoviews

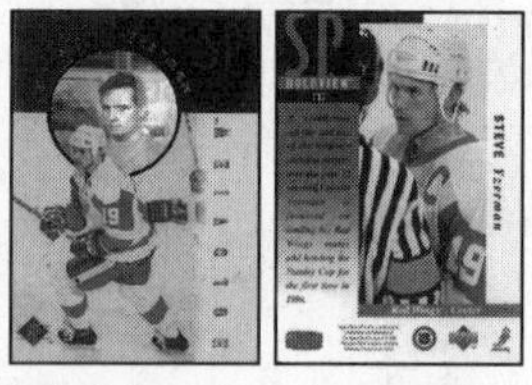

Randomly inserted in packs at a rate of 1:5, this 20-card set utilizes UD's Holoview technology to great effect. There also exists a die-cut parallel version of this set (known as Special FX), issued 1:75 packs. Special FX cards are enhanced by rainbow foil, as well as the die-cutting. Multipliers to determine the value of these cards are listed below.

| | MINT | NRMT |
|---|---|---|
| COMPLETE SET (20) | 100.00 | 45.00 |
| COMMON CARD (FX1-FX20) | 1.50 | .70 |
| COMPLETE SPECIAL FX SET (20) | 700.00 | 325.00 |
| COMMON SPEC.FX (FX1-FX20) | 8.00 | 3.60 |

*STARS: 2.5X TO 5X BASIC CARDS
*YOUNG STARS: 2X TO 4X BASIC CARDS

❑ FX1 Teemu Selanne 1.50 .70
❑ FX2 Paul Kariya 3.00 1.35
❑ FX3 Chris Chelios 3.00 1.35
❑ FX4 Peter Forsberg 3.00 1.35
❑ FX5 Sergei Fedorov 3.00 1.35
❑ FX6 Paul Coffey 3.00 1.35
❑ FX7 Steve Yzerman 3.00 1.35
❑ FX8 Jason Arnott 2.00 .90
❑ FX9 Doug Weight 2.00 .90
❑ FX10 Wayne Gretzky 3.00 1.35
❑ FX11 Vitali Yachmenev 1.50 .70
❑ FX12 Martin Brodeur 3.00 1.35
❑ FX13 Scott Stevens 1.50 .70
❑ FX14 Mark Messier 3.00 1.35
❑ FX15 Daniel Alfredsson 3.00 1.35
❑ FX16 Eric Lindros 3.00 1.35
❑ FX17 Mario Lemieux 3.00 1.35
❑ FX18 Jaromir Jagr 3.00 1.35
❑ FX19 Shayne Corson 1.50 .70
❑ FX20 Pavel Bure 3.00 1.35

## 1995-96 SP Stars/Etoiles

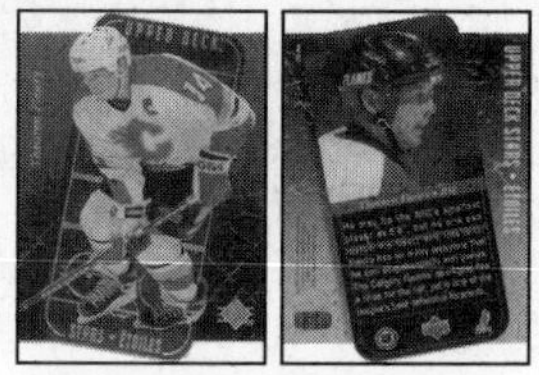

Randomly inserted in packs at a rate of 1:3, this 30-card set uses a double die-cut design to highlight the top athletes in the NHL. This version uses silver foil as it's primary element. There also is a gold foil parallel version, which is significantly tougher to pull. These cards were randomly inserted 1:61 packs.

| | MINT | NRMT |
|---|---|---|
| COMPLETE SET (30) | 80.00 | 36.00 |
| COMMON CARD (E1-E30) | 1.00 | .45 |
| COMP.GOLD SET (30) | 600.00 | 275.00 |

*GOLD: 4X TO 8X BASIC CARDS

❑ E1 Paul Kariya 2.00 .90
❑ E2 Teemu Selanne 2.00 .90
❑ E3 Ray Bourque 2.00 .90
❑ E4 Cam Neely 1.50 .70
❑ E5 Pat LaFontaine 1.00 .45
❑ E6 Theoren Fleury 1.50 .70
❑ E7 Jeremy Roenick 2.00 .90
❑ E8 Joe Sakic 2.00 .90
❑ E9 Patrick Roy 2.00 .90
❑ E10 Peter Forsberg 2.00 .90
❑ E11 Mike Modano 1.50 .70
❑ E12 Sergei Fedorov 2.00 .90
❑ E13 Paul Coffey 2.00 .90
❑ E14 Steve Yzerman 2.00 .90
❑ E15 Pierre Turgeon 1.50 .70
❑ E16 Brendan Shanahan 2.00 .90
❑ E17 Wayne Gretzky 2.00 .90
❑ E18 Martin Brodeur 2.00 .90
❑ E19 Mark Messier 2.00 .90
❑ E20 Brian Leetch 2.00 .90
❑ E21 Eric Lindros 2.00 .90
❑ E22 Mario Lemieux 2.00 .90
❑ E23 Jaromir Jagr 2.00 .90
❑ E24 Brett Hull 2.00 .90
❑ E25 Roman Hamrlik 1.50 .70
❑ E26 Mats Sundin 1.50 .70
❑ E27 Felix Potvin 2.00 .90
❑ E28 Alexander Mogilny 1.50 .70
❑ E29 Pavel Bure 2.00 .90
❑ E30 Keith Tkachuk 2.00 .90

## 1996-97 SP

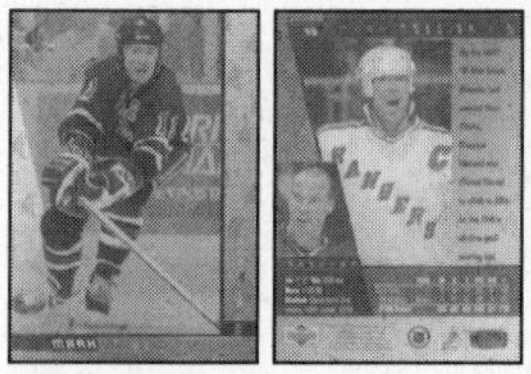

The 1996-97 SP set was issued in one series totalling 188 cards. The eight-card packs had a suggested retail price of $3.49 each. Printed on 20 pt. card stock, this set featured color action photos of 168 regular players from all 26 NHL teams and included a subset of 20 premier prospects. The backs carried player information and statistics. Key rookies include Sergei Berezin, Mike Grier, Ethan Moreau, and Dainius Zubrus. The Gretzky promo was distributed to dealers; it mirrors the regular issue save for the word SAMPLE written across the back.

| | MINT | NRMT |
|---|---|---|
| COMPLETE SET (188) | 50.00 | 22.00 |
| COMMON CARD (1-188) | .20 | .09 |

❑ 1 Paul Kariya 3.00 1.35
❑ 2 Teemu Selanne 1.50 .70
❑ 3 Jari Kurri .40 .18
❑ 4 Darren Van Impe .20 .09
❑ 5 Guy Hebert .40 .18
❑ 6 Steve Rucchin .20 .09
❑ 7 Ray Bourque .75 .35
❑ 8 Kyle McLaren .20 .09
❑ 9 Bill Ranford .40 .18
❑ 10 Don Sweeney .20 .09
❑ 11 Adam Oates .40 .18
❑ 12 Rick Tocchet .40 .18
❑ 13 Ted Donato .20 .09
❑ 14 Curtis Brown .20 .09
❑ 15 Pat LaFontaine .40 .18

❑ 16 Derek Plante .20 .09
❑ 17 Dominik Hasek 1.50 .70
❑ 18 Brian Holzinger .40 .18
❑ 19 Alexei Zhitnik .20 .09
❑ 20 Theoren Fleury .40 .18
❑ 21 Trevor Kidd .40 .18
❑ 22 Steve Chiasson .20 .09
❑ 23 Jarome Iginla .75 .35
❑ 24 German Titov .20 .09
❑ 25 Zarley Zalapski .20 .09
❑ 26 Eric Daze .40 .18
❑ 27 Chris Chelios .75 .35
❑ 28 Ed Belfour .75 .35
❑ 29 Gary Suter .20 .09
❑ 30 Alexei Zhamnov .40 .18
❑ 31 Ethan Moreau .75 .35
❑ 32 Tony Amonte .40 .18
❑ 33 Peter Forsberg 2.50 1.10
❑ 34 Joe Sakic 1.50 .70
❑ 35 Patrick Roy 4.00 1.80
❑ 36 Adam Deadmarsh .40 .18
❑ 37 Mike Ricci .20 .09
❑ 38 Adam Foote .20 .09
❑ 39 Claude Lemieux .40 .18
❑ 40 Mike Modano 1.00 .45
❑ 41 Pat Verbeek .20 .09
❑ 42 Todd Harvey .20 .09
❑ 43 Sergei Zubov .20 .09
❑ 44 Andy Moog .40 .18
❑ 45 Derian Hatcher .20 .09
❑ 46 Jamie Langenbrunner .20 .09
❑ 47 Steve Yzerman 2.50 1.10
❑ 48 Sergei Fedorov 1.50 .70
❑ 49 Slava Kozlov .40 .18
❑ 50 Brendan Shanahan 1.50 .70
❑ 51 Chris Osgood .75 .35
❑ 52 Nicklas Lidstrom .40 .18
❑ 53 Vladimir Konstantinov .20 .09
❑ 54 Curtis Joseph .75 .35
❑ 55 Jason Arnott .40 .18
❑ 56 Ryan Smyth .75 .35
❑ 57 Doug Weight .40 .18
❑ 58 Andrei Kovalenko .20 .09
❑ 59 Mariusz Czerkawski .20 .09
❑ 60 Ed Jovanovski .40 .18
❑ 61 John Vanbiesbrouck 1.25 .55
❑ 62 Rob Niedermayer .40 .18
❑ 63 Robert Svehla .20 .09
❑ 64 Brian Skrudland .20 .09
❑ 65 Scott Mellanby .40 .18
❑ 66 Ray Sheppard .40 .18
❑ 67 Jeff O'Neill .20 .09
❑ 68 Keith Primeau .40 .18
❑ 69 Geoff Sanderson .40 .18
❑ 70 Sean Burke .40 .18
❑ 71 Kevin Dineen .20 .09
❑ 72 Andrew Cassels .20 .09
❑ 73 Kevin Stevens .20 .09
❑ 74 Rob Blake .20 .09
❑ 75 Ed Olczyk .20 .09
❑ 76 Mattias Norstrom .20 .09
❑ 77 Stephane Fiset .40 .18
❑ 78 Vitali Yachmenev .20 .09
❑ 79 Saku Koivu 1.25 .55
❑ 80 Valeri Bure .40 .18
❑ 81 Jocelyn Thibault .75 .35
❑ 82 David Wilkie .20 .09
❑ 83 Stephane Richer .40 .18
❑ 84 Shayne Corson .20 .09
❑ 85 Mark Recchi .40 .18
❑ 86 Martin Brodeur 2.00 .90
❑ 87 Bobby Holik .20 .09
❑ 88 Petr Sykora .20 .09
❑ 89 Scott Stevens .40 .18
❑ 90 Scott Niedermayer .20 .09
❑ 91 Bill Guerin .20 .09
❑ 92 Eric Fichaud .40 .18
❑ 93 Kenny Jonsson .20 .09
❑ 94 Travis Green .40 .18
❑ 95 Derek King .20 .09
❑ 96 Todd Bertuzzi .20 .09
❑ 97 Zigmund Palffy .75 .35
❑ 98 Mark Messier 1.00 .45
❑ 99 Wayne Gretzky 6.00 2.70
❑ 100 Mike Richter .75 .35
❑ 101 Brian Leetch .75 .35
❑ 102 Luc Robitaille .40 .18
❑ 103 Adam Graves .40 .18
❑ 104 Alexei Kovalev .20 .09
❑ 105 Radek Bonk .20 .09
❑ 106 Alexandre Daigle .20 .09
❑ 107 Daniel Alfredsson .40 .18
❑ 108 Alexei Yashin .40 .18
❑ 109 Andreas Dackell .20 .09
❑ 110 Damian Rhodes .40 .18
❑ 111 Petr Svoboda .20 .09
❑ 112 John LeClair 1.25 .55
❑ 113 Eric Desjardins .20 .09
❑ 114 Eric Lindros 2.50 1.10
❑ 115 Mikael Renberg .40 .18
❑ 116 Ron Hextall .40 .18
❑ 117 Dainius Zubrus 1.50 .70
❑ 118 Keith Tkachuk 1.00 .45
❑ 119 Jeremy Roenick .75 .35
❑ 120 Nikolai Khabibulin .40 .18
❑ 121 Oleg Tverdovsky .40 .18
❑ 122 Teppo Numminen .20 .09
❑ 123 Mike Gartner .40 .18
❑ 124 Cliff Ronning .20 .09
❑ 125 Mario Lemieux 4.00 1.80
❑ 126 Jaromir Jagr 2.50 1.10
❑ 127 Ron Francis .40 .18
❑ 128 Petr Nedved .40 .18
❑ 129 Darius Kasparaitis .20 .09
❑ 130 Kevin Hatcher .20 .09
❑ 131 Joe Mullen .40 .18
❑ 132 Joe Murphy .20 .09
❑ 133 Grant Fuhr .40 .18
❑ 134 Harry York .75 .35
❑ 135 Chris Pronger .40 .18
❑ 136 Brett Hull 1.00 .45
❑ 137 Pierre Turgeon .40 .18
❑ 138 Owen Nolan .40 .18
❑ 139 Bernie Nicholls .20 .09
❑ 140 Tony Granato .20 .09
❑ 141 Kelly Hrudey .40 .18
❑ 142 Darren Turcotte .20 .09
❑ 143 Jeff Friesen .40 .18
❑ 144 Roman Hamrlik .40 .18
❑ 145 Chris Gratton .40 .18
❑ 146 Daymond Langkow .20 .09
❑ 147 Dino Ciccarelli .40 .18
❑ 148 Alexander Selivanov .20 .09
❑ 149 Brian Bradley .20 .09
❑ 150 Wendel Clark .40 .18
❑ 151 Mats Sundin .40 .18
❑ 152 Doug Gilmour .75 .35
❑ 153 Felix Potvin .75 .35
❑ 154 Larry Murphy .40 .18
❑ 155 Mathieu Schneider .20 .09
❑ 156 Kirk Muller .20 .09
❑ 157 Pavel Bure 1.50 .70
❑ 158 Alexander Mogilny .40 .18
❑ 159 Corey Hirsch .40 .18
❑ 160 Jyrki Lumme .20 .09
❑ 161 Russ Courtnall .20 .09
❑ 162 Mike Fountain .20 .09
❑ 163 Peter Bondra .75 .35
❑ 164 Jim Carey .75 .35
❑ 165 Sergei Gonchar .20 .09
❑ 166 Joe Juneau .20 .09
❑ 167 Phil Housley .40 .18
❑ 168 Jason Allison .20 .09
❑ 169 Ruslan Salei .20 .09
❑ 170 Mattias Timander .20 .09
❑ 171 Vaclav Varada .40 .18
❑ 172 Jonas Hoglund .20 .09
❑ 173 Jason Podollan .40 .18
❑ 174 Jose Theodore .40 .18
❑ 175 Roman Turek .75 .35
❑ 176 Anders Eriksson .20 .09
❑ 177 Mike Grier 1.50 .70
❑ 178 Rem Murray .40 .18
❑ 179 Per Gustafsson .20 .09
❑ 180 Jay Pandolfo .20 .09
❑ 181 Kai Nurminen .20 .09
❑ 182 Bryan Berard .75 .35
❑ 183 Christian Dube .20 .09
❑ 184 Daniel Goneau .40 .18
❑ 185 Wade Redden .20 .09
❑ 186 Janne Niinimaa .75 .35
❑ 187 Jim Campbell .20 .09
❑ 188 Sergei Berezin 1.25 .55
❑ P99 Wayne Gretzky PROMO 5.00 2.20

## 1996-97 SP Clearcut Winner

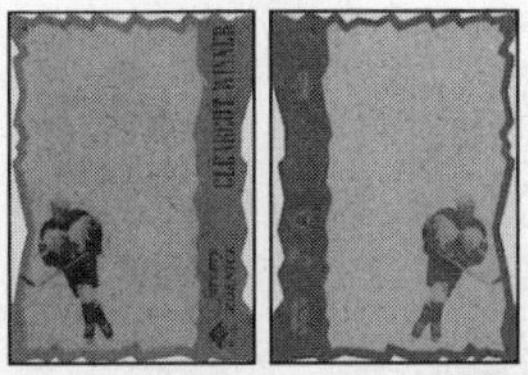

Randomly inserted in packs at a rate of one in 91, this 20-card set featured color player images in a chiseled-out ice block, die-cut card displaying a full body transparent Hologram.

| | MINT | NRMT |
|---|---|---|
| COMPLETE SET (20) | 800.00 | 350.00 |
| COMMON CARD (CW1-CW20) | 12.00 | 5.50 |

❑ CW1 Wayne Gretzky 150.00 70.00
❑ CW2 Saku Koivu 30.00 13.50
❑ CW3 Mario Lemieux 100.00 45.00
❑ CW4 Sergei Fedorov 40.00 18.00
❑ CW5 Paul Kariya 80.00 36.00
❑ CW6 Patrick Roy 100.00 45.00
❑ CW7 Jeremy Roenick 25.00 11.00
❑ CW8 Brendan Shanahan 40.00 18.00
❑ CW9 John Vanbiesbrouck 30.00 13.50
❑ CW10 Doug Weight 15.00 6.75
❑ CW11 Mark Messier 30.00 13.50
❑ CW12 Mats Sundin 15.00 6.75
❑ CW13 Paul Coffey 25.00 11.00
❑ CW14 Theoren Fleury 15.00 6.75
❑ CW15 Steve Yzerman 60.00 27.00
❑ CW16 Pavel Bure 40.00 18.00
❑ CW17 Adam Deadmarsh 12.00 5.50
❑ CW18 Chris Chelios 25.00 11.00
❑ CW19 Joe Sakic 40.00 18.00
❑ CW20 Eric Daze 12.00 5.50

## 1996-97 SP Holoview Collection

Randomly inserted in packs at a rate of one in nine, this 30-card set featured color player photos of some of the NHL's most elite stars printed on an all new design Holoview die-cut card.

| | MINT | NRMT |
|---|---|---|
| COMPLETE SET (30) | 150.00 | 70.00 |
| COMMON CARD (HC1-HC30) | 4.00 | 1.80 |

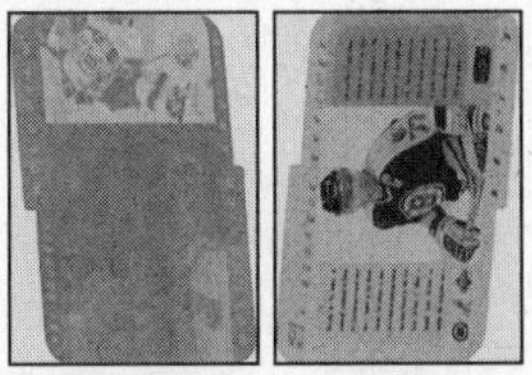

❑ HC1 Wayne Gretzky 30.00 13.50
❑ HC2 Eric Daze 4.00 1.80
❑ HC3 Doug Gilmour 5.00 2.20
❑ HC4 Jason Arnott 5.00 2.20
❑ HC5 Sergei Fedorov 10.00 4.50
❑ HC6 Chris Chelios 5.00 2.20
❑ HC7 Alexei Kovalev 4.00 1.80
❑ HC8 Pat LaFontaine 4.00 1.80
❑ HC9 Daniel Alfredsson 4.00 1.80
❑ HC10 Chris Pronger 4.00 1.80
❑ HC11 Jocelyn Thibault 5.00 2.20
❑ HC12 Chris Gratton 4.00 1.80
❑ HC13 Alexei Yashin 4.00 1.80
❑ HC14 Peter Bondra 5.00 2.20
❑ HC15 Saku Koivu 8.00 3.60
❑ HC16 Valeri Bure 4.00 1.80
❑ HC17 Joe Juneau 4.00 1.80
❑ HC18 Tony Amonte 4.00 1.80
❑ HC19 Brian Holzinger 4.00 1.80
❑ HC20 Mats Sundin 5.00 2.20
❑ HC21 Chris Osgood 5.00 2.20
❑ HC22 Roman Hamrlik 5.00 2.20
❑ HC23 Ray Bourque 5.00 2.20
❑ HC24 Doug Weight 5.00 2.20
❑ HC25 Mike Modano 6.00 2.70
❑ HC26 Niklas Sundstrom 4.00 1.80
❑ HC27 Mike Richter 5.00 2.20
❑ HC28 Zigmund Palffy 5.00 2.20
❑ HC29 Adam Oates 4.00 1.80
❑ HC30 Dominik Hasek 10.00 4.50

## 1996-97 SP Inside Info

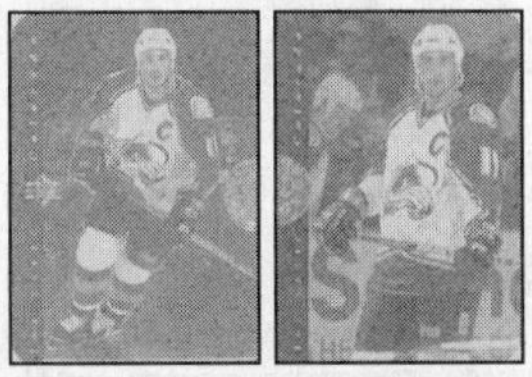

Randomly inserted at the rate of one per box, this eight-card set featured color action player photos with a special pull-out panel that displayed another photo of the same player and statistics. A gold version was also available and was seeded one in every two cases. Values for these cards can be determined by using the multipliers listed below.

| | MINT | NRMT |
|---|---|---|
| COMPLETE SET (8) | 100.00 | 45.00 |
| COMMON CARD (IN1-IN8) | 5.00 | 2.20 |

*GOLD: 3X TO 6X BASIC CARDS

❑ IN1 Wayne Gretzky 40.00 18.00
❑ IN2 Keith Tkachuk 8.00 3.60
❑ IN3 Brendan Shanahan 12.00 5.50
❑ IN4 Teemu Selanne 12.00 5.50
❑ IN5 Ray Bourque 5.00 2.20
❑ IN6 Joe Sakic 12.00 5.50
❑ IN7 Felix Potvin 5.00 2.20
❑ IN8 Steve Yzerman 20.00 9.00

## 1996-97 SP Game Film

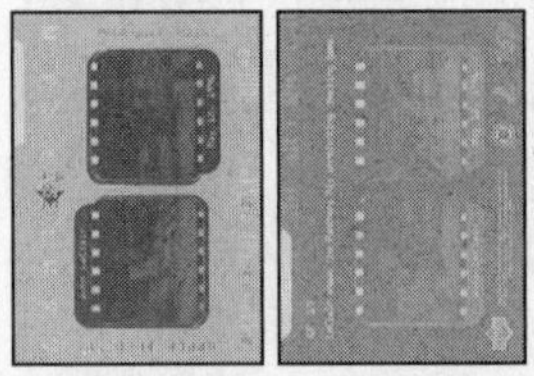

Randomly inserted in packs at a rate of one in 30, this 20-card set carried actual game photography featuring film footage of favorite NHL players.

| | MINT | NRMT |
|---|---|---|
| COMPLETE SET (20) | 300.00 | 135.00 |
| COMMON CARD (GF1-GF20) | 8.00 | 3.60 |

❑ GF1 Wayne Gretzky 60.00 27.00
❑ GF2 Peter Forsberg 30.00 13.50
❑ GF3 Patrick Roy 50.00 22.00
❑ GF4 Brett Hull 12.00 5.50
❑ GF5 Keith Tkachuk 12.00 5.50
❑ GF6 Eric Lindros 30.00 13.50
❑ GF7 Felix Potvin 10.00 4.50
❑ GF8 John Vanbiesbrouck 15.00 6.75
❑ GF9 Paul Kariya 40.00 18.00
❑ GF10 Mark Messier 12.00 5.50
❑ GF11 Ed Belfour 10.00 4.50
❑ GF12 Alexander Mogilny 12.00 5.50
❑ GF13 Jim Carey 10.00 4.50
❑ GF14 Ed Jovanovski 8.00 3.60
❑ GF15 Theoren Fleury 12.00 5.50
❑ GF16 Doug Gilmour 12.00 5.50
❑ GF17 John LeClair 15.00 6.75
❑ GF18 Pat LaFontaine 8.00 3.60
❑ GF19 Paul Coffey 10.00 4.50
❑ GF20 Daniel Alfredsson 8.00 3.60

## 1996-97 SP SPx Force

Randomly inserted in packs at a rate of one in 360, this five-card set featured top NHL players on a multi-image Holoview card. Each of the first four cards displayed a center, winger, goalie and rookie. The last card carried the top player from each of the previous cards.

| | MINT | NRMT |
|---|---|---|
| COMPLETE SET (5) | 500.00 | 220.00 |
| COMMON CARD (SPX1-SPX5) | 25.00 | 11.00 |

❑ 1 Eric Lindros 150.00 70.00
Mario Lemieux
Peter Forsberg
Wayne Gretzky
❑ 2 Brett Hull 100.00 45.00
Jaromir Jagr
Pavel Bure
Teemu Selanne
❑ 3 Chris Osgood 100.00 45.00
Dominik Hasek
Martin Brodeur
Mike Richter
❑ 4 Anders Eriksson 25.00 11.00
Bryan Berard
Jarome Iginla
Sergei Berezin
❑ 5 Jarome Iginla 150.00 70.00
Jaromir Jagr
Wayne Gretzky
Martin Brodeur

## 1996-97 SP SPx Force Autographs

These four different autograph cards were randomly inserted one in 2,500 packs of 1996-97 SP. Besides the player's signature, the cards are parallel to the more common, unsigned SPx Force inserts. Only 100 cards were signed by each player.

| | MINT | NRMT |
|---|---|---|
| COMPLETE SET (4) | 2000.00 | 900.00 |
| COMMON CARD (SPX1-SPX4) | 100.00 | 45.00 |

❑ 1 Wayne Gretzky AU 1200.00 550.00
❑ 2 Jaromir Jagr AU 600.00 275.00
❑ 3 Martin Brodeur AU 300.00 135.00
❑ 4 Jarome Iginla AU 100.00 45.00

## 1997-98 SP Authentic

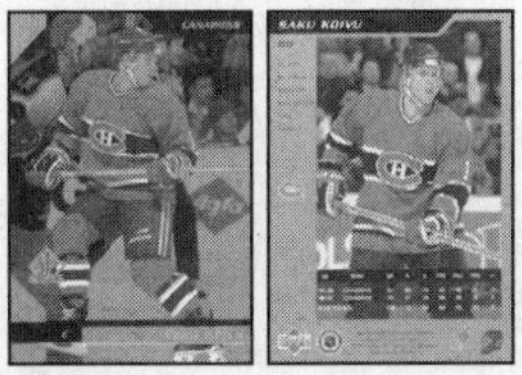

The 1997-98 SP Authentic set was issued in one series totalling 198 cards and was distributed in five-card packs with a suggested retail price of $4.99. The fronts features color player photos printed on 24 pt. card stock. The backs carry player information. The set contains the topical subset: Future Watch (169-198).

| | MINT | NRMT |
|---|---|---|
| COMPLETE SET (198) | 60.00 | 27.00 |
| COMMON CARD (1-198) | .25 | .11 |

❑ 1 Teemu Selanne 1.50 .70
❑ 2 Sean Pronger .25 .11
❑ 3 Joe Sacco .25 .11
❑ 4 Tomas Sandstrom .25 .11
❑ 5 Steve Rucchin .25 .11
❑ 6 Paul Kariya 3.00 1.35
❑ 7 Ted Donato .25 .11
❑ 8 Ray Bourque .75 .35
❑ 9 Tim Taylor .25 .11
❑ 10 Jason Allison .60 .25
❑ 11 Kyle McLaren .25 .11
❑ 12 Dimitri Khristich .25 .11
❑ 13 Jason Dawe .25 .11
❑ 14 Dominik Hasek 1.50 .70
❑ 15 Miroslav Satan .25 .11
❑ 16 Brian Holzinger .25 .11
❑ 17 Alexei Zhitnik .25 .11
❑ 18 Theoren Fleury .60 .25
❑ 19 Cory Stillman .25 .11
❑ 20 Jarome Iginla .60 .25
❑ 21 Sandy McCarthy .25 .11
❑ 22 German Titov .25 .11
❑ 23 Glen Wesley .25 .11
❑ 24 Keith Primeau .25 .11
❑ 25 Geoff Sanderson .60 .25
❑ 26 Gary Roberts .25 .11
❑ 27 Sami Kapanen .60 .25
❑ 28 Jeff O'Neill .25 .11
❑ 29 Tony Amonte .60 .25
❑ 30 Chris Chelios .75 .35
❑ 31 Eric Daze .60 .25
❑ 32 Alexei Zhamnov .25 .11
❑ 33 Chris Terreri .60 .25
❑ 34 Sergei Krivokrasov .25 .11
❑ 35 Joe Sakic 1.50 .70
❑ 36 Peter Forsberg 2.50 1.10
❑ 37 Patrick Roy 4.00 1.80
❑ 38 Claude Lemieux .60 .25
❑ 39 Valeri Kamensky .60 .25
❑ 40 Adam Deadmarsh .60 .25
❑ 41 Sandis Ozolinsh .60 .25
❑ 42 Jari Kurri .60 .25
❑ 43 Mike Modano 1.00 .45
❑ 44 Ed Belfour .75 .35
❑ 45 Derian Hatcher .25 .11
❑ 46 Sergei Zubov .25 .11
❑ 47 Jamie Langenbrunner .25 .11
❑ 48 Jere Lehtinen .25 .11
❑ 49 Joe Nieuwendyk .60 .25
❑ 50 Vyacheslav Kozlov .25 .11
❑ 51 Chris Osgood .75 .35
❑ 52 Steve Yzerman 2.50 1.10
❑ 53 Nicklas Lidstrom .60 .25
❑ 54 Igor Larionov .25 .11
❑ 55 Brendan Shanahan 1.50 .70
❑ 56 Anders Eriksson .25 .11
❑ 57 Darren McCarty .25 .11
❑ 58 Doug Weight .60 .25
❑ 59 Jason Arnott .60 .25
❑ 60 Curtis Joseph .75 .35
❑ 61 Ryan Smyth .60 .25
❑ 62 Dean McAmmond .25 .11
❑ 63 Mike Grier .25 .11
❑ 64 Kelly Buchberger .25 .11
❑ 65 Ed Jovanovski .60 .25
❑ 66 Ray Whitney .25 .11
❑ 67 Rob Niedermayer .25 .11
❑ 68 Scott Mellanby .25 .11
❑ 69 John Vanbiesbrouck 1.25 .55
❑ 70 Viktor Kozlov .25 .11
❑ 71 Jozef Stumpel .60 .25
❑ 72 Rob Blake .25 .11
❑ 73 Garry Galley .25 .11
❑ 74 Vladimir Tsyplakov .25 .11
❑ 75 Yanic Perreault .25 .11
❑ 76 Stephane Fiset .60 .25
❑ 77 Luc Robitaille .60 .25
❑ 78 Valeri Bure .25 .11
❑ 79 Mark Recchi .60 .25
❑ 80 Saku Koivu 1.25 .55
❑ 81 Andy Moog .60 .25
❑ 82 Vincent Damphousse .60 .25
❑ 83 Vladimir Malakhov .25 .11
❑ 84 Shayne Corson .25 .11
❑ 85 Scott Stevens .25 .11
❑ 86 Bill Guerin .60 .25
❑ 87 Martin Brodeur 2.00 .90
❑ 88 Doug Gilmour .75 .35
❑ 89 Bobby Holik .25 .11
❑ 90 Petr Sykora .25 .11
❑ 91 Zigmund Palffy .75 .35
❑ 92 Bryan Berard .60 .25
❑ 93 Tommy Salo .60 .25
❑ 94 Travis Green .25 .11
❑ 95 Kenny Jonsson .25 .11
❑ 96 Todd Bertuzzi .25 .11
❑ 97 Robert Reichel .25 .11
❑ 98 Pat LaFontaine .60 .25
❑ 99 Wayne Gretzky 5.00 2.20
❑ 100 Brian Leetch .75 .35
❑ 101 Mike Richter .75 .35
❑ 102 Alexei Kovalev .60 .25
❑ 103 Adam Graves .60 .25
❑ 104 Niklas Sundstrom .25 .11
❑ 105 Alexei Yashin .60 .25
❑ 106 Daniel Alfredsson .60 .25
❑ 107 Alexandre Daigle .25 .11
❑ 108 Wade Redden .25 .11
❑ 109 Andreas Dackell .25 .11
❑ 110 Shawn McEachern .25 .11
❑ 111 Eric Lindros 2.50 1.10
❑ 112 Chris Gratton .60 .25
❑ 113 Paul Coffey .75 .35
❑ 114 John LeClair 1.25 .55
❑ 115 Rod Brind'Amour .60 .25
❑ 116 Ron Hextall .60 .25
❑ 117 Dainius Zubrus .75 .35
❑ 118 Jeremy Roenick .75 .35
❑ 119 Keith Tkachuk 1.00 .45
❑ 120 Nikolai Khabibulin .60 .25
❑ 121 Rick Tocchet .60 .25
❑ 122 Teppo Numminen .25 .11
❑ 123 Craig Janney .25 .11
❑ 124 Mike Gartner .60 .25
❑ 125 Jaromir Jagr 2.50 1.10
❑ 126 Ron Francis .60 .25
❑ 127 Kevin Hatcher .25 .11
❑ 128 Robert Dome .25 .11
❑ 129 Martin Straka .25 .11
❑ 130 Peter Skudra .25 .11
❑ 131 Owen Nolan .60 .25
❑ 132 Bernie Nicholls .25 .11
❑ 133 Mike Vernon .60 .25
❑ 134 Jeff Friesen .60 .25
❑ 135 Tony Granato .25 .11
❑ 136 Mike Ricci .25 .11
❑ 137 Jim Campbell .25 .11
❑ 138 Brett Hull 1.00 .45
❑ 139 Chris Pronger .60 .25
❑ 140 Al MacInnis .60 .25
❑ 141 Pierre Turgeon .60 .25
❑ 142 Pavol Demitra .25 .11
❑ 143 Grant Fuhr .60 .25
❑ 144 Steve Duchesne .25 .11
❑ 145 Daymond Langkow .25 .11

❑ 146 Alexander Selivanov .25 .11
❑ 147 Daren Puppa .60 .25
❑ 148 Dino Ciccarelli .25 .11
❑ 149 Roman Hamrlik .25 .11
❑ 150 Mats Sundin .75 .35
❑ 151 Felix Potvin .75 .35
❑ 152 Wendel Clark .60 .25
❑ 153 Sergei Berezin .25 .11
❑ 154 Steve Sullivan .25 .11
❑ 155 Alexander Mogilny .60 .25
❑ 156 Pavel Bure 1.50 .70
❑ 157 Mark Messier 1.00 .45
❑ 158 Bret Hedican .25 .11
❑ 159 Kirk McLean .60 .25
❑ 160 Trevor Linden .60 .25
❑ 161 Dave Scatchard .25 .11
❑ 162 Adam Oates .60 .25
❑ 163 Joe Juneau .60 .25
❑ 164 Peter Bondra .75 .35
❑ 165 Bill Ranford .60 .25
❑ 166 Sergei Gonchar .25 .11
❑ 167 Calle Johansson .25 .11
❑ 168 Phil Housley .25 .11
❑ 169 Espen Knutsen FW .25 .11
❑ 170 Pavel Trnka FW .25 .11
❑ 171 Joe Thornton FW 1.50 .70
❑ 172 Sergei Samsonov FW 2.00 .90
❑ 173 Erik Rasmussen FW .25 .11
❑ 174 Tyler Moss FW .25 .11
❑ 175 Derek Morris FW .25 .11
❑ 176 Craig Mills FW .25 .11
❑ 177 Daniel Cleary FW .60 .25
❑ 178 Eric Messier FW .60 .25
❑ 179 Kevin Hodson FW .60 .25
❑ 180 Mike Knuble FW .25 .11
❑ 181 Boyd Deveraux FW .25 .11
❑ 182 Craig Millar FW .25 .11
❑ 183 Kevin Weekes FW .25 .11
❑ 184 Donald MacLean FW .25 .11
❑ 185 Patrik Elias FW 1.00 .45
❑ 186 Zdeno Chara FW RC .50 .23
❑ 187 Chris Phillips FW .25 .11
❑ 188 Vaclav Prospal FW 1.00 .45
❑ 189 Brad Isbister FW .25 .11
❑ 190 Alexei Morozov FW .60 .25
❑ 191 Patrick Marleau FW 1.50 .70
❑ 192 Marco Sturm FW 1.25 .55
❑ 193 Brendan Morrison FW 1.00 .45
❑ 194 Mike Johnson FW 1.00 .45
❑ 195 Alyn McCauley FW .60 .25
❑ 196 Mattias Ohlund FW .60 .25
❑ 197 Richard Zednik FW .25 .11
❑ 198 Jan Bulis FW .25 .11

## 1997-98 SP Authentic Authentics

Randomly inserted in packs at the rate of one in 288, these special "trade" cards could be redeemed for an assortment of Wayne Gretzky's signed memorabilia from Upper Deck Authenticated such as autographed jerseys, pucks, sticks and other items. Only three "SP Authentics Collection" cards were produced that could be redeemed for Wayne Gretzky's entire collection of autographed memorabilia.

MINT NRMT
COMMON CARD 50.00 22.00

❑ 1 W.Gretzky Jersey AU 600.00 275.00
❑ 2 W.Gretzky 802 Jersey AU 600.00 275.00
❑ 3 W.Gretzky Stick AU(40) 400.00 180.00
❑ 4 Wayne Gretzky 120.00 55.00
Rangers Puck AU(399)
❑ 5 Wayne Gretzky 150.00 70.00
Kings Puck AU(200)
❑ 6 W.Gretzky Photo AU(250) 100.00 45.00
❑ 7 Wayne Gretzky 100.00 45.00
802 Photo AU(249)
❑ 8 Wayne Gretzky 150.00 70.00
Blues Puck AU(200)
❑ 9 W.Gretzky Standee (249) 50.00 22.00
❑ 10 W.Gretzky 802 Card (184) 50.00 22.00
❑ 11 W.Gretzky Motiv.Photo (185) 60.00 27.00

## 1997-98 SP Authentic Icons

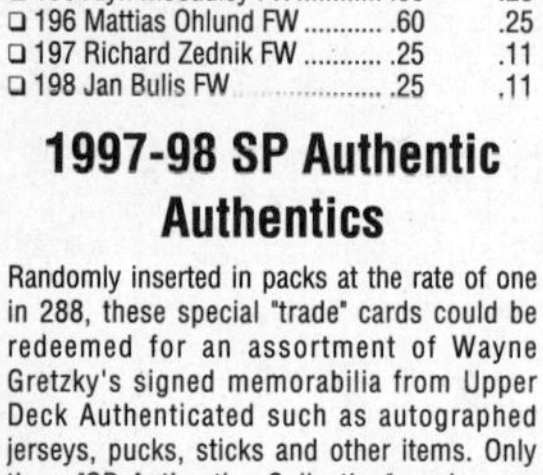

Randomly inserted in packs at the rate of one in five, this 40-card set features color action photos of the most respected players of the NHL.

MINT NRMT
COMPLETE SET (40) 120.00 55.00
COMMON CARD (I1-I40) .60 .25

❑ I1 Pat LaFontaine 1.50 .70
❑ I2 Brett Hull 2.50 1.10
❑ I3 Chris Chelios 2.00 .90
❑ I4 Joe Sakic 4.00 1.80
❑ I5 John Vanbiesbrouck 3.00 1.35
❑ I6 Patrik Elias 2.00 .90
❑ I7 Eric Lindros 6.00 2.70
❑ I8 Jaromir Jagr 6.00 2.70
❑ I9 Joe Thornton 3.00 1.35
❑ I10 Brendan Shanahan 4.00 1.80
❑ I11 Paul Kariya 8.00 3.60
❑ I12 Peter Forsberg 6.00 2.70
❑ I13 Ed Belfour 2.00 .90
❑ I14 Martin Brodeur 5.00 2.20
❑ I15 Alexei Morozov 1.50 .70
❑ I16 Mark Messier 2.50 1.10
❑ I17 John LeClair 3.00 1.35
❑ I18 Luc Robitaille 1.50 .70
❑ I19 Teemu Selanne 4.00 1.80
❑ I20 Theoren Fleury 1.50 .70
❑ I21 Steve Yzerman 6.00 2.70
❑ I22 Chris Phillips .60 .25
❑ I23 Keith Tkachuk 2.50 1.10
❑ I24 Patrick Roy 10.00 4.50
❑ I25 Mark Recchi 1.50 .70
❑ I26 Wayne Gretzky 12.00 5.50
❑ I27 Dino Ciccarelli .60 .25
❑ I28 Ray Bourque 2.00 .90
❑ I29 Tony Amonte 1.50 .70
❑ I30 Daniel Alfredsson 1.50 .70
❑ I31 Saku Koivu 3.00 1.35
❑ I32 Doug Weight 1.50 .70
❑ I33 Mats Sundin 2.00 .90
❑ I34 Dominik Hasek 4.00 1.80
❑ I35 Scott Stevens .60 .25
❑ I36 Pavel Bure 4.00 1.80
❑ I37 Mike Modano 2.50 1.10
❑ I38 Zigmund Palffy 2.00 .90
❑ I39 Brian Leetch 2.00 .90
❑ I40 Marco Sturm 2.50 1.10

## 1997-98 SP Authentic Icons Die-Cuts

Randomly inserted in packs, this 40-card set is a die-cut parallel version of the 1997-98 SP Authentic Icons insert set. Each card is sequentially numbered to just 100.

MINT NRMT
COMPLETE SET (40) 6000.00 2700.00
COMMON CARD (I1-I40) 25.00 11.00

❑ I1 Pat LaFontaine 60.00 27.00
❑ I2 Brett Hull 100.00 45.00
❑ I3 Chris Chelios 80.00 36.00
❑ I4 Joe Sakic 150.00 70.00
❑ I5 John Vanbiesbrouck 100.00 45.00
❑ I6 Patrik Elias 60.00 27.00
❑ I7 Eric Lindros 250.00 110.00
❑ I8 Jaromir Jagr 250.00 110.00
❑ I9 Joe Thornton 80.00 36.00
❑ I10 Brendan Shanahan 150.00 70.00
❑ I11 Paul Kariya 300.00 135.00
❑ I12 Peter Forsberg 250.00 110.00
❑ I13 Ed Belfour 80.00 36.00
❑ I14 Martin Brodeur 200.00 90.00
❑ I15 Alexei Morozov 60.00 27.00
❑ I16 Mark Messier 100.00 45.00
❑ I17 John LeClair 100.00 45.00
❑ I18 Luc Robitaille 60.00 27.00
❑ I19 Teemu Selanne 150.00 70.00
❑ I20 Theoren Fleury 80.00 36.00
❑ I21 Steve Yzerman 250.00 110.00
❑ I22 Chris Phillips 25.00 11.00
❑ I23 Keith Tkachuk 100.00 45.00
❑ I24 Patrick Roy 400.00 180.00
❑ I25 Mark Recchi 60.00 27.00
❑ I26 Wayne Gretzky 500.00 220.00
❑ I27 Dino Ciccarelli 60.00 27.00
❑ I28 Ray Bourque 80.00 36.00
❑ I29 Tony Amonte 60.00 27.00
❑ I30 Daniel Alfredsson 60.00 27.00
❑ I31 Saku Koivu 100.00 45.00
❑ I32 Doug Weight 60.00 27.00
❑ I33 Mats Sundin 80.00 36.00
❑ I34 Dominik Hasek 150.00 70.00
❑ I35 Scott Stevens 25.00 11.00
❑ I36 Pavel Bure 150.00 70.00
❑ I37 Mike Modano 100.00 45.00
❑ I38 Zigmund Palffy 80.00 36.00
❑ I39 Brian Leetch 80.00 36.00
❑ I40 Marco Sturm 60.00 27.00

## 1997-98 SP Authentic Icons Embossed

Randomly inserted in packs at the rate of one in 12, this 40-card set is an embossed parallel version of the 1997-98 SP Authentic Icons insert set.

MINT NRMT
COMPLETE SET (40) 300.00 135.00
COMMON CARD (I1-I40) 1.50 .70
*EMBOSSED: 1X TO 2X ICONS

## 1997-98 SP Authentic Mark of a Legend

Randomly inserted in packs at the rate of one in 198, this six-card set features autographed color portraits of six of the NHL's greatest all-time players.

MINT NRMT
COMPLETE SET (6) 1400.00 650.00
COMMON CARD (M1-M6) 50.00 22.00

❑ M1 Gordie Howe/112 500.00 220.00
❑ M2 Billy Smith/560 50.00 22.00
❑ M3 Cam Neely/560 60.00 27.00
❑ M4 Bryan Trottier/560 50.00 22.00
❑ M5 Bobby Hull/560 80.00 36.00
❑ M6 Wayne Gretzky/560 600.00 275.00

## 1997-98 SP Authentic Sign of the Times

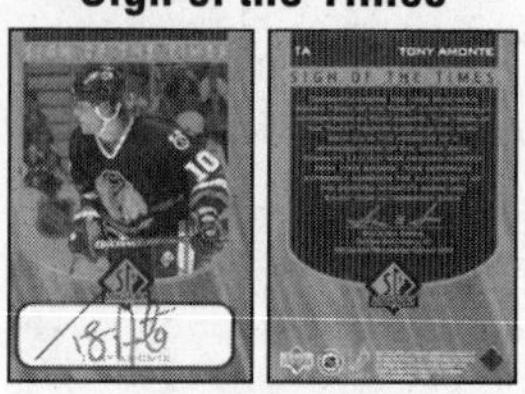

Randomly inserted in packs at the rate of one in 23, this 29-card set features autographed color action photos of top players in the NHL.

MINT NRMT
COMPLETE SET (29) 2000.00 900.00
COMMON CARD (S1-S29) 8.00 3.60
EXCH EXPIRATION 3/16/99

❑ BB Bryan Berard 20.00 9.00
❑ BH Brian Holzinger 8.00 3.60
❑ BH Brett Hull 60.00 27.00
❑ CC Chris Chelios 50.00 22.00
❑ DM Darren McCarty 20.00 9.00
❑ DW Doug Weight 20.00 9.00
❑ DZ Dainius Zubrus 8.00 3.60
❑ GF Grant Fuhr 30.00 13.50
❑ GH Guy Hebert 20.00 9.00
❑ JI Jarome Iginla 8.00 3.60
❑ JL Jamie Langenbrunner 8.00 3.60
❑ JS Jaroslav Svejkovsky 8.00 3.60
❑ JT Joe Thornton 40.00 18.00
❑ JTH Jose Theodore 8.00 3.60
❑ MB Martin Brodeur 120.00 55.00
❑ MG Mike Grier 8.00 3.60
❑ MS Mats Sundin 30.00 13.50
❑ NK Nikolai Khabibulin 8.00 3.60
❑ NL Nicklas Lidstrom 30.00 13.50
❑ PB Peter Bondra 40.00 18.00
❑ PR Patrick Roy 250.00 110.00
❑ RB Ray Bourque 80.00 36.00
❑ RN Rob Niedermayer 8.00 3.60
❑ SB Sergei Berezin 8.00 3.60
❑ SS Sergei Samsonov 50.00 22.00
❑ SY Steve Yzerman 200.00 90.00
❑ TA Tony Amonte 8.00 3.60
❑ WG Wayne Gretzky 400.00 180.00
❑ YP Yanic Perreault 8.00 3.60

## 1997-98 SP Authentic Tradition

Randomly inserted in packs at the rate of one in 340, this six-card set features color action dual photos and autographs of a current star and NHL legend from the same team.

MINT NRMT
COMPLETE SET (6) 2000.00 900.00
COMMON CARD (T1-T6) 70.00 32.00

❑ T1 Wayne Gretzky 1000.00 450.00
Gordie Howe
❑ T2 Patrick Roy 300.00 135.00
Billy Smith/333
❑ T3 Joe Thornton 100.00 45.00
Cam Neely/352
❑ T4 Bryan Berard 60.00 27.00
Bryan Trottier/352
❑ T5 Brett Hull 200.00 90.00
Bobby Hull/352
❑ T6 Ray Bourque 200.00 90.00
Cam Neely/140

## 1998-99 SP Authentic

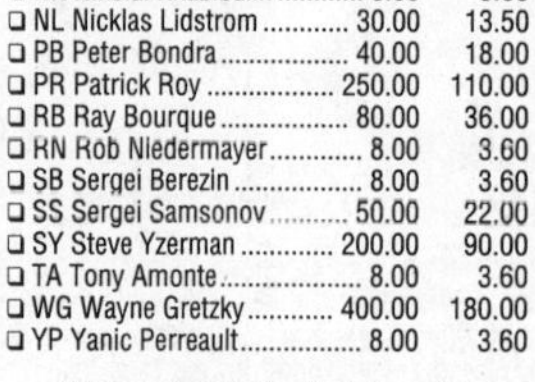

The 1998-99 SP Authentic set was issued in one series totalling 135 cards and was distributed in five-card packs with a suggested retail price of $4.99. The set features action color photos of 90 superstars of the NHL (1-90) and 45 top prospects (91-135) which are numbered to just 2000.

MINT NRMT
COMPLETE SET (135) 300.00 135.00
COMMON CARD (1-90) .25 .11
COMMON SP (91-135) 5.00 2.20

❑ 1 Paul Kariya 3.00 1.35
❑ 2 Teemu Selanne 1.50 .70
❑ 3 Guy Hebert .60 .25
❑ 4 Sergei Samsonov 1.25 .55
❑ 5 Joe Thornton .75 .35
❑ 6 Jason Allison .60 .25
❑ 7 Ray Bourque .75 .35
❑ 8 Dominik Hasek 1.50 .70
❑ 9 Michael Peca .25 .11
❑ 10 Michal Grosek .25 .11
❑ 11 Derek Morris .25 .11
❑ 12 Theoren Fleury .75 .35
❑ 13 Jarome Iginla .25 .11
❑ 14 Ron Francis .60 .25
❑ 15 Keith Primeau .60 .25
❑ 16 Sami Kapanen .60 .25
❑ 17 Tony Amonte .60 .25
❑ 18 Doug Gilmour .75 .35
❑ 19 Chris Chelios .75 .35
❑ 20 Peter Forsberg 2.50 1.10
❑ 21 Patrick Roy 4.00 1.80
❑ 22 Joe Sakic 1.50 .70
❑ 23 Adam Deadmarsh .60 .25
❑ 24 Brett Hull 1.00 .45
❑ 25 Mike Modano 1.00 .45
❑ 26 Ed Belfour .75 .35
❑ 27 Jere Lehtinen .25 .11
❑ 28 Sergei Fedorov 1.50 .70
❑ 29 Brendan Shanahan 1.50 .70
❑ 30 Chris Osgood .75 .35
❑ 31 Steve Yzerman 2.50 1.10
❑ 32 Nicklas Lidstrom .60 .25
❑ 33 Doug Weight .60 .25
❑ 34 Bill Guerin .60 .25
❑ 35 Tom Poti .25 .11
❑ 36 Rob Niedermayer .25 .11
❑ 37 Ed Jovanovski .25 .11
❑ 38 Luc Robitaille .60 .25
❑ 39 Rob Blake .60 .25
❑ 40 Glen Murray .25 .11
❑ 41 Saku Koivu 1.25 .55
❑ 42 Mark Recchi .60 .25
❑ 43 Vincent Damphousse .60 .25
❑ 44 Mike Dunham .60 .25
❑ 45 Sergei Krivokrasov .25 .11
❑ 46 Andrew Brunette .25 .11
❑ 47 Brendan Morrison .25 .11
❑ 48 Martin Brodeur 2.00 .90
❑ 49 Scott Stevens .25 .11
❑ 50 Patrik Elias .60 .25
❑ 51 Trevor Linden .60 .25
❑ 52 Zigmund Palffy .75 .35
❑ 53 Bryan Berard .25 .11
❑ 54 Robert Reichel .25 .11
❑ 55 Mike Richter .75 .35
❑ 56 Wayne Gretzky 5.00 2.20
❑ 57 Brian Leetch .25 .11
❑ 58 Wade Redden .25 .11
❑ 59 Alexei Yashin .60 .25
❑ 60 Daniel Alfredsson .25 .11
❑ 61 Eric Lindros 2.50 1.10
❑ 62 John Vanbiesbrouck 1.25 .55
❑ 63 John LeClair 1.25 .55
❑ 64 Rod Brind'Amour .60 .25
❑ 65 Jeremy Roenick .75 .35
❑ 66 Keith Tkachuk 1.00 .45
❑ 67 Nikolai Khabibulin .60 .25
❑ 68 German Titov .25 .11
❑ 69 Martin Straka .25 .11
❑ 70 Jaromir Jagr 2.50 1.10
❑ 71 Chris Pronger .60 .25
❑ 72 Al MacInnis .60 .25
❑ 73 Pierre Turgeon .60 .25
❑ 74 Pavol Demitra .60 .25
❑ 75 Patrick Marleau .25 .11
❑ 76 Jeff Friesen .25 .11
❑ 77 Owen Nolan .25 .11
❑ 78 Bill Ranford .25 .11
❑ 79 Wendel Clark .60 .25
❑ 80 Craig Janney .25 .11
❑ 81 Mike Johnson .25 .11
❑ 82 Curtis Joseph .75 .35
❑ 83 Mats Sundin .75 .35
❑ 84 Mattias Ohlund .60 .25
❑ 85 Mark Messier 1.00 .45
❑ 86 Pavel Bure 1.50 .70
❑ 87 Olaf Kolzig .60 .25
❑ 88 Peter Bondra .75 .35
❑ 89 Joe Juneau .60 .25
❑ 90 Adam Oates .60 .25
❑ 91 Johan Davidsson SP 5.00 2.20
❑ 92 Rico Fata SP 10.00 4.50
❑ 93 Mike Maneluk SP 12.00 5.50
❑ 94 J.P. Dumont SP 5.00 2.20
❑ 95 Milan Hejduk 20.00 9.00
❑ 96 Chris Drury SP 12.00 5.50
❑ 97 Mark Parrish 20.00 9.00
❑ 98 Oleg Kvasha SP 12.00 5.50
❑ 99 Josh Green SP 6.00 2.70
❑ 100 Olli Jokinen SP 5.00 2.20
❑ 101 Manny Malhotra SP 15.00 6.75
❑ 102 Eric Brewer SP 5.00 2.20
❑ 103 Mike Watt SP 5.00 2.20
❑ 104 Daniel Briere SP 5.00 2.20
❑ 105 J.S. Aubin SP 10.00 4.50
❑ 106 Jan Hrdina 10.00 4.50
❑ 107 Marty Reasoner SP 5.00 2.20
❑ 108 Michal Handzus 10.00 4.50
❑ 109 Vincent Lecavalier SP 25.00 11.00
❑ 110 Tomas Kaberle SP 5.00 2.20
❑ 111 Bill Muckalt SP 15.00 6.75
❑ 112 Josh Holden SP 5.00 2.20
❑ 113 Matt Herr SP 5.00 2.20
❑ 114 Brian Finley SP 20.00 9.00
❑ 115 Maxime Ouellet SP 15.00 6.75
❑ 116 Kurtis Foster SP 5.00 2.20
❑ 117 Barrett Jackman SP 5.00 2.20
❑ 118 Ross Lupaschuk SP 5.00 2.20
❑ 119 Steven McCarthy SP 10.00 4.50
❑ 120 Peter Reynolds SP .50 .23
❑ 121 Bart Rushmer SP 5.00 2.20
❑ 122 Jonathon Zion SP 5.00 2.20
❑ 123 Kris Beech SP 20.00 9.00
❑ 124 Brandin Cote SP 5.00 2.20
❑ 125 Scott Kelman SP 10.00 4.50
❑ 126 Jamie Lundmark SP 15.00 6.75
❑ 127 Derek MacKenzie SP 5.00 2.20
❑ 128 Rory McDade SP 5.00 2.20
❑ 129 David Morisset SP 10.00 4.50
❑ 130 Mirko Murovic SP 10.00 4.50
❑ 131 Taylor Pyatt SP 20.00 9.00
❑ 132 Charlie Stephens SP 5.00 2.20
❑ 133 Kyle Wanvig SP 12.00 5.50
❑ 134 Krzystof Wieckowski SP 5.00 2.20
❑ 135 Michael Zigomanis SP 15.00 6.75

## 1998-99 SP Authentic Power Shift

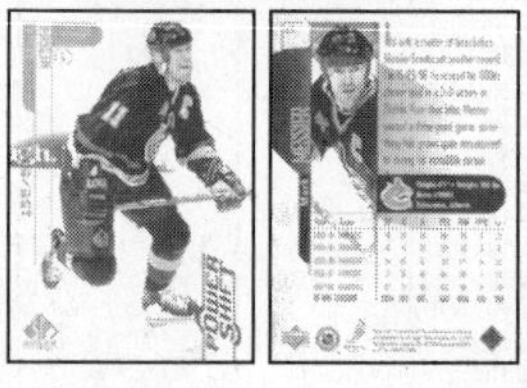

Randomly inserted into packs, this 135-card set is parallel to the base set. Only 500 sets were made.

MINT NRMT
COMPLETE SET (135) 2500.00 1100.00
COMMON CARD (1-135) 2.50 1.10
*STARS: 5X TO 10X BASIC CARDS
*YOUNG STARS: 4X TO 8X
*SP's: .75X TO 1.5X

## 1998-99 SP Authentic Authentics

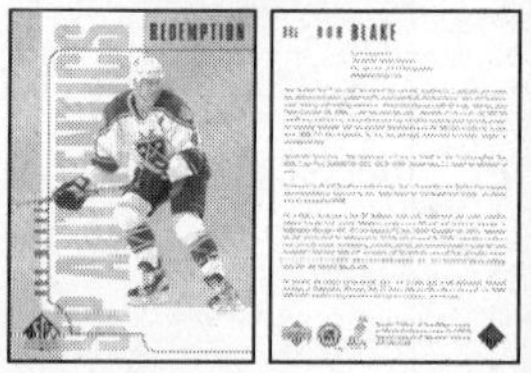

Randomly inserted into packs at the rate of one in 697, this set features hand numbered redemption cards for autographed merchandise and game used memorabilia. The number of each item available is indicated after each listed name. The cards expire on February 23, 2000

MINT NRMT
COMMON CARD (1-17) 25.00 11.00
TRADE CARD EXPIRES 2/23/00

❑ 1 W.Gretzky GW Piece/1
❑ 2 P.Roy GW Piece/1
❑ 3 S.Yzerman GW Piece/1
❑ 4 D.Weight GW Piece/1
❑ 5 D.Gilmour GW Piece/1
❑ 6 R.Blake Puck/75 25.00 11.00
❑ 7 R.Blake Photo/100 25.00 11.00
❑ 8 C.Chelios Photo/75 60.00 27.00
❑ 9 C.Chelios Puck/75 60.00 27.00
❑ 10 W.Gretzky Puck/50 250.00 110.00
❑ 11 W.Gretzky Photo/50 250.00 110.00
❑ 12 B.Hull Puck/90 80.00 36.00
❑ 13 K.Tkachuk Photo/75 80.00 36.00
❑ 14 K.Tkachuk Puck/75 80.00 36.00
❑ 15 S.Yzerman Card/50 100.00 45.00
❑ 16 S.Yzerman 2-card REDEMPT 150.00
70.00
❑ 17 S.Yzerman '98 BD Card/50 150.00 70.00

## 1998-99 SP Authentic Sign of the Times

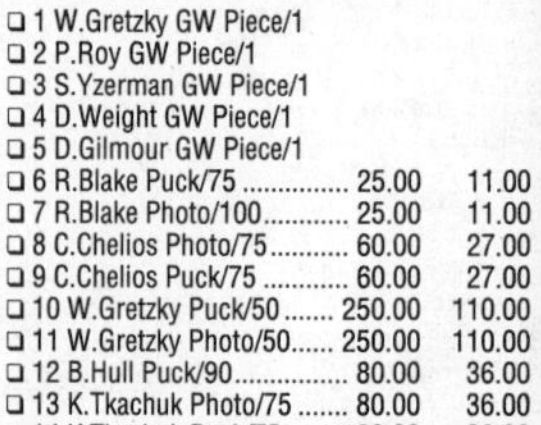

Randomly inserted into packs at the rate of one in 23, this 50-card set features autographed color photos of top players and future stars of the NHL. Some of the autographs were obtained through redemption cards.

MINT NRMT
COMPLETE SET (50) 1200.00 550.00
COMMON CARD 6.00 2.70

❑ AD Adam Deadmarsh 6.00 2.70
❑ AM Alexander Mogilny EXCH 20.00 9.00

❑ AS Alex Selivanov 6.00 2.70
❑ BB Bates Battaglia 6.00 2.70
❑ BD Byron Dafoe 20.00 9.00
❑ BF Brian Finley EXCH 25.00 11.00
❑ BH Brett Hull 50.00 22.00
❑ BJ Barrett Jackman EXCH 15.00 6.75
❑ CJ Curtis Joseph 25.00 11.00
❑ CS Charlie Stephens 12.00 5.50
❑ DA Daniel Alfredsson 6.00 2.70
❑ DM David Morisset 12.00 5.50
❑ DW Doug Weight 6.00 2.70
❑ EJ Ed Jovanovski EXCH 6.00 2.70
❑ JA Jason Allison 15.00 6.75
❑ JJ Joe Juneau 6.00 2.70
❑ JS Jozef Stumpel 6.00 2.70
❑ JT Joe Thornton 20.00 9.00
❑ KB Kris Beech EXCH 25.00 11.00
❑ KF Kurtis Foster 12.00 5.50
❑ KT Keith Tkachuk 25.00 11.00
❑ MB Matthew Barnaby 6.00 2.70
❑ MH Marian Hossa 6.00 2.70
❑ MM Manny Malhotra 20.00 9.00
❑ MO Mattias Ohlund 6.00 2.70
❑ MS Mats Sundin 25.00 11.00
❑ MZ Michael Zigomanis 25.00 11.00
❑ NL Nicklas Lidstrom 20.00 9.00
❑ ON Owen Nolan 6.00 2.70
❑ PR Patrick Roy 120.00 55.00
❑ RB Rob Blake 6.00 2.70
❑ RL Ross Lupaschuk 15.00 6.75
❑ RM Rory McDade EXCH 15.00 6.75
❑ RN Rumun Ndur 6.00 2.70
❑ RS Ryan Smyth 6.00 2.70
❑ SG Sergei Gonchar 6.00 2.70
❑ SK Scott Kelman EXCH 15.00 6.75
❑ SM Steven McCarthy 15.00 6.75
❑ SY Steve Yzerman EXCH 120.00 55.00
❑ TH Tomas Holmstrom 6.00 2.70
❑ TP Taylor Pyatt 25.00 11.00
❑ VL Vincent Lecavalier 40.00 18.00
❑ WG Wayne Gretzky 300.00 135.00
❑ DMA Derek Mackenzie 12.00 5.50
❑ MAO Maxime Ouellet 15.00 6.75
❑ MIM Mirko Murovic 15.00 6.75
❑ MMC Marty McSorley 6.00 2.70
❑ PBO Peter Bondra 25.00 11.00
❑ PRE Peter Reynolds EXCH 12.00 5.50
❑ PB Pavel Bure 50.00 22.00

## 1998-99 SP Authentic Sign of the Times Gold

Randomly inserted into packs, this set is a parallel version of the regular SP Authentic Sign of the Times insert set with each card hand-numbered to the pictured player's jersey number. These numbers follow the player's name in the checklist below.

MINT NRMT
COMMON CARD 40.00 18.00

❑ AD Adam Deadmarsh/18 100.00 45.00
❑ AM A.Mogilny/89 EXCH 50.00 22.00
❑ AS Alex Selivanov/29 50.00 22.00
❑ BB Bates Battaglia/33 40.00 18.00
❑ BD Byron Dafoe/34 80.00 36.00
❑ BF Brian Finley/100 EXCH 100.00 45.00
❑ BH Brett Hull/22 250.00 110.00
❑ BJ Barrett Jackman/100 EXCH 50.00 22.00
❑ CJ Curtis Joseph/31 100.00 45.00
❑ CS Charlie Stephens/100 40.00 18.00
❑ DA Daniel Alfredsson/11 120.00 55.00
❑ DM David Morisset/100 50.00 22.00
❑ DW Doug Weight/39 60.00 27.00
❑ EJ E.Jovanovski/55 EXCH 40.00 18.00
❑ JA Jason Allison/41 60.00 27.00
❑ JJ Joe Juneau/49 60.00 27.00
❑ JS Jozef Stumpel/16 125.00 55.00
❑ JT Joe Thornton/10 200.00 90.00
❑ KB Kris Beech/100 EXCH 100.00 45.00
❑ KF Kurtis Foster/100 50.00 22.00
❑ KT Keith Tkachuk/10 350.00 160.00
❑ MB Matthew Barnaby/36 60.00 27.00
❑ MH Marian Hossa/18 100.00 45.00
❑ MM Manny Malhotra/10 120.00 55.00
❑ MO Mattias Ohlund/10 120.00 55.00
❑ MS Mats Sundin/13 300.00 135.00
❑ MZ Michael Zigomanis/100 100.00 45.00
❑ NL Nicklas Lidstrom/10 150.00 70.00
❑ ON Owen Nolan/11 120.00 55.00
❑ PR Patrick Roy/33 EXCH 800.00 350.00
❑ RB Rob Blake/10 120.00 55.00
❑ RL Ross Lupaschuk/100 60.00 27.00
❑ RM Rory McDade/100 EXCH 50.00 22.00
❑ RN Rumun Ndur/40 40.00 18.00
❑ RS Ryan Smyth/94 50.00 22.00
❑ SG Sergei Gonchar/55 40.00 18.00
❑ SK Scott Kelman/100 EXCH. 60.00 27.00
❑ SM Steven McCarthy/100 60.00 27.00
❑ SY Steve Yzerman/19 EXCH 1000.00 450.00
❑ TH Tomas Holmstrom/96 40.00 18.00
❑ TP Taylor Pyatt/100 100.00 45.00
❑ VL Vincent Lecavalier/14 300.00 135.00
❑ WG Wayne Gretzky/99 1000.00 450.00
❑ DMA Derek Mackenzie/100 50.00 22.00
❑ MAO Maxime Ouellet/100 80.00 36.00
❑ MIM Mirko Murovic/100 60.00 27.00
❑ MMC Marty McSorley/33 40.00 18.00
❑ PBO Peter Bondra/12 300.00 135.00
❑ PRE Peter Reynolds EXCH/100 50.00 22.00
❑ PB Pavel Bure/10 400.00 180.00

## 1998-99 SP Authentic Snapshots

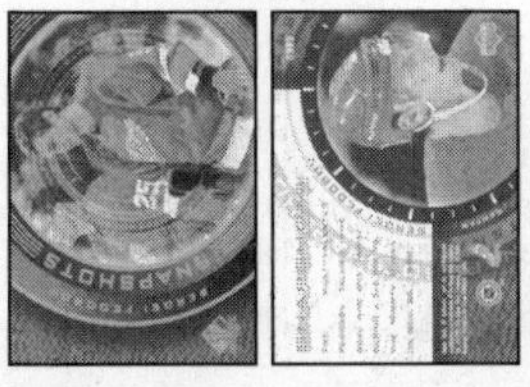

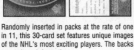

Randomly inserted in packs at the rate of one in 11, this 30-card set features unique images of the NHL's most exciting players. The backs carry player information.

MINT NRMT
COMPLETE SET (30) 150.00 70.00
COMMON CARD (1-30) 2.00 .90

❑ SS1 Wayne Gretzky 15.00 6.75
❑ SS2 Patrick Roy 12.00 5.50
❑ SS3 Steve Yzerman 8.00 3.60
❑ SS4 Brett Hull 3.00 1.35
❑ SS5 Jaromir Jagr 8.00 3.60
❑ SS6 Peter Forsberg 8.00 3.60
❑ SS7 Dominik Hasek 5.00 2.20
❑ SS8 Paul Kariya 10.00 4.50
❑ SS9 Eric Lindros 8.00 3.60
❑ SS10 Teemu Selanne 5.00 2.20
❑ SS11 John LeClair 4.00 1.80
❑ SS12 Mike Modano 3.00 1.35
❑ SS13 Martin Brodeur 6.00 2.70
❑ SS14 Brendan Shanahan 5.00 2.20
❑ SS15 Ray Bourque 2.50 1.10
❑ SS16 John Vanbiesbrouck 4.00 1.80
❑ SS17 Brian Leetch 2.50 1.10
❑ SS18 Vincent Lecavalier 6.00 2.70
❑ SS19 Joe Sakic 3.00 1.35
❑ SS20 Chris Drury 3.00 1.35
❑ SS21 Eric Brewer 2.00 .90
❑ SS22 Jeremy Roenick 2.50 1.10
❑ SS23 Mats Sundin 2.50 1.10
❑ SS24 Zigmund Palffy 2.50 1.10
❑ SS25 Keith Tkachuk 3.00 1.35
❑ SS26 Sergei Samsonov 4.00 1.80
❑ SS27 Curtis Joseph 2.50 1.10
❑ SS28 Peter Bondra 2.50 1.10
❑ SS29 Sergei Fedorov 5.00 2.20
❑ SS30 Doug Gilmour 2.50 1.10

## 1998-99 SP Authentic Stat Masters

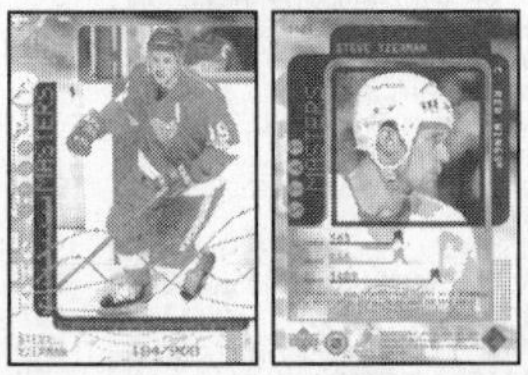

Randomly inserted into packs, this 30-card set features color photos of the NHL's best players printed on sequentially numbered cards based on the achievements of the player featured. Each player's card is sequentially numbered to the player's key accomplishment. These numbers follow the player's name in the checklist below.

MINT NRMT
COMPLETE SET (30) 1600.00 700.00
COMMON CARD (1-30) 6.00 2.70

❑ S1 Brendan Shanahan/400 30.00 13.50
❑ S2 Brett Hull/1000 12.00 5.50
❑ S3 Dominik Hasek/200 60.00 27.00
❑ S4 Doug Gilmour/1200 6.00 2.70
❑ S5 Doug Weight/500 12.00 5.50
❑ S6 Eric Lindros/115 200.00 90.00
❑ S7 Jaromir Jagr/301 60.00 27.00
❑ S8 Joe Sakic/900 20.00 9.00
❑ S9 John LeClair/500 25.00 11.00
❑ S10 John Vanbiesbrouck/306 30.00 13.50
❑ S11 Keith Tkachuk/250 30.00 13.50
❑ S12 Mark Messier/600 15.00 6.75
❑ S13 Martin Brodeur/200 100.00 45.00
❑ S14 Mike Modano/650 15.00 6.75
❑ S15 Patrick Roy/400 60.00 27.00
❑ S16 Paul Kariya/108 250.00 110.00
❑ S17 Pavel Bure/500 30.00 13.50
❑ S18 Peter Bondra/300 20.00 9.00
❑ S19 Peter Forsberg/400 40.00 18.00
❑ S20 Ray Bourque/1500 8.00 3.60
❑ S21 Ron Francis/1500 6.00 2.70
❑ S22 Sergei Fedorov/600 25.00 11.00
❑ S23 Steve Yzerman/1500 25.00 11.00
❑ S24 Steve Yzerman/900 30.00 13.50
❑ S25 Steve Yzerman/500 50.00 22.00
❑ S26 Teemu Selanne/300 40.00 18.00
❑ S27 Vincent Lecavalier/1998 15.00 6.75
❑ S28 Wayne Gretzky/92 400.00 180.00
❑ S29 Wayne Gretzky/900 40.00 18.00
❑ S30 Wayne Gretzky/2000 25.00 11.00

## 1996-97 SPx

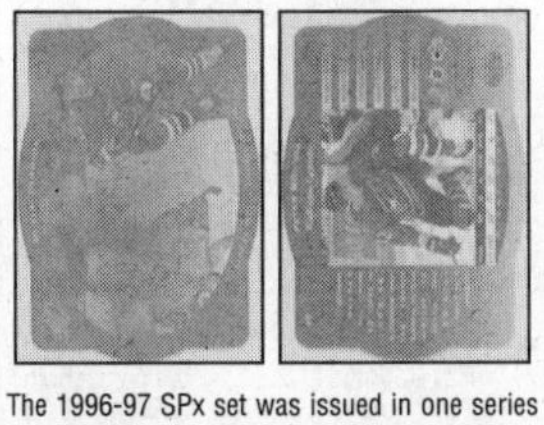

The 1996-97 SPx set was issued in one series totalling 50 cards. The one-card packs retailed for $3.49 each. Each die-cut card features a full-motion hologram. Two special cards of Wayne Gretzky were randomly inserted, including a tribute (found 1:95), and an autographed tribute (found just one in 1297 packs). An additional special insert is the Great Futures card, which includes holoview images of four young stars (Eric Daze, Daniel Alfredsson, Vitali Yachmenev, and Saku Koivu) and was randomly inserted at a rate of 1:75 packs.

MINT NRMT
COMPLETE SET (50) 80.00 36.00
COMMON CARD (1-50) 1.00 .45

❑ 1 Paul Kariya 6.00 2.70
❑ 2 Teemu Selanne 3.00 1.35
❑ 3 Ray Bourque 1.50 .70
❑ 4 Cam Neely 1.25 .55
❑ 5 Theoren Fleury 1.25 .55
❑ 6 Chris Chelios 1.50 .70
❑ 7 Jeremy Roenick 1.50 .70
❑ 8 Peter Forsberg 5.00 2.20
❑ 9 Joe Sakic 3.00 1.35
❑ 10 Patrick Roy 8.00 3.60
❑ 11 Mike Modano 2.00 .90
❑ 12 Joe Nieuwendyk 1.25 .55
❑ 13 Sergei Fedorov 3.00 1.35
❑ 14 Steve Yzerman 5.00 2.20
❑ 15 Paul Coffey 1.50 .70
❑ 16 Chris Osgood 1.50 .70
❑ 17 Doug Weight 1.25 .55
❑ 18 Pat LaFontaine 1.25 .55
❑ 19 Brendan Shanahan 3.00 1.35
❑ 20 Vitali Yachmenev 1.00 .45
❑ 21 Saku Koivu 2.50 1.10
❑ 22 Pierre Turgeon 1.25 .55
❑ 23 Petr Sykora 1.00 .45
❑ 24 Scott Stevens 1.25 .55
❑ 25 Martin Brodeur 4.00 1.80
❑ 26 Brian Leetch 1.50 .70
❑ 27 Mark Messier 2.00 .90
❑ 28 Mike Richter 1.50 .70
❑ 29 Zigmund Palffy 1.50 .70
❑ 30 Todd Bertuzzi 1.00 .45
❑ 31 Alexei Yashin 1.25 .55
❑ 32 Daniel Alfredsson 1.25 .55
❑ 33 Eric Lindros 5.00 2.20
❑ 34 John LeClair 2.50 1.10
❑ 35 Keith Tkachuk 2.00 .90
❑ 36 Alexei Zhamnov 1.25 .55
❑ 37 Mario Lemieux 8.00 3.60
❑ 38 Jaromir Jagr 5.00 2.20
❑ 39 Wayne Gretzky 12.00 5.50
❑ 40 Brett Hull 2.00 .90
❑ 41 Owen Nolan 1.25 .55
❑ 42 Roman Hamrlik 1.25 .55
❑ 43 Mats Sundin 1.25 .55
❑ 44 Felix Potvin 1.50 .70
❑ 45 Doug Gilmour 1.50 .70
❑ 46 Pavel Bure 3.00 1.35
❑ 47 Alexander Mogilny 1.25 .55
❑ 48 Jim Carey 1.50 .70
❑ 49 Peter Bondra 1.50 .70
❑ 50 Eric Daze 1.25 .55
❑ P39 Wayne Gretzky PROMO 10.00 4.50
❑ GF1 Wayne Gretzky 12.00 5.50
Daniel Alfredsson
Eric Daze
Saku Koivu
Vitali Yachmenev
❑ GS1 W.Gretzky Tribute AU. 300.00 135.00
❑ GT1 Wayne Gretzky Tribute 25.00 11.00

## 1996-97 SPx Gold

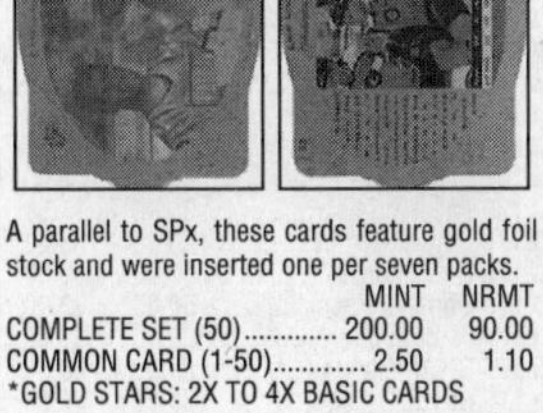

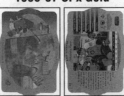

A parallel to SPx, these cards feature gold foil stock and were inserted one per seven packs.

MINT NRMT
COMPLETE SET (50) 200.00 90.00
COMMON CARD (1-50) 2.50 1.10
*GOLD STARS: 2X TO 4X BASIC CARDS

## 1996-97 SPx Holoview Heroes

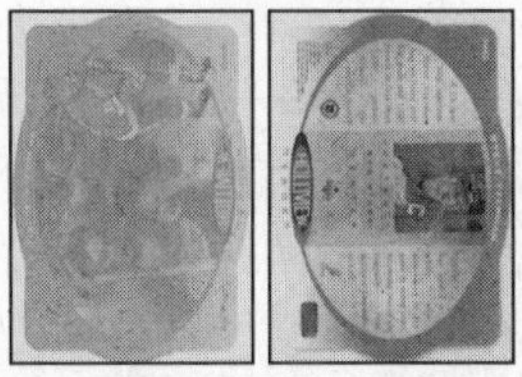

Randomly inserted in packs at a rate of one in 24, this 10-card set also was die-cut with a full-motion hologram.

MINT NRMT
COMPLETE SET (10) 150.00 70.00
COMMON CARD (HH1-HH10) 6.00 2.70

❑ HH1 Ray Bourque 8.00 3.60
❑ HH2 Patrick Roy 30.00 13.50
❑ HH3 Steve Yzerman 20.00 9.00
❑ HH4 Paul Coffey 8.00 3.60
❑ HH5 Mark Messier 8.00 3.60
❑ HH6 Mario Lemieux 30.00 13.50
❑ HH7 Wayne Gretzky 40.00 18.00
❑ HH8 Brett Hull 8.00 3.60
❑ HH9 Doug Gilmour 6.00 2.70
❑ HH10 Grant Fuhr 6.00 2.70

## 1997-98 SPx

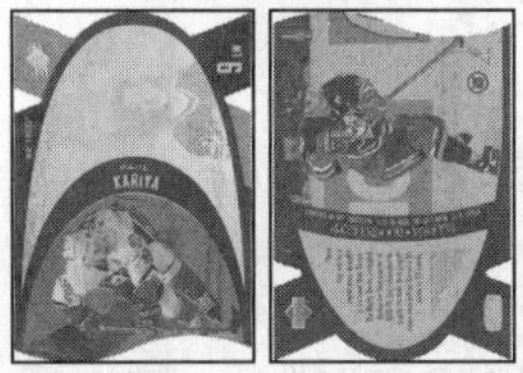

The 1997-98 SPx set was issued in one series totalling 50 cards and was distributed in three-card packs with a suggested retail price of $5.99. The fronts features color action player photos printed on 32-point card stock utilizing decorative foil on the exclusive Light F/X/Holoview cards.

MINT NRMT
COMPLETE SET (50) 60.00 27.00
COMMON CARD (1-50) .50 .23

❑ 1 Paul Kariya 4.00 1.80
❑ 2 Teemu Selanne 2.00 .90
❑ 3 Ray Bourque 1.00 .45
❑ 4 Dominik Hasek 2.00 .90
❑ 5 Pat LaFontaine .75 .35
❑ 6 Theoren Fleury .75 .35
❑ 7 Jarome Iginla .75 .35
❑ 8 Tony Amonte .75 .35
❑ 9 Chris Chelios 1.00 .45
❑ 10 Patrick Roy 5.00 2.20
❑ 11 Peter Forsberg 3.00 1.35
❑ 12 Joe Sakic 2.00 .90
❑ 13 Mike Modano 1.25 .55
❑ 14 Steve Yzerman 3.00 1.35
❑ 15 Sergei Fedorov 2.00 .90
❑ 16 Brendan Shanahan 2.00 .90
❑ 17 Doug Weight .75 .35
❑ 18 Jason Arnott .75 .35
❑ 19 Curtis Joseph 1.00 .45
❑ 20 John Vanbiesbrouck 1.50 .70
❑ 21 Ed Jovanovski .75 .35
❑ 22 Geoff Sanderson .75 .35
❑ 23 Rob Blake .50 .23
❑ 24 Saku Koivu 1.50 .70
❑ 25 Doug Gilmour 1.00 .45
❑ 26 Scott Stevens .50 .23
❑ 27 Martin Brodeur 2.50 1.10
❑ 28 Zigmund Palffy 1.00 .45
❑ 29 Bryan Berard .75 .35
❑ 30 Wayne Gretzky 6.00 2.70
❑ 30S Wayne Gretzky SAMPLE. 5.00 2.20
❑ 31 Mike Richter 1.00 .45
❑ 32 Mark Messier 1.25 .55
❑ 33 Brian Leetch 1.00 .45
❑ 34 Daniel Alfredsson .75 .35
❑ 35 Alexei Yashin .75 .35
❑ 36 Eric Lindros 3.00 1.35
❑ 37 Janne Niinimaa .75 .35
❑ 38 John LeClair 1.50 .70
❑ 39 Jeremy Roenick 1.00 .45
❑ 40 Keith Tkachuk 1.25 .55
❑ 41 Ron Francis .75 .35
❑ 42 Jaromir Jagr 3.00 1.35
❑ 43 Brett Hull 1.25 .55
❑ 44 Owen Nolan .75 .35
❑ 45 Chris Gratton .75 .35
❑ 46 Mats Sundin 1.00 .45
❑ 47 Pavel Bure 2.00 .90
❑ 48 Adam Oates .75 .35
❑ 49 Joe Juneau .75 .35
❑ 50 Peter Bondra 1.00 .45

## 1997-98 SPx Bronze

Randomly inserted in packs at the rate of one in three, this 50-card set is parallel to the base set and is similar in design. The difference is found in the bronze foil enhancements of the cards.

MINT NRMT
COMPLETE SET (50) 200.00 90.00
COMMON CARD (1-50) 1.50 .70
*BRONZE STARS: 1.5X TO 3X BASIC CARDS

## 1997-98 SPx Gold

Randomly inserted in packs at the rate of one in 17, this 50-card set is parallel to the base set and is similar in design. The difference is found in the gold foil enhancements of the cards.

MINT NRMT
COMPLETE SET (50) 800.00 350.00
COMMON CARD (1-50) 5.00 2.20
*GOLD STARS: 5X TO 10X BASIC CARDS

## 1997-98 SPx Silver

Randomly inserted in packs at the rate of one in six, this 50-card set is parallel to the base set and is similar in design. The difference is found in the silver foil enhancements of the cards.

MINT NRMT
COMPLETE SET (50) 250.00 110.00
COMMON CARD (1-50) 2.00 .90
*SILVER STARS: 2X TO 4X BASIC CARDS

## 1997-98 SPx Steel

Randomly inserted one in every pack, this 50-card set is parallel to the base set and is similar in design. The difference is found in the gray foil enhancements of the cards.

MINT NRMT
COMPLETE SET (50) 120.00 55.00
COMMON CARD (1-50) 1.00 .45
*STEEL STARS: 1X TO 2X BASIC CARDS

## 1997-98 SPx Dimension

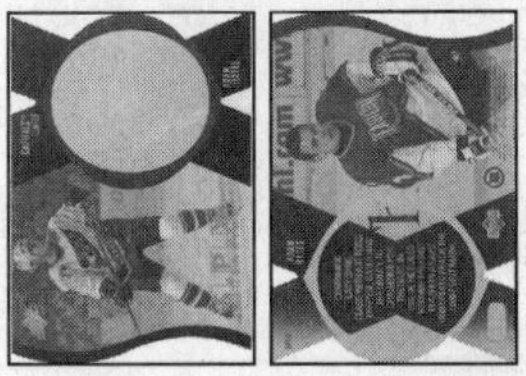

Randomly inserted in packs at the rate of one in 54, this 20-card set features color action player photos printed with a rainbow Light F/X and Litho combination.

MINT NRMT
COMPLETE SET (20) 900.00 400.00
COMMON CARD (SPX1-SPX20) 20.00 9.00

❑ SPX1 Wayne Gretzky 150.00 70.00
❑ SPX2 Jeremy Roenick 25.00 11.00
❑ SPX3 Mark Messier 30.00 13.50
❑ SPX4 Eric Lindros 80.00 36.00
❑ SPX5 Doug Gilmour 20.00 9.00
❑ SPX6 Pavel Bure 50.00 22.00
❑ SPX7 Brendan Shanahan 50.00 22.00
❑ SPX8 Bryan Berard 20.00 9.00
❑ SPX9 Curtis Joseph 25.00 11.00
❑ SPX10 Chris Chelios 25.00 11.00
❑ SPX11 Sergei Fedorov 50.00 22.00
❑ SPX12 Adam Oates 20.00 9.00
❑ SPX13 Zigmund Palffy 25.00 11.00
❑ SPX14 Theoren Fleury 20.00 9.00
❑ SPX15 Keith Tkachuk 30.00 13.50
❑ SPX16 Peter Forsberg 80.00 36.00
❑ SPX17 Mats Sundin 25.00 11.00
❑ SPX18 Teemu Selanne 50.00 22.00
❑ SPX19 Paul Kariya 100.00 45.00
❑ SPX20 Brett Hull 30.00 13.50

## 1997-98 SPx DuoView

Randomly inserted in packs at the rate of one in 252, this 10-card set features two different holoview images of the player depicted on the card front in a unique silver and gold combination printed on Light F/X holoview cards.

MINT NRMT
COMPLETE SET (10) 1300.00 575.00
COMMON CARD (1-10) 40.00 18.00

❑ 1 Wayne Gretzky 300.00 135.00
❑ 2 Jaromir Jagr 150.00 70.00
❑ 3 Martin Brodeur 125.00 55.00
❑ 4 Jarome Iginla 40.00 18.00
❑ 5 Steve Yzerman 150.00 70.00
❑ 6 Patrick Roy 250.00 110.00
❑ 7 Doug Weight 40.00 18.00
❑ 8 John Vanbiesbrouck 80.00 36.00
❑ 9 Dominik Hasek 100.00 45.00
❑ 10 Joe Sakic 100.00 45.00

## 1997-98 SPx DuoView Autographs

Randomly inserted in packs, this six-card set is a partial parallel version of the DuoView insert set featuring gold foil enhancements and

the pictured player's autograph. Only 100 of each each card was produced and are sequentially hand numbered.

MINT NRMT
COMPLETE SET (6)............ 2500.00 1100.00
COMMON CARD (1-6)............ 80.00 36.00

❑ 1 Wayne Gretzky............ 1000.00 450.00
❑ 2 Jaromir Jagr............ 500.00 220.00
❑ 3 Martin Brodeur............ 250.00 110.00
❑ 4 Jarome Iginla............ 100.00 45.00
❑ 5 Patrick Roy............ 800.00 350.00
❑ 6 Doug Weight............ 100.00 45.00

## 1997-98 SPx Grand Finale

Randomly inserted in packs, this 50-card set is parallel to the base set and is similar in design. The difference is found in the gold foil enhancements and gold Holoview/Hologram on the cards. Only 50 of each card of this set was produced.

MINT NRMT
COMMON CARD (1-50)........... 80.00 36.00
*STARS: 75X TO 125X HI COLUMN

## 1998-99 SPx Finite

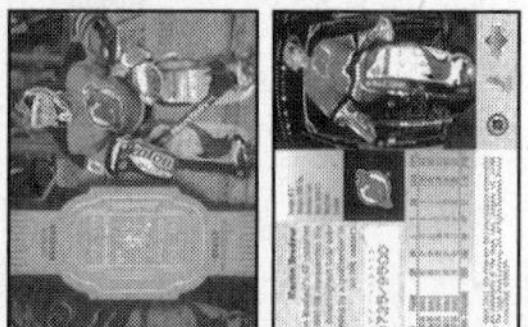

The 1998-99 SPx Finite hobby-only Series One was issued with a total of 180 cards. The three-card packs retail for $5.99 each. The 90 regular player cards (1-90) are sequentially numbered to 9,500 and feature color action player photos with a unique bronze foil emblem embedded in the center of the cards. The set contains the subsets: Global Impact (91-120) sequentially numbered to 6,950, NHL Sure Shots, (121-150) numbered to 3,900, Marquee Performers (151-170) numbered to 2,625, and Living Legends (171-180) numbered to 1,620.

MINT NRMT
COMPLETE SET (180)........... 900.00 400.00
COMP.BASE SET (90)........... 100.00 45.00
COMMON CARD (1-90)........... .50 .23
COMP.GLOB.IMPACT.SET (30) 120.00 55.00
COMMON GLOB.IMP.(91-120) . 2.00 .90
COMP.SURE SHOTS SET (30) 60.00 27.00
COMMON SURE SHOT (121-150) 1.50 .70
COMP. MARQ.PERF.SET (20) 250.00 110.00
COMMON MARQ.PERF. (151-170) 6.00 2.70
COMP.LIVING.LEG.SET (10). 400.00 180.00
COMMON LIV.LEG. (171-180) 15.00 6.75

❑ 1 Teemu Selanne............ 3.00 1.35
❑ 2 Guy Hebert............ 1.25 .55
❑ 3 Josef Marha............ .50 .23
❑ 4 Travis Green............ .50 .23
❑ 5 Sergei Samsonov............ 3.00 1.35
❑ 6 Jason Allison............ 1.25 .55
❑ 7 Byron Dafoe............ 1.25 .55
❑ 8 Dominik Hasek............ 3.00 1.35
❑ 9 Michael Peca............ .50 .23
❑ 10 Erik Rasmussen............ .50 .23
❑ 11 Matthew Barnaby............ .50 .23
❑ 12 Theoren Fleury............ 1.50 .70
❑ 13 Derek Morris............ .50 .23
❑ 14 Valeri Bure............ .50 .23
❑ 15 Trevor Kidd............ 1.25 .55
❑ 16 Sami Kapanen............ 1.25 .55
❑ 17 Bates Battaglia............ .50 .23
❑ 18 Tony Amonte............ 1.25 .55
❑ 19 Dmitri Nabokov............ .50 .23
❑ 20 Daniel Cleary............ .50 .23
❑ 21 Jeff Hackett............ 1.25 .55
❑ 22 Joe Sakic............ 3.00 1.35
❑ 23 Valeri Kamensky............ 1.25 .55
❑ 24 Patrick Roy............ 8.00 3.60
❑ 25 Wade Belak............ .50 .23
❑ 26 Joe Nieuwendyk............ 1.25 .55
❑ 27 Mike Keane............ .50 .23
❑ 28 Jere Lehtinen............ .50 .23
❑ 29 Ed Belfour............ 1.50 .70
❑ 30 Steve Yzerman............ 5.00 2.20
❑ 31 Dmitri Mironov............ .50 .23
❑ 32 Brendan Shanahan............ 3.00 1.35
❑ 33 Nicklas Lidstrom............ 1.25 .55
❑ 34 Doug Weight............ 1.25 .55
❑ 35 Janne Niinimaa............ .50 .23
❑ 36 Bill Guerin............ 1.25 .55
❑ 37 Ray Whitney............ .50 .23
❑ 38 Robert Svehla............ .50 .23
❑ 39 Ed Jovanovski............ .50 .23
❑ 40 Vladimir Tsyplakov............ .50 .23
❑ 41 Josef Stumpel............ 1.25 .55
❑ 42 Rob Blake............ 1.25 .55
❑ 43 Mark Recchi............ 1.25 .55
❑ 44 Andy Moog............ 1.25 .55
❑ 45 Matt Higgins............ .50 .23
❑ 46 Martin Brodeur............ 4.00 1.80
❑ 47 Doug Gilmour............ 1.50 .70
❑ 48 Brendan Morrison............ 1.25 .55
❑ 49 Patrik Elias............ 1.25 .55
❑ 50 Trevor Linden............ 1.25 .55
❑ 51 Bryan Berard............ .50 .23
❑ 52 Zdeno Chara............ .50 .23
❑ 53 Wayne Gretzky............ 10.00 4.50
❑ 54 Marc Savard............ .50 .23
❑ 55 Daniel Goneau............ .50 .23
❑ 56 Pat Lafontaine............ 1.25 .55
❑ 57 Alexei Yashin............ 1.25 .55
❑ 58 Marian Hossa............ .50 .23
❑ 59 Wade Redden............ .50 .23
❑ 60 John LeClair............ 2.50 1.10
❑ 61 Alexandre Daigle............ .50 .23
❑ 62 Rod Brind'Amour............ 1.25 .55
❑ 63 Chris Therien............ .50 .23
❑ 64 Keith Tkachuk............ 2.00 .90
❑ 65 Brad Isbister............ .50 .23
❑ 66 Nikolai Khabibulin............ 1.25 .55
❑ 67 Robert Dome............ .50 .23
❑ 68 Alexei Morozov............ .50 .23
❑ 69 Stu Barnes............ .50 .23
❑ 70 Tom Barrasso............ 1.25 .55
❑ 71 Owen Nolan............ 1.25 .55
❑ 72 Marco Sturm............ 1.25 .55
❑ 73 Patrick Marleau............ .50 .23
❑ 74 Pierre Turgeon............ 1.25 .55
❑ 75 Chris Pronger............ 1.25 .55
❑ 76 Pavol Demitra............ 1.25 .55
❑ 77 Grant Fuhr............ 1.25 .55
❑ 78 Stephane Richer............ 1.25 .55
❑ 79 Zac Bierk RC............ 1.25 .55
❑ 80 Alexander Selivanov............ .50 .23
❑ 81 Mike Johnson............ 1.25 .55
❑ 82 Mats Sundin............ 1.50 .70
❑ 83 Alyn McAuley............ .50 .23
❑ 84 Pavel Bure............ 3.00 1.35
❑ 85 Todd Bertuzzi............ .50 .23
❑ 86 Garth Snow............ 1.25 .55
❑ 87 Peter Bondra............ 1.50 .70
❑ 88 Olaf Kolzig............ 1.25 .55
❑ 89 Jan Bulis............ .50 .23
❑ 90 Sergei Gonchar............ .50 .23
❑ 91 Pavel Bure GI............ 5.00 2.20
❑ 92 Joe Sakic GI............ 5.00 2.20
❑ 93 Steve Yzerman GI............ 8.00 3.60
❑ 94 Jaromir Jagr GI............ 8.00 3.60
❑ 95 Peter Forsberg GI............ 8.00 3.60
❑ 96 Brendan Shanahan GI............ 5.00 2.20
❑ 97 Brett Hull GI............ 3.00 1.35
❑ 98 Alexei Yashin GI............ 2.00 .90
❑ 99 Wayne Gretzky GI............ 15.00 6.75
❑ 100 Eric Lindros GI............ 8.00 3.60
❑ 101 Sergei Samsonov GI............ 4.00 1.80
❑ 102 John LeClair GI............ 4.00 1.80
❑ 103 Dominik Hasek GI............ 5.00 2.20
❑ 104 Teemu Selanne GI............ 5.00 2.20
❑ 105 Martin Brodeur GI............ 6.00 2.70
❑ 106 Tony Amonte GI............ 2.00 .90
❑ 107 Theoren Fleury GI............ 2.50 1.10
❑ 108 Rob Blake GI............ 2.00 .90
❑ 109 Mike Modano GI............ 3.00 1.35
❑ 110 Peter Bondra GI............ 2.50 1.10
❑ 111 Brian Leetch GI............ 2.50 1.10
❑ 112 Nicklas Lidstrom GI............ 2.00 .90
❑ 113 Doug Weight GI............ 2.00 .90
❑ 114 Zigmund Palffy GI............ 2.50 1.10
❑ 115 Saku Koivu GI............ 4.00 1.80
❑ 116 Paul Kariya GI............ 10.00 4.50
❑ 117 Ray Bourque GI............ 2.50 1.10
❑ 118 Mats Sundin GI............ 2.50 1.10
❑ 119 Patrick Roy GI............ 12.00 5.50
❑ 120 Chris Chelios GI............ 2.50 1.10
❑ 121 Sergei Samsonov SS............ 8.00 3.60
❑ 122 Mike Johnson SS............ 4.00 1.80
❑ 123 Patrik Elias SS............ 4.00 1.80
❑ 124 Josef Marha SS............ .50 .23
❑ 125 Dan Cloutier SS............ .50 .23
❑ 126 Cameron Mann SS............ .50 .23
❑ 127 Mattias Ohlund SS............ .50 .23
❑ 128 Daniel Cleary SS............ .50 .23
❑ 129 Anders Eriksson SS............ .50 .23
❑ 130 Patrick Marleau SS............ .50 .23
❑ 131 Jan Bulis SS............ .50 .23
❑ 132 Alyn McAuley SS............ .50 .23
❑ 133 Joe Thornton SS............ .50 .23
❑ 134 Andrei Zyuzin SS............ .50 .23
❑ 135 Richard Zednik SS............ .50 .23
❑ 136 Derek Morris SS............ .50 .23
❑ 137 Bates Battaglia SS............ .50 .23
❑ 138 Mike Watt SS............ .50 .23
❑ 139 Olli Jokinen SS............ .50 .23
❑ 140 Marian Hossa SS............ 4.00 1.80
❑ 141 Daniel Goneau SS............ .50 .23
❑ 142 Erik Rasmussen SS............ .50 .23
❑ 143 Daniel Briere SS............ .50 .23
❑ 144 Norm Maracle RC SS............ 8.00 3.60
❑ 145 Brendan Morrison SS............ 4.00 1.80
❑ 146 Brad Isbister SS............ .50 .23
❑ 147 Robert Dome SS............ .50 .23
❑ 148 Zac Bierk SS............ .50 .23
❑ 149 Alexei Morozov SS............ .50 .23
❑ 150 Marco Sturm SS............ .50 .23
❑ 151 Wayne Gretzky MP............ 40.00 18.00
❑ 152 Eric Lindros MP............ 20.00 9.00
❑ 153 Paul Kariya MP............ 25.00 11.00
❑ 154 Patrick Roy MP............ 30.00 13.50
❑ 155 Sergei Samsonov MP............ 10.00 4.50
❑ 156 Steve Yzerman MP............ 20.00 9.00
❑ 157 Teemu Selanne MP............ 12.00 5.50
❑ 158 Brendan Shanahan MP............ 12.00 5.50
❑ 159 Dominik Hasek MP............ 12.00 5.50
❑ 160 Mark Messier MP............ 8.00 3.60
❑ 161 Martin Brodeur MP............ 15.00 6.75
❑ 162 Mats Sundin MP............ 6.00 2.70
❑ 163 Joe Sakic MP............ 12.00 5.50
❑ 164 John LeClair MP............ 10.00 4.50
❑ 165 Jaromir Jagr MP............ 20.00 9.00
❑ 166 Peter Forsberg MP............ 20.00 9.00
❑ 167 Theoren Fleury MP............ 6.00 2.70
❑ 168 Peter Bondra MP............ 6.00 2.70
❑ 169 Mike Modano MP............ 8.00 3.60
❑ 170 Pavel Bure MP............ 12.00 5.50
❑ 171 Patrick Roy LL............ 60.00 27.00
❑ 172 Eric Lindros LL............ 40.00 18.00
❑ 173 Dominik Hasek LL............ 25.00 11.00
❑ 174 Jaromir Jagr LL............ 40.00 18.00
❑ 175 Steve Yzerman LL............ 40.00 18.00
❑ 176 Martin Brodeur LL............ 30.00 13.50
❑ 177 Ray Bourque LL............ 15.00 6.75
❑ 178 Peter Forsberg LL............ 40.00 18.00
❑ 179 Paul Kariya LL............ 50.00 22.00
❑ 180 Wayne Gretzky LL............ 80.00 36.00
❑ S99 Wayne Gretzky SAMPLE. 6.00 2.70

## 1998-99 SPx Finite Radiance

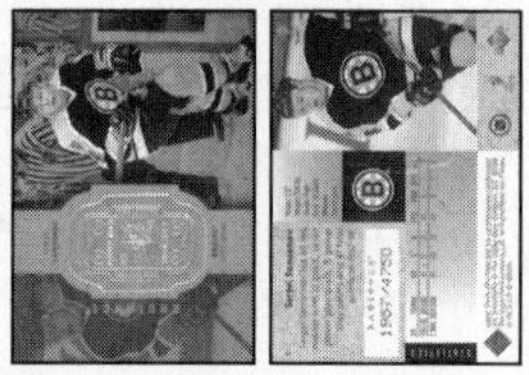

Sequentially numbered to 7000, this 180-card silver foil parallel features the same players as in the SPx Finite base set, but with an extra added altered technology.

MINT NRMT
COMPLETE SET (180)......... 2000.00 900.00
COMP.BASE SET (90)......... 200.00 90.00
COMMON CARD (1-90)......... 1.00 .45
COMP.GLOB.IMPACT.SET (30) 250.00 110.00
COMMON GLOB.IMP. (91-120) 1.50 .70
COMP.SURE SHOTS SET (30) 120.00 55.00
COMMON SURE SHOT (121-150) 2.50 1.10
COMP. MARQ.PERF.SET (20) 700.00 325.00
COMMON MARQ.PERF. (151-170) 12.00 5.50
COMP.LIVING.LEG.SET (10). 800.00 350.00
COMMON LIV.LEG. (171-180) 25.00 11.00

❑ 1 Teemu Selanne............ 6.00 2.70
❑ 5 Sergei Samsonov............ 5.00 2.20
❑ 8 Dominik Hasek............ 6.00 2.70
❑ 22 Joe Sakic............ 6.00 2.70
❑ 24 Patrick Roy............ 15.00 6.75
❑ 30 Steve Yzerman............ 10.00 4.50
❑ 32 Brendan Shanahan............ 6.00 2.70
❑ 40 Vladimir Tsyplakov............ 1.00 .45
❑ 46 Martin Brodeur............ 8.00 3.60
❑ 53 Wayne Gretzky............ 20.00 9.00
❑ 60 John LeClair............ 5.00 2.20
❑ 64 Keith Tkachuk............ 4.00 1.80
❑ 73 Patrick Marleau............ 1.00 .45
❑ 84 Pavel Bure............ 6.00 2.70
❑ 91 Pavel Bure GI............ 10.00 4.50
❑ 92 Joe Sakic GI............ 10.00 4.50
❑ 93 Steve Yzerman GI............ 15.00 6.75
❑ 94 Jaromir Jagr GI............ 15.00 6.75
❑ 95 Peter Forsberg GI............ 15.00 6.75
❑ 96 Brendan Shanahan GI............ 10.00 4.50
❑ 97 Brett Hull GI............ 6.00 2.70
❑ 99 Wayne Gretzky GI............ 30.00 13.50
❑ 100 Eric Lindros GI............ 15.00 6.75
❑ 101 Sergei Samsonov GI............ 8.00 3.60
❑ 102 John LeClair GI............ 8.00 3.60
❑ 103 Dominik Hasek GI............ 10.00 4.50
❑ 104 Teemu Selanne GI............ 10.00 4.50
❑ 105 Martin Brodeur GI............ 12.00 5.50
❑ 109 Mike Modano GI............ 6.00 2.70
❑ 115 Saku Koivu GI............ 8.00 3.60
❑ 116 Paul Kariya GI............ 20.00 9.00
❑ 119 Patrick Roy GI............ 25.00 11.00
❑ 121 Sergei Samsonov SS............ 15.00 6.75
❑ 130 Patrick Marleau SS............ 1.00 .45
❑ 133 Joe Thornton SS............ 1.00 .45
❑ 144 Norm Maracle SS............ 12.00 5.50
❑ 151 Wayne Gretzky MP............ 100.00 45.00
❑ 152 Eric Lindros MP............ 50.00 22.00
❑ 153 Paul Kariya MP............ 60.00 27.00
❑ 154 Patrick Roy MP............ 80.00 36.00
❑ 155 Sergei Samsonov MP............ 25.00 11.00
❑ 156 Steve Yzerman MP............ 50.00 22.00
❑ 157 Teemu Selanne MP............ 30.00 13.50
❑ 158 Brendan Shanahan MP............ 30.00 13.50
❑ 159 Dominik Hasek MP............ 30.00 13.50
❑ 160 Mark Messier MP............ 20.00 9.00
❑ 161 Martin Brodeur MP............ 40.00 18.00
❑ 163 Joe Sakic MP............ 30.00 13.50
❑ 164 John LeClair MP............ 25.00 11.00
❑ 165 Jaromir Jagr MP............ 50.00 22.00
❑ 166 Peter Forsberg MP............ 50.00 22.00
❑ 169 Mike Modano MP............ 20.00 9.00
❑ 170 Pavel Bure MP............ 30.00 13.50
❑ 171 Patrick Roy LL............ 120.00 55.00
❑ 172 Eric Lindros LL............ 80.00 36.00
❑ 173 Dominik Hasek LL............ 50.00 22.00
❑ 174 Jaromir Jagr LL............ 80.00 36.00
❑ 175 Steve Yzerman LL............ 80.00 36.00
❑ 176 Martin Brodeur LL............ 60.00 27.00
❑ 178 Peter Forsberg LL............ 80.00 36.00
❑ 179 Paul Kariya LL............ 100.00 45.00
❑ 180 Wayne Gretzky LL............ 150.00 70.00

## 1998-99 SPx Finite Spectrum

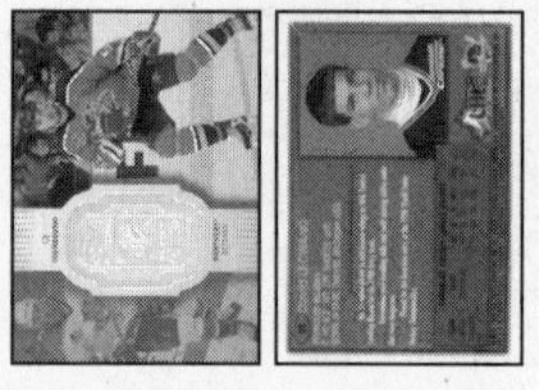

Sequentially numbered to 5500, this 180-card rainbow foil parallel again offers the same players as in the SPx Finite base set, but with an even further modified technology.

MINT NRMT
COMP.BASE SET (90)......... 2500.00 1100.00
COMMON CARD (1-90)......... 12.00 5.50
SEMISTARS/GOALIES......... 30.00 13.50
UNLISTED STARS......... 40.00 18.00
COMP.GLOB.IMPACT.SET (30) 3000.00 1350.00
COMMON GLOB.IMPACT (91-120) 15.00 6.75
GLOB.IMP.SEMIS/GOALIES.... 40.00 18.00
GLOB.IMP.UNLISTED STARS . 50.00 22.00
COMP.SURE SHOTS SET (30)
COMMON SURE SHOT (121-150) 25.00 11.00
SURE SHOT SEMISTARS/GOALIES 60.00 27.00
SURE SHOT UNLISTED STARS 80.00 36.00
COMP. MARQ.PERF.SET (20)
COMMON MARQ.PERF. (151-170) 150.00 70.00

❑ 1 Teemu Selanne............ 80.00 36.00
❑ 5 Sergei Samsonov............ 60.00 27.00
❑ 8 Dominik Hasek............ 80.00 36.00
❑ 22 Joe Sakic............ 80.00 36.00
❑ 24 Patrick Roy............ 200.00 90.00
❑ 30 Steve Yzerman............ 120.00 55.00
❑ 32 Brendan Shanahan............ 80.00 36.00
❑ 46 Martin Brodeur............ 100.00 45.00
❑ 53 Wayne Gretzky............ 250.00 110.00
❑ 60 John LeClair............ 60.00 27.00
❑ 64 Keith Tkachuk............ 50.00 22.00
❑ 73 Patrick Marleau............ 12.00 5.50
❑ 84 Pavel Bure............ 80.00 36.00
❑ 91 Pavel Bure GI............ 100.00 45.00
❑ 92 Joe Sakic GI............ 100.00 45.00
❑ 93 Steve Yzerman GI............ 150.00 70.00
❑ 94 Jaromir Jagr GI............ 150.00 70.00
❑ 95 Peter Forsberg GI............ 150.00 70.00
❑ 96 Brendan Shanahan GI............ 100.00 45.00
❑ 97 Brett Hull GI............ 60.00 27.00
❑ 99 Wayne Gretzky GI............ 300.00 135.00
❑ 100 Eric Lindros GI............ 150.00 70.00
❑ 101 Sergei Samsonov GI............ 80.00 36.00
❑ 102 John LeClair GI............ 80.00 36.00
❑ 103 Dominik Hasek GI............ 100.00 45.00
❑ 104 Teemu Selanne GI............ 100.00 45.00
❑ 105 Martin Brodeur GI............ 120.00 55.00
❑ 109 Mike Modano GI............ 60.00 27.00
❑ 115 Saku Koivu GI............ 80.00 36.00
❑ 116 Paul Kariya GI............ 200.00 90.00
❑ 119 Patrick Roy GI............ 250.00 110.00
❑ 121 Sergei Samsonov SS............ 120.00 55.00
❑ 130 Patrick Marleau SS............ 12.00 5.50
❑ 133 Joe Thornton SS............ 12.00 5.50
❑ 144 Norm Maracle SS............ 100.00 45.00
❑ 151 Wayne Gretzky MP............ 1000.00 450.00
❑ 152 Eric Lindros MP............ 500.00 220.00
❑ 153 Paul Kariya MP............ 600.00 275.00
❑ 154 Patrick Roy MP............ 800.00 350.00
❑ 155 Sergei Samsonov MP. 250.00 110.00
❑ 156 Steve Yzerman MP............ 500.00 220.00
❑ 157 Teemu Selanne MP............ 300.00 135.00
❑ 158 Brendan Shanahan MP 300.00 135.00
❑ 159 Dominik Hasek MP............ 300.00 135.00
❑ 160 Mark Messier MP............ 200.00 90.00
❑ 161 Martin Brodeur MP............ 400.00 180.00
❑ 163 Joe Sakic MP............ 300.00 135.00
❑ 164 John LeClair MP............ 250.00 110.00
❑ 165 Jaromir Jagr MP............ 500.00 220.00
❑ 166 Peter Forsberg MP............ 500.00 220.00
❑ 169 Mike Modano MP............ 200.00 90.00
❑ 170 Pavel Bure MP............ 300.00 135.00

## 1998-99 SPx Top Prospects

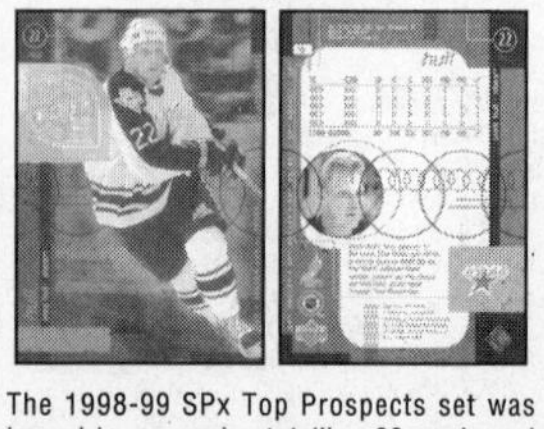

The 1998-99 SPx Top Prospects set was issued in one series totalling 90 cards and features action color player photos with player information on the backs. Only 1,999 of cards numbered 61-90 were printed. Cards numbered 79 and 80 were only available signed.

MINT NRMT
COMPLETE SET (90)............ 300.00 135.00
COMMON CARD (1-60)............ .30 .14
COMMON SP (61-90)............ 5.00 2.20

❑ 1 Paul Kariya............ 6.00 2.70
❑ 2 Teemu Selanne............ 3.00 1.35
❑ 3 Ray Bourque............ 1.50 .70
❑ 4 Sergei Samsonov............ 2.50 1.10
❑ 5 Joe Thornton............ .30 .14
❑ 6 Dominik Hasek............ 3.00 1.35
❑ 7 Theoren Fleury............ 1.50 .70
❑ 8 Keith Primeau............ 1.25 .55
❑ 9 Tony Amonte............ 1.25 .55
❑ 10 Doug Gilmour............ 1.50 .70
❑ 11 J.P. Dumont............ 1.50 .70
❑ 12 Chris Chelios............ 1.50 .70
❑ 13 Peter Forsberg............ 5.00 2.20
❑ 14 Patrick Roy............ 8.00 3.60
❑ 15 Joe Sakic............ 3.00 1.35
❑ 16 Milan Hedjuk............ 2.00 .90
❑ 17 Chris Drury............ 2.00 .90
❑ 18 Mike Modano............ 2.00 .90
❑ 19 Brett Hull............ 2.00 .90
❑ 20 Ed Belfour............ 1.50 .70
❑ 21 Steve Yzerman............ 5.00 2.20
❑ 22 Brendan Shanahan............ 3.00 1.35
❑ 23 Sergei Fedorov............ 3.00 1.35
❑ 24 Chris Osgood............ 1.50 .70
❑ 25 Nicklas Lidstrom............ 1.25 .55
❑ 26 Bill Guerin............ 1.25 .55
❑ 27 Doug Weight............ 1.25 .55
❑ 28 Tom Poti............ .30 .14
❑ 29 Mark Parrish............ 2.00 .90
❑ 30 Rob Blake............ 1.25 .55
❑ 31 Pavel Rosa............ 1.25 .55
❑ 32 Vincent Damphousse............ 1.25 .55
❑ 33 Saku Koivu............ 2.50 1.10
❑ 34 Mike Dunham............ 1.25 .55
❑ 35 Martin Brodeur............ 4.00 1.80
❑ 36 Zigmund Palffy............ 1.25 .55
❑ 37 Eric Brewer............ .30 .14
❑ 38 Wayne Gretzky............ 10.00 4.50
❑ 39 Brian Leetch............ 1.50 .70
❑ 40 Manny Malhotra............ 1.25 .55
❑ 41 Petr Nedved............ 1.25 .55
❑ 42 Alexei Yashin............ 1.25 .55
❑ 43 Eric Lindros............ 5.00 2.20
❑ 44 John LeClair............ 2.50 1.10
❑ 45 John Vanbiesbrouck............ 2.50 1.10
❑ 46 Keith Tkachuk............ 2.00 .90
❑ 47 Jeremy Roenick............ 1.50 .70
❑ 48 Daniel Briere............ .30 .14
❑ 49 Jaromir Jagr............ 5.00 2.20
❑ 50 Patrick Marleau............ .30 .14
❑ 51 Al MacInnis............ 1.25 .55
❑ 52 Chris Pronger............ 1.25 .55
❑ 53 Vincent Lecavalier............ 4.00 1.80
❑ 54 Curtis Joseph............ 1.50 .70
❑ 55 Mats Sundin............ 1.50 .70
❑ 56 Tomas Kaberle............ 1.25 .55
❑ 57 Mark Messier............ 2.00 .90
❑ 58 Pavel Bure............ 3.00 1.35
❑ 59 Bill Muckalt............ 1.50 .70
❑ 60 Peter Bondra............ 1.50 .70
❑ 61 Brian Finley SP............ 10.00 4.50
❑ 62 Roberto Luongo SP............ 8.00 3.60
❑ 63 Mike Van Ryn SP............ 5.00 2.20
❑ 64 Harold Druken SP............ 5.00 2.20
❑ 65 Daniel Tkaczuk SP............ 5.00 2.20
❑ 66 Brenden Morrow SP............ 6.00 2.70
❑ 67 Jani Rita SP............ 15.00 6.75
❑ 68 Tommi Santala SP............ 5.00 2.20
❑ 69 Teemu Virkkunen SP............ 5.00 2.20
❑ 70 Arto Laaktikainen SP............ 5.00 2.20
❑ 71 Ilkka Mikkola SP............ 5.00 2.20
❑ 72 Miko Jokela SP............ 5.00 2.20
❑ 73 Kirill Safronov SP............ 8.00 3.60
❑ 74 Denis Shvidky SP............ 6.00 2.70
❑ 75 Denis Arkhipov SP............ 6.00 2.70
❑ 76 Maxim Afinogenov SP............ 5.00 2.20
❑ 77 Alexander Zevakhin SP............ 5.00 2.20
❑ 78 Alexei Volkov SP............ 6.00 2.70
❑ 79 Daniel Sedin SP AU............ 60.00 27.00
❑ 80 Henrik Sedin SP AU............ 50.00 22.00
❑ 81 Jimmie Olvestad SP............ 5.00 2.20
❑ 82 Mattias Weinhandl SP............ 5.00 2.20
❑ 83 Mathias Tjarnqvist SP............ 5.00 2.20
❑ 84 Jakob Johansson SP............ 5.00 2.20
❑ 85 Barrett Heisten SP............ 5.00 2.20
❑ 86 Tim Connolly............ 12.00 5.50
❑ 87 Andy Hilbert SP............ 5.00 2.20
❑ 88 David Legwand SP............ 10.00 4.50
❑ 89 Joe Blackburn SP............ 5.00 2.20
❑ 90 Dave Tanabe SP............ 5.00 2.20

## 1998-99 SPx Top Prospects Radiance

Randomly inserted in Finite Radiance hot packs only, this 90-card set is parallel to the base SPx Top Prospects set and is crash numbered to 100. A crash numbered 1 of 1 Spectrum parallel was also available and found only in Finite Spectrum hot packs.

MINT NRMT
COMMON CARD (1-90)............ 12.00 5.50
*STARS: 20X TO 40X BASIC CARDS
*YOUNG STARS: 12.5X TO 25X
*SP's: 5X TO 10X
1/1 SPECTRUM PARALLEL AVAILABLE

❑ 79 Daniel Sedin AU............ 300.00 135.00
❑ 80 Henrik Sedin AU............ 250.00 110.00

## 1998-99 SPx Top Prospects Highlight Heroes

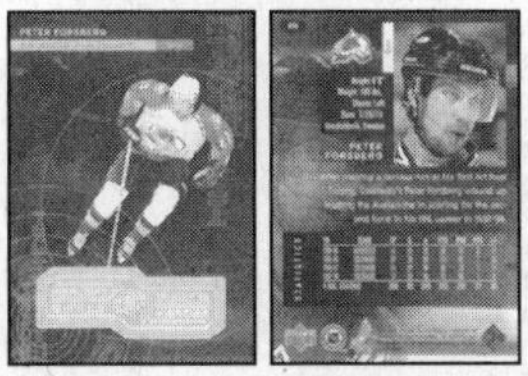

Randomly inserted in packs at the rate of one in eight, this 30-card set features action color photos of top NHL players who are most likely to appear on the nightly highlight reels.

| | MINT | NRMT |
|---|---|---|
| COMPLETE SET (30) | 200.00 | 90.00 |
| COMMON CARD (H1-H30) | 3.00 | 1.35 |
| ❑ H1 Paul Kariya | 15.00 | 6.75 |
| ❑ H2 Teemu Selanne | 8.00 | 3.60 |
| ❑ H3 Ray Bourque | 3.00 | 1.35 |
| ❑ H4 Sergei Samsonov | 6.00 | 2.70 |
| ❑ H5 Dominik Hasek | 8.00 | 3.60 |
| ❑ H6 Theoren Fleury | 3.00 | 1.35 |
| ❑ H7 Doug Gilmour | 3.00 | 1.35 |
| ❑ H8 Joe Sakic | 8.00 | 3.60 |
| ❑ H9 Patrick Roy | 20.00 | 9.00 |
| ❑ H10 Peter Forsberg | 12.00 | 5.50 |
| ❑ H11 Mike Modano | 4.00 | 1.80 |
| ❑ H12 Brett Hull | 4.00 | 1.80 |
| ❑ H13 Brendan Shanahan | 8.00 | 3.60 |
| ❑ H14 Steve Yzerman | 12.00 | 5.50 |
| ❑ H15 Sergei Fedorov | 8.00 | 3.60 |
| ❑ H16 Saku Koivu | 6.00 | 2.70 |
| ❑ H17 Martin Brodeur | 10.00 | 4.50 |
| ❑ H18 Wayne Gretzky | 25.00 | 11.00 |
| ❑ H19 Zigmund Palffy | 3.00 | 1.35 |
| ❑ H20 John Vanbiesbrouck | 6.00 | 2.70 |
| ❑ H21 Eric Lindros | 12.00 | 5.50 |
| ❑ H22 John LeClair | 6.00 | 2.70 |
| ❑ H23 Keith Tkachuk | 4.00 | 1.80 |
| ❑ H24 Jeremy Roenick | 3.00 | 1.35 |
| ❑ H25 Jaromir Jagr | 12.00 | 5.50 |
| ❑ H26 Vincent Lecavalier | 8.00 | 3.60 |
| ❑ H27 Mats Sundin | 3.00 | 1.35 |
| ❑ H28 Curtis Joseph | 3.00 | 1.35 |
| ❑ H29 Pavel Bure | 8.00 | 3.60 |
| ❑ H30 Peter Bondra | 3.00 | 1.35 |

## 1998-99 SPx Top Prospects Lasting Impressions

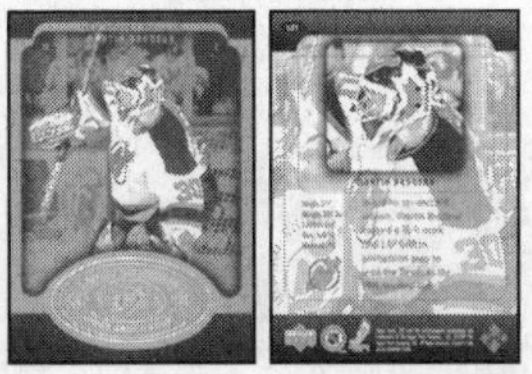

Randomly inserted into packs at the rate of one in three, this 30-card set features action color photos of some of the league's top players with player information on the backs.

| | MINT | NRMT |
|---|---|---|
| COMPLETE SET (30) | 120.00 | 55.00 |
| COMMON CARD (L1-L30) | 2.00 | .90 |
| ❑ L1 Vincent Lecavalier | 4.00 | 1.80 |
| ❑ L2 John Vanbiesbrouck | 3.00 | 1.35 |
| ❑ L3 Paul Kariya | 8.00 | 3.60 |
| ❑ L4 Keith Tkachuk | 2.50 | 1.10 |
| ❑ L5 Mike Modano | 2.50 | 1.10 |
| ❑ L6 Dominik Hasek | 4.00 | 1.80 |
| ❑ L7 Teemu Selanne | 4.00 | 1.80 |
| ❑ L8 Mats Sundin | 2.00 | .90 |
| ❑ L9 Brendan Shanahan | 4.00 | 1.80 |
| ❑ L10 Pavel Bure | 4.00 | 1.80 |
| ❑ L11 Theoren Fleury | 2.00 | .90 |
| ❑ L12 Curtis Joseph | 2.00 | .90 |
| ❑ L13 Joe Sakic | 4.00 | 1.80 |
| ❑ L14 Eric Lindros | 6.00 | 2.70 |
| ❑ L15 Peter Bondra | 2.00 | .90 |
| ❑ L16 Brett Hull | 2.50 | 1.10 |
| ❑ L17 Ray Bourque | 2.00 | .90 |
| ❑ L18 Jaromir Jagr | 6.00 | 2.70 |
| ❑ L19 Steve Yzerman | 6.00 | 2.70 |
| ❑ L20 Jeremy Roenick | 2.00 | .90 |
| ❑ L21 Martin Brodeur | 5.00 | 2.20 |
| ❑ L22 Saku Koivu | 3.00 | 1.35 |
| ❑ L23 Patrick Roy | 10.00 | 4.50 |
| ❑ L24 John LeClair | 3.00 | 1.35 |
| ❑ L25 Doug Gilmour | 2.00 | .90 |
| ❑ L26 Sergei Fedorov | 4.00 | 1.80 |
| ❑ L27 Wayne Gretzky | 12.00 | 5.50 |
| ❑ L28 Peter Forsberg | 6.00 | 2.70 |
| ❑ L29 Zigmund Palffy | 2.00 | .90 |
| ❑ L30 Sergei Samsonov | 3.00 | 1.35 |

## 1998-99 SPx Top Prospects Premier Stars

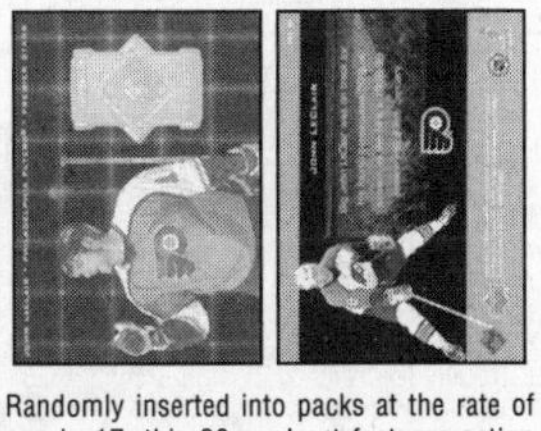

Randomly inserted into packs at the rate of one in 17, this 30-card set features action color photos of the NHL's most exciting and established players with player information on the backs.

| | MINT | NRMT |
|---|---|---|
| COMPLETE SET (30) | 400.00 | 180.00 |
| COMMON CARD (PS1-PS30) | 5.00 | 2.20 |
| ❑ PS1 Wayne Gretzky | 40.00 | 18.00 |
| ❑ PS2 Sergei Samsonov | 10.00 | 4.50 |
| ❑ PS3 Ray Bourque | 6.00 | 2.70 |
| ❑ PS4 Dominik Hasek | 12.00 | 5.50 |
| ❑ PS5 Martin Brodeur | 15.00 | 6.75 |
| ❑ PS6 Brian Leetch | 6.00 | 2.70 |
| ❑ PS7 Mike Richter | 6.00 | 2.70 |
| ❑ PS8 Eric Lindros | 20.00 | 9.00 |
| ❑ PS9 John LeClair | 10.00 | 4.50 |
| ❑ PS10 John Vanbiesbrouck | 10.00 | 4.50 |
| ❑ PS11 Jaromir Jagr | 20.00 | 9.00 |
| ❑ PS12 Vincent Lecavalier | 12.00 | 5.50 |
| ❑ PS13 Mats Sundin | 6.00 | 2.70 |
| ❑ PS14 Curtis Joseph | 6.00 | 2.70 |
| ❑ PS15 Peter Bondra | 6.00 | 2.70 |
| ❑ PS16 Wayne Gretzky | 40.00 | 18.00 |
| ❑ PS17 Teemu Selanne | 12.00 | 5.50 |
| ❑ PS18 Paul Kariya | 25.00 | 11.00 |
| ❑ PS19 Theoren Fleury | 6.00 | 2.70 |
| ❑ PS20 Tony Amonte | 5.00 | 2.20 |
| ❑ PS21 Patrick Roy | 30.00 | 13.50 |
| ❑ PS22 Joe Sakic | 12.00 | 5.50 |
| ❑ PS23 Peter Forsberg | 20.00 | 9.00 |
| ❑ PS24 Mike Modano | 8.00 | 3.60 |
| ❑ PS25 Brett Hull | 8.00 | 3.60 |
| ❑ PS26 Steve Yzerman | 20.00 | 9.00 |
| ❑ PS27 Brendan Shanahan | 12.00 | 5.50 |
| ❑ PS28 Doug Weight | 5.00 | 2.20 |
| ❑ PS29 Keith Tkachuk | 8.00 | 3.60 |
| ❑ PS30 Mark Messier | 8.00 | 3.60 |

## 1998-99 SPx Top Prospects Winning Materials

Randomly inserted into packs at the rate of one in 251, this 12-card set features color player photos with pieces of the pictured player's game-used jersey and stick cut and affixed to the card.

| | MINT | NRMT |
|---|---|---|
| COMPLETE SET (12) | 3000.00 | 1350.00 |
| COMMON CARD | 150.00 | 70.00 |
| ❑ CJ Curtis Joseph | 200.00 | 90.00 |
| ❑ CO Chris Osgood | 200.00 | 90.00 |
| ❑ EL Eric Lindros | 300.00 | 135.00 |
| ❑ FP Felix Potvin | 150.00 | 70.00 |
| ❑ JJ Jaromir Jagr | 300.00 | 135.00 |
| ❑ JL John LeClair | 250.00 | 110.00 |
| ❑ JS Joe Sakic | 300.00 | 135.00 |
| ❑ JV John Vanbiesbrouck | 200.00 | 90.00 |
| ❑ MR Mike Richter | 175.00 | 80.00 |
| ❑ MS Mats Sundin | 175.00 | 80.00 |
| ❑ PR Patrick Roy | 400.00 | 180.00 |
| ❑ RB Ray Bourque | 200.00 | 90.00 |

## 1998-99 SPx Top Prospects Year of the Great One

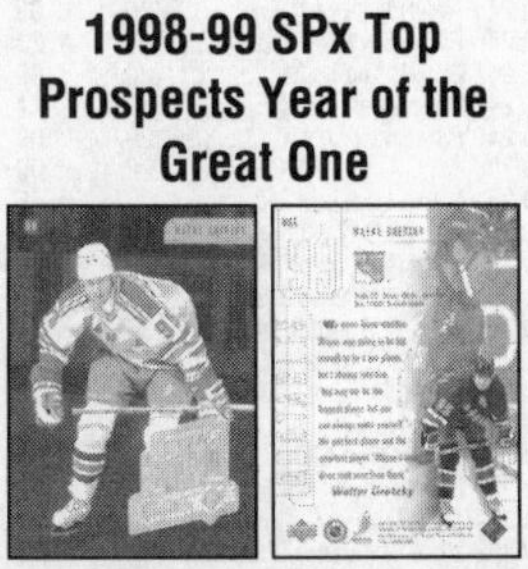

Randomly inserted into packs at the rate of one in 17, this 30-card set features unique photos of Wayne Gretzky with notable quotes about his career from his father, various coaches, NHL greats and former teammates.

| | MINT | NRMT |
|---|---|---|
| COMPLETE SET (30) | 300.00 | 135.00 |
| COMMON CARD (WG1-WG30) | 12.00 | 5.50 |

## 1992 Sport-Flash

This 15-card standard-size set was produced by Sport-Flash as the first series of "Hockey

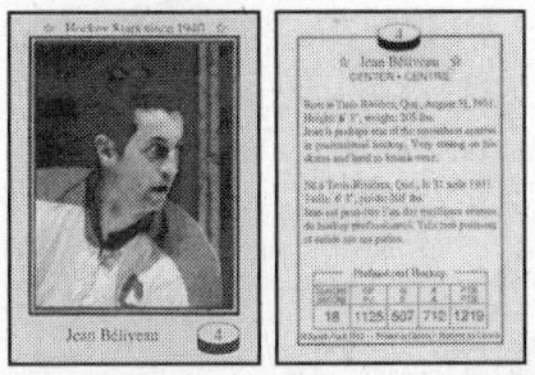

Stars since 1940". The accompanying certification of limited edition claims that the production run was 200,000 sets. Each set contained one autographed hockey card signed by the player. On a bright yellow card face, the fronts display close-up color photos enclosed by blue and black border stripes. The player's name appears in the bottom yellow border. The backs are bilingual and present biography, player profile, and career statistics. The cards are numbered on both sides. Autographed cards are valued at five to eight times the prices below.

| | MINT | NRMT |
|---|---|---|
| COMPLETE SET (15) | 10.00 | 4.50 |
| COMMON CARD (1-15) | .10 | .05 |
| ❑ 1 Jacques Laperriere | .60 | .25 |
| ❑ 2 Larry Carriere | .50 | .23 |
| ❑ 3 Chuck Rayner | .75 | .35 |
| ❑ 4 Jean Beliveau | 2.00 | .90 |
| ❑ 5 BoomBoom Geoffrion | 1.50 | .70 |
| ❑ 6 Gilles Gilbert | .75 | .35 |
| ❑ 7 Marcel Bonin | .50 | .23 |
| ❑ 8 Leon Rochefort | .50 | .23 |
| ❑ 9 Maurice Richard | 3.00 | 1.35 |
| ❑ 10 Rejean Houle | .50 | .23 |
| ❑ 11 Pierre Mondou | .50 | .23 |
| ❑ 12 Yvan Cournoyer | .75 | .35 |
| ❑ 13 Henri Richard | 1.00 | .45 |
| ❑ 14 Checklist Card | .10 | .05 |
| ❑ 15 Certification of Limited Edition | .10 | .05 |

## 1991-92 Stadium Club

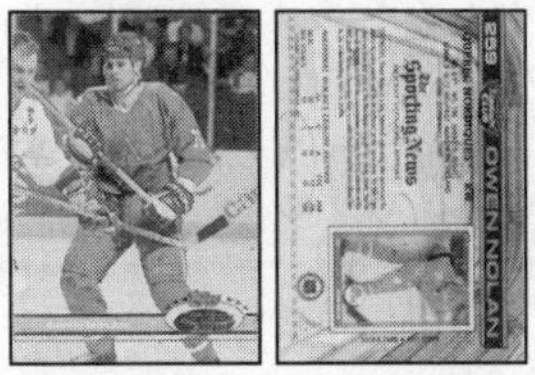

The 1991-92 Topps Stadium Club hockey set contains 400 standard-size cards. The fronts feature full-bleed glossy color player photos. At the bottom, the player's name appears in an aqua stripe that is bordered in gold. In the lower left or right corner the Stadium Club logo overlays the stripe. Against the background of a colorful drawing of a hockey rink, the horizontally oriented backs have a biography, The Sporting News Hockey Scouting Report (which consists of strengths and evaluative comments), statistics (last season and career totals), and a miniature photo of the player's first Topps card. There are many cards in the set that can be found with or without "The Sporting News" on the card back; these variations (no added premium) are 13, 16, 22, 46, 50, 60, 68, 149, 190, 204, 230, 249, 264, 276, 297, 298, 307, 320, 332, 339, 341, 342, 348, 351, and 362. There are no key Rookie Cards in this set.

| | MINT | NRMT |
|---|---|---|
| COMPLETE SET (400) | 25.00 | 11.00 |
| COMMON CARD (1-400) | .10 | .05 |
| ❑ 1 Wayne Gretzky | 2.50 | 1.10 |
| ❑ 2 Randy Moller | .10 | .05 |
| ❑ 3 Ray Ferraro | .10 | .05 |
| ❑ 4 Craig Wolanin | .10 | .05 |
| ❑ 5 Shayne Corson | .10 | .05 |
| ❑ 6 Chris Chelios | .40 | .18 |
| ❑ 7 Joe Mullen | .25 | .11 |
| ❑ 8 Ken Wregget | .25 | .11 |
| ❑ 9 Rob Cimetta | .10 | .05 |
| ❑ 10 Mike Liut | .25 | .11 |
| ❑ 11 Martin Gelinas | .10 | .05 |
| ❑ 12 Mario Marois | .10 | .05 |
| ❑ 13 Rick Vaive | .10 | .05 |
| ❑ 14 Brad McCrimmon | .10 | .05 |
| ❑ 15 Mark Hunter | .10 | .05 |
| ❑ 16 Jim Wiemer | .10 | .05 |
| ❑ 17 Sergio Momesso | .10 | .05 |
| ❑ 18 Claude Lemieux | .25 | .11 |
| ❑ 19 Brian Hayward | .25 | .11 |
| ❑ 20 Pat Flatley | .10 | .05 |
| ❑ 21 Mark Osborne | .10 | .05 |
| ❑ 22 Mike Hudson | .10 | .05 |
| ❑ 23 Rejean Lemelin | .25 | .11 |
| ❑ 24 Slava Fetisov | .10 | .05 |
| ❑ 25 Bobby Smith | .25 | .11 |
| ❑ 26 Kris King | .10 | .05 |
| ❑ 27 Randy Velischek | .10 | .05 |
| ❑ 28 Steve Bozek | .10 | .05 |
| ❑ 29 Mike Foligno | .10 | .05 |
| ❑ 30 Scott Arniel | .10 | .05 |
| ❑ 31 Sergei Makarov | .10 | .05 |
| ❑ 32 Rick Zombo | .10 | .05 |
| ❑ 33 Christian Ruuttu | .10 | .05 |
| ❑ 34 Gino Cavallini | .10 | .05 |
| ❑ 35 Rick Tocchet | .25 | .11 |
| ❑ 36 Jiri Hrdina | .10 | .05 |
| ❑ 37 Peter Bondra | .40 | .18 |
| ❑ 38 Craig Ludwig | .10 | .05 |
| ❑ 39 Mikael Andersson | .10 | .05 |
| ❑ 40 Bob Kudelski | .10 | .05 |
| ❑ 41 Guy Carbonneau | .25 | .11 |
| ❑ 42 Geoff Smith | .10 | .05 |
| ❑ 43 Russ Courtnall | .10 | .05 |
| ❑ 44 Michal Pivonka | .10 | .05 |
| ❑ 45 Todd Krygier | .10 | .05 |
| ❑ 46 Jeremy Roenick | .50 | .23 |
| ❑ 47 Doug Brown | .10 | .05 |
| ❑ 48 Paul Cavallini | .10 | .05 |
| ❑ 49 Ron Sutter | .10 | .05 |
| ❑ 50 Paul Ranheim | .10 | .05 |
| ❑ 51 Mike Gartner | .25 | .11 |
| ❑ 52 Greg Adams | .10 | .05 |
| ❑ 53 Dave Capuano | .10 | .05 |
| ❑ 54 Mike Krushelnyski | .10 | .05 |
| ❑ 55 Ulf Dahlen | .10 | .05 |
| ❑ 56 Steven Finn | .10 | .05 |
| ❑ 57 Ed Olczyk | .10 | .05 |
| ❑ 58 Steve Duchesne | .10 | .05 |
| ❑ 59 Bob Probert | .25 | .11 |
| ❑ 60 Joe Nieuwendyk | .25 | .11 |
| ❑ 61 Petr Klima | .10 | .05 |
| ❑ 62 Uwe Krupp | .10 | .05 |
| ❑ 63 Jay Miller | .10 | .05 |
| ❑ 64 Cam Neely | .25 | .11 |
| ❑ 65 Phil Housley | .25 | .11 |
| ❑ 66 Michel Goulet | .25 | .11 |
| ❑ 67 Brett Hull | .60 | .25 |
| ❑ 68 Mike Ridley | .10 | .05 |
| ❑ 69 Esa Tikkanen | .10 | .05 |
| ❑ 70 Kjell Samuelsson | .10 | .05 |
| ❑ 71 Corey Millen | .10 | .05 |
| ❑ 72 Doug Lidster | .10 | .05 |
| ❑ 73 Ron Francis | .25 | .11 |
| ❑ 74 Scott Young | .10 | .05 |
| ❑ 75 Bob Sweeney | .10 | .05 |
| ❑ 76 Sean Burke | .25 | .11 |
| ❑ 77 Pierre Turgeon | .25 | .11 |
| ❑ 78 David Reid | .10 | .05 |
| ❑ 79 Al MacInnis | .25 | .11 |
| ❑ 80 Mike Hough | .10 | .05 |
| ❑ 81 Steve Yzerman | 1.00 | .45 |
| ❑ 82 Derek King | .10 | .05 |
| ❑ 83 Brad Shaw | .10 | .05 |
| ❑ 84 Trevor Linden | .25 | .11 |
| ❑ 85 Rick Meagher | .10 | .05 |
| ❑ 86 Stephane Richer | .25 | .11 |
| ❑ 87 Brian Bellows | .10 | .05 |
| ❑ 88 Pete Peeters | .25 | .11 |
| ❑ 89 Adam Creighton | .10 | .05 |
| ❑ 90 Brent Ashton | .10 | .05 |
| ❑ 91 Bryan Trottier | .25 | .11 |
| ❑ 92 Mike Richter | .50 | .23 |
| ❑ 93 Dave Andreychuk | .25 | .11 |
| ❑ 94 Randy Carlyle | .10 | .05 |
| ❑ 95 Dave Christian | .10 | .05 |
| ❑ 96 Doug Gilmour | .40 | .18 |
| ❑ 97 Tony Granato | .10 | .05 |
| ❑ 98 Jeff Norton | .10 | .05 |
| ❑ 99 Neal Broten | .25 | .11 |
| ❑ 100 Jody Hull | .10 | .05 |
| ❑ 101 Shawn Burr | .10 | .05 |
| ❑ 102 Pat Verbeek | .10 | .05 |
| ❑ 103 Ken Daneyko | .10 | .05 |
| ❑ 104 Peter Zezel | .10 | .05 |
| ❑ 105 Kirk McLean | .25 | .11 |
| ❑ 106 Kelly Miller | .10 | .05 |
| ❑ 107 Patrick Roy | 2.00 | .90 |
| ❑ 108 Adam Oates | .25 | .11 |
| ❑ 109 Steve Thomas | .10 | .05 |
| ❑ 110 Scott Mellanby | .25 | .11 |
| ❑ 111 Mark Messier | .60 | .25 |
| ❑ 112 Larry Murphy | .25 | .11 |
| ❑ 113 Mark Janssens | .10 | .05 |
| ❑ 114 Doug Bodger | .10 | .05 |
| ❑ 115 Ron Tugnutt | .25 | .11 |
| ❑ 116 Glenn Anderson | .25 | .11 |
| ❑ 117 Dave Gagner | .25 | .11 |
| ❑ 118 Dino Ciccarelli | .25 | .11 |
| ❑ 119 Randy Burridge | .10 | .05 |
| ❑ 120 Kelly Hrudey | .25 | .11 |
| ❑ 121 Jimmy Carson | .10 | .05 |
| ❑ 122 Bruce Driver | .10 | .05 |
| ❑ 123 Pat LaFontaine | .25 | .11 |
| ❑ 124 Wendel Clark | .25 | .11 |
| ❑ 125 Peter Sidorkiewicz | .25 | .11 |
| ❑ 126 Gary Roberts | .10 | .05 |
| ❑ 127 Petr Svoboda | .10 | .05 |
| ❑ 128 Vincent Riendeau | .25 | .11 |
| ❑ 129 Brian Skrudland | .10 | .05 |
| ❑ 130 Tim Kerr | .10 | .05 |
| ❑ 131 Doug Wilson | .25 | .11 |
| ❑ 132 Pat Elynuik | .10 | .05 |
| ❑ 133 Craig MacTavish | .10 | .05 |
| ❑ 134 Troy Mallette | .10 | .05 |
| ❑ 135 Mike Ramsey | .10 | .05 |
| ❑ 136 Tony Hrkac | .10 | .05 |
| ❑ 137 Craig Simpson | .10 | .05 |
| ❑ 138 Jon Casey | .25 | .11 |
| ❑ 139 Steve Kasper | .10 | .05 |
| ❑ 140 Kevin Hatcher | .10 | .05 |
| ❑ 141 Dave Barr | .10 | .05 |
| ❑ 142 Brad Lauer | .10 | .05 |
| ❑ 143 Gary Suter | .10 | .05 |
| ❑ 144 John MacLean | .25 | .11 |
| ❑ 145 Dean Evason | .10 | .05 |
| ❑ 146 Vincent Damphousse | .25 | .11 |
| ❑ 147 Craig Janney | .25 | .11 |
| ❑ 148 Jeff Brown | .10 | .05 |
| ❑ 149 Geoff Courtnall | .10 | .05 |
| ❑ 150 Igor Larionov | .10 | .05 |
| ❑ 151 Jan Erixon | .10 | .05 |
| ❑ 152 Bob Essensa | .25 | .11 |
| ❑ 153 Gaetan Duchesne | .10 | .05 |
| ❑ 154 Jyrki Lumme | .10 | .05 |
| ❑ 155 Tom Barrasso | .25 | .11 |
| ❑ 156 Curtis Leschyshyn | .10 | .05 |
| ❑ 157 Benoit Hogue | .10 | .05 |
| ❑ 158 Gary Leeman | .10 | .05 |
| ❑ 159 Luc Robitaille | .25 | .11 |
| ❑ 160 Jamie Macoun | .10 | .05 |
| ❑ 161 Bob Carpenter | .10 | .05 |
| ❑ 162 Kevin Dineen | .10 | .05 |
| ❑ 163 Gary Nylund | .10 | .05 |
| ❑ 164 Dale Hunter | .10 | .05 |
| ❑ 165 Gerard Gallant | .10 | .05 |
| ❑ 166 Jacques Cloutier | .25 | .11 |
| ❑ 167 Troy Murray | .10 | .05 |
| ❑ 168 Phil Bourque | .10 | .05 |
| ❑ 169 Grant Ledyard | .10 | .05 |
| ❑ 170 Joel Otto | .10 | .05 |
| ❑ 171 Paul Ysebaert UER (Photo actually Mike Sillinger) | .10 | .05 |
| ❑ 172 Luke Richardson | .10 | .05 |
| ❑ 173 Ron Hextall | .25 | .11 |
| ❑ 174 Mario Lemieux | 2.00 | .90 |
| ❑ 175 Garry Galley | .10 | .05 |
| ❑ 176 Murray Craven | .10 | .05 |
| ❑ 177 Walt Poddubny | .10 | .05 |
| ❑ 178 Scott Pearson | .10 | .05 |
| ❑ 179 Kevin Lowe | .10 | .05 |
| ❑ 180 Brent Sutter | .10 | .05 |
| ❑ 181 Dirk Graham | .10 | .05 |
| ❑ 182 Pelle Eklund | .10 | .05 |
| ❑ 183 Sylvain Cote | .10 | .05 |
| ❑ 184 Rod Brind'Amour | .25 | .11 |
| ❑ 185 Fredrik Olausson | .10 | .05 |
| ❑ 186 Kelly Kisio | .10 | .05 |
| ❑ 187 Mike Modano | .50 | .23 |
| ❑ 188 Calle Johansson | .10 | .05 |
| ❑ 189 John Tonelli | .10 | .05 |
| ❑ 190 Glen Wesley | .10 | .05 |
| ❑ 191 Bob Errey | .10 | .05 |
| ❑ 192 Rich Sutter | .10 | .05 |
| ❑ 193 Kirk Muller | .10 | .05 |
| ❑ 194 Rob Zettler | .10 | .05 |
| ❑ 195 Alexander Mogilny | .50 | .23 |
| ❑ 196 Adrien Plavsic | .10 | .05 |
| ❑ 197 Daniel Marois | .10 | .05 |
| ❑ 198 Yves Racine | .10 | .05 |
| ❑ 199 Brendan Shanahan | .75 | .35 |
| ❑ 200 Rob Brown | .10 | .05 |
| ❑ 201 Brian Leetch | .40 | .18 |
| ❑ 202 Dave McLlwain | .10 | .05 |
| ❑ 203 Charlie Huddy | .10 | .05 |
| ❑ 204 David Volek | .10 | .05 |
| ❑ 205 Trent Yawney | .10 | .05 |
| ❑ 206 Brian MacLellan | .10 | .05 |
| ❑ 207 Thomas Steen | .10 | .05 |
| ❑ 208 Sylvain Lefebvre | .10 | .05 |
| ❑ 209 Tomas Sandstrom | .10 | .05 |
| ❑ 210 Mike McPhee | .10 | .05 |
| ❑ 211 Andy Moog | .25 | .11 |
| ❑ 212 Paul Coffey | .40 | .18 |
| ❑ 213 Denis Savard | .25 | .11 |
| ❑ 214 Eric Desjardins | .10 | .05 |
| ❑ 215 Wayne Presley | .10 | .05 |
| ❑ 216 Stephane Morin UER (Photo actually Jeff Jackson) | .10 | .05 |
| ❑ 217 Ric Nattress | .10 | .05 |
| ❑ 218 Troy Gamble | .25 | .11 |
| ❑ 219 Terry Carkner | .10 | .05 |
| ❑ 220 Dave Hannan | .10 | .05 |
| ❑ 221 Randy Wood | .10 | .05 |
| ❑ 222 Brian Mullen | .10 | .05 |
| ❑ 223 Garth Butcher | .10 | .05 |
| ❑ 224 Tim Cheveldae | .25 | .11 |
| ❑ 225 Rod Langway | .10 | .05 |
| ❑ 226 Stephen Leach | .10 | .05 |
| ❑ 227 Perry Berezan | .10 | .05 |
| ❑ 228 Zarley Zalapski | .10 | .05 |
| ❑ 229 Patrik Sundstrom | .10 | .05 |
| ❑ 230 Steve Smith | .10 | .05 |
| ❑ 231 Daren Puppa | .25 | .11 |
| ❑ 232 Dave Taylor | .25 | .11 |
| ❑ 233 Ray Bourque | .40 | .18 |
| ❑ 234 Kevin Stevens | .10 | .05 |
| ❑ 235 Frank Musil | .10 | .05 |
| ❑ 236 Mike Keane | .10 | .05 |
| ❑ 237 Brian Propp | .10 | .05 |
| ❑ 238 Brent Fedyk | .10 | .05 |
| ❑ 239 Rob Ramage | .10 | .05 |
| ❑ 240 Robert Kron | .10 | .05 |
| ❑ 241 Mike McNeil | .10 | .05 |
| ❑ 242 Greg Gilbert | .10 | .05 |
| ❑ 243 Dan Quinn | .10 | .05 |
| ❑ 244 Chris Nilan | .10 | .05 |
| ❑ 245 Bernie Nicholls | .25 | .11 |
| ❑ 246 Don Beaupre | .25 | .11 |
| ❑ 247 Keith Acton | .10 | .05 |
| ❑ 248 Gord Murphy | .10 | .05 |
| ❑ 249 Bill Ranford | .25 | .11 |
| ❑ 250 Dave Chyzowski | .10 | .05 |
| ❑ 251 Clint Malarchuk | .25 | .11 |
| ❑ 252 Larry Robinson | .25 | .11 |
| ❑ 253 Dave Poulin | .10 | .05 |
| ❑ 254 Paul MacDermid | .10 | .05 |
| ❑ 255 Doug Smail | .10 | .05 |
| ❑ 256 Mark Recchi | .25 | .11 |
| ❑ 257 Brian Bradley | .10 | .05 |

❑ 258 Grant Fuhr .25 .11
❑ 259 Owen Nolan .25 .11
❑ 260 Hubie McDonough .10 .05
❑ 261 Mikko Makela .10 .05
❑ 262 Mathieu Schneider .10 .05
❑ 263 Peter Stastny .25 .11
❑ 264 Jim Hrivnak .25 .11
❑ 265 Scott Stevens .25 .11
❑ 266 Mike Tomlak .10 .05
❑ 267 Marty McSorley .10 .05
❑ 268 Johan Garpenlov .10 .05
❑ 269 Mike Vernon .25 .11
❑ 270 Steve Larmer .25 .11
❑ 271 Phil Sykes .10 .05
❑ 272 Jay Mazur .10 .05
❑ 273 John Ogrodnick .10 .05
❑ 274 Dave Ellett .10 .05
❑ 275 Randy Gilhen .10 .05
❑ 276 Tom Chorske .10 .05
❑ 277 James Patrick .10 .05
❑ 278 Darin Kimble .10 .05
❑ 279 Paul Cyr .10 .05
❑ 280 Petr Nedved .25 .11
❑ 281 Tony McKegney .10 .05
❑ 282 Alexei Kasatonov .10 .05
❑ 283 Stephen Lebeau .10 .05
❑ 284 Everett Sanipass .10 .05
❑ 285 Tony Tanti .10 .05
❑ 286 Kevin Miller .10 .05
❑ 287 Moe Mantha .10 .05
❑ 288 Alan May .10 .05
❑ 289 John Cullen .10 .05
❑ 290 Daniel Berthiaume .25 .11
❑ 291 Mark Pederson .10 .05
❑ 292 Laurie Boschman .10 .05
❑ 293 Neil Wilkinson .10 .05
❑ 294 Rick Wamsley .25 .11
❑ 295 Ken Linseman .10 .05
❑ 296 Jamie Leach .10 .05
❑ 297 Chris Terreri .25 .11
❑ 298 Cliff Ronning .10 .05
❑ 299 Bobby Holik .10 .05
❑ 300 Mats Sundin .50 .23
❑ 301 Carey Wilson .10 .05
❑ 302 Teppo Numminen .10 .05
❑ 303 Dave Lowry .10 .05
❑ 304 Joe Reekie .10 .05
❑ 305 Keith Primeau .25 .11
❑ 306 David Shaw .10 .05
❑ 307 Nick Kypreos .10 .05
❑ 308 Dave Manson .10 .05
❑ 309 Mick Vukota .10 .05
❑ 310 Todd Flik .10 .05
❑ 311 Michel Petit .10 .05
❑ 312 Dale Hawerchuk .25 .11
❑ 313 Joe Murphy .10 .05
❑ 314 Chris Dahlquist .10 .05
❑ 315 Petri Skriko .10 .05
❑ 316 Sergei Fedorov .75 .35
❑ 317 Lee Norwood .10 .05
❑ 318 Garry Valk .10 .05
❑ 319 Glen Featherstone .10 .05
❑ 320 Dave Snuggerud .10 .05
❑ 321 Doug Evans .10 .05
❑ 322 Marc Bureau .10 .05
❑ 323 John Vanbiesbrouck .60 .25
❑ 324 John McIntyre .10 .05
❑ 325 Wes Walz .10 .05
❑ 326 Daryl Reaugh .10 .05
❑ 327 Paul Fenton .10 .05
❑ 328 Ulf Samuelsson .10 .05
❑ 329 Andrew Cassels .10 .05
❑ 330 Alexei Gusarov .10 .05
❑ 331 John Druce .10 .05
❑ 332 Adam Graves .25 .11
❑ 333 Ed Belfour .50 .23
❑ 334 Murray Baron .10 .05
❑ 335 John Tucker .10 .05
❑ 336 Todd Gill .10 .05
❑ 337 Martin Hostak .10 .05
❑ 338 Gino Odjick .10 .05
❑ 339 Eric Weinrich .10 .05
❑ 340 Todd Ewen .10 .05
❑ 341 Mike Hartman .10 .05
❑ 342 Danton Cole .10 .05
❑ 343 Jaromir Jagr 1.25 .55
❑ 344 Mike Craig .10 .05
❑ 345 Mark Fitzpatrick .25 .11
❑ 346 Darren Turcotte .10 .05
❑ 347 Ron Wilson .10 .05
❑ 348 Rob Blake .25 .11
❑ 349 Dale Kushner .10 .05
❑ 350 Jeff Beukeboom .10 .05
❑ 351 Tim Bergland .10 .05
❑ 352 Peter Ing .25 .11
❑ 353 Wayne McBean .10 .05
❑ 354 Jim McKenzie .10 .05
❑ 355 Theoren Fleury .25 .11
❑ 356 Jocelyn Lemieux .10 .05
❑ 357 Ken Hodge Jr. .10 .05
❑ 358 Shawn Anderson .10 .05
❑ 359 Dimitri Khristich .10 .05
❑ 360 Jon Morris .10 .05
❑ 361 Darrin Shannon .10 .05
❑ 362 Chris Joseph .10 .05
❑ 363 Normand Lacombe .10 .05
❑ 364 Frank Pietrangelo .25 .11
❑ 365 Joey Kocur .10 .05
❑ 366 Anatoli Semenov .10 .05
❑ 367 Bob Bassen .10 .05
❑ 368 Brad Jones .10 .05
❑ 369 Glenn Healy .25 .11
❑ 370 Don Sweeney .10 .05
❑ 371 Brad Dalgarno .10 .05
❑ 372 Al Iafrate .25 .11
❑ 373 Patrick Lebeau UER .10 .05
(Photo actually
Brent Gilchrist)
❑ 374 Terry Yake .10 .05
❑ 375 Roger Johansson .10 .05
❑ 376 Paul Broten .10 .05
❑ 377 Andre Racicot .25 .11
❑ 378 Scott Thornton .10 .05
❑ 379 Zdeno Ciger .10 .05
❑ 380 Paul Stanton .10 .05
❑ 381 Ray Sheppard .25 .11
❑ 382 Kevin Haller .10 .05
❑ 383 Vladimir Ruzicka .10 .05
❑ 384 Bryan Marchment .10 .05
❑ 385 Bill Berg .10 .05
❑ 386 Mike Ricci .10 .05
❑ 387 Pat Conacher .10 .05
❑ 388 Brian Glynn .10 .05
❑ 389 Joe Sakic .75 .35
❑ 390 Mikhail Tatarinov .10 .05
❑ 391 Stephane Matteau .10 .05
❑ 392 Mark Tinordi .10 .05
❑ 393 Robert Reichel .10 .05
❑ 394 Tim Sweeney .10 .05
❑ 395 Rick Tabaracci .25 .11
❑ 396 Ken Sabourin .10 .05
❑ 397 Jeff Lazaro .10 .05
❑ 398 Checklist 1-133 .10 .05
❑ 399 Checklist 134-266 .10 .05
❑ 400 Checklist 267-400 .10 .05

## 1992-93 Stadium Club

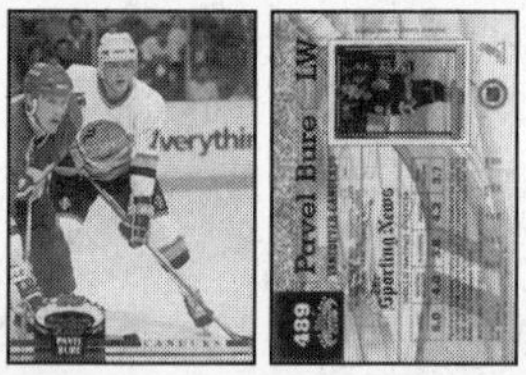

This 501-card standard-size set features full-bleed color action player photos. The Stadium Club logo appears at the bottom and intersects a gold foil double stripe carrying the team name. The horizontal backs show an artist's rendering of a hockey rink as the background. A mini-reproduction of the player's first Topps card is shown as well as biography, statistics, and The Sporting News Skills Rating System. The Members Choice (241-250 and 251-260) subsets, showing full-bleed color photos, closes the first series and opens the second series. These backs have the same art work background with 1991-92 season statistics. The only notable Rookie Card is Guy Hebert.

| | MINT | NRMT |
|---|---|---|
| COMPLETE SET (501) | 20.00 | 9.00 |
| COMPLETE SERIES 1 (250) | 10.00 | 4.50 |
| COMPLETE SERIES 2 (251) | 10.00 | 4.50 |
| COMMON CARD (1-501) | .10 | .05 |

❑ 1 Brett Hull .50 .23
❑ 2 Theoren Fleury .20 .09
❑ 3 Joe Sakic .60 .25
❑ 4 Mike Modano .40 .18
❑ 5 Dmitri Mironov .10 .05
❑ 6 Yves Racine .10 .05
❑ 7 Igor Kravchuk .10 .05
❑ 8 Philippe Bozon .10 .05
❑ 9 Stephane Richer .20 .09
❑ 10 Dave Lowry .10 .05
❑ 11 Dean Evason .10 .05
❑ 12 Mark Fitzpatrick .20 .09
❑ 13 Dave Poulin .10 .05
❑ 14 Phil Housley .20 .09
❑ 15 Adrien Plavsic .10 .05
❑ 16 Claude Boivin .10 .05
❑ 17 Bill Guerin .10 .05
❑ 18 Wayne Gretzky 2.00 .90
❑ 19 Steve Yzerman 1.00 .45
❑ 20 Joe Mullen .20 .09
❑ 21 Brad McCrimmon .10 .05
❑ 22 Dan Quinn .10 .05
❑ 23 Rob Blake .20 .09
❑ 24 Wayne Presley .10 .05
❑ 25 Zarley Zalapski .10 .05
❑ 26 Bryan Trottier .20 .09
❑ 27 Peter Sidorkiewicz .20 .09
❑ 28 John MacLean .20 .09
❑ 29 Brad Schlegel .10 .05
❑ 30 Marc Bureau .10 .05
❑ 31 Troy Murray .10 .05
❑ 32 Tony Amonte .20 .09
❑ 33 Rob DiMaio .10 .05
❑ 34 Joe Murphy .10 .05
❑ 35 Jim Waite .20 .09
❑ 36 Ron Sutter .10 .05
❑ 37 Joe Nieuwendyk .20 .09
❑ 38 Kevin Haller .10 .05
❑ 39 Andrew Cassels .10 .05
❑ 40 Dale Hunter .10 .05
❑ 41 Craig Janney .20 .09
❑ 42 Sergio Momesso .10 .05
❑ 43 Nicklas Lidstrom .20 .09
❑ 44 Luc Robitaille .20 .09
❑ 45 Adam Creighton .10 .05
❑ 46 Norm Maciver .10 .05
❑ 47 Mikhail Tatarinov .10 .05
❑ 48 Gary Roberts .10 .05
❑ 49 Gord Hynes .10 .05
❑ 50 Claude Lemieux .20 .09
❑ 51 Brad May .20 .09
❑ 52 Paul Stanton .10 .05
❑ 53 Rick Wamsley .20 .09
❑ 54 Steve Larmer .20 .09
❑ 55 Darrin Shannon .10 .05
❑ 56 Pat Falloon .10 .05
❑ 57 Chris Dahlquist .10 .05
❑ 58 John Vanbiesbrouck .50 .23
❑ 59 Sylvain Turgeon .10 .05
❑ 60 Jay More .10 .05
❑ 61 Randy Burridge .10 .05
❑ 62 Slava Kozlov UER .20 .09
❑ 63 Daniel Marois .10 .05
❑ 64 Curt Giles .10 .05
❑ 65 Brad Shaw .10 .05
❑ 66 Bill Ranford .20 .09
❑ 67 Frank Musil .10 .05
❑ 68 Steve Leach .10 .05
❑ 69 Michel Goulet .20 .09
❑ 70 Mathieu Schneider .10 .05
❑ 71 Steve Kasper .10 .05
❑ 72 Darryl Sydor .10 .05
❑ 73 Brian Leetch .30 .14
❑ 74 Chris Terreri .20 .09
❑ 75 Jim Johnson .10 .05
❑ 76 Rick Tocchet .20 .09
❑ 77 Teppo Numminen .10 .05
❑ 78 Owen Nolan .20 .09
❑ 79 Grant Ledyard .10 .05
❑ 80 Trevor Linden .20 .09
❑ 81 Luciano Borsato .10 .05
❑ 82 Derek King .10 .05
❑ 83 Robert Cimetta .10 .05
❑ 84 Geoff Smith .10 .05
❑ 85 Ray Sheppard .20 .09
❑ 86 Dimitri Khristich .10 .05
❑ 87 Chris Chelios .30 .14
❑ 88 Alexander Godynyuk .10 .05
❑ 89 Perry Anderson .10 .05
❑ 90 Neal Broten .20 .09
❑ 91 Brian Benning .10 .05
❑ 92 Brent Thompson .10 .05
❑ 93 Claude LaPointe .10 .05
❑ 94 Mario Lemieux 1.50 .70
❑ 95 Pat LaFontaine .20 .09
❑ 96 Frank Pietrangelo .20 .09
❑ 97 Gerald Diduck .10 .05
❑ 98 Paul DiPietro .10 .05
❑ 99 Valeri Zelepukin .10 .05
❑ 100 Rick Zombo .10 .05
❑ 101 Daniel Berthiaume .20 .09
❑ 102 Tom Fitzgerald .10 .05
❑ 103 Ken Baumgartner .10 .05
❑ 104 Esa Tikkanen .10 .05
❑ 105 Steve Chiasson .10 .05
❑ 106 Bobby Holik .10 .05
❑ 107 Dominik Hasek 1.00 .45
❑ 108 Jeff Hackett .20 .09
❑ 109 Paul Broten .10 .05
❑ 110 Kevin Stevens .10 .05
❑ 111 Geoff Sanderson .20 .09
❑ 112 Donald Audette .20 .09
❑ 113 Jarmo Myllys .10 .05
❑ 114 Brian Skrudland .10 .05
❑ 115 Andrei Lomakin .10 .05
❑ 116 Keith Tkachuk .75 .35
❑ 117 John McIntyre .10 .05
❑ 118 Jacques Cloutier .20 .09
❑ 119 Michel Picard .10 .05
❑ 120 Dave Babych .10 .05
❑ 121 Dave Gagner .20 .09
❑ 122 Bob Carpenter .10 .05
❑ 123 Ray Ferraro .10 .05
❑ 124 Glenn Anderson .20 .09
❑ 125 Craig MacTavish .10 .05
❑ 126 Shawn Burr .10 .05
❑ 127 Tim Bergland .10 .05
❑ 128 Al MacInnis .20 .09
❑ 129 Jeff Beukeboom .10 .05
❑ 130 Ken Wregget .20 .09
❑ 131 Arturs Irbe .20 .09
❑ 132 Dave Andreychuk .20 .09
❑ 133 Patrick Roy 1.50 .70
❑ 134 Benoit Brunet .10 .05
❑ 135 Rick Tabaracci .20 .09
❑ 136 Jamie Baker .10 .05
❑ 137 Yanic Dupre .10 .05
❑ 138 Jari Kurri .20 .09
❑ 139 Adam Burt .10 .05
❑ 140 Peter Stastny .20 .09
❑ 141 Brad Jones .10 .05
❑ 142 Jeff Odgers .10 .05
❑ 143 Anatoli Semenov UER .10 .05
(Goalie stat headings)
❑ 144 Paul Ranheim .10 .05
❑ 145 Sylvain Cote .10 .05
❑ 146 Brent Ashton .10 .05
❑ 147 Doug Bodger .10 .05
❑ 148 Bryan Marchment .10 .05
❑ 149 Bob Kudelski .10 .05
❑ 150 Adam Graves .20 .09
❑ 151 Scott Stevens .20 .09
❑ 152 Russ Courtnall .10 .05
❑ 153 Darcy Wakaluk .20 .09
❑ 154 Pelle Eklund .10 .05
❑ 155 Robert Kron .10 .05
❑ 156 Randy Ladouceur .10 .05
❑ 157 Ed Olczyk .10 .05
❑ 158 Jiri Hrdina .10 .05
❑ 159 John Tonelli .10 .05
❑ 160 John Cullen .10 .05
❑ 161 Jan Erixon .10 .05
❑ 162 David Shaw .10 .05
❑ 163 Brian Bradley .10 .05
❑ 164 Russ Romaniuk .10 .05
❑ 165 Eric Weinrich .10 .05
❑ 166 Steve Heinze .10 .05
❑ 167 Jeremy Roenick .30 .14
❑ 168 Mark Pederson .10 .05
❑ 169 Paul Coffey .30 .14
❑ 170 Bob Errey .10 .05
❑ 171 Brian Lawton .10 .05
❑ 172 Vincent Riendeau .20 .09
❑ 173 Marc Fortier .10 .05
❑ 174 Marc Bergevin .10 .05
❑ 175 Jim Sandlak .10 .05
❑ 176 Bob Bassen .10 .05
❑ 177 Uwe Krupp .10 .05
❑ 178 Paul MacDermid .10 .05
❑ 179 Bob Corkum .10 .05
❑ 180 Robert Reichel .10 .05
❑ 181 John LeClair .75 .35
❑ 182 Mike Hudson .10 .05
❑ 183 Mark Recchi .20 .09
❑ 184 Rollie Melanson .20 .09
❑ 185 Gordie Roberts .10 .05
❑ 186 Clint Malarchuk .20 .09
❑ 187 Kris King .10 .05
❑ 188 Adam Oates .20 .09
❑ 189 Jarrod Skalde .10 .05
❑ 190 Mike Lalor .10 .05
❑ 191 Vincent Damphousse .20 .09
❑ 192 Peter Ahola .10 .05
❑ 193 Kirk McLean .20 .09
❑ 194 Murray Baron .10 .05
❑ 195 Michel Petit .10 .05
❑ 196 Stephane Fiset .20 .09
❑ 197 Pat Verbeek .10 .05
❑ 198 Jon Casey .20 .09
❑ 199 Tim Cheveldae .20 .09
❑ 200 Mike Ridley .10 .05
❑ 201 Scott Lachance .10 .05
❑ 202 Rod Brind'Amour .20 .09
❑ 203 Bret Hedican UER .10 .05
(Misspelled Brett
on both sides)
❑ 204 Wendel Clark .20 .09
❑ 205 Shawn McEachern .10 .05
❑ 206 Randy Wood .10 .05
❑ 207 Ulf Dahlen .10 .05
❑ 208 Andy Brickley .10 .05
❑ 209 Scott Niedermayer UER .20 .09
(Rookie card reported to be 1985
on back; should be 1991)
❑ 210 Bob Essensa .20 .09
❑ 211 Patrick Poulin .10 .05
❑ 212 Johan Garpenlov .10 .05
❑ 213 Marty McInnis .10 .05
❑ 214 Josef Beranek .10 .05
❑ 215 Rod Langway .10 .05
❑ 216 Dave Christian .10 .05
❑ 217 Sergei Makarov .10 .05
❑ 218 Gerard Gallant .10 .05
❑ 219 Neil Wilkinson UER .10 .05
Missing personal bio on back)
❑ 220 Tomas Sandstrom .10 .05
❑ 221 Shane Corson .10 .05
❑ 222 John Ogrodnick .10 .05
❑ 223 Keith Acton .10 .05
❑ 224 Paul Brown .10 .05
❑ 225 Rob Zettler .10 .05
❑ 226 Todd Elik .10 .05
❑ 227 Petr Svoboda .10 .05
❑ 228 Zdeno Ciger .10 .05
❑ 229 Kevin Miller .10 .05
❑ 230 Rich Pilon .10 .05
❑ 231 Pat Jablonski .20 .09
❑ 232 Greg Adams .10 .05
❑ 233 Martin Brodeur 1.25 .55
❑ 234 Dave Taylor .20 .09
❑ 235 Kelly Buchberger .10 .05
❑ 236 Steve Konroyd .10 .05
❑ 237 Guy Larose .10 .05
❑ 238 Patrice Brisebois .10 .05
❑ 239 Checklist 1-125 .10 .05
❑ 240 Checklist 126-250 .10 .05
❑ 241 Mark Messier MC .30 .14
❑ 242 Mike Richter MC .30 .14
❑ 243 Ed Belfour MC .20 .09
❑ 244 Sergei Fedorov MC .50 .23
❑ 245 Adam Oates MC .20 .09
❑ 246 Pavel Bure MC .50 .23
❑ 247 Luc Robitaille MC .20 .09
❑ 248 Brian Leetch MC .30 .14
❑ 249 Ray Bourque MC .20 .09
❑ 250 Tony Amonte MC .20 .09
❑ 251 Mario Lemieux MC 1.00 .45
❑ 252 Patrick Roy MC 1.00 .45
❑ 253 Nicklas Lidstrom MC .20 .09
❑ 254 Steve Yzerman MC .60 .25
❑ 255 Jeremy Roenick MC .30 .14
❑ 256 Wayne Gretzky MC 1.50 .70
❑ 257 Kevin Stevens MC .10 .05
❑ 258 Brett Hull MC .30 .14
❑ 259 Pat Falloon MC .10 .05
❑ 260 Guy Carbonneau MC .20 .09
❑ 261 Todd Gill .10 .05
❑ 262 Mike Sullivan .10 .05
❑ 263 Jeff Brown .10 .05
❑ 264 Joe Reekie .10 .05
❑ 265 Geoff Courtnall .10 .05
❑ 266 Mike Richter .30 .14
❑ 267 Ray Bourque .30 .14
❑ 268 Mike Craig .10 .05
❑ 269 Scott King .10 .05
❑ 270 Don Beaupre .20 .09
❑ 271 Ted Donato .10 .05
❑ 272 Gary Leeman .10 .05
❑ 273 Steve Weeks .20 .09
❑ 274 Keith Brown .10 .05
❑ 275 Greg Paslawski .10 .05
❑ 276 Pierre Turgeon .20 .09
❑ 277 Jimmy Carson .10 .05
❑ 278 Tom Fergus .10 .05
❑ 279 Glen Wesley .10 .05
❑ 280 Tomas Forslund .10 .05
❑ 281 Tony Granato .10 .05
❑ 282 Phil Bourque .10 .05
❑ 283 Dave Ellett .10 .05
❑ 284 David Bruce .10 .05
❑ 285 Stu Barnes .10 .05
❑ 286 Peter Bondra .30 .14
❑ 287 Garth Butcher .10 .05
❑ 288 Ron Hextall .20 .09
❑ 289 Guy Carbonneau .20 .09
❑ 290 Louie DeBrusk .10 .05
❑ 291 Dave Barr .10 .05
❑ 292 Ken Sutton .10 .05
❑ 293 Brian Bellows .10 .05
❑ 294 Mike McNeill .10 .05
❑ 295 Rob Brown .10 .05
❑ 296 Corey Millen .10 .05
❑ 297 Joe Juneau UER .20 .09
(Shoots left, not right)
❑ 298 Jeff Chychrun UER .10 .05
(Misspelled Chychurn
on card front)
❑ 299 Igor Larionov .10 .05
❑ 300 Sergei Fedorov .60 .25
❑ 301 Kevin Hatcher .10 .05
❑ 302 Al Iafrate .20 .09
❑ 303 James Black .10 .05
❑ 304 Steph Beauregard .20 .09
❑ 305 Joel Otto .10 .05
❑ 306 Nelson Emerson .10 .05
❑ 307 Gaetan Duchesne .10 .05
❑ 308 J.J. Daigneault .10 .05
❑ 309 Jamie Macoun .10 .05
❑ 310 Laurie Boschman .10 .05
❑ 311 Mike Gartner .20 .09
❑ 312 Tony Tanti .10 .05
❑ 313 Steve Duchesne .10 .05
❑ 314 Martin Gelinas .10 .05
❑ 315 Dominic Roussel .20 .09
❑ 316 Cam Neely .20 .09
❑ 317 Craig Wolanin .10 .05
❑ 318 Randy Gilhen .10 .05
❑ 319 David Volek .10 .05
❑ 320 Alexander Mogilny .20 .09
❑ 321 Jyrki Lumme .10 .05
❑ 322 Jeff Reese .10 .05
❑ 323 Greg Gilbert .10 .05
❑ 324 Jeff Norton .10 .05
❑ 325 Jim Hrivnak .20 .09
❑ 326 Eric Desjardins .10 .05
❑ 327 Curtis Joseph .30 .14
❑ 328 Ric Nattress .10 .05
❑ 329 Jamie Leach .10 .05
❑ 330 Christian Ruuttu .10 .05
❑ 331 Doug Brown .10 .05
❑ 332 Randy Carlyle .10 .05
❑ 333 Ed Belfour .30 .14
❑ 334 Doug Smail .10 .05
❑ 335 Hubie McDonough .10 .05
❑ 336 Pat MacLeod .10 .05
❑ 337 Don Sweeney .10 .05
❑ 338 Felix Potvin .30 .14
❑ 339 Kent Manderville .10 .05
❑ 340 Sergei Nemchinov .10 .05
❑ 341 Calle Johansson .10 .05
❑ 342 Dirk Graham .10 .05
❑ 343 Craig Billington .20 .09
❑ 344 Valeri Kamensky .20 .09
❑ 345 Mike Vernon .20 .09
❑ 346 Fredrik Olausson .10 .05
❑ 347 Peter Ing .20 .09
❑ 348 Mikael Andersson .10 .05
❑ 349 Mike Keane .10 .05
❑ 350 Stephane Quintal .10 .05
❑ 351 Tom Chorske .10 .05
❑ 352 Ron Francis .20 .09
❑ 353 Dana Murzyn .10 .05
❑ 354 Craig Ludwig .10 .05
❑ 355 Bob Probert .20 .09
❑ 356 Glenn Healy .20 .09
❑ 357 Troy Loney .10 .05
❑ 358 Vladimir Ruzicka .10 .05
❑ 359 Doug Gilmour .30 .14
❑ 360 Darren Turcotte .10 .05
❑ 361 Kelly Miller .10 .05
❑ 362 Dennis Vaske .10 .05
❑ 363 Stephane Matteau .10 .05
❑ 364 Brian Hayward .20 .09
❑ 365 Kevin Dineen .10 .05
❑ 366 Igor Ulanov .10 .05
❑ 367 Sylvain Lefebvre .10 .05
❑ 368 Petr Klima .10 .05
❑ 369 Steve Thomas .10 .05
❑ 370 Daren Puppa .20 .09
❑ 371 Brendan Shanahan .60 .25
❑ 372 Charlie Huddy .10 .05
❑ 373 Cliff Ronning .10 .05
❑ 374 Brian Propp .10 .05
❑ 375 Larry Murphy .20 .09
❑ 376 Bruce Driver .10 .05
❑ 377 Rob Pearson .10 .05
❑ 378 Paul Ysebaert .10 .05
❑ 379 Mark Osborne .10 .05
❑ 380 Doug Weight .20 .09
❑ 381 Kerry Huffman UER .10 .05
(Team name on front
is Flyers)
❑ 382 Michal Pivonka .10 .05
❑ 383 Steve Smith .10 .05
❑ 384 Steven Finn .10 .05
❑ 385 Kevin Lowe .10 .05
❑ 386 Mike Ramsey .10 .05
❑ 387 Kirk Muller .10 .05

❑ 388 John LeBlanc .10 .05
❑ 389 Rich Sutter .10 .05
❑ 390 Brent Fedyk .10 .05
❑ 391 Kelly Hrudey .20 .09
❑ 392 Slava Fetisov .10 .05
❑ 393 Glen Murray UER .10 .05
(Misspelled Glenn
on both sides)
❑ 394 James Patrick .10 .05
❑ 395 Tom Draper .20 .09
❑ 396 Mark Hunter .10 .05
❑ 397 Wayne McBean .10 .05
❑ 398 Joe Sacco .10 .05
❑ 399 Dino Ciccarelli .20 .09
❑ 400 Brian Noonan .10 .05
❑ 401 Guy Hebert 1.00 .45
❑ 402 Peter Douris .10 .05
❑ 403 Gilbert Dionne .10 .05
❑ 404 Doug Lidster .10 .05
❑ 405 John Druce .10 .05
❑ 406 Alexei Kasatonov .10 .05
❑ 407 Chris Lindberg .10 .05
❑ 408 Mike Ricci .10 .05
❑ 409 Tom Kurvers .10 .05
❑ 410 Pat Elynuik .10 .05
❑ 411 Mike Donnelly .10 .05
❑ 412 Grant Fuhr .20 .09
❑ 413 Curtis Leschyshyn .10 .05
❑ 414 Derian Hatcher .10 .05
❑ 415 Michel Mongeau .10 .05
❑ 416 Tom Barrasso .20 .09
❑ 417 Joey Kocur .10 .05
❑ 418 Vladimir Konstantinov .10 .05
❑ 419 Dale Hawerchuk .20 .09
❑ 420 Brian Mullen .10 .05
❑ 421 Mark Greig .10 .05
❑ 422 Claude Vilgrain .10 .05
❑ 423 Gary Suter .10 .05
❑ 424 Garry Galley .10 .05
❑ 425 Benoit Hogue .10 .05
❑ 426 Jeff Finley .10 .05
❑ 427 Bobby Smith .20 .09
❑ 428 Brent Sutter .10 .05
❑ 429 Ron Wilson .10 .05
❑ 430 Andy Moog .20 .09
❑ 431 Stephan Lebeau .10 .05
❑ 432 Troy Mallette .10 .05
❑ 433 Peter Zezel .10 .05
❑ 434 Mike Hough .10 .05
❑ 435 Mark Tinordi .10 .05
❑ 436 Dave Manson .10 .05
❑ 437 Jim Paek .10 .05
❑ 438 Frantisek Kucera .10 .05
❑ 439 Rob Zamuner .10 .05
❑ 440 Ulf Samuelsson .10 .05
❑ 441 Perry Berezan .10 .05
❑ 442 Murray Craven .10 .05
❑ 443 Mark Messier .50 .23
❑ 444 Alexander Semak .10 .05
❑ 445 Gord Murphy .10 .05
❑ 446 Jocelyn Lemieux .10 .05
❑ 447 Paul Cavallini .10 .05
❑ 448 Bernie Nicholls .20 .09
❑ 449 Brent Gilchrist .10 .05
❑ 450 Randy McKay .10 .05
❑ 451 Alexei Gusarov .10 .05
❑ 452 Mike McPhee .10 .05
❑ 453 Kimbi Daniels .10 .05
❑ 454 Kelly Kisio .10 .05
❑ 455 Bob Sweeney .10 .05
❑ 456 Luke Richardson .10 .05
❑ 457 Petr Nedved .20 .09
❑ 458 Craig Berube .10 .05
❑ 459 Kay Whitmore .20 .09
❑ 460 Randy Velischek .10 .05
❑ 461 David Williams .10 .05
❑ 462 Scott Mellanby .20 .09
❑ 463 Terry Carkner .10 .05
❑ 464 Dale Craigwell .10 .05
❑ 465 Kevin Todd .10 .05
❑ 466 Kjell Samuelsson .10 .05
❑ 467 Denis Savard .20 .09
❑ 468 Adam Foote .10 .05
❑ 469 Stephane Morin .10 .05
❑ 470 Doug Wilson .20 .09
❑ 471 Shawn Cronin .10 .05
❑ 472 Brian Glynn UER .10 .05
(Oilers misspelled Oiolers on back)
❑ 473 Craig Simpson .10 .05
❑ 474 Todd Krygier .10 .05
❑ 475 Brad Miller .10 .05
❑ 476 Yvon Corriveau .10 .05
❑ 477 Patrick Flatley .10 .05
❑ 478 Mats Sundin .30 .14
❑ 479 Joe Cirella .10 .05
❑ 480 Gino Cavallini .10 .05
❑ 481 Marty McSorley .10 .05
❑ 482 Brad Marsh .10 .05
❑ 483 Bob McGill .10 .05
❑ 484 Randy Moller .10 .05
❑ 485 Keith Primeau .20 .09
❑ 486 Darin Kimble .10 .05
❑ 487 Mike Krushelnyski .10 .05
❑ 488 Sutter Brothers .10 .05
❑ 489 Pavel Bure .60 .25
❑ 490 Ray Whitney .10 .05
❑ 491 Dave McLlwain .10 .05
❑ 492 Per Djoos .10 .05
❑ 493 Garry Valk .10 .05
❑ 494 Mike Bullard .10 .05
❑ 495 Greg Hawgood .10 .05
❑ 496 Terry Yake .10 .05
❑ 497 Mike Hartman .10 .05
❑ 498 Jaromir Jagr 1.00 .45
❑ 499 Checklist 251-384 .10 .05
❑ 500 Checklist 385-500 .10 .05
❑ 501 Eric Lindros 2.50 1.10

## 1993-94 Stadium Club

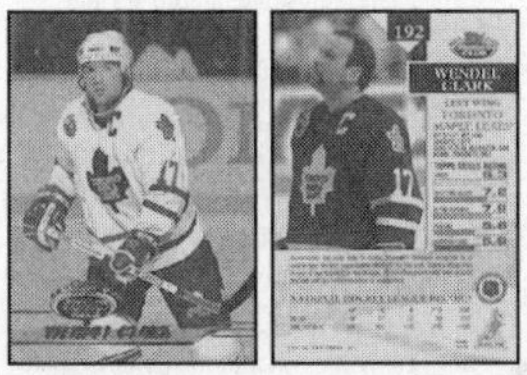

This 500-card standard-size set features borderless color player action shots on the card fronts. The set was issued in two series of 250 cards each. Cards were printed for both the Canadian and U.S. markets. The O-Pee-Chee version has a U.S.A. copyright on back for series one cards only. The player's name appears in gold foil at the bottom, atop blue and gold foil stripes. Using an out-of-focus photo of the ice and sideboards for background, the back features a color player photo at the upper left. His name, position, and team, along with a player skills rating, are displayed alongside. At the bottom, the player's career highlights and stats, and the NHL and NHLPA logos, round out the card. Included is a ten-card Award Winners subset (141-150) that features the 1992-93 NHL Trophy winners. Rookie Cards include Jason Arnott, Chris Osgood, Jocelyn Thibault and German Titov.

| | MINT | NRMT |
|---|---|---|
| COMPLETE SET (500) | 30.00 | 13.50 |
| COMPLETE SERIES 1 (250) | 15.00 | 6.75 |
| COMPLETE SERIES 2 (250) | 15.00 | 6.75 |
| COMMON CARD (1-500) | .05 | .02 |

❑ 1 Guy Carbonneau .05 .02
❑ 2 Joe Cirella .05 .02
❑ 3 Laurie Boschman .05 .02
❑ 4 Arturs Irbe .10 .05
❑ 5 Adam Creighton .05 .02
❑ 6 Mike McPhee .05 .02
❑ 7 Jeff Beukeboom .05 .02
❑ 8 Kevin Todd .05 .02
❑ 9 Yvon Corriveau .05 .02
❑ 10 Eric Lindros 1.00 .45
❑ 11 Martin Rucinsky .05 .02
❑ 12 Michel Goulet .10 .05
❑ 13 Scott Pellerin .05 .02
❑ 14 Mike Eagles .05 .02
❑ 15 Steve Heinze .05 .02
❑ 16 Gerard Gallant .05 .02
❑ 17 Kelly Miller .05 .02
❑ 18 Petr Nedved .10 .05
❑ 19 Joe Mullen .10 .05
❑ 20 Pat LaFontaine .10 .05
❑ 21 Garth Butcher .05 .02
❑ 22 Jeff Reese .05 .02
❑ 23 Dave Andreychuk .10 .05
❑ 24 Patrick Flatley .05 .02
❑ 25 Tomas Sandstrom .05 .02
❑ 26 Andre Racicot .10 .05
❑ 27 Patrice Brisebois .05 .02
❑ 28 Neal Broten .10 .05
❑ 29 Mark Freer .05 .02
❑ 30 Kelly Kisio .05 .02
❑ 31 Scott Mellanby .10 .05
❑ 32 Joe Sakic .50 .23
❑ 33 Kerry Huffman .05 .02
❑ 34 Evgeny Davydov .05 .02
❑ 35 Mark Messier .30 .14
❑ 36 Pat Verbeek .05 .02
❑ 37 Greg Gilbert .05 .02
❑ 38 John Tucker .05 .02
❑ 39 Claude Lemieux .10 .05
❑ 40 Shayne Corson .05 .02
❑ 41 Gordie Roberts .05 .02
❑ 42 Jiri Slegr .05 .02
❑ 43 Kevin Dineen .05 .02
❑ 44 Johan Garpenlov .05 .02
❑ 45 Sergei Fedorov .50 .23
❑ 46 Rich Sutter .05 .02
❑ 47 Dave Hannan .05 .02
❑ 48 Sylvain Lefebvre .05 .02
❑ 49 Pat Elynuik .05 .02
❑ 50 Ray Ferraro .05 .02
❑ 51 Brent Ashton .05 .02
❑ 52 Paul Stanton .05 .02
❑ 53 Kevin Haller .05 .02
❑ 54 Kelly Hrudey .10 .05
❑ 55 Russ Courtnall .05 .02
❑ 56 Alexei Zhamnov .10 .05
❑ 57 Andrei Lomakin .05 .02
❑ 58 Keith Brown .05 .02
❑ 59 Glen Murray .05 .02
❑ 60 Kay Whitmore .10 .05
❑ 61 Stephane Richer .10 .05
❑ 62 Todd Gill .05 .02
❑ 63 Bob Sweeney .05 .02
❑ 64 Mike Richter .25 .11
❑ 65 Brett Hull .30 .14
❑ 66 Sylvain Cote .05 .02
❑ 67 Kirk Muller .05 .02
❑ 68 Ronnie Stern .05 .02
❑ 69 Josef Beranek .05 .02
❑ 70 Steve Yzerman .75 .35
❑ 71 Don Beaupre .10 .05
❑ 72 Ed Courtenay .05 .02
❑ 73 Zdeno Ciger .05 .02
❑ 74 Andrew Cassels .05 .02
❑ 75 Roman Hamrlik .10 .05
❑ 76 Benoit Hogue .05 .02
❑ 77 Andrei Kovalenko .05 .02
❑ 78 Rod Brind'Amour .10 .05
❑ 79 Tom Barrasso .10 .05
❑ 80 Al Iafrate .05 .02
❑ 81 Brett Hedican .05 .02
❑ 82 Peter Bondra .25 .11
❑ 83 Ted Donato .05 .02
❑ 84 Chris Lindberg .05 .02
❑ 85 John Vanbiesbrouck .40 .18
❑ 86 Ron Sutter .05 .02
❑ 87 Luc Robitaille .10 .05
❑ 88 Brian Leetch .25 .11
❑ 89 Randy Wood .05 .02
❑ 90 Dirk Graham .05 .02
❑ 91 Alexander Mogilny .10 .05
❑ 92 Mike Keane .05 .02
❑ 93 Adam Oates .10 .05
❑ 94 Viacheslav Butsayev .05 .02
❑ 95 John LeClair .40 .18
❑ 96 Joe Nieuwendyk .10 .05
❑ 97 Mikael Andersson .05 .02
❑ 98 Jaromir Jagr .75 .35
❑ 99 Ed Belfour .25 .11
❑ 100 David Reid .05 .02
❑ 101 Darius Kasparaitis .05 .02
❑ 102 Zarley Zalapski .05 .02
❑ 103 Christian Ruuttu .05 .02
❑ 104 Phil Housley .10 .05
❑ 105 Al MacInnis .10 .05
❑ 106 Tommy Sjodin .05 .02
❑ 107 Richard Smehlik .05 .02
❑ 108 Jyrki Lumme .05 .02
❑ 109 Dominic Roussel .10 .05
❑ 110 Mike Gartner .10 .05
❑ 111 Bernie Nicholls .05 .02
❑ 112 Mark Howe .05 .02
❑ 113 Rich Pilon .05 .02
❑ 114 Jeff Odgers .05 .02
❑ 115 Gilbert Dionne .05 .02
❑ 116 Peter Zezel .05 .02
❑ 117 Don Sweeney .05 .02
❑ 118 Jimmy Carson .05 .02
❑ 119 Igor Korolev .05 .02
❑ 120 Bob Kudelski .05 .02
❑ 121 Dave Lowry .05 .02
❑ 122 Steve Kasper .05 .02
❑ 123 Mike Ridley .05 .02
❑ 124 Dave Tippett .05 .02
❑ 125 Cliff Ronning .05 .02
❑ 126 Bruce Driver .05 .02
❑ 127 Stephane Matteau .05 .02
❑ 128 Joel Otto .05 .02
❑ 129 Alexei Kovalev .10 .05
❑ 130 Mike Modano .30 .14
❑ 131 Bill Ranford .10 .05
❑ 132 Petr Svoboda .05 .02
❑ 133 Roger Johansson .05 .02
❑ 134 Marc Bureau .05 .02
❑ 135 Keith Tkachuk .30 .14
❑ 136 Mark Recchi .10 .05
❑ 137 Bob Probert .10 .05
❑ 138 Uwe Krupp .05 .02
❑ 139 Mike Sullivan .05 .02
❑ 140 Doug Gilmour .25 .11
❑ 141 Teemu Selanne .30 .14
Calder Trophy Winner
❑ 142 Dave Poulin .05 .02
Clancy Trophy Winner
❑ 143 Mario Lemieux .60 .25
Hart Trophy Winner
❑ 144 Ed Belfour .25 .11
Jennings Trophy Winner
❑ 145 Pierre Turgeon .10 .05
Lady Byng Trophy
Winner
❑ 146 Mario Lemieux .60 .25
Masterton Trophy
Winner
❑ 147 Chris Chelios .25 .11
Norris Trophy Winner
❑ 148 Mario Lemieux .60 .25
Art Ross Trophy Winner
❑ 149 Doug Gilmour .25 .11
Selke Trophy Winner
❑ 150 Ed Belfour .25 .11
Vezina Trophy Winner
❑ 151 Paul Ranheim .05 .02
❑ 152 Gino Cavallini .05 .02
❑ 153 Kevin Hatcher .05 .02
❑ 154 Marc Bergevin .05 .02
❑ 155 Marty McSorley .05 .02
❑ 156 Brian Bellows .05 .02
❑ 157 Patrick Poulin .05 .02
❑ 158 Kevin Stevens .05 .02
❑ 159 Bobby Holik .05 .02
❑ 160 Ray Bourque .25 .11
❑ 161 Bryan Marchment .05 .02
❑ 162 Curtis Joseph .25 .11
❑ 163 Kirk McLean .10 .05
❑ 164 Teppo Numminen .05 .02
❑ 165 Kevin Lowe .05 .02
❑ 166 Tim Cheveldae .10 .05
❑ 167 Brad Dalgarno .05 .02
❑ 168 Glenn Anderson .10 .05
❑ 169 Frank Musil .05 .02
❑ 170 Eric Desjardins .05 .02
❑ 171 Doug Zmolek .05 .02
❑ 172 Mark Lamb .05 .02
❑ 173 Craig Ludwig .05 .02
❑ 174 Rob Gaudreau .05 .02
❑ 175 Bob Carpenter .05 .02
❑ 176 Mike Ricci .05 .02
❑ 177 Brian Skrudland .05 .02
❑ 178 Dominik Hasek .75 .35
❑ 179 Pat Conacher .05 .02
❑ 180 Mark Janssens .05 .02
❑ 181 Brent Fedyk .05 .02
❑ 182 Rob DiMaio .05 .02
❑ 183 Dave Manson .05 .02
❑ 184 Janne Ojanen .05 .02
❑ 185 Ryan Walter .05 .02
❑ 186 Michael Nylander .05 .02
❑ 187 Steve Leach .05 .02
❑ 188 Jeff Brown .05 .02
❑ 189 Shawn McEachern .05 .02
❑ 190 Jeremy Roenick .25 .11
❑ 191 Darrin Shannon .05 .02
❑ 192 Wendel Clark .10 .05
❑ 193 Kevin Miller .05 .02
❑ 194 Paul DiPietro .05 .02
❑ 195 Steve Thomas .05 .02
❑ 196 Nicklas Lidstrom .10 .05
❑ 197 Ed Olczyk .05 .02
❑ 198 Robert Reichel .05 .02
❑ 199 Neil Brady .05 .02
❑ 200 Wayne Gretzky 1.50 .70
❑ 201 Adrien Plavsic .05 .02
❑ 202 Joe Juneau .10 .05
❑ 203 Brad May .10 .05
❑ 204 Igor Kravchuk .05 .02
❑ 205 Keith Acton .05 .02
❑ 206 Ken Daneyko .05 .02
❑ 207 Sean Burke .10 .05
❑ 208 Jay More .05 .02
❑ 209 John Cullen .05 .02
❑ 210 Teemu Selanne .60 .25
❑ 211 Brent Sutter .05 .02
❑ 212 Brian Bradley .05 .02
❑ 213 Donald Audette .10 .05
❑ 214 Philippe Bozon .05 .02
❑ 215 Derek King .05 .02
❑ 216 Cam Neely .10 .05
❑ 217 Keith Primeau .10 .05
❑ 218 Steve Smith .05 .02
❑ 219 Ken Sutton .05 .02
❑ 220 Dale Hawerchuk .10 .05
❑ 221 Alexei Zhitnik .05 .02
❑ 222 Glen Wesley .05 .02
❑ 223 Nelson Emerson .05 .02
❑ 224 Pat Falloon .05 .02
❑ 225 Darryl Sydor .05 .02
❑ 226 Tony Amonte .10 .05
❑ 227 Brian Mullen .05 .02
❑ 228 Gary Suter .05 .02
❑ 229 David Shaw .05 .02
❑ 230 Troy Murray .05 .02
❑ 231 Patrick Roy 1.25 .55
❑ 232 Mitchel Petit .05 .02
❑ 233 Wayne Presley .05 .02
❑ 234 Keith Jones .05 .02
❑ 235 Gary Roberts .05 .02
❑ 236 Steve Larmer .10 .05
❑ 237 Valeri Kamensky .10 .05
❑ 238 Ulf Dahlen .05 .02
❑ 239 Danton Cole .05 .02
❑ 240 Vincent Damphousse .10 .05
❑ 241 Yuri Khmylev .05 .02
❑ 242 Stephane Quintal .05 .02
❑ 243 Peter Taglianetti .05 .02
❑ 244 Gary Leeman .05 .02
❑ 245 Sergei Nemchinov .05 .02
❑ 246 Rob Blake .05 .02
❑ 247 Steve Chiasson .05 .02
❑ 248 Vladimir Malakhov .05 .02
❑ 249 Checklist 1-125 .05 .02
❑ 250 Checklist 126-250 .05 .02
❑ 251 Kjell Samuelsson .05 .02
❑ 252 Terry Carkner .05 .02
❑ 253 Bill Lindsay .05 .02
❑ 254 Bob Essensa .10 .05
❑ 255 Jocelyn Lemieux .05 .02
❑ 256 Joe Sacco .05 .02
❑ 257 Marty McInnis .05 .02
❑ 258 Warren Rychel .05 .02
❑ 259 David Maley .05 .02
❑ 260 Grant Fuhr .10 .05
❑ 261 Scott Young .05 .02
❑ 262 Ed Ronan .05 .02
❑ 263 Micah Aivazoff .05 .02
❑ 264 Murray Craven .05 .02
❑ 265 Slava Fetisov .05 .02
❑ 266 Chris Dahlquist .05 .02
❑ 267 Norm Maciver .05 .02
❑ 268 Alexander Godynyuk .05 .02
❑ 269 Mikael Renberg .25 .11
❑ 270 Adam Graves .10 .05
❑ 271 Randy Ladouceur .05 .02
❑ 272 Frank Pietrangelo .10 .05
❑ 273 Basil McRae .05 .02
❑ 274 Bryan Smolinski .05 .02
❑ 275 Daren Puppa .10 .05
❑ 276 Darcy Wakaluk .10 .05
❑ 277 Dimitri Khristich .05 .02
❑ 278 Vladimir Vujtek .05 .02
❑ 279 Tom Kurvers .05 .02
❑ 280 Felix Potvin .25 .11
❑ 281 Keith Brown .05 .02
❑ 282 Thomas Steen .05 .02
❑ 283 Larry Murphy .10 .05
❑ 284 Bob Corkum .05 .02
❑ 285 Tony Granato .05 .02
❑ 286 Cam Russell .05 .02
❑ 287 John MacLean .10 .05
❑ 288 Shawn Antoski .05 .02
❑ 289 Pelle Eklund .05 .02
❑ 290 Chris Pronger .10 .05
❑ 291 Alexander Karpovtsev .05 .02
❑ 292 Paul Laus .05 .02
❑ 293 Jaroslav Otevrel .05 .02
❑ 294 Dino Ciccarelli .10 .05
❑ 295 Guy Hebert .10 .05
❑ 296 Dave Karpa .05 .02
❑ 297 Denis Savard .10 .05
❑ 298 Jim Johnson .05 .02
❑ 299 Kirk Maltby .05 .02
❑ 300 Alexandre Daigle .05 .02
❑ 301 Dave Poulin .05 .02
❑ 302 James Patrick .05 .02
❑ 303 Jon Casey .10 .05
❑ 304 Yves Racine .05 .02
❑ 305 Craig Simpson .05 .02
❑ 306 Mike Krushelnyski .05 .02
❑ 307 Mark Fitzpatrick .10 .05
❑ 308 Charlie Huddy .05 .02
❑ 309 Todd Ewen .05 .02
❑ 310 Mario Lemieux 1.25 .55
❑ 311 Dan Keczmer .05 .02
❑ 312 Sergei Zubov .05 .02
❑ 313 Shawn Burr .05 .02
❑ 314 Valeri Zelepukin .05 .02
❑ 315 Stephane Fiset .10 .05
❑ 316 C.J. Young .05 .02
❑ 317 Luciano Borsato .05 .02
❑ 318 Darcy Loewen .05 .02
❑ 319 Mike Vernon .10 .05
❑ 320 Chris Gratton .10 .05
❑ 321 Matthew Barnaby .10 .05
❑ 322 Mike Rathje .05 .02
❑ 323 Sergio Momesso .05 .02
❑ 324 David Volek .05 .02
❑ 325 Ron Tugnutt .10 .05
❑ 326 Jeff Hackett .10 .05
❑ 327 Robb Stauber .10 .05
❑ 328 Chris Terreri .10 .05
❑ 329 Rick Tocchet .10 .05
❑ 330 John Vanbiesbrouck .40 .18
❑ 331 Drake Berehowsky .05 .02
❑ 332 Alexei Kasatonov .05 .02
❑ 333 Vladimir Konstantinov .05 .02
❑ 334 John Blue .10 .05
❑ 335 Craig Janney .10 .05
❑ 336 Curtis Leschyshyn .05 .02
❑ 337 Todd Krygier .05 .02
❑ 338 Boris Mironov .05 .02
❑ 339 Joby Messier .05 .02
❑ 340 Tommy Soderstrom .10 .05
❑ 341 Randy Cunneyworth .05 .02
❑ 342 Mark Ferner .05 .02
❑ 343 Stephan Lebeau .05 .02
❑ 344 Jody Hull .05 .02
❑ 345 Jason Arnott .75 .35
❑ 346 Gerard Gallant .05 .02
❑ 347 Stephane Richer .10 .05
❑ 348 Jeff Shantz .05 .02
❑ 349 Brian Skrudland .05 .02
❑ 350 Chris Osgood 1.50 .70
❑ 351 Gary Shuchuk .05 .02
❑ 352 Martin Brodeur .75 .35
❑ 353 Bob Rouse .05 .02
❑ 354 Doug Bodger .05 .02
❑ 355 Mike Craig .05 .02
❑ 356 Ulf Samuelsson .05 .02
❑ 357 Trevor Linden .10 .05
❑ 358 Dennis Vaske .05 .02
❑ 359 Alexei Yashin .10 .05
❑ 360 Paul Ysebaert .05 .02
❑ 361 Shaun Van Allen .05 .02
❑ 362 Sandis Ozolinsh .10 .05
❑ 363 Todd Elik .05 .02
❑ 364 German Titov .05 .02
❑ 365 Alexander Semak .05 .02
❑ 366 Allen Pedersen .05 .02
❑ 367 Greg Johnson .05 .02
❑ 368 Anatoli Semenov .05 .02
❑ 369 Scott Mellanby .10 .05
❑ 370 Mats Sundin .10 .05
❑ 371 Mattias Norstrom .05 .02
❑ 372 Glen Featherstone .05 .02
❑ 373 Sergei Petrenko .05 .02
❑ 374 Mike Donnelly .05 .02
❑ 375 Nikolai Borschevsky .05 .02
❑ 376 Rob Zamuner .05 .02
❑ 377 Steven King .05 .02
❑ 378 Rick Tabaracci .10 .05
❑ 379 Dave Lowry .05 .02
❑ 380 Pierre Turgeon .10 .05
❑ 381 Garry Galley .05 .02
❑ 382 Doug Weight .10 .05
❑ 383 Scott Stevens .10 .05
❑ 384 Mark Tinordi .05 .02
❑ 385 Ron Francis .10 .05
❑ 386 Mark Greig .05 .02
❑ 387 Sean Hill .05 .02
❑ 388 Slava Kozlov .10 .05
❑ 389 Brendan Shanahan .50 .23
❑ 390 Theoren Fleury .10 .05
❑ 391 Mathieu Schneider .05 .02
❑ 392 Tom Fitzgerald .05 .02
❑ 393 Markus Naslund .05 .02
❑ 394 Travis Green .10 .05
❑ 395 Troy Loney .05 .02
❑ 396 Gord Donnelly .05 .02
❑ 397 Owen Nolan .10 .05
❑ 398 Steve Larmer .10 .05
❑ 399 Dave Archibald .05 .02
❑ 400 Jari Kurri .10 .05
❑ 401 Jim Paek .05 .02
❑ 402 Andrei Lomakin .05 .02
❑ 403 Scott Niedermayer .05 .02
❑ 404 Bob Errey .05 .02
❑ 405 Michal Pivonka .05 .02
❑ 406 Doug Lidster .05 .02
❑ 407 Garry Valk .05 .02
❑ 408 Geoff Sanderson .10 .05

| | | |
|---|---|---|
| ❑ 409 Stewart Malgunas | .05 | .02 |
| ❑ 410 Craig MacTavish | .05 | .02 |
| ❑ 411 Jaroslav Modry | .05 | .02 |
| ❑ 412 Shawn Chambers | .05 | .02 |
| ❑ 413 Geoff Courtnall | .05 | .02 |
| ❑ 414 Mark Hardy | .05 | .02 |
| ❑ 415 Martin Straka | .05 | .02 |
| ❑ 416 Randy Burridge | .05 | .02 |
| ❑ 417 Kent Manderville | .05 | .02 |
| ❑ 418 Darren Rumble | .05 | .02 |
| ❑ 419 Bill Houlder | .05 | .02 |
| ❑ 420 Chris Chelios | .25 | .11 |
| ❑ 421 Jim Hrivnak | .10 | .05 |
| ❑ 422 Benoit Brunet | .05 | .02 |
| ❑ 423 Aaron Ward | .05 | .02 |
| ❑ 424 Alexei Gusarov | .05 | .02 |
| ❑ 425 Mats Sundin | .10 | .05 |
| ❑ 426 Kjell Samuelsson | .05 | .02 |
| ❑ 427 Mikael Andersson | .05 | .02 |
| ❑ 428 Ulf Dahlen | .05 | .02 |
| ❑ 429 Nicklas Lidstrom | .10 | .05 |
| ❑ 430 Tommy Soderstrom | .10 | .05 |
| ❑ 431 Darrin Madeley | .05 | .02 |
| ❑ 432 Kevin Dahl | .05 | .02 |
| ❑ 433 Ron Hextall | .10 | .05 |
| ❑ 434 Patrick Carnback | .05 | .02 |
| ❑ 435 Randy Moller | .05 | .02 |
| ❑ 436 Dave Gagner | .10 | .05 |
| ❑ 437 Corey Millen | .05 | .02 |
| ❑ 438 Olaf Kolzig | .10 | .05 |
| ❑ 439 Gord Murphy | .05 | .02 |
| ❑ 440 Cam Stewart | .05 | .02 |
| ❑ 441 Darren McCarty | .30 | .14 |
| ❑ 442 Frantisek Kucera | .05 | .02 |
| ❑ 443 Ted Drury | .05 | .02 |
| ❑ 444 Troy Mallette | .05 | .02 |
| ❑ 445 Robin Bawa | .05 | .02 |
| ❑ 446 Steven Rice | .05 | .02 |
| ❑ 447 Pat Elynuik | .05 | .02 |
| ❑ 448 Jim Cummins | .05 | .02 |
| ❑ 449 Rob Niedermayer | .10 | .05 |
| ❑ 450 Paul Coffey | .25 | .11 |
| ❑ 451 Calle Johansson | .05 | .02 |
| ❑ 452 Mike Needham | .05 | .02 |
| ❑ 453 Glenn Healy | .10 | .05 |
| ❑ 454 Dixon Ward | .05 | .02 |
| ❑ 455 Al Iafrate | .05 | .02 |
| ❑ 456 Jon Casey | .10 | .05 |
| ❑ 457 Kevin Stevens | .05 | .02 |
| ❑ 458 Tony Amonte | .10 | .05 |
| ❑ 459 Chris Chelios | .25 | .11 |
| ❑ 460 Pat LaFontaine | .10 | .05 |
| ❑ 461 Jamie Baker | .05 | .02 |
| ❑ 462 Andre Faust | .05 | .02 |
| ❑ 463 Bobby Dollas | .05 | .02 |
| ❑ 464 Steven Finn | .05 | .02 |
| ❑ 465 Scott Lachance | .05 | .02 |
| ❑ 466 Mike Hough | .05 | .02 |
| ❑ 467 Bill Guerin | .05 | .02 |
| ❑ 468 Dimitri Filimonov | .05 | .02 |
| ❑ 469 Dave Ellett | .05 | .02 |
| ❑ 470 Andy Moog | .10 | .05 |
| ❑ 471 Scott Thomas | .05 | .02 |
| ❑ 472 Trent Yawney | .05 | .02 |
| ❑ 473 Tim Sweeney | .05 | .02 |
| ❑ 474 Shjon Podein | .05 | .02 |
| ❑ 475 J.J. Daigneault | .05 | .02 |
| ❑ 476 Darren Turcotte | .05 | .02 |
| ❑ 477 Esa Tikkanen | .05 | .02 |
| ❑ 478 Vitali Karamnov | .05 | .02 |
| ❑ 479 Jocelyn Thibault | 1.00 | .45 |
| ❑ 480 Pavel Bure | .50 | .23 |
| ❑ 481 Steve Konowalchuk | .05 | .02 |
| ❑ 482 Sylvain Turgeon | .05 | .02 |
| ❑ 483 Jeff Daniels | .05 | .02 |
| ❑ 484 Dallas Drake | .05 | .02 |
| ❑ 485 Iain Fraser | .05 | .02 |
| ❑ 486 Joe Reekie | .05 | .02 |
| ❑ 487 Evgeny Davydov | .05 | .02 |
| ❑ 488 Jozef Stumpel | .05 | .02 |
| ❑ 489 Brent Thompson | .05 | .02 |
| ❑ 490 Terry Yake | .05 | .02 |
| ❑ 491 Derek Plante | .05 | .02 |
| ❑ 492 Dimitri Yushkevich | .05 | .02 |
| ❑ 493 Wayne McBean | .05 | .02 |
| ❑ 494 Derian Hatcher | .05 | .02 |
| ❑ 495 Jeff Norton | .05 | .02 |
| ❑ 496 Adam Foote | .05 | .02 |
| ❑ 497 Mike Peluso | .05 | .02 |
| ❑ 498 Rob Pearson | .05 | .02 |
| ❑ 499 Checklist 251-375 | .05 | .02 |
| ❑ 500 Checklist 376-500 | .05 | .02 |

## 1993-94 Stadium Club First Day Issue

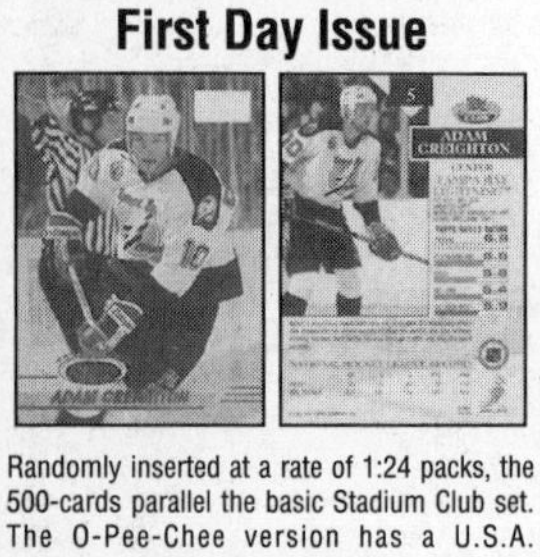

Randomly inserted at a rate of 1:24 packs, the 500-cards parallel the basic Stadium Club set. The O-Pee-Chee version has a U.S.A. copyright on back for series one cards only. The cards of Wayne Gretzky, Vincent Damphousse, Luc Robitaille and Wayne Presley can be found with the logo in either upper corner.

| | MINT | NRMT |
|---|---|---|
| COMPLETE SET (500) | 2500.00 | 1100.00 |
| COMPLETE SERIES 1 (250) | 1250.00 | 550.00 |
| COMPLETE SERIES 2 (250) | 1250.00 | 550.00 |
| COMMON CARD (1-500) | 2.50 | 1.10 |

*STARS: 30X TO 80X BASIC CARDS
*YOUNG STARS: 20X TO 50X BASIC CARDS
*RCs: 12X TO 30X BASIC CARDS
*SER.1 OPC CARDS: 1X TO 1.25X HI

| | | |
|---|---|---|
| ❑ 10 Eric Lindros | 80.00 | 36.00 |
| ❑ 32 Joe Sakic | 40.00 | 18.00 |
| ❑ 70 Steve Yzerman | 60.00 | 27.00 |
| ❑ 98 Jaromir Jagr | 60.00 | 27.00 |
| ❑ 200 Wayne Gretzky | 150.00 | 70.00 |
| ❑ 210 Teemu Selanne | 50.00 | 22.00 |
| ❑ 231 Patrick Roy | 120.00 | 55.00 |
| ❑ 310 Mario Lemieux | 120.00 | 55.00 |

## 1993-94 Stadium Club All-Stars

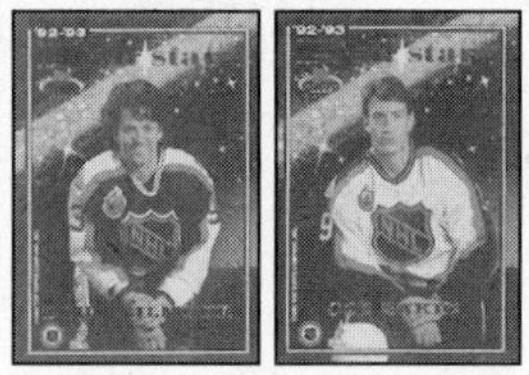

Randomly inserted at the rate of 1:24 first-series packs, each of these 23 standard-size cards features two 1992-93 All-Stars, one from each conference. Both sides carry a posed color player photo superimposed over a stellar background. The player's name in gold foil appears on the bottom, while the words "NHL All-Star" are printed at the top. The cards are unnumbered and checklisted below in alphabetical order.

| | MINT | NRMT |
|---|---|---|
| COMPLETE SET (23) | 120.00 | 55.00 |
| COMMON CARD (1-23) | 2.00 | .90 |

| | | |
|---|---|---|
| ❑ 1 Patrick Roy | 20.00 | 9.00 |
| Ed Belfour | | |
| ❑ 2 Ray Bourque | 6.00 | 2.70 |
| Paul Coffey | | |
| ❑ 3 Al Iafrate | 4.00 | 1.80 |
| Chris Chelios | | |
| ❑ 4 Jaromir Jagr | 12.00 | 5.50 |
| Brett Hull | | |
| ❑ 5 Pat LaFontaine | 10.00 | 4.50 |
| Steve Yzerman | | |
| ❑ 6 Kevin Stevens | 6.00 | 2.70 |
| Pavel Bure | | |
| ❑ 7 Craig Billington | 2.00 | .90 |
| Jon Casey | | |
| ❑ 8 Steve Duchesne | 2.00 | .90 |
| Steve Chiasson | | |
| ❑ 9 Scott Stevens | 2.00 | .90 |
| Phil Housley | | |
| ❑ 10 Peter Bondra | 3.00 | 1.35 |
| Kelly Kisio | | |
| ❑ 11 Adam Oates | 4.00 | 1.80 |
| Brian Bradley | | |
| ❑ 12 Alexander Mogilny | 4.00 | 1.80 |
| Jari Kurri | | |
| ❑ 13 Peter Sidorkiewicz | 2.00 | .90 |
| Mike Vernon | | |
| ❑ 14 Zarley Zalapski | 2.00 | .90 |
| Dave Manson | | |
| ❑ 15 Brad Marsh | 2.00 | .90 |
| Randy Carlyle | | |
| ❑ 16 Kirk Muller | 2.00 | .90 |
| Gary Roberts | | |
| ❑ 17 Joe Sakic | 8.00 | 3.60 |
| Doug Gilmour | | |
| ❑ 18 Mark Recchi | 4.00 | 1.80 |
| Luc Robitaille | | |
| ❑ 19 Kevin Lowe | 2.00 | .90 |
| Garth Butcher | | |
| ❑ 20 Rick Tocchet | 6.00 | 2.70 |
| Jeremy Roenick | | |
| ❑ 21 Pierre Turgeon | 5.00 | 2.20 |
| Mike Modano | | |
| ❑ 22 Mike Gartner | 6.00 | 2.70 |
| Teemu Selanne | | |
| ❑ 23 Mario Lemieux | 30.00 | 13.50 |
| Wayne Gretzky | | |

## 1993-94 Stadium Club Finest

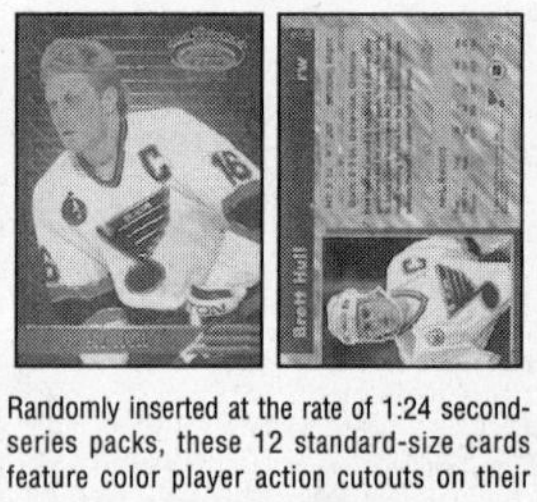

Randomly inserted at the rate of 1:24 second-series packs, these 12 standard-size cards feature color player action cutouts on their multicolored metallic fronts. The player's name in gold lettering appears on a silver bar at the lower left. The horizontal back carries a color player photo on the left. The player's name and position appear at the top, with biography, career highlights, and statistics following below on a background that resembles blue ruffled silk. The cards are numbered on the back as "X of 12."

| | MINT | NRMT |
|---|---|---|
| COMPLETE SET (12) | 50.00 | 22.00 |
| COMMON CARD (1-12) | 1.50 | .70 |

| | | |
|---|---|---|
| ❑ 1 Wayne Gretzky | 15.00 | 6.75 |
| ❑ 2 Jeff Brown | 1.50 | .70 |
| ❑ 3 Brett Hull | 3.00 | 1.35 |
| ❑ 4 Paul Coffey | 2.50 | 1.10 |
| ❑ 5 Felix Potvin | 2.50 | 1.10 |
| ❑ 6 Mike Gartner | 2.00 | .90 |
| ❑ 7 Luc Robitaille | 2.00 | .90 |
| ❑ 8 Marty McSorley | 1.50 | .70 |
| ❑ 9 Gary Roberts | 1.50 | .70 |
| ❑ 10 Mario Lemieux | 12.00 | 5.50 |
| ❑ 11 Patrick Roy | 12.00 | 5.50 |
| ❑ 12 Ray Bourque | 2.50 | 1.10 |
| ❑ NNO Redemption Single | 1.00 | .45 |
| ❑ NNO Redemption Set | 4.00 | 1.80 |

## 1993-94 Stadium Club Master Photos

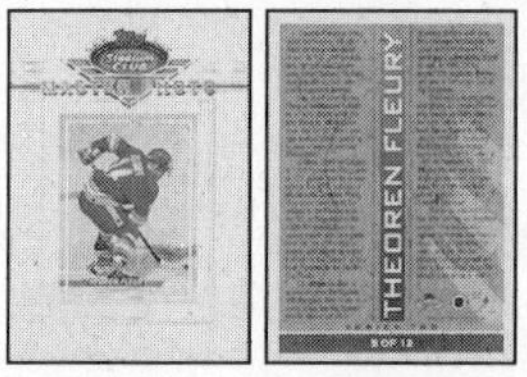

Inserted one per U.S. box, and issued in two 12-card series, these 24 oversized cards measure 5" by 7". The fronts feature color player action shots framed by prismatic foil lines and set on a white card face. The player's name appears in prismatic-foil lettering atop a blue bar near the bottom of the photo. The white-bordered back carries the player's name in white lettering within the vertical red stripe in the middle. Career highlights are printed in the blue areas to the left and right. The cards are numbered on the back for both series as "X of 12," but are listed below as 1-24 to avoid confusion. Winner cards, which could be redeemed for one 5" X 7" card of each of the three players listed on the reverse, were inserted 1:24 packs of '93-94 Stadium Club

| | MINT | NRMT |
|---|---|---|
| COMPLETE SET (24) | 30.00 | 13.50 |
| COMPLETE SERIES 1 (12) | 20.00 | 9.00 |
| COMPLETE SERIES 2 (12) | 10.00 | 4.50 |
| COMMON CARD (1-24) | .50 | .23 |
| COMP.WINNER SET (24) | 40.00 | 18.00 |

*WINNER CARDS: 1.25X JUMBOS

| | | |
|---|---|---|
| ❑ 1 Pat LaFontaine | 1.50 | .70 |
| ❑ 2 Doug Gilmour | 1.50 | .70 |
| ❑ 3 Ray Bourque | 1.50 | .70 |
| ❑ 4 Teemu Selanne | 2.50 | 1.10 |
| ❑ 5 Eric Lindros | 4.00 | 1.80 |
| ❑ 6 Ray Ferraro | .50 | .23 |
| ❑ 7 Patrick Roy | 5.00 | 2.20 |
| ❑ 8 Wayne Gretzky | 6.00 | 2.70 |
| ❑ 9 Brett Hull | 1.50 | .70 |
| ❑ 10 John Vanbiesbrouck | 2.00 | .90 |
| ❑ 11 Adam Oates | 1.50 | .70 |
| ❑ 12 Tom Barrasso | 1.50 | .70 |
| ❑ 13 Esa Tikkanen | .50 | .23 |
| ❑ 14 Jari Kurri | 1.50 | .70 |
| ❑ 15 Grant Fuhr | .50 | .23 |
| ❑ 16 Scott Lachance | .50 | .23 |
| ❑ 17 Theoren Fleury | 1.50 | .70 |
| ❑ 18 Adam Graves | 1.50 | .70 |
| ❑ 19 Rick Tabaracci | .50 | .23 |
| ❑ 20 Pierre Turgeon | 1.50 | .70 |
| ❑ 21 Steven Finn | .50 | .23 |
| ❑ 22 Craig Janney | .50 | .23 |
| ❑ 23 Mathieu Schneider | .50 | .23 |
| ❑ 24 Felix Potvin | 2.00 | .90 |

## 1993-94 Stadium Club Team USA

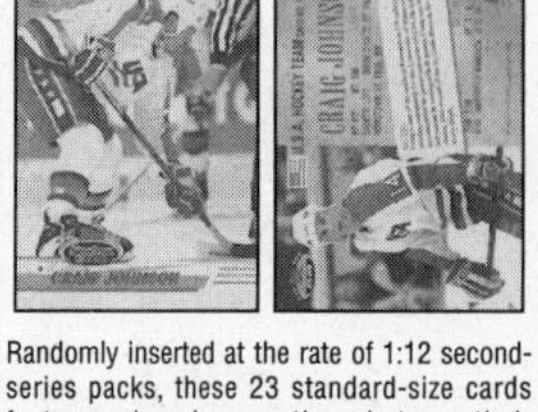

Randomly inserted at the rate of 1:12 second-series packs, these 23 standard-size cards feature color player action shots on their borderless fronts. The player's name appears in gold-foil lettering over a blue stripe near the bottom. The gold foil USA Hockey logo appears in an upper corner. The horizontal back carries a color player photo on the left. The player's name, position, biography, career highlights, and statistics appear on a blue background on the right. The cards are numbered on the back as "X of 23."

| | MINT | NRMT |
|---|---|---|
| COMPLETE SET (23) | 20.00 | 9.00 |
| COMMON CARD (1-23) | 1.00 | .45 |

| | | |
|---|---|---|
| ❑ 1 Mark Beaufait | 1.00 | .45 |
| ❑ 2 Jim Campbell | 1.00 | .45 |
| ❑ 3 Ted Crowley | 1.00 | .45 |
| ❑ 4 Mike Dunham | 1.50 | .70 |
| ❑ 5 Chris Ferraro | 1.50 | .70 |
| ❑ 6 Peter Ferraro | 1.50 | .70 |
| ❑ 7 Brett Hauer | 1.00 | .45 |
| ❑ 8 Darby Hendrickson | 1.00 | .45 |
| ❑ 9 Jon Hillebrandt | 1.50 | .70 |
| ❑ 10 Chris Imes | 1.00 | .45 |
| ❑ 11 Craig Johnson | 1.00 | .45 |
| ❑ 12 Peter Laviolette | 1.00 | .45 |
| ❑ 13 Jeff Lazaro | 1.00 | .45 |
| ❑ 14 John Lilley | 1.00 | .45 |
| ❑ 15 Todd Marchant | 1.50 | .70 |
| ❑ 16 Matt Martin | 1.00 | .45 |
| ❑ 17 Ian Moran | 1.00 | .45 |
| ❑ 18 Travis Richards | 1.00 | .45 |
| ❑ 19 Barry Richter | 1.00 | .45 |
| ❑ 20 David Roberts | 1.00 | .45 |
| ❑ 21 Brian Rolston | 1.50 | .70 |
| ❑ 22 David Sacco | 1.00 | .45 |
| ❑ 23 Jim Storm | 1.00 | .45 |

## 1994 Stadium Club Members Only

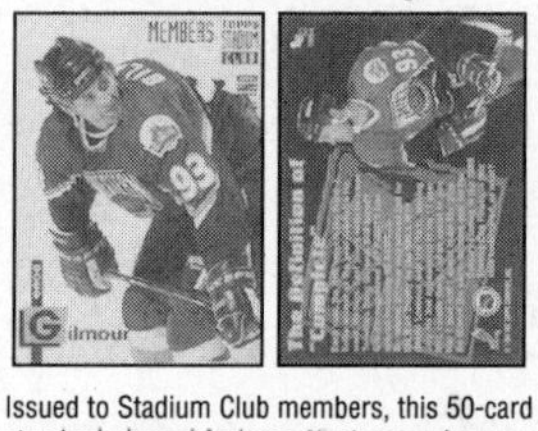

Issued to Stadium Club members, this 50-card standard-size set features 45 players who were involved with the 1994 All-Star game, Western Conference All-Stars (1-22), Eastern Conference All-Stars (23-45), and five Stadium Club Finest cards. The fronts have full-bleed color action player photos. The player's name is printed in the bottom left corner, the words "Topps Stadium Club Members Only" in gold foil appear in one of the top corners. On a black background, the horizontal backs carry a color player close-up shot, along with a player profile.

| | MINT | NRMT |
|---|---|---|
| COMPLETE SET (50) | 25.00 | 11.00 |
| COMMON CARD (1-50) | .10 | .05 |

| | | |
|---|---|---|
| ❑ 1 Felix Potvin | .75 | .35 |
| ❑ 2 Chris Chelios | .75 | .35 |
| ❑ 3 Paul Coffey | .75 | .35 |
| ❑ 4 Pavel Bure | 1.25 | .55 |
| ❑ 5 Wayne Gretzky | 4.00 | 1.80 |
| ❑ 6 Brett Hull | 1.00 | .45 |
| ❑ 7 Al MacInnis | .20 | .09 |
| ❑ 8 Rob Blake | .10 | .05 |
| ❑ 9 Alexei Kasatonov | .10 | .05 |
| ❑ 10 Teemu Selanne | 1.25 | .55 |
| ❑ 11 Sandis Ozolinsh | .25 | .11 |
| ❑ 12 Shayne Corson | .15 | .07 |
| ❑ 13 Dave Andreychuk | .15 | .07 |
| ❑ 14 Dave Taylor | .10 | .05 |
| ❑ 15 Sergei Fedorov | 1.25 | .55 |
| ❑ 16 Brendan Shanahan | 1.25 | .55 |
| ❑ 17 Arturs Irbe | .25 | .11 |
| ❑ 18 Joe Nieuwendyk | .25 | .11 |
| ❑ 19 Russ Courtnall | .10 | .05 |
| ❑ 20 Jeremy Roenick | .75 | .35 |
| ❑ 21 Doug Gilmour | .75 | .35 |
| ❑ 22 Curtis Joseph | .75 | .35 |
| ❑ 23 Patrick Roy | 3.00 | 1.35 |
| ❑ 24 Brian Leetch | .75 | .35 |
| ❑ 25 Ray Bourque | .75 | .35 |
| ❑ 26 Alexander Mogilny | .50 | .23 |
| ❑ 27 Mark Messier | 1.00 | .45 |
| ❑ 28 Eric Lindros | 2.00 | .90 |
| ❑ 29 Garry Galley | .10 | .05 |
| ❑ 30 Scott Stevens | .15 | .07 |
| ❑ 31 Al Iafrate | .10 | .05 |
| ❑ 32 Larry Murphy | .15 | .07 |
| ❑ 33 Joe Mullen | .10 | .05 |
| ❑ 34 Mark Recchi | .35 | .16 |
| ❑ 35 Adam Graves | .15 | .07 |
| ❑ 36 Geoff Sanderson | .15 | .07 |
| ❑ 37 Adam Oates | .35 | .16 |
| ❑ 38 Pierre Turgeon | .35 | .16 |
| ❑ 39 Joe Sakic | 1.25 | .55 |
| ❑ 40 John Vanbiesbrouck | 1.00 | .45 |
| ❑ 41 Brian Bradley | .10 | .05 |
| ❑ 42 Alexei Yashin | .75 | .35 |
| ❑ 43 Bob Kudelski | .10 | .05 |
| ❑ 44 Jaromir Jagr | 2.00 | .90 |
| ❑ 45 Mike Richter | .75 | .35 |
| ❑ 46 Martin Brodeur | 2.00 | .90 |
| ❑ 47 Mikael Renberg | .75 | .35 |
| ❑ 48 Derek Plante | .20 | .09 |
| ❑ 49 Jason Arnott | .50 | .23 |
| ❑ 50 Alexandre Daigle | .50 | .23 |

## 1994-95 Stadium Club

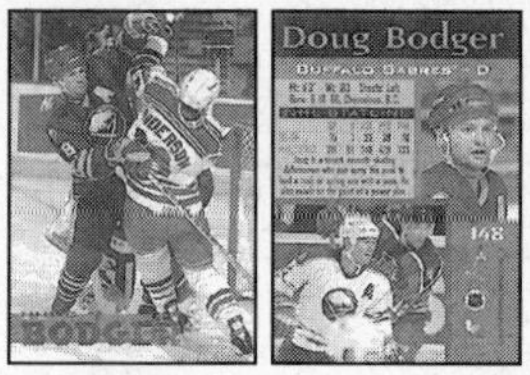

This 270-card standard-size set was issued in one series. Due to the NHL lock-out, series two was replaced on the production schedule by Finest; therefore, this set does not have a comprehensive player selection. There are 12 cards per pack and 24 packs per box. The card fronts feature a full-bleed photo with the player's name and set name printed in gold foil along the bottom. The backs feature two player photos and previous year stats. Subsets include Power Players (55-60), Great Expectations (110-119), Shutouts (178-190), Rink Report (201-204), and Trophy Winners (264-270). There are no key Rookie Cards in this set. A parallel "Member's Only" set was made available to collectors through the Topps Stadium Club. This set contains all regular and insert cards from the 1994-95 Stadium Club series; the cards are distinguished by a gold foil Member's Only icon. These cards tend to trade for 3X to 5X the values listed below for regular cards; superstars can be somewhat higher. Insert cards are valued at 1.5X to 2X the values listed under the appropriate header.

| | MINT | NRMT |
|---|---|---|
| COMPLETE SET (270) | 30.00 | 13.50 |
| COMMON CARD (1-270) | .10 | .05 |

| | | |
|---|---|---|
| ❑ 1 Mark Messier | .40 | .18 |
| ❑ 2 Brad May | .15 | .07 |
| ❑ 3 Mike Ricci | .10 | .05 |
| ❑ 4 Scott Stevens | .15 | .07 |
| ❑ 5 Keith Tkachuk | .40 | .18 |
| ❑ 6 Guy Hebert | .15 | .07 |
| ❑ 7 Jason Arnott | .15 | .07 |
| ❑ 8 Cam Neely | .15 | .07 |
| ❑ 9 Adam Graves | .15 | .07 |
| ❑ 10 Pavel Bure | .60 | .25 |
| ❑ 11 Jeff Odgers | .10 | .05 |
| ❑ 12 Dimitri Khristich | .10 | .05 |
| ❑ 13 Patrick Poulin | .10 | .05 |
| ❑ 14 Mike Donnelly | .10 | .05 |
| ❑ 15 Felix Potvin | .30 | .14 |
| ❑ 16 Keith Primeau | .15 | .07 |
| ❑ 17 Fred Knipscheer | .10 | .05 |
| ❑ 18 Mike Keane | .10 | .05 |
| ❑ 19 Vitali Prokhorov | .10 | .05 |
| ❑ 20 Ray Ferraro | .10 | .05 |
| ❑ 21 Shane Churla | .10 | .05 |
| ❑ 22 Rob Niedermayer | .15 | .07 |
| ❑ 23 Adam Creighton | .10 | .05 |
| ❑ 24 Tommy Soderstrom | .15 | .07 |
| ❑ 25 Theoren Fleury | .15 | .07 |
| ❑ 26 Jim Storm | .10 | .05 |
| ❑ 27 Bret Hedican | .10 | .05 |
| ❑ 28 Sean Hill | .10 | .05 |
| ❑ 29 Bill Ranford | .15 | .07 |
| ❑ 30 Derek Plante | .10 | .05 |
| ❑ 31 Dave McLlwain | .10 | .05 |
| ❑ 32 Iain Fraser | .10 | .05 |
| ❑ 33 Patrick Roy | 1.50 | .70 |
| ❑ 34 Martin Straka | .10 | .05 |
| ❑ 35 Bruce Driver | .10 | .05 |
| ❑ 36 Brian Skrudland | .10 | .05 |
| ❑ 37 Bob Errey | .10 | .05 |
| ❑ 38 Randy Cunneyworth | .10 | .05 |
| ❑ 39 John Slaney | .10 | .05 |
| ❑ 40 Ray Sheppard | .15 | .07 |
| ❑ 41 Sergei Nemchinov | .10 | .05 |
| ❑ 42 Dave Ellett | .10 | .05 |
| ❑ 43 Vincent Riendeau | .15 | .07 |
| ❑ 44 Trent Yawney | .10 | .05 |
| ❑ 45 Dave Gagner | .15 | .07 |
| ❑ 46 Igor Korolev | .10 | .05 |
| ❑ 47 Gary Shuchuk | .10 | .05 |
| ❑ 48 Rob Zamuner | .10 | .05 |
| ❑ 49 Frantisek Kucera | .10 | .05 |
| ❑ 50 Joe Mullen | .15 | .07 |
| ❑ 51 Ron Hextall | .15 | .07 |
| ❑ 52 J.J. Daigneault | .10 | .05 |
| ❑ 53 Patrik Carnback | .10 | .05 |
| ❑ 54 Steven Rice | .10 | .05 |
| ❑ 55 Brian Leetch PP | .30 | .14 |
| ❑ 56 Al MacInnis PP | .15 | .07 |
| ❑ 57 Luc Robitaille PP | .15 | .07 |
| ❑ 58 Dave Andreychuk PP | .15 | .07 |
| ❑ 59 Jeremy Roenick PP | .30 | .14 |
| ❑ 60 Mario Lemieux PP | 1.50 | .70 |
| ❑ 61 Dave Manson | .10 | .05 |
| ❑ 62 Pat Falloon | .10 | .05 |
| ❑ 63 Jesse Belanger | .10 | .05 |
| ❑ 64 Philippe Boucher | .10 | .05 |
| ❑ 65 Sergio Momesso | .10 | .05 |
| ❑ 66 Evgeny Davydov | .10 | .05 |
| ❑ 67 Alexei Gusarov | .10 | .05 |

❑ 68 Jaromir Jagr 1.00 .45
❑ 69 Randy Ladouceur .10 .05
❑ 70 Chris Chelios .30 .14
❑ 71 John Druce .10 .05
❑ 72 Kris Draper .10 .05
❑ 73 Joey Kocur .10 .05
❑ 74 Rich Tabarraci .15 .07
❑ 75 Mikael Andersson .10 .05
❑ 76 Mark Osborne .10 .05
❑ 77 Ray Bourque .30 .14
❑ 78 Dimitri Yushkevich .10 .05
❑ 79 Mike Vernon .15 .07
❑ 80 Steve Thomas .10 .05
❑ 81 Steve Duchesne .10 .05
❑ 82 Dean Evason .10 .05
❑ 83 Jason Smith .10 .05
❑ 84 Bryan Marchment .10 .05
❑ 85 Boris Mironov .10 .05
❑ 86 Jeff Norton .10 .05
❑ 87 Donald Audette .15 .07
❑ 88 Eric Lindros 1.25 .55
❑ 89 Garry Valk .10 .05
❑ 90 Mats Sundin .15 .07
❑ 91 Gerald Diduck .10 .05
❑ 92 Jeff Shantz .10 .05
❑ 93 Scott Niedermayer .10 .05
❑ 94 Troy Mallette .10 .05
❑ 95 John Vanbiesbrouck .50 .23
❑ 96 Ron Francis .15 .07
❑ 97 Slava Kozlov .15 .07
❑ 98 Ken Baumgartner .10 .05
❑ 99 Wayne Gretzky 2.00 .90
❑ 100 Brett Hull .40 .18
❑ 101 Marc Bergevin .10 .05
❑ 102 Owen Nolan .15 .07
❑ 103 Bryan Smolinski .10 .05
❑ 104 Lyle Odelein .10 .05
❑ 105 Mike Ridley .10 .05
❑ 106 Trevor Kidd .15 .07
❑ 107 Derian Hatcher .10 .05
❑ 108 Derek King .10 .05
❑ 109 Rob Zettler .10 .05
❑ 110 Alexandre Daigle GE .10 .05
❑ 111 Chris Pronger GE .15 .07
❑ 112 Chris Gratton GE .15 .07
❑ 113 John Slaney GE .10 .05
❑ 114 Jocelyn Thibault GE .30 .14
❑ 115 Jason Arnott GE .15 .07
❑ 116 Alexei Yashin GE .15 .07
❑ 117 Rob Niedermayer GE .15 .07
❑ 118 Jason Allison GE .10 .05
❑ 119 Martin Brodeur GE .75 .35
❑ 120 Pat Verbeek .10 .05
❑ 121 Kelly Buchberger .10 .05
❑ 122 Doug Lidster .10 .05
❑ 123 Sergei Makarov .10 .05
❑ 124 Kris King .10 .05
❑ 125 Dominik Hasek .60 .25
❑ 126 Martin Rucinsky .10 .05
❑ 127 Kerry Huffman .10 .05
❑ 128 Gord Murphy .10 .05
❑ 129 Bobby Holik .10 .05
❑ 130 Kirk Muller .10 .05
❑ 131 Christian Ruuttu .10 .05
❑ 132 Jyrki Lumme .10 .05
❑ 133 Ken Wregget .15 .07
❑ 134 Dale Hunter .10 .05
❑ 135 Rob Blake .10 .05
❑ 136 Petr Klima .10 .05
❑ 137 Steve Heinze .10 .05
❑ 138 Chris Osgood .50 .23
❑ 139 John Lilley .10 .05
❑ 140 Dave Andreychuk .15 .07
❑ 141 Zarley Zalapski .10 .05
❑ 142 Curtis Joseph .30 .14
❑ 143 Brent Gilchrist .10 .05
❑ 144 Vladimir Malakhov .10 .05
❑ 145 Mikael Renberg .15 .07
❑ 146 Robert Kron .10 .05
❑ 147 Dean McAmmond .10 .05
❑ 148 Doug Bodger .10 .05
❑ 149 Ray Whitney .10 .05
❑ 150 Brian Leetch .30 .14
❑ 151 Martin Lapointe .10 .05
❑ 152 Teppo Numminen .10 .05
❑ 153 Scott Young .10 .05
❑ 154 Nick Kypreos .10 .05
❑ 155 Ed Belfour .30 .14
❑ 156 Greg Adams .10 .05
❑ 157 Brian Benning .10 .05
❑ 158 Bob Carpenter .10 .05
❑ 159 Vladimir Konstantinov .10 .05
❑ 160 Rick Tocchet .15 .07
❑ 161 Joe Sacco .10 .05
❑ 162 Daren Puppa .15 .07
❑ 163 Randy Burridge .10 .05
❑ 164 Darryl Sydor .10 .05
❑ 165 Jay More .10 .05
❑ 166 Joe Nieuwendyk .15 .07
❑ 167 Mike Eastwood .10 .05
❑ 168 Murray Baron .10 .05
❑ 169 Brent Fedyk .10 .05
❑ 170 Russ Courtnall .10 .05
❑ 171 Sean Burke .15 .07
❑ 172 Uwe Krupp .10 .05
❑ 173 Kevin Lowe .10 .05
❑ 174 Guy Carbonneau .10 .05
❑ 175 Alexei Yashin .15 .07
❑ 176 Thomas Steen .10 .05
❑ 177 Sandis Ozolinsh .15 .07
❑ 178 Patrick Roy SO 1.00 .45
❑ 179 Dominik Hasek SO .40 .18
❑ 180 Ed Belfour SO .30 .14
❑ 181 Mike Richter SO .30 .14
❑ 182 Ron Hextall SO .15 .07
❑ 183 Daren Puppa SO .15 .07
❑ 184 Jon Casey SO .15 .07
❑ 185 Felix Potvin SO .30 .14
❑ 186 Martin Brodeur SO .75 .35
❑ 187 Darcy Wakaluk SO .15 .07
❑ 188 Kirk McLean SO .15 .07
❑ 189 Mike Vernon SO .15 .07
❑ 190 Arturs Irbe SO .15 .07
❑ 191 Dino Ciccarelli .15 .07
❑ 192 Steven Finn .10 .05
❑ 193 Pierre Sevigny .10 .05
❑ 194 Jim Dowd .10 .05
❑ 195 Chris Gratton .15 .07
❑ 196 Wayne Presley .10 .05
❑ 197 Joel Otto .10 .05
❑ 198 Fredrik Olausson .10 .05
❑ 199 Jody Hull .10 .05
❑ 200 Cliff Ronning .10 .05
❑ 201 Darren Turcotte RR .10 .05
❑ 202 Al Iafrate RR .10 .05
❑ 203 Eric Lindros RR .75 .35
❑ 204 Sandis Ozolinsh RR .15 .07
❑ 205 Petr Nedved .15 .07
❑ 206 Mark Lamb .10 .05
❑ 207 Shaun Van Allen .10 .05
❑ 208 Kelly Hrudey .15 .07
❑ 209 Nikolai Borschevsky .10 .05
❑ 210 Glen Wesley .10 .05
❑ 211 Shawn McEachern .10 .05
❑ 212 Mark Janssens .10 .05
❑ 213 Brian Mullen .10 .05
❑ 214 Craig Ludwig .10 .05
❑ 215 Mike Rathje .10 .05
❑ 216 Stephane Matteau .10 .05
❑ 217 Tim Cheveldae .15 .07
❑ 218 Brent Sutter .15 .07
❑ 219 Gord Dineen UER .10 .05
(Listed as born in Toronto, Quebec; should be Toronto, Ontario)
❑ 220 Kevin Hatcher .10 .05
❑ 221 Todd Simon .10 .05
❑ 222 Bill Lindsay .10 .05
❑ 223 Kirk McLean .15 .07
❑ 224 Chris Joseph .10 .05
❑ 225 Valeri Zelepukin .10 .05
❑ 226 Terry Yake .10 .05
❑ 227 Benoit Brunet .10 .05
❑ 228 Nicklas Lidstrom .15 .07
❑ 229 Zdeno Ciger .10 .05
❑ 230 Gary Roberts .10 .05
❑ 231 Andy Moog .15 .07
❑ 232 Ed Patterson .10 .05
❑ 233 Philippe Bozon .10 .05
❑ 234 Brent Hughes .10 .05
❑ 235 Chris Pronger .15 .07
❑ 236 Travis Green .15 .07
❑ 237 Pat Conacher .10 .05
❑ 238 Bob Rouse .10 .05
❑ 239 Yves Racine .10 .05
❑ 240 Nelson Emerson .10 .05
❑ 241 Oleg Petrov .10 .05
❑ 242 Steve Larmer .15 .07
❑ 243 Dan Laperriere .10 .05
❑ 244 John McIntyre .10 .05
❑ 245 Alexander Semak .10 .05
❑ 246 Stephane Fiset UER .15 .07
(Listed as being born in Montreal, Ontario;
should be Montreal, Quebec)
❑ 247 Peter Bondra .30 .14
❑ 248 Dale Hawerchuk .15 .07
❑ 249 Jamie Baker .10 .05
❑ 250 Sergei Fedorov .60 .25
❑ 251 Derek Mayer .10 .05
❑ 252 Ivan Droppa .10 .05
❑ 253 Kent Manderville .10 .05
❑ 254 Sergei Zholtok .10 .05
❑ 255 Murray Craven .10 .05
❑ 256 Todd Krygier .10 .05
❑ 257 Brent Grieve .10 .05
❑ 258 Esa Tikkanen .10 .05
❑ 259 Brad Dalgarno .10 .05
❑ 260 Russ Romaniuk .15 .07
❑ 261 Stu Barnes .10 .05
❑ 262 Dan Keczmer .10 .05
❑ 263 Eric Desjardins .10 .05
❑ 264 Martin Brodeur TW .75 .35
❑ 265 Adam Graves TW .15 .07
❑ 266 Cam Neely TW .15 .07
❑ 267 Ray Bourque TW .30 .14
❑ 268 Sergei Fedorov TW .40 .18
❑ 269 Dominik Hasek TW .40 .18
❑ 270 Wayne Gretzky TW 1.50 .70

## 1994-95 Stadium Club First Day Issue

This is a parallel to the 270 card basic set, inserted at a rate of 1:24 packs. The only difference is the silver foil "First Day Issue" logo on the card front.

| | MINT | NRMT |
|---|---|---|
| COMPLETE SET (270) | 1000.00 | 450.00 |
| COMMON CARD (1-270) | 2.50 | 1.10 |

*STARS: 30X TO 60X BASIC CARDS
*YOUNG STARS: 20X TO 40X BASIC CARDS

## 1994-95 Stadium Club Dynasty and Destiny

According to published odds, the five cards in this set were randomly inserted at the rate of 1:24 packs. Collector and dealer reports suggest they are available at a much easier rate than listed. Each card features two

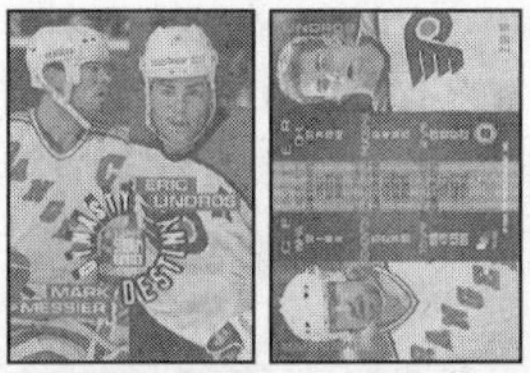

players; one veteran and an up and coming player with the same type of skills. Photos and stats for each player are on the backs. Each card is numbered out of ten, signifying that five more cards were to be included in the never-produced second series.

| | MINT | NRMT |
|---|---|---|
| COMPLETE SET (5) | 25.00 | 11.00 |
| COMMON CARD (1-5) | 2.50 | 1.10 |

❑ 1 Tom Barrasso 2.50 1.10
Arturs Irbe
❑ 2 Mark Messier 10.00 4.50
Eric Lindros
❑ 3 Brett Hull 8.00 3.60
Pavel Bure
❑ 4 Luc Robitaille 4.00 1.80
Mikael Renberg
❑ 5 Chris Chelios 4.00 1.80
Chris Pronger

## 1994-95 Stadium Club Finest Inserts

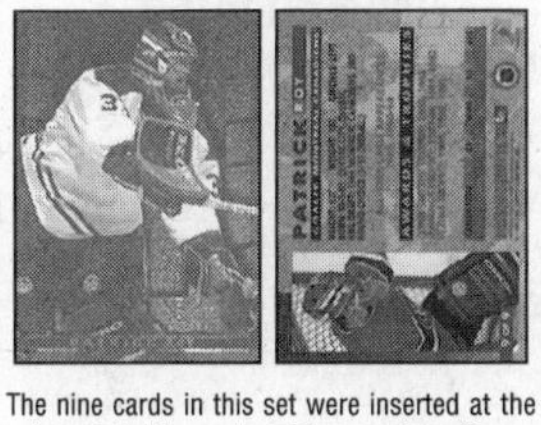

The nine cards in this set were inserted at the rate of 1:12 packs. The cards offer a completely different design from those of the basic Finest set which was released later in the season. These cards feature a cut-out player photo on a blue textured background. The player name is printed on a multi-color bar on the bottom of the card. Backs feature a small photo on the left with text information and limited stats. Cards are numbered out of nine.

| | MINT | NRMT |
|---|---|---|
| COMPLETE SET (9) | 60.00 | 27.00 |
| COMMON CARD (1-9) | 1.50 | .70 |

❑ 1 Mario Lemieux 12.00 5.50
❑ 2 Brett Hull 3.00 1.35
❑ 3 Mark Messier 3.00 1.35
❑ 4 Wayne Gretzky 15.00 6.75
❑ 5 Pavel Bure 5.00 2.20
❑ 6 Sergei Fedorov 5.00 2.20
❑ 7 Brian Leetch 1.50 .70
❑ 8 Ray Bourque 1.50 .70
❑ 9 Patrick Roy 12.00 5.50

## 1994-95 Stadium Club Super Teams

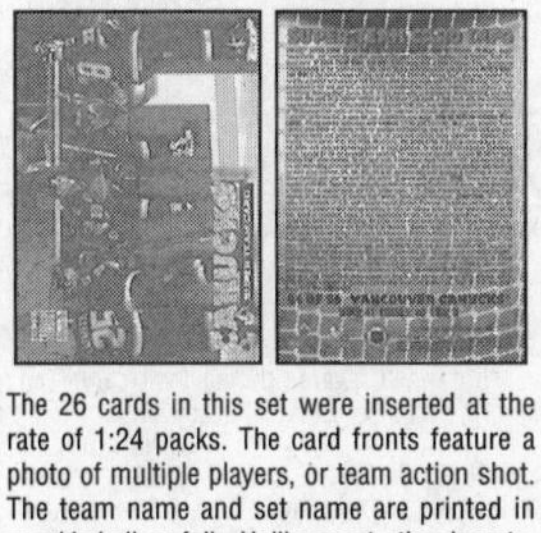

The 26 cards in this set were inserted at the rate of 1:24 packs. The card fronts feature a photo of multiple players, or team action shot. The team name and set name are printed in speckled silver foil. Unlike most other inserts, these cards were part of an interactive game which allowed the holder to redeem the card for prizes if the pictured team won a division, conference or Stanley Cup championship. The backs have contest information and the teams record from the 1993-94 season. Holders of the New Jersey Devils card were able to redeem it for complete, specially stamped sets of Stadium Club and Finest. Winning division (Calgary, Detroit, Philadelphia, Quebec) and conference (Detroit, New Jersey) team cards were redeemable for packages of special stamped cards featuring members of that team. Since individual Division and Conference Winner team sets are generally traded in complete set form, values are listed in the header as such.

| | MINT | NRMT |
|---|---|---|
| COMPLETE SET (26) | 100.00 | 45.00 |
| COMMON CARD (1-26) | 4.00 | 1.80 |
| COMP.DEVILS CONF.W.SET | 10.00 | 4.50 |
| COMP.FLAMES DIV.W.SET | 5.00 | 2.20 |
| COMP.FLYERS DIV.W.SET | 15.00 | 6.75 |
| COMP.NORDIQUES DIV.W.SET | 15.00 | 6.75 |
| COMP.RED WINGS CONF.W.SET | 12.00 | 5.50 |
| COMP.RED WINGS DIV.W.SET | 12.00 | 5.50 |

❑ 1 Anaheim Mighty Ducks 4.00 1.80
(Bob Corkum et al.)
❑ 2 Boston Bruins 5.00 2.20
(Adam Oates/Ray Bourque)
❑ 3 Buffalo Sabres 4.00 1.80
(Dominik Hasek et al.)
❑ 4 Calgary Flames 4.00 1.80
(Andrei Trefilov/Theoren Fleury)
❑ 5 Chicago Blackhawks 5.00 2.20
(Ed Belfour et al.)
❑ 6 Dallas Stars 4.00 1.80
(Mike Modano/Trent Klatt/
Paul Broten)
❑ 7 Detroit Red Wings 12.00 5.50
(Bench)
❑ 8 Edmonton Oilers 4.00 1.80
(Bill Ranford/Bob Beers)
❑ 9 Florida Panthers 4.00 1.80
(Line change)
❑ 10 Hartford Whalers 4.00 1.80
(Sean Burke/Jim Storm/
Ted Crowley)
❑ 11 Los Angeles Kings 4.00 1.80
(Lined up for anthem)
❑ 12 Montreal Canadiens 8.00 3.60
(Patrick Roy)
❑ 13 New Jersey Devils 15.00 6.75
(Martin Brodeur)
❑ 14 New York Islanders 4.00 1.80
(Darius Kasparaitis/Yan Kaminsky)
❑ 15 New York Rangers 6.00 2.70
(Stanley Cup parade with
Mark Messier raising cup)
❑ 16 Ottawa Senators 4.00 1.80
(Practice session)
❑ 17 Philadelphia Flyers 8.00 3.60
(Eric Lindros/Mark Recchi/Jason Bowen)
❑ 18 Pittsburgh Penguins 5.00 2.20
(Ron Francis/Joe Mullen)
❑ 19 Quebec Nordiques 6.00 2.70
(Joe Sakic et al.)
❑ 20 St. Louis Blues 5.00 2.20
(Curtis Joseph)
❑ 21 San Jose Sharks 4.00 1.80
(Tom Pederson/Sergei Makarov)
❑ 22 Tampa Bay Lightning 4.00 1.80
(Denis Savard/Petr Klima)
❑ 23 Toronto Maple Leafs 5.00 2.20
(Doug Gilmour/Dave Andreychuk)
❑ 24 Vancouver Canucks 6.00 2.70
(Pavel Bure et al.)
❑ 25 Washington Capitals 4.00 1.80
(Byron Dafoe/Dave Poulin/
Kevin Hatcher/Calle Johansson)
❑ 26 Winnipeg Jets 6.00 2.70
(Teemu Selanne/Alexei Zhamnov)

## 1995 Stadium Club Members Only

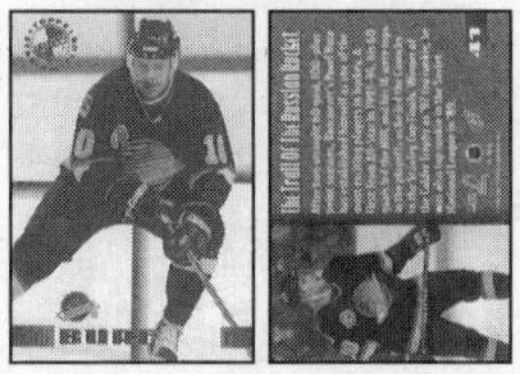

Topps produced a 50-card boxed set for each of the four major sports. With their club membership, members received one set of their choice and had the option of purchasing additional sets for $10.00 each. The five Finest cards (46-50) represent Topps' selection of the top 1994-95 rookies. The color action photos on the fronts have brightly-colored backgrounds and carry the distinctive Topps Stadium Club Members Only gold foil seal. The backs present a second color photo and player profile.

| | MINT | NRMT |
|---|---|---|
| COMPLETE SET (50) | 25.00 | 11.00 |
| COMMON CARD (1-50) | .10 | .05 |

❑ 1 Patrick Roy 2.50 1.10
❑ 2 Ray Bourque .50 .23
❑ 3 Brian Leetch .50 .23
❑ 4 Cam Neely .35 .16
❑ 5 Jaromir Jagr 1.50 .70
❑ 6 Alexander Mogilny .35 .16
❑ 7 John Vanbiesbrouck 1.00 .45
❑ 8 Geoff Sanderson .15 .07
❑ 9 Mark Recchi .25 .11
❑ 10 Scott Stevens .10 .05
❑ 11 Roman Hamrlik .15 .07
❑ 12 Dominik Hasek 1.00 .45
❑ 13 Joe Sakic 1.00 .45
❑ 14 Alexei Yashin .50 .23
❑ 15 Eric Lindros 1.50 .70
❑ 16 Adam Oates .25 .11
❑ 17 Ulf Samuelsson .10 .05
❑ 18 Wendel Clark .15 .07
❑ 19 Mark Messier .75 .35
❑ 20 Pierre Turgeon .25 .11
❑ 21 Mark Tinordi .10 .05
❑ 22 Ron Francis .25 .11
❑ 23 Jeff Brown .10 .05
❑ 24 Tom Kurvers .10 .05
❑ 25 Mike Modano .75 .35
❑ 26 Mats Sundin .50 .23
❑ 27 Jeremy Roenick .50 .23
❑ 28 Kevin Hatcher .10 .05
❑ 29 Curtis Joseph .50 .23
❑ 30 Paul Coffey .50 .23
❑ 31 Jason Arnott .25 .11
❑ 32 Wayne Gretzky 3.00 1.35
❑ 33 Theoren Fleury .50 .23
❑ 34 Al MacInnis .20 .09
❑ 35 Ed Belfour .50 .23
❑ 36 Sergei Fedorov 1.00 .45
❑ 37 Brett Hull .75 .35
❑ 38 Chris Chelios .50 .23
❑ 39 Keith Tkachuk .75 .35
❑ 40 Felix Potvin .50 .23
❑ 41 Pavel Bure 1.00 .45
❑ 42 Ulf Dahlen .10 .05
❑ 43 Teemu Selanne 1.00 .45
❑ 44 Doug Gilmour .50 .23
❑ 45 Phil Housley .15 .07
❑ 46 Paul Kariya FIN 6.00 2.70
❑ 47 Peter Forsberg FIN 5.00 2.20
❑ 48 Jim Carey FIN 1.50 .70
❑ 49 Todd Marchant FIN .50 .23
❑ 50 Blaine Lacher FIN .75 .35

## 1995-96 Stadium Club

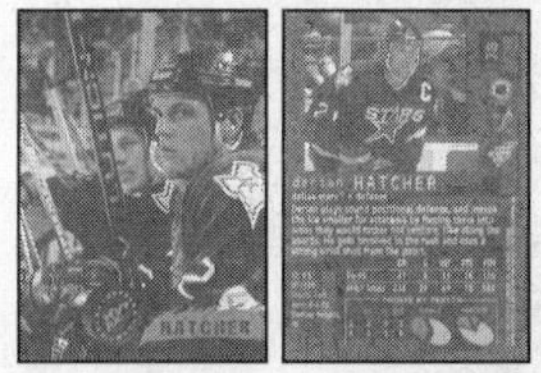

The 1995-96 Stadium Club set was issued in one series totalling 225 cards. The 10-card packs retail for $2.50. The set features two subsets: Extreme Corps (163-189) and Extreme Rookies (190-207). One EC or ER subset card was included per hobby or retail pack (1:2 canadian packs), making them somewhat more difficult to obtain than regular singles. Of note is the Stadium Club logo on the card fronts, which features the brand name translated into the primary language of the player featured. Rookie Cards in this set include Daniel Alfredsson.

| | MINT | NRMT |
|---|---|---|
| COMPLETE SET (225) | 50.00 | 22.00 |
| COMMON CARD (1-162/208-225) | .10 | .05 |
| COMMON EC/ER SP (163-207) | .50 | .23 |

❑ 1 Alexander Mogilny .15 .07
❑ 2 Ray Bourque .20 .09
❑ 3 Garry Galley .10 .05
❑ 4 Glen Wesley .10 .05
❑ 5 Dave Andreychuk .15 .07
❑ 6 Daren Puppa .15 .07
❑ 7 Shayne Corson .10 .05
❑ 8 Kelly Hrudey .15 .07
❑ 9 Russ Courtnall .10 .05
❑ 10 Chris Chelios .20 .09
❑ 11 Ulf Samuelsson .10 .05
❑ 12 Mike Vernon .15 .07
❑ 13 Al MacInnis .15 .07
❑ 14 Joel Otto .10 .05
❑ 15 Patrick Roy 1.50 .70
❑ 16 Steve Thomas .10 .05
❑ 17 Pat Verbeek .10 .05
❑ 18 Joe Nieuwendyk .15 .07
❑ 19 Todd Krygier .10 .05
❑ 20 Steve Yzerman 1.00 .45
❑ 21 Bill Ranford UER .15 .07
misnumbered #2
❑ 22 Ron Francis .15 .07
❑ 23 Sylvain Cote .10 .05
❑ 24 Grant Fuhr .15 .07
❑ 25 Brendan Shanahan .60 .25
❑ 26 John MacLean .15 .07
❑ 27 Darren Turcotte .10 .05
❑ 28 Bernie Nicholls .10 .05
❑ 29 Sean Burke .15 .07
❑ 30 Brian Leetch .20 .09
❑ 31 Dave Gagner .15 .07
❑ 32 Rick Tocchet .15 .07
❑ 33 Ron Hextall .15 .07
❑ 34 Paul Coffey .20 .09
❑ 35 John Vanbiesbrouck .50 .23
❑ 36 Rod Brind'Amour .15 .07
❑ 37 Brian Savage .15 .07
❑ 38 Nelson Emerson .10 .05
❑ 39 Brian Bradley .10 .05
❑ 40 Adam Oates .15 .07
❑ 41 Kirk McLean .15 .07
❑ 42 Kevin Hatcher .10 .05
❑ 43 Mike Keane .10 .05
❑ 44 Don Beaupre .15 .07
❑ 45 Scott Stevens .15 .07
❑ 46 Dale Hawerchuk .15 .07
❑ 47 Scott Young .10 .05
❑ 48 Mark Recchi .15 .07
❑ 49 Mike Richter .20 .09
❑ 50 Kevin Stevens .10 .05

| | | |
|---|---|---|
| ❑ 51 Mike Ridley | .10 | .05 |
| ❑ 52 Joe Murphy | .10 | .05 |
| ❑ 53 Stephane Fiset | .15 | .07 |
| ❑ 54 Donald Audette | .15 | .07 |
| ❑ 55 Ed Belfour | .20 | .09 |
| ❑ 56 Rob Blake | .10 | .05 |
| ❑ 57 Adam Graves | .15 | .07 |
| ❑ 58 Arturs Irbe | .15 | .07 |
| ❑ 59 Mathieu Schneider | .10 | .05 |
| ❑ 60 Dominik Hasek | .60 | .25 |
| ❑ 61 Andrew Cassels | .10 | .05 |
| ❑ 62 Johan Garpenlov | .10 | .05 |
| ❑ 63 Kyle McLaren | .10 | .05 |
| ❑ 64 Petr Nedved | .15 | .07 |
| ❑ 65 Owen Nolan | .15 | .07 |
| ❑ 66 Keith Primeau | .15 | .07 |
| ❑ 67 Mark Tinordi | .10 | .05 |
| ❑ 68 Dimitri Khristich | .10 | .05 |
| ❑ 69 Chris Pronger | .15 | .07 |
| ❑ 70 Jaromir Jagr | 1.00 | .45 |
| ❑ 71 Mike Ricci | .10 | .05 |
| ❑ 72 Trevor Kidd | .15 | .07 |
| ❑ 73 Stu Barnes | .10 | .05 |
| ❑ 74 Doug Weight | .15 | .07 |
| ❑ 75 Mats Sundin | .15 | .07 |
| ❑ 76 Scott Niedermayer | .10 | .05 |
| ❑ 77 John LeClair | .50 | .23 |
| ❑ 78 Derian Hatcher | .10 | .05 |
| ❑ 79 Brad May | .15 | .07 |
| ❑ 80 Felix Potvin | .20 | .09 |
| ❑ 81 Derek King | .10 | .05 |
| ❑ 82 Guy Hebert | .15 | .07 |
| ❑ 83 Shawn McEachern | .10 | .05 |
| ❑ 84 Slava Kozlov | .15 | .07 |
| ❑ 85 Martin Brodeur | .75 | .35 |
| ❑ 86 Ray Whitney | .10 | .05 |
| ❑ 87 Martin Straka | .10 | .05 |
| ❑ 88 Keith Jones | .10 | .05 |
| ❑ 89 Roman Hamrlik | .15 | .07 |
| ❑ 90 Keith Tkachuk | .40 | .18 |
| ❑ 91 Jim Dowd | .10 | .05 |
| ❑ 92 Sergei Zubov | .10 | .05 |
| ❑ 93 Bryan McCabe | .10 | .05 |
| ❑ 94 Rob Niedermayer | .15 | .07 |
| ❑ 95 Alexei Zhamnov | .15 | .07 |
| ❑ 96 Zarley Zalapski | .10 | .05 |
| ❑ 97 Alexandre Daigle | .10 | .05 |
| ❑ 98 Jocelyn Thibault | .20 | .09 |
| ❑ 99 Zigmund Palffy | .15 | .07 |
| ❑ 100 Luc Robitaille | .15 | .07 |
| ❑ 101 Radek Bonk | .10 | .05 |
| ❑ 102 Todd Marchant | .10 | .05 |
| ❑ 103 Todd Harvey | .10 | .05 |
| ❑ 104 Blaine Lacher | .15 | .07 |
| ❑ 105 Peter Forsberg | 1.00 | .45 |
| ❑ 106 Jeff Friesen | .15 | .07 |
| ❑ 107 Kenny Jonsson | .10 | .05 |
| ❑ 108 Brett Lindros | .10 | .05 |
| ❑ 109 David Oliver | .10 | .05 |
| ❑ 110 Mikael Renberg | .15 | .07 |
| ❑ 111 Alexander Selivanov | .10 | .05 |
| ❑ 112 Stanislav Neckar | .10 | .05 |
| ❑ 113 Oleg Tverdovsky | .15 | .07 |
| ❑ 114 Shean Donovan | .10 | .05 |
| ❑ 115 Jim Carey | .20 | .09 |
| ❑ 116 Tony Granato | .10 | .05 |
| ❑ 117 Tony Amonte | .15 | .07 |
| ❑ 118 Tomas Sandstrom | .10 | .05 |
| ❑ 119 Rick Tabaracci | .15 | .07 |
| ❑ 120 Ray Ferraro | .10 | .05 |
| ❑ 121 Brian Noonan | .10 | .05 |
| ❑ 122 Miroslav Satan | 1.50 | .70 |
| ❑ 123 Sergio Momesso | .10 | .05 |
| ❑ 124 Gary Suter | .10 | .05 |
| ❑ 125 Eric Desjardins | .10 | .05 |
| ❑ 126 Steve Duchesne | .10 | .05 |
| ❑ 127 Zdeno Ciger | .10 | .05 |
| ❑ 128 Cliff Ronning | .10 | .05 |
| ❑ 129 Nicklas Lidstrom | .15 | .07 |
| ❑ 130 Bill Guerin | .10 | .05 |
| ❑ 131 Igor Korolev | .10 | .05 |
| ❑ 132 Roman Oksiuta | .10 | .05 |
| ❑ 133 Jesse Belanger | .10 | .05 |
| ❑ 134 Chris Gratton | .15 | .07 |
| ❑ 135 Chris Osgood | .20 | .09 |
| ❑ 136 Pat Peake | .10 | .05 |
| ❑ 137 Viktor Kozlov | .10 | .05 |
| ❑ 138 Aaron Gavey | .10 | .05 |
| ❑ 139 Zdenek Nedved | .10 | .05 |
| ❑ 140 Rhett Warrener | .10 | .05 |
| ❑ 141 Marko Kiprusoff | .10 | .05 |
| ❑ 142 Dan Quinn | .10 | .05 |
| ❑ 143 Alexei Zhitnik | .10 | .05 |
| ❑ 144 Larry Murphy | .15 | .07 |
| ❑ 145 Phil Housley | .15 | .07 |
| ❑ 146 Don Sweeney | .10 | .05 |
| ❑ 147 Jason Dawe | .10 | .05 |
| ❑ 148 Marcus Ragnarsson | .10 | .05 |
| ❑ 149 Andrei Nikolishin | .10 | .05 |
| ❑ 150 Dino Ciccarelli | .15 | .07 |
| ❑ 151 Jari Kurri | .15 | .07 |
| ❑ 152 Bob Probert | .15 | .07 |
| ❑ 153 Randy McKay | .10 | .05 |
| ❑ 154 Michael Nylander | .10 | .05 |
| ❑ 155 Wendel Clark | .15 | .07 |
| ❑ 156 Antti Tormanen | .10 | .05 |
| ❑ 157 Nikolai Khabibulin | .15 | .07 |
| ❑ 158 Tom Barrasso | .15 | .07 |
| ❑ 159 Vincent Damphousse | .15 | .07 |
| ❑ 160 Trevor Linden | .15 | .07 |
| ❑ 161 Valeri Kamensky | .15 | .07 |
| ❑ 162 Mike Gartner | .15 | .07 |
| ❑ 163 Cam Neely EC SP | .20 | .09 |
| ❑ 164 Pat LaFontaine EC SP | .50 | .23 |
| ❑ 165 Theoren Fleury EC SP | .50 | .23 |
| ❑ 166 Jeremy Roenick EC SP | .75 | .35 |
| ❑ 167 Joe Sakic EC SP | 2.50 | 1.10 |
| ❑ 168 Mike Modano EC SP | 1.25 | .55 |
| ❑ 169 Sergei Fedorov EC SP | 2.00 | .90 |
| ❑ 170 Scott Mellanby EC SP | .50 | .23 |
| ❑ 171 Jason Arnott EC SP | .60 | .25 |
| ❑ 172 Geoff Sanderson EC SP | .60 | .25 |
| ❑ 173 Wayne Gretzky EC SP | 8.00 | 3.60 |
| ❑ 174 Paul Kariya EC SP | 5.00 | 2.20 |
| ❑ 175 Pierre Turgeon EC SP | .50 | .23 |
| ❑ 176 Stephane Richer EC SP | .50 | .23 |
| ❑ 177 Kirk Muller EC SP | .10 | .05 |
| ❑ 178 Mark Messier EC SP | 1.25 | .55 |
| ❑ 179 Craig Janney EC SP | .50 | .23 |
| ❑ 180 Mario Lemieux EC SP | 6.00 | 2.70 |
| ❑ 181 Eric Lindros EC SP | 4.00 | 1.80 |
| ❑ 182 Alexei Yashin EC SP | .50 | .23 |
| ❑ 183 Brett Hull EC SP | 1.25 | .55 |
| ❑ 184 Doug Gilmour EC SP | .60 | .25 |
| ❑ 185 Petr Klima EC SP | .50 | .23 |
| ❑ 186 Pavel Bure EC SP | 2.50 | 1.10 |
| ❑ 187 Joe Juneau EC SP | .50 | .23 |
| ❑ 188 Teemu Selanne EC SP | 2.50 | 1.10 |
| ❑ 189 Claude Lemieux EC SP | .50 | .23 |
| ❑ 190 Vitali Yachmenev ER SP | .50 | .23 |
| ❑ 191 Jason Bonsignore ER SP | .50 | .23 |
| ❑ 192 Jeff O'Neill ER SP | .50 | .23 |
| ❑ 193 Brendan Witt ER SP | .50 | .23 |
| ❑ 194 Brian Holzinger ER SP | .50 | .23 |
| ❑ 195 Eric Daze ER SP | .50 | .23 |
| ❑ 196 Ed Jovanovski ER SP | .50 | .23 |
| ❑ 197 Deron Quint ER SP | .50 | .23 |
| ❑ 198 Marty Murray ER SP | .50 | .23 |
| ❑ 199 Jere Lehtinen ER SP | .50 | .23 |
| ❑ 200 Radek Dvorak ER | .50 | .23 |
| ❑ 201 Aki-Petteri Berg ER | .10 | .05 |
| ❑ 202 Chad Kilger ER | .50 | .23 |
| ❑ 203 Saku Koivu ER SP | 2.00 | .90 |
| ❑ 204 Todd Bertuzzi ER | .50 | .23 |
| ❑ 205 Niklas Sundstrom ER SP | .50 | .23 |
| ❑ 206 Daniel Alfredsson ER | 2.00 | .90 |
| ❑ 207 Shane Doan ER | .50 | .23 |
| ❑ 208 Richard Park | .10 | .05 |
| ❑ 209 Peter Bondra | .20 | .09 |
| ❑ 210 Bryan Smolinski | .10 | .05 |
| ❑ 211 Tommy Salo | .15 | .07 |
| ❑ 212 Patrick Poulin | .10 | .05 |
| ❑ 213 Mathieu Dandenault | .10 | .05 |
| ❑ 214 Steve Rucchin | .10 | .05 |
| ❑ 215 Ray Sheppard | .15 | .07 |
| ❑ 216 Robert Svehla | .10 | .05 |
| ❑ 217 Olaf Kolzig | .15 | .07 |
| ❑ 218 Alexei Kovalev | .10 | .05 |
| ❑ 219 Ian Moran | .10 | .05 |
| ❑ 220 Valeri Bure | .15 | .07 |
| ❑ 221 Dean Malkoc | .10 | .05 |
| ❑ 222 Jason Doig | .10 | .05 |
| ❑ 223 David Nemirovsky | .10 | .05 |
| ❑ 224 Jamie Pushor | .10 | .05 |
| ❑ 225 Ricard Persson | .10 | .05 |

## 1995-96 Stadium Club Members Only Master Set

Parallel to base set that was only available to members of Topps Stadium Club. Cards are distinguishable by an embossed Members only logo.

| | MINT | NRMT |
|---|---|---|
| COMPLETE SET (225) | 800.00 | 350.00 |
| COMMON CARD (1-162/208-225) | 2.00 | .90 |
| COMMON EC/ER SP (163-207) | 10.00 | 4.50 |

*STARS: 10X TO 20X BASIC CARDS
*YOUNG STARS: 7.5X TO 15X BASIC CARDS
*RC's: 5X TO 10X BASIC CARDS

## 1995-96 Stadium Club Extreme North

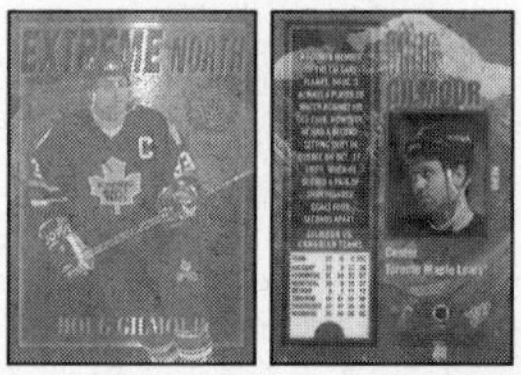

Randomly inserted in packs at a rate of 1:48, this 9-card set focuses on some of the best players on Canadian teams. The cards are printed on diffraction foil.

| | MINT | NRMT |
|---|---|---|
| COMPLETE SET (9) | 70.00 | 32.00 |
| COMMON CARD (EN1-EN9) | 4.00 | 1.80 |
| ❑ EN1 Pavel Bure | 12.00 | 5.50 |
| ❑ EN2 Teemu Selanne | 12.00 | 5.50 |
| ❑ EN3 Felix Potvin | 5.00 | 2.20 |
| ❑ EN4 Patrick Roy | 30.00 | 13.50 |
| ❑ EN5 Theoren Fleury | 4.00 | 1.80 |
| ❑ EN6 Bill Ranford | 4.00 | 1.80 |
| ❑ EN7 Pierre Turgeon | 4.00 | 1.80 |
| ❑ EN8 Doug Gilmour | 4.00 | 1.80 |
| ❑ EN9 Alexander Mogilny | 4.00 | 1.80 |

## 1995-96 Stadium Club Fearless

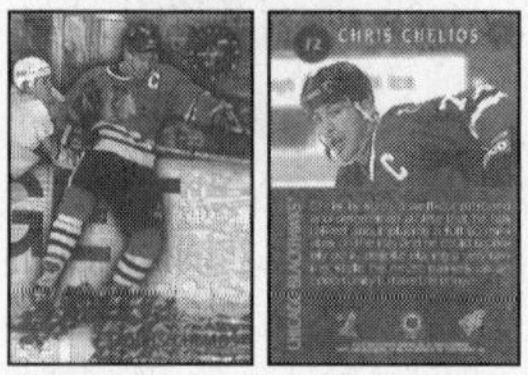

Randomly inserted at a rate of 1:24 retail, and 1:48 hobby and Canadian packs, this 9-card set features hockey's toughest players on double diffraction foil-stamped cards.

| | MINT | NRMT |
|---|---|---|
| COMPLETE SET (9) | 30.00 | 13.50 |
| COMMON CARD (NF1-NF9) | 2.00 | .90 |
| ❑ F1 Brendan Shanahan | 12.00 | 5.50 |
| ❑ F2 Chris Chelios | 4.00 | 1.80 |
| ❑ F3 Keith Primeau | 4.00 | 1.80 |
| ❑ F4 Scott Stevens | 2.00 | .90 |
| ❑ F5 Rick Tocchet | 2.00 | .90 |
| ❑ F6 Kevin Stevens | 2.00 | .90 |
| ❑ F7 Ulf Samuelsson | 2.00 | .90 |
| ❑ F8 Wendel Clark | 2.00 | .90 |
| ❑ F9 Keith Tkachuk | 8.00 | 3.60 |

## 1995-96 Stadium Club Generation TSC

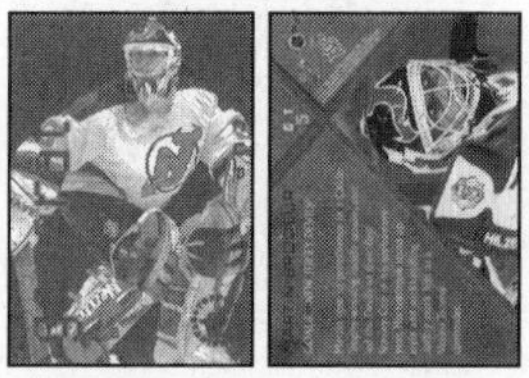

Randomly inserted at a rate of 1:36 hobby and retail, and 1:72 Canadian packs, this 9-card set introduces some up-and-coming youngsters using an interesting textured foil design element.

| | MINT | NRMT |
|---|---|---|
| COMPLETE SET (9) | 85.00 | 38.00 |
| COMMON CARD (GT1-GT9) | 2.50 | 1.10 |
| ❑ GT1 Paul Kariya | 20.00 | 9.00 |
| ❑ GT2 Teemu Selanne | 10.00 | 4.50 |
| ❑ GT3 Jaromir Jagr | 15.00 | 6.75 |
| ❑ GT4 Peter Forsberg | 15.00 | 6.75 |
| ❑ GT5 Martin Brodeur | 12.00 | 5.50 |
| ❑ GT6 Jim Carey | 6.00 | 2.70 |
| ❑ GT7 Mikael Renberg | 5.00 | 2.20 |
| ❑ GT8 Scott Niedermayer | 2.50 | 1.10 |
| ❑ GT9 Ed Jovanovski | 5.00 | 2.20 |

## 1995-96 Stadium Club Metalists

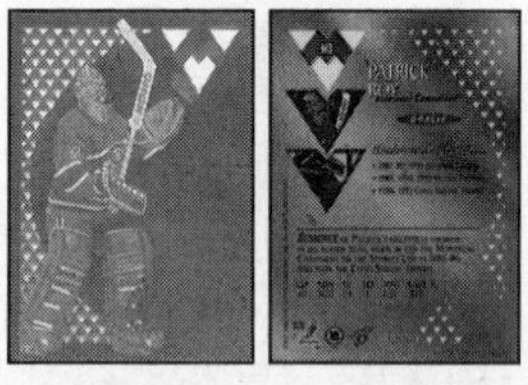

Randomly inserted at a rate of 1:48 hobby, 1:96 retail, and 1:192 Canadian packs, this 12-card set showcases players who have won two or more major awards during their career on the first ever laser-cut foil hockey cards.

| | MINT | NRMT |
|---|---|---|
| COMPLETE SET (12) | 150.00 | 70.00 |
| COMMON CARD (M1-M12) | 2.50 | 1.10 |
| ❑ M1 Wayne Gretzky | 40.00 | 18.00 |
| ❑ M2 Mario Lemieux | 30.00 | 13.50 |
| ❑ M3 Patrick Roy | 30.00 | 13.50 |
| ❑ M4 Ray Bourque | 6.00 | 2.70 |
| ❑ M5 Ed Belfour | 6.00 | 2.70 |
| ❑ M6 Tom Barrasso | 4.00 | 1.80 |
| ❑ M7 Joe Mullen | 2.50 | 1.10 |
| ❑ M8 Brian Leetch | 6.00 | 2.70 |
| ❑ M9 Mark Messier | 8.00 | 3.60 |
| ❑ M10 Dominik Hasek | 15.00 | 6.75 |
| ❑ M11 Paul Coffey | 6.00 | 2.70 |
| ❑ M12 Guy Carbonneau | 2.50 | 1.10 |

## 1995-96 Stadium Club Nemeses

Randomly inserted at a rate of 1:24 hobby, 1:48 retail, and 1:96 Canadian packs, this 9-card set highlights two rival players together on one card. The cards use etched foil on each side.

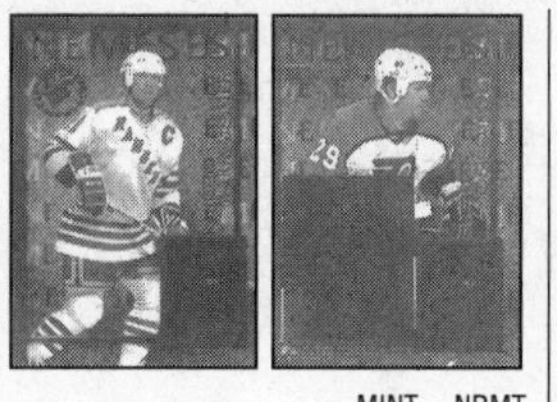

| | MINT | NRMT |
|---|---|---|
| COMPLETE SET (9) | 120.00 | 55.00 |
| COMMON CARD (N1-N9) | 5.00 | 2.20 |
| ❑ N1 Eric Lindros<br>Scott Stevens | 20.00 | 9.00 |
| ❑ N2 Wayne Gretzky<br>Mario Lemieux | 50.00 | 22.00 |
| ❑ N3 Claude Lemieux<br>Cam Neely | 5.00 | 2.20 |
| ❑ N4 Pavel Bure<br>Mike Richter | 12.00 | 5.50 |
| ❑ N5 Brian Leetch<br>Ray Bourque | 6.00 | 2.70 |
| ❑ N6 Martin Brodeur<br>Dominik Hasek | 15.00 | 6.75 |
| ❑ N7 Doug Gilmour<br>Sergei Fedorov | 12.00 | 5.50 |
| ❑ N8 Mark Messier<br>Joel Otto | 6.00 | 2.70 |
| ❑ N9 Paul Kariya<br>Peter Forsberg | 30.00 | 13.50 |

## 1995-96 Stadium Club Power Streak

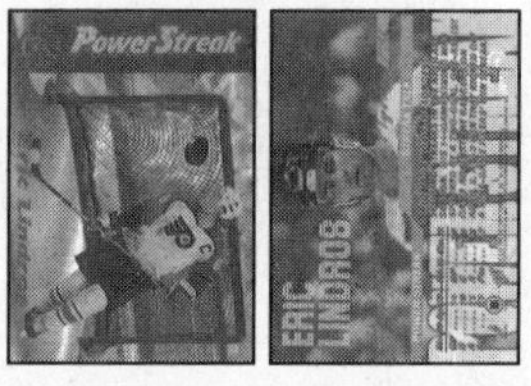

Randomly inserted at a rate of 1:12 retail, and 1:24 hobby and Canadian packs, this set features 10 players who have sustained prolonged goal scoring streaks. The cards are printed using Power Matrix technology.

| | MINT | NRMT |
|---|---|---|
| COMPLETE SET (10) | 40.00 | 18.00 |
| COMMON CARD (PS1-PS10) | 2.00 | .90 |
| ❑ PS1 Pierre Turgeon | 2.00 | .90 |
| ❑ PS2 Eric Lindros | 12.00 | 5.50 |
| ❑ PS3 Ron Francis | 3.00 | 1.35 |
| ❑ PS4 Paul Coffey | 5.00 | 2.20 |
| ❑ PS5 Mikael Renberg | 3.00 | 1.35 |
| ❑ PS6 John LeClair | 6.00 | 2.70 |
| ❑ PS7 Dino Ciccarelli | 3.00 | 1.35 |
| ❑ PS8 Wendel Clark | 3.00 | 1.35 |
| ❑ PS9 Brett Hull | 5.00 | 2.20 |
| ❑ PS10 Stephane Richer | 2.00 | .90 |

## 1995-96 Stadium Club Master Photo Test

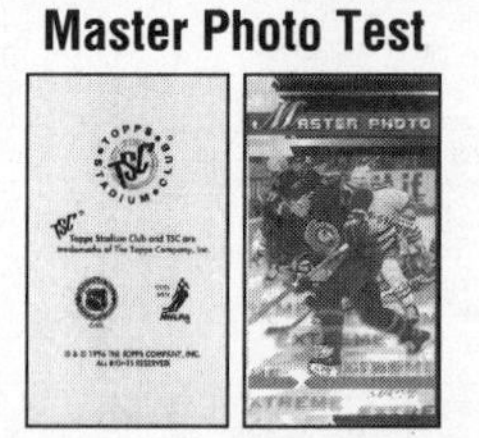

This nine-card set measures approximately 3" by 5" and features color action player photos from the 1995-96 Stadium Club set inside a black border bearing the words Master Photo. The backs carry the TSC, NHL, and NHLPA logos. No further information on origin or distribution is available.The cards are unnumbered and checklisted below in alphabetical order. This may be an incomplete checklist; additional information would be appreciated.

| | MINT | NRMT |
|---|---|---|
| COMPLETE SET (9) | 30.00 | 13.50 |
| COMMON CARD (1-9) | 2.00 | .90 |
| ❑ 1 Jason Arnott | 3.00 | 1.35 |
| ❑ 2 Theoren Fleury | 5.00 | 2.20 |
| ❑ 3 Doug Gilmour | 5.00 | 2.20 |
| ❑ 4 Trevor Linden | 2.00 | .90 |
| ❑ 5 Kirk McLean | 2.00 | .90 |
| ❑ 6 Alexander Mogilny | 4.00 | 1.80 |
| ❑ 7 Felix Potvin | 5.00 | 2.20 |
| ❑ 8 Mats Sundin | 5.00 | 2.20 |
| ❑ 9 Alexei Yashin | 5.00 | 2.20 |

## 1996 Stadium Club Members Only

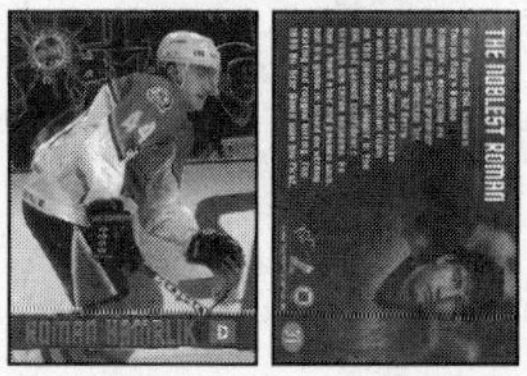

This 50-card set was available through the direct marketing arm of the Topps Stadium Club. The first 45 cards feature the competitors in the 1996 NHL All-Star Game. The players are pictured in their AS sweaters over a stylized background. the back includes a portrait and player profile. The final five cards in the set picture some of the year's top rookies on Finest-style technology.

| | MINT | NRMT |
|---|---|---|
| COMPLETE SET (50) | 20.00 | 9.00 |
| COMMON CARD (1-50) | .10 | .05 |
| ❑ 1 Wayne Gretzky | 3.00 | 1.35 |
| ❑ 2 Paul Kariya | 2.00 | .90 |
| ❑ 3 Brett Hull | .75 | .35 |
| ❑ 4 Chris Chelios | .60 | .25 |
| ❑ 5 Paul Coffey | .60 | .25 |
| ❑ 6 Ed Belfour | .60 | .25 |
| ❑ 7 Theoren Fleury | .60 | .25 |
| ❑ 8 Owen Nolan | .25 | .11 |
| ❑ 9 Al MacInnis | .25 | .11 |
| ❑ 10 Alexander Mogilny | .60 | .25 |
| ❑ 11 Kevin Hatcher | .10 | .05 |
| ❑ 12 Doug Weight | .35 | .16 |
| ❑ 13 Felix Potvin | .75 | .35 |
| ❑ 14 Teemu Selanne | 1.00 | .45 |
| ❑ 15 Sergei Fedorov | 1.00 | .45 |
| ❑ 16 Larry Murphy | .10 | .05 |
| ❑ 17 Joe Sakic | 1.00 | .45 |
| ❑ 18 Mats Sundin | .60 | .25 |
| ❑ 19 Nicklas Lidstrom | .25 | .11 |
| ❑ 20 Peter Forsberg | 1.50 | .70 |
| ❑ 21 Chris Osgood | .60 | .25 |
| ❑ 22 Mike Gartner | .15 | .07 |
| ❑ 23 Denis Savard<br>Craig MacTavish | .15 | .07 |
| ❑ 24 Mario Lemieux | 2.00 | .90 |
| ❑ 25 Jaromir Jagr | 1.50 | .70 |
| ❑ 26 Brendan Shanahan | 1.00 | .45 |
| ❑ 27 Scott Stevens | .15 | .07 |
| ❑ 28 Ray Bourque | .60 | .25 |
| ❑ 29 Martin Brodeur | 1.25 | .55 |
| ❑ 30 Eric Lindros | 1.50 | .70 |
| ❑ 31 Peter Bondra | .60 | .25 |
| ❑ 32 Scott Mellanby | .10 | .05 |
| ❑ 33 Brian Leetch | .60 | .25 |
| ❑ 34 John Vanbiesbrouck | .75 | .35 |
| ❑ 35 Pat Verbeek | .20 | .09 |
| ❑ 36 Cam Neely | .50 | .23 |
| ❑ 37 Roman Hamrlik | .35 | .16 |
| ❑ 38 Daniel Alfredsson | .60 | .25 |
| ❑ 39 Pierre Turgeon | .50 | .23 |
| ❑ 40 Mark Messier | .75 | .35 |
| ❑ 41 Eric Desjardins | .10 | .05 |
| ❑ 42 Dominik Hasek | 1.00 | .45 |
| ❑ 43 John LeClair | .75 | .35 |
| ❑ 44 Mathieu Schneider | .10 | .05 |
| ❑ 45 Ron Francis | .50 | .23 |
| ❑ 46 Saku Koivu | 3.00 | 1.35 |
| ❑ 47 Ed Jovanovski | 2.00 | .90 |
| ❑ 48 Vitali Yachmenev | 1.00 | .45 |
| ❑ 49 Petr Sykora | 2.00 | .90 |
| ❑ 50 Eric Daze | 3.00 | 1.35 |

## 1994-95 Stars HockeyKaps

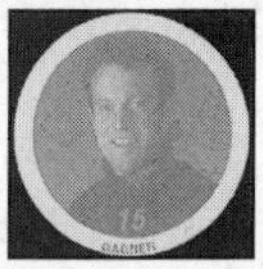

Measuring approximately 1 3/4" in diameter, this set of 25 caps features the Dallas Stars. The caps were given away at Stars games on February 6, 9, 16 and 18. Additional caps could be obtained through a mail-in offer by sending a SASE along with proof-of-purchase from one 46 oz. or one six-pack of 10 oz. Tropicana Twister. A HockeyKap collector game board was also available through a mail-in offer for two proofs-of-purchase of the above-mentioned products. The fronts feature color head shots with a white border. The player's last name is printed in the white border. The backs are blank. The caps are unnumbered and checklisted below in alphabetical order.

| | MINT | NRMT |
|---|---|---|
| COMPLETE SET (25) | 7.00 | 3.10 |
| COMMON CARD (1-25) | .10 | .05 |
| ❑ 1 Dave Barr | .25 | .11 |

| | | |
|---|---|---|
| ❑ 2 Brad Berry | .25 | .11 |
| ❑ 3 Neal Broten | .50 | .23 |
| ❑ 4 Paul Broten | .25 | .11 |
| ❑ 5 Paul Cavallini | .25 | .11 |
| ❑ 6 Shane Churla | .50 | .23 |
| ❑ 7 Russ Courtnall | .35 | .16 |
| ❑ 8 Mike Craig | .25 | .11 |
| ❑ 9 Ulf Dahlen | .35 | .16 |
| ❑ 10 Dean Evason | .25 | .11 |
| ❑ 11 Dave Gagner | .35 | .16 |
| ❑ 12 Bob Gainey CO | .35 | .16 |
| ❑ 13 Brent Gilchrist | .25 | .11 |
| ❑ 14 Derian Hatcher | .35 | .16 |
| ❑ 15 Doug Jarvis ACO | .10 | .05 |
| ❑ 16 Jim Johnson | .25 | .11 |
| ❑ 17 Trent Klatt | .25 | .11 |
| ❑ 18 Grant Ledyard | .25 | .11 |
| ❑ 19 Craig Ludwig | .25 | .11 |
| ❑ 20 Mike McPhee | .25 | .11 |
| ❑ 21 Mike Modano | 1.50 | .70 |
| ❑ 22 Andy Moog | 1.00 | .45 |
| ❑ 23 Mark Tinordi | .25 | .11 |
| ❑ 24 Darcy Wakaluk | .35 | .16 |
| ❑ 25 Rick Wilson ACO | .10 | .05 |

## 1994-95 Stars Pinnacle Sheet

Produced by Pinnacle, this promo sheet was given out at Reunion Arena for the Dallas Stars game vs. the Red Wings on April 1, 1995. The sheet measures approximately 12 1/2" by 10 1/2". The left, perforated portion displays nine standard-size player cards, while the right portion consists of an advertisement to purchase 12-packs of Coke products at participating Texaco retailers. The design is the same as the 1994-95 Pinnacle hockey series, with the same numbering. The cards are listed below, beginning at the upper left of the sheet and moving toward the lower right corner.

| | MINT | NRMT |
|---|---|---|
| COMPLETE SET (9) | 5.00 | 2.20 |
| COMMON PANEL | 5.00 | 2.20 |
| ❑ 3 Mike.Modano | 1.50 | .70 |
| ❑ 55 Derian Hatcher | .50 | .23 |
| ❑ 133 Russ Courtnall | .50 | .23 |
| ❑ 157 Darcy Wakaluk | .50 | .23 |
| ❑ 185 Brent Gilchrist | .25 | .11 |
| ❑ 262 Todd Harvey | .50 | .23 |
| ❑ 315 Andy Moog | 1.00 | .45 |
| ❑ 334 Dave Gagner | .50 | .23 |
| ❑ 433 Paul Broten | .25 | .11 |

## 1994-95 Stars Postcards

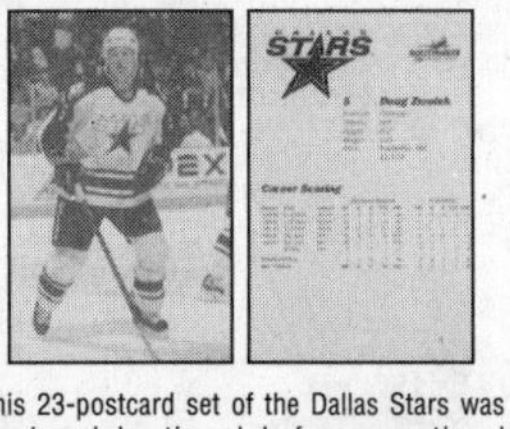

This 23-postcard set of the Dallas Stars was produced by the club for promotional giveaways and autograph signings. The cards feature full-bleed action photos on the fronts, while the backs contain biographical and statistical information. As the cards are unnumbered, they are listed below in alphabetical order.

| | MINT | NRMT |
|---|---|---|
| COMPLETE SET (23) | 14.00 | 6.25 |
| COMMON POSTCARD (1-23) | .50 | .23 |
| ❑ 1 Paul Broten | .50 | .23 |
| ❑ 2 Paul Cavallini | .50 | .23 |
| ❑ 3 Shane Churla | .75 | .35 |
| ❑ 4 Gord Donnelly | .50 | .23 |
| ❑ 5 Mike Donnelly | .50 | .23 |
| ❑ 6 Dean Evason | .50 | .23 |
| ❑ 7 Dave Gagner | .75 | .35 |
| ❑ 8 Brent Gilchrist | .50 | .23 |
| ❑ 9 Todd Harvey | .75 | .35 |
| ❑ 10 Derian Hatcher | .75 | .35 |
| ❑ 11 Kevin Hatcher | .60 | .25 |
| ❑ 12 Mike Kennedy | .50 | .23 |
| ❑ 13 Trent Klatt | .60 | .25 |
| ❑ 14 Mike Lalor | .50 | .23 |
| ❑ 15 Grant Ledyard | .50 | .23 |
| ❑ 16 Craig Ludwig | .50 | .23 |
| ❑ 17 Richard Matvichuk | .75 | .35 |
| ❑ 18 Corey Millen | .50 | .23 |
| ❑ 19 Mike Modano | 3.00 | 1.35 |
| ❑ 20 Andy Moog | 2.00 | .90 |
| ❑ 21 Darcy Wakaluk | .75 | .35 |
| ❑ 22 Peter Zezel | .50 | .23 |
| ❑ 23 Doug Zmolek | .50 | .23 |

## 1994-95 Stars Score Sheet

This perforated sheet was given away February 2, 1995, at the Dallas Stars' home game against the San Jose Sharks. The sheet measures approximately 12 1/2" by 10 1/2"; the larger left portion consists of nine standard-size cards, while the smaller right portion presents an advertisement for 1994-95 Score hockey first series. The back of the ad portion mentions Tom Thumb grocery stores as a place to buy Score cards. The cards have the same design as the regular issue cards. Note, however, that Shane Churla does not have a card in the regular series; this is his only appearance on a 1994-95 Score card. The cards are listed below beginning in the upper left and moving across and down toward the lower right.

| | MINT | NRMT |
|---|---|---|
| COMPLETE SET (9) | 5.00 | 2.20 |
| COMMON PANEL | 5.00 | 2.20 |
| ❑ 17 Mike McPhee | .25 | .11 |
| ❑ 43 Russ Courtnall | .25 | .11 |
| ❑ 68 Mark Tinordi | .25 | .11 |
| ❑ 94 Paul Cavallini | .25 | .11 |
| ❑ 113 Neal Broten | .50 | .23 |
| ❑ 148 Derian Hatcher | .50 | .23 |
| ❑ 173 Andy Moog | 1.00 | .45 |
| ❑ 188 Mike Modano | 1.50 | .70 |
| ❑ NNO Shane Churla | 1.00 | .45 |

## 1995-96 Stars Score Sheet

This perforated sheet was given away at a Dallas Stars game at Reunion Arena and measures approximately 12 1/2" by 10 1/2". The left portion displays nine cards with color action player photos while the right consists of sponsor logos and an advertisement to purchase six packs of Coke products at participating Texaco retailers. The cards are listed below beginning at the upper left of the sheet and moving toward the lower right corner.

| | MINT | NRMT |
|---|---|---|
| COMPLETE SET (1) | 5.00 | 2.20 |
| COMMON PANEL | 5.00 | 2.20 |
| ❑ 12 Kevin Hatcher | .25 | .11 |
| ❑ 38 Todd Harvey | .50 | .23 |
| ❑ 64 Andy Moog | 1.00 | .45 |
| ❑ 89 Greg Adams | .50 | .23 |
| ❑ 120 Mike Modano | 1.50 | .70 |
| ❑ 197 Darcy Wakaluk | .50 | .23 |
| ❑ 225 Derian Hatcher | .50 | .23 |
| ❑ 229 Joe Nieuwendyk | .75 | .35 |
| ❑ 261 Brent Gilchrist | .25 | .11 |

## 1996-97 Stars Postcards

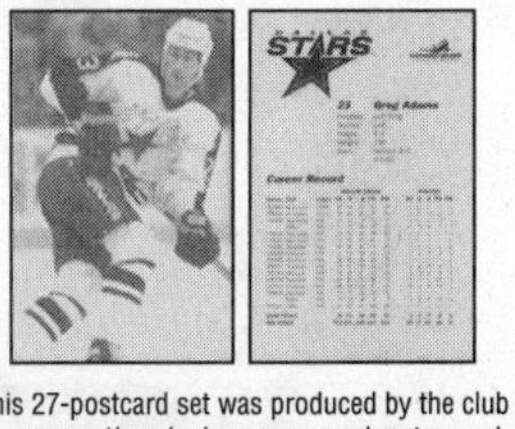

This 27-postcard set was produced by the club for promotional giveaways and autograph signings. The cards feature full color action photos on the front; the backs have biographical information and complete career stats. As the cards are unnumbered, they are listed below alphabetically.

| | MINT | NRMT |
|---|---|---|
| COMPLETE SET | 15.00 | 6.75 |
| COMMON POSTCARD (1-27) | .50 | .23 |
| ❑ 1 Greg Adams | .50 | .23 |
| ❑ 2 Bob Bassen | .50 | .23 |
| ❑ 3 Neal Broten | .75 | .35 |
| ❑ 4 Guy Carbonneau | .50 | .23 |
| ❑ 5 Bob Gainey | .50 | .23 |
| ❑ 6 Brent Gilchrist | .50 | .23 |
| ❑ 7 Todd Harvey | .75 | .35 |
| ❑ 8 Derian Hatcher | .75 | .35 |
| ❑ 9 Ken Hitchcock CO | .50 | .23 |
| ❑ 10 Benoit Hogue | .50 | .23 |
| ❑ 11 Bill Huard | .50 | .23 |
| ❑ 12 Arturs Irbe | .75 | .35 |
| ❑ 13 Mike Kennedy | .50 | .23 |
| ❑ 14 Mike Lalor | .50 | .23 |
| ❑ 15 Jamie Langenbrunner | .75 | .35 |
| ❑ 16 Grant Ledyard | .50 | .23 |
| ❑ 17 Jere Lehtinen | .75 | .35 |
| ❑ 18 Craig Ludwig | .50 | .23 |
| ❑ 19 Grant Marshall | .50 | .23 |
| ❑ 20 Richard Matvichuk | .50 | .23 |
| ❑ 21 Mike Modano | 2.50 | 1.10 |
| ❑ 22 Joe Nieuwendyk | .75 | .35 |
| ❑ 23 Andy Moog | 1.50 | .70 |
| ❑ 24 Dave Reid | .50 | .23 |
| ❑ 25 Darryl Sydor | .50 | .23 |
| ❑ 26 Pat Verbeek | .75 | .35 |
| ❑ 27 Sergei Zubov | .50 | .23 |

## 1996-97 Stars Score Sheet

For the third straight season, Score and the Stars teamed up to distribute a special, perforated card sheet, this time at a match against the Edmonton Oilers on Sunday, February 23, as well as at a local card show the weekend following. The majority of the cards mirror those found in the 1996-97 Score set. Of note are the cards of Pat Verbeek and Sergei Zubov, which were updated to show them as members of the Stars; Jere Lehtinen, which features green ink on the back instead of red; and Derian Hatcher, who is not included in the regular Score set. Although it typically is sold in sheet form, it is listed below as singles because the unique cards have led to many dealers breaking it up.

| | MINT | NRMT |
|---|---|---|
| COMPLETE SET | 5.00 | 2.20 |
| COMMON CARD | .50 | .23 |
| ❑ 39 Greg Adams | .50 | .23 |
| ❑ 72 Mike Modano | 2.00 | .90 |
| ❑ 86 Todd Harvey | .50 | .23 |
| ❑ 94 Pat Verbeek | .50 | .23 |
| ❑ 104 Andy Moog | 1.00 | .45 |
| ❑ 152 Joe Nieuwendyk | .75 | .35 |
| ❑ 171 Sergei Zubov | .50 | .23 |
| ❑ 246 Jere Lehtinen | .50 | .23 |
| ❑ NNO Derian Hatcher | .50 | .23 |

## 1975-76 Stingers Kahn's

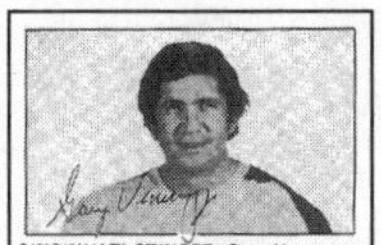

CINCINNATI STINGER: Gary Veneruzzo

This set of 14 photos was issued on wrappers of Kahn's Wieners and Beef Franks and features players of the Cincinnati Stingers of the WHA. The wrappers are approximately 2 11/16" wide and 11 5/8" long. The wiener wrappers are predominantly yellow and carry a 2" by 1 1/4" black-and-white posed photo of the player with a facsimile autograph inscribed across the picture. The beef frank wrappers are identical in design but predominantly red in color. The wrappers are unnumbered and checklisted below in alphabetical order.

| | NRMT-MT | EXC |
|---|---|---|
| COMPLETE SET (14) | 125.00 | 55.00 |
| COMMON CARD (1-14) | 10.00 | 4.50 |
| ❑ 1 Serge Aubry | 10.00 | 4.50 |
| ❑ 2 Bryan Campbell | 10.00 | 4.50 |
| ❑ 3 Rick Dudley | 15.00 | 6.75 |
| ❑ 4 Pierre Guite | 10.00 | 4.50 |
| ❑ 5 John Hughes | 10.00 | 4.50 |
| ❑ 6 Claude Larose | 12.00 | 5.50 |
| ❑ 7 Jacques Locas UER (Misspelled Jacque) | 10.00 | 4.50 |
| ❑ 8 Bernie MacNeil | 10.00 | 4.50 |
| ❑ 9 Mike Pelyk | 10.00 | 4.50 |
| ❑ 10 Ron Plumb | 10.00 | 4.50 |
| ❑ 11 Dave Smedsmo | 10.00 | 4.50 |
| ❑ 12 Dennis Sobchuk | 10.00 | 4.50 |
| ❑ 13 Gene Sobchuk | 10.00 | 4.50 |
| ❑ 14 Gary Veneruzzo | 10.00 | 4.50 |

## 1976-77 Stingers Kahn's

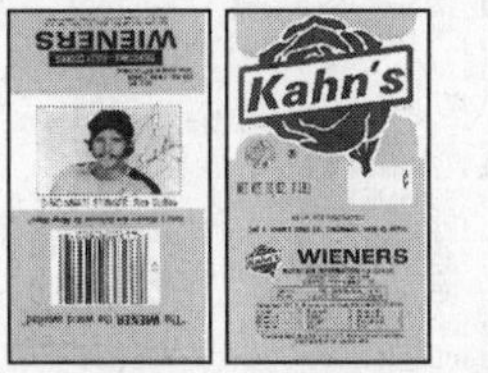

This set of six photos was issued on wrappers of Kahn's Wieners and features players of the Cincinnati Stingers of the WHA. The wrappers are approximately 2 11/16" wide and 11 5/8" long. On a predominantly yellow wrapper with red lettering, a 2" by 1 1/4" black and white player action photo appears, with a facsimile autograph inscribed across the picture. The wrappers are unnumbered and checklisted below in alphabetical order. This set is distinguished from the previous year by the fact that these card photo poses (for the players in both sets) appear to be taken in an action sequence compared to the posed photographs taken the previous year.

| | NRMT-MT | EXC |
|---|---|---|
| COMPLETE SET (6) | 125.00 | 55.00 |
| COMMON CARD (1-6) | 20.00 | 9.00 |
| ❑ 1 Rick Dudley | 30.00 | 13.50 |
| ❑ 2 Dave Inkpen | 25.00 | 11.00 |
| ❑ 3 John Hughes | 20.00 | 9.00 |
| ❑ 4 Claude Larose | 25.00 | 11.00 |
| ❑ 5 Jacques Locas | 20.00 | 9.00 |
| ❑ 6 Ron Plumb | 20.00 | 9.00 |
| ❑ 7 Dennis Sobchuk | 20.00 | 9.00 |

## 1997-98 Studio

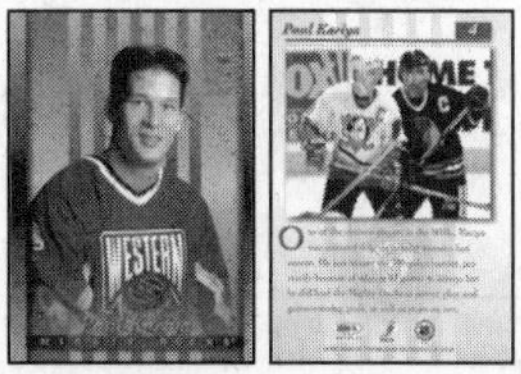

The 1997-98 Studio set was issued in one series totalling 110 cards and was distributed in five-card packs with an 8x10 Studio Portrait enclosed. The fronts feature color player portraits, while the backs carry an action player photos and player information.

| | MINT | NRMT |
|---|---|---|
| COMPLETE SET (110) | 40.00 | 18.00 |
| COMMON CARD (1-110) | .10 | .05 |
| ❑ 1 Wayne Gretzky | 2.50 | 1.10 |
| ❑ 2 Dominik Hasek | .75 | .35 |
| ❑ 3 Eric Lindros | 1.25 | .55 |
| ❑ 4 Paul Kariya | 1.50 | .70 |
| ❑ 5 Jaromir Jagr | 1.25 | .55 |
| ❑ 6 Brendan Shanahan | .75 | .35 |
| ❑ 7 Patrick Roy | 2.00 | .90 |
| ❑ 8 Keith Tkachuk | .50 | .23 |
| ❑ 9 Mark Messier | .50 | .23 |
| ❑ 10 Steve Yzerman | 1.25 | .55 |
| ❑ 11 Brett Hull | .50 | .23 |
| ❑ 12 Jarome Iginla | .30 | .14 |
| ❑ 13 Mike Modano | .50 | .23 |
| ❑ 14 Pavel Bure | .75 | .35 |
| ❑ 15 Peter Forsberg | 1.25 | .55 |
| ❑ 16 Ryan Smyth | .30 | .14 |
| ❑ 17 John Vanbiesbrouck | .60 | .25 |
| ❑ 18 Teemu Selanne | .75 | .35 |
| ❑ 19 Saku Koivu | .60 | .25 |
| ❑ 20 Martin Brodeur | 1.00 | .45 |
| ❑ 21 Sergei Fedorov | .75 | .35 |
| ❑ 22 John LeClair | .60 | .25 |
| ❑ 23 Joe Sakic | .75 | .35 |
| ❑ 24 Jose Theodore | .30 | .14 |
| ❑ 25 Marc Denis | .30 | .14 |
| ❑ 26 Dainius Zubrus | .40 | .18 |
| ❑ 27 Bryan Berard | .30 | .14 |
| ❑ 28 Ray Bourque | .40 | .18 |
| ❑ 29 Curtis Joseph | .40 | .18 |
| ❑ 30 Chris Chelios | .40 | .18 |
| ❑ 31 Alexei Yashin | .30 | .14 |
| ❑ 32 Adam Oates | .30 | .14 |
| ❑ 33 Anson Carter | .10 | .05 |
| ❑ 34 Jim Campbell | .10 | .05 |
| ❑ 35 Jason Arnott | .30 | .14 |
| ❑ 36 Derek Plante | .10 | .05 |
| ❑ 37 Guy Hebert | .30 | .14 |
| ❑ 38 Oleg Tverdovsky | .10 | .05 |
| ❑ 39 Ed Jovanovski | .30 | .14 |
| ❑ 40 Jeremy Roenick | .40 | .18 |
| ❑ 41 Scott Mellanby | .10 | .05 |
| ❑ 42 Keith Primeau | .10 | .05 |
| ❑ 43 Ron Hextall | .30 | .14 |
| ❑ 44 Daren Puppa | .30 | .14 |
| ❑ 45 Jim Carey | .30 | .14 |
| ❑ 46 Zigmund Palffy | .40 | .18 |
| ❑ 47 Jaroslav Svejkovsky | .30 | .14 |
| ❑ 48 Daymond Langkow | .10 | .05 |
| ❑ 49 Mikael Renberg | .30 | .14 |
| ❑ 50 Pat LaFontaine | .30 | .14 |
| ❑ 51 Mike Grier | .10 | .05 |
| ❑ 52 Stephane Fiset | .30 | .14 |
| ❑ 53 Luc Robitaille | .30 | .14 |
| ❑ 54 Joe Thornton | .75 | .35 |
| ❑ 55 Joe Nieuwendyk | .30 | .14 |
| ❑ 56 Mike Dunham | .30 | .14 |
| ❑ 57 Mark Recchi | .30 | .14 |
| ❑ 58 Ed Belfour | .40 | .18 |
| ❑ 59 Mike Richter | .40 | .18 |
| ❑ 60 Peter Bondra | .40 | .18 |
| ❑ 61 Trevor Kidd | .30 | .14 |
| ❑ 62 Sean Burke | .30 | .14 |
| ❑ 63 Nikolai Khabibulin | .30 | .14 |
| ❑ 64 Pierre Turgeon | .30 | .14 |
| ❑ 65 Dino Ciccarelli | .10 | .05 |
| ❑ 66 Felix Potvin | .40 | .18 |
| ❑ 67 Mats Sundin | .40 | .18 |
| ❑ 68 Joe Juneau | .30 | .14 |
| ❑ 69 Mike Vernon | .30 | .14 |
| ❑ 70 Adam Deadmarsh | .30 | .14 |
| ❑ 71 Damian Rhodes | .30 | .14 |
| ❑ 72 Mike Peca | .10 | .05 |
| ❑ 73 Jean-Sebastien Giguere | .30 | .14 |
| ❑ 74 Ron Francis | .30 | .14 |
| ❑ 75 Roman Hamrlik | .10 | .05 |
| ❑ 76 Vincent Damphousse | .30 | .14 |
| ❑ 77 Jocelyn Thibault | .30 | .14 |
| ❑ 78 Claude Lemieux | .30 | .14 |
| ❑ 79 Steve Shields | .30 | .14 |
| ❑ 80 Dimitri Khristich | .10 | .05 |
| ❑ 81 Theoren Fleury | .30 | .14 |
| ❑ 82 Sandis Ozolinsh | .30 | .14 |
| ❑ 83 Ethan Moreau | .10 | .05 |
| ❑ 84 Geoff Sanderson | .30 | .14 |
| ❑ 85 Paul Coffey | .40 | .18 |
| ❑ 86 Brian Leetch | .40 | .18 |
| ❑ 87 Chris Osgood | .40 | .18 |
| ❑ 88 Kirk McLean | .30 | .14 |
| ❑ 89 Mike Gartner | .30 | .14 |
| ❑ 90 Chris Gratton | .30 | .14 |
| ❑ 91 Eric Fichaud | .30 | .14 |
| ❑ 92 Alexandre Daigle | .30 | .14 |
| ❑ 93 Doug Gilmour | .40 | .18 |
| ❑ 94 Daniel Alfredsson | .30 | .14 |
| ❑ 95 Doug Weight | .30 | .14 |
| ❑ 96 Derian Hatcher | .10 | .05 |
| ❑ 97 Wade Redden | .10 | .05 |
| ❑ 98 Jeff Friesen | .30 | .14 |
| ❑ 99 Tony Amonte | .30 | .14 |
| ❑ 100 Janne Niinimaa | .30 | .14 |
| ❑ 101 Trevor Linden | .30 | .14 |
| ❑ 102 Grant Fuhr | .30 | .14 |
| ❑ 103 Chris Phillips | .10 | .05 |
| ❑ 104 Sergei Berezin | .10 | .05 |
| ❑ 105 Brendan Shanahan CL | .30 | .14 |
| ❑ 106 Steve Yzerman CL | .40 | .18 |
| ❑ 107 Teemu Selanne CL | .40 | .18 |
| ❑ 108 Eric Lindros CL | .40 | .18 |
| ❑ 109 Wayne Gretzky CL | .40 | .18 |
| ❑ 110 Patrick Roy CL | .40 | .18 |
| ❑ P3 Eric Lindros PROMO | 3.00 | 1.35 |

## 1997-98 Studio Press Proofs Silver

Randomly inserted in packs, this 110-card set is parallel to the base set. The difference is found in the silver holographic foil and micro-etched borders. Each card is numbered 1 of 1000.

| | MINT | NRMT |
|---|---|---|
| COMPLETE SET (110) | 1500.00 | 700.00 |
| COMMON CARD (1-110) | 6.00 | 2.70 |

*STARS: 25X TO 60X BASIC CARDS
*YOUNG STARS: 20X TO 50X

## 1997-98 Studio Press Proofs Gold

Randomly inserted in packs, this 110-card set is parallel to the regular Studio set. The difference is found in the special gold holographic foil and micro-etched borders. Each card is numbered as 1 of 250.

| | MINT | NRMT |
|---|---|---|
| COMMON CARD (1-110) | 12.00 | 5.50 |

*STARS: 30X TO 60X BASIC CARDS
*YOUNG STARS: 25X TO 50X BASIC CARDS

## 1997-98 Studio Hard Hats

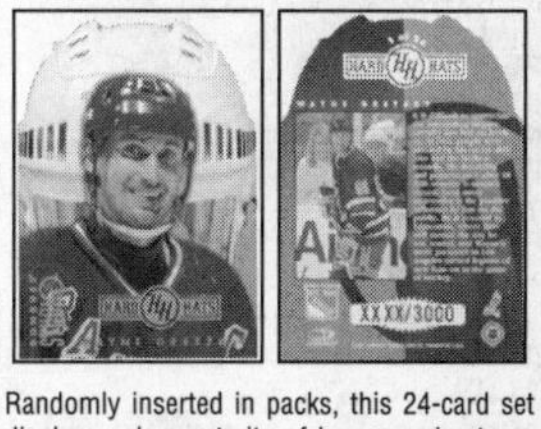

Randomly inserted in packs, this 24-card set displays color portraits of houng and veteran stars printed on plastic card stock and featuring a die-cut helmet in the background. The cards are individually numbered to 3000.

| | MINT | NRMT |
|---|---|---|
| COMPLETE SET (24) | 400.00 | 180.00 |
| COMMON CARD (1-24) | 3.00 | 1.35 |
| ❑ 1 Wayne Gretzky | 50.00 | 22.00 |
| ❑ 2 Eric Lindros | 25.00 | 11.00 |
| ❑ 3 Paul Kariya | 30.00 | 13.50 |
| ❑ 4 Bryan Berard | 6.00 | 2.70 |
| ❑ 5 Dainius Zubrus | 6.00 | 2.70 |
| ❑ 6 Daymond Langkow | 3.00 | 1.35 |
| ❑ 7 Keith Tkachuk | 10.00 | 4.50 |
| ❑ 8 Ryan Smyth | 6.00 | 2.70 |
| ❑ 9 Brendan Shanahan | 15.00 | 6.75 |
| ❑ 10 Steve Yzerman | 25.00 | 11.00 |
| ❑ 11 Teemu Selanne | 15.00 | 6.75 |
| ❑ 12 Jarome Iginla | 6.00 | 2.70 |
| ❑ 13 Zigmund Palffy | 8.00 | 3.60 |
| ❑ 14 Sergei Berezin | 6.00 | 2.70 |
| ❑ 15 Saku Koivu | 12.00 | 5.50 |
| ❑ 16 Peter Forsberg | 25.00 | 11.00 |
| ❑ 17 Joe Sakic | 15.00 | 6.75 |
| ❑ 18 Pavel Bure | 15.00 | 6.75 |
| ❑ 19 Jaromir Jagr | 25.00 | 11.00 |
| ❑ 20 Brett Hull | 10.00 | 4.50 |
| ❑ 21 Sergei Fedorov | 15.00 | 6.75 |
| ❑ 22 Mike Grier | 3.00 | 1.35 |
| ❑ 23 Ethan Moreau | 3.00 | 1.35 |
| ❑ 24 Mats Sundin | 8.00 | 3.60 |

## 1997-98 Studio Portraits

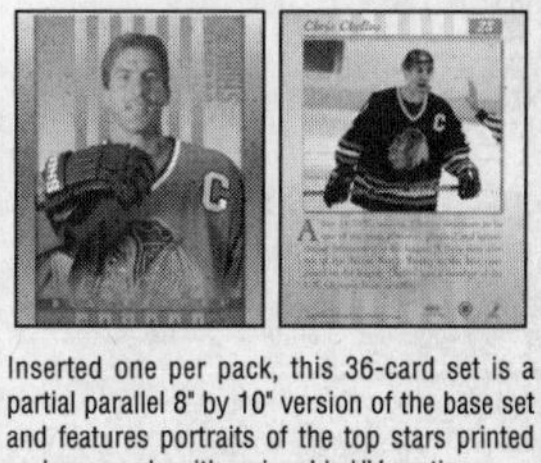

Inserted one per pack, this 36-card set is a partial parallel 8" by 10" version of the base set and features portraits of the top stars printed on large cards with a signable UV coating.

| | MINT | NRMT |
|---|---|---|
| COMPLETE SET (36) | 60.00 | 27.00 |
| COMMON CARD (1-36) | .75 | .35 |
| ❑ 1 Wayne Gretzky | 6.00 | 2.70 |
| ❑ 2 Dominik Hasek | 2.00 | .90 |
| ❑ 3 Eric Lindros | 3.00 | 1.35 |
| ❑ 4 Paul Kariya | 4.00 | 1.80 |
| ❑ 5 Jaromir Jagr | 3.00 | 1.35 |
| ❑ 6 Brendan Shanahan | 2.00 | .90 |
| ❑ 7 Patrick Roy | 5.00 | 2.20 |
| ❑ 8 Keith Tkachuk | 1.25 | .55 |
| ❑ 9 Mark Messier | 1.25 | .55 |
| ❑ 10 Steve Yzerman | 3.00 | 1.35 |
| ❑ 11 Brett Hull | 1.25 | .55 |
| ❑ 12 Jarome Iginla | .75 | .35 |
| ❑ 13 Mike Modano | 1.25 | .55 |
| ❑ 14 Pavel Bure | 2.00 | .90 |
| ❑ 15 Peter Forsberg | 3.00 | 1.35 |
| ❑ 16 Ryan Smyth | .75 | .35 |
| ❑ 17 John Vanbiesbrouck | 1.50 | .70 |
| ❑ 18 Teemu Selanne | 2.00 | .90 |
| ❑ 19 Saku Koivu | 1.50 | .70 |
| ❑ 20 Martin Brodeur | 2.50 | 1.10 |
| ❑ 21 Sergei Fedorov | 2.00 | .90 |
| ❑ 22 Joe Thornton | 2.00 | .90 |
| ❑ 23 Joe Sakic | 2.00 | .90 |
| ❑ 24 Bryan Berard | .75 | .35 |
| ❑ 25 John LeClair | 1.50 | .70 |
| ❑ 26 Marc Denis | .75 | .35 |
| ❑ 27 Dainius Zubrus | .75 | .35 |
| ❑ 28 Chris Chelios | 1.00 | .45 |
| ❑ 29 Jason Arnott | .75 | .35 |
| ❑ 30 Jeremy Roenick | 1.00 | .45 |
| ❑ 31 Zigmund Palffy | 1.00 | .45 |
| ❑ 32 Jaroslav Svejkovsky | .75 | .35 |
| ❑ 33 Mike Richter | 1.00 | .45 |
| ❑ 34 Felix Potvin | 1.00 | .45 |
| ❑ 35 Brian Leetch | 1.00 | .45 |
| ❑ 36 Chris Osgood | 1.00 | .45 |
| ❑ NNO Martin Brodeur AU/700 | 100.00 | 45.00 |
| ❑ NNO Jarome Iginla AU/1000 | 20.00 | 9.00 |
| ❑ NNO Ryan Smyth AU/1000 | 25.00 | 11.00 |

## 1997-98 Studio Silhouettes

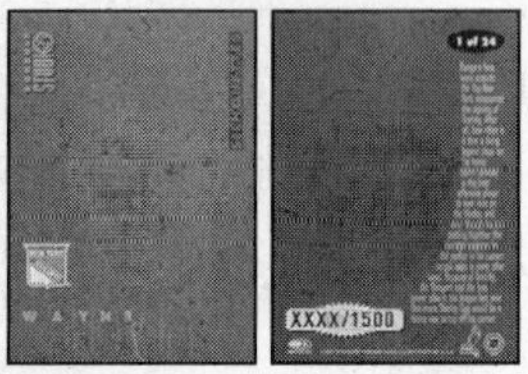

Randomly inserted in packs, this 24-card set features laser die-cutting of star players' facial features. The cards are sequentially numbered to 1,500.

| | MINT | NRMT |
|---|---|---|
| COMPLETE SET (24) | 600.00 | 275.00 |
| COMMON CARD (1-24) | 8.00 | 3.60 |
| ❑ 1 Wayne Gretzky | 60.00 | 27.00 |
| ❑ 2 Eric Lindros | 30.00 | 13.50 |
| ❑ 3 Patrick Roy | 50.00 | 22.00 |
| ❑ 4 Martin Brodeur | 25.00 | 11.00 |
| ❑ 5 Paul Kariya | 40.00 | 18.00 |
| ❑ 6 Mark Messier | 12.00 | 5.50 |
| ❑ 7 Dominik Hasek | 20.00 | 9.00 |
| ❑ 8 Brett Hull | 12.00 | 5.50 |
| ❑ 9 Pavel Bure | 20.00 | 9.00 |
| ❑ 10 Steve Yzerman | 30.00 | 13.50 |
| ❑ 11 Brendan Shanahan | 20.00 | 9.00 |
| ❑ 12 Joe Sakic | 20.00 | 9.00 |
| ❑ 13 Peter Forsberg | 30.00 | 13.50 |
| ❑ 14 Sergei Fedorov | 20.00 | 9.00 |
| ❑ 15 John LeClair | 15.00 | 6.75 |
| ❑ 16 John Vanbiesbrouck | 15.00 | 6.75 |
| ❑ 17 Teemu Selanne | 20.00 | 9.00 |
| ❑ 18 Keith Tkachuk | 12.00 | 5.50 |
| ❑ 19 Mike Modano | 12.00 | 5.50 |
| ❑ 20 Felix Potvin | 10.00 | 4.50 |
| ❑ 21 Ryan Smyth | 8.00 | 3.60 |
| ❑ 22 Jaromir Jagr | 30.00 | 13.50 |
| ❑ 23 Brian Leetch | 10.00 | 4.50 |
| ❑ 24 Jarome Iginla | 8.00 | 3.60 |

## 1997-98 Studio Silhouettes 8 x 10

Randomly inserted in packs, this 24-card set is an 8" by 10" parallel version of the regular Studio Silhouettes set. Each card is individually numbered to 3,000.

| | MINT | NRMT |
|---|---|---|
| COMPLETE SET (24) | 350.00 | 160.00 |
| COMMON CARD (1-24) | 5.00 | 2.20 |

*STARS: .3X TO .5X BASIC CARDS

## 1995-96 Summit

The 1995-96 Summit set was issued in one series totalling 200 cards. The 7-card packs had a suggested retail of $1.99 each. The set was highlighted by a double thick 24-point card stock. The Cool Trade redemption card was randomly inserted in 1:72 packs, and was redeemable for NHL Cool Trade Upgrade cards

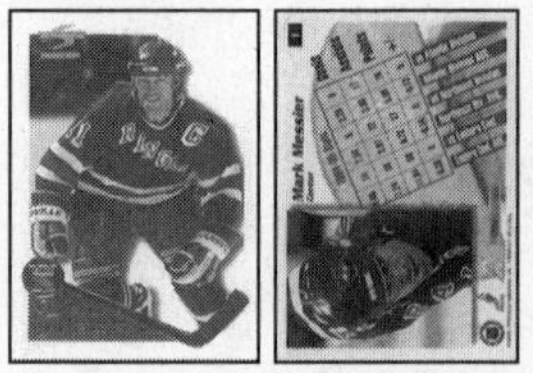

of Patrick Roy, Chris Chelios, Ray Bourque and Cam Neely. Rookie Cards include Daniel Alfredsson, Radek Dvorak, Chad Kilger, and Kyle McLaren.

| | MINT | NRMT |
|---|---|---|
| COMPLETE SET (200) | 20.00 | 9.00 |
| COMMON CARD (1-200) | .10 | .05 |
| ❑ 1 Mark Messier | .40 | .18 |
| ❑ 2 Paul Kariya | 1.25 | .55 |
| ❑ 3 Alexei Zhamnov | .15 | .07 |
| ❑ 4 Adam Oates | .15 | .07 |
| ❑ 5 Dale Hunter | .10 | .05 |
| ❑ 6 Valeri Kamensky | .15 | .07 |
| ❑ 7 Pavel Bure | .60 | .25 |
| ❑ 8 Theoren Fleury | .15 | .07 |
| ❑ 9 Mats Sundin | .15 | .07 |
| ❑ 10 Joe Murphy | .10 | .05 |
| ❑ 11 Brian Bellows | .10 | .05 |
| ❑ 12 Owen Nolan | .15 | .07 |
| ❑ 13 Brett Hull | .40 | .18 |
| ❑ 14 Mike Modano | .40 | .18 |
| ❑ 15 Ulf Dahlen | .10 | .05 |
| ❑ 16 Paul Coffey | .30 | .14 |
| ❑ 17 Jaromir Jagr | 1.00 | .45 |
| ❑ 18 Jason Arnott | .15 | .07 |
| ❑ 19 Eric Lindros | 1.00 | .45 |
| ❑ 20 Jesse Belanger | .10 | .05 |
| ❑ 21 Alexandre Daigle | .10 | .05 |
| ❑ 22 Darren Turcotte | .10 | .05 |
| ❑ 23 Brian Leetch | .30 | .14 |
| ❑ 24 Wayne Gretzky | 2.00 | .90 |
| ❑ 25 Mathieu Schneider | .10 | .05 |
| ❑ 26 Mark Recchi | .15 | .07 |
| ❑ 27 Martin Brodeur | .75 | .35 |
| ❑ 28 Igor Korolev | .10 | .05 |
| ❑ 29 Jocelyn Thibault | .30 | .14 |
| ❑ 30 Chris Pronger | .15 | .07 |
| ❑ 31 Sergei Fedorov | .50 | .23 |
| ❑ 32 Jari Kurri | .15 | .07 |
| ❑ 33 Ray Bourque | .30 | .14 |
| ❑ 34 Pat LaFontaine | .15 | .07 |
| ❑ 35 Don Beaupre | .15 | .07 |
| ❑ 36 Dave Andreychuk | .15 | .07 |
| ❑ 37 Oleg Tverdovsky | .15 | .07 |
| ❑ 38 Geoff Sanderson | .15 | .07 |
| ❑ 39 Chris Chelios | .30 | .14 |
| ❑ 40 Phil Housley | .15 | .07 |
| ❑ 41 Kevin Hatcher | .10 | .05 |
| ❑ 42 Ron Francis | .15 | .07 |
| ❑ 43 Pierre Turgeon | .15 | .07 |
| ❑ 44 Mikael Renberg | .15 | .07 |
| ❑ 45 Chris Gratton | .15 | .07 |
| ❑ 46 Tommy Soderstrom | .15 | .07 |
| ❑ 47 Stu Barnes | .10 | .05 |
| ❑ 48 Alexander Mogilny | .15 | .07 |
| ❑ 49 Craig Janney | .15 | .07 |
| ❑ 50 Scott Niedermayer | .10 | .05 |
| ❑ 51 Jim Carey | .30 | .14 |
| ❑ 52 Stephane Richer | .15 | .07 |
| ❑ 53 Dave Gagner | .15 | .07 |
| ❑ 54 Teemu Selanne | .60 | .25 |
| ❑ 55 Kelly Hrudey | .15 | .07 |
| ❑ 56 Roman Hamrlik | .15 | .07 |
| ❑ 57 Scott Mellanby | .15 | .07 |
| ❑ 58 Guy Hebert | .15 | .07 |
| ❑ 59 Gary Suter | .10 | .05 |
| ❑ 60 Travis Green | .15 | .07 |
| ❑ 61 Joe Sakic | .60 | .25 |
| ❑ 62 Doug Gilmour | .30 | .14 |
| ❑ 63 Peter Bondra | .30 | .14 |
| ❑ 64 Vincent Damphousse | .15 | .07 |
| ❑ 65 Dino Ciccarelli | .15 | .07 |
| ❑ 66 Adam Graves | .15 | .07 |
| ❑ 67 Kevin Stevens | .10 | .05 |
| ❑ 68 Jeff Friesen | .15 | .07 |
| ❑ 69 Kirk McLean | .15 | .07 |
| ❑ 70 Brad May | .15 | .07 |
| ❑ 71 Bill Ranford | .15 | .07 |
| ❑ 72 Derian Hatcher | .10 | .05 |
| ❑ 73 Glen Wesley | .10 | .05 |
| ❑ 74 Sergei Zubov | .10 | .05 |
| ❑ 75 John LeClair | .50 | .23 |
| ❑ 76 Igor Larionov | .10 | .05 |
| ❑ 77 Ray Sheppard | .15 | .07 |
| ❑ 78 Ulf Samuelsson | .10 | .05 |
| ❑ 79 Rod Brind'Amour | .15 | .07 |
| ❑ 80 Felix Potvin | .30 | .14 |
| ❑ 81 Cam Neely | .15 | .07 |
| ❑ 82 Jeremy Roenick | .30 | .14 |
| ❑ 83 Slava Kozlov | .15 | .07 |
| ❑ 84 Arturs Irbe | .15 | .07 |
| ❑ 85 Daren Puppa | .15 | .07 |
| ❑ 86 Rob Blake | .10 | .05 |
| ❑ 87 Steve Heinze | .10 | .05 |
| ❑ 88 Tom Barrasso | .15 | .07 |
| ❑ 89 Luc Robitaille | .15 | .07 |
| ❑ 90 Al MacInnis | .15 | .07 |
| ❑ 91 Petr Nedved | .15 | .07 |
| ❑ 92 Joe Mullen | .15 | .07 |
| ❑ 93 Mark Tinordi | .10 | .05 |
| ❑ 94 Tomas Sandstrom | .10 | .05 |
| ❑ 95 Dale Hawerchuk | .15 | .07 |
| ❑ 96 Andy Moog | .15 | .07 |
| ❑ 97 Alexei Kovalev | .10 | .05 |
| ❑ 98 David Oliver | .10 | .05 |
| ❑ 99 Patrick Poulin | .10 | .05 |
| ❑ 100 Tony Granato | .10 | .05 |
| ❑ 101 Alexei Yashin | .15 | .07 |
| ❑ 102 Trevor Linden | .15 | .07 |
| ❑ 103 Rick Tocchet | .15 | .07 |
| ❑ 104 Brett Lindros | .10 | .05 |
| ❑ 105 Rob Niedermayer | .15 | .07 |
| ❑ 106 John MacLean | .15 | .07 |
| ❑ 107 Pat Verbeek | .10 | .05 |
| ❑ 108 Ray Ferraro | .10 | .05 |
| ❑ 109 Mike Ricci | .10 | .05 |
| ❑ 110 Doug Weight | .15 | .07 |
| ❑ 111 Bill Guerin | .10 | .05 |
| ❑ 112 Ken Wregget | .15 | .07 |
| ❑ 113 Teppo Numminen | .10 | .05 |
| ❑ 114 Mike Vernon | .15 | .07 |
| ❑ 115 Mike Richter | .30 | .14 |
| ❑ 116 Dan Quinn | .10 | .05 |
| ❑ 117 Peter Forsberg | 1.00 | .45 |
| ❑ 118 Mario Lemieux | 1.50 | .70 |
| ❑ 119 Geoff Courtnall | .10 | .05 |
| ❑ 120 Ed Belfour | .30 | .14 |
| ❑ 121 Kirk Muller | .10 | .05 |
| ❑ 122 Chris Osgood | .30 | .14 |
| ❑ 123 Radek Bonk | .10 | .05 |
| ❑ 124 Brendan Shanahan | .60 | .25 |
| ❑ 125 Sean Burke | .15 | .07 |
| ❑ 126 Larry Murphy | .15 | .07 |
| ❑ 127 Blaine Lacher | .15 | .07 |
| ❑ 128 Russ Courtnall | .10 | .05 |
| ❑ 129 Claude Lemieux | .15 | .07 |
| ❑ 130 John Vanbiesbrouck | .50 | .23 |
| ❑ 131 Wendel Clark | .15 | .07 |
| ❑ 132 Nelson Emerson | .10 | .05 |
| ❑ 133 Ron Hextall | .15 | .07 |
| ❑ 134 Scott Stevens | .15 | .07 |
| ❑ 135 Bernie Nicholls | .10 | .05 |
| ❑ 136 Brian Skrudland | .10 | .05 |
| ❑ 137 Sandis Ozolinsh | .15 | .07 |
| ❑ 138 Trevor Kidd | .15 | .07 |
| ❑ 139 Joe Juneau | .10 | .05 |
| ❑ 140 Keith Primeau | .15 | .07 |
| ❑ 141 Petr Klima | .10 | .05 |
| ❑ 142 Viktor Kozlov | .10 | .05 |
| ❑ 143 Mike Gartner | .15 | .07 |
| ❑ 144 Zigmund Palffy | .15 | .07 |
| ❑ 145 Steve Duchesne | .10 | .05 |
| ❑ 146 Brian Bradley | .10 | .05 |
| ❑ 147 Michal Pivonka | .10 | .05 |
| ❑ 148 Todd Harvey | .10 | .05 |
| ❑ 149 Patrick Roy | 1.50 | .70 |
| ❑ 150 Gary Roberts | .10 | .05 |
| ❑ 151 Shayne Corson | .10 | .05 |
| ❑ 152 Keith Tkachuk | .40 | .18 |
| ❑ 153 Dimitri Khristich | .10 | .05 |
| ❑ 154 Steve Yzerman | 1.00 | .45 |
| ❑ 155 Shawn McEachern | .10 | .05 |
| ❑ 156 Bryan Smolinski | .10 | .05 |
| ❑ 157 Vladimir Malakhov | .10 | .05 |
| ❑ 158 Andrew Cassels | .10 | .05 |
| ❑ 159 Dominik Hasek | .60 | .25 |
| ❑ 160 Stephane Fiset | .15 | .07 |
| ❑ 161 Steve Thomas | .10 | .05 |
| ❑ 162 Joe Nieuwendyk | .15 | .07 |
| ❑ 163 Sergio Momesso | .10 | .05 |
| ❑ 164 Jyrki Lumme | .10 | .05 |
| ❑ 165 Tony Amonte | .15 | .07 |
| ❑ 166 Yanic Perreault | .10 | .05 |
| ❑ 167 Brian Savage | .10 | .05 |
| ❑ 168 Brian Holzinger | .30 | .14 |
| ❑ 169 Radek Dvorak | .10 | .05 |
| ❑ 170 Jamie Langenbrunner | .10 | .05 |
| ❑ 171 Ed Jovanovski | .30 | .14 |
| ❑ 172 Bryan McCabe | .10 | .05 |
| ❑ 173 Jere Lehtinen | .10 | .05 |
| ❑ 174 Antti Tormanen | .10 | .05 |
| ❑ 175 Aki-Petteri Berg | .10 | .05 |
| ❑ 176 Ryan Smyth | .10 | .05 |
| ❑ 177 Shean Donovan | .10 | .05 |
| ❑ 178 Darby Hendrickson | .10 | .05 |
| ❑ 179 Chad Kilger | .10 | .05 |
| ❑ 180 Vitali Yachmenev | .10 | .05 |
| ❑ 181 Deron Quint | .10 | .05 |
| ❑ 182 Daniel Alfredsson | .60 | .25 |
| ❑ 183 Jeff O'Neill | .10 | .05 |
| ❑ 184 Corey Hirsch | .15 | .07 |
| ❑ 185 Sandy Moger | .10 | .05 |
| ❑ 186 Saku Koivu | .50 | .23 |
| ❑ 187 Niklas Sundstrom | .10 | .05 |
| ❑ 188 Shane Doan | .10 | .05 |
| ❑ 189 Brendan Witt | .10 | .05 |
| ❑ 190 Eric Daze | .30 | .14 |
| ❑ 191 Marty Murray | .10 | .05 |
| ❑ 192 Byron Dafoe | .15 | .07 |
| ❑ 193 Todd Bertuzzi | .15 | .07 |
| ❑ 194 Kyle McLaren | .30 | .14 |
| ❑ 195 Marcus Ragnarsson | .10 | .05 |
| ❑ 196 Robert Svehla | .10 | .05 |
| ❑ 197 Valeri Bure | .15 | .07 |
| ❑ 198 Paul Coffey | .30 | .14 |
| ❑ 199 Checklist (1-198) | .10 | .05 |
| ❑ 200 Checklist (inserts) | .10 | .05 |
| ❑ NNO Cool Trade Exchange | 2.00 | .90 |

## 1995-96 Summit Artist's Proofs

This set is a parallel version of the regular Summit issue. The card fronts use a gold prismatic foil background, while the words "Artist's Proof" are stamped on the back. The cards were randomly inserted 1:36 packs.

| | MINT | NRMT |
|---|---|---|
| COMPLETE SET (200) | 2000.00 | 900.00 |
| COMMON CARD (1-200) | 4.00 | 1.80 |

*STARS: 40X TO 100X BASIC CARDS
*YOUNG STARS: 20X TO 50X BASIC CARDS
*RCs: 12X TO 30X BASIC CARDS

## 1995-96 Summit Ice

This lower end parallel set of the basic Summit issue features silver prismatic foil print technology on the front, and the words "Summit Ice" on the back. The cards were randomly inserted at a rate of 1:7 packs.

| | MINT | NRMT |
|---|---|---|
| COMPLETE SET (200) | 500.00 | 220.00 |
| COMMON CARD (1-200) | 1.50 | .70 |

*STARS: 7.5X TO 15X BASIC CARDS
*YOUNG STARS: 6X TO 12X BASIC CARDS
*RCs: 5X TO 10X BASIC CARDS

## 1995-96 Summit GM's Choice

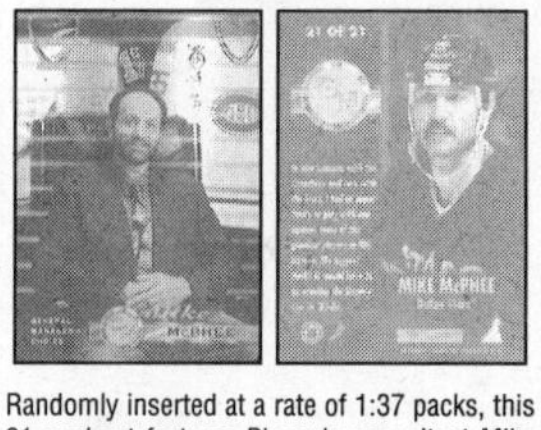

Randomly inserted at a rate of 1:37 packs, this 21-card set features Pinnacle consultant Mike McPhee selecting his top choices for an all-star "dream team". The appearance of the cards is boosted by the use of a holographic gold-foil background.

| | MINT | NRMT |
|---|---|---|
| COMPLETE SET (21) | 300.00 | 135.00 |
| COMMON CARD (1-21) | 2.50 | 1.10 |
| ❑ 1 Patrick Roy | 40.00 | 18.00 |
| ❑ 2 Martin Brodeur | 20.00 | 9.00 |
| ❑ 3 Chris Chelios | 6.00 | 2.70 |
| ❑ 4 Brian Leetch | 6.00 | 2.70 |
| ❑ 5 Eric Lindros | 25.00 | 11.00 |
| ❑ 6 Keith Tkachuk | 10.00 | 4.50 |
| ❑ 7 Pavel Bure | 15.00 | 6.75 |
| ❑ 8 Scott Stevens | 2.50 | 1.10 |
| ❑ 9 Paul Coffey | 6.00 | 2.70 |
| ❑ 10 Mario Lemieux | 40.00 | 18.00 |
| ❑ 11 Jaromir Jagr | 25.00 | 11.00 |
| ❑ 12 Cam Neely | 5.00 | 2.20 |
| ❑ 13 Ray Bourque | 6.00 | 2.70 |
| ❑ 14 Al MacInnis | 2.50 | 1.10 |
| ❑ 15 Sergei Fedorov | 15.00 | 6.75 |
| ❑ 16 Mark Messier | 10.00 | 4.50 |
| ❑ 17 Brett Hull | 10.00 | 4.50 |
| ❑ 18 Wayne Gretzky | 50.00 | 22.00 |
| ❑ 19 Paul Kariya | 30.00 | 13.50 |
| ❑ 20 Brendan Shanahan | 15.00 | 6.75 |
| ❑ 21 Mike McPhee | 2.50 | 1.10 |

## 1995-96 Summit In The Crease

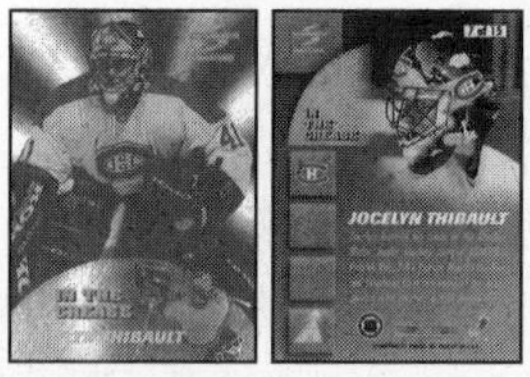

Randomly inserted at a rate of 1:91 packs, this 15-card set showcases some of the hottest goaltenders in the league on cards utilizing Spectroetch technology.

| | MINT | NRMT |
|---|---|---|
| COMPLETE SET (15) | 400.00 | 180.00 |
| COMMON CARD (1-15) | 15.00 | 6.75 |
| ❑ 1 Martin Brodeur | 50.00 | 22.00 |
| ❑ 2 Dominik Hasek | 40.00 | 18.00 |
| ❑ 3 Patrick Roy | 80.00 | 36.00 |
| ❑ 4 Ed Belfour | 20.00 | 9.00 |
| ❑ 5 Felix Potvin | 15.00 | 6.75 |
| ❑ 6 Jim Carey | 15.00 | 6.75 |
| ❑ 7 Jocelyn Thibault | 15.00 | 6.75 |
| ❑ 8 Stephane Fiset | 15.00 | 6.75 |
| ❑ 9 Chris Osgood | 20.00 | 9.00 |
| ❑ 10 Ron Hextall | 15.00 | 6.75 |
| ❑ 11 Mike Richter | 20.00 | 9.00 |
| ❑ 12 Andy Moog | 15.00 | 6.75 |
| ❑ 13 Sean Burke | 15.00 | 6.75 |
| ❑ 14 Kirk McLean | 15.00 | 6.75 |
| ❑ 15 John Vanbiesbrouck | 30.00 | 13.50 |

## 1995-96 Summit Mad Hatters

Randomly inserted at a rate of 1:23 packs, this 15-card set pays tribute -- not surprisingly -- to some of the top hat trick artists of the 1994-95 season on Spectroetched cards.

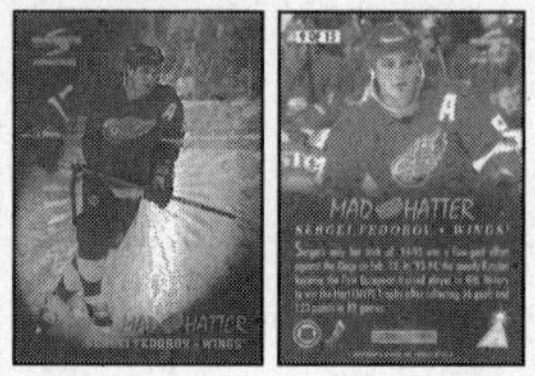

| | MINT | NRMT |
|---|---|---|
| COMPLETE SET (15) | 60.00 | 27.00 |
| COMMON CARD (1-15) | 2.00 | .90 |
| ❑ 1 Eric Lindros<br>Owen Nolan<br>Bernie Nicholls | 12.00 | 5.50 |
| ❑ 2 Brett Hull | 6.00 | 2.70 |
| ❑ 3 John LeClair | 6.00 | 2.70 |
| ❑ 4 Cam Neely | 4.00 | 1.80 |
| ❑ 5 Alexei Zhamnov | 4.00 | 1.80 |
| ❑ 6 Jason Arnott | 4.00 | 1.80 |
| ❑ 7 Pavel Bure | 8.00 | 3.60 |
| ❑ 8 Wendel Clark | 2.00 | .90 |
| ❑ 9 Sergei Fedorov | 8.00 | 3.60 |
| ❑ 10 Jaromir Jagr | 12.00 | 5.50 |
| ❑ 11 Peter Bondra | 4.00 | 1.80 |
| ❑ 12 Alexei Yashin | 2.00 | .90 |
| ❑ 13 Joe Nieuwendyk | 2.00 | .90 |
| ❑ 14 Luc Robitaille | 2.00 | .90 |
| ❑ 15 Todd Harvey | 2.00 | .90 |

## 1996-97 Summit

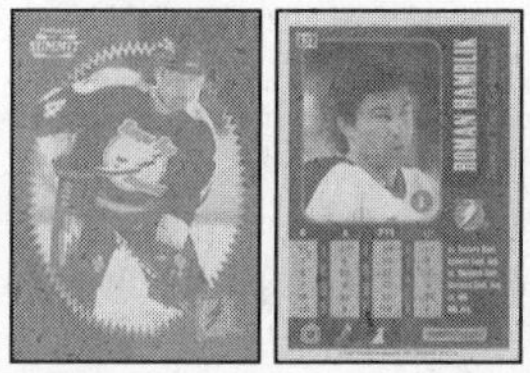

This 200-card set was distributed in seven-card packs with a suggested retail price of $2.99. The fronts featured color action player photos while the backs carried player information. A 25-card "Rookies" subset and three checklists were included in this set. Key rookies include Kevin Hodson and Ethan Moreau.

| | MINT | NRMT |
|---|---|---|
| COMPLETE SET (200) | 30.00 | 13.50 |
| COMMON CARD (1-200) | .10 | .05 |
| COMP.PRM.STOCK SET (200) | 125.00 | 55.00 |
| COMMON PRM.STOCK (1-200) | .25 | .11 |
| *PRM.STOCK: 2X TO 4X BASIC CARDS | | |
| COMP.METAL SET (200) | 125.00 | 55.00 |
| COMMON METAL (1-200) | .25 | .11 |
| *METAL: 2X TO 4X BASIC CARDS | | |
| METAL DIST.ONLY TO MAG.OUTLETS | | |
| ❑ 1 Joe Sakic | .75 | .35 |
| ❑ 2 Dominik Hasek | .75 | .35 |
| ❑ 3 Paul Coffey | .40 | .18 |
| ❑ 4 Todd Gill | .10 | .05 |
| ❑ 5 Pat Verbeek | .10 | .05 |
| ❑ 6 John LeClair | .60 | .25 |
| ❑ 7 Joe Juneau | .10 | .05 |
| ❑ 8 Scott Mellanby | .25 | .11 |
| ❑ 9 Scott Stevens | .25 | .11 |
| ❑ 10 Ron Francis | .25 | .11 |
| ❑ 11 Larry Murphy | .25 | .11 |
| ❑ 12 Sandis Ozolinsh | .25 | .11 |
| ❑ 13 Luc Robitaille | .25 | .11 |
| ❑ 14 Grant Fuhr | .25 | .11 |
| ❑ 15 Adam Oates | .25 | .11 |
| ❑ 16 Keith Primeau | .25 | .11 |
| ❑ 17 Mark Recchi | .25 | .11 |
| ❑ 18 Brian Bradley | .10 | .05 |
| ❑ 19 Zdeno Ciger | .10 | .05 |
| ❑ 20 Zigmund Palffy | .40 | .18 |
| ❑ 21 Damian Rhodes | .25 | .11 |
| ❑ 22 Russ Courtnall | .10 | .05 |
| ❑ 23 Mike Modano | .50 | .23 |
| ❑ 24 Geoff Sanderson | .25 | .11 |
| ❑ 25 Michal Pivonka | .10 | .05 |
| ❑ 26 Randy Burridge | .10 | .05 |
| ❑ 27 Dimitri Khristich | .10 | .05 |
| ❑ 28 Mike Gartner | .25 | .11 |
| ❑ 29 Cam Neely | .25 | .11 |
| ❑ 30 Mathieu Schneider | .10 | .05 |
| ❑ 31 Steve Thomas | .10 | .05 |
| ❑ 32 Mario Lemieux | 2.00 | .90 |
| ❑ 33 Darryl Sydor | .10 | .05 |
| ❑ 34 Alexei Yashin | .25 | .11 |
| ❑ 35 Brett Hull | .50 | .23 |
| ❑ 36 Trevor Kidd | .25 | .11 |
| ❑ 37 Alexei Zhamnov | .25 | .11 |
| ❑ 38 Uwe Krupp | .10 | .05 |
| ❑ 39 Brian Skrudland | .10 | .05 |
| ❑ 40 Igor Larionov | .10 | .05 |
| ❑ 41 Nikolai Khabibulin | .25 | .11 |
| ❑ 42 Pavel Bure | .75 | .35 |
| ❑ 43 Chris Chelios | .40 | .18 |
| ❑ 44 Andrew Cassels | .10 | .05 |
| ❑ 45 Owen Nolan | .25 | .11 |
| ❑ 46 Todd Harvey | .10 | .05 |
| ❑ 47 Jari Kurri | .25 | .11 |
| ❑ 48 Olaf Kolzig | .25 | .11 |
| ❑ 49 Greg Johnson | .10 | .05 |

❑ 50 Dominic Roussel .25 .11
❑ 51 Mats Sundin .25 .11
❑ 52 Robert Svehla .10 .05
❑ 53 Sandy Moger .10 .05
❑ 54 Darren Turcotte .10 .05
❑ 55 Teppo Numminen .10 .05
❑ 56 Benoit Hogue .10 .05
❑ 57 Scott Niedermayer .10 .05
❑ 58 Alexander Selivanov .10 .05
❑ 59 Valeri Kamensky .25 .11
❑ 60 Ken Wregget .25 .11
❑ 61 Travis Green .25 .11
❑ 62 Peter Bondra .40 .18
❑ 63 Vladimir Konstantinov .10 .05
❑ 64 Craig Janney .25 .11
❑ 65 Joe Nieuwendyk .25 .11
❑ 66 John Vanbiesbrouck .60 .25
❑ 67 Wayne Gretzky 3.00 1.35
❑ 68 Kirk McLean .25 .11
❑ 69 Alexei Zhitnik .10 .05
❑ 70 Mike Ricci .10 .05
❑ 71 Jeff Beukeboom .10 .05
❑ 72 Felix Potvin .40 .18
❑ 73 Mikael Renberg .25 .11
❑ 74 Jamie Baker .10 .05
❑ 75 Guy Hebert .25 .11
❑ 76 Steve Yzerman 1.25 .55
❑ 77 Daren Puppa .25 .11
❑ 78 Scott Young .10 .05
❑ 79 Martin Gelinas .10 .05
❑ 80 Dave Gagner .25 .11
❑ 81 Tomas Sandstrom .10 .05
❑ 82 Alexei Kovalev .10 .05
❑ 83 Ray Whitney .10 .05
❑ 84 Vyacheslav Kozlov .10 .05
❑ 85 Jaromir Jagr 1.25 .55
❑ 86 Joe Murphy .10 .05
❑ 87 Patrick Roy 2.00 .90
❑ 88 Ray Sheppard .25 .11
❑ 89 Chris Terreri .25 .11
❑ 90 Pierre Turgeon .25 .11
❑ 91 Theoren Fleury .25 .11
❑ 92 Doug Weight .25 .11
❑ 93 Tom Barrasso .25 .11
❑ 94 Jim Carey .40 .18
❑ 95 Greg Adams .10 .05
❑ 96 Brian Leetch .40 .18
❑ 97 Ed Belfour .40 .18
❑ 98 Stephane Fiset .25 .11
❑ 99 Stephane Richer .25 .11
❑ 100 Ron Hextall .25 .11
❑ 101 Mike Vernon .25 .11
❑ 102 Jocelyn Thibault .40 .18
❑ 103 Jason Arnott .25 .11
❑ 104 Keith Tkachuk .50 .23
❑ 105 Sergei Fedorov .60 .25
❑ 106 Alexandre Daigle .10 .05
❑ 107 Alexander Mogilny .25 .11
❑ 108 German Titov .10 .05
❑ 109 Sean Burke .25 .11
❑ 110 Arturs Irbe .25 .11
❑ 111 Mark Messier .50 .23
❑ 112 Nicklas Lidstrom .25 .11
❑ 113 Claude Lemieux .25 .11
❑ 114 Martin Brodeur 1.00 .45
❑ 115 Bernie Nicholls .10 .05
❑ 116 Paul Kariya 1.50 .70
❑ 117 Eric Lindros 1.25 .55
❑ 118 Doug Gilmour .40 .18
❑ 119 Sergei Zubov .25 .11
❑ 120 Adam Graves .25 .11
❑ 121 Phil Housley .25 .11
❑ 122 Bob Bassen .10 .05
❑ 123 Rod Brind'Amour .25 .11
❑ 124 Dave Andreychuk .25 .11
❑ 125 Corey Hirsch .25 .11
❑ 126 Kelly Hrudey .25 .11
❑ 127 Pat LaFontaine .25 .11
❑ 128 Viacheslav Fetisov .10 .05
❑ 129 Oleg Tverdovsky .25 .11
❑ 130 Andy Moog .25 .11
❑ 131 Stu Barnes .10 .05
❑ 132 Roman Hamrlik .25 .11
❑ 133 Teemu Selanne .75 .35
❑ 134 Trevor Linden .25 .11
❑ 135 Chris Osgood .40 .18
❑ 136 Vincent Damphousse .25 .11
❑ 137 Shayne Corson .10 .05
❑ 138 Jeremy Roenick .40 .18
❑ 139 Brendan Shanahan .75 .35
❑ 140 Wendel Clark .25 .11
❑ 141 Ray Bourque .40 .18
❑ 142 Peter Forsberg 1.25 .55
❑ 143 John MacLean .25 .11
❑ 144 Jeff Friesen .25 .11
❑ 145 Mike Richter .40 .18
❑ 146 Dave Reid .10 .05
❑ 147 Rob Niedermayer .25 .11
❑ 148 Petr Nedved .25 .11
❑ 149 Sylvain Lefebvre .10 .05
❑ 150 Curtis Joseph .40 .18
❑ 151 Eric Daze .25 .11
❑ 152 Saku Koivu .60 .25
❑ 153 Jere Lehtinen .10 .05
❑ 154 Todd Bertuzzi .10 .05
❑ 155 Chad Kilger .10 .05
❑ 156 Stephane Yelle .10 .05
❑ 157 Bryan McCabe .10 .05
❑ 158 Aaron Gavey .10 .05
❑ 159 Kyle McLaren .10 .05
❑ 160 Valeri Bure .25 .11
❑ 161 Antti Tormanen .10 .05
❑ 162 Brendan Witt .10 .05
❑ 163 Ed Jovanovski .25 .11
❑ 164 Aki-Petteri Berg .10 .05
❑ 165 Marcus Ragnarsson .10 .05
❑ 166 Miroslav Satan .10 .05
❑ 167 Daniel Alfredsson .25 .11
❑ 168 Jeff O'Neill .10 .05
❑ 169 Radek Dvorak .10 .05
❑ 170 Petr Sykora .10 .05
❑ 171 Vitali Yachmenev .10 .05
❑ 172 Niklas Andersson .10 .05
❑ 173 Nolan Baumgartner .10 .05
❑ 174 Brandon Convery .10 .05
❑ 175 Ralph Intranuovo .10 .05
❑ 176 Niklas Sundblad .10 .05
❑ 177 Patrick Labrecque .25 .11
❑ 178 Eric Fichaud .25 .11
❑ 179 Martin Biron .25 .11
❑ 180 Steve Sullivan .10 .05
❑ 181 Peter Ferraro .10 .05
❑ 182 Jose Theodore .25 .11
❑ 183 Kevin Hodson .40 .18
❑ 184 Ethan Moreau .40 .18
❑ 185 Curtis Brown .10 .05
❑ 186 Daymond Langkow .10 .05
❑ 187 Jan Caloun .10 .05
❑ 188 Landon Wilson .10 .05
❑ 189 Tommy Salo .25 .11
❑ 190 Anders Eriksson .10 .05
❑ 191 David Nemirovsky .10 .05
❑ 192 Jamie Langenbrunner .10 .05
❑ 193 Zdenek Nedved .10 .05
❑ 194 Todd Hlushko .10 .05
❑ 195 Alexei Yegorov .10 .05
❑ 196 Jamie Pushor .10 .05
❑ 197 Anders Myrvold .10 .05
❑ 198 Mark Messier CL .40 .18
❑ 199 Brett Hull CL .40 .18
❑ 200 Pavel Bure CL .40 .18

## 1996-97 Summit Artist's Proofs

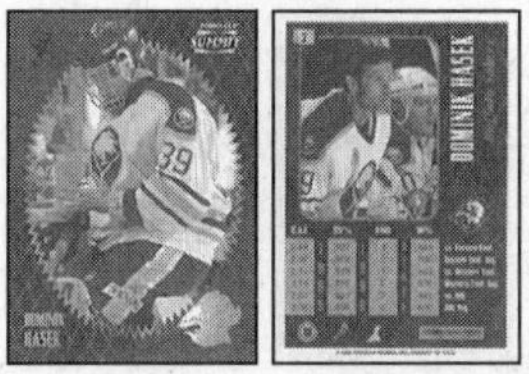


Randomly inserted in packs at a rate of one in 35, this 200-card parallel set to the regular 1996-97 Summit set was distinguished in design by a holographic foil stamped Artist's Proof logo on the front. Values are listed below for only the most heavily traded singles. Values for all other cards can be determined by using the multipliers listed in the header below against the base set.

| | MINT | NRMT |
|---|---|---|
| COMPLETE SET (200) | 2000.00 | 900.00 |
| COMMON CARD (1-200) | 4.00 | 1.80 |

*STARS: 40X TO 80X BASIC CARDS
*YOUNG STARS: 25X TO 50X BASIC CARDS
*RCs: 15X TO 30X BASIC CARDS

## 1996-97 Summit Ice

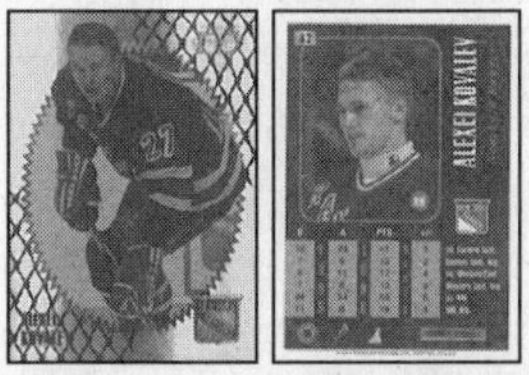


Randomly inserted in packs at the rate of one in six, this 200-card parellel set featured prismatic foil printing which distinguished it from the regular Summit set. Values for all singles can be determined by using the multipliers below on the correpsonding card from the base set.

| | MINT | NRMT |
|---|---|---|
| COMPLETE SET (200) | 500.00 | 220.00 |
| COMMON CARD (1-200) | 2.00 | .90 |

*STARS: 6X TO 15X BASIC CARDS
*YOUNG STARS: 4X TO 10X BASIC CARDS

## 1996-97 Summit High Voltage

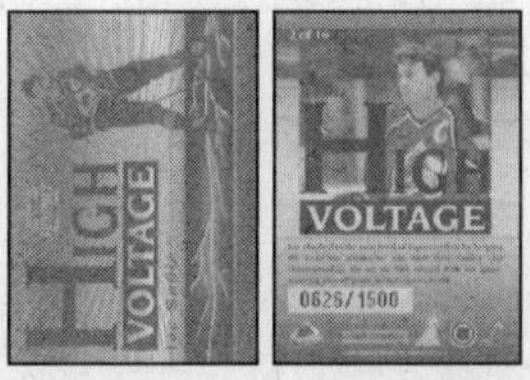


This 16-card Spectroetch insert set spotlighted the high-energy play of the NHL's superstar elite. The fronts featured a color player image on a silver and black lightning displayed background. The backs carried another player photo with player information. Just 1,500 copies of each card in this set were produced and sequentially numbered. A parallel "Mirage" version of these cards was randomly inserted into packs and sequentially numbered to 600.

| | MINT | NRMT |
|---|---|---|
| COMPLETE SET (16) | 500.00 | 220.00 |
| COMMON CARD (1-16) | 12.00 | 5.50 |

*MIRAGE STARS: 1.25X TO 2.5X BASIC CARDS

❑ 1 Mark Messier 15.00 6.75
❑ 2 Joe Sakic 25.00 11.00
❑ 3 Paul Kariya 50.00 22.00
❑ 4 Daniel Alfredsson 12.00 5.50
❑ 5 Wayne Gretzky 80.00 36.00
❑ 6 Peter Forsberg 40.00 18.00
❑ 7 Eric Daze 12.00 5.50
❑ 8 Mario Lemieux 60.00 27.00
❑ 9 Eric Lindros 40.00 18.00
❑ 10 Jeremy Roenick 20.00 9.00
❑ 11 Alexander Mogilny 12.00 5.50
❑ 12 Teemu Selanne 25.00 11.00
❑ 13 Sergei Fedorov 25.00 11.00
❑ 14 Saku Koivu 20.00 9.00
❑ 15 Jaromir Jagr 40.00 18.00
❑ 16 Brett Hull 15.00 6.75
❑ P16 Eric Lindros 10.00 4.50

## 1996-97 Summit In The Crease

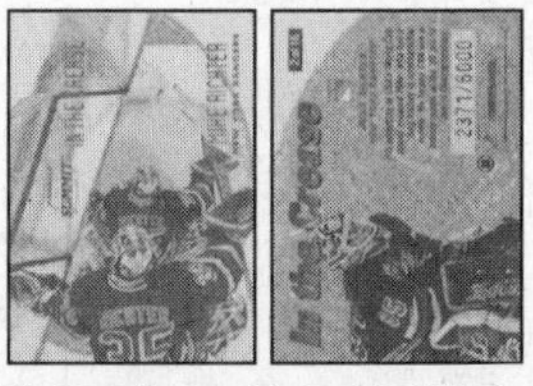

This 16-card insert set featured the NHL's top goalies. A gold-foil stamped print technology was utilized which gave the cards a distinctive feel and look, and created a sense of depth in the cards. 6,000 copies of each of the cards in this set were produced and sequentially numbered.

| | MINT | NRMT |
|---|---|---|
| COMPLETE SET (16) | 200.00 | 90.00 |
| COMMON CARD (1-16) | 8.00 | 3.60 |

❑ 1 Patrick Roy 50.00 22.00
❑ 2 Mike Richter 12.00 5.50
❑ 3 Ed Belfour 12.00 5.50
❑ 4 Daren Puppa 8.00 3.60
❑ 5 Curtis Joseph 12.00 5.50
❑ 6 Jim Carey 12.00 5.50
❑ 7 Damian Rhodes 8.00 3.60
❑ 8 Martin Brodeur 30.00 13.50
❑ 9 Felix Potvin 20.00 9.00
❑ 10 John Vanbiesbrouck 20.00 9.00
❑ 11 Jocelyn Thibault 12.00 5.50
❑ 12 Nikolai Khabibulin 8.00 3.60
❑ 13 Chris Osgood 12.00 5.50
❑ 14 Dominik Hasek 25.00 11.00
❑ 15 Corey Hirsch 8.00 3.60
❑ 16 Ron Hextall 8.00 3.60

## 1996-97 Summit In The Crease Premium Stock

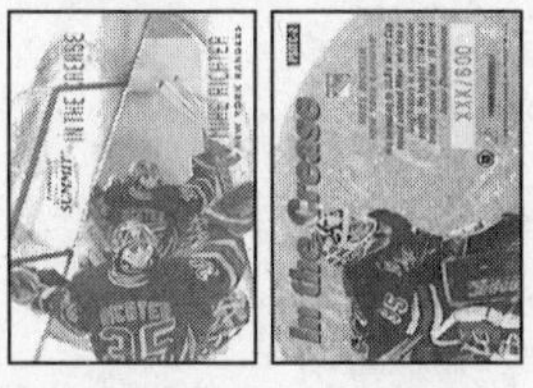

Paralleling the standard "In The Crease" set, these inserts were randomly seeded in Premium Stock packs and were serially numbered out of 600. Unlike the regular version, the premium stock version has an enhanced foil background and is numbered with the prefix PSITC.

| | MINT | NRMT |
|---|---|---|
| COMPLETE SET (16) | 800.00 | 350.00 |
| COMMON CARD (1-16) | 30.00 | 13.50 |

*PRM.STOCK STARS: 2X TO 4X BASIC CARDS

## 1996-97 Summit Untouchables

This 18-card insert set was an all-foil version of the regular series which honored 12 skaters who amassed 100 or more points and six goaltenders who notched 30 wins during the 1995-96 season. Although the cards were intended to mention this fact, all the goalie cards read 100 points along the bottom front,

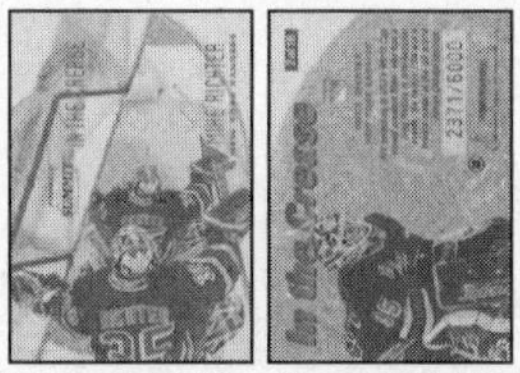

the same as the skaters. No corrected versions were produced. Just 1,000 copies of this set were produced and each card was sequentially numbered.

| | MINT | NRMT |
|---|---|---|
| COMPLETE SET (18) | 800.00 | 350.00 |
| COMMON CARD (1-18) | 15.00 | 6.75 |

❑ 1 Mario Lemieux 100.00 45.00
❑ 2 Jaromir Jagr 60.00 27.00
❑ 3 Joe Sakic 40.00 18.00
❑ 4 Ron Francis 15.00 6.75
❑ 5 Peter Forsberg 60.00 27.00
❑ 6 Eric Lindros 60.00 27.00
❑ 7 Paul Kariya 80.00 36.00
❑ 8 Teemu Selanne 40.00 18.00
❑ 9 Alexander Mogilny 20.00 9.00
❑ 10 Sergei Fedorov 40.00 18.00
❑ 11 Doug Weight 15.00 6.75
❑ 12 Wayne Gretzky 120.00 55.00
❑ 13 Chris Osgood 20.00 9.00
❑ 14 Jim Carey 20.00 9.00
❑ 15 Patrick Roy 100.00 45.00
❑ 16 Martin Brodeur 50.00 22.00
❑ 17 Felix Potvin 20.00 9.00
❑ 18 Ron Hextall 15.00 6.75

## 1910-11 Sweet Caporal Postcards

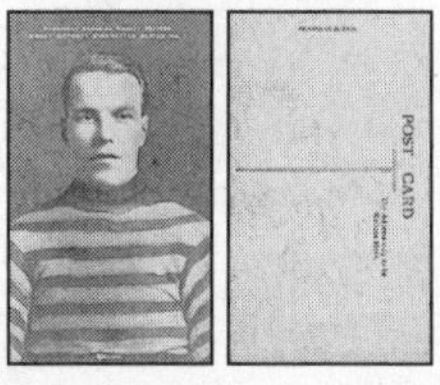

These black-and-white photo postcards apparently were used by the artists working on the C55 cards of the next year, 1911-12. Printed by the British American Tobacco Co. in England, these cards were distributed by Imperial Tobacco of Canada. One card was reportedly packed in each 50-cigarette tin of Sweet Caporal cigarettes. The backs show the postcard design. The cards are checklisted below according to teams as follows: Quebec Bulldogs (1-8), Ottawa Senators (10-17), Renfrew Millionaires (18-26), Montreal Wanderers (27-36), and Montreal Canadiens (37-45).

| | EX-MT | VG-E |
|---|---|---|
| COMPLETE SET (45) | 18000.00 | 9000.00 |
| COMMON CARD (1-45) | 200.00 | 100.00 |

❑ 1 Paddy Moran 500.00 250.00
❑ 2 Joe Hall 350.00 180.00
❑ 3 Barney Holden 200.00 100.00
❑ 4 Joe Malone 1000.00 500.00
❑ 5 Ed Oatman 200.00 100.00
❑ 6 Tom Dunderdale 350.00 180.00
❑ 7 Ken Mallen 200.00 100.00
❑ 8 Jack MacDonald 200.00 100.00
❑ 9 Fred Lake 200.00 100.00
❑ 10 Albert Kerr 200.00 100.00
❑ 11 Marty Walsh 350.00 180.00
❑ 12 Hamby Shore 200.00 100.00
❑ 13 Alex Currie 200.00 100.00
❑ 14 Bruce Ridpath 200.00 100.00
❑ 15 Bruce Stuart 350.00 180.00
❑ 16 Percy Lesueur 350.00 180.00
❑ 17 Jack Darragh 350.00 180.00
❑ 18 Steve Vair 200.00 100.00
❑ 19 Don Smith 200.00 100.00
❑ 20 Cyclone Taylor 1200.00 600.00
❑ 21 Bert Lindsay 250.00 125.00
❑ 22 H.L.(Larry) Gilmour 350.00 180.00
❑ 23 Bobby Rowe 200.00 100.00
❑ 24 Sprague Cleghorn 600.00 300.00
❑ 25 Odie Cleghorn 250.00 125.00
❑ 26 Skein Ronan 200.00 100.00
❑ 27 Walter Smaill 250.00 125.00
❑ 28 Ernest(Moose) Johnson 400.00 200.00
❑ 29 Jack Marshall 350.00 180.00
❑ 30 Harry Hyland 350.00 180.00
❑ 31 Art Ross 1200.00 600.00
❑ 32 Riley Hern 350.00 180.00
❑ 33 Gordon Roberts 350.00 180.00
❑ 34 Frank Glass 200.00 100.00
❑ 35 Ernest Russell 400.00 200.00
❑ 36 James Gardner 350.00 180.00
❑ 37 Art Bernier 200.00 100.00
❑ 38 Georges Vezina 4000.00 2000.00
❑ 39 G.(Henri) Dallaire 200.00 100.00
❑ 40 R.(Rocket) Power 200.00 100.00
❑ 41 Didier(Pit) Pitre 350.00 180.00
❑ 42 Newsy Lalonde 1200.00 600.00
❑ 43 Eugene Payan 200.00 100.00
❑ 44 George Poulin 200.00 100.00
❑ 45 Jack Laviolette 400.00 200.00

## 1934-35 Sweet Caporal

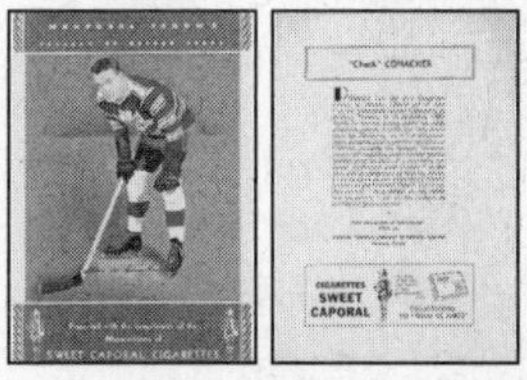

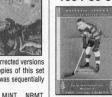

This colorful set of 48 large (approximately 6 3/4" by 10 1/2") pictures were actually inserts in Montreal Forum programs during Canadiens and Maroons home games during the 1934-35 season. Apparently a different photo was inserted each game. Players in the checklist below are identified as part of the following teams, Montreal Canadiens (MC), Montreal Maroons (MM), Boston Bruins (BB), Chicago Blackhawks (CBH), Detroit Red Wings (DRW), New York Rangers (NYR), and Toronto Maple Leafs (TML). Card backs contain player biography and an ad for Sweet Caporal Cigarettes, both in French. The cards are unnumbered.

| | EX-MT | VG-E |
|---|---|---|
| COMPLETE SET (48) | 5000.00 | 2500.00 |
| COMMON CARD | 50.00 | 25.00 |

❑ 1 Gerald Carson MC 50.00 25.00
❑ 2 Nels Crutchfield MC 50.00 25.00
❑ 3 Wilfrid Cude MC 60.00 30.00
❑ 4 Roger Jenkins MC 50.00 25.00
❑ 5 Aurel Joliat MC 350.00 180.00
❑ 6 Joe Lamb MC 50.00 25.00
❑ 7 Wildor Larochelle MC 50.00 25.00
❑ 8 Pete Lepine MC 50.00 25.00
❑ 9 Georges Mantha MC 50.00 25.00
❑ 10 Sylvio Mantha MC 100.00 50.00
❑ 11 Jack McGill MC 50.00 25.00
❑ 12 Armand Mondou MC 50.00 25.00
❑ 13 Paul Marcel Raymond MC 50.00 25.00
❑ 14 Jack Riley MC 50.00 25.00
❑ 15 Russ Blinco MM 50.00 25.00
❑ 16 Herb Cain MM 80.00 40.00
❑ 17 Lionel Conacher MM 250.00 125.00
❑ 18 Alex Connell MM 125.00 60.00
❑ 19 Stewart Evans MM 50.00 25.00
❑ 20 Norman Gainor MM 50.00 25.00
❑ 21 Paul Haynes MM 50.00 25.00
❑ 22 Gus Marker MM 50.00 25.00
❑ 23 Baldy Northcott MM 60.00 30.00
❑ 24 Earl Robinson MM 50.00 25.00
❑ 25 Hooley Smith MM 100.00 50.00
❑ 26 Dave Trottier MM 50.00 25.00
❑ 27 Jimmy Ward MM 50.00 25.00
❑ 28 Cy Wentworth MM 60.00 30.00
❑ 29 Eddie Shore BB 500.00 250.00
❑ 30 Babe Siebert BB 125.00 60.00
❑ 31 Nels Stewart BB 150.00 75.00
❑ 32 Cecil(Tiny) Thompson BB 150.00 75.00
❑ 33 Lorne Chabot CBH 100.00 50.00
❑ 34 Harold March CBH 50.00 25.00
❑ 35 Howie Morenz CBH 800.00 400.00
❑ 36 Larry Aurie DRW 50.00 25.00
❑ 37 Ebbie Goodfellow DRW 100.00 50.00
❑ 38 Herbie Lewis DRW 50.00 25.00
❑ 39 Cooney Weiland DRW 100.00 50.00
❑ 40 Bill Cook NYR 100.00 50.00
❑ 41 Fred(Bun) Cook NYR 100.00 50.00
❑ 42 Ivan(Ching) Johnson NYR 135.00 70.00
❑ 43 Dave Kerr NYR 80.00 40.00
❑ 44 Frank(King) Clancy TML 400.00 200.00
❑ 45 Chuck Conacher TML 400.00 200.00
❑ 46 Red Horner TML 125.00 60.00
❑ 47 Busher Jackson TML 150.00 75.00
❑ 48 Joe Primeau TML 200.00 100.00

## 1981-82 TCMA

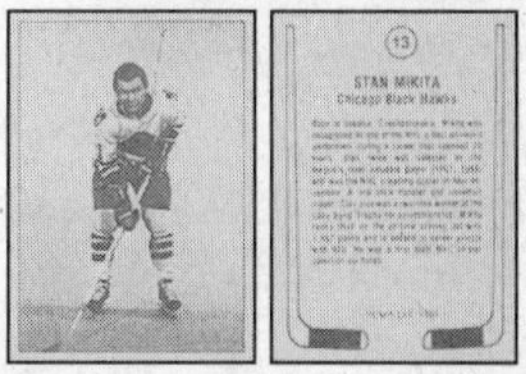

This 13-card set measures the standard size. The front features a color posed photo, with a thin black border on white card stock. The cards are numbered on the back and have biographical information as well as career highlights between two hockey sticks drawn on the sides of the card backs. Supposedly there were only 3000 sets produced. Eleven Hockey Hall of Famers are included in the set.

| | NRMT-MT | EXC |
|---|---|---|
| COMPLETE SET (13) | 60.00 | 27.00 |
| COMMON CARD (1-13) | 1.50 | .70 |

❑ 1 Norm Ullman 3.00 1.35
❑ 2 Gump Worsley 5.00 2.20
❑ 3 J.C. Tremblay 1.50 .70

| | | |
|---|---|---|
| ❑ 4 Lou Fontinato | 1.50 | .70 |
| ❑ 5 Johnny Bucyk | 3.00 | 1.35 |
| ❑ 6 Harry Howell | 2.00 | .90 |
| ❑ 7 Henri Richard | 5.00 | 2.20 |
| ❑ 8 Andy Bathgate | 3.00 | 1.35 |
| ❑ 9 Bobby Orr | 25.00 | 11.00 |
| ❑ 10 Frank Mahovlich | 5.00 | 2.20 |
| ❑ 11 Jean Beliveau | 10.00 | 4.50 |
| ❑ 12 Jacques Plante | 10.00 | 4.50 |
| ❑ 13 Stan Mikita | 7.00 | 3.10 |

## 1974 Team Canada L'Equipe WHA

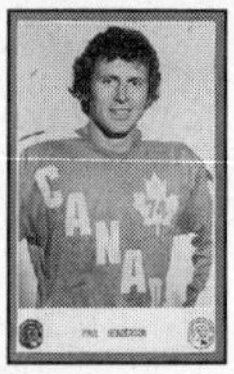

This 24-photo set measures approximately 4 1/8" by 7 1/2" and features posed, glossy, black-and-white player photos on thin stock. The pictures are attached to red posterboard. The player's name and two Team Canada L'Equipe logos appear in the white margin at the bottom. The backs are blank. The cards are unnumbered and checklisted below in alphabetical order.

| | NRMT-MT | EXC |
|---|---|---|
| COMPLETE SET (24) | 50.00 | 22.00 |
| COMMON CARD (1-24) | 1.00 | .45 |
| ❑ 1 Ralph Backstrom | 2.00 | .90 |
| ❑ 2 Serge Bernier | 1.50 | .70 |
| ❑ 3 Gerry Cheevers | 10.00 | 4.50 |
| ❑ 4 Al Hamilton | 2.00 | .90 |
| ❑ 5 Billy Harris CO | 1.00 | .45 |
| ❑ 6 Jim Harrison | 1.50 | .70 |
| ❑ 7 Ben Hatzkin | 1.50 | .70 |
| ❑ 8 Paul Henderson | 4.00 | 1.80 |
| ❑ 9 Rejean Houle | 2.00 | .90 |
| ❑ 10 Mark Howe | 8.00 | 3.60 |
| ❑ 11 Marty Howe | 2.00 | .90 |
| ❑ 12 Bill Hunter | 1.00 | .45 |
| ❑ 13 Gordon W. Jukes | 1.00 | .45 |
| ❑ 14 Rick Ley | 2.00 | .90 |
| ❑ 15 Frank Mahovlich | 8.00 | 3.60 |
| ❑ 16 John McKenzie | 2.00 | .90 |
| ❑ 17 Don McLeod | 1.50 | .70 |
| ❑ 18 Rick Noonan | 1.50 | .70 |
| ❑ 19 Brad Selwood | 1.50 | .70 |
| ❑ 20 Rick Smith | 1.50 | .70 |
| ❑ 21 Pat Stapleton | 2.00 | .90 |
| ❑ 22 Marc Tardif | 2.00 | .90 |
| ❑ 23 Mike Walton | 2.00 | .90 |
| ❑ 24 Tom Webster | 2.00 | .90 |

## 1996-97 Team Out

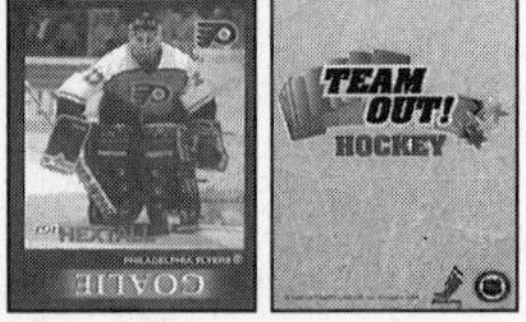


The 1996-97 Team Out set was issued in one series totalling 89 cards. The cards were intended for use in a game, which is explained in the instructions included with the set. While the game itself never quite took off, the cards were quite popular with superstar and team collectors, which led to a fairly wide break of the product.

| | MINT | NRMT |
|---|---|---|
| COMPLETE SET (89) | 25.00 | 11.00 |
| COMMON CARD (1-89) | .10 | .05 |
| ❑ 1 Paul Kariya | 2.00 | .90 |
| ❑ 2 Luc Robitaille | .25 | .11 |
| ❑ 3 John LeClair | .75 | .35 |
| ❑ 4 Theoren Fleury | .50 | .23 |
| ❑ 5 Scott Mellanby | .25 | .11 |
| ❑ 6 Adam Graves | .25 | .11 |
| ❑ 7 Esa Tikkanen | .10 | .05 |
| ❑ 8 Slava Kozlov | .10 | .05 |
| ❑ 9 Eric Daze | .25 | .11 |
| ❑ 10 Ryan Smyth | .25 | .11 |
| ❑ 11 Shayne Corson | .10 | .05 |
| ❑ 12 Kevin Stevens | .10 | .05 |
| ❑ 13 Murray Craven | .10 | .05 |
| ❑ 14 Keith Tkachuk | .60 | .25 |
| ❑ 15 Zigmund Palffy | .50 | .23 |
| ❑ 16 Eric Lindros | 1.50 | .70 |
| ❑ 17 Mario Lemieux | 2.50 | 1.10 |
| ❑ 18 Joe Sakic | 1.00 | .45 |
| ❑ 19 Wayne Gretzky | 3.00 | 1.35 |
| ❑ 20 Mark Messier | .60 | .25 |
| ❑ 21 Sergei Fedorov | 1.00 | .45 |
| ❑ 22 Jason Arnott | .25 | .11 |
| ❑ 23 Chris Gratton | .20 | .09 |
| ❑ 24 Pierre Turgeon | .25 | .11 |
| ❑ 25 Mike Modano | .60 | .25 |
| ❑ 26 Saku Koivu | .75 | .35 |
| ❑ 27 Alexei Yashin | .50 | .23 |
| ❑ 28 Steve Yzerman | 1.50 | .70 |
| ❑ 29 Peter Forsberg | 1.50 | .70 |
| ❑ 30 Adam Oates | .25 | .11 |
| ❑ 31 Brett Hull | .60 | .25 |
| ❑ 32 Jaromir Jagr | 1.50 | .70 |
| ❑ 33 Pavel Bure | 1.00 | .45 |
| ❑ 34 Teemu Selanne | 1.00 | .45 |
| ❑ 35 Stephane Richer | .10 | .05 |
| ❑ 36 Mike Gartner | .25 | .11 |
| ❑ 37 Claude Lemieux | .25 | .11 |
| ❑ 38 Rick Tocchet | .25 | .11 |
| ❑ 39 Alexander Mogilny | .40 | .18 |
| ❑ 40 Peter Bondra | .50 | .23 |
| ❑ 41 Mats Sundin | .50 | .23 |
| ❑ 42 Daniel Alfredsson | .25 | .11 |
| ❑ 43 Owen Nolan | .25 | .11 |
| ❑ 44 Joe Juneau | .25 | .11 |
| ❑ 45 Mikael Renberg | .25 | .11 |
| ❑ 46 Chris Chelios | .50 | .23 |
| ❑ 47 Ray Bourque | .50 | .23 |
| ❑ 48 Scott Stevens | .25 | .11 |
| ❑ 49 Paul Coffey | .50 | .23 |
| ❑ 50 Glen Wesley | .10 | .05 |
| ❑ 51 Nicklas Lidstrom | .25 | .11 |
| ❑ 52 Scott Niedermayer | .25 | .11 |
| ❑ 53 Larry Murphy | .25 | .11 |
| ❑ 54 Sandis Ozolinsh | .25 | .11 |
| ❑ 55 Vladimir Malakhov | .10 | .05 |
| ❑ 56 Robert Svehla | .10 | .05 |
| ❑ 57 Steve Duchesne | .10 | .05 |
| ❑ 58 Sergei Gonchar | .10 | .05 |
| ❑ 59 Darius Kasparaitis | .25 | .11 |
| ❑ 60 Patrick Roy | 2.50 | 1.10 |
| ❑ 61 Martin Brodeur | 1.25 | .55 |
| ❑ 62 Mike Richter | .50 | .23 |
| ❑ 63 John Vanbiesbrouck | .75 | .35 |
| ❑ 64 Ron Hextall | .25 | .11 |
| ❑ 65 Nikolai Khabibulin | .25 | .11 |
| ❑ 66 Grant Fuhr | .25 | .11 |
| ❑ 67 Kirk McLean | .25 | .11 |
| ❑ 68 Jim Carey | .30 | .14 |
| ❑ 69 Dominik Hasek | 1.00 | .45 |
| ❑ 70 Ed Belfour | .50 | .23 |
| ❑ 71 Chris Osgood | .50 | .23 |
| ❑ 72 Guy Hebert | .25 | .11 |
| ❑ 73 Trevor Kidd | .25 | .11 |
| ❑ 74 Felix Potvin | .50 | .23 |
| ❑ 75 Roman Hamrlik | .10 | .05 |
| ❑ 76 Alexei Zhitnik | .10 | .05 |
| ❑ 77 Al MacInnis | .25 | .11 |
| ❑ 78 Brian Leetch | .50 | .23 |
| ❑ 79 Rob Blake | .10 | .05 |
| ❑ 80 Derian Hatcher | .10 | .05 |
| ❑ 81 Mathieu Schneider | .10 | .05 |
| ❑ 82 Gary Suter | .10 | .05 |
| ❑ 83 Jeff Brown | .10 | .05 |
| ❑ 84 Jyrki Lumme | .10 | .05 |
| ❑ 85 Ed Jovanovski | .25 | .11 |
| ❑ 86 Eric Desjardins | .10 | .05 |
| ❑ 87 Stephane Quintal | .10 | .05 |
| ❑ 88 Marcus Ragnarsson | .10 | .05 |
| ❑ 89 Zarley Zalapski | .10 | .05 |

## 1993 Titrex Guy Lafleur Insert

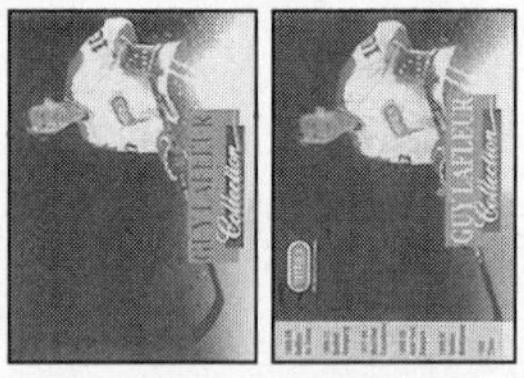


This standard-size card was inserted in Canadian packages of Power Bar, made by Titrex International, a firm specializing in dietary products. Also included in the package was an order form in French for ordering the 24-card Guy Lafleur Collection set. The card features on its front and back a horizontal borderless shot of Guy Lafleur on ice wearing a Titrex jersey, with the Guy Lafleur Collection logo appearing at the bottom. The front has a glossy finish, and Lafleur's name is highlighted in gold foil. The unglossy back carries the Titrex logo at the upper left, and also has the years Lafleur played for each hockey team within a gray stripe down the left edge. The card is unnumbered.

| | MINT | NRMT |
|---|---|---|
| COMPLETE SET (1) | 3.00 | 1.35 |
| COMMON CARD | 3.00 | 1.35 |
| ❑ 1 Guy Lafleur (Wearing Titrex jersey) | 3.00 | 1.35 |

## 1994 Titrex Guy Lafleur

This 24-card standard size set presents the progression of Guy Lafleur's career. The cards were printed on heavier card stock and came with a card storage album measuring approximately 6 1/4" by 8" and a certificate of authenticity. The borderless fronts feature both horizontal and vertical black-and-white photos.

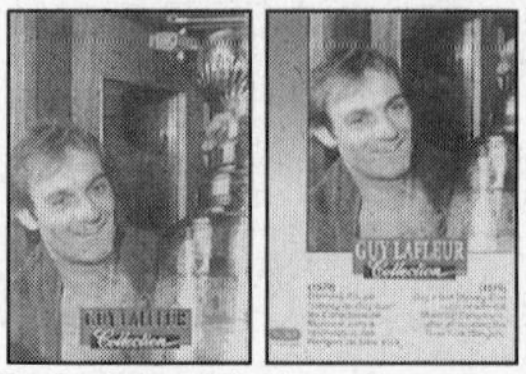


The Guy Lafleur Collection emblem appears inside a red rectangle at the bottom. On a white background with a fading red stripe to the left, the backs carry horizontal and vertical black-and-white photos with the date and a brief photo description (in French and English) below. The cards are unnumbered and checklisted below in chronological order. The set could be obtained by mailing in the order form (plus 24.95 Canadian) that accompanied the 1993 Titrex Guy Lafleur Power Bar Insert in packages of Titrex's Power Bar.

| | MINT | NRMT |
|---|---|---|
| COMPLETE SET (24) | 25.00 | 11.00 |
| COMMON LAFLEUR (1-24) | 1.50 | .70 |
| ❑ 1 Guy Lafleur 1956, Thurso | 2.00 | .90 |
| ❑ 2 Guy Lafleur 1961-1962, Thurso | 1.50 | .70 |
| ❑ 3 Guy Lafleur 1961-1962 (Mosquito's Team Trophy) | 1.50 | .70 |
| ❑ 4 Guy Lafleur 1962 (Guy Wins The Red Story Trophy) | 1.50 | .70 |
| ❑ 5 Guy Lafleur 1962, Hawkesbury | 1.50 | .70 |
| ❑ 6 Guy Lafleur 1962 (First Participation In Quebec Pee-Wee International Hockey Tournament) | 1.50 | .70 |
| ❑ 7 Guy Lafleur 1963-1964 | 1.50 | .70 |
| ❑ 8 Guy Lafleur 1964-1965 | 1.50 | .70 |
| ❑ 9 Guy Lafleur 1966-1967 | 1.50 | .70 |
| ❑ 10 Guy Lafleur 1967-1968 | 1.50 | .70 |
| ❑ 11 Guy Lafleur 1970 (His 75th Goal) | 1.50 | .70 |
| ❑ 12 Guy Lafleur 1970 (After 76th Goal) | 1.50 | .70 |
| ❑ 13 Guy Lafleur 1970-1971 (Holding Paul Lebel Trophy) | 1.50 | .70 |
| ❑ 14 Guy Lafleur 1970-1971 (Last Season With Quebec Remparts) | 1.50 | .70 |
| ❑ 15 Guy Lafleur 1970-1971, Quebec Winning The Memorial Cup) | 1.50 | .70 |
| ❑ 16 Guy Lafleur Rejean Giroux Andre Savard 1970-1971 | 1.50 | .70 |
| ❑ 17 Guy Lafleur Rejean Lafleur, 1970-1971 | 1.50 | .70 |
| ❑ 18 Guy Lafleur Rejean Lafleur, 1971 | 1.50 | .70 |
| ❑ 19 Guy Lafleur 1971 (His Last Year With Quebec Remparts) | 1.50 | .70 |
| ❑ 20 Guy Lafleur 1971 (Carrying The Memorial Cup) | 1.50 | .70 |
| ❑ 21 Guy Lafleur Lieutenant Governor Roland Mitchener, 1971 | 1.50 | .70 |
| ❑ 22 Guy Lafleur 1971 (Leaving The Quebec Remparts) | 1.50 | .70 |
| ❑ 23 Guy Lafleur 1971 (Holding The Memorial Cup) | 1.50 | .70 |
| ❑ 24 Guy Lafleur 1979 | 2.00 | .90 |

## 1954-55 Topps

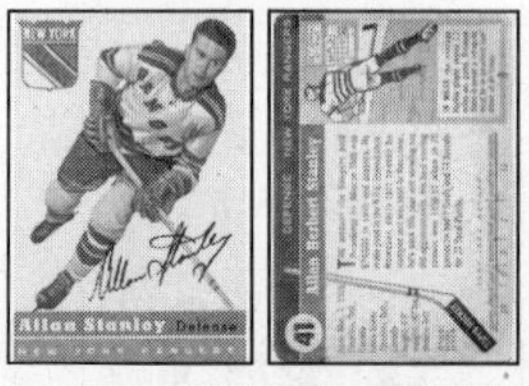


Topps introduced its first hockey set in 1954-55. The issue includes 60 cards of players on the four American (Boston, Chicago, Detroit and New York) teams. Cards measure approximately 2 5/8" by 3 3/4". Color fronts feature the player on a white background with facsimile autograph and team logo. The player's name, team name and position appear in bottom borders that are in team colors. The backs, printed in red and blue, contain player biographies, 1953-54 statistics and a hockey fact section. The cards were printed in the USA. Rookie Cards include Camille Henry and Doug Mohns. An early and very popular card of Gordie Howe is the main attraction in this set.

| | NRMT | VG-E |
|---|---|---|
| COMPLETE SET (60) | 4500.00 | 2000.00 |
| COMMON CARD (1-60) | 30.00 | 13.50 |
| ❑ 1 Dick Gamble | 125.00 | 31.00 |
| ❑ 2 Bob Chrystal | 30.00 | 13.50 |
| ❑ 3 Harry Howell | 100.00 | 45.00 |
| ❑ 4 Johnny Wilson | 30.00 | 13.50 |
| ❑ 5 Red Kelly | 150.00 | 70.00 |
| ❑ 6 Real Chevrefils | 30.00 | 13.50 |
| ❑ 7 Bob Armstrong | 30.00 | 13.50 |
| ❑ 8 Gordie Howe | 1800.00 | 800.00 |
| ❑ 9 Benny Woit | 30.00 | 13.50 |
| ❑ 10 Gump Worsley | 200.00 | 90.00 |
| ❑ 11 Andy Bathgate | 100.00 | 45.00 |
| ❑ 12 Bucky Hollingworth | 30.00 | 13.50 |
| ❑ 13 Ray Timgren | 30.00 | 13.50 |
| ❑ 14 Jack Evans | 30.00 | 13.50 |
| ❑ 15 Paul Ronty | 30.00 | 13.50 |
| ❑ 16 Glen Skov | 30.00 | 13.50 |
| ❑ 17 Gus Mortson | 30.00 | 13.50 |
| ❑ 18 Doug Mohns | 100.00 | 45.00 |
| ❑ 19 Leo Labine | 35.00 | 16.00 |
| ❑ 20 Bill Gadsby | 80.00 | 36.00 |
| ❑ 21 Jerry Toppazzini | 35.00 | 16.00 |
| ❑ 22 Wally Hergesheimer | 30.00 | 13.50 |
| ❑ 23 Danny Lewicki | 30.00 | 13.50 |
| ❑ 24 Metro Prystai | 30.00 | 13.50 |
| ❑ 25 Fern Flaman | 50.00 | 22.00 |
| ❑ 26 Al Rollins | 80.00 | 36.00 |
| ❑ 27 Marcel Pronovost | 50.00 | 22.00 |
| ❑ 28 Lou Jankowski | 30.00 | 13.50 |
| ❑ 29 Nick Mickoski | 30.00 | 13.50 |
| ❑ 30 Frank Martin | 30.00 | 13.50 |
| ❑ 31 Lorne Ferguson | 30.00 | 13.50 |
| ❑ 32 Camille Henry | 50.00 | 22.00 |
| ❑ 33 Pete Conacher | 35.00 | 16.00 |
| ❑ 34 Marty Pavelich | 30.00 | 13.50 |
| ❑ 35 Don McKenney | 50.00 | 22.00 |
| ❑ 36 Fleming Mackell | 30.00 | 13.50 |
| ❑ 37 Jim Henry | 80.00 | 36.00 |
| ❑ 38 Hal Laycoe | 30.00 | 13.50 |
| ❑ 39 Alex Delvecchio | 150.00 | 70.00 |
| ❑ 40 Larry Wilson | 30.00 | 13.50 |
| ❑ 41 Allan Stanley | 100.00 | 45.00 |
| ❑ 42 George Sullivan | 30.00 | 13.50 |
| ❑ 43 Jack McIntyre | 30.00 | 13.50 |
| ❑ 44 Ivan Irwin | 30.00 | 13.50 |
| ❑ 45 Tony Leswick | 30.00 | 13.50 |
| ❑ 46 Bob Goldham | 30.00 | 13.50 |
| ❑ 47 Cal Gardner | 35.00 | 16.00 |
| ❑ 48 Ed Sandford | 30.00 | 13.50 |
| ❑ 49 Bill Quackenbush | 80.00 | 36.00 |
| ❑ 50 Warren Godfrey | 30.00 | 13.50 |
| ❑ 51 Ted Lindsay | 150.00 | 70.00 |
| ❑ 52 Earl Reibel | 35.00 | 16.00 |
| ❑ 53 Don Raleigh | 30.00 | 13.50 |
| ❑ 54 Bill Mosienko | 60.00 | 27.00 |
| ❑ 55 Larry Popein | 30.00 | 13.50 |
| ❑ 56 Edgar Laprade | 40.00 | 18.00 |
| ❑ 57 Bill Dineen | 35.00 | 16.00 |
| ❑ 58 Terry Sawchuk | 700.00 | 325.00 |
| ❑ 59 Marcel Bonin | 30.00 | 13.50 |
| ❑ 60 Milt Schmidt | 200.00 | 50.00 |

## 1957-58 Topps

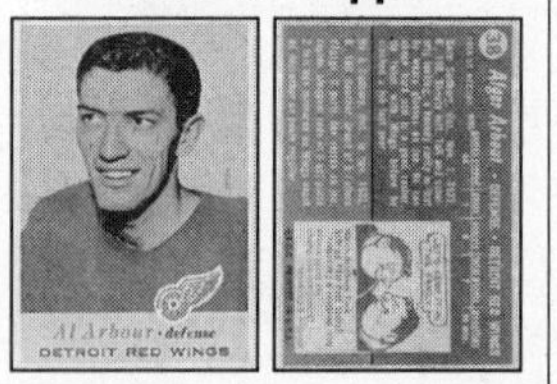


After a two year hiatus, Topps returned to producing hockey cards for 1957-58. Reportedly, Topps spent the interim evaluating the hockey card market. Cards in this 66-card set were reduced to measure the standard 2 1/2" by 3 1/2". The players in this set are from the four U.S. based teams. The cards are in team order: Boston 1-18, Chicago 19-33, Detroit 34-50 and New York 51-66. Bilingual backs feature 1956-57 statistics, a short player biography and a cartoon question and answer section. Rookie Cards in this include Johnny Bucyk, Glenn Hall, Pierre Pilote, and Norm Ullman.

| | NRMT | VG-E |
|---|---|---|
| COMPLETE SET (66) | 2000.00 | 900.00 |
| COMMON CARD (1-66) | 20.00 | 9.00 |
| ❑ 1 Real Chevrefils | 50.00 | 12.50 |
| ❑ 2 Jack Bionda | 20.00 | 9.00 |
| ❑ 3 Bob Armstrong | 20.00 | 9.00 |
| ❑ 4 Fern Flaman | 20.00 | 9.00 |
| ❑ 5 Jerry Toppazzini | 20.00 | 9.00 |
| ❑ 6 Larry Regan | 20.00 | 9.00 |
| ❑ 7 Bronco Horvath | 25.00 | 11.00 |
| ❑ 8 Jack Caffery | 20.00 | 9.00 |
| ❑ 9 Leo Labine | 18.00 | 8.00 |
| ❑ 10 Johnny Bucyk | 225.00 | 100.00 |
| ❑ 11 Vic Stasiuk | 20.00 | 9.00 |
| ❑ 12 Doug Mohns | 25.00 | 11.00 |
| ❑ 13 Don McKenney | 20.00 | 9.00 |
| ❑ 14 Don Simmons | 25.00 | 11.00 |
| ❑ 15 Allan Stanley | 30.00 | 13.50 |
| ❑ 16 Fleming Mackell | 20.00 | 9.00 |
| ❑ 17 Larry Hillman | 20.00 | 9.00 |
| ❑ 18 Leo Boivin | 20.00 | 9.00 |
| ❑ 19 Bob Bailey | 20.00 | 9.00 |
| ❑ 20 Glenn Hall | 400.00 | 180.00 |
| ❑ 21 Ted Lindsay | 50.00 | 22.00 |
| ❑ 22 Pierre Pilote | 100.00 | 45.00 |
| ❑ 23 Jim Thomson | 20.00 | 9.00 |
| ❑ 24 Eric Nesterenko | 20.00 | 9.00 |
| ❑ 25 Gus Mortson | 20.00 | 9.00 |
| ❑ 26 Ed Litzenberger | 25.00 | 11.00 |
| ❑ 27 Elmer Vasko | 25.00 | 11.00 |
| ❑ 28 Jack McIntyre | 20.00 | 9.00 |
| ❑ 29 Ron Murphy | 20.00 | 9.00 |
| ❑ 30 Glen Skov | 20.00 | 9.00 |
| ❑ 31 Hec Lalande | 20.00 | 9.00 |
| ❑ 32 Nick Mickoski | 20.00 | 9.00 |
| ❑ 33 Wally Hergesheimer | 20.00 | 9.00 |
| ❑ 34 Alex Delvecchio | 50.00 | 22.00 |
| ❑ 35 Terry Sawchuk UER (Misspelled Sawchuck on card front) | 200.00 | 90.00 |
| ❑ 36 Guyle Fielder | 25.00 | 11.00 |
| ❑ 37 Tom McCarthy | 20.00 | 9.00 |
| ❑ 38 Al Arbour | 40.00 | 18.00 |
| ❑ 39 Billy Dea | 20.00 | 9.00 |
| ❑ 40 Lorne Ferguson | 20.00 | 9.00 |
| ❑ 41 Warren Godfrey | 20.00 | 9.00 |
| ❑ 42 Gordie Howe | 500.00 | 220.00 |
| ❑ 43 Marcel Pronovost | 25.00 | 11.00 |
| ❑ 44 Bill McNeil | 20.00 | 9.00 |
| ❑ 45 Earl Reibel | 20.00 | 9.00 |
| ❑ 46 Norm Ullman | 225.00 | 100.00 |
| ❑ 47 Johnny Wilson | 20.00 | 9.00 |
| ❑ 48 Red Kelly | 50.00 | 22.00 |
| ❑ 49 Bill Dineen | 20.00 | 9.00 |
| ❑ 50 Forbes Kennedy | 25.00 | 11.00 |
| ❑ 51 Harry Howell | 40.00 | 18.00 |
| ❑ 52 Jean-Guy Gendron | 20.00 | 9.00 |
| ❑ 53 Gump Worsley | 100.00 | 45.00 |
| ❑ 54 Larry Popein | 20.00 | 9.00 |
| ❑ 55 Jack Evans | 20.00 | 9.00 |
| ❑ 56 George Sullivan | 20.00 | 9.00 |
| ❑ 57 Gerry Foley | 20.00 | 9.00 |
| ❑ 58 Andy Hebenton | 25.00 | 11.00 |
| ❑ 59 Larry Cahan | 20.00 | 9.00 |
| ❑ 60 Andy Bathgate | 40.00 | 18.00 |
| ❑ 61 Danny Lewicki | 20.00 | 9.00 |
| ❑ 62 Dean Prentice | 20.00 | 9.00 |
| ❑ 63 Camille Henry | 25.00 | 11.00 |
| ❑ 64 Lou Fontinato | 40.00 | 18.00 |
| ❑ 65 Bill Gadsby | 25.00 | 11.00 |
| ❑ 66 Dave Creighton | 40.00 | 10.00 |

## 1958-59 Topps

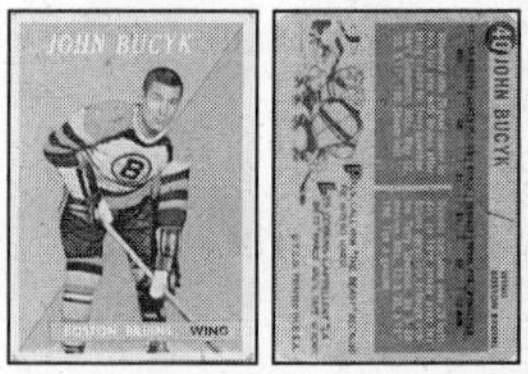


The 1958-59 Topps set contains 66 color standard-size cards of players from the four U.S. based teams. Bilingual backs feature 1957-58 statistics, player biographies and a cartoon information section on the player. The set features the Rookie Card of Bobby Hull. Due to being the last card and subject to wear as well as being chronically off-center, the Hull card is quite scarce in top grades. Other Rookie Cards include Eddie Shack and Ken Wharram.

| | NRMT | VG-E |
|---|---|---|
| COMPLETE SET (66) | 4500.00 | 2000.00 |
| COMMON CARD (1-66) | 20.00 | 9.00 |
| ❑ 1 Bob Armstrong | 40.00 | 10.00 |
| ❑ 2 Terry Sawchuk | 175.00 | 80.00 |
| ❑ 3 Glen Skov | 20.00 | 9.00 |
| ❑ 4 Leo Labine | 18.00 | 8.00 |
| ❑ 5 Dollard St.Laurent | 20.00 | 9.00 |
| ❑ 6 Danny Lewicki | 20.00 | 9.00 |
| ❑ 7 John Hanna | 20.00 | 9.00 |
| ❑ 8 Gordie Howe UER (Misspelled Gordy on card front) | 500.00 | 220.00 |
| ❑ 9 Vic Stasiuk | 20.00 | 9.00 |
| ❑ 10 Larry Regan | 20.00 | 9.00 |
| ❑ 11 Forbes Kennedy | 20.00 | 9.00 |
| ❑ 12 Elmer Vasko | 20.00 | 9.00 |
| ❑ 13 Glenn Hall | 150.00 | 70.00 |
| ❑ 14 Ken Wharram | 25.00 | 11.00 |
| ❑ 15 Len Lunde | 20.00 | 9.00 |
| ❑ 16 Ed Litzenberger | 20.00 | 9.00 |
| ❑ 17 Norm Johnson | 20.00 | 9.00 |
| ❑ 18 Earl Ingarfield | 20.00 | 9.00 |
| ❑ 19 Les Colwill | 20.00 | 9.00 |
| ❑ 20 Leo Boivin | 20.00 | 9.00 |
| ❑ 21 Andy Bathgate | 30.00 | 13.50 |
| ❑ 22 Johnny Wilson | 20.00 | 9.00 |
| ❑ 23 Larry Cahan | 20.00 | 9.00 |
| ❑ 24 Marcel Pronovost | 20.00 | 9.00 |
| ❑ 25 Larry Hillman | 20.00 | 9.00 |
| ❑ 26 Jim Bartlett | 20.00 | 9.00 |

❑ 27 Nick Mickoski .................. 20.00 9.00
❑ 28 Larry Popein .................. 20.00 9.00
❑ 29 Fleming Mackell.............. 20.00 9.00
❑ 30 Eddie Shack.................. 250.00 110.00
❑ 31 Jack Evans..................... 20.00 9.00
❑ 32 Dean Prentice ................ 20.00 9.00
❑ 33 Claude Laforge .............. 20.00 9.00
❑ 34 Bill Gadsby ................... 25.00 11.00
❑ 35 Bronco Horvath .............. 20.00 9.00
❑ 36 Pierre Pilote .................. 50.00 22.00
❑ 37 Earl Balfour.................... 20.00 9.00
❑ 38 Gus Mortson................... 20.00 9.00
❑ 39 Gump Worsley................ 80.00 36.00
❑ 40 Johnny Bucyk.............. 125.00 55.00
❑ 41 Lou Fontinato ................ 20.00 9.00
❑ 42 Tod Sloan ...................... 20.00 9.00
❑ 43 Charlie Burns.................. 20.00 9.00
❑ 44 Don Simmons................. 20.00 9.00
❑ 45 Jerry Toppazzini ............. 20.00 9.00
❑ 46 Andy Hebenton .............. 20.00 9.00
❑ 47 Pete Goegan UER ........... 20.00 9.00
(Misspelled Geogan
on card front)
❑ 48 George Sullivan .............. 20.00 9.00
❑ 49 Hank Ciesla .................... 20.00 9.00
❑ 50 Doug Mohns................... 20.00 9.00
❑ 51 Jean-Guy Gendron.......... 20.00 9.00
❑ 52 Alex Delvecchio ............. 40.00 18.00
❑ 53 Eric Nesterenko .............. 20.00 9.00
❑ 54 Camille Henry ................. 20.00 9.00
❑ 55 Lorne Ferguson .............. 20.00 9.00
❑ 56 Fern Flaman.................... 20.00 9.00
❑ 57 Earl Reibel ..................... 20.00 9.00
❑ 58 Warren Godfrey .............. 20.00 9.00
❑ 59 Ron Murphy .................... 20.00 9.00
❑ 60 Harry Howell................... 30.00 13.50
❑ 61 Red Kelly ....................... 40.00 18.00
❑ 62 Don McKenney ................ 20.00 9.00
❑ 63 Ted Lindsay .................... 40.00 18.00
❑ 64 Al Arbour ........................ 25.00 11.00
❑ 65 Norm Ullman ................ 100.00 45.00
❑ 66 Bobby Hull.................. 3000.00 750.00

## 1959-60 Topps

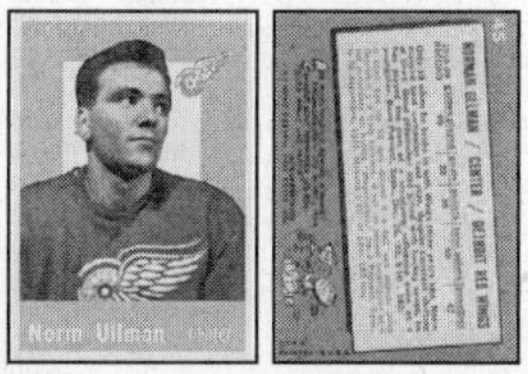


The 1959-60 Topps set contains 66 color standard-size cards of players from the four U.S. based teams. The fronts have the player's name and position at the bottom with team name and logo at the top. Bilingual backs feature 1958-59 statistics, a short biography and a cartoon question section.

| | NRMT | VG-E |
|---|---|---|
| COMPLETE SET (66) | 2000.00 | 900.00 |
| COMMON CARD (1-66) | 20.00 | 9.00 |

❑ 1 Eric Nesterenko ................ 40.00 10.00
❑ 2 Pierre Pilote.................... 40.00 18.00
❑ 3 Elmer Vasko .................... 20.00 9.00
❑ 4 Peter Goegan................... 20.00 9.00
❑ 5 Lou Fontinato .................. 18.00 8.00
❑ 6 Ted Lindsay ..................... 25.00 11.00
❑ 7 Leo Labine....................... 18.00 8.00
❑ 8 Alex Delvecchio ............... 30.00 13.50
❑ 9 Don McKenney UER ......... 20.00 9.00
(Misspelled McKenny
on card front)
❑ 10 Earl Ingarfield ................. 20.00 9.00
❑ 11 Don Simmons.................. 20.00 9.00
❑ 12 Glen Skov ...................... 20.00 9.00
❑ 13 Tod Sloan ....................... 20.00 9.00
❑ 14 Vic Stasiuk..................... 20.00 9.00
❑ 15 Gump Worsley................ 60.00 27.00
❑ 16 Andy Hebenton ............... 20.00 9.00
❑ 17 Dean Prentice ................. 20.00 9.00
❑ 18 Action picture ................. 15.00 6.75
❑ 19 Fleming Mackell.............. 20.00 9.00
❑ 20 Harry Howell................... 25.00 11.00
❑ 21 Larry Popein ................... 20.00 9.00
❑ 22 Len Lunde....................... 20.00 9.00
❑ 23 Johnny Bucyk.................. 60.00 27.00
❑ 24 Jean-Guy Gendron........... 20.00 9.00
❑ 25 Barry Cullen.................... 20.00 9.00
❑ 26 Leo Boivin....................... 20.00 9.00
❑ 27 Warren Godfrey ............... 20.00 9.00
❑ 28 Action Picture................. 30.00 13.50
(Glenn Hall and
Camille Henry)
❑ 29 Fern Flaman.................... 20.00 9.00
❑ 30 Jack Evans...................... 20.00 9.00
❑ 31 John Hanna ..................... 20.00 9.00
❑ 32 Glenn Hall .................... 100.00 45.00
❑ 33 Murray Balfour ................ 20.00 9.00
❑ 34 Andy Bathgate ................. 25.00 11.00
❑ 35 Al Arbour ........................ 25.00 11.00
❑ 36 Jim Morrison.................... 20.00 9.00
❑ 37 Nick Mickoski .................. 20.00 9.00
❑ 38 Jerry Toppazzini .............. 20.00 9.00
❑ 39 Bob Armstrong................. 20.00 9.00
❑ 40 Charlie Burns UER........... 20.00 9.00
(Misspelled Charley
on card front)
❑ 41 Bill McNeil ...................... 20.00 9.00
❑ 42 Terry Sawchuk.............. 150.00 70.00
❑ 43 Dollard St.Laurent .......... 20.00 9.00
❑ 44 Marcel Pronovost ........... 20.00 9.00
❑ 45 Norm Ullman ................. 60.00 27.00
❑ 46 Camille Henry ................. 20.00 9.00
❑ 47 Bobby Hull .................. 600.00 275.00
❑ 48 Action Picture ................ 80.00 36.00
(Gordie Howe and
Jack Evans)
❑ 49 Lou Marcon .................... 20.00 9.00
❑ 50 Earl Balfour .................... 20.00 9.00
❑ 51 Jim Bartlett ..................... 20.00 9.00
❑ 52 Forbes Kennedy .............. 20.00 9.00
❑ 53 Action Picture ................. 15.00 6.75
(Nick Mickoski and
Johnny Hanna)
❑ 54 Action Picture ................. 25.00 11.00
(Norm Johnson,
Gump Worsley, and
Harry Howell)
❑ 55 Brian Cullen .................... 20.00 9.00
❑ 56 Bronco Horvath .............. 20.00 9.00
❑ 57 Eddie Shack ................. 100.00 45.00
❑ 58 Doug Mohns.................... 20.00 9.00
❑ 59 George Sullivan .............. 20.00 9.00
❑ 60 Pierre Pilote/Flem Mackell IA 20.00 9.00
❑ 61 Ed Litzenberger............... 20.00 9.00
❑ 62 Bill Gadsby .................... 25.00 11.00
❑ 63 Gordie Howe................ 400.00 180.00
❑ 64 Claude Laforge ............... 20.00 9.00
❑ 65 Red Kelly ....................... 30.00 13.50
❑ 66 Ron Murphy .................... 40.00 10.00

## 1960-61 Topps

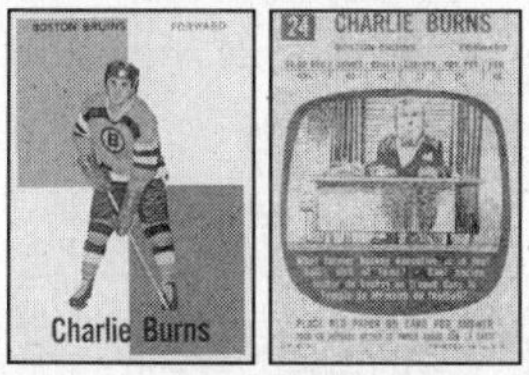


The 1960-61 Topps set contains 66 color standard-size cards featuring players from Boston (1-20), Chicago (23-42) and New York (45-63). In addition to player and team names, the typical card front features color patterns according to the player's team. The backs are bilingual and have 1959-60 statistics and a cartoon trivia quiz. Cards titled "All-Time Greats" are an attractive feature to this set and include the likes of Georges Vezina and Eddie Shore. The All-Time Great players are indicated by ATG in the checklist below. Stan Mikita's Rookie Card is part of this set. The existence of an album issued by Topps to store this set has recently been confirmed. It is valued at approximately $150.

| | NRMT | VG-E |
|---|---|---|
| COMPLETE SET (66) | 1800.00 | 800.00 |
| COMMON CARD (1-66) | 12.00 | 5.50 |
| A-T GREAT'S | 15.00 | 6.75 |

❑ 1 Lester Patrick ATG........... 80.00 20.00
❑ 2 Paddy Moran ATG ............ 20.00 9.00
❑ 3 Joe Malone ATG .............. 30.00 13.50
❑ 4 Ernest (Moose) Johnson ATG 15.00 6.75
❑ 5 Nels Stewart ATG............. 25.00 11.00
❑ 6 Bill(Red) Hay ................... 15.00 6.75
❑ 7 Eddie Shack..................... 80.00 36.00
❑ 8 Cy Denneny ATG.............. 15.00 6.75
❑ 9 Jim Morrison.................... 12.00 5.50
❑ 10 Bill Cook ATG.................. 15.00 6.75
❑ 11 Johnny Bucyk.................. 50.00 22.00
❑ 12 Murray Balfour ................ 12.00 5.50
❑ 13 Leo Labine...................... 12.00 5.50
❑ 14 Stan Mikita .................. 400.00 180.00
❑ 15 George Hay ATG.............. 15.00 6.75
❑ 16 Mervyn(Red) Dutton ATG 15.00 6.75
❑ 17 Dickie Boon ATG UER..... 15.00 6.75
(Misspelled Boone
on card front)
❑ 18 George Sullivan .............. 12.00 5.50
❑ 19 Georges Vezina ATG ....... 80.00 36.00
❑ 20 Eddie Shore ATG ............ 60.00 27.00
❑ 21 Ed Litzenberger............... 12.00 5.50
❑ 22 Bill Gadsby ..................... 15.00 6.75
❑ 23 Elmer Vasko ................... 12.00 5.50
❑ 24 Charlie Burns................... 12.00 5.50
❑ 25 Glenn Hall ...................... 80.00 36.00
❑ 26 Dit Clapper ATG .............. 25.00 11.00
❑ 27 Art Ross ATG .................. 50.00 22.00
❑ 28 Jerry Toppazzini .............. 12.00 5.50
❑ 29 Frank Boucher ATG.......... 15.00 6.75
❑ 30 Jack Evans...................... 12.00 5.50
❑ 31 Jean-Guy Gendron........... 12.00 5.50
❑ 32 Chuck Gardiner ATG ........ 25.00 11.00
❑ 33 Ab McDonald................... 12.00 5.50
❑ 34 Frank Frederickson ATG.. 15.00 6.75
UER (Misspelled
Fredrickson
on front)
❑ 35 Frank Nighbor ATG .......... 20.00 9.00
❑ 36 Gump Worsley................. 50.00 22.00
❑ 37 Dean Prentice ................. 14.00 6.25
❑ 38 Hugh Lehman ATG ........... 15.00 6.75
❑ 39 Jack McCartan................. 12.00 5.50
❑ 40 Don McKenney UER ........ 12.00 5.50
(Misspelled McKenny
on card front)
❑ 41 Ron Murphy .................... 12.00 5.50
❑ 42 Andy Hebenton ............... 12.00 5.50
❑ 43 Don Simmons.................. 15.00 6.75
❑ 44 Herb Gardiner ATG .......... 15.00 6.75
❑ 45 Andy Bathgate ................. 20.00 9.00
❑ 46 Cyclone Taylor ATG ......... 30.00 13.50
❑ 47 King Clancy ATG.............. 50.00 22.00
❑ 48 Newsy Lalonde ATG......... 30.00 13.50
❑ 49 Harry Howell................... 20.00 9.00
❑ 50 Ken Schinkel RC ............. 12.00 5.50
❑ 51 Tod Sloan ....................... 12.00 5.50
❑ 52 Doug Mohns.................... 15.00 6.75
❑ 53 Camille Henry ................. 15.00 6.75
❑ 54 Bronco Horvath .............. 12.00 5.50
❑ 55 Tiny Thompson ATG........ 30.00 13.50
❑ 56 Bob Armstrong................ 12.00 5.50
❑ 57 Fern Flaman.................... 12.00 5.50
❑ 58 Bobby Hull.................... 500.00 220.00
❑ 59 Howie Morenz ATG .......... 60.00 27.00
❑ 60 Dick Irvin ATG ................ 30.00 13.50
❑ 61 Lou Fontinato ................. 12.00 5.50
❑ 62 Leo Boivin....................... 15.00 6.75
❑ 63 Moose Goheen ATG......... 15.00 6.75
❑ 64 Al Arbour ........................ 20.00 9.00
❑ 65 Pierre Pilote.................... 30.00 13.50
❑ 66 Vic Stasiuk..................... 30.00 7.50

## 1960-61 Topps Stamps

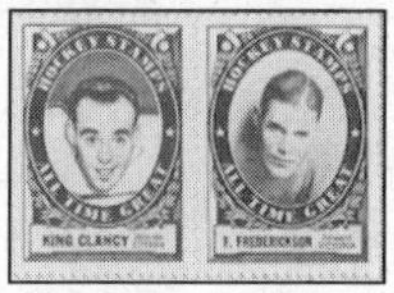


There are 52 stamps in this scarce set. They were issued as pairs as an insert in with the 1960-61 Topps Hockey regular issue cards. The players in the set are either members of the Boston Bruins (BB), Chicago Blackhawks (CBH), New York Rangers (NYR), or All-Time Greats (ATG). The stamps are unnumbered, so they are listed below alphabetically. Stan Mikita's stamp is notable in that it appears in Stan's Rookie Card year. Dallas Smith's stamp precedes his RC by one year. Intact pairs of stamps with tabs are more difficult to find and would be valued 50 percent higher than the sum of the two players.

| | NRMT | VG-E |
|---|---|---|
| COMPLETE SET (52) | 1800.00 | 800.00 |
| COMMON CARD (1-52) | 15.00 | 6.75 |

❑ 1 Murray Balfour CBH.......... 15.00 6.75
❑ 2 Andy Bathgate NYR .......... 30.00 13.50
❑ 3 Leo Boivin BB.................. 25.00 11.00
❑ 4 Dickie Boon ATG.............. 25.00 11.00
❑ 5 Frank Boucher ATG........... 25.00 11.00
❑ 6 Johnny Bucyk BB.............. 40.00 18.00
❑ 7 Charlie Burns BB ............. 15.00 6.75
❑ 8 King Clancy ATG.............. 60.00 27.00
❑ 9 Dit Clapper ATG .............. 40.00 18.00
❑ 10 Sprague Cleghorn ATG ... 40.00 18.00
❑ 11 Alex Connell ATG ............ 30.00 13.50
❑ 12 Bill Cook ATG.................. 30.00 13.50
❑ 13 Cy Denneny ATG.............. 30.00 13.50
❑ 14 Jack Evans CBH............... 15.00 6.75
❑ 15 Frank Frederickson ATG.. 25.00 11.00
❑ 16 Chuck Gardiner ATG ....... 30.00 13.50
❑ 17 Herb Gardiner ATG .......... 25.00 11.00
❑ 18 Eddie Gerard ATG ........... 25.00 11.00
❑ 19 Moose Goheen ATG ......... 25.00 11.00
❑ 20 Glenn Hall CBH ............... 60.00 27.00
❑ 21 Doug Harvey NYR............ 50.00 22.00
❑ 22 Bill(Red) Hay CBH ........... 15.00 6.75
❑ 23 George Hay ATG.............. 30.00 13.50
❑ 24 Andy Hebenton NYR........ 15.00 6.75
❑ 25 Camille Henry NYR ......... 15.00 6.75
❑ 26 Bronco Horvath CBH ....... 20.00 9.00
❑ 27 Harry Howell NYR............ 25.00 11.00
❑ 28 Bobby Hull CBH............ 200.00 90.00
❑ 29 Dick Irvin ATG ................ 40.00 18.00
❑ 30 Ernest(Moose) Johnson . 25.00 11.00
ATG
❑ 31 Newsy Lalonde ATG........ 50.00 22.00
❑ 32 Albert Langlois NYR ....... 15.00 6.75
❑ 33 Hugh Lehman ATG .......... 25.00 11.00
❑ 34 Joe Malone ATG ............. 50.00 22.00
❑ 35 Don McKenney BB........... 15.00 6.75
❑ 36 Stan Mikita CBH........... 125.00 55.00
❑ 37 Doug Mohns BB .............. 20.00 9.00
❑ 38 Paddy Moran ATG ........... 30.00 13.50
❑ 39 Howie Morenz ATG....... 100.00 45.00
❑ 40 Ron Murphy CBH............. 15.00 6.75
❑ 41 Frank Nighbor ATG.......... 30.00 13.50
❑ 42 Murray Oliver BB ............ 15.00 6.75
❑ 43 Pierre Pilote CBH ............ 30.00 13.50
❑ 44 Dean Prentice NYR ......... 20.00 9.00
❑ 45 Andre Pronovost BB ....... 15.00 6.75
❑ 46 Art Ross ATG................... 60.00 27.00
❑ 47 Dallas Smith BB............... 25.00 11.00
❑ 48 Nels Stewart ATG............ 30.00 13.50
❑ 49 Cyclone Taylor ATG ........ 30.00 13.50
❑ 50 Elmer Vasko CBH............ 15.00 6.75
❑ 51 Georges Vezina ATG ..... 100.00 45.00
❑ 52 Gump Worsley NYR......... 50.00 22.00

## 1961-62 Topps

The 1961-62 Topps set contains 66 color standard-size cards featuring players from Boston, Chicago and New York. The card

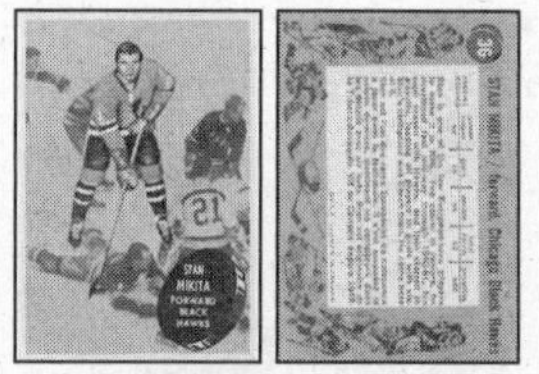

numbering in this set is basically by team order, e.g., Boston Bruins (1-22), Chicago Blackhawks (23-44), and New York Rangers (45-65). Bilingual backs contain 1960-61 statistics and brief career highlights. For the first time, Topps cards were printed in Canada. Rookie Cards include New York Ranger stars Rod Gilbert and Jean Ratelle. The set marks the debut of team and checklist cards within Topps hockey card sets.

| | NRMT | VG-E |
|---|---|---|
| COMPLETE SET (66) | 1500.00 | 700.00 |
| COMMON CARD (1-66) | 12.00 | 5.50 |

❑ 1 Phil Watson CO ................ 25.00 6.25
❑ 2 Ted Green ........................ 40.00 18.00
❑ 3 Earl Balfour..................... 12.00 5.50
❑ 4 Dallas Smith .................... 25.00 11.00
❑ 5 Andre Pronovost UER....... 12.00 5.50
(Misspelled Provonost
on card back)
❑ 6 Dick Meissner................... 12.00 5.50
❑ 7 Leo Boivin....................... 15.00 6.75
❑ 8 Johnny Bucyk.................. 40.00 18.00
❑ 9 Jerry Toppazzini .............. 12.00 5.50
❑ 10 Doug Mohns................... 15.00 6.75
❑ 11 Charlie Burns.................. 12.00 5.50
❑ 12 Don McKenney ............... 12.00 5.50
❑ 13 Bob Armstrong ............... 12.00 5.50
❑ 14 Murray Oliver.................. 12.00 5.50
❑ 15 Orland Kurtenbach.......... 20.00 9.00
❑ 16 Terry Gray....................... 12.00 5.50
❑ 17 Don Head........................ 15.00 6.75
❑ 18 Pat Stapleton .................. 25.00 11.00
❑ 19 Cliff Pennington............... 12.00 5.50
❑ 20 Team Picture .................. 40.00 18.00
❑ 21 Action Picture................. 14.00 6.25
(Earl Balfour and
Fern Flaman)
❑ 22 Action Picture................. 25.00 11.00
(Andy Bathgate
and Glenn Hall)
❑ 23 Rudy Pilous CO .............. 15.00 6.75
❑ 24 Pierre Pilote.................... 25.00 11.00
❑ 25 Elmer Vasko ................... 12.00 5.50
❑ 26 Reg Fleming ................... 15.00 6.75
❑ 27 Ab McDonald.................. 12.00 5.50
❑ 28 Eric Nesterenko ............... 15.00 6.75
❑ 29 Bobby Hull................... 350.00 160.00
❑ 30 Ken Wharram .................. 15.00 6.75
❑ 31 Dollard St.Laurent ........... 12.00 5.50
❑ 32 Glenn Hall ....................... 60.00 27.00
❑ 33 Murray Balfour ................ 12.00 5.50
❑ 34 Ron Murphy .................... 12.00 5.50
❑ 35 Bill(Red) Hay .................. 12.00 5.50
❑ 36 Stan Mikita ................... 200.00 90.00
❑ 37 Denis DeJordy ................. 40.00 18.00
❑ 38 Wayne Hillman ............... 15.00 6.75
❑ 39 Rino Robazzo .................. 12.00 5.50
❑ 40 Bronco Horvath ............... 12.00 5.50
❑ 41 Bob Turner ...................... 12.00 5.50
❑ 42 Blackhawks Team ........... 40.00 18.00
❑ 43 Action Picture................. 14.00 6.25
(Ken Wharram)
❑ 44 Action Picture................. 25.00 11.00
(Dollard St.Laurent
helps Glenn Hall)
❑ 45 Doug Harvey CO ............. 40.00 18.00
❑ 46 Junior Langlois................ 12.00 5.50
❑ 47 Irv Spencer..................... 12.00 5.50
❑ 48 George Sullivan .............. 12.00 5.50
❑ 49 Earl Ingarfield ................. 12.00 5.50
❑ 50 Gump Worsley................. 40.00 18.00
❑ 51 Harry Howell................... 20.00 9.00
❑ 52 Larry Cahan ..................... 12.00 5.50
❑ 53 Andy Bathgate ................. 20.00 9.00
❑ 54 Dean Prentice ................. 15.00 6.75
❑ 55 Andy Hebenton ............... 12.00 5.50
❑ 56 Camille Henry ................. 15.00 6.75
❑ 57 Jean-Guy Gendron........... 12.00 5.50
❑ 58 Pat Hannigan .................. 12.00 5.50
❑ 59 Ted Hampson .................. 12.00 5.50
❑ 60 Jean Ratelle ................. 125.00 55.00
❑ 61 Al Lebrun........................ 12.00 5.50
❑ 62 Rod Gilbert .................. 125.00 55.00
❑ 63 Team Picture .................. 40.00 18.00
❑ 64 Action Picture................. 20.00 9.00
(Dick Meissner and
Gump Worsley)
❑ 65 Action Picture................. 20.00 9.00
(Gump Worsley)
❑ 66 Checklist Card............... 300.00 75.00

## 1962-63 Topps

The 1962-63 Topps set contains 66 color standard-size cards featuring players from Boston, Chicago, and New York. The card numbering in this set is by team order, e.g., Boston Bruins (1-22), Chicago Blackhawks (23-44), and New York Rangers (45-65). Included within the numbering sequence are team cards. Bilingual backs feature 1961-62

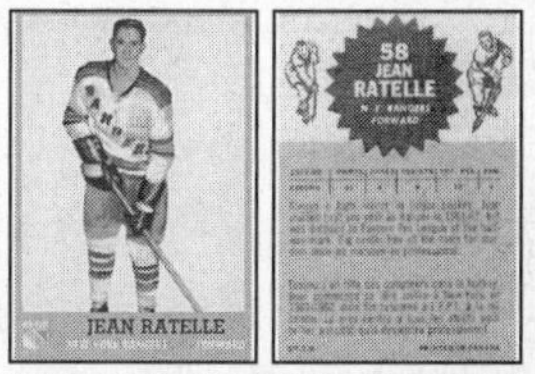


statistics and career highlights. The cards were printed in Canada. Rookie Cards include Vic Hadfield, Chico Maki, and Jim "The Chief" Neilson.

| | NRMT | VG-E |
|---|---|---|
| COMPLETE SET (66) | 1200.00 | 550.00 |
| COMMON CARD (1-66) | 10.00 | 4.50 |

❑ 1 Phil Watson CO ................ 25.00 6.25
❑ 2 Bob Perreault................... 12.00 5.50
❑ 3 Bruce Gamble................... 20.00 9.00
❑ 4 Warren Godfrey ............... 10.00 4.50
❑ 5 Leo Boivin........................ 12.00 5.50
❑ 6 Doug Mohns..................... 12.00 5.50
❑ 7 Ted Green ........................ 15.00 6.75
❑ 8 Pat Stapleton ................... 15.00 6.75
❑ 9 Dallas Smith .................... 15.00 6.75
❑ 10 Don McKenney ............... 10.00 4.50
❑ 11 Johnny Bucyk................. 30.00 13.50
❑ 12 Murray Oliver.................. 10.00 4.50
❑ 13 Jerry Toppazzini ............. 10.00 4.50
❑ 14 Cliff Pennington.............. 10.00 4.50
❑ 15 Charlie Burns.................. 10.00 4.50
❑ 16 Jean-Guy Gendron.......... 10.00 4.50
❑ 17 Irv Spencer..................... 10.00 4.50
❑ 18 Wayne Connelly.............. 10.00 4.50
❑ 19 Andre Pronovost............. 10.00 4.50
❑ 20 Terry Gray....................... 10.00 4.50
❑ 21 Tom Williams .................. 15.00 6.75
❑ 22 Bruins Team ................... 40.00 18.00
❑ 23 Rudy Pilous CO .............. 12.00 5.50
❑ 24 Glenn Hall ...................... 50.00 22.00
❑ 25 Denis DeJordy................. 15.00 6.75
❑ 26 Jack Evans...................... 10.00 4.50
❑ 27 Elmer Vasko ................... 10.00 4.50
❑ 28 Pierre Pilote.................... 20.00 9.00
❑ 29 Bob Turner ...................... 10.00 4.50
❑ 30 Dollard St.Laurent .......... 10.00 4.50
❑ 31 Wayne Hillman ............... 12.00 5.50
❑ 32 Al McNeil ........................ 10.00 4.50
❑ 33 Bobby Hull................... 350.00 160.00
❑ 34 Stan Mikita .................. 125.00 55.00
❑ 35 Bill(Red) Hay .................. 10.00 4.50
❑ 36 Murray Balfour ............... 10.00 4.50
❑ 37 Chico Maki...................... 20.00 9.00
❑ 38 Ab McDonald.................. 10.00 4.50
❑ 39 Ken Wharram .................. 12.00 5.50
❑ 40 Ron Murphy .................... 10.00 4.50
❑ 41 Eric Nesterenko ............... 12.00 5.50
❑ 42 Reg Fleming ................... 12.00 5.50
❑ 43 Murray Hall..................... 10.00 4.50
❑ 44 Blackhawks Team ........... 40.00 18.00
❑ 45 Gump Worsley................ 40.00 18.00
❑ 46 Harry Howell................... 15.00 6.75
❑ 47 Albert Langlois ............... 10.00 4.50
❑ 48 Larry Cahan .................... 10.00 4.50
❑ 49 Jim Neilson..................... 20.00 9.00
❑ 50 Al Lebrun........................ 10.00 4.50
❑ 51 Earl Ingarfield ................. 10.00 4.50
❑ 52 Andy Bathgate ................ 15.00 6.75
❑ 53 Dean Prentice ................. 12.00 5.50
❑ 54 Andy Hebenton ............... 10.00 4.50
❑ 55 Ted Hampson .................. 10.00 4.50
❑ 56 Dave Balon ..................... 10.00 4.50
❑ 57 Bert Olmstead................. 12.00 5.50
❑ 58 Jean Ratelle ................... 50.00 22.00
❑ 59 Rod Gilbert .................... 50.00 22.00
❑ 60 Vic Hadfield ................... 50.00 22.00
❑ 61 Frank Paice..................... 10.00 4.50
❑ 62 Camille Henry ................. 12.00 5.50
❑ 63 Bronco Horvath ............... 10.00 4.50
❑ 64 Pat Hannigan .................. 10.00 4.50
❑ 65 Rangers Team ................. 40.00 18.00
❑ 66 Checklist Card.............. 250.00 60.00

## 1962-63 Topps Hockey Bucks

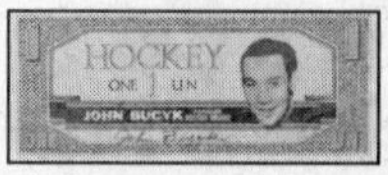


These "bucks" are actually inserts printed to look like Canadian currency on thin paper stock. They were distributed as an inserted folded in one buck per wax pack. Since these bucks are unnumbered, they are ordered below in alphabetical order by player's name. The bucks are approximately 4 1/16" by 1 11/16"; there is no information on the backs, just a green-patterned design.

| | NRMT | VG-E |
|---|---|---|
| COMPLETE SET (24) | 1000.00 | 450.00 |
| COMMON CARD (1-24) | 25.00 | 11.00 |
| COMMON CARD DP | 25.00 | 11.00 |

❑ 1 Dave Balon DP................. 25.00 11.00
❑ 2 Andy Bathgate ................. 50.00 22.00
❑ 3 Leo Boivin....................... 40.00 18.00
❑ 4 Johnny Bucyk DP ............ 50.00 22.00
❑ 5 Reg Fleming DP............... 25.00 11.00

❑ 6 Warren Godfrey DP 25.00 11.00
❑ 7 Ted Green 40.00 18.00
❑ 8 Glenn Hall DP 60.00 27.00
❑ 9 Bill(Red) Hay 25.00 11.00
❑ 10 Andy Hebenton DP 25.00 11.00
❑ 11 Harry Howell DP 25.00 11.00
❑ 12 Bobby Hull 200.00 90.00
❑ 13 Earl Ingarfield 25.00 11.00
❑ 14 Albert Langlois 25.00 11.00
❑ 15 Ab McDonald DP 25.00 11.00
❑ 16 Don McKenney 25.00 11.00
❑ 17 Stan Mikita 100.00 45.00
❑ 18 Doug Mohns 40.00 18.00
❑ 19 Murray Oliver DP 25.00 11.00
❑ 20 Pierre Pilote 50.00 22.00
❑ 21 Dean Prentice 40.00 18.00
❑ 22 Jerry Toppazzini DP 25.00 11.00
❑ 23 Elmer Vasko DP 25.00 11.00
❑ 24 Gump Worsley DP 60.00 27.00

## 1963-64 Topps

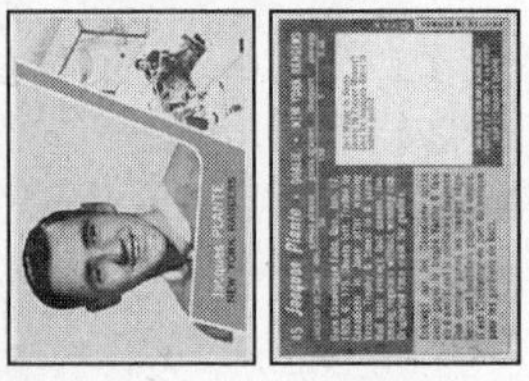

The 1963-64 Topps set contains 66 color cards featuring players and team cards from Boston (1-21), Chicago (22-43) and New York (44-65). Cards in the set measure 2 1/2" by 3 1/2". Bilingual backs contain 1962-63 statistics and a short player biography. A question section, the answer for which could be obtained by rubbing the edge of a coin over a blank space under the question, also appears on the card backs. The cards were printed in Canada. The notable Rookie Cards in this set are Ed Johnston, Gilles Villemure, and Ed Westfall. Jacques Plante makes his first appearance in a Topps set.

NRMT VG-E
COMPLETE SET (66) 1000.00 450.00
COMMON CARD (1-66) 10.00 4.50

❑ 1 Milt Schmidt CO 25.00 6.25
❑ 2 Ed Johnston 40.00 18.00
❑ 3 Doug Mohns 12.00 5.50
❑ 4 Tom Johnson 12.00 5.50
❑ 5 Leo Boivin 12.00 5.50
❑ 6 Bob McCord 10.00 4.50
❑ 7 Ted Green 12.00 5.50
❑ 8 Ed Westfall 30.00 13.50
❑ 9 Charlie Burns 10.00 4.50
❑ 10 Murray Oliver 12.00 5.50
❑ 11 Johnny Bucyk 25.00 11.00
❑ 12 Tom Williams 12.00 5.50
❑ 13 Dean Prentice 12.00 5.50
❑ 14 Bob Leiter 10.00 4.50
❑ 15 Andy Hebenton 10.00 4.50
❑ 16 Jean-Guy Gendron 10.00 4.50
❑ 17 Wayne Rivers 10.00 4.50
❑ 18 Jerry Toppazzini 10.00 4.50
❑ 19 Forbes Kennedy 10.00 4.50
❑ 20 Orland Kurtenbach 12.00 5.50
❑ 21 Bruins Team 35.00 16.00
❑ 22 Billy Reay CO 12.00 5.50
❑ 23 Glenn Hall 40.00 18.00
❑ 24 Denis DeJordy 12.00 5.50
❑ 25 Pierre Pilote 15.00 6.75
❑ 26 Elmer Vasko 10.00 4.50
❑ 27 Wayne Hillman 12.00 5.50
❑ 28 Al McNeil 10.00 4.50
❑ 29 Howie Young 10.00 4.50
❑ 30 Ed Van Impe 15.00 6.75
❑ 31 Reg Fleming 15.00 6.75
(Gordie Howe also shown)
❑ 32 Bob Turner 10.00 4.50
❑ 33 Bobby Hull 250.00 110.00
❑ 34 Bill(Red) Hay 10.00 4.50
❑ 35 Murray Balfour 10.00 4.50
❑ 36 Stan Mikita 100.00 45.00
❑ 37 Ab McDonald 10.00 4.50
❑ 38 Ken Wharram 12.00 5.50
❑ 39 Eric Nesterenko 12.00 5.50
❑ 40 Ron Murphy 10.00 4.50
❑ 41 Chico Maki 10.00 4.50
❑ 42 John McKenzie 15.00 6.75
❑ 43 Blackhawks Team 35.00 16.00
❑ 44 George Sullivan 10.00 4.50
❑ 45 Jacques Plante 125.00 55.00
❑ 46 Gilles Villemure 30.00 13.50
❑ 47 Doug Harvey 30.00 13.50
❑ 48 Harry Howell 12.00 5.50
❑ 49 Albert Langlois 10.00 4.50
❑ 50 Jim Neilson 12.00 5.50
❑ 51 Larry Cahan 10.00 4.50
❑ 52 Andy Bathgate 12.00 5.50
❑ 53 Don McKenney 10.00 4.50
❑ 54 Vic Hadfield 15.00 6.75
❑ 55 Earl Ingarfield 10.00 4.50
❑ 56 Camille Henry 10.00 4.50
❑ 57 Rod Gilbert 30.00 13.50
❑ 58 Phil Goyette 15.00 6.75
(Gordie Howe also shown in background)
❑ 59 Don Marshall 12.00 5.50
❑ 60 Dick Meissner 10.00 4.50
❑ 61 Val Fonteyne 10.00 4.50
❑ 62 Ken Schinkel 10.00 4.50
❑ 63 Jean Ratelle 30.00 13.50
❑ 64 Don Johns 10.00 4.50
❑ 65 Rangers Team 35.00 16.00
❑ 66 Checklist Card 200.00 50.00

## 1964-65 Topps

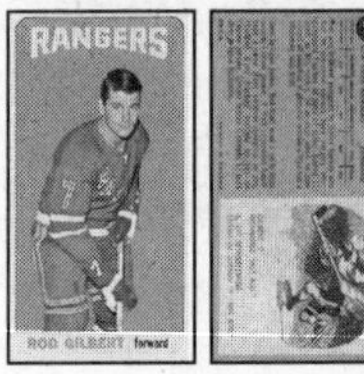

The 1964-65 Topps hockey set features 110 color cards of players from all six NHL teams. The size of the card is larger than in previous years at 2 1/2" by 4 11/16". Colorful fronts contain a solid player background with team name at the top and player name and position at the bottom. Bilingual backs have 1963-64 statistics, a brief player bio and a cartoon section featuring a fact about the player. The cards were printed in Canada. Eleven of the numbers in the last series (56-110) appear to have been short printed. They are designated SP below. Rookie Cards include single prints of Gary Dornhoefer and Marcel Paille found in the last series. Other Rookie Cards include Roger Crozier, Jim Pappin, Pit Martin, Rod Seiling and Lou Angotti.

NRMT VG-E
COMPLETE SET (110) 6000.00 2700.00
COMMON CARD (1-55) 20.00 9.00
COMMON CARD (56-110) 45.00 20.00

❑ 1 Pit Martin 80.00 20.00
❑ 2 Gilles Tremblay 22.00 10.00
❑ 3 Terry Harper 25.00 11.00
❑ 4 John Ferguson 40.00 18.00
❑ 5 Elmer Vasko 20.00 9.00
❑ 6 Terry Sawchuk UER 100.00 45.00
(Misspelled Sawchuck on card back)
❑ 7 Bill(Red) Hay 20.00 9.00
❑ 8 Gary Bergman 25.00 11.00
❑ 9 Doug Barkley 20.00 9.00
❑ 10 Bob McCord 20.00 9.00
❑ 11 Parker MacDonald 20.00 9.00
❑ 12 Glenn Hall 60.00 27.00
❑ 13 Albert Langlois 20.00 9.00
❑ 14 Camille Henry 20.00 9.00
❑ 15 Norm Ullman 30.00 13.50
❑ 16 Ab McDonald 20.00 9.00
❑ 17 Charlie Hodge 22.00 10.00
❑ 18 Orland Kurtenbach 20.00 9.00
❑ 19 Dean Prentice 22.00 10.00
❑ 20 Bobby Hull 350.00 160.00
❑ 21 Ed Johnston 25.00 11.00
❑ 22 Denis DeJordy 22.00 10.00
❑ 23 Claude Provost 20.00 9.00
❑ 24 Rod Gilbert 40.00 18.00
❑ 25 Doug Mohns 22.00 10.00
❑ 26 Al McNeil 20.00 9.00
❑ 27 Billy Harris 20.00 9.00
❑ 28 Ken Wharram 22.00 10.00
❑ 29 George Sullivan 20.00 9.00
❑ 30 John McKenzie 25.00 11.00
❑ 31 Stan Mikita 100.00 45.00
❑ 32 Ted Green 22.00 10.00
❑ 33 Jean Beliveau 100.00 45.00
❑ 34 Arnie Brown 20.00 9.00
❑ 35 Reg Fleming 20.00 9.00
❑ 36 Jim Mikol 20.00 9.00
❑ 37 Dave Balon 20.00 9.00
❑ 38 Billy Reay CO 22.00 10.00
❑ 39 Marcel Pronovost 22.00 10.00
❑ 40 Johnny Bower 60.00 27.00
❑ 41 Wayne Hillman 20.00 9.00
❑ 42 Floyd Smith 20.00 9.00
❑ 43 Toe Blake CO 30.00 13.50
❑ 44 Red Kelly 30.00 13.50
❑ 45 Punch Imlach CO 25.00 11.00
❑ 46 Dick Duff 22.00 10.00
❑ 47 Roger Crozier 60.00 27.00
❑ 48 Henri Richard 80.00 36.00
❑ 49 Larry Jeffrey 20.00 9.00
❑ 50 Leo Boivin 22.00 10.00
❑ 51 Ed Westfall 22.00 10.00
❑ 52 Jean-Guy Talbot 20.00 9.00
❑ 53 Jacques Laperriere 25.00 11.00
❑ 54 1st Series Checklist 300.00 75.00
❑ 55 2nd Series Checklist 400.00 100.00
❑ 56 Ron Murphy 45.00 20.00
❑ 57 Bob Baun 50.00 22.00
❑ 58 Tom Williams SP 150.00 70.00
❑ 59 Pierre Pilote SP 250.00 110.00
❑ 60 Bob Pulford 50.00 22.00
❑ 61 Red Berenson 50.00 22.00
❑ 62 Vic Hadfield 50.00 22.00
❑ 63 Bob Leiter 45.00 20.00
❑ 64 Jim Pappin 60.00 27.00
❑ 65 Earl Ingarfield 45.00 20.00
❑ 66 Lou Angotti 50.00 22.00
❑ 67 Rod Seiling 50.00 22.00
❑ 68 Jacques Plante 175.00 80.00
❑ 69 George Armstrong UER 60.00 27.00
❑ 70 Milt Schmidt CO 50.00 22.00
❑ 71 Eddie Shack 100.00 45.00
❑ 72 Gary Dornhoefer SP 200.00 90.00
❑ 73 Chico Maki SP 200.00 90.00
❑ 74 Gilles Villemure SP 200.00 90.00
❑ 75 Carl Brewer 50.00 22.00
❑ 76 Bruce MacGregor 45.00 20.00
❑ 77 Bob Nevin 50.00 22.00
❑ 78 Ralph Backstrom 50.00 22.00
❑ 79 Murray Oliver 45.00 20.00
❑ 80 Bobby Rousseau SP 150.00 70.00
❑ 81 Don McKenney 45.00 20.00
❑ 82 Ted Lindsay 75.00 34.00
❑ 83 Harry Howell 60.00 27.00
❑ 84 Doug Robinson 45.00 20.00
❑ 85 Frank Mahovlich 125.00 55.00
❑ 86 Andy Bathgate 60.00 27.00
❑ 87 Phil Goyette 45.00 20.00
❑ 88 J.C. Tremblay 60.00 27.00
❑ 89 Gordie Howe 500.00 220.00
❑ 90 Murray Balfour 45.00 20.00
❑ 91 Eric Nesterenko SP 150.00 70.00
❑ 92 Marcel Paille SP 250.00 110.00
❑ 93 Sid Abel CO 45.00 20.00
❑ 94 Dave Keon 100.00 45.00
❑ 95 Alex Delvecchio 75.00 34.00
❑ 96 Bill Gadsby 50.00 22.00
❑ 97 Don Marshall 50.00 22.00
❑ 98 Bill Hicke SP 150.00 70.00
❑ 99 Ron Stewart 45.00 20.00
❑ 100 Johnny Bucyk 75.00 34.00
❑ 101 Tom Johnson 50.00 22.00
❑ 102 Tim Horton 150.00 70.00
❑ 103 Jim Neilson 50.00 22.00
❑ 104 Allan Stanley 50.00 22.00
❑ 105 Tim Horton AS SP 300.00 135.00
❑ 106 Stan Mikita AS SP 300.00 135.00
❑ 107 Bobby Hull AS 200.00 90.00
❑ 108 Ken Wharram AS 45.00 20.00
❑ 109 Pierre Pilote AS 60.00 27.00
❑ 110 Glenn Hall AS 150.00 38.00

## 1965-66 Topps

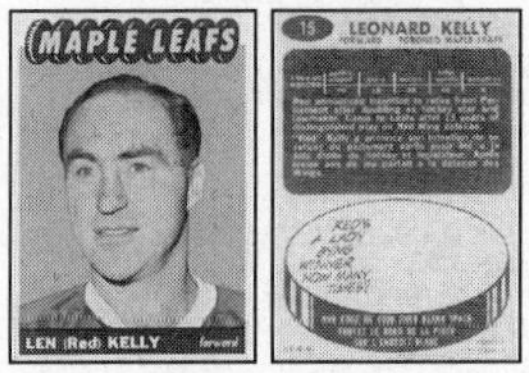

The 1965-66 Topps set contains 128 cards. Cards measure the standard 2 1/2" by 3 1/2". Bilingual backs contain 1964-65 statistics, a short biography and a scratch-off question section. The cards were printed in Canada. The cards are grouped by team: Montreal (1-10, 67-76), Toronto (11-20, 77-86), New York (21-30, 87-95), Boston (31-40, 96-105), Detroit (41-53, 106-112) and Chicago (54-65, 113-120). Cards 122-128 are quite scarce and considered single prints. The seven cards were not included on checklist card 121. Rookie Cards include Gerry Cheevers, Yvan Cournoyer, Phil Esposito, Ed Giacomin, Paul Henderson, Ken Hodge and Dennis Hull. Eleven cards in the set were double printed including Cournoyer's Rookie Card.

NRMT-MT EXC
COMPLETE SET (128) 2700.00 1200.00
COMMON CARD (1-128) 8.00 3.60
COMMON DP's 6.00 2.70

❑ 1 Toe Blake CO 25.00 6.25
❑ 2 Gump Worsley 30.00 13.50
❑ 3 Jacques Laperriere 15.00 6.75
❑ 4 Jean-Guy Talbot 8.00 3.60
❑ 5 Ted Harris 8.00 3.60
❑ 6 Jean Beliveau 60.00 27.00
❑ 7 Dick Duff 10.00 4.50
❑ 8 Claude Provost DP 6.00 2.70
❑ 9 Red Berenson 10.00 4.50
❑ 10 John Ferguson 10.00 4.50
❑ 11 Punch Imlach CO 10.00 4.50
❑ 12 Terry Sawchuk 75.00 34.00
❑ 13 Bob Baun 10.00 4.50
❑ 14 Kent Douglas 8.00 3.60
❑ 15 Red Kelly 15.00 6.75
❑ 16 Jim Pappin 10.00 4.50
❑ 17 Dave Keon 50.00 22.00
❑ 18 Bob Pulford 8.00 3.60
❑ 19 George Armstrong 10.00 4.50
❑ 20 Orland Kurtenbach 8.00 3.60
❑ 21 Ed Giacomin 150.00 70.00
❑ 22 Harry Howell 10.00 4.50
❑ 23 Rod Seiling 8.00 3.60
❑ 24 Mike McMahon 8.00 3.60
❑ 25 Jean Ratelle 25.00 11.00
❑ 26 Doug Robinson 8.00 3.60
❑ 27 Vic Hadfield 10.00 4.50
❑ 28 Garry Peters UER 8.00 3.60
(Misspelled Gary on card front)
❑ 29 Don Marshall 10.00 4.50
❑ 30 Bill Hicke 8.00 3.60
❑ 31 Gerry Cheevers 150.00 70.00
❑ 32 Leo Boivin 10.00 4.50
❑ 33 Albert Langlois 8.00 3.60
❑ 34 Murray Oliver DP 6.00 2.70
❑ 35 Tom Williams 8.00 3.60
❑ 36 Ron Schock 8.00 3.60
❑ 37 Ed Westfall 10.00 4.50
❑ 38 Gary Dornhoefer 10.00 4.50
❑ 39 Bob Dillabough 8.00 3.60
❑ 40 Paul Popiel 8.00 3.60
❑ 41 Sid Abel CO 10.00 4.50
❑ 42 Roger Crozier 15.00 6.75
❑ 43 Doug Barkley 8.00 3.60
❑ 44 Bill Gadsby 8.00 3.60
❑ 45 Bryan Watson 15.00 6.75
❑ 46 Bob McCord 8.00 3.60
❑ 47 Alex Delvecchio 15.00 6.75
❑ 48 Andy Bathgate 10.00 4.50
❑ 49 Norm Ullman 20.00 9.00
❑ 50 Ab McDonald 8.00 3.60
❑ 51 Paul Henderson 50.00 22.00
❑ 52 Pit Martin 10.00 4.50
❑ 53 Billy Harris DP 6.00 2.70
❑ 54 Billy Reay CO 10.00 4.50
❑ 55 Glenn Hall 30.00 13.50
❑ 56 Pierre Pilote 10.00 4.50
❑ 57 Al McNeil 8.00 3.60
❑ 58 Camille Henry 8.00 3.60
❑ 59 Bobby Hull 200.00 90.00
❑ 60 Stan Mikita 60.00 27.00
❑ 61 Ken Wharram 10.00 4.50
❑ 62 Bill(Red) Hay 8.00 3.60
❑ 63 Fred Stanfield 10.00 4.50
❑ 64 Dennis Hull DP 30.00 13.50
❑ 65 Ken Hodge 30.00 13.50
❑ 66 Checklist Card 200.00 50.00
❑ 67 Charlie Hodge 10.00 4.50
❑ 68 Terry Harper 8.00 3.60
❑ 69 J.C. Tremblay 10.00 4.50
❑ 70 Bobby Rousseau DP 6.00 2.70
❑ 71 Henri Richard 50.00 22.00
❑ 72 Dave Balon 8.00 3.60
❑ 73 Ralph Backstrom 10.00 4.50
❑ 74 Jim Roberts 10.00 4.50
❑ 75 Claude Larose 10.00 4.50
❑ 76 Yvan Cournoyer UER DP 100.00 45.00
❑ 77 Johnny Bower DP 25.00 11.00
❑ 78 Carl Brewer 10.00 4.50
❑ 79 Tim Horton 50.00 22.00
❑ 80 Marcel Pronovost 8.00 3.60
❑ 81 Frank Mahovlich 40.00 18.00
❑ 82 Ron Ellis 30.00 13.50
❑ 83 Larry Jeffrey 8.00 3.60
❑ 84 Pete Stemkowski 10.00 4.50
❑ 85 Eddie Joyal 8.00 3.60
❑ 86 Mike Walton 10.00 4.50
❑ 87 George Sullivan 8.00 3.60
❑ 88 Don Simmons 10.00 4.50
❑ 89 Jim Neilson 10.00 4.50
❑ 90 Arnie Brown 8.00 3.60
❑ 91 Rod Gilbert 25.00 11.00
❑ 92 Phil Goyette 8.00 3.60
❑ 93 Bob Nevin 10.00 4.50
❑ 94 John McKenzie 10.00 4.50
❑ 95 Ted Taylor 8.00 3.60
❑ 96 Milt Schmidt CO DP 10.00 4.50
❑ 97 Ed Johnston 10.00 4.50
❑ 98 Ted Green 10.00 4.50
❑ 99 Don Awrey 10.00 4.50
❑ 100 Bob Woytowich DP 6.00 2.70
❑ 101 Johnny Bucyk 20.00 9.00
❑ 102 Dean Prentice 10.00 4.50
❑ 103 Ron Stewart 8.00 3.60
❑ 104 Reg Fleming 8.00 3.60
❑ 105 Parker MacDonald 8.00 3.60
❑ 106 Hank Bassen 10.00 4.50
❑ 107 Gary Bergman 8.00 3.60
❑ 108 Gordie Howe DP 150.00 70.00
❑ 109 Floyd Smith 8.00 3.60
❑ 110 Bruce MacGregor 8.00 3.60
❑ 111 Ron Murphy 8.00 3.60
❑ 112 Don McKenney 8.00 3.60
❑ 113 Denis DeJordy DP 6.00 2.70
❑ 114 Elmer Vasko 8.00 3.60
❑ 115 Matt Ravlich 8.00 3.60
❑ 116 Phil Esposito 400.00 180.00
❑ 117 Chico Maki 8.00 3.60
❑ 118 Doug Mohns 10.00 4.50
❑ 119 Eric Nesterenko 10.00 4.50
❑ 120 Pat Stapleton 10.00 4.50
❑ 121 Checklist Card 200.00 90.00
❑ 122 Gordie Howe SP 400.00 180.00
(600 Goals)
❑ 123 Toronto Maple Leafs 80.00 36.00
Team Card SP
❑ 124 Chicago Blackhawks 70.00 32.00
Team Card SP
❑ 125 Detroit Red Wings 70.00 32.00
Team Card SP
❑ 126 Montreal Canadiens 80.00 36.00
Team Card SP
❑ 127 New York Rangers 70.00 32.00
Team Card SP
❑ 128 Boston Bruins 200.00 50.00
Team Card SP

## 1966-67 Topps

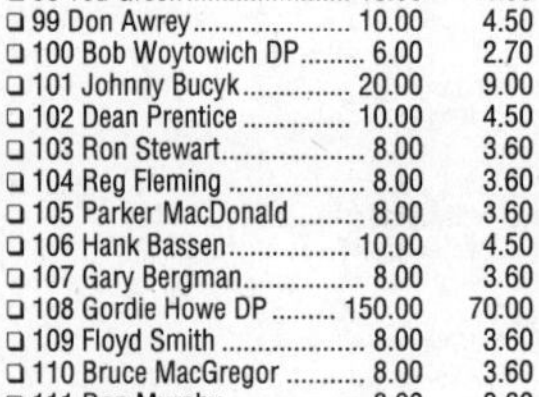

At 132 standard-size cards, the 1966-67 issue was the largest Topps set to date. The front features a distinctive wood grain border with a television screen look. Bilingual backs feature a short biography, 1965-66 and career statistics. The cards are grouped by team: Montreal (1-10/67-75), Toronto (11-20/76-84), New York (21-30/85-93), Boston (31-41/94-101), Detroit (42-52/102-109) and Chicago (53-64/110-117). The cards were printed in Canada. The key card in the set is Bobby Orr's Rookie Card. Other Rookie Cards include Emile Francis, Harry Sinden and Peter Mahovlich. The backs of card numbers 127-132 form a puzzle of Bobby Orr.

NRMT-MT EXC
COMPLETE SET (132) 4000.00 1800.00
COMMON CARD (1-132) 10.00 4.50

❑ 1 Toe Blake CO 25.00 6.25
❑ 2 Gump Worsley 20.00 9.00
❑ 3 Jean-Guy Talbot 10.00 4.50
❑ 4 Gilles Tremblay 10.00 4.50
❑ 5 J.C. Tremblay 10.00 4.50
❑ 6 Jim Roberts 10.00 4.50
❑ 7 Bobby Rousseau 10.00 4.50
❑ 8 Henri Richard 35.00 16.00
❑ 9 Claude Provost 10.00 4.50
❑ 10 Claude Larose 10.00 4.50
❑ 11 Punch Imlach CO 10.00 4.50
❑ 12 Johnny Bower 25.00 11.00
❑ 13 Terry Sawchuk 65.00 29.00
❑ 14 Mike Walton 10.00 4.50
❑ 15 Pete Stemkowski 10.00 4.50
❑ 16 Allan Stanley 10.00 4.50
❑ 17 Eddie Shack 30.00 13.50
❑ 18 Brit Selby 12.00 5.50
❑ 19 Bob Pulford 10.00 4.50
❑ 20 Marcel Pronovost 10.00 4.50
❑ 21 Emile Francis 20.00 9.00
❑ 22 Rod Seiling 10.00 4.50
❑ 23 Ed Giacomin 45.00 20.00
❑ 24 Don Marshall 10.00 4.50
❑ 25 Orland Kurtenbach 10.00 4.50
❑ 26 Rod Gilbert 20.00 9.00
❑ 27 Bob Nevin 10.00 4.50
❑ 28 Phil Goyette 10.00 4.50
❑ 29 Jean Ratelle 20.00 9.00
❑ 30 Earl Ingarfield 10.00 4.50
❑ 31 Harry Sinden 40.00 18.00
❑ 32 Ed Westfall 10.00 4.50
❑ 33 Joe Watson 12.00 5.50
❑ 34 Bob Woytowich 10.00 4.50
❑ 35 Bobby Orr 2500.00 1100.00
❑ 36 Gilles Marotte 12.00 5.50
❑ 37 Ted Green 10.00 4.50
❑ 38 Tom Williams 10.00 4.50
❑ 39 Johnny Bucyk 15.00 6.75
❑ 40 Wayne Connelly 10.00 4.50
❑ 41 Pit Martin 10.00 4.50
❑ 42 Sid Abel CO 10.00 4.50
❑ 43 Roger Crozier 12.00 5.50
❑ 44 Andy Bathgate 10.00 4.50
❑ 45 Dean Prentice 10.00 4.50
❑ 46 Paul Henderson 15.00 6.75
❑ 47 Gary Bergman 10.00 4.50
❑ 48 Bryan Watson 10.00 4.50
❑ 49 Bob Wall 10.00 4.50
❑ 50 Leo Boivin 10.00 4.50
❑ 51 Bert Marshall 10.00 4.50
❑ 52 Norm Ullman 15.00 6.75
❑ 53 Billy Reay CO 10.00 4.50
❑ 54 Glenn Hall 25.00 11.00
❑ 55 Wally Boyer 10.00 4.50
❑ 56 Fred Stanfield 10.00 4.50
❑ 57 Pat Stapleton 10.00 4.50
❑ 58 Matt Ravlich 10.00 4.50
❑ 59 Pierre Pilote 10.00 4.50
❑ 60 Eric Nesterenko 10.00 4.50
❑ 61 Doug Mohns 10.00 4.50
❑ 62 Stan Mikita 50.00 22.00
❑ 63 Phil Esposito 125.00 55.00
❑ 64 Leading Scorer 75.00 34.00
(Bobby Hull)
❑ 65 Vezina Trophy 25.00 11.00
(Charlie Hodge/
Gump Worsley)
❑ 66 Checklist Card 225.00 55.00
❑ 67 Jacques Laperriere 12.00 5.50
❑ 68 Terry Harper 10.00 4.50
❑ 69 Ted Harris 10.00 4.50
❑ 70 John Ferguson 10.00 4.50
❑ 71 Dick Duff 10.00 4.50
❑ 72 Yvan Cournoyer 50.00 22.00
❑ 73 Jean Beliveau 50.00 22.00
❑ 74 Dave Balon 10.00 4.50
❑ 75 Ralph Backstrom 10.00 4.50
❑ 76 Jim Pappin 10.00 4.50
❑ 77 Frank Mahovlich 30.00 13.50
❑ 78 Dave Keon 30.00 13.50
❑ 79 Red Kelly 15.00 6.75
❑ 80 Tim Horton 40.00 18.00
❑ 81 Ron Ellis 12.00 5.50
❑ 82 Kent Douglas 10.00 4.50
❑ 83 Bob Baun 10.00 4.50
❑ 84 George Armstrong 10.00 4.50
❑ 85 Bernie Geoffrion 25.00 11.00
❑ 86 Vic Hadfield 10.00 4.50
❑ 87 Wayne Hillman 10.00 4.50
❑ 88 Jim Neilson 10.00 4.50
❑ 89 Al McNeil 10.00 4.50
❑ 90 Arnie Brown 10.00 4.50
❑ 91 Harry Howell 10.00 4.50
❑ 92 Red Berenson 10.00 4.50
❑ 93 Reg Fleming 10.00 4.50
❑ 94 Ron Stewart 10.00 4.50

❑ 95 Murray Oliver 10.00 4.50
❑ 96 Ron Murphy 10.00 4.50
❑ 97 John McKenzie 10.00 4.50
❑ 98 Bob Dillabough 10.00 4.50
❑ 99 Ed Johnston 10.00 4.50
❑ 100 Ron Schock 10.00 4.50
❑ 101 Dallas Smith 10.00 4.50
❑ 102 Alex Delvecchio 15.00 6.75
❑ 103 Peter Mahovlich 30.00 13.50
❑ 104 Bruce MacGregor 10.00 4.50
❑ 105 Murray Hall 10.00 4.50
❑ 106 Floyd Smith 10.00 4.50
❑ 107 Hank Bassen 10.00 4.50
❑ 108 Val Fonteyne 10.00 4.50
❑ 109 Gordie Howe 200.00 90.00
❑ 110 Chico Maki 10.00 4.50
❑ 111 Doug Jarrett 10.00 4.50
❑ 112 Bobby Hull 150.00 70.00
❑ 113 Dennis Hull 12.00 5.50
❑ 114 Ken Hodge 12.00 5.50
❑ 115 Denis DeJordy 10.00 4.50
❑ 116 Lou Angotti 10.00 4.50
❑ 117 Ken Wharram 10.00 4.50
❑ 118 Montreal Canadiens Team Card 25.00 11.00
❑ 119 Detroit Red Wings Team Card 25.00 11.00
❑ 120 Checklist Card 225.00 55.00
❑ 121 Gordie Howe AS 100.00 45.00
❑ 122 Jacques Laperriere AS 10.00 4.50
❑ 123 Pierre Pilote AS 10.00 4.50
❑ 124 Stan Mikita AS 35.00 16.00
❑ 125 Bobby Hull AS 75.00 34.00
❑ 126 Glenn Hall AS 20.00 9.00
❑ 127 Jean Beliveau AS 25.00 11.00
❑ 128 Allan Stanley AS 10.00 4.50
❑ 129 Pat Stapleton AS 10.00 4.50
❑ 130 Gump Worsley AS 20.00 9.00
❑ 131 Frank Mahovlich AS 20.00 9.00
❑ 132 Bobby Rousseau AS 20.00 5.00

## 1966-67 Topps USA Test

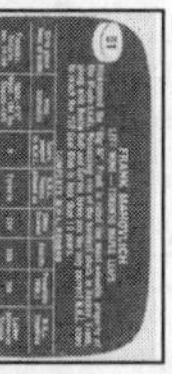

This 66-card standard-size set was apparently a test issue with limited distribution solely in America as it is quite scarce. The cards feature the same format as the 1966-67 Topps regular hockey cards. The primary difference is that the card backs in this scarce issue are only printed in English, i.e., no French. The card numbering has some similarities to the regular issue, e.g., Bobby Orr is number 35 in both sets, however there are also many differences from the regular Topps Canadian version which was mass produced. The wood grain border on the front of the cards is slightly lighter than that of the regular issue.

| | NRMT-MT | EXC |
|---|---|---|
| COMPLETE SET (66) | 12000.00 | 5400.00 |
| COMMON CARD (1-66) | 30.00 | 13.50 |

❑ 1 Dennis Hull 50.00 22.00
❑ 2 Gump Worsley 125.00 55.00
❑ 3 Dallas Smith 30.00 13.50
❑ 4 Gilles Tremblay 30.00 13.50
❑ 5 J.C. Tremblay 40.00 18.00
❑ 6 Ralph Backstrom 40.00 18.00
❑ 7 Bobby Rousseau 30.00 13.50
❑ 8 Henri Richard 200.00 90.00
❑ 9 Claude Provost 40.00 18.00
❑ 10 Red Berenson 40.00 18.00
❑ 11 Punch Imlach CO 40.00 18.00
❑ 12 Johnny Bower 125.00 55.00
❑ 13 Yvan Cournoyer 150.00 70.00
❑ 14 Mike Walton 40.00 18.00
❑ 15 Pete Stemkowski 40.00 18.00
❑ 16 Allan Stanley 60.00 27.00
❑ 17 George Armstrong 60.00 27.00
❑ 18 Harry Howell 60.00 27.00
❑ 19 Vic Hadfield 40.00 18.00
❑ 20 Marcel Pronovost 50.00 22.00
❑ 21 Pete Mahovlich 50.00 22.00
❑ 22 Rod Seiling 30.00 13.50
❑ 23 Gordie Howe 800.00 350.00
❑ 24 Don Marshall 30.00 13.50
❑ 25 Orland Kurtenbach 40.00 18.00
❑ 26 Rod Gilbert 80.00 36.00
❑ 27 Bob Nevin 40.00 18.00
❑ 28 Phil Goyette 30.00 13.50
❑ 29 Jean Ratelle 100.00 45.00
❑ 30 Dave Keon 150.00 70.00
❑ 31 Jean Beliveau 300.00 135.00
❑ 32 Ed Westfall 30.00 13.50
❑ 33 Ron Murphy 30.00 13.50
❑ 34 Wayne Hillman 30.00 13.50
❑ 35 Bobby Orr 8000.00 3600.00
❑ 36 Boom Boom Geoffrion 150.00 70.00
❑ 37 Ted Green 40.00 18.00
❑ 38 Tom Williams 30.00 13.50
❑ 39 Johnny Bucyk 80.00 36.00
❑ 40 Bobby Hull 600.00 275.00
❑ 41 Ted Harris 30.00 13.50
❑ 42 Red Kelly 80.00 36.00
❑ 43 Roger Crozier 50.00 22.00
❑ 44 Ken Wharram 30.00 13.50
❑ 45 Dean Prentice 40.00 18.00
❑ 46 Paul Henderson 80.00 36.00
❑ 47 Gary Bergman 30.00 13.50
❑ 48 Arnie Brown 30.00 13.50
❑ 49 Jim Pappin 30.00 13.50
❑ 50 Denis DeJordy 50.00 22.00
❑ 51 Frank Mahovlich 150.00 70.00
❑ 52 Norm Ullman 80.00 36.00
❑ 53 Chico Maki 40.00 18.00
❑ 54 Reg Fleming 30.00 13.50
❑ 55 Jim Neilson 30.00 13.50
❑ 56 Bruce MacGregor 30.00 13.50
❑ 57 Pat Stapleton 40.00 18.00
❑ 58 Matt Ravlich 30.00 13.50
❑ 59 Pierre Pilote 60.00 27.00
❑ 60 Eric Nesterenko 40.00 18.00
❑ 61 Doug Mohns 40.00 18.00
❑ 62 Stan Mikita 300.00 135.00
❑ 63 Alex Delvecchio 100.00 45.00
❑ 64 Ed Johnston 50.00 22.00
❑ 65 John Ferguson 50.00 22.00
❑ 66 John McKenzie 50.00 22.00

## 1967-68 Topps

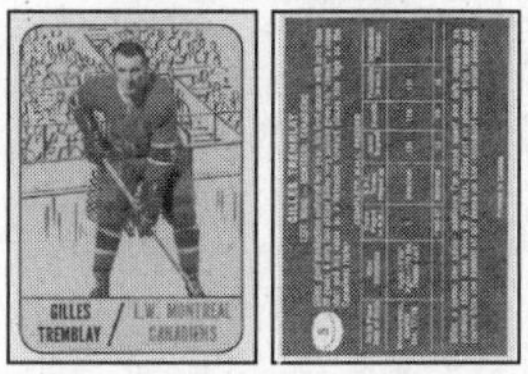


The 1967-68 Topps set features 132 standard-size cards. Players on the six expansion teams (Los Angeles, Minnesota, Oakland, Philadelphia, Pittsburgh, and St. Louis) were not included until 1968-69. Bilingual backs feature a short biography, 1966-67 and career records. The backs are identical in format to the 1966-67 cards. The cards are grouped by team: Montreal (1-10/67-75), Toronto (11-20/76-83), New York (21-31/84-91), Boston (32-42/92-100), Detroit (43-52/101-108) and Chicago (53-63/109-117). The cards were printed in Canada. Rookie Cards include Jacques Lemaire, Derek Sanderson, Glen Sather, and Rogatien Vachon.

| | NRMT-MT | EXC |
|---|---|---|
| COMPLETE SET (132) | 3000.00 | 1350.00 |
| COMMON CARD (1-132) | 8.00 | 3.60 |

❑ 1 Gump Worsley 40.00 10.00
❑ 2 Dick Duff 10.00 4.50
❑ 3 Jacques Lemaire 60.00 27.00
❑ 4 Claude Larose 9.00 4.00
❑ 5 Gilles Tremblay 8.00 3.60
❑ 6 Terry Harper 8.00 3.60
❑ 7 Jacques Laperriere 10.00 4.50
❑ 8 Garry Monahan 8.00 3.60
❑ 9 Carol Vadnais 10.00 4.50
❑ 10 Ted Harris 8.00 3.60
❑ 11 Dave Keon 20.00 9.00
❑ 12 Pete Stemkowski 8.00 3.60
❑ 13 Allan Stanley 9.00 4.00
❑ 14 Ron Ellis 9.00 4.00
❑ 15 Mike Walton 9.00 4.00
❑ 16 Tim Horton 35.00 16.00
❑ 17 Brian Conacher 8.00 3.60
❑ 18 Bruce Gamble 10.00 4.50
❑ 19 Bob Pulford 8.00 3.60
❑ 20 Duane Rupp 8.00 3.60
❑ 21 Larry Jeffrey 8.00 3.60
❑ 22 Wayne Hillman 8.00 3.60
❑ 23 Don Marshall 9.00 4.00
❑ 24 Red Berenson 9.00 4.00
❑ 25 Phil Goyette 8.00 3.60
❑ 26 Camille Henry 8.00 3.60
❑ 27 Rod Seiling 8.00 3.60
❑ 28 Bob Nevin 9.00 4.00
❑ 29 Bernie Geoffrion 20.00 9.00
❑ 30 Reg Fleming 8.00 3.60
❑ 31 Jean Ratelle 15.00 6.75
❑ 32 Phil Esposito 75.00 34.00
❑ 33 Derek Sanderson 80.00 36.00
❑ 34 Eddie Shack 25.00 11.00
❑ 35 Ross Lonsberry 10.00 4.50
❑ 36 Fred Stanfield 8.00 3.60
❑ 37 Don Awrey UER (Photo actually Skip Krake) 8.00 3.60
❑ 38 Glen Sather 30.00 13.50
❑ 39 John McKenzie 9.00 4.00
❑ 40 Tom Williams 8.00 3.60
❑ 41 Dallas Smith 8.00 3.60
❑ 42 Johnny Bucyk 15.00 6.75
❑ 43 Gordie Howe 150.00 70.00
❑ 44 Gary Jarrett 8.00 3.60
❑ 45 Dean Prentice 8.00 3.60
❑ 46 Bert Marshall 8.00 3.60
❑ 47 Gary Bergman 8.00 3.60
❑ 48 Roger Crozier 10.00 4.50
❑ 49 Howie Young 8.00 3.60
❑ 50 Doug Roberts 8.00 3.60
❑ 51 Alex Delvecchio 15.00 6.75
❑ 52 Floyd Smith 8.00 3.60
❑ 53 Doug Shelton 8.00 3.60
❑ 54 Gerry Goyer 8.00 3.60
❑ 55 Wayne Maki 8.00 3.60
❑ 56 Dennis Hull 10.00 4.50
❑ 57 Dave Dryden 15.00 6.75
❑ 58 Paul Terbenche 8.00 3.60
❑ 59 Gilles Marotte 8.00 3.60
❑ 60 Eric Nesterenko 9.00 4.00
❑ 61 Pat Stapleton 9.00 4.00
❑ 62 Pierre Pilote 9.00 4.00
❑ 63 Doug Mohns 8.00 3.60
❑ 64 Triple Winner (Stan Mikita) 30.00 13.50
❑ 65 Vezina Trophy (Glenn Hall/ Denis DeJordy) 20.00 9.00
❑ 66 Checklist Card 175.00 45.00
❑ 67 Ralph Backstrom 9.00 4.00
❑ 68 Bobby Rousseau 8.00 3.60
❑ 69 John Ferguson 9.00 4.00
❑ 70 Yvan Cournoyer 30.00 13.50
❑ 71 Claude Provost 8.00 3.60
❑ 72 Henri Richard 25.00 11.00
❑ 73 J.C. Tremblay 9.00 4.00
❑ 74 Jean Beliveau 40.00 18.00
❑ 75 Rogatien Vachon 80.00 36.00
❑ 76 Johnny Bower 20.00 9.00
❑ 77 Wayne Carleton 8.00 3.60
❑ 78 Jim Pappin 8.00 3.60
❑ 79 Frank Mahovlich 25.00 11.00
❑ 80 Larry Hillman 8.00 3.60
❑ 81 Marcel Pronovost 8.00 3.60
❑ 82 Murray Oliver 8.00 3.60
❑ 83 George Armstrong 10.00 4.50
❑ 84 Harry Howell 9.00 4.00
❑ 85 Ed Giacomin 30.00 13.50
❑ 86 Gilles Villemure 10.00 4.50
❑ 87 Orland Kurtenbach 8.00 3.60
❑ 88 Vic Hadfield 9.00 4.00
❑ 89 Arnie Brown 8.00 3.60
❑ 90 Rod Gilbert 15.00 6.75
❑ 91 Jim Neilson 8.00 3.60
❑ 92 Bobby Orr 700.00 325.00
❑ 93 Skip Krake UER (Photo actually Don Awrey) 8.00 3.60
❑ 94 Ted Green 9.00 4.00
❑ 95 Ed Westfall 9.00 4.00
❑ 96 Ed Johnston 10.00 4.50
❑ 97 Gary Doak 10.00 4.50
❑ 98 Ken Hodge 9.00 4.00
❑ 99 Gerry Cheevers 50.00 22.00
❑ 100 Ron Murphy 8.00 3.60
❑ 101 Norm Ullman 15.00 6.75
❑ 102 Bruce MacGregor 8.00 3.60
❑ 103 Paul Henderson 10.00 4.50
❑ 104 Jean-Guy Talbot 8.00 3.60
❑ 105 Bart Crashley 8.00 3.60
❑ 106 Roy Edwards 10.00 4.50
❑ 107 Jim Watson 8.00 3.60
❑ 108 Ted Hampson 8.00 3.60
❑ 109 Bill Orban 8.00 3.60
❑ 110 Geoffrey Powis 8.00 3.60
❑ 111 Chico Maki 8.00 3.60
❑ 112 Doug Jarrett 8.00 3.60
❑ 113 Bobby Hull 125.00 55.00
❑ 114 Stan Mikita 40.00 18.00
❑ 115 Denis DeJordy 10.00 4.50
❑ 116 Pit Martin 9.00 4.00
❑ 117 Ken Wharram 8.00 3.60
❑ 118 Calder Trophy (Bobby Orr) 300.00 135.00
❑ 119 Norris Trophy (Harry Howell) 8.00 3.60
❑ 120 Checklist Card 175.00 45.00
❑ 121 Harry Howell AS 8.00 3.60
❑ 122 Pierre Pilote AS 8.00 3.60
❑ 123 Ed Giacomin AS 15.00 6.75
❑ 124 Bobby Hull AS 80.00 36.00
❑ 125 Ken Wharram AS 8.00 3.60
❑ 126 Stan Mikita AS 25.00 11.00
❑ 127 Tim Horton AS 20.00 9.00
❑ 128 Bobby Orr AS 300.00 135.00
❑ 129 Glenn Hall AS 20.00 9.00
❑ 130 Don Marshall AS 8.00 3.60
❑ 131 Gordie Howe AS 100.00 45.00
❑ 132 Norm Ullman AS 20.00 5.00

## 1968-69 Topps

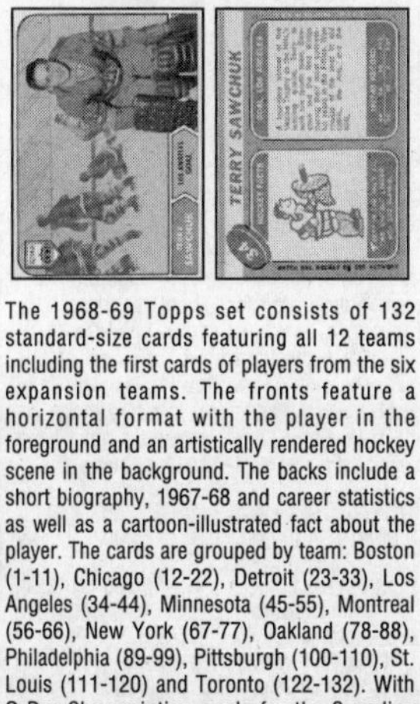


The 1968-69 Topps set consists of 132 standard-size cards featuring all 12 teams including the first cards of players from the six expansion teams. The fronts feature a horizontal format with the player in the foreground and an artistically rendered hockey scene in the background. The backs include a short biography, 1967-68 and career statistics as well as a cartoon-illustrated fact about the player. The cards are grouped by team: Boston (1-11), Chicago (12-22), Detroit (23-33), Los Angeles (34-44), Minnesota (45-55), Montreal (56-66), New York (67-77), Oakland (78-88), Philadelphia (89-99), Pittsburgh (100-110), St. Louis (111-120) and Toronto (122-132). With O-Pee-Chee printing cards for the Canadian market, text on back is English only. For the first time since 1960-61, Topps cards were printed in the U.S. The only Rookie Card of consequence is Bernie Parent.

| | NRMT-MT | EXC |
|---|---|---|
| COMPLETE SET (132) | 750.00 | 350.00 |
| COMMON CARD (1-132) | 4.00 | 1.80 |

❑ 1 Gerry Cheevers 20.00 5.00
❑ 2 Bobby Orr 225.00 100.00
❑ 3 Don Awrey UER (Photo actually Skip Krake) 4.00 1.80
❑ 4 Ted Green 5.00 2.20
❑ 5 Johnny Bucyk 6.00 2.70
❑ 6 Derek Sanderson 25.00 11.00
❑ 7 Phil Esposito 30.00 13.50
❑ 8 Ken Hodge 5.00 2.20
❑ 9 John McKenzie 5.00 2.20
❑ 10 Fred Stanfield 4.00 1.80
❑ 11 Tom Williams 4.00 1.80
❑ 12 Denis DeJordy 5.00 2.20
❑ 13 Doug Jarrett 4.00 1.80
❑ 14 Gilles Marotte 4.00 1.80
❑ 15 Pat Stapleton 5.00 2.20
❑ 16 Bobby Hull 50.00 22.00
❑ 17 Chico Maki 4.00 1.80
❑ 18 Pit Martin 5.00 2.20
❑ 19 Doug Mohns 4.00 1.80
❑ 20 Stan Mikita 20.00 9.00
❑ 21 Jim Pappin 4.00 1.80
❑ 22 Ken Wharram 4.00 1.80
❑ 23 Roger Crozier 5.00 2.20
❑ 24 Bob Baun 5.00 2.20
❑ 25 Gary Bergman 4.00 1.80
❑ 26 Kent Douglas 4.00 1.80
❑ 27 Ron Harris 4.00 1.80
❑ 28 Alex Delvecchio 6.00 2.70
❑ 29 Gordie Howe 70.00 32.00
❑ 30 Bruce MacGregor 4.00 1.80
❑ 31 Frank Mahovlich 12.00 5.50
❑ 32 Dean Prentice 4.00 1.80
❑ 33 Pete Stemkowski 4.00 1.80
❑ 34 Terry Sawchuk 40.00 18.00
❑ 35 Larry Cahan 4.00 1.80
❑ 36 Real Lemieux 4.00 1.80
❑ 37 Bill White 6.00 2.70
❑ 38 Gord Labossière 4.00 1.80
❑ 39 Ted Irvine 4.00 1.80
❑ 40 Eddie Joyal 4.00 1.80
❑ 41 Dale Rolfe 4.00 1.80
❑ 42 Lowell MacDonald 6.00 2.70
❑ 43 Skip Krake UER (Photo actually Don Awrey) 4.00 1.80
❑ 44 Terry Gray 4.00 1.80
❑ 45 Cesare Maniago 5.00 2.20
❑ 46 Mike McMahon 4.00 1.80
❑ 47 Wayne Hillman 4.00 1.80
❑ 48 Larry Hillman 4.00 1.80
❑ 49 Bob Woytowich 4.00 1.80
❑ 50 Wayne Connelly 4.00 1.80
❑ 51 Claude Larose 4.00 1.80
❑ 52 Danny Grant 6.00 2.70
❑ 53 Andre Boudrias 4.00 1.80
❑ 54 Ray Cullen 4.00 1.80
❑ 55 Parker MacDonald 4.00 1.80
❑ 56 Gump Worsley 10.00 4.50
❑ 57 Terry Harper 4.00 1.80
❑ 58 Jacques Laperriere 5.00 2.20
❑ 59 J.C. Tremblay 5.00 2.20
❑ 60 Ralph Backstrom 5.00 2.20
❑ 61 Jean Beliveau 15.00 6.75
❑ 62 Yvan Cournoyer 12.00 5.50
❑ 63 Jacques Lemaire 15.00 6.75
❑ 64 Henri Richard 12.00 5.50
❑ 65 Bobby Rousseau 4.00 1.80
❑ 66 Gilles Tremblay 4.00 1.80
❑ 67 Ed Giacomin 12.00 5.50
❑ 68 Arnie Brown 4.00 1.80
❑ 69 Harry Howell 5.00 2.20
❑ 70 Jim Neilson 4.00 1.80
❑ 71 Rod Seiling 4.00 1.80
❑ 72 Rod Gilbert 7.00 3.10
❑ 73 Phil Goyette 4.00 1.80
❑ 74 Vic Hadfield 5.00 2.20
❑ 75 Don Marshall 5.00 2.20
❑ 76 Bob Nevin 5.00 2.20
❑ 77 Jean Ratelle 7.00 3.10
❑ 78 Charlie Hodge 5.00 2.20
❑ 79 Bert Marshall 4.00 1.80
❑ 80 Billy Harris 4.00 1.80
❑ 81 Carol Vadnais 5.00 2.20
❑ 82 Howie Young 4.00 1.80
❑ 83 John Brenneman 4.00 1.80
❑ 84 Gerry Ehman 4.00 1.80
❑ 85 Ted Hampson 4.00 1.80
❑ 86 Bill Hicke 4.00 1.80
❑ 87 Gary Jarrett 4.00 1.80
❑ 88 Doug Roberts 4.00 1.80
❑ 89 Bernie Parent 60.00 27.00
❑ 90 Joe Watson 4.00 1.80
❑ 91 Ed Van Impe 4.00 1.80
❑ 92 Larry Zeidel 4.00 1.80
❑ 93 John Miszuk 4.00 1.80
❑ 94 Gary Dornhoefer 5.00 2.20
❑ 95 Leon Rochefort 4.00 1.80
❑ 96 Brit Selby 4.00 1.80
❑ 97 Forbes Kennedy 4.00 1.80
❑ 98 Ed Hoekstra 4.00 1.80
❑ 99 Garry Peters 4.00 1.80
❑ 100 Les Binkley 8.00 3.60
❑ 101 Leo Boivin 5.00 2.20
❑ 102 Earl Ingarfield 4.00 1.80
❑ 103 Lou Angotti 4.00 1.80
❑ 104 Andy Bathgate 5.00 2.20
❑ 105 Wally Boyer 4.00 1.80
❑ 106 Ken Schinkel 4.00 1.80
❑ 107 Ab McDonald 4.00 1.80
❑ 108 Charlie Burns 4.00 1.80
❑ 109 Val Fonteyne 4.00 1.80
❑ 110 Noel Price 4.00 1.80
❑ 111 Glenn Hall 10.00 4.50
❑ 112 Bob Plager 6.00 2.70
❑ 113 Jim Roberts 5.00 2.20
❑ 114 Red Berenson 5.00 2.20
❑ 115 Larry Keenan 4.00 1.80
❑ 116 Camille Henry 4.00 1.80
❑ 117 Gary Sabourin 4.00 1.80
❑ 118 Ron Schock 4.00 1.80
❑ 119 Gary Veneruzzo 4.00 1.80
❑ 120 Gerry Melnyk 4.00 1.80
❑ 121 Checklist Card 75.00 19.00
❑ 122 Johnny Bower 10.00 4.50
❑ 123 Tim Horton 15.00 6.75
❑ 124 Pierre Pilote 5.00 2.20
❑ 125 Marcel Pronovost 4.00 1.80
❑ 126 Ron Ellis 5.00 2.20
❑ 127 Paul Henderson 5.00 2.20
❑ 128 Dave Keon 7.00 3.10
❑ 129 Bob Pulford 5.00 2.20
❑ 130 Floyd Smith 4.00 1.80
❑ 131 Norm Ullman 6.00 2.70
❑ 132 Mike Walton 5.00 1.25

## 1969-70 Topps

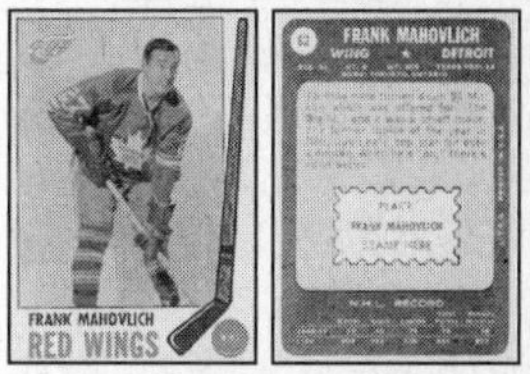


The 1969-70 Topps set consists of 132 standard-size cards. The backs contain 1968-69 and career statistics, a short biography and a cartoon-illustrated fact about the player. Those players in this set who were also included in the insert set of stamps have a place on the card back for placing that player's stamp. This is not recommended as it would be considered a means of defacing the card and lowering its grade. The cards are grouped by team: Montreal (1-11), St. Louis (12-21), Boston (22-32), New York (33-43), Toronto (44-54), Detroit (55-65), Chicago (66-76), Oakland (77-87), Philadelphia (88-98), Los Angeles (99-109), Pittsburgh (110-120) and Minnesota (121-131). The only notable Rookie Card in the set is Serge Savard.

| | NRMT-MT | EXC |
|---|---|---|
| COMPLETE SET (132) | 500.00 | 220.00 |
| COMMON CARD (1-132) | 2.50 | 1.10 |

❑ 1 Gump Worsley 15.00 3.70
❑ 2 Ted Harris 2.50 1.10
❑ 3 Jacques Laperriere 3.00 1.35
❑ 4 Serge Savard 20.00 9.00
❑ 5 J.C. Tremblay 3.00 1.35
❑ 6 Yvan Cournoyer 8.00 3.60
❑ 7 John Ferguson 3.00 1.35
❑ 8 Jacques Lemaire 10.00 4.50
❑ 9 Bobby Rousseau 2.50 1.10
❑ 10 Jean Beliveau 12.00 5.50
❑ 11 Henri Richard 8.00 3.60
❑ 12 Glenn Hall 8.00 3.60
❑ 13 Bob Plager 3.00 1.35
❑ 14 Jim Roberts 3.00 1.35
❑ 15 Jean-Guy Talbot 2.50 1.10
❑ 16 Andre Boudrias 2.50 1.10
❑ 17 Camille Henry 2.50 1.10
❑ 18 Ab McDonald 2.50 1.10
❑ 19 Gary Sabourin 2.50 1.10
❑ 20 Red Berenson 3.00 1.35
❑ 21 Phil Goyette 2.50 1.10
❑ 22 Gerry Cheevers 10.00 4.50
❑ 23 Ted Green 3.00 1.35
❑ 24 Bobby Orr 125.00 55.00
❑ 25 Dallas Smith 2.50 1.10
❑ 26 Johnny Bucyk 5.00 2.20
❑ 27 Ken Hodge 3.00 1.35
❑ 28 John McKenzie 3.00 1.35
❑ 29 Ed Westfall 3.00 1.35
❑ 30 Phil Esposito 20.00 9.00
❑ 31 Derek Sanderson 15.00 6.75
❑ 32 Fred Stanfield 2.50 1.10
❑ 33 Ed Giacomin 10.00 4.50
❑ 34 Arnie Brown 2.50 1.10
❑ 35 Jim Neilson 2.50 1.10
❑ 36 Rod Seiling 2.50 1.10
❑ 37 Rod Gilbert 5.00 2.20
❑ 38 Vic Hadfield 3.00 1.35
❑ 39 Don Marshall 3.00 1.35
❑ 40 Bob Nevin 3.00 1.35
❑ 41 Ron Stewart 2.50 1.10
❑ 42 Jean Ratelle 5.00 2.20
❑ 43 Walt Tkaczuk 5.00 2.20
❑ 44 Bruce Gamble 3.00 1.35
❑ 45 Tim Horton 12.00 5.50
❑ 46 Ron Ellis 3.00 1.35
❑ 47 Paul Henderson 3.00 1.35
❑ 48 Brit Selby 2.50 1.10
❑ 49 Floyd Smith 2.50 1.10
❑ 50 Mike Walton 3.00 1.35
❑ 51 Dave Keon 5.00 2.20

❑ 52 Murray Oliver 2.50 1.10
❑ 53 Bob Pulford 3.00 1.35
❑ 54 Norm Ullman 5.00 2.20
❑ 55 Roger Crozier 3.00 1.35
❑ 56 Roy Edwards 3.00 1.35
❑ 57 Bob Baun 3.00 1.35
❑ 58 Gary Bergman 2.50 1.10
❑ 59 Carl Brewer 3.00 1.35
❑ 60 Wayne Connelly 2.50 1.10
❑ 61 Gordie Howe 50.00 22.00
❑ 62 Frank Mahovlich 8.00 3.60
❑ 63 Bruce MacGregor 2.50 1.10
❑ 64 Alex Delvecchio 5.00 2.20
❑ 65 Pete Stemkowski 2.50 1.10
❑ 66 Denis DeJordy 3.00 1.35
❑ 67 Doug Jarrett 2.50 1.10
❑ 68 Gilles Marotte 2.50 1.10
❑ 69 Pat Stapleton 3.00 1.35
❑ 70 Bobby Hull 40.00 18.00
❑ 71 Dennis Hull 3.00 1.35
❑ 72 Doug Mohns 2.50 1.10
❑ 73 Jim Pappin 2.50 1.10
❑ 74 Ken Wharram 2.50 1.10
❑ 75 Pit Martin 3.00 1.35
❑ 76 Stan Mikita 12.00 5.50
❑ 77 Charlie Hodge 3.00 1.35
❑ 78 Gary Smith 3.00 1.35
❑ 79 Harry Howell 3.00 1.35
❑ 80 Bert Marshall 2.50 1.10
❑ 81 Doug Roberts 2.50 1.10
❑ 82 Carol Vadnais 3.00 1.35
❑ 83 Gerry Ehman 2.50 1.10
❑ 84 Bill Hicke 2.50 1.10
❑ 85 Gary Jarrett 2.50 1.10
❑ 86 Ted Hampson 2.50 1.10
❑ 87 Earl Ingarfield 2.50 1.10
❑ 88 Doug Favell 10.00 4.50
❑ 89 Bernie Parent 25.00 11.00
❑ 90 Larry Hillman 2.50 1.10
❑ 91 Wayne Hillman 2.50 1.10
❑ 92 Ed Van Impe 2.50 1.10
❑ 93 Joe Watson 2.50 1.10
❑ 94 Gary Dornhoefer 3.00 1.35
❑ 95 Reg Fleming 2.50 1.10
❑ 96 Jean-Guy Gendron 2.50 1.10
❑ 97 Jim Johnson 2.50 1.10
❑ 98 Andre Lacroix 3.00 1.35
❑ 99 Gerry Desjardins 8.00 3.60
❑ 100 Dale Rolfe 2.50 1.10
❑ 101 Bill White 2.50 1.10
❑ 102 Bill Flett 2.50 1.10
❑ 103 Ted Irvine 2.50 1.10
❑ 104 Ross Lonsberry 3.00 1.35
❑ 105 Leon Rochefort 2.50 1.10
❑ 106 Eddie Shack 8.00 3.60
❑ 107 Dennis Hextall 3.50 1.55
❑ 108 Eddie Joyal 2.50 1.10
❑ 109 Gord Labossiere 2.50 1.10
❑ 110 Les Binkley 3.00 1.35
❑ 111 Tracy Pratt 2.50 1.10
❑ 112 Bryan Watson 2.50 1.10
❑ 113 Bob Woytowich 2.50 1.10
❑ 114 Keith McCreary 2.50 1.10
❑ 115 Dean Prentice 2.50 1.10
❑ 116 Glen Sather 4.00 1.80
❑ 117 Ken Schinkel 2.50 1.10
❑ 118 Wally Boyer 2.50 1.10
❑ 119 Val Fonteyne 2.50 1.10
❑ 120 Ron Schock 2.50 1.10
❑ 121 Cesare Maniago 3.00 1.35
❑ 122 Leo Boivin 3.00 1.35
❑ 123 Bob McCord 2.50 1.10
❑ 124 John Miszuk 2.50 1.10
❑ 125 Danny Grant 3.00 1.35
❑ 126 Claude Larose 2.50 1.10
❑ 127 Jean-Paul Parise 3.00 1.35
❑ 128 Tom Williams 2.50 1.10
❑ 129 Charlie Burns 2.50 1.10
❑ 130 Ray Cullen 2.50 1.10
❑ 131 Danny O'Shea 2.50 1.10
❑ 132 Checklist Card 60.00 15.00

## 1970-71 Topps

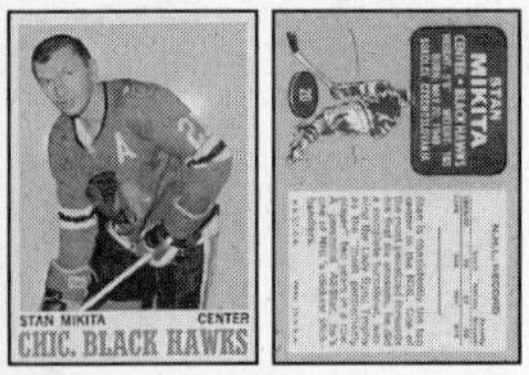


The 1970-71 Topps set consists of 132 standard-size cards. Card fronts have solid player backgrounds that differ in color according to team. The player's name, team and position are at the bottom. The backs feature the player's 1969-70 and career statistics as well as a short biography. Players from the expansion Buffalo Sabres and Vancouver Canucks are included. For the most part, cards are grouped by team. However, team names on front are updated on some cards to reflect transactions that occurred late in the off-season. Rookie Cards include Wayne Cashman, Brad Park and Gilbert Perreault.

| | NRMT-MT | EXC |
|---|---|---|
| COMPLETE SET (132) | 400.00 | 180.00 |
| COMMON CARD (1-132) | 1.50 | .70 |

❑ 1 Gerry Cheevers 15.00 3.70
❑ 2 Johnny Bucyk 4.00 1.80
❑ 3 Bobby Orr 75.00 34.00
❑ 4 Don Awrey 1.50 .70
❑ 5 Fred Stanfield 1.50 .70
❑ 6 John McKenzie 2.50 1.10
❑ 7 Wayne Cashman 8.00 3.60
❑ 8 Ken Hodge 2.50 1.10
❑ 9 Wayne Carleton 1.50 .70
❑ 10 Garnet Bailey 1.50 .70
❑ 11 Phil Esposito 20.00 9.00
❑ 12 Lou Angotti 1.50 .70
❑ 13 Jim Pappin 1.50 .70
❑ 14 Dennis Hull 2.50 1.10
❑ 15 Bobby Hull 40.00 18.00
❑ 16 Doug Mohns 1.50 .70
❑ 17 Pat Stapleton 2.50 1.10
❑ 18 Pit Martin 2.50 1.10
❑ 19 Eric Nesterenko 2.50 1.10
❑ 20 Stan Mikita 12.00 5.50
❑ 21 Roy Edwards 2.50 1.10
❑ 22 Frank Mahovlich 6.00 2.70
❑ 23 Ron Harris 1.50 .70
❑ 24 Bob Baun 2.50 1.10
❑ 25 Pete Stemkowski 1.50 .70
❑ 26 Garry Unger 2.50 1.10
❑ 27 Bruce MacGregor 1.50 .70
❑ 28 Larry Jeffrey 1.50 .70
❑ 29 Gordie Howe 50.00 22.00
❑ 30 Billy Dea 1.50 .70
❑ 31 Denis DeJordy 2.50 1.10
❑ 32 Matt Ravlich 1.50 .70
❑ 33 Dave Amadio 1.50 .70
❑ 34 Gilles Marotte 1.50 .70
❑ 35 Eddie Shack 6.00 2.70
❑ 36 Bob Pulford 2.50 1.10
❑ 37 Ross Lonsberry 2.50 1.10
❑ 38 Gord Labossiere 1.50 .70
❑ 39 Eddie Joyal 1.50 .70
❑ 40 Gump Worsley 6.00 2.70
❑ 41 Bob McCord 1.50 .70
❑ 42 Leo Boivin 2.50 1.10
❑ 43 Tom Reid 1.50 .70
❑ 44 Charlie Burns 1.50 .70
❑ 45 Bob Barlow 1.50 .70
❑ 46 Bill Goldsworthy 2.50 1.10
❑ 47 Danny Grant 2.50 1.10
❑ 48 Norm Beaudin 1.50 .70
❑ 49 Rogatien Vachon 6.00 2.70
❑ 50 Yvan Cournoyer 5.00 2.20
❑ 51 Serge Savard 6.00 2.70
❑ 52 Jacques Laperriere 2.50 1.10
❑ 53 Terry Harper 1.50 .70
❑ 54 Ralph Backstrom 2.50 1.10
❑ 55 Jean Beliveau 10.00 4.50
❑ 56 Claude Larose UER 1.50 .70
(Misspelled LaRose on both sides)
❑ 57 Jacques Lemaire 6.00 2.70
❑ 58 Peter Mahovlich 2.50 1.10
❑ 59 Tim Horton 10.00 4.50
❑ 60 Bob Nevin 1.50 .70
❑ 61 Dave Balon 1.50 .70
❑ 62 Vic Hadfield 2.50 1.10
❑ 63 Rod Gilbert 4.00 1.80
❑ 64 Ron Stewart 1.50 .70
❑ 65 Ted Irvine 1.50 .70
❑ 66 Arnie Brown 1.50 .70
❑ 67 Brad Park 25.00 11.00
❑ 68 Ed Giacomin 6.00 2.70
❑ 69 Gary Smith 2.50 1.10
❑ 70 Carol Vadnais 2.50 1.10
❑ 71 Doug Roberts 1.50 .70
❑ 72 Harry Howell 2.50 1.10
❑ 73 Joe Szura 1.50 .70
❑ 74 Mike Laughton 1.50 .70
❑ 75 Gary Jarrett 1.50 .70
❑ 76 Bill Hicke 1.50 .70
❑ 77 Paul Andrea 1.50 .70
❑ 78 Bernie Parent 15.00 6.75
❑ 79 Joe Watson 1.50 .70
❑ 80 Ed Van Impe 1.50 .70
❑ 81 Larry Hillman 1.50 .70
❑ 82 George Swarbrick 1.50 .70
❑ 83 Bill Sutherland 1.50 .70
❑ 84 Andre Lacroix 2.50 1.10
❑ 85 Gary Dornhoefer 2.50 1.10
❑ 86 Jean-Guy Gendron 1.50 .70
❑ 87 Al Smith 2.50 1.10
❑ 88 Bob Woytowich 1.50 .70
❑ 89 Duane Rupp 1.50 .70
❑ 90 Jim Morrison 1.50 .70
❑ 91 Ron Schock 1.50 .70
❑ 92 Ken Schinkel 1.50 .70
❑ 93 Keith McCreary 1.50 .70
❑ 94 Bryan Hextall 2.50 1.10
❑ 95 Wayne Hicks 1.50 .70
❑ 96 Gary Sabourin 1.50 .70
❑ 97 Ernie Wakely 2.50 1.10
❑ 98 Bob Wall 1.50 .70
❑ 99 Barclay Plager 2.50 1.10
❑ 100 Jean-Guy Talbot 1.50 .70
❑ 101 Gary Veneruzzo 1.50 .70
❑ 102 Tim Ecclestone 1.50 .70
❑ 103 Red Berenson 2.50 1.10
❑ 104 Larry Keenan 1.50 .70
❑ 105 Bruce Gamble 2.50 1.10
❑ 106 Jim Dorey 1.50 .70
❑ 107 Mike Pelyk 1.50 .70
❑ 108 Rick Ley 1.50 .70
❑ 109 Mike Walton 1.50 .70
❑ 110 Norm Ullman 4.00 1.80
❑ 111 Brit Selby 1.50 .70
❑ 112 Garry Monahan 1.50 .70
❑ 113 George Armstrong 2.50 1.10
❑ 114 Gary Doak 1.50 .70
❑ 115 Darryl Sly 1.50 .70
❑ 116 Wayne Maki 1.50 .70
❑ 117 Orland Kurtenbach 1.50 .70
❑ 118 Murray Hall 1.50 .70
❑ 119 Marc Reaume 1.50 .70
❑ 120 Pat Quinn 4.00 1.80
❑ 121 Andre Boudrias 1.50 .70
❑ 122 Paul Popiel 1.50 .70
❑ 123 Paul Terbenche 1.50 .70
❑ 124 Howie Menard 1.50 .70
❑ 125 Gerry Meehan 4.00 1.80
❑ 126 Skip Krake 1.50 .70
❑ 127 Phil Goyette 1.50 .70
❑ 128 Reg Fleming 1.50 .70
❑ 129 Don Marshall 2.50 1.10
❑ 130 Bill Inglis 1.50 .70
❑ 131 Gilbert Perreault 50.00 22.00
❑ 132 Checklist Card 60.00 15.00

## 1970-71 Topps/OPC Sticker Stamps

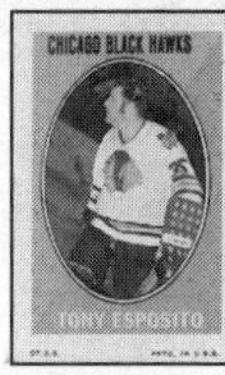


This set consists of 33 unnumbered, full-color sticker stamps measuring 2 1/2" by 3 1/2". The backs are blank. The checklist below is ordered alphabetically for convenience. The sticker cards were issued as an insert in the regular issue wax packs of the 1970-71 Topps hockey as well as in first series wax packs of 1970-71 O-Pee-Chee.

| | NRMT-MT | EXC |
|---|---|---|
| COMPLETE SET (33) | 275.00 | 125.00 |
| COMMON CARD (1-33) | 2.00 | .90 |

❑ 1 Jean Beliveau 25.00 11.00
❑ 2 Red Berenson 3.00 1.35
❑ 3 Wayne Carleton 2.00 .90
❑ 4 Tim Ecclestone 2.00 .90
❑ 5 Ron Ellis 3.00 1.35
❑ 6 Phil Esposito 25.00 11.00
❑ 7 Tony Esposito 25.00 11.00
❑ 8 Bill Flett 2.00 .90
❑ 9 Ed Giacomin 8.00 3.60
❑ 10 Rod Gilbert 8.00 3.60
❑ 11 Danny Grant 3.00 1.35
❑ 12 Bill Hicke 2.00 .90
❑ 13 Gordie Howe 60.00 27.00
❑ 14 Bobby Hull 40.00 18.00
❑ 15 Earl Ingarfield 2.00 .90
❑ 16 Eddie Joyal 2.00 .90
❑ 17 Dave Keon 7.00 3.10
❑ 18 Andre Lacroix 3.00 1.35
❑ 19 Jacques Laperriere 3.00 1.35
❑ 20 Jacques Lemaire 8.00 3.60
❑ 21 Frank Mahovlich 12.00 5.50
❑ 22 Keith McCreary 2.00 .90
❑ 23 Stan Mikita 15.00 6.75
❑ 24 Bobby Orr 75.00 34.00
❑ 25 Jean-Paul Parise 2.00 .90
❑ 26 Jean Ratelle 8.00 3.60
❑ 27 Derek Sanderson 10.00 4.50
❑ 28 Frank St.Marseille 2.00 .90
❑ 29 Ron Schock 2.00 .90
❑ 30 Garry Unger 3.00 1.35
❑ 31 Carol Vadnais 2.00 .90
❑ 32 Ed Van Impe 2.00 .90
❑ 33 Bob Woytowich 2.00 .90

## 1971-72 Topps

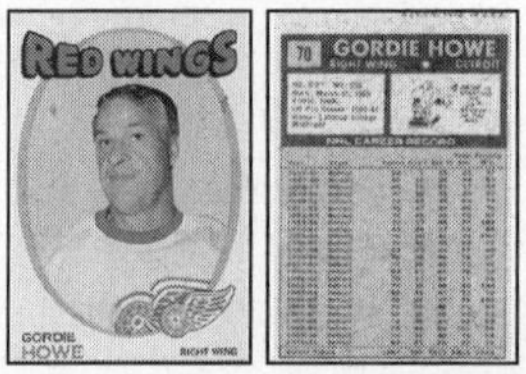


The 1971-72 Topps set consists of 132 standard-size cards. For the first time, Topps included the player's NHL year-by-year career record on back. A short player biography and a cartoon-illustrated fact about the player also appear on back. A League Leaders (1-6) subset is exclusive to the Topps set of this year. The only noteworthy Rookie Card is of Ken Dryden. An additional key card in the set is Gordie Howe (70). Howe does not have a basic card in the 1971-72 O-Pee-Chee set.

| | NRMT-MT | EXC |
|---|---|---|
| COMPLETE SET (132) | 350.00 | 160.00 |
| COMMON CARD (1-132) | 1.00 | .45 |

❑ 1 Goal Leaders 20.00 5.00
Phil Esposito
Johnny Bucyk
Bobby Hull
❑ 2 Assists Leaders 15.00 6.75
Bobby Orr
Phil Esposito
Johnny Bucyk
❑ 3 Scoring Leaders 15.00 6.75
Phil Esposito
Bobby Orr
Johnny Bucyk
❑ 4 Goalies Win Leaders 10.00 4.50
Tony Esposito
Ed Johnston
Gerry Cheevers
Ed Giacomin
❑ 5 Shutouts Leaders 6.00 2.70
Ed Giacomin
Tony Esposito
Cesare Maniago
❑ 6 Goals Against 12.00 5.50
Average Leaders
Jacques Plante
Ed Giacomin
Tony Esposito
❑ 7 Fred Stanfield 1.00 .45
❑ 8 Mike Robitaille 1.00 .45
❑ 9 Vic Hadfield 2.00 .90
❑ 10 Jacques Plante 15.00 6.75
❑ 11 Bill White 1.00 .45
❑ 12 Andre Boudrias 1.00 .45
❑ 13 Jim Lorentz 1.00 .45
❑ 14 Arnie Brown 1.00 .45
❑ 15 Yvan Cournoyer 4.00 1.80
❑ 16 Bryan Hextall 2.00 .90
❑ 17 Gary Croteau 1.00 .45
❑ 18 Gilles Villemure 2.00 .90
❑ 19 Serge Bernier 2.00 .90
❑ 20 Phil Esposito 12.00 5.50
❑ 21 Charlie Burns 1.00 .45
❑ 22 Doug Barrie 1.00 .45
❑ 23 Eddie Joyal 1.00 .45
❑ 24 Rosaire Paiement 1.00 .45
❑ 25 Pat Stapleton 2.00 .90
❑ 26 Garry Unger 2.00 .90
❑ 27 Al Smith 2.00 .90
❑ 28 Bob Woytowich 1.00 .45
❑ 29 Marc Tardif 2.00 .90
❑ 30 Norm Ullman 3.00 1.35
❑ 31 Tom Williams 1.00 .45
❑ 32 Ted Harris 1.00 .45
❑ 33 Andre Lacroix 2.00 .90
❑ 34 Mike Byers 1.00 .45
❑ 35 Johnny Bucyk 3.00 1.35
❑ 36 Roger Crozier 2.00 .90
❑ 37 Alex Delvecchio 4.00 1.80
❑ 38 Frank St.Marseille 1.00 .45
❑ 39 Pit Martin 2.00 .90
❑ 40 Brad Park 10.00 4.50
❑ 41 Greg Polis 1.00 .45
❑ 42 Orland Kurtenbach 1.00 .45
❑ 43 Jim McKenny 1.00 .45
❑ 44 Bob Nevin 1.00 .45
❑ 45 Ken Dryden 125.00 55.00
❑ 46 Carol Vadnais 2.00 .90
❑ 47 Bill Flett 1.00 .45
❑ 48 Jim Johnson 1.00 .45
❑ 49 Al Hamilton 1.00 .45
❑ 50 Bobby Hull 25.00 11.00
❑ 51 Chris Bordeleau 1.00 .45
❑ 52 Tim Ecclestone 1.00 .45
❑ 53 Rod Seiling 1.00 .45
❑ 54 Gerry Cheevers 6.00 2.70
❑ 55 Bill Goldsworthy 2.00 .90
❑ 56 Ron Schock 1.00 .45
❑ 57 Jim Dorey 1.00 .45
❑ 58 Wayne Maki 1.00 .45
❑ 59 Terry Harper 1.00 .45
❑ 60 Gilbert Perreault 15.00 6.75
❑ 61 Ernie Hicke 1.00 .45
❑ 62 Wayne Hillman 1.00 .45
❑ 63 Denis DeJordy 2.00 .90
❑ 64 Ken Schinkel 1.00 .45
❑ 65 Derek Sanderson 6.00 2.70
❑ 66 Barclay Plager 2.00 .90
❑ 67 Paul Henderson 2.00 .90
❑ 68 Jude Drouin 1.00 .45
❑ 69 Keith Magnuson 2.00 .90
❑ 70 Gordie Howe 50.00 22.00
❑ 71 Jacques Lemaire 4.00 1.80
❑ 72 Doug Favell 2.00 .90
❑ 73 Bert Marshall 1.00 .45
❑ 74 Gerry Meehan 2.00 .90
❑ 75 Walt Tkaczuk 2.00 .90
❑ 76 Bob Berry 3.00 1.35
❑ 77 Syl Apps 3.00 1.35
❑ 78 Tom Webster 2.00 .90
❑ 79 Danny Grant 2.00 .90
❑ 80 Dave Keon 3.00 1.35
❑ 81 Ernie Wakely 2.00 .90
❑ 82 John McKenzie 2.00 .90
❑ 83 Doug Roberts 1.00 .45
❑ 84 Peter Mahovlich 2.00 .90
❑ 85 Dennis Hull 2.00 .90
❑ 86 Juha Widing 1.00 .45
❑ 87 Gary Doak 1.00 .45
❑ 88 Phil Goyette 1.00 .45
❑ 89 Gary Dornhoefer 2.00 .90
❑ 90 Ed Giacomin 6.00 2.70
❑ 91 Red Berenson 2.00 .90
❑ 92 Mike Pelyk 1.00 .45
❑ 93 Gary Jarrett 1.00 .45
❑ 94 Bob Pulford 2.00 .90
❑ 95 Dale Tallon 2.00 .90
❑ 96 Eddie Shack 5.00 2.20
❑ 97 Jean Ratelle 3.00 1.35
❑ 98 Jim Pappin 1.00 .45
❑ 99 Roy Edwards 2.00 .90
❑ 100 Bobby Orr 50.00 22.00
❑ 101 Ted Hampson 1.00 .45
❑ 102 Mickey Redmond 3.00 1.35
❑ 103 Bob Plager 2.00 .90
❑ 104 Bruce Gamble 2.00 .90
❑ 105 Frank Mahovlich 5.00 2.20
❑ 106 Tony Featherstone 1.00 .45
❑ 107 Tracy Pratt 1.00 .45
❑ 108 Ralph Backstrom 2.00 .90
❑ 109 Murray Hall 1.00 .45
❑ 110 Tony Esposito 20.00 9.00
❑ 111 Checklist Card 60.00 15.00
❑ 112 Jim Neilson 1.00 .45
❑ 113 Ron Ellis 2.00 .90
❑ 114 Bobby Clarke 30.00 13.50
❑ 115 Ken Hodge 2.00 .90
❑ 116 Jim Roberts 2.00 .90
❑ 117 Cesare Maniago 2.00 .90
❑ 118 Jean Pronovost 2.00 .90
❑ 119 Gary Bergman 1.00 .45
❑ 120 Henri Richard 5.00 2.20
❑ 121 Ross Lonsberry 1.00 .45
❑ 122 Pat Quinn 2.00 .90
❑ 123 Rod Gilbert 3.00 1.35
❑ 124 Gary Smith 2.00 .90
❑ 125 Stan Mikita 10.00 4.50
❑ 126 Ed Van Impe 1.00 .45
❑ 127 Wayne Connelly 1.00 .45
❑ 128 Dennis Hextall 2.00 .90
❑ 129 Wayne Cashman 3.00 1.35
❑ 130 J.C. Tremblay 2.00 .90
❑ 131 Bernie Parent 10.00 4.50
❑ 132 Dunc McCallum 4.00 1.00

## 1972-73 Topps

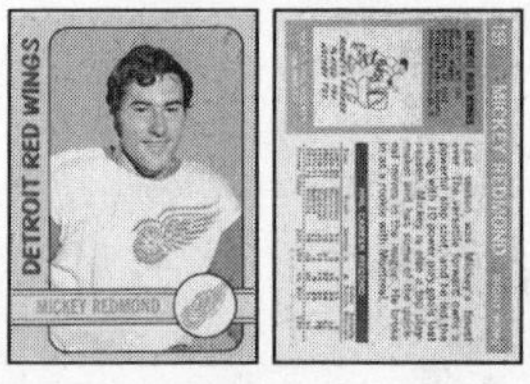


The 1972-73 production marked Topps' largest set to date at 176 standard-size cards. Expansion plays a part in the increase as the Atlanta Flames and New York Islanders join the league. Tan borders include team name down the left side. A tan colored bar that crosses the bottom portion of the player photo includes the player's name and team logo. The back contains the year-by-year NHL career record of the player, a short biography and a cartoon illustrated fact about the player. The key cards in the set are the first Topps cards of Marcel Dionne and Guy Lafleur. The set was printed on two sheets of 132 cards creating 88 double-printed cards. The double prints are noted in the checklist below by DP. Topps gives collectors a look at the various NHL hardware in the Trophy subset (170-176).

| | NRMT-MT | EXC |
|---|---|---|
| COMPLETE SET (176) | 350.00 | 160.00 |
| COMMON CARD (1-176) | .75 | .35 |
| COMMON CARD DP | .50 | .23 |

❑ 1 World Champions DP 6.00 1.50
Boston Bruins Team
❑ 2 Playoff Game 1 1.00 .45
Bruins 6
Rangers 5
❑ 3 Playoff Game 2 1.00 .45
Bruins 2
Rangers 1
❑ 4 Playoff Game 3 1.00 .45
Rangers 5
Bruins 2
❑ 5 Playoff Game 4 DP 1.00 .45
Bruins 3
Rangers 2
❑ 6 Playoff Game 5 DP 1.00 .45
Rangers 3
Bruins 2
❑ 7 Playoff Game 6 DP 1.00 .45
Bruins 3
Rangers 0
❑ 8 Stanley Cup Trophy 5.00 2.20
❑ 9 Ed Van Impe DP .50 .23
❑ 10 Yvan Cournoyer DP 2.50 1.10
❑ 11 Syl Apps DP .50 .23
❑ 12 Bill Plager 1.50 .70
❑ 13 Ed Johnston DP .50 .23
❑ 14 Walt Tkaczuk 1.00 .45
❑ 15 Dale Tallon DP .50 .23
❑ 16 Gerry Meehan 1.00 .45
❑ 17 Reggie Leach 3.00 1.35
❑ 18 Marcel Dionne DP 12.00 5.50
❑ 19 Andre Dupont 1.50 .70
❑ 20 Tony Esposito 12.00 5.50
❑ 21 Bob Berry DP .50 .23
❑ 22 Craig Cameron .75 .35
❑ 23 Ted Harris .75 .35
❑ 24 Jacques Plante 12.00 5.50
❑ 25 Jacques Lemaire DP 1.50 .70
❑ 26 Simon Nolet DP .50 .23
❑ 27 Keith McCreary DP .50 .23
❑ 28 Duane Rupp .75 .35
❑ 29 Wayne Cashman 1.50 .70
❑ 30 Brad Park 6.00 2.70
❑ 31 Roger Crozier 2.50 1.10
❑ 32 Wayne Maki .75 .35
❑ 33 Tim Ecclestone .75 .35
❑ 34 Rick Smith .75 .35

❑ 35 Garry Unger DP .50 .23
❑ 36 Serge Bernier DP .50 .23
❑ 37 Brian Glennie .75 .35
❑ 38 Gerry Desjardins DP .50 .23
❑ 39 Danny Grant 1.00 .45
❑ 40 Bill White DP .50 .23
❑ 41 Gary Dornhoefer DP .50 .23
❑ 42 Peter Mahovlich 1.00 .45
❑ 43 Greg Polis DP .50 .23
❑ 44 Larry Hale DP .50 .23
❑ 45 Dallas Smith .75 .35
❑ 46 Orland Kurtenbach DP .50 .23
❑ 47 Steve Atkinson .75 .35
❑ 48 Joey Johnston DP .50 .23
❑ 49 Gary Bergman .75 .35
❑ 50 Jean Ratelle 3.00 1.35
❑ 51 Rogatien Vachon DP 2.50 1.10
❑ 52 Phil Roberto DP .50 .23
❑ 53 Brian Spencer DP .50 .23
❑ 54 Jim McKenny DP .50 .23
❑ 55 Gump Worsley 4.00 1.80
❑ 56 Stan Mikita DP 5.00 2.20
❑ 57 Guy Lapointe 1.50 .70
❑ 58 Lew Morrison DP .50 .23
❑ 59 Ron Schock DP .50 .23
❑ 60 Johnny Bucyk 2.50 1.10
❑ 61 Goals Leaders 10.00 4.50
Phil Esposito
Vic Hadfield
Bobby Hull
❑ 62 Assists Leaders DP 12.00 5.50
Bobby Orr
Phil Esposito
Jean Ratelle
❑ 63 Scoring Leaders DP 12.00 5.50
Phil Esposito
Bobby Orr
Jean Ratelle
❑ 64 Goals Against 6.00 2.70
Average Leaders
Tony Esposito
Gilles Villemure
Gump Worsley
❑ 65 Penalty Minutes 1.50 .70
Leaders DP
Bryan Watson
Keith Magnuson
Gary Dornhoefer
❑ 66 Jim Neilson .75 .35
❑ 67 Nick Libett DP .50 .23
❑ 68 Jim Lorentz .75 .35
❑ 69 Gilles Meloche 5.00 2.20
❑ 70 Pat Stapleton 1.00 .45
❑ 71 Frank St.Marseille DP .50 .23
❑ 72 Butch Goring 1.50 .70
❑ 73 Paul Henderson DP .50 .23
❑ 74 Doug Favell 1.00 .45
❑ 75 Jocelyn Guevremont DP .50 .23
❑ 76 Tom Miller .75 .35
❑ 77 Bill MacMillan .75 .35
❑ 78 Doug Mohns .75 .35
❑ 79 Guy Lafleur DP 20.00 9.00
❑ 80 Rod Gilbert DP 1.50 .70
❑ 81 Gary Doak .75 .35
❑ 82 Dave Burrows DP .50 .23
❑ 83 Gary Croteau .75 .35
❑ 84 Tracy Pratt DP .50 .23
❑ 85 Carol Vadnais DP .50 .23
❑ 86 Jacques Caron DP .50 .23
❑ 87 Keith Magnuson 1.50 .70
❑ 88 Dave Keon 1.50 .70
❑ 89 Mike Corrigan .75 .35
❑ 90 Bobby Clarke 15.00 6.75
❑ 91 Dunc Wilson DP .50 .23
❑ 92 Gerry Hart .75 .35
❑ 93 Lou Nanne 1.00 .45
❑ 94 Checklist 1-176 DP 25.00 6.25
❑ 95 Red Berenson DP .50 .23
❑ 96 Bob Plager 1.00 .45
❑ 97 Jim Rutherford 6.00 2.70
❑ 98 Rick Foley DP .50 .23
❑ 99 Pit Martin DP .50 .23
❑ 100 Bobby Orr DP 30.00 13.50
❑ 101 Stan Gilbertson .75 .35
❑ 102 Barry Wilkins .75 .35
❑ 103 Terry Crisp DP .50 .23
❑ 104 Cesare Maniago DP .50 .23
❑ 105 Marc Tardif .75 .35
❑ 106 Don Luce DP .50 .23
❑ 107 Mike Pelyk .75 .35
❑ 108 Juha Widing DP .50 .23
❑ 109 Phil Myre DP 3.00 1.35
❑ 110 Vic Hadfield 1.00 .45
❑ 111 Arnie Brown DP .50 .23
❑ 112 Ross Lonsberry DP .50 .23
❑ 113 Dick Redmond .75 .35
❑ 114 Gary Smith 1.00 .45
❑ 115 Bill Goldsworthy 1.00 .45
❑ 116 Bryan Watson .75 .35
❑ 117 Dave Balon DP .50 .23
❑ 118 Bill Mikkelson DP .50 .23
❑ 119 Terry Harper DP .50 .23
❑ 120 Gilbert Perreault DP 6.00 2.70
❑ 121 Tony Esposito AS1 6.00 2.70
❑ 122 Bobby Orr AS1 20.00 9.00
❑ 123 Brad Park AS1 3.00 1.35
❑ 124 Phil Esposito AS1 5.00 2.20
(Brother Tony pic-
tured in background)
❑ 125 Rod Gilbert AS1 1.50 .70
❑ 126 Bobby Hull AS1 15.00 6.75
❑ 127 Ken Dryden AS2 DP 10.00 4.50
❑ 128 Bill White AS2 DP .75 .35
❑ 129 Pat Stapleton AS2 DP .50 .23
❑ 130 Jean Ratelle AS2 DP 1.50 .70
❑ 131 Yvan Cournoyer AS2 DP 1.50 .70
❑ 132 Vic Hadfield AS2 DP .50 .23
❑ 133 Ralph Backstrom DP .50 .23
❑ 134 Bob Baun DP .50 .23
❑ 135 Fred Stanfield DP .50 .23
❑ 136 Barclay Plager DP .50 .23
❑ 137 Gilles Villemure 1.00 .45
❑ 138 Ron Harris DP .50 .23
❑ 139 Bill Flett DP .50 .23
❑ 140 Frank Mahovlich 4.00 1.80
❑ 141 Alex Delvecchio DP 1.50 .70
❑ 142 Paul Popiel .75 .35
❑ 143 Jean Pronovost DP .50 .23
❑ 144 Denis DeJordy DP .50 .23
❑ 145 Richard Martin DP 3.00 1.35
❑ 146 Ivan Boldirev 1.50 .70
❑ 147 Jack Egers .75 .35
❑ 148 Jim Pappin .75 .35
❑ 149 Rod Seiling .75 .35
❑ 150 Phil Esposito 10.00 4.50
❑ 151 Gary Edwards 1.00 .45
❑ 152 Ron Ellis DP .50 .23
❑ 153 Jude Drouin .75 .35
❑ 154 Ernie Hicke DP .50 .23
❑ 155 Mickey Redmond 1.50 .70
❑ 156 Joe Watson DP .50 .23
❑ 157 Bryan Hextall .75 .35
❑ 158 Andre Boudrias .75 .35
❑ 159 Ed Westfall 1.00 .45
❑ 160 Ken Dryden 30.00 13.50
❑ 161 Rene Robert DP 2.50 1.10
❑ 162 Bert Marshall DP .50 .23
❑ 163 Gary Sabourin .75 .35
❑ 164 Dennis Hull 1.00 .45
❑ 165 Ed Giacomin DP 2.50 1.10
❑ 166 Ken Hodge 1.00 .45
❑ 167 Gilles Marotte DP .50 .23
❑ 168 Norm Ullman DP 1.50 .70
❑ 169 Barry Gibbs .75 .35
❑ 170 Art Ross Trophy 1.50 .70
❑ 171 Hart Memorial Trophy 1.50 .70
❑ 172 James Norris Trophy 1.50 .70
❑ 173 Vezina Trophy DP 1.00 .45
❑ 174 Calder Trophy DP 1.00 .45
❑ 175 Lady Byng Trophy DP 1.00 .45
❑ 176 Conn Smythe Trophy DP 3.00 .75

## 1973-74 Topps

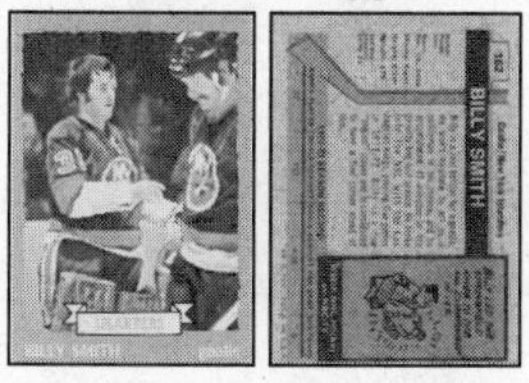

Once again increasing in size, the 1973-74 Topps set consists of 198 standard-size cards. The fronts of the cards have distinct colored borders including blue and green. This differs from O-Pee-Chee which used red borders for cards 1-198. The backs contain the player's 1972-73 season record, career numbers, a short biography and a cartoon-illustrated fact about the player. Team cards (92-107) give team and player records on the back. Since the set was printed on two 132-card sheets, there are 66 double-printed cards. These double prints are noted in the checklist below by DP. Rookie Cards include Bill Barber, Billy Smith and Dave Schultz. Ken Dryden (10) is only in the Topps set.

| | NRMT-MT | EXC |
|---|---|---|
| COMPLETE SET (198) | 200.00 | 90.00 |
| COMMON CARD (1-198) | .50 | .23 |
| COMMON DP | .40 | .18 |

❑ 1 Goal Leaders 5.00 1.25
Phil Esposito
Rick MacLeish
❑ 2 Assists Leaders 5.00 2.20
Phil Esposito
Bobby Clarke
❑ 3 Scoring Leaders 5.00 2.20
Phil Esposito
Bobby Clarke
❑ 4 Goals Against 6.00 2.70
Average Leaders
Ken Dryden
Tony Esposito
❑ 5 Penalty Min. Leaders 2.00 .90
Jim Schoenfeld
Dave Schultz
❑ 6 Power Play Goals 3.00 1.35
Leaders
Phil Esposito
Rick MacLeish
❑ 7 Paul Henderson DP .40 .18
❑ 8 Gregg Sheppard DP UER .40 .18
(Misspelled Greg
on card front)
❑ 9 Rod Seiling DP .40 .18
❑ 10 Ken Dryden 40.00 18.00
❑ 11 Jean Pronovost DP .40 .18
❑ 12 Dick Redmond .50 .23
❑ 13 Keith McCreary DP .40 .18
❑ 14 Ted Harris DP .40 .18
❑ 15 Garry Unger .75 .35
❑ 16 Neil Komadoski .50 .23
❑ 17 Marcel Dionne 10.00 4.50
❑ 18 Ernie Hicke DP .40 .18
❑ 19 Andre Boudrias .50 .23
❑ 20 Bill Flett .50 .23
❑ 21 Marshall Johnston .50 .23
❑ 22 Gerry Meehan .50 .23
❑ 23 Ed Johnston DP .40 .18
❑ 24 Serge Savard 1.25 .55
❑ 25 Walt Tkaczuk .75 .35
❑ 26 Johnny Bucyk 2.00 .90
❑ 27 Dave Burrows .50 .23
❑ 28 Cliff Koroll .50 .23
❑ 29 Rey Comeau DP .40 .18
❑ 30 Barry Gibbs .50 .23
❑ 31 Wayne Stephenson .75 .35
❑ 32 Dan Maloney DP .40 .18
❑ 33 Henry Boucha DP .40 .18
❑ 34 Gerry Hart .50 .23
❑ 35 Bobby Schmautz .50 .23
❑ 36 Ross Lonsberry DP .40 .18
❑ 37 Ted McAneeley .50 .23
❑ 38 Don Luce DP .40 .18
❑ 39 Jim McKenny DP .40 .18
❑ 40 Frank Mahovlich 4.00 1.80
❑ 41 Bill Fairbairn .50 .23
❑ 42 Dallas Smith .50 .23
❑ 43 Bryan Hextall .50 .23
❑ 44 Keith Magnuson .75 .35
❑ 45 Dan Bouchard .75 .35
❑ 46 Jean-Paul Parise DP .40 .18
❑ 47 Barclay Plager .75 .35
❑ 48 Mike Corrigan .50 .23
❑ 49 Nick Libett DP .40 .18
❑ 50 Bobby Clarke 12.00 5.50
❑ 51 Bert Marshall DP .40 .18
❑ 52 Craig Patrick .75 .35
❑ 53 Richard Lemieux .50 .23
❑ 54 Tracy Pratt DP .40 .18
❑ 55 Ron Ellis DP .40 .18
❑ 56 Jacques Lemaire 2.00 .90
❑ 57 Steve Vickers DP .40 .18
❑ 58 Carol Vadnais .50 .23
❑ 59 Jim Rutherford DP .40 .18
❑ 60 Dennis Hull .75 .35
❑ 61 Pat Quinn DP .40 .18
❑ 62 Bill Goldsworthy DP .40 .18
❑ 63 Fran Huck .50 .23
❑ 64 Rogatien Vachon DP 2.00 .90
❑ 65 Gary Bergman DP .40 .18
❑ 66 Bernie Parent 6.00 2.70
❑ 67 Ed Westfall .75 .35
❑ 68 Ivan Boldirev .75 .35
❑ 69 Don Tannahill DP .40 .18
❑ 70 Gilbert Perreault DP 6.00 2.70
❑ 71 Mike Pelyk DP .40 .18
❑ 72 Guy Lafleur DP 15.00 6.75
❑ 73 Jean Ratelle 1.25 .55
❑ 74 Gilles Gilbert DP 4.00 1.80
❑ 75 Greg Polis .50 .23
❑ 76 Doug Jarrett DP .40 .18
❑ 77 Phil Myre DP .40 .18
❑ 78 Fred Harvey DP .40 .18
❑ 79 Jack Egers .50 .23
❑ 80 Terry Harper .50 .23
❑ 81 Bill Barber 10.00 4.50
❑ 82 Roy Edwards DP .40 .18
❑ 83 Brian Spencer .75 .35
❑ 84 Reggie Leach DP 1.25 .55
❑ 85 Dave Keon 2.50 1.10
❑ 86 Jim Schoenfeld 2.00 .90
❑ 87 Henri Richard DP 2.50 1.10
❑ 88 Rod Gilbert DP 1.25 .55
❑ 89 Don Marcotte DP .40 .18
❑ 90 Tony Esposito 6.00 2.70
❑ 91 Joe Watson .50 .23
❑ 92 Flames Team 1.50 .70
❑ 93 Bruins Team 1.50 .70
❑ 94 Sabres Team DP 1.50 .70
❑ 95 Golden Seals Team DP 1.50 .70
❑ 96 Blackhawks Team 1.50 .70
❑ 97 Red Wings Team DP 1.50 .70
❑ 98 Kings Team DP 1.50 .70
❑ 99 North Stars Team 1.50 .70
❑ 100 Canadiens Team 1.50 .70
❑ 101 Islanders Team 1.50 .70
❑ 102 Rangers Team DP 1.50 .70
❑ 103 Flyers Team DP 1.50 .70
❑ 104 Penguins Team 1.50 .70
❑ 105 Blues Team 1.50 .70
❑ 106 Maple Leafs Team 1.50 .70
❑ 107 Canucks Team 1.50 .70
❑ 108 Roger Crozier DP .40 .18
❑ 109 Tom Reid .50 .23
❑ 110 Hilliard Graves .50 .23
❑ 111 Don Lever .75 .35
❑ 112 Jim Pappin .50 .23
❑ 113 Ron Schock DP .40 .18
❑ 114 Gerry Desjardins .75 .35
❑ 115 Yvan Cournoyer DP 2.00 .90
❑ 116 Checklist Card 20.00 5.00
❑ 117 Bob Leiter .50 .23
❑ 118 Ab DeMarco .50 .23
❑ 119 Doug Favell .75 .35
❑ 120 Phil Esposito 6.00 2.70
❑ 121 Mike Robitaille .50 .23
❑ 122 Real Lemieux .50 .23
❑ 123 Jim Neilson .50 .23
❑ 124 Tim Ecclestone DP .40 .18
❑ 125 Jude Drouin .50 .23
❑ 126 Gary Smith DP .40 .18
❑ 127 Walt McKechnie .50 .23
❑ 128 Lowell MacDonald .50 .23
❑ 129 Dale Tallon DP .40 .18
❑ 130 Billy Harris .75 .35
❑ 131 Randy Manery DP .40 .18
❑ 132 Darryl Sittler DP 6.00 2.70
❑ 133 Ken Hodge .75 .35
❑ 134 Bob Plager .75 .35
❑ 135 Rick MacLeish 2.00 .90
❑ 136 Dennis Hextall .50 .23
❑ 137 Jacques Laperriere DP .40 .18
❑ 138 Butch Goring .75 .35
❑ 139 Rene Robert .75 .35
❑ 140 Ed Giacomin 2.50 1.10
❑ 141 Alex Delvecchio DP 1.25 .55
❑ 142 Jocelyn Guevremont .50 .23
❑ 143 Joey Johnston .50 .23
❑ 144 Bryan Watson DP .40 .18
❑ 145 Stan Mikita 5.00 2.20
❑ 146 Cesare Maniago .75 .35
❑ 147 Craig Cameron .50 .23
❑ 148 Norm Ullman DP 1.25 .55
❑ 149 Dave Schultz 12.00 5.50
❑ 150 Bobby Orr 30.00 13.50
❑ 151 Phil Roberto .50 .23
❑ 152 Curt Bennett .50 .23
❑ 153 Gilles Villemure DP .40 .18
❑ 154 Chuck Lefley .50 .23
❑ 155 Richard Martin 2.50 1.10
❑ 156 Juha Widing .50 .23
❑ 157 Orland Kurtenbach .50 .23
❑ 158 Bill Collins DP .40 .18
❑ 159 Bob Stewart .50 .23
❑ 160 Syl Apps .75 .35
❑ 161 Danny Grant .75 .35
❑ 162 Billy Smith 25.00 11.00
❑ 163 Brian Glennie .50 .23
❑ 164 Pit Martin DP .40 .18
❑ 165 Brad Park 4.00 1.80
❑ 166 Wayne Cashman DP .40 .18
❑ 167 Gary Dornhoefer .50 .23
❑ 168 Steve Durbano .50 .23
❑ 169 Jacques Richard .50 .23
❑ 170 Guy Lapointe .75 .35
❑ 171 Jim Lorentz .50 .23
❑ 172 Bob Berry DP .40 .18
❑ 173 Dennis Kearns .50 .23
❑ 174 Red Berenson .75 .35
❑ 175 Gilles Meloche DP .40 .18
❑ 176 Al McDonough .50 .23
❑ 177 Dennis O'Brien .50 .23
❑ 178 Germaine Gagnon UER DP .40 .18
❑ 179 Rick Kehoe DP .40 .18
❑ 180 Bill White .50 .23
❑ 181 Vic Hadfield DP .40 .18
❑ 182 Derek Sanderson 3.00 1.35
❑ 183 Andre Dupont DP .40 .18
❑ 184 Gary Sabourin .50 .23
❑ 185 Larry Romanchych .50 .23
❑ 186 Peter Mahovlich .75 .35
❑ 187 Dave Dryden .75 .35
❑ 188 Gilles Marotte .50 .23
❑ 189 Bobby Lalonde .50 .23
❑ 190 Mickey Redmond .75 .35
❑ 191 Series A .75 .35
Canadiens 4
Sabres 2
❑ 192 Series B .75 .35
Flyers 4
North Stars 2
❑ 193 Series C .75 .35
Blackhawks 4
Blues 1
❑ 194 Series D .75 .35
Rangers 4
Bruins
❑ 195 Series E .75 .35
Canadiens 4
Flyers 1
❑ 196 Series F .75 .35
Blackhawks 4
Rangers 1
❑ 197 Series G .75 .35
Canadiens 4
Blackhawks 2
❑ 198 Stanley Cup Champs 2.50 .60

## 1974-75 Topps

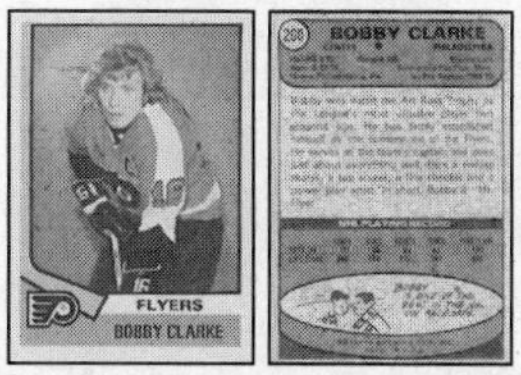


Topps produced a set of 264 standard-size cards for 1974-75. Design of card fronts offers a hockey stick down the left side. The team name, player name and team logo appear at the bottom in a border that features one of the team colors. The backs feature the player's 1973-74 and career statistics, a short biography and a cartoon-illustrated fact about the player. Players from the 1974-75 expansion Washington Capitals and Kansas City Scouts (presently New Jersey Devils) appear in this set. The set marks the return of coach cards, including Don Cherry and Scotty Bowman. Rookie Cards include John Davidson, Lanny McDonald, Denis Potvin and Borje Salming.

| | NRMT-MT | EXC |
|---|---|---|
| COMPLETE SET (264) | 200.00 | 90.00 |
| COMMON CARD (1-264) | .40 | .18 |

❑ 1 Goal Leaders 3.00 .75
Phil Esposito
Bill Goldsworthy
❑ 2 Assists Leaders 5.00 2.20
Bobby Orr
Dennis Hextall
❑ 3 Scoring Leaders 4.00 1.80
Phil Esposito
Bobby Clarke
❑ 4 Goals Against Average 1.50 .70
Leaders
Doug Favell
Bernie Parent
❑ 5 Penalty Min. Leaders .75 .35
Bryan Watson
Dave Schultz
❑ 6 Power Play Goal .75 .35
Leaders
Mickey Redmond
Rick MacLeish
❑ 7 Gary Bromley .75 .35
❑ 8 Bill Barber 4.00 1.80
❑ 9 Emile Francis CO .40 .18
❑ 10 Gilles Gilbert 1.50 .70
❑ 11 John Davidson 8.00 3.60
❑ 12 Ron Ellis .75 .35
❑ 13 Syl Apps .40 .18
❑ 14 Flames Leaders .75 .35
Jacques Richard
Tom Lysiak
Keith McCreary
❑ 15 Dan Bouchard .75 .35
❑ 16 Ivan Boldirev .75 .35
❑ 17 Gary Coalter .40 .18
❑ 18 Bob Berry .40 .18
❑ 19 Red Berenson .75 .35
❑ 20 Stan Mikita 4.00 1.80
❑ 21 Fred Shero CO 2.50 1.10
❑ 22 Gary Smith .75 .35
❑ 23 Bill Mikkelson .40 .18
❑ 24 Jacques Lemaire UER 2.00 .90
(Shown in Sabres
sweater)
❑ 25 Gilbert Perreault 4.00 1.80
❑ 26 Cesare Maniago .75 .35
❑ 27 Bobby Schmautz .40 .18
❑ 28 Bruins Leaders 8.00 3.60
Phil Esposito
Bobby Orr
Johnny Bucyk
❑ 29 Steve Vickers .75 .35
❑ 30 Lowell MacDonald .40 .18
❑ 31 Fred Stanfield .40 .18
❑ 32 Ed Westfall .75 .35
❑ 33 Curt Bennett .40 .18
❑ 34 Bep Guidolin CO .40 .18
❑ 35 Cliff Koroll .40 .18
❑ 36 Gary Croteau .40 .18
❑ 37 Mike Corrigan .40 .18
❑ 38 Henry Boucha .40 .18
❑ 39 Ron Low .75 .35
❑ 40 Darryl Sittler 5.00 2.20
❑ 41 Tracy Pratt .40 .18
❑ 42 Sabres Leaders .75 .35
Richard Martin
Rene Robert
❑ 43 Larry Carriere .40 .18
❑ 44 Gary Dornhoefer .75 .35
❑ 45 Denis Herron 2.50 1.10
❑ 46 Doug Favell .75 .35
❑ 47 Dave Gardner .40 .18
❑ 48 Morris Mott .40 .18
❑ 49 Marc Boileau CO .40 .18
❑ 50 Brad Park 3.00 1.35
❑ 51 Bob Leiter .40 .18
❑ 52 Tom Reid .40 .18
❑ 53 Serge Savard .40 .18
❑ 54 Checklist 1-132 12.00 3.00
❑ 55 Terry Harper .40 .18
❑ 56 Golden Seals .50 .23
Leaders
Joey Johnston
Walt McKechnie
❑ 57 Guy Charron .40 .18
❑ 58 Pit Martin .40 .18
❑ 59 Chris Evans .40 .18
❑ 60 Bernie Parent 3.00 1.35
❑ 61 Jim Lorentz .40 .18
❑ 62 Dave Kryskow .40 .18
❑ 63 Lou Angotti CO .40 .18
❑ 64 Bill Flett .40 .18
❑ 65 Vic Hadfield .75 .35
❑ 66 Wayne Merrick .40 .18
❑ 67 Andre Dupont .40 .18
❑ 68 Tom Lysiak 1.50 .70
❑ 69 Blackhawks Leaders .75 .35
Jim Pappin
Stan Mikita
J.P. Bordeleau
❑ 70 Guy Lapointe .75 .35
❑ 71 Gerry O'Flaherty .40 .18
❑ 72 Marcel Dionne 6.00 2.70
❑ 73 Brent Hughes .40 .18
❑ 74 Butch Goring .75 .35
❑ 75 Keith Magnuson .40 .18
❑ 76 Red Kelly CO .40 .18
❑ 77 Pete Stemkowski .40 .18
❑ 78 Jim Roberts .40 .18
❑ 79 Don Luce .40 .18
❑ 80 Don Awrey .40 .18
❑ 81 Rick Kehoe .75 .35
❑ 82 Billy Smith 6.00 2.70
❑ 83 Jean-Paul Parise .40 .18
❑ 84 Red Wings Leaders 1.50 .70
Mickey Redmond
Marcel Dionne
Bill Hogaboam
❑ 85 Ed Van Impe .40 .18

❑ 86 Randy Manery .40 .18
❑ 87 Barclay Plager .75 .35
❑ 88 Inge Hammarstrom .40 .18
❑ 89 Ab DeMarco .40 .18
❑ 90 Bill White .40 .18
❑ 91 Al Arbour CO 1.50 .70
❑ 92 Bob Stewart .40 .18
❑ 93 Jack Egers .40 .18
❑ 94 Don Lever .40 .18
❑ 95 Reggie Leach .75 .35
❑ 96 Dennis O'Brien .40 .18
❑ 97 Peter Mahovlich .75 .35
❑ 98 Kings Leaders .75 .35
Butch Goring
Frank St.Marseille
Don Kozak
❑ 99 Gerry Meehan .40 .18
❑ 100 Bobby Orr 25.00 11.00
❑ 101 Jean Potvin .40 .18
❑ 102 Rod Seiling .40 .18
❑ 103 Keith McCreary .40 .18
❑ 104 Phil Maloney CO .40 .18
❑ 105 Denis Dupere .40 .18
❑ 106 Steve Durbano .40 .18
❑ 107 Bob Plager UER .75 .35
(Photo actually
Barclay Plager)
❑ 108 Chris Oddleifson .40 .18
❑ 109 Jim Neilson .40 .18
❑ 110 Jean Pronovost .75 .35
❑ 111 Don Kozak .40 .18
❑ 112 North Stars .75 .35
Leaders
Bill Goldsworthy
Dennis Hextall
Danny Grant
❑ 113 Jim Pappin .40 .18
❑ 114 Richard Lemieux .40 .18
❑ 115 Dennis Hextall .40 .18
❑ 116 Bill Hogaboam .40 .18
❑ 117 Canucks Leaders .75 .35
Dennis Ververgaert
Bob Schmautz
Andre Boudrias
Don Tannahill
❑ 118 Jimmy Anderson CO .40 .18
❑ 119 Walt Tkaczuk .75 .35
❑ 120 Mickey Redmond .75 .35
❑ 121 Jim Schoenfeld 1.50 .70
❑ 122 Jocelyn Guevremont .40 .18
❑ 123 Bob Nystrom 1.50 .70
❑ 124 Canadiens Leaders 2.00 .90
Yvan Cournoyer
Frank Mahovlich
Claude Larose
❑ 125 Lew Morrison .40 .18
❑ 126 Terry Murray .75 .35
❑ 127 Richard Martin AS .75 .35
❑ 128 Ken Hodge AS .40 .18
❑ 129 Phil Esposito AS 2.50 1.10
❑ 130 Bobby Orr AS 12.00 5.50
❑ 131 Brad Park AS 1.50 .70
❑ 132 Gilles Gilbert AS .75 .35
❑ 133 Lowell MacDonald AS .40 .18
❑ 134 Bill Goldsworthy AS .40 .18
❑ 135 Bobby Clarke AS 4.00 1.80
❑ 136 Bill White AS .40 .18
❑ 137 Dave Burrows AS .40 .18
❑ 138 Bernie Parent AS 1.50 .70
❑ 139 Jacques Richard .40 .18
❑ 140 Yvan Cournoyer 2.00 .90
❑ 141 Rangers Leaders 1.50 .70
Rod Gilbert
Brad Park
❑ 142 Rene Robert .75 .35
❑ 143 J. Bob Kelly .40 .18
❑ 144 Ross Lonsberry .40 .18
❑ 145 Jean Ratelle 1.50 .70
❑ 146 Dallas Smith .40 .18
❑ 147 Bernie Geoffrion CO 2.50 1.10
❑ 148 Ted McAneeley .40 .18
❑ 149 Pierre Plante .40 .18
❑ 150 Dennis Hull .75 .35
❑ 151 Dave Keon 1.50 .70
❑ 152 Dave Dunn .40 .18
❑ 153 Michel Belhumeur .75 .35
❑ 154 Flyers Leaders 2.00 .90
Bobby Clarke
Dave Schultz
❑ 155 Ken Dryden 15.00 6.75
❑ 156 John Wright .40 .18
❑ 157 Larry Romanchych .40 .18
❑ 158 Ralph Stewart .40 .18
❑ 159 Mike Robitaille .40 .18
❑ 160 Ed Giacomin 2.00 .90
❑ 161 Don Cherry CO 25.00 11.00
❑ 162 Checklist 133-264 12.00 3.00
❑ 163 Rick MacLeish 1.50 .70
❑ 164 Greg Polis .40 .18
❑ 165 Carol Vadnais .40 .18
❑ 166 Pete Laframboise .40 .18
❑ 167 Ron Schock .40 .18
❑ 168 Lanny McDonald 12.00 5.50
❑ 169 Scouts Emblem 1.00 .45
Draft Selections
on back
❑ 170 Tony Esposito 5.00 2.20
❑ 171 Pierre Jarry .40 .18
❑ 172 Dan Maloney .75 .35
❑ 173 Peter McDuffe .75 .35
❑ 174 Danny Grant .75 .35
❑ 175 John Stewart .40 .18
❑ 176 Floyd Smith CO .40 .18
❑ 177 Bert Marshall .40 .18
❑ 178 Chuck Lefley UER .40 .18
(Photo actually
Pierre Bouchard)
❑ 179 Gilles Villemure .75 .35
❑ 180 Borje Salming 12.00 5.50
❑ 181 Doug Mohns .40 .18
❑ 182 Barry Wilkins .40 .18
❑ 183 Penguins Leaders .75 .35
Lowell MacDonald
Syl Apps
❑ 184 Gregg Sheppard .40 .18
❑ 185 Joey Johnston .40 .18
❑ 186 Dick Redmond .40 .18
❑ 187 Simon Nolet .40 .18
❑ 188 Ron Stackhouse .40 .18
❑ 189 Marshall Johnston .40 .18
❑ 190 Richard Martin 1.50 .70
❑ 191 Andre Boudrias .40 .18
❑ 192 Steve Atkinson .40 .18
❑ 193 Nick Libett .40 .18
❑ 194 Bob Murdoch .40 .18
❑ 195 Denis Potvin 20.00 9.00
❑ 196 Dave Schultz 2.00 .90
❑ 197 Blues Leaders .75 .35
Garry Unger
Pierre Plante
❑ 198 Jim McKenny .40 .18
❑ 199 Gerry Hart .40 .18
❑ 200 Phil Esposito 4.00 1.80
❑ 201 Rod Gilbert 1.50 .70
❑ 202 Jacques Laperriere .75 .35
❑ 203 Barry Gibbs .40 .18
❑ 204 Billy Reay CO .75 .35
❑ 205 Gilles Meloche .75 .35
❑ 206 Wayne Cashman .75 .35
❑ 207 Dennis Ververgaert .40 .18
❑ 208 Phil Roberto .40 .18
❑ 209 Quarter Finals .75 .35
Flyers sweep
Flames
❑ 210 Quarter Finals .75 .35
Rangers over
Canadiens
❑ 211 Quarter Finals .75 .35
Bruins sweep
Maple Leafs
❑ 212 Quarter Finals .75 .35
Blackhawks over
L.A. Kings
❑ 213 Stanley Cup Semifinals .75 .35
Flyers over Rangers
❑ 214 Stanley Cup Semifinals .75 .35
Bruins over
Blackhawks
❑ 215 Stanley Cup Finals .75 .35
Flyers over Bruins
❑ 216 Stanley Cup Champions 1.50 .70
❑ 217 Joe Watson .40 .18
❑ 218 Wayne Stephenson .75 .35
❑ 219 Maple Leaf Leaders 1.50 .70
Darryl Sittler
Norm Ullman
Paul Henderson
Denis Dupere
❑ 220 Bill Goldsworthy .75 .35
❑ 221 Don Marcotte .40 .18
❑ 222 Alex Delvecchio CO .40 .18
❑ 223 Stan Gilbertson .40 .18
❑ 224 Mike Murphy .40 .18
❑ 225 Jim Rutherford .75 .35
❑ 226 Phil Russell .40 .18
❑ 227 Lynn Powis .40 .18
❑ 228 Billy Harris .40 .18
❑ 229 Bob Pulford CO .75 .35
❑ 230 Ken Hodge .75 .35
❑ 231 Bill Fairbairn .40 .18
❑ 232 Guy Lafleur 12.00 5.50
❑ 233 Islanders Leaders 2.50 1.10
Billy Harris
Ralph Stewart
Denis Potvin
❑ 234 Fred Barrett .40 .18
❑ 235 Rogatien Vachon 2.50 1.10
❑ 236 Norm Ullman 1.50 .70
❑ 237 Garry Unger .75 .35
❑ 238 Jack Gordon CO .40 .18
❑ 239 Johnny Bucyk 1.50 .70
❑ 240 Bob Dailey .40 .18
❑ 241 Dave Burrows .40 .18
❑ 242 Len Frig .40 .18
❑ 243 Masterson Trophy 1.50 .70
Henri Richard
❑ 244 Hart Trophy 2.50 1.10
Phil Esposito
❑ 245 Byng Trophy 1.00 .45
Johnny Bucyk
❑ 246 Ross Trophy 2.50 1.10
Phil Esposito
❑ 247 Prince of Wales .75 .35
Trophy
❑ 248 Norris Trophy 12.00 5.50
Bobby Orr
❑ 249 Vezina Trophy 1.50 .70
Bernie Parent
❑ 250 Stanley Cup .75 .35
❑ 251 Smythe Trophy 1.50 .70
Bernie Parent
❑ 252 Calder Trophy 6.00 2.70
Denis Potvin
❑ 253 Campbell Trophy .75 .35
❑ 254 Pierre Bouchard .40 .18
❑ 255 Jude Drouin .40 .18
❑ 256 Capitals Emblem 1.00 .45
(Draft Selections
on back)
❑ 257 Michel Plasse .75 .35
❑ 258 Juha Widing .40 .18
❑ 259 Bryan Watson .40 .18
❑ 260 Bobby Clarke 8.00 3.60
❑ 261 Scotty Bowman CO 25.00 11.00
❑ 262 Craig Patrick .75 .35
❑ 263 Craig Cameron .40 .18
❑ 264 Ted Irvine 1.50 .35

## 1975-76 Topps

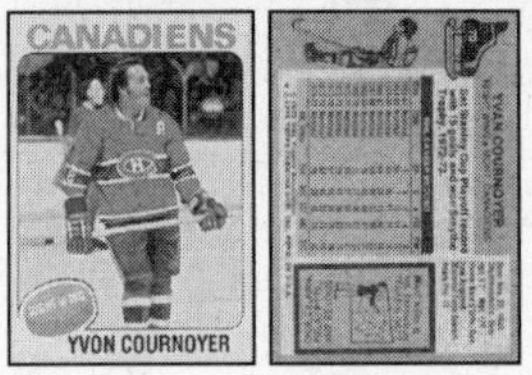


At 330 standard-size cards, the 1975-76 Topps set stands as the company's largest until 1990-91. Fronts feature team name at top and player name at the bottom. The player's position appears in a puck at the bottom. The backs contain year-by-year and NHL career records, a short biography and a cartoon-illustrated hockey fact or referee's signal with interpretation. For the first time, team cards (81-98) with team checklist on back appear in a Topps set. Rookie Cards include Clark Gillies, Ron Greschner, Pierre Larouche, Peter McNab and Mario Tremblay.

| | NRMT-MT | EXC |
|---|---|---|
| COMPLETE SET (330) | 150.00 | 70.00 |
| COMMON CARD (1-330) | .30 | .14 |

❑ 1 Stanley Cup Finals 1.50 .35
Philadelphia 4
Buffalo 2
❑ 2 Semi-Finals .50 .23
Philadelphia 4
N.Y. Islanders 3
❑ 3 Semi-Finals .50 .23
Buffalo 4
Montreal 2
❑ 4 Quarter Finals .50 .23
N.Y. Islanders 4
Pittsburgh 2
❑ 5 Quarter Finals .50 .23
Montreal 4
Vancouver 1
❑ 6 Quarter Finals .50 .23
Buffalo 4
Chicago 1
❑ 7 Quarter Finals .50 .23
Philadelphia 4
Toronto 0
❑ 8 Curt Bennett .30 .14
❑ 9 Johnny Bucyk 1.00 .45
❑ 10 Gilbert Perreault 3.00 1.35
❑ 11 Darryl Edestrand .30 .14
❑ 12 Ivan Boldirev .30 .14
❑ 13 Nick Libett .30 .14
❑ 14 Jim McElmury .30 .14
❑ 15 Frank St.Marseille .30 .14
❑ 16 Blake Dunlop .30 .14
❑ 17 Yvon Lambert .50 .23
❑ 18 Gerry Hart .30 .14
❑ 19 Steve Vickers .30 .14
❑ 20 Rick MacLeish .50 .23
❑ 21 Bob Paradise .30 .14
❑ 22 Red Berenson .50 .23
❑ 23 Lanny McDonald 4.00 1.80
❑ 24 Mike Robitaille .30 .14
❑ 25 Ron Low .50 .23
❑ 26 Bryan Hextall .30 .14
❑ 27 Carol Vadnais .30 .14
❑ 28 Jim Lorentz .30 .14
❑ 29 Gary Simmons .50 .23
❑ 30 Stan Mikita 3.00 1.35
❑ 31 Bryan Watson .30 .14
❑ 32 Guy Charron .30 .14
❑ 33 Bob Murdoch .30 .14
❑ 34 Norm Gratton .30 .14
❑ 35 Ken Dryden 15.00 6.75
❑ 36 Jean Potvin .30 .14
❑ 37 Rick Middleton 3.00 1.35
❑ 38 Ed Van Impe .30 .14
❑ 39 Rick Kehoe .50 .23
❑ 40 Garry Unger .50 .23
❑ 41 Ian Turnbull .50 .23
❑ 42 Dennis Ververgaert .30 .14
❑ 43 Mike Marson .30 .14
❑ 44 Randy Manery .30 .14
❑ 45 Gilles Gilbert .50 .23
❑ 46 Rene Robert .50 .23
❑ 47 Bob Stewart .30 .14
❑ 48 Pit Martin .30 .14
❑ 49 Danny Grant .50 .23
❑ 50 Peter Mahovlich .50 .23
❑ 51 Dennis Patterson .30 .14
❑ 52 Mike Murphy .30 .14
❑ 53 Dennis O'Brien .30 .14
❑ 54 Garry Howatt .30 .14
❑ 55 Ed Giacomin 1.50 .70
❑ 56 Andre Dupont .30 .14
❑ 57 Chuck Arnason .30 .14
❑ 58 Bob Gassoff .30 .14
❑ 59 Ron Ellis .50 .23
❑ 60 Andre Boudrias .30 .14
❑ 61 Yvon Labre .30 .14
❑ 62 Hilliard Graves .30 .14
❑ 63 Wayne Cashman .50 .23
❑ 64 Danny Gare 2.00 .90
❑ 65 Rick Hampton .30 .14
❑ 66 Darcy Rota .30 .14
❑ 67 Bill Hogaboam .30 .14
❑ 68 Dennis Herron .50 .23
❑ 69 Sheldon Kannegiesser .30 .14
❑ 70 Yvan Cournoyer UER 1.50 .70
(Misspelled Yvon
on card front)
❑ 71 Ernie Hicke .30 .14
❑ 72 Bert Marshall .30 .14
❑ 73 Derek Sanderson 2.00 .90
❑ 74 Tom Bladon .50 .23
❑ 75 Ron Schock .30 .14
❑ 76 Larry Sacharuk .30 .14
❑ 77 George Ferguson .30 .14
❑ 78 Ab DeMarco .30 .14
❑ 79 Tom Williams .30 .14
❑ 80 Phil Roberto .30 .14
❑ 81 Bruins Team 2.50 1.10
(Checklist back)
❑ 82 Seals Team 2.50 1.10
(Checklist back)
❑ 83 Sabres Team UER 2.50 1.10
(Gary Desjardins, sic;
checklist back)
❑ 84 Blackhawks Team UER 2.50 1.10
(Germain Gagnon, sic;
checklist back)
❑ 85 Flames Team 2.50 1.10
(Checklist back)
❑ 86 Kings Team 2.50 1.10
(Checklist back)
❑ 87 Red Wings Team 2.50 1.10
(Checklist back)
❑ 88 Scouts Team UER 2.50 1.10
(Dennis Dupere, sic;
checklist back)
❑ 89 North Stars Team 2.50 1.10
(Checklist back)
❑ 90 Canadiens Team 2.50 1.10
(Checklist back)
❑ 91 Maple Leafs Team 2.50 1.10
(Checklist back)
❑ 92 Islanders Team 2.50 1.10
(Checklist back)
❑ 93 Penguins Team 2.50 1.10
(Checklist back)
❑ 94 Rangers Team 2.50 1.10
(Checklist back)
❑ 95 Flyers Team UER 2.50 1.10
(Philadelphia mis-
spelled on card back;
checklist back)
❑ 96 Blues Team 2.50 1.10
(Checklist back)
❑ 97 Canucks Team UER 2.50 1.10
(242 Robitaille should
be 24 and 42 Ververgaert
not shown;
checklist back)
❑ 98 Capitals Team 2.50 1.10
(Checklist back)
❑ 99 Checklist 1-110 10.00 2.50
❑ 100 Bobby Orr 20.00 9.00
❑ 101 Germaine Gagnon UER .30 .14
(Misspelled Germain
on both sides)
❑ 102 Phil Russell .30 .14
❑ 103 Billy Lochead .30 .14
❑ 104 Robin Burns .30 .14
❑ 105 Gary Edwards .50 .23
❑ 106 Dwight Bialowas .30 .14
❑ 107 Doug Risebrough UER 2.00 .90
(Photo actually
Bob Gainey)
❑ 108 Dave Lewis .30 .14
❑ 109 Bill Fairbairn .30 .14
❑ 110 Ross Lonsberry .30 .14
❑ 111 Ron Stackhouse .30 .14
❑ 112 Claude Larose .30 .14
❑ 113 Don Luce .30 .14
❑ 114 Errol Thompson .30 .14
❑ 115 Gary Smith .50 .23
❑ 116 Jack Lynch .30 .14
❑ 117 Jacques Richard .30 .14
❑ 118 Dallas Smith .30 .14
❑ 119 Dave Gardner .30 .14
❑ 120 Mickey Redmond .50 .23
❑ 121 John Marks .30 .14
❑ 122 Dave Hudson .30 .14
❑ 123 Bob Nevin .30 .14
❑ 124 Fred Barrett .30 .14
❑ 125 Gerry Desjardins .50 .23
❑ 126 Guy Lafleur UER 10.00 4.50
(Listed as Defense
on card front)
❑ 127 Jean-Paul Parise .30 .14
❑ 128 Walt Tkaczuk .50 .23
❑ 129 Gary Dornhoefer .50 .23
❑ 130 Syl Apps .30 .14
❑ 131 Bob Plager .50 .23
❑ 132 Stan Weir .30 .14
❑ 133 Tracy Pratt .30 .14
❑ 134 Jack Egers .30 .14
❑ 135 Eric Vail .30 .14
❑ 136 Al Sims .30 .14
❑ 137 Larry Patey .30 .14
❑ 138 Jim Schoenfeld .50 .23
❑ 139 Cliff Koroll .30 .14
❑ 140 Marcel Dionne 4.00 1.80
❑ 141 Jean-Guy Lagace .30 .14
❑ 142 Juha Widing .30 .14
❑ 143 Lou Nanne .50 .23
❑ 144 Serge Savard .30 .14
❑ 145 Glenn Resch 3.00 1.35
❑ 146 Ron Greschner 2.00 .90
❑ 147 Dave Schultz .50 .23
❑ 148 Barry Wilkins .30 .14
❑ 149 Floyd Thomson .30 .14
❑ 150 Darryl Sittler 4.00 1.80
❑ 151 Paulin Bordeleau .30 .14
❑ 152 Ron Lalonde .30 .14
❑ 153 Larry Romanchych .30 .14
❑ 154 Larry Carriere .30 .14
❑ 155 Andre Savard .30 .14
❑ 156 Dave Hrechkosy .30 .14
❑ 157 Bill White .30 .14
❑ 158 Dave Kryskow .30 .14
❑ 159 Denis Dupere .30 .14
❑ 160 Rogatien Vachon 1.50 .70
❑ 161 Doug Rombough .30 .14
❑ 162 Murray Wilson .30 .14
❑ 163 Bob Bourne 1.50 .70
❑ 164 Gilles Marotte .30 .14
❑ 165 Vic Hadfield .50 .23
❑ 166 Reggie Leach .50 .23
❑ 167 Jerry Butler .30 .14
❑ 168 Inge Hammarstrom .30 .14
❑ 169 Chris Oddleifson .30 .14
❑ 170 Greg Joly .30 .14
❑ 171 Checklist 111-220 10.00 2.50
❑ 172 Pat Quinn .50 .23
❑ 173 Dave Forbes .30 .14
❑ 174 Len Frig .30 .14
❑ 175 Richard Martin .50 .23
❑ 176 Keith Magnuson .30 .14
❑ 177 Dan Maloney .30 .14
❑ 178 Craig Patrick .50 .23
❑ 179 Tom Williams .30 .14
❑ 180 Bill Goldsworthy .50 .23
❑ 181 Steve Shutt 3.00 1.35
❑ 182 Ralph Stewart .30 .14
❑ 183 John Davidson 3.00 1.35
❑ 184 Bob Kelly .30 .14
❑ 185 Ed Johnston .50 .23
❑ 186 Dave Burrows .30 .14
❑ 187 Dave Dunn .30 .14
❑ 188 Dennis Kearns .30 .14
❑ 189 Bill Clement 2.50 1.10
❑ 190 Gilles Meloche .50 .23
❑ 191 Bob Leiter .30 .14
❑ 192 Jerry Korab .30 .14
❑ 193 Joey Johnston .30 .14
❑ 194 Walt McKechnie .30 .14
❑ 195 Wilf Paiement .30 .14
❑ 196 Bob Berry .30 .14
❑ 197 Dean Talafous .30 .14
❑ 198 Guy Lapointe .50 .23
❑ 199 Clark Gillies 4.00 1.80
❑ 200 Phil Esposito 3.00 1.35
❑ 201 Greg Polis .30 .14
❑ 202 Jim Watson .50 .23
❑ 203 Gord McRae .50 .23
❑ 204 Lowell MacDonald .30 .14
❑ 205 Barclay Plager .50 .23
❑ 206 Don Lever .30 .14
❑ 207 Bill Mikkelson .30 .14
❑ 208 Goals Leaders 3.00 1.35
Phil Esposito
Guy Lafleur
Richard Martin
❑ 209 Assists Leaders 4.00 1.80
Bobby Clarke
Bobby Orr
Pete Mahovlich
❑ 210 Scoring Leaders 5.00 2.20
Bobby Orr
Phil Esposito
Marcel Dionne
❑ 211 Penalty Min. Leaders .50 .23
Dave Schultz
Andre Dupont
Phil Russell
❑ 212 Power Play 1.50 .70
Goal Leaders
Phil Esposito
Richard Martin
Danny Grant
❑ 213 Goals Against 5.00 2.20
Average Leaders
Bernie Parent
Rogatien Vachon
Ken Dryden
❑ 214 Barry Gibbs .30 .14
❑ 215 Ken Hodge .50 .23
❑ 216 Jocelyn Guevremont .30 .14
❑ 217 Warren Williams .30 .14
❑ 218 Dick Redmond .30 .14
❑ 219 Jim Rutherford .50 .23
❑ 220 Simon Nolet .30 .14
❑ 221 Butch Goring .50 .23
❑ 222 Glen Sather .30 .14
❑ 223 Mario Tremblay 2.50 1.10
❑ 224 Jude Drouin .30 .14
❑ 225 Rod Gilbert 1.00 .45
❑ 226 Bill Barber 2.50 1.10
❑ 227 Gary Inness .50 .23
❑ 228 Wayne Merrick .30 .14
❑ 229 Rod Seiling .30 .14
❑ 230 Tom Lysiak .50 .23
❑ 231 Bob Dailey .30 .14
❑ 232 Michel Belhumeur .50 .23
❑ 233 Bill Hajt .30 .14
❑ 234 Jim Pappin .30 .14
❑ 235 Gregg Sheppard .30 .14
❑ 236 Gary Bergman .30 .14
❑ 237 Randy Rota .30 .14
❑ 238 Neil Komadoski .30 .14
❑ 239 Craig Cameron .30 .14
❑ 240 Tony Esposito 3.00 1.3
❑ 241 Larry Robinson 6.00 2.7
❑ 242 Billy Harris .30 .1

❑ 243 Jean Ratelle 1.00 .45
❑ 244 Ted Irvine UER .30 .14
(Photo actually
Ted Harris)
❑ 245 Bob Neely .30 .14
❑ 246 Bobby Lalonde .30 .14
❑ 247 Ron Jones .30 .14
❑ 248 Rey Comeau .30 .14
❑ 249 Michel Plasse .50 .23
❑ 250 Bobby Clarke 6.00 2.70
❑ 251 Bobby Schmautz .30 .14
❑ 252 Peter McNab 2.50 1.10
❑ 253 Al MacAdam .30 .14
❑ 254 Dennis Hull .50 .23
❑ 255 Terry Harper .30 .14
❑ 256 Peter McDuffe .50 .23
❑ 257 Jean Hamel .30 .14
❑ 258 Jacques Lemaire 1.00 .45
❑ 259 Bob Nystrom .50 .23
❑ 260 Brad Park 2.00 .90
❑ 261 Cesare Maniago .50 .23
❑ 262 Don Saleski .30 .14
❑ 263 J. Bob Kelly .30 .14
❑ 264 Bob Hess .30 .14
❑ 265 Blaine Stoughton .50 .23
❑ 266 John Gould .30 .14
❑ 267 Checklist 221-330 10.00 2.50
❑ 268 Dan Bouchard .50 .23
❑ 269 Don Marcotte .30 .14
❑ 270 Jim Neilson .30 .14
❑ 271 Craig Ramsay .30 .14
❑ 272 Grant Mulvey .50 .23
❑ 273 Larry Giroux .30 .14
❑ 274 Real Lemieux .30 .14
❑ 275 Denis Potvin 6.00 2.70
❑ 276 Don Kozak .30 .14
❑ 277 Tom Reid .30 .14
❑ 278 Bob Gainey 4.00 1.80
❑ 279 Nick Beverley .30 .14
❑ 280 Jean Pronovost .50 .23
❑ 281 Joe Watson .30 .14
❑ 282 Chuck Lefley .30 .14
❑ 283 Borje Salming 5.00 2.20
❑ 284 Garnet Bailey .30 .14
❑ 285 Gregg Boddy .30 .14
❑ 286 Bobby Clarke AS1 3.00 1.35
❑ 287 Denis Potvin AS1 3.00 1.35
❑ 288 Bobby Orr AS1 10.00 4.50
❑ 289 Richard Martin AS1 .30 .14
❑ 290 Guy Lafleur AS1 4.00 1.80
❑ 291 Bernie Parent AS1 1.00 .45
❑ 292 Phil Esposito AS2 2.00 .90
❑ 293 Guy Lapointe AS2 .30 .14
❑ 294 Borje Salming AS2 2.50 1.10
❑ 295 Steve Vickers AS2 .30 .14
❑ 296 Rene Robert AS2 .30 .14
❑ 297 Rogatien Vachon AS2 1.00 .45
❑ 298 Buster Harvey .30 .14
❑ 299 Gary Sabourin .30 .14
❑ 300 Bernie Parent 2.50 1.10
❑ 301 Terry O'Reilly .50 .23
❑ 302 Ed Westfall .50 .23
❑ 303 Pete Stemkowski .30 .14
❑ 304 Pierre Bouchard .30 .14
❑ 305 Pierre Larouche 4.00 1.80
❑ 306 Lee Fogolin .30 .14
❑ 307 Gerry O'Flaherty .30 .14
❑ 308 Phil Myre .50 .23
❑ 309 Pierre Plante .30 .14
❑ 310 Dennis Hextall .30 .14
❑ 311 Jim McKenny .30 .14
❑ 312 Vic Venasky .30 .14
❑ 313 Flames Leaders .40 .18
Eric Vail
Tom Lysiak
Tom Lysiak
Tom Lysiak
❑ 314 Bruins Leaders 5.00 2.20
Phil Esposito
Bobby Orr
Phil Esposito
Johnny Bucyk
❑ 315 Sabres Leaders .40 .18
Richard Martin
Rene Robert
Rene Robert
Richard Martin
❑ 316 Seals Leaders .40 .18
Dave Hrechkosy
Larry Patey
Stan Weir
Stan Weir
Larry Patey
Dave Hrechkosy
❑ 317 Blackhawks Leaders .50 .23
Stan Mikita
Jim Pappin
Stan Mikita
Stan Mikita
Stan Mikita
❑ 318 Red Wings Leaders .40 .18
Danny Grant
Marcel Dionne
Marcel Dionne
Danny Grant
❑ 319 Scouts Leaders .40 .18
Simon Nolet
Wilf Paiement
Simon Nolet
Guy Charron
Simon Nolet
320 Kings Leaders .40 .18
Bob Nevin
Bob Nevin
Bob Nevin
Bob Nevin
Juha Widing
Bob Berry
❑ 321 North Stars Leaders .40 .18
Bill Goldsworthy
Dennis Hextall
Dennis Hextall
Bill Goldsworthy
❑ 322 Canadiens Leaders 1.50 .70
Guy Lafleur
Pete Mahovlich
Guy Lafleur
Guy Lafleur
❑ 323 Islanders Leaders 1.50 .70
Bob Nystrom
Denis Potvin
Denis Potvin
Clark Gillies
❑ 324 Rangers Leaders .50 .23
Steve Vickers
Steve Vickers
Rod Gilbert
Rod Gilbert
Jean Ratelle
❑ 325 Flyers Leaders 1.00 .45
Reggie Leach
Bobby Clarke
Bobby Clarke
Reggie Leach
❑ 326 Penguins Leaders .40 .18
Jean Pronovost
Ron Schock
Ron Schock
Jean Pronovost
❑ 327 Blues Leaders .40 .18
Garry Unger
Garry Unger
Garry Unger
Garry Unger
Larry Sacharuk
❑ 328 Maple Leafs Leaders 1.50 .70
Darryl Sittler
Darryl Sittler
Darryl Sittler
Darryl Sittler
❑ 329 Canucks Leaders .40 .18
Don Lever
Don Lever
Andre Boudrias
Andre Boudrias
❑ 330 Capitals Leaders .50 .12
Tommy Williams
Garnet Bailey
Tommy Williams
Garnet Bailey
Tommy Williams

## 1976-77 Topps

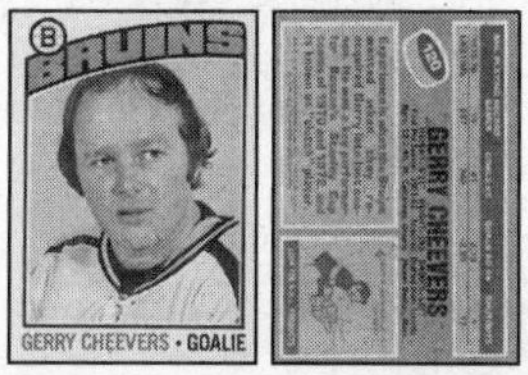


The 1976-77 Topps set contains 264 color standard-size cards. The fronts contain team name and logo at the top with player name and position at the bottom. The backs feature 1975-76 and career statistics, career highlights and a cartoon-illustrated fact. The first cards of Colorado Rockies (formerly Kansas City) players appear this year. Rookie Cards in this set include Bryan Trottier and Dennis Maruk.

| | NRMT-MT | EXC |
|---|---|---|
| COMPLETE SET (264) | 125.00 | 55.00 |
| COMMON CARD (1-264) | .25 | .11 |

❑ 1 Goals Leaders 2.00 .50
Reggie Leach
Guy Lafleur
Pierre Larouche
❑ 2 Assists Leaders 2.00 .90
Bobby Clarke
Peter Mahovlich
Guy Lafleur
Gilbert Perrault
Jean Ratelle
❑ 3 Scoring Leaders 2.00 .90
Guy Lafleur
Bobby Clarke
Gilbert Perrault
❑ 4 Penalty Min. Leaders .25 .11
Steve Durbano
Bryan Watson
Dave Schultz
❑ 5 Power Play Goals 2.00 .90
Leaders
Phil Esposito
Guy Lafleur
Richard Martin
Pierre Larouche
Denis Potvin
❑ 6 Goals Against 3.00 1.35
Average Leaders
Ken Dryden
Glenn Resch
Michel Larocque
❑ 7 Gary Doak .25 .11
❑ 8 Jacques Richard .25 .11
❑ 9 Wayne Dillon .25 .11
❑ 10 Bernie Parent 2.00 .90
❑ 11 Ed Westfall .40 .18
❑ 12 Dick Redmond .25 .11
❑ 13 Bryan Hextall .25 .11
❑ 14 Jean Pronovost .40 .18
❑ 15 Peter Mahovlich .40 .18
❑ 16 Danny Grant .40 .18
❑ 17 Phil Myre .40 .18
❑ 18 Wayne Merrick .25 .11
❑ 19 Steve Durbano .25 .11
❑ 20 Derek Sanderson 1.50 .70
❑ 21 Mike Murphy .25 .11
❑ 22 Borje Salming 2.50 1.10
❑ 23 Mike Walton .25 .11
❑ 24 Randy Manery .25 .11
❑ 25 Ken Hodge .40 .18
❑ 26 Mel Bridgman .75 .35
❑ 27 Jerry Korab .25 .11
❑ 28 Gilles Gratton .40 .18
❑ 29 Andre St.Laurent .25 .11
❑ 30 Yvan Cournoyer .75 .35
❑ 31 Phil Russell .25 .11
❑ 32 Dennis Hextall .25 .11
❑ 33 Lowell MacDonald .25 .11
❑ 34 Dennis O'Brien .25 .11
❑ 35 Gerry Meehan .25 .11
❑ 36 Gilles Meloche .40 .18
❑ 37 Wilf Paiement .40 .18
❑ 38 Bob MacMillan .75 .35
❑ 39 Ian Turnbull .40 .18
❑ 40 Rogatien Vachon .75 .35
❑ 41 Nick Beverley .25 .11
❑ 42 Rene Robert .40 .18
❑ 43 Andre Savard .25 .11
❑ 44 Bob Gainey 2.50 1.10
❑ 45 Joe Watson .25 .11
❑ 46 Billy Smith 2.50 1.10
❑ 47 Darcy Rota .25 .11
❑ 48 Rick Lapointe .25 .11
❑ 49 Pierre Jarry .25 .11
❑ 50 Syl Apps .25 .11
❑ 51 Eric Vail .25 .11
❑ 52 Greg Joly .25 .11
❑ 53 Don Lever .25 .11
❑ 54 Bob Murdoch .25 .11
Seals Right Wing
❑ 55 Denis Herron .40 .18
❑ 56 Mike Bloom .25 .11
❑ 57 Bill Fairbairn .25 .11
❑ 58 Fred Stanfield .25 .11
❑ 59 Steve Shutt 2.00 .90
❑ 60 Brad Park 1.50 .70
❑ 61 Gilles Villemure .40 .18
❑ 62 Bert Marshall .25 .11
❑ 63 Chuck Lefley .25 .11
❑ 64 Simon Nolet .25 .11
❑ 65 Reggie Leach RB .40 .18
Most Goals, Playoffs
❑ 66 Darryl Sittler RB .75 .35
Most Points, Game
❑ 67 Bryan Trottier RB 5.00 2.20
Most Points,
Season, Rookie
❑ 68 Garry Unger RB .40 .18
Most Consecutive
Games, Lifetime
❑ 69 Ron Low .40 .18
❑ 70 Bobby Clarke 4.00 1.80
❑ 71 Michel Bergeron .25 .11
❑ 72 Ron Stackhouse .25 .11
❑ 73 Bill Hogaboam .25 .11
❑ 74 Bob Murdoch .25 .11
Kings Defenseman
❑ 75 Steve Vickers .25 .11
❑ 76 Pit Martin .25 .11
❑ 77 Gerry Hart .25 .11
❑ 78 Craig Ramsay .25 .11
❑ 79 Michel Larocque .40 .18
❑ 80 Jean Ratelle .75 .35
❑ 81 Don Saleski .25 .11
❑ 82 Bill Clement .75 .35
❑ 83 Dave Burrows .25 .11
❑ 84 Wayne Thomas .40 .18
❑ 85 John Gould .25 .11
❑ 86 Dennis Maruk 2.00 .90
❑ 87 Ernie Hicke .25 .11
❑ 88 Jim Rutherford .40 .18
❑ 89 Dale Tallon .25 .11
❑ 90 Rod Gilbert .75 .35
❑ 91 Marcel Dionne 3.00 1.35
❑ 92 Chuck Arnason .25 .11
❑ 93 Jean Potvin .25 .11
❑ 94 Don Luce .25 .11
❑ 95 Johnny Bucyk .75 .35
❑ 96 Larry Goodenough .25 .11
❑ 97 Mario Tremblay .40 .18
❑ 98 Nelson Pyatt .25 .11
❑ 99 Brian Glennie .25 .11
❑ 100 Tony Esposito 2.00 .90
❑ 101 Dan Maloney .25 .11
❑ 102 Barry Wilkins .25 .11
❑ 103 Dean Talafous .25 .11
❑ 104 Ed Staniowski .25 .11
❑ 105 Dallas Smith .25 .11
❑ 106 Jude Drouin .25 .11
❑ 107 Pat Hickey .25 .11
❑ 108 Jocelyn Guevremont .25 .11
❑ 109 Doug Risebrough .75 .35
❑ 110 Reggie Leach .40 .18
❑ 111 Dan Bouchard .40 .18
❑ 112 Chris Oddleifson .25 .11
❑ 113 Rick Hampton .25 .11
❑ 114 John Marks .25 .11
❑ 115 Bryan Trottier 30.00 13.50
❑ 116 Checklist 1-132 6.00 1.50
❑ 117 Greg Polis .25 .11
❑ 118 Peter McNab .75 .35
❑ 119 Jim Roberts .25 .11
❑ 120 Gerry Cheevers 2.00 .90
❑ 121 Rick MacLeish .40 .18
❑ 122 Billy Lochead .25 .11
❑ 123 Tom Reid .25 .11
❑ 124 Rick Kehoe .40 .18
❑ 125 Keith Magnuson .25 .11
❑ 126 Clark Gillies .75 .35
❑ 127 Rick Middleton 2.00 .90
❑ 128 Bill Hajt .25 .11
❑ 129 Jacques Lemaire .75 .35
❑ 130 Terry O'Reilly .75 .35
❑ 131 Andre Dupont .25 .11
❑ 132 Flames Team 2.00 .90
(Checklist back)
❑ 133 Bruins Team 2.00 .90
(Checklist back)
❑ 134 Sabres Team 2.00 .90
(Checklist back)
❑ 135 Seals Team 2.00 .90
(Checklist back)
❑ 136 Blackhawks Team 2.00 .90
(Checklist back)
❑ 137 Red Wings Team 2.00 .90
(Checklist back)
❑ 138 Scouts Team 2.00 .90
(Checklist back)
❑ 139 Kings Team 2.00 .90
(Checklist back)
❑ 140 North Stars Team 2.00 .90
(Checklist back)
❑ 141 Canadiens Team 2.00 .90
(Checklist back)
❑ 142 Islanders Team 2.00 .90
(Checklist back)
❑ 143 Rangers Team 2.00 .90
(Checklist back)
❑ 144 Flyers Team 2.00 .90
(Checklist back)
❑ 145 Penguins Team 2.00 .90
(Checklist back)
❑ 146 Blues Team 2.00 .90
(Checklist back)
❑ 147 Maple Leafs Team 2.00 .90
(Checklist back)
❑ 148 Canucks Team 2.00 .90
(Checklist back)
❑ 149 Capitals Team 2.00 .90
(Checklist back)
❑ 150 Dave Schultz .75 .35
❑ 151 Larry Robinson 4.00 1.80
❑ 152 Al Smith .40 .18
❑ 153 Bob Nystrom .40 .18
❑ 154 Ron Greschner UER .25 .11
(Shown as Penguin on
front, should be Ranger)
❑ 155 Gregg Sheppard .25 .11
❑ 156 Alain Daigle .25 .11
❑ 157 Ed Van Impe .25 .11
❑ 158 Tim Young .40 .18
❑ 159 Gary Bergman .25 .11
❑ 160 Ed Giacomin 1.50 .70
❑ 161 Yvon Labre .25 .11
❑ 162 Jim Lorentz .25 .11
❑ 163 Guy Lafleur 6.00 2.70
❑ 164 Tom Bladon .40 .18
❑ 165 Wayne Cashman .40 .18
❑ 166 Pete Stemkowski .25 .11
❑ 167 Grant Mulvey .25 .11
❑ 168 Yves Belanger .40 .18
❑ 169 Bill Goldsworthy .40 .18
❑ 170 Denis Potvin 4.00 1.80
❑ 171 Nick Libett .25 .11
❑ 172 Michel Plasse .40 .18
❑ 173 Lou Nanne .25 .11
❑ 174 Tom Lysiak .40 .18
❑ 175 Dennis Ververgaert .25 .11
❑ 176 Gary Simmons .40 .18
❑ 177 Pierre Bouchard .25 .11
❑ 178 Bill Barber 1.50 .70
❑ 179 Darryl Edestrand .25 .11
❑ 180 Gilbert Perreault 2.00 .90
❑ 181 Dave Maloney .75 .35
❑ 182 Jean-Paul Parise .25 .11
❑ 183 Bobby Sheehan .25 .11
❑ 184 Pete Lopresti .40 .18
❑ 185 Don Kozak .25 .11
❑ 186 Guy Charron .25 .11
❑ 187 Stan Gilbertson .25 .11
❑ 188 Bill Nyrop .25 .11
❑ 189 Bobby Schmautz .25 .11
❑ 190 Wayne Stephenson .40 .18
❑ 191 Brian Spencer .25 .11
❑ 192 Gilles Marotte .25 .11
❑ 193 Lorne Henning .25 .11
❑ 194 Bob Neely .25 .11
❑ 195 Dennis Hull .40 .18
❑ 196 Walt McKechnie .25 .11
❑ 197 Curt Ridley .25 .11
❑ 198 Dwight Bialowas .25 .11
❑ 199 Pierre Larouche .75 .35
❑ 200 Ken Dryden 12.00 5.50
❑ 201 Ross Lonsberry .25 .11
❑ 202 Curt Bennett .25 .11
❑ 203 Hartland Monahan .25 .11
❑ 204 John Davidson 2.00 .90
❑ 205 Serge Savard .25 .11
❑ 206 Garry Howatt .25 .11
❑ 207 Darryl Sittler 3.00 1.35
❑ 208 J.P. Bordeleau .25 .11
❑ 209 Henry Boucha .25 .11
❑ 210 Richard Martin .40 .18
❑ 211 Vic Venasky .25 .11
❑ 212 Buster Harvey .25 .11
❑ 213 Bobby Orr 20.00 9.00
❑ 214 French Connection 2.00 .90
Richard Martin
Gilbert Perreault
Rene Robert
❑ 215 LCB Line 2.50 1.10
Reggie Leach
Bobby Clarke
Bill Barber
❑ 216 Long Island Lightning 3.00 1.35
Clark Gillies
Bryan Trottier
Billy Harris
❑ 217 Checking Line .75 .35
Bob Gainey
Doug Jarvis
Jim Roberts
❑ 218 Bicentennial Line .40 .18
Lowell MacDonald
Syl Apps
Jean Pronovost
❑ 219 Bob Kelly .25 .11
❑ 220 Walt Tkaczuk .40 .18
❑ 221 Dave Lewis .25 .11
❑ 222 Danny Gare .75 .35
❑ 223 Guy Lapointe .40 .18
❑ 224 Hank Nowak .25 .11
❑ 225 Stan Mikita 2.50 1.10
❑ 226 Vic Hadfield .40 .18
❑ 227 Bernie Wolfe .40 .18
❑ 228 Bryan Watson .25 .11
❑ 229 Ralph Stewart .25 .11
❑ 230 Gerry Desjardins .40 .18
❑ 231 John Bednarski .25 .11
❑ 232 Yvon Lambert .25 .11
❑ 233 Orest Kindrachuk .25 .11
❑ 234 Don Marcotte .25 .11
❑ 235 Bill White .25 .11
❑ 236 Red Berenson .40 .18
❑ 237 Al MacAdam .25 .11
❑ 238 Rick Blight .25 .11
❑ 239 Butch Goring .40 .18
❑ 240 Cesare Maniago .40 .18
❑ 241 Jim Schoenfeld .40 .18
❑ 242 Cliff Koroll .25 .11
❑ 243 Mickey Redmond .40 .18
❑ 244 Rick Chartraw .25 .11
❑ 245 Phil Esposito 2.50 1.10
❑ 246 Dave Forbes .25 .11
❑ 247 Joe Watson .25 .11
❑ 248 Ron Schock .25 .11
❑ 249 Fred Barrett .25 .11
❑ 250 Glenn Resch 2.00 .90
❑ 251 Ivan Boldirev .25 .11
❑ 252 Billy Harris .25 .11
❑ 253 Lee Fogolin .25 .11
❑ 254 Murray Wilson .25 .11
❑ 255 Gilles Gilbert .40 .18
❑ 256 Gary Dornhoefer .40 .18
❑ 257 Carol Vadnais .25 .11
❑ 258 Checklist 133-264 6.00 1.50
❑ 259 Errol Thompson .25 .11
❑ 260 Garry Unger .40 .18
❑ 261 J. Bob Kelly .25 .11
❑ 262 Terry Harper .25 .11
❑ 263 Blake Dunlop .25 .11
❑ 264 Stanley Cup Champs 1.50 .35

## 1976-77 Topps Glossy Inserts

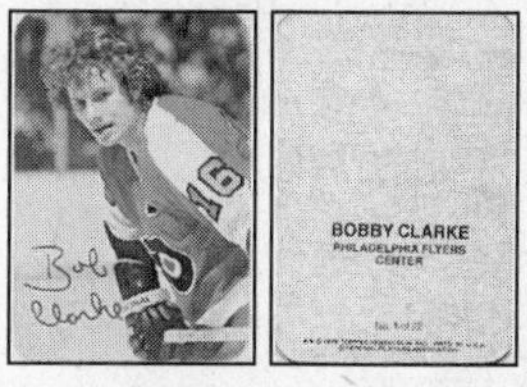


This 22-card insert set was issued with the 1976-77 Topps hockey card set but not with the O-Pee-Chee hockey cards unlike the glossy insert produced "jointly" by Topps and O-Pee-Chee the next year. This set is very similar to (but much more difficult to find than) the glossy insert set of the following year. The cards were printed in the United States. These rounded-corner cards are approximately 2 1/4" by 3 1/4".

| | NRMT-MT | EXC |
|---|---|---|
| COMPLETE SET (22) | 80.00 | 36.00 |
| COMMON CARD (1-22) | 1.00 | .45 |

❑ 1 Bobby Clarke 4.00 1.80
❑ 2 Brad Park 2.50 1.10
❑ 3 Tony Esposito 3.00 1.35
❑ 4 Marcel Dionne 4.00 1.80
❑ 5 Ken Dryden 15.00 6.75
❑ 6 Glenn Resch 2.00 .90
❑ 7 Phil Esposito 5.00 2.20
❑ 8 Darryl Sittler 3.00 1.35
❑ 9 Gilbert Perreault 2.00 .90
❑ 10 Denis Potvin 4.00 1.80
❑ 11 Guy Lafleur 8.00 3.60
❑ 12 Bill Barber 2.00 .90
❑ 13 Syl Apps 1.00 .45
❑ 14 Johnny Bucyk 2.00 .90
❑ 15 Bryan Trottier 15.00 6.75
❑ 16 Dennis Hull 1.00 .45
❑ 17 Guy Lapointe 1.50 .70
❑ 18 Rod Gilbert 2.50 1.10

❑ 19 Richard Martin 1.50 .70
❑ 20 Bobby Orr 25.00 11.00
❑ 21 Reggie Leach 1.50 .70
❑ 22 Jean Ratelle 2.50 1.10

## 1977-78 Topps

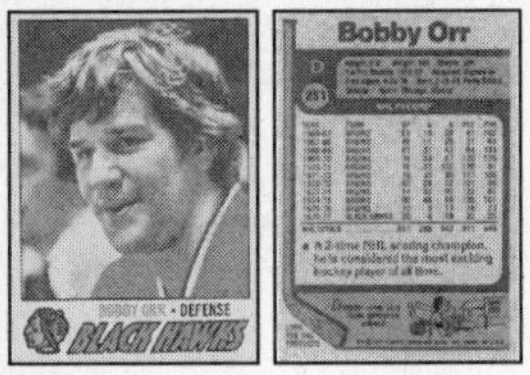


The 1977-78 Topps set consists of 264 standard-size cards. Cards 203 (Stan Gilbertson) and 255 (Bill Fairbairn) differ from those of O-Pee-Chee. Card fronts have team name and logo, player name and position at the bottom. Yearly statistics including minor league numbers are featured on the back along with a short biography and a cartoon-illustrated fact about the player. After the initial print run, Topps changed the photos on card numbers 131, 138, 149 and 152. Two of the changes (138 and 149) were necessary corrections. Rookie Cards include Mike Milbury and Mike Palmateer. This set marks Bobby Orr's last Topps appearance.

| | NRMT-MT | EXC |
|---|---|---|
| COMPLETE SET (264) | 90.00 | 40.00 |
| COMMON CARD (1-264) | .20 | .09 |

❑ 1 Goals Leaders 2.50 .60
Steve Shutt
Guy Lafleur
Marcel Dionne
❑ 2 Assists Leaders 1.50 .70
Guy Lafleur
Marcel Dionne
Larry Robinson
Borje Salming
Tim Young
❑ 3 Scoring Leaders 2.00 .90
Guy Lafleur
Marcel Dionne
Steve Shutt
❑ 4 Penalty Min. Leaders .35 .16
Dave(Tiger) Williams
Dennis Polonich
Bob Gassoff
❑ 5 Power Play Goals .75 .35
Leaders
Lanny McDonald
Phil Esposito
Tom Williams
❑ 6 Goals Against 2.50 1.10
Average Leaders
Michel Larocque
Ken Dryden
Glenn Resch
❑ 7 Game Winning 1.50 .70
Goals Leaders
Gilbert Perreault
Steve Shutt
Guy Lafleur
Rick MacLeish
Peter McNab
❑ 8 Shutouts Leaders 3.00 1.35
Ken Dryden
Rogatien Vachon
Bernie Parent
Dunc Wilson
❑ 9 Brian Spencer .20 .09
❑ 10 Denis Potvin AS2 2.50 1.10
❑ 11 Nick Fotiu .75 .35
❑ 12 Bob Murray .20 .09
❑ 13 Pete Lopresti .35 .16
❑ 14 J. Bob Kelly .20 .09
❑ 15 Rick MacLeish .75 .35
❑ 16 Terry Harper .20 .09
❑ 17 Willi Plett .75 .35
❑ 18 Peter McNab .35 .16
❑ 19 Wayne Thomas .35 .16
❑ 20 Pierre Bouchard .20 .09
❑ 21 Dennis Maruk .75 .35
❑ 22 Mike Murphy .20 .09
❑ 23 Cesare Maniago .35 .16
❑ 24 Paul Gardner .20 .09
❑ 25 Rod Gilbert .75 .35
❑ 26 Orest Kindrachuk .20 .09
❑ 27 Bill Hajt .20 .09
❑ 28 John Davidson .75 .35
❑ 29 Jean-Paul Parise .20 .09
❑ 30 Larry Robinson AS1 3.00 1.35
❑ 31 Yvon Labre .20 .09
❑ 32 Walt McKechnie .20 .09
❑ 33 Rick Kehoe .35 .16
❑ 34 Randy Holt .20 .09
❑ 35 Garry Unger .35 .16
❑ 36 Lou Nanne .20 .09
❑ 37 Dan Bouchard .35 .16
❑ 38 Darryl Sittler 2.00 .90
❑ 39 Bob Murdoch .20 .09
❑ 40 Jean Ratelle .75 .35
❑ 41 Dave Maloney .20 .09
❑ 42 Danny Gare .75 .35
❑ 43 Jim Watson .20 .09
❑ 44 Tom Williams .20 .09
❑ 45 Serge Savard .20 .09
❑ 46 Derek Sanderson .75 .35
❑ 47 John Marks .20 .09
❑ 48 Al Cameron .20 .09
❑ 49 Dean Talafous .20 .09
❑ 50 Glenn Resch .75 .35
❑ 51 Ron Schock .20 .09
❑ 52 Gary Croteau .20 .09
❑ 53 Gerry Meehan .20 .09
❑ 54 Ed Staniowski .20 .09
❑ 55 Phil Esposito 2.00 .90
❑ 56 Dennis Ververgaert .20 .09
❑ 57 Rick Wilson .20 .09
❑ 58 Jim Lorentz .20 .09
❑ 59 Bobby Schmautz .20 .09
❑ 60 Guy Lapointe AS2 .35 .16
❑ 61 Ivan Boldirev .20 .09
❑ 62 Bob Nystrom .20 .09
❑ 63 Rick Hampton .20 .09
❑ 64 Jack Valiquette .20 .09
❑ 65 Bernie Parent 1.50 .70
❑ 66 Dave Burrows .20 .09
❑ 67 Butch Goring .35 .16
❑ 68 Checklist 1-132 4.00 1.00
❑ 69 Murray Wilson .20 .09
❑ 70 Ed Giacomin .75 .35
❑ 71 Flames Team 1.25 .55
(checklist back)
❑ 72 Bruins Team 1.25 .55
(checklist back)
❑ 73 Sabres Team 1.25 .55
(checklist back)
❑ 74 Blackhawks Team 1.25 .55
(checklist back)
❑ 75 Barons Team 1.25 .55
(checklist back)
❑ 76 Rockies Team 1.25 .55
(checklist back)
❑ 77 Red Wings Team 1.25 .55
(checklist back)
❑ 78 Kings Team 1.25 .55
(checklist back)
❑ 79 North Stars Team 1.25 .55
(checklist back)
❑ 80 Canadiens Team 1.25 .55
(checklist back)
❑ 81 Islanders Team 1.25 .55
(checklist back)
❑ 82 Rangers Team 1.25 .55
(checklist back)
❑ 83 Flyers Team 1.25 .55
(checklist back)
❑ 84 Penguins Team 1.25 .55
(checklist back)
❑ 85 Blues Team 1.25 .55
(checklist back)
❑ 86 Maple Leafs Team 1.25 .55
(checklist back)
❑ 87 Canucks Team 1.25 .55
(checklist back)
❑ 88 Capitals Team 1.25 .55
(checklist back)
❑ 89 Keith Magnuson .20 .09
❑ 90 Walt Tkaczuk .35 .16
❑ 91 Bill Nyrop .20 .09
❑ 92 Michel Plasse .35 .16
❑ 93 Bob Bourne .35 .16
❑ 94 Lee Fogolin .20 .09
❑ 95 Gregg Sheppard .20 .09
❑ 96 Hartland Monahan .20 .09
❑ 97 Curt Bennett .20 .09
❑ 98 Bob Dailey .20 .09
❑ 99 Bill Goldsworthy .35 .16
❑ 100 Ken Dryden AS1 8.00 3.60
❑ 101 Grant Mulvey .20 .09
❑ 102 Pierre Larouche .75 .35
❑ 103 Nick Libett .20 .09
❑ 104 Rick Smith .20 .09
❑ 105 Bryan Trottier 8.00 3.60
❑ 106 Pierre Jarry .20 .09
❑ 107 Red Berenson .35 .16
❑ 108 Jim Schoenfeld .35 .16
❑ 109 Gilles Meloche .35 .16
❑ 110 Lanny McDonald AS2 1.50 .70
❑ 111 Don Lever .20 .09
❑ 112 Greg Polis .20 .09
❑ 113 Gary Sargent .20 .09
❑ 114 Earl Anderson .20 .09
❑ 115 Bobby Clarke 3.00 1.35
❑ 116 Dave Lewis .20 .09
❑ 117 Darcy Rota .20 .09
❑ 118 Andre Savard .20 .09
❑ 119 Denis Herron .35 .16
❑ 120 Steve Shutt AS1 .75 .35
❑ 121 Mel Bridgman .20 .09
❑ 122 Buster Harvey .20 .09
❑ 123 Roland Eriksson .20 .09
❑ 124 Dale Tallon .20 .09
❑ 125 Gilles Gilbert .35 .16
❑ 126 Billy Harris .20 .09
❑ 127 Tom Lysiak .35 .16
❑ 128 Jerry Korab .20 .09
❑ 129 Bob Gainey 1.50 .70
❑ 130 Wilf Paiement .35 .16
❑ 131A Tom Bladon 2.00 .90
(Standing)
❑ 131B Tom Bladon .20 .09
(Crouched for face off)
❑ 132 Ernie Hicke .20 .09
❑ 133 J.P. LeBlanc .20 .09
❑ 134 Mike Milbury 5.00 2.20
❑ 135 Pit Martin .20 .09
❑ 136 Steve Vickers .20 .09
❑ 137 Don Awrey .20 .09
❑ 138A Bernie Wolfe ERR 2.00 .90
(Photo actually
Al MacAdam looking
straight ahead)
❑ 138B Bernie Wolfe COR .20 .09
❑ 139 Doug Jarvis .75 .35
❑ 140 Borje Salming AS1 1.50 .70
❑ 141 Bob MacMillan .20 .09
❑ 142 Wayne Stephenson .35 .16
❑ 143 Dave Forbes .20 .09
❑ 144 Jean Potvin .20 .09
❑ 145 Guy Charron .20 .09
❑ 146 Cliff Koroll .20 .09
❑ 147 Danny Grant .35 .16
❑ 148 Bill Hogaboam UER .20 .09
(Photo actually
Michel Bergeron)
❑ 149A Al MacAdam ERR 2.00 .90
(Photo actually
Bernie Wolfe,
looking left)
❑ 149B Al MacAdam COR .20 .09
❑ 150 Gerry Desjardins .35 .16
❑ 151 Yvon Lambert .20 .09
❑ 152A Rick Lapointe 2.00 .90
(Shooting, facing right,
without mustache)
❑ 152B Rick Lapointe .20 .09
(With mustache)
❑ 153 Ed Westfall .35 .16
❑ 154 Carol Vadnais .20 .09
❑ 155 Johnny Bucyk .75 .35
❑ 156 J.P. Bordeleau .20 .09
❑ 157 Ron Stackhouse .20 .09
❑ 158 Glen Sharpley .20 .09
❑ 159 Michel Bergeron .20 .09
❑ 160 Rogatien Vachon AS2 .75 .35
❑ 161 Fred Stanfield .20 .09
❑ 162 Gerry Hart .20 .09
❑ 163 Mario Tremblay .35 .16
❑ 164 Andre Dupont .20 .09
❑ 165 Don Marcotte .20 .09
❑ 166 Wayne Dillon .20 .09
❑ 167 Claude Larose .20 .09
❑ 168 Eric Vail .20 .09
❑ 169 Tom Edur .20 .09
❑ 170 Tony Esposito 1.50 .70
❑ 171 Andre St.Laurent .20 .09
❑ 172 Dan Maloney .20 .09
❑ 173 Dennis O'Brien .20 .09
❑ 174 Blair Chapman .20 .09
❑ 175 Dennis Kearns .20 .09
❑ 176 Wayne Merrick .20 .09
❑ 177 Michel Larocque .35 .16
❑ 178 Bob Kelly .20 .09
❑ 179 Dave Farrish .20 .09
❑ 180 Richard Martin AS2 .75 .35
❑ 181 Gary Doak .20 .09
❑ 182 Jude Drouin .20 .09
❑ 183 Barry Dean .20 .09
❑ 184 Gary Smith .35 .16
❑ 185 Reggie Leach .75 .35
❑ 186 Ian Turnbull .35 .16
❑ 187 Vic Venasky .20 .09
❑ 188 Wayne Bianchin .20 .09
❑ 189 Doug Risebrough .35 .16
❑ 190 Brad Park .75 .35
❑ 191 Craig Ramsay .20 .09
❑ 192 Ken Hodge .35 .16
❑ 193 Phil Myre .35 .16
❑ 194 Garry Howatt .20 .09
❑ 195 Stan Mikita 2.00 .90
❑ 196 Garnet Bailey .20 .09
❑ 197 Dennis Hextall .20 .09
❑ 198 Nick Beverley .20 .09
❑ 199 Larry Patey .20 .09
❑ 200 Guy Lafleur AS1 5.00 2.20
❑ 201 Don Edwards 2.00 .90
❑ 202 Gary Dornhoefer .35 .16
❑ 203 Stan Gilbertson .20 .09
❑ 204 Alex Pirus .20 .09
❑ 205 Peter Mahovlich .35 .16
❑ 206 Bert Marshall .20 .09
❑ 207 Gilles Gratton .35 .16
❑ 208 Alain Daigle .20 .09
❑ 209 Chris Oddleifson .20 .09
❑ 210 Gilbert Perreault AS2 1.50 .70
❑ 211 Mike Palmateer 4.00 1.80
❑ 212 Billy Lochead .20 .09
❑ 213 Dick Redmond .20 .09
❑ 214 Guy Lafleur RB 1.50 .70
Most Points,
RW, Season
❑ 215 Ian Turnbull RB .20 .09
Most Goals,
Defenseman, Game
❑ 216 Guy Lafleur RB 1.50 .70
Longest Point
Scoring Streak
❑ 217 Steve Shutt RB .75 .35
Most Goals,
LW, Season
❑ 218 Guy Lafleur RB 1.50 .70
Most Assists,
RW, Season
❑ 219 Lorne Henning .20 .09
❑ 220 Terry O'Reilly .75 .35
❑ 221 Pat Hickey .20 .09
❑ 222 Rene Robert .35 .16
❑ 223 Tim Young .20 .09
❑ 224 Dunc Wilson .35 .16
❑ 225 Dennis Hull .35 .16
❑ 226 Rod Seiling .20 .09
❑ 227 Bill Barber .75 .35
❑ 228 Dennis Polonich .20 .09
❑ 229 Billy Smith 1.50 .70
❑ 230 Yvan Cournoyer .75 .35
❑ 231 Don Luce .20 .09
❑ 232 Mike McEwen .20 .09
❑ 233 Don Saleski .20 .09
❑ 234 Wayne Cashman .75 .35
❑ 235 Phil Russell .20 .09
❑ 236 Mike Corrigan .20 .09
❑ 237 Guy Chouinard .35 .16
❑ 238 Steve Jensen .20 .09
❑ 239 Jim Rutherford .35 .16
❑ 240 Marcel Dionne AS1 2.50 1.10
❑ 241 Rejean Houle .20 .09
❑ 242 Jocelyn Guevremont .20 .09
❑ 243 Jim Harrison .20 .09
❑ 244 Don Murdoch .20 .09
❑ 245 Rick Green .75 .35
❑ 246 Rick Middleton .75 .35
❑ 247 Joe Watson .20 .09
❑ 248 Syl Apps .20 .09
❑ 249 Checklist 133-264 4.00 1.00
❑ 250 Clark Gillies .75 .35
❑ 251 Bobby Orr 15.00 6.75
❑ 252 Nelson Pyatt .20 .09
❑ 253 Gary McAdam .20 .09
❑ 254 Jacques Lemaire .75 .35
❑ 255 Bill Fairbairn .20 .09
❑ 256 Ron Greschner .35 .16
❑ 257 Ross Lonsberry .20 .09
❑ 258 Dave Gardner .20 .09
❑ 259 Rick Blight .20 .09
❑ 260 Gerry Cheevers .75 .35
❑ 261 Jean Pronovost .35 .16
❑ 262 Semi-Finals .35 .16
Canadiens Skate
Past Islanders
❑ 263 Semi-Finals .35 .16
Bruins Advance
to Finals
❑ 264 Finals .75 .19
Canadiens Win
20th Stanley Cup

## 1977-78 Topps/O-Pee-Chee Glossy

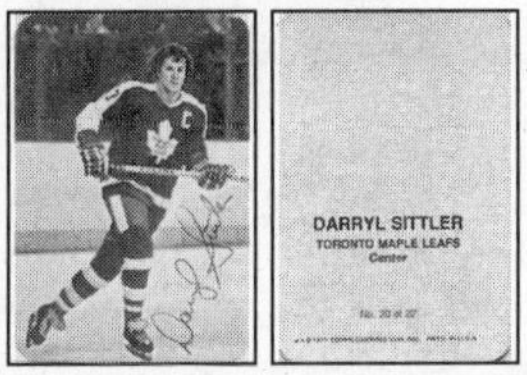


This set of 22 numbered cards was issued with either square or round corners as an insert with both the Topps and O-Pee-Chee hockey cards of 1977-78. Cards were numbered on the back and measure 2 1/4" by 3 1/4". They are essentially the same as the O-Pee-Chee insert issue of the same year. The O-Pee-Chee inserts have the same card numbers and pictures, same values, but different copyright lines on the reverses. The cards are priced below for the round cornered version; the square cornered cards are worth approximately 10 percent more than the the prices below.

| | NRMT-MT | EXC |
|---|---|---|
| COMPLETE SET (22) | 15.00 | 6.75 |
| COMMON CARD (1-22) | .25 | .11 |

❑ 1 Wayne Cashman .40 .18
❑ 2 Gerry Cheevers 1.50 .70
❑ 3 Bobby Clarke 1.50 .70
❑ 4 Marcel Dionne 1.50 .70
❑ 5 Ken Dryden 4.00 1.80
❑ 6 Clark Gillies .40 .18
❑ 7 Guy Lafleur 2.50 1.10
❑ 8 Reggie Leach .35 .16
❑ 9 Rick MacLeish .50 .23
❑ 10 Dave Maloney .25 .11
❑ 11 Richard Martin .40 .18
❑ 12 Don Murdoch .25 .11
❑ 13 Brad Park .75 .35
❑ 14 Gilbert Perreault 1.00 .45
❑ 15 Denis Potvin 1.50 .70
❑ 16 Jean Ratelle .75 .35
❑ 17 Glenn Resch .75 .35
❑ 18 Larry Robinson 1.50 .70
❑ 19 Steve Shutt .75 .35
❑ 20 Darryl Sittler 1.25 .55
❑ 21 Rogatien Vachon .75 .35
❑ 22 Tim Young .25 .11

## 1978-79 Topps

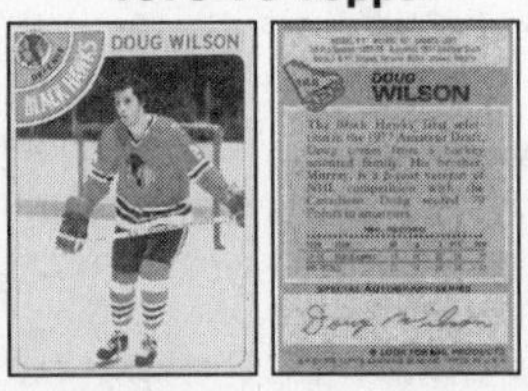


The 1978-79 Topps set consists of 264 standard-size cards. Card fronts have team name, logo and player position in the top left corner. The player's name is within the top border. A short biography, yearly statistics including minor leagues and a facsimile autograph are included on the back. The key Rookie Cards in this set are Mike Bossy, Bernie Federko, and Doug Wilson.

| | NRMT-MT | EXC |
|---|---|---|
| COMPLETE SET (264) | 60.00 | 27.00 |
| COMMON CARD (1-264) | .15 | .07 |

❑ 1 Mike Bossy HL 5.00 1.25
Goals by Rookie
❑ 2 Phil Esposito HL 1.00 .45
29th Hat Trick
❑ 3 Guy Lafleur HL 1.00 .45
Scores Against
Every Team
❑ 4 Darryl Sittler HL .60 .25
Goals In Nine
Straight Games
❑ 5 Garry Unger HL .20 .09
803 Consecutive Games
❑ 6 Gary Edwards .25 .11
❑ 7 Rick Blight .15 .07
❑ 8 Larry Patey .15 .07
❑ 9 Craig Ramsay .15 .07
❑ 10 Bryan Trottier AS1 5.00 2.20
❑ 11 Don Murdoch .15 .07
❑ 12 Phil Russell .15 .07
❑ 13 Doug Jarvis .25 .11
❑ 14 Gene Carr .15 .07
❑ 15 Bernie Parent 1.00 .45
❑ 16 Perry Miller .15 .07
❑ 17 Kent-Erik Andersson .15 .07
❑ 18 Gregg Sheppard .15 .07
❑ 19 Dennis Owchar .15 .07
❑ 20 Rogatien Vachon .60 .25
❑ 21 Dan Maloney .15 .07
❑ 22 Guy Charron .15 .07
❑ 23 Dick Redmond .15 .07
❑ 24 Checklist 1-132 2.50 .60
❑ 25 Anders Hedberg .25 .11
❑ 26 Mel Bridgman .25 .11
❑ 27 Lee Fogolin .15 .07
❑ 28 Gilles Meloche .25 .11
❑ 29 Garry Howatt .15 .07
❑ 30 Darryl Sittler AS2 1.50 .70
❑ 31 Curt Bennett .15 .07
❑ 32 Andre St.Laurent .15 .07
❑ 33 Blair Chapman .15 .07
❑ 34 Keith Magnuson .15 .07
❑ 35 Pierre Larouche .60 .25
❑ 36 Michel Plasse .25 .11
❑ 37 Gary Sargent .15 .07
❑ 38 Mike Walton .15 .07
❑ 39 Robert Picard .15 .07
❑ 40 Terry O'Reilly AS2 .25 .11
❑ 41 Dave Farrish .15 .07
❑ 42 Gary McAdam .15 .07
❑ 43 Joe Watson .15 .07
❑ 44 Yves Belanger .25 .11
❑ 45 Steve Jensen .15 .07
❑ 46 Bob Stewart .15 .07
❑ 47 Darcy Rota .15 .07
❑ 48 Dennis Hextall .15 .07
❑ 49 Bert Marshall .15 .07
❑ 50 Ken Dryden AS1 6.00 2.70
❑ 51 Peter Mahovlich .25 .11
❑ 52 Dennis Ververgaert .15 .07
❑ 53 Inge Hammarstrom .15 .07
❑ 54 Doug Favell .25 .11
❑ 55 Steve Vickers .15 .07
❑ 56 Syl Apps .15 .07
❑ 57 Errol Thompson .15 .07
❑ 58 Don Luce .15 .07
❑ 59 Mike Milbury .60 .25
❑ 60 Yvan Cournoyer .60 .25
❑ 61 Kirk Bowman .15 .07
❑ 62 Billy Smith .60 .25
❑ 63 Goal Leaders 2.50 1.10
Guy Lafleur
Mike Bossy
Steve Shutt
❑ 64 Assist Leaders 1.50 .70
Bryan Trottier
Guy Lafleur
Darryl Sittler
❑ 65 Scoring Leaders 1.50 .70
Guy Lafleur
Bryan Trottier
Darryl Sittler
❑ 66 Penalty Minutes .30 .14
Leaders
Dave Schultz
Dave(Tiger) Williams
Dennis Polonich
❑ 67 Power Play Goal 2.00 .90
Leaders
Mike Bossy
Phil Esposito
Steve Shutt
❑ 68 Goals Against 2.50 1.10
Average Leaders
Ken Dryden
Bernie Parent
Gilles Gilbert
❑ 69 Game Winning 1.25 .55
Goal Leaders
Guy Lafleur
Bill Barber
Darryl Sittler
Bob Bourne
❑ 70 Shutout Leaders 2.50 1.10
Bernie Parent
Ken Dryden
Don Edwards
Tony Esposito
Mike Palmateer

❑ 71 Bob Kelly .15 .07
❑ 72 Ron Stackhouse .15 .07
❑ 73 Wayne Dillon .15 .07
❑ 74 Jim Rutherford .25 .11
❑ 75 Stan Mikita 1.50 .70
❑ 76 Bob Gainey 1.00 .45
❑ 77 Gerry Hart .15 .07
❑ 78 Lanny McDonald 1.00 .45
❑ 79 Brad Park 1.00 .45
❑ 80 Richard Martin .60 .25
❑ 81 Bernie Wolfe .25 .11
❑ 82 Bob MacMillan .15 .07
❑ 83 Brad Maxwell .15 .07
❑ 84 Mike Fidler .15 .07
❑ 85 Carol Vadnais .15 .07
❑ 86 Don Lever .15 .07
❑ 87 Phil Myre .25 .11
❑ 88 Paul Gardner .15 .07
❑ 89 Bob Murray .15 .07
❑ 90 Guy Lafleur AS1 4.00 1.80
❑ 91 Bob Murdoch .15 .07
❑ 92 Ron Ellis .25 .11
❑ 93 Jude Drouin .15 .07
❑ 94 Jocelyn Guevremont .15 .07
❑ 95 Gilles Gilbert .25 .11
❑ 96 Bob Sirois .15 .07
❑ 97 Tom Lysiak .25 .11
❑ 98 Andre Dupont .15 .07
❑ 99 Per-Olov Brasar .15 .07
❑ 100 Phil Esposito 2.00 .90
❑ 101 J.P. Bordeleau .15 .07
❑ 102 Pierre Mondou .60 .25
❑ 103 Wayne Bianchin .15 .07
❑ 104 Dennis O'Brien .15 .07
❑ 105 Glenn Resch .60 .25
❑ 106 Dennis Polonich .15 .07
❑ 107 Kris Manery .15 .07
❑ 108 Bill Hajt .15 .07
❑ 109 Jere Gillis .15 .07
❑ 110 Garry Unger .25 .11
❑ 111 Nick Beverley .15 .07
❑ 112 Pat Hickey .15 .07
❑ 113 Rick Middleton .60 .25
❑ 114 Orest Kindrachuk .15 .07
❑ 115 Mike Bossy 30.00 13.50
❑ 116 Pierre Bouchard .15 .07
❑ 117 Alain Daigle .15 .07
❑ 118 Terry Martin .15 .07
❑ 119 Tom Edur .15 .07
❑ 120 Marcel Dionne 2.00 .90
❑ 121 Barry Beck 1.00 .45
❑ 122 Billy Lochead .15 .07
❑ 123 Paul Harrison .25 .11
❑ 124 Wayne Cashman .60 .25
❑ 125 Rick MacLeish .60 .25
❑ 126 Bob Bourne .25 .11
❑ 127 Ian Turnbull .15 .07
❑ 128 Gerry Meehan .15 .07
❑ 129 Eric Vail .15 .07
❑ 130 Gilbert Perreault .60 .25
❑ 131 Bob Dailey .15 .07
❑ 132 Dale McCourt .60 .25
❑ 133 John Wensink .60 .25
❑ 134 Bill Nyrop .15 .07
❑ 135 Ivan Boldirev .15 .07
❑ 136 Lucien DeBlois .15 .07
❑ 137 Brian Spencer .15 .07
❑ 138 Tim Young .15 .07
❑ 139 Ron Sedlbauer .15 .07
❑ 140 Gerry Cheevers 1.00 .45
❑ 141 Dennis Maruk .25 .11
❑ 142 Barry Dean .15 .07
❑ 143 Bernie Federko 6.00 2.70
❑ 144 Stefan Persson .15 .07
❑ 145 Wilf Paiement .25 .11
❑ 146 Dale Tallon .15 .07
❑ 147 Yvon Lambert .15 .07
❑ 148 Greg Joly .15 .07
❑ 149 Dean Talafous .15 .07
❑ 150 Don Edwards AS2 .15 .07
❑ 151 Butch Goring .25 .11
❑ 152 Tom Bladon .15 .07
❑ 153 Bob Nystrom .15 .07
❑ 154 Ron Greschner .25 .11
❑ 155 Jean Ratelle .60 .25
❑ 156 Russ Anderson .15 .07
❑ 157 John Marks .15 .07
❑ 158 Michel Larocque .25 .11
❑ 159 Paul Woods .15 .07
❑ 160 Mike Palmateer .25 .11
❑ 161 Jim Lorentz .15 .07
❑ 162 Dave Lewis .15 .07
❑ 163 Harvey Bennett .15 .07
❑ 164 Rick Smith .15 .07
❑ 165 Reggie Leach .60 .25
❑ 166 Wayne Thomas .25 .11
❑ 167 Dave Forbes .15 .07
❑ 168 Doug Wilson 6.00 2.70
❑ 169 Dan Bouchard .25 .11
❑ 170 Steve Shutt AS2 .60 .25
❑ 171 Mike Kaszycki .15 .07
❑ 172 Denis Herron .25 .11
❑ 173 Rick Bowness .25 .11
❑ 174 Rick Hampton .15 .07
❑ 175 Glen Sharpley .15 .07
❑ 176 Bill Barber .60 .25
❑ 177 Ron Duguay 2.00 .90
❑ 178 Jim Schoenfeld .25 .11
❑ 179 Pierre Plante .15 .07
❑ 180 Jacques Lemaire .60 .25
❑ 181 Stan Jonathan .15 .07
❑ 182 Billy Harris .15 .07
❑ 183 Chris Oddleifson .15 .07
❑ 184 Jean Pronovost .25 .11
❑ 185 Fred Barrett .15 .07
❑ 186 Ross Lonsberry .15 .07
❑ 187 Mike McEwen .15 .07
❑ 188 Rene Robert .25 .11
❑ 189 J. Bob Kelly .15 .07
❑ 190 Serge Savard AS2 .25 .11
❑ 191 Dennis Kearns .15 .07
❑ 192 Flames Team .50 .23
(checklist back)
❑ 193 Bruins Team .50 .23
(checklist back)
❑ 194 Sabres Team .50 .23
(checklist back)
❑ 195 Blackhawks Team .50 .23
(checklist back)
❑ 196 Rockies Team .50 .23
(checklist back)
❑ 197 Red Wings Team .50 .23
(checklist back)
❑ 198 Kings Team .50 .23
(checklist back)
❑ 199 North Stars Team .50 .23
(checklist back)
❑ 200 Canadiens Team .50 .23
(checklist back)
❑ 201 Islanders Team .50 .23
(checklist back)
❑ 202 Rangers Team .50 .23
(checklist back)
❑ 203 Flyers Team .50 .23
(checklist back)
❑ 204 Penguins Team .50 .23
(checklist back)
❑ 205 Blues Team .50 .23
(checklist back)
❑ 206 Maple Leafs Team .50 .23
(checklist back)
❑ 207 Canucks Team .50 .23
(checklist back)
❑ 208 Capitals Team .50 .23
(checklist back)
❑ 209 Danny Gare .25 .11
❑ 210 Larry Robinson AS1 1.50 .70
❑ 211 John Davidson .60 .25
❑ 212 Peter McNab .25 .11
❑ 213 Rick Kehoe .25 .11
❑ 214 Terry Harper .15 .07
❑ 215 Bobby Clarke 2.00 .90
❑ 216 Bryan Maxwell UER .15 .07
(Photo actually
Brad Maxwell)
❑ 217 Ted Bulley .15 .07
❑ 218 Red Berenson .25 .11
❑ 219 Ron Grahame .25 .11
❑ 220 Clark Gillies AS1 .25 .11
❑ 221 Dave Maloney .15 .07
❑ 222 Derek Smith .15 .07
❑ 223 Wayne Stephenson .25 .11
❑ 224 John Van Boxmeer .15 .07
❑ 225 Dave Schultz .25 .11
❑ 226 Reed Larson .60 .25
❑ 227 Rejean Houle .15 .07
❑ 228 Doug Hicks .15 .07
❑ 229 Mike Murphy .15 .07
❑ 230 Pete Lopresti .25 .11
❑ 231 Jerry Korab .15 .07
❑ 232 Ed Westfall .25 .11
❑ 233 Greg Malone .15 .07
❑ 234 Paul Holmgren .60 .25
❑ 235 Walt Tkaczuk .25 .11
❑ 236 Don Marcotte .15 .07
❑ 237 Ron Low .25 .11
❑ 238 Rick Chartraw .15 .07
❑ 239 Cliff Koroll .15 .07
❑ 240 Borje Salming AS1 1.00 .45
❑ 241 Roland Eriksson .15 .07
❑ 242 Ric Seiling .15 .07
❑ 243 Jim Bedard .25 .11
❑ 244 Peter Lee .25 .11
❑ 245 Denis Potvin AS2 1.50 .70
❑ 246 Greg Polis .15 .07
❑ 247 Jim Watson .15 .07
❑ 248 Bobby Schmautz .15 .07
❑ 249 Doug Risebrough .25 .11
❑ 250 Tony Esposito 1.25 .55
❑ 251 Nick Libett .15 .07
❑ 252 Ron Zanussi .15 .07
❑ 253 Andre Savard .15 .07
❑ 254 Dave Burrows .15 .07
❑ 255 Ulf Nilsson .60 .25
❑ 256 Richard Mulhern .15 .07
❑ 257 Don Saleski .15 .07
❑ 258 Wayne Merrick .15 .07
❑ 259 Checklist 133-264 2.50 .60
❑ 260 Guy Lapointe .25 .11
❑ 261 Grant Mulvey .15 .07
❑ 262 Stanley Cup: Semis .30 .14
Canadiens sweep
Maple Leafs
❑ 263 Stanley Cup: Semis .30 .14
Bruins skate
past Flyers
❑ 264 Stanley Cup: Finals 1.00 .25
Canadiens win 3rd
Straight Cup

## 1978-79 Topps Team Inserts

This set of 17 team inserts measures the standard size. Each team insert consists of two decals: a team logo and a second decal consisting of three mini-decals. The mini-decals picture hockey equipment (mask, stick(s), or puck), a hockey word (center, defense, goal!, goalie, score! or wing), and a number between zero and nine. The backs are blank. Several different combinations of the stickers are known to exist.

| | NRMT-MT | EXC |
|---|---|---|
| COMPLETE SET (17) | 15.00 | 6.75 |
| COMMON CARD (1-17) | 1.00 | .45 |

❑ 1 Atlanta Flames 1.50 .70
❑ 2 Boston Bruins 1.50 .70
❑ 3 Buffalo Sabres 1.00 .45
❑ 4 Chicago Blackhawks 1.50 .70
❑ 5 Colorado Rockies 1.50 .70
❑ 6 Detroit Red Wings 1.50 .70
❑ 7 Los Angeles Kings 1.00 .45
❑ 8 Minnesota North Stars 1.00 .45
❑ 9 Montreal Canadiens 1.50 .70
❑ 10 New York Islanders 1.00 .45
❑ 11 New York Rangers 1.50 .70
❑ 12 Philadelphia Flyers 1.00 .45
❑ 13 Pittsburgh Penguins 1.00 .45
❑ 14 St. Louis Blues 1.00 .45
❑ 15 Toronto Maple Leafs 1.50 .70
❑ 16 Vancouver Canucks 1.00 .45
❑ 17 Washington Capitals 1.00 .45

## 1979-80 Topps

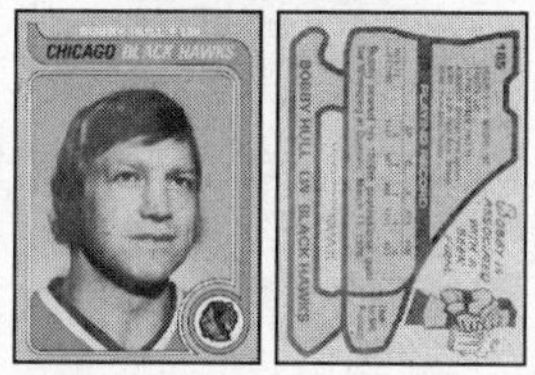

The 1979-80 Topps set consists of 264 standard-size cards. Card numbers 81 and 82 (Stanley Cup Playoffs), 163 (Ulf Nilsson RB) and 261 (NHL Entries) differ from those of O-Pee-Chee. Unopened packs consist of ten cards plus a piece of bubble gum. The fronts contain a blue border that is prone to chipping. The player's name, team and position are at the top with team logo at the bottom. Career and 1978-79 statistics, short biography and a cartoon-illustrated fact about the player appear on the back. Included in this set are players from the four remaining WHA franchises that were absorbed by the NHL. The franchises are the Edmonton Oilers, Hartford Whalers, Quebec Nordiques and Winnipeg Jets. The set features the Rookie Card of Wayne Gretzky and the last cards of a Hall of Fame crop including Gordie Howe, Bobby Hull, Ken Dryden and Stan Mikita. In additon to Gretzky, Rookie Cards include Ken Linseman, Charlie Simmer, Bobby Smith, and John Tonelli.

| | NRMT-MT | EXC |
|---|---|---|
| COMPLETE SET (264) | 600.00 | 275.00 |
| COMMON CARD (1-264) | .35 | .16 |

❑ 1 Goal Leaders 2.50 1.10
Mike Bossy
Marcel Dionne
Guy Lafleur
❑ 2 Assist Leaders 1.50 .70
Bryan Trottier
Guy Lafleur
Marcel Dionne
Bob MacMillan
❑ 3 Scoring Leaders 1.50 .70
Bryan Trottier
Marcel Dionne
Guy Lafleur
❑ 4 Penalty Minutes .40 .18
Leaders
Dave(Tiger) Williams
Randy Holt
Dave Schultz
❑ 5 Power Play 1.50 .70
Goal Leaders
Mike Bossy
Marcel Dionne
Paul Gardner
Lanny McDonald
❑ 6 Goals Against 2.50 1.10
Average Leaders
Ken Dryden
Glenn Resch
Bernie Parent
❑ 7 Game Winning 2.00 .90
Goals Leaders
Guy Lafleur
Mike Bossy
Bryan Trottier
Jean Pronovost
Ted Bulley
❑ 8A Shutout Leaders ERR 8.00 3.60
Ken Dryden
Tony Esposito
Mario Lessard
Mike Palmateer
Bernie Parent
(Palmateer and Lessard
photos switched)
❑ 8B Shutout Leaders COR 3.00 1.35
Ken Dryden
Tony Esposito
Mario Lessard
Mike Palmateer
Bernie Parent
❑ 9 Greg Malone .35 .16
❑ 10 Rick Middleton .60 .25
❑ 11 Greg Smith .35 .16
❑ 12 Rene Robert .60 .25
❑ 13 Doug Risebrough .60 .25
❑ 14 Bob Kelly .35 .16
❑ 15 Walt Tkaczuk .60 .25
❑ 16 John Marks .35 .16
❑ 17 Willie Huber .35 .16
❑ 18 Wayne Gretzky UER 500.00 220.00
(Games played should
be 80, not 60)
❑ 19 Ron Sedlbauer .35 .16
❑ 20 Glenn Resch AS2 .60 .25
❑ 21 Blair Chapman .35 .16
❑ 22 Ron Zanussi .35 .16
❑ 23 Brad Park .60 .25
❑ 24 Yvon Lambert .35 .16
❑ 25 Andre Savard .35 .16
❑ 26 Jim Watson .35 .16
❑ 27 Hal Philipoff .35 .16
❑ 28 Dan Bouchard .60 .25
❑ 29 Bob Sirois .35 .16
❑ 30 Ulf Nilsson .60 .25
❑ 31 Mike Murphy .35 .16
❑ 32 Stefan Persson .35 .16
❑ 33 Garry Unger .60 .25
❑ 34 Rejean Houle .35 .16
❑ 35 Barry Beck .60 .25
❑ 36 Tim Young .35 .16
❑ 37 Rick Dudley .35 .16
❑ 38 Wayne Stephenson .60 .25
❑ 39 Peter McNab .60 .25
❑ 40 Borje Salming AS2 .60 .25
❑ 41 Tom Lysiak .35 .16
❑ 42 Don Maloney 1.00 .45
❑ 43 Mike Rogers .60 .25
❑ 44 Dave Lewis .35 .16
❑ 45 Peter Lee .35 .16
❑ 46 Marty Howe .60 .25
❑ 47 Serge Bernier .35 .16
❑ 48 Paul Woods .35 .16
❑ 49 Bob Sauve .60 .25
❑ 50 Larry Robinson AS1 1.50 .70
❑ 51 Tom Gorence .35 .16
❑ 52 Gary Sargent .35 .16
❑ 53 Thomas Gradin 1.00 .45
❑ 54 Dean Talafous .35 .16
❑ 55 Bob Murray .35 .16
❑ 56 Bob Bourne .60 .25
❑ 57 Larry Patey .35 .16
❑ 58 Ross Lonsberry .35 .16
❑ 59 Rick Smith .35 .16
❑ 60 Guy Chouinard .60 .25
❑ 61 Danny Gare .60 .25
❑ 62 Jim Bedard .60 .25
❑ 63 Dale McCourt .35 .16
❑ 64 Steve Payne .35 .16
❑ 65 Pat Hughes .35 .16
❑ 66 Mike McEwen .35 .16
❑ 67 Reg Kerr .35 .16
❑ 68 Walt McKechnie .35 .16
❑ 69 Michel Plasse .60 .25
❑ 70 Denis Potvin AS1 1.25 .55
❑ 71 Dave Dryden .60 .25
❑ 72 Gary McAdam .35 .16
❑ 73 Andre St.Laurent .35 .16
❑ 74 Jerry Korab .35 .16
❑ 75 Rick MacLeish 1.00 .45
❑ 76 Dennis Kearns .35 .16
❑ 77 Jean Pronovost .60 .25
❑ 78 Ron Greschner .60 .25
❑ 79 Wayne Cashman 1.00 .45
❑ 80 Tony Esposito 1.25 .55
❑ 81 Cup Semi-Finals .40 .18
Canadiens squeak
past Bruins
❑ 82 Cup Semi-Finals .40 .18
Rangers upset
Islanders in Six
❑ 83 Stanley Cup Finals 1.00 .45
Canadiens Make It
Four Straight Cups
❑ 84 Brian Sutter 2.00 .90
❑ 85 Gerry Cheevers 1.00 .45
❑ 86 Pat Hickey .35 .16
❑ 87 Mike Kaszycki .35 .16
❑ 88 Grant Mulvey .35 .16
❑ 89 Derek Smith .35 .16
❑ 90 Steve Shutt 1.00 .45
❑ 91 Robert Picard .35 .16
❑ 92 Dan Labraaten .35 .16
❑ 93 Glen Sharpley .35 .16
❑ 94 Denis Herron .60 .25
❑ 95 Reggie Leach 1.00 .45
❑ 96 John Van Boxmeer .35 .16
❑ 97 Dave(Tiger) Williams .60 .25
❑ 98 Butch Goring .60 .25
❑ 99 Don Marcotte .35 .16
❑ 100 Bryan Trottier AS1 2.50 1.10
❑ 101 Serge Savard AS2 .60 .25
❑ 102 Cliff Koroll .35 .16
❑ 103 Gary Smith .60 .25
❑ 104 Al MacAdam .35 .16
❑ 105 Don Edwards .60 .25
❑ 106 Errol Thompson .35 .16
❑ 107 Andre Lacroix .60 .25
❑ 108 Marc Tardif .60 .25
❑ 109 Rick Kehoe .60 .25
❑ 110 John Davidson .60 .25
❑ 111 Behn Wilson .35 .16
❑ 112 Doug Jarvis .60 .25
❑ 113 Tom Rowe .35 .16
❑ 114 Mike Milbury .60 .25
❑ 115 Billy Harris .35 .16
❑ 116 Greg Fox .35 .16
❑ 117 Curt Fraser .35 .16
❑ 118 Jean-Paul Parise .35 .16
❑ 119 Ric Seiling .35 .16
❑ 120 Darryl Sittler 1.00 .45
❑ 121 Rick Lapointe .35 .16
❑ 122 Jim Rutherford .60 .25
❑ 123 Mario Tremblay .60 .25
❑ 124 Randy Carlyle 1.00 .45
❑ 125 Bobby Clarke 1.50 .70
❑ 126 Wayne Thomas .60 .25
❑ 127 Ivan Boldirev .35 .16
❑ 128 Ted Bulley .35 .16
❑ 129 Dick Redmond .35 .16
❑ 130 Clark Gillies AS1 .60 .25
❑ 131 Checklist 1-132 4.00 1.80
❑ 132 Vaclav Nedomansky .35 .16
❑ 133 Richard Mulhern .35 .16
❑ 134 Dave Schultz .60 .25
❑ 135 Guy Lapointe .60 .25
❑ 136 Gilles Meloche .60 .25
❑ 137 Randy Pierce UER .35 .16
(Photo actually
Ron Delorme)
❑ 138 Cam Connor .35 .16
❑ 139 George Ferguson .35 .16
❑ 140 Bill Barber .60 .25
❑ 141 Mike Walton .35 .16
❑ 142 Wayne Babych .35 .16
❑ 143 Phil Russell .35 .16
❑ 144 Bobby Schmautz .35 .16
❑ 145 Carol Vadnais .35 .16
❑ 146 John Tonelli 4.00 1.80
❑ 147 Peter Marsh .35 .16
❑ 148 Thommie Bergman .35 .16
❑ 149 Richard Martin 1.00 .45
❑ 150 Ken Dryden AS1 5.00 2.20
❑ 151 Kris Manery .35 .16
❑ 152 Guy Charron .35 .16
❑ 153 Lanny McDonald .60 .25
❑ 154 Ron Stackhouse .35 .16
❑ 155 Stan Mikita 1.50 .70
❑ 156 Paul Holmgren .60 .25
❑ 157 Perry Miller .35 .16
❑ 158 Gary Croteau .35 .16
❑ 159 Dave Maloney .35 .16
❑ 160 Marcel Dionne AS2 2.00 .90
❑ 161 Mike Bossy RB 2.00 .90
Most Goals,
RW Season
❑ 162 Don Maloney RB .40 .18
Rookie Most Points,
Playoff Series
❑ 163 Ulf Nilsson RB .40 .18
Highest Scoring
Percentage, Season
❑ 164 Brad Park RB .40 .18
Most Career Playoff
Goals, Defenseman
❑ 165 Bryan Trottier RB 1.00 .45
Most Points, Period
❑ 166 Al Hill .35 .16
❑ 167 Gary Bromley .60 .25
❑ 168 Don Murdoch .35 .16
❑ 169 Wayne Merrick .35 .16
❑ 170 Bob Gainey 1.00 .45
❑ 171 Jim Schoenfeld .60 .25
❑ 172 Gregg Sheppard .35 .16
❑ 173 Dan Bolduc .35 .16
❑ 174 Blake Dunlop .35 .16
❑ 175 Gordie Howe 20.00 9.00
❑ 176 Richard Brodeur .60 .25
❑ 177 Tom Younghans .35 .16
❑ 178 Andre Dupont .35 .16
❑ 179 Ed Johnstone .35 .16
❑ 180 Gilbert Perreault 1.00 .45
❑ 181 Bob Lorimer .35 .16
❑ 182 John Wensink .35 .16
❑ 183 Lee Fogolin .35 .16
❑ 184 Greg Carroll .35 .16
❑ 185 Bobby Hull 15.00 6.75
❑ 186 Harold Snepsts .35 .16
❑ 187 Peter Mahovlich .60 .25
❑ 188 Eric Vail .35 .16
❑ 189 Phil Myre .60 .25
❑ 190 Wilf Paiement .60 .25
❑ 191 Charlie Simmer 4.00 1.80
❑ 192 Per-Olov Brasar .35 .16
❑ 193 Lorne Henning .35 .16
❑ 194 Don Luce .35 .16
❑ 195 Steve Vickers .35 .16
❑ 196 Bob Miller .35 .16
❑ 197 Mike Palmateer .60 .25
❑ 198 Nick Libett .35 .16
❑ 199 Pat Ribble .35 .16
❑ 200 Guy Lafleur AS1 3.00 1.35
❑ 201 Mel Bridgman .60 .25
❑ 202 Morris Lukowich .35 .16
❑ 203 Don Lever .35 .16
❑ 204 Tom Bladon .35 .16
❑ 205 Garry Howatt .35 .16
❑ 206 Bobby Smith 4.00 1.80
❑ 207 Craig Ramsay .60 .25
❑ 208 Ron Duguay .60 .25
❑ 209 Gilles Gilbert .60 .25
❑ 210 Bob MacMillan .35 .16
❑ 211 Pierre Mondou .35 .16
❑ 212 J.P. Bordeleau .35 .16
❑ 213 Reed Larson .60 .25
❑ 214 Dennis Ververgaert .35 .16
❑ 215 Bernie Federko 3.00 1.35
❑ 216 Mark Howe 2.00 .90
❑ 217 Bob Nystrom .35 .16
❑ 218 Orest Kindrachuk .35 .16
❑ 219 Mike Fidler .35 .16
❑ 220 Phil Esposito 1.00 .45
❑ 221 Bill Hajt .35 .16
❑ 222 Mark Napier .60 .25

❑ 223 Dennis Maruk .60 .25
❑ 224 Dennis Polonich .35 .16
❑ 225 Jean Ratelle .60 .25
❑ 226 Bob Dailey .35 .16
❑ 227 Alain Daigle .35 .16
❑ 228 Ian Turnbull .35 .16
❑ 229 Jack Valiquette .35 .16
❑ 230 Mike Bossy AS2 8.00 3.60
❑ 231 Brad Maxwell .35 .16
❑ 232 Dave Taylor 5.00 2.20
❑ 233 Pierre Larouche 1.00 .45
❑ 234 Rod Schutt .35 .16
❑ 235 Rogatien Vachon .60 .25
❑ 236 Ryan Walter 1.00 .45
❑ 237 Checklist 133-264 4.00 1.80
❑ 238 Terry O'Reilly .60 .25
❑ 239 Real Cloutier .60 .25
❑ 240 Anders Hedberg .60 .25
❑ 241 Ken Linseman 2.50 1.10
❑ 242 Billy Smith .60 .25
❑ 243 Rick Chartraw .35 .16
❑ 244 Flames Team 1.50 .70
(checklist back)
❑ 245 Bruins Team 1.50 .70
(checklist back)
❑ 246 Sabres Team 1.50 .70
(checklist back)
❑ 247 Blackhawks Team 1.50 .70
(checklist back)
❑ 248 Rockies Team 1.50 .70
(checklist back)
❑ 249 Red Wings Team 1.50 .70
(checklist back)
❑ 250 Kings Team 1.50 .70
(checklist back)
❑ 251 North Stars Team 1.50 .70
(checklist back)
❑ 252 Canadiens Team 1.50 .70
(checklist back)
❑ 253 Islanders Team 1.50 .70
(checklist back)
❑ 254 Rangers Team 1.50 .70
(checklist back)
❑ 255 Flyers Team 1.50 .70
(checklist back)
❑ 256 Penguins Team 1.50 .70
(checklist back)
❑ 257 Blues Team 1.50 .70
(checklist back)
❑ 258 Maple Leafs Team 1.50 .70
(checklist back)
❑ 259 Canucks Team 1.50 .70
(checklist back)
❑ 260 Capitals Team 1.50 .70
(checklist back)
❑ 261 New NHL Entries 12.00 5.50
(checklist back)
❑ 262 Jean Hamel .35 .16
❑ 263 Stan Jonathan .35 .16
❑ 264 Russ Anderson 1.00 .45

## 1979-80 Topps Team Inserts

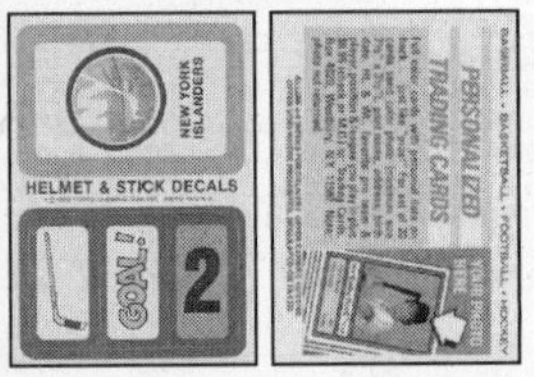

This set of 21 team inserts measures the standard size, 2 1/2" by 3 1/2". They were issued one per wax pack. Each team insert consists of two decals: a team logo decal, and a second decal that is subdivided into three mini-decals. The three mini-decals picture a pair of hockey sticks, a hockey word (goal, wing, score, defense), and a one-digit number. The horizontally oriented back has an offer for personalized trading cards which expires as of 12/31/80.

| | NRMT-MT | EXC |
|---|---|---|
| COMPLETE SET (21) | 18.00 | 8.00 |
| COMMON CARD (1-21) | 1.00 | .45 |

❑ 1 Atlanta Flames 1.50 .70
❑ 2 Boston Bruins 1.50 .70
❑ 3 Buffalo Sabres 1.00 .45
❑ 4 Chicago Blackhawks 1.50 .70
❑ 5 Colorado Rockies 1.50 .70
❑ 6 Detroit Red Wings 1.50 .70
❑ 7 Edmonton Oilers 1.50 .70
❑ 8 Hartford Whalers 1.00 .45
❑ 9 Los Angeles Kings 1.00 .45
❑ 10 Minnesota North Stars 1.00 .45
❑ 11 Montreal Canadiens 1.50 .70
❑ 12 New York Islanders 1.00 .45
❑ 13 New York Rangers 1.50 .70
❑ 14 Philadelphia Flyers 1.00 .45
❑ 15 Pittsburgh Penguins UER 1.50 .70
(Triangle in Penguins logo is upside down)
❑ 16 Quebec Nordiques 1.50 .70
❑ 17 St. Louis Blues 1.00 .45
❑ 18 Toronto Maple Leafs 1.50 .70
❑ 19 Vancouver Canucks 1.00 .45
❑ 20 Washington Capitals 1.00 .45
❑ 21 Winnipeg Jets 1.00 .45

## 1980-81 Topps

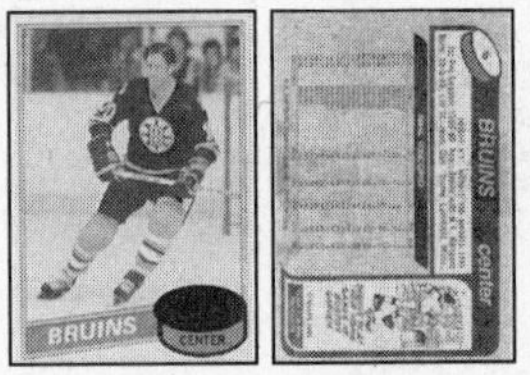

The 1980-81 Topps set features 264 standard-size cards. The fronts contain a puck (black ink) at the bottom right which can be scratched-off to reveal the player's name. Cards that have been scratched are considered to be, at best, half the value of the Mint price below. Yearly statistics including minor leagues, a short biography and a cartoon-illustrated hockey fact are included on the back. Members of the U.S. Olympic team are designated by USA. Rookie Cards in this set include Ray Bourque, Dave Christian, Mike Foligno, Mike Gartner, Michel Goulet, Mike Liut, Kent Nilsson, Brian Propp, Rob Ramage and Rick Vaive.

| | NRMT-MT | EXC |
|---|---|---|
| COMPLETE SET (264) | 275.00 | 125.00 |
| COMMON CARD (1-264) | .20 | .09 |

❑ 1 Phila. Flyers RB .75 .35
35 Game Streak, Longest in Sports History
❑ 2 Ray Bourque RB 6.00 2.70
65 Pts.; Record for Rookie Defenseman
❑ 3 Wayne Gretzky RB 20.00 9.00
Youngest Ever, 50-goal Scorer
❑ 4 Charlie Simmer RB .30 .14
Scores in 13th Straight Game, NHL Record
❑ 5 Billy Smith RB .30 .14
First Goalie to Score a Goal
❑ 6 Jean Ratelle .40 .18
❑ 7 Dave Maloney .20 .09
❑ 8 Phil Myre .40 .18
❑ 9 Ken Morrow USA 1.00 .45
❑ 10 Guy Lafleur 2.00 .90
❑ 11 Bill Derlago .20 .09
❑ 12 Doug Wilson .75 .35
❑ 13 Craig Ramsay .20 .09
❑ 14 Pat Boutette .20 .09
❑ 15 Eric Vail .20 .09
❑ 16 Mike Foligno .40 .18
Red Wings Scoring Leaders
(checklist back)
❑ 17 Bobby Smith 1.25 .55
❑ 18 Rick Kehoe .40 .18
❑ 19 Joel Quenneville .20 .09
❑ 20 Marcel Dionne 1.00 .45
❑ 21 Kevin McCarthy .20 .09
❑ 22 Jim Craig USA 1.00 .45
❑ 23 Steve Vickers .20 .09
❑ 24 Ken Linseman .40 .18
❑ 25 Mike Bossy 4.00 1.80
❑ 26 Serge Savard .40 .18
❑ 27 Grant Mulvey .40 .18
Blackhawks Scoring Leaders
(checklist back)
❑ 28 Pat Hickey .20 .09
❑ 29 Peter Sullivan .20 .09
❑ 30 Blaine Stoughton .40 .18
❑ 31 Mike Liut 4.00 1.80
❑ 32 Blair MacDonald .20 .09
❑ 33 Rick Green .20 .09
❑ 34 Al MacAdam .20 .09
❑ 35 Robbie Ftorek .20 .09
❑ 36 Dick Redmond .20 .09
❑ 37 Ron Duguay .20 .09
❑ 38 Danny Gare .40 .18
Sabres Scoring Leaders
(checklist back)
❑ 39 Brian Propp 4.00 1.80
❑ 40 Bryan Trottier 1.50 .70
❑ 41 Rich Preston .20 .09
❑ 42 Pierre Mondou .20 .09
❑ 43 Reed Larson .20 .09
❑ 44 George Ferguson .20 .09
❑ 45 Guy Chouinard .40 .18
❑ 46 Billy Harris .20 .09
❑ 47 Gilles Meloche .40 .18
❑ 48 Blair Chapman .20 .09
❑ 49 Mike Gartner 4.00 1.80
Capitals Scoring Leaders
(checklist back)
❑ 50 Darryl Sittler .75 .35
❑ 51 Richard Martin .40 .18
❑ 52 Ivan Boldirev .20 .09
❑ 53 Craig Norwich .20 .09
❑ 54 Dennis Polonich .20 .09
❑ 55 Bobby Clarke 1.00 .45
❑ 56 Terry O'Reilly .40 .18
❑ 57 Carol Vadnais .20 .09
❑ 58 Bob Gainey .75 .35
❑ 59 Blaine Stoughton .40 .18
Whalers Scoring Leaders
(checklist back)
❑ 60 Billy Smith .40 .18
❑ 61 Mike O'Connell .40 .18
❑ 62 Lanny McDonald .40 .18
❑ 63 Lee Fogolin .20 .09
❑ 64 Rocky Saganiuk .20 .09
❑ 65 Rolf Edberg .20 .09
❑ 66 Paul Shmyr .20 .09
❑ 67 Michel Goulet 10.00 4.50
❑ 68 Dan Bouchard .40 .18
❑ 69 Mark Johnson USA .40 .18
❑ 70 Reggie Leach .40 .18
❑ 71 Bernie Federko .40 .18
Blues Scoring Leaders
(checklist back)
❑ 72 Peter Mahovlich .40 .18
❑ 73 Anders Hedberg .40 .18
❑ 74 Brad Park .40 .18
❑ 75 Clark Gillies .40 .18
❑ 76 Doug Jarvis .20 .09
❑ 77 John Garrett .40 .18
❑ 78 Dave Hutchinson .20 .09
❑ 79 John Anderson .20 .09
❑ 80 Gilbert Perreault .75 .35
❑ 81 Marcel Dionne AS1 .75 .35
❑ 82 Guy Lafleur AS1 1.00 .45
❑ 83 Charlie Simmer AS1 .30 .14
❑ 84 Larry Robinson AS1 .30 .14
❑ 85 Borje Salming AS1 .30 .14
❑ 86 Tony Esposito AS1 .75 .35
❑ 87 Wayne Gretzky AS2 25.00 11.00
❑ 88 Danny Gare AS2 .30 .14
❑ 89 Steve Shutt AS2 .30 .14
❑ 90 Barry Beck AS2 .30 .14
❑ 91 Mark Howe AS2 .40 .18
❑ 92 Don Edwards AS2 .30 .14
❑ 93 Tom McCarthy .20 .09
❑ 94 Peter McNab/Rick Middleton .40 .18
Bruins Scoring Leaders
(checklist back)
❑ 95 Mike Palmateer .40 .18
❑ 96 Jim Schoenfeld .40 .18
❑ 97 Jordy Douglas .20 .09
❑ 98 Keith Brown .20 .09
❑ 99 Dennis Ververgaert .20 .09
❑ 100 Phil Esposito .75 .35
❑ 101 Jack Brownschidle .20 .09
❑ 102 Bob Nystrom .20 .09
❑ 103 Steve Christoff USA .30 .14
❑ 104 Rob Palmer .20 .09
❑ 105 Dave(Tiger) Williams .40 .18
❑ 106 Kent Nilsson .40 .18
Flames Scoring Leaders
checklist back)
❑ 107 Morris Lukowich .40 .18
❑ 108 Jack Valiquette .20 .09
❑ 109 Richie Dunn .20 .09
❑ 110 Rogatien Vachon .40 .18
❑ 111 Mark Napier .20 .09
❑ 112 Gordie Roberts .20 .09
❑ 113 Stan Jonathan .20 .09
❑ 114 Brett Callighen .20 .09
❑ 115 Rick MacLeish .40 .18
❑ 116 Ulf Nilsson .40 .18
❑ 117 Rick Kehoe .40 .18
Penguins Scoring Leaders
(checklist back)
❑ 118 Dan Maloney .20 .09
❑ 119 Terry Ruskowski .20 .09
❑ 120 Denis Potvin 1.00 .45
❑ 121 Wayne Stephenson .40 .18
❑ 122 Rich Leduc .20 .09
❑ 123 Checklist 1-132 3.00 1.35
❑ 124 Don Lever .20 .09
❑ 125 Jim Rutherford .40 .18
❑ 126 Ray Allison .20 .09
❑ 127 Mike Ramsey USA 2.00 .90
❑ 128 Stan Smyl .40 .18
Canucks Scoring Leaders
(checklist back)
❑ 129 Al Secord 2.00 .90
❑ 130 Denis Herron .40 .18
❑ 131 Bob Dailey .20 .09
❑ 132 Dean Talafous .20 .09
❑ 133 Ian Turnbull .20 .09
❑ 134 Ron Sedlbauer .20 .09
❑ 135 Tom Bladon .20 .09
❑ 136 Bernie Federko 1.50 .70
❑ 137 Dave Taylor 2.00 .90
❑ 138 Bob Lorimer .20 .09
❑ 139 Al MacAdam/Steve Payne .40 .18
North Stars Scoring Leaders
(checklist back)
❑ 140 Ray Bourque 65.00 29.00
❑ 141 Glen Hanlon .40 .18
❑ 142 Willy Lindstrom .20 .09
❑ 143 Mike Rogers .20 .09
❑ 144 Tony McKegney .20 .09
❑ 145 Behn Wilson .20 .09
❑ 146 Lucien DeBlois .20 .09
❑ 147 Dave Burrows .20 .09
❑ 148 Paul Woods .20 .09
❑ 149 Phil Esposito .75 .35
Rangers Scoring Leaders
(checklist back)
❑ 150 Tony Esposito 1.00 .45
❑ 151 Pierre Larouche .40 .18
❑ 152 Brad Maxwell .20 .09
❑ 153 Stan Weir .20 .09
❑ 154 Ryan Walter .20 .09
❑ 155 Dale Hoganson .20 .09
❑ 156 Anders Kallur .20 .09
❑ 157 Paul Reinhart .75 .35
❑ 158 Greg Millen .40 .18
❑ 159 Ric Seiling .20 .09
❑ 160 Mark Howe 1.00 .45
❑ 161 Goals Leaders .30 .14
Danny Gare (1)
Charlie Simmer (1)
Blaine Stoughton (1)
❑ 162 Assists Leaders 10.00 4.50
Wayne Gretzky (1)
Marcel Dionne (2)
Guy Lafleur (3)
❑ 163 Scoring Leaders 10.00 4.50
Marcel Dionne (1)
Wayne Gretzky (1)
Guy Lafleur (3)
❑ 164 Penalty Minutes .30 .14
Leaders
Jimmy Mann (1)
Dave(Tiger) Williams (2)
Paul Holmgren (3)
❑ 165 Power Play Goals .30 .14
Leaders
Charlie Simmer (1)
Marcel Dionne (2)
Danny Gare (2)
Steve Shutt (2)
Darryl Sittler (2)
❑ 166 Goals Against Average .30 .14
Leaders
Bob Sauve (1)
Denis Herron (2)
Don Edwards (3)
❑ 167 Game-Winning Goals .30 .14
Leaders
Danny Gare (1)
Peter McNab (2)
Blaine Stoughton (2)
❑ 168 Shutout Leaders 1.00 .45
Tony Esposito (1)
Gerry Cheevers (2)
Bob Sauve (2)
Rogatien Vachon (2)
❑ 169 Perry Turnbull .20 .09
❑ 170 Barry Beck .40 .18
❑ 171 Charlie Simmer .40 .18
Kings Scoring Leaders
(checklist back)
❑ 172 Paul Holmgren .40 .18
❑ 173 Willie Huber .20 .09
❑ 174 Tim Young .20 .09
❑ 175 Gilles Gilbert .40 .18
❑ 176 Dave Christian USA 2.00 .90
❑ 177 Lars Lindgren .20 .09
❑ 178 Real Cloutier .20 .09
❑ 179 Laurie Boschman .20 .09
❑ 180 Steve Shutt .20 .09
❑ 181 Bob Murray .20 .09
❑ 182 Wayne Gretzky 15.00 6.75
Oilers Scoring Leaders
(checklist back)
❑ 183 John Van Boxmeer .20 .09
❑ 184 Nick Fotiu .40 .18
❑ 185 Mike McEwen .20 .09
❑ 186 Greg Malone .20 .09
❑ 187 Mike Foligno 2.50 1.10
❑ 188 Dave Langevin .20 .09
❑ 189 Mel Bridgman .20 .09
❑ 190 John Davidson .40 .18
❑ 191 Mike Milbury .40 .18
❑ 192 Ron Zanussi .20 .09
❑ 193 Darryl Sittler .40 .18
Maple Leafs Scoring Leaders
(checklist back)
❑ 194 John Marks .20 .09
❑ 195 Mike Gartner 30.00 13.50
❑ 196 Dave Lewis .20 .09
❑ 197 Kent Nilsson 3.00 1.35
❑ 198 Rick Ley .20 .09
❑ 199 Derek Smith .20 .09
❑ 200 Bill Barber .40 .18
❑ 201 Guy Lapointe .20 .09
❑ 202 Vaclav Nedomansky .20 .09
❑ 203 Don Murdoch .20 .09
❑ 204 Mike Bossy 1.00 .45
Islanders Scoring Leaders
(checklist back)
❑ 205 Pierre Hamel .75 .35
❑ 206 Mike Eaves .20 .09
❑ 207 Doug Halward .20 .09
❑ 208 Stan Smyl .75 .35
❑ 209 Mike Zuke .20 .09
❑ 210 Borje Salming .40 .18
❑ 211 Walt Tkaczuk .40 .18
❑ 212 Grant Mulvey .20 .09
❑ 213 Rob Ramage 2.00 .90
❑ 214 Tom Rowe .20 .09
❑ 215 Don Edwards .20 .09
❑ 216 Guy Lafleur .75 .35
Pierre Larouche
Canadiens Scoring Leaders
(checklist back)
❑ 217 Dan Labraaten .20 .09
❑ 218 Glen Sharpley .20 .09
❑ 219 Stefan Persson .20 .09
❑ 220 Peter McNab .20 .09
❑ 221 Doug Hicks .20 .09
❑ 222 Bengt Gustafsson .20 .09
❑ 223 Michel Dion .40 .18
❑ 224 Jim Watson .20 .09
❑ 225 Wilf Paiement .20 .09
❑ 226 Phil Russell .20 .09
❑ 227 Morris Lukowich .40 .18
Jets Scoring Leaders
(checklist back)
❑ 228 Ron Stackhouse .20 .09
❑ 229 Ted Bulley .20 .09
❑ 230 Larry Robinson .75 .35
❑ 231 Don Maloney .20 .09
❑ 232 Rob McClanahan USA .30 .14
❑ 233 Al Sims .20 .09
❑ 234 Errol Thompson .20 .09
❑ 235 Glenn Resch .40 .18
❑ 236 Bob Miller .20 .09
❑ 237 Gary Sargent .20 .09
❑ 238 Real Cloutier .40 .18
Nordiques Scoring Leaders
(checklist back)
❑ 239 Rene Robert .40 .18
❑ 240 Charlie Simmer 1.25 .55
❑ 241 Thomas Gradin .20 .09
❑ 242 Rick Vaive 2.00 .90
❑ 243 Ron Wilson .20 .09
❑ 244 Brian Sutter .40 .18
❑ 245 Dale McCourt .20 .09
❑ 246 Yvon Lambert .20 .09
❑ 247 Tom Lysiak .20 .09
❑ 248 Ron Greschner .20 .09
❑ 249 Reggie Leach .40 .18
Flyers Scoring Leaders
(checklist back)
❑ 250 Wayne Gretzky UER 80.00 36.00
(1978-79 GP should be 80, not 60)
❑ 251 Rick Middleton .40 .18
❑ 252 Al Smith .40 .18
❑ 253 Fred Barrett .20 .09
❑ 254 Butch Goring .40 .18
❑ 255 Robert Picard .20 .09
❑ 256 Marc Tardif .20 .09
❑ 257 Checklist 133-264 3.00 1.35
❑ 258 Barry Long .20 .09
❑ 259 Rene Robert .40 .18
Rockies Scoring Leaders
(checklist back)
❑ 260 Danny Gare .40 .18
❑ 261 Rejean Houle .20 .09
❑ 262 Stanley Cup Semifinals .30 .14
Islanders-Sabres
❑ 263 Stanley Cup Semifinals .30 .14
Flyers-North Stars
❑ 264 Stanley Cup Finals 1.00 .45
Islanders win 1st

## 1980-81 Topps Team Posters

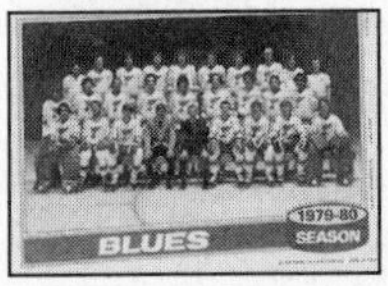

The 1980-81 Topps pin-up posters were issued as folded inserts (approximately 5" by 7" horizontal) to the 1980-81 Topps regular hockey issue. These 16 numbered posters are in full color with a white border on very thin stock. The posters feature posed shots (on ice) of the entire 1979-80 hockey team. The name of the team is indicated in large letters to the left of the hockey puck, which contains the designation 1979-80 Season. Fold lines or creases are natural and do not detract from the condition of the poster. For some reason the Edmonton Oilers, Quebec Nordiques, and Winnipeg Jets were not included in this set.

| | NRMT-MT | EXC |
|---|---|---|
| COMPLETE SET (16) | 25.00 | 11.00 |
| COMMON TEAM (1-16) | 1.50 | .70 |

❑ 1 New York Islanders 1.50 .70
❑ 2 New York Rangers 2.00 .90
❑ 3 Philadelphia Flyers 1.50 .70
❑ 4 Boston Bruins 2.50 1.10
❑ 5 Hartford Whalers 4.00 1.80
(Gordie Howe included)
❑ 6 Buffalo Sabres 1.50 .70
❑ 7 Chicago Blackhawks 2.50 1.10
❑ 8 Detroit Red Wings 2.50 1.10
❑ 9 Minn. North Stars 2.00 .90
❑ 10 Toronto Maple Leafs 2.50 1.10
❑ 11 Montreal Canadiens 2.50 1.10
❑ 12 Colorado Rockies 2.50 1.10
❑ 13 Los Angeles Kings 3.00 1.35
(Jack Carlson)
❑ 14 Vancouver Canucks 1.50 .70
❑ 15 St. Louis Blues 1.50 .70
❑ 16 Washington Capitals 1.50 .70

## 1981-82 Topps

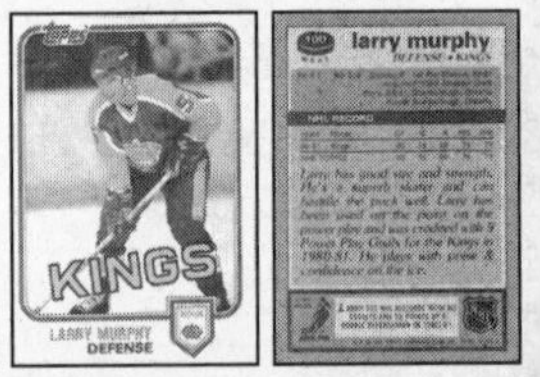

Topps regionalized distribution of its 198-card standard-size set for 1981-82, and issued two types of wax boxes, commonly referred to as either "East" boxes or "West" boxes. There is no way to differentiate which type of box you have without opening the packs. While the first 66 cards of the set were distributed nationally in both pack types, cards numbered 67 East through 132 East and 67 West through 132 West were distributed regionally. The

card fronts contain the Topps logo at the top, with team logo, player name and position at the bottom. The team name appears in large letters placed over the bottom portion of the photo. The backs feature player biographies and yearly statistics including minor leagues. As for the regionally distributed portions of the set, the card numbering is according to team: Boston Bruins (E67-E74), Buffalo Sabres (E75-E80), Pittsburgh Penguins (E81, E112-E114, E116), Hartford Whalers (E82-E86, E108, E115), New York Islanders (E87-E93), New York Rangers (E94-E102), Philadelphia Flyers (E103-E110), Pittsburgh Penguins (E112-E116), Washington Capitals (E117-E122), Chicago Blackhawks (W67-W72), Winnipeg Jets (W79), Colorado Rockies (W80-W85), Detroit Red Wings (W87-W95), Los Angeles Kings (W96-W98, W100-W101), Toronto Maple Leafs (W99), Minnesota North Stars (W102-113) and St. Louis Blues (W114-W119, W121-W124). Super Action subsets (SA) are E123-E132 and W125-W132. Rookie Cards include Dave Babych, Don Beaupre, Dino Ciccarelli, Steve Kasper, Jari Kurri, Larry Murphy, Denis Savard, Peter Stastny and Darryl Sutter.

| | NRMT-MT | EXC |
|---|---|---|
| COMPLETE SET (198) | 70.00 | 32.00 |
| COMMON CARD (1-66) | .10 | .05 |
| COMMON CARD (E67-E132) | .10 | .05 |
| COMMON CARD (W67-W132) | .15 | .07 |

❑ 1 Dave Babych .50 .23
❑ 2 Bill Barber .25 .11
❑ 3 Barry Beck .25 .11
❑ 4 Mike Bossy 2.00 .90
❑ 5 Ray Bourque 4.00 1.80
❑ 6 Guy Chouinard .10 .05
❑ 7 Dave Christian .25 .11
❑ 8 Bill Derlago .10 .05
❑ 9 Marcel Dionne .50 .23
❑ 10 Brian Engblom .10 .05
❑ 11 Tony Esposito .50 .23
❑ 12 Bernie Federko .50 .23
❑ 13 Bob Gainey .50 .23
❑ 14 Danny Gare .10 .05
❑ 15 Thomas Gradin .25 .11
❑ 16 Wayne Gretzky UER 10.00 4.50
(1978-79 GP should be 80, not 60)
❑ 17 Rick Kehoe .10 .05
❑ 18 Jari Kurri 6.00 2.70
❑ 19 Guy Lafleur 1.00 .45
❑ 20 Mike Liut .50 .23
❑ 21 Dale McCourt .10 .05
❑ 22 Rick Middleton .10 .05
❑ 23 Mark Napier .10 .05
❑ 24 Kent Nilsson .25 .11
❑ 25 Wilf Paiement .10 .05
❑ 26 Willi Plett .10 .05
❑ 27 Denis Potvin .50 .23
❑ 28 Paul Reinhart .10 .05
❑ 29 Jacques Richard .10 .05
❑ 30 Pat Riggin .25 .11
❑ 31 Larry Robinson .25 .11
❑ 32 Mike Rogers .10 .05
❑ 33 Borje Salming .25 .11
❑ 34 Steve Shutt .10 .05
❑ 35 Charlie Simmer .50 .23
❑ 36 Darryl Sittler .50 .23
❑ 37 Bobby Smith .25 .11
❑ 38 Stan Smyl .10 .05
❑ 39 Peter Stastny 4.00 1.80
❑ 40 Dave Taylor .50 .23
❑ 41 Bryan Trottier .50 .23
❑ 42 Ian Turnbull .10 .05
❑ 43 Eric Vail .10 .05
❑ 44 Rick Vaive .25 .11
❑ 45 Behn Wilson .10 .05
❑ 46 Rick Middleton .25 .11
Bruins Leaders
❑ 47 Danny Gare .10 .05
Sabres Leaders
❑ 48 Kent Nilsson .10 .05
Flames Leaders
❑ 49 Tom Lysiak .10 .05
Blackhawks Leaders
❑ 50 Lanny McDonald .25 .11
Rockies Leaders
❑ 51 Dale McCourt .10 .05
Red Wings Leaders
❑ 52 Wayne Gretzky 3.00 1.35
Oilers Leaders
❑ 53 Mike Rogers .10 .05
Whalers Leaders
❑ 54 Marcel Dionne .25 .11
Kings Leaders
❑ 55 Bobby Smith .25 .11
North Stars Leaders
❑ 56 Steve Shutt .25 .11
Canadiens Leaders
❑ 57 Mike Bossy .10 .05
Islanders Leaders
❑ 58 Anders Hedberg .10 .05
Rangers Leaders
❑ 59 Bill Barber .10 .05
Flyers Leaders
❑ 60 Rick Kehoe .10 .05
Penguins Leaders
❑ 61 Peter Stastny .10 .05
Nordiques Leaders
❑ 62 Bernie Federko .25 .11
Blues Leaders
❑ 63 Wilf Paiement .10 .05
Maple Leafs Leaders
❑ 64 Thomas Gradin .10 .05
Canucks Leaders
❑ 65 Dennis Maruk .10 .05
Capitals Leaders
❑ 66 Dave Christian .10 .05
Jets Leaders
❑ E67 Dwight Foster .10 .05
❑ E68 Steve Kasper 1.00 .45
❑ E69 Peter McNab .10 .05
❑ E70 Mike O'Connell .25 .11
❑ E71 Terry O'Reilly .25 .11
❑ E72 Brad Park .25 .11
❑ E73 Dick Redmond .10 .05
❑ E74 Rogatien Vachon .25 .11
❑ E75 Don Edwards .10 .05
❑ E76 Tony McKegney .10 .05
❑ E77 Bob Sauve .25 .11
❑ E78 Andre Savard .10 .05
❑ E79 Derek Smith .10 .05
❑ E80 John Van Boxmeer .10 .05
❑ E81 Pat Boutette .10 .05
❑ E82 Mark Howe .50 .23
❑ E83 Dave Keon .25 .11
❑ E84 Warren Miller .10 .05
❑ E85 Al Sims .10 .05
❑ E86 Blaine Stoughton .25 .11
❑ E87 Bob Bourne .10 .05
❑ E88 Clark Gillies .25 .11
❑ E89 Butch Goring .25 .11
❑ E90 Anders Kallur .10 .05
❑ E91 Ken Morrow .25 .11
❑ E92 Stefan Persson .10 .05
❑ E93 Billy Smith .25 .11
❑ E94 Mike Allison .10 .05
❑ E95 John Davidson .25 .11
❑ E96 Ron Duguay .10 .05
❑ E97 Ron Greschner .10 .05
❑ E98 Anders Hedberg .25 .11
❑ E99 Ed Johnstone .10 .05
❑ E100 Dave Maloney .10 .05
❑ E101 Don Maloney .10 .05
❑ E102 Ulf Nilsson .25 .11
❑ E103 Bobby Clarke .50 .23
❑ E104 Bob Dailey .10 .05
❑ E105 Paul Holmgren .10 .05
❑ E106 Reggie Leach .25 .11
❑ E107 Ken Linseman .25 .11
❑ E108 Rick MacLeish .25 .11
❑ E109 Pete Peeters .50 .23
❑ E110 Brian Propp .50 .23
❑ E111 Checklist 1-132 1.00 .45
❑ E112 Randy Carlyle .25 .11
❑ E113 Paul Gardner .10 .05
❑ E114 Peter Lee .10 .05
❑ E115 Greg Millen .25 .11
❑ E116 Rod Schutt .10 .05
❑ E117 Mike Gartner 5.00 2.20
❑ E118 Rick Green .10 .05
❑ E119 Bob Kelly .10 .05
❑ E120 Dennis Maruk .25 .11
❑ E121 Mike Palmateer .25 .11
❑ E122 Ryan Walter .10 .05
❑ E123 Bill Barber SA .10 .05
❑ E124 Barry Beck SA .10 .05
❑ E125 Mike Bossy SA .50 .23
❑ E126 Ray Bourque SA 2.00 .90
❑ E127 Danny Gare SA .10 .05
❑ E128 Rick Kehoe SA .10 .05
❑ E129 Rick Middleton SA .25 .11
❑ E130 Denis Potvin SA .50 .23
❑ E131 Mike Rogers SA .10 .05
❑ E132 Bryan Trottier SA .50 .23
❑ W67 Keith Brown .15 .07
❑ W68 Ted Bulley .15 .07
❑ W69 Tim Higgins .15 .07
❑ W70 Reg Kerr .15 .07
❑ W71 Tom Lysiak .15 .07
❑ W72 Grant Mulvey .15 .07
❑ W73 Bob Murray .15 .07
❑ W74 Terry Ruskowski .15 .07
❑ W75 Denis Savard 10.00 4.50
❑ W76 Glen Sharpley .15 .07
❑ W77 Darryl Sutter .50 .23
❑ W78 Doug Wilson .50 .23
❑ W79 Lucien DeBlois .15 .07
❑ W80 Paul Gagne .15 .07
❑ W81 Merlin Malinowski .15 .07
❑ W82 Lanny McDonald .25 .11
❑ W83 Joel Quenneville .15 .07
❑ W84 Rob Ramage .15 .07
❑ W85 Glenn Resch .25 .11
❑ W86 Steve Tambellini .15 .07
❑ W87 Mike Foligno .50 .23
❑ W88 Gilles Gilbert .25 .11
❑ W89 Willie Huber .15 .07
❑ W90 Mark Kirton .15 .07
❑ W91 Jim Korn .15 .07
❑ W92 Reed Larson .10 .05
❑ W93 Gary McAdam .15 .07
❑ W94 Vaclav Nedomansky .15 .07
❑ W95 John Ogrodnick .50 .23
❑ W96 Billy Harris .15 .07
❑ W97 Jerry Korab .15 .07
❑ W98 Mario Lessard .25 .11
❑ W99 Don Luce .15 .07
❑ W100 Larry Murphy 10.00 4.50
❑ W101 Mike Murphy .15 .07
❑ W102 Kent-Erik Andersson .15 .07
❑ W103 Don Beaupre 3.00 1.35
❑ W104 Steve Christoff .15 .07
❑ W105 Dino Ciccarelli 10.00 4.50
❑ W106 Craig Hartsburg .15 .07
❑ W107 Al MacAdam .15 .07
❑ W108 Tom McCarthy .15 .07
❑ W109 Gilles Meloche .25 .11
❑ W110 Steve Payne .15 .07
❑ W111 Gordie Roberts .10 .05
❑ W112 Greg Smith .15 .07
❑ W113 Tim Young .15 .07
❑ W114 Wayne Babych .15 .07
❑ W115 Blair Chapman .15 .07
❑ W116 Tony Currie .15 .07
❑ W117 Blake Dunlop .15 .07
❑ W118 Ed Kea .15 .07
❑ W119 Rick Lapointe .15 .07
❑ W120 Checklist 1-132 1.50 .70
❑ W121 Jorgen Pettersson .15 .07
❑ W122 Brian Sutter .25 .11
❑ W123 Perry Turnbull .15 .07
❑ W124 Mike Zuke .15 .07
❑ W125 Marcel Dionne SA .50 .23
❑ W126 Tony Esposito SA .50 .23
❑ W127 Bernie Federko SA .25 .11
❑ W128 Mike Liut SA .50 .23
❑ W129 Dale McCourt SA .15 .07
❑ W130 Charlie Simmer SA .25 .11
❑ W131 Bobby Smith SA .15 .07
❑ W132 Dave Taylor SA .50 .23

## 1984-85 Topps

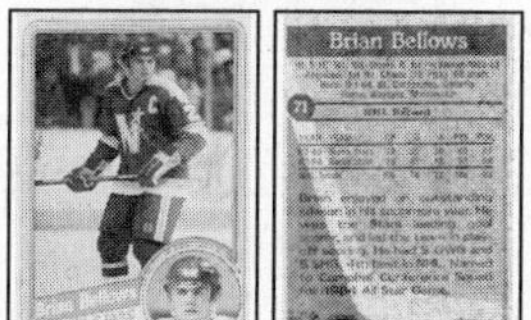


After a two year hiatus, Topps returned to hockey with a set of 165 standard size cards. The set contains 66 single print cards which are noted in the checklist by SP. Teams from the United States have a greater player representation than the Canadian teams. Card fronts (much like 1983 Topps baseball) are color coordinated by team and feature two photos. A small photo at bottom right has player name, position and team name to the left. Card backs contain complete career statistics. Cards are in team order: Boston (1-12), Buffalo (13-23), Calgary (24-26), Chicago (27-37), Detroit (38-49), Edmonton (50-52), Hartford (53-63), Los Angeles (64-69), Minnesota (70-80), Montreal (81-83), New Jersey (84-90), New York Islanders (91-104), New York Rangers (105-116), Philadelphia (117-122), Pittsburgh (123-127), Quebec (128-130), St. Louis (131-135), Toronto (136-138), Vancouver (139-141), Washington (142-149) and Winnipeg (150-152). Rookie Cards include Dave Andreychuk, Tom Barrasso, Pat LaFontaine, Dave Poulin, Pat Verbeek and Steve Yzerman.

| | MINT | NRMT |
|---|---|---|
| COMPLETE SET (165) | 40.00 | 18.00 |
| COMMON CARD (1-165) | .10 | .05 |

❑ 1 Ray Bourque 1.50 .70
❑ 2 Keith Crowder SP .10 .05
❑ 3 Tom Fergus .10 .05
❑ 4 Doug Keans .10 .05
❑ 5 Gord Kluzak SP .10 .05
❑ 6 Mike Krushelnyski SP .10 .05
❑ 7 Nevin Markwart .10 .05
❑ 8 Rick Middleton .15 .07
❑ 9 Mike O'Connell .10 .05
❑ 10 Terry O'Reilly SP .10 .05
❑ 11 Barry Pederson .10 .05
❑ 12 Pete Peeters .15 .07
❑ 13 Dave Andreychuk SP 4.00 1.80
❑ 14 Tom Barrasso 3.00 1.35
❑ 15 Real Cloutier SP .10 .05
❑ 16 Mike Foligno .15 .07
❑ 17 Bill Hajt SP .10 .05
❑ 18 Phil Housley SP 1.00 .45
❑ 19 Gilbert Perreault .15 .07
❑ 20 Larry Playfair SP .10 .05
❑ 21 Craig Ramsay SP .10 .05
❑ 22 Mike Ramsey .10 .05
❑ 23 Lindy Ruff SP .10 .05
❑ 24 Ed Beers .10 .05
❑ 25 Rejean Lemelin SP .15 .07
❑ 26 Lanny McDonald .15 .07
❑ 27 Murray Bannerman .15 .07
❑ 28 Keith Brown SP .10 .05
❑ 29 Curt Fraser .10 .05
❑ 30 Steve Larmer 1.50 .70
❑ 31 Tom Lysiak .10 .05
❑ 32 Bob Murray .10 .05
❑ 33 Jack O'Callahan SP .10 .05
❑ 34 Rich Preston .10 .05
❑ 35 Denis Savard .25 .11
❑ 36 Darryl Sutter .10 .05
❑ 37 Doug Wilson .15 .07
❑ 38 Ivan Boldirev .10 .05
❑ 39 Colin Campbell SP .10 .05
❑ 40 Ron Duguay SP .10 .05
❑ 41 Dwight Foster SP .10 .05
❑ 42 Danny Gare SP .10 .05
❑ 43 Ed Johnstone .10 .05
❑ 44 Reed Larson SP .10 .05
❑ 45 Eddie Mio SP .10 .05
❑ 46 John Ogrodnick .10 .05
❑ 47 Brad Park .15 .07
❑ 48 Greg Stefan SP .10 .05
❑ 49 Steve Yzerman 25.00 11.00
❑ 50 Paul Coffey 2.00 .90
❑ 51 Wayne Gretzky 8.00 3.60
❑ 52 Jari Kurri 1.25 .55
❑ 53 Bob Crawford .10 .05
❑ 54 Ron Francis 1.50 .70
❑ 55 Marty Howe .10 .05
❑ 56 Mark Johnson SP .10 .05
❑ 57 Greg Malone SP .10 .05
❑ 58 Greg Millen SP .10 .05
❑ 59 Ray Neufeld .10 .05
❑ 60 Joel Quenneville SP .10 .05
❑ 61 Risto Siltanen .10 .05
❑ 62 Sylvain Turgeon .15 .07
❑ 63 Mike Zuke SP .10 .05
❑ 64 Marcel Dionne .25 .11
❑ 65 Brian Engblom SP .10 .05
❑ 66 Jim Fox SP .10 .05
❑ 67 Bernie Nicholls .75 .35
❑ 68 Terry Ruskowski SP .10 .05
❑ 69 Charlie Simmer .15 .07
❑ 70 Don Beaupre .15 .07
❑ 71 Brian Bellows .50 .23
❑ 72 Neal Broten SP .10 .05
❑ 73 Dino Ciccarelli .25 .11
❑ 74 Paul Holmgren SP .10 .05
❑ 75 Al MacAdam SP .10 .05
❑ 76 Dennis Maruk .15 .07
❑ 77 Brad Maxwell SP .10 .05
❑ 78 Tom McCarthy SP .10 .05
❑ 79 Gilles Meloche SP .10 .05
❑ 80 Steve Payne .10 .05
❑ 81 Guy Lafleur .25 .11
❑ 82 Larry Robinson .15 .07
❑ 83 Bobby Smith .15 .07
❑ 84 Mel Bridgman .10 .05
❑ 85 Joe Cirella .10 .05
❑ 86 Don Lever .10 .05
❑ 87 Dave Lewis .10 .05
❑ 88 Jan Ludvig .10 .05
❑ 89 Glenn Resch .15 .07
❑ 90 Pat Verbeek 5.00 2.20
❑ 91 Mike Bossy .25 .11
❑ 92 Bob Bourne .10 .05
❑ 93 Greg Gilbert .10 .05
❑ 94 Clark Gillies SP .10 .05
❑ 95 Butch Goring SP .10 .05
❑ 96 Pat LaFontaine SP 6.00 2.70
❑ 97 Ken Morrow .10 .05
❑ 98 Bob Nystrom SP .10 .05
❑ 99 Stefan Persson SP .10 .05
❑ 100 Denis Potvin .15 .07
❑ 101 Billy Smith SP .15 .07
❑ 102 Brent Sutter SP .25 .11
❑ 103 John Tonelli .15 .07
❑ 104 Bryan Trottier .25 .11
❑ 105 Barry Beck .10 .05
❑ 106 Glen Hanlon SP .10 .05
❑ 107 Anders Hedberg SP .10 .05
❑ 108 Pierre Larouche SP .15 .07
❑ 109 Don Maloney SP .10 .05
❑ 110 Mark Osborne SP .10 .05
❑ 111 Larry Patey .10 .05
❑ 112 James Patrick .25 .11
❑ 113 Mark Pavelich SP .10 .05
❑ 114 Mike Rogers SP .10 .05
❑ 115 Reijo Ruotsalainen SP .10 .05
❑ 116 Peter Sundstrom SP .10 .05
❑ 117 Bob Froese .15 .07
❑ 118 Mark Howe .15 .07
❑ 119 Tim Kerr SP .15 .07
❑ 120 Dave Poulin 1.00 .45
❑ 121 Darryl Sittler SP .25 .11
❑ 122 Ron Sutter .25 .11
❑ 123 Mike Bullard SP .10 .05
❑ 124 Ron Flockhart SP .10 .05
❑ 125 Rick Kehoe .15 .07
❑ 126 Kevin McCarthy SP .10 .05
❑ 127 Mark Taylor .10 .05
❑ 128 Dan Bouchard SP .10 .05
❑ 129 Michel Goulet .25 .11
❑ 130 Peter Stastny SP .25 .11
❑ 131 Bernie Federko .15 .07
❑ 132 Mike Liut .15 .07
❑ 133 Joe Mullen SP .60 .25
❑ 134 Rob Ramage .10 .05
❑ 135 Brian Sutter .15 .07
❑ 136 John Anderson SP .10 .05
❑ 137 Dan Daoust .10 .05
❑ 138 Rick Vaive .10 .05
❑ 139 Darcy Rota SP .10 .05
❑ 140 Stan Smyl SP .10 .05
❑ 141 Tony Tanti .10 .05
❑ 142 Dave Christian SP .10 .05
❑ 143 Mike Gartner SP 1.50 .70
❑ 144 Bengt Gustafsson SP .10 .05
❑ 145 Doug Jarvis .10 .05
❑ 146 Al Jensen .10 .05
❑ 147 Rod Langway .25 .11
❑ 148 Pat Riggin .15 .07
❑ 149 Scott Stevens SP 1.50 .70
❑ 150 Dave Babych .10 .05
❑ 151 Laurie Boschman .10 .05
❑ 152 Dale Hawerchuk 1.00 .45
❑ 153 Michel Goulet AS .15 .07
❑ 154 Wayne Gretzky AS 2.50 1.10
❑ 155 Mike Bossy AS .25 .11
❑ 156 Rod Langway AS .10 .05
❑ 157 Ray Bourque AS .25 .11
❑ 158 Tom Barrasso AS .50 .23
❑ 159 Mark Messier AS 1.50 .70
❑ 160 Bryan Trottier AS .25 .11
❑ 161 Jari Kurri AS .25 .11
❑ 162 Denis Potvin AS .15 .07
❑ 163 Paul Coffey AS .25 .11
❑ 164 Pat Riggin AS .10 .05
❑ 165 Checklist 1-165 SP 1.50 .70

## 1985-86 Topps

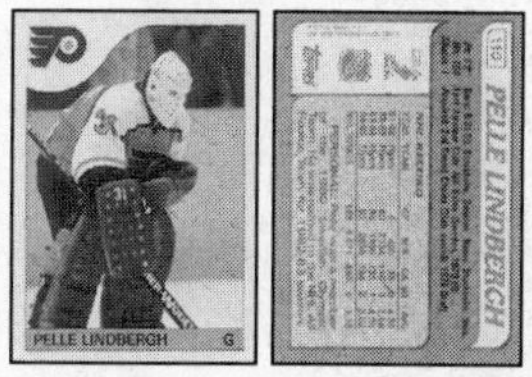


This set of 165 standard-size cards is very similar to Topps' hockey set of the previous season in that there are 66 single prints. The single prints are noted in the checklist by SP. Unopened packs consist of 12 cards plus one sticker and a piece of bubble gum. The fronts have player name and position at the bottom with the team logo at the top right or left. Backs contain complete career statistics and personal notes. The key Rookie Card is Mario Lemieux. Other Rookie Cards include Kevin Dineen, Kelly Hrudey, Kirk Muller, Tomas Sandstrom and Peter Zezel.

| | MINT | NRMT |
|---|---|---|
| COMPLETE SET (165) | 225.00 | 100.00 |
| COMMON CARD (1-165) | .25 | .11 |

❑ 1 Lanny McDonald 1.00 .45
❑ 2 Mike O'Connell SP .50 .23
❑ 3 Curt Fraser SP .50 .23
❑ 4 Steve Penney .25 .11
❑ 5 Brian Engblom .25 .11
❑ 6 Ron Sutter .25 .11
❑ 7 Joe Mullen 1.00 .45
❑ 8 Rod Langway .50 .23
❑ 9 Mario Lemieux 150.00 70.00
❑ 10 Dave Babych .25 .11
❑ 11 Bob Nystrom .25 .11
❑ 12 Andy Moog SP 2.50 1.10
❑ 13 Dino Ciccarelli 1.00 .45
❑ 14 Dwight Foster SP .50 .23
❑ 15 James Patrick SP 1.00 .45
❑ 16 Thomas Gradin SP .50 .23
❑ 17 Mike Foligno .50 .23
❑ 18 Mario Gosselin .50 .23
❑ 19 Mike Zuke SP .50 .23
❑ 20 John Anderson SP .50 .23
❑ 21 Dave Pichette .25 .11
❑ 22 Nick Fotiu SP .50 .23
❑ 23 Tom Lysiak .25 .11
❑ 24 Peter Zezel 1.00 .45
❑ 25 Denis Potvin .50 .23
❑ 26 Bob Carpenter .25 .11
❑ 27 Murray Bannerman SP .50 .23
❑ 28 Gordie Roberts SP .50 .23
❑ 29 Steve Yzerman 15.00 6.75
❑ 30 Phil Russell .25 .11
❑ 31 Peter Stastny 1.00 .45
❑ 32 Craig Ramsay SP .50 .23
❑ 33 Terry Ruskowski SP .50 .23
❑ 34 Kevin Dineen SP 3.00 1.35
❑ 35 Mark Howe .50 .23
❑ 36 Glenn Resch .50 .23
❑ 37 Danny Gare SP .50 .23
❑ 38 Doug Bodger .50 .23
❑ 39 Mike Rogers .25 .11
❑ 40 Ray Bourque 3.00 1.35
❑ 41 John Tonelli .50 .23
❑ 42 Mel Bridgman .25 .11
❑ 43 Sylvain Turgeon SP .50 .23
❑ 44 Mark Johnson .25 .11
❑ 45 Doug Wilson .50 .23
❑ 46 Mike Gartner 1.00 .45
❑ 47 Brent Peterson .25 .11
❑ 48 Paul Reinhart SP .50 .23
❑ 49 Mike Krushelnyski .25 .11
❑ 50 Brian Bellows 1.00 .45
❑ 51 Chris Chelios 4.00 1.80
❑ 52 Barry Pederson SP .50 .23
❑ 53 Murray Craven SP .50 .23
❑ 54 Pierre Larouche SP .50 .23
❑ 55 Reed Larson .25 .11
❑ 56 Pat Verbeek SP 1.00 .45
❑ 57 Randy Carlyle .25 .11
❑ 58 Ray Neufeld SP .50 .23
❑ 59 Keith Brown SP .50 .23
❑ 60 Bryan Trottier 1.00 .45
❑ 61 Jim Fox SP .50 .23
❑ 62 Scott Stevens 1.00 .45
❑ 63 Phil Housley 1.00 .45
❑ 64 Rick Middleton .50 .23
❑ 65 Steve Payne .25 .11
❑ 66 Dave Lewis .25 .11
❑ 67 Mike Bullard .25 .11
❑ 68 Stan Smyl SP .50 .23
❑ 69 Mark Pavelich SP .50 .23
❑ 70 John Ogrodnick .25 .11
❑ 71 Bill Derlago SP .50 .23
❑ 72 Brad Marsh SP 1.00 .45
❑ 73 Denis Savard 1.00 .45
❑ 74 Mark Fusco .25 .11
❑ 75 Pete Peeters .25 .11
❑ 76 Doug Gilmour 6.00 2.70
❑ 77 Mike Ramsey .25 .11
❑ 78 Anton Stastny SP .50 .23
❑ 79 Steve Kasper SP .50 .23
❑ 80 Bryan Erickson SP .50 .23

❑ 81 Clark Gillies .50 .23
❑ 82 Keith Acton .25 .11
❑ 83 Pat Flatley .50 .23
❑ 84 Kirk Muller 2.50 1.10
❑ 85 Paul Coffey 3.00 1.35
❑ 86 Ed Olczyk .50 .23
❑ 87 Charlie Simmer SP 1.00 .45
❑ 88 Mike Liut .50 .23
❑ 89 Dave Maloney .25 .11
❑ 90 Marcel Dionne .50 .23
❑ 91 Tim Kerr .50 .23
❑ 92 Ivan Boldirev SP .50 .23
❑ 93 Ken Morrow SP .50 .23
❑ 94 Don Maloney SP .50 .23
❑ 95 Rejean Lemelin .50 .23
❑ 96 Curt Giles .25 .11
❑ 97 Bob Bourne .25 .11
❑ 98 Joe Cirella .25 .11
❑ 99 Dave Christian SP .50 .23
❑ 100 Darryl Sutter .25 .11
❑ 101 Kelly Kisio .50 .23
❑ 102 Mats Naslund .50 .23
❑ 103 Joel Quenneville SP .50 .23
❑ 104 Bernie Federko .50 .23
❑ 105 Tom Barrasso 1.00 .45
❑ 106 Rick Vaive .25 .11
❑ 107 Brent Sutter .25 .11
❑ 108 Wayne Babych .25 .11
❑ 109 Dale Hawerchuk 1.00 .45
❑ 110 Pelle Lindbergh SP 10.00 4.50
❑ 111 Dennis Maruk SP 1.00 .45
❑ 112 Reijo Ruotsalainen SP .50 .23
❑ 113 Tom Fergus SP .50 .23
❑ 114 Bob Murray SP .50 .23
❑ 115 Patrick Sundstrom .25 .11
❑ 116 Ron Duguay SP 1.00 .45
❑ 117 Alan Haworth SP .50 .23
❑ 118 Greg Malone .25 .11
❑ 119 Bill Hajt .25 .11
❑ 120 Wayne Gretzky 20.00 9.00
❑ 121 Craig Redmond .25 .11
❑ 122 Kelly Hrudey 3.00 1.35
❑ 123 Tomas Sandstrom 3.00 1.35
❑ 124 Neal Broten .50 .23
❑ 125 Moe Mantha SP .50 .23
❑ 126 Greg Gilbert SP .50 .23
❑ 127 Bruce Driver SP 1.00 .45
❑ 128 Dave Poulin .50 .23
❑ 129 Morris Lukowich SP .50 .23
❑ 130 Mike Bossy 1.00 .45
❑ 131 Larry Playfair SP .50 .23
❑ 132 Steve Larmer 1.00 .45
❑ 133 Doug Keans SP .50 .23
❑ 134 Bob Manno .25 .11
❑ 135 Brian Sutter .50 .23
❑ 136 Pat Riggin .50 .23
❑ 137 Pat LaFontaine 3.00 1.35
❑ 138 Barry Beck SP .50 .23
❑ 139 Rich Preston SP .50 .23
❑ 140 Ron Francis 2.50 1.10
❑ 141 Brian Propp SP 1.00 .45
❑ 142 Don Beaupre .50 .23
❑ 143 Dave Andreychuk SP 1.00 .45
❑ 144 Ed Beers .25 .11
❑ 145 Paul MacLean .25 .11
❑ 146 Troy Murray SP .50 .23
❑ 147 Larry Robinson .50 .23
❑ 148 Bernie Nicholls 1.00 .45
❑ 149 Glen Hanlon SP 1.00 .45
❑ 150 Michel Goulet 1.00 .45
❑ 151 Doug Jarvis SP .50 .23
❑ 152 Warren Young .25 .11
❑ 153 Tony Tanti .25 .11
❑ 154 Tomas Jonsson SP .50 .23
❑ 155 Jari Kurri 2.00 .90
❑ 156 Tony McKegney .25 .11
❑ 157 Greg Stefan SP 1.00 .45
❑ 158 Brad McCrimmon SP 1.00 .45
❑ 159 Keith Crowder SP .50 .23
❑ 160 Gilbert Perreault .50 .23
❑ 161 Tim Bothwell SP .50 .23
❑ 162 Bob Crawford SP .50 .23
❑ 163 Paul Gagne SP .50 .23
❑ 164 Dan Daoust SP .50 .23
❑ 165 Checklist 1-165 SP 2.50 1.10

## 1985-86 Topps Box Bottoms

This 16-card standard-size set was issued in sets of four on the bottom of the 1985-86 Topps wax pack boxes. Complete box bottom panels are valued at a 25 percent premium above the prices listed below. The back, written in English, includes statistical information. The cards are lettered rather than numbered. The key card in the set is Mario Lemieux, pictured in his Rookie Card year.

| | MINT | NRMT |
|---|---|---|
| COMPLETE SET (16) | 65.00 | 29.00 |
| COMMON CARD (A-P) | .40 | .18 |

❑ A Brian Bellows .60 .25
❑ B Ray Bourque 2.50 1.10
❑ C Bob Carpenter .40 .18
❑ D Chris Chelios 4.00 1.80
❑ E Marcel Dionne 1.25 .55
❑ F Ron Francis 2.50 1.10
❑ G Wayne Gretzky 25.00 11.00
❑ H Tim Kerr .40 .18
❑ I Mario Lemieux 50.00 22.00
❑ J John Ogrodnick .40 .18
❑ K Gilbert Perreault .75 .35
❑ L Glenn Resch .60 .25
❑ M Reijo Ruotsalainen .40 .18
❑ N Brian Sutter .60 .25
❑ O John Tonelli .40 .18
❑ P Doug Wilson .60 .25

## 1985-86 Topps Sticker Inserts

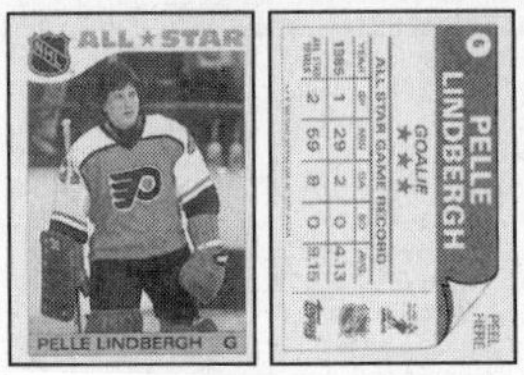


This set of 33 "Hockey Helmet Stickers" features stickers of 12 All-Star players (1-12) and 21 stickers of team logos, pucks, and numbers. The stickers were inserted in with the 1985-86 Topps hockey regular issue wax packs and as such are also 2 1/2" by 3 1/2". The card backs are printed in blue and red on white card stock. These inserts were also included in some O-Pee-Chee packs that year, which may explain why this particular year of stickers is relatively plentiful. The last seven team stickers can be found with the team logos on the top or bottom.

| | MINT | NRMT |
|---|---|---|
| COMPLETE SET (33) | 20.00 | 9.00 |
| COMMON CARD (1-12) | .25 | .11 |
| COMMON TEAM (13-33) | .15 | .07 |

❑ 1 John Ogrodnick .25 .11
❑ 2 Wayne Gretzky 10.00 4.50
❑ 3 Jari Kurri 1.00 .45
❑ 4 Paul Coffey 1.50 .70
❑ 5 Ray Bourque 1.50 .70
❑ 6 Pelle Lindbergh 4.00 1.80
❑ 7 John Tonelli .25 .11
❑ 8 Dale Hawerchuk .75 .35
❑ 9 Mike Bossy 1.00 .45
❑ 10 Rod Langway .25 .11
❑ 11 Doug Wilson .25 .11
❑ 12 Tom Barrasso .35 .16
❑ 13 Toronto Maple Leafs .25 .11
❑ 14 Buffalo Sabres .15 .07
❑ 15 Detroit Red Wings .25 .11
❑ 16 Pittsburgh Penguins .15 .07
❑ 17 New York Rangers .25 .11
❑ 18 Calgary Flames .15 .07
❑ 19 Winnipeg Jets .15 .07
❑ 20 Quebec Nordiques .15 .07
❑ 21 Chicago Blackhawks .25 .11
❑ 22 Los Angeles Kings .15 .07
❑ 23 Montreal Canadiens .25 .11
❑ 24 Vancouver Canucks .15 .07
❑ 25 Hartford Whalers .15 .07
❑ 26 Philadelphia Flyers .15 .07
❑ 27 New Jersey Devils .15 .07
❑ 28 St. Louis Blues .15 .07
❑ 29 Minnesota North Stars .15 .07
❑ 30 Washington Capitals .15 .07
❑ 31 Boston Bruins .25 .11
❑ 32 New York Islanders .15 .07
❑ 33 Edmonton Oilers .15 .07

## 1986-87 Topps

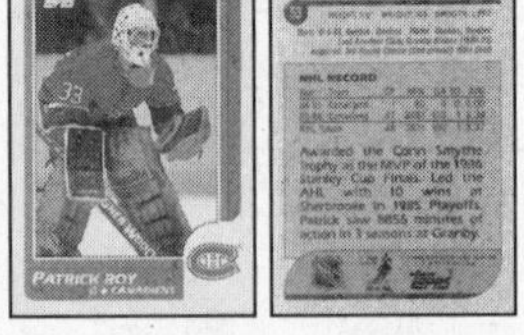


This set of 198 cards measures the standard size. There are 66 double prints that are noted in the checklist by DP. Card fronts feature player name, team, team logo and position at the bottom with a team colored stripe up the right border. Card backs contain complete career statistics and career highlights. The key Rookie Card in this set is Patrick Roy. Other Rookie Cards include Greg Adams, Wendel Clark, Russ Courtnall, Ray Ferraro, Dirk Graham, Petr Klima, John MacLean, Craig MacTavish, Mike Ridley, Gary Suter and John Vanbiesbrouck.

| | MINT | NRMT |
|---|---|---|
| COMPLETE SET (198) | 150.00 | 70.00 |
| COMMON CARD (1-198) | .15 | .07 |
| COMMON CARD DP | .10 | .05 |

❑ 1 Ray Bourque 2.00 .90
❑ 2 Pat LaFontaine DP 1.50 .70
❑ 3 Wayne Gretzky 18.00 8.00
❑ 4 Lindy Ruff .15 .07
❑ 5 Brad McCrimmon .15 .07
❑ 6 Dave(Tiger) Williams .40 .18
❑ 7 Denis Savard DP .40 .18
❑ 8 Lanny McDonald .15 .07
❑ 9 John Vanbiesbrouck DP 20.00 9.00
❑ 10 Greg Adams 1.00 .45
❑ 11 Steve Yzerman 12.00 5.50
❑ 12 Craig Hartsburg .15 .07
❑ 13 John Anderson DP .10 .05
❑ 14 Bob Bourne DP .10 .05
❑ 15 Kjell Dahlin .15 .07
❑ 16 Dave Andreychuk 1.00 .45
❑ 17 Rob Ramage DP .10 .05
❑ 18 Ron Greschner DP .10 .05
❑ 19 Bruce Driver .15 .07
❑ 20 Peter Stastny .40 .18
❑ 21 Dave Christian .15 .07
❑ 22 Doug Keans .15 .07
❑ 23 Scott Bjugstad .15 .07
❑ 24 Doug Bodger DP .10 .05
❑ 25 Troy Murray DP .10 .05
❑ 26 Al Iafrate 1.00 .45
❑ 27 Kelly Hrudey 1.00 .45
❑ 28 Doug Jarvis .15 .07
❑ 29 Rich Sutter .15 .07
❑ 30 Marcel Dionne .40 .18
❑ 31 Curt Fraser .15 .07
❑ 32 Doug Lidster .15 .07
❑ 33 Brian MacLellan .15 .07
❑ 34 Barry Pederson .15 .07
❑ 35 Craig Laughlin .15 .07
❑ 36 Ilkka Sinisalo DP .10 .05
❑ 37 John MacLean 2.50 1.10
❑ 38 Brian Mullen .15 .07
❑ 39 Duane Sutter DP .10 .05
❑ 40 Brian Engblom .15 .07
❑ 41 Chris Cichocki .15 .07
❑ 42 Gordie Roberts .15 .07
❑ 43 Ron Francis 1.50 .70
❑ 44 Joe Mullen 1.00 .45
❑ 45 Moe Mantha DP .10 .05
❑ 46 Pat Verbeek 1.00 .45
❑ 47 Clint Malarchuk 1.00 .45
❑ 48 Bob Brooke DP .10 .05
❑ 49 Darryl Sutter DP .10 .05
❑ 50 Stan Smyl DP .10 .05
❑ 51 Greg Stefan .40 .18
❑ 52 Bill Hajt DP .10 .05
❑ 53 Patrick Roy 100.00 45.00
❑ 54 Gord Kluzak .15 .07
❑ 55 Bob Froese DP .10 .05
❑ 56 Grant Fuhr 2.50 1.10
❑ 57 Mark Hunter DP .10 .05
❑ 58 Dana Murzyn .15 .07
❑ 59 Mike Gartner 1.00 .45
❑ 60 Dennis Maruk .15 .07
❑ 61 Rich Preston .15 .07
❑ 62 Larry Robinson DP .10 .05
❑ 63 Dave Taylor DP .10 .05
❑ 64 Bob Murray DP .10 .05
❑ 65 Ken Morrow .15 .07
❑ 66 Mike Ridley 1.00 .45
❑ 67 John Tucker .15 .07
❑ 68 Miroslav Frycer .15 .07
❑ 69 Danny Gare .40 .18
❑ 70 Randy Burridge 1.00 .45
❑ 71 Dave Poulin .15 .07
❑ 72 Brian Sutter .40 .18
❑ 73 Dave Babych .15 .07
❑ 74 Dale Hawerchuk DP 1.00 .45
❑ 75 Brian Bellows .15 .07
❑ 76 Dave Pasin DP .10 .05
❑ 77 Pete Peeters DP .10 .05
❑ 78 Tomas Jonsson DP .10 .05
❑ 79 Gilbert Perreault DP .10 .05
❑ 80 Glenn Anderson DP 1.00 .45
❑ 81 Don Maloney .15 .07
❑ 82 Ed Olczyk DP .10 .05
❑ 83 Mike Bullard DP .10 .05
❑ 84 Tom Fergus .15 .07
❑ 85 Dave Lewis .15 .07
❑ 86 Brian Propp .40 .18
❑ 87 John Ogrodnick .15 .07
❑ 88 Kevin Dineen DP 1.00 .45
❑ 89 Don Beaupre .40 .18
❑ 90 Mike Bossy DP 1.00 .45
❑ 91 Tom Barrasso DP 1.00 .45
❑ 92 Michel Goulet DP .10 .05
❑ 93 Doug Gilmour 3.00 1.35
❑ 94 Kirk Muller 1.00 .45
❑ 95 Larry Melnyk DP .10 .05
❑ 96 Bob Gainey DP 1.00 .45
❑ 97 Steve Kasper .15 .07
❑ 98 Petr Klima .40 .18
❑ 99 Neal Broten DP .15 .07
❑ 100 Al Secord DP .10 .05
❑ 101 Bryan Erickson DP .10 .05
❑ 102 Rejean Lemelin .15 .07
❑ 103 Sylvain Turgeon .15 .07
❑ 104 Bob Nystrom .15 .07
❑ 105 Bernie Federko .40 .18
❑ 106 Doug Wilson DP .10 .05
❑ 107 Alan Haworth .15 .07
❑ 108 Jari Kurri 1.50 .70
❑ 109 Ron Sutter .15 .07
❑ 110 Reed Larson DP .10 .05
❑ 111 Terry Ruskowski DP .10 .05
❑ 112 Mark Johnson DP .10 .05
❑ 113 James Patrick .15 .07
❑ 114 Paul MacLean .15 .07
❑ 115 Mike Ramsey DP .10 .05
❑ 116 Kelly Kisio DP .10 .05
❑ 117 Brent Sutter .15 .07
❑ 118 Joel Quenneville .15 .07
❑ 119 Curt Giles DP .10 .05
❑ 120 Tony Tanti DP .10 .05
❑ 121 Doug Sulliman DP .10 .05
❑ 122 Mario Lemieux 30.00 13.50
❑ 123 Mark Howe DP .10 .05
❑ 124 Bob Sauve .40 .18
❑ 125 Anton Stastny .15 .07
❑ 126 Scott Stevens DP 1.00 .45
❑ 127 Mike Foligno .15 .07
❑ 128 Reijo Ruotsalainen DP .10 .05
❑ 129 Denis Potvin .40 .18
❑ 130 Keith Crowder .15 .07
❑ 131 Bob Janecyk DP .10 .05
❑ 132 John Tonelli .15 .07
❑ 133 Mike Liut DP .10 .05
❑ 134 Tim Kerr DP .10 .05
❑ 135 Al Jensen .15 .07
❑ 136 Mel Bridgman .15 .07
❑ 137 Paul Coffey DP 1.50 .70
❑ 138 Dino Ciccarelli DP .40 .18
❑ 139 Steve Larmer 1.00 .45
❑ 140 Mike O'Connell .15 .07
❑ 141 Clark Gillies .40 .18
❑ 142 Phil Russell DP .10 .05
❑ 143 Dirk Graham DP 1.00 .45
❑ 144 Randy Carlyle .10 .05
❑ 145 Charlie Simmer .15 .07
❑ 146 Ron Flockhart DP .10 .05
❑ 147 Tom Laidlaw .15 .07
❑ 148 Dave Tippett .15 .07
❑ 149 Wendel Clark DP 15.00 6.75
❑ 150 Bob Carpenter DP .10 .05
❑ 151 Bill Watson .15 .07
❑ 152 Roberto Romano DP .10 .05
❑ 153 Doug Shedden .15 .07
❑ 154 Phil Housley 1.00 .45
❑ 155 Bryan Trottier 1.00 .45
❑ 156 Patrik Sundstrom DP .10 .05
❑ 157 Rick Middleton DP .10 .05
❑ 158 Glenn Resch .40 .18
❑ 159 Bernie Nicholls DP 1.00 .45
❑ 160 Ray Ferraro 2.50 1.10
❑ 161 Mats Naslund DP .10 .05
❑ 162 Pat Flatley DP .10 .05
❑ 163 Joe Cirella .15 .07
❑ 164 Rod Langway DP .10 .05
❑ 165 Checklist 1-99 1.00 .45
❑ 166 Carey Wilson .15 .07
❑ 167 Murray Craven .15 .07
❑ 168 Paul Gillis .15 .07
❑ 169 Borje Salming .15 .07
❑ 170 Perry Turnbull .15 .07
❑ 171 Chris Chelios 3.00 1.35
❑ 172 Keith Acton .15 .07
❑ 173 Al MacInnis 5.00 2.20
❑ 174 Russ Courtnall 2.50 1.10
❑ 175 Brad Marsh .15 .07
❑ 176 Guy Carbonneau .40 .18
❑ 177 Ray Neufeld .15 .07
❑ 178 Craig MacTavish 1.00 .45
❑ 179 Rick Lanz .15 .07
❑ 180 Murray Bannerman .15 .07
❑ 181 Brent Ashton .15 .07
❑ 182 Jim Peplinski .15 .07
❑ 183 Mark Napier .15 .07
❑ 184 Laurie Boschman .15 .07
❑ 185 Larry Murphy .40 .18
❑ 186 Mark Messier 3.50 1.55
❑ 187 Risto Siltanen .15 .07
❑ 188 Bobby Smith .40 .18
❑ 189 Gary Suter 2.00 .90
❑ 190 Peter Zezel .15 .07
❑ 191 Rick Vaive .15 .07
❑ 192 Dale Hunter .40 .18
❑ 193 Mike Krushelnyski .15 .07
❑ 194 Scott Arniel .15 .07
❑ 195 Larry Playfair .15 .07
❑ 196 Doug Risebrough .15 .07
❑ 197 Kevin Lowe .15 .07
❑ 198 Checklist 100-198 1.00 .45

## 1986-87 Topps Box Bottoms

This sixteen-card standard-size set was issued in sets of four on the bottom of the 1986-87 Topps wax pack boxes. Complete box bottom panels are valued at a 25 percent premium above the prices listed below. The front presents a color action photo with various color borders, with the team's logo in the lower right hand corner. The back includes statistical information, is written in English, and is printed on blue with black ink. The cards are lettered rather than numbered.

| | MINT | NRMT |
|---|---|---|
| COMPLETE SET (16) | 35.00 | 16.00 |
| COMMON CARD (A-P) | .25 | .11 |

❑ A Greg Adams .50 .23
❑ B Mike Bossy 1.00 .45
❑ C Dave Christian .25 .11
❑ D Mike Foligno .25 .11
❑ E Michel Goulet .50 .23
❑ F Wayne Gretzky 15.00 6.75
❑ G Tim Kerr .25 .11
❑ H Jari Kurri 1.50 .70
❑ I Mario Lemieux 20.00 9.00
❑ J Lanny McDonald .50 .23
❑ K Bernie Nicholls .50 .23
❑ L Mike Ridley .50 .23
❑ M Larry Robinson .50 .23
❑ N Denis Savard .50 .23
❑ O Brian Sutter .25 .11
❑ P Bryan Trottier .75 .35

## 1986-87 Topps Sticker Inserts

This set of 33 "Hockey Helmet Stickers" features stickers of 12 All-Star players (1-12) and 21 stickers of team logos, pucks, and

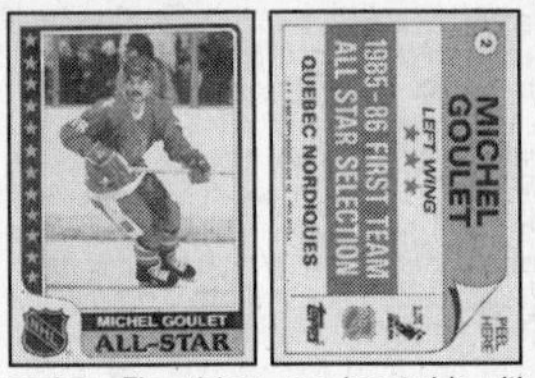


numbers. The stickers were inserted in with the 1986-87 Topps hockey regular issue wax packs and as such are also 2 1/2" by 3 1/2". The card backs are printed in blue and red on white card stock. The last seven team stickers can be found with the team logos on the top or bottom.

| | MINT | NRMT |
|---|---|---|
| COMPLETE SET (33) | 30.00 | 13.50 |
| COMMON CARD (1-12) | .35 | .16 |
| COMMON TEAM (13-33) | .15 | .07 |

❑ 1 John Vanbiesbrouck 6.00 2.70
❑ 2 Michel Goulet .50 .23
❑ 3 Wayne Gretzky 10.00 4.50
❑ 4 Mike Bossy 1.00 .45
❑ 5 Paul Coffey 1.50 .70
❑ 6 Mark Howe .35 .16
❑ 7 Bob Froese .35 .16
❑ 8 Mats Naslund .35 .16
❑ 9 Mario Lemieux 10.00 4.50
❑ 10 Jari Kurri 1.50 .70
❑ 11 Ray Bourque 1.50 .70
❑ 12 Larry Robinson .50 .23
❑ 13 Toronto Maple Leafs .25 .11
❑ 14 Buffalo Sabres .15 .07
❑ 15 Detroit Red Wings .25 .11
❑ 16 Pittsburgh Penguins .15 .07
❑ 17 New York Rangers .25 .11
❑ 18 Calgary Flames .15 .07
❑ 19 Winnipeg Jets .15 .07
❑ 20 Quebec Nordiques .15 .07
❑ 21 Chicago Blackhawks .25 .11
❑ 22 Los Angeles Kings .15 .07
❑ 23 Montreal Canadiens .25 .11
❑ 24 Vancouver Canucks .15 .07
❑ 25 Hartford Whalers .15 .07
❑ 26 Philadelphia Flyers .15 .07
❑ 27 New Jersey Devils .15 .07
❑ 28 St. Louis Blues .15 .07
❑ 29 Minnesota North Stars .15 .07
❑ 30 Washington Capitals .15 .07
❑ 31 Boston Bruins .25 .11
❑ 32 New York Islanders .15 .07
❑ 33 Edmonton Oilers .15 .07

## 1987-88 Topps

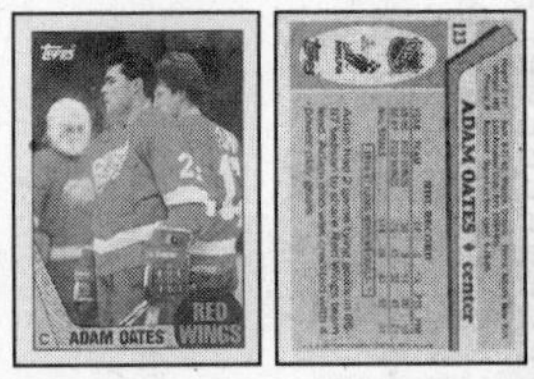


The 1987-88 Topps hockey set contains 198 standard size cards. There are 66 double printed cards which are indicated by DP below. Again, unopened packs had 12 cards plus one sticker and a piece of gum. The fronts feature a design that includes a hockey stick at the bottom with which the player's name is located. At bottom right, the team name appears in a large puck. The card backs contain career statistics, game winning goals from 1986-87 and highlights. Rookie Cards in this set include Kevin Hatcher, Ron Hextall, Adam Oates, Bill Ranford, Luc Robitaille, Ulf Samuelsson, Esa Tikkanen, and Rick Tocchet.

| | MINT | NRMT |
|---|---|---|
| COMPLETE SET (198) | 120.00 | 55.00 |
| COMMON CARD (1-198) | .10 | .05 |
| COMMON CARD DP | .05 | .02 |

❑ 1 Denis Potvin DP .25 .11
❑ 2 Rick Tocchet 6.00 2.70
❑ 3 Dave Andreychuk .50 .23
❑ 4 Stan Smyl .25 .11
❑ 5 Dave Babych DP .05 .02
❑ 6 Pat Verbeek .50 .23
❑ 7 Esa Tikkanen 5.00 2.20
❑ 8 Mike Ridley .25 .11
❑ 9 Randy Carlyle .25 .11
❑ 10 Greg Paslawski .10 .05
❑ 11 Neal Broten .25 .1
❑ 12 Wendel Clark DP 2.50 1.10
❑ 13 Bill Ranford DP UER 5.00 2.20
(Date of birth is 12-12-66; should be 12-14-66)
❑ 14 Doug Wilson .25 .1
❑ 15 Mario Lemieux 15.00 6.7
❑ 16 Mats Naslund .25 .1
❑ 17 Mel Bridgman .10 .0
❑ 18 James Patrick DP .05 .0
❑ 19 Rollie Melanson .25 .1
❑ 20 Lanny McDonald .25 .1
❑ 21 Peter Stastny .25 .1
❑ 22 Murray Craven .10 .0

| | | |
|---|---|---|
| ❑ 23 Ulf Samuelsson DP | 2.50 | 1.10 |
| ❑ 24 Michael Thelven DP UER (Misspelled Thelvin on card front) | .05 | .02 |
| ❑ 25 Scott Stevens | .50 | .23 |
| ❑ 26 Petr Klima | .25 | .11 |
| ❑ 27 Brent Sutter DP | .05 | .02 |
| ❑ 28 Tomas Sandstrom | .50 | .23 |
| ❑ 29 Tim Bothwell | .10 | .05 |
| ❑ 30 Bob Carpenter DP | .05 | .02 |
| ❑ 31 Brian MacLellan DP | .05 | .02 |
| ❑ 32 John Chabot | .10 | .05 |
| ❑ 33 Phil Housley DP | .25 | .11 |
| ❑ 34 Patrik Sundstrom DP | .05 | .02 |
| ❑ 35 Dave Ellett | .25 | .11 |
| ❑ 36 John Vanbiesbrouck | 10.00 | 4.50 |
| ❑ 37 Dave Lewis | .10 | .05 |
| ❑ 38 Tom McCarthy DP | .05 | .02 |
| ❑ 39 Dave Poulin | .25 | .11 |
| ❑ 40 Mike Foligno | .25 | .11 |
| ❑ 41 Gordie Roberts | .10 | .05 |
| ❑ 42 Luc Robitaille | 15.00 | 6.75 |
| ❑ 43 Duane Sutter | .10 | .05 |
| ❑ 44 Pete Peeters | .25 | .11 |
| ❑ 45 John Anderson | .10 | .05 |
| ❑ 46 Aaron Broten | .10 | .05 |
| ❑ 47 Keith Brown | .10 | .05 |
| ❑ 48 Bobby Smith | .25 | .11 |
| ❑ 49 Don Maloney | .10 | .05 |
| ❑ 50 Mark Hunter | .10 | .05 |
| ❑ 51 Moe Mantha | .10 | .05 |
| ❑ 52 Charlie Simmer | .25 | .11 |
| ❑ 53 Wayne Gretzky | 15.00 | 6.75 |
| ❑ 54 Mark Howe | .25 | .11 |
| ❑ 55 Bob Gould | .10 | .05 |
| ❑ 56 Steve Yzerman DP | 5.00 | 2.20 |
| ❑ 57 Larry Playfair | .10 | .05 |
| ❑ 58 Alain Chevrier | .25 | .11 |
| ❑ 59 Steve Larmer | .50 | .23 |
| ❑ 60 Bryan Trottier | .50 | .23 |
| ❑ 61 Stewart Gavin DP | .05 | .02 |
| ❑ 62 Russ Courtnall DP | .50 | .23 |
| ❑ 63 Mike Ramsey DP | .05 | .02 |
| ❑ 64 Bob Brooke | .10 | .05 |
| ❑ 65 Rick Wamsley DP | .05 | .02 |
| ❑ 66 Ken Morrow DP | .05 | .02 |
| ❑ 67 Gerard Gallant UER (Misspelled Gerald on card front) | .10 | .05 |
| ❑ 68 Kevin Hatcher | 1.50 | .70 |
| ❑ 69 Cam Neely | 2.00 | .90 |
| ❑ 70 Sylvain Turgeon DP | .05 | .02 |
| ❑ 71 Peter Zezel | .10 | .05 |
| ❑ 72 Al MacInnis | 2.50 | 1.10 |
| ❑ 73 Terry Ruskowski DP | .05 | .02 |
| ❑ 74 Troy Murray | .10 | .05 |
| ❑ 75 Jim Fox DP | .05 | .02 |
| ❑ 76 Kelly Kisio | .10 | .05 |
| ❑ 77 Michel Goulet DP | .25 | .11 |
| ❑ 78 Tom Barrasso DP | .25 | .11 |
| ❑ 79 Bruce Driver DP | .05 | .02 |
| ❑ 80 Craig Simpson DP | .25 | .11 |
| ❑ 81 Dino Ciccarelli | .25 | .11 |
| ❑ 82 Gary Nylund DP | .05 | .02 |
| ❑ 83 Bernie Federko | .25 | .11 |
| ❑ 84 John Tonelli DP | .05 | .02 |
| ❑ 85 Brad McCrimmon DP | .05 | .02 |
| ❑ 86 Dave Tippett DP | .05 | .02 |
| ❑ 87 Ray Bourque DP | 1.00 | .45 |
| ❑ 88 Dave Christian | .25 | .11 |
| ❑ 89 Glen Hanlon | .25 | .11 |
| ❑ 90 Brian Curran | .10 | .05 |
| ❑ 91 Paul MacLean | .25 | .11 |
| ❑ 92 Jimmy Carson | .25 | .11 |
| ❑ 93 Willie Huber | .10 | .05 |
| ❑ 94 Brian Bellows | .25 | .11 |
| ❑ 95 Doug Jarvis DP | .05 | .02 |
| ❑ 96 Clark Gillies | .25 | .11 |
| ❑ 97 Tony Tanti | .10 | .05 |
| ❑ 98 Pelle Eklund DP | .25 | .11 |
| ❑ 99 Paul Coffey | 1.50 | .70 |
| ❑ 100 Brent Ashton DP | .05 | .02 |
| ❑ 101 Mark Johnson | .10 | .05 |
| ❑ 102 Greg Johnston | .10 | .05 |
| ❑ 103 Ron Flockhart | .10 | .05 |
| ❑ 104 Ed Olczyk | .10 | .05 |
| ❑ 105 Mike Bossy | .40 | .18 |
| ❑ 106 Chris Chelios | 1.50 | .70 |
| ❑ 107 Gilles Meloche | .25 | .11 |
| ❑ 108 Rod Langway | .25 | .11 |
| ❑ 109 Ray Ferraro DP | .50 | .23 |
| ❑ 110 Ron Duguay DP | .05 | .02 |
| ❑ 111 Al Secord DP | .05 | .02 |
| ❑ 112 Mark Messier | 2.50 | 1.10 |
| ❑ 113 Ron Sutter | .10 | .05 |
| ❑ 114 Darren Veitch | .10 | .05 |
| ❑ 115 Rick Middleton DP | .05 | .02 |
| ❑ 116 Doug Sulliman | .10 | .05 |
| ❑ 117 Dennis Maruk DP | .05 | .02 |
| ❑ 118 Dave Taylor | .25 | .11 |
| ❑ 119 Kelly Hrudey | .50 | .23 |
| ❑ 120 Tom Fergus | .10 | .05 |
| ❑ 121 Christian Ruuttu | .10 | .05 |
| ❑ 122 Brian Benning | .10 | .05 |
| ❑ 123 Adam Oates | 10.00 | 4.50 |
| ❑ 124 Kevin Dineen | .40 | .18 |
| ❑ 125 Doug Bodger DP | .05 | .02 |
| ❑ 126 Joe Mullen | .50 | .23 |
| ❑ 127 Denis Savard | .25 | .11 |
| ❑ 128 Brad Marsh | .25 | .11 |
| ❑ 129 Marcel Dionne DP | .25 | .11 |
| ❑ 130 Bryan Erickson | .10 | .05 |
| ❑ 131 Reed Larson DP | .05 | .02 |
| ❑ 132 Don Beaupre | .25 | .11 |
| ❑ 133 Larry Murphy DP | .25 | .11 |
| ❑ 134 John Ogrodnick DP | .05 | .02 |
| ❑ 135 Greg Adams DP | .05 | .02 |
| ❑ 136 Pat Flatley | .10 | .05 |
| ❑ 137 Scott Arniel DP | .05 | .02 |
| ❑ 138 Dana Murzyn | .10 | .05 |
| ❑ 139 Greg C. Adams | .10 | .05 |
| ❑ 140 Bob Sauve | .25 | .11 |
| ❑ 141 Mike O'Connell | .10 | .05 |
| ❑ 142 Walt Poddubny DP | .05 | .02 |
| ❑ 143 Paul Reinhart | .10 | .05 |
| ❑ 144 Tim Kerr DP | .25 | .11 |
| ❑ 145 Brian Lawton | .10 | .05 |
| ❑ 146 Gino Cavallini | .10 | .05 |
| ❑ 147 Doug Keans DP | .05 | .02 |
| ❑ 148 Jari Kurri | .50 | .23 |
| ❑ 149 Dale Hawerchuk | .50 | .23 |
| ❑ 150 Randy Cunneyworth | .10 | .05 |
| ❑ 151 Jay Wells | .10 | .05 |
| ❑ 152 Mike Liut DP | .25 | .11 |
| ❑ 153 Steve Konroyd | .10 | .05 |
| ❑ 154 John Tucker | .10 | .05 |
| ❑ 155 Rick Vaive DP | .05 | .02 |
| ❑ 156 Bob Murray | .10 | .05 |
| ❑ 157 Kirk Muller DP | .50 | .23 |
| ❑ 158 Brian Propp | .10 | .05 |
| ❑ 159 Ron Greschner | .10 | .05 |
| ❑ 160 Bob Ramage | .10 | .05 |
| ❑ 161 Craig Laughlin | .10 | .05 |
| ❑ 162 Steve Kasper DP | .05 | .02 |
| ❑ 163 Patrick Roy | 25.00 | 11.00 |
| ❑ 164 Shawn Burr DP | .25 | .11 |
| ❑ 165 Craig Hartsburg DP | .05 | .02 |
| ❑ 166 Dean Evason | .25 | .11 |
| ❑ 167 Bob Bourne | .10 | .05 |
| ❑ 168 Mike Gartner | .50 | .23 |
| ❑ 169 Ron Hextall | 6.00 | 2.70 |
| ❑ 170 Joe Cirella | .10 | .05 |
| ❑ 171 Dan Quinn DP | .05 | .02 |
| ❑ 172 Tony McKegney | .10 | .05 |
| ❑ 173 Pat LaFontaine DP | .50 | .23 |
| ❑ 174 Allen Pedersen DP | .05 | .02 |
| ❑ 175 Doug Gilmour | 2.00 | .90 |
| ❑ 176 Gary Suter DP | .10 | .05 |
| ❑ 177 Barry Pederson DP | .05 | .02 |
| ❑ 178 Grant Fuhr DP | .50 | .23 |
| ❑ 179 Wayne Presley | .25 | .11 |
| ❑ 180 Wilf Paiement | .25 | .11 |
| ❑ 181 Doug Smail | .10 | .05 |
| ❑ 182 Doug Crossman DP | .05 | .02 |
| ❑ 183 Bernie Nicholls UER (Misspelled Nichols on card front) | .25 | .11 |
| ❑ 184 Dirk Graham UER (Misspelled Dick on card front) | .25 | .11 |
| ❑ 185 Anton Stastny | .10 | .05 |
| ❑ 186 Greg Stefan | .25 | .11 |
| ❑ 187 Ron Francis | .50 | .23 |
| ❑ 188 Steve Thomas DP | .40 | .18 |
| ❑ 189 Kelly Miller | .25 | .11 |
| ❑ 190 Tomas Jonsson | .10 | .05 |
| ❑ 191 John MacLean | .50 | .23 |
| ❑ 192 Larry Robinson DP | .25 | .11 |
| ❑ 193 Doug Wickenheiser DP | .05 | .02 |
| ❑ 194 Keith Crowder DP | .05 | .02 |
| ❑ 195 Bob Froese | .25 | .11 |
| ❑ 196 Jim Johnson | .10 | .05 |
| ❑ 197 Checklist 1-99 | .75 | .35 |
| ❑ 198 Checklist 100-198 | .75 | .35 |

## 1987-88 Topps Box Bottoms

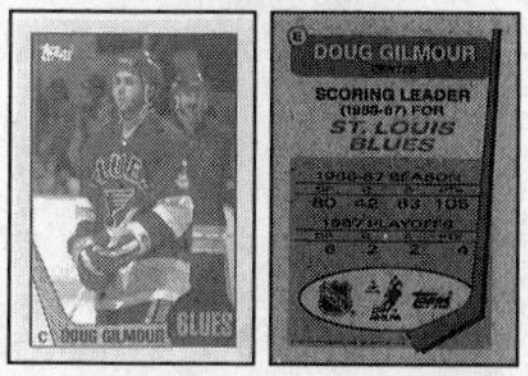


This sixteen-card standard-size set was issued in sets of four on the bottom of the 1987-88 Topps wax pack boxes. The cards feature team scoring leaders. Complete box bottom panels are valued at a 25 percent premium above the prices listed below. The cards are in the same design as the 1987-88 Topps regular issues except they are bordered in yellow. The backs are printed in red and black ink and give statistical information. The cards are lettered rather than numbered. This set features NHL luminaries such as Ray Bourque, Wayne Gretzky, and Steve Yzerman. The key card in the set is Luc Robitaille, appearing in the same year as his Rookie Card.

| | MINT | NRMT |
|---|---|---|
| COMPLETE SET (16) | 25.00 | 11.00 |
| COMMON CARD (A-P) | .15 | .07 |
| ❑ A Wayne Gretzky | 10.00 | 4.50 |
| ❑ B Tim Kerr | .25 | .11 |
| ❑ C Steve Yzerman | 5.00 | 2.20 |
| ❑ D Luc Robitaille | 4.00 | 1.80 |
| ❑ E Doug Gilmour | 1.00 | .45 |
| ❑ F Ray Bourque | 1.00 | .45 |
| ❑ G Joe Mullen | .50 | .23 |
| ❑ H Larry Murphy | .50 | .23 |
| ❑ I Dale Hawerchuk | .60 | .25 |
| ❑ J Ron Francis | 1.00 | .45 |
| ❑ K Walt Poddubny | .15 | .07 |
| ❑ L Mats Naslund | .35 | .16 |
| ❑ M Michel Goulet | .50 | .23 |
| ❑ N Denis Savard | .50 | .23 |
| ❑ O Bryan Trottier | .60 | .25 |
| ❑ P Russ Courtnall | .50 | .23 |

## 1987-88 Topps Sticker Inserts

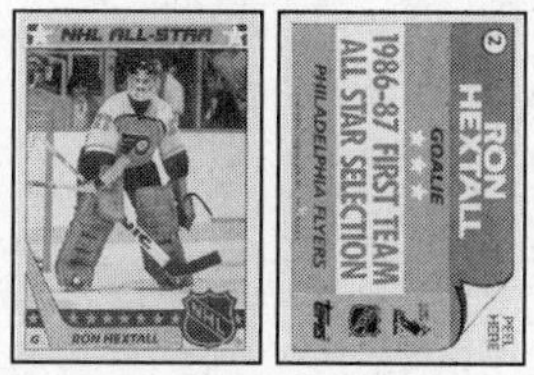


This set of 33 "Hockey Helmet Stickers" features stickers of 12 All-Star players (1-12) and 21 stickers of team logos, pucks, and numbers. The stickers were inserted in with the 1987-88 Topps hockey regular issue wax packs and as such are also 2 1/2" by 3 1/2". The card backs are printed in blue and red on white card stock. The last seven team stickers can be found with the team logos on the top or bottom.

| | MINT | NRMT |
|---|---|---|
| COMPLETE SET (33) | 20.00 | 9.00 |
| COMMON CARD (1-12) | .25 | .11 |
| COMMON TEAM (13-33) | .15 | .07 |
| ❑ 1 Ray Bourque | 1.25 | .55 |
| ❑ 2 Ron Hextall | 2.50 | 1.10 |
| ❑ 3 Mark Howe | .35 | .16 |
| ❑ 4 Jari Kurri | .75 | .35 |
| ❑ 5 Wayne Gretzky | 8.00 | 3.60 |
| ❑ 6 Michel Goulet | .35 | .16 |
| ❑ 7 Larry Murphy | .35 | .16 |
| ❑ 8 Mike Liut | .35 | .16 |
| ❑ 9 Al MacInnis | .50 | .23 |
| ❑ 10 Tim Kerr | .25 | .11 |
| ❑ 11 Mario Lemieux | 10.00 | 4.50 |
| ❑ 12 Luc Robitaille | 4.00 | 1.80 |
| ❑ 13 Toronto Maple Leafs | .25 | .11 |
| ❑ 14 Buffalo Sabres | .15 | .07 |
| ❑ 15 Detroit Red Wings | .25 | .11 |
| ❑ 16 Pittsburgh Penguins | .15 | .07 |
| ❑ 17 New York Rangers | .25 | .11 |
| ❑ 18 Calgary Flames | .15 | .07 |
| ❑ 19 Winnipeg Jets | .15 | .07 |
| ❑ 20 Quebec Nordiques | .15 | .07 |
| ❑ 21 Chicago Blackhawks | .15 | .07 |
| ❑ 22 Los Angeles Kings | .15 | .07 |
| ❑ 23 Montreal Canadiens | .25 | .11 |
| ❑ 24 Vancouver Canucks | .15 | .07 |
| ❑ 25 Hartford Whalers | .15 | .07 |
| ❑ 26 Philadelphia Flyers | .15 | .07 |
| ❑ 27 New Jersey Devils | .15 | .07 |
| ❑ 28 St. Louis Blues | .15 | .07 |
| ❑ 29 Minnesota North Stars | .15 | .07 |
| ❑ 30 Washington Capitals | .15 | .07 |
| ❑ 31 Boston Bruins | .25 | .11 |
| ❑ 32 New York Islanders | .15 | .07 |
| ❑ 33 Edmonton Oilers | .15 | .07 |

## 1988-89 Topps

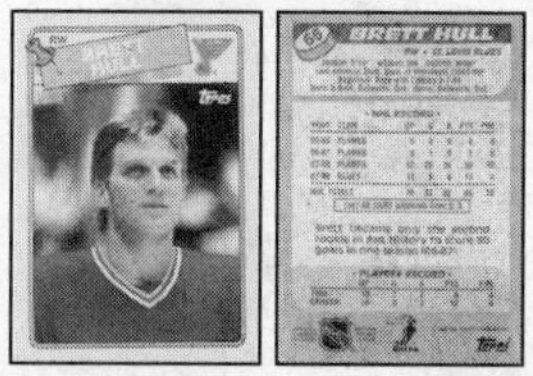


The 1988-89 Topps hockey set contains 198 standard size cards. There are 66 double printed cards that are indicated by DP in the checklist below. The fronts feature colored borders and each player's team logo. The backs contain yearly statistics, playoff statistics, game winning goals from 1987-88 and highlights. Wayne Gretzky (120) appears as a King for the first time. The press conference photo has Gretzky holding his new Kings jersey. Rookie Cards in this set include Sean Burke, Ulf Dahlen, Steve Duchesne, Brett Hull, Joe Nieuwendyk, Bob Probert, Brendan Shanahan, Ray Sheppard, Pierre Turgeon and Glen Wesley.

| | MINT | NRMT |
|---|---|---|
| COMPLETE SET (198) | 80.00 | 36.00 |
| COMMON CARD (1-198) | .10 | .05 |
| COMMON CARD DP | .05 | .02 |
| ❑ 1 Mario Lemieux DP | 4.00 | 1.80 |
| ❑ 2 Bob Joyce DP | .05 | .02 |
| ❑ 3 Joel Quenneville DP | .05 | .02 |
| ❑ 4 Tony McKegney | .10 | .05 |
| ❑ 5 Stephane Richer DP | .50 | .23 |
| ❑ 6 Mark Howe DP | .05 | .02 |
| ❑ 7 Brent Sutter DP | .05 | .02 |
| ❑ 8 Gilles Meloche DP | .05 | .02 |
| ❑ 9 Jimmy Carson DP | .05 | .02 |
| ❑ 10 John MacLean | .25 | .11 |
| ❑ 11 Gary Leeman | .10 | .05 |
| ❑ 12 Gerard Gallant DP | .05 | .02 |
| ❑ 13 Marcel Dionne | .25 | .11 |
| ❑ 14 Dave Christian DP | .05 | .02 |
| ❑ 15 Gary Nylund | .10 | .05 |
| ❑ 16 Joe Nieuwendyk | 5.00 | 2.20 |
| ❑ 17 Billy Smith DP | .25 | .11 |
| ❑ 18 Christian Ruuttu | .10 | .05 |
| ❑ 19 Randy Cunneyworth | .10 | .05 |
| ❑ 20 Brian Lawton | .10 | .05 |
| ❑ 21 Scott Mellanby DP | 1.00 | .45 |
| ❑ 22 Peter Stastny DP | .05 | .02 |
| ❑ 23 Gord Kluzak | .10 | .05 |
| ❑ 24 Sylvain Turgeon | .10 | .05 |
| ❑ 25 Clint Malarchuk | .25 | .11 |
| ❑ 26 Denis Savard | .25 | .11 |
| ❑ 27 Craig Simpson | .10 | .05 |
| ❑ 28 Petr Klima | .10 | .05 |
| ❑ 29 Pat Verbeek | .10 | .05 |
| ❑ 30 Moe Mantha | .10 | .05 |
| ❑ 31 Chris Nilan | .10 | .05 |
| ❑ 32 Barry Pederson | .10 | .05 |
| ❑ 33 Randy Burridge | .10 | .05 |
| ❑ 34 Ron Hextall | 1.00 | .45 |
| ❑ 35 Gaston Gingras | .10 | .05 |
| ❑ 36 Kevin Dineen DP | .05 | .02 |
| ❑ 37 Tom Laidlaw | .10 | .05 |
| ❑ 38 Paul MacLean DP | .05 | .02 |
| ❑ 39 John Chabot DP | .05 | .02 |
| ❑ 40 Lindy Ruff | .10 | .05 |
| ❑ 41 Dan Quinn DP | .05 | .02 |
| ❑ 42 Don Beaupre | .25 | .11 |
| ❑ 43 Gary Suter | .10 | .05 |
| ❑ 44 Mikko Makela DP | .05 | .02 |
| ❑ 45 Mark Johnson DP | .05 | .02 |
| ❑ 46 Dave Taylor | .25 | .11 |
| ❑ 47 Ulf Dahlen DP | .50 | .23 |
| ❑ 48 Jeff Sharples | .10 | .05 |
| ❑ 49 Chris Chelios | 1.00 | .45 |
| ❑ 50 Mike Gartner DP | .25 | .11 |
| ❑ 51 Darren Pang DP | .50 | .23 |
| ❑ 52 Ron Francis | .50 | .23 |
| ❑ 53 Ken Morrow | .10 | .05 |
| ❑ 54 Michel Goulet | .25 | .11 |
| ❑ 55 Ray Sheppard | 1.50 | .70 |
| ❑ 56 Doug Gilmour | 1.25 | .55 |
| ❑ 57 David Shaw DP | .05 | .02 |
| ❑ 58 Cam Neely DP | .25 | .11 |
| ❑ 59 Grant Fuhr DP | .50 | .23 |
| ❑ 60 Scott Stevens | .25 | .11 |
| ❑ 61 Bob Brooke | .10 | .05 |
| ❑ 62 Dave Hunter | .10 | .05 |
| ❑ 63 Alan Kerr | .10 | .05 |
| ❑ 64 Brad Marsh | .10 | .05 |
| ❑ 65 Dale Hawerchuk DP | .25 | .11 |
| ❑ 66 Brett Hull DP | 20.00 | 9.00 |
| ❑ 67 Patrik Sundstrom DP | .05 | .02 |
| ❑ 68 Greg Stefan | .25 | .11 |
| ❑ 69 James Patrick | .10 | .05 |
| ❑ 70 Dale Hunter DP | .05 | .02 |
| ❑ 71 Al Iafrate | .25 | .11 |
| ❑ 72 Bob Carpenter | .10 | .05 |
| ❑ 73 Ray Bourque DP | .75 | .35 |
| ❑ 74 John Tucker DP | .05 | .02 |
| ❑ 75 Carey Wilson | .10 | .05 |
| ❑ 76 Joe Mullen | .25 | .11 |
| ❑ 77 Rick Vaive | .10 | .05 |
| ❑ 78 Shawn Burr DP | .05 | .02 |
| ❑ 79 Murray Craven DP | .05 | .02 |
| ❑ 80 Clark Gillies | .25 | .11 |
| ❑ 81 Bernie Federko | .25 | .11 |
| ❑ 82 Tony Tanti | .10 | .05 |
| ❑ 83 Greg Gilbert | .10 | .05 |
| ❑ 84 Kirk Muller | .25 | .11 |
| ❑ 85 Dave Tippett | .10 | .05 |
| ❑ 86 Kevin Hatcher DP | .25 | .11 |
| ❑ 87 Rick Middleton DP | .05 | .02 |
| ❑ 88 Bobby Smith | .25 | .11 |
| ❑ 89 Doug Wilson DP | .05 | .02 |
| ❑ 90 Scott Arniel | .10 | .05 |
| ❑ 91 Brian Mullen | .10 | .05 |
| ❑ 92 Mike O'Connell DP | .05 | .02 |
| ❑ 93 Mark Messier DP | 1.25 | .55 |
| ❑ 94 Sean Burke | 1.50 | .70 |
| ❑ 95 Brian Bellows DP | .05 | .02 |
| ❑ 96 Doug Bodger | .10 | .05 |
| ❑ 97 Bryan Trottier | .50 | .23 |
| ❑ 98 Anton Stastny | .10 | .05 |
| ❑ 99 Checklist 1-99 | .50 | .23 |
| ❑ 100 Dave Poulin DP | .05 | .02 |
| ❑ 101 Bob Bourne DP | .05 | .02 |
| ❑ 102 John Vanbiesbrouck | 4.00 | 1.80 |
| ❑ 103 Allen Pedersen | .10 | .05 |
| ❑ 104 Mike Ridley | .10 | .05 |
| ❑ 105 Andrew McBain | .10 | .05 |
| ❑ 106 Troy Murray DP | .05 | .02 |
| ❑ 107 Tom Barrasso | .25 | .11 |
| ❑ 108 Tomas Jonsson | .10 | .05 |
| ❑ 109 Rob Brown | .10 | .05 |
| ❑ 110 Hakan Loob DP | .05 | .02 |
| ❑ 111 Ilkka Sinisalo DP | .05 | .02 |
| ❑ 112 Dave Archibald | .10 | .05 |
| ❑ 113 Doug Halward | .10 | .05 |
| ❑ 114 Ray Ferraro | .10 | .05 |
| ❑ 115 Doug Brown | .10 | .05 |
| ❑ 116 Patrick Roy DP | 4.00 | 1.80 |
| ❑ 117 Greg Millen | .25 | .11 |
| ❑ 118 Ken Linseman | .10 | .05 |
| ❑ 119 Phil Housley DP | .15 | .07 |
| ❑ 120 Wayne Gretzky (Holding up Kings sweater) | 20.00 | 9.00 |
| ❑ 121 Tomas Sandstrom | .25 | .11 |
| ❑ 122 Brendan Shanahan | 20.00 | 9.00 |
| ❑ 123 Pat LaFontaine | .50 | .23 |
| ❑ 124 Luc Robitaille DP | 1.50 | .70 |
| ❑ 125 Ed Olczyk DP | .05 | .02 |
| ❑ 126 Ron Sutter | .10 | .05 |
| ❑ 127 Mike Liut | .25 | .11 |
| ❑ 128 Brent Ashton DP | .05 | .02 |
| ❑ 129 Tony Hrkac | .10 | .05 |
| ❑ 130 Kelly Miller | .10 | .05 |
| ❑ 131 Alan Haworth | .10 | .05 |
| ❑ 132 Dave McLlwain | .10 | .05 |
| ❑ 133 Mike Ramsey | .10 | .05 |
| ❑ 134 Bob Sweeney | .10 | .05 |
| ❑ 135 Dirk Graham DP | .05 | .02 |
| ❑ 136 Ulf Samuelsson | .50 | .23 |
| ❑ 137 Petri Skriko | .10 | .05 |
| ❑ 138 Aaron Broten DP | .05 | .02 |
| ❑ 139 Jim Fox | .10 | .05 |
| ❑ 140 Randy Wood DP | .05 | .02 |
| ❑ 141 Larry Murphy | .25 | .11 |
| ❑ 142 Daniel Berthiaume DP | .05 | .02 |
| ❑ 143 Kelly Kisio | .10 | .05 |
| ❑ 144 Neal Broten | .10 | .05 |
| ❑ 145 Reed Larson | .10 | .05 |
| ❑ 146 Peter Zezel DP | .05 | .02 |
| ❑ 147 Jari Kurri | .50 | .23 |
| ❑ 148 Jim Johnson | .10 | .05 |
| ❑ 149 Gino Cavallini DP | .05 | .02 |
| ❑ 150 Glen Hanlon DP | .25 | .11 |
| ❑ 151 Bengt Gustafsson | .10 | .05 |
| ❑ 152 Mike Bullard DP | .05 | .02 |
| ❑ 153 John Ogrodnick | .10 | .05 |
| ❑ 154 Steve Larmer | .25 | .11 |
| ❑ 155 Kelly Hrudey | .25 | .11 |
| ❑ 156 Mats Naslund | .10 | .05 |
| ❑ 157 Bruce Driver | .10 | .05 |
| ❑ 158 Randy Hillier | .10 | .05 |
| ❑ 159 Craig Hartsburg | .10 | .05 |
| ❑ 160 Rollie Melanson | .25 | .11 |
| ❑ 161 Adam Oates DP | 1.50 | .70 |
| ❑ 162 Greg Adams DP | .05 | .02 |
| ❑ 163 Dave Andreychuk DP | .25 | .11 |
| ❑ 164 Dave Babych | .10 | .05 |
| ❑ 165 Brian Noonan | .10 | .05 |
| ❑ 166 Glen Wesley | .10 | .05 |
| ❑ 167 Dave Ellett | .10 | .05 |
| ❑ 168 Brian Propp | .10 | .05 |
| ❑ 169 Bernie Nicholls | .25 | .11 |
| ❑ 170 Walt Poddubny | .10 | .05 |
| ❑ 171 Steve Konroyd | .10 | .05 |
| ❑ 172 Doug Sulliman DP | .05 | .02 |
| ❑ 173 Mario Gosselin | .25 | .11 |
| ❑ 174 Brian Benning | .10 | .05 |
| ❑ 175 Dino Ciccarelli | .25 | .11 |
| ❑ 176 Steve Kasper | .10 | .05 |
| ❑ 177 Rick Tocchet | 1.00 | .45 |
| ❑ 178 Brad McCrimmon | .10 | .05 |
| ❑ 179 Paul Coffey | 1.00 | .45 |
| ❑ 180 Pete Peeters | .25 | .11 |
| ❑ 181 Bob Probert DP | 1.50 | .70 |
| ❑ 182 Steve Duchesne DP | 1.25 | .55 |
| ❑ 183 Russ Courtnall | .25 | .11 |
| ❑ 184 Mike Foligno DP | .05 | .02 |
| ❑ 185 Wayne Presley DP | .05 | .02 |
| ❑ 186 Rejean Lemelin | .25 | .11 |
| ❑ 187 Mark Hunter | .10 | .05 |
| ❑ 188 Joe Cirella | .10 | .05 |
| ❑ 189 Glenn Anderson DP | .25 | .11 |
| ❑ 190 John Anderson | .10 | .05 |
| ❑ 191 Pat Flatley | .10 | .05 |
| ❑ 192 Rod Langway | .10 | .05 |
| ❑ 193 Brian MacLellan | .10 | .05 |
| ❑ 194 Pierre Turgeon | 10.00 | 4.50 |
| ❑ 195 Brian Hayward | .25 | .11 |
| ❑ 196 Steve Yzerman DP | 2.50 | 1.10 |
| ❑ 197 Doug Crossman | .10 | .05 |
| ❑ 198 Checklist 100-198 | .50 | .23 |

## 1988-89 Topps Box Bottoms

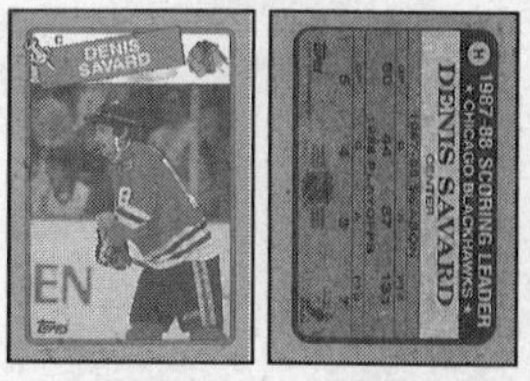


This sixteen-card standard-size set was issued in sets of four on the bottom of the 1988-89 Topps wax pack boxes. The cards featue team scoring leaders. Complete box bottom panels are valued at a 25 percent premium above the prices listed below. The cards are in the same design as the 1988-89 Topps regular issues except they are bordered only in gray. The backs are printed in purple on orange background and give statistical information. The cards are lettered rather than numbered and include stars such as Ray Bourque, Wayne Gretzky, Pat LaFontaine, Luc Robitaille, and Steve Yzerman.

| | MINT | NRMT |
|---|---|---|
| COMPLETE SET (16) | 14.00 | 6.25 |
| COMMON CARD (A-P) | .15 | .07 |
| ❑ A Ron Francis | .75 | .35 |
| ❑ B Wayne Gretzky | 6.00 | 2.70 |
| ❑ C Pat LaFontaine | .75 | .35 |
| ❑ D Bobby Smith | .25 | .11 |
| ❑ E Bernie Federko | .25 | .11 |
| ❑ F Kirk Muller | .50 | .23 |

❑ G Ed Olczyk .15 .07
❑ H Denis Savard .50 .23
❑ I Ray Bourque 1.00 .45
❑ J Murray Craven and .15 .07
Brian Propp
❑ K Dale Hawerchuk .50 .23
❑ L Steve Yzerman 3.00 1.35
❑ M Dave Andreychuk .35 .16
❑ N Mike Gartner .50 .23
❑ O Hakan Loob .25 .11
❑ P Luc Robitaille 1.00 .45

## 1988-89 Topps Sticker Inserts

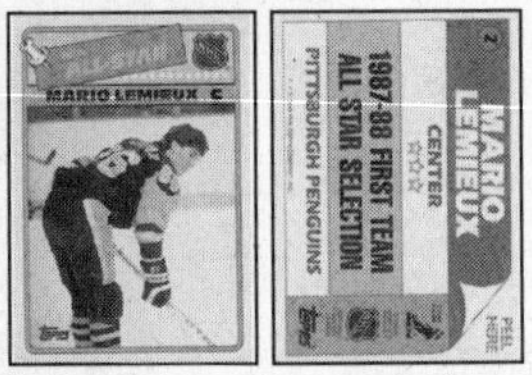

This set of 33 "Hockey Helmet Stickers" features stickers of 12 All-Star players (1-12) and 21 stickers of team logos, pucks, and numbers. The stickers were inserted in with the 1988-89 Topps hockey regular issue wax packs and as such are also 2 1/2" by 3 1/2". The card backs are printed in blue and red on white card stock. The last seven team stickers can be found with the team logos on the top or bottom.

| | MINT | NRMT |
|---|---|---|
| COMPLETE SET (33) | 15.00 | 6.75 |
| COMMON CARD (1-12) | .25 | .11 |
| COMMON TEAM (13-33) | .15 | .07 |

❑ 1 Luc Robitaille 1.50 .70
❑ 2 Mario Lemieux 4.00 1.80
❑ 3 Hakan Loob .25 .11
❑ 4 Scott Stevens .35 .16
❑ 5 Ray Bourque .75 .35
❑ 6 Grant Fuhr .50 .23
❑ 7 Michel Goulet .35 .16
❑ 8 Wayne Gretzky 5.00 2.20
❑ 9 Cam Neely .75 .35
❑ 10 Brad McCrimmon .25 .11
❑ 11 Gary Suter .25 .11
❑ 12 Patrick Roy 5.00 2.20
❑ 13 Toronto Maple Leafs .25 .11
❑ 14 Buffalo Sabres .15 .07
❑ 15 Detroit Red Wings .25 .11
❑ 16 Pittsburgh Penguins .15 .07
❑ 17 New York Rangers .25 .11
❑ 18 Calgary Flames .15 .07
❑ 19 Winnipeg Jets .15 .07
❑ 20 Quebec Nordiques .15 .07
❑ 21 Chicago Blackhawks .25 .11
❑ 22 Los Angeles Kings .15 .07
❑ 23 Montreal Canadiens .25 .11
❑ 24 Vancouver Canucks .15 .07
❑ 25 Hartford Whalers .15 .07
❑ 26 Philadelphia Flyers .15 .07
❑ 27 New Jersey Devils .15 .07
❑ 28 St. Louis Blues .15 .07
❑ 29 Minnesota North Stars .15 .07
❑ 30 Washington Capitals .15 .07
❑ 31 Boston Bruins .25 .11
❑ 32 New York Islanders .15 .07
❑ 33 Edmonton Oilers .15 .07

## 1989-90 Topps

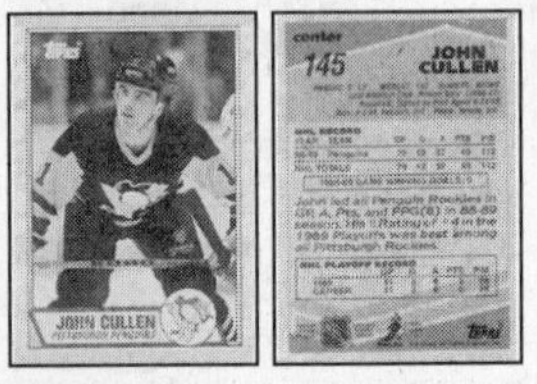

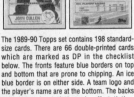

The 1989-90 Topps set contains 198 standard-size cards. There are 66 double-printed cards which are marked as DP in the checklist below. The fronts feature blue borders on top and bottom that are prone to chipping. An ice blue border is on either side. A team logo and the player's name are at the bottom. The backs contain yearly statistics, playoff statistics, game-winning goals from 1988-89 and highlights. The key Rookie Card in this set is Joe Sakic. Other Rookie Cards in this set include Geoff Courtnall, Craig Janney, Derek King, Trevor Linden, Brian Leetch, Dave Manson, Kirk McLean, and Cliff Ronning.

| | MINT | NRMT |
|---|---|---|
| COMPLETE SET (198) | 35.00 | 16.00 |
| COMMON CARD (1-198) | .10 | .05 |

❑ 1 Mario Lemieux 3.00 1.35
❑ 2 Ulf Dahlen DP .10 .05
❑ 3 Terry Carkner .10 .05
❑ 4 Tony McKegney .10 .05
❑ 5 Denis Savard .25 .11
❑ 6 Derek King DP .50 .23
❑ 7 Lanny McDonald .25 .11
❑ 8 John Tonelli .10 .05
❑ 9 Tom Kurvers DP .10 .05
❑ 10 Dave Archibald .10 .05
❑ 11 Peter Sidorkiewicz .25 .11
❑ 12 Esa Tikkanen .25 .11
❑ 13 Dave Barr .10 .05
❑ 14 Brent Sutter .25 .11
❑ 15 Cam Neely .25 .11
❑ 16 Calle Johansson .25 .11
❑ 17 Patrick Roy DP 2.00 .90
❑ 18 Dale DeGray DP .10 .05
❑ 19 Phil Bourque .10 .05
❑ 20 Kevin Dineen .10 .05
❑ 21 Mike Bullard DP .10 .05
❑ 22 Gary Leeman .10 .05
❑ 23 Greg Stefan DP .25 .11
❑ 24 Brian Mullen .10 .05
❑ 25 Pierre Turgeon DP .75 .35
❑ 26 Bob Rouse DP .10 .05
❑ 27 Peter Zezel .10 .05
❑ 28 Jeff Brown DP .50 .23
❑ 29 Andy Brickley DP .10 .05
❑ 30 Mike Gartner .25 .11
❑ 31 Darren Pang .25 .11
❑ 32 Pat Verbeek .10 .05
❑ 33 Petri Skriko DP .10 .05
❑ 34 Tom Laidlaw .10 .05
❑ 35 Randy Wood .10 .05
❑ 36 Tom Barrasso DP .25 .11
❑ 37 John Tucker DP .10 .05
❑ 38 Andrew McBain .10 .05
❑ 39 David Shaw DP .10 .05
❑ 40 Rejean Lemelin .25 .11
❑ 41 Dino Ciccarelli DP .25 .11
❑ 42 Jeff Sharples .10 .05
❑ 43 Jari Kurri .50 .23
❑ 44 Murray Craven DP .10 .05
❑ 45 Cliff Ronning DP .50 .23
❑ 46 Dave Babych .10 .05
❑ 47 Bernie Nicholls DP .25 .11
❑ 48 Jon Casey .25 .11
❑ 49 Al MacInnis .25 .11
❑ 50 Bob Errey DP .25 .11
❑ 51 Glen Wesley .10 .05
❑ 52 Dirk Graham .10 .05
❑ 53 Guy Carbonneau DP .25 .11
❑ 54 Tomas Sandstrom .25 .11
❑ 55 Rod Langway DP .10 .05
❑ 56 Patrik Sundstrom .10 .05
❑ 57 Michel Goulet .25 .11
❑ 58 Dave Taylor .25 .11
❑ 59 Phil Housley .25 .11
❑ 60 Pat LaFontaine DP .50 .23
❑ 61 Kirk McLean DP 1.00 .45
❑ 62 Ken Linseman .10 .05
❑ 63A Randy Cunneyworth ERR 6.00 2.70
(Pittsburgh Penguins)
❑ 63B Randy Cunneyworth COR. .10 .05
(Winnipeg Jets)
❑ 64 Tony Hrkac DP .10 .05
❑ 65 Mark Messier DP .60 .25
❑ 66 Carey Wilson DP .10 .05
❑ 67 Stephen Leach .10 .05
❑ 68 Christian Ruuttu .10 .05
❑ 69 Dave Ellett .10 .05
❑ 70 Ray Ferraro .10 .05
❑ 71 Colin Patterson .10 .05
❑ 72 Tim Kerr .25 .11
❑ 73 Bob Joyce .25 .11
❑ 74 Doug Gilmour DP .50 .23
❑ 75 Lee Norwood DP .10 .05
❑ 76 Dale Hunter .25 .11
❑ 77 Jim Johnson DP .10 .05
❑ 78 Mike Foligno DP .10 .05
❑ 79 Al Iafrate DP .25 .11
❑ 80 Rick Tocchet DP .25 .11
❑ 81 Greg Hawgood DP .10 .05
❑ 82 Steve Thomas .25 .11
❑ 83 Steve Yzerman DP 1.25 .55
❑ 84 Mike McPhee .10 .05
❑ 85 David Volek DP .10 .05
❑ 86 Brian Benning .10 .05
❑ 87 Neal Broten .25 .11
❑ 88 Luc Robitaille .50 .23
❑ 89 Trevor Linden 2.50 1.10
❑ 90 James Patrick DP .10 .05
❑ 91 Brian Lawton .10 .05
❑ 92 Sean Burke DP .25 .11
❑ 93 Scott Stevens .25 .11
❑ 94 Pat Elynuik DP .25 .11
❑ 95 Paul Coffey .50 .23
❑ 96 Jan Erixon DP .10 .05
❑ 97 Mike Liut .25 .11
❑ 98 Wayne Presley .10 .05
❑ 99 Craig Simpson .25 .11
❑ 100 Kjell Samuelsson .25 .11
❑ 101 Shawn Burr DP .10 .05
❑ 102 John MacLean .25 .11
❑ 103 Tom Fergus .10 .05
❑ 104 Mike Krushelnyski .10 .05
❑ 105 Gary Nylund .10 .05
❑ 106 Dave Andreychuk .25 .11
❑ 107 Bernie Federko .25 .11
❑ 108 Gary Suter .10 .05
❑ 109 Dave Gagner DP .25 .11
❑ 110 Ray Bourque .50 .23
❑ 111 Geoff Courtnall 1.25 .55
❑ 112 Doug Wilson .25 .11
❑ 113 Joe Sakic 12.00 5.50
❑ 114 John Vanbiesbrouck 1.50 .70
❑ 115 Dave Poulin .10 .05
❑ 116 Rick Meagher .10 .05
❑ 117 Kirk Muller DP .25 .11
❑ 118 Mats Naslund .10 .05
❑ 119 Ray Sheppard .50 .23
❑ 120 Jeff Norton .10 .05
❑ 121 Randy Burridge DP .10 .05
❑ 122 Dale Hawerchuk DP .25 .11
❑ 123 Steve Duchesne .25 .11
❑ 124 John Anderson .10 .05
❑ 125 Rick Vaive DP .10 .05
❑ 126 Randy Hillier .10 .05
❑ 127 Jimmy Carson .10 .05
❑ 128 Larry Murphy .25 .11
❑ 129 Paul MacLean DP .10 .05
❑ 130 Joe Cirella .10 .05
❑ 131 Kelly Miller DP .10 .05
❑ 132 Alain Chevrier DP .25 .11
❑ 133 Ed Olczyk .10 .05
❑ 134 Dave Tippett .10 .05
❑ 135 Bob Sweeney .10 .05
❑ 136 Brian Leetch 6.00 2.70
❑ 137 Greg Millen .25 .11
❑ 138 Joe Nieuwendyk .50 .23
❑ 139 Brian Propp .10 .05
❑ 140 Mike Ramsey .10 .05
❑ 141 Mike Allison .10 .05
❑ 142 Shawn Chambers .10 .05
❑ 143 Peter Stastny DP .25 .11
❑ 144 Glen Hanlon .25 .11
❑ 145 John Cullen .25 .11
❑ 146 Kevin Hatcher .10 .05
❑ 147 Brendan Shanahan 4.00 1.80
❑ 148 Paul Reinhart .10 .05
❑ 149 Bryan Trottier .50 .23
❑ 150 Dave Manson .50 .23
❑ 151 Marc Habscheid DP .10 .05
❑ 152 Dan Quinn .10 .05
❑ 153 Stephane Richer DP .25 .11
❑ 154 Doug Bodger DP .10 .05
❑ 155 Ron Hextall .50 .23
❑ 156 Wayne Gretzky 4.00 1.80
❑ 157 Steve Tuttle DP .10 .05
❑ 158 Charlie Huddy DP .10 .05
❑ 159 Dave Christian DP .10 .05
❑ 160 Andy Moog .25 .11
❑ 161 Tony Granato .50 .23
❑ 162 Sylvain Cote .10 .05
❑ 163 Mike Vernon .75 .35
❑ 164 Steve Chiasson .50 .23
❑ 165 Mike Ridley .10 .05
❑ 166 Kelly Hrudey .25 .11
❑ 167 Bob Carpenter DP .10 .05
❑ 168 Zarley Zalapski .50 .23
❑ 169 Derek Laxdal .10 .05
❑ 170 Clint Malarchuk DP .25 .11
❑ 171 Kelly Kisio .10 .05
❑ 172 Gerard Gallant .10 .05
❑ 173 Ron Sutter .10 .05
❑ 174 Chris Chelios .50 .23
❑ 175 Ron Francis .50 .23
❑ 176 Gino Cavallini .10 .05
❑ 177 Brian Bellows DP .10 .05
❑ 178 Greg C. Adams DP .10 .05
❑ 179 Steve Larmer .25 .11
❑ 180 Aaron Broten .10 .05
❑ 181 Brent Ashton DP .10 .05
❑ 182 Gerald Diduck DP .10 .05
❑ 183 Paul MacDermid .10 .05
❑ 184 Walt Poddubny DP .10 .05
❑ 185 Adam Oates .50 .23
❑ 186 Brett Hull 3.00 1.35
❑ 187 Scott Arniel .10 .05
❑ 188 Bobby Smith .25 .11
❑ 189 Guy Lafleur .25 .11
❑ 190 Craig Janney 1.00 .45
❑ 191 Mark Howe .25 .11
❑ 192 Grant Fuhr DP .50 .23
❑ 193 Rob Brown .10 .05
❑ 194 Steve Kasper DP .10 .05
❑ 195 Pete Peeters .25 .11
❑ 196 Joe Mullen .25 .11
❑ 197 Checklist 1-99 .10 .05
❑ 198 Checklist 100-198 DP .10 .05

## 1989-90 Topps Box Bottoms

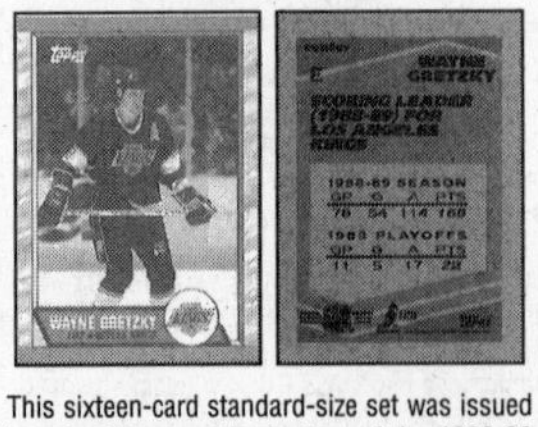

This sixteen-card standard-size set was issued in sets of four on the bottom of the 1989-90 Topps wax pack boxes. The cards feature sixteen NHL star players who were scoring leaders on their teams. Complete box bottom panels are valued at a 25 percent premium above the prices listed below. A color action photo appears on the front and the player's name, team, and team logo at the bottom of the picture. The back is printed in red and black ink and gives the player's position and statistical information. The cards are lettered rather than numbered. The set features such NHL stars as Wayne Gretzky, Brett Hull, and Mario Lemieux.

| | MINT | NRMT |
|---|---|---|
| COMPLETE SET (16) | 10.00 | 4.50 |
| COMMON CARD (A-P) | .25 | .11 |

❑ A Mario Lemieux 4.00 1.80
❑ B Mike Ridley .25 .11
❑ C Tomas Sandstrom .25 .11
❑ D Petri Skriko .25 .11
❑ E Wayne Gretzky 4.00 1.80
❑ F Brett Hull 2.00 .90
❑ G Tim Kerr .25 .11
❑ H Mats Naslund .25 .11
❑ I Jari Kurri .50 .23
❑ J Steve Larmer .50 .23
❑ K Cam Neely .75 .35
❑ L Steve Yzerman 2.00 .90
❑ M Kevin Dineen .25 .11
❑ N Dave Gagner .35 .16
❑ O Joe Mullen .35 .16
❑ P Pierre Turgeon .75 .35

## 1989-90 Topps Sticker Inserts

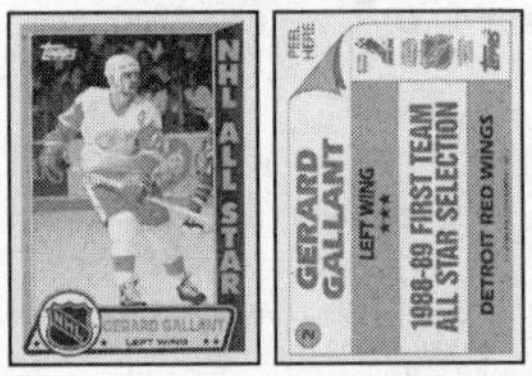

This 33-card standard-size set was issued as a one per pack insert in the 1989-90 Topps Hockey packs. This set is divided into the first 12 cards being the 1989-90 NHL all-stars and the next 21 cards being the various team logos along with some number stickers and stickers of hockey pucks. For some reason Topps apparently printed these sticker cards on sheets in such a way that there were three complete sets of 33 and then three more rows of 11 double-printed cards instead of merely printing four complete sets on the printing sheet.

| | MINT | NRMT |
|---|---|---|
| COMPLETE SET (33) | 10.00 | 4.50 |
| COMMON CARD (1-12) | .25 | .11 |
| COMMON DP (2/5/9/10) | .15 | .07 |
| COMMON TEAM (13-26) | .15 | .07 |
| COMMON TEAM DP (27-33) | .10 | .05 |

❑ 1 Chris Chelios .75 .35
❑ 2 Gerard Gallant DP .15 .07
❑ 3 Mario Lemieux 5.00 2.20
❑ 4 Al MacInnis .50 .23
❑ 5 Joe Mullen DP .25 .11
❑ 6 Patrick Roy 4.00 1.80
❑ 7 Ray Bourque .75 .35
❑ 8 Rob Brown .25 .11
❑ 9 Geoff Courtnall DP .25 .11
❑ 10 Steve Duchesne DP .15 .07
❑ 11 Wayne Gretzky 5.00 2.20
❑ 12 Mike Vernon .35 .16
❑ 13 Toronto Maple Leafs .15 .07
❑ 14 Buffalo Sabres .15 .07
❑ 15 Detroit Red Wings .15 .07
❑ 16 Pittsburgh Penguins .15 .07
❑ 17 New York Rangers .15 .07
❑ 18 Calgary Flames .15 .07
❑ 19 Winnipeg Jets .15 .07
❑ 20 Quebec Nordiques .15 .07
❑ 21 Chicago Blackhawks .15 .07
❑ 22 Los Angeles Kings .15 .07
❑ 23 Montreal Canadiens .15 .07
❑ 24 Vancouver Canucks .15 .07
❑ 25 Hartford Whalers .15 .07
❑ 26 Philadelphia Flyers .15 .07
❑ 27 New Jersey Devils DP .10 .05
❑ 28 St. Louis Blues DP .10 .05
❑ 29 Minn. North Stars DP .10 .05
❑ 30 Washington Capitals DP .10 .05
❑ 31 Boston Bruins DP .10 .05
❑ 32 New York Islanders DP .10 .05
❑ 33 Edmonton Oilers DP .10 .05

## 1990-91 Topps

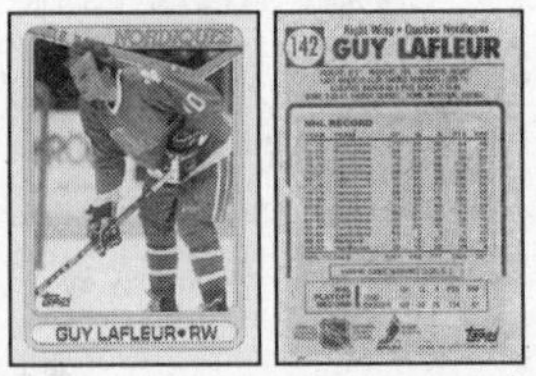

The 1990-91 Topps hockey set contains 396 standard-size cards. The fronts feature color action photos with color borders (according to team) on all four sides. A hockey stick is superimposed over the picture at the top border. The backs have yearly statistics, playoff statistics, and game winning goals from 1989-90. Included in the set is a three-card Tribute to Wayne Gretzky (1-3). Team cards have action scenes with the team's previous season standings and power play stats on back. The set was also produced in a high-gloss Tiffany version with supposedly just 3000 sets produced; the values for the Tiffany version are approximately five to ten times the values listed below, although superstar players such as Gretzky, Lemieux and Roy may go for twenty times or more. Rookie Cards in this set include Rod Brind'Amour, Stephane Fiset, Curtis Joseph, Mike Modano, Alexander Mogilny, Mark Recchi, Mike Richter, Jeremy Roenick, and Kevin Stevens.

| | MINT | NRMT |
|---|---|---|
| COMPLETE SET (396) | 15.00 | 6.75 |
| COMP.FACT.SET (396) | 15.00 | 6.75 |
| COMMON CARD (1-396) | .05 | .02 |

❑ 1 Gretzky Tribute .60 .25
Indianapolis Racers
❑ 2 Gretzky Tribute .50 .23
❑ 3 Gretzky Tribute .50 .23
❑ 4 Brett Hull HL .25 .11
❑ 5 Jari Kurri HL UER .05 .02
(Jari, not Jarri)
❑ 6 Bryan Trottier HL .10 .05
❑ 7 Jeremy Roenick .75 .35
❑ 8 Brian Propp .05 .02
❑ 9 Jim Hrivnak .10 .05
❑ 10 Mick Vukota .05 .02
❑ 11 Tom Kurvers .05 .02
❑ 12 Ulf Dahlen .05 .02
❑ 13 Bernie Nicholls .10 .05
❑ 14 Peter Sidorkiewicz .10 .05
❑ 15 Peter Zezel .05 .02
❑ 16 Mike Hartman .05 .02
❑ 17 Kings Team .05 .02
(Marty McSorley et al.)
❑ 18 Jim Sandlak .05 .02
❑ 19 Rob Brown .05 .02
❑ 20 Paul Ranheim .05 .02
❑ 21 Rick Zombo .05 .02
❑ 22 Paul Gillis .05 .02
❑ 23 Brian Hayward .10 .05
❑ 24 Brent Ashton .05 .02
❑ 25 Mark Lamb .05 .02
❑ 26 Rick Tocchet .10 .05
❑ 27 Slava Fetisov .05 .02
❑ 28 Denis Savard .10 .05
❑ 29 Chris Chelios .25 .11
❑ 30 Janne Ojanen .05 .02
❑ 31 Don Maloney .05 .02
❑ 32 Allan Bester .10 .05
❑ 33 Geoff Smith .05 .02
❑ 34 Daniel Shank .05 .02
❑ 35 Mikael Andersson .05 .02
❑ 36 Gino Cavallini .05 .02
❑ 37 Rob Murphy .05 .02
❑ 38 Flames Team .05 .02
(Goal celebration)
❑ 39 Laurie Boschman .05 .02
❑ 40 Craig Wolanin .05 .02
❑ 41 Phil Bourque .05 .02
❑ 42 Alexander Mogilny .75 .35
❑ 43 Ray Bourque .25 .11
❑ 44 Mike Liut .10 .05
❑ 45 Ron Sutter .05 .02
❑ 46 Bob Kudelski .05 .02
❑ 47 Larry Murphy .10 .05
❑ 48 Darren Turcotte .05 .02
❑ 49 Paul Ysebaert .05 .02
❑ 50 Alan Kerr .05 .02
❑ 51 Randy Carlyle .05 .02
❑ 52 Iiro Jarvi .05 .02
❑ 53 Don Barber .05 .02
❑ 54 Carey Wilson UER .05 .02
(Misspelled Cary
on both sides)
❑ 55 Joey Kocur .05 .02
❑ 56 Steve Larmer .10 .05
❑ 57 Paul Cavallini .05 .02
❑ 58 Shayne Corson .05 .02
❑ 59 Canucks Team .05 .02
(Brian Bradley)
❑ 60 Sergei Makarov .05 .02
❑ 61 Kjell Samuelsson .05 .02
❑ 62 Tony Granato .05 .02
❑ 63 Tom Fergus .05 .02
❑ 64 Martin Gelinas .30 .14
❑ 65 Tom Barrasso .10 .05
❑ 66 Pierre Turgeon .10 .05
❑ 67 Randy Cunneyworth .05 .02
❑ 68 Michal Pivonka .05 .02
❑ 69 Cam Neely .10 .05
❑ 70 Brian Bellows .05 .02
❑ 71 Pat Elynuik .05 .02
❑ 72 Doug Crossman .05 .02
❑ 73 Sylvain Turgeon .05 .02
❑ 74 Shawn Burr .05 .02
❑ 75 John Vanbiesbrouck .50 .23
❑ 76 Steve Bozek .05 .02
❑ 77 Brett Hull .50 .23
❑ 78 Zarley Zalapski .05 .02
❑ 79 Wendel Clark .10 .05
❑ 80 Flyers Team .05 .02
(Wendell Young/Kjell Samuelsson)
❑ 81 Kelly Miller .05 .02
❑ 82 Mark Pederson .05 .02
❑ 83 Adam Creighton .05 .02
❑ 84 Scott Young .05 .02
❑ 85 Petr Klima .05 .02
❑ 86 Steve Duchesne .05 .02
❑ 87 Joe Nieuwendyk .10 .05
❑ 88 Andy Brickley .05 .02
❑ 89 Phil Housley .10 .05
❑ 90 Neal Broten .10 .05
❑ 91 Al Iafrate .10 .05
❑ 92 Steve Thomas .05 .02
❑ 93 Guy Carbonneau .10 .05

❑ 94 Steve Chiasson .05 .02
❑ 95 Mike Tomlak .05 .02
❑ 96 Roger Johansson .05 .02
❑ 97 Randy Wood .05 .02
❑ 98 Jim Johnson .05 .02
❑ 99 Bob Sweeney .05 .02
❑ 100 Dino Ciccarelli .10 .05
❑ 101 Rangers Team .05 .02
(Goal Celebration)
❑ 102 Mike Ramsey .05 .02
❑ 103 Kelly Hrudey .10 .05
❑ 104 Dave Ellett .05 .02
❑ 105 Bob Brooke .05 .02
❑ 106 Greg Adams .05 .02
❑ 107 Joe Cirella .05 .02
❑ 108 Jari Kurri .10 .05
❑ 109 Pete Peeters .10 .05
❑ 110 Paul MacLean .05 .02
❑ 111 Doug Wilson .10 .05
❑ 112 Pat Verbeek .05 .02
❑ 113 Bob Beers .05 .02
❑ 114 Mike O'Connell .05 .02
❑ 115 Brian Bradley .05 .02
❑ 116 Paul Coffey .25 .11
❑ 117 Doug Brown .05 .02
❑ 118 Aaron Broten .05 .02
❑ 119 Bob Essensa .10 .05
❑ 120 Wayne Gretzky UER 1.25 .55
(1302 career assists,
not 13102)
❑ 121 Vincent Damphousse .10 .05
❑ 122 Nordiques Team .05 .02
(Paul Gillis)
❑ 123 Mike Foligno .05 .02
❑ 124 Russ Courtnall .05 .02
❑ 125 Rick Meagher .05 .02
❑ 126 Craig Fisher .05 .02
❑ 127 Al MacInnis .10 .05
❑ 128 Derek King .05 .02
❑ 129 Dale Hunter .05 .02
❑ 130 Mark Messier UER .30 .14
(Shown as LW,
should be C)
❑ 131 James Patrick UER .05 .02
(Orange border,
should be blue)
❑ 132 Checklist 1-132 UER .05 .02
(54 Cary Wilson,
should be Carey)
❑ 133 Red Wings Team .25 .11
(Steve Yzerman)
❑ 134 Barry Pederson .05 .02
❑ 135 Gary Leeman .05 .02
❑ 136 Doug Gilmour .25 .11
❑ 137 Mike McPhee .05 .02
❑ 138 Bob Murray .05 .02
❑ 139 Bob Carpenter .05 .02
❑ 140 Sean Burke .10 .05
❑ 141 Dale Hawerchuk .10 .05
❑ 142 Guy Lafleur .25 .11
❑ 143 Lindy Ruff .05 .02
❑ 144 Whalers Team .05 .02
(Brad Shaw)
❑ 145 Glenn Anderson .10 .05
❑ 146 Dave Chyzowski .05 .02
❑ 147 Kevin Hatcher .05 .02
❑ 148 Rick Vaive .05 .02
❑ 149 Adam Oates .10 .05
❑ 150 Garth Butcher .05 .02
❑ 151 Basil McRae .05 .02
❑ 152 Ilkka Sinisalo .05 .02
❑ 153 Steve Kasper .05 .02
❑ 154 Greg Paslawski .05 .02
❑ 155 Brad Marsh .05 .02
❑ 156 Esa Tikkanen .05 .02
❑ 157 Tony Tanti .05 .02
❑ 158 Mario Marois .05 .02
(oi in last name line
below rest of name)
❑ 159 Sylvain Lefebvre .05 .02
❑ 160 Troy Murray .05 .02
❑ 161 Gary Roberts .05 .02
❑ 162 Randy Ladouceur .05 .02
❑ 163 John Chabot .05 .02
❑ 164 Calle Johansson .05 .02
❑ 165 Bruins Team .05 .02
(Goal celebration)
❑ 166 Jeff Norton .05 .02
❑ 167 Mike Krushelnyski .05 .02
❑ 168 Dave Gagner .10 .05
❑ 169 Dave Andreychuk .10 .05
❑ 170 Dave Capuano .05 .02
❑ 171 Curtis Joseph .75 .35
❑ 172 Bruce Driver .05 .02
❑ 173 Scott Mellanby .10 .05
❑ 174 John Ogrodnick .05 .02
❑ 175 Mario Lemieux 1.00 .45
❑ 176 Marc Fortier .05 .02
❑ 177 Vincent Riendeau .10 .05
❑ 178 Mark Johnson .05 .02
❑ 179 Dirk Graham .05 .02
❑ 180 Jets Team .05 .02
(Keith Acton breaking in on
Daniel Berthiaume)
❑ 181 Robb Stauber .10 .05
❑ 182 Christian Ruuttu .05 .02
❑ 183 Dave Tippett .05 .02
❑ 184 Pat LaFontaine .10 .05
❑ 185 Mark Howe .05 .02
❑ 186 Stephane Richer .10 .05
❑ 187 Jan Erixon .05 .02
❑ 188 Neil Sheehy .05 .02
❑ 189 Craig MacTavish .05 .02
❑ 190 Randy Burridge .05 .02
❑ 191 Bernie Federko .10 .05
❑ 192 Shawn Chambers .05 .02
❑ 193 Mark Messier AS1 .25 .11
❑ 194 Luc Robitaille AS1 .05 .02
❑ 195 Brett Hull AS1 .10 .05
❑ 196 Ray Bourque AS1 .10 .05
❑ 197 Al MacInnis AS1 .10 .05
❑ 198 Patrick Roy AS1 .50 .23
❑ 199 Wayne Gretzky AS2 .60 .25
❑ 200 Brian Bellows AS2 .05 .02
❑ 201 Cam Neely AS2 .05 .02
❑ 202 Paul Coffey AS2 .05 .02
❑ 203 Doug Wilson AS2 .05 .02
❑ 204 Daren Puppa AS2 UER .10 .05
(Misspelled Darren
on front and back)
❑ 205 Gary Suter .05 .02
❑ 206 Ed Olczyk .05 .02
❑ 207 Doug Lidster .05 .02
❑ 208 John Cullen .05 .02
❑ 209 Luc Robitaille .10 .05
❑ 210 Tim Kerr .05 .02
❑ 211 Scott Stevens .10 .05
❑ 212 Craig Janney .10 .05
❑ 213 Kevin Dineen .05 .02
❑ 214 Jimmy Waite .10 .05
❑ 215 Benoit Hogue .05 .02
❑ 216 Curtis Leschyshyn .05 .02
❑ 217 Brad Lauer .05 .02
❑ 218 Joe Mullen .10 .05
❑ 219 Patrick Roy 1.00 .45
❑ 220 Blues Team .05 .02
(Gathering at bench)
❑ 221 Brian Leetch .35 .16
❑ 222 Steve Yzerman .60 .25
❑ 223 Stephane Beauregard .10 .05
❑ 224 John MacLean .10 .05
❑ 225 Trevor Linden .10 .05
❑ 226 Bill Ranford .10 .05
❑ 227 Mark Osborne .05 .02
❑ 228 Curt Giles .05 .02
❑ 229 Mikko Makela .05 .02
❑ 230 Bob Errey .05 .02
❑ 231 Jimmy Carson .05 .02
❑ 232 Kay Whitmore .10 .05
❑ 233 Gary Nylund .05 .02
❑ 234 Jiri Hrdina .05 .02
❑ 235 Stephen Leach .05 .02
❑ 236 Greg Hawgood UER .05 .02
(Photo actually
Don Sweeney)
❑ 237 Jocelyn Lemieux .05 .02
❑ 238 Daren Puppa .10 .05
❑ 239 Kelly Kisio .05 .02
❑ 240 Craig Simpson .05 .02
❑ 241 Maple Leafs Team .10 .05
(Vincent Damphousse)
❑ 242 Fredrik Olausson .05 .02
❑ 243 Ron Hextall .10 .05
❑ 244 Sergio Momesso .05 .02
❑ 245 Kirk Muller .05 .02
❑ 246 Petr Svoboda .05 .02
❑ 247 Daniel Berthiaume .10 .05
❑ 248 Andrew McBain .05 .02
❑ 249 Jeff Jackson UER .05 .02
(Game total for
'89-90 is 65, not 0)
❑ 250 Randy Gilhen .05 .02
❑ 251 Oilers Team .05 .02
(Adam Graves)
❑ 252 Rick Bennett .05 .02
❑ 253 Don Beaupre .10 .05
❑ 254 Pelle Eklund .05 .02
❑ 255 Greg Gilbert .05 .02
❑ 256 Gordie Roberts .05 .02
❑ 257 Kirk McLean .10 .05
❑ 258 Brent Sutter .05 .02
❑ 259 Brendan Shanahan .60 .25
❑ 260 Todd Krygier .05 .02
❑ 261 Larry Robinson UER .10 .05
(No '80-81 stats on
card, totals wrong)
❑ 262 Sabres Team .05 .02
(Phil Housley celebrating goal)
❑ 263 Dave Christian .05 .02
❑ 264 Checklist 133-264 .05 .02
❑ 265 Jamie Macoun .05 .02
❑ 266 Glen Hanlon .10 .05
❑ 267 Daniel Marois .05 .02
❑ 268 Doug Smail .05 .02
❑ 269 Jon Casey .10 .05
❑ 270 Brian Skrudland .05 .02
❑ 271 Michel Petit .05 .02
❑ 272 Dan Quinn .05 .02
❑ 273 Geoff Courtnall .05 .02
❑ 274 Mike Bullard .05 .02
❑ 275 Randy Gregg .05 .02
❑ 276 Keith Brown .05 .02
❑ 277 Troy Mallette .05 .02
❑ 278 Steve Tuttle .05 .02
❑ 279 Brad Shaw .05 .02
❑ 280 Mark Recchi .50 .23
❑ 281 John Tonelli .05 .02
❑ 282 Doug Bodger .05 .02
❑ 283 Thomas Steen .05 .02
❑ 284 Devils Team .05 .02
(Terreri making save)
❑ 285 Lee Norwood .05 .02
❑ 286 Brian MacLellan .05 .02
❑ 287 Bobby Smith .10 .05
❑ 288 Rob Cimetta .05 .02
❑ 289 Rob Zettler .05 .02
❑ 290 David Reid .05 .02
❑ 291 Bryan Trottier .10 .05
❑ 292 Brian Mullen .05 .02
❑ 293 Paul Reinhart .05 .02
❑ 294 Andy Moog .10 .05
❑ 295 Jeff Brown .05 .02
❑ 296 Ryan Walter .05 .02
❑ 297 Trent Yawney .05 .02
❑ 298 John Druce .05 .02
❑ 299 Dave McLlwain UER .05 .02
(Card says shoots
right, should be left)
❑ 300 David Volek .05 .02
❑ 301 Tomas Sandstrom .05 .02
❑ 302 Gord Murphy .05 .02
❑ 303 Lou Franceschetti .05 .02
❑ 304 Dana Murzyn .05 .02
❑ 305 North Stars Team .05 .02
❑ 306 Patrik Sundstrom .05 .02
❑ 307 Kevin Lowe .05 .02
❑ 308 Dave Barr .05 .02
❑ 309 Wendell Young .10 .05
❑ 310 Darrin Shannon .05 .02
❑ 311 Ron Francis .10 .05
❑ 312 Stephane Fiset .50 .23
❑ 313 Paul Fenton .05 .02
❑ 314 Dave Taylor .10 .05
❑ 315 Islanders Team .05 .02
(Pat LaFontaine)
❑ 316 Petri Skriko .05 .02
❑ 317 Rob Ramage .05 .02
❑ 318 Murray Craven .05 .02
❑ 319 Gaetan Duchesne .05 .02
❑ 320 Brad McCrimmon .05 .02
❑ 321 Grant Fuhr .10 .05
❑ 322 Gerard Gallant .05 .02
❑ 323 Tommy Albelin .05 .02
❑ 324 Scott Arniel .05 .02
❑ 325 Mike Keane .05 .02
❑ 326 Penguins Team .05 .02
❑ 327 Mike Ridley .05 .02
❑ 328 Dave Babych .05 .02
❑ 329 Michel Goulet .10 .05
❑ 330 Mike Richter .75 .35
❑ 331 Garry Galley .05 .02
❑ 332 Rod Brind'Amour .50 .23
❑ 333 Tony McKegney .05 .02
❑ 334 Peter Stastny .10 .05
❑ 335 Greg Millen .10 .05
❑ 336 Ray Ferraro .05 .02
❑ 337 Miloslav Horava .05 .02
❑ 338 Paul MacDermid .05 .02
❑ 339 Craig Coxe .05 .02
❑ 340 Dave Snuggerud .05 .02
❑ 341 Mike Lalor .05 .02
❑ 342 Marc Habscheid .05 .02
❑ 343 Rejean Lemelin .10 .05
❑ 344 Charlie Huddy .05 .02
❑ 345 Ken Linseman .05 .02
❑ 346 Canadiens Team .05 .02
(Goal celebration)
❑ 347 Troy Loney .05 .02
❑ 348 Mike Modano 1.00 .45
❑ 349 Jeff Reese .05 .02
❑ 350 Pat Flatley .05 .02
❑ 351 Mike Vernon .10 .05
❑ 352 Todd Elik .05 .02
❑ 353 Rod Langway .05 .02
❑ 354 Moe Mantha .05 .02
❑ 355 Keith Acton .05 .02
❑ 356 Scott Pearson .05 .02
❑ 357 Perry Berezan .05 .02
❑ 358 Alexei Kasatonov .05 .02
❑ 359 Igor Larionov .40 .18
❑ 360 Kevin Stevens .05 .02
❑ 361 Yves Racine .05 .02
❑ 362 Dave Poulin .05 .02
❑ 363 Blackhawks Team .05 .02
(Manson et al.)
❑ 364 Yvon Corriveau .05 .02
❑ 365 Brian Benning .05 .02
❑ 366 Hubie McDonough .05 .02
❑ 367 Ron Tugnutt .10 .05
❑ 368 Steve Smith .05 .02
❑ 369 Joel Otto .05 .02
❑ 370 Dave Lowry .05 .02
❑ 371 Clint Malarchuk .10 .05
❑ 372 Mathieu Schneider .05 .02
❑ 373 Mike Gartner .10 .05
❑ 374 John Tucker .05 .02
❑ 375 Chris Terreri .10 .05
❑ 376 Dean Evason .05 .02
❑ 377 Jamie Leach .05 .02
❑ 378 Jacques Cloutier .10 .05
❑ 379 Glen Wesley .05 .02
❑ 380 Vladimir Krutov .10 .05
❑ 381 Terry Carkner .05 .02
❑ 382 John McIntyre .05 .02
❑ 383 Ville Siren .05 .02
❑ 384 Joe Sakic .60 .25
❑ 385 Teppo Numminen .05 .02
❑ 386 Theoren Fleury .10 .05
❑ 387 Glen Featherstone .05 .02
❑ 388 Stephan Lebeau .05 .02
❑ 389 Kevin McClelland .05 .02
❑ 390 Uwe Krupp .05 .02
❑ 391 Mark Janssens .05 .02
❑ 392 Marty McSorley .05 .02
❑ 393 Vladimir Ruzicka .05 .02
❑ 394 Capitals Team .05 .02
(Scott Stevens\Kirk Muller)
❑ 395 Mark Fitzpatrick .10 .05
❑ 396 Checklist 265-396 .05 .02

## 1990-91 Topps Tiffany

Parallel to base set, Topps only produced 3000 sets. Cards can be distinguished by a glossy coating not found on regular issued cards.

| | MINT | NRMT |
|---|---|---|
| COMPLETE SET (396) | 150.00 | 70.00 |
| COMMON CARD (1-396) | 1.25 | .55 |

*STARS: 12.5X TO 25X BASIC CARDS

## 1990-91 Topps Box Bottoms

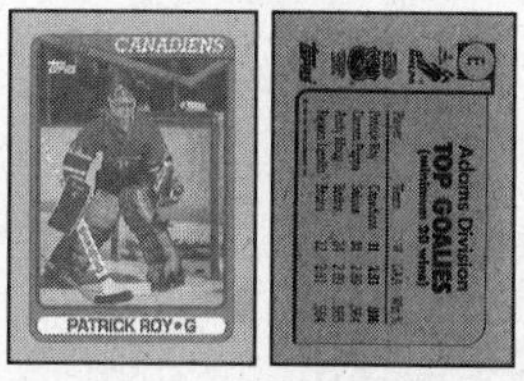

This 16-card standard-size set was issued in sets of four on the bottom of the 1990-91 Topps wax pack boxes. The cards are lettered rather than numbered. Complete box bottom panels are valued at a 25 percent premium above the prices listed below. The front design of these cards is essentially the same as the regular issue cards. The horizontally oriented backs have special statistics in blue lettering on a pale green background. The checklist does not agree with the actual grouping of the players in the four sets.

| | MINT | NRMT |
|---|---|---|
| COMPLETE SET (16) | 8.00 | 3.60 |
| COMMON CARD (A-P) | .25 | .11 |

❑ A Alexander Mogilny 1.25 .55
❑ B Jon Casey .40 .18
❑ C Paul Coffey .60 .25
❑ D Wayne Gretzky 2.50 1.10
❑ E Patrick Roy 1.50 .70
❑ F Mike Modano .75 .35
❑ G Mario Lemieux 1.50 .70
❑ H Al MacInnis .40 .18
❑ I Ray Bourque .60 .25
❑ J Steve Yzerman 1.00 .45
❑ K Darren Turcotte .25 .11
❑ L Mike Vernon .40 .18
❑ M Pierre Turgeon .50 .23
❑ N Doug Wilson .25 .11
❑ O Don Beaupre .40 .18
❑ P Sergei Makarov .25 .11

## 1990-91 Topps Team Scoring Leaders

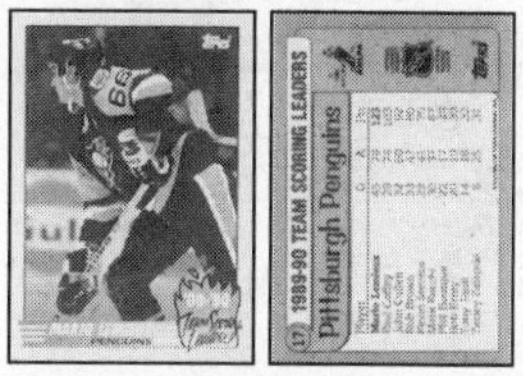

The 21-cards in this standard size set was included as a one per pack insert in the 1990-91 Topps hockey packs. This set has a glossy front with a full color action shot of the team's leading scorer while the back of the card has a list of the ten leading scorers for each team.

| | MINT | NRMT |
|---|---|---|
| COMPLETE SET (21) | 7.50 | 3.40 |
| COMMON CARD (1-21) | .10 | .05 |

❑ 1 Steve Larmer .20 .09
❑ 2 Brett Hull .75 .35
❑ 3 Cam Neely .50 .23
❑ 4 Stephane Richer .25 .11
❑ 5 Paul Reinhart .10 .05
❑ 6 Dino Ciccarelli .25 .11
❑ 7 Kirk Muller .25 .11
❑ 8 Joe Nieuwendyk .30 .14
❑ 9 Rick Tocchet .25 .11
❑ 10 Pat LaFontaine .25 .11
❑ 11 Dale Hawerchuk .50 .23
❑ 12 Wayne Gretzky 2.00 .90
❑ 13 Gary Leeman .10 .05
❑ 14 Joe Sakic 1.00 .45
❑ 15 Brian Bellows .15 .07
❑ 16 Mark Messier .75 .35
❑ 17 Mario Lemieux 1.50 .70
❑ 18 John Ogrodnick .10 .05
❑ 19 Steve Yzerman 1.00 .45
❑ 20 Pierre Turgeon .50 .23
❑ 21 Ron Francis .50 .23

## 1991-92 Topps/Bowman Preview Sheet

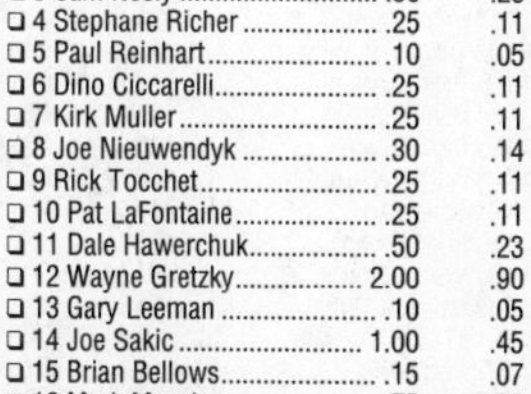


This nine-card unperforated sheet of Topps and Bowman hockey cards was sent to dealers to show them the graphic design of the coming year's hockey cards. The fronts of these preview cards are identical to the regular issue. In blue lettering, the backs have the player's name, the words "Pre-Production Sample", "1991 Topps (or as the case may be, Bowman) Card", and a tagline. The cards are unnumbered on the back and hence are listed below beginning with the upper left corner, counting across, and ending with the lower right corner. The cards are arranged so that Topps and Bowman cards alternate with one another.

| | MINT | NRMT |
|---|---|---|
| COMPLETE SET (9) | 10.00 | 4.50 |
| COMMON CARD (1-9) | .50 | .23 |

❑ 1 Mario Lemieux 2.50 1.10
(Topps)
❑ 2 Wayne Gretzky 3.00 1.35
(Bowman)
❑ 3 Joe Sakic 1.25 .55
(Topps)
❑ 4 Ray Bourque .75 .35
(Bowman)
❑ 5 Ed Belfour .75 .35
(Topps)
❑ 6 Mark Messier 1.00 .45
(Bowman)
❑ 7 Pat LaFontaine .50 .23
(Topps)
❑ 8 Steve Yzerman 1.50 .70
(Bowman)
❑ 9 Brett Hull 1.00 .45
(Topps)

## 1991-92 Topps Team Scoring Leaders

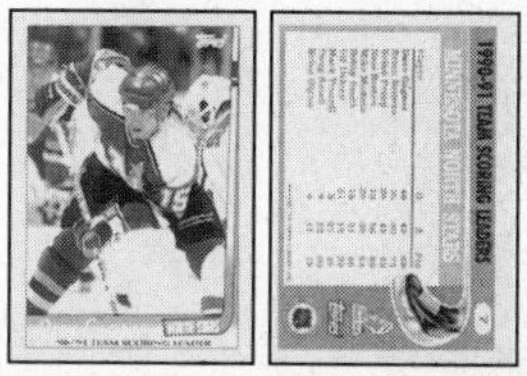

This 21-card standard-size set was inserted at a rate of one per '91-92 Topps pack and features the top scorer from every team on the front, while the back ranks the top 10 point leaders for that team.

| | MINT | NRMT |
|---|---|---|
| COMPLETE SET (21) | 7.00 | 3.10 |
| COMMON CARD (1-21) | .10 | .05 |

❑ 1 Pat Verbeek .10 .05
❑ 2 Dale Hawerchuk .40 .18
❑ 3 Steve Yzerman 1.50 .70
❑ 4 Brian Leetch .50 .23
❑ 5 Mark Recchi .40 .18
❑ 6 Esa Tikkanen .10 .05
❑ 7 Dave Gagner .10 .05
❑ 8 Joe Sakic 1.25 .55
❑ 9 Vincent Damphousse .40 .18
❑ 10 Wayne Gretzky 3.00 1.35
❑ 11 Phil Housley .10 .05
❑ 12 Pat LaFontaine .40 .18
❑ 13 Rick Tocchet .40 .18
❑ 14 Theoren Fleury UER .40 .18
(Misspelled Fluery
on card back)
❑ 15 John MacLean .10 .05
❑ 16 Kevin Hatcher .10 .05
❑ 17 Trevor Linden .40 .18
❑ 18 Russ Courtnall .10 .05
❑ 19 Ray Bourque .50 .23
❑ 20 Brett Hull .60 .25
❑ 21 Steve Larmer .10 .05

## 1992-93 Topps

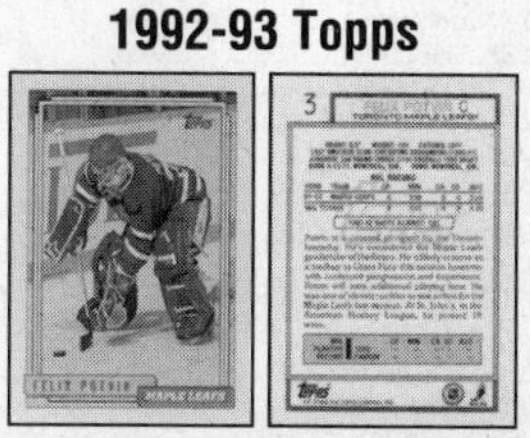

The 1992-93 Topps set contains 529 standard-size cards. Topps switched to white card stock this year allowing for a better looking product. Card fronts have team and player name at the bottom. Colorful backs include yearly statistics, playoff statistics and game- winning goals from 1991-92. The early print-run cards of Randy Moller (407) suffer from a print flaw which appears to be large finger impression on the card face. The only Rookie Card of note is Guy Hebert.

| | MINT | NRMT |
|---|---|---|
| COMPLETE SET (529) | 20.00 | 9.00 |
| COMP.FACT.SET (549) | 30.00 | 13.50 |
| COMMON CARD (1-529) | .05 | .02 |

❑ 1 Wayne Gretzky 1.50 .70
❑ 2 Brett Hull .30 .14
❑ 3 Felix Potvin .25 .11
❑ 4 Mark Tinordi .05 .02
❑ 5 Paul Coffey HL .25 .11
❑ 6 Tony Amonte .10 .05
❑ 7 Pat Falloon .05 .02
❑ 8 Pavel Bure .40 .18
❑ 9 Nicklas Lidstrom .10 .05
❑ 10 Dominic Roussel .10 .05
❑ 11 Nelson Emerson .05 .02
❑ 12 Donald Audette .10 .05
❑ 13 Gilbert Dionne .05 .02
❑ 14 Vladimir Konstantinov .05 .02
❑ 15 Kevin Todd .05 .02
❑ 16 Steve Leach .05 .02
❑ 17 Ed Olczyk .05 .02
❑ 18 Jim Hrivnak .10 .05
❑ 19 Gilbert Dionne .05 .02
❑ 20 Mike Vernon .10 .05
❑ 21 Dave Christian .05 .02
❑ 22 Ed Belfour .25 .11
❑ 23 Andrew Cassels .05 .02
❑ 24 Jaromir Jagr .60 .25
❑ 25 Arturs Irbe .10 .05
❑ 26 Petr Klima .05 .02
❑ 27 Randy Gilhen .05 .02
❑ 28 Ulf Dahlen .05 .02
❑ 29 Kelly Hrudey .10 .05
❑ 30 Dave Ellett .05 .02
❑ 31 Tom Fitzgerald .05 .02
❑ 32 Cam Neely .10 .05
❑ 33 Greg Paslawski .05 .02
❑ 34 Brad May .10 .05
❑ 35 Slava Kozlov .10 .05
❑ 36 Mark Hunter .05 .02
❑ 37 Steve Chiasson .05 .02
❑ 38 Joe Murphy .05 .02
❑ 39 Darryl Sydor .05 .02
❑ 40 Ron Hextall .10 .05
❑ 41 Jim Sandlak .05 .02
❑ 42 Dave Lowry .05 .02
❑ 43 Claude Lemieux .10 .05
❑ 44 Gerald Diduck .05 .02
❑ 45 Mike McPhee .05 .02
❑ 46 Rod Langway .05 .02
❑ 47 Guy Larose .05 .02
❑ 48 Craig Billington .10 .05
❑ 49 Daniel Marois .05 .02
❑ 50 Todd Nelson .05 .02
❑ 51 Jari Kurri .10 .05
❑ 52 Keith Brown .05 .02
❑ 53 Valeri Kamensky .10 .05
❑ 54 Jim Johnson .05 .02
❑ 55 Vincent Damphousse .10 .05
❑ 56 Pat Elynuik .05 .02
❑ 57 Jeff Beukeboom .05 .02
❑ 58 Paul Ysebaert .05 .02
❑ 59 Ken Sutton .05 .02
❑ 60 Dale Craigwell .05 .02
❑ 61 Marc Bergevin .05 .02
❑ 62 Stephane Beauregard .10 .05
❑ 63 Bob Probert .10 .05
❑ 64 Jergus Baca .05 .02
❑ 65 Brian Propp .05 .02
❑ 66 Jacques Cloutier .10 .05
❑ 67 Jim Thomson .05 .02
❑ 68 Anatoli Semenov .05 .02
❑ 69 Stephan Lebeau .05 .02
❑ 70 Rick Tocchet .10 .05
❑ 71 James Patrick .05 .02
❑ 72 Rob Brown .05 .02
❑ 73 Peter Ahola .05 .02
❑ 74 Bob Corkum .05 .02
❑ 75 Brent Sutter .05 .02
❑ 76 Neil Wilkinson .05 .02
❑ 77 Mark Osborne .05 .02
❑ 78 Ron Wilson .05 .02
❑ 79 Todd Richards .05 .02
❑ 80 Robert Kron .05 .02
❑ 81 Cliff Ronning .05 .02
❑ 82 Zarley Zalapski .05 .02
❑ 83 Randy Burridge .05 .02
❑ 84 Jarrod Skalde .05 .02
❑ 85 Gary Leeman .05 .02
❑ 86 Mike Ricci .05 .02
❑ 87 Dennis Vaske .05 .02
❑ 88 John LeBlanc .05 .02
❑ 89 Brad Shaw .05 .02
❑ 90 Rod Brind'Amour .10 .05
❑ 91 Colin Patterson .05 .02
❑ 92 Gerard Gallant .05 .02
❑ 93 Per Djoos .05 .02
❑ 94 Claude Lapointe .05 .02
❑ 95 Bob Errey .05 .02
❑ 96 Norm Maciver .05 .02
❑ 97 Todd Elik .05 .02
❑ 98 Chris Chelios .25 .11
❑ 99 Keith Primeau .10 .05
❑ 100 Jim Waite .10 .05
❑ 101 Luc Robitaille .10 .05
❑ 102 Keith Tkachuk .50 .23
❑ 103 Benoit Hogue .05 .02
❑ 104 Brian Mullen .05 .02
❑ 105 Joe Nieuwendyk .10 .05
❑ 106 Randy McKay .05 .02
❑ 107 Michal Pivonka .05 .02
❑ 108 Darcy Wakaluk .10 .05
❑ 109 Andy Brickley .05 .02
❑ 110 Patrick Roy .50 .23
Goals Against
Average Leader
❑ 111 Bob Sweeney .05 .02
❑ 112 Guy Hebert .60 .25
❑ 113 Joe Mullen .10 .05
❑ 114 Gord Murphy .05 .02
❑ 115 Evgeny Davydov .05 .02
❑ 116 Gary Roberts .05 .02
❑ 117 Pelle Eklund .05 .02
❑ 118 Tom Kurvers .05 .02
❑ 119 John Tonelli .05 .02
❑ 120 Fredrik Olausson .05 .02
❑ 121 Mike Donnelly .05 .02
❑ 122 Doug Gilmour .25 .11
❑ 123 Wayne Gretzky .75 .35
Assists Leader
❑ 124 Curtis Leschyshyn .05 .02
❑ 125 Guy Carbonneau .10 .05
❑ 126 Bill Ranford .10 .05
❑ 127 Ulf Samuelsson .05 .02
❑ 128 Joey Kocur .05 .02
❑ 129 Kevin Miller .05 .02
❑ 130 Kirk McLean .10 .05
❑ 131 Kevin Dineen .05 .02
❑ 132 John Cullen .05 .02
❑ 133 Al Iafrate .10 .05
❑ 134 Craig Janney .10 .05
❑ 135 Patrick Flatley .05 .02
❑ 136 Dominik Hasek .75 .35
❑ 137 Benoit Brunet .05 .02
❑ 138 Dave Babych .05 .02
❑ 139 Doug Brown .05 .02
❑ 140 Mike Lalor .05 .02
❑ 141 Thomas Steen .05 .02
❑ 142 Frank Musil .05 .02
❑ 143 Dan Quinn .05 .02
❑ 144 Dmitri Mironov .05 .02
❑ 145 Bob Kudelski .05 .02
❑ 146 Mike Bullard .05 .02
❑ 147 Randy Carlyle .05 .02
❑ 148 Kent Manderville .05 .02
❑ 149 Kevin Hatcher .05 .02
❑ 150 Steve Kasper .05 .02
❑ 151 Mikael Andersson .05 .02
❑ 152 Alexei Kasatonov .05 .02
❑ 153 Jan Erixon .05 .02
❑ 154 Craig Ludwig .05 .02
❑ 155 Dave Poulin .05 .02
❑ 156 Scott Stevens .10 .05
❑ 157 Robert Reichel .05 .02
❑ 158 Uwe Krupp .05 .02
❑ 159 Brian Noonan .05 .02
❑ 160 Stephane Richer .10 .05
❑ 161 Brent Thompson .05 .02
❑ 162 Glenn Anderson .10 .05
❑ 163 Joe Cirella .05 .02
❑ 164 Dave Andreychuk .10 .05
❑ 165 Vladimir Konstantinov .05 .02
❑ 166 Mike McNeill .05 .02
❑ 167 Darrin Shannon .05 .02
❑ 168 Rob Pearson .05 .02
❑ 169 John Vanbiesbrouck .30 .14
❑ 170 Randy Wood .05 .02
❑ 171 Marty McSorley .05 .02
❑ 172 Mike Hudson .05 .02
❑ 173 Paul Fenton .05 .02
❑ 174 Jeff Brown .05 .02
❑ 175 Mark Greig .05 .02
❑ 176 Gordie Roberts .05 .02
❑ 177 Josef Beranek .05 .02
❑ 178 Shawn Burr .05 .02
❑ 179 Marc Bureau .05 .02
❑ 180 Mikhail Tatarinov .05 .02
❑ 181 Robert Cimetta .05 .02
❑ 182 Paul Coffey UER .25 .11
(Still pictured
as a Penguin)
❑ 183 Bob Essensa .10 .05
❑ 184 Joe Reekie .05 .02
❑ 185 Jeff Hackett .10 .05
❑ 186 Tomas Forslund .05 .02
❑ 187 Claude Vilgrain .05 .02
❑ 188 John Druce .05 .02
❑ 189 Patrice Brisebois .05 .02
❑ 190 Peter Douris .05 .02
❑ 191 Brent Ashton .05 .02
❑ 192 Eric Desjardins .05 .02
❑ 193 Nick Kypreos .05 .02
❑ 194 Dana Murzyn .05 .02
❑ 195 Don Beaupre .10 .05
❑ 196 Jeff Chychrun .05 .02
❑ 197 Dave Barr .05 .02
❑ 198 Brian Glynn .05 .02
❑ 199 Keith Acton .05 .02
❑ 200 Igor Kravchuk .05 .02
❑ 201 Shayne Corson .05 .02
❑ 202 Curt Giles .05 .02
❑ 203 Darren Turcotte .05 .02
❑ 204 David Volek .05 .02
❑ 205 Ray Whitney .05 .02
❑ 206 Donald Audette .10 .05
❑ 207 Steve Yzerman .60 .25
❑ 208 Craig Berube .05 .02
❑ 209 Bob McGill .05 .02
❑ 210 Stu Barnes .05 .02
❑ 211 Rob Blake .10 .05
❑ 212 Mario Lemieux 1.00 .45
❑ 213 Dominic Roussel .10 .05
❑ 214 Sergio Momesso .05 .02
❑ 215 Brad Marsh .05 .02
❑ 216 Mark Fitzpatrick .10 .05
❑ 217 Ken Baumgartner .05 .02
❑ 218 Greg Gilbert .05 .02
❑ 219 Ric Nattress .05 .02
❑ 220 Theoren Fleury .10 .05
❑ 221 Ray Bourque .25 .11
❑ 222 Steve Thomas .05 .02
❑ 223 Scott Niedermayer .10 .05
❑ 224 Jeff Lazaro .05 .02
❑ 225 Tim Cheveldae .10 .05
Kirk McLean
Wins Leaders
❑ 226 Marc Fortier .05 .02
❑ 227 Rob Zettler .05 .02
❑ 228 Kevin Todd .05 .02
❑ 229 Tony Amonte .10 .05
❑ 230 Mark Lamb .05 .02
❑ 231 Chris Dahlquist .05 .02
❑ 232 James Black .05 .02
❑ 233 Paul Cavallini .05 .02
❑ 234 Gino Cavallini .05 .02
❑ 235 Tony Tanti .05 .02
❑ 236 Mike Ridley .05 .02
❑ 237 Curtis Joseph .25 .11
❑ 238 Mike Craig .05 .02
❑ 239 Luciano Borsato .05 .02
❑ 240 Brian Bellows .05 .02
❑ 241 Barry Pederson .05 .02
❑ 242 Tony Granato .05 .02
❑ 243 Jim Paek .05 .02
❑ 244 Tim Bergland .05 .02
❑ 245 Jay More .05 .02
❑ 246 Laurie Boschman .05 .02
❑ 247 Doug Bodger .05 .02
❑ 248 Murray Craven .05 .02
❑ 249 Kris Draper .05 .02
❑ 250 Brian Benning .05 .02
❑ 251 Jarmo Myllys .05 .02
❑ 252 Sergei Fedorov .40 .18
❑ 253 Mathieu Schneider .05 .02
❑ 254 Dave Gagner .10 .05
❑ 255 Michel Goulet .10 .05
❑ 256 Alexander Godynyuk .05 .02
❑ 257 Ray Sheppard .10 .05
❑ 258 Mark Messier AS .25 .11
❑ 259 Kevin Stevens AS .05 .02
❑ 260 Brett Hull AS .25 .11
❑ 261 Brian Leetch AS .25 .11
❑ 262 Ray Bourque AS .10 .05
❑ 263 Patrick Roy AS .50 .23
❑ 264 Mike Gartner HL .10 .05
❑ 265 Mario Lemieux AS .50 .23
❑ 266 Luc Robitaille AS .10 .05
❑ 267 Mark Recchi AS .10 .05
❑ 268 Phil Housley AS .10 .05
❑ 269 Scott Stevens AS .10 .05
❑ 270 Kirk McLean AS .10 .05
❑ 271 Steve Duchesne .05 .02
❑ 272 Jiri Hrdina .05 .02
❑ 273 John MacLean .10 .05
❑ 274 Mark Messier .30 .14
❑ 275 Geoff Smith .05 .02
❑ 276 Russ Courtnall .05 .02
❑ 277 Yves Racine .05 .02
❑ 278 Tom Draper .10 .05
❑ 279 Charlie Huddy .05 .02
❑ 280 Trevor Kidd .10 .05
❑ 281 Garth Butcher .05 .02
❑ 282 Mike Sullivan .05 .02
❑ 283 Adam Burt .05 .02
❑ 284 Troy Murray .05 .02
❑ 285 Stephane Fiset .10 .05
❑ 286 Perry Anderson .05 .02
❑ 287 Sergei Nemchinov .05 .02
❑ 288 Rick Zombo .05 .02
❑ 289 Pierre Turgeon .10 .05
❑ 290 Kevin Lowe .05 .02
❑ 291 Brian Bradley .05 .02
❑ 292 Martin Gelinas UER .05 .02
(Transaction date should
be 8-9-88, not 8-9-89)
❑ 293 Brian Leetch .25 .11
❑ 294 Peter Bondra .25 .11
❑ 295 Brendan Shanahan .40 .18
❑ 296 Dale Hawerchuk .10 .05
❑ 297 Mike Hough .05 .02
❑ 298 Rollie Melanson .10 .05
❑ 299 Brad Jones .05 .02
❑ 300 Jocelyn Lemieux .05 .02
❑ 301 Brad McCrimmon .05 .02
❑ 302 Marty McInnis .05 .02
❑ 303 Chris Terreri .10 .05
❑ 304 Dean Evason .05 .02
❑ 305 Glenn Healy .10 .05
❑ 306 Ken Hodge Jr. .05 .02
❑ 307 Mike Liut .10 .05
❑ 308 Gary Suter .05 .02
❑ 309 Neal Broten .10 .05
❑ 310 Tim Cheveldae .10 .05
❑ 311 Tom Fergus .05 .02
❑ 312 Petr Svoboda .05 .02
❑ 313 Tom Chorske .05 .02
❑ 314 Paul Ysebaert .05 .02
Plus/Minus Leader
❑ 315 Steve Smith .05 .02
❑ 316 Stephane Morin .05 .02
❑ 317 Pat MacLeod .05 .02
❑ 318 Dino Ciccarelli .10 .05
❑ 319 Peter Zezel .05 .02
❑ 320 Chris Lindberg .05 .02
❑ 321 Grant Ledyard .05 .02
❑ 322 Ron Francis .10 .05
❑ 323 Adrien Plavsic .05 .02
❑ 324 Ray Ferraro .05 .02
❑ 325 Wendel Clark .10 .05
❑ 326 Corey Millen .05 .02
❑ 327 Mark Pederson .05 .02
❑ 328 Patrick Poulin .05 .02
❑ 329 Adam Graves .10 .05
❑ 330 Bobby Holik .05 .02
❑ 331 Kelly Kisio .05 .02
❑ 332 Peter Sidorkiewicz .10 .05
❑ 333 Vladimir Ruzicka .05 .02
❑ 334 J.J. Daigneault .05 .02
❑ 335 Troy Mallette .05 .02
❑ 336 Craig MacTavish .05 .02
❑ 337 Michel Petit .05 .02
❑ 338 Claude Loiselle .05 .02
❑ 339 Teppo Numminen .05 .02
❑ 340 Brett Hull .25 .11
Goal Scoring Leader
❑ 341 Sylvain Lefebvre .05 .02
❑ 342 Perry Berezan .05 .02
❑ 343 Kevin Stevens .05 .02
❑ 344 Randy Ladouceur .05 .02
❑ 345 Pat LaFontaine .10 .05
❑ 346 Glen Wesley .05 .02
❑ 347 Michel Goulet HL .10 .05
❑ 348 Jamie Macoun .05 .02
❑ 349 Owen Nolan .10 .05
❑ 350 Grant Fuhr .10 .05
❑ 351 Tim Kerr .05 .02
❑ 352 Kjell Samuelsson .05 .02
❑ 353 Pavel Bure .40 .18
❑ 354 Murray Baron .05 .02
❑ 355 Paul Broten .05 .02
❑ 356 Craig Simpson .05 .02
❑ 357 Ken Daneyko .05 .02
❑ 358 Greg Hawgood .05 .02
❑ 359 Johan Garpenlov .05 .02
❑ 360 Garry Galley .05 .02
❑ 361 Paul DiPietro .05 .02
❑ 362 Jamie Leach .05 .02
❑ 363 Clint Malarchuk .10 .05
❑ 364 Dan Lambert .05 .02
❑ 365 Joe Juneau UER .10 .05
(Shoots left, not right)
❑ 366 Scott Lachance .05 .02
❑ 367 Mike Richter .25 .11
❑ 368 Sheldon Kennedy .05 .02
❑ 369 John McIntyre .05 .02
❑ 370 Glen Murray UER .05 .02
(Misspelled Glenn
on both sides)
❑ 371 Ron Sutter .05 .02
❑ 372 David Williams .05 .02
❑ 373 Bill Lindsay .05 .02
❑ 374 Todd Gill .05 .02
❑ 375 Sylvain Turgeon .05 .02
❑ 376 Dirk Graham .05 .02
❑ 377 Brad Schlegel .05 .02
❑ 378 Bob Carpenter .05 .02
❑ 379 Jon Casey .10 .05
❑ 380 Andrei Lomakin .05 .02
❑ 381 Kay Whitmore .10 .05
❑ 382 Alexander Mogilny .10 .05
❑ 383 Garry Valk .05 .02
❑ 384 Bruce Driver .05 .02
❑ 385 Jeff Reese .05 .02
❑ 386 Brent Gilchrist .05 .02
❑ 387 Kerry Huffman .05 .02
❑ 388 Bobby Smith .10 .05
❑ 389 Dave Manson .05 .02
❑ 390 Russ Romaniuk .05 .02
❑ 391 Paul MacDermid .05 .02
❑ 392 Louie DeBrusk .05 .02
❑ 393 Dave McLlwain .05 .02
❑ 394 Andy Moog .10 .05
❑ 395 Tie Domi .10 .05
❑ 396 Pat Jablonski .10 .05
❑ 397 Troy Loney .05 .02
❑ 398 Jimmy Carson .05 .02
❑ 399 Eric Weinrich .05 .02
❑ 400 Jeremy Roenick .25 .11
❑ 401 Brent Fedyk .05 .02
❑ 402 Geoff Sanderson .10 .05
❑ 403 Doug Lidster .05 .02
❑ 404 Mike Gartner .10 .05
❑ 405 Derian Hatcher .05 .02
❑ 406 Gaetan Duchesne .05 .02
❑ 407 Randy Moller .05 .02
❑ 408 Brian Skrudland .05 .02
❑ 409 Luke Richardson .05 .02
❑ 410 Mark Recchi .10 .05
❑ 411 Steve Konroyd .05 .02
❑ 412 Troy Gamble .10 .05
❑ 413 Greg Johnston .05 .02
❑ 414 Denis Savard .10 .05
❑ 415 Mats Sundin .25 .11
❑ 416 Bryan Trottier .10 .05
❑ 417 Don Sweeney .05 .02
❑ 418 Pat Falloon .05 .02
❑ 419 Alexander Semak .05 .02
❑ 420 David Shaw .05 .02
❑ 421 Tomas Sandstrom .05 .02
❑ 422 Petr Nedved .10 .05
❑ 423 Peter Ing .10 .05
❑ 424 Wayne Presley .05 .02
❑ 425 Rick Wamsley .10 .05
❑ 426 Rob Zamuner .05 .02
❑ 427 Claude Boivin .05 .02
❑ 428 Sylvain Cote .05 .02
❑ 429 Kevin Stevens HL .05 .02
❑ 430 Randy Velischek .05 .02
❑ 431 Derek King .05 .02
❑ 432 Terry Yake .05 .02
❑ 433 Philippe Bozon .05 .02
❑ 434 Rich Sutter .05 .02
❑ 435 Brian Lawton .05 .02
❑ 436 Brian Hayward .10 .05
❑ 437 Robert Dirk .05 .02
❑ 438 Bernie Nicholls .10 .05
❑ 439 Michel Picard .05 .02
❑ 440 Nicklas Lidstrom .10 .05
❑ 441 Mike Modano .30 .14
❑ 442 Phil Bourque .05 .02
❑ 443 Wayne McBean .05 .02
❑ 444 Scott Mellanby .10 .05
❑ 445 Kevin Haller .05 .02
❑ 446 Dave Taylor UER .10 .05
(Games played total
***, should be 1,030)
❑ 447 Larry Murphy .10 .05
❑ 448 David Bruce .05 .02
❑ 449 Steven Finn .05 .02
❑ 450 Mike Krushelnyski .05 .02
❑ 451 Adam Creighton .05 .02
❑ 452 Al MacInnis .10 .05
❑ 453 Rick Tabaracci .10 .05
❑ 454 Bob Bassen .05 .02
❑ 455 Kelly Buchberger .05 .02
❑ 456 Phil Housley .10 .05
❑ 457 Daren Puppa .10 .05
❑ 458 Slava Fetisov .05 .02
❑ 459 Doug Smail .05 .02
❑ 460 Paul Stanton .05 .02
❑ 461 Steve Weeks .10 .05
❑ 462 Valeri Zelepukin .05 .02
❑ 463 Stephane Matteau .05 .02
❑ 464 Dale Hunter .05 .02
❑ 465 Terry Carkner .05 .02
❑ 466 Vincent Riendeau .10 .05
❑ 467 Sergei Makarov .05 .02
❑ 468 Igor Ulanov .05 .02
❑ 469 Peter Stastny .10 .05
❑ 470 Dimitri Khristich .05 .02
❑ 471 Joel Otto .05 .02
❑ 472 Geoff Courtnall .05 .02
❑ 473 Mike Ramsey .05 .02
❑ 474 Yvon Corriveau .05 .02
❑ 475 Adam Oates .10 .05
❑ 476 Esa Tikkanen .05 .02
❑ 477 Doug Weight .10 .05
❑ 478 Mike Keane .05 .02
❑ 479 Kelly Miller .05 .02
❑ 480 Nelson Emerson .05 .02
❑ 481 Shawn McEachern .05 .02
❑ 482 Doug Wilson .10 .05
❑ 483 Jeff Odgers .05 .02
❑ 484 Stephane Quintal .05 .02
❑ 485 Christian Ruuttu .05 .02
❑ 486 Paul Ranheim .05 .02
❑ 487 Craig Wolanin .05 .02
❑ 488 Rob DiMaio .05 .02
❑ 489 Shawn Cronin .05 .02
❑ 490 Kirk Muller .05 .02
❑ 491 Patrick Roy .50 .23
Save Pct. Leader
❑ 492 Rich Pilon .05 .02
❑ 493 Pat Verbeek .05 .02
❑ 494 Ken Wregget .10 .05
❑ 495 Joe Sakic .40 .18
❑ 496 Zdeno Ciger .05 .02
❑ 497 Steve Larmer .10 .05
❑ 498 Calle Johansson .05 .02
❑ 499 Trevor Linden .10 .05
❑ 500 John LeClair .50 .23
❑ 501 Bryan Marchment .05 .02
❑ 502 Todd Krygler .05 .02
❑ 503 Tom Barrasso .10 .05
❑ 504 Mario Lemieux .50 .23
Points Leader
❑ 505 Daniel Berthiaume UER .10 .05
(Headings on back are
for non-goalies)
❑ 506 Jamie Baker .05 .02
❑ 507 Greg Adams .05 .02
❑ 508 Patrick Roy 1.00 .45
❑ 509 Kris King .05 .02
❑ 510 Jyrki Lumme .05 .02
❑ 511 Darin Kimble .05 .02
❑ 512 Igor Larionov .05 .02
❑ 513 Martin Brodeur .75 .35
❑ 514 Denny Felsner .05 .02
❑ 515 Yanic Dupre .05 .02
❑ 516 Bill Guerin .05 .02
❑ 517 Bret Hedican UER .05 .02
(Misspelled Brett
on both sides)
❑ 518 Mike Hartman .05 .02
❑ 519 Steve Heinze UER .05 .02
(Photo actually
Gord Hynes)
❑ 520 Frantisek Kucera .05 .02
❑ 521 David Reid .05 .02
❑ 522 Frank Pietrangelo .10 .05
❑ 523 Martin Rucinsky .05 .02
❑ 524 Tony Hrkac .05 .02
❑ 525 Checklist 1-132 .05 .02
❑ 526 Checklist 133-264 .05 .02
❑ 527 Checklist 265-396 .05 .02
❑ 528 Checklist 397-528 UER .05 .02
(529 not listed)
❑ 529 Eric Lindros UER 2.00 .90
(Acquired 6-30-92,
not 6-20-92)

## 1992-93 Topps Gold

Gold foil versions of all 529 cards in the 1992-93 Topps Hockey set were produced: one was inserted in each foil pack, three in each jumbo pack, and 20 were included in factory sets as a bonus. Deciding against producing Gold checklists, Topps made cards 525-528 of players not featured in the basic set. On a white card face, the fronts display color action player photos inside a two-color picture frame. The player's name and team name appear in two short colored bars toward the bottom of the picture. The backs carry biography, statistics, and player profile. The following cards were printed in a horizontal format and carry a premium: 90, 164, 195, 225, 272, 307, 324, 337, 350, 366, 413 and 420.

| | MINT | NRMT |
|---|---|---|
| COMPLETE SET (529) | 350.00 | 160.00 |
| COMMON CARD (1G-529G) | .25 | .11 |

*STARS: 5X TO 10X BASIC CARDS

*YOUNG STARS: 3X TO 6X BASIC CARDS
*RC's: 2X TO 4X BASIC CARDS

❑ 1G Wayne Gretzky 50.00 22.00
❑ 2G Brett Hull 10.00 4.50
❑ 24G Jaromir Jagr 25.00 11.00
❑ 110G Patrick Roy 12.00 5.50
GAA Leader
❑ 123G Wayne Gretzky 20.00 9.00
Assists Leader
❑ 169G John Vanbiesbrouck 10.00 4.50
❑ 207G Steve Yzerman 20.00 9.00
❑ 212G Mario Lemieux 30.00 13.50
❑ 263G Patrick Roy AS 12.00 5.50
❑ 265G Mario Lemieux AS 12.00 5.50
❑ 353G Pavel Bure 15.00 6.75
❑ 491G Patrick Roy 12.00 5.50
Save Percentage Leader
❑ 495G Joe Sakic 12.00 5.50
❑ 504G Mario Lemieux 12.00 5.50
Points Leader
❑ 508G Patrick Roy 30.00 13.50
❑ 513G Martin Brodeur 15.00 6.75
❑ 529G Eric Lindros UER 25.00 11.00
(Acquired 6-30-92, not 6-20-92)

## 1993-94 Topps Premier Promo Sheet

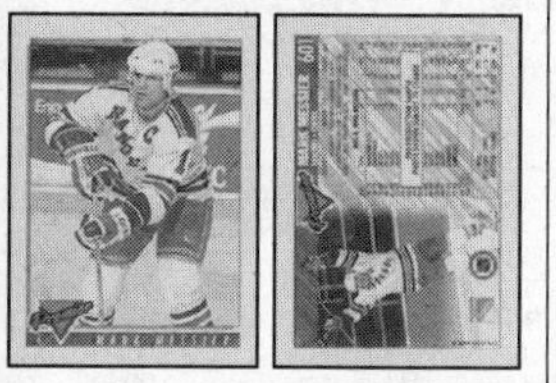

This nine-card promo sheet measures approximately 7 3/4" by 10 3/4" and features white-bordered color player photos on the front. The player's name and position appear at the bottom of each card within a team color-coded stripe, and the Premier logo is displayed in the lower left. The horizontal backs carry color player action shots on their left sides. At the top, the player's name, uniform number, team, and position appear within a team color-coded stripe. Below this, and to the right of the player photo, appear the player's biography and stats on a background that resembles white ruffled silk. The team, NHL, and NHLPA logos in the lower left round out the back.

MINT NRMT
COMPLETE SET (9) 4.00 1.80
COMMON CARD .25 .11

❑ 1 Patrick Roy 1.50 .70
❑ 15 Mike Vernon .35 .16
❑ 22 Jamie Baker .25 .11
❑ 100 Theoren Fleury .35 .16
❑ 156 Geoff Sanderson .35 .16
❑ 244 Dave Lowry .25 .11
❑ 257 Scott Lachance .25 .11
❑ 601 Mark Messier .50 .23
❑ 602 Ray Bourque .50 .23

## 1993-94 Topps/OPC Premier

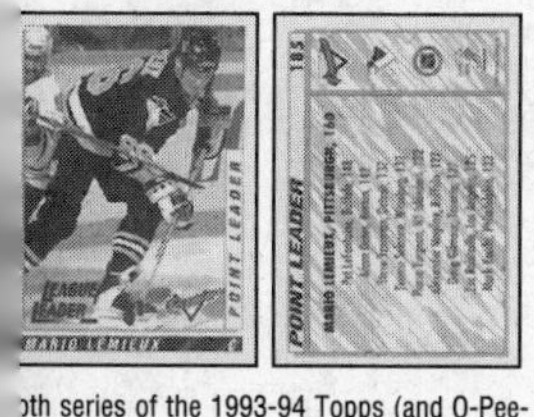

...oth series of the 1993-94 Topps (and O-Pee-...hee) Premier hockey set consisted of 264 ...andard-size cards. The fronts feature white-...ordered color player photos. The player's ...ame and position appear at the bottom of ...ch card within a team color-coded stripe, ...d the Premier logo is displayed in the lower ...t. The horizontal backs carry color player ...tion shots on their left sides. At the top, the ...ayer's name, uniform number, team, and ...sition appear within a team color-coded ...ipe. Below this, and to the right of the player ...oto, appear the player's biography and stats ...a background that resembles white ruffled ...k. The team, NHL, and NHLPA logos in the ...wer left round out the back. Topical subsets ...tured are Super Rookies (121-130), and 1st ...am All-Stars, 2nd Team All-Stars, and ...ague Leaders scattered throughout the set. ...cept for some information in French on the ...cks, the 1993-94 O-Pee-Chee Premier set is ...ntical to the 1993-94 Topps Premier set. A ...mium of up to 1.25 times the prices below ...plies to all OPC version cards. The only Rookie Card of note is Jocelyn Thibault.

MINT NRMT
COMPLETE SET (528) 20.00 9.00
COMPLETE SERIES 1 (264) 10.00 4.50
COMPLETE SERIES 2 (264) 10.00 4.50
COMMON CARD (1-528) .05 .02

❑ 1 Patrick Roy 1.00 .45
❑ 2 Alexei Zhitnik .05 .02
❑ 3 Uwe Krupp .05 .02
❑ 4 Todd Gill .05 .02
❑ 5 Paul Stanton .05 .02
❑ 6 Petr Nedved .10 .05
❑ 7 Dale Hawerchuk .10 .05
❑ 8 Kevin Miller .05 .02
❑ 9 Nicklas Lidstrom .10 .05
❑ 10 Joe Sakic .40 .18
❑ 11 Thomas Steen .05 .02
❑ 12 Peter Bondra .20 .09
❑ 13 Brian Noonan .05 .02
❑ 14 Glen Featherstone .05 .02
❑ 15 Mike Vernon .10 .05
❑ 16 Janne Ojanen .05 .02
❑ 17 Neil Brady .05 .02
❑ 18 Dimitri Yushkevich .05 .02
❑ 19 Bob Zamuner .05 .02
❑ 20 Zarley Zalapski .05 .02
❑ 21 Mike Sullivan .05 .02
❑ 22 Jamie Baker .05 .02
❑ 23 Craig MacTavish .05 .02
❑ 24 Mark Tinordi .05 .02
❑ 25 Brian Leetch .20 .09
❑ 26 Brian Skrudland .05 .02
❑ 27 Keith Tkachuk .25 .11
❑ 28 Patrick Flatley .05 .02
❑ 29 Doug Bodger .05 .02
❑ 30 Felix Potvin .20 .09
❑ 31 Shawn Antoski .05 .02
❑ 32 Eric Desjardins .05 .02
❑ 33 Mike Donnelly .05 .02
❑ 34 Kjell Samuelsson .05 .02
❑ 35 Nelson Emerson .05 .02
❑ 36 Phil Housley .10 .05
❑ 37 Mario Lemieux .50 .23
❑ 38 Shayne Corson .05 .02
❑ 39 Steve Smith .05 .02
❑ 40 Bob Kudelski .05 .02
❑ 41 Joe Cirella .05 .02
❑ 42 Sergei Nemchinov .05 .02
❑ 43 Kerry Huffman .05 .02
❑ 44 Bob Beers .05 .02
❑ 45 Al Iafrate .05 .02
❑ 46 Mike Modano .25 .11
❑ 47 Pat Verbeek .05 .02
❑ 48 Joel Otto .05 .02
❑ 49 Dino Ciccarelli .10 .05
❑ 50 Adam Oates .10 .05
❑ 51 Pat Elynuik .05 .02
❑ 52 Bobby Holik .05 .02
❑ 53 Johan Garpenlov .05 .02
❑ 54 Jeff Beukeboom .05 .02
❑ 55 Tommy Soderstrom .10 .05
❑ 56 Rob Blake .05 .02
❑ 57 Marty McInnis .05 .02
❑ 58 Dixon Ward .05 .02
❑ 59 Patrice Brisebois .05 .02
❑ 60 Ed Belfour .20 .09
❑ 61 Donald Audette .10 .05
❑ 62 Mike Ricci .05 .02
❑ 63 Fredrik Olausson .05 .02
❑ 64 Norm Maciver .05 .02
❑ 65 Andrew Cassels .05 .02
❑ 66 Tim Cheveldae .10 .05
❑ 67 David Reid .05 .02
❑ 68 Philippe Bozon .05 .02
❑ 69 Drake Berehowsky .05 .02
❑ 70 Tony Amonte .10 .05
❑ 71 Dave Manson .05 .02
❑ 72 Rick Tocchet .10 .05
❑ 73 Steve Kasper .05 .02
❑ 74 Assist Leader .10 .05
Adam Oates
❑ 75 Ulf Dahlen .05 .02
❑ 76 Chris Lindberg .05 .02
❑ 77 Doug Wilson .10 .05
❑ 78 Mike Ridley .05 .02
❑ 79 Viacheslav Butsayev .05 .02
❑ 80 Scott Stevens .10 .05
❑ 81 Cliff Ronning .05 .02
❑ 82 Andrei Lomakin .05 .02
❑ 83 Shawn Burr .05 .02
❑ 84 Benoit Brunet .05 .02
❑ 85 Valeri Kamensky .10 .05
❑ 86 Randy Carlyle .05 .02
❑ 87 Chris Joseph .05 .02
❑ 88 Dirk Graham .05 .02
❑ 89 Ken Sutton .05 .02
❑ 90 Luc Robitaille AS .10 .05
❑ 91 Mario Lemieux AS .50 .23
❑ 92 Teemu Selanne AS .25 .11
❑ 93 Ray Bourque AS .20 .09
❑ 94 Chris Chelios AS .20 .09
❑ 95 Ed Belfour AS .20 .09
❑ 96 Keith Jones .05 .02
❑ 97 Sylvain Turgeon .05 .02
❑ 98 Jim Johnson .05 .02
❑ 99 Michael Nylander .05 .02
❑ 100 Theoren Fleury .10 .05
❑ 101 Shawn Chambers .05 .02
❑ 102 Alexander Semak .05 .02
❑ 103 Ron Sutter .05 .02
❑ 104 Glenn Anderson .10 .05
❑ 105 Jaromir Jagr .60 .25
❑ 106 Adam Graves .10 .05
❑ 107 Nikolai Borschevsky .05 .02
❑ 108 Vladimir Konstantinov .05 .02
❑ 109 Robb Stauber .10 .05
❑ 110 Arturs Irbe .10 .05
❑ 111 Felix Potvin .20 .09
G.A.A. Leader
❑ 112 Darius Kasparaitis .05 .02
❑ 113 Kirk McLean .10 .05
❑ 114 Glen Wesley .05 .02
❑ 115 Rod Brind'Amour .10 .05
❑ 116 Mike Eagles .05 .02
❑ 117 Brian Bradley .05 .02
❑ 118 Dave Christian .05 .02
❑ 119 Randy Wood .05 .02
❑ 120 Craig Janney .10 .05
❑ 121 Eric Lindros SR .60 .25
❑ 122 Tommy Soderstrom SR .10 .05
❑ 123 Shawn McEachern SR .05 .02
❑ 124 Andrei Kovalenko SR .05 .02
❑ 125 Joe Juneau SR .10 .05
❑ 126 Felix Potvin SR .20 .09
❑ 127 Dixon Ward SR .05 .02
❑ 128 Alexei Zhamnov SR .10 .05
❑ 129 Vladimir Malakhov SR .05 .02
❑ 130 Teemu Selanne SR .25 .11
❑ 131 Neal Broten .10 .05
❑ 132 Ulf Samuelsson .05 .02
❑ 133 Mark Janssens .05 .02
❑ 134 Claude Lemieux .10 .05
❑ 135 Mike Richter .20 .09
❑ 136 Doug Weight .10 .05
❑ 137 Rob Pearson .05 .02
❑ 138 Sylvain Cote .05 .02
❑ 139 Mike Keane .05 .02
❑ 140 Benoit Hogue .05 .02
❑ 141 Michel Petit .05 .02
❑ 142 Mark Freer .05 .02
❑ 143 Doug Zmolek .05 .02
❑ 144 Tony Granato .05 .02
❑ 145 Paul Coffey .20 .09
❑ 146 Ted Donato .05 .02
❑ 147 Brent Sutter .05 .02
❑ 148 Alexander Mogilny .20 .09
Teemu Selanne
Goal Scoring Leaders
❑ 149 James Patrick .05 .02
❑ 150 Mikael Andersson .05 .02
❑ 151 Steve Duchesne .05 .02
❑ 152 Terry Carkner .05 .02
❑ 153 Russ Courtnall .05 .02
❑ 154 Brian Mullen .05 .02
❑ 155 Martin Straka .05 .02
❑ 156 Geoff Sanderson .10 .05
❑ 157 Mark Howe .05 .02
❑ 158 Stephane Richer .10 .05
❑ 159 Doug Crossman .05 .02
❑ 160 John Vanbiesbrouck .30 .14
❑ 161 Bob Essensa .10 .05
❑ 162 Wayne Presley .05 .02
❑ 163 Mathieu Schneider .05 .02
❑ 164 Jiri Slegr .05 .02
❑ 165 Stephane Fiset .10 .05
❑ 166 Wendell Young .10 .05
❑ 167 Kevin Dineen .05 .02
❑ 168 Sandis Ozolinsh .10 .05
❑ 169 Mike Krushelnyski .05 .02
❑ 170 Kevin Stevens AS .05 .02
❑ 171 Pat LaFontaine AS .10 .05
❑ 172 Alexander Mogilny AS .10 .05
❑ 173 Larry Murphy AS .10 .05
❑ 174 Al Iafrate AS .05 .02
❑ 175 Tom Barrasso AS .10 .05
❑ 176 Derek King .05 .02
❑ 177 Bob Probert .10 .05
❑ 178 Gary Suter .05 .02
❑ 179 David Shaw .05 .02
❑ 180 Luc Robitaille .10 .05
❑ 181 John LeClair .30 .14
❑ 182 Troy Murray .05 .02
❑ 183 Dave Gagner .10 .05
❑ 184 Darcy Loewen .05 .02
❑ 185 Mario Lemieux .50 .23
Points Leader
❑ 186 Pat Jablonski .10 .05
❑ 187 Alexei Kovalev .10 .05
❑ 188 Todd Krygier .05 .02
❑ 189 Larry Murphy .10 .05
❑ 190 Pierre Turgeon .10 .05
❑ 191 Craig Ludwig .05 .02
❑ 192 Brad May .10 .05
❑ 193 John MacLean .10 .05
❑ 194 Ron Wilson .05 .02
❑ 195 Eric Weinrich .05 .02
❑ 196 Steve Chiasson .05 .02
❑ 197 Dmitri Kvartalnov .05 .02
❑ 198 Andrei Kovalenko .05 .02
❑ 199 Rob Gaudreau .05 .02
❑ 200 Evgeny Davydov .05 .02
❑ 201 Adrien Plavsic .05 .02
❑ 202 Brian Bellows .05 .02
❑ 203 Doug Evans .05 .02
❑ 204 Tom Barrasso .10 .05
Wins Leader
❑ 205 Joe Nieuwendyk .10 .05
❑ 206 Jari Kurri .10 .05
❑ 207 Bob Rouse .05 .02
❑ 208 Yvon Corriveau .05 .02
❑ 209 John Blue .10 .05
❑ 210 Dimitri Khristich .05 .02
❑ 211 Brent Fedyk .05 .02
❑ 212 Jody Hull .05 .02
❑ 213 Chris Terreri .10 .05
❑ 214 Mike McPhee .05 .02
❑ 215 Chris Kontos .05 .02
❑ 216 Greg Gilbert .05 .02
❑ 217 Sergei Zubov .10 .05
❑ 218 Grant Fuhr .10 .05
❑ 219 Charlie Huddy .05 .02
❑ 220 Mario Lemieux 1.00 .45
❑ 221 Sheldon Kennedy .05 .02
❑ 222 Curtis Joseph .20 .09
Save Pct. Leader
❑ 223 Brad Dalgarno .05 .02
❑ 224 Bret Hedican .05 .02
❑ 225 Trevor Linden .10 .05
❑ 226 Darryl Sydor .05 .02
❑ 227 Jay More .05 .02
❑ 228 Dave Poulin .05 .02
❑ 229 Frank Musil .05 .02
❑ 230 Mark Recchi .10 .05
❑ 231 Craig Simpson .05 .02
❑ 232 Gino Cavallini .05 .02
❑ 233 Vincent Damphousse .10 .05
❑ 234 Luciano Borsato .05 .02
❑ 235 Dave Andreychuk .10 .05
❑ 236 Ken Daneyko .05 .02
❑ 237 Chris Chelios .20 .09
❑ 238 Andrew McBain .05 .02
❑ 239 Rick Tabaracci .10 .05
❑ 240 Steve Larmer .10 .05
❑ 241 Sean Burke .10 .05
❑ 242 Rob DiMaio .05 .02
❑ 243 Jim Paek .05 .02
❑ 244 Dave Lowry .05 .02
❑ 245 Alexander Mogilny .10 .05
❑ 246 Darren Turcotte .05 .02
❑ 247 Brendan Shanahan .40 .18
❑ 248 Peter Taglianetti .05 .02
❑ 249 Scott Mellanby .10 .05
❑ 250 Guy Carbonneau .05 .02
❑ 251 Claude LaPointe .05 .02
❑ 252 Pat Conacher .05 .02
❑ 253 Roger Johansson .05 .02
❑ 254 Cam Neely .10 .05
❑ 255 Garry Galley .05 .02
❑ 256 Keith Primeau .10 .05
❑ 257 Scott Lachance .05 .02
❑ 258 Bill Ranford .10 .05
❑ 259 Pat Falloon .05 .02
❑ 260 Pavel Bure .40 .18
❑ 261 Darrin Shannon .05 .02
❑ 262 Mike Foligno .05 .02
❑ 263 Checklist 1-132 .05 .02
❑ 264 Checklist 133-264 .05 .02
❑ 265 Peter Douris .05 .02
❑ 266 Warren Rychel .05 .02
❑ 267 Owen Nolan .10 .05
❑ 268 Mark Osborne .05 .02
❑ 269 Teppo Numminen .05 .02
❑ 270 Rob Niedermayer .10 .05
❑ 271 Mark Lamb .05 .02
❑ 272 Curtis Joseph .20 .09
❑ 273 Joe Murphy .05 .02
❑ 274 Bernie Nicholls .05 .02
❑ 275 Gord Roberts .05 .02
❑ 276 Al MacInnis .10 .05
❑ 277 Ken Wregget .10 .05
❑ 278 Calle Johansson .05 .02
❑ 279 Tom Kurvers .05 .02
❑ 280 Steve Yzerman .60 .25
❑ 281 Roman Hamrlik .10 .05
❑ 282 Esa Tikkanen .05 .02
❑ 283 Darrin Madeley .05 .02
❑ 284 Robert Dirk .05 .02
❑ 285 Derek Plante .05 .02
❑ 286 Ron Tugnutt .10 .05
❑ 287 Frank Pietrangelo .10 .05
❑ 288 Paul DiPietro .05 .02
❑ 289 Alexander Godynyuk .05 .02
❑ 290 Kirk Maltby .05 .02
❑ 291 Olaf Kolzig .10 .05
❑ 292 Vitali Karamnov .05 .02
❑ 293 Alexei Gusarov .05 .02
❑ 294 Bryan Erickson .05 .02
❑ 295 Jocelyn Lemieux .05 .02
❑ 296 Bryan Trottier .10 .05
❑ 297 Dave Ellett .05 .02
❑ 298 Tim Watters .05 .02
❑ 299 Joe Juneau .10 .05
❑ 300 Steve Thomas .05 .02
❑ 301 Mark Greig .05 .02
❑ 302 Jeff Reese .05 .02
❑ 303 Steven King .05 .02
❑ 304 Don Beaupre .10 .05
❑ 305 Denis Savard .10 .05
❑ 306 Greg Smyth .05 .02
❑ 307 Jaroslav Modry .05 .02
❑ 308 Petr Svoboda .05 .02
❑ 309 Mike Craig .05 .02
❑ 310 Eric Lindros .75 .35
❑ 311 Dana Murzyn .05 .02
❑ 312 Sean Hill .05 .02
❑ 313 Andre Racicot .10 .05
❑ 314 John Vanbiesbrouck .30 .14
❑ 315 Doug Lidster .05 .02
❑ 316 Garth Butcher .05 .02
❑ 317 Alexei Yashin .10 .05
❑ 318 Sergei Fedorov .40 .18
❑ 319 Louie DeBrusk .05 .02
❑ 320 Dominik Hasek .25 .11
❑ 321 Michal Pivonka .05 .02
❑ 322 Bobby Holik .05 .02
❑ 323 Roman Hamrlik .10 .05
❑ 324 Petr Svoboda .05 .02
❑ 325 Jaromir Jagr .30 .14
❑ 326 Steven Finn .05 .02
❑ 327 Stephane Richer .10 .05
❑ 328 Claude Loiselle .05 .02
❑ 329 Joe Sacco .05 .02
❑ 330 Wayne Gretzky 1.25 .55
❑ 331 Sylvain Lefebvre .05 .02
❑ 332 Sergei Bautin .05 .02
❑ 333 Craig Simpson .05 .02
❑ 334 Don Sweeney .05 .02
❑ 335 Dominic Roussel .10 .05
❑ 336 Scott Thomas .05 .02
❑ 337 Geoff Courtnall .05 .02
❑ 338 Tom Fitzgerald .05 .02
❑ 339 Kevin Haller .05 .02
❑ 340 Troy Loney .05 .02
❑ 341 Ronnie Stern .05 .02
❑ 342 Mark Astley .05 .02
❑ 343 Jeff Daniels .05 .02
❑ 344 Marc Bureau .05 .02
❑ 345 Micah Aivazoff .05 .02
❑ 346 Matthew Barnaby .10 .05
❑ 347 C.J. Young .05 .02
❑ 348 Dale Craigwell .05 .02
❑ 349 Ray Ferraro .05 .02
❑ 350 Ray Bourque .20 .09
❑ 351 Stu Barnes .05 .02
❑ 352 Allan Conroy .05 .02
❑ 353 Shawn McEachern .05 .02
❑ 354 Garry Valk .05 .02
❑ 355 Christian Ruuttu .05 .02
❑ 356 Darren Rumble .05 .02
❑ 357 Stu Grimson .05 .02
❑ 358 Alexander Karpovtsev .05 .02
❑ 359 Wendel Clark .10 .05
❑ 360 Michal Pivonka .05 .02
❑ 361 Peter Popovic .05 .02
❑ 362 Kevin Dahl .05 .02
❑ 363 Jeff Brown .05 .02
❑ 364 Daren Puppa .10 .05
❑ 365 Dallas Drake .05 .02
❑ 366 Dean McAmmond .05 .02
❑ 367 Martin Rucinsky .05 .02
❑ 368 Shane Churla .05 .02
❑ 369 Todd Ewen .05 .02
❑ 370 Kevin Stevens .05 .02
❑ 371 David Volek .05 .02
❑ 372 J.J. Daigneault .05 .02
❑ 373 Marc Bergevin .05 .02
❑ 374 Craig Billington .10 .05
❑ 375 Mike Gartner .10 .05
❑ 376 Jimmy Carson .05 .02
❑ 377 Bruce Driver .05 .02
❑ 378 Steve Heinze .05 .02
❑ 379 Patrick Carnback .05 .02
❑ 380 Wayne Gretzky CAN 1.25 .55
❑ 381 Jeff Brown CAN .05 .02
❑ 382 Gary Roberts CAN .05 .02
❑ 383 Ray Bourque CAN .20 .09
❑ 384 Mike Gartner CAN .10 .05
❑ 385 Felix Potvin CAN .20 .09
❑ 386 Michel Goulet .10 .05
❑ 387 Dave Tippett .05 .02
❑ 388 Jim Waite .10 .05
❑ 389 Yuri Khmylev .05 .02
❑ 390 Doug Gilmour .20 .09
❑ 391 Brad McCrimmon .05 .02
❑ 392 Brent Severyn .05 .02
❑ 393 Jocelyn Thibault .75 .35
❑ 394 Boris Mironov .05 .02
❑ 395 Marty McSorley .05 .02
❑ 396 Shaun Van Allen .05 .02
❑ 397 Gary Leeman .05 .02
❑ 398 Ed Olczyk .05 .02
❑ 399 Darcy Wakaluk .10 .05
❑ 400 Murray Craven .05 .02
❑ 401 Martin Brodeur .50 .23
❑ 402 Paul Laus .05 .02
❑ 403 Bill Houlder .05 .02
❑ 404 Robert Reichel .05 .02
❑ 405 Alexandre Daigle .05 .02
❑ 406 Brent Thompson .05 .02
❑ 407 Keith Acton .05 .02
❑ 408 Dave Karpa .05 .02
❑ 409 Igor Korolev .05 .02
❑ 410 Chris Gratton .10 .05
❑ 411 Vincent Riendeau .10 .05
❑ 412 Darren McCarty .25 .11
❑ 413 Bob Carpenter .05 .02
❑ 414 Joe Cirella .05 .02
❑ 415 Stephane Matteau .05 .02
❑ 416 Jozef Stumpel .05 .02
❑ 417 Rich Pilon .05 .02
❑ 418 Mattias Norstrom .05 .02
❑ 419 Dmitri Moronov .05 .02
❑ 420 Alexei Zhamnov .10 .05
❑ 421 Bill Guerin .05 .02
❑ 422 Greg Hawgood .05 .02
❑ 423 Randy Cunneyworth .05 .02
❑ 424 Ron Francis .10 .05
❑ 425 Brett Hull .25 .11
❑ 426 Tim Sweeney .05 .02
❑ 427 Mike Rathje .05 .02
❑ 428 Dave Babych .05 .02
❑ 429 Chris Tancill .05 .02
❑ 430 Mark Messier .25 .11
❑ 431 Bob Sweeney .05 .02
❑ 432 Terry Yake .05 .02
❑ 433 Joe Reekie .05 .02
❑ 434 Tomas Sandstrom .05 .02
❑ 435 Kevin Hatcher .05 .02
❑ 436 Bill Lindsay .05 .02
❑ 437 Jon Casey .10 .05
❑ 438 Dennis Vaske .05 .02
❑ 439 Allen Pedersen .05 .02
❑ 440 Pavel Bure .20 .09
❑ 441 Sergei Fedorov .20 .09
❑ 442 Arturs Irbe .10 .05
❑ 443 Darius Kasparaitis .05 .02
❑ 444 Evgeny Davydov .05 .02
❑ 445 Vladimir Malakhov .05 .02
❑ 446 Tom Barrasso .10 .05
❑ 447 Jeff Norton .05 .02
❑ 448 David Emma .05 .02
❑ 449 Pelle Eklund .05 .02
❑ 450 Jeremy Roenick .20 .09

□ 451 Jesse Belanger .05 .02
□ 452 Vitali Prokhorov .05 .02
□ 453 Arto Blomsten .05 .02
□ 454 Peter Zezel .05 .02
□ 455 Kelly Kisio .05 .02
□ 456 Zdeno Ciger .05 .02
□ 457 Greg Johnson .05 .02
□ 458 Dave Archibald .05 .02
□ 459 Vladimir Vujtek .05 .02
□ 460 Mats Sundin .10 .05
□ 461 Dan Keczmer .05 .02
□ 462 Stephan Lebeau .05 .02
□ 463 Dominik Hasek .50 .23
□ 464 Kevin Lowe .05 .02
□ 465 Gord Murphy .05 .02
□ 466 Bryan Smolinski .05 .02
□ 467 Josef Beranek .05 .02
□ 468 Ron Hextall .10 .05
□ 469 Randy Ladouceur .05 .02
□ 470 Scott Niedermayer .05 .02
□ 471 Kelly Hrudey .10 .05
□ 472 Mike Needham .05 .02
□ 473 John Tucker .05 .02
□ 474 Kelly Miller .05 .02
□ 475 Jyrki Lumme .05 .02
□ 476 Andy Moog .10 .05
□ 477 Glen Murray .05 .02
□ 478 Mark Ferner .05 .02
□ 479 John Cullen .05 .02
□ 480 Gilbert Dionne .05 .02
□ 481 Paul Ranheim .05 .02
□ 482 Mike Hough .05 .02
□ 483 Teemu Selanne .50 .23
□ 484 Aaron Ward .05 .02
□ 485 Chris Pronger .10 .05
□ 486 Glenn Healy .10 .05
□ 487 Curtis Leschyshyn .05 .02
□ 488 Jim Montgomery .05 .02
□ 489 Travis Green .10 .05
□ 490 Pat LaFontaine .10 .05
□ 491 Bobby Dollas .05 .02
□ 492 Alexei Kasatonov .05 .02
□ 493 Corey Millen .05 .02
□ 494 Slava Kozlov .10 .05
□ 495 Igor Kravchuk .05 .02
□ 496 Dimitri Filimonov .05 .02
□ 497 Jeff Odgers .05 .02
□ 498 Joe Mullen .10 .05
□ 499 Gary Shuchuk .05 .02
□ 500 Jeremy Roenick USA .20 .09
□ 501 Tom Barrasso USA .10 .05
□ 502 Keith Tkachuk USA .20 .09
□ 503 Phil Housley USA .10 .05
□ 504 Tony Granato USA .05 .02
□ 505 Brian Leetch USA .20 .09
□ 506 Anatoli Semenov .05 .02
□ 507 Steve Leach .05 .02
□ 508 Brian Skrudland .05 .02
□ 509 Kirk Muller .05 .02
□ 510 Gary Roberts .05 .02
□ 511 Gerard Gallant .05 .02
□ 512 Joey Kocur .05 .02
□ 513 Tie Domi .10 .05
□ 514 Kay Whitmore .10 .05
□ 515 Vladimir Malakhov .05 .02
□ 516 Stewart Malgunas .05 .02
□ 517 Jamie Macoun .05 .02
□ 518 Alan May .05 .02
□ 519 Guy Hebert .10 .05
□ 520 Derian Hatcher .05 .02
□ 521 Richard Smehlik .05 .02
□ 522 Joby Messier .05 .02
□ 523 Trent Klatt .05 .02
□ 524 Tom Chorske .05 .02
□ 525 Iain Fraser .05 .02
□ 526 Dan Laperriere .05 .02
□ 527 Checklist 265-396 .05 .02
□ 528 Checklist 397-528 .05 .02

## 1993-94 Topps/OPC Premier Gold

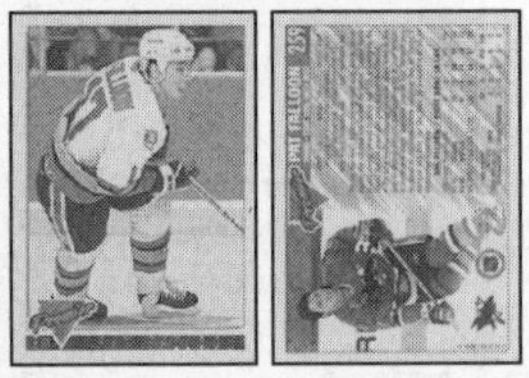

This parallel insert set to the regular issue '93-94 Topps/OPC Premier set comprises 528 standard-size cards. Every regular Premier 12-card pack included 11 regular cards plus one Premier Gold card. Also, one in four packs contained 10 regular cards plus two Premier Gold cards; and four Gold cards were inserted in every Topps jumbo pack. Aside from the gold-foil, the Premier Gold cards are identical to their regular issue counterparts. The four regular issue Premier checklists (263, 264, 527, and 528) were replaced by Gold cards of players not included in the basic set. The cards are numbered on the back. Except for some information in French on the backs, the 1993-94 O-Pee-Chee Premier Gold set is identical to the 1993-94 Topps Premier Gold set.

| | MINT | NRMT |
|---|---|---|
| COMPLETE TOPPS SET (528) | 150.00 | 70.00 |
| COMP.TOPPS SER.1 (264) | 75.00 | 34.00 |
| COMP.TOPPS SER.2 (264) | 75.00 | 34.00 |
| *TOPPS STARS: 2X TO 5X BASIC CARDS | | |
| *TOPPS YNG.STARS: 1.5X TO 4X BASIC CARDS | | |
| COMPLETE OPC SET (528) | 200.00 | 90.00 |
| COMP.OPC SER.1 (264) | 100.00 | 45.00 |
| COMP.OPC SER.2 (264) | 100.00 | 45.00 |
| *OPC STARS: 3X TO 6X BASIC CARDS | | |
| *OPC YNG.STARS: 2.5X TO 5X BASIC CARDS | | |
| COMMON GOLD (1G-528G) | .25 | .11 |
| CL REPLACE (263G-264G) | 1.00 | .45 |
| CL REPLACE (527G-528G) | 1.00 | .45 |

## 1993-94 Topps Premier Black Gold

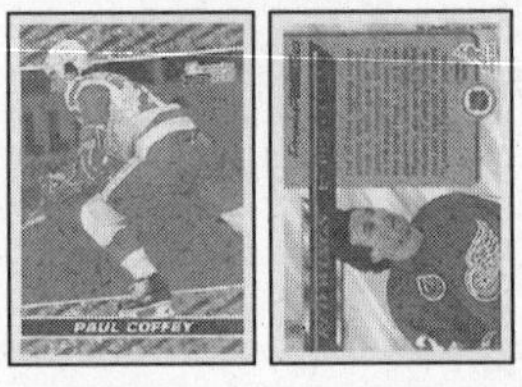

Randomly inserted in Topps packs, these 24 standard-size cards feature on their white-bordered fronts color player action shots set on ghosted and darkened backgrounds. Gold foil inner borders at the top and bottom carry multiple Premier Black Gold logos. The player's name appears in white lettering within a black stripe across the lower gold-foil inner margin. The horizontal back carries a color action cutout set on a bluish background on the left. Career highlights appear within a purple area on the right. The player's name and team name appear within a black bar across the top. The cards are numbered on the back. Collectors could also find in packs a Winner Card A, redeemable for the entire 12-card first-series set; a Winner Card B, redeemable for the 12-card second series; and a Winner Card AB, redeemable for the entire 24 card set. The Winner cards expired May 31, 1994.

| | MINT | NRMT |
|---|---|---|
| COMPLETE SET (24) | 50.00 | 22.00 |
| COMPLETE SERIES 1 (12) | 25.00 | 11.00 |
| COMPLETE SERIES 2 (12) | 25.00 | 11.00 |
| COMMON CARD (1-24) | 1.00 | .45 |

□ 1 Teemu Selanne 3.00 1.35
□ 2 Steve Duchesne 1.00 .45
□ 3 Felix Potvin 1.50 .70
□ 4 Shawn McEachern 1.00 .45
□ 5 Adam Oates 1.25 .55
□ 6 Paul Coffey 1.50 .70
□ 7 Wayne Gretzky 10.00 4.50
□ 8 Alexei Zhamnov 1.25 .55
□ 9 Mario Lemieux 8.00 3.60
□ 10 Gary Suter 1.00 .45
□ 11 Tom Barrasso 1.25 .55
□ 12 Joe Juneau 1.25 .55
□ 13 Eric Lindros 8.00 3.60
□ 14 Ed Belfour 1.50 .70
□ 15 Ray Bourque 1.50 .70
□ 16 Steve Yzerman 5.00 2.20
□ 17 Andrei Kovalenko 1.00 .45
□ 18 Curtis Joseph 1.50 .70
□ 19 Phil Housley 1.00 .45
□ 20 Pierre Turgeon 1.25 .55
□ 21 Brett Hull 2.00 .90
□ 22 Patrick Roy 8.00 3.60
□ 23 Larry Murphy 1.00 .45
□ 24 Pat LaFontaine 1.25 .55
□ A Winner 1-12 Expired 1.00 .45
□ B Winner 13-24 Expired 1.00 .45
□ AB Winner 1-24 Expired 1.00 .45

## 1993-94 Topps Premier Finest

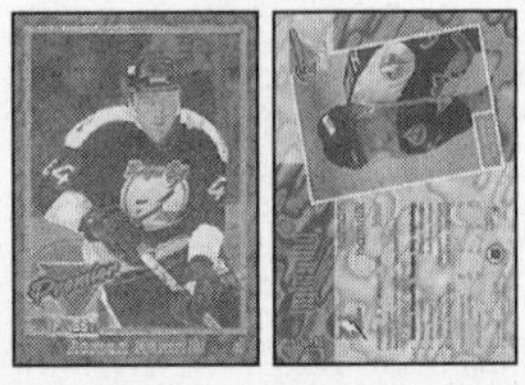

Randomly inserted in both Topps and OPC second-series packs, these 12 standard-size cards feature on their metallic fronts color player action shots framed by a gold line and bordered in blue. The player's name and position appear in gold lettering in the lower blue margin. The horizontal blue and gray back carries a color player action shot on the right, which carries the date of the player's NHL debut in its lower left corner. On the left are displayed the team name, player name, position, biography, and statistics. The cards are numbered on the back as "X of 12."

| | MINT | NRMT |
|---|---|---|
| COMPLETE SET (12) | 40.00 | 18.00 |
| COMMON CARD (1-12) | 2.00 | .90 |

□ 1 Alexandre Daigle 2.00 .90
□ 2 Roman Hamrlik 2.00 .90
□ 3 Eric Lindros 15.00 6.75
□ 4 Owen Nolan 3.00 1.35
□ 5 Mats Sundin 4.00 1.80
□ 6 Mike Modano 5.00 2.20
□ 7 Pierre Turgeon 3.00 1.35
□ 8 Joe Murphy 2.00 .90
□ 9 Wendel Clark 2.00 .90
□ 10 Mario Lemieux 15.00 6.75
□ 11 Dale Hawerchuk 2.00 .90
□ 12 Rob Ramage 2.00 .90
□ NNO OPC Redemption Single 1.00 .45
□ NNO OPC Redemption Set 6.00 2.70
□ NNO Topps Redemption Single .50 .23
□ NNO Topps Redemption Set 4.00 1.80

## 1993-94 Topps Premier Team USA

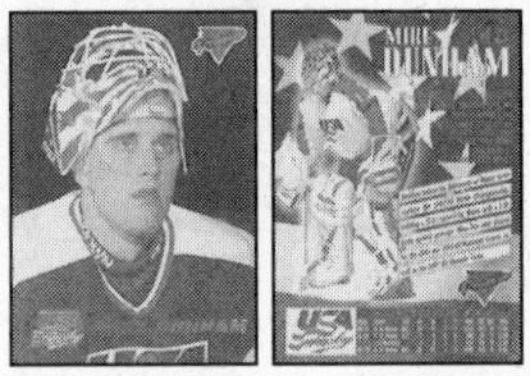

Randomly inserted at a rate of 1:12 second-series Topps Premier packs, these 23 standard-size cards feature borderless color player photos on their fronts. The player's name and the USA Hockey logo appear at the bottom in gold foil. The red, white, and blue back carries the player's name and position at the top, followed below by biography, player photo, career highlights, and statistics. The cards are numbered on the back as "X of 23."

| | MINT | NRMT |
|---|---|---|
| COMPLETE SET (23) | 20.00 | 9.00 |
| COMMON CARD (1-23) | 1.00 | .45 |

□ 1 Mike Dunham 1.50 .70
□ 2 Ian Moran 1.00 .45
□ 3 Peter Laviolette 1.00 .45
□ 4 Darby Hendrickson 1.00 .45
□ 5 Brian Rolston 1.50 .70
□ 6 Mark Beaufait 1.00 .45
□ 7 Travis Richards 1.00 .45
□ 8 John Lilley 1.00 .45
□ 9 Chris Ferraro 1.50 .70
□ 10 Jon Hillebrandt 1.50 .70
□ 11 Chris Imes 1.00 .45
□ 12 Ted Crowley 1.00 .45
□ 13 David Sacco 1.00 .45
□ 14 Todd Marchant 1.50 .70
□ 15 Peter Ferraro 1.50 .70
□ 16 David Roberts 1.00 .45
□ 17 Jim Campbell 2.00 .90
□ 18 Barry Richter 1.00 .45
□ 19 Craig Johnson 1.00 .45
□ 20 Brett Hauer 1.00 .45
□ 21 Jeff Lazaro 1.00 .45
□ 22 Jim Storm 1.00 .45
□ 23 Matt Martin 1.00 .45

## 1994-95 Topps/OPC Premier

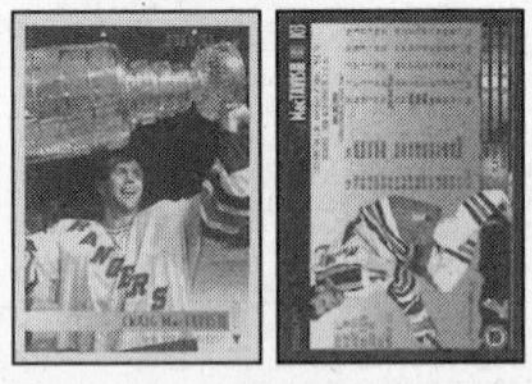

This 550-card set was issued in two series of 275 cards each. OPC packs contain 14 cards and Topps packs contain 12 cards. Both boxes contain 36 packs. It was announced in press material that no more than 2,000 cases of each series of the OPC version were printed. Because of this shorter quantity, OPC versions earn a slight premium. Card fronts feature a full white border with a color bar enclosing the player's name near the bottom. Position runs vertically down the right side of the name, team name directly below it. All text is printed in silver foil. Backs have a black border with a cutout player photo, full stats including playoffs, and personal information. The OPC back text is in French and English. The Topps version is in English only. Since some of the cards have no written text, such as the All-Star cards, they are impossible to positively identify as being from one set or the other. Both versions have "The Topps Company, Inc." printed on the back. Several subsets appear scattered throughout the set, including All-Stars, Goaltending Duos, League Leaders, Rookie Sensations, Team of the Future, Tools of the Game, The Trade and Power. Rookie cards include Mariusz Czerkawski, Ian Laperriere, Jason Wiemer and Eric Fichaud.

| | MINT | NRMT |
|---|---|---|
| COMPLETE SET (550) | 40.00 | 18.00 |
| COMPLETE SERIES 1 (275) | 15.00 | 6.75 |
| COMPLETE SERIES 2 (275) | 25.00 | 11.00 |
| COMMON CARD (1-550) | .05 | .02 |

□ 1 Mark Messier .30 .14
□ 2 Darren Turcotte .05 .02
□ 3 Mikhail Shtalenkov .05 .02
□ 4 Rob Gaudreau .05 .02
□ 5 Tony Amonte .10 .05
□ 6 Stephane Quintal .05 .02
□ 7 Iain Fraser .05 .02
□ 8 Doug Weight .10 .05
□ 9 German Titov .05 .02
□ 10 Larry Murphy .10 .05
□ 11 Danton Cole .05 .02
□ 12 Pat Peake .05 .02
□ 13 Chris Terreri .10 .05
□ 14 Yuri Khmylev .05 .02
□ 15 Paul Coffey .25 .11
□ 16 Brian Savage .05 .02
□ 17 Rod Brind'Amour .10 .05
□ 18 Nathan Lafayette .05 .02
□ 19 Gord Murphy .05 .02
□ 20 Al Iafrate .05 .02
□ 21 Kevin Miller .05 .02
□ 22 Peter Zezel .05 .02
□ 23 Sylvain Turgeon .05 .02
□ 24 Mark Tinordi .05 .02
□ 25 Jari Kurri .10 .05
□ 26 Benoit Hogue .05 .02
□ 27 Jeff Reese .05 .02
□ 28 Brian Noonan .05 .02
□ 29 Denis Tsygurov .05 .02
□ 30 James Patrick .05 .02
□ 31 Bob Corkum .05 .02
□ 32 Valeri Kamensky .10 .05
□ 33 Ray Whitney .05 .02
□ 34 Joe Murphy .05 .02
□ 35 Dominik Hasek AS .25 .11
□ 36 Ray Bourque AS .25 .11
□ 37 Brian Leetch AS .25 .11
□ 38 Dave Andreychuk AS .10 .05
□ 39 Pavel Bure AS .25 .11
□ 40 Sergei Fedorov AS .25 .11
□ 41 Bob Beers .05 .02
□ 42 Byron Dafoe .10 .05
□ 43 Lyle Odelein .05 .02
□ 44 Markus Naslund .05 .02
□ 45 Dean Chynoweth .05 .02
□ 46 Trent Klatt .05 .02
□ 47 Murray Craven .05 .02
□ 48 Dave Mackey .05 .02
□ 49 Norm Maciver .05 .02
□ 50 Alexander Mogilny .10 .05
□ 51 David Reid .05 .02
□ 52 Nicklas Lidstrom .10 .05
□ 53 Tom Fitzgerald .05 .02
□ 54 Roman Hamrlik .10 .05
□ 55 Wendel Clark .10 .05
□ 56 Dominic Roussel .10 .05
□ 57 Alexei Zhitnik .05 .02
□ 58 Valeri Zelepukin .05 .02
□ 59 Calle Johansson .05 .02
□ 60 Craig Janney .10 .05
□ 61 Randy Wood .05 .02
□ 62 Curtis Leschyshyn .05 .02
□ 63 Stephan Lebeau .05 .02
□ 64 Dallas Drake .05 .02
□ 65 Vincent Damphousse .10 .05
□ 66 Scott Lachance .05 .02
□ 67 Dirk Graham .05 .02
□ 68 Kevin Smyth .05 .02
□ 69 Denis Savard .10 .05
□ 70 Mike Richter .25 .11
□ 71 Ronnie Stern .05 .02
□ 72 Kirk Maltby .05 .02
□ 73 Kjell Samuelsson .05 .02
□ 74 Neal Broten .10 .05
□ 75 Trevor Linden .10 .05
□ 76 Todd Elik .05 .02
□ 77 Andrew McBain .05 .02
□ 78 Alexei Kudashov .05 .02
□ 79 Ken Daneyko .05 .02
□ 80 Dominik Hasek .25 .11
Grant Fuhr DUO
□ 81 Andy Moog .10 .05
Darcy Wakaluk DUO
□ 82 John Vanbiesbrouck .25 .11
Mark Fitzpatrick DUO
□ 83 Martin Brodeur .25 .11
Chris Terreri DUO
□ 84 Tom Barrasso .10 .05
Ken Wregget DUO
□ 85 Kirk McLean .10 .05
Kay Whitmore DUO
□ 86 Darryl Sydor .05 .02
□ 87 Chris Osgood .40 .18
□ 88 Ted Donato .05 .02
□ 89 Dave Lowry .05 .02
□ 90 Mark Recchi .10 .05
□ 91 Jim Montgomery .05 .02
□ 92 Bill Houlder .05 .02
□ 93 Richard Smehlik .05 .02
□ 94 Benoit Brunet .05 .02
□ 95 Teemu Selanne .50 .23
□ 96 Paul Ranheim .05 .02
□ 97 Andrei Kovalenko .05 .02
□ 98 Grant Ledyard .05 .02
□ 99 Brent Grieve .05 .02
□ 100 Joe Juneau .10 .05
□ 101 Martin Gelinas .05 .02
□ 102 Jamie Macoun .05 .02
□ 103 Craig MacTavish .05 .02
□ 104 Micah Aivazoff .05 .02
□ 105 Stephane Richer .10 .05
□ 106 Eric Weinrich .05 .02
□ 107 Pat Elynuik .05 .02
□ 108 Tomas Sandstrom .05 .02
□ 109 Darrin Madeley .05 .02
□ 110 Al MacInnis .10 .05
□ 111 Cam Stewart .05 .02
□ 112 Dixon Ward .05 .02
□ 113 Vlastimil Kroupa .05 .02
□ 114 Rob DiMaio .05 .02
□ 115 Pierre Turgeon .10 .05
□ 116 Mike Hough .05 .02
□ 117 John LeClair .40 .18
□ 118 Dave Hannan .05 .02
□ 119 Todd Ewen .05 .02
□ 120 Stanley Cup Card .10 .05
□ 121 Dave Manson .05 .02
□ 122 Jocelyn Lemieux .05 .02
□ 123 Jocelyn Thibault .25 .11
□ 124 Scott Pearson .05 .02
□ 125 Patrick Roy AS .50 .23
□ 126 Scott Stevens AS .10 .05
□ 127 Al MacInnis AS .10 .05
□ 128 Adam Graves AS .10 .05
□ 129 Cam Neely AS .10 .05
□ 130 Wayne Gretzky AS .75 .35
□ 131 Tom Chorske .05 .02
□ 132 John Tucker .05 .02
□ 133 Steve Smith .05 .02
□ 134 Kay Whitmore .10 .05
□ 135 Adam Oates .10 .05
□ 136 Bill Berg .05 .02
□ 137 Wes Walz .05 .02
□ 138 Jeff Beukeboom .05 .02
□ 139 Ron Francis .10 .05
□ 140 Alexandre Daigle .05 .02
□ 141 Josef Beranek .05 .02
□ 142 Tom Pederson .05 .02
□ 143 Jamie McLennan .05 .02
□ 144 Scott Mellanby .10 .05
□ 145 Slava Kozlov .10 .05
□ 146 Marty McSorley .05 .02
□ 147 Tim Sweeney .05 .02
□ 148 Luciano Borsato .05 .02
□ 149 Jason Dawe .05 .02
□ 150 Wayne Gretzky LL .75 .35
□ 151 Pavel Bure LL .25 .11
□ 152 Dominik Hasek LL .25 .11
□ 153 Scott Stevens LL .10 .05
□ 154 Wayne Gretzky LL .75 .35
□ 155 Mike Richter LL .25 .11
□ 156 Dominik Hasek LL .25 .11
□ 157 Ted Drury .05 .02
□ 158 Peter Popovic .05 .02
□ 159 Alexei Kasatonov .05 .02
□ 160 Mats Sundin .10 .05
□ 161 Brad Shaw .05 .02
□ 162 Bret Hedican .05 .02
□ 163 Mike McPhee .05 .02
□ 164 Martin Straka .05 .02
□ 165 Dmitri Mironov .05 .02
□ 166 Andrei Trefilov .05 .02
□ 167 Joe Reekie .05 .02
□ 168 Gary Suter .05 .02
□ 169 Greg Gilbert .05 .02
□ 170 Igor Larionov .05 .02
□ 171 Mike Sillinger .05 .02
□ 172 Igor Kravchuk .05 .02
□ 173 Glen Murray .05 .02
□ 174 Shawn Chambers .05 .02
□ 175 John MacLean .10 .05
□ 176 Yves Racine .05 .02
□ 177 Andrei Lomakin .05 .02
□ 178 Patrick Flatley .05 .02
□ 179 Igor Ulanov .05 .02
□ 180 Pat LaFontaine .10 .05
□ 181 Mathieu Schneider .05 .02
□ 182 Peter Stastny .10 .05
□ 183 Tony Granato .05 .02
□ 184 Peter Douris .05 .02
□ 185 Alexei Kovalev .10 .05
□ 186 Geoff Courtnall .05 .02
□ 187 Richard Matvichuk .05 .02
□ 188 Troy Murray .05 .02
□ 189 Todd Gill .05 .02
□ 190 Martin Brodeur RS .25 .11
□ 191 Mikael Renberg RS .10 .05
□ 192 Alexei Yashin RS .10 .05
□ 193 Jason Arnott RS .10 .05
□ 194 Derek Plante RS .05 .02
□ 195 Alexandre Daigle RS .05 .02
□ 196 Bryan Smolinski RS .05 .02
□ 197 Jesse Belanger RS .05 .02
□ 198 Chris Pronger RS .10 .05
□ 199 Chris Osgood RS .25 .1
□ 200 Jeremy Roenick .25 .1
□ 201 Johan Garpenlov .05 .0
□ 202 Dave Karpa .05 .0
□ 203 Darren McCarty .05 .0
□ 204 Claude Lemieux .10 .0
□ 205 Geoff Sanderson .10 .0
□ 206 Tom Barrasso .10 .0
□ 207 Kevin Dineen .05 .0
□ 208 Sylvain Cote .05 .0
□ 209 Brent Gretzky .05 .0
□ 210 Shayne Corson .05 .0
□ 211 Darius Kasparaitis .05 .0
□ 212 Peter Andersson .05 .0
□ 213 Robert Reichel .05 .0
□ 214 Jozef Stumpel .05 .0
□ 215 Brendan Shanahan .50 .2

❑ 216 Craig Muni .05 .02
❑ 217 Alexei Zhamnov .10 .05
❑ 218 Robert Lang .05 .02
❑ 219 Brian Bellows .05 .02
❑ 220 Steven King .05 .02
❑ 221 Sergei Zubov .05 .02
❑ 222 Kelly Miller .05 .02
❑ 223 Ilya Byakin .05 .02
❑ 224 Chris Tamer .05 .02
❑ 225 Doug Gilmour .25 .11
❑ 226 Shawn Antoski .05 .02
❑ 227 Andrew Cassels .05 .02
❑ 228 Craig Wolanin .05 .02
❑ 229 Jon Casey .10 .05
❑ 230 Mike Modano .10 .05
❑ 231 Bill Guerin .05 .02
❑ 232 Gaetan Duchesne .05 .02
❑ 233 Steve Dubinsky .05 .02
❑ 234 Jason Bowen .05 .02
❑ 235 Steve Yzerman .75 .35
❑ 236 Dave Poulin .05 .02
❑ 237 Michael Nylander .05 .02
❑ 238 Felix Potvin FUT .25 .11
❑ 239 Sandis Ozolinsh FUT .10 .05
❑ 240 Scott Niedermayer FUT .05 .02
❑ 241 Eric Lindros FUT .50 .23
❑ 242 Keith Tkachuk FUT .25 .11
❑ 243 Teemu Selanne FUT .25 .11
❑ 244 Marty McInnis .05 .02
❑ 245 Bob Kudelski .05 .02
❑ 246 Paul Cavallini .05 .02
❑ 247 Brian Bradley .05 .02
❑ 248 Robb Stauber .10 .05
❑ 249 Jay Wells .05 .02
❑ 250 Mario Lemieux 1.25 .55
❑ 251 Tommy Albelin .05 .02
❑ 252 Paul DiPietro .05 .02
❑ 253 Mike Gartner .10 .05
❑ 254 Darrin Shannon .05 .02
❑ 255 Alexander Karpovtsev .05 .02
❑ 256 Dave Babych .05 .02
❑ 257 Greg Johnson .05 .02
❑ 258 Frank Musil .05 .02
❑ 259 Michal Pivonka .05 .02
❑ 260 Arturs Irbe .10 .05
❑ 261 Paul Broten .05 .02
❑ 262 Don Sweeney .05 .02
❑ 263 Doug Brown .05 .02
❑ 264 Bobby Dollas .05 .02
❑ 265 Brian Skrudland .05 .02
❑ 266 Dan Plante .05 .02
❑ 267 Chad Penney .05 .02
❑ 268 Steve Leach .05 .02
❑ 269 Damian Rhodes .10 .05
❑ 270 Glenn Anderson .10 .05
❑ 271 Randy McKay .05 .02
❑ 272 Jeff Brown .05 .02
❑ 273 Steve Konowalchuk .05 .02
❑ 274 Checklist 1-136 .05 .02
❑ 275 Checklist 137-275 .05 .02
❑ 276 Sergei Fedorov .25 .11
❑ 277 Adam Oates .10 .05
❑ 278 Mark Messier .25 .11
❑ 279 Doug Gilmour .25 .11
❑ 280 Wayne Gretzky .75 .35
❑ 281 Rick Tocchet .10 .05
❑ 282 Guy Carbonneau .05 .02
❑ 283 Peter Bondra .25 .11
❑ 284 Valeri Karpov .05 .02
❑ 285 Ed Belfour .25 .11
❑ 286 Petr Nedved .10 .05
❑ 287 Mikael Andersson .05 .02
❑ 288 Boris Mironov .05 .02
❑ 289 Donald Audette .10 .05
❑ 290 Kevin Stevens .05 .02
❑ 291 Cliff Ronning .05 .02
❑ 292 Bruce Driver .05 .02
❑ 293 Mariusz Czerkawski .05 .02
❑ 294 Mikael Renberg .10 .05
❑ 295 Theoren Fleury .10 .05
❑ 296 Robert Kron .05 .02
❑ 297 Wendel Clark .10 .05
❑ 298 Dave Gagner .10 .05
❑ 299 Ulf Dahlen .05 .02
❑ 300 Keith Tkachuk .30 .14
❑ 301 Mike Ridley .05 .02
❑ 302 Mike Vernon .10 .05
❑ 303 Troy Mallette .05 .02
❑ 304 Derek King .05 .02
❑ 305 Kirk Muller .05 .02
❑ 306 Rob Niedermayer .10 .05
❑ 307 Ian Laperriere .05 .02
❑ 308 Mike Donnelly .05 .02
❑ 309 Joe Sacco .05 .02
❑ 310 Patrick Roy .50 .23
❑ 311 Tom Barrasso .10 .05
❑ 312 Dominik Hasek .25 .11
❑ 313 Felix Potvin .25 .11
❑ 314 Mike Richter .25 .11
❑ 315 Bobby Holik .05 .02
❑ 316 Patrick Poulin .05 .02
❑ 317 Stephane Matteau .05 .02
❑ 318 Petr Klima .05 .02
❑ 319 Fredrik Olausson .05 .02
❑ 320 Dale Hawerchuk .10 .05
❑ 321 Jim Dowd .05 .02
❑ 322 Chris Therien .05 .02
❑ 323 Ravil Gusmanov .05 .02
❑ 324 Vincent Riendeau .10 .05
❑ 325 Pavel Bure .50 .23
❑ 326 Jimmy Carson .05 .02
❑ 327 Steve Chiasson .05 .02
❑ 328 Ken Wregget .10 .05
❑ 329 Kenny Jonsson .05 .02
❑ 330 Keith Primeau .10 .05
❑ 331 Bob Errey .05 .02
❑ 332 Derian Hatcher .05 .02
❑ 333 Stephane Fiset .10 .05
❑ 334 Brent Severyn .05 .02
❑ 335 Ray Ferraro .05 .02
❑ 336 Pavol Demitra .05 .02
❑ 337 Valeri Bure .10 .05
❑ 338 Guy Hebert .10 .05
❑ 339 Matt Johnson .05 .02
❑ 340 Curtis Joseph .25 .11
❑ 341 Rob Pearson .05 .02
❑ 342 Jeff Shantz .05 .02
❑ 343 Eric Charron .05 .02
❑ 344 Jason Smith .05 .02
❑ 345 Mats Sundin .10 .05
Wendel Clark
❑ 346 Rick Tocchet .10 .05
Luc Robitaille
❑ 347 Al MacInnis .10 .05
Phil Housley
❑ 348 Mike Vernon .10 .05
Steve Chiasson
❑ 349 Craig Simpson .05 .02
❑ 350 Adam Graves .10 .05
❑ 351 Kevin Haller .05 .02
❑ 352 Nelson Emerson .05 .02
❑ 353 Phil Housley .10 .05
❑ 354 Shawn McEachern .05 .02
❑ 355 Felix Potvin .25 .11
❑ 356 Sergio Momesso .05 .02
❑ 357 Glen Wesley .05 .02
❑ 358 David Shaw .05 .02
❑ 359 Terry Carkner .05 .02
❑ 360 John Vanbiesbrouck .40 .18
❑ 361 Dean Evason .05 .02
❑ 362 Michal Sykora .05 .02
❑ 363 Troy Loney .05 .02
❑ 364 Sylvain Lefebvre .05 .02
❑ 365 Alexei Yashin .10 .05
❑ 366 Gilbert Dionne .05 .02
❑ 367 Rick Tabaracci .10 .05
❑ 368 Paul Ysebaert .05 .02
❑ 369 Craig Johnson .05 .02
❑ 370 Scott Stevens .10 .05
❑ 371 Philippe Boucher .05 .02
❑ 372 Garry Valk .05 .02
❑ 373 Jason Muzzatti .10 .05
❑ 374 Chris Joseph .05 .02
❑ 375 Wayne Gretzky 1.50 .70
❑ 376 Teppo Numminen .05 .02
❑ 377 Oleg Petrov .05 .02
❑ 378 Patrik Juhlin .05 .02
❑ 379 Zarley Zalapski .05 .02
❑ 380 Martin Brodeur .25 .11
❑ 381 Chris Pronger .10 .05
❑ 382 Sergei Zubov .05 .02
❑ 383 Mikael Renberg .10 .05
❑ 384 Brett Lindros .05 .02
❑ 385 Peter Forsberg .50 .23
❑ 386 Brandon Convery .05 .02
❑ 387 Steve Heinze .05 .02
❑ 388 Glenn Healy .10 .05
❑ 389 Brian Benning .05 .02
❑ 390 Pat Verbeek .05 .02
❑ 391 Ulf Samuelsson .05 .02
❑ 392 Turner Stevenson .05 .02
❑ 393 Bob Rouse .05 .02
❑ 394 Steve Konroyd .05 .02
❑ 395 Russ Courtnall .05 .02
❑ 396 Sergei Makarov .05 .02
❑ 397 Kirk McLean .10 .05
❑ 398 Steven Finn .05 .02
❑ 399 Yan Kaminsky .05 .02
❑ 400 Eric Lindros .75 .35
❑ 401 Steve Duchesne .05 .02
❑ 402 John Slaney .05 .02
❑ 403 Bernie Nicholls .05 .02
❑ 404 Kelly Buchberger .05 .02
❑ 405 Paul Kariya 1.25 .55
❑ 406 Michel Petit .05 .02
❑ 407 Cale Hulse .05 .02
❑ 408 Sheldon Kennedy .05 .02
❑ 409 Brad May .10 .05
❑ 410 Daren Puppa .10 .05
❑ 411 Janne Laukkanen .05 .02
❑ 412 Mats Sundin .10 .05
❑ 413 Trevor Kidd .10 .05
❑ 414 Greg Adams .05 .02
❑ 415 Pavel Bure .25 .11
❑ 416 Teemu Selanne .25 .11
❑ 417 Brett Hull .25 .11
❑ 418 Steve Larmer .10 .05
❑ 419 Cam Neely .10 .05
❑ 420 Ray Bourque .25 .11
❑ 421 Andrei Nikolishin .05 .02
❑ 422 Jim Paek .05 .02
❑ 423 John Cullen .05 .02
❑ 424 Darcy Wakaluk .10 .05
❑ 425 Peter Forsberg 1.00 .45
❑ 426 Yves Racine .05 .02
❑ 427 Jody Hull .05 .02
❑ 428 Ron Sutter .05 .02
❑ 429 Ray Sheppard .10 .05
❑ 430 Sandis Ozolinsh .10 .05
❑ 431 Brent Grieve .05 .02
❑ 432 Shaun Van Allen .05 .02
❑ 433 Craig Berube .05 .02
❑ 434 Vladislav Boulin .05 .02
❑ 435 Bill Ranford .10 .05
❑ 436 Denny Felsner .05 .02
❑ 437 Jamie Storr .10 .05
❑ 438 Brian Rolston .05 .02
❑ 439 Chris Gratton .10 .05
❑ 440 Dominik Hasek .50 .23
❑ 441 Garth Butcher .05 .02
❑ 442 Jyrki Lumme .05 .02
❑ 443 Sergei Nemchinov .05 .02
❑ 444 Tie Domi .10 .05
❑ 445 Gary Roberts .05 .02
❑ 446 Dave McLlwain .05 .02
❑ 447 John Gruden .05 .02
❑ 448 Vladimir Konstantinov .05 .02
❑ 449 Adam Deadmarsh .10 .05
❑ 450 Brian Leetch .25 .11
❑ 451 Scott Stevens .10 .05
❑ 452 Mark Tinordi .05 .02
❑ 453 Al Iafrate .05 .02
❑ 454 Ray Bourque .25 .11
❑ 455 Patrick Roy 1.00 .45
❑ 456 Viktor Gordiouk .05 .02
❑ 457 Owen Nolan .10 .05
❑ 458 Stu Barnes .05 .02
❑ 459 Zigmund Palffy .10 .05
❑ 460 Jaromir Jagr .75 .35
❑ 461 Andrei Nazarov .05 .02
❑ 462 Kelly Hrudey .10 .05
❑ 463 Jason Wiemer .05 .02
❑ 464 Oleg Tverdovsky .10 .05
❑ 465 Brett Hull .30 .14
❑ 466 Luke Richardson .05 .02
❑ 467 Jason Allison .05 .02
❑ 468 Dimitri Yushkevich .05 .02
❑ 469 Todd Simon .05 .02
❑ 470 Martin Brodeur .60 .25
❑ 471 Thomas Steen .05 .02
❑ 472 Vesa Viitakoski .05 .02
❑ 473 Todd Harvey .05 .02
❑ 474 Kent Manderville .05 .02
❑ 475 Chris Chelios .25 .11
❑ 476 Joby Messier .05 .02
❑ 477 Jassen Cullimore .05 .02
❑ 478 Jamie Pushor .05 .02
❑ 479 Bryan Smolinski .05 .02
❑ 480 Joe Sakic .50 .23
❑ 481 David Wilkie .05 .02
❑ 482 Craig Billington .10 .05
❑ 483 Pat Neaton .05 .02
❑ 484 Chris Pronger .10 .05
❑ 485 Brian Leetch .25 .11
❑ 486 Chris Chelios .25 .11
❑ 487 Jeff Brown .05 .02
❑ 488 Al MacInnis .10 .05
❑ 489 Paul Coffey .25 .11
❑ 490 Ray Bourque .25 .11
❑ 491 Phil Housley .10 .05
❑ 492 Larry Murphy .10 .05
❑ 493 Sergei Zubov .05 .02
❑ 494 Scott Stevens .10 .05
❑ 495 Steve Thomas .05 .02
❑ 496 Jim Waite .10 .05
❑ 497 Mike Keane .05 .02
❑ 498 Rob Blake .05 .02
❑ 499 John Lilley .05 .02
❑ 500 Brian Leetch .25 .11
❑ 501 Derek Plante .05 .02
❑ 502 Tim Cheveldae .10 .05
❑ 503 Vladimir Vujtek .05 .02
❑ 504 Esa Tikkanen .05 .02
❑ 505 Cam Neely .10 .05
❑ 506 Dale Hunter .05 .02
❑ 507 Marc Bergevin .05 .02
❑ 508 Joel Otto .05 .02
❑ 509 Brent Fedyk .05 .02
❑ 510 Dave Andreychuk .10 .05
❑ 511 Andy Moog .10 .05
❑ 512 Jaroslav Modry .05 .02
❑ 513 Sergei Krivokrasov .05 .02
❑ 514 Brett Lindros .05 .02
❑ 515 Cory Stillman .05 .02
❑ 516 Jon Rohloff .05 .02
❑ 517 Joe Mullen .10 .05
❑ 518 Evgeny Davydov .05 .02
❑ 519 Scott Young .05 .02
❑ 520 Sergei Fedorov .40 .18
❑ 521 Pat Falloon .05 .02
❑ 522 Bill Lindsay .05 .02
❑ 523 Ron Tugnutt .10 .05
❑ 524 Anatoli Semenov .05 .02
❑ 525 Geoff Courtnall .05 .02
❑ 526 Luc Robitaille .10 .05
❑ 527 Geoff Sanderson .10 .05
❑ 528 Esa Tikkanen .05 .02
❑ 529 Brendan Shanahan .25 .11
❑ 530 Jason Arnott .10 .05
❑ 531 Michal Grosek .05 .02
❑ 532 Steve Larmer .10 .05
❑ 533 Eric Fichaud .40 .18
❑ 534 Dimitri Khristich .05 .02
❑ 535 Garry Galley .05 .02
❑ 536 Aaron Gavey .05 .02
❑ 537 Joe Nieuwendyk .10 .05
❑ 538 Mike Craig .05 .02
❑ 539 Scott Niedermayer .05 .02
❑ 540 Luc Robitaille .10 .05
❑ 541 Dino Ciccarelli .10 .05
❑ 542 Sean Burke .10 .05
❑ 543 Jiri Slegr .05 .02
❑ 544 Jesse Belanger .05 .02
❑ 545 Sean Hill .05 .02
❑ 546 Vladimir Malakhov .05 .02
❑ 547 Jeff Friesen .10 .05
❑ 548 Mike Ricci .05 .02
❑ 549 Checklist 276-414 .05 .02
❑ 550 Checklist 415-550 .05 .02

## 1994-95 Topps/OPC Premier Special Effects

One card from this parallel set was issued in every other pack of OPC and Topps Premier. The cards can be differentiated from the basic set by the reflective rainbow foil which appears

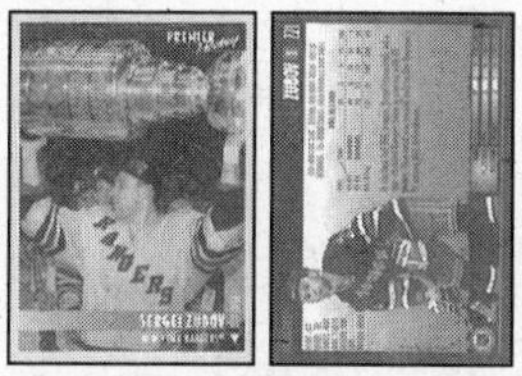

in the card background when held at an angle to a light source. Card backs are the same. The OPC versions are slightly more desirable because they were printed in smaller quantities than the Topps cards. Cards 274, 275, 549 and 550 replaced the checklists with players not featured in the basic set.

MINT NRMT
COMPLETE TOPPS SET (550) 400.00 180.00
COMP.TOPPS SER.1 (275) ... 150.00 70.00
COMP.TOPPS SER.2 (275) ... 250.00 110.00
COMMON TOPPS FX (1-550) ...... .35 .16
TOPPS SEMISTARS/GOALIES
*TOPPS SER.1 STARS: 5X TO 10X BASIC CARDS
*TOPPS SER.1 YNG.STARS: 2.5X TO 5X BASIC CARDS
*TOPPS SER.2 STARS: 7.5X TO 15X BASIC CARDS
*TOPPS SER.2 YOUNG STARS: 5X TO 10X BASIC CARDS
COMPLETE OPC SET (550) ... 600.00 275.00
COMP.OPC SER.1 (275) ....... 225.00 100.00
COMP.OPC SER.2 (275) ....... 375.00 170.00
COMMON OPC FX (1-550) .......... .50 .23
*OPC STARS: 7.5X TO 15X BASIC CARDS
*OPC YNG.STARS: 5X TO 10X BASIC CARDS

## 1994-95 Topps Finest Inserts

The 23 cards in this set were randomly inserted at a rate of 1:36 Topps Premier series one packs. The set includes all players who scored at least 40 goals in 1993-94. Cards feature an isolated player photo over a textured rainbow background. A reflective rainbow border is broken up by the player name and his goal scoring mark. Premier Finest is written across the top of the card. Backs have a small player photo with brief personal information, and scoring breakdown by division. Cards are numbered "X" of 23.

MINT NRMT
COMPLETE SET (23) 90.00 40.00
COMMON CARD (1-23) 1.00 .45

❑ 1 Pavel Bure 10.00 4.50
❑ 2 Brett Hull 6.00 2.70
❑ 3 Sergei Fedorov 10.00 4.50
❑ 4 Dave Andreychuk 1.00 .45
❑ 5 Brendan Shanahan 10.00 4.50
❑ 6 Ray Sheppard 1.00 .45
❑ 7 Adam Graves 2.00 .90
❑ 8 Cam Neely 2.00 .90
❑ 9 Mike Modano 6.00 2.70
❑ 10 Wendel Clark 1.00 .45
❑ 11 Jeremy Roenick 5.00 2.20
❑ 12 Eric Lindros 20.00 9.00
❑ 13 Luc Robitaille 1.00 .45
❑ 14 Steve Thomas 1.00 .45
❑ 15 Geoff Sanderson 2.00 .90
❑ 16 Gary Roberts 1.00 .45
❑ 17 Kevin Stevens 1.00 .45
❑ 18 Keith Tkachuk 6.00 2.70
❑ 19 Theoren Fleury 2.00 .90
❑ 20 Robert Reichel 1.00 .45
❑ 21 Mark Recchi 1.00 .45
❑ 22 Vincent Damphousse 2.00 .90
❑ 23 Bob Kudelski 1.00 .45

## 1994-95 Topps/OPC Premier The Go To Guy

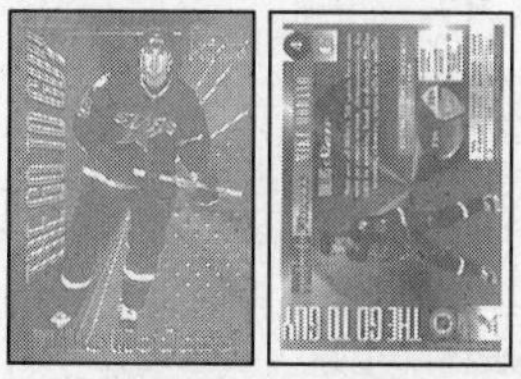

This 15-card set was issued in both Topps and OPC Premier series two product at the rate of 1:36 packs. There is no difference between the cards inserted in each product. Card fronts have a cut out player photo over a background that can best be described as pockmarked. "The Go To Guy" is along the left side of the card. Premier Finest is printed on the upper right corner. Player name appears along the bottom. Backs are horizontal with an impressive array of statistical information demonstrating the player's impact on total team offense crowded in around a player photo. "1994 Topps Company, Inc." trademark is on back.

MINT NRMT
COMPLETE SET (15) 100.00 45.00
COMMON CARD (1-15) 1.50 .70

❑ 1 Wayne Gretzky 20.00 9.00
❑ 2 Joe Sakic 8.00 3.60
❑ 3 Brett Hull 4.00 1.80
❑ 4 Mike Modano 4.00 1.80
❑ 5 Pavel Bure 6.00 2.70
❑ 6 Pat LaFontaine 2.50 1.10
❑ 7 Theoren Fleury 2.50 1.10
❑ 8 Jeremy Roenick 3.00 1.35
❑ 9 Sergei Fedorov 6.00 2.70
❑ 10 Eric Lindros 15.00 6.75
❑ 11 Kirk Muller 1.50 .70
❑ 12 Steve Yzerman 10.00 4.50
❑ 13 Alexander Mogilny 2.50 1.10
❑ 14 Doug Gilmour 2.50 1.10
❑ 15 Mark Messier 4.00 1.80

## 1994-96 Topps Finest Bronze

This trio of sets were made available to collectors exclusively through Topps Stadium Club program. The sets cost approximately $95 each, including shipping, from the club. Each bronze card features embossed color action player images on a metallic background of the team logo in a marbleized black border and thin gold frame. The gold backs carry player information and career statistics. Cards 1-6 were issued as a first series in 1994.

MINT NRMT
COMPLETE SERIES 1 (6) 175.00 80.00
COMPLETE SERIES 2 (8) 135.00 60.00
COMPLETE SERIES 3 (8) 150.00 70.00
COMMON CARD SERIES 1 (1-6) 15.00 6.75
COMMON CARD SERIES 2 (7-14) 12.00 5.50
COMMON CARD SERIES 3 (15-22) 12.00 5.50

❑ 1 Jaromir Jagr 40.00 18.00
❑ 2 Eric Lindros 40.00 18.00
❑ 3 Patrick Roy 50.00 22.00
❑ 4 Pavel Bure 25.00 11.00
❑ 5 Teemu Selanne 25.00 11.00
❑ 6 Doug Gilmour 15.00 6.75
❑ 7 Sergei Fedorov 25.00 11.00
❑ 8 Brett Hull 20.00 9.00
❑ 9 Paul Kariya 40.00 18.00
❑ 10 Cam Neely 12.00 5.50
❑ 11 Mats Sundin 12.00 5.50
❑ 12 Martin Brodeur 25.00 11.00
❑ 13 Jeremy Roenick 15.00 6.75
❑ 14 Brian Leetch 15.00 6.75
❑ 15 Mark Messier 20.00 9.00
❑ 16 Mario Lemieux 50.00 22.00
❑ 17 Peter Forsberg 40.00 18.00
❑ 18 Felix Potvin 25.00 11.00
❑ 19 Alexander Mogilny 15.00 6.75
❑ 20 Ray Bourque 15.00 6.75
❑ 21 Ed Jovanovski 15.00 6.75
❑ 22 Mikael Renberg 12.00 5.50

## 1995-96 Topps

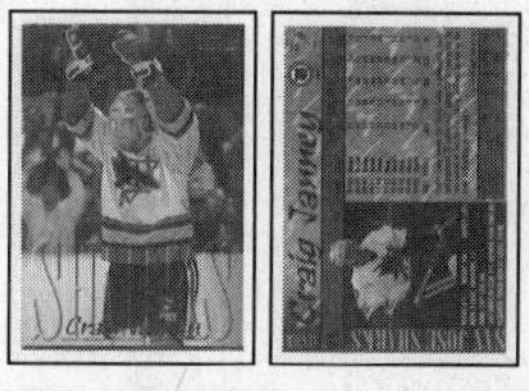

The 385-card set was issued in two series of 220 and 165 cards, respectively. The 13-card packs had an SRP of $1.29. Top rookies in the set include Daniel Alfredsson, Todd Bertuzzi, Chad Kilger and Kyle McLaren; all four of these players appeared in the second series.

MINT NRMT
COMPLETE SET (385) 25.00 11.00
COMPLETE SERIES 1 (220) 15.00 6.75
COMPLETE SERIES 2 (165) 10.00 4.50
COMMON CARD (1-385) .05 .02

❑ 1 Eric Lindros MM .50 .23
❑ 2 Dominik Hasek MM .20 .09
❑ 3 Jeremy Roenick MM .20 .09
❑ 4 Paul Coffey MM .20 .09
❑ 5 Mark Messier MM .20 .09
❑ 6 Peter Bondra MM .20 .09
❑ 7 Paul Kariya MM .60 .25
❑ 8 Chris Chelios .20 .09
❑ 9 Martin Brodeur MM .20 .09
❑ 10 Brett Hull MM .20 .09
❑ 11 Mike Vernon MM .10 .05
❑ 12 Trevor Linden MM .10 .05
❑ 13 Pat LaFontaine MM .10 .05
❑ 14 Geoff Sanderson MM .10 .05
❑ 15 Cam Neely MM .10 .05
❑ 16 Brendan Shanahan MM .20 .09
❑ 17 Jason Arnott MM .10 .05
❑ 18 Mikael Renberg MM .10 .05
❑ 19 Mats Sundin MM .10 .05
❑ 20 Pavel Bure MM .20 .09
❑ 21 Pierre Turgeon MM .10 .05
❑ 22 Alexei Zhamnov MM .10 .05
❑ 23 Blaine Lacher .10 .05
❑ 24 Brian Holzinger .20 .09

❑ 25 Theoren Fleury .10 .05
❑ 26 Eric Daze .20 .09
❑ 27 Mike Kennedy .05 .02
❑ 28 Darren McCarty .05 .02
❑ 29 Todd Marchant .05 .02
❑ 30 Andrew Cassels .05 .02
❑ 31 Rob Niedermayer .10 .05
❑ 32 Eric Lacroix .05 .02
❑ 33 Steve Rucchin .05 .02
❑ 34 Turner Stevenson .05 .02
❑ 35 Sergei Brylin .05 .02
❑ 36 Mathieu Schneider .05 .02
❑ 37 Pat Verbeek .05 .02
❑ 38 Steve Larouche .05 .02
❑ 39 Rod Brind'Amour .10 .05
❑ 40 Luc Robitaille .10 .05
❑ 41 Brett Lindros .05 .02
❑ 42 Shean Donovan .05 .02
❑ 43 David Roberts .05 .02
❑ 44 Cory Cross .05 .02
❑ 45 Todd Warriner .05 .02
❑ 46 Yevgeny Namestnikov .05 .02
❑ 47 Sergei Gonchar .05 .02
❑ 48 Nikolai Khabibulin .10 .05
❑ 49 Alexei Zhitnik .05 .02
❑ 50 Ray Bourque .20 .09
❑ 51 Paul Kruse .05 .02
❑ 52 Murray Craven .05 .02
❑ 53 Andy Moog .10 .05
❑ 54 Keith Primeau .10 .05
❑ 55 Shayne Corson .05 .02
❑ 56 Johan Garpenlov .05 .02
❑ 57 Marek Malik .05 .02
❑ 58 Tony Granato .05 .02
❑ 59 Bob Corkum .05 .02
❑ 60 Patrick Roy 1.00 .45
❑ 61 Chris McAlpine .05 .02
❑ 62 Chris Marinucci .05 .02
❑ 63 Jeff Beukeboom .05 .02
❑ 64 Radek Bonk .05 .02
❑ 65 John LeClair .30 .14
❑ 66 Len Barrie .05 .02
❑ 67 Teppo Numminen .05 .02
❑ 68 Ray Whitney .05 .02
❑ 69 Jeff Norton .05 .02
❑ 70 Chris Gratton .10 .05
❑ 71 Benoit Hogue .05 .02
❑ 72 Bret Hedican .05 .02
❑ 73 Keith Jones .05 .02
❑ 74 John Cullen .05 .02
❑ 75 Brian Leetch .20 .09
❑ 76 Dave Reid .05 .02
❑ 77 Dino Ciccarelli .10 .05
❑ 78 Gary Roberts .05 .02
❑ 79 Tony Amonte .10 .05
❑ 80 Mike Modano .30 .14
❑ 81 Doug Brown .05 .02
❑ 82 Scott Thornton .05 .02
❑ 83 Bill Lindsay .05 .02
❑ 84 Frantisek Kucera .05 .02
❑ 85 Wayne Gretzky 1.50 .70
❑ 86 Joe Sacco .05 .02
❑ 87 Benoit Brunet .05 .02
❑ 88 Bill Guerin .05 .02
❑ 89 Travis Green .10 .05
❑ 90 Alexei Kovalev .05 .02
❑ 91 Stanislav Neckar .05 .02
❑ 92 Rob Dimaio .05 .02
❑ 93 Chris Joseph .05 .02
❑ 94 Craig Martin .05 .02
❑ 95 Craig Janney .10 .05
❑ 96 Greg Gilbert .05 .02
❑ 97 Alexander Semak .05 .02
❑ 98 Mike Gartner .10 .05
❑ 99 Cliff Ronning .05 .02
❑ 100 Mario Lemieux 1.00 .45
❑ 101 Jassen Cullimore .05 .02
❑ 102 Steve Duchesne .05 .02
❑ 103 Derek Plante .05 .02
❑ 104 John Gruden .05 .02
❑ 105 Michal Sykora .05 .02
❑ 106 Trent Klatt .05 .02
❑ 107 Nicklas Lidstrom .10 .05
❑ 108 Luke Richardson .05 .02
❑ 109 Steven Rice .05 .02
❑ 110 Stu Barnes .05 .02
❑ 111 John Druce .05 .02
❑ 112 Guy Hebert .10 .05
❑ 113 Vladimir Malakhov .05 .02
❑ 114 Claude Lemieux .10 .05
❑ 115 Kirk Muller .05 .02
❑ 116 Darren Langdon .05 .02
❑ 117 Rob Gaudreau .05 .02
❑ 118 Karl Dykhuis .05 .02
❑ 119 Richard Park .05 .02
❑ 120 Dave Manson .05 .02
❑ 121 Andrei Nazarov .05 .02
❑ 122 Bernie Nicholls .05 .02
❑ 123 Mikael Andersson .05 .02
❑ 124 Todd Gill .05 .02
❑ 125 Trevor Linden .10 .05
❑ 126 Kelly Miller .05 .02
❑ 127 Don Sweeney .05 .02
❑ 128 Jason Dawe .05 .02
❑ 129 Steve Chiasson .05 .02
❑ 130 Ed Belfour .20 .09
❑ 131 Kerry Huffman .05 .02
❑ 132 Tim Taylor .05 .02
❑ 133 Kirk Maltby .05 .02
❑ 134 Jody Hull .05 .02
❑ 135 Sean Burke .10 .05
❑ 136 Philippe Boucher .05 .02
❑ 137 Valeri Karpov .05 .02
❑ 138 Yves Racine .05 .02
❑ 139 Patrick Flatley .05 .02
❑ 140 John MacLean .10 .05
❑ 141 Sergei Nemchinov .05 .02
❑ 142 Don Beaupre .10 .05
❑ 143 Kevin Dineen .05 .02
❑ 144 Ulf Samuelsson .05 .02
❑ 145 Al MacInnis .10 .05
❑ 146 Igor Korolev .05 .02
❑ 147 Pat Falloon .05 .02
❑ 148 Brian Bradley .05 .02
❑ 149 Josef Beranek .05 .02
❑ 150 Mats Sundin .10 .05
❑ 152 Keith Tkachuk .25 .11
❑ 153 Mariusz Czerkawski .05 .02
❑ 154 Trevor Kidd .10 .05
❑ 155 Garry Galley .05 .02
❑ 156 Gary Suter .05 .02
❑ 157 Grant Ledyard .05 .02
❑ 158 Doug Weight .10 .05
❑ 159 Jesse Belanger .05 .02
❑ 160 Mike Vernon .10 .05
❑ 161 Robert Kron .05 .02
❑ 162 Marty McSorley .05 .02
❑ 163 Todd Krygier .05 .02
❑ 164 Scott Niedermayer .05 .02
❑ 165 Mark Recchi .10 .05
❑ 166 Phil Housley .10 .05
❑ 167 Ron Hextall .10 .05
❑ 168 Richard Smehlik .05 .02
❑ 169 Chris Tamer .05 .02
❑ 170 Alexei Yashin .10 .05
❑ 171 Sergei Makarov .05 .02
❑ 172 Patrice Tardif .05 .02
❑ 173 Milos Holan .05 .02
❑ 174 J.C. Bergeron .05 .02
❑ 175 Dave Andreychuk .10 .05
❑ 176 Martin Gelinas .05 .02
❑ 177 Dale Hunter .05 .02
❑ 178 Kevin Haller .05 .02
❑ 179 Jeff Shantz .05 .02
❑ 180 Adam Oates .10 .05
❑ 181 Ronnie Stern .05 .02
❑ 182 Jamie Langenbrunner .05 .02
❑ 183 Mark Fitzpatrick .10 .05
❑ 184 Adam Burt .05 .02
❑ 185 Sergei Fedorov .40 .18
❑ 186 Robert Lang .05 .02
❑ 187 Craig Conroy .05 .02
❑ 188 Ken Daneyko .05 .02
❑ 189 Marko Tuomainen .05 .02
❑ 190 Ken Wregget .10 .05
❑ 191 Mike Rathje .05 .02
❑ 192 Dimitri Yushkevich .05 .02
❑ 193 Roman Hamrlik .10 .05
❑ 194 Russ Courtnall .05 .02
❑ 195 Teemu Selanne .40 .18
❑ 196 Jon Rohloff .05 .02
❑ 197 Derian Hatcher .05 .02
❑ 198 Mark Tinordi .05 .02
❑ 199 Patrice Brisebois .05 .02
❑ 200 Jaromir Jagr .60 .25
❑ 201 Randy McKay .05 .02
❑ 202 Derek King .05 .02
❑ 203 Tony Twist .05 .02
❑ 204 Jyrki Lumme .05 .02
❑ 205 Steve Smith .05 .02
❑ 206 Bob Rouse .05 .02
❑ 207 Dave Ellett .05 .02
❑ 208 Kevin Dean .05 .02
❑ 209 Rusty Fitzgerald .05 .02
❑ 210 Jim Carey .20 .09
❑ 211 Kenny Jonsson .05 .02
❑ 212 Mike Richter .20 .09
❑ 213 Glen Wesley .05 .02
❑ 214 Donald Audette .10 .05
❑ 215 Curtis Joseph .20 .09
❑ 216 Joe Juneau .05 .02
❑ 217 Paul Kariya .75 .35
❑ 218 1995 Stanley Cup .10 .05
Champions Card
❑ 219 Checklist 1-110 .05 .02
❑ 220 Checklist 111-220 .05 .02
❑ 221 Cam Neely .10 .05
❑ 222 Wayne Primeau .05 .02
❑ 223 Yanic Perreault .05 .02
❑ 224 Pierre Turgeon .10 .05
❑ 225 Alexander Mogilny .10 .05
❑ 226 Daren Puppa .10 .05
❑ 227 Ulf Dahlen .05 .02
❑ 228 Tomas Sandstrom .05 .02
❑ 229 Shayne Corson .05 .02
❑ 230 Chris Chelios .20 .09
❑ 231 Stephane Richer .10 .05
❑ 232 Paul Ranheim .05 .02
❑ 233 Joe Nieuwendyk .10 .05
❑ 234 Doug Gilmour .20 .09
❑ 235 Jeremy Roenick .20 .09
❑ 236 Joel Otto .05 .02
❑ 237 Steve Yzerman .60 .25
❑ 238 Petr Klima .05 .02
❑ 239 Jari Kurri .10 .05
❑ 240 Mark Messier .30 .14
❑ 241 Bill Ranford .10 .05
❑ 242 Grant Fuhr .10 .05
❑ 243 Brent Severyn .05 .02
❑ 244 Ron Francis .10 .05
❑ 245 Ray Ferraro .05 .02
❑ 246 Martin Straka .05 .02
❑ 247 Gerald Diduck .05 .02
❑ 248 Dimitri Khristich .05 .02
❑ 249 Wade Flaherty .10 .05
❑ 250 Pat LaFontaine .10 .05
❑ 251 Darren Turcotte .05 .02
❑ 252 John Vanbiesbrouck .30 .14
❑ 253 Brian Bellows .05 .02
❑ 254 Dave Gagner .10 .05
❑ 255 Larry Murphy .10 .05
❑ 256 Steve Thomas .05 .02
❑ 257 Robert Svehla .05 .02
❑ 258 Deron Quint .05 .02
❑ 259 Kjell Samuelsson .05 .02
❑ 260 Scott Mellanby .10 .05
❑ 261 Dan Quinn .05 .02
❑ 262 Tom Barrasso .10 .05
❑ 263 Zarley Zalapski .05 .02
❑ 264 Rick Tocchet .10 .05
❑ 265 Paul Coffey .20 .09
❑ 266 Joe Sakic .40 .18
❑ 267 Aki-Petteri Berg .05 .02
❑ 268 Jeff Brown .05 .02
❑ 269 Wendel Clark .10 .05
❑ 270 Vincent Damphousse .10 .05
❑ 271 Dale Hawerchuk .10 .05
❑ 272 Rhett Warrener .05 .02
❑ 273 Kevin Hatcher .05 .02
❑ 274 Calle Johansson .05 .02
❑ 275 Scott Stevens .10 .05
❑ 276 Geoff Courtnall .05 .02
❑ 277 Kirk McLean .10 .05
❑ 278 Steve Heinze .05 .02
❑ 279 Sylvain Lefebvre .05 .02
❑ 280 Joe Murphy .05 .02
❑ 281 Mike Keane .05 .02
❑ 282 Kevin Stevens .05 .02
❑ 283 Miroslav Satan 1.00 .45
❑ 284 Stephane Fiset .10 .05
❑ 285 Jeff O'Neill .05 .02
❑ 286 Denny Lambert .05 .02
❑ 287 Marcus Ragnarsson .05 .02
❑ 288 Adam Deadmarsh .10 .05
❑ 289 Eric Weinrich .05 .02
❑ 290 Eric Desjardins .05 .02
❑ 291 Tim Cheveldae .10 .05
❑ 292 Glenn Healy .10 .05
❑ 293 Byron Dafoe .10 .05
❑ 294 Tom Fitzgerald .05 .02
❑ 295 Adam Graves .10 .05
❑ 296 Arturs Irbe UER .10 .05
front reads "Aturs"
❑ 297 Shaun Van Allen .05 .02
❑ 298 Kelly Buchberger .05 .02
❑ 299 Bob Probert .10 .05
❑ 300 Pavel Bure .40 .18
❑ 301 Chad Kilger .05 .02
❑ 302 Dominik Hasek .40 .18
❑ 303 Bobby Holik .05 .02
❑ 304 Petr Nedved .10 .05
❑ 305 Owen Nolan .10 .05
❑ 306 Saku Koivu .40 .18
❑ 307 Rob Blake .05 .02
❑ 308 Chris Pronger .10 .05
❑ 309 Kyle McLaren .25 .11
❑ 310 Peter Bondra .20 .09
❑ 311 Nelson Emerson .05 .02
❑ 312 Bryan McCabe .05 .02
❑ 313 Darcy Wakaluk .10 .05
❑ 314 Shane Doan .05 .02
❑ 315 Felix Potvin .20 .09
❑ 316 Jim Dowd .05 .02
❑ 317 Roman Oksiuta .05 .02
❑ 318 Geoff Sanderson .10 .05
❑ 319 Radek Dvorak .05 .02
❑ 320 Paul Ysebaert .05 .02
❑ 321 Shawn McEachern .05 .02
❑ 322 Vyacheslav Kozlov .05 .02
❑ 323 Marty McInnis .05 .02
❑ 324 Ted Donato .05 .02
❑ 325 Martin Brodeur .50 .23
❑ 326 Patrick Poulin .05 .02
❑ 327 Eric Lindros .60 .25
❑ 328 Dallas Drake .05 .02
❑ 329 Sean Hill .05 .02
❑ 330 Michal Pivonka .05 .02
❑ 331 Alexei Zhamnov .10 .05
❑ 332 Cory Stillman .05 .02
❑ 333 Sergei Zubov .05 .02
❑ 334 Tommy Soderstrom .10 .05
❑ 335 Patrik Carnback .05 .02
❑ 336 Joe Dziedzic .05 .02
❑ 337 Steve Duchesne .05 .02
❑ 338 Marty Murray .05 .02
❑ 339 Todd Bertuzzi .10 .05
❑ 340 Jason Arnott .10 .05
❑ 341 Niklas Sundstrom .05 .02
❑ 342 Alexandre Daigle .05 .02
❑ 343 Jocelyn Thibault .25 .11
❑ 344 Mikhail Shtalenkov .05 .02
❑ 345 Chris Osgood .20 .09
❑ 346 Brendan Witt .05 .02
❑ 347 Ian Laperriere .05 .02
❑ 348 Zigmund Palffy .20 .09
❑ 349 Brian Savage .05 .02
❑ 350 Mike Peca .05 .02
❑ 351 Vitali Yachmenev .05 .02
❑ 352 Luc Robitaille .10 .05
❑ 353 Mikael Renberg .10 .05
❑ 354 Ed Jovanovski .20 .09
❑ 355 Jason Doig .05 .02
❑ 356 Todd Harvey .05 .02
❑ 357 Viktor Kozlov .05 .02
❑ 358 Valeri Bure .05 .02
❑ 359 Peter Forsberg .60 .25
❑ 360 Jeff Friesen .10 .05
❑ 361 Andrei Nikolishin .05 .02
❑ 362 Brian Rolston .05 .02
❑ 363 Jamie Storr .10 .05
❑ 364 Chris Therien .05 .02
❑ 365 Oleg Tverdovsky .10 .05
❑ 366 David Oliver .05 .02
❑ 367 Alexander Selivanov .05 .02
❑ 368 Alex Stojanov .05 .02
❑ 369 Daniel Alfredsson .50 .23
❑ 370 Brendan Shanahan .40 .18
❑ 371 Yuri Khmylev .05 .02
❑ 372 Brett Hull .30 .14
❑ 373 Sergei Fedorov MM .20 .09
❑ 374 Jaromir Jagr MM .20 .09
❑ 375 Wayne Gretzky MM 1.00 .45
❑ 376 Alexander Mogilny MM .10 .05
❑ 377 Patrick Roy MM .75 .35
❑ 378 Ed Belfour MM .20 .09
❑ 379 Luc Robitaille MM .10 .05
❑ 380 Peter Forsberg MM .20 .09
❑ 381 Adam Oates MM .10 .05
❑ 382 Theoren Fleury MM .10 .05
❑ 383 Jim Carey MM .20 .09
❑ 384 Checklist 221-304 .05 .02
❑ 385 Checklist 305-385 .05 .02

## 1995-96 Topps OPC Inserts

The 1995-96 OPC Insert set is a parallel to the 1995-96 Topps set. The set is identical save for the silver foil OPC logo in place of the gold foil Topps. The cards were inserted one per second series Canadian foil pack; cards from both series were included in this manner and were not available in separate packs as in the past. Several of the cards on the D printing sheet were shortprinted according to Topps Canada. These cards have been designated below with an SP suffix. Although Topps officials claim that there are no further shortprints, all remaining cards from the D printing sheet are in much higher demand than their non-D sheet counterparts.

| | MINT | NRMT |
|---|---|---|
| COMPLETE SET (385) | 600.00 | 275.00 |
| COMMON CARD (1-385) | .40 | .18 |
| COMMON D SHEET CARD | 5.00 | 2.20 |

*STARS: 7X TO 15X BASIC CARDS
*YOUNG STARS: 5X TO 10X BASIC CARDS
*RCs: 3X TO 6X BASIC CARDS

❑ 1 Eric Lindros MM 6.00 2.70
❑ 7 Paul Kariya MM 8.00 3.60
❑ 20 Pavel Bure MM 5.00 2.20
❑ 60 Patrick Roy 20.00 9.00
❑ 85 Wayne Gretzky 30.00 13.50
❑ 100 Mario Lemieux 20.00 9.00
❑ 200 Jaromir Jagr 10.00 4.50
❑ 217 Paul Kariya 12.00 5.50
❑ 300 Pavel Bure 6.00 2.70
❑ 327 Eric Lindros D 12.00 5.50
❑ 359 Peter Forsberg SP 40.00 18.00
❑ 373 Sergei Fedorov MM SP 20.00 9.00
❑ 374 Jaromir Jagr MM SP 50.00 22.00
❑ 375 Wayne Gretzky MM SP 125.00 55.00
❑ 376 Alexander Mogilny MM SP 10.00 4.50
❑ 377 Patrick Roy MM SP 60.00 27.00
❑ 378 Ed Belfour MM SP 15.00 6.75
❑ 379 Luc Robitaille MM SP 10.00 4.50
❑ 380 Peter Forsberg MM SP 30.00 13.50
❑ 381 Adam Oates MM SP 10.00 4.50
❑ 382 Theoren Fleury MM SP 12.00 5.50
❑ 384 Checklist 221-304 SP 10.00 4.50
❑ 385 Checklist 305-385 SP 10.00 4.50

## 1995-96 Topps Canadian Gold

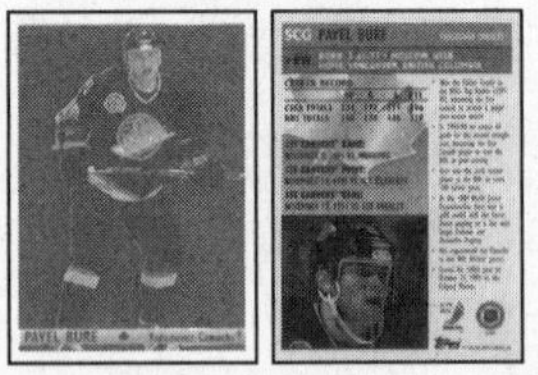

These ten cards featuring some of the top players who don their whites in Canadian rinks were randomly inserted at a rate of 1:36 series 1 Canadian retail packs. These packs, unlike the American ones, contained just five cards each.

| | MINT | NRMT |
|---|---|---|
| COMPLETE SET (10) | 120.00 | 55.00 |
| COMMON CARD (1CG-10CG) | 5.00 | 2.20 |

❑ 1CG Patrick Roy 50.00 22.00
❑ 2CG Alexei Yashin 5.00 2.20
❑ 3CG Jason Arnott 8.00 3.60
❑ 4CG Trevor Kidd 5.00 2.20
❑ 5CG Pavel Bure 20.00 9.00
❑ 6CG Theoren Fleury 8.00 3.60
❑ 7CG Pierre Turgeon 8.00 3.60
❑ 8CG Felix Potvin 10.00 4.50
❑ 9CG Teemu Selanne 20.00 9.00
❑ 10CG Mats Sundin 10.00 4.50

## 1995-96 Topps Canadian World Juniors

The cards in this set, featuring the member of the World Champion Canadian junior team, could be found randomly inserted at a rate of 1:18 series one Canadian Topps packs.

| | MINT | NRMT |
|---|---|---|
| COMPLETE SET (22) | 30.00 | 13.50 |
| COMMON CARD (1CJ-22CJ) | 1.00 | .45 |

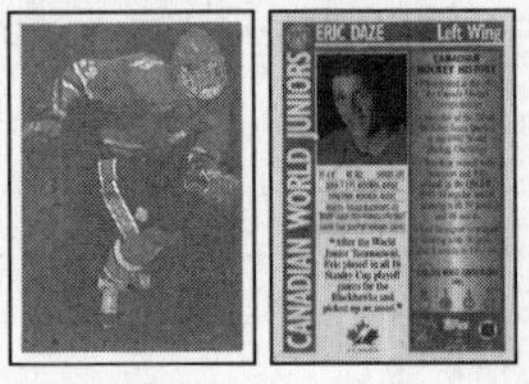

❑ 1CJ Wade Redden 1.50 .70
❑ 2CJ Jamie Storr 1.50 .70
❑ 3CJ Larry Courville 1.00 .45
❑ 4CJ Jason Allison 1.00 .45
❑ 5CJ Alexandre Daigle 1.50 .70
❑ 6CJ Marty Murray 1.00 .45
❑ 7CJ Bryan McCabe 1.00 .45
❑ 8CJ Ryan Smyth 4.00 1.80
❑ 9CJ Lee Sorochan 1.00 .45
❑ 10CJ Todd Harvey 1.00 .45
❑ 11CJ Nolan Baumgartner 1.00 .45
❑ 12CJ Denis Pederson 1.50 .70
❑ 13CJ Shean Donovan 1.00 .45
❑ 14CJ Jason Botterill 1.00 .45
❑ 15CJ Jeff Friesen 1.50 .70
❑ 16CJ Darcy Tucker 1.00 .45
❑ 17CJ Chad Allan 1.00 .45
❑ 18CJ Dan Cloutier 1.00 .45
❑ 19CJ Eric Daze 3.00 1.35
❑ 20CJ Jeff O'Neill 1.50 .70
❑ 21CJ Jamie Rivers 1.00 .45
❑ 22CJ Ed Jovanovski 2.00 .90

## 1995-96 Topps Hidden Gems

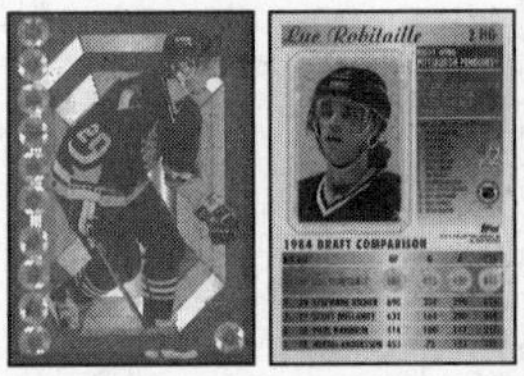

The cards in this chase set focus on star players who were mined in the sixth round or later of the NHL entry draft. The cards were randomly inserted in series 1 packs at a rate of 1:24.

| | MINT | NRMT |
|---|---|---|
| COMPLETE SET (15) | 50.00 | 22.00 |
| COMMON CARD (1HG-15HG) | 1.00 | .45 |

❑ 1HG Theoren Fleury 2.50 1.10
❑ 2HG Luc Robitaille 2.50 1.10
❑ 3HG Doug Gilmour 1.00 .45
❑ 4HG Dominik Hasek 10.00 4.50
❑ 5HG Pavel Bure 10.00 4.50
❑ 6HG Peter Bondra 2.50 1.10
❑ 7HG Steve Larmer 2.50 1.10
❑ 8HG David Oliver 1.00 .45
❑ 9HG Gary Suter 1.00 .45
❑ 10HG Brett Hull 6.00 2.70
❑ 11HG Kevin Stevens 1.00 .45
❑ 12HG Ron Hextall 2.50 1.10
❑ 13HG Kirk McLean 2.50 1.10
❑ 14HG Andy Moog 2.50 1.10
❑ 15HG Rick Tocchet 2.50 1.10

## 1995-96 Topps Home Grown Canada

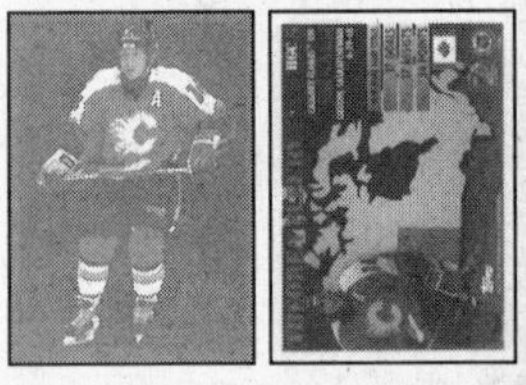

These cards, randomly inserted in Canadian series two retail packs only (HGC1-HGC15) at a rate of 1:36 and randomly inserted in Canadian series 2 hobby packs only (HGC16-HGC30) at a rate of 1:36, feature players born in the Great White North. The hobby-only cards are somewhat harder to find, as Topps announced that an indeterminite number of the 1-15 cards were inserted in their place, resulting in fewer of the 16-30 cards being released.

| | MINT | NRMT |
|---|---|---|
| COMPLETE SET (30) | 500.00 | 220.00 |
| COMMON CARD (HGC1-HGC15) | 2.50 | 1.10 |
| COMMON CARD (HGC16-HGC30) | 4.00 | 1.80 |

❑ HGC1 Patrick Roy 40.00 18.00
❑ HGC2 Wendel Clark 2.50 1.10
❑ HGC3 Pierre Turgeon 2.50 1.10
❑ HGC4 Doug Gilmour 6.00 2.70
❑ HGC5 Theoren Fleury 2.50 1.10
❑ HGC6 Eric Lindros 25.00 11.00
❑ HGC7 Paul Kariya 30.00 13.50
❑ HGC8 Bill Ranford 2.50 1.10

❑ HGC9 Ray Bourque 6.00 2.70
❑ HGC10 Brendan Shanahan 15.00 6.75
❑ HGC11 Paul Coffey 6.00 2.70
❑ HGC12 Trevor Linden 2.50 1.10
❑ HGC13 Trevor Kidd 2.50 1.10
❑ HGC14 Alexandre Daigle 2.50 1.10
❑ HGC15 Chris Pronger 2.50 1.10
❑ HGC16 Steve Yzerman 60.00 27.00
❑ HGC17 Todd Harvey 4.00 1.80
❑ HGC18 Felix Potvin 6.00 2.70
❑ HGC19 Luc Robitaille 6.00 2.70
❑ HGC20 Wayne Gretzky 120.00 55.00
❑ HGC21 Keith Primeau 4.00 1.80
❑ HGC22 Al MacInnis 4.00 1.80
❑ HGC23 Cam Neely 4.00 1.80
❑ HGC24 Ed Belfour 6.00 2.70
❑ HGC25 Joe Juneau 4.00 1.80
❑ HGC26 Adam Graves 4.00 1.80
❑ HGC27 Mark Recchi 6.00 2.70
❑ HGC28 Stephane Richer 4.00 1.80
❑ HGC29 Mark Messier 25.00 11.00
❑ HGC30 Mario Lemieux 100.00 45.00

## 1995-96 Topps Home Grown USA

This 10-card set features some of the top US-born players in the NHL. The cards were randomly inserted at a rate of 1:36 series two US packs.

| | MINT | NRMT |
|---|---|---|
| COMPLETE SET (10) | 40.00 | 18.00 |
| COMMON CARD (HGA1-HGA10) | 2.00 | .90 |

❑ HGA1 Brian Leetch 5.00 2.20
❑ HGA2 Jeremy Roenick 5.00 2.20
❑ HGA3 Mike Modano 6.00 2.70
❑ HGA4 Pat LaFontaine 3.00 1.35
❑ HGA5 Keith Tkachuk 6.00 2.70
❑ HGA6 Chris Chelios 5.00 2.20
❑ HGA7 Darren Turcotte 2.00 .90
❑ HGA8 John Vanbiesbrouck 8.00 3.60
❑ HGA9 John LeClair 8.00 3.60
❑ HGA10 Mike Richter 5.00 2.20

## 1995-96 Topps Marquee Men Power Boosters

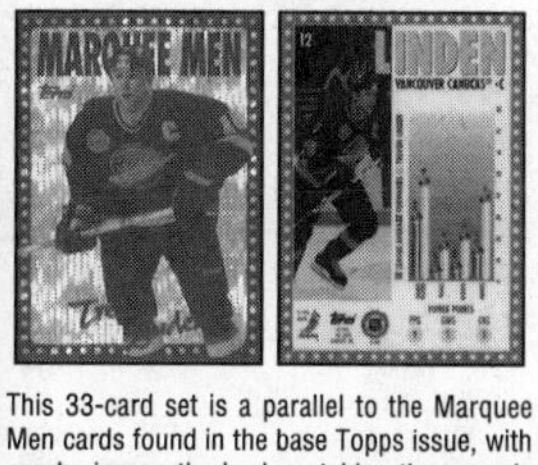

This 33-card set is a parallel to the Marquee Men cards found in the base Topps issue, with numbering on the back matching those cards as well. Cards 1-22 were randomly inserted in series 1 packs at a rate of 1:36; cards 373-383 used the same odds in series 2 packs. Because there were more cards distributed throughout the series 1 production run (22 to 11) the series one cards are somewhat more difficult to acquire. These cards can be differentiated from the base issues by the use of much thicker 28-point card stock and the prismatic foil front.

| | MINT | NRMT |
|---|---|---|
| COMPLETE SET (33) | 230.00 | 105.00 |
| COMPLETE SERIES 1 (22) | 140.00 | 65.00 |
| COMPLETE SERIES 2 (11) | 90.00 | 40.00 |
| COMMON CARD (1-22/373-383) | 2.00 | .90 |

❑ 1 Eric Lindros 20.00 9.00
❑ 2 Dominik Hasek 10.00 4.50
❑ 3 Jeremy Roenick 5.00 2.20
❑ 4 Paul Coffey 5.00 2.20
❑ 5 Mark Messier 6.00 2.70
❑ 6 Peter Bondra 5.00 2.20
❑ 7 Paul Kariya 20.00 9.00
❑ 8 Chris Chelios 5.00 2.20
❑ 9 Martin Brodeur 12.00 5.50
❑ 10 Brett Hull 6.00 2.70
❑ 11 Mike Vernon 3.00 1.35
❑ 12 Trevor Linden 2.00 .90
❑ 13 Pat LaFontaine 3.00 1.35
❑ 14 Geoff Sanderson 3.00 1.35
❑ 15 Cam Neely 3.00 1.35
❑ 16 Brendan Shanahan 10.00 4.50
❑ 17 Jason Arnott 3.00 1.35
❑ 18 Mikael Renberg 3.00 1.35
❑ 19 Mats Sundin 5.00 2.20
❑ 20 Pavel Bure 10.00 4.50
❑ 21 Pierre Turgeon 3.00 1.35
❑ 22 Alexei Zhamnov 2.00 .90
❑ 373 Sergei Fedorov 10.00 4.50
❑ 374 Jaromir Jagr 15.00 6.75
❑ 375 Wayne Gretzky 30.00 13.50
❑ 376 Alexander Mogilny 3.00 1.35
❑ 377 Patrick Roy 20.00 9.00
❑ 378 Ed Belfour 5.00 2.20
❑ 379 Luc Robitaille 3.00 1.35
❑ 380 Peter Forsberg 15.00 6.75
❑ 381 Adam Oates 3.00 1.35
❑ 382 Theoren Fleury 3.00 1.35
❑ 383 Jim Carey 2.00 .90

## 1995-96 Topps Mystery Finest

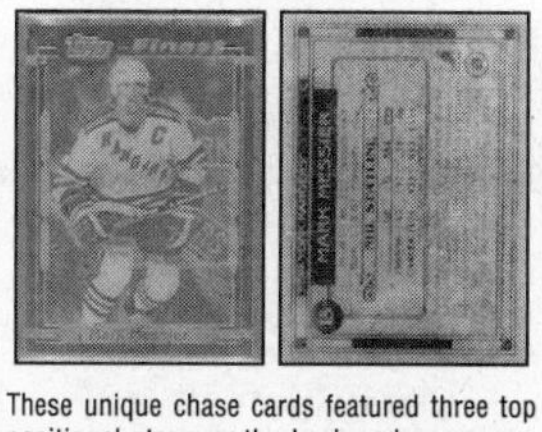

These unique chase cards featured three top positional stars on the back and an opaque protective foil covering on the front. When removed, it would reveal a full frontal shot of one of the three players on the back, hence the mystery. The cards, which utilized the Finest technology, were randomly inserted 1:36 series 2 packs. A parallel refractor version of the set also existed. These cards were much more difficult to pull, coming out of 1:216 packs. Multipliers for these cards are included in the headers below.

| | MINT | NRMT |
|---|---|---|
| COMPLETE SET (22) | 200.00 | 90.00 |
| COMMON CARD (M1-M22) | 3.00 | 1.35 |
| COMP.REFRACTOR SET (22) | 800.00 | 350.00 |
| COMMON REF. (M1-M22) | 15.00 | 6.75 |
| *STARS: 2X TO 4X BASIC CARDS | | |

❑ M1 Wayne Gretzky 30.00 13.50
❑ M2 Mario Lemieux 25.00 11.00
❑ M3 Mark Messier 6.00 2.70
❑ M4 Eric Lindros 15.00 6.75
❑ M5 Sergei Fedorov 10.00 4.50
❑ M6 Joe Sakic 10.00 4.50
❑ M7 Brett Hull 6.00 2.70
❑ M8 Jaromir Jagr 15.00 6.75
❑ M9 Teemu Selanne 10.00 4.50
❑ M10 Brendan Shanahan 10.00 4.50
❑ M11 Cam Neely 3.00 1.35
❑ M12 Mikael Renberg 3.00 1.35
❑ M13 Paul Kariya 20.00 9.00
❑ M14 Keith Tkachuk 6.00 2.70
❑ M15 Pavel Bure 10.00 4.50
❑ M16 Brian Leetch 5.00 2.20
❑ M17 Scott Stevens 3.00 1.35
❑ M18 Chris Chelios 5.00 2.20
❑ M19 Dominik Hasek 10.00 4.50
❑ M20 Patrick Roy 25.00 11.00
❑ M21 Martin Brodeur 12.00 5.50
❑ M22 Felix Potvin 5.00 2.20

## 1995-96 Topps New To The Game

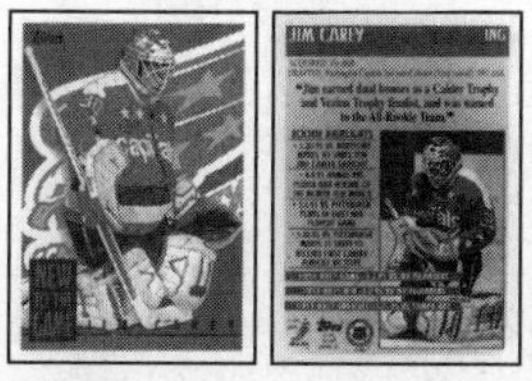

This 22-card set featured some of the top players just beginning to make their marks in the NHL. The cards were inserted one per US series 1 retail packs.

| | MINT | NRMT |
|---|---|---|
| COMPLETE SET (22) | 30.00 | 13.50 |
| COMMON CARD (1NG-22NG) | .75 | .35 |

❑ 1NG Jim Carey 2.00 .90
❑ 2NG Sergei Brylin .75 .35
❑ 3NG Todd Marchant .75 .35
❑ 4NG Oleg Tverdovsky 1.50 .70
❑ 5NG Paul Kariya 2.00 .90
❑ 6NG Adam Deadmarsh 1.50 .70
❑ 7NG Mike Kennedy .75 .35
❑ 8NG Roman Oksiuta .75 .35
❑ 9NG Kenny Jonsson .75 .35
❑ 10NG Peter Forsberg 2.00 .90
❑ 11NG Alexander Selivanov .75 .35
❑ 12NG Chris Therien .75 .35
❑ 13NG Brian Rolston .75 .35
❑ 14NG David Oliver .75 .35
❑ 15NG Blaine Lacher 1.50 .70
❑ 16NG Sergei Krivokrasov .75 .35
❑ 17NG Todd Harvey .75 .35
❑ 18NG Jeff Friesen 1.50 .70
❑ 19NG Mariusz Czerkawski .75 .35
❑ 20NG Ian Laperriere .75 .35
❑ 21NG Brian Savage 1.50 .70
❑ 22NG Andrei Nikolishin .75 .35

## 1995-96 Topps Power Lines

These ten three player-cards feature the top lines of the 1994-95 NHL season. The cards were randomly inserted in 1:12 series 1 packs.

| | MINT | NRMT |
|---|---|---|
| COMPLETE SET (10) | 25.00 | 11.00 |
| COMMON CARD (1PL-10PL) | .50 | .23 |

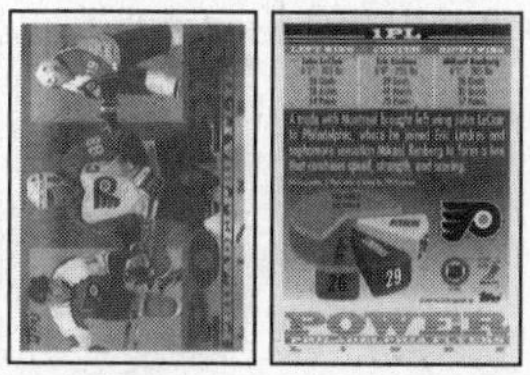

❑ 1PL Eric Lindros 5.00 2.20
John LeClair
Mikael Renberg
❑ 2PL Keith Tkachuk 4.00 1.80
Teemu Selanne
Alexei Zhamnov
❑ 3PL Adam Graves 3.00 1.35
Mark Messier
Pat Verbeek
❑ 4PL Pat Poulin 1.50 .70
Jeremy Roenick
Tony Amonte
❑ 5PL Kevin Stevens 4.00 1.80
Jaromir Jagr
Ron Francis
❑ 6PL Jason Dawe 1.00 .45
Pat Lafontaine
Alexander Mogilny
❑ 7PL Adam Oates 1.00 .45
Cam Neely
Mariusz Czerkawski
❑ 8PL Slava Kozlov 4.00 1.80
Sergei Fedorov
Doug Brown
❑ 9PL Vin Damphousse 1.00 .45
Pierre Turgeon
Mark Recchi
❑ 10PL Mike Peluso .50 .23
Bobby Holik
Randy McKay

## 1995-96 Topps Profiles

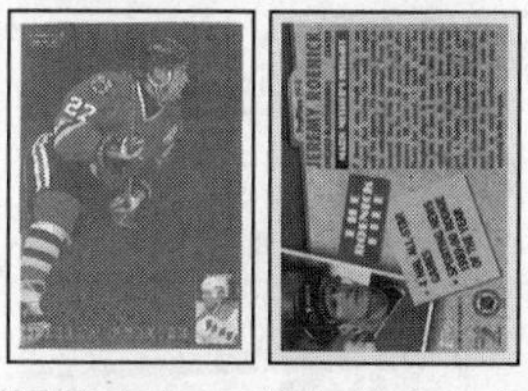

Mark Messier knows a bit about hockey, as he demonstrates here with his choices of and commentary on some of the game's finest. The cards were inserted in both series 1 (1-10) and series 2 (11-20) packs at a rate of 1:12.

| | MINT | NRMT |
|---|---|---|
| COMPLETE SET (20) | 70.00 | 32.00 |
| COMPLETE SERIES 1 (10) | 40.00 | 18.00 |
| COMPLETE SERIES 2 (10) | 30.00 | 13.50 |
| COMMON CARD (PS1-PS20) | 1.50 | .70 |

❑ PF1 Wayne Gretzky 12.00 5.50
❑ PF2 Brian Leetch 2.00 .90
❑ PF3 Patrick Roy 10.00 4.50
❑ PF4 Jaromir Jagr 6.00 2.70
❑ PF5 Sergei Fedorov 4.00 1.80
❑ PF6 Martin Brodeur 5.00 2.20
❑ PF7 Eric Lindros 6.00 2.70
❑ PF8 Jeremy Roenick 2.00 .90
❑ PF9 John Vanbiesbrouck 2.50 1.10
❑ PF10 Cam Neely 1.50 .70
❑ PF11 Pavel Bure 4.00 1.80
❑ PF12 Paul Coffey 2.00 .90
❑ PF13 Scott Stevens 1.50 .70
❑ PF14 Dominik Hasek 4.00 1.80
❑ PF15 Mario Lemieux 10.00 4.50
❑ PF16 Ed Belfour 2.00 .90
❑ PF17 Doug Gilmour 2.00 .90
❑ PF18 Teemu Selanne 4.00 1.80
❑ PF19 Brett Hull 2.50 1.10
❑ PF20 Joe Sakic 3.00 1.35

## 1995-96 Topps Rink Leaders

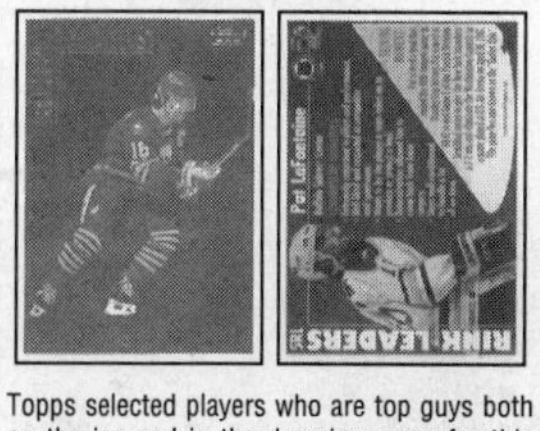

Topps selected players who are top guys both on the ice and in the dressing room for this ten-card tribute. The cards were randomly inserted in series 1 hobby packs at a rate of 1:36.

| | MINT | NRMT |
|---|---|---|
| COMPLETE SET (10) | 75.00 | 34.00 |
| COMMON CARD (1RL-10RL) | 1.50 | .70 |

❑ 1RL Mark Messier 6.00 2.70
❑ 2RL Mario Lemieux 25.00 11.00
❑ 3RL Ray Bourque 4.00 1.80
❑ 4RL Brett Hull 6.00 2.70
❑ 5RL Pat LaFontaine 1.50 .70
❑ 6RL Scott Stevens 1.50 .70
❑ 7RL Keith Tkachuk 6.00 2.70
❑ 8RL Doug Gilmour 3.00 1.35
❑ 9RL Chris Chelios 4.00 1.80
❑ 10RL Wayne Gretzky 30.00 13.50

## 1995-96 Topps Young Stars

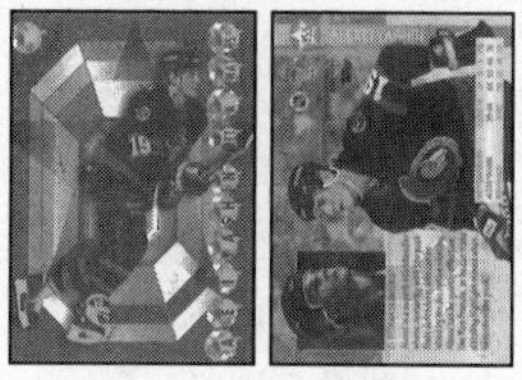

Topps honors fifteen of the brightest young stars in the game with this set which utilizes the Power Matrix printing technology. The cards were randomly inserted to the tune of 1:24 series 2 packs.

| | MINT | NRMT |
|---|---|---|
| COMPLETE SET (15) | 50.00 | 22.00 |
| COMMON CARD (YS1-YS15) | 1.50 | .70 |

❑ YS1 Paul Kariya 10.00 4.50
❑ YS2 Martin Brodeur 6.00 2.70
❑ YS3 Mikael Renberg 2.50 1.10
❑ YS4 Peter Forsberg 8.00 3.60
❑ YS5 Alexei Yashin UER 2.50 1.10
front reads "Alexi"
❑ YS6 Jeff Friesen 2.50 1.10
❑ YS7 Oleg Tverdovsky 1.50 .70
❑ YS8 Jim Carey 2.50 1.10
❑ YS9 Alexei Kovalev 1.50 .70
❑ YS10 Jason Arnott 2.50 1.10
❑ YS11 Teemu Selanne 5.00 2.20
❑ YS12 Chris Osgood 3.00 1.35
❑ YS13 Roman Hamrlik 2.50 1.10
❑ YS14 Scott Niedermayer 1.50 .70
❑ YS15 Jaromir Jagr 8.00 3.60

## 1998-99 Topps

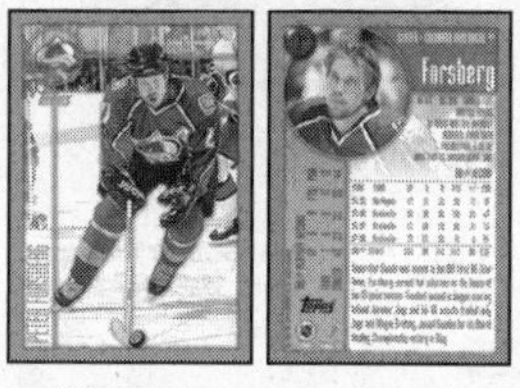

The 1998-99 Topps set was issued in one series totalling 242 cards. The 11-card packs retail for $1.29 each. The fronts feature color action photos of the most important hockey stars of today. The backs carry player information and statistics.

| | MINT | NRMT |
|---|---|---|
| COMPLETE SET (242) | 25.00 | 11.00 |
| COMMON CARD (1-242) | .15 | .07 |

❑ 1 Peter Forsberg 1.00 .45
❑ 2 Petr Sykora .15 .07
❑ 3 Byron Dafoe .25 .11
❑ 4 Ron Francis .25 .11
❑ 5 Alexei Yashin .25 .11
❑ 6 Dave Ellett .15 .07
❑ 7 Jamie Langenbrunner .15 .07
❑ 8 Doug Weight .25 .11
❑ 9 Jason Woolley .15 .07
❑ 10 Paul Coffey .30 .14
❑ 11 Uwe Krupp .15 .07
❑ 12 Tomas Sandstrom .15 .07
❑ 13 Scott Mellanby .15 .07
❑ 14 Vladimir Tsyplakov .15 .07
❑ 15 Martin Rucinsky .15 .07
❑ 16 Mikael Renberg .25 .11
❑ 17 Marco Sturm .15 .07
❑ 18 Eric Lindros 1.00 .45
❑ 19 Sean Burke .15 .07
❑ 20 Martin Brodeur .75 .35
❑ 21 Boyd Devereaux .15 .07
❑ 22 Kelly Buchberger .15 .07
❑ 23 Scott Stevens .15 .07
❑ 24 Jamie Storr .25 .11
❑ 25 Anders Eriksson .15 .07
❑ 26 Gary Suter .15 .07
❑ 27 Theoren Fleury .30 .14
❑ 28 Steve Leach .15 .07
❑ 29 Felix Potvin .30 .14
❑ 30 Brett Hull .40 .18
❑ 31 Mike Grier .15 .07
❑ 32 Cale Hulse .15 .07
❑ 33 Larry Murphy .25 .11
❑ 34 Rick Tocchet .25 .11
❑ 35 Eric Desjardins .15 .07
❑ 36 Igor Kravchuk .15 .07
❑ 37 Rob Niedermayer .15 .07
❑ 38 Bryan Smolinski .15 .07
❑ 39 Valeri Kamensky .15 .07
❑ 40 Ryan Smyth .25 .11
❑ 41 Bruce Driver .15 .07
❑ 42 Mike Johnson .15 .07
❑ 43 Rob Zamuner .15 .07
❑ 44 Steve Duchesne .15 .07
❑ 45 Martin Straka .15 .07
❑ 46 Bill Houlder .15 .07
❑ 47 Craig Conroy .15 .07
❑ 48 Guy Hebert .25 .11
❑ 49 Colin Forbes .15 .07
❑ 50 Mike Modano .40 .18
❑ 51 Jamie Pushor .15 .07
❑ 52 Jarome Iginla .15 .07
❑ 53 Paul Kariya 1.25 .55
❑ 54 Mattias Ohlund .25 .11
❑ 55 Sergei Berezin .25 .11
❑ 56 Peter Zezel .15 .07
❑ 57 Teppo Numminen .15 .07
❑ 58 Dale Hunter .15 .07
❑ 59 Sandy Moger .15 .07
❑ 60 John LeClair .50 .23
❑ 61 Wade Redden .15 .07
❑ 62 Patrik Elias .25 .11
❑ 63 Rob Blake .25 .11
❑ 64 Todd Marchant .15 .07
❑ 65 Claude Lemieux .25 .11
❑ 66 Trevor Kidd .25 .11
❑ 67 Sergei Fedorov .60 .25
❑ 68 Joe Sakic .60 .25
❑ 69 Derek Morris .15 .07
❑ 70 Alexei Morozov .15 .07
❑ 71 Mats Sundin .30 .14
❑ 72 Daymond Langkow .15 .07
❑ 73 Kevin Hatcher .15 .07
❑ 74 Damian Rhodes .25 .11
❑ 75 Brian Leetch .30 .14
❑ 76 Saku Koivu .50 .23
❑ 77 Rick Tabaracci .15 .07
❑ 78 Bernie Nicholls .15 .07
❑ 79 Alyn McCauley .15 .07
❑ 80 Patrice Brisebois .15 .07
❑ 81 Bret Hedican .15 .07
❑ 82 Sandy McCarthy .15 .07
❑ 83 Viktor Kozlov .15 .07
❑ 84 Derek King .15 .07
❑ 85 Alexander Selivanov .15 .07
❑ 86 Mike Vernon .25 .11
❑ 87 Jeff Beukeboom .15 .07
❑ 88 Tommy Salo .25 .11
❑ 89 Adam Graves .25 .11
❑ 90 Randy McKay .15 .07
❑ 91 Rich Pilon .15 .07
❑ 92 Richard Zednik .15 .07
❑ 93 Jeff Hackett .25 .11
❑ 94 Michael Peca .15 .07
❑ 95 Brent Gilchrist .15 .07
❑ 96 Stu Grimson .15 .07
❑ 97 Bob Probert .15 .07
❑ 98 Stu Barnes .15 .07
❑ 99 Ruslan Salei .15 .07
❑ 100 Al MacInnis .25 .11
❑ 101 Ken Daneyko .15 .07
❑ 102 Paul Ranheim .15 .07
❑ 103 Marty McInnis .15 .07
❑ 104 Marian Hossa .25 .11
❑ 105 Darren McCarty .15 .07
❑ 106 Guy Carbonneau .15 .07
❑ 107 Dallas Drake .15 .07
❑ 108 Sergei Samsonov .50 .23
❑ 109 Teemu Selanne .60 .25
❑ 110 Checklist .15 .07
❑ 111 Jaromir Jagr 1.00 .45
❑ 112 Joe Thornton .30 .14
❑ 113 Jon Klemm .15 .07
❑ 114 Grant Fuhr .25 .11
❑ 115 Nikolai Khabibulin .25 .11
❑ 116 Rod Brind'Amour .25 .11
❑ 117 Trevor Linden .25 .11
❑ 118 Vincent Damphousse .25 .11
❑ 119 Dino Ciccarelli .25 .11
❑ 120 Pat Verbeek .15 .07
❑ 121 Sandis Ozolinsh .25 .11
❑ 122 Garth Snow .25 .11
❑ 123 Ed Belfour .30 .14
❑ 124 Keith Primeau .25 .11
❑ 125 Jason Allison .25 .11
❑ 126 Peter Bondra .30 .14
❑ 127 Ulf Samuelsson .15 .07
❑ 128 Jeff Friesen .25 .11
❑ 129 Jason Bonsignore .15 .07
❑ 130 Daniel Alfredsson .25 .11
❑ 131 Bobby Holik .15 .07
❑ 132 Jozef Stumpel .25 .11
❑ 133 Brian Bellows .15 .07
❑ 134 Chris Osgood .30 .14
❑ 135 Alexei Zhamnov .15 .07
❑ 136 Mattias Norstrom .15 .07
❑ 137 Drake Berehowsky .15 .07
❑ 138 Mark Messier .40 .18
❑ 139 Geoff Courtnall .15 .07
❑ 140 Marc Bureau .15 .07
❑ 141 Don Sweeney .15 .07
❑ 142 Wendel Clark .25 .11
❑ 143 Scott Niedermayer .15 .07
❑ 144 Chris Therien .15 .07
❑ 145 Kirk Muller .15 .07
❑ 146 Wayne Primeau .15 .07
❑ 147 Tony Granato .15 .07
❑ 148 Derian Hatcher .15 .07
❑ 149 Daniel Briere .15 .07
❑ 150 Fredrik Olausson .15 .07
❑ 151 Joe Juneau .25 .11
❑ 152 Michal Grosek .15 .07
❑ 153 Janne Laukkanen .15 .07
❑ 154 Keith Tkachuk .40 .18
❑ 155 Marty McSorley .15 .07
❑ 156 Owen Nolan .25 .11
❑ 157 Mark Tinordi .15 .07

❑ 158 Steve Washburn .15 .07
❑ 159 Luke Richardson .15 .07
❑ 160 Kris King .15 .07
❑ 161 Joe Nieuwendyk .25 .11
❑ 162 Travis Green .15 .07
❑ 163 Dominik Hasek .60 .25
❑ 164 Dimitri Khristich .15 .07
❑ 165 Dave Manson .15 .07
❑ 166 Chris Chelios .30 .14
❑ 167 Claude LaPointe .15 .07
❑ 168 Kris Draper .15 .07
❑ 169 Brad Isbister .15 .07
❑ 170 Patrick Marleau .15 .07
❑ 171 Jeremy Roenick .30 .14
❑ 172 Darren Langdon .15 .07
❑ 173 Kevin Dineen .15 .07
❑ 174 Luc Robitaille .25 .11
❑ 175 Steve Yzerman 1.00 .45
❑ 176 Sergei Zubov .15 .07
❑ 177 Ed Jovanovski .15 .07
❑ 178 Sami Kapanen .25 .11
❑ 179 Adam Oates .25 .11
❑ 180 Pavel Bure .60 .25
❑ 181 Chris Pronger .25 .11
❑ 182 Pat Falloon .15 .07
❑ 183 Darcy Tucker .15 .07
❑ 184 Zigmund Palffy .30 .14
❑ 185 Curtis Brown .15 .07
❑ 186 Curtis Joseph .30 .14
❑ 187 Valeri Zelepukin .15 .07
❑ 188 Russ Courtnall .15 .07
❑ 189 Adam Foote .15 .07
❑ 190 Patrick Roy 1.50 .70
❑ 191 Cory Stillman .15 .07
❑ 192 Alexei Zhitnik .15 .07
❑ 193 Olaf Kolzig .25 .11
❑ 194 Mark Fitzpatrick .15 .07
❑ 195 Eric Daze .15 .07
❑ 196 Zarley Zalapski .15 .07
❑ 197 Niklas Sundstrom .15 .07
❑ 198 Bryan Berard .25 .11
❑ 199 Jason Arnott .25 .11
❑ 200 Mike Richter .30 .14
❑ 201 Ken Baumgartner .15 .07
❑ 202 Jason Dawe .15 .07
❑ 203 Nicklas Lidstrom .25 .11
❑ 204 Tony Amonte .25 .11
❑ 205 Kjell Samuelsson .15 .07
❑ 206 Ray Bourque .30 .14
❑ 207 Alexander Mogilny .25 .11
❑ 208 Pierre Turgeon .25 .11
❑ 209 Tom Barrasso .25 .11
❑ 210 Richard Matvichuk .15 .07
❑ 211 Sergei Krivokrasov .15 .07
❑ 212 Ted Drury .15 .07
❑ 213 Matthew Barnaby .15 .07
❑ 214 Denis Pederson .15 .07
❑ 215 John Vanbiesbrouck .50 .23
❑ 216 Brendan Shanahan .60 .25
❑ 217 Jocelyn Thibault .25 .11
❑ 218 Nelson Emerson .15 .07
❑ 219 Wayne Gretzky 2.00 .90
❑ 220 Checklist .15 .07
❑ 221 Ramzi Abid .60 .25
❑ 222 Mark Bell .60 .25
❑ 223 Michael Henrich .60 .25
❑ 224 Vincent Lecavalier 1.00 .45
❑ 225 Rico Fata .50 .23
❑ 226 Bryan Allen .15 .07
❑ 227 Daniel Tkaczuk .25 .11
❑ 228 Brad Stuart .25 .11
❑ 229 Derrick Walser .25 .11
❑ 230 Jonathan Cheechoo .60 .25
❑ 231 Sergei Varlamov .50 .23
❑ 232 Scott Gomez .50 .23
❑ 233 Jeff Heerema .40 .18
❑ 234 David Legwand .60 .25
❑ 236 Michael Rupp .50 .23
❑ 237 Alex Tanguay .60 .25
❑ 238 Mathieu Biron .40 .18
❑ 239 Bujar Amidovski .50 .23
❑ 240 Brian Finley .60 .25
❑ 241 Philippe Sauve .15 .07
❑ 242 Jiri Fischer .25 .11

## 1998-99 Topps O-Pee-Chee

This 242-card parallel set, offered only in Canadian hobby packs, offers the same players as the Topps base set, but was emblazoned with the O-Pee-Chee foil stamp logo. Some players included were Martin Brodeur, Sergei Fedorov, Peter Forsberg and Eric Lindros.

| | MINT | NRMT |
|---|---|---|
| COMPLETE SET (242) | 300.00 | 135.00 |
| COMMON CARD (1-242) | .75 | .35 |

*STARS: 6X TO 12X BASIC CARDS
*YOUNG STARS: 5X TO 10X
*RC's: 4X TO 8X

## 1998-99 Topps Blast From The Past

Randomly inserted in packs at a rate of one in 23, this 10-card insert features color photos of the true heroes of the game including Gordie Howe, Phil Esposito and Stan Mikita.

| | MINT | NRMT |
|---|---|---|
| COMPLETE SET (10) | 60.00 | 27.00 |
| COMMON CARD (1-10) | 5.00 | 2.20 |

❑ 1 Wayne Gretzky 12.00 5.50

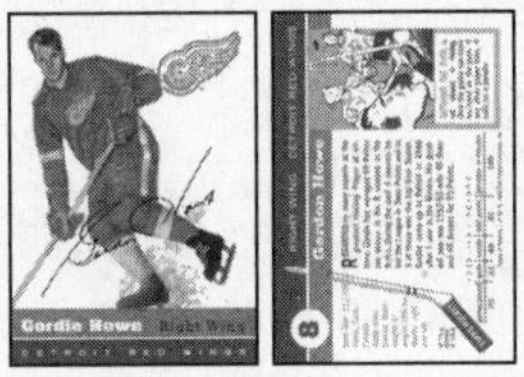

❑ 2 Mark Messier 5.00 2.20
❑ 3 Ray Bourque 5.00 2.20
❑ 4 Patrick Roy 10.00 4.50
❑ 5 Grant Fuhr 5.00 2.20
❑ 6 Brett Hull 5.00 2.20
❑ 7 Gordie Howe 12.00 5.50
❑ 8 Stan Mikita 6.00 2.70
❑ 9 Bobby Hull 8.00 3.60
❑ 10 Phil Esposito 6.00 2.70

## 1998-99 Topps Blast From The Past Autographs

Randomly inserted into packs at the rate of one in 1,878, this four card set features autographed photos of great retired players. Stan Mikita has insertion odds of 1:3,756.

| | MINT | NRMT |
|---|---|---|
| COMPLETE SET (4) | 700.00 | 325.00 |
| COMMON CARD (1-4) | 150.00 | 70.00 |

❑ 7 Gordie Howe 250.00 110.00
❑ 8 Stan Mikita 150.00 70.00
❑ 9 Bobby Hull 150.00 70.00
❑ 10 Phil Esposito 150.00 70.00

## 1998-99 Topps Board Members

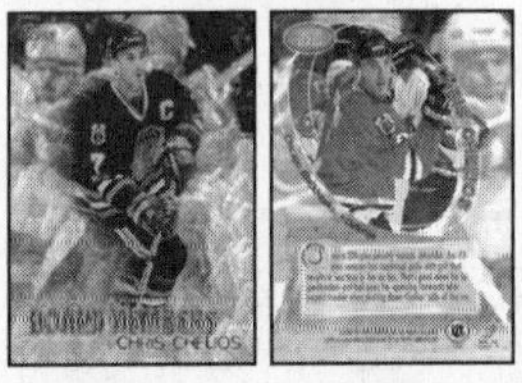

Randomly inserted in packs at a rate of one in 36, this 15-card insert features color action photography of superstar defensemen on vibrant foilboard. Superstars included were Chris Chelios, Brian Leetch, and Ray Bourque.

| | MINT | NRMT |
|---|---|---|
| COMPLETE SET (15) | 50.00 | 22.00 |
| COMMON CARD (B1-B15) | 2.00 | .90 |

❑ B1 Chris Pronger 4.00 1.80
❑ B2 Chris Chelios 6.00 2.70
❑ B3 Brian Leetch 6.00 2.70
❑ B4 Ray Bourque 6.00 2.70
❑ B5 Mattias Ohlund 4.00 1.80
❑ B6 Nicklas Lidstrom 4.00 1.80
❑ B7 Sergei Zubov 4.00 1.80
❑ B8 Scott Niedermayer 4.00 1.80
❑ B9 Larry Murphy 4.00 1.80
❑ B10 Sandis Ozolinsh 4.00 1.80
❑ B11 Rob Blake 2.00 .90
❑ B12 Scott Stevens 2.00 .90
❑ B13 Derian Hatcher 2.00 .90
❑ B14 Kevin Hatcher 2.00 .90
❑ B15 Wade Redden 2.00 .90

## 1998-99 Topps Ice Age 2000

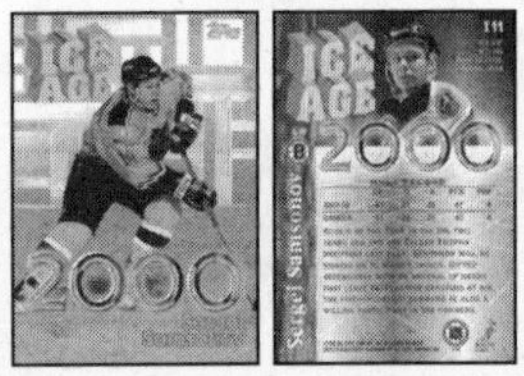

Randomly inserted in packs at a rate of one in 12, this 15-card insert printed with dot-matrix technology features color player photos of such players as Paul Kariya and Sergei Samsonov.

| | MINT | NRMT |
|---|---|---|
| COMPLETE SET (15) | 30.00 | 13.50 |
| COMMON CARD (I1-I15) | .75 | .35 |

❑ I1 Paul Kariya 6.00 2.70
❑ I2 Marco Sturm 1.25 .55
❑ I3 Jarome Iginla .75 .35
❑ I4 Denis Pederson .75 .35
❑ I5 Wade Redden .75 .35
❑ I6 Jason Allison 1.25 .55
❑ I7 Chris Pronger 1.25 .55
❑ I8 Peter Forsberg 5.00 2.20
❑ I9 Saku Koivu 2.50 1.10
❑ I10 Eric Lindros 5.00 2.20
❑ I11 Sergei Samsonov 2.50 1.10
❑ I12 Mattias Ohlund 1.25 .55
❑ I13 Joe Thornton .75 .35
❑ I14 Mike Johnson .75 .35
❑ I15 Nikolai Khabibulin 1.25 .55

## 1998-99 Topps Local Legends

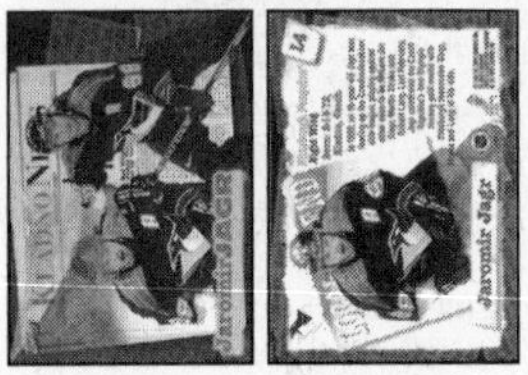

Randomly inserted in packs at a rate of one in 18, this worldly 15-card insert honors players on foilboard cards that actually depict that player's country of origin. Some players included were Joe Sakic, Mike Modano, and Patrick Roy.

| | MINT | NRMT |
|---|---|---|
| COMPLETE SET (15) | 90.00 | 40.00 |
| COMMON CARD (L1-L15) | 2.50 | 1.10 |

❑ L1 Peter Forsberg 8.00 3.60
❑ L2 Mats Sundin 2.50 1.10
❑ L3 Zigmund Palffy 2.50 1.10
❑ L4 Jaromir Jagr 8.00 3.60
❑ L5 Dominik Hasek 5.00 2.20
❑ L6 Martin Brodeur 6.00 2.70
❑ L7 Wayne Gretzky 15.00 6.75
❑ L8 Patrick Roy 12.00 5.50
❑ L9 Eric Lindros 8.00 3.60
❑ L10 Joe Sakic 5.00 2.20
❑ L11 Mark Messier 3.00 1.35
❑ L12 Mike Modano 3.00 1.35
❑ L13 Sergei Fedorov 5.00 2.20
❑ L14 Pavel Bure 5.00 2.20
❑ L15 Teemu Selanne 5.00 2.20

## 1998-99 Topps Mystery Finest Bronze

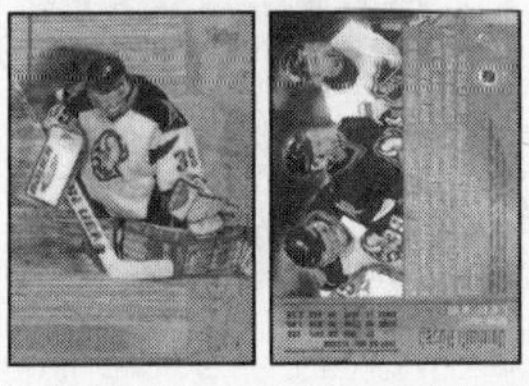

Sequentially numbered and arranged by jersey (home, away and All-Star), this 20-card insert honors the 20 best players in the NHL today. The set was also grouped and randomly inserted in Bronze 1:36; Silver 1:72; and Gold 1:108 variations.

| | MINT | NRMT |
|---|---|---|
| COMPLETE SET (20) | 150.00 | 70.00 |
| COMMON CARD (M1-M20) | 3.00 | 1.35 |
| COMP.REFRACTOR SET (20) | 300.00 | 135.00 |
| COMMON REFRACTOR (1-20) | 6.00 | 2.70 |

*REFRACTOR STARS: 1X TO 2X BASIC CARDS

| | | |
|---|---|---|
| COMP.SILVER SET (20) | 225.00 | 100.00 |
| COMMON SILVER (1-20) | 5.00 | 2.20 |

*SILVER STARS: .75X TO 1.5X BASIC CARDS
SILVER STATED ODDS 1:72

| | | |
|---|---|---|
| COMP.SILVER.REF.SET (20) | 600.00 | 275.00 |
| COMMON SILVER.REF (1-20) | 12.00 | 5.50 |

*SIL.REF.STARS: 2X TO 4X BASIC CARDS
SILVER REF.STATED ODDS 1:216

| | | |
|---|---|---|
| COMP.GOLD SET (20) | 300.00 | 135.00 |
| COMMON GOLD (1-20) | 6.00 | 2.70 |

*GOLD STARS: 1X TO 2X BASIC CARDS
GOLD STATED ODDS 1:108

| | | |
|---|---|---|
| COMP.GOLD.REF.SET (20) | 1800.00 | 800.00 |
| COMMON GOLD.REF. (1-20) | 30.00 | 13.50 |

*GOLD.REF.STARS: 6X TO 12X BASIC CARDS

❑ M1 Teemu Selanne 8.00 3.60
❑ M2 Olaf Kolzig 3.00 1.35
❑ M3 Pavel Bure 8.00 3.60
❑ M4 Wayne Gretzky 25.00 11.00
❑ M5 Mike Modano 5.00 2.20
❑ M6 Jaromir Jagr 12.00 5.50
❑ M7 Dominik Hasek 8.00 3.60
❑ M8 Peter Forsberg 12.00 5.50
❑ M9 Eric Lindros 12.00 5.50
❑ M10 John LeClair 6.00 2.70
❑ M11 Zigmund Palffy 3.00 1.35
❑ M12 Martin Brodeur 10.00 4.50
❑ M13 Keith Tkachuk 5.00 2.20
❑ M14 Peter Bondra 3.00 1.35
❑ M15 Nicklas Lidstrom 3.00 1.35
❑ M16 Patrick Roy 20.00 9.00
❑ M17 Chris Chelios 3.00 1.35
❑ M18 Saku Koivu 6.00 2.70
❑ M19 Mark Messier 5.00 2.20
❑ M20 Joe Sakic 8.00 3.60

## 1998-99 Topps Season's Best

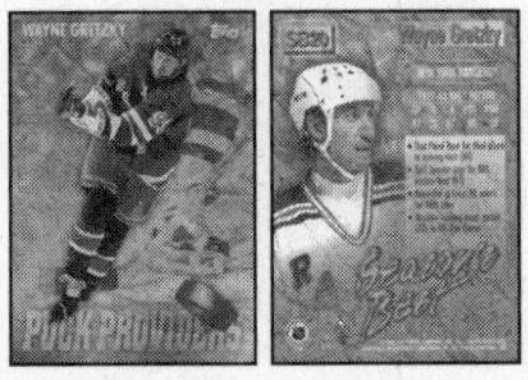

Randomly inserted in packs at a rate of one in eight, this 30-card insert features color action photography in five distinct categories: NetMinders salutes the league's top goalies, Sharpshooters features the top scoring leaders, Puck Providers showcases assist leaders, Performers Plus features those that lead ice time by plus/minus ratio, and Ice Hot introduces the poweful rookies.

| | MINT | NRMT |
|---|---|---|
| COMPLETE SET (30) | 80.00 | 36.00 |
| COMMON CARD (SB1-SB30) | .75 | .35 |

❑ SB1 Dominik Hasek 4.00 1.80
❑ SB2 Martin Brodeur 5.00 2.20
❑ SB3 Ed Belfour 2.00 .90
❑ SB4 Curtis Joseph 2.00 .90
❑ SB5 Jeff Hackett 1.50 .70
❑ SB6 Tom Barrasso 1.50 .70
❑ SB7 Mike Johnson 1.50 .70
❑ SB8 Sergei Samsonov 3.00 1.35
❑ SB9 Patrik Elias 1.50 .70
❑ SB10 Patrick Marleau 2.00 .90
❑ SB11 Mattias Ohlund 1.50 .70
❑ SB12 Marco Sturm 1.50 .70
❑ SB13 Teemu Selanne 4.00 1.80
❑ SB14 Peter Bondra 2.00 .90
❑ SB15 Pavel Bure 4.00 1.80
❑ SB16 John LeClair 3.00 1.35
❑ SB17 Zigmund Palffy 2.00 .90
❑ SB18 Keith Tkachuk 2.50 1.10
❑ SB19 Jaromir Jagr 6.00 2.70
❑ SB20 Wayne Gretzky 12.00 5.50
❑ SB21 Peter Forsberg 6.00 2.70
❑ SB22 Ron Francis 1.50 .70
❑ SB23 Adam Oates 1.50 .70
❑ SB24 Jozef Stumpel 1.50 .70
❑ SB25 Chris Pronger 1.50 .70
❑ SB26 Larry Murphy 1.50 .70
❑ SB27 Jason Allison 1.50 .70
❑ SB28 John LeClair 3.00 1.35
❑ SB29 Randy McKay .75 .35
❑ SB30 Dainius Zubrus 1.50 .70

## 1995-96 Topps SuperSkills

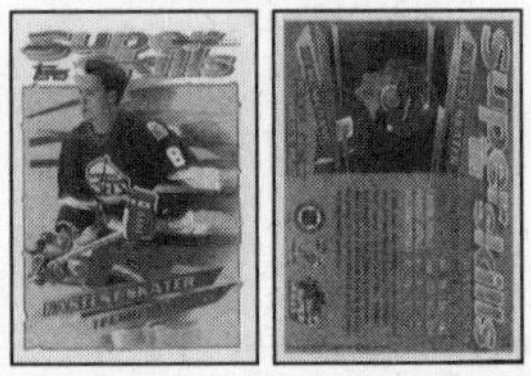

The 1995-96 Topps SuperSkills set was issued in one series totalling 90 cards. The 11-card packs originally retailed for $3.99. The set was a special one-off project designed to capitalize on Topps sponsorship of the SuperSkills program held in conjunction with the 1996 All-Star Game in Boston. The set features the players who were expected to compete in the following categories: Puck Control (1-18), Fastest Skater (19-36), Hardest Shot (37-54), Accuracy Shooting (55-72) and Rapid Fire/Breakaway Relay (73-90). The packs clearly identified which conference and event the cards inside would picture. A one-card-per-pack parallel set, "Platinum", is identical to the basic set save for a platinum trim along the edges of the cards. Multipliers can be found in the header below to determine values for these.

| | MINT | NRMT |
|---|---|---|
| COMPLETE SET (90) | 20.00 | 9.00 |
| COMMON CARD (1-90) | .05 | .02 |
| COMPLETE PLATINUM SET (90) | 45.00 | 20.00 |
| COMMON PLATINUM CARD (1-90) | .15 | .07 |

*STARS: 2X to 3X BASIC CARDS
*YOUNG STARS: 1.5X to 2X BASIC CARDS

❑ 1 Mario Lemieux 2.50 1.10
❑ 2 Adam Oates .15 .07
❑ 3 Donald Audette .05 .02
❑ 4 Andrew Cassels .05 .02
❑ 5 Pat LaFontaine .15 .07
❑ 6 Mathieu Schneider .05 .02
❑ 7 Scott Stevens .05 .02
❑ 8 Mikael Renberg .15 .07
❑ 9 Pierre Turgeon .15 .07
❑ 10 Steve Yzerman 1.50 .70
❑ 11 Russ Courtnall .05 .02
❑ 12 Oleg Tverdovsky .15 .07
❑ 13 Craig Janney .10 .05
❑ 14 Doug Gilmour .35 .16
❑ 15 Wayne Gretzky 3.00 1.35
❑ 16 Paul Kariya 2.00 .90
❑ 17 Joe Sakic 1.00 .45
❑ 18 Peter Forsberg 1.50 .70
❑ 19 Brian Leetch .35 .16
❑ 20 Jaromir Jagr 1.50 .70
❑ 21 Geoff Sanderson .10 .05
❑ 22 Rob Niedermayer .15 .07
❑ 23 Ray Ferraro .05 .02
❑ 24 Alexandre Daigle .10 .05
❑ 25 Joe Juneau .10 .05
❑ 26 Don Sweeney .05 .02
❑ 27 Scott Niedermayer .10 .05
❑ 28 Mike Gartner .10 .05
❑ 29 Paul Coffey .35 .16
❑ 30 Pavel Bure 1.00 .45
❑ 31 Teemu Selanne 1.00 .45
❑ 32 Mats Sundin .35 .16
❑ 33 Trevor Linden .10 .05
❑ 34 Sergei Fedorov 1.00 .45
❑ 35 Theoren Fleury .35 .16
❑ 36 Alexander Mogilny .20 .09
❑ 37 Garry Galley .05 .02
❑ 38 Stu Barnes .05 .02
❑ 39 Glen Wesley .05 .02
❑ 40 Eric Lindros 1.50 .70
❑ 41 Stephane Richer .05 .02
❑ 42 John LeClair .75 .35
❑ 43 Pat Verbeek .15 .07
❑ 44 Bill Guerin .05 .02
❑ 45 Wendel Clark .15 .07
❑ 46 Mike Modano .60 .25
❑ 47 Keith Primeau .10 .05
❑ 48 Brett Hull .60 .25
❑ 49 Al MacInnis .15 .07
❑ 50 Chris Chelios .35 .16
❑ 51 Keith Tkachuk .60 .25
❑ 52 Dave Andreychuk .10 .05
❑ 53 Kevin Hatcher .05 .02
❑ 54 Chris Pronger .10 .05
❑ 55 Brendan Shanahan 1.00 .45
❑ 56 Luc Robitaille .15 .07
❑ 57 Ray Bourque .35 .16
❑ 58 Mark Recchi .15 .07
❑ 59 Brian Bradley .10 .05
❑ 60 Mark Messier .60 .25
❑ 61 Kevin Stevens .10 .05
❑ 62 John MacLean .10 .05
❑ 63 Cam Neely .20 .09
❑ 64 Rick Tocchet .10 .05
❑ 65 Jeremy Roenick .35 .16
❑ 66 Phil Housley .05 .02
❑ 67 Jason Arnott .20 .09
❑ 68 Todd Harvey .05 .02
❑ 69 Jeff Friesen .10 .05
❑ 70 Alexei Zhamnov .10 .05
❑ 71 David Oliver .05 .02
❑ 72 Bernie Nicholls .10 .05
❑ 73 Jim Carey .20 .09
❑ 74 Mike Richter .35 .16
❑ 75 Dominik Hasek 1.00 .45
❑ 76 Sean Burke .10 .05
❑ 77 Ron Hextall .15 .07
❑ 78 John Vanbiesbrouck .75 .35
❑ 79 Tom Barrasso .10 .05
❑ 80 Martin Brodeur 1.25 .55
❑ 81 Patrick Roy 2.50 1.10
❑ 82 Trevor Kidd .10 .05
❑ 83 Andy Moog .15 .07
❑ 84 Mike Vernon .10 .05
❑ 85 Felix Potvin .35 .16
❑ 86 Bill Ranford .15 .07
❑ 87 Kelly Hrudey .10 .05
❑ 88 Grant Fuhr .20 .09
❑ 89 Kirk McLean .10 .05
❑ 90 Ed Belfour .35 .16

## 1995-96 Topps SuperSkills Super Rookies

Inserted one per Topps SuperSkills pack, this 15-card set features the cream of the 1995-96 rookie crop on 20 point all-foil board stock with gild-edge technology.

| | MINT | NRMT |
|---|---|---|
| COMPLETE SET (15) | 20.00 | 9.00 |
| COMMON CARD (SR1-SR15) | .50 | .23 |

❑ SR1 Ed Jovanovski 1.50 .70
❑ SR2 Jason Bonsignore .50 .23
❑ SR3 Jeff O'Neill 1.00 .45
❑ SR4 Cory Stillman .50 .23
❑ SR5 Chad Kilger 1.50 .70
❑ SR6 Aki-Petteri Berg 1.00 .45
❑ SR7 Todd Bertuzzi 1.50 .70
❑ SR8 Shane Doan .75 .35
❑ SR9 Kyle McLaren 1.50 .70
❑ SR10 Radek Dvorak 1.50 .70
❑ SR11 Saku Koivu 5.00 2.20
❑ SR12 Daniel Alfredsson 3.00 1.35
❑ SR13 Antti Tormanen .50 .23
❑ SR14 Niklas Sundstrom 1.50 .70
❑ SR15 Vitali Yachmenev .75 .35

## 1998-99 Topps Gold Label Class 2

Randomly inserted into packs at the rate of one in six, this 100-card set features colo

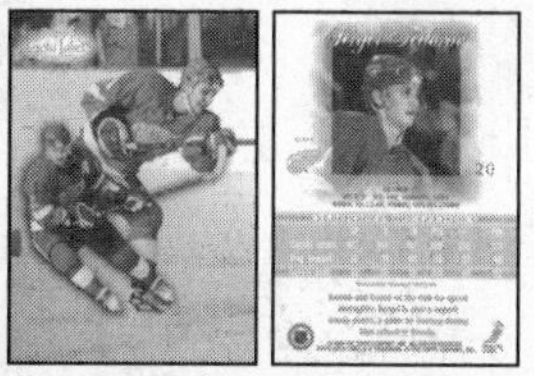

player photos printed on 35-point spectral-reflective rainbow polycarbonate stock with gold stamping. Each card showcases an NHL player on three different version of his base card. Displayed in the foreground of the Class 2 set is a photo of the player with an action shot appearing in the background featuring players shooting and goalies sprawling. Three parallel versions of this set were also produced: The Black Label Parallel with the Black Topps Gold Label logo, the Red Label Parallel identified by the Red Topps Gold Label logo and sequentially numbered to 50, and the One to One Parallel printed on special silver foil backs and numbered 1 of 1.

| | MINT | NRMT |
|---|---|---|
| COMPLETE SET (100) | 250.00 | 110.00 |
| COMMON CARD (1-100) | .75 | .35 |
| STATED ODDS 1:6 | | |
| COMP.BLACK SET (100) | 1000.00 | 450.00 |
| COMMON BLACK (1-100) | 3.00 | 1.35 |
| *CLASS 2 BLACK: 2X TO 4X HI COLUMN | | |
| CLASS 2 BLACK STATED ODDS 1:36 | | |
| COMP.RED SET (1000 | 10000.00 | 4500.00 |
| COMMON RED (1-100) | 30.00 | 13.50 |
| *CLASS 2 RED: 20X TO 40X HI COLUMN | | |
| CLASS 2 RED STATED ODDS 1:146 | | |
| CLASS 2 RED PRINT RUN 50 SETS | | |

| | | |
|---|---|---|
| ❑ 1 Brendan Shanahan | 6.00 | 2.70 |
| ❑ 2 Mike Modano | 4.00 | 1.80 |
| ❑ 3 Chris Chelios | 3.00 | 1.35 |
| ❑ 4 Wayne Gretzky | 20.00 | 9.00 |
| ❑ 5 Jaromir Jagr | 10.00 | 4.50 |
| ❑ 6 Mark Messier | 4.00 | 1.80 |
| ❑ 7 Teemu Selanne | 6.00 | 2.70 |
| ❑ 8 Theoren Fleury | 3.00 | 1.35 |
| ❑ 9 Ray Bourque | 3.00 | 1.35 |
| ❑ 10 Martin Brodeur | 8.00 | 3.60 |
| ❑ 11 Alexei Yashin | 2.50 | 1.10 |
| ❑ 12 Keith Tkachuk | 4.00 | 1.80 |
| ❑ 13 Eric Lindros | 10.00 | 4.50 |
| ❑ 14 Owen Nolan | 2.50 | 1.10 |
| ❑ 15 Al MacInnis | 2.50 | 1.10 |
| ❑ 16 Peter Bondra | 3.00 | 1.35 |
| ❑ 17 Saku Koivu | 5.00 | 2.20 |
| ❑ 18 Doug Weight | 2.50 | 1.10 |
| ❑ 19 Robert Reichel | .75 | .35 |
| ❑ 20 Sergei Fedorov | 6.00 | 2.70 |
| ❑ 21 Peter Forsberg | 10.00 | 4.50 |
| ❑ 22 Ron Francis | 2.50 | 1.10 |
| ❑ 23 Dimitri Khristich | .75 | .35 |
| ❑ 24 Ed Belfour | 3.00 | 1.35 |
| ❑ 25 Oleg Kvasha | 3.00 | 1.35 |
| ❑ 26 Ray Whitney | .75 | .35 |
| ❑ 27 Kenny Jonsson | .75 | .35 |
| ❑ 28 Randy McKay | .75 | .35 |
| ❑ 29 Pavol Demitra | 2.50 | 1.10 |
| ❑ 30 Pierre Turgeon | 2.50 | 1.10 |
| ❑ 31 Steve Yzerman | 10.00 | 4.50 |
| ❑ 32 Ryan Smyth | 2.50 | 1.10 |
| ❑ 33 Tony Amonte | 2.50 | 1.10 |
| ❑ 34 Dominik Hasek | 6.00 | 2.70 |
| ❑ 35 Jarome Iginla | .75 | .35 |
| ❑ 36 Sami Kapanen | 2.50 | 1.10 |
| ❑ 37 Patrik Elias | .75 | .35 |
| ❑ 38 Daniel Cleary | .75 | .35 |
| ❑ 39 Curtis Joseph | 3.00 | 1.35 |
| ❑ 40 Joe Juneau | .75 | .35 |
| ❑ 41 Adam Graves | 2.50 | 1.10 |
| ❑ 42 Trevor Linden | 2.50 | 1.10 |
| ❑ 43 Olli Jokinen | .75 | .35 |
| ❑ 44 Joe Nieuwendyk | 2.50 | 1.10 |
| ❑ 45 Sergei Samsonov | 5.00 | 2.20 |
| ❑ 46 Rico Fata | 4.00 | 1.80 |
| ❑ 47 Mark Recchi | 2.50 | 1.10 |
| ❑ 48 Rick Tocchet | 2.50 | 1.10 |
| ❑ 49 Chris Pronger | 2.50 | 1.10 |
| ❑ 50 Jason Allison | 2.50 | 1.10 |
| ❑ 51 Paul Kariya | 12.00 | 5.50 |
| ❑ 52 Stu Barnes | .75 | .35 |
| ❑ 53 Mats Sundin | 3.00 | 1.35 |
| ❑ 54 Mike Richter | 3.00 | 1.35 |
| ❑ 55 Cliff Ronning | .75 | .35 |
| ❑ 56 Keith Primeau | 2.50 | 1.10 |
| ❑ 57 Guy Hebert | 2.50 | 1.10 |
| ❑ 58 Nicklas Lidstrom | 2.50 | 1.10 |
| ❑ 59 John Vanbiesbrouck | 5.00 | 2.20 |
| ❑ 60 Jeff Friesen | .75 | .35 |
| ❑ 61 Vincent Lecavalier | 6.00 | 2.70 |
| ❑ 62 Alexander Mogilny | 2.50 | 1.10 |
| ❑ 63 Olaf Kolzig | 2.50 | 1.10 |
| ❑ 64 Doug Gilmour | 3.00 | 1.35 |
| ❑ 65 Joe Sakic | 6.00 | 2.70 |
| ❑ 66 Mike Johnson | .75 | .35 |
| ❑ 67 Vincent Damphousse | 2.50 | 1.10 |
| ❑ 68 Eric Brewer | .75 | .35 |
| ❑ 69 Daniel Alfredsson | 2.50 | 1.10 |
| ❑ 70 Nikolai Khabibulin | 2.50 | 1.10 |
| ❑ 71 Marco Sturm | .75 | .35 |
| ❑ 72 Marty Reasoner | .75 | .35 |
| ❑ 73 Bill Muckalt | 4.00 | 1.80 |
| ❑ 74 Pavel Bure | 6.00 | 2.70 |
| ❑ 75 Bill Guerin | .75 | .35 |
| ❑ 76 Chris Osgood | 3.00 | 1.35 |
| ❑ 77 Patrick Roy | 15.00 | 6.75 |
| ❑ 78 Tom Barrasso | 2.50 | 1.10 |
| ❑ 79 Alyn McCauley | .75 | .35 |
| ❑ 80 Adam Oates | 2.50 | 1.10 |
| ❑ 81 Joe Thornton | .75 | .35 |
| ❑ 82 Brendan Morrison | 2.50 | 1.10 |
| ❑ 83 Mike Dunham | 2.50 | 1.10 |
| ❑ 84 Jeremy Roenick | 3.00 | 1.35 |
| ❑ 85 Brian Leetch | 3.00 | 1.35 |
| ❑ 86 John LeClair | 5.00 | 2.20 |
| ❑ 87 Mattias Ohlund | 2.50 | 1.10 |
| ❑ 88 Wade Redden | .75 | .35 |
| ❑ 89 Mark Parrish | 5.00 | 2.20 |
| ❑ 90 Milan Hejduk | 5.00 | 2.20 |
| ❑ 91 Michael Peca | 2.50 | 1.10 |
| ❑ 92 Brett Hull | 4.00 | 1.80 |
| ❑ 94 Patrick Marleau | 2.50 | 1.10 |
| ❑ 95 Grant Fuhr | 2.50 | 1.10 |
| ❑ 96 Rob Blake | 2.50 | 1.10 |
| ❑ 97 Damian Rhodes | 2.50 | 1.10 |
| ❑ 98 Eric Daze | .75 | .35 |
| ❑ 99 Rod Brind'Amour | 2.50 | 1.10 |
| ❑ 100 Scott Stevens | .75 | .35 |

## 1998-99 Topps Gold Label Class 3

Randomly inserted into packs at the rate of one in 12, this 100-card set features color player photos printed on 35-point spectral-reflective rainbow polycarbonate stock with gold stamping. Each card showcases an NHL player on three different version of his base card. Displayed in the foreground of the Class 3 set is a photo of the player with an action shot appearing in the background featuring players celebrating and goalies with their masks off. Three parallel versions of this set were also produced: The Black Label Parallel with the Black Topps Gold Label logo, the Red Label Parallel identified by the Red Topps Gold Label logo and sequentially numbered to 25 and the One to One Parallel printed on special silver foil backs and numbered 1 of 1.

| | MINT | NRMT |
|---|---|---|
| COMPLETE SET (100) | 400.00 | 180.00 |
| COMMON CARD (1-100) | 1.25 | .55 |
| STATED ODDS 1:12 | | |
| COMP.BLACK SET (100) | 4500.00 | 2000.00 |
| COMMON BLACK (1-100) | 15.00 | 6.75 |
| *CLASS 3 BLACK: 6X TO 12X HI COLUMN | | |
| CLASS 3 BLACK STATED ODDS 1:72 | | |
| COMMON RED (1-100) | 40.00 | 18.00 |
| *CLASS 3 RED: 20X TO 35X HI COLUMN | | |
| CLASS 3 RED STATED ODDS 1:293 | | |
| CLASS 3 RED PRINT RUN 25 SETS | | |

| | | |
|---|---|---|
| ❑ 1 Brendan Shanahan | 10.00 | 4.50 |
| ❑ 2 Mike Modano | 6.00 | 2.70 |
| ❑ 3 Chris Chelios | 5.00 | 2.20 |
| ❑ 4 Wayne Gretzky | 30.00 | 13.50 |
| ❑ 5 Jaromir Jagr | 15.00 | 6.75 |
| ❑ 6 Mark Messier | 6.00 | 2.70 |
| ❑ 7 Teemu Selanne | 10.00 | 4.50 |
| ❑ 8 Theoren Fleury | 5.00 | 2.20 |
| ❑ 9 Ray Bourque | 5.00 | 2.20 |
| ❑ 10 Martin Brodeur | 12.00 | 5.50 |
| ❑ 11 Alexei Yashin | 4.00 | 1.80 |
| ❑ 12 Keith Tkachuk | 6.00 | 2.70 |
| ❑ 13 Eric Lindros | 15.00 | 6.75 |
| ❑ 14 Owen Nolan | 4.00 | 1.80 |
| ❑ 15 Al MacInnis | 4.00 | 1.80 |
| ❑ 16 Peter Bondra | 5.00 | 2.20 |
| ❑ 17 Saku Koivu | 8.00 | 3.60 |
| ❑ 18 Doug Weight | 4.00 | 1.80 |
| ❑ 19 Robert Reichel | 1.25 | .55 |
| ❑ 20 Sergei Fedorov | 10.00 | 4.50 |
| ❑ 21 Peter Forsberg | 15.00 | 6.75 |
| ❑ 22 Ron Francis | 4.00 | 1.80 |
| ❑ 23 Dimitri Khristich | 1.25 | .55 |
| ❑ 24 Ed Belfour | 5.00 | 2.20 |
| ❑ 25 Oleg Kvasha | 5.00 | 2.20 |
| ❑ 26 Ray Whitney | 1.25 | .55 |
| ❑ 27 Kenny Jonsson | 1.25 | .55 |
| ❑ 28 Randy McKay | 1.25 | .55 |
| ❑ 29 Pavol Demitra | 4.00 | 1.80 |
| ❑ 30 Pierre Turgeon | 4.00 | 1.80 |
| ❑ 31 Steve Yzerman | 15.00 | 6.75 |
| ❑ 32 Ryan Smyth | 4.00 | 1.80 |
| ❑ 33 Tony Amonte | 4.00 | 1.80 |
| ❑ 34 Dominik Hasek | 10.00 | 4.50 |
| ❑ 35 Jarome Iginla | 1.25 | .55 |
| ❑ 36 Sami Kapanen | 4.00 | 1.80 |
| ❑ 37 Patrik Elias | 1.25 | .55 |
| ❑ 38 Daniel Cleary | 1.25 | .55 |
| ❑ 39 Curtis Joseph | 5.00 | 2.20 |
| ❑ 40 Joe Juneau | 1.25 | .55 |
| ❑ 41 Adam Graves | 4.00 | 1.80 |
| ❑ 42 Trevor Linden | 4.00 | 1.80 |
| ❑ 43 Olli Jokinen | 1.25 | .55 |
| ❑ 44 Joe Nieuwendyk | 4.00 | 1.80 |
| ❑ 45 Sergei Samsonov | 8.00 | 3.60 |
| ❑ 46 Rico Fata | 6.00 | 2.70 |
| ❑ 47 Mark Recchi | 4.00 | 1.80 |
| ❑ 48 Rick Tocchet | 4.00 | 1.80 |
| ❑ 49 Chris Pronger | 4.00 | 1.80 |
| ❑ 50 Jason Allison | 4.00 | 1.80 |
| ❑ 51 Paul Kariya | 20.00 | 9.00 |
| ❑ 52 Stu Barnes | 1.25 | .55 |
| ❑ 53 Mats Sundin | 5.00 | 2.20 |
| ❑ 54 Mike Richter | 5.00 | 2.20 |
| ❑ 55 Cliff Ronning | 1.25 | .55 |
| ❑ 56 Keith Primeau | 4.00 | 1.80 |
| ❑ 57 Guy Hebert | 4.00 | 1.80 |
| ❑ 58 Nicklas Lidstrom | 4.00 | 1.80 |
| ❑ 59 John Vanbiesbrouck | 8.00 | 3.60 |
| ❑ 60 Jeff Friesen | 1.25 | .55 |
| ❑ 61 Vincent Lecavalier | 10.00 | 4.50 |
| ❑ 62 Alexander Mogilny | 4.00 | 1.80 |
| ❑ 63 Olaf Kolzig | 4.00 | 1.80 |
| ❑ 64 Doug Gilmour | 5.00 | 2.20 |
| ❑ 65 Joe Sakic | 10.00 | 4.50 |
| ❑ 66 Mike Johnson | 1.25 | .55 |
| ❑ 67 Vincent Damphousse | 4.00 | 1.80 |
| ❑ 68 Eric Brewer | 1.25 | .55 |
| ❑ 69 Daniel Alfredsson | 4.00 | 1.80 |
| ❑ 70 Nikolai Khabibulin | 4.00 | 1.80 |
| ❑ 71 Marco Sturm | 1.25 | .55 |
| ❑ 72 Marty Reasoner | 1.25 | .55 |
| ❑ 73 Bill Muckalt | 6.00 | 2.70 |
| ❑ 74 Pavel Bure | 10.00 | 4.50 |
| ❑ 75 Bill Guerin | 1.25 | .55 |
| ❑ 76 Chris Osgood | 5.00 | 2.20 |
| ❑ 77 Patrick Roy | 25.00 | 11.00 |
| ❑ 78 Tom Barrasso | 4.00 | 1.80 |
| ❑ 79 Alyn McCauley | 1.25 | .55 |
| ❑ 80 Adam Oates | 4.00 | 1.80 |
| ❑ 81 Joe Thornton | 1.25 | .55 |
| ❑ 82 Brendan Morrison | 4.00 | 1.80 |
| ❑ 83 Mike Dunham | 4.00 | 1.80 |
| ❑ 84 Jeremy Roenick | 5.00 | 2.20 |
| ❑ 85 Brian Leetch | 5.00 | 2.20 |
| ❑ 86 John LeClair | 8.00 | 3.60 |
| ❑ 87 Mattias Ohlund | 4.00 | 1.80 |
| ❑ 88 Wade Redden | 1.25 | .55 |
| ❑ 89 Mark Parrish | 8.00 | 3.60 |
| ❑ 90 Milan Hejduk | 8.00 | 3.60 |
| ❑ 91 Michael Peca | 4.00 | 1.80 |
| ❑ 92 Brett Hull | 6.00 | 2.70 |
| ❑ 94 Patrick Marleau | 4.00 | 1.80 |
| ❑ 95 Grant Fuhr | 4.00 | 1.80 |
| ❑ 96 Rob Blake | 4.00 | 1.80 |
| ❑ 97 Damian Rhodes | 4.00 | 1.80 |
| ❑ 98 Eric Daze | 1.25 | .55 |
| ❑ 99 Rod Brind'Amour | 4.00 | 1.80 |
| ❑ 100 Scott Stevens | 1.25 | .55 |

## 1998-99 Topps Gold Label Goal Race '99

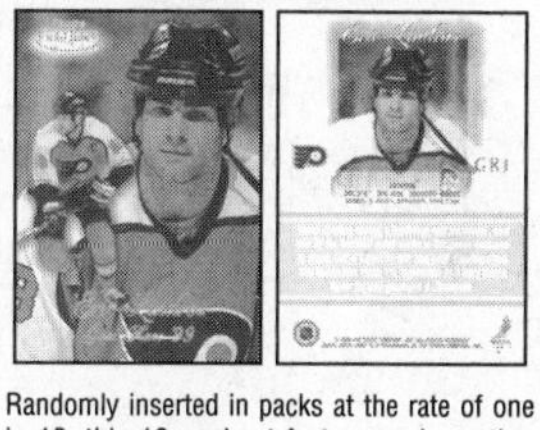

Randomly inserted in packs at the rate of one in 18, this 10-card set features color action photos of the top players who strike fear in the hearts of goalies night after night. Three parallel versions of this set were also produced: Black Label Parallel with the Black Topps Gold Label logo and insertion rate of 1:54; Red Label Parallel with the Red Topps Gold Label logo, insertion rate of 1:795, and sequentially numbered to 92; and One of One parallel version printed on special silver foil backs and sequentially numbered 1 of 1.

| | MINT | NRMT |
|---|---|---|
| COMPLETE SET (10) | 120.00 | 55.00 |
| COMMON CARD (GR1-GR10) | 5.00 | 2.20 |
| COMP.BLACK SET (10) | 300.00 | 135.00 |
| COMMON BLACK (1-10) | 12.00 | 5.50 |
| *BLACK: 1.25X TO 2.5X HI COLUMN | | |
| BLACK STATED ODDS 1:54 | | |
| COMP.RED SET (10) | 1500.00 | 700.00 |
| COMMON RED (1-10) | 60.00 | 27.00 |
| *RED: 6X TO 12X HI COLUMN | | |
| RED STATED ODDS 1:795 | | |
| STATED PRINT RUN 92 SERIAL #'d SETS | | |
| GOLD, BLACK, RED 1/1 PARALLELS EXIST | | |

| | | |
|---|---|---|
| ❑ GR1 Eric Lindros | 20.00 | 9.00 |
| ❑ GR2 John LeClair | 10.00 | 4.50 |
| ❑ GR3 Teemu Selanne | 12.00 | 5.50 |
| ❑ GR4 Paul Kariya | 25.00 | 11.00 |
| ❑ GR5 Jaromir Jagr | 20.00 | 9.00 |
| ❑ GR6 Keith Tkachuk | 8.00 | 3.60 |
| ❑ GR7 Theoren Fleury | 6.00 | 2.70 |
| ❑ GR8 Brendan Shanahan | 12.00 | 5.50 |
| ❑ GR9 Tony Amonte | 5.00 | 2.20 |
| ❑ GR10 Joe Sakic | 12.00 | 5.50 |

## 1996-97 Topps Picks

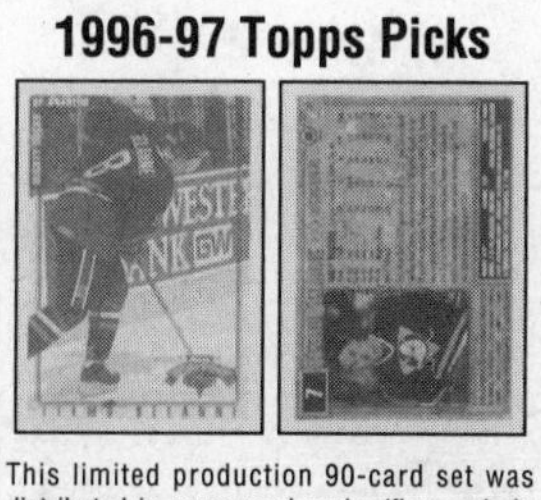

This limited production 90-card set was distributed in seven-card packs (five-cards in Canadian packs) with a suggested retail price of $.99. Topps and Fleer card companies joined together to each select a team of 90 hockey players. The cards in Topps set all have odd numbers because Topps had the first pick of players. Each card features color player photos with player career statistics, biographical information, and a "Topps Prediction" section which gave the upcoming season's goals, assists, wins and shutouts totals for each player as predicted by the Topps Sports Department. Each pack contained an official NHL/NHLPA Draft Game registration form which allowed the collectors the chance to draft their own players and create teams in order to win prizes in a fantasy league.

| | MINT | NRMT |
|---|---|---|
| COMPLETE SET (90) | 15.00 | 6.75 |
| COMMON CARD | .05 | .02 |

| | | |
|---|---|---|
| ❑ 1 Jaromir Jagr | 1.00 | .45 |
| ❑ 3 Mario Lemieux | 1.50 | .70 |
| ❑ 5 Peter Forsberg | 1.00 | .45 |
| ❑ 7 Teemu Selanne | .60 | .25 |
| ❑ 9 Alexander Mogilny | .15 | .07 |
| ❑ 11 Patrick Roy | 1.50 | .70 |
| ❑ 13 Jim Carey | .30 | .14 |
| ❑ 15 Pavel Bure | .60 | .25 |
| ❑ 17 Sergei Fedorov | .50 | .23 |
| ❑ 19 Chris Chelios | .30 | .14 |
| ❑ 21 Sandis Ozolinsh | .15 | .07 |
| ❑ 23 Doug Weight | .15 | .07 |
| ❑ 25 Mark Messier | .40 | .18 |
| ❑ 27 Martin Brodeur | .75 | .35 |
| ❑ 29 Brett Hull | .40 | .18 |
| ❑ 31 Steve Yzerman | 1.00 | .45 |
| ❑ 33 Kevin Hatcher | .05 | .02 |
| ❑ 35 Roman Hamrlik | .15 | .07 |
| ❑ 37 Petr Nedved | .15 | .07 |
| ❑ 39 Valeri Kamensky | .15 | .07 |
| ❑ 41 Gary Suter | .05 | .02 |
| ❑ 43 Mats Sundin | .15 | .07 |
| ❑ 45 Trevor Linden | .15 | .07 |
| ❑ 47 Jeremy Roenick | .30 | .14 |
| ❑ 49 Al MacInnis | .15 | .07 |
| ❑ 51 Mike Modano | .40 | .18 |
| ❑ 53 Mathieu Schneider | .05 | .02 |
| ❑ 55 Michal Pivonka | .05 | .02 |
| ❑ 57 Owen Nolan | .15 | .07 |
| ❑ 59 Martin Rucinsky | .05 | .02 |
| ❑ 61 Joe Nieuwendyk | .15 | .07 |
| ❑ 63 Mark Recchi | .15 | .07 |
| ❑ 65 Geoff Sanderson | .15 | .07 |
| ❑ 67 Vyacheslav Kozlov | .05 | .02 |
| ❑ 69 Pat Verbeek | .05 | .02 |
| ❑ 71 Brian Bradley | .05 | .02 |
| ❑ 73 Steve Duchesne | .05 | .02 |
| ❑ 75 Steve Thomas | .05 | .02 |
| ❑ 77 Eric Daze | .15 | .07 |
| ❑ 79 Alexei Kovalev | .05 | .02 |
| ❑ 81 Kevin Stevens | .05 | .02 |
| ❑ 83 Curtis Joseph | .30 | .14 |
| ❑ 85 Bill Ranford | .15 | .07 |
| ❑ 87 Luc Robitaille | .15 | .07 |
| ❑ 89 Claude Lemieux | .15 | .07 |
| ❑ 91 Sergei Gonchar | .05 | .02 |
| ❑ 93 Eric Desjardins | .05 | .02 |
| ❑ 95 Garry Galley | .05 | .02 |
| ❑ 97 Oleg Tverdovsky | .15 | .07 |
| ❑ 99 Rob Niedermayer | .15 | .07 |
| ❑ 101 Scott Mellanby | .15 | .07 |
| ❑ 103 Adam Deadmarsh | .15 | .07 |
| ❑ 105 Cliff Ronning | .05 | .02 |
| ❑ 107 Russ Courtnall | .05 | .02 |
| ❑ 109 Keith Primeau | .15 | .07 |
| ❑ 111 Rick Tocchet | .15 | .07 |
| ❑ 113 Scott Young | .05 | .02 |
| ❑ 115 Scott Stevens | .15 | .07 |
| ❑ 117 Al Iafrate | .05 | .02 |
| ❑ 119 Ray Ferraro | .05 | .02 |
| ❑ 121 Todd Bertuzzi | .05 | .02 |
| ❑ 123 Alexander Selivanov | .05 | .02 |
| ❑ 125 Steve Chiasson | .05 | .02 |
| ❑ 127 Dave Andreychuk | .15 | .07 |
| ❑ 129 Ray Sheppard | .15 | .07 |
| ❑ 131 Bernie Nicholls | .05 | .02 |
| ❑ 133 Tony Amonte | .15 | .07 |
| ❑ 135 Nelson Emerson | .05 | .02 |
| ❑ 137 Cam Neely | .15 | .07 |
| ❑ 139 Shayne Corson | .05 | .02 |
| ❑ 141 Bill Guerin | .05 | .02 |
| ❑ 143 Joe Murphy | .05 | .02 |
| ❑ 145 Cory Stillman | .05 | .02 |
| ❑ 147 Radek Bonk | .05 | .02 |
| ❑ 149 Geoff Courtnall | .05 | .02 |
| ❑ 151 Chad Kilger | .05 | .02 |
| ❑ 153 Sylvain Cote | .05 | .02 |
| ❑ 155 Glen Wesley | .05 | .02 |
| ❑ 157 Jeff Norton | .05 | .02 |
| ❑ 159 Rob Blake | .05 | .02 |
| ❑ 161 Calle Johansson | .05 | .02 |
| ❑ 163 Uwe Krupp | .05 | .02 |
| ❑ 165 James Patrick | .05 | .02 |
| ❑ 167 Dmitri Mironov | .05 | .02 |
| ❑ 169 Vladimir Konstantinov | .05 | .02 |
| ❑ 171 Mattias Norstrom | .05 | .02 |
| ❑ 173 David Wilkie | .05 | .02 |
| ❑ 175 Bryan McCabe | .05 | .02 |
| ❑ 177 Barry Richter | .05 | .02 |
| ❑ 179 Ed Belfour | .30 | .14 |

## 1996-97 Topps Picks OPC Inserts

Randomly inserted in Canadian packs only at

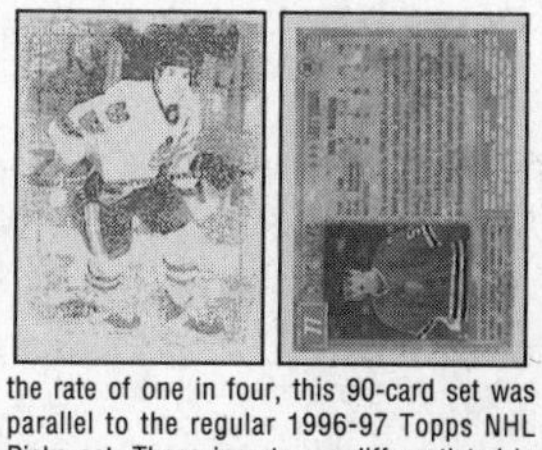

the rate of one in four, this 90-card set was parallel to the regular 1996-97 Topps NHL Picks set. These inserts are differentiated in that OPC cards have foil backgrounds and feature the OPC logo on the front. Values for the cards can be determined by using the multipliers below on the base cards.

| | MINT | NRMT |
|---|---|---|
| COMPLETE SET (90) | 125.00 | 55.00 |
| COMMON CARD (1-179) | .50 | .23 |
| *OPC STARS: 5X TO 10X BASIC CARDS | | |

## 1996-97 Topps Picks Fantasy Team

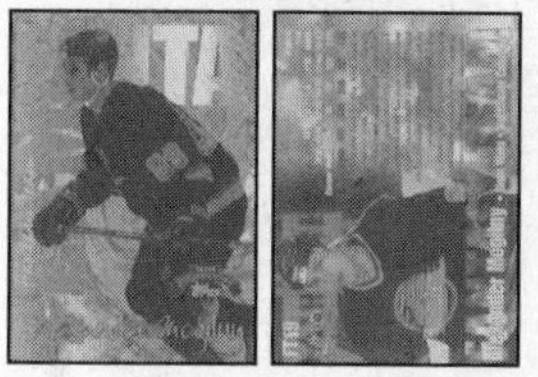

Randomly inserted at the rate of one in every 24 packs, this 22 card set featured a dream team made up of the elite hockey stars which any NHL general manager would want playing for him. Printed with Power Matrix technology, the fronts displayed color player photos while the backs carried player information.

| | MINT | NRMT |
|---|---|---|
| COMPLETE SET (7) | 120.00 | 55.00 |
| COMMON CARD (1-7) | 2.00 | .90 |

| | | |
|---|---|---|
| ❑ FT1 Patrick Roy | 15.00 | 6.75 |
| ❑ FT2 Chris Osgood | 3.00 | 1.35 |
| ❑ FT3 Martin Brodeur | 8.00 | 3.60 |
| ❑ FT4 Ray Bourque | 3.00 | 1.35 |
| ❑ FT5 Brian Leetch | 3.00 | 1.35 |
| ❑ FT6 Chris Chelios | 3.00 | 1.35 |
| ❑ FT7 Paul Coffey | 3.00 | 1.35 |
| ❑ FT8 Ed Jovanovski | 2.00 | .90 |
| ❑ FT9 Roman Hamrlik | 2.00 | .90 |
| ❑ FT10 Wayne Gretzky | 25.00 | 11.00 |
| ❑ FT11 Paul Kariya | 12.00 | 5.50 |
| ❑ FT12 Brett Hull | 4.00 | 1.80 |
| ❑ FT13 Pavel Bure | 6.00 | 2.70 |
| ❑ FT14 Jaromir Jagr | 10.00 | 4.50 |
| ❑ FT15 Mario Lemieux | 15.00 | 6.75 |
| ❑ FT16 Peter Forsberg | 10.00 | 4.50 |
| ❑ FT17 Sergei Fedorov | 6.00 | 2.70 |
| ❑ FT18 Jeremy Roenick | 3.00 | 1.35 |
| ❑ FT19 Alexander Mogilny | 2.00 | .90 |
| ❑ FT20 Joe Sakic | 6.00 | 2.70 |
| ❑ FT21 Teemu Selanne | 6.00 | 2.70 |
| ❑ FT22 Eric Lindros | 10.00 | 4.50 |

## 1996-97 Topps Picks 500 Club

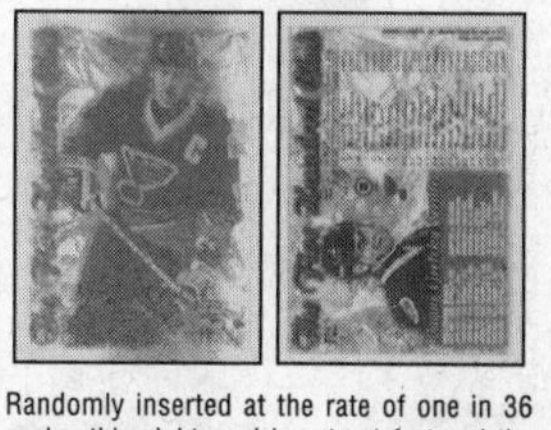

Randomly inserted at the rate of one in 36 packs, this eight-card insert set featured the eight active players who had scored their 500th career goal by the end of the 1995-96 season. The set featured color player photos and player information printed on rainbow diffraction foilboard.

| | MINT | NRMT |
|---|---|---|
| COMPLETE SET (8) | 90.00 | 40.00 |
| COMMON CARD (FC1-FC8) | 4.00 | 1.80 |

| | | |
|---|---|---|
| ❑ FC1 Wayne Gretzky | 30.00 | 13.50 |
| ❑ FC2 Mike Gartner | 4.00 | 1.80 |
| ❑ FC3 Jari Kurri | 4.00 | 1.80 |
| ❑ FC4 Dino Ciccarelli | 4.00 | 1.80 |
| ❑ FC5 Mario Lemieux | 25.00 | 11.00 |
| ❑ FC6 Mark Messier | 6.00 | 2.70 |
| ❑ FC7 Steve Yzerman | 15.00 | 6.75 |
| ❑ FC8 Dale Hawerchuk | 4.00 | 1.80 |

## 1996-97 Topps Picks Ice D

Randomly inserted at the rate of one in 24 packs, this 15-card set featured five of the best defensemen and ten top goalies. Color player

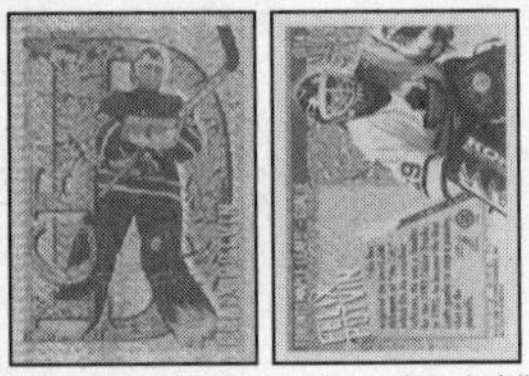

photos were printed on rainbow prismatic foil with player information on the backs.

| | MINT | NRMT |
|---|---|---|
| COMPLETE SET (15) | 120.00 | 55.00 |
| COMMON CARD (ID1-ID15) | 2.50 | 1.10 |

| | | |
|---|---|---|
| ❑ ID1 Brian Leetch | 6.00 | 2.70 |
| ❑ ID2 Ray Bourque | 6.00 | 2.70 |
| ❑ ID3 Chris Chelios | 6.00 | 2.70 |
| ❑ ID4 Scott Stevens | 2.50 | 1.10 |
| ❑ ID5 Ed Jovanovski | 4.00 | 1.80 |
| ❑ ID6 Martin Brodeur | 15.00 | 6.75 |
| ❑ ID7 Patrick Roy | 30.00 | 13.50 |
| ❑ ID8 Chris Osgood | 6.00 | 2.70 |
| ❑ ID9 Jim Carey | 6.00 | 2.70 |
| ❑ ID10 Dominik Hasek | 12.00 | 5.50 |
| ❑ ID11 Ron Hextall | 4.00 | 1.80 |
| ❑ ID12 John Vanbiesbrouck | 10.00 | 4.50 |
| ❑ ID13 Mike Richter | 6.00 | 2.70 |
| ❑ ID14 Felix Potvin | 6.00 | 2.70 |
| ❑ ID15 Grant Fuhr | 4.00 | 1.80 |

## 1996-97 Topps Picks Rookie Stars

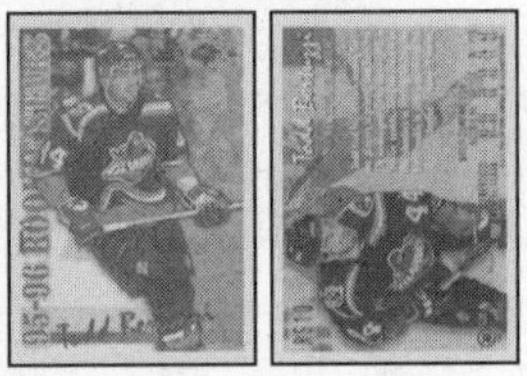

Inserted at the rate of one per pack, this 18-card set showcased hockey's best and brightest young stars. The fronts displayed color player photos while the back carried player information.

| | MINT | NRMT |
|---|---|---|
| COMPLETE SET (18) | 10.00 | 4.50 |
| COMMON CARD (RS1-RS18) | .25 | .11 |
| *OPC: 5X TO 10X BASIC CARDS | | |

| | | |
|---|---|---|
| ❑ RS1 Daniel Alfredsson | .75 | .35 |
| ❑ RS2 Jere Lehtinen | .25 | .11 |
| ❑ RS3 Vitali Yachmenev | .25 | .11 |
| ❑ RS4 Eric Daze | .25 | .11 |
| ❑ RS5 Saku Koivu | 2.00 | .90 |
| ❑ RS6 Petr Sykora | .25 | .11 |
| ❑ RS7 Marcus Ragnarsson | .25 | .11 |
| ❑ RS8 Valeri Bure | .25 | .11 |
| ❑ RS9 Cory Stillman | .25 | .11 |
| ❑ RS10 Todd Bertuzzi | .25 | .11 |
| ❑ RS11 Ed Jovanovski | .75 | .35 |
| ❑ RS12 Miroslav Satan | .25 | .11 |
| ❑ RS13 Kyle McLaren | .25 | .11 |
| ❑ RS14 Byron Dafoe | .75 | .35 |
| ❑ RS15 Eric Fichaud | .75 | .35 |
| ❑ RS16 Corey Hirsch | .25 | .11 |
| ❑ RS17 Jeff O'Neill | .25 | .11 |
| ❑ RS18 Niklas Sundstrom | .25 | .11 |

## 1996-97 Topps Picks Top Shelf

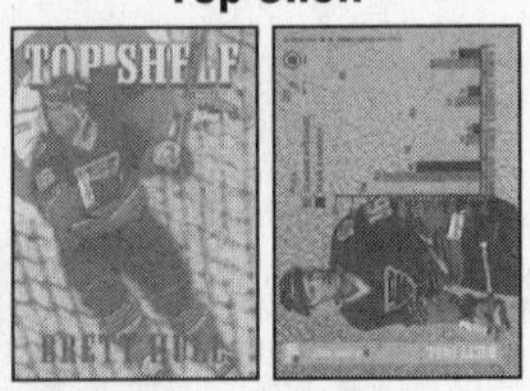

Randomly inserted at the rate of one in 12 packs, this 15-card set featured red foil-stamped cards of the league's top scorers and award winners of the 1995-96 season. The fronts displayed color player photos while the backs carried player information.

| | MINT | NRMT |
|---|---|---|
| COMPLETE SET (15) | 100.00 | 45.00 |
| COMMON CARD (TS1-TS15) | 2.50 | 1.10 |

| | | |
|---|---|---|
| ❑ TS1 John LeClair | 5.00 | 2.20 |
| ❑ TS2 Wayne Gretzky | 20.00 | 9.00 |
| ❑ TS3 Eric Lindros | 10.00 | 4.50 |
| ❑ TS4 Paul Kariya | 12.00 | 5.50 |
| ❑ TS5 Mark Messier | 4.00 | 1.80 |
| ❑ TS6 Jaromir Jagr | 10.00 | 4.50 |
| ❑ TS7 Peter Forsberg | 10.00 | 4.50 |
| ❑ TS8 Teemu Selanne | 6.00 | 2.70 |
| ❑ TS9 Alexander Mogilny | 2.50 | 1.10 |
| ❑ TS10 Brett Hull | 4.00 | 1.80 |
| ❑ TS11 Sergei Fedorov | 6.00 | 2.70 |
| ❑ TS12 Joe Sakic | 6.00 | 2.70 |
| ❑ TS13 Mats Sundin | 2.50 | 1.10 |
| ❑ TS14 Theoren Fleury | 2.50 | 1.10 |
| ❑ TS15 Steve Yzerman | 10.00 | 4.50 |

## 1963-64 Toronto Star

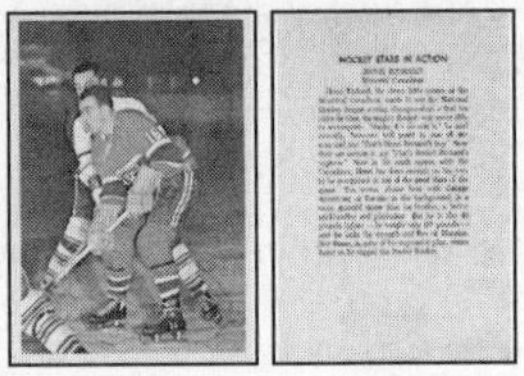

This set of 42 photos was distributed one per week with the Toronto Star and was also available as a complete set directly. The photos measure approximately 4 3/4" by 6 3/4" and are entitled, "Hockey Stars in Action." There is a short write-up on the back of each photo. The player's team is identified in the checklist below, Boston Bruins (BB), Chicago Blackhawks (CBH), Detroit Red Wings (DRW), Montreal Canadiens (MC), New York Rangers (NYR), and Toronto Maple Leafs (TML). Since the photos are unnumbered, they are listed below in alphabetical order.

| | NRMT | VG-E |
|---|---|---|
| COMPLETE SET (42) | 300.00 | 135.00 |
| COMMON CARD (1-42) | 4.00 | 1.80 |

| | | |
|---|---|---|
| ❑ 1 George Armstrong TML | 8.00 | 3.60 |
| ❑ 2 Andy Bathgate NYR | 8.00 | 3.60 |
| ❑ 3 Bob Baun TML | 5.00 | 2.20 |
| ❑ 4 Jean Beliveau MC | 15.00 | 6.75 |
| ❑ 5 Leo Boivin BB | 5.00 | 2.20 |
| ❑ 6 Johnny Bower TML | 10.00 | 4.50 |
| ❑ 7 Carl Brewer TML | 5.00 | 2.20 |
| ❑ 8 Johnny Bucyk BB | 8.00 | 3.60 |
| ❑ 9 Alex Delvecchio DRW | 10.00 | 4.50 |
| ❑ 10 Kent Douglas TML | 4.00 | 1.80 |
| ❑ 11 Dick Duff TML | 5.00 | 2.20 |
| ❑ 12 Bill Gadsby DRW | 6.00 | 2.70 |
| ❑ 13 Jean-Guy Gendron BB | 4.00 | 1.80 |
| ❑ 14 BoomBoom Geoffrion MC | 15.00 | 6.75 |
| ❑ 15 Glenn Hall CBH | 12.00 | 5.50 |
| ❑ 16 Doug Harvey NYR | 10.00 | 4.50 |
| ❑ 17 Bill(Red) Hay CBH | 5.00 | 2.20 |
| ❑ 18 Camille Henry NYR | 5.00 | 2.20 |
| ❑ 19 Tim Horton TML | 15.00 | 6.75 |
| ❑ 20 Gordie Howe DRW | 50.00 | 22.00 |
| ❑ 21 Bobby Hull CBH | 30.00 | 13.50 |
| ❑ 22 Red Kelly TML | 10.00 | 4.50 |
| ❑ 23 Dave Keon TML | 15.00 | 6.75 |
| ❑ 24 Parker MacDonald DRW | 4.00 | 1.80 |
| ❑ 25 Frank Mahovlich TML | 15.00 | 6.75 |
| ❑ 26 Stan Mikita CBH | 15.00 | 6.75 |
| ❑ 27 Dickie Moore MC | 10.00 | 4.50 |
| ❑ 28 Eric Nesterenko CBH | 5.00 | 2.20 |
| ❑ 29 Marcel Pronovost DRW | 5.00 | 2.20 |
| ❑ 30 Claude Provost MC | 5.00 | 2.20 |
| ❑ 31 Bob Pulford TML | 6.00 | 2.70 |
| ❑ 32 Henri Richard MC | 15.00 | 6.75 |
| ❑ 33 Terry Sawchuk DRW | 20.00 | 9.00 |
| ❑ 34 Eddie Shack TML | 10.00 | 4.50 |
| ❑ 35 Allan Stanley TML | 6.00 | 2.70 |
| ❑ 36 Ron Stewart TML | 4.00 | 1.80 |
| ❑ 37 Jean-Guy Talbot MC | 5.00 | 2.20 |
| ❑ 38 Gilles Tremblay MC | 4.00 | 1.80 |
| ❑ 39 J.C. Tremblay MC | 5.00 | 2.20 |
| ❑ 40 Norm Ullman DRW | 8.00 | 3.60 |
| ❑ 41 Elmer(Moose) Vasko CBH | 4.00 | 1.80 |
| ❑ 42 Ken Wharram CBH | 5.00 | 2.20 |

## 1964-65 Toronto Star

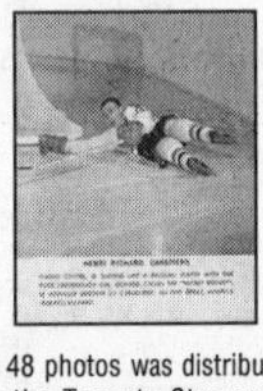

This set of 48 photos was distributed one per week with the Toronto Star and was also available as a complete set directly. The direct complete sets also included a booklet and glossy photo of Dave Keon in the mail-away package. These blank-backed photos measure approximately 4 1/8" by 5 1/8". The player's team is identified in the checklist below, Boston Bruins (BB), Chicago Blackhawks (CBH), Detroit Red Wings (DRW), Montreal Canadiens (MC), New York Rangers (NYR), and Toronto Maple Leafs (TML). Since the photos are unnumbered, they are listed below in alphabetical order. There was an album (actually a folder) available for each team to slot in cards. However when the cards were placed in the album it rendered the card's caption unreadable as only the action photo was visible.

| | NRMT | VG-E |
|---|---|---|
| COMPLETE SET (48) | 300.00 | 135.00 |
| COMMON CARD (1-48) | 4.00 | 1.80 |

| | | |
|---|---|---|
| ❑ 1 Dave Balon MC | 4.00 | 1.80 |
| ❑ 2 Andy Bathgate TML | 8.00 | 3.60 |
| ❑ 3 Bob Baun TML | 6.00 | 2.70 |
| ❑ 4 Jean Beliveau MC | 15.00 | 6.75 |
| ❑ 5 Red Berenson MC | 5.00 | 2.20 |
| ❑ 6 Leo Boivin BB | 6.00 | 2.70 |
| ❑ 7 Carl Brewer TML | 5.00 | 2.20 |
| ❑ 8 Alex Delvecchio DRW | 8.00 | 3.60 |
| ❑ 9 Rod Gilbert NYR | 8.00 | 3.60 |
| ❑ 10 Ted Green BB | 5.00 | 2.20 |
| ❑ 11 Glenn Hall CBH | 10.00 | 4.50 |
| ❑ 12 Billy Harris TML | 4.00 | 1.80 |
| ❑ 13 Bill(Red) Hay CBH | 4.00 | 1.80 |
| ❑ 14 Paul Henderson DRW | 6.00 | 2.70 |
| ❑ 15 Wayne Hillman CBH | 4.00 | 1.80 |
| ❑ 16 Charlie Hodge MC | 6.00 | 2.70 |
| ❑ 17 Tim Horton TML | 15.00 | 6.75 |
| ❑ 18 Gordie Howe DRW | 40.00 | 18.00 |
| ❑ 19 Harry Howell NYR | 6.00 | 2.70 |
| ❑ 20 Bobby Hull CBH | 25.00 | 11.00 |
| ❑ 21 Larry Jeffrey DRW | 4.00 | 1.80 |
| ❑ 22 Tom Johnson BB | 6.00 | 2.70 |
| ❑ 23 Forbes Kennedy BB | 4.00 | 1.80 |
| ❑ 24 Dave Keon TML | 12.00 | 5.50 |
| ❑ 25 Orland Kurtenbach BB | 5.00 | 2.20 |
| ❑ 26 Jacques Laperriere MC | 5.00 | 2.20 |
| ❑ 27 Parker MacDonald DRW | 4.00 | 1.80 |
| ❑ 28 Al MacNeil CBH | 4.00 | 1.80 |
| ❑ 29 Frank Mahovlich TML | 12.00 | 5.50 |
| ❑ 30 Chico Maki CBH | 4.00 | 1.80 |
| ❑ 31 Don McKenney TML | 4.00 | 1.80 |
| ❑ 32 John McKenzie CBH | 5.00 | 2.20 |
| ❑ 33 Stan Mikita CBH | 12.00 | 5.50 |
| ❑ 34 Jim Neilson NYR | 4.00 | 1.80 |
| ❑ 35 Jim Pappin TML | 4.00 | 1.80 |
| ❑ 36 Pierre Pilote CBH | 6.00 | 2.70 |
| ❑ 37 Jacques Plante NYR | 20.00 | 9.00 |
| ❑ 38 Marcel Pronovost DRW | 6.00 | 2.70 |
| ❑ 39 Claude Provost MC | 5.00 | 2.20 |
| ❑ 40 Bob Pulford TML | 6.00 | 2.70 |
| ❑ 41 Henri Richard MC | 12.00 | 5.50 |
| ❑ 42 Wayne Rivers BB | 4.00 | 1.80 |
| ❑ 43 Floyd Smith DRW | 4.00 | 1.80 |
| ❑ 44 Allan Stanley TML | 8.00 | 3.60 |
| ❑ 45 Ron Stewart TML | 4.00 | 1.80 |
| ❑ 46 J.C. Tremblay MC | 5.00 | 2.20 |
| ❑ 47 Norm Ullman DRW | 8.00 | 3.60 |
| ❑ 48 Elmer Vasko CBH | 4.00 | 1.80 |
| ❑ xx Album/Folder | 25.00 | 11.00 |

## 1971-72 Toronto Sun

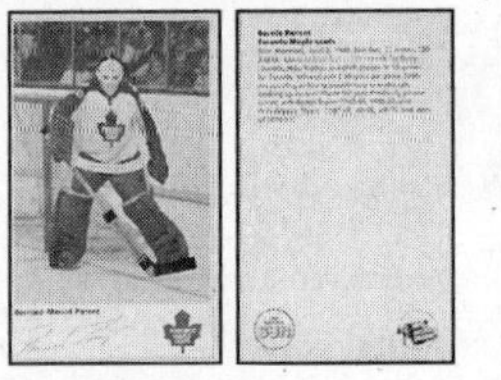

This set of 294 photo cards with two punch holes has never been very popular with collectors. The photos are quite fragile, printed on thin paper, and measure approximately 5" by 7". The checklist below is in team order as follows: Boston Bruins (1-21), Buffalo Sabres (22-41), California Golden Seals (42-61), Chicago Blackhawks (62-82), Detroit Red Wings (83-103), Los Angeles Kings (104-124), Minnesota North Stars (125-145), Montreal Canadiens (146-166), New York Rangers (167-186), Philadelphia Flyers (187-208), Pittsburgh Penguins (209-230), St. Louis Blues (231-252), Toronto Maple Leafs (253-274), and Vancouver Canucks (275-294). The cards were intended to fit in a two-ring binder specially made to hold the cards. Also included was and introduction photo, with text by Scott Young.

| | NRMT-MT | EXC |
|---|---|---|
| COMPLETE SET (294) | 600.00 | 275.00 |
| COMMON CARD (1-294) | 1.00 | .45 |

| | | |
|---|---|---|
| ❑ 1 Boston Bruins Team Crest | 3.00 | 1.35 |
| ❑ 2 Don Awrey | 1.00 | .45 |
| ❑ 3 Garnet Bailey | 1.00 | .45 |
| ❑ 4 Ivan Boldirev | 1.00 | .45 |
| ❑ 5 Johnny Bucyk | 6.00 | 2.70 |
| ❑ 6 Wayne Cashman | 1.50 | .70 |
| ❑ 7 Gerry Cheevers | 8.00 | 3.60 |
| ❑ 8 Phil Esposito | 20.00 | 9.00 |
| ❑ 9 Ted Green | 1.50 | .70 |
| ❑ 10 Ken Hodge | 1.50 | .70 |
| ❑ 11 Ed Johnston | 3.00 | 1.35 |
| ❑ 12 Reggie Leach | 3.00 | 1.35 |
| ❑ 13 Don Marcotte | 1.00 | .45 |
| ❑ 14 John McKenzie | 1.00 | .45 |
| ❑ 15 Bobby Orr | 60.00 | 27.00 |
| ❑ 16 Derek Sanderson | 8.00 | 3.60 |
| ❑ 17 Dallas Smith | 1.00 | .45 |
| ❑ 18 Richard Allan Smith | 1.00 | .45 |
| ❑ 19 Fred Stanfield | 1.00 | .45 |
| ❑ 20 Mike Walton | 1.50 | .70 |
| ❑ 21 Ed Westfall | 1.50 | .70 |
| ❑ 22 Buffalo Sabres Team Crest | 2.00 | .90 |
| ❑ 23 Doug Barrie | 1.00 | .45 |
| ❑ 24 Roger Crozier | 4.00 | 1.80 |
| ❑ 25 Dave Dryden | 2.00 | .90 |
| ❑ 26 Dick Duff | 1.50 | .70 |
| ❑ 27 Phil Goyette | 1.00 | .45 |
| ❑ 28 Al Hamilton | 1.00 | .45 |
| ❑ 29 Larry Keenan | 1.00 | .45 |
| ❑ 30 Danny Lawson | 1.00 | .45 |
| ❑ 31 Don Luce | 1.00 | .45 |
| ❑ 32 Richard Martin | 2.00 | .90 |
| ❑ 33 Ray McKay | 1.00 | .45 |
| ❑ 34 Gerry Meehan | 1.50 | .70 |
| ❑ 35 Kevin O'Shea | 1.00 | .45 |
| ❑ 36 Gilbert Perreault | 8.00 | 3.60 |
| ❑ 37 Tracy Pratt | 1.00 | .45 |
| ❑ 38 Mike Robitaille | 1.00 | .45 |
| ❑ 39 Eddie Shack | 4.00 | 1.80 |
| ❑ 40 Jim Watson | 1.00 | .45 |
| ❑ 41 Rod Zaine | 1.00 | .45 |
| ❑ 42 California Seals Team Crest | 3.00 | 1.35 |
| ❑ 43 Wayne Carleton | 1.00 | .45 |
| ❑ 44 Lyle Carter | 1.00 | .45 |
| ❑ 45 Gary Croteau | 1.00 | .45 |
| ❑ 46 Norm Ferguson | 1.00 | .45 |
| ❑ 47 Stan Gilbertson | 1.00 | .45 |
| ❑ 48 Ernie Hicke | 1.00 | .45 |
| ❑ 49 Gary Jarrett | 2.00 | .90 |
| ❑ 50 Joey Johnston | 1.00 | .45 |
| ❑ 51 Marshall Johnston | 1.00 | .45 |
| ❑ 52 Bert Marshall | 1.00 | .45 |
| ❑ 53 Walt McKechnie | 1.00 | .45 |
| ❑ 54 Don O'Donoghue | 1.00 | .45 |
| ❑ 55 Gerry Pinder | 1.50 | .70 |
| ❑ 56 Dick Redmond | 1.00 | .45 |
| ❑ 57 Robert Sheehan | 1.00 | .45 |
| ❑ 58 Paul Shmyr | 1.00 | .45 |
| ❑ 59 Ron Stackhouse SP | 12.00 | 5.50 |
| ❑ 60 Carol Vadnais | 1.00 | .45 |
| ❑ 61 Tom Williams | 1.00 | .45 |
| ❑ 62 Chicago Blackhawks Team Crest | 3.00 | 1.35 |
| ❑ 63 Lou Angotti | 1.00 | .45 |
| ❑ 64 Bryan Campbell | 1.00 | .45 |
| ❑ 65 Tony Esposito | 20.00 | 9.00 |
| ❑ 66 Bobby Hull | 30.00 | 13.50 |
| ❑ 67 Dennis Hull | 2.00 | .90 |
| ❑ 68 Doug Jarrett | 1.00 | .45 |
| ❑ 69 Jerry Korab | 1.00 | .45 |
| ❑ 70 Cliff Koroll | 1.00 | .45 |
| ❑ 71 Darryl Maggs | 1.00 | .45 |
| ❑ 72 Keith Magnuson | 1.50 | .70 |
| ❑ 73 Chico Maki | 1.50 | .70 |
| ❑ 74 Dan Maloney | 1.00 | .45 |
| ❑ 75 Pit Martin | 1.50 | .70 |
| ❑ 76 Stan Mikita | 12.00 | 5.50 |
| ❑ 77 Eric Nesterenko | 1.00 | .45 |
| ❑ 78 Danny O'Shea | 1.00 | .45 |
| ❑ 79 Jim Pappin | 1.00 | .45 |
| ❑ 80 Gary Smith | 2.00 | .90 |
| ❑ 81 Pat Stapleton | 1.00 | .45 |
| ❑ 82 Bill White | 1.00 | .45 |
| ❑ 83 Detroit Red Wings Team Crest | 3.00 | 1.35 |
| ❑ 84 Red Berenson | 1.50 | .70 |
| ❑ 85 Gary Bergman | 1.50 | .70 |
| ❑ 86 Arnie Brown | 1.00 | .45 |
| ❑ 87 Guy Charron | 1.00 | .45 |
| ❑ 88 Bill Collins | 1.00 | .45 |
| ❑ 89 Brian Conacher | 1.00 | .45 |
| ❑ 90 Joe Daley | 3.00 | 1.35 |
| ❑ 91 Alex Delvecchio | 6.00 | 2.70 |
| ❑ 92 Marcel Dionne | 15.00 | 6.75 |
| ❑ 93 Tim Ecclestone | 1.00 | .45 |
| ❑ 94 Ron Harris | 1.00 | .45 |
| ❑ 95 Gerry Hart | 1.00 | .45 |
| ❑ 96 Gordie Howe | 50.00 | 22.00 |
| ❑ 97 Al Karlander | 1.00 | .45 |
| ❑ 98 Nick Libett | 1.50 | .70 |
| ❑ 99 Ab McDonald | 1.00 | .45 |
| ❑ 100 James Niekamp | 1.00 | .45 |
| ❑ 101 Mickey Redmond | 4.00 | 1.80 |
| ❑ 102 Leon Rochefort | 1.00 | .45 |
| ❑ 103 Al Smith | 1.50 | .70 |
| ❑ 104 Los Angeles Kings Team Crest | 2.00 | .90 |
| ❑ 105 Ralph Backstrom | 1.50 | .70 |
| ❑ 106 Bob Berry | 1.50 | .70 |
| ❑ 107 Mike Byers | 1.00 | .45 |
| ❑ 108 Larry Cahan | 1.00 | .45 |
| ❑ 109 Paul Curtis | 1.00 | .45 |
| ❑ 110 Denis DeJordy | 3.00 | 1.35 |
| ❑ 111 Gary Edwards | 2.00 | .90 |
| ❑ 112 Bill Flett | 1.00 | .45 |
| ❑ 113 Butch Goring | 1.50 | .70 |
| ❑ 114 Lucien Grenier | 1.00 | .45 |
| ❑ 115 Larry Hillman | 1.00 | .45 |
| ❑ 116 Dale Hoganson | 1.00 | .45 |
| ❑ 117 Harry Howell | 3.00 | 1.35 |
| ❑ 118 Eddie Joyal | 1.00 | .45 |
| ❑ 119 Real Lemieux | 1.00 | .45 |
| ❑ 120 Ross Lonsberry | 1.00 | .45 |
| ❑ 121 Al McDonough | 1.00 | .45 |
| ❑ 122 Jean Potvin | 1.00 | .45 |
| ❑ 123 Bob Pulford | 3.00 | 1.35 |
| ❑ 124 Juha Widing | 1.50 | .70 |
| ❑ 125 Minnesota North Stars Team Crest | 2.00 | .90 |
| ❑ 126 Fred Barrett | 1.00 | .45 |
| ❑ 127 Charlie Burns | 1.00 | .45 |
| ❑ 128 Jude Drouin | 1.00 | .45 |
| ❑ 129 Barry Gibbs | 1.00 | .45 |
| ❑ 130 Gilles Gilbert | 4.00 | 1.80 |
| ❑ 131 Bill Goldsworthy | 2.00 | .90 |
| ❑ 132 Danny Grant | 1.50 | .70 |
| ❑ 133 Ted Hampson | 1.00 | .45 |
| ❑ 134 Ted Harris | 1.00 | .45 |
| ❑ 135 Fred Harvey | 1.00 | .45 |
| ❑ 136 Cesare Maniago | 4.00 | 1.80 |
| ❑ 137 Doug Mohns | 1.50 | .70 |
| ❑ 138 Lou Nanne | 1.50 | .70 |
| ❑ 139 Bob Nevin | 1.50 | .70 |
| ❑ 140 Dennis O'Brien | 1.00 | .45 |
| ❑ 141 Murray Oliver | 1.00 | .45 |
| ❑ 142 Jean-Paul Parise | 1.50 | .70 |
| ❑ 143 Dean Prentice | 1.50 | .70 |
| ❑ 144 Tom Reid | 1.00 | .45 |
| ❑ 145 Gump Worsley | 6.00 | 2.70 |
| ❑ 146 Montreal Canadiens Team Crest | 3.00 | 1.35 |
| ❑ 147 Pierre Bouchard | 1.00 | .45 |
| ❑ 148 Yvan Cournoyer | 6.00 | 2.70 |
| ❑ 149 Ken Dryden | 50.00 | 22.00 |
| ❑ 150 Terry Harper | 1.50 | .70 |
| ❑ 151 Rejean Houle | 1.50 | .70 |
| ❑ 152 Guy Lafleur | 30.00 | 13.50 |
| ❑ 153 Jacques Laperriere | 2.00 | .90 |
| ❑ 154 Guy Lapointe | 3.00 | 1.35 |
| ❑ 155 Claude Larose | 1.00 | .45 |
| ❑ 156 Jacques Lemaire | 4.00 | 1.80 |
| ❑ 157 Frank Mahovlich | 12.00 | 5.50 |
| ❑ 158 Pete Mahovlich | 1.50 | .70 |
| ❑ 159 Phil Myre | 3.00 | 1.35 |
| ❑ 160 Larry Pleau | 1.50 | .70 |
| ❑ 161 Henri Richard | 12.00 | 5.50 |
| ❑ 162 Phil Roberto | 1.00 | .45 |
| ❑ 163 Serge Savard | 3.00 | 1.35 |
| ❑ 164 Marc Tardif | 1.50 | .70 |
| ❑ 165 J.C. Tremblay | 1.50 | .70 |
| ❑ 166 Rogatien Vachon | 6.00 | 2.70 |
| ❑ 167 New York Rangers Team Crest | 3.00 | 1.35 |
| ❑ 168 Dave Balon | 1.00 | .45 |
| ❑ 169 Ab DeMarco | 1.00 | .45 |
| ❑ 170 Jack Egers | 1.00 | .45 |
| ❑ 171 Bill Fairbairn | 1.00 | .45 |
| ❑ 172 Ed Giacomin | 8.00 | 3.60 |
| ❑ 173 Rod Gilbert | 4.00 | 1.80 |
| ❑ 174 Vic Hadfield | 1.50 | .70 |
| ❑ 175 Ted Irvine | 1.00 | .45 |
| ❑ 176 Bruce MacGregor | 1.00 | .45 |
| ❑ 177 Jim Neilson | 1.00 | .45 |
| ❑ 178 Brad Park | 6.00 | 2.70 |
| ❑ 179 Jean Ratelle | 4.00 | 1.80 |
| ❑ 180 Dale Rolfe | 1.00 | .45 |
| ❑ 181 Bobby Rousseau | 1.50 | .70 |
| ❑ 182 Glen Sather | 3.00 | 1.35 |
| ❑ 183 Rod Seiling | 1.00 | .45 |
| ❑ 184 Pete Stemkowski | 1.50 | .70 |
| ❑ 185 Walt Tkaczuk | 1.50 | .70 |
| ❑ 186 Gilles Villemure | 3.00 | 1.35 |
| ❑ 187 Philadelphia Flyers Team Crest | 3.00 | 1.35 |
| ❑ 188 Barry Ashbee | 2.00 | .90 |
| ❑ 189 Serge Bernier | 1.00 | .45 |
| ❑ 190 Larry Brown | 1.00 | .45 |
| ❑ 191 Bobby Clarke | 20.00 | 9.00 |
| ❑ 192 Gary Dornhoefer | 1.50 | .70 |
| ❑ 193 Doug Favell | 3.00 | 1.35 |
| ❑ 194 Bruce Gamble | 4.00 | 1.80 |
| ❑ 195 Jean-Guy Gendron | 1.00 | .45 |
| ❑ 196 Larry Hale | 1.00 | .45 |
| ❑ 197 Wayne Hillman | 1.00 | .45 |
| ❑ 198 Brent Hughes | 1.00 | .45 |
| ❑ 199 Jim Johnson | 1.00 | .45 |
| ❑ 200 Bob Kelly | 1.00 | .45 |
| ❑ 201 Andre Lacroix | 1.50 | .70 |
| ❑ 202 Bill Lesuk | 1.00 | .45 |
| ❑ 203 Rick MacLeish | 2.00 | .90 |
| ❑ 204 Larry Mickey | 1.00 | .45 |
| ❑ 205 Simon Nolet | 1.00 | .45 |
| ❑ 206 Pierre Plante | 1.00 | .45 |
| ❑ 207 Ed Van Impe | 1.00 | .45 |
| ❑ 208 Joe Watson | 1.00 | .45 |
| ❑ 209 Pittsburgh Penguins Team Crest | 2.00 | .90 |
| ❑ 210 Syl Apps | 1.50 | .70 |
| ❑ 211 Les Binkley | 3.00 | 1.35 |
| ❑ 212 Wally Boyer | 1.00 | .45 |
| ❑ 213 Darryl Edestrand | 1.00 | .45 |
| ❑ 214 Roy Edwards | 3.00 | 1.35 |
| ❑ 215 Nick Harbaruk | 1.00 | .45 |
| ❑ 216 Bryan Hextall | 1.50 | .70 |
| ❑ 217 Bill Hicke | 1.00 | .45 |
| ❑ 218 Tim Horton | 10.00 | 4.50 |
| ❑ 219 Sheldon Kannegiesser | 1.00 | .45 |
| ❑ 220 Bob Leiter | 1.00 | .45 |
| ❑ 221 Keith McCreary | 1.00 | .45 |
| ❑ 222 Joe Noris | 1.00 | .45 |
| ❑ 223 Greg Polis | 1.00 | .45 |
| ❑ 224 Jean Pronovost | 1.50 | .70 |
| ❑ 225 Rene Robert | 1.50 | .70 |
| ❑ 226 Duane Rupp | 1.00 | .4 |
| ❑ 227 Ken Schinkel | 1.00 | .4 |
| ❑ 228 Ron Schock | 1.00 | .4 |
| ❑ 229 Bryan Watson | 1.50 | .7 |
| ❑ 230 Bob Woytowich | 1.00 | .4 |
| ❑ 231 St. Louis Blues Team Crest | 2.00 | .9 |
| ❑ 232 Al Arbour | 3.00 | 1.3 |
| ❑ 233 John Arbour | 1.00 | .4 |
| ❑ 234 Chris Bordeleau | 1.00 | .4 |
| ❑ 235 Carl Brewer | 1.50 | .7 |
| ❑ 236 Gene Carr | 1.00 | .4 |
| ❑ 237 Wayne Connelly | 1.00 | .4 |
| ❑ 238 Terry Crisp | 1.50 | .7 |
| ❑ 239 Jim Lorentz | 1.00 | .4 |
| ❑ 240 Peter McDuffe | 2.00 | .9 |
| ❑ 241 George Morrison | 1.00 | .4 |
| ❑ 242 Michel Parizeau | 1.00 | .4 |
| ❑ 243 Noel Picard | 1.00 | .4 |
| ❑ 244 Barclay Plager | 1.50 | .7 |
| ❑ 245 Bob Plager | 1.50 | .7 |
| ❑ 246 Jim Roberts | 1.00 | .4 |
| ❑ 247 Gary Sabourin | 1.00 | .4 |
| ❑ 248 Jim Shires | 1.00 | .4 |

❑ 249 Frank St.Marseille .......... 1.00 .45
❑ 250 Bill Sutherland .......... 1.00 .45
❑ 251 Garry Unger .......... 2.00 .90
❑ 252 Ernie Wakely .......... 3.00 1.35
❑ 253 Toronto Maple Leafs .......... 3.00 1.35
Team Crest
❑ 254 Bob Baun .......... 1.50 .70
❑ 255 Jim Dorey .......... 1.00 .45
❑ 256 Denis Dupere .......... 1.00 .45
❑ 257 Ron Ellis .......... 1.50 .70
❑ 258 Brian Glennie .......... 1.00 .45
❑ 259 Jim Harrison .......... 1.00 .45
❑ 260 Paul Henderson .......... 2.00 .90
❑ 261 Dave Keon .......... 6.00 2.70
❑ 262 Rick Ley .......... 1.00 .45
❑ 263 Billy MacMillan .......... 1.00 .45
❑ 264 Don Marshall .......... 1.00 .45
❑ 265 Jim McKenny .......... 1.00 .45
❑ 266 Garry Monahan .......... 1.00 .45
❑ 267 Bernie Parent .......... 12.00 5.50
❑ 268 Mike Pelyk .......... 1.00 .45
❑ 269 Jacques Plante .......... 20.00 9.00
❑ 270 Brad Selwood .......... 1.00 .45
❑ 271 Darryl Sittler .......... 12.00 5.50
❑ 272 Brian Spencer .......... 2.00 .90
❑ 273 Guy Trottier .......... 1.00 .45
❑ 274 Norm Ullman .......... 5.00 2.20
❑ 275 Vancouver Canucks .......... 2.00 .90
Team Crest
❑ 276 Andre Boudrias .......... 1.00 .45
❑ 277 George Gardiner .......... 1.00 .45
❑ 278 Jocelyn Guevremont .......... 1.50 .70
❑ 279 Murray Hall .......... 1.00 .45
❑ 280 Danny Johnson .......... 1.00 .45
❑ 281 Dennis Kearns .......... 1.00 .45
❑ 282 Orland Kurtenbach .......... 1.50 .70
❑ 283 Bobby Lalonde .......... 1.00 .45
❑ 284 Wayne Maki .......... 1.00 .45
❑ 285 Rosaire Paiement .......... 1.50 .70
❑ 286 Paul Popiel .......... 1.00 .45
❑ 287 Pat Quinn .......... 2.00 .90
❑ 288 John Schella .......... 1.00 .45
❑ 289 Bobby Schmautz .......... 1.50 .70
❑ 290 Fred Speck .......... 1.00 .45
❑ 291 Dale Tallon .......... 1.50 .70
❑ 292 Ron Ward .......... 1.00 .45
❑ 293 Barry Wilkins .......... 1.00 .45
❑ 294 Dunc Wilson .......... 3.00 1.35
❑ xx Binder .......... 25.00 11.00
❑ NNO Introduction Card .......... 4.00 1.80
(Written by Scott Young)

## 1936 Triumph Postcards

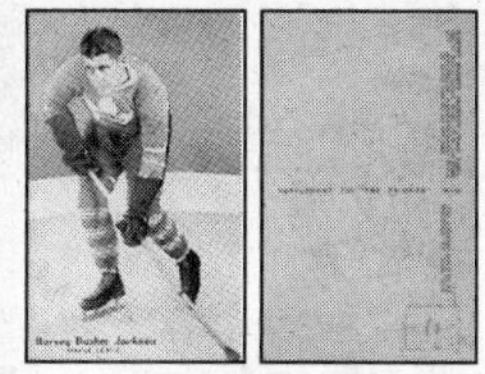

This eleven-card set was issued as a supplement to The Triumph (a newspaper). The cards measure approximately 3 1/2" by 5 1/2" and are in the postcard format. The borderless fronts feature full-length black and white posed action shots. The player's name and team name appear in the lower left corner. The back carries the typical postcard design with each player's name and biographical information in the upper corner. Different dates appear on the back of the cards, which represent the date each card was distributed. The cards were issued three the first week with The Triumph, then one per week thereafter. The cards are unnumbered and checklisted below in alphabetical order. The date mentioned below is the issue date as noted on the card back in Canadian style, day/month/year.

EX-MT VG-E
COMPLETE SET (11) .......... 1300.00 650.00
COMMON CARD .......... 80.00 40.00

1 Lionel Conacher .......... 250.00 125.00
22/2/36
2 Harvey(Busher) Jackson. 250.00 125.00
18/1/36
3 Ivan(Ching) Johnson .......... 125.00 60.00
8/2/36
4 Herbie Lewis .......... 80.00 40.00
7/3/36
5 Sylvio Mantha .......... 125.00 60.00
18/1/36
6 Nick Metz .......... 80.00 40.00
15/2/36
7 Baldy Northcott .......... 90.00 45.00
Montreal Maroons
1/2/36
8 Eddie Shore .......... 500.00 250.00
25/1/36
9 Paul Thompson .......... 80.00 40.00
29/2/36
10 Roy Worters .......... 125.00 60.00
New York Americans
18/1/36
11 Charley Conacher .......... 80.00 40.00

## 1998-99 UD Choice Preview

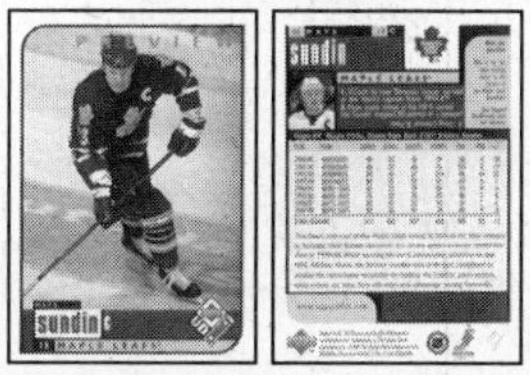

The 1998-99 UD Choice Preview set was issued in one series totalling 60 cards. The 6-card packs retail for $.79 each. Set is skip numbered.

MINT NRMT
COMPLETE SET (60) .......... 10.00 4.50
COMMON CARD .......... .15 .07

❑ 1 Guy Hebert .......... .30 .14
❑ 5 Travis Green .......... .15 .07
❑ 11 Ted Donato .......... .15 .07
❑ 13 Sergei Samsonov .......... .60 .25
❑ 15 Ray Bourque .......... .40 .18
❑ 21 Brian Holzinger .......... .15 .07
❑ 23 Dominik Hasek .......... .75 .35
❑ 25 Erik Rasmussen .......... .15 .07
❑ 31 Valeri Bure .......... .15 .07
❑ 33 Cory Stillman .......... .15 .07
❑ 35 Jarome Iginla .......... .15 .07
❑ 41 Glen Wesley .......... .15 .07
❑ 43 Nelson Emerson .......... .15 .07
❑ 45 Eric Daze .......... .15 .07
❑ 51 Tony Amonte .......... .30 .14
❑ 53 Eric Messier .......... .15 .07
❑ 55 Claude Lemieux .......... .15 .07
❑ 61 Jamie Langenbrunner .......... .15 .07
❑ 63 Ed Belfour .......... .40 .18
❑ 65 Derian Hatcher .......... .15 .07
❑ 71 Igor Larionov .......... .15 .07
❑ 73 Steve Yzerman .......... 1.25 .55
❑ 75 Sergei Fedorov .......... .75 .35
❑ 78 Slava Kozlov .......... .15 .07
❑ 81 Curtis Joseph .......... .15 .07
❑ 83 Boris Mironov .......... .15 .07
❑ 85 Doug Weight .......... .30 .14
❑ 90 Scott Mellanby .......... .15 .07
❑ 91 Ed Jovanovski .......... .15 .07
❑ 93 Dino Ciccarelli .......... .30 .14
❑ 95 Rob Blake .......... .30 .14
❑ 101 Vladimir Tsyplakov .......... .15 .07
❑ 103 Shayne Corson .......... .15 .07
❑ 105 Saku Koivu .......... .60 .25
❑ 111 Brian Savage .......... .15 .07
❑ 113 Scott Stevens .......... .15 .07
❑ 115 Bobby Holik .......... .15 .07
❑ 121 Zigmund Palffy .......... .40 .18
❑ 123 Bryan Berard .......... .15 .07
❑ 125 Kenny Jonsson .......... .15 .07
❑ 131 Dan Cloutier .......... .15 .07
❑ 133 Marc Savard .......... .15 .07
❑ 135 Mike Richter .......... .40 .18
❑ 141 Alexei Yashin .......... .30 .14
❑ 143 Chris Phillips .......... .15 .07
❑ 151 Paul Coffey .......... .40 .18
❑ 153 John LeClair .......... .60 .25
❑ 161 Brad Isbister .......... .15 .07
❑ 163 Daniel Briere .......... .15 .07
❑ 171 Robert Dome .......... .15 .07
❑ 173 Patrick Marleau .......... .15 .07
❑ 181 Marco Sturm .......... .15 .07
❑ 183 Brett Hull .......... .50 .23
❑ 190 Geoff Courtnall .......... .15 .07
❑ 191 Daren Puppa .......... .15 .07
❑ 193 Stephane Richer .......... .30 .14
❑ 201 Sergei Berezin .......... .30 .14
❑ 203 Mats Sundin .......... .40 .18
❑ 211 Mark Messier .......... .50 .23
❑ 213 Peter Bondra .......... .40 .18

## 1998-99 UD Choice

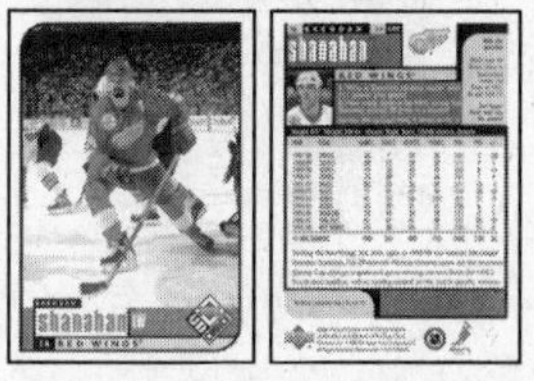

The 1998-99 Upper Deck UD Choice set was issued with a total of 220 cards. The 12-card packs retail for $1.29 each. The set contains the subsets: GM's Choice (221-242), Crease Lightning (244-252), and Jr. Showcase (253-307). The fronts feature color action photos surrounded by a white border.

MINT NRMT
COMPLETE SET (310) .......... 30.00 13.50
COMMON CARD (1-310) .......... .10 .05

❑ 1 Guy Hebert .......... .25 .11
❑ 2 Mikhail Shtalenkov .......... .10 .05
❑ 3 Josef Marha .......... .10 .05
❑ 4 Paul Kariya .......... 1.25 .55
❑ 5 Travis Green .......... .10 .05
❑ 6 Steve Rucchin .......... .10 .05
❑ 7 Matt Cullen .......... .10 .05
❑ 8 Teemu Selanne .......... .60 .25
❑ 9 Antti Aalto .......... .10 .05
❑ 10 Byron Dafoe .......... .25 .11
❑ 11 Ted Donato .......... .10 .05
❑ 12 Dimitri Khristich .......... .10 .05
❑ 13 Sergei Samsonov .......... .50 .23
❑ 14 Jason Allison .......... .25 .11
❑ 15 Ray Bourque .......... .30 .14
❑ 16 Kyle McLaren .......... .10 .05
❑ 17 Cameron Mann .......... .10 .05
❑ 18 Shawn Bates .......... .10 .05
❑ 19 Joe Thornton .......... .30 .14
❑ 20 Vaclav Varada .......... .10 .05
❑ 21 Brian Holzinger .......... .10 .05
❑ 22 Miroslav Satan .......... .25 .11
❑ 23 Dominik Hasek .......... .60 .25
❑ 24 Michael Peca .......... .10 .05
❑ 25 Erik Rasmussen .......... .10 .05
❑ 26 Alexei Zhitnik .......... .10 .05
❑ 27 Geoff Sanderson .......... .25 .11
❑ 28 Donald Audette .......... .10 .05
❑ 29 Derek Morris .......... .10 .05
❑ 30 German Titov .......... .10 .05
❑ 31 Valeri Bure .......... .10 .05
❑ 32 Michael Nylander .......... .10 .05
❑ 33 Cory Stillman .......... .10 .05
❑ 34 Theoren Fleury .......... .30 .14
❑ 35 Jarome Iginla .......... .10 .05
❑ 36 Gary Roberts .......... .10 .05
❑ 37 Jeff O'Neill .......... .10 .05
❑ 38 Bates Battaglia RC .......... .25 .11
❑ 39 Keith Primeau .......... .25 .11
❑ 40 Sami Kapanen .......... .25 .11
❑ 41 Glen Wesley .......... .10 .05
❑ 42 Trevor Kidd .......... .25 .11
❑ 43 Nelson Emerson .......... .10 .05
❑ 44 Daniel Cleary .......... .10 .05
❑ 45 Eric Daze .......... .10 .05
❑ 46 Chris Chelios .......... .30 .14
❑ 47 Gary Suter .......... .10 .05
❑ 48 Alexei Zhamnov .......... .10 .05
❑ 49 Jeff Hackett .......... .25 .11
❑ 50 Dmitri Nabokov .......... .10 .05
❑ 51 Tony Amonte .......... .25 .11
❑ 52 Jean-Yves Leroux .......... .10 .05
❑ 53 Eric Messier .......... .10 .05
❑ 54 Patrick Roy .......... 1.50 .70
❑ 55 Claude Lemieux .......... .25 .11
❑ 56 Peter Forsberg .......... 1.00 .45
❑ 57 Adam Deadmarsh .......... .25 .11
❑ 58 Valeri Kamensky .......... .10 .05
❑ 59 Joe Sakic .......... .60 .25
❑ 60 Sandis Ozolinsh .......... .25 .11
❑ 61 Jamie Langenbrunner .......... .10 .05
❑ 62 Joe Nieuwendyk .......... .25 .11
❑ 63 Ed Belfour .......... .30 .14
❑ 64 Juha Lind .......... .10 .05
❑ 65 Derian Hatcher .......... .10 .05
❑ 66 Sergei Zubov .......... .10 .05
❑ 67 Darryl Sydor .......... .10 .05
❑ 68 Jere Lehtinen .......... .10 .05
❑ 69 Mike Modano .......... .40 .18
❑ 70 Larry Murphy .......... .25 .11
❑ 71 Igor Larionov .......... .10 .05
❑ 72 Darren McCarty .......... .10 .05
❑ 73 Steve Yzerman .......... 1.00 .45
❑ 74 Chris Osgood .......... .30 .14
❑ 75 Sergei Fedorov .......... .60 .25
❑ 76 Brendan Shanahan .......... .60 .25
❑ 77 Nicklas Lidstrom .......... .25 .11
❑ 78 Vyacheslav Kozlov .......... .10 .05
❑ 79 Dean McAmmond .......... .10 .05
❑ 80 Roman Hamrlik .......... .10 .05
❑ 81 Curtis Joseph .......... .30 .14
❑ 82 Ryan Smyth .......... .25 .11
❑ 83 Boris Mironov .......... .10 .05
❑ 84 Bill Guerin .......... .25 .11
❑ 85 Doug Weight .......... .25 .11
❑ 86 Janne Niinimaa .......... .10 .05
❑ 87 Ray Whitney .......... .10 .05
❑ 88 Robert Svehla .......... .10 .05
❑ 89 John Vanbiesbrouck .......... .50 .23
❑ 90 Scott Mellanby .......... .10 .05
❑ 91 Ed Jovanovski .......... .10 .05
❑ 92 Dave Gagner .......... .10 .05
❑ 93 Dino Ciccarelli .......... .25 .11
❑ 94 Rob Niedermayer .......... .10 .05
❑ 95 Rob Blake .......... .25 .11
❑ 96 Yanic Perreault .......... .10 .05
❑ 97 Stephane Fiset .......... .25 .11
❑ 98 Luc Robitaille .......... .25 .11
❑ 99 Glen Murray .......... .10 .05
❑ 100 Jozef Stumpel .......... .25 .11
❑ 101 Vladimir Tsyplakov .......... .10 .05
❑ 102 Donald MacLean .......... .10 .05
❑ 103 Shayne Corson .......... .10 .05
❑ 104 Vladimir Malakhov .......... .10 .05
❑ 105 Saku Koivu .......... .50 .23
❑ 106 Andy Moog .......... .25 .11
❑ 107 Matt Higgins .......... .10 .05
❑ 108 Dave Manson .......... .10 .05
❑ 109 Mark Recchi .......... .25 .11
❑ 110 Vincent Damphousse .......... .25 .11
❑ 111 Brian Savage .......... .10 .05
❑ 112 Petr Sykora .......... .10 .05
❑ 113 Scott Stevens .......... .10 .05
❑ 114 Patrik Elias .......... .25 .11
❑ 115 Bobby Holik .......... .10 .05
❑ 116 Martin Brodeur .......... .75 .35
❑ 117 Doug Gilmour .......... .25 .11
❑ 118 Jason Arnott .......... .25 .11
❑ 119 Scott Niedermayer .......... .10 .05
❑ 120 Brendan Morrison .......... .10 .05
❑ 121 Zigmund Palffy .......... .30 .14
❑ 122 Trevor Linden .......... .25 .11
❑ 123 Bryan Berard .......... .25 .11
❑ 124 Zdeno Chara .......... .10 .05
❑ 125 Kenny Jonsson .......... .10 .05
❑ 126 Robert Reichel .......... .10 .05
❑ 127 Bryan Smolinski .......... .10 .05
❑ 128 Wayne Gretzky .......... 2.00 .90
❑ 129 Brian Leetch .......... .30 .14
❑ 130 Pat Lafontaine .......... .25 .11
❑ 131 Dan Cloutier .......... .10 .05
❑ 132 Niklas Sundstrom .......... .10 .05
❑ 133 Marc Savard .......... .10 .05
❑ 134 Adam Graves .......... .25 .11
❑ 135 Mike Richter .......... .30 .14
❑ 136 Jeff Beukeboom .......... .10 .05
❑ 137 Daniel Goneau .......... .10 .05
❑ 138 Shawn McEachern .......... .10 .05
❑ 139 Damian Rhodes .......... .25 .11
❑ 140 Wade Redden .......... .10 .05
❑ 141 Alexei Yashin .......... .25 .11
❑ 142 Marian Hossa .......... .25 .11
❑ 143 Chris Phillips .......... .10 .05
❑ 144 Daniel Alfredsson .......... .25 .11
❑ 145 Vaclav Prospal .......... .10 .05
❑ 146 Andreas Dackell .......... .10 .05
❑ 147 Sean Burke .......... .10 .05
❑ 148 Alexandre Daigle .......... .10 .05
❑ 149 Rod Brind'Amour .......... .25 .11
❑ 150 Chris Gratton .......... .25 .11
❑ 151 Paul Coffey .......... .30 .14
❑ 152 Eric Lindros .......... 1.00 .45
❑ 153 John LeClair .......... .50 .23
❑ 154 Chris Therien .......... .10 .05
❑ 155 Keith Carney .......... .10 .05
❑ 156 Craig Janney .......... .10 .05
❑ 157 Teppo Numminen .......... .10 .05
❑ 158 Jeremy Roenick .......... .30 .14
❑ 159 Oleg Tverdovsky .......... .10 .05
❑ 160 Keith Tkachuk .......... .40 .18
❑ 161 Brad Isbister .......... .10 .05
❑ 162 Nikolai Khabibulin .......... .25 .11
❑ 163 Daniel Briere .......... .10 .05
❑ 164 Juha Ylonen .......... .10 .05
❑ 165 Tom Barrasso .......... .25 .11
❑ 166 Alexei Morozov .......... .10 .05
❑ 167 Stu Barnes .......... .10 .05
❑ 168 Jaromir Jagr .......... 1.00 .45
❑ 169 Ron Francis .......... .25 .11
❑ 170 Peter Skudra .......... .10 .05
❑ 171 Robert Dome .......... .10 .05
❑ 172 Kevin Hatcher .......... .10 .05
❑ 173 Patrick Marleau .......... .10 .05
❑ 174 Jeff Friesen .......... .25 .11
❑ 175 Owen Nolan .......... .25 .11
❑ 176 John MacLean .......... .10 .05
❑ 177 Mike Vernon .......... .25 .11
❑ 178 Marcus Ragnarsson .......... .10 .05
❑ 179 Andrei Zyuzin .......... .10 .05
❑ 180 Mike Ricci .......... .25 .11
❑ 181 Marco Sturm .......... .10 .05
❑ 182 Steve Duchesne .......... .10 .05
❑ 183 Brett Hull .......... .40 .18
❑ 184 Pierre Turgeon .......... .25 .11
❑ 185 Chris Pronger .......... .25 .11
❑ 186 Pavol Demitra .......... .25 .11
❑ 187 Jamie McLennan .......... .10 .05
❑ 188 Al MacInnis .......... .25 .11
❑ 189 Jim Campbell .......... .10 .05
❑ 190 Geoff Courtnall .......... .10 .05
❑ 191 Daren Puppa .......... .25 .11
❑ 192 Daymond Langkow .......... .10 .05
❑ 193 Stephane Richer .......... .25 .11
❑ 194 Paul Ysebaert .......... .10 .05
❑ 195 Alexander Selivanov .......... .10 .05
❑ 196 Rob Zamuner .......... .10 .05
❑ 197 Mikael Renberg .......... .25 .11
❑ 198 Mathieu Schneider .......... .10 .05
❑ 199 Mike Johnson .......... .10 .05
❑ 200 Alyn McCauley .......... .10 .05
❑ 201 Sergei Berezin .......... .25 .11
❑ 202 Wendel Clark .......... .25 .11
❑ 203 Mats Sundin .......... .30 .14
❑ 204 Tie Domi .......... .10 .05
❑ 205 Jyrki Lumme .......... .10 .05
❑ 206 Mattias Ohlund .......... .25 .11
❑ 207 Garth Snow .......... .25 .11
❑ 208 Pavel Bure .......... .60 .25
❑ 209 Dave Scatchard .......... .10 .05
❑ 210 Alexander Mogilny .......... .25 .11
❑ 211 Mark Messier .......... .40 .18
❑ 212 Todd Bertuzzi .......... .10 .05
❑ 213 Peter Bondra .......... .30 .14
❑ 214 Joe Juneau .......... .25 .11
❑ 215 Olaf Kolzig .......... .25 .11
❑ 216 Jan Bulis .......... .10 .05
❑ 217 Adam Oates .......... .25 .11
❑ 218 Richard Zednik .......... .10 .05
❑ 219 Calle Johansson .......... .10 .05
❑ 220 Phil Housley .......... .10 .05
❑ 221 Dominik Hasek GM .......... .30 .14
❑ 222 Ray Bourque GM .......... .10 .05
❑ 223 Chris Chelios GM .......... .30 .14
❑ 224 Paul Kariya GM .......... .60 .25
❑ 225 Wayne Gretzky GM .......... 1.00 .45
❑ 226 Jaromir Jagr GM .......... .50 .23
❑ 227 Rob Blake GM .......... .10 .05
❑ 228 Adam Foote GM .......... .10 .05
❑ 229 Peter Forsberg GM .......... .50 .23
❑ 230 Joe Sakic GM .......... .25 .11
❑ 231 Mark Recchi GM .......... .25 .11
❑ 232 Patrick Roy GM .......... .75 .35
❑ 233 Nicklas Lidstrom GM .......... .10 .05
❑ 234 Rob Blake GM .......... .10 .05
❑ 235 John LeClair GM .......... .25 .11
❑ 236 Wayne Gretzky GM .......... 1.00 .45
❑ 237 Eric Lindros GM .......... .60 .25
❑ 238 Brian Leetch GM .......... .30 .14
❑ 239 Scott Stevens GM .......... .10 .05
❑ 240 Paul Kariya GM .......... .60 .25
❑ 241 Peter Forsberg GM .......... .50 .23
❑ 242 Teemu Selanne GM .......... .30 .14
❑ 243 Patrick Roy CRL .......... .75 .35
❑ 244 Dominik Hasek CRL .......... .30 .14
❑ 245 Martin Brodeur CRL .......... .40 .18
❑ 246 Mike Richter CRL .......... .15 .07
❑ 247 John Vanbiesbrouck CRL .......... .25 .11
❑ 248 Chris Osgood CRL .......... .30 .14
❑ 249 Ed Belfour CRL .......... .30 .14
❑ 250 Tom Barrasso CRL .......... .25 .11
❑ 251 Curtis Joseph CRL .......... .30 .14
❑ 252 Sean Burke CRL .......... .10 .05
❑ 253 Josh Holden .......... .25 .11
❑ 254 Daniel Tkaczuk .......... .25 .11
❑ 256 Eric Brewer .......... .25 .11
❑ 257 Alex Tanguay .......... .30 .14
❑ 258 Roberto Luongo .......... .50 .23
❑ 259 Vincent Lecavalier .......... 1.00 .45
❑ 260 Mathieu Garon .......... .10 .05
❑ 261 Brad Ference .......... .10 .05
❑ 262 Jesse Wallin .......... .10 .05
❑ 263 Zenith Komarniski .......... .10 .05
❑ 264 Sean Blanchard .......... .10 .05
❑ 265 Cory Sarich .......... .10 .05
❑ 266 Mike Van Ryn .......... .10 .05
❑ 267 Steve Begin .......... .10 .05
❑ 268 Matt Cooke .......... .10 .05
❑ 269 Daniel Corso .......... .10 .05
❑ 270 Brett McLean .......... .10 .05
❑ 271 Jean-Pierre Dumont .......... .10 .05
❑ 272 Jason Ward .......... .10 .05
❑ 273 Brian Willsie .......... .10 .05
❑ 274 Matt Bradley .......... .10 .05
❑ 275 Olli Jokinen .......... .10 .05
❑ 276 Teemu Elomo .......... .10 .05
❑ 277 Timo Vertala .......... .10 .05
❑ 278 Mika Noronen .......... .10 .05
❑ 279 Pasi Petrilainen .......... .10 .05
❑ 280 Timo Ahmaoja .......... .10 .05
❑ 281 Eero Somervuori .......... .10 .05
❑ 282 Maxim Afinogenov .......... .40 .18
❑ 283 Maxim Balmochnykh .......... .10 .05
❑ 284 Artem Chubarov .......... .10 .05
❑ 285 Vitali Vishnevsky .......... .10 .05
❑ 286 Denis Shvidky .......... .40 .18
❑ 287 Dmitri Vlasenkov .......... .10 .05
❑ 288 Magnus Nilsson .......... .10 .05
❑ 289 Mikael Holmqvist .......... .10 .05
❑ 290 Mattias Karlin .......... .10 .05
❑ 291 Pierre Hedin .......... .10 .05
❑ 292 Henrik Petre .......... .10 .05
❑ 293 Johan Forsander .......... .10 .05
❑ 294 Daniel Sedin .......... .30 .14
❑ 295 Henrik Sedin .......... .30 .14
❑ 296 Marcus Nilsson .......... .10 .05
❑ 297 Paul Mara .......... .10 .05
❑ 298 Brian Gionta .......... .10 .05
❑ 299 Chris Hajt .......... .10 .05
❑ 300 Mike Mottau .......... .10 .05
❑ 301 Jean-Marc Pelletier .......... .10 .05
❑ 302 David Legwand .......... .60 .25
❑ 303 Ty Jones .......... .10 .05
❑ 304 Nikos Tselios .......... .10 .05
❑ 305 Jesse Boulerice .......... .10 .05
❑ 306 Jeff Farkas .......... .10 .05
❑ 307 Toby Petersen .......... .10 .05
❑ 308 Wayne Gretzky CL .......... 1.00 .45
❑ 309 Patrick Roy CL .......... .75 .35
❑ 310 Steve Yzerman CL .......... .50 .23

## 1998-99 UD Choice Prime Choice Reserve

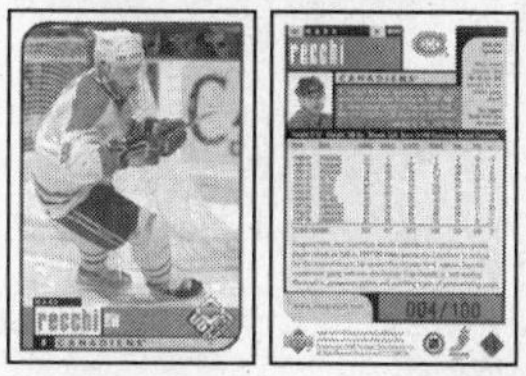

This hobby-only parallel showcases the same players found in the UD Choice base set, except each card is foil-stamped with the words "Prime Choice Reserve". The set is sequentially numbered to 100.

MINT NRMT
COMMON CARD (1-310) .......... 10.00 4.50
*STARS: 75X TO 150X BASIC CARDS
*YOUNG STARS: 60X TO 120X
*RC's: 40X TO 80X

## 1998-99 UD Choice Reserve

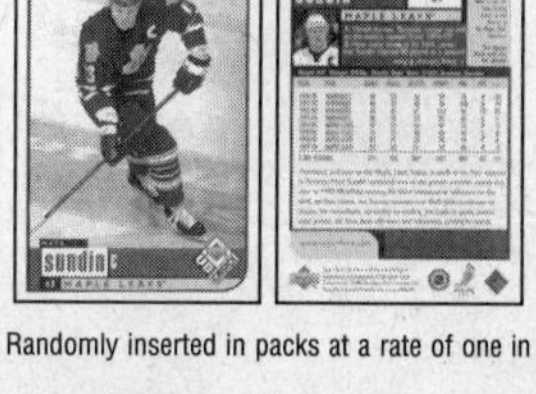

Randomly inserted in packs at a rate of one in

6, this 310-card parallel showcases the same players found in the UD Choice base set, except each card sports a distinctive foil treatment.

| | MINT | NRMT |
|---|---|---|
| COMPLETE SET (310) | 200.00 | 90.00 |
| COMMON CARD (1-310) | .60 | .25 |

*STARS: 3X TO 6X BASIC CARDS
*YOUNG STARS: 2.5X TO 5X
*RC's: 2X TO 4X

## 1998-99 UD Choice Mini Bobbing Head

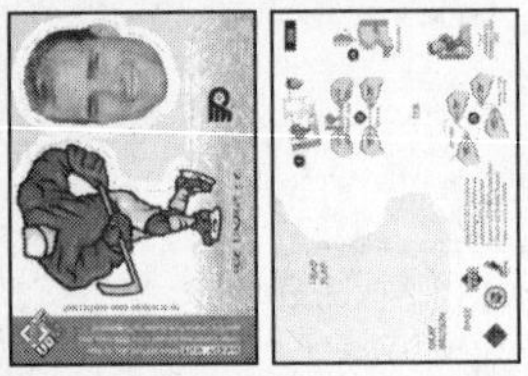

Randomly inserted in packs at a rate of one in 4, this 30-card insert features specially enhanced miniatures that fold into a stand-up figure with a removable bobbing head.

| | MINT | NRMT |
|---|---|---|
| COMPLETE SET (30) | 40.00 | 18.00 |
| COMMON CARD (BH1-BH30) | .60 | .25 |

| | | |
|---|---|---|
| ❑ BH1 Wayne Gretzky | 5.00 | 2.20 |
| ❑ BH2 Keith Tkachuk | 1.00 | .45 |
| ❑ BH3 Ray Bourque | .75 | .35 |
| ❑ BH4 Brett Hull | 1.00 | .45 |
| ❑ BH5 Jaromir Jagr | 2.50 | 1.10 |
| ❑ BH6 John Leclair | 1.25 | .55 |
| ❑ BH7 Martin Brodeur | 2.00 | .90 |
| ❑ BH8 Eric Lindros | 2.50 | 1.10 |
| ❑ BH9 Mark Messier | 1.00 | .45 |
| ❑ BH10 John Vanbiesbrouck | 1.25 | .55 |
| ❑ BH11 Paul Kariya | 3.00 | 1.35 |
| ❑ BH12 Luc Robitaille | .60 | .25 |
| ❑ BH13 Zigmund Palffy | 1.00 | .45 |
| ❑ BH14 Peter Forsberg | 2.50 | 1.10 |
| ❑ BH15 Teemu Selanne | 1.50 | .70 |
| ❑ BH16 Mike Modano | 1.00 | .45 |
| ❑ BH17 Mats Sundin | .75 | .35 |
| ❑ BH18 Dominik Hasek | 1.50 | .70 |
| ❑ BH19 Joe Sakic | 1.50 | .70 |
| ❑ BH20 Rob Blake | .60 | .25 |
| ❑ BH21 Patrick Roy | 4.00 | 1.80 |
| ❑ BH22 Sergei Samsonov | 1.25 | .55 |
| ❑ BH23 Chris Chelios | .75 | .35 |
| ❑ BH24 Brendan Shanahan | 1.50 | .70 |
| ❑ BH25 Theoren Fleury | .75 | .35 |
| ❑ BH26 Ed Belfour | .75 | .35 |
| ❑ BH27 Steve Yzerman | 2.50 | 1.10 |
| ❑ BH28 Saku Koivu | 1.25 | .55 |
| ❑ BH29 Brian Leetch | .75 | .35 |
| ❑ BH30 Pavel Bure | 1.50 | .70 |

## 1998-99 UD Choice StarQuest Blue

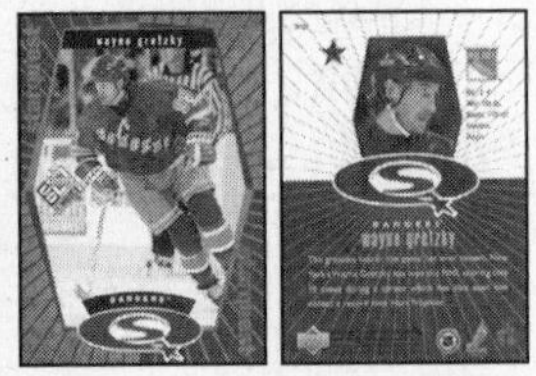

The 1998-99 UD Choice StarQuest insert set salutes 30 of the NHL's top players with each of four 30-card tiers representing a different insert ratio. The cards feature color action player photos in different colored borders and with a different number of stars in the left bottom corner according to which tier the card is from. StarQuest Blue has one star and is inserted one per pack; StarQuest Green has two stars with an insertion rate of 1:7; StarQuest Red features three stars and an insertion rate of 1:23; StarQuest Gold is a limited-edition set and displays four stars. Only 100 sequentially numbered Gold sets were made.

| | MINT | NRMT |
|---|---|---|
| COMPLETE SET (30) | 30.00 | 13.50 |
| COMMON CARD (SQ1-SQ30) | .40 | .18 |

*GREEN: 1.5X TO 3X BASIC CARDS
GREEN STATED ODDS 1:7
*RED: 4X TO 8X BASIC CARDS
RED STATED ODDS 1:23
*GOLD: 50X TO 100X BASIC CARDS
GOLD: RANDOM INSERTS IN PACKS

| | | |
|---|---|---|
| ❑ SQ1 Wayne Gretzky | 3.00 | 1.35 |
| ❑ SQ2 Pavel Bure | 1.00 | .45 |
| ❑ SQ3 Patrick Roy | 2.50 | 1.10 |
| ❑ SQ4 Dominik Hasek | 1.00 | .45 |
| ❑ SQ5 Teemu Selanne | 1.00 | .45 |
| ❑ SQ6 Sergei Samsonov | .75 | .35 |
| ❑ SQ7 Brian Leetch | .50 | .23 |
| ❑ SQ8 Saku Koivu | .75 | .35 |
| ❑ SQ9 Brendan Shanahan | 1.00 | .45 |
| ❑ SQ10 Alexei Yashin | .40 | .18 |
| ❑ SQ11 Joe Sakic | 1.00 | .45 |
| ❑ SQ12 Patrik Elias | .40 | .18 |
| ❑ SQ13 Theoren Fleury | .50 | .23 |
| ❑ SQ14 Peter Bondra | .50 | .23 |
| ❑ SQ15 John LeClair | .75 | .35 |
| ❑ SQ16 Jaromir Jagr | 1.50 | .70 |
| ❑ SQ17 Ed Belfour | .50 | .23 |
| ❑ SQ18 Steve Yzerman | 1.50 | .70 |
| ❑ SQ19 Mats Sundin | .50 | .23 |
| ❑ SQ20 Peter Forsberg | 1.50 | .70 |
| ❑ SQ21 Ray Bourque | .50 | .23 |
| ❑ SQ22 Brett Hull | .60 | .25 |
| ❑ SQ23 Martin Brodeur | 1.25 | .55 |
| ❑ SQ24 Mike Modano | .60 | .25 |
| ❑ SQ25 Paul Kariya | 2.00 | .90 |
| ❑ SQ26 Tony Amonte | .40 | .18 |
| ❑ SQ27 Mike Johnson | .40 | .18 |
| ❑ SQ28 Eric Lindros | 1.50 | .70 |
| ❑ SQ29 Mark Messier | .60 | .25 |
| ❑ SQ30 Keith Tkachuk | .60 | .25 |

## 1998-99 UD3

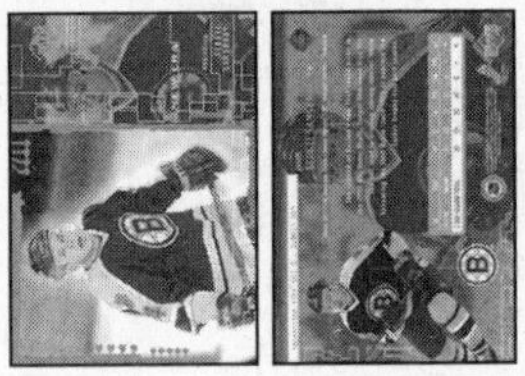

The 1998-99 UD3 set is comprised of six 30-card subsets each printed with three different technologies and features color action player photos. The Embossed technology subsets include New Era (1-30) inserted 1:1 and Three Star Spotlight (151-180) inserted 1:23. The Light F/X technology subsets include new Era (61-90) inserted 1:1 and Three Star Spotlight (91-120). The Rainbow Foil technology subsets include New Era (121-150) inserted 1:5 and Three Star Spotlight (31-60) inserted 1:1.

| | MINT | NRMT |
|---|---|---|
| COMPLETE SET (180) | 700.00 | 325.00 |
| COMP.NEW.ERA.EMB.SET (30) | 20.00 | 9.00 |
| COMMON NEW.ERA.EMB. (1-30) | .75 | .35 |
| NEW ERA EMB.SEMIS./GOALIES | 1.00 | .45 |
| NEW ERA EMB.UNLISTED STARS | 1.00 | .45 |
| NEW ERA EMB.ODDS 1:1 | | |
| COMP.3STAR.SEL.RAIN.SET(30) | 50.00 | 22.00 |
| COMMON 3ST.SEL.RAIN(31-60) | 1.00 | .45 |
| 3.STAR.SEL.SEMIS./GOALIES | 1.00 | .45 |
| 3.STAR.SEL.UNLISTED STARS. | 1.00 | .45 |
| 3.STAR.SEL.ODDS 1:1 | | |
| COMP.NEW ERA FX.SET (30) | 20.00 | 9.00 |
| COMMON NEW ERA FX. (61-90) | .75 | .35 |
| NEW ERA FX.SEMIS./GOALIES | 1.00 | .45 |
| NEW ERA FX.UNLISTED STARS | 1.00 | .45 |
| NEW ERA FX.ODDS 1:1 | | |
| COMP.3.ST.SEL.FX.SET (30) | 80.00 | 36.00 |
| COMM.3STAR.SEL.FX.(91-120) | 1.50 | .70 |
| 3.STAR.SEL.FX.SEMIS./GOALIES | 2.00 | .90 |
| 3.STAR.SEL.FX.UNLISTED STARS | | |
| 3.STAR.SEL.FX.ODDS 1:3 | | |
| COMP.NEWERA RAIN.SET(30) | 60.00 | 27.00 |
| COMM.NEWERA.RAIN(121-150) | 2.50 | 1.10 |
| NEW ERA RAIN.SEMIS/GOALIES | 3.00 | 1.35 |
| NEW ERA RAIN.UNLISTED STARS | 3.00 | 1.35 |
| NEW ERA RAIN.ODDS 1:5 | | |
| COMP.3.STAR.SEL.EMB.SET (30) | 500.00 | 220.00 |
| COMM.3ST.SEL.EMB(151-180) | 10.00 | 4.50 |
| 3.STAR.SEL.EMB.SEMIS./GOALIES | | |
| 3.STAR.SEL.EMB.UNLISTED STARS | | |
| 3.STAR.SEL.EMB.ODDS 1:23 | | |

| | | |
|---|---|---|
| ❑ 1 Sergei Samsonov NE | 3.00 | 1.35 |
| ❑ 2 Ryan Johnson NE | .75 | .35 |
| ❑ 3 Josef Marha NE | .75 | .35 |
| ❑ 4 Patrick Marleau NE | .75 | .35 |
| ❑ 5 Derek Morris NE | .75 | .35 |
| ❑ 6 Jamie Storr NE | 1.00 | .45 |
| ❑ 7 Richard Zednik NE | .75 | .35 |
| ❑ 8 Alyn McCauley NE | .75 | .35 |
| ❑ 9 Robert Dome NE | .75 | .35 |
| ❑ 10 Patrik Elias NE | 1.00 | .45 |
| ❑ 11 Olli Jokinen NE | 1.00 | .45 |
| ❑ 12 Warren Luhning NE | .75 | .35 |
| ❑ 13 Chris Phillips NE | .75 | .35 |
| ❑ 14 Mattias Ohlund NE | 1.00 | .45 |
| ❑ 15 Joe Thornton NE | .75 | .35 |
| ❑ 16 Matt Cullen NE | .75 | .35 |
| ❑ 17 Bates Battaglia NE | .75 | .35 |
| ❑ 18 Andrei Zyuzin NE | .75 | .35 |
| ❑ 19 Cameron Mann NE | .75 | .35 |
| ❑ 20 Zdeno Chara NE | .75 | .35 |
| ❑ 21 Marc Savard NE | .75 | .35 |
| ❑ 22 Alexei Morozov NE | .75 | .35 |
| ❑ 23 Mike Johnson NE | 1.00 | .45 |
| ❑ 24 Vaclav Varada NE | .75 | .35 |
| ❑ 25 Dan Cloutier NE | .75 | .35 |
| ❑ 26 Brad Isbister NE | .75 | .35 |
| ❑ 27 Marco Sturm NE | .75 | .35 |
| ❑ 28 Anders Eriksson NE | .75 | .35 |
| ❑ 29 Jan Bulis NE | .75 | .35 |
| ❑ 30 Brendan Morrison NE | 1.50 | .70 |
| ❑ 31 Wayne Gretzky TR | 6.00 | 2.70 |
| ❑ 32 Jaromir Jagr TR | 3.00 | 1.35 |
| ❑ 33 Peter Forsberg TR | 3.00 | 1.35 |
| ❑ 34 Paul Kariya TR | 4.00 | 1.80 |
| ❑ 35 Brett Hull TR | 1.25 | .55 |
| ❑ 36 Martin Brodeur TR | 2.50 | 1.10 |
| ❑ 37 Eric Lindros TR | 3.00 | 1.35 |
| ❑ 38 Peter Bondra TR | 1.00 | .45 |
| ❑ 39 Mike Modano TR | 1.25 | .55 |
| ❑ 40 Theoren Fleury TR | 1.00 | .45 |
| ❑ 41 Curtis Joseph TR | 1.00 | .45 |
| ❑ 42 Sergei Fedorov TR | 2.00 | .90 |
| ❑ 43 Saku Koivu TR | 1.50 | .70 |
| ❑ 44 Zigmund Palffy TR | 1.00 | .45 |
| ❑ 45 Ed Belfour TR | 1.00 | .45 |
| ❑ 46 Patrick Roy TR | 5.00 | 2.20 |
| ❑ 47 Brendan Shanahan TR | 2.00 | .90 |
| ❑ 48 Mats Sundin TR | 1.00 | .45 |
| ❑ 49 Alexei Yashin TR | 1.00 | .45 |
| ❑ 50 Doug Gilmour TR | 1.00 | .45 |
| ❑ 51 Chris Osgood TR | 1.00 | .45 |
| ❑ 52 Keith Tkachuk TR | 1.25 | .55 |
| ❑ 53 Mark Messier TR | 1.25 | .55 |
| ❑ 54 John Vanbiesbrouck TR | 1.50 | .70 |
| ❑ 55 Ray Bourque TR | 1.00 | .45 |
| ❑ 56 John LeClair TR | 1.50 | .70 |
| ❑ 57 Dominik Hasek TR | 2.00 | .90 |
| ❑ 58 Teemu Selanne TR | 2.00 | .90 |
| ❑ 59 Joe Sakic TR | 2.00 | .90 |
| ❑ 60 Steve Yzerman TR | 3.00 | 1.35 |
| ❑ 61 Sergei Samsonov NF | 3.00 | 1.35 |
| ❑ 62 Ryan Johnson NF | .75 | .35 |
| ❑ 63 Josef Marha NF | .75 | .35 |
| ❑ 64 Patrick Marleau NF | .75 | .35 |
| ❑ 65 Derek Morris NF | .75 | .35 |
| ❑ 66 Jamie Storr NF | 1.00 | .45 |
| ❑ 67 Richard Zednik NF | .75 | .35 |
| ❑ 68 Alyn McCauley NF | .75 | .35 |
| ❑ 69 Robert Dome NF | .75 | .35 |
| ❑ 70 Patrik Elias NF | 1.00 | .45 |
| ❑ 71 Olli Jokinen NF | 1.00 | .45 |
| ❑ 72 Warren Luhning NF | .75 | .35 |
| ❑ 73 Chris Phillips NF | .75 | .35 |
| ❑ 74 Mattias Ohlund NF | 1.00 | .45 |
| ❑ 75 Joe Thornton NF | .75 | .35 |
| ❑ 76 Matt Cullen NF | .75 | .35 |
| ❑ 77 Bates Battaglia NF | .75 | .35 |
| ❑ 78 Andrei Zyuzin NF | .75 | .35 |
| ❑ 79 Cameron Mann NF | 1.00 | .45 |
| ❑ 80 Zdeno Chara NF | .75 | .35 |
| ❑ 81 Marc Savard NF | .75 | .35 |
| ❑ 82 Alexei Morozov NF | 1.00 | .45 |
| ❑ 83 Mike Johnson NF | 1.00 | .45 |
| ❑ 84 Vaclav Varada NF | .75 | .35 |
| ❑ 85 Dan Cloutier NF | .75 | .35 |
| ❑ 86 Brad Isbister NF | .75 | .35 |
| ❑ 87 Marco Sturm NF | 1.00 | .45 |
| ❑ 88 Anders Eriksson NF | .75 | .35 |
| ❑ 89 Jan Bulis NF | .75 | .35 |
| ❑ 90 Brendan Morrison NF | 1.50 | .70 |
| ❑ 91 Wayne Gretzky TF | 10.00 | 4.50 |
| ❑ 92 Jaromir Jagr TF | 5.00 | 2.20 |
| ❑ 93 Peter Forsberg TF | 5.00 | 2.20 |
| ❑ 94 Paul Kariya TF | 6.00 | 2.70 |
| ❑ 95 Brett Hull TF | 2.00 | .90 |
| ❑ 96 Martin Brodeur TF | 4.00 | 1.80 |
| ❑ 97 Eric Lindros TF | 5.00 | 2.20 |
| ❑ 98 Peter Bondra TF | 2.00 | .90 |
| ❑ 99 Mike Modano TF | 2.00 | .90 |
| ❑ 100 Theoren Fleury TF | 2.00 | .90 |
| ❑ 101 Curtis Joseph TF | 2.00 | .90 |
| ❑ 102 Sergei Fedorov TF | 3.00 | 1.35 |
| ❑ 103 Saku Koivu TF | 2.50 | 1.10 |
| ❑ 104 Zigmund Palffy TF | 2.00 | .90 |
| ❑ 105 Ed Belfour TF | 2.00 | .90 |
| ❑ 106 Patrick Roy TF | 8.00 | 3.60 |
| ❑ 107 Brendan Shanahan TF | 3.00 | 1.35 |
| ❑ 108 Mats Sundin TF | 2.00 | .90 |
| ❑ 109 Alexei Yashin TF | 2.00 | .90 |
| ❑ 110 Doug Gilmour TF | 2.00 | .90 |
| ❑ 111 Chris Osgood TF | 2.00 | .90 |
| ❑ 112 Keith Tkachuk TF | 2.00 | .90 |
| ❑ 113 Mark Messier TF | 2.00 | .90 |
| ❑ 114 John Vanbiesbrouck TF | 2.50 | 1.10 |
| ❑ 115 Ray Bourque TF | 2.00 | .90 |
| ❑ 116 John LeClair TF | 2.50 | 1.10 |
| ❑ 117 Dominik Hasek TF | 3.00 | 1.35 |
| ❑ 118 Teemu Selanne TF | 3.00 | 1.35 |
| ❑ 119 Joe Sakic TF | 3.00 | 1.35 |
| ❑ 120 Steve Yzerman TF | 5.00 | 2.20 |
| ❑ 121 Sergei Samsonov NR | 10.00 | 4.50 |
| ❑ 122 Ryan Johnson NR | 2.50 | 1.10 |
| ❑ 123 Josef Marha NR | 2.50 | 1.10 |
| ❑ 124 Patrick Marleau NR | .75 | .35 |
| ❑ 125 Derek Morris NR | 2.50 | 1.10 |
| ❑ 126 Jamie Storr NR | 3.00 | 1.35 |
| ❑ 127 Richard Zednik NR | 2.50 | 1.10 |
| ❑ 128 Alyn McCauley NR | 2.50 | 1.10 |
| ❑ 129 Robert Dome NR | 2.50 | 1.10 |
| ❑ 130 Patrik Elias NR | 3.00 | 1.35 |
| ❑ 131 Olli Jokinen NR | 3.00 | 1.35 |
| ❑ 132 Warren Luhning NR | 2.50 | 1.10 |
| ❑ 133 Chris Phillips NR | 2.50 | 1.10 |
| ❑ 134 Mattias Ohlund NR | 3.00 | 1.35 |
| ❑ 135 Joe Thornton NR | .75 | .35 |
| ❑ 136 Matt Cullen NR | 2.50 | 1.10 |
| ❑ 137 Bates Battglia NR | 2.50 | 1.10 |
| ❑ 138 Andrei Zyuzin NR | 2.50 | 1.10 |
| ❑ 139 Cameron Mann NR | 2.50 | 1.10 |
| ❑ 140 Zdeno Chara NR | 2.50 | 1.10 |
| ❑ 141 Marc Savard NR | 2.50 | 1.10 |
| ❑ 142 Alexei Morozov NR | 3.00 | 1.35 |
| ❑ 143 Mike Johnson NR | 3.00 | 1.35 |
| ❑ 144 Vaclav Varada NR | 2.50 | 1.10 |
| ❑ 145 Dan Cloutier NR | 2.50 | 1.10 |
| ❑ 146 Brad Isbister NR | 2.50 | 1.10 |
| ❑ 147 Marco Sturm NR | 3.00 | 1.35 |
| ❑ 148 Anders Eriksson NR | 2.50 | 1.10 |
| ❑ 149 Jan Bulis NR | 2.50 | 1.10 |
| ❑ 150 Brendan Morrison NR | 5.00 | 2.20 |
| ❑ 151 Wayne Gretzky TE | 60.00 | 27.00 |
| ❑ 152 Jaromir Jagr TE | 30.00 | 13.50 |
| ❑ 153 Peter Forsberg TE | 30.00 | 13.50 |
| ❑ 154 Paul Kariya TE | 40.00 | 18.00 |
| ❑ 155 Brett Hull TE | 12.00 | 5.50 |
| ❑ 156 Martin Brodeur TE | 25.00 | 11.00 |
| ❑ 157 Eric Lindros TE | 30.00 | 13.50 |
| ❑ 158 Peter Bondra TE | 10.00 | 4.50 |
| ❑ 159 Mike Modano TE | 12.00 | 5.50 |
| ❑ 160 Theoren Fleury TE | 10.00 | 4.50 |
| ❑ 161 Curtis Joseph TE | 10.00 | 4.50 |
| ❑ 162 Sergei Fedorov TE | 20.00 | 9.00 |
| ❑ 163 Saku Koivu TE | 15.00 | 6.75 |
| ❑ 164 Zigmund Palffy TE | 10.00 | 4.50 |
| ❑ 165 Ed Belfour TE | 10.00 | 4.50 |
| ❑ 166 Patrick Roy TE | 50.00 | 22.00 |
| ❑ 167 Brendan Shanahan TE | 20.00 | 9.00 |
| ❑ 168 Mats Sundin TE | 10.00 | 4.50 |
| ❑ 169 Alexei Yashin TE | 10.00 | 4.50 |
| ❑ 170 Doug Gilmour TE | 10.00 | 4.50 |
| ❑ 171 Chris Osgood TE | 10.00 | 4.50 |
| ❑ 172 Keith Tkachuk TE | 12.00 | 5.50 |
| ❑ 173 Mark Messier TE | 12.00 | 5.50 |
| ❑ 174 John Vanbiesbrouck TE | 15.00 | 6.75 |
| ❑ 175 Ray Bourque TE | 10.00 | 4.50 |
| ❑ 176 John LeClair TE | 15.00 | 6.75 |
| ❑ 177 Dominik Hasek TE | 20.00 | 9.00 |
| ❑ 178 Teemu Selanne TE | 20.00 | 9.00 |
| ❑ 179 Joe Sakic TE | 20.00 | 9.00 |
| ❑ 180 Steve Yzerman TE | 30.00 | 13.50 |

## 1998-99 UD3 Die Cuts

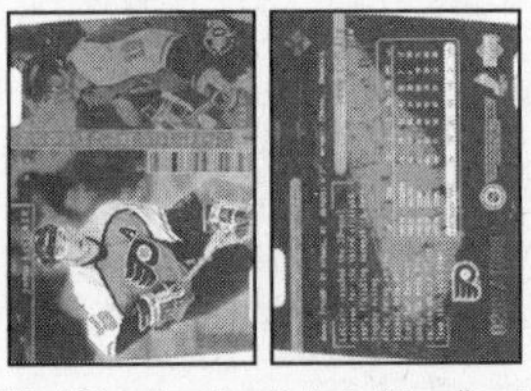

This 180-card set is a limited edition die-cut parallel version of the base set. The New Era and Three Star Spotlight SE Light F/X card versions (61-120) are sequentially numbered to 1,000. The New Era Embossed cards (1-30) are sequentially numbered to 200 with the Three Star Spotlight Embossed ones (151-180) sequentially numbered to 100. The New Era Rainbow cards (121-150) are sequentially numbered to 50. The Three Star Spotlight Rainbow ones (31-60) are numbered 1 of 1.

| | MINT | NRMT |
|---|---|---|
| COMP.EMB.SET (60) | 4000.00 | 1800.00 |
| COMMON CARD (1-30) | 15.00 | 6.75 |
| COMMON CARD (151-180) | 80.00 | 36.00 |
| *DIECUTS 1-30: 10X TO 20X BASIC 1-30 | | |
| *DIECUTS 151-180: 4X TO 8X BASIC 151-180 | | |
| 1-30 EMB.PRINT RUN 200 SETS | | |
| 151-180 EMB.PRINT RUN 100 SETS | | |
| COMMON CARD (121-150) | 60.00 | 27.00 |
| *DIECUTS 121-150: 15X to 30X BASIC 121-150 | | |
| 121-150 RAINBOW PRINT RUN 50 SETS | | |
| COMP.F/X.SET (60) | 500.00 | 220.00 |
| COMMON CARD (61-90/ | 4.00 | 1.80 |
| *DIECUTS 61-90: 2.5X TO 5X BASIC 61-90 | | |
| *DIECUTS 91-120: 2.5X TO 5X BASIC 91-120 | | |
| 61-120 F/S PRINT RUN 1000 SETS | | |

## 1991-92 Ultimate Original Six

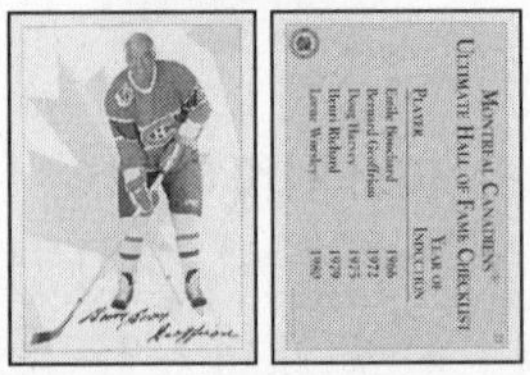

Produced by the Ultimate Trading Card Company, this 100-card standard-size set celebrates the 75th anniversary of the NHL by featuring players from the original six teams in the NHL. The cards were available only in foil packs, with a production run reportedly of 25,000 foil cases. Each foil pack included a sweepstake card; prizes offered included 250 autographed Bobby Hull holograms and 500 sets autographed by those players living at the time. The fronts feature color action photos with white borders, with the player's name in a silver bar at the top and the left lower corner of the picture rolled back to allow space for the producer's logo. The backs have a career summary presented in the format of a newspaper article (with different headlines), with biography and career statistics appearing in a silver box toward the bottom of the card. The cards are numbered on the back and checklisted below as follows: Team Checklists (1-6), Montreal Canadiens (7-17), New York Rangers (18-29), Toronto Maple Leafs (30-46), Boston Bruins (47-56), Chicago Blackhawks (57-65), Detroit Red Wings (66-72), Ultimate Hall of Fame (73-78), All Ultimate Team (79-84), Referees (85-87), Bobby Hull (88-92), and Great Moments (93-97). The cards were produced in both English and French versions. Either version is valued the same.

| | MINT | NRMT |
|---|---|---|
| COMPLETE SET (100) | 6.00 | 2.70 |
| COMMON CARD (1-100) | .05 | .02 |

*FRENCH: SAME VALUE

| | | |
|---|---|---|
| ❑ 1 Montreal Canadiens Checklist | .10 | .05 |
| ❑ 2 New York Rangers Checklist | .05 | .02 |
| ❑ 3 Toronto Maple Leafs Checklist | .05 | .02 |
| ❑ 4 Boston Bruins Checklist | .05 | .02 |
| ❑ 5 Chicago Blackhawks Checklist | .05 | .02 |
| ❑ 6 Detroit Red Wings Checklist | .05 | .02 |
| ❑ 7 Ralph Backstrom | .05 | .02 |
| ❑ 8 Emile(Butch) Bouchard | .15 | .07 |
| ❑ 9 John Ferguson | .10 | .05 |
| ❑ 10 BoomBoom Geoffrion | .60 | .25 |
| ❑ 11 Phil Goyette | .05 | .02 |
| ❑ 12 Doug Harvey | .40 | .18 |
| ❑ 13 Don Marshall | .10 | .05 |
| ❑ 14 Henri Richard | .50 | .23 |
| ❑ 15 Dollard St.Laurent | .05 | .02 |
| ❑ 16 Jean-Guy Talbot | .10 | .05 |
| ❑ 17 Gump Worsley | .35 | .16 |
| ❑ 18 Andy Bathgate | .20 | .09 |
| ❑ 19 Lou Fontinato | .05 | .02 |
| ❑ 20 Ed Giacomin | .20 | .09 |
| ❑ 21 Vic Hadfield | .10 | .05 |
| ❑ 22 Camille Henry | .05 | .02 |
| ❑ 23 Harry Howell | .15 | .07 |
| ❑ 24 Orland Kurtenbach | .10 | .05 |
| ❑ 25 Jim Neilson | .05 | .02 |
| ❑ 26 Bob Nevin | .05 | .02 |
| ❑ 27 Dean Prentice | .10 | .05 |
| ❑ 28 Leo Reise Jr. | .05 | .02 |
| ❑ 29 George Sullivan | .05 | .02 |
| ❑ 30 Bob Baun | .10 | .05 |
| ❑ 31 Gus Bodnar | .05 | .02 |
| ❑ 32 Johnny Bower | .20 | .09 |
| ❑ 33 Bob Davidson | .05 | .02 |
| ❑ 34 Ron Ellis | .10 | .05 |
| ❑ 35 Billy Harris | .05 | .02 |
| ❑ 36 Larry Hillman | .05 | .02 |
| ❑ 37 Tim Horton | .75 | .35 |
| ❑ 38 Red Kelly | .30 | .14 |
| ❑ 39 Dave Keon | .20 | .09 |
| ❑ 40 Frank Mahovlich | .50 | .23 |
| ❑ 41 Eddie Shack | .20 | .09 |
| ❑ 42 Tod Sloan | .05 | .02 |
| ❑ 43 Sid Smith | .10 | .05 |
| ❑ 44 Allan Stanley | .20 | .09 |
| ❑ 45 Gaye Stewart | .05 | .02 |
| ❑ 46 Harry Watson | .15 | .07 |
| ❑ 47 Wayne Carleton | .05 | .02 |
| ❑ 48 Fern Flaman | .10 | .05 |
| ❑ 49 Ken Hodge UER (Photo actually Ed Westfall) | .10 | .05 |
| ❑ 50 Leo Labine | .05 | .02 |
| ❑ 51 Harry Lumley | .20 | .09 |
| ❑ 52 John McKenzie | .10 | .05 |
| ❑ 53 Doug Mohns | .10 | .05 |
| ❑ 54 Fred Stanfield | .05 | .02 |
| ❑ 55 Jerry Toppazzini | .05 | .02 |
| ❑ 56 Ed Westfall | .10 | .05 |
| ❑ 57 Bobby Hull | 1.00 | .45 |
| ❑ 58 Ed Litzenberger | .05 | .02 |
| ❑ 59 Gilles Marotte | .05 | .02 |
| ❑ 60 Ab McDonald | .05 | .02 |
| ❑ 61 Bill Mosienko | .15 | .07 |
| ❑ 62 Jim Pappin | .05 | .02 |
| ❑ 63 Pierre Pilote | .15 | .07 |
| ❑ 64 Elmer Vasko | .05 | .02 |
| ❑ 65 Johnny Wilson | .05 | .02 |
| ❑ 66 Sid Abel | .20 | .09 |
| ❑ 67 Gary Bergman | .05 | .02 |
| ❑ 68 Alex Delvecchio | .30 | .14 |
| ❑ 69 Bill Gadsby | .20 | .09 |
| ❑ 70 Ted Lindsay | .40 | .18 |
| ❑ 71 Marcel Pronovost | .15 | .07 |
| ❑ 72 Norm Ullman | .20 | .09 |
| ❑ 73 BoomBoom Geoffrion | .60 | .25 |
| ❑ 74 Andy Bathgate | .20 | .09 |
| ❑ 75 Allan Stanley | .20 | .09 |
| ❑ 76 Fern Flaman | .15 | .07 |
| ❑ 77 Bobby Hull | 1.00 | .45 |
| ❑ 78 Norm Ullman | .20 | .09 |
| ❑ 79 Red Kelly | .30 | .14 |
| ❑ 80 Johnny Bower | .30 | .14 |
| ❑ 81 Henri Richard | .50 | .23 |
| ❑ 82 Bobby Hull | 1.00 | .45 |
| ❑ 83 BoomBoom Geoffrion | .60 | .25 |
| ❑ 84 Tim Horton | .75 | .35 |
| ❑ 85 Bill Friday REF | .05 | .02 |
| ❑ 86 Bruce Hood REF | .05 | .02 |
| ❑ 87 Ron Wicks REF | .05 | .02 |
| ❑ 88 Bobby Hull Electric Slap Shot | .50 | .23 |
| ❑ 89 Bobby Hull The Point Race | .50 | .2 |
| ❑ 90 Bobby Hull 1960-61 Stanley Cup | .50 | .2 |
| ❑ 91 Bobby Hull | .50 | .2 |

The Curse of Muldoon
is lifted
❑ 92 Bobby Hull .50 .23
Million Dollar Man
❑ 93 Bobby Baun .05 .02
Baun's Heroics
❑ 94 Ted Lindsay .15 .07
Lindsay's comeback
❑ 95 Henri Richard .15 .07
Richard's 99-year record
❑ 96 Bobby Hull .50 .23
Hull breaks 50 goal
barrier
❑ 97 Tim Horton .25 .11
A Tribute to Horton
❑ 98 Keith McCreary .05 .02
❑ 99 Checklist 1 .05 .02
❑ 100 Checklist 2 .05 .02
❑ NNO Bobby Hull Hologram .. 25.00 11.00

## 1991-92 Ultimate Original Six Box Bottoms

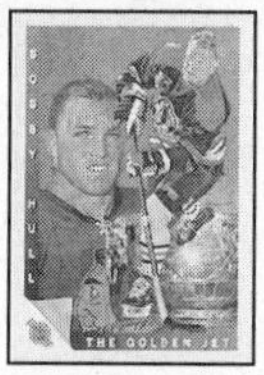

This four-card standard-size set was issued on the bottom of foil boxes. The cards feature on the fronts four-color or black and white action photos, with the lower left corner turned upward to allow space for the Ultimate logo. The player's name appears in black in a silver border at the top and the NHL logo is placed toward the end of the silver bar. Bobby Hull's card features red to black screened bars on two sides enclosing an artwork collage. The cards are unnumbered and checklisted below in alphabetical order.

| | MINT | NRMT |
|---|---|---|
| COMPLETE SET (4) | 1.50 | .70 |
| COMMON CARD (1-4) | .25 | .11 |

❑ 1 Ed Giacomin .50 .23
❑ 2 Bobby Hull 1.00 .45
The Golden Jet
❑ 3 Marcel Pronovost .25 .11
❑ 4 Eddie Shack .25 .11

## 1992-93 Ultra

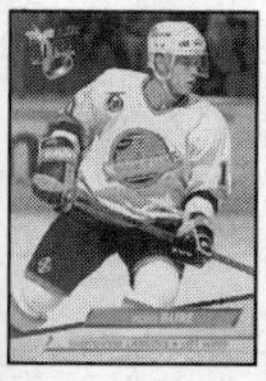

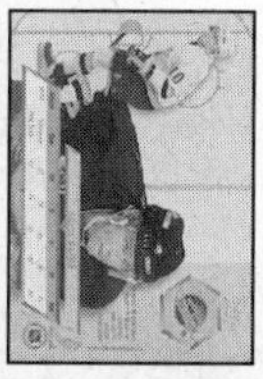

The 1992-93 Fleer Ultra hockey set consists of 450 standard-size cards. The fronts have glossy color action player photos that are full-bleed except at the bottom where a diagonal gold-foil stripe edges a "blue ice" border. The player's name and team appear on two team color-coded bars that overlay the bottom border. The horizontally oriented backs display action and close-up cut-out player photos against a hockey rink background. The team logo and biographical information appear in a blue ice bar edging the right side, while the player's name and statistics are given in bars running across the card bottom. The cards are numbered on the back and checklisted below alphabetically according to team. Rookie Cards include Roman Hamrlik, Guy Hebert, Andrei Kovalenko, Chris Osgood, Tommy Soderstrom, Martin Straka, Chris Therien and Sergei Zubov.

| | MINT | NRMT |
|---|---|---|
| COMPLETE SET (450) | 30.00 | 13.50 |
| COMPLETE SERIES 1 (250) | 20.00 | 9.00 |
| COMPLETE SERIES 2 (200) | 10.00 | 4.50 |
| COMMON CARD (1-450) | .10 | .05 |

❑ 1 Brent Ashton .10 .05
❑ 2 Ray Bourque .30 .14
❑ 3 Steve Heinze .10 .05
❑ 4 Joe Juneau UER .20 .09
(Shoots left, not right)
❑ 5 Stephen Leach .10 .05
❑ 6 Andy Moog .20 .09
❑ 7 Cam Neely .20 .09
❑ 8 Adam Oates .20 .09
❑ 9 Dave Poulin .10 .05
❑ 10 Vladimir Ruzicka .10 .05
❑ 11 Glen Wesley .10 .05
❑ 12 Dave Andreychuk .20 .09
❑ 13 Keith Carney .10 .05
❑ 14 Tom Draper .10 .05
❑ 15 Dale Hawerchuk .20 .09
❑ 16 Pat LaFontaine .20 .09
❑ 17 Brad May .20 .09
❑ 18 Alexander Mogilny .20 .09
❑ 19 Mike Ramsey .10 .05
❑ 20 Ken Sutton .10 .05
❑ 21 Theoren Fleury .20 .09
❑ 22 Gary Leeman .10 .05
❑ 23 Al MacInnis .20 .09
❑ 24 Sergei Makarov .10 .05
❑ 25 Joe Nieuwendyk .20 .09
❑ 26 Joel Otto .10 .05
❑ 27 Paul Ranheim .10 .05
❑ 28 Robert Reichel .10 .05
❑ 29 Gary Roberts .10 .05
❑ 30 Gary Suter .10 .05
❑ 31 Mike Vernon .20 .09
❑ 32 Ed Belfour .30 .14
❑ 33 Rob Brown .10 .05
❑ 34 Chris Chelios .30 .14
❑ 35 Michel Goulet .20 .09
❑ 36 Dirk Graham .10 .05
❑ 37 Mike Hudson .10 .05
❑ 38 Igor Kravchuk .10 .05
❑ 39 Steve Larmer .20 .09
❑ 40 Dean McAmmond .10 .05
❑ 41 Jeremy Roenick .30 .14
❑ 42 Steve Smith .10 .05
❑ 43 Brent Sutter .10 .05
❑ 44 Shawn Burr .10 .05
❑ 45 Jimmy Carson .10 .05
❑ 46 Tim Cheveldae .20 .09
❑ 47 Dino Ciccarelli .20 .09
❑ 48 Sergei Fedorov .60 .25
❑ 49 Vladimir Konstantinov .10 .05
❑ 50 Slava Kozlov .20 .09
❑ 51 Nicklas Lidstrom .20 .09
❑ 52 Brad McCrimmon .10 .05
❑ 53 Bob Probert .20 .09
❑ 54 Paul Ysebaert .10 .05
❑ 55 Steve Yzerman 1.00 .45
❑ 56 Josef Beranek .10 .05
❑ 57 Shayne Corson .10 .05
❑ 58 Brian Glynn .10 .05
❑ 59 Petr Klima .10 .05
❑ 60 Kevin Lowe .10 .05
❑ 61 Norm Maciver .10 .05
❑ 62 Dave Manson .10 .05
❑ 63 Joe Murphy .10 .05
❑ 64 Bernie Nicholls .20 .09
❑ 65 Bill Ranford .20 .09
❑ 66 Craig Simpson .10 .05
❑ 67 Esa Tikkanen .10 .05
❑ 68 Sean Burke .20 .09
❑ 69 Adam Burt .10 .05
❑ 70 Andrew Cassels .10 .05
❑ 71 Murray Craven .10 .05
❑ 72 John Cullen .10 .05
❑ 73 Randy Cunneyworth .10 .05
❑ 74 Tim Kerr .10 .05
❑ 75 Geoff Sanderson .20 .09
❑ 76 Eric Weinrich .10 .05
❑ 77 Zarley Zalapski .10 .05
❑ 78 Peter Ahola .10 .05
❑ 79 Rob Blake .20 .09
❑ 80 Paul Coffey .30 .14
❑ 81 Mike Donnelly .10 .05
❑ 82 Tony Granato .10 .05
❑ 83 Wayne Gretzky 2.00 .90
❑ 84 Kelly Hrudey .20 .09
❑ 85 Jari Kurri .20 .09
❑ 86 Corey Millen .10 .05
❑ 87 Luc Robitaille .20 .09
❑ 88 Tomas Sandstrom .10 .05
❑ 89 Neal Broten .20 .09
❑ 90 Jon Casey .20 .09
❑ 91 Russ Courtnall .10 .05
❑ 92 Ulf Dahlen .10 .05
❑ 93 Todd Elik .10 .05
❑ 94 Dave Gagner .20 .09
❑ 95 Jim Johnson .10 .05
❑ 96 Mike Modano UER .40 .18
(Born in Livonia,
Michigan, not Minnesota)
❑ 97 Bobby Smith .20 .09
❑ 98 Mark Tinordi .10 .05
❑ 99 Darcy Wakaluk .20 .09
❑ 100 Brian Bellows .10 .05
❑ 101 Benoit Brunet .10 .05
❑ 102 Guy Carbonneau .20 .09
❑ 103 Vincent Damphousse .20 .09
❑ 104 Eric Desjardins .10 .05
❑ 105 Gilbert Dionne .10 .05
❑ 106 Mike Keane .10 .05
❑ 107 Kirk Muller .10 .05
❑ 108 Patrick Roy 1.50 .70
❑ 109 Denis Savard .20 .09
❑ 110 Mathieu Schneider .10 .05
❑ 111 Brian Skrudland .10 .05
❑ 112 Tom Chorske .10 .05
❑ 113 Zdeno Ciger .10 .05
❑ 114 Claude Lemieux .20 .09
❑ 115 John MacLean .20 .09
❑ 116 Scott Niedermayer .20 .09
❑ 117 Stephane Richer .20 .09
❑ 118 Peter Stastny .20 .09
❑ 119 Scott Stevens .20 .09
❑ 120 Chris Terreri .20 .09
❑ 121 Kevin Todd .10 .05
❑ 122 Valeri Zelepukin .20 .09
❑ 123 Ray Ferraro .10 .05
❑ 124 Mark Fitzpatrick .20 .09
❑ 125 Patrick Flatley .10 .05
❑ 126 Glenn Healy .20 .09
❑ 127 Benoit Hogue .10 .05
❑ 128 Derek King .10 .05
❑ 129 Uwe Krupp .10 .05
❑ 130 Scott Lachance .10 .05
❑ 131 Steve Thomas .10 .05
❑ 132 Pierre Turgeon .20 .09
❑ 133 Tony Amonte .20 .09
❑ 134 Paul Broten .10 .05
❑ 135 Mike Gartner .20 .09
❑ 136 Adam Graves .20 .09
❑ 137 Alexei Kovalev .20 .09
❑ 138 Brian Leetch .30 .14
❑ 139 Mark Messier .50 .23
❑ 140 Sergei Nemchinov .10 .05
❑ 141 James Patrick .10 .05
❑ 142 Mike Richter .30 .14
❑ 143 Darren Turcotte .10 .05
❑ 144 John Vanbiesbrouck .50 .23
❑ 145 Dominic Lavoie .10 .05
❑ 146 Lonnie Loach .10 .05
❑ 147 Andrew McBain .10 .05
❑ 148 Darren Rumble .10 .05
❑ 149 Sylvain Turgeon .10 .05
❑ 150 Peter Sidorkiewicz .20 .09
❑ 151 Brian Benning .10 .05
❑ 152 Rod Brind'Amour .20 .09
❑ 153 Viacheslav Butsayev .10 .05
❑ 154 Kevin Dineen .10 .05
❑ 155 Pelle Eklund .10 .05
❑ 156 Garry Galley .10 .05
❑ 157 Eric Lindros 2.50 1.10
❑ 158 Mark Recchi .20 .09
❑ 159 Dominic Roussel .20 .09
❑ 160 Tommy Soderstrom .20 .09
❑ 161 Dimitri Yushkevich .10 .05
❑ 162 Tom Barrasso .20 .09
❑ 163 Ron Francis .20 .09
❑ 164 Jaromir Jagr 1.00 .45
❑ 165 Mario Lemieux 1.50 .70
❑ 166 Joe Mullen .20 .09
❑ 167 Larry Murphy .20 .09
❑ 168 Jim Paek .10 .05
❑ 169 Kjell Samuelsson .10 .05
❑ 170 Ulf Samuelsson .10 .05
❑ 171 Kevin Stevens .10 .05
❑ 172 Rick Tocchet .20 .09
❑ 173 Alexei Gusarov .10 .05
❑ 174 Ron Hextall .20 .09
❑ 175 Mike Hough .10 .05
❑ 176 Claude Lapointe .10 .05
❑ 177 Owen Nolan .20 .09
❑ 178 Mike Ricci .10 .05
❑ 179 Joe Sakic .60 .25
❑ 180 Mats Sundin .30 .14
❑ 181 Mikhail Tatarinov .10 .05
❑ 182 Bob Bassen .10 .05
❑ 183 Jeff Brown .10 .05
❑ 184 Garth Butcher .10 .05
❑ 185 Paul Cavallini .10 .05
❑ 186 Brett Hull .50 .23
❑ 187 Craig Janney .20 .09
❑ 188 Curtis Joseph .30 .14
❑ 189 Brendan Shanahan .60 .25
❑ 190 Ron Sutter .10 .05
❑ 191 David Bruce .10 .05
❑ 192 Dale Craigwell .10 .05
❑ 193 Dean Evason .10 .05
❑ 194 Pat Falloon .10 .05
❑ 195 Jeff Hackett .20 .09
❑ 196 Kelly Kisio .10 .05
❑ 197 Brian Lawton .10 .05
❑ 198 Neil Wilkinson .10 .05
❑ 199 Doug Wilson .20 .09
❑ 200 Marc Bergevin .10 .05
❑ 201 Roman Hamrlik .50 .23
❑ 202 Pat Jablonski .20 .09
❑ 203 Michel Mongeau .10 .05
❑ 204 Peter Taglianetti .10 .05
❑ 205 Steve Tuttle .10 .05
❑ 206 Wendell Young .20 .09
❑ 207 Glenn Anderson .20 .09
❑ 208 Wendel Clark .20 .09
❑ 209 Dave Ellett .10 .05
❑ 210 Grant Fuhr .20 .09
❑ 211 Doug Gilmour .30 .14
❑ 212 Jamie Macoun .10 .05
❑ 213 Felix Potvin .30 .14
❑ 214 Bob Rouse .10 .05
❑ 215 Joe Sacco .10 .05
❑ 216 Peter Zezel .10 .05
❑ 217 Greg Adams .10 .05
❑ 218 Dave Babych .10 .05
❑ 219 Pavel Bure .60 .25
❑ 220 Geoff Courtnall .10 .05
❑ 221 Doug Lidster .10 .05
❑ 222 Trevor Linden .20 .09
❑ 223 Jyrki Lumme .10 .05
❑ 224 Kirk McLean .20 .09
❑ 225 Sergio Momesso .10 .05
❑ 226 Petr Nedved .20 .09
❑ 227 Cliff Ronning .10 .05
❑ 228 Jim Sandlak .10 .05
❑ 229 Don Beaupre .20 .09
❑ 230 Peter Bondra .30 .14
❑ 231 Kevin Hatcher .10 .05
❑ 232 Dale Hunter .20 .09
❑ 233 Al Iafrate .20 .09
❑ 234 Calle Johansson .10 .05
❑ 235 Dimitri Khristich .10 .05
❑ 236 Kelly Miller .10 .05
❑ 237 Michal Pivonka .10 .05
❑ 238 Mike Ridley .10 .05
❑ 239 Luciano Borsato .10 .05
❑ 240 Bob Essensa .20 .09
❑ 241 Phil Housley .20 .09
❑ 242 Troy Murray .10 .05
❑ 243 Teppo Numminen .10 .05
❑ 244 Fredrik Olausson .10 .05
❑ 245 Ed Olczyk .10 .05
❑ 246 Darrin Shannon .10 .05
❑ 247 Thomas Steen .10 .05
❑ 248 Checklist 1 .10 .05
❑ 249 Checklist 2 .10 .05
❑ 250 Checklist 3 .10 .05
❑ 251 Ted Donato .10 .05
❑ 252 Dmitri Kvartalnov .10 .05
❑ 253 Gord Murphy .10 .05
❑ 254 Gregori Panteleyev .10 .05
❑ 255 Gordie Roberts .10 .05
❑ 256 David Shaw .10 .05
❑ 257 Don Sweeney .10 .05
❑ 258 Doug Bodger .10 .05
❑ 259 Gord Donnelly .10 .05
❑ 260 Yuri Khmylev .10 .05
❑ 261 Daren Puppa .20 .09
❑ 262 Richard Smehlik .10 .05
❑ 263 Petr Svoboda .10 .05
❑ 264 Bob Sweeney .10 .05
❑ 265 Randy Wood .10 .05
❑ 266 Kevin Dahl .10 .05
❑ 267 Chris Dahlquist .10 .05
❑ 268 Roger Johansson .10 .05
❑ 269 Chris Lindberg .10 .05
❑ 270 Frank Musil .10 .05
❑ 271 Ronnie Stern .10 .05
❑ 272 Carey Wilson .10 .05
❑ 273 Dave Christian .10 .05
❑ 274 Karl Dykhuis .10 .05
❑ 275 Greg Gilbert .10 .05
❑ 276 Sergei Krivokrasov .10 .05
❑ 277 Frantisek Kucera .10 .05
❑ 278 Bryan Marchment .10 .05
❑ 279 Stephane Matteau .10 .05
❑ 280 Brian Noonan .10 .05
❑ 281 Christian Ruuttu .10 .05
❑ 282 Steve Chiasson .10 .05
❑ 283 Dino Ciccarelli .20 .09
❑ 284 Gerard Gallant .10 .05
❑ 285 Mark Howe .10 .05
❑ 286 Keith Primeau .20 .09
❑ 287 Yves Racine .10 .05
❑ 288 Vincent Riendeau .20 .09
❑ 289 Ray Sheppard .20 .09
❑ 290 Mike Sillinger .10 .05
❑ 291 Kelly Buchberger .10 .05
❑ 292 Shayne Corson .10 .05
❑ 293 Brent Gilchrist .10 .05
❑ 294 Craig MacTavish .10 .05
❑ 295 Scott Mellanby .20 .09
❑ 296 Craig Muni .10 .05
❑ 297 Luke Richardson .10 .05
❑ 298 Ron Tugnutt .20 .09
❑ 299 Shaun Van Allen .10 .05
❑ 300 Steve Konroyd .10 .05
❑ 301 Nick Kypreos .10 .05
❑ 302 Robert Petrovicky .10 .05
❑ 303 Frank Pietrangelo .20 .09
❑ 304 Patrick Poulin .10 .05
❑ 305 Pat Verbeek .10 .05
❑ 306 Eric Weinrich .10 .05
❑ 307 Jim Hiller .10 .05
❑ 308 Charlie Huddy .10 .05
❑ 309 Lonnie Loach .10 .05
❑ 310 Marty McSorley .10 .05
❑ 311 Robb Stauber .20 .09
❑ 312 Darryl Sydor .10 .05
❑ 313 Dave Taylor .20 .09
❑ 314 Alexei Zhitnik .10 .05
❑ 315 Shane Churla .10 .05
❑ 316 Russ Courtnall .10 .05
❑ 317 Mike Craig .10 .05
❑ 318 Gaetan Duchesne .10 .05
❑ 319 Derian Hatcher .10 .05
❑ 320 Craig Ludwig .10 .05
❑ 321 Richard Matvichuk .10 .05
❑ 322 Mike McPhee .10 .05
❑ 323 Tommy Sjodin .10 .05
❑ 324 Brian Bellows .10 .05
❑ 325 Patrice Brisebois .10 .05
❑ 326 J.J.Daigneault .10 .05
❑ 327 Kevin Haller .10 .05
❑ 328 Sean Hill .10 .05
❑ 329 Stephan Lebeau .10 .05
❑ 330 John LeClair .75 .35
❑ 331 Lyle Odelein .10 .05
❑ 332 Andre Racicot .20 .09
❑ 333 Ed Ronan .10 .05
❑ 334 Craig Billington .20 .09
❑ 335 Ken Daneyko .10 .05
❑ 336 Bruce Driver .10 .05
❑ 337 Slava Fetisov .10 .05
❑ 338 Bill Guerin .10 .05
❑ 339 Bobby Holik .10 .05
❑ 340 Alexei Kasatonov .10 .05
❑ 341 Alexander Semak .10 .05
❑ 342 Tom Fitzgerald .10 .05
❑ 343 Travis Green .20 .09
❑ 344 Darius Kasparaitis .10 .05
❑ 345 Danny Lorenz .10 .05
❑ 346 Vladimir Malakhov .10 .05
❑ 347 Marty McInnis .10 .05
❑ 348 Brian Mullen .10 .05
❑ 349 Jeff Norton .10 .05
❑ 350 David Volek .10 .05
❑ 351 Jeff Beukeboom .10 .05
❑ 352 Phil Bourque .10 .05
❑ 353 Paul Broten .10 .05
❑ 354 Mark Hardy .10 .05
❑ 355 Steven King .10 .05
❑ 356 Kevin Lowe .10 .05
❑ 357 Ed Olczyk .10 .05
❑ 358 Doug Weight .20 .09
❑ 359 Sergei Zubov .75 .35
❑ 360 Jamie Baker .10 .05
❑ 361 Daniel Berthiaume .20 .09
❑ 362 Chris Luongo .10 .05
❑ 363 Norm Maciver .10 .05
❑ 364 Brad Marsh .10 .05
❑ 365 Mike Peluso .10 .05
❑ 366 Brad Shaw .10 .05
❑ 367 Peter Sidorkiewicz .20 .09
❑ 368 Keith Acton .10 .05
❑ 369 Stephane Beauregard .20 .09
❑ 370 Terry Carkner .10 .05
❑ 371 Brent Fedyk .10 .05
❑ 372 Andrei Lomakin .10 .05
❑ 373 Ryan McGill .10 .05
❑ 374 Ric Nattress .10 .05
❑ 375 Greg Paslawski .10 .05
❑ 376 Peter Ahola .10 .05
❑ 377 Jeff Daniels .10 .05
❑ 378 Troy Loney .10 .05
❑ 379 Shawn McEachern .10 .05
❑ 380 Mike Needham .10 .05
❑ 381 Paul Stanton .10 .05
❑ 382 Martin Straka .50 .23
❑ 383 Ken Wregget .20 .09
❑ 384 Steve Duchesne .10 .05
❑ 385 Ron Hextall .20 .09
❑ 386 Kerry Huffman .10 .05
❑ 387 Andrei Kovalenko .10 .05
❑ 388 Bill Lindsay .10 .05
❑ 389 Mike Ricci .10 .05
❑ 390 Martin Rucinsky .10 .05
❑ 391 Scott Young .10 .05
❑ 392 Philippe Bozon .10 .05
❑ 393 Nelson Emerson .10 .05
❑ 394 Guy Hebert 1.00 .45
❑ 395 Igor Korolev .10 .05
❑ 396 Kevin Miller .10 .05
❑ 397 Vitali Prokhorov .10 .05
❑ 398 Rich Sutter .10 .05
❑ 399 John Carter .10 .05
❑ 400 Johan Garpenlov .10 .05
❑ 401 Arturs Irbe .20 .09
❑ 402 Sandis Ozolinsh .20 .09
❑ 403 Tom Pederson .10 .05
❑ 404 Michel Picard .10 .05
❑ 405 Doug Zmolek .10 .05
❑ 406 Mikael Andersson .10 .05
❑ 407 Bob Beers .10 .05
❑ 408 Brian Bradley .10 .05
❑ 409 Adam Creighton .10 .05
❑ 410 Doug Crossman .10 .05
❑ 411 Ken Hodge .10 .05
❑ 412 Chris Kontos .10 .05
❑ 413 Rob Ramage .10 .05
❑ 414 John Tucker .10 .05
❑ 415 Rob Zamuner .10 .05
❑ 416 Ken Baumgartner .10 .05
❑ 417 Drake Berehowsky .10 .05
❑ 418 Nikolai Borschevsky .10 .05
❑ 419 John Cullen .10 .05
❑ 420 Mike Foligno .10 .05
❑ 421 Mike Krushelnyski .10 .05
❑ 422 Dmitri Mironov .10 .05
❑ 423 Rob Pearson .10 .05
❑ 424 Gerald Diduck .10 .05
❑ 425 Robert Dirk .10 .05
❑ 426 Tom Fergus .10 .05
❑ 427 Gino Odjick .10 .05
❑ 428 Adrien Plavsic .10 .05
❑ 429 Anatoli Semenov .10 .05
❑ 430 Jiri Slegr .10 .05
❑ 431 Dixon Ward .10 .05
❑ 432 Paul Cavallini .10 .05
❑ 433 Sylvain Cote .10 .05
❑ 434 Pat Elynuik .10 .05
❑ 435 Jim Hrivnak .20 .09
❑ 436 Keith Jones .40 .18
❑ 437 Steve Konowalchuk .10 .05
❑ 438 Todd Krygier .10 .05
❑ 439 Paul MacDermid .10 .05
❑ 440 Sergei Bautin .10 .05
❑ 441 Evgeny Davydov .10 .05
❑ 442 John Druce .10 .05
❑ 443 Troy Murray .10 .05
❑ 444 Teemu Selanne 1.50 .70
❑ 445 Rick Tabaracci .20 .09
❑ 446 Keith Tkachuk .75 .35
❑ 447 Alexei Zhamnov .20 .09
❑ 448 Checklist 4 .10 .05
❑ 449 Checklist 5 .10 .05
❑ 450 Checklist 6 .10 .05

## 1992-93 Ultra All-Stars

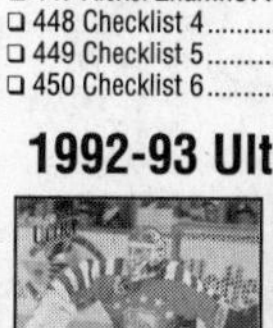

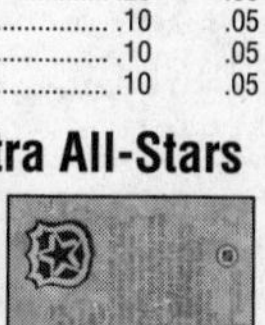

This 12-card standard-size set was randomly inserted in 1992-93 Ultra first series foil packs. The cards depict First Team All-Stars by conference. The glossy color action player photos on the fronts are full-bleed except at the bottom where a diagonal gold-foil stripe edges a beige marbleized border. A gold-foil insignia with a star is superimposed on the beige border. The fronts feature color, action player photos from the 1992 All-Star Game. A brown marbleized border runs diagonally

across the bottom. This border is separated from the photo by a thin gold foil stripe. The player's name and the words "NHL All-Star" are printed in gold foil on the marbleized border. On a gray marbleized background, the horizontal backs feature a cut-out color close-up player photo and a season summary.

| | MINT | NRMT |
|---|---|---|
| COMPLETE SET (12) | 25.00 | 11.00 |
| COMMON CARD (1-12) | 1.00 | .45 |
| ❑ 1 Paul Coffey UER (Photo on back actually Kevin Stevens) | 1.50 | .70 |
| ❑ 2 Ray Bourque | 3.00 | 1.35 |
| ❑ 3 Patrick Roy | 6.00 | 2.70 |
| ❑ 4 Mario Lemieux | 6.00 | 2.70 |
| ❑ 5 Kevin Stevens UER (Photo on back actually Paul Coffey) | 1.00 | .45 |
| ❑ 6 Jaromir Jagr | 4.00 | 1.80 |
| ❑ 7 Chris Chelios | 1.50 | .70 |
| ❑ 8 Al MacInnis | 1.00 | .45 |
| ❑ 9 Ed Belfour | 3.00 | 1.35 |
| ❑ 10 Wayne Gretzky | 8.00 | 3.60 |
| ❑ 11 Luc Robitaille | 1.00 | .45 |
| ❑ 12 Brett Hull | 2.00 | .90 |

## 1992-93 Ultra Award Winners

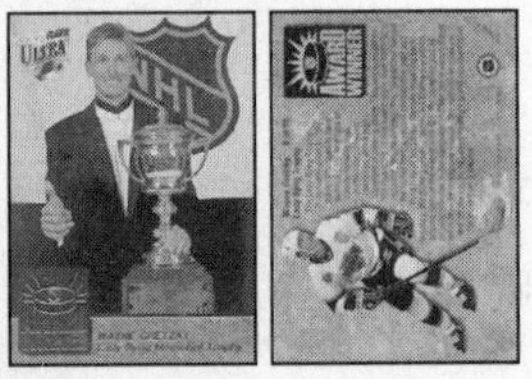

This ten-card standard-size set was randomly inserted in 1992-93 Ultra first series foil packs. The cards feature 1991-92 award winners. The glossy color action player photos on the fronts are full-bleed except at the bottom where a gold-foil stripe edges into a marbleized border.

| | MINT | NRMT |
|---|---|---|
| COMPLETE SET (10) | 25.00 | 11.00 |
| COMMON CARD (1-10) | .75 | .35 |
| ❑ 1 Mark Messier | 2.00 | .90 |
| ❑ 2 Brian Leetch | 1.50 | .70 |
| ❑ 3 Guy Carbonneau | .75 | .35 |
| ❑ 4 Patrick Roy | 6.00 | 2.70 |
| ❑ 5 Mario Lemieux | 6.00 | 2.70 |
| ❑ 6 Wayne Gretzky | 8.00 | 3.60 |
| ❑ 7 Mark Fitzpatrick | 1.25 | .55 |
| ❑ 8 Ray Bourque | 1.50 | .70 |
| ❑ 9 Pavel Bure | 2.50 | 1.10 |
| ❑ 10 Mark Messier | 2.00 | .90 |

## 1992-93 Ultra Imports

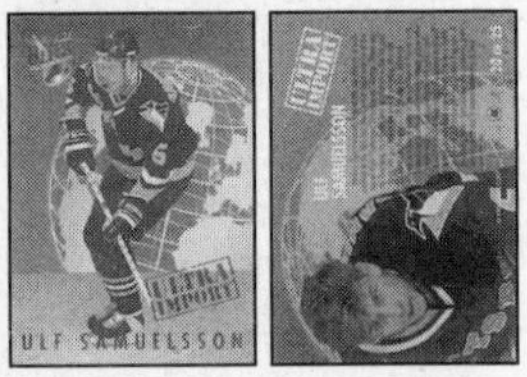

Randomly inserted in second series 1992-93 Ultra foil packs, this 25-card set measures the standard size. The cards depict foreign players in the National Hockey League. Fronts feature color action cut-out player photos against a purple surreal background showing the player on ice with a globe design in the distance. The player's name is silver foil stamped at the bottom. The horizontal backs carry a close-up of the player, the player's name, and player information. The background is similar to the front.

| | MINT | NRMT |
|---|---|---|
| COMPLETE SET (25) | 50.00 | 22.00 |
| COMMON CARD (1-25) | 1.00 | .45 |
| ❑ 1 Nikolai Borschevsky | 1.00 | .45 |
| ❑ 2 Pavel Bure | 5.00 | 2.20 |
| ❑ 3 Sergei Fedorov | 5.00 | 2.20 |
| ❑ 4 Roman Hamrlik | 3.00 | 1.35 |
| ❑ 5 Arturs Irbe | 1.00 | .45 |
| ❑ 6 Jaromir Jagr | 6.00 | 2.70 |
| ❑ 7 Dimitri Khristich | 3.00 | 1.35 |
| ❑ 8 Petr Klima | 1.00 | .45 |
| ❑ 9 Andrei Kovalenko | 1.00 | .45 |
| ❑ 10 Alexei Kovalev | 1.00 | .45 |
| ❑ 11 Jari Kurri | 3.00 | 1.35 |
| ❑ 12 Dmitri Kvartalnov | 1.00 | .45 |
| ❑ 13 Nicklas Lidstrom | 3.00 | 1.35 |
| ❑ 14 Vladimir Malakhov | 3.00 | 1.35 |
| ❑ 15 Dmitri Mironov | 1.00 | .45 |
| ❑ 16 Alexander Mogilny | 3.00 | 1.35 |
| ❑ 17 Petr Nedved | 3.00 | 1.35 |
| ❑ 18 Fredrik Olausson | 1.00 | .45 |
| ❑ 19 Sandis Ozolinsh | 3.00 | 1.35 |
| ❑ 20 Ulf Samuelsson | 1.00 | .45 |
| ❑ 21 Teemu Selanne | 8.00 | 3.60 |
| ❑ 22 Richard Smehlik | 1.00 | .45 |
| ❑ 23 Tommy Soderstrom | 3.00 | 1.35 |
| ❑ 24 Peter Stastny | 3.00 | 1.35 |
| ❑ 25 Mats Sundin | 3.00 | 1.35 |

## 1992-93 Ultra Jeremy Roenick

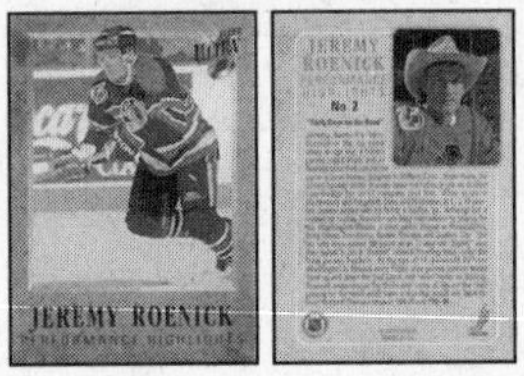

Randomly inserted in first series 1992-93 Ultra foil packs, this 12-card set measures the standard size. Two of the cards (11, 12) were available through a mail-in offer which was not available in Canada. The set, which features color action photos on front and career highlights on back, spotlights the career of Chicago Blackhawks' Jeremy Roenick. Roenick personally autographed more than 2,000 of his cards. Stated odds suggest the likelihood of pulling an autographed card at 1:8,000 packs.

| | MINT | NRMT |
|---|---|---|
| COMPLETE SET (10) | 20.00 | 9.00 |
| COMMON ROENICK (1-10) | 2.50 | 1.10 |
| CERTIFIED AUTO | 120.00 | 55.00 |
| ❑ 1 Jeremy Roenick Blast From The Past | 2.50 | 1.10 |
| ❑ 2 Jeremy Roenick Early Days on the Road | 2.50 | 1.10 |
| ❑ 3 Jeremy Roenick Prep School Phenom | 2.50 | 1.10 |
| ❑ 4 Jeremy Roenick Blackhawk-Bound | 2.50 | 1.10 |
| ❑ 5 Jeremy Roenick Breakfast With A Champion | 2.50 | 1.10 |
| ❑ 6 Jeremy Roenick The Fast Track | 2.50 | 1.10 |
| ❑ 7 Jeremy Roenick Boy To Man | 2.50 | 1.10 |
| ❑ 8 Jeremy Roenick Great Expectations | 2.50 | 1.10 |
| ❑ 9 Jeremy Roenick Changing of the Guard | 2.50 | 1.10 |
| ❑ 10 Jeremy Roenick Superstar | 2.50 | 1.10 |
| ❑ 11 Jeremy Roenick Impressive Impressions (Skating, front shot) | 3.00 | 1.35 |
| ❑ 12 Jeremy Roenick Roenick on Roenick (Skating, side view) | 3.00 | 1.35 |

## 1992-93 Ultra Rookies

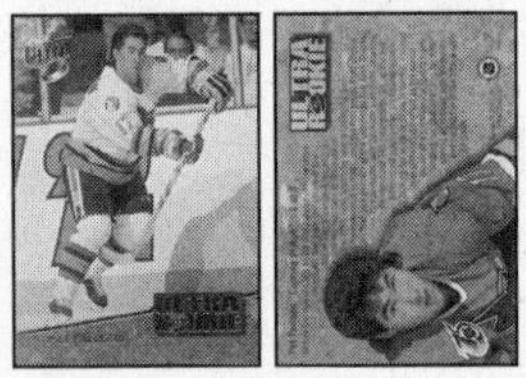

This eight-card standard-size set was randomly inserted in 1992-93 Ultra series one foil packs. The card fronts feature color, action player photos. A brown marbleized border runs diagonally across the bottom. This border is separated from the photo by a thin gold foil stripe. The player's name and the words "Ultra Rookie" are printed in gold foil on the marbleized border. The backs show a close-up picture with a player profile against a gray marbleized background.

| | MINT | NRMT |
|---|---|---|
| COMPLETE SET (8) | 10.00 | 4.50 |
| COMMON CARD (1-8) | 1.00 | .45 |
| ❑ 1 Tony Amonte | 1.50 | .70 |
| ❑ 2 Donald Audette | 1.25 | .55 |
| ❑ 3 Pavel Bure | 5.00 | 2.20 |
| ❑ 4 Gilbert Dionne | 1.00 | .45 |
| ❑ 5 Nelson Emerson | 1.00 | .45 |
| ❑ 6 Pat Falloon | 1.00 | .45 |
| ❑ 7 Nicklas Lidstrom | 1.25 | .55 |
| ❑ 8 Kevin Todd | 1.00 | .45 |

## 1993-94 Ultra Promo Sheet

This (approximately) 11" by 8 1/2" sheet features some of the cards of the 1993-94 Ultra set. It is arranged in three rows with three cards each, the middle card in the middle row is not a player's card but a title card. The backs are also identical to the cards' backs.

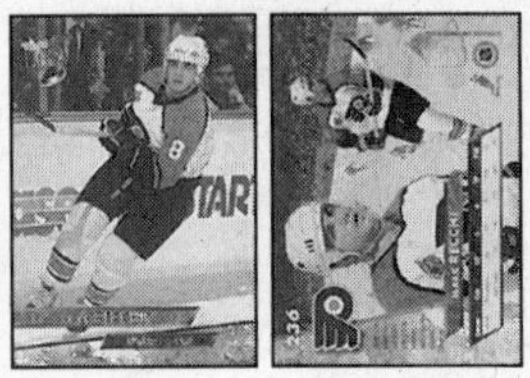

| | MINT | NRMT |
|---|---|---|
| COMPLETE SET (1) | 5.00 | 2.20 |
| COMMON PANEL | 5.00 | 2.20 |
| ❑ NNO Joe Juneau, Sergei Fedorov, Mats Sundin, Mark Recchi, Jeremy Roenick, Alexei Kovalev | 5.00 | 2.20 |

## 1993-94 Ultra

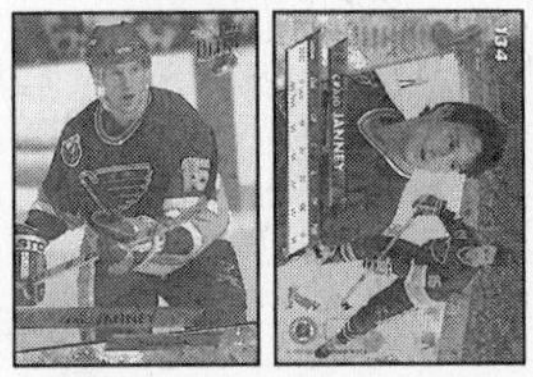

The 1993-94 Ultra hockey set consists of 500 standard-size cards. Both the first and second series contained 250 cards. The color action player photos on the fronts are full-bleed except at the bottom where a diagonal gold foil stripe separates the picture from a gray ice border. The player's name, team name, and position are gold foil-stamped on team color-coded bars. The horizontal backs display two color player cut-outs superimposed on a hockey stadium background, with biography, statistics, and team logo overprinted. Rookie Cards include Jason Arnott, Chris Osgood, Brian Savage, Chris Therien and Jocelyn Thibault

| | MINT | NRMT |
|---|---|---|
| COMPLETE SET (500) | 40.00 | 18.00 |
| COMPLETE SERIES 1 (250) | 20.00 | 9.00 |
| COMPLETE SERIES 2 (250) | 20.00 | 9.00 |
| COMMON CARD (1-500) | .10 | .05 |
| ❑ 1 Ray Bourque | .30 | .14 |
| ❑ 2 Andy Moog | .15 | .07 |
| ❑ 3 Brian Benning | .10 | .05 |
| ❑ 4 Brian Bellows | .10 | .05 |
| ❑ 5 Claude Lemieux | .15 | .07 |
| ❑ 6 Jamie Baker | .10 | .05 |
| ❑ 7 Steve Duchesne | .10 | .05 |
| ❑ 8 Ed Courtenay | .10 | .05 |
| ❑ 9 Glenn Anderson | .15 | .07 |
| ❑ 10 Sergei Bautin | .10 | .05 |
| ❑ 11 Al Iafrate | .10 | .05 |
| ❑ 12 Gary Shuchuk | .10 | .05 |
| ❑ 13 Matthew Barnaby | .15 | .07 |
| ❑ 14 Tim Cheveldae | .15 | .07 |
| ❑ 15 Sean Burke | .15 | .07 |
| ❑ 16 Ray Ferraro | .10 | .05 |
| ❑ 17 Josef Beranek | .10 | .05 |
| ❑ 18 Bob Beers | .10 | .05 |
| ❑ 19 Greg Adams | .10 | .05 |
| ❑ 20 John Cullen | .10 | .05 |
| ❑ 21 Kirk Muller | .10 | .05 |
| ❑ 22 Ed Belfour | .30 | .14 |
| ❑ 23 Kevin Dahl | .10 | .05 |
| ❑ 24 Rob Blake | .10 | .05 |
| ❑ 25 Mike Gartner | .15 | .07 |
| ❑ 26 Tom Barrasso | .15 | .07 |
| ❑ 27 Garth Butcher | .10 | .05 |
| ❑ 28 Don Beaupre | .15 | .07 |
| ❑ 29 Kirk McLean | .15 | .07 |
| ❑ 30 Felix Potvin | .30 | .14 |
| ❑ 31 Doug Bodger | .10 | .05 |
| ❑ 32 Dino Ciccarelli | .15 | .07 |
| ❑ 33 Andrew Cassels | .10 | .05 |
| ❑ 34 Patrick Flatley | .10 | .05 |
| ❑ 35 Jason Bowen | .10 | .05 |
| ❑ 36 Brian Bradley | .10 | .05 |
| ❑ 37 Pavel Bure | .60 | .25 |
| ❑ 38 Dave Ellett | .10 | .05 |
| ❑ 39 Patrick Roy | 1.50 | .70 |
| ❑ 40 Chris Chelios | .30 | .14 |
| ❑ 41 Theoren Fleury | .15 | .07 |
| ❑ 42 Jimmy Carson | .10 | .05 |
| ❑ 43 Adam Graves | .15 | .07 |
| ❑ 44 Ron Francis | .15 | .07 |
| ❑ 45 Nelson Emerson | .10 | .05 |
| ❑ 46 Peter Bondra | .30 | .14 |
| ❑ 47 Sergio Momesso | .10 | .05 |
| ❑ 48 Teemu Selanne | .75 | .35 |
| ❑ 49 Joe Juneau | .15 | .07 |
| ❑ 50 Russ Courtnall | .10 | .05 |
| ❑ 51 Shayne Corson | .10 | .05 |
| ❑ 52 Patrice Brisebois | .10 | .05 |
| ❑ 53 John MacLean | .15 | .07 |
| ❑ 54 Daniel Berthiaume | .15 | .07 |
| ❑ 55 Stephane Fiset | .15 | .07 |
| ❑ 56 Pat Falloon | .10 | .05 |
| ❑ 57 Dave Andreychuk | .15 | .07 |
| ❑ 58 Evgeny Davydov | .10 | .05 |
| ❑ 59 Dimitri Khristich | .10 | .05 |
| ❑ 60 Darryl Sydor | .10 | .05 |
| ❑ 61 Dirk Graham | .10 | .05 |
| ❑ 62 Chris Lindberg | .10 | .05 |
| ❑ 63 Tony Granato | .10 | .05 |
| ❑ 64 Corey Hirsch | .15 | .07 |
| ❑ 65 Jaromir Jagr | 1.00 | .45 |
| ❑ 66 Bret Hedican | .10 | .05 |
| ❑ 67 Pat Elynuik | .10 | .05 |
| ❑ 68 Petr Nedved | .15 | .07 |
| ❑ 69 Thomas Steen | .10 | .05 |
| ❑ 70 Philippe Boucher | .10 | .05 |
| ❑ 71 Paul Coffey | .30 | .14 |
| ❑ 72 Mike Lenarduzzi | .10 | .05 |
| ❑ 73 Iain Fraser | .10 | .05 |
| ❑ 74 Rod Brind'Amour | .15 | .07 |
| ❑ 75 Shawn Chambers | .10 | .05 |
| ❑ 76 Geoff Courtnall | .10 | .05 |
| ❑ 77 Todd Gill | .10 | .05 |
| ❑ 78 Mathieu Schneider | .10 | .05 |
| ❑ 79 Vincent Damphousse | .15 | .07 |
| ❑ 80 Igor Kravchuk | .10 | .05 |
| ❑ 81 Ulf Dahlen | .10 | .05 |
| ❑ 82 Dmitri Kvartalnov | .10 | .05 |
| ❑ 83 Johan Garpenlov | .10 | .05 |
| ❑ 84 Valeri Kamensky | .15 | .07 |
| ❑ 85 Bob Kudelski | .10 | .05 |
| ❑ 86 Bernie Nicholls | .10 | .05 |
| ❑ 87 Alexei Zhitnik | .10 | .05 |
| ❑ 88 Kelly Miller | .10 | .05 |
| ❑ 89 Bob Essensa | .15 | .07 |
| ❑ 90 Drake Berehowsky | .10 | .05 |
| ❑ 91 Jon Casey | .15 | .07 |
| ❑ 92 Dave Gagner | .15 | .07 |
| ❑ 93 Dave Manson | .10 | .05 |
| ❑ 94 Eric Desjardins | .10 | .05 |
| ❑ 95 Scott Niedermayer | .10 | .05 |
| ❑ 96 Chris Luongo | .10 | .05 |
| ❑ 97 Dave Karpa | .10 | .05 |
| ❑ 98 Rob Gaudreau | .10 | .05 |
| ❑ 99 Nikolai Borschevsky | .10 | .05 |
| ❑ 100 Phil Housley | .15 | .07 |
| ❑ 101 Michal Pivonka | .10 | .05 |
| ❑ 102 Dixon Ward | .10 | .05 |
| ❑ 103 Grant Fuhr | .15 | .07 |
| ❑ 104 Dallas Drake | .10 | .05 |
| ❑ 105 Michael Nylander | .10 | .05 |
| ❑ 106 Glenn Healy | .15 | .07 |
| ❑ 107 Kevin Dineen | .10 | .05 |
| ❑ 108 Roman Hamrlik | .15 | .07 |
| ❑ 109 Trevor Linden | .15 | .07 |
| ❑ 110 Doug Gilmour | .30 | .14 |
| ❑ 111 Keith Tkachuk | .40 | .18 |
| ❑ 112 Sergei Krivokrasov | .10 | .05 |
| ❑ 113 Al MacInnis | .15 | .07 |
| ❑ 114 Wayne Gretzky | 2.00 | .90 |
| ❑ 115 Alexei Kovalev | .15 | .07 |
| ❑ 116 Mario Lemieux | 1.50 | .70 |
| ❑ 117 Brett Hull | .40 | .18 |
| ❑ 118 Kevin Hatcher | .10 | .05 |
| ❑ 119 Cliff Ronning | .10 | .05 |
| ❑ 120 Viktor Gordiouk | .10 | .05 |
| ❑ 121 Sergei Fedorov | .60 | .25 |
| ❑ 122 Patrick Poulin | .10 | .05 |
| ❑ 123 Benoit Hogue | .10 | .05 |
| ❑ 124 Garry Galley | .10 | .05 |
| ❑ 125 Pat Jablonski | .15 | .07 |
| ❑ 126 Jyrki Lumme | .10 | .05 |
| ❑ 127 Dimitri Mironov | .10 | .05 |
| ❑ 128 Alexei Zhamnov | .15 | .07 |
| ❑ 129 Steve Larmer | .15 | .07 |
| ❑ 130 Joe Nieuwendyk | .15 | .07 |
| ❑ 131 Kelly Hrudey | .15 | .07 |
| ❑ 132 Brian Leetch | .30 | .14 |
| ❑ 133 Shawn McEachern | .10 | .05 |
| ❑ 134 Craig Janney | .15 | .07 |
| ❑ 135 Dale Hunter | .10 | .05 |
| ❑ 136 Jiri Slegr | .10 | .05 |
| ❑ 137 Mats Sundin | .15 | .07 |
| ❑ 138 Cam Neely | .15 | .07 |
| ❑ 139 Derian Hatcher | .10 | .05 |
| ❑ 140 Shjon Podein | .10 | .05 |
| ❑ 141 Gilbert Dionne | .10 | .05 |
| ❑ 142 Scott Pellerin | .10 | .05 |
| ❑ 143 Norm Maciver | .10 | .05 |
| ❑ 144 Andrei Kovalenko | .10 | .05 |
| ❑ 145 Arturs Irbe | .15 | .07 |
| ❑ 146 Wendel Clark | .15 | .07 |
| ❑ 147 Fredrik Olausson | .10 | .05 |
| ❑ 148 Mike Ridley | .10 | .05 |
| ❑ 149 Dale Hawerchuk | .15 | .07 |
| ❑ 150 Vladimir Konstantinov | .10 | .05 |
| ❑ 151 Geoff Sanderson | .15 | .07 |
| ❑ 152 Stephane Richer | .15 | .07 |
| ❑ 153 Darren Rumble | .10 | .05 |
| ❑ 154 Owen Nolan | .15 | .07 |
| ❑ 155 Kelly Kisio | .10 | .05 |
| ❑ 156 Adam Oates | .15 | .07 |
| ❑ 157 Trent Klatt | .15 | .07 |
| ❑ 158 Bill Ranford | .15 | .07 |
| ❑ 159 Paul DiPietro | .10 | .05 |
| ❑ 160 Darius Kasparaitis | .10 | .05 |
| ❑ 161 Eric Lindros | 1.25 | .55 |
| ❑ 162 Chris Kontos | .10 | .05 |
| ❑ 163 Joe Murphy | .10 | .05 |
| ❑ 164 Robert Reichel | .10 | .05 |
| ❑ 165 Jari Kurri | .15 | .07 |
| ❑ 166 Alexander Semak | .10 | .05 |
| ❑ 167 Brad Shaw | .10 | .05 |
| ❑ 168 Mike Ricci | .10 | .05 |
| ❑ 169 Sandis Ozolinsh | .15 | .07 |
| ❑ 170 Joby Messier | .10 | .05 |
| ❑ 171 Joe Mullen | .15 | .07 |
| ❑ 172 Curtis Joseph | .30 | .14 |
| ❑ 173 Yuri Khmylev | .10 | .05 |
| ❑ 174 Slava Kozlov | .15 | .07 |
| ❑ 175 Pat Verbeek | .10 | .05 |
| ❑ 176 Derek King | .10 | .05 |
| ❑ 177 Ryan McGill | .10 | .05 |
| ❑ 178 Chris LiPuma | .10 | .05 |
| ❑ 179 Grigori Pantaleyev | .10 | .05 |
| ❑ 180 Richard Matvichuk | .10 | .05 |
| ❑ 181 Steven Rice | .10 | .05 |
| ❑ 182 Sean Hill | .10 | .05 |
| ❑ 183 Mark Messier | .40 | .18 |
| ❑ 184 Larry Murphy | .15 | .07 |
| ❑ 185 Igor Korolev | .10 | .05 |
| ❑ 186 Jeremy Roenick | .30 | .14 |
| ❑ 187 Gary Roberts | .10 | .05 |
| ❑ 188 Robert Lang | .10 | .05 |
| ❑ 189 Scott Stevens | .15 | .07 |
| ❑ 190 Sylvain Turgeon | .10 | .05 |
| ❑ 191 Martin Rucinsky | .10 | .05 |
| ❑ 192 J.F. Quintin | .10 | .05 |
| ❑ 193 Dave Poulin | .10 | .05 |
| ❑ 194 Mike Modano | .40 | .18 |
| ❑ 195 Doug Weight | .15 | .07 |
| ❑ 196 Mike Keane | .10 | .05 |
| ❑ 197 Pierre Turgeon | .15 | .07 |
| ❑ 198 Dimitri Yushkevich | .10 | .05 |
| ❑ 199 Rob Zamuner | .10 | .05 |
| ❑ 200 Richard Smehlik | .10 | .05 |
| ❑ 201 Steve Yzerman | 1.00 | .45 |
| ❑ 202 Tony Amonte | .15 | .07 |
| ❑ 203 Sergei Nemchinov | .10 | .05 |
| ❑ 204 Ulf Samuelsson | .10 | .05 |
| ❑ 205 Kevin Miehm | .10 | .05 |
| ❑ 206 Brent Sutter | .10 | .05 |
| ❑ 207 Mike Vernon | .15 | .07 |
| ❑ 208 Luc Robitaille | .15 | .07 |
| ❑ 209 Chris Terreri | .15 | .07 |
| ❑ 210 Philippe Bozon | .10 | .05 |
| ❑ 211 John Tucker | .10 | .05 |
| ❑ 212 Jozef Stumpel | .10 | .05 |
| ❑ 213 Mark Tinordi | .10 | .05 |
| ❑ 214 Bruce Driver | .10 | .05 |
| ❑ 215 John LeClair | .50 | .23 |
| ❑ 216 Steve Thomas | .10 | .05 |
| ❑ 217 Tommy Soderstrom | .15 | .07 |
| ❑ 218 Kevin Miller | .10 | .05 |
| ❑ 219 Pat LaFontaine | .15 | .07 |
| ❑ 220 Nicklas Lidstrom | .15 | .07 |
| ❑ 221 Terry Yake | .10 | .05 |
| ❑ 222 Valeri Zelepukin | .10 | .05 |
| ❑ 223 Jeff Brown | .10 | .05 |
| ❑ 224 Chris Simon | .10 | .05 |
| ❑ 225 Rick Tocchet | .15 | .07 |
| ❑ 226 Gary Suter | .10 | .05 |
| ❑ 227 Marty McSorley | .10 | .05 |
| ❑ 228 Mike Richter | .30 | .14 |
| ❑ 229 Kevin Stevens | .10 | .05 |
| ❑ 230 Doug Wilson | .15 | .07 |
| ❑ 231 Steve Smith | .10 | .05 |
| ❑ 232 Bryan Smolinski | .10 | .05 |
| ❑ 233 Tommy Sjodin | .10 | .05 |
| ❑ 234 Zarley Zalapski | .10 | .05 |
| ❑ 235 Vladimir Malakhov | .10 | .05 |
| ❑ 236 Mark Recchi | .15 | .07 |
| ❑ 237 David Littman | .10 | .05 |
| ❑ 238 Alexander Mogilny | .15 | .07 |
| ❑ 239 Keith Primeau | .15 | .07 |
| ❑ 240 Tyler Wright | .10 | .05 |
| ❑ 241 Stephan Lebeau | .10 | .05 |
| ❑ 242 Joe Sakic | .60 | .25 |
| ❑ 243 Sergei Zubov | .10 | .05 |
| ❑ 244 Martin Straka | .10 | .05 |
| ❑ 245 Brendan Shanahan | .60 | .25 |
| ❑ 246 Tomas Sandstrom | .10 | .05 |
| ❑ 247 Milan Tichy | .10 | .05 |
| ❑ 248 C.J. Young | .10 | .05 |
| ❑ 249 Checklist Eric Lindros | .40 | .18 |
| ❑ 250 Checklist Teemu Selanne | .30 | .14 |
| ❑ 251 Patrick Carnback | .10 | .05 |
| ❑ 252 Todd Ewen | .10 | .05 |
| ❑ 253 Stu Grimson | .10 | .05 |
| ❑ 254 Guy Hebert | .15 | .07 |
| ❑ 255 Sean Hill | .10 | .05 |
| ❑ 256 Bill Houlder | .10 | .05 |
| ❑ 257 Alexei Kasatonov | .10 | .05 |
| ❑ 258 Steven King | .10 | .05 |
| ❑ 259 Troy Loney | .10 | .05 |
| ❑ 260 Joe Sacco | .10 | .05 |
| ❑ 261 Anatoli Semenov | .10 | .05 |
| ❑ 262 Tim Sweeney | .10 | .05 |
| ❑ 263 Ron Tugnutt | .15 | .07 |
| ❑ 264 Shaun Van Allen | .10 | .05 |
| ❑ 265 Terry Yake | .10 | .05 |
| ❑ 266 Jon Casey | .15 | .07 |
| ❑ 267 Ted Donato | .10 | .05 |
| ❑ 268 Steve Leach | .10 | .05 |
| ❑ 269 David Reid | .10 | .05 |
| ❑ 270 Cam Stewart | .10 | .05 |
| ❑ 271 Don Sweeney | .10 | .05 |
| ❑ 272 Glen Wesley | .10 | .05 |
| ❑ 273 Donald Audette | .15 | .07 |
| ❑ 274 Dominik Hasek | 1.00 | .45 |
| ❑ 275 Sergei Petrenko | .10 | .05 |
| ❑ 276 Derek Plante | .10 | .05 |
| ❑ 277 Craig Simpson | .10 | .05 |
| ❑ 278 Bob Sweeney | .10 | .05 |
| ❑ 279 Randy Wood | .10 | .05 |
| ❑ 280 Ted Drury | .10 | .05 |
| ❑ 281 Trevor Kidd | .15 | .07 |
| ❑ 282 Kelly Kisio | .10 | .05 |
| ❑ 283 Frank Musil | .10 | .05 |
| ❑ 284 Jason Muzzatti | .15 | .07 |
| ❑ 285 Joel Otto | .10 | .05 |
| ❑ 286 Paul Ranheim | .10 | .05 |
| ❑ 287 Wes Walz | .10 | .05 |

| | | |
|---|---|---|
| ❑ 288 Ivan Droppa | .10 | .05 |
| ❑ 289 Michel Goulet | .15 | .07 |
| ❑ 290 Stephane Matteau | .10 | .05 |
| ❑ 291 Brian Noonan | .10 | .05 |
| ❑ 292 Patrick Poulin | .10 | .05 |
| ❑ 293 Rich Sutter | .10 | .05 |
| ❑ 294 Kevin Todd | .10 | .05 |
| ❑ 295 Eric Weinrich | .10 | .05 |
| ❑ 296 Neal Broten | .15 | .07 |
| ❑ 297 Mike Craig | .10 | .05 |
| ❑ 298 Dean Evason | .10 | .05 |
| ❑ 299 Grant Ledyard | .10 | .05 |
| ❑ 300 Mike McPhee | .10 | .05 |
| ❑ 301 Andy Moog | .15 | .07 |
| ❑ 302 Jarkko Varvio | .10 | .05 |
| ❑ 303 Micah Aivazoff | .10 | .05 |
| ❑ 304 Terry Carkner | .10 | .05 |
| ❑ 305 Steve Chiasson | .10 | .05 |
| ❑ 306 Greg Johnson | .10 | .05 |
| ❑ 307 Darren McCarty | .40 | .18 |
| ❑ 308 Chris Osgood | 2.00 | .90 |
| ❑ 309 Bob Probert | .15 | .07 |
| ❑ 310 Ray Sheppard | .15 | .07 |
| ❑ 311 Mike Sillinger | .10 | .05 |
| ❑ 312 Jason Arnott | 1.00 | .45 |
| ❑ 313 Fred Brathwaite | .15 | .07 |
| ❑ 314 Kelly Buchberger | .10 | .05 |
| ❑ 315 Zdeno Ciger | .10 | .05 |
| ❑ 316 Craig MacTavish | .10 | .05 |
| ❑ 317 Dean McAmmond | .10 | .05 |
| ❑ 318 Luke Richardson | .10 | .05 |
| ❑ 319 Vladimir Vujtek | .10 | .05 |
| ❑ 320 Jesse Belanger | .10 | .05 |
| ❑ 321 Brian Benning | .10 | .05 |
| ❑ 322 Keith Brown | .10 | .05 |
| ❑ 323 Evgeny Davydov | .10 | .05 |
| ❑ 324 Tom Fitzgerald | .10 | .05 |
| ❑ 325 Alexander Godynyuk | .10 | .05 |
| ❑ 326 Scott Levins | .10 | .05 |
| ❑ 327 Andrei Lomakin | .10 | .05 |
| ❑ 328 Scott Mellanby | .15 | .07 |
| ❑ 329 Gord Murphy | .10 | .05 |
| ❑ 330 Rob Niedermayer | .15 | .07 |
| ❑ 331 Brent Severyn | .10 | .05 |
| ❑ 332 Brian Skrudland | .10 | .05 |
| ❑ 333 John Vanbiesbrouck | .50 | .23 |
| ❑ 334 Mark Greig | .10 | .05 |
| ❑ 335 Bryan Marchment | .10 | .05 |
| ❑ 336 James Patrick | .10 | .05 |
| ❑ 337 Robert Petrovicky | .10 | .05 |
| ❑ 338 Frank Pietrangelo | .15 | .07 |
| ❑ 339 Chris Pronger | .15 | .07 |
| ❑ 340 Brian Propp | .10 | .05 |
| ❑ 341 Darren Turcotte | .10 | .05 |
| ❑ 342 Pat Conacher | .10 | .05 |
| ❑ 343 Mark Hardy | .10 | .05 |
| ❑ 344 Charlie Huddy | .10 | .05 |
| ❑ 345 Shawn McEachern | .10 | .05 |
| ❑ 346 Warren Rychel | .10 | .05 |
| ❑ 347 Robb Stauber | .15 | .07 |
| ❑ 348 Dave Taylor | .15 | .07 |
| ❑ 349 Benoit Brunet | .10 | .05 |
| ❑ 350 Guy Carbonneau | .10 | .05 |
| ❑ 351 J.J. Daigneault | .10 | .05 |
| ❑ 352 Kevin Haller | .10 | .05 |
| ❑ 353 Gary Leeman | .10 | .05 |
| ❑ 354 Lyle Odelein | .10 | .05 |
| ❑ 355 Andre Racicot | .15 | .07 |
| ❑ 356 Ron Wilson | .10 | .05 |
| ❑ 357 Martin Brodeur | 1.00 | .45 |
| ❑ 358 Ken Daneyko | .10 | .05 |
| ❑ 359 Bill Guerin | .10 | .05 |
| ❑ 360 Bobby Holik | .10 | .05 |
| ❑ 361 Corey Millen | .10 | .05 |
| ❑ 362 Jaroslav Modry | .10 | .05 |
| ❑ 363 Jason Smith | .10 | .05 |
| ❑ 364 Brad Dalgarno | .10 | .05 |
| ❑ 365 Travis Green | .15 | .07 |
| ❑ 366 Ron Hextall | .15 | .07 |
| ❑ 367 Steve Junker | .10 | .05 |
| ❑ 368 Tom Kurvers | .10 | .05 |
| ❑ 369 Scott Lachance | .10 | .05 |
| ❑ 370 Marty McInnis | .10 | .05 |
| ❑ 371 Glenn Healy | .15 | .07 |
| ❑ 372 Alexander Karpovtsev | .10 | .05 |
| ❑ 373 Steve Larmer | .15 | .07 |
| ❑ 374 Doug Lidster | .10 | .05 |
| ❑ 375 Kevin Lowe | .10 | .05 |
| ❑ 376 Mattias Norstrom | .10 | .05 |
| ❑ 377 Esa Tikkanen | .10 | .05 |
| ❑ 378 Craig Billington | .15 | .07 |
| ❑ 379 Robert Burakovsky | .10 | .05 |
| ❑ 380 Alexandre Daigle | .10 | .05 |
| ❑ 381 Dmitri Filimonov | .10 | .05 |
| ❑ 382 Darrin Madeley | .10 | .05 |
| ❑ 383 Vladimir Ruzicka | .10 | .05 |
| ❑ 384 Alexei Yashin | .15 | .07 |
| ❑ 385 Viacheslav Butsayev | .10 | .05 |
| ❑ 386 Pelle Eklund | .10 | .05 |
| ❑ 387 Brent Fedyk | .10 | .05 |
| ❑ 388 Greg Hawgood | .10 | .05 |
| ❑ 389 Milos Holan | .10 | .05 |
| ❑ 390 Stewart Malgunas | .10 | .05 |
| ❑ 391 Mikael Renberg | .30 | .14 |
| ❑ 392 Dominic Roussel | .15 | .07 |
| ❑ 393 Doug Brown | .10 | .05 |
| ❑ 394 Marty McSorley | .10 | .05 |
| ❑ 395 Markus Naslund | .10 | .05 |
| ❑ 396 Mike Ramsey | .10 | .05 |
| ❑ 397 Peter Taglianetti | .10 | .05 |
| ❑ 398 Bryan Trottier | .15 | .07 |
| ❑ 399 Ken Wregget | .15 | .07 |
| ❑ 400 Iain Fraser | .10 | .05 |
| ❑ 401 Martin Gelinas | .10 | .05 |
| ❑ 402 Kerry Huffman | .10 | .05 |
| ❑ 403 Claude Lapointe | .10 | .05 |
| ❑ 404 Curtis Leschyshyn | .10 | .05 |
| ❑ 405 Chris Lindberg | .10 | .05 |
| ❑ 406 Jocelyn Thibault | 1.25 | .55 |
| ❑ 407 Murray Baron | .10 | .05 |
| ❑ 408 Bob Bassen | .10 | .05 |
| ❑ 409 Phil Housley | .15 | .07 |
| ❑ 410 Jim Hrivnak | .15 | .07 |
| ❑ 411 Tony Hrkac | .10 | .05 |
| ❑ 412 Vitali Karamnov | .10 | .05 |
| ❑ 413 Jim Montgomery | .10 | .05 |
| ❑ 414 Vlastimil Kroupa | .10 | .05 |
| ❑ 415 Igor Larionov | .10 | .05 |
| ❑ 416 Sergei Makarov | .10 | .05 |
| ❑ 417 Jeff Norton | .10 | .05 |
| ❑ 418 Mike Rathje | .10 | .05 |
| ❑ 419 Jim Waite | .15 | .07 |
| ❑ 420 Ray Whitney | .10 | .05 |
| ❑ 421 Mikael Andersson | .10 | .05 |
| ❑ 422 Donald Dufresne | .10 | .05 |
| ❑ 423 Chris Gratton | .15 | .07 |
| ❑ 424 Brent Gretzky | .10 | .05 |
| ❑ 425 Petr Klima | .10 | .05 |
| ❑ 426 Bill McDougall | .10 | .05 |
| ❑ 427 Daren Puppa | .15 | .07 |
| ❑ 428 Denis Savard | .15 | .07 |
| ❑ 429 Ken Baumgartner | .10 | .05 |
| ❑ 430 Sylvain Lefebvre | .10 | .05 |
| ❑ 431 Jamie Macoun | .10 | .05 |
| ❑ 432 Matt Martin | .10 | .05 |
| ❑ 433 Mark Osborne | .10 | .05 |
| ❑ 434 Rob Pearson | .10 | .05 |
| ❑ 435 Damian Rhodes | .15 | .07 |
| ❑ 436 Peter Zezel | .10 | .05 |
| ❑ 437 Shawn Antoski | .10 | .05 |
| ❑ 438 Jose Charbonneau | .10 | .05 |
| ❑ 439 Murray Craven | .10 | .05 |
| ❑ 440 Gerald Diduck | .10 | .05 |
| ❑ 441 Dana Murzyn | .10 | .05 |
| ❑ 442 Gino Odjick | .10 | .05 |
| ❑ 443 Kay Whitmore | .15 | .07 |
| ❑ 444 Randy Burridge | .10 | .05 |
| ❑ 445 Sylvain Cote | .10 | .05 |
| ❑ 446 Keith Jones | .10 | .05 |
| ❑ 447 Olaf Kolzig | .15 | .07 |
| ❑ 448 Todd Krygier | .10 | .05 |
| ❑ 449 Pat Peake | .10 | .05 |
| ❑ 450 Dave Poulin | .10 | .05 |
| ❑ 451 Stephane Beauregard | .15 | .07 |
| ❑ 452 Luciano Borsato | .10 | .05 |
| ❑ 453 Nelson Emerson | .10 | .05 |
| ❑ 454 Boris Mironov | .10 | .05 |
| ❑ 455 Teppo Numminen | .10 | .05 |
| ❑ 456 Stephane Quintal | .10 | .05 |
| ❑ 457 Paul Ysebaert | .10 | .05 |
| ❑ 458 Adrian Aucoin | .10 | .05 |
| ❑ 459 Todd Brost | .10 | .05 |
| ❑ 460 Martin Gendron | .10 | .05 |
| ❑ 461 David Harlock | .10 | .05 |
| ❑ 462 Corey Hirsch | .15 | .07 |
| ❑ 463 Todd Hlushko | .10 | .05 |
| ❑ 464 Fabian Joseph | .10 | .05 |
| ❑ 465 Paul Kariya | 8.00 | 3.60 |
| ❑ 466 Brett Lindros | .10 | .05 |
| ❑ 467 Ken Lovsin | .10 | .05 |
| ❑ 468 Jason Marshall | .10 | .05 |
| ❑ 469 Derek Mayer | .10 | .05 |
| ❑ 470 Dwayne Norris | .10 | .05 |
| ❑ 471 Russ Romaniuk | .10 | .05 |
| ❑ 472 Brian Savage | .30 | .14 |
| ❑ 473 Trevor Sim | .10 | .05 |
| ❑ 474 Chris Therien | .10 | .05 |
| ❑ 475 Brad Turner | .10 | .05 |
| ❑ 476 Todd Warriner | .10 | .05 |
| ❑ 477 Craig Woodcroft | .10 | .05 |
| ❑ 478 Mark Beaufait | .10 | .05 |
| ❑ 479 Jim Campbell | .10 | .05 |
| ❑ 480 Ted Crowley | .10 | .05 |
| ❑ 481 Mike Dunham | .15 | .07 |
| ❑ 482 Chris Ferraro | .10 | .05 |
| ❑ 483 Peter Ferraro | .10 | .05 |
| ❑ 484 Brett Hauer | .10 | .05 |
| ❑ 485 Darby Hendrickson | .10 | .05 |
| ❑ 486 Chris Imes | .10 | .05 |
| ❑ 487 Craig Johnson | .10 | .05 |
| ❑ 488 Peter Laviolette | .10 | .05 |
| ❑ 489 Jeff Lazaro | .10 | .05 |
| ❑ 490 John Lilley | .10 | .05 |
| ❑ 491 Todd Marchant | .10 | .05 |
| ❑ 492 Ian Moran | .10 | .05 |
| ❑ 493 Travis Richards | .15 | .07 |
| ❑ 494 Barry Richter | .10 | .05 |
| ❑ 495 David Roberts | .10 | .05 |
| ❑ 496 Brian Rolston | .10 | .05 |
| ❑ 497 David Sacco | .10 | .05 |
| ❑ 498 Checklist Card | .10 | .05 |
| ❑ 499 Checklist Card | .10 | .05 |
| ❑ 500 Checklist Card | .10 | .05 |

## 1993-94 Ultra All-Rookies

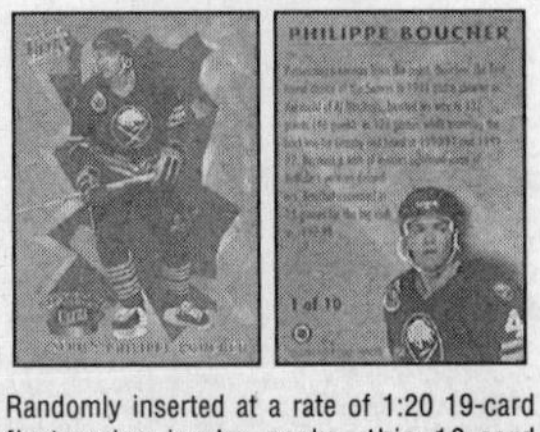


Randomly inserted at a rate of 1:20 19-card first-series jumbo packs, this 10-card standard-size set features on its borderless fronts color player action cutouts "breaking out" of their simulated ice backgrounds. The player's name appears in gold-foil lettering at a lower corner. The blue back carries the player's name at the top in gold-foil lettering, followed below by career highlights and a color player action cutout. The cards are numbered on the back as "X of 10."

| | MINT | NRMT |
|---|---|---|
| COMPLETE SET (10) | 50.00 | 22.00 |
| COMMON CARD (1-10) | 4.00 | 1.80 |
| ❑ 1 Philippe Boucher | 4.00 | 1.80 |
| ❑ 2 Viktor Gordiouk | 4.00 | 1.80 |
| ❑ 3 Corey Hirsch | 8.00 | 3.60 |
| ❑ 4 Chris LiPuma | 4.00 | 1.80 |
| ❑ 5 David Littman | 4.00 | 1.80 |
| ❑ 6 Joby Messier | 4.00 | 1.80 |
| ❑ 7 Chris Simon | 4.00 | 1.80 |
| ❑ 8 Bryan Smolinski | 8.00 | 3.60 |
| ❑ 9 Jozef Stumpel | 5.00 | 2.20 |
| ❑ 10 Milan Tichy | 4.00 | 1.80 |

## 1993-94 Ultra All-Stars

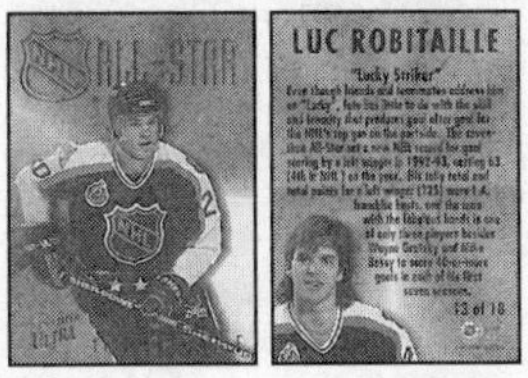


Randomly inserted into all first series packs, this 18-card standard-size set focuses on 18 of the NHL's best players. The set numbering is by conference All-Stars, Wales (1-9) and Campbell (10-18).

| | MINT | NRMT |
|---|---|---|
| COMPLETE SET (18) | 30.00 | 13.50 |
| COMMON CARD (1-18) | .75 | .35 |
| ❑ 1 Patrick Roy | 6.00 | 2.70 |
| ❑ 2 Ray Bourque | 1.25 | .55 |
| ❑ 3 Pierre Turgeon | 1.00 | .45 |
| ❑ 4 Pat LaFontaine | 1.00 | .45 |
| ❑ 5 Alexander Mogilny | 1.00 | .45 |
| ❑ 6 Kevin Stevens | .75 | .35 |
| ❑ 7 Adam Oates | 1.00 | .45 |
| ❑ 8 Al Iafrate | .75 | .35 |
| ❑ 9 Kirk Muller | .75 | .35 |
| ❑ 10 Ed Belfour | 1.25 | .55 |
| ❑ 11 Teemu Selanne | 3.00 | 1.35 |
| ❑ 12 Steve Yzerman | 4.00 | 1.80 |
| ❑ 13 Luc Robitaille | 1.00 | .45 |
| ❑ 14 Chris Chelios | 1.25 | .55 |
| ❑ 15 Wayne Gretzky | 10.00 | 4.50 |
| ❑ 16 Doug Gilmour | 1.00 | .45 |
| ❑ 17 Pavel Bure | 3.00 | 1.35 |
| ❑ 18 Phil Housley | .75 | .35 |

## 1993-94 Ultra Award Winners

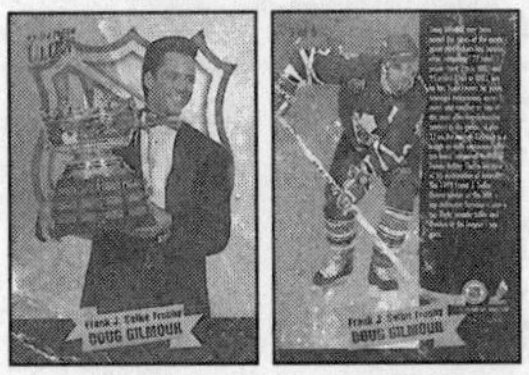


Randomly inserted into all first series packs, this six-card standard-size set honors NHL award winners of the previous season. Each borderless front features the player with his award. The back has an action photo and career highlights. The cards are numbered "X of 6".

| | MINT | NRMT |
|---|---|---|
| COMPLETE SET (6) | 20.00 | 9.00 |
| COMMON CARD (1-6) | 1.50 | .70 |
| ❑ 1 Ed Belfour<br>Jennings/Vezina Trophies | 2.50 | 1.10 |
| ❑ 2 Chris Chelios<br>Norris Trophy | 2.50 | 1.10 |
| ❑ 3 Doug Gilmour<br>Selke Trophy | 2.50 | 1.10 |
| ❑ 4 Mario Lemieux<br>Masterton Memorial/ Ross/Hart Memorial Trophies | 8.00 | 3.60 |
| ❑ 5 Dave Poulin<br>King Clancy Trophy | 1.50 | .70 |
| ❑ 6 Teemu Selanne<br>Calder Trophy | 4.00 | 1.80 |

## 1993-94 Ultra Adam Oates

As part of Ultra's Signature series, this 12-card standard-size set presents career highlights of

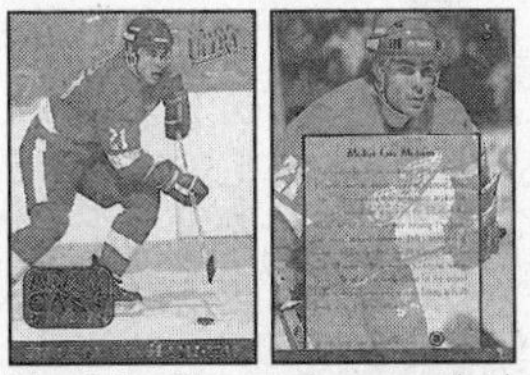

Adam Oates. These cards were randomly inserted throughout all packs, and Oates autographed more than 2,000 of his cards. Stated odds suggest the likelihood of pulling an autographed card at 1:10,000 packs. Two additional cards (11, 12) were available only by mail for ten Ultra wrappers plus 1.00.

| | MINT | NRMT |
|---|---|---|
| COMPLETE SET (10) | 4.00 | 1.80 |
| COMMON OATES (1-10) | .50 | .23 |
| CERTIFIED AUTO | 80.00 | 36.00 |
| ❑ 1 Adam Oates<br>A Challenge Met | .50 | .23 |
| ❑ 2 Adam Oates<br>Sowing His Oates | .50 | .23 |
| ❑ 3 Adam Oates<br>Wanted Man | .50 | .23 |
| ❑ 4 Adam Oates<br>Making the Grade | .50 | .23 |
| ❑ 5 Adam Oates<br>Motor City Motion | .50 | .23 |
| ❑ 6 Adam Oates<br>Hello and Goodbye | .50 | .23 |
| ❑ 7 Adam Oates<br>Blues Brother | .50 | .23 |
| ❑ 8 Adam Oates<br>Hit the Ignition | .50 | .23 |
| ❑ 9 Adam Oates<br>The Breakup | .50 | .23 |
| ❑ 10 Adam Oates<br>The Spotlight Shines | .50 | .23 |
| ❑ 11 Adam Oates<br>North American Dream | .50 | .23 |
| ❑ 12 Adam Oates<br>Giving 'till it Hurts | .50 | .23 |

## 1993-94 Ultra Premier Pivots

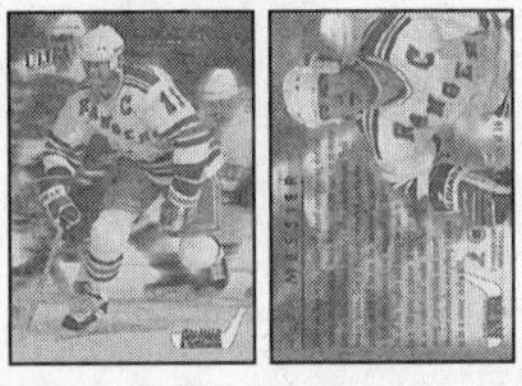

Randomly inserted in all series II packs, these ten standard-size cards feature some of the NHL's greatest centers. The borderless fronts have color player action shots on motion-streaked backgrounds. The player's name appears in silver foil at the upper right. The horizontal back carries another borderless color player action shot offset to the right. The on-ice background is ghosted and again motion-streaked. The player's name appears in silver foil at the upper left, followed below by career highlights. The cards are numbered on the back as "X of 10."

| | MINT | NRMT |
|---|---|---|
| COMPLETE SET (10) | 20.00 | 9.00 |
| COMMON CARD (1-10) | .50 | .23 |
| ❑ 1 Doug Gilmour | .50 | .23 |
| ❑ 2 Wayne Gretzky | 6.00 | 2.70 |
| ❑ 3 Pat LaFontaine | .50 | .23 |
| ❑ 4 Mario Lemieux | 5.00 | 2.20 |
| ❑ 5 Eric Lindros | 4.00 | 1.80 |
| ❑ 6 Mark Messier | 1.25 | .55 |
| ❑ 7 Adam Oates | .50 | .23 |
| ❑ 8 Jeremy Roenick | 1.00 | .45 |
| ❑ 9 Pierre Turgeon | .50 | .23 |
| ❑ 10 Steve Yzerman | 3.00 | 1.35 |

## 1993-94 Ultra Prospects

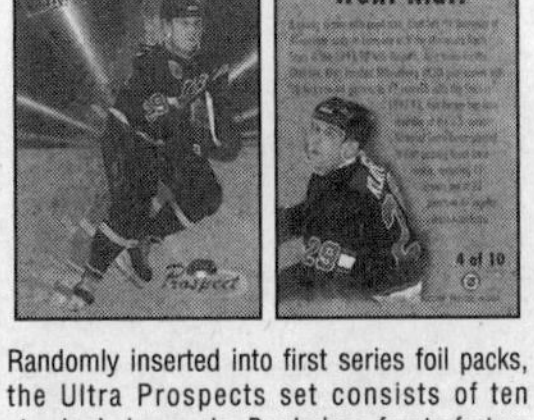


Randomly inserted into first series foil packs, the Ultra Prospects set consists of ten standard-size cards. Borderless fronts feature the player emerging from a solid background. The backs contain a photo and career highlights. The cards are numbered as "X of 10".

| | MINT | NRMT |
|---|---|---|
| COMPLETE SET (10) | 8.00 | 3.60 |
| COMMON CARD (1-10) | 1.00 | .45 |
| ❑ 1 Iain Fraser | 1.00 | .45 |
| ❑ 2 Rob Gaudreau | 1.00 | .45 |
| ❑ 3 Dave Karpa | 1.00 | .45 |
| ❑ 4 Trent Klatt | 1.00 | .45 |
| ❑ 5 Mike Lenarduzzi | 1.25 | .55 |
| ❑ 6 Kevin Miehm | 1.00 | .45 |
| ❑ 7 Michael Nylander | 1.25 | .55 |
| ❑ 8 J.F. Quintin | 1.00 | .45 |
| ❑ 9 Gary Shuchuk | 1.00 | .45 |
| ❑ 10 Tyler Wright | 1.00 | .45 |

## 1993-94 Ultra Red Light Specials

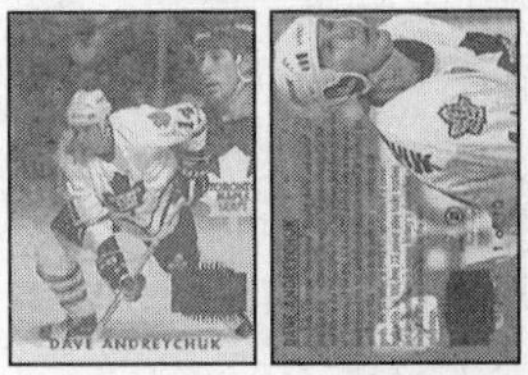


Randomly inserted in series 2 packs, this ten-card standard-size set highlights some of the NHL's best goal scorers. The borderless fronts feature two color player action shots, one superimposed upon the other. The player's name appears in red foil at the bottom. The horizontal back carries an on-ice closeup of the player set off to the right. The player's name appears in red foil at the upper left, followed below by the player's goal-scoring highlights, all on the red-screened background from the player closeup. The cards are numbered on the back as "X of 10."

| | MINT | NRMT |
|---|---|---|
| COMPLETE SET (10) | 30.00 | 13.50 |
| COMMON CARD (1-10) | .50 | .23 |
| ❑ 1 Dave Andreychuk | .50 | .23 |
| ❑ 2 Pavel Bure | 4.00 | 1.80 |
| ❑ 3 Mike Gartner | .50 | .23 |
| ❑ 4 Brett Hull | 2.50 | 1.10 |
| ❑ 5 Jaromir Jagr | 6.00 | 2.70 |
| ❑ 6 Mario Lemieux | 10.00 | 4.50 |
| ❑ 7 Alexander Mogilny | .75 | .35 |
| ❑ 8 Mark Recchi | .50 | .23 |
| ❑ 9 Luc Robitaille | .50 | .23 |
| ❑ 10 Teemu Selanne | 5.00 | 2.20 |

## 1993-94 Ultra Scoring Kings

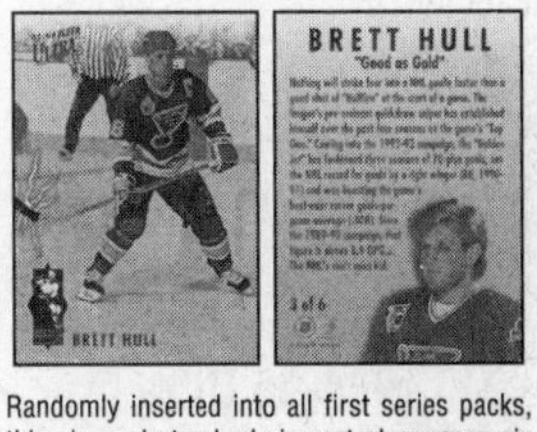


Randomly inserted into all first series packs, this six-card standard-size set showcases six of the NHL's top scorers. Borderless fronts have action player photos. Backs feature a player photo and career highlights. The player's name appears in gold at the top. The card are numbered "X of 6".

| | MINT | NRMT |
|---|---|---|
| COMPLETE SET (6) | 25.00 | 11.00 |
| COMMON CARD (1-6) | 1.50 | .70 |
| ❑ 1 Pat LaFontaine | 1.50 | .70 |
| ❑ 2 Wayne Gretzky | 10.00 | 4.50 |
| ❑ 3 Brett Hull | 2.50 | 1.10 |
| ❑ 4 Mario Lemieux | 8.00 | 3.60 |
| ❑ 5 Pierre Turgeon | 1.50 | .70 |
| ❑ 6 Steve Yzerman | 5.00 | 2.20 |

## 1993-94 Ultra Speed Merchants

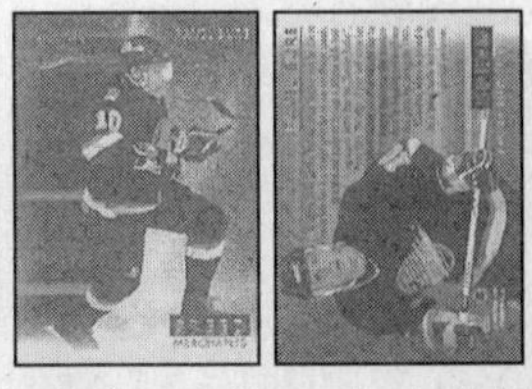

Randomly inserted in second series jumbo packs, this 10-card standard-size set sports fronts of motion-streaked color player action cutouts set on borderless indigo backgrounds highlighted by ice spray. The horizontal borderless back carries a motion-streaked

color player action cutout on one side, with the player's name in silver foil and career highlights on the other, all on a grayish background. The cards are numbered on the back as "X of 10."

| | MINT | NRMT |
|---|---|---|
| COMPLETE SET (10) | 80.00 | 36.00 |
| COMMON CARD (1-10) | 5.00 | 2.20 |
| ❑ 1 Pavel Bure | 15.00 | 6.75 |
| ❑ 2 Russ Courtnall | 5.00 | 2.20 |
| ❑ 3 Sergei Fedorov | 15.00 | 6.75 |
| ❑ 4 Mike Gartner | 5.00 | 2.20 |
| ❑ 5 Al Iafrate | 5.00 | 2.20 |
| ❑ 6 Pat LaFontaine | 6.00 | 2.70 |
| ❑ 7 Alexander Mogilny | 6.00 | 2.70 |
| ❑ 8 Rob Niedermayer | 8.00 | 3.60 |
| ❑ 9 Geoff Sanderson | 5.00 | 2.20 |
| ❑ 10 Teemu Selanne | 20.00 | 9.00 |

## 1993-94 Ultra Wave of the Future

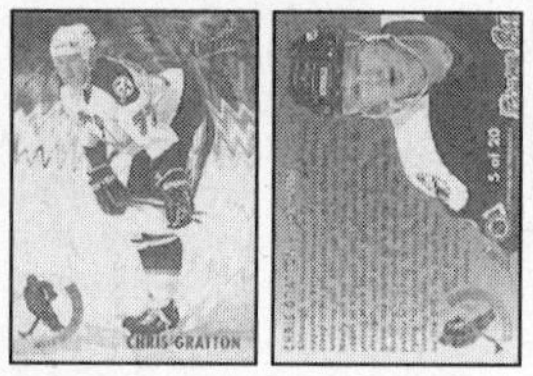


Randomly inserted in series II packs, these 20 standard-size cards highlight players in their first or second NHL season. The borderless fronts feature color player action shots with "rippled" on-ice backgrounds. The player's name appears in gold foil at a lower corner. The borderless horizontal back carries a player color closeup on the right. The player's name, and the card's descriptive title, appear in gold foil at the upper left; below are career highlights. The "rippled" background is a solid team color. The cards are numbered on the back as "X of 20."

| | MINT | NRMT |
|---|---|---|
| COMPLETE SET (20) | 30.00 | 13.50 |
| COMMON CARD (1-20) | .50 | .23 |
| ❑ 1 Jason Arnott | 4.00 | 1.80 |
| ❑ 2 Martin Brodeur | 5.00 | 2.20 |
| ❑ 3 Alexandre Daigle | 1.50 | .70 |
| ❑ 4 Ted Drury | .50 | .23 |
| ❑ 5 Chris Gratton | 1.50 | .70 |
| ❑ 6 Milos Holan | .50 | .23 |
| ❑ 7 Greg Johnson | .50 | .23 |
| ❑ 8 Boris Mironov | .50 | .23 |
| ❑ 9 Jaroslav Modry | .50 | .23 |
| ❑ 10 Markus Naslund | .50 | .23 |
| ❑ 11 Rob Niedermayer | 2.00 | .90 |
| ❑ 12 Chris Osgood | 8.00 | 3.60 |
| ❑ 13 Derek Plante | 2.00 | .90 |
| ❑ 14 Chris Pronger | 1.50 | .70 |
| ❑ 15 Mike Rathje | .50 | .23 |
| ❑ 16 Mikael Renberg | 2.00 | .90 |
| ❑ 17 Jason Smith | .50 | .23 |
| ❑ 18 Jocelyn Thibault | 5.00 | 2.20 |
| ❑ 19 Jarkko Varvio | .50 | .23 |
| ❑ 20 Alexei Yashin | 1.50 | .70 |

## 1994-95 Ultra

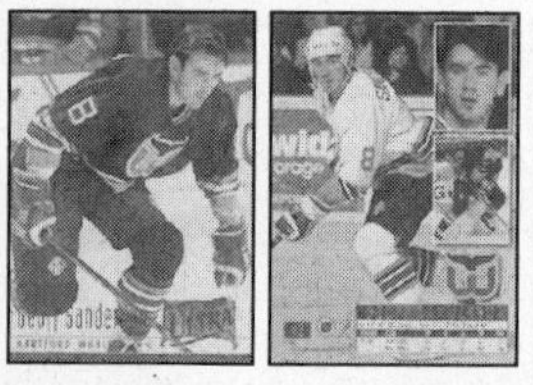

The 1994-95 Ultra hockey set consists of two series of 200 and 150 cards, for a total of 350 standard-size cards. The suggested retail price for 12-card packs was $1.99, and $2.69 for 15-card packs. Every pack included one insert card, and one "Hot Pack" consisting exclusively of insert cards was seeded once every two boxes (or 1:72 packs). Full-bleed card fronts have the player's name, team and Ultra logo in gold foil at the bottom. The backs also have a full-bleed photo with two smaller inset photos. Stats are at the bottom. Each series is arranged alphabetically by team and the player's within each team alphabetized. Rookie Cards include Mariusz Czerkawski and Eric Fichaud.

| | MINT | NRMT |
|---|---|---|
| COMPLETE SET (400) | 35.00 | 16.00 |
| COMPLETE SERIES 1 (250) | 20.00 | 9.00 |
| COMPLETE SERIES 2 (150) | 15.00 | 6.75 |
| COMMON CARD (1-400) | .10 | .05 |
| ❑ 1 Bob Corkum | .10 | .05 |
| ❑ 2 Todd Ewen | .10 | .05 |
| ❑ 3 Guy Hebert | .15 | .07 |
| ❑ 4 Bill Houlder | .10 | .05 |
| ❑ 5 Stephan Lebeau | .10 | .05 |
| ❑ 6 Joe Sacco | .10 | .05 |
| ❑ 7 Anatoli Semenov | .10 | .05 |
| ❑ 8 Tim Sweeney | .10 | .05 |
| ❑ 9 Terry Yake | .10 | .05 |
| ❑ 10 Ray Bourque | .30 | .14 |
| ❑ 11 Mariusz Czerkawski | .10 | .05 |
| ❑ 12 Ted Donato | .10 | .05 |
| ❑ 13 Cam Neely | .15 | .07 |
| ❑ 14 Adam Oates | .15 | .07 |
| ❑ 15 Vincent Riendeau | .15 | .07 |
| ❑ 16 Bryan Smolinski | .10 | .05 |
| ❑ 17 Don Sweeney | .10 | .05 |
| ❑ 18 Glen Wesley | .10 | .05 |
| ❑ 19 Donald Audette | .15 | .07 |
| ❑ 20 Doug Bodger | .10 | .05 |
| ❑ 21 Jason Dawe | .10 | .05 |
| ❑ 22 Dominik Hasek | .60 | .25 |
| ❑ 23 Dale Hawerchuk | .15 | .07 |
| ❑ 24 Pat LaFontaine | .15 | .07 |
| ❑ 25 Brad May | .15 | .07 |
| ❑ 26 Alexander Mogilny | .15 | .07 |
| ❑ 27 Derek Plante | .10 | .05 |
| ❑ 28 Richard Smehlik | .10 | .05 |
| ❑ 29 Theoren Fleury | .15 | .07 |
| ❑ 30 Trevor Kidd | .15 | .07 |
| ❑ 31 Frank Musil | .10 | .05 |
| ❑ 32 Michael Nylander | .10 | .05 |
| ❑ 33 James Patrick | .10 | .05 |
| ❑ 34 Robert Reichel | .10 | .05 |
| ❑ 35 Gary Roberts | .10 | .05 |
| ❑ 36 German Titov | .10 | .05 |
| ❑ 37 Wes Walz | .10 | .05 |
| ❑ 38 Zarley Zalapski | .10 | .05 |
| ❑ 39 Ed Belfour | .30 | .14 |
| ❑ 40 Chris Chelios | .30 | .14 |
| ❑ 41 Dirk Graham | .10 | .05 |
| ❑ 42 Bernie Nicholls | .15 | .07 |
| ❑ 43 Patrick Poulin | .10 | .05 |
| ❑ 44 Jeremy Roenick | .30 | .14 |
| ❑ 45 Steve Smith | .10 | .05 |
| ❑ 46 Gary Suter | .10 | .05 |
| ❑ 47 Brent Sutter | .10 | .05 |
| ❑ 48 Neal Broten | .15 | .07 |
| ❑ 49 Paul Cavallini | .10 | .05 |
| ❑ 50 Dean Evason | .10 | .05 |
| ❑ 51 Dave Gagner | .15 | .07 |
| ❑ 52 Derian Hatcher | .10 | .05 |
| ❑ 53 Trent Klatt | .10 | .05 |
| ❑ 54 Grant Ledyard | .10 | .05 |
| ❑ 55 Mike Modano | .40 | .18 |
| ❑ 56 Andy Moog | .15 | .07 |
| ❑ 57 Mark Tinordi | .10 | .05 |
| ❑ 58 Dino Ciccarelli | .15 | .07 |
| ❑ 59 Paul Coffey | .30 | .14 |
| ❑ 60 Sergei Fedorov | .60 | .25 |
| ❑ 61 Vladimir Konstantinov | .10 | .05 |
| ❑ 62 Nicklas Lidstrom | .15 | .07 |
| ❑ 63 Darren McCarty | .10 | .05 |
| ❑ 64 Chris Osgood | .50 | .23 |
| ❑ 65 Keith Primeau | .15 | .07 |
| ❑ 66 Ray Sheppard | .15 | .07 |
| ❑ 67 Steve Yzerman | 1.00 | .45 |
| ❑ 68 Jason Arnott | .15 | .07 |
| ❑ 69 Bob Beers | .10 | .05 |
| ❑ 70 Ilya Byakin | .10 | .05 |
| ❑ 71 Zdeno Ciger | .10 | .05 |
| ❑ 72 Igor Kravchuk | .10 | .05 |
| ❑ 73 Boris Mironov | .10 | .05 |
| ❑ 74 Fredrik Olausson | .10 | .05 |
| ❑ 75 Scott Pearson | .10 | .05 |
| ❑ 76 Bill Ranford | .15 | .07 |
| ❑ 77 Doug Weight | .15 | .07 |
| ❑ 78 Stu Barnes | .10 | .05 |
| ❑ 79 Jesse Belanger | .10 | .05 |
| ❑ 80 Bob Kudelski | .10 | .05 |
| ❑ 81 Andrei Lomakin | .10 | .05 |
| ❑ 82 Dave Lowry | .10 | .05 |
| ❑ 83 Gord Murphy | .10 | .05 |
| ❑ 84 Rob Niedermayer | .15 | .07 |
| ❑ 85 Brian Skrudland | .10 | .05 |
| ❑ 86 John Vanbiesbrouck | .50 | .23 |
| ❑ 87 Sean Burke | .15 | .07 |
| ❑ 88 Ted Drury | .10 | .05 |
| ❑ 89 Alexander Godynyuk | .10 | .05 |
| ❑ 90 Robert Kron | .10 | .05 |
| ❑ 91 Chris Pronger | .15 | .07 |
| ❑ 92 Brian Propp | .10 | .05 |
| ❑ 93 Geoff Sanderson | .15 | .07 |
| ❑ 94 Darren Turcotte | .10 | .05 |
| ❑ 95 Pat Verbeek | .10 | .05 |
| ❑ 96 Rob Blake | .10 | .05 |
| ❑ 97 Mike Donnelly | .10 | .05 |
| ❑ 98 John Druce | .10 | .05 |
| ❑ 99 Kelly Hrudey | .15 | .07 |
| ❑ 100 Jari Kurri | .15 | .07 |
| ❑ 101 Robert Lang | .10 | .05 |
| ❑ 102 Marty McSorley | .10 | .05 |
| ❑ 103 Luc Robitaille | .15 | .07 |
| ❑ 104 Alexei Zhitnik | .10 | .05 |
| ❑ 105 Brian Bellows | .10 | .05 |
| ❑ 106 Patrice Brisebois | .10 | .05 |
| ❑ 107 Vincent Damphousse | .15 | .07 |
| ❑ 108 Eric Desjardins | .10 | .05 |
| ❑ 109 Gilbert Dionne | .10 | .05 |
| ❑ 110 Mike Keane | .10 | .05 |
| ❑ 111 John LeClair | .50 | .23 |
| ❑ 112 Lyle Odelein | .10 | .05 |
| ❑ 113 Patrick Roy | 1.50 | .70 |
| ❑ 114 Mathieu Schneider | .10 | .05 |
| ❑ 115 Martin Brodeur | .75 | .35 |
| ❑ 116 Jim Dowd | .10 | .05 |
| ❑ 117 Bill Guerin | .10 | .05 |
| ❑ 118 Claude Lemieux | .15 | .07 |
| ❑ 119 John MacLean | .15 | .07 |
| ❑ 120 Corey Millen | .10 | .05 |
| ❑ 121 Scott Niedermayer | .10 | .05 |
| ❑ 122 Stephane Richer | .15 | .07 |
| ❑ 123 Scott Stevens | .15 | .07 |
| ❑ 124 Valeri Zelepukin | .10 | .05 |
| ❑ 125 Patrick Flatley | .10 | .05 |
| ❑ 126 Travis Green | .15 | .07 |
| ❑ 127 Ron Hextall | .15 | .07 |
| ❑ 128 Benoit Hogue | .10 | .05 |
| ❑ 129 Darius Kasparaitis | .10 | .05 |
| ❑ 130 Vladimir Malakhov | .10 | .05 |
| ❑ 131 Marty McInnis | .10 | .05 |
| ❑ 132 Steve Thomas | .10 | .05 |
| ❑ 133 Pierre Turgeon | .15 | .07 |
| ❑ 134 Dennis Vaske | .10 | .05 |
| ❑ 135 Glenn Anderson | .15 | .07 |
| ❑ 136 Jeff Beukeboom | .10 | .05 |
| ❑ 137 Adam Graves | .15 | .07 |
| ❑ 138 Steve Larmer | .15 | .07 |
| ❑ 139 Brian Leetch | .30 | .14 |
| ❑ 140 Mark Messier | .40 | .18 |
| ❑ 141 Petr Nedved | .15 | .07 |
| ❑ 142 Sergei Nemchinov | .10 | .05 |
| ❑ 143 Mike Richter | .30 | .14 |
| ❑ 144 Sergei Zubov | .10 | .05 |
| ❑ 145 Craig Billington | .15 | .07 |
| ❑ 146 Alexandre Daigle | .10 | .05 |
| ❑ 147 Evgeny Davydov | .10 | .05 |
| ❑ 148 Scott Levins | .10 | .05 |
| ❑ 149 Norm Maciver | .10 | .05 |
| ❑ 150 Troy Mallette | .10 | .05 |
| ❑ 151 Brad Shaw | .10 | .05 |
| ❑ 152 Alexei Yashin | .15 | .07 |
| ❑ 153 Josef Beranek | .10 | .05 |
| ❑ 154 Jason Bowen | .10 | .05 |
| ❑ 155 Rod Brind'Amour | .15 | .07 |
| ❑ 156 Kevin Dineen | .10 | .05 |
| ❑ 157 Garry Galley | .10 | .05 |
| ❑ 158 Mark Recchi | .15 | .07 |
| ❑ 159 Mikael Renberg | .15 | .07 |
| ❑ 160 Tommy Soderstrom | .15 | .07 |
| ❑ 161 Dimitri Yushkevich | .10 | .05 |
| ❑ 162 Tom Barrasso | .15 | .07 |
| ❑ 163 Ron Francis | .15 | .07 |
| ❑ 164 Jaromir Jagr | 1.00 | .45 |
| ❑ 165 Mario Lemieux | 1.50 | .70 |
| ❑ 166 Shawn McEachern | .10 | .05 |
| ❑ 167 Joe Mullen | .15 | .07 |
| ❑ 168 Larry Murphy | .15 | .07 |
| ❑ 169 Ulf Samuelsson | .10 | .05 |
| ❑ 170 Kevin Stevens | .10 | .05 |
| ❑ 171 Martin Straka | .10 | .05 |
| ❑ 172 Wendel Clark | .15 | .07 |
| ❑ 173 Stephane Fiset | .15 | .07 |
| ❑ 174 Iain Fraser | .10 | .05 |
| ❑ 175 Andrei Kovalenko | .10 | .05 |
| ❑ 176 Sylvain Lefebvre | .10 | .05 |
| ❑ 177 Owen Nolan | .15 | .07 |
| ❑ 178 Mike Ricci | .10 | .05 |
| ❑ 179 Martin Rucinsky | .10 | .05 |
| ❑ 180 Joe Sakic | .60 | .25 |
| ❑ 181 Scott Young | .10 | .05 |
| ❑ 182 Steve Duchesne | .10 | .05 |
| ❑ 183 Brett Hull | .40 | .18 |
| ❑ 184 Curtis Joseph | .30 | .14 |
| ❑ 185 Al MacInnis | .15 | .07 |
| ❑ 186 Kevin Miller | .10 | .05 |
| ❑ 187 Jim Montgomery | .10 | .05 |
| ❑ 188 Vitali Prokhorov | .10 | .05 |
| ❑ 189 Brendan Shanahan | .60 | .25 |
| ❑ 190 Peter Stastny | .15 | .07 |
| ❑ 191 Esa Tikkanen | .10 | .05 |
| ❑ 192 Ulf Dahlen | .10 | .05 |
| ❑ 193 Todd Elik | .10 | .05 |
| ❑ 194 Johan Garpenlov | .10 | .05 |
| ❑ 195 Arturs Irbe | .15 | .07 |
| ❑ 196 Vlastimil Kroupa | .10 | .05 |
| ❑ 197 Igor Larionov | .10 | .05 |
| ❑ 198 Sergei Makarov | .10 | .05 |
| ❑ 199 Jeff Norton | .10 | .05 |
| ❑ 200 Sandis Ozolinsh | .15 | .07 |
| ❑ 201 Mike Rathje | .10 | .05 |
| ❑ 202 Brian Bradley | .10 | .05 |
| ❑ 203 Shawn Chambers | .10 | .05 |
| ❑ 204 Danton Cole | .10 | .05 |
| ❑ 205 Chris Gratton | .15 | .07 |
| ❑ 206 Roman Hamrlik | .15 | .07 |
| ❑ 207 Chris Joseph | .10 | .05 |
| ❑ 208 Petr Klima | .10 | .05 |
| ❑ 209 Daren Puppa | .15 | .07 |
| ❑ 210 John Tucker | .10 | .05 |
| ❑ 211 Dave Andreychuk | .15 | .07 |
| ❑ 212 Ken Baumgartner | .10 | .05 |
| ❑ 213 Dave Ellett | .10 | .05 |
| ❑ 214 Mike Gartner | .15 | .07 |
| ❑ 215 Todd Gill | .10 | .05 |
| ❑ 216 Doug Gilmour | .30 | .14 |
| ❑ 217 Jamie Macoun | .10 | .05 |
| ❑ 218 Dmitri Mironov | .10 | .05 |
| ❑ 219 Felix Potvin | .30 | .14 |
| ❑ 220 Mats Sundin | .15 | .07 |
| ❑ 221 Jeff Brown | .10 | .05 |
| ❑ 222 Pavel Bure | .60 | .25 |
| ❑ 223 Murray Craven | .10 | .05 |
| ❑ 224 Bret Hedican | .10 | .05 |
| ❑ 225 Nathan Lafayette | .10 | .05 |
| ❑ 226 Trevor Linden | .15 | .07 |
| ❑ 227 Jyrki Lumme | .10 | .05 |
| ❑ 228 Kirk McLean | .15 | .07 |
| ❑ 229 Gino Odjick | .10 | .05 |
| ❑ 230 Cliff Ronning | .10 | .05 |
| ❑ 231 Peter Bondra | .30 | .14 |
| ❑ 232 Sylvain Cote | .10 | .05 |
| ❑ 233 Kevin Hatcher | .10 | .05 |
| ❑ 234 Dale Hunter | .10 | .05 |
| ❑ 235 Calle Johansson | .10 | .05 |
| ❑ 236 Dimitri Khristich | .10 | .05 |
| ❑ 237 Pat Peake | .10 | .05 |
| ❑ 238 Michal Pivonka | .10 | .05 |
| ❑ 239 Rick Tabaracci | .15 | .07 |
| ❑ 240 Tim Cheveldae | .15 | .07 |
| ❑ 241 Dallas Drake | .10 | .05 |
| ❑ 242 Nelson Emerson | .10 | .05 |
| ❑ 243 Dave Manson | .10 | .05 |
| ❑ 244 Teppo Numminen | .10 | .05 |
| ❑ 245 Stephane Quintal | .10 | .05 |
| ❑ 246 Teemu Selanne | .60 | .25 |
| ❑ 247 Keith Tkachuk | .40 | .18 |
| ❑ 248 Checklist | .10 | .05 |
| ❑ 249 Checklist | .10 | .05 |
| ❑ 250 Checklist | .10 | .05 |
| ❑ 251 John Lilley | .10 | .05 |
| ❑ 252 Mikhail Shtalenkov | .10 | .05 |
| ❑ 253 Garry Valk | .10 | .05 |
| ❑ 254 John Gruden | .10 | .05 |
| ❑ 255 Brent Hughes | .10 | .05 |
| ❑ 256 Al Iafrate | .10 | .05 |
| ❑ 257 Alexei Kasatonov | .10 | .05 |
| ❑ 258 Mikko Makela | .10 | .05 |
| ❑ 259 Marc Potvin | .10 | .05 |
| ❑ 260 Jon Rohloff | .10 | .05 |
| ❑ 261 Jozef Stumpel | .10 | .05 |
| ❑ 262 Grant Fuhr | .15 | .07 |
| ❑ 263 Viktor Gordiouk | .10 | .05 |
| ❑ 264 Yuri Khmylev | .10 | .05 |
| ❑ 265 Craig Muni | .10 | .05 |
| ❑ 266 Craig Simpson | .10 | .05 |
| ❑ 267 Denis Tsygurov | .10 | .05 |
| ❑ 268 Steve Chiasson | .10 | .05 |
| ❑ 269 Phil Housley | .15 | .07 |
| ❑ 270 Joel Otto | .10 | .05 |
| ❑ 271 Andrei Trefilov | .10 | .05 |
| ❑ 272 Vesa Viitakoski | .10 | .05 |
| ❑ 273 Tony Amonte | .15 | .07 |
| ❑ 274 Brent Grieve | .10 | .05 |
| ❑ 275 Bernie Nicholls | .10 | .05 |
| ❑ 276 Christian Soucy | .15 | .07 |
| ❑ 277 Paul Ysebaert | .10 | .05 |
| ❑ 278 Shane Churla | .10 | .05 |
| ❑ 279 Russ Courtnall | .10 | .05 |
| ❑ 280 Craig Ludwig | .10 | .05 |
| ❑ 281 Jarkko Varvio | .10 | .05 |
| ❑ 282 Darcy Wakaluk | .15 | .07 |
| ❑ 283 Greg Johnson | .10 | .05 |
| ❑ 284 Slava Kozlov | .15 | .07 |
| ❑ 285 Martin Lapointe | .10 | .05 |
| ❑ 286 Tim Taylor | .10 | .05 |
| ❑ 287 Mike Vernon | .15 | .07 |
| ❑ 288 Jason York | .10 | .05 |
| ❑ 289 Fred Brathwaite | .15 | .07 |
| ❑ 290 Kelly Buchberger | .10 | .05 |
| ❑ 291 Shayne Corson | .10 | .05 |
| ❑ 292 Dean McAmmond | .10 | .05 |
| ❑ 293 Vladimir Vujtek | .10 | .05 |
| ❑ 294 Doug Barrault | .10 | .05 |
| ❑ 295 Keith Brown | .10 | .05 |
| ❑ 296 Mark Fitzpatrick | .15 | .07 |
| ❑ 297 Mike Hough | .10 | .05 |
| ❑ 298 Scott Mellanby | .15 | .07 |
| ❑ 299 Jimmy Carson | .10 | .05 |
| ❑ 300 Andrew Cassels | .10 | .05 |
| ❑ 301 Andrei Nikolishin | .10 | .05 |
| ❑ 302 Steven Rice | .10 | .05 |
| ❑ 303 Glen Wesley | .10 | .05 |
| ❑ 304 Rob Brown | .10 | .05 |
| ❑ 305 Tony Granato | .10 | .05 |
| ❑ 306 Wayne Gretzky | 2.00 | .90 |
| ❑ 307 Dan Quinn | .10 | .05 |
| ❑ 308 Darryl Sydor | .10 | .05 |
| ❑ 309 Rick Tocchet | .15 | .07 |
| ❑ 310 Donald Brashear | .10 | .05 |
| ❑ 311 Valeri Bure | .15 | .07 |
| ❑ 312 Jim Montgomery | .10 | .05 |
| ❑ 313 Kirk Muller | .10 | .05 |
| ❑ 314 Oleg Petrov | .10 | .05 |
| ❑ 315 Peter Popovic | .10 | .05 |
| ❑ 316 Yves Racine | .10 | .05 |
| ❑ 317 Turner Stevenson | .10 | .05 |
| ❑ 318 Ken Daneyko | .10 | .05 |
| ❑ 319 David Emma | .10 | .05 |
| ❑ 320 Brian Rolston | .10 | .05 |
| ❑ 321 Alexander Semak | .10 | .05 |
| ❑ 322 Jason Smith | .10 | .05 |
| ❑ 323 Chris Terreri | .15 | .07 |
| ❑ 324 Ray Ferraro | .10 | .05 |
| ❑ 325 Derek King | .10 | .05 |
| ❑ 326 Scott Lachance | .10 | .05 |
| ❑ 327 Brett Lindros | .10 | .05 |
| ❑ 328 Jamie McLennan | .10 | .05 |
| ❑ 329 Zigmund Palffy | .30 | .14 |
| ❑ 330 Corey Hirsch | .15 | .07 |
| ❑ 331 Alexei Kovalev | .15 | .07 |
| ❑ 332 Stephane Matteau | .10 | .05 |
| ❑ 333 Petr Nedved | .15 | .07 |
| ❑ 334 Mattias Norstrom | .10 | .05 |
| ❑ 335 Mark Osborne | .10 | .05 |
| ❑ 336 Randy Cunneyworth | .10 | .05 |
| ❑ 337 Pavol Demitra | .10 | .05 |
| ❑ 338 Pat Elynuik | .10 | .05 |
| ❑ 339 Sean Hill | .10 | .05 |
| ❑ 340 Darrin Madeley | .10 | .05 |
| ❑ 341 Sylvain Turgeon | .10 | .05 |
| ❑ 342 Vladislav Boulin | .15 | .07 |
| ❑ 343 Ron Hextall | .15 | .07 |
| ❑ 344 Patrik Juhlin | .10 | .05 |
| ❑ 345 Eric Lindros | 1.25 | .55 |
| ❑ 346 Shjon Podein | .10 | .05 |
| ❑ 347 Chris Therien | .10 | .05 |
| ❑ 348 John Cullen | .10 | .05 |
| ❑ 349 Markus Naslund | .10 | .05 |
| ❑ 350 Luc Robitaille | .15 | .07 |
| ❑ 351 Kjell Samuelsson | .10 | .05 |
| ❑ 352 Tomas Sandstrom | .10 | .05 |
| ❑ 353 Ken Wregget | .15 | .07 |
| ❑ 354 Wendel Clark | .15 | .07 |
| ❑ 355 Adam Deadmarsh | .15 | .07 |
| ❑ 356 Peter Forsberg | 1.50 | .70 |
| ❑ 357 Valeri Kamensky | .15 | .07 |
| ❑ 358 Uwe Krupp | .10 | .05 |
| ❑ 359 Janne Laukkanen | .10 | .05 |
| ❑ 360 Sylvain Lefebvre | .10 | .05 |
| ❑ 361 Jocelyn Thibault | .30 | .14 |
| ❑ 362 Bill Houlder | .10 | .05 |
| ❑ 363 Craig Janney | .15 | .07 |
| ❑ 364 Pat Falloon | .10 | .05 |
| ❑ 365 Jeff Friesen | .15 | .07 |
| ❑ 366 Viktor Kozlov | .10 | .05 |
| ❑ 367 Andrei Nazarov | .10 | .05 |
| ❑ 368 Jeff Odgers | .10 | .05 |
| ❑ 369 Michal Sykora | .10 | .05 |
| ❑ 370 Mikael Andersson | .10 | .05 |
| ❑ 371 Eric Charron | .10 | .05 |
| ❑ 372 Chris LiPuma | .10 | .05 |
| ❑ 373 Denis Savard | .15 | .07 |
| ❑ 374 Jason Wiemer | .10 | .05 |
| ❑ 375 Nikolai Borschevsky | .10 | .05 |
| ❑ 376 Eric Fichaud | .60 | .25 |
| ❑ 377 Kenny Jonsson | .10 | .05 |
| ❑ 378 Mike Ridley | .10 | .05 |
| ❑ 379 Mats Sundin | .15 | .07 |
| ❑ 380 Greg Adams | .10 | .05 |
| ❑ 381 Shawn Antoski | .10 | .05 |
| ❑ 382 Geoff Courtnall | .10 | .05 |
| ❑ 383 Martin Gelinas | .10 | .05 |
| ❑ 384 Sergio Momesso | .10 | .05 |
| ❑ 385 Jiri Slegr | .10 | .05 |
| ❑ 386 Jason Allison | .10 | .05 |
| ❑ 387 Don Beaupre | .15 | .07 |
| ❑ 388 Joe Juneau | .15 | .07 |
| ❑ 389 Steve Konowalchuk | .10 | .05 |
| ❑ 390 Kelly Miller | .10 | .05 |
| ❑ 391 Dave Poulin | .10 | .05 |
| ❑ 392 Tie Domi | .15 | .07 |
| ❑ 393 Michal Grosek | .10 | .05 |
| ❑ 394 Russ Romaniuk | .10 | .05 |
| ❑ 395 Darrin Shannon | .10 | .05 |
| ❑ 396 Thomas Steen | .10 | .05 |
| ❑ 397 Igor Ulanov | .10 | .05 |
| ❑ 398 Alexei Zhamnov | .15 | .07 |
| ❑ 399 Checklist | .10 | .05 |
| ❑ 400 Checklist | .10 | .05 |

## 1994-95 Ultra All-Rookies

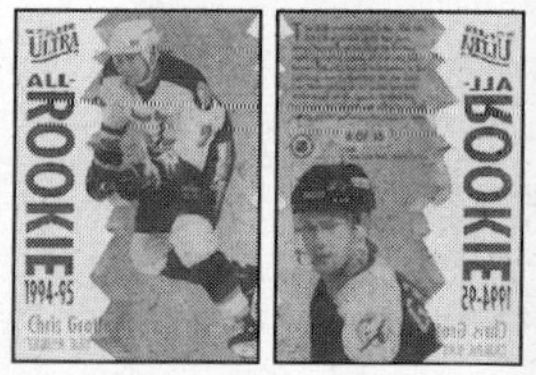


Randomly inserted in first series jumbo packs, this 10-card standard-size set reflects top rookies from the 1993-94 campaign. On acetate stock, the player is on the right superimposed over an ice-like surface. The left side is clear with the set title. The left portion of the back has a brief write-up and photo. Two distinct versions of each card in this set exist; one version carries the words "All-Rookie 1994-95" in a dark, greyish silver tint; the other in a bright, sparkling silver tint.

| | MINT | NRMT |
|---|---|---|
| COMPLETE SET (10) | 80.00 | 36.00 |
| COMMON CARD (1-10) | 4.00 | 1.80 |
| ❑ 1 Jason Arnott | 15.00 | 6.75 |
| ❑ 2 Martin Brodeur | 40.00 | 18.00 |
| ❑ 3 Alexandre Daigle | 8.00 | 3.60 |
| ❑ 4 Chris Gratton | 8.00 | 3.60 |
| ❑ 5 Boris Mironov | 4.00 | 1.80 |
| ❑ 6 Derek Plante | 4.00 | 1.80 |
| ❑ 7 Chris Pronger | 8.00 | 3.60 |
| ❑ 8 Mikael Renberg | 8.00 | 3.60 |
| ❑ 9 Bryan Smolinski | 4.00 | 1.80 |
| ❑ 10 Alexei Yashin | 4.00 | 1.80 |

## 1994-95 Ultra All-Stars

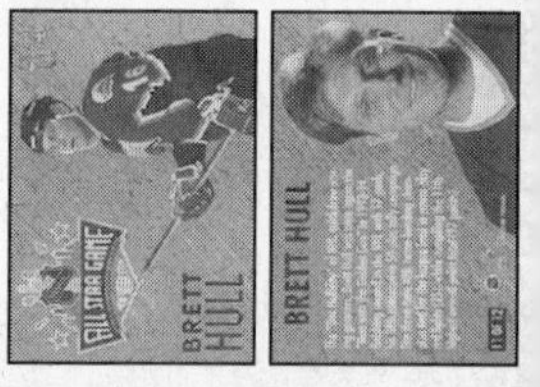


Randomly inserted into first series foil packs at a rate of 1:2, this standard-size set focuses on 12 players who participated in the 1994 NHL All-Star Game in New York. The set is arranged according to Eastern (1-6) and Western Conferences (7-12). Horizontally designed, the front features the player in his All-Star jersey. The background is colorful and flashy. The All-Star logo also appears on front. The backs are much the same with an up-close player photo.

| | MINT | NRMT |
|---|---|---|
| COMPLETE SET (12) | 10.00 | 4.50 |
| COMMON CARD (1-12) | .25 | .11 |
| ❑ 1 Ray Bourque | .40 | .18 |
| ❑ 2 Brian Leetch | .40 | .18 |
| ❑ 3 Eric Lindros | 2.00 | .90 |
| ❑ 4 Mark Messier | .50 | .23 |
| ❑ 5 Alexander Mogilny | .25 | .11 |
| ❑ 6 Patrick Roy | 2.00 | .90 |
| ❑ 7 Pavel Bure | .75 | .35 |
| ❑ 8 Chris Chelios | .40 | .18 |
| ❑ 9 Paul Coffey | .40 | .18 |
| ❑ 10 Wayne Gretzky | 2.50 | 1.10 |
| ❑ 11 Brett Hull | .50 | .23 |
| ❑ 12 Felix Potvin | .40 | .18 |

## 1994-95 Ultra Award Winners

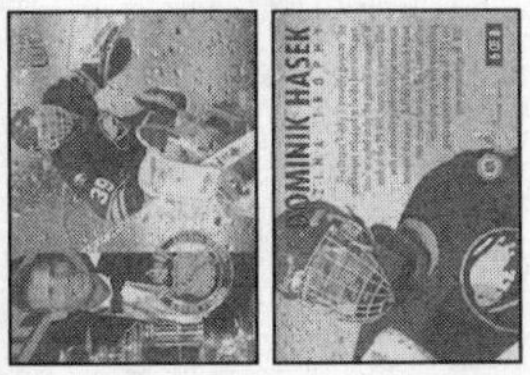

Randomly inserted into first series foil packs, this 8-card standard-size set honors NHL award winners of the previous season. Horizontally designed, the fronts have an action photo and, to the left, the player in his tux at the awards ceremony. The backs have a write-up and a player photo.

| | MINT | NRMT |
|---|---|---|
| COMPLETE SET (8) | 12.00 | 5.50 |
| COMMON CARD (1-8) | .75 | .35 |
| ❑ 1 Ray Bourque | 1.00 | .45 |
| James Norris Trophy | | |
| ❑ 2 Martin Brodeur | 2.50 | 1.10 |
| Calder Trophy | | |
| ❑ 3 Sergei Fedorov | 2.00 | .90 |
| Hart Trophy | | |
| ❑ 4 Adam Graves | .75 | .35 |
| King Clancy Trophy | | |
| ❑ 5 Wayne Gretzky | 6.00 | 2.70 |
| Art Ross Trophy | | |
| ❑ 6 Dominik Hasek | 2.00 | .90 |
| Vezina Trophy | | |
| ❑ 7 Brian Leetch | 1.00 | .45 |
| Cann Smythe Trophy | | |
| ❑ 8 Cam Neely | .75 | .35 |
| Bill Masterton Trophy | | |

## 1994-95 Ultra Sergei Fedorov

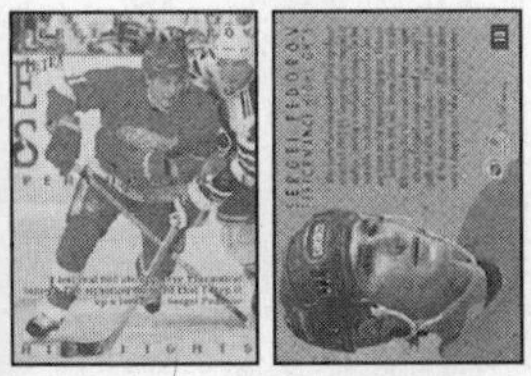

Measuring the standard-size, the first ten cards were randomly inserted in first series foil packs. Card Nos. 11 and 12 were available through a mail-in offer. The set chronicles various stages of Fedorov's career and his abilities. The front offers a photo with a quote from an opposing player, teammate or executive. In addition to providing career information, horizontal backs contain a player photo. An indeterminite number of cards were autographed by Fedorov, and randomly inserted in series one packs.

| | MINT | NRMT |
|---|---|---|
| COMPLETE SET (10) | 10.00 | 4.50 |
| COMMON FEDOROV (1-10) | 1.50 | .70 |
| CERTIFIED AUTO | 200.00 | 90.00 |
| COMMON MAIL-IN (11-12) | 2.00 | .90 |
| ❑ 1 Sergei Fedorov | 1.50 | .70 |
| Ray Bourque quote | | |
| ❑ 2 Sergei Fedorov | 1.50 | .70 |
| Fedorov quote | | |
| ❑ 3 Sergei Fedorov | 1.50 | .70 |
| Fedorov quote | | |
| ❑ 4 Sergei Fedorov | 1.50 | .70 |
| Jim Lites quote | | |
| ❑ 5 Sergei Fedorov | 1.50 | .70 |
| Jim Lites quote | | |
| ❑ 6 Sergei Fedorov | 1.50 | .70 |
| Igor Larionov quote | | |
| ❑ 7 Sergei Fedorov | 1.50 | .70 |
| Ken Daneyko quote | | |
| ❑ 8 Sergei Fedorov | 1.50 | .70 |
| Mark Howe quote | | |
| ❑ 9 Sergei Fedorov | 1.50 | .70 |
| Bryan Murray quote | | |
| ❑ 10 Sergei Fedorov | 1.50 | .70 |
| Fedorov quote | | |
| ❑ 11 Sergei Fedorov | 2.00 | .90 |
| Tim Cheveldae quote | | |
| ❑ 12 Sergei Fedorov | 2.00 | .90 |
| Ken Daneyko quote | | |

## 1994-95 Ultra Global Greats

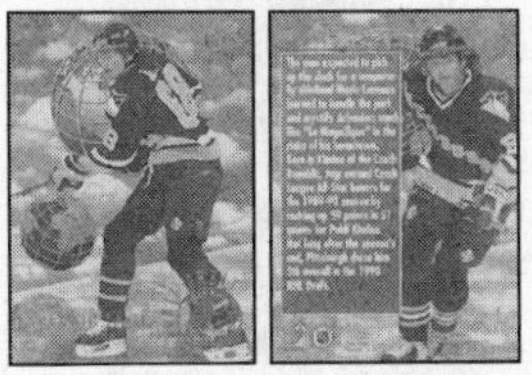

Randomly inserted in second series 15-card jumbo packs at a rate of 1:12, this 10-card standard-size set features superstars who hail from outside North America. On the front, a player photo is superimposed over a background of colorful globes. The back features a write-up and a photo over the same background.

| | MINT | NRMT |
|---|---|---|
| COMPLETE SET (10) | 125.00 | 55.00 |
| COMMON CARD (1-10) | 5.00 | 2.20 |
| ❑ 1 Sergei Fedorov | 20.00 | 9.00 |
| ❑ 2 Dominik Hasek | 20.00 | 9.00 |
| ❑ 3 Arturs Irbe | 5.00 | 2.20 |
| ❑ 4 Jaromir Jagr | 30.00 | 13.50 |
| ❑ 5 Jari Kurri | 5.00 | 2.20 |
| ❑ 6 Alexander Mogilny | 10.00 | 4.50 |
| ❑ 7 Petr Nedved | 5.00 | 2.20 |
| ❑ 8 Mikael Renberg | 10.00 | 4.50 |
| ❑ 9 Teemu Selanne | 20.00 | 9.00 |
| ❑ 10 Alexei Yashin | 5.00 | 2.20 |

## 1994-95 Ultra Power

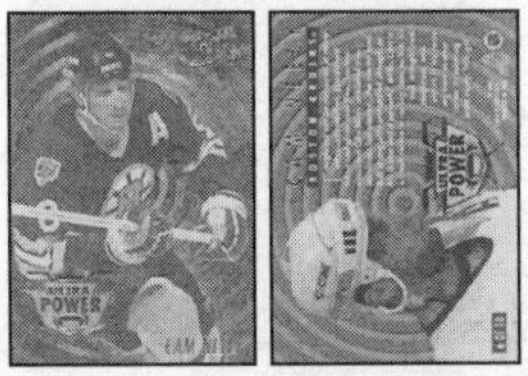

Randomly inserted in first series foil packs and distributed one set per hobby case, this 10-card standard-size set focuses on high scoring forwards. The card fronts contain a player photo superimposed over a glossy and circular background. The backs are horizontal with a player photo, highlights and a similar background.

| | MINT | NRMT |
|---|---|---|
| COMPLETE SET (10) | 50.00 | 22.00 |
| COMMON CARD (1-10) | 2.50 | 1.10 |
| ❑ 1 Dave Andreychuk | 2.50 | 1.10 |
| ❑ 2 Jason Arnott | 3.00 | 1.35 |
| ❑ 3 Chris Gratton | 3.00 | 1.35 |
| ❑ 4 Adam Graves | 3.00 | 1.35 |
| ❑ 5 Eric Lindros | 20.00 | 9.00 |
| ❑ 6 Cam Neely | 2.50 | 1.10 |
| ❑ 7 Mikael Renberg | 3.00 | 1.35 |
| ❑ 8 Jeremy Roenick | 4.00 | 1.80 |
| ❑ 9 Brendan Shanahan | 8.00 | 3.60 |
| ❑ 10 Keith Tkachuk | 5.00 | 2.20 |

## 1994-95 Ultra Premier Pad Men

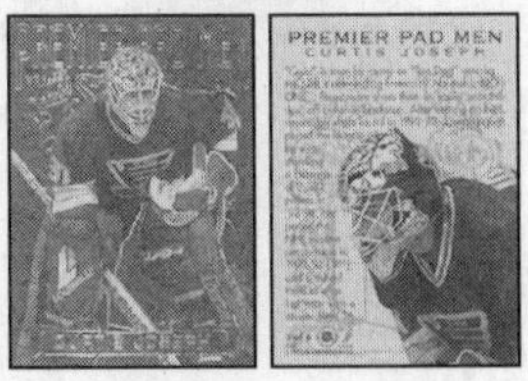

Randomly inserted in first series foil packs at a rate of 1:37, this 6-card standard-size set spotlights leading goaltenders. On front, a gold embossed design serves as background to the player photo. The backs have a solid color background that coordinates with the player's team. A player photo and write-up are in the foreground.

| | MINT | NRMT |
|---|---|---|
| COMPLETE SET (6) | 60.00 | 27.00 |
| COMMON CARD (1-6) | 5.00 | 2.20 |
| ❑ 1 Dominik Hasek | 15.00 | 6.75 |
| ❑ 2 Arturs Irbe | 5.00 | 2.20 |
| ❑ 3 Curtis Joseph | 10.00 | 4.50 |
| ❑ 4 Felix Potvin | 10.00 | 4.50 |
| ❑ 5 Mike Richter | 10.00 | 4.50 |
| ❑ 6 Patrick Roy | 25.00 | 11.00 |

## 1994-95 Ultra Premier Pivots

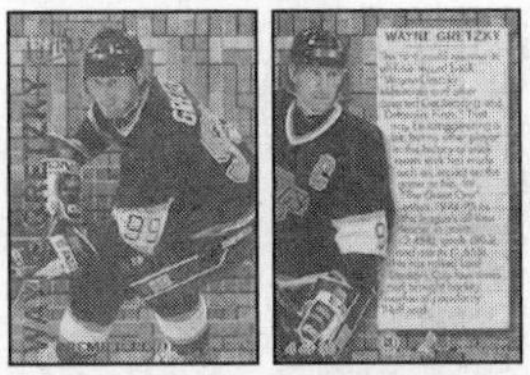

Randomly inserted in second series foil packs at a rate of 1:4, this 10-card standard-size set spotlights leading NHL centers. The fronts contain a player photo superimposed over a brown checkered background. The backs are similar except for the addition of some player highlights.

| | MINT | NRMT |
|---|---|---|
| COMPLETE SET (10) | 15.00 | 6.75 |
| COMMON CARD (1-10) | .50 | .23 |
| ❑ 1 Jason Arnott | .75 | .35 |
| ❑ 2 Sergei Fedorov | 2.00 | .90 |
| ❑ 3 Doug Gilmour | .75 | .35 |
| ❑ 4 Wayne Gretzky | 6.00 | 2.70 |
| ❑ 5 Pat LaFontaine | .50 | .23 |
| ❑ 6 Eric Lindros | 5.00 | 2.20 |
| ❑ 7 Mark Messier | 1.25 | .55 |
| ❑ 8 Mike Modano | 1.25 | .55 |
| ❑ 9 Adam Oates | .75 | .35 |
| ❑ 10 Steve Yzerman | 3.00 | 1.35 |

## 1994-95 Ultra Prospects

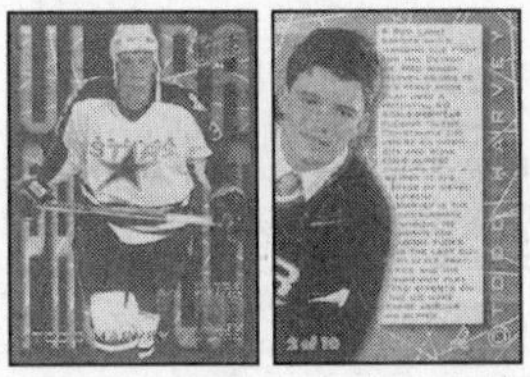

Randomly inserted in second series 12-card foil packs at a rate of 1:12, this 10-card standard-size set focuses on some of the rookie crop from the 1994-95 season. The fronts have an embossed player photo superimposed over a background containing the set name. The backs have a photo and write-up.

| | MINT | NRMT |
|---|---|---|
| COMPLETE SET (10) | 40.00 | 18.00 |
| COMMON CARD (1-10) | 2.00 | .90 |
| ❑ 1 Peter Forsberg | 15.00 | 6.75 |
| ❑ 2 Todd Harvey | 2.00 | .90 |
| ❑ 3 Paul Kariya | 15.00 | 6.75 |
| ❑ 4 Viktor Kozlov | 2.00 | .90 |
| ❑ 5 Brett Lindros | 2.00 | .90 |
| ❑ 6 Mike Peca | 2.00 | .90 |
| ❑ 7 Brian Rolston | 2.00 | .90 |
| ❑ 8 Jamie Storr | 4.00 | 1.80 |
| ❑ 9 Oleg Tverdovsky | 2.00 | .90 |
| ❑ 10 Jason Wiemer | 2.00 | .90 |

## 1994-95 Ultra Red Light Specials

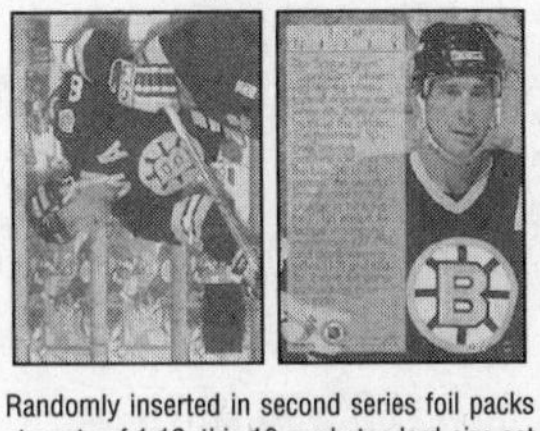

Randomly inserted in second series foil packs at a rate of 1:12, this 10-card standard-size set presents top goal scorers. The fronts are horizontally designed with a player photo superimposed over three action strips of the player. The set logo is in red foil at bottom left. The backs offer a photo and highlights.

| | MINT | NRMT |
|---|---|---|
| COMPLETE SET (10) | 20.00 | 9.00 |
| COMMON CARD (1-10) | .75 | .35 |
| ❑ 1 Dave Andreychuk | .75 | .35 |
| ❑ 2 Pavel Bure | 4.00 | 1.80 |
| ❑ 3 Mike Gartner | .75 | .35 |
| ❑ 4 Adam Graves | 1.00 | .45 |
| ❑ 5 Brett Hull | 2.50 | 1.10 |
| ❑ 6 Cam Neely | 1.00 | .45 |
| ❑ 7 Gary Roberts | .75 | .35 |
| ❑ 8 Teemu Selanne | 4.00 | 1.80 |
| ❑ 9 Brendan Shanahan | 4.00 | 1.80 |
| ❑ 10 Kevin Stevens | .75 | .35 |

## 1994-95 Ultra Scoring Kings

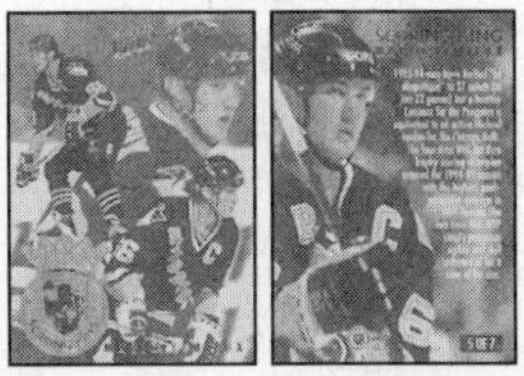

Randomly inserted in first series foil packs, this 7-card standard-size set showcases seven of the NHL's top scorers. The fronts provide three player photos with a gold foil set logo at bottom left. The backs have a player photo and write-up.

| | MINT | NRMT |
|---|---|---|
| COMPLETE SET (7) | 20.00 | 9.00 |
| COMMON CARD (1-7) | 1.50 | .70 |
| ❑ 1 Pavel Bure | 2.50 | 1.10 |
| ❑ 2 Sergei Fedorov | 2.50 | 1.10 |
| ❑ 3 Doug Gilmour | 1.50 | .70 |
| ❑ 4 Wayne Gretzky | 8.00 | 3.60 |
| ❑ 5 Mario Lemieux | 6.00 | 2.70 |
| ❑ 6 Eric Lindros | 6.00 | 2.70 |
| ❑ 7 Steve Yzerman | 4.00 | 1.80 |

## 1994-95 Ultra Speed Merchants

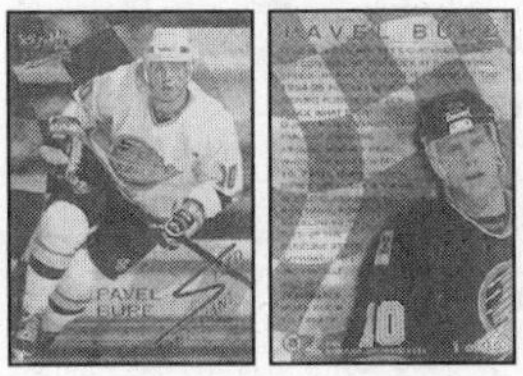

Randomly inserted in second series foil packs at the rate of 1:2, this 10-card standard-size set salutes the league's fastest and hardest-to-defend skaters. A player photo is superimposed over an action-oriented background with the player's name and set title in gold foil at the bottom. The backs contain a checkered flag background with a photo and highlights.

| | MINT | NRMT |
|---|---|---|
| COMPLETE SET (10) | 12.00 | 5.50 |
| COMMON CARD (1-10) | .50 | .23 |
| ❑ 1 Pavel Bure | 2.50 | 1.10 |
| ❑ 2 Russ Courtnall | .50 | .23 |
| ❑ 3 Sergei Fedorov | 2.50 | 1.10 |
| ❑ 4 Al Iafrate | .50 | .23 |
| ❑ 5 Pat LaFontaine | .75 | .35 |
| ❑ 6 Brian Leetch | 1.25 | .55 |
| ❑ 7 Mike Modano | 1.50 | .70 |
| ❑ 8 Alexander Mogilny | .75 | .35 |
| ❑ 9 Jeremy Roenick | 1.25 | .55 |
| ❑ 10 Geoff Sanderson | .75 | .35 |

## 1995-96 Ultra

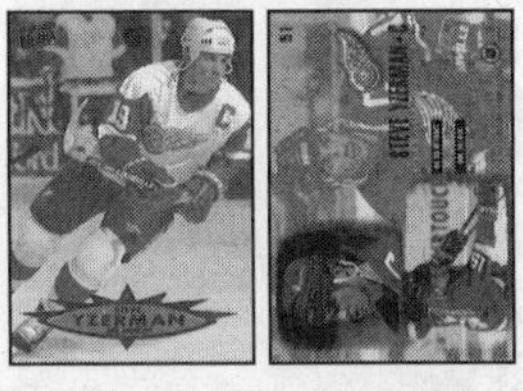

These 400 standard-size cards represent the two series release of the 1995-96 Ultra issue. Issued in 12-card packs, the suggested retail price per pack was $2.49. Each series one pack contains two insert cards. One was a Gold Medallion parallel insert while the other was from one of the five series one Ultra insert sets. Second series packs did not guarantee an insert per pack. The cards are printed on 20-point stock. Key RCs in the set include Daniel Alfredsson, Todd Bertuzzi, Chad Kilger and Kyle McLaren. The Cool Trade Exchange card was randomly inserted 1:360 series two packs, making it the hardest to pull of the five available. The card could be redeemed, until the expiration date of 3/1/97, for special Emotion cards of Jeremy Roenick, Paul Kariya, Saku Koivu and Martin Brodeur.

| | MINT | NRMT |
|---|---|---|
| COMPLETE SET (400) | 50.00 | 22.00 |
| COMPLETE SERIES 1 (200) | 25.00 | 11.00 |
| COMPLETE SERIES 2 (200) | 25.00 | 11.00 |
| COMMON CARD (1-400) | .10 | .05 |
| ❑ 1 Guy Hebert | .15 | .07 |
| ❑ 2 Milos Holan | .10 | .05 |
| ❑ 3 Paul Kariya | 1.25 | .55 |
| ❑ 4 Denny Lambert | .10 | .05 |
| ❑ 5 Stephan Lebeau | .10 | .05 |
| ❑ 6 Oleg Tverdovsky | .15 | .07 |
| ❑ 7 Shaun Van Allen | .10 | .05 |
| ❑ 8 Ray Bourque | .30 | .14 |
| ❑ 9 Mariusz Czerkawski | .10 | .05 |
| ❑ 10 Blaine Lacher | .15 | .07 |
| ❑ 11 Sandy Moger | .10 | .05 |
| ❑ 12 Cam Neely | .15 | .07 |
| ❑ 13 Adam Oates | .15 | .07 |
| ❑ 14 Bryan Smolinski | .10 | .05 |
| ❑ 15 Donald Audette | .15 | .07 |
| ❑ 16 Jason Dawe | .10 | .05 |
| ❑ 17 Garry Galley | .10 | .05 |
| ❑ 18 Dominik Hasek | .60 | .25 |
| ❑ 19 Brian Holzinger RC | .15 | .07 |
| ❑ 20 Pat LaFontaine | .15 | .07 |
| ❑ 21 Alexander Mogilny | .15 | .07 |
| ❑ 22 Alexei Zhitnik | .10 | .05 |
| ❑ 23 Steve Chiasson | .10 | .05 |
| ❑ 24 Theoren Fleury | .15 | .07 |
| ❑ 25 Phil Housley | .15 | .07 |
| ❑ 26 Trevor Kidd | .15 | .07 |
| ❑ 27 Joel Otto | .10 | .05 |
| ❑ 28 Gary Roberts | .10 | .05 |
| ❑ 29 Zarley Zalapski | .10 | .05 |
| ❑ 30 Ed Belfour | .30 | .14 |
| ❑ 31 Chris Chelios | .30 | .14 |
| ❑ 32 Eric Daze | .30 | .14 |
| ❑ 33 Sergei Krivokrasov | .10 | .05 |
| ❑ 34 Bernie Nicholls | .10 | .05 |
| ❑ 35 Jeremy Roenick | .30 | .14 |
| ❑ 36 Gary Suter | .10 | .05 |
| ❑ 37 Todd Harvey | .10 | .05 |
| ❑ 38 Derian Hatcher | .10 | .05 |
| ❑ 39 Mike Kennedy | .10 | .05 |
| ❑ 40 Grant Ledyard | .10 | .05 |
| ❑ 41 Mike Modano | .40 | .18 |
| ❑ 42 Andy Moog | .15 | .07 |
| ❑ 43 Mike Torchia | .15 | .07 |
| ❑ 44 Paul Coffey | .30 | .14 |
| ❑ 45 Sergei Fedorov | .60 | .25 |
| ❑ 46 Vladimir Konstantinov | .10 | .05 |
| ❑ 47 Slava Kozlov | .15 | .07 |
| ❑ 48 Keith Primeau | .15 | .07 |
| ❑ 49 Ray Sheppard | .15 | .07 |
| ❑ 50 Mike Vernon | .15 | .07 |
| ❑ 51 Steve Yzerman | 1.00 | .45 |
| ❑ 52 Jason Arnott | .15 | .07 |
| ❑ 53 Shayne Corson | .10 | .05 |
| ❑ 54 Igor Kravchuk | .10 | .05 |
| ❑ 55 Todd Marchant | .10 | .05 |
| ❑ 56 David Oliver | .10 | .05 |
| ❑ 57 Bill Ranford | .15 | .07 |
| ❑ 58 Doug Weight | .15 | .07 |
| ❑ 59 Stu Barnes | .10 | .05 |
| ❑ 60 Jesse Belanger | .10 | .05 |
| ❑ 61 Gord Murphy | .10 | .05 |
| ❑ 62 Rob Niedermayer | .15 | .07 |
| ❑ 63 Brian Skrudland | .10 | .05 |
| ❑ 64 John Vanbiesbrouck | .50 | .23 |
| ❑ 65 Sean Burke | .15 | .07 |
| ❑ 66 Andrew Cassels | .10 | .05 |
| ❑ 67 Frantisek Kucera | .10 | .05 |
| ❑ 68 Andrei Nikolishin | .10 | .05 |
| ❑ 69 Chris Pronger | .15 | .07 |
| ❑ 70 Geoff Sanderson | .15 | .07 |
| ❑ 71 Kevin Smyth | .10 | .05 |
| ❑ 72 Darren Turcotte | .10 | .05 |
| ❑ 73 Rob Blake | .10 | .05 |
| ❑ 74 Wayne Gretzky | 2.00 | .90 |
| ❑ 75 Kelly Hrudey | .15 | .07 |
| ❑ 76 Marty McSorley | .10 | .05 |
| ❑ 77 Jamie Storr | .15 | .07 |
| ❑ 78 Darryl Sydor | .10 | .05 |
| ❑ 79 Rick Tocchet | .15 | .07 |
| ❑ 80 Vincent Damphousse | .15 | .07 |
| ❑ 81 Vladimir Malakhov | .10 | .05 |
| ❑ 82 Mark Recchi | .15 | .07 |
| ❑ 83 Patrick Roy | 1.50 | .70 |
| ❑ 84 Brian Savage | .10 | .05 |
| ❑ 85 Pierre Turgeon | .15 | .07 |
| ❑ 86 Martin Brodeur | .75 | .35 |
| ❑ 87 Neal Broten | .15 | .07 |
| ❑ 88 Sergei Brylin | .10 | .05 |
| ❑ 89 John MacLean | .15 | .07 |
| ❑ 90 Scott Niedermayer | .10 | .05 |
| ❑ 91 Stephane Richer | .15 | .07 |
| ❑ 92 Scott Stevens | .15 | .07 |
| ❑ 93 Ray Ferraro | .10 | .05 |
| ❑ 94 Scott Lachance | .10 | .05 |
| ❑ 95 Brett Lindros | .10 | .05 |
| ❑ 96 Kirk Muller | .10 | .05 |
| ❑ 97 Zigmund Palffy | .15 | .07 |
| ❑ 98 Tommy Salo RC | .15 | .07 |
| ❑ 99 Mathieu Schneider | .10 | .05 |
| ❑ 100 Tommy Soderstrom | .15 | .07 |
| ❑ 101 Glenn Healy | .15 | .07 |
| ❑ 102 Darren Langdon | .10 | .05 |
| ❑ 103 Steve Larmer | .15 | .07 |
| ❑ 104 Brian Leetch | .30 | .14 |
| ❑ 105 Mark Messier | .40 | .18 |
| ❑ 106 Mattias Norstrom | .10 | .05 |
| ❑ 107 Pat Verbeek | .10 | .05 |
| ❑ 108 Sergei Zubov | .10 | .05 |
| ❑ 109 Don Beaupre | .15 | .07 |
| ❑ 110 Radek Bonk | .10 | .05 |
| ❑ 111 Alexandre Daigle | .10 | .05 |
| ❑ 112 Steve Larouche | .10 | .05 |
| ❑ 113 Stanislav Neckar | .10 | .05 |
| ❑ 114 Alexei Yashin | .15 | .07 |
| ❑ 115 Rod Brind'Amour | .15 | .07 |
| ❑ 116 Eric Desjardins | .10 | .05 |
| ❑ 117 Ron Hextall | .15 | .07 |
| ❑ 118 John LeClair | .50 | .23 |

❑ 119 Eric Lindros 1.00 .45
❑ 120 Mikael Renberg .15 .07
❑ 121 Chris Therien .10 .05
❑ 122 Ron Francis .15 .07
❑ 123 Jaromir Jagr 1.00 .45
❑ 124 Joe Mullen .15 .07
❑ 125 Larry Murphy .15 .07
❑ 126 Ulf Samuelsson .10 .05
❑ 127 Kevin Stevens .10 .05
❑ 128 Ken Wregget .15 .07
❑ 129 Wendel Clark .15 .07
❑ 130 Adam Deadmarsh .15 .07
❑ 131 Stephane Fiset .15 .07
❑ 132 Peter Forsberg 1.00 .45
❑ 133 Curtis Leschyshyn .10 .05
❑ 134 Owen Nolan .15 .07
❑ 135 Mike Ricci .10 .05
❑ 136 Joe Sakic .60 .25
❑ 137 Denis Chasse .10 .05
❑ 138 Steve Duchesne .10 .05
❑ 139 Brett Hull .40 .18
❑ 140 Curtis Joseph .30 .14
❑ 141 Ian Laperriere .10 .05
❑ 142 Brendan Shanahan .60 .25
❑ 143 Esa Tikkanen .10 .05
❑ 144 Ulf Dahlen .10 .05
❑ 145 Jeff Friesen .15 .07
❑ 146 Arturs Irbe .15 .07
❑ 147 Craig Janney .15 .07
❑ 148 Sergei Makarov .10 .05
❑ 149 Sandis Ozolinsh .15 .07
❑ 150 Ray Whitney .10 .05
❑ 151 Chris Gratton .15 .07
❑ 152 Roman Hamrlik .15 .07
❑ 153 Petr Klima .10 .05
❑ 154 Brantt Myhres .10 .05
❑ 155 Daren Puppa .15 .07
❑ 156 Jason Wiemer .10 .05
❑ 157 Paul Ysebaert .10 .05
❑ 158 Dave Andreychuk .15 .07
❑ 159 Tie Domi .15 .07
❑ 160 Doug Gilmour .30 .14
❑ 161 Kenny Jonsson .10 .05
❑ 162 Felix Potvin .30 .14
❑ 163 Mike Ridley .10 .05
❑ 164 Mats Sundin .15 .07
❑ 165 Jeff Brown .10 .05
❑ 166 Pavel Bure .60 .25
❑ 167 Geoff Courtnall .10 .05
❑ 168 Russ Courtnall .10 .05
❑ 169 Trevor Linden .15 .07
❑ 170 Kirk McLean .15 .07
❑ 171 Roman Oksiuta .10 .05
❑ 172 Peter Bondra .30 .14
❑ 173 Jim Carey .30 .14
❑ 174 Martin Gendron .10 .05
❑ 175 Dale Hunter .10 .05
❑ 176 Calle Johansson .10 .05
❑ 177 Michal Pivonka .10 .05
❑ 178 Mark Tinordi .10 .05
❑ 179 Nelson Emerson .10 .05
❑ 180 Nikolai Khabibulin .15 .07
❑ 181 Dave Manson .10 .05
❑ 182 Teppo Numminen .10 .05
❑ 183 Teemu Selanne .60 .25
❑ 184 Keith Tkachuk .40 .18
❑ 185 Alexei Zhamnov .15 .07
❑ 186 Martin Brodeur .40 .18
Stanley Cup Champions
❑ 187 Neal Broten .15 .07
❑ 188 Bob Carpenter .10 .05
❑ 189 Ken Daneyko .10 .05
❑ 190 Bruce Driver .10 .05
❑ 191 Bill Guerin .10 .05
❑ 192 Claude Lemieux .15 .07
❑ 193 John MacLean .15 .07
❑ 194 Scott Niedermayer .10 .05
❑ 195 Stephane Richer .15 .07
❑ 196 Scott Stevens .15 .07
❑ 197 Presentation Card .15 .07
Stanley Cup Champions
❑ 198 Checklist (1-83) .10 .05
❑ 199 Checklist (84-169) .10 .05
❑ 200 Checklist (170-200) .10 .05
❑ 201 Todd Krygier .10 .05
❑ 202 Steve Rucchin .10 .05
❑ 203 Mike Sillinger .10 .05
❑ 204 Ted Donato .10 .05
❑ 205 Shawn McEachern .10 .05
❑ 206 Joe Mullen .15 .07
❑ 207 Kevin Stevens .10 .05
❑ 208 Don Sweeney .10 .05
❑ 209 Mark Astley .10 .05
❑ 210 Randy Burridge .10 .05
❑ 211 Jason Dawe .10 .05
❑ 212 Mike Peca .10 .05
❑ 213 Michael Nylander .10 .05
❑ 214 Cory Stillman .10 .05
❑ 215 Pavel Torgajev .10 .05
❑ 216 Tony Amonte .15 .07
❑ 217 Joe Murphy .10 .05
❑ 218 Bob Probert .15 .07
❑ 219 Denis Savard .15 .07
❑ 220 Stephane Fiset .15 .07
❑ 221 Valeri Kamensky .15 .07
❑ 222 Sylvain Lefebvre .10 .05
❑ 223 Claude Lemieux .15 .07
❑ 224 Sandis Ozolinsh .15 .07
❑ 225 Patrick Roy 1.50 .70
❑ 226 Scott Young .10 .05
❑ 227 Greg Adams .10 .05
❑ 228 Guy Carbonneau .10 .05
❑ 229 Dave Gagner .15 .07
❑ 230 Kevin Hatcher .10 .05
❑ 231 Darcy Wakaluk .10 .05
❑ 232 Dino Ciccarelli .15 .07
❑ 233 Greg Johnson .10 .05
❑ 234 Igor Larionov .10 .05
❑ 235 Darren McCarty .10 .05
❑ 236 Chris Osgood .30 .14
❑ 237 Zdeno Ciger .10 .05
❑ 238 Bryan Marchment .10 .05
❑ 239 Boris Mironov .10 .05
❑ 240 Peter White .10 .05
❑ 241 Jody Hull .10 .05
❑ 242 Scott Mellanby .15 .07
❑ 243 Gord Murphy .10 .05
❑ 244 Jason Woolley .10 .05
❑ 245 Gerald Diduck .10 .05
❑ 246 Nelson Emerson .10 .05
❑ 247 Brendan Shanahan .60 .25
❑ 248 Glen Wesley .10 .05
❑ 249 Tony Granato .10 .05
❑ 250 Dimitri Khristich .10 .05
❑ 251 Jari Kurri .15 .07
❑ 252 Eric Lacroix .10 .05
❑ 253 Yanic Perreault .10 .05
❑ 254 Patrice Brisebois .10 .05
❑ 255 Benoit Brunet .10 .05
❑ 256 Valeri Bure .15 .07
❑ 257 Stephane Quintal .10 .05
❑ 258 Jocelyn Thibault .30 .14
❑ 259 Shawn Chambers .10 .05
❑ 260 Jim Dowd .10 .05
❑ 261 Bill Guerin .10 .05
❑ 262 Bobby Holik .10 .05
❑ 263 Steve Thomas .10 .05
❑ 264 Esa Tikkanen .10 .05
❑ 265 Wendel Clark .15 .07
❑ 266 Travis Green .15 .07
❑ 267 Brett Lindros .10 .05
❑ 268 Kirk Muller .10 .05
❑ 269 Zigmund Palffy .15 .07
❑ 270 Mathieu Schneider .10 .05
❑ 271 Alexander Semak .10 .05
❑ 272 Dennis Vaske .10 .05
❑ 273 Ray Ferraro .10 .05
❑ 274 Adam Graves .15 .07
❑ 275 Alexei Kovalev .10 .05
❑ 276 Mike Richter .30 .14
❑ 277 Luc Robitaille .15 .07
❑ 278 Ulf Samuelsson .10 .05
❑ 279 Steve Duchesne .10 .05
❑ 280 Trent McCleary .10 .05
❑ 281 Dan Quinn .10 .05
❑ 282 Martin Straka .10 .05
❑ 283 Karl Dykhuis .10 .05
❑ 284 Pat Falloon .10 .05
❑ 285 Joel Otto .10 .05
❑ 286 Kjell Samuelsson .10 .05
❑ 287 Garth Snow .15 .07
❑ 288 Mario Lemieux 1.50 .70
❑ 289 Norm Maciver .10 .05
❑ 290 Dmitri Mironov .10 .05
❑ 291 Markus Naslund .10 .05
❑ 292 Petr Nedved .15 .07
❑ 293 Tomas Sandstrom .10 .05
❑ 294 Bryan Smolinski .10 .05
❑ 295 Sergei Zubov .10 .05
❑ 296 Shayne Corson .10 .05
❑ 297 Geoff Courtnall .10 .05
❑ 298 Grant Fuhr .15 .07
❑ 299 Dale Hawerchuk .15 .07
❑ 300 Al MacInnis .15 .07
❑ 301 Brian Noonan .10 .05
❑ 302 Chris Pronger .15 .07
❑ 303 Andrei Nazarov .10 .05
❑ 304 Owen Nolan .15 .07
❑ 305 Ray Sheppard .15 .07
❑ 306 Chris Terreri .15 .07
❑ 307 Brian Bellows .10 .05
❑ 308 Brian Bradley .10 .05
❑ 309 John Cullen .10 .05
❑ 310 Alexander Selivanov .10 .05
❑ 311 Mike Gartner .15 .07
❑ 312 Benoit Hogue .10 .05
❑ 313 Sergio Momesso .10 .05
❑ 314 Larry Murphy .15 .07
❑ 315 Dave Babych .10 .05
❑ 316 Bret Hedican .10 .05
❑ 317 Alexander Mogilny .15 .07
❑ 318 Mike Ridley .10 .05
❑ 319 Peter Bondra .30 .14
❑ 320 Jim Carey .30 .14
❑ 321 Sylvain Cote .10 .05
❑ 322 Sergei Gonchar .10 .05
❑ 323 Joe Juneau .10 .05
❑ 324 Steve Konowalchuk .10 .05
❑ 325 Pat Peake .10 .05
❑ 326 Dallas Drake .10 .05
❑ 327 Igor Korolev .10 .05
❑ 328 Darren Turcotte .10 .05
❑ 329 Daniel Alfredsson .60 .25
❑ 330 Aki-Petteri Berg .10 .05
❑ 331 Todd Bertuzzi .15 .07
❑ 332 Jason Bonsignore .10 .05
❑ 333 Curtis Brown .10 .05
❑ 334 Byron Dafoe .15 .07
❑ 335 Eric Daze .30 .14
❑ 336 Shane Doan .10 .05
❑ 337 Jason Doig .10 .05
❑ 338 Radek Dvorak .10 .05
❑ 339 Joe Dziedzic .10 .05
❑ 340 Darby Hendrickson .10 .05
❑ 341 Brian Holzinger .30 .14
❑ 342 Ed Jovanovski .30 .14
❑ 343 Chad Kilger .10 .05
❑ 344 Saku Koivu .50 .23
❑ 345 Darren Langdon .10 .05
❑ 346 Jamie Langenbrunner .10 .05
❑ 347 Jere Lehtinen .10 .05
❑ 348 Bryan McCabe .10 .05
❑ 349 Kyle McLaren .10 .05
❑ 350 Marty Murray .10 .05
❑ 351 Jeff O'Neill .10 .05
❑ 352 Deron Quint .10 .05
❑ 353 Marcus Ragnarsson .10 .05
❑ 354 Tommy Salo .15 .07
❑ 355 Miroslav Satan 1.25 .55
❑ 356 Jamie Storr .15 .07
❑ 357 Niklas Sundstrom .10 .05
❑ 358 Robert Svehla .10 .05
❑ 359 Denis Pederson .10 .05
❑ 360 Antti Tormanen .10 .05
❑ 361 Brendan Witt .10 .05
❑ 362 Vitali Yachmenev .10 .05
❑ 363 Stephane Yelle .10 .05
❑ 364 Tom Barrasso NE .15 .07
❑ 365 Ed Belfour NE .30 .14
❑ 366 Martin Brodeur NE .40 .18
❑ 367 Sean Burke NE .15 .07
❑ 368 Jim Carey NE .30 .14
❑ 369 Stephane Fiset NE .15 .07
❑ 370 Dominik Hasek NE .60 .25
❑ 371 Ron Hextall NE .15 .07
❑ 372 Nikolai Khabibulin NE .15 .07
❑ 373 Kirk McLean NE .15 .07
❑ 374 Chris Osgood NE .30 .14
❑ 375 Felix Potvin NE .30 .14
❑ 376 Daren Puppa NE .15 .07
❑ 377 Patrick Roy NE 1.50 .70
❑ 378 John Vanbiesbrouck NE .30 .14
❑ 379 Pavel Bure UC .60 .25
❑ 380 Chris Chelios UC .30 .14
❑ 381 Sergei Fedorov UC .60 .25
❑ 382 Theoren Fleury UC .15 .07
❑ 383 Peter Forsberg UC 1.00 .45
❑ 384 Ron Francis UC .15 .07
❑ 385 Wayne Gretzky UC 2.50 1.10
❑ 386 Brett Hull UC .50 .23
❑ 387 Jaromir Jagr UC 1.00 .45
❑ 388 Paul Kariya UC 1.25 .55
❑ 389 Pat LaFontaine UC .15 .07
❑ 390 Brian Leetch UC .30 .14
❑ 391 Mario Lemieux UC 1.50 .70
❑ 392 Eric Lindros UC 1.00 .45
❑ 393 Mark Messier UC .50 .23
❑ 394 Mike Modano UC .15 .07
❑ 395 Adam Oates UC .15 .07
❑ 396 Jeremy Roenick UC .30 .14
❑ 397 Joe Sakic UC .60 .25
❑ 398 Alexei Zhamnov UC .15 .07
❑ 399 Checklist .10 .05
❑ 400 Checklist .10 .05
❑ NNO Cool Trade Exchange 2.00 .90

## 1995-96 Ultra Gold Medallion

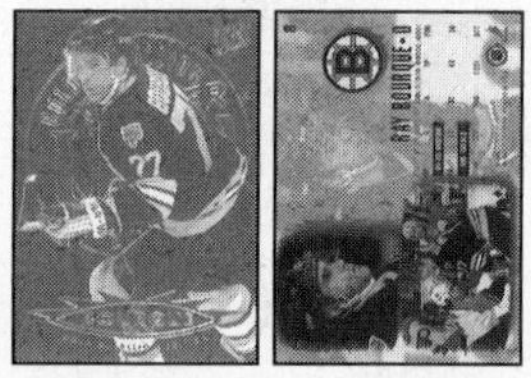

This 200-card standard-size set is a parallel to the basic Ultra series one issue. These cards were issued one per series one pack. No Gold Medallion version exists for series two cards. The fronts have the same photos as the regular cards except the entire background is gold. The Ultra Gold Medallion logo is in the middle of the card and is embossed for effect. The words "Gold Medallion Edition" are located under the player's name. The backs are identical to the regular cards. Gold Medallion version also could be found for series one insert cards. Values for those are included under the appropriate insert header.

| | MINT | NRMT |
|---|---|---|
| COMPLETE SET (200) | 175.00 | 80.00 |
| COMMON CARD (1-200) | .25 | .11 |

*STARS: 3X TO 6X BASIC CARDS
*YOUNG STARS: 2X TO 4X BASIC CARDS
*RCs: 1.5X TO 3X BASIC CARDS

## 1995-96 Ultra All-Rookies

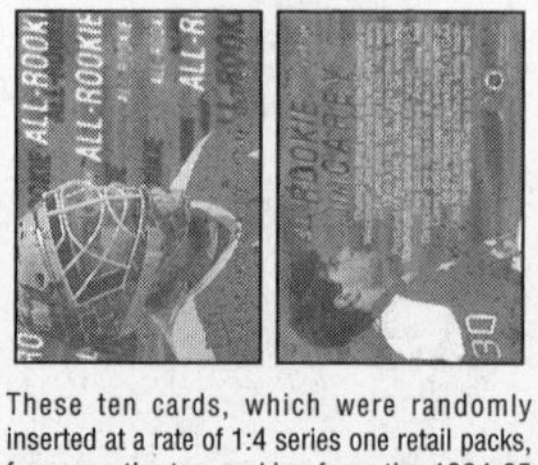

These ten cards, which were randomly inserted at a rate of 1:4 series one retail packs, focus on the top rookies from the 1994-95 campaign. Gold Medallion parallel versions of these cards also were available, at indeterminate odds. Multipliers can be found in the header below to determine values for these.

| | MINT | NRMT |
|---|---|---|
| COMPLETE SET (10) | 40.00 | 18.00 |
| COMMON CARD (1-10) | 2.50 | 1.10 |

*GOLD MEDALLION: 12.5X TO 25X BASIC CARDS

❑ 1 Jim Carey 3.00 1.35
❑ 2 Mariusz Czerkawski 2.50 1.10
❑ 3 Peter Forsberg 12.00 5.50
❑ 4 Jeff Friesen 3.00 1.35
❑ 5 Paul Kariya 15.00 6.75
❑ 6 Blaine Lacher 3.00 1.35
❑ 7 Ian Laperriere 2.50 1.10
❑ 8 Todd Marchant 2.50 1.10
❑ 9 Roman Oksiuta 2.50 1.10
❑ 10 David Oliver 2.50 1.10

## 1995-96 Ultra Crease Crashers

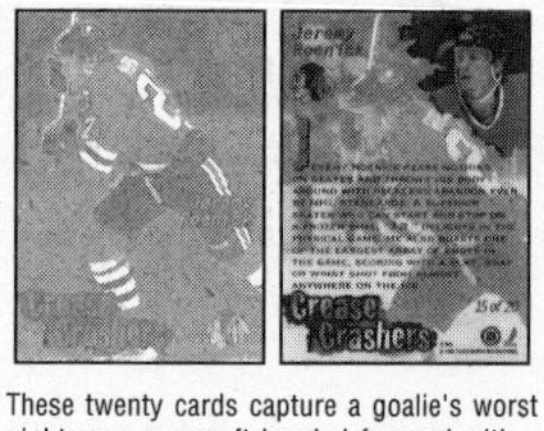

These twenty cards capture a goalie's worst nightmare -- a soft-handed forward with a propensity for invading a netminder's home turf. The cards were randomly inserted in series two retail packs only at a rate of 1:18.

| | MINT | NRMT |
|---|---|---|
| COMPLETE SET (20) | 225.00 | 100.00 |
| COMMON CARD (1-20) | 4.00 | 1.80 |

❑ 1 Jason Arnott 8.00 3.60
❑ 2 Rod Brind'Amour 8.00 3.60
❑ 3 Theoren Fleury 8.00 3.60
❑ 4 Todd Harvey 4.00 1.80
❑ 5 John LeClair 25.00 11.00
❑ 6 Claude Lemieux 8.00 3.60
❑ 7 Trevor Linden 8.00 3.60
❑ 8 Eric Lindros 50.00 22.00
❑ 9 Darren McCarty 4.00 1.80
❑ 10 Scott Mellanby 8.00 3.60
❑ 11 Mark Messier 20.00 9.00
❑ 12 Cam Neely 8.00 3.60
❑ 13 Owen Nolan 8.00 3.60
❑ 14 Keith Primeau 8.00 3.60
❑ 15 Jeremy Roenick 15.00 6.75
❑ 16 Tomas Sandstrom 4.00 1.80
❑ 17 Brendan Shanahan 30.00 13.50
❑ 18 Kevin Stevens 4.00 1.80
❑ 19 Rick Tocchet 4.00 1.80
❑ 20 Keith Tkachuk 20.00 9.00

## 1995-96 Ultra Extra Attackers

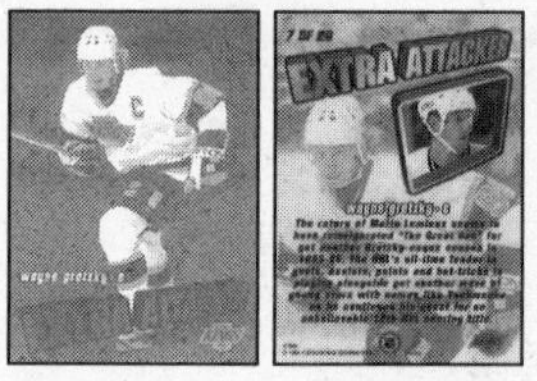

When pulling the goalie and down late in the game, these are the guys you'd love to tap on the shoulder. The cards were randomly inserted in series two hobby packs only at a rate of 1:18.

| | MINT | NRMT |
|---|---|---|
| COMPLETE SET (20) | 200.00 | 90.00 |
| COMMON CARD (1-20) | 2.50 | 1.10 |

❑ 1 Peter Bondra 4.00 1.80
❑ 2 Eric Daze 6.00 2.70
❑ 3 Radek Dvorak 2.50 1.10
❑ 4 Sergei Fedorov 12.00 5.50
❑ 5 Peter Forsberg 20.00 9.00
❑ 6 Ron Francis 4.00 1.80
❑ 7 Wayne Gretzky 40.00 18.00
❑ 8 Brett Hull 8.00 3.60
❑ 9 Jaromir Jagr 20.00 9.00
❑ 10 Ed Jovanovski 6.00 2.70
❑ 11 Paul Kariya 25.00 11.00
❑ 12 Saku Koivu 10.00 4.50
❑ 13 Mario Lemieux 30.00 13.50
❑ 14 Mike Modano 8.00 3.60
❑ 15 Alexander Mogilny 4.00 1.80
❑ 16 Adam Oates 4.00 1.80
❑ 17 Joe Sakic 12.00 5.50
❑ 18 Niklas Sundstrom 2.50 1.10
❑ 19 Mats Sundin 4.00 1.80
❑ 20 Steve Yzerman 20.00 9.00

## 1995-96 Ultra High Speed

Young stars in a hurry to reach the upper echelon of the NHL pay scale, and some already there trying to prove they're worth it,

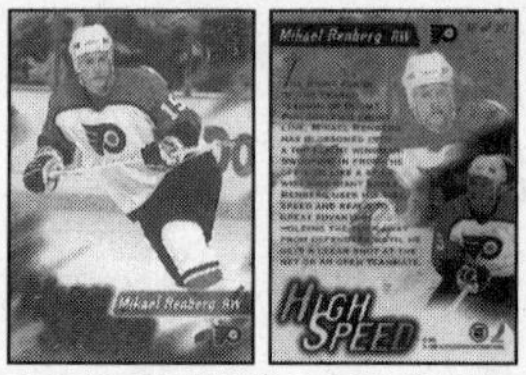

are featured in this 20-card set. Collectors could find these cards randomly inserted at a rate of 1:5 series two packs.

| | MINT | NRMT |
|---|---|---|
| COMPLETE SET (20) | 30.00 | 13.50 |
| COMMON CARD (1-20) | .50 | .23 |

❑ 1 Daniel Alfredsson 1.50 .70
❑ 2 Jason Arnott 1.50 .70
❑ 3 Todd Bertuzzi .50 .23
❑ 4 Radek Bonk .50 .23
❑ 5 Martin Brodeur 5.00 2.20
❑ 6 Alexandre Daigle .50 .23
❑ 7 Shane Doan .50 .23
❑ 8 Peter Forsberg 6.00 2.70
❑ 9 Roman Hamrlik 1.50 .70
❑ 10 Todd Harvey .50 .23
❑ 11 Paul Kariya 1.50 .70
❑ 12 Travis Green .50 .23
❑ 13 Chris Osgood 1.50 .70
❑ 14 Zigmund Palffy 1.50 .70
❑ 15 Marcus Ragnarsson .50 .23
❑ 16 Mikael Renberg 1.50 .70
❑ 17 Brian Savage .50 .23
❑ 18 Robert Svehla .50 .23
❑ 19 Jocelyn Thibault 1.50 .70
❑ 20 Brendan Witt .50 .23

## 1995-96 Ultra Premier Pad Men

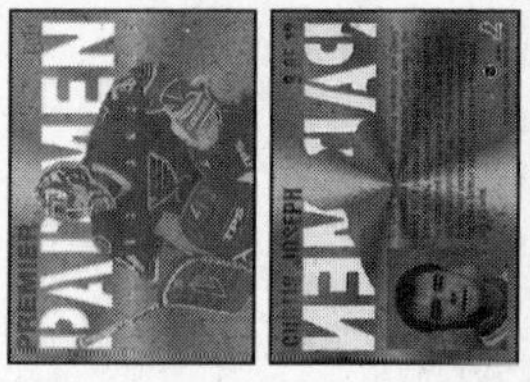

Cards from this 12-card standard-size set was inserted 1:36 series one packs. This set features leading NHL goaltenders on a special gold foil embossed design. There is also a Gold Medallion parallel version of each card. Multipliers can be found in the header below to determine values for these.

| | MINT | NRMT |
|---|---|---|
| COMPLETE SET (12) | 150.00 | 70.00 |
| COMMON CARD (1-12) | 8.00 | 3.60 |

*GOLD MEDALLION: 1.25X TO 2X BASIC CARDS

❑ 1 Ed Belfour 10.00 4.50
❑ 2 Martin Brodeur 25.00 11.00
❑ 3 Sean Burke 8.00 3.60
❑ 4 Jim Carey 10.00 4.50
❑ 5 Dominik Hasek 25.00 11.00
❑ 6 Curtis Joseph 10.00 4.50
❑ 7 Blaine Lacher 8.00 3.60
❑ 8 Andy Moog 8.00 3.60
❑ 9 Felix Potvin 10.00 4.50
❑ 10 Patrick Roy 40.00 18.00
❑ 11 John Vanbiesbrouck 15.00 6.75
❑ 12 Mike Vernon 8.00 3.60

## 1995-96 Ultra Premier Pivots

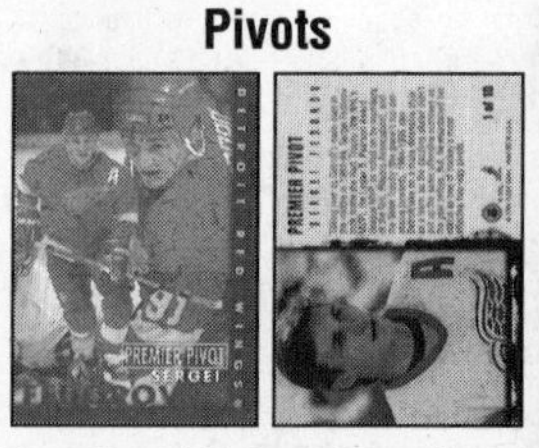

These 10 standard-size cards were inserted into first series packs at a rate of 1:4. Leading NHL centers are showcased on these cards. There also are Gold Medallion versions of each of these cards which were inserted at indeterminate odds. Multipliers can be found in the header below to determine values for these.

| | MINT | NRMT |
|---|---|---|
| COMPLETE SET (10) | 20.00 | 9.00 |
| COMMON CARD (1-10) | .75 | .35 |

*GOLD MEDALLION: 4X TO 8X BASIC CARDS

❑ 1 Sergei Fedorov 3.00 1.35
❑ 2 Ron Francis 1.00 .45
❑ 3 Wayne Gretzky 100.00 45.00
❑ 4 Eric Lindros 6.00 2.70
❑ 5 Mark Messier 2.00 .90

❑ 6 Adam Oates 1.00 .45
❑ 7 Jeremy Roenick 1.50 .70
❑ 8 Joe Sakic 4.00 1.80
❑ 9 Mats Sundin 1.00 .45
❑ 10 Alexei Zhamnov .75 .35

## 1995-96 Ultra Red Light Specials

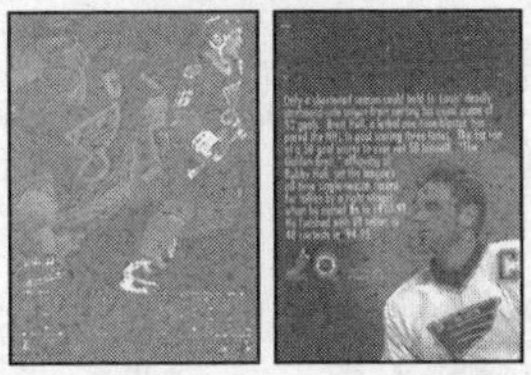

These 10 standard-size cards were inserted into series one packs at a rate of 1:3. These cards feature players who lit the lamp on a regular basis during the '94-95 season. There is also a Gold Medallion parallel version of each card. Multipliers can be found in the header below to determine values for these.

| | MINT | NRMT |
|---|---|---|
| COMPLETE SET (10) | 12.00 | 5.50 |
| COMMON CARD (1-10) | .25 | .11 |

*GOLD MEDALLION: 3X TO 6X BASIC CARDS

❑ 1 Peter Bondra 1.00 .45
❑ 2 Theoren Fleury .75 .35
❑ 3 Brett Hull 1.25 .55
❑ 4 Jaromir Jagr 3.00 1.35
❑ 5 John LeClair 1.50 .70
❑ 6 Eric Lindros 4.00 1.80
❑ 7 Cam Neely .75 .35
❑ 8 Owen Nolan .75 .35
❑ 9 Ray Sheppard .25 .11
❑ 10 Alexei Zhamnov .75 .35

## 1995-96 Ultra Rising Stars

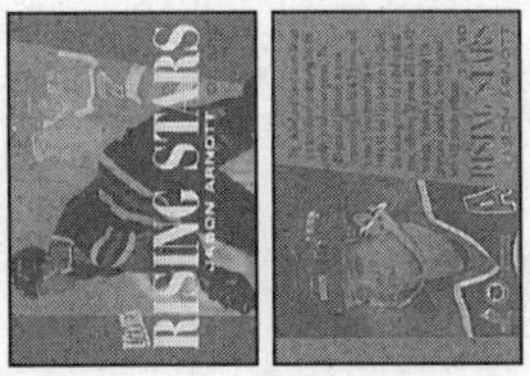


These 10 standard-size cards were randomly inserted 1:4 series onepacks. There are also Gold Medallion parallel versions of these cards which were randomly inserted at indeterminate odds. Multipliers can be found in the header below to determine values for these.

| | MINT | NRMT |
|---|---|---|
| COMPLETE SET (10) | 6.00 | 2.70 |
| COMMON CARD (1-10) | .25 | .11 |

*GOLD MEDALLION: 5X TO 10X BASIC CARDS

❑ 1 Jason Arnott .75 .35
❑ 2 Alexandre Daigle .75 .35
❑ 3 Roman Hamrlik .75 .35
❑ 4 Trevor Kidd .75 .35
❑ 5 Scott Niedermayer .25 .11
❑ 6 Keith Primeau .75 .35
❑ 7 Mikael Renberg .75 .35
❑ 8 Jocelyn Thibault .75 .35
❑ 9 Alexei Yashin .75 .35
❑ 10 Alexei Zhitnik .25 .11

## 1995-96 Ultra Ultraview

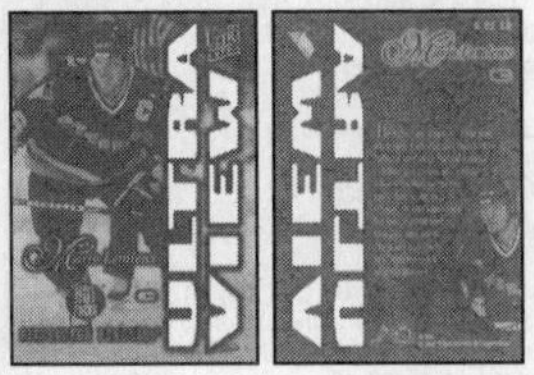


This 10-card set features the NHL's best on clear acrylic. The cards were randomly inserted at a rate of 1:55 series two packs. A parallel version of these cards could be found in complete set form in randomly inserted Ultraview Hot Packs. These sets, which bore the Hot Pack logo, were found in 1:360 packs. Because they were found in complete set form, dealers tended to discount them slightly at time of sale. Multipliers can be found in the header below to determine value for these.

| | MINT | NRMT |
|---|---|---|
| COMPLETE SET (10) | 150.00 | 70.00 |
| COMMON CARD (1-10) | 5.00 | 2.20 |
| COMPLETE HOT PACK SET (10) | 80.00 | 36.00 |

*HOT PACK VERSION: .25X TO .5X BASIC CARDS

❑ 1 Sergei Fedorov 12.00 5.50
❑ 2 Wayne Gretzky 40.00 18.00
❑ 3 Dominik Hasek 12.00 5.50
❑ 4 Jaromir Jagr 20.00 9.00
❑ 5 Brian Leetch 6.00 2.70
❑ 6 Mario Lemieux 30.00 13.50
❑ 7 Eric Lindros 20.00 9.00
❑ 8 Jeremy Roenick 6.00 2.70
❑ 9 Joe Sakic 12.00 5.50
❑ 10 Alexei Zhamnov 5.00 2.20

## 1996-97 Ultra

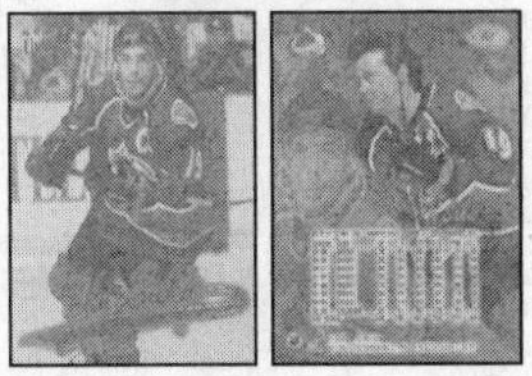

The 1996-97 Ultra set was issued in one series totaling 180 cards. Ten-card packs retailed for $2.49. Key rookies include Dainius Zubrus, Patrick Lalime, and Sergei Berezin. Card fronts feature a color action photo with player information on the back.

| | MINT | NRMT |
|---|---|---|
| COMPLETE SET (180) | 30.00 | 13.50 |
| COMMON CARD (1-180) | .10 | .05 |

❑ 1 Guy Hebert .25 .11
❑ 2 Paul Kariya 1.50 .70
❑ 3 Jari Kurri .25 .11
❑ 4 Roman Oksiuta .10 .05
❑ 5 Ruslan Salei .10 .05
❑ 6 Teemu Selanne .75 .35
❑ 7 Darren Van Impe .10 .05
❑ 8 Ray Bourque .40 .18
❑ 9 Kyle McLaren .10 .05
❑ 10 Adam Oates .25 .11
❑ 11 Bill Ranford .25 .11
❑ 12 Rick Tocchet .25 .11
❑ 13 Donald Audette .25 .11
❑ 14 Curtis Brown .10 .05
❑ 15 Jason Dawe .10 .05
❑ 16 Dominik Hasek .75 .35
❑ 17 Pat LaFontaine .25 .11
❑ 18 Jay McKee .10 .05
❑ 19 Derek Plante .10 .05
❑ 20 Wayne Primeau .10 .05
❑ 21 Theoren Fleury .25 .11
❑ 22 Dave Gagner .25 .11
❑ 23 Jonas Hoglund .10 .05
❑ 24 Jarome Iginla .40 .18
❑ 25 Trevor Kidd .25 .11
❑ 26 Robert Reichel .10 .05
❑ 27 German Titov .10 .05
❑ 28 Tony Amonte .25 .11
❑ 29 Ed Belfour .40 .18
❑ 30 Chris Chelios .40 .18
❑ 31 Eric Daze .25 .11
❑ 32 Ethan Moreau .40 .18
❑ 33 Gary Suter .10 .05
❑ 34 Adam Deadmarsh .25 .11
❑ 35 Peter Forsberg 1.25 .55
❑ 36 Valeri Kamensky .25 .11
❑ 37 Claude Lemieux .25 .11
❑ 38 Sandis Ozolinsh .25 .11
❑ 39 Patrick Roy 2.00 .90
❑ 40 Joe Sakic .75 .35
❑ 41 Landon Wilson .10 .05
❑ 42 Derian Hatcher .10 .05
❑ 43 Jamie Langenbrunner .10 .05
❑ 44 Mike Modano .50 .23
❑ 45 Andy Moog .25 .11
❑ 46 Joe Nieuwendyk .25 .11
❑ 47 Pat Verbeek .10 .05
❑ 48 Sergei Zubov .10 .05
❑ 49 Anders Eriksson .10 .05
❑ 50 Sergei Fedorov .60 .25
❑ 51 Vladimir Konstantinov .10 .05
❑ 52 Slava Kozlov .25 .11
❑ 53 Nicklas Lidstrom .25 .11
❑ 54 Chris Osgood .40 .18
❑ 55 Brendan Shanahan .75 .35
❑ 56 Steve Yzerman 1.25 .55
❑ 57 Jason Arnott .25 .11
❑ 58 Mike Grier .75 .35
❑ 59 Curtis Joseph .40 .18
❑ 60 Rem Murray .10 .05
❑ 61 Jeff Norton .10 .05
❑ 62 Miroslav Satan .10 .05
❑ 63 Doug Weight .25 .11
❑ 64 Radek Dvorak .10 .05
❑ 65 Ed Jovanovski .25 .11
❑ 66 Scott Mellanby .25 .11
❑ 67 Rob Niedermayer .25 .11
❑ 68 Ray Sheppard .25 .11
❑ 69 Robert Svehla .10 .05
❑ 70 John Vanbiesbrouck .60 .25
❑ 71 Steve Washburn .10 .05
❑ 72 Jeff Brown .10 .05
❑ 73 Sean Burke .25 .11
❑ 74 Hnat Domenichelli .10 .05
❑ 75 Keith Primeau .25 .11
❑ 76 Geoff Sanderson .25 .11
❑ 77 Rob Blake .10 .05
❑ 78 Stephane Fiset .25 .11
❑ 79 Dimitri Khristich .10 .05
❑ 80 Mattias Norstrom .10 .05
❑ 81 Ed Olczyk .10 .05
❑ 82 Jamie Storr .25 .11
❑ 83 Jan Vopat .10 .05
❑ 84 Vitali Yachmenev .10 .05
❑ 85 Shayne Corson .10 .05
❑ 86 Vincent Damphousse .25 .11
❑ 87 Saku Koivu .60 .25
❑ 88 Mark Recchi .25 .11
❑ 89 Stephane Richer .25 .11
❑ 90 Jocelyn Thibault .40 .18
❑ 91 David Wilkie .10 .05
❑ 92 Dave Andreychuk .25 .11
❑ 93 Martin Brodeur 1.00 .45
❑ 94 Scott Niedermayer .10 .05
❑ 95 Scott Stevens .25 .11
❑ 96 Petr Sykora .10 .05
❑ 97 Steve Thomas .10 .05
❑ 98 Bryan Berard .40 .18
❑ 99 Todd Bertuzzi .10 .05
❑ 100 Eric Fichaud .25 .11
❑ 101 Travis Green .25 .11
❑ 102 Kenny Jonsson .10 .05
❑ 103 Zigmund Palffy .40 .18
❑ 104 Christian Dube .10 .05
❑ 105 Daniel Goneau .10 .05
❑ 106 Wayne Gretzky 3.00 1.35
❑ 107 Alexei Kovalev .10 .05
❑ 108 Brian Leetch .40 .18
❑ 109 Mark Messier .50 .23
❑ 110 Mike Richter .40 .18
❑ 111 Luc Robitaille .25 .11
❑ 112 Niklas Sundstrom .10 .05
❑ 113 Daniel Alfredsson .25 .11
❑ 114 Radek Bonk .10 .05
❑ 115 Andreas Dackell .10 .05
❑ 116 Alexandre Daigle .10 .05
❑ 117 Steve Duchesne .10 .05
❑ 118 Wade Redden .10 .05
❑ 119 Damian Rhodes .25 .11
❑ 120 Alexei Yashin .25 .11
❑ 121 Rod Brind'Amour .25 .11
❑ 122 Paul Coffey .40 .18
❑ 123 Eric Desjardins .10 .05
❑ 124 Ron Hextall .25 .11
❑ 125 John LeClair .60 .25
❑ 126 Eric Lindros 1.25 .55
❑ 127 Janne Niinimaa .40 .18
❑ 128 Mikael Renberg .25 .11
❑ 129 Dainius Zubrus .75 .35
❑ 130 Mike Gartner .25 .11
❑ 131 Craig Janney .25 .11
❑ 132 Nikolai Khabibulin .25 .11
❑ 133 Dave Manson .10 .05
❑ 134 Teppo Numminen .10 .05
❑ 135 Jeremy Roenick .40 .18
❑ 136 Keith Tkachuk .50 .23
❑ 137 Oleg Tverdovsky .25 .11
❑ 138 Tom Barrasso .25 .11
❑ 139 Ron Francis .25 .11
❑ 140 Kevin Hatcher .10 .05
❑ 141 Jaromir Jagr 1.25 .55
❑ 142 Patrick Lalime .40 .18
❑ 143 Mario Lemieux 2.00 .90
❑ 144 Jim Campbell .10 .05
❑ 145 Grant Fuhr .25 .11
❑ 146 Brett Hull .50 .23
❑ 147 Al MacInnis .25 .11
❑ 148 Pierre Turgeon .25 .11
❑ 149 Harry York .40 .18
❑ 150 Kelly Hrudey .25 .11
❑ 151 Al Iafrate .10 .05
❑ 152 Bernie Nicholls .10 .05
❑ 153 Owen Nolan .25 .11
❑ 154 Darren Turcotte .10 .05
❑ 155 Brian Bradley .10 .05
❑ 156 Dino Ciccarelli .25 .11
❑ 157 Roman Hamrlik .25 .11
❑ 158 Daymond Langkow .10 .05
❑ 159 Daren Puppa .25 .11
❑ 160 Alexander Selivanov .10 .05
❑ 161 Sergei Berezin .60 .25
❑ 162 Wendel Clark .25 .11
❑ 163 Doug Gilmour .40 .18
❑ 164 Larry Murphy .25 .11
❑ 165 Felix Potvin .40 .18
❑ 166 Mats Sundin .25 .11
❑ 167 Pavel Bure .75 .35
❑ 168 Trevor Linden .25 .11
❑ 169 Kirk McLean .25 .11
❑ 170 Alexander Mogilny .25 .11
❑ 171 Esa Tikkanen .10 .05
❑ 172 Peter Bondra .40 .18
❑ 173 Andrew Brunette .10 .05
❑ 174 Jim Carey .40 .18
❑ 175 Sergei Gonchar .10 .05
❑ 176 Phil Housley .25 .11
❑ 177 Joe Juneau .10 .05
❑ 178 Michal Pivonka .10 .05
❑ 179 Checklist (1-143) .10 .05
❑ 180 Checklist (143-180/inserts) .10 .05
❑ S125 John LeClair promo 2.00 .90

## 1996-97 Ultra Gold Medallion

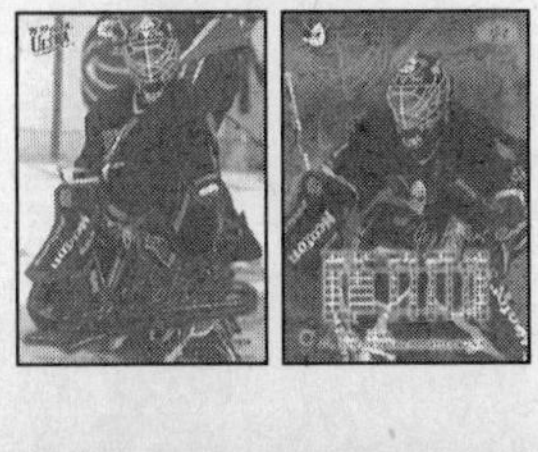

A one-per-pack parallel, these cards differ from the base cards by the use of gold foil to highlight the player's name on the card front. The words "Gold Medallion" are also included. Values for the cards can be determined by using the multipliers below on the corresponding base card.

| | MINT | NRMT |
|---|---|---|
| COMPLETE SET (180) | 175.00 | 80.00 |
| COMMON CARD (1-180) | .25 | .11 |

*STARS: 3X TO 6X BASIC CARDS
*YOUNG STARS: 2.5X TO 5X BASIC CARDS
*RC'S: 2X TO 4X BASIC CARDS

## 1996-97 Ultra Clear the Ice

Ten players recognized as some of the elite at their position are the subject of this set, which was randomly inserted in packs at the stingy rate of one in 350.

| | MINT | NRMT |
|---|---|---|
| COMPLETE SET (10) | 700.00 | 325.00 |
| COMMON CARD (1-10) | 30.00 | 13.50 |

❑ 1 Jim Carey 30.00 13.50
❑ 2 Peter Forsberg 100.00 45.00
❑ 3 Dominik Hasek 60.00 27.00
❑ 4 Jaromir Jagr 100.00 45.00
❑ 5 John LeClair 50.00 22.00
❑ 6 Eric Lindros 100.00 45.00
❑ 7 Mark Messier 40.00 18.00
❑ 8 Patrick Roy 150.00 70.00
❑ 9 Brendan Shanahan 60.00 27.00
❑ 10 Keith Tkachuk 40.00 18.00

## 1996-97 Ultra Mr. Momentum

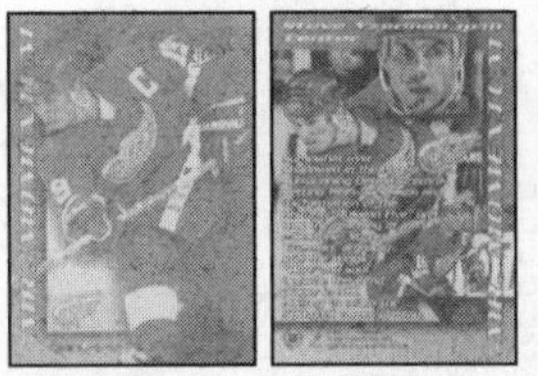

Randomly inserted in retail packs only at a rate of one in 36, these ten cards offer simple fronts and three-photo, text-laden backs.

| | MINT | NRMT |
|---|---|---|
| COMPLETE SET (10) | 275.00 | 125.00 |
| COMMON CARD (1-10) | 12.00 | 5.50 |

❑ 1 Peter Bondra 12.00 5.50
❑ 2 Pavel Bure 30.00 13.50
❑ 3 Ron Francis 12.00 5.50
❑ 4 Brett Hull 20.00 9.00
❑ 5 Jaromir Jagr 40.00 18.00
❑ 6 Pat LaFontaine 12.00 5.50
❑ 7 Eric Lindros 50.00 22.00
❑ 8 Mark Messier 20.00 9.00
❑ 9 Mats Sundin 15.00 6.75
❑ 10 Steve Yzerman 50.00 22.00

## 1996-97 Ultra Power

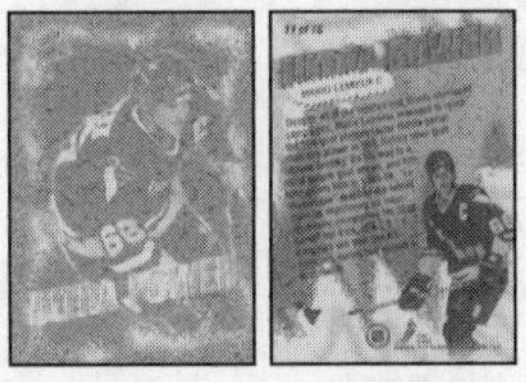

The 16 cards in this set were randomly inserted in packs at a rate of 1:16. The cards feature fiery lettering and a glitter-enhanced design. Card fronts also featrure a color action photo, with biographical info on the back. The checklist was mirrored in the Red Line and Blue Line sets, although photo choice and card numbering varied slightly.

| | MINT | NRMT |
|---|---|---|
| COMPLETE SET (16) | 200.00 | 90.00 |
| COMMON CARD (1-16) | 6.00 | 2.70 |

❑ 1 Ray Bourque 10.00 4.50
❑ 2 Chris Chelios 10.00 4.50
❑ 3 Paul Coffey 10.00 4.50
❑ 4 Sergei Fedorov 15.00 6.75
❑ 5 Wayne Gretzky 50.00 22.00
❑ 6 Roman Hamrlik 8.00 3.60
❑ 7 Ed Jovanovski 10.00 4.50
❑ 8 Paul Kariya 30.00 13.50
❑ 9 Vladimir Konstantinov 8.00 3.60
❑ 10 Brian Leetch 10.00 4.50
❑ 11 Mario Lemieux 40.00 18.00
❑ 12 Nicklas Lidstrom 6.00 2.70
❑ 13 Alexander Mogilny 8.00 3.60
❑ 14 Adam Oates 8.00 3.60
❑ 15 Joe Sakic 15.00 6.75
❑ 16 Teemu Selanne 15.00 6.75

## 1996-97 Ultra Power Blue Line

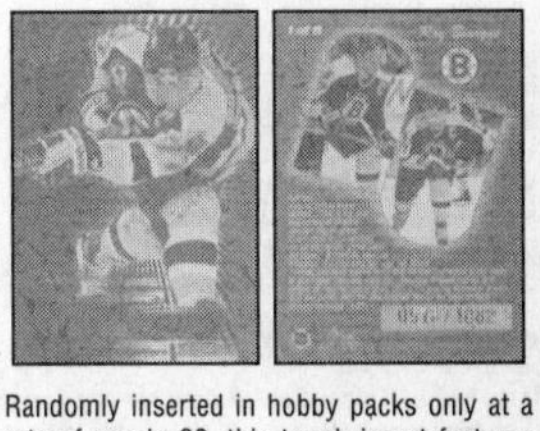

Randomly inserted in hobby packs only at a rate of one in 90, this tough insert features eight top defensive players. The cards are sequentially numbered on the back out of 1,082.

| | MINT | NRMT |
|---|---|---|
| COMPLETE SET (8) | 100.00 | 45.00 |
| COMMON CARD (1-8) | 10.00 | 4.50 |

❑ 1 Ray Bourque 20.00 9.00
❑ 2 Chris Chelios 20.00 9.00
❑ 3 Paul Coffey 20.00 9.00
❑ 4 Roman Hamrlik 10.00 4.50
❑ 5 Ed Jovanovski 15.00 6.75
❑ 6 Vladimir Konstantinov 10.00 4.50
❑ 7 Brian Leetch 20.00 9.00
❑ 8 Nicklas Lidstrom 10.00 4.50

## 1996-97 Ultra Power Red Line

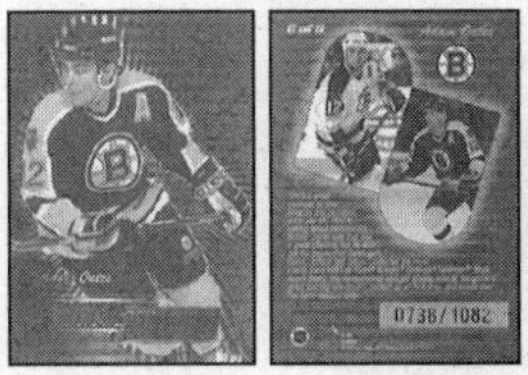

Eight of the absolute best offensive weapons grace this tough insert set, randomly seeded only in hobby packs at a rate of one in 90. The cards are sequentially numbered on the back out of 1,082.

| | MINT | NRMT |
|---|---|---|
| COMPLETE SET (8) | 400.00 | 180.00 |
| COMMON CARD (1-8) | 20.00 | 9.00 |

❑ 1 Sergei Fedorov 40.00 18.00
❑ 2 Wayne Gretzky 120.00 55.00
❑ 3 Paul Kariya 80.00 36.00
❑ 4 Mario Lemieux 100.00 45.00
❑ 5 Alexander Mogilny 25.00 11.00
❑ 6 Adam Oates 20.00 9.00
❑ 7 Joe Sakic 40.00 18.00
❑ 8 Teemu Selanne 40.00 18.00

## 1996-97 Ultra Rookies

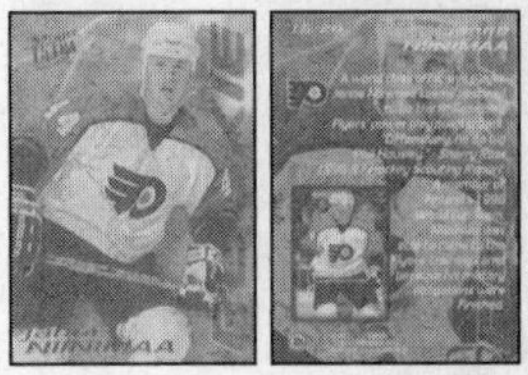

Randomly inserted in packs at a rate of 1:9, these cards offer a single player photo with the player's name with "Rookie" written on the left-hand side. Flip sides give a smaller photo with several pieces of information about each athlete.

| | MINT | NRMT |
|---|---|---|
| COMPLETE SET (20) | 60.00 | 27.00 |
| COMMON CARD (1-20) | 2.00 | .90 |

❑ 1 Bryan Berard 6.00 2.70
❑ 2 Sergei Berezin 6.00 2.70
❑ 3 Curtis Brown 2.00 .90
❑ 4 Jim Campbell 6.00 2.70
❑ 5 Christian Dube 2.00 .90
❑ 6 Anders Eriksson 2.00 .90
❑ 7 Eric Fichaud 6.00 2.70
❑ 8 Daniel Goneau 4.00 1.80
❑ 9 Mike Grier 6.00 2.70
❑ 10 Jarome Iginla 6.00 2.70
❑ 11 Jamie Langenbrunner 4.00 1.80
❑ 12 Jay McKee 2.00 .90
❑ 13 Ethan Moreau 4.00 1.80
❑ 14 Rem Murray 2.00 .90
❑ 15 Janne Niinimaa 6.00 2.70
❑ 16 Wayne Primeau 2.00 .90
❑ 17 Wade Redden 4.00 1.80
❑ 18 Jamie Storr 4.00 1.80
❑ 19 David Wilkie 2.00 .90
❑ 20 Landon Wilson 2.00 .90

## 1990-91 Upper Deck Promos

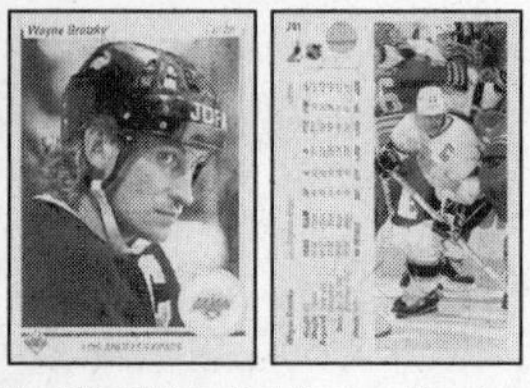

The 1990-91 Upper Deck Promo set is a two-card set featuring Wayne Gretzky and Patrick Roy both numbered as card number 241. The cards were first handed out as samples at the 1990 National Sports Collectors Convention in Arlington. The Arlington National promos were issued as a set in a special screw-down holder commemorating the National; these sets are much more limited and are rarely offered for sale. The photos on the front and back of both of the cards were changed in the regular set, as were the card numbers.

| | MINT | NRMT |
|---|---|---|
| COMPLETE SET (2) | 50.00 | 22.00 |
| COMMON CARD | 20.00 | 9.00 |

❑ 241A Wayne Gretzky UER .... 30.00 13.50
(Wrong height, feet and inches reversed)
❑ 241B Patrick Roy UER ......... 20.00 9.00
(Wrong height, feet and inches reversed)

## 1990-91 Upper Deck

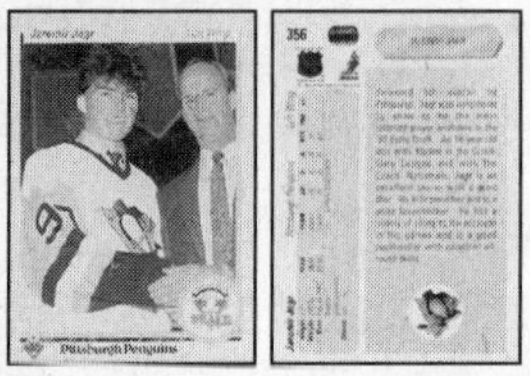

The 1990-91 Upper Deck Hockey set contains 550 standard-size cards. The set was released in two series of 400 and 150 cards, respectively. The card fronts feature color action photos, bordered on the right and bottom in the team's colors with the team logo in the lower right hand corner. The player's name and position in black lettering appear in a pale blue bar at the top of the card front. Two-thirds of back shows another color action photo, while the remaining third presents biographical information and career statistics in pale blue box running the length of the card. The second (or extended) series contains 150 cards and includes newest rookies, traded players, All Stars, Heroes of the NHL, and members of the Canadian National Junior Team. It should also be noted that the Canada's Captains card (473) shows Eric Lindros along with Kris Draper and Steven Rice. The French version of 1990-91 Upper Deck was produced in smaller quantities compared to the English version; multipliers can be found in the header below to determine values for these. A solid Rookie Card crop includes Ed Belfour, Peter Bondra, Rod Brind'Amour, Pavel Bure, Sergei Fedorov, Slava Fetisov, Adam Graves, Jaromir Jagr, Trevor Kidd, Curtis Joseph, Igor Larionov, Sergei Makarov, Mike Modano, Alexander Mogilny, Joe Murphy, Petr Nedved, Scott Niedermayer, Owen Nolan, Felix Potvin, Keith Primeau, Mark Recchi, Mike Ricci, Mike Richter, Jeremy Roenick, Kevin Stevens, Mats Sundin and Chris Terreri.

| | MINT | NRMT |
|---|---|---|
| COMPLETE SET (550) | 60.00 | 27.00 |
| COMPLETE LO SERIES (400) | 30.00 | 13.50 |
| COMPLETE HI SERIES (150) | 30.00 | 13.50 |
| COMP.HI FACT.SERIES (150) | 30.00 | 13.50 |
| COMMON CARD (1-550) | .10 | .05 |

❑ 1 David Volek .10 .05
❑ 2 Brian Propp .10 .05
❑ 3 Wendel Clark .20 .09
❑ 4 Adam Creighton .10 .05
❑ 5 Mark Osborne .10 .05
❑ 6 Murray Craven .10 .05
❑ 7 Doug Crossman .10 .05
❑ 8 Mario Marois .10 .05
❑ 9 Curt Giles .10 .05
❑ 10 Rick Wamsley .20 .09
❑ 11 Troy Mallette .10 .05
❑ 12 John Cullen .10 .05
❑ 13 Miloslav Horava .10 .05
❑ 14 Kevin Stevens .10 .05
❑ 15 David Shaw .10 .05
❑ 16 Randy Wood .10 .05
❑ 17 Peter Zezel .10 .05
❑ 18 Glenn Healy .20 .09
❑ 19 Sergio Momesso .10 .05
❑ 20 Don Maloney .10 .05
❑ 21 Craig Muni .10 .05
❑ 22 Phil Housley .20 .09
❑ 23 Martin Gelinas .50 .23
❑ 24 Alexander Mogilny 1.25 .55
❑ 25 John Byce .10 .05
❑ 26 Joe Nieuwendyk .20 .09
❑ 27 Ron Tugnutt .20 .09
❑ 28 Don Barber .10 .05
❑ 29 Gary Roberts .10 .05
❑ 30 Basil McRae .10 .05
❑ 31 Phil Bourque .10 .05
❑ 32 Mike Richter 1.50 .70
❑ 33 Zarley Zalapski .10 .05
❑ 34 Bernie Nicholls .20 .09
❑ 35 Bob Corkum .10 .05
❑ 36 Rod Brind'Amour 1.00 .45
❑ 37 Mark Fitzpatrick UER .20 .09
(Back says catches right, not left)
❑ 38 Gino Cavallini .10 .05
❑ 39 Mick Vukota .10 .05
❑ 40 Mike Lalor .10 .05
❑ 41 Dave Andreychuk .20 .09
❑ 42 Bill Ranford .20 .09
❑ 43 Pierre Turgeon .20 .09
❑ 44 Mark Messier .50 .23
❑ 45 Rob Blake .60 .25
❑ 46 Mike Modano 3.00 1.35
❑ 47 Theoren Fleury .20 .09
❑ 48 Neal Broten .20 .09
❑ 49 Paul Gillis .10 .05
❑ 50 Doug Bodger UER .10 .05
(Birthplace should be Chemainus)
❑ 51 Stephan Lebeau .10 .05
❑ 52 Larry Robinson .20 .09
❑ 53 Dale Hawerchuk .20 .09
❑ 54 Wayne Gretzky 2.00 .90
❑ 55 Ed Belfour UER 2.50 1.10
(Turned pro with Gears, should be Generals)
❑ 56 Steve Yzerman 1.00 .45
❑ 57 Rod Langway .10 .05
❑ 58 Bernie Federko .20 .09
❑ 59 Mario Lemieux Streak .75 .35
❑ 60 Doug Lidster .10 .05
❑ 61 Dave Christian .10 .05
❑ 62 Rob Ramage .10 .05
❑ 63 Jeremy Roenick 1.50 .70
❑ 64 Ray Bourque .40 .18
❑ 65 Jon Morris .10 .05
❑ 66 Sean Burke .20 .09
❑ 67 Ron Francis .20 .09
❑ 68 Ron Sutter .10 .05
❑ 69 Peter Sidorkiewicz .20 .09
❑ 70 Sylvain Turgeon .10 .05
❑ 71 Dave Ellett .10 .05
❑ 72 Bobby Smith .20 .09
❑ 73 Luc Robitaille .20 .09
❑ 74 Pat Elynuik .10 .05
❑ 75 Jason Soules .10 .05
❑ 76 Dino Ciccarelli .20 .09
❑ 77 Vladimir Krutov .20 .09
❑ 78 Lee Norwood .10 .05
❑ 79 Brian Bradley .10 .05
❑ 80 Michal Pivonka .10 .05
❑ 81 Mark LaForest .10 .05
❑ 82 Trent Yawney .10 .05
❑ 83 Tom Fergus .10 .05
❑ 84 Andy Brickley .10 .05
❑ 85 Dave Manson .10 .05
❑ 86 Gord Murphy .10 .05
❑ 87 Scott Young .10 .05
❑ 88 Tommy Albelin .10 .05
❑ 89 Ken Wregget .20 .09
❑ 90 Brad Shaw .10 .05
❑ 91 Mario Gosselin .20 .09
❑ 92 Paul Fenton .10 .05
❑ 93 Brian Skrudland .10 .05
❑ 94 Thomas Steen .10 .05
❑ 95 John Tonelli .10 .05
❑ 96 Steve Chiasson UER .10 .05
(Back photo actually Yves Racine)
❑ 97 Mike Ridley .10 .05
❑ 98 Garth Butcher .10 .05
❑ 99 Daniel Shank .10 .05
❑ 100 Checklist 1-100 .10 .05
❑ 101 Jamie Macoun .10 .05
❑ 102 Wendell Young .20 .09
❑ 103 Laurie Boschman .10 .05
❑ 104 Paul Ranheim .10 .05
❑ 105 Doug Smail .10 .05
❑ 106 Shawn Chambers .10 .05
❑ 107 Steve Weeks .20 .09
❑ 108 Gaetan Duchesne .10 .05
❑ 109 Kevin Hatcher .10 .05
❑ 110 Paul Reinhart .10 .05
❑ 111 Shawn Burr .10 .05
❑ 112 Troy Murray .10 .05
❑ 113 John Chabot .10 .05
❑ 114 Jacques Cloutier .20 .09
❑ 115 Rick Zombo .10 .05
❑ 116 Kjell Samuelsson .10 .05
❑ 117 Tim Watters .10 .05
❑ 118 Pat Flatley .10 .05
❑ 119 Tom Laidlaw .10 .05
❑ 120 Ilkka Sinisalo .10 .05
❑ 121 Tom Barrasso .20 .09
❑ 122 Bob Essensa .20 .09
❑ 123 Sergei Makarov .50 .23
❑ 124 Paul Coffey .40 .18
❑ 125 Bob Beers .10 .05
❑ 126 Brian Bellows .10 .05
❑ 127 Mike Liut .20 .09
❑ 128 Igor Larionov 1.00 .45
❑ 129 Craig Simpson .10 .05
❑ 130 Kelly Miller .10 .05
❑ 131 Dirk Graham .10 .05
❑ 132 Jimmy Carson .10 .05
❑ 133 Michel Goulet .20 .09
❑ 134 Gerard Gallant .10 .05
❑ 135 Bruce Hoffort .10 .05
❑ 136 Steve Duchesne .10 .05
❑ 137 Bryan Trottier .20 .09
❑ 138 Pelle Eklund .10 .05
❑ 139 Gary Nylund .10 .05
❑ 140 Steve Kasper .10 .05
❑ 141 Joel Otto .10 .05
❑ 142 Rob Brown .10 .05
❑ 143 Al MacInnis .20 .09
❑ 144 Mario Lemieux 1.50 .70
❑ 145 Peter Eriksson UER .10 .05
(Photo actually Tommy Lehmann)
❑ 146 Jari Kurri .20 .09
❑ 147 Petri Skriko .10 .05
❑ 148 Steve Smith .10 .05
❑ 149 Calle Johansson .10 .05
❑ 150 Stewart Gavin .10 .05
❑ 151 Randy Ladouceur .10 .05
❑ 152 Vincent Riendeau .20 .09
❑ 153 Patrick Roy UER 1.50 .70
(Feet and inches reversed in stat table)
❑ 154 Brett Hull .75 .35
❑ 155 Craig Fisher UER .10 .05
(Photo actually Jay Wells)
❑ 156 Cam Neely .20 .09
❑ 157 Al Iafrate .20 .09
❑ 158 Bob Carpenter .10 .05
❑ 159 Doug Brown .10 .05
❑ 160 Tom Kurvers .10 .05
❑ 161 John MacLean .20 .09
❑ 162 Guy Lafleur .40 .18
❑ 163 Peter Stastny .20 .09
❑ 164 Joe Sakic 1.00 .45
❑ 165 Robb Stauber .20 .09
❑ 166 Daren Puppa .20 .09
❑ 167 Esa Tikkanen .10 .05
❑ 168 Mike Ramsey .10 .05
❑ 169 Craig MacTavish .10 .05
❑ 170 Christian Ruuttu .10 .05
❑ 171 Brian Hayward .20 .09
❑ 172 Pat Verbeek .10 .05
❑ 173 Adam Oates .20 .09
❑ 174 Chris Chelios .40 .18
❑ 175 Curtis Joseph 1.50 .70
❑ 176 Slava Fetisov .50 .23
❑ 177 Dave Poulin .10 .05
❑ 178 Mark Recchi 1.00 .45
❑ 179 Daniel Marois .10 .05
❑ 180 Mark Johnson .10 .05
❑ 181 Michel Petit .10 .05
❑ 182 Brian Mullen .10 .05
❑ 183 Chris Terreri .20 .09
❑ 184 Tony Hrkac .10 .05
❑ 185 James Patrick .10 .05
❑ 186 Craig Ludwig .10 .05
❑ 187 Uwe Krupp .10 .05
❑ 188 Guy Carbonneau .20 .09
❑ 189 Dave Snuggerud .10 .05
❑ 190 Joe Murphy .10 .05
❑ 191 Jeff Brown .10 .05
❑ 192 Dean Evason .10 .05
❑ 193 Petr Svoboda .10 .05
❑ 194 Dave Babych .10 .05
❑ 195 Steve Tuttle .10 .05
❑ 196 Randy Burridge .10 .05
❑ 197 Tony Tanti .10 .05
❑ 198 Bob Sweeney .10 .05
❑ 199 Brad Marsh .10 .05
❑ 200 Checklist 101-200 .10 .05
❑ 201 Conn Smythe Trophy .20 .09
Bill Ranford
❑ 202 Calder Trophy .10 .05
Sergei Makarov
❑ 203 Lady Byng Trophy .40 .18
Brett Hull
❑ 204 Norris Trophy .20 .09
Ray Bourque
❑ 205 Art Ross Trophy 1.00 .45
Wayne Gretzky
❑ 206 Hart Trophy .20 .09
Mark Messier
❑ 207 Vezina Trophy .75 .35
Patrick Roy
❑ 208 Frank Selke Trophy .10 .05
Rick Meagher
❑ 209 William Jennings .10 .05
Trophy
Andy Moog and Reggie Lemelin
❑ 210 Aaron Broten .10 .05
❑ 211 John Carter .10 .05
❑ 212 Marty McSorley .10 .05
❑ 213 Greg Millen .20 .09
❑ 214 Dave Taylor .20 .09
❑ 215 Rejean Lemelin .20 .09
❑ 216 Dave McLlwain UER .10 .05
(Shoots left, not right)
❑ 217 Don Beaupre .20 .09
❑ 218 Paul MacDermid .10 .05
❑ 219 Dale Hunter .10 .05
❑ 220 Brent Ashton .10 .05
❑ 221 Steve Thomas .10 .05
❑ 222 Ed Olczyk .10 .05
❑ 223 Doug Wilson .20 .09
❑ 224 Vincent Damphousse .20 .09
❑ 225 Rob DiMaio .10 .05
❑ 226 Hubie McDonough .10 .05
❑ 227 Ron Hextall .20 .09
❑ 228 Dave Chyzowski .10 .05
❑ 229 Larry Murphy .20 .09
❑ 230 Mike Bullard .10 .05
❑ 231 Kelly Hrudey .20 .09
❑ 232 Andy Moog .20 .09
❑ 233 Todd Elik .10 .05
❑ 234 Craig Janney .20 .09
❑ 235 Peter Lappin .10 .05
❑ 236 Scott Stevens .20 .09
❑ 237 Fredrik Olausson .10 .05
❑ 238 Geoff Courtnall .10 .05
❑ 239 Greg Paslawski .10 .05
❑ 240 Alan May .10 .05
❑ 241 Allan Bester .20 .09
❑ 242 Steve Larmer .20 .09
❑ 243 Gary Leeman .10 .05
❑ 244 Denis Savard .20 .09
❑ 245 Eric Weinrich .10 .05
❑ 246 Pat LaFontaine .20 .09
❑ 247 Tim Kerr .10 .05
❑ 248 Dave Gagner .20 .09
❑ 249 Brent Sutter .10 .05
❑ 250 Claude Vilgrain .10 .05
❑ 251 Tomas Sandstrom .10 .05
❑ 252 Joe Mullen .20 .09
❑ 253 Brian Leetch .60 .25
❑ 254 Mike Vernon .20 .09
❑ 255 Daniel Dore .10 .05
❑ 256 Trevor Linden .20 .09
❑ 257 Dave Barr .10 .05
❑ 258 John Ogrodnick .10 .05
❑ 259 Russ Courtnall .10 .05
❑ 260 Dan Quinn .10 .05
❑ 261 Mark Howe .10 .05
❑ 262 Kevin Lowe .10 .05
❑ 263 Rick Tocchet .20 .09
❑ 264 Grant Fuhr .20 .09
❑ 265 Andrew Cassels .10 .05
❑ 266 Kevin Dineen .10 .05
❑ 267 Kirk Muller .10 .05
❑ 268 Randy Cunneyworth .10 .05
❑ 269 Brendan Shanahan 1.00 .45
❑ 270 Dave Tippett .10 .05
❑ 271 Doug Gilmour .40 .18
❑ 272 Tony Granato .10 .05
❑ 273 Gary Suter .10 .05
❑ 274 Darren Turcotte .10 .05
❑ 275 Murray Baron .10 .05
❑ 276 Stephane Richer .20 .09
❑ 277 Mike Gartner .20 .09
❑ 278 Kirk McLean .20 .09
❑ 279 John Vanbiesbrouck .75 .35
❑ 280 Shayne Corson .10 .05
❑ 281 Paul Cavallini .10 .05
❑ 282 Petr Klima .10 .05
❑ 283 Ulf Dahlen .10 .05
❑ 284 Glenn Anderson .20 .09
❑ 285 Rick Meagher .10 .05
❑ 286 Alexei Kasatonov .10 .05
❑ 287 Ulf Samuelsson .10 .05
❑ 288 Patrik Sundstrom .10 .05
❑ 289 Ray Ferraro .10 .05
❑ 290 Janne Ojanen .10 .05
❑ 291 Jeff Jackson .10 .05
❑ 292 Jiri Hrdina .10 .05
❑ 293 Joe Cirella .10 .05
❑ 294 Brad McCrimmon .10 .05
❑ 295 Curtis Leschyshyn .10 .05
❑ 296 Kelly Kisio .10 .05
❑ 297 Jyrki Lumme .10 .05
❑ 298 Mark Janssens .10 .05
❑ 299 Stan Smyl .10 .05
❑ 300 Checklist 201-300 .10 .05
❑ 301 Joe Sakic .40 .18
(Quebec Nordiques TC)
❑ 302 Petri Skriko .10 .05
(Vancouver Canucks TC)
❑ 303 Steve Yzerman .40 .18
(Detroit Red Wings TC)
❑ 304 Tim Kerr .10 .05
(Philadelphia Flyers TC)
❑ 305 Mario Lemieux .75 .35
(Pittsburgh Penguins TC)
❑ 306 Pat LaFontaine .20 .09
(New York Islanders TC)
❑ 307 Wayne Gretzky 1.00 .45
(Los Angeles Kings TC)
❑ 308 Brian Bellows .10 .05
(Minnesota North Stars TC)
❑ 309 Rod Langway .10 .05
(Washington Capitals TC)
❑ 310 Gary Leeman .10 .05
(Toronto Maple Leafs TC)
❑ 311 Kirk Muller .10 .05
(New Jersey Devils TC)
❑ 312 Brett Hull .20 .09
(St. Louis Blues TC)
❑ 313 Thomas Steen .10 .05
(Winnipeg Jets TC)
❑ 314 Ron Francis .20 .09
(Hartford Whalers TC)
❑ 315 Brian Leetch .20 .09
(New York Rangers TC)
❑ 316 Jeremy Roenick .40 .18
(Chicago Blackhawks TC)
❑ 317 Patrick Roy .75 .35
(Montreal Canadiens TC)
❑ 318 Pierre Turgeon .20 .09
(Buffalo Sabres TC)
❑ 319 Al MacInnis .20 .09
(Calgary Flames TC)
❑ 320 Ray Bourque .20 .09
(Boston Bruins TC)
❑ 321 Mark Messier .20 .09
(Edmonton Oilers TC)
❑ 322 Jody Hull .10 .05
❑ 323 Chris Joseph .10 .05
❑ 324 Adam Burt .10 .05
❑ 325 Jason Herter .10 .05
❑ 326 Geoff Smith ART .10 .05
❑ 327 Brad Shaw ART .10 .05
❑ 328 Rich Sutter .10 .05
❑ 329 Barry Pederson .10 .05
❑ 330 Paul MacLean .10 .05
❑ 331 Randy Carlyle .10 .05
❑ 332 Donald Dufresne UER .10 .05
(Says shoots right, should say left)
❑ 333 Brent Hughes .10 .05
❑ 334 Mathieu Schneider .10 .05
❑ 335 Jason Miller .10 .05
❑ 336 Sergei Makarov ART .10 .05
❑ 337 Bob Essensa ART .20 .09
❑ 338 Claude Loiselle .10 .05
❑ 339 Wayne Presley .10 .05
❑ 340 Tony McKegney .10 .05
❑ 341 Charlie Huddy .10 .05
❑ 342 Greg Adams UER .10 .05
(Front photo actually Igor Larionov)
❑ 343 Mike Thomas .10 .05
❑ 344 Adam Graves 1.00 .45
❑ 345 Michel Mongeau .10 .05
❑ 346 Mike Modano UER ART .20 .09
('89 Entry Draft, should say '88)
❑ 347 Rod Brind'Amour ART .20 .09
❑ 348 Dana Murzyn .10 .05
❑ 349 Dave Lowry RC .10 .05
❑ 350 Star Rookie CL .10 .05
❑ 351 First Four Picks .50 .23
Owen Nolan
Keith Primeau
Petr Nedved
Mike Ricci
Top Ten Draft Pick CL
❑ 352 Owen Nolan FDP 1.00 .45
❑ 353 Petr Nedved 1.00 .45
❑ 354 Keith Primeau .60 .25
❑ 355 Mike Ricci UER .20 .09
(Born October, not November 27)
❑ 356 Jaromir Jagr 5.00 2.20
(With Penguins General Manager Craig Patrick)
❑ 357 Scott Scissons .10 .05
❑ 358 Darryl Sydor .75 .35
❑ 359 Derian Hatcher .10 .05
(With North Stars Owner Norman Green)
❑ 360 John Slaney .10 .05
❑ 361 Drake Berehowsky .10 .05
❑ 362 Luke Richardson .10 .05
❑ 363 Lucien DeBlois .10 .05
❑ 364 David Reid .10 .05
❑ 365 Mats Sundin 1.50 .70
❑ 366 Jan Erixon .10 .05
❑ 367 Troy Loney .10 .05
❑ 368 Chris Nilan .10 .05
❑ 369 Gord Dineen .10 .05
❑ 370 Jeff Bloemberg .10 .05
❑ 371 John Druce .10 .05
❑ 372 Brian MacLellan .10 .05
❑ 373 Bruce Driver .10 .05
❑ 374 Marc Habscheid .10 .05
❑ 375 Paul Ysebaert .10 .05
❑ 376 Rick Vaive .10 .05
❑ 377 Glen Wesley .10 .05
❑ 378 Mike Foligno .10 .05
❑ 379 Garry Galley .10 .05
❑ 380 Dean Kennedy .10 .05
❑ 381 Daniel Berthiaume .20 .09
❑ 382 Mike Keane .10 .05
❑ 383 Frank Musil .10 .05
❑ 384 Mike McPhee .10 .05
❑ 385 Jon Casey .20 .09
❑ 386 Jeff Norton .10 .05
❑ 387 John Tucker .10 .05
❑ 388 Alan Kerr .10 .05
❑ 389 Bob Rouse .10 .05
❑ 390 Gerald Diduck .10 .05
❑ 391 Greg Hawgood .10 .05
❑ 392 Randy Velischek .10 .05
❑ 393 Tim Cheveldae .20 .09
❑ 394 Mike Krushelnyski .10 .05
❑ 395 Glen Hanlon .20 .09
❑ 396 Lou Franceschetti .10 .05
❑ 397 Scott Arniel .10 .05
❑ 398 Terry Carkner .10 .05
❑ 399 Clint Malarchuk .20 .09
❑ 400 Checklist 301-400 .10 .05
❑ 401 Mikhail Tatarinov .10 .05
❑ 402 Benoit Hogue .10 .05
❑ 403 Frank Pietrangelo .20 .09
❑ 404 Paul Stanton .10 .05
❑ 405 Anatoli Semenov .10 .05
❑ 406 Bobby Smith .20 .09
❑ 407 Derek King .10 .05
❑ 408 J.C. Bergeron .10 .05
❑ 409 Brian Propp .10 .05
❑ 410 Jiri Latal .10 .05
❑ 411 Joey Kocur .50 .23
❑ 412 Daniel Berthiaume .20 .09
❑ 413 Dave Ellett .10 .05
❑ 414 Jay Miller .10 .05
❑ 415 Stephane Beauregard .20 .09
❑ 416 Mark Hardy .10 .05
❑ 417 Todd Krygier .10 .05
❑ 418 Randy Moller .10 .05

❑ 419 Doug Crossman .10 .05
❑ 420 Ray Sheppard .20 .09
❑ 421 Sylvain Lefebvre .10 .05
❑ 422 Chris Chelios .40 .18
❑ 423 Joe Mullen .20 .09
❑ 424 Pete Peeters .20 .09
❑ 425 Bryan Trottier .20 .09
❑ 426 Denis Savard .20 .09
❑ 427 Ken Daneyko .10 .05
❑ 428 Eric Desjardins .60 .25
❑ 429 Zdeno Ciger .10 .05
❑ 430 Brad McCrimmon .10 .05
❑ 431 Ed Olczyk .10 .05
❑ 432 Peter Ing .20 .09
❑ 433 Bob Kudelski .10 .05
❑ 434 Troy Gamble .20 .09
❑ 435 Phil Housley .20 .09
❑ 436 Scott Stevens .20 .09
❑ 437 Normand Rochefort .10 .05
❑ 438 Geoff Courtnall .10 .05
❑ 439 Ken Baumgartner .10 .05
❑ 440 Kris King .10 .05
❑ 441 Troy Crowder .10 .05
❑ 442 Chris Nilan .10 .05
❑ 443 Dale Hawerchuk .20 .09
❑ 444 Kevin Miller .10 .05
❑ 445 Keith Acton .10 .05
❑ 446 Jeff Chychrun .10 .05
❑ 447 Claude Lemieux .20 .09
❑ 448 Bob Probert .20 .09
❑ 449 Brian Hayward .20 .09
❑ 450 Craig Berube .10 .05
❑ 451 Team Canada .40 .18
❑ 452 Mike Sillinger .10 .05
❑ 453 Jason Marshall .10 .05
❑ 454 Patrice Brisebois .10 .05
❑ 455 Brad May .50 .23
❑ 456 Pierre Sevigny .10 .05
❑ 457 John Slaney .10 .05
❑ 458 Felix Potvin 3.00 1.35
❑ 459 Scott Thornton .10 .05
❑ 460 Greg Johnson .10 .05
❑ 461 Scott Niedermayer 1.00 .45
❑ 462 Steven Rice .10 .05
❑ 463 Trevor Kidd 1.00 .45
❑ 464 Dale Craigwell .10 .05
❑ 465 Kent Manderville .10 .05
❑ 466 Kris Draper .50 .23
❑ 467 Martin Lapointe .50 .23
❑ 468 Chris Snell .10 .05
❑ 469 Pat Falloon .10 .05
❑ 470 David Harlock .10 .05
❑ 471 Karl Dykhuis .10 .05
❑ 472 Mike Craig .10 .05
❑ 473 Canada's Captains 3.00 1.35
Kris Draper
Steven Rice
Eric Lindros
❑ 474 Brett Hull AS .40 .18
❑ 475 Darren Turcotte AS .10 .05
❑ 476 Wayne Gretzky AS 1.00 .45
❑ 477 Steve Yzerman AS .50 .23
❑ 478 Theoren Fleury AS .20 .09
❑ 479 Pat LaFontaine AS .20 .09
❑ 480 Trevor Linden AS .20 .09
❑ 481 Jeremy Roenick AS .40 .18
❑ 482 Scott Stevens AS .20 .09
❑ 483 Adam Oates AS .20 .09
❑ 484 Vincent Damphousse AS .20 .09
❑ 485 Brian Leetch AS .40 .18
❑ 486 Kevin Hatcher AS .10 .05
❑ 487 Mark Recchi AS .20 .09
❑ 488 Rick Tocchet AS .20 .09
❑ 489 Ray Bourque AS .20 .09
❑ 490 Joe Sakic AS .50 .23
❑ 491 Chris Chelios AS .20 .09
❑ 492 John Cullen AS .10 .05
❑ 493 Cam Neely AS .20 .09
❑ 494 Mark Messier AS .40 .18
❑ 495 Mike Vernon AS .20 .09
❑ 496 Patrick Roy AS .75 .35
❑ 497 Al MacInnis AS .20 .09
❑ 498 Paul Coffey AS .20 .09
❑ 499 Steve Larmer AS .20 .09
❑ 500 Checklist 401-500 .10 .05
❑ 501 Heroes Checklist .10 .05
❑ 502 Red Kelly HERO .10 .05
❑ 503 Eric Nesterenko HERO .10 .05
❑ 504 Darryl Sittler HERO .10 .05
❑ 505 Jim Schoenfeld HERO .10 .05
❑ 506 Serge Savard HERO .10 .05
❑ 507 Glenn Resch HERO .20 .09
❑ 508 Lanny McDonald HERO .10 .05
❑ 509 Bobby Clarke HERO .20 .09
❑ 510 Phil Esposito HERO .20 .09
❑ 511 Harry Howell HERO .10 .05
❑ 512 Rod Gilbert HERO .10 .05
❑ 513 Pit Martin HERO .10 .05
❑ 514 Jimmy Watson HERO .10 .05
❑ 515 Denis Potvin HERO .10 .05
❑ 516 Robert Ray .10 .05
❑ 517 Danton Cole .10 .05
❑ 518 Gino Odjick .10 .05
❑ 519 Donald Audette .20 .09
❑ 520 Rick Tabaracci .20 .09
❑ 521 Sergei Fedorov 1.00 .45
Johan Garpenlov
(Young Guns Checklist)
❑ 522 Kip Miller YG .10 .05
❑ 523 Johan Garpenlov YG .10 .05
❑ 524 Stephane Morin YG .10 .05
❑ 525 Sergei Fedorov YG UER 8.00 3.60
(Birthplace listed
as Pskow, should be
Appatity)
❑ 526 Pavel Bure YG 10.00 4.50
❑ 527 Wes Walz YG .10 .05
❑ 528 Robert Kron YG .10 .05
❑ 529 Ken Hodge Jr. YG .10 .05
❑ 530 Garry Valk YG .10 .05
❑ 531 Tim Sweeney YG .10 .05
❑ 532 Mark Pederson YG .10 .05
❑ 533 Robert Reichel YG .50 .23
❑ 534 Bobby Holik YG .10 .05
❑ 535 Stephane Matteau YG .10 .05
❑ 536 Peter Bondra YG 2.00 .90
❑ 537 Dimitri Khristich .10 .05
❑ 538 Vladimir Ruzicka .10 .05
❑ 539 Al Iafrate .20 .09
❑ 540 Rick Bennett .10 .05
❑ 541 Daryl Reaugh .10 .05
❑ 542 Martin Hostak .10 .05
❑ 543 Kari Takko .20 .09
❑ 544 Jocelyn Lemieux .10 .05
❑ 545 Gretzky's 2000th 1.00 .45
Point
❑ 546 Hull's 50 Goals .40 .18
❑ 547 Neil Wilkinson .10 .05
❑ 548 Bryan Fogarty .10 .05
❑ 549 Zamboni Machine .20 .09
(Frank J. Zamboni)
❑ 550 Checklist 501-550 .10 .05

## 1990-91 Upper Deck Holograms

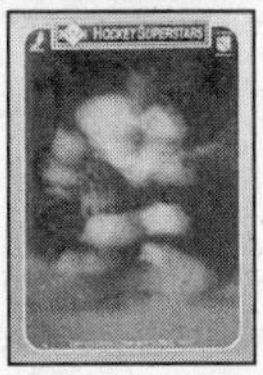

The nine standard-size cards in this set were randomly inserted in 1990-91 Upper Deck foil packs (low and high series). The cards are best described as stereograms because the players show movement when the cards are slowly rotated. On the fronts, the stereograms are enclosed by a frame with rounded corners. The Upper Deck logo and title line "Hockey Superstars" appear in a bar at the top. The backs are blank and can be peeled off to stick the stereogram on a surface. The cards are unnumbered and checklisted below in alphabetical order.

| | MINT | NRMT |
|---|---|---|
| COMPLETE SET (9) | 10.00 | 4.50 |
| COMMON CARD (1-9) | .75 | .35 |

❑ 1 Wayne Gretzky 2.00 .90
Stopping
❑ 2 Wayne Gretzky 2.00 .90
Shooting
❑ 3 Wayne Gretzky 2.00 .90
Standing
❑ 4 Brett Hull .75 .35
❑ 5 Mark Messier .75 .35
❑ 6 Mark Messier and .75 .35
Brett Hull
❑ 7 Mark Messier and 1.00 .45
Steve Yzerman
❑ 8 Steve Yzerman 1.00 .45
❑ 9 Steve Yzerman 1.00 .45

## 1990-91 Upper Deck Sheets

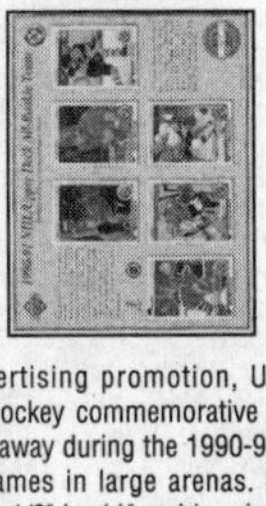

As an advertising promotion, Upper Deck produced hockey commemorative sheets that were given away during the 1990-91 season at selected games in large arenas. Each sheet measures 8 1/2" by 11" and is printed on card stock. The fronts of the team commemorative sheets feature the team logo and a series of Upper Deck cards of star players on that team. Some of these sheets have a brief history of the team, which is tied in with an Upper Deck advertisement. The All-Star game sheet is distinguished by a hockey stick facsimile autographed by those All-Star players whose cards are displayed. All the sheets have an Upper Deck stamp indicating the production quota; in addition, some of the sheets have the serial number. The backs are blank. The sheets are listed below in chronological order.

| | MINT | NRMT |
|---|---|---|
| COMPLETE SET (11) | 160.00 | 70.00 |
| COMMON CARD (1-11) | 10.00 | 4.50 |

❑ 1 Toronto Maple Leafs 25.00 11.00
vs. Detroit Red Wings
Nov. 17, 1990 (20,000)
Al Iafrate
Ed Olczyk
Vincent Damphousse
Wendel Clark
Gary Leeman
Drake Berehowsky
❑ 2 Detroit Red Wings I 15.00 6.75
vs. Boston Bruins
Dec. 4, 1990 (22,000)
Keith Primeau
Shawn Burr
Steve Yzerman
Jimmy Carson
Tim Cheveldae
Steve Chiasson
❑ 3 Los Angeles Kings 15.00 6.75
vs. Calgary Flames
Dec. 13, 1990 (19,500)
Steve Duchesne
Luc Robitaille
Rob Blake
Wayne Gretzky
Tony Granato
Tomas Sandstrom
❑ 4 New York Rangers I 10.00 4.50
vs. Hartford Whalers
Jan. 13, 1991 (25,700)
Mike Richter
Ray Sheppard
Troy Mallette
Normand Rochefort
Mark Janssens
Dennis Vial
John Ogrodnick
Lindy Ruff
Brian Leetch
❑ 5 New York Rangers II 12.00 5.50
vs. Chicago Blackhawks
Jan. 17, 1991 (25,700)
David Shaw
Miloslav Horava
Darren Turcotte
Jan Erixon
Kelly Kisio
Brian Mullen
Bernie Nicholls
John Vanbiesbrouck
James Patrick
❑ 6 Campbell All-Stars 30.00 13.50
Chicago Stadium
Jan. 19, 1991 (15,100)
Wayne Gretzky
Chris Chelios
Luc Robitaille
Brett Hull
Al MacInnis
Mike Vernon
❑ 7 Wales All-Stars 25.00 11.00
Chicago Stadium
Jan. 19, 1991 (15,100)
Ray Bourque
Rick Tocchet
Joe Sakic
Paul Coffey
Cam Neely
Patrick Roy
❑ 8 St. Louis Blues 10.00 4.50
vs. Buffalo Sabres
Jan. 29, 1991 (21,000)
Jeff Brown
Vincent Riendeau
Brent Hull
Paul Cavallini
Curtis Joseph
Gino Cavallini
Adam Oates
Scott Stevens
Rod Brind'Amour
❑ 9 Detroit Red Wings II 12.00 5.50
vs. Minnesota North Stars
Feb. 16, 1991 (23,000)
Joey Kocur
Rick Zombo
Sergei Fedorov
Gerard Gallant
Johan Garpenlov
Glen Hanlon
Dave Barr
John Chabot
Bob Probert
❑ 10 New York Rangers III 10.00 4.50
vs. New York Islanders
Feb. 18, 1991 (25,700)
Tie Domi
Randy Moller
Mike Gartner
Kevin Miller
Mark Hardy
Jody Hull
Kris King
Bob Froese
Paul Broten
❑ 11 All-Rookie Team 20.00 9.00
June 21, 1991 (16,000)
Eric Weinrich
Jaromir Jagr
Ed Belfour
Sergei Fedorov
Rob Blake
Ken Hodge

## 1991-92 Upper Deck

The 1991-92 Upper Deck hockey set contains 700 standard-size cards. The set was released

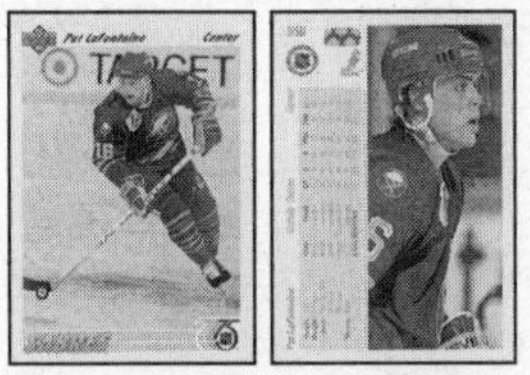

in two series of 500 and 200 cards, respectively. The front design features action photos with white borders. The player's name and position appear in the top white border, while the team name is given in the bottom white border. Biographical information, statistics, or player profile are displayed on the back alongside a second color photo. The set includes several distinctive subsets. The teams that played in the Canada Cup are represented as follows: Soviet Union (1-6), Canada (8-15), Czechoslovakia (16-20), Finland (21-25), Sweden (26-31), and United States (32-37). Cards 1-6 even have the phrase "Soviet Stars" translated into Russian on both sides. Other subsets include All-Rookie Team (39-44), first round draft picks (64-77), team checklists illustrated by artist Steve Cusano (78-99), and Star Rookies (441-462). The All-Rookie Team and the Star Rookies are marked by the abbreviations ART and SR respectively in the list below. A randomly inserted Glasnost card (SP1) featuring Wayne Gretzky, Brett Hull and Valeri Kamensky and ballots by which fans could vote for their favorite NHL All-Stars were included in foil packs. Special subsets include Canada Cup players (Canada 502-507 and USA 508-513), Young Guns (584-599), All-Stars (611-634), Heroes (635-643), Bloodlines (644-648), and members of the teams that participated in the IIHF World Junior Championships. The WJC teams include Commonwealth of Independent States (650-662), Switzerland (663-670), Finland (671-677), Germany (678-683), Canada (684-691), and USA (692-699). Rookie Cards in this set include Tony Amonte, Josef Beranek, Peter Forsberg, Dominik Hasek, Valeri Kamensky, Nikolai Khabibulin, Alexei Kovalev, Slava Kozlov, Sergei Krivokrasov, John LeClair, Nicklas Lidstrom, Vladimir Malakhov, Sandis Ozolinsh, Zigmund Palffy, Geoff Sanderson, Teemu Selanne, Keith Tkachuk, Doug Weight, Alexei Yashin, Alexei Zhamnov, and Alexei Zhitnik.

| | MINT | NRMT |
|---|---|---|
| COMPLETE SET (700) | 35.00 | 16.00 |
| COMPLETE LO SET (500) | 25.00 | 11.00 |
| COMPLETE HI SET (200) | 10.00 | 4.50 |
| COMP.HI FACT.SET (200) | 10.00 | 4.50 |
| COMMON CARD (1-700) | .05 | .02 |
| *FRENCH: SAME VALUE | | |

❑ 1 Vladimir Malakhov SS .25 .11
❑ 2 Alexei Zhamnov SS .75 .35
❑ 3 Dimitri Filiminov SS .05 .02
❑ 4 Alexander Semak SS .15 .07
❑ 5 Slava Kozlov SS .75 .35
❑ 6 Sergei Fedorov SS .30 .14
❑ 7 Canada Cup Checklist .75 .35
Eric Lindros and
Brett Hull
❑ 8 Al MacInnis CC .15 .07
❑ 9 Eric Lindros CC 3.00 1.35
❑ 10 Bill Ranford CC .15 .07
❑ 11 Paul Coffey CC .15 .07
❑ 12 Dale Hawerchuk CC .15 .07
❑ 13 Wayne Gretzky CC 1.25 .55
❑ 14 Mark Messier CC .25 .11
❑ 15 Steve Larmer CC .15 .07
❑ 16 Zigmund Palffy CC 2.50 1.10
❑ 17 Josef Beranek CC .05 .02
❑ 18 Jiri Slegr CC .05 .02
❑ 19 Martin Rucinsky CC .50 .23
❑ 20 Jaromir Jagr CC .40 .18
❑ 21 Teemu Selanne CC 6.00 2.70
❑ 22 Janne Laukkanen CC .05 .02
❑ 23 Markus Ketterer CC .05 .02
❑ 24 Jari Kurri CC .15 .07
❑ 25 Janne Ojanen CC .05 .02
❑ 26 Nicklas Lidstrom CC 1.25 .55
❑ 27 Tomas Forslund CC .05 .02
❑ 28 Johan Garpenlov CC .05 .02
❑ 29 Niclas Andersson CC .05 .02
❑ 30 Tomas Sandstrom CC .05 .02
❑ 31 Mats Sundin CC .15 .07
❑ 32 Mike Modano CC .15 .07
❑ 33 Brett Hull CC .25 .11
❑ 34 Mike Richter CC .15 .07
❑ 35 Brian Leetch CC .25 .11
❑ 36 Jeremy Roenick CC .25 .11
❑ 37 Chris Chelios CC .15 .07
❑ 38 Wayne Gretzky 99 1.00 .45
❑ 39 Ed Belfour ART .15 .07
❑ 40 Sergei Fedorov ART .30 .14
❑ 41 Ken Hodge Jr. ART .05 .02
❑ 42 Jaromir Jagr ART .40 .18
❑ 43 Rob Blake ART .15 .07
❑ 44 Eric Weinrich ART .05 .02
❑ 45 The 50/50 Club .75 .35
Mario Lemieux
Wayne Gretzky
Brett Hull
❑ 46 Russ Romaniuk .05 .02
❑ 47 White House Welcome .50 .23
George Bush
Mario Lemieux
❑ 48 Michel Picard .05 .02
❑ 49 Dennis Vaske .05 .02
❑ 50 Eric Murano .05 .02
❑ 51 Enrico Ciccone .05 .02
❑ 52 Shaun Van Allen .05 .02
❑ 53 Stu Barnes .05 .02
❑ 54 Pavel Bure .75 .35
❑ 55 Neil Wilkinson .05 .02
❑ 56 Tony Hrkac .05 .02
❑ 57 Brian Mullen .05 .02
❑ 58 Jeff Hackett .15 .07
❑ 59 Brian Hayward .15 .07
❑ 60 Craig Coxe .05 .02
❑ 61 Rob Zettler .05 .02
❑ 62 Bob McGill .05 .02
❑ 63 Draft Picks Checklist .05 .02
(Martin Lapointe
and Jamie Pushor)
❑ 64 Peter Forsberg 6.00 2.70
❑ 65 Patrick Poulin .05 .02
❑ 66 Martin Lapointe .05 .02
❑ 67 Tyler Wright .05 .02
❑ 68 Philippe Boucher .05 .02
❑ 69 Glen Murray .05 .02
❑ 70 Martin Rucinsky .50 .23
❑ 71 Zigmund Palffy 2.50 1.10
❑ 72 Jassen Cullimore .05 .02
❑ 73 Jamie Pushor .05 .02
❑ 74 Andrew Verner .05 .02
❑ 75 Jason Dawe .05 .02
❑ 76 Jamie Matthews .05 .02
❑ 77 Sandy McCarthy .05 .02
❑ 78 Cam Neely .15 .07
(Boston Bruins TC)
❑ 79 Dale Hawerchuk .15 .07
(Buffalo Sabres TC)
❑ 80 Theoren Fleury .15 .07
(Calgary Flames TC)
❑ 81 Ed Belfour .15 .07
(Chicago Blackhawks TC)
❑ 82 Sergei Fedorov .25 .11
(Detroit Red Wings TC)
❑ 83 Esa Tikkanen .05 .02
(Edmonton Oilers TC)
❑ 84 John Cullen .05 .02
(Hartford Whalers TC)
❑ 85 Tomas Sandstrom .05 .02
(Los Angeles Kings TC)
❑ 86 Dave Gagner .15 .07
(Minnesota North Stars TC)
❑ 87 Russ Courtnall .05 .02
(Montreal Canadiens TC)
❑ 88 John MacLean .15 .07
(New Jersey Devils TC)
❑ 89 David Volek .05 .02
(New York Islanders TC)
❑ 90 Darren Turcotte .05 .02
(New York Rangers TC)
❑ 91 Rick Tocchet .15 .07
(Philadelphia Flyers TC)
❑ 92 Mark Recchi .15 .07
(Pittsburgh Penguins TC)
❑ 93 Mats Sundin .15 .07
(Quebec Nordiques TC)
❑ 94 Adam Oates .15 .07
(St. Louis Blues TC)
❑ 95 Neil Wilkinson .05 .02
(San Jose Sharks TC)
❑ 96 Dave Ellett .05 .02
(Toronto Maple Leafs TC)
❑ 97 Trevor Linden .15 .07
(Vancouver Canucks TC)
❑ 98 Kevin Hatcher .05 .02
(Washington Capitals TC)
❑ 99 Ed Olczyk .05 .02
(Winnipeg Jets TC)
❑ 100 Checklist 1-100 .05 .02
❑ 101 Bob Essensa .15 .07
❑ 102 Uwe Krupp .05 .02
❑ 103 Pelle Eklund .05 .02
❑ 104 Christian Ruuttu .05 .02
❑ 105 Kevin Dineen .05 .02
❑ 106 Phil Housley .15 .07
❑ 107 Pat Jablonski .15 .07
❑ 108 Jarmo Kekalainen .05 .02
❑ 109 Pat Elynuik .05 .02
❑ 110 Corey Millen .05 .02
❑ 111 Petr Klima .05 .02
❑ 112 Mike Ridley .05 .02
❑ 113 Peter Stastny .15 .07
❑ 114 Jyrki Lumme .15 .07
❑ 115 Chris Terreri .15 .07
❑ 116 Tom Barrasso .15 .07
❑ 117 Bill Ranford .15 .07
❑ 118 Peter Ing .15 .07
❑ 119 John Tanner .05 .02
❑ 120 Troy Gamble .15 .07
❑ 121 Stephane Matteau .05 .02
❑ 122 Rick Tocchet .15 .07
❑ 123 Wes Walz .05 .02
❑ 124 Dave Andreychuk .15 .07
❑ 125 Mike Craig .05 .02
❑ 126 Dale Hawerchuk .15 .07
❑ 127 Dean Evason .05 .02
❑ 128 Craig Janney .15 .07
❑ 129 Tim Cheveldae .15 .07
❑ 130 Rick Wamsley .15 .07
❑ 131 Peter Bondra .25 .11
❑ 132 Scott Stevens .15 .07
❑ 133 Kelly Miller .05 .02

❑ 134 Mats Sundin .30 .14
❑ 135 Mick Vukota .05 .02
❑ 136 Vincent Damphousse .15 .07
❑ 137 Patrick Roy 1.25 .55
❑ 138 Hubie McDonough .05 .02
❑ 139 Curtis Joseph .30 .14
❑ 140 Brent Sutter .05 .02
❑ 141 Tomas Sandstrom .05 .02
❑ 142 Kevin Miller .05 .02
❑ 143 Mike Ricci .05 .02
❑ 144 Sergei Fedorov .60 .25
❑ 145 Luc Robitaille .15 .07
❑ 146 Steve Yzerman .75 .35
❑ 147 Andy Moog .15 .07
❑ 148 Rob Blake .15 .07
❑ 149 Kirk Muller .05 .02
❑ 150 Daniel Berthiaume .15 .07
❑ 151 John Druce .05 .02
❑ 152 Garry Valk .05 .02
❑ 153 Brian Leetch .25 .11
❑ 154 Kevin Stevens .05 .02
❑ 155 Darren Turcotte .05 .02
❑ 156 Mario Lemieux 1.25 .55
❑ 157 Dimitri Khristich .05 .02
❑ 158 Brian Glynn .05 .02
❑ 159 Benoit Hogue UER .05 .02
(Back photo actually Dean Kennedy)
❑ 160 Mike Modano .30 .14
❑ 161 Jimmy Carson .05 .02
❑ 162 Steve Thomas .05 .02
❑ 163 Mike Vernon .15 .07
❑ 164 Ed Belfour .30 .14
❑ 165 Joel Otto .05 .02
❑ 166 Jeremy Roenick .30 .14
❑ 167 Johan Garpenlov .05 .02
❑ 168 Russ Courtnall .05 .02
❑ 169 John MacLean .15 .07
❑ 170 J.J. Daigneault .05 .02
❑ 171 Sylvain Lefebvre .05 .02
❑ 172 Tony Granato .05 .02
❑ 173 David Volek .05 .02
❑ 174 Trevor Linden .15 .07
❑ 175 Mike Richter .30 .14
❑ 176 Pierre Turgeon .15 .07
❑ 177 Paul Coffey .25 .11
❑ 178 Jan Erixon .05 .02
❑ 179 Rick Vaive .05 .02
❑ 180 Dave Gagner .15 .07
❑ 181 Thomas Steen .05 .02
❑ 182 Esa Tikkanen .05 .02
❑ 183 Sean Burke .15 .07
❑ 184 Paul Cavallini .05 .02
❑ 185 Alexei Kasatonov .05 .02
❑ 186 Kevin Lowe .05 .02
❑ 187 Gino Cavallini .05 .02
❑ 188 Doug Gilmour .25 .11
❑ 189 Rod Brind'Amour .15 .07
❑ 190 Gary Roberts .05 .02
❑ 191 Kirk McLean .15 .07
❑ 192 Kevin Haller .05 .02
❑ 193 Pat Verbeek .05 .02
❑ 194 Dave Snuggerud .05 .02
❑ 195 Gino Odjick .05 .02
❑ 196 Dave Ellett .05 .02
❑ 197 Don Beaupre .15 .07
❑ 198 Rob Brown .05 .02
❑ 199 Marty McSorley .05 .02
❑ 200 Checklist 101-200 .05 .02
❑ 201 Joe Mullen .15 .07
❑ 202 Dave Capuano .05 .02
❑ 203 Paul Stanton .05 .02
❑ 204 Terry Carkner .05 .02
❑ 205 Jon Casey .15 .07
❑ 206 Ken Wregget .15 .07
❑ 207 Gaetan Duchesne .05 .02
❑ 208 Cliff Ronning .05 .02
❑ 209 Dale Hunter .05 .02
❑ 210 Danton Cole .05 .02
❑ 211 Jeff Brown .05 .02
❑ 212 Mike Foligno .05 .02
❑ 213 Michel Mongeau .05 .02
❑ 214 Doug Brown .05 .02
❑ 215 Todd Krygier .05 .02
❑ 216 Jon Morris .05 .02
❑ 217 David Reid .05 .02
❑ 218 John McIntyre .05 .02
❑ 219 Guy Lafleur's Farewell .15 .07
❑ 220 Vincent Riendeau .15 .07
❑ 221 Tim Hunter .05 .02
❑ 222 Dave McLlwain .05 .02
❑ 223 Robert Reichel .05 .02
❑ 224 Glenn Healy .15 .07
❑ 225 Robert Kron .05 .02
❑ 226 Pat Flatley .05 .02
❑ 227 Petr Nedved .15 .07
❑ 228 Mark Janssens .05 .02
❑ 229 Michal Pivonka .05 .02
❑ 230 Ulf Samuelsson .05 .02
❑ 231 Zarley Zalapski .05 .02
❑ 232 Neal Broten .15 .07
❑ 233 Bobby Holik .05 .02
❑ 234 Cam Neely .15 .07
❑ 235 John Cullen .05 .02
❑ 236 Brian Bellows .05 .02
❑ 237 Chris Nilan .05 .02
❑ 238 Mikael Andersson .05 .02
❑ 239 Bob Probert .15 .07
❑ 240 Teppo Numminen .05 .02
❑ 241 Peter Zezel .05 .02
❑ 242 Denis Savard .15 .07
❑ 243 Al MacInnis .15 .07
❑ 244 Stephane Richer .15 .07
❑ 245 Theoren Fleury .15 .07
❑ 246 Mark Messier .40 .18
❑ 247 Mike Gartner .15 .07
❑ 248 Daren Puppa .15 .07
❑ 249 Louie DeBrusk .05 .02
❑ 250 Glenn Anderson .15 .07
❑ 251 Ken Hodge Jr. .05 .02
❑ 252 Adam Oates .15 .07
❑ 253 Pat LaFontaine .15 .07
❑ 254 Adam Creighton .05 .02
❑ 255 Ray Bourque .25 .11
❑ 256 Jaromir Jagr .75 .35
❑ 257 Steve Larmer .15 .07
❑ 258 Keith Primeau .15 .07
❑ 259 Mike Liut .15 .07
❑ 260 Brian Propp .05 .02
❑ 261 Stephan Lebeau .05 .02
❑ 262 Kelly Hrudey .15 .07
❑ 263 Joe Nieuwendyk .15 .07
❑ 264 Grant Fuhr .15 .07
❑ 265 Guy Carbonneau .15 .07
❑ 266 Martin Gelinas .05 .02
❑ 267 Alexander Mogilny .30 .14
❑ 268 Adam Graves .15 .07
❑ 269 Anatoli Semenov .05 .02
❑ 270 Dave Taylor .15 .07
❑ 271 Dirk Graham .05 .02
❑ 272 Gary Leeman .05 .02
❑ 273 Valeri Kamensky .75 .35
❑ 274 Marc Bureau .05 .02
❑ 275 James Patrick .05 .02
❑ 276 Dino Ciccarelli .15 .07
❑ 277 Ron Tugnutt .15 .07
❑ 278 Paul Ysebaert .05 .02
❑ 279 Laurie Boschman .05 .02
❑ 280 Dave Manson .05 .02
❑ 281 Dave Chyzowski .05 .02
❑ 282 Shayne Corson .05 .02
❑ 283 Steve Chiasson .05 .02
❑ 284 Craig MacTavish .05 .02
❑ 285 Petr Svoboda .05 .02
❑ 286 Craig Simpson .05 .02
❑ 287 Ron Hoover .05 .02
❑ 288 Vladimir Ruzicka .05 .02
❑ 289 Randy Wood .05 .02
❑ 290 Doug Lidster .05 .02
❑ 291 Kay Whitmore .15 .07
❑ 292 Bruce Driver .05 .02
❑ 293 Bobby Smith .15 .07
❑ 294 Claude Lemieux .15 .07
❑ 295 Mark Tinordi .05 .02
❑ 296 Mark Osborne .05 .02
❑ 297 Brad Shaw .05 .02
❑ 298 Igor Larionov .05 .02
❑ 299 Ron Francis .15 .07
❑ 300 Checklist 201-300 .05 .02
❑ 301 Bob Kudelski .05 .02
❑ 302 Larry Murphy .15 .07
❑ 303 Brent Ashton .05 .02
❑ 304 Brad Jones .05 .02
❑ 305 Gord Donnelly .05 .02
❑ 306 Murray Craven .05 .02
❑ 307 Chris Dahlquist .05 .02
❑ 308 Jim Paek .05 .02
❑ 309 Ron Sutter .05 .02
❑ 310 Mike Tomlak .05 .02
❑ 311 Ray Ferraro .05 .02
❑ 312 Dave Hannan .05 .02
❑ 313 Randy McKay .05 .02
❑ 314 Rod Langway .05 .02
❑ 315 Shawn Burr .05 .02
❑ 316 Calle Johansson .05 .02
❑ 317 Rich Sutter .05 .02
❑ 318 Al Iafrate .15 .07
❑ 319 Bob Bassen .05 .02
❑ 320 Mike Krushelnyski .05 .02
❑ 321 Sergei Makarov .05 .02
❑ 322 Darrin Shannon .05 .02
❑ 323 Terry Yake .05 .02
❑ 324 John Vanbiesbrouck .50 .23
❑ 325 Peter Sidorkiewicz .15 .07
❑ 326 Troy Mallette .05 .02
❑ 327 Ron Hextall .15 .07
❑ 328 Mathieu Schneider .05 .02
❑ 329 Bryan Trottier .15 .07
❑ 330 Kris King .05 .02
❑ 331 Daniel Marois .05 .02
❑ 332 Shayne Stevenson .05 .02
❑ 333 Joe Sakic .60 .25
❑ 334 Petri Skriko .05 .02
❑ 335 Dominik Hasek 6.00 2.70
❑ 336 Scott Pearson .05 .02
❑ 337 Bryan Fogarty .05 .02
❑ 338 Don Sweeney .05 .02
❑ 339 Rick Tabaracci .15 .07
❑ 340 Steven Finn .05 .02
❑ 341 Gary Suter .05 .02
❑ 342 Troy Crowder .05 .02
❑ 343 Jim Hrivnak .15 .07
❑ 344 Eric Weinrich .05 .02
❑ 345 John LeClair 4.00 1.80
❑ 346 Mark Recchi .15 .07
❑ 347 Dan Currie .05 .02
❑ 348 Ulf Dahlen .05 .02
❑ 349 Robert Ray .05 .02
❑ 350 Steve Smith .05 .02
❑ 351 Shawn Antoski .05 .02
❑ 352 Cam Russell .05 .02
❑ 353 Scott Thornton .05 .02
❑ 354 Chris Chelios .25 .11
❑ 355 Sergei Nemchinov .05 .02
❑ 356 Bernie Nicholls .15 .07
❑ 357 Jeff Norton .05 .02
❑ 358 Dan Quinn .05 .02
❑ 359 Michel Petit .05 .02
❑ 360 Eric Desjardins .05 .02
❑ 361 Kevin Hatcher .05 .02
❑ 362 Jiri Sejba .05 .02
❑ 363 Mark Pederson .05 .02
❑ 364 Jeff Lazaro .05 .02
❑ 365 Alexei Gusarov .05 .02
❑ 366 Jari Kurri .15 .07
❑ 367 Owen Nolan .15 .07
❑ 368 Clint Malarchuk .15 .07
❑ 369 Patrik Sundstrom .05 .02
❑ 370 Glen Wesley .05 .02
❑ 371 Wayne Presley .05 .02
❑ 372 Craig Muni .05 .02
❑ 373 Brent Fedyk .05 .02
❑ 374 Michel Goulet .15 .07
❑ 375 Tim Sweeney .05 .02
❑ 376 Gary Shuchuk .05 .02
❑ 377 Andre Racicot .15 .07
❑ 378 Jay Mazur .05 .02
❑ 379 Andrew Cassels .05 .02
❑ 380 Brian Noonan .05 .02
❑ 381 Sergei Kharin .05 .02
❑ 382 Derek King .05 .02
❑ 383 Fredrik Olausson .05 .02
❑ 384 Tom Fergus .05 .02
❑ 385 Zdeno Ciger .05 .02
❑ 386 Wendel Clark .15 .07
❑ 387 Ed Olczyk .05 .02
❑ 388 Basil McRae .05 .02
❑ 389 Tom Fitzgerald .05 .02
❑ 390 Ray Sheppard .15 .07
❑ 391 Bob Sweeney .05 .02
❑ 392 Gord Murphy .05 .02
❑ 393 John Chabot .05 .02
❑ 394 Jeff Beukeboom .05 .02
❑ 395 Rick Zombo .05 .02
❑ 396 Kjell Samuelsson .05 .02
❑ 397 Garth Butcher .05 .02
❑ 398 Phil Bourque .05 .02
❑ 399 Lou Franceschetti .05 .02
❑ 400 Checklist 301-400 .05 .02
❑ 401 Kevin Todd .05 .02
❑ 402 Ken Baumgartner .05 .02
❑ 403 Peter Douris .05 .02
❑ 404 Jiri Latal .05 .02
❑ 405 Marc Potvin .05 .02
❑ 406 Gary Nylund .05 .02
❑ 407 Yvon Corriveau .05 .02
❑ 408 Sheldon Kennedy .05 .02
❑ 409 David Shaw .05 .02
❑ 410 Slava Fetisov .05 .02
❑ 411 Mario Doyon .05 .02
❑ 412 Jamie Macoun .05 .02
❑ 413 Curtis Leschyshyn .05 .02
❑ 414 Mike Peluso .05 .02
❑ 415 Brian Benning .05 .02
❑ 416 Stu Grimson .15 .07
❑ 417 Ken Sabourin .05 .02
❑ 418 Luke Richardson .05 .02
❑ 419 Ken Quinney .05 .02
❑ 420 Mike Donnelly .05 .02
❑ 421 Darcy Loewen .05 .02
❑ 422 Brian Skrudland .05 .02
❑ 423 Joel Savage .05 .02
❑ 424 Adrien Plavsic .05 .02
❑ 425 Jergus Baca .05 .02
❑ 426 Greg Adams .05 .02
❑ 427 Tom Chorske .05 .02
❑ 428 Scott Scissons .05 .02
❑ 429 Dale Kushner .05 .02
❑ 430 Todd Richards .05 .02
❑ 431 Kip Miller .05 .02
❑ 432 Jason Prosofsky .05 .02
❑ 433 Stephane Morin .05 .02
❑ 434 Brian McReynolds .05 .02
❑ 435 Ken Daneyko .05 .02
❑ 436 Chris Joseph .05 .02
❑ 437 Wayne Gretzky 1.50 .70
❑ 438 Jocelyn Lemieux .05 .02
❑ 439 Garry Galley .05 .02
❑ 440 Super Rookie Checklist .30 .14
Tony Amonte,
Doug Weight,
and Steven Rice
❑ 441 Steven Rice SR .05 .02
❑ 442 Patrice Brisebois SR .05 .02
❑ 443 Jimmy Waite SR .15 .07
❑ 444 Doug Weight SR 1.25 .55
❑ 445 Nelson Emerson SR .05 .02
❑ 446 Jarrod Skalde SR .05 .02
❑ 447 Jamie Leach SR .05 .02
❑ 448 Gilbert Dionne SR .05 .02
❑ 449 Trevor Kidd SR .25 .11
❑ 450 Tony Amonte SR 1.25 .55
❑ 451 Pat Murray SR .05 .02
❑ 452 Stephane Fiset SR .25 .11
❑ 453 Patrick Lebeau SR .05 .02
❑ 454 Chris Taylor SR .05 .02
❑ 455 Chris Tancill SR .05 .02
❑ 456 Mark Greig SR .05 .02
❑ 457 Mike Sillinger SR .05 .02
❑ 458 Ken Sutton SR .05 .02
❑ 459 Len Barrie SR .05 .02
❑ 460 Felix Potvin SR .75 .35
❑ 461 Brian Sakic SR .05 .02
❑ 462 Slava Kozlov SR .75 .35
❑ 463 Matt DelGuidice .05 .02
❑ 464 Brett Hull .50 .23
❑ 465 Norm Foster .05 .02
❑ 466 Alexander Godynyuk .05 .02
❑ 467 Geoff Courtnall .05 .02
❑ 468 Frantisek Kucera .05 .02
❑ 469 Benoit Brunet .05 .02
❑ 470 Mark Vermette .05 .02
❑ 471 Tim Watters .05 .02
❑ 472 Paul Ranheim .05 .02
❑ 473 Martin Hostak .05 .02
❑ 474 Joe Murphy .05 .02
❑ 475 Claude Boivin .05 .02
❑ 476 John Ogrodnick .05 .02
❑ 477 Doug Bodger .05 .02
❑ 478 Shawn Cronin .05 .02
❑ 479 Mark Hunter .05 .02
❑ 480 Dave Tippett .05 .02
❑ 481 Rob DiMaio .05 .02
❑ 482 Lyle Odelein .05 .02
❑ 483 Joe Reekie .05 .02
❑ 484 Randy Velischek .05 .02
❑ 485 Myles O'Connor .05 .02
❑ 486 Craig Wolanin .05 .02
❑ 487 Mike McPhee .05 .02
❑ 488 Claude Lapointe .05 .02
❑ 489 Troy Loney .05 .02
❑ 490 Bob Beers .05 .02
❑ 491 Sylvain Couturier .05 .02
❑ 492 Kimbi Daniels .05 .02
❑ 493 Darryl Shannon .05 .02
❑ 494 Jim McKenzie .05 .02
❑ 495 Don Gibson .05 .02
❑ 496 Ralph Barahona .05 .02
❑ 497 Murray Baron .05 .02
❑ 498 Yves Racine .05 .02
❑ 499 Larry Robinson .15 .07
❑ 500 Checklist 401-500 .05 .02
❑ 501 Canada Cup Checklist .75 .35
Paul Coffey and
Wayne Gretzky
❑ 502 Dirk Graham CC .05 .02
❑ 503 Rick Tocchet CC .15 .07
❑ 504 Eric Desjardins CC .05 .02
❑ 505 Shayne Corson CC .05 .02
❑ 506 Theoren Fleury CC .15 .07
❑ 507 Luc Robitaille CC .15 .07
❑ 508 Tony Granato CC .05 .02
❑ 509 Eric Weinrich CC .05 .02
❑ 510 Gary Suter CC .05 .02
❑ 511 Kevin Hatcher CC .05 .02
❑ 512 Craig Janney CC .15 .07
❑ 513 Darren Turcotte CC .05 .02
❑ 514 Chris Winnes .05 .02
❑ 515 Kelly Kisio .05 .02
❑ 516 Joe Day .05 .02
❑ 517 Ed Courtenay .05 .02
❑ 518 Andrei Lomakin .05 .02
❑ 519 Kirk Muller .05 .02
❑ 520 Rick Lessard .05 .02
❑ 521 Scott Thornton .05 .02
❑ 522 Luke Richardson .05 .02
❑ 523 Mike Eagles .05 .02
❑ 524 Mike McNeill .05 .02
❑ 525 Ken Priestlay .05 .02
❑ 526 Louie DeBrusk .05 .02
❑ 527 Dave McLlwain .05 .02
❑ 528 Gary Leeman .05 .02
❑ 529 Adam Foote .40 .18
❑ 530 Kevin Dineen .05 .02
❑ 531 David Reid .05 .02
❑ 532 Arturs Irbe .15 .07
❑ 533 Mark Osiecki .05 .02
❑ 534 Steve Thomas .05 .02
❑ 535 Vincent Damphousse .15 .07
❑ 536 Stephane Richer .15 .07
❑ 537 Jarmo Myllys .05 .02
❑ 538 Carey Wilson .05 .02
❑ 539 Scott Stevens .15 .07
❑ 540 Uwe Krupp .05 .02
❑ 541 Dave Christian .05 .02
❑ 542 Scott Mellanby .15 .07
❑ 543 Peter Ahola .05 .02
❑ 544 Todd Elik .05 .02
❑ 545 Mark Messier .40 .18
❑ 546 Derian Hatcher .05 .02
❑ 547 Rod Brind'Amour .15 .07
❑ 548 Dave Manson .05 .02
❑ 549 Darryl Sydor .05 .02
❑ 550 Paul Broten .05 .02
❑ 551 Andrew Cassels .05 .02
❑ 552 Tom Draper .15 .07
❑ 553 Grant Fuhr .15 .07
❑ 554 Pierre Turgeon .15 .07
❑ 555 Pavel Bure .75 .35
❑ 556 Pat LaFontaine .15 .07
❑ 557 Dave Thomlinson .05 .02
❑ 558 Doug Gilmour .25 .11
❑ 559 Craig Billington .15 .07
❑ 560 Dean Evason .05 .02
❑ 561 Brendan Shanahan .60 .25
❑ 562 Mike Hough .05 .02
❑ 563 Dan Quinn .05 .02
❑ 564 Jeff Daniels .05 .02
❑ 565 Troy Murray .05 .02
❑ 566 Bernie Nicholls .15 .07
❑ 567 Randy Burridge .05 .02
❑ 568 Todd Hartje .05 .02
❑ 569 Charlie Huddy .05 .02
❑ 570 Steve Duchesne .05 .02
❑ 571 Sergio Momesso .05 .02
❑ 572 Brian Lawton .05 .02
❑ 573 Ray Sheppard .15 .07
❑ 574 Adam Graves .15 .07
❑ 575 Rollie Melanson .15 .07
❑ 576 Steve Kasper .05 .02
❑ 577 Jim Sandlak .05 .02
❑ 578 Pat MacLeod .05 .02
❑ 579 Sylvain Turgeon .05 .02
❑ 580 James Black .05 .02
❑ 581 Darrin Shannon .05 .02
❑ 582 Todd Krygier .05 .02
❑ 583 Dominic Roussel .15 .07
❑ 584 Young Guns Checklist .15 .07
Nicklas Lidstrom
❑ 585 Donald Audette YG .15 .07
❑ 586 Tomas Forslund YG .05 .02
❑ 587 Nicklas Lidstrom YG .25 .11
❑ 588 Geoff Sanderson YG .60 .25
❑ 589 Valeri Zelepukin YG .05 .02
❑ 590 Igor Ulanov YG .05 .02
❑ 591 Corey Foster YG .05 .02
❑ 592 Dan Lambert YG .05 .02
❑ 593 Pat Falloon YG .05 .02
❑ 594 Vladimir Konstantinov YG .40 .18
❑ 595 Josef Beranek YG .05 .02
❑ 596 Brad May YG .15 .07
❑ 597 Jeff Odgers YG .05 .02
❑ 598 Rob Pearson YG .05 .02
❑ 599 Luciano Borsato YG .05 .02
❑ 600 Checklist 501-600 .05 .02
❑ 601 Peter Douris .05 .02
❑ 602 Mark Fitzpatrick .15 .07
❑ 603 Randy Gilhen .05 .02
❑ 604 Corey Millen .05 .02
❑ 605 Jason Cirone .05 .02
❑ 606 Kyosti Karjalainen .05 .02
❑ 607 Garry Galley .05 .02
❑ 608 Brent Thompson .05 .02
❑ 609 Alexander Godynyuk .05 .02
❑ 610 All-Star Checklist .40 .18
Mark Messier
Mike Richter
Brian Leetch
❑ 611 Mario Lemieux AS .60 .25
❑ 612 Brian Leetch AS .15 .07
❑ 613 Kevin Stevens AS .05 .02
❑ 614 Patrick Roy AS .50 .23
❑ 615 Paul Coffey AS .15 .07
❑ 616 Joe Sakic AS .30 .14
❑ 617 Jaromir Jagr AS .40 .18
❑ 618 Alexander Mogilny AS .15 .07
❑ 619 Owen Nolan AS .15 .07
❑ 620 Mark Messier AS .25 .11
❑ 621 Wayne Gretzky AS .75 .35
❑ 622 Brett Hull AS .25 .11
❑ 623 Luc Robitaille AS .15 .07
❑ 624 Phil Housley AS .15 .07
❑ 625 Ed Belfour AS .15 .07
❑ 626 Steve Yzerman AS .40 .18
❑ 627 Adam Oates AS .15 .07
❑ 628 Trevor Linden AS .15 .07
❑ 629 Jeremy Roenick AS .25 .11
❑ 630 Theoren Fleury AS .15 .07
❑ 631 Sergei Fedorov AS .30 .14
❑ 632 Al MacInnis AS .15 .07
❑ 633 Ray Bourque AS .15 .07
❑ 634 Mike Richter AS .15 .07
❑ 635 Al Secord HERO .05 .02
❑ 636 Marcel Dionne HERO .05 .02
❑ 637 Ken Morrow HERO .05 .02
❑ 638 Guy Lafleur HERO .15 .07
❑ 639 Ed Mio HERO .05 .02
❑ 640 Clark Gillies HERO .05 .02
❑ 641 Dob Nystrom HERO .05 .02
❑ 642 Pete Peeters HERO .15 .07
❑ 643 Ulf Nilsson HERO .05 .02
❑ 644 Stephan Lebeau and .05 .02
Patrick Lebeau
❑ 645 The Sutter Brothers .05 .02
Brian Sutter
Duane Sutter
Darryl Sutter
Brent Sutter
Rich Sutter
Ron Sutter
❑ 646 Gino Cavallini and .05 .02
Paul Cavallini
❑ 647 Valeri Bure .75 .35
and Pavel Bure
❑ 648 Chris Ferraro and .15 .07
Peter Ferraro
❑ 649 World Jr. Checklist .15 .07
CCCP Team Photo
❑ 650 Darius Kasparaitis .50 .23
❑ 651 Alexei Yashin 2.50 1.10
❑ 652 Nikolai Khabibulin 1.50 .70
❑ 653 Denis Metlyuk .05 .02
❑ 654 Konstantin Korotkov .05 .02
❑ 655 Alexei Kovalev .75 .35
❑ 656 Alexander Kuzminsky .05 .02
❑ 657 Alexander Cherbayev .05 .02
❑ 658 Sergei Krivokrasov .15 .07
❑ 659 Sergei Zholtok .05 .02
❑ 660 Alexei Zhitnik .05 .02
❑ 661 Sandis Ozolinch 1.50 .70
❑ 662 Boris Mironov .05 .02
❑ 663 Pauli Jaks .15 .07
❑ 664 Gaetan Voisard .05 .02
❑ 665 Nicola Celio .05 .02
❑ 666 Marc Weber .05 .02
❑ 667 Bernhard Schumperli .05 .02
❑ 668 Laurent Bucher .05 .02
❑ 669 Michael Blaha .05 .02
❑ 670 Tiziano Gianini .05 .02
❑ 671 Marko Kiprusoff .15 .07
❑ 672 Janne Gronvall .05 .02
❑ 673 Juha Ylonen .05 .02
❑ 674 Sami Kapanen 1.25 .55
❑ 675 Marko Tuomainen .05 .02
❑ 676 Jarkko Varvio .05 .02
❑ 677 Tuomas Gronman .05 .02
❑ 678 Andreas Naumann .05 .02
❑ 679 Steffen Ziesche .05 .02
❑ 680 Jens Schwabe .05 .02
❑ 681 Thomas Schubert .05 .02
❑ 682 Hans-Jorg Mayer .05 .02
❑ 683 Marc Seliger .05 .02
❑ 684 Trevor Kidd .15 .07
❑ 685 Martin Lapointe .05 .02
❑ 686 Tyler Wright .05 .02
❑ 687 Kimbi Daniels .05 .02
❑ 688 Karl Dykhuis .05 .02
❑ 689 Jeff Nelson .05 .02
❑ 690 Jassen Cullimore .05 .02
❑ 691 Turner Stevenson .05 .02

❑ 692 Scott Lachance .05 .02
❑ 693 Mike Dunham .15 .07
❑ 694 Brent Bilodeau .05 .02
❑ 695 Ryan Sittler .05 .02
❑ 696 Peter Ferraro .40 .18
❑ 697 Pat Peake .05 .02
❑ 698 Keith Tkachuk 2.50 1.10
❑ 699 Brian Rolston .40 .18
❑ 700 Checklist 601-700 .05 .02
❑ SP1 Glasnost On Ice 4.00 1.80
Wayne Gretzky
Valeri Kamensky
Brett Hull

## 1991-92 Upper Deck Award Winner Holograms

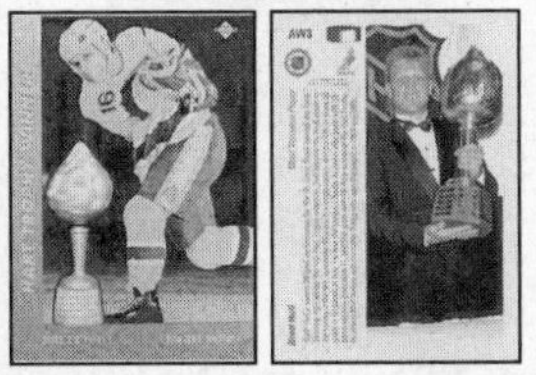

This nine-card standard-size hologram set features award-winning hockey players with their respective trophies for most outstanding performance. The name of the award appears in the left border stripe, while the player's name and position are printed in the bottom border stripe. The backs have a color photo of the player with the trophy as well as biographical information. The holograms were randomly inserted into foil packs and subdivided into three groups: AW1-AW3 (low series); AW5-AW7 (late winter, low series); and AW4, AW8, and AW9 (high series). The holograms are numbered on the back with an "AW" prefix.

| | MINT | NRMT |
|---|---|---|
| COMPLETE SET (9) | 8.00 | 3.60 |
| COMMON CARD (AW1-AW9) | .50 | .23 |

❑ AW1 Wayne Gretzky 2.00 .90
Art Ross Trophy
❑ AW2 Ed Belfour .60 .25
William M. Jennings Trophy
❑ AW3 Brett Hull .75 .35
Hart Trophy
❑ AW4 Ed Belfour .60 .25
Calder Trophy
❑ AW5A Ray Bourque ERR .60 .25
Norris Trophy
(No best defenseman notation on back)
❑ AW5B Ray Bourque COR .60 .25
Norris Trophy
(Best defenseman notation on back)
❑ AW6 Wayne Gretzky 2.00 .90
Lady Byng Trophy
❑ AW7 Ed Belfour .60 .25
Vezina Trophy
❑ AW8 Dirk Graham .50 .23
Frank J. Selke Trophy
❑ AW9 Mario Lemieux 2.00 .90
Conn Smythe Trophy

## 1991-92 Upper Deck Box Bottoms

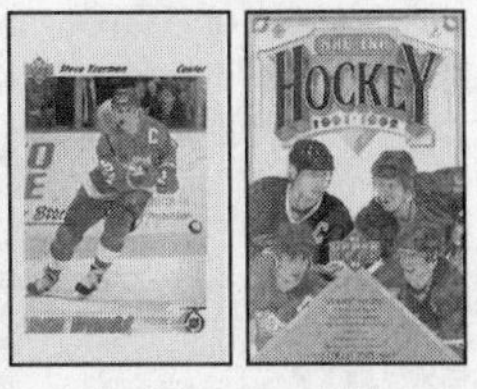

These five box bottoms are printed on glossy cover stock and measure approximately 5 1/2" by 9". Though they were issued with both French and English hockey sets, the New York Rangers' Mark Messier box bottom was available only with the high series. Each bottom features a four-color action photo enclosed by white borders. The Upper Deck logo, player's name, and position appear above the photo while the team name and the 75th NHL Anniversary logo appear beneath the picture superimposed on small black lines. The box bottoms are unnumbered and checklisted below alphabetically.

| | MINT | NRMT |
|---|---|---|
| COMPLETE SET (5) | 5.00 | 2.20 |
| COMMON CARD (1-5) | .60 | .25 |

❑ 1 Wayne Gretzky 3.00 1.35
❑ 2 Brett Hull .75 .35
❑ 3 Mark Messier .75 .35
❑ 4 Mark Messier .75 .35
❑ 5 Steve Yzerman 1.50 .70

## 1991-92 Upper Deck Euro-Stars

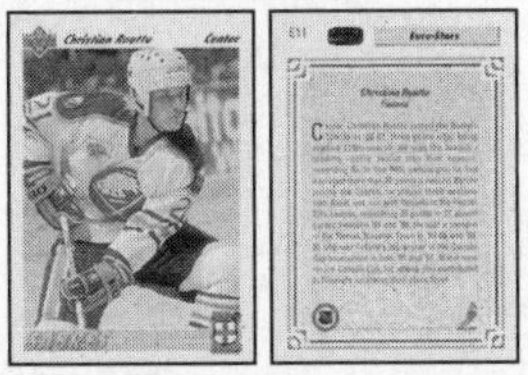

This 18-card standard-size set spotlights NHL players from Finland, the former Soviet Union, Czechoslovakia, and Sweden. One Euro-Star card was inserted in each 1991-92 Upper Deck Hockey jumbo pack in both English and French editions. The front design of the cards is the same as the regular issue except that a Euro-Stars emblem featuring a segment of the player's homeland flag, appears in the lower right corner. On a textured background, the backs present career summary.

| | MINT | NRMT |
|---|---|---|
| COMPLETE SET (18) | 10.00 | 4.50 |
| COMMON CARD (1-18) | .25 | .11 |

*FRENCH VERSION: SAME VALUE

❑ 1 Jarmo Kekalainen .25 .11
❑ 2 Alexander Mogilny 1.00 .45
❑ 3 Bobby Holik .25 .11
❑ 4 Anatoli Semenov .25 .11
❑ 5 Petr Nedved .75 .35
❑ 6 Jaromir Jagr 2.50 1.10
❑ 7 Tomas Sandstrom .25 .11
❑ 8 Robert Kron .25 .11
❑ 9 Sergei Fedorov 2.50 1.10
❑ 10 Esa Tikkanen .75 .35
❑ 11 Christian Ruuttu .25 .11
❑ 12 Peter Bondra 1.25 .55
❑ 13 Mats Sundin 1.25 .55
❑ 14 Dominik Hasek 5.00 2.20
❑ 15 Johan Garpenlov .25 .11
❑ 16 Alexander Godynyuk .25 .11
❑ 17 Ulf Samuelsson .25 .11
❑ 18 Igor Larionov .75 .35

## 1991-92 Upper Deck Brett Hull Heroes

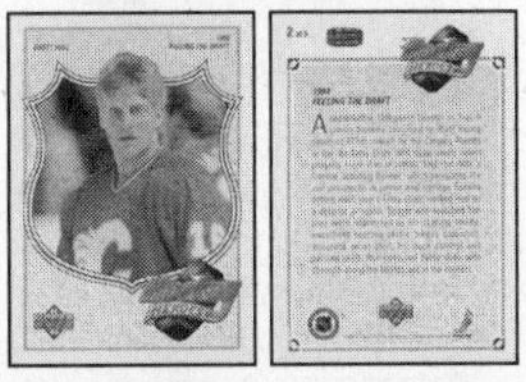

This ten-card standard-size set was inserted in 1991-92 Upper Deck low series foil packs (French as well as English editions). On a light gray textured background, the fronts have color player photos cut out and superimposed on an emblem. The textured background is enclosed by thin tan border stripes. On the same textured background, the backs summarize various moments in Hull's career. Brett Hull personally signed and numbered 2,500 of the checklist card number 9; these autographed cards were randomly inserted in packs. The signed cards are numbered by hand on the front.

| | MINT | NRMT |
|---|---|---|
| COMPLETE SET (10) | 12.00 | 5.50 |
| COMMON HULL HEROES (1-9) | 1.00 | .45 |

❑ 1 Brett Hull 1.00 .45
Penticton's 105-Goal Man
❑ 2 Brett Hull 1.00 .45
Feeling the Draft
❑ 3 Brett Hull 1.00 .45
NCAA's Goal-Scoring Leader
❑ 4 Brett Hull 1.00 .45
AHL's Rookie-of-the-Year
❑ 5 Brett Hull 1.00 .45
A Full-Time Flame
❑ 6 Brett Hull 1.00 .45
40-Goal Plateau
❑ 7 Brett Hull 1.00 .45
NHL's New 70-Goal Scorer
❑ 8 Brett Hull 1.00 .45
A Season With Hart
❑ 9 Brett Hull 1.00 .45
(Vernon Wells Artwork)
❑ AU1 Brett Hull 150.00 70.00
(Certified autograph)
❑ NNO Hull Header SP 5.00 2.20

## 1991-92 Upper Deck Sheets

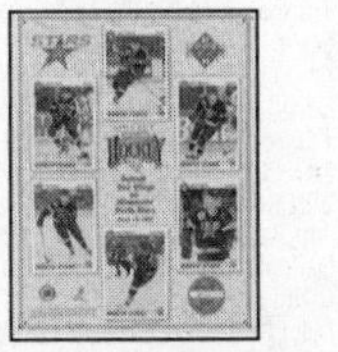

For the second straight year, Upper Deck produced hockey commemorative sheets that were given away during the 1991-92 season at selected games in large arenas. Each sheet measures approximately 8 1/2" by 11" and is printed on card stock. The fronts of the team commemorative sheets feature the team logo and a series of Upper Deck cards of star players on that team. The Alumni sheet features player portraits by sports artist Alan Studt. All the sheets have an Upper Deck stamp indicating the production quota and the serial number. The backs are blank. The sheets are listed below in chronological order.

| | MINT | NRMT |
|---|---|---|
| COMPLETE SET (19) | 225.00 | 100.00 |
| COMMON CARD (1-19) | 10.00 | 4.50 |

❑ 1 Los Angeles Kings 25th 15.00 6.75
vs. Edmonton Oilers
Oct. 8, 1991 (20,000)
Rob Blake
Jari Kurri
Tomas Sandstrom
Wayne Gretzky
Marty McSorley
Kelly Hrudey
❑ 2 New York Rangers I 10.00 4.50
vs. Calgary Flames
Nov. 4, 1991 (21,500)
Randy Moller
Paul Broten
Jody Hull
Jan Erixon
Mark Janssens
Brian Leetch
Mike Gartner
Joey Kocur
Mark Hardy
❑ 3 St. Louis Blues 10.00 4.50
vs. Philadelphia Flyers
Nov. 5, 1991 (21,500)
Adam Oates
Nelson Emerson
Paul Cavallini
Curtis Joseph
Brett Hull
Jeff Brown
❑ 4 New Jersey Devils 10th 10.00 4.50
vs. Chicago Blackhawks
Dec. 21, 1991 (24,000)
(New Jersey Devils Tenth Anniversary)
Walt Poddubny
John MacLean
Scott Stevens
Peter Stastny
Claude Lemieux
Stephane Richer
❑ 5 Calgary Flames I 12.00 5.50
Tenth Annual Clinic
Dec. 27, 1991 (26,000)
Robert Reichel
Doug Gilmour
Theoren Fleury
Al MacInnis
Joel Otto
Gary Roberts
❑ 6 New York Rangers II 10.00 4.50
vs. St. Louis Blues
Jan. 8, 1992 (23,000)
Mike Richter
Kris King
Tie Domi
Tony Amonte
Mark Messier
Joe Cirella
James Patrick
Sergei Nemchinov
❑ 7 Philadelphia Flyers I 10.00 4.50
Alumni vs. NHL Heroes
Jan. 17, 1992 (21,000)
Bill Barber
Bill Clement
Keith Allen
Joe Watson
Bobby Clarke
Bernie Parent
❑ 8 Campbell All-Stars 25.00 11.00
Philadelphia Spectrum
Jan. 18, 1992 (13,500)
Brett Hull
Al MacInnis
Luc Robitaille
Chris Chelios
Wayne Gretzky
Ed Belfour
❑ 9 Wales All-Stars 25.00 11.00
Philadelphia Spectrum
Jan. 18, 1992 (13,500)
Mario Lemieux
Patrick Roy
Kevin Stevens
Paul Coffey
Jaromir Jagr
Ray Bourque
❑ 10 Detroit Red Wings I 12.00 5.50
vs. Toronto Maple Leafs
Feb. 7, 1992 (25,000)
Niklas Lidstrom
Steve Yzerman
Tim Cheveldae
Bob Probert
Steve Chiasson
Sergei Fedorov
❑ 11 Washington Capitals 10.00 4.50
vs. New York Rangers
Feb. 7, 1992 (20,500)
Kevin Hatcher
Dimitri Khristich
Calle Johansson
Michal Pivonka
Al Iafrate
Dino Ciccarelli
❑ 12 Minnesota North Stars 20.00 9.00
Dream Team
Feb.15, 1992 (19,000)
Brian Bellows
Neal Broten
Bill Goldsworthy
Curt Giles
Jon Casey
Craig Hartsburg
❑ 13 Pittsburgh Penguins 20.00 9.00
vs. Toronto Maple Leafs
Feb. 18, 1992 (21,000)
Kevin Stevens
Jaromir Jagr
Ulf Samuelsson
Tom Barrasso
Mark Recchi
Joe Mullen
❑ 14 New York Rangers III 10.00 4.50
vs. Philadelphia Flyers
Feb. 23, 1992 (23,000)
John Vanbiesbrouck
Kris King
Normand Rochefort
John Ogrodnick
Mark Messier
Jeff Beukeboom
Adam Graves
Darren Turcotte
❑ 15 Edmonton Oilers 12.00 5.50
vs. Philadelphia Flyers
Feb. 28, 1992 (22,000)
Kevin Lowe
Craig MacTavish
Esa Tikkanen
Bill Ranford
Craig Simpson
Vincent Damphousse
❑ 16 Minnesota North Stars 20.00 9.00
vs. Detroit Red Wings
March 14, 1992 (19,000)
Bobby Smith
Dave Gagner
Mike Modano
Ulf Dahlen
Mark Tinordi
Basil McRae
❑ 17 Calgary Flames II 12.00 5.50
vs. Minnesota North Stars
Eighth Fan Appreciation Night
March 28, 1992 (24,000)
Mike Vernon
Joe Nieuwendyk
Gary Suter
Paul Ranheim
Sergei Makarov
Carey Wilson
❑ 18 Detroit Red Wings II 10.00 4.50
vs. Chicago Blackhawks
March 31, 1992 (25,000)
Paul Ysebaert
Yves Racine
Vladimir Konstantinov
Ray Sheppard
Kevin Miller
Jimmy Carson
❑ 19 Philadelphia Flyers II 10.00 4.50
April 5, 1992 (21,000)
Mike Ricci
Kevin Dineen
Garry Galley
Steve Duchesne
Rod Brind'Amour
Claude Boivin

## 1991-92 Upper Deck Czech World Juniors

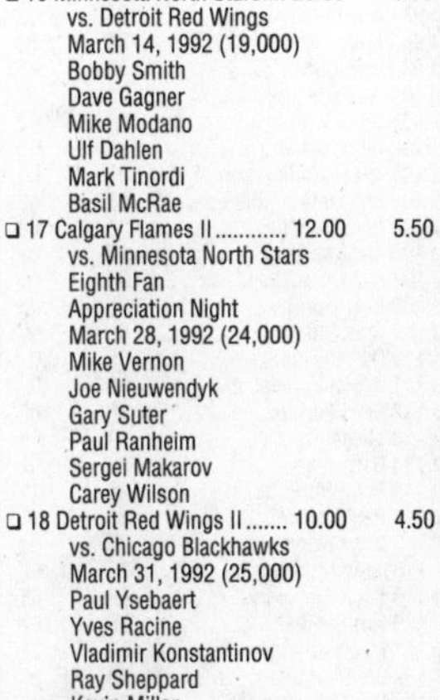

This 100 card standard-size set feature players from the 1991 World Junior Championships. Two Wayne Gretzky Holograms were inserted into the set. They are priced at the end of the listings but are not included in the set price. Inside white borders, the fronts display glossy color action photos of the players in their national team uniforms. The player's name and position appear on the top, while the World Junior Tournament logo and an emblem of their national flag overlay the bottom. The backs have a second color player photo; alongside in a gray box, the player's position and a brief profile are printed in English and Czech. The cards are sequenced in this way: C.I.S. (1-23), Switzerland (24-31), Finland (32-40), Germany (41-46), Canada (47-65), U.S.A. (66-86), Czechoslovakia (87-99). These cards were designed for distribution in Eastern Europe. An album (valued at about $5) was also made to house the set.

| | MINT | NRMT |
|---|---|---|
| COMPLETE SET (100) | 50.00 | 22.00 |
| COMMON CARD (1-100) | .10 | .05 |

❑ 1 Description Card .10 .05
❑ 2 Vladislav Buljin .10 .05
❑ 3 Ravil Gusmanov .10 .05
❑ 4 Denis Vinokurov .10 .05
❑ 5 Mikhail Volkov .10 .05
❑ 6 Alexei Troschinsky .10 .05
❑ 7 Andrei Nikolishin .75 .35
❑ 8 Alexander Sverztov .10 .05
❑ 9 Artem Kopot .25 .11
❑ 10 Ildar Mukhometov .25 .11
❑ 11 Darius Kasparaitis .50 .23
❑ 12 Alexei Yashin 6.00 2.70
❑ 13 Nikolai Khabibulin 4.00 1.80
❑ 14 Denis Metlyuk .10 .05
❑ 15 Konstantin Korotkov .10 .05
❑ 16 Alexei Kovalev 3.00 1.35
❑ 17 Alexander Kuzminsky .10 .05
❑ 18 Alexander Cherbayev .10 .05
❑ 19 Sergei Krivokrasov .75 .35
❑ 20 Sergei Zholtok .50 .23
❑ 21 Alexei Zhitnik 1.00 .45
❑ 22 Sandis Ozolinsh 3.00 1.35
❑ 23 Boris Mironov .50 .23
❑ 24 Pauli Jaks .10 .05
❑ 25 Gaetan Voisard .10 .05
❑ 26 Nicola Celio .10 .05
❑ 27 Marc Weber .10 .05
❑ 28 Bernhard Schumperli .10 .05
❑ 29 Laurent Bucher .10 .05
❑ 30 Michael Blaha .10 .05
❑ 31 Tiziano Gianini .10 .05
❑ 32 Tero Lehtera .10 .05
❑ 33 Mikko Luovi .10 .05
❑ 34 Marko Kiprusoff .25 .11
❑ 35 Janne Gronvall .25 .11
❑ 36 Juha Ylonen .25 .11
❑ 37 Sami Kapanen 1.00 .45
❑ 38 Marko Tuomainen .25 .11
❑ 39 Jarkko Varvio .25 .11
❑ 40 Tuomas Gronman .25 .11
❑ 41 Andreas Naumann .10 .05
❑ 42 Steffen Ziesche .10 .05
❑ 43 Jens Schwabe .25 .11
❑ 44 Thomas Schubert .10 .05
❑ 45 Hans-Jorg Mayer .10 .05
❑ 46 Marc Seliger .25 .11
❑ 47 Ryan Hughes .10 .05
❑ 48 Richard Matvichuk .50 .23
❑ 49 David St. Pierre .10 .05
❑ 50 Paul Kariya 25.00 11.00
❑ 51 Patrick Poulin .50 .23
❑ 52 Mike Fountain .10 .05
❑ 53 Scott Niedermayer 1.50 .70
❑ 54 John Slaney .10 .05
❑ 55 Brad Bombardir .10 .05
❑ 56 Andy Schneider .10 .05
❑ 57 Steve Junker .10 .05
❑ 58 Trevor Kidd 2.00 .90
❑ 59 Martin Lapointe .50 .23
❑ 60 Tyler Wright .10 .05
❑ 61 Kimbi Daniels .10 .05
❑ 62 Karl Dykhuis .50 .23
❑ 63 Jeff Nelson .10 .05
❑ 64 Jassen Cullimore .50 .23
❑ 65 Turner Stevenson .10 .05
❑ 66 Brian Mueller .10 .05
❑ 67 Chris Tucker .10 .05
❑ 68 Marty Schriner .10 .05
❑ 69 Mike Prendergast .10 .05
❑ 70 John Lilley .10 .05
❑ 71 Jim Campbell 2.00 .90
❑ 72 Brian Holzinger 1.00 .45
❑ 73 Steve Konowalchuk .50 .23
❑ 74 Chris Ferraro .50 .23
❑ 75 Chris Imes .10 .05
❑ 76 Rich Brennan .10 .05
❑ 77 Todd Hall .10 .05
❑ 78 Brian Rafalski .10 .05
❑ 79 Scott Lachance .50 .23
❑ 80 Mike Dunham 1.00 .45
❑ 81 Brent Bilodeau .25 .11
❑ 82 Ryan Sittler .50 .23
❑ 83 Peter Ferraro .50 .23
❑ 84 Pat Peake .25 .11
❑ 85 Keith Tkachuk 8.00 3.60
❑ 86 Brian Rolston .50 .23
❑ 87 Milan Hnilicka .10 .05
❑ 88 Roman Hamrlik 2.00 .90
❑ 89 Milan Nedoma .10 .05
❑ 90 Patrik Luza .10 .05

❑ 91 Jan Caloun .50 .23
❑ 92 Viktor Ujcik .10 .05
❑ 93 Robert Petrovicky .50 .23
❑ 94 Roman Meluzin .10 .05
❑ 95 Jan Vopat .50 .23
❑ 96 Martin Prochazka .50 .23
❑ 97 Zigmund Palffy 6.00 2.70
❑ 98 Ivan Droppa .10 .05
❑ 99 Martin Straka 2.00 .90
❑ 100 Checklist 1-100 .10 .05
❑ NNO1 W.Gretzky Hologram 5.00 2.20
❑ NNO2 W.Gretzky Hologram 5.00 2.20

## 1992-93 Upper Deck

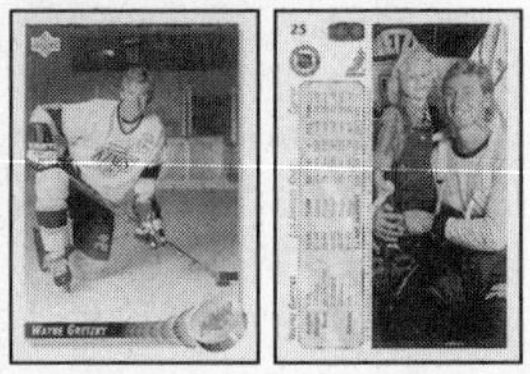

The 1992-93 Upper Deck hockey set contains 640 standard-size cards. The set was released in two series of 440 and 200 cards, respectively. Action photos on the fronts are bordered by the player's name and team logo at the bottom. Special subsets featured include Team Checklists (1-24), Bloodlines (35-39), '92 World Juniors (222-236), Russian Stars from Moscow Dynamo (333-353), Rookie Report (354-368), '92 World Championships (369-386), Team USA (392-397), Star Rookies (398-422), and Award Winners (431-440). Pavel Bure is showcased on a special card (SP2) that was randomly inserted in first series foil and jumbo packs. Another special card (SP3) titled "World Champions", honors Canada's 1993 IIHF World Junior Champions team. High series subsets featured are Lethal Lines (453-456), Young Guns (554-583), and World Junior Champions (584-619). The World Junior Champions subset is grouped according to national teams as follows: Canada (585-594), Sweden (595-599), Czechoslovakia (600-604), USA (605-609), Russia (610-614), and Finland (615-619). An Upper Deck Profiles (620-640) subset closes out the set. Rookie Cards include Alexandre Daigle, Adam Deadmarsh, Chris Gratton, Roman Hamrlik, Kenny Jonsson, Paul Kariya, Saku Koivu, Viktor Kozlov, Todd Marchant, Martin Straka, Rob Niedermayer, Chris Pronger, Mikael Renberg, Tommy Soderstrom, Nicklas Sundstrom and Sergei Zubov. Card No. 88, Eric Lindros, was short-printed (SP) as it was not included in second series packaging. This was brought about because of a controversy over Lindros' head being superimposed on a teammate's body.

| | MINT | NRMT |
|---|---|---|
| COMPLETE SET (640) | 50.00 | 22.00 |
| COMPLETE LO SET (440) | 20.00 | 9.00 |
| COMPLETE HI SET (200) | 30.00 | 13.50 |
| COMMON CARD (1-640) | .05 | .02 |

❑ 1 Andy Moog TC .10 .05
❑ 2 Donald Audette TC .10 .05
❑ 3 Tomas Forslund TC .05 .02
❑ 4 Steve Larmer TC .10 .05
❑ 5 Tim Cheveldae TC .10 .05
❑ 6 Vincent Damphousse TC .10 .05
❑ 7 Pat Verbeek TC .05 .02
❑ 8 Luc Robitaille TC .10 .05
❑ 9 Mike Modano TC .10 .05
❑ 10 Denis Savard TC .10 .05
❑ 11 Kevin Todd TC .05 .02
❑ 12 Ray Ferraro TC .05 .02
❑ 13 Tony Amonte TC .10 .05
❑ 14 Peter Sidorkiewicz TC .10 .05
❑ 15 Rod Brind'Amour TC .05 .02
❑ 16 Jaromir Jagr TC .40 .18
❑ 17 Owen Nolan TC .10 .05
❑ 18 Nelson Emerson TC .05 .02
❑ 19 Pat Falloon TC .05 .02
❑ 20 Anatoli Semenov TC .05 .02
❑ 21 Doug Gilmour TC .25 .11
❑ 22 Kirk McLean TC .10 .05
❑ 23 Don Beaupre TC .10 .05
❑ 24 Phil Housley TC .10 .05
❑ 25 Wayne Gretzky 1.50 .70
❑ 26 Mario Lemieux 1.25 .55
❑ 27 Valeri Kamensky .10 .05
❑ 28 Jaromir Jagr .75 .35
❑ 29 Brett Hull .40 .18
❑ 30 Neil Wilkinson .05 .02
❑ 31 Dominic Roussel .10 .05
❑ 32 Kent Manderville .05 .02
❑ 33 Gretzky 1500 .75 .35
❑ 34 Presidents' Cup .25 .11
❑ 35 Kip Miller BL .05 .02
Kevin Miller
Kelly Miller
❑ 36 Brian Sakic BL .25 .11
Joe Sakic
❑ 37 Wayne Gretzky BL .75 .35
Keith Gretzky
Brent Gretzky
❑ 38 Jamie Linden BL .10 .05
Trevor Linden
❑ 39 Geoff Courtnall BL .05 .02
Russ Courtnall
❑ 40 Dale Craigwell .05 .02
❑ 41 Peter Ahola .05 .02
❑ 42 Robert Reichel .05 .02
❑ 43 Chris Terreri .10 .05
❑ 44 John Vanbiesbrouck .40 .18
❑ 45 Alexander Semak .05 .02
❑ 46 Mike Sullivan .05 .02
❑ 47 Bob Sweeney .05 .02
❑ 48 Corey Millen .05 .02
❑ 49 Murray Craven .05 .02
❑ 50 Dennis Vaske .05 .02
❑ 51 David Williams .05 .02
❑ 52 Tom Fitzgerald .05 .02
❑ 53 Corey Foster .05 .02
❑ 54 Al Iafrate .10 .05
❑ 55 John LeClair .60 .25
❑ 56 Stephane Richer .10 .05
❑ 57 Claude Boivin .05 .02
❑ 58 Rick Tabaracci .10 .05
❑ 59 Johan Garpenlov .05 .02
❑ 60 Checklist 1-110 .05 .02
❑ 61 Steve Leach .05 .02
❑ 62 Trent Klatt .05 .02
❑ 63 Darryl Sydor .05 .02
❑ 64 Brian Glynn .05 .02
❑ 65 Mike Craig .05 .02
❑ 66 Gary Leeman .05 .02
❑ 67 Jim Waite .10 .05
❑ 68 Jason Marshall .05 .02
❑ 69 Robert Kron .05 .02
❑ 70 Yanic Perreault .05 .02
❑ 71 Daniel Marois .05 .02
❑ 72 Mark Osborne .05 .02
❑ 73 Mark Tinordi .05 .02
❑ 74 Brad May .10 .05
❑ 75 Kimbi Daniels .05 .02
❑ 76 Kay Whitmore .10 .05
❑ 77 Luciano Borsato .05 .02
❑ 78 Kris King .05 .02
❑ 79 Felix Potvin .25 .11
❑ 80 Benoit Brunet .05 .02
❑ 81 Shawn Antoski .05 .02
❑ 82 Randy Gilhen .05 .02
❑ 83 Dimitri Mironov .05 .02
❑ 84 Dave Manson .05 .02
❑ 85 Sergio Momesso .05 .02
❑ 86 Cam Neely .10 .05
❑ 87 Mike Krushelnyski .05 .02
❑ 88 Eric Lindros UER SP 2.50 1.10
(8 games with Canadian
Olympic Team, not 7)
❑ 89 Wendel Clark .10 .05
❑ 90 Enrico Ciccone .05 .02
❑ 91 Jarrod Skalde .05 .02
❑ 92 Dominik Hasek 1.00 .45
❑ 93 Dave McLlwain .05 .02
❑ 94 Russ Courtnall .05 .02
❑ 95 Tim Sweeney .05 .02
❑ 96 Alexei Kasatonov .05 .02
❑ 97 Chris Lindberg .05 .02
❑ 98 Steven Rice .05 .02
❑ 99 Tie Domi .10 .05
❑ 100 Paul Stanton .05 .02
❑ 101 Brad Schlegel .05 .02
❑ 102 David Bruce .05 .02
❑ 103 Mikael Andersson .05 .02
❑ 104 Shawn Chambers .05 .02
❑ 105 Rob Ramage .05 .02
❑ 106 Joe Reekie .05 .02
❑ 107 Sylvain Turgeon .05 .02
❑ 108 Rob Murphy .05 .02
❑ 109 Brad Shaw .05 .02
❑ 110 Darren Rumble .05 .02
❑ 111 Kyosti Karjalainen .05 .02
❑ 112 Mike Vernon .10 .05
❑ 113 Michel Goulet .10 .05
❑ 114 Garry Valk .05 .02
❑ 115 Peter Bondra .25 .11
❑ 116 Paul Coffey .25 .11
❑ 117 Brian Noonan .05 .02
❑ 118 John McIntyre .05 .02
❑ 119 Scott Mellanby .10 .05
❑ 120 Jim Sandlak .05 .02
❑ 121 Mats Sundin .25 .11
❑ 122 Brendan Shanahan .50 .23
❑ 123 Kelly Buchberger .05 .02
❑ 124 Doug Smail .05 .02
❑ 125 Craig Janney .10 .05
❑ 126 Mike Gartner .10 .05
❑ 127 Alexei Gusarov .05 .02
❑ 128 Joe Nieuwendyk .10 .05
❑ 129 Troy Murray .05 .02
❑ 130 Jamie Baker .05 .02
❑ 131 Dale Hunter .05 .02
❑ 132 Darrin Shannon .05 .02
❑ 133 Adam Oates .10 .05
❑ 134 Trevor Kidd .10 .05
❑ 135 Steve Larmer .10 .05
❑ 136 Fredrik Olausson .05 .02
❑ 137 Jyrki Lumme .05 .02
❑ 138 Tony Amonte .10 .05
❑ 139 Calle Johansson .05 .02
❑ 140 Rob Blake .10 .05
❑ 141 Phil Bourque .05 .02
❑ 142 Yves Racine .05 .02
❑ 143 Rich Sutter .05 .02
❑ 144 Joe Mullen .10 .05
❑ 145 Mike Richter .25 .11
❑ 146 Pat MacLeod .05 .02
❑ 147 Claude Lapointe .05 .02
❑ 148 Paul Broten .05 .02
❑ 149 Patrick Roy 1.25 .55
❑ 150 Doug Wilson .10 .05
❑ 151 Jim Hrivnak .10 .05
❑ 152 Joe Murphy .05 .02
❑ 153 Randy Burridge .05 .02
❑ 154 Thomas Steen .05 .02
❑ 155 Steve Yzerman .75 .35
❑ 156 Pavel Bure .50 .23
❑ 157 Sergei Fedorov .50 .23
❑ 158 Trevor Linden .10 .05
❑ 159 Chris Chelios .25 .11
❑ 160 Cliff Ronning .05 .02
❑ 161 Jeff Beukeboom .05 .02
❑ 162 Denis Savard .10 .05
❑ 163 Claude Lemieux .10 .05
❑ 164 Mike Keane .05 .02
❑ 165 Pat LaFontaine .10 .05
❑ 166 Nelson Emerson .05 .02
❑ 167 Alexander Mogilny .10 .05
❑ 168 Jamie Leach .05 .02
❑ 169 Darren Turcotte .05 .02
❑ 170 Checklist 111-220 .05 .02
❑ 171 Steve Thomas .05 .02
❑ 172 Brian Bellows .05 .02
❑ 173 Mike Ridley .05 .02
❑ 174 Dave Gagner .10 .05
❑ 175 Pierre Turgeon .10 .05
❑ 176 Paul Ysebaert .05 .02
❑ 177 Brian Propp .05 .02
❑ 178 Nicklas Lidstrom .10 .05
❑ 179 Kelly Miller .05 .02
❑ 180 Kirk Muller .05 .02
❑ 181 Bob Bassen .05 .02
❑ 182 Tony Tanti .05 .02
❑ 183 Mikhail Tatarinov .05 .02
❑ 184 Ron Sutter .05 .02
❑ 185 Tony Granato .05 .02
❑ 186 Curtis Joseph .25 .11
❑ 187 Uwe Krupp .05 .02
❑ 188 Esa Tikkanen .05 .02
❑ 189 Ulf Samuelsson .05 .02
❑ 190 Jon Casey .10 .05
❑ 191 Derek King .05 .02
❑ 192 Greg Adams .05 .02
❑ 193 Ray Ferraro .05 .02
❑ 194 Dave Christian .05 .02
❑ 195 Eric Weinrich .05 .02
❑ 196 Josef Beranek .05 .02
❑ 197 Tim Cheveldae .10 .05
❑ 198 Kevin Hatcher .05 .02
❑ 199 Brent Sutter .05 .02
❑ 200 Bruce Driver .05 .02
❑ 201 Tom Draper .10 .05
❑ 202 Ted Donato .05 .02
❑ 203 Ed Belfour .25 .11
❑ 204 Pat Verbeek .05 .02
❑ 205 John Druce .05 .02
❑ 206 Neal Broten .10 .05
❑ 207 Doug Bodger .05 .02
❑ 208 Troy Loney .05 .02
❑ 209 Mark Pederson .05 .02
❑ 210 Todd Elik .05 .02
❑ 211 Ed Olczyk .05 .02
❑ 212 Paul Cavallini .05 .02
❑ 213 Stephan Lebeau .05 .02
❑ 214 Dave Ellett .05 .02
❑ 215 Doug Gilmour .25 .11
❑ 216 Luc Robitaille .10 .05
❑ 217 Bob Essensa .10 .05
❑ 218 Jari Kurri .10 .05
❑ 219 Dimitri Khristich .05 .02
❑ 220 Joel Otto .05 .02
❑ 221 Checklist 221-280 .05 .02
❑ 222 Jonas Hoglund .05 .02
❑ 223 Rolf Wanhainen .05 .02
❑ 224 Stefan Klockare .05 .02
❑ 225 Johan Norgren .05 .02
❑ 226 Roger Kyro .05 .02
❑ 227 Niklas Sundblad .05 .02
❑ 228 Calle Carlsson .05 .02
❑ 229 Jakob Karlsson .05 .02
❑ 230 Fredrik Jax .05 .02
❑ 231 Bjorn Nord .05 .02
❑ 232 Kristian Gahn .05 .02
❑ 233 Mikael Renberg 2.00 .90
❑ 234 Markus Naslund .50 .23
❑ 235 Peter Forsberg .75 .35
❑ 236 Michael Nylander .05 .02
❑ 237 Stanley Cup Centennial .05 .02
❑ 238 Rick Tocchet .10 .05
❑ 239 Igor Kravchuk .05 .02
❑ 240 Geoff Courtnall .05 .02
❑ 241 Larry Murphy .10 .05
❑ 242 Mark Messier .40 .18
❑ 243 Tom Barrasso .10 .05
❑ 244 Glen Wesley .05 .02
❑ 245 Randy Wood .05 .02
❑ 246 Gerard Gallant .05 .02
❑ 247 Kip Miller .05 .02
❑ 248 Bob Probert .10 .05
❑ 249 Gary Suter .05 .02
❑ 250 Ulf Dahlen .05 .02
❑ 251 Dan Lambert .05 .02
❑ 252 Bobby Holik .05 .02
❑ 253 Jimmy Carson .05 .02
❑ 254 Ken Hodge Jr. .05 .02
❑ 255 Joe Sakic .50 .23
❑ 256 Kevin Dineen .10 .05
❑ 257 Al MacInnis .10 .05
❑ 258 Vladimir Ruzicka .05 .02
❑ 259 Ken Daneyko .05 .02
❑ 260 Guy Carbonneau .10 .05
❑ 261 Michal Pivonka .05 .02
❑ 262 Bill Ranford .10 .05
❑ 263 Petr Nedved .10 .05
❑ 264 Rod Brind'Amour .10 .05
❑ 265 Ray Bourque .25 .11
❑ 266 Joe Sacco .05 .02
❑ 267 Vladimir Konstantinov .05 .02
❑ 268 Eric Desjardins .05 .02
❑ 269 Dave Andreychuk .10 .05
❑ 270 Kelly Hrudey .10 .05
❑ 271 Grant Fuhr .10 .05
❑ 272 Dirk Graham .05 .02
❑ 273 Frank Pietrangelo .10 .05
❑ 274 Jeremy Roenick .25 .11
❑ 275 Kevin Stevens .05 .02
❑ 276 Phil Housley .10 .05
❑ 277 Patrice Brisebois .05 .02
❑ 278 Slava Fetisov .05 .02
❑ 279 Doug Weight .10 .05
❑ 280 Checklist 281-330 .05 .02
❑ 281 Dean Evason .05 .02
❑ 282 Martin Gelinas .05 .02
❑ 283 Philippe Bozon .05 .02
❑ 284 Brian Leetch .25 .11
❑ 285 Theoren Fleury .10 .05
❑ 286 Pat Falloon .05 .02
❑ 287 Derian Hatcher .05 .02
❑ 288 Andrew Cassels .05 .02
❑ 289 Gary Roberts .05 .02
❑ 290 Bernie Nicholls .10 .05
❑ 291 Ron Francis .10 .05
❑ 292 Tom Kurvers .05 .02
❑ 293 Geoff Sanderson .10 .05
❑ 294 Slava Kozlov .10 .05
❑ 295 Valeri Zelepukin .05 .02
❑ 296 Ray Sheppard .10 .05
❑ 297 Scott Stevens .10 .05
❑ 298 Sergei Nemchinov .05 .02
❑ 299 Kirk McLean .10 .05
❑ 300 Igor Ulanov .05 .02
❑ 301 Brian Benning .05 .02
❑ 302 Dale Hawerchuk .10 .05
❑ 303 Kevin Todd .05 .02
❑ 304 John Cullen .05 .02
❑ 305 Mike Modano .30 .14
❑ 306 Donald Audette .10 .05
❑ 307 Vincent Damphousse .10 .05
❑ 308 Jeff Hackett .10 .05
❑ 309 Craig Simpson .05 .02
❑ 310 Don Beaupre .10 .05
❑ 311 Adam Creighton .05 .02
❑ 312 Pat Elynuik .05 .02
❑ 313 David Volek .05 .02
❑ 314 Sergei Makarov .05 .02
❑ 315 Craig Billington .10 .05
❑ 316 Zarley Zalapski .05 .02
❑ 317 Brian Mullen .05 .02
❑ 318 Rob Pearson .05 .02
❑ 319 Garry Galley .05 .02
❑ 320 James Patrick .05 .02
❑ 321 Owen Nolan .10 .05
❑ 322 Marty McSorley .05 .02
❑ 323 James Black .05 .02
❑ 324 Jacques Cloutier .10 .05
❑ 325 Benoit Hogue .05 .02
❑ 326 Teppo Numminen .05 .02
❑ 327 Mark Recchi .10 .05
❑ 328 Paul Ranheim .05 .02
❑ 329 Andy Moog .10 .05
❑ 330 Shayne Corson .05 .02
❑ 331 J.J. Daigneault .05 .02
❑ 332 Mark Fitzpatrick .10 .05
❑ 333 Russian Stars CL .05 .02
Alexander Yudin
Dmitri Yushkevich
Yan Kaminsky
Alexander Andriyevski
❑ 334 Alexei Yashin RS .10 .05
❑ 335 Darius Kasparaitis RS .05 .02
❑ 336 Alexander Yudin RS .05 .02
❑ 337 Sergei Bautin RS .05 .02
❑ 338 Igor Korolev RS .05 .02
❑ 339 Sergei Klimovich RS .10 .05
❑ 340 Andrei Nikolishin RS .05 .02
❑ 341 Vitali Karamnov RS .05 .02
❑ 342 Alex. Andriyevski RS .05 .02
❑ 343 Sergei Sorokin RS .05 .02
❑ 344 Yan Kaminsky RS .05 .02
❑ 345 Andrei Trefilov RS .05 .02
❑ 346 Sergei Petrenko RS .05 .02
❑ 347 Ravil Khaidarov RS .05 .02
❑ 348 Dmitri Frolov RS .05 .02
❑ 349 Ravil Yakubov RS .05 .02
❑ 350 Dmitri Yushkevich RS .05 .02
❑ 351 Alexander Karpovtsev .05 .02
RS
❑ 352 Igor Dorofeyev RS .05 .02
❑ 353 Alexander Galchenyuk .05 .02
RS
❑ 354 Joe Juneau RR .10 .05
❑ 355 Pat Falloon RR .05 .02
❑ 356 Gilbert Dionne RR .05 .02
❑ 357 Vladimir Konstantinov .05 .02
RR
❑ 358 Rick Tabaracci RR .10 .05
❑ 359 Tony Amonte RR .10 .05
❑ 360 Scott Lachance RR .05 .02
❑ 361 Tom Draper RR .10 .05
❑ 362 Pavel Bure RR .25 .11
❑ 363 Nicklas Lidstrom RR .10 .05
❑ 364 Keith Tkachuk RR .40 .18
❑ 365 Kevin Todd RR .05 .02
❑ 366 Dominik Hasek RR .50 .23
❑ 367 Igor Kravchuk RR .05 .02
❑ 368 Shawn McEachern RR .05 .02
❑ 369 '92 World Champion- .40 .18
ships Checklist
Arto Blomsten
Peter Forsberg
❑ 370 Dieter Hegen .05 .02
❑ 371 Stefan Ustorf .05 .02
❑ 372 Ernst Kopf .05 .02
❑ 373 Raimond Hilger .05 .02
❑ 374 Mats Sundin .25 .11
❑ 375 Peter Forsberg .75 .35
❑ 376 Arto Blomsten .05 .02
❑ 377 Tommy Soderstom .10 .05
❑ 378 Michael Nylander .05 .02
❑ 379 David Jensen .05 .02
❑ 380 Chris Winnes .05 .02
❑ 381 Ray LeBlanc .10 .05
❑ 382 Joe Sacco .05 .02
❑ 383 Dennis Vaske .05 .02
❑ 384 Jorg Eberle .05 .02
❑ 385 Trevor Kidd .10 .05
❑ 386 Pat Falloon .05 .02
❑ 387 Rob Brown .05 .02
❑ 388 Adam Graves .10 .05
❑ 389 Peter Zezel .05 .02
❑ 390 Checklist 391-440 .05 .02
❑ 391 Don Sweeney .05 .02
❑ 392 Sean Hill .05 .02
❑ 393 Ted Donato .05 .02
❑ 394 Marty McInnis .05 .02
❑ 395 C.J. Young .05 .02
❑ 396 Ted Drury .05 .02
❑ 397 Scott Young .05 .02
❑ 398 Star Rookie CL .10 .05
Scott Lachance
Keith Tkachuk
❑ 399 Joe Juneau SR UER .05 .02
(Olympic stats should
read 8 games, 9 assists,
15 points, and 4 PIM)
❑ 400 Steve Heinze SR .05 .02
❑ 401 Glen Murray SR .05 .02
❑ 402 Keith Carney SR .05 .02
❑ 403 Dean McAmmond SR .05 .02
❑ 404 Karl Dykhuis SR .05 .02
❑ 405 Martin Lapointe SR .05 .02
❑ 406 Scott Niedermayer SR .10 .05
❑ 407 Ray Whitney SR .05 .02
❑ 408 Martin Brodeur SR 1.00 .45
❑ 409 Scott Lachance SR .05 .02
❑ 410 Marty McInnis SR .05 .02
❑ 411 Bill Guerin SR .05 .02
❑ 412 Shawn McEachern SR .05 .02
❑ 413 Denny Felsner SR .05 .02
❑ 414 Bret Hedican SR .05 .02
❑ 415 Drake Berehowsky SR .05 .02
❑ 416 Patrick Poulin SR .05 .02
❑ 417 Vladimir Vujtek SR .05 .02
❑ 418 Steve Konowalchuk SR .05 .02
❑ 419 Keith Tkachuk SR .60 .25
❑ 420 Evgeny Davydov SR .05 .02
❑ 421 Yanick Dupre SR .05 .02
❑ 422 Jason Woolley SR .05 .02
❑ 423 Back-to-Back .75 .35
Brett Hull
Wayne Gretzky
❑ 424 Tomas Sandstrom .05 .02
❑ 425 Craig MacTavish .05 .02
❑ 426 Stu Barnes .05 .02
❑ 427 Gilbert Dionne .05 .02
❑ 428 Andrei Lomakin .05 .02
❑ 429 Tomas Forslund .05 .02
❑ 430 Andre Racicot .10 .05
❑ 431 Pavel Bure AW .25 .11
Calder Memorial
❑ 432 Mark Messier AW .25 .11
Lester B. Pearson
❑ 433 Mario Lemieux AW .60 .25
Art Ross
❑ 434 Brian Leetch AW .25 .11
Norris
❑ 435 Wayne Gretzky AW .75 .35
Lady Byng
❑ 436 Mario Lemieux AW .60 .25
Conn Smythe
❑ 437 Mark Messier AW .25 .11
Hart
❑ 438 Patrick Roy AW .60 .25
Vezina
❑ 439 Guy Carbonneau AW .10 .05
Frank J. Selke
❑ 440 Patrick Roy AW .60 .25
William M. Jennings
❑ 441 Russ Courtnall .05 .02
❑ 442 Jeff Reese .05 .02
❑ 443 Brent Fedyk .05 .02
❑ 444 Kerry Huffman .05 .02
❑ 445 Mark Freer .05 .02
❑ 446 Christian Ruuttu .05 .02
❑ 447 Nick Kypreos .05 .02
❑ 448 Mike Hurlbut .05 .02
❑ 449 Bob Sweeney .05 .02
❑ 450 Checklist 491-540 .05 .02
❑ 451 Perry Berezan .05 .02
❑ 452 Phil Bourque .05 .02
❑ 453 New York Rangers LL .25 .11
Mark Messier
Tony Amonte
Adam Graves
❑ 454 Pittsburgh Penguins LL .40 .18
Mario Lemieux
Kevin Stevens
Rick Tocchet
❑ 455 Boston Bruins LL .10 .05
Adam Oates
Joe Juneau
Dmitri Kvartalnov
❑ 456 Buffalo Sabres LL .10 .05
Pat LaFontaine
Dave Andreychuk
Alexander Mogilny
❑ 457 Zdeno Ciger .05 .02
❑ 458 Pat Jablonski .10 .05

❑ 459 Brent Gilchrist .05 .02
❑ 460 Yvon Corriveau .05 .02
❑ 461 Dino Ciccarelli .10 .05
❑ 462 David Emma .05 .02
❑ 463 Corey Hirsch .60 .25
❑ 464 Jamie Baker .05 .02
❑ 465 John Cullen .05 .02
❑ 466 Lonnie Loach .05 .02
❑ 467 Louie DeBrusk .05 .02
❑ 468 Brian Mullen .05 .02
❑ 469 Gaeten Duchesne .05 .02
❑ 470 Eric Lindros 2.00 .90
❑ 471 Brian Bellows .05 .02
❑ 472 Bill Lindsay .05 .02
❑ 473 Dave Archibald .05 .02
❑ 474 Reggie Savage .05 .02
❑ 475 Tommy Soderstrom .10 .05
❑ 476 Vincent Damphousse .10 .05
❑ 477 Mike Ricci .05 .02
❑ 478 Bob Carpenter .05 .02
❑ 479 Kevin Haller .05 .02
❑ 480 Peter Sidorkiewicz .10 .05
❑ 481 Peter Andersson .05 .02
❑ 482 Kevin Miller .05 .02
❑ 483 Jean-Francois Quintin .05 .02
❑ 484 Philippe Boucher .05 .02
❑ 485 Jozef Stumpel .05 .02
❑ 486 Vitali Prokhorov .05 .02
❑ 487 Stan Drulia .05 .02
❑ 488 Jay More .05 .02
❑ 489 Mike Needham .05 .02
❑ 490 Glenn Mulvenna .05 .02
❑ 491 Ed Ronan .05 .02
❑ 492 Grigori Panteleyev .05 .02
❑ 493 Kevin Dahl .05 .02
❑ 494 Ryan McGill .05 .02
❑ 495 Robb Stauber .10 .05
❑ 496 Vladimir Vujtek .05 .02
❑ 497 Tomas Jelinek .05 .02
❑ 498 Patrik Kjellberg .05 .02
❑ 499 Sergei Bautin .05 .02
❑ 500 Bobby Holik .05 .02
❑ 501 Guy Hebert 1.00 .45
❑ 502 Chris Kontos .05 .02
❑ 503 Vyatcheslav Butsayev .05 .02
❑ 504 Yuri Khymlev .05 .02
❑ 505 Richard Matvichuk .05 .02
❑ 506 Dominik Hasek .75 .35
❑ 507 Ed Courtenay .05 .02
❑ 508 Jeff Daniels .05 .02
❑ 509 Doug Zmolek .05 .02
❑ 510 Vitali Karamnov .05 .02
❑ 511 Norm Maciver .05 .02
❑ 512 Terry Yake .05 .02
❑ 513 Steve Duchesne .05 .02
❑ 514 Andrei Trefilov .05 .02
❑ 515 Jiri Slegr .05 .02
❑ 516 Sergei Zubov .60 .25
❑ 517 Dave Karpa .05 .02
❑ 518 Sean Burke .10 .05
❑ 519 Adrien Plavsic .05 .02
❑ 520 Michael Nylander .05 .02
❑ 521 John MacLean .10 .05
❑ 522 Jason Ruff .05 .02
❑ 523 Sean Hill .05 .02
❑ 524 Mike Sillinger .05 .02
❑ 525 Dan Laperriere .05 .02
❑ 526 Peter Ahola .05 .02
❑ 527 Guy Larose .05 .02
❑ 528 Tommy Sjodin .05 .02
❑ 529 Rob DiMaio .05 .02
❑ 530 Mark Howe .05 .02
❑ 531 Greg Paslawski .05 .02
❑ 532 Ron Hextall .10 .05
❑ 533 Keith Jones .50 .23
❑ 534 Chris Luongo .05 .02
❑ 535 Anatoli Semenov .05 .02
❑ 536 Stephane Beauregard .10 .05
❑ 537 Pat Elynuik .05 .02
❑ 538 Mike McPhee .05 .02
❑ 539 Jody Hull .05 .02
❑ 540 Stephane Matteau .05 .02
❑ 541 Shayne Corson .05 .02
❑ 542 Mikhail Kravets .05 .02
❑ 543 Kevin Miehm .05 .02
❑ 544 Brian Bradley .05 .02
❑ 545 Mathieu Schneider .05 .02
❑ 546 Steve Chiasson .05 .02
❑ 547 Warren Rychel .05 .02
❑ 548 John Tucker .05 .02
❑ 549 Todd Ewen .05 .02
❑ 550 Checklist 591-640 .05 .02
❑ 551 Petr Klima .05 .02
❑ 552 Robert Lang .05 .02
❑ 553 Eric Weinrich .05 .02
❑ 554 Young Guns Checklist .05 .02
❑ 555 Roman Hamrlik YG .75 .35
❑ 556 Martin Rucinsky YG .05 .02
❑ 557 Patrick Poulin YG .05 .02
❑ 558 Tyler Wright YG .05 .02
❑ 559 Martin Straka YG 1.25 .55
❑ 560 Jim Hiller YG .05 .02
❑ 561 Dmitri Kvartalnov YG .05 .02
❑ 562 Scott Niedermayer YG .10 .05
❑ 563 Darius Kasparaitis YG .05 .02
❑ 564 Richard Smehlik YG .05 .02
❑ 565 Shawn McEachern YG .05 .02
❑ 566 Alexei Zhitnik YG .05 .02
❑ 567 Andrei Kovalenko YG .05 .02
❑ 568 Sandis Ozolinsh YG .10 .05
❑ 569 Robert Petrovicky YG .05 .02
❑ 570 Dimitri Yushkevich YG .05 .02
❑ 571 Scott Lachance YG .05 .02
❑ 572 Nikolai Borschevsky YG .05 .02
❑ 573 Alexei Kovalev YG .10 .05
❑ 574 Teemu Selanne YG 1.25 .55
❑ 575 Steven King YG .05 .02
❑ 576 Guy Leveque YG .05 .02
❑ 577 Vladimir Malakhov YG .05 .02
❑ 578 Alexei Zhamnov YG .10 .05
❑ 579 Viktor Gordiouk YG .05 .02
❑ 580 Dixon Ward YG .05 .02
❑ 581 Igor Korolev YG .05 .02
❑ 582 Sergei Krivokrasov YG .05 .02
❑ 583 Rob Zamuner YG .05 .02
❑ 584 World Jr. Championship Checklist .05 .02
❑ 585 Manny Legace .50 .23
❑ 586 Paul Kariya 20.00 9.00
❑ 587 Alexandre Daigle 1.00 .45
❑ 588 Nathan Lafeyette .05 .02
❑ 589 Mike Rathje .05 .02
❑ 590 Chris Gratton 1.00 .45
❑ 591 Chris Pronger 1.25 .55
❑ 592 Brent Tully .05 .02
❑ 593 Rob Niedermayer UER 1.50 .70
(Hometown is Cassiar, not Kassier)
❑ 594 Darcy Werenka .05 .02
❑ 595 Peter Forsberg .75 .35
❑ 596 Kenny Jonsson .05 .02
❑ 597 Niklas Sundstrom .75 .35
❑ 598 Reine Rauhala .05 .02
❑ 599 Daniel Johansson .05 .02
❑ 600 David Vyborny .05 .02
❑ 601 Jan Vopat .10 .05
❑ 602 Pavol Demitra 4.00 1.80
❑ 603 Michal Cerny .05 .02
❑ 604 Ondrej Steiner .05 .02
❑ 605 Jim Campbell 1.50 .70
❑ 606 Todd Marchant .05 .02
❑ 607 Mike Pomichter .10 .05
❑ 608 John Emmons .05 .02
❑ 609 Adam Deadmarsh 2.00 .90
❑ 610 Nikolai Semin .05 .02
❑ 611 Igor Alexandrov .05 .02
❑ 612 Vadim Sharifjanov .10 .05
❑ 613 Viktor Kozlov .50 .23
❑ 614 Nikolai Tsulygin .05 .02
❑ 615 Jere Lehtinen 1.50 .70
❑ 616 Ville Peltonen .25 .11
❑ 617 Saku Koivu 6.00 2.70
❑ 618 Kimmo Rintanen .05 .02
❑ 619 Jonni Vauhkonen .05 .02
❑ 620 Brett Hull .25 .11
❑ 621 Wayne Gretzky .75 .35
❑ 622 Jaromir Jagr .40 .18
❑ 623 Darius Kasparaitis .05 .02
❑ 624 Bernie Nicholls .05 .02
❑ 625 Gilbert Dionne .05 .02
❑ 626 Ray Bourque .25 .11
❑ 627 Mike Ricci .05 .02
❑ 628 Phil Housley .10 .05
❑ 629 Chris Chelios .25 .11
❑ 630 Kevin Stevens .25 .11
❑ 631 Roman Hamrlik .10 .05
❑ 632 Sergei Fedorov .25 .11
❑ 633 Alexei Kovalev .10 .05
❑ 634 Shawn McEachern .05 .02
❑ 635 Tony Amonte .10 .05
❑ 636 Brian Bellows .05 .02
❑ 637 Adam Oates .10 .05
❑ 638 Denis Savard .10 .05
❑ 639 Doug Gilmour .25 .11
❑ 640 Brian Leetch .25 .11
❑ SP2 Pavel Bure 4.00 1.80
All-Rookie Team
❑ SP3 World Jr. Champs 4.00 1.80
Gold medal winner
Canada

## 1992-93 Upper Deck All-Rookie Team

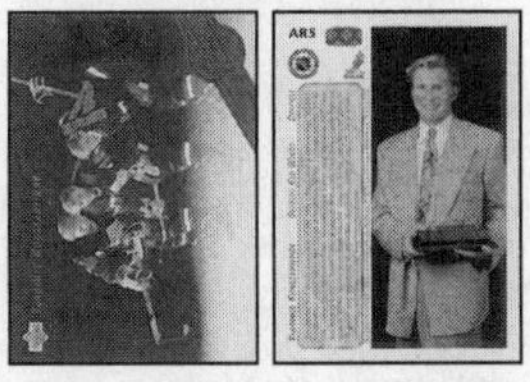

This seven-card set was inserted only in low series U.S. foil packs and features six of the NHL's brighest rookies from the 1991-92 season. The fronts show a triple-pose player photo and have a diagonal silver foil stripe in the lower right corner with the words "All-Rookie Team". The backs provide biographical information and a color photo of the player in civilian dress. The checklist card has a group photo of all six players. The cards are numbered on the back with an "AR" prefix.

| | MINT | NRMT |
|---|---|---|
| COMPLETE SET (7) | 30.00 | 13.50 |
| COMMON CARD (AR1-AR7) | 3.00 | 1.35 |

❑ AR1 Tony Amonte 4.00 1.80
❑ AR2 Gilbert Dionne 3.00 1.35
❑ AR3 Kevin Todd 3.00 1.35
❑ AR4 Nicklas Lidstrom 3.00 1.35
❑ AR5 Vladimir Konstantinov 4.00 1.80
❑ AR6 Dominik Hasek 12.00 5.50
❑ AR7 Checklist Card 12.00 5.50
Tony Amonte
Gilbert Dionne
Kevin Todd
Nicklas Lidstrom
Vladimir Konstantinov
Dominik Hasek

## 1992-93 Upper Deck All-World Team

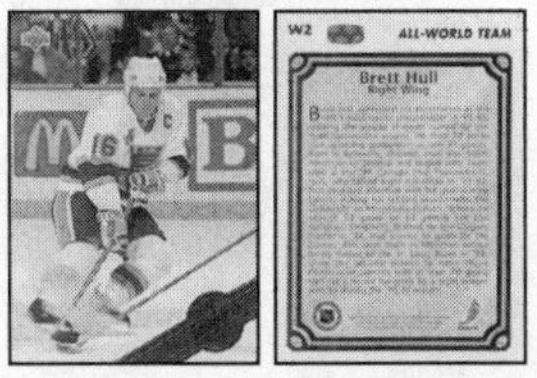

This six-card set was randomly inserted only in Canadian low series foil packs. These standard size cards are full bleed with a gold "All-World Team" logo at the bottom of the card. The cards are numbered on the back with a "W" prefix.

| | MINT | NRMT |
|---|---|---|
| COMPLETE SET (6) | 25.00 | 11.00 |
| COMMON CARD (W1-W6) | .75 | .35 |

❑ W1 Wayne Gretzky 8.00 3.60
❑ W2 Brett Hull 1.50 .70
❑ W3 Jaromir Jagr 4.00 1.80
❑ W4 Nicklas Lidstrom .75 .35
❑ W5 Vladimir Konstantinov .75 .35
❑ W6 Patrick Roy 6.00 2.70

## 1992-93 Upper Deck Ameri/Can Holograms

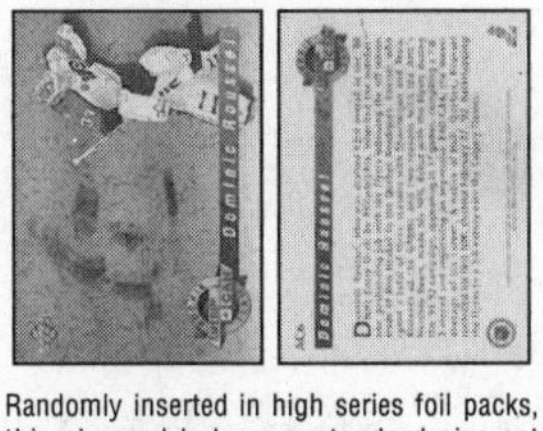

Randomly inserted in high series foil packs, this six-card hologram standard-size set spotlights the top rookies of either U.S. or Canadian heritage at each position. The cards have the photo superimposed over the hologram.

| | MINT | NRMT |
|---|---|---|
| COMPLETE SET (6) | 12.00 | 5.50 |
| COMMON CARD (1-6) | 1.00 | .45 |

❑ 1 Joe Juneau 2.00 .90
❑ 2 Keith Tkachuk 6.00 2.70
❑ 3 Steve Heinze 1.00 .45
❑ 4 Scott Lachance 1.00 .45
❑ 5 Scott Niedermayer 1.00 .45
❑ 6 Dominic Roussel 2.00 .90

## 1992-93 Upper Deck Calder Candidates

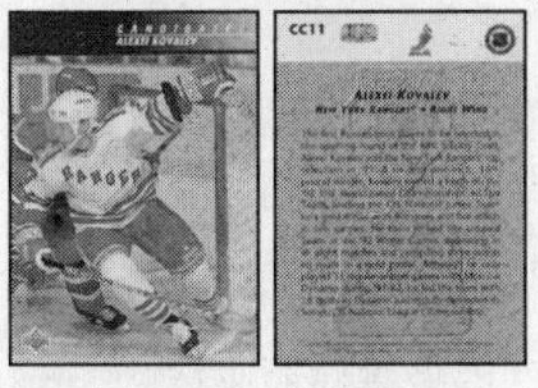

Randomly inserted into 1992-93 Upper Deck U.S. high series retail foil packs only, this 20-card standard-size set spotlights top rookies eligible to win the Calder Memorial Trophy for the 1992-93 season. The full-bleed photos on the front are bordered on the top by a gold foil stripe. The team name and player's name appears in bar that shades from black to white. On a background consisting of a stone slab carved with an image of the Calder trophy, the backs present a career summary. The card number appears in a white stripe that cuts across the top of the card. The cards are numbered with a "CC" prefix.

| | MINT | NRMT |
|---|---|---|
| COMPLETE SET (20) | 60.00 | 27.00 |
| COMMON CARD (CC1-CC20) | 2.00 | .90 |

❑ CC1 Dixon Ward 2.00 .90
❑ CC2 Igor Korolev 2.00 .90
❑ CC3 Felix Potvin 5.00 2.20
❑ CC4 Rob Zamuner 2.00 .90
❑ CC5 Scott Niedermayer 3.00 1.35
❑ CC6 Eric Lindros 12.00 5.50
❑ CC7 Alexei Zhitnik 2.00 .90
❑ CC8 Roman Hamrlik 5.00 2.20
❑ CC9 Joe Juneau 3.00 1.35
❑ CC10 Teemu Selanne 10.00 4.50
❑ CC11 Alexei Kovalev 2.00 .90
❑ CC12 Vladimir Malakhov 2.00 .90
❑ CC13 Darius Kasparaitis 2.00 .90
❑ CC14 Shawn McEachern 2.00 .90
❑ CC15 Keith Tkachuk 8.00 3.60
❑ CC16 Scott Lachance 2.00 .90
❑ CC17 Andrei Kovalenko 2.00 .90
❑ CC18 Patrick Poulin 2.00 .90
❑ CC19 Evgeny Davydov 2.00 .90
❑ CC20 Dimitri Yushkevich 2.00 .90

## 1992-93 Upper Deck Euro-Rookie Team

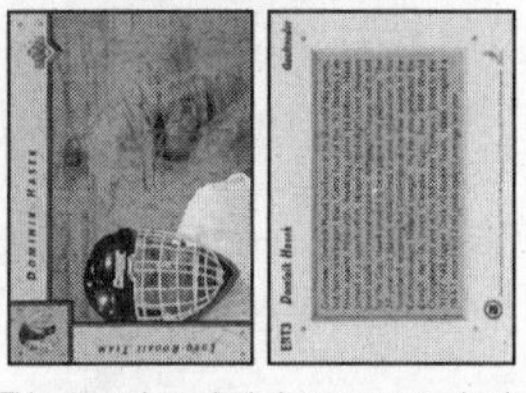

This six-card standard-size set was randomly inserted in 1992-93 Upper Deck low series packs. The cards feature cut-out color player photos superimposed on a hologram that shows the player in action. The horizontal fronts are bordered on the left and top by gray wood-textured panels. The team logo appears at the top left on a tan wood-textured panel. The horizontal backs feature a player profile on a tan background bordered by gray wood-textured panels. The cards are numbered on the back with an "ERT" prefix.

| | MINT | NRMT |
|---|---|---|
| COMPLETE SET (6) | 15.00 | 6.75 |
| COMMON CARD (ERT1-ERT6) | 1.00 | .45 |

❑ ERT1 Pavel Bure 5.00 2.20
❑ ERT2 Nicklas Lidstrom 1.00 .45
❑ ERT3 Dominik Hasek 6.00 2.70
❑ ERT4 Peter Ahola 1.00 .45
❑ ERT5 Alexander Semak 1.00 .45
❑ ERT6 Tomas Forslund 1.00 .45

## 1992-93 Upper Deck Euro-Rookies

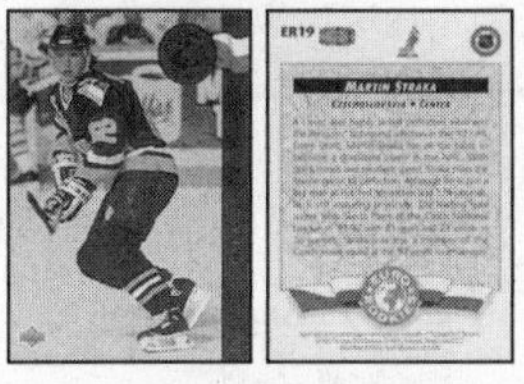

One per high series jumbo pack, this 20-card standard-size set spotlights European born rookies. The color action player photos on the fronts are full-bleed except on the right side, where a black stripe carries the player's name in bronze foil lettering. At the upper right corner appears a bronze foil "Euro-Rookies" seal, with the flag of the player's country immediately to the right. The cards are numbered on the back with an "ER" prefix.

| | MINT | NRMT |
|---|---|---|
| COMPLETE SET (20) | 25.00 | 11.00 |
| COMMON CARD (ER1-ER20) | .75 | .35 |

❑ ER1 Richard Smehlik .75 .35
❑ ER2 Michael Nylander .75 .35
❑ ER3 Igor Korolev .75 .35
❑ ER4 Robert Lang .75 .35
❑ ER5 Sergei Krivokrasov .75 .35
❑ ER6 Teemu Selanne 6.00 2.70
❑ ER7 Darius Kasparaitis .75 .35
❑ ER8 Alexei Zhamnov 1.50 .70
❑ ER9 Jiri Slegr .75 .35
❑ ER10 Alexei Kovalev .75 .35
❑ ER11 Roman Hamrlik 1.50 .70
❑ ER12 Dimitri Yushkevich .75 .35
❑ ER13 Alexei Zhitnik .75 .35
❑ ER14 Andrei Kovalenko .75 .35
❑ ER15 Vladimir Malakhov .75 .35
❑ ER16 Sandis Ozolinsh 3.00 1.35
❑ ER17 Evgeny Davydov .75 .35
❑ ER18 Viktor Gordiouk .75 .35
❑ ER19 Martin Straka .75 .35
❑ ER20 Robert Petrovicky .75 .35

## 1992-93 Upper Deck Euro-Stars

This 20-card standard-size set, issued one per low series jumbo pack, features action color player photos with a silver foil border. The borders are prone to chipping. The pictures are silver-foil stamped with the player's name and with the "Euro Stars" emblem which hangs down from a white, red, and blue ribbon at the upper right corner. The backs display player profile information against a light gray panel with a black, silver, and gold frame design.

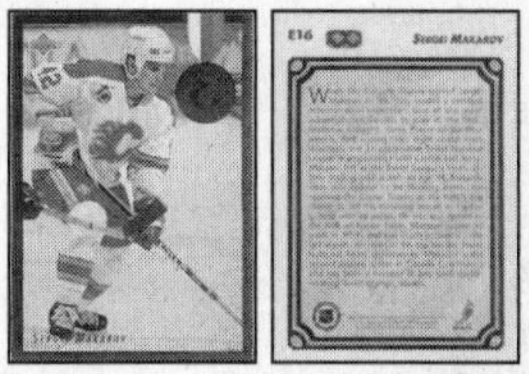

The cards are numbered on the back with an "E" prefix.

| | MINT | NRMT |
|---|---|---|
| COMPLETE SET (20) | 30.00 | 13.50 |
| COMMON CARD (E1-E20) | 1.00 | .45 |

❑ E1 Sergei Fedorov 3.00 1.35
❑ E2 Pavel Bure 3.00 1.35
❑ E3 Dominik Hasek 5.00 2.20
❑ E4 Vladimir Ruzicka 1.00 .45
❑ E5 Peter Ahola 1.00 .45
❑ E6 Kyosti Karjalainen 1.00 .45
❑ E7 Igor Kravchuk 1.00 .45
❑ E8 Evgeny Davydov 1.00 .45
❑ E9 Nicklas Lidstrom 1.00 .45
❑ E10 Vlad. Konstantinov 2.00 .90
❑ E11 Josef Beranek 1.00 .45
❑ E12 Valeri Zelepukin 1.00 .45
❑ E13 Sergei Nemchinov 1.00 .45
❑ E14 Jaromir Jagr 5.00 2.20
❑ E15 Igor Ulanov 1.00 .45
❑ E16 Sergei Makarov 1.00 .45
❑ E17 Andrei Lomakin 1.00 .45
❑ E18 Mats Sundin 2.00 .90
❑ E19 Jarmo Myllys 1.00 .45
❑ E20 Valeri Kamensky 2.00 .90

## 1992-93 Upper Deck Wayne Gretzky Heroes

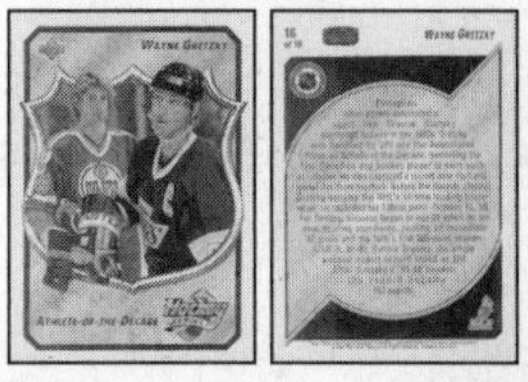

Randomly inserted in low series foil packs, this ten-card "Hockey Heroes" standard-size set pays tribute to Wayne Gretzky by chronicling his career. Inside white borders on a gray ice background, the fronts display color photos that are cut out to fit a emblem design. On a gray ice background accented by black, the backs (which continue the numbering from where the Hull Heroes left off) capture highlights in Gretzky's career.

| | MINT | NRMT |
|---|---|---|
| COMPLETE SET (10) | 40.00 | 18.00 |
| COMMON GRETZKY (10-18) | 5.00 | 2.20 |
| GRETZKY HEADER SP (NNO) | 10.00 | 4.50 |

❑ 10 The Untouchable Greyhound 5.00 2.20
❑ 11 17-Year-Old Pro 5.00 2.20
❑ 12 Hart Trophy in NHL Debut 5.00 2.20
❑ 13 Four Cups in Five Seasons 5.00 2.20
❑ 14 Wrapped In The Maple Leaf 5.00 2.20
❑ 15 The Trade That Rocked Sports 5.00 2.20
❑ 16 Athlete-Of-The-Decade 5.00 2.20
❑ 17 New Goals 5.00 2.20
❑ 18 Checklist 5.00 2.20

## 1992-93 Upper Deck Gordie Howe Heroes

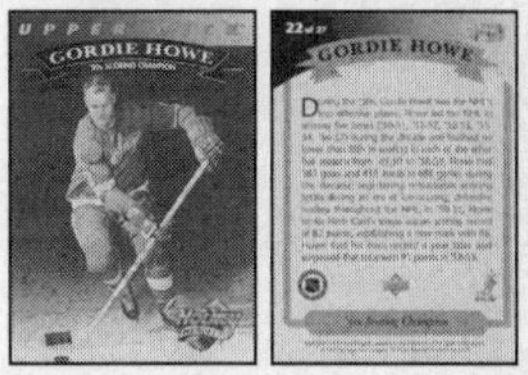

Randomly inserted in high series foil packs, this 10-card "Hockey Heroes" standard-size set showcases Gordie Howe, the NHL's former all-time leader in goals, assists, and points. The backs capture highlights in Howe's career. The cards are numbered on the back and continue from where the Gretzky Heroes left off.

| | MINT | NRMT |
|---|---|---|
| COMPLETE SET (10) | 15.00 | 6.75 |
| COMMON HOWE (19-27) | 2.00 | .90 |
| HOWE HEADER SP (NNO) | 4.00 | 1.80 |

❑ 19 Gordie Howe 2.00 .90
The Early Years
❑ 20 Gordie Howe 2.00 .90

Dynasty in Detroit
❑ 21 Gordie Howe 2.00 .90
The First Production Line
❑ 22 Gordie Howe 2.00 .90
'50s Scoring Champion
❑ 23 Gordie Howe 2.00 .90
Six-time Hart
Trophy Winner
❑ 24 Gordie Howe 2.00 .90
Hall of Fame
❑ 25 Gordie Howe 2.00 .90
The Comeback
❑ 26 Gordie Howe 2.00 .90
Wayne Gretzky
"Mr. Hockey" and
"The Great One"
❑ 27 Checklist Card 2.00 .90

## 1992-93 Upper Deck Gordie Howe Selects

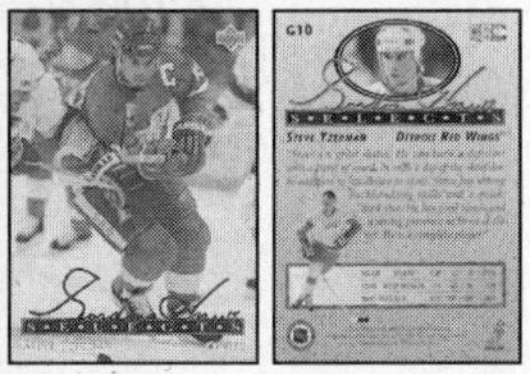

Randomly inserted throughout U.S. high series hobby packs only, this 20-card set standard-size features Gordie Howe's selections of ten current NHL superstars and ten rookies who he believes are the NHL's best. The fronts carry full-bleed color player photos. Howe's signature in gold foil sits on top of a black bar (carrying the word "Selects") toward the bottom of the picture, with the player's name and position immediately below. The backs have a color head shot in an oval and a quote of Howe's evaluation of the player's strengths. A small color player cut-out of Howe and the player's statistics complete the back. The cards are numbered on the back with a "G" prefix.

| | MINT | NRMT |
|---|---|---|
| COMPLETE SET (20) | 50.00 | 22.00 |
| COMMON CARD (G1-G20) | 2.00 | .90 |

❑ G1 Brian Bellows 2.00 .90
❑ G2 Luc Robitaille 2.50 1.10
❑ G3 Pat LaFontaine 2.50 1.10
❑ G4 Kevin Stevens 2.00 .90
❑ G5 Wayne Gretzky 12.00 5.50
❑ G6 Steve Larmer 2.00 .90
❑ G7 Brett Hull 3.00 1.35
❑ G8 Jeremy Roenick 2.50 1.10
❑ G9 Mario Lemieux 10.00 4.50
❑ G10 Steve Yzerman 6.00 2.70
❑ G11 Joe Juneau 2.50 1.10
❑ G12 Vladimir Malakhov 2.00 .90
❑ G13 Alexei Kovalev 2.00 .90
❑ G14 Eric Lindros 8.00 3.60
❑ G15 Teemu Selanne 6.00 2.70
❑ G16 Patrick Poulin 2.00 .90
❑ G17 Shawn McEachern 2.00 .90
❑ G18 Keith Tkachuk 5.00 2.20
❑ G19 Andrei Kovalenko 2.00 .90
❑ G20 Ted Donato 2.00 .90

## 1992-93 Upper Deck World Junior Grads

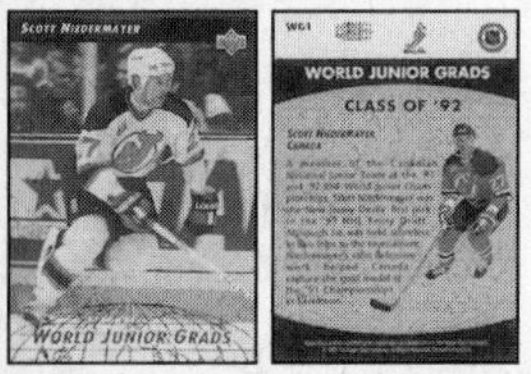

Randomly inserted in Canadian high series foil packs, this 20-card standard-size set features top players in the world who have participated in the IIHF Junior Championships. Beneath a black stripe carrying the player's name, the fronts display full-bleed color action player photos. The top portion of a globe and the words "World Junior Grads" are silver foil-stamped at the bottom of the picture. On the backs, a full-size globe serves as a panel for displaying a career summary and a color action player cut-out. The back also includes the year the player participated in the IIHF World Junior Championships. The cards are numbered on the back with a "WG" prefix.

| | MINT | NRMT |
|---|---|---|
| COMPLETE SET (20) | 100.00 | 45.00 |
| COMMON CARD (WG1-WG20) | 2.00 | .90 |

❑ WG1 Scott Niedermayer 2.00 .90
❑ WG2 Slava Kozlov 3.00 1.35
❑ WG3 Chris Chelios 4.00 1.80
❑ WG4 Jari Kurri 3.00 1.35
❑ WG5 Pavel Bure 8.00 3.60
❑ WG6 Jaromir Jagr 10.00 4.50
❑ WG7 Steve Yzerman 12.00 5.50
❑ WG8 Joe Sakic 6.00 2.70
❑ WG9 Alexei Kovalev 2.00 .90
❑ WG10 Wayne Gretzky 25.00 11.00
❑ WG11 Mario Lemieux 20.00 9.00
❑ WG12 Eric Lindros 15.00 6.75
❑ WG13 Pat Falloon 2.00 .90
❑ WG14 Trevor Linden 3.00 1.35
❑ WG15 Brian Leetch 4.00 1.80
❑ WG16 Sergei Fedorov 8.00 3.60
❑ WG17 Mats Sundin 4.00 1.80
❑ WG18 Alexander Mogilny 3.00 1.35
❑ WG19 Jeremy Roenick 4.00 1.80
❑ WG20 Luc Robitaille 3.00 1.35

## 1992-93 Upper Deck Sheets

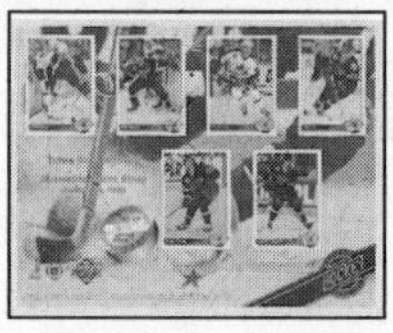

For the third straight year, Upper Deck produced hockey commemorative sheets that were given away during the 1992-93 season at selected games in large arenas. Each sheet measures 8 1/2" by 11" and is printed on card stock. The fronts of the team commemorative sheets feature a series of Upper Deck cards of star players on a particular team and the team logo. The 1993 All-Star Game sheets feature a series of Upper Deck cards of players that participated in the All-Star Game. All the sheets have an Upper Deck stamp indicating the production quota and the serial number. Sheets without a production quantity number are listed as NNO. The backs of the sheets are blank. The players are listed as they appear from left to right.

| | MINT | NRMT |
|---|---|---|
| COMPLETE SET (17) | 175.00 | 80.00 |
| COMMON SHEET (1-17) | 8.00 | 3.60 |

❑ 1 '91-92 All-Rookie Team 15.00 6.75
June 1992 (17,000)
Gilbert Dionne
Kevin Todd
Vladimir Konstantinov
Tony Amonte
Nicklas Lidstrom
Dominik Hasek
❑ 2 New York Rangers 10.00 4.50
Defending Season Champs
Undated (18,000)
Peter Andersson
Phil Bourque
Joe Kocur
Doug Weight
Randy Gilhen
John Vanbiesbrouck
Adam Graves
Mark Messier
❑ 3 Gordie Howe Birthday 10.00 4.50
Undated (NNO)
65th Birthday
Celebration Tour
(Nine Howe Hockey Heroes
Cards Pictured)
❑ 4 Gordie Howe Birthday 10.00 4.50
Undated (NNO)
Hamilton McDonald's
❑ 5 Wayne Gretzky Heroes 15.00 6.75
Mail-In (NNO)
❑ 6 New York Rangers 8.00 3.60
vs. Quebec Nordiques
Oct. 29, 1992 (18,000)
Paul Broten
Mike Richter
Sergei Nemchinov
Tie Domi
Kris King
Jeff Beukeboom
Brian Leetch Norris
Tony Amonte
❑ 7 Los Angeles Kings 10.00 4.50
vs. Vancouver Canucks
Nov. 12, 1992 (18,000)
Luc Robitaille
Paul Coffey
Tony Granato
Rob Blake
Tomas Sandstrom
Kelly Hrudey
❑ 8 Minnesota North Stars 20.00 9.00
vs. San Jose Sharks
Nov. 28, 1992 (16,500)
❑ 9 Edmonton Oilers 8.00 3.60
vs. Calgary Flames
Dec. 8, 1992 (18,500)
Brian Glynn
Scott Mellanby
Dave Manson
Craig MacTavish
Bernie Nicholls
Bill Ranford
❑ 10 Philadelphia Flyers 8.00 3.60
vs. Pittsburgh Penguins
Dec. 17, 1992 (19,000)
Kevin Dineen
Mark Recchi
Garry Galley
Dominic Roussel
Brian Benning
Rod Brind'Amour
❑ 11 Minnesota North Stars 18.00 8.00
vs. Tampa Bay Lightning
Jan. 30, 1993 (16,500)
Dave Gagner
Neal Broten
Ulf Dahlen
Todd Elik
Tommy Sjodin
Gaetan Duchesne
❑ 12 Campbell All-Stars 12.00 5.50
Montreal Forum
Feb. 6, 1993 (NNO)
Ed Belfour
Paul Coffey
Chris Chelios
Steve Yzerman
Brett Hull
Pavel Bure
❑ 13 Wales All-Stars 12.00 5.50
Montreal Forum
Feb. 6, 1993 (NNO)
Patrick Roy
Brian Leetch
Ray Bourque
Kevin Stevens
Mario Lemieux
Jaromir Jagr
❑ 14 Washington Capitals 10.00 4.50
vs. St. Louis Blues
Feb. 21, 1993 (17,000)
Jim Hrivnak
Mike Ridley
Peter Bondra
Dale Hunter
Kelly Miller
Don Beaupre
❑ 15 Los Angeles Kings 12.00 5.50
vs. Ottawa Senators
Mar. 4, 1993 (18,000)
Jari Kurri
Corey Millen
Marty McSorley
Darryl Sydor
Wayne Gretzky
Robb Stauber
❑ 16 Quebec Nordiques 15.00 6.75
vs. Hartford Whalers
Mar. 8, 1993 (15,000)
❑ 17 St.Louis Blues 8.00 3.60
vs. Vancouver Canucks
Mar. 30, 1993 (17,500)

## 1993 Upper Deck Locker All-Stars

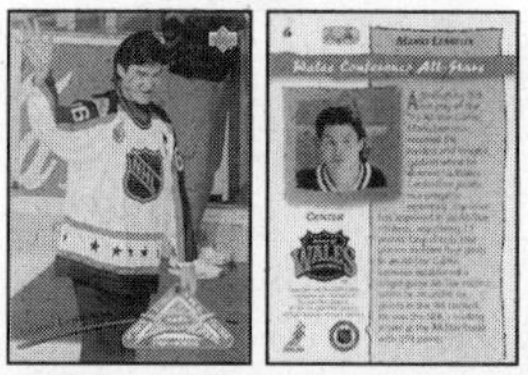

This 60-card standard-size set was issued as the 1992-93 Upper Deck NHL All-Star Locker Series. The set came in a plastic locker box. Personally signed Gordie Howe "Hockey Heroes" cards were randomly inserted throughout the locker boxes; the odds of finding one are one in 120 boxes. The fronts feature full-bleed, color, action player photos. The player's name is printed in gold foil above a blue and gold-foil curving stripe at the bottom. The 44th NHL All-Star game logo overlaps the stripe and is printed in the lower right corner. The backs carry a small, close-up picture within a bright blue rough-edged border that gives the effect of torn paper. This photo overlaps a gray panel with the same rough-edge look. This panel carries player profile information. After presenting the NHL All-Stars by conference, Campbell Conference All-Stars (1-18) and Wales Conference All-Stars (19-36), the set features the following special subsets, All-Star Skills Winners (37-40), All-Star Heroes (41-50), and Future All-Stars (51-60). The card pictures for this set were taken during the 1993 NHL All-Star Weekend in Montreal.

| | MINT | NRMT |
|---|---|---|
| COMPLETE SET (60) | 15.00 | 6.75 |
| COMMON CARD (1-60) | .05 | .02 |

❑ 1 Peter Bondra .40 .18
❑ 2 Steve Duchesne .05 .02
❑ 3 Jaromir Jagr 1.25 .55
❑ 4 Pat LaFontaine .25 .11
❑ 5 Brian Leetch .35 .16
❑ 6 Mario Lemieux 2.00 .90
❑ 7 Mark Messier .60 .25
❑ 8 Alexander Mogilny .40 .18
❑ 9 Kirk Muller .10 .05
❑ 10 Adam Oates .25 .11
❑ 11 Mark Recchi .25 .11
❑ 12 Patrick Roy 2.00 .90
❑ 13 Joe Sakic 1.00 .45
❑ 14 Kevin Stevens .10 .05
❑ 15 Scott Stevens .10 .05
❑ 16 Rick Tocchet .10 .05
❑ 17 Pierre Turgeon .25 .11
❑ 18 Zarley Zalapski .05 .02
❑ 19 Ed Belfour .50 .23
❑ 20 Brian Bradley .10 .05
❑ 21 Pavel Bure .60 .25
❑ 22 Chris Chelios .35 .16
❑ 23 Paul Coffey .35 .16
❑ 24 Doug Gilmour .40 .18
❑ 25 Wayne Gretzky 2.50 1.10
❑ 26 Phil Housley .10 .05
❑ 27 Brett Hull .50 .23
❑ 28 Kelly Kisio .05 .02
❑ 29 Jari Kurri .15 .07
❑ 30 Dave Manson .05 .02
❑ 31 Mike Modano .25 .11
❑ 32 Gary Roberts .10 .05
❑ 33 Luc Robitaille .25 .11
❑ 34 Jeremy Roenick .40 .18
❑ 35 Teemu Selanne .75 .35
❑ 36 Steve Yzerman 1.00 .45
❑ 37 Al Iafrate .10 .05
❑ 38 Mike Gartner .15 .07
❑ 39 Ray Bourque .35 .16
❑ 40 Jon Casey .10 .05
❑ 41 Bob Gainey .10 .05
❑ 42 Gordie Howe .60 .25
❑ 43 Bobby Hull .50 .23
❑ 44 Frank Mahovlich .25 .11
❑ 45 Lanny McDonald .20 .09
❑ 46 Stan Mikita .25 .11
❑ 47 Henri Richard .25 .11
❑ 48 Larry Robinson .15 .07
❑ 49 Glen Sather .10 .05
❑ 50 Bryan Trottier .20 .09
❑ 51 Tony Amonte .20 .09
❑ 52 Pat Falloon .05 .02
❑ 53 Joe Juneau .10 .05
❑ 54 Alexei Kovalev .25 .11
❑ 55 Dmitri Kvartalnov .05 .02
❑ 56 Eric Lindros 1.25 .55
❑ 57 Vladimir Malakhov .05 .02
❑ 58 Felix Potvin .60 .25
❑ 59 Mats Sundin .40 .18
❑ 60 Alexei Zhamnov .20 .09
❑ AU Gordie Howe AU 150.00 70.00
(Certified autograph)

## 1993-94 Upper Deck

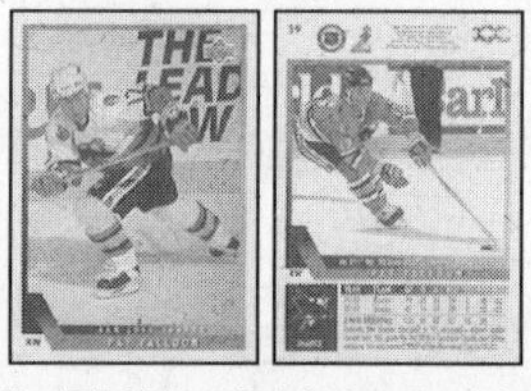

The 1993-94 Upper Deck hockey set contains 575 standard-size cards. The set was released in two series of 310 and 265 cards, respectively. The fronts feature a photo with team color-coded inner borders. The player's name, position and team name are at the bottom. The backs have a photo in the upper half with yearly statistics in the bottom portion. The following subsets are included: 100-Point Club (220-235), NHL Star Rookies (236-249), World Jr. Championships - which include Canada (250-260/531-550), Czechoslovakia (261-267/573), Finland (268-271), Russia (272-279/571/574) and USA (551-568) - All-Rookie Team (280-285) and Team Point Leaders (286-309). The set closes with an All-World Junior Team subset (569-574). A special card (SP4) was randomly inserted in Upper Deck series one packs commemorating Teemu Selanne's record-breaking 76 goal rookie season. A Wayne Gretzky card commemorating his 802nd NHL goal was randomly inserted at a rate of 1:36 Parkhurst series two packs. This card is identical to his regular Upper Deck card for '93-94, with the exception of a gold foil stamp that indicates his 802nd goal. The silver version of this card was handed out to Canadian dealers as a promotion for Parkhurst series two, and also given to each of the 16,005 fans attending the next game at the Great Western Forum following the event. Rookie Cards include Jason Arnott, Valeri Bure, Jeff Friesen, Todd Harvey, Chris Osgood, Jamie Storr and Jocelyn Thibault.

| | MINT | NRMT |
|---|---|---|
| COMPLETE SET (575) | 30.00 | 13.50 |
| COMPLETE SERIES 1 (310) | 15.00 | 6.75 |
| COMPLETE SERIES 2 (265) | 15.00 | 6.75 |
| COMMON CARD (1-575) | .05 | .02 |

❑ 1 Guy Hebert .10 .05
❑ 2 Bob Bassen .05 .02
❑ 3 Theoren Fleury .10 .05
❑ 4 Ray Whitney .05 .02
❑ 5 Donald Audette .10 .05
❑ 6 Martin Rucinsky .05 .02
❑ 7 Lyle Odelein .05 .02
❑ 8 John Vanbiesbrouck .40 .18
❑ 9 Tim Cheveldae .10 .05
❑ 10 Jock Callander .05 .02
❑ 11 Nick Kypreos .05 .02
❑ 12 Jarrod Skalde .05 .02
❑ 13 Gary Shuchuk .05 .02
❑ 14 Kris King .05 .02
❑ 15 Josef Beranek .05 .02
❑ 16 Sean Hill .05 .02
❑ 17 Bob Kudelski .05 .02
❑ 18 Jiri Slegr .05 .02
❑ 19 Dmitri Kvartalnov .05 .02
❑ 20 Drake Berehowsky .05 .02
❑ 21 Jean-Francois Quintin .05 .02
❑ 22 Randy Wood .05 .02
❑ 23 Jim McKenzie .05 .02
❑ 24 Steven King .05 .02
❑ 25 Scott Niedermayer .05 .02
❑ 26 Alexander Andrijevski .05 .02
❑ 27 Alexei Kovalev .10 .05
❑ 28 Steve Konowalchuk .05 .02
❑ 29 Vladimir Malakhov .05 .02
❑ 30 Eric Lindros 1.00 .45
❑ 31 Mathieu Schneider .05 .02
❑ 32 Russ Courtnall .05 .02
❑ 33 Ron Sutter .05 .02
❑ 34 Radek Hamr .05 .02
❑ 35 Pavel Bure .50 .23
❑ 36 Joe Sacco .05 .02
❑ 37 Robert Petrovicky .05 .02
❑ 38 Anatoli Fedotov .05 .02
❑ 39 Pat Falloon .05 .02
❑ 40 Martin Straka .05 .02
❑ 41 Brad Werenka .05 .02
❑ 42 Mike Richter .25 .11
❑ 43 Mike McPhee .05 .02
❑ 44 Sylvain Turgeon .05 .02
❑ 45 Tom Barrasso .10 .05
❑ 46 Anatoli Semenov .05 .02
❑ 47 Joe Murphy .05 .02
❑ 48 Rob Pearson .05 .02
❑ 49 Patrick Roy 1.25 .55
❑ 50 Dallas Drake .05 .02
❑ 51 Mark Messier .30 .14
❑ 52 Scott Pellerin .05 .02
❑ 53 Teppo Numminen .05 .02
❑ 54 Chris Kontos .05 .02
❑ 55 Richard Matvichuk .05 .02
❑ 56 Dale Craigwell .05 .02
❑ 57 Mike Eastwood .05 .02
❑ 58 Bernie Nicholls .05 .02
❑ 59 Travis Green .10 .05
❑ 60 Shjon Podein .05 .02
❑ 61 Darrin Madeley .05 .02
❑ 62 Dixon Ward .05 .02
❑ 63 Andre Faust .05 .02
❑ 64 Tony Amonte .10 .05
❑ 65 Joe Cirella .05 .02
❑ 66 Michel Petit .05 .02
❑ 67 David Lowry .05 .02
❑ 68 Shawn Chambers .05 .02
❑ 69 Joe Sakic .50 .23
❑ 70 Michael Nylander .05 .02
❑ 71 Peter Andersson .05 .02
❑ 72 Sandis Ozolinsh UER .10 .05
(Petri Skriko on back)
❑ 73 Joby Messier .05 .02
❑ 74 John Blue .10 .05
❑ 75 Pat Elynuik .05 .02
❑ 76 Keith Osborne .05 .02
❑ 77 Greg Adams .05 .02
❑ 78 Chris Gratton .10 .05
❑ 79 Louie DeBrusk .05 .02
❑ 80 Todd Harkins .05 .02
❑ 81 Neil Brady .05 .02
❑ 82 Philippe Boucher .05 .02
❑ 83 Darryl Sydor .05 .02
❑ 84 Oleg Petrov .05 .02
❑ 85 Andrei Kovalenko .05 .02
❑ 86 Dave Andreychuk .10 .05
❑ 87 Jeff Daniels .05 .02
❑ 88 Kevin Todd .05 .02
❑ 89 Mark Tinordi .05 .02
❑ 90 Garry Galley .05 .02
❑ 91 Shawn Burr .05 .02
❑ 92 Tom Pederson .05 .02
❑ 93 Warren Rychel .05 .02
❑ 94 Stu Barnes .05 .02
❑ 95 Peter Bondra .25 .11
❑ 96 Brian Skrudland .05 .02
❑ 97 Doug MacDonald .05 .02
❑ 98 Rob Niedermayer .10 .05
❑ 99 Wayne Gretzky 1.50 .70
❑ 100 Peter Taglianetti .05 .02
❑ 101 Don Sweeney .05 .02
❑ 102 Andrei Lomakin .05 .02
❑ 103 Checklist 1-103 .05 .02
❑ 104 Sergio Momesso .05 .02
❑ 105 Dave Archibald .05 .02
❑ 106 Karl Dykhuis .05 .02
❑ 107 Scott Mellanby .10 .05
❑ 108 Paul DiPietro .05 .02
❑ 109 Neal Broten .10 .05
❑ 110 Chris Terreri .10 .05
❑ 111 Craig MacTavish .05 .02
❑ 112 Jody Hull .05 .02
❑ 113 Philippe Bozon .05 .02
❑ 114 Geoff Courtnall .05 .02
❑ 115 Ed Olczyk .05 .02
❑ 116 Ray Bourque .25 .11
❑ 117 Gilbert Dionne .05 .02
❑ 118 Valeri Kamensky .10 .05

❑ 119 Scott Stevens .10 .05
❑ 120 Pelle Eklund .05 .02
❑ 121 Brian Bradley .05 .02
❑ 122 Steve Thomas .05 .02
❑ 123 Don Beaupre .10 .05
❑ 124 Joel Otto .05 .02
❑ 125 Arturs Irbe .10 .05
❑ 126 Kevin Stevens .05 .02
❑ 127 Dimitri Yushkevich .05 .02
❑ 128 Adam Graves .10 .05
❑ 129 Chris Chelios .25 .11
❑ 130 Jeff Brown .05 .02
❑ 131 Paul Ranheim .05 .02
❑ 132 Shayne Corson .05 .02
❑ 133 Curtis Leschyshyn .05 .02
❑ 134 John MacLean .10 .05
❑ 135 Dimitri Khristich .05 .02
❑ 136 Dino Ciccarelli .10 .05
❑ 137 Pat LaFontaine .10 .05
❑ 138 Patrick Poulin .05 .02
❑ 139 Jaromir Jagr .75 .35
❑ 140 Kevin Hatcher .05 .02
❑ 141 Christian Ruuttu .05 .02
❑ 142 Ulf Samuelsson .05 .02
❑ 143 Ted Donato .05 .02
❑ 144 Bob Essensa .10 .05
❑ 145 Dave Gagner .10 .05
❑ 146 Tony Granato .05 .02
❑ 147 Ed Belfour .25 .11
❑ 148 Kirk Muller .05 .02
❑ 149 Rob Gaudreau .05 .02
❑ 150 Nicklas Lidstrom .10 .05
❑ 151 Gary Roberts .05 .02
❑ 152 Trent Klatt .05 .02
❑ 153 Ray Ferraro .05 .02
❑ 154 Michal Pivonka .05 .02
❑ 155 Mike Foligno .05 .02
❑ 156 Kirk McLean .10 .05
❑ 157 Curtis Joseph .25 .11
❑ 158 Roman Hamrlik .05 .02
❑ 159 Felix Potvin .25 .11
❑ 160 Brett Hull .30 .14
❑ 161 Alexei Zhitnik UER .05 .02
(Listed as being drafted in 1990; should be 1991)
❑ 162 Alexei Zhamnov .10 .05
❑ 163 Grant Fuhr .10 .05
❑ 164 Nikolai Borschevsky .05 .02
❑ 165 Tomas Jelinek .05 .02
❑ 166 Thomas Steen .05 .02
❑ 167 John LeClair .40 .18
❑ 168 Vladimir Vujtek .05 .02
❑ 169 Richard Smehlik .05 .02
❑ 170 Alexandre Daigle .05 .02
❑ 171 Sergei Fedorov .50 .23
❑ 172 Steve Larmer .10 .05
❑ 173 Darius Kasparaitis .05 .02
❑ 174 Igor Kravchuk .05 .02
❑ 175 Owen Nolan .10 .05
❑ 176 Rob DiMaio .05 .02
❑ 177 Mike Vernon .10 .05
❑ 178 Alexander Semak .05 .02
❑ 179 Rick Tocchet .10 .05
❑ 180 Bill Ranford .10 .05
❑ 181 Sergei Zubov .05 .02
❑ 182 Tommy Soderstrom .10 .05
❑ 183 Al Iafrate .05 .02
❑ 184 Eric Desjardins .05 .02
❑ 185 Bret Hedican .05 .02
❑ 186 Joe Mullen .10 .05
❑ 187 Doug Bodger .05 .02
❑ 188 Tomas Sandstrom .05 .02
❑ 189 Glen Murray .05 .02
❑ 190 Chris Pronger .10 .05
❑ 191 Mike Craig .05 .02
❑ 192 Jim Paek .05 .02
❑ 193 Doug Zmolek .05 .02
❑ 194 Yves Racine .05 .02
❑ 195 Keith Tkachuk .30 .14
❑ 196 Chris Lindberg .05 .02
❑ 197 Kelly Buchberger .05 .02
❑ 198 Mark Janssens .05 .02
❑ 199 Peter Zezel .05 .02
❑ 200 Bob Probert .10 .05
❑ 201 Brad May .10 .05
❑ 202 Rob Zamuner .05 .02
❑ 203 Stephane Fiset .10 .05
❑ 204 Derian Hatcher .05 .02
❑ 205 Mike Gartner .10 .05
❑ 206 Checklist 104-206 .05 .02
❑ 207 Todd Krygier .05 .02
❑ 208 Glen Wesley .05 .02
❑ 209 Fredrik Olausson .05 .02
❑ 210 Patrick Flatley .05 .02
❑ 211 Cliff Ronning .05 .02
❑ 212 Kevin Dineen .05 .02
❑ 213 Zarley Zalapski .05 .02
❑ 214 Stephane Matteau .05 .02
❑ 215 Dave Ellett .05 .02
❑ 216 Kelly Hrudey .10 .05
❑ 217 Steve Duchesne .05 .02
❑ 218 Bobby Holik .05 .02
❑ 219 Brad Dalgarno .05 .02
❑ 220 Mats Sundin 100 CL .10 .05
❑ 221 Pat LaFontaine 100 .10 .05
❑ 222 Mark Recchi 100 .10 .05
❑ 223 Joe Sakic 100 .25 .11
❑ 224 Pierre Turgeon 100 .10 .05
❑ 225 Craig Janney 100 .10 .05
❑ 226 Adam Oates 100 .10 .05
❑ 227 Steve Yzerman 100 .40 .18
❑ 228 Mats Sundin 100 .10 .05
❑ 229 Theoren Fleury 100 .10 .05
❑ 230 Kevin Stevens 100 .10 .05
❑ 231 Luc Robitaille 100 .10 .05
❑ 232 Brett Hull 100 .10 .05
❑ 233 Rick Tocchet 100 .10 .05
❑ 234 Alexander Mogilny 100 .10 .05
❑ 235 Jeremy Roenick 100 .10 .05
❑ 236 Guy Leveque .05 .02
Turner Stevenson
SR CL
❑ 237 Adam Bennett SR .05 .02
❑ 238 Dody Wood SR .05 .02
❑ 239 Niclas Andersson SR .05 .02
❑ 240 Jason Bowen SR .05 .02
❑ 241 Steve Junker SR .05 .02
❑ 242 Bryan Smolinski SR .05 .02
❑ 243 Chris Simon SR .05 .02
❑ 244 Sergei Zholtok SR .05 .02
❑ 245 Dan Ratushny SR .05 .02
❑ 246 Guy Leveque SR .05 .02
❑ 247 Scott Thomas SR .05 .02
❑ 248 Turner Stevenson SR .05 .02
❑ 249 Dan Keczmer SR .05 .02
❑ 250 Alexandre Daigle WJC .05 .02
Checklist
❑ 251 Adrian Aucoin WJC .05 .02
❑ 252 Jason Smith .05 .02
❑ 253 Ralph Intranouvo WJC .05 .02
❑ 254 Jason Dawe .05 .02
❑ 255 Jeff Bes WJC .05 .02
❑ 256 Tyler Wright .05 .02
❑ 257 Martin Lapointe .05 .02
❑ 258 Jeff Shantz WJC .05 .02
❑ 259 Martin Gendron WJC .05 .02
❑ 260 Philippe DeRouville .05 .02
WJC
❑ 261 Frantisek Kaberle WJC .10 .05
❑ 262 Radim Bicanek WJC .10 .05
❑ 263 Tomas Klimt WJC .10 .05
❑ 264 Tomas Nemcicky WJC .10 .05
❑ 265 Richard Kapus WJC .10 .05
❑ 266 Patrik Krisak WJC .10 .05
❑ 267 Roman Kadera WJC .10 .05
❑ 268 Kimmo Timonen WJC .10 .05
❑ 269 Jukka Ollila WJC .10 .05
❑ 270 Tuomas Gronman .05 .02
❑ 271 Mikko Luovi WJC .10 .05
❑ 272 Sergei Gonchar WJC .05 .02
❑ 273 Maxim Golanov WJC .10 .05
❑ 274 Oleg Belov WJC .10 .05
❑ 275 Sergei Klimovich WJC .10 .05
❑ 276 Sergei Brylin WJC .05 .02
❑ 277 Alexei Yashin .05 .02
❑ 278 Vitali Tomilin WJC .10 .05
❑ 279 Alexander Cherbaev .05 .02
WJC
❑ 280 Eric Lindros ART .60 .25
❑ 281 Teemu Selanne ART .30 .14
❑ 282 Joe Juneau ART .10 .05
❑ 283 Vladimir Malakhov ART .05 .02
❑ 284 Scott Niedermayer ART .05 .02
❑ 285 Felix Potvin ART .10 .05
❑ 286 Adam Oates TL .10 .05
❑ 287 Pat LaFontaine TL .10 .05
❑ 288 Theoren Fleury TL .10 .05
❑ 289 Jeremy Roenick TL .10 .05
❑ 290 Steve Yzerman TL .40 .18
❑ 291 Petr Klima TL .05 .02
Doug Weight TL
❑ 292 Geoff Sanderson TL .10 .05
❑ 293 Luc Robitaille TL .10 .05
❑ 294 Mike Modano TL .10 .05
❑ 295 Vincent Damphousse TL .10 .05
❑ 296 Claude Lemieux TL .10 .05
❑ 297 Pierre Turgeon TL .10 .05
❑ 298 Mark Messier TL .10 .05
❑ 299 Norm Maciver TL .05 .02
❑ 300 Mark Recchi TL .10 .05
❑ 301 Mario Lemieux TL .60 .25
❑ 302 Mats Sundin TL .10 .05
❑ 303 Craig Janney TL .10 .05
❑ 304 Kelly Kisio TL .05 .02
❑ 305 Brian Bradley TL .05 .02
❑ 306 Doug Gilmour TL .10 .05
❑ 307 Pavel Bure TL .10 .05
❑ 308 Peter Bondra TL .10 .05
❑ 309 Teemu Selanne TL .30 .14
❑ 310 Checklist 207-310 .05 .02
❑ 311 Terry Yake .05 .02
❑ 312 Bob Sweeney .05 .02
❑ 313 Robert Reichel .05 .02
❑ 314 Jeremy Roenick .25 .11
❑ 315 Paul Coffey .25 .11
❑ 316 Geoff Sanderson .10 .05
❑ 317 Rob Blake .05 .02
❑ 318 Patrice Brisebois .05 .02
❑ 319 Jaroslav Modry .05 .02
❑ 320 Scott Lachance .05 .02
❑ 321 Glenn Healy .10 .05
❑ 322 Martin Gelinas .05 .02
❑ 323 Craig Janney .10 .05
❑ 324 Bill McDougall .05 .02
❑ 325 Shawn Antoski .05 .02
❑ 326 Olaf Kolzig .10 .05
❑ 327 Adam Oates .10 .05
❑ 328 Dirk Graham .05 .02
❑ 329 Brent Gilchrist .05 .02
❑ 330 Zdeno Ciger .05 .02
❑ 331 Pat Verbeek .05 .02
❑ 332 Jari Kurri .10 .05
❑ 333 Kevin Haller .05 .02
❑ 334 Martin Brodeur .75 .35
❑ 335 Norm Maciver .05 .02
❑ 336 Dominic Roussel .10 .05
❑ 337 Iain Fraser .05 .02
❑ 338 Vitali Karamnov .05 .02
❑ 339 Rene Corbet .05 .02
❑ 340 Wendel Clark .10 .05
❑ 341 Mike Ridley .05 .02
❑ 342 Nelson Emerson .05 .02
❑ 343 Joe Juneau .10 .05
❑ 344 Vesa Viitakoski .05 .02
❑ 345 Steve Chiasson .05 .02
❑ 346 Andrew Cassels .05 .02
❑ 347 Pierre Turgeon .10 .05
❑ 348 Brian Leetch .25 .11
❑ 349 Alexei Yashin .10 .05
❑ 350 Mark Recchi .10 .05
❑ 351 Ron Francis .10 .05
❑ 352 Mike Ricci .05 .02
❑ 353 Igor Korolev .05 .02
❑ 354 Brent Gretzky .05 .02
❑ 355 Dave Poulin .05 .02
❑ 356 Cam Neely .10 .05
❑ 357 Gary Suter .05 .02
❑ 358 Dave Manson .05 .02
❑ 359 Robert Kron .05 .02
❑ 360 Ulf Dahlen .05 .02
❑ 361 Rod Brind'Amour .10 .05
❑ 362 Alexei Gusarov .05 .02
❑ 363 Vitali Prokhorov .05 .02
❑ 364 Damian Rhodes .10 .05
❑ 365 Paul Ysebaert .05 .02
❑ 366 Vladimir Konstantinov .05 .02
❑ 367 Steven Rice .05 .02
❑ 368 Brian Propp .05 .02
❑ 369 Valeri Zelepukin .05 .02
❑ 370 David Volek .05 .02
❑ 371 Sergei Nemchinov .05 .02
❑ 372 Pavol Demitra .05 .02
❑ 373 Brent Fedyk .05 .02
❑ 374 Larry Murphy .10 .05
❑ 375 Dave Karpa .05 .02
❑ 376 Dave Babych .05 .02
❑ 377 Keith Jones .05 .02
❑ 378 Neil Wilkinson .05 .02
❑ 379 Jozef Stumpel .05 .02
❑ 380 Vincent Damphousse .10 .05
❑ 381 Tom Kurvers .05 .02
❑ 382 Doug Gilmour .25 .11
❑ 383 Trevor Linden .10 .05
❑ 384 Kelly Miller .05 .02
❑ 385 Tim Sweeney .05 .02
❑ 386 Mikhail Tatarinov .05 .02
❑ 387 Dominic Hasek .75 .35
❑ 388 Steve Yzerman .75 .35
❑ 389 Scott Pearson .05 .02
❑ 390 Brian Bellows .05 .02
❑ 391 Claude Lemieux .10 .05
❑ 392 Marty McInnis .05 .02
❑ 393 Jim Sandlak .05 .02
❑ 394 Jocelyn Thibault 1.00 .45
❑ 395 John Cullen .05 .02
❑ 396 Joe Nieuwendyk .10 .05
❑ 397 Mike Modano .30 .14
❑ 398 Ray Sheppard .10 .05
❑ 399 Trevor Kidd .10 .05
❑ 400 Checklist .05 .02
❑ 401 Frank Pietrangelo .10 .05
❑ 402 Stephan Lebeau .05 .02
❑ 403 Stephane Richer .10 .05
❑ 404 Greg Gilbert .05 .02
❑ 405 Dmitri Filimonov .05 .02
❑ 406 Vyachaslav Butsayev .05 .02
❑ 407 Mario Lemieux 1.25 .55
❑ 408 Kevin Miller .05 .02
❑ 409 John Tucker .05 .02
❑ 410 Murray Craven .05 .02
❑ 411 Dale Hawerchuk .10 .05
❑ 412 Al MacInnis .10 .05
❑ 413 Keith Primeau .10 .05
❑ 414 Luc Robitaille .10 .05
❑ 415 Benoit Brunet .05 .02
❑ 416 Tom Chorske .05 .02
❑ 417 Derek King .05 .02
❑ 418 Troy Mallette .05 .02
❑ 419 Mats Sundin .10 .05
❑ 420 Kent Manderville .05 .02
❑ 421 Kip Miller .05 .02
❑ 422 Jarkko Varvio .05 .02
❑ 423 Jason Arnott .75 .35
❑ 424 Craig Billington .10 .05
❑ 425 Stewart Malgunas .05 .02
❑ 426 Ron Tugnutt .10 .05
❑ 427 Alexei Kudashov .05 .02
❑ 428 Harijs Vitolinsh .05 .02
❑ 429 Bill Houlder .05 .02
❑ 430 Craig Simpson .05 .02
❑ 431 Wes Walz .05 .02
❑ 432 Micah Aivazoff .05 .02
❑ 433 Scott Levins .05 .02
❑ 434 Ron Hextall .10 .05
❑ 435 Fred Brathwaite .10 .05
❑ 436 Chad Penney .05 .02
❑ 437 Vlastimil Kroupa .05 .02
❑ 438 Troy Loney .05 .02
❑ 439 Matthew Barnaby .10 .05
❑ 440 Kevin Todd .05 .02
❑ 441 Paul Cavallini .05 .02
❑ 442 Doug Weight .10 .05
❑ 443 Evgeny Davydov .05 .02
❑ 444 Dominic Lavoie .05 .02
❑ 445 Peter Popovic .05 .02
❑ 446 Sergei Makarov .05 .02
❑ 447 Matt Martin .05 .02
❑ 448 Teemu Selanne .60 .25
❑ 449 Todd Ewen .05 .02
❑ 450 Sergei Petrenko .05 .02
❑ 451 Jeff Shantz .05 .02
❑ 452 Greg Johnson .05 .02
❑ 453 Brent Severyn .05 .02
❑ 454 Shawn McEachern .05 .02
❑ 455 Pierre Sevigny .05 .02
❑ 456 Benoit Hogue .05 .02
❑ 457 Esa Tikkanen .05 .02
❑ 458 Brian Glynn .05 .02
❑ 459 Doug Brown .05 .02
❑ 460 Mike Rathje .05 .02
❑ 461 Rudy Poeschek .05 .02
❑ 462 Jason Woolley .05 .02
❑ 463 Patrick Carnback .05 .02
❑ 464 Cam Stewart .05 .02
❑ 465 Petr Svoboda .05 .02
❑ 466 Ted Drury .05 .02
❑ 467 Ladislav Karabin .05 .02
❑ 468 Paul Broten .05 .02
❑ 469 Alexander Godynyuk .05 .02
❑ 470 Bob Jay .05 .02
❑ 471 Steve Larmer .10 .05
❑ 472 Jim Montgomery .05 .02
❑ 473 Darren Puppa .05 .02
❑ 474 Alexei Kasatonov .05 .02
❑ 475 Derek Plante .05 .02
❑ 476 German Titov .05 .02
❑ 477 Steve Dubinsky .05 .02
❑ 478 Andy Moog .10 .05
❑ 479 Aaron Ward .05 .02
❑ 480 Dean McAmmond .05 .02
❑ 481 Randy Gilhen .05 .02
❑ 482 Jason Muzzatti .10 .05
❑ 483 Corey Millen .05 .02
❑ 484 Alexander Karpovtsev .05 .02
❑ 485 Bill Huard .05 .02
❑ 486 Mikael Renberg .25 .11
❑ 487 Marty McSorley .05 .02
❑ 488 Alexander Mogilny .10 .05
❑ 489 Michal Sykora .05 .02
❑ 490 Checklist .05 .02
❑ 491 Tom Tilley .05 .02
❑ 492 Boris Mironov .05 .02
❑ 493 Sandy McCarthy .05 .02
❑ 494 Mark Astley .05 .02
❑ 495 Slava Kozlov .10 .05
❑ 496 Brian Benning .05 .02
❑ 497 Eric Weinrich .05 .02
❑ 498 Robert Burakovsky .05 .02
❑ 499 Patrick Lebeau .05 .02
❑ 500 Markus Naslund .05 .02
❑ 501 Jimmy Waite .10 .05
❑ 502 Denis Savard .10 .05
❑ 503 Jose Charbonneau .05 .02
❑ 504 Randy Burridge .05 .02
❑ 505 Arto Blomsten .05 .02
❑ 506 Shaun Van Allen .05 .02
❑ 507 Jon Casey .10 .05
❑ 508 Darren McCarty .30 .14
❑ 509 Roman Oksiuta .05 .02
❑ 510 Jody Hull .05 .02
❑ 511 Scott Scissons .05 .02
❑ 512 Jeff Norton .05 .02
❑ 513 Dmitri Mironov .05 .02
❑ 514 Sergei Bautin .05 .02
❑ 515 Garry Valk .05 .02
❑ 516 Keith Carney .05 .02
❑ 517 James Black .05 .02
❑ 518 Pat Peake .05 .02
❑ 519 Chris Osgood 1.50 .70
❑ 520 Kirk Maltby .05 .02
❑ 521 Gord Murphy .05 .02
❑ 522 Mattias Norstrom .05 .02
❑ 523 Milos Holan .05 .02
❑ 524 Dave McLlwain .05 .02
❑ 525 Phil Housley .10 .05
❑ 526 Petr Klima .05 .02
❑ 527 John McIntyre .05 .02
❑ 528 Enrico Ciccone .05 .02
❑ 529 Stephane Quintal .05 .02
❑ 530 World Junior .10 .05
Checklist
❑ 531 Anson Carter .25 .11
❑ 532 Jeff Friesen .60 .25
❑ 533 Yanick Dube .05 .02
❑ 534 Jason Botterill .25 .11
❑ 535 Todd Harvey .05 .02
❑ 536 Manny Fernandez .10 .05
❑ 537 Jason Allison .50 .23
❑ 538 Jamie Storr .40 .18
❑ 539 Rick Girrard .05 .02
❑ 540 Martin Gendron .05 .02
❑ 541 Joel Bouchard .05 .02
❑ 542 Mike Peca 1.00 .45
❑ 543 Nick Stajduhar .05 .02
❑ 544 Brendan Witt .05 .02
❑ 545 Aaron Gavey .05 .02
❑ 546 Chris Armstrong .05 .02
❑ 547 Curtis Bowen .05 .02
❑ 548 Brandon Convery .05 .02
❑ 549 Bryan McCabe .30 .14
❑ 550 Marty Murray .05 .02
❑ 551 Ryan Sittler .05 .02
❑ 552 Jason McBain .05 .02
❑ 553 Richard Park .05 .02
❑ 554 Aaron Ellis .10 .05
❑ 555 Toby Kvalevog .10 .05
❑ 556 Jay Pandolfo .05 .02
❑ 557 John Emmons .05 .02
❑ 558 David Wilkie .05 .02
❑ 559 John Varga .05 .02
❑ 560 Jason Bonsignore .05 .02
❑ 561 Blake Sloan .05 .02
❑ 562 Adam Deadmarsh .10 .05
❑ 563 Jon Coleman .05 .02
❑ 564 Bob Lachance .05 .02
❑ 565 Chris O'Sullivan .05 .02
❑ 566 Jamie Langenbrunner .75 .35
❑ 567 Kevin Hilton .05 .02
❑ 568 Kevyn Adams .05 .02
❑ 569 Saku Koivu 1.25 .55
❑ 570 Mats Lindgren .05 .02
❑ 571 Nikolai Tsulygin .05 .02
❑ 572 Edvin Frylen .05 .02
❑ 573 Jaroslav Miklenda .10 .05
❑ 574 Vadim Sharifjanov .10 .05
❑ 575 Checklist Card .05 .02
❑ *99B W.Gretzky 802 Silver 25.00 11.00
❑ *99B W.Gretzky 802 Gold 10.00 4.50
❑ SP4 Teemu Selanne Hologram 3.00 1.35

## 1993-94 Upper Deck Award Winners

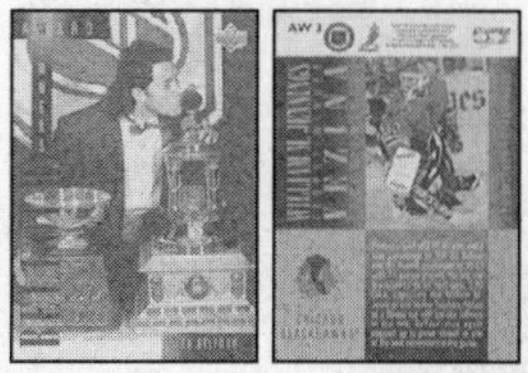

Randomly inserted at a rate of 1:30 Canadian first-series foil packs, this eight-card set measures the standard size. The fronts feature a black-and-white photo of the player and his trophy. The player's name appears at the bottom and in silver-foil letters on the left side. The backs carry a color action photo, along with the player's name, position, profile, team logo and the name of the trophy. The cards are numbered on the back with an "AW" prefix.

| | MINT | NRMT |
|---|---|---|
| COMPLETE SET (8) | 40.00 | 18.00 |
| COMMON CARD (AW1-AW8) | 2.00 | .90 |

❑ AW1 Mario Lemieux 15.00 6.75
Hart Trophy
Art Ross Trophy
Lester B. Pearson Award
Bill Master Trophy
❑ AW2 Teemu Selanne 8.00 3.60
Calder Trophy
❑ AW3 Ed Belfour 3.00 1.35
Jennings Trophy
Vezina Trophy
❑ AW4 Patrick Roy 15.00 6.75
Conn Smythe Trophy
❑ AW5 Chris Chelios 3.00 1.35
Jack Norris Trophy
❑ AW6 Doug Gilmour 3.00 1.35
Frank J. Selke Trophy
❑ AW7 Pierre Turgeon 3.00 1.35
Lady Byng Trophy
❑ AW8 Dave Poulin 2.00 .90
King Clancy

## 1993-94 Upper Deck Future Heroes

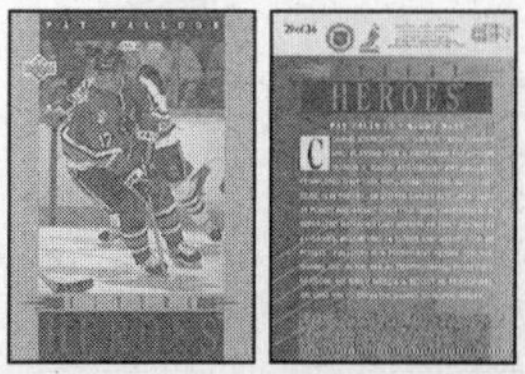

Randomly inserted at a rate of 1:30 first-series U.S. hobby packs, this 10-card set measures the standard size. The tan-bordered fronts feature sepia-toned action player photos with the player's name in white lettering within a black bar above the photo. The set's title appears below the photo, with the word "Heroes" printed in copper foil. On a gray background, the back carries a player profile. The cards are numbered on the back and continue where the Howe Heroes left off.

| | MINT | NRMT |
|---|---|---|
| COMPLETE SET (10) | 120.00 | 55.00 |
| COMMON CARD (28-36) | 4.00 | 1.80 |

❑ 28 Felix Potvin 6.00 2.70
❑ 29 Pat Falloon 4.00 1.80
❑ 30 Pavel Bure 15.00 6.75
❑ 31 Eric Lindros 25.00 11.00
❑ 32 Teemu Selanne 15.00 6.75
❑ 33 Jaromir Jagr 20.00 9.00
❑ 34 Alexander Mogilny 5.00 2.20
❑ 35 Joe Juneau 5.00 2.20
❑ 36 Checklist 20.00 9.00
❑ NNO Header Card 10.00 4.50

## 1993-94 Upper Deck Gretzky's Great Ones

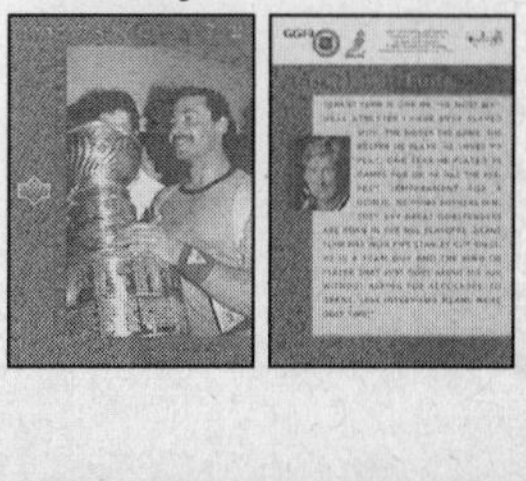

Randomly inserted in series one packs and one per series one jumbo, this 10-card set measures the standard size. The fronts feature color player photos with blue and gray bars above, below, and to the left. The player's name and the words "Gretzky's Great Ones" in copper-foil letters appear below and above the photo, respectively. The backs carry a small head shot of Wayne Gretzky along with his comments on the featured player. The cards are numbered on the back with a "GG" prefix.

| | MINT | NRMT |
|---|---|---|
| COMPLETE SET (10) | 10.00 | 4.50 |
| COMMON CARD (GG1-GG10) | .60 | .25 |

| | | |
|---|---|---|
| ❑ GG1 Denis Savard | .60 | .25 |
| ❑ GG2 Chris Chelios | 1.00 | .45 |
| ❑ GG3 Brett Hull | 1.25 | .55 |
| ❑ GG4 Mario Lemieux | 5.00 | 2.20 |
| ❑ GG5 Mark Messier | 1.25 | .55 |
| ❑ GG6 Paul Coffey | 1.00 | .45 |
| ❑ GG7 Theoren Fleury | .60 | .25 |
| ❑ GG8 Luc Robitaille | .60 | .25 |
| ❑ GG9 Marty McSorley | .60 | .25 |
| ❑ GG10 Grant Fuhr | .60 | .25 |

## 1993-94 Upper Deck Hat Tricks

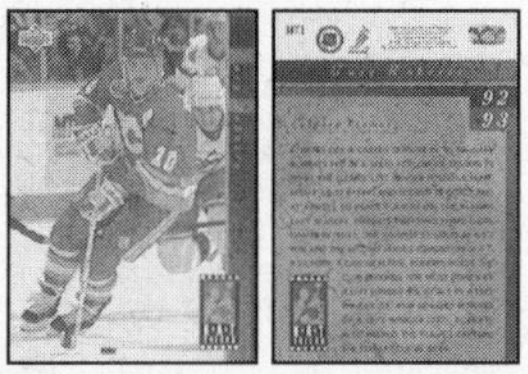

Inserted one per series one jumbo pack, this 20-card set measures the standard size. The fronts feature color player photos that are borderless, except on the right, where a strip that fades from brown to black carries the player's name. The backs carry the player's name, team name, and description of his hat trick performances. The cards are numbered on the back with an "HT" prefix.

| | MINT | NRMT |
|---|---|---|
| COMPLETE SET (20) | 10.00 | 4.50 |
| COMMON CARD (HT1-HT20) | .25 | .11 |

| | | |
|---|---|---|
| ❑ HT1 Adam Graves | .50 | .23 |
| ❑ HT2 Geoff Sanderson | .50 | .23 |
| ❑ HT3 Gary Roberts | .25 | .11 |
| ❑ HT4 Robert Reichel | .25 | .11 |
| ❑ HT5 Adam Oates | .50 | .23 |
| ❑ HT6 Steve Yzerman | 2.50 | 1.10 |
| ❑ HT7 Alexei Kovalev | .50 | .23 |
| ❑ HT8 Vincent Damphousse | .50 | .23 |
| ❑ HT9 Rob Gaudreau | .25 | .11 |
| ❑ HT10 Pat LaFontaine | .50 | .23 |
| ❑ HT11 Pierre Turgeon | .50 | .23 |
| ❑ HT12 Rick Tocchet | .25 | .11 |
| ❑ HT13 Michael Nylander | .25 | .11 |
| ❑ HT14 Steve Larmer | .25 | .11 |
| ❑ HT15 Alexander Mogilny | .50 | .23 |
| ❑ HT16 Owen Nolan | .25 | .11 |
| ❑ HT17 Luc Robitaille | .50 | .23 |
| ❑ HT18 Jeremy Roenick | .75 | .35 |
| ❑ HT19 Kevin Stevens | .25 | .11 |
| ❑ HT20 Mats Sundin | .50 | .23 |

## 1993-94 Upper Deck Next In Line

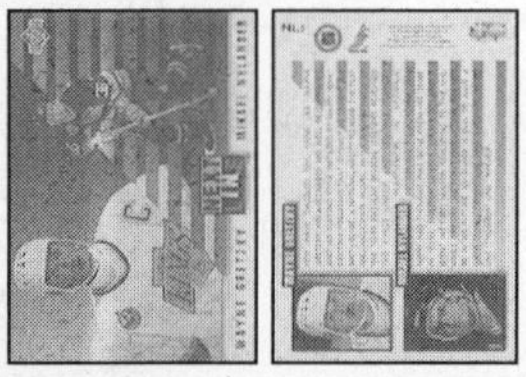

Randomly inserted in all first-series packs, this six-card set measures the standard-size. The horizontal metallic and prismatic fronts feature photos of two NHL players, diagonally divided in the middle. The players' names appear under the photos. The horizontal backs carry small head shots of both players, along with player profiles. The cards are numbered on the back with an "NL" prefix.

| | MINT | NRMT |
|---|---|---|
| COMPLETE SET (6) | 15.00 | 6.75 |
| COMMON PAIR (NL1-NL6) | 2.00 | .90 |

| | | |
|---|---|---|
| ❑ NL1 Wayne Gretzky<br>Michael Nylander | 6.00 | 2.70 |
| ❑ NL2 Brett Hull<br>Patrick Poulin | 2.00 | .90 |
| ❑ NL3 Steve Yzerman<br>Joe Sakic | 5.00 | 2.20 |
| ❑ NL4 Ray Bourque<br>Brian Leetch | 2.00 | .90 |
| ❑ NL5 Doug Gilmour<br>Keith Tkachuk | 3.00 | 1.35 |
| ❑ NL6 Patrick Roy<br>Felix Potvin | 6.00 | 2.70 |

## 1993-94 Upper Deck NHL's Best

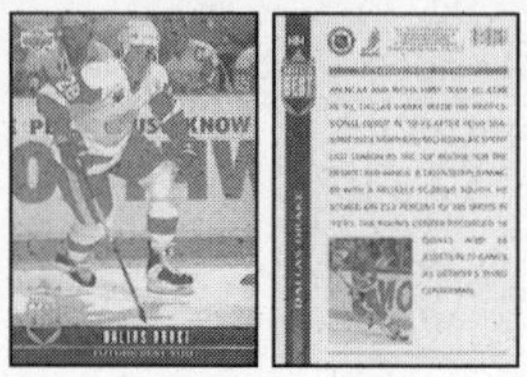

Randomly inserted at a rate of 1:30 first-series U.S. retail packs, this 10-card set measures the standard size. The fronts feature color action player photos that are borderless, except at the bottom, where a black bar carries the player's name. On a white background, the backs carry a small color action player photo, along with career highlights. The player's name appears vertically in the black bar to the left. The cards are numbered on the back with an "HB" prefix.

| | MINT | NRMT |
|---|---|---|
| COMPLETE SET (10) | 120.00 | 55.00 |
| COMMON CARD (HB1-HB10) | 4.00 | 1.80 |

| | | |
|---|---|---|
| ❑ HB1 Alexander Mogilny | 5.00 | 2.20 |
| ❑ HB2 Rob Gaudreau | 4.00 | 1.80 |
| ❑ HB3 Brett Hull | 10.00 | 4.50 |
| ❑ HB4 Dallas Drake | 4.00 | 1.80 |
| ❑ HB5 Pavel Bure | 12.00 | 5.50 |
| ❑ HB6 Alexei Kovalev | 4.00 | 1.80 |
| ❑ HB7 Mario Lemieux | 30.00 | 13.50 |
| ❑ HB8 Eric Lindros | 25.00 | 11.00 |
| ❑ HB9 Wayne Gretzky | 40.00 | 18.00 |
| ❑ HB10 Joe Juneau | 4.00 | 1.80 |

## 1993-94 Upper Deck Program of Excellence

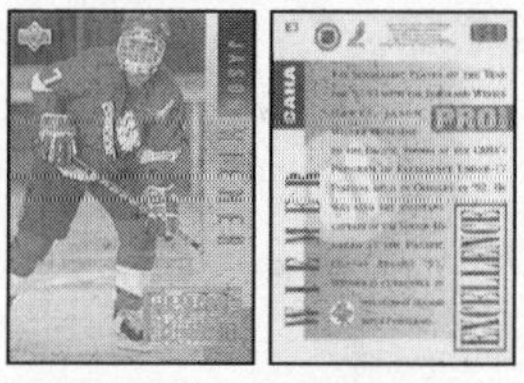

Randomly inserted at a rate of 1:30 Canadian second series packs, this 15-card set measures the standard size. The fronts feature color action player photos that are borderless, except at the right, where the margin carries the player's name in silver-foil letters. The silver-foil "Program of Excellence" logo rests at the lower right. The backs carry the player's name and career highlights. The cards are numbered on the back with an "E" prefix.

| | MINT | NRMT |
|---|---|---|
| COMPLETE SET (15) | 250.00 | 110.00 |
| COMMON CARD (E1-E15) | 8.00 | 3.60 |

| | | |
|---|---|---|
| ❑ E1 Adam Smith | 8.00 | 3.60 |
| ❑ E2 Jason Podollan | 10.00 | 4.50 |
| ❑ E3 Jason Wiemer | 10.00 | 4.50 |
| ❑ E4 Jeff O'Neill | 15.00 | 6.75 |
| ❑ E5 Daniel Goneau | 15.00 | 6.75 |
| ❑ E6 Christian Laflamme | 8.00 | 3.60 |
| ❑ E7 Daymond Langkow | 15.00 | 6.75 |
| ❑ E8 Jeff Friesen | 15.00 | 6.75 |
| ❑ E9 Wayne Primeau | 10.00 | 4.50 |
| ❑ E10 Paul Kariya | 60.00 | 27.00 |
| ❑ E11 Rob Niedermayer | 15.00 | 6.75 |
| ❑ E12 Eric Lindros | 50.00 | 22.00 |
| ❑ E13 Mario Lemieux | 60.00 | 27.00 |
| ❑ E14 Steve Yzerman | 40.00 | 18.00 |
| ❑ E15 Alexandre Daigle | 15.00 | 6.75 |

## 1993-94 Upper Deck Silver Skates

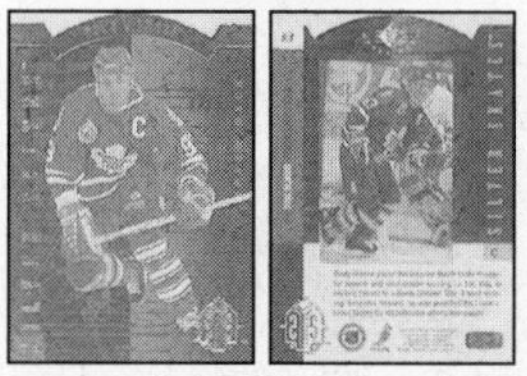

The first ten standard-size die-cut cards (H1-H10) listed below were randomly inserted in U.S. second-series hobby packs, while the second ten (R1-R10) were inserted in U.S. retail packs. The fronts feature color player action cutouts set on red and black backgrounds. The player's name appears in black lettering within the die-cut silver-foil top edge. The back carries a color action shot and career highlights. The trade cards were randomly inserted in both hobby and jumbo packs and could be redeemed for a silver or gold retail set. These cards picture Gretzky, and because the majority were redeemed, they have become highly sought after in their own right.

| | MINT | NRMT |
|---|---|---|
| COMPLETE HOBBY SET (10) | 60.00 | 27.00 |
| COMMON CARD (H1-H10) | 2.00 | .90 |
| COMPLETE RETAIL SET (10) | 60.00 | 27.00 |
| COMMON CARD (R1-R10) | 2.00 | .90 |
| COMP.GOLD EXCH.SET (10) | 100.00 | 45.00 |

*RETAIL GOLD EXCH: .75X TO 1.5X BASIC SILVER SKATES

| | | |
|---|---|---|
| ❑ H1 Mario Lemieux | 15.00 | 6.75 |
| ❑ H2 Pavel Bure | 6.00 | 2.70 |
| ❑ H3 Eric Lindros | 12.00 | 5.50 |
| ❑ H4 Rob Niedermayer | 2.00 | .90 |
| ❑ H5 Chris Pronger | 2.00 | .90 |
| ❑ H6 Adam Oates | 3.00 | 1.35 |
| ❑ H7 Pierre Turgeon | 3.00 | 1.35 |
| ❑ H8 Alexei Yashin | 2.00 | .90 |
| ❑ H9 Joe Sakic | 8.00 | 3.60 |
| ❑ H10 Alexander Mogilny | 3.00 | 1.35 |
| ❑ R1 Wayne Gretzky | 20.00 | 9.00 |
| ❑ R2 Teemu Selanne | 6.00 | 2.70 |
| ❑ R3 Alexandre Daigle | 2.00 | .90 |
| ❑ R4 Chris Gratton | 2.00 | .90 |
| ❑ R5 Brett Hull | 4.00 | 1.80 |
| ❑ R6 Steve Yzerman | 10.00 | 4.50 |
| ❑ R7 Doug Gilmour | 3.00 | 1.35 |
| ❑ R8 Jaromir Jagr | 12.00 | 5.50 |
| ❑ R9 Jason Arnott | 3.00 | 1.35 |
| ❑ R10 Jeremy Roenick | 4.00 | 1.80 |

## 1993-94 Upper Deck SP

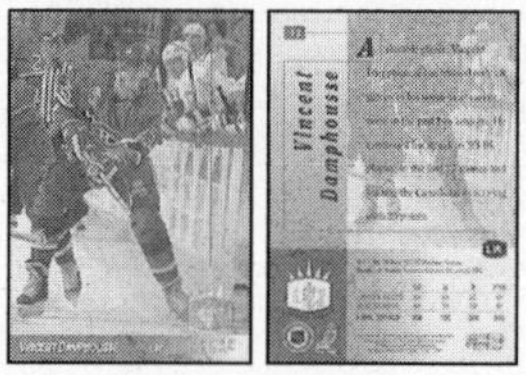

Inserted one per second-series pack and two per second-series jumbo, these 180 standard-size cards feature color player action shots on their fronts. The photos are borderless, except at the bottom, where a team color-coded margin carries the player's name and position in white lettering. The player's team name appears in a silver-foil arc above him. The silver-foil set logo rests at the lower right. The back carries a ghosted and team color-screened action shot at the upper right, overprinted with player profile. Biography and statistics appear below. The cards are numbered on the back, and grouped alphabetically within teams.

| | MINT | NRMT |
|---|---|---|
| COMPLETE SET (180) | 75.00 | 34.00 |
| COMMON CARD (1-180) | .25 | .11 |

| | | |
|---|---|---|
| ❑ 1 Sean Hill | .25 | .11 |
| ❑ 2 Troy Loney | .25 | .11 |
| ❑ 3 Joe Sacco | .25 | .11 |
| ❑ 4 Anatoli Semenov | .25 | .11 |
| ❑ 5 Ron Tugnutt | .40 | .18 |
| ❑ 6 Terry Yake | .25 | .11 |
| ❑ 7 Ray Bourque | .75 | .35 |
| ❑ 8 Jon Casey | .40 | .18 |
| ❑ 9 Joe Juneau | .40 | .18 |
| ❑ 10 Cam Neely | .40 | .18 |
| ❑ 11 Adam Oates | .40 | .18 |
| ❑ 12 Bryan Smolinski | .40 | .18 |
| ❑ 13 Matthew Barnaby | .40 | .18 |
| ❑ 14 Philippe Boucher | .25 | .11 |
| ❑ 15 Grant Fuhr | .40 | .18 |
| ❑ 16 Dale Hawerchuk | .40 | .18 |
| ❑ 17 Pat LaFontaine | .40 | .18 |
| ❑ 18 Alexander Mogilny | .40 | .18 |
| ❑ 19 Craig Simpson | .25 | .11 |
| ❑ 20 Ted Drury | .25 | .11 |
| ❑ 21 Theoren Fleury | .40 | .18 |
| ❑ 22 Al MacInnis | .40 | .18 |
| ❑ 23 Joe Nieuwendyk | .40 | .18 |
| ❑ 24 Joel Otto | .25 | .11 |
| ❑ 25 Gary Roberts | .25 | .11 |
| ❑ 26 Vesa Viitakoski | .25 | .11 |
| ❑ 27 Ed Belfour | .75 | .35 |
| ❑ 28 Chris Chelios | .75 | .35 |
| ❑ 29 Joe Murphy | .25 | .11 |
| ❑ 30 Patrick Poulin | .25 | .11 |
| ❑ 31 Jeremy Roenick | .75 | .35 |
| ❑ 32 Jeff Shantz | .25 | .11 |
| ❑ 33 Kevin Todd | .25 | .11 |
| ❑ 34 Neal Broten | .25 | .11 |
| ❑ 35 Paul Cavallini | .25 | .11 |
| ❑ 36 Russ Courtnall | .25 | .11 |
| ❑ 37 Derian Hatcher | .25 | .11 |
| ❑ 38 Mike Modano | 1.50 | .70 |
| ❑ 39 Andy Moog | .40 | .18 |
| ❑ 40 Jarkko Varvio | .25 | .11 |
| ❑ 41 Dino Ciccarelli | .25 | .11 |
| ❑ 42 Paul Coffey | .75 | .35 |
| ❑ 43 Dallas Drake | .25 | .11 |
| ❑ 44 Sergei Fedorov | 2.50 | 1.10 |
| ❑ 45 Keith Primeau | .40 | .18 |
| ❑ 46 Bob Probert | .25 | .11 |
| ❑ 47 Steve Yzerman | 4.00 | 1.80 |
| ❑ 48 Jason Arnott | 2.00 | .90 |
| ❑ 49 Shayne Corson | .25 | .11 |
| ❑ 50 Dave Manson | .25 | .11 |
| ❑ 51 Dean McAmmond | .25 | .11 |
| ❑ 52 Bill Ranford | .40 | .18 |
| ❑ 53 Doug Weight | .40 | .18 |
| ❑ 54 Brad Werenka | .25 | .11 |
| ❑ 55 Egeny Davydov | .25 | .11 |
| ❑ 56 Scott Levins | .25 | .11 |
| ❑ 57 Scott Mellanby | .40 | .18 |
| ❑ 58 Rob Niedermayer | .40 | .18 |
| ❑ 59 Brian Skrudland | .25 | .11 |
| ❑ 60 John Vanbiesbrouck | 2.00 | .90 |
| ❑ 61 Robert Kron | .25 | .11 |
| ❑ 62 Michael Nylander | .25 | .11 |
| ❑ 63 Robert Petrovicky | .25 | .11 |
| ❑ 64 Chris Pronger | .40 | .18 |
| ❑ 65 Geoff Sanderson | .40 | .18 |
| ❑ 66 Darren Turcotte | .25 | .11 |
| ❑ 67 Pat Verbeek | .25 | .11 |
| ❑ 68 Rob Blake | .25 | .11 |
| ❑ 69 Tony Granato | .25 | .11 |
| ❑ 70 Wayne Gretzky | 10.00 | 4.50 |
| ❑ 71 Kelly Hrudey | .40 | .18 |
| ❑ 72 Shawn McEachern | .25 | .11 |
| ❑ 73 Luc Robitaille | .40 | .18 |
| ❑ 74 Darryl Sydor | .25 | .11 |
| ❑ 75 Alexei Zhitnik | .25 | .11 |
| ❑ 76 Brian Bellows | .25 | .11 |
| ❑ 77 Vincent Damphousse | .40 | .18 |
| ❑ 78 Stephan Lebeau | .25 | .11 |
| ❑ 79 John LeClair | 2.00 | .90 |
| ❑ 80 Kirk Muller | .25 | .11 |
| ❑ 81 Patrick Roy | 6.00 | 2.70 |
| ❑ 82 Pierre Sevigny | .25 | .11 |
| ❑ 83 Claude Lemieux | .40 | .18 |
| ❑ 84 Corey Millen | .25 | .11 |
| ❑ 85 Bernie Nicholls | .25 | .11 |
| ❑ 86 Scott Niedermayer | .40 | .18 |
| ❑ 87 Stephane Richer | .25 | .11 |
| ❑ 88 Alexander Semak | .25 | .11 |
| ❑ 89 Scott Stevens | .25 | .11 |
| ❑ 90 Ray Ferraro | .25 | .11 |
| ❑ 91 Darius Kasparaitis | .25 | .11 |
| ❑ 92 Scott Lachance | .25 | .11 |
| ❑ 93 Vladimir Malakhov | .25 | .11 |
| ❑ 94 Scott Scissons | .25 | .11 |
| ❑ 95 Steve Thomas | .25 | .11 |
| ❑ 96 Pierre Turgeon | .40 | .18 |
| ❑ 97 Tony Amonte | .40 | .18 |
| ❑ 98 Mike Gartner | .40 | .18 |
| ❑ 99 Adam Graves | .40 | .18 |
| ❑ 100 Alexander Karpovtsev | .25 | .11 |
| ❑ 101 Alexei Kovalev | .40 | .18 |
| ❑ 102 Brian Leetch | .75 | .35 |
| ❑ 103 Mark Messier | 1.50 | .70 |
| ❑ 104 Esa Tikkanen | .25 | .11 |
| ❑ 105 Craig Billington | .40 | .18 |
| ❑ 106 Robert Burakovsky | .25 | .11 |
| ❑ 107 Alexandre Daigle | .40 | .18 |
| ❑ 108 Pavol Demitra | .25 | .11 |
| ❑ 109 Dmitri Filimonov | .25 | .11 |
| ❑ 110 Bob Kudelski | .25 | .11 |
| ❑ 111 Norm Maciver | .25 | .11 |
| ❑ 112 Alexei Yashin | .40 | .18 |
| ❑ 113 Josef Beranek | .25 | .11 |
| ❑ 114 Rod Brind'Amour | .40 | .18 |
| ❑ 115 Milos Holan | .25 | .11 |
| ❑ 116 Eric Lindros | 5.00 | 2.20 |
| ❑ 117 Mark Recchi | .40 | .18 |
| ❑ 118 Mikael Renberg | .40 | .18 |
| ❑ 119 Dimitri Yushkevich | .25 | .11 |
| ❑ 120 Tom Barrasso | .40 | .18 |
| ❑ 121 Jaromir Jagr | 4.00 | 1.80 |
| ❑ 122 Mario Lemieux | 6.00 | 2.70 |
| ❑ 123 Markus Naslund | .25 | .11 |
| ❑ 124 Kevin Stevens | .40 | .18 |
| ❑ 125 Martin Straka | .25 | .11 |
| ❑ 126 Rick Tocchet | .40 | .18 |
| ❑ 127 Martin Gelinas | .25 | .11 |
| ❑ 128 Owen Nolan | .25 | .11 |
| ❑ 129 Mike Ricci | .40 | .18 |
| ❑ 130 Joe Sakic | 2.50 | 1.10 |
| ❑ 131 Chris Simon | .25 | .11 |
| ❑ 132 Mats Sundin | .40 | .18 |
| ❑ 133 Jocelyn Thibault | 2.50 | 1.10 |
| ❑ 134 Philippe Bozon | .25 | .11 |
| ❑ 135 Jeff Brown | .25 | .11 |
| ❑ 136 Phil Housley | .25 | .11 |
| ❑ 137 Brett Hull | 1.50 | .70 |
| ❑ 138 Craig Janney | .40 | .18 |
| ❑ 139 Curtis Joseph | .75 | .35 |
| ❑ 140 Brendan Shanahan | 2.50 | 1.10 |
| ❑ 141 Pat Falloon | .25 | .11 |
| ❑ 142 Johan Garpenlov | .25 | .11 |
| ❑ 143 Rob Gaudreau | .25 | .11 |
| ❑ 144 Vlastimil Kroupa | .25 | .11 |
| ❑ 145 Sergei Makarov | .25 | .11 |
| ❑ 146 Sandis Ozolinsh | .40 | .18 |
| ❑ 147 Mike Rathje | .25 | .11 |
| ❑ 148 Brian Bradley | .25 | .11 |
| ❑ 149 Chris Gratton | .40 | .18 |
| ❑ 150 Brent Gretzky | .25 | .11 |
| ❑ 151 Roman Hamrlik | .40 | .18 |
| ❑ 152 Petr Klima | .25 | .11 |
| ❑ 153 Denis Savard | .25 | .11 |
| ❑ 154 Rob Zamuner | .25 | .11 |
| ❑ 155 Dave Andreychuk | .40 | .18 |
| ❑ 156 Nikolai Borschevsky | .25 | .11 |
| ❑ 157 Dave Ellett | .25 | .11 |
| ❑ 158 Doug Gilmour | .40 | .18 |
| ❑ 159 Alexei Kudashov | .25 | .11 |
| ❑ 160 Felix Potvin | .75 | .35 |
| ❑ 161 Greg Adams | .25 | .11 |
| ❑ 162 Pavel Bure | 2.50 | 1.10 |
| ❑ 163 Geoff Courtnall | .25 | .11 |
| ❑ 164 Trevor Linden | .40 | .18 |
| ❑ 165 Kirk McLean | .40 | .18 |
| ❑ 166 Jiri Slegr | .25 | .11 |
| ❑ 167 Dixon Ward | .25 | .11 |
| ❑ 168 Peter Bondra | .40 | .18 |
| ❑ 169 Kevin Hatcher | .25 | .11 |
| ❑ 170 Al Lafrate | .25 | .11 |
| ❑ 171 Dimitri Khristich | .25 | .11 |
| ❑ 172 Pat Peake | .25 | .11 |
| ❑ 173 Mike Ridley | .25 | .11 |
| ❑ 174 Arto Blomsten | .25 | .11 |
| ❑ 175 Nelson Emerson | .25 | .11 |
| ❑ 176 Boris Mironov | .25 | .11 |
| ❑ 177 Teemu Selanne | 3.00 | 1.35 |
| ❑ 178 Keith Tkachuk | 1.50 | .70 |
| ❑ 179 Paul Ysebaert | .25 | .11 |
| ❑ 180 Alexei Zhamnov | .40 | .18 |

## 1993-94 Upper Deck Gretzky Box Bottom

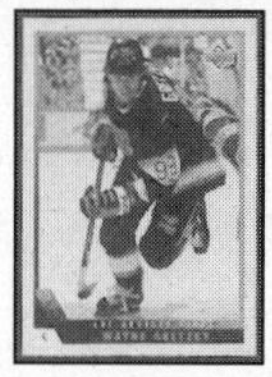

Issued on the bottom of Upper Deck boxes, this card measures approximately 5" by 7" and features Wayne Gretzky on the front. The design is the same as his regular issue card. The back is blank. The card is unnumbered.

| | MINT | NRMT |
|---|---|---|
| COMPLETE SET (1) | 1.00 | .45 |
| COMMON CARD | 1.00 | .45 |

| | | |
|---|---|---|
| ❑ 1 Wayne Gretzky | 1.00 | .45 |

## 1993-94 Upper Deck Gretzky Sheet

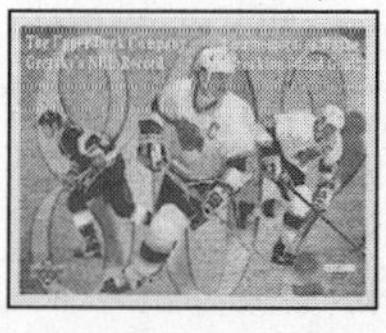

This sheet was mailed to collectors who ordered Wayne Gretzky's 24-Karat Gold Card commemorating his NHL record breaking 802nd goal after Upper Deck had unexpected production difficulties. It could also be ordered through the Upper Deck Authenticated catalog. It measures 8 1/2" by 11". The front features a white border and three color action photos of Wayne Gretzky set against a background with the number "802". A seal on the front carries the serial number and the production figure (30,000). The back is blank.

| | MINT | NRMT |
|---|---|---|
| COMPLETE SET (1) | 20.00 | 9.00 |
| COMMON SHEET | 20.00 | 9.00 |

| | | |
|---|---|---|
| ❑ 1 Upper Deck Commemorates<br>Wayne Gretzky's NHL<br>Record 802nd Goal | 20.00 | 9.00 |

## 1993-94 Upper Deck NHLPA/Roots

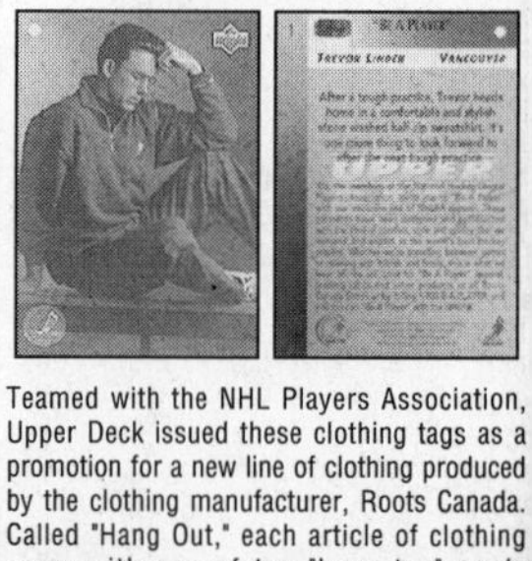

Teamed with the NHL Players Association, Upper Deck issued these clothing tags as a promotion for a new line of clothing produced by the clothing manufacturer, Roots Canada. Called "Hang Out," each article of clothing came with one of ten "hang tag" cards featuring on their fronts a full-bleed photo of the NHL player wearing the clothing. The clothing tags measure the standard size and are punchholed in the upper left corner. Versions of these cards without the punchhole also exist. With a faded and enlarged Upper Deck logo, the backs carry the player's name and an advertisement for the NHLPA apparel. The cards are numbered on the back. The

entire set could also be purchased by mail. The first series came out in 1993, while the second series came out in 1994. Reportedly 5,000 sets of the third series were produced. The backs of cards 21-30 also have a NHLPA apparel advertisement but sport a different design than cards 1-20.

| | MINT | NRMT |
|---|---|---|
| COMPLETE SET (30) | 40.00 | 18.00 |
| COMPLETE SERIES 1 (10) | 15.00 | 6.75 |
| COMPLETE SERIES 2 (10) | 12.00 | 5.50 |
| COMPLETE SERIES 3 (10) | 14.00 | 6.25 |
| COMMON CARD (1-30) | .25 | .11 |

| | | |
|---|---|---|
| ❑ 1 Trevor Linden | .50 | .23 |
| ❑ 2 Patrick Roy | 8.00 | 3.60 |
| ❑ 3 Felix Potvin | 1.50 | .70 |
| ❑ 4 Steve Yzerman | 5.00 | 2.20 |
| ❑ 5 Doug Gilmour | 1.50 | .70 |
| ❑ 6 Wendel Clark | .75 | .35 |
| ❑ 7 Kirk McLean | .35 | .16 |
| ❑ 8 Larry Murphy | .25 | .11 |
| ❑ 9 Guy Carbonneau | .25 | .11 |
| ❑ 10 Mike Ricci | .25 | .11 |
| ❑ 11 Doug Gilmour | 1.50 | .70 |
| ❑ 12 Sergei Fedorov | 3.00 | 1.35 |
| ❑ 13 Shayne Corson | .35 | .16 |
| ❑ 14 Alexei Yashin | 1.50 | .70 |
| ❑ 15 Pavel Bure | 3.00 | 1.35 |
| ❑ 16 Joe Sakic | 3.00 | 1.35 |
| ❑ 17 Teemu Selanne | 3.00 | 1.35 |
| ❑ 18 Dave Andreychuk | .35 | .16 |
| ❑ 19 Al MacInnis | .35 | .16 |
| ❑ 20 Rob Blake | .25 | .11 |
| ❑ 21 Doug Gilmour | 1.50 | .70 |
| ❑ 22 Steve Larmer | .35 | .16 |
| ❑ 23 Eric Lindros | 6.00 | 2.70 |
| ❑ 24 Mike Modano | 2.00 | .90 |
| ❑ 25 Vincent Damphousse | .35 | .16 |
| ❑ 26 Mike Gartner | .35 | .16 |
| ❑ 27 John Vanbiesbrouck | 2.50 | 1.10 |
| ❑ 28 Theoren Fleury | 1.50 | .70 |
| ❑ 29 Ken Baumgartner | .25 | .11 |
| ❑ 30 Jeremy Roenick | 1.50 | .70 |

## 1994 Upper Deck Gretzky 24K Gold

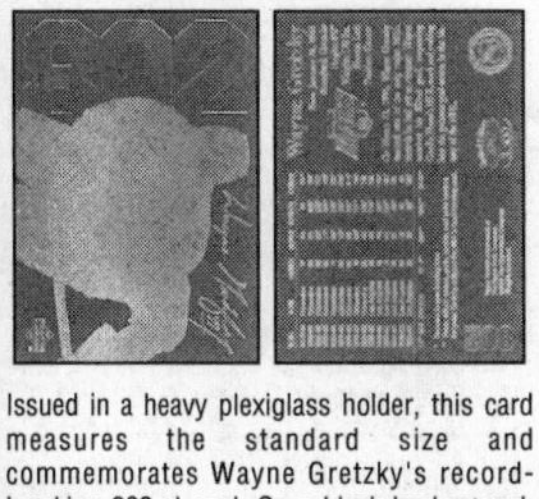

Issued in a heavy plexiglass holder, this card measures the standard size and commemorates Wayne Gretzky's record-breaking 802nd goal. On a black background, the horizontal front features a 24-karat gold photo and a facsimile autograph of Gretzky, along with "802" printed in large silver numbers on the left. On the same black background, the horizontal back carries Gretzky's biography and stats in gold print. The card's serial number and the production run figure (3,500) round out the back.

| | MINT | NRMT |
|---|---|---|
| COMPLETE SET (1) | 150.00 | 70.00 |
| COMMON CARD | 150.00 | 70.00 |
| ❑ 1 Wayne Gretzky | 150.00 | 70.00 |

## 1994 Upper Deck NHLPA/Be A Player

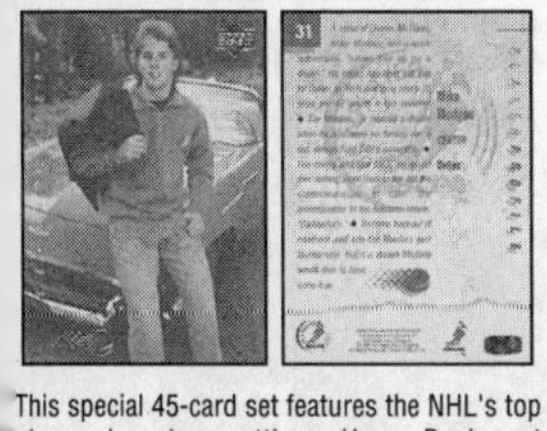

This special 45-card set features the NHL's top players in unique settings. Upper Deck sent three top photographers, including Walter Iooss, to capture on film players in off-ice situations. The first 18 cards bear Iooss' photos (Walter Iooss Collection) and are arranged alphabetically. Cards 19-40 are also arranged alphabetically and carry photos of the other photographers. The final five cards feature Doug Gilmour: A Canadian Hero (41-45). The cards promote the NHLPA line of clothing. All NHLPA clothing proceeds benefit a Special Assistance Fund for former NHL Players. The front of each card features a borderless posed shot of the player relaxing in NHLPA clothing. The gold-foil Upper Deck logo appears in an upper corner. A gold-foil and motion-streaked hockey puck icon rests in a lower corner. The words "Be a Player" appear vertically in white lettering near the left edge. The back carries the player's name, position and team, along with information about the NHLPA clothes and Special Assistance Fund. The left side of the card back has either a quote from Iooss or personal information about the player. The set was issued in a box with a checklist on its back.

| | MINT | NRMT |
|---|---|---|
| COMPLETE SET (45) | 30.00 | 13.50 |
| COMMON CARD (1-45) | .25 | .11 |

| | | |
|---|---|---|
| ❑ 1 Tony Amonte | .50 | .23 |
| ❑ 2 Chris Chelios | .75 | .35 |
| ❑ 3 Alexandre Daigle | .25 | .11 |
| ❑ 4 Dave Ellett | .25 | .11 |
| ❑ 5 Sergei Fedorov | 1.75 | .80 |
| ❑ 6 Chris Gratton | .50 | .23 |
| ❑ 7 Wayne Gretzky | 5.00 | 2.20 |
| ❑ 8 Brett Hull | 1.00 | .45 |
| ❑ 9 Brian Leetch | .75 | .35 |
| ❑ 10 Rob Niedermayer | .50 | .23 |
| ❑ 11 Felix Potvin | .75 | .35 |
| ❑ 12 Luc Robitaille | .50 | .23 |
| ❑ 13 Jeremy Roenick | .75 | .35 |
| ❑ 14 Joe Sakic | 1.75 | .80 |
| ❑ 15 Teemu Selanne | 1.75 | .80 |
| ❑ 16 Brendan Shanahan | 1.75 | .80 |
| ❑ 17 Alexei Yashin | .75 | .35 |
| ❑ 18 Steve Yzerman | 2.50 | 1.10 |
| ❑ 19 Jason Arnott | .50 | .23 |
| ❑ 20 Pavel Bure | 1.75 | .80 |
| ❑ 21 Theoren Fleury | .75 | .35 |
| ❑ 22 Mike Gartner | .35 | .16 |
| ❑ 23 Kevin Haller | .25 | .11 |
| ❑ 24 Derian Hatcher | .25 | .11 |
| ❑ 25 Mark Howe<br>Gordie Howe | .75 | .35 |
| ❑ 26 Al Iafrate | .25 | .11 |
| ❑ 27 Joe Juneau | .35 | .16 |
| ❑ 28 Pat LaFontaine | .50 | .23 |
| ❑ 29 Eric Lindros | 2.50 | 1.10 |
| ❑ 30 Dave Manson | .25 | .11 |
| ❑ 31 Mike Modano | 1.00 | .45 |
| ❑ 32 Scott Niedermayer | .25 | .11 |
| ❑ 33 Owen Nolan | .50 | .23 |
| ❑ 34 Joel Otto | .25 | .11 |
| ❑ 35 Chris Pronger | .25 | .11 |
| ❑ 36 Scott Stevens | .25 | .11 |
| ❑ 37 Pierre Turgeon | .50 | .23 |
| ❑ 38 Pat Verbeek | .25 | .11 |
| ❑ 39 Doug Weight | .50 | .23 |
| ❑ 40 Terry Yake | .25 | .11 |
| ❑ 41 Doug Gilmour<br>(Two-Year Old Doug With A Hockey Stick) | .35 | .16 |
| ❑ 42 Doug Gilmour<br>(Nine-Year Old Doug On The Ice) | .35 | .16 |
| ❑ 43 Doug Gilmour<br>(Standing Next To A Little Girl) | .35 | .16 |
| ❑ 44 Doug Gilmour<br>(Sitting On Motorcycle) | .35 | .16 |
| ❑ 45 Doug Gilmour<br>(With Fishing Rod) | .35 | .16 |

## 1994-95 Upper Deck

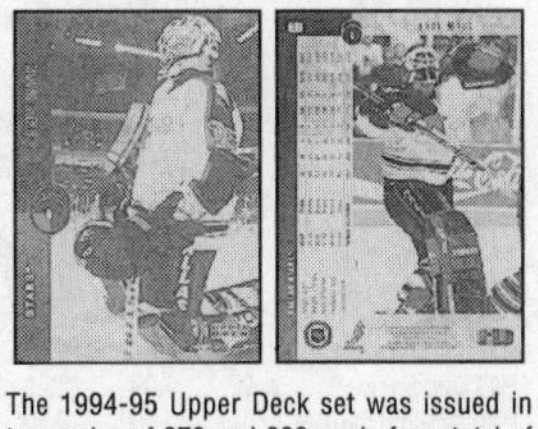

The 1994-95 Upper Deck set was issued in two series of 270 and 300 cards for a total of 570 standard-size cards. The product was available in three packaging versions per series: US Hobby, US Retail and Canadian. The fronts have a team color coded bar on the left border. The team name, position and player name are within the bar in gold foil. Due to a printing error, card numbers 22, 65, 85 and 200 each appear with two different numbers. Each variation was printed in the same quantity, so neither version carries a premium. Subsets include Shooter's Edge (227-234), Super Rookies (235-270), World Junior Championship teams including Canada (496-505), Czech Republic (506-509), Finland (510-512), Russia (513-517), Sweden (518-521) and USA (522-525), as well as Calder Candidates (526-540), and 1994 World Tour (541-570). Rookie Cards include Bryan Berard, Radek Bonk, Mariusz Czerkawski, Eric Daze, Eric Fichaud, Ed Jovanovski, Blaine Lacher, Ian Laperriere, Wade Redden, Jason Wiemer, and Vitali Yachmenev.

| | MINT | NRMT |
|---|---|---|
| COMPLETE SET (570) | 50.00 | 22.00 |
| COMPLETE SERIES 1 (270) | 25.00 | 11.00 |
| COMPLETE SERIES 2 (300) | 25.00 | 11.00 |
| COMMON CARD (1-570) | .10 | .05 |

| | | |
|---|---|---|
| ❑ 1 Wayne Gretzky | 2.00 | .90 |
| ❑ 2 German Titov | .10 | .05 |
| ❑ 3 Guy Hebert | .15 | .07 |
| ❑ 4 Tony Amonte | .15 | .07 |
| ❑ 5 Dino Ciccarelli | .15 | .07 |
| ❑ 6 Geoff Sanderson | .15 | .07 |
| ❑ 7 Alexei Zhamnov | .15 | .07 |
| ❑ 8 John MacLean | .15 | .07 |
| ❑ 9 Brent Fedyk | .10 | .05 |
| ❑ 10 Adam Graves | .15 | .07 |
| ❑ 11 Adam Oates | .15 | .07 |
| ❑ 12 Ron Francis | .15 | .07 |
| ❑ 13 Bobby Dollas | .10 | .05 |
| ❑ 14 Ray Ferraro | .10 | .05 |
| ❑ 15 Paul Broten | .10 | .05 |
| ❑ 16 Ulf Dahlen | .10 | .05 |
| ❑ 17 Pat LaFontaine | .15 | .07 |
| ❑ 18 Craig Janney | .15 | .07 |
| ❑ 19 Garry Galley | .10 | .05 |
| ❑ 20 Gary Roberts | .10 | .05 |
| ❑ 21 Bill Ranford | .15 | .07 |
| ❑ 22 Mario Lemieux | 1.50 | .70 |
| ❑ 23 Glen Murray | .10 | .05 |
| ❑ 24 Paul Coffey | .30 | .14 |
| ❑ 25 Corey Millen | .10 | .05 |
| ❑ 26 Chris Chelios | .30 | .14 |
| ❑ 27 Ronnie Stern | .10 | .05 |
| ❑ 28 Zdeno Ciger | .10 | .05 |
| ❑ 29 Tony Granato | .10 | .05 |
| ❑ 30 Donald Audette | .15 | .07 |
| ❑ 31 Russ Courtnall | .10 | .05 |
| ❑ 32 Mike Gartner | .15 | .07 |
| ❑ 33 Marty McSorley | .10 | .05 |
| ❑ 34 Jeff Brown | .10 | .05 |
| ❑ 35 Mark Janssens | .10 | .05 |
| ❑ 36 Patrick Poulin | .10 | .05 |
| ❑ 37 Sergei Fedorov | .60 | .25 |
| ❑ 38 Tim Sweeney | .10 | .05 |
| ❑ 39 John Slaney | .10 | .05 |
| ❑ 40 Steve Larmer | .15 | .07 |
| ❑ 41 Dave Karpa | .10 | .05 |
| ❑ 42 Esa Tikkanen | .10 | .05 |
| ❑ 43 Joel Otto | .10 | .05 |
| ❑ 44 Doug Weight | .15 | .07 |
| ❑ 45 Murray Craven | .10 | .05 |
| ❑ 46 John Vanbiesbrouck | .50 | .23 |
| ❑ 47 Nelson Emerson | .10 | .05 |
| ❑ 48 Dean Evason | .10 | .05 |
| ❑ 49 Evgeny Davydov | .10 | .05 |
| ❑ 50 Craig Simpson | .10 | .05 |
| ❑ 51 Mats Sundin | .15 | .07 |
| ❑ 52 Chris Pronger | .15 | .07 |
| ❑ 53 Stephan Lebeau | .10 | .05 |
| ❑ 54 Martin Gelinas | .10 | .05 |
| ❑ 55 Bob Rouse | .10 | .05 |
| ❑ 56 Christian Ruuttu | .10 | .05 |
| ❑ 57 Gilbert Dionne | .10 | .05 |
| ❑ 58 Mike Modano | .40 | .18 |
| ❑ 59 Derek King | .10 | .05 |
| ❑ 60 Peter Stastny | .15 | .07 |
| ❑ 61 Ted Donato | .10 | .05 |
| ❑ 62 Mark Messier | .40 | .18 |
| ❑ 63 Dave Manson | .10 | .05 |
| ❑ 64 Johan Garpenlov | .10 | .05 |
| ❑ 65 Sergio Momesso | .10 | .05 |
| ❑ 66 Kirk Muller | .10 | .05 |
| ❑ 67 Dave Ellett | .10 | .05 |
| ❑ 68 Dale Hunter | .10 | .05 |
| ❑ 69 Brent Gretzky | .10 | .05 |
| ❑ 70 Tom Barrasso | .15 | .07 |
| ❑ 71 Philippe Boucher | .10 | .05 |
| ❑ 72 Jesse Belanger | .10 | .05 |
| ❑ 73 Scott Stevens | .15 | .07 |
| ❑ 74 Gary Suter | .10 | .05 |
| ❑ 75 Tim Cheveldae | .15 | .07 |
| ❑ 76 Dimitri Khristich | .10 | .05 |
| ❑ 77 Pierre Turgeon | .15 | .07 |
| ❑ 78 Mike Richter | .30 | .14 |
| ❑ 79 Michael Nylander | .10 | .05 |
| ❑ 80 Sergei Krivokrasov | .10 | .05 |
| ❑ 81 Andy Moog UER<br>(Darcy Wakaluk on back) | .15 | .07 |
| ❑ 82 Al Iafrate | .10 | .05 |
| ❑ 83 Bernie Nicholls | .10 | .05 |
| ❑ 84 Darren Turcotte | .10 | .05 |
| ❑ 85 Igor Larionov | .10 | .05 |
| ❑ 86 Petr Klima | .10 | .05 |
| ❑ 87 Alexandre Daigle | .10 | .05 |
| ❑ 88 Joe Juneau | .15 | .07 |
| ❑ 89 Glen Wesley | .10 | .05 |
| ❑ 90 Teemu Selanne | .60 | .25 |
| ❑ 91 Curtis Joseph | .30 | .14 |
| ❑ 92 Scott Mellanby | .15 | .07 |
| ❑ 93 Jaromir Jagr | 1.00 | .45 |
| ❑ 94 Mark Recchi | .15 | .07 |
| ❑ 95 Jiri Slegr | .10 | .05 |
| ❑ 96 Martin Brodeur | .75 | .35 |
| ❑ 97 Scott Pearson | .10 | .05 |
| ❑ 98 Eric Lindros | 1.25 | .55 |
| ❑ 99 Larry Murphy | .15 | .07 |
| ❑ 100 Sergei Zubov | .10 | .05 |
| ❑ 101 Mathieu Schneider | .10 | .05 |
| ❑ 102 Dale Hawerchuk | .15 | .07 |
| ❑ 103 Owen Nolan | .15 | .07 |
| ❑ 104 Darryl Sydor | .10 | .05 |
| ❑ 105 Anatoli Semenov | .10 | .05 |
| ❑ 106 Marty McInnis | .10 | .05 |
| ❑ 107 Derek Mayer | .10 | .05 |
| ❑ 108 Steve Duchesne | .10 | .05 |
| ❑ 109 Geoff Smith | .10 | .05 |
| ❑ 110 Zarley Zalapski | .10 | .05 |
| ❑ 111 Rod Brind'Amour | .15 | .07 |
| ❑ 112 Nicklas Lidstrom | .15 | .07 |
| ❑ 113 Teppo Numminen | .10 | .05 |
| ❑ 114 Denny Felsner | .10 | .05 |
| ❑ 115 Wendel Clark | .15 | .07 |
| ❑ 116 Arturs Irbe | .15 | .07 |
| ❑ 117 Josef Beranek | .10 | .05 |
| ❑ 118 Brian Bradley | .10 | .05 |
| ❑ 119 Eric Weinrich | .10 | .05 |
| ❑ 120 Kevin Todd | .10 | .05 |
| ❑ 121 Patrick Roy | 1.50 | .70 |
| ❑ 122 Guy Carbonneau | .10 | .05 |
| ❑ 123 Tom Kurvers | .10 | .05 |
| ❑ 124 Sergei Makarov | .10 | .05 |
| ❑ 125 Pat Peake | .10 | .05 |
| ❑ 126 Danton Cole | .10 | .05 |
| ❑ 127 Derian Hatcher | .10 | .05 |
| ❑ 128 Kjell Samuelsson | .10 | .05 |
| ❑ 129 Alexei Yashin | .15 | .07 |
| ❑ 130 Chris Osgood | .50 | .23 |
| ❑ 131 Kent Manderville | .10 | .05 |
| ❑ 132 Jim Montgomery | .10 | .05 |
| ❑ 133 Kirk McLean | .15 | .07 |
| ❑ 134 Kelly Buchberger | .10 | .05 |
| ❑ 135 Peter Bondra | .30 | .14 |
| ❑ 136 Stephane Matteau | .10 | .05 |
| ❑ 137 Oleg Petrov | .10 | .05 |
| ❑ 138 Doug Gilmour | .30 | .14 |
| ❑ 139 Vladimir Malakhov | .10 | .05 |
| ❑ 140 Peter Zezel | .10 | .05 |
| ❑ 141 Mike Vernon | .15 | .07 |
| ❑ 142 Derek Plante | .10 | .05 |
| ❑ 143 Valeri Zelepukin | .10 | .05 |
| ❑ 144 Kevin Haller | .10 | .05 |
| ❑ 145 Keith Tkachuk | .40 | .18 |
| ❑ 146 Claude Boivin | .10 | .05 |
| ❑ 147 Jocelyn Thibault | .30 | .14 |
| ❑ 148 Jyrki Lumme | .10 | .05 |
| ❑ 149 Ray Whitney | .10 | .05 |
| ❑ 150 Al MacInnis | .15 | .07 |
| ❑ 151 Kelly Miller | .10 | .05 |
| ❑ 152 Ray Sheppard | .15 | .07 |
| ❑ 153 Aaron Ward | .10 | .05 |
| ❑ 154 Damian Rhodes | .15 | .07 |
| ❑ 155 Josef Stumpel | .10 | .05 |
| ❑ 156 Sergei Nemchinov | .10 | .05 |
| ❑ 157 Richard Matvichuk | .10 | .05 |
| ❑ 158 Sean Burke | .15 | .07 |
| ❑ 159 Todd Marchant | .10 | .05 |
| ❑ 160 Ryan McGill | .10 | .05 |
| ❑ 161 Sean Hill | .10 | .05 |
| ❑ 162 Iain Fraser | .10 | .05 |
| ❑ 163 Shawn McEachern | .10 | .05 |
| ❑ 164 Petr Nedved | .15 | .07 |
| ❑ 165 John Lilley | .10 | .05 |
| ❑ 166 Joe Sacco | .10 | .05 |
| ❑ 167 Jason Dawe | .10 | .05 |
| ❑ 168 Mike Rathje | .10 | .05 |
| ❑ 169 Phil Housley | .15 | .07 |
| ❑ 170 Ron Hextall | .15 | .07 |
| ❑ 171 Yves Racine | .10 | .05 |
| ❑ 172 Boris Mironov | .10 | .05 |
| ❑ 173 Vitali Prokhorov | .10 | .05 |
| ❑ 174 Roman Hamrlik | .15 | .07 |
| ❑ 175 Robert Lang | .10 | .05 |
| ❑ 176 Jody Hull | .10 | .05 |
| ❑ 177 Mike Ridley | .10 | .05 |
| ❑ 178 Dmitri Filimonov | .10 | .05 |
| ❑ 179 Rene Corbet | .10 | .05 |
| ❑ 180 Rob Pearson | .10 | .05 |
| ❑ 181 Richard Smehlik | .10 | .05 |
| ❑ 182 Rob Gaudreau | .10 | .05 |
| ❑ 183 Bill Houlder | .10 | .05 |
| ❑ 184 Igor Korolev | .10 | .05 |
| ❑ 185 Chris Joseph | .10 | .05 |
| ❑ 186 Shane Churla | .10 | .05 |
| ❑ 187 Rick Tabaracci | .15 | .07 |
| ❑ 188 Alexander Godynyuk | .10 | .05 |
| ❑ 189 Vladimir Konstantinov | .10 | .05 |
| ❑ 190 Markus Naslund | .10 | .05 |
| ❑ 191 Tom Chorske | .10 | .05 |
| ❑ 192 Thomas Steen | .10 | .05 |
| ❑ 193 Patrice Brisebois | .10 | .05 |
| ❑ 194 Luc Robitaille | .15 | .07 |
| ❑ 195 Michal Sykora | .10 | .05 |
| ❑ 196 Troy Mallette | .10 | .05 |
| ❑ 197 Steve Chiasson | .10 | .05 |
| ❑ 198 Jimmy Carson | .10 | .05 |
| ❑ 199 Mike Donnelly | .10 | .05 |
| ❑ 200 Mike Sillinger | .10 | .05 |
| ❑ 201 Martin Rucinsky | .10 | .05 |
| ❑ 202 Adam Bennett | .10 | .05 |
| ❑ 203 Matt Johnson | .10 | .05 |
| ❑ 204 Daren Puppa | .15 | .07 |
| ❑ 205 Ted Drury | .10 | .05 |
| ❑ 206 Jon Casey | .15 | .07 |
| ❑ 207 Alexei Kovalev | .15 | .07 |
| ❑ 208 Alexei Kasatonov | .10 | .05 |
| ❑ 209 Ulf Samuelsson | .10 | .05 |
| ❑ 210 Justin Hocking | .10 | .05 |
| ❑ 211 Greg Adams | .10 | .05 |
| ❑ 212 Greg Johnson | .10 | .05 |
| ❑ 213 Mike Craig | .10 | .05 |
| ❑ 214 Steve Konowalchuk | .10 | .05 |
| ❑ 215 Luke Richardson | .10 | .05 |
| ❑ 216 Pavol Demitra | .10 | .05 |
| ❑ 217 Brian Benning | .10 | .05 |
| ❑ 218 Corey Hirsch | .15 | .07 |
| ❑ 219 Alexander Semak | .10 | .05 |
| ❑ 220 Travis Green | .15 | .07 |
| ❑ 221 Turner Stevenson | .10 | .05 |
| ❑ 222 Dimitri Mironov | .10 | .05 |
| ❑ 223 Christian Soucy | .15 | .07 |
| ❑ 224 Rick Tocchet | .15 | .07 |
| ❑ 225 Craig MacTavish | .10 | .05 |
| ❑ 226 Wayne Gretzky 802<br>Record Breaker | 2.00 | .90 |
| ❑ 227 Pavel Bure | .30 | .14 |
| ❑ 228 Wayne Gretzky | 1.00 | .45 |
| ❑ 229 Brett Hull | .30 | .14 |
| ❑ 230 Mike Gartner | .15 | .07 |
| ❑ 231 Brian Leetch | .30 | .14 |
| ❑ 232 Al MacInnis | .15 | .07 |
| ❑ 233 Dominik Hasek | .30 | .14 |
| ❑ 234 Mark Messier | .30 | .14 |
| ❑ 235 Paul Kariya | 2.00 | .90 |
| ❑ 236 Jamie Storr | .15 | .07 |
| ❑ 237 Jeff Friesen | .15 | .07 |
| ❑ 238 Kenny Jonsson | .10 | .05 |
| ❑ 239 Mariusz Czerkawski | .10 | .05 |
| ❑ 240 Brett Lindros | .10 | .05 |
| ❑ 241 Andrei Nikolishin | .10 | .05 |
| ❑ 242 Jason Allison | .10 | .05 |
| ❑ 243 Oleg Tverdovsky | .15 | .07 |
| ❑ 244 Brian Savage | .10 | .05 |
| ❑ 245 Peter Forsberg | 1.50 | .70 |
| ❑ 246 Patrik Juhlin | .10 | .05 |
| ❑ 247 Jassen Cullimore | .10 | .05 |
| ❑ 248 Chris Therien | .10 | .05 |
| ❑ 249 Kevin Brown | .10 | .05 |
| ❑ 250 Jeff Nelson | .10 | .05 |
| ❑ 251 Janne Laukkanen | .10 | .05 |
| ❑ 252 Jamie McLennan | .10 | .05 |
| ❑ 253 Craig Johnson | .10 | .05 |
| ❑ 254 Ravil Gusmanov | .10 | .05 |
| ❑ 255 Valeri Bure | .15 | .07 |
| ❑ 256 Valeri Karpov | .10 | .05 |
| ❑ 257 Mike Peca | .10 | .05 |
| ❑ 258 Brian Rolston | .10 | .05 |
| ❑ 259 Brandon Convery | .10 | .05 |
| ❑ 260 Mark Lawrence | .10 | .05 |
| ❑ 261 Adam Deadmarsh | .15 | .07 |
| ❑ 262 Jason Wiemer | .10 | .05 |
| ❑ 263 Alexander Cherbayev | .10 | .05 |
| ❑ 264 Sergei Gonchar | .10 | .05 |
| ❑ 265 Viktor Kozlov | .10 | .05 |
| ❑ 266 Vladislav Boulin | .10 | .05 |
| ❑ 267 Todd Harvey | .10 | .05 |
| ❑ 268 Cory Stillman | .10 | .05 |
| ❑ 269 David Oliver | .10 | .05 |
| ❑ 270 Andrei Nazarov | .10 | .05 |
| ❑ 271 Mikael Renberg | .15 | .07 |
| ❑ 272 Andrei Kovalenko | .10 | .05 |
| ❑ 273 Neal Broten | .15 | .07 |
| ❑ 274 Ed Olczyk | .10 | .05 |
| ❑ 275 Steve Thomas | .10 | .05 |
| ❑ 276 Joe Nieuwendyk | .15 | .07 |
| ❑ 277 Rob Gaudreau | .10 | .05 |
| ❑ 278 Pat Verbeek | .10 | .05 |
| ❑ 279 Eric Desjardins | .10 | .05 |
| ❑ 280 Vincent Damphousse | .15 | .07 |
| ❑ 281 John Cullen | .10 | .05 |
| ❑ 282 Garry Valk | .10 | .05 |
| ❑ 283 Daniel Lacroix | .10 | .05 |
| ❑ 284 Mike Ricci | .10 | .05 |
| ❑ 285 Dominik Hasek | .60 | .25 |
| ❑ 286 Geoff Courtnall | .10 | .05 |
| ❑ 287 Rob Niedermayer | .15 | .07 |
| ❑ 288 Alexander Karpovtsev | .10 | .05 |
| ❑ 289 Martin Straka | .10 | .05 |
| ❑ 290 Ed Belfour | .30 | .14 |
| ❑ 291 Dave Lowry | .10 | .05 |
| ❑ 292 Brendan Shanahan | .60 | .25 |
| ❑ 293 Jari Kurri | .15 | .07 |
| ❑ 294 Steven Rice | .10 | .05 |
| ❑ 295 Scott Levins | .10 | .05 |
| ❑ 296 Ray Bourque | .30 | .14 |
| ❑ 297 Mikael Andersson | .10 | .05 |
| ❑ 298 Darius Kasparaitis | .10 | .05 |
| ❑ 299 Chris Simon | .10 | .05 |
| ❑ 300 Steve Yzerman | 1.00 | .45 |
| ❑ 301 Don McSween | .10 | .05 |
| ❑ 302 Brian Noonan | .10 | .05 |
| ❑ 303 Claude Lemieux | .15 | .07 |
| ❑ 304 Radek Bonk | .10 | .05 |
| ❑ 305 Jason Arnott | .15 | .07 |
| ❑ 306 Ian Laperriere | .10 | .05 |
| ❑ 307 Pat Falloon | .10 | .05 |
| ❑ 308 Kris King | .10 | .05 |
| ❑ 309 Brian Bellows | .10 | .05 |
| ❑ 310 Uwe Krupp | .10 | .05 |
| ❑ 311 Paul Cavallini | .10 | .05 |
| ❑ 312 Shaun Van Allen | .10 | .05 |
| ❑ 313 Dave Andreychuk | .15 | .07 |
| ❑ 314 Bobby Holik | .10 | .05 |
| ❑ 315 Theoren Fleury | .15 | .07 |
| ❑ 316 Mark Osborne | .10 | .05 |
| ❑ 317 Andrew Cassels | .10 | .05 |
| ❑ 318 Chris Tamer | .10 | .05 |
| ❑ 319 Trevor Linden | .15 | .07 |
| ❑ 320 Tom Fitzgerald | .10 | .05 |
| ❑ 321 Ron Tugnutt | .15 | .07 |
| ❑ 322 Jeremy Roenick | .30 | .14 |
| ❑ 323 Todd Marchant | .10 | .05 |
| ❑ 324 Scott Niedermayer | .10 | .05 |
| ❑ 325 Tim Taylor | .10 | .05 |
| ❑ 326 Mike Kennedy | .10 | .05 |
| ❑ 327 Steve Heinze | .10 | .05 |
| ❑ 328 David Sacco | .10 | .05 |
| ❑ 329 Sergei Brylin | .10 | .05 |
| ❑ 330 John LeClair | .50 | .23 |
| ❑ 331 Brian Skrudland | .10 | .05 |
| ❑ 332 Kevin Hatcher | .10 | .05 |
| ❑ 333 Brett Hull | .40 | .18 |
| ❑ 334 Alexander Mogilny | .15 | .07 |
| ❑ 335 Sylvain Lefebvre | .10 | .05 |
| ❑ 336 Sylvain Turgeon | .10 | .05 |
| ❑ 337 Keith Primeau | .15 | .07 |
| ❑ 338 Eric Fichaud | .60 | .25 |
| ❑ 339 Jeff Beukeboom | .10 | .05 |
| ❑ 340 Cory Cross | .10 | .05 |
| ❑ 341 J.J. Daigneault | .10 | .05 |
| ❑ 342 Stephen Leach | .10 | .05 |
| ❑ 343 Zigmund Palffy | .30 | .14 |
| ❑ 344 Igor Korolev | .10 | .05 |
| ❑ 345 Chris Gratton | .15 | .07 |
| ❑ 346 Joe Mullen | .15 | .07 |
| ❑ 347 Brent Gilchrist | .10 | .05 |
| ❑ 348 Adam Creighton | .10 | .05 |
| ❑ 349 Dimitri Yushkevich | .10 | .05 |

| | | |
|---|---|---|
| ❑ 350 Wes Walz | .10 | .05 |
| ❑ 351 Shayne Corson | .10 | .05 |
| ❑ 352 Eric Lacroix | .10 | .05 |
| ❑ 353 Maxim Bets | .10 | .05 |
| ❑ 354 Sylvain Cote | .10 | .05 |
| ❑ 355 Valeri Kamensky | .15 | .07 |
| ❑ 356 Shjon Podein | .10 | .05 |
| ❑ 357 Robert Reichel | .10 | .05 |
| ❑ 358 Cliff Ronning | .10 | .05 |
| ❑ 359 Bill Guerin | .10 | .05 |
| ❑ 360 Dallas Drake | .10 | .05 |
| ❑ 361 Robert Petrovicky | .10 | .05 |
| ❑ 362 Ken Wregget | .15 | .07 |
| ❑ 363 Todd Elik | .10 | .05 |
| ❑ 364 Cam Neely | .15 | .07 |
| ❑ 365 Darren McCarty | .10 | .05 |
| ❑ 366 Shean Donovan | .10 | .05 |
| ❑ 367 Felix Potvin | .30 | .14 |
| ❑ 368 Yuri Khmylev | .10 | .05 |
| ❑ 369 Mark Tinordi | .10 | .05 |
| ❑ 370 Craig Billington | .15 | .07 |
| ❑ 371 Patrick Flatley | .10 | .05 |
| ❑ 372 Jocelyn Lemieux | .10 | .05 |
| ❑ 373 Slava Kozlov | .15 | .07 |
| ❑ 374 Trent Klatt | .10 | .05 |
| ❑ 375 Geoff Sarjeant | .10 | .05 |
| ❑ 376 Bob Kudelski | .10 | .05 |
| ❑ 377 Stanislav Neckar | .10 | .05 |
| ❑ 378 Jon Rohloff | .10 | .05 |
| ❑ 379 Jeff Shantz | .10 | .05 |
| ❑ 380 Dale Craigwell | .10 | .05 |
| ❑ 381 Adrien Plavsic | .10 | .05 |
| ❑ 382 Dave Gagner | .15 | .07 |
| ❑ 383 Dave Archibald | .10 | .05 |
| ❑ 384 Gilbert Dionne | .10 | .05 |
| ❑ 385 Troy Loney | .10 | .05 |
| ❑ 386 Dean McAmmond | .10 | .05 |
| ❑ 387 Pauli Jaks | .15 | .07 |
| ❑ 388 Stephane Richer | .15 | .07 |
| ❑ 389 Don Beaupre | .15 | .07 |
| ❑ 390 Kevin Stevens | .10 | .05 |
| ❑ 391 Brad May | .15 | .07 |
| ❑ 392 Neil Wilkinson | .10 | .05 |
| ❑ 393 Kevin Lowe | .10 | .05 |
| ❑ 394 Fredrik Olausson | .10 | .05 |
| ❑ 395 Trevor Kidd | .15 | .07 |
| ❑ 396 Brent Grieve | .10 | .05 |
| ❑ 397 Dominic Roussel | .15 | .07 |
| ❑ 398 Bret Hedican | .10 | .05 |
| ❑ 399 Bryan Smolinski | .10 | .05 |
| ❑ 400 Doug Lidster | .10 | .05 |
| ❑ 401 Bob Errey | .10 | .05 |
| ❑ 402 Pierre Sevigny | .10 | .05 |
| ❑ 403 Rob Brown | .10 | .05 |
| ❑ 404 Joe Sakic | .60 | .25 |
| ❑ 405 Nikolai Borschevsky | .10 | .05 |
| ❑ 406 Martin Lapointe | .10 | .05 |
| ❑ 407 Jean-Yves Roy | .10 | .05 |
| ❑ 408 Robert Kron | .10 | .05 |
| ❑ 409 Tie Domi | .15 | .07 |
| ❑ 410 Jim Dowd | .10 | .05 |
| ❑ 411 Keith Jones | .10 | .05 |
| ❑ 412 Scott Lachance | .10 | .05 |
| ❑ 413 Bob Corkum | .10 | .05 |
| ❑ 414 Denis Chasse | .10 | .05 |
| ❑ 415 Denis Savard | .15 | .07 |
| ❑ 416 Joe Murphy | .10 | .05 |
| ❑ 417 Vyacheslav Butsayev | .10 | .05 |
| ❑ 418 Mattias Norstrom | .10 | .05 |
| ❑ 419 Sergei Zholtok | .10 | .05 |
| ❑ 420 Nikolai Khabibulin | .15 | .07 |
| ❑ 421 Pat Elynuik | .10 | .05 |
| ❑ 422 Doug Brown | .10 | .05 |
| ❑ 423 Dave McLlwain | .10 | .05 |
| ❑ 424 James Patrick | .10 | .05 |
| ❑ 425 Alexander Selivanov | .10 | .05 |
| ❑ 426 Scott Thornton | .10 | .05 |
| ❑ 427 Todd Ewen | .10 | .05 |
| ❑ 428 Peter Popovic | .10 | .05 |
| ❑ 429 Jarkko Varvio | .10 | .05 |
| ❑ 430 Paul Ranheim | .10 | .05 |
| ❑ 431 Kevin Dineen | .10 | .05 |
| ❑ 432 Kelly Hrudey | .15 | .07 |
| ❑ 433 Michal Grosek | .10 | .05 |
| ❑ 434 Slava Fetisov | .10 | .05 |
| ❑ 435 Ivan Droppa | .10 | .05 |
| ❑ 436 Benoit Hogue | .10 | .05 |
| ❑ 437 Sheldon Kennedy | .10 | .05 |
| ❑ 438 Gord Murphy | .10 | .05 |
| ❑ 439 Jamie Baker | .10 | .05 |
| ❑ 440 Todd Gill | .10 | .05 |
| ❑ 441 Mark Recchi | .15 | .07 |
| ❑ 442 Ted Crowley | .10 | .05 |
| ❑ 443 Ryan Smyth | 1.50 | .70 |
| ❑ 444 Brian Leetch | .30 | .14 |
| ❑ 445 Bob Sweeney | .10 | .05 |
| ❑ 446 Don Sweeney | .10 | .05 |
| ❑ 447 Byron Dafoe | 1.50 | .70 |
| ❑ 448 Nathan Lafayette | .10 | .05 |
| ❑ 449 Keith Carney | .10 | .05 |
| ❑ 450 Stephane Fiset | .15 | .07 |
| ❑ 451 Kevin Miller | .10 | .05 |
| ❑ 452 Craig Darby | .10 | .05 |
| ❑ 453 Vlastimil Kroupa | .10 | .05 |
| ❑ 454 Rob Zettler | .10 | .05 |
| ❑ 455 Glenn Healy | .15 | .07 |
| ❑ 456 Todd Simon | .10 | .05 |
| ❑ 457 Mark Fitzpatrick | .15 | .07 |
| ❑ 458 Drake Berehowsky | .10 | .05 |
| ❑ 459 Darcy Wakaluk | .15 | .07 |
| ❑ 460 Enrico Ciccone | .10 | .05 |
| ❑ 461 Tomas Sandstrom | .10 | .05 |
| ❑ 462 Mikhail Shtalenkov | .10 | .05 |
| ❑ 463 Igor Kravchuk | .10 | .05 |
| ❑ 464 Jamie Allison | .10 | .05 |
| ❑ 465 Gino Odjick | .10 | .05 |
| ❑ 466 Norm Maciver | .10 | .05 |
| ❑ 467 Terry Carkner | .10 | .05 |
| ❑ 468 Rob Zamuner | .10 | .05 |
| ❑ 469 Pavel Bure | .60 | .25 |
| ❑ 470 Patrice Tardif | .10 | .05 |
| ❑ 471 Andrei Lomakin | .10 | .05 |
| ❑ 472 Kirk Maltby | .10 | .05 |
| ❑ 473 Jaroslav Modry | .10 | .05 |
| ❑ 474 Tommy Soderstrom | .15 | .07 |
| ❑ 475 Patrik Carnback | .10 | .05 |
| ❑ 476 Jeff Reese | .10 | .05 |
| ❑ 477 Todd Krygier | .10 | .05 |
| ❑ 478 John McIntyre | .10 | .05 |
| ❑ 479 Joey Kocur | .10 | .05 |
| ❑ 480 Steve Rucchin | .50 | .23 |
| ❑ 481 Bob Bassen | .10 | .05 |
| ❑ 482 Marek Malik | .10 | .05 |
| ❑ 483 Darrin Shannon | .10 | .05 |
| ❑ 484 Shawn Burr | .10 | .05 |
| ❑ 485 Louie DeBrusk | .10 | .05 |
| ❑ 486 Olaf Kolzig | .15 | .07 |
| ❑ 487 Cam Stewart | .10 | .05 |
| ❑ 488 Rob Blake | .10 | .05 |
| ❑ 489 Eric Charron | .10 | .05 |
| ❑ 490 Sandis Ozolinsh | .15 | .07 |
| ❑ 491 Paul Ysebaert | .10 | .05 |
| ❑ 492 Kris Draper | .10 | .05 |
| ❑ 493 Stu Barnes | .10 | .05 |
| ❑ 494 Doug Bodger | .10 | .05 |
| ❑ 495 Blaine Lacher | .15 | .07 |
| ❑ 496 Ed Jovanovski | .50 | .23 |
| ❑ 497 Eric Daze | 1.25 | .55 |
| ❑ 498 Dan Cloutier | .40 | .18 |
| ❑ 499 Chad Allen | .10 | .05 |
| ❑ 500 Todd Harvey | .10 | .05 |
| ❑ 501 Jamie Rivers | .10 | .05 |
| ❑ 502 Bryan McCabe | .10 | .05 |
| ❑ 503 Darcy Tucker | .10 | .05 |
| ❑ 504 Wade Redden | .50 | .23 |
| ❑ 505 Nolan Baumgartner | .10 | .05 |
| ❑ 506 Marek Malik | .10 | .05 |
| ❑ 507 Petr Cajanek | .10 | .05 |
| ❑ 508 Jan Hlavac | .15 | .07 |
| ❑ 509 Ladislav Kohn | .10 | .05 |
| ❑ 510 Kimmo Timonen | .15 | .07 |
| ❑ 511 Antti Aalto | .15 | .07 |
| ❑ 512 Tommi Rajamaki | .15 | .07 |
| ❑ 513 Vitali Yachmenev | .10 | .05 |
| ❑ 514 Vadim Epantchinsev | .15 | .07 |
| ❑ 515 Dmitri Klevakin | .15 | .07 |
| ❑ 516 Nikolai Zavaroukhine | .10 | .05 |
| ❑ 517 Alexandre Koroliouk | .10 | .05 |
| ❑ 518 Anders Eriksson | .10 | .05 |
| ❑ 519 Jesper Mattsson | .15 | .07 |
| ❑ 520 Mattias Ohlund | 1.00 | .45 |
| ❑ 521 Anders Soderberg | .10 | .05 |
| ❑ 522 Bryan Berard | 2.50 | 1.10 |
| ❑ 523 Jason Bonsignore | .10 | .05 |
| ❑ 524 Deron Quint | .10 | .05 |
| ❑ 525 Richard Park | .10 | .05 |
| ❑ 526 Jeff Friesen | .15 | .07 |
| ❑ 527 Paul Kariya | 1.00 | .45 |
| ❑ 528 Peter Forsberg | 1.00 | .45 |
| ❑ 529 Zigmund Palffy CC | .30 | .14 |
| ❑ 530 Kenny Jonsson | .10 | .05 |
| ❑ 531 Jamie Storr | .15 | .07 |
| ❑ 532 Alexander Selivanov | .10 | .05 |
| ❑ 533 Mike Peca CC | .10 | .05 |
| ❑ 534 Mariusz Czerkawski | .10 | .05 |
| ❑ 535 Jason Allison | .10 | .05 |
| ❑ 536 Todd Harvey | .10 | .05 |
| ❑ 537 Brett Lindros | .10 | .05 |
| ❑ 538 Radek Bonk | .10 | .05 |
| ❑ 539 Blaine Lacher | .15 | .07 |
| ❑ 540 Oleg Tverdovsky | .15 | .07 |
| ❑ 541 Wayne Gretzky | 1.00 | .45 |
| ❑ 542 Radek Bonk | .10 | .05 |
| ❑ 543 Mariusz Czerkawski | .10 | .05 |
| ❑ 544 Jaromir Jagr | .50 | .23 |
| ❑ 545 Dominik Hasek | .30 | .14 |
| ❑ 546 Todd Harvey | .10 | .05 |
| ❑ 547 Mike Peca WT | .10 | .05 |
| ❑ 548 Mats Sundin | .15 | .07 |
| ❑ 549 Doug Weight WT | .15 | .07 |
| ❑ 550 Steve Yzerman | .50 | .23 |
| ❑ 551 Brett Lindros | .10 | .05 |
| ❑ 552 Alexander Mogilny | .15 | .07 |
| ❑ 553 Patrik Juhlin WT | .10 | .05 |
| ❑ 554 Alexei Yashin | .15 | .07 |
| ❑ 555 Peter Forsberg | 1.00 | .45 |
| ❑ 556 Michael Nylander WT | .10 | .05 |
| ❑ 557 Teemu Selanne | .30 | .14 |
| ❑ 558 Marek Malik | .10 | .05 |
| ❑ 559 Jari Kurri WT | .15 | .07 |
| ❑ 560 Kenny Jonsson | .10 | .05 |
| ❑ 561 Mikael Renberg | .15 | .07 |
| ❑ 562 Adam Deadmarsh WT | .15 | .07 |
| ❑ 563 Mark Messier | .30 | .14 |
| ❑ 564 Rob Blake WT | .10 | .05 |
| ❑ 565 Janne Laukkanen WT | .10 | .05 |
| ❑ 566 Theoren Fleury WT | .15 | .07 |
| ❑ 567 Alexei Kovalev | .15 | .07 |
| ❑ 568 Jamie Storr | .15 | .07 |
| ❑ 569 Brett Hull | .30 | .14 |
| ❑ 570 Valeri Karpov | .10 | .05 |

## 1994-95 Upper Deck Electric Ice

This is a parallel set to the regular Upper Deck issue and is inserted in packs at the rate of 1:35. The backs are identical to the regular set. The only difference on the front is that the words "Electric Ice" are at the bottom which, along with the player's name and bar

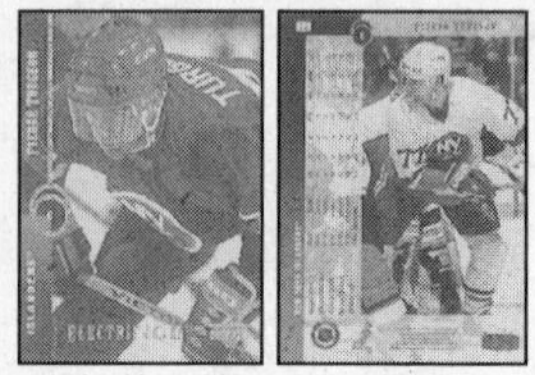

enclosing his position, are all in electric foil.

| | MINT | NRMT |
|---|---|---|
| COMPLETE SET (570) | 2200.00 | 1000.00 |
| COMPLETE SERIES 1 (270) | 1000.00 | 450.00 |
| COMPLETE SERIES 2 (300) | 1200.00 | 550.00 |
| COMMON CARD (1-570) | 2.00 | .90 |

*STARS: 15X TO 40X BASIC CARDS
*YOUNG STARS: 12X TO 30X BASIC CARDS

## 1994-95 Upper Deck Ice Gallery

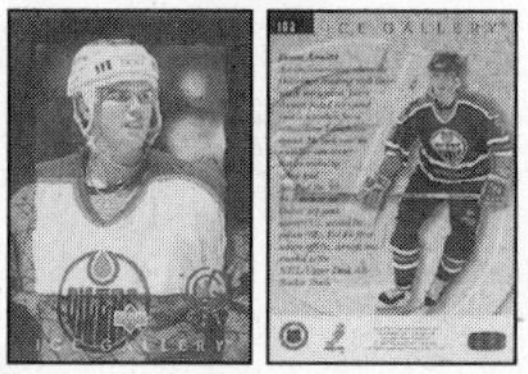

This 15-card set features some of the NHL's top players, along with a few journeymen. The cards were inserted 1:25 packs in Upper Deck series one. The cards feature a close-up headshot with a wide black and gray border. An action photo and text appear on the back. The cards are numbered with an "IG" prefix.

| | MINT | NRMT |
|---|---|---|
| COMPLETE SET (15) | 50.00 | 22.00 |
| COMMON CARD (IG1-IG15) | 1.00 | .45 |
| ❑ IG1 Steve Yzerman | 8.00 | 3.60 |
| ❑ IG2 Jason Arnott | 2.00 | .90 |
| ❑ IG3 Jeremy Roenick | 2.50 | 1.10 |
| ❑ IG4 Brendan Shanahan | 5.00 | 2.20 |
| ❑ IG5 Scott Stevens | 1.00 | .45 |
| ❑ IG6 Scott Niedermayer | 1.00 | .45 |
| ❑ IG7 Adam Graves | 2.00 | .90 |
| ❑ IG8 Mike Modano | 3.00 | 1.35 |
| ❑ IG9 Kirk Muller | 1.00 | .45 |
| ❑ IG10 Alexandre Daigle | 2.00 | .90 |
| ❑ IG11 Martin Brodeur | 6.00 | 2.70 |
| ❑ IG12 Garry Valk | 1.00 | .45 |
| ❑ IG13 Teemu Selanne | 5.00 | 2.20 |
| ❑ IG14 Pat LaFontaine | 2.00 | .90 |
| ❑ IG15 Wayne Gretzky | 15.00 | 6.75 |

## 1994-95 Upper Deck Predictor Canadian

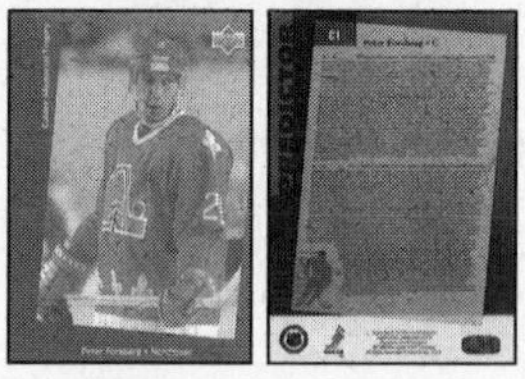

The Calder Predictors (C1-C15) were inserted at a rate of 1:20 first series Canadian packs, while the Pearson/Norris cards (C16-C35) were inserted at a rate of 1:20 series two Canadian packs. C1 (Peter Forsberg) was the winning card that could be redeemed for a gold foil Calder set, while C15 (Long Shot) could be redeemed for a silver version. Either C23 (Eric Lindros) or C31 (Paul Coffey) could be redeemed for a 20-card gold foil Pearson/Norris set, while C24 (Jaromir Jagr) netted the collector a silver version of cards C16-C25, and C29 (Chris Chelios) could be redeemed for a silver version of cards C26-C35.

| | MINT | NRMT |
|---|---|---|
| COMPLETE SET (35) | 175.00 | 80.00 |
| COMMON CARD (C1-C35) | 2.00 | .90 |
| COMP.CALD.EXCH.SET (15) | 25.00 | 11.00 |
| COMP.PEAR.EXCH.SET (10) | 40.00 | 18.00 |
| COMP.NORR.EXCH.SET (10) | 15.00 | 6.75 |

*EXCH.CARDS: .25X TO .5X HI COLUMN
*GOLD/SILVER CALDER EXCH: EQUAL VALUE

| | | |
|---|---|---|
| ❑ C1 Peter Forsberg | 12.00 | 5.50 |
| ❑ C2 Paul Kariya | 12.00 | 5.50 |
| ❑ C3 Viktor Kozlov | 2.00 | .90 |
| ❑ C4 Jason Allison | 2.00 | .90 |
| ❑ C5 Mariusz Czerkawski | 2.00 | .90 |
| ❑ C6 Valeri Karpov | 2.00 | .90 |
| ❑ C7 Brett Lindros | 2.00 | .90 |
| ❑ C8 Valeri Bure | 2.00 | .90 |
| ❑ C9 Andrei Nikolishin | 2.00 | .90 |
| ❑ C10 Mike Peca | 2.00 | .90 |
| ❑ C11 Kenny Jonsson | 2.00 | .90 |
| ❑ C12 Alexander Cherbayev | 2.00 | .90 |
| ❑ C13 Brian Rolston | 2.00 | .90 |
| ❑ C14 Oleg Tverdovsky | 2.00 | .90 |
| ❑ C15 Calder Long Shot | 2.00 | .90 |
| ❑ C16 Wayne Gretzky | 20.00 | 9.00 |
| ❑ C17 Brett Hull | 4.00 | 1.80 |
| ❑ C18 Doug Gilmour | 3.00 | 1.35 |
| ❑ C19 Jeremy Roenick | 3.00 | 1.35 |
| ❑ C20 John Vanbiesbrouck | 5.00 | 2.20 |
| ❑ C21 Sergei Fedorov | 6.00 | 2.70 |
| ❑ C22 Mark Messier | 4.00 | 1.80 |
| ❑ C23 Eric Lindros | 12.00 | 5.50 |
| ❑ C24 Jaromir Jagr | 10.00 | 4.50 |
| ❑ C25 Pearson Long Shot | 2.00 | .90 |
| ❑ C26 Ray Bourque | 3.00 | 1.35 |
| ❑ C27 Sandis Ozolinsh | 2.00 | .90 |
| ❑ C28 Brian Leetch | 3.00 | 1.35 |
| ❑ C29 Chris Chelios | 3.00 | 1.35 |
| ❑ C30 Scott Stevens | 2.00 | .90 |
| ❑ C31 Paul Coffey | 3.00 | 1.35 |
| ❑ C32 Rob Blake | 2.00 | .90 |
| ❑ C33 Al MacInnis | 2.00 | .90 |
| ❑ C34 Scott Niedermayer | 2.00 | .90 |
| ❑ C35 Norris Long Shot | 2.00 | .90 |

## 1994-95 Upper Deck Predictor Hobby

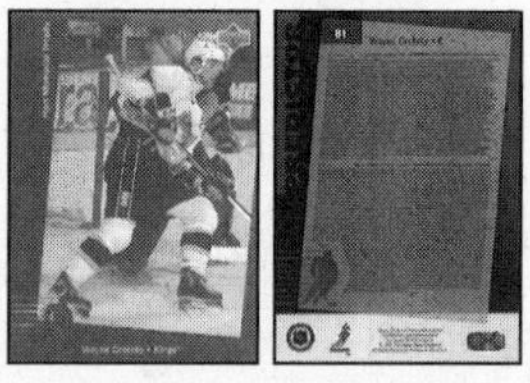

The Hart Predictors (H1-H15) were inserted at a rate of 1:20 first series U.S. hobby packs, while the Art Ross/Vezina cards (H16-H35) were inserted at a rate of 1:20 second series U.S. hobby packs. H8 (Eric Lindros) was redeemable for a gold foil version of the Hart set, while card H15 (Long Shot) was redeemable for a silver version. Either H24 (Jaromir Jagr) or H31 (Dominik Hasek) could be redeemed for a 20-card gold foil version of the Art Ross/Vezina set, while H23 (Eric Lindros) and H27 (Ed Belfour) won gold foil versions of cards H16-H25, and H26-H35, respectively.

| | MINT | NRMT |
|---|---|---|
| COMPLETE SET (35) | 225.00 | 100.00 |
| COMMON CARD (H1-H35) | 2.00 | .90 |
| COMP.HART EXCH.SET (15) | 50.00 | 22.00 |
| COMP.ROSS EXCH.SET (10) | 30.00 | 13.50 |
| COMP.VEZ.EXCH SET (10) | 20.00 | 9.00 |

*EXCH.CARDS: .25X TO .5X HI COLUMN
*GOLD/SILVER HART EXCH: EQUAL VALUE

| | | |
|---|---|---|
| ❑ H1 Wayne Gretzky | 20.00 | 9.00 |
| ❑ H2 Pavel Bure | 6.00 | 2.70 |
| ❑ H3 Doug Gilmour | 2.50 | 1.10 |
| ❑ H4 Mark Messier | 4.00 | 1.80 |
| ❑ H5 Patrick Roy | 15.00 | 6.75 |
| ❑ H6 Sergei Fedorov | 6.00 | 2.70 |
| ❑ H7 Chris Chelios | 3.00 | 1.35 |
| ❑ H8 Eric Lindros | 12.00 | 5.50 |
| ❑ H9 Alexander Mogilny | 2.50 | 1.10 |
| ❑ H10 Peter Forsberg | 10.00 | 4.50 |
| ❑ H11 Brian Leetch | 3.00 | 1.35 |
| ❑ H12 Martin Brodeur | 8.00 | 3.60 |
| ❑ H13 Jeremy Roenick | 3.00 | 1.35 |
| ❑ H14 Paul Kariya | 12.00 | 5.50 |
| ❑ H15 Hart Long Shot | 2.00 | .90 |
| ❑ H16 Wayne Gretzky | 20.00 | 9.00 |
| ❑ H17 Joe Sakic | 5.00 | 2.20 |
| ❑ H18 Sergei Fedorov | 6.00 | 2.70 |
| ❑ H19 Pavel Bure | 6.00 | 2.70 |
| ❑ H20 Adam Oates | 2.50 | 1.10 |
| ❑ H21 Doug Gilmour | 2.50 | 1.10 |
| ❑ H22 Steve Yzerman | 8.00 | 3.60 |
| ❑ H23 Eric Lindros | 12.00 | 5.50 |
| ❑ H24 Jaromir Jagr | 10.00 | 4.50 |
| ❑ H25 Art Ross Long Shot | 2.00 | .90 |
| ❑ H26 Patrick Roy | 15.00 | 6.75 |
| ❑ H27 Ed Belfour | 3.00 | 1.35 |
| ❑ H28 Felix Potvin | 3.00 | 1.35 |
| ❑ H29 Martin Brodeur | 8.00 | 3.60 |
| ❑ H30 Mike Richter | 3.00 | 1.35 |
| ❑ H31 Dominik Hasek | 6.00 | 2.70 |
| ❑ H32 John Vanbiesbrouck | 5.00 | 2.20 |
| ❑ H33 Curtis Joseph | 3.00 | 1.35 |
| ❑ H34 Kirk McLean | 2.00 | .90 |
| ❑ H35 Vezina Long Shot | 2.00 | .90 |

## 1994-95 Upper Deck Predictor Retail

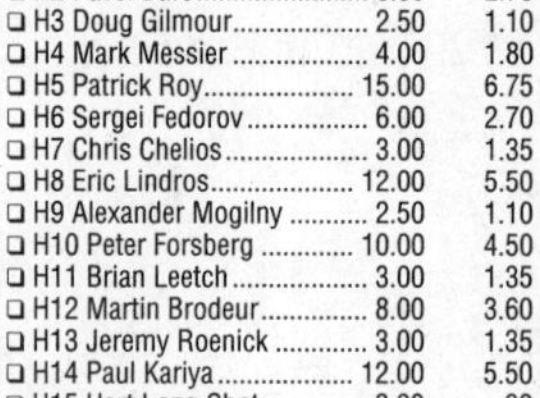

The Scoring Predictors (R1-R30) were inserted at a rate of 1:20 series one U.S. retail packs, while the Playoff Scoring cards (R31-R60) were inserted at a rate of 1:20 series two U.S. retail packs. Cards R10 (Goals Long Shot), R20 (Assists Long Shot), R28 (Eric Lindros), R29 (Jaromir Jagr), and R30 (Points Long shot) were all redeemable for a 30 card gold foil version of Scoring Predictors. Cards R40 (Goals Long Shot), R50 (Assists Long Shot), and R52 (Sergei Fedorov) were all redeemable for a 30 card gold foil version of the Playoff Scoring Predictors. Cards R39 (Jaromir Jagr), and R60 (Points Long Shot) won gold foil versions of cards R31-40, and R51-60, respectively.

| | MINT | NRMT |
|---|---|---|
| COMPLETE SET (60) | 350.00 | 160.00 |
| COMMON CARD (R1-R60) | 2.00 | .90 |
| COMP.SCOR.EXCH.SET (30) | 70.00 | 32.00 |
| COMP.GOALS EXCH.SET (10) | 20.00 | 9.00 |
| COMP.ASST.EXCH.SET (10) | 20.00 | 9.00 |
| COMP.PTS.EXCH.SET (10) | 25.00 | 11.00 |

*EXCH.CARDS: .25X TO .5X HI COLUMN

| | | |
|---|---|---|
| ❑ R1 Pavel Bure | 6.00 | 2.70 |
| ❑ R2 Brett Hull | 4.00 | 1.80 |
| ❑ R3 Teemu Selanne | 6.00 | 2.70 |
| ❑ R4 Sergei Fedorov | 6.00 | 2.70 |
| ❑ R5 Adam Graves | 3.00 | 1.35 |
| ❑ R6 Dave Andreychuk | 2.00 | .90 |
| ❑ R7 Brendan Shanahan | 6.00 | 2.70 |
| ❑ R8 Jeremy Roenick | 3.00 | 1.35 |
| ❑ R9 Eric Lindros | 12.00 | 5.50 |
| ❑ R10 Goals Long Shot | 2.00 | .90 |
| ❑ R11 Doug Gilmour | 3.00 | 1.35 |
| ❑ R12 Adam Oates | 2.00 | .90 |
| ❑ R13 Brian Leetch | 3.00 | 1.35 |
| ❑ R14 Ray Bourque | 3.00 | 1.35 |
| ❑ R15 Joe Juneau | 2.00 | .90 |
| ❑ R16 Craig Janney | 2.00 | .90 |
| ❑ R17 Pat LaFontaine | 2.00 | .90 |
| ❑ R18 Jaromir Jagr | 10.00 | 4.50 |
| ❑ R19 Wayne Gretzky | 20.00 | 9.00 |
| ❑ R20 Assists Long Shot | 2.00 | .90 |
| ❑ R21 Wayne Gretzky | 20.00 | 9.00 |
| ❑ R22 Pat LaFontaine | 2.00 | .90 |
| ❑ R23 Sergei Fedorov | 6.00 | 2.70 |
| ❑ R24 Steve Yzerman | 10.00 | 4.50 |
| ❑ R25 Pavel Bure | 6.00 | 2.70 |
| ❑ R26 Adam Oates | 2.00 | .90 |
| ❑ R27 Doug Gilmour | 3.00 | 1.35 |
| ❑ R28 Eric Lindros | 12.00 | 5.50 |
| ❑ R29 Jaromir Jagr | 10.00 | 4.50 |
| ❑ R30 Points Long Shot | 2.00 | .90 |
| ❑ R31 Pavel Bure | 6.00 | 2.70 |
| ❑ R32 Brett Hull | 4.00 | 1.80 |
| ❑ R33 Cam Neely | 2.00 | .90 |
| ❑ R34 Mark Messier | 4.00 | 1.80 |
| ❑ R35 Dave Andreychuk | 2.00 | .90 |
| ❑ R36 Sergei Fedorov | 6.00 | 2.70 |
| ❑ R37 Mike Modano | 4.00 | 1.80 |
| ❑ R38 Adam Graves | 2.00 | .90 |
| ❑ R39 Jaromir Jagr | 10.00 | 4.50 |
| ❑ R40 Playoff Goals Long Shot | 2.00 | .90 |
| ❑ R41 Theoren Fleury | 3.00 | 1.35 |
| ❑ R42 Wayne Gretzky | 20.00 | 9.00 |
| ❑ R43 Steve Yzerman | 10.00 | 4.50 |
| ❑ R44 Adam Oates | 2.00 | .90 |
| ❑ R45 Brian Leetch | 3.00 | 1.35 |
| ❑ R46 Al MacInnis | 2.00 | .90 |
| ❑ R47 Pat LaFontaine | 2.00 | .90 |
| ❑ R48 Scott Stevens | 2.00 | .90 |
| ❑ R49 Doug Gilmour | 3.00 | 1.35 |
| ❑ R50 Playoff Assists Long Shot | 2.00 | .90 |
| ❑ R51 Brian Leetch | 3.00 | 1.35 |
| ❑ R52 Sergei Fedorov | 6.00 | 2.70 |
| ❑ R53 Pavel Bure | 6.00 | 2.70 |
| ❑ R54 Mark Messier | 4.00 | 1.80 |
| ❑ R55 Pat LaFontaine | 2.00 | .90 |
| ❑ R56 Doug Gilmour | 3.00 | 1.35 |
| ❑ R57 Brett Hull | 4.00 | 1.80 |
| ❑ R58 Theoren Fleury | 3.00 | 1.35 |
| ❑ R59 Wayne Gretzky | 20.00 | 9.00 |
| ❑ R60 Playoff Points Long Shot | 2.00 | .90 |

## 1994-95 Upper Deck SP Inserts

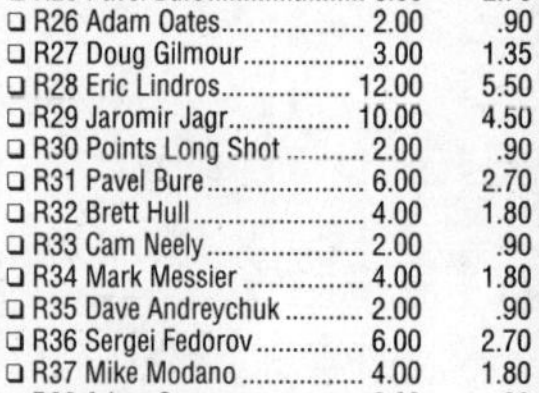

The 1994-95 Upper Deck SP Insert set was released in two series of 90 cards for a total of 180. One SP Insert was found in each Upper Deck hobby pack, with two per retail pack. The cards feature a gold metallic foil front, with the SP logo running down either side of the card front. The cards are numbered with an SP prefix, and have a silver hologram on the back. The cards are grouped alphabetically within teams.

| | MINT | NRMT |
|---|---|---|
| COMPLETE SET (180) | 100.00 | 45.00 |

COMPLETE SERIES 1 (90) 50.00 22.00
COMPLETE SERIES 2 (90) 50.00 22.00
COMMON CARD (SP1-SP180) .25 .11

□ SP1 Maxim Bets .25 .11
□ SP2 Stephan Lebeau .25 .11
□ SP3 Garry Valk .25 .11
□ SP4 Ray Bourque .75 .35
□ SP5 Mariusz Czerkawski .25 .11
□ SP6 Cam Neely .40 .18
□ SP7 Adam Oates .40 .18
□ SP8 Dominik Hasek .75 .35
□ SP9 Dale Hawerchuk .40 .18
□ SP10 Alexander Mogilny .40 .18
□ SP11 Theoren Fleury .40 .18
□ SP12 Trevor Kidd .40 .18
□ SP13 Joe Nieuwendyk .40 .18
□ SP14 Gary Roberts .25 .11
□ SP15 Ed Belfour .75 .35
□ SP16 Chris Chelios .75 .35
□ SP17 Jeremy Roenick .75 .35
□ SP18 Neal Broten .25 .11
□ SP19 Russ Courtnall .25 .11
□ SP20 Derian Hatcher .25 .11
□ SP21 Mike Modano .40 .18
□ SP22 Paul Coffey .75 .35
□ SP23 Slava Kozlov .40 .18
□ SP24 Keith Primeau .25 .11
□ SP25 Steve Yzerman .75 .35
□ SP26 Jason Arnott .40 .18
□ SP27 Bill Ranford .40 .18
□ SP28 Doug Weight .40 .18
□ SP29 Bob Kudelski .25 .11
□ SP30 Rob Niedermayer .40 .18
□ SP31 John Vanbiesbrouck .75 .35
□ SP32 Andrew Cassels .25 .11
□ SP33 Chris Pronger .40 .18
□ SP34 Geoff Sanderson .40 .18
□ SP35 Rob Blake .25 .11
□ SP36 Wayne Gretzky .75 .35
□ SP37 Jari Kurri .25 .11
□ SP38 Alexei Zhitnik .25 .11
□ SP39 Vincent Damphousse .40 .18
□ SP40 Kirk Muller .25 .11
□ SP41 Oleg Petrov .25 .11
□ SP42 Patrick Roy .75 .35
□ SP43 Martin Brodeur .75 .35
□ SP44 Stephane Richer .25 .11
□ SP45 Scott Stevens .25 .11
□ SP46 Darius Kasparaitis .25 .11
□ SP47 Vladimir Malakhov .25 .11
□ SP48 Pierre Turgeon .40 .18
□ SP49 Alexei Kovalev .25 .11
□ SP50 Brian Leetch .75 .35
□ SP51 Mark Messier .75 .35
□ SP52 Mike Richter .75 .35
□ SP53 Craig Billington .25 .11
□ SP54 Alexandre Daigle .25 .11
□ SP55 Alexei Yashin .25 .11
□ SP56 Josef Beranek .25 .11
□ SP57 Rod Brind'Amour .25 .11
□ SP58 Mark Recchi .25 .11
□ SP59 Mikael Renberg .40 .18
□ SP60 Jaromir Jagr .75 .35
□ SP61 Mario Lemieux .75 .35
□ SP62 Kevin Stevens .25 .11
□ SP63 Owen Nolan .25 .11
□ SP64 Mike Ricci .25 .11
□ SP65 Joe Sakic .75 .35
□ SP66 Brett Hull .75 .35
□ SP67 Craig Janney .25 .11
□ SP68 Curtis Joseph .75 .35
□ SP69 Brendan Shanahan .75 .35
□ SP70 Ulf Dahlen .25 .11
□ SP71 Arturs Irbe .40 .18
□ SP72 Sergei Makarov .25 .11
□ SP73 Sandis Ozolinsh .40 .18
□ SP74 Brian Bradley .25 .11
□ SP75 Chris Gratton .40 .18
□ SP76 Denis Savard .40 .18
□ SP77 Dave Andreychuk .25 .11
□ SP78 Mike Gartner .40 .18
□ SP79 Dimitri Mironov .25 .11
□ SP80 Felix Potvin .75 .35
□ SP81 Jeff Brown .25 .11
□ SP82 Geoff Courtnall .25 .11
□ SP83 Trevor Linden .40 .18
□ SP84 Kirk McLean .40 .18
□ SP85 Peter Bondra .40 .18
□ SP86 Kevin Hatcher .40 .18
□ SP87 Dimitri Khristich .25 .11
□ SP88 Teemu Selanne .75 .35
□ SP89 Keith Tkachuk .75 .35
□ SP90 Alexei Zhamnov .40 .18
□ SP91 Paul Kariya .75 .35
□ SP92 Valeri Karpov .25 .11
□ SP93 Oleg Tverdovsky .25 .11
□ SP94 Al Iafrate .25 .11
□ SP95 Blaine Lacher .40 .18
□ SP96 Bryan Smolinski .25 .11
□ SP97 Donald Audette .40 .18
□ SP98 Yuri Khymlev .25 .11
□ SP99 Pat LaFontaine .40 .18
□ SP100 Derek Plante .25 .11
□ SP101 Steve Chiasson .25 .11
□ SP102 Phil Housley .25 .11
□ SP103 Michael Nylander .25 .11
□ SP104 Robert Reichel .25 .11
□ SP105 Tony Amonte .40 .18
□ SP106 Bernie Nicholls .25 .11
□ SP107 Gary Suter .25 .11
□ SP108 Paul Cavallini .25 .11
□ SP109 Todd Harvey .25 .11
□ SP110 Kevin Hatcher .25 .11
□ SP111 Andy Moog .40 .18
□ SP112 Dino Ciccarelli .25 .11
□ SP113 Sergei Fedorov .75 .35
□ SP114 Nicklas Lidstrom .40 .18
□ SP115 Mike Vernon .40 .18
□ SP116 Shayne Corson .25 .11
□ SP117 David Oliver .25 .11
□ SP118 Ryan Smyth .75 .35
□ SP119 Jesse Belanger .25 .11
□ SP120 Mark Fitzpatrick .40 .18
□ SP121 Scott Mellanby .40 .18
□ SP122 Andrei Nikolishin .25 .11
□ SP123 Darren Turcotte .25 .11
□ SP124 Pat Verbeek .25 .11
□ SP125 Glen Wesley .25 .11
□ SP126 Tony Granato .25 .11
□ SP127 Marty McSorley .25 .11
□ SP128 Jamie Storr .40 .18
□ SP129 Rick Tocchet .25 .11
□ SP130 Brian Bellows .25 .11
□ SP131 Valeri Bure .25 .11
□ SP132 Turner Stevenson .25 .11
□ SP133 John MacLean .25 .11
□ SP134 Scott Niedermayer .25 .11
□ SP135 Brian Rolston .25 .11
□ SP136 Brett Lindros .25 .11
□ SP137 Jamie McLennan .25 .11
□ SP138 Zigmund Palffy .75 .35
□ SP139 Steve Thomas .25 .11
□ SP140 Adam Graves .40 .18
□ SP141 Petr Nedved .40 .18
□ SP142 Sergei Zubov .40 .18
□ SP143 Don Beaupre .40 .18
□ SP144 Radek Bonk .40 .18
□ SP145 Pavol Demitra .25 .11
□ SP146 Sylvain Turgeon .25 .11
□ SP147 Ron Hextall .40 .18
□ SP148 Patrik Juhlin .25 .11
□ SP149 Eric Lindros .75 .35
□ SP150 Ron Francis .40 .18
□ SP151 Markus Naslund .25 .11
□ SP152 Luc Robitaille .25 .11
□ SP153 Martin Straka .25 .11
□ SP154 Wendel Clark .25 .11
□ SP155 Adam Deadmarsh .40 .18
□ SP156 Peter Forsberg .75 .35
□ SP157 Janne Laukkanen .25 .11
□ SP158 Steve Duchesne .25 .11
□ SP159 Al MacInnis .25 .11
□ SP160 Esa Tikkanen .25 .11
□ SP161 Jeff Friesen .25 .11
□ SP162 Viktor Kozlov .25 .11
□ SP163 Ray Whitney .25 .11
□ SP164 Roman Hamrlik .40 .18
□ SP165 Alexander Selivanov .25 .11
□ SP166 Jason Wiemer .25 .11
□ SP167 Doug Gilmour .40 .18
□ SP168 Kenny Jonsson .25 .11
□ SP169 Mike Ridley .25 .11
□ SP170 Mats Sundin .40 .18
□ SP171 Pavel Bure .75 .35
□ SP172 Martin Gelinas .25 .11
□ SP173 Mike Peca .25 .11
□ SP174 Jason Allison .25 .11
□ SP175 Joe Juneau .25 .11
□ SP176 Pat Peake .25 .11
□ SP177 Mark Tinordi .25 .11
□ SP178 Tim Cheveldae .40 .18
□ SP179 Nelson Emerson .25 .11
□ SP180 Dave Manson .25 .11

## 1994-95 Upper Deck SP Inserts Die Cuts

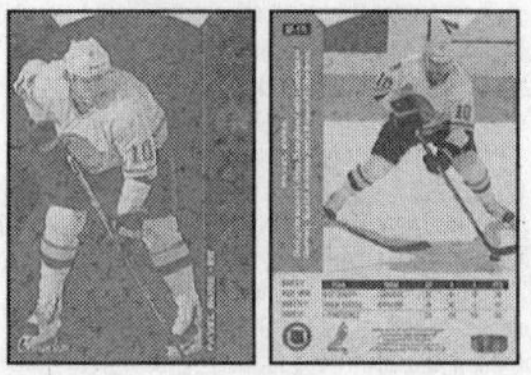

The 1994-95 Upper Deck SP Die-cut inserts are a parallel of the SP inserts. This 180-card set was issued only in Upper Deck series two packs, but featured specially cut versions of the inserts found in either series. To ensure that you have an actual die-cut insert, note that the hologram on the back is gold instead of the silver used on regular cards.

MINT NRMT
COMPLETE DIE CUT SET (180) 400.00 180.00
COMMON CARD (SP1-SP180).. 1.00 .45
*STARS: 2X TO 4X BASIC CARDS
*YOUNG STARS: 1.5X TO 3X BASIC CARDS

## 1995 Upper Deck World Junior Alumni

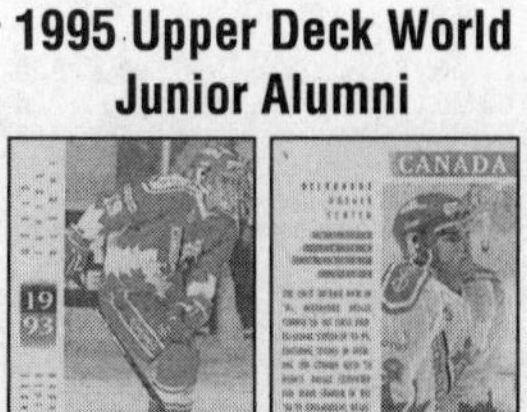

Produced by Upper Deck in conjunction with the Canadian Amateur Hockey Association, this 15-card set features players from the 1992, 1993, and 1994 Canadian World Junior Championship teams. The sets were offered at Esso service stations in Alberta, Canada for 2.99 with a gasoline purchase. The offer ran from December 20, 1994 through January 4, 1995, during the 1995 World Junior Hockey Championships, which were headquartered in Red Deer, Alberta. The fronts display color action shots that are full-bleed except on the left, where a white stripe carries player identification, year and the set title. The backs present a second color action shot and a player profile.

MINT NRMT
COMPLETE SET (15) 8.00 3.60
COMMON CARD (1-15) .25 .11

□ 1 Title Card .25 .11
□ 2 Manny Legace .40 .18
□ 3 Jeff Nelson .25 .11
□ 4 Alexandre Daigle .40 .18
□ 5 Paul Kariya 5.00 2.20
□ 6 Turner Stevenson .25 .11
□ 7 Mike Peca 1.00 .45
□ 8 Tyler Wright .25 .11
□ 9 Brent Tully .25 .11
□ 10 Trevor Kidd .50 .23
□ 11 Martin Lapointe .40 .18
□ 12 Scott Niedermayer .50 .23
□ 13 Jeff Friesen .75 .35
□ 14 Todd Harvey .50 .23
□ 15 Jamie Storr .50 .23

## 1995-96 Upper Deck

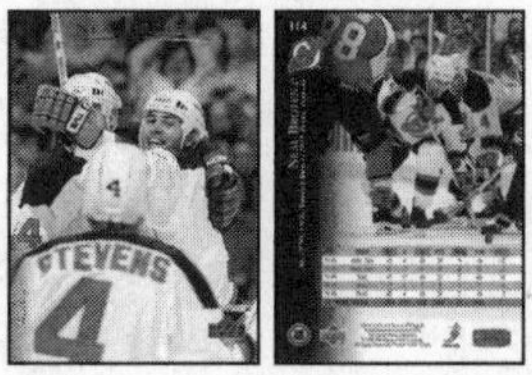

The 1995-96 Upper Deck set was issued in two series totalling 570 cards. The set is distinguished primarily through the inclusion of a number of noteworthy rookie cards in the the Star Rookie (496-507) and Program of Excellence (508-525) subsets including Daniel Alfredsson, Daniel Cleary, Chris Phillips, Marc Denis, Jose Theodore, Hnat Domenichelli, Marcus Nilsson and Niklas Anger. The Cool Trade Exchange card was randomly inserted in 1:82 series 2 packs. The card could be redeemed for special die-cut cards of Wayne Gretzky, Sergei Fedorov, Peter Forsberg and Doug Gilmour.

MINT NRMT
COMPLETE SET (570) 60.00 27.00
COMPLETE SERIES 1 (270) 20.00 9.00
COMPLETE SERIES 2 (300) 40.00 18.00
COMMON CARD (1-570) .10 .05

□ 1 Cam Neely .15 .07
□ 2 Donald Audette .15 .07
□ 3 Derian Hatcher .10 .05
□ 4 Mike Vernon .15 .07
□ 5 Darryl Sydor .10 .05
□ 6 Patrice Brisebois .10 .05
□ 7 John LeClair .50 .23
□ 8 Luc Robitaille .15 .07
□ 9 Todd Krygier .10 .05
□ 10 Steve Chiasson .10 .05
□ 11 Sergei Krivokrasov .10 .05
□ 12 Marko Tuomainen .10 .05
□ 13 Paul Ranheim .10 .05
□ 14 Brian Rolston .10 .05
□ 15 Alexei Yashin .15 .07
□ 16 Joe Mullen .15 .07
□ 17 Dallas Drake .10 .05
□ 18 Tony Amonte .15 .07
□ 19 Gary Roberts .10 .05
□ 20 Geoff Sanderson .15 .07
□ 21 Gord Murphy .10 .05
□ 22 Dean Evason .10 .05
□ 23 Brantt Myhres .10 .05
□ 24 Sergei Makarov .10 .05
□ 25 Joe Juneau .10 .05
□ 26 Greg Adams .10 .05
□ 27 Yuri Khmylev .10 .05
□ 28 Yanic Perreault .10 .05
□ 29 Jason Arnott .15 .07
□ 30 Glenn Healy .15 .07
□ 31 Sergei Brylin .10 .05
□ 32 Ian Laperriere .10 .05
□ 33 Trevor Linden .15 .07
□ 34 Nicklas Lidstrom .15 .07
□ 35 Don Sweeney .10 .05
□ 36 Brian Savage .10 .05
□ 37 Richard Matvichuk .10 .05
□ 38 Dale Hawerchuk .15 .07
□ 39 Patrick Roy 1.50 .70
□ 40 Alexander Semak .10 .05
□ 41 Kirk Maltby .10 .05
□ 42 Jiri Slegr .10 .05
□ 43 Joe Sacco .10 .05
□ 44 Claude Lemieux .15 .07
□ 45 Eric Weinrich .10 .05
□ 46 Ron Francis .15 .07
□ 47 Jamie Storr .15 .07
□ 48 Felix Potvin .30 .14
□ 49 Steve Duchesne .10 .05
□ 50 Jody Hull .10 .05
□ 51 Dave Manson .10 .05
□ 52 Marty McInnis .10 .05
□ 53 James Patrick .10 .05
□ 54 Joe Sakic .60 .25
□ 55 Andrei Nikolishin .10 .05
□ 56 Adrian Aucoin .10 .05
□ 57 Wade Flaherty .15 .07
□ 58 Marek Malik .10 .05
□ 59 Jason Allison .10 .05
□ 60 Stephane Matteau .10 .05
□ 61 Jason Dawe .10 .05
□ 62 Ray Whitney .10 .05
□ 63 Bill Lindsay .10 .05
□ 64 Alexei Zhamnov .15 .07
□ 65 Adam Deadmarsh .15 .07
□ 66 Vincent Damphousse .15 .07
□ 67 Josef Beranek .10 .05
□ 68 Stanislav Neckar .10 .05
□ 69 Alexei Kasatonov .10 .05
□ 70 Jon Casey .15 .07
□ 71 Todd Marchant .10 .05
□ 72 Mike Sillinger .10 .05
□ 73 Markus Naslund .10 .05
□ 74 John MacLean .15 .07
□ 75 Mike Ridley .10 .05
□ 76 Petr Svoboda .10 .05
□ 77 Milos Holan .10 .05
□ 78 John Tucker .10 .05
□ 79 Doug Brown .10 .05
□ 80 Ted Donato .10 .05
□ 81 Dimitri Yushkevich .10 .05
□ 82 Brett Lindros .10 .05
□ 83 Brian Bradley .10 .05
□ 84 Mario Lemieux 1.50 .70
□ 85 Nikolai Khabibulin .15 .07
□ 86 Larry Murphy .15 .07
□ 87 Mike Donnelly .10 .05
□ 88 Brian Holzinger .30 .14
□ 89 Steve Larouche .10 .05
□ 90 Ray Ferraro .10 .05
□ 91 Mikhail Shtalenkov .10 .05
□ 92 Viktor Kozlov .10 .05
□ 93 Jon Klemm .10 .05
□ 94 Mark Tinordi .10 .05
□ 95 Bret Hedican .10 .05
□ 96 Kevin Stevens .10 .05
□ 97 Bernie Nicholls .10 .05
□ 98 Pat Verbeek .10 .05
□ 99 Wayne Gretzky 2.00 .90
□ 100 Rene Corbet .10 .05
□ 101 Shayne Corson .10 .05
□ 102 Cliff Ronning .10 .05
□ 103 Olaf Kolzig .15 .07
□ 104 Dominik Hasek .60 .25
□ 105 Corey Millen .10 .05
□ 106 Patrick Flatley .10 .05
□ 107 Chris Therien .10 .05
□ 108 Ken Wregget .15 .07
□ 109 Paul Ysebaert .10 .05
□ 110 Mike Gartner .15 .07
□ 111 Michal Grosek .10 .05
□ 112 Craig Billington .15 .07
□ 113 Steve Yzerman 1.00 .45
□ 114 Neal Broten .15 .07
□ 115 Tom Barrasso .15 .07
□ 116 Brent Fedyk .10 .05
□ 117 Todd Gill .10 .05
□ 118 Petr Klima .10 .05
□ 119 Dave Karpa .10 .05
□ 120 Geoff Courtnall .10 .05
□ 121 Kelly Buchberger .10 .05
□ 122 Eric LaCroix .10 .05
□ 123 Janne Laukkanen .10 .05
□ 124 Radek Bonk .10 .05
□ 125 Sergio Momesso .10 .05
□ 126 Esa Tikkanen .10 .05
□ 127 Jon Rohloff .10 .05
□ 128 Ken Klee .10 .05
□ 129 Johan Garpenlov .10 .05
□ 130 Sean Burke .15 .07
□ 131 Shean Donovan .10 .05
□ 132 Alexei Kovalev .10 .05
□ 133 Sylvain Cote .10 .05
□ 134 Jeff Friesen .15 .07
□ 135 Scott Pearson .10 .05
□ 136 Kirk McLean .15 .07
□ 137 Glen Wesley .10 .05
□ 138 Bob Kudelski .10 .05
□ 139 Craig Johnson .10 .05
□ 140 Zigmund Palffy .30 .14
□ 141 Kris King .10 .05
□ 142 Rusty Fitzgerald .10 .05
□ 143 Trevor Kidd .15 .07
□ 144 Dave Ellett .10 .05
□ 145 Kelly Hrudey .15 .07
□ 146 Igor Kravchuk .10 .05
□ 147 Mats Sundin .15 .07
□ 148 Shawn Chambers .10 .05
□ 149 Bob Corkum .10 .05
□ 150 Shjon Podein .10 .05
□ 151 Murray Craven .15 .07
□ 152 Roman Hamrlik .15 .07
□ 153 Lyle Odelein .10 .05
□ 154 Vyacheslav Kozlov .10 .05
□ 155 David Emma .10 .05
□ 156 Benoit Brunet .10 .05
□ 157 Jozef Stumpel .10 .05
□ 158 Darrin Madeley .10 .05
□ 159 Keith Primeau .15 .07
□ 160 Jeff Norton .15 .07
□ 161 Mathieu Schneider .10 .05
□ 162 Trent Klatt .10 .05
□ 163 Pat Peake .10 .05
□ 164 Rob Gaudreau .10 .05
□ 165 Doug Bodger .10 .05
□ 166 Sergei Nemchinov .10 .05
□ 167 David Oliver .10 .05
□ 168 Sandis Ozolinsh .15 .07
□ 169 Mark Messier .40 .18
□ 170 Chris Chelios .30 .14
□ 171 Teemu Selanne .60 .25
□ 172 Robert Svehla .10 .05
□ 173 Nikolai Borschevsky .10 .05
□ 174 Chris Pronger .15 .07
□ 175 Dave Lowry .10 .05
□ 176 Owen Nolan .15 .07
□ 177 Sylvain Turgeon .10 .05
□ 178 Nelson Emerson .10 .05
□ 179 Theoren Fleury .15 .07
□ 180 Patrik Carnback .10 .05
□ 181 Kevin Smyth .10 .05
□ 182 Jeff Shantz .10 .05
□ 183 Bob Carpenter .10 .05
□ 184 Brendan Shanahan .60 .25
□ 185 Tomas Sandstrom .10 .05
□ 186 Eric Desjardins .10 .05
□ 187 Alexei Zhitnik .10 .05
□ 188 Alexander Mogilny .15 .07
□ 189 Mariusz Czerkawski .10 .05
□ 190 Vladimir Konstantinov .10 .05
□ 191 Andy Moog .15 .07
□ 192 Peter Popovic .10 .05
□ 193 Marty McSorley .10 .05
□ 194 Mikael Renberg .15 .07
□ 195 Alek Stojanov .10 .05
□ 196 Rick Tabaracci .15 .07
□ 197 Adam Oates .15 .07
□ 198 Garry Galley .10 .05
□ 199 Todd Harvey .10 .05
□ 200 Martin Lapointe .10 .05
□ 201 Tony Granato .10 .05
□ 202 Turner Stevenson .10 .05
□ 203 Jeff Beukeboom .10 .05
□ 204 Adam Foote .10 .05
□ 205 Daren Puppa .15 .07
□ 206 Paul Kariya 1.25 .55
□ 207 German Titov .10 .05
□ 208 Patrick Poulin .10 .05
□ 209 Jesse Belanger .10 .05
□ 210 Steven Rice .10 .05
□ 211 Martin Brodeur .75 .35
□ 212 Rob Pearson .10 .05
□ 213 Igor Larionov .10 .05
□ 214 Pavel Bure .30 .14
□ 215 Sergei Fedorov .30 .14
□ 216 Ed Belfour .30 .14
□ 217 Mark Messier .30 .14
□ 218 Steve Yzerman .50 .23
□ 219 Mats Sundin .15 .07
□ 220 Mike Modano .40 .18
□ 221 Alexander Mogilny .15 .07
□ 222 Wayne Gretzky 1.00 .45
□ 223 Keith Primeau .15 .07
□ 224 Adam Graves .15 .07
□ 225 Owen Nolan .15 .07
□ 226 Paul Coffey .30 .14
□ 227 Jeremy Roenick .30 .14
□ 228 Felix Potvin .30 .14
□ 229 Trevor Kidd .15 .07
□ 230 Ray Bourque .30 .14
□ 231 Mario Lemieux .75 .35
□ 232 Peter Bondra .30 .14
□ 233 Brett Hull .30 .14
□ 234 Alexei Zhamnov .15 .07
□ 235 Theoren Fleury .15 .07
□ 236 Brian Leetch .30 .14
□ 237 Cam Neely .15 .07
□ 238 Chris Chelios .30 .14
□ 239 Adam Graves .15 .07
□ 240 Doug Gilmour .30 .14
□ 241 Jeremy Roenick .30 .14
□ 242 Joe Sakic .30 .14
□ 243 Keith Tkachuk .30 .14
□ 244 Luc Robitaille .15 .07
□ 245 Paul Kariya .75 .35
□ 246 Owen Nolan .15 .07
□ 247 John LeClair .30 .14
□ 248 Paul Coffey .30 .14
□ 249 Peter Bondra .30 .14
□ 250 Ray Bourque .30 .14
□ 251 Brett Hull .30 .14
□ 252 Wayne Gretzky 1.00 .45
□ 253 Teemu Selanne .30 .14
□ 254 Ray Sheppard .15 .07
□ 255 Ron Francis .15 .07
□ 256 Kevin Hatcher .10 .05
□ 257 Brett Lindros .10 .05
□ 258 Claude Lemieux .15 .07
□ 259 Saku Koivu .50 .23
□ 260 Radek Dvorak .10 .05
□ 261 Niklas Sundstrom .10 .05
□ 262 Chad Kilger .20 .09
□ 263 Vitali Yachmenev .10 .05
□ 264 Jeff O'Neill .10 .05
□ 265 Brendan Witt .10 .05
□ 266 Jason Bonsignore .10 .05
□ 267 Aki-Petteri Berg .20 .09
□ 268 Eric Daze .30 .14
□ 269 Shane Doan .20 .09
□ 270 Daymond Langkow .30 .14
□ 272 Brian Noonan .10 .05
□ 273 Guy Carbonneau .10 .05
□ 274 Rick Tocchet .15 .07
□ 275 Teppo Numminen .10 .05
□ 276 Brian Skrudland .10 .05
□ 277 Andrei Trefilov .10 .05
□ 278 Joe Murphy .10 .05

| | | |
|---|---|---|
| ❑ 279 Sergei Fedorov | .60 | .25 |
| ❑ 280 Doug Weight | .15 | .07 |
| ❑ 281 Robert Lang | .10 | .05 |
| ❑ 282 Darryl Shannon | .10 | .05 |
| ❑ 283 Cory Stillman | .10 | .05 |
| ❑ 284 Gary Suter | .10 | .05 |
| ❑ 285 Joe Nieuwendyk | .15 | .07 |
| ❑ 286 Terry Carkner | .10 | .05 |
| ❑ 287 Dimitri Khristich | .10 | .05 |
| ❑ 288 Alexander Karpovtsev | .10 | .05 |
| ❑ 289 Garth Snow | .15 | .07 |
| ❑ 290 Al MacInnis | .15 | .07 |
| ❑ 291 Doug Gilmour | .30 | .14 |
| ❑ 292 Mike Eastwood | .10 | .05 |
| ❑ 293 Steve Heinze | .10 | .05 |
| ❑ 294 Phil Housley | .15 | .07 |
| ❑ 295 Tim Taylor | .10 | .05 |
| ❑ 296 Curtis Joseph | .30 | .14 |
| ❑ 297 Patrick Roy | 1.50 | .70 |
| ❑ 298 Ted Drury | .10 | .05 |
| ❑ 299 Igor Korolev | .10 | .05 |
| ❑ 300 Ray Bourque | .30 | .14 |
| ❑ 301 Darren McCarty | .10 | .05 |
| ❑ 302 Miroslav Satan | 2.00 | .90 |
| ❑ 303 Adam Burt | .10 | .05 |
| ❑ 304 Valeri Bure | .15 | .07 |
| ❑ 305 Sergei Gonchar | .10 | .05 |
| ❑ 306 Jason York | .10 | .05 |
| ❑ 307 Brent Grieve | .10 | .05 |
| ❑ 308 Greg Johnson | .10 | .05 |
| ❑ 309 Kevin Hatcher | .10 | .05 |
| ❑ 310 Rob Niedermayer | .15 | .07 |
| ❑ 311 Nelson Emerson | .10 | .05 |
| ❑ 312 Mark Janssens | .10 | .05 |
| ❑ 313 Tommy Soderstrom | .15 | .07 |
| ❑ 314 Joey Kocur | .10 | .05 |
| ❑ 315 Craig Janney | .15 | .07 |
| ❑ 316 Alexander Selivanov | .10 | .05 |
| ❑ 317 Russ Courtnall | .10 | .05 |
| ❑ 318 Petr Sykora | .40 | .18 |
| ❑ 319 Rick Zombo | .10 | .05 |
| ❑ 320 Randy Burridge | .10 | .05 |
| ❑ 321 John Vanbiesbrouck | .50 | .23 |
| ❑ 322 Dmitri Mironov | .10 | .05 |
| ❑ 323 Sean Hill | .10 | .05 |
| ❑ 324 Rod Brind'Amour | .15 | .07 |
| ❑ 325 Wendel Clark | .15 | .07 |
| ❑ 326 Brent Gilchrist | .10 | .05 |
| ❑ 327 Tyler Wright | .10 | .05 |
| ❑ 328 Scott Daniels | .10 | .05 |
| ❑ 329 Adam Graves | .15 | .07 |
| ❑ 330 Dean Malkoc | .10 | .05 |
| ❑ 331 Jamie Macoun | .10 | .05 |
| ❑ 332 Sandy Moger | .10 | .05 |
| ❑ 333 Mike Peca | .10 | .05 |
| ❑ 334 Greg Johnson | .10 | .05 |
| ❑ 335 Jason Woolley | .10 | .05 |
| ❑ 336 Rob Dimaio | .10 | .05 |
| ❑ 337 Damian Rhodes | .15 | .07 |
| ❑ 338 Gino Odjick | .10 | .05 |
| ❑ 339 Peter Bondra | .30 | .14 |
| ❑ 340 Todd Ewen | .10 | .05 |
| ❑ 341 Matthew Barnaby | .15 | .07 |
| ❑ 342 Sylvain Lefebvre | .10 | .05 |
| ❑ 343 Oleg Petrov | .10 | .05 |
| ❑ 344 Jim Carey | .30 | .14 |
| ❑ 345 Stu Barnes | .10 | .05 |
| ❑ 346 Kelly Miller | .10 | .05 |
| ❑ 347 Antti Tormanen | .10 | .05 |
| ❑ 348 Ray Sheppard | .15 | .07 |
| ❑ 349 Igor Larionov | .10 | .05 |
| ❑ 350 Kjell Samuelsson | .10 | .05 |
| ❑ 351 Benoit Hogue | .10 | .05 |
| ❑ 352 Jeff Brown | .10 | .05 |
| ❑ 353 Nolan Baumgartner | .10 | .05 |
| ❑ 354 Denis Pederson | .10 | .05 |
| ❑ 355 Shawn Burr | .10 | .05 |
| ❑ 356 Jyrki Lumme | .10 | .05 |
| ❑ 357 Kevin Haller | .10 | .05 |
| ❑ 358 John Cullen | .10 | .05 |
| ❑ 359 Martin Gelinas | .10 | .05 |
| ❑ 360 Shawn McEachern | .10 | .05 |
| ❑ 361 Sandy McCarthy | .10 | .05 |
| ❑ 362 Grant Marshall | .10 | .05 |
| ❑ 363 Dean McAmmond | .10 | .05 |
| ❑ 364 Kevin Todd | .10 | .05 |
| ❑ 365 Bobby Holik | .10 | .05 |
| ❑ 366 Joel Otto | .10 | .05 |
| ❑ 367 Dave Andreychuk | .15 | .07 |
| ❑ 368 Ronnie Stern | .10 | .05 |
| ❑ 369 Jocelyn Thibault | .30 | .14 |
| ❑ 370 Dave Gagner | .15 | .07 |
| ❑ 371 Bryan Marchment | .10 | .05 |
| ❑ 372 Jari Kurri | .15 | .07 |
| ❑ 373 Bill Guerin | .10 | .05 |
| ❑ 374 Eric Lindros | 1.00 | .45 |
| ❑ 375 Adam Creighton | .10 | .05 |
| ❑ 376 Dimitri Yushkevich | .10 | .05 |
| ❑ 377 Peter Zezel | .10 | .05 |
| ❑ 378 Valeri Karpov | .10 | .05 |
| ❑ 379 Patrick Labrecque | .10 | .05 |
| ❑ 380 Mick Vukota | .10 | .05 |
| ❑ 381 Ulf Dahlen | .10 | .05 |
| ❑ 382 Enrico Ciccone | .10 | .05 |
| ❑ 383 Scott Niedermayer | .10 | .05 |
| ❑ 384 Ville Peltonen | .10 | .05 |
| ❑ 385 Blaine Lacher | .15 | .07 |
| ❑ 386 Pat LaFontaine | .15 | .07 |
| ❑ 387 Jeff Hackett | .15 | .07 |
| ❑ 388 Mike Keane | .10 | .05 |
| ❑ 389 Pierre Turgeon | .15 | .07 |
| ❑ 390 Scott Lachance | .10 | .05 |
| ❑ 391 Jason Wiemer | .10 | .05 |
| ❑ 392 Michal Pivonka | .10 | .05 |
| ❑ 393 Dennis Bonvie | .10 | .05 |
| ❑ 394 Glen Murray | .10 | .05 |
| ❑ 395 Bobby Dollas | .10 | .05 |
| ❑ 396 Paul Coffey | .30 | .14 |
| ❑ 397 Stephane Fiset | .15 | .07 |
| ❑ 398 Jere Lehtinen | .10 | .05 |
| ❑ 399 Scott Mellanby | .15 | .07 |
| ❑ 400 Robert Kron | .10 | .05 |
| ❑ 401 Doug Lidster | .10 | .05 |
| ❑ 402 Don Beaupre | .15 | .07 |
| ❑ 403 Arturs Irbe | .15 | .07 |
| ❑ 404 Brian Bellows | .10 | .05 |
| ❑ 405 Corey Hirsch | .15 | .07 |
| ❑ 406 Pavel Bure | .60 | .25 |
| ❑ 407 Chris Gratton | .15 | .07 |
| ❑ 408 Oleg Tverdovsky | .15 | .07 |
| ❑ 409 Derek Plante | .10 | .05 |
| ❑ 410 Dan Keczmer | .10 | .05 |
| ❑ 411 Donald Brashear | .10 | .05 |
| ❑ 412 Andrei Vasilyev | .10 | .05 |
| ❑ 413 Tommy Salo | .40 | .18 |
| ❑ 414 Kevin Lowe | .10 | .05 |
| ❑ 415 Dody Wood | .10 | .05 |
| ❑ 416 Denis Chasse | .10 | .05 |
| ❑ 417 Aaron Gavey | .10 | .05 |
| ❑ 418 Scott Walker | .10 | .05 |
| ❑ 419 Richard Park | .10 | .05 |
| ❑ 420 Mike Modano | .15 | .07 |
| ❑ 421 Kyle McLaren | .30 | .14 |
| ❑ 422 Jeremy Roenick | .30 | .14 |
| ❑ 423 Mark Fitzpatrick | .15 | .07 |
| ❑ 424 Landon Wilson | .10 | .05 |
| ❑ 425 Steve Rucchin | .10 | .05 |
| ❑ 426 Stephane Richer | .15 | .07 |
| ❑ 427 Martin Straka | .10 | .05 |
| ❑ 428 Ron Hextall | .15 | .07 |
| ❑ 429 Joe Dziedzic | .10 | .05 |
| ❑ 430 Peter Forsberg | 1.00 | .45 |
| ❑ 431 Dino Ciccarelli | .15 | .07 |
| ❑ 432 Robert Dirk | .10 | .05 |
| ❑ 433 Wayne Primeau | .10 | .05 |
| ❑ 434 Denis Savard | .15 | .07 |
| ❑ 435 Keith Carney | .10 | .05 |
| ❑ 436 Tom Fitzgerald | .10 | .05 |
| ❑ 437 Cale Hulse | .10 | .05 |
| ❑ 438 Mike Richter | .30 | .14 |
| ❑ 439 Marcus Ragnarsson | .10 | .05 |
| ❑ 440 Roman Vopat | .10 | .05 |
| ❑ 441 Zdenek Nedved | .10 | .05 |
| ❑ 442 Dale Hunter | .10 | .05 |
| ❑ 443 Bob Sweeney | .10 | .05 |
| ❑ 444 Randy McKay | .10 | .05 |
| ❑ 445 Chris Osgood | .30 | .14 |
| ❑ 446 Andrei Kovalenko | .10 | .05 |
| ❑ 447 Darius Kasparaitis | .10 | .05 |
| ❑ 448 Ulf Samuelsson | .10 | .05 |
| ❑ 449 Chris Joseph | .10 | .05 |
| ❑ 450 Chris Terreri | .15 | .07 |
| ❑ 451 Keith Jones | .10 | .05 |
| ❑ 452 Tim Cheveldae | .15 | .07 |
| ❑ 453 Stephen Leach | .10 | .05 |
| ❑ 454 Michael Nylander | .10 | .05 |
| ❑ 455 Ed Belfour | .30 | .14 |
| ❑ 456 Claude Lemieux | .15 | .07 |
| ❑ 457 Mike Ricci | .10 | .05 |
| ❑ 458 Shane Churla | .10 | .05 |
| ❑ 459 Kris Draper | .10 | .05 |
| ❑ 460 Byron Dafoe | .15 | .07 |
| ❑ 461 Troy Mallette | .10 | .05 |
| ❑ 462 Petr Nedved | .15 | .07 |
| ❑ 463 Kenny Jonsson | .10 | .05 |
| ❑ 464 Keith Tkachuk | .40 | .18 |
| ❑ 465 Jaromir Jagr | 1.00 | .45 |
| ❑ 466 Vladimir Malakhov | .10 | .05 |
| ❑ 467 Guy Hebert | .15 | .07 |
| ❑ 468 Brad May | .10 | .05 |
| ❑ 469 Bob Probert | .15 | .07 |
| ❑ 470 Sandis Ozolinsh | .15 | .07 |
| ❑ 471 Oleg Mikulchik | .10 | .05 |
| ❑ 472 Steve Thomas | .10 | .05 |
| ❑ 473 Travis Green | .15 | .07 |
| ❑ 474 Sergei Zubov | .10 | .05 |
| ❑ 475 Bill Houlder | .10 | .05 |
| ❑ 476 Roman Oksiuta | .10 | .05 |
| ❑ 477 Jamie Rivers | .10 | .05 |
| ❑ 478 Rob Blake | .10 | .05 |
| ❑ 479 Todd Elik | .10 | .05 |
| ❑ 480 Zarley Zalapski | .10 | .05 |
| ❑ 481 Darren Turcotte | .10 | .05 |
| ❑ 482 Scott Stevens | .15 | .07 |
| ❑ 483 Pat Falloon | .15 | .07 |
| ❑ 484 Grant Fuhr | .15 | .07 |
| ❑ 485 Martin Rucinsky | .10 | .05 |
| ❑ 486 Brett Hull | .40 | .18 |
| ❑ 487 Brian Leetch | .30 | .14 |
| ❑ 488 Shaun Van Allen | .10 | .05 |
| ❑ 489 Valeri Kamensky | .15 | .07 |
| ❑ 490 Mark Recchi | .15 | .07 |
| ❑ 491 Jason Muzzatti | .15 | .07 |
| ❑ 492 Andrew Cassels | .15 | .07 |
| ❑ 493 Nick Kypreos | .10 | .05 |
| ❑ 494 Bryan Smolinski | .10 | .05 |
| ❑ 495 Owen Nolan | .15 | .07 |
| ❑ 496 Bryan McCabe | .10 | .05 |
| ❑ 497 Mathieu Dandenault | .10 | .05 |
| ❑ 498 Deron Quint | .10 | .05 |
| ❑ 499 Jason Doig | .10 | .05 |
| ❑ 500 Marty Murray | .10 | .05 |
| ❑ 501 Ed Jovanovski | .30 | .14 |
| ❑ 502 Stefan Ustorf | .10 | .05 |
| ❑ 503 Jamie Langenbrunner | .10 | .05 |
| ❑ 504 Daniel Alfredsson | .75 | .35 |
| ❑ 505 Darby Hendrickson | .10 | .05 |
| ❑ 506 Brett McLean | .15 | .07 |
| ❑ 507 Daniel Cleary | 3.00 | 1.35 |
| ❑ 508 Todd Robinson | .10 | .05 |
| ❑ 509 Arron Asham | .15 | .07 |
| ❑ 510 Daniel Corso | .30 | .14 |
| ❑ 511 Darren Van Oene | .10 | .05 |
| ❑ 512 Trevor Wasyluk | .30 | .14 |
| ❑ 513 Josh Holden | .60 | .25 |
| ❑ 514 Etienne Drapeau | .15 | .07 |
| ❑ 515 Matt Osborne | .10 | .05 |
| ❑ 516 Zenith Komarniski | .15 | .07 |
| ❑ 517 Chris Phillips | .60 | .25 |
| ❑ 518 Chris Fleury | .10 | .05 |
| ❑ 519 Cory Sarich | .60 | .25 |
| ❑ 520 Glenn Crawford | .10 | .05 |
| ❑ 521 Francois Methot | .10 | .05 |
| ❑ 522 Geoff Peters | .20 | .09 |
| ❑ 523 Joey Tetarenko | .15 | .07 |
| ❑ 524 Randy Petruk | .15 | .07 |
| ❑ 525 Mathieu Garon | .60 | .25 |
| ❑ 526 Daymond Langkow | .30 | .14 |
| ❑ 527 Craig Mills | .10 | .05 |
| ❑ 528 Rhett Warrener | .10 | .05 |
| ❑ 529 Marc Denis | 2.00 | .90 |
| ❑ 530 Jose Theodore | 1.50 | .70 |
| ❑ 531 Curtis Brown | .10 | .05 |
| ❑ 532 Chad Allen | .10 | .05 |
| ❑ 533 Denis Gauthier | .10 | .05 |
| ❑ 534 Brad Larsen | .10 | .05 |
| ❑ 535 Jamie Wright | .15 | .07 |
| ❑ 536 Mike Watt | .15 | .07 |
| ❑ 537 Jason Holland | .15 | .07 |
| ❑ 538 Robb Gordon | .10 | .05 |
| ❑ 539 Hnat Domenichelli | .30 | .14 |
| ❑ 540 Ondrej Kratena | .15 | .07 |
| ❑ 541 Michal Bros | .15 | .07 |
| ❑ 542 Marek Posmyk | .15 | .07 |
| ❑ 543 Marek Melanovsky | .15 | .07 |
| ❑ 544 Jan Tomajko | .15 | .07 |
| ❑ 545 Ales Pisa | .15 | .07 |
| ❑ 546 Miika Elomo | .15 | .07 |
| ❑ 547 Timo Salonen | .15 | .07 |
| ❑ 548 Teemu Riihijarvi | .15 | .07 |
| ❑ 549 Antti-Jussi Niemi | .15 | .07 |
| ❑ 550 Pasi Petrilainen | .15 | .07 |
| ❑ 551 Toni Lydman | .15 | .07 |
| ❑ 552 Dmitri Nabokov | .15 | .07 |
| ❑ 553 Alexei Morozov | .60 | .25 |
| ❑ 554 Sergei Samsonov | 1.25 | .55 |
| ❑ 555 Alexei Vasilyev | .15 | .07 |
| ❑ 556 Andrei Petrunin | .10 | .05 |
| ❑ 557 Dimitri Rybkin | .15 | .07 |
| ❑ 558 Sergei Zimakov | .15 | .07 |
| ❑ 559 Peter Nylander | .10 | .05 |
| ❑ 560 Marcus Nilsson UER | .10 | .05 |
| ❑ 561 Niklas Anger | .15 | .07 |
| ❑ 562 Per Anton Lundstrom | .15 | .07 |
| ❑ 563 Patrik Wallenberg | .15 | .07 |
| ❑ 564 Per Ragnar Bergkvist | .15 | .07 |
| ❑ 565 Mike Sylvia | .10 | .05 |
| ❑ 566 Marty Reasoner | .15 | .07 |
| ❑ 567 Reg Berg | .10 | .05 |
| ❑ 568 Tom Poti | .10 | .05 |
| ❑ 569 Chris Drury | 10.00 | 4.50 |
| ❑ 570 Michael McBain | .10 | .05 |
| ❑ NNO Cool Trade Exchange | 2.00 | .90 |

## 1995-96 Upper Deck Electric Ice

The Electric Ice cards were inserted one per every retail pack, or two per jumbo. These cards featured the Electric Ice logo on a silver foil background.

| | MINT | NRMT |
|---|---|---|
| COMPLETE SET (570) | 300.00 | 135.00 |
| COMPLETE SERIES 1 (270) | 120.00 | 55.00 |
| COMPLETE SERIES 2 (300) | 180.00 | 80.00 |
| COMMON CARD (1-570) | .25 | .11 |

*STARS: 5X TO 10X BASIC CARDS
*YOUNG STARS: 3X TO 6X BASIC CARDS
*RC'S: 20X TO 40X BASIC CARDS

## 1995-96 Upper Deck Electric Ice Gold

These cards were inserted at the rate of 1:35 retail packs only, and could be differentiated from basic UD cards by the inclusion of the words Electric Ice embossed in gold down the side of the card front.

| | MINT | NRMT |
|---|---|---|
| COMPLETE SET (570) | 5200.00 | 2300.00 |
| COMPLETE SERIES 1 (270) | 2200.00 | 1000.00 |
| COMPLETE SERIES 2 (300) | 3000.00 | 1350.00 |
| COMMON CARD (1-570) | 5.00 | 2.20 |

*STARS: 50X TO 100X BASIC CARDS
*YOUNG STARS: 25X TO 50X BASIC CARDS

| | | |
|---|---|---|
| ❑ 39 Patrick Roy | 150.00 | 70.00 |
| ❑ 54 Joe Sakic | 60.00 | 27.00 |
| ❑ 84 Mario Lemieux | 150.00 | 70.00 |
| ❑ 99 Wayne Gretzky | 225.00 | 100.00 |
| ❑ 113 Steve Yzerman | 100.00 | 45.00 |
| ❑ 206 Paul Kariya | 120.00 | 55.00 |
| ❑ 222 Wayne Gretzky | 100.00 | 45.00 |
| ❑ 231 Mario Lemieux | 80.00 | 36.00 |
| ❑ 252 Wayne Gretzky | 100.00 | 45.00 |
| ❑ 297 Patrick Roy | 150.00 | 70.00 |
| ❑ 374 Eric Lindros | 100.00 | 45.00 |
| ❑ 430 Peter Forsberg | 100.00 | 45.00 |
| ❑ 465 Jaromir Jagr | 100.00 | 45.00 |
| ❑ 507 Daniel Cleary | 80.00 | 36.00 |
| ❑ 529 Marc Denis | 50.00 | 22.00 |
| ❑ 554 Sergei Samsonov | 60.00 | 27.00 |
| ❑ 569 Chris Drury RC | 150.00 | 70.00 |

## 1995-96 Upper Deck Freeze Frame

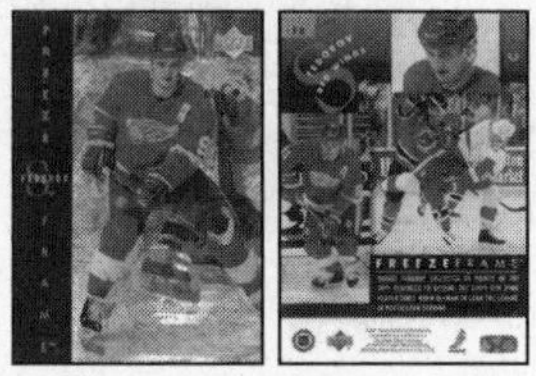

Twenty top stars are featured in this multiple photo insert set which utilizes Upper Deck's Light FX foil printing technology. The cards were randomly inserted at a rate of 1:34 series one packs. Jumbo versions of these cards, measuring 3 1/2" by 6", were inserted one per series one box. Multipliers can be found in the header below to determine values for these.

| | MINT | NRMT |
|---|---|---|
| COMPLETE SET (20) | 200.00 | 90.00 |
| COMMON CARD (F1-F20) | 2.50 | 1.10 |

*JUMBOS: .5X TO 1X BASIC CARDS

| | | |
|---|---|---|
| ❑ F1 Peter Forsberg | 15.00 | 6.75 |
| ❑ F2 Wayne Gretzky | 30.00 | 13.50 |
| ❑ F3 Eric Lindros | 20.00 | 9.00 |
| ❑ F4 Jaromir Jagr | 15.00 | 6.75 |
| ❑ F5 Cam Neely | 2.50 | 1.10 |
| ❑ F6 Jeremy Roenick | 2.50 | 1.10 |
| ❑ F7 Mark Messier | 6.00 | 2.70 |
| ❑ F8 Sergei Fedorov | 10.00 | 4.50 |
| ❑ F9 Paul Kariya | 20.00 | 9.00 |
| ❑ F10 Pavel Bure | 10.00 | 4.50 |
| ❑ F11 Dominik Hasek | 10.00 | 4.50 |
| ❑ F12 Theoren Fleury | 4.00 | 1.80 |
| ❑ F13 Alexei Zhamnov | 4.00 | 1.80 |
| ❑ F14 Martin Brodeur | 12.00 | 5.50 |
| ❑ F15 Brett Hull | 6.00 | 2.70 |
| ❑ F16 Mario Lemieux | 25.00 | 11.00 |
| ❑ F17 Paul Coffey | 2.50 | 1.10 |
| ❑ F18 Brian Leetch | 2.50 | 1.10 |
| ❑ F19 Ray Bourque | 2.50 | 1.10 |
| ❑ F20 Jim Carey | 4.00 | 1.80 |

## 1995-96 Upper Deck Gretzky Collection

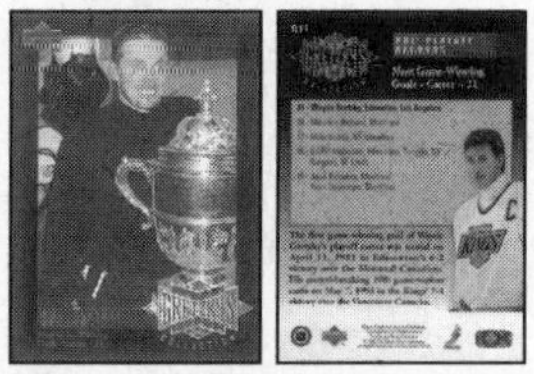

This 24 card set, which focuses on the many remarkable achievements in the career of Wayne Gretzky, was released through four separate products. Cards G1-G9, along with an NNO header card, could be found in 1995-96 Collector's Choice retail and hobby packs at a rate of 1:11. Cards G10-G13 and an NNO header card were randomly inserted in packs of Upper Deck series 1 at a rate of 1:29. Cards G14-17 along with an NNO header card were randomly inserted in packs of Upper Deck series 2 at a rate of 1:29. Finally, cards G18-G20, along with an NNO header card, were randomly inserted at a rate of 1:45 packs of SP. The cards share a similar design element, but with added foil enhancements for each step up the premium ladder. A jumbo version of cards G1-G10 were produced and inserted into some Collector's Choice boxes. Multipliers can be found in the header below to determine value for these.

| | MINT | NRMT |
|---|---|---|
| COMPLETE SET (24) | 200.00 | 90.00 |
| COMP.CC SET (10) | 40.00 | 18.00 |
| COMP.SP SET (4) | 90.00 | 40.00 |
| COMP.UD SER.1 (5) | 40.00 | 18.00 |
| COMP.UD SER.2 (5) | 40.00 | 18.00 |
| COMMON CC (G1-G9/HDR) | 5.00 | 2.20 |
| COMMON UD (G10-G17/HDR'S) | 10.00 | 4.50 |
| COMMON SP (G18-G20/HDR) | 25.00 | 11.00 |

*G1-G10 JUMBOS: .75X TO 1.5X BASIC CARDS

| | | |
|---|---|---|
| ❑ G1 Most Goals In One Season | 5.00 | 2.20 |
| ❑ G2 Most Assists in One Season | 5.00 | 2.20 |
| ❑ G3 Most Points in One Season | 5.00 | 2.20 |
| ❑ G4 Most Three-or-more Goal Games | 5.00 | 2.20 |
| ❑ G5 Longest Consecutive Point-Score | 5.00 | 2.20 |
| ❑ G6 Longest Consecutive Assist-Score | 5.00 | 2.20 |
| ❑ G7 Most Assists in One Game in Finals | 5.00 | 2.20 |
| ❑ G8 Most Goals in One Season | 5.00 | 2.20 |
| ❑ G9 Most Points in One Season | 5.00 | 2.20 |
| ❑ G10 Most Points-Career | 10.00 | 4.50 |
| ❑ G11 Most Game-Winning Goals Career | 10.00 | 4.50 |
| ❑ G12 Most Points in One Playoff Year | 10.00 | 4.50 |
| ❑ G13 Most Points in Final Series | 10.00 | 4.50 |
| ❑ G14 Most Goals-Career | 10.00 | 4.50 |
| ❑ G15 Most Points-Career | 10.00 | 4.50 |
| ❑ G16 Most Goals in One All-Star Game | 10.00 | 4.50 |
| ❑ G17 Most Goals in One Period | 10.00 | 4.50 |
| ❑ G18 Most Goals | 25.00 | 11.00 |
| ❑ G19 Most Assists | 25.00 | 11.00 |
| ❑ G20 Most Points | 25.00 | 11.00 |

## 1995-96 Upper Deck NHL All-Stars

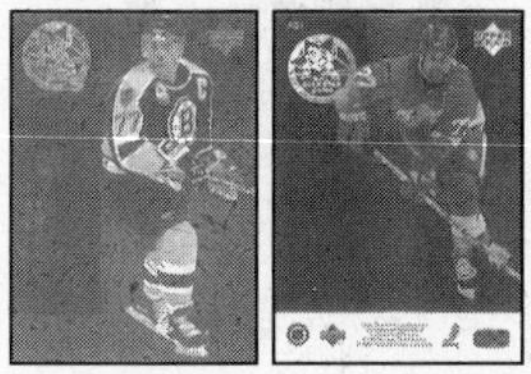

Randomly inserted in packs at a rate of 1:34 series 2 packs, these twenty two-sided cards highlight the participants in the 1995-96 All-Star Game. The cards utilize the UD Light FX technology. Players from the Western Conference have a teal left border, while players from the Eastern Conference have purple left border. There also were jumbo version of these cards inserted one per series 2 box. Multipliers can be found in the header below to determine value for these.

| | MINT | NRMT |
|---|---|---|
| COMPLETE SET (20) | 200.00 | 90.00 |
| COMMON CARD (AS1-AS20) | 2.00 | .90 |

*JUMBOS: .5X TO 1X BASIC ALL-STARS

| | | |
|---|---|---|
| ❑ AS1 Ray Bourque / Paul Coffey | 5.00 | 2.20 |
| ❑ AS2 Scott Stevens / Chris Chelios | 5.00 | 2.20 |
| ❑ AS3 Jaromir Jagr / Brett Hull | 15.00 | 6.75 |
| ❑ AS4 Brendan Shanahan / Pavel Bure | 10.00 | 4.50 |
| ❑ AS5 Mario Lemieux / Wayne Gretzky | 50.00 | 22.00 |
| ❑ AS6 Martin Brodeur / Ed Belfour | 10.00 | 4.50 |
| ❑ AS7 Brian Leetch / Nicklas Lidstrom | 5.00 | 2.20 |
| ❑ AS8 Roman Hamrlik / Gary Suter | 2.00 | .90 |
| ❑ AS9 Eric Desjardins / Al MacInnis | 2.00 | .90 |
| ❑ AS10 Cam Neely / Alexander Mogilny | 4.00 | 1.80 |
| ❑ AS11 Peter Bondra / Theoren Fleury | 4.00 | 1.80 |
| ❑ AS12 Daniel Alfredsson / Teemu Selanne | 8.00 | 3.60 |
| ❑ AS13 Pat Verbeek / Owen Nolan | 2.00 | .90 |
| ❑ AS14 John LeClair / Paul Kariya | 25.00 | 11.00 |
| ❑ AS15 Pierre Turgeon / Sergei Fedorov | 10.00 | 4.50 |
| ❑ AS16 Mark Messier / Doug Weight | 8.00 | 3.60 |
| ❑ AS17 Eric Lindros / Peter Forsberg | 25.00 | 11.00 |
| ❑ AS18 Ron Francis / Mats Sundin | 4.00 | 1.80 |
| ❑ AS19 John Vanbiesbrouck / Chris Osgood | 10.00 | 4.50 |
| ❑ AS20 Dominik Hasek / Felix Potvin | 5.00 | 2.20 |

## 1995-96 Upper Deck Predictor Hobby

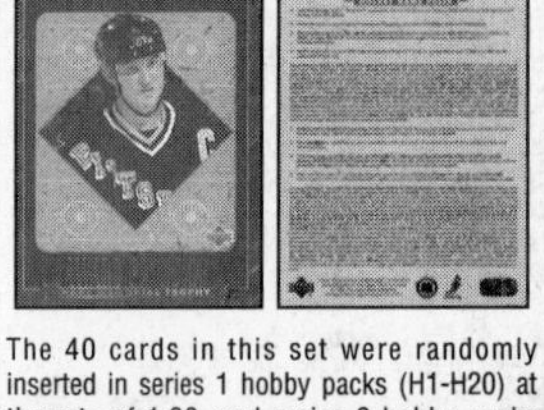

The 40 cards in this set were randomly inserted in series 1 hobby packs (H1-H20) at the rate of 1:30, and series 2 hobby packs (H21-H40) at the rate of 1:23. Each card was a potential winner in an interactive game based on season-end award recipients: if the player pictured on your card came in first or second in the voting for that award, you could redeem your card for a complete set of Predictors from that distribution category. Cards H1-H10 were contestants for the Hart Trophy, cards H11-H20 were goalies competing for the Vezina Trophy, cards H21-H30 were

contestants for the Calder Trophy, and cards H31-H40 were vying for the James Norris Trophy. The cards of Mario Lemieux, Mark Messier, Jim Carey, Vezina Long Shot, Daniel Alfredsson, Eric Daze, Chris Chelios and Ray Bourque may be somewhat harder to locate now, because, as winners, many of them were redeemed and destroyed.

| | MINT | NRMT |
|---|---|---|
| COMPLETE SET (40) | 200.00 | 90.00 |
| COMMON CARD (H1-H40) | 2.00 | .90 |
| ❑ H1 Eric Lindros | 12.00 | 5.50 |
| ❑ H2 Jaromir Jagr | 12.00 | 5.50 |
| ❑ H3 Paul Coffey | 3.00 | 1.35 |
| ❑ H4 Mario Lemieux | 15.00 | 6.75 |
| ❑ H5 Martin Brodeur | 8.00 | 3.60 |
| ❑ H6 Sergei Fedorov | 6.00 | 2.70 |
| ❑ H7 Wayne Gretzky | 20.00 | 9.00 |
| ❑ H8 Peter Forsberg | 12.00 | 5.50 |
| ❑ H9 Mark Messier | 5.00 | 2.20 |
| ❑ H10 Hart Long Shot | 2.00 | .90 |
| ❑ H11 Martin Brodeur | 8.00 | 3.60 |
| ❑ H12 Mike Richter | 3.00 | 1.35 |
| ❑ H13 Dominik Hasek | 6.00 | 2.70 |
| ❑ H14 Patrick Roy | 15.00 | 6.75 |
| ❑ H15 Blaine Lacher | 2.00 | .90 |
| ❑ H16 Jim Carey | 2.00 | .90 |
| ❑ H17 Felix Potvin | 3.00 | 1.35 |
| ❑ H18 Ed Belfour | 3.00 | 1.35 |
| ❑ H19 John Vanbiesbrouck | 5.00 | 2.20 |
| ❑ H20 Vezina Long Shot | 2.00 | .90 |
| ❑ H21 Vitali Yachmenev | 2.00 | .90 |
| ❑ H22 Saku Koivu | 6.00 | 2.70 |
| ❑ H23 Daniel Alfredsson | 2.50 | 1.10 |
| ❑ H24 Ed Jovanovski | 2.50 | 1.10 |
| ❑ H25 Aki Berg | 2.00 | .90 |
| ❑ H26 Radek Dvorak | 2.00 | .90 |
| ❑ H27 Shane Doan | 2.00 | .90 |
| ❑ H28 Nicklas Sundstrom | 2.50 | 1.10 |
| ❑ H29 Eric Daze | 2.50 | 1.10 |
| ❑ H30 Calder Long Shot | 2.00 | .90 |
| ❑ H31 Paul Coffey | 3.00 | 1.35 |
| ❑ H32 Ray Bourque | 3.00 | 1.35 |
| ❑ H33 Brian Leetch | 3.00 | 1.35 |
| ❑ H34 Chris Chelios | 3.00 | 1.35 |
| ❑ H35 Scott Stevens | 2.00 | .90 |
| ❑ H36 Nicklas Lidstrom | 2.50 | 1.10 |
| ❑ H37 Sergei Zubov | 2.00 | .90 |
| ❑ H38 Larry Murphy | 2.00 | .90 |
| ❑ H39 Roman Hamrlik | 2.00 | .90 |
| ❑ H40 Norris Long Shot | 2.00 | .90 |

## 1995-96 Upper Deck Predictor Retail

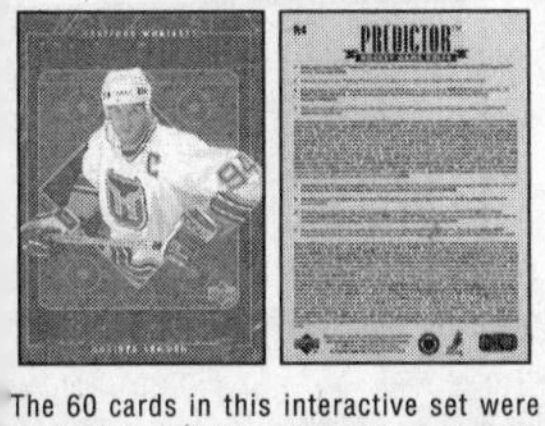

The 60 cards in this interactive set were randomly inserted in retail packs from both series. R1-R30 were inserted at a rate of 1:30 series 1 retail packs, and 1:17 Value Added retail packs, while cards R31-R60 were inserted at a rate of 1:23 retail series 2 packs. A card could be redeemed if the player pictured finished first or second in the race for the scoring category featured. Cards R1-R10 battled for the assists crown, R11-R20 aimed to be the most prolific snipers, R21-R30 aimed to reach the top of the point scoring heap, R31-R40 were shooting for Art Ross, R41-R50 were in search of Lester B. Pearson, and R51-R60 were players looking to be awarded the Conn Smythe. However, a printing error at the printing plant reversed the intended categories on cards R1-R10 and R11-R20. In light of this, Upper Deck decided to honour a card as a winner if the player pictured won in either category. The cards of Mario Lemieux (R32, R42), Jaromir Jagr, Patrick Roy, Ron Francis and the Long Shots in the Assists, Goals, Points, and Smythe categories may be somewhat harder to find, as many were redeemed as winners.

| | MINT | NRMT |
|---|---|---|
| COMPLETE SET (60) | 400.00 | 180.00 |
| COMMON CARD (R1-R60) | 2.00 | .90 |
| COMP.ASST.EXCH.SET (10) | 25.00 | 11.00 |
| COMP.GOAL.EXCH.SET (10) | 25.00 | 11.00 |
| COMP.SCOR.EXCH.SET (10) | 30.00 | 13.50 |
| COMP.ROSS.EXCH.SET (10) | 40.00 | 18.00 |
| COMP.PEAR.EXCH.SET (10) | 30.00 | 13.50 |
| COMP.SMYTH.EXCH.SET (10) | 40.00 | 18.00 |
| ❑ R1 Cam Neely | 2.00 | .90 |
| ❑ R2 Eric Lindros | 12.00 | 5.50 |
| ❑ R3 Jaromir Jagr | 10.00 | 4.50 |
| ❑ R4 Brendan Shanahan | 6.00 | 2.70 |
| ❑ R5 Brett Hull | 4.00 | 1.80 |
| ❑ R6 Alexander Mogilny | 2.50 | 1.10 |
| ❑ R7 Owen Nolan | 2.00 | .90 |
| ❑ R8 Theoren Fleury | 2.50 | 1.10 |
| ❑ R9 Pavel Bure | 6.00 | 2.70 |
| ❑ R10 Assists Long Shot | 2.00 | .90 |
| ❑ R11 Ron Francis | 2.00 | .90 |
| ❑ R12 Paul Coffey | 3.00 | 1.35 |
| ❑ R13 Wayne Gretzky | 20.00 | 9.00 |
| ❑ R14 Joe Sakic | 8.00 | 3.60 |
| ❑ R15 Steve Yzerman | 10.00 | 4.50 |
| ❑ R16 Adam Oates | 2.50 | 1.10 |
| ❑ R17 Joe Juneau | 2.50 | 1.10 |
| ❑ R18 Brian Leetch | 3.00 | 1.35 |
| ❑ R19 Pat LaFontaine | 2.00 | .90 |
| ❑ R20 Goals Long Shot | 2.00 | .90 |
| ❑ R21 Eric Lindros | 12.00 | 5.50 |
| ❑ R22 Jaromir Jagr | 10.00 | 4.50 |
| ❑ R23 Wayne Gretzky | 20.00 | 9.00 |
| ❑ R24 Sergei Fedorov | 6.00 | 2.70 |
| ❑ R25 Peter Forsberg | 10.00 | 4.50 |
| ❑ R26 Pavel Bure | 6.00 | 2.70 |
| ❑ R27 Joe Sakic | 8.00 | 3.60 |
| ❑ R28 Alexei Zhamnov | 2.50 | 1.10 |
| ❑ R29 Pat LaFontaine | 2.50 | 1.10 |
| ❑ R30 Points Long Shot | 4.00 | 1.80 |
| ❑ R31 Wayne Gretzky | 20.00 | 9.00 |
| ❑ R32 Mario Lemieux | 15.00 | 6.75 |
| ❑ R33 Eric Lindros | 12.00 | 5.50 |
| ❑ R34 Sergei Fedorov | 6.00 | 2.70 |
| ❑ R35 Alexander Mogilny | 2.50 | 1.10 |
| ❑ R36 Joe Sakic | 8.00 | 3.60 |
| ❑ R37 Peter Forsberg | 10.00 | 4.50 |
| ❑ R38 Jaromir Jagr | 10.00 | 4.50 |
| ❑ R39 Mark Messier | 4.00 | 1.80 |
| ❑ R40 Ross Long Shot | 2.00 | .90 |
| ❑ R41 Wayne Gretzky | 20.00 | 9.00 |
| ❑ R42 Mario Lemieux | 15.00 | 6.75 |
| ❑ R43 Paul Kariya | 12.00 | 5.50 |
| ❑ R44 Sergei Fedorov | 6.00 | 2.70 |
| ❑ R45 Joe Sakic | 8.00 | 3.60 |
| ❑ R46 Jaromir Jagr | 10.00 | 4.50 |
| ❑ R47 Jeremy Roenick | 3.00 | 1.35 |
| ❑ R48 Ray Bourque | 3.00 | 1.35 |
| ❑ R49 Teemu Selanne | 6.00 | 2.70 |
| ❑ R50 Pearson Long Shot | 2.00 | .90 |
| ❑ R51 Wayne Gretzky | 20.00 | 9.00 |
| ❑ R52 Eric Lindros | 12.00 | 5.50 |
| ❑ R53 Mario Lemieux | 15.00 | 6.75 |
| ❑ R54 Peter Forsberg | 10.00 | 4.50 |
| ❑ R55 Patrick Roy | 15.00 | 6.75 |
| ❑ R56 Mark Messier | 4.00 | 1.80 |
| ❑ R57 Martin Brodeur | 8.00 | 3.60 |
| ❑ R58 Steve Yzerman | 10.00 | 4.50 |
| ❑ R59 Mike Modano | 2.50 | 1.10 |
| ❑ R60 Smythe Long Shot | 2.00 | .90 |

## 1995-96 Upper Deck Special Edition

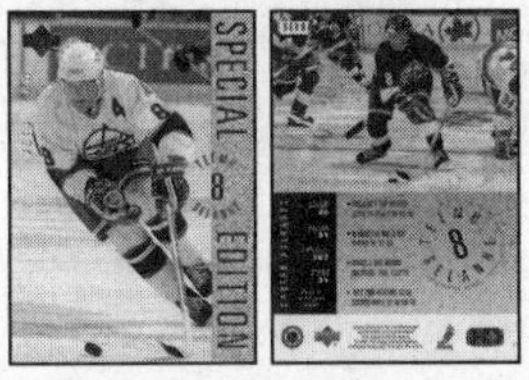

This 180-card set was inserted one per hobby pack over both series of 1995-96 Upper Deck cards. Cards 1-90 were found in series 1 packs, while 91-180 were in series 2. The cards featured a nearly full-bleed photo on the front, with a silver foil Special Edition logo down the right border.

| | MINT | NRMT |
|---|---|---|
| COMPLETE SET (180) | 90.00 | 40.00 |
| COMPLETE SERIES 1 (90) | 30.00 | 13.50 |
| COMPLETE SERIES 2 (90) | 60.00 | 27.00 |
| COMMON CARD (1-180) | .25 | .11 |
| ❑ SE1 Paul Kariya | 5.00 | 2.20 |
| ❑ SE2 Oleg Tverdovsky | .25 | .11 |
| ❑ SE3 Guy Hebert | .50 | .23 |
| ❑ SE4 Ray Bourque | 1.25 | .55 |
| ❑ SE5 Adam Oates | .50 | .23 |
| ❑ SE6 Mariusz Czerkawski | .25 | .11 |
| ❑ SE7 Blaine Lacher | .50 | .23 |
| ❑ SE8 Garry Galley | .25 | .11 |
| ❑ SE9 Donald Audette | .25 | .11 |
| ❑ SE10 Pat LaFontaine | .50 | .23 |
| ❑ SE11 Alexei Zhitnik | .25 | .11 |
| ❑ SE12 Joe Nieuwendyk | .50 | .23 |
| ❑ SE13 Phil Housley | .50 | .23 |
| ❑ SE14 German Titov | .25 | .11 |
| ❑ SE15 Trevor Kidd | .50 | .23 |
| ❑ SE16 Bernie Nicholls | .25 | .11 |
| ❑ SE17 Chris Chelios | 1.25 | .55 |
| ❑ SE18 Tony Amonte | .50 | .23 |
| ❑ SE19 Ed Belfour | 1.25 | .55 |
| ❑ SE20 Jon Klemm | .25 | .11 |
| ❑ SE21 Peter Forsberg | 4.00 | 1.80 |
| ❑ SE22 Adam Deadmarsh | .50 | .23 |
| ❑ SE23 Stephane Fiset | .50 | .23 |
| ❑ SE24 Dave Gagner | .25 | .11 |
| ❑ SE25 Kevin Hatcher | .25 | .11 |
| ❑ SE26 Mike Modano | .50 | .23 |
| ❑ SE27 Keith Primeau | .25 | .11 |
| ❑ SE28 Dino Ciccarelli | .25 | .11 |
| ❑ SE29 Nicklas Lidstrom | .50 | .23 |
| ❑ SE30 Steve Yzerman | 4.00 | 1.80 |
| ❑ SE31 Doug Weight | .50 | .23 |
| ❑ SE32 Bill Ranford | .50 | .23 |
| ❑ SE33 Stu Barnes | .25 | .11 |
| ❑ SE34 Scott Mellanby | .50 | .23 |
| ❑ SE35 Rob Niedermayer | .50 | .23 |
| ❑ SE36 Andrew Cassels | .25 | .11 |
| ❑ SE37 Darren Turcotte | .25 | .11 |
| ❑ SE38 Andrei Nikolishin | .25 | .11 |
| ❑ SE39 Sean Burke | .50 | .23 |
| ❑ SE40 Rick Tocchet | .50 | .23 |
| ❑ SE41 Jari Kurri | .50 | .23 |
| ❑ SE42 Rob Blake | .25 | .11 |
| ❑ SE43 Mark Recchi | .50 | .23 |
| ❑ SE44 Pierre Turgeon | .50 | .23 |
| ❑ SE45 Vladimir Malakhov | .25 | .11 |
| ❑ SE46 Valeri Bure | .25 | .11 |
| ❑ SE47 Stephane Richer | .25 | .11 |
| ❑ SE48 Bill Guerin | .25 | .11 |
| ❑ SE49 Scott Stevens | .50 | .23 |
| ❑ SE50 Claude Lemieux | .50 | .23 |
| ❑ SE51 Zigmund Palffy | 1.50 | .70 |
| ❑ SE52 Kirk Muller | .25 | .11 |
| ❑ SE53 Todd Bertuzzi | .25 | .11 |
| ❑ SE54 Brett Lindros | .25 | .11 |
| ❑ SE55 Brian Leetch | 1.25 | .55 |
| ❑ SE56 Alexei Kovalev | .25 | .11 |
| ❑ SE57 Adam Graves | .50 | .23 |
| ❑ SE58 Mike Richter | 1.25 | .55 |
| ❑ SE59 Alexei Yashin | .50 | .23 |
| ❑ SE60 Alexandre Daigle | .50 | .23 |
| ❑ SE61 Don Beaupre | .50 | .23 |
| ❑ SE62 Radek Bonk | .25 | .11 |
| ❑ SE63 John LeClair | 2.00 | .90 |
| ❑ SE64 Rod Brind'Amour | .50 | .23 |
| ❑ SE65 Ron Hextall | .50 | .23 |
| ❑ SE66 Ron Francis | .25 | .11 |
| ❑ SE67 Markus Naslund | .25 | .11 |
| ❑ SE68 Tom Barrasso | .50 | .23 |
| ❑ SE69 Ian Laperriere | .25 | .11 |
| ❑ SE70 Esa Tikkanen | .25 | .11 |
| ❑ SE71 Al MacInnis | .25 | .11 |
| ❑ SE72 Ulf Dahlen | .25 | .11 |
| ❑ SE73 Craig Janney | .25 | .11 |
| ❑ SE74 Jeff Friesen | .50 | .23 |
| ❑ SE75 Chris Gratton | .25 | .11 |
| ❑ SE76 Roman Hamrlik | .50 | .23 |
| ❑ SE77 Alexander Selivanov | .25 | .11 |
| ❑ SE78 Daren Puppa | .50 | .23 |
| ❑ SE79 Dave Andreychuk | .50 | .23 |
| ❑ SE80 Doug Gilmour | .50 | .23 |
| ❑ SE81 Kenny Jonsson | .25 | .11 |
| ❑ SE82 Trevor Linden | .50 | .23 |
| ❑ SE83 Kirk McLean | .50 | .23 |
| ❑ SE84 Jeff Brown | .25 | .11 |
| ❑ SE85 Keith Jones | .50 | .23 |
| ❑ SE86 Joe Juneau | .50 | .23 |
| ❑ SE87 Jim Carey | .50 | .23 |
| ❑ SE88 Keith Tkachuk | 1.50 | .70 |
| ❑ SE89 Teemu Selanne | 2.50 | 1.10 |
| ❑ SE90 Igor Korolev | .25 | .11 |
| ❑ SE91 Mike Sillinger | .25 | .11 |
| ❑ SE92 Steve Rucchin | .25 | .11 |
| ❑ SE93 Valeri Karpov | .25 | .11 |
| ❑ SE94 Cam Neely | .50 | .23 |
| ❑ SE95 Shawn McEachern | .25 | .11 |
| ❑ SE96 Kevin Stevens | .25 | .11 |
| ❑ SE97 Ted Donato | .25 | .11 |
| ❑ SE98 Dominik Hasek | 2.50 | 1.10 |
| ❑ SE99 Randy Burridge | .25 | .11 |
| ❑ SE100 Jason Dawe | .25 | .11 |
| ❑ SE101 Theoren Fleury | .50 | .23 |
| ❑ SE102 Michael Nylander | .25 | .11 |
| ❑ SE103 Rick Tabaracci | .25 | .11 |
| ❑ SE104 Jeremy Roenick | 1.25 | .55 |
| ❑ SE105 Bob Probert | .50 | .23 |
| ❑ SE106 Patrick Poulin | .25 | .11 |
| ❑ SE107 Gary Suter | .25 | .11 |
| ❑ SE108 Claude Lemieux | .50 | .23 |
| ❑ SE109 Sandis Ozolinsh | .50 | .23 |
| ❑ SE110 Patrick Roy | 6.00 | 2.70 |
| ❑ SE111 Joe Sakic | 3.00 | 1.35 |
| ❑ SE112 Derian Hatcher | .25 | .11 |
| ❑ SE113 Greg Adams | .25 | .11 |
| ❑ SE114 Todd Harvey | .25 | .11 |
| ❑ SE115 Sergei Fedorov | 2.50 | 1.10 |
| ❑ SE116 Chris Osgood | 1.25 | .55 |
| ❑ SE117 Vyacheslav Kozlov | .50 | .23 |
| ❑ SE118 Paul Coffey | 1.25 | .55 |
| ❑ SE119 Jason Arnott | .50 | .23 |
| ❑ SE120 David Oliver | .25 | .11 |
| ❑ SE121 Todd Marchant | .25 | .11 |
| ❑ SE122 John Vanbiesbrouck | 3.00 | 1.35 |
| ❑ SE123 Jody Hull | .25 | .11 |
| ❑ SE124 Jason Woolley | .25 | .11 |
| ❑ SE125 Brendan Shanahan | 2.50 | 1.10 |
| ❑ SE126 Nelson Emerson | .25 | .11 |
| ❑ SE127 Geoff Sanderson | .50 | .23 |
| ❑ SE128 Wayne Gretzky | 8.00 | 3.60 |
| ❑ SE129 Marty McSorley | .25 | .11 |
| ❑ SE130 Yanic Perreault | .25 | .11 |
| ❑ SE131 Jocelyn Thibault | 1.25 | .55 |
| ❑ SE132 Brian Savage | .25 | .11 |
| ❑ SE133 Vincent Damphousse | .50 | .23 |
| ❑ SE134 John MacLean | .25 | .11 |
| ❑ SE135 Martin Brodeur | 3.00 | 1.35 |
| ❑ SE136 Steve Thomas | .25 | .11 |
| ❑ SE137 Esa Tikkanen | .25 | .11 |
| ❑ SE138 Travis Green | .50 | .23 |
| ❑ SE139 Wendel Clark | .25 | .11 |
| ❑ SE140 Tommy Soderstrom | .25 | .11 |
| ❑ SE141 Mark Messier | 2.00 | .90 |
| ❑ SE142 Ulf Samuelsson | .25 | .11 |
| ❑ SE143 Ray Ferraro | .25 | .11 |
| ❑ SE144 Luc Robitaille | .25 | .11 |
| ❑ SE145 Daniel Alfredsson | 1.25 | .55 |
| ❑ SE146 Martin Straka | .25 | .11 |
| ❑ SE147 Steve Duchesne | .25 | .11 |
| ❑ SE148 Eric Lindros | 5.00 | 2.20 |
| ❑ SE149 Mikael Renberg | .50 | .23 |
| ❑ SE150 Eric Desjardins | .25 | .11 |
| ❑ SE151 Joel Otto | .25 | .11 |
| ❑ SE152 Mario Lemieux | 6.00 | 2.70 |
| ❑ SE153 Jaromir Jagr | 4.00 | 1.80 |
| ❑ SE154 Petr Nedved | .50 | .23 |
| ❑ SE155 Sergei Zubov | .25 | .11 |
| ❑ SE156 Tomas Sandstrom | .25 | .11 |
| ❑ SE157 Brett Hull | 1.50 | .70 |
| ❑ SE158 Grant Fuhr | .50 | .23 |
| ❑ SE159 Shayne Corson | .25 | .11 |
| ❑ SE160 Chris Pronger | .50 | .23 |
| ❑ SE161 Ray Sheppard | .25 | .11 |
| ❑ SE162 Arturs Irbe | .50 | .23 |
| ❑ SE163 Owen Nolan | .50 | .23 |
| ❑ SE164 Andrei Nazarov | .25 | .11 |
| ❑ SE165 Paul Ysebaert | .25 | .11 |
| ❑ SE166 Brian Bradley | .25 | .11 |
| ❑ SE167 Petr Klima | .25 | .11 |
| ❑ SE168 Felix Potvin | 1.25 | .55 |
| ❑ SE169 Mats Sundin | .50 | .23 |
| ❑ SE170 Larry Murphy | .25 | .11 |
| ❑ SE171 Benoit Hogue | .25 | .11 |
| ❑ SE172 Pavel Bure | 2.50 | 1.10 |
| ❑ SE173 Alexander Mogilny | .50 | .23 |
| ❑ SE174 Cliff Ronning | .25 | .11 |
| ❑ SE175 Pat Peake | .25 | .11 |
| ❑ SE176 Sylvain Cote | .25 | .11 |
| ❑ SE177 Peter Bondra | .50 | .23 |
| ❑ SE178 Dallas Drake | .25 | .11 |
| ❑ SE179 Tim Cheveldae | .25 | .11 |
| ❑ SE180 Darren Turcotte | .25 | .11 |

## 1995-96 Upper Deck Special Edition Gold

This 180-card set was randomly inserted at a rate of 1:35 hobby packs across both series. Series 1 contained cards SE1-SE90, while series 2 contained cards SE91-SE180. These cards featured the words, "Special Edition" in gold down the right side of the card. Multipliers in the header below to determine value for these are to be used with regular Special Edition cards.

| | MINT | NRMT |
|---|---|---|
| COMPLETE SET (180) | 750.00 | 350.00 |
| COMPLETE SERIES 1 (90) | 250.00 | 110.00 |
| COMPLETE SERIES 2 (90) | 500.00 | 220.00 |
| COMMON CARD (SE1-SE180) | 2.50 | 1.10 |

*VETERAN STARS: 5X TO 10X BASIC CARDS
*YOUNG STARS: 3X TO 6X BASIC CARDS

## 1995-96 Upper Deck All-Star Game Predictors

The thirty cards in this set were handed out one per person at the Upper Deck booth at the All-Star FanFest in Boston. The winning card, no. 21 Ray Bourque, was redeemable for a full thirty card set of All-Star game Predictors that contained different photos than the original give-aways. Prices below are for the cards handed out at the All-Star game. Superstars like Gretzky, Lemieux, etc. trade at higher levels than other stars, thus separate multipliers to determine values for the redeemed versions can be found in the header below. The redeemed Bourque card is actually worth about 25 percent of the game card; this is due to the mass redemption of the Bourque game card, making it extremely difficult to locate in the secondary market.

| | MINT | NRMT |
|---|---|---|
| COMPLETE SET (30) | 1200.00 | 550.00 |
| COMMON CARD (1-30) | 10.00 | 4.50 |

*REDEEMED STARS: 2X TO 3X BASIC PREDICTORS

| | MINT | NRMT |
|---|---|---|
| ❑ 1 Wayne Gretzky | 150.00 | 70.00 |
| ❑ 2 Sergei Fedorov | 40.00 | 18.00 |
| ❑ 3 Brett Hull | 30.00 | 13.50 |
| ❑ 4 Alexander Mogilny | 20.00 | 9.00 |
| ❑ 5 Joe Sakic | 60.00 | 27.00 |
| ❑ 6 Paul Kariya | 100.00 | 45.00 |
| ❑ 7 Teemu Selanne | 40.00 | 18.00 |
| ❑ 8 Paul Coffey | 20.00 | 9.00 |
| ❑ 9 Chris Chelios | 20.00 | 9.00 |
| ❑ 10 Doug Gilmour | 20.00 | 9.00 |
| ❑ 11 Peter Forsberg | 75.00 | 34.00 |
| ❑ 12 Jeremy Roenick | 25.00 | 11.00 |
| ❑ 13 Theoren Fleury | 20.00 | 9.00 |
| ❑ 14 Mike Modano | 25.00 | 11.00 |
| ❑ 15 Steve Yzerman | 60.00 | 27.00 |
| ❑ 16 Mario Lemieux | 100.00 | 45.00 |
| ❑ 17 Jaromir Jagr | 75.00 | 34.00 |
| ❑ 18 Eric Lindros | 100.00 | 45.00 |
| ❑ 19 Mark Messier | 30.00 | 13.50 |
| ❑ 20 Brendan Shanahan | 50.00 | 22.00 |
| ❑ 21 Ray Bourque | 75.00 | 34.00 |
| ❑ 22 Cam Neely | 25.00 | 11.00 |
| ❑ 23 Ron Francis | 15.00 | 6.75 |
| ❑ 24 John LeClair | 40.00 | 18.00 |
| ❑ 25 Brian Leetch | 20.00 | 9.00 |
| ❑ 26 Peter Bondra | 20.00 | 9.00 |
| ❑ 27 Scott Stevens | 15.00 | 6.75 |
| ❑ 28 Adam Oates | 20.00 | 9.00 |
| ❑ 29 Martin Brodeur | 60.00 | 27.00 |
| ❑ 30 Longshot | 10.00 | 4.50 |

## 1996-97 Upper Deck

This two-series, 390-card set was distributed in 12-card packs with the suggested retail price of $2.49. The set was highlighted by the

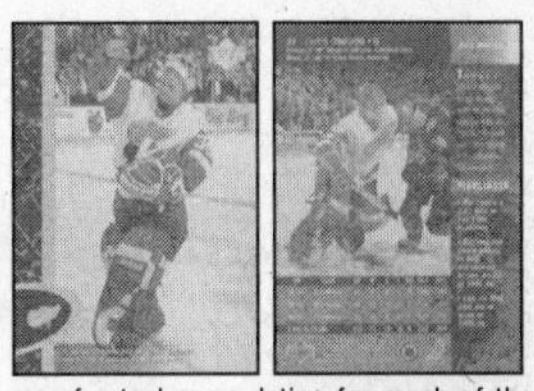

use of actual game dating for much of the photography, the selection of which included some of the most memorable moments of the '96 season. The set is noteworthy for including Wayne Gretzky in his new uniform as a New York Ranger both in the set and on all packaging. The set also contained a 15-card Star Rookie subset (#181-195), a 13-card Through the Glass subset (#196-208), a 10-card On-Ice Insight subset (359-368) and four checklist cards. Several key rookies appeared in this set, including Joe Thornton, Patrick Marleau, Daniel Tkaczuk, and Dainius Zubrus. The "Meet the Stars" promotion was continued in this set, which gave the collector an opportunity to win a chance to meet "The Great One" himself. Trivia cards were inserted one in every four packs and Instant Win cards one in every 56 packs. These cards are not widely traded, but are now worth about ten cents each.

| | MINT | NRMT |
|---|---|---|
| COMPLETE SET (390) | 65.00 | 29.00 |
| COMPLETE SERIES 1 (210) | 25.00 | 11.00 |
| COMPLETE SERIES 2 (180) | 40.00 | 18.00 |
| COMMON CARD (1-390) | .10 | .05 |
| ❑ 1 Paul Kariya | 1.50 | .70 |
| ❑ 2 Guy Hebert | .25 | .11 |
| ❑ 3 J.F. Jomphe | .10 | .05 |
| ❑ 4 Joe Sacco | .10 | .05 |
| ❑ 5 Jason York | .10 | .05 |
| ❑ 6 Alex Hicks | .10 | .05 |
| ❑ 7 Mikhail Shtalenkov | .10 | .05 |
| ❑ 8 Bill Ranford | .25 | .11 |
| ❑ 9 Kyle McLaren | .10 | .05 |
| ❑ 10 Rick Tocchet | .25 | .11 |
| ❑ 11 Jon Rohloff | .10 | .05 |
| ❑ 12 Jozef Stumpel | .10 | .05 |
| ❑ 13 Cam Neely | .25 | .11 |
| ❑ 14 Ray Bourque | .40 | .18 |
| ❑ 15 Pat LaFontaine | .25 | .11 |
| ❑ 16 Brian Holzinger | .25 | .11 |
| ❑ 17 Alexei Zhitnik | .10 | .05 |
| ❑ 18 Donald Audette | .25 | .11 |
| ❑ 19 Jason Dawe | .10 | .05 |
| ❑ 20 Wayne Primeau | .10 | .05 |
| ❑ 21 Mike Peca | .10 | .05 |
| ❑ 22 Theoren Fleury | .25 | .11 |
| ❑ 23 Sandy McCarthy | .10 | .05 |
| ❑ 24 Zarley Zalapski | .10 | .05 |
| ❑ 25 Trevor Kidd | .25 | .11 |
| ❑ 26 Steve Chiasson | .10 | .05 |
| ❑ 27 Michael Nylander | .10 | .05 |
| ❑ 28 Ronnie Stern | .10 | .05 |
| ❑ 29 Eric Daze | .25 | .11 |
| ❑ 30 Jeff Hackett | .25 | .11 |
| ❑ 31 Chris Chelios | .40 | .18 |
| ❑ 32 Tony Amonte | .25 | .11 |
| ❑ 33 Bob Probert | .25 | .11 |
| ❑ 34 Eric Weinrich | .10 | .05 |
| ❑ 35 Jeremy Roenick | .40 | .18 |
| ❑ 36 Mike Ricci | .10 | .05 |
| ❑ 37 Sandis Ozolinsh | .25 | .11 |
| ❑ 38 Patrick Roy | 2.00 | .90 |
| ❑ 39 Uwe Krupp | .10 | .05 |
| ❑ 40 Stephane Yelle | .10 | .05 |
| ❑ 41 Adam Deadmarsh | .25 | .11 |
| ❑ 42 Scott Young | .10 | .05 |
| ❑ 43 Mike Modano | .50 | .23 |
| ❑ 44 Derian Hatcher | .10 | .05 |
| ❑ 45 Todd Harvey | .10 | .05 |
| ❑ 46 Brent Fedyk | .10 | .05 |
| ❑ 47 Grant Marshall | .10 | .05 |
| ❑ 48 Jamie Langenbrunner | .10 | .05 |
| ❑ 49 Jere Lehtinen | .10 | .05 |
| ❑ 50 Steve Yzerman | 1.25 | .55 |
| ❑ 51 Igor Larionov | .10 | .05 |
| ❑ 52 Vladimir Konstantinov | .10 | .05 |
| ❑ 53 Chris Osgood | .40 | .18 |
| ❑ 54 Jamie Pushor | .10 | .05 |
| ❑ 55 Darren McCarty | .10 | .05 |
| ❑ 56 Nicklas Lidstrom | .25 | .11 |
| ❑ 57 Jason Arnott | .25 | .11 |
| ❑ 58 Doug Weight | .25 | .11 |
| ❑ 59 Todd Marchant | .10 | .05 |
| ❑ 60 David Oliver | .10 | .05 |
| ❑ 61 Luke Richardson | .10 | .05 |
| ❑ 62 Jason Bonsignore | .10 | .05 |
| ❑ 63 John Vanbiesbrouck | .60 | .25 |
| ❑ 64 Stu Barnes | .10 | .05 |
| ❑ 65 Martin Straka | .10 | .05 |
| ❑ 66 Ed Jovanovski | .25 | .11 |
| ❑ 67 Robert Svehla | .10 | .05 |
| ❑ 68 Gord Murphy | .10 | .05 |
| ❑ 69 Tom Fitzgerald | .10 | .05 |
| ❑ 70 Jeff O'Neill | .10 | .05 |
| ❑ 71 Jason Muzzatti | .25 | .11 |
| ❑ 72 Sean Burke | .25 | .11 |
| ❑ 73 Jeff Brown | .10 | .05 |
| ❑ 74 Andrew Cassels | .10 | .05 |
| ❑ 75 Geoff Sanderson | .25 | .11 |
| ❑ 76 Dimitri Khristich | .10 | .05 |

| | | |
|---|---|---|
| □ 77 Vitali Yachmenev | .10 | .05 |
| □ 78 Kevin Stevens | .10 | .05 |
| □ 79 Yanic Perreault | .10 | .05 |
| □ 80 Craig Johnson | .10 | .05 |
| □ 81 John Slaney | .10 | .05 |
| □ 82 Saku Koivu | .60 | .25 |
| □ 83 Jocelyn Thibault | .40 | .18 |
| □ 84 Vladimir Malakhov | .10 | .05 |
| □ 85 Turner Stevenson | .10 | .05 |
| □ 86 Vincent Damphousse | .25 | .11 |
| □ 87 Mark Recchi | .25 | .11 |
| □ 88 Patrice Brisebois | .10 | .05 |
| □ 89 Dave Andreychuk | .25 | .11 |
| □ 90 Bill Guerin | .10 | .05 |
| □ 91 Martin Brodeur | 1.00 | .45 |
| □ 92 Scott Niedermayer | .10 | .05 |
| □ 93 Petr Sykora | .10 | .05 |
| □ 94 Stephane Richer | .25 | .11 |
| □ 95 John MacLean | .25 | .11 |
| □ 96 Eric Fichaud | .25 | .11 |
| □ 97 Zigmund Palffy | .40 | .18 |
| □ 98 Alexander Semak | .10 | .05 |
| □ 99 Bryan McCabe | .10 | .05 |
| □ 100 Darby Hendrickson | .10 | .05 |
| □ 101 Kenny Jonsson | .10 | .05 |
| □ 102 Marty McInnis | .10 | .05 |
| □ 103 Alexei Kovalev | .10 | .05 |
| □ 104 Ulf Samuelsson | .10 | .05 |
| □ 105 Jeff Beukeboom | .10 | .05 |
| □ 106 Marty McSorley | .10 | .05 |
| □ 107 Niklas Sundstrom | .10 | .05 |
| □ 108 Wayne Gretzky | 4.00 | 1.80 |
| □ 109 Mike Richter | .40 | .18 |
| □ 110 Alexei Yashin | .25 | .11 |
| □ 111 Randy Cunneyworth | .10 | .05 |
| □ 112 Damian Rhodes | .25 | .11 |
| □ 113 Daniel Alfredsson | .25 | .11 |
| □ 114 Antti Tormanen | .10 | .05 |
| □ 115 Ted Drury | .10 | .05 |
| □ 116 Janne Laukkanen | .10 | .05 |
| □ 117 Sean Hill | .10 | .05 |
| □ 118 John LeClair | .60 | .25 |
| □ 119 Ron Hextall | .25 | .11 |
| □ 120 Dale Hawerchuk | .25 | .11 |
| □ 121 Rod Brind'Amour | .25 | .11 |
| □ 122 Pat Falloon | .10 | .05 |
| □ 123 Eric Desjardins | .10 | .05 |
| □ 124 Joel Otto | .10 | .05 |
| □ 125 Alexei Zhamnov | .25 | .11 |
| □ 126 Nikolai Khabibulin | .25 | .11 |
| □ 127 Craig Janney | .25 | .11 |
| □ 128 Deron Quint | .10 | .05 |
| □ 129 Oleg Tverdovsky | .25 | .11 |
| □ 130 Chad Kilger | .10 | .05 |
| □ 131 Teppo Numminen | .10 | .05 |
| □ 132 Tom Barrasso | .25 | .11 |
| □ 133 Ron Francis | .25 | .11 |
| □ 134 Petr Nedved | .25 | .11 |
| □ 135 Ken Wregget | .25 | .11 |
| □ 136 Joe Dziedzic | .10 | .05 |
| □ 137 Tomas Sandstrom | .10 | .05 |
| □ 138 Dmitri Mironov | .10 | .05 |
| □ 139 Shayne Corson | .10 | .05 |
| □ 140 Grant Fuhr | .25 | .11 |
| □ 141 Al MacInnis | .25 | .11 |
| □ 142 Stephen Leach | .10 | .05 |
| □ 143 Murray Baron | .10 | .05 |
| □ 144 Chris Pronger | .25 | .11 |
| □ 145 Jamie Rivers | .10 | .05 |
| □ 146 Owen Nolan | .25 | .11 |
| □ 147 Chris Terreri | .25 | .11 |
| □ 148 Marcus Ragnarsson | .10 | .05 |
| □ 149 Shean Donovan | .10 | .05 |
| □ 150 Ray Whitney | .10 | .05 |
| □ 151 Michal Sykora | .10 | .05 |
| □ 152 Viktor Kozlov | .10 | .05 |
| □ 153 Roman Hamrlik | .25 | .11 |
| □ 154 Bill Houlder | .10 | .05 |
| □ 155 Mikael Andersson | .10 | .05 |
| □ 156 Petr Klima | .10 | .05 |
| □ 157 Jason Wiemer | .10 | .05 |
| □ 158 Rob Zamuner | .10 | .05 |
| □ 159 Paul Ysebaert | .10 | .05 |
| □ 160 Mats Sundin | .25 | .11 |
| □ 161 Larry Murphy UER (bio info that of Mats Sundin) | .25 | .11 |
| □ 162 Doug Gilmour | .40 | .18 |
| □ 163 Todd Warriner | .10 | .05 |
| □ 164 Dmitri Yushkevich | .10 | .05 |
| □ 165 Kirk Muller | .10 | .05 |
| □ 166 Jamie Macoun | .10 | .05 |
| □ 167 Alexander Mogilny | .25 | .11 |
| □ 168 Corey Hirsch | .25 | .11 |
| □ 169 Trevor Linden | .25 | .11 |
| □ 170 Markus Naslund | .10 | .05 |
| □ 171 Martin Gelinas | .10 | .05 |
| □ 172 Jyrki Lumme | .10 | .05 |
| □ 173 Bret Hedican | .10 | .05 |
| □ 174 Jim Carey | .40 | .18 |
| □ 175 Sergei Gonchar | .10 | .05 |
| □ 176 Joe Juneau | .10 | .05 |
| □ 177 Brendan Witt | .10 | .05 |
| □ 178 Dale Hunter | .10 | .05 |
| □ 179 Steve Konowalchuk | .10 | .05 |
| □ 180 Peter Bondra | .40 | .18 |
| □ 181 Jarome Iginla | .40 | .18 |
| □ 182 Ralph Intranuovo | .10 | .05 |
| □ 183 Anders Eriksson | .10 | .05 |
| □ 184 Andrew Brunette | .10 | .05 |
| □ 185 Steve Sullivan | .10 | .05 |
| □ 186 Brandon Convery | .10 | .05 |
| □ 187 Ethan Moreau | .40 | .18 |
| □ 188 Marko Kiprusoff | .10 | .05 |
| □ 189 Jason McBain | .10 | .05 |
| □ 190 Mark Kolesar | .10 | .05 |
| □ 191 Greg DeVries | .10 | .05 |
| □ 192 Alexei Yegorov | .10 | .05 |
| □ 193 Sebastien Bordeleau | .10 | .05 |
| □ 194 Nick Stajduhar | .10 | .05 |
| □ 195 Jan Caloun | .10 | .05 |
| □ 196 Dino Ciccarelli TTG | .25 | .11 |
| □ 197 Ron Hextall TTG | .25 | .11 |
| □ 198 Murray Baron TTG | .10 | .05 |
| □ 199 Patrick Roy TTG | .40 | .18 |
| □ 200 Scott Mellanby TTG | .25 | .11 |
| □ 201 Tie Domi TTG | .25 | .11 |
| □ 202 Glenn Healy TTG | .25 | .11 |
| □ 203 Keith Primeau | .25 | .11 |
| □ 204 Joe Sakic TTG | .40 | .18 |
| □ 205 Jeremy Roenick TTG | .40 | .18 |
| □ 206 Sergei Fedorov TTG | .40 | .18 |
| □ 207 Claude Lemieux TTG | .25 | .11 |
| □ 208 Theoren Fleury TTG | .25 | .11 |
| □ 209 Checklist (1-104) | .10 | .05 |
| □ 210 Checklist (105-210) | .10 | .05 |
| □ 211 Teemu Selanne | .75 | .35 |
| □ 212 Jari Kurri | .25 | .11 |
| □ 213 Darren Van Impe | .10 | .05 |
| □ 214 Steve Rucchin | .10 | .05 |
| □ 215 Ruslan Salei | .10 | .05 |
| □ 216 Adam Oates | .25 | .11 |
| □ 217 Don Sweeney | .10 | .05 |
| □ 218 Steve Staios | .10 | .05 |
| □ 219 Barry Richter | .10 | .05 |
| □ 220 Mattias Timander | .10 | .05 |
| □ 221 Ted Donato | .10 | .05 |
| □ 222 Dominik Hasek | .75 | .35 |
| □ 223 Derek Plante | .10 | .05 |
| □ 224 Vaclav Varada | .10 | .05 |
| □ 225 Andrei Trefilov | .10 | .05 |
| □ 226 Curtis Brown | .10 | .05 |
| □ 227 German Titov | .10 | .05 |
| □ 228 Robert Reichel | .10 | .05 |
| □ 229 Cory Stillman | .10 | .05 |
| □ 230 Chris O'Sullivan | .10 | .05 |
| □ 231 Corey Millen | .10 | .05 |
| □ 232 Jonas Hoglund | .10 | .05 |
| □ 233 Alexei Zhamnov | .25 | .11 |
| □ 234 Ed Belfour | .40 | .18 |
| □ 235 Gary Suter | .10 | .05 |
| □ 236 Kevin Miller | .10 | .05 |
| □ 237 Tuomas Gronman | .10 | .05 |
| □ 238 Enrico Ciccone | .10 | .05 |
| □ 239 Peter Forsberg | 1.25 | .55 |
| □ 240 Joe Sakic | .75 | .35 |
| □ 241 Valeri Kamensky | .25 | .11 |
| □ 242 Landon Wilson | .10 | .05 |
| □ 243 Claude Lemieux | .25 | .11 |
| □ 244 Eric Lacroix | .10 | .05 |
| □ 245 Joe Nieuwendyk UER (front Joe Nieuwendky) | .25 | .11 |
| □ 246 Sergei Zubov | .10 | .05 |
| □ 247 Benoit Hogue | .10 | .05 |
| □ 248 Arturs Irbe | .25 | .11 |
| □ 249 Pat Verbeek | .10 | .05 |
| □ 250 Sergei Fedorov | .60 | .25 |
| □ 251 Vyacheslav Kozlov | .10 | .05 |
| □ 252 Brendan Shanahan | .75 | .35 |
| □ 253 Kevin Hodson | .40 | .18 |
| □ 254 Greg Johnson | .10 | .05 |
| □ 255 Tomas Holmstrom | .10 | .05 |
| □ 256 Curtis Joseph | .40 | .18 |
| □ 257 Dean McAmmond | .10 | .05 |
| □ 258 Ryan Smyth | .40 | .18 |
| □ 259 Mike Grier | .75 | .35 |
| □ 260 Miroslav Satan | .10 | .05 |
| □ 261 Rem Murray | .10 | .05 |
| □ 262 Rob Niedermayer | .25 | .11 |
| □ 263 Ray Sheppard | .25 | .11 |
| □ 264 Dave Lowry | .10 | .05 |
| □ 265 Scott Mellanby | .25 | .11 |
| □ 266 Rhett Warrener | .10 | .05 |
| □ 267 Per Gustafsson | .10 | .05 |
| □ 268 Paul Coffey | .40 | .18 |
| □ 269 Nelson Emerson | .10 | .05 |
| □ 270 Kevin Dineen | .10 | .05 |
| □ 271 Keith Primeau | .25 | .11 |
| □ 272 Hnat Domenichelli | .10 | .05 |
| □ 273 Ray Ferraro | .10 | .05 |
| □ 274 Stephane Fiset | .25 | .11 |
| □ 275 Kai Nurminen | .10 | .05 |
| □ 276 Dan Bylsma | .10 | .05 |
| □ 277 Mattias Norstrom | .10 | .05 |
| □ 278 Rob Blake | .10 | .05 |
| □ 279 Jose Theodore | .25 | .11 |
| □ 280 Martin Rucinsky | .10 | .05 |
| □ 281 Darcy Tucker | .10 | .05 |
| □ 282 David Wilkie | .10 | .05 |
| □ 283 Valeri Bure | .25 | .11 |
| □ 284 Steve Thomas | .10 | .05 |
| □ 285 Brian Rolston | .10 | .05 |
| □ 286 Scott Stevens | .25 | .11 |
| □ 287 Shawn Chambers | .10 | .05 |
| □ 288 Denis Pederson | .10 | .05 |
| □ 289 Lyle Odelein | .10 | .05 |
| □ 290 Travis Green | .25 | .11 |
| □ 291 Todd Bertuzzi | .10 | .05 |
| □ 292 Niclas Andersson | .10 | .05 |
| □ 293 Darius Kasparaitis | .10 | .05 |
| □ 294 Bryan Berard | .40 | .18 |
| □ 295 Daniel Goneau | .10 | .05 |
| □ 296 Christian Dube | .10 | .05 |
| □ 297 Adam Graves | .25 | .11 |
| □ 298 Sergei Nemchinov | .10 | .05 |
| □ 299 Mark Messier | .50 | .23 |
| □ 300 Brian Leetch | .40 | .18 |
| □ 301 Radek Bonk | .10 | .05 |
| □ 302 Alexandre Daigle | .10 | .05 |
| □ 303 Andreas Dackell | .10 | .05 |
| □ 304 Steve Duchesne | .10 | .05 |
| □ 305 Wade Redden | .10 | .05 |
| □ 306 Eric Lindros | 1.25 | .55 |
| □ 307 Mikael Renberg | .25 | .11 |
| □ 308 Shjon Podein | .10 | .05 |
| □ 309 Dainius Zubrus | .75 | .35 |
| □ 310 Janne Niinimaa | .40 | .18 |
| □ 311 Karl Dykhuis | .10 | .05 |
| □ 312 Jeremy Roenick | .40 | .18 |
| □ 313 Keith Tkachuk | .50 | .23 |
| □ 314 Shane Doan | .10 | .05 |
| □ 315 Cliff Ronning | .10 | .05 |
| □ 316 Mike Gartner | .25 | .11 |
| □ 317 Dave Manson | .10 | .05 |
| □ 318 Shawn Antoski | .10 | .05 |
| □ 319 Kevin Hatcher | .10 | .05 |
| □ 320 Jaromir Jagr | 1.25 | .55 |
| □ 321 Mario Lemieux | 2.00 | .90 |
| □ 322 Bryan Smolinski | .10 | .05 |
| □ 323 Stefan Bergkvist | .10 | .05 |
| □ 324 Brett Hull | .50 | .23 |
| □ 325 Joe Murphy | .10 | .05 |
| □ 326 Stephane Matteau | .10 | .05 |
| □ 327 Geoff Courtnall | .10 | .05 |
| □ 328 Jim Campbell | .10 | .05 |
| □ 329 Harry York | .40 | .18 |
| □ 330 Kelly Hrudey | .25 | .11 |
| □ 331 Al Iafrate | .10 | .05 |
| □ 332 Jeff Friesen | .25 | .11 |
| □ 333 Darren Turcotte | .10 | .05 |
| □ 334 Bernie Nicholls | .10 | .05 |
| □ 335 Ville Peltonen | .10 | .05 |
| □ 336 Dino Ciccarelli | .25 | .11 |
| □ 337 Chris Gratton | .25 | .11 |
| □ 338 Daren Puppa | .25 | .11 |
| □ 339 Alexander Selivanov | .10 | .05 |
| □ 340 Daymond Langkow | .10 | .05 |
| □ 341 Felix Potvin | .40 | .18 |
| □ 342 Wendel Clark | .25 | .11 |
| □ 343 Mathieu Schneider | .10 | .05 |
| □ 344 Dave Ellet | .10 | .05 |
| □ 345 Fredrik Modin | .10 | .05 |
| □ 346 Sergei Berezin | .60 | .25 |
| □ 347 Pavel Bure | .75 | .35 |
| □ 348 Kirk McLean | .25 | .11 |
| □ 349 Mike Sillinger | .10 | .05 |
| □ 350 Russ Courtnall | .10 | .05 |
| □ 351 Scott Walker | .10 | .05 |
| □ 352 Esa Tikkanen | .10 | .05 |
| □ 353 Pat Peake | .10 | .05 |
| □ 354 Olaf Kolzig | .25 | .11 |
| □ 355 Michal Pivonka | .10 | .05 |
| □ 356 Richard Zednik | .10 | .05 |
| □ 357 Phil Housley | .25 | .11 |
| □ 358 Anson Carter | .10 | .05 |
| □ 359 Eric Daze OII | .25 | .11 |
| □ 360 Folix Potvin OII | .40 | .18 |
| □ 361 Wayne Gretzky OII | .40 | .18 |
| □ 362 Ed Jovanovski OII | .25 | .11 |
| □ 363 Mike Modano OII | .25 | .11 |
| □ 364 Peter Bondra OII | .40 | .18 |
| □ 365 Patrick Roy OII | .40 | .18 |
| □ 366 Ray Bourque OII | .40 | .18 |
| □ 367 Roman Hamrlik OII | .25 | .11 |
| □ 368 John LeClair OII | .40 | .18 |
| □ 369 Adam Colagiacomo | .75 | .35 |
| □ 370 Joe Thornton | 6.00 | 2.70 |
| □ 371 Patrick Desrochers | 1.00 | .45 |
| □ 372 Pierre-Luc Therrien | .25 | .11 |
| □ 373 Nick Boynton | .75 | .35 |
| □ 374 Andrew Ference | .25 | .11 |
| □ 375 Jean-Francois Fortin | .10 | .05 |
| □ 376 Daniel Tetrault | .25 | .11 |
| □ 377 Luc Theoret | .25 | .11 |
| □ 378 Mike Van Ryn | .25 | .11 |
| □ 379 Scott Barney | .50 | .23 |
| □ 380 Harold Druken | .25 | .11 |
| □ 381 Dylan Gyori | .25 | .11 |
| □ 382 Chris Heron | .25 | .11 |
| □ 383 Chad Hinz | .25 | .11 |
| □ 384 Patrick Marleau | 6.00 | 2.70 |
| □ 385 Serge Payer | .25 | .11 |
| □ 386 Jeremy Reich | .10 | .05 |
| □ 387 Daniel Tkaczuk | 2.00 | .90 |
| □ 388 Jason Ward | .75 | .35 |
| □ 389 Checklist (211-298) | .10 | .05 |
| □ 390 Checklist (299-390) | .10 | .05 |

## 1996-97 Upper Deck Game Jerseys

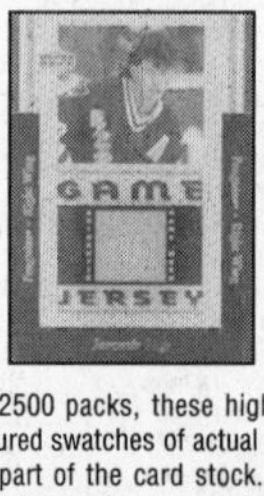

Inserted 1:2500 packs, these highly popular inserts featured swatches of actual game-worn jerseys as part of the card stock. Five cards were inserted in series one packs, while the remaining eight cards were distributed with series two. In some cases, there were premiums attached to cards which featured swatches with two colors, stick marks, or other unique distinguishing characteristics.

| | MINT | NRMT |
|---|---|---|
| COMPLETE SET (13) | 4400.00 | 2000.00 |
| COMPLETE SERIES 1 (5) | 1500.00 | 700.00 |
| COMPLETE SERIES 2 (8) | 2900.00 | 1300.00 |
| COMMON CARD (GJ1-GJ13) | 175.00 | 80.00 |

| | | |
|---|---|---|
| □ GJ1 Steve Yzerman | 400.00 | 180.00 |
| □ GJ2 Brett Hull | 250.00 | 110.00 |
| □ GJ3 Doug Gilmour | 200.00 | 90.00 |
| □ GJ4 Jaromir Jagr | 500.00 | 220.00 |
| □ GJ5 Ray Bourque | 250.00 | 110.00 |
| □ GJ6 Mario Lemieux | 650.00 | 300.00 |
| □ GJ7 John Vanbiesbrouck | 250.00 | 110.00 |
| □ GJ8 Eric Lindros | 500.00 | 220.00 |
| □ GJ9 Mike Modano | 275.00 | 125.00 |
| □ GJ10 Pavel Bure | 300.00 | 135.00 |
| □ GJ11 Mark Messier | 275.00 | 125.00 |
| □ GJ12 Theoren Fleury | 200.00 | 90.00 |
| □ GJ13 Mats Sundin UER | 200.00 | 90.00 |

## 1996-97 Upper Deck Generation Next

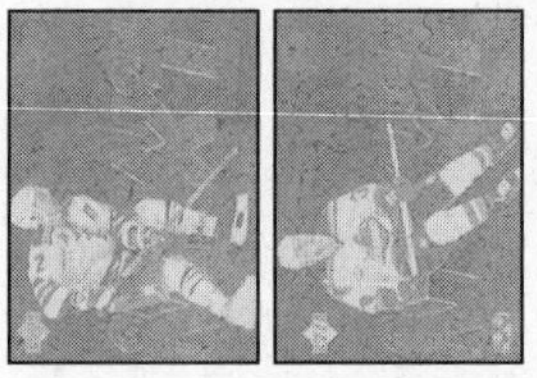

Randomly inserted in packs at a rate of one in four, this double-fronted, series two insert paired up two top players on each card. Both sides were enhanced with silver and gold foil.

| | MINT | NRMT |
|---|---|---|
| COMPLETE SET (40) | 120.00 | 55.00 |
| COMMON CARD (X1-X40) | 1.00 | .45 |

| | | |
|---|---|---|
| □ X1 Paul Kariya / Wayne Gretzky | 15.00 | 6.75 |
| □ X2 Trevor Linden / Peter Forsberg | 6.00 | 2.70 |
| □ X3 Joe Sakic / Rob Niedermayer | 4.00 | 1.80 |
| □ X4 Chris O'Sullivan / Eric Weinrich | 1.00 | .45 |
| □ X5 Jocelyn Thibault / Patrick Roy | 10.00 | 4.50 |
| □ X6 Brett Hull / Daniel Alfredsson | 3.00 | 1.35 |
| □ X7 Chris Osgood / John Vanbiesbrouck | 4.00 | 1.80 |
| □ X8 Ray Bourque / Roman Hamrlik | 3.00 | 1.35 |
| □ X9 Paul Coffey / Sandis Ozolinsh | 3.00 | 1.35 |
| □ X10 Doug Gilmour / Sergei Fedorov | 4.00 | 1.80 |
| □ X11 Chris Chelios / Ed Jovanovski | 3.00 | 1.35 |
| □ X12 Jason Arnott / Jeremy Roenick | 3.00 | 1.35 |
| □ X13 Doug Weight / Steve Yzerman | 6.00 | 2.70 |
| □ X14 Brendan Shanahan / Todd Bertuzzi | 5.00 | 2.20 |
| □ X15 Wendel Clark / Keith Tkachuk | 3.00 | 1.35 |
| □ X16 Saku Koivu / Teemu Selanne | 5.00 | 2.20 |
| □ X17 Jaromir Jagr / Zigmund Palffy | 6.00 | 2.70 |
| □ X18 Ed Belfour / Martin Brodeur | 4.00 | 1.80 |
| □ X19 Eric Daze / Owen Nolan | 2.00 | .90 |
| □ X20 Valeri Kamensky / Vitali Yachmenev | 1.00 | .45 |
| □ X21 Jarome Iginla / Mike Modano | 5.00 | 2.20 |
| □ X22 Anders Eriksson / Niklas Lidstrom | 2.00 | .90 |
| □ X23 Brian Leetch / Bryan Berard | 3.00 | 1.35 |
| □ X24 Jari Kurri / Niklas Sundstrom | 1.00 | .45 |
| □ X25 Adam Deadmarsh / Scott Mellanby | 2.00 | .90 |
| □ X26 Peter Bondra/Petr Sykora | 2.00 | .90 |
| □ X27 Curtis Joseph / Eric Fichaud | 3.00 | 1.35 |
| □ X28 Dominik Hasek / Roman Turek | 4.00 | 1.80 |
| □ X29 Alexander Mogilny / Valeri Bure | 2.00 | .90 |
| □ X30 Daymond Langkow / Theo Fleury | 2.00 | .90 |
| □ X31 Bernie Nicholls / Sergei Berezin | 2.00 | .90 |
| □ X32 Chris Gratton / Rick Tocchet | 2.00 | .90 |
| □ X33 Felix Potvin / Grant Fuhr | 3.00 | 1.35 |
| □ X34 Keith Primeau / Kevin Stevens | 2.00 | .90 |
| □ X35 Rob Blake / Wade Redden | 2.00 | .90 |
| □ X36 Chris Pronger / Scott Stevens | 2.00 | .90 |
| □ X37 Gary Suter / Kyle McLaren | 1.00 | .45 |
| □ X38 Jonas Hoglund / Mats Sundin | 2.00 | .90 |
| □ X39 Larry Murphy / Sergei Zubov | 1.00 | .45 |
| □ X40 Adam Oates / Joe Juneau | 2.00 | .90 |

## 1996-97 Upper Deck Hart Hopefuls Bronze

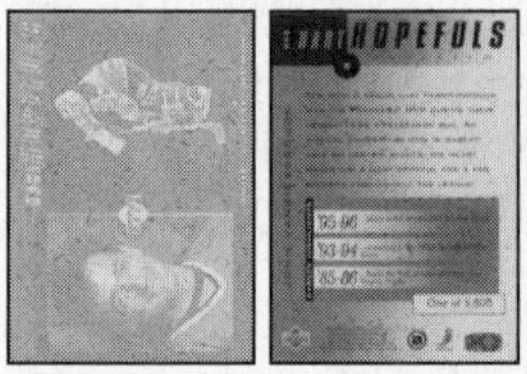

Randomly inserted in packs at a rate of one in 30, this series two-only insert consisted of twenty players vying for the title of league MVP and the chance to take home the Hart Trophy. Cards were numbered "One of 5000" on the back.

| | MINT | NRMT |
|---|---|---|
| COMPLETE SET (20) | 300.00 | 135.00 |
| COMMON CARD (HH1-HH20) | 6.00 | 2.70 |

SILVER STATED PRINT RUN 1000 SETS

| | | |
|---|---|---|
| □ HH1 Wayne Gretzky | 40.00 | 18.00 |
| □ HH2 Mark Messier | 10.00 | 4.50 |
| □ HH3 Eric Lindros | 20.00 | 9.00 |
| □ HH4 Sergei Fedorov | 12.00 | 5.50 |
| □ HH5 Saku Koivu | 10.00 | 4.50 |
| □ HH6 John Vanbiesbrouck | 10.00 | 4.50 |
| □ HH7 Peter Forsberg | 20.00 | 9.00 |
| □ HH8 Keith Tkachuk | 10.00 | 4.50 |
| □ HH9 Paul Kariya | 25.00 | 11.00 |
| □ HH10 Martin Brodeur | 15.00 | 6.75 |
| □ HH11 Patrick Roy | 30.00 | 13.50 |
| □ HH12 Alexander Mogilny | 6.00 | 2.70 |
| □ HH13 Brett Hull | 10.00 | 4.50 |
| □ HH14 Pavel Bure | 12.00 | 5.50 |
| □ HH15 Teemu Selanne | 12.00 | 5.50 |
| □ HH16 Mario Lemieux | 30.00 | 13.50 |
| □ HH17 Jeremy Roenick | 6.00 | 2.70 |
| □ HH18 Jaromir Jagr | 20.00 | 9.00 |
| □ HH19 Steve Yzerman | 20.00 | 9.00 |
| □ HH20 Joe Sakic | 12.00 | 5.50 |

## 1996-97 Upper Deck Hart Hopefuls Gold

Ultra rare and serially numbered to just 100, these parallels were randomly inserted in packs at a rate of one in 1500. The cards can be differentiated from the more common versions by the use of gold foil.

| | MINT | NRMT |
|---|---|---|
| COMPLETE SET (20) | 4000.00 | 1800.00 |
| COMMON CARD (HH1-HH20) | 100.00 | 45.00 |

*STARS: 6X TO 12X BRONZE

## 1996-97 Upper Deck Hart Hopefuls Silver

Randomly inserted in packs at a rate of one in 150, these parallel inserts were numbered "one of 1000" cards, and were distinguished by their silver foil treatment.

| | MINT | NRMT |
|---|---|---|
| COMPLETE SET (20) | 1200.00 | 550.00 |
| COMMON CARD (HH1-HH20) | 25.00 | 11.00 |

*SILVER STARS: 1.5X TO 4X BRONZE

## 1996-97 Upper Deck Lord Stanley's Heroes Finals

Randomly inserted in packs at a rate of one in 1,850, this 20-card parallel set featured serially numbered inserts out of 100 using cel chrome technology with a perimeter die cut. A player's head photo was displayed on this acetate on a die-cut replica of the trophy.

| | MINT | NRMT |
|---|---|---|
| COMPLETE SET (20) | 7000.00 | 3200.00 |
| COMMON CARD (LS1-LS20) | 120.00 | 55.00 |

*STARS: 10X TO 20X QUARTERS

## 1996-97 Upper Deck Lord Stanley's Heroes Quarterfinals

Randomly inserted in series one packs at a rate of one in 37, this 20-card set featured numbered inserts (one of 5,000) on cel chrome technology. A player's head photo was displayed on acetate in the middle of the trophy.

| | MINT | NRMT |
|---|---|---|
| COMPLETE SET (20) | 300.00 | 135.00 |
| COMMON CARD (LS1-LS20) | 6.00 | 2.70 |

| | | |
|---|---|---|
| □ LS1 Wayne Gretzky | 40.00 | 18.00 |
| □ LS2 Mark Messier | 8.00 | 3.60 |
| □ LS3 Mario Lemieux | 30.00 | 13.50 |
| □ LS4 Jaromir Jagr | 20.00 | 9.00 |
| □ LS5 Martin Brodeur | 15.00 | 6.75 |
| □ LS6 Patrick Roy | 30.00 | 13.50 |

| | | |
|---|---|---|
| ❑ LS7 Joe Sakic | 12.00 | 5.50 |
| ❑ LS8 Peter Forsberg | 20.00 | 9.00 |
| ❑ LS9 Theoren Fleury | 6.00 | 2.70 |
| ❑ LS10 Paul Coffey | 6.00 | 2.70 |
| ❑ LS11 Doug Gilmour | 6.00 | 2.70 |
| ❑ LS12 Paul Kariya | 25.00 | 11.00 |
| ❑ LS13 Eric Lindros | 20.00 | 9.00 |
| ❑ LS14 Sergei Fedorov | 12.00 | 5.50 |
| ❑ LS15 Eric Daze | 6.00 | 2.70 |
| ❑ LS16 Teemu Selanne | 12.00 | 5.50 |
| ❑ LS17 Keith Tkachuk | 8.00 | 3.60 |
| ❑ LS18 Pavel Bure | 12.00 | 5.50 |
| ❑ LS19 Mats Sundin | 6.00 | 2.70 |
| ❑ LS20 Saku Koivu | 10.00 | 4.50 |

## 1996-97 Upper Deck Lord Stanley's Heroes Semifinals

Randomly inserted in packs at a rate of one in 185, this 20-card set was numbered "one of 1,000" on cel chrome technology. A player's head photo was displayed on acetate, while the top and bottom of the trophy were die-cut.

| | MINT | NRMT |
|---|---|---|
| COMPLETE SET (20) | 1200.00 | 550.00 |
| COMMON CARD (LS1-LS20) | 25.00 | 11.00 |

*SEMI-FINALS STARS: 1.5X TO 4X QUARTERS

## 1996-97 Upper Deck Power Performers

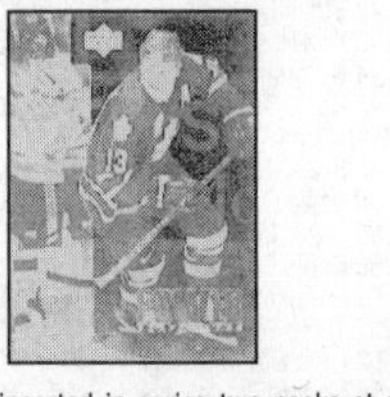

Randomly inserted in series two packs at a rate of one in 13, these cards featured a layered design on gold foil. Thirty of the league's toughest physical competitors were highlighted in the set.

| | MINT | NRMT |
|---|---|---|
| COMPLETE SET (30) | 80.00 | 36.00 |
| COMMON CARD (P1-P30) | 2.50 | 1.10 |

| | | |
|---|---|---|
| ❑ P1 Brendan Shanahan | 12.00 | 5.50 |
| ❑ P2 Mikael Renberg | 5.00 | 2.20 |
| ❑ P3 John LeClair | 10.00 | 4.50 |
| ❑ P4 Keith Primeau | 5.00 | 2.20 |
| ❑ P5 Adam Graves | 5.00 | 2.20 |
| ❑ P6 Jason Arnott | 5.00 | 2.20 |
| ❑ P7 Todd Bertuzzi | 2.50 | 1.10 |
| ❑ P8 Ed Jovanovski | 5.00 | 2.20 |
| ❑ P9 Scott Stevens | 2.50 | 1.10 |
| ❑ P10 Chris Gratton | 2.50 | 1.10 |
| ❑ P11 Bill Guerin | 2.50 | 1.10 |
| ❑ P12 Vladimir Konstantinov | 2.50 | 1.10 |
| ❑ P13 Mike Grier | 6.00 | 2.70 |
| ❑ P14 Theoren Fleury | 5.00 | 2.20 |
| ❑ P15 Chris Chelios | 6.00 | 2.70 |
| ❑ P16 Trevor Linden | 5.00 | 2.20 |
| ❑ P17 Claude Lemieux | 5.00 | 2.20 |
| ❑ P18 Owen Nolan | 5.00 | 2.20 |
| ❑ P19 Jarome Iginla | 6.00 | 2.70 |
| ❑ P20 Joe Nieuwendyk | 2.50 | 1.10 |
| ❑ P21 Kevin Hatcher | 2.50 | 1.10 |
| ❑ P22 Dino Ciccarelli | 5.00 | 2.20 |
| ❑ P23 Adam Deadmarsh | 5.00 | 2.20 |
| ❑ P24 Chris Pronger | 2.50 | 1.10 |
| ❑ P25 Mike Ricci | 2.50 | 1.10 |
| ❑ P26 Rod Brind'Amour | 5.00 | 2.20 |
| ❑ P27 Derian Hatcher | 2.50 | 1.10 |
| ❑ P28 Mats Sundin | 6.00 | 2.70 |
| ❑ P29 Doug Gilmour | 6.00 | 2.70 |
| ❑ P30 Todd Harvey | 2.50 | 1.10 |

## 1996-97 Upper Deck Superstar Showdown

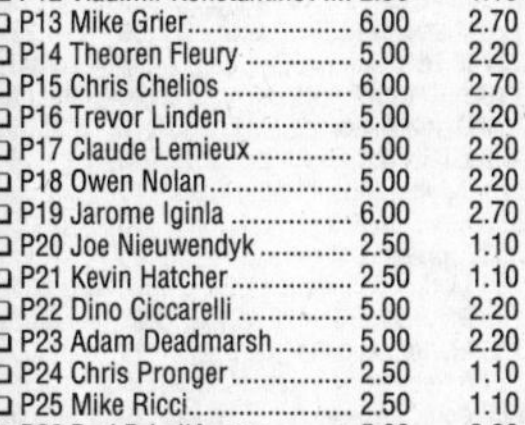

Randomly inserted in first series packs at a rate of one in 4, this 60-card set featured 30 different one-on-one match-ups of the NHL's top stars. Each of the card fronts displayed a single player photo with a die-cut design that eanbled the cards to be matched together in pairs.

| | MINT | NRMT |
|---|---|---|
| COMPLETE SET (60) | 175.00 | 80.00 |
| COMMON CARD (SS1-SS30) | 1.50 | .70 |

| | | |
|---|---|---|
| ❑ SS1A Pavel Bure | 5.00 | 2.20 |
| ❑ SS1B Paul Kariya | 10.00 | 4.50 |
| ❑ SS2A Patrick Roy | 12.00 | 5.50 |
| ❑ SS2B John Vanbiesbrouck | 4.00 | 1.80 |
| ❑ SS3A Eric Lindros | 8.00 | 3.60 |
| ❑ SS3B Ed Jovanovski | 2.00 | .90 |
| ❑ SS4A Theoren Fleury | 2.00 | .90 |
| ❑ SS4B Doug Gilmour | 2.00 | .90 |
| ❑ SS5A Wayne Gretzky | 15.00 | 6.75 |
| ❑ SS5B Mario Lemieux | 12.00 | 5.50 |
| ❑ SS6A Keith Tkachuk | 4.00 | 1.80 |
| ❑ SS6B Brendan Shanahan | 5.00 | 2.20 |
| ❑ SS7A Ray Bourque | 2.50 | 1.10 |
| ❑ SS7B Brian Leetch | 2.50 | 1.10 |
| ❑ SS8A Peter Forsberg | 8.00 | 3.60 |
| ❑ SS8B Sergei Fedorov | 5.00 | 2.20 |
| ❑ SS9A Mark Messier | 3.00 | 1.35 |
| ❑ SS9B Scott Stevens | 1.50 | .70 |
| ❑ SS10A Teemu Selanne | 5.00 | 2.20 |
| ❑ SS10B Alexander Mogilny | 2.00 | .90 |
| ❑ SS11A Felix Potvin | 2.50 | 1.10 |
| ❑ SS11B Jocelyn Thibault | 2.50 | 1.10 |
| ❑ SS12A Martin Brodeur | 6.00 | 2.70 |
| ❑ SS12B Eric Fichaud | 2.00 | .90 |
| ❑ SS13A Roman Hamrlik | 2.00 | .90 |
| ❑ SS13B Jaromir Jagr | 8.00 | 3.60 |
| ❑ SS14A Jim Carey | 2.50 | 1.10 |
| ❑ SS14B Saku Koivu | 4.00 | 1.80 |
| ❑ SS15A Jeremy Roenick | 2.50 | 1.10 |
| ❑ SS15B Brett Hull | 3.00 | 1.35 |
| ❑ SS16A Joe Sakic | 5.00 | 2.20 |
| ❑ SS16B Steve Yzerman | 8.00 | 3.60 |
| ❑ SS17A Doug Weight | 2.00 | .90 |
| ❑ SS17B Pat LaFontaine | 1.50 | .70 |
| ❑ SS18A Daniel Alfredsson | 2.00 | .90 |
| ❑ SS18B Eric Daze | 2.00 | .90 |
| ❑ SS19A Mike Modano | 3.00 | 1.35 |
| ❑ SS19B Jason Arnott | 2.00 | .90 |
| ❑ SS20A Paul Coffey | 2.50 | 1.10 |
| ❑ SS20B Sandis Ozolinsh | 2.00 | .90 |
| ❑ SS21A Zigmund Palffy | 2.50 | 1.10 |
| ❑ SS21B Petr Sykora | 1.50 | .70 |
| ❑ SS22A Ed Belfour | 2.50 | 1.10 |
| ❑ SS22B Ron Hextall | 2.00 | .90 |
| ❑ SS23A Mats Sundin | 2.00 | .90 |
| ❑ SS23B Mikael Renberg | 2.00 | .90 |
| ❑ SS24A Vitali Yachmenev | 1.50 | .70 |
| ❑ SS24B Alexei Zhamnov | 2.00 | .90 |
| ❑ SS25A Oleg Tverdovsky | 1.50 | .70 |
| ❑ SS25B Kyle McLaren | 1.50 | .70 |
| ❑ SS26A Dominik Hasek | 6.00 | 2.70 |
| ❑ SS26B Petr Nedved | 1.50 | .70 |
| ❑ SS27A Chris Chelios | 2.50 | 1.10 |
| ❑ SS27B Chris Pronger | 2.00 | .90 |
| ❑ SS28A Rob Niedermayer | 1.50 | .70 |
| ❑ SS28B Scott Niedermayer | 1.50 | .70 |
| ❑ SS29A Keith Primeau | 2.00 | .90 |
| ❑ SS29B Bob Probert | 1.50 | .70 |
| ❑ SS30A Bill Ranford | 2.00 | .90 |
| ❑ SS30B Chris Osgood | 2.50 | 1.10 |

## 1997-98 Upper Deck

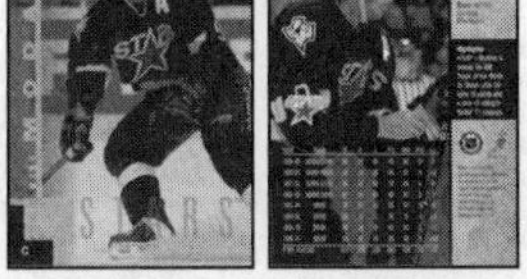

The 1997-98 Upper Deck set was issued in two series totaling 420 cards and was distributed in 12-card packs with a suggested retail price of $2.49. The fronts feature color player photos, while the backs carry player information and career statistics. Series 1 contains the following subsets: Star Rookie (181-195), Fan Favorites (196-208) and two checklists (209-210). Series 2 contains the following subsets: Physical Force (389-398), Program of Excellence (399-418) and two checklists (419-420).

| | MINT | NRMT |
|---|---|---|
| COMPLETE SET (420) | 55.00 | 25.00 |
| COMP.SER. 1 (210) | 20.00 | 9.00 |
| COMP.SER. 2 (210) | 35.00 | 16.00 |
| COMMON CARD (1-420) | .10 | .05 |

| | | |
|---|---|---|
| ❑ 1 Teemu Selanne | .75 | .35 |
| ❑ 2 Steve Rucchin | .10 | .05 |
| ❑ 3 Kevin Todd | .10 | .05 |
| ❑ 4 Darren Van Impe | .10 | .05 |
| ❑ 5 Mark Janssens | .10 | .05 |
| ❑ 6 Guy Hebert | .25 | .11 |
| ❑ 7 Sean Pronger | .10 | .05 |
| ❑ 8 Jason Allison | .25 | .11 |
| ❑ 9 Ray Bourque | .40 | .18 |
| ❑ 10 Landon Wilson | .10 | .05 |
| ❑ 11 Anson Carter | .10 | .05 |
| ❑ 12 Jean-Yves Roy | .10 | .05 |
| ❑ 13 Kyle McLaren | .10 | .05 |
| ❑ 14 Don Sweeney | .10 | .05 |
| ❑ 15 Brian Holzinger | .10 | .05 |
| ❑ 16 Matthew Barnaby | .10 | .05 |
| ❑ 17 Wayne Primeau | .10 | .05 |
| ❑ 18 Steve Shields | .25 | .11 |
| ❑ 19 Jason Dawe | .10 | .05 |
| ❑ 20 Donald Audette | .10 | .05 |
| ❑ 21 Dixon Ward | .10 | .05 |
| ❑ 22 Hnat Domenichelli | .10 | .05 |
| ❑ 23 Trevor Kidd | .25 | .11 |
| ❑ 24 Jarome Iginla | .25 | .11 |
| ❑ 25 Sandy McCarthy | .10 | .05 |
| ❑ 26 Marty McInnis | .10 | .05 |
| ❑ 27 Jonas Hoglund | .10 | .05 |
| ❑ 28 Aaron Gavey | .10 | .05 |
| ❑ 29 Keith Primeau | .10 | .05 |
| ❑ 30 Geoff Sanderson | .25 | .11 |
| ❑ 31 Sean Burke | .25 | .11 |
| ❑ 32 Steven Rice | .10 | .05 |
| ❑ 33 Stu Grimson | .10 | .05 |
| ❑ 34 Jeff O'Neill | .10 | .05 |
| ❑ 35 Curtis Leschyshyn | .10 | .05 |
| ❑ 36 Chris Chelios | .40 | .18 |
| ❑ 37 Sergei Krivokrasov | .10 | .05 |
| ❑ 38 Jeff Hackett | .25 | .11 |
| ❑ 39 Bob Probert | .10 | .05 |
| ❑ 40 Chris Terreri | .25 | .11 |
| ❑ 41 Eric Daze | .25 | .11 |
| ❑ 42 Alexei Zhamnov | .10 | .05 |
| ❑ 43 Patrick Roy | 2.00 | .90 |
| ❑ 44 Sandis Ozolinsh | .25 | .11 |
| ❑ 45 Eric Messier | .25 | .11 |
| ❑ 46 Adam Deadmarsh | .25 | .11 |
| ❑ 47 Claude Lemieux | .25 | .11 |
| ❑ 48 Mike Ricci | .10 | .05 |
| ❑ 49 Stephane Yelle | .10 | .05 |
| ❑ 50 Joe Nieuwendyk | .25 | .11 |
| ❑ 51 Derian Hatcher | .10 | .05 |
| ❑ 52 Jere Lehtinen | .10 | .05 |
| ❑ 53 Roman Turek | .25 | .11 |
| ❑ 54 Darryl Sydor | .10 | .05 |
| ❑ 55 Todd Harvey | .10 | .05 |
| ❑ 56 Mike Modano | .50 | .23 |
| ❑ 57 Steve Yzerman | 1.25 | .55 |
| ❑ 58 Martin Lapointe | .10 | .05 |
| ❑ 59 Darren McCarty | .10 | .05 |
| ❑ 60 Mike Vernon | .25 | .11 |
| ❑ 61 Kirk Maltby | .10 | .05 |
| ❑ 62 Kris Draper | .10 | .05 |
| ❑ 63 Vladimir Konstantinov | .10 | .05 |
| ❑ 64 Todd Marchant | .10 | .05 |
| ❑ 65 Doug Weight | .25 | .11 |
| ❑ 66 Jason Arnott | .25 | .11 |
| ❑ 67 Mike Grier | .10 | .05 |
| ❑ 68 Mats Lindgren | .10 | .05 |
| ❑ 69 Bryan Marchment | .10 | .05 |
| ❑ 70 Rem Murray | .10 | .05 |
| ❑ 71 Radek Dvorak | .10 | .05 |
| ❑ 72 John Vanbiesbrouck | .60 | .25 |
| ❑ 73 Robert Svehla | .10 | .05 |
| ❑ 74 Bill Lindsay | .10 | .05 |
| ❑ 75 Paul Laus | .10 | .05 |
| ❑ 76 Kirk Muller | .10 | .05 |
| ❑ 77 Dave Nemirovsky | .10 | .05 |
| ❑ 78 Roman Vopat | .10 | .05 |
| ❑ 79 Jan Vopat | .10 | .05 |
| ❑ 80 Dimitri Khristich | .10 | .05 |
| ❑ 81 Glen Murray | .10 | .05 |
| ❑ 82 Mattias Norstrom | .10 | .05 |
| ❑ 83 Ian Laperriere | .10 | .05 |
| ❑ 84 Mark Recchi | .25 | .11 |
| ❑ 85 Jose Theodore | .25 | .11 |
| ❑ 86 Vincent Damphousse | .25 | .11 |
| ❑ 87 Sebastien Bordeleau | .10 | .05 |
| ❑ 88 Darcy Tucker | .10 | .05 |
| ❑ 89 Martin Rucinsky | .10 | .05 |
| ❑ 90 Jocelyn Thibault | .25 | .11 |
| ❑ 91 Doug Gilmour | .40 | .18 |
| ❑ 92 Brian Rolston | .10 | .05 |
| ❑ 93 Jay Pandolfo | .10 | .05 |
| ❑ 94 John MacLean | .10 | .05 |
| ❑ 95 Scott Stevens | .10 | .05 |
| ❑ 96 Dave Andreychuk | .10 | .05 |
| ❑ 97 Denis Pederson | .10 | .05 |
| ❑ 98 Bryan Berard | .25 | .11 |
| ❑ 99 Zigmund Palffy | .40 | .18 |
| ❑ 100 Bryan McCabe | .10 | .05 |
| ❑ 101 Rich Pilon | .10 | .05 |
| ❑ 102 Eric Fichaud | .25 | .11 |
| ❑ 103 Todd Bertuzzi | .10 | .05 |
| ❑ 104 Robert Reichel | .10 | .05 |
| ❑ 105 Christian Dube | .10 | .05 |
| ❑ 106 Niklas Sundstrom | .10 | .05 |
| ❑ 107 Mike Richter | .40 | .18 |
| ❑ 108 Adam Graves | .25 | .11 |
| ❑ 109 Wayne Gretzky | 2.50 | 1.10 |
| ❑ 110 Bruce Driver | .10 | .05 |
| ❑ 111 Esa Tikkanen | .10 | .05 |
| ❑ 112 Daniel Alfredsson | .25 | .11 |
| ❑ 113 Ron Tugnutt | .25 | .11 |
| ❑ 114 Steve Duchesne | .10 | .05 |
| ❑ 115 Bruce Gardiner | .10 | .05 |
| ❑ 116 Sergei Zholtok | .10 | .05 |
| ❑ 117 Alexandre Daigle | .25 | .11 |
| ❑ 118 Wade Redden | .10 | .05 |
| ❑ 119 Mikael Renberg | .25 | .11 |
| ❑ 120 Trent Klatt | .10 | .05 |
| ❑ 121 Rod Brind'Amour | .25 | .11 |
| ❑ 122 Dainius Zubrus | .40 | .18 |
| ❑ 123 John LeClair | .60 | .25 |
| ❑ 124 Janne Niinimaa | .25 | .11 |
| ❑ 125 Vaclav Prospal | 1.25 | .55 |
| ❑ 126 Keith Tkachuk | .50 | .23 |
| ❑ 127 Jeremy Roenick | .40 | .18 |
| ❑ 128 Mike Gartner | .25 | .11 |
| ❑ 129 Nikolai Khabibulin | .25 | .11 |
| ❑ 130 Chad Kilger | .10 | .05 |
| ❑ 131 Shane Doan | .10 | .05 |
| ❑ 132 Cliff Ronning | .25 | .11 |
| ❑ 133 Patrick Lalime | .25 | .11 |
| ❑ 134 Greg Johnson | .10 | .05 |
| ❑ 135 Ron Francis | .25 | .11 |
| ❑ 136 Darius Kasparaitis | .10 | .05 |
| ❑ 137 Petr Nedved | .25 | .11 |
| ❑ 138 Jason Woolley | .10 | .05 |
| ❑ 139 Fredrik Olausson | .10 | .05 |
| ❑ 140 Harry York | .10 | .05 |
| ❑ 141 Brett Hull | .50 | .23 |
| ❑ 142 Chris Pronger | .25 | .11 |
| ❑ 143 Jim Campbell | .10 | .05 |
| ❑ 144 Libor Zabransky | .10 | .05 |
| ❑ 145 Grant Fuhr | .25 | .11 |
| ❑ 146 Pavol Demitra | .10 | .05 |
| ❑ 147 Owen Nolan | .25 | .11 |
| ❑ 148 Stephen Guolla | .10 | .05 |
| ❑ 149 Marcus Ragnarsson | .10 | .05 |
| ❑ 150 Bernie Nicholls | .10 | .05 |
| ❑ 151 Todd Gill | .10 | .05 |
| ❑ 152 Shean Donovan | .10 | .05 |
| ❑ 153 Corey Schwab | .25 | .11 |
| ❑ 154 Dino Ciccarelli | .10 | .05 |
| ❑ 155 Chris Gratton | .25 | .11 |
| ❑ 156 Alexander Selivanov | .10 | .05 |
| ❑ 157 Roman Hamrlik | .10 | .05 |
| ❑ 158 Daymond Langkow | .10 | .05 |
| ❑ 159 Paul Ysebaert | .10 | .05 |
| ❑ 160 Steve Sullivan | .10 | .05 |
| ❑ 161 Sergei Berezin | .10 | .05 |
| ❑ 162 Fredrik Modin | .10 | .05 |
| ❑ 163 Todd Warriner | .10 | .05 |
| ❑ 164 Wendel Clark | .25 | .11 |
| ❑ 165 Jason Podollan | .10 | .05 |
| ❑ 166 Darby Hendrickson | .10 | .05 |
| ❑ 167 Martin Gelinas | .10 | .05 |
| ❑ 168 Pavel Bure | .75 | .35 |
| ❑ 169 Trevor Linden | .25 | .11 |
| ❑ 170 Mike Sillinger | .10 | .05 |
| ❑ 171 Corey Hirsch | .25 | .11 |
| ❑ 172 Lonny Bohonos | .10 | .05 |
| ❑ 173 Markus Naslund | .10 | .05 |
| ❑ 174 Steve Konowalchuk | .10 | .05 |
| ❑ 175 Dale Hunter | .10 | .05 |
| ❑ 176 Joe Juneau | .25 | .11 |
| ❑ 177 Adam Oates | .25 | .11 |
| ❑ 178 Bill Ranford | .25 | .11 |
| ❑ 179 Pat Peake | .10 | .05 |
| ❑ 180 Sergei Gonchar | .10 | .05 |
| ❑ 181 Mike Leclerc | .10 | .05 |
| ❑ 182 Randy Robitaille | .10 | .05 |
| ❑ 183 Paxton Schafer | .10 | .05 |
| ❑ 184 Rumun Ndur | .10 | .05 |
| ❑ 185 Christian Laflamme | .10 | .05 |
| ❑ 186 Wade Belak | .25 | .11 |
| ❑ 187 Mike Knuble | .10 | .05 |
| ❑ 188 Steve Kelly | .10 | .05 |
| ❑ 189 Patrik Elias | 1.25 | .55 |
| ❑ 190 Ken Belanger | .10 | .05 |
| ❑ 191 Colin Forbes | .10 | .05 |
| ❑ 192 Juha Ylonen | .10 | .05 |
| ❑ 193 David Cooper | .10 | .05 |
| ❑ 194 D.J. Smith | .10 | .05 |
| ❑ 195 Jaroslav Svejkovsky | .25 | .11 |
| ❑ 196 Tie Domi | .10 | .05 |
| ❑ 197 Bob Probert | .10 | .05 |
| ❑ 198 Doug Gilmour | .40 | .18 |
| ❑ 199 Dino Ciccarelli | .10 | .05 |
| ❑ 200 Martin Gelinas | .10 | .05 |
| ❑ 201 Tony Twist | .25 | .11 |
| ❑ 202 Claude Lemieux | .25 | .11 |
| ❑ 203 Vladimir Konstantinov | .10 | .05 |
| ❑ 204 Ulf Samuelsson | .10 | .05 |
| ❑ 205 Chris Simon | .10 | .05 |
| ❑ 206 Gino Odjick | .10 | .05 |
| ❑ 207 Mike Grier | .10 | .05 |
| ❑ 208 Tony Amonte | .25 | .11 |
| ❑ 209 Wayne Gretzky CL | .40 | .18 |
| ❑ 210 Patrick Roy CL | .40 | .18 |
| ❑ 211 Paul Kariya | 1.50 | .70 |
| ❑ 212 J.J. Daigneault | .10 | .05 |
| ❑ 213 Dmitri Mironov | .10 | .05 |
| ❑ 214 Joe Sacco | .10 | .05 |
| ❑ 215 Richard Park | .10 | .05 |
| ❑ 216 Espen Knutsen | .10 | .05 |
| ❑ 217 Dave Karpa | .10 | .05 |
| ❑ 218 Joe Thornton | .75 | .35 |
| ❑ 219 Sergei Samsonov | 1.00 | .45 |
| ❑ 220 P.J. Axelsson | .10 | .05 |
| ❑ 221 Ted Donato | .10 | .05 |
| ❑ 222 Dean Chynoweth | .10 | .05 |
| ❑ 223 Rob Tallas | .10 | .05 |
| ❑ 224 Mattias Timander | .10 | .05 |
| ❑ 225 Dominik Hasek | .75 | .35 |
| ❑ 226 Erik Rasmussen | .10 | .05 |
| ❑ 227 Mike Peca | .10 | .05 |
| ❑ 228 Rob Ray | .10 | .05 |
| ❑ 229 Vaclav Varada | .10 | .05 |
| ❑ 230 Curtis Brown | .10 | .05 |
| ❑ 231 Jay McKee | .10 | .05 |
| ❑ 232 Theoren Fleury | .25 | .11 |
| ❑ 233 Derek Morris | .10 | .05 |
| ❑ 234 Chris Dingman | .10 | .05 |
| ❑ 235 Chris O'Sullivan | .10 | .05 |
| ❑ 236 Rick Tabaracci | .25 | .11 |
| ❑ 237 Tommy Albelin | .10 | .05 |
| ❑ 238 Todd Simpson | .10 | .05 |
| ❑ 239 Sami Kapanen | .25 | .11 |
| UER numbered 229 | | |
| ❑ 240 Gary Roberts | .10 | .05 |
| ❑ 241 Kevin Dineen | .10 | .05 |
| ❑ 242 Kevin Haller | .10 | .05 |
| ❑ 243 Nelson Emerson | .10 | .05 |
| ❑ 244 Glen Wesley | .10 | .05 |
| ❑ 245 Tony Amonte | .25 | .11 |
| ❑ 246 Eric Weinrich | .10 | .05 |
| ❑ 247 Daniel Cleary | .25 | .11 |
| ❑ 248 Jeff Shantz | .10 | .05 |
| ❑ 249 Jean-Yves Leroux | .10 | .05 |
| ❑ 250 Ethan Moreau | .10 | .05 |
| ❑ 251 Craig Mills | .10 | .05 |
| ❑ 252 Peter Forsberg | 1.25 | .55 |
| ❑ 253 Joe Sakic | .75 | .35 |
| ❑ 254 Valeri Kamensky | .25 | .11 |
| ❑ 255 Adam Foote | .10 | .05 |
| ❑ 256 Josef Marha | .10 | .05 |
| ❑ 257 Christian Matte | .10 | .05 |
| ❑ 258 Aaron Miller | .10 | .05 |
| ❑ 259 Ed Belfour | .40 | .18 |
| ❑ 260 Jamie Langenbrunner | .10 | .05 |
| ❑ 261 Juha Lind | .10 | .05 |
| ❑ 262 Pat Verbeek | .10 | .05 |
| ❑ 263 Sergei Zubov | .10 | .05 |
| ❑ 264 Dave Reid | .10 | .05 |
| ❑ 265 Greg Adams | .10 | .05 |
| ❑ 266 Sergei Fedorov | .75 | .35 |
| ❑ 267 Nicklas Lidstrom | .25 | .11 |
| ❑ 268 Brendan Shanahan | .75 | .35 |
| ❑ 269 Chris Osgood | .40 | .18 |
| ❑ 270 Aaron Ward | .10 | .05 |
| ❑ 271 Vyacheslav Kozlov | .10 | .05 |
| ❑ 272 Kevin Hodson | .25 | .11 |
| ❑ 273 Curtis Joseph | .40 | .18 |
| ❑ 274 Ryan Smyth | .25 | .11 |
| ❑ 275 Dean McAmmond | .10 | .05 |
| ❑ 276 Boris Mironov | .10 | .05 |
| ❑ 277 Dennis Bonvie | .10 | .05 |
| ❑ 278 Kelly Buchberger | .10 | .05 |
| ❑ 279 Kevin Lowe | .10 | .05 |
| ❑ 280 Ray Sheppard | .10 | .05 |
| ❑ 281 Rob Niedermayer | .10 | .05 |
| ❑ 282 Scott Mellanby | .10 | .05 |
| ❑ 283 Terry Carkner | .10 | .05 |
| ❑ 284 Ed Jovanovski | .25 | .11 |
| ❑ 285 Gord Murphy | .10 | .05 |
| ❑ 286 Tom Fitzgerald | .10 | .05 |
| ❑ 287 Jamie Storr | .25 | .11 |
| ❑ 288 Olli Jokinen | 1.25 | .55 |
| ❑ 289 Vladimir Tsyplakov | .10 | .05 |
| ❑ 290 Luc Robitaille | .25 | .11 |
| ❑ 291 Vitali Yachmenev | .10 | .05 |
| ❑ 292 Donald MacLean | .10 | .05 |
| ❑ 293 Saku Koivu | .60 | .25 |
| ❑ 294 Andy Moog | .25 | .11 |
| ❑ 295 Patrice Brisebois | .10 | .05 |
| ❑ 296 Brad Brown | .10 | .05 |
| ❑ 297 Turner Stevenson | .10 | .05 |
| ❑ 298 Shayne Corson | .10 | .05 |
| ❑ 299 Brian Savage | .10 | .05 |
| ❑ 300 Martin Brodeur | 1.00 | .45 |
| ❑ 301 Scott Niedermayer | .10 | .05 |
| ❑ 302 Krzysztof Oliwa | .10 | .05 |
| ❑ 303 Valeri Zelepukin | .10 | .05 |
| ❑ 304 Bobby Holik | .10 | .05 |
| ❑ 305 Ken Daneyko | .10 | .05 |
| ❑ 306 Lyle Odelein | .10 | .05 |
| ❑ 307 Travis Green | .10 | .05 |
| ❑ 308 Steve Webb | .10 | .05 |
| ❑ 309 Dan Plante | .10 | .05 |
| ❑ 310 Bryan Smolinski | .10 | .05 |
| ❑ 311 Claude Lapointe | .10 | .05 |
| ❑ 312 Kenny Jonsson | .10 | .05 |
| ❑ 313 Ulf Samuelsson | .10 | .05 |
| ❑ 314 Jeff Beukeboom | .10 | .05 |
| ❑ 315 Mike Keane | .10 | .05 |
| ❑ 316 Brian Leetch | .40 | .18 |
| ❑ 317 Shane Churla | .10 | .05 |
| ❑ 318 Pat LaFontaine | .25 | .11 |
| ❑ 319 Alexei Kovalev | .10 | .05 |
| ❑ 320 Radek Bonk | .10 | .05 |
| ❑ 321 Alexei Yashin | .25 | .11 |
| ❑ 322 Damian Rhodes | .25 | .11 |
| ❑ 323 Andreas Dackell | .10 | .05 |
| ❑ 324 Magnus Arvedson | .10 | .05 |
| ❑ 325 Chris Phillips | .10 | .05 |
| ❑ 326 Marian Hossa | 4.00 | 1.80 |
| ❑ 327 Chris Gratton | .25 | .11 |
| ❑ 328 Shjon Podein | .10 | .05 |
| ❑ 329 Paul Coffey | .40 | .18 |
| ❑ 330 Luke Richardson | .10 | .05 |
| ❑ 331 Eric Lindros | 1.25 | .55 |
| ❑ 332 Eric Desjardins | .10 | .05 |
| ❑ 333 Joel Otto | .10 | .05 |
| ❑ 334 Craig Janney | .10 | .05 |
| ❑ 335 Oleg Tverdovsky | .10 | .05 |
| ❑ 336 Teppo Numminen | .10 | .05 |
| ❑ 337 Jim McKenzie | .10 | .05 |
| ❑ 338 Dallas Drake | .10 | .05 |
| ❑ 339 Rick Tocchet | .25 | .11 |
| ❑ 340 Brad Isbister | .10 | .05 |
| ❑ 341 Alexei Morozov | .25 | .11 |
| ❑ 342 Jaromir Jagr | 1.25 | .55 |
| ❑ 343 Kevin Hatcher | .10 | .05 |
| ❑ 344 Ken Wregget | .25 | .11 |
| ❑ 345 Chris Tamer | .10 | .05 |
| ❑ 346 Robert Dome | .10 | .05 |
| ❑ 347 Neil Wilkinson | .10 | .05 |
| ❑ 348 Chris McAlpine | .10 | .05 |
| ❑ 349 Joe Murphy | .10 | .05 |
| ❑ 350 Robert Petrovicky | .10 | .05 |
| ❑ 351 Marc Bergevin | .10 | .05 |
| ❑ 352 Al MacInnis | .25 | .11 |
| ❑ 353 Pierre Turgeon | .25 | .11 |
| ❑ 354 Patrick Marleau | .75 | .35 |
| ❑ 355 Marco Sturm | 1.25 | .55 |
| ❑ 356 Mike Vernon | .25 | .11 |
| ❑ 357 Al Iafrate | .10 | .05 |
| ❑ 358 Jeff Friesen | .25 | .11 |
| ❑ 359 Viktor Kozlov | .25 | .11 |
| ❑ 360 Tony Granato | .10 | .05 |
| ❑ 361 Mikael Renberg | .25 | .11 |
| ❑ 362 Daren Puppa | .25 | .11 |
| ❑ 363 Roman Hamrlik | .10 | .05 |
| ❑ 364 Rob Zamuner | .10 | .05 |
| ❑ 365 Cory Cross | .10 | .05 |
| ❑ 366 Patrick Poulin | .10 | .05 |
| ❑ 367 Felix Potvin | .40 | .18 |
| ❑ 368 Tie Domi | .10 | .05 |
| ❑ 369 Mats Sundin | .40 | .18 |

□ 370 Jeff Ware .10 .05
□ 371 Alyn McCauley .25 .11
□ 372 Mathieu Schneider .10 .05
□ 373 Craig Wolanin .10 .05
□ 374 Mark Messier .50 .23
□ 375 Kirk McLean .25 .11
□ 376 Donald Brashear .10 .05
□ 377 Arturs Irbe .25 .11
□ 378 Jyrki Lumme .10 .05
□ 379 Gino Odjick .10 .05
□ 380 Mattias Ohlund .25 .11
□ 381 Jan Bulis .10 .05
□ 382 Andrew Brunette .10 .05
□ 383 Calle Johansson .10 .05
□ 384 Brendan Witt .10 .05
□ 385 Mark Tinordi .10 .05
□ 386 Ken Klee .10 .05
□ 387 Chris Simon .10 .05
□ 388 Richard Zednik .10 .05
□ 389 Ed Jovanovski .25 .11
□ 390 Darren McCarty .10 .05
□ 391 Darius Kasparaitis .10 .05
□ 392 Bryan Marchment .10 .05
□ 393 Matthew Barnaby .10 .05
□ 394 Chris Chelios .40 .18
□ 395 Ulf Samuelsson .10 .05
□ 396 Scott Stevens .10 .05
□ 397 Derian Hatcher .10 .05
□ 398 Chris Pronger .25 .11
□ 399 Mathieu Chouinard 1.50 .70
□ 400 Jake McCracken 1.50 .70
□ 401 Bryan Allen .75 .35
□ 402 Christian Chartier .10 .05
□ 403 Jonathan Girard .10 .05
□ 404 Abe Herbst .10 .05
□ 405 Stephen Peat .10 .05
□ 406 Robyn Regehr .10 .05
□ 407 Blair Betts .10 .05
□ 408 Eric Chouinard .50 .23
□ 409 Brett DeCecco .10 .05
□ 410 Rico Fata 3.00 1.35
□ 411 Simon Gagne 5.00 2.20
□ 412 Vincent Lecavalier 12.00 5.50
□ 413 Manny Malhotra 3.00 1.35
□ 414 Norm Milley 1.50 .70
□ 415 Justin Papineau 1.50 .70
□ 416 Garrett Prosofsky 1.25 .55
□ 417 Mike Ribeiro 2.00 .90
□ 418 Brad Richards .10 .05
□ 419 Wayne Gretzky CL .40 .18
□ 420 Patrick Roy CL .40 .18

## 1997-98 Upper Deck Game Dated Moments

Randomly inserted in packs at the rate of one in 1500, this 60-card set features color player photos of their top moments of last year and printed on 24 pt. embossed Light F/X cards. The set is skip numbered.

| | MINT | NRMT |
|---|---|---|
| COMPLETE SET (60) | 7500.00 | 3400.00 |
| COMMON CARD | 30.00 | 13.50 |

## 1997-98 Upper Deck Game Jerseys

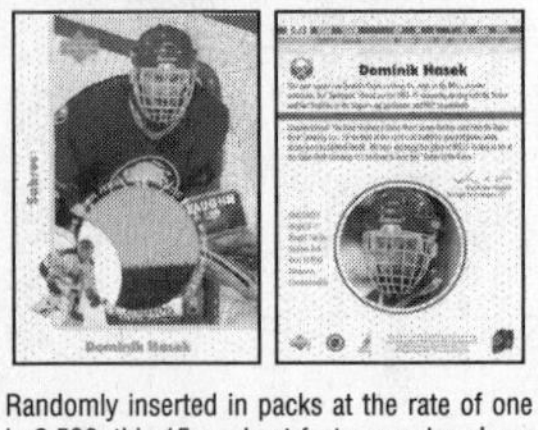

Randomly inserted in packs at the rate of one in 2,500, this 15-card set features color player photos with an actual piece of the player's game-worn jersey embedded in the card. Patrick Roy autographed 33 special Game Jersey cards inserted in Series 1 packs, and Wayne Gretzky has signed 99 cards containing remnants of his 1997 All-Star Game jersey inserted in Series 2 packs.

| | MINT | NRMT |
|---|---|---|
| COMPLETE SET (13) | 5400.00 | 2400.00 |
| COMP.SERIES 1 (7) | 2700.00 | 1200.00 |
| COMP.SERIES 2 (6) | 2700.00 | 1200.00 |
| COMMON CARD | 120.00 | 55.00 |

SET PRICE DOES NOT INCLUDE SIGNED CARDS

□ GJ1 Patrick Roy HOME 600.00 275.00
□ GJ2 Patrick Roy AWAY 600.00 275.00
□ GJ3 Dominik Hasek 300.00 135.00
□ GJ4 Jarome Iginla 120.00 55.00
□ GJ5 Sergei Fedorov 300.00 135.00
□ GJ6 Tony Amonte 150.00 70.00
□ GJ7 Joe Sakic 300.00 135.00
□ GJ8 Wayne Gretzky 1000.00 450.00
□ GJ9 Saku Koivu 200.00 90.00
□ GJ11 Mike Richter 175.00 80.00
□ GJ12 Doug Weight 120.00 55.00
□ GJ13 Brendan Shanahan 300.00 135.00
□ GJ14 Brian Leetch 175.00 80.00
□ GJ1S Patrick Roy AU 2000.00 900.00
□ GJ8S Wayne Gretzky AU 2500.00 1100.00

## 1997-98 Upper Deck Sixth Sense Masters

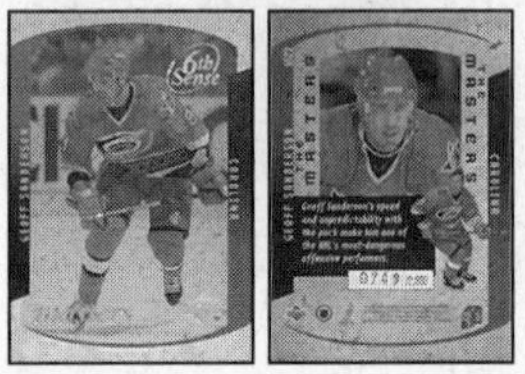

Randomly inserted in Series 2 packs, this 30-card set features color photos of the NHL's brightest stars. Only 2,000 of each card were produced and are sequentially numbered.

| | MINT | NRMT |
|---|---|---|
| COMPLETE SET (30) | 550.00 | 250.00 |
| COMMON CARD (SS1-SS30) | 8.00 | 3.60 |

□ SS1 Wayne Gretzky 60.00 27.00
□ SS2 Jaromir Jagr 30.00 13.50
□ SS3 Sergei Fedorov 20.00 9.00
□ SS4 Brett Hull 12.00 5.50
□ SS5 Brian Leetch 10.00 4.50
□ SS6 Joe Thornton 20.00 9.00
□ SS7 Ray Bourque 10.00 4.50
□ SS8 Teemu Selanne 20.00 9.00
□ SS9 Paul Kariya 40.00 18.00
□ SS10 Doug Weight 8.00 3.60
□ SS11 Mark Messier 12.00 5.50
□ SS12 Adam Oates 8.00 3.60
□ SS13 Mats Sundin 10.00 4.50
□ SS14 Brendan Shanahan 20.00 9.00
□ SS15 Saku Koivu 15.00 6.75
□ SS16 Doug Gilmour 8.00 3.60
□ SS17 Eric Lindros 30.00 13.50
□ SS18 Tony Amonte 8.00 3.60
□ SS19 Joe Sakic 20.00 9.00
□ SS20 Steve Yzerman 30.00 13.50
□ SS21 Peter Forsberg 30.00 13.50
□ SS22 Geoff Sanderson 8.00 3.60
□ SS23 Keith Tkachuk 12.00 5.50
□ SS24 Pavel Bure 20.00 9.00
□ SS25 Ron Francis 8.00 3.60
□ SS26 Zigmund Palffy 10.00 4.50
□ SS27 Daniel Alfredsson 8.00 3.60
□ SS28 Bryan Berard 8.00 3.60
□ SS29 Mike Modano 12.00 5.50
□ SS30 Patrick Roy 50.00 22.00

## 1997-98 Upper Deck Sixth Sense Wizards

Randomly inserted in Series 2 packs, this 30-card set is a holographic die-cut parallel version of the Sixth Sense Masters insert set. Only 100 of each card was produced.

| | MINT | NRMT |
|---|---|---|
| COMPLETE SET (30) | 5000.00 | 2200.00 |
| COMMON CARD (SS1-SS30) | 60.00 | 27.00 |

*STARS: 4X TO 8X MASTERS

## 1997-98 Upper Deck Smooth Grooves

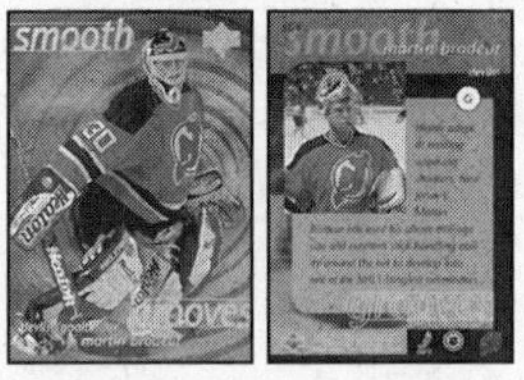

Randomly inserted in Series 2 packs at the rate of one in four, this 60-card set features color photos of the league's top performers with skating grooves as the background.

| | MINT | NRMT |
|---|---|---|
| COMPLETE SET (60) | 150.00 | 70.00 |
| COMMON CARD (SG1-SG60) | .60 | .25 |

□ SG1 Wayne Gretzky 12.00 5.50
□ SG2 Patrick Roy 10.00 4.50
□ SG3 Patrick Marleau 4.00 1.80
□ SG4 Martin Brodeur 5.00 2.20
□ SG5 Zigmund Palffy 2.00 .90
□ SG6 Joe Thornton 4.00 1.80
□ SG7 Chris Chelios 2.00 .90
□ SG8 Teemu Selanne 4.00 1.80
□ SG9 Paul Kariya 8.00 3.60
□ SG10 Tony Amonte 1.50 .70
□ SG11 Mark Messier 2.50 1.10
□ SG12 Jarome Iginla 1.50 .70
□ SG13 Mats Sundin 2.00 .90
□ SG14 Brendan Shanahan 4.00 1.80
□ SG15 Ed Jovanovski 1.50 .70
□ SG16 Brett Hull 2.50 1.10
□ SG17 Brian Rolston .60 .25
□ SG18 Saku Koivu 3.00 1.35
□ SG19 Steve Yzerman 6.00 2.70
□ SG20 Doug Weight 1.50 .70
□ SG21 Peter Forsberg 6.00 2.70
□ SG22 Brian Leetch 2.00 .90
□ SG23 Alexei Yashin 1.50 .70
□ SG24 Owen Nolan 1.50 .70
□ SG25 Mike Grier .60 .25
□ SG26 Jere Lehtinen .60 .25
□ SG27 Vaclav Prospal 2.50 1.10
□ SG28 Sandis Ozolinsh 1.50 .70
□ SG29 Mike Modano 2.50 1.10
□ SG30 Sergei Samsonov 5.00 2.20
□ SG31 Curtis Joseph 2.00 .90
□ SG32 Daymond Langkow .60 .25
□ SG33 Doug Gilmour 1.50 .70
□ SG34 Bryan Berard 1.50 .70
□ SG35 Joe Sakic 4.00 1.80
□ SG36 Wade Redden .60 .25
□ SG37 Keith Tkachuk 2.50 1.10
□ SG38 Jaromir Jagr 6.00 2.70
□ SG39 Dominik Hasek 4.00 1.80
□ SG40 Patrick Lalime 1.50 .70
□ SG41 Janne Niinima 1.50 .70
□ SG42 Oleg Tverdovsky .60 .25
□ SG43 Vitali Yachmenev .60 .25
□ SG44 Rob Niedermayer .60 .25
□ SG45 Nicklas Lidstrom .60 .25
□ SG46 Jim Campbell .60 .25
□ SG47 Roman Hamrlik .60 .25
□ SG48 Eric Lindros 6.00 2.70
□ SG49 Brian Holzinger .60 .25
□ SG50 John LeClair 3.00 1.35
□ SG51 Sergei Berezin 1.50 .70
□ SG52 Jaroslav Svejkovsky 1.50 .70
□ SG53 Mike Richter 2.00 .90
□ SG54 John Vanbiesbrouck 3.00 1.35
□ SG55 Keith Primeau 1.50 .70
□ SG56 Adam Oates 1.50 .70
□ SG57 Jeremy Roenick 2.00 .90
□ SG58 Pavel Bure 4.00 1.80
□ SG59 Dainius Zubrus 2.00 .90
□ SG60 Jose Theodore 1.50 .70

## 1997-98 Upper Deck The Specialists

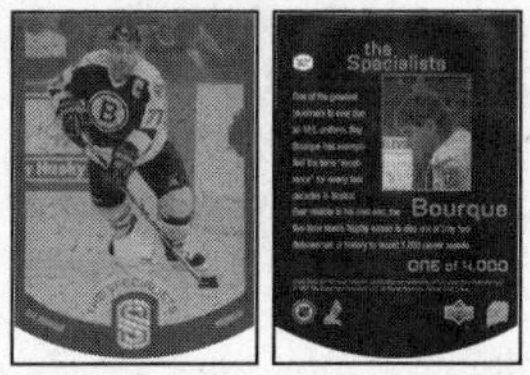

Randomly inserted in Series 1 packs, this 30-card set features black-and-white action photos of the NHL brightest stars. Only 4,000 of each card were produced and numbered.

| | MINT | NRMT |
|---|---|---|
| COMPLETE SET (30) | 350.00 | 160.00 |
| COMMON CARD (1-30) | 5.00 | 2.20 |

□ 1 Wayne Gretzky 40.00 18.00
□ 2 Patrick Roy 30.00 13.50
□ 3 Jaromir Jagr 20.00 9.00
□ 4 Joe Sakic 12.00 5.50
□ 5 Mark Messier 8.00 3.60
□ 6 Eric Lindros 20.00 9.00
□ 7 John Vanbiesbrouck 10.00 4.50
□ 8 Teemu Selanne 12.00 5.50
□ 9 Paul Kariya 25.00 11.00
□ 10 Pavel Bure 12.00 5.50
□ 11 Sergei Fedorov 12.00 5.50
□ 12 Peter Bondra 6.00 2.70
□ 13 Mats Sundin 6.00 2.70
□ 14 Brendan Shanahan 12.00 5.50
□ 15 Keith Tkachuk 8.00 3.60
□ 16 Brett Hull 8.00 3.60
□ 17 Jeremy Roenick 6.00 2.70
□ 18 Dominik Hasek 12.00 5.50
□ 19 Steve Yzerman 20.00 9.00
□ 20 John LeClair 10.00 4.50
□ 21 Peter Forsberg 20.00 9.00
□ 22 Zigmund Palffy 6.00 2.70
□ 23 Tony Amonte 5.00 2.20
□ 24 Jarome Iginla 5.00 2.20
□ 25 Curtis Joseph 6.00 2.70
□ 26 Mike Modano 8.00 3.60
□ 27 Ray Bourque 6.00 2.70
□ 28 Brian Leetch 6.00 2.70
□ 29 Bryan Berard 5.00 2.20
□ 30 Martin Brodeur 15.00 6.75

## 1997-98 Upper Deck The Specialists Level 2

Randomly inserted in Series 1 packs, this 30-card set is a crash numbered, laser die-cut parallel version of The Specialists Level 1 set. Only 100 of each card was produced and serially numbered.

| | MINT | NRMT |
|---|---|---|
| COMPLETE SET (30) | 5000.00 | 2200.00 |
| COMMON CARD (1-30) | 60.00 | 27.00 |

*STARS: 6X TO 12X BASIC CARDS

## 1997-98 Upper Deck Three Star Selects

Randomly inserted in Series 1 packs at the rate of one in four, this 60-card set features color photos on die-cut cards of three top players that fit together to form 20 different sets.

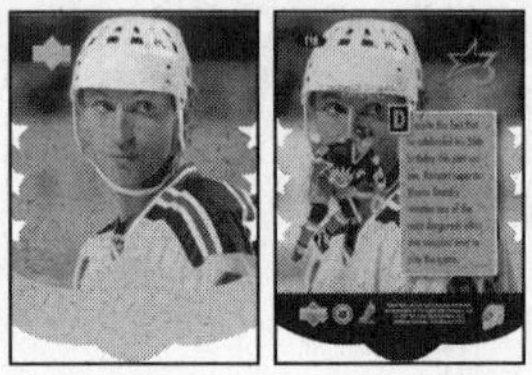

| | MINT | NRMT |
|---|---|---|
| COMPLETE SET (60) | 150.00 | 70.00 |
| COMMON CARD (1A-20C) | .60 | .25 |

□ 1A Eric Lindros 6.00 2.70
□ 1B Wayne Gretzky 12.00 5.50
□ 1C Peter Forsberg 6.00 2.70
□ 2A Dominik Hasek 4.00 1.80
□ 2B Patrick Roy 10.00 4.50
□ 2C John Vanbiesbrouck 3.00 1.35
□ 3A Joe Sakic 4.00 1.80
□ 3B Steve Yzerman 6.00 2.70
□ 3C Paul Kariya 8.00 3.60
□ 4A Bryan Berard 1.50 .70
□ 4B Brian Leetch 2.00 .90
□ 4C Chris Chelios 2.00 .90
□ 5A Teemu Selanne 4.00 1.80
□ 5B Jaromir Jagr 6.00 2.70
□ 5C Pavel Bure 4.00 1.80
□ 6A Owen Nolan 1.50 .70
□ 6B Brendan Shanahan 4.00 1.80
□ 6C Keith Tkachuk 2.50 1.10
□ 7A Sergei Fedorov 4.00 1.80
□ 7B Niklas Sundstrom .60 .25
□ 7C Mike Peca 1.50 .70
□ 8A Janne Niinimaa 1.50 .70
□ 8B Saku Koivu 3.00 1.35
□ 8C Jere Lehtinen .60 .25
□ 9A Tony Amonte 1.50 .70
□ 9B John LeClair 3.00 1.35
□ 9C Brett Hull 2.50 1.10
□ 10A Martin Brodeur 5.00 2.20
□ 10B Curtis Joseph 2.00 .90
□ 10C Mike Richter 2.00 .90
□ 11A Ray Bourque 2.00 .90
□ 11B Mark Messier 2.50 1.10
□ 11C Scott Stevens 1.50 .70
□ 12A Patrick Lalime 1.50 .70
□ 12B Marc Denis 1.50 .70
□ 12C Jose Theodore 1.50 .70
□ 13A Adam Deadmarsh 1.50 .70
□ 13B Doug Weight 1.50 .70
□ 13C Bill Guerin 1.50 .70
□ 14A Daniel Alfredsson 1.50 .70
□ 14B Mats Sundin 2.00 .90
□ 14C Nicklas Lidstrom .60 .25
□ 15A Jim Campbell .60 .25
□ 15B Dainius Zubrus 2.00 .90
□ 15C Daymond Langkow .60 .25
□ 16A Mike Grier .60 .25
□ 16B Mike Modano 2.50 1.10
□ 16C Jeremy Roenick 2.00 .90
□ 17A Jason Arnott 1.50 .70
□ 17B Trevor Linden 1.50 .70
□ 17C Rod Brind'Amour 1.50 .70
□ 18A Adam Oates 1.50 .70
□ 18B Doug Gilmour 1.50 .70
□ 18C Joe Juneau .60 .25
□ 19A Sergei Berezin 1.50 .70
□ 19B Alexander Mogilny 1.50 .70
□ 19C Alexei Zhamnov .60 .25
□ 20A Derian Hatcher .60 .25
□ 20B Wade Redden .60 .25
□ 20C Sandis Ozolinsh 1.50 .70

## 1998-99 Upper Deck

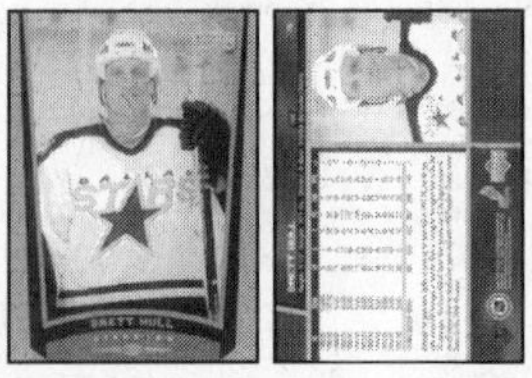

The 1998-99 Upper Deck set was issued in two series of 210 cards each for a total of 420 cards and was distributed in 10-card packs with a suggested retail price of $2.49. The fronts feature a color action player photo with player information on the backs. Series 1 contains the following subsets: Star Rookies, Rookie Rewind, and three Checklist cards. Series 2 contains the subset Program of Excellence which consists of the top Canadian prospects, eight Calder Candidates, and three Checklist cards.

| | MINT | NRMT |
|---|---|---|
| COMPLETE SET (420) | 250.00 | 110.00 |
| COMP.SER 1 (1-210) | 125.00 | 55.00 |
| COMP.SER 2 (211-420) | 125.00 | 55.00 |
| COMMON CARD (31-420) | .10 | .05 |
| COMMON SR,RR (1-15,16-30) | 2.00 | .90 |
| COMMON PE,CC (391-420) | 2.00 | .90 |

□ 1 Antti Aalto SR 2.00 .90
□ 2 Cameron Mann SR 2.00 .90
□ 3 Norm Maracle SR 6.00 2.70
□ 4 Daniel Cleary SR 2.00 .90
□ 5 Brendan Morrison SR 4.00 1.80
□ 6 Marian Hossa SR 2.00 .90
□ 7 Daniel Briere SR 2.00 .90
□ 8 Mike Crowley .25 .11
□ 9 Darryl Laplante 2.00 .90
□ 10 Suem Butenschen SR 2.00 .90
□ 11 Yan Golubovsky 2.00 .90
□ 12 Olli Jokinen SR 4.00 1.80
□ 13 Jean-Sebastien Giguere 2.00 .90
□ 14 Mike Watt SR 2.00 .90
□ 15 Ryan Johnson SR 2.00 .90
□ 16 Teemu Selanne RR 6.00 2.70
□ 17 Paul Kariya RR 12.00 5.50
□ 18 Pavel Bure RR 6.00 2.70
□ 19 Joe Thornton RR 2.00 .90
□ 20 Dominik Hasek RR 6.00 2.70
□ 21 Bryan Berard RR 2.00 .90
□ 22 Chris Phillips RR 2.00 .90
□ 23 Sergei Fedorov RR 6.00 2.70
□ 24 Sergei Samsonov RR 5.00 2.20
□ 25 Marc Denis RR 2.00 .90
□ 26 Patrick Marleau RR 2.00 .90
□ 27 Jaromir Jagr RR 10.00 4.50
□ 28 Saku Koivu RR 5.00 2.20
□ 29 Peter Forsberg RR 10.00 4.50
□ 30 Mike Modano RR 4.00 1.80
□ 31 Paul Kariya 1.50 .70
□ 32 Matt Cullen .10 .05
□ 33 Josef Marha .10 .05
□ 34 Teemu Selanne .75 .35
□ 35 Pavel Trnka .10 .05
□ 36 Tom Askey .10 .05
□ 37 Tim Taylor .10 .05
□ 38 Ray Bourque .10 .05
□ 39 Sergei Samsonov .60 .25
□ 40 Don Sweeney .10 .05
□ 41 Jason Allison .25 .11
□ 42 Steve Heinze .10 .05
□ 43 Erik Rasmussen .10 .05
□ 44 Dominik Hasek .75 .35
□ 45 Geoff Sanderson .25 .11
□ 46 Michael Peca .10 .05
□ 47 Brian Holzinger .10 .05
□ 48 Vaclav Varada .10 .05
□ 49 Steve Begin .10 .05
□ 50 Denis Gauthier .10 .05
□ 51 Derek Morris .10 .05
□ 52 Valeri Bure .10 .05
□ 53 Hnat Domenichelli .10 .05
□ 54 Cory Stillman .10 .05
□ 55 Jarome Iginla .10 .05
□ 56 Tyler Moss .10 .05
□ 57 Sami Kapanen .10 .05
□ 58 Trevor Kidd .10 .05
□ 59 Glen Wesley .10 .05
□ 60 Nelson Emerson .10 .05
□ 61 Jeff O'Neill .10 .05
□ 62 Bates Battaglia .10 .05
□ 63 Doug Gilmour .40 .18
□ 64 Christian LaFlamme .10 .05
□ 65 Chris Chelios .40 .18
□ 66 Paul Coffey .10 .05
□ 67 Eric Weinrich .10 .05
□ 68 Eric Daze .10 .05
□ 69 Peter Forsberg 1.25 .55
□ 70 Eric Messier .10 .05
□ 71 Eric Lacroix .10 .05
□ 72 Adam Deadmarsh .25 .11
□ 73 Claude Lemieux .25 .11
□ 74 Patrick Roy 2.00 .90
□ 75 Marc Denis .25 .11
□ 76 Brett Hull .50 .23
□ 77 Mike Keane .10 .05
□ 78 Joe Nieuwendyk .25 .11
□ 79 Darryl Sydor .10 .05
□ 80 Ed Belfour .40 .18
□ 81 Jamie Langenbrunner .10 .05
□ 82 Petr Buzek .10 .05
□ 83 Nicklas Lidstrom .25 .11
□ 84 Mathieu Dandenault .10 .05
□ 85 Steve Yzerman 1.25 .55
□ 86 Martin Lapointe .10 .05
□ 87 Brendan Shanahan .75 .35
□ 88 Anders Eriksson .10 .05
□ 89 Tomas Holmstrom .10 .05
□ 90 Doug Weight .25 .11
□ 91 Janne Niinimaa .10 .05
□ 92 Bill Guerin .25 .11
□ 93 Kelly Buchberger .10 .05
□ 94 Mike Grier .10 .05
□ 95 Craig Millar .10 .05
□ 96 Roman Hamrlik .10 .05
□ 97 Ray Whitney .10 .05
□ 98 Viktor Kozlov .10 .05
□ 99 Peter Worrell .10 .05
□ 100 Kevin Weekes .25 .11
□ 101 Ed Jovanovski .10 .05
□ 102 Bill Lindsay .10 .05
□ 103 Jozef Stumpel .25 .11
□ 104 Luc Robitaille .25 .11
□ 105 Yanic Perreault .10 .05
□ 106 Donald MacLean .10 .05
□ 107 Jamie Storr .25 .11
□ 108 Ian Laperriere .10 .05
□ 109 Jason Morgan .10 .05
□ 110 Vincent Damphousse .25 .11
□ 111 Mark Recchi .25 .11
□ 112 Vladimir Malakhov .10 .05
□ 113 Dave Manson .10 .05
□ 114 Jose Theodore .10 .05
□ 115 Brian Savage .10 .05
□ 116 Jonas Hoglund .10 .05
□ 117 Krzysztof Oliwa .10 .05
□ 118 Martin Brodeur 1.00 .45
□ 119 Patrik Elias .10 .05
□ 120 Jason Arnott .25 .11
□ 121 Scott Stevens .10 .05

| | | |
|---|---|---|
| ❑ 122 Sheldon Souray | .10 | .05 |
| ❑ 123 Brian Rolston | .10 | .05 |
| ❑ 124 Trevor Linden | .25 | .11 |
| ❑ 125 Warren Luhning | .10 | .05 |
| ❑ 126 Zdeno Chara | .10 | .05 |
| ❑ 127 Bryan Berard | .25 | .11 |
| ❑ 128 Bryan Smolinski | .10 | .05 |
| ❑ 129 Jason Dawe | .10 | .05 |
| ❑ 130 Kevin Stevens | .10 | .05 |
| ❑ 131 P.J. Stock | .10 | .05 |
| ❑ 132 Marc Savard | .10 | .05 |
| ❑ 133 Pat LaFontaine | .25 | .11 |
| ❑ 134 Dan Cloutier | .10 | .05 |
| ❑ 135 Wayne Gretzky | 2.50 | 1.10 |
| ❑ 136 Niklas Sundstrom | .10 | .05 |
| ❑ 137 Damian Rhodes | .25 | .11 |
| ❑ 138 Magnus Arvedson | .10 | .05 |
| ❑ 139 Alexei Yashin | .25 | .11 |
| ❑ 140 Chris Phillips | .10 | .05 |
| ❑ 141 Janne Laukkanen | .10 | .05 |
| ❑ 142 Shawn McEachern | .10 | .05 |
| ❑ 143 John LeClair | .60 | .25 |
| ❑ 144 Alexandre Daigle | .10 | .05 |
| ❑ 145 Dainius Zubrus | .10 | .05 |
| ❑ 146 Joel Otto | .10 | .05 |
| ❑ 147 Mike Sillinger | .10 | .05 |
| ❑ 148 John Vanbiesbrouck | .50 | .23 |
| ❑ 149 Chris Gratton | .25 | .11 |
| ❑ 150 Eric Desjardins | .10 | .05 |
| ❑ 151 Juha Ylonen | .10 | .05 |
| ❑ 152 Brad Isbister | .10 | .05 |
| ❑ 153 Oleg Tverdovsky | .10 | .05 |
| ❑ 154 Keith Tkachuk | .50 | .23 |
| ❑ 155 Teppo Numminen | .10 | .05 |
| ❑ 156 Cliff Ronning | .10 | .05 |
| ❑ 157 Nikolai Khabibulin | .25 | .11 |
| ❑ 158 Alexei Morozov | .10 | .05 |
| ❑ 159 Kevin Hatcher | .10 | .05 |
| ❑ 160 Darius Kasparaitis | .10 | .05 |
| ❑ 161 Jaromir Jagr | 1.25 | .55 |
| ❑ 162 Tom Barrasso | .25 | .11 |
| ❑ 163 Tuomas Gronman | .10 | .05 |
| ❑ 164 Robert Dome | .10 | .05 |
| ❑ 165 Peter Skudra | .10 | .05 |
| ❑ 166 Marcus Ragnarsson | .10 | .05 |
| ❑ 167 Mike Vernon | .25 | .11 |
| ❑ 168 Andrei Zyuzin | .10 | .05 |
| ❑ 169 Marco Sturm | .10 | .05 |
| ❑ 170 Mike Ricci | .10 | .05 |
| ❑ 171 Patrick Marleau | .10 | .05 |
| ❑ 172 Pierre Turgeon | .10 | .05 |
| ❑ 173 Pavol Demitra | .10 | .05 |
| ❑ 174 Chris Pronger | .25 | .11 |
| ❑ 175 Pascal Rheaume | .10 | .05 |
| ❑ 176 Al MacInnis | .25 | .11 |
| ❑ 177 Tony Twist | .10 | .05 |
| ❑ 178 Jim Campbell | .10 | .05 |
| ❑ 179 Mikael Renberg | .25 | .11 |
| ❑ 180 Jason Bonsignore | .10 | .05 |
| ❑ 181 Zac Bierk | .10 | .05 |
| ❑ 182 Alexander Selivanov | .10 | .05 |
| ❑ 183 Stephane Richer | .10 | .05 |
| ❑ 184 Sandy McCarthy | .10 | .05 |
| ❑ 185 Alyn McCauley | .10 | .05 |
| ❑ 186 Sergei Berezin | .25 | .11 |
| ❑ 187 Mike Johnson | .10 | .05 |
| ❑ 188 Wendel Clark | .25 | .11 |
| ❑ 189 Tie Domi | .10 | .05 |
| ❑ 190 Yannick Trembley | .10 | .05 |
| ❑ 191 Curtis Joseph | .40 | .18 |
| ❑ 192 Fredrik Modin | .10 | .05 |
| ❑ 193 Pavel Bure | .75 | .35 |
| ❑ 194 Todd Bertuzzi | .10 | .05 |
| ❑ 195 Mark Messier | .50 | .23 |
| ❑ 196 Bret Hedican | .10 | .05 |
| ❑ 197 Mattias Ohlund | .10 | .05 |
| ❑ 198 Garth Snow | .25 | .11 |
| ❑ 199 Adam Oates | .25 | .11 |
| ❑ 200 Peter Bondra | .10 | .05 |
| ❑ 201 Sergei Gonchar | .10 | .05 |
| ❑ 202 Jan Bulis | .10 | .05 |
| ❑ 203 Joe Juneau | .25 | .11 |
| ❑ 204 Brian Bellows | .10 | .05 |
| ❑ 205 Olaf Kolzig | .25 | .11 |
| ❑ 206 Richard Zednik | .10 | .05 |
| ❑ 207 Wayne Gretzky CL | 1.25 | .55 |
| ❑ 208 Patrick Roy CL | 1.00 | .45 |
| ❑ 209 Steve Yzerman CL | .60 | .25 |
| ❑ 210 Mike Dunham | .25 | .11 |
| ❑ 211 Johan Davidsson | .10 | .05 |
| ❑ 212 Guy Hebert | .25 | .11 |
| ❑ 213 Mike Leclerc | .10 | .05 |
| ❑ 214 Steve Rucchin | .10 | .05 |
| ❑ 215 Travis Green | .10 | .05 |
| ❑ 216 Josef Marha | .10 | .05 |
| ❑ 217 Ted Donato | .10 | .05 |
| ❑ 218 Joe Thornton | .40 | .18 |
| ❑ 219 Kyle McLaren | .10 | .05 |
| ❑ 220 Peter Nordstrom | .10 | .05 |
| ❑ 221 Byron Dafoe | .25 | .11 |
| ❑ 222 Jonathon Girard | .10 | .05 |
| ❑ 223 Antti Laaksonen | .10 | .05 |
| ❑ 224 Jason Holland | .10 | .05 |
| ❑ 225 Miroslav Satan | .10 | .05 |
| ❑ 226 Alexei Zhitnik | .10 | .05 |
| ❑ 227 Donald Audette | .10 | .05 |
| ❑ 228 Matthew Barnaby | .10 | .05 |
| ❑ 229 Rumun Ndur | .10 | .05 |
| ❑ 230 Ken Wregget | .25 | .11 |
| ❑ 231 Andrew Cassels | .10 | .05 |
| ❑ 232 Theoren Fleury | .40 | .18 |
| ❑ 233 Phil Housley | .25 | .11 |
| ❑ 234 Martin St. Louis | .25 | .11 |
| ❑ 235 Mike Rucinski | .10 | .05 |
| ❑ 236 Gary Roberts | .10 | .05 |
| ❑ 237 Keith Primeau | .25 | .11 |
| ❑ 238 Martin Gelinas | .10 | .05 |
| ❑ 239 Nolan Pratt | .10 | .05 |
| ❑ 240 Ray Sheppard | .10 | .05 |
| ❑ 241 Ron Francis | .25 | .11 |
| ❑ 242 Ty Jones | .10 | .05 |
| ❑ 243 Tony Amonte | .25 | .11 |
| ❑ 244 Chad Kilger | .10 | .05 |
| ❑ 245 Alexei Zhamnov | .25 | .11 |
| ❑ 246 Remi Royer | .10 | .05 |
| ❑ 247 Milan Hejduk | .75 | .35 |
| ❑ 248 Joe Sakic | .75 | .35 |
| ❑ 249 Valeri Kamensky | .25 | .11 |
| ❑ 250 Sandis Ozolinsh | .25 | .11 |
| ❑ 251 Shean Donovan | .10 | .05 |
| ❑ 252 Wade Belak | .10 | .05 |
| ❑ 253 Jamie Wright | .10 | .05 |
| ❑ 254 Sergei Zubov | .10 | .05 |
| ❑ 255 Richard Matvichuk | .10 | .05 |
| ❑ 256 Mike Modano | .50 | .23 |
| ❑ 257 Pat Verbeek | .10 | .05 |
| ❑ 258 Jere Lehtinen | .25 | .11 |
| ❑ 259 Derian Hatcher | .10 | .05 |
| ❑ 260 Jason Botterill | .10 | .05 |
| ❑ 261 Igor Larionov | .10 | .05 |
| ❑ 262 Sergei Fedorov | .75 | .35 |
| ❑ 263 Chris Osgood | .40 | .18 |
| ❑ 264 Vyacheslav Kozlov | .25 | .11 |
| ❑ 265 Larry Murphy | .25 | .11 |
| ❑ 266 Darren McCarty | .10 | .05 |
| ❑ 267 Doug Brown | .10 | .05 |
| ❑ 268 Kris Draper | .10 | .05 |
| ❑ 269 Uwe Krupp | .10 | .05 |
| ❑ 270 Fredrik Lindquist | .10 | .05 |
| ❑ 271 Dean McAmmond | .10 | .05 |
| ❑ 272 Ryan Smyth | .25 | .11 |
| ❑ 273 Boris Mironov | .10 | .05 |
| ❑ 274 Tom Poti | .10 | .05 |
| ❑ 275 Todd Marchant | .10 | .05 |
| ❑ 276 Sean Brown | .10 | .05 |
| ❑ 277 Rob Niedermayer | .10 | .05 |
| ❑ 278 Robert Svehla | .10 | .05 |
| ❑ 279 Scott Mellanby | .10 | .05 |
| ❑ 280 Radek Dvorak | .10 | .05 |
| ❑ 281 Jaroslav Spacek | .10 | .05 |
| ❑ 282 Mark Parrish | .75 | .35 |
| ❑ 283 Ryan Johnson | .10 | .05 |
| ❑ 284 Glen Murray | .10 | .05 |
| ❑ 285 Rob Blake | .25 | .11 |
| ❑ 286 Steve Duchesne | .25 | .11 |
| ❑ 287 Vladimir Tsyplakov | .10 | .05 |
| ❑ 288 Stephane Fiset | .25 | .11 |
| ❑ 289 Mattias Norstrom | .10 | .05 |
| ❑ 290 Saku Koivu | .60 | .25 |
| ❑ 291 Shayne Corson | .25 | .11 |
| ❑ 292 Brad Brown | .10 | .05 |
| ❑ 293 Patrice Brisebois | .10 | .05 |
| ❑ 294 Terry Ryan | .10 | .05 |
| ❑ 295 Jocelyn Thibault | .25 | .11 |
| ❑ 296 Miroslav Guren | .10 | .05 |
| ❑ 297 Darren Turcotte | .25 | .11 |
| ❑ 298 Sebastien Bordeleau | .10 | .05 |
| ❑ 299 Jan Vopat | .10 | .05 |
| ❑ 300 Blair Atcheynum | .10 | .05 |
| ❑ 301 Andrew Brunette | .10 | .05 |
| ❑ 302 Sergei Krivokrasov | .10 | .05 |
| ❑ 303 Marian Cisar | .10 | .05 |
| ❑ 304 Patrick Cote | .10 | .05 |
| ❑ 305 J.J. Daigneault | .10 | .05 |
| ❑ 306 Greg Johnson | .10 | .05 |
| ❑ 307 Chris Terreri | .25 | .11 |
| ❑ 308 Scott Niedermayer | .10 | .05 |
| ❑ 309 Vadim Sharifijanov | .10 | .05 |
| ❑ 310 Petr Sykora | .10 | .05 |
| ❑ 311 Sergei Brylin | .10 | .05 |
| ❑ 312 Denis Pederson | .10 | .05 |
| ❑ 313 Bobby Holik | .10 | .05 |
| ❑ 314 Bryan Muir | .10 | .05 |
| ❑ 315 Zigmund Palffy | .40 | .18 |
| ❑ 316 Mike Watt | .10 | .05 |
| ❑ 317 Tommy Salo | .25 | .11 |
| ❑ 318 Kenny Jonsson | .10 | .05 |
| ❑ 319 Dimitri Nabakov | .10 | .05 |
| ❑ 320 John MacLean | .10 | .05 |
| ❑ 321 Zarley Zalapski | .10 | .05 |
| ❑ 322 Brian Leetch | .40 | .18 |
| ❑ 323 Todd Harvey | .10 | .05 |
| ❑ 324 Mike Richter | .40 | .18 |
| ❑ 325 Mike Knuble | .10 | .05 |
| ❑ 326 Jeff Beukeboom | .10 | .05 |
| ❑ 327 Daniel Alfredsson | .25 | .11 |
| ❑ 328 Vaclav Prospal | .10 | .05 |
| ❑ 329 Wade Redden | .10 | .05 |
| ❑ 330 Igor Kravchuk | .10 | .05 |
| ❑ 331 Andreas Dackell | .10 | .05 |
| ❑ 332 Mike Maneluk | .75 | .35 |
| ❑ 333 Eric Lindros | 1.25 | .55 |
| ❑ 334 Rod Brind'Amour | .25 | .11 |
| ❑ 335 Colin Forbes | .10 | .05 |
| ❑ 336 Dimitri Tertyshny | .10 | .05 |
| ❑ 337 Shjon Podein | .10 | .05 |
| ❑ 338 Chris Therien | .10 | .05 |
| ❑ 339 Jeremy Roenick | .40 | .18 |
| ❑ 340 Jyrki Lumme | .10 | .05 |
| ❑ 341 Rick Tocchet | .25 | .11 |
| ❑ 342 Dallas Drake | .10 | .05 |
| ❑ 343 Keith Carney | .10 | .05 |
| ❑ 344 Greg Adams | .10 | .05 |
| ❑ 345 Jan Hrdina | .50 | .23 |
| ❑ 346 German Titov | .10 | .05 |
| ❑ 347 Stu Barnes | .10 | .05 |
| ❑ 348 Kevin Hatcher | .10 | .05 |
| ❑ 349 Martin Straka | .10 | .05 |
| ❑ 350 Jean-Sebastien Robin | .10 | .05 |
| ❑ 351 Jeff Friesen | .25 | .11 |
| ❑ 352 Tony Granato | .10 | .05 |
| ❑ 353 Scott Hannan | .10 | .05 |
| ❑ 354 Owen Nolan | .25 | .11 |
| ❑ 355 Stephane Matteau | .10 | .05 |
| ❑ 356 Bryan Marchment | .10 | .05 |
| ❑ 357 Geoff Courtnall | .25 | .11 |
| ❑ 358 Brent Johnson | .10 | .05 |
| ❑ 359 Jamie Rivers | .10 | .05 |
| ❑ 360 Terry Yake | .10 | .05 |
| ❑ 361 Jamie McLennan | .10 | .05 |
| ❑ 362 Grant Fuhr | .25 | .11 |
| ❑ 363 Michal Handzus | .50 | .23 |
| ❑ 364 Bill Ranford | .25 | .11 |
| ❑ 365 John Cullen | .10 | .05 |
| ❑ 366 Craig Janney | .10 | .05 |
| ❑ 367 Daren Puppa | .25 | .11 |
| ❑ 368 Pavel Kubina | .50 | .23 |
| ❑ 369 Wendel Clark | .25 | .11 |
| ❑ 370 Mats Sundin | .40 | .18 |
| ❑ 371 Felix Potvin | .40 | .18 |
| ❑ 372 Daniil Markov | .10 | .05 |
| ❑ 373 Derek King | .10 | .05 |
| ❑ 374 Steve Thomas | .10 | .05 |
| ❑ 375 Tomas Kaberle | .25 | .11 |
| ❑ 376 Alexander Mogilny | .25 | .11 |
| ❑ 377 Bill Muckalt | .60 | .25 |
| ❑ 378 Brian Noonan | .10 | .05 |
| ❑ 379 Markus Naslund | .10 | .05 |
| ❑ 380 Brad May | .10 | .05 |
| ❑ 381 Matt Cooke | .10 | .05 |
| ❑ 382 Calle Johansson | .10 | .05 |
| ❑ 383 Dale Hunter | .10 | .05 |
| ❑ 384 Jaroslav Svejkovsky | .10 | .05 |
| ❑ 385 Dmitri Mironov | .10 | .05 |
| ❑ 386 Matt Herr | .10 | .05 |
| ❑ 387 Nolan Baumgartner | .10 | .05 |
| ❑ 388 Wayne Gretzky CL | .10 | .05 |
| ❑ 389 Steve Yzerman CL | .10 | .05 |
| ❑ 390 Wayne Gretzky<br>Steve Yzerman CL | .10 | .05 |
| ❑ 391 Brian Finley PE | 8.00 | 3.60 |
| ❑ 392 Maxime Ouellet PE | 5.00 | 2.20 |
| ❑ 393 Kurtis Foster PE | 2.00 | .90 |
| ❑ 394 Barrett Jackman PE | 2.00 | .90 |
| ❑ 395 Ross Lupaschuk PE | 3.00 | 1.35 |
| ❑ 396 Steven McCarthy PE | 3.00 | 1.35 |
| ❑ 397 Peter Reynolds PE | 2.00 | .90 |
| ❑ 398 Bart Rushmer PE | 2.00 | .90 |
| ❑ 399 Jonathan Zion PE | 2.00 | .90 |
| ❑ 400 Kris Beech PE | 8.00 | 3.60 |
| ❑ 401 Brandin Cote PE | 2.00 | .90 |
| ❑ 402 Scott Kelman PE | 3.00 | 1.35 |
| ❑ 403 Jamie Lundmark PE | 4.00 | 1.80 |
| ❑ 404 Derek MacKenzie PE | 2.00 | .90 |
| ❑ 405 Rory McDade PE | 2.00 | .90 |
| ❑ 406 David Morisset PE | 4.00 | 1.80 |
| ❑ 407 Mirko Murovic PE | 3.00 | 1.35 |
| ❑ 408 Taylor Pyatt PE | 6.00 | 2.70 |
| ❑ 409 Charlie Stephens PE | 2.00 | .90 |
| ❑ 410 Kyle Wanvig PE | 4.00 | 1.80 |
| ❑ 411 Krzystof Wieckows PE | 2.00 | .90 |
| ❑ 412 Michael Zigomanis PE | 4.00 | 1.80 |
| ❑ 413 Rico Fata CC | 3.00 | 1.35 |
| ❑ 414 Vincent Lecavalier CC | 6.00 | 2.70 |
| ❑ 415 Chris Drury CC | 4.00 | 1.80 |
| ❑ 416 Oleg Kvasha CC | 5.00 | 2.20 |
| ❑ 417 Eric Brewer CC | 2.00 | .90 |
| ❑ 418 Josh Green CC | 3.00 | 1.35 |
| ❑ 419 Marty Reasoner CC | 2.00 | .90 |
| ❑ 420 Manny Malhotra CC | 4.00 | 1.80 |

## 1998-99 Upper Deck Exclusive

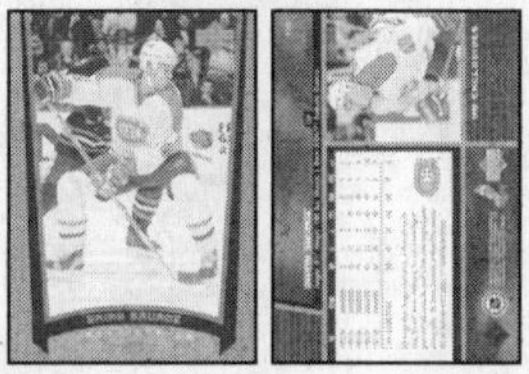

Randomly inserted into hobby packs only, this 420-card set is parallel to the base set. Cards are serial numbered to only 100 copies. An exclusive 1 of 1 parallel also exists and randomly inserted into packs.

| | MINT | NRMT |
|---|---|---|
| COMMON CARD (1-420) | 20.00 | 9.00 |

*STARS: 100X TO 200X BASIC CARDS
*YOUNG STARS: 75X TO 150X
*RC's: 50X TO 100X HI
*SR, RR STARS: 7.5X TO 15X HI
*SR,RR,PE,CC RC's: 6X TO 12X HI
EXCLUSIVE 1 OF 1 PARALLELS EXIST

## 1998-99 Upper Deck Fantastic Finishers

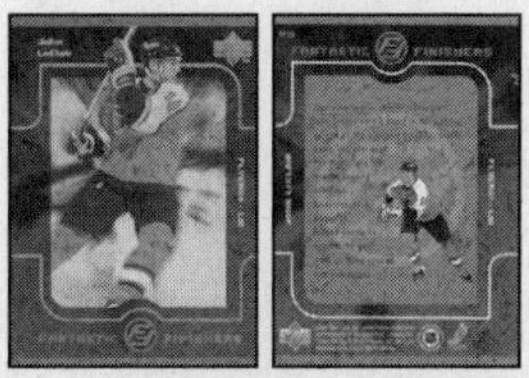

Randomly inserted into Series 1 packs at a rate of one in 12, this 30-card set features color action photos of players considered to be the more prolific and gifted finishers in the NHL. Three Tier Quantum parallel versions of this insert set were also produced and inserted into Series 1 packs. Tier 1 cards were sequentially numbered to 1,500; Tier 2 cards were sequentially numbered to 50; and Tier 3 cards were sequentially numbered to 1.

| | MINT | NRMT |
|---|---|---|
| COMPLETE SET (30) | 100.00 | 45.00 |
| COMMON CARD (FF1-FF30) | 2.00 | .90 |
| COMP.F.F.QUANTUM 1 SET (30) | 200.00 | 90.00 |
| COMMON F.F.QUANTUM 1 (1-30) | 4.00 | 1.80 |

*F.F.QUANT.1 STARS: 1X TO 2X BASIC CARDS
F.F.QUANT.1 RANDOMS INS.IN PACKS
F.F.QUANT.1 STATED PRINT RUN 1500 SETS

| | | |
|---|---|---|
| COMP.F.F.QUANT.2 SET (30) | 4000.00 | 1800.00 |
| COMMON F.F.QUANT.2 (1-30) | 80.00 | 36.00 |

*F.F.QUANT.2 STARS: 20X TO 40X BASIC CARDS
F.F.QUANT.2 RANDOMS INS.IN PACKS
F.F.QUANT.2 STATED PRINT RUN 50 SETS
F.F. 1 OF 1 PARALLEL EXISTS

| | | |
|---|---|---|
| ❑ FF1 Wayne Gretzky | 15.00 | 6.75 |
| ❑ FF2 Peter Bondra | 2.00 | .90 |
| ❑ FF3 Sergei Samsonov | 3.00 | 1.35 |
| ❑ FF4 Jaromir Jagr | 8.00 | 3.60 |
| ❑ FF5 Brendan Shanahan | 5.00 | 2.20 |
| ❑ FF6 Joe Sakic | 5.00 | 2.20 |
| ❑ FF7 Brett Hull | 3.00 | 1.35 |
| ❑ FF8 Paul Kariya | 10.00 | 4.50 |
| ❑ FF9 Keith Tkachuk | 3.00 | 1.35 |
| ❑ FF10 Zigmund Palffy | 2.00 | .90 |
| ❑ FF11 Eric Lindros | 8.00 | 3.60 |
| ❑ FF12 Mike Modano | 3.00 | 1.35 |
| ❑ FF13 Pavel Bure | 5.00 | 2.20 |
| ❑ FF14 Mats Sundin | 2.00 | .90 |
| ❑ FF15 Patrik Elias | 2.00 | .90 |
| ❑ FF16 Tony Amonte | 2.00 | .90 |
| ❑ FF17 Peter Forsberg | 8.00 | 3.60 |
| ❑ FF18 Alexei Yashin | 2.00 | .90 |
| ❑ FF19 Mark Recchi | 2.00 | .90 |
| ❑ FF20 Steve Yzerman | 8.00 | 3.60 |
| ❑ FF21 Doug Weight | 2.00 | .90 |
| ❑ FF22 Jeremy Roenick | 2.00 | .90 |
| ❑ FF23 Teemu Selanne | 5.00 | 2.20 |
| ❑ FF24 Owen Nolan | 2.00 | .90 |
| ❑ FF25 John LeClair | 4.00 | 1.80 |
| ❑ FF26 Jason Allison | 2.00 | .90 |
| ❑ FF27 Mike Johnson | 2.00 | .90 |
| ❑ FF28 Theoren Fleury | 2.00 | .90 |
| ❑ FF29 Nicklas Lidstrom | 2.00 | .90 |
| ❑ FF30 Joe Nieuwendyk | 2.00 | .90 |

## 1998-99 Upper Deck Frozen In Time

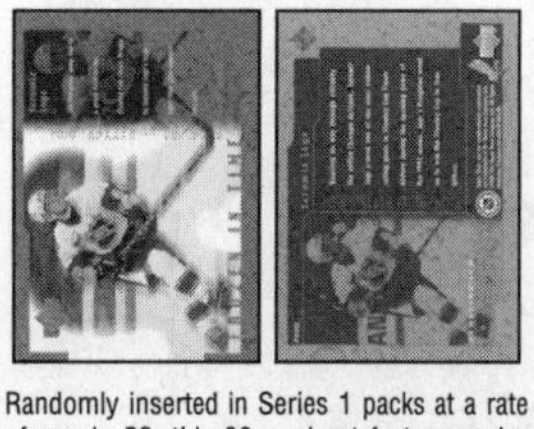

Randomly inserted in Series 1 packs at a rate of one in 23, this 30-card set features color action photos of some of the key moments throughout the careers of the highlighted players. Three Tier Quantum parallel versions of this insert set were also produced and inserted into Series 1 packs. Tier 1 cards were sequentially numbered to 1,000; Tier 2 cards were sequentially numbered to 25; and Tier 3 cards were numbered to 1.

| | MINT | NRMT |
|---|---|---|
| COMPLETE SET (30) | 200.00 | 90.00 |
| COMMON CARD (FT1-FT30) | 2.00 | .90 |
| COMP.F.I.T.QUANT.1 SET (30) | 400.00 | 180.00 |
| COMMON F.I.T.QUANT.1 (1-30) | 4.00 | 1.80 |

*FIT.QUANT.1 STARS: 1X TO 2X BASIC CARDS
RANDOM INSERTS IN PACKS
F.I.T.QUANT.1 STATED PRINT RUN 1000 SETS

| | | |
|---|---|---|
| COMMON F.I.T.QUANT.2 (1-30) | 120.00 | 55.00 |

*F.I.T.QUANT.2 STARS: 30X TO 60X BASIC CARDS
RANDOM INSERTS IN PACKS
F.I.T.QUANT.2 STATED PRINT RUN 25 SETS
F.I.T. 1 OF 1 PARALLEL EXISTS

| | | |
|---|---|---|
| ❑ FT1 Steve Yzerman | 12.00 | 5.50 |
| ❑ FT2 Peter Forsberg | 12.00 | 5.50 |
| ❑ FT3 Sergei Samsonov | 6.00 | 2.70 |
| ❑ FT4 Martin Brodeur | 10.00 | 4.50 |
| ❑ FT5 Theoren Fleury | 4.00 | 1.80 |
| ❑ FT6 Paul Kariya | 15.00 | 6.75 |
| ❑ FT7 Rob Blake | 2.00 | .90 |
| ❑ FT8 Jari Kurri | 2.00 | .90 |
| ❑ FT9 Eric Lindros | 12.00 | 5.50 |
| ❑ FT10 Dominik Hasek | 8.00 | 3.60 |
| ❑ FT11 Patrick Roy | 20.00 | 9.00 |
| ❑ FT12 Saku Koivu | 6.00 | 2.70 |
| ❑ FT13 Mike Modano | 5.00 | 2.20 |
| ❑ FT14 Alexei Morozov | 2.00 | .90 |
| ❑ FT15 Chris Osgood | 4.00 | 1.80 |
| ❑ FT16 Doug Gilmour | 4.00 | 1.80 |
| ❑ FT17 Owen Nolan | 3.00 | 1.35 |
| ❑ FT18 Mike Johnson | 3.00 | 1.35 |
| ❑ FT19 Keith Tkachuk | 5.00 | 2.20 |
| ❑ FT20 Adam Oates | 3.00 | 1.35 |
| ❑ FT21 Chris Chelios | 4.00 | 1.80 |
| ❑ FT22 Brendan Shanahan | 8.00 | 3.60 |
| ❑ FT23 Joe Sakic | 8.00 | 3.60 |
| ❑ FT24 Pavel Bure | 8.00 | 3.60 |
| ❑ FT25 Ray Bourque | 4.00 | 1.80 |
| ❑ FT26 Ed Belfour | 4.00 | 1.80 |
| ❑ FT27 John LeClair | 6.00 | 2.70 |
| ❑ FT28 Teemu Selanne | 8.00 | 3.60 |
| ❑ FT29 Jaromir Jagr | 12.00 | 5.50 |
| ❑ FT30 Wayne Gretzky | 25.00 | 11.00 |

## 1998-99 Upper Deck Generation Next

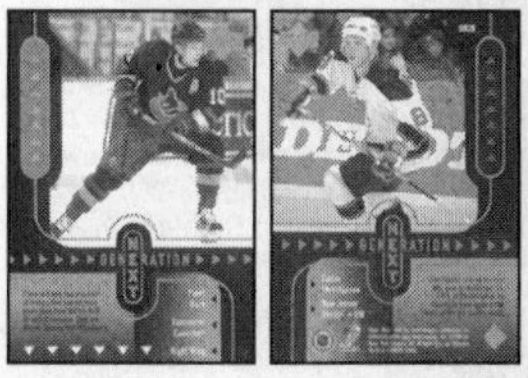

Randomly inserted in Series 2 packs at the rate of one in 23, this 30-card set features color action photos of ten of the top players in the NHL on one side with one of three heir apparents pictured on the other. Three Tier Quantum parallel versions of this insert set were also produced and inserted into Series 2 packs. Tier 1 featured ten cards sequentially numbered to 1,000; ten numbered to 500; and ten cards sequentially numbered to 250. Tier 2 contained ten cards sequentially numbered to 75; ten numbered to 25; and ten cards sequentially numbered to 10. Tier 3 had ten cards sequentially numbered to 3; ten sequentially numbered to 2; and ten cards numbered to 1.

| | MINT | NRMT |
|---|---|---|
| COMPLETE SET (30) | 450.00 | 200.00 |
| COMMON CARD (GN1-GN30) | 5.00 | 2.20 |

SEMISTARS/GOALIES
UNLISTED STARS

| | | |
|---|---|---|
| COMP.G.N.QUANT.1 SET (30) | 1200.00 | 550.00 |
| COMMON G.N.QUANT.1 (1-30) | 8.00 | 3.60 |

*TIER 1: .75X TO 1.5X BASIC CARDS
*TIER 2: 1.5X TO 3X
*TIER 3: 2.5X TO 5X
TIER 1 PRINT RUN 1000 SERIAL #'d SETS
TIER 2 PRINT RUN 500 SERIAL #'d SETS
TIER 3 PRINT RUN 250 SERIAL #'d SETS

| | | |
|---|---|---|
| COMMON G.N.QUANT.2 (1-30) | 100.00 | 45.00 |

*TIER 1: 10X TO 20X BASIC CARDS
*TIER 2: 25X TO 50X
TIER 1 PRINT RUN 75 SERIAL #'d SETS
TIER 2 PRINT RUN 25 SERIAL #'d SETS
TIER 3 PRINT RUN 10 SERIAL #'d SETS
TIER 1 CARDS: 1,4,7,10,13,16,19,22,25,28
TIER 2 CARDS: 2,5,8,11,14,17,20,23,26,29
TIER 3 CARDS: 3,6,9,12,15,18,21,24,27,30
G.N. 1 OF 1 PARALLEL EXISTS

| | | |
|---|---|---|
| ❑ GN1 Wayne Gretzky<br>Sergei Samsonov | 30.00 | 13.50 |
| ❑ GN2 Wayne Gretzky<br>Marian Hossa | 30.00 | 13.50 |
| ❑ GN3 Wayne Gretzky<br>Vincent Lecavalier | 30.00 | 13.50 |
| ❑ GN4 Steve Yzerman<br>Brendan Morrison | 15.00 | 6.75 |
| ❑ GN5 Steve Yzerman<br>Marty Reasoner | 15.00 | 6.75 |
| ❑ GN6 Steve Yzerman<br>Manny Malhotra | 15.00 | 6.75 |
| ❑ GN7 Patrick Roy<br>Jean Sebastien Giguere | 25.00 | 11.00 |
| ❑ GN8 Patrick Roy<br>Jose Theodore | 25.00 | 11.00 |
| ❑ GN9 Patrick Roy<br>Marc Denis | 25.00 | 11.00 |
| ❑ GN10 Eric Lindros<br>Patrick Marleau | 15.00 | 6.75 |
| ❑ GN11 Eric Lindros<br>Brad Isbister | 15.00 | 6.75 |
| ❑ GN12 Eric Lindros<br>Joe Thornton | 15.00 | 6.75 |
| ❑ GN13 Brendan Shanahan<br>Josh Green | 10.00 | 4.50 |
| ❑ GN14 Brendan Shanahan<br>Ty Jones | 10.00 | 4.50 |
| ❑ GN15 Brendan Shanahan<br>Mike Watt | 10.00 | 4.50 |
| ❑ GN16 Ray Bourque<br>Mattias Ohlund | 5.00 | 2.20 |
| ❑ GN17 Ray Bourque<br>Tom Poti | 5.00 | 2.20 |
| ❑ GN18 Ray Bourque<br>Eric Brewer | 5.00 | 2.20 |
| ❑ GN19 Paul Kariya<br>Daniel Briere | 20.00 | 9.00 |
| ❑ GN20 Paul Kariya<br>Rico Fata | 20.00 | 9.00 |
| ❑ GN21 Paul Kariya<br>Chris Drury | 25.00 | 11.00 |
| ❑ GN22 Jaromir Jagr | 15.00 | 6.75 |

Robert Dome
❑ GN23 Jaromir Jagr ............. 15.00 6.75
Richard Zednik
❑ GN24 Jaromir Jagr ............. 15.00 6.75
Oleg Kvasha
❑ GN25 Peter Forsberg ........... 15.00 6.75
Olli Jokinen
❑ GN26 Peter Forsberg ........... 15.00 6.75
Niklas Sundstrom
❑ GN27 Peter Forsberg ........... 15.00 6.75
Brendan Morrison
❑ GN28 Pavel Bure ................ 10.00 4.50
Vadim Sharifijanov
❑ GN29 Pavel Bure ................ 10.00 4.50
Dimitri Nabakov
❑ GN30 Pavel Bure ................ 12.00 5.50
Sergei Samsonov

## 1998-99 Upper Deck Game Jerseys

Randomly inserted into Series 1 and Series 2 packs at the rate of one in 2,500, this 24-card set features color action player photos with a piece from an actual game-worn jersey embedded in the cards. Four of the player's autographed some of their cards. The set price does not include these cards. The number of cards each player autographed follow the player's name in the checklist below.

| | MINT | NRMT |
|---|---|---|
| COMPLETE SET (24) | 5000.00 | 2200.00 |
| COMP.SER 1 (1-14) | 3000.00 | 1350.00 |
| COMP.SER 2 (15-24) | 2000.00 | 900.00 |
| COMMON CARD (GJ1-GJ24) | 60.00 | 27.00 |
| SEMISTARS/GOALIES | | |
| UNLISTED STARS | | |
| SET PRICE DOES NOT INCLUDE GJA1-GJA4 | | |

❑ GJ1 Wayne Gretzky ......... 1000.00 450.00
❑ GJ2 Vincent Lecavalier ...... 300.00 135.00
❑ GJ3 Bobby Hull ................. 300.00 135.00
❑ GJ4 Curtis Joseph ............ 200.00 90.00
❑ GJ5 Roberto Luongo ......... 150.00 70.00
❑ GJ6 Martin Brodeur ........... 300.00 135.00
❑ GJ7 Ed Belfour ................... 175.00 80.00
❑ GJ8 Al MacInnis ................ 100.00 45.00
❑ GJ9 Derian Hatcher ............ 60.00 27.00
❑ GJ10 Daniel Tkaczuk ........... 60.00 27.00
❑ GJ11 Manny Malhotra ....... 100.00 45.00
❑ GJ12 Eric Brewer ................ 80.00 36.00
❑ GJ13 Alex Tanguay ............ 100.00 45.00
❑ GJ14 Brendan Shanahan ... 200.00 90.00
❑ GJ15 Jaromir Jagr ............ 400.00 180.00
❑ GJ16 Chris Osgood ........... 150.00 70.00
❑ GJ17 Dominik Hasek ......... 250.00 110.00
❑ GJ18 Doug Gilmour ........... 200.00 90.00
❑ GJ19 Mats Sundin ............. 150.00 70.00
❑ GJ20 Darryl Sydor .............. 60.00 27.00
❑ GJ21 Chris Therien ............. 60.00 27.00
❑ GJ22 Darius Kasparaitis ....... 60.00 27.00
❑ GJ23 Alexei Zhamnov .......... 60.00 27.00
❑ GJ24 Joe Nieuwendyk ......... 80.00 36.00
❑ GJA1 Bobby Hull AU/9..... 2500.00 1100.00
❑ GJA2 W.Gretzky AU/99.... 2000.00 900.00
❑ GJA3 V.Lecavalier AU/100. 700.00 325.00
❑ GJA4 Gretzky 2Swatch AU/99 2200.00 1000.00

## 1998-99 Upper Deck Lord Stanley Heroes

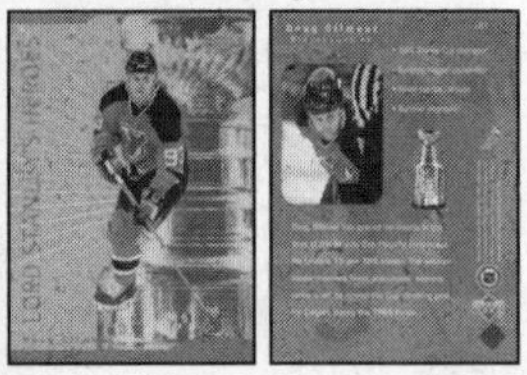

Randomly inserted into Series 1 packs at a rate of one in six, this 30-card set features color action photos of players vying for their chance at claiming the Stanley Cup. Three Tier Quantum parallel versions of this insert set were also produced and inserted into Series 1 packs. Tier 1 cards were sequentially numbered to 2,000; Tier 2 cards were sequentially numbered to 100; and Tier 3 cards were numbered to 1.

| | MINT | NRMT |
|---|---|---|
| COMPLETE SET (30) | 90.00 | 40.00 |
| COMMON CARD (LS1-LS30) | 1.25 | .55 |
| COMP.L.S.H.QUANT.1 SET (30) | 180.00 | 80.00 |
| COMMON L.S.H.QUANT.1 (1-30) | 2.50 | 1.10 |
| *LSH.QUANT.1 STARS: 1X TO 2X BASIC CARDS | | |
| L.S.H.QUANT.1 PRINT RUN 2000 SETS | | |
| COMP.L.S.H.QUANT.2 SET (30) | 450.00 | 200.00 |
| COMMON L.S.H.QUANT.2 (1-30) | 60.00 | 27.00 |
| *L.S.H.QUANT.2 STARS: 25X TO 50X BASIC CARDS | | |
| L.S.H.QUANT.2 PRINT RUN 100 SETS | | |
| L.S.H 1 OF 1 PARALLEL EXISTS | | |

❑ LS1 Wayne Gretzky ............ 10.00 4.50
❑ LS2 Joe Sakic .................... 3.00 1.35
❑ LS3 Jaromir Jagr.................. 5.00 2.20
❑ LS4 Brendan Shanahan ......... 3.00 1.35
❑ LS5 Martin Brodeur .............. 4.00 1.80
❑ LS6 Theoren Fleury ............... 1.50 .70
❑ LS7 Doug Gilmour.................. 1.50 .70
❑ LS8 Ron Francis .................... 1.25 .55
❑ LS9 Sergei Fedorov ............... 3.00 1.35
❑ LS10 Patrick Roy.................... 8.00 3.60
❑ LS11 Mark Messier ................ 2.00 .90
❑ LS12 Peter Forsberg............... 5.00 2.20
❑ LS13 Brian Leetch ................. 1.50 .70
❑ LS14 Steve Yzerman .............. 5.00 2.20
❑ LS15 Sergei Samsonov ........... 2.50 1.10
❑ LS16 Eric Lindros................... 5.00 2.20
❑ LS17 Paul Kariya .................... 6.00 2.70
❑ LS18 Saku Koivu .................... 2.50 1.10
❑ LS19 Bryan Berard .................. 1.25 .55
❑ LS20 Chris Pronger................. 1.25 .55
❑ LS21 Keith Tkachuk................ 2.00 .90
❑ LS22 Doug Weight .................. 1.25 .55
❑ LS23 Ed Belfour...................... 1.50 .70
❑ LS24 Mats Sundin ................... 1.50 .70
❑ LS25 John LeClair ................... 2.50 1.10
❑ LS26 Pavel Bure...................... 3.00 1.35
❑ LS27 Dominik Hasek ............... 3.00 1.35
❑ LS28 Mike Modano ................. 2.00 .90
❑ LS29 Curtis Joseph ................. 1.50 .70
❑ LS30 Teemu Selanne............... 3.00 1.35

## 1998-99 Upper Deck Profiles

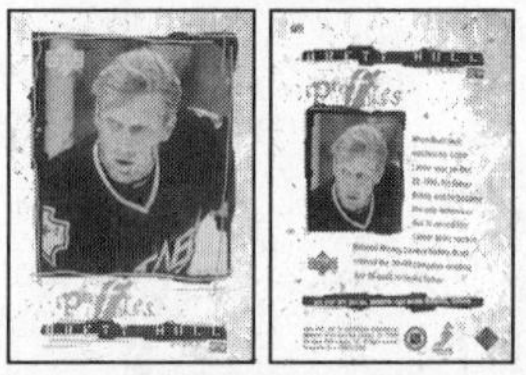

Randomly inserted into Series 2 packs at the rate of one in 12, this 30-card set features color action photos of some of the greatest current players in the NHL. Three Tier Quantum parallel versions of this insert set were also produced and inserted into Series 2 packs. Tier 1 cards were sequentially numbered to 1,500; Tier 2 cards were sequentially numbered to 50; and Tier 3 cards were numbered to 1.

| | MINT | NRMT |
|---|---|---|
| COMPLETE SET (30) | 175.00 | 80.00 |
| COMMON CARD (P1-P30) | 1.50 | .70 |
| COMP.PROF.QUANT.1 SET (30) | 350.00 | 160.00 |
| COMMON PROF.QUANT.1 (1-30) | 3.00 | 1.35 |
| *PROF.QUANT.1 STARS: 1X TO 2X BASIC CARDS | | |
| PROF.QUANTUM 1 PRINT RUN 1500 SETS | | |
| COMP.PROF.QUANT.2 SET (30) | 5000.00 | 2200.00 |
| COMMON PROF.QUANT.2 (1-30) | 50.00 | 22.00 |
| *PROF.QUANT.2 STARS: 15X TO 30X BASIC CARDS | | |
| PROF.QUANTUM 2 PRINT RUN 50 SETS | | |
| PROFILES 1 OF 1 PARALLEL EXISTS | | |

❑ P1 Marty Reasoner................ 1.50 .70
❑ P2 Brett Hull ......................... 4.00 1.80
❑ P3 Steve Yzerman ............... 10.00 4.50
❑ P4 Eric Lindros.................... 10.00 4.50
❑ P5 Eric Brewer...................... 1.50 .70
❑ P6 Martin Brodeur ................ 8.00 3.60
❑ P7 John Vanbiesbrouck......... 4.00 1.80
❑ P8 Teemu Selanne................. 6.00 2.70
❑ P9 Wayne Gretzky ............... 20.00 9.00
❑ P10 Jaromir Jagr .................. 10.00 4.50
❑ P11 Peter Forsberg............... 10.00 4.50
❑ P12 Manny Malhotra ............. 1.50 .70
❑ P13 Sergei Samsonov ............ 5.00 2.20
❑ P14 Brendan Shanahan .......... 6.00 2.70
❑ P15 Doug Gilmour.................. 1.50 .70
❑ P16 Vincent Lecavalier .......... 6.00 2.70
❑ P17 Dominik Hasek ................ 6.00 2.70
❑ P18 Mike Modano .................. 4.00 1.80
❑ P19 Saku Koivu ..................... 5.00 2.20
❑ P20 Curtis Joseph .................. 1.50 .70
❑ P21 Paul Kariya .................... 12.00 5.50
❑ P22 Doug Weight ................... 1.50 .70
❑ P23 Ray Bourque.................... 1.50 .70
❑ P24 Patrick Roy.................... 15.00 6.75
❑ P25 John LeClair .................... 5.00 2.20
❑ P26 Chris Drury...................... 4.00 1.80
❑ P27 Theoren Fleury ................ 1.50 .70
❑ P28 Mats Sundin .................... 1.50 .70
❑ P29 Sergei Fedorov ................ 6.00 2.70
❑ P30 Rico Fata ........................ 1.50 .70

## 1998-99 Upper Deck Wayne Gretzky Game Jersey Autographs

This set was inserted in Upper Deck Black Diamond packs, Upper Deck MVP packs, SP Authentic packs, and SPx Top Prospects. Each card was numbered out of 40, and each product has 40 cards. The cards contain an actual piece of a game worn Wayne Gretzy jersey embedded in the cards.

| | MINT | NRMT |
|---|---|---|
| COMMON CARD | 3000.00 | 1350.00 |
| EACH CARD NUMBERED OUT OF 40 | | |
| EACH PRODUCT HAS 40 CARDS | | |
| AVAILABLE IN BLACK DIAMOND | | |
| AVAILABLE IN MVP | | |
| AVAILABLE IN SP AUTHENTIC | | |
| AVAILABLE IN SPX TOP PROSPECTS | | |

## 1998-99 Upper Deck Year of the Great One

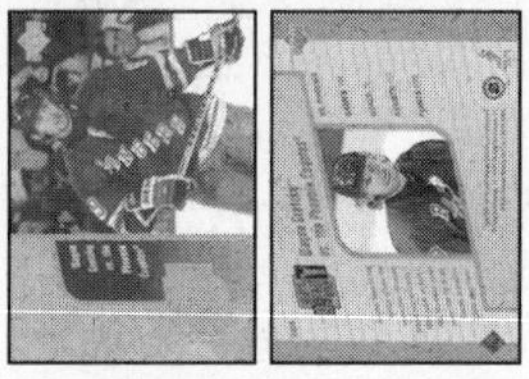

Randomly inserted into Series 2 packs at the rate of one in six, this 30-card set features color photos of Hockey great, Wayne Gretzky. Three Tier Quantum parallel versions of this insert set were also produced and inserted into Series 2 packs. Tier 1 cards were sequentially numbered to 1,999; Tier 2 cards were sequentially numbered to 99; and Tier 3 cards were numbered to 1.

| | MINT | NRMT |
|---|---|---|
| COMPLETE SET (30) | 100.00 | 45.00 |
| COMMON CARD (G01-G030) | 4.00 | 1.80 |
| COMP.QUANT.1 SET (30) | 500.00 | 220.00 |
| COMMON QUANTUM 1 (1-30) | 15.00 | 6.75 |
| QUANTUM 1 PRINT RUN 1999 SETS | | |
| COMP.QUANT.2 SET (30) | 7500.00 | 3400.00 |
| COMMON QUANTUM 2 (1-30) | 250.00 | 110.00 |
| QUANTUM 2 PRINT RUN 99 SETS | | |
| COMP.QUANTUM 3 SET (30) | | |
| COMMON QUANTUM 3 (1-30) | | |
| QUANTUM 3 PRINT RUN 1 SET | 4.00 | 1.80 |
| Y.O.T.G. 1 OF 1 PARALLEL EXISTS | | |

## 1997 Upper Deck Crash the All-Star Game

Distributed one per attendee of the 1997 NHL All-Star Game in San Jose, these one-off Crash the Game cards were redeemable for a special set if the player pictured scored a goal in the contest. The Western Conference cards (1-11) were rumored to be the only ones distributed, although a few copies of each of the Eastern Conference cards have surfaced as well. The complete set price below includes both conferences. The winners are numbered AR1 thru AR20, and feature gold foil and a record of the player's performance in the game.

| | MINT | NRMT |
|---|---|---|
| COMPLETE SET (20) | 2200.00 | 1000.00 |
| COMMON CARD (1-20) | 40.00 | 18.00 |
| COMPLETE WINNER SET (20) | 750.00 | 350.00 |
| COMMON WINNER CARD (AR1-AR20) | 20.00 | 9.00 |

❑ 1 Tony Amonte .................... 40.00 18.00
❑ 2 Paul Kariya .................... 250.00 110.00
❑ 3 Brett Hull ......................... 80.00 36.00
❑ 4 Teemu Selanne .............. 120.00 55.00
❑ 5 Steve Yzerman............... 200.00 90.00
❑ 6 Owen Nolan ..................... 40.00 18.00
❑ 7 Mats Sundin ..................... 60.00 27.00
❑ 8 Pavel Bure ..................... 120.00 55.00
❑ 9 Brendan Shanahan .......... 120.00 55.00
❑ 10 Sandis Ozolinsh............... 40.00 18.00
❑ 11 Keith Tkachuk................. 80.00 36.00
❑ 12 Ray Bourque................... 50.00 22.00
❑ 13 Eric Lindros .................. 300.00 135.00
❑ 14 Mark Messier.................. 80.00 36.00
❑ 15 John LeClair.................. 100.00 45.00
❑ 16 Jaromir Jagr.................. 200.00 90.00
❑ 17 Dino Ciccarelli................. 40.00 18.00
❑ 18 Peter Bondra.................... 60.00 27.00
❑ 19 Brian Leetch .................... 80.00 36.00
❑ 20 Wayne Gretzky.............. 400.00 180.00
❑ AR1 Tony Amonte ................ 20.00 9.00
❑ AR2 Paul Kariya ................. 100.00 45.00
❑ AR3 Brett Hull...................... 30.00 13.50
❑ AR4 Teemu Selanne ............. 50.00 22.00
❑ AR5 Steve Yzerman .............. 75.00 34.00
❑ AR6 Owen Nolan .................. 30.00 13.50
❑ AR7 Mats Sundin................... 40.00 18.00
❑ AR8 Pavel Bure..................... 50.00 22.00
❑ AR9 Brendan Shanahan......... 50.00 22.00
❑ AR10 Sandis Ozolinsh ........... 20.00 9.00
❑ AR11 Keith Tkachuk .............. 30.00 13.50
❑ AR12 Ray Bourque ................ 20.00 9.00
❑ AR13 Eric Lindros ............... 100.00 45.00
❑ AR14 Mark Messier ............... 30.00 13.50
❑ AR15 John LeClair................. 40.00 18.00
❑ AR16 Jaromir Jagr ................. 75.00 34.00
❑ AR17 Dino Ciccarelli .............. 20.00 9.00
❑ AR18 Peter Bondra................. 25.00 11.00
❑ AR19 Brian Leetch ................. 25.00 11.00
❑ AR20 Wayne Gretzky ........... 150.00 70.00

## 1996-97 Upper Deck Black Diamond

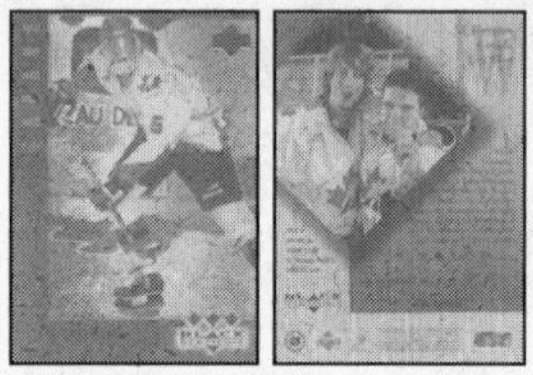

This hobby-only set was issued in one series totalling 180 cards, with three varying levels of difficulty: Single Black Diamond (1-90), Double Black Diamond (91-150), and Triple Black Diamond (151-180). Doubles were inserted 1:4 packs and Triples 1:30 packs. Packs of six cards retailed for $3.49. Numerous rookies are included, such as Joe Thornton, Patrick Marleau, Patrick Lalime, Dainius Zubrus and Sergei Berezin. The Gretzky promo mirrors the regular issue, aside from the word SAMPLE which runs across his portrait on the card back.

| | MINT | NRMT |
|---|---|---|
| COMPLETE SET (180) | 950.00 | 425.00 |
| COMP.SINGLE SET (90) | 25.00 | 11.00 |
| COMMON SINGLE (1-90) | .25 | .11 |
| COMP.DOUBLE SET (60) | 120.00 | 55.00 |
| COMMON DOUBLE (91-150) | 1.50 | .70 |
| COMP.TRIPLE SET (30) | 700.00 | 325.00 |
| COMMON TRIPLE (151-180) | 5.00 | 2.20 |

❑ 1 Roman Turek ...................... 1.25 .55
❑ 2 Vyacheslav Fetisov .............. .25 .11
❑ 3 Mike Dunham ....................... .50 .23
❑ 4 Jean-Francois Fortin ............ .25 .11
❑ 5 Keith Primeau ...................... .25 .11
❑ 6 Zigmund Palffy .................. 1.00 .45
❑ 7 Curtis Leschyshyn ................ .25 .11
❑ 8 Vladimir Tsyplakov ............... .25 .11
❑ 9 Adam Graves ........................ .25 .11
❑ 10 Ian Laperriere ..................... .25 .11
❑ 11 Bill Lindsay.......................... .25 .11
❑ 12 Brian Leetch ..................... 1.00 .45
❑ 13 Martin Lapointe .................. .25 .11
❑ 14 Scott Barney ..................... 1.00 .45
❑ 15 Mike Grier......................... 2.00 .90
❑ 16 Vladimir Konstantinov ......... .50 .23
❑ 17 Rem Murray ........................ .25 .11
❑ 18 Ed Jovanovski..................... .50 .23
❑ 19 Chris O'Sullivan .................. .25 .11
❑ 20 Steve Rucchin...................... .25 .11
❑ 21 Jay Pandolfo........................ .25 .11
❑ 22 Nick Boynton .................... 1.50 .70
❑ 23 Greg Adams......................... .25 .11
❑ 24 Adam Colagiacomo........... 1.25 .55
❑ 25 Vincent Damphousse........... .50 .23
❑ 26 Shane Willis...................... 1.00 .45
❑ 27 Alexei Kovalev..................... .25 .11
❑ 28 Doug Gilmour ...................... .50 .23
❑ 29 Joel Otto ............................. .25 .11
❑ 30 Donald Audette .................... .25 .11
❑ 31 Tommy Salo ........................ .50 .23
❑ 32 Rob Ray............................... .25 .11
❑ 33 Kris Draper .......................... .25 .11
❑ 34 Ed Belfour......................... 1.00 .45
❑ 35 Mike Richter ...................... 1.00 .45
❑ 36 Nikolai Khabibulin................ .50 .23
❑ 37 Eric Desjardins .................... .25 .11
❑ 38 Daniel Tkaczuk................... 3.00 1.35
❑ 39 Keith Jones........................... .50 .23
❑ 40 Per Gustafsson ..................... .25 .11
❑ 41 Jocelyn Thibault ................ 1.00 .45
❑ 42 Mike Gartner......................... .50 .23
❑ 43 Vitali Yachmenev .................. .25 .11
❑ 44 Jonas Hoglund ...................... .25 .11
❑ 45 Craig Janney......................... .25 .11
❑ 46 Daymond Langkow................ .25 .11
❑ 47 Mattias Timander................... .25 .11
❑ 48 Scott Young........................... .25 .11
❑ 49 Mikael Renberg...................... .25 .11
❑ 50 Nicklas Lidstrom.................... .25 .11
❑ 51 Andrei Kovalenko................... .25 .11
❑ 52 Adam Foote ........................... .25 .11
❑ 53 Guy Hebert ............................ .50 .23
❑ 54 Kevin Hatcher ........................ .25 .11
❑ 55 Rick Tocchet.......................... .25 .11
❑ 56 Sergei Zubov ......................... .25 .11
❑ 57 Chris Phillips ......................... .25 .11
❑ 58 Denis Savard ......................... .50 .23
❑ 59 Bernie Nicholls ...................... .25 .11
❑ 60 Jozef Stumpel........................ .25 .11
❑ 61 Darius Kasparaitis.................. .25 .11
❑ 62 Kelly Hrudey .......................... .50 .23
❑ 63 Marcel Cousineau ............... 1.00 .45
❑ 64 Brian Skrudland ..................... .25 .11
❑ 65 Byron Dafoe........................... .50 .23
❑ 66 Ray Sheppard ........................ .25 .11
❑ 67 Chris Simon............................ .25 .11
❑ 68 Dainius Zubrus ................... 2.00 .90
❑ 69 Ethan Moreau ..................... 1.00 .45
❑ 70 Theoren Fleury....................... .50 .23
❑ 71 Damian Rhodes ..................... .50 .23
❑ 72 Kevin Dineen.......................... .25 .11
❑ 73 Kenny Jonsson....................... .25 .11
❑ 74 Ray Ferraro............................ .25 .11
❑ 75 Jaromir Jagr ....................... 3.00 1.35
❑ 76 Wayne Primeau ..................... .25 .11
❑ 77 Chris Gratton ......................... .25 .11
❑ 78 Alyn McCauley ................... 1.00 .45
❑ 79 Christian Dube....................... .50 .23
❑ 80 Bill Ranford............................ .50 .23
❑ 81 Adam Deadmarsh .................. .50 .23
❑ 82 Dale Hunter............................ .50 .23
❑ 83 Derek Plante .......................... .25 .11
❑ 84 Todd Bertuzzi.......................... .25 .11
❑ 85 Stephane Fiset ........................ .50 .23
❑ 86 Boyd Devereaux.................. 2.50 1.10
❑ 87 Jere Lehtinen ........................... .25 .11
❑ 88 Peter Schaefer ..................... 3.00 1.35
❑ 89 Alexander Mogilny.................. .50 .23
❑ 90 Joe Juneau .............................. .50 .23
❑ 91 Alexandre Daigle................. 1.50 .70
❑ 92 Jeff O'Neill .......................... 1.50 .70
❑ 93 Todd Warriner ...................... 1.50 .70
❑ 94 Sergei Berezin...................... 4.00 1.80
❑ 95 Petr Nedved.......................... 1.50 .70
❑ 96 Phil Housley ......................... 1.50 .70
❑ 97 Jason Arnott ......................... 3.00 1.35
❑ 98 Sandis Ozolinsh.................... 3.00 1.35
❑ 99 Mike Modano........................ 6.00 2.70
❑ 100 Mark Messier...................... 6.00 2.70
❑ 101 Ron Francis ........................ 1.50 .70
❑ 102 Oleg Tverdovsky.................. 1.50 .70
❑ 103 Patrick Marleau.............. 20.00 9.00
❑ 104 Brian Bellows ...................... 1.50 .70
❑ 105 Eric Fichaud ........................ 3.00 1.35
❑ 106 Alexei Zhamnov .................. 3.00 1.35
❑ 107 Wendel Clark ...................... 1.50 .70
❑ 108 Dimitri Khristich .................. 1.50 .70
❑ 109 Mike Ricci ........................... 1.50 .70
❑ 110 John LeClair........................ 8.00 3.60
❑ 111 Owen Nolan ........................ 3.00 1.35
❑ 112 Bill Guerin............................ 1.50 .70
❑ 113 Vyacheslav Kozlov .............. 1.50 .70
❑ 114 Brendan Shanahan ........... 10.00 4.50
❑ 115 Trevor Linden ...................... 1.50 .70
❑ 116 Jose Theodore..................... 3.00 1.35
❑ 117 Rod Brind'Amour................. 3.00 1.35
❑ 118 Brian Holzinger.................... 1.50 .70
❑ 119 Shayne Corson .................... 1.50 .70
❑ 120 Bryan Smolinski ................... 1.50 .70
❑ 121 Tony Granato....................... 1.50 .70
❑ 122 Mariusz Czerkawski ............. 1.50 .70
❑ 123 Andrew Cassels ................... 1.50 .70
❑ 124 Scott Stevens ...................... 1.50 .70
❑ 125 Mike Ridley .......................... 1.50 .70
❑ 126 Jamie Langenbrunner........... 1.50 .70
❑ 127 Scott Mellanby...................... 1.50 .70
❑ 128 Grant Fuhr ........................... 1.50 .70
❑ 129 Felix Potvin .......................... 3.00 1.35
❑ 130 Marc Denis .......................... 6.00 2.70
❑ 131 Corey Hirsch ........................ 3.00 1.35
❑ 132 Chris Osgood ....................... 5.00 2.20
❑ 133 Peter Bondra ........................ 3.00 1.35
❑ 134 Martin Brodeur ................. 12.00 5.50
❑ 135 Pierre Turgeon...................... 3.00 1.35
❑ 136 Pat Verbeek ......................... 1.50 .70
❑ 137 Scott Niedermayer................ 1.50 .70
❑ 138 Geoff Sanderson .................. 1.50 .70
❑ 139 Jason Dawe .......................... 1.50 .70
❑ 140 Rob Niedermayer.................. 1.50 .70
❑ 141 Daniel Alfredsson ................. 3.00 1.35
❑ 142 Jim Campbell......................... 1.50 .70
❑ 143 Roman Hamrlik...................... 1.50 .70
❑ 144 Rob Blake ............................. 1.50 .70
❑ 145 Chris Chelios ........................ 5.00 2.20
❑ 146 Teemu Selanne................. 10.00 4.50
❑ 147 Jim Carey ............................. 5.00 2.20
❑ 148 Dino Ciccarelli...................... 1.50 .70
❑ 149 Mark Recchi ......................... 1.50 .70
❑ 150 Chris Pronger ....................... 1.50 .70
❑ 151 Paul Coffey ....................... 12.00 5.50
❑ 152 Adam Oates ......................... 5.00 2.20
❑ 153 Keith Tkachuk ................... 15.00 6.75
❑ 154 Janne Niinimaa .................. 12.00 5.50
❑ 155 Sergei Fedorov .................. 25.00 11.00
❑ 156 Dominik Hasek ................... 25.00 11.00
❑ 157 Eric Lindros ....................... 40.00 18.00
❑ 158 Curtis Joseph ..................... 12.00 5.50
❑ 159 Alexei Yashin ....................... 5.00 2.20
❑ 160 Joe Thornton ...................... 25.00 11.00
❑ 161 Bryan Berard ........................ 6.00 2.70
❑ 162 Steve Yzerman................... 40.00 18.00
❑ 163 Mats Sundin ....................... 12.00 5.50
❑ 164 Jarome Iginla...................... 12.00 5.50
❑ 165 John Vanbiesbrouck ........... 20.00 9.00
❑ 166 Mario Lemieux.................... 60.00 27.00
❑ 167 Jeremy Roenick.................. 12.00 5.50
❑ 168 Patrick Lalime ..................... 12.00 5.50
❑ 169 Joe Sakic ............................ 25.00 11.00
❑ 170 Brett Hull ............................ 20.00 9.00
❑ 171 Peter Forsberg.................... 40.00 18.00
❑ 172 Doug Weight ........................ 5.00 2.20
❑ 173 Tony Amonte ........................ 5.00 2.20
❑ 174 Patrick Roy......................... 60.00 27.00
❑ 175 Paul Kariya ......................... 50.00 22.00
❑ 176 Pavel Bure .......................... 25.00 11.00
❑ 177 Ray Bourque....................... 12.00 5.50
❑ 178 Saku Koivu ......................... 20.00 9.00
❑ 179 Wade Redden ....................... 5.00 2.20
❑ 180 Wayne Gretzky.................... 80.00 36.00
❑ P180 Wayne Gretzky Promo 10.00 4.50

## 1996-97 Upper Deck Black Diamond Gold

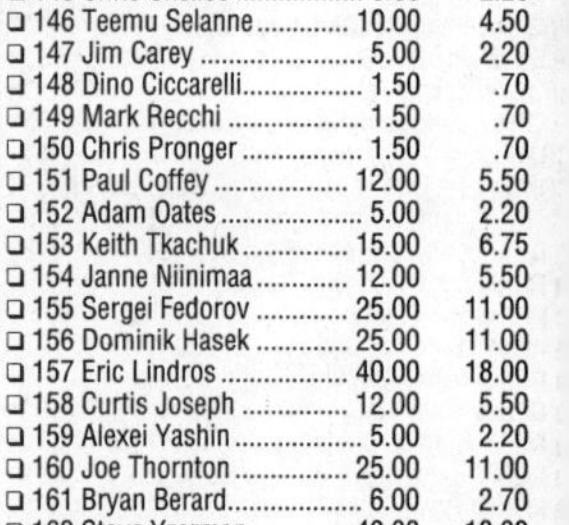

This was a gold-foil parallel to the three-tiered

Upper Deck Black Diamond set. Single golds were inserted 1:15 packs, Doubles 1:46, and Triples, for which an insertion ratio was not announced, were limited to just 50 sets.

| | MINT | NRMT |
|---|---|---|
| COMP.SINGLE SET (90) | 400.00 | 180.00 |
| COMMON SINGLE (1-90) | 3.00 | 1.35 |
| *SINGLE DIAM.STARS: 3X TO 8X BASIC CARDS | | |
| *SINGLE DIAM.YNG.STARS: 2.5X TO 6X BASIC CARDS | | |
| *SINGLE DIAM.RC's: 2X TO 5X BASIC CARDS | | |
| COMP.DOUBLE SET (60) | 600.00 | 275.00 |
| COMMON DOUBLE (91-150) | 6.00 | 2.70 |
| *DOUBLE DIAM.STARS: 1.5X TO 3X BASIC CARDS | | |
| *DOUBLE DIAM.YOUNG STARS: 2X TO 4X BASIC CARDS | | |
| *DOUBLE DIAM.RCs: 1.5X TO 4X BASIC CARDS | | |
| COMP.TRIPLE SET (30) | 4500.00 | 2000.00 |
| COMMON TRIPLE (151-180) | 50.00 | 22.00 |
| TRIPLE SEMIS/GOALIES | 60.00 | 27.00 |
| TRIPLE UNLISTED STARS | 80.00 | 36.00 |

| | | |
|---|---|---|
| ❑ 153 Keith Tkachuk | 100.00 | 45.00 |
| ❑ 154 Janne Niinimaa | 100.00 | 45.00 |
| ❑ 155 Sergei Fedorov | 150.00 | 70.00 |
| ❑ 156 Dominik Hasek | 150.00 | 70.00 |
| ❑ 157 Eric Lindros | 300.00 | 135.00 |
| ❑ 160 Joe Thornton | 150.00 | 70.00 |
| ❑ 162 Steve Yzerman | 250.00 | 110.00 |
| ❑ 165 John Vanbiesbrouck | 120.00 | 55.00 |
| ❑ 166 Mario Lemieux | 400.00 | 180.00 |
| ❑ 169 Joe Sakic | 200.00 | 90.00 |
| ❑ 170 Brett Hull | 100.00 | 45.00 |
| ❑ 171 Peter Forsberg | 250.00 | 110.00 |
| ❑ 174 Patrick Roy | 400.00 | 180.00 |
| ❑ 175 Paul Kariya | 300.00 | 135.00 |
| ❑ 176 Pavel Bure | 150.00 | 70.00 |
| ❑ 178 Saku Koivu | 150.00 | 70.00 |
| ❑ 180 Wayne Gretzky | 600.00 | 275.00 |

## 1996-97 Upper Deck Black Diamond Run for the Cup

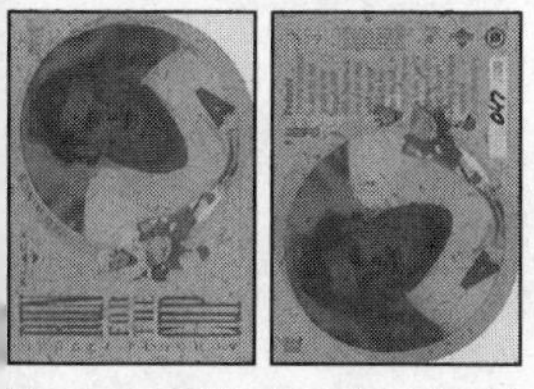

Ultra-rare and individually crash-numbered to just 100 sets, these 20 cel-chrome inserts featured high profile players with their eyes set on the Stanley Cup.

| | MINT | NRMT |
|---|---|---|
| COMPLETE SET (20) | 5000.00 | 2200.00 |
| COMMON CARD (RC1-RC20) | 60.00 | 27.00 |
| ❑ RC1 Wayne Gretzky | 500.00 | 220.00 |
| ❑ RC2 Saku Koivu | 120.00 | 55.00 |
| ❑ RC3 Mario Lemieux | 400.00 | 180.00 |
| ❑ RC4 Patrick Roy | 400.00 | 180.00 |
| ❑ RC5 Jaromir Jagr | 200.00 | 90.00 |
| ❑ RC6 John Vanbiesbrouck | 120.00 | 55.00 |
| ❑ RC7 Peter Forsberg | 200.00 | 90.00 |
| ❑ RC8 Paul Kariya | 300.00 | 135.00 |
| ❑ RC9 Steve Yzerman | 200.00 | 90.00 |
| ❑ RC10 Joe Sakic | 150.00 | 70.00 |
| ❑ RC11 Mark Messier | 100.00 | 45.00 |
| ❑ RC12 Sergei Fedorov | 150.00 | 70.00 |
| ❑ RC13 Mats Sundin | 80.00 | 36.00 |
| ❑ RC14 Pavel Bure | 150.00 | 70.00 |
| ❑ RC15 Ed Jovanovski | 60.00 | 27.00 |
| ❑ RC16 Mike Modano | 100.00 | 45.00 |
| ❑ RC17 Curtis Joseph | 80.00 | 36.00 |
| ❑ RC18 Teemu Selanne | 150.00 | 70.00 |
| ❑ RC19 Jarome Iginla | 60.00 | 27.00 |
| ❑ RC20 Eric Lindros | 200.00 | 90.00 |

## 1997-98 Upper Deck Black Diamond

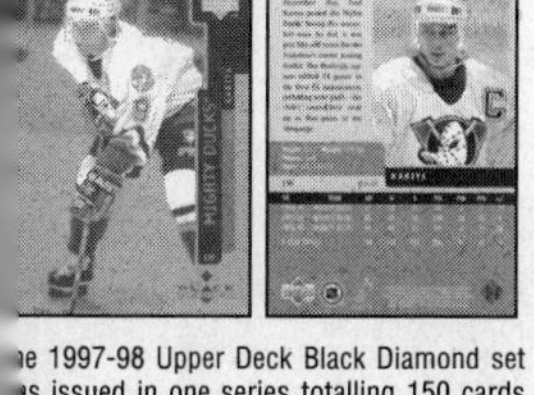

The 1997-98 Upper Deck Black Diamond set was issued in one series totalling 150 cards and distributed in six-card packs with a suggested retail price of $3.49. The fronts feature color action player photos reproduced on Light F/X card stock with foil treatment and one, two, three, or four Black Diamonds on the front designating its rarity. The backs carry player information and statistics.

| | MINT | NRMT |
|---|---|---|
| COMPLETE SET (150) | 100.00 | 45.00 |
| COMMON CARD (1-150) | .20 | .09 |
| ❑ 1 Alexei Zhitnik | .20 | .09 |
| ❑ 2 Adam Graves | .50 | .23 |
| ❑ 3 Keith Primeau | .20 | .09 |
| ❑ 4 Mike Richter | .60 | .25 |
| ❑ 5 Felix Potvin | .60 | .25 |
| ❑ 6 Valeri Bure | .20 | .09 |
| ❑ 7 Mark Messier | .75 | .35 |
| ❑ 8 Dainius Zubrus | .60 | .25 |
| ❑ 9 Owen Nolan | .50 | .23 |
| ❑ 10 Kenny Jonsson | .20 | .09 |
| ❑ 11 Ron Francis | .50 | .23 |
| ❑ 12 Bryan Berard | .20 | .09 |
| ❑ 13 Eric Messier | .50 | .23 |
| ❑ 14 Paul Kariya | 2.50 | 1.10 |
| ❑ 15 Teemu Elomo | 1.00 | .45 |
| ❑ 16 Joe Nieuwendyk | .20 | .09 |
| ❑ 17 Scott Stevens | .20 | .09 |
| ❑ 18 Zigmund Palffy | .60 | .25 |
| ❑ 19 Brett Hull | .75 | .35 |
| ❑ 20 Dominik Hasek | 1.25 | .55 |
| ❑ 21 Dino Ciccarelli | .20 | .09 |
| ❑ 22 Rob Niedermayer | .20 | .09 |
| ❑ 23 Mark Recchi | .50 | .23 |
| ❑ 24 Brad Isbister | .20 | .09 |
| ❑ 25 Timo Vertala | 1.00 | .45 |
| ❑ 26 Mika Noronen RC | 3.00 | 1.35 |
| ❑ 27 Sandis Ozolinsh | .50 | .23 |
| ❑ 28 Chris Phillips | .20 | .09 |
| ❑ 29 Chris Chelios | .60 | .25 |
| ❑ 30 Jason Dawe | .20 | .09 |
| ❑ 31 Kirk McLean | .50 | .23 |
| ❑ 32 Jason Allison | .50 | .23 |
| ❑ 33 Brian Leetch | .60 | .25 |
| ❑ 34 Guy Hebert | .20 | .09 |
| ❑ 35 David Legwand | 10.00 | 4.50 |
| ❑ 36 Pierre Hedin | .50 | .23 |
| ❑ 37 Sergei Samsonov | 1.50 | .70 |
| ❑ 38 Bill Guerin | .50 | .23 |
| ❑ 39 Chris Osgood | .60 | .25 |
| ❑ 40 Jere Lehtinen | .20 | .09 |
| ❑ 41 Patrick Roy | 3.00 | 1.35 |
| ❑ 42 John Vanbiesbrouck | 1.00 | .45 |
| ❑ 43 Maxim Afinogenov | 3.00 | 1.35 |
| ❑ 44 Patrik Elias | 2.00 | .90 |
| ❑ 45 Josh Holden | .20 | .09 |
| ❑ 46 Saku Koivu | 1.00 | .45 |
| ❑ 47 Maxim Balmochnykh | .75 | .35 |
| ❑ 48 Pasi Petrilainen | 1.00 | .45 |
| ❑ 49 Robert Reichel | .20 | .09 |
| ❑ 50 Wade Redden | .20 | .09 |
| ❑ 51 Richard Zednik | .20 | .09 |
| ❑ 52 Ty Jones | .75 | .35 |
| ❑ 53 Nikolai Khabibulin | .50 | .23 |
| ❑ 54 Kyle McLaren | .20 | .09 |
| ❑ 55 Daniel Tkaczuk | .60 | .25 |
| ❑ 56 Alexei Zhamnov | .20 | .09 |
| ❑ 57 Donald MacLean | .20 | .09 |
| ❑ 58 Dave Gagner | .20 | .09 |
| ❑ 59 Jeremy Roenick | .60 | .25 |
| ❑ 60 Ray Bourque | .60 | .25 |
| ❑ 61 Rod Brind'Amour | .50 | .23 |
| ❑ 62 Miroslav Satan | .20 | .09 |
| ❑ 63 Eric Daze | .50 | .23 |
| ❑ 64 Mike Ricci | .20 | .09 |
| ❑ 65 John LeClair | 1.00 | .45 |
| ❑ 66 Bryan Marchment | .20 | .09 |
| ❑ 67 Henrik Petre RC | .50 | .23 |
| ❑ 68 John MacLean | .20 | .09 |
| ❑ 69 Artem Chubarov | .50 | .23 |
| ❑ 70 Doug Gilmour | .60 | .25 |
| ❑ 71 Marco Sturm | 2.50 | 1.10 |
| ❑ 72 Jaromir Jagr | 2.00 | .90 |
| ❑ 73 Daniel Alfredsson | .50 | .23 |
| ❑ 74 Daren Puppa | .50 | .23 |
| ❑ 75 Adam Deadmarsh | .50 | .23 |
| ❑ 76 Luc Robitaille | .50 | .23 |
| ❑ 77 Mats Sundin | .60 | .25 |
| ❑ 78 Dan Cloutier | .20 | .09 |
| ❑ 79 Manny Malhotra | 4.00 | 1.80 |
| ❑ 80 Mike Modano | .75 | .35 |
| ❑ 81 Espen Knutsen | .20 | .09 |
| ❑ 82 Sergei Fedorov | 1.25 | .55 |
| ❑ 83 Chris Pronger | .50 | .23 |
| ❑ 84 Doug Weight | .50 | .23 |
| ❑ 85 Dmitri Nabokov | .20 | .09 |
| ❑ 86 Gary Roberts | .20 | .09 |
| ❑ 87 Peter Bondra | .60 | .25 |
| ❑ 88 Robert Dome | .20 | .09 |
| ❑ 89 Jan Bulis | .20 | .09 |
| ❑ 90 Eric Brewer | 1.50 | .70 |
| ❑ 91 Nikos Tselios | .20 | .09 |
| ❑ 92 Scott Mellanby | .20 | .09 |
| ❑ 93 Vitali Vishnevsky | .75 | .35 |
| ❑ 94 Derian Hatcher | .20 | .09 |
| ❑ 95 Teemu Selanne | 1.25 | .55 |
| ❑ 96 Joe Sakic | 1.25 | .55 |
| ❑ 97 Alexander Mogilny | .50 | .23 |
| ❑ 98 Jesse Boulerice | .50 | .23 |
| ❑ 99 Johan Forsander | .50 | .23 |
| ❑ 100 Pierre Turgeon | .50 | .23 |
| ❑ 101 Tony Amonte | .50 | .23 |
| ❑ 102 Timo Ahmaoja | .50 | .23 |
| ❑ 103 Rob Blake | .20 | .09 |
| ❑ 104 Derek Morris | .20 | .09 |
| ❑ 105 Alex Tanguay | 6.00 | 2.70 |
| ❑ 106 Peter Forsberg | 2.00 | .90 |
| ❑ 107 Shayne Corson | .20 | .09 |
| ❑ 108 Tyler Moss | .20 | .09 |
| ❑ 109 Adam Oates | .50 | .23 |
| ❑ 110 Keith Tkachuk | .75 | .35 |
| ❑ 111 Alexei Yashin | .50 | .23 |
| ❑ 112 Joe Thornton | 1.25 | .55 |
| ❑ 113 Andy Moog | .50 | .23 |
| ❑ 114 Daniel Sedin | 10.00 | 4.50 |
| ❑ 115 Pavel Bure | 1.25 | .55 |
| ❑ 116 Denis Shvidky RC | 2.50 | 1.10 |
| ❑ 117 Jason Arnott | .20 | .09 |
| ❑ 118 Mike Johnson | 2.00 | .90 |
| ❑ 119 Nicklas Lidstrom | .50 | .23 |
| ❑ 120 Mattias Ohlund | .50 | .23 |
| ❑ 121 Alexander Selivanov | .20 | .09 |
| ❑ 122 Martin Brodeur | 1.50 | .70 |
| ❑ 123 Steve Yzerman | 2.00 | .90 |
| ❑ 124 Dimitri Vlassenkov | .50 | .23 |
| ❑ 125 Jeff Farkas | .50 | .23 |
| ❑ 126 Curtis Joseph | .60 | .25 |
| ❑ 127 Yanic Perreault | .20 | .09 |
| ❑ 128 Alyn McCauley | .50 | .23 |
| ❑ 129 Vyacheslav Kozlov | .20 | .09 |
| ❑ 130 Alexei Morozov | .50 | .23 |
| ❑ 131 Roberto Luongo | 6.00 | 2.70 |
| ❑ 132 Jarome Iginla | .50 | .23 |
| ❑ 133 Pat LaFontaine | .50 | .23 |
| ❑ 134 Ed Belfour | .60 | .25 |
| ❑ 135 Toby Peterson | .50 | .23 |
| ❑ 136 Henrik Sedin RC | 8.00 | 3.60 |
| ❑ 137 Marcus Nilson | .20 | .09 |
| ❑ 138 Cameron Mann | .60 | .25 |
| ❑ 139 Eero Somervuori | 1.00 | .45 |
| ❑ 140 Patrick Marleau | 1.25 | .55 |
| ❑ 141 Ed Jovanovski | .50 | .23 |
| ❑ 142 Roman Hamrlik | .20 | .09 |
| ❑ 143 Theoren Fleury | .50 | .23 |
| ❑ 144 Wayne Gretzky | 4.00 | 1.80 |
| ❑ 145 Eric Lindros | 2.00 | .90 |
| ❑ 146 Boyd Deveraux | .20 | .09 |
| ❑ 147 Sami Kapanen | .50 | .23 |
| ❑ 148 Grant Fuhr | .20 | .09 |
| ❑ 149 Brendan Shanahan | 1.25 | .55 |
| ❑ 150 Vincent Lecavalier | 20.00 | 9.00 |

## 1997-98 Upper Deck Black Diamond Double Diamond

Inserted one in every pack, this 150-card set is a two black diamond parallel version of the Upper Deck Black Diamond base set.

| | MINT | NRMT |
|---|---|---|
| COMPLETE SET (150) | 250.00 | 110.00 |
| COMMON CARD (1-150) | .40 | .18 |
| *STARS: 1X TO 2X BASIC CARDS | | |
| *YOUNG STARS: .75 X TO 1.5X | | |
| *RC's: .5X TO 1.25X | | |

## 1997-98 Upper Deck Black Diamond Triple Diamond

Randomly inserted in packs at the rate of one in three, this 150-card set is an all-gold Light F/X parallel version of the base set with three black diamonds printed on the card fronts.

| | MINT | NRMT |
|---|---|---|
| COMPLETE SET (150) | 1000.00 | 450.00 |
| COMMON CARD (1-150) | 1.50 | .70 |
| *STARS: 4X TO 8X BASIC CARDS | | |
| *YOUNG STARS: 3X TO 6X BASIC CARDS | | |
| *RC's: 2X TO 4X BASIC CARDS | | |

## 1997-98 Upper Deck Black Diamond Quadruple Diamond

Randomly inserted in packs, this 150-card set is an all-black Light F/X parallel version of the base set with four black diamonds printed on the card fronts. Only 50 sets were produced.

| | MINT | NRMT |
|---|---|---|
| COMMON CARD (1-150) | 20.00 | 9.00 |
| SEMISTARS/GOALIES | 50.00 | 22.00 |
| UNLISTED STARS | 60.00 | 27.00 |
| *STARS: 50X TO 100X BASIC CARDS | | |
| *YOUNG STARS: 40X TO 80X BASIC CARDS | | |
| *RC's: 10X TO 20X BASIC CARDS | | |

## 1997-98 Upper Deck Black Diamond Premium Cut

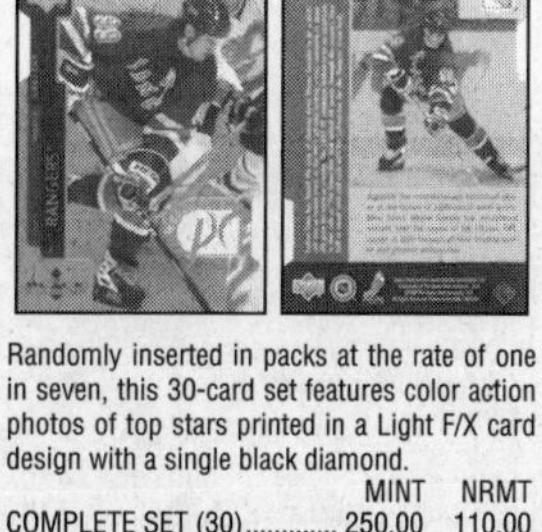

Randomly inserted in packs at the rate of one in seven, this 30-card set features color action photos of top stars printed in a Light F/X card design with a single black diamond.

| | MINT | NRMT |
|---|---|---|
| COMPLETE SET (30) | 250.00 | 110.00 |
| COMMON CARD (PC1-PC30) | 4.00 | 1.80 |
| ❑ PC1 Wayne Gretzky | 30.00 | 13.50 |
| ❑ PC2 Patrick Roy | 25.00 | 11.00 |
| ❑ PC3 Brendan Shanahan | 10.00 | 4.50 |
| ❑ PC4 Ray Bourque | 5.00 | 2.20 |
| ❑ PC5 Alexei Morozov | 4.00 | 1.80 |
| ❑ PC6 John LeClair | 8.00 | 3.60 |
| ❑ PC7 Steve Yzerman | 15.00 | 6.75 |
| ❑ PC8 Patrik Elias | 5.00 | 2.20 |
| ❑ PC9 Pavel Bure | 10.00 | 4.50 |
| ❑ PC10 Brian Leetch | 5.00 | 2.20 |
| ❑ PC11 Peter Forsberg | 15.00 | 6.75 |
| ❑ PC12 Marco Sturm | 5.00 | 2.20 |
| ❑ PC13 Eric Lindros | 15.00 | 6.75 |
| ❑ PC14 Keith Tkachuk | 6.00 | 2.70 |
| ❑ PC15 Teemu Selanne | 10.00 | 4.50 |
| ❑ PC16 Bryan Berard | 4.00 | 1.80 |
| ❑ PC17 Joe Thornton | 6.00 | 2.70 |
| ❑ PC18 Brett Hull | 6.00 | 2.70 |
| ❑ PC19 Nicklas Lidstrom | 4.00 | 1.80 |
| ❑ PC20 Jaromir Jagr | 15.00 | 6.75 |
| ❑ PC21 Vaclav Prospal | 5.00 | 2.20 |
| ❑ PC22 Pat LaFontaine | 4.00 | 1.80 |
| ❑ PC23 Mark Messier | 6.00 | 2.70 |
| ❑ PC24 Martin Brodeur | 12.00 | 5.50 |
| ❑ PC25 Mike Modano | 6.00 | 2.70 |
| ❑ PC26 Paul Kariya | 20.00 | 9.00 |
| ❑ PC27 Mike Johnson | 5.00 | 2.20 |
| ❑ PC28 Sergei Samsonov | 10.00 | 4.50 |
| ❑ PC29 Joe Sakic | 10.00 | 4.50 |
| ❑ PC30 Mats Sundin | 5.00 | 2.20 |

## 1997-98 Upper Deck Black Diamond Premium Cut Double Diamond

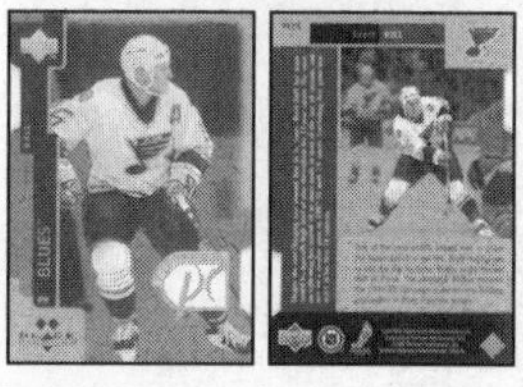

Randomly inserted in packs at the rate of one in 15, this 30-card set is a parallel version of the regular insert set with two black diamonds on the card fronts.

| | MINT | NRMT |
|---|---|---|
| COMPLETE SET (30) | 400.00 | 180.00 |
| COMMON CARD (PC1-PC30) | 6.00 | 2.70 |
| *DOUBLE DIAMONDS: .75X TO 1.5X BASIC CARDS | | |

## 1997-98 Upper Deck Black Diamond Premium Cut Quadruple Diamond Horizontal

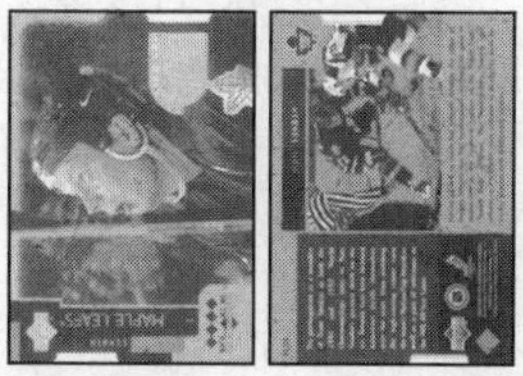

This 30-card hobby only set is a special black Light F/X, embossed, horizontal, die-cut version of the regular insert set with various insertion rates. Cards #8, 10, 16, 17, 18, 19, 23, 27, 29 and 30 have an insertion rate of 1:30; #4, 5, 7, 12, 14, 15, 21, 22, 25 and 26 have a 1:90 insertion rate; #6, 9, 11, 20, 24 and 28 have a 1:2000 insertion rate; #3 and 13 have a 1:15,000 insertion rate; and #1 and 2 have a 1:30,000 insertion rate.

| | MINT | NRMT |
|---|---|---|
| COMPLETE SET (30) | 5000.00 | 2200.00 |
| COMMON CARD (PC1-PC30) | 4.00 | 1.80 |
| ❑ PC1 Wayne Gretzky | 1500.00 | 700.00 |
| ❑ PC2 Patrick Roy | 1000.00 | 450.00 |
| ❑ PC3 Brendan Shanahan | 400.00 | 180.00 |
| ❑ PC4 Ray Bourque | 12.00 | 5.50 |
| ❑ PC5 Alexei Morozov | 10.00 | 4.50 |
| ❑ PC6 John LeClair | 150.00 | 70.00 |
| ❑ PC7 Steve Yzerman | 40.00 | 18.00 |
| ❑ PC8 Patrik Elias | 6.00 | 2.70 |
| ❑ PC9 Pavel Bure | 200.00 | 90.00 |
| ❑ PC10 Brian Leetch | 5.00 | 2.20 |
| ❑ PC11 Peter Forsberg | 300.00 | 135.00 |
| ❑ PC12 Marco Sturm | 20.00 | 9.00 |
| ❑ PC13 Eric Lindros | 500.00 | 220.00 |
| ❑ PC14 Keith Tkachuk | 15.00 | 6.75 |
| ❑ PC15 Teemu Selanne | 25.00 | 11.00 |
| ❑ PC16 Bryan Berard | 4.00 | 1.80 |
| ❑ PC17 Joe Thornton | 10.00 | 4.50 |
| ❑ PC18 Brett Hull | 6.00 | 2.70 |
| ❑ PC19 Nicklas Lidstrom | 4.00 | 1.80 |
| ❑ PC20 Jaromir Jagr | 300.00 | 135.00 |
| ❑ PC21 Vaclav Prospal | 20.00 | 9.00 |
| ❑ PC22 Pat LaFontaine | 10.00 | 4.50 |
| ❑ PC23 Mark Messier | 6.00 | 2.70 |
| ❑ PC24 Martin Brodeur | 250.00 | 110.00 |
| ❑ PC25 Mike Modano | 15.00 | 6.75 |
| ❑ PC26 Paul Kariya | 50.00 | 22.00 |
| ❑ PC27 Mike Johnson | 6.00 | 2.70 |
| ❑ PC28 Sergei Samsonov | 150.00 | 70.00 |
| ❑ PC29 Joe Sakic | 10.00 | 4.50 |
| ❑ PC30 Mats Sundin | 5.00 | 2.20 |

## 1997-98 Upper Deck Black Diamond Premium Cut Triple Diamond

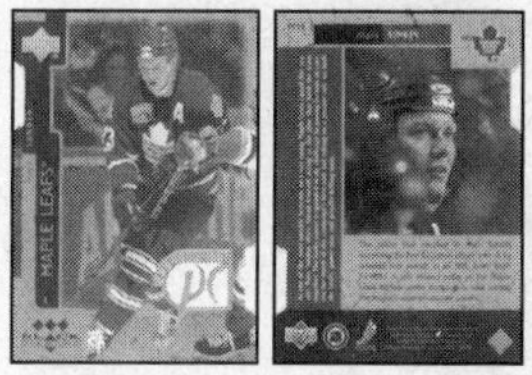

Randomly inserted in packs at the rate of one in 30, this 30-card set is a parallel version of the regular insert set with three black diamonds on the card fronts.

| | MINT | NRMT |
|---|---|---|
| COMPLETE SET (30) | 600.00 | 275.00 |
| COMMON CARD (PC1-PC30) | 10.00 | 4.50 |
| *TRIPLE DIAMONDS: 1.25X TO 2.5X BASIC CARDS | 10.00 | 4.50 |

## 1997-98 Upper Deck Black Diamond Premium Cut Quadruple Diamond Verticals

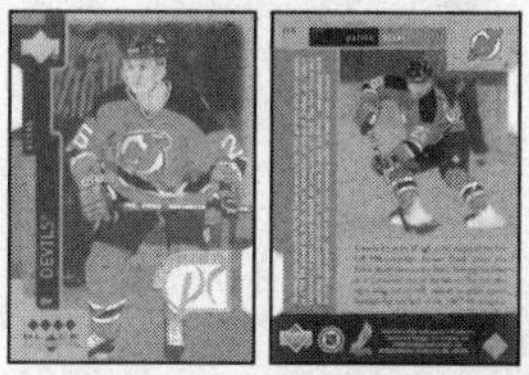

Randomly inserted in packs at the rate of one in 180, this 30-card set is a parallel version of the regular insert set with four black diamonds on the card fronts.

| | MINT | NRMT |
|---|---|---|
| COMPLETE SET (30) | 2500.00 | 1100.00 |
| COMMON CARD (PC1-PC30) | 40.00 | 18.00 |
| *QUAD.VERT.STARS: 4X TO 10X BASIC CARDS | | |

## 1998-99 Upper Deck Black Diamond

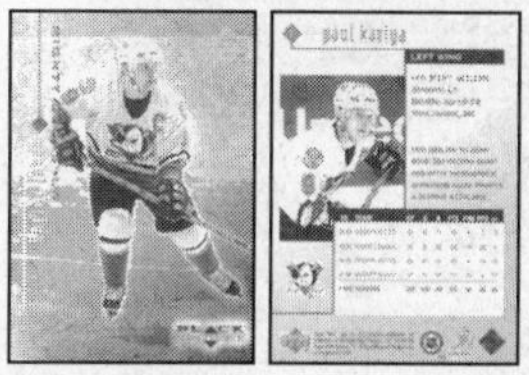

The 1998-99 Upper Deck Black Diamond set was issued in one series for a total of 120 cards and was distributed in six-card packs with a suggested retail price of $3.99. The fronts feature color action player photos reproduced on Light F/X card stock with foil treatment and one, two, three, or four Black Diamonds designating its rarity. Cards 1-90 are regular player cards with cards 91-120 displaying top prospect players and an insertion rate of 1:4 for the single diamond cards. The backs carry player information and statistics. Only 2,000 Double Diamond sets were produced, 1,000 Triple Diamond sets, and 100 Quadruple Diamond sets.

| | MINT | NRMT |
|---|---|---|
| COMPLETE SET (120) | 200.00 | 90.00 |
| COMMON CARD (1-90) | .25 | .11 |
| COMMON SP (91-120) | 3.00 | 1.35 |
| COMP.DBL.SET (120) | 700.00 | 325.00 |
| COMMON DBL.(1-120) | 1.25 | .55 |
| *DOUBLE STARS: 2.5X TO 5X BASIC CARDS | | |
| *DOUBLE YNG.STARS:1.5 X TO 3X | | |
| *DOUBLE RC's:.75 X TO 1.5X | | |
| DOUBLE STATED PRINT RUN 2000 SETS | | |
| COMP.TRPL.SET (120) | 1500.00 | 700.00 |
| COMMON TRPL.(1-120) | 2.50 | 1.10 |
| *TRIPLE STARS: 5X TO 10X BASIC CARDS | | |
| *TRIPLE YNG.STARS: 3X TO 6X | | |
| *TRIPLE RC's: 1.5X TO 3X | | |
| TRIPLE STATED PRINT RUN 1000 SETS | | |
| COMP.QUAD.SET (120) | 12000.00 | 5400.00 |
| COMMON QUAD. (1-120) | 20.00 | 9.00 |

*QUAD STARS: 40X TO 80X BASIC CARDS
*QUAD YNG.STARS: 25X TO 50X
*QUAD SP's: 6X TO 12X
QUAD.STATED PRINT RUN 100 SETS

| | | |
|---|---|---|
| ❑ 1 Paul Kariya | 2.50 | 1.10 |
| ❑ 2 Teemu Selanne | 1.25 | .55 |
| ❑ 3 Johan Davidsson | .25 | .11 |
| ❑ 4 Ray Bourque | .60 | .25 |
| ❑ 5 Sergei Samsonov | 1.00 | .45 |
| ❑ 6 Jason Allison | .50 | .23 |
| ❑ 7 Joe Thornton | .25 | .11 |
| ❑ 8 Miroslav Satan | .50 | .23 |
| ❑ 9 Brian Holzinger | .25 | .11 |
| ❑ 10 Dominik Hasek | 1.25 | .55 |
| ❑ 11 Rico Fata | .25 | .11 |
| ❑ 12 Jarome Iginla | .25 | .11 |
| ❑ 13 Theoren Fleury | .60 | .25 |
| ❑ 14 Ron Francis | .50 | .23 |
| ❑ 15 Gary Roberts | .25 | .11 |
| ❑ 16 Keith Primeau | .50 | .23 |
| ❑ 17 Sami Kapanen | .50 | .23 |
| ❑ 18 Doug Gilmour | .60 | .25 |
| ❑ 19 Chris Chelios | .60 | .25 |
| ❑ 20 Tony Amonte | .50 | .23 |
| ❑ 21 Peter Forsberg | 2.00 | .90 |
| ❑ 22 Patrick Roy | 3.00 | 1.35 |
| ❑ 23 Joe Sakic | 1.25 | .55 |
| ❑ 24 Chris Drury | .50 | .23 |
| ❑ 25 Brett Hull | .75 | .35 |
| ❑ 26 Ed Belfour | .60 | .25 |
| ❑ 27 Mike Modano | .75 | .35 |
| ❑ 28 Darryl Sydor | .25 | .11 |
| ❑ 29 Sergei Fedorov | 1.25 | .55 |
| ❑ 30 Steve Yzerman | 2.00 | .90 |
| ❑ 31 Nicklas Lidstrom | .50 | .23 |
| ❑ 32 Chris Osgood | .60 | .25 |
| ❑ 33 Brendan Shanahan | 1.25 | .55 |
| ❑ 34 Doug Weight | .50 | .23 |
| ❑ 35 Bill Guerin | .25 | .11 |
| ❑ 36 Tom Poti | .25 | .11 |
| ❑ 37 Ed Jovanovski | .25 | .11 |
| ❑ 38 Mark Parrish | 2.00 | .90 |
| ❑ 39 Rob Niedermayer | .25 | .11 |
| ❑ 40 Pavel Rosa | .25 | .11 |
| ❑ 41 Rob Blake | .25 | .11 |
| ❑ 42 Olli Jokinen | .50 | .23 |
| ❑ 43 Vincent Damphousse | .50 | .23 |
| ❑ 44 Mark Recchi | .50 | .23 |
| ❑ 45 Terry Ryan | .25 | .11 |
| ❑ 46 Saku Koivu | 1.00 | .45 |
| ❑ 47 Mike Dunham | .50 | .23 |
| ❑ 48 Sergei Krivokrasov | .25 | .11 |
| ❑ 49 Scott Stevens | .25 | .11 |
| ❑ 50 Martin Brodeur | 1.50 | .70 |
| ❑ 51 Brendan Morrison | .50 | .23 |
| ❑ 52 Eric Brewer | .25 | .11 |
| ❑ 53 Zigmund Palffy | .60 | .25 |
| ❑ 54 Bryan Berard | .25 | .11 |
| ❑ 55 Wayne Gretzky | 4.00 | 1.80 |
| ❑ 56 Brian Leetch | .60 | .25 |
| ❑ 58 Mike Richter | .60 | .25 |
| ❑ 59 Alexei Yashin | .50 | .23 |
| ❑ 60 Wade Redden | .25 | .11 |
| ❑ 61 Daniel Alfredsson | .50 | .23 |
| ❑ 62 Eric Lindros | 2.00 | .90 |
| ❑ 63 John LeClair | 1.00 | .45 |
| ❑ 64 John Vanbiesbrouck | 1.00 | .45 |
| ❑ 65 Rod Brind'Amour | .50 | .23 |
| ❑ 66 Keith Tkachuk | .75 | .35 |
| ❑ 67 Daniel Briere | .25 | .11 |
| ❑ 68 Jeremy Roenick | .60 | .25 |
| ❑ 69 Jaromir Jagr | 2.00 | .90 |
| ❑ 70 German Titov | .25 | .11 |
| ❑ 71 Alexei Morozov | .50 | .23 |
| ❑ 72 Patrick Marleau | .25 | .11 |
| ❑ 73 Andrei Zyuzin | .25 | .11 |
| ❑ 74 Mike Vernon | .50 | .23 |
| ❑ 75 Owen Nolan | .50 | .23 |
| ❑ 76 Marty Reasoner | .25 | .11 |
| ❑ 77 Al MacInnis | .50 | .23 |
| ❑ 78 Chris Pronger | .50 | .23 |
| ❑ 79 Wendel Clark | .50 | .23 |
| ❑ 80 Vincent Lecavalier | 1.50 | .70 |
| ❑ 81 Craig Janney | .25 | .11 |
| ❑ 82 Tomas Kaberle | .50 | .23 |
| ❑ 83 Curtis Joseph | .60 | .25 |
| ❑ 84 Mats Sundin | .60 | .25 |
| ❑ 85 Mark Messier | .75 | .35 |
| ❑ 86 Bill Muckalt RC | 1.50 | .70 |
| ❑ 87 Mattias Ohlund | .50 | .23 |
| ❑ 88 Peter Bondra | .60 | .25 |
| ❑ 89 Olaf Kolzig | .50 | .23 |
| ❑ 90 Richard Zednik | .25 | .11 |
| ❑ 91 Harold Druken SP | 3.00 | 1.35 |
| ❑ 92 Roberto Luongo SP | 10.00 | 4.50 |
| ❑ 93 Daniel Tkaczuk SP | 3.00 | 1.35 |
| ❑ 94 Brenden Morrow SP | 8.00 | 3.60 |
| ❑ 95 Mike Van Ryn SP | 3.00 | 1.35 |
| ❑ 96 Brian Finley SP | 12.00 | 5.50 |
| ❑ 97 Jani Rita SP | 10.00 | 4.50 |
| ❑ 98 Iikka Mikkola SP | 3.00 | 1.35 |
| ❑ 99 Mikko Jokela SP | 3.00 | 1.35 |
| ❑ 100 Tommi Santala SP | 3.00 | 1.35 |
| ❑ 101 Teemu Virkkunnen SP | 3.00 | 1.35 |
| ❑ 102 Arto Laatikainen SP | 3.00 | 1.35 |
| ❑ 103 Kirill Safronov SP | 8.00 | 3.60 |
| ❑ 104 Alexei Volkov SP | 8.00 | 3.60 |
| ❑ 105 Denis Arkhipov SP | 8.00 | 3.60 |
| ❑ 106 Alexander Zevakhi SP | 3.00 | 1.35 |
| ❑ 107 Denis Shvidki SP | 8.00 | 3.60 |
| ❑ 108 Maxim Afinogenov SP | 10.00 | 4.50 |
| ❑ 109 Daniel Sedin SP | 8.00 | 3.60 |
| ❑ 110 Henrik Sedin SP | 6.00 | 2.70 |
| ❑ 111 Jimmie Olvestad SP | 3.00 | 1.35 |
| ❑ 112 Mattias Weinhandl SP | 3.00 | 1.35 |
| ❑ 113 Mathias Tjarnqvist SP | 3.00 | 1.35 |
| ❑ 114 Jakob Johnansson SP | 3.00 | 1.35 |
| ❑ 115 David Legwand SP | 12.00 | 5.50 |
| ❑ 116 Barrett Heisten SP | 6.00 | 2.70 |
| ❑ 117 Tim Connolly SP | 10.00 | 4.50 |
| ❑ 118 Andy Hilbert SP | 3.00 | 1.35 |
| ❑ 119 Joe Blackburn SP | 6.00 | 2.70 |
| ❑ 120 Dave Tanabe SP | 3.00 | 1.35 |

## 1998-99 Upper Deck Black Diamond Myriad 1

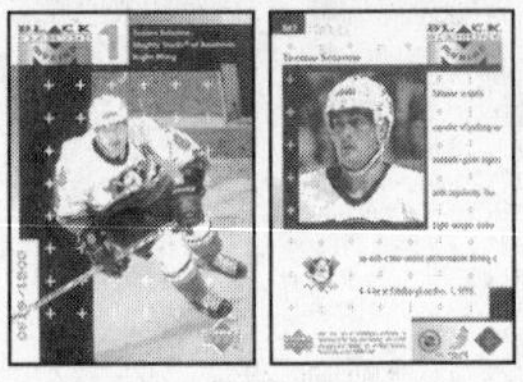

Randomly inserted into packs, this 30-card set features color action photos of the current top NHL's superstars. Only 1,500 serially numbered sets were produced. A limited edition parallel version of this set, Myriad 2, was produced and numbered 1 of 1.

| | MINT | NRMT |
|---|---|---|
| COMPLETE SET (30) | 400.00 | 180.00 |
| COMMON CARD (M1-M30) | 4.00 | 1.80 |

MYRIAD 2 ONE OF ONE PARALLEL EXISTS

| | | |
|---|---|---|
| ❑ M1 Vincent Lecavalier | 15.00 | 6.75 |
| ❑ M2 John Vanbiesbrouck | 10.00 | 4.50 |
| ❑ M3 Paul Kariya | 25.00 | 11.00 |
| ❑ M4 Keith Tkachuk | 8.00 | 3.60 |
| ❑ M5 Mike Modano | 8.00 | 3.60 |
| ❑ M6 Dominik Hasek | 12.00 | 5.50 |
| ❑ M7 Teemu Selanne | 12.00 | 5.50 |
| ❑ M9 Brendan Shanahan | 12.00 | 5.50 |
| ❑ M10 Pavel Bure | 12.00 | 5.50 |
| ❑ M11 Chris Drury | 8.00 | 3.60 |
| ❑ M12 Curtis Joseph | 6.00 | 2.70 |
| ❑ M13 Joe Sakic | 12.00 | 5.50 |
| ❑ M14 Eric Lindros | 20.00 | 9.00 |
| ❑ M15 Peter Bondra | 6.00 | 2.70 |
| ❑ M16 Brett Hull | 8.00 | 3.60 |
| ❑ M17 Ray Bourque | 6.00 | 2.70 |
| ❑ M18 Jaromir Jagr | 20.00 | 9.00 |
| ❑ M19 Steve Yzerman | 20.00 | 9.00 |
| ❑ M20 Mark Parrish | 15.00 | 6.75 |
| ❑ M21 Martin Brodeur | 15.00 | 6.75 |
| ❑ M22 Saku Koivu | 10.00 | 4.50 |
| ❑ M23 Patrick Roy | 30.00 | 13.50 |
| ❑ M24 John LeClair | 10.00 | 4.50 |
| ❑ M25 Doug Gilmour | 6.00 | 2.70 |
| ❑ M26 Sergei Fedorov | 12.00 | 5.50 |
| ❑ M27 Wayne Gretzky | 40.00 | 18.00 |
| ❑ M28 Peter Forsberg | 20.00 | 9.00 |
| ❑ M29 Eric Brewer | 4.00 | 1.80 |
| ❑ M30 Sergei Samsonov | 10.00 | 4.50 |

## 1998-99 Upper Deck Black Diamond Winning Formula Gold

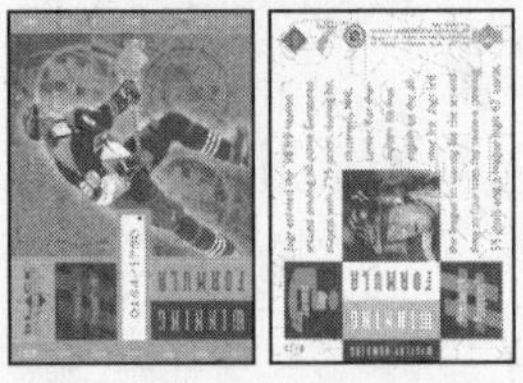

Randomly inserted into hobby packs only, this 30-card set features color photos of top players and goalies. Each card is sequentially numbered to the pictured player's goals or goalie's wins multiplied times 50.

| | MINT | NRMT |
|---|---|---|
| COMPLETE SET (30) | 500.00 | 220.00 |
| COMMON CARD (WF1-WF30) | 6.00 | 2.70 |

| | | |
|---|---|---|
| ❑ WF1 Paul Kariya/850 | 50.00 | 22.00 |
| ❑ WF2 Teemu Selanne/2600 | 12.00 | 5.50 |
| ❑ WF3 Sergei Samsonov/1100 | 20.00 | 9.00 |
| ❑ WF4 Dominik Hasek/1650 | 15.00 | 6.75 |
| ❑ WF5 Vincent Lecavalier/2200 | 15.00 | 6.75 |
| ❑ WF6 Patrick Roy/1550 | 40.00 | 18.00 |
| ❑ WF7 Peter Forsberg/1250 | 25.00 | 11.00 |
| ❑ WF8 Joe Sakic/1350 | 20.00 | 9.00 |
| ❑ WF9 Ed Belfour/1850 | 8.00 | 3.60 |
| ❑ WF10 Brendan Shanahan/1400 | 20.00 | 9.00 |
| ❑ WF11 Steve Yzerman/1200 | 30.00 | 13.50 |
| ❑ WF12 Chris Osgood/1650 | 8.00 | 3.60 |
| ❑ WF13 Curtis Joseph/1450 | 8.00 | 3.60 |
| ❑ WF14 Manny Malhotra/800 | 15.00 | 6.75 |
| ❑ WF15 Martin Brodeur/2150 | 15.00 | 6.75 |
| ❑ WF16 Chris Drury/1400 | 8.00 | 3.60 |
| ❑ WF17 Zigmund Palffy/2250 | 6.00 | 2.70 |
| ❑ WF18 Wayne Gretzky/1150 | 60.00 | 27.00 |
| ❑ WF19 Theoren Fleury/1350 | 10.00 | 4.50 |
| ❑ WF20 Alexei Yashin/1650 | 8.00 | 3.60 |
| ❑ WF21 Eric Lindros/1500 | 30.00 | 13.50 |
| ❑ WF22 John LeClair/2550 | 8.00 | 3.60 |
| ❑ WF23 Keith Tkachuk/2000 | 10.00 | 4.50 |
| ❑ WF24 Mark Messier/1100 | 15.00 | 6.75 |
| ❑ WF25 Jaromir Jagr/1750 | 30.00 | 13.50 |
| ❑ WF26 Brett Hull/1350 | 12.00 | 5.50 |
| ❑ WF27 Mats Sundin/1650 | 10.00 | 4.50 |
| ❑ WF28 Pavel Bure/2550 | 12.00 | 5.50 |
| ❑ WF29 Peter Bondra/2600 | 6.00 | 2.70 |
| ❑ WF30 Mike Modano/1050 | 15.00 | 6.75 |

## 1998-99 Upper Deck Black Diamond Winning Formula Platinum

Randomly inserted into packs, this 30-card set is a platinum foil parallel version of the regular Winning Formula set. Each card is numbered to the player's actual accomplishments.

| | MINT | NRMT |
|---|---|---|
| COMPLETE SET (30) | 8000.00 | 3600.00 |
| COMMON CARD (WF1-WF30) | 100.00 | 45.00 |

| | | |
|---|---|---|
| ❑ WF1 Paul Kariya/17 | 800.00 | 350.00 |
| ❑ WF2 Teemu Selanne/52 | 150.00 | 70.00 |
| ❑ WF3 Sergei Samsonov/22 | 250.00 | 110.00 |
| ❑ WF4 Dominik Hasek/33 | 250.00 | 110.00 |
| ❑ WF5 Vincent Lecavalier/44 | 200.00 | 90.00 |
| ❑ WF6 Patrick Roy/31 | 600.00 | 275.00 |
| ❑ WF7 Peter Forsberg/25 | 500.00 | 220.00 |
| ❑ WF8 Joe Sakic/27 | 250.00 | 110.00 |
| ❑ WF9 Ed Belfour/37 | 120.00 | 55.00 |
| ❑ WF10 Brendan Shanahan/28 | 250.00 | 110.00 |
| ❑ WF11 Steve Yzerman/24 | 500.00 | 220.00 |
| ❑ WF12 Chris Osgood/33 | 120.00 | 55.00 |
| ❑ WF13 Curtis Joseph/29 | 120.00 | 55.00 |
| ❑ WF14 Manny Malhotra/16 | 100.00 | 45.00 |
| ❑ WF15 Martin Brodeur/43 | 250.00 | 110.00 |
| ❑ WF16 Chris Drury/28 | 100.00 | 45.00 |
| ❑ WF17 Zigmund Palffy/45 | 120.00 | 55.00 |
| ❑ WF18 Wayne Gretzky/23 | 1000.00 | 450.00 |
| ❑ WF19 Theoren Fleury/27 | 120.00 | 55.00 |
| ❑ WF20 Alexei Yashin/33 | 100.00 | 45.00 |
| ❑ WF21 Eric Lindros/30 | 400.00 | 180.00 |
| ❑ WF22 John LeClair/51 | 150.00 | 70.00 |
| ❑ WF23 Keith Tkachuk/40 | 150.00 | 70.00 |
| ❑ WF24 Mark Messier/22 | 200.00 | 90.00 |
| ❑ WF25 Jaromir Jagr/35 | 400.00 | 180.00 |
| ❑ WF26 Brett Hull/27 | 150.00 | 70.00 |
| ❑ WF27 Mats Sundin/33 | 120.00 | 55.00 |
| ❑ WF28 Pavel Bure/51 | 200.00 | 90.00 |
| ❑ WF29 Peter Bondra/52 | 100.00 | 45.00 |
| ❑ WF30 Mike Modano/21 | 200.00 | 90.00 |

## 1998-99 Upper Deck Black Diamond Year of the Great One

Randomly inserted into packs, this 99-card set features color photos of the great Wayne Gretzky. Cards 1-45 are marked with a single diamond; 46-75 display double diamonds; 76-90 show triple diamonds; and 91-99 carry quadruple diamonds. Each card is sequentially numbered to 99.

| | MINT | NRMT |
|---|---|---|
| COMMON YOTG (1-99) | 400.00 | 180.00 |

CARDS 1-45: SINGLE DIAMOND
CARDS 46-75: DOUBLE DIAMOND
CARDS 76-90: TRIPLE DIAMOND
CARDS 91-99: QUADRUPLE DIAMOND

## 1997-98 Upper Deck Diamond Vision

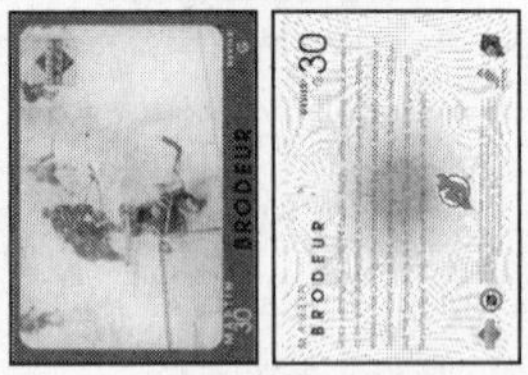

This 25-card set was distributed in one-card packs with a suggested retail price of $7.99. The cards feature actual NHL game footage of the named player on each card combined with the latest technology to create fluid action sequences. Inserted one in every 500 packs is a Wayne Gretzky REEL Time card which displays his greatest moments in frame-by-frame action imagery.

| | MINT | NRMT |
|---|---|---|
| COMPLETE SET (25) | 250.00 | 110.00 |
| COMMON CARD (1-25) | 4.00 | 1.80 |

| | | |
|---|---|---|
| ❑ 1 Wayne Gretzky | 30.00 | 13.50 |
| ❑ 2 Patrick Roy | 25.00 | 11.00 |
| ❑ 3 Jaromir Jagr | 15.00 | 6.75 |
| ❑ 4 Steve Yzerman | 15.00 | 6.75 |
| ❑ 5 Martin Brodeur | 12.00 | 5.50 |
| ❑ 6 Paul Kariya | 20.00 | 9.00 |
| ❑ 7 John Vanbiesbrouck | 8.00 | 3.60 |
| ❑ 8 Ray Bourque | 5.00 | 2.20 |
| ❑ 9 Theoren Fleury | 4.00 | 1.80 |
| ❑ 10 Pavel Bure | 10.00 | 4.50 |
| ❑ 11 Brendan Shanahan | 10.00 | 4.50 |
| ❑ 12 Brian Leetch | 5.00 | 2.20 |
| ❑ 13 Owen Nolan | 4.00 | 1.80 |
| ❑ 14 Peter Forsberg | 15.00 | 6.75 |
| ❑ 15 Doug Weight | 4.00 | 1.80 |
| ❑ 16 Teemu Selanne | 10.00 | 4.50 |
| ❑ 17 Mats Sundin | 5.00 | 2.20 |
| ❑ 18 Keith Tkachuk | 6.00 | 2.70 |
| ❑ 19 Tony Amonte | 4.00 | 1.80 |
| ❑ 20 Joe Sakic | 10.00 | 4.50 |
| ❑ 21 Zigmund Palffy | 5.00 | 2.20 |
| ❑ 22 Eric Lindros | 15.00 | 6.75 |
| ❑ 23 Sergei Fedorov | 10.00 | 4.50 |
| ❑ 24 Dominik Hasek | 10.00 | 4.50 |
| ❑ 25 Brett Hull | 6.00 | 2.70 |
| ❑ RT1 W. Gretzky REEL TIME | 250.00 | 110.00 |

## 1997-98 Upper Deck Diamond Vision Signature Moves

Randomly inserted in packs at the rate of one in five, this 25-card set is parallel to the regular Diamond Vision set only with a facsimile signature of the player pictured on the card.

| | MINT | NRMT |
|---|---|---|
| COMPLETE SET (25) | 500.00 | 220.00 |
| COMMON CARD (1-25) | 8.00 | 3.60 |

*SIGNATURE MOVES: 1X TO 2X BASIC CARDS

## 1997-98 Upper Deck Diamond Vision Defining Moments

Randomly inserted in packs at the rate of one in 40, this six-card set features incredible action technology to show the memorable highlights of the pictured player's career.

| | MINT | NRMT |
|---|---|---|
| COMPLETE SET (6) | 400.00 | 180.00 |
| COMMON CARD (1-6) | 40.00 | 18.00 |

| | | |
|---|---|---|
| ❑ DM1 Wayne Gretzky | 120.00 | 55.00 |
| ❑ DM2 Patrick Roy | 100.00 | 45.00 |
| ❑ DM3 Steve Yzerman | 60.00 | 27.00 |
| ❑ DM4 Jaromir Jagr | 60.00 | 27.00 |
| ❑ DM5 Joe Sakic | 40.00 | 18.00 |
| ❑ DM6 Brendan Shanahan | 40.00 | 18.00 |

## 1998-99 Upper Deck Gold Reserve

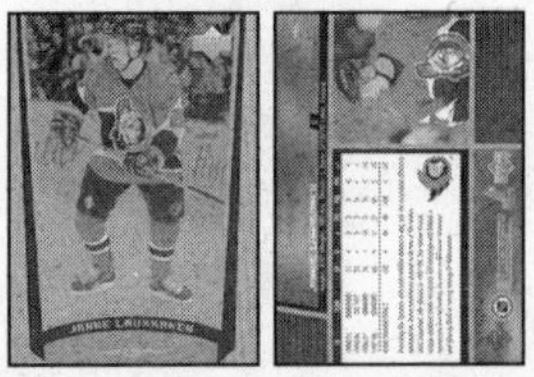

Randomly inserted into packs, this 420-card set is a gold foil parallel version of the base set.

| | MINT | NRMT |
|---|---|---|
| COMPLETE SET (420) | 250.00 | 110.00 |
| COMP.SER.1 SET (210) | 150.00 | 70.00 |
| COMP.SER.2 SET (210) | 100.00 | 45.00 |
| COMMON CARD (1-420) | .40 | .18 |
| COMMON SR,RR (1-15,16-30) | 2.00 | .90 |
| COMMON PE,CC (391-420) | 2.50 | 1.10 |

| | | |
|---|---|---|
| ❑ 1 Antti Aalto SR | 2.00 | .90 |
| ❑ 2 Cameron Mann SR | 2.00 | .90 |
| ❑ 3 Norm Maracle SR | 6.00 | 2.70 |
| ❑ 4 Daniel Cleary SR | 2.00 | .90 |
| ❑ 5 Brendan Morrison SR | 6.00 | 2.70 |
| ❑ 6 Marian Hossa SR | 2.00 | .90 |
| ❑ 7 Daniel Briere SR | 2.00 | .90 |
| ❑ 8 Mike Crowley SR | 2.00 | .90 |
| ❑ 9 Darryl Laplante SR | 2.00 | .90 |
| ❑ 10 Suem Butenschen SR | 2.00 | .90 |
| ❑ 11 Yan Golubovsky SR | 2.00 | .90 |
| ❑ 12 Olli Jokinen SR | 6.00 | 2.70 |
| ❑ 13 Jean-Sebastien Giguere SR | 2.00 | .90 |
| ❑ 14 Mike Watt SR | 2.00 | .90 |
| ❑ 15 Ryan Johnson SR | 2.00 | .90 |
| ❑ 16 Teemu Selanne RR | 10.00 | 4.50 |
| ❑ 17 Paul Kariya RR | 20.00 | 9.00 |
| ❑ 18 Pavel Bure RR | 10.00 | 4.50 |
| ❑ 19 Joe Thornton RR | 2.00 | .90 |
| ❑ 20 Dominik Hasek RR | 10.00 | 4.50 |
| ❑ 21 Bryan Berard RR | 2.00 | .90 |
| ❑ 22 Chris Phillips RR | 2.00 | .90 |
| ❑ 23 Sergei Fedorov RR | 10.00 | 4.50 |
| ❑ 24 Sergei Samsonov RR | 8.00 | 3.60 |
| ❑ 25 Marc Denis RR | 2.00 | .90 |
| ❑ 26 Patrick Marleau RR | 2.00 | .90 |
| ❑ 27 Jaromir Jagr RR | 15.00 | 6.75 |
| ❑ 28 Saku Koivu RR | 8.00 | 3.60 |
| ❑ 29 Peter Forsberg RR | 15.00 | 6.75 |
| ❑ 30 Mike Modano RR | 6.00 | 2.70 |
| ❑ 31 Paul Kariya | 5.00 | 2.20 |
| ❑ 32 Matt Cullen | .40 | .18 |
| ❑ 33 Josef Marha | .40 | .18 |
| ❑ 34 Teemu Selanne | 2.50 | 1.10 |
| ❑ 35 Pavel Trnka | .40 | .18 |
| ❑ 36 Tom Askey | .40 | .18 |
| ❑ 37 Tim Taylor | .40 | .18 |
| ❑ 38 Ray Bourque | .40 | .18 |
| ❑ 39 Sergei Samsonov | 2.00 | .90 |
| ❑ 40 Don Sweeney | .40 | .18 |
| ❑ 41 Jason Allison | 1.00 | .45 |
| ❑ 42 Steve Heinze | .40 | .18 |
| ❑ 43 Erik Rasmussen | .40 | .18 |
| ❑ 44 Dominik Hasek | 2.50 | 1.10 |
| ❑ 45 Geoff Sanderson | 1.00 | .45 |
| ❑ 46 Michael Peca | .40 | .18 |
| ❑ 47 Brian Holzinger | .40 | .18 |
| ❑ 48 Vaclav Varada | .40 | .18 |
| ❑ 49 Steve Begin | .40 | .18 |
| ❑ 50 Denis Gauthier | .40 | .18 |
| ❑ 51 Derek Morris | .40 | .18 |
| ❑ 52 Valeri Bure | .40 | .18 |
| ❑ 53 Hnat Domenichelli | .40 | .18 |
| ❑ 54 Corey Stillman | .40 | .18 |
| ❑ 55 Jarome Iginla | .40 | .18 |
| ❑ 56 Tyler Moss | .40 | .18 |
| ❑ 57 Sami Kapanen | .40 | .18 |
| ❑ 58 Trevor Kidd | .40 | .18 |
| ❑ 59 Glen Wesley | .40 | .18 |
| ❑ 60 Nelson Emerson | .40 | .18 |
| ❑ 61 Jeff O'Neill | .40 | .18 |
| ❑ 62 Bates Battaglia | .40 | .18 |
| ❑ 63 Doug Gilmour | 1.25 | .55 |
| ❑ 64 Christian LaFlamme | .40 | .18 |
| ❑ 65 Chris Chelios | 1.25 | .55 |
| ❑ 66 Paul Coffey | .40 | .18 |
| ❑ 67 Eric Weinrich | .40 | .18 |
| ❑ 68 Eric Daze | .40 | .18 |
| ❑ 69 Peter Forsberg | 4.00 | 1.80 |
| ❑ 70 Eric Messier | .40 | .18 |
| ❑ 71 Eric Lacroix | .40 | .18 |
| ❑ 72 Adam Deadmarsh | 1.00 | .45 |
| ❑ 73 Claude Lemieux | 1.00 | .45 |
| ❑ 74 Patrick Roy | 6.00 | 2.70 |
| ❑ 75 Marc Denis | 1.00 | .45 |
| ❑ 76 Brett Hull | 1.50 | .70 |
| ❑ 77 Mike Keane | .40 | .18 |
| ❑ 78 Joe Nieuwendyk | 1.00 | .45 |
| ❑ 79 Darryl Sydor | .40 | .18 |
| ❑ 80 Ed Belfour | 1.25 | .55 |
| ❑ 81 Jamie Langenbrunner | .40 | .18 |
| ❑ 82 Petr Buzek | .40 | .18 |
| ❑ 83 Nicklas Lidstrom | 1.00 | .45 |
| ❑ 84 Mathieu Dandenault | .40 | .18 |
| ❑ 85 Steve Yzerman | 4.00 | 1.80 |
| ❑ 86 Martin Lapointe | .40 | .18 |
| ❑ 87 Brendan Shanahan | 2.50 | 1.10 |
| ❑ 88 Anders Erikkson | .40 | .18 |
| ❑ 89 Tomas Holmstrom | .40 | .18 |
| ❑ 90 Doug Weight | 1.00 | .45 |
| ❑ 91 Janne Ninnimaa | .40 | .18 |
| ❑ 92 Bill Guerin | 1.00 | .45 |
| ❑ 93 Kelly Buchberger | .40 | .18 |
| ❑ 94 Mike Grier | .40 | .18 |
| ❑ 95 Craig Millar | .40 | .18 |
| ❑ 96 Roman Hamrlik | .40 | .18 |
| ❑ 97 Ray Whitney | .40 | .18 |
| ❑ 98 Viktor Kozlov | .40 | .18 |
| ❑ 99 Peter Worrell | .40 | .18 |
| ❑ 100 Kevin Weekes | 1.00 | .45 |
| ❑ 101 Ed Jovanovski | .40 | .18 |
| ❑ 102 Bill Lindsay | .40 | .18 |
| ❑ 103 Jozef Stumpel | 1.00 | .45 |
| ❑ 104 Luc Robitaille | 1.00 | .45 |
| ❑ 105 Yanic Perreault | .40 | .18 |
| ❑ 106 Donald MacLean | .40 | .18 |
| ❑ 107 Jamie Storr | 1.00 | .45 |
| ❑ 108 Ian Laperriere | .40 | .18 |
| ❑ 109 Jason Morgan | .40 | .18 |
| ❑ 110 Vincent Damphousse | 1.00 | .45 |
| ❑ 111 Mark Recchi | 1.00 | .45 |
| ❑ 112 Vladimir Malakhov | .40 | .18 |
| ❑ 113 Dave Manson | .40 | .18 |
| ❑ 114 Jose Theodore | .40 | .18 |
| ❑ 115 Brian Savage | .40 | .18 |
| ❑ 116 Jonas Hoglund | .40 | .18 |
| ❑ 117 Krzysztof Oliwa | .40 | .18 |
| ❑ 118 Martin Brodeur | 3.00 | 1.35 |
| ❑ 119 Patrik Elias | .40 | .18 |
| ❑ 120 Jason Arnott | 1.00 | .45 |
| ❑ 121 Scott Stevens | .40 | .18 |
| ❑ 122 Sheldon Souray | .40 | .18 |
| ❑ 123 Brian Rolston | .40 | .18 |
| ❑ 124 Trevor Linden | 1.00 | .45 |
| ❑ 125 Warren Luhning | .40 | .18 |
| ❑ 126 Zdeno Chara | .40 | .18 |
| ❑ 127 Bryan Berard | 1.00 | .45 |
| ❑ 128 Bryan Smolinski | .40 | .18 |
| ❑ 129 Jason Dawe | .40 | .18 |
| ❑ 130 Kevin Stevens | .40 | .18 |
| ❑ 131 P.J. Stock | .40 | .18 |
| ❑ 132 Marc Savard | .40 | .18 |
| ❑ 133 Pat LaFontaine | 1.00 | .45 |
| ❑ 134 Dan Cloutier | .40 | .18 |
| ❑ 135 Wayne Gretzky | 8.00 | 3.60 |
| ❑ 136 Niklas Sundstrom | .40 | .18 |
| ❑ 137 Damian Rhodes | 1.00 | .45 |
| ❑ 138 Magnus Arvedson | .40 | .18 |
| ❑ 139 Alexei Yashin | 1.00 | .45 |
| ❑ 140 Chris Phillips | .40 | .18 |
| ❑ 141 Janne Laukkanen | .40 | .18 |
| ❑ 142 Shawn McEachern | .40 | .18 |
| ❑ 143 John LeClair | 2.00 | .90 |
| ❑ 144 Alexandre Daigle | .40 | .18 |
| ❑ 145 Dainius Zubrus | .40 | .18 |
| ❑ 146 Joel Otto | .40 | .18 |
| ❑ 147 Mike Sillinger | .40 | .18 |
| ❑ 148 John Vanbiesbrouck | .40 | .18 |
| ❑ 149 Chris Gratton | 1.00 | .45 |
| ❑ 150 Eric Desjardins | .40 | .18 |
| ❑ 151 Juha Ylonen | .40 | .18 |
| ❑ 152 Brad Isbister | .40 | .18 |
| ❑ 153 Oleg Tverdovsky | .40 | .18 |

❑ 154 Keith Tkachuk 1.50 .70
❑ 155 Teppo Numminen .40 .18
❑ 156 Cliff Ronning .40 .18
❑ 157 Nikolai Khabibulin 1.00 .45
❑ 158 Alexei Morozov .40 .18
❑ 159 Kevin Hatcher .40 .18
❑ 160 Darius Kasparaitis .40 .18
❑ 161 Jaromir Jagr 4.00 1.80
❑ 162 Tom Barrasso 1.00 .45
❑ 163 Tuomas Gronman .40 .18
❑ 164 Robert Dome .40 .18
❑ 165 Peter Skudra .40 .18
❑ 166 Marcus Ragnarsson .40 .18
❑ 167 Mike Vernon 1.00 .45
❑ 168 Andrei Zyuzin .40 .18
❑ 169 Marco Sturm .40 .18
❑ 170 Mike Ricci .40 .18
❑ 171 Patrick Marleau .40 .18
❑ 172 Pierre Turgeon .40 .18
❑ 173 Pavol Demitra .40 .18
❑ 174 Chris Pronger 1.00 .45
❑ 175 Pascal Rheaume .40 .18
❑ 176 Al MacInnis 1.00 .45
❑ 177 Tony Twist .40 .18
❑ 178 Jim Campbell .40 .18
❑ 179 Mikael Renberg 1.00 .45
❑ 180 Jason Bonsignore .40 .18
❑ 181 Zac Bierk .40 .18
❑ 182 Alexander Selivanov .40 .18
❑ 183 Stephane Richer .40 .18
❑ 184 Sandy McCarthy .40 .18
❑ 185 Alyn McCauley .40 .18
❑ 186 Sergei Berezin 1.00 .45
❑ 187 Mike Johnson .40 .18
❑ 188 Wendel Clark 1.00 .45
❑ 189 Tie Domi .40 .18
❑ 190 Yannick Trembley .40 .18
❑ 191 Curtis Joseph 1.25 .55
❑ 192 Fredrik Modin .40 .18
❑ 193 Pavel Bure 2.50 1.10
❑ 194 Todd Bertuzzi .40 .18
❑ 195 Mark Messier 1.50 .70
❑ 196 Bret Hedican .40 .18
❑ 197 Mattias Ohlund .40 .18
❑ 198 Garth Snow 1.00 .45
❑ 199 Adam Oates 1.00 .45
❑ 200 Peter Bondra .40 .18
❑ 201 Sergei Gonchar .40 .18
❑ 202 Jan Bulis .40 .18
❑ 203 Joe Juneau 1.00 .45
❑ 204 Brian Bellows .40 .18
❑ 205 Olaf Kolzig 1.00 .45
❑ 206 Richard Zednik .40 .18
❑ 207 Wayne Gretzky CL 4.00 1.80
❑ 208 Patrick Roy CL 3.00 1.35
❑ 209 Steve Yzerman CL 2.00 .90
❑ 210 Mike Dunham 1.00 .45
❑ 211 Johan Davidsson .40 .18
❑ 212 Guy Hebert 1.00 .45
❑ 213 Mike LeClerc .40 .18
❑ 214 Steve Rucchin .40 .18
❑ 215 Travis Green .40 .18
❑ 216 Josef Marha .40 .18
❑ 217 Ted Donato .40 .18
❑ 218 Joe Thornton 1.25 .55
❑ 219 Kyle McLaren .40 .18
❑ 220 Peter Nordstrom .40 .18
❑ 221 Byron Dafoe 1.00 .45
❑ 222 Jonathan Girard .40 .18
❑ 223 Antti Laaksonen .40 .18
❑ 224 Jason Holland .40 .18
❑ 225 Miroslav Satan .40 .18
❑ 226 Alexei Zhitnik .40 .18
❑ 227 Donald Audette .40 .18
❑ 228 Matthew Barnaby .40 .18
❑ 229 Rumun Ndur .40 .18
❑ 230 Ken Wregget 1.00 .45
❑ 231 Andrew Cassels .40 .18
❑ 232 Theoren Fleury 1.25 .55
❑ 233 Phil Housley 1.00 .45
❑ 234 Martin St. Louis 1.00 .45
❑ 235 Mike Rucinski .40 .18
❑ 236 Gary Roberts .40 .18
❑ 237 Keith Primeau 1.00 .45
❑ 238 Martin Gelinas .40 .18
❑ 239 Nolan Pratt RC .40 .18
❑ 240 Ray Sheppard .40 .18
❑ 241 Ron Francis 1.00 .45
❑ 242 Ty Jones .40 .18
❑ 243 Tony Amonte 1.00 .45
❑ 244 Chad Kilger .40 .18
❑ 245 Alexei Zhamnov .40 .18
❑ 246 Remi Royer .40 .18
❑ 247 Milan Hejduk 3.00 1.35
❑ 248 Joe Sakic 3.00 1.35
❑ 249 Valeri Kamensky 1.00 .45
❑ 250 Sandis Ozolinsh 1.00 .45
❑ 251 Shean Donovan .40 .18
❑ 252 Wade Belak .40 .18
❑ 253 Jamie Wright .40 .18
❑ 254 Sergei Zubov .40 .18
❑ 255 Richard Matvichuk .40 .18
❑ 256 Mike Modano 2.00 .90
❑ 257 Pat Verbeek .40 .18
❑ 258 Jere Lehtinen 1.00 .45
❑ 259 Derian Hatcher .40 .18
❑ 260 Jason Botterill .40 .18
❑ 261 Igor Larionov .40 .18
❑ 262 Sergei Fedorov 3.00 1.35
❑ 263 Chris Osgood 1.25 .55
❑ 264 Vyacheslav Kozlov .40 .18
❑ 265 Larry Murphy 1.00 .45
❑ 266 Darren McCarty .40 .18
❑ 267 Doug Brown .40 .18
❑ 268 Kris Draper .40 .18
❑ 269 Uwe Krupp .40 .18
❑ 270 Fredrik Lindquist .40 .18
❑ 271 Dean McAmmond .40 .18
❑ 272 Ryan Smyth 1.00 .45
❑ 273 Boris Mironov .40 .18
❑ 274 Tom Poti .40 .18
❑ 275 Todd Marchant .40 .18
❑ 276 Sean Brown .40 .18
❑ 277 Rob Niedermayer .40 .18
❑ 278 Robert Svehla .40 .18
❑ 279 Scott Mellanby .40 .18
❑ 280 Radek Dvorak .40 .18
❑ 281 Jaroslav Spacek .40 .18
❑ 282 Mark Parrish 3.00 1.35
❑ 283 Ryan Johnson .40 .18
❑ 284 Glen Murray .40 .18
❑ 285 Rob Blake 1.00 .45
❑ 286 Steve Duchesne 1.00 .45
❑ 287 Vladimir Tsyplakov .40 .18
❑ 288 Stephane Fiset 1.00 .45
❑ 289 Mattias Norstrom .40 .18
❑ 290 Saku Koivu 2.50 1.10
❑ 291 Shayne Corson 1.00 .45
❑ 292 Brad Brown .40 .18
❑ 293 Patrice Brisebois .40 .18
❑ 294 Terry Ryan .40 .18
❑ 295 Jocelyn Thibault 1.00 .45
❑ 296 Miroslav Guren .40 .18
❑ 297 Darren Turcotte 1.00 .45
❑ 298 Sebastien Bordeleau .40 .18
❑ 299 Jan Vopat .40 .18
❑ 300 Blair Atcheynum .40 .18
❑ 301 Andrew Brunette .40 .18
❑ 302 Sergei Krivokrasov .40 .18
❑ 303 Marian Cisar .40 .18
❑ 304 Patrick Cote .40 .18
❑ 305 J.J. Daigneault .40 .18
❑ 306 Greg Johnson .40 .18
❑ 307 Chris Terreri 1.00 .45
❑ 308 Scott Niedermayer .40 .18
❑ 309 Vadim Sharifijanov .40 .18
❑ 310 Petr Sykora .40 .18
❑ 311 Sergei Brylin .40 .18
❑ 312 Denis Pederson .40 .18
❑ 313 Bobby Holik .40 .18
❑ 314 Bryan Muir .40 .18
❑ 315 Zigmund Palffy 1.25 .55
❑ 316 Mike Watt .40 .18
❑ 317 Tommy Salo 1.00 .45
❑ 318 Kenny Jonsson .40 .18
❑ 319 Dimitri Nabakov .40 .18
❑ 320 John Maclean .40 .18
❑ 321 Zarley Zalapski .40 .18
❑ 322 Brian Leetch 1.25 .55
❑ 323 Todd Harvey .40 .18
❑ 324 Mike Richter 1.25 .55
❑ 325 Mike Knuble .40 .18
❑ 326 Jeff Beukeboom .40 .18
❑ 327 Daniel Alfredsson 1.00 .45
❑ 328 Vaclav Prospal .40 .18
❑ 329 Wade Redden .40 .18
❑ 330 Igor Kravchuk .40 .18
❑ 331 Andreas Dackell .40 .18
❑ 332 Mike Maneluk 2.00 .90
❑ 333 Eric Lindros 4.00 1.80
❑ 334 Rod Brind'Amour 1.00 .45
❑ 335 Colin Forbes .40 .18
❑ 336 Dimitri Tertyshny .40 .18
❑ 337 Shjon Podein .40 .18
❑ 338 Chris Therien .40 .18
❑ 339 Jeremy Roenick 1.25 .55
❑ 340 Jyrki Lumme .40 .18
❑ 341 Rick Tocchet 1.00 .45
❑ 342 Dallas Drake .40 .18
❑ 343 Keith Carney .40 .18
❑ 344 Greg Adams .40 .18
❑ 345 Jan Hrdina 1.50 .70
❑ 346 German Titov .40 .18
❑ 347 Stu Barnes .40 .18
❑ 348 Kevin Hatcher .40 .18
❑ 349 Martin Straka .40 .18
❑ 350 Jean-Sebastien Aubin .40 .18
❑ 351 Jeff Friesen 1.00 .45
❑ 352 Tony Granato .40 .18
❑ 353 Scott Hannan .40 .18
❑ 354 Owen Nolan 1.00 .45
❑ 355 Stephane Matteau .40 .18
❑ 356 Bryan Marchment .40 .18
❑ 357 Geoff Courtnall 1.00 .45
❑ 358 Brent Johnson .40 .18
❑ 359 Jamie Rivers .40 .18
❑ 360 Terry Yake .40 .18
❑ 361 Jamie McLennan .40 .18
❑ 362 Grant Fuhr 1.00 .45
❑ 363 Michal Handzus 1.50 .70
❑ 364 Bill Ranford 1.00 .45
❑ 365 John Cullen .40 .18
❑ 366 Craig Janney .40 .18
❑ 367 Daren Puppa 1.00 .45
❑ 368 Pavel Kubina 1.50 .70
❑ 369 Wendel Clark 1.00 .45
❑ 370 Mats Sundin 1.25 .55
❑ 371 Felix Potvin 1.25 .55
❑ 372 Daniil Markov .40 .18
❑ 373 Derek King .40 .18
❑ 374 Steve Thomas .40 .18
❑ 375 Tomas Kaberle 1.00 .45
❑ 376 Alexander Mogilny 1.00 .45
❑ 377 Bill Muckalt .40 .18
❑ 378 Brian Noonan .40 .18
❑ 379 Markus Naslund .40 .18
❑ 380 Brad May .40 .18
❑ 381 Matt Cooke .40 .18
❑ 382 Calle Johansson .40 .18
❑ 383 Dale Hunter .40 .18
❑ 384 Jaroslav Svejkovsky .40 .18
❑ 385 Dmitri Mironov .40 .18
❑ 386 Matt Herr .40 .18
❑ 387 Nolan Baumgartner .40 .18
❑ 388 Wayne Gretzky CL .40 .18
❑ 389 Steve Yzerman CL .40 .18
❑ 390 W.Gretzky/S.Yzerman CL .40 .18
❑ 391 Brian Finley PE 8.00 3.60
❑ 392 Maxime Ouellet PE 5.00 2.20
❑ 393 Kurtis Foster PE 2.00 .90
❑ 394 Barrett Jackman PE 2.00 .90
❑ 395 Ross Lupaschuk PE 3.00 1.35
❑ 396 Steven McCarthy PE 3.00 1.35
❑ 397 Peter Reynolds PE 2.00 .90
❑ 398 Bart Rushmer PE 2.00 .90
❑ 399 Jonathan Zion PE 2.00 .90
❑ 400 Kris Beech PE 8.00 3.60
❑ 401 Brandin Cote PE 2.00 .90
❑ 402 Scott Kelman PE 3.00 1.35
❑ 403 Jamie Lundmark PE 4.00 1.80
❑ 404 Derek Mackenzie PE 2.00 .90
❑ 405 Rory McDade PE 2.00 .90
❑ 406 David Morisset PE 4.00 1.80
❑ 407 Mirko Murovic PE 3.00 1.35
❑ 408 Taylor Pyatt PE 6.00 2.70
❑ 409 Charlie Stephens PE 2.00 .90
❑ 410 Kyle Wanvig PE 4.00 1.80
❑ 411 Krzystof Wieckowk PE 2.00 .90
❑ 412 Michael Zigomanis PE 4.00 1.80
❑ 413 Rico Fata CC 3.00 1.35
❑ 414 Vincent Lecavalier CC 6.00 2.70
❑ 415 Chris Drury CC 4.00 1.80
❑ 416 Oleg Kvasha CC 5.00 2.20
❑ 417 Eric Brewer CC 2.00 .90
❑ 418 Josh Green CC 3.00 1.35
❑ 419 Marty Reasoner CC 2.00 .90
❑ 420 Manny Malhotra CC 2.00 .90
❑ NNO W.Gretzky AU/200 800.00 350.00
❑ NNO W.Gretzky Stick/200 800.00 350.00
❑ NNO W.Gretzky Stick AU/99 2000.00 900.00
❑ NNO S.Yzerman AU/200 500.00 220.00
❑ NNO S.Yzerman Stick/200 400.00 180.00
❑ NNO S.Yzerman Stick AU/19 1000.00 450.00

## 1996-97 Upper Deck Ice

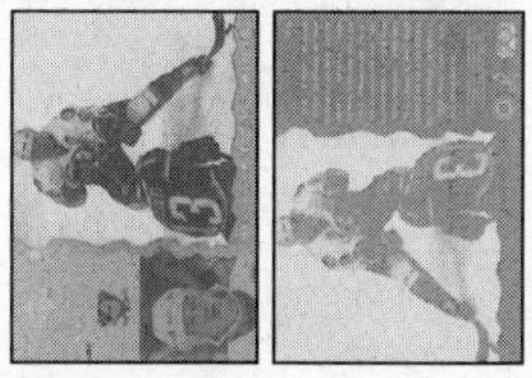

This retail-only set was issued in one series totalling 150 cards. Each pack contained three see-through cel cards and carried a suggested retail price of $3.99. The set is broken down into four subsets: Ice Performers (1-75), Ice Phenoms (76-105), Ice Legends (106-115), and World Juniors (116-150). Many rookies were included, with Joe Thornton, Patrick Marleau, Dainius Zubrus, Patrick Lalime, Mike Grier and Cameron Mann highlighting the potential-laden cast.

| | MINT | NRMT |
|---|---|---|
| COMPLETE SET (150) | 150.00 | 70.00 |
| COMMON CARD (1-115) | .50 | .23 |
| COMMON WORLD JR. (116-150) | 1.00 | .45 |

❑ 1 Kevin Todd .50 .23
❑ 2 Adam Oates 1.00 .45
❑ 3 Bill Ranford 1.00 .45
❑ 4 Rick Tocchet 1.00 .45
❑ 5 Dominik Hasek 3.00 1.35
❑ 6 Richard Smehlik .50 .23
❑ 7 Derek Plante .50 .23
❑ 8 Joel Bouchard .50 .23
❑ 9 Theoren Fleury 1.00 .45
❑ 10 Chris Chelios 1.50 .70
❑ 11 Ed Belfour 1.50 .70
❑ 12 Eric Weinrich .50 .23
❑ 13 Tony Amonte 1.00 .45
❑ 14 Greg Adams .50 .23
❑ 15 Jamie Langenbrunner .50 .23
❑ 16 Sergei Zubov .50 .23
❑ 17 Pat Verbeek .50 .23
❑ 18 Chris Osgood 1.50 .70
❑ 19 Rem Murray .50 .23
❑ 20 Jason Arnott 1.00 .45
❑ 21 Curtis Joseph 1.50 .70
❑ 22 Bill Lindsay .50 .23
❑ 23 Ray Sheppard .50 .23
❑ 24 Martin Straka .50 .23
❑ 25 Jean Sebastien Giguere 3.00 1.35
❑ 26 Sean Burke 1.00 .45
❑ 27 Keith Primeau 1.00 .45
❑ 28 Geoff Sanderson .50 .23
❑ 29 Rob Blake .50 .23
❑ 30 Ian Laperriere .50 .23
❑ 31 Byron Dafoe 1.00 .45
❑ 32 Vincent Damphousse 1.00 .45
❑ 33 Darcy Tucker .50 .23
❑ 34 Brian Savage .50 .23
❑ 35 Bill Guerin .50 .23
❑ 36 Scott Niedermayer .50 .23
❑ 37 Steve Thomas .50 .23
❑ 38 Valeri Zelepukin .50 .23
❑ 39 Bryan Smolinski .50 .23
❑ 40 Derek King .50 .23
❑ 41 Mike Richter 1.50 .70
❑ 42 Daniel Goneau .50 .23
❑ 43 Brian Leetch 1.50 .70
❑ 44 Adam Graves 1.00 .45
❑ 45 Damian Rhodes 1.00 .45
❑ 46 Mikael Renberg 1.00 .45
❑ 47 Eric Desjardins .50 .23
❑ 48 Rod Brind'Amour 1.00 .45
❑ 49 Janne Niinimaa 1.50 .70
❑ 50 Dale Hawerchuk 1.00 .45
❑ 51 Jeremy Roenick 1.50 .70
❑ 52 Mike Gartner 1.00 .45
❑ 53 Cliff Ronning .50 .23
❑ 54 Patrick Lalime 1.50 .70
❑ 55 Ron Francis 1.00 .45
❑ 56 Petr Nedved 1.00 .45
❑ 57 Bernie Nicholls .50 .23
❑ 58 Jeff Friesen 1.00 .45
❑ 59 Owen Nolan 1.00 .45
❑ 60 Marty McSorley .50 .23
❑ 61 Pierre Turgeon 1.00 .45
❑ 62 Grant Fuhr 1.00 .45
❑ 63 Chris Pronger 1.00 .45
❑ 64 Jim Campbell .50 .23
❑ 65 Chris Gratton .50 .23
❑ 66 Dino Ciccarelli 1.00 .45
❑ 67 Felix Potvin 1.50 .70
❑ 68 Tie Domi .50 .23
❑ 69 Doug Gilmour 1.50 .70
❑ 70 Trevor Linden 1.00 .45
❑ 71 Corey Hirsch 1.00 .45
❑ 72 Jim Carey 1.50 .70
❑ 73 Chris Simon .50 .23
❑ 74 Mark Tinordi .50 .23
❑ 75 Sergei Gonchar .50 .23
❑ 76 Paul Kariya 6.00 2.70
❑ 77 Teemu Selanne 3.00 1.35
❑ 78 Jarome Iginla 1.50 .70
❑ 79 Eric Daze .50 .23
❑ 80 Sandis Ozolinsh 1.00 .45
❑ 81 Peter Forsberg 5.00 2.20
❑ 82 Mike Modano 2.50 1.10
❑ 83 Anders Eriksson .50 .23
❑ 84 Sergei Fedorov 3.00 1.35
❑ 85 Brendan Shanahan 3.00 1.35
❑ 86 Mike Grier 3.00 1.35
❑ 87 Doug Weight 1.00 .45
❑ 88 Ed Jovanovski 1.00 .45
❑ 89 Saku Koivu 2.50 1.10
❑ 90 Jose Theodore 1.00 .45
❑ 91 Jocelyn Thibault 1.50 .70
❑ 92 Martin Brodeur 4.00 1.80
❑ 93 Bryan Berard 1.50 .70
❑ 94 Zigmund Palffy 1.50 .70
❑ 95 Daniel Alfredsson 1.00 .45
❑ 96 Alexei Yashin 1.00 .45
❑ 97 Wade Redden 1.00 .45
❑ 98 John LeClair 2.50 1.10
❑ 99 Oleg Tverdovsky .50 .23
❑ 100 Keith Tkachuk 2.00 .90
❑ 101 Jaromir Jagr 5.00 2.20
❑ 102 Roman Hamrlik 1.00 .45
❑ 103 Sergei Berezin 2.50 1.10
❑ 104 Alexander Mogilny 1.00 .45
❑ 105 Pavel Bure 3.00 1.35
❑ 106 Ray Bourque 1.50 .70
❑ 107 Patrick Roy 8.00 3.60
❑ 108 Joe Sakic 3.00 1.35
❑ 109 Steve Yzerman 5.00 2.20
❑ 110 John Vanbiesbrouck 2.50 1.10
❑ 111 Mark Messier 2.00 .90
❑ 112 Wayne Gretzky 10.00 4.50
❑ 113 Eric Lindros 5.00 2.20
❑ 114 Mario Lemieux 8.00 3.60
❑ 115 Brett Hull 2.00 .90
❑ 116 Joe Thornton 12.00 5.50
❑ 117 Marc Denis 4.00 1.80
❑ 118 Martin Biron 1.50 .70
❑ 119 Jason Doig 1.00 .45
❑ 120 Daniel Briere 4.00 1.80
❑ 121 Trevor Letowski 1.00 .45
❑ 122 Boyd Devereaux 3.00 1.35
❑ 123 Dwayne Hay 1.50 .70
❑ 124 Hugh Hamilton 1.00 .45
❑ 125 Brad Isbister 1.50 .70
❑ 126 Shane Willis 1.50 .70
❑ 127 Trent Whitfield 1.50 .70
❑ 128 Jesse Wallin 1.50 .70
❑ 129 Alyn McCauley 1.50 .70
❑ 130 Cameron Mann 4.00 1.80
❑ 131 Jeff Ware 1.50 .70
❑ 132 Corey Sarich 1.50 .70
❑ 133 Richard Jackman 2.50 1.10
❑ 134 Brad Larsen 1.00 .45
❑ 135 Peter Schaefer 4.00 1.80
❑ 136 Christian Dube 1.50 .70
❑ 137 Chris Phillips 1.50 .70
❑ 138 Sergei Samsonov 5.00 2.20
❑ 139 Alexei Morozov 3.00 1.35
❑ 140 Sergei Fedotov 1.00 .45
❑ 141 Denis Khlopotnov 1.50 .70
❑ 142 Andrei Markov 1.00 .45
❑ 143 Andrei Petrunin 1.00 .45
❑ 144 Roman Liachenko RC 1.50 .70
❑ 145 Joe Corvo 1.50 .70
❑ 146 Erik Rasmussen 2.00 .90
❑ 147 Mike York 1.50 .70
❑ 148 Brian Boucher 2.00 .90
❑ 149 Paul Mara 3.00 1.35
❑ 150 Marty Reasoner 1.50 .70

## 1996-97 Upper Deck Ice Parallel

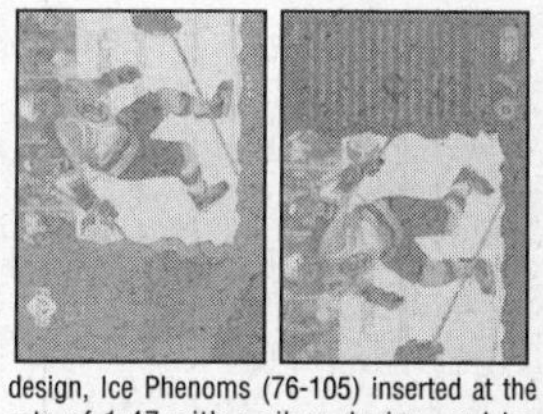

This 115-card set is a partial parallel version of the regular Upper Deck Ice set and features a special Light F/X acetate card design. The set contains three subsets: Ice Performers (1-75) inserted at the rate of 1:9 with a bronze design, Ice Phenoms (76-105) inserted at the rate of 1:47 with a silver design, and Ice Legends (106-115) inserted at the rate of 1:325 with a gold design. The World Juniors subset, present in the regular issue, is not included in the parallel version, leaving the set complete at 115 cards.

| | MINT | NRMT |
|---|---|---|
| COMP.PERF.SET (75) | 300.00 | 135.00 |
| COMMON PERF. (1-75) | 4.00 | 1.80 |
| *PERF.STARS: 3X TO 8X BASIC CARDS | | |
| *PERF.YOUNG STARS: 1.5X TO 4X BASIC CARDS | | |
| COMP.PHENOM SET (30) | 600.00 | 275.00 |
| COMMON PHENOM (76-105) | 8.00 | 3.60 |
| *PHENOMS: 6X TO 15X BASIC CARDS | | |
| PHENOMS STATED ODDS 1:47 | | |
| COMP.LEGENDS SET (10) | 1500.00 | 700.00 |
| COMMON LEGENDS (106-115) | 50.00 | 22.00 |

❑ 106 Ray Bourque 50.00 22.00
❑ 107 Patrick Roy 300.00 135.00
❑ 108 Joe Sakic 150.00 70.00
❑ 109 Steve Yzerman 200.00 90.00
❑ 110 John Vanbiesbrouck 100.00 45.00
❑ 111 Mark Messier 80.00 36.00
❑ 112 Wayne Gretzky 400.00 180.00
❑ 113 Eric Lindros 300.00 135.00
❑ 114 Mario Lemieux 300.00 135.00
❑ 115 Brett Hull 80.00 36.00

## 1996-97 Upper Deck Ice Stanley Cup Foundation

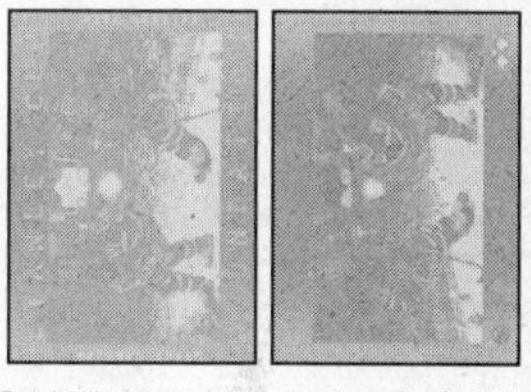

Randomly inserted in packs at a rate of one in 96, this 10-card set features color player photos of winning teammate pairs in colored borders on an acetate card.

| | MINT | NRMT |
|---|---|---|
| COMPLETE SET (10) | 600.00 | 275.00 |
| COMMON CARD (S1-S10) | 15.00 | 6.75 |

❑ S1 Wayne Gretzky 120.00 55.00
Mark Messier
❑ S2 Brendan Shanahan 80.00 36.00
Steve Yzerman
❑ S3 John Vanbiesbrouck 15.00 6.75
Ed Jovanovski
❑ S4 Joceyln Thibault 25.00 11.00
Saku Koivu
❑ S5 Joe Sakic 100.00 45.00
Patrick Roy
❑ S6 Paul Kariya 80.00 36.00
Teemu Selanne
❑ S7 Mario Lemieux 100.00 45.00
Jaromir Jagr
❑ S8 Jeremy Roenick 30.00 13.50
Keith Tkachuk
❑ S9 Doug Weight 15.00 6.75
Jason Arnott
❑ S10 John LeClair 60.00 27.00
Eric Lindros

## 1996-97 Upper Deck Ice Dynasty Foundation

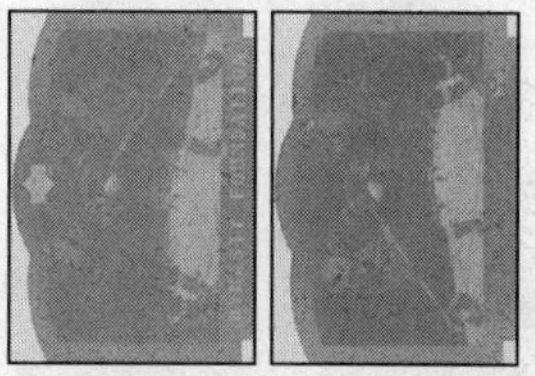

Randomly inserted in packs at a rate of one in 960, this 10-card set is a parallel to the Upper Deck Ice Stanley Cup Foundation set. The distinctions between the two are the unique die-cut border and the wording Dynasty Foundation on front.

| | MINT | NRMT |
|---|---|---|
| COMPLETE SET (10) | 3000.00 | 1350.00 |
| COMMON CARD (S1-S10) | 100.00 | 45.00 |
| *DYNASTY: 2.5X TO 5X BASIC CARDS | | |

## 1997-98 Upper Deck Ice

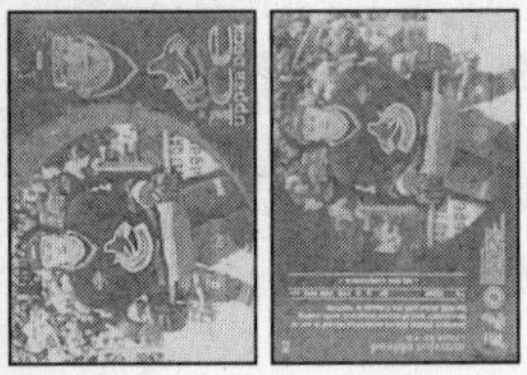

The 1997-98 Upper Deck Ice set was issued in one series totalling 90 cards and was distributed in three-card packs with a suggested retail price of $4.99. The fronts feature color action player photos printed on acetate card stock. The backs carry player information.

| | MINT | NRMT |
|---|---|---|
| COMPLETE SET (90) | 100.00 | 45.00 |
| COMMON CARD (1-90) | .40 | .18 |

| | | |
|---|---|---|
| □ 1 Nelson Emerson | .40 | .18 |
| □ 2 Derian Hatcher | .40 | .18 |
| □ 3 Mike Richter | 1.25 | .55 |
| □ 4 Sergei Berezin | .40 | .18 |
| □ 5 Nicklas Lidstrom | 1.00 | .45 |
| □ 6 Ryan Smyth | 1.00 | .45 |
| □ 7 Martin Brodeur | 3.00 | 1.35 |
| □ 8 Geoff Sanderson | 1.00 | .45 |
| □ 9 Doug Weight | 1.00 | .45 |
| □ 10 Owen Nolan | 1.00 | .45 |
| □ 11 Daniel Alfredsson | 1.00 | .45 |
| □ 12 Peter Bondra | 1.25 | .55 |
| □ 13 Jim Campbell | .40 | .18 |
| □ 14 Rob Niedermayer | .40 | .18 |
| □ 15 Daymond Langkow | .40 | .18 |
| □ 16 Zigmund Palffy | 1.25 | .55 |
| □ 17 Adam Oates | 1.00 | .45 |
| □ 18 Adam Deadmarsh | 1.00 | .45 |
| □ 19 Brian Holzinger | .40 | .18 |
| □ 20 Jarome Iginla | 1.00 | .45 |
| □ 21 Janne Niinimaa | 1.00 | .45 |
| □ 22 Dino Ciccarelli | .40 | .18 |
| □ 23 Mark Recchi | 1.00 | .45 |
| □ 24 Sandis Ozolinsh | 1.00 | .45 |
| □ 25 Keith Primeau | .40 | .18 |
| □ 26 Ed Jovanovski | 1.00 | .45 |
| □ 27 Jeremy Roenick | 1.25 | .55 |
| □ 28 Alexei Yashin | 1.00 | .45 |
| □ 29 Felix Potvin | 1.25 | .55 |
| □ 30 Chris Osgood | 1.25 | .55 |
| □ 31 Marc Denis | 1.00 | .45 |
| □ 32 Tyler Moss | .40 | .18 |
| □ 33 Kevin Hodson | 1.00 | .45 |
| □ 34 Jamie Storr | 1.00 | .45 |
| □ 35 Roman Turek | 1.00 | .45 |
| □ 36 Jose Theodore | 1.00 | .45 |
| □ 37 Magnus Arvedson | .40 | .18 |
| □ 38 Dan Cleary | .40 | .18 |
| □ 39 Mike Knuble | .40 | .18 |
| □ 40 Jaroslav Svejkovsky | 1.00 | .45 |
| □ 41 Patrick Marleau | 2.50 | 1.10 |
| □ 42 Mattias Ohlund | 1.00 | .45 |
| □ 43 Sergei Samsonov | 3.00 | 1.35 |
| □ 44 Espen Knutsen | .40 | .18 |
| □ 45 Vaclav Prospal | 1.50 | .70 |
| □ 46 Joe Thornton | 2.50 | 1.10 |
| □ 47 Chris Phillips | .40 | .18 |
| □ 48 Mike Johnson | 1.50 | .70 |
| □ 49 Dainius Zubrus | 1.25 | .55 |
| □ 50 Wade Redden | .40 | .18 |
| □ 51 Derek Morris | .40 | .18 |
| □ 52 Marco Sturm | 2.00 | .90 |
| □ 53 Don MacLean | .40 | .18 |
| □ 54 Bryan Berard | .40 | .18 |
| □ 55 Richard Zednik | .40 | .18 |
| □ 56 Alexei Morozov | 1.00 | .45 |
| □ 57 Erik Rasmussen | .40 | .18 |
| □ 58 Olli Jokinen | 2.00 | .90 |
| □ 59 Jan Bulis | .40 | .18 |
| □ 60 Patrik Elias | 1.50 | .70 |
| □ 61 Peter Forsberg | 4.00 | 1.80 |
| □ 62 Mike Modano | 1.25 | .55 |
| □ 63 Tony Amonte | 1.00 | .45 |
| □ 64 Theoren Fleury | 1.00 | .45 |
| □ 65 Ron Francis | 1.00 | .45 |
| □ 66 Brett Hull | 1.50 | .70 |
| □ 67 Chris Chelios | 1.25 | .55 |
| □ 68 Jaromir Jagr | 4.00 | 1.80 |
| □ 69 Sergei Fedorov | 2.50 | 1.10 |
| □ 70 Keith Tkachuk | 1.50 | .70 |
| □ 71 Mark Messier | 2.00 | .90 |
| □ 72 Pat LaFontaine | 1.00 | .45 |
| □ 73 Mats Sundin | 1.25 | .55 |
| □ 74 John Vanbiesbrouck | 2.00 | .90 |
| □ 75 John LeClair | 2.00 | .90 |
| □ 76 Brian Leetch | 1.25 | .55 |
| □ 77 Ray Bourque | 1.25 | .55 |
| □ 78 Saku Koivu | 2.00 | .90 |
| □ 79 Joe Sakic | 2.50 | 1.10 |
| □ 80 Teemu Selanne | 2.50 | 1.10 |
| □ 81 Curtis Joseph | 1.25 | .55 |
| □ 82 Doug Gilmour | 1.25 | .55 |
| □ 83 Patrick Roy | 6.00 | 2.70 |
| □ 84 Brendan Shanahan | 2.50 | 1.10 |
| □ 85 Paul Kariya | 5.00 | 2.20 |
| □ 86 Pavel Bure | 2.50 | 1.10 |
| □ 87 Dominik Hasek | 2.50 | 1.10 |
| □ 88 Eric Lindros | 4.00 | 1.80 |
| □ 89 Steve Yzerman | 4.00 | 1.80 |
| □ 90 Wayne Gretzky | 8.00 | 3.60 |

## 1997-98 Upper Deck Ice Parallel

This 90-card set is a parallel version of the base set and is divided into three partial parallel sets. Ice Performers consists of cards 1-30 with an insertion rate of 1:2; Ice Phenoms consists of cards 31-60 with an insertion rate of 1:5; Ice Legends consists of the top 30 NHL players whose cards are 61-90 and have an insertion rate of 1:11.

| | MINT | NRMT |
|---|---|---|
| COMPLETE SET (90) | 400.00 | 180.00 |
| COMP.PERF.SET (30) | 20.00 | 9.00 |
| COMMON PERF. (1-30) | .60 | .25 |
| *PERF.STARS: .75X TO 1.5X BASIC CARDS | | |
| COMP.PHENOM SET (30) | 80.00 | 36.00 |
| COMMON PHENOM (31-60) | 1.25 | .55 |
| *PHEN.STARS: 1X TO 2X BASIC CARDS | | |
| COMP.LEGENDS SET (30) | 300.00 | 135.00 |
| COMMON LEGENDS (61-90) | 5.00 | 2.20 |
| *LEGENDS STARS: 2X TO 5X BASIC CARDS | | |

## 1997-98 Upper Deck Ice Power Shift

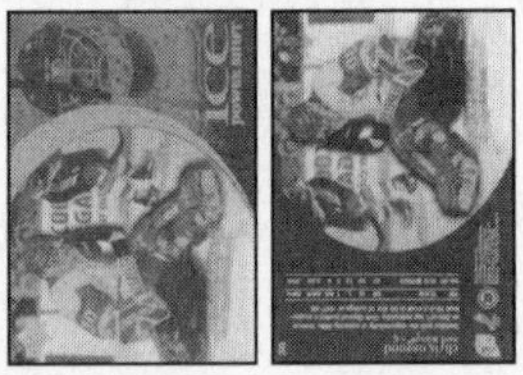

Randomly inserted in packs at the rate of one in 23, this 90-card set is a gold foil parallel version of the base set.

| | MINT | NRMT |
|---|---|---|
| COMPLETE SET (90) | 1200.00 | 550.00 |
| COMMON CARD (1-90) | 5.00 | 2.20 |
| *STARS: 6X TO 12X BASIC CARDS | | |
| *YOUNG STARS: 5X TO 10X BASIC CARDS | | |

## 1997-98 Upper Deck Ice Champions

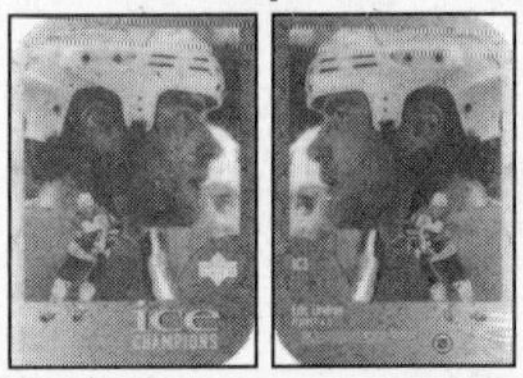

Randomly inserted in packs at the rate of one in 47, this 20-card set features color player head photos and action images printed with a Light FX/litho/acetate combination.

| | MINT | NRMT |
|---|---|---|
| COMPLETE SET (20) | 600.00 | 275.00 |
| COMMON CARD (IC1-IC20) | 12.00 | 5.50 |
| COMP.ICE CHAMP.2 SET (20 | 5000.00 | 2200.00 |
| COMMON ICE CHAMP.2 (1-20) | 100.00 | 45.00 |
| *ICE CHAMP.2 STARS: 4X TO 8X BASIC CARDS | | |
| *ICE CHAMP.2 YNG.STARS: 3X TO 6X BASIC CARDS | | |

| | | |
|---|---|---|
| □ IC1 Wayne Gretzky | 80.00 | 36.00 |
| □ IC2 Patrick Roy | 60.00 | 27.00 |
| □ IC3 Eric Lindros | 40.00 | 18.00 |
| □ IC4 Saku Koivu | 20.00 | 9.00 |
| □ IC5 Dominik Hasek | 25.00 | 11.00 |
| □ IC6 Joe Thornton | 20.00 | 9.00 |
| □ IC7 Martin Brodeur | 30.00 | 13.50 |
| □ IC8 Teemu Selanne | 25.00 | 11.00 |
| □ IC9 Paul Kariya | 50.00 | 22.00 |
| □ IC10 Joe Sakic | 25.00 | 11.00 |
| □ IC11 Mark Messier | 20.00 | 9.00 |
| □ IC12 Peter Forsberg | 40.00 | 18.00 |
| □ IC13 Mats Sundin | 12.00 | 5.50 |
| □ IC14 Brendan Shanahan | 25.00 | 11.00 |
| □ IC15 Keith Tkachuk | 15.00 | 6.75 |
| □ IC16 Brett Hull | 15.00 | 6.75 |
| □ IC17 John Vanbiesbrouck | 20.00 | 9.00 |
| □ IC18 Jaromir Jagr | 40.00 | 18.00 |
| □ IC19 Steve Yzerman | 40.00 | 18.00 |
| □ IC20 Sergei Samsonov | 20.00 | 9.00 |

## 1997-98 Upper Deck Ice Lethal Lines

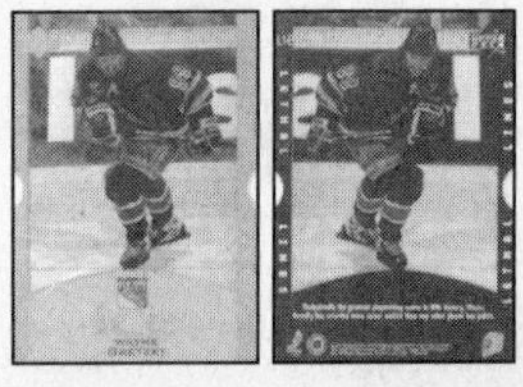

Randomly inserted in packs at the rate of one in 11, this 30-card set features ten sets of three cards each displaying an action player photo which create an interlocking complete die-cut "lethal line" card when placed side-by-side in the correct order.

| | MINT | NRMT |
|---|---|---|
| COMPLETE SET (30) | 300.00 | 135.00 |
| COMMON CARD (L1A-L10C) | 2.00 | .90 |
| COMP.LETHAL LINE 2 (30) | 1500.00 | 700.00 |
| COMMON LETHAL LINE 2 (1-30) | 10.00 | 4.50 |
| *LETH.LINE 2 STARS: 2.5X TO 5X BASIC CARDS | | |
| *LETH.LINE 2 YNG.STARS: 2X TO 4X BASIC CARDS | | |

| | | |
|---|---|---|
| □ L1A Paul Kariya | 25.00 | 11.00 |
| □ L1B Wayne Gretzky | 40.00 | 18.00 |
| □ L1C Joe Thornton | 6.00 | 2.70 |
| □ L2A Brendan Shanahan | 12.00 | 5.50 |
| □ L2B Eric Lindros | 20.00 | 9.00 |
| □ L2C Jaromir Jagr | 20.00 | 9.00 |
| □ L3A Keith Tkachuk | 8.00 | 3.60 |
| □ L3B Mark Messier | 8.00 | 3.60 |
| □ L3C Owen Nolan | 5.00 | 2.20 |
| □ L4A Daniel Alfredsson | 5.00 | 2.20 |
| □ L4B Peter Forsberg | 20.00 | 9.00 |
| □ L4C Mats Sundin | 6.00 | 2.70 |
| □ L5A Ryan Smyth | 5.00 | 2.20 |
| □ L5B Steve Yzerman | 20.00 | 9.00 |
| □ L5C Jarome Iginla | 5.00 | 2.20 |
| □ L6A Sergei Samsonov | 6.00 | 2.70 |
| □ L6B Igor Larionov | 2.00 | .90 |
| □ L6C Sergei Fedorov | 12.00 | 5.50 |
| □ L7A Patrik Elias | 6.00 | 2.70 |
| □ L7B Alexei Morozov | 5.00 | 2.20 |
| □ L7C Vaclav Prospal | 5.00 | 2.20 |
| □ L8A John LeClair | 10.00 | 4.50 |
| □ L8B Mike Modano | 8.00 | 3.60 |
| □ L8C Brett Hull | 8.00 | 3.60 |
| □ L9A Olli Jokinen | 5.00 | 2.20 |
| □ L9B Saku Koivu | 10.00 | 4.50 |
| □ L9C Teemu Selanne | 12.00 | 5.50 |
| □ L10A Brian Leetch | 6.00 | 2.70 |
| □ L10B Patrick Roy | 30.00 | 13.50 |
| □ L10C Nicklas Lidstrom | 2.00 | .90 |

## 1998-99 Upper Deck MVP

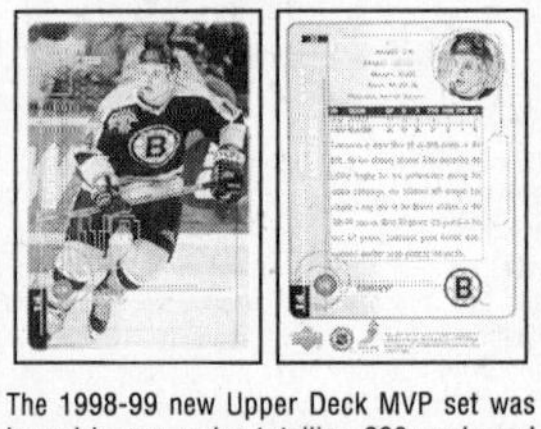

The 1998-99 new Upper Deck MVP set was issued in one series totalling 220 cards and distributed in ten-card packs with a suggested retail price of $1.59. The fronts feature color action player photos printed on internally die-cut, double laminated cards with player information on the backs.

| | MINT | NRMT |
|---|---|---|
| COMPLETE SET (220) | 30.00 | 13.50 |
| COMMON CARD (1-220) | .15 | .07 |
| GRETZKY RETIREMENT CARD/99 | 400.00 | 180.00 |

| | | |
|---|---|---|
| □ 1 Paul Kariya | 1.25 | .55 |
| □ 2 Teemu Selanne | .60 | .25 |
| □ 3 Tomas Sandstrom | .15 | .07 |
| □ 4 Johan Davidsson | .15 | .07 |
| □ 5 Mike Crowley | .15 | .07 |
| □ 6 Guy Hebert | .25 | .11 |
| □ 7 Marty McInnis | .15 | .07 |
| □ 8 Steve Rucchin | .15 | .07 |
| □ 9 Ray Bourque | .30 | .14 |
| □ 10 Sergei Samsonov | .50 | .23 |
| □ 11 Cameron Mann | .15 | .07 |
| □ 12 Joe Thornton | .15 | .07 |
| □ 13 Jason Allison | .25 | .11 |
| □ 14 Byron Dafoe | .25 | .11 |
| □ 15 Kyle McLaren | .15 | .07 |
| □ 16 Dmitri Khristich | .15 | .07 |
| □ 17 Hal Gill | .15 | .07 |
| □ 18 Anson Carter | .15 | .07 |
| □ 19 Miroslav Satan | .25 | .11 |
| □ 20 Brian Holzinger | .15 | .07 |
| □ 21 Dominik Hasek | .60 | .25 |
| □ 22 Matthew Barnaby | .15 | .07 |
| □ 23 Erik Rasmussen | .15 | .07 |
| □ 24 Geoff Sanderson | .25 | .11 |
| □ 25 Michal Grosek | .15 | .07 |
| □ 26 Michael Peca | .25 | .11 |
| □ 27 Rico Fata | .40 | .18 |
| □ 28 Derek Morris | .15 | .07 |
| □ 29 Phil Housley | .15 | .07 |
| □ 30 Valeri Bure | .15 | .07 |
| □ 31 Ed Ward | .15 | .07 |
| □ 32 Jean-Sebastian Giguere | .25 | .11 |
| □ 33 Jeff Shantz | .15 | .07 |
| □ 34 Jarome Iginla | .15 | .07 |
| □ 35 Ron Francis | .25 | .11 |
| □ 36 Trevor Kidd | .25 | .11 |
| □ 37 Keith Primeau | .25 | .11 |
| □ 38 Sami Kapanen | .15 | .07 |
| □ 39 Martin Gelinas | .15 | .07 |
| □ 40 Jeff O'Neill | .15 | .07 |
| □ 41 Gary Roberts | .15 | .07 |
| □ 42 Jocelyn Thibault | .25 | .11 |
| □ 43 Doug Gilmour | .30 | .14 |
| □ 44 Chris Chelios | .30 | .14 |
| □ 45 Tony Amonte | .25 | .11 |
| □ 46 Bob Probert | .15 | .07 |
| □ 47 Daniel Cleary | .15 | .07 |
| □ 48 Eric Daze | .15 | .07 |
| □ 49 Mike Maneluk RC | .40 | .18 |
| □ 50 Remi Royer | .15 | .07 |
| □ 51 Peter Forsberg | 1.00 | .45 |
| □ 52 Patrick Roy | 1.50 | .70 |
| □ 53 Joe Sakic | .60 | .25 |
| □ 54 Chris Drury | .40 | .18 |
| □ 55 Milan Hejduk RC | .50 | .23 |
| □ 56 Greg DeVries | .15 | .07 |
| □ 57 Theoren Fleury | .30 | .14 |
| □ 58 Adam Deadmarsh | .25 | .11 |
| □ 59 Brett Hull | .40 | .18 |
| □ 60 Ed Belfour | .30 | .14 |
| □ 61 Mike Modano | .40 | .18 |
| □ 62 Darryl Sydor | .15 | .07 |
| □ 63 Joe Nieuwendyk | .25 | .11 |
| □ 64 Grant Marshall | .15 | .07 |
| □ 65 Sergei Zubov | .15 | .07 |
| □ 66 Derian Hatcher | .15 | .07 |
| □ 67 Jere Lehtinen | .25 | .11 |
| □ 68 Sergei Fedorov | .60 | .25 |
| □ 69 Steve Yzerman | 1.00 | .45 |
| □ 70 Nicklas Lidstrom | .25 | .11 |
| □ 71 Chris Osgood | .30 | .14 |
| □ 72 Brendan Shanahan | .60 | .25 |
| □ 73 Darren McCarty | .15 | .07 |
| □ 74 Tomas Holmstrom | .15 | .07 |
| □ 75 Norm Maracle RC | .50 | .23 |
| □ 76 Doug Brown | .15 | .07 |
| □ 77 Doug Weight | .25 | .11 |
| □ 78 Janne Niinimaa | .15 | .07 |
| □ 79 Tom Poti | .15 | .07 |
| □ 80 Bill Guerin | .25 | .11 |
| □ 81 Mike Grier | .15 | .07 |
| □ 82 Ryan Smyth | .25 | .11 |
| □ 83 Roman Hamrlik | .15 | .07 |
| □ 84 Kevin Brown | .15 | .07 |
| □ 85 Pavel Bure | .60 | .25 |
| □ 86 Jaroslav Spacek | .15 | .07 |
| □ 87 Rob Niedermayer | .15 | .07 |
| □ 88 Robert Svehla | .15 | .07 |
| □ 89 Ray Whitney | .15 | .07 |
| □ 90 Peter Worrell RC | .25 | .11 |
| □ 91 Mark Parrish RC | .50 | .23 |
| □ 92 Oleg Kvasha RC | .30 | .14 |
| □ 93 Steve Duchesne | .25 | .11 |
| □ 94 Rob Blake | .15 | .07 |
| □ 95 Olli Jokinen | .25 | .11 |
| □ 96 Donald Audette | .15 | .07 |
| □ 97 Luc Robitaille | .25 | .11 |
| □ 98 Josh Green | .25 | .11 |
| □ 99 Philippe Boucher | .15 | .07 |
| □ 100 Matt Johnson | .15 | .07 |
| □ 101 Vincent Damphousse | .25 | .11 |
| □ 102 Dainius Zubrus | .15 | .07 |
| □ 103 Terry Ryan | .15 | .07 |
| □ 104 Saku Koivu | .50 | .23 |
| □ 105 Brett Clark | .15 | .07 |
| □ 106 Dave Morrisette | .15 | .07 |
| □ 107 Eric Weinrich | .15 | .07 |
| □ 108 Brian Savage | .15 | .07 |
| □ 109 Shayne Corson | .15 | .07 |
| □ 110 Mike Dunham | .25 | .11 |
| □ 111 Greg Johnson | .15 | .07 |
| □ 112 Cliff Ronning | .15 | .07 |
| □ 113 Andrew Brunette | .15 | .07 |
| □ 114 Sergei Krivokrasov | .15 | .07 |
| □ 115 Sebastien Bordeleau | .15 | .07 |
| □ 116 Scott Stevens | .15 | .07 |
| □ 117 Martin Brodeur | .75 | .35 |
| □ 118 Brendan Morrison | .25 | .11 |
| □ 119 Patrik Elias | .25 | .11 |
| □ 120 Scott Niedermayer | .15 | .07 |
| □ 121 Bobby Holik | .15 | .07 |
| □ 122 Jason Arnott | .25 | .11 |
| □ 123 Jay Pandolfo | .15 | .07 |
| □ 124 Eric Brewer | .15 | .07 |
| □ 125 Zigmund Palffy | .30 | .14 |
| □ 126 Felix Potvin | .30 | .14 |
| □ 127 Robert Reichel | .15 | .07 |
| □ 128 Mike Watt | .15 | .07 |
| □ 129 Tommy Salo | .25 | .11 |
| □ 130 Kenny Jonsson | .15 | .07 |
| □ 131 Trevor Linden | .25 | .11 |
| □ 132 Wayne Gretzky | 2.00 | .90 |
| □ 133 Brian Leetch | .30 | .14 |
| □ 134 Manny Malhotra | .25 | .11 |
| □ 135 Mike Richter | .30 | .14 |
| □ 136 Mike Knuble | .15 | .07 |
| □ 137 Niklas Sundstrom | .15 | .07 |
| □ 138 Todd Harvey | .15 | .07 |
| □ 139 Alexei Yashin | .25 | .11 |
| □ 140 Damian Rhodes | .25 | .11 |
| □ 141 Daniel Alfredsson | .25 | .11 |
| □ 142 Magnus Arvedson | .15 | .07 |
| □ 143 Shawn McEachern | .15 | .07 |
| □ 144 Chris Phillips | .15 | .07 |
| □ 145 Vaclav Prospal | .15 | .07 |
| □ 146 Wade Redden | .15 | .07 |
| □ 147 Eric Lindros | 1.00 | .45 |
| □ 148 John LeClair | .50 | .23 |
| □ 149 John Vanbiesbrouck | .50 | .23 |
| □ 150 Keith Jones | .25 | .11 |
| □ 151 Colin Forbes | .15 | .07 |
| □ 152 Mark Recchi | .25 | .11 |
| □ 153 Dan McGillis | .15 | .07 |
| □ 154 Eric Desjardins | .15 | .07 |
| □ 155 Rod Brind'Amour | .25 | .11 |
| □ 156 Keith Tkachuk | .40 | .18 |
| □ 157 Daniel Briere | .15 | .07 |
| □ 158 Nikolai Khabibulin | .25 | .11 |
| □ 159 Brad Isbister | .15 | .07 |
| □ 160 Jeremy Roenick | .30 | .14 |
| □ 161 Oleg Tverdovsky | .15 | .07 |
| □ 162 Rick Tocchet | .25 | .11 |
| □ 163 Jaromir Jagr | 1.00 | .45 |
| □ 164 Tom Barrasso | .25 | .11 |
| □ 165 Alexei Morozov | .25 | .11 |
| □ 166 Robert Dome | .15 | .07 |
| □ 167 Stu Barnes | .15 | .07 |
| □ 168 Martin Straka | .15 | .07 |
| □ 169 German Titov | .15 | .07 |
| □ 170 Patrick Marleau | .15 | .07 |
| □ 171 Andrei Zyuzin | .15 | .07 |
| □ 172 Marco Sturm | .25 | .11 |
| □ 173 Owen Nolan | .25 | .11 |
| □ 174 Jeff Friesen | .15 | .07 |
| □ 175 Bob Rouse | .15 | .07 |
| □ 176 Mike Vernon | .25 | .11 |
| □ 177 Mike Ricci | .25 | .11 |
| □ 178 Marty Reasoner | .15 | .07 |
| □ 179 Al MacInnis | .15 | .07 |
| □ 180 Chris Pronger | .25 | .11 |
| □ 181 Pierre Turgeon | .25 | .11 |
| □ 182 Michal Handzus | .30 | .14 |
| □ 183 Jim Campbell | .15 | .07 |
| □ 184 Tony Twist | .15 | .07 |
| □ 185 Pavol Demitra | .25 | .11 |
| □ 186 Daren Puppa | .25 | .11 |
| □ 187 Vincent Lecavalier | .75 | .35 |
| □ 188 Bill Ranford | .25 | .11 |
| □ 189 Alexandre Daigle | .15 | .07 |
| □ 190 Wendel Clark | .25 | .11 |
| □ 191 Rob Zamuner | .15 | .07 |
| □ 192 Chris Gratton | .15 | .07 |
| □ 193 Fredrik Modin | .15 | .07 |
| □ 194 Curtis Joseph | .30 | .14 |
| □ 195 Mats Sundin | .30 | .14 |
| □ 196 Steve Thomas | .15 | .07 |
| □ 197 Tomas Kaberle RC | .25 | .11 |
| □ 198 Alyn McCauley | .15 | .07 |
| □ 199 Mike Johnson | .25 | .11 |
| □ 200 Bryan Berard | .15 | .07 |
| □ 201 Mark Messier | .40 | .18 |
| □ 202 Jason Strudwick | .15 | .07 |
| □ 203 Mattias Ohlund | .25 | .11 |
| □ 204 Alexander Mogilny | .25 | .11 |
| □ 205 Bill Muckalt RC | .40 | .18 |
| □ 206 Ed Jovanovski | .25 | .11 |
| □ 207 Josh Holden | .15 | .07 |
| □ 208 Peter Schaefer | .15 | .07 |
| □ 209 Peter Bondra | .30 | .14 |
| □ 210 Olaf Kolzig | .25 | .11 |
| □ 211 Sergei Gonchar | .15 | .07 |
| □ 212 Adam Oates | .25 | .11 |
| □ 213 Brian Bellows | .15 | .07 |
| □ 214 Matt Herr | .15 | .07 |
| □ 215 Richard Zednik | .15 | .07 |
| □ 216 Joe Juneau | .15 | .07 |
| □ 217 Jaroslav Svejkovski | .15 | .07 |
| □ 218 Wayne Gretzky CL | 1.00 | .45 |
| □ 219 Wayne Gretzky CL | 1.00 | .45 |
| □ 220 Wayne Gretzky CL | 1.00 | .45 |

## 1998-99 Upper Deck MVP Silver Script

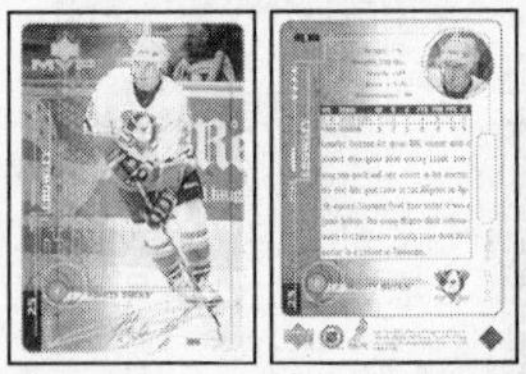

Randomly inserted into packs at the rate of one in two, this 220-card set is a silver foil parallel version of the base set.

| | MINT | NRMT |
|---|---|---|
| COMPLETE SET (220) | 120.00 | 55.00 |
| COMMON CARD (1-220) | .60 | .25 |
| *STARS: 2X TO 4X BASIC CARD | | |
| *YOUNG STARS: 1.5X TO 3X | | |
| *RC's: 1X TO 2X | | |

## 1998-99 Upper Deck MVP Gold Script

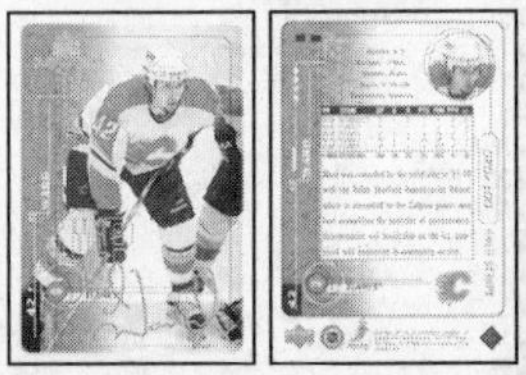

Randomly inserted in hobby packs only, this 220-card set is a gold foil hobby parallel version of the base set. Only 100 sequentially numbered sets were produced.

| | MINT | NRMT |
|---|---|---|
| COMPLETE SET (220) | 5000.00 | 2200.00 |
| COMMON CARD (1-220) | 20.00 | 9.00 |
| *STARS: 75X TO 150X BASIC CARD | | |

*YOUNG STARS: 50X TO 100X
*RC's: 40X TO 80X

## 1998-99 Upper Deck MVP Super Script

Randomly inserted into hobby packs only, this 220-card set is a hobby limited edition, holographic foil parallel version of the base set. Only 25 sequentially numbered sets were produced.

| | MINT | NRMT |
|---|---|---|
| COMMON CARD (1-220) | 40.00 | 18.00 |
| *STARS: 200X TO 400X BASIC CARDS | | |
| *YOUNG STARS: 150X TO 300X | | |
| *RC's: 125X TO 250X | | |

## 1998-99 Upper Deck MVP Dynamics

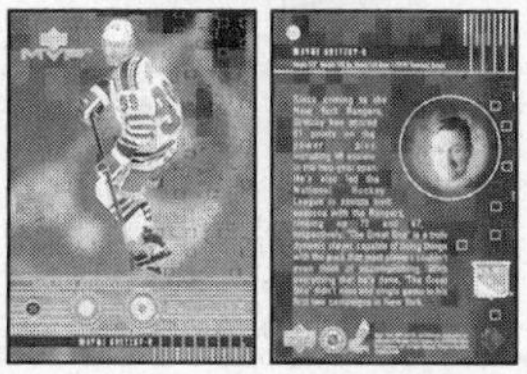

Randomly inserted into packs at a ratio of one in 28, this set commemorates the brilliant career of Wayne Gretzky.

| | MINT | NRMT |
|---|---|---|
| COMPLETE SET (15) | 175.00 | 80.00 |
| COMMON CARD (D1-D15) | 12.00 | 5.50 |

## 1998-99 Upper Deck MVP Game Souvenirs

Randomly inserted in hobby packs only at the rate of one in 144, this 10-card set features color action player photos with actual pieces of game used memorabilia right on the cards.

| | MINT | NRMT |
|---|---|---|
| COMPLETE SET (10) | 800.00 | 350.00 |
| COMMON CARD | 60.00 | 27.00 |
| STATED ODDS 1:144 | | |
| ❑ BH Brett Hull | 50.00 | 22.00 |
| ❑ BS Brendan Shanahan | 80.00 | 36.00 |
| ❑ EL Eric Lindros | 100.00 | 45.00 |
| ❑ JL John LeClair | 60.00 | 27.00 |
| ❑ MM Mike Modano | 50.00 | 22.00 |
| ❑ PR Patrick Roy | 120.00 | 55.00 |
| ❑ RB Ray Bourque | 50.00 | 22.00 |
| ❑ SF Sergei Fedorov | 80.00 | 36.00 |
| ❑ SS Sergei Samsonov | 50.00 | 22.00 |
| ❑ SY Steve Yzerman | 100.00 | 45.00 |
| ❑ VL Vincent Lecavalier | 50.00 | 22.00 |
| ❑ WG Wayne Gretzky | 150.00 | 70.00 |
| ❑ SYA S.Yzerman AU/19 | 1000.00 | 450.00 |
| ❑ VLA V.Lecavalier AU/14 | 500.00 | 220.00 |

## 1998-99 Upper Deck MVP OT Heroes

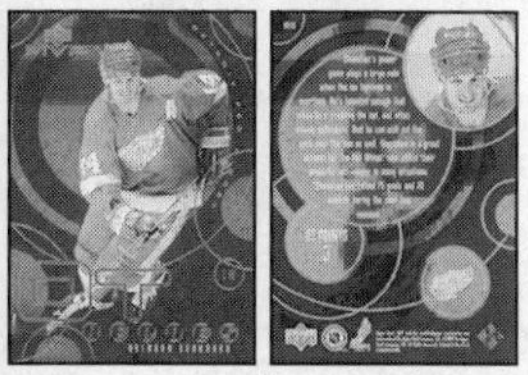

Randomly inserted into packs at the rate of one in nine, this 15-card set features color action photos of top Hockey players and goalies who usually come through especially in overtime situations.

| | MINT | NRMT |
|---|---|---|
| COMPLETE SET (15) | 80.00 | 36.00 |
| COMMON CARD (OT1-OT15) | 2.00 | .90 |
| ❑ OT1 Steve Yzerman | 6.00 | 2.70 |
| ❑ OT2 Patrick Roy | 10.00 | 4.50 |
| ❑ OT3 Jaromir Jagr | 6.00 | 2.70 |
| ❑ OT4 Ray Bourque | 2.00 | .90 |
| ❑ OT5 Wayne Gretzky | 12.00 | 5.50 |
| ❑ OT6 Sergei Samsonov | 3.00 | 1.35 |
| ❑ OT7 Dominik Hasek | 4.00 | 1.80 |
| ❑ OT8 Peter Forsberg | 6.00 | 2.70 |
| ❑ OT9 Paul Kariya | 8.00 | 3.60 |
| ❑ OT10 Eric Lindros | 6.00 | 2.70 |
| ❑ OT11 Pavel Bure | 4.00 | 1.80 |
| ❑ OT12 Keith Tkachuk | 2.50 | 1.10 |
| ❑ OT13 Brendan Shanahan | 4.00 | 1.80 |
| ❑ OT14 John LeClair | 3.00 | 1.35 |
| ❑ OT15 Joe Sakic | 4.00 | 1.80 |

## 1998-99 Upper Deck MVP Power Game

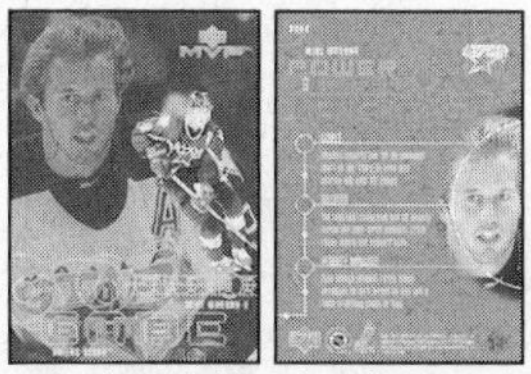

Randomly inserted into packs at the rate of one in nine, this 15-card set features color action photos of some of the biggest and most talented power forwards in the NHL.

| | MINT | NRMT |
|---|---|---|
| COMPLETE SET (15) | 50.00 | 22.00 |
| COMMON CARD (PG1-PG15) | 1.50 | .70 |
| ❑ PG1 Brendan Shanahan | 4.00 | 1.80 |
| ❑ PG2 Keith Tkachuk | 2.50 | 1.10 |
| ❑ PG3 Eric Lindros | 6.00 | 2.70 |
| ❑ PG4 Mike Modano | 2.50 | 1.10 |
| ❑ PG5 Vincent Lecavalier | 4.00 | 1.80 |
| ❑ PG6 John LeClair | 3.00 | 1.35 |
| ❑ PG7 Mark Messier | 2.50 | 1.10 |
| ❑ PG8 Mats Sundin | 1.50 | .70 |
| ❑ PG9 Peter Forsberg | 6.00 | 2.70 |
| ❑ PG10 Jaromir Jagr | 6.00 | 2.70 |
| ❑ PG11 Keith Primeau | 1.50 | .70 |
| ❑ PG12 Mark Parrish | 1.50 | .70 |
| ❑ PG13 Patrick Marleau | 1.50 | .70 |
| ❑ PG14 Bill Guerin | 1.50 | .70 |
| ❑ PG15 Jeremy Roenick | 1.50 | .70 |

## 1998-99 Upper Deck MVP ProSign

Randomly inserted in retail packs only at the rate of one in 216, this 23-card set features color action photos of the NHL's superstars with the player's autograph in the wide bottom margin. These cards were among this years toughest autograph pulls.

| | MINT | NRMT |
|---|---|---|
| COMMON CARD | 12.00 | 5.50 |
| ❑ AM Alyn McCauley | 15.00 | 6.75 |
| ❑ BB Brian Bellows | 12.00 | 5.50 |
| ❑ BM Brendan Morrison | 20.00 | 9.00 |
| ❑ CD Chris Drury | 30.00 | 13.50 |
| ❑ DN Dmitri Nabokov | 20.00 | 9.00 |
| ❑ DW Doug Weight | 20.00 | 9.00 |
| ❑ EB Eric Brewer | 15.00 | 6.75 |
| ❑ ER Erik Rasmussen | 20.00 | 9.00 |
| ❑ JA Jason Allison | 12.00 | 5.50 |
| ❑ JI Jarome Iginla | 15.00 | 6.75 |
| ❑ JT Jose Theodore | 15.00 | 6.75 |
| ❑ MD Mike Dunham | 12.00 | 5.50 |
| ❑ MJ Mike Johnson | 15.00 | 6.75 |
| ❑ MM Manny Malhotra | 20.00 | 9.00 |
| ❑ MP Mark Parrish | 25.00 | 11.00 |
| ❑ OT Oleg Tverdovsky | 12.00 | 5.50 |
| ❑ RF Rico Fata | 15.00 | 6.75 |
| ❑ RN Rob Niedermayer | 12.00 | 5.50 |
| ❑ SY Steve Yzerman | 200.00 | 90.00 |
| ❑ VL Vincent Lecavalier | 30.00 | 13.50 |
| ❑ WG Wayne Gretzky | 400.00 | 180.00 |
| ❑ WR Wade Redden | 15.00 | 6.75 |
| ❑ JAR Jason Arnott | 15.00 | 6.75 |

## 1998-99 Upper Deck MVP Snipers

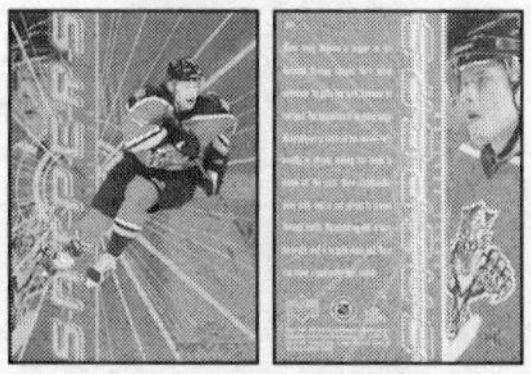

Randomly inserted into packs at the rate of one in six, this 12-card set features color action photos of some of the NHL's top sharpshooters printed on geometric backgrounds.

| | MINT | NRMT |
|---|---|---|
| COMPLETE SET (12) | 30.00 | 13.50 |
| COMMON CARD (S1-S12) | 1.25 | .55 |
| ❑ S1 Vincent Lecavalier | 2.50 | 1.10 |
| ❑ S2 Wayne Gretzky | 8.00 | 3.60 |
| ❑ S3 Sergei Samsonov | 2.00 | .90 |
| ❑ S4 Teemu Selanne | 2.50 | 1.10 |
| ❑ S5 Peter Forsberg | 4.00 | 1.80 |
| ❑ S6 Paul Kariya | 5.00 | 2.20 |
| ❑ S7 Eric Lindros | 4.00 | 1.80 |
| ❑ S8 Pavel Bure | 2.50 | 1.10 |
| ❑ S9 Peter Bondra | 1.25 | .55 |
| ❑ S10 Joe Sakic | 2.50 | 1.10 |
| ❑ S11 Steve Yzerman | 4.00 | 1.80 |
| ❑ S12 Sergei Fedorov | 2.50 | 1.10 |

## 1998-99 Upper Deck MVP Special Forces

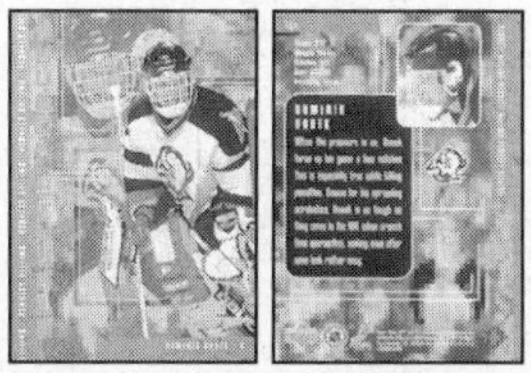

Randomly inserted into packs at the rate of one in 14, this 15-card set features color action images of some of the NHL's special players who are key to penalty killing and powerplays printed on backgrounds using the same image in a close-up black-and-white version.

| | MINT | NRMT |
|---|---|---|
| COMPLETE SET (15) | 100.00 | 45.00 |
| COMMON CARD (F1-F15) | 4.00 | 1.80 |
| ❑ F1 Brett Hull | 3.00 | 1.35 |
| ❑ F2 Sergei Samsonov | 4.00 | 1.80 |
| ❑ F3 Vincent Lecavalier | 5.00 | 2.20 |
| ❑ F4 Dominik Hasek | 5.00 | 2.20 |
| ❑ F5 Eric Lindros | 8.00 | 3.60 |
| ❑ F6 Paul Kariya | 10.00 | 4.50 |
| ❑ F7 Steve Yzerman | 8.00 | 3.60 |
| ❑ F8 Brendan Shanahan | 5.00 | 2.20 |
| ❑ F9 Martin Brodeur | 6.00 | 2.70 |
| ❑ F10 Teemu Selanne | 5.00 | 2.20 |
| ❑ F11 Jaromir Jagr | 8.00 | 3.60 |
| ❑ F12 Wayne Gretzky | 15.00 | 6.75 |
| ❑ F13 Patrick Roy | 12.00 | 5.50 |
| ❑ F14 Peter Forsberg | 8.00 | 3.60 |
| ❑ F15 Joe Sakic | 5.00 | 2.20 |

## 1998 Upper Deck Willie O'Ree Commemorative Card

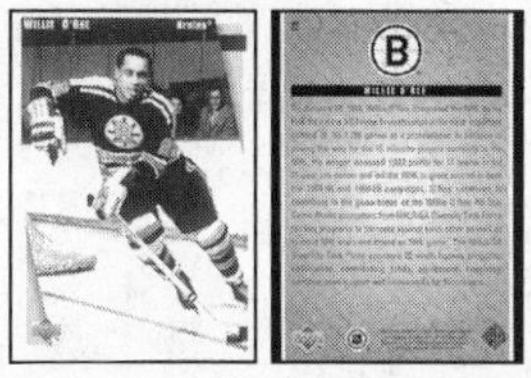

This card was issued by Upper Deck of the 1998 NHL All-Stars game in Vancouver. It was available at All-Star activies throughout the weekend.

| | MINT | NRMT |
|---|---|---|
| ❑ 22 Willie O'Ree | 3.00 | 1.35 |

## 1980 USA Olympic Team Mini Pics

Cards measure 1 3/4" x 2 3/4". Card fronts feature a black and white photo, players name, and position. Card backs feature card number and the words MINI PICS and 1980 GOLD MEDAL WINNERS.

| | MINT | NRMT |
|---|---|---|
| COMPLETE SET (15) | 35.00 | 16.00 |
| COMMON CARD (1-15) | 1.50 | .70 |
| ❑ 1 Jim Craig | 3.00 | 1.35 |
| ❑ 2 Mike Eruzione | 5.00 | 2.20 |
| ❑ 3 John Harrington | 1.50 | .70 |
| ❑ 4 Mark Johnson | 1.50 | .70 |
| ❑ 5 Rob McClanahan | 1.50 | .70 |
| ❑ 6 Jack O'Callahan | 2.00 | .90 |
| ❑ 7 Phil Verchota | 1.50 | .70 |
| ❑ 8 Bob Suter | 1.50 | .70 |
| ❑ 9 Eric Strobel | 1.50 | .70 |
| ❑ 10 Dave Silk | 1.50 | .70 |
| ❑ 11 Mike Ramsey | 1.50 | .70 |
| ❑ 12 Marty Pavelich | 1.50 | .70 |
| ❑ 13 Steve Christoff | 1.50 | .70 |
| ❑ 14 Dave Christian | 2.50 | 1.10 |
| ❑ 15 Herb Brooks CO | 2.00 | .90 |
| ❑ NNO Score Card | 6.00 | 2.70 |

## 1980 USSR Olympic Team Mini Pics

| | MINT | NRMT |
|---|---|---|
| COMPLETE SET (10) | 20.00 | 9.00 |
| COMMON CARD (1-10) | 1.50 | .70 |
| ❑ 1 Juri Federov | 1.50 | .70 |
| ❑ 2 Irek Gimayev | 1.50 | .70 |
| ❑ 3 Alexander Golikov | 1.50 | .70 |
| ❑ 4 Sergei Kapustin | 1.50 | .70 |
| ❑ 5 V.Kovin | 1.50 | .70 |
| ❑ 6 Boris Mikhailov | 1.50 | .70 |
| ❑ 7 V.Myshkin | 1.50 | .70 |
| ❑ 8 Vladimir Petrov | 2.00 | .90 |
| ❑ 9 Vladislav Tretiak | 6.00 | 2.70 |
| ❑ 10 Valeri Vasilijev | 1.50 | .70 |

## 1923-24 V128-1 Paulin's Candy

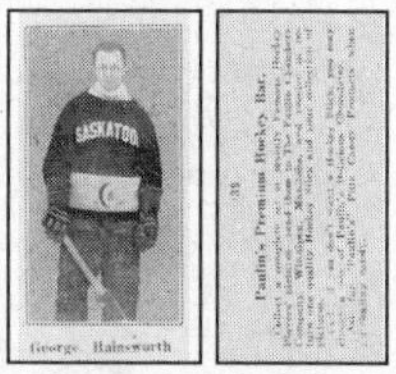

This 70-card set was issued during the 1923-24 season and featured players from the WCHL. The horizontal back explains how to obtain either a hockey stick or a box of Paulin's chocolates by collecting and sending in the complete Famous Hockey Players set. The cards were to be returned to the collector with the hockey stick or chocolates. The cards are in black and white and measure approximately 1 3/8" by 2 3/4".

| | EX-MT | VG-E |
|---|---|---|
| COMPLETE SET (70) | 9000.00 | 4500.00 |
| COMMON CARD (1-70) | 100.00 | 50.00 |
| ❑ 1 Bill Borland | 150.00 | 75.00 |
| ❑ 2 Pete Speirs | 100.00 | 50.00 |
| ❑ 3 Jack Hughes | 100.00 | 50.00 |
| ❑ 4 Errol Gillis | 100.00 | 50.00 |
| ❑ 5 Cecil Browne | 100.00 | 50.00 |
| ❑ 6 W. Roberts | 100.00 | 50.00 |
| ❑ 7 Howard Brandon | 100.00 | 50.00 |
| ❑ 8 Fred Comfort | 100.00 | 50.00 |
| ❑ 9 Cliff O'Meara | 100.00 | 50.00 |
| ❑ 10 Leo Benard | 100.00 | 50.00 |
| ❑ 11 Lloyd Harvey | 100.00 | 50.00 |
| ❑ 12 Bobby Connors | 100.00 | 50.00 |
| ❑ 13 Daddy Dalman | 100.00 | 50.00 |
| ❑ 14 Dub Mackie | 100.00 | 50.00 |
| ❑ 15 Lorne Chabot | 250.00 | 125.00 |
| ❑ 16 Phat Wilson | 125.00 | 60.00 |
| ❑ 17 Wilf L'Heureux | 100.00 | 50.00 |
| ❑ 18 Danny Cox | 100.00 | 50.00 |
| ❑ 19 Bill Brydge | 100.00 | 50.00 |
| ❑ 20 Alex Gray | 100.00 | 50.00 |
| ❑ 21 Albert Pudas | 100.00 | 50.00 |
| ❑ 22 Jack Irwin | 100.00 | 50.00 |
| ❑ 23 Puss Traub | 100.00 | 50.00 |
| ❑ 24 Red McCusker | 125.00 | 60.00 |
| ❑ 25 Jack Asseltine | 125.00 | 60.00 |
| ❑ 26 Duke Dutkowski | 100.00 | 50.00 |
| ❑ 27 Charley McVeigh | 100.00 | 50.00 |
| ❑ 28 George Hay | 250.00 | 125.00 |
| ❑ 29 Amby Moran | 100.00 | 50.00 |
| ❑ 30 Barney Stanley | 300.00 | 150.00 |
| ❑ 31 Art Gagne | 100.00 | 50.00 |
| ❑ 32 Louis Berlinquette | 100.00 | 50.00 |
| ❑ 33 P.C. Stevens | 100.00 | 50.00 |
| ❑ 34 W.D. Elmer | 100.00 | 50.00 |
| ❑ 35 Bill Cook | 350.00 | 180.00 |
| ❑ 36 Leo Reise | 100.00 | 50.00 |
| ❑ 37 Curly Headley | 250.00 | 125.00 |
| ❑ 38 Newsy Lalonde | 600.00 | 300.00 |
| ❑ 39 George Hainsworth | 600.00 | 300.00 |
| ❑ 40 Laurie Scott | 100.00 | 50.00 |
| ❑ 41 Joe Simpson | 350.00 | 180.00 |
| ❑ 42 Bob Trapp | 100.00 | 50.00 |
| ❑ 43 Joe McCormick | 100.00 | 50.00 |
| ❑ 44 Ty Arbour | 100.00 | 50.00 |
| ❑ 45 Duke Keats | 125.00 | 60.00 |
| ❑ 46 Hal Winkler | 100.00 | 50.00 |
| ❑ 47 Johnny Sheppard | 100.00 | 50.00 |
| ❑ 48 Crutchy Morrison | 100.00 | 50.00 |
| ❑ 49 Spunk Sparrow | 100.00 | 50.00 |
| ❑ 50 Percy McGregor | 100.00 | 50.00 |
| ❑ 51 Harry Tuckwell | 100.00 | 50.00 |
| ❑ 52 Chubby Scott | 100.00 | 50.00 |
| ❑ 53 Scotty Fraser | 100.00 | 50.00 |
| ❑ 54 Bob Davis | 100.00 | 50.00 |
| ❑ 55 Clucker White | 100.00 | 50.00 |
| ❑ 56 Bob Armstrong | 100.00 | 50.00 |
| ❑ 57 Doc Longtry | 100.00 | 50.00 |
| ❑ 58 Darb Sommers | 100.00 | 50.00 |
| ❑ 59 Frank Hacquoil | 100.00 | 50.00 |
| ❑ 60 Stan Evans | 100.00 | 50.00 |
| ❑ 61 Ed Oatman | 100.00 | 50.00 |
| ❑ 62 Mervyn(Red) Dutton | 400.00 | 200.00 |
| ❑ 63 Herb Gardiner | 250.00 | 125.00 |
| ❑ 64 Bernie Morris | 100.00 | 50.00 |
| ❑ 65 Bobbie Benson | 100.00 | 50.00 |
| ❑ 66 Ernie Anderson | 100.00 | 50.00 |
| ❑ 67 Cully Wilson | 100.00 | 50.00 |
| ❑ 68 Charlie Reid | 125.00 | 60.00 |
| ❑ 69 Harry Oliver | 250.00 | 125.00 |
| ❑ 70 Rusty Crawford | 200.00 | 100.00 |

## 1928-29 V128-2 Paulins Candy

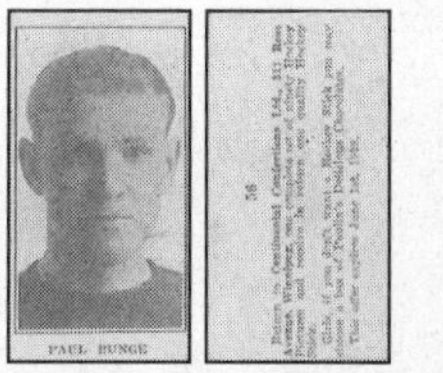

This scarce set of 90 black and white cards was produced and distributed in Western Canada and features Western Canadian teams and players. The cards are numbered on the back and measure approximately 1 3/8" by 2 5/8". The card back details an offer (expiring June 1st, 1929) of a hockey stick prize (or box of chocolates for girls) if someone could bring in a complete set of 90 cards. Players on the Calgary Jimmies are not explicitly identified on the card so they are listed below without a specific player name.

| | EX-MT | VG-E |
|---|---|---|
| COMPLETE SET (90) | 5500.00 | 2800.00 |
| COMMON TEAM (1-40) | 75.00 | 38.00 |
| COMMON CARD (41-90) | 50.00 | 25.00 |
| ❑ 1 Univ. of Man. Girls Hockey Team | 100.00 | 50.00 |
| ❑ 2 Elgin Hockey Team | 75.00 | 38.00 |
| ❑ 3 Brandon Schools Boy Champions | 75.00 | 38.00 |
| ❑ 4 Port Arthur Hockey Team | 75.00 | 38.00 |
| ❑ 5 Enderby Hockey Team | 75.00 | 38.00 |
| ❑ 6 Humboldt High School Team | 75.00 | 38.00 |
| ❑ 7 Regina Collegiate Hockey Team | 75.00 | 38.00 |
| ❑ 8 Weyburn Beavers | 75.00 | 38.00 |
| ❑ 9 Moose Jaw College Junior Hockey Team | 100.00 | 50.00 |
| ❑ 10 M.A.C. Junior Hockey | 75.00 | 38.00 |
| ❑ 11 Vermillion Agri-cultural School | 75.00 | 38.00 |
| ❑ 12 Rovers, Cranbrook, B.C. | 75.00 | 38.00 |
| ❑ 13 Empire School, Moose Jaw | 75.00 | 38.00 |
| ❑ 14 Arts Senior Hockey | 75.00 | 38.00 |
| ❑ 15 Juvenile Varsity Hockey | 75.00 | 38.00 |
| ❑ 16 St. Peter's College Hockey | 75.00 | 38.00 |
| ❑ 17 Arts Girls Hockey | 100.00 | 50.00 |
| ❑ 18 Swan River Hockey Team | 75.00 | 38.00 |
| ❑ 19 U.M.S.U. Junior Hockey Team | 75.00 | 38.00 |
| ❑ 20 Campion College Hockey Team | 100.00 | 50.00 |
| ❑ 21 Drinkwater Hockey Team | 75.00 | 38.00 |
| ❑ 22 Elks Hockey Team, Biggar, Saskatchewan | 75.00 | 38.00 |
| ❑ 23 South Calgary High School | 75.00 | 38.00 |
| ❑ 24 Meota Hockey | 75.00 | 38.00 |
| ❑ 25 Chartered Accountants | 100.00 | 50.00 |
| ❑ 26 Nutana Collegiate Hockey Team | 75.00 | 38.00 |
| ❑ 27 MacLeod Hockey Team | 100.00 | 50.00 |
| ❑ 28 Arts Junior Hockey | 75.00 | 38.00 |
| ❑ 29 Fort William Juniors | 75.00 | 38.00 |
| ❑ 30 Swan Lake Hockey Team | 75.00 | 38.00 |
| ❑ 31 Dauphin Hockey Team | 75.00 | 38.00 |
| ❑ 32 Mount Royal Hockey Team | 75.00 | 38.00 |
| ❑ 33 Port Arthur W. End Junior Hockey | 75.00 | 38.00 |
| ❑ 34 Hanna Hockey Club | 75.00 | 38.00 |
| ❑ 35 Vermillion Junior Hockey | 75.00 | 38.00 |
| ❑ 36 Smithers Hockey Team | 75.00 | 38.00 |
| ❑ 37 Lloydminster High School | 75.00 | 38.00 |
| ❑ 38 Winnipeg Rangers | 100.00 | 50.00 |
| ❑ 39 Delisle Intermediate Hockey | 75.00 | 38.00 |
| ❑ 40 Moose Jaw College Senior Hockey | 75.00 | 38.00 |
| ❑ 41 Art Bonneyman | 50.00 | 25.00 |
| ❑ 42 Jimmy Graham | 50.00 | 25.00 |
| ❑ 43 Pat O'Hunter | 50.00 | 25.00 |
| ❑ 44 Leo Moret | 50.00 | 25.00 |
| ❑ 45 Blondie McLennen | 50.00 | 25.00 |
| ❑ 46 Red Beattie | 75.00 | 38.00 |
| ❑ 47 Frank Peters | 50.00 | 25.00 |
| ❑ 48 Lloyd McIntyre | 50.00 | 25.00 |
| ❑ 49 Art Somers | 75.00 | 38.00 |
| ❑ 50 Ikey Morrison | 50.00 | 25.00 |
| ❑ 51 Calgary Jimmies | 50.00 | 25.00 |
| ❑ 52 Don Cummings | 50.00 | 25.00 |
| ❑ 53 Calgary Jimmies | 50.00 | 25.00 |
| ❑ 54 P. Gerlitz | 50.00 | 25.00 |
| ❑ 55 A. Kay | 50.00 | 25.00 |
| ❑ 56 Paul Runge | 75.00 | 38.00 |
| ❑ 57 J. Gerlitz | 50.00 | 25.00 |
| ❑ 58 H. Gerlitz | 50.00 | 25.00 |
| ❑ 59 C. Biles | 50.00 | 25.00 |
| ❑ 60 Jimmy Evans | 50.00 | 25.00 |
| ❑ 61 Ira Stuart | 50.00 | 25.00 |
| ❑ 62 Berg Irving | 100.00 | 50.00 |
| ❑ 63 Cecil Browne | 75.00 | 38.00 |
| ❑ 64 Nick Wasnie | 75.00 | 38.00 |
| ❑ 65 Gordon Teal | 75.00 | 38.00 |
| ❑ 66 Jack Hughes | 75.00 | 38.00 |
| ❑ 67 D. Yeatman | 75.00 | 38.00 |
| ❑ 68 Connie Johanneson | 50.00 | 25.00 |
| ❑ 69 S. Walters | 50.00 | 25.00 |
| ❑ 70 Harold McMunn | 75.00 | 38.00 |
| ❑ 71 Smokey Harris | 50.00 | 25.00 |
| ❑ 72 Calgary Jimmies | 50.00 | 25.00 |
| ❑ 73 Bernie Morris | 50.00 | 25.00 |
| ❑ 74 J. Fowler | 75.00 | 38.00 |
| ❑ 75 Calgary Jimmies | 50.00 | 25.00 |
| ❑ 76 Pete Spiers | 50.00 | 25.00 |

| | | |
|---|---|---|
| ❑ 77 Bill Borland | 75.00 | 38.00 |
| ❑ 78 Cliff O'Meara | 75.00 | 38.00 |
| ❑ 79 F. Porteous | 75.00 | 38.00 |
| ❑ 80 W. Brooks | 75.00 | 38.00 |
| ❑ 81 Everett McGowan | 50.00 | 25.00 |
| ❑ 82 Calgary Jimmies | 50.00 | 25.00 |
| ❑ 83 George Dame | 50.00 | 25.00 |
| ❑ 84 Calgary Jimmies | 50.00 | 25.00 |
| ❑ 85 Calgary Jimmies | 50.00 | 25.00 |
| ❑ 86 Calgary Jimmies | 50.00 | 25.00 |
| ❑ 87 Heck Fowler | 75.00 | 38.00 |
| ❑ 88 Jimmy Hoyle | 50.00 | 25.00 |
| ❑ 89 Charlie Gardiner | 150.00 | 75.00 |
| ❑ 90 Calgary Jimmies | 75.00 | 38.00 |

## 1933-34 V129

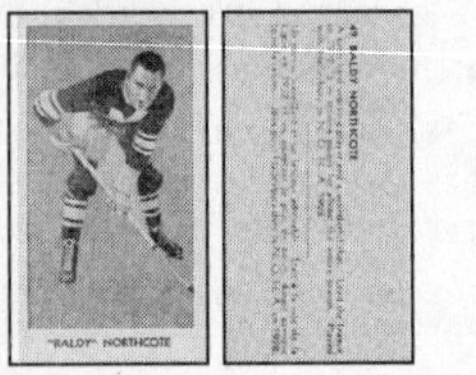

This 50-card set was issued anonymously during the 1933-34 season. Recent research may link the cards' distribution to British Consul Cigarettes. This has yet to be confirmed. The cards are sepia toned and measure approximately 1 5/8" by 2 7/8". The cards are numbered on the back with the capsule biography both in French and in English. Card number 39 is now known to exist but is quite scarce as it was the card that the company (allegedly) short-printed in order to make it difficult to complete the set. The short-printed Oliver card is not included in the complete set price below.

| | EX-MT | VG-E |
|---|---|---|
| COMPLETE SET (49) | 15000.00 | 7500.00 |
| COMMON CARD (1-50) | 150.00 | 75.00 |
| ❑ 1 Red Horner | 500.00 | 250.00 |
| ❑ 2 Clarence(Hap) Day | 350.00 | 180.00 |
| ❑ 3 Ace Bailey | 500.00 | 250.00 |
| ❑ 4 Buzz Bull | 150.00 | 75.00 |
| ❑ 5 Charlie Conacher | 1000.00 | 500.00 |
| ❑ 6 Harvey(Busher) Jackson | 500.00 | 250.00 |
| ❑ 7 Joe Primeau | 500.00 | 250.00 |
| ❑ 8 King Clancy | 1000.00 | 500.00 |
| ❑ 9 Alex Levinsky | 200.00 | 100.00 |
| ❑ 10 Bill Thoms | 150.00 | 75.00 |
| ❑ 11 Andy Blair | 150.00 | 75.00 |
| ❑ 12 Harold Cotton | 200.00 | 100.00 |
| ❑ 13 George Hainsworth | 500.00 | 250.00 |
| ❑ 14 Ken Doraty | 150.00 | 75.00 |
| ❑ 15 Fred Robertson | 150.00 | 75.00 |
| ❑ 16 Charlie Sands | 150.00 | 75.00 |
| ❑ 17 Hec Kilrea | 150.00 | 75.00 |
| ❑ 18 John Ross Roach | 200.00 | 100.00 |
| ❑ 19 Larry Aurie | 150.00 | 75.00 |
| ❑ 20 Ebbie Goodfellow | 300.00 | 150.00 |
| ❑ 21 Normie Himes | 200.00 | 100.00 |
| ❑ 22 Bill Brydge | 150.00 | 75.00 |
| ❑ 23 Mervyn(Red) Dutton | 300.00 | 150.00 |
| ❑ 24 Cooney Weiland | 300.00 | 150.00 |
| ❑ 25 Bill Beveridge | 200.00 | 100.00 |
| ❑ 26 Frank Finnigan | 200.00 | 100.00 |
| ❑ 27 Albert Leduc | 200.00 | 100.00 |
| ❑ 28 Babe Siebert | 400.00 | 200.00 |
| ❑ 29 Murray Murdoch | 150.00 | 75.00 |
| ❑ 30 Butch Keeling | 150.00 | 75.00 |
| ❑ 31 Bill Cook | 300.00 | 150.00 |
| ❑ 32 Cecil Dillon | 150.00 | 75.00 |
| ❑ 33 Ivan(Ching) Johnson | 450.00 | 220.00 |
| ❑ 34 Ott Heller | 150.00 | 75.00 |
| ❑ 35 Red Beattie | 150.00 | 75.00 |
| ❑ 36 Dit Clapper | 600.00 | 300.00 |
| ❑ 37 Eddie Shore | 2000.00 | 1000.00 |
| ❑ 38 Marty Barry | 300.00 | 150.00 |
| ❑ 39 Harry Oliver SP | 12000.00 | 6000.00 |
| ❑ 40 Bob Gracie | 150.00 | 75.00 |
| ❑ 41 Howie Morenz | 2750.00 | 1400.00 |
| ❑ 42 Pit Lepine | 150.00 | 75.00 |
| ❑ 43 Johnny Gagnon | 150.00 | 75.00 |
| ❑ 44 Armand Mondou | 150.00 | 75.00 |
| ❑ 45 Lorne Chabot | 300.00 | 150.00 |
| ❑ 46 Bun Cook | 300.00 | 150.00 |
| ❑ 47 Alex Smith | 150.00 | 75.00 |
| ❑ 48 Danny Cox | 150.00 | 75.00 |
| ❑ 49 Baldy Northcott UER | 200.00 | 100.00 |
| ❑ 50 Paul Thompson | 200.00 | 100.00 |

## 1924-25 V130 Maple Crispette

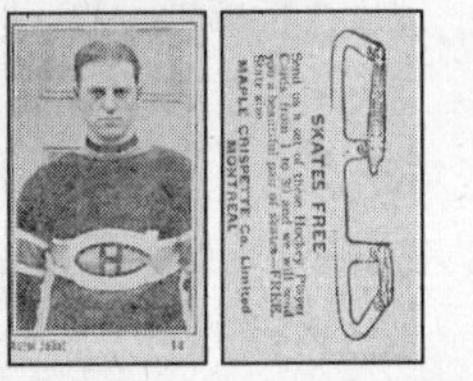

This 30-card set was issued during the 1924-25 season in the Montreal area. The cards are in black and white and measure approximately 1 3/8" by 2 3/8". There was a prize offer detailed on the reverse of every card offering a pair of hockey skates for a complete set of the cards. Card number 15 apparently was the "impossible" card that prevented most collectors of that day from ever getting the skates. The cards are numbered on the front in the lower right hand corner. The set is considered complete without the short-printed Cleghorn.

| | EX-MT | VG-E |
|---|---|---|
| COMPLETE SET (29) | 8000.00 | 4000.00 |
| COMMON CARD (1-30) | 150.00 | 75.00 |
| ❑ 1 Capt. Dunc Munro | 200.00 | 100.00 |
| ❑ 2 Clint Benedict | 400.00 | 200.00 |
| ❑ 3 Norman Fowler | 200.00 | 100.00 |
| ❑ 4 Curly Headley | 150.00 | 75.00 |
| ❑ 5 Alf Skinner | 150.00 | 75.00 |
| ❑ 6 Bill Cook | 300.00 | 150.00 |
| ❑ 7 Smokey Harris | 150.00 | 75.00 |
| ❑ 8 Jim Herberts | 150.00 | 75.00 |
| ❑ 9 Carson Cooper | 150.00 | 75.00 |
| ❑ 10 Red Green | 150.00 | 75.00 |
| ❑ 11 Billy Boucher | 150.00 | 75.00 |
| ❑ 12 Howie Morenz | 2000.00 | 1000.00 |
| ❑ 13 Georges Vezina | 1400.00 | 700.00 |
| ❑ 14 Aurel Joliat | 800.00 | 400.00 |
| ❑ 15 Sprague Cleghorn SP | 12000.00 | 6000.00 |
| ❑ 16 Dutch Cain | 150.00 | 75.00 |
| ❑ 17 Charlie Dinsmore | 150.00 | 75.00 |
| ❑ 18 Punch Broadbent | 300.00 | 150.00 |
| ❑ 19 Sam Rothschild | 150.00 | 75.00 |
| ❑ 20 George Carroll | 150.00 | 75.00 |
| ❑ 21 Billy Burch | 300.00 | 150.00 |
| ❑ 22 Shorty Green | 300.00 | 150.00 |
| ❑ 23 Mickey Roach | 150.00 | 75.00 |
| ❑ 24 Ken Randall | 150.00 | 75.00 |
| ❑ 25 Vernon Forbes | 200.00 | 100.00 |
| ❑ 26 Charlie Langlois | 150.00 | 75.00 |
| ❑ 27 Newsy Lalonde | 600.00 | 300.00 |
| ❑ 28 Fred (Frock) Lowrey | 150.00 | 75.00 |
| ❑ 29 Ganton Scott | 150.00 | 75.00 |
| ❑ 30 Louis Berlinguette | 200.00 | 100.00 |

## 1923-24 V145-1

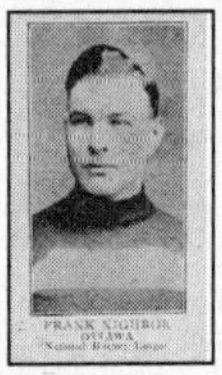

This relatively unattractive 40-card set is printed in sepia tone. The cards measure approximately 2" by 3 1/4". The cards have blank backs. The cards are numbered on the front in the lower left corner. The player's name, team, and National Hockey League are at the bottom of each card. The issuer of the set is not indicated in any way on the card, although speculation suggests it was William Patterson, Ltd, a Canadian confectioner. This set is easily confused with the other V145 set. Except for the tint and size differences and the different card name/number correspondence, these sets are essentially the same. Thankfully the only player with the same number in both sets is number 3 King Clancy. The Bert Corbeau card (#25) is extremely difficult to find in any condition, as it most likely was short printed. It is not included in the complete set price below.

| | EX-MT | VG-E |
|---|---|---|
| COMPLETE SET (40) | 12000.00 | 6000.00 |
| COMMON CARD (1-40) | 100.00 | 50.00 |
| ❑ 1 Eddie Gerard | 250.00 | 125.00 |
| ❑ 2 Frank Nighbor | 300.00 | 150.00 |
| ❑ 3 King Clancy | 1600.00 | 800.00 |
| ❑ 4 Jack Darragh | 200.00 | 100.00 |
| ❑ 5 Harry Helman | 100.00 | 50.00 |
| ❑ 6 George (Buck) Boucher | 200.00 | 100.00 |
| ❑ 7 Clint Benedict | 250.00 | 125.00 |
| ❑ 8 Lionel Hitchman | 150.00 | 75.00 |
| ❑ 9 Punch Broadbent | 250.00 | 125.00 |
| ❑ 10 Cy Denneny | 400.00 | 200.00 |
| ❑ 11 Sprague Cleghorn | 300.00 | 150.00 |
| ❑ 12 Sylvio Mantha | 250.00 | 125.00 |
| ❑ 13 Joe Malone | 400.00 | 200.00 |
| ❑ 14 Aurel Joliat | 1300.00 | 650.00 |
| ❑ 15 Howie Morenz | 2800.00 | 1400.00 |
| ❑ 16 Billy Boucher | 125.00 | 60.00 |
| ❑ 17 Billy Coutu | 125.00 | 60.00 |
| ❑ 18 Odie Cleghorn | 125.00 | 60.00 |
| ❑ 19 Georges Vezina | 1200.00 | 600.00 |
| ❑ 20 Amos Arbour | 100.00 | 50.00 |
| ❑ 21 Lloyd Andrews | 100.00 | 50.00 |
| ❑ 22 Red Stuart | 125.00 | 60.00 |
| ❑ 23 Cecil (Babe) Dye | 300.00 | 150.00 |
| ❑ 24 Jack Adams | 400.00 | 200.00 |
| ❑ 25 Bert Corbeau SP | 18000.00 | 9000.00 |
| ❑ 26 Reg Noble | 200.00 | 100.00 |
| ❑ 27 Stan Jackson | 100.00 | 50.00 |
| ❑ 28 John Ross Roach | 125.00 | 60.00 |
| ❑ 29 Vernon Forbes | 125.00 | 60.00 |
| ❑ 30 Shorty Green | 200.00 | 100.00 |
| ❑ 31 Red Green | 100.00 | 50.00 |
| ❑ 32 Goldie Prodgers | 100.00 | 50.00 |
| ❑ 33 Leo Reise | 100.00 | 50.00 |
| ❑ 34 Ken Randall | 100.00 | 50.00 |
| ❑ 35 Billy Burch | 200.00 | 100.00 |
| ❑ 36 Jesse Spring | 100.00 | 50.00 |
| ❑ 37 Eddie Bouchard | 100.00 | 50.00 |
| ❑ 38 Mickey Roach | 100.00 | 50.00 |
| ❑ 39 Chas. Fraser | 100.00 | 50.00 |
| ❑ 40 Corbett Denneny | 200.00 | 100.00 |

## 1924-25 V145-2

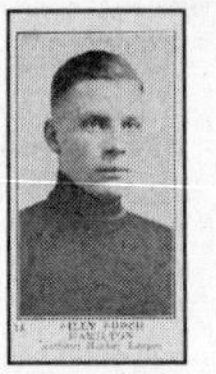

This 60-card set was issued anonymously during the 1924-25 season. The cards have a green-black tint and measure approximately 1 3/4" by 3 1/4". Cards are numbered in the lower left corner and have a blank back. The player's name, team, and National Hockey League are at the bottom of each card. The issuer of the set is not indicated in any way on the card, although speculation points to William Patterson, Ltd., a Canadian confectioner. This set is easily confused with the other V145 set. Except for the tint and size differences and the different card name/number correspondence, these sets are essentially the same. Thankfully the only player with the same number in both sets is number 3 King Clancy.

| | EX-MT | VG-E |
|---|---|---|
| COMPLETE SET (60) | 12000.00 | 6000.00 |
| COMMON CARD (1-60) | 100.00 | 50.00 |
| ❑ 1 Joe Ironstone | 250.00 | 125.00 |
| ❑ 2 George (Buck) Boucher | 200.00 | 100.00 |
| ❑ 3 King Clancy | 1500.00 | 750.00 |
| ❑ 4 Lionel Hitchman | 150.00 | 75.00 |
| ❑ 5 Hooley Smith | 250.00 | 125.00 |
| ❑ 6 Frank Nighbor | 200.00 | 100.00 |
| ❑ 7 Cy Denneny | 250.00 | 125.00 |
| ❑ 8 Spiff Campbell | 100.00 | 50.00 |
| ❑ 9 Frank Finnigan | 150.00 | 75.00 |
| ❑ 10 Alex Connell | 250.00 | 125.00 |
| ❑ 11 Vernon Forbes | 125.00 | 60.00 |
| ❑ 12 Ken Randall | 100.00 | 50.00 |
| ❑ 13 Billy Burch | 200.00 | 100.00 |
| ❑ 14 Shorty Green | 200.00 | 100.00 |
| ❑ 15 Red Green | 100.00 | 50.00 |
| ❑ 16 Alex McKinnon | 100.00 | 50.00 |
| ❑ 17 Charlie Langlois | 100.00 | 50.00 |
| ❑ 18 Mickey Roach | 100.00 | 50.00 |
| ❑ 19 Eddie Bouchard | 100.00 | 50.00 |
| ❑ 20 Jesse Spring | 100.00 | 50.00 |
| ❑ 21 Carson Cooper | 100.00 | 50.00 |
| ❑ 22 Smokey Harris | 100.00 | 50.00 |
| ❑ 23 Gopher Headley | 100.00 | 50.00 |
| ❑ 24 Bill Cook | 300.00 | 150.00 |
| ❑ 25 Jim Herberts | 100.00 | 50.00 |
| ❑ 26 Werner Schnarr | 100.00 | 50.00 |
| ❑ 27 Alf Skinner | 100.00 | 50.00 |
| ❑ 28 George Redding | 100.00 | 50.00 |
| ❑ 29 Herbie Mitchell | 100.00 | 50.00 |
| ❑ 30 Hek Fowler | 125.00 | 60.00 |
| ❑ 31 Red Stuart | 100.00 | 50.00 |
| ❑ 32 Clint Benedict | 200.00 | 100.00 |
| ❑ 33 Gerald Munro | 100.00 | 50.00 |
| ❑ 34 Dunc Munro | 125.00 | 60.00 |
| ❑ 35 Dutch Cain | 100.00 | 50.00 |
| ❑ 36 Fred (Frock) Lowrey | 100.00 | 50.00 |
| ❑ 37 Sam Rothschild | 100.00 | 50.00 |
| ❑ 38 Ganton Scott | 100.00 | 50.00 |
| ❑ 39 Punch Broadbent | 250.00 | 125.00 |
| ❑ 40 Charlie Dinsmore | 100.00 | 50.00 |
| ❑ 41 Louis Berlinquette | 100.00 | 50.00 |
| ❑ 42 George Carroll | 100.00 | 50.00 |
| ❑ 43 Georges Vezina | 1200.00 | 600.00 |
| ❑ 44 Billy Coutu | 100.00 | 50.00 |
| ❑ 45 Odie Cleghorn | 125.00 | 60.00 |
| ❑ 46 Billy Boucher | 150.00 | 75.00 |
| ❑ 47 Howie Morenz | 2000.00 | 1000.00 |
| ❑ 48 Aurel Joliat | 1000.00 | 500.00 |
| ❑ 49 Sprague Cleghorn | 250.00 | 125.00 |
| ❑ 50 Billy Mantha | 100.00 | 50.00 |
| ❑ 51 Reg Noble | 200.00 | 100.00 |
| ❑ 52 John Ross Roach | 125.00 | 60.00 |
| ❑ 53 Jack Adams | 250.00 | 125.00 |
| ❑ 54 Cecil (Babe) Dye | 200.00 | 100.00 |
| ❑ 55 Reg Reid | 100.00 | 50.00 |
| ❑ 56 Albert Holway | 100.00 | 50.00 |
| ❑ 57 Bert McCaffery | 100.00 | 50.00 |
| ❑ 58 Bert Corbeau | 200.00 | 100.00 |
| ❑ 59 Lloyd Andrews | 100.00 | 50.00 |
| ❑ 60 Stan Jackson | 150.00 | 75.00 |

## 1933-34 V252 Canadian Gum

This unnumbered set of 50 cards was designated V252 by the American Card Catalog. Cards are black and white pictures

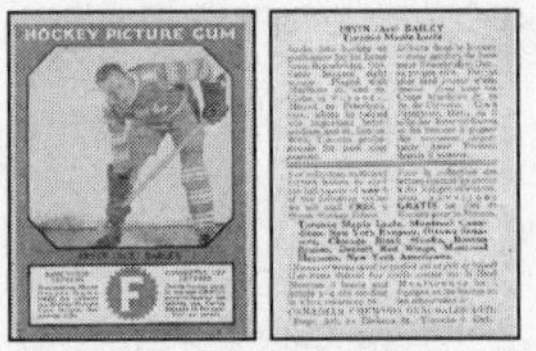


with a red border. Backs are written in both French and English. Cards measure approximately 2 1/2" by 3 1/4" including a 3/4" tab at the bottom describing a premium (contest) offer and containing one large letter. When enough of these letters were saved so that the collector could spell out the names of five NHL teams, they could be redeemed for a free home hockey game according to the details given on the card backs. The cards are checklisted in alphabetical order.

| | EX-MT | VG-E |
|---|---|---|
| COMPLETE SET (50) | 9000.00 | 4500.00 |
| COMMON CARD | 90.00 | 45.00 |
| ❑ 1 Clarence(Taffy) Abel | 150.00 | 75.00 |
| ❑ 2 Larry Aurie | 90.00 | 45.00 |
| ❑ 3 Ace Bailey | 400.00 | 200.00 |
| ❑ 4 Helge Bostrom | 90.00 | 45.00 |
| ❑ 5 Bill Brydge | 90.00 | 45.00 |
| ❑ 6 Glyn Brydson | 90.00 | 45.00 |
| ❑ 7 Marty Burke | 90.00 | 45.00 |
| ❑ 8 Gerald Carson | 90.00 | 45.00 |
| ❑ 9 Lorne Chabot | 200.00 | 100.00 |
| ❑ 10 King Clancy | 800.00 | 400.00 |
| ❑ 11 Dit Clapper | 300.00 | 150.00 |
| ❑ 12 Charlie Conacher | 750.00 | 375.00 |
| ❑ 13 Lionel Conacher | 400.00 | 200.00 |
| ❑ 14 Alex Connell | 175.00 | 90.00 |
| ❑ 15 Bun Cook | 175.00 | 90.00 |
| ❑ 16 Danny Cox | 90.00 | 45.00 |
| ❑ 17 Clarence(Hap) Day | 200.00 | 100.00 |
| ❑ 18 Cecil Dillon | 90.00 | 45.00 |
| ❑ 19 Lorne Duguid | 125.00 | 60.00 |
| ❑ 20 Duke Dutkowski | 90.00 | 45.00 |
| ❑ 21 Mervyn(Red) Dutton | 175.00 | 90.00 |
| ❑ 22 Happy Emms | 125.00 | 60.00 |
| ❑ 23 Frank Finnigan | 125.00 | 60.00 |
| ❑ 24 Chuck Gardiner | 175.00 | 90.00 |
| ❑ 25 Ebbie Goodfellow | 175.00 | 90.00 |
| ❑ 26 Johnny Gottselig | 125.00 | 60.00 |
| ❑ 27 Bob Gracie | 90.00 | 45.00 |
| ❑ 28 George Hainsworth | 400.00 | 200.00 |
| ❑ 29 Ott Heller | 90.00 | 45.00 |
| ❑ 30 Normie Hlmes | 125.00 | 60.00 |
| ❑ 31 Red Horner | 300.00 | 150.00 |
| ❑ 32 Harvey(Busher) Jackson | 400.00 | 200.00 |
| ❑ 33 Walter(Red) Jackson | 90.00 | 45.00 |
| ❑ 34 Aurel Joliat | 700.00 | 350.00 |
| ❑ 35 Dave Kerr | 125.00 | 60.00 |
| ❑ 36 Pit Lepine | 90.00 | 45.00 |
| ❑ 37 Georges Mantha | 90.00 | 45.00 |
| ❑ 38 Howie Morenz | 2000.00 | 1000.00 |
| ❑ 39 Murray Murdoch | 90.00 | 45.00 |
| ❑ 40 Baldy Northcott | 125.00 | 60.00 |
| ❑ 41 John Ross Roach | 125.00 | 60.00 |
| ❑ 42 Johnny Sheppard | 90.00 | 45.00 |
| ❑ 43 Babe Siebert | 250.00 | 125.00 |
| ❑ 44 Alex Smith | 90.00 | 45.00 |
| ❑ 45 John Sorrell | 90.00 | 45.00 |
| ❑ 46 Nelson Stewart | 400.00 | 200.00 |
| ❑ 47 Dave Trottier | 90.00 | 45.00 |
| ❑ 48 Bill Touhey | 90.00 | 45.00 |
| ❑ 49 Jimmy Ward | 90.00 | 45.00 |
| ❑ 50 Nick Wasnie | 90.00 | 45.00 |

## 1933-34 V288 Hamilton Gum

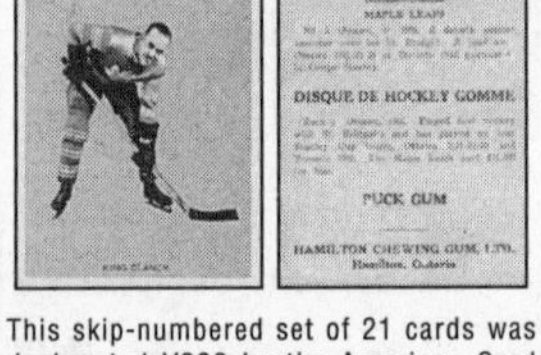

This skip-numbered set of 21 cards was designated V288 by the American Card Catalog. Cards are black and white pictures with a beige, blue, green, or orange background. Backs are written in both French and English. Cards measure approximately 2 3/8" by 2 3/4".

| | EX-MT | VG-E |
|---|---|---|
| COMPLETE SET (21) | 6000.00 | 3000.00 |
| COMMON CARD (1-49) | 90.00 | 45.00 |
| ❑ 1 Nick Wasnie | 125.00 | 60.00 |
| ❑ 2 Joe Primeau | 400.00 | 200.00 |
| ❑ 3 Marty Burke | 90.00 | 45.00 |
| ❑ 7 Bill Thoms | 90.00 | 45.00 |
| ❑ 8 Howie Morenz | 2000.00 | 1000.00 |
| ❑ 9 Andy Blair | 90.00 | 45.00 |
| ❑ 11 Ace Bailey | 350.00 | 180.00 |
| ❑ 14 Wildor Larochelle | 100.00 | 50.00 |
| ❑ 17 King Clancy | 800.00 | 400.00 |
| ❑ 18 Sylvio Mantha | 175.00 | 90.00 |
| ❑ 21 Red Horner | 300.00 | 150.00 |
| ❑ 23 Pit Lepine | 90.00 | 45.00 |
| ❑ 27 Aurel Joliat | 800.00 | 400.00 |
| ❑ 29 Harvey(Busher) Jackson | 350.00 | 180.00 |
| ❑ 30 Lorne Chabot | 200.00 | 100.00 |
| ❑ 33 Clarence(Hap) Day | 200.00 | 100.00 |
| ❑ 36 Alex Levinsky | 125.00 | 60.00 |
| ❑ 39 Harold Cotton | 150.00 | 75.00 |
| ❑ 42 Ebbie Goodfellow | 175.00 | 90.00 |
| ❑ 44 Larry Aurie | 90.00 | 45.00 |
| ❑ 49 Charlie Conacher | 800.00 | 400.00 |

## 1936-37 V356 Worldwide Gum

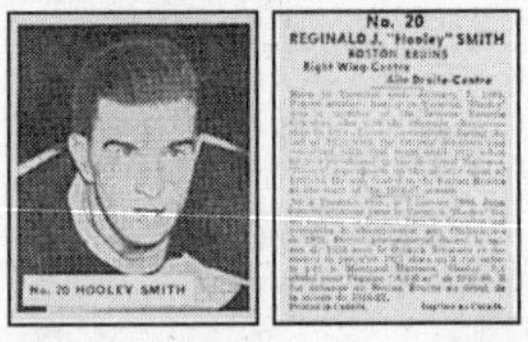

These rather crude greenish-gray cards feature the player's name and card number on the front and the card number, the player's name, his position and biographical data (in both English and French) on the back. Cards are approximately 2 3/8" by 2 7/8". Although the backs of the cards state that the cards were printed in Canada, no mention of the issuer, World Wide Gum, is apparent anywhere on the card.

| | EX-MT | VG-E |
|---|---|---|
| COMPLETE SET (135) | 22000.00 | 11000.00 |
| COMMON CARD (1-135) | 100.00 | 50.00 |
| ❑ 1 Charlie Conacher | 900.00 | 450.00 |
| ❑ 2 Jimmy Ward | 100.00 | 50.00 |
| ❑ 3 Babe Siebert | 350.00 | 180.00 |
| ❑ 4 Marty Barry | 200.00 | 100.00 |
| ❑ 5 Eddie Shore | 1500.00 | 750.00 |
| ❑ 6 Paul Thompson | 100.00 | 50.00 |
| ❑ 7 Roy Worters | 300.00 | 150.00 |
| ❑ 8 Red Horner | 200.00 | 100.00 |
| ❑ 9 Wilfred Cude | 150.00 | 75.00 |
| ❑ 10 Lionel Conacher | 350.00 | 180.00 |
| ❑ 11 Ebbie Goodfellow | 225.00 | 110.00 |
| ❑ 12 Tiny Thompson | 300.00 | 150.00 |
| ❑ 13 Harold(Mush) March | 125.00 | 60.00 |
| ❑ 14 Mervyn(Red) Dutton | 200.00 | 100.00 |
| ❑ 15 Butch Keeling | 100.00 | 50.00 |
| ❑ 16 Frank Boucher | 200.00 | 100.00 |
| ❑ 17 Tommy Gorman | 100.00 | 50.00 |
| ❑ 18 Howie Morenz | 2500.00 | 1250.00 |
| ❑ 19 Marvin Wentworth | 150.00 | 75.00 |
| ❑ 20 Hooley Smith | 200.00 | 100.00 |
| ❑ 21 Ivan(Ching) Johnson | 300.00 | 150.00 |
| ❑ 22 Baldy Northcott | 150.00 | 75.00 |
| ❑ 23 Syl Apps | 750.00 | 375.00 |
| ❑ 24 Hec Kilrea | 100.00 | 50.00 |
| ❑ 25 John Sorrell | 100.00 | 50.00 |
| ❑ 26 Lorne Carr | 100.00 | 50.00 |
| ❑ 27 Charlie Sands | 100.00 | 50.00 |
| ❑ 28 Nick Metz | 100.00 | 50.00 |
| ❑ 29 King Clancy | 1000.00 | 500.00 |
| ❑ 30 Russ Blinco | 100.00 | 50.00 |
| ❑ 31 Pete Martin | 100.00 | 50.00 |
| ❑ 32 Walter Buswell | 100.00 | 50.00 |
| ❑ 33 Paul Haynes | 100.00 | 50.00 |
| ❑ 34 Wildor Larochelle | 125.00 | 60.00 |
| ❑ 35 Harold Cotton | 125.00 | 60.00 |
| ❑ 36 Dit Clapper | 350.00 | 180.00 |
| ❑ 37 Joe Lamb | 100.00 | 50.00 |
| ❑ 38 Bob Gracie | 100.00 | 50.00 |
| ❑ 39 Jack Shill | 100.00 | 50.00 |
| ❑ 40 Buzz Boll | 100.00 | 50.00 |
| ❑ 41 John Gallagher | 100.00 | 50.00 |
| ❑ 42 Art Chapman | 100.00 | 50.00 |
| ❑ 43 Tom Cook | 100.00 | 50.00 |
| ❑ 44 Bill MacKenzie | 100.00 | 50.00 |
| ❑ 45 Georges Mantha | 100.00 | 50.00 |
| ❑ 46 Herb Cain | 125.00 | 60.00 |
| ❑ 47 Mud Bruneteau | 150.00 | 75.00 |
| ❑ 48 Bob Davidson | 100.00 | 50.00 |
| ❑ 49 Doug Young | 100.00 | 50.00 |
| ❑ 50 Paul Drouin | 100.00 | 50.00 |
| ❑ 51 Harvey(Busher) Jackson | 350.00 | 180.00 |
| ❑ 52 Clarence(Hap) Day | 300.00 | 150.00 |
| ❑ 53 Dave Kerr | 200.00 | 100.00 |
| ❑ 54 Al Murray | 100.00 | 50.00 |
| ❑ 55 Johnny Gottselig | 125.00 | 60.00 |
| ❑ 56 Andy Blair | 100.00 | 50.00 |
| ❑ 57 Lynn Patrick | 400.00 | 200.00 |
| ❑ 58 Sweeney Schriner | 250.00 | 125.00 |
| ❑ 59 Happy Emms | 125.00 | 60.00 |
| ❑ 60 Allan Shields | 100.00 | 50.00 |
| ❑ 61 Alex Levinsky | 125.00 | 60.00 |
| ❑ 62 Flash Hollett | 100.00 | 50.00 |
| ❑ 63 Peggy O'Neil | 100.00 | 50.00 |
| ❑ 64 Herbie Lewis | 200.00 | 100.00 |
| ❑ 65 Aurel Joliat | 750.00 | 375.00 |
| ❑ 66 Carl Voss | 200.00 | 100.00 |
| ❑ 67 Stewart Evans | 100.00 | 50.00 |
| ❑ 68 Bun Cook | 225.00 | 110.00 |
| ❑ 69 Cooney Weiland | 250.00 | 125.00 |
| ❑ 70 Dave Trottier | 100.00 | 50.00 |
| ❑ 71 Louis Trudel | 100.00 | 50.00 |
| ❑ 72 Marty Burke | 100.00 | 50.00 |
| ❑ 73 Leroy Goldsworthy | 100.00 | 50.00 |
| ❑ 74 Normie Smith | 100.00 | 50.00 |
| ❑ 75 Syd Howe | 300.00 | 150.00 |
| ❑ 76 Gordon Pettinger | 100.00 | 50.00 |
| ❑ 77 Jack McGill | 100.00 | 50.00 |

❑ 78 Pit Lepine 100.00 50.00
❑ 79 Sammy McManus 100.00 50.00
❑ 80 Phil Watson 150.00 75.00
❑ 81 Paul Runge 100.00 50.00
❑ 82 Bill Beveridge 125.00 60.00
❑ 83 Johnny Gagnon 100.00 50.00
❑ 84 Bucko MacDonald 125.00 60.00
❑ 85 Earl Robinson 100.00 50.00
❑ 86 Pep Kelly 100.00 50.00
❑ 87 Ott Heller 100.00 50.00
❑ 88 Murray Murdoch 100.00 50.00
❑ 89 Mac Colville 100.00 50.00
❑ 90 Alex Shibicky 150.00 75.00
❑ 91 Neil Colville 225.00 110.00
❑ 92 Normie Himes 125.00 60.00
❑ 93 Charley McVeigh 100.00 50.00
❑ 94 Lester Patrick 350.00 180.00
❑ 95 Connie Smythe 400.00 200.00
❑ 96 Art Ross 400.00 200.00
❑ 97 Cecil M.Hart 250.00 125.00
❑ 98 Dutch Gainor 100.00 50.00
❑ 99 Jack Adams 300.00 150.00
❑ 100 Howie Morenz Jr. 300.00 150.00
❑ 101 Buster Mundy 100.00 50.00
❑ 102 Johnny Wing 100.00 50.00
❑ 103 Morris Croghan 100.00 50.00
❑ 104 Pete Jotkus 100.00 50.00
❑ 105 Doug MacQuisten 100.00 50.00
❑ 106 Lester Brennan 100.00 50.00
❑ 107 Jack O'Connell 100.00 50.00
❑ 108 Ray Malenfant 100.00 50.00
❑ 109 Ken Murray 100.00 50.00
❑ 110 Frank Stangle 100.00 50.00
❑ 111 Dave Neville 100.00 50.00
❑ 112 Claude Burke 100.00 50.00
❑ 113 Herman Murray 100.00 50.00
❑ 114 Buddy O'Connor 250.00 125.00
❑ 115 Albert Perreault 100.00 50.00
❑ 116 Johnny Taugher 100.00 50.00
❑ 117 Rene Boudreau 100.00 50.00
❑ 118 Kenny McKinnon 100.00 50.00
❑ 119 Alex Bolduc 100.00 50.00
❑ 120 Jimmy Keiller 100.00 50.00
❑ 121 Lloyd McIntyre 100.00 50.00
❑ 122 Emile Fortin 100.00 50.00
❑ 123 Mike Karakas 125.00 60.00
❑ 124 Art Wiebe 100.00 50.00
❑ 125 Louis St. Denis 100.00 50.00
❑ 126 Stan Pratt 100.00 50.00
❑ 127 Jules Cholette 100.00 50.00
❑ 128 Jimmy Muir 100.00 50.00
❑ 129 Pete Morin 100.00 50.00
❑ 130 Jimmy Heffernan 100.00 50.00
❑ 131 Morris Bastien 100.00 50.00
❑ 132 Tuffy Griffiths 100.00 50.00
❑ 133 Johnny Mahaffey 100.00 50.00
❑ 134 Trueman Donnelly 100.00 50.00
❑ 135 Bill Stewart 150.00 75.00

## 1933-34 V357 Ice Kings

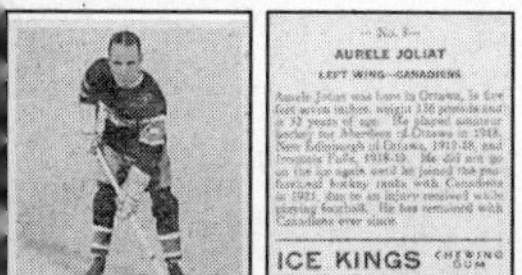

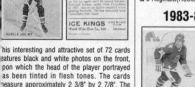

his interesting and attractive set of 72 cards eatures black and white photos on the front, pon which the head of the player portrayed as been tinted in flesh tones. The cards neasure approximately 2 3/8" by 2 7/8". The layer's name appears on the front of the card. he card number, position, team and player's ame is listed on the back as are brief iographies in both French and English. Some ards appear with the resumes in English only. rinted in Canada and issued by World Wide um, the catalog designation for this set is 357.

EX-MT VG-E
OMPLETE SET (72) 10000.00 5000.00
OMMON CARD (1-48) 80.00 40.00
OMMON CARD (49-72) 100.00 50.00

1 Dit Clapper 400.00 200.00
2 Bill Brydge 80.00 40.00
3 Aurel Joliat UER 600.00 300.00
4 Andy Blair 80.00 40.00
5 Earl Robinson 80.00 40.00
6 Paul Haynes 80.00 40.00
7 Ronnie Martin 80.00 40.00
8 Babe Siebert 200.00 100.00
9 Archie Wilcox 80.00 40.00
10 Clarence(Hap) Day 200.00 100.00
11 Roy Worters 250.00 125.00
12 Nelson Stewart 400.00 200.00
13 King Clancy 700.00 350.00
14 Marty Burke 150.00 75.00
15 Cecil Dillon 80.00 40.00
16 Red Horner 250.00 125.00
17 Armand Mondou 80.00 40.00
18 Paul Raymond 80.00 40.00
19 Dave Kerr 100.00 50.00
20 Butch Keeling 80.00 40.00
21 Johnny Gagnon 80.00 40.00
22 Ace Bailey 400.00 200.00
23 Harry Oliver 200.00 100.00
24 Gerald Carson 80.00 40.00
25 Mervyn(Red) Dutton 200.00 100.00

❑ 26 Georges Mantha 80.00 40.00
❑ 27 Marty Barry 200.00 100.00
❑ 28 Wildor Larochelle 100.00 50.00
❑ 29 Red Beattie 80.00 40.00
❑ 30 Bill Cook 200.00 100.00
❑ 31 Hooley Smith 200.00 100.00
❑ 32 Art Chapman 80.00 40.00
❑ 33 Harold Cotton 150.00 75.00
❑ 34 Lionel Hitchman 150.00 75.00
❑ 35 George Patterson 80.00 40.00
❑ 36 Howie Morenz 1600.00 800.00
❑ 37 Jimmy Ward 80.00 40.00
❑ 38 Charley McVeigh 100.00 50.00
❑ 39 Glen Brydson 100.00 50.00
❑ 40 Joe Primeau 300.00 150.00
❑ 41 Joe Lamb 125.00 60.00
❑ 42 Sylvio Mantha 175.00 90.00
❑ 43 Cy Wentworth 100.00 50.00
❑ 44 Normie Himes 100.00 50.00
❑ 45 Doug Brennan 80.00 40.00
❑ 46 Pit Lepine 80.00 40.00
❑ 47 Alex Levinsky 100.00 50.00
❑ 48 Baldy Northcott 100.00 50.00
❑ 49 Ken Doraty 100.00 50.00
❑ 50 Bill Thoms 100.00 50.00
❑ 51 Vernon Ayers 100.00 50.00
❑ 52 Lorne Duguid 100.00 50.00
❑ 53 Wally Kilrea 100.00 50.00
❑ 54 Vic Ripley 100.00 50.00
❑ 55 Happy Emms 125.00 60.00
❑ 56 Duke Dutkowski 100.00 50.00
❑ 57 Tiny Thompson 300.00 150.00
❑ 58 Charlie Sands 100.00 50.00
❑ 59 Larry Aurie 100.00 50.00
❑ 60 Bill Beveridge 100.00 50.00
❑ 61 Bill McKenzie 100.00 50.00
❑ 62 Earl Roche 100.00 50.00
❑ 63 Bob Gracie 100.00 50.00
❑ 64 Hec Kilrea 100.00 50.00
❑ 65 Cooney Weiland 250.00 125.00
❑ 66 Bun Cook 250.00 125.00
❑ 67 John Ross Roach 125.00 60.00
❑ 68 Murray Murdoch 100.00 50.00
❑ 69 Danny Cox 100.00 50.00
❑ 70 Desse Roche 100.00 50.00
❑ 71 Lorne Chabot 200.00 100.00
❑ 72 Syd Howe 350.00 180.00

## 1933-34 V357-2 Ice Kings Premiums

These six black-and-white large cards are actually premiums. The cards measure approximately 7" by 9". The cards are unnumbered and rather difficult to find now.

EX-MT VG-E
COMPLETE SET (6) 5000.00 2500.00
COMMON CARD (1-6) 150.00 75.00

❑ 1 King Clancy 1200.00 600.00
❑ 2 Clarence(Hap) Day 350.00 180.00
❑ 3 Aurel Joliat 1000.00 500.00
❑ 4 Howie Morenz 2500.00 1250.00
❑ 5 Allan Shields 150.00 75.00
❑ 6 Reginald(Hooley) Smith 250.00 125.00

## 1983-84 Vachon

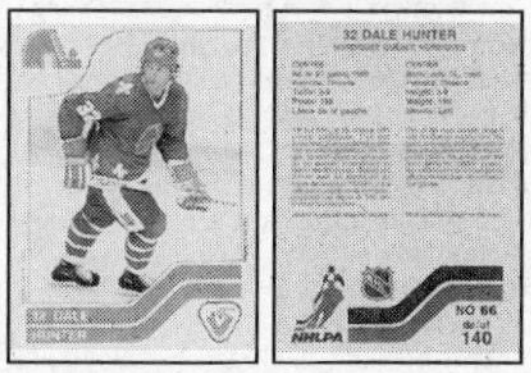

This set of 140 standard-size cards was issued by Vachon Foods as panels of two cards cards. The set includes players from the seven Canadian NHL teams. The cards were also available as a set directly from Vachon. The first printing contained an error in that number 96 pictures Peter Ihnacek instead of Walt Poddubny. The error was corrected for the second printing. The card backs are written in French and English. The Vachon logo is on the front of every card in the lower right corner. The set is difficult to collect in uncut panels of two; the prices below are for individual cards, the panel prices are 50 percent greater than the prices listed below.

MINT NRMT
COMPLETE SET (140) 200.00 90.00
COMMON CARD (1-140) .50 .23

❑ 1 Paul Baxter .75 .35
❑ 2 Ed Beers .50 .23
❑ 3 Steve Bozek .50 .23
❑ 4 Mike Eaves .50 .23
❑ 5 Don Edwards 1.00 .45
❑ 6 Kari Eloranta .50 .23
❑ 7 Dave Hindmarch .50 .23
❑ 8 Jamie Hislop .50 .23
❑ 9 Steve Konroyd .50 .23
❑ 10 Reggie Lemelin 1.00 .45
❑ 11 Hakan Loob 2.00 .90
❑ 12 Jamie Macoun .50 .23
❑ 13 Lanny McDonald 3.00 1.35
❑ 14 Kent Nilsson 2.00 .90
❑ 15 Colin Patterson .50 .23
❑ 16 Jim Peplinski 1.00 .45
❑ 17 Paul Reinhart 1.00 .45
❑ 18 Doug Risebrough 1.00 .45
❑ 19 Steve Tambellini .50 .23
❑ 20 Mickey Volcan .50 .23
❑ 21 Glenn Anderson 4.00 1.80
❑ 22 Paul Coffey 12.00 5.50
❑ 23 Lee Fogolin .50 .23
❑ 24 Grant Fuhr 5.00 2.20
❑ 25 Randy Gregg .50 .23
❑ 26 Wayne Gretzky 50.00 22.00
❑ 27 Charlie Huddy .75 .35
❑ 28 Pat Hughes .50 .23
❑ 29 Dave Hunter .50 .23
❑ 30 Don Jackson .50 .23
❑ 31 Jari Kurri 8.00 3.60
❑ 32 Willy Lindstrom .50 .23
❑ 33 Ken Linseman .75 .35
❑ 34 Kevin Lowe 1.50 .70
❑ 35 Dave Lumley .50 .23
❑ 36 Mark Messier 25.00 11.00
❑ 37 Andy Moog 5.00 2.20
❑ 38 Jaroslav Pouzar .50 .23
❑ 39 Tom Roulston .50 .23
❑ 40 Dave Semenko .75 .35
❑ 41 Guy Carbonneau 3.00 1.35
❑ 42 Kent Carlson .50 .23
❑ 43 Gilbert Delorme .50 .23
❑ 44 Bob Gainey 2.00 .90
❑ 45 Jean Hamel .50 .23
❑ 46 Mark Hunter .50 .23
❑ 47 Guy Lafleur 6.00 2.70
❑ 48 Craig Ludwig .50 .23
❑ 49 Pierre Mondou .50 .23
❑ 50 Mats Naslund 2.00 .90
❑ 51 Chris Nilan 1.00 .45
❑ 52 Greg Paslawski .50 .23
❑ 53 Larry Robinson 2.00 .90
❑ 54 Richard Sevigny 1.00 .45
❑ 55 Steve Shutt 2.00 .90
❑ 56 Bobby Smith 1.00 .45
❑ 57 Mario Tremblay .75 .35
❑ 58 Ryan Walter .75 .35
❑ 59 Rick Wamsley 1.00 .45
❑ 60 Doug Wickenheiser .50 .23
❑ 61 Bo Berglund .50 .23
❑ 62 Dan Bouchard 1.00 .45
❑ 63 Alain Cote .50 .23
❑ 64 Brian Ford .50 .23
❑ 65 Michel Goulet 2.50 1.10
❑ 66 Dale Hunter 2.00 .90
❑ 67 Mario Marois .75 .35
❑ 68 Tony McKegney .75 .35
❑ 69 Randy Moller .50 .23
❑ 70 Wilf Paiement 1.00 .45
❑ 71 Pat Price .50 .23
❑ 72 Normand Rochefort .50 .23
❑ 73 Andre Savard .50 .23
❑ 74 Louis Sleigher .50 .23
❑ 75 Anton Stastny .75 .35
❑ 76 Marian Stastny .75 .35
❑ 77 Peter Stastny 6.00 2.70
❑ 78 John Van Boxmeer .50 .23
❑ 79 Wally Weir .50 .23
❑ 80 Blake Wesley .50 .23
❑ 81 John Anderson .50 .23
❑ 82 Jim Benning .50 .23
❑ 83 Dan Daoust .50 .23
❑ 84 Bill Derlago .75 .35
❑ 85 Dave Farrish .50 .23
❑ 86 Miroslav Frycer .50 .23
❑ 87 Stewart Gavin .75 .35
❑ 88 Gaston Gingras .50 .23
❑ 89 Billy Harris .50 .23
❑ 90 Peter Inhacak 1.00 .45
❑ 91 Jim Korn .50 .23
❑ 92 Terry Martin .50 .23
❑ 93 Dale McCourt .50 .23
❑ 94 Gary Nylund .50 .23
❑ 95 Mike Palmateer 2.00 .90
❑ 96A Walt Poddubny ERR 10.00 4.50
(Photo actually
Peter Inhacek,
no mustache)
❑ 96B Walt Poddubny COR 2.50 1.10
(With mustache)
❑ 97 Borje Salming 3.00 1.35
❑ 98 Rick St.Croix 1.00 .45
❑ 99 Greg P. Terrion .50 .23
❑ 100 Rick Vaive 1.00 .45
❑ 101 Richard Brodeur 1.50 .70
❑ 102 Jiri Bubla .50 .23
❑ 103 Garth Butcher .50 .23
❑ 104 Ron Delorme .50 .23
❑ 105 John Garrett 1.50 .70
❑ 106 Jere Gillis .50 .23
❑ 107 Thomas Gradin 1.00 .45
❑ 108 Doug Halward .50 .23
❑ 109 Mark Kirton .50 .23
❑ 110 Rick Lanz .50 .23
❑ 111 Gary Lupul .50 .23
❑ 112 Kevin McCarthy .50 .23
❑ 113 Lars Molin .50 .23
❑ 114 Jim Nill .50 .23
❑ 115 Darcy Rota .50 .23
❑ 116 Stan Smyl 1.00 .45
❑ 117 Harold Snepsts 1.50 .70
❑ 118 Patrik Sundstrom 1.00 .45
❑ 119 Tony Tanti 1.00 .45
❑ 120 Dave(Tiger) Williams 2.00 .90
❑ 121 Scott Arniel .50 .23
❑ 122 Dave Babych 1.00 .45
❑ 123 Laurie Boschman .50 .23
❑ 124 Wade Campbell .50 .23
❑ 125 Lucien DeBlois .50 .23
❑ 126 Dale Hawerchuk 7.50 3.40
❑ 127 Brian Hayward 1.00 .45
❑ 128 Jim Kyte .75 .35
❑ 129 Morris Lukowich .50 .23
❑ 130 Bengt Lundholm .50 .23
❑ 131 Paul MacLean 1.00 .45
❑ 132 Moe Mantha .50 .23
❑ 133 Andrew McBain .50 .23
❑ 134 Brian Mullen .50 .23
❑ 135 Robert Picard .50 .23
❑ 136 Doug Smail 1.00 .45
❑ 137 Doug Soetaert 1.00 .45
❑ 138 Thomas Steen 1.50 .70
❑ 139 Tim Watters .50 .23
❑ 140 Tim Young .75 .35

## 1972-73 Whalers New England WHA

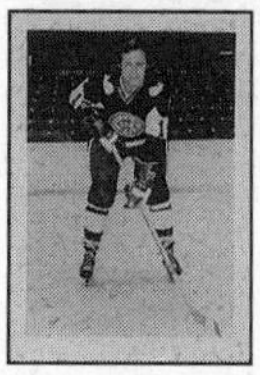

This 17-photo card set measures 3 3/4" by 5". The fronts feature black-and-white posed player photographs. The backs are blank. The cards are unnumbered and checklisted below in alphabetical order.

NRMT-MT EXC
COMPLETE SET (15) 35.00 16.00
COMMON CARD (1-15) 2.00 .90

❑ 1 Mike Byers 2.00 .90
❑ 2 Terry Caffery 2.00 .90
❑ 3 John Cunniff 3.00 1.35
❑ 4 John Danby 2.00 .90
❑ 5 Jim Dorey 2.00 .90
❑ 6 Tom Earl 2.00 .90
❑ 7 John French 2.00 .90
❑ 8 Ted Green 4.00 1.80
❑ 9 Ric Jordan 2.00 .90
❑ 10 Bruce Landon 2.00 .90
❑ 11 Rick Ley 4.00 1.80
❑ 12 Larry Pleau 3.00 1.35
❑ 13 Brad Selwood 2.00 .90
❑ 14 Tim Sheehy 2.00 .90
❑ 15 Al Smith 4.00 1.80
❑ 16 Tom Webster 3.00 1.35
❑ 17 Tom Williams 3.00 1.35

## 1982-83 Whalers Junior Hartford Courant

Sponsored by the Hartford Courant, this 23-card set measures approximately 3 1/4" by 6 3/8". The fronts feature borderless color action player photos. At the bottom is a blue stripe containing an oval that is divided in half horizontally with the top half being white and the bottom green. The design contains the sponsor's name in the top portion in black letters, while the team name appears in the bottom portion in white letters. The white backs carry a black-and-white headshot, player's name, jersey number, biography, career information, and statistics. The cards are unnumbered and checklisted below in alphabetical order. The card of Ron Francis appears in his rookie card year.

MINT NRMT
COMPLETE SET (22) 35.00 16.00
COMMON CARD (1-22) 1.00 .45

❑ 1 Greg Adams 2.50 1.10
❑ 2 Russ Anderson 1.00 .45
❑ 3 Ron Francis 10.00 4.50
❑ 4 Michel Galarneau 1.00 .45
❑ 5 Dan Fridgen 1.00 .45
❑ 6 Archie Henderson 1.00 .45
❑ 7 Ed Hospodar 1.00 .45
❑ 8 Mark Johnson 2.00 .90
❑ 9 Chris Kotsopoulos 1.00 .45
❑ 10 Pierre Larouche 2.50 1.10
❑ 11 George Lyle 1.00 .45
❑ 12 Greg Millen 3.00 1.35
❑ 13 Warren Miller 1.00 .45
❑ 14 Ray Neufeld 1.50 .70
❑ 15 Mark Renaud 1.00 .45
❑ 16 Risto Siltanen 1.50 .70
❑ 17 Stuart Smith 1.00 .45
❑ 18 Blaine Stoughton 2.50 1.10
❑ 19 Doug Sulliman 1.00 .45
❑ 20 Bob Sullivan 1.00 .45
❑ 21 Mike Veisor 1.50 .70
❑ 22 Mickey Volcan 1.00 .45
❑ 23 Blake Wesley 1.00 .45

## 1983-84 Whalers Junior Hartford Courant

Sponsored by the Hartford Courant, this 22-card set measures approximately 3 3/4" by 8 1/4". The fronts feature color action player photos. At the bottom is a blue stripe

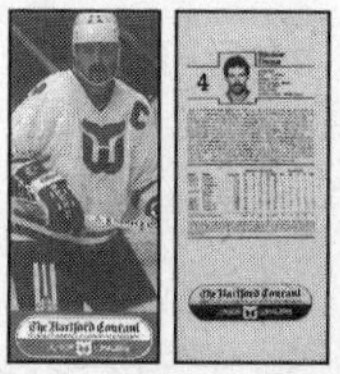

containing an oval that is divided in half horizontally with the top half being white and the bottom green. The design contains the sponsor's name in the top portion in black letters, while the team name appears in the bottom portion in white letters. The white backs carry a black-and-white headshot, player's name, jersey number, biography, career and personal information, and statistics. The oval design is repeated on the back in black-and-white. The cards are unnumbered and checklisted below in alphabetical order.

MINT NRMT
COMPLETE SET (22) 25.00 11.00
COMMON CARD (1-22) 1.00 .45

❑ 1 Bob Crawford 1.00 .45
❑ 2 Mike Crombeen 1.00 .45
❑ 3 Richie Dunn 1.00 .45
❑ 4 Normand Dupont 1.00 .45
❑ 5 Ron Francis 8.00 3.60
❑ 6 Ed Hospodar 1.00 .45
❑ 7 Marty Howe 2.00 .90
❑ 8 Mark Johnson 1.50 .70
❑ 9 Chris Kotsopoulos 1.00 .45
❑ 10 Pierre Lacroix 1.50 .70
❑ 11 Greg Malone 1.50 .70
❑ 12 Greg Malone 1.50 .70
❑ 13 Ray Neufeld 1.00 .45
❑ 14 Joel Quenneville 1.50 .70
❑ 15 Torrie Robertson 1.50 .70
❑ 16 Risto Siltanen 1.00 .45
❑ 17 Blaine Stoughton 2.00 .90
❑ 18 Steve Stoyanovich 1.00 .45
❑ 19 Doug Sulliman 1.00 .45
❑ 20 Sylvain Turgeon 1.50 .70
❑ 21 Mike Veisor 1.50 .70
❑ 22 Mike Zuke 1.00 .45

## 1984-85 Whalers Junior Wendy's

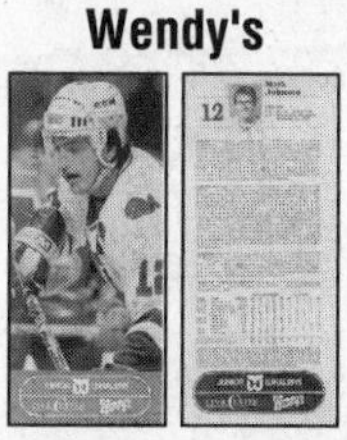

This 22-card set was sponsored by Wendy's and The Civic Center Mall. The cards measure approximately 3 1/4" by 8 1/4" and feature color action player photos. The pictures are full-bleed except for a bright blue bottom border that contains an oval that is divided in half horizontally with the top half being green and the bottom red. The design contains the team name and sponsors in white print. The backs have a black and white head shot, biography, 1983-84 season summary, career summary, miscellaneous player information, and statistics. The oval design is repeated on the back in black. The cards are unnumbered and checklisted below in alphabetical order.

MINT NRMT
COMPLETE SET (22) 25.00 11.00
COMMON CARD (1-22) 1.00 .45

❑ 1 Jack Brownschidle 1.00 .45
❑ 2 Sylvain Cote 1.00 .45
❑ 3 Bob Crawford 1.00 .45
❑ 4 Mike Crombeen 1.00 .45
❑ 5 Tony Currie 1.00 .45
❑ 6 Ron Francis 6.00 2.70
❑ 7 Mark Fusco 1.00 .45
❑ 8 Dave Jensen 1.00 .45
❑ 9 Mark Johnson 1.50 .70
❑ 10 Chris Kotsopoulos 1.00 .45
❑ 11 Greg Malone 1.50 .70
❑ 12 Greg Millen 2.00 .90
❑ 13 Ray Neufeld 1.00 .45
❑ 14 Randy Pierce 1.00 .45
❑ 15 Joel Quenneville 1.50 .70
❑ 16 Torrie Robertson 1.50 .70
❑ 17 Ulf Samuelsson 4.00 1.80
❑ 18 Risto Siltanen 1.00 .45
❑ 19 Dave Tippett 1.00 .45
❑ 20 Sylvain Turgeon 1.00 .45
❑ 21 Steve Weeks 2.00 .90
❑ 22 Mike Zuke 1.50 .70

## 1985-86 Whalers Junior Wendy's

Sponsored by Wendy's, this 23-card set measures approximately 3 3/4" by 8 1/4". The

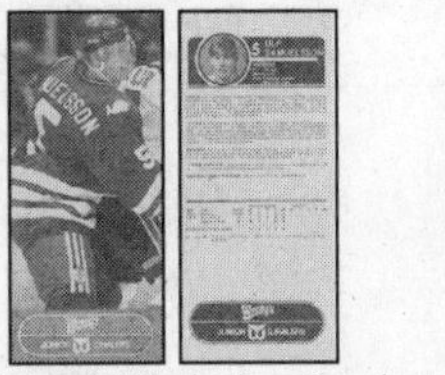

fronts feature full-bleed color action player photos, except at the bottom where a bright blue stripe contains an oval that is divided in half horizontally with the top half being green and the bottom red. The design contains the sponsor's name in the top portion, while the team name appears in the bottom portion, both in white letters. The white backs carry a black-and-white headshot, biography, 1984-85 season summary, career summary, personal information, and statistics. The oval design is repeated on the back in black-and-white. The cards are unnumbered and checklisted below in alphabetical order.

| | MINT | NRMT |
|---|---|---|
| COMPLETE SET (23) | 30.00 | 13.50 |
| COMMON CARD (1-23) | 1.00 | .45 |
| ❑ 1 Jack Brownschidle | 1.00 | .45 |
| ❑ 2 Sylvain Cote | 1.00 | .45 |
| ❑ 3 Bob Crawford | 1.00 | .45 |
| ❑ 4 Kevin Dineen | 4.00 | 1.80 |
| ❑ 5 Paul Fenton | 1.00 | .45 |
| ❑ 6 Ray Ferraro | 3.00 | 1.35 |
| ❑ 7 Ron Francis | 5.00 | 2.20 |
| ❑ 8 Scott Kleinendorst | 1.00 | .45 |
| ❑ 9 Paul Lawless | 1.00 | .45 |
| ❑ 10 Mike Liut | 3.00 | 1.35 |
| ❑ 11 Paul MacDermid | 1.00 | .45 |
| ❑ 12 Greg Malone | 1.00 | .45 |
| ❑ 13 Dana Murzyn | 1.00 | .45 |
| ❑ 14 Ray Neufeld | 1.00 | .45 |
| ❑ 15 Jorgen Pettersson | 1.00 | .45 |
| ❑ 16 Joel Quenneville | 1.00 | .45 |
| ❑ 17 Torrie Robertson | 1.50 | .70 |
| ❑ 18 Ulf Samuelsson | 3.00 | 1.35 |
| ❑ 19 Risto Siltanen | 1.00 | .45 |
| ❑ 20 Dave Tippett | 1.00 | .45 |
| ❑ 21 Sylvain Turgeon | 1.50 | .70 |
| ❑ 22 Steve Weeks | 1.50 | .70 |
| ❑ 23 Mike Zuke | 1.00 | .45 |

## 1986-87 Whalers Junior Thomas'

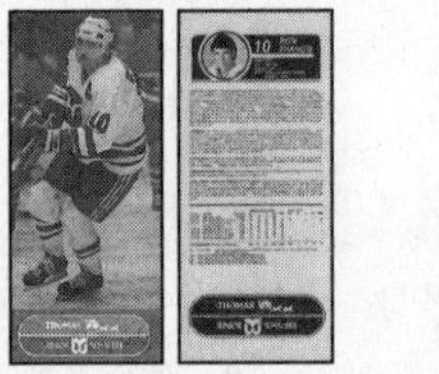

Sponsored by Thomas', this 23-card set measures approximately 3 3/4" by 8 1/4". The fronts feature color action player photos. At the bottom is a blue stripe containing an oval that is divided in half horizontally with the top half being orange and the bottom green. The design contains the sponsor's name in the top portion, while the team name appears in the bottom portion, both in white letters. The white backs carry a black-and-white headshot, player's name, jersey number, biography, 1985-86 season summary, career summary, personal information, and statistics. The oval design is repeated on the back in black-and-white. The cards are unnumbered and checklisted below in alphabetical order.

| | MINT | NRMT |
|---|---|---|
| COMPLETE SET (23) | 30.00 | 13.50 |
| COMMON CARD (1-23) | 1.00 | .45 |
| ❑ 1 John Anderson | 1.00 | .45 |
| ❑ 2 Dave Babych | 2.00 | .90 |
| ❑ 3 Wayne Babych | 1.00 | .45 |
| ❑ 4 Sylvain Cote | 1.00 | .45 |
| ❑ 5 Kevin Dineen | 3.00 | 1.35 |
| ❑ 6 Dean Evason | 1.00 | .45 |
| ❑ 7 Ray Ferraro | 1.00 | .45 |
| ❑ 8 Ron Francis | 6.00 | 2.70 |
| ❑ 9 Bill Gardner | 1.00 | .45 |
| ❑ 10 Stewart Gavin | 1.00 | .45 |
| ❑ 11 Doug Jarvis | 1.00 | .45 |
| ❑ 12 Scot Kleinendorst | 1.00 | .45 |
| ❑ 13 Paul Lawless | 1.00 | .45 |
| ❑ 14 Mike Liut | 3.00 | 1.35 |
| ❑ 15 Paul MacDermid | 1.00 | .45 |
| ❑ 16 Mike McEwen | 1.00 | .45 |
| ❑ 17 Dana Murzyn | 1.00 | .45 |
| ❑ 18 Joel Quenneville | 1.00 | .45 |
| ❑ 19 Torrie Robertson | 1.25 | .55 |
| ❑ 20 Ulf Samuelsson | 3.00 | 1.35 |
| ❑ 21 Dave Tippett | 1.00 | .45 |
| ❑ 22 Sylvain Turgeon | 1.00 | .45 |
| ❑ 23 Steve Weeks | 1.50 | .70 |

## 1987-88 Whalers Jr. Burger King/Pepsi

This 21-card set was sponsored by Burger King restaurants and Pepsi Cola and measures approximately 3 3/4" by 8 1/4". The fronts feature color action player photos with the team name and sponsors' logos at the bottom. The backs carry a small headshot, biography, season summary, career summary, miscellaneous player information, and statistics. The cards are unnumbered and checklisted below in alphabetical order.

| | MINT | NRMT |
|---|---|---|
| COMPLETE SET (21) | 25.00 | 11.00 |
| COMMON CARD (1-21) | 1.00 | .45 |
| ❑ 1 John Anderson | 1.00 | .45 |
| ❑ 2 Dave Babych | 2.00 | .90 |
| ❑ 3 Sylvain Cote | 1.00 | .45 |
| ❑ 4 Kevin Dineen | 2.50 | 1.10 |
| ❑ 5 Dean Evason | 1.00 | .45 |
| ❑ 6 Ray Ferraro | 2.50 | 1.10 |
| ❑ 7 Ron Francis | 4.00 | 1.80 |
| ❑ 8 Stew Gavin | 1.00 | .45 |
| ❑ 9 Doug Jarvis | 1.00 | .45 |
| ❑ 10 Scott Kleinendorst | 1.00 | .45 |
| ❑ 11 Randy Ladouceur | 1.00 | .45 |
| ❑ 12 Paul Lawless | 1.00 | .45 |
| ❑ 13 Mike Liut | 2.50 | 1.10 |
| ❑ 14 Paul MacDermid | 1.00 | .45 |
| ❑ 15 Dana Murzyn | 1.00 | .45 |
| ❑ 16 Joel Quenneville | 1.00 | .45 |
| ❑ 17 Torrie Robertson | 1.00 | .45 |
| ❑ 18 Ulf Samuelsson | 2.00 | .90 |
| ❑ 19 Dave Tippett | 1.00 | .45 |
| ❑ 20 Sylvain Turgeon | 1.00 | .45 |
| ❑ 21 Steve Weeks | 1.50 | .70 |

## 1988-89 Whalers Junior Ground Round

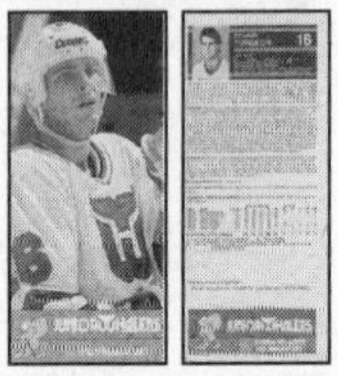

This 18-card set of Hartford Whalers was sponsored by Ground Round restaurants. The cards measure approximately 3 11/16" by 8 1/4". The front features a borderless full color photo of the player. The team logo and a Ground Round advertisement appear in the blue and green stripes that cut across the bottom of the card face. The back has a black and white head shot of the player at the upper left hand corner as well as extensive player information and career statistics. Another Ground Round advertisement and a Ground Round Drug Tip (an anti-drug and alcohol message) appear at the bottom of the card. The cards are unnumbered and hence are checklisted below in alphabetical order.

| | MINT | NRMT |
|---|---|---|
| COMPLETE SET (18) | 20.00 | 9.00 |
| COMMON CARD (1-18) | 1.00 | .45 |
| ❑ 1 John Anderson | 1.00 | .45 |
| ❑ 2 Dave Babych | 1.50 | .70 |
| ❑ 3 Sylvain Cote | 1.00 | .45 |
| ❑ 4 Kevin Dineen | 2.00 | .90 |
| ❑ 5 Dean Evason | 1.00 | .45 |
| ❑ 6 Ray Ferraro | 2.00 | .90 |
| ❑ 7 Ron Francis | 3.50 | 1.55 |
| ❑ 8 Scot Kleinendorst | 1.00 | .45 |
| ❑ 9 Randy Ladouceur | 1.00 | .45 |
| ❑ 10 Mike Liut | 2.00 | .90 |
| ❑ 11 Paul MacDermid | 1.00 | .45 |
| ❑ 12 Brent Peterson | 1.00 | .45 |
| ❑ 13 Joel Quenneville | 1.00 | .45 |
| ❑ 14 Torrie Robertson | 1.00 | .45 |
| ❑ 15 Ulf Samuelsson | 2.00 | .90 |
| ❑ 16 Dave Tippett | 1.00 | .45 |
| ❑ 17 Sylvain Turgeon | 1.00 | .45 |
| ❑ 18 Carey Wilson | 1.00 | .45 |

## 1989-90 Whalers Junior Milk

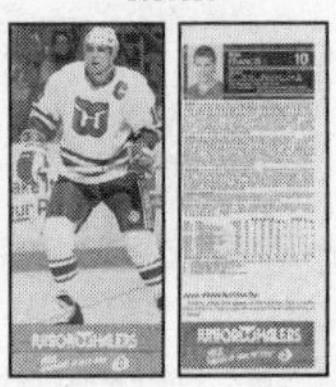

This 23-card set of Hartford Whalers was sponsored by Milk, America's Health Kick. The cards measure approximately 3 11/16" by 8 1/4". The front features a borderless full color photo of the player. The team logo and a Milk advertisement appear in the blue and green stripes that cut across the bottom of the card face. The back has a black and white head shot of the player at the upper left hand corner as well as extensive player information and career statistics. A Junior Whaler Nutrition Tip and another Milk advertisement appear at the bottom of the card's reverse. The cards are unnumbered and hence are checklisted below in alphabetical order. Three cards (11, 12, 21) were added to the set at the end of the season and are marked as SP in the checklist below.

| | MINT | NRMT |
|---|---|---|
| COMPLETE SET (23) | 20.00 | 9.00 |
| COMMON CARD (1-23) | .50 | .23 |
| ❑ 1 Mikael Andersson | .50 | .23 |
| ❑ 2 Dave Babych | .75 | .35 |
| ❑ 3 Sylvain Cote | .50 | .23 |
| ❑ 4 Randy Cunneyworth | .50 | .23 |
| ❑ 5 Kevin Dineen | 1.50 | .70 |
| ❑ 6 Dean Evason | .50 | .23 |
| ❑ 7 Ray Ferraro | 1.00 | .45 |
| ❑ 8 Ron Francis | 3.00 | 1.35 |
| ❑ 9 Jody Hull | .50 | .23 |
| ❑ 10 Grant Jennings | .50 | .23 |
| ❑ 11 Ed Kastelic SP | 2.00 | .90 |
| ❑ 12 Todd Krygier SP | 2.00 | .90 |
| ❑ 13 Randy Ladouceur | .50 | .23 |
| ❑ 14 Mike Liut | 1.50 | .70 |
| ❑ 15 Paul MacDermid | .50 | .23 |
| ❑ 16 Joel Quenneville | .50 | .23 |
| ❑ 17 Ulf Samuelsson | 1.50 | .70 |
| ❑ 18 Brad Shaw | .75 | .35 |
| ❑ 19 Peter Sidorkiewicz | .75 | .35 |
| ❑ 20 Dave Tippett | .50 | .23 |
| ❑ 21 Mike Tomlak SP | 2.00 | .90 |
| ❑ 22 Pat Verbeek | 1.50 | .70 |
| ❑ 23 Scott Young | 1.00 | .45 |

## 1990-91 Whalers Jr. 7-Eleven

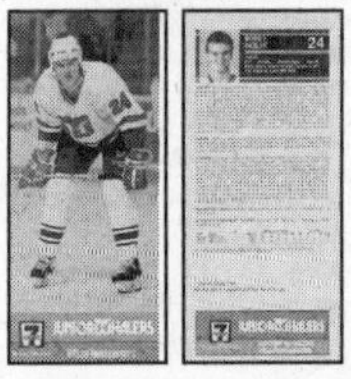

This 27-card set of Hartford Whalers was issued by 7-Eleven and sent out as a premium to all members of the Hartford Junior Whalers. This set features full-color photographs on the front while the backs contain the same information about the players that is available in the media guides. The set has been checklisted alphabetically for convenient reference. The set measures approximately 3 3/4" by 8 1/4" and has the players of the Hartford Whalers along with a special Gordie Howe card. Four cards (3, 12, 19, 20) were added to the set at the end of the season and their backs are blank.

| | MINT | NRMT |
|---|---|---|
| COMPLETE SET (27) | 20.00 | 9.00 |
| COMMON CARD (1-27) | .50 | .23 |
| COMMON CARD SP | 2.00 | .90 |
| ❑ 1 Mikael Andersson | .50 | .23 |
| ❑ 2 Dave Babych | .75 | .35 |
| ❑ 3 Rob Brown SP | 2.00 | .90 |
| ❑ 4 Yvon Corriveau | .50 | .23 |
| ❑ 5 Sylvain Cote | .50 | .23 |
| ❑ 6 Doug Crossman | .50 | .23 |
| ❑ 7 Randy Cunneyworth | .50 | .23 |
| ❑ 8 Paul Cyr | .50 | .23 |
| ❑ 9 Kevin Dineen | 1.00 | .45 |
| ❑ 10 Dean Evason | .50 | .23 |
| ❑ 11 Ron Francis | 2.00 | .90 |
| ❑ 12 Chris Govedaris SP | 2.00 | .90 |
| ❑ 13 Bobby Holik | 1.00 | .45 |
| ❑ 14 Gordie Howe | 5.00 | 2.20 |
| ❑ 15 Grant Jennings | .50 | .23 |
| ❑ 16 Ed Kastelic | .50 | .23 |
| ❑ 17 Todd Krygier | .50 | .23 |
| ❑ 18 Randy Ladouceur | .50 | .23 |
| ❑ 19 Jim McKenzie SP | 2.00 | .90 |
| ❑ 20 Daryl Reaugh SP | 2.50 | 1.10 |
| ❑ 21 Ulf Samuelsson | 1.00 | .45 |
| ❑ 22 Brad Shaw | .75 | .35 |
| ❑ 23 Peter Sidorkiewicz | .75 | .35 |
| ❑ 24 Mike Tomlak | .50 | .23 |
| ❑ 25 Pat Verbeek | 1.50 | .70 |
| ❑ 26 Carey Wilson | .50 | .23 |
| ❑ 27 Scott Young | .75 | .35 |

## 1991-92 Whalers Jr. 7-Eleven

This 28-card set of Hartford Whalers was issued by 7-Eleven and sent out as a premium to all members of the Hartford Junior Whalers. This set features full-color photographs on the front while the backs contain the same

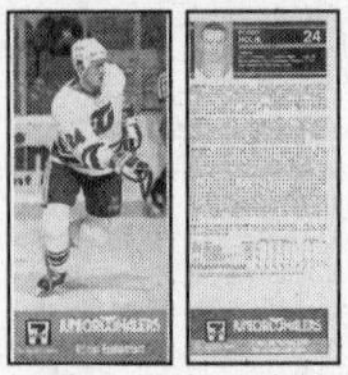

information about the players that is available in the media guides. The set has been checklisted alphabetically for convenient reference. The set measures approximately 3 3/4" by 8 1/4" and contains the players of the Hartford Whalers. Six cards (3, 6, 10, 12, 18, 19) were issued late in the season and their backs are blank.

| | MINT | NRMT |
|---|---|---|
| COMPLETE SET (28) | 20.00 | 9.00 |
| COMMON CARD (1-28) | .50 | .23 |
| COMMON CARD SP | 1.50 | .70 |
| ❑ 1 Mikael Andersson | .50 | .23 |
| ❑ 2 Marc Bergevin | .50 | .23 |
| ❑ 3 James Black SP | 1.50 | .70 |
| ❑ 4 Rob Brown | .50 | .23 |
| ❑ 5 Adam Burt | .50 | .23 |
| ❑ 6 Andrew Cassels SP | 3.00 | 1.35 |
| ❑ 7 Murray Craven | .75 | .35 |
| ❑ 8 John Cullen | 1.00 | .45 |
| ❑ 9 Randy Cunneyworth | .50 | .23 |
| ❑ 10 Paul Cyr SP | 1.50 | .70 |
| ❑ 11 Joe Day | .50 | .23 |
| ❑ 12 Paul Gillis SP | 1.50 | .70 |
| ❑ 13 Mark Greig | .50 | .23 |
| ❑ 14 Bobby Holik | .75 | .35 |
| ❑ 15 Doug Houda | .50 | .23 |
| ❑ 16 Mark Hunter | .50 | .23 |
| ❑ 17 Ed Kastelic | .50 | .23 |
| ❑ 18 Dan Keczmer SP | 2.00 | .90 |
| ❑ 19 Steve Konroyd SP | 1.50 | .70 |
| ❑ 20 Randy Ladouceur | .50 | .23 |
| ❑ 21 Jim McKenzie | .50 | .23 |
| ❑ 22 Michel Picard | .50 | .23 |
| ❑ 23 Geoff Sanderson | 5.00 | 2.20 |
| ❑ 24 Brad Shaw | .60 | .25 |
| ❑ 25 Peter Sidorkiewicz | .75 | .35 |
| ❑ 26 Pat Verbeek | 1.50 | .70 |
| ❑ 27 Kay Whitmore | .75 | .35 |
| ❑ 28 Zarley Zalapski | .75 | .35 |

## 1992-93 Whalers Dairymart

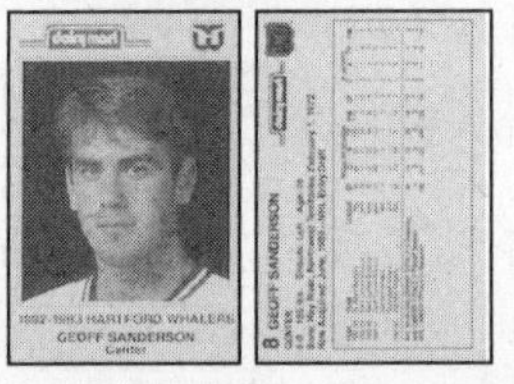

Sponsored by Dairymart, this 26-card set features white-bordered glossy color studio head shots on cards that measure approximately 2 3/8" by 3 1/2". The Dairymart and Whalers logos are displayed above the player photo, and the player's name and position, along with "1992-93 Hartford Whalers," appear beneath his image. The white horizontal back carries the player's name, uniform number, position, and biography above a stat table. The Dairymart and Whalers logos in the upper right complete the card. The cards are unnumbered and checklisted below in alphabetical order.

| | MINT | NRMT |
|---|---|---|
| COMPLETE SET (26) | 18.00 | 8.00 |
| COMMON CARD (1-26) | .25 | .11 |
| ❑ 1 Jim Agnew | .50 | .23 |
| ❑ 2 Sean Burke | 1.50 | .70 |
| ❑ 3 Adam Burt | .50 | .23 |
| ❑ 4 Andrew Cassels | 1.00 | .45 |
| ❑ 5 Murray Craven | .60 | .25 |
| ❑ 6 Randy Cunneyworth | .50 | .23 |
| ❑ 7 Paul Gillis | .50 | .23 |
| ❑ 8 Paul Holmgren CO | .50 | .23 |
| ❑ 9 Doug Houda | .50 | .23 |
| ❑ 10 Mark Janssens | .50 | .23 |
| ❑ 11 Tim Kerr | .75 | .35 |
| ❑ 12 Steve Konroyd | .50 | .23 |
| ❑ 13 Nick Kypreos | .50 | .23 |
| ❑ 14 Randy Ladouceur | .50 | .23 |
| ❑ 15 Jim McKenzie | .50 | .23 |
| ❑ 16 Michael Nylander | 1.00 | .45 |
| ❑ 17 Allen Pedersen | .50 | .23 |
| ❑ 18 Robert Petrovicky | .50 | .23 |
| ❑ 19 Frank Pietrangelo | .75 | .35 |
| ❑ 20 Patrick Poulin | .50 | .23 |
| ❑ 21 Geoff Sanderson | 4.00 | 1.80 |
| ❑ 22 Pat Verbeek | 1.50 | .70 |
| ❑ 23 Eric Weinrich | .50 | .23 |
| ❑ 24 Terry Yake | .50 | .23 |
| ❑ 25 Zarley Zalapski | .50 | .23 |
| ❑ 26 Junior Whalers Member Card | .25 | .11 |

## 1993-94 Whalers Coke

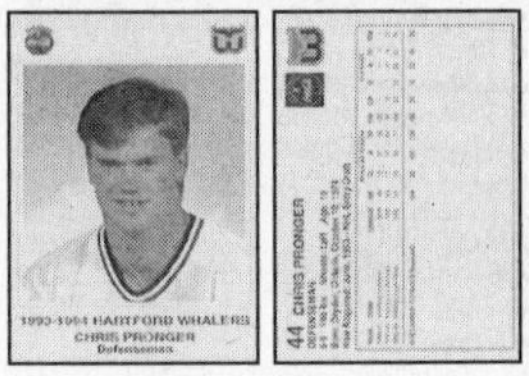

Sponsored by Coca-Cola, this 24-card set features white-bordered color studio head shots on cards that measure approximately 2 3/8" by 3 1/2". The Coca-Cola and Whalers logos are displayed above the player photo, while the player's name and position appear beneath his image. The white horizontal backs carry the player's name, uniform number, position, and biography above a stat table. The Coca-Cola and Whalers logos in the upper right corner complete the backs. The cards are unnumbered and checklisted below in alphabetical order.

| | MINT | NRMT |
|---|---|---|
| COMPLETE SET (24) | 18.00 | 8.00 |
| COMMON CARD (1-24) | .25 | .11 |
| ❑ 1 Sean Burke | 2.00 | .90 |
| ❑ 2 Adam Burt | .50 | .23 |
| ❑ 3 Andrew Cassels | 1.00 | .45 |
| ❑ 4 Randy Cunneyworth | .50 | .23 |
| ❑ 5 Alexander Godynyuk | .50 | .23 |
| ❑ 6 Mark Greig | .50 | .23 |
| ❑ 7 Mark Janssens | .50 | .23 |
| ❑ 8 Robert Kron | .50 | .23 |
| ❑ 9 Bryan Marchment | .50 | .23 |
| ❑ 10 Brad McCrimmon | .50 | .23 |
| ❑ 11 Pierre McGuire CO | .25 | .11 |
| ❑ 12 Michael Nylander | .75 | .35 |
| ❑ 13 James Patrick | .50 | .23 |
| ❑ 14 Frank Pietrangelo | .75 | .35 |
| ❑ 15 Marc Potvin | .50 | .23 |
| ❑ 16 Chris Pronger | 3.00 | 1.35 |
| ❑ 17 Brian Propp | .75 | .35 |
| ❑ 18 Jeff Reese | .75 | .35 |
| ❑ 19 Geoff Sanderson | 2.00 | .90 |
| ❑ 20 Jim Sandlak | .50 | .23 |
| ❑ 21 Jim Storm | .50 | .23 |
| ❑ 22 Darren Turcotte | .75 | .35 |
| ❑ 23 Pat Verbeek | 1.50 | .70 |
| ❑ 24 Zarley Zalapski | .50 | .23 |

## 1995-96 Whalers Bob's Stores

| | MINT | NRMT |
|---|---|---|
| COMPLETE SET (27) | 12.00 | 5.50 |
| COMMON CARD (1-27) | .10 | .05 |
| ❑ 1 Sean Burke | .75 | .35 |
| ❑ 2 Adam Burke | .40 | .18 |
| ❑ 3 Andrew Cassels | .40 | .18 |
| ❑ 4 Kelly Chase | .40 | .18 |
| ❑ 5 Scott Daniels | .40 | .18 |
| ❑ 6 Gerald Diduck | .40 | .18 |
| ❑ 7 Nelson Emerson | .60 | .25 |
| ❑ 8 Glen Featherstone | .40 | .18 |
| ❑ 9 Brian Glynn | .40 | .18 |
| ❑ 10 Mark Janssens | .40 | .18 |
| ❑ 11 Robert Kron | .40 | .18 |
| ❑ 12 Frantisek Kucera | .40 | .18 |
| ❑ 13 Jocelyn Lemieux | .40 | .18 |
| ❑ 14 Marek Malik | .40 | .18 |
| ❑ 15 Steve Martins | .40 | .18 |
| ❑ 16 Paul Maurice CO | .25 | .11 |
| ❑ 17 Brad McCrimmon | .40 | .18 |
| ❑ 18 Jason Muzzatti | .40 | .18 |
| ❑ 19 Andrei Nikolishin | .40 | .18 |
| ❑ 20 Jeff O'Neill | .40 | .18 |
| ❑ 21 Paul Ranheim | .40 | .18 |
| ❑ 22 Steven Rice | .40 | .18 |
| ❑ 23 Geoff Sanderson | .60 | .25 |
| ❑ 24 Brendan Shanahan | 3.00 | 1.35 |
| ❑ 25 Kevin Smyth | .40 | .18 |
| ❑ 26 Glen Wesley | .60 | .25 |
| ❑ 27 Kids Club Discount Card | .10 | .05 |

## 1960-61 Wonder Bread Premium Photos

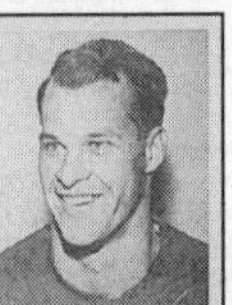

Produced and issued in Canada, the 1960-6 Wonder Bread set features four hockey star. This set of premium photos measu approximately 5" by 7" and are unnumberec There were actually two sets produced: Brea Labels and Premium Photos. The bread labe are valued at 50 to 100 percent of the value

listed below. Reportedly the premium photo was inside the bread package and there was also a small picture of the player on the end of the bread wrapper. Keon's photo is noteworthy for preceding his RC by one year.

| | NRMT | VG-E |
|---|---|---|
| COMPLETE SET (4) | 600.00 | 275.00 |
| COMMON CARD (1-4) | 80.00 | 36.00 |
| ❑ 1 Gordie Howe | 300.00 | 135.00 |
| ❑ 2 Bobby Hull | 200.00 | 90.00 |
| ❑ 3 Dave Keon | 80.00 | 36.00 |
| ❑ 4 Maurice Richard | 150.00 | 70.00 |

## 1960-61 York Premium Photos

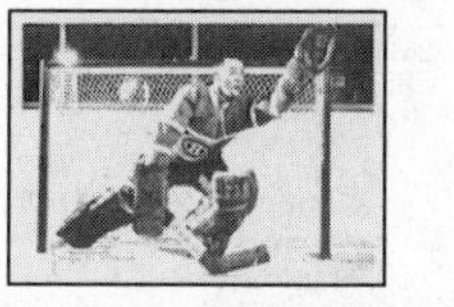

This set of 37 photos is very difficult to put together. These unnumbered photos measure approximately 5" by 7" and feature members of the Montreal Canadiens (MC) and Toronto Maple Leafs (TML). The checklist below is ordered alphabetically. These large black and white cards were supposedly available from York Peanut Butter as a mail-in premium in return for two proofs of purchase; unfortunately there are no identifying marking on the photo that indicate the producer or the year of issue. The photos are action shots with a facsimile autograph of the player on the photo. The cards were apparently issued very late in the 1960-61 season since the set includes Eddie Shack as a Maple Leaf (he was acquired by Toronto from the Rangers during the 1960-61 season), Gilles Tremblay (his first NHL season was 1960-61 with the Canadiens), and several players (Jean-Guy Gendron, Larry Regan, Bob Turner) who were with other teams for the 1961-62 season.

| | NRMT | VG-E |
|---|---|---|
| COMPLETE SET (37) | 2000.00 | 900.00 |
| COMMON CARD (1-37) | 30.00 | 13.50 |
| ❑ 1 George Armstrong TML | 50.00 | 22.00 |
| ❑ 2 Ralph Backstrom MC | 40.00 | 18.00 |
| ❑ 3 Bob Baun TML | 50.00 | 22.00 |
| ❑ 4 Jean Beliveau MC | 150.00 | 70.00 |
| ❑ 5 Marcel Bonin MC | 30.00 | 13.50 |
| ❑ 6 Johnny Bower TML | 100.00 | 45.00 |
| ❑ 7 Carl Brewer TML | 40.00 | 18.00 |
| ❑ 8 Dick Duff TML | 40.00 | 18.00 |
| ❑ 9 Jean-Guy Gendron MC | 30.00 | 13.50 |
| ❑ 10 Boom Boom Geoffrion MC | 80.00 | 36.00 |
| ❑ 11 Phil Goyette MC | 30.00 | 13.50 |
| ❑ 12 Billy Harris TML | 30.00 | 13.50 |
| ❑ 13 Doug Harvey MC | 80.00 | 36.00 |
| ❑ 14 Bill Hicke MC | 30.00 | 13.50 |
| ❑ 15 Larry Hillman TML | 30.00 | 13.50 |
| ❑ 16 Charlie Hodge MC | 40.00 | 18.00 |
| ❑ 17 Tim Horton TML | 150.00 | 70.00 |
| ❑ 18 Tom Johnson MC | 40.00 | 18.00 |
| ❑ 19 Red Kelly TML | 50.00 | 22.00 |
| ❑ 20 Dave Keon TML | 100.00 | 45.00 |
| ❑ 21 Albert Langlois MC | 30.00 | 13.50 |
| ❑ 22 Frank Mahovlich TML | 100.00 | 45.00 |
| ❑ 23 Don Marshall MC | 40.00 | 18.00 |
| ❑ 24 Dickie Moore MC | 50.00 | 22.00 |
| ❑ 25 Bob Nevin TML | 30.00 | 13.50 |
| ❑ 26 Bert Olmstead TML | 50.00 | 22.00 |
| ❑ 27 Jacques Plante MC | 300.00 | 135.00 |
| ❑ 28 Claude Provost MC | 40.00 | 18.00 |
| ❑ 29 Bob Pulford TML | 50.00 | 22.00 |
| ❑ 30 Larry Regan TML | 30.00 | 13.50 |
| ❑ 31 Henri Richard MC | 100.00 | 45.00 |
| ❑ 32 Eddie Shack TML | 80.00 | 36.00 |
| ❑ 33 Allan Stanley TML | 50.00 | 22.00 |
| ❑ 34 Ron Stewart TML | 30.00 | 13.50 |
| ❑ 35 Jean-Guy Talbot MC | 40.00 | 18.00 |
| ❑ 36 Gilles Tremblay MC | 40.00 | 18.00 |
| ❑ 37 Bob Turner MC | 30.00 | 13.50 |

## 1961-62 York Yellow Backs

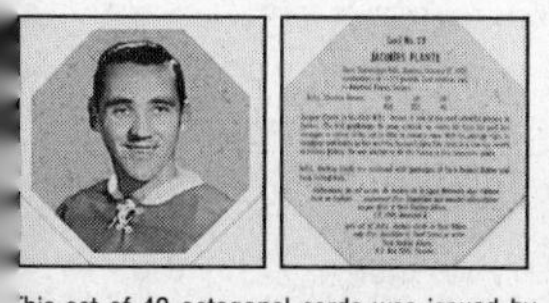

This set of 42 octagonal cards was issued by York Peanut Butter. The cards are numbered on the backs at the top. An album was originally available as a send-in offer or at certain food stores for 25 cents. The cards measure approximately 2 1/2" in diameter. The set can be dated as a 1961-62 set by referring to the career totals given on the back of each player's cards. The card backs were written in both French and English. The set is considered complete without the album.

| | NRMT | VG-E |
|---|---|---|
| COMPLETE SET (42) | 600.00 | 275.00 |
| COMMON CARD (1-42) | 10.00 | 4.50 |
| ❑ 1 Bob Baun | 15.00 | 6.75 |
| ❑ 2 Dick Duff | 12.00 | 5.50 |
| ❑ 3 Frank Mahovlich | 25.00 | 11.00 |
| ❑ 4 Gilles Tremblay | 10.00 | 4.50 |
| ❑ 5 Dickie Moore | 15.00 | 6.75 |
| ❑ 6 Don Marshall | 10.00 | 4.50 |
| ❑ 7 Tim Horton | 30.00 | 13.50 |
| ❑ 8 Johnny Bower | 20.00 | 9.00 |
| ❑ 9 Allan Stanley | 15.00 | 6.75 |
| ❑ 10 Jean Beliveau | 40.00 | 18.00 |
| ❑ 11 Tom Johnson | 15.00 | 6.75 |
| ❑ 12 Jean-Guy Talbot | 12.00 | 5.50 |
| ❑ 13 Carl Brewer | 10.00 | 4.50 |
| ❑ 14 Bob Pulford | 15.00 | 6.75 |
| ❑ 15 Billy Harris | 10.00 | 4.50 |
| ❑ 16 Bill Hicke | 10.00 | 4.50 |
| ❑ 17 Claude Provost | 12.00 | 5.50 |
| ❑ 18 Henri Richard | 25.00 | 11.00 |
| ❑ 19 Bert Olmstead | 15.00 | 6.75 |
| ❑ 20 Ron Stewart | 10.00 | 4.50 |
| ❑ 21 Red Kelly | 15.00 | 6.75 |
| ❑ 22 Hector(Toe) Blake CO | 15.00 | 6.75 |
| ❑ 23 Jacques Plante | 50.00 | 22.00 |
| ❑ 24 Ralph Backstrom | 12.00 | 5.50 |
| ❑ 25 Eddie Shack | 20.00 | 9.00 |
| ❑ 26 Bob Nevin | 10.00 | 4.50 |
| ❑ 27 Dave Keon | 40.00 | 18.00 |
| ❑ 28 Boom Boom Geoffrion | 20.00 | 9.00 |
| ❑ 29 Marcel Bonin | 10.00 | 4.50 |
| ❑ 30 Phil Goyette | 10.00 | 4.50 |
| ❑ 31 Larry Hillman | 10.00 | 4.50 |
| ❑ 32 Larry Keenan | 10.00 | 4.50 |
| ❑ 33 Al Arbour | 15.00 | 6.75 |
| ❑ 34 J.C. Tremblay | 12.00 | 5.50 |
| ❑ 35 Bobby Rousseau | 10.00 | 4.50 |
| ❑ 36 Al McNeil | 10.00 | 4.50 |
| ❑ 37 George Armstrong | 15.00 | 6.75 |
| ❑ 38 Punch Imlach CO | 12.00 | 5.50 |
| ❑ 39 King Clancy | 20.00 | 9.00 |
| ❑ 40 Lou Fontinato | 10.00 | 4.50 |
| ❑ 41 Cesare Maniago | 15.00 | 6.75 |
| ❑ 42 Jean Gauthier | 10.00 | 4.50 |
| ❑ xx Album | 40.00 | 18.00 |

## 1962-63 York Iron-On Transfers

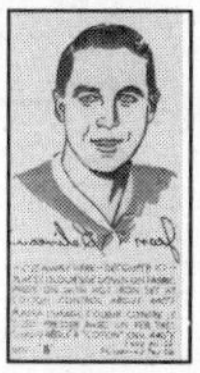

These iron-on transfers are very difficult to find. They measure approximately 2 1/4" by 4 1/4". There is some dispute with regard to the year of issue but the 1962-63 season seems to be a likely date based on the careers of the players selected for and included in the set. These transfers are numbered at the bottom.

| | NRMT | VG-E |
|---|---|---|
| COMPLETE SET (36) | 1800.00 | 800.00 |
| COMMON CARD (1-36) | 25.00 | 11.00 |
| ❑ 1 Johnny Bower | 50.00 | 22.00 |
| ❑ 2 Jacques Plante | 150.00 | 70.00 |
| ❑ 3 Tim Horton | 100.00 | 45.00 |
| ❑ 4 Jean-Guy Talbot | 30.00 | 13.50 |
| ❑ 5 Carl Brewer | 30.00 | 13.50 |
| ❑ 6 J.C. Tremblay | 30.00 | 13.50 |
| ❑ 7 Dick Duff | 30.00 | 13.50 |
| ❑ 8 Jean Beliveau | 100.00 | 45.00 |
| ❑ 9 Dave Keon | 50.00 | 22.00 |
| ❑ 10 Henri Richard | 80.00 | 36.00 |
| ❑ 11 Frank Mahovlich | 80.00 | 36.00 |
| ❑ 12 BoomBoom Geoffrion | 50.00 | 22.00 |
| ❑ 13 Kent Douglas | 25.00 | 11.00 |
| ❑ 14 Claude Provost | 30.00 | 13.50 |
| ❑ 15 Bob Pulford | 30.00 | 13.50 |
| ❑ 16 Ralph Backstrom | 30.00 | 13.50 |
| ❑ 17 George Armstrong | 40.00 | 18.00 |
| ❑ 18 Bobby Rousseau | 25.00 | 11.00 |
| ❑ 19 Gordie Howe | 250.00 | 110.00 |
| ❑ 20 Red Kelly | 40.00 | 18.00 |
| ❑ 21 Alex Delvecchio | 40.00 | 18.00 |
| ❑ 22 Dickie Moore | 40.00 | 18.00 |
| ❑ 23 Marcel Pronovost | 30.00 | 13.50 |
| ❑ 24 Doug Barkley | 25.00 | 11.00 |
| ❑ 25 Terry Sawchuk | 100.00 | 45.00 |
| ❑ 26 Billy Harris | 25.00 | 11.00 |
| ❑ 27 Parker MacDonald | 25.00 | 11.00 |
| ❑ 28 Don Marshall | 25.00 | 11.00 |
| ❑ 29 Norm Ullman | 50.00 | 22.00 |
| ❑ 30A Andre Pronovost | 25.00 | 11.00 |
| ❑ 30B Vic Stasiuk | 25.00 | 11.00 |
| ❑ 31 Bill Gadsby | 30.00 | 13.50 |
| ❑ 32 Eddie Shack | 50.00 | 22.00 |
| ❑ 33 Larry Jeffrey | 25.00 | 11.00 |
| ❑ 34 Gilles Tremblay | 25.00 | 11.00 |
| ❑ 35 Howie Young | 25.00 | 11.00 |
| ❑ 36 Bruce MacGregor | 25.00 | 11.00 |

## 1963-64 York White Backs

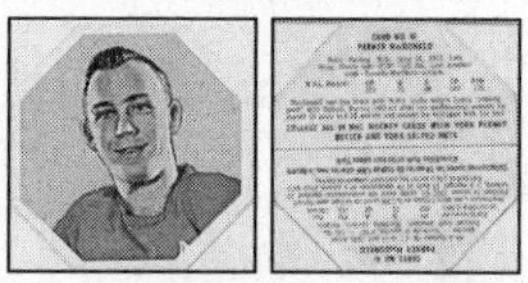

This set of 54 octagonal cards was issued with York Peanut Butter and York Salted Nuts. The cards are numbered on the backs at the top. The cards measure approximately 2 1/2" in diameter. The set can be dated as a 1963-64 set by referring to the career totals given on the back of each player's cards. The card backs were written in both French and English. An album was originally available for holding the set; the set is considered complete without the album.

| | NRMT | VG-E |
|---|---|---|
| COMPLETE SET (54) | 750.00 | 350.00 |
| COMMON CARD (1-54) | 10.00 | 4.50 |
| ❑ 1 Tim Horton | 40.00 | 18.00 |
| ❑ 2 Johnny Bower | 20.00 | 9.00 |
| ❑ 3 Ron Stewart | 10.00 | 4.50 |
| ❑ 4 Eddie Shack | 20.00 | 9.00 |
| ❑ 5 Frank Mahovlich | 25.00 | 11.00 |
| ❑ 6 Dave Keon | 30.00 | 13.50 |
| ❑ 7 Bob Baun | 12.00 | 5.50 |
| ❑ 8 Bob Nevin | 10.00 | 4.50 |
| ❑ 9 Dick Duff | 12.00 | 5.50 |
| ❑ 10 Billy Harris | 10.00 | 4.50 |
| ❑ 11 Larry Hillman | 10.00 | 4.50 |
| ❑ 12 Red Kelly | 15.00 | 6.75 |
| ❑ 13 Kent Douglas | 10.00 | 4.50 |
| ❑ 14 Allan Stanley | 12.00 | 5.50 |
| ❑ 15 Don Simmons | 12.00 | 5.50 |
| ❑ 16 George Armstrong | 15.00 | 6.75 |
| ❑ 17 Carl Brewer | 12.00 | 5.50 |
| ❑ 18 Bob Pulford | 12.00 | 5.50 |
| ❑ 19 Henri Richard | 25.00 | 11.00 |
| ❑ 20 BoomBoom Geoffrion | 20.00 | 9.00 |
| ❑ 21 Gilles Tremblay | 10.00 | 4.50 |
| ❑ 22 Gump Worsley | 20.00 | 9.00 |
| ❑ 23 Jean-Guy Talbot | 12.00 | 5.50 |
| ❑ 24 J.C. Tremblay | 12.00 | 5.50 |
| ❑ 25 Bobby Rousseau | 10.00 | 4.50 |
| ❑ 26 Jean Beliveau | 40.00 | 18.00 |
| ❑ 27 Ralph Backstrom | 12.00 | 5.50 |
| ❑ 28 Claude Provost | 12.00 | 5.50 |
| ❑ 29 Jean Gauthier | 10.00 | 4.50 |
| ❑ 30 Bill Hicke | 10.00 | 4.50 |
| ❑ 31 Terry Harper | 12.00 | 5.50 |
| ❑ 32 Marc Reaume | 10.00 | 4.50 |
| ❑ 33 Dave Balon | 10.00 | 4.50 |
| ❑ 34 Jacques Laperriere | 15.00 | 6.75 |
| ❑ 35 John Ferguson | 15.00 | 6.75 |
| ❑ 36 Red Berenson | 12.00 | 5.50 |
| ❑ 37 Terry Sawchuk | 50.00 | 22.00 |
| ❑ 38 Marcel Pronovost | 12.00 | 5.50 |
| ❑ 39 Bill Gadsby | 15.00 | 6.75 |
| ❑ 40 Parker MacDonald | 10.00 | 4.50 |
| ❑ 41 Larry Jeffrey | 10.00 | 4.50 |
| ❑ 42 Floyd Smith | 10.00 | 4.50 |
| ❑ 43 Andre Pronovost | 10.00 | 4.50 |
| ❑ 44 Art Stratton | 10.00 | 4.50 |
| ❑ 45 Gordie Howe | 100.00 | 45.00 |
| ❑ 46 Doug Barkley | 10.00 | 4.50 |
| ❑ 47 Norm Ullman | 15.00 | 6.75 |
| ❑ 48 Eddie Joyal | 10.00 | 4.50 |
| ❑ 49 Alex Faulkner | 25.00 | 11.00 |
| ❑ 50 Alex Delvecchio | 15.00 | 6.75 |
| ❑ 51 Bruce MacGregor | 10.00 | 4.50 |
| ❑ 52 Ted Hampson | 10.00 | 4.50 |
| ❑ 53 Pete Goegan | 10.00 | 4.50 |
| ❑ 54 Ron Ingram | 10.00 | 4.50 |
| ❑ xx Album | 40.00 | 18.00 |

## 1967-68 York Action Octagons

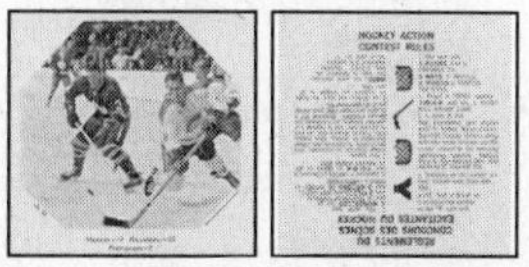

This 36-card set was issued by York Peanut Butter. Only cards 13-36 are numbered. The twelve unnumbered cards have been assigned the numbers 1-12 based on alphabetizing the names of the first player listed on each card. Each card shows an action scene involving two or three players. Uniform numbers are also given on the cards. The card backs give the details of a send-in contest ending June 30, 1968. Collecting four cards spelling "YORK" entitled one to receive a Bobby Hull Hockey Game. These octagonal cards measure approximately 2 7/8" in diameter. The card backs were written in both French and English.

| | NRMT-MT | EXC |
|---|---|---|
| COMPLETE SET (36) | 600.00 | 275.00 |
| COMMON CARD (1-36) | 10.00 | 4.50 |
| ❑ 1 Brian Conacher 22<br>Allan Stanley 26<br>Leon Rochefort 25 | 12.00 | 5.50 |
| ❑ 2 Terry Harper 19<br>Gump Worsley 30<br>Mike Walton 16 | 20.00 | 9.00 |
| ❑ 3 Tim Horton 7<br>George Armstrong 10<br>Jean Beliveau 4 | 40.00 | 18.00 |
| ❑ 4 Dave Keon 14<br>George Armstrong 10<br>Claude Provost 14 | 20.00 | 9.00 |
| ❑ 5 Jacques Laperriere 2<br>Rogatien Vachon 29<br>Bob Pulford 20 | 20.00 | 9.00 |
| ❑ 6 Bob Pulford 20<br>Brian Conacher 22<br>Claude Provost 14 | 12.00 | 5.50 |
| ❑ 7 Bob Pulford 20<br>Jim Pappin 18<br>Terry Harper 19 | 12.00 | 5.50 |
| ❑ 8 Pete Stemkowski 12<br>Jim Pappin 18<br>Harris 10 | 12.00 | 5.50 |
| ❑ 9 J.C. Tremblay 3<br>Rogatien Vachon 29<br>Pete Stemkowski 12 | 15.00 | 6.75 |
| ❑ 10 Rogatien Vachon 29<br>Ralph Backstrom 6<br>Bob Pulford 20 | 20.00 | 9.00 |
| ❑ 11 Rogatien Vachon 29<br>Jacques Laperriere 2<br>Mike Walton 16 | 20.00 | 9.00 |
| ❑ 12 Mike Walton 16<br>Pete Stemkowski 12<br>J.C. Tremblay 3 | 12.00 | 5.50 |
| ❑ 13 Dave Keon 14<br>Mike Walton 16<br>J.C. Tremblay 3 | 12.00 | 5.50 |
| ❑ 14 Pete Stemkowski 12<br>Ralph Backstrom 6 | 10.00 | 4.50 |
| ❑ 15 Rogatien Vachon 29<br>Bob Pulford 20 | 15.00 | 6.75 |
| ❑ 16 Johnny Bower 1<br>Ron Ellis 8<br>John Ferguson 22 | 15.00 | 6.75 |
| ❑ 17 Ron Ellis 8<br>Gump Worsley 30 | 15.00 | 6.75 |
| ❑ 18 Gump Worsley 30<br>Jacques Laperriere 2<br>Frank Mahovlich 27 | 25.00 | 11.00 |
| ❑ 19 J.C. Tremblay 3<br>Dave Keon 14 | 12.00 | 5.50 |
| ❑ 20 Claude Provost 14<br>Frank Mahovlich 27 | 20.00 | 9.00 |
| ❑ 21 John Ferguson 22<br>Tim Horton 7 | 20.00 | 9.00 |
| ❑ 22 Gump Worsley 30<br>Ron Ellis 8 | 15.00 | 6.75 |
| ❑ 23 Johnny Bower 1<br>Mike Walton 16<br>Jean Beliveau 4 | 20.00 | 9.00 |
| ❑ 24 J.C. Tremblay 3<br>Gump Worsley 30<br>Bob Pulford 20 | 15.00 | 6.75 |
| ❑ 25 Tim Horton 7<br>Johnny Bower 1<br>Jean Beliveau 4 | 30.00 | 13.50 |
| ❑ 26 Allan Stanley 26<br>Johnny Bower 1<br>Dick Duff 8 | 15.00 | 6.75 |
| ❑ 27 Ralph Backstrom 6<br>Johnny Bower 1 | 15.00 | 6.75 |
| ❑ 28 Yvan Cournoyer 12<br>Jean Beliveau 4<br>Frank Mahovlich 27 | 40.00 | 18.00 |
| ❑ 29 Johnny Bower 1<br>Larry Hillman 2<br>Yvan Cournoyer 12 | 20.00 | 9.00 |
| ❑ 30 Johnny Bower 1<br>Yvan Cournoyer 12 | 20.00 | 9.00 |
| ❑ 31 Tim Horton 7<br>Rogatien Vachon 29 | 20.00 | 9.00 |
| ❑ 32 Jim Pappin 18<br>Bob Pulford 20<br>Rogatien Vachon 29 | 15.00 | 6.75 |
| ❑ 33 Terry Harper 19<br>Bobby Rousseau 15<br>Pronovost 3 | 10.00 | 4.50 |
| ❑ 34 Johnny Bower 1<br>Pronovost 3<br>Ralph Backstrom 6 | 12.00 | 5.50 |
| ❑ 35 Frank Mahovlich 27<br>Gump Worsley 30 | 25.00 | 11.00 |
| ❑ 36 Claude Provost 14<br>Johnny Bower 1 | 12.00 | 5.50 |

## 1992-93 Zellers Masters of Hockey

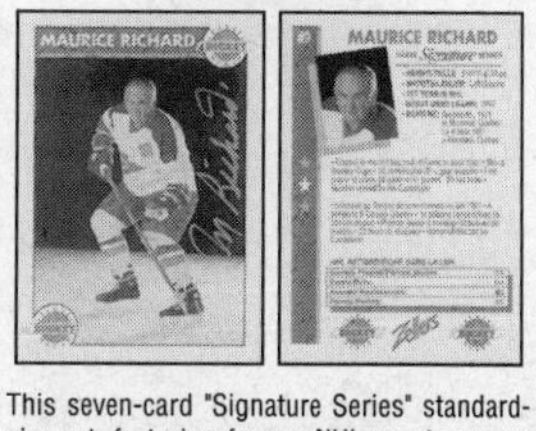

This seven-card "Signature Series" standard-size set, featuring former NHL greats, was a promotion by Zellers. According to the certificate of authenticity, the production run was 1,000 sets. The cards have posed color player photos inside white borders. A blue stripe above the picture carries the player's name and is accented by a thin mustard stripe. A silver foil facsimile signature is inscribed across the picture. The backs have the blue and mustard stripes running down the left side and carrying the player's jersey number. In English and French, biography, career highlights, and statistics are included on a white background. A close-up color player photo with a shadow border partially overlaps the stripe near the top. The cards are unnumbered and checklisted below in alphabetical order. There was also a large Marcel Dionne card reportedly given out at various store signings.

| | MINT | NRMT |
|---|---|---|
| COMPLETE SET (7) | 20.00 | 9.00 |
| COMMON CARD (1-7) | 2.00 | .90 |
| ❑ 1 Johnny Bower | 3.00 | 1.35 |
| ❑ 2 Rod Gilbert | 3.00 | 1.35 |
| ❑ 3 Ted Lindsay | 3.00 | 1.35 |
| ❑ 4 Frank Mahovlich | 4.00 | 1.80 |
| ❑ 5 Stan Mikita | 4.00 | 1.80 |
| ❑ 6 Maurice Richard | 6.00 | 2.70 |
| ❑ 7 Certificate of Authenticity | 2.00 | .90 |

## 1993-94 Zellers Masters of Hockey

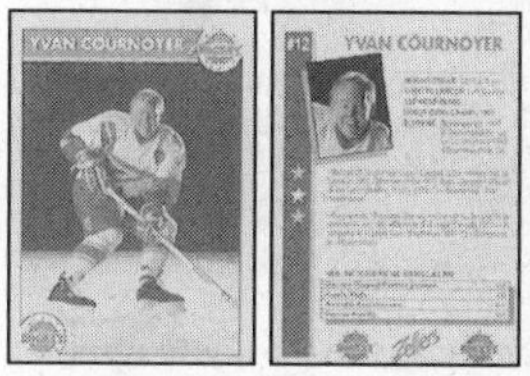

Featuring former NHL greats, this 8-card "Signature Series" marks the second consecutive year a promotion was issued by Zellers. The cards measure the standard size and have posed color player photos inside white borders. A blue stripe above the picture carries the player's name and is accented by a thin mustard stripe. A silver foil facsimile signature is inscribed across the picture. The backs have the blue and mustard stripes running down the left side and carrying the player's jersey number. In English and French, biography, career highlights, and statistics are included on a white background. A close-up color player photo with a shadow border partially overlaps the stripe near the top. The cards are unnumbered and checklisted below in alphabetical order.

| | MINT | NRMT |
|---|---|---|
| COMPLETE SET (8) | 15.00 | 6.75 |
| COMMON CARD (1-8) | 1.00 | .45 |
| ❑ 1 Andy Bathgate | 1.00 | .45 |
| ❑ 2 Johnny Bucyk | 2.00 | .90 |
| ❑ 3 Yvan Cournoyer | 2.00 | .90 |
| ❑ 4 Marcel Dionne | 2.00 | .90 |
| ❑ 5 Bobby Hull | 4.00 | 1.80 |
| ❑ 6 Brad Park | 2.00 | .90 |
| ❑ 7 Jean Ratelle | 2.00 | .90 |
| ❑ 8 Gump Worsley | 2.50 | 1.10 |
| ❑ NNO Marcel Dionne Large | 1.00 | .45 |

## 1994-95 Zellers Masters of Hockey

For the third consecutive year, Zellers issued an 8-card "Signature Series" set, featuring former NHL greats. The cards measure the standard size and have posed color player photos inside white borders. A blue stripe above the picture carries the player's name and is accented by a thin mustard stripe. A silver foil facsimile signature is inscribed across the picture. The backs have the blue and mustard stripes running down the left side and carrying the player's jersey number. In English and French, biography, career highlights, and statistics are included on a white background. A close-up color player photo with a shadow border partially overlaps the stripe near the top. The cards are unnumbered and checklisted below in alphabetical order.

| | MINT | NRMT |
|---|---|---|
| COMPLETE SET (8) | 10.00 | 4.50 |
| COMMON CARD (1-8) | 1.00 | .45 |
| ❑ 1 Jean Beliveau | 4.00 | 1.80 |
| ❑ 2 Gerry Cheevers | 2.00 | .90 |
| ❑ 3 Red Kelly | 2.00 | .90 |
| ❑ 4 Dave Keon | 2.00 | .90 |
| ❑ 5 Lanny McDonald | 1.00 | .45 |
| ❑ 6 Pierre Pilote | 1.00 | .45 |

❑ 7 Henri Richard 2.00 .90
❑ 8 Norm Ullman 2.00 .90
❑ NNO Jean Beliveau Large 1.00 .45

## 1995-96 Zellers Masters of Hockey Signed

Cards are only available signed and were limited to 3500 copies. Each card came with a certificate of authenticity.

| | MINT | NRMT |
|---|---|---|
| COMPLETE SET (8) | 175.00 | 80.00 |
| COMMON CARD (1-8) | 15.00 | 6.75 |

❑ 1 Mike Bossy 25.00 11.00
❑ 2 Eddie Giacomin 15.00 6.75
❑ 3 Gordie Howe 50.00 22.00
❑ 4 Jacques Laperriere 15.00 6.75
❑ 5 Gilbert Perreault 20.00 9.00
❑ 6 Serge Savard 15.00 6.75
❑ 7 Steve Shutt 15.00 6.75
❑ 8 Darryl Sittler 20.00 9.00

## 1995-96 Zenith

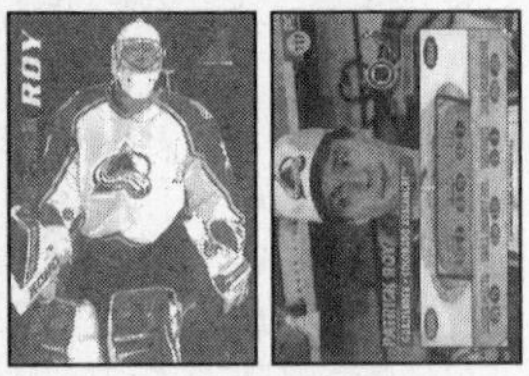

The 1995-96 Zenith set was issued in one series totalling 150 standard-size cards. The 6-card packs had a suggested retail of $3.99. The set features 24-point card stock with exclusive Dufex all-foil printing. Rookie Cards in this set include Daniel Alfredsson, Miroslav Satan, Todd Bertuzzi, Chad Kilger, Daymond Langkow and Radek Dvorak.

| | MINT | NRMT |
|---|---|---|
| COMPLETE SET (150) | 60.00 | 27.00 |
| COMMON CARD (1-150) | .25 | .11 |

❑ 1 Brett Hull 1.50 .70
❑ 2 Paul Coffey .60 .25
❑ 3 Jaromir Jagr 4.00 1.80
❑ 4 Joe Murphy .25 .11
❑ 5 Jim Carey .60 .25
❑ 6 Eric Lindros 4.00 1.80
❑ 7 Ulf Dahlen .25 .11
❑ 8 Mark Recchi .40 .18
❑ 9 Pavel Bure 2.50 1.10
❑ 10 Adam Oates .40 .18
❑ 11 Theoren Fleury .40 .18
❑ 12 Martin Brodeur 3.00 1.35
❑ 13 Wayne Gretzky 8.00 3.60
❑ 14 Geoff Sanderson .40 .18
❑ 15 Chris Gratton .40 .18
❑ 16 Owen Nolan .40 .18
❑ 17 Paul Kariya 5.00 2.20
❑ 18 Mark Messier 1.50 .70
❑ 19 Mats Sundin .40 .18
❑ 20 Brian Savage .25 .11
❑ 21 Mathieu Schneider .25 .11
❑ 22 Alexandre Daigle .25 .11
❑ 23 Jason Arnott .40 .18
❑ 24 Mike Modano 1.50 .70
❑ 25 Scott Mellanby .40 .18
❑ 26 Alexei Zhamnov .40 .18
❑ 27 Scott Niedermayer .25 .11
❑ 28 Chris Pronger .40 .18
❑ 29 Ray Bourque .60 .25
❑ 30 Sergei Fedorov 2.00 .90
❑ 31 Alexander Mogilny .40 .18
❑ 32 Brian Leetch .60 .25
❑ 33 Adam Graves .40 .18
❑ 34 Jocelyn Thibault .60 .25
❑ 35 Ron Francis .40 .18
❑ 36 John Vanbiesbrouck 2.00 .90
❑ 37 Chris Chelios .60 .25
❑ 38 Pierre Turgeon .40 .18
❑ 39 Stephane Richer .40 .18
❑ 40 Al MacInnis .40 .18
❑ 41 Dave Andreychuk .40 .18
❑ 42 Mikael Renberg .40 .18
❑ 43 Nelson Emerson .25 .11
❑ 44 Kevin Hatcher .25 .11
❑ 45 Kirk Muller .25 .11
❑ 46 Bernie Nicholls .25 .11
❑ 47 Bill Ranford .40 .18
❑ 48 Luc Robitaille .40 .18
❑ 49 Peter Bondra .60 .25
❑ 50 Jari Kurri .40 .18
❑ 51 Dino Ciccarelli .40 .18
❑ 52 Kevin Stevens .25 .11
❑ 53 Mike Richter .60 .25
❑ 54 Doug Gilmour .60 .25
❑ 55 Kelly Hrudey .40 .18
❑ 56 Dave Gagner .40 .18
❑ 57 Kirk McLean .40 .18
❑ 58 Geoff Courtnall .25 .11
❑ 59 John LeClair 2.00 .90
❑ 60 Mike Vernon .40 .18
❑ 61 Cam Neely .40 .18
❑ 62 Mike Gartner .40 .18
❑ 63 Igor Korolev .25 .11
❑ 64 Joe Sakic 2.50 1.10
❑ 65 Jeff Friesen .40 .18
❑ 66 Sergei Zubov .25 .11
❑ 67 Trevor Kidd .40 .18
❑ 68 Rod Brind'Amour .40 .18
❑ 69 John MacLean .40 .18
❑ 70 Peter Forsberg 4.00 1.80
❑ 71 Oleg Tverdovsky .40 .18
❑ 72 Jeremy Roenick .60 .25
❑ 73 Gary Suter .25 .11
❑ 74 Keith Tkachuk 1.50 .70
❑ 75 Todd Harvey .25 .11
❑ 76 Felix Potvin .60 .25
❑ 77 Vincent Damphousse .40 .18
❑ 78 Blaine Lacher .40 .18
❑ 79 Tomas Sandstrom .25 .11
❑ 80 Chris Osgood .60 .25
❑ 81 Arturs Irbe .40 .18
❑ 82 Pat Verbeek .25 .11
❑ 83 Keith Primeau .40 .18
❑ 84 Brett Lindros .25 .11
❑ 85 Pat LaFontaine .40 .18
❑ 86 Brendan Shanahan 2.50 1.10
❑ 87 Trevor Linden .40 .18
❑ 88 Rob Blake .25 .11
❑ 89 Scott Stevens .40 .18
❑ 90 Tom Barrasso .40 .18
❑ 91 Mike Ricci .25 .11
❑ 92 Ray Sheppard .40 .18
❑ 93 Steve Yzerman 4.00 1.80
❑ 94 Wendel Clark .40 .18
❑ 95 Ed Belfour .60 .25
❑ 96 Joe Juneau .25 .11
❑ 97 Ron Hextall .40 .18
❑ 98 Shayne Corson .25 .11
❑ 99 Guy Hebert .40 .18
❑ 100 Sean Burke .40 .18
❑ 101 Sandis Ozolinsh .40 .18
❑ 102 Teemu Selanne 2.50 1.10
❑ 103 Petr Nedved .40 .18
❑ 104 Phil Housley .40 .18
❑ 105 Andy Moog .40 .18
❑ 106 Larry Murphy .40 .18
❑ 107 Grant Fuhr .40 .18
❑ 108 Mario Lemieux 6.00 2.70
❑ 109 Dominik Hasek 2.50 1.10
❑ 110 Rob Niedermayer .40 .18
❑ 111 Steve Duchesne .25 .11
❑ 112 Joe Nieuwendyk .40 .18
❑ 113 Yanic Perreault .25 .11
❑ 114 Steve Thomas .25 .11
❑ 115 Russ Courtnall .25 .11
❑ 116 Claude Lemieux .40 .18
❑ 117 Patrick Roy 6.00 2.70
❑ 118 Rick Tocchet .40 .18
❑ 119 Stephane Fiset .40 .18
❑ 120 Daren Puppa .40 .18
❑ 121 Ed Jovanovski .60 .25
❑ 122 Eric Daze .60 .25
❑ 123 Cory Stillman .25 .11
❑ 124 Brendan Witt .25 .11
❑ 125 Valeri Bure .40 .18
❑ 126 Brian Holzinger .40 .18
❑ 127 Kyle McLaren .25 .11
❑ 128 Niklas Sundstrom .25 .11
❑ 129 Jamie Langenbrunner .25 .11
❑ 130 Jeff O'Neill .25 .11
❑ 131 Vitali Yachmenev .25 .11
❑ 132 Shane Doan .25 .11
❑ 133 Byron Dafoe .40 .18
❑ 134 Corey Hirsch .40 .18
❑ 135 Antti Tormanen .25 .11
❑ 136 Jason Bonsignore .25 .11
❑ 137 Ryan Smyth .25 .11
❑ 138 Bryan McCabe .25 .11
❑ 139 Chad Kilger .25 .11
❑ 140 Todd Bertuzzi .40 .18
❑ 141 Marcus Ragnarsson .25 .11
❑ 142 Marty Murray .25 .11
❑ 143 Daymond Langkow .60 .25
❑ 144 Saku Koivu 2.00 .90
❑ 145 Jere Lehtinen .25 .11
❑ 146 Aki-Petteri Berg .25 .11
❑ 147 Radek Dvorak .25 .11
❑ 148 Robert Svehla .25 .11
❑ 149 Daniel Alfredsson 2.00 .90
❑ 150 Miroslav Satan 3.00 1.35

## 1995-96 Zenith Gifted Grinders

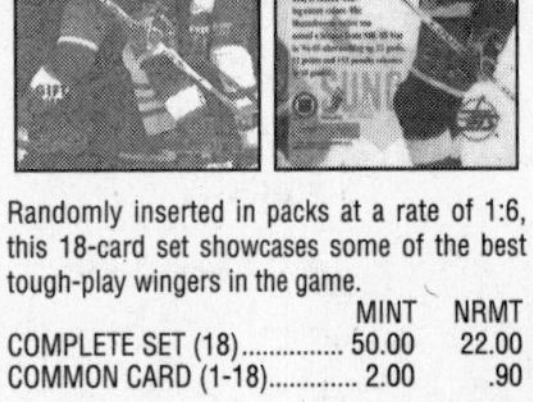

Randomly inserted in packs at a rate of 1:6, this 18-card set showcases some of the best tough-play wingers in the game.

| | MINT | NRMT |
|---|---|---|
| COMPLETE SET (18) | 50.00 | 22.00 |
| COMMON CARD (1-18) | 2.00 | .90 |

❑ 1 Keith Tkachuk 6.00 2.70
❑ 2 Kevin Stevens 2.00 .90
❑ 3 Wendel Clark 2.00 .90
❑ 4 Claude Lemieux 4.00 1.80
❑ 5 Rick Tocchet 4.00 1.80
❑ 6 Trevor Linden 4.00 1.80
❑ 7 John LeClair 8.00 3.60
❑ 8 Mikael Renberg 4.00 1.80
❑ 9 Owen Nolan 4.00 1.80
❑ 10 Todd Harvey 2.00 .90
❑ 11 Dave Gagner 2.00 .90
❑ 12 Dale Hunter 2.00 .90
❑ 13 Dave Andreychuk 2.00 .90
❑ 14 Mark Recchi 4.00 1.80
❑ 15 Jason Arnott 4.00 1.80
❑ 16 Dino Ciccarelli 2.00 .90
❑ 17 Adam Graves 4.00 1.80
❑ 18 Steve Thomas 2.00 .90

## 1995-96 Zenith Rookie Roll Call

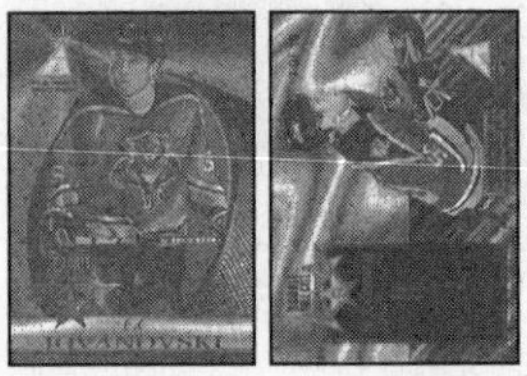

Randomly inserted in packs at a rate of 1:24, this 18-card set features the hottest 1995-96 rookies highlighted by the Dufex technology. A note on the card backs alluded to the total production run of these cards being no greater than 1,200 total sets.

| | MINT | NRMT |
|---|---|---|
| COMPLETE SET (18) | 200.00 | 90.00 |
| COMMON CARDS (1-18) | 10.00 | 4.50 |

❑ 1 Saku Koivu 20.00 9.00
❑ 2 Radek Dvorak 10.00 4.50
❑ 3 Brendan Witt 10.00 4.50
❑ 4 Antti Tormanen 10.00 4.50
❑ 5 Brian Holzinger 10.00 4.50
❑ 6 Aki-Petteri Berg 10.00 4.50
❑ 7 Ed Jovanovski 15.00 6.75
❑ 8 Marcus Ragnarsson 15.00 6.75
❑ 9 Todd Bertuzzi 15.00 6.75
❑ 10 Daniel Alfredsson 15.00 6.75
❑ 11 Vitali Yachmenev 10.00 4.50
❑ 12 Chad Kilger 10.00 4.50
❑ 13 Eric Daze 15.00 6.75
❑ 14 Niklas Sundstrom 10.00 4.50
❑ 15 Shane Doan 10.00 4.50
❑ 16 Cory Stillman 10.00 4.50
❑ 17 Kyle McLaren 10.00 4.50
❑ 18 Jeff O'Neill 10.00 4.50

## 1995-96 Zenith Z-Team

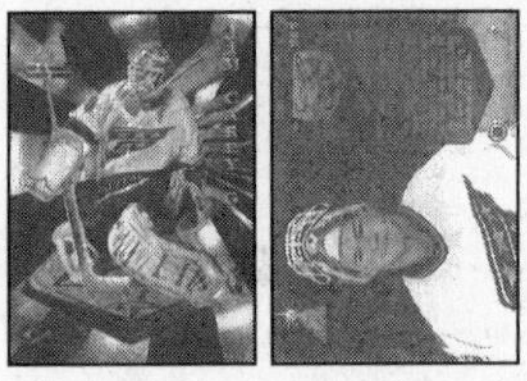

Randomly inserted in packs at a rate of 1:72, this 18-card set depicts the best players in hockey, using a modified Dufex-type foil style. Based on stated insertion odds and the information given on the backs of the Rookie Roll Call singles, it is believed that no more than 400 of each Z-Team card is in existence.

| | MINT | NRMT |
|---|---|---|
| COMPLETE SET (18) | 1200.00 | 550.00 |
| COMMON CARD (1-18) | 20.00 | 9.00 |

❑ 1 Patrick Roy 150.00 70.00
❑ 2 Martin Brodeur 30.00 13.50
❑ 3 Mario Lemieux 150.00 70.00
❑ 4 Wayne Gretzky 200.00 90.00
❑ 5 Mark Messier 40.00 18.00
❑ 6 Jeremy Roenick 30.00 13.50
❑ 7 Eric Lindros 100.00 45.00
❑ 8 Peter Forsberg 100.00 45.00
❑ 9 Sergei Fedorov 60.00 27.00
❑ 10 Mike Modano 40.00 18.00
❑ 11 Jaromir Jagr 100.00 45.00
❑ 12 Pavel Bure 60.00 27.00
❑ 13 Joe Sakic 60.00 27.00
❑ 14 Paul Kariya 120.00 55.00
❑ 15 Brett Hull 40.00 18.00
❑ 16 Brendan Shanahan 60.00 27.00
❑ 17 Felix Potvin 30.00 13.50
❑ 18 Jim Carey 30.00 13.50
❑ S2 Martin Brodeur-SAMPLE 20.00 9.00

## 1996-97 Zenith

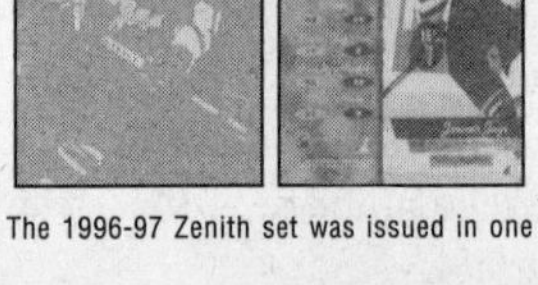

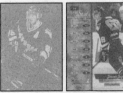

The 1996-97 Zenith set was issued in one series totalling 150 cards and was distributed in six-card packs. Printed on thick card stock, the fronts feature color action player images on a gold foil background. The backs carry in-depth player statistics. Dainius Zubrus and Sergei Berezin are the key rookies in the set.

| | MINT | NRMT |
|---|---|---|
| COMPLETE SET (150) | 40.00 | 18.00 |
| COMMON CARD (1-150) | .15 | .07 |

❑ 1 Mike Modano 1.00 .45
❑ 2 Martin Brodeur 2.00 .90
❑ 3 Pavel Bure 1.50 .70
❑ 4 Ray Bourque .75 .35
❑ 5 Steve Yzerman 2.50 1.10
❑ 6 Keith Tkachuk 1.00 .45
❑ 7 Jim Carey .75 .35
❑ 8 Valeri Kamensky .40 .18
❑ 9 Valeri Bure .40 .18
❑ 10 Ron Francis .40 .18
❑ 11 Trevor Kidd .40 .18
❑ 12 Doug Weight .40 .18
❑ 13 Wayne Gretzky 6.00 2.70
❑ 14 Todd Gill .15 .07
❑ 15 Dominik Hasek 1.50 .70
❑ 16 Scott Mellanby .40 .18
❑ 17 John LeClair 1.25 .55
❑ 18 Al MacInnis .40 .18
❑ 19 Derian Hatcher .15 .07
❑ 20 Stephane Fiset .40 .18
❑ 21 Alexander Selivanov .15 .07
❑ 22 Vyacheslav Kozlov .15 .07
❑ 23 Alexei Yashin .40 .18
❑ 24 Wendel Clark .40 .18
❑ 25 Ed Belfour .75 .35
❑ 26 Travis Green .40 .18
❑ 27 Joe Juneau .15 .07
❑ 28 Teemu Selanne 1.50 .70
❑ 29 Jeff O'Neill .15 .07
❑ 30 Jeremy Roenick .75 .35
❑ 31 Felix Potvin .75 .35
❑ 32 Bernie Nicholls .15 .07
❑ 33 Steve Thomas .15 .07
❑ 34 Alexander Mogilny .40 .18
❑ 35 Patrick Roy 4.00 1.80
❑ 36 Luc Robitaille .40 .18
❑ 37 Owen Nolan .40 .18
❑ 38 Sergei Zubov .15 .07
❑ 39 Pierre Turgeon .40 .18
❑ 40 Nikolai Khabibulin .40 .18
❑ 41 Adam Oates .40 .18
❑ 42 Stephane Richer .40 .18
❑ 43 Daren Puppa .40 .18
❑ 44 Joe Sakic 1.50 .70
❑ 45 Ed Jovanovski .40 .18
❑ 46 Ron Hextall .40 .18
❑ 47 Doug Gilmour .75 .35
❑ 48 Paul Coffey .75 .35
❑ 49 Craig Janney .40 .18
❑ 50 Brendan Witt .15 .07
❑ 51 Jere Lehtinen .15 .07
❑ 52 Vitali Yachmenev .15 .07
❑ 53 Damian Rhodes .40 .18
❑ 54 Petr Nedved .40 .18
❑ 55 Theoren Fleury .40 .18
❑ 56 Petr Sykora .15 .07
❑ 57 Kelly Hrudey .40 .18
❑ 58 Saku Koivu 1.25 .55
❑ 59 Brian Bradley .15 .07
❑ 60 Arturs Irbe .40 .18
❑ 61 Eric Lindros 2.50 1.10
❑ 62 Michal Pivonka .15 .07
❑ 63 Joe Nieuwendyk .40 .18
❑ 64 Mats Sundin .40 .18
❑ 65 Jason Arnott .40 .18
❑ 66 Mike Richter .75 .35
❑ 67 Brett Hull 1.00 .45
❑ 68 Chris Chelios .75 .35
❑ 69 Jocelyn Thibault .75 .35
❑ 70 Oleg Tverdovsky .40 .18
❑ 71 Peter Bondra .75 .35
❑ 72 Bill Ranford .40 .18
❑ 73 Scott Stevens .40 .18
❑ 74 Jaromir Jagr 2.50 1.10
❑ 75 Corey Hirsch .40 .18
❑ 76 Peter Forsberg 2.50 1.10
❑ 77 Brendan Shanahan 1.50 .70
❑ 78 Antti Tormanen .15 .07
❑ 79 Marcus Ragnarsson .15 .07
❑ 80 Sergei Fedorov 1.50 .70
❑ 81 Todd Bertuzzi .15 .07
❑ 82 Grant Fuhr .40 .18
❑ 83 Pat LaFontaine .40 .18
❑ 84 Rob Niedermayer .40 .18
❑ 85 Brian Leetch .75 .35
❑ 86 Yanic Perreault .15 .07
❑ 87 Dino Ciccarelli .40 .18
❑ 88 Dimitri Khristich .15 .07
❑ 89 Jeff Friesen .40 .18
❑ 90 Paul Kariya 3.00 1.35
❑ 91 John Vanbiesbrouck 1.25 .55
❑ 92 Roman Hamrlik .40 .18
❑ 93 Pat Verbeek .15 .07
❑ 94 Mark Messier 1.00 .45
❑ 95 Trevor Linden .40 .18
❑ 96 Igor Larionov .15 .07
❑ 97 Zigmund Palffy .75 .35
❑ 98 Tom Barrasso .40 .18
❑ 99 Eric Daze .40 .18
❑ 100 Vincent Damphousse .40 .18
❑ 101 Keith Primeau .40 .18
❑ 102 Claude Lemieux .40 .18
❑ 103 Daniel Alfredsson .40 .18
❑ 104 Ryan Smyth .75 .35
❑ 105 Chris Osgood .75 .35
❑ 106 Bill Guerin .15 .07
❑ 107 Shayne Corson .15 .07
❑ 108 Alexei Zhamnov .40 .18
❑ 109 Mikael Renberg .40 .18
❑ 110 Andy Moog .40 .18
❑ 111 Larry Murphy .40 .18
❑ 112 Curtis Joseph .75 .35
❑ 113 Cory Stillman .15 .07
❑ 114 Mario Lemieux 4.00 1.80
❑ 115 Scott Young .15 .07
❑ 116 Eric Fichaud .40 .18
❑ 117 Jonas Hoglund .15 .07
❑ 118 Tomas Holmstrom .15 .07
❑ 119 Jarome Iginla .75 .35
❑ 120 Richard Zednik .15 .07
❑ 121 Andreas Dackell .15 .07
❑ 122 Anson Carter .15 .07
❑ 123 Dainius Zubrus 1.50 .70
❑ 124 Janne Niinimaa .75 .35
❑ 125 Jason Allison .15 .07
❑ 126 Bryan Berard .75 .35
❑ 127 Sergei Berezin 1.25 .55
❑ 128 Wade Redden .15 .07
❑ 129 Jim Campbell .15 .07
❑ 130 Darcy Tucker .15 .07
❑ 131 Harry York .75 .35
❑ 132 Brandon Convery .15 .07
❑ 133 Ethan Moreau .75 .35
❑ 134 Mattias Timander .15 .07
❑ 135 Christian Dube .15 .07
❑ 136 Kevin Hodson .75 .35
❑ 137 Anders Eriksson .15 .07
❑ 138 Chris O'Sullivan .15 .07
❑ 139 Jamie Langenbrunner .15 .07
❑ 140 Steve Sullivan .25 .11
❑ 141 Daymond Langkow .15 .07
❑ 142 Landon Wilson .15 .07
❑ 143 Scott Bailey .25 .11
❑ 144 Terry Ryan .25 .11
❑ 145 Curtis Brown .15 .07
❑ 146 Rem Murray .25 .11
❑ 147 Jamie Pushor .15 .07
❑ 148 Daniel Goneau .25 .11
❑ 149 Mike Prokopec .15 .07
❑ 150 Brad Smyth .15 .07

## 1996-97 Zenith Artist's Proofs

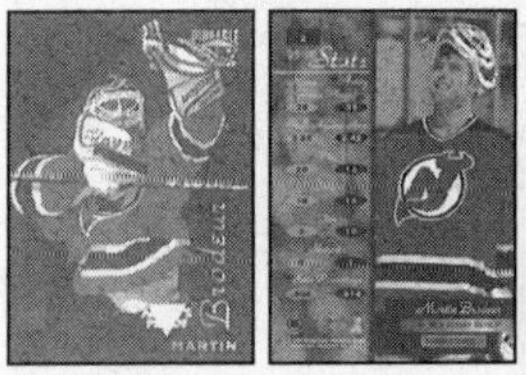

Randomly inserted in packs at a rate of one in 48, this 150-card set is parallel to the regular set and is similar in design. The difference is found in the gold, rainbow holographic foil stamp on each card.

| | MINT | NRMT |
|---|---|---|
| COMPLETE SET (150) | 3500.00 | 1600.00 |
| COMMON CARD (1-150) | 4.00 | 1.80 |

*STARS: 25X TO 50X BASIC CARDS
*YOUNG STARS: 15X TO 30X BASIC CARDS
*RCs: 10X TO 20X BASIC CARDS

## 1996-97 Zenith Assailants

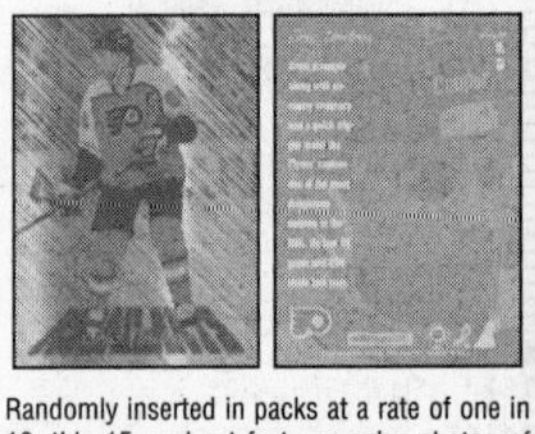

Randomly inserted in packs at a rate of one in 10, this 15-card set features color photos of some of the NHL's most deadly snipers (as well as a couple of guys who couldn't hit water from the beach) and is printed on silver, micro-etched, poly-laminate card stock.

| | MINT | NRMT |
|---|---|---|
| COMPLETE SET (15) | 60.00 | 27.00 |
| COMMON CARD (1-15) | 4.00 | 1.80 |

❑ 1 Alexei Yashin 4.00 1.80
❑ 2 Mike Modano 6.00 2.70
❑ 3 Jason Arnott 5.00 2.20
❑ 4 Mikael Renberg 5.00 2.20
❑ 5 Saku Koivu 8.00 3.60
❑ 6 Todd Bertuzzi 4.00 1.80
❑ 7 Zigmund Palffy 6.00 2.70
❑ 8 Eric Lindros 15.00 6.75
❑ 9 Pat LaFontaine 4.00 1.80
❑ 10 John LeClair 8.00 3.60
❑ 11 Theoren Fleury 5.00 2.20
❑ 12 Pierre Turgeon 5.00 2.20
❑ 13 Petr Nedved 4.00 1.80
❑ 14 Owen Nolan 5.00 2.20
❑ 15 Valeri Bure 4.00 1.80

## 1996-97 Zenith Champion Salute

Randomly inserted in packs at a rate of one in 23, this special commemorative insert set honors superstar veteran players who have played on a Stanley Cup championship team. The fronts feature color player photos printed on micro-etched, silver poly-laminate card stock, along with a faux "diamond" chip embedded in the Stanley Cup ring icon. A parallel to this set, entitled Champion Salute Extra, included an actual diamond chip.

| | MINT | NRMT |
|---|---|---|
| COMPLETE SET (15) | 150.00 | 70.00 |
| COMMON CARD (1-15) | 4.00 | 1.80 |
| COMP.DIAMOND SET (15) | 1000.00 | 450.00 |
| *DIAMOND STARS: 3X TO 6X BASIC CARDS | | |

| | | MINT | NRMT |
|---|---|---|---|
| □ 1 Mark Messier | | 6.00 | 2.70 |
| □ 2 Wayne Gretzky | | 30.00 | 13.50 |
| □ 3 Grant Fuhr | | 6.00 | 2.70 |
| □ 4 Paul Coffey | | 8.00 | 3.60 |
| □ 5 Mario Lemieux | | 25.00 | 11.00 |
| □ 6 Jaromir Jagr | | 15.00 | 6.75 |
| □ 7 Ron Francis | | 4.00 | 1.80 |
| □ 8 Joe Sakic | | 10.00 | 4.50 |
| □ 9 Peter Forsberg | | 15.00 | 6.75 |
| □ 10 Claude Lemieux | | 6.00 | 2.70 |
| □ 11 Patrick Roy | | 25.00 | 11.00 |
| □ 12 Chris Chelios | | 8.00 | 3.60 |
| □ 13 Doug Gilmour | | 6.00 | 2.70 |
| □ 14 Mike Richter | | 8.00 | 3.60 |
| □ 15 Martin Brodeur | | 12.00 | 5.50 |
| □ P3 Grant Fuhr promo | | 4.00 | 1.80 |
| □ P15 Martin Brodeur promo | | 10.00 | 4.50 |

## 1996-97 Zenith Z-Team

Randomly inserted packs at a rate of one in 71, this 18-card set honors some of the NHL superstars by combining embossing, micro-etching, rainbow holographic and gold foil stamping on clear plastic card stock.

| | MINT | NRMT |
|---|---|---|
| COMPLETE SET (18) | 700.00 | 325.00 |
| COMMON CARD (1-18) | 15.00 | 6.75 |

| | MINT | NRMT |
|---|---|---|
| □ 1 Eric Lindros | 80.00 | 36.00 |
| □ 2 Paul Kariya | 100.00 | 45.00 |
| □ 3 Teemu Selanne | 50.00 | 22.00 |
| □ 4 Brendan Shanahan | 50.00 | 22.00 |
| □ 5 Sergei Fedorov | 50.00 | 22.00 |
| □ 6 Steve Yzerman | 80.00 | 36.00 |
| □ 7 Brett Hull | 30.00 | 13.50 |
| □ 8 Pavel Bure | 50.00 | 22.00 |
| □ 9 Alexander Mogilny | 15.00 | 6.75 |
| □ 10 Jeremy Roenick | 25.00 | 11.00 |
| □ 11 Jocelyn Thibault | 25.00 | 11.00 |
| □ 12 Keith Tkachuk | 30.00 | 13.50 |
| □ 13 Daniel Alfredsson | 15.00 | 6.75 |
| □ 14 Eric Daze | 15.00 | 6.75 |
| □ 15 Jim Carey | 25.00 | 11.00 |
| □ 16 Felix Potvin | 25.00 | 11.00 |
| □ 17 John Vanbiesbrouck | 40.00 | 18.00 |
| □ 18 Chris Osgood | 25.00 | 11.00 |

## 1997-98 Zenith

The 1997-98 Zenith set was issued in one series totalling 100 cards and was distributed in packs of three 5" by 7" cards with one regular size card inside each of the jumbo cards. The jumbo cards had to be torn open to get to the regular cards inside. The fronts feature action color player photos. The backs carry player information and another photo.

| | MINT | NRMT |
|---|---|---|
| COMPLETE SET (100) | 150.00 | 70.00 |
| COMMON CARD (1-100) | .50 | .23 |

| | MINT | NRMT |
|---|---|---|
| □ 1 Jarome Iginla | 1.00 | .45 |
| □ 2 Peter Forsberg | 4.00 | 1.80 |
| □ 3 Brendan Shanahan | 2.50 | 1.10 |
| □ 4 Wayne Gretzky | 8.00 | 3.60 |
| □ 5 Steve Yzerman | 4.00 | 1.80 |
| □ 6 Eric Lindros | 4.00 | 1.80 |
| □ 7 Keith Tkachuk | 1.50 | .70 |
| □ 8 John LeClair | 2.00 | .90 |
| □ 9 John Vanbiesbrouck | 2.00 | .90 |
| □ 10 Patrick Roy | 6.00 | 2.70 |
| □ 11 Ray Bourque | 1.25 | .55 |
| □ 12 Theoren Fleury | 1.00 | .45 |
| □ 13 Brian Leetch | 1.25 | .55 |
| □ 14 Chris Chelios | 1.25 | .55 |
| □ 15 Paul Kariya | 5.00 | 2.20 |
| □ 16 Mark Messier | 1.50 | .70 |
| □ 17 Curtis Joseph | 1.25 | .55 |
| □ 18 Mike Richter | 1.25 | .55 |
| □ 19 Jeremy Roenick | 1.25 | .55 |
| □ 20 Dominik Hasek | 2.50 | 1.10 |
| □ 21 Martin Brodeur | 3.00 | 1.35 |
| □ 22 Sergei Fedorov | 2.50 | 1.10 |
| □ 23 Pierre Turgeon | 1.00 | .45 |
| □ 24 Teemu Selanne | 2.50 | 1.10 |
| □ 25 Brett Hull | 1.50 | .70 |
| □ 26 Saku Koivu | 2.00 | .90 |
| □ 27 Owen Nolan | 1.00 | .45 |
| □ 28 Jozef Stumpel | 1.00 | .45 |
| □ 29 Joe Sakic | 2.50 | 1.10 |
| □ 30 Zigmund Palffy | 1.25 | .55 |
| □ 31 Jaromir Jagr | 4.00 | 1.80 |
| □ 32 Adam Oates | 1.00 | .45 |
| □ 33 Jeff Friesen | 1.00 | .45 |
| □ 34 Pavel Bure | 2.50 | 1.10 |
| □ 35 Chris Osgood | 1.25 | .55 |
| □ 36 Mark Recchi | 1.00 | .45 |
| □ 37 Mike Modano | 1.50 | .70 |
| □ 38 Felix Potvin | 1.25 | .55 |
| □ 39 Vincent Damphousse | 1.00 | .45 |
| □ 40 Byron Dafoe | 1.00 | .45 |
| □ 41 Luc Robitaille | 1.00 | .45 |
| □ 42 Peter Bondra | 1.25 | .55 |
| □ 43 Daniel Alfredsson | 1.00 | .45 |
| □ 44 Pat LaFontaine | 1.00 | .45 |
| □ 45 Mikael Renberg | 1.00 | .45 |
| □ 46 Doug Gilmour | 1.25 | .55 |
| □ 47 Dino Ciccarelli | .50 | .23 |
| □ 48 Mats Sundin | 1.00 | .45 |
| □ 49 Ed Belfour | 1.25 | .55 |
| □ 50 Ron Francis | 1.00 | .45 |
| □ 51 Miroslav Satan | .50 | .23 |
| □ 52 Cory Stillman | .50 | .23 |
| □ 53 Bryan Berard | 1.00 | .45 |
| □ 54 Keith Primeau | 1.00 | .45 |
| □ 55 Eric Daze | 1.00 | .45 |
| □ 56 Chris Gratton | 1.00 | .45 |
| □ 57 Claude Lemieux | 1.00 | .45 |
| □ 58 Nicklas Lidstrom | 1.00 | .45 |
| □ 59 Olaf Kolzig | 1.00 | .45 |
| □ 60 Grant Fuhr | .50 | .23 |
| □ 61 Jamie Langenbrunner | .50 | .23 |
| □ 62 Doug Weight | .50 | .23 |
| □ 63 Joe Nieuwendyk | .50 | .23 |
| □ 64 Yanic Perreault | .50 | .23 |
| □ 65 Jocelyn Thibault | 1.00 | .45 |
| □ 66 Guy Hebert | .50 | .23 |
| □ 67 Shayne Corson | .50 | .23 |
| □ 68 Bobby Holik | .50 | .23 |
| □ 69 Sami Kapanen | 1.00 | .45 |
| □ 70 Robert Reichel | .50 | .23 |
| □ 71 Ryan Smyth | 1.00 | .45 |
| □ 72 Alexei Yashin | 1.00 | .45 |
| □ 73 Trevor Linden | 1.00 | .45 |
| □ 74 Rod Brind'Amour | 1.00 | .45 |
| □ 75 Dave Gagner | .50 | .23 |
| □ 76 Nikolai Khabibulin | 1.00 | .45 |
| □ 77 Tom Barrasso | 1.00 | .45 |
| □ 78 Tony Amonte | 1.00 | .45 |
| □ 79 Alexander Mogilny | 1.00 | .45 |
| □ 80 Jason Allison | 1.00 | .45 |
| □ 81 Patrik Elias | 2.50 | 1.10 |
| □ 82 Mike Johnson | 2.50 | 1.10 |
| □ 83 Richard Zednik | .50 | .23 |
| □ 84 Patrick Marleau | 3.00 | 1.35 |
| □ 85 Mattias Ohlund | 1.00 | .45 |
| □ 86 Sergei Samsonov | 4.00 | 1.80 |
| □ 87 Marco Sturm | 3.00 | 1.35 |
| □ 88 Alyn McCauley | 1.00 | .45 |
| □ 89 Chris Phillips | | .23 |
| □ 90 Brendan Morrison | 3.00 | 1.35 |
| □ 91 Vaclav Prospal | 2.00 | .90 |
| □ 92 Joe Thornton | 3.00 | 1.35 |
| □ 93 Boyd Devereaux | 1.00 | .45 |
| □ 94 Alexei Morozov | 1.00 | .45 |
| □ 95 Vincent LeCavalier | 40.00 | 18.00 |
| □ 96 Manny Malhotra | 6.00 | 2.70 |
| □ 97 Roberto Luongo | 10.00 | 4.50 |
| □ 98 Mathieu Garon | 1.25 | .55 |
| □ 99 Alex Tanguay | 8.00 | 3.60 |
| UER front Tanquay | | |
| □ 100 Josh Holden | 1.25 | .55 |

## 1997-98 Zenith Z-Gold

Randomly inserted in packs, this 100-card set is a parallel version of the base set printed on gold-foil card stock and sequentially numbered to 100.

| | MINT | NRMT |
|---|---|---|
| COMMON CARD (1-100) | 25.00 | 11.00 |
| *STARS: 25X TO 60X BASIC CARDS | | |
| *YNG.STARS: 20X TO 50X BASIC CARDS | | |

*RC's: 5X TO 10X BASIC CARDS

## 1997-98 Zenith Z-Silver

Randomly inserted in packs at the rate of one in seven, this 100-card set is a parallel version of the base set printed on silver-foil board.

| | MINT | NRMT |
|---|---|---|
| COMPLETE SET (100) | 800.00 | 350.00 |
| COMMON CARD (1-100) | 2.00 | .90 |
| *STARS: 2.5X TO 5X BASIC CARDS | | |
| *YOUNG STARS: 2X TO 4X | | |
| *RC's: 1.5X TO 3X | | |

## 1997-98 Zenith 5 x 7

This 80-card set measuring 5" by 7" was distributed in three-card packs with a regular size card inside each jumbo card. The fronts feature color action player photos with another photo and player information on the backs.

| | MINT | NRMT |
|---|---|---|
| COMPLETE SET (80) | 150.00 | 70.00 |
| COMMON CARD (1-80) | .60 | .25 |

| | MINT | NRMT |
|---|---|---|
| □ 1 Wayne Gretzky | 10.00 | 4.50 |
| □ 2 Eric Lindros | 5.00 | 2.20 |
| □ 3 Patrick Roy | 8.00 | 3.60 |
| □ 4 John Vanbiesbrouck | 2.50 | 1.10 |
| □ 5 Martin Brodeur | 4.00 | 1.80 |
| □ 6 Teemu Selanne | 3.00 | 1.35 |
| □ 7 Joe Sakic | 3.00 | 1.35 |
| □ 8 Jaromir Jagr | 5.00 | 2.20 |
| □ 9 Brendan Shanahan | 3.00 | 1.35 |
| □ 10 Ed Belfour | 1.50 | .70 |
| □ 11 Guy Hebert | 1.25 | .55 |
| □ 12 Doug Gilmour | 1.25 | .55 |
| □ 13 Keith Primeau | 1.25 | .55 |
| □ 14 Grant Fuhr | 1.25 | .55 |
| □ 15 Joe Nieuwendyk | 1.25 | .55 |
| □ 16 Ryan Smyth | 1.25 | .55 |
| □ 17 Chris Osgood | 1.50 | .70 |
| □ 18 Keith Tkachuk | 2.00 | .90 |
| □ 19 Peter Forsberg | 5.00 | 2.20 |
| □ 20 Jarome Iginla | 1.25 | .55 |
| □ 21 Steve Yzerman | 5.00 | 2.20 |
| □ 22 Jeremy Roenick | 1.50 | .70 |
| □ 23 Jozef Stumpel | 1.25 | .55 |
| □ 24 Mark Recchi | 1.25 | .55 |
| □ 25 Daniel Alfredsson | 1.25 | .55 |
| □ 26 Pat LaFontaine | 1.25 | .55 |
| □ 27 Zigmund Palffy | 1.50 | .70 |
| □ 28 Jason Allison | 1.25 | .55 |
| □ 29 Yanic Perreault | .60 | .25 |
| □ 30 Olaf Kolzig | 1.25 | .55 |
| □ 31 Mikael Renberg | 1.25 | .55 |
| □ 32 Bryan Berard | 1.25 | .55 |
| □ 33 Jocelyn Thibault | 1.25 | .55 |
| □ 34 Shayne Corson | 1.25 | .55 |
| □ 35 Dave Gagner | .60 | .25 |
| □ 36 Claude Lemieux | 1.25 | .55 |
| □ 37 Saku Koivu | 2.50 | 1.10 |
| □ 38 Curtis Joseph | 1.50 | .70 |
| □ 39 Chris Chelios | 1.50 | .70 |
| □ 40 Ray Bourque | 1.50 | .70 |
| □ 41 Adam Oates | 1.25 | .55 |
| □ 42 Felix Potvin | 1.50 | .70 |
| □ 43 Peter Bondra | 1.50 | .70 |
| □ 44 Sergei Fedorov | 3.00 | 1.35 |
| □ 45 Paul Kariya | 6.00 | 2.70 |
| □ 46 Theoren Fleury | 1.25 | .55 |
| □ 47 John LeClair | 2.50 | 1.10 |
| □ 48 Brett Hull | 2.00 | .90 |
| □ 49 Rod Brind'Amour | 1.25 | .55 |
| □ 50 Doug Weight | 1.25 | .55 |
| □ 51 Jamie Langenbrunner | .60 | .25 |
| □ 52 Mats Sundin | 1.50 | .70 |
| □ 53 Ron Francis | 1.25 | .55 |
| □ 54 Eric Daze | 1.25 | .55 |
| □ 55 Nicklas Lidstrom | 1.25 | .55 |
| □ 56 Luc Robitaille | 1.25 | .55 |
| □ 57 Vincent Damphousse | 1.25 | .55 |
| □ 58 Mike Modano | 2.00 | .90 |
| □ 59 Pavel Bure | 3.00 | 1.35 |
| □ 60 Owen Nolan | 1.25 | .55 |
| □ 61 Pierre Turgeon | 1.25 | .55 |
| □ 62 Dominik Hasek | 3.00 | 1.35 |
| □ 63 Mike Richter | 1.50 | .70 |
| □ 64 Mark Messier | 2.00 | .90 |
| □ 65 Brian Leetch | 1.50 | .70 |
| □ 66 Sergei Samsonov | 4.00 | 1.80 |
| □ 67 Alexei Morozov | 1.25 | .55 |
| □ 68 Marco Sturm RC | 3.00 | 1.35 |
| □ 69 Patrik Elias RC | 3.00 | 1.35 |
| □ 70 Eric Messier RC | 1.50 | .70 |
| □ 71 Alyn McCauley | 1.25 | .55 |
| □ 72 Richard Zednik | .60 | .25 |
| □ 73 Mattias Ohlund | 1.25 | .55 |
| □ 74 Joe Thornton | 3.00 | 1.35 |
| □ 75 Vincent LeCavalier RC | 30.00 | 13.50 |
| □ 76 Manny Malhotra RC | 5.00 | 2.20 |
| □ 77 Roberto Luongo RC | 10.00 | 4.50 |
| □ 78 Mathieu Garon RC | 1.50 | .70 |
| □ 79 Alex Tanguay RC | 6.00 | 2.70 |
| □ 80 Josh Holden | 1.50 | .70 |

## 1997-98 Zenith 5 x 7 Gold Impulse

Randomly inserted in packs, this 80-card set is a gold foil parallel version of the base set and is sequentially numbered to 100.

| | MINT | NRMT |
|---|---|---|
| COMMON CARD (1-80) | 25.00 | 11.00 |
| SEMISTARS/GOALIES | 60.00 | 27.00 |
| UNLISTED STARS | 80.00 | 36.00 |
| *STARS: 20X TO 50X BASIC CARDS | | |
| *YNG.STARS: 15X TO 40X BASIC CARDS | | |
| *RC's: 5X TO 10X BASIC CARDS | | |

## 1997-98 Zenith 5 x 7 Silver Impulse

Randomly inserted in packs at the rate of one in seven, this 80-card set is a silver foil parallel version of the base set.

| | MINT | NRMT |
|---|---|---|
| COMPLETE SET (80) | 800.00 | 350.00 |
| COMMON CARD (1-80) | 2.50 | 1.10 |
| *STARS: 2.5X TO 5X BASIC CARDS | | |
| *YOUNG STARS: 2X TO 4X | | |
| *RC's: 1.5X TO 3X | | |

## 1997-98 Zenith Chasing The Cup

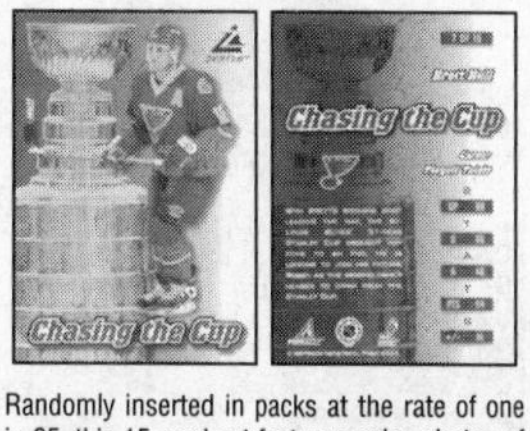

Randomly inserted in packs at the rate of one in 25, this 15-card set features color photos of top players printed on rainbow-hued holographic foil with an image of the trophy in the background.

| | MINT | NRMT |
|---|---|---|
| COMPLETE SET (15) | 300.00 | 135.00 |
| COMMON CARD (1-15) | 6.00 | 2.70 |

| | MINT | NRMT |
|---|---|---|
| □ 1 Patrick Roy | 40.00 | 18.00 |
| □ 2 Wayne Gretzky | 50.00 | 22.00 |
| □ 3 Jaromir Jagr | 25.00 | 11.00 |
| □ 4 Eric Lindros | 25.00 | 11.00 |
| □ 5 Mike Modano | 10.00 | 4.50 |
| □ 6 Brendan Shanahan | 15.00 | 6.75 |
| □ 7 Brett Hull | 10.00 | 4.50 |
| □ 8 John LeClair | 12.00 | 5.50 |
| □ 9 Jocelyn Thibault | 6.00 | 2.70 |
| □ 10 Ed Belfour | 6.00 | 2.70 |
| □ 11 Martin Brodeur | 20.00 | 9.00 |
| □ 12 Peter Forsberg | 25.00 | 11.00 |

## 1997-98 Zenith Rookie Reign

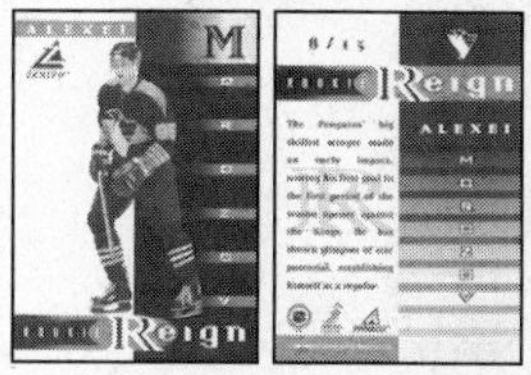

Randomly inserted in packs at the rate of one in 25, this 15-card set features color photos of top young players printed on holographic foil.

| | MINT | NRMT |
|---|---|---|
| COMPLETE SET (15) | 200.00 | 90.00 |
| COMMON CARD (1-15) | 8.00 | 3.60 |

| | MINT | NRMT |
|---|---|---|
| □ 1 Sergei Samsonov | 25.00 | 11.00 |
| □ 2 Joe Thornton | 25.00 | 11.00 |
| □ 3 Erik Rasmussen | 8.00 | 3.60 |
| □ 4 Brendan Morrison | 8.00 | 3.60 |
| □ 5 Magnus Arvedson | 8.00 | 3.60 |
| □ 6 Vaclav Prospal | 8.00 | 3.60 |
| □ 7 Brad Isbister | 8.00 | 3.60 |
| □ 8 Alexei Morozov | 8.00 | 3.60 |
| □ 9 Marco Sturm | 8.00 | 3.60 |
| □ 10 Patrick Marleau | 25.00 | 11.00 |
| □ 11 Alyn McCauley | 8.00 | 3.60 |
| □ 12 Mike Johnson | 8.00 | 3.60 |
| □ 13 Mattias Ohlund | 8.00 | 3.60 |
| □ 14 Patrik Elias | 8.00 | 3.60 |
| □ 15 Richard Zednik | 8.00 | 3.60 |

## 1997-98 Zenith Z-Team

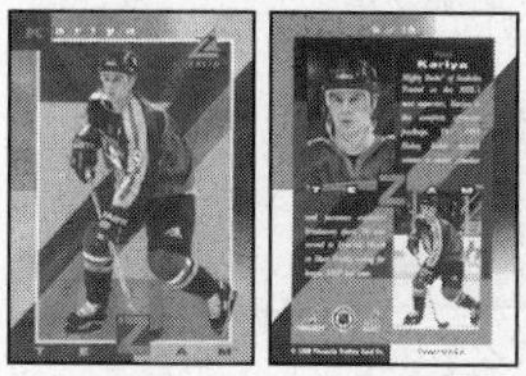

Randomly inserted in packs at the rate of one in 35 for cards #1-9 and one in 58 for #10-18, this 18-card set features color action photos of top NHL players and rookies in white, black, and colored borders. The backs carry player information.

| | MINT | NRMT |
|---|---|---|
| COMPLETE SET (18) | 700.00 | 325.00 |
| COMMON CARD (1-18) | 10.00 | 4.50 |

| | MINT | NRMT |
|---|---|---|
| □ 1 Teemu Selanne | 30.00 | 13.50 |
| □ 2 Wayne Gretzky | 100.00 | 45.00 |
| □ 3 Patrick Roy | 80.00 | 36.00 |
| □ 4 Eric Lindros | 50.00 | 22.00 |
| □ 5 Peter Forsberg | 50.00 | 22.00 |
| □ 6 Paul Kariya | 60.00 | 27.00 |
| □ 7 John LeClair | 25.00 | 11.00 |
| □ 8 Martin Brodeur | 40.00 | 18.00 |
| □ 9 Brendan Shanahan | 30.00 | 13.50 |
| □ 10 Joe Thornton | 40.00 | 18.00 |
| □ 11 Mattias Ohlund | 20.00 | 9.00 |
| □ 12 Mike Johnson | 25.00 | 11.00 |
| □ 13 Vaclav Prospal | 30.00 | 13.50 |
| □ 14 Sergei Samsonov | 40.00 | 18.00 |
| □ 15 Marco Sturm | 30.00 | 13.50 |
| □ 16 Patrik Elias | 25.00 | 11.00 |
| □ 17 Richard Zednik | 10.00 | 4.50 |
| □ 18 Alexei Morozov | 20.00 | 9.00 |

## 1997-98 Zenith Z-Team Gold

Randomly inserted in packs at the rate of one in 175, this 18-card set is a gold parallel version of the regular Z-Team set printed on gold micro-etched foil.

| | MINT | NRMT |
|---|---|---|
| COMPLETE SET (18) | 3500.00 | 1600.00 |
| COMMON CARD (1-18) | 50.00 | 22.00 |
| *STARS: 2.5X TO 5X BASIC CARDS | | |
| *YOUNG STARS: 2X TO 4X | | |

## 1997-98 Zenith Z-Team 5 x 7

Randomly inserted in packs at the rate of one in 35, this nine-card set features color action photos of top NHL players printed on jumbo 5" by 7" cards.

| | MINT | NRMT |
|---|---|---|
| COMPLETE SET (9) | 600.00 | 275.00 |
| COMMON CARD (1-9) | 30.00 | 13.50 |
| *STARS: 1X TO 1.5X BASIC CARDS | | |

## 1991-92 Air Canada SJHL

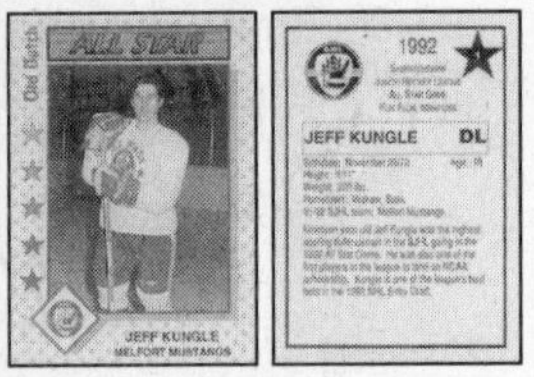


This 250-card standard-size set features players in the Saskatchewan Junior Hockey League. The set included an entry form for a contest sponsored by Air Canada and Old Dutch, which entitled the winner to a trip for two to anywhere in North America. The cards features posed color player photos with team color-coded shadow borders. The pictures are set on thin, white card stock with the team name in a yellow bar at the top. The player's name appears in the white margin at the bottom. The backs are white and carry biographical information and a player profile. The cards are numbered on the back and were issued in five series denoted by the letters A, B, C, D, and E as card number prefixes.

| | MINT | NRMT |
|---|---|---|
| COMPLETE SET (250) | 35.00 | 16.00 |
| COMMON CARD (A1-A49) | .20 | .09 |
| COMMON CARD (B1-B51) | .20 | .09 |
| COMMON CARD (C1-C50) | .20 | .09 |
| COMMON CARD (D1-D50) | .20 | .09 |
| COMMON CARD (E1-E50) | .20 | .09 |

❑ A1 Dean Normand .30 .14
❑ A2 Dan Meyers .25 .11
❑ A3 Tyson Balog .20 .09
❑ A4 Tyler McMillan .20 .09
❑ A5 Jason Selkirk .20 .09
❑ A6 Bryce Bohun .20 .09
❑ A7 Blaire Hornung .20 .09
❑ A8 Craig McKechnie .20 .09
❑ A9 Rejean Stringer .20 .09
❑ A10 Corri Moffat .20 .09
❑ A11 Dion Johnson .20 .09
❑ A12 Rod Krushel .20 .09
❑ A13 Mike Langen .20 .09
❑ A14 Jeff Hassman .20 .09
❑ A15 Dean Moore .20 .09
❑ A16 Trevor Wathen .20 .09
❑ A17 Curtis Knight .20 .09
❑ A18 Chris Morgan .20 .09
❑ A19 Trevor Thurstan .20 .09
❑ A20 Wayne Filipenko .20 .09
❑ A21 Jason Feiffer .20 .09
❑ A22 Layne Douglas .20 .09
❑ A23 Dave Gardner .20 .09
❑ A24 Ryan Sandholm .20 .09
❑ A25 Corey McKee .20 .09
❑ A26 Trevor Schmiess .20 .09
❑ A27 Todd Hollinger .50 .23
❑ A28 Jay Dunn .20 .09
❑ A29 Jamie Ling .30 .14
❑ A30 Todd Small .20 .09
❑ A31 Barret Kropf .20 .09
❑ A32 Dean Gerard .20 .09
❑ A33 Christian Dutil .20 .09
❑ A34 Tyler Scheidt .20 .09
Aaron Campbell
❑ A35 Dean Sideroff .20 .09
❑ A36 Dan Dufresne .20 .09
❑ A37 Cam Yager .20 .09
❑ A38 Richard Nagy .25 .11
❑ A39 Aaron Cain .50 .23
❑ A40 Rob Beck .20 .09
❑ A41 Blair Wagar .20 .09
❑ A42 Kim Maier .20 .09
❑ A43 Brent Hoiness .20 .09
❑ A44 Troy Edwards .20 .09
❑ A45 Evan Anderson .20 .09
❑ A46 Carlin Nordstrom .20 .09
❑ A47 Dean Seymour .20 .09
❑ A48 Scott Wotton .30 .14
❑ A49 Curtis Joseph 5.00 2.20
SJHL All Star
❑ B1 Richard Boscher .20 .09
❑ B2 James Schaeffler .20 .09
❑ B3 Wes Rommel .20 .09
❑ B4 Corey Thompson .20 .09
❑ B5 Rob Phillips .30 .14
❑ B6 Jim McLean .20 .09
❑ B7 Trevor Warrener .50 .23
❑ B8 Peter Boake .20 .09
❑ B9 Kevin Riffel .20 .09
❑ B10 Tom Perry .20 .09
❑ B11 Mark Baird .20 .09
❑ B12 Stacy Prevost .20 .09
❑ B13 Taras Lendzyk .20 .09
❑ B14 Shawn Reis .20 .09
❑ B15 Shawn Thompson .20 .09
❑ B16 Curtis Kleisinger .20 .09
❑ B17 Kent Rogers .20 .09
❑ B18 Scott Christion .30 .14
❑ B19 Gerald Tallaire .30 .14
❑ B20 Kelly Hollingshead .30 .14
❑ B21 Mike Savard .20 .09
❑ B22 Darren Maloney .20 .09
❑ B23 Jason Hynd .20 .09
❑ B24 Scott Stewart .20 .09
❑ B25 Scott Beattie .30 .14
SJHL All Star
❑ B26 Dave McAmmond .20 .09
❑ B27 Myles Gibb .20 .09
❑ B28 Ryan Bach .50 .23
❑ B29 Martin Smith .20 .09
❑ B30 Leigh Brookbank .20 .09
❑ B31 Todd Markus .20 .09
❑ B32 The Boys From PA .30 .14
Dean Gerard
Darryn Listwan
Scott Rogers
Brad Federenko
Derek Simonson
Jeff Greenwood
❑ B33 Randy Muise .20 .09
❑ B34 George Gervais .20 .09
❑ B35 Keith Harris .20 .09
❑ B36 Jamie Stelmak .20 .09
❑ B37 Bart Vanstaalduinen .20 .09
❑ B38 Scott Murray .20 .09
❑ B39 Danny Galarneau .20 .09
❑ B40 Keith Murphy .20 .09
❑ B41 Jeff Kungle .30 .14
❑ B42 Michel Cook .20 .09
❑ B43 Daryl Krauss .20 .09
❑ B44 Derek Wynne .20 .09
❑ B45 Derek Crimin .20 .09
❑ B46 Jason Brown .20 .09
❑ B47 Bruce Matatall .20 .09
❑ B48 Chris Hatch .20 .09
❑ B49 Kurtise Souchotte .20 .09
❑ B50 Michael Brennan .20 .09
❑ B51 Orrin Hergott .20 .09
❑ C1 Craig Matatall .20 .09
❑ C2 Brad Prefontaine .20 .09
❑ C3 Mike Evans .20 .09
❑ C4 Jody Reiter .20 .09
❑ C5 Jeremy Mylymok .20 .09
❑ C6 Dave Doucet .30 .14
❑ C7 Randy Kerr .20 .09
❑ C8 Gordon McCann .20 .09
❑ C9 Quinn Fair .20 .09
❑ C10 Kyle Niemegeers .20 .09
❑ C11 Ryan Smith .30 .14
❑ C12 Mike Hillock .20 .09
❑ C13 Vern Anderson .20 .09
❑ C14 Trent Hamm .20 .09
❑ C15 Curtis Folkett ACO .20 .09
❑ C16 Warren Pickford .20 .09
❑ C17 Craig Volstad .20 .09
❑ C18 Sean Tallaire .30 .14
❑ C19 Jason Yaganiski .20 .09
❑ C20 Jim McLarty .20 .09
❑ C21 Jamie Fyfuglien .20 .09
❑ C22 Terry Metro .20 .09
❑ C23 Todd Kozak .20 .09
❑ C24 Jeff Huckle .20 .09
❑ C25 Darren McLean .20 .09
❑ C26 Bret Mohninger .20 .09
❑ C27 Tim Slukynsky .20 .09
❑ C28 Roman Mrhalek .20 .09
❑ C29 Joel Martinson .20 .09
❑ C30 Ron Patterson .20 .09
❑ C31 Mark Gorgi .20 .09
❑ C32 Tom Thomson .20 .09
❑ C33 Greg Wahl .20 .09
❑ C34 Craig Perrett .20 .09
❑ C35 Mike Harder .20 .09
❑ C36 Jeff Cole .20 .09
❑ C37 Justin Christoffer .20 .09
❑ C38 Nolan Weir .20 .09
❑ C39 Jeff Knight .20 .09
❑ C40 Lyle Vaughan .20 .09
❑ C41 Scott Bellefontaine .20 .09
❑ C42 Trevor Mathias .20 .09
❑ C43 Chris Schinkel .30 .14
❑ C44 Scott Rogers .20 .09
❑ C45 Shane Holunga .20 .09
❑ C46 Dwayne Rhinehart .20 .09
❑ C47 Eddy Marchant .20 .09
❑ C48 Travis Smith .20 .09
❑ C49 Not Known .20 .09
❑ C50 Mike Hidlebaugh .20 .09
❑ D1 Darcy Herlick .20 .09
❑ D2 Joel Appleton .20 .09
❑ D3 Bobby Standish .20 .09
❑ D4 Kory Karlander .30 .14
❑ D5 Brett Kinaschuk .20 .09
❑ D6 Kevin Messer .20 .09
❑ D7 Jason Martin .20 .09
❑ D8 Devin Zimmer .20 .09
❑ D9 David Foster .20 .09
❑ D10 Bob Schwark .20 .09
❑ D11 Ted Grayling .20 .09
❑ D12 Travis Vantighem .30 .14
❑ D13 Darren Houghton .20 .09
❑ D14 Wade Welte .20 .09
❑ D15 1991 NB All Stars .50 .23
Martin Smith
Ron Gunville
Derek Knorr
Geoff McMaster
Trevor Converse
❑ D16 Kevin Powell .20 .09
❑ D17 Returning Hounds .20 .09
Dave Lovesin
Bernie Adlys
Bart Vanstaalduinen
Scott Christion
Bob MacIntosh
Rice Thompson
Adam Thompson
❑ D18 Dennis Budeau .20 .09
❑ D19 Darren Opp .20 .09
❑ D20 Jeff Greenwood .20 .09
❑ D21 Mark Daniels .50 .23
❑ D22 Todd Murphy .20 .09
❑ D23 Scott Weaver .20 .09
❑ D24 Robby Bear .20 .09
❑ D25 Nigel Werenka .30 .14
❑ D26 Sean Timmins .20 .09
❑ D27 Ken Malenfant .20 .09
❑ D28 Greg Taylor .20 .09
❑ D29 Sheldon Bylsma .20 .09
❑ D30 Clint Hooge .20 .09
❑ D31 Bob McIntosh .20 .09
❑ D32 Dave Lovsin .20 .09
❑ D33 Jeremy Mathies .20 .09
❑ D34 Blaine Fomradas .20 .09
❑ D35 Cory Borys .20 .09
❑ D36 Brad Purdie .20 .09
❑ D37 J. Sotropa .20 .09
❑ D38 Duane Vardale .20 .09
❑ D39 Jim Nellis .20 .09
❑ D40 Brent Sheppard .20 .09
❑ D41 Cam Bristow .20 .09
❑ D42 Steven Brent .20 .09
❑ D43 Mike Matteucci .20 .09
❑ D44 Bryan Cossette .20 .09
❑ D45 Tyler Kuhn .20 .09
❑ D46 Dave Debusschere .20 .09
❑ D47 Darryl Dickson .20 .09
❑ D48 Derek Meikle .20 .09
❑ D49 Parris Duffus .50 .23
Ex SJHLer
❑ D50 Lance Wakefield .30 .14
❑ E1 Brooke Battersby .20 .09
❑ E2 Jay Dobrescu .20 .09
❑ E3 Blair Allison .20 .09
❑ E4 Shane Johnson .20 .09
❑ E5 Carson Cardinal .20 .09
❑ E6 Dean Pooyak .20 .09
❑ E7 Mark Loeppky .20 .09
❑ E8 Travis Cheyne .20 .09
❑ E9 Karl Johnson .20 .09
❑ E10 Jason Ahenakew .20 .09
❑ E11 Darren Schmidt .30 .14
❑ E12 Larry Empey .20 .09
❑ E13 Colin Froese .20 .09
❑ E14 Darryn Listwan .20 .09
❑ E15 Todd MacMillan .20 .09
❑ E16 Ken Ruddock .20 .09
❑ E17 Derek Simonson .20 .09
❑ E18 Lyle Ehrmantraut .20 .09
❑ E19 Jody Weller .20 .09
❑ E20 Danny Dennis .20 .09
❑ E21 Trent Harper .20 .09
❑ E22 Jason Prokopetz .30 .14
❑ E23 Tom Thomson .20 .09
❑ E24 Trent Dumaine .20 .09
❑ E25 Mike Wevers .20 .09
❑ E26 Darren Duncalfe .20 .09
❑ E27 Regan Simpson .20 .09
❑ E28 Jeff Bloski .20 .09
❑ E29 Blake Sutton .20 .09
❑ E30 Darcy Blair .30 .14
❑ E31 Marty Craigdallie .20 .09
❑ E32 Jason Krug .20 .09
❑ E33 Mark Hansen .20 .09
❑ E34 Bernie Adlys .20 .09
❑ E35 Brett Colborne .20 .09
❑ E36 Tony Bergin .20 .09
❑ E37 Ian Adamson .20 .09
❑ E38 Darren MacMillan .20 .09
❑ E39 Rob Neighbour .20 .09
❑ E40 Jeff Lawson .20 .09
❑ E41 Derrick Brucks .20 .09
❑ E42 Todd Schoenroth .20 .09
❑ E43 Jody Forseth .20 .09
❑ E44 Derek Beuselinck .20 .09
❑ E45 Clint Wensley .20 .09
❑ E46 Darren Donald .20 .09
❑ E47 Shane Stangby .20 .09
❑ E48 Jamie Dunn .20 .09
❑ E49 Steve Sabo .20 .09
❑ E50 Anthony Toth .20 .09

## 1991-92 Air Canada SJHL All-Stars

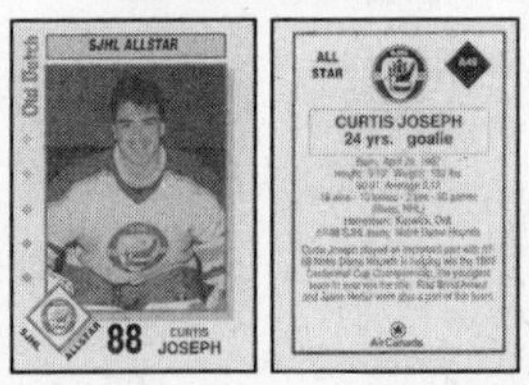


This 50-card standard-size set features Saskatchewan Junior Hockey League All-Stars. The set included an entry form for a contest sponsored by Air Canada and Old Dutch, which entitled the winner to a trip for two to anywhere in North America. The cards feature posed color player photos with yellow shadow borders. The pictures are set against a white card face accented with an screened pale purple star pattern. The words "All Star" appear in red within a yellow and black striped bar at the top, while the player's name is printed below the photo. The backs carry the player's name, biographical information, and a player profile.

| | MINT | NRMT |
|---|---|---|
| COMPLETE SET (50) | 12.00 | 5.50 |
| COMMON CARD (1-50) | .25 | .11 |

❑ 1 Jeff Kungle .35 .16
❑ 2 Jay Dunn .25 .11
❑ 3 Kevin Dickie .25 .11
❑ 4 Martin Smith .25 .11
❑ 5 Jeff Cole .25 .11
❑ 6 Trent Hamm .25 .11
❑ 7 Kent Rogers .25 .11
❑ 8 Dean Gerard .25 .11
❑ 9 Jim McLarty .25 .11
❑ 10 Malcolm Kostuchenko .25 .11
❑ 11 Mark Scollan .25 .11
❑ 12 Brad Federenko .50 .23
❑ 13 Rob Beck .25 .11
❑ 14 Bryce Bohun .25 .11
❑ 15 Kory Karlander .35 .16
❑ 16 Scott Christion .35 .16
❑ 17 Tyler Kuhn .25 .11
❑ 18 Corri Moffatt .25 .11
❑ 19 Layne Douglas .25 .11
❑ 20 Shane Holunga .25 .11
❑ 21 Mike Matteucci .25 .11
❑ 22 Bart Vanstaalduinen .25 .11
❑ 23 Brad McEwen .25 .11
❑ 24 Kim Maier .25 .11
❑ 25 Jamie Ling .50 .23
❑ 26 Dean Seymour .25 .11
❑ 27 Derek Crimin .25 .11
❑ 28 Evan Anderson .25 .11
❑ 29 Craig Matatall .25 .11
❑ 30 Keith Murphy .25 .11
❑ 31 Jason Feiffer .25 .11
❑ 32 Michel Cook .25 .11
❑ 33 Rod Krushel .25 .11
❑ 34 Tyler Rice .35 .16
❑ 35 Gerald Tallaire .50 .23
❑ 36 Richard Nagy .25 .11
❑ 37 Taras Lendzyk .25 .11
❑ 38 Jeff Knight .25 .11
❑ 39 Darren Opp .25 .11
❑ 40 Dwayne Rhinehart .25 .11
❑ 41 Minot Americans .25 .11
Layne Douglas
Derek Crimin
❑ 42 Scott Bellefontaine .25 .11
❑ 43 Darren Maloney .25 .11
❑ 44 North Division .50 .23
All-Star Team
Team Photo
❑ 45 Yorkton Terriers .50 .23
All Stars
Michel Cook
Dean Seymour
Scott Bellefontaine
❑ 46 Melville Millionaires .50 .23
All Stars
Team Photo
❑ 47 Best 1992 All-Stars .50 .23
Kevin Dickie CO
Mike Matteucci
Kory Karlander
Kim Maier
Darren Opp
Richard Nagy
Mark Scollan
❑ 48 Estevan Bruins .50 .23
All Stars
Gerald Tallaire
Kim Maier
Mike Matteucci
Evan Anderson
❑ 49 Notre Dame Hounds .50 .23
All Stars
Tyler Rice
Scott Christion
Bart Van Staalduinen
Jamie Ling
Craig Matatall
❑ 50 Bob Robson CO .25 .11

## 1991-92 British Columbia JHL

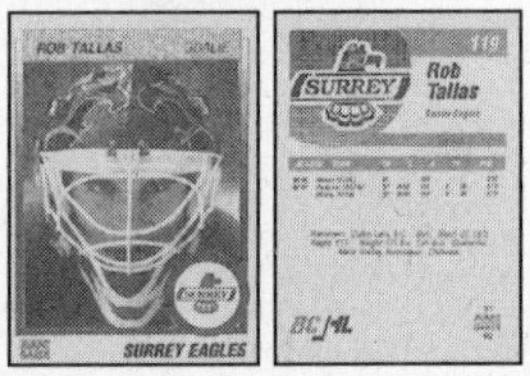


This 172-card standard-size set features players of the British Columbia Junior Hockey League The card design features action and posed color player photos. A border design that frames the picture is royal blue at the bottom and fades to pale blue and white at the top. Overlapping this frame at the top is a bar with a blue speckled pattern, which contains the player's name, team name, or card title. The team logo appears within a royal blue circle that is superimposed over the lower right corner of the picture. The backs carry a black-and-white close-up, statistics, and biographical information. Topical subsets featured are Stars of the Future (81, 91, 93, 106, 146-147, 164, 166, 168-169), Coastal All-Stars (151-154, 163), and Interior All-Stars (155-162). The cards are numbered on the back and checklisted below according to teams as follows: Vernon Lakers (1-17, 23-25), Kelowna Spartans (18-22, 26-41), Nanaimo Clippers (42-62, 79-80, 153), Merritt Centennials (63-78, 82, 107), Chilliwack Chiefs (81, 127-145), Surrey Eagles (83, 106, 108-117, 119-126), and Penticton Panthers (85-105, 118, 147).

| | MINT | NRMT |
|---|---|---|
| COMPLETE SET (173) | 75.00 | 34.00 |
| COMMON CARD (1-170) | .15 | .07 |

❑ 1 Vernon Lakers .25 .11
Team Photo
❑ 2 Scott Longstaff .15 .07
❑ 3 Rick Crowe .15 .07
❑ 4 Sheldon Wolitski .15 .07
❑ 5 Kevan Rilcof .15 .07
❑ 6 Greg Buchanan .15 .07
❑ 7 Vernon Lakers .15 .07
Executives
❑ 8 Murray Caton .15 .07
❑ 9 Adrian Bubola .15 .07
❑ 10 Troy Becker .15 .07
❑ 11 Shawn Potyok .15 .07
❑ 12 John Morabito .15 .07
❑ 13 Peter Zurba .15 .07
❑ 14 Chad Schraeder .15 .07
❑ 15 Shawn Bourgeois .15 .07
❑ 16 Michal Sup .15 .07
❑ 17 Rick Eremenko .15 .07
❑ 18 David Lemanowicz .15 .07
❑ 19 Daniel Blasko .15 .07
❑ 20 Gary Audette .15 .07
❑ 21 Graham Harder .15 .07
❑ 22 Ryan Nessman .15 .07
❑ 23 Jason Switzer .15 .07
❑ 24 Roland Ramoser .15 .07
❑ 25 Dusty McLellan .15 .07
❑ 26 Dustin Green .15 .07
❑ 27 Steve Roberts .15 .07
❑ 28 Jason Lowe .15 .07
❑ 29 Brad Knight .15 .07
❑ 30 Pavel Suchanek .15 .07
❑ 31 Ken Crockett .15 .07
❑ 32 Adam Smith .35 .16
❑ 33 Glen Pullishy .15 .07
❑ 34 Mike Zambon .15 .07
❑ 35 Scott Chartier .35 .16
❑ 36 Donny Hearn .15 .07
❑ 37 Jeff Denham .15 .07
❑ 38 Jamie Marriott .15 .07
❑ 39 Silverio Mirao .15 .07
❑ 40 Darren Tymchyshyn .15 .07
❑ 41 Mark Basanta .15 .07
❑ 42 Trevor Prest .15 .07
❑ 43 Jim Lessard .15 .07
❑ 44 Jade Kersey .15 .07
❑ 45 Geordie Young .15 .07
❑ 46 Darren Holmes .15 .07
❑ 47 Wade Dayley .15 .07
❑ 48 Dan Murphy .15 .07
❑ 49 Paul Taylor .15 .07
❑ 50 Sjon Wynia .15 .07
❑ 51 Ryan Loxam .15 .07
❑ 52 Andy Faulkner .15 .07
❑ 53 Scott Kowalski .15 .07
❑ 54 Mickey McGuire .15 .07
❑ 55 Jason Disiewich .15 .07
❑ 56 Jim Ingram .15 .07
❑ 57 Ryan Keller .15 .07
❑ 58 Brian Schiebel .15 .07
❑ 59 Shawn York .15 .07
❑ 60 Sean Krause .15 .07
❑ 61 Casey Hungle .15 .07
❑ 62 Chris Jones .15 .07
❑ 63 Doug Stewart .15 .07
❑ 64 Jason Sirota .25 .11
❑ 65 Dave Dunnigan .15 .07
❑ 66 Aaron Hoffman .15 .07
❑ 67 Jason Timewell .15 .07
❑ 68 Pat Meehan .15 .07
❑ 69 Mike Leduc .15 .07
❑ 70 Brad Koopmans .15 .07
❑ 71 Guy Prince .15 .07
❑ 72 Dorel Gecse .15 .07
❑ 73 Scott Salmond .15 .07
❑ 74 Brian Zakall .15 .07
❑ 75 Mike Josephson .15 .07
❑ 76 Derek Harper .15 .07
❑ 77 John Graham .50 .23
❑ 78 Dan Morrissey .35 .16
❑ 79 Glenn Calder .15 .07
❑ 80 Jason Northard .15 .07
❑ 81 Chris Kerr .15 .07
❑ 82 Bill Muckalt .25 .11
❑ 83 Greg Hunt .15 .07
❑ 84 Paul Kariya 20.00 9.00
1990-91 All-Star Team
❑ 85 Dean Rowland .15 .07
❑ 86 Paul Kariya 20.00 9.00
(Skating)
❑ 87 David Kilduff .15 .07
❑ 88 Jeff Tory .15 .07
❑ 89 Mike Newman .15 .07
❑ 90 Tyler Boucher .15 .07
❑ 91 Paul Kariya 20.00 9.00
(Skating with stick)
❑ 92 Phil Valk .15 .07
❑ 93 Paul Kariya 15.00 6.75
(Passing)
❑ 94 Bob Lewis .15 .07
❑ 95 Steve Williams .15 .07
❑ 96 James Pelzer .15 .07
❑ 97 Shawn Carter .15 .07
❑ 98 Ryan Erasmas .35 .16

❑ 99 John Dehart .15 .07
❑ 100 David Green .15 .07
❑ 101 Derek Gecse .15 .07
❑ 102 Brian Barnes .15 .07
❑ 103 Jason Given .15 .07
❑ 104 Jason Podollan 1.50 .70
❑ 105 Brian Veale .15 .07
❑ 106 Rob Tallas 1.00 .45
❑ 107 Bob McBurnie .15 .07
❑ 108 Paul McMillan .15 .07
❑ 109 Ryan Donovan .15 .07
❑ 110 Kevin Robertson .15 .07
❑ 111 Milt Mastad .25 .11
❑ 112 Kees Roodbol .15 .07
❑ 113 Carey Causey .15 .07
❑ 114 Patrick O'Flaherty .15 .07
❑ 115 Chad Vestergaard .15 .07
❑ 116 Tyler Quiring .35 .16
❑ 117 Loui Mellios .15 .07
❑ 118 Bob Bell .15 .07
❑ 119 Rob Tallas 1.00 .45
❑ 120 Clint MacDonald .15 .07
❑ 121 Bart Taylor .15 .07
❑ 122 Mark Basanta .15 .07
❑ 123 Don McCusker .15 .07
❑ 124 Jason Howse .15 .07
❑ 125 Mike McKinlay .15 .07
❑ 126 Trevor Pennock .15 .07
❑ 127 Dean Shmyr .25 .11
❑ 128 Chris Kerr .15 .07
❑ 129 Erin Thornton .15 .07
❑ 130 Dennis Archibald .15 .07
❑ 131 Brian McDonald .15 .07
❑ 132 Bob Quinnell .15 .07
❑ 133 Clint Black .15 .07
❑ 134 Jason Peters .15 .07
❑ 135 Doug Ast .15 .07
❑ 136 Jason Bilous .35 .16
❑ 137 Lee Schill .15 .07
❑ 138 Jason Sanford .15 .07
❑ 139 Jeff Hokanson .15 .07
❑ 140 Marc Gagnon .15 .07
❑ 141 Gunnar Henrikson .15 .07
❑ 142 Jamie Lund .15 .07
❑ 143 Jason White .15 .07
❑ 144 Jag Bal .15 .07
❑ 145 Brad Loring .15 .07
❑ 146 Mark Gagnon .15 .07
❑ 147 Brian Veale .15 .07
❑ 148 Checklist 1 .15 .07
❑ 149 Checklist 2 .15 .07
❑ 150 The Centennial Cup .25 .11
❑ 151 Brian Law .15 .07
❑ 152 Al Radke .15 .07
❑ 153 Andy Faulkner .25 .11
Jason Disiewich
Darren Holmes
Casey Hungle
Chris Jones
❑ 154 1982 Coastal Division .25 .11
Team Photo
❑ 155 Dusty McLellan .25 .11
Roland Ramoser
Rick Eremenko
Sheldon Wolitski
Shawn Potyok
Scott Longstaff
❑ 156 Hendrikson .25 .11
Anchikoski
Marc Gagnon
Jason White
❑ 157 John Graham .35 .16
Dave Dunnigan
❑ 158 Scott Chartier .35 .16
Mike Zambon
Paul Taylor
Jason Lowe
❑ 159 Jeff Tory .25 .11
Tyler Boucher
David Kilduff
Lee Davidson
John Dehart
Burns
160 Didmon .25 .11
Bentham
Marsh
Walsh
161 Lipsett .25 .11
McNeill
Klyn
Edgington
162 1991 Interior .35 .16
All-Stars Team
Photo
163 Johnson .25 .11
Meek
Welker
Fitzpatrick
Collins
Sofikitas
Hutson
Herman
164 John Dehart .15 .07
165 John Craighead .25 .11
166 Mike Josephson .15 .07
167 Wayne Anchikoski .15 .07
168 Paul Kariya 20.00 9.00
(Stars of the Future
on the front)
169 Jim Lessard .15 .07
170 Tommi Virkgunen .15 .07
NNO Wayne Anchikoski .15 .07
NNO John Craighead .25 .11
NNO Tommi Virkgunen .35 .16

## 1992-93 British Columbia JHL

This 246-card standard-size set showcases players in the British Columbia Junior Hockey League. The cards feature color, action player photos with white borders. The player's name and position appear at the top. The team name is at the bottom. The backs carry the team logo in orange and black, statistics, and biographical information. The cards are numbered on the back and are in team order as follows: Bellingham Ice Hawks (1-23), Chilliwack Chiefs (24-45), Kelowna Spartans (46-70), Merritt Centennials (71-92), Nanaimo Clippers (93-116, 240), Penticton Panthers (117-140), Powell River Paper Kings (141-163, 245), Surrey Eagles (164-188), Vernon Lakers (189-211), and Victoria Warriors (212-233). The set closes with an Alumni of the BCJHL subset (234-239, 241) and other miscellaneous cards (242-246).

| | MINT | NRMT |
|---|---|---|
| COMPLETE SET (246) | 25.00 | 11.00 |
| COMMON CARD (1-246) | .15 | .07 |

❑ 1 Tom Wittenberg .25 .11
❑ 2 Kendel Kelly .15 .07
❑ 3 Gus Rettschlag .15 .07
❑ 4 Don Barr .15 .07
❑ 5 Dave Kirkpatrick .25 .11
❑ 6 Josh Flett .15 .07
❑ 7 Paul McKenna .15 .07
❑ 8 Brad Wingfield .25 .11
❑ 9 Derek Gesce .15 .07
❑ 10 Garry Gulash .15 .07
❑ 11 Tim Bell .15 .07
❑ 12 Dean Stork .15 .07
❑ 13 Wes Reusse .25 .11
❑ 14 Jason Peipmann .15 .07
❑ 15 Tyler Johnston .15 .07
❑ 16 Jason Delesoy .15 .07
❑ 17 The Ice Man .25 .11
❑ 18 Don Barr .15 .07
❑ 19 Brad Swain .15 .07
❑ 20 Wes Rudy .15 .07
❑ 21 Michael Sigouin .15 .07
❑ 22 Kevan Rilcof .15 .07
❑ 23 Brian Preston .15 .07
❑ 24 Doug Ast .15 .07
❑ 25 Knut Engqvist .15 .07
❑ 26 Zac George .15 .07
❑ 27 Clint Black .15 .07
❑ 28 Cameron Campbell .15 .07
❑ 29 Dan Davies .15 .07
❑ 30 Bryce Munro .15 .07
❑ 31 Ryan Dayman .15 .07
❑ 32 Kevin Kimura .15 .07
❑ 33 Paul Nicolls .15 .07
❑ 34 Thomas Kraft .15 .07
❑ 35 Erin Thornton .15 .07
❑ 36 Brad Loring .15 .07
❑ 37 Jag Bal .15 .07
❑ 38 Jeff Grabinsky .15 .07
❑ 39 Johan Ahrgren .15 .07
❑ 40 The Lethal Weapon .15 .07
❑ 41 Two Unidentified .15 .07
Players
❑ 42 Judd Lambert .15 .07
❑ 43 Brian Schiebel .15 .07
❑ 44 Dennis Archibald .25 .11
❑ 45 David Longbroek .15 .07
❑ 46 Silverio Mirao .15 .07
❑ 47 Jason Haakstad .15 .07
❑ 48 Lee Grant .15 .07
❑ 49 Ryan Esselmont .15 .07
❑ 50 Steve Roberts .15 .07
❑ 51 Curtis Fry .15 .07
❑ 52 David Dollard .15 .07
❑ 53 Diano Zol .15 .07
❑ 54 Bob Needham .15 .07
❑ 55 Dustin Green .15 .07
❑ 56 Darren Tymchyshyn .15 .07
❑ 57 Peter Arvanitis .15 .07
❑ 58 Don Hearn .15 .07
❑ 59 Title Card .25 .11
(Unnumbered)
❑ 60 Martin Masa .25 .11
❑ 61 Steffon Walby .35 .16
❑ 62 Joel Irwin .15 .07
❑ 63 Brent Bradford .15 .07
❑ 64 Dieter Kochan .15 .07
❑ 65 Brendan Kenny .15 .07
❑ 66 Marty Craigdallie .15 .07
❑ 67 Graeme Harder .15 .07
❑ 68 Pavel Suchanek .15 .07
❑ 69 Shane Johnson .15 .07
❑ 70 Burt Henderson .15 .07
❑ 71 Tyler Willis .50 .23
❑ 72 Mike Olaski .15 .07
❑ 73 David Green .15 .07
❑ 74 Tom Mix .25 .11
❑ 75 Walter(Guy) Prince .15 .07
❑ 76 Joseph Rybar .15 .07
❑ 77 Bill Muckalt .25 .11
❑ 78 Jason Mansoff .15 .07
❑ 79 Duane Puga .15 .07
❑ 80 Aaron Hoffman .15 .07
❑ 81 Dan Blasko .15 .07
❑ 82 Rob Szatmary .15 .07
❑ 83 Mike Minnis .15 .07
❑ 84 Pat Meehan .15 .07
❑ 85 Andre Robichaud .15 .07
❑ 86 The Terminator .25 .11
❑ 87 Derrek Harper .15 .07
❑ 88 Dan Morrissey .15 .07
❑ 89 Joey Kennedy .15 .07
❑ 90 Derrek Harper .15 .07
❑ 91 Lawrence Klyne .15 .07
❑ 92 Ryan Beamin .15 .07
❑ 93 Sjon Wynia .15 .07
❑ 94 Jason Disiewich .15 .07
❑ 95 Jason Sanford .15 .07
❑ 96 Casey Hungle .15 .07
❑ 97 Brent Murcheson .15 .07
❑ 98 Glenn Calder .25 .11
❑ 99 Jade Kersey .15 .07
❑ 100 Shawn York .15 .07
❑ 101 Bob Quinnell .15 .07
❑ 102 Geordie Dunstan .15 .07
❑ 103 Cory Crowther .15 .07
❑ 104 Jason Hodson .15 .07
❑ 105 Chris Jones .15 .07
❑ 106 Cory Green .15 .07
❑ 107 Chris Buie .15 .07
❑ 108 Shaun Peet .15 .07
❑ 109 Jason Wood .15 .07
❑ 110 Dan Murphy .15 .07
❑ 111 Jason Disiewich .15 .07
❑ 112 Cory Dayley .15 .07
❑ 113 Brian Veale .15 .07
❑ 114 Jason Northard .15 .07
❑ 115 Phil Valk .25 .11
❑ 116 Wade Dayley .15 .07
❑ 117 Brendan Morrison 2.00 .90
❑ 118 Marcel Sakac .15 .07
❑ 119 Tyler Boucher .15 .07
❑ 120 Ray Guze .15 .07
❑ 121 Brian Barnes .25 .11
❑ 122 Jason Given .15 .07
❑ 123 Michael Dairon .15 .07
❑ 124 Mike Newman .15 .07
❑ 125 Craig Fletcher .15 .07
❑ 126 Ty Davidson .15 .07
❑ 127 Miki Antonik .15 .07
❑ 128 Rob Pennoyer .15 .07
❑ 129 Dave Whitworth .15 .07
❑ 130 Steve Williams .15 .07
❑ 131 Robbie Trampuh .15 .07
❑ 132 Mark Filipenko .15 .07
❑ 133 Clint MacDonald .15 .07
❑ 134 Colin Ryder .15 .07
❑ 135 David Kilduff .25 .11
❑ 136 Mickey McGuire .15 .07
❑ 137 Randy Polacik .15 .07
❑ 138 Jeff Tory .25 .11
❑ 139 Chris Buckman .15 .07
❑ 140 Bill Moody .15 .07
❑ 141 Rick McLarren .15 .07
❑ 142 The Phantom .25 .11
❑ 143 Jason Zaichkowski .15 .07
❑ 144 Tony Hrycuik .15 .07
❑ 145 Cameron Knox .15 .07
❑ 146 Mike Warriner .15 .07
❑ 147 Robb Gordon .75 .35
❑ 148 Mike Pawluk .35 .16
❑ 149 Tim Harris .15 .07
❑ 150 Mike Bzdel .15 .07
❑ 151 Chad Wilson .15 .07
❑ 152 Andrew Plumb .15 .07
❑ 153 Andy MacIntosh .15 .07
❑ 154 Stefan Brannare .15 .07
❑ 155 Matt Sharrers .15 .07
❑ 156 Brent Berry .15 .07
❑ 157 Ryan Douglas .15 .07
❑ 158 Heath Dennison .15 .07
❑ 159 Chad Vizzutti .15 .07
❑ 160 Adam Lord .15 .07
❑ 161 Brad Klyn .15 .07
❑ 162 Andrew Young .15 .07
❑ 163 Casey Lemanski .15 .07
❑ 164 Mike McKinlay .15 .07
❑ 165 Derek Robinson .15 .07
❑ 166 Kees Roodbol .15 .07
❑ 167 Scott Boucher .15 .07
❑ 168 Shawn Gervais .15 .07
❑ 169 Ryan Schaffer .15 .07
❑ 170 Kevin Robertson .15 .07
❑ 171 Ryan Donovan .15 .07
❑ 172 Bart Taylor .15 .07
❑ 173 Greg Hunt .15 .07
❑ 174 Darcy George .15 .07
❑ 175 Shane Tidsbury .15 .07
❑ 176 Rob Smillie .15 .07
❑ 177 Chad Vestergaard .15 .07
❑ 178 Al Kinisky .15 .07
❑ 179 Patrick O'Flaherty .15 .07
❑ 180 Loui Mellios .15 .07
❑ 181 Lorin Murdock .25 .11
(Unnumbered)
❑ 182 Jason Genik .15 .07
❑ 183 Rob Herrington .15 .07
❑ 184 Loui Mellios .15 .07
❑ 185 Cal Benazic .25 .11
❑ 186 Richard Kraus .15 .07
❑ 187 Geoff White .15 .07
❑ 188 Kirk Buchanan .15 .07
❑ 189 Peter Zurba .15 .07
❑ 190 John Morabito .15 .07
❑ 191 Corey Kruchkowski .15 .07
❑ 192 Spencer Ward .15 .07
❑ 193 Danny Shermerhorn .15 .07
❑ 194 Mark Davies .15 .07
❑ 195 Jason Rushton .15 .07
❑ 196 Chad Buckle .15 .07
❑ 197 Serge Beauchesne .15 .07
❑ 198 Todd Kelman .15 .07
❑ 199 Jason Switzer .15 .07
❑ 200 Eon MacFarlane .15 .07
❑ 201 Terry Ryan 2.00 .90
❑ 202 Shawn Bourgeois .15 .07
❑ 203 Chad Schraeder .15 .07
❑ 204 Dusty McLellan .15 .07
❑ 205 The Predator .25 .11
❑ 206 Danny Shermerhorn .15 .07
❑ 207 Chris Godard .15 .07
❑ 208 Jason Chipman .15 .07
❑ 209 Christian Twomey .25 .11
❑ 210 Ryan Loxam .15 .07
❑ 211 Greg Buchanan .15 .07
❑ 212 Kees Roodbol .15 .07
❑ 213 Ryan Keller .15 .07
❑ 214 Kevin Paschal .15 .07
❑ 215 David Hebky .15 .07
❑ 216 Vince Devlin .15 .07
❑ 217 Mike Cole .15 .07
❑ 218 Daljit Takhar .15 .07
❑ 219 Scott Hall .15 .07
❑ 220 Derek Lawrence .15 .07
❑ 221 Mark Basanta .15 .07
❑ 222 Jan Kloboucek .15 .07
❑ 223 Randy Barker .15 .07
❑ 224 Kris Gailloux .15 .07
❑ 225 Tyson Scheuer .15 .07
❑ 226 Brent Wormald .15 .07
❑ 227 Vince Devlin .15 .07
❑ 228 Gus Miller .15 .07
❑ 229 Todd McKave .15 .07
❑ 230 Lawrence Oliver .15 .07
❑ 231 Scott Garvin .15 .07
❑ 232 Rob Milliken .15 .07
❑ 233 Roman Kobrc .15 .07
❑ 234 Dan Skene .15 .07
❑ 235 Blair Marsh .15 .07
❑ 236 Maco Balkovec .15 .07
❑ 237 Scott Kirton .15 .07
❑ 238 Blaine Moore .15 .07
❑ 239 Nigel Creightney .15 .07
❑ 240 Bill Zapt .15 .07
❑ 241 Jason Elders .15 .07
❑ 242 BCJHL Officials .15 .07
(Unidentified Referee)
❑ 243 Masks of the BCJHL .75 .35
The Black Panther
❑ 244 Masks of the BCJHL .75 .35
The Puck Pirate
(Unnumbered)
❑ 245 Mike Pawluk .35 .16
BCJHL MVP
❑ 246 Steffon Walby .35 .16
Captains of the BCJHL

## 1991 Arena Draft Picks

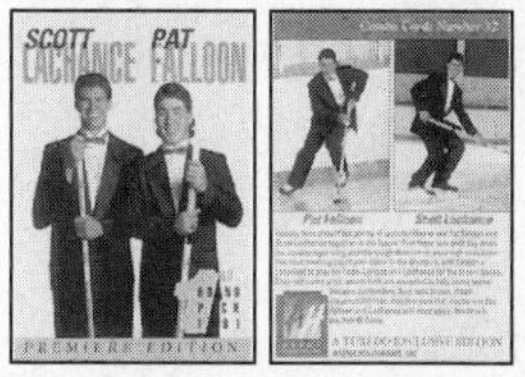

The 1991 Arena Draft Picks boxed set consists of 33 standard-size cards. The set was produced in English as well as French versions, with both versions currently carrying the same values. One thousand cards (numbered out of 667 for the English version, 333 for the French) signed by each player were randomly inserted throughout the sets with one autograph per approximately ten sets or two per case. These autographed cards are valued at 25 to 50 times the values listed below. Moreover, a Pat Falloon hologram was produced in conjunction with this set, although its release came much later. The Falloon hologram is not included in the complete set price below. The production run was reported to be 198,000 English and 99,000 French sets, and each set was issued with a numbered certificate of authenticity. The full-bleed fronts have a white background and show the hockey player in an action pose wearing a tuxedo.

| | MINT | NRMT |
|---|---|---|
| COMPLETE SET (33) | 3.00 | 1.35 |
| COMMON CARD (1-32) | .05 | .02 |

❑ 1 Pat Falloon .15 .07
❑ 2 Scott Niedermayer .25 .11
❑ 3 Scott Lachance .10 .05
❑ 4 Peter Forsberg UER 1.00 .45
❑ 5 Alek Stojanov .05 .02
❑ 6 Richard Matvichuk .15 .07
❑ 7 Patrick Poulin .05 .02
❑ 8 Martin Lapointe .20 .09
❑ 9 Tyler Wright .05 .02
❑ 10 Philippe Boucher .10 .05
❑ 11 Pat Peake .10 .05
❑ 12 Markus Naslund UER .15 .07
❑ 13 Brent Bilodeau .05 .02
❑ 14 Glen Murray .10 .05
❑ 15 Niklas Sundblad .05 .02
❑ 16 Trevor Halverson .05 .02
❑ 17 Dean McAmmond .10 .05
❑ 18 Rene Corbet .10 .05
❑ 19 Eric Lavigne .05 .02
❑ 20 Steve Staios .05 .02
❑ 21 Jim Campbell .25 .11
❑ 22 Jassen Cullimore .05 .02
❑ 23 Jamie Pushor .10 .05
❑ 24 Donevan Hextall .05 .02
❑ 25 Andrew Verner .10 .05
❑ 26 Jason Dawe .15 .07
❑ 27 Jeff Nelson .05 .02
❑ 28 Darcy Werenka .05 .02
❑ 29 Francois Groleau .05 .02
❑ 30 Guy Leveque .05 .02
❑ 31 Yanic Perreault .15 .07
❑ 32 Pat Falloon and .15 .07
Scott Lachance
❑ NNO Checklist Card .05 .02
❑ HOLO Pat Falloon .50 .23
Hologram

## 1997 Bowman CHL

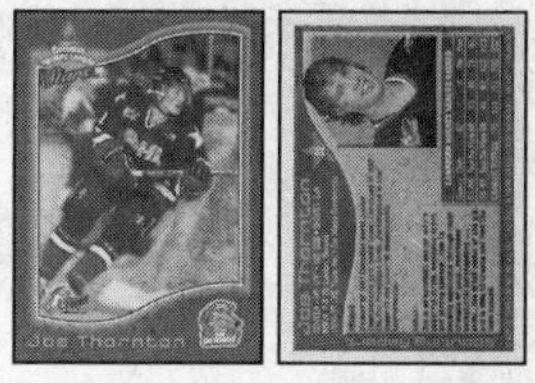

The 1997-98 Bowman CHL set was issued in one series totalling 165 cards and was distributed in eight-card packs with a suggested retail price of $1.89. It marks Topps first venture into minor league hockey. The set features color photos of established CHL stars as well as 40 NHL 1997 Draft Prospects. The 40 Draft Prospects each autographed cards that were distributed at the rate of one in 24 to form the Bowman CHL Prospects Autographs insert set. Each of these cards is authenticated by the Topps Certified Autograph Issue stamp.

| | MINT | NRMT |
|---|---|---|
| COMPLETE SET (160) | 40.00 | 18.00 |
| COMMON CARD (1-160) | .20 | .09 |

❑ 1 Jan Bulis .75 .35
❑ 2 Daniel Cleary 1.50 .70
❑ 3 Dave Duerden .20 .09
❑ 4 Cameron Mann 1.50 .70
❑ 5 Alyn McCauley .50 .23
❑ 6 Tyler Rennette .20 .09
❑ 7 Marc Savard .50 .23
❑ 8 Daniel Tkaczuk 1.50 .70
❑ 9 John Tripp .20 .09
❑ 10 Joel Trottier .20 .09
❑ 11 Sean Venedam .20 .09
❑ 12 Alexandre Volchkov .20 .09
❑ 13 Sean Blanchard .20 .09
❑ 14 Kevin Bolibruck .20 .09
❑ 15 Nick Boynton .50 .23
❑ 16 Paul Mara .50 .23
❑ 17 Marc Moro .20 .09
❑ 18 Marty Wilford .20 .09
❑ 19 Zac Bierk .50 .23
❑ 20 Kory Cooper .20 .09
❑ 21 Richard Rochefort .20 .09
❑ 22 Matt Cooke .50 .23
❑ 23 Boyd Devereaux .20 .09
❑ 24 Rico Fata 3.00 1.35
❑ 25 Dwayne Hay .20 .09
❑ 26 Trevor Letowski .50 .23
❑ 27 Ryan Mougenel .20 .09
❑ 28 Todd Norman .20 .09
❑ 29 Larry Paleczny .20 .09
❑ 30 Colin Pepperall .20 .09
❑ 31 Jonathan Sim .50 .23
❑ 32 Joe Thornton 4.00 1.80
❑ 33 Brian Wesenberg .20 .09
❑ 34 Andy Delmore .20 .09
❑ 35 Chris Hajt .50 .23
❑ 36 Richard Jackman .50 .23
❑ 37 Denis Smith .50 .23
❑ 38 Jamie Sokolsky .20 .09
❑ 39 Paul Traynor .20 .09
❑ 40 Patrick DesRochers 1.50 .70
❑ 41 Robert Esche .75 .35
❑ 42 Roberto Luongo 6.00 2.70
❑ 43 Frederic Henry .20 .09
❑ 44 Marc Olivier Roy .20 .09
❑ 45 Samy Nasreddine .50 .23
❑ 46 Jean-Francois Fortin .50 .23
❑ 47 Martin Ethier .20 .09
❑ 48 Jason Doig .50 .23
❑ 49 Dominic Perna .20 .09
❑ 50 Daniel Briere 1.50 .70
❑ 51 Pavel Rosa .75 .35
❑ 52 Philippe Audet .50 .23
❑ 53 Gordie Dwyer .20 .09
❑ 54 Martin Menard .20 .09
❑ 55 Jonathan Delisle .20 .09
❑ 56 Peter Worrell .50 .23
❑ 57 Francois Methot .20 .09
❑ 58 Steve Begin .20 .09
❑ 59 Karol Bartanus .50 .23
❑ 60 Jean-Pierre Dumont 1.00 .45
❑ 61 Marc Denis 1.50 .70
❑ 62 Jean-Sebastien Giguere .75 .35
❑ 63 Jason Gorleau .20 .09
❑ 64 Radoslav Suchy .20 .09
❑ 65 Stephane Robidas .20 .09
❑ 66 Marc-Andre Gaudet .20 .09
❑ 67 Eric Drouin .50 .23
❑ 68 Derrick Walser .20 .09
❑ 69 Vincent Lecavalier 6.00 2.70
❑ 70 Denis Hamel .20 .09
❑ 71 Daniel Corso .75 .35

❑ 72 Martin Moise .20 .09
❑ 73 Eric Belanger .50 .23
❑ 74 Olivier Morin .20 .09
❑ 75 Jerome Tremblay .20 .09
❑ 76 Jody Shelley .20 .09
❑ 77 Eric Normandin .20 .09
❑ 78 David Thibeault .20 .09
❑ 79 Christian Daigle .50 .23
❑ 80 Alexandre Jacques .50 .23
❑ 81 Brian Boucher 2.00 .90
❑ 82 Randy Petruk .50 .23
❑ 83 Hugh Hamilton .50 .23
❑ 84 Joel Kwiatkowski .20 .09
❑ 85 Zenith Komarniski .20 .09
❑ 86 Joey Tetarenko .20 .09
❑ 87 Tyler Willis .20 .09
❑ 88 Patrick Marleau 4.00 1.80
❑ 89 Trent Whitfield .20 .09
❑ 90 Martin Cerven .20 .09
❑ 91 Donnie Kinney .20 .09
❑ 92 Brad Isbister 1.00 .45
❑ 93 Todd Robinson .20 .09
❑ 94 Greg Leeb .20 .09
❑ 95 John Cirjak .20 .09
❑ 96 Randy Perry .20 .09
❑ 97 Derek Schutz .20 .09
❑ 98 Brenden Morrow .50 .23
❑ 99 Shawn McNeil .20 .09
❑ 100 Brad Ference .50 .23
❑ 101 Ryan Hoople .20 .09
❑ 102 Brian Elder .20 .09
❑ 103 Mike McBain .20 .09
❑ 104 Jesse Wallin .75 .35
❑ 105 Chris Phillips 1.25 .55
❑ 106 Kelly Smart .20 .09
❑ 107 Arron Asham .20 .09
❑ 108 Byron Ritchie .50 .23
❑ 109 Derek Morris .20 .09
❑ 110 Travis Brigley .20 .09
❑ 111 Justin Kurtz .20 .09
❑ 112 B.J. Young .20 .09
❑ 113 Shane Willis .50 .23
❑ 114 Josh Holden .50 .23
❑ 115 Cory Sarich .50 .23
❑ 116 Brad Larsen .50 .23
❑ 117 Stefan Cherneski .50 .23
❑ 118 Peter Schaefer .75 .35
❑ 119 Dmitri Nabokov .75 .35
❑ 120 Sergei Varlamov .50 .23
❑ 121 Daniel Cleary TP .20 .09
❑ 122 Jarrett Smith TP .20 .09
❑ 123 Alexandre Mathieu TP .20 .09
❑ 124 Matt Elich TP .20 .09
❑ 125 Joe Thornton TP 2.00 .90
❑ 126 Mike Brown TP .20 .09
❑ 127 Derek Schutz TP .20 .09
❑ 128 Benoit Cote TP .20 .09
❑ 129 Jason Ward TP .20 .09
❑ 130 Karol Bartanus TP .20 .09
❑ 131 Tyler Rennette TP .20 .09
❑ 132 Matt Zultek TP .20 .09
❑ 133 Brad Ference TP .20 .09
❑ 134 Daniel Tetrault TP .20 .09
❑ 135 Ryan Bonni TP .20 .09
❑ 136 Kevin Grimes TP .20 .09
❑ 137 Paul Mara TP .20 .09
❑ 138 Nikos Tselios TP .20 .09
❑ 139 Curtis Cruickshank TP .20 .09
❑ 140 Pierre-Luc Therrien TP .20 .09
❑ 141 Patrick Marleau TP 2.00 .90
❑ 142 Ty Jones TP .20 .09
❑ 143 Jeremy Reich TP .20 .09
❑ 144 Adam Mair TP .20 .09
❑ 145 Adam Colagiacomo TP .20 .09
❑ 146 Harold Druken TP .20 .09
❑ 147 Brenden Morrow TP .20 .09
❑ 148 Jay Legault TP .20 .09
❑ 149 Jeff Zehr TP .20 .09
❑ 150 Scott Barney TP .20 .09
❑ 151 Gregor Baumgartner TP .20 .09
❑ 152 Daniel Tkaczuk TP .20 .09
❑ 153 Eric Brewer TP .20 .09
❑ 154 Nick Boynton TP .20 .09
❑ 155 Vratislav Cech TP .20 .09
❑ 156 Kyle Kos TP .20 .09
❑ 157 Jean-Francois Fortin TP .20 .09
❑ 158 Wes Jarvis TP .20 .09
❑ 159 Roberto Luongo TP 3.00 1.35
❑ 160 Jean-Francois Damphousse TP .20 .09
❑ NNO B.B.Redempt. 3.00 1.35
❑ NNO Ref.Redempt. 5.00 2.20
❑ NNO Ato.Ref.Redempt. 10.00 4.50
❑ NNO Auto.Redempt. 12.00 5.50

## 1997 Bowman CHL Autographs

Randomly inserted at the rate of one in 46, this 40-card set features cards signed by the top NHL draft picks. Each of these cards is authenticated by the Topps Certified Autograph Issue stamp.

| | MINT | NRMT |
|---|---|---|
| COMPLETE SET (40) | 300.00 | 135.00 |
| COMMON CARD (1-40) | 8.00 | 3.60 |

❑ 2 Jarrett Smith 12.00 5.50
❑ 3 Alexandre Mathieu 12.00 5.50
❑ 4 Matt Elich 12.00 5.50
❑ 6 Mike Brown 12.00 5.50
❑ 7 Derek Schultz 12.00 5.50
❑ 8 Benoit Cote 12.00 5.50
❑ 10 Karol Bartanus 12.00 5.50
❑ 11 Tyler Rennette 12.00 5.50
❑ 13 Brad Ference 12.00 5.50
❑ 14 Daniel Tetrault 12.00 5.50
❑ 15 Ray Bonni 12.00 5.50
❑ 16 Kevin Grimes 12.00 5.50
❑ 18 Nikos Tselios 12.00 5.50
❑ 19 Curtis Cruickshank 12.00 5.50
❑ 20 Pierre-Luc Therrien 12.00 5.50
❑ 22 Ty Jones 12.00 5.50
❑ 23 Jeremy Reich 12.00 5.50
❑ 24 Adam Mair 12.00 5.50
❑ 25 Adam Colagiacomo 12.00 5.50
❑ 26 Harold Druken 12.00 5.50
❑ 27 Brenden Morrow 12.00 5.50
❑ 28 Jay Legault 12.00 5.50
❑ 29 Jeff Zehr 12.00 5.50
❑ 30 Scott Barney 12.00 5.50
❑ 31 Gregor Baumgartner 12.00 5.50
❑ 33 Eric Brewer 12.00 5.50
❑ 34 Nick Boynton 12.00 5.50
❑ 35 Vratislav Cech 12.00 5.50
❑ 36 Kyle Kos 12.00 5.50
❑ 37 Jean Francois Fortin 12.00 5.50
❑ 38 Wes Jarvis 12.00 5.50
❑ 39 Roberto Luongo 12.00 5.50
❑ 121 Daniel Cleary 20.00 9.00
❑ 125 Joe Thornton 50.00 22.00
❑ 129 Jason Ward 15.00 6.75
❑ 132 Matt Zultek 15.00 6.75
❑ 160 Jean Francois Damphousse 15.00 6.75

## 1997 Bowman CHL Bowman's Best

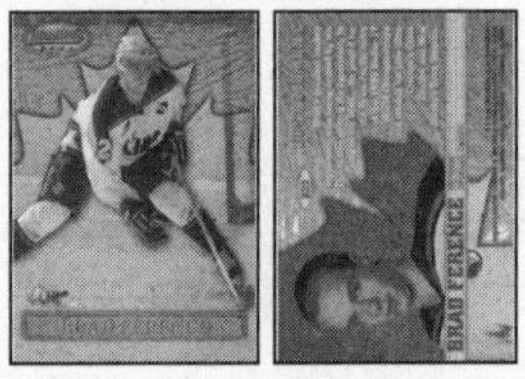

This 20-card set was randomly inserted in packs at the rate of one in 12 and features color player photos printed on laser-cut cards using chromium technology.

| | MINT | NRMT |
|---|---|---|
| COMPLETE SET (20) | 50.00 | 22.00 |
| COMMON CARD (1-20) | 1.50 | .70 |
| COMP.REF.SET (20) | 150.00 | 70.00 |
| COMMON REF. (1-20) | 5.00 | 2.20 |
| *REF.STARS: 1.5X TO 3X BASIC BOWMAN'S BEST | | |
| REF.STATED ODDS: 1:24 | | |
| COMP.ATOMIC SET (20) | 250.00 | 110.00 |
| COMMON ATOMIC (1-20) | 8.00 | 3.60 |
| *ATOMIC STARS: 2.5X TO 5X BASIC BOWMAN'S BEST | | |
| ATOMIC STATED ODDS: 1:48 | | |

❑ 1 Joe Thornton 8.00 3.60
❑ 2 Patrick Marleau 8.00 3.60
❑ 3 Paul Mara 1.50 .70
❑ 4 Daniel Tkaczuk 4.00 1.80
❑ 5 Jason Ward 2.00 .90
❑ 6 Nick Boynton 1.50 .70
❑ 7 Daniel Cleary 4.00 1.80
❑ 8 Eric Brewer 1.50 .70
❑ 9 Brad Ference 1.50 .70
❑ 10 Stefan Cherneski 1.50 .70
❑ 11 Ryan Bonni 1.50 .70
❑ 12 Adam Colagiacomo 1.50 .70
❑ 13 Mike Brown 1.50 .70
❑ 14 Scott Barney 1.50 .70
❑ 15 Jarrett Smith 1.50 .70
❑ 16 Brenden Morrow 1.50 .70
❑ 17 Jean-Francois Fortin 1.50 .70
❑ 18 Roberto Luongo 12.00 5.50
❑ 19 Curtis Cruickshank 1.50 .70
❑ 20 Pierre-Luc Therrien 1.50 .70

## 1997 Bowman CHL OPC

Randomly inserted in packs at the rate of one in six, this 160 card set is an O-Pee-Chee parallel version of the basic Bowman CHL issue.

| | MINT | NRMT |
|---|---|---|
| COMPLETE SET (160) | 600.00 | 275.00 |
| COMMON CARD (1-160) | 2.00 | .90 |
| *STARS: 5X TO 10X BASIC CARDS | | |

## 1998 Bowman CHL

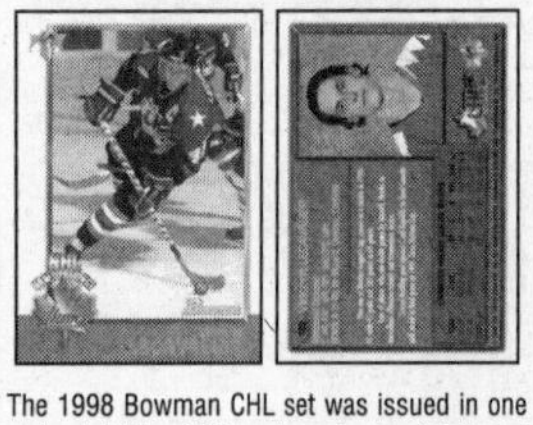

The 1998 Bowman CHL set was issued in one series totalling 165 cards and was distributed in eight-card packs with a suggested retail price of $1.89. The set features action color photos of established CHL stars as well as 40 NHL 1998 Draft Prospects. The backs carry player information and statistics.

| | MINT | NRMT |
|---|---|---|
| COMPLETE SET (165) | 50.00 | 22.00 |
| COMMON CARD (1-165) | .20 | .09 |

❑ 1 Robert Esche .50 .23
❑ 2 Chris Hajt .20 .09
❑ 3 Mark McMahon .20 .09
❑ 4 Jeff Brown .20 .09
❑ 5 Richard Jackman .50 .23
❑ 6 Greg Labenski .20 .09
❑ 7 Marek Posmyk .20 .09
❑ 8 Brian Willsie .20 .09
❑ 9 Jason Ward 1.50 .70
❑ 10 Manny Malhotra 3.00 1.35
❑ 11 Matt Cooke .50 .23
❑ 12 Mike Gorman .20 .09
❑ 13 Rodney Richard .20 .09
❑ 14 David Legwand 4.00 1.80
❑ 15 Jon Sim .50 .23
❑ 16 Peter Sarno .20 .09
❑ 17 Andrew Long .20 .09
❑ 18 Peter Cava .20 .09
❑ 19 Colin Pepperall .20 .09
❑ 20 Jay Legault 1.50 .70
❑ 21 Brian Finley 2.50 1.10
❑ 22 Martin Skoula 1.50 .70
❑ 23 Brian Campbell .20 .09
❑ 24 Sean Blanchard .20 .09
❑ 25 Bryan Allen 1.50 .70
❑ 26 Peter Hogan .20 .09
❑ 27 Nick Boynton .50 .23
❑ 28 Matt Bradley .20 .09
❑ 29 Jeremy Adduono .20 .09
❑ 30 Mike Henrich 1.50 .70
❑ 31 Justin Papineau 1.50 .70
❑ 32 Bujar Amidovski 1.00 .45
❑ 33 Robert Mailloux .20 .09
❑ 34 Daniel Tkaczuk 1.50 .70
❑ 35 Sean Avery .20 .09
❑ 36 Mark Bell 1.50 .70
❑ 37 Kevin Colley .20 .09
❑ 38 Norm Milley 2.00 .90
❑ 39 Scott Barney .50 .23
❑ 40 Joel Trottier .20 .09
❑ 41 Brent Belecki .20 .09
❑ 42 Randy Petruk .20 .09
❑ 43 Brad Ference 1.00 .45
❑ 44 Perry Johnson .20 .09
❑ 45 Joel Kwiatkowski .20 .09
❑ 46 Zenith Komarniski .20 .09
❑ 47 Greg Kuznik .20 .09
❑ 48 Andrew Ference .20 .09
❑ 49 Jason Deleurme .20 .09
❑ 50 Trent Whitfield .20 .09
❑ 51 Dylan Gyori .20 .09
❑ 52 Todd Robinson .20 .09
❑ 53 Marian Hossa 2.00 .90
❑ 54 Mike Hurley .20 .09
❑ 55 Greg Leeb .20 .09
❑ 56 Andrej Podkonicky .20 .09
❑ 57 Quinn Hancock .20 .09
❑ 58 Marian Cisar 1.00 .45
❑ 59 Bret DeCecco .20 .09
❑ 60 Brenden Morrow 1.50 .70
❑ 61 Evan Lindsay .20 .09
❑ 62 Terry Friesen .20 .09
❑ 63 Ryan Shannon .20 .09
❑ 64 Michal Rozsival .20 .09
❑ 65 Luc Theoret .20 .09
❑ 66 Brad Stuart 2.00 .90
❑ 67 Burke Henry .20 .09
❑ 68 Cory Sarich .50 .23
❑ 69 Martin Sonnenberg .20 .09
❑ 70 Mark Smith .20 .09
❑ 71 Shawn McNeil .20 .09
❑ 72 Brad Moran .20 .09
❑ 73 Josh Holden .50 .23
❑ 74 Cory Cyrenne .20 .09
❑ 75 Shane Willis .50 .23
❑ 76 Stefan Cherneski 1.50 .70
❑ 77 Jay Henderson .20 .09
❑ 78 Ronald Petrovicky .20 .09
❑ 79 Sergei Varlamov 1.00 .45
❑ 80 Chad Hinz .20 .09
❑ 81 Mathieu Garon 1.00 .45
❑ 82 Mathieu Chouinard 2.00 .90
❑ 83 Dominic Perna .20 .09
❑ 84 Didier Tremblay 4.00 1.80
❑ 85 Mike Ribeiro 2.00 .90
❑ 86 Marty Johnston .20 .09
❑ 87 Remi Royer 1.50 .70
❑ 88 Patrick Pelchat .20 .09
❑ 89 Daniel Corso .50 .23
❑ 90 Francois Fortier .20 .09
❑ 91 Marc-Andre Gaudet .20 .09
❑ 92 Francois Beauchemin .20 .09
❑ 93 Michel Tremblay .20 .09
❑ 94 Jean-Philippe Pare .20 .09
❑ 95 Francois Methot .20 .09
❑ 96 David Thibeault .20 .09
❑ 97 Jonathan Girard Jr. 1.50 .70
❑ 98 Karol Bartanus .50 .23
❑ 99 Peter Ratchuk .20 .09
❑ 100 Pierre Dagenais 1.50 .70
❑ 101 Philippe Sauve 2.00 .90
❑ 102 Remi Bergeron .20 .09
❑ 103 Vincent Lecavalier 6.00 2.70
❑ 104 Eric Chouinard 1.50 .70
❑ 105 Oleg Timchenko .20 .09
❑ 106 Sebastien Roger .20 .09
❑ 107 Simon Gagne 2.00 .90
❑ 108 Alex Tanguay 2.50 1.10
❑ 109 David Gosselin .20 .09
❑ 110 Ramzi Abid 1.50 .70
❑ 111 Eric Drouin .20 .09
❑ 112 Dominic Auger .20 .09
❑ 113 Martin Moise .20 .09
❑ 114 Randy Copley 1.50 .70
❑ 115 Alexandre Mathieu .20 .09
❑ 116 Brad Richards 1.50 .70
❑ 117 Dmitri Tolkunov .20 .09
❑ 118 Alexei Tezikov .20 .09
❑ 119 Derrick Walser .20 .09
❑ 120 Adam Borzecki .20 .09
❑ 121 Ramzi Abid 1.50 .70
❑ 122 Brett Allan 1.50 .70
❑ 123 Mark Bell 1.50 .70
❑ 124 Blair Betts .20 .09
❑ 125 Randy Copley .20 .09
❑ 126 Simon Gagne 2.00 .90
❑ 127 Michael Henrich 1.50 .70
❑ 128 Vincent Lecavalier 6.00 2.70
❑ 129 Norman Milley 1.50 .70
❑ 130 Chris Neilsen .20 .09
❑ 131 Rico Fata 3.00 1.35
❑ 132 Mike Ribeiro 1.50 .70
❑ 133 Bryan Allen 1.50 .70
❑ 134 John Erskine .20 .09
❑ 135 Jonathan Girard Jr. 1.50 .70
❑ 136 Stephen Peat .20 .09
❑ 137 Robyn Regehr .20 .09
❑ 138 Brad Stuart 1.50 .70
❑ 139 Patrick Desrochers 2.00 .90
❑ 140 Jason Labarbera .20 .09
❑ 141 David Cameron 1.50 .70
❑ 142 Jonathan Cheechoo 1.00 .45
❑ 143 Eric Chouinard 1.50 .70
❑ 144 Brent Gauvreau 1.50 .70
❑ 145 Scott Gomez 1.00 .45
❑ 146 Jeff Heerema 1.50 .70
❑ 147 David Legwand 4.00 1.80
❑ 148 Manny Malhotra 3.00 1.35
❑ 149 Justin Papineau 1.50 .70
❑ 150 Andrew Peters .20 .09
❑ 151 Michael Rupp 1.00 .45
❑ 152 Alex Tanguay 2.50 1.10
❑ 153 Francois Beauchemin .20 .09
❑ 154 Mathieu Biron .50 .23
❑ 155 Jiri Fisher .50 .23
❑ 156 Alex Henry .20 .09
❑ 157 Kyle Rossiter .20 .09
❑ 158 Martin Skoula 1.50 .70
❑ 159 Mathieu Chouinard 2.00 .90
❑ 160 Philippe Sauve 2.00 .90
❑ 161 Brian Finley 1.50 .70
❑ 162 Brent Belecki .20 .09
❑ 163 Dominic Perna .20 .09
❑ 164 Jonathan Cheechoo 1.00 .45
❑ 165 Checklist .20 .09

## 1998 Bowman CHL Golden Anniversary

Randomly inserted in packs at the rate of one in 57, this 165-card set is a gold-foil parallel version of the base set and is sequentially numbered to 50 in honor of the 50 years of Bowman cards.

| | MINT | NRMT |
|---|---|---|
| COMMON CARD (1-165) | 6.00 | 2.70 |
| *STARS: 15X TO 30X BASIC CARDS | | |
| STATED ODDS 1:57 | | |

## 1998 Bowman CHL OPC International

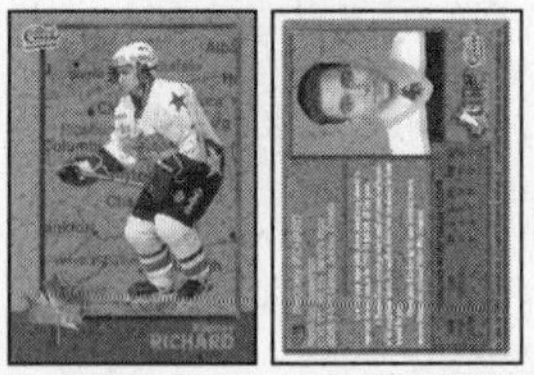

Inserted one in every pack, this 165-card set is parallel to the base set and features color player photos with a national indication in the background by way of a map printed on 16 pt. mirrorboard. Each back is written in the language of that player's native country.

| | MINT | NRMT |
|---|---|---|
| COMPLETE SET (165) | 100.00 | 45.00 |
| COMMON CARD (1-165) | .40 | .18 |
| *STARS: .75X TO 2X BASIC CARDS | | |
| STATED ODDS 1:1 | | |

## 1998 Bowman CHL Certified Autographs Blue

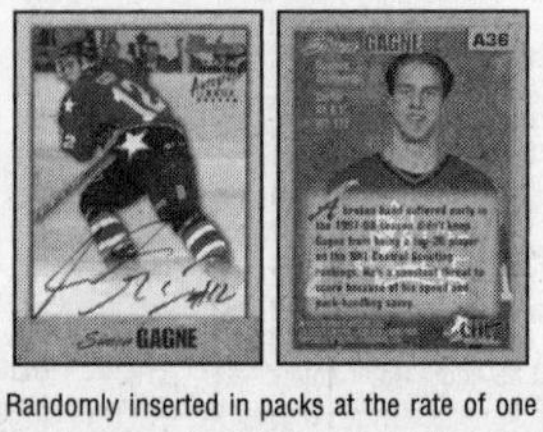

Randomly inserted in packs at the rate of one in 59, this 40-card set features cards signed by the top 40 NHL draft prospects and authenticated by a blue foil "Topps Certified Issue" stamp.

| | MINT | NRMT |
|---|---|---|
| COMPLETE SET (40) | 500.00 | 220.00 |
| COMMON CARD (A1-A40) | 6.00 | 2.70 |
| *SILVER AU's: 1X TO 2X BASIC AU | | |
| SILVER AU's STATED ODDS 1:157 | | |
| *GOLD AU's: 2X TO 5X BASIC AU | | |
| GOLD AU's STATED ODDS 1:470 | | |

❑ A1 Justin Papineau 15.00 6.75
❑ A2 Jason Labarbera 6.00 2.70
❑ A3 Michael Rupp 15.00 6.75
❑ A4 Stephen Peat 6.00 2.70
❑ A5 Manny Malhotra 30.00 13.50
❑ A6 Michael Henrich 15.00 6.75
❑ A7 Kyle Rossiter 6.00 2.70
❑ A8 Mark Bell 15.00 6.75
❑ A9 Mathieu Chouinard 20.00 9.00
❑ A10 Vincent Lecavalier 60.00 27.00
❑ A11 David Legwand 40.00 18.00
❑ A12 Bryan Allen 10.00 4.50
❑ A13 Francois Beauchemin 6.00 2.70
❑ A14 Robyn Regehr 10.00 4.50
❑ A15 Eric Chouinard 15.00 6.75
❑ A16 Norman Milley 15.00 6.75
❑ A17 Alex Henry 10.00 4.50
❑ A18 Ramzi Abid 15.00 6.75
❑ A19 Jiri Fischer 10.00 4.50
❑ A20 Patrick Desrochers 20.00 9.00
❑ A21 Mathieu Biron 10.00 4.50
❑ A22 Brad Stuart 10.00 4.50
❑ A23 Philippe Sauve 20.00 9.00
❑ A24 John Erskine 6.00 2.70
❑ A25 Jonathan Cheechoo 15.00 6.75
❑ A26 Brett Allan 6.00 2.70
❑ A27 Scott Gomez 15.00 6.75
❑ A28 Chris Neilsen 6.00 2.70
❑ A29 David Cameron 6.00 2.70
❑ A30 Jonathan Girard Jr. 10.00 4.50
❑ A31 Jeff Heerema 12.00 5.50
❑ A32 Blair Betts 6.00 2.70
❑ A33 Andrew Peters 6.00 2.70
❑ A34 Randy Copley 6.00 2.70
❑ A35 Alex Tanguay 25.00 11.00
❑ A36 Simon Gagne 30.00 13.50
❑ A37 Brent Gauvreau 6.00 2.70
❑ A38 Mike Ribeiro 15.00 6.75
❑ A39 Martin Skoula 10.00 4.50
❑ A40 Rico Fata 30.00 13.50

## 1998 Bowman CHL Scout's Choice

Randomly inserted in packs at the rate of one in 12, this 21-card set features color photos of players picked by Bowman Hockey Scouts and printed on borderless, double-ethced foil cards.

| | MINT | NRMT |
|---|---|---|
| COMPLETE SET (21) | 90.00 | 40.00 |
| COMMON CARD (SC1-SC21) | 1.50 | .70 |
| STATED ODDS 1:12 | | |

❑ SC1 Bryan Allen 3.00 1.35
❑ SC2 Manny Malhotra 6.00 2.70
❑ SC3 Daniel Tkaczuk 3.00 1.35
❑ SC4 Bujar Amidovski 3.00 1.35
❑ SC5 Patrick Desrochers 6.00 2.70
❑ SC6 Brad Ference 2.50 1.10
❑ SC7 Marian Hossa 5.00 2.20
❑ SC8 Brad Stuart 2.50 1.10
❑ SC9 Sergei Varlamov 2.50 1.10
❑ SC10 Randy Petruk 1.50 .70
❑ SC11 Karol Bartanus 1.50 .70
❑ SC12 Vincent LeCavalier 15.00 6.75
❑ SC13 Jonathan Girard 2.50 1.10
❑ SC14 Peter Ratchuk 1.50 .70
❑ SC15 Alex Tanguay 6.00 2.70
❑ SC16 Rico Fata 6.00 2.70
❑ SC17 Brian Finley 5.00 2.20
❑ SC18 Jonathan Cheechoo 5.00 2.20
❑ SC19 Scott Gomez 5.00 2.20
❑ SC20 Michal Rozsival 1.50 .70
❑ SC21 Mathieu Garon 5.00 2.20

## 1998 Bowman Chrome CHL

The 1998-99 Bowman Chrome CHL hobby only set was issued in one series totalling 165 cards. The 4-card packs retail for $3.00 each. The fronts feature color action photography on chromium technology. The Bowman Rookie Card stamp appears on all cards for players making their first appearance in the set. The scheduled release date was September, 1998.

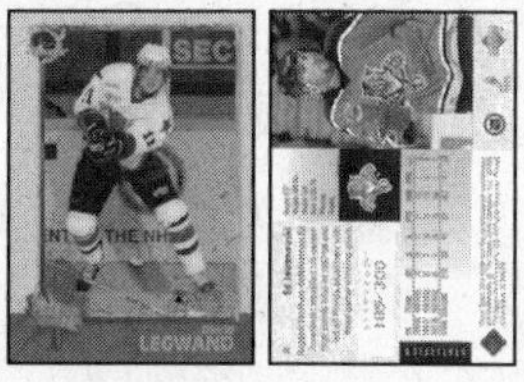

| | MINT | NRMT |
|---|---|---|
| COMPLETE SET (165) | 150.00 | 70.00 |
| COMMON CARD (1-165) | .40 | .18 |
| COMP.REF.SET (165) | 1500.00 | 700.00 |
| COMMON REFRACTOR (1-165) | 4.00 | 1.80 |

*REF.STARS: 4X TO 10X BASIC CARD
REFRACTOR STATED ODDS 1:12

| | | |
|---|---|---|
| ❑ 1 Robert Esche | 1.00 | .45 |
| ❑ 2 Chris Hajt | .40 | .18 |
| ❑ 3 Mark McMahon | .40 | .18 |
| ❑ 4 Jeff Brown | .40 | .18 |
| ❑ 5 Richard Jackman | 1.00 | .45 |
| ❑ 6 Greg Labenski | .40 | .18 |
| ❑ 7 Marek Posmyk | .40 | .18 |
| ❑ 8 Brian Willsie | .40 | .18 |
| ❑ 9 Jason Ward | 1.50 | .70 |
| ❑ 10 Manny Malhotra | 6.00 | 2.70 |
| ❑ 11 Matt Cooke | 1.00 | .45 |
| ❑ 12 Mike Gorman | .40 | .18 |
| ❑ 13 Rodney Richard | .40 | .18 |
| ❑ 14 David Legwand | 8.00 | 3.60 |
| ❑ 15 Jon Sim | 1.00 | .45 |
| ❑ 16 Peter Sarno | .40 | .18 |
| ❑ 17 Andrew Long | .40 | .18 |
| ❑ 18 Peter Cava | .40 | .18 |
| ❑ 19 Colin Pepperall | .40 | .18 |
| ❑ 20 Jay Legault | 1.50 | .70 |
| ❑ 21 Brian Finley | 2.50 | 1.10 |
| ❑ 22 Martin Skoula | 1.50 | .70 |
| ❑ 23 Brian Campbell | .40 | .18 |
| ❑ 24 Sean Blanchard | .40 | .18 |
| ❑ 25 Bryan Allen | 1.50 | .70 |
| ❑ 26 Peter Hogan | .40 | .18 |
| ❑ 27 Nick Boynton | 1.00 | .45 |
| ❑ 28 Matt Bradley | .40 | .18 |
| ❑ 29 Jeremy Adduono | .40 | .18 |
| ❑ 30 Mike Henrich | 3.00 | 1.35 |
| ❑ 31 Justin Papineau | 3.00 | 1.35 |
| ❑ 32 Bujar Amidovski | 2.00 | .90 |
| ❑ 33 Robert Mailloux | .40 | .18 |
| ❑ 34 Daniel Tkaczuk | 3.00 | 1.35 |
| ❑ 35 Sean Avery | .40 | .18 |
| ❑ 36 Mark Bell | 3.00 | 1.35 |
| ❑ 37 Kevin Colley | .40 | .18 |
| ❑ 38 Norman Milley | 3.00 | 1.35 |
| ❑ 39 Scott Barney | 1.00 | .45 |
| ❑ 40 Joel Trottier | .40 | .18 |
| ❑ 41 Brent Belecki | .40 | .18 |
| ❑ 42 Randy Petruk | .40 | .18 |
| ❑ 43 Brad Ference | 2.00 | .90 |
| ❑ 44 Perry Johnson | .40 | .18 |
| ❑ 45 Joel Kwiatkowski | .40 | .18 |
| ❑ 46 Zenith Komarniski | .40 | .18 |
| ❑ 47 Greg Kuznik | .40 | .18 |
| ❑ 48 Andrew Ference | 1.00 | .45 |
| ❑ 49 Jason Deleurme | .40 | .18 |
| ❑ 50 Trent Whitfield | .40 | .18 |
| ❑ 51 Dylan Gyori | .40 | .18 |
| ❑ 52 Todd Robinson | .40 | .18 |
| ❑ 53 Marian Hossa | 4.00 | 1.80 |
| ❑ 54 Mike Hurley | .40 | .18 |
| ❑ 55 Greg Leeb | .40 | .18 |
| ❑ 56 Andrej Podkonicky | .40 | .18 |
| ❑ 57 Quinn Hancock | .40 | .18 |
| ❑ 58 Marian Cisar | 2.00 | .90 |
| ❑ 59 Bret DeCecco | .40 | .18 |
| ❑ 60 Brenden Morrow | 1.50 | .70 |
| ❑ 61 Evan Lindsay | .40 | .18 |
| ❑ 62 Terry Friesen | .40 | .18 |
| ❑ 63 Ryan Shannon | .40 | .18 |
| ❑ 64 Michal Rozsival | .40 | .18 |
| ❑ 65 Luc Theoret | .40 | .18 |
| ❑ 66 Brad Stuart | 2.00 | .90 |
| ❑ 67 Burke Henry | .40 | .18 |
| ❑ 68 Cory Sarich | 1.00 | .45 |
| ❑ 69 Martin Sonnenberg | .40 | .18 |
| ❑ 70 Mark Smith | .40 | .18 |
| ❑ 71 Shawn McNeil | .40 | .18 |
| ❑ 72 Brad Moran | .40 | .18 |
| ❑ 73 Josh Holden | 1.00 | .45 |
| ❑ 74 Cory Cyrenne | .40 | .18 |
| ❑ 75 Shane Willis | 1.00 | .45 |
| ❑ 76 Stefan Cherneski | 3.00 | 1.35 |
| ❑ 77 Jay Henderson | .40 | .18 |
| ❑ 78 Ronald Petrovicky | 1.00 | .45 |
| ❑ 79 Sergei Varlamov | 2.00 | .90 |
| ❑ 80 Chad Hinz | .40 | .18 |
| ❑ 81 Mathieu Garon | 2.00 | .90 |
| ❑ 82 Mathieu Chouinard | 4.00 | 1.80 |
| ❑ 83 Dominic Perna | .40 | .18 |
| ❑ 84 Didier Tremblay | .40 | .18 |
| ❑ 85 Mike Ribeiro | 3.00 | 1.35 |
| ❑ 86 Marty Johnston | .40 | .18 |
| ❑ 87 Remi Royer | 1.50 | .70 |
| ❑ 88 Patrick Pelchat | .40 | .18 |
| ❑ 89 Daniel Corso | 1.00 | .45 |
| ❑ 90 Francois Fortier | .40 | .18 |
| ❑ 91 Marc-Andre Gaudet | .40 | .18 |
| ❑ 92 Francois Beauchemin | .40 | .18 |
| ❑ 93 Michel Tremblay | .40 | .18 |
| ❑ 94 Jean-Philippe Pare | .40 | .18 |
| ❑ 95 Francois Methot | .40 | .18 |
| ❑ 96 David Thibeault | .40 | .18 |
| ❑ 97 Jonathan Girard Jr. | 1.50 | .70 |
| ❑ 98 Karol Bartanus | 1.00 | .45 |
| ❑ 99 Peter Ratchuk | .40 | .18 |
| ❑ 100 Pierre Dagenais | 1.50 | .70 |
| ❑ 101 Philippe Sauve | 4.00 | 1.80 |
| ❑ 102 Remi Bergeron | .40 | .18 |
| ❑ 103 Vincent Lecavalier | 12.00 | 5.50 |
| ❑ 104 Eric Chouinard | 3.00 | 1.35 |
| ❑ 105 Oleg Timchenko | .40 | .18 |
| ❑ 106 Sebastien Roger | .40 | .18 |
| ❑ 107 Simon Gagne | 3.00 | 1.35 |
| ❑ 108 Alex Tanguay | 6.00 | 2.70 |
| ❑ 109 David Gosselin | .40 | .18 |
| ❑ 110 Ramzi Abid | 3.00 | 1.35 |
| ❑ 111 Eric Drouin | 1.00 | .45 |
| ❑ 112 Dominic Auger | .40 | .18 |
| ❑ 113 Martin Moise | .40 | .18 |
| ❑ 114 Randy Copley | 1.50 | .70 |
| ❑ 115 Alexandre Mathieu | .40 | .18 |
| ❑ 116 Brad Richards | 1.50 | .70 |
| ❑ 117 Dmitri Tolkunov | .40 | .18 |
| ❑ 118 Alexei Tezikov | .40 | .18 |
| ❑ 119 Derrick Walser | .40 | .18 |
| ❑ 120 Adam Borzecki | .40 | .18 |
| ❑ 121 Ramzi Abid | 3.00 | 1.35 |
| ❑ 122 Brett Allan | 1.50 | .70 |
| ❑ 123 Mark Bell | 3.00 | 1.35 |
| ❑ 124 Blair Betts | .40 | .18 |
| ❑ 125 Randy Copley | .40 | .18 |
| ❑ 126 Simon Gagne | 3.00 | 1.35 |
| ❑ 127 Michael Henrich | 3.00 | 1.35 |
| ❑ 128 Vincent Lecavalier | 12.00 | 5.50 |
| ❑ 129 Norman Milley | 3.00 | 1.35 |
| ❑ 130 Chris Nielsen | .40 | .18 |
| ❑ 131 Rico Fata | 6.00 | 2.70 |
| ❑ 132 Mike Ribeiro | 3.00 | 1.35 |
| ❑ 133 Bryan Allen | 1.50 | .70 |
| ❑ 134 John Erskine | .40 | .18 |
| ❑ 135 Jonathan Girard Jr. | 1.50 | .70 |
| ❑ 136 Stephen Peat | .40 | .18 |
| ❑ 137 Robyn Regehr | .40 | .18 |
| ❑ 138 Brad Stuart | 1.50 | .70 |
| ❑ 139 Patrick Desrochers | 4.00 | 1.80 |
| ❑ 140 Jason Labarbera | .40 | .18 |
| ❑ 141 David Cameron | 1.50 | .70 |
| ❑ 142 Jonathan Cheechoo | 2.00 | .90 |
| ❑ 143 Eric Chouinard | 3.00 | 1.35 |
| ❑ 144 Brent Gauvreau | 1.50 | .70 |
| ❑ 145 Scott Gomez | 2.00 | .90 |
| ❑ 146 Jeff Heerema | 1.50 | .70 |
| ❑ 147 David Legwand | 8.00 | 3.60 |
| ❑ 148 Manny Malhotra | 6.00 | 2.70 |
| ❑ 149 Justin Papineau | 3.00 | 1.35 |
| ❑ 150 Andrew Peters | .40 | .18 |
| ❑ 151 Michael Rupp | 2.00 | .90 |
| ❑ 152 Alex Tanguay | 6.00 | 2.70 |
| ❑ 153 Francois Beauchemin | .40 | .18 |
| ❑ 154 Mathieu Biron | 1.00 | .45 |
| ❑ 155 Jiri Fisher | .40 | .18 |
| ❑ 156 Alex Henry | .40 | .18 |
| ❑ 157 Kyle Rossiter | .40 | .18 |
| ❑ 158 Martin Skoula | 1.50 | .70 |
| ❑ 159 Mathieu Chouinard | 4.00 | 1.80 |
| ❑ 160 Philippe Sauve | 4.00 | 1.80 |
| ❑ 161 Brian Finley | 2.50 | 1.10 |
| ❑ 162 Brent Belecki | .40 | .18 |
| ❑ 163 Dominic Perna | .40 | .18 |
| ❑ 164 Jonathan Cheechoo | 2.00 | .90 |
| ❑ 165 Checklist | .40 | .18 |

## 1998 Bowman Chrome CHL Golden Anniversary

Randomly inserted in packs at a rate of one in 39, this 165-card parallel offers the same players as in the Bowman Chrome CHL base set. The set is sequentially numbered to 50. Cards are randomly inserted into packs.

| | MINT | NRMT |
|---|---|---|
| COMMON CARD (1-165) | 10.00 | 4.50 |

*STARS: 12.5X TO 25X BASIC CARDS

## 1998 Bowman Chrome CHL OPC International

Randomly inserted in packs at a rate of one in 8, this 165-card parallel features the same players as in the Bowman Chrome CHL base set. The set also offers background map designs of the player's homeland and vital statistics written in that player's native language.

| | MINT | NRMT |
|---|---|---|
| COMPLETE SET (165) | 800.00 | 350.00 |
| COMMON CARD (1-165) | 2.00 | .90 |

*STARS: 2.5X TO 5X BASIC CARD

| | | |
|---|---|---|
| COMMON REFRACTOR (1-165) | 40.00 | 18.00 |

*STARS: 8X TO 20X BASIC CARDS
REF.STATED ODDS 1:48

## 1994-95 Central Hockey League

This 127-card standard-size set features the seven teams of the Central Hockey League. Reportedly only 13,000 of each card were produced. The cards were available in pack form only, either at team rinks or from the league for 3.00 by mail. The fronts feature borderless color action player photos except on the left, where a gray bar edges the picture

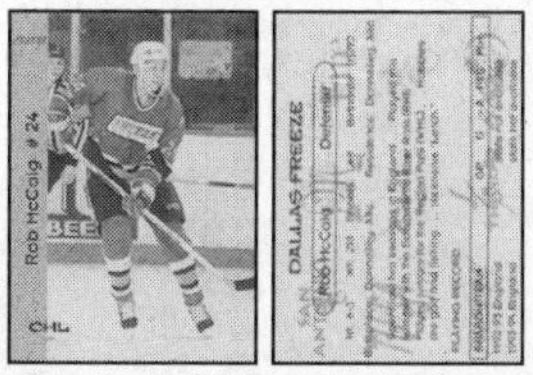

and carries the CHL logo, the player's name and number, and the team logo. On a white background with light gray team logos, the horizontal backs carry a short player biography, profile and stats. The cards are unnumbered, grouped alphabetically within teams and checklisted below alphabetically according to teams as follows: Dallas Freeze (1-18), Ft. Worth Fire (19-36), Memphis Riverkings (37-54), Oklahoma City Blazers (55-72), San Antonio Iguanas (73-90), Tulsa Oilers (91-108), and Wichita Thunder (109-126).

| | MINT | NRMT |
|---|---|---|
| COMPLETE SET (127) | 35.00 | 16.00 |
| COMMON CARD (1-127) | .40 | .18 |

| | | |
|---|---|---|
| ❑ 1 Jamie Adams | .40 | .18 |
| ❑ 2 Wayne Anchikoski | .50 | .23 |
| ❑ 3 Jeff Beaudin | .40 | .18 |
| ❑ 4 Troy Binnie | .50 | .23 |
| ❑ 5 Don Burke | .40 | .18 |
| ❑ 6 Derek Crawford | .40 | .18 |
| ❑ 7 Ray Desouza | .40 | .18 |
| ❑ 8 Ron Flockhart CO | .40 | .18 |
| ❑ 9 Jon Gustafson | .50 | .23 |
| ❑ 10 Jason Heiland | .40 | .18 |
| ❑ 11 James Jensen | .40 | .18 |
| ❑ 12 Frank LaScala | .40 | .18 |
| ❑ 13 Ryan Leschasin | .40 | .18 |
| ❑ 14 Rob Madia | .40 | .18 |
| ❑ 15 Rob McCaig | .40 | .18 |
| ❑ 16 Jim McGeough | .50 | .23 |
| ❑ 17 Doug Roberts | .40 | .18 |
| ❑ 18 Jason Taylor | .40 | .18 |
| ❑ 19 Scott Allen | .40 | .18 |
| ❑ 20 Bruce Bell | .50 | .23 |
| ❑ 21 Francois Bourdeau | .40 | .18 |
| ❑ 22 Troy Frederick | .40 | .18 |
| ❑ 23 Steve Harrison CO | .40 | .18 |
| ❑ 24 Alex Kholomeyev | .50 | .23 |
| ❑ 25 Dominic Maltais | .50 | .23 |
| ❑ 26 Martin Masa | .50 | .23 |
| ❑ 27 Jeff Massey | .40 | .18 |
| ❑ 28 Mike McCormick | .40 | .18 |
| ❑ 29 Pat McGarry | .50 | .23 |
| ❑ 30 Dwight Mullins | .40 | .18 |
| ❑ 31 Eric Ricard | .40 | .18 |
| ❑ 32 Sean Rowe | .40 | .18 |
| ❑ 33 Bryan Schoen | .40 | .18 |
| ❑ 34 Darren Srochenski | .40 | .18 |
| ❑ 35 Andy Stewart | .40 | .18 |
| ❑ 36 Stephen Tepper | .40 | .18 |
| ❑ 37 Denis Beauchamp | .40 | .18 |
| ❑ 38 Herb Boxer CO | .40 | .18 |
| ❑ 39 Nicolas Brousseau | .40 | .18 |
| ❑ 40 Scott Brower | .50 | .23 |
| ❑ 41 Dan Brown | .40 | .18 |
| ❑ 42 Brian Cook | .40 | .18 |
| ❑ 43 Brent Fleetwood | .40 | .18 |
| ❑ 44 Francois Gagon | .40 | .18 |
| ❑ 45 Dominic Grand-Maison | .40 | .18 |
| ❑ 46 Kyle Haviland | .40 | .18 |
| ❑ 47 Jamie Hearn | .40 | .18 |
| ❑ 48 Mike Jackson | .50 | .23 |
| ❑ 49 Paul Krake | .50 | .23 |
| ❑ 50 Layne LeBel | .40 | .18 |
| ❑ 51 Steve Magnusson | .40 | .18 |
| ❑ 52 Mark McGinn | .40 | .18 |
| ❑ 53 Darren Miciak | .40 | .18 |
| ❑ 54 Bobby Wallwork | .50 | .23 |
| ❑ 55 Ron Aubrey | .50 | .23 |
| ❑ 56 Joe Burton | .50 | .23 |
| ❑ 57 George Dupont | .50 | .23 |
| ❑ 58 Tom Gomes | .40 | .18 |
| ❑ 59 Sean Gorman | .40 | .18 |
| ❑ 60 Viktor Ignatjev | .50 | .23 |
| ❑ 61 Chris Laganas | .40 | .18 |
| ❑ 62 Michael McEwen CO | .50 | .23 |
| ❑ 63 Chris McMurtry | .40 | .18 |
| ❑ 64 Derry Menard | .40 | .18 |
| ❑ 65 Sergei Naumov | .50 | .23 |
| ❑ 66 Trent Pankewicz | .40 | .18 |
| ❑ 67 Alan Perry | .75 | .35 |
| ❑ 68 Eric Plante | .40 | .18 |
| ❑ 69 Dave Slifka | .40 | .18 |
| ❑ 70 Steve Simoni | .40 | .18 |
| ❑ 71 Michel St. Jacques | .40 | .18 |
| ❑ 72 Tom Thornbury | .40 | .18 |
| ❑ 73 Trevor Buchanan | .40 | .18 |
| ❑ 74 Link Gaetz | .75 | .35 |
| ❑ 75 Sean Goldsworthy | .40 | .18 |
| ❑ 76 Fred Goltz | .40 | .18 |
| ❑ 77 Sheldon Gorski | .40 | .18 |
| ❑ 78 Ross Harris | .40 | .18 |
| ❑ 79 Dale Henry | .50 | .23 |
| ❑ 80 Paul Jackson | .75 | .35 |
| ❑ 81 Scot Kelsey | .40 | .18 |
| ❑ 82 John Klaers | .40 | .18 |
| ❑ 83 Stu Kulak | .50 | .23 |
| ❑ 84 Ken Plaquin | .40 | .18 |
| ❑ 85 Brian Shantz | .50 | .23 |
| ❑ 86 Dean Shmyr | .40 | .18 |
| ❑ 87 Adam Thompson | .40 | .18 |
| ❑ 88 John Torchetti | .40 | .18 |
| ❑ 89 Ken Venis | .40 | .18 |
| ❑ 90 Mike Williams | .40 | .18 |
| ❑ 91 Colin Baustad | .40 | .18 |
| ❑ 92 Luc Beausoleil | .50 | .23 |
| ❑ 93 Mike Berger | .40 | .18 |
| ❑ 94 Mark Cavallin | .40 | .18 |
| ❑ 95 Shaun Clouston | .40 | .18 |
| ❑ 96 Michel Couvrette | .40 | .18 |
| ❑ 97 Taylor Hall | .40 | .18 |
| ❑ 98 Ryan Harrison | .40 | .18 |
| ❑ 99 Sasha Lakovic | .75 | .35 |
| ❑ 100 Chuck Loreto | .40 | .18 |
| ❑ 101 Tony Martino | .50 | .23 |
| ❑ 102 David Moore | .40 | .18 |
| ❑ 103 Sylvain Naud | .50 | .23 |
| ❑ 104 Dan O'Rourke | .40 | .18 |
| ❑ 105 Jody Praznik | .40 | .18 |
| ❑ 106 Andy Ross | .40 | .18 |
| ❑ 107 Mike Shea | .40 | .18 |
| ❑ 108 Garry Unger CO | .75 | .35 |
| ❑ 109 Bob Berg | .40 | .18 |
| ❑ 110 John DePourcq | .50 | .23 |
| ❑ 111 Dave Doucette | .50 | .23 |
| ❑ 112 Ron Handy | .50 | .23 |
| ❑ 113 Mark Hilton | .40 | .18 |
| ❑ 114 Darcy Kaminski | .40 | .18 |
| ❑ 115 Mark Karpen | .40 | .18 |
| ❑ 116 Jim Latos | .40 | .18 |
| ❑ 117 George Maneluk | .50 | .23 |
| ❑ 118 Greg Neish | .40 | .18 |
| ❑ 119 Brent Sapergia | .75 | .35 |
| ❑ 120 Doug Shedden CO | .50 | .23 |
| ❑ 121 Greg Smith | .40 | .18 |
| ❑ 122 Conrade Thomas | .40 | .18 |
| ❑ 123 John Vary | .40 | .18 |
| ❑ 124 Rob Weingartner | .40 | .18 |
| ❑ 125 Brian Wells | .40 | .18 |
| ❑ 126 Jack Williams | .40 | .18 |
| ❑ 127 Title Card CL | .40 | .18 |

## 1995-96 Central Hockey League

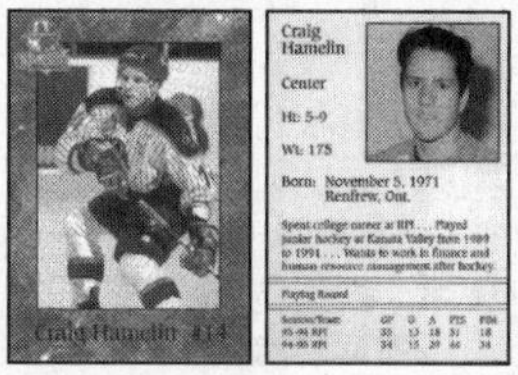

This set features the players of the Central Hockey League. The cards feature action photography on the front ensconced in a gray marble border, highlighted by the team logo in the top left corner. The backs contain another photo, and player information. The cards are unnumbered, so they are listed alphabetically by team, and then by name. Each of the team sets contains eighteen cards. They were available in packs at CHL games.

| | MINT | NRMT |
|---|---|---|
| COMPLETE SET (90) | 35.00 | 16.00 |
| COMMON CARD (1-90) | .40 | .18 |

| | | |
|---|---|---|
| ❑ 1 Scott Allen | .40 | .18 |
| ❑ 2 Trevor Burgess | .40 | .18 |
| ❑ 3 Brian Caruso | .40 | .18 |
| ❑ 4 Trevor Converse | .40 | .18 |
| ❑ 5 Steve Dykstra | .50 | .23 |
| ❑ 6 Troy Frederick | .40 | .18 |
| ❑ 7 Phil Groeneveld | .40 | .18 |
| ❑ 8 Mark Hilton | .40 | .18 |
| ❑ 9 Jeff Massey | .40 | .18 |
| ❑ 10 Dennis Miller | .40 | .18 |
| ❑ 11 Dwight Mullins | .40 | .18 |
| ❑ 12 Steve Plouffe | .50 | .23 |
| ❑ 13 Vern Ray | .40 | .18 |
| ❑ 14 Kyle Reeves | .50 | .23 |
| ❑ 15 Troy Stephens | .40 | .18 |
| ❑ 16 Sean Whyte | .50 | .23 |
| ❑ 17 Scorch | .40 | .18 |
| ❑ 18 Bill McDonald | .40 | .18 |
| ❑ 19 Scott Brower | .50 | .23 |
| ❑ 20 Dan Brown | .40 | .18 |
| ❑ 21 Jamie Cooke | .40 | .18 |
| ❑ 22 Kevin Evans | .40 | .18 |
| ❑ 23 Brent Fleetwood | .40 | .18 |
| ❑ 24 Ron Fogarty | .40 | .18 |
| ❑ 25 Trent Gleason | .40 | .18 |
| ❑ 26 Derek Grant | .40 | .18 |
| ❑ 27 Mike Jackson | .50 | .23 |
| ❑ 28 Scot Kelsey | .40 | .18 |
| ❑ 29 Steve Magnusson | .40 | .18 |
| ❑ 30 Carl Menard | .50 | .23 |
| ❑ 31 Chris Morque | .40 | .18 |
| ❑ 32 Rick Robus | .40 | .18 |
| ❑ 33 Andy Ross | .40 | .18 |
| ❑ 34 Stephane Roy | .75 | .35 |
| ❑ 35 Doug Strombeck | .40 | .18 |
| ❑ 36 Herb Boxer | .40 | .18 |
| ❑ 37 Kevin Barrett | .40 | .18 |
| ❑ 38 Carl Boudreau | .50 | .23 |
| ❑ 39 Joe Burton | .50 | .23 |
| ❑ 40 George Dupont | .50 | .23 |
| ❑ 41 Dominic Fafard | .40 | .18 |
| ❑ 42 Jean-Ian Filiatrault | .40 | .18 |
| ❑ 43 Tom Gomes | .40 | .18 |
| ❑ 44 Todd Harris | .40 | .18 |
| ❑ 45 Mervin Kopeck | .40 | .18 |
| ❑ 46 Doug Lawrence | .75 | .35 |
| ❑ 47 Kevin Lune | .40 | .18 |
| ❑ 48 Steve Moore | .40 | .18 |
| ❑ 49 Simon Olivier | .40 | .18 |
| ❑ 50 Darren Pengelly | .40 | .18 |
| ❑ 51 Steve Simoni | .40 | .18 |
| ❑ 52 Barkley Swenson | .40 | .18 |
| ❑ 53 Serge Tkachenko | .50 | .23 |
| ❑ 54 Doug Sauter | .40 | .18 |
| ❑ 55 Colin Baustad | .40 | .18 |
| ❑ 56 Mike Berger | .40 | .18 |
| ❑ 57 Mike Chase | .40 | .18 |
| ❑ 58 Trevor Ellerman | .40 | .18 |
| ❑ 59 Bryan Forslund | .40 | .18 |
| ❑ 60 Taylor Hall | .40 | .18 |
| ❑ 61 Craig Hamelin | .40 | .18 |
| ❑ 62 Ryan Harrison | .40 | .18 |
| ❑ 63 John Laan | .40 | .18 |
| ❑ 64 Glen Lang | .40 | .18 |
| ❑ 65 Dave Larouche | .40 | .18 |
| ❑ 66 Tony Martino | .50 | .23 |
| ❑ 67 Sylvain Naud | .50 | .23 |
| ❑ 68 Jim Peters | .40 | .18 |
| ❑ 69 Cory Peterson | .40 | .18 |
| ❑ 70 Chris Robertson | .40 | .18 |
| ❑ 71 Kyuin Shim | .40 | .18 |
| ❑ 72 Garry Unger | .75 | .35 |
| ❑ 73 Clint Black | .40 | .18 |
| ❑ 74 Mike Chighisola | .40 | .18 |
| ❑ 75 Leonard Devuono | .40 | .18 |
| ❑ 76 Ty Eigner | .50 | .23 |
| ❑ 77 Anton Fedorov | .50 | .23 |
| ❑ 78 Paul Krake | .50 | .23 |
| ❑ 79 Antonin Necas | .40 | .18 |
| ❑ 80 Ryan Pisiak | .40 | .18 |
| ❑ 81 Richard Roesler | .40 | .18 |
| ❑ 82 Jason Rushton | .40 | .18 |
| ❑ 83 Art Saran | .40 | .18 |
| ❑ 84 Stefan Simoes | .40 | .18 |
| ❑ 85 Greg Smith | .40 | .18 |
| ❑ 86 Dale Turnbull | .40 | .18 |
| ❑ 87 Rob Weingartner | .40 | .18 |
| ❑ 88 Bryan Wells | .40 | .18 |
| ❑ 89 Jack Williams | .40 | .18 |
| ❑ 90 Don Jackson | .50 | .23 |

## 1991 Classic Promos

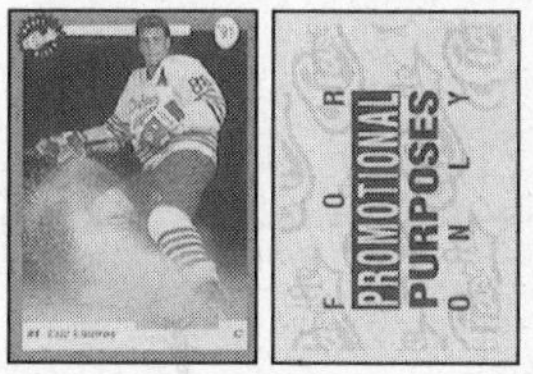

The two standard size promo cards were issued by Classic to show collectors and dealers the style of their new hockey draft picks set.

| | MINT | NRMT |
|---|---|---|
| COMPLETE SET (2) | 4.00 | 1.80 |
| COMMON CARD (1-2) | .25 | .11 |

| | | |
|---|---|---|
| ❑ 1 Eric Lindros | 4.00 | 1.80 |
| ❑ 2 Pat Falloon | .25 | .11 |

## 1991 Classic

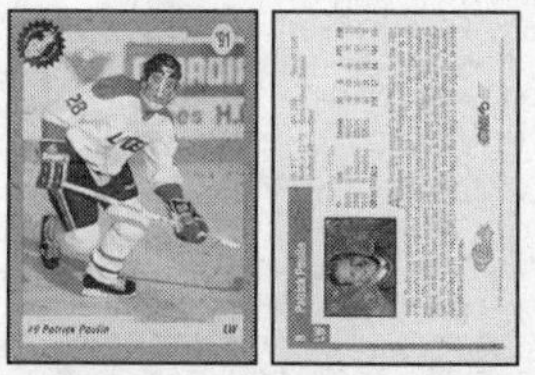

The premier edition of Classic's 1991 Hockey Draft Pick set includes 50 standard-size cards featuring 50 of the top 60 NHL draft picks. The set was issued in a run of 360,000 factory sets and included an individually numbered certificate of authenticity. The front has glossy color action player photos, with blue-green borders. The "Classic Draft Picks" logo appears in the upper left corner, and player information appears in a lemon yellow stripe below the picture. The backs have the player's current statistics and biography. The cards were issued in both English and French and carry the same value.

| | MINT | NRMT |
|---|---|---|
| COMPLETE SET (50) | 3.00 | 1.35 |
| COMMON CARD (1-50) | .10 | .05 |

| | | |
|---|---|---|
| ❑ 1 Eric Lindros | 3.00 | 1.35 |
| ❑ 2 Pat Falloon | .25 | .11 |
| ❑ 3 Scott Niedermayer | .40 | .18 |
| ❑ 4 Scott Lachance | .10 | .05 |
| ❑ 5 Peter Forsberg | 2.00 | .90 |
| ❑ 6 Alek Stojanov | .10 | .05 |
| ❑ 7 Richard Matvichuk | .10 | .05 |
| ❑ 8 Patrick Poulin | .10 | .05 |
| ❑ 9 Martin Lapointe | .10 | .05 |
| ❑ 10 Tyler Wright | .10 | .05 |
| ❑ 11 Philippe Boucher | .10 | .05 |
| ❑ 12 Pat Peake | .10 | .05 |

| | | |
|---|---|---|
| ❑ 13 Markus Naslund | .10 | .05 |
| ❑ 14 Brent Bilodeau | .10 | .05 |
| ❑ 15 Glen Murray | .10 | .05 |
| ❑ 16 Niklas Sundblad | .10 | .05 |
| ❑ 17 Martin Rucinsky | .10 | .05 |
| ❑ 18 Trevor Halverson | .10 | .05 |
| ❑ 19 Dean McAmmond | .10 | .05 |
| ❑ 20 Ray Whitney | .25 | .11 |
| ❑ 21 Rene Corbet | .10 | .05 |
| ❑ 22 Eric Lavigne | .10 | .05 |
| ❑ 23 Zigmund Palffy | .40 | .18 |
| ❑ 24 Steve Staios | .10 | .05 |
| ❑ 25 Jim Campbell | .10 | .05 |
| ❑ 26 Jassen Cullimore | .10 | .05 |
| ❑ 27 Martin Hamrlik | .10 | .05 |
| ❑ 28 Jamie Pushor | .10 | .05 |
| ❑ 29 Donevan Hextall | .10 | .05 |
| ❑ 30 Andrew Verner | .10 | .05 |
| ❑ 31 Jason Dawe | .10 | .05 |
| ❑ 32 Jeff Nelson | .10 | .05 |
| ❑ 33 Darcy Werenka | .10 | .05 |
| ❑ 34 Jozef Stumpel | .10 | .05 |
| ❑ 35 Francois Groleau | .10 | .05 |
| ❑ 36 Guy Leveque | .10 | .05 |
| ❑ 37 Jamie Matthews | .10 | .05 |
| ❑ 38 Dody Wood | .10 | .05 |
| ❑ 39 Yanic Perreault | .10 | .05 |
| ❑ 40 Jamie McLennan | .10 | .05 |
| ❑ 41 Yanic Dupre UER | .10 | .05 |
| ❑ 42 Sandy McCarthy | .10 | .05 |
| ❑ 43 Chris Osgood | .40 | .18 |
| ❑ 44 Fredrik Lindquist | .10 | .05 |
| ❑ 45 Jason Young | .10 | .05 |
| ❑ 46 Steve Konowalchuk | .10 | .05 |
| ❑ 47 Michael Nylander UER | .10 | .05 |
| ❑ 48 Shane Peacock | .10 | .05 |
| ❑ 49 Yves Sarault | .10 | .05 |
| ❑ 50 Marcel Cousineau | .10 | .05 |
| ❑ NNO Rocket On Ice | .30 | .14 |

## 1992 Classic Promos

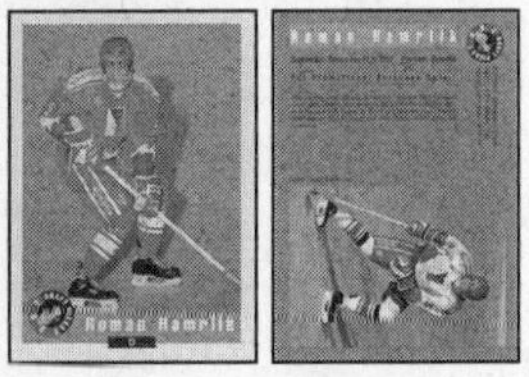

These three cards measure the standard size and feature color action player photos with white borders, except for the Lemieux card, which has a black and white picture with the words "Flash Back 92" printed at the top. The player's name is printed in a gold stripe at the bottom, which intersects the Classic logo at the lower left corner. The gold backs have horizontally oriented player photos, again the Lemieux being black and white and the others color. The text on the back is vertically oriented, except for the biography, and includes draft information, career highlights, and the words "For Promotional Purposes Only". The cards are unnumbered and checklisted below in alphabetical order.

| | MINT | NRMT |
|---|---|---|
| COMPLETE SET (3) | 6.00 | 2.70 |
| COMMON CARD (1-3) | .50 | .23 |
| ❑ 1 Roman Hamrlik | .50 | .23 |
| ❑ 2 Mario Lemieux (Flash Back 92) | 5.00 | 2.20 |
| ❑ 3 Ray Whitney | .50 | .23 |

## 1992 Classic

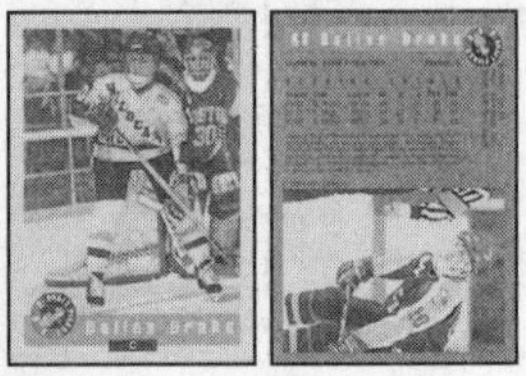

The 1992 Classic Hockey Draft Picks set consists of 120 standard-size cards. Mario Lemieux was featured on a regular issue flashback card, an autograph card, and a special card individually numbered 1-10,000, all of which were randomly inserted throughout the production run. Also randomly inserted throughout the foil packs were 1,366 instant winner cards that entitled the holder to win autographed memorabilia from Mario Lemieux and other hockey stars. The production run for the regular issue cards was reportedly 9,966 ten-box cases. Classic also issued the 1992 Draft Pick set in a Gold version. The Gold factory sets were packaged in a walnut display case. The Gold sets also included an individually numbered card signed by Valeri and Pavel Bure. The set included draft picks and minor leaguers from the American and International hockey leagues as well as the first card of female goaltender Manon Rheaume.

| | MINT | NRMT |
|---|---|---|
| COMPLETE SET (120) | 10.00 | 4.50 |
| COMMON CARD (1-120) | .05 | .02 |
| ❑ 1 Roman Hamrlik | .40 | .18 |
| ❑ 2 Alexei Yashin | .40 | .18 |
| ❑ 3 Mike Rathje | .05 | .02 |
| ❑ 4 Darius Kasparaitis | .05 | .02 |
| ❑ 5 Cory Stillman | .05 | .02 |
| ❑ 6 Robert Petrovicky | .05 | .02 |
| ❑ 7 Andrei Nazarov | .05 | .02 |
| ❑ 8 Cory Stillman CL | .05 | .02 |
| ❑ 9 Jason Bowen | .05 | .02 |
| ❑ 10 Jason Smith | .05 | .02 |
| ❑ 11 David Wilkie | .05 | .02 |
| ❑ 12 Curtis Bowen | .05 | .02 |
| ❑ 13 Grant Marshall | .05 | .02 |
| ❑ 14 Valeri Bure | .25 | .11 |
| ❑ 15 Jeff Shantz | .05 | .02 |
| ❑ 16 Justin Hocking | .05 | .02 |
| ❑ 17 Mike Peca | .50 | .23 |
| ❑ 18 Marc Hussey | .05 | .02 |
| ❑ 19 Sandy Allan | .05 | .02 |
| ❑ 20 Kirk Maltby | .05 | .02 |
| ❑ 21 Cale Hulse | .05 | .02 |
| ❑ 22 Sylvain Cloutier | .05 | .02 |
| ❑ 23 Martin Gendron | .05 | .02 |
| ❑ 24 Kevin Smyth | .05 | .02 |
| ❑ 25 Jason McBain | .05 | .02 |
| ❑ 26 Lee J. Leslie | .05 | .02 |
| ❑ 27 Ralph Intranuovo | .05 | .02 |
| ❑ 28 Martin Reichel | .05 | .02 |
| ❑ 29 Stefan Ustorf | .05 | .02 |
| ❑ 30 Jarkko Varvio | .05 | .02 |
| ❑ 31 Jere Lehtinen | .05 | .02 |
| ❑ 32 Janne Gronvall | .05 | .02 |
| ❑ 33 Martin Straka | .40 | .18 |
| ❑ 34 Libor Polasek | .05 | .02 |
| ❑ 35 Jozef Cierny | .05 | .02 |
| ❑ 36 Jan Vopat | .05 | .02 |
| ❑ 37 Ondrej Steiner | .05 | .02 |
| ❑ 38 Jan Caloun | .05 | .02 |
| ❑ 39 Petr Hrbek | .05 | .02 |
| ❑ 40 Richard Smehlik | .05 | .02 |
| ❑ 41 Sergei Gonchar CL | .05 | .02 |
| ❑ 42 Sergei Krivokrasov | .05 | .02 |
| ❑ 43 Sergei Gonchar | .05 | .02 |
| ❑ 44 Boris Mironov | .05 | .02 |
| ❑ 45 Denis Metlyuk | .05 | .02 |
| ❑ 46 Sergei Klimovich | .05 | .02 |
| ❑ 47 Sergei Brylin | .05 | .02 |
| ❑ 48 Andrei Nikolishin | .05 | .02 |
| ❑ 49 Alexander Cherbayev | .05 | .02 |
| ❑ 50 Sergei Zholtok | .05 | .02 |
| ❑ 51 Vitali Prokhorov | .05 | .02 |
| ❑ 52 Nikolai Borschevsky | .05 | .02 |
| ❑ 53 Vitali Tomilin | .05 | .02 |
| ❑ 54 Alexander Alexeyev | .05 | .02 |
| ❑ 55 Roman Zolotov | .05 | .02 |
| ❑ 56 Konstantin Korotkov | .05 | .02 |
| ❑ 57 Laperriere Family | .05 | .02 |
| ❑ 58 Lacroix Family | .05 | .02 |
| ❑ 59 Manon Rheaume | 4.00 | 1.80 |
| ❑ 60 Hamrlik/Yashin/Rathje CL | .05 | .02 |
| ❑ 61 Viktor Kozlov CL | .05 | .02 |
| ❑ 62 Viktor Kozlov | .25 | .11 |
| ❑ 63 Denny Felsner CL | .05 | .02 |
| ❑ 64 Denny Felsner | .05 | .02 |
| ❑ 65 Darrin Madeley | .05 | .02 |
| ❑ 66 Mario Lemieux FLB | 1.00 | .45 |
| ❑ 67 Sandy Moger | .05 | .02 |
| ❑ 68 Dave Karpa | .05 | .02 |
| ❑ 69 Martin Jiranek | .05 | .02 |
| ❑ 70 Dwayne Norris | .05 | .02 |
| ❑ 71 Michael Stewart | .05 | .02 |
| ❑ 72 Joby Messier | .05 | .02 |
| ❑ 73 Mike Bales | .05 | .02 |
| ❑ 74 Scott Thomas | .05 | .02 |
| ❑ 75 Dan Laperriere | .05 | .02 |
| ❑ 76 Mike Lappin | .05 | .02 |
| ❑ 77 Eric Lacroix | .05 | .02 |
| ❑ 78 Martin Lacroix | .05 | .02 |
| ❑ 79 Scott LaGrand | .05 | .02 |
| ❑ 80 Jean-Yves Roy | .05 | .02 |
| ❑ 81 Scott Pellerin | .05 | .02 |
| ❑ 82 Rob Gaudreau | .05 | .02 |
| ❑ 83 Mike Boback | .05 | .02 |
| ❑ 84 Dixon Ward | .05 | .02 |
| ❑ 85 Jeff McLean | .05 | .02 |
| ❑ 86 Dallas Drake | .05 | .02 |
| ❑ 87 Bret Hedican | .05 | .02 |
| ❑ 88 Doug Zmolek | .05 | .02 |
| ❑ 89 Trent Klatt | .05 | .02 |
| ❑ 90 Larry Olimb | .05 | .02 |
| ❑ 91 Duane Derksen | .05 | .02 |
| ❑ 92 Doug MacDonald | .05 | .02 |
| ❑ 93 Dmitri Kvartalnov CL | .05 | .02 |
| ❑ 94 Jim Cummins | .05 | .02 |
| ❑ 95 Lonnie Loach | .05 | .02 |
| ❑ 96 Keith Jones | .05 | .02 |
| ❑ 97 Jason Woolley | .05 | .02 |
| ❑ 98 Rob Zamuner | .05 | .02 |
| ❑ 99 Brad Werenka | .05 | .02 |
| ❑ 100 Brent Grieve | .05 | .02 |
| ❑ 101 Sean Hill | .05 | .02 |
| ❑ 102 Keith Carney | .05 | .02 |
| ❑ 103 Peter Ciavaglia | .05 | .02 |
| ❑ 104 David Littman | .05 | .02 |
| ❑ 105 Bill Guerin | .25 | .11 |
| ❑ 106 Mikhail Kravets | .05 | .02 |
| ❑ 107 J.F. Quintin | .05 | .02 |
| ❑ 108 Mike Needham | .05 | .02 |
| ❑ 109 Jason Ruff | .05 | .02 |
| ❑ 110 Mike Vukonich | .05 | .02 |
| ❑ 111 Shawn McCosh | .05 | .02 |
| ❑ 112 Dave Tretowicz | .05 | .02 |
| ❑ 113 Todd Harkins | .05 | .02 |
| ❑ 114 Jason Muzzatti | .05 | .02 |
| ❑ 115 Paul Kruse | .05 | .02 |
| ❑ 116 Kevin Wortman | .05 | .02 |
| ❑ 117 Sean Burke | .05 | .02 |
| ❑ 118 Keith Gretzky | .05 | .02 |
| ❑ 119 Ray Whitney | .05 | .02 |
| ❑ 120 Dmitri Kvartalnov | .05 | .02 |
| ❑ SP Mario Lemieux FLB | 25.00 | 11.00 |
| ❑ AU2 Bure Brothers AU6000 | 40.00 | 18.00 |

## 1992 Classic Gold Promo

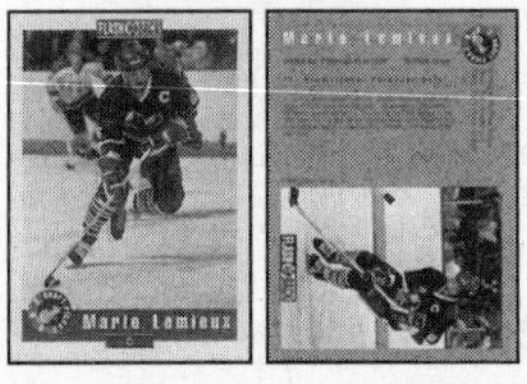

The front features a black-and-white action player photo bordered in white. The player's name is printed in a gold foil stripe beneath the picture, with the position given on a short black bar. On a gold background, the back has draft information, statistics, player profile, and a second black-and-white photo that is horizontally oriented. The card is unnumbered and has the disclaimer "For Promotional Purposes Only" printed on the back.

| | MINT | NRMT |
|---|---|---|
| COMPLETE SET (1) | 6.00 | 2.70 |
| COMMON CARD | 6.00 | 2.70 |
| ❑ NNO Mario Lemieux | 6.00 | 2.70 |

## 1992 Classic Gold

Classic also issued the 1992 Draft Picks set in a Gold version. The singles sell for between three and eight times the corresponding regular cards. Reportedly only 6,000 sets and 7,500 uncut sheets were produced. The sets were packaged in a walnut display case. The fronts feature posed and action color player photos bordered in white. The player's name is printed in a gold stripe beneath the picture, with the position given on a short black bar. On a gold background, the backs have draft information, statistics, player profile, and a second color photo that is horizontally oriented. The Gold factory sets also included an individually numbered card signed by Valeri and Pavel Bure.

| | MINT | NRMT |
|---|---|---|
| COMPLETE SET(121) | 75.00 | 34.00 |
| COMMON GOLD CARD (1-120) | .25 | .11 |
| *GOLD STARS: 3X TO 5X BASIC CARDS | | |
| ❑ AU Bure Brothers AU/6000 Pavel Bure Valeri Bure (Only Available In Gold Sets) | 40.00 | 18.00 |

## 1992 Classic LPs

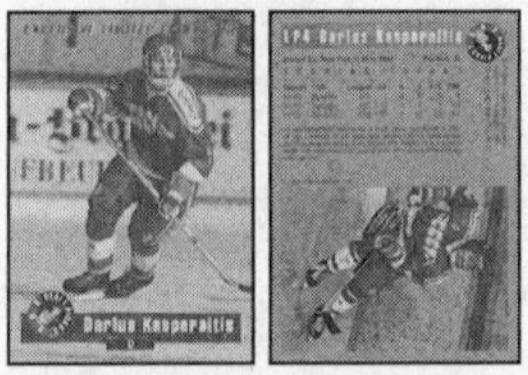

This ten-card standard-size set features hockey draft picks. The cards are numbered on the back with an "LP" prefix. The cards were random inserts in packs of 1992 Classic Hockey Draft Picks.

| | MINT | NRMT |
|---|---|---|
| COMPLETE SET (10) | 15.00 | 6.75 |
| COMMON CARD (1-10) | 1.00 | .45 |
| ❑ LP1 Roman Hamrlik | 2.00 | .90 |
| ❑ LP2 Alexei Yashin | 5.00 | 2.20 |
| ❑ LP3 Mike Rathje | 1.00 | .45 |
| ❑ LP4 Darius Kasparaitis | 1.00 | .45 |
| ❑ LP5 Cory Stillman | 1.00 | .45 |
| ❑ LP6 Dmitri Kvartalnov | 1.00 | .45 |
| ❑ LP7 David Wilkie | 1.00 | .45 |
| ❑ LP8 Curtis Bowen | 1.00 | .45 |
| ❑ LP9 Valeri Bure | 1.00 | .45 |
| ❑ LP10 Joby Messier | 1.00 | .45 |

## 1992-93 Classic Manon Rheaume C3 Presidential

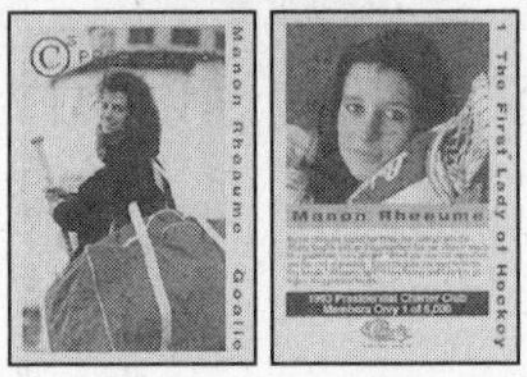

This standard-size card pictures Rheaume holding a hockey stick and carrying an equipment bag over her shoulder. The picture is bordered in white, and her name and position are printed on the wider right border. The Classic "C3 Presidential" logo is gold foil stamped across the top of the picture. The back has a color close-up photo and a player quote. Reportedly only 5,000 of these cards were produced.

| | MINT | NRMT |
|---|---|---|
| COMPLETE SET (1) | 10.00 | 4.50 |
| COMMON CARD | 10.00 | 4.50 |
| ❑ 1 Manon Rheaume | 10.00 | 4.50 |

## 1992-93 Classic Manon Rheaume Promo

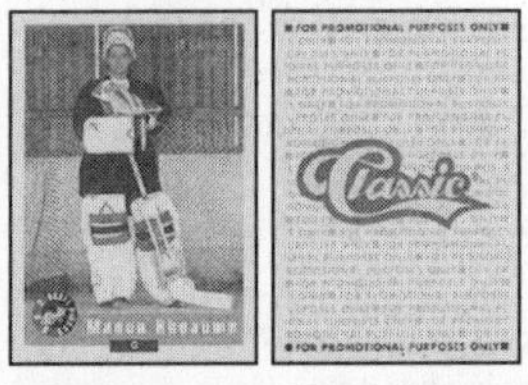

Manon Rheaume, professional hockey's first female player, signed her trading card for fans before the Atlanta Braves playoff game Wednesday, October 7, 1992. Sponsored by Power 99, a local radio station, this promotion was aimed at benefiting "Pennies from Heaven," an urban renewal movement championed by former President Jimmy Carter and Atlanta Braves third baseman Terry Pendleton. Fans who brought a jar of pennies or a 10.00 donation were given the autographed Rheaume promotional card; close to 1,000 cards were signed and about 2,500 promo bags were given away. The front of this standard size card features a posed color player photo with white borders. Her name appears in a gold stripe across the bottom of the picture. The words "A Classic First" are printed in gold at the upper right corner of the picture. The center back shows the yellow and green Classic logo. The disclaimer "For Promotional Purposes Only" is printed in black at the top and bottom and in gray over the rest of the card back.

| | MINT | NRMT |
|---|---|---|
| COMPLETE SET (1) | 10.00 | 4.50 |
| COMMON CARD | 10.00 | 4.50 |
| ❑ NNO Manon Rheaume | 10.00 | 4.50 |

## 1993 Classic Previews

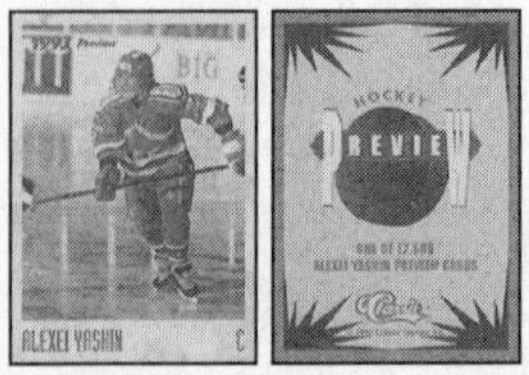

These five standard-size cards were inserted on an average of three per case of 1993 Classic Basketball Draft Picks. The fronts have a color action photo with the player's name at the bottom in the icy border. The backs say "preview" and tells that it is one of 17,500 preview cards of that player. The cards are unnumbered.

| | MINT | NRMT |
|---|---|---|
| COMPLETE SET (5) | 15.00 | 6.75 |
| COMMON CARD (HK1-HK5) | 1.00 | .45 |
| ❑ HK1 Alexandre Daigle | 1.00 | .45 |
| ❑ HK2 Manon Rheaume | 8.00 | 3.60 |
| ❑ HK3 Barry Richter | 1.00 | .45 |
| ❑ HK4 Teemu Selanne | 6.00 | 2.70 |
| ❑ HK5 Alexei Yashin | 2.00 | .90 |

## 1993 Classic Promos

These four standard-size promo cards feature gray-bordered glossy color player action shots on the fronts. The player's name and position appears in blue lettering within the bottom border. The back carries another color player action shot, but bordered in white. The player's biography and draft status are printed in black lettering within the broad lower border. The unnumbered Paul Kariya card was distributed at the San Francisco Labor Day Sports Collectors Convention, held in September 1993. The cards are numbered on the back with a "PR" prefix.

| | MINT | NRMT |
|---|---|---|
| COMPLETE SET (4) | 15.00 | 6.75 |
| COMMON CARD (1-3) | 2.00 | .90 |
| ❑ 1 Alexandre Daigle | 2.00 | .90 |
| ❑ 2 Jeff O'Neill Jason Bonsignore Jeff Friesen The Class of '94 | 2.00 | .90 |
| ❑ 3 Pavel Bure | 5.00 | 2.20 |
| ❑ NNO Paul Kariya | 7.50 | 3.40 |

## 1993 Classic

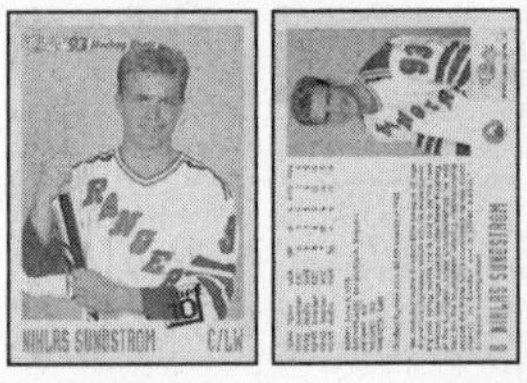

The 1993 Classic Hockey Draft set consists of 150 standard-size cards. Production was reported to be 14,500 sequentially-numbered ten-box cases. More than 15,000 autographed cards from Manon Rheaume, Doug Gilmour, Mark Recchi, Mike Bossy, Jeff O'Neill and other hockey stars were randomly inserted throughout the packs. Subsets featuring foil-stamped cards are Top 10, The Class of '94, The Daigle File, Flashbacks, College Champions, Manon Rheaume, and Hockey Art.

| | MINT | NRMT |
|---|---|---|
| COMPLETE SET (150) | 6.00 | 2.70 |
| COMMON CARD (1-150) | .05 | .02 |
| ❑ 1 Alexandre Daigle | .15 | .07 |
| ❑ 2 Chris Pronger | .15 | .07 |
| ❑ 3 Chris Gratton | .15 | .07 |
| ❑ 4 Paul Kariya | 1.50 | .70 |
| ❑ 5 Rob Niedermayer | .15 | .07 |
| ❑ 6 Viktor Kozlov | .05 | .02 |
| ❑ 7 Jason Arnott | .15 | .07 |
| ❑ 8 Niklas Sundstrom | .15 | .07 |
| ❑ 9 Todd Harvey | .05 | .02 |
| ❑ 10 Jocelyn Thibault | .75 | .35 |
| ❑ 11 Checklist 1 Top Draft Picks | .05 | .02 |
| ❑ 12 Pat Peake 1993 CHL POY | .05 | .02 |
| ❑ 13 Jason Allison | .50 | .23 |
| ❑ 14 Todd Bertuzzi | .15 | .07 |
| ❑ 15 Maxim Bets | .05 | .02 |
| ❑ 16 Curtis Bowen | .05 | .02 |
| ❑ 17 Kevin Brown | .05 | .02 |
| ❑ 18 Valeri Bure | .05 | .02 |
| ❑ 19 Jason Dawe | .05 | .02 |
| ❑ 20 Adam Deadmarsh | .05 | .02 |
| ❑ 21 Aaron Gavey | .05 | .02 |
| ❑ 22 Nathan Lafayette | .05 | .02 |
| ❑ 23 Eric Lecompte | .05 | .02 |
| ❑ 24 Manny Legace | .05 | .02 |
| ❑ 25 Mike Peca | .05 | .02 |
| ❑ 26 Denis Pederson | .05 | .02 |
| ❑ 27 Jeff Shantz | .05 | .02 |
| ❑ 28 Nick Stadjuhar | .05 | .02 |
| ❑ 29 Cory Stillman | .05 | .02 |
| ❑ 30 Michal Sykora | .05 | .02 |
| ❑ 31 Brent Tully | .05 | .02 |
| ❑ 32 Mike Wilson | .05 | .02 |
| ❑ 33 Junior Production Line Kevin Brown Pat Peake Bob Wren | .05 | .02 |
| ❑ 34 Checklist 2 Dynamic Duo Alexandre Daigle Alexei Yashin | .15 | .07 |
| ❑ 35 Antti Aalto | .05 | .02 |
| ❑ 36 Radim Bicanek | .05 | .02 |
| ❑ 37 Vladimir Chebaturkin | .05 | .02 |
| ❑ 38 Alexander Cherbayev | .05 | .02 |
| ❑ 39 Markus Ketterer | .05 | .02 |
| ❑ 40 Saku Koivu | .75 | .35 |
| ❑ 41 Vladimir Krechin | .05 | .02 |
| ❑ 42 Alexei Kudashov | .05 | .02 |
| ❑ 43 Janne Laukkanen | .05 | .02 |
| ❑ 44 Janne Niinimaa | .50 | .23 |
| ❑ 45 Juha Riihijarvi | .05 | .02 |
| ❑ 46 Nikolai Tsulygin | .05 | .02 |
| ❑ 47 Vesa Viitakoski | .05 | .02 |
| ❑ 48 David Vyborny | .05 | .02 |
| ❑ 49 Nikolai Zavarukhin | .05 | .02 |
| ❑ 50 Alexandre Daigle | .35 | .16 |

1991 QMJHL Draft
❑ 51 Alexandre Daigle .35 .16
1991-92 QMJHL Rookie
❑ 52 Alexandre Daigle .35 .16
1992 CHL ROY
❑ 53 Alexandre Daigle .35 .16
Emerging Superstar
1992-93
❑ 54 Alexandre Daigle .35 .16
First Draft Pick
❑ 55 Jim Montgomery .05 .02
❑ 56 Mike Dunham .05 .02
❑ 57 Matt Martin .05 .02
❑ 58 Garth Snow .15 .07
❑ 59 Shawn Walsh .05 .02
❑ 60 Mark Bavis .05 .02
Mike Davis
❑ 61 Scott Chartier .05 .02
❑ 62 Craig Darby .05 .02
❑ 63 Ted Drury .05 .02
❑ 64 Steve Dubinsky .05 .02
❑ 65 Joe Frederick .05 .02
❑ 66 Cammi Granato 1.50 .70
❑ 67 Brett Hauer .05 .02
❑ 68 Jon Hillebrandt .05 .02
❑ 69 Ryan Hughes .05 .02
❑ 70 Dean Hulett .05 .02
❑ 71 Kevin O'Sullivan .05 .02
❑ 72 Dan Plante .05 .02
❑ 73 Derek Plante .05 .02
❑ 74 Travis Richards .05 .02
❑ 75 Barry Richter .05 .02
❑ 76 David Roberts .05 .02
❑ 77 Chris Rogles .05 .02
❑ 78 Jon Rohloff .05 .02
❑ 79 Brian Rolston .05 .02
❑ 80 David Sacco .05 .02
❑ 81 Brian Savage .05 .02
❑ 82 Mike Smith .05 .02
❑ 83 Chris Tamer .05 .02
❑ 84 Chris Therien .05 .02
❑ 85 Aaron Ward .05 .02
❑ 86 Russian Celebration .05 .02
❑ 87 Vyacheslav Butsayev .05 .02
❑ 88 Jan Kaminsky .05 .02
❑ 89 Alexander Karpovtsev .05 .02
❑ 90 Valeri Karpov .05 .02
❑ 91 Sergei Petrenko .05 .02
❑ 92 Andrei Sapozhnikov .05 .02
❑ 93 Sergei Sorokin .05 .02
❑ 94 German Titov .05 .02
❑ 95 Andrei Trefilov .05 .02
❑ 96 Alexei Yashin .15 .07
❑ 97 Dimitri Yushkevich .05 .02
❑ 98 Radek Bonk .15 .07
❑ 99 Jason Bonsignore .05 .02
❑ 100 Brad Brown .05 .02
❑ 101 Chris Drury 2.00 .90
❑ 102 Jeff Friesen .15 .07
❑ 103 Sean Haggerty .05 .02
❑ 104 Jeff Kealty .05 .02
❑ 105 Alexander Kharlamov .05 .02
❑ 106 Stanislav Neckar .05 .02
❑ 107 Tom O'Connor .05 .02
❑ 108 Jeff O'Neill .15 .07
❑ 109 Deron Quint .15 .07
❑ 110 Vadim Sharifianov .05 .02
❑ 111 Oleg Tverdovsky .15 .07
❑ 112 Manon Rheaume COMIC .75 .35
❑ 113 Paul Kariya COMIC .75 .35
❑ 114 Alexandre Daigle COMIC .15 .07
❑ 115 Jeff O'Neill COMIC .15 .07
❑ 116 Mike Bossy .05 .02
❑ 117 Pavel Bure .75 .35
❑ 118 Chris Chelios .15 .07
❑ 119 Doug Gilmour .15 .07
❑ 120 Roman Hamrlik .15 .07
❑ 121 Jari Kurri .05 .02
❑ 122 Alexander Mogilny .15 .07
❑ 123 Felix Potvin 1.00 .45
❑ 124 Teemu Selanne 1.00 .45
❑ 125 Tommy Soderstrom .05 .02
❑ 126 Mike Bales .05 .02
❑ 127 Jozef Cierny .05 .02
❑ 128 Ivan Droppa .05 .02
❑ 129 Anders Eriksson .15 .07
❑ 130 Anatoli Fedotov .05 .02
❑ 131 Martin Gendron .05 .02
❑ 132 Daniel Guerard .05 .02
❑ 133 Corey Hirsch .15 .07
❑ 134 Milos Holan .05 .02
❑ 135 Kenny Jonsson .15 .07
❑ 136 Steven King .05 .02
❑ 137 Alexei Kovalev .15 .07
❑ 138 Sergei Krivokrasov .05 .02
❑ 139 Mats Lindgren .05 .02
❑ 140 Grant Marshall .05 .02
❑ 141 Jesper Mattsson .05 .02
❑ 142 Sandy McCarthy .05 .02
❑ 143 Dean Melanson .05 .02
❑ 144 Robert Petrovicky .05 .02
❑ 145 Mike Rathje .05 .02
❑ 146 Manon Rheaume 2.00 .90
❑ 147 Claude Savoie .05 .02
❑ 148 Mikhail Shtalenkov .15 .07
❑ 149 Manon Rheaume 2.00 .90
A Season To Remember
❑ 150 Manon Rheaume 2.00 .90
Up Close And Personal
❑ MR1 Manon Rheaume Acetate 25.00 11.00
❑ AU1 Mike Bossy AU/975 30.00 13.50
❑ AU2 Pavel Bure AU/900 80.00 36.00
❑ AU3 Chris Chelios AU/1800 40.00 18.00
❑ AU4 Doug Gilmour AU/1850 40.00 18.00
❑ AU5 Alexander Mogilny/950 40.00 18.00
❑ AU6 Jim Montgomery AU/1800 6.00 2.70
❑ AU7 Rob Niedermayer AU/2500 30.00 13.50
❑ AU8 Jeff O'Neill AU/2225 25.00 11.00
❑ AU9 Pat Peake AU/790 10.00 4.50
❑ AU10 Mark Recchi AU/1725 30.00 13.50
❑ AU11 Manon Rheaume AU/1500 80.00 36.00
❑ AU12 Geoff Sanderson AU/875 25.00 11.00

## 1993 Classic Class of '94

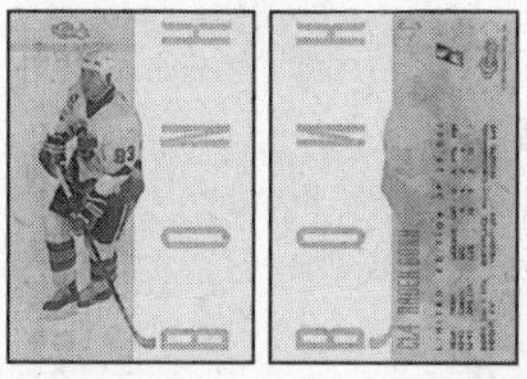

These standard size cards were randomly inserted throughout the foil packs. The cards are acetates and the player's last name is in capital letters in the clear potion. The fronts also have a color action photo of the player. The backs have player statistics. The cards are numbered on the back with a "CL" prefix.

| | MINT | NRMT |
|---|---|---|
| COMPLETE SET (7) | 12.00 | 5.50 |
| COMMON CARD (CL1-CL7) | 1.50 | .70 |

❑ CL1 Jeff O'Neill 2.00 .90
❑ CL2 Jason Bonsignore 1.50 .70
❑ CL3 Jeff Friesen 4.00 1.80
❑ CL4 Radek Bonk 1.50 .70
❑ CL5 Deron Quint 2.50 1.10
❑ CL6 Vadim Sharifianov 1.50 .70
❑ CL7 Tom O'Connor 1.50 .70

## 1993 Classic Crash Numbered

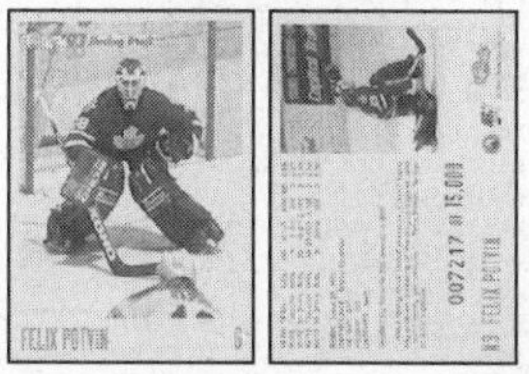

This 10-card standard-size set was randomly inserted throughout the foil packs and 15,000 individually numbered copies were made of each. The fronts have a color action photo with the player's name at the bottom in the icy border. The backs have a color photo on the right-side and player information and statistics on the left. The cards are numbered on the back with a "N" prefix.

| | MINT | NRMT |
|---|---|---|
| COMPLETE SET (10) | 120.00 | 55.00 |
| COMMON CARD (N1-N10) | 3.00 | 1.35 |

❑ N1 Alexandre Daigle 8.00 3.60
❑ N2 Paul Kariya 25.00 11.00
❑ N3 Jeff O'Neill 3.00 1.35
❑ N4 Jason Bonsignore 3.00 1.35
❑ N5 Teemu Selanne 15.00 6.75
❑ N6 Pavel Bure 20.00 9.00
❑ N7 Alexander Mogilny 8.00 3.60
❑ N8 Manon Rheaume 25.00 11.00
❑ N9 Felix Potvin 10.00 4.50
❑ N10 Radek Bonk 3.00 1.35

## 1993 Classic Team Canada

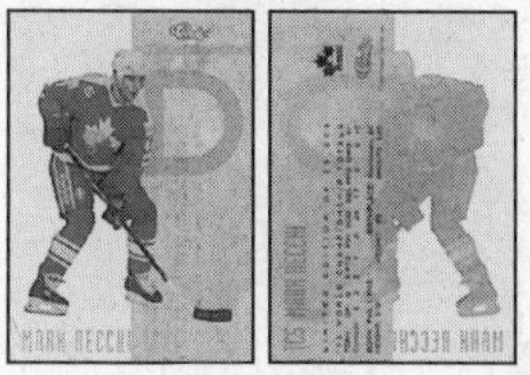

This seven-card standard size set was randomly inserted throughout the foil packs. These acetate cards have a color action photo on the left clear portion with player name at the bottom. The right-side has a letter so the complete set spells Canada. The backs have the player's name and statistics. The cards are numbered on the back with a "TC" prefix.

| | MINT | NRMT |
|---|---|---|
| COMPLETE SET (7) | 15.00 | 6.75 |
| COMMON CARD (TC1-TC7) | 2.00 | .90 |

❑ TC1 Greg Johnson 2.00 .90
❑ TC2 Paul Kariya 8.00 3.60
❑ TC3 Brian Savage 2.00 .90
❑ TC4 Bill Ranford 2.00 .90
❑ TC5 Mark Recchi 2.00 .90
❑ TC6 Geoff Sanderson 2.00 .90
❑ TC7 Adam Graves 2.00 .90

## 1993 Classic Top Ten

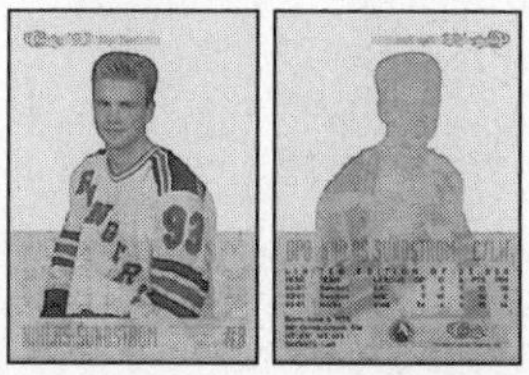

Measuring the standard-size, these ten acetate cards were randomly inserted throughout the foil packs. The cards have a color action photo, visible on both sides. the backs also have player statistics. The cards are numbered on the back with a "DP" prefix.

| | MINT | NRMT |
|---|---|---|
| COMPLETE SET (10) | 20.00 | 9.00 |
| COMMON CARD (DP1-DP10) | 1.00 | .45 |

❑ DP1 Alexandre Daigle 2.00 .90
❑ DP2 Chris Pronger 1.50 .70
❑ DP3 Chris Gratton 2.00 .90
❑ DP4 Paul Kariya 8.00 3.60
❑ DP5 Rob Niedermayer 2.50 1.10
❑ DP6 Viktor Kozlov 1.00 .45
❑ DP7 Jason Arnott 2.50 1.10
❑ DP8 Niklas Sundstrom 2.50 1.10
❑ DP9 Todd Harvey 1.00 .45
❑ DP10 Jocelyn Thibault 5.00 2.20

## 1993 Classic Pro Prospects Prototypes

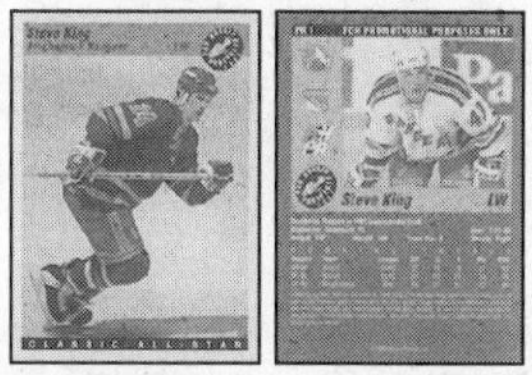

These three standard-size promo cards were issued to show the design of the 1993 Classic Pro Hockey Prospects set. Inside white borders, the fronts display color action player photos. A color bar edges the top of each picture and carries the player's name, team, and position. Also a black bar edges the bottom of each picture. On a gray background, the backs feature a color close-up photo, logos, biographical information, statistics, and career summary. A black bar that accents the top carries the card number and the disclaimer "For Promotional Purposes Only".

| | MINT | NRMT |
|---|---|---|
| COMPLETE SET (3) | 8.00 | 3.60 |
| COMMON CARD (PR1-PR3) | 1.50 | .70 |

❑ PR1 Steve King 1.50 .70
❑ PR2 Manon Rheaume 6.00 2.70
❑ PR3 Rob Gaudreau 1.50 .70

## 1993 Classic Pro Prospects

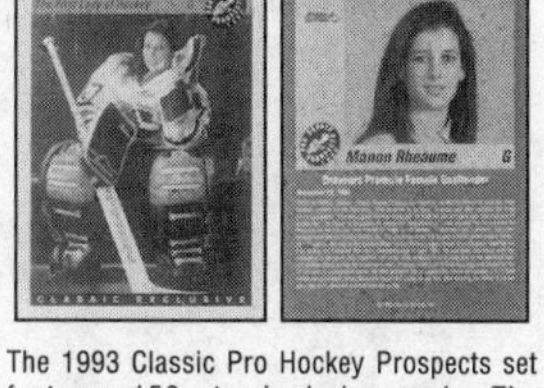

The 1993 Classic Pro Hockey Prospects set features 150 standard-size cards. The production run was 6,500 sequentially numbered cases, and female hockey phenom Manon Rheaume autographed 6,500 cards for random insertion into the foil packs. Inside white borders, the fronts display color action player photos. A color bar edges the top of each picture and carries the player's name, team, and position. On the subset cards, a black bar edges the bottom of the picture. On a gray background, the backs feature a color close-up photo, logos, biographical information, statistics, and career summary. The set includes a Manon Rheaume subset (1-7), a Minor League Graduate subset (31-34), a 1993 Draft Prospect subset (93-98), and, scattered throughout the set, 24 cards of the hottest AHL and IHL All-Stars of the 1992-93 season.

| | MINT | NRMT |
|---|---|---|
| COMPLETE SET (150) | 10.00 | 4.50 |
| COMMON CARD (1-150) | .05 | .02 |

❑ 1 Manon Rheaume 2.00 .90
Draveurs Promote
Female Goaltender
❑ 2 Manon Rheaume 2.00 .90
Quebec League Welcomes
Female Netminder
❑ 3 Manon Rheaume 2.00 .90
Woman Plays
Preseason Game
❑ 4 Manon Rheaume 2.00 .90
Atlanta Knights Sign
Female Netminder
❑ 5 Manon Rheaume 2.00 .90
Rheaume Makes Pro
Hockey History
❑ 6 Manon Rheaume 2.00 .90
Standing Ovation For
Hockey Pioneer
❑ 7 Manon Rheaume 2.00 .90
Rheaume Has Golden
Touch In Finland
❑ 8 Oleg Petrov .05 .02
❑ 9 Shjon Podein .05 .02
❑ 10 Alexei Kovalev AS .25 .11
❑ 11 Roman Oksiuta .05 .02
❑ 12 Dave Tomlinson .05 .02
❑ 13 Jason Miller .05 .02
❑ 14 Andrew McKim .05 .02
❑ 15 Dallas Drake .05 .02
❑ 16 Rob Gaudreau .05 .02
❑ 17 Darrin Madeley .05 .02
❑ 18 Scott Pellerin .05 .02
❑ 19 Scott Thomas .05 .02
❑ 20 Chris Tancill AS .05 .02
❑ 21 Patrick Kjellberg .05 .02
❑ 22 Jim Dowd .05 .02
❑ 23 Daniel Gauthier .05 .02
❑ 24 Mark Beaufait .05 .02
❑ 25 Milan Tichy AS .05 .02
❑ 26 Chris Osgood .75 .35
❑ 27 Charles Poulin .05 .02
❑ 28 Patrick Lebeau .05 .02
❑ 29 Chris Govedaris .05 .02
❑ 30 Andrei Trefilov AS .05 .02
❑ 31 Kevin Stevens MLG .05 .02
❑ 32 Dmitri Kvartalnov MLG .05 .02
❑ 33 Patrick Roy MLG 1.50 .70
❑ 34 Mark Recchi MLG .05 .02
❑ 35 Adam Oates MLG .20 .09
❑ 36 Patrick Augusta .05 .02
❑ 37 Gerry Fleming .05 .02
❑ 38 Sergei Krivokrasov .05 .02
❑ 39 Mike O'Neill .05 .02
❑ 40 Darrin Madeley AS .05 .02
❑ 41 Lindsay Vallis .05 .02
❑ 42 Todd Nelson .05 .02
❑ 43 Keith Jones .05 .02
❑ 44 Howie Rosenblatt .05 .02
❑ 45 Jason Ruff AS .05 .02
❑ 46 Robert Lang .05 .02
❑ 47 Andre Faust .05 .02
❑ 48 Steve Bancroft .05 .02
❑ 49 Iain Fraser .05 .02
❑ 50 Roman Hamrlik AS .25 .11
❑ 51 Pierre Sevigny .05 .02
❑ 52 Jeff Levy .05 .02
❑ 53 Len Barrie .05 .02
❑ 54 David Goverde .05 .02
❑ 55 Vladimir Malakhov AS .05 .02
❑ 56 Scott White .05 .02
❑ 57 Dmitri Motkov .05 .02
❑ 58 Jason Herter .05 .02
❑ 59 Drake Berehowsky .05 .02
❑ 60 Steve King AS .05 .02
❑ 61 Doug Barrault .05 .02
❑ 62 Martin Hamrlik .05 .02
❑ 63 Kevin Miehm .05 .02
❑ 64 Shaun Van Allen .05 .02
❑ 65 Corey Hirsch AS .25 .11
❑ 66 Dwayne Norris .05 .02
❑ 67 Petr Hrbek .05 .02
❑ 68 Philippe Boucher .05 .02
❑ 69 Denis Chervyakov .05 .02
❑ 70 Sergei Zubov AS .20 .09
❑ 71 Geoff Sarjeant .05 .02
❑ 72 Les Kuntar .05 .02
❑ 73 Byron Dafoe .75 .35
❑ 74 Checklist .05 .02
Alexei Kovalev
Sergei Zubov
Steve King
Corey Hirsch
❑ 75 Alexander Andrievski AS .05 .02
❑ 76 Checklist .05 .02
Joby Messier
Mitch Messier
❑ 77 Brian Sullivan .05 .02
❑ 78 Steve Larouche .05 .02
❑ 79 Denis Chasse .05 .02
❑ 80 Felix Potvin AS .75 .35
❑ 81 Josef Beranek .05 .02
❑ 82 Ken Klee .05 .02
❑ 83 Jozef Stumpel .05 .02
❑ 84 Andrew Verner .05 .02
❑ 85 Keith Osborne AS .05 .02
❑ 86 Igor Malykhin .05 .02
❑ 87 Gilbert Dionne .05 .02
❑ 88 Viktor Gordiouk .05 .02
❑ 89 Glen Murray .05 .02
❑ 90 Scott Pellerin AS .05 .02
❑ 91 Tommy Soderstrom .05 .02
❑ 92 Terry Chitaroni .05 .02
❑ 93 Viktor Kozlov .05 .02
❑ 94 Mikhail Shtalenkov .20 .09
❑ 95 Leonid Toropchenko .05 .02
❑ 96 Alex Galchenyuk .05 .02
❑ 97 Anatoli Fedotov .05 .02
❑ 98 Igor Chibirev .05 .02
❑ 99 Keith Gretzky .05 .02
❑ 100 Manon Rheaume 2.50 1.10
❑ 101 Sean Whyte .05 .02
❑ 102 Steve Konowalchuk .05 .02
❑ 103 Richard Borgo .05 .02
❑ 104 Paul DiPietro .05 .02
❑ 105 Patrik Carnback AS .05 .02
❑ 106 Mike Fountain .05 .02
❑ 107 Jamie Heward .05 .02
❑ 108 David St. Pierre .05 .02
❑ 109 Sean O'Donnell .05 .02
❑ 110 Greg Andrusak AS .05 .02
❑ 111 Damian Rhodes .20 .09
❑ 112 Ted Crowley .05 .02
❑ 113 Chris Taylor .05 .02
❑ 114 Terran Sandwith .05 .02
❑ 115 Jesse Belanger AS .05 .02
❑ 116 Justin Duberman .05 .02
❑ 117 Arturs Irbe .25 .11
❑ 118 Chris LiPuma .05 .02
❑ 119 Mike Torchia .05 .02
❑ 120 Niclas Andersson AS .05 .02
❑ 121 Rick Knickle .05 .02
❑ 122 Scott Gruhl .05 .02
❑ 123 Dave Michayluk .05 .02
❑ 124 Guy Leveque .05 .02
❑ 125 Scott Thomas AS .05 .02
❑ 126 Travis Green .05 .02
❑ 127 Joby Messier .05 .02
❑ 128 Victor Ignatjev .05 .02
❑ 129 Brad Tiley .05 .02
❑ 130 Grigori Panteleyev AS .05 .02
❑ 131 Vyatcheslav Butsayev .05 .02
❑ 132 Danny Lorenz .05 .02
❑ 133 Marty McInnis .05 .02
❑ 134 Ed Ronan .05 .02
❑ 135 Slava Kozlov AS .25 .11
❑ 136 Kevin St. Jacques .05 .02
❑ 137 Pavel Kostichkin .05 .02
❑ 138 Mike Hurlbut .05 .02
❑ 139 Tomas Forslund .05 .02
❑ 140 Rob Gaudreau AS .05 .02
❑ 141 Shawn Heaphy .05 .02
❑ 142 Radek Hamr .05 .02
❑ 143 Jaroslav Otevrel .05 .02
❑ 144 Keith Redmond .05 .02
❑ 145 Tom Pederson AS .05 .02
❑ 146 Jaroslav Modry .05 .02
❑ 147 Darren McCarty .05 .02
❑ 148 Terry Yake .05 .02
❑ 149 Ivan Droppa .05 .02
❑ 150 The VCR Line .05 .02
Shaun Van Allen
Dan Currie
Steven Rice
❑ AU1 Dmitri Kvartalnov 8.00 3.60
AU/4000
(Certified Autograph)
❑ AU2 Manon Rheaume 75.00 34.00
AU/6500
(Certified Autograph)

## 1993 Classic Pro Prospects BCs

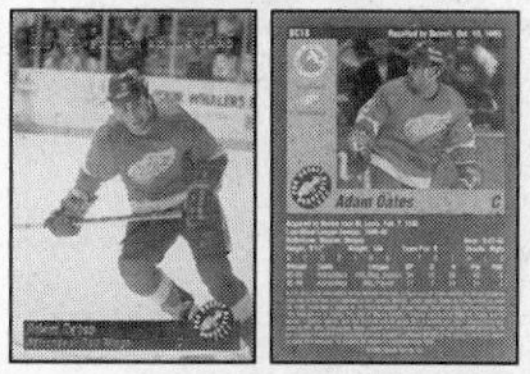

This 20-card standard-size set features full-bleed, color, action player photos. One BC card was inserted in each jumbo pack. A silver foil bar at the bottom contains the player's name, team, and position. According to the silver-foil print near the top of the photo, each card is one of 40,000 limited edition bonus cards. The backs are gray and display a player picture, biographical information, statistics, and career highlights. The cards are numbered on the back with a "BC" prefix.

| | MINT | NRMT |
|---|---|---|
| COMPLETE SET (20) | 30.00 | 13.50 |
| COMMON CARD (BC1-BC20) | .50 | .23 |

❑ BC1 Alexei Kovalev 1.50 .70
❑ BC2 Andrei Trefilov .50 .23
❑ BC3 Roman Hamrlik 1.50 .70
❑ BC4 Vladimir Malakhov .50 .23
❑ BC5 Corey Hirsch 1.00 .45
❑ BC6 Sergei Zubov 1.00 .45
❑ BC7 Felix Potvin 5.00 2.20
❑ BC8 Tommy Soderstrom .50 .23
❑ BC9 Viktor Kozlov .50 .23
❑ BC10 Manon Rheaume 8.00 3.60
❑ BC11 Jesse Belanger .50 .23
❑ BC12 Rick Knickle .50 .23
❑ BC13 Joby Messier .50 .23
❑ BC14 Vyacheslav Butsayev .50 .23
❑ BC15 Tomas Forslund .50 .23
❑ BC16 Jozef Stumpel 1.50 .70
❑ BC17 Dmitri Kvartalnov MLG .50 .23
❑ BC18 Adam Oates MLG 2.00 .90
❑ BC19 Dallas Drake .50 .23
❑ BC20 Mark Recchi MLG 2.00 .90

## 1993 Classic Pro Prospects LPs

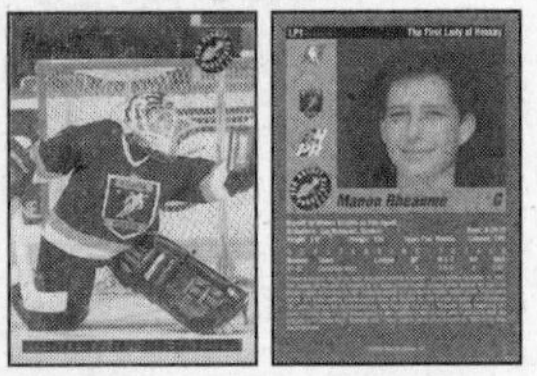

These five limited-print standard-size cards were randomly inserted throughout each case. The fronts feature full-bleed, color, posed and action player photos. A metallic aqua stripe across the top carries the player's name, team, and position. The Classic logo overlaps this stripe and the photo. In a black stripe at the bottom are the words, "Limited Edition 1 of 26,000." The backs display a small player photo that is bordered on two sides by a light gray area containing hockey organizations logos and the player's name and position. Below the picture are statistics, biographical information, and career highlights. This information is printed in white against a dark gray background. The cards are numbered on the back with an "LP" prefix.

| | MINT | NRMT |
|---|---|---|
| COMPLETE SET (5) | 30.00 | 13.50 |
| COMMON CARD (LP1-LP5) | 3.00 | 1.35 |
| ❑ LP1 Manon Rheaume | 20.00 | 9.00 |
| ❑ LP2 Alexei Kovalev | 5.00 | 2.20 |
| ❑ LP3 Rob Gaudreau | 3.00 | 1.35 |
| ❑ LP4 Viktor Kozlov | 3.00 | 1.35 |
| ❑ LP5 Dallas Drake | 3.00 | 1.35 |

## 1994 Classic Previews

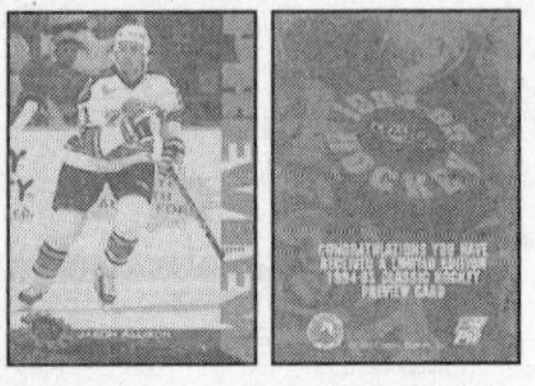

Randomly inserted in 1994 Classic basketball packs, this 5-card set measures the standard-size. The fronts feature full-bleed color action photos, except at the bottom where a color stripe carries the player's name. The word "PREVIEW" is printed vertically in large block letters running down the right edge. On a purple-tinted action photo, the backs display the Classic logo and a short congratulatory message. The cards are unnumbered and checklisted below in alphabetical order.

| | MINT | NRMT |
|---|---|---|
| COMPLETE SET (5) | 20.00 | 9.00 |
| COMMON CARD (HK1-HK5) | 2.00 | .90 |
| ❑ HK1 Jason Allison | 5.00 | 2.20 |
| ❑ HK2 Radek Bonk | 5.00 | 2.20 |
| ❑ HK3 Xavier Majic | 2.00 | .90 |
| ❑ HK4 Manon Rheaume | 15.00 | 6.75 |
| ❑ HK5 Oleg Tverdovsky | 5.00 | 2.20 |

## 1994 Classic

The 1994 Classic Hockey set consists of 120 standard-size cards. Production was reported at 6,000 U.S. and 2,000 Canadian 10-box foil cases. The fronts feature borderless color action player photos, with the player's name in a purple bar at the bottom. The city name of the player's drafting team is printed in large red letters alongside the right. The backs carry the player's name in large red letters alongside the left, as well as stats, biography and a short player profile. Subsets featured are 1994 First Round Picks (1-22) and College All-Americans (50-63). The Jason Arnott Canada World Champs card (numbered TC1) was randomly inserted into Canadian packs. Classic also offered a redemption program in which a collector sending in wrappers received various prizes. For each 216 wrappers redeemed a collector received either a Cam Neely or a Doug Gilmour autographed card. For each 360 wrappers redeemed, a Manon Rheaume autograph card was sent by Classic. The wrapper redemption ended December 1, 1994.

| | MINT | NRMT |
|---|---|---|
| COMPLETE SET (120) | 10.00 | 4.50 |
| COMMON CARD (1-120) | .05 | .02 |
| ❑ 1 Ed Jovanovski | .50 | .23 |
| ❑ 2 Oleg Tverdovsky | .20 | .09 |
| ❑ 3 Radek Bonk | .20 | .09 |
| ❑ 4 Jason Bonsignore | .05 | .02 |
| ❑ 5 Jeff O'Neill | .20 | .09 |
| ❑ 6 Ryan Smyth | .75 | .35 |
| ❑ 7 Jamie Storr | .40 | .18 |
| ❑ 8 Jason Wiemer | .20 | .09 |
| ❑ 9 Nolan Baumgartner | .05 | .02 |
| ❑ 10 Jeff Friesen | .30 | .14 |
| ❑ 11 Wade Belak | .05 | .02 |
| ❑ 12 Ethan Moreau | .05 | .02 |
| ❑ 13 Alexander Kharlamov | .05 | .02 |
| ❑ 14 Eric Fichaud | .50 | .23 |
| ❑ 15 Wayne Primeau | .05 | .02 |
| ❑ 16 Brad Brown | .05 | .02 |
| ❑ 17 Chris Dingman | .05 | .02 |
| ❑ 18 Evgeni Ryabchikov | .05 | .02 |
| ❑ 19 Yan Golubovsky | .05 | .02 |
| ❑ 20 Chris Wells | .05 | .02 |
| ❑ 21 Vadim Sharifjanov | .05 | .02 |
| ❑ 22 Dan Cloutier | .20 | .09 |
| ❑ 23 Checklist | .05 | .02 |
| ❑ 24 Jamie Langenbrunner | .05 | .02 |
| ❑ 25 Kenny Jonsson | .20 | .09 |
| ❑ 26 Curtis Bowen | .05 | .02 |
| ❑ 27 Sergei Gonchar | .05 | .02 |
| ❑ 28 Stefan Bergqvist | .05 | .02 |
| ❑ 29 Vaclav Prospal | .05 | .02 |
| ❑ 30 Valeri Bure | .05 | .02 |
| ❑ 31 Richard Shulmistra | .05 | .02 |
| ❑ 32 Chris Armstrong | .05 | .02 |
| ❑ 33 Brian Farrell | .05 | .02 |
| ❑ 34 Brian Savage | .05 | .02 |
| ❑ 35 Blaine Lacher | .25 | .11 |
| ❑ 36 Kevin Brown | .05 | .02 |
| ❑ 37 Joe Dziedzic | .05 | .02 |
| ❑ 38 Peter Ferraro | .05 | .02 |
| ❑ 39 Chris Ferraro | .05 | .02 |
| ❑ 40 Todd Harvey | .05 | .02 |
| ❑ 41 Eric Lecompte | .05 | .02 |
| ❑ 42 Dean Grillo | .05 | .02 |
| ❑ 43 Valeri Karpov | .05 | .02 |
| ❑ 44 Andrew Shier | .05 | .02 |
| ❑ 45 Vesa Viitakoski | .05 | .02 |
| ❑ 46 Xavier Majic | .05 | .02 |
| ❑ 47 Kevin Smyth | .05 | .02 |
| ❑ 48 Jeff Nelson | .05 | .02 |
| ❑ 49 Cory Stillman | .05 | .02 |
| ❑ 50 Clayton Beddoes | .05 | .02 |
| ❑ 51 Craig Conroy | .05 | .02 |
| ❑ 52 Dean Fedorchuk | .05 | .02 |
| ❑ 53 John Gruden | .05 | .02 |
| ❑ 54 Chris McAlpine | .05 | .02 |
| ❑ 55 Sean McCann | .05 | .02 |
| ❑ 56 Derek Maguire | .05 | .02 |
| ❑ 57 David Oliver | .10 | .05 |
| ❑ 58 Mike Pomichter | .05 | .02 |
| ❑ 59 Jamie Ram | .05 | .02 |
| ❑ 60 Shawn Reid | .05 | .02 |
| ❑ 61 Dwayne Roloson | .05 | .02 |
| ❑ 62 Steve Shields | .05 | .02 |
| ❑ 63 Brian Wiseman | .05 | .02 |
| ❑ 64 Drew Bannister | .05 | .02 |
| ❑ 65 Matt Johnson | .05 | .02 |
| ❑ 66 Scott Malone | .05 | .02 |
| ❑ 67 Sergei Berezin | .05 | .02 |
| ❑ 68 Chad Penney | .05 | .02 |
| ❑ 69 Ian Laperriere | .05 | .02 |
| ❑ 70 Andrei Nikolishin | .05 | .02 |
| ❑ 71 Kelly Fairchild | .05 | .02 |
| ❑ 72 Jere Lehtinen | .05 | .02 |
| ❑ 73 Ravil Gusmanov | .05 | .02 |
| ❑ 74 Checklist | .05 | .02 |
| ❑ 75 Neil Little | .05 | .02 |
| ❑ 76 Brian Rolston | .05 | .02 |
| ❑ 77 David Vyborny | .05 | .02 |
| ❑ 78 Nikolai Tsulygin | .05 | .02 |
| ❑ 79 Niklas Sundstrom | .05 | .02 |
| ❑ 80 Patrik Juhlin | .05 | .02 |
| ❑ 81 Dan Plante | .05 | .02 |
| ❑ 82 Brandon Convery | .05 | .02 |
| ❑ 83 Nick Stajduhar | .05 | .02 |
| ❑ 84 Garth Snow | .05 | .02 |
| ❑ 85 Corey Hirsch | .20 | .09 |
| ❑ 86 Craig Darby | .05 | .02 |
| ❑ 87 Andrei Nazarov | .05 | .02 |
| ❑ 88 Todd Marchant | .05 | .02 |
| ❑ 89 Jeff Neilson | .05 | .02 |
| ❑ 90 Brendan Witt | .05 | .02 |
| ❑ 91 Denis Metlyuk | .05 | .02 |
| ❑ 92 Maxim Bets | .05 | .02 |
| ❑ 93 Sean Pronger | .05 | .02 |
| ❑ 94 Chris Tamer | .05 | .02 |
| ❑ 95 Saku Koivu | .75 | .35 |
| ❑ 96 Mattias Norstrom | .05 | .02 |
| ❑ 97 Ville Peltonen | .05 | .02 |
| ❑ 98 Rene Corbet | .05 | .02 |
| ❑ 99 Brent Gretzky | .05 | .02 |
| ❑ 100 Chris Marinucci | .05 | .02 |
| ❑ 101 Ian Moran | .05 | .02 |
| ❑ 102 Janne Laukkanen | .05 | .02 |
| ❑ 103 Todd Bertuzzi | .05 | .02 |
| ❑ 104 Darby Hendrickson | .05 | .02 |
| ❑ 105 Janne Niinimaa | .50 | .23 |
| ❑ 106 David Roberts | .05 | .02 |
| ❑ 107 Pat Neaton | .05 | .02 |
| ❑ 108 Mats Lindgren | .05 | .02 |
| ❑ 109 Todd Warriner | .05 | .02 |
| ❑ 110 Jason Allison | .05 | .02 |
| ❑ 111 Radim Bicanek | .05 | .02 |
| ❑ 112 Denis Pederson | .05 | .02 |
| ❑ 113 Viktor Kozlov | .05 | .02 |
| ❑ 114 Mike Murray | .05 | .02 |
| ❑ 115 Aaron Gavey | .05 | .02 |
| ❑ 116 Mike Peca | .05 | .02 |
| ❑ 117 Jason Zent | .05 | .02 |
| ❑ 118 Jason MacDonald | .05 | .02 |
| ❑ 119 Aaron Israel | .05 | .02 |
| ❑ 120 Manon Rheaume | 1.50 | .70 |
| ❑ TC1 Jason Arnott CWC | 15.00 | 6.75 |

## 1994 Classic Draft Gold

Each of the 120 regular issue cards was issued as a parallel set with a gold-foil stamp and inserted at a rate of one gold card per pack. The card design is identical to the regular issue, except that the city name is printed in gold-foil stamped letters. In addition, collectors could acquire gold cards by mail. If Classic received either 36 or 54 wrappers in their redemption program from any collector, the collector received 10 gold cards. If a collector mailed in 108 wrappers, there were 25 gold cards sent from Classic. The wrapper redemption program expired on December 1, 1994. Also, a complete gold factory set was available to collectors who redeemed the Field card from the "Rookie of the Year?" insert set/contest.

| | MINT | NRMT |
|---|---|---|
| COMPLETE SET (120) | 50.00 | 22.00 |
| COMMON GOLD CARD (1-120) | .20 | .09 |

*STARS: 1.5X TO 3X BASIC CARDS.

## 1994 Classic All-Americans

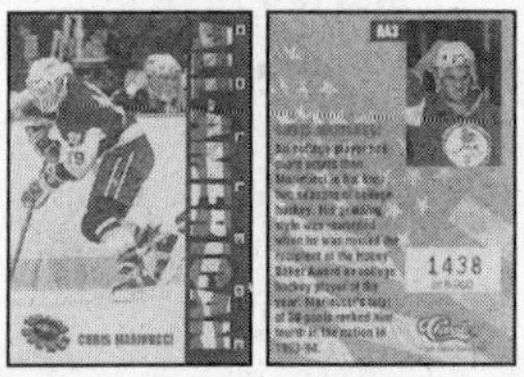

Found only in U.S. cases and inserted at a rate of one card per box, this ten-card standard-size set spotlights first team NCAA All-Americans. The fronts feature color action player photos, with the words "College All-American" in a black bar alongside the right. The player's name appears at the bottom. On a ghosted U.S. flag background, the backs carry a small color player photo with a short player profile. The cards are serially numbered out of 6,000 on the back.

| | MINT | NRMT |
|---|---|---|
| COMPLETE SET (10) | 20.00 | 9.00 |
| COMMON CARD (AA1-AA10) | 2.00 | .90 |
| ❑ AA1 Craig Conroy | 2.00 | .90 |
| ❑ AA2 John Gruden | 2.00 | .90 |
| ❑ AA3 Chris Marinucci | 2.00 | .90 |
| ❑ AA4 Chris McAlpine | 2.00 | .90 |
| ❑ AA5 Sean McCann | 2.00 | .90 |
| ❑ AA6 David Oliver | 2.00 | .90 |
| ❑ AA7 Mike Pomichter | 2.00 | .90 |
| ❑ AA8 Jamie Ram | 2.00 | .90 |
| ❑ AA9 Shawn Reid | 2.00 | .90 |
| ❑ AA10 Dwayne Roloson | 2.00 | .90 |

## 1994 Classic All-Rookie Team

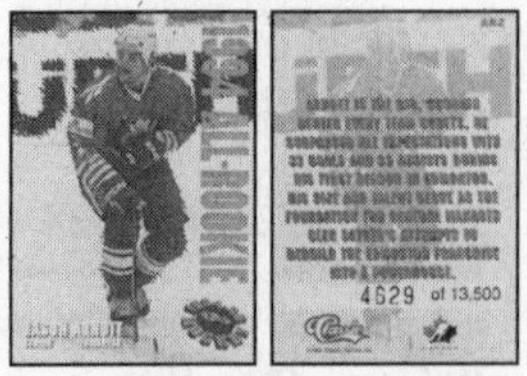

Inserted in both U.S. and Canadian cases at a rate of one card per box, this six-card set measures the standard size. The fronts have borderless color action player photos with the words "1994 All-Rookie" printed alongside the right, while the player's name, position and city appear on the bottom. On a ghosted background, the backs carry a player profile in big red letters. Each card is serially numbered out of 13,500.

| | MINT | NRMT |
|---|---|---|
| COMPLETE SET (6) | 25.00 | 11.00 |
| COMMON CARD (AR1-AR6) | 1.00 | .45 |
| ❑ AR1 Martin Brodeur | 15.00 | 6.75 |
| ❑ AR2 Jason Arnott | 4.00 | 1.80 |
| ❑ AR3 Alexei Yashin | 5.00 | 2.20 |
| ❑ AR4 Oleg Petrov | 1.00 | .45 |
| ❑ AR5 Chris Pronger | 4.00 | 1.80 |
| ❑ AR6 Alexander Karpovtsev | 1.00 | .45 |

## 1994 Classic Autographs

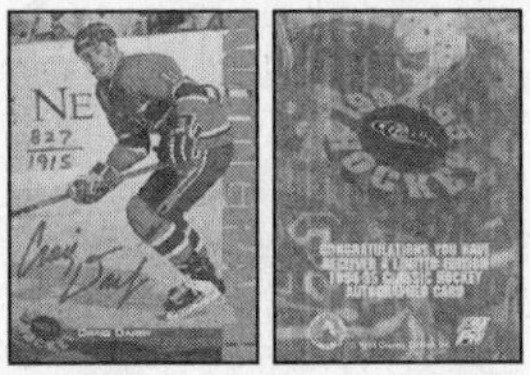

Inserted at a rate of one card per box, this 36-card set measures the standard size. The fronts feature borderless color action player photos with the word "Autograph" printed in big red letters along the right. The player's name appears in a purple bar at the bottom. Each player signed and hand numbered a certain amount of cards indicated in the checklist below. The backs carry a congratulatory message which serves to authenticate the signature. The autograph cards that correspond to the regular draft cards are listed in numerical order while those autograph cards not in the regular set are listed in alphabetical order. In addition to the insertion of one per box, these cards were redeemable on a random basis in exchange for sending 72 wrappers to Classic. The deadline for wrapper redemption was December 1, 1994.

| | MINT | NRMT |
|---|---|---|
| COMPLETE SET (36) | 350.00 | 160.00 |
| COMMON CARD | 5.00 | 2.20 |
| ❑ 3 Radek Bonk/4940 | 20.00 | 9.00 |
| ❑ 4 Jason Bonsignore/4300 | 10.00 | 4.50 |
| ❑ 5 Jeff O'Neill/5380 | 20.00 | 9.00 |
| ❑ 10 Jeff Friesen/6145 | 15.00 | 6.75 |
| ❑ 34 Brian Savage/4930 | 8.00 | 3.60 |
| ❑ 38 Peter Ferraro/4875 | 10.00 | 4.50 |
| ❑ 39 Chris Ferraro/4770 | 5.00 | 2.20 |
| ❑ 76 Brian Rolston/2400 | 12.00 | 5.50 |
| ❑ 86 Craig Darby/1915 | 5.00 | 2.20 |
| ❑ 94 Chris Tamer/1900 | 5.00 | 2.20 |
| ❑ 106 David Roberts/1970 | 5.00 | 2.20 |
| ❑ NNO Barry Richter/1935 | 5.00 | 2.20 |
| ❑ NNO Doug Gilmour/1950 | 30.00 | 13.50 |
| ❑ NNO Chris Gratton/2000 | 15.00 | 6.75 |
| ❑ NNO Rob Niedermayer/950 | 20.00 | 9.00 |
| ❑ NNO Derek Plante/1970 | 10.00 | 4.50 |
| ❑ NNO Manon Rheaume/2400 | 60.00 | 27.00 |
| ❑ NNO Mike Dunham/1955 | 15.00 | 6.75 |
| ❑ NNO Travis Richards/1950 | 5.00 | 2.20 |
| ❑ NNO Brett Hauer/1930 | 5.00 | 2.20 |
| ❑ NNO Jon Hillebrandt/1570 | 5.00 | 2.20 |
| ❑ NNO Ryan Hughes/1940 | 5.00 | 2.20 |
| ❑ NNO Dean Hulett/1955 | 5.00 | 2.20 |
| ❑ NNO Mark Bavis/1955 | 5.00 | 2.20 |
| ❑ NNO Brett Harkins/1885 | 5.00 | 2.20 |
| ❑ NNO Chris Rogles/1920 | 5.00 | 2.20 |
| ❑ NNO Fred Knipscheer/1945 | 5.00 | 2.20 |
| ❑ NNO Jon Rohloff/2010 | 5.00 | 2.20 |
| ❑ NNO David Sacco/1975 | 5.00 | 2.20 |
| ❑ NNO Cam Stewart/970 | 5.00 | 2.20 |
| ❑ NNO Jim Storm/1950 | 5.00 | 2.20 |
| ❑ NNO Aaron Ward/1965 | 5.00 | 2.20 |
| ❑ NNO Cam Neely | 30.00 | 13.50 |
| ❑ NNO John Lilley/2460 | 5.00 | 2.20 |
| ❑ NNO Ted Drury/1920 | 5.00 | 2.20 |
| ❑ NNO Dallas Drake/960 | 5.00 | 2.20 |
| ❑ NNO Scott Chartier/1930 | 5.00 | 2.20 |
| ❑ NNO Stanislav Neckar/4645 | 5.00 | 2.20 |
| ❑ NNO Eric Fenton/1845 | 5.00 | 2.20 |

## 1994 Classic CHL All-Stars

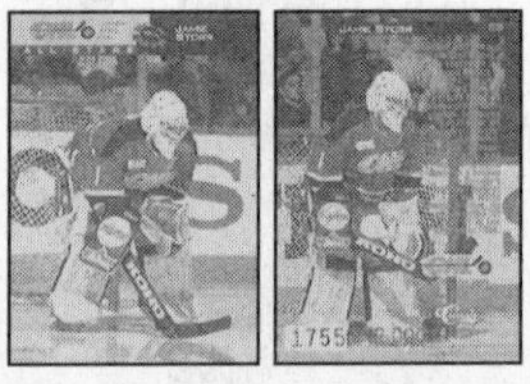

This 10-card standard-size set was randomly inserted in Canadian foil packs only. The fronts have a color action photo with the player's name at the top along with the CHL emblem. The backs have a full-color action photo with player information and the number printed out of 2,000. The cards are numbered on the back with a "C" prefix.

| | MINT | NRMT |
|---|---|---|
| COMPLETE SET (10) | 50.00 | 22.00 |
| COMMON CARD (C1-C10) | 3.00 | 1.35 |
| ❑ C1 Jason Allison | 8.00 | 3.60 |
| ❑ C2 Yanick Dube | 3.00 | 1.35 |
| ❑ C3 Eric Fichaud | 8.00 | 3.60 |
| ❑ C4 Jeff Friesen | 6.00 | 2.70 |
| ❑ C5 Aaron Gavey | 3.00 | 1.35 |
| ❑ C6 Ed Jovanovski | 8.00 | 3.60 |
| ❑ C7 Jeff O'Neill | 3.00 | 1.35 |
| ❑ C8 Ryan Smyth | 8.00 | 3.60 |
| ❑ C9 Jamie Storr | 6.00 | 2.70 |
| ❑ C10 Brendan Witt | 3.00 | 1.35 |

## 1994 Classic CHL Previews

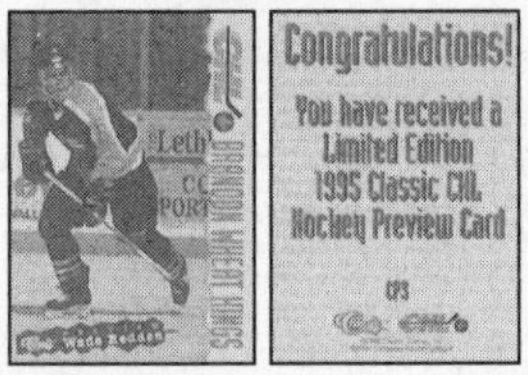

Randomly inserted in Canadian foil packs only, this six-card standard-size set was created to preview Classic's 1995 CHL set. Unfortunately, the company was unable to complete negotiations with the league, and the full set was never created.

| | MINT | NRMT |
|---|---|---|
| COMPLETE SET (6) | 15.00 | 6.75 |
| COMMON CARD (CP1-CP6) | 3.00 | 1.35 |
| ❑ CP1 Wayne Primeau | 3.00 | 1.35 |
| ❑ CP2 Eric Fichaud | 3.00 | 1.35 |
| ❑ CP3 Wade Redden | 3.00 | 1.35 |
| ❑ CP4 Jason Doig | 3.00 | 1.35 |
| ❑ CP5 Vitali Yachmenev | 3.00 | 1.35 |
| ❑ CP6 Nolan Baumgartner | 3.00 | 1.35 |

## 1994 Classic Enforcers

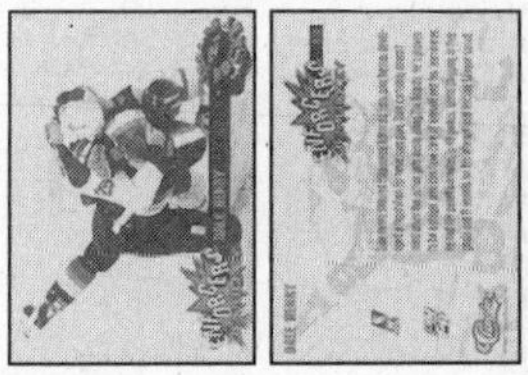

Featured in both U.S. and Canadian cases and inserted on average of three cards per box, this ten-card standard-size set captures the toughest players in the minor leagues. The horizontal fronts feature color action player photos with the player's name in a black bar at the bottom. The set name also appears at the bottom. On a background consisting of a crude drawing of the front photo, the back carries a player profile.

| | MINT | NRMT |
|---|---|---|
| COMPLETE SET (10) | 12.00 | 5.50 |
| COMMON CARD (E1-E10) | 1.50 | .70 |
| ❑ E1 Donald Brashear | 2.00 | .90 |
| ❑ E2 Daniel Lacroix | 1.50 | .70 |
| ❑ E3 Dale Henry | 1.50 | .70 |
| ❑ E4 John Badduke | 1.50 | .70 |
| ❑ E5 Corey Schwab | 1.50 | .70 |
| ❑ E6 Craig Martin | 1.50 | .70 |
| ❑ E7 Kerry Clark | 1.50 | .70 |
| ❑ E8 Kevin Kaminski | 1.50 | .70 |
| ❑ E9 Jim Kyte | 1.50 | .70 |
| ❑ E10 Mark DeSantis | 1.50 | .70 |

## 1994 Classic Enforcers Promo

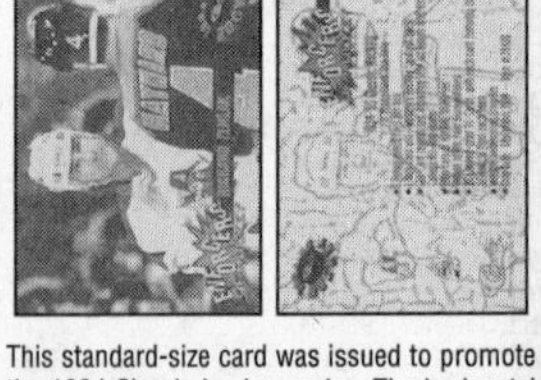

This standard-size card was issued to promote the 1994 Classic hockey series. The horizontal front features Richard Zemlak preparing to fight another player. On a background consisting of a crude drawing of the front photo, the back presents an advertisement for Classic hockey cards. The card is numbered on the back in the upper right corner.

| | MINT | NRMT |
|---|---|---|
| COMPLETE SET (1) | 1.00 | .45 |
| COMMON CARD | 1.00 | .45 |
| ❑ PR1 Richard Zemlak | 1.00 | .45 |

## 1994 Classic Draft Prospects

Found only in U.S. cases and inserted at a rate of one card per box, this ten-card standard-size set features players expected to be selected early in the 1995 NHL entry draft. The fronts feature the player's name in capital

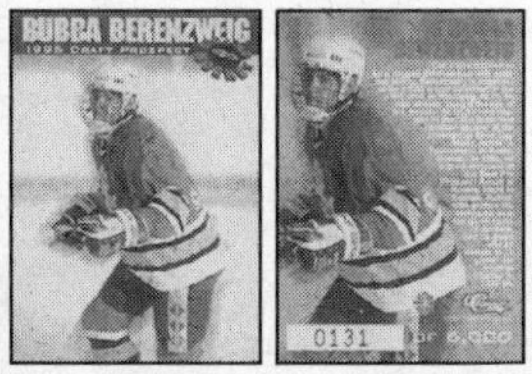

letters on the top with a small notation underneath that he is a 1995 Draft Prospect. The majority of the card is devoted to the player's photo. The reverse of the card features the player's photo on the left side of the cards with a biography on the right side. The cards are numbered in the top left corner. Each card is serially numbered out of 6,000 on the bottom.

| | MINT | NRMT |
|---|---|---|
| COMPLETE SET (10) | 30.00 | 13.50 |
| COMMON CARD (DP1-DP10) | 2.00 | .90 |
| ❑ DP1 Bubba Berenzweig | 2.00 | .90 |
| ❑ DP2 Aki-Petteri Berg | 2.00 | .90 |
| ❑ DP3 Chad Kilger | 2.00 | .90 |
| ❑ DP4 Daymond Langkow | 2.00 | .90 |
| ❑ DP5 Alyn McCauley | 10.00 | 4.50 |
| ❑ DP6 Igor Melyakov | 2.00 | .90 |
| ❑ DP7 Erik Rasmussen | 8.00 | 3.60 |
| ❑ DP8 Marty Reasoner | 6.00 | 2.70 |
| ❑ DP9 Scott Roche | 2.00 | .90 |
| ❑ DP10 Petr Sykora | 8.00 | 3.60 |

## 1994 Classic Picks

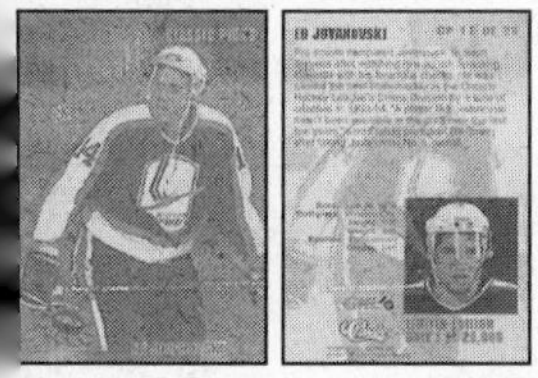

his five-card standard-size set was randomly nserted in packs. The fronts feature color ction photos with the player's name and the lassic logo at the bottom. The backs carry the layer's name in the upper left, card number in he upper right, career and biographical nformation, logos, and a small color player hoto.

| | MINT | NRMT |
|---|---|---|
| OMPLETE SET (5) | 25.00 | 11.00 |
| OMMON CARD (CP11-CP15).. | 2.00 | .90 |
| CP11 Ed Jovanovski | 5.00 | 2.20 |
| CP12 Oleg Tverdovsky | 4.00 | 1.80 |
| CP13 Radek Bonk | 2.00 | .90 |
| CP14 Jason Allison | 5.00 | 2.20 |
| CP15 Manon Rheaume | 15.00 | 6.75 |

## 1994 Classic ROY Sweepstakes

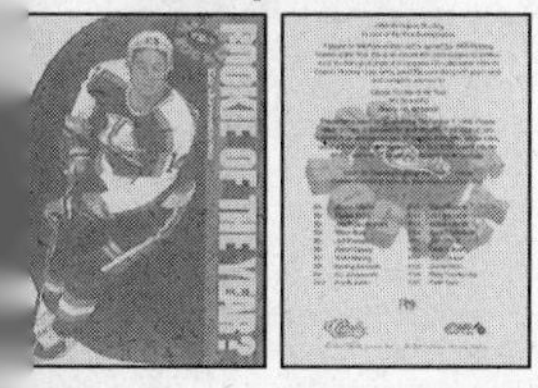

is 20-card standard-size set was featured in S. and Canadian cases and inserted on erage of five cards per case. Holders of the nning Field Card could redeem it for a mplete set of 1994 Classic Hockey Gold rds. The fronts feature a color action player tout superimposed over a large hockey ck. The words "Rookie of the Year?" and the ayer's name appear along the right. The cks carry the checklist, along with formation on how to claim the prize. The adline for redeeming cards was September 1995.

| | MINT | NRMT |
|---|---|---|
| MPLETE SET (20) | 60.00 | 27.00 |
| MMON CARD (R1-R20) | 1.00 | .45 |
| R1 Jason Allison | 5.00 | 2.20 |
| R2 Radek Bonk | 2.00 | .90 |
| R3 Jason Bonsignore | 1.00 | .45 |
| R4 Valeri Bure | 2.00 | .90 |
| R5 Jeff Friesen | 6.00 | 2.70 |
| R6 Aaron Gavey | 1.00 | .45 |
| R7 Todd Harvey | 2.00 | .90 |
| R8 Kenny Jonsson | 2.00 | .90 |
| R9 Ed Jovanovski | 5.00 | 2.20 |
| R10 Patrik Juhlin | 1.00 | .45 |
| R11 Valeri Karpov | 1.00 | .45 |
| R12 Viktor Kozlov | 2.00 | .90 |
| R13 Blaine Lacher | 2.00 | .90 |
| R14 Andrei Nikolishin | 1.00 | .45 |
| ❑ R15 Jeff O'Neill | 4.00 | 1.80 |
| ❑ R16 David Oliver | 1.00 | .45 |
| ❑ R17 Garth Snow | 3.00 | 1.35 |
| ❑ R18 Jamie Storr | 4.00 | 1.80 |
| ❑ R19 Oleg Tverdovsky | 4.00 | 1.80 |
| ❑ R20 Field Card WIN G | 1.00 | .45 |

## 1994 Classic Tri-Cards

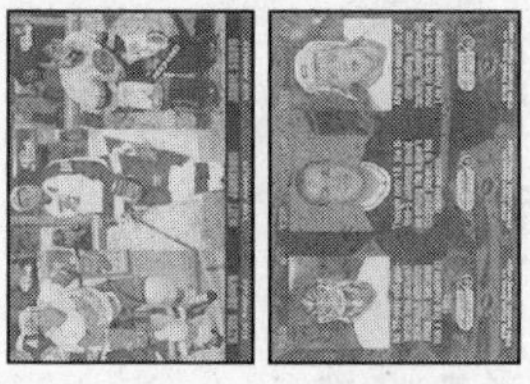

Featured in both U.S. and Canadian cases and inserted at a rate of two cards per box, this 26-card standard-size set showcases the top three prospects from each NHL city. The horizontal fronts feature three borderless color player photos next to each other, with the player's name in a black bar under each photo, and the team name in a purple bar directly below. The backs carry three small color player portraits with a brief player profile. The cards are arranged alphabetically by city name. Each card has three numbers.

| | MINT | NRMT |
|---|---|---|
| COMPLETE SET (26) | | |
| COMMON PANEL (T1-T78) | | |
| ❑ T1 Valeri Karpov | 2.00 | .90 |
| T2)Nikolai Tsulygin | | |
| T3)Oleg Tverdovsky | | |
| ❑ T4 Fred Knipscheer | 2.00 | .90 |
| T5)Blaine Lacher | | |
| T6)Evgeni Ryabchikov | | |
| ❑ T7 David Cooper | 2.00 | .90 |
| T8)Wayne Primeau | | |
| T9)Steve Shields | | |
| ❑ T10 Chris Dingman | 2.00 | .90 |
| T11)Cory Stillman | | |
| T12)Vesa Viitakoski | | |
| ❑ T13 Eric Lecompte | 2.00 | .90 |
| T14)Ethan Moreau | | |
| T15)Mike Pomichter | | |
| ❑ T16 Todd Harvey | 2.00 | .90 |
| T17)Jamie Langenbrunner | | |
| T18)Jere Lehtinen | | |
| ❑ T19 Curtis Bowen | 2.00 | .90 |
| T20)Yan Golubovsky | | |
| T21)Kevin Hodson | | |
| ❑ T22 Jason Bonsignore | 2.00 | .90 |
| T23)Mats Lindgren | | |
| T24)David Oliver | | |
| ❑ T25 Chris Armstrong | 4.00 | 1.80 |
| T26)Ed Jovanovski | | |
| T27)Jason Podollan | | |
| ❑ T28 Andrei Nikolishin | 2.00 | .90 |
| T29)Jeff O'Neill | | |
| T30)Kevin Smyth | | |
| ❑ T31 Kevin Brown | 2.00 | .90 |
| T32)Matt Johnson | | |
| T33)Jamie Storr | | |
| ❑ T34 Valeri Bure | 5.00 | 2.20 |
| T35)Saku Koivu | | |
| T36)Brian Savage | | |
| ❑ T37 Denis Pederson | 2.00 | .90 |
| T38)Brian Rolston | | |
| T39)Vadim Sharifijanov | | |
| ❑ T40 Todd Bertuzzi | 2.00 | .90 |
| T41) Chris Marinucci | | |
| T42)Dan Plante | | |
| ❑ T43 Corey Hirsch | 2.00 | .90 |
| T44)Niklas Sundstrom#} T45)Scott Malone | | |
| ❑ T46 Radim Bicanek | 2.00 | .90 |
| T47)Radek Bonk | | |
| T48)Chad Penney | | |
| ❑ T49 Patrik Juhlin | 2.00 | .90 |
| T50)Denis Metlyuk | | |
| T51)Janne Niinimaa | | |
| ❑ T52 Greg Andrusak | 2.00 | .90 |
| T53)Pat Neaton | | |
| T54)Chris Wells | | |
| ❑ T55 Rene Corbet | 2.00 | .90 |
| T56)Adam Deadmarsh | | |
| T57)Garth Snow | | |
| ❑ T58 David Roberts | 2.00 | .90 |
| T59)Ian Laperriere | | |
| T60)Patrice Tardiff | | |
| ❑ T61 Jeff Friesen | 4.00 | 1.80 |
| T62)Viktor Kozlov | | |
| T63)Ville Peltonen | | |
| ❑ T64 Aaron Gavey | 2.00 | .90 |
| T65)Brent Gretzky | | |
| T66)Jason Weimer | | |
| ❑ T67 Brandon Convery | 4.00 | 1.80 |
| T68)Eric Fichaud | | |
| T69)Kenny Jonsson | | |
| ❑ T70 Mike Fountain | 2.00 | .90 |
| T71)Rick Girard | | |
| T72)Mike Peca | | |
| ❑ T73 Jason Allison | 2.00 | .90 |
| T74)Alexander Kharlamov | | |
| T75)Brendan Witt | | |
| ❑ T76 Mika Alatalo | 2.00 | .90 |
| T77)Ravil Gusmanov | | |
| T78)Deron Quint | | |

## 1994 Classic Women of Hockey

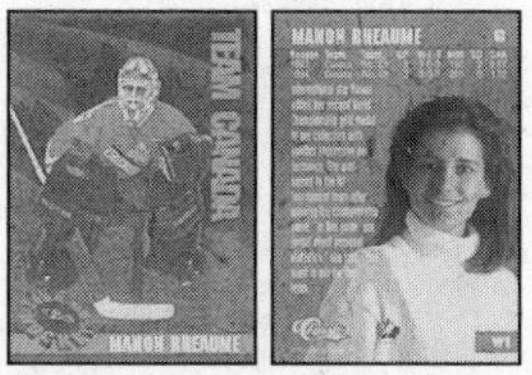

Inserted in both U.S. and Canadian product at a rate of one card per pack, this 40-card standard-size set features female hockey players who represented Canada (1-21) and the U.S.A. (22-40) at the 1994 World Women's Ice Hockey Championships. The fronts have color action player cutouts superimposed over a Canadian or American flag with a metallic sheen. The words "Team Canada Women" or "Team USA Women" appear alongside the right, while the player's name is printed at the bottom. The backs carry a close-up color player photo, along with stats from the tournament (won by Canada) and player profile.

| | MINT | NRMT |
|---|---|---|
| COMPLETE SET (40) | 15.00 | 6.75 |
| COMMON CARD (W1-W40) | .25 | .11 |
| ❑ W1 Manon Rheaume | 4.00 | 1.80 |
| ❑ W2 France St. Louis | .25 | .11 |
| ❑ W3 Cheryl Pounder | .25 | .11 |
| ❑ W4 Therese Brisson | .25 | .11 |
| ❑ W5 Cassie Campbell | .75 | .35 |
| ❑ W6 Angela James | .25 | .11 |
| ❑ W7 Danielle Goyette | .25 | .11 |
| ❑ W8 Jane Robinson | .25 | .11 |
| ❑ W9 Stacy Wilson | .25 | .11 |
| ❑ W10 Margot Page | .25 | .11 |
| ❑ W11 Laura Leslie | .25 | .11 |
| ❑ W12 Judy Diduck | .25 | .11 |
| ❑ W13 Hayley Wickenheiser | .75 | .35 |
| ❑ W14 Nathalie Picard | .25 | .11 |
| ❑ W15 Leslie Reddon | .25 | .11 |
| ❑ W16 Marianne Grnak | .25 | .11 |
| ❑ W17 Andria Hunter | .25 | .11 |
| ❑ W18 Nancy Drolet | .25 | .11 |
| ❑ W19 Geraldine Heaney | .25 | .11 |
| ❑ W20 Karen Nystrom | .25 | .11 |
| ❑ W21 Manon Rheaume CL | 1.50 | .70 |
| ❑ W22 Kelly Dyer | .75 | .35 |
| ❑ W23 Vicki Movsessian | .25 | .11 |
| ❑ W24 Lisa Brown | .25 | .11 |
| ❑ W25 Shawna Davidson | .25 | .11 |
| ❑ W26 Colleen Coyne | .25 | .11 |
| ❑ W27 Karyn Bye | .25 | .11 |
| ❑ W28 Suzanne Merz | .25 | .11 |
| ❑ W29 Gretchen Ulion | .25 | .11 |
| ❑ W30 Sandra Whyte | .25 | .11 |
| ❑ W31 Cindy Curley | .25 | .11 |
| ❑ W32 Michele DiFronzo | .25 | .11 |
| ❑ W33 Stephanie Boyd | .25 | .11 |
| ❑ W34 Shelley Looney | .25 | .11 |
| ❑ W35 Jeanine Sobek | .25 | .11 |
| ❑ W36 Beth Beagan | .25 | .11 |
| ❑ W37 Cammi Granato | .25 | .11 |
| ❑ W38 Christina Bailey | .25 | .11 |
| ❑ W39 Kelly O'Leary | .25 | .11 |
| ❑ W40 Erin Whitten | 1.00 | .45 |

## 1994 Classic Draft Day

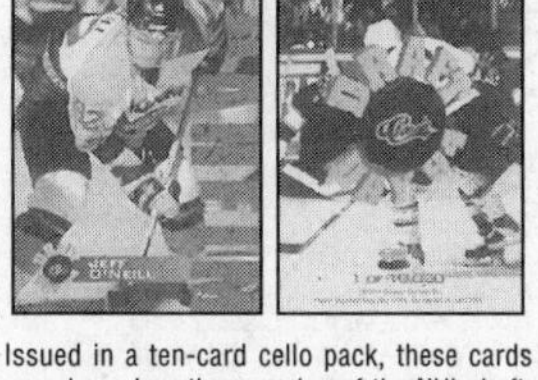

Issued in a ten-card cello pack, these cards were issued on the occasion of the NHL draft, which took place on June 28-29, 1994. The cards measure the standard size, and were available through a wrapper redemption offer. The fronts feature borderless color action player photos; the player's name is printed in a bar at the bottom that intersects the Classic logo at the lower left corner. The city (or state) of the teams that were likely to draft the player is printed vertically in block lettering along the right edge. The backs carry the "Draft Day 94" logo superimposed over a color painting of a hockey player. A tagline at the bottom rounds out the back and gives the production figures "1 of 10,000". The cards are unnumbered and checklisted below in alphabetical order.

| | MINT | NRMT |
|---|---|---|
| COMPLETE SET (10) | 25.00 | 11.00 |
| COMMON CARD (1-10) | 2.00 | .90 |
| ❑ 1 Radek Bonk | 2.00 | .90 |
| Anaheim Mighty Ducks | | |
| ❑ 2 Radek Bonk | 2.00 | .90 |
| Florida Panthers | | |
| ❑ 3 Radek Bonk | 2.00 | .90 |
| Ottawa Senators | | |
| ❑ 4 Jason Bonsignore | 2.00 | .90 |
| Edmonton Oilers | | |
| ❑ 5 Ed Jovanovski | 3.00 | 1.35 |
| Anaheim Mighty Ducks | | |
| ❑ 6 Ed Jovanovski | 3.00 | 1.35 |
| Florida Panthers | | |
| ❑ 7 Ed Jovanovski | 3.00 | 1.35 |
| Ottawa Senators | | |
| ❑ 8 Jeff O'Neill | 3.00 | 1.35 |
| Anaheim Mighty Ducks | | |
| ❑ 9 Jeff O'Neill | 3.00 | 1.35 |
| Florida Panthers | | |
| ❑ 10 Jeff O'Neill | 3.00 | 1.35 |
| Ottawa Senators | | |

## 1994 Classic Pro Prospects Promo

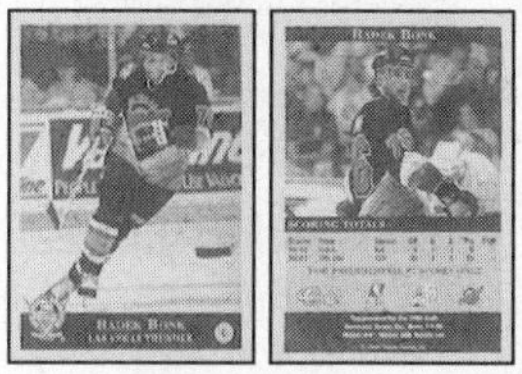

This standard-size promo card was issued to show the design of the 1994 Classic Pro Hockey Prospects set. Inside white borders, the front displays a color action player photo. The player's name, team, and position appear in a black bar at the bottom of the card. Also inside white borders, the back features another color player photo, logos, biographical information, and scoring totals. The disclaimer "For Promotional Purposes Only" is printed on the back.

| | MINT | NRMT |
|---|---|---|
| COMPLETE SET (1) | 2.00 | .90 |
| COMMON CARD | 2.00 | .90 |
| ❑ 1 Radek Bonk | 2.00 | .90 |

## 1994 Classic Pro Prospects Prototype

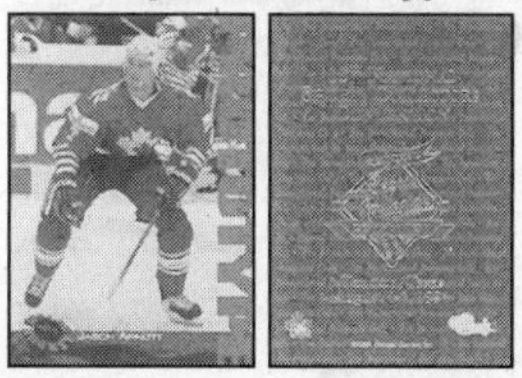

Given away at the 1994 National Sports Convention in Houston, this prototype card measures the standard size. The front features a borderless color action player photo, with the player's name on the bottom. The word "PROTOTYPE" is written vertically in red block lettering along the right edge. On a screened background, the back carries an advertisement for the convention in gold foil lettering. The card is unnumbered.

| | MINT | NRMT |
|---|---|---|
| COMPLETE SET (1) | 2.00 | .90 |
| COMMON CARD | 2.00 | .90 |
| ❑ NNO Jason Arnott | 2.00 | .90 |

## 1994 Classic Pro Prospects

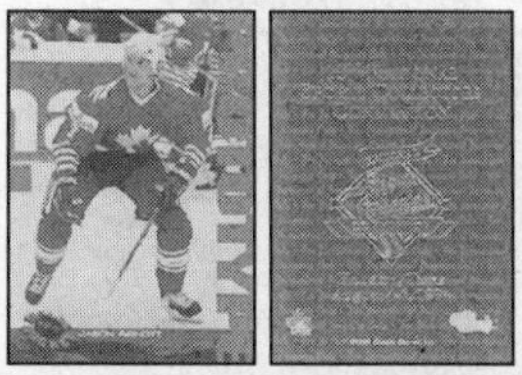

This 250-card set includes more than 100 foil-stamped subset cards. Randomly inserted throughout the foil packs were 25 limited print clear acetate cards and over 10,000 randomly inserted autographed cards of Radek Bonk, Alexei Yashin, Chris Pronger, Manon Rheaume, Joe Juneau, and more.

| | MINT | NRMT |
|---|---|---|
| COMPLETE SET (250) | 8.00 | 3.60 |
| COMMON CARD (1-250) | .05 | .02 |
| ❑ 1 Radek Bonk | .50 | .23 |
| ❑ 2 Radek Bonk | .50 | .23 |
| ❑ 3 Radek Bonk | .50 | .23 |
| ❑ 4 Vlastimil Kroupa | .05 | .02 |
| ❑ 5 Mattias Norstrom | .05 | .02 |
| ❑ 6 Jaroslav Nedved | .05 | .02 |
| ❑ 7 Steve Dubinsky | .05 | .02 |
| ❑ 8 Christian Proulx | .05 | .02 |
| ❑ 9 Michal Grosek | .05 | .02 |
| ❑ 10 Pat Neaton | .05 | .02 |
| ❑ 11 Jason Arnott | .50 | .23 |
| ❑ 12 Martin Brodeur | 1.00 | .45 |
| ❑ 13 Alexandre Daigle | .30 | .14 |
| ❑ 14 Ted Drury | .05 | .02 |
| ❑ 15 Iain Fraser | .05 | .02 |
| ❑ 16 Chris Gratton | .30 | .14 |
| ❑ 17 Greg Johnson | .05 | .02 |
| ❑ 18 Paul Kariya | 1.50 | .70 |
| ❑ 19 Alexander Karpovtsev | .05 | .02 |
| ❑ 20 Chris Lipuma | .05 | .02 |
| ❑ 21 Kirk Maltby | .05 | .02 |
| ❑ 22 Sandy McCarthy | .05 | .02 |
| ❑ 23 Darren McCarty | .05 | .02 |
| ❑ 24 Jaroslav Modry | .05 | .02 |
| ❑ 25 Jim Montgomery | .05 | .02 |
| ❑ 26 Markus Naslund | .05 | .02 |
| ❑ 27 Rob Niedermayer | .75 | .35 |
| ❑ 28 Chris Osgood | .75 | .35 |
| ❑ 29 Pat Peake | .05 | .02 |
| ❑ 30 Derek Plante | .25 | .11 |
| ❑ 31 Chris Pronger | .25 | .11 |
| ❑ 32 Mike Rathje | .05 | .02 |
| ❑ 33 Mikael Renberg | .50 | .23 |
| ❑ 34 Damian Rhodes | .25 | .11 |
| ❑ 35 Garth Snow | .05 | .02 |
| ❑ 36 Cam Stewart | .05 | .02 |
| ❑ 37 Jim Storm | .05 | .02 |
| ❑ 38 Michal Sykora | .05 | .02 |
| ❑ 39 Jocelyn Thibault | .50 | .23 |
| ❑ 40 Alexei Yashin | .25 | .11 |
| ❑ 41 Checklist 1 | .05 | .02 |
| ❑ 42 Vesa Viitakoski | .05 | .02 |
| ❑ 43 Jake Grimes | .05 | .02 |
| ❑ 44 Jim Dowd | .05 | .02 |
| ❑ 45 Craig Ferguson | .05 | .02 |
| ❑ 46 Mike Boback | .05 | .02 |
| ❑ 47 Francois Groleau | .05 | .02 |
| ❑ 48 Juha Riihijarvi | .05 | .02 |
| ❑ 49 Mikhail Shtalenkov | .25 | .11 |
| ❑ 50 Zigmund Palffy | .50 | .23 |
| ❑ 51 Felix Potvin | .50 | .23 |
| ❑ 52 Alexei Kovalev | .25 | .11 |
| ❑ 53 Larry Robinson | .05 | .02 |
| ❑ 54 John LeClair | 1.00 | .45 |
| ❑ 55 Dominic Roussel | .05 | .02 |
| ❑ 56 Geoff Sanderson | .05 | .02 |
| ❑ 57 Greg Pankewicz | .05 | .02 |
| ❑ 58 Brent Bilodeau | .05 | .02 |
| ❑ 59 Brandon Convery | .05 | .02 |
| ❑ 60 Fred Knipscheer | .05 | .02 |
| ❑ 61 Igor Chibirev | .05 | .02 |
| ❑ 62 Anatoli Fedotov | .05 | .02 |
| ❑ 63 Bob Kellogg | .05 | .02 |
| ❑ 64 Mike Maurice | .05 | .02 |
| ❑ 65 Chad Penney | .05 | .02 |
| ❑ 66 Mike Bavis | .05 | .02 |
| ❑ 67 Eric Veilleux | .05 | .02 |
| ❑ 68 Parris Duffus | .05 | .02 |
| ❑ 69 Daniel Lacroix | .05 | .02 |
| ❑ 70 Milos Holan | .05 | .02 |
| ❑ 71 Mike Muller | .05 | .02 |
| ❑ 72 Micah Aivazoff | .05 | .02 |
| ❑ 73 Krzysztof Oliwa | .05 | .02 |
| ❑ 74 Ryan Hughes | .05 | .02 |
| ❑ 75 Christian Soucy | .05 | .02 |
| ❑ 76 Keith Redmond | .05 | .02 |
| ❑ 77 Mark De Santis | .05 | .02 |
| ❑ 78 Craig Martin | .05 | .02 |
| ❑ 79 Mike Kennedy | .05 | .02 |
| ❑ 80 Pauli Jaks | .05 | .02 |
| ❑ 81 Colin Chin | .05 | .02 |
| ❑ 82 Jody Gage | .05 | .02 |
| ❑ 83 Don Biggs | .05 | .02 |
| ❑ 84 Tim Tookey | .05 | .02 |
| ❑ 85 Clint Malarchuk | .05 | .02 |
| ❑ 86 Jozef Cierny | .05 | .02 |
| ❑ 87 Radek Hamr | .05 | .02 |
| ❑ 88 Jason Dawe | .05 | .02 |
| ❑ 89 Chris Longo | .05 | .02 |
| ❑ 90 Brian Rolston | .05 | .02 |
| ❑ 91 Mike McKee | .05 | .02 |
| ❑ 92 Vitali Prokhorov | .05 | .02 |
| ❑ 93 Chris Snell | .05 | .02 |
| ❑ 94 Martin Brochu | .05 | .02 |
| ❑ 95 Dan Plante | .05 | .02 |
| ❑ 96 Darcy Werenka | .05 | .02 |
| ❑ 97 Steffon Walby | .05 | .02 |
| ❑ 98 David Emma | .05 | .02 |
| ❑ 99 Dan Stiver | .05 | .02 |
| ❑ 100 Radek Bonk | .25 | .11 |
| ❑ 101 Mark Visheau | .05 | .02 |
| ❑ 102 Dean Melanson | .05 | .02 |
| ❑ 103 Vladimir Tsyplakov | .05 | .02 |
| ❑ 104 Mikhail Volkov | .05 | .02 |
| ❑ 105 Aaron Miller | .05 | .02 |
| ❑ 106 Alexei Kudashov | .05 | .02 |
| ❑ 107 Shawn Rivers | .05 | .02 |
| ❑ 108 Ladislav Karabin | .05 | .02 |
| ❑ 109 Matt Mallgrave | .05 | .02 |
| ❑ 110 Craig Darby | .05 | .02 |
| ❑ 111 Marcel Cousineau | .05 | .02 |
| ❑ 112 Jamie McLennan | .05 | .02 |
| ❑ 113 Yanic Perreault | .05 | .02 |
| ❑ 114 Zac Boyer | .05 | .02 |
| ❑ 115 Sergei Zubov | .05 | .02 |
| ❑ 116 Dan Kesa | .05 | .02 |
| ❑ 117 Jim Hiller | .05 | .02 |
| ❑ 118 Dmitri Starostenko | .05 | .02 |
| ❑ 119 Chris Tamer | .05 | .02 |
| ❑ 120 Aaron Ward | .05 | .02 |
| ❑ 121 Claude Savoie | .05 | .02 |

❑ 122 Jamie Black .05 .02
❑ 123 Jean-Francois Jomphe .05 .02
❑ 124 Paxton Schulte .05 .02
❑ 125 Jarkko Varvio .05 .02
❑ 126 Jaroslav Otevrel .05 .02
❑ 127 Dane Jackson .05 .02
❑ 128 Brent Grieve .05 .02
❑ 129 Checklist .75 .35
Pascal Rheaume
Manon Rheaume
❑ 130 Rene Corbet .05 .02
❑ 131 Joe Frederick .05 .02
❑ 132 Martin Tanguay .05 .02
❑ 133 Fredrik Jax .05 .02
❑ 134 Jamie Linden .05 .02
❑ 135 Jason Smith .05 .02
❑ 136 Rick Kowalsky .05 .02
❑ 137 Dino Grossi .05 .02
❑ 138 Aris Brimanis .05 .02
❑ 139 Jeff McLean .05 .02
❑ 140 Tyler Wright .05 .02
❑ 141 Roman Gorev .05 .02
❑ 142 Dean Hulett .05 .02
❑ 143 Niklas Sundblad .05 .02
❑ 144 Jeff Bes .05 .02
❑ 145 Pascal Rheaume .05 .02
❑ 146 Donald Brashear .05 .02
❑ 147 Hugo Belanger .05 .02
❑ 148 Blair Scott .05 .02
❑ 149 Steve Staios .05 .02
❑ 150 Matt Martin .05 .02
❑ 151 Richard Matvichuk .05 .02
❑ 152 Paul Brousseau .05 .02
❑ 153 Evgeny Namestnikov .05 .02
❑ 154 Mike Peca .05 .02
❑ 155 Jeff Nelson .05 .02
❑ 156 Greg Andrusak .05 .02
❑ 157 Norm Batherson .05 .02
❑ 158 Martin Bakula .05 .02
❑ 159 Ed Patterson .05 .02
❑ 160 Steve Larouche .05 .02
❑ 161 Libor Polasek .05 .02
❑ 162 Jon Hillebrandt .05 .02
❑ 163 Guy Leveque .05 .02
❑ 164 Eric Lacroix .05 .02
❑ 165 Scott Walker .05 .02
❑ 166 Robert Burakovsky .05 .02
❑ 167 Markus Ketterer .05 .02
❑ 168 Mike Speer .05 .02
❑ 169 Martin Jiranek .05 .02
❑ 170 Andy Schneider .05 .02
❑ 171 Terry Hollinger .05 .02
❑ 172 Mark Lawrence .05 .02
❑ 173 Martin Lapointe .05 .02
❑ 174 Vaclav Prospal .05 .02
❑ 175 Mike Fountain .05 .02
❑ 176 Alexander Kerch .05 .02
❑ 177 Oleg Petrov .05 .02
❑ 178 Derek Armstrong .05 .02
❑ 179 Matthew Barnaby .05 .02
❑ 180 Andrei Nazarov .05 .02
❑ 181 Andrei Trefilov .05 .02
❑ 182 Jean-Yves Roy .05 .02
❑ 183 Boris Rousson .05 .02
❑ 184 Dan Laperriere .05 .02
❑ 185 Yan Kaminsky .05 .02
❑ 186 Ralph Intranuovo .05 .02
❑ 187 Sandy Moger .05 .02
❑ 188 Grant Marshall .05 .02
❑ 189 Denny Felsner .05 .02
❑ 190 Cory Stillman .05 .02
❑ 191 Eric Lavigne .05 .02
❑ 192 Jarrod Skalde .05 .02
❑ 193 Steve Junker .05 .02
❑ 194 Alexander Cherbayev .05 .02
❑ 195 Nathan Lafayette .05 .02
❑ 196 Ed Ward .05 .02
❑ 197 Harijs Vitolinsh .05 .02
❑ 198 Jarmo Kekalainen .05 .02
❑ 199 Neil Eisenhut .05 .02
❑ 200 Radek Bonk .25 .11
❑ 201 Jason Bonsignore .05 .02
❑ 202 Jeff Friesen .40 .18
❑ 203 Ed Jovanovski .50 .23
❑ 204 Brett Lindros .05 .02
❑ 205 Jeff O'Neill .25 .11
❑ 206 Deron Quint .05 .02
❑ 207 Vadim Sharifjanov .05 .02
❑ 208 Oleg Tverdovsky .25 .11
❑ 209 Checklist .25 .11
Jeff O'Neill
Jeff Friesen
❑ 210 David Cooper .05 .02
❑ 211 Doug McDonald .05 .02
❑ 212 Leonid Toropchenko .05 .02
❑ 213 Chris Rogles .05 .02
❑ 214 Slava Kozlov .25 .11
❑ 215 Denis Metlyuk .05 .02
❑ 216 Scott McKay .05 .02
❑ 217 Brian Loney .05 .02
❑ 218 Kevin Hodson .05 .02
❑ 219 Bobby House .05 .02
❑ 220 Sergei Krivokrasov .05 .02
❑ 221 Brett Harkins .05 .02
❑ 222 Cale Hulse .05 .02
❑ 223 Marc Tardif .05 .02
❑ 224 Jon Rohloff .05 .02
❑ 225 Kevin Smyth .05 .02
❑ 226 Jason Young .05 .02
❑ 227 Sergei Zholtok .05 .02
❑ 228 Todd Simon .05 .02
❑ 229 Jerome Bechard .05 .02
❑ 230 Matt Robbins .05 .02
❑ 231 Joe Cook .05 .02
❑ 232 John Brill .05 .02
❑ 233 Dan Goldie .05 .02
❑ 234 Dan Gravelle .05 .02
❑ 235 Shawn Wheeler .05 .02
❑ 236 Brad Harrison .05 .02
❑ 237 Joe Dragon .05 .02
❑ 238 Jason Jennings .05 .02
❑ 239 Manon Rheaume 2.00 .90
❑ 240 Jamie Steer .05 .02
❑ 241 Scott Rogers .05 .02
❑ 242 Lyle Wildgoose .05 .02
❑ 243 Darren Colbourne .05 .02
❑ 244 Mike Smith .05 .02
❑ 245 Chris Bright .05 .02
❑ 246 Chris Belanger .05 .02
❑ 247 Darren Schwartz .05 .02
❑ 248 Cammi Granato 1.50 .70
❑ 249 Erin Whitten .50 .23
❑ 250 Manon Rheaume 2.00 .90
❑ AU1 Radek Bonk AU/2400 10.00 4.50
❑ AU2 Jason Bonsignore AU/2450 10.00 4.50
❑ AU3 Jeff Friesen AU/2450 30.00 13.50
❑ AU4 Joe Juneau AU/1370 30.00 13.50
❑ AU5 Alexei Kovalev AU/1900 20.00 9.00
❑ AU6 Chris Pronger AU/1400 30.00 13.50
❑ AU7 Manon Rheaume AU/1900 80.00 36.00
❑ AU8 Erin Whitten AU/1800 30.00 13.50
❑ AU9 Alexei Yashin AU/1400 40.00 18.00
❑ NNO Arnott/Yashin ROY? 3.00 1.35

## 1994 Classic Pro Prospects Ice Ambassadors

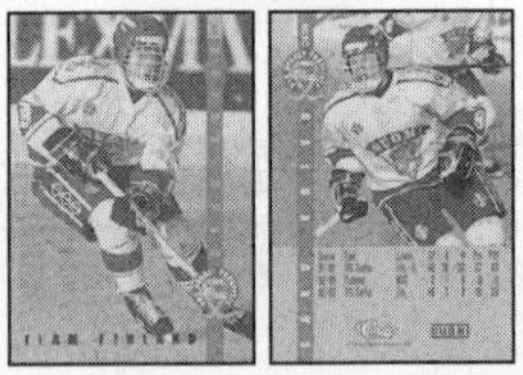

This standard-size set features young players from all over the world. The cards were inserted one per jumbo sheet in a late-season, retail-only repackaging configuration. The fronts feature a player photo with a stripe down the right side carrying the player's name. On the bottom of the card in gold lettering is the identification of the team. The reverse of the card features a player photo on the top half with statistical information on the bottom half.

| | MINT | NRMT |
|---|---|---|
| COMPLETE SET (20) | 8.00 | 3.60 |
| COMMON CARD (IA1-IA20) | .25 | .11 |

❑ IA1 Adrian Aucoin .25 .11
❑ IA2 Corey Hirsch .75 .35
❑ IA3 Paul Kariya 4.00 1.80
❑ IA4 David Harlock .25 .11
❑ IA5 Manny Legace .25 .11
❑ IA6 Chris Therien .25 .11
❑ IA7 Todd Warriner .25 .11
❑ IA8 Todd Marchant .25 .11
❑ IA9 Matt Martin .25 .11
❑ IA10 Peter Ferraro .25 .11
❑ IA11 Brian Rolston .40 .18
❑ IA12 Jim Campbell .25 .11
❑ IA13 Mike Dunham .25 .11
❑ IA14 Craig Johnson .25 .11
❑ IA15 Saku Koivu 2.50 1.10
❑ IA16 Jere Lehtinen .25 .11
❑ IA17 Viktor Kozlov .40 .18
❑ IA18 Andrei Nikolishin .25 .11
❑ IA19 Sergei Gonchar .25 .11
❑ IA20 Valeri Karpov .25 .11

## 1994 Classic Pro Prospects International Heroes

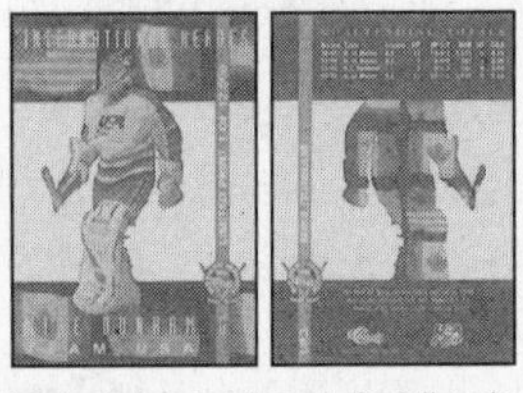

Randomly inserted through the foil packs, these 25 clear acetate standard-size cards predominantly feature the U.S. and Canadian National Teams. The cards are numbered on the back with an "LP" prefix. The nationalities of the players are as follows: U.S. (1-10); Canadian (11-20, 24); Czech (21); Russian (22, 25); and Finnish (23).

| | MINT | NRMT |
|---|---|---|
| COMPLETE SET (25) | 50.00 | 22.00 |
| COMMON CARD (LP1-LP25) | 2.00 | .90 |

❑ LP1 Jim Campbell 2.00 .90
❑ LP2 Ted Drury 2.00 .90
❑ LP3 Mike Dunham 2.00 .90
❑ LP4 Chris Ferraro 2.00 .90
❑ LP5 Peter Ferraro 2.00 .90
❑ LP6 Darby Hendrickson 2.00 .90
❑ LP7 Craig Johnson 2.00 .90
❑ LP8 Todd Marchant 2.00 .90
❑ LP9 Matt Martin 2.00 .90
❑ LP10 Brian Rolston 3.00 1.35
❑ LP11 Adrian Aucoin 2.00 .90
❑ LP12 Martin Gendron 2.00 .90
❑ LP13 David Harlock 2.00 .90
❑ LP14 Corey Hirsch 3.00 1.35
❑ LP15 Paul Kariya 10.00 4.50
❑ LP16 Manny Legace 2.00 .90
❑ LP17 Brett Lindros 2.00 .90
❑ LP18 Brian Savage 2.00 .90
❑ LP19 Chris Therien 2.00 .90
❑ LP20 Todd Warriner 2.00 .90
❑ LP21 Radek Bonk 2.00 .90
❑ LP22 Pavel Bure 8.00 3.60
❑ LP23 Teemu Selanne 8.00 3.60
❑ LP24 Mark Recchi 3.00 1.35
❑ LP25 Alexei Yashin 4.00 1.80

## 1995 Classic

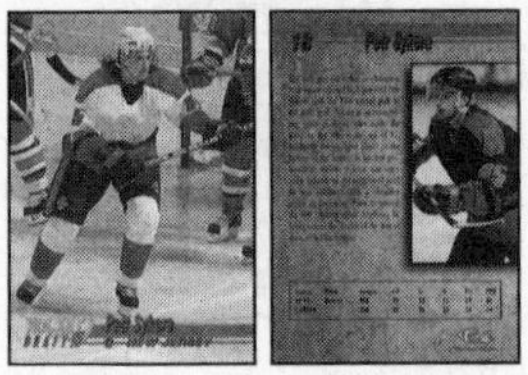

This 100-card standard-size set marked the conclusion of the fifth (and so far, final) set Classic issued featuring hockey prospects. 3,990 sequentially numbered American cases and 999 Canadian cases were issued with 12 boxes in a case, 36 packs in a box and 10 cards in a pack. There were also a special Manon Rheaume autograph card issued on the average of one per case. One Hot Box, containing nothing but inserts, was inserted one every five cases.

| | MINT | NRMT |
|---|---|---|
| COMPLETE SET (100) | 8.00 | 3.60 |
| COMMON CARD (1-100) | .05 | .02 |
| COMMON NHLer | .25 | .11 |

❑ 1 Bryan Berard .75 .35
❑ 2 Wade Redden .05 .02
❑ 3 Aki-Petteri Berg .05 .02
❑ 4 Chad Kilger .05 .02
❑ 5 Daymond Langkow .05 .02
❑ 6 Steve Kelly .05 .02
❑ 7 Shane Doan .05 .02
❑ 8 Terry Ryan .05 .02
❑ 9 Mike Martin .05 .02
❑ 10 Radek Dvorak .40 .18
❑ 11 Jarome Iginla .60 .25
❑ 12 Teemu Riihijarvi .05 .02
❑ 13 Jean-Sebastien Giguere .40 .18
❑ 14 Peter Schaefer .05 .02
❑ 15 Jeff Ware .05 .02
❑ 16 Martin Biron .40 .18
❑ 17 Brad Church .05 .02
❑ 18 Petr Sykora .75 .35
❑ 19 Denis Gauthier .05 .02
❑ 20 Sean Brown .05 .02
❑ 21 Brad Isbister .05 .02
❑ 22 Miikka Elomo .05 .02
❑ 23 Mathieu Sunderland .05 .02
❑ 24 Marc Moro .05 .02
❑ 25 Jan Hlavac .05 .02
❑ 26 Brian Wesenberg .05 .02
❑ 27 Mike McBain .05 .02
❑ 28 Georges Laraque .05 .02
❑ 29 Marc Chouinard .05 .02
❑ 30 Donald MacLean .05 .02
❑ 31 Jason Doig .05 .02
❑ 32 Aaron MacDonald .05 .02
❑ 33 Patrick Cote .05 .02
❑ 34 Christian Dube .05 .02
❑ 35 Chris McAllister .05 .02
❑ 36 Denis Smith .05 .02
❑ 37 Mark Dutiaume .05 .02
❑ 38 Dwayne Hay .05 .02
❑ 39 Nathan Perrott .05 .02
❑ 40 Christian Laflamme .05 .02
❑ 41 Paxton Schafer .05 .02
❑ 42 Shane Kenny .05 .02
❑ 43 Nic Beaudoin .05 .02
❑ 44 Philippe Audet .05 .02
❑ 45 Brad Larsen .05 .02
❑ 46 Ryan Pepperall .05 .02
❑ 47 Mike Leclere .05 .02
❑ 48 Shane Willis .05 .02
❑ 49 Darryl Laplante .05 .02
❑ 50 Larry Courville .05 .02
❑ 51 Mike O'Grady .05 .02
❑ 52 Petr Buzek .05 .02
❑ 53 Alyn McCauley .60 .25
❑ 54 Scott Roche .05 .02
❑ 55 John Tripp .05 .02
❑ 56 Johnathan Aitken .05 .02
❑ 57 Blake Bellefeuille .05 .02
❑ 58 Daniel Briere .50 .23
❑ 59 Josh DeWolf .05 .02
❑ 60 Josh Green .05 .02
❑ 61 Chris Hajt .05 .02
❑ 62 Josh Holden .05 .02
❑ 63 Henry Kuster .05 .02
❑ 64 Dan Lacouture .05 .02
❑ 65 Oleg Orekhovsky .05 .02
❑ 66 Andrei Petrunin .05 .02
❑ 67 Tom Poti .05 .02
❑ 68 Peter Ratchuk .05 .02
❑ 69 Andrei Zyuzin .40 .18
❑ 70 George Breen .05 .02
❑ 71 Greg Bullock .05 .02
❑ 72 Kent Fearns .05 .02
❑ 73 Eric Flinton .05 .02
❑ 74 Brian Holzinger .05 .02
❑ 75 Chris Kenady .05 .02
❑ 76 Kaj Linna .05 .02
❑ 77 Brian Mueller .05 .02
❑ 78 Brent Peterson .05 .02
❑ 79 Chad Quenneville .05 .02
❑ 80 Randy Stevens .05 .02
❑ 81 Adam Wiesel .05 .02
❑ 82 Barrie Colts .10 .05
❑ 83 Belleville Bulls .05 .02
❑ 84 Detroit Jr. Whalers .05 .02
❑ 85 Guelph Storm .05 .02
❑ 86 Kingston Frontenacs .05 .02
❑ 87 Kitchener Rangers .05 .02
❑ 88 London Knights .10 .05
❑ 89 Niagara Falls Thunder .10 .05
❑ 90 North Bay Centennials .05 .02
❑ 91 Oshawa Generals .10 .05
❑ 92 Ottawa 67's .05 .02
❑ 93 Owen Sound Platers .10 .05
❑ 94 Peterborough Petes .10 .05
❑ 95 S.S. Marie Greyhounds 1.00 .45
❑ 96 Sarnia Sting .10 .05
❑ 97 Sudbury Wolves .05 .02
❑ 98 Windsor Spitfires .05 .02
❑ 99 Bryan Berard CL .05 .02
❑ 100 Wade Redden CL .05 .02

## 1995 Classic Gold

This 100 card set is a parallel to the regular Classic issue. The cards are inserted one per American pack.

| | MINT | NRMT |
|---|---|---|
| COMPLETE SET (100) | 40.00 | 18.00 |
| COMMON GOLD (1-100) | .15 | .07 |

*STARS:3X BASIC CARDS

## 1995 Classic Printer's Proofs

These cards were insered approximately one per box. The cards are numbered out of 749.

| | MINT | NRMT |
|---|---|---|
| COMPLETE SET (100) | 300.00 | 135.00 |
| COMMON CARD (1-100) | 2.00 | .90 |

*STARS: 20X TO 40X BASIC CARDS

## 1995 Classic Printer's Proofs Gold

These 100 cards are a parallel to the Classic Gold set. The cards were inserted one every three boxes and are numbered out of 249.

| | MINT | NRMT |
|---|---|---|
| COMPLETE SET (100) | 500.00 | 220.00 |
| COMMON CARD (1-100) | 5.00 | 2.20 |

*STARS:15X TO 35X BASIC CARDS

## 1995 Classic Silver

This 100 card standard-size set is a parallel to the regular Classic issue. The cards were inserted one per Canadian pack.

| | MINT | NRMT |
|---|---|---|
| COMPLETE SET (100) | 50.00 | 22.00 |
| COMMON SILVER (1-100) | .25 | .11 |

*STARS:2X TO 5X BASIC CARDS

## 1995 Classic Autographs

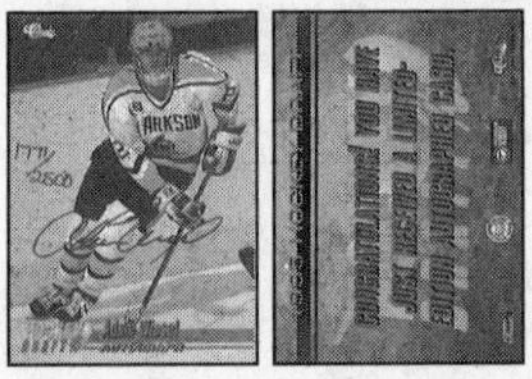

These 24 standard-size cards were inserted on the average of one per box. Classic guaranteed that there would be one autographed card in each box. The front is a picture of the card along with the signature. The back is a congratulatory message that you have received an authentic signed card.

| | MINT | NRMT |
|---|---|---|
| COMPLETE SET (25) | 350.00 | 160.00 |
| COMMON CARD (1-24) | 5.00 | 2.20 |

❑ 1 George Breen/2400 6.00 2.70
❑ 2 Greg Bullock/2485 6.00 2.70
❑ 3 Petr Buzek/3978 8.00 3.60
❑ 4 Radek Dvorak/4022 30.00 13.50
❑ 5 Kent Fearns/4034 6.00 2.70
❑ 6 Eric Flinton/2495 8.00 3.60
❑ 7 Josh Green/4293 20.00 9.00
❑ 8 Josh Holden/4994 15.00 6.75
❑ 9 Brian Holzinger/2599 20.00 9.00
❑ 10 Ed Jovanovski/2584 20.00 9.00
❑ 11 Chris Kenady/2480 6.00 2.70
❑ 12 Henry Kuster/2490 8.00 3.60
❑ 13 Josef Marha/2584 10.00 4.50
❑ 14 Brian Mueller/2488 10.00 4.50
❑ 15 Angel Nikolov/2500 8.00 3.60
❑ 16 Oleg Orekhovsky/5090 6.00 2.70
❑ 17 Brent Peterson/2468 6.00 2.70
❑ 18 Andrei Petrunin/4764 20.00 9.00
❑ 19 Chad Quenneville/2594 6.00 2.70
❑ 20 Miroslav Satan/2487 30.00 13.50
❑ 21 Randy Stevens/2591 6.00 2.70
❑ 22 Petr Sykora/792 30.00 13.50
❑ 23 Adam Wiesel/2511 6.00 2.70
❑ 24 Andrei Zyuzin/5076 25.00 11.00
❑ NNO Manon Rheaume/6300 30.00 13.50

## 1995 Classic CHL All-Stars

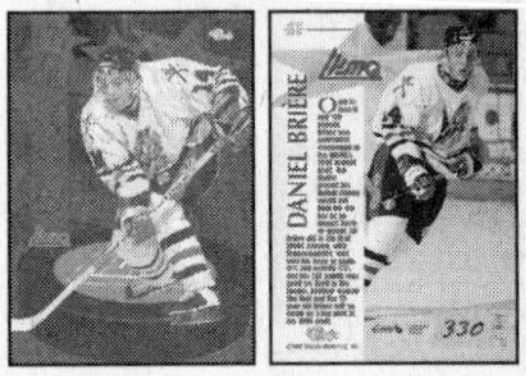

These cards feature all-stars of the CHL. They were inserted into Canadian packs at a ratio of one every 72. The cards are numbered with a "AS" prefix.

| | MINT | NRMT |
|---|---|---|
| COMPLETE SET (18) | 150.00 | 70.00 |
| COMMON CARD (AS1-AS18) | 4.00 | 1.80 |
| COMMON PROSPECT | 8.00 | 3.60 |

❑ AS1 Nolan Baumgartner 4.00 1.80
❑ AS2 Wade Redden 10.00 4.50
❑ AS3 Henry Kuster 4.00 1.80
❑ AS4 Daymond Langkow 10.00 4.50
❑ AS5 Shane Doan 8.00 3.60
❑ AS6 Steve Kelly 6.00 2.70
❑ AS7 Tyler Moss 4.00 1.80
❑ AS8 Bryan Berard 20.00 9.00
❑ AS9 Ed Jovanovski 12.00 5.50
❑ AS10 Chad Kilger 10.00 4.50
❑ AS11 Daniel Cleary 12.00 5.50
❑ AS12 Ethan Moreau 6.00 2.70
❑ AS13 Jean-Sebastien Giguere 10.00 4.50
❑ AS14 Denis Gauthier 4.00 1.80
❑ AS15 Jason Doig 4.00 1.80
❑ AS16 Etienne Drapeau 4.00 1.80
❑ AS17 Daniel Briere 12.00 5.50
❑ AS18 Mark Chouinard 4.00 1.80

## 1995 Classic Ice Breakers

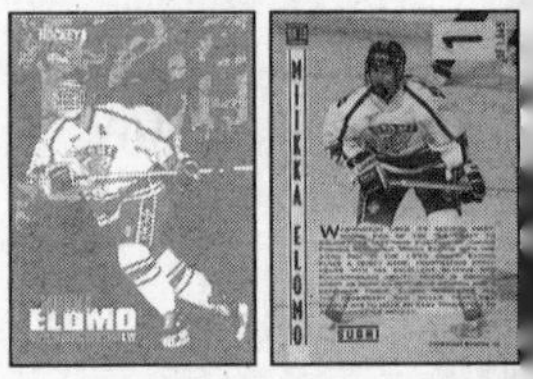

These cards were randolmy inserted int packs at a ratio of approximately one ever other box. The cards are sequentiall numbered an less than 2,000 of each car were printed. The cards feature some of th leading prospects which included Brya Berard, Nolan Baumgartner and Wade Redde A die-cut version of these cards were issue as well. These cards were sequentiall numbered to 495. The cards are numbere with a "BK" prefix.

| | MINT | NRM |
|---|---|---|
| COMPLETE SET (20) | 120.00 | 55.0 |
| COMMON CARD (BK1-BK20) | 3.00 | 1.3 |

*DIE CUT STARS: 2X TO 4X BASIC CARDS

❑ BK1 Bryan Berard 15.00 6.7
❑ BK2 Wade Redden 10.00 4.5
❑ BK3 Aki-Petteri Berg 6.00 2.7
❑ BK4 Chad Kilger 10.00 4.5
❑ BK5 Daymond Langkow 10.00 4.5
❑ BK6 Steve Kelly 6.00 2.7
❑ BK7 Shane Doan 6.00 2.7
❑ BK8 Terry Ryan 6.00 2.7
❑ BK9 Radek Dvorak 12.00 5.5
❑ BK10 Miikka Elomo 5.00 2.2
❑ BK11 Teemu Riihijarvi 5.00 2.2
❑ BK12 Jean-Sebastien Giguere 8.00 3.6
❑ BK13 Martin Biron 8.00 3.6
❑ BK14 Jeff Ware 4.00 1.8
❑ BK15 Brad Church 6.00 2.7
❑ BK16 Petr Sykora 10.00 4.5
❑ BK17 Jason Bonsignore 4.00 1.8
❑ BK18 Brian Holzinger 4.00 1.8
❑ BK19 Ed Jovanovski 10.00 4.5
❑ BK20 Nolan Baumgartner 4.00 1.8

## 1995-96 Collector's Edge Ice Promos

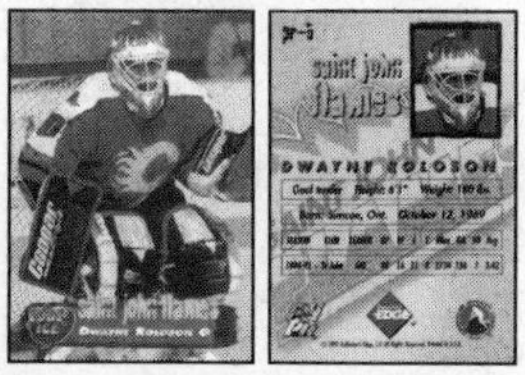

This 7-card set was issued as a promotional device to entice dealers to purchase the upcoming Collector's Edge Ice set of minor league stars. The cards mirror the design of the regular issue cards, save for the numbering, which comes with a PR-prefix.

| | MINT | NRMT |
|---|---|---|
| COMPLETE SET (7) | 2.00 | .90 |
| COMMON CARD (PR1-PR6) | .25 | .11 |
| ❑ PR1 Todd Marchant | .25 | .11 |
| ❑ PR2 Tommy Salo | .50 | .23 |
| ❑ PR3 Michael Dunham | .50 | .23 |
| ❑ PR4 Viktor Kozlov | .35 | .16 |
| ❑ PR5 Dwayne Roloson | .35 | .16 |
| ❑ PR6 Tony Hrkac | .25 | .11 |
| ❑ NNO Title Card | .50 | .23 |

## 1995-96 Collector's Edge Ice

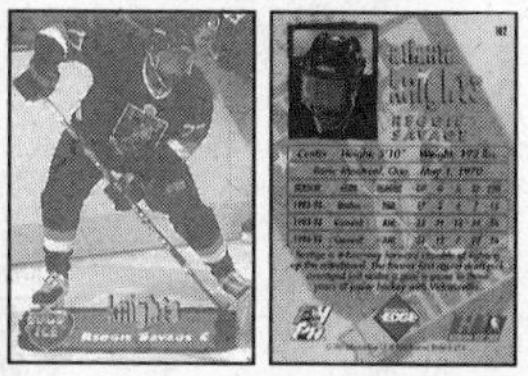

This 200-card set was the first offering by Collector's Edge for minor league hockey. The set features players from both the American and the International leagues in action shots with team and player name and company logo along the bottom. The card backs offers a limited stats package over a ghosted image of the team's logo. The cards came in regular and regional boxes. The latter were designed to increase sales in this obviously locally-slanted issue by inserting a number of prismatic parallel cards of players from your home team. These boxes could only be ordered from within specified regions. These prismatic cards are serially numbered on the back (presumably out of 1,000) and are valued at 3 to 5 times the regular card values below. Furthermore, this product was laced with redemption cards and offers for autographed cards, photos and memorabilia. Now expired, these redemption cards are worth fifty cents to one dollar each.

| | MINT | NRMT |
|---|---|---|
| COMPLETE SET (200) | 30.00 | 13.50 |
| COMMON CARD (1-200) | .10 | .05 |
| ❑ 1 Curtis Bowen | .20 | .09 |
| ❑ 2 Anders Eriksson | .50 | .23 |
| ❑ 3 Kevin Hodson | 1.00 | .45 |
| ❑ 4 Martin LaPointe | .20 | .09 |
| ❑ 5 Aaron Ward | .50 | .23 |
| ❑ 6 Mike Dunham | .20 | .09 |
| ❑ 7 Chris McAlpine | .10 | .05 |
| ❑ 8 Brian Rolston | .20 | .09 |
| ❑ 9 Corey Schwab | .40 | .18 |
| ❑ 10 Steve Sullivan | .30 | .14 |
| ❑ 11 Petr Sykora | 2.00 | .90 |
| ❑ 12 Darren Van Impe | .10 | .05 |
| ❑ 13 Mike Maneluk | .10 | .05 |
| ❑ 14 David Sacco | .10 | .05 |
| ❑ 15 Jarrod Skalde | .10 | .05 |
| ❑ 16 Nikolai Tsulygin | .10 | .05 |
| ❑ 17 Peter Ferraro | .30 | .14 |
| ❑ 18 Chris Ferraro | .20 | .09 |
| ❑ 19 Corey Hirsch | .50 | .23 |
| ❑ 20 Mattias Norstrom | .30 | .14 |
| ❑ 21 Jamie Ram | .30 | .14 |
| ❑ 22 Chris Armstrong | .10 | .05 |
| ❑ 23 Alexei Kudashov | .10 | .05 |
| ❑ 24 Todd MacDonald | .10 | .05 |
| ❑ 25 Steve Washburn | .10 | .05 |
| ❑ 26 Kevin Weekes | .20 | .09 |
| ❑ 27 Rene Corbet | .20 | .09 |
| ❑ 28 Janne Laukkanen | .10 | .05 |
| ❑ 29 Aaron Miller | .10 | .05 |
| ❑ 30 Landon Wilson | .40 | .18 |
| ❑ 31 Fred Brathwaite | .20 | .09 |
| ❑ 32 Ryan Haggerty | .10 | .05 |
| ❑ 33 Ralph Intranuovo | .10 | .05 |
| ❑ 34 Todd Marchant | .20 | .09 |
| ❑ 35 David Oliver | .20 | .09 |
| ❑ 36 Marko Tuomainen | .10 | .05 |
| ❑ 37 Peter White | .10 | .05 |
| ❑ 38 Sebastien Bordeleau | .10 | .05 |
| ❑ 39 Martin Brochu | .20 | .09 |
| ❑ 40 Valeri Bure | .40 | .18 |
| ❑ 41 Craig Conroy | .10 | .05 |
| ❑ 42 Darcy Tucker | .20 | .09 |
| ❑ 43 David Wilkie | .30 | .14 |
| ❑ 44 Paul Healey | .10 | .05 |
| ❑ 45 Chris Herperger | .10 | .05 |
| ❑ 46 Jim Montgomery | .10 | .05 |
| ❑ 47 Chris Therien | .20 | .09 |
| ❑ 48 Pavol Demitra | .40 | .18 |
| ❑ 49 Michel Picard | .10 | .05 |
| ❑ 50 Jason Zent | .10 | .05 |
| ❑ 51 Patrick Boileau | .10 | .05 |
| ❑ 52 Jim Carey | 2.50 | 1.10 |
| ❑ 53 Sergei Gonchar | .20 | .09 |
| ❑ 54 Jeff Nelson | .10 | .05 |
| ❑ 55 Stefan Ustorf | .30 | .14 |
| ❑ 56 Alexander Kharlamov | .40 | .18 |
| ❑ 57 Ron Tugnutt | .20 | .09 |
| ❑ 58 Scott Bailey | .40 | .18 |
| ❑ 59 Clayton Beddoes | .10 | .05 |
| ❑ 60 Andre Roy | .10 | .05 |
| ❑ 61 Evgeny Ryabchikov | .20 | .09 |
| ❑ 62 Mark Astley | .10 | .05 |
| ❑ 63 Jody Gage | .10 | .05 |
| ❑ 64 Sergei Klimentiev | .10 | .05 |
| ❑ 65 Barrie Moore | .10 | .05 |
| ❑ 66 Mike Wilson | .10 | .05 |
| ❑ 67 Shayne Wright | .10 | .05 |
| ❑ 68 Michal Grosek | .10 | .05 |
| ❑ 69 Tavis Hansen | .10 | .05 |
| ❑ 70 Nikolai Khabibulin | 1.00 | .45 |
| ❑ 71 Scott Langkow | .40 | .18 |
| ❑ 72 Jason McBain | .10 | .05 |
| ❑ 73 Dwayne Roloson | .20 | .09 |
| ❑ 74 Cory Stillman | .30 | .14 |
| ❑ 75 Jamie Allison | .30 | .14 |
| ❑ 76 Jesper Mattsson | .30 | .14 |
| ❑ 77 David Ling | .30 | .14 |
| ❑ 78 Brandon Convery | .20 | .09 |
| ❑ 79 Darby Hendrickson | .10 | .05 |
| ❑ 80 Janne Gronvall | .10 | .05 |
| ❑ 81 Jason Saal | .20 | .09 |
| ❑ 82 Brent Gretzky | .20 | .09 |
| ❑ 83 Kent Manderville | .10 | .05 |
| ❑ 84 Shayne Toporowski | .10 | .05 |
| ❑ 85 Paul Vincent | .10 | .05 |
| ❑ 86 Mark Kolesar | .10 | .05 |
| ❑ 87 Lonny Bohonos | .10 | .05 |
| ❑ 88 Larry Courville | .10 | .05 |
| ❑ 89 Jassen Cullimore | .10 | .05 |
| ❑ 90 Scott Walker | .10 | .05 |
| ❑ 91 Mike Buzak | .10 | .05 |
| ❑ 92 Craig Darby | .10 | .05 |
| ❑ 93 Eric Fichaud | .75 | .35 |
| ❑ 94 Andreas Johansson | .10 | .05 |
| ❑ 95 Jamie Rivers | .20 | .09 |
| ❑ 96 Jason Strudwick | .10 | .05 |
| ❑ 97 Patrice Tardif | .10 | .05 |
| ❑ 98 Alexander Vasilevskii | .10 | .05 |
| ❑ 99 Drew Bannister | .10 | .05 |
| ❑ 100 Stan Drulia | .20 | .09 |
| ❑ 101 Aaron Gavey | .20 | .09 |
| ❑ 102 Reggie Savage | .10 | .05 |
| ❑ 103 Derek Wilkinson | .10 | .05 |
| ❑ 104 Rob Brown | .10 | .05 |
| ❑ 105 Dan Currie | .10 | .05 |
| ❑ 106 Kevin MacDonald | .10 | .05 |
| ❑ 107 Steve Maltais | .20 | .09 |
| ❑ 108 Shawn Rivers | .10 | .05 |
| ❑ 109 Wendell Young | .20 | .09 |
| ❑ 110 Don Biggs | .10 | .05 |
| ❑ 111 Dale DeGray | .10 | .05 |
| ❑ 112 Paul Lawless | .10 | .05 |
| ❑ 113 Danny Lorenz | .20 | .09 |
| ❑ 114 Dave Tomlinson | .10 | .05 |
| ❑ 115 Jock Callander | .10 | .05 |
| ❑ 116 Phillipe DeRouville | .30 | .14 |
| ❑ 117 Ryan Savoia | .10 | .05 |
| ❑ 118 Mike Stevens | .10 | .05 |
| ❑ 119 Chris Tamer | .10 | .05 |
| ❑ 120 Peter Bondra | 1.00 | .45 |
| ❑ 121 Peter Ciavaglia | .10 | .05 |
| ❑ 122 Rick Knickle | .20 | .09 |
| ❑ 123 Lonnie Loach | .20 | .09 |
| ❑ 124 Michal Pivonka | .30 | .14 |
| ❑ 125 Andy Bezeau | .10 | .05 |
| ❑ 126 Bob Essensa | .20 | .09 |
| ❑ 127 Andrew McBain | .10 | .05 |
| ❑ 128 Kevin Miehm | .10 | .05 |
| ❑ 129 Scott Arniel | .10 | .05 |
| ❑ 130 Kevin Dineen | .20 | .09 |
| ❑ 131 Robert Dopson | .20 | .09 |
| ❑ 132 Mark Freer | .10 | .05 |
| ❑ 133 Troy Gamble | .20 | .09 |
| ❑ 134 Ethan Moreau | .20 | .09 |
| ❑ 135 Sergei Klimovich | .10 | .05 |
| ❑ 136 Eric LeCompte | .10 | .05 |
| ❑ 137 Eric Manlow | .10 | .05 |
| ❑ 138 Kip Miller | .10 | .05 |
| ❑ 139 Manny Fernandez | .40 | .18 |
| ❑ 140 Mike Kennedy | .10 | .05 |
| ❑ 141 Jamie Langenbrunner | .40 | .18 |
| ❑ 142 Derrick Smith | .10 | .05 |
| ❑ 143 Jordan Willis | .20 | .09 |
| ❑ 144 Jan Caloun | .40 | .18 |
| ❑ 145 Viktor Kozlov | .40 | .18 |
| ❑ 146 Andrei Nazarov | .10 | .05 |
| ❑ 147 Geoff Sarjeant | .20 | .09 |
| ❑ 148 Patrik Augusta | .10 | .05 |
| ❑ 149 Victor Gordiouk | .10 | .05 |
| ❑ 150 Dave Littman | .20 | .09 |
| ❑ 151 Todd Gillingham | .10 | .05 |
| ❑ 152 Greg Hawgood | .10 | .05 |
| ❑ 153 Patrice Lefebvre | .20 | .09 |
| ❑ 154 Pokey Reddick | .20 | .09 |
| ❑ 155 Manon Rheaume | 3.00 | 1.35 |
| ❑ 156 Jeff Sharples | .10 | .05 |
| ❑ 157 Todd Simon | .10 | .05 |
| ❑ 158 Radek Bonk | .50 | .23 |
| ❑ 159 Gino Cavallini | .10 | .05 |
| ❑ 160 Tom Draper | .20 | .09 |
| ❑ 161 Tony Hrkac | .10 | .05 |
| ❑ 162 Fabian Joseph | .10 | .05 |
| ❑ 163 Mark LaForest | .20 | .09 |
| ❑ 164 Dave Christian | .10 | .05 |
| ❑ 165 Bryan Fogarty | .10 | .05 |
| ❑ 166 Chris Govedaris | .10 | .05 |
| ❑ 167 Mike Hurlbut | .10 | .05 |
| ❑ 168 Chris Imes | .10 | .05 |
| ❑ 169 Stephane Morin | .10 | .05 |
| ❑ 170 Allan Bester | .20 | .09 |
| ❑ 171 Kerry Clark | .10 | .05 |
| ❑ 172 Neil Eisenhut | .10 | .05 |
| ❑ 173 Craig Fisher | .10 | .05 |
| ❑ 174 Patrick Neaton | .10 | .05 |
| ❑ 175 Todd Richards | .10 | .05 |
| ❑ 176 Jon Casey | .20 | .09 |
| ❑ 177 Doug Evans | .10 | .05 |
| ❑ 178 Michel Mongeau | .10 | .05 |
| ❑ 179 Greg Paslawski | .10 | .05 |
| ❑ 180 Darren Veitch | .10 | .05 |
| ❑ 181 Frederick Beaubien | .20 | .09 |
| ❑ 182 Kevin Brown | .10 | .05 |
| ❑ 183 Rob Cowie | .10 | .05 |
| ❑ 184 Yanic Perreault | .20 | .09 |
| ❑ 185 Chris Snell | .10 | .05 |
| ❑ 186 Jan Vopat | .10 | .05 |
| ❑ 187 Robin Bawa | .10 | .05 |
| ❑ 188 Stephane Beauregard | .20 | .09 |
| ❑ 189 Dale Craigwell | .10 | .05 |
| ❑ 190 John Purves | .10 | .05 |
| ❑ 191 Jeff Madill | .10 | .05 |
| ❑ 192 Gord Dineen | .10 | .05 |
| ❑ 193 Chris Marinucci | .30 | .14 |
| ❑ 194 Mark McArthur | .20 | .09 |
| ❑ 195 Zigmund Palffy | 1.25 | .55 |
| ❑ 196 Tommy Salo | .60 | .25 |
| ❑ 197 Checklist | .10 | .05 |
| ❑ 198 Checklist | .10 | .05 |
| ❑ 199 Checklist | .10 | .05 |
| ❑ 200 Checklist | .10 | .05 |

## 1995-96 Collector's Edge Ice Crucibles

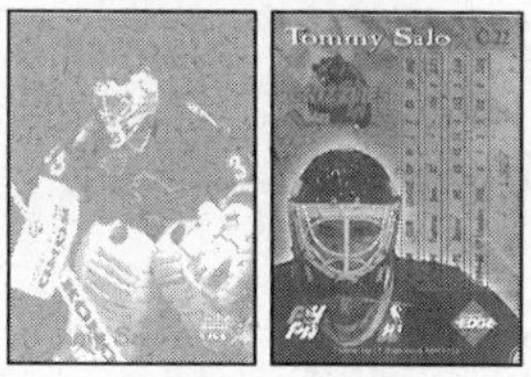

Randomly inserted at a rate of 1:20 packs, this 24-card features players who perform best in the heat of battle. The fronts utilize a metallic-foil background; the backs offer another photo and an expanded stats package. The cards are serially numbered, presumably out of 2,000.

| | MINT | NRMT |
|---|---|---|
| COMPLETE SET (24) | 60.00 | 27.00 |
| COMMON CARD (C1-C24) | 1.00 | .45 |
| ❑ C1 David Roberts | 1.00 | .45 |
| ❑ C2 Ian Laperriere | 2.00 | .90 |
| ❑ C3 Kevin Dineen | 2.00 | .90 |
| ❑ C4 Kenny Jonsson | 2.00 | .90 |
| ❑ C5 Jim Carey | 6.00 | 2.70 |
| ❑ C6 Todd Marchant | 2.00 | .90 |
| ❑ C7 David Oliver | 2.00 | .90 |
| ❑ C8 Yanic Perreault | 2.00 | .90 |
| ❑ C9 Chris Therien | 1.00 | .45 |
| ❑ C10 Viktor Kozlov | 2.00 | .90 |
| ❑ C11 Valeri Bure | 2.00 | .90 |
| ❑ C12 Nikolai Khabibulin | 8.00 | 3.60 |
| ❑ C13 Steven Rice | 1.00 | .45 |
| ❑ C14 Mike Kennedy | 1.00 | .45 |
| ❑ C15 Peter Bondra | 8.00 | 3.60 |
| ❑ C16 Sergei Zubov | 2.00 | .90 |
| ❑ C17 Slava Kozlov | 2.00 | .90 |
| ❑ C18 Chris Osgood | 15.00 | 6.75 |
| ❑ C19 Darren McCarty | 2.00 | .90 |
| ❑ C20 Jason Dawe | 1.00 | .45 |
| ❑ C21 Trevor Kidd | 2.00 | .90 |
| ❑ C22 Tommy Salo | 2.00 | .90 |
| ❑ C23 Michal Pivonka | 1.00 | .45 |
| ❑ C24 Zigmund Palffy | 8.00 | 3.60 |

## 1995-96 Collector's Edge Ice Livin' Large

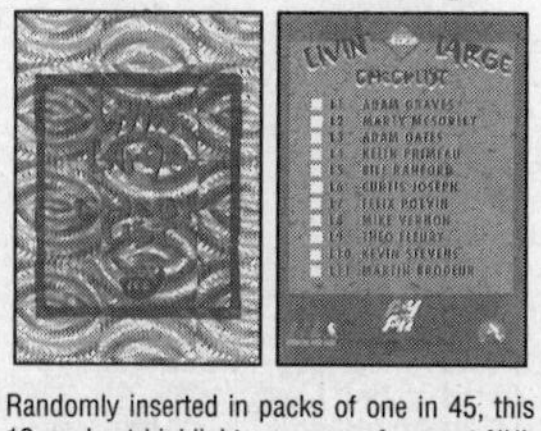

Randomly inserted in packs of one in 45, this 12-card set highlights a group of current NHL stars who earned their stripes playing in the minor leagues. The players are featured in their AHL or IHL togs. The twelfth card is an NNO checklist.

| | MINT | NRMT |
|---|---|---|
| COMPLETE SET (12) | 50.00 | 22.00 |
| COMMON CARD (L1-L11) | 4.00 | 1.80 |
| ❑ L1 Adam Graves | 4.00 | 1.80 |
| ❑ L2 Marty McSorley | 4.00 | 1.80 |
| ❑ L3 Adam Oates | 4.00 | 1.80 |
| ❑ L4 Keith Primeau | 4.00 | 1.80 |
| ❑ L5 Bill Ranford | 6.00 | 2.70 |
| ❑ L6 Curtis Joseph | 8.00 | 3.60 |
| ❑ L7 Felix Potvin | 8.00 | 3.60 |
| ❑ L8 Mike Vernon | 6.00 | 2.70 |
| ❑ L9 Theo Fleury | 6.00 | 2.70 |
| ❑ L10 Kevin Stevens | 4.00 | 1.80 |
| ❑ L11 Martin Brodeur | 25.00 | 11.00 |
| ❑ NNO Checklist | 2.00 | .90 |

## 1995-96 Collector's Edge Ice QuantumMotion

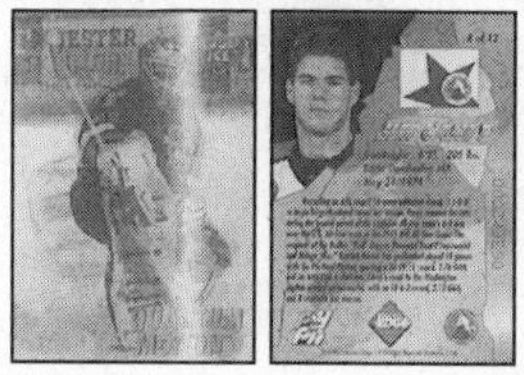

Randomly inserted in packs at a rate of 1:75 packs, this 12-card set celebrates top minor leaguers using QuantumMotion technology that gives the action the appearance of movement on the card front.

| | MINT | NRMT |
|---|---|---|
| COMPLETE SET (12) | 30.00 | 13.50 |
| COMMON CARD (IR1-IR12) | 2.00 | .90 |
| ❑ IR1 Manny Fernandez | 4.00 | 1.80 |
| ❑ IR2 Pokey Reddick | 2.00 | .90 |
| ❑ IR3 Yanic Perreault | 2.00 | .90 |
| ❑ IR4 Rob Brown | 2.00 | .90 |
| ❑ IR5 Hubie McDonough | 2.00 | .90 |
| ❑ IR6 Stan Drulia | 2.00 | .90 |
| ❑ IR7 Michel Picard | 2.00 | .90 |
| ❑ IR8 Jim Carey | 10.00 | 4.50 |
| ❑ IR9 Martin Lapointe | 2.00 | .90 |
| ❑ IR10 Valeri Bure | 2.00 | .90 |
| ❑ IR11 Martin Brochu | 2.00 | .90 |
| ❑ IR12 Corey Schwab | 4.00 | 1.80 |

## 1995-96 Collector's Edge Ice The Wall

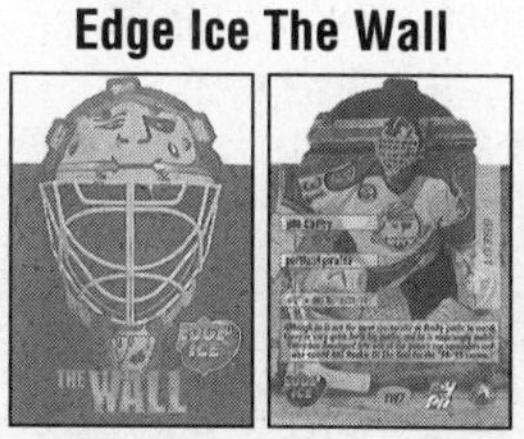

Randomly inserted in packs at a rate of 1:15, this 12-card die-cut set focuses on some of the colorful masks being worn by goalies in the minors. These cards also were distributed in complete set form in cellophane wrap with each box. Many other singles were given away as promotional cards; these cards do not vary in any way from those which were randomly inserted.

| | MINT | NRMT |
|---|---|---|
| COMPLETE SET (12) | 12.00 | 5.50 |
| COMMON CARD (G1-G12) | 1.00 | .45 |
| ❑ G1 Ray LeBlanc | 1.00 | .45 |
| ❑ G2 Manny Fernandez | 2.00 | .90 |
| ❑ G3 Rick Knickle | 1.00 | .45 |
| ❑ G4 Troy Gamble | 1.00 | .45 |
| ❑ G5 Pokey Reddick | 1.00 | .45 |
| ❑ G6 Wendell Young | 1.00 | .45 |
| ❑ G7 Jim Carey | 2.00 | .90 |
| ❑ G8 Dwayne Roloson | 1.00 | .45 |
| ❑ G9 Les Kuntar | 1.00 | .45 |
| ❑ G10 Mike Dunham | 2.00 | .90 |
| ❑ G11 Eric Fichaud | 2.00 | .90 |
| ❑ G12 Kevin Hodson | 3.00 | 1.35 |

## 1995 Images

This 100-card set features top NHL prospects currently playing in the juniors, minors or overseas. The standard-sized cards feature full-bleed color photography over a metallic sheen background. The Classic logo is in the upper left corner, while the Images logo, player name and postion rest on a blue and silver bar near the bottom. The backs feature another color photo, stats and the logos of the licensing bodies. One autographed card was found in each box. A total of 1995 individually numbered 12-box cases were produced.

| | MINT | NRMT |
|---|---|---|
| COMPLETE SET (100) | 12.00 | 5.50 |
| COMMON CARD (1-100) | .10 | .05 |
| ❑ 1 Bryan Berard | 1.00 | .45 |
| ❑ 2 Jeff Friesen | .50 | .23 |
| ❑ 3 Tommy Salo | .50 | .23 |
| ❑ 4 Jim Carey | 1.00 | .45 |
| ❑ 5 Wade Redden | .60 | .25 |
| ❑ 6 Jocelyn Thibault | 1.00 | .45 |
| ❑ 7 Ian Laperriere | .10 | .05 |
| ❑ 8 Todd Marchant | .10 | .05 |
| ❑ 9 Blaine Lacher | .40 | .18 |
| ❑ 10 Pavel Bure | 2.00 | .90 |
| ❑ 11 Alex Vasilevskii | .10 | .05 |
| ❑ 12 Jason Doig | .25 | .11 |
| ❑ 13 Eric Fichaud | .75 | .35 |
| ❑ 14 Eric Daze | .75 | .35 |
| ❑ 15 Ed Jovanovski | 1.50 | .70 |
| ❑ 16 Alexander Selivanov | .20 | .09 |
| ❑ 17 Brent Gretzky | .20 | .09 |
| ❑ 18 Terry Ryan | .40 | .18 |
| ❑ 19 Chris Wells | .10 | .05 |
| ❑ 20 Wade Belak | .10 | .05 |
| ❑ 21 Kevin Dineen | .10 | .05 |
| ❑ 22 Craig Fisher | .10 | .05 |
| ❑ 23 Jan Caloun | .10 | .05 |
| ❑ 24 Manny Fernandez | .25 | .11 |
| ❑ 25 Radek Bonk | .40 | .18 |
| ❑ 26 Dave Christian | .10 | .05 |
| ❑ 27 Patrice Tardif | .10 | .05 |
| ❑ 28 Kevin Brown | .10 | .05 |
| ❑ 29 Hubie McDonough | .10 | .05 |
| ❑ 30 Yan Golubovsky | .10 | .05 |
| ❑ 31 Steve Larouche | .10 | .05 |
| ❑ 32 Chris Therien | .10 | .05 |
| ❑ 33 Craig Darby | .10 | .05 |
| ❑ 34 Dwayne Norris | .10 | .05 |
| ❑ 35 Roman Oksiuta | .10 | .05 |
| ❑ 36 Steve Washburn | .10 | .05 |
| ❑ 37 Todd Bertuzzi | .25 | .11 |
| ❑ 38 Cory Stillman | .15 | .07 |
| ❑ 39 Steve Kelly | .40 | .18 |
| ❑ 40 Nathan LaFayette | .10 | .05 |
| ❑ 41 Dwayne Roloson | .20 | .09 |
| ❑ 42 Nikolai Khabibulin | .75 | .35 |
| ❑ 43 Radim Bicanek | .10 | .05 |
| ❑ 44 Jeff O'Neill | .40 | .18 |
| ❑ 45 Jason Bonsignore | .10 | .05 |
| ❑ 46 Shean Donovan | .10 | .05 |
| ❑ 47 Wayne Primeau | .15 | .07 |
| ❑ 48 Jamie Langenbrunner | .75 | .35 |
| ❑ 49 Dan Cloutier | .50 | .23 |
| ❑ 50 Ethan Moreau | .50 | .23 |
| ❑ 51 Brad Bombardir | .10 | .05 |
| ❑ 52 Jason Muzzatti | .25 | .11 |
| ❑ 53 Jassen Cullimore | .10 | .05 |
| ❑ 54 Jason Zent | .10 | .05 |
| ❑ 55 Sergei Gonchar | .15 | .07 |
| ❑ 56 Steve Rucchin | .25 | .11 |
| ❑ 57 Rob Cowie | .10 | .05 |
| ❑ 58 Miroslav Satan | 1.00 | .45 |
| ❑ 59 Kenny Jonsson | .40 | .18 |
| ❑ 60 Adam Deadmarsh | .60 | .25 |
| ❑ 61 Mike Dunham | .60 | .25 |
| ❑ 62 Corey Hirsch | .50 | .23 |
| ❑ 63 Janne Laukkanen | .15 | .07 |
| ❑ 64 Craig Conroy | .10 | .05 |
| ❑ 65 Ryan Sittler | .10 | .05 |
| ❑ 66 Jeff Nelson | .10 | .05 |
| ❑ 67 Michel Picard | .10 | .05 |
| ❑ 68 Mark Astley | .10 | .05 |
| ❑ 69 Lonny Bohonos | .20 | .09 |
| ❑ 70 Evgeny Ryabchikov | .20 | .09 |
| ❑ 71 Chris Osgood | 1.50 | .70 |
| ❑ 72 Manon Rheaume | 2.50 | 1.10 |
| ❑ 73 Mike Kennedy | .10 | .05 |
| ❑ 74 Deron Quint | .25 | .11 |
| ❑ 75 Jamie Storr | .60 | .25 |
| ❑ 76 Aris Brimanis | .10 | .05 |
| ❑ 77 Valeri Bure | .25 | .11 |
| ❑ 78 Rene Corbet | .15 | .07 |
| ❑ 79 David Oliver | .10 | .05 |
| ❑ 80 Chris McAlpine | .10 | .05 |
| ❑ 81 Petr Sykora | .75 | .35 |
| ❑ 82 Brad Church | .40 | .18 |
| ❑ 83 Daymond Langkow | .60 | .25 |
| ❑ 84 Chad Kilger | .60 | .25 |
| ❑ 85 Shane Doan | .40 | .18 |
| ❑ 86 Jeff Ware | .10 | .05 |
| ❑ 87 Christian Laflamme | .10 | .05 |
| ❑ 88 Cory Cross | .10 | .05 |
| ❑ 89 Al Secord | .10 | .05 |
| ❑ 90 Jason Woolley | .20 | .09 |
| ❑ 91 Bryan McCabe | .20 | .09 |
| ❑ 92 Travis Richards | .10 | .05 |
| ❑ 93 Andrei Nazarov | .10 | .05 |
| ❑ 94 Mike Pomichter | .10 | .05 |
| ❑ 95 Chris Marinucci | .10 | .05 |
| ❑ 96 Jean-Yves Roy | .10 | .05 |
| ❑ 97 Brian Rolston | .25 | .11 |
| ❑ 98 Aaron Ward | .15 | .07 |
| ❑ 99 Jim Carey CL | .60 | .25 |
| ❑ 100 Pavel Bure CL | .40 | .18 |

## 1995 Images Gold

These 100 standard-size cards were issued as a one-per-pack parallel to the Images set. The card design is identical to the standard Images card, except for the metallic background being a golden tone rather than the standard silver.

| | MINT | NRMT |
|---|---|---|
| COMPLETE SET (100) | 40.00 | 18.00 |

| | | |
|---|---|---|
| COMMON CARD (1-100) | .25 | .11 |
| *STARS: 1.5X TO 2.5X BASIC CARDS | | |

## 1995 Images Autographs

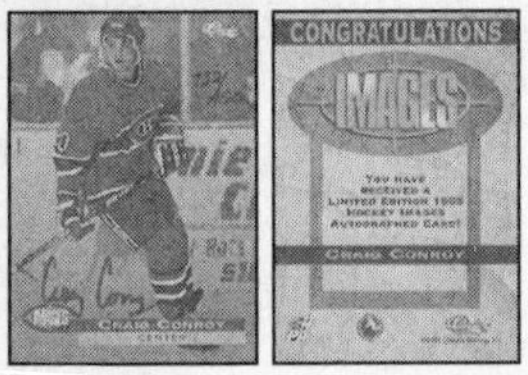

These 22 standard-size cards were random inserts throughout the packs. The card design is identical to the standard Images card except for the facsimile autograph inscribed across the picture. The number of cards signed is indicated in parenthesis.

| | MINT | NRMT |
|---|---|---|
| COMPLETE SET (22) | 350.00 | 160.00 |
| COMMON AUTOGRAPH | 8.00 | 3.60 |
| ❑ 2A Jeff Friesen/1500 | 30.00 | 13.50 |
| ❑ 6A Jocelyn Thibault/1185 | 30.00 | 13.50 |
| ❑ 9A Blaine Lacher/1500 | 15.00 | 6.75 |
| ❑ 25A Radek Bonk/970 | 15.00 | 6.75 |
| ❑ 30A Yan Golubovsky/1500 | 10.00 | 4.50 |
| ❑ 36A Steve Washburn/1500 | 10.00 | 4.50 |
| ❑ 41A Dwayne Roloson/1115 | 12.00 | 5.50 |
| ❑ 45A Jason Bonsignore/1500 | 15.00 | 6.75 |
| ❑ 46A Shean Donovan/1500 | 12.00 | 5.50 |
| ❑ 48A Jamie Langenbrunner/1500 | 30.00 | 13.50 |
| ❑ 54A Jason Zent/1125 | 10.00 | 4.50 |
| ❑ 59A Kenny Jonsson/1180 | 15.00 | 6.75 |
| ❑ 60A Adam Deadmarsh/1500 | 40.00 | 18.00 |
| ❑ 64A Craig Conroy/1170 | 10.00 | 4.50 |
| ❑ 74A Deron Quint/1500 | 15.00 | 6.75 |
| ❑ 76A Aris Brimanis/1500 | 10.00 | 4.50 |
| ❑ 79A David Oliver/1500 | 10.00 | 4.50 |
| ❑ 80A Chris McAlpine/1185 | 10.00 | 4.50 |
| ❑ 81A Petr Sykora/1500 | 25.00 | 11.00 |
| ❑ 94A Mike Pomichter/1175 | 10.00 | 4.50 |
| ❑ 95A Chris Marinucci/1500 | 12.00 | 5.50 |
| ❑ 98A Aaron Ward/1190 | 12.00 | 5.50 |

## 1995 Images Clear Excitement

This 20-card standard-size set was randomly inserted only in Hot boxes. Essentially, the odds of finding one of these cards was 1, 152 packs. Each pack in a Hot box has 3 cards from any of the five insert sets. These clear cards feature color player action cutouts on their fronts. The player's name appears in a blue bar on the left. The backs carry the reverse image as a shadow with the player's name in an oval across it. The blue bar on the left contains information about the player and the card number at the top.

| | MINT | NRMT |
|---|---|---|
| COMPLETE SET (20) | 350.00 | 160.00 |
| COMMON CARD (CE1-CE20) | 8.00 | 3.60 |
| ❑ CE1 Bryan Berard | 30.00 | 13.50 |
| ❑ CE2 Jeff Friesen | 15.00 | 6.75 |
| ❑ CE3 Tommy Salo | 15.00 | 6.75 |
| ❑ CE4 Jim Carey | 15.00 | 6.75 |
| ❑ CE5 Wade Redden | 8.00 | 3.60 |
| ❑ CE6 Jocelyn Thibault | 30.00 | 13.50 |
| ❑ CE7 Ian Laperriere | 8.00 | 3.60 |
| ❑ CE8 Todd Marchant | 8.00 | 3.60 |
| ❑ CE9 Blaine Lacher | 15.00 | 6.75 |
| ❑ CE10 Pavel Bure | 50.00 | 22.00 |
| ❑ CE11 Petr Sykora | 15.00 | 6.75 |
| ❑ CE12 Daymond Langkow | 15.00 | 6.75 |
| ❑ CE13 Radek Bonk | 15.00 | 6.75 |
| ❑ CE14 Patrice Tardif | 8.00 | 3.60 |
| ❑ CE15 Jeff Nelson | 8.00 | 3.60 |
| ❑ CE16 Jeff O'Neill | 15.00 | 6.75 |
| ❑ CE17 Ed Jovanovski | 20.00 | 9.00 |
| ❑ CE18 Jason Doig | 8.00 | 3.60 |
| ❑ CE19 Chris Marinucci | 8.00 | 3.60 |
| ❑ CE20 Manon Rheaume | 80.00 | 36.00 |

## 1995 Images Platinum Players

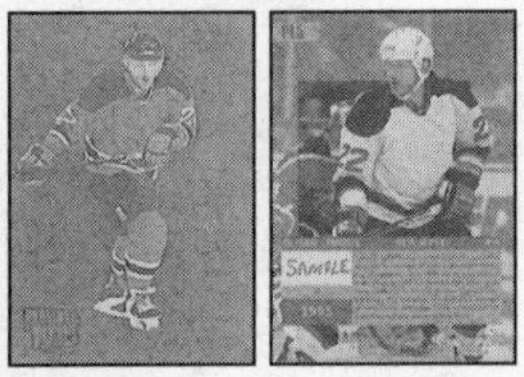

The cards in this 10 card standard-size set were randomly inserted at a rate of one per 36 packs. The fronts have a color action photo with a green and silver foil background. The word "Images" is at the top and "Platinum Player" is at the bottom. The backs have a color action photo with a green tint in the background. Player information appears at the bottom and each card is numbered out of 1,995.

| | MINT | NRMT |
|---|---|---|
| COMPLETE SET (10) | 30.00 | 13.50 |
| COMMON CARD (PL1-PL10) | 2.00 | .90 |
| ❑ PL1 Pavel Bure | 15.00 | 6.75 |
| ❑ PL2 Tony Granato | 2.00 | .90 |
| ❑ PL3 Kevin Dineen | 2.00 | .90 |
| ❑ PL4 Ron Hextall | 4.00 | 1.80 |
| ❑ PL5 Claude Lemieux | 3.00 | 1.35 |
| ❑ PL6 Mark Recchi | 5.00 | 2.20 |
| ❑ PL7 Benoit Hogue | 2.00 | .90 |
| ❑ PL8 Tim Cheveldae | 2.00 | .90 |
| ❑ PL9 Darcy Wakaluk | 2.00 | .90 |
| ❑ PL10 Todd Gill | 2.00 | .90 |

## 1995 Images Platinum Premier Draft Choice

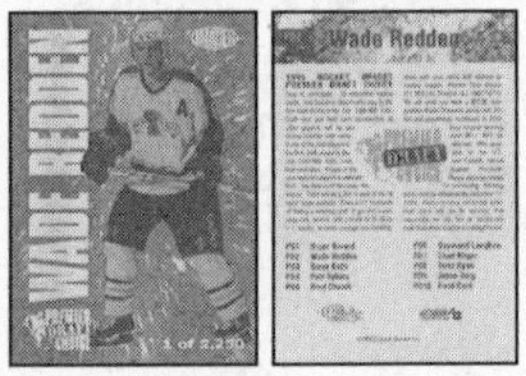

One card from this 10 standard-size set was randomly inserted in every 48 packs. The card of Bryan Berard, the no. 1 draft choice, was redeemable for a 25.00 Manon Rheaume autographed phone card. The offer expired 12/31/95. The fronts feature a player action photo on a borderless blue and silver background with the player's name printed vertically down the left side. The backs carry the card number and players name in a marble blue stripe at the top with the redemption directions below. A checklist of the 10 cards is printed at the bottom.

| | MINT | NRMT |
|---|---|---|
| COMPLETE SET (10) | 50.00 | 22.00 |
| COMMON CARD (PD1-PD10) | 2.00 | .90 |
| ❑ PD1 Bryan Berard | 15.00 | 6.75 |
| ❑ PD2 Wade Redden | 8.00 | 3.60 |
| ❑ PD3 Steve Kelly | 8.00 | 3.60 |
| ❑ PD4 Petr Sykora | 8.00 | 3.60 |
| ❑ PD5 Brad Church | 8.00 | 3.60 |
| ❑ PD6 Daymond Langkow | 8.00 | 3.60 |
| ❑ PD7 Chad Kilger | 8.00 | 3.60 |
| ❑ PD8 Terry Ryan | 8.00 | 3.60 |
| ❑ PD9 Jason Doig | 4.00 | 1.80 |
| ❑ PD10 Field Card | 2.00 | .90 |

## 1995 Images Platinum Prospects

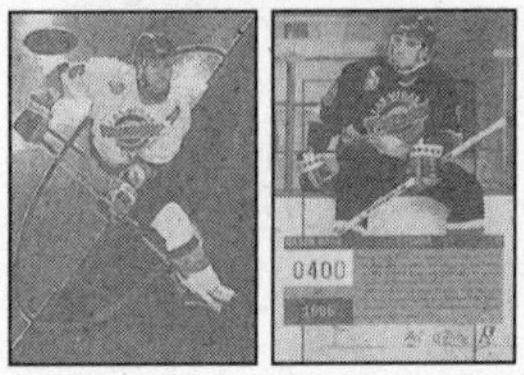

The ten cards in this set (found 1:36 packs) feature some of the top prospects for NHL stardom. The cards feature a color player photo over a diagonally split silver and blue metallic background. The Images logo is in the top left corner, while the Platinum Prospects logo rests in the bottom right, beside the player's name in stylized script. The backs feature another color photo and a blurb assessing the player's chances. Each card is serially numbered out of 1,995 at the bottom left corner.

| | MINT | NRMT |
|---|---|---|
| COMPLETE SET (10) | 30.00 | 13.50 |
| COMMON CARD (PR1-PR10) | 1.00 | .45 |
| ❑ PR1 Jeff Nelson | 1.00 | .45 |
| ❑ PR2 Jim Carey | 2.50 | 1.10 |
| ❑ PR3 Ian Laperriere | 1.00 | .45 |
| ❑ PR4 Chris Osgood | 15.00 | 6.75 |
| ❑ PR5 Todd Marchant | 1.00 | .45 |
| ❑ PR6 Radek Bonk | 2.50 | 1.10 |
| ❑ PR7 Chris Marinucci | 1.00 | .45 |
| ❑ PR8 Tommy Salo | 2.50 | 1.10 |
| ❑ PR9 Manny Fernandez | 2.50 | 1.10 |
| ❑ PR10 Jan Caloun | 1.00 | .45 |

## 1952-53 Juniors Blue Tint

The 1952-53 Junior set contains 182 cards measuring approximately 2" by 3". The cards have a blue tint and are numbered on the back. It is not known at this time who sponsored this set. Key cards in this set are "Pre-Rookie

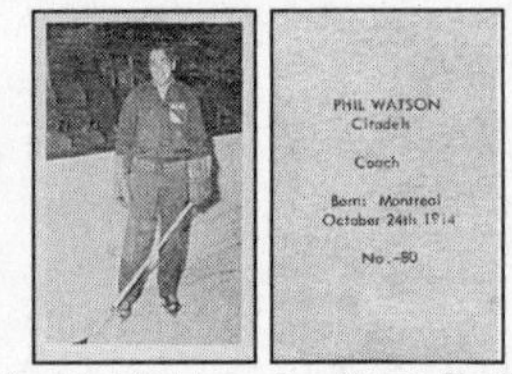


Cards" of Al Arbour, Don Cherry, Charlie Hodge, John Muckler, Henri Richard, and Harry Sinden.

| | EX-MT | VG-E |
|---|---|---|
| COMPLETE SET (182) | 2000.00 | 900.00 |
| COMMON CARD (1-182) | 8.00 | 3.60 |
| ❑ 1 Dennis Riggin | 15.00 | 6.75 |
| ❑ 2 Joe Zorica | 8.00 | 3.60 |
| ❑ 3 Larry Hillman | 15.00 | 6.75 |
| ❑ 4 Edward(Ted) Reid | 8.00 | 3.60 |
| ❑ 5 Al Arbour | 60.00 | 27.00 |
| ❑ 6 Marlin McAlendin | 8.00 | 3.60 |
| ❑ 7 Ross Graham | 8.00 | 3.60 |
| ❑ 8 Cumming Burton | 8.00 | 3.60 |
| ❑ 9 Ed Palamar | 8.00 | 3.60 |
| ❑ 10 Elmer Skov | 10.00 | 4.50 |
| ❑ 11 Eddie Louttit | 8.00 | 3.60 |
| ❑ 12 Gerry Price | 8.00 | 3.60 |
| ❑ 13 Lou Dietrich | 8.00 | 3.60 |
| ❑ 14 Gaston Marcotte | 8.00 | 3.60 |
| ❑ 15 Bob Brown | 8.00 | 3.60 |
| ❑ 16 Archie Burton | 8.00 | 3.60 |
| ❑ 17 Marv Edwards | 20.00 | 9.00 |
| ❑ 18 Norman Defelice | 10.00 | 4.50 |
| ❑ 19 Pete Kamula | 8.00 | 3.60 |
| ❑ 20 Charles Marshall | 8.00 | 3.60 |
| ❑ 21 Alex Leslie | 8.00 | 3.60 |
| ❑ 22 Minpy Roberts | 8.00 | 3.60 |
| ❑ 23 Danny Poliziani | 8.00 | 3.60 |
| ❑ 24 Allen Kellogg | 8.00 | 3.60 |
| ❑ 25 Brian Cullen | 20.00 | 9.00 |
| ❑ 26 Ken Schinkel | 10.00 | 4.50 |
| ❑ 27 W. Hass | 8.00 | 3.60 |
| ❑ 28 Don Nash | 8.00 | 3.60 |
| ❑ 29 Robert Maxwell | 8.00 | 3.60 |
| ❑ 30 Eddie Mateka | 8.00 | 3.60 |
| ❑ 31 Joe Kastelic | 7.00 | 3.10 |
| ❑ 32 Hank Ciesla | 10.00 | 4.50 |
| ❑ 33 Hugh Barlow | 8.00 | 3.60 |
| ❑ 34 Claude Roy | 8.00 | 3.60 |
| ❑ 35 Jean-Guy Gamache | 8.00 | 3.60 |
| ❑ 36 Leon Michelin | 8.00 | 3.60 |
| ❑ 37 Gerard Bergeron | 8.00 | 3.60 |
| ❑ 38 Herve Lalonde | 8.00 | 3.60 |
| ❑ 39 J.M. Cossette | 8.00 | 3.60 |
| ❑ 40 Jean-Guy Gendron | 15.00 | 6.75 |
| ❑ 41 Gamill Bedard | 8.00 | 3.60 |
| ❑ 42 Alfred Soucy | 8.00 | 3.60 |
| ❑ 43 Jean Leclerc | 8.00 | 3.60 |
| ❑ 44 Raymond St.Cyr | 10.00 | 4.50 |
| ❑ 45 Lester Lahaye | 8.00 | 3.60 |
| ❑ 46 Yvan Houle | 8.00 | 3.60 |
| ❑ 47 Louis Desrosiers | 8.00 | 3.60 |
| ❑ 48 Douglas Lessor | 8.00 | 3.60 |
| ❑ 49 Irvin Scott | 8.00 | 3.60 |
| ❑ 50 Danny Blair | 8.00 | 3.60 |
| ❑ 51 Jim Connelly | 10.00 | 4.50 |
| ❑ 52 William Chalmers | 8.00 | 3.60 |
| ❑ 53 Frank Bettiol | 8.00 | 3.60 |
| ❑ 54 James Holmes | 8.00 | 3.60 |
| ❑ 55 Birley Dimme | 8.00 | 3.60 |
| ❑ 56 Donald Beattie | 8.00 | 3.60 |
| ❑ 57 Terrance Chattington | 8.00 | 3.60 |
| ❑ 58 Bruce Wallace | 8.00 | 3.60 |
| ❑ 59 William McCreary | 10.00 | 4.50 |
| ❑ 60 Fred Brady | 8.00 | 3.60 |
| ❑ 61 Ronald Murphy | 10.00 | 4.50 |
| ❑ 62 Lavi Purola | 8.00 | 3.60 |
| ❑ 63 George Whyte | 8.00 | 3.60 |
| ❑ 64 Marcel Paille | 40.00 | 18.00 |
| ❑ 65 Maurice Collins | 8.00 | 3.60 |
| ❑ 66 Gerard(Butch) Houle | 10.00 | 4.50 |
| ❑ 67 Gilles Laperriere | 8.00 | 3.60 |
| ❑ 68 Robert Chevalier | 8.00 | 3.60 |
| ❑ 69 Bertrand Lepage | 8.00 | 3.60 |
| ❑ 70 Michel Labadie | 8.00 | 3.60 |
| ❑ 71 Gabriel Alain | 8.00 | 3.60 |
| ❑ 72 Jean-Jacques Pichette | 10.00 | 4.50 |
| ❑ 73A Camille Henry (Citadelles) | 25.00 | 11.00 |
| ❑ 73B Camille Henry (New York) | 200.00 | 90.00 |
| ❑ 74 Jean-Guy Gignac | 8.00 | 3.60 |
| ❑ 75 Leo Amadio | 10.00 | 4.50 |
| ❑ 76 Gilles Thibault | 10.00 | 4.50 |
| ❑ 77 Gaston Pelletier | 10.00 | 4.50 |
| ❑ 78 Adolph Kukulowicz | 10.00 | 4.50 |
| ❑ 79 Roland Leclerc | 8.00 | 3.60 |
| ❑ 80 Phil Watson CO | 40.00 | 18.00 |
| ❑ 81 Raymond Cyr | 10.00 | 4.50 |
| ❑ 82 Jacques Marcotte | 8.00 | 3.60 |
| ❑ 83 Floyd(Bud) Hillman | 10.00 | 4.50 |
| ❑ 84 Bob Attersley | 8.00 | 3.60 |
| ❑ 85 Harry Sinden | 60.00 | 27.00 |
| ❑ 86 Stan Parker | 8.00 | 3.60 |
| ❑ 87 Bob Mader | 8.00 | 3.60 |
| ❑ 88 Roger Maisonneuve | 8.00 | 3.60 |
| ❑ 89 Phil Chapman | 8.00 | 3.60 |
| ❑ 90 Don McIntosh | 8.00 | 3.60 |
| ❑ 91 Jack Armstrong | 8.00 | 3.60 |
| ❑ 92 Carlo Montemurro | 8.00 | 3.60 |
| ❑ 93 Ken Courtney | 8.00 | 3.60 |
| ❑ 94 Bill Stewart | 10.00 | 4.50 |
| ❑ 95 Gerald Casey | 8.00 | 3.60 |
| ❑ 96 Fred Etcher | 8.00 | 3.60 |
| ❑ 97 Orrin Carver | 8.00 | 3.60 |
| ❑ 98 Ralph Willis | 8.00 | 3.60 |
| ❑ 99 Kenneth Robertson | 8.00 | 3.60 |
| ❑ 100 Don Cherry | 350.00 | 160.00 |
| ❑ 101 Fred Pletsch | 8.00 | 3.60 |
| ❑ 102 Larry Thibault | 8.00 | 3.60 |
| ❑ 103 James Robertson | 8.00 | 3.60 |
| ❑ 104 Orval Tessier | 15.00 | 6.75 |
| ❑ 105 Jack Higgins | 8.00 | 3.60 |
| ❑ 106 Robert White | 8.00 | 3.60 |
| ❑ 107 Doug Mohns | 30.00 | 13.50 |
| ❑ 108 William Sexton | 8.00 | 3.60 |
| ❑ 109 John Martan | 8.00 | 3.60 |
| ❑ 110 Tony Poeta | 10.00 | 4.50 |
| ❑ 111 Don McKenney | 15.00 | 6.75 |
| ❑ 112 Bill Harrington | 8.00 | 3.60 |
| ❑ 113 Allen(Skip) Peal | 8.00 | 3.60 |
| ❑ 114 John Ford | 8.00 | 3.60 |
| ❑ 115 Ken Collins | 10.00 | 4.50 |
| ❑ 116 Marc Boileau | 10.00 | 4.50 |
| ❑ 117 Doug Vaughan | 8.00 | 3.60 |
| ❑ 118 Gilles Boisvert | 8.00 | 3.60 |
| ❑ 119 Buddy Horne | 8.00 | 3.60 |
| ❑ 120 Graham Joyce | 8.00 | 3.60 |
| ❑ 121 Gary Collins | 8.00 | 3.60 |
| ❑ 122 Roy Greenan | 8.00 | 3.60 |
| ❑ 123 Beryl Klynck | 8.00 | 3.60 |
| ❑ 124 Grieg Hicks | 8.00 | 3.60 |
| ❑ 125 Jack(Red) Novak | 8.00 | 3.60 |
| ❑ 126 Ken Tennant | 8.00 | 3.60 |
| ❑ 127 Glen Cressman | 8.00 | 3.60 |
| ❑ 128 Curly Davies | 8.00 | 3.60 |
| ❑ 129 Charlie Hodge | 75.00 | 34.00 |
| ❑ 130 Bob McCord | 10.00 | 4.50 |
| ❑ 131 Gordie Hollinworth | 8.00 | 3.60 |
| ❑ 132 Ronald Pilon | 8.00 | 3.60 |
| ❑ 133 Brian Mackay | 8.00 | 3.60 |
| ❑ 134 Yvon Chasle | 8.00 | 3.60 |
| ❑ 135 Denis Boucher | 10.00 | 4.50 |
| ❑ 136 Claude Boileau | 8.00 | 3.60 |
| ❑ 137 Claude Vinet | 8.00 | 3.60 |
| ❑ 138 Claude Provost | 40.00 | 18.00 |
| ❑ 139 Henri Richard | 250.00 | 110.00 |
| ❑ 140 Les Lilley | 8.00 | 3.60 |
| ❑ 141 Phil Goyette | 25.00 | 11.00 |
| ❑ 142 Guy Rousseau | 8.00 | 3.60 |
| ❑ 143 Paul Knox | 8.00 | 3.60 |
| ❑ 144 Bill Lee | 8.00 | 3.60 |
| ❑ 145 Ted Topazzini | 10.00 | 4.50 |
| ❑ 146 Marc Reaume | 10.00 | 4.50 |
| ❑ 147 Bill Dineen | 35.00 | 16.00 |
| ❑ 148 Ed Plata | 8.00 | 3.60 |
| ❑ 149 Noel Price | 10.00 | 4.50 |
| ❑ 150 Mike Ratchford | 8.00 | 3.60 |
| ❑ 151 Jim Logan | 8.00 | 3.60 |
| ❑ 152 Art Clune | 8.00 | 3.60 |
| ❑ 153 Jerry MacNamara | 8.00 | 3.60 |
| ❑ 154 Jack Caffery | 12.00 | 5.50 |
| ❑ 155 Less Duff | 8.00 | 3.60 |
| ❑ 156 Murray Costello | 12.00 | 5.50 |
| ❑ 157 Ed Chadwick | 80.00 | 36.00 |
| ❑ 158 Mike Desilets | 8.00 | 3.60 |
| ❑ 159 Ross Watson | 8.00 | 3.60 |
| ❑ 160 Roger Landry | 8.00 | 3.60 |
| ❑ 161 Terry O'Connor | 8.00 | 3.60 |
| ❑ 162 Ovila Gagnon | 8.00 | 3.60 |
| ❑ 163 Dave Broadbelt | 8.00 | 3.60 |
| ❑ 164 Sandy Monrisson | 8.00 | 3.60 |
| ❑ 165 John MacGillvray | 8.00 | 3.60 |
| ❑ 166 Claude Beaupre | 8.00 | 3.60 |
| ❑ 167 Eddie Eustache | 8.00 | 3.60 |
| ❑ 168 Stan Rodek | 8.00 | 3.60 |
| ❑ 169 Maurice Mantha | 10.00 | 4.50 |
| ❑ 170 Hector Lalande | 10.00 | 4.50 |
| ❑ 171 Bob Wilson | 8.00 | 3.60 |
| ❑ 172 Frank Bonello | 8.00 | 3.60 |
| ❑ 173 Peter Kowalchuch | 8.00 | 3.60 |
| ❑ 174 Les Binkley | 40.00 | 18.00 |
| ❑ 175 John Muckler | 40.00 | 18.00 |
| ❑ 176 Ken Wharram | 25.00 | 11.00 |
| ❑ 177 John Sleaver | 8.00 | 3.60 |
| ❑ 178 Ralph Markarian | 8.00 | 3.60 |
| ❑ 179 Ken McMeekin | 8.00 | 3.60 |
| ❑ 180 Ron Boomer | 8.00 | 3.60 |
| ❑ 181 Kenneth(Red) Crawford | 8.00 | 3.60 |
| ❑ 182 Jim McBurney | 15.00 | 6.75 |

## 1951-52 Laval Dairy QSHL

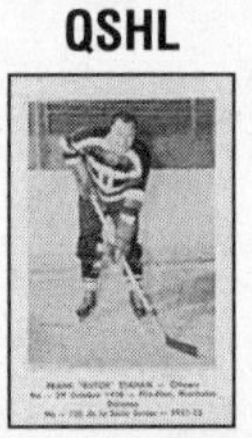

The 1951-52 Laval Dairy QSHL set includes 109 black and white blank-back cards measuring approximately 1 3/4" by 2 1/2". These cards were issued in the province of Quebec and the Ottawa region. The cards are numbered and dated on the front. Key cards in this set are "Pre-Rookie Cards" of Jean Beliveau and Jacques Plante. The card numbering is organized by team as follows: Aces de Quebec (1-18 and 37), Chicoutimi (19-36), Sherbrooke (38-51), Shawinigan Falls (52-67), Valleyfield (68-84), Royals de Montreal (85-100), and Ottawa (101-109).

| | EX-MT | VG-E |
|---|---|---|
| COMPLETE SET (109) | 2000.00 | 900.00 |
| COMMON CARD (1-109) | 8.00 | 3.60 |
| ❑ 1 Jean Beliveau | 600.00 | 275.00 |
| ❑ 2 Jean Marois | 8.00 | 3.60 |
| ❑ 3 Joe Crozier | 15.00 | 6.75 |
| ❑ 4 Jack Gelineau | 8.00 | 3.60 |
| ❑ 5 Murdo McKay | 10.00 | 4.50 |
| ❑ 6 Arthur Leyte | 8.00 | 3.60 |
| ❑ 7 W.(Bill) Leblanc | 8.00 | 3.60 |
| ❑ 8 Robert Hayes | 8.00 | 3.60 |
| ❑ 9 Yogi Kraiger | 10.00 | 4.50 |
| ❑ 10 Frank King | 8.00 | 3.60 |
| ❑ 11 Ludger Tremblay | 10.00 | 4.50 |
| ❑ 12 Jackie Leclair | 30.00 | 13.50 |
| ❑ 13 Martial Pruneau | 8.00 | 3.60 |
| ❑ 14 Armand Gaudreault | 8.00 | 3.60 |
| ❑ 15 Marcel Bonin | 30.00 | 13.50 |
| ❑ 16 Herbie Carnegie | 40.00 | 18.00 |
| ❑ 17 Claude Robert | 8.00 | 3.60 |
| ❑ 18 Phil Renaud | 8.00 | 3.60 |
| ❑ 19 Roland Hebert | 8.00 | 3.60 |
| ❑ 20 Donat Duschene | 8.00 | 3.60 |
| ❑ 21 Jacques Gagnon | 8.00 | 3.60 |
| ❑ 22 Normand Dussault | 10.00 | 4.50 |
| ❑ 23 Stan Smrke | 15.00 | 6.75 |
| ❑ 24 Louis Smrke | 10.00 | 4.50 |
| ❑ 25 Floyd Crawford | 8.00 | 3.60 |
| ❑ 26 Germain Leger | 8.00 | 3.60 |
| ❑ 27 Delphis Franche | 8.00 | 3.60 |
| ❑ 28 Dick Wray | 8.00 | 3.60 |
| ❑ 29 Guildor Levesque | 8.00 | 3.60 |
| ❑ 30 Georges Roy | 8.00 | 3.60 |
| ❑ 31 J.P. Lamirande | 8.00 | 3.60 |
| ❑ 32 Gerard Glaude | 8.00 | 3.60 |
| ❑ 33 Marcel Pelletier | 15.00 | 6.75 |
| ❑ 34 Pete Tkachuck | 8.00 | 3.60 |
| ❑ 35 Sherman White | 8.00 | 3.60 |
| ❑ 36 Jimmy Moore | 8.00 | 3.60 |
| ❑ 37 Punch Imlach | 80.00 | 36.00 |
| ❑ 38 Alex Sandalax | 8.00 | 3.60 |
| ❑ 39 William Kyle | 8.00 | 3.60 |
| ❑ 40 Kenneth Biggs | 8.00 | 3.60 |
| ❑ 41 Peter Wright | 8.00 | 3.60 |
| ❑ 42 Rene Pepin | 8.00 | 3.60 |
| ❑ 43 Tod Campeau | 10.00 | 4.50 |
| ❑ 44 John Smith | 8.00 | 3.60 |
| ❑ 45 Thomas McDougall | 8.00 | 3.60 |
| ❑ 46 Jos. Lepine | 8.00 | 3.60 |
| ❑ 47 Guy Labrie | 8.00 | 3.60 |
| ❑ 48 Roger Bessette | 8.00 | 3.60 |
| ❑ 49 Yvan Dugre | 10.00 | 4.50 |
| ❑ 50 James Planche | 8.00 | 3.60 |
| ❑ 51 Nils Tremblay | 8.00 | 3.60 |
| ❑ 52 Bill MacDonagh | 8.00 | 3.60 |
| ❑ 53 Georges Ouellet | 8.00 | 3.60 |
| ❑ 54 Billy Arcand | 8.00 | 3.60 |
| ❑ 55 Johnny Mahaffy | 10.00 | 4.50 |
| ❑ 56 Bucky Buchanan | 15.00 | 6.75 |
| ❑ 57 Al Miller | 8.00 | 3.60 |
| ❑ 58 Don Penniston | 8.00 | 3.60 |
| ❑ 59 Spike Laliberte | 8.00 | 3.60 |
| ❑ 60 Ernie Oakley | 8.00 | 3.60 |
| ❑ 61 Jack Bownass | 8.00 | 3.60 |
| ❑ 62 Ted Hodgson | 8.00 | 3.60 |
| ❑ 63 Lyall Wiseman | 8.00 | 3.60 |
| ❑ 64 Erwin Grosse | 8.00 | 3.60 |
| ❑ 65 Mel Read | 8.00 | 3.60 |
| ❑ 66 Lloyd Henchberger | 8.00 | 3.60 |
| ❑ 67 Jack Taylor | 8.00 | 3.60 |
| ❑ 68 Marcel Bessette | 8.00 | 3.60 |
| ❑ 69 Jack Schmidt | 8.00 | 3.60 |
| ❑ 70 Paul Saindon | 8.00 | 3.60 |
| ❑ 71 J.P. Bisaillon | 8.00 | 3.60 |
| ❑ 72 Eddie Redmond | 8.00 | 3.60 |
| ❑ 73 Larry Kwong | 15.00 | 6.75 |
| ❑ 74 Andre Corriveau | 8.00 | 3.60 |
| ❑ 75 Kitoute Joanette | 8.00 | 3.60 |
| ❑ 76 Toe Blake | 125.00 | 55.00 |
| ❑ 77 Georges Bougie | 8.00 | 3.60 |
| ❑ 78 Jack Irvine | 8.00 | 3.60 |
| ❑ 79 Paul Larivee | 8.00 | 3.60 |
| ❑ 80 Paul Leclerc | 8.00 | 3.60 |
| ❑ 81 Bertrand Bourassa | 8.00 | 3.60 |
| ❑ 82 Jacques Deslauriers | 8.00 | 3.60 |
| ❑ 83 Bingo Ernst | 8.00 | 3.60 |
| ❑ 84 Gaston Gervais | 8.00 | 3.60 |
| ❑ 85 Gerry Plamondon | 10.00 | 4.50 |
| ❑ 86 Glen Harmon | 8.00 | 3.60 |
| ❑ 87 Bob Friday | 8.00 | 3.60 |
| ❑ 88 Rolland Rousseau | 8.00 | 3.60 |
| ❑ 89 Billy Goold | 8.00 | 3.60 |
| ❑ 90 Lloyd Finkbeiner | 8.00 | 3.60 |
| ❑ 91 Cliff Malone | 8.00 | 3.60 |
| ❑ 92 Jacques Plante | 600.00 | 275.00 |
| ❑ 93 Gerard Desaulniers | 10.00 | 4.50 |
| ❑ 94 Arthur Rose | 8.00 | 3.60 |
| ❑ 95 Jacques Locas | 8.00 | 3.60 |
| ❑ 96 Walter Clune | 8.00 | 3.60 |
| ❑ 97 Louis Denis | 8.00 | 3.60 |
| ❑ 98 Fernand Perreault | 8.00 | 3.60 |
| ❑ 99 Douglas McNeil | 10.00 | 4.50 |
| ❑ 100 Les Douglas | 8.00 | 3.60 |
| ❑ 101 Howard Riopelle | 10.00 | 4.50 |
| ❑ 102 Vic Grigg | 8.00 | 3.60 |
| ❑ 103 Bobby Roberts | 8.00 | 3.60 |
| ❑ 104 Legs Fraser | 8.00 | 3.60 |
| ❑ 105 Butch Stahan | 8.00 | 3.60 |
| ❑ 106 Fritz Frazer | 8.00 | 3.60 |
| ❑ 107 Bill Robinson | 8.00 | 3.60 |
| ❑ 108 Eddie Emberg | 8.00 | 3.60 |
| ❑ 109 Leo Gravelle | 20.00 | 9.00 |

## 1951-52 Laval Dairy Subset

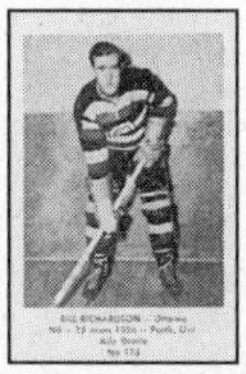

The 1951-52 Laval Dairy Subset includes 66 skip-numbered black and white blank-back cards measuring approximately 1 3/4" by 2 1/2". Apparently, this set was intended to update the QSHL set and was issued after the QSHL set perhaps even as late as the 1952-53 season. The card numbering is organized by team as follows: Aces de Quebec (7-15 and 117), Chicoutimi (25-38), Sherbrooke (39-57), Shawinigan Falls (59-67, 89-90, 94-95, 115, 118, and 120), Valleyfield (68-84 and 116), Royals de Montreal (85-86, 92-93, and 96-97), and Ottawa (98-114, 119, and 121).

| | EX-MT | VG-E |
|---|---|---|
| COMPLETE SET (66) | 1500.00 | 700.00 |
| COMMON CARD | 15.00 | 6.75 |
| □ 4 Jack Gelineau SP | 40.00 | 18.00 |
| □ 7 Al Miller | 15.00 | 6.75 |
| □ 8 Walter Pawlyshyn | 15.00 | 6.75 |
| □ 9 Yogi Kraiger SP | 40.00 | 18.00 |
| □ 10 Al Baccari | 15.00 | 6.75 |
| □ 12 Denis Smith | 15.00 | 6.75 |
| □ 13 Pierre Brillant | 15.00 | 6.75 |
| □ 14 Frank Mario | 15.00 | 6.75 |
| □ 15 Danny Nixon | 15.00 | 6.75 |
| □ 25 Leon Bouchard | 15.00 | 6.75 |
| □ 26 Pete Taillefer | 15.00 | 6.75 |
| □ 29 Bucky Buchanan | 20.00 | 9.00 |
| □ 36 Marius Groleau | 15.00 | 6.75 |
| □ 38 Fernand Perreault | 15.00 | 6.75 |
| □ 39 Robert Drainville | 15.00 | 6.75 |
| □ 40 Ronnie Matthews | 15.00 | 6.75 |
| □ 44 Roger Roberge | 15.00 | 6.75 |
| □ 46 Pete Wywrot | 15.00 | 6.75 |
| □ 50 Gilles Dube | 15.00 | 6.75 |
| □ 51 Nils Tremblay SP | 40.00 | 18.00 |
| □ 52 Bob Pepin | 15.00 | 6.75 |
| □ 53 Dewar Thompson | 15.00 | 6.75 |
| □ 55 Irene St.Hilaire | 15.00 | 6.75 |
| □ 56 Martial Pruneau | 15.00 | 6.75 |
| □ 57 Jacques Locas | 15.00 | 6.75 |
| □ 59 Nelson Podolsky | 15.00 | 6.75 |
| □ 60 Bert Giesebrecht | 15.00 | 6.75 |
| □ 61 Steve Brklaicich | 15.00 | 6.75 |
| □ 65 Jack Hamilton | 15.00 | 6.75 |
| □ 66 Dave Gatherum | 15.00 | 6.75 |
| □ 67 Jean-Marie Plante | 15.00 | 6.75 |
| □ 68 Gordie Haworth | 20.00 | 9.00 |
| □ 69 Jack Schmidt SP | 40.00 | 18.00 |
| □ 70 Bruce Cline | 20.00 | 9.00 |
| □ 72 Phil Vitale | 15.00 | 6.75 |
| □ 81 Carl Smelle | 15.00 | 6.75 |
| □ 84 Tom Smelle | 15.00 | 6.75 |
| □ 85 Gerry Plamondon | 20.00 | 9.00 |
| □ 86 Glen Harmon | 15.00 | 6.75 |
| □ 89 Frank Bathgate | 15.00 | 6.75 |
| □ 90 Bernie Lemonde | 15.00 | 6.75 |
| □ 92 Jacques Plante | 600.00 | 275.00 |
| □ 93 Gerard Desaulniers | 15.00 | 6.75 |
| □ 94 J.C. Lebrun | 15.00 | 6.75 |
| □ 95 Bob Leger | 15.00 | 6.75 |
| □ 96 Walter Clune | 15.00 | 6.75 |
| □ 97 Louis Denis | 15.00 | 6.75 |
| □ 98 Jackie Leclair | 25.00 | 11.00 |
| □ 99 John Arundel | 15.00 | 6.75 |
| □ 100 Leslie(Les) Douglas | 15.00 | 6.75 |
| □ 103 Bobby Robertson | 15.00 | 6.75 |
| □ 104 Ray Fredericks | 15.00 | 6.75 |
| □ 106 Emile Dagenais | 15.00 | 6.75 |
| □ 108 Al Kuntz | 15.00 | 6.75 |
| □ 110 Red Johnson | 15.00 | 6.75 |
| □ 111 John O'Flaherty | 15.00 | 6.75 |
| □ 112 Jack Giesebrecht | 20.00 | 9.00 |
| □ 113 Bill Richardson | 15.00 | 6.75 |
| □ 114 Bep Guidolin | 30.00 | 13.50 |
| □ 115 Roger Bedard | 15.00 | 6.75 |
| □ 116 Renald Lacroix | 15.00 | 6.75 |
| □ 117 Gordie Hudson | 15.00 | 6.75 |
| □ 118 Dick Wray | 15.00 | 6.75 |
| □ 119 Ronnie Hurst | 15.00 | 6.75 |
| □ 120 Eddie Joss | 15.00 | 6.75 |
| □ 121 Lyall Wiseman | 15.00 | 6.75 |

## 1951-52 Laval Dairy Lac St. Jean

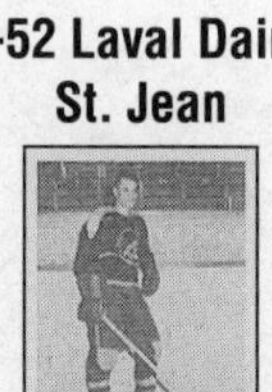

The 1951-52 Laval Dairy Lac St. Jean set includes 59 green-and-white tinted cards measuring approximately 1 3/4" by 2 1/2". The backs are blank. The cards are numbered on the front.

| | EX-MT | VG-E |
|---|---|---|
| COMPLETE SET (59) | 1500.00 | 700.00 |
| COMMON CARD (1-59) | 30.00 | 13.50 |
| □ 1 Eddy Daoust | 40.00 | 18.00 |
| □ 2 Guy Gareau | 30.00 | 13.50 |
| □ 3 Gilles Desrosiers | 30.00 | 13.50 |
| □ 4 Robert Desbiens | 30.00 | 13.50 |
| □ 5 James Hayes | 30.00 | 13.50 |
| □ 6 Paul Gagnon | 30.00 | 13.50 |
| □ 7 Gerry Perreault | 30.00 | 13.50 |
| □ 8 Marcel Dufour | 30.00 | 13.50 |
| □ 9 Armand Bourdon | 30.00 | 13.50 |
| □ 10 Jean-Marc Pichette | 40.00 | 18.00 |
| □ 11 Gerry Gagnon | 30.00 | 13.50 |
| □ 12 Jules Racette | 30.00 | 13.50 |
| □ 13 Real Marcotte | 30.00 | 13.50 |
| □ 14 Gerry Theberge | 30.00 | 13.50 |
| □ 15 Rene Harvey | 30.00 | 13.50 |
| □ 16 Joseph Lacoursiere | 30.00 | 13.50 |
| □ 17 Fernand Benaquez | 30.00 | 13.50 |
| □ 18 Andre Boisvert | 30.00 | 13.50 |
| □ 19 Claude Chretien | 30.00 | 13.50 |
| □ 20 Norbert Clark | 30.00 | 13.50 |
| □ 21 Sylvio Lambert | 30.00 | 13.50 |
| □ 22 Lucien Roy | 30.00 | 13.50 |
| □ 23 Gerard Audet | 30.00 | 13.50 |
| □ 24 Jacques Lalancette | 30.00 | 13.50 |
| □ 25 Maurice St.Jean | 30.00 | 13.50 |
| □ 26 Camille Lupien | 30.00 | 13.50 |
| □ 27 Rodrigue Pelchat | 30.00 | 13.50 |
| □ 28 Conrad L'Heureux | 30.00 | 13.50 |
| □ 29 Paul Tremblay | 30.00 | 13.50 |
| □ 30 Robert Vincent | 30.00 | 13.50 |
| □ 31 Charles Lamirande | 30.00 | 13.50 |
| □ 32 Leon Gaudreault | 30.00 | 13.50 |
| □ 33 Maurice Thiffault | 30.00 | 13.50 |
| □ 34 Marc-Aurele Tremblay | 30.00 | 13.50 |
| □ 35 Rene Pronovost | 30.00 | 13.50 |
| □ 36 Victor Corbin | 30.00 | 13.50 |
| □ 37 Tiny Tamminen | 40.00 | 18.00 |
| □ 38 Guildor Levesque | 30.00 | 13.50 |
| □ 39 Gaston Lamirande | 30.00 | 13.50 |
| □ 40 Guy Gervais | 30.00 | 13.50 |
| □ 41 Rayner Makila | 40.00 | 18.00 |
| □ 42 Jules Tremblay | 30.00 | 13.50 |
| □ 43 Roland Girard | 30.00 | 13.50 |
| □ 44 Germain Bergeron | 30.00 | 13.50 |
| □ 45 Paul Duchesne | 30.00 | 13.50 |
| □ 46 Roger Beaudoin | 30.00 | 13.50 |
| □ 47 Georges Archibal | 30.00 | 13.50 |
| □ 48 Claude Basque | 30.00 | 13.50 |
| □ 49 Roger Sarda | 30.00 | 13.50 |
| □ 50 Edgard Gendron | 30.00 | 13.50 |
| □ 51 Gaston Labossiere | 30.00 | 13.50 |
| □ 52 Roland Clantara | 30.00 | 13.50 |
| □ 53 Florian Gravel | 30.00 | 13.50 |
| □ 54 Jean-Guy Thompson | 30.00 | 13.50 |
| □ 55 Yvan Forton | 30.00 | 13.50 |
| □ 56 Yves Laporte | 30.00 | 13.50 |
| □ 57 Claude Germain | 30.00 | 13.50 |
| □ 58 Gerry Brunet | 30.00 | 13.50 |
| □ 59 Maurice Courteau | 40.00 | 18.00 |

## 1992-93 MPS Photographics SJHL

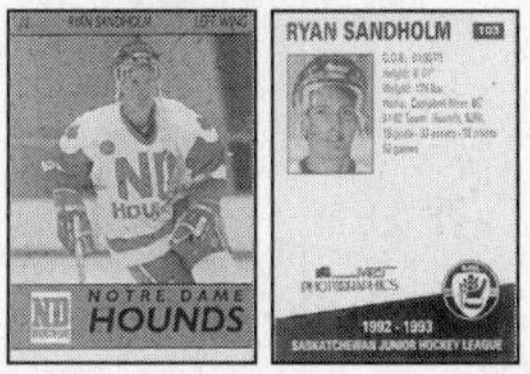


This 168-card set features players in the Saskatchewan Junior Hockey League. The cards are slightly larger than standard size, measuring 2 9/16" by 3 9/16." The fronts feature color action player photos with team color-coded borders at the top and bottom. The player's name and position appear in the top border. The team name and logo appear in the wider bottom border. The backs are white and carry a black-and-white close-up picture, biographical information, and a brief player profile. The sponsor logos are printed at the bottom of the card. The cards are numbered on the back and checklisted below according to teams: Estevan Bruins (1-14), Flin Flon Bombers (15-28, 58), Humboldt Broncos (29-42), Melfort Mustangs (43, 45-57, 59-70, 126), Melville Millionaires (44, 71-84, 95), North Battleford North Stars (85-91, 94, 96-98), Wilkie Youngbloods (92), Notre Dame Hounds (99-112), Nipawin Hawks (113-125), Saskatoon Titans (127-140), Weyburn Red Wings (93/141-154), and Yorkton Terriers (155-168).

| | MINT | NRMT |
|---|---|---|
| COMPLETE SET (168) | 20.00 | 9.00 |
| COMMON CARD (1-168) | .15 | .07 |
| □ 1 Troy Edwards | .15 | .07 |
| □ 2 Simon Oliver | .15 | .07 |
| □ 3 Gerald Tallaire | .15 | .07 |
| □ 4 Blair Allison | .15 | .07 |
| □ 5 Mads True | .15 | .07 |
| □ 6 Steve Brent | .15 | .07 |
| □ 7 Jay Dobrescu | .15 | .07 |
| □ 8 Dave Debusschere | .15 | .07 |
| □ 9 Bryan Cossette | .15 | .07 |
| □ 10 Brooke Battersby | .15 | .07 |
| □ 11 Kyle Niemegeers | .15 | .07 |
| □ 12 Darren McLean | .15 | .07 |
| □ 13 Carson Cardinal | .15 | .07 |
| □ 14 Bill McKay | .15 | .07 |
| □ 15 Chris Hatch | .15 | .07 |
| □ 16 Nolan Weir | .15 | .07 |
| □ 17 Karl Johnson | .15 | .07 |
| □ 18 Jason Brown | .15 | .07 |
| □ 19 Tyler Kuhn | .15 | .07 |
| □ 20 Daniel Dennis | .15 | .07 |
| □ 21 Wally Spence | .15 | .07 |
| □ 22 Rob Beck | .15 | .07 |
| □ 23 Aaron Cain | .50 | .23 |
| □ 24 Darryl Dickson | .15 | .07 |
| □ 25 Travis Cheyne | .15 | .07 |
| □ 26 Mark Leoppky | .15 | .07 |
| □ 27 Jason Ahenakew | .15 | .07 |
| □ 28 Kyle Paul | .15 | .07 |
| □ 29 Dean Normand | .15 | .07 |
| □ 30 Brett Kinaschuk | .15 | .07 |
| □ 31 Darren Schmidt | .15 | .07 |
| □ 32 Chris Schinkel | .15 | .07 |
| □ 33 David Foster | .15 | .07 |
| □ 34 Jason Zimmerman | .15 | .07 |
| □ 35 Tom Perry | .15 | .07 |
| □ 36 Kent Kinaschuk | .15 | .07 |
| □ 37 Colin Froese | .15 | .07 |
| □ 38 Shawn Zimmerman | .15 | .07 |
| □ 39 Larry Empey | .15 | .07 |
| □ 40 Curtis Knight | .15 | .07 |
| □ 41 Blake Shipley | .15 | .07 |
| □ 42 Cory Heon | .15 | .07 |
| □ 43 Steve Pashulka | .15 | .07 |
| □ 44 Rob Kinch | .15 | .07 |
| □ 45 Dean Gerard | .15 | .07 |
| □ 46 Matt Desmarais | .15 | .07 |
| □ 47 Chad Rusnak | .15 | .07 |
| □ 48 Brad Bagu | .15 | .07 |
| □ 49 Cam Bristow | .15 | .07 |
| □ 50 Derek Simonson | .15 | .07 |
| □ 51 Ken Ruddock | .15 | .07 |
| □ 52 Tyler Deis | .15 | .07 |
| □ 53 Steve Tansowny | .15 | .07 |
| □ 54 Bill Stait | .15 | .07 |
| □ 55 Garfield Henderson | .15 | .07 |
| □ 56 Lonny Deobald | .15 | .07 |
| □ 57 Lyle Ehrmantraut | .15 | .07 |
| □ 58 Layne Humenny | .15 | .07 |
| □ 59 Darren Balcombe | .15 | .07 |
| □ 60 Jeff McCutheon | .15 | .07 |
| □ 61 Trevor Wathen | .15 | .07 |
| □ 62 Derek Wynne | .15 | .07 |
| □ 63 Matt Russo | .15 | .07 |
| □ 64 Bruce Matatall | .15 | .07 |
| □ 65 Derek Crimin | .15 | .07 |
| □ 66 Chad Crumley | .15 | .07 |
| □ 67 Mike Hillock | .15 | .07 |
| □ 68 Art Houghton | .15 | .07 |
| □ 69 Lee Materi | .15 | .07 |
| □ 70 Nick Dyhr | .15 | .07 |
| □ 71 Darren Maloney | .15 | .07 |
| □ 72 Kurtise Souchotte | .15 | .07 |
| □ 73 Noel Kamel | .15 | .07 |
| □ 74 Trent Harper | .15 | .07 |
| □ 75 Ted Grayling | .15 | .07 |
| □ 76 Keith Harris | .15 | .07 |
| □ 77 Corri Moffat | .15 | .07 |
| □ 78 Travis Vantighem | .15 | .07 |
| □ 79 Darren Houghton | .15 | .07 |
| □ 80 Wade Welte | .15 | .07 |
| □ 81 Dave Doucet | .15 | .07 |
| □ 82 Jason Prokopetz | .15 | .07 |
| □ 83 Gordon McCann | .15 | .07 |
| □ 84 Clint Hooge | .15 | .07 |
| □ 85 Glen McGillvary | .15 | .07 |
| □ 86 Regan Simpson | .15 | .07 |
| □ 87 Mike Masse | .15 | .07 |
| □ 88 Jeremy Procyshyn | .15 | .07 |
| □ 89 Jim Nellis | .15 | .07 |
| □ 90 Todd Kozak | .15 | .07 |
| □ 91 Brent Hoiness | .15 | .07 |
| □ 92 Josh Welter<br>Jason Welter | .15 | .07 |
| □ 93 Eldon Barker | .15 | .07 |
| □ 94 Duane Vandale | .15 | .07 |
| □ 95 Brad McEwen | .15 | .07 |
| □ 96 Trent Tibbatts | .15 | .07 |
| □ 97 Jody Reiter | .15 | .07 |
| □ 98 Greg Moore | .15 | .07 |
| □ 99 Jon Rowe | .15 | .07 |
| □ 100 Mike Evans | .15 | .07 |
| □ 101 Jason Krug | .15 | .07 |
| □ 102 Jon Bracco | .15 | .07 |
| □ 103 Ryan Sandholm | .15 | .07 |
| □ 104 Darryl Sangster | .15 | .07 |
| □ 105 Brett Colborne | .15 | .07 |
| □ 106 Dean Moore | .15 | .07 |
| □ 107 Chris Dechaine | .15 | .07 |
| □ 108 Steve McKenna | .15 | .07 |
| □ 109 Tony Bergin | .15 | .07 |
| □ 110 Tim Murray | .15 | .07 |
| □ 111 Casey Kesselring | .15 | .07 |
| □ 112 Todd Barth | .15 | .07 |
| □ 113 Ryan McConnell | .15 | .07 |
| □ 114 Ian Adamson | .15 | .07 |
| □ 115 Warren Pickford | .15 | .07 |
| □ 116 Todd Murphy | .15 | .07 |
| □ 117 Rob Phillips | .15 | .07 |
| □ 118 Trevor Demmans | .15 | .07 |
| □ 119 Jeff Greenwood | .15 | .07 |
| □ 120 Kevin Messer | .15 | .07 |
| □ 121 Dion Johnson | .15 | .07 |
| □ 122 Rejean Stringer | .15 | .07 |
| □ 123 Scott Mead | .15 | .07 |
| □ 124 Jeff Lawson | .15 | .07 |
| □ 125 Scot Newberry | .15 | .07 |
| □ 126 Bill Reid | .15 | .07 |
| □ 127 Chris Winkler | .15 | .07 |
| □ 128 Kyle Girgan | .15 | .07 |
| □ 129 Trevor Warrener | .15 | .07 |
| □ 130 Richard Boscher | .15 | .07 |
| □ 131 Tom Thomson | .15 | .07 |
| □ 132 Mike Wevers | .15 | .07 |
| □ 133 Barton Holt | .15 | .07 |
| □ 134 Kent Rogers | .15 | .07 |
| □ 135 Richard Gibbs | .15 | .07 |
| □ 136 Jared Witt | .15 | .07 |
| □ 137 Jamie Stelmak | .15 | .07 |
| □ 138 Greg Wahl | .15 | .07 |
| □ 139 J. Sotropa | .15 | .07 |
| □ 140 Mark Pivetz | .15 | .07 |
| □ 141 Travis Kirby | .15 | .07 |
| □ 142 Jason Scanzano | .15 | .07 |
| □ 143 Tyson Balog | .15 | .07 |
| □ 144 Daryl Krauss | .15 | .07 |
| □ 145 Mike Harder | .15 | .07 |
| □ 146 Tyler McMillan | .15 | .07 |
| □ 147 Darcy Herlick | .15 | .07 |
| □ 148 Dave Zwyer | .15 | .07 |
| □ 149 Craig McKechnie | .15 | .07 |
| □ 150 Cam Cook | .15 | .07 |
| □ 151 Derek Bruselinck | .15 | .07 |
| □ 152 Travis Smith | .15 | .07 |
| □ 153 Daryl Jones | .15 | .07 |
| □ 154 Mike Savard | .15 | .07 |
| □ 155 Jeremy Matthies | .15 | .07 |
| □ 156 Michel Cook | .15 | .07 |
| □ 157 Leigh Brookbank | .15 | .07 |
| □ 158 Christian Dutil | .15 | .07 |
| □ 159 Scott Heshka | .15 | .07 |
| □ 160 Danny Galarneau | .15 | .07 |
| □ 161 Jamie Dunn | .15 | .07 |
| □ 162 Nigel Werenka | .15 | .07 |
| □ 163 Steve Sabo | .15 | .07 |
| □ 164 Tony Toth | .15 | .07 |
| □ 165 Sebastien Moreau | .15 | .07 |
| □ 166 Tim Slukynsky | .15 | .07 |
| □ 167 Sheldon Bylsma | .15 | .07 |
| □ 168 Stacy Prevost | .30 | .14 |

## 1988-89 ProCards AHL

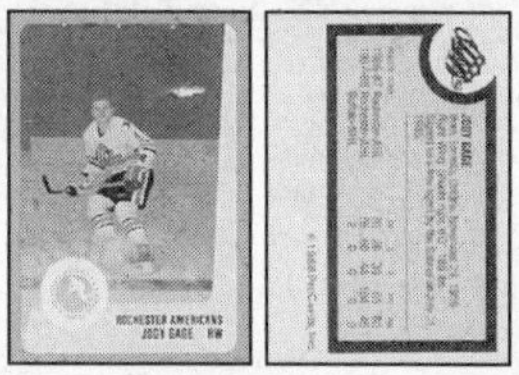


This set of 348 cards features the 14 teams of the American Hockey League. The cards measure the standard size, 2 1/2" by 3 1/2". The fronts feature color player photos accented by a beige-colored hockey stick superimposed on the right and lower sides of the picture. The AHL logo appears in the lower left corner, and the photo is bordered on all sides by red. The back has player information in a black box, with the upper left corner cut out for the team logo. The cards are unnumbered and checklisted below alphabetically according to teams as follows (teams in alphabetical order and players listed alphabetically within each team): Adirondack Red Wings (1-25), Baltimore Skipjacks (26-48), Binghamton Whalers (49-72), Cape Breton Oilers (73-96), Halifax Citadels (97-119), Hershey Bears (120-147), Maine Mariners (148-169), Moncton Hawks (170-190), New Haven Nighthawks (191-222), Newmarket Saints (223-244), Rochester Americans (245-268), Sherbrooke Canadiens (269-299), Springfield Indians (300-324), and Utica Devils (325-348). Of all the teams, on the Hershey cards alone they failed to put the team name. Although the team sets were originally sold with a suggested retail price of 3.00 per team set and packaged individually, they are listed below as one giant set. In many cases that was the way they were advertised and sold, i.e., as a complete set of all the teams in the AHL.

| | MINT | NRMT |
|---|---|---|
| COMPLETE SET (348) | 80.00 | 36.00 |
| COMMON CARD (1-348) | .05 | .02 |
| □ 1 Rob Nichols | .20 | .09 |
| □ 2 Bill Dineen CO | .25 | .11 |
| □ 3 Tim Paris Asst.TR | .05 | .02 |
| □ 4 Glenn Merkosky | .15 | .07 |
| □ 5 Mike Gober | .20 | .09 |
| □ 6 Dave Casey TR | .05 | .02 |
| □ 7 Sam St.Laurent | .50 | .23 |
| □ 8 Mark Reimer | .25 | .11 |
| □ 9 Dennis Smith | .20 | .09 |
| □ 10 Lou Crawford | .20 | .09 |
| □ 11 John Mokosak | .20 | .09 |
| □ 12 Murray Eaves | .20 | .09 |
| □ 13 Dave Korol | .20 | .09 |
| □ 14 Miroslav Ihnacak | .50 | .23 |
| □ 15 Dale Krentz | .20 | .09 |
| □ 16 Brent Fedyk | .50 | .23 |
| □ 17 Dean Morton | .20 | .09 |
| □ 18 Jeff Brubaker | .35 | .16 |
| □ 19 Tim Cheveldae | 1.50 | .70 |
| □ 20 Randy McKay | .75 | .35 |
| □ 21 Peter Dineen | .20 | .09 |
| □ 22 Rob Doyle | .20 | .09 |
| □ 23 Daniel Shank | .50 | .23 |
| □ 24 Joe Ferras | .20 | .09 |
| □ 25 John Blum | .25 | .11 |
| □ 26 Tim Bergland | .20 | .09 |
| □ 27 Robin Bawa | .20 | .09 |
| □ 28 Shawn Simpson | .20 | .09 |
| □ 29 Chris Felix | .25 | .11 |
| □ 30 Jeff Greenlaw | .20 | .09 |
| □ 31 Frank Dimuzio | .20 | .09 |
| □ 32 Tyler Larter | .20 | .09 |
| □ 33 Rob Whistle | .20 | .09 |
| □ 34 Dallas Eakins | .20 | .09 |
| □ 35 Mark Hatcher | .20 | .09 |
| □ 36 Dave Farrish | .25 | .11 |
| □ 37 Bill Houlder | .75 | .35 |
| □ 38 Doug Keans | .50 | .23 |
| □ 39 Lou Franceschetti | .25 | .11 |
| □ 40 Rob Murray | .15 | .07 |
| □ 41 Terry Murray GM/CO | .50 | .23 |
| □ 42 Steve Seftel | .20 | .09 |
| □ 43 J.P. Mattingly TR | .05 | .02 |
| □ 44 Mike Richard | .20 | .09 |
| □ 45 Shawn Cronin | .50 | .23 |
| □ 46 Scott McCrory | .20 | .09 |
| □ 47 Mike Millar | .20 | .09 |
| □ 48 Dave Sherrid TR | .05 | .02 |
| □ 49 Marc Laforge | .20 | .09 |
| □ 50 David O'Brien | .20 | .09 |
| □ 51 Dave Rowbotham | .20 | .09 |
| □ 52 Kay Whitmore | 1.00 | .45 |
| □ 53 Richard Brodeur | 1.00 | .45 |
| □ 54 Mike Vellucci | .20 | .09 |
| □ 55 Terry Yake | .50 | .23 |
| □ 56 Roger Kortko | .20 | .09 |
| □ 57 Jon Smith TR | .05 | .02 |
| □ 58 Lindsay Carson UER<br>(Misspelled Lindsy<br>on card front) | .20 | .09 |
| □ 59 Chris Brant | .20 | .09 |
| □ 60 Claude Larose CO | .25 | .11 |
| □ 61 Dallas Gaume | .20 | .09 |
| □ 62 Charlie Bourgeois | .20 | .09 |
| □ 63 Todd Krygier | .50 | .23 |
| □ 64 Gary Callahan | .20 | .09 |
| □ 65 Mark Reeds | .20 | .09 |
| □ 66 Al Tuer | .20 | .09 |
| □ 67 Brian Chapman | .20 | .09 |
| □ 68 Mark Lavarre | .20 | .09 |
| □ 69 Mark Dumas | .20 | .09 |
| □ 70 Jim Culhane | .20 | .09 |
| □ 71 Larry Trader | .20 | .09 |
| □ 72 Tom Mitchell GM | .05 | .02 |
| □ 73 Rob MacInnis | .20 | .09 |
| □ 74 John B. Hanna | .20 | .09 |
| □ 75 Dan Currie | .50 | .23 |
| □ 76 Dave Roach | .20 | .09 |
| □ 77 Jamie Nicolls | .20 | .09 |
| □ 78 Alan May | .25 | .11 |
| □ 79 David Haas | .20 | .09 |
| □ 80 Daryl Reaugh | .50 | .23 |
| □ 81 Mike Ware | .20 | .09 |
| □ 82 Mike Glover | .20 | .09 |
| □ 83 Nick Beaulieu | .20 | .09 |
| □ 84 Mario Barbe | .20 | .09 |
| □ 85 Darren Beals | .20 | .09 |
| □ 86 Kim Issel | .20 | .09 |
| □ 87 Shaun Van Allen | .50 | .23 |
| □ 88 Jim Ennis | .20 | .09 |
| □ 89 Mark Lamb | .50 | .23 |
| □ 90 Larry Floyd | .20 | .09 |
| □ 91 Ron Shudra | .20 | .09 |
| □ 92 Fabian Joseph | .25 | .11 |
| □ 93 Selmar Odelein | .25 | .11 |
| □ 94 Don Martin | .20 | .09 |
| □ 95 Jim Wiemer | .25 | .11 |
| □ 96 Brad MacGregor | .20 | .09 |
| □ 97 Gerald Bzdel | .20 | .09 |
| □ 98 Mike Hough | .50 | .23 |
| □ 99 Ken McRae | .25 | .11 |
| □ 100 Bobby Dollas | .25 | .11 |
| □ 101 Joel Baillargeon | .20 | .09 |
| □ 102 Ladislav Tresl | .15 | .07 |
| □ 103 Jacques Mailhot | .20 | .09 |
| □ 104 Dean Hopkins | .20 | .09 |
| □ 105 Claude Julien | .20 | .09 |
| □ 106 Brent Severyn | .50 | .23 |
| □ 107 Keith Miller | .20 | .09 |
| □ 108 Scott Shaunessy | .20 | .09 |
| □ 109 Jaroslav Sevcik | .20 | .09 |
| □ 110 Darin Kimble | .50 | .23 |
| □ 111 Jean-Marc Routhier | .20 | .09 |
| □ 112 Ken Quinney | .20 | .09 |
| □ 113 Max Middendorf | .20 | .09 |
| □ 114 Marc Fortier | .35 | .16 |
| □ 115 Jean-Marc Richard | .20 | .09 |
| □ 116 Mike Natyshak | .20 | .09 |
| □ 117 Ron Tugnutt | 2.50 | 1.10 |
| □ 118 Scott Gordon | .25 | .11 |
| □ 119 Doug Carpenter CO/GM | .10 | .05 |
| □ 120 Jeff Harding | .20 | .09 |
| □ 121 Jocelyn Perrault | .20 | .09 |
| □ 122 Darryl Gilmour | .25 | .11 |
| □ 123 John Stevens | .20 | .09 |
| □ 124 Warren Harper | .20 | .09 |

❑ 125 Chris Jensen .20 .09
❑ 126 Mark Freer .25 .11
❑ 127 Gordon Paddock .20 .09
❑ 128 Bruce Randall .20 .09
❑ 129 Glen Seabrooke .20 .09
❑ 130 Mike Stothers .20 .09
❑ 131 Dave Fenyves .25 .11
❑ 132 Mark Lofthouse .20 .09
❑ 133 Marc D'Amour .25 .11
❑ 134 Shaun Sabol .20 .09
❑ 135 Craig Kitteringham .20 .09
❑ 136 J.J. Daigneault .50 .23
❑ 137 Don Biggs .25 .11
❑ 138 Kent Hawley .20 .09
❑ 139 Tony Horacek .20 .09
❑ 140 Al Hill .25 .11
❑ 141 Don Nachbaur .20 .09
❑ 142 John Paddock CO .20 .09
❑ 143 Kevin McCarthy CO .20 .09
❑ 144 Dan Stuck TR .05 .02
❑ 145 Doug Yingst .20 .09
❑ 146 Frank Mathers PR/GM .20 .09
❑ 147 Brian Bucciarelli TR .05 .02
❑ 148 Terry Taillefer .20 .09
❑ 149 Paul Beraldo .20 .09
❑ 150 Jeff Lamb .20 .09
❑ 151 Mitch Molloy .20 .09
❑ 152 Darren Lowe .20 .09
❑ 153 Stephane Quintal 1.00 .45
❑ 154 Norm Foster .25 .11
❑ 155 Jean-Marc Lanthier .20 .09
❑ 156 Carl Mokosak .20 .09
❑ 157 Mike Neill .20 .09
❑ 158 Mike Jeffrey .20 .09
❑ 159 Steve Tsujiura .20 .09
❑ 160 Scott Drevitch .20 .09
❑ 161 Paul Guay .25 .11
❑ 162 Scott Wykoff ANN .05 .02
❑ 163 John Carter .25 .11
❑ 164 Phil Degaetano .20 .09
❑ 165 Doug Foerster PB/TKTS .05 .02
❑ 166 Bruce Shoebottom .25 .11
❑ 167 Ray Podloski .20 .09
❑ 168 Greg Hawgood .50 .23
❑ 169 Joe Flaherty .20 .09
❑ 170 Todd Flichel .20 .09
❑ 171 Steven Fletcher .20 .09
❑ 172 Len Nielson .20 .09
❑ 173 Neil Meadmore .20 .09
❑ 174 Gilles Hamel .25 .11
❑ 175 Ron Wilson .50 .23
❑ 176 Stu Kulak .25 .11
❑ 177 Scott Schneider .20 .09
❑ 178 Mike Warus .20 .09
❑ 179 Jamie Husgen .20 .09
❑ 180 Tom Draper .50 .23
❑ 181 Guy Gosselin .20 .09
❑ 182 Guy Larose .25 .11
❑ 183 Stephane Beauregard .50 .23
❑ 184 Brent Hughes .35 .16
❑ 185 Sean Clement .20 .09
❑ 186 Matt Hervey .15 .07
❑ 187 Chris Norton .20 .09
❑ 188 Rob Snitzer THER .05 .02
❑ 189 Rick Bowness CO .50 .23
❑ 190 Wayne Flemming MG .05 .02
❑ 191 Tim Tookey .25 .11
❑ 192 Ken Baumgartner 1.50 .70
❑ 193 John English .20 .09
❑ 194 Darryl Williams .20 .09
❑ 195 Hubie McDonough .50 .23
❑ 196 Brad Hyatt .20 .09
❑ 197 Phil Sykes .15 .07
❑ 198 Mario Chitaroni .20 .09
❑ 199 Tom Pratt .20 .09
❑ 200 Sal Lombardi TR .05 .02
❑ 201 Rick Dudley CO .25 .11
❑ 202 John Tortorella CO .05 .02
❑ 203 Chris Panek .20 .09
❑ 204 Scott Green TR .05 .02
❑ 205 Eric Germain .20 .09
❑ 206 Bob Kudelski .50 .23
❑ 207 Joe Paterson .20 .09
❑ 208 Al Loring .20 .09
❑ 209 Mark Fitzpatrick 3.00 1.35
❑ 210 Dan Gratton .20 .09
❑ 211 Sylvain Couturier .20 .09
❑ 212 Pat Hickey DIR .05 .02
❑ 213 Petr Prajsler .15 .07
❑ 214 Lyle Phair .20 .09
❑ 215 Bob Logan .20 .09
❑ 216 Francois Breault .20 .09
❑ 217 Paul Kelly .20 .09
❑ 218 Steve Richmond .20 .09
❑ 219 Denis Larocque .20 .09
❑ 220 Brian Wilks .20 .09
❑ 221 Dave Pasin .20 .09
❑ 222 Gordie Walker .20 .09
❑ 223 Marty Dallman .20 .09
❑ 224 Jim Ralph 1.00 .45
❑ 225 Mike Blaisdell .50 .23
❑ 226 Sean McKenna .20 .09
❑ 227 Mark Kirton .25 .11
❑ 228 Greg Hotham .20 .09
❑ 229 Bill Root .25 .11
❑ 230 Wes Jarvis .20 .09
❑ 231 Daryl Evans .20 .09
❑ 232 Jack Capuano .20 .09
❑ 233 Tim Armstrong .20 .09
❑ 234 Alan Hepple .20 .09
❑ 235 Brian Blad .20 .09
❑ 236 Ken Yaremchuk .25 .11
❑ 237 Paul Gagne .35 .16
❑ 238 Doug Shedden .50 .23
❑ 239 Brian Hoard .20 .09
❑ 240 Greg Terrion .35 .16
❑ 241 Trevor Jobe .05 .02
❑ 242 Jeff Reese 1.00 .45
❑ 243 Darryl Shannon .75 .35
❑ 244 Tim Bernhardt .50 .23
❑ 245 The Moose Mascot .20 .09
❑ 246 Paul Brydges .20 .09
❑ 247 Ken Priestlay .25 .11
❑ 248 Jacques Cloutier .75 .35
❑ 249 Steve Smith .20 .09
❑ 250 Jim Jackson .25 .11
❑ 251 Grant Tkachuk .20 .09
❑ 252 Kevin Kerr .20 .09
❑ 253 Mark Ferner .25 .11
❑ 254 Jeff Parker .20 .09
❑ 255 Don McSween .25 .11
❑ 256 Jim Hofford .20 .09
❑ 257 Darcy Wakaluk 1.50 .70
❑ 258 Scott Metcalfe .20 .09
❑ 259 Richie Dunn .20 .09
❑ 260 Wayne Van Dorp .35 .16
❑ 261 Shawn Anderson .25 .11
❑ 262 Jeff Capello .20 .09
❑ 263 Mike Donnelly .50 .23
❑ 264 Mikael Andersson .50 .23
❑ 265 Robert Ray 3.00 1.35
❑ 266 Jody Gage .50 .23
❑ 267 Francois Guay .15 .07
❑ 268 John Van Boxmeer CO .25 .11
❑ 269 Jim Nesich .20 .09
❑ 271 J.J. Daigneault .50 .23
❑ 272 Randy Exelby .25 .11
❑ 273 Jyrki Lumme 1.50 .70
❑ 275 Francois Gravel .20 .09
❑ 276 Jacques Parent THER .05 .02
❑ 277 Bobby Boulanger MG .05 .02
❑ 278 Benoit Brunet 1.00 .45
❑ 279 Martin Nicoletti .20 .09
❑ 280 Mark Pederson .25 .11
❑ 281 Stephan Lebeau 1.00 .45
❑ 282 Claude Larose CO .25 .11
❑ 283 Steve Bisson .20 .09
❑ 284 Scott Sandelin .20 .09
❑ 285 Rocky Dundas .20 .09
❑ 286 Serge Roberge .20 .09
❑ 287 Rob Bryden .20 .09
❑ 288 Marc Saumier .20 .09
❑ 289 Jean Hamel CO .20 .09
❑ 290 Mario Roberge .25 .11
❑ 291 Jocelyn Lemieux .75 .35
❑ 292 Ron Chyzowski .20 .09
❑ 293 Martin Desjardins .20 .09
❑ 294 Steven Martinson .20 .09
❑ 295 Jose Charbonneau .25 .11
❑ 296 Stephane J.G. Richer .15 .07
❑ 297 Sylvain Lefebvre 2.00 .90
❑ 298 Donald Dufresne .25 .11
❑ 299 Luc Gauthier .20 .09
❑ 300 Shawn Evans .15 .07
❑ 301 Mike Stevens .15 .07
❑ 302 Bruce Boudreau .50 .23
❑ 303 Todd McLellan .20 .09
❑ 304 Jeff Hackett 4.00 1.80
❑ 305 Bill Berg .50 .23
❑ 306 Stu Burnie .20 .09
❑ 307 Duncan McPherson .20 .09
❑ 308 Jeff Finley .25 .11
❑ 309 Ralph Calvanese MG .05 .02
❑ 310 Rob DiMaio 1.00 .45
❑ 311 Chris Pryor .20 .09
❑ 312 Jim Roberts CO .20 .09
❑ 313 Vern Smith .20 .09
❑ 314 Mike Walsh .20 .09
❑ 315 Ed Tyburski TR .05 .02
❑ 316 Rod Dallman .20 .09
❑ 317 George Maneluk .25 .11
❑ 318 Richard Kromm .25 .11
❑ 319 Kerry Clark .20 .09
❑ 320 Hank Lammens .25 .11
❑ 321 Tom Fitzgerald .50 .23
❑ 322 Dale Henry .20 .09
❑ 323 Shawn Byram .20 .09
❑ 324 Doug Weiss .20 .09
❑ 325 John Walker .20 .09
❑ 326 Paul Ysebaert .75 .35
❑ 327 Chris Cichocki .20 .09
❑ 328 Marc Laniel .20 .09
❑ 329 Kevin Todd .50 .23
❑ 330 Dan Delianedis .20 .09
❑ 331 Robert Bill TR .05 .02
❑ 332 Jeff Croop TR .05 .02
❑ 333 Craig Billington 2.00 .90
❑ 334 Alan Stewart .20 .09
❑ 335 Jeff Madill .25 .11
❑ 336 Scott Moon TR .05 .02
❑ 337 Neil Brady .25 .11
❑ 338 Murray Brumwell .20 .09
❑ 339 Anders Carlsson .20 .09
❑ 340 Dan Dorion .20 .09
❑ 341 Tom McVie CO .25 .11
❑ 342 David Marcinyshyn .20 .09
❑ 343 John Blessman .20 .09
❑ 344 Chris Terreri 2.00 .90
❑ 345 Eric Weinrich .75 .35
❑ 346 Janne Ojanen .50 .23
❑ 347 Tim Lenardon .20 .09
❑ 348 Jamie Huscroft .50 .23

## 1988-89 ProCards IHL

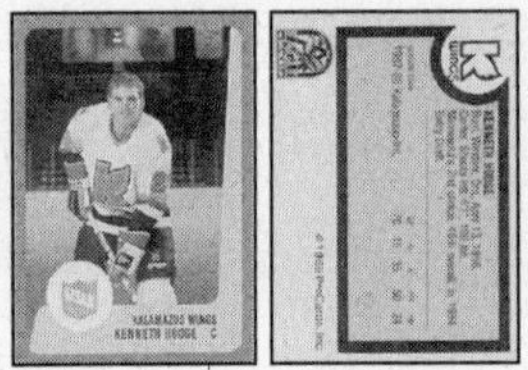

This set of 119 cards features players from the teams of the International Hockey League. The cards measure the standard size 2 1/2" by 3 1/2". The fronts feature color player photos accented by a beige-colored hockey stick superimposed on the right and lower sides of the picture. The IHL logo appears in a circle in the lower left corner, and the photo is bordered on all sides by red. The back has player information in a black box, with the upper left corner cut out for the team logo. The cards are unnumbered and checklisted below alphabetically according to teams as follows: Indianapolis Ice (1-22), Kalamazoo Wings (23-42), Muskegon Lumberjacks (43-65), Peoria Rivermen (66-94), and Saginaw Hawks (95-119). Although the team sets were originally sold with a suggested retail price of 3.00 per team set and packaged individually, they are listed below as one giant set. In many cases that was the way they were advertised and sold, i.e., as a complete set of all the teams in the IHL.

| | MINT | NRMT |
|---|---|---|
| COMPLETE SET (119) | 50.00 | 22.00 |
| COMMON CARD (1-119) | .05 | .02 |

❑ 1 Bob Lakso .20 .09
❑ 2 Rick Boyd .20 .09
❑ 3 Alan Perry .35 .16
❑ 4 Mark Teevens .20 .09
❑ 5 Gary Stewart .20 .09
❑ 6 Randy Taylor .20 .09
❑ 7 Scott Clements .20 .09
❑ 8 Chris McSorley .50 .23
❑ 9 Dave Allison .20 .09
❑ 10 Shane Doyle .20 .09
❑ 11 Darwin McCutcheon .20 .09
❑ 12 Geoff Benic .20 .09
❑ 13 Rich Oberlin TR .05 .02
❑ 14 Glen Johannesen .20 .09
❑ 15 Graeme Bonar .20 .09
❑ 16 Ron Handy .20 .09
❑ 17 Archie Henderson .25 .11
❑ 18 Brent Sapergia .20 .09
❑ 19 Brad Beck .20 .09
❑ 20 Paul Houck .20 .09
❑ 21 Jimmy Mann .50 .23
❑ 22 Rick Barkovich .20 .09
❑ 23 Scott McCrady .20 .09
❑ 24 Andy Akervik .20 .09
❑ 25 Rob Zettler .50 .23
❑ 26 Jarmo Myllys .75 .35
❑ 27 D'Arcy Norton .20 .09
❑ 28 Ken Hodge Jr. .50 .23
❑ 29 Emanuel Viveiros .20 .09
❑ 30 Scott Bjugstad .20 .09
❑ 31 Mike Berger .20 .09
❑ 32 Joe Lockwood .20 .09
❑ 33 Stephane Roy .25 .11
❑ 34 Randy Smith .25 .11
❑ 35 Mike McHugh .20 .09
❑ 36 Warren Babe .20 .09
❑ 37 Gary McColgan .20 .09
❑ 38 Darin Baker .20 .09
❑ 39 Neil Wilkinson 1.00 .45
❑ 40 Kirk Tomlinson .20 .09
❑ 41 Larry Dyck .35 .16
❑ 42 Dave Schofield .20 .09
❑ 43 Brad Aitken .20 .09
❑ 44 Jock Callander .50 .23
❑ 45 Todd Charlesworth .20 .09
❑ 46 Jeff Cooper .20 .09
❑ 47 Jeff Daniels .50 .23
❑ 48 Greg Davies .20 .09
❑ 49 Lee Giffin .20 .09
❑ 50 Dave Goertz .20 .09
❑ 51 Steve Gotaas .20 .09
❑ 52 Scott Gruhl .50 .23
❑ 53 Doug Hobson .20 .09
❑ 54 Kevin MacDonald .20 .09
❑ 55 Pat Mayer .20 .09
❑ 56 Dave McLlwain .75 .35
❑ 57 Dave Michayluk .20 .09
❑ 58 Glenn Mulvenna .20 .09
❑ 59 Jim Paek .50 .23
❑ 60 Frank Pietrangelo .75 .35
❑ 61 Bruce Racine .35 .16
❑ 62 Mark Recchi 8.00 3.60
❑ 63 Troy Vollhoffer .20 .09
❑ 64 Jeff Waver .20 .09
❑ 65 Mitch Wilson .20 .09
❑ 66 Mitch Messier .25 .11
❑ 67 Dave Lowry .50 .23
❑ 68 Tim Bothwell .25 .11
❑ 69 Sheryl Reeves ADM .05 .02
❑ 70 Shane MacEachern .25 .11
❑ 71 Glen Featherstone .50 .23
❑ 72 Charlie Thompson MGR .05 .02
❑ 73 Wayne Thomas CO .25 .11
❑ 74 Dominic Lavoie .25 .11
❑ 75 Team Photo .50 .23
Peoria Rivermen
❑ 76 Scott Paluch .20 .09
❑ 77 Wayne Gagne .20 .09
❑ 78 Dave Thomlinson .50 .23
❑ 79 Tony Twist 4.00 1.80
❑ 80 Brad McCaughey .20 .09
❑ 81 Kelly Chase .75 .35
❑ 82 Scott Harlow .20 .09
❑ 83 Peter Douris .50 .23
❑ 84 Cliff Ronning 2.50 1.10
❑ 85 Lyle Odelein 1.50 .70
❑ 86 Terry MacLean .20 .09
❑ 87 Darin Smith .20 .09
❑ 88 Skip Probst .20 .09
❑ 89 Ed McMurray MGR .05 .02
❑ 90 Greg Eberle TR .05 .02
❑ 91 Jim Vesey .20 .09
❑ 92 Toby Ducolon .20 .09
❑ 93 Pat Jablonski 1.50 .70
❑ 94 Darrell May .20 .09
❑ 95 Ed Belfour 25.00 11.00
❑ 96 Bruce Cassidy .25 .11
❑ 97 Chris Clifford .20 .09
❑ 98 Mario Doyon .20 .09
❑ 99 Bill Gardner .20 .09
❑ 100 Mark Kurzawski .20 .09
❑ 101 Lonnie Loach .50 .23
❑ 102 Steve Ludzik .25 .11
❑ 103 David Mackey .20 .09
❑ 104 Dale Marquette .20 .09
❑ 105 Gary Moscaluk .20 .09
❑ 106 Marty Nanne .20 .09
❑ 107 Brian Noonan 1.00 .45
❑ 108 Mark Paterson .20 .09
❑ 109 Kent Paynter .20 .09
❑ 110 Guy Phillips .20 .09
❑ 111 John Reid .20 .09
❑ 112 Mike Rucinski .20 .09
❑ 113 Warren Rychel .75 .35
❑ 114 Everett Sanipass .50 .23
❑ 115 Mike Stapleton .25 .11
❑ 116 Darryl Sutter 1.00 .45
❑ 117 Jari Torkki .20 .09
❑ 118 Bill Watson .25 .11
❑ 119 Sean Williams .25 .11

## 1989-90 ProCards AHL

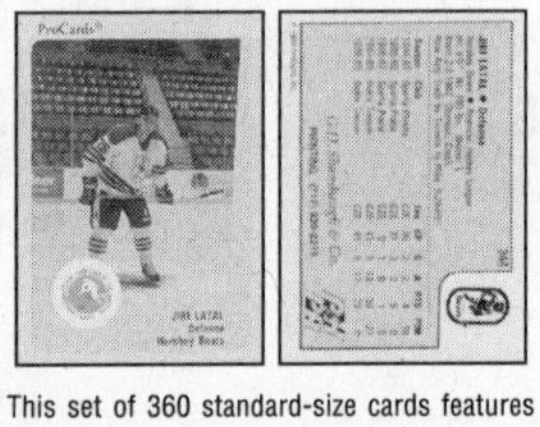

This set of 360 standard-size cards features the 14 teams of the American Hockey League. Although the team sets were originally sold with a suggested retail price of 3.00 per team set and packaged individually, they are listed below as one giant set. In many cases that was the way they were advertised and sold, i.e., as a complete set of all the teams in the AHL. The numbering is by teams as follows: New Haven Nighthawks (1-27), Moncton Hawks (28-52), Maine Mariners (53-76), Baltimore Skipjacks (77-103), Newmarket Saints (104-128), Cape Breton Oilers (129-151), Halifax Citadels (152-178), Sherbrooke Canadiens (179-201), Utica Devils (202-228), Springfield Indians (229-254), Rochester Americans (255-282), Birmingham Whalers (283-305), Adirondack Red Wings (306-329), and Hershey Bears (330-360).

| | MINT | NRMT |
|---|---|---|
| COMPLETE SET (360) | 90.00 | 40.00 |
| COMMON CARD (1-360) | .05 | .02 |

❑ 1 New Haven Checklist .05 .02
❑ 2 Francois Breault .25 .11
❑ 3 Paul Kelly .25 .11
❑ 4 Phil Sykes .35 .16
❑ 5 Ron Scott .35 .16
❑ 6 Micah Aivazoff .35 .16
❑ 7 Sylvain Couturier .25 .11
❑ 8 Carl Repp .25 .11
❑ 9 Murray Brumwell .25 .11
❑ 10 Todd Elik .75 .35
❑ 11 Darwin Bozek .25 .11
❑ 12 Eric Germain .25 .11
❑ 13 Scott Young 1.50 .70
❑ 14 Chris Kontos .50 .23
❑ 15 Scott Bjugstad .35 .16
❑ 16 Eric Ricard .25 .11
❑ 17 Ross Wilson .25 .11
❑ 18 Graham Stanley .25 .11
❑ 19 Chris Panek .25 .11
❑ 20 Nick Fotiu .75 .35
❑ 21 Rene Chapdelaine .25 .11
❑ 22 Gordie Walker .25 .11
❑ 23 Tim Bothwell .35 .16
❑ 24 Kevin MacDonald .25 .11
❑ 25 Darryl Williams .25 .11
❑ 26 John Van Kessel .25 .11
❑ 27 Paul Brydges .25 .11
❑ 28 Moncton Checklist .05 .02
❑ 29 Guy Larose .35 .16
❑ 30 Danton Cole .35 .16
❑ 31 Brent Hughes .35 .16
❑ 32 Larry Bernard .25 .11
❑ 33 Stu Kulak .25 .11
❑ 34 Bob Essensa 1.50 .70
❑ 35 Luciano Borsato .35 .16
❑ 36 Guy Gosselin .25 .11
❑ 37 Todd Flichel .25 .11
❑ 38 Brian Hunt .25 .11
❑ 39 Neil Meadmore .25 .11
❑ 40 Matt Hervey .25 .11
❑ 41 Dallas Eakins .25 .11
❑ 42 Brad Jones .25 .11
❑ 43 Chris Norton .25 .11
❑ 44 Bryan Marchment .75 .35
❑ 45 Rick Tabaracci 1.50 .70
❑ 46 Grant Richison .25 .11
❑ 47 Brian McReynolds .25 .11
❑ 48 Tony Joseph .25 .11
❑ 49 Dave Farrish .35 .16
❑ 50 Rob Snitzer .05 .02
❑ 51 Ron Wilson .35 .16
❑ 52 Scott Schneider .25 .11
❑ 53 Maine Checklist .05 .02
❑ 54 Dave Buda .25 .11
❑ 55 Paul Beraldo .25 .11
❑ 56 Lou Crawford .25 .11
❑ 57 Mark Montanari .25 .11
❑ 58 Don Sweeney 2.00 .90
❑ 59 Jeff Sirkka .25 .11
❑ 60 Norm Foster .50 .23
❑ 61 Greg Poss .25 .11
❑ 62 Gord Cruickshank .25 .11
❑ 63 Bruce Shoebottom .25 .11
❑ 64 Mark Ziliotto .25 .11
❑ 65 Ron Hoover .25 .11
❑ 66 Scott Harlow .25 .11
❑ 67 Mike Millar .25 .11
❑ 68 Bob Beers .50 .23
❑ 69 Ray Neufeld .35 .16
❑ 70 Graeme Townshend .50 .23
❑ 71 Billy O'Dwyer .25 .11
❑ 72 Frank Caprice .50 .23
❑ 73 John Blum .25 .11
❑ 74 Jerry Foster .25 .11
❑ 75 Bill Sutherland and Rick Bowness .25 .11
❑ 76 Scott Drevitch .25 .11
❑ 77 Baltimore Checklist .05 .02
❑ 78 John Purves .25 .11
❑ 79 Jeff Greenlaw .25 .11
❑ 80 Jim Taylor .25 .11
❑ 81 Alfie Turcotte .25 .11
❑ 82 Dan Redmond .05 .02
❑ 83 Chris Felix .25 .11
❑ 84 Bobby Babcock .25 .11
❑ 85 Steve Maltais .25 .11
❑ 86 Mike Richard .25 .11
❑ 87 Team Picture .25 .11
❑ 88 Bob Mason .75 .35
❑ 89 Mark Ferner .35 .16
❑ 90 Steve Seftel .25 .11
❑ 91 Brian Tutt .25 .11
❑ 92 Terry Murray .35 .16
❑ 93 Jim Hrivnak 1.00 .45
❑ 94 Tyler Larter .25 .11
❑ 95 Tim Bergland .25 .11
❑ 96 Dennis Smith .25 .11
❑ 97 Steve Hollett .25 .11
❑ 98 Shawn Simpson .25 .11
❑ 99 Robin Bawa .25 .11
❑ 100 John Druce .50 .23
❑ 101 Kent Paynter .25 .11
❑ 102 Alain Cote .35 .16
❑ 103 J.P. Mattingly .05 .02
❑ 104 Newmarket Checklist .05 .02
❑ 105 Dean Anderson .25 .11
❑ 106 Wes Jarvis .25 .11
❑ 107 Brian Blad .25 .11
❑ 108 Derek Laxdal .25 .11
❑ 109 Kent Hulst .25 .11
❑ 110 Tim Bernhardt .35 .16
❑ 111 Brian Hoard .25 .11
❑ 112 Bill Root .35 .16
❑ 113 Paul Gardner .25 .11
❑ 114 Tim Armstrong .25 .11
❑ 115 Sean McKenna .25 .11
❑ 116 Tim Bean .25 .11
❑ 117 Alan Hepple .25 .11
❑ 118 Greg Hotham .25 .11
❑ 119 Scott Pearson .50 .23
❑ 120 Peter Ihnacak .35 .16
❑ 121 John McIntyre .35 .16
❑ 122 Paul Gagne .25 .11
❑ 123 Darren Veitch .35 .16
❑ 124 Mark LaForest .35 .16
❑ 125 Doug Shedden .35 .16
❑ 126 Bobby Reynolds .25 .11
❑ 127 Tie Domi 4.00 1.80
❑ 128 Ken Hammond .35 .16
❑ 129 Cape Breton Checklist .05 .02
❑ 130 Wade Campbell .25 .11
❑ 131 Chris Joseph .35 .16
❑ 132 Mario Barbe .25 .11
❑ 133 Mike Greenlay .35 .16
❑ 134 Peter Soberlak .25 .11
❑ 135 Bruce Bell .35 .16
❑ 136 Dan Currie .25 .11
❑ 137 Fabian Joseph .35 .16
❑ 138 Stan Drulia .35 .16
❑ 139 Todd Charlesworth .25 .11
❑ 140 Norm Maciver .75 .35
❑ 141 David Haas .25 .11
❑ 142 Tim Tisdale .25 .11
❑ 143 Eldon Reddick .50 .23
❑ 144 Alexander Tyznych .25 .11
❑ 145 Kim Issel .25 .11
❑ 146 Corey Foster .25 .11
❑ 147 Tomas Kapusta .25 .11
❑ 148 Brian Wilks .25 .11
❑ 149 John LeBlanc .25 .11
❑ 150 Ivan Matulik .25 .11
❑ 151 Shaun Van Allen .50 .23
❑ 152 Halifax Checklist .05 .02
❑ 153 Scott Gordon .35 .16
❑ 154 Trevor Steinburg .25 .11
❑ 155 Miroslav Ihnacak .35 .16
❑ 156 Jamie Baker .35 .16

- ☐ 157 Robbie Ftorek .......... .50 .23
- ☐ 158 C. McQuaid and .......... .05 .02
  B.Smith
- ☐ 159 Mario Brunetta .......... .35 .16
- ☐ 160 Jean-Marc Routhier .......... .25 .11
- ☐ 161 David Espe .......... .25 .11
- ☐ 162 Ken Quinney .......... .25 .11
- ☐ 163 Mark Vermette .......... .25 .11
- ☐ 164 Dean Hopkins .......... .25 .11
- ☐ 165 Claude Julien .......... .25 .11
- ☐ 166 Claude Lapointe .......... .50 .23
- ☐ 167 Stephane Morin .......... .50 .23
- ☐ 168 Bryan Fogarty .......... .50 .23
- ☐ 169 Dave Pichette .......... .25 .11
- ☐ 170 Kevin Kaminski .......... .35 .16
- ☐ 171 Brent Severyn .......... .35 .16
- ☐ 172 Max Middendorf .......... .25 .11
- ☐ 173 Jean-Marc Richard .......... .25 .11
- ☐ 174 Gerald Bzdel .......... .25 .11
- ☐ 175 Ladislav Tresl .......... .25 .11
- ☐ 176 Jaroslav Sevcik .......... .25 .11
- ☐ 177 Greg Smyth .......... .35 .16
- ☐ 178 Joel Baillargeon .......... .25 .11
- ☐ 179 Sherbrooke Checklist .......... .05 .02
- ☐ 180 Andre Racicot .......... 1.00 .45
- ☐ 181 Jean-Claude Bergeron .......... .50 .23
- ☐ 182 Jim Nesich .......... .25 .11
- ☐ 183 Todd Richards .......... .25 .11
- ☐ 184 Francois Gravel .......... .25 .11
- ☐ 185 Lyle Odelein .......... 1.50 .70
- ☐ 186 Benoit Brunet .......... .75 .35
- ☐ 187 Mario Roberge .......... .35 .16
- ☐ 188 Marc Saumier .......... .25 .11
- ☐ 189 Norman Desjardins .......... .25 .11
- ☐ 190 Dan Woodley .......... .25 .11
- ☐ 191 Andrew Cassels .......... 2.00 .90
- ☐ 192 Roy Mitchell .......... .25 .11
- ☐ 193 Guy Darveau .......... .25 .11
- ☐ 194 Ed Cristofoli .......... .25 .11
- ☐ 195 Stephane J.G. Richer .......... .25 .11
- ☐ 196 Jacques Parent .......... .05 .02
- ☐ 197 Luc Gauthier .......... .25 .11
- ☐ 198 John Ferguson .......... .25 .11
- ☐ 199 Mathieu Schneider .......... 2.50 1.10
- ☐ 200 Serge Roberge .......... .25 .11
- ☐ 201 Jean Hamel .......... .25 .11
- ☐ 202 Utica Checklist .......... .05 .02
- ☐ 203 Jason Simon .......... .25 .11
- ☐ 204 Jeff Madill .......... .25 .11
- ☐ 205 Kevin Todd .......... .50 .23
- ☐ 206 Myles O'Connor .......... .25 .11
- ☐ 207 Jon Morris .......... .35 .16
- ☐ 208 Bob Hoffmeyer .......... .25 .11
- ☐ 209 Paul Ysebaert .......... .75 .35
- ☐ 210 Steve Rooney .......... .35 .16
- ☐ 211 Claude Vilgrain .......... .25 .11
- ☐ 212 Paul Guay .......... .25 .11
- ☐ 213 Roland Melanson .......... .75 .35
- ☐ 214 Tom McVie .......... .35 .16
- ☐ 215 David Marcinyshyn .......... .25 .11
- ☐ 216 Perry Anderson .......... .25 .11
- ☐ 217 Jamie Huscroft .......... .50 .23
- ☐ 218 Bob Woods .......... .25 .11
- ☐ 219 Pat Conacher .......... .50 .23
- ☐ 220 Jean-Marc Lanthier .......... .25 .11
- ☐ 221 Chris Kiene .......... .25 .11
- ☐ 222 Eric Weinrich .......... .50 .23
- ☐ 223 Brian Fitzgerald .......... .05 .02
- ☐ 224 Craig Billington .......... 1.50 .70
- ☐ 225 Jim Thomson .......... .35 .16
- ☐ 226 Tim Budy .......... .25 .11
- ☐ 227 Marc Laniel .......... .25 .11
- ☐ 228 Robert Bill .......... .05 .02
- ☐ 229 Springfield Checklist .......... .05 .02
- ☐ 230 Mike Walsh .......... .25 .11
- ☐ 231 Dale Henry .......... .25 .11
- ☐ 232 Bill Berg .......... .50 .23
- ☐ 233 Hank Lammens .......... .25 .11
- ☐ 234 Rob DiMaio .......... .75 .35
- ☐ 235 Shawn Byram .......... .25 .11
- ☐ 236 Jeff Hackett .......... 3.00 1.35
- ☐ 237 Wayne McBean .......... .35 .16
- ☐ 238 Tim Hanley .......... .25 .11
- ☐ 239 Tom Fitzgerald .......... .35 .16
- ☐ 240 Mike Stevens .......... .25 .11
- ☐ 241 George Maneluk .......... .25 .11
- ☐ 242 Dean Ewen .......... .25 .11
- ☐ 243 Dale Kushner .......... .25 .11
- ☐ 244 Shawn Evans .......... .25 .11
- ☐ 245 Rod Dallman .......... .25 .11
- ☐ 246 Mike Kelfer .......... .25 .11
- ☐ 247 Sean LeBrun .......... .25 .11
- ☐ 248 Kerry Clark .......... .25 .11
- ☐ 249 Ed Tyburski .......... .05 .02
- ☐ 250 Derek King .......... 2.00 .90
- ☐ 251 Marc Bergevin .......... .50 .23
- ☐ 252 Jeff Finley .......... .35 .16
- ☐ 253 Jim Roberts .......... .25 .11
- ☐ 254 Chris Pryor .......... .25 .11
- ☐ 255 Rochester Checklist .......... .05 .02
- ☐ 256 Robert Ray .......... 2.50 1.10
- ☐ 257 Ken Priestlay .......... .35 .16
- ☐ 258 Darcy Wakaluk .......... 1.00 .45
- ☐ 259 Richie Dunn .......... .25 .11
- ☐ 260 Ken Sutton .......... .50 .23
- ☐ 261 Terry Martin .......... .25 .11
- ☐ 262 Scott Metcalfe .......... .25 .11
- ☐ 263 Joel Savage .......... .25 .11
- ☐ 264 Brad Miller .......... .25 .11
- ☐ 265 Donald Audette .......... 2.00 .90
- ☐ 266 John Van Boxmeer .......... .05 .02
- ☐ 267 The Moose .......... .05 .02
- ☐ 268 Brian Ford .......... .25 .11
- ☐ 269 Darcy Loewen .......... .25 .11
- ☐ 270 Bob Halkidis .......... .35 .16
- ☐ 271 Steve Ludzik .......... .35 .16


- ☐ 272 Steve Smith .......... .25 .11
- ☐ 273 Francis Guay .......... .25 .11
- ☐ 274 Mike Donnelly .......... .50 .23
- ☐ 275 Darrin Shannon .......... 1.00 .45
- ☐ 276 Jody Gage .......... .75 .35
- ☐ 277 Dave Baseggio .......... .25 .11
- ☐ 278 Bob Corkum .......... .75 .35
- ☐ 279 Jim Jackson .......... .25 .11
- ☐ 280 Don McSween .......... .25 .11
- ☐ 281 Jim Hofford .......... .25 .11
- ☐ 282 Scott McCrory .......... .25 .11
- ☐ 283 Binghamton Checklist .......... .05 .02
- ☐ 284 Raymond Saumier .......... .25 .11
- ☐ 285 Mike Berger .......... .25 .11
- ☐ 286 Corey Beaulieu .......... .25 .11
- ☐ 287 Doug McKay .......... .25 .11
- ☐ 288 Blair Atcheynum .......... .25 .11
- ☐ 289 Al Tuer .......... .25 .11
- ☐ 290 Chris Lindberg .......... .35 .16
- ☐ 291 Daryl Reaugh .......... .50 .23
- ☐ 292 James Black .......... .25 .11
- ☐ 293 Vern Smith .......... .25 .11
- ☐ 294 Todd Krygier .......... .50 .23
- ☐ 295 Bob Bodak .......... .25 .11
- ☐ 296 Jon Smith .......... .05 .02
- ☐ 297 Michel Picard .......... .35 .16
- ☐ 298 Jim Culhane .......... .25 .11
- ☐ 299 Brian Chapman .......... .25 .11
- ☐ 300 Jim Ennis .......... .25 .11
- ☐ 301 Jacques Caron .......... .25 .11
- ☐ 302 Jim McKenzie .......... .35 .16
- ☐ 303 Kay Whitmore .......... .75 .35
- ☐ 304 Terry Yake .......... .35 .16
- ☐ 305 Mike Moller .......... .25 .11
- ☐ 306 Adirondack Checklist .......... .05 .02
- ☐ 307 Bob Wilkie .......... .25 .11
- ☐ 308 Chris McRae .......... .25 .11
- ☐ 309 Chris Kotsopoulos .......... .35 .16
- ☐ 310 Steve Sumner .......... .05 .02
- ☐ 311 Timothy Abbott .......... .05 .02
- ☐ 312 Gord Kruppke .......... .25 .11
- ☐ 313 Mike Gober .......... .25 .11
- ☐ 314 Al Conroy .......... .25 .11
- ☐ 315 Sam St.Laurent .......... .35 .16
- ☐ 316 Dave Casey .......... .05 .02
- ☐ 317 Yves Racine .......... .50 .23
- ☐ 318 Randy McKay .......... .50 .23
- ☐ 319 Dale Krentz .......... .25 .11
- ☐ 320 Sheldon Kennedy .......... .75 .35
- ☐ 321 Barry Melrose .......... 2.00 .90
- ☐ 322 Dennis Holland .......... .25 .11
- ☐ 323 Glenn Merkosky .......... .25 .11
- ☐ 324 Murray Eaves .......... .25 .11
- ☐ 325 Mark Reimer .......... .35 .16
- ☐ 326 Tim Cheveldae .......... 1.00 .45
- ☐ 327 Peter Dineen .......... .25 .11
- ☐ 328 Dean Morton .......... .25 .11
- ☐ 329 Derek Mayer .......... .35 .16
- ☐ 330 Hershey Checklist .......... .05 .02
- ☐ 331 Don Biggs .......... .25 .11
- ☐ 332 Scott Sandelin .......... .25 .11
- ☐ 333 Shaun Sabol .......... .25 .11
- ☐ 334 Murray Baron .......... .35 .16
- ☐ 335 Dave Fenyves .......... .25 .11
- ☐ 336 Glen Seabrooke .......... .25 .11
- ☐ 337 Mark Freer .......... .35 .16
- ☐ 338 Ray Allison .......... .25 .11
- ☐ 339 Chris Jensen .......... .25 .11
- ☐ 340 Ross Fitzpatrick .......... .25 .11
- ☐ 341 Brian Dobbin .......... .25 .11
- ☐ 342 Darren Rumble .......... .25 .11
- ☐ 343 Mike Stothers .......... .25 .11
- ☐ 344 Jiri Latal .......... .25 .11
- ☐ 345 Don Nachbaur .......... .25 .11
- ☐ 346 John Stevens .......... .25 .11
- ☐ 347 Steven Fletcher .......... .25 .11
- ☐ 348 Kent Hawley .......... .25 .11
- ☐ 349 Bill Armstrong .......... .25 .11
- ☐ 350 Bruce Hoffort .......... .35 .16
- ☐ 351 Gordon Paddock .......... .25 .11
- ☐ 352 Marc D'Amour .......... .35 .16
- ☐ 353 Tim Tookey .......... .25 .11
- ☐ 354 Reid Simpson .......... .25 .11
- ☐ 355 Mark Bassen .......... .25 .11
- ☐ 356 Rocky Trottier .......... .25 .11
- ☐ 357 Harry Bricker .......... .05 .02
- ☐ 358 Dan Stuck .......... .05 .02
- ☐ 359 Al Hill .......... .25 .11
- ☐ 360 Kevin McCarthy .......... .25 .11

## 1989-90 ProCards IHL

This set of 208 standard-size cards features the nine teams of the International Hockey League. Although the team sets were originally sold with a suggested retail price of 3.00 per team set and packaged individually, they are listed below as one giant set. In many cases that was the way they were advertised and sold, i.e., as a complete set of all the teams in the IHL. The numbering is by teams as follows, Peoria Rivermen (1-23), Flint Spirits (24-48), Indianapolis Ice (49-73), Kalamazoo


Wings (74-98), Phoenix Roadrunners (99-121), Fort Wayne Komets (122-141), Muskegon Lumberjacks (142-164), Milwaukee Admirals (165-189), and Salt Lake City Golden Eagles (190-208).

|  | MINT | NRMT |
|---|---|---|
| COMPLETE SET (208) | 70.00 | 32.00 |
| COMMON CARD (1-208) | .05 | .02 |

- ☐ 1 Peoria Checklist .......... .05 .02
- ☐ 2 Darwin McPherson .......... .25 .11
- ☐ 3 Pat Jablonski .......... .75 .35
- ☐ 4 Scott Paluch .......... .25 .11
- ☐ 5 Guy Hebert .......... 8.00 3.60
- ☐ 6 Richard Pilon .......... .35 .16
- ☐ 7 Curtis Joseph .......... 15.00 6.75
- ☐ 8 Robert Dirk .......... .50 .23
- ☐ 9 Darin Smith .......... .25 .11
- ☐ 10 Terry McLean .......... .25 .11
- ☐ 11 Kevin Miehm .......... .35 .16
- ☐ 12 Toby Ducolon .......... .25 .11
- ☐ 13 Mike Wolak .......... .25 .11
- ☐ 14 Adrien Plavsic .......... .50 .23
- ☐ 15 Dave Thomlinson .......... .35 .16
- ☐ 16 Jim Vesey .......... .25 .11
- ☐ 17 Michel Mongeau .......... .50 .23
- ☐ 18 Tom Nash .......... .05 .02
- ☐ 19 David O'Brien .......... .25 .11
- ☐ 20 Dominic Lavoie .......... .50 .23
- ☐ 21 Keith Osborne .......... .25 .11
- ☐ 22 Rob Robinson .......... .25 .11
- ☐ 23 Wayne Thomas .......... .35 .16
- ☐ 24 Flint Checklist .......... .05 .02
- ☐ 25 Jason Lafreniere .......... .35 .16
- ☐ 26 Rick Knickle .......... .75 .35
- ☐ 27 Jerry Tarrant .......... .25 .11
- ☐ 28 Paul Broten .......... .50 .23
- ☐ 29 Kevin Miller .......... 1.50 .70
- ☐ 30 Jim Latos .......... .25 .11
- ☐ 31 Daniel Lacroix .......... .35 .16
- ☐ 32 Dennis Vial .......... .25 .11
- ☐ 33 Denis Larocque .......... .25 .11
- ☐ 34 Mike Golden .......... .25 .11
- ☐ 35 Mike Hurlbut .......... .25 .11
- ☐ 36 Scott Browter .......... .25 .11
- ☐ 37 Lee Giffin .......... .25 .11
- ☐ 38 Jeff Bloemberg .......... .25 .11
- ☐ 39 Simon Wheeldon .......... .25 .11
- ☐ 40 Rob Zamuner .......... 1.50 .70
- ☐ 41 Joe Paterson .......... .25 .11
- ☐ 42 Barry Chyzowski .......... .25 .11
- ☐ 43 Peter Laviolette .......... .25 .11
- ☐ 44 Corey Millen .......... .75 .35
- ☐ 45 Darren Lowe .......... .25 .11
- ☐ 46 Peter Fiorentino .......... .25 .11
- ☐ 47 Soren True .......... .25 .11
- ☐ 48 Mike Richter .......... 15.00 6.75
- ☐ 49 Ice Checklist .......... .05 .02
- ☐ 50 Sean Williams .......... .25 .11
- ☐ 51 Bruce Cassidy .......... .25 .11
- ☐ 52 Mark Kurawski .......... .25 .11
- ☐ 53 Bob Bassen .......... .75 .35
- ☐ 54 Marty Nanne .......... .25 .11
- ☐ 55 Jari Torkki .......... .25 .11
- ☐ 56 Ryan McGill .......... .35 .16
- ☐ 57 Mike Peluso .......... 1.00 .45
- ☐ 58 Darryl Sutter .......... .75 .35
- ☐ 59 Dan Vincelette .......... .25 .11
- ☐ 60 Lonnie Loach .......... .25 .11
- ☐ 61 Mike Rucinski .......... .25 .11
- ☐ 62 Jim Playfair .......... .25 .11
- ☐ 63 Everett Sanipass .......... .25 .11
- ☐ 64 Dale Marquette .......... .25 .11
- ☐ 65 Gary Moscaluk .......... .25 .11
- ☐ 66 Mario Doyon .......... .25 .11
- ☐ 67 Ray LeBlanc .......... 1.00 .45
- ☐ 68 Mike Eagles .......... .35 .16
- ☐ 69 Warren Rychel .......... .75 .35
- ☐ 70 Jim Johannson .......... .35 .16
- ☐ 71 Cam Russell .......... .50 .23
- ☐ 72 Mike McNeil .......... .25 .11
- ☐ 73 Jimmy Waite .......... .75 .35
- ☐ 74 Kalamazoo Checklist .......... .05 .02
- ☐ 75 Kevin Schamehorn .......... .25 .11
- ☐ 76 Kevin Evans .......... .25 .11
- ☐ 77 D'Arcy Norton .......... .25 .11
- ☐ 78 Scott Robinson .......... .25 .11
- ☐ 79 Larry DePalma .......... .25 .11
- ☐ 80 Ed Courtenay .......... .35 .16
- ☐ 81 Rob Zettler .......... .50 .23
- ☐ 82 Dusan Pasek .......... .25 .11
- ☐ 83 Gary Emmons .......... .25 .11
- ☐ 84 Peter Lappin .......... .25 .11
- ☐ 85 Mario Thyer .......... .25 .11
- ☐ 86 Mike McHugh .......... .25 .11
- ☐ 87 Randy Smith .......... .35 .16
- ☐ 88 Link Gaetz .......... .50 .23
- ☐ 89 Ken Hodge Jr. .......... .35 .16
- ☐ 90 Pat MacLeod .......... .50 .23
- ☐ 91 Neil Wilkinson .......... .75 .35
- ☐ 92 Brett Barnett .......... .25 .11
- ☐ 93 Larry Dyck .......... .25 .11
- ☐ 94 Dean Kolstad .......... .25 .11
- ☐ 95 Jarmo Myllys .......... .50 .23
- ☐ 96 Paul Jerrard .......... .25 .11
- ☐ 97 Jean-Francois Quintin .......... .35 .16
- ☐ 98 Mitch Messier .......... .25 .11
- ☐ 99 Phoenix Checklist UER .......... .05 .02
  (110 Jeff Lamb
  not listed)
- ☐ 100 Bryant Perrier .......... .25 .11
- ☐ 101 Rob Gretzky .......... 1.00 .45
- ☐ 102 Don Martin .......... .25 .11
- ☐ 103 David Littman .......... .35 .16
- ☐ 104 Mike DeCarle .......... .25 .11
- ☐ 105 Grant Tkachuk .......... .25 .11


- ☐ 106 Richard Novak .......... .25 .11
- ☐ 107 Chris Luongo .......... .25 .11
- ☐ 108 Bruce Boudreau .......... .35 .16
- ☐ 109 Nick Beaulieu .......... .25 .11
- ☐ 110 Jeff Lamb .......... .25 .11
- ☐ 111 Rob Nichols .......... .25 .11
- ☐ 112 Garry Unger .......... .50 .23
- ☐ 113 Larry Floyd .......... .25 .11
- ☐ 114 Brent Sapergia .......... .25 .11
- ☐ 115 Randy Exelby .......... .35 .16
- ☐ 116 Jim McGeough .......... .25 .11
- ☐ 117 Tom Karalis .......... .25 .11
- ☐ 118 Ken Spangler .......... .25 .11
- ☐ 119 Jacques Mailhot .......... .25 .11
- ☐ 120 Shawn Dineen .......... .25 .11
- ☐ 121 Dave Korol .......... .25 .11
- ☐ 122 Fort Wayne Checklist .......... .05 .02
- ☐ 123 Colin Chin .......... .25 .11
- ☐ 124 Scott Shaunessy .......... .25 .11
- ☐ 125 Bob Lakso .......... .25 .11
- ☐ 126 Duane Joyce .......... .25 .11
- ☐ 127 Joe Stephan .......... .25 .11
- ☐ 128 Ron Shudra .......... .25 .11
- ☐ 129 Bob Fowler .......... .25 .11
- ☐ 130 Steve Bisson .......... .25 .11
- ☐ 131 Craig Endean .......... .25 .11
- ☐ 132 Carl Mokosak .......... .25 .11
- ☐ 133 Carey Lucyk .......... .25 .11
- ☐ 134 Craig Channell .......... .25 .11
- ☐ 135 Frederic Chabot .......... .50 .23
- ☐ 136 Brian Hannon .......... .25 .11
- ☐ 137 Keith Miller .......... .25 .11
- ☐ 138 Al Sims .......... .50 .23
- ☐ 139 Stephane Beauregard .......... .75 .35
- ☐ 140 Ron Handy .......... .25 .11
- ☐ 141 Byron Lomow .......... .25 .11
- ☐ 142 Muskegon Checklist .......... .05 .02
- ☐ 143 Jamie Leach .......... .25 .11
- ☐ 144 Chris Clifford .......... .25 .11
- ☐ 145 Dave Capuano .......... .35 .16
- ☐ 146 Jeff Daniels .......... .25 .11
- ☐ 147 Dave Goertz .......... .25 .11
- ☐ 148 Perry Ganchar .......... .25 .11
- ☐ 149 Mitch Wilson .......... .25 .11
- ☐ 150 Scott Gruhl .......... .35 .16
- ☐ 151 Randy Taylor .......... .25 .11
- ☐ 152 Bruce Racine .......... .35 .16
- ☐ 153 Dave Michayluk .......... .35 .16
- ☐ 154 Richard Zemlak .......... .35 .16
- ☐ 155 Brad Aitken .......... .25 .11
- ☐ 156 Paul Stanton .......... .35 .16
- ☐ 157 Darren Stolk .......... .25 .11
- ☐ 158 Jim Paek .......... .50 .16
- ☐ 159 Mark Kachowski .......... .25 .11
- ☐ 160 Dan Frawley .......... .25 .11
- ☐ 161 Mike Mersch .......... .25 .11
- ☐ 162 Glenn Mulvenna .......... .25 .11
- ☐ 163 Phil Russell .......... .35 .16
- ☐ 164 Blair McDonald .......... .25 .11
- ☐ 165 Milwaukee Checklist .......... .05 .02
- ☐ 166 Shaun Clouston .......... .25 .11
- ☐ 167 Steve Veilleux .......... .25 .11
- ☐ 168 Peter Bakovic .......... .25 .11
- ☐ 169 Peter DeBoer .......... .25 .11
- ☐ 170 Ernie Vargas .......... .25 .11
- ☐ 171 Keith Street .......... .25 .11
- ☐ 172 Rob Murphy .......... .35 .16
- ☐ 173 David Bruce .......... .50 .23
- ☐ 174 Shannon Travis .......... .25 .11
- ☐ 175 Jeff Rohlicek .......... .35 .16
- ☐ 176 Jay Mazur .......... .25 .11
- ☐ 177 Kevan Guy .......... .25 .11
- ☐ 178 Troy Gamble .......... 1.00 .45
- ☐ 179 Ronnie Stern .......... .50 .23
- ☐ 180 Jim Revenberg .......... .25 .11
- ☐ 181 Jose Charbonneau .......... .25 .11
- ☐ 182 Ian Kidd .......... .25 .11
- ☐ 183 Todd Hawkins .......... .25 .11
- ☐ 184 Carl Valimont .......... .25 .11
- ☐ 185 Jim Agnew .......... .25 .11
- ☐ 186 Curtis Hunt .......... .25 .11
- ☐ 187 Dean Cook .......... .25 .11
- ☐ 188 Ron Wilson .......... .35 .16
- ☐ 189 Ron Lapointe .......... .25 .11
- ☐ 190 Salt Lake City .......... .05 .02
  Checklist
- ☐ 191 Brian Glynn .......... .35 .16
- ☐ 192 Stephane Matteau .......... .75 .35
- ☐ 193 Rick Barkovich .......... .25 .11
- ☐ 194 Jeff Wenaas .......... .25 .11
- ☐ 195 Darryl Olsen .......... .25 .11
- ☐ 196 Rick Lessard .......... .25 .11
- ☐ 197 Kevin Grant .......... .25 .11
- ☐ 198 Rich Chernomaz .......... .25 .11
- ☐ 199 Stu Grimson .......... 1.00 .45
- ☐ 200 Jamie Hislop and .......... .25 .11
  Bob Francis
- ☐ 201 Doug Pickell .......... .25 .11
- ☐ 202 Chris Biotti .......... .25 .11
- ☐ 203 Tim Sweeney .......... .50 .23
- ☐ 204 Ken Sabourin .......... .35 .16
- ☐ 205 Randy Bucyk .......... .25 .11
- ☐ 206 Wayne Cowley .......... .35 .16
- ☐ 207 Rick Hayward .......... .25 .11
- ☐ 208 Marc Bureau .......... .75 .35

## 1990-91 ProCards AHL/IHL

This 629-card standard-size set features players who started or were expected to start the 1990-91 season in the minors. Players from the American Hockey League and the International Hockey League are included in this set. This set features red borders with a


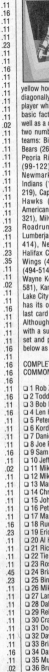

yellow hockey stick on the left side of the card diagonally framing a full-color picture of the player while the backs of the cards feature the basic factual information about the player as well as a complete statistical history. There are two number 99's and the set is arranged by teams: Binghamton Rangers (1-25), Hershey Bears (26-53), Fredericton Canadiens (54-75), Peoria Riverman (76-99) Kalamazoo Wings (99-122), Maine Mariners (123-145), Newmarket Saints (146-170), Springfield Indians (171-194), Baltimore Skipjacks (195-219), Cape Breton Oilers (220-242), Moncton Hawks (243-264, 343-344), Rochester Americans (265-295), San Diego Gulls (296-321), Milwaukee Admirals (322-342), Phoenix Roadrunner (345-369), Muskegon Lumberjacks (370-392), Indianapolis Ice (393-414), New Haven Nighthawks (415-441), Halifax Citadels (442-468), Adirondack Red Wings (469-493), Capital District Islanders (494-514), Albany Choppers (515-535), Fort Wayne Komets (536-556), Utica Devils (557-581), Kansas City Blades (582-602), and Salt Lake City Golden Eagles (603-628). Each team has its own team checklist (TC) card as the last card in the team's numbering sequence. Although the team sets were originally sold with a suggested retail price of 4.00 per team set and packaged individually, they are listed below as one giant set.

|  | MINT | NRMT |
|---|---|---|
| COMPLETE SET (629) | 100.00 | 45.00 |
| COMMON CARD (1-628) | .05 | .02 |

- ☐ 1 Rob Zamuner .......... .75 .35
- ☐ 2 Todd Charlesworth .......... .15 .07
- ☐ 3 Bob Bodak .......... .15 .07
- ☐ 4 Len Hachborn .......... .25 .11
- ☐ 5 Peter Fiorentino .......... .15 .07
- ☐ 6 Kord Cernich .......... .15 .07
- ☐ 7 Daniel Lacroix .......... .50 .23
- ☐ 8 Joe Paterson .......... .15 .07
- ☐ 9 Sam St.Laurent .......... .50 .23
- ☐ 10 Jeff Bloemberg .......... .15 .07
- ☐ 11 Mike Golden .......... .15 .07
- ☐ 12 Mike Hurlbut .......... .25 .11
- ☐ 13 Mark LaForest .......... .50 .23
- ☐ 14 Chris Cichocki .......... .15 .07
- ☐ 15 John Paddock .......... .25 .11
- ☐ 16 Peter Laviolette .......... .25 .11
- ☐ 17 Martin Bergeron .......... .15 .07
- ☐ 18 Rudy Poeschek .......... .50 .23
- ☐ 19 Eric Germain .......... .15 .07
- ☐ 20 Al Hill ACO .......... .15 .07
- ☐ 21 Rick Bennett .......... .25 .11
- ☐ 22 Tie Domi .......... 2.50 1.10
- ☐ 23 Ross Fitzpatrick .......... .15 .07
- ☐ 24 Brian McReynolds .......... .25 .11
- ☐ 25 Binghamton Rangers TC .......... .05 .02
- ☐ 26 Mike Eaves CO .......... .15 .07
- ☐ 27 Lance Pitlick .......... .40 .18
- ☐ 28 Dale Kushner .......... .15 .07
- ☐ 29 Reid Simpson .......... .25 .11
- ☐ 30 Craig Fisher .......... .25 .11
- ☐ 31 Dominic Roussel .......... 1.00 .45
- ☐ 32 Dave Fenyves .......... .15 .07
- ☐ 33 Brian Dobbin .......... .15 .07
- ☐ 34 Darren Rumble .......... .40 .18
- ☐ 35 Murray Baron .......... .40 .18
- ☐ 36 Bruce Hoffort .......... .25 .11
- ☐ 37 Steve Beadle .......... .15 .07
- ☐ 38 Chris Jensen .......... .15 .07
- ☐ 39 Mike Stothers .......... .15 .07
- ☐ 40 Kent Hawley .......... .15 .07
- ☐ 41 Scott Sandelin .......... .15 .07
- ☐ 42 Guy Phillips .......... .15 .07
- ☐ 43 Mark Bassen .......... .15 .07
- ☐ 44 Steve Scheifele .......... .15 .07
- ☐ 45 Bill Armstrong .......... .15 .07
- ☐ 46 Shaun Sabol .......... .15 .07
- ☐ 47 Mark Freer .......... .15 .07
- ☐ 48 Claude Boivin .......... .25 .11
- ☐ 49 Len Barrie .......... .25 .11
- ☐ 50 Bill Armstrong .......... .15 .07
- ☐ 51 Tim Tookey .......... .15 .07
- ☐ 52 Harry Bricker ACO .......... .05 .02
- ☐ 53 Hershey Bears TC .......... .05 .02
- ☐ 54 Alain Cote .......... .15 .07
- ☐ 55 Luc Gauthier .......... .15 .07
- ☐ 56 Eric Charron .......... .25 .11
- ☐ 57 Mario Roberge .......... .15 .07
- ☐ 58 Tom Sagissor .......... .15 .07
- ☐ 59 Brent Bobyck .......... .15 .07
- ☐ 60 John Ferguson .......... .15 .07
- ☐ 61 Jim Nesich .......... .15 .07
- ☐ 62 Gilbert Dionne .......... .40 .18
- ☐ 63 Herbert Hohenberger .......... .15 .07
- ☐ 64 Dan Woodley .......... .15 .07
- ☐ 65 Roy Mitchell .......... .15 .07
- ☐ 66 Frederic Chabot .......... .50 .23
- ☐ 67 Andre Racicot .......... .50 .23

❑ 68 Paul DiPietro .50 .23
❑ 69 Norman Desjardins .15 .07
❑ 70 Martin St.Amour .15 .07
❑ 71 Jesse Belanger .50 .23
❑ 72 Ed Cristofoli .15 .07
❑ 73 Patrick Lebeau .25 .11
❑ 74 Paulin Bordeleau CO .15 .07
❑ 75 Fredericton Canadiens TC .05 .02
❑ 76 Keith Osborne .15 .07
❑ 77 Richard Pilon .40 .18
❑ 78 Alain Raymond .15 .07
❑ 79 Rob Robinson .15 .07
❑ 80 Andy Rymsha .15 .07
❑ 81 Randy Skarda .25 .11
❑ 82 Dave Thomlinson .25 .11
❑ 83 Tom Tilley .40 .18
❑ 84 Steve Tuttle .15 .07
❑ 85 Tony Twist 1.00 .45
❑ 86 David Bruce .25 .11
❑ 87 Kelly Chase .50 .23
❑ 88 Nelson Emerson 2.00 .90
❑ 89 Guy Hebert 5.00 2.20
❑ 90 Tony Hejna .15 .07
❑ 91 Michel Mongeau .40 .18
❑ 92 David O'Brien .15 .07
❑ 93 Kevin Miehm .25 .11
❑ 94 Darwin McPherson .15 .07
❑ 95 Dominic Lavoie .15 .07
❑ 96 Yves Heroux .15 .07
❑ 97 Pat Jablonski .75 .35
❑ 98 Bob Plager CO .50 .23
❑ 99A Peoria Rivermen TC .05 .02
❑ 99B Jayson More .25 .11
❑ 100 Kevin Evans .15 .07
❑ 101 Warren Babe .15 .07
❑ 102 Mitch Messier .15 .07
❑ 103 John Blue .50 .23
❑ 104 Larry Dyck .25 .11
❑ 105 Duane Joyce .15 .07
❑ 106 Kari Takko .40 .18
❑ 107 Brett Barnett .15 .07
❑ 108 Pat MacLeod .25 .11
❑ 109 Peter Lappin .15 .07
❑ 110 Link Gaetz .40 .18
❑ 111 Larry DePalma .15 .07
❑ 112 Steve Gotaas .15 .07
❑ 113 Mike McHugh .15 .07
❑ 114 Dan Keczmer .25 .11
❑ 115 Jackson Penney .15 .07
❑ 116 Ed Courtenay .40 .18
❑ 117 Jean-Francois Quintin .15 .07
❑ 118 Scott Robinson .15 .07
❑ 119 Mario Thyer .15 .07
❑ 120 Enrico Ciccone .75 .35
❑ 121 Kevin Constantine and John Marks .40 .18
❑ 122 Kalamazoo Wings TC .05 .02
❑ 123 Shayne Stevenson .15 .07
❑ 124 Jeff Lazaro .25 .11
❑ 125 Matt DelGuidice .25 .11
❑ 126 Ron Hoover .15 .07
❑ 127 John Mokosak .15 .07
❑ 128 John Blum .15 .07
❑ 129 Mike Parson .25 .11
❑ 130 Bruce Shoebottom .15 .07
❑ 131 Dave Donnelly .15 .07
❑ 132 Ralph Barahona .15 .07
❑ 133 Graeme Townshend .25 .11
❑ 134 Ken Hodge Jr. .40 .18
❑ 135 Norm Foster .25 .11
❑ 136 Greg Poss .15 .07
❑ 137 Brad James .15 .07
❑ 138 Lou Crawford .15 .07
❑ 139 Rick Allain .15 .07
❑ 140 Bob Beers .40 .18
❑ 141 Ken Hammond .25 .11
❑ 142 Mark Montanari .15 .07
❑ 143 Rick Bowness CO .25 .11
❑ 144 Bob Gould P/CO .15 .07
❑ 145 Maine Mariners TC .05 .02
❑ 146 Mike Stevens .15 .07
❑ 147 Greg Walters .15 .07
❑ 148 Mike Moes .15 .07
❑ 149 Kent Hulst .15 .07
❑ 150 Len Esau .15 .07
❑ 151 Darryl Shannon .40 .18
❑ 152 Bobby Reynolds .15 .07
❑ 153 Derek Langille .15 .07
❑ 154 Jeff Serowik .25 .11
❑ 155 Darren Veitch .40 .18
❑ 156 Joe Sacco .40 .18
❑ 157 Alan Hepple .15 .07
❑ 158 Doug Shedden .40 .18
❑ 159 Steve Bancroft .15 .07
❑ 160 Greg Johnston .40 .18
❑ 161 Trevor Jobe .15 .07
❑ 162 Bill Root .40 .18
❑ 163 Tim Bean .15 .07
❑ 164 Brian Blad .15 .07
❑ 165 Robert Hornya .15 .07
❑ 166 Dean Anderson .15 .07
❑ 167 Damian Rhodes 4.00 1.80
❑ 168 Mike Millar .15 .07
❑ 169 Mike Jackson .15 .07
❑ 170 Newmarket Saints TC .05 .02
❑ 171 Cal Brown .15 .07
❑ 172 Michel Picard .40 .18
❑ 173 Cam Brauer .15 .07
❑ 174 Jim Burke .15 .07
❑ 175 Jim McKenzie .40 .18
❑ 176 Mike Tomlak .15 .07
❑ 177 Ross McKay .15 .07
❑ 178 Blair Atcheynum .15 .07
❑ 179 Chris Tancill .25 .11
❑ 180 Mark Greig .25 .11
❑ 181 Joe Day .15 .07
❑ 182 Jim Roberts CO .15 .07
❑ 183 Emanuel Viveiros .15 .07
❑ 184 Daryl Reaugh .40 .18
❑ 185 Tommie Eriksen .15 .07
❑ 186 Terry Yake .40 .18
❑ 187 Chris Govedaris .15 .07
❑ 188 Chris Bright .15 .07
❑ 189 John Stevens .15 .07
❑ 190 Brian Chapman .15 .07
❑ 191 James Black .25 .11
❑ 192 Scott Daniels .15 .07
❑ 193 Kelly Ens .15 .07
❑ 194 Springfield Indians TC .05 .02
❑ 195 Ken Lovsin .15 .07
❑ 196 Kent Paynter .15 .07
❑ 197 Jim Mathieson .20 .09
❑ 198 Bob Mendel .15 .07
❑ 199 Reggie Savage .25 .11
❑ 200 Alfie Turcotte .15 .07
❑ 201 Victor Gervais .15 .07
❑ 202 Todd Hlushko .50 .23
❑ 203 Steve Seftel .15 .07
❑ 204 Thomas Sjogren .15 .07
❑ 205 Steve Maltais .25 .11
❑ 206 Bob Joyce .50 .23
❑ 207 Tyler Larter .15 .07
❑ 208 Mark Ferner .25 .11
❑ 209 Bobby Babcock .15 .07
❑ 210 Jeff Greenlaw .15 .07
❑ 211 Tim Taylor .75 .35
❑ 212 John Purves .15 .07
❑ 213 Chris Felix .40 .18
❑ 214 Jiri Vykoukal .15 .07
❑ 215 Shawn Simpson .15 .07
❑ 216 Jim Hrivnak .75 .35
❑ 217 Rob Laird CO/GM .05 .02
❑ 218 Barry Trotz Asst.CO .05 .02
❑ 219 Baltimore Skipjacks TC .05 .02
❑ 220 David Haas .15 .07
❑ 221 Wade Campbell .15 .07
❑ 222 Dan Currie .15 .07
❑ 223 Shaun Van Allen .40 .18
❑ 224 Norm Maciver .50 .23
❑ 225 Mike Greenlay .25 .11
❑ 226 Peter Soberlak .15 .07
❑ 227 Tim Tisdale .15 .07
❑ 228 Mario Barbe .15 .07
❑ 229 Shjon Podein .75 .35
❑ 230 Trevor Sim .15 .07
❑ 231 Corey Foster .25 .11
❑ 232 Mike Ware .15 .07
❑ 233 Marc Laforge .15 .07
❑ 234 Bruce Bell .25 .11
❑ 235 Tomas Kapusta .15 .07
❑ 236 Alexander Tyjynch .25 .11
❑ 237 Tomas Srsen .15 .07
❑ 238 Collin Bauer .15 .07
❑ 239 Francois Leroux .50 .23
❑ 240 Don MacAdam CO .05 .02
❑ 241 Norm Ferguson ACO .05 .02
❑ 242 Cape Breton Oilers TC .05 .02
❑ 243 Tony Joseph .15 .07
❑ 244 Brent Hughes .40 .18
❑ 245 Larry Bernard .15 .07
❑ 246 Simon Wheeldon .15 .07
❑ 247 Todd Flichel .15 .07
❑ 248 Craig Duncanson .15 .07
❑ 249 Iain Duncan .15 .07
❑ 250 Bryan Marchment .50 .23
❑ 251 Matt Hervey .15 .07
❑ 252 Chris Norton .15 .07
❑ 253 Dallas Eakins .15 .07
❑ 254 Peter Hankinson .15 .07
❑ 255 Grant Richison .15 .07
❑ 256 Lee Davidson .15 .07
❑ 257 Denis Larocque .15 .07
❑ 258 Scott Levins .40 .18
❑ 259 Guy Larose .25 .11
❑ 260 Scott Schneider .15 .07
❑ 261 Sergei Kharin .15 .07
❑ 262 Hawk .05 .02
❑ 263 Dave Farrish CO .15 .07
❑ 264 Moncton Hawks TC .05 .02
❑ 265 Kevin Haller .50 .23
❑ 266 Joel Savage .15 .07
❑ 267 Scott Metcalfe .15 .07
❑ 268 Ian Boyce .15 .07
❑ 269 David Littman .25 .11
❑ 270 Dave Baseggio .15 .07
❑ 271 Ken Sutton .40 .18
❑ 272 Brad Miller .15 .07
❑ 273 Bill Houlder .50 .23
❑ 274 Dan Frawley .40 .18
❑ 275 Scott McCrory .15 .07
❑ 276 Steve Ludzik .40 .18
❑ 277 Robert Ray 1.00 .45
❑ 278 Darrin Shannon .75 .35
❑ 279 Dale Degray .15 .07
❑ 280 Bob Corkum .75 .35
❑ 281 Grant Tkachuk .15 .07
❑ 282 Kevin Kerr .15 .07
❑ 283 Mitch Molloy .15 .07
❑ 284 Darcy Loewen .25 .11
❑ 285 Jody Gage .50 .23
❑ 286 Jiri Sejba .15 .07
❑ 287 Steve Smith .15 .07
❑ 288 Darcy Wakaluk .75 .35
❑ 289 Donald Audette 2.00 .90
❑ 290 Don McSween .25 .11
❑ 291 Francois Guay .15 .07
❑ 292 Terry Martin ACO .05 .02
❑ 293 Don Lever CO .15 .07
❑ 294 The Moose .05 .02
❑ 295 Rochester Americans TC .05 .02
❑ 296 Mike O'Connell CO .40 .18
❑ 297 Paul Marshall .15 .07
❑ 298 Darin Bannister .15 .07
❑ 299 Rob Nichols .15 .07
❑ 300 Charlie Simmer P/CO .50 .23
❑ 301 Bob Jones .15 .07
❑ 302 Scott Brower .15 .07
❑ 303 Taylor Hall .15 .07
❑ 304 Carl Mokosak .15 .07
❑ 305 Glen Hanlon .50 .23
❑ 306 Peter Dineen .15 .07
❑ 307 Mike Sullivan .40 .18
❑ 308 Steven Martinson .15 .07
❑ 309 Dave Korol .15 .07
❑ 310 Darren Lowe .15 .07
❑ 311 Mark Reimer .25 .11
❑ 312 Mike Gober .15 .07
❑ 313 Al Tuer .15 .07
❑ 314 Dean Morton .15 .07
❑ 315 Jim McGeough .15 .07
❑ 316 Clark Donatelli .15 .07
❑ 317 Steven Dykstra .15 .07
❑ 318 Brent Sapergia .15 .07
❑ 319 Lloyd Floyd .15 .07
❑ 320 D'Arcy Norton .15 .07
❑ 321 San Diego Gulls TC .05 .02
❑ 322 Garry Valk .50 .23
❑ 323 Ian Kidd .15 .07
❑ 324 Todd Hawkins .15 .07
❑ 325 Carl Valimont .15 .07
❑ 326 Peter Bakovic .15 .07
❑ 327 Curt Fraser ACO .40 .18
❑ 328 David Mackey .15 .07
❑ 329 Jim Benning .50 .23
❑ 330 Peter DeBoer .25 .11
❑ 331 Steve Weeks .50 .23
❑ 332 Steve Veilleux .15 .07
❑ 333 Shaun Clouston .15 .07
❑ 334 Gino Odjick 1.00 .45
❑ 335 Mike Murphy CO .25 .11
❑ 336 Cam Brown .15 .07
❑ 337 Patrice LeFebvre .25 .11
❑ 338 Eric Murano .15 .07
❑ 339 Jim Revenberg .15 .07
❑ 340 Don Gibson .15 .07
❑ 341 Steve McKichan .15 .07
❑ 342 Milwaukee Admirals TC .05 .02
❑ 343 Rick Tabaracci 1.00 .45
❑ 344 Mike O'Neill .40 .18
❑ 345 Rick Hayward .15 .07
❑ 346 Sean Whyte .15 .07
❑ 347 Petr Prajsler .15 .07
❑ 348 John Van Kessel .15 .07
❑ 349 Mario Gosselin .40 .18
❑ 350 Kyosti Karjalainen .15 .07
❑ 351 Mikael Lindholm .15 .07
❑ 352 David Goverde .25 .11
❑ 353 Graham Stanley .15 .07
❑ 354 Stephane J.G. Richer Defenseman .15 .07
❑ 355 Brian Lawton .40 .18
❑ 356 Jerome Bechard .15 .07
❑ 357 Jeff Rohlicek .15 .07
❑ 358 Steve Jacques .15 .07
❑ 359 Chris Kontos .50 .23
❑ 360 Sylvain Couturier .15 .07
❑ 361 Peter Sentner .15 .07
❑ 362 Steve Graves .15 .07
❑ 363 Daryn McBride .15 .07
❑ 364 Steve Rooney .40 .18
❑ 365 Mickey Volcan .15 .07
❑ 366 Kevin MacDonald .15 .07
❑ 367 Ralph Backstrom CO .50 .23
❑ 368 Garry Unger ACO .50 .23
❑ 369 Phoenix Roadrunners TC .05 .02
❑ 370 Rob Dopson .40 .18
❑ 371 Jock Callander .40 .18
❑ 372 Chris Clifford .15 .07
❑ 373 Sandy Smith .15 .07
❑ 374 Jim Kyte .40 .18
❑ 375 Mike Needham .40 .18
❑ 376 Mitch Wilson .15 .07
❑ 377 Dave Goertz .15 .07
❑ 378 Mark Kachowski .15 .07
❑ 379 Perry Ganchar .15 .07
❑ 380 Mark Major .25 .11
❑ 381 Joel Gardner .15 .07
❑ 382 Scott Gruhl .40 .18
❑ 383 Todd Nelson .15 .07
❑ 384 Darren Stolk .15 .07
❑ 385 Scott Shaunessy .15 .07
❑ 386 Mike Mersch .15 .07
❑ 387 Glenn Mulvenna .15 .07
❑ 388 Brad Aitken .15 .07
❑ 389 Dave Michayluk .15 .07
❑ 390 Blair MacDonald CO .15 .07
❑ 391 Phil Russell ACO .25 .11
❑ 392 Muskegon Lumberjacks TC .05 .02
❑ 393 Sean Williams .15 .07
❑ 394 Ryan McGill .15 .07
❑ 395 Mike Eagles .40 .18
❑ 396 Jim Johannson .40 .18
❑ 397 Marty Nanne .15 .07
❑ 398 Jim Playfair .15 .07
❑ 399 Warren Rychel .75 .35
❑ 400 Cam Russell .50 .23
❑ 401 Jimmy Waite .75 .35
❑ 402 Mike Stapleton .15 .07
❑ 403 Trevor Dam .15 .07
❑ 404 Tracy Egeland .15 .07
❑ 405 Owen Lessard .15 .07
❑ 406 Jeff Sirkka .15 .07
❑ 407 Mike Dagenais .15 .07
❑ 408 Alex Roberts .15 .07
❑ 409 Dominik Hasek 25.00 11.00
❑ 410 Martin Desjardins .15 .07
❑ 411 Frantisek Kucera .40 .18
❑ 412 Carl Mokosak .15 .07
❑ 413 Dave McDowell .15 .07
❑ 414 Indianapolis Ice TC .05 .02
❑ 415 Paul Saundercock .15 .07
❑ 416 Darryl Williams .15 .07
❑ 417 Micah Aivazoff .15 .07
❑ 418 Robb Stauber .75 .35
❑ 419 Tom Martin .15 .07
❑ 420 Billy O'Dwyer .15 .07
❑ 421 Scott Harlow .15 .07
❑ 422 Jim Thomson .15 .07
❑ 423 Jim Pavese .15 .07
❑ 424 Ron Scott .15 .07
❑ 425 Dave Pasin .15 .07
❑ 426 Serge Roy .15 .07
❑ 427 Darryl Gilmour .40 .18
❑ 428 Mike Donnelly .50 .23
❑ 429 Rene Chapdelaine .15 .07
❑ 430 Brandy Semchuk .15 .07
❑ 431 Paul Holden .15 .07
❑ 432 Bob Berg .15 .07
❑ 433 Ladislav Tresl .15 .07
❑ 434 Eric Ricard .15 .07
❑ 435 Murray Brumwell .15 .07
❑ 436 Shawn McCosh .15 .07
❑ 437 Ross Wilson .15 .07
❑ 438 Scott Young 1.00 .45
❑ 439 David Moylan .15 .07
❑ 440 Marcel Comeau CO .15 .07
❑ 441 New Haven Nighthawks TC .05 .02
❑ 442 David Espe .15 .07
❑ 443 Mario Doyon .15 .07
❑ 444 Gerald Bzdel .15 .07
❑ 445 Claude Lapointe .50 .23
❑ 446 Dean Hopkins .15 .07
❑ 447 Clement Jodoin .15 .07
❑ 448 Kevin Kaminski .25 .11
❑ 449 Jamie Baker .40 .18
❑ 450 Mark Vermette .15 .07
❑ 451 Iiro Jarvi .40 .18
❑ 452 Kip Miller .50 .23
❑ 453 Greg Smyth .25 .11
❑ 454 Serge Roberge .15 .07
❑ 455 Stephane Morin .50 .23
❑ 456 Brent Severyn .40 .18
❑ 457 Jean-Marc Richard .15 .07
❑ 458 Ken Quinney .15 .07
❑ 459 Jeff Jackson .40 .18
❑ 460 Jaroslav Sevcik .15 .07
❑ 461 David Latta .15 .07
❑ 462 Trevor Steinburg .15 .07
❑ 463 Miroslav Ihnacak .15 .07
❑ 464 Jim Sprott .15 .07
❑ 465 Mike Bishop .15 .07
❑ 466 Stephane Fiset 4.00 1.80
❑ 467 Scott Gordon .25 .11
❑ 468 Halifax Citadels TC .05 .02
❑ 469 Gord Kruppke .15 .07
❑ 470 Glenn Merkosky .40 .18
❑ 471 Dennis Holland .15 .07
❑ 472 Chris McRae .15 .07
❑ 473 Al Conroy .15 .07
❑ 474 Yves Racine .50 .23
❑ 475 Jim Nill P/CO .15 .07
❑ 476 Barry Melrose CO 1.50 .70
❑ 477 Bob Wilkie .15 .07
❑ 478 Guy Dupuis .15 .07
❑ 479 Doug Houda .40 .18
❑ 480 Tom Bissett .15 .07
❑ 481 Bill McDougall .25 .11
❑ 482 Glen Goodall .15 .07
❑ 483 Kory Kocur .15 .07
❑ 484 Chris Luongo .15 .07
❑ 485 Serge Anglehart .15 .07
❑ 486 Marc Potvin .40 .18
❑ 487 Stewart Malgunas .15 .07
❑ 488 John Chabot .40 .18
❑ 489 Daniel Shank .40 .18
❑ 490 Randy Hansch .25 .11
❑ 491 Dave Gagnon .25 .11
❑ 492 Scott King .15 .07
❑ 493 Adirondack Red Wings TC .05 .02
❑ 494 Derek Laxdal .15 .07
❑ 495 Sean LeBrun .15 .07
❑ 496 Shawn Bryan .15 .07
❑ 497 Wayne Doucet .15 .07
❑ 498 Rich Kromm .15 .07
❑ 499 Chris Pryor P/CO .15 .07
❑ 500 George Maneluk .15 .07
❑ 501 Brad Lauer .25 .11
❑ 502 Wayne McBean .25 .11
❑ 503 Jeff Finley .40 .18
❑ 504 Jim Culhane .15 .07
❑ 505 Paul Cohen .15 .07
❑ 506 Brent Grieve .25 .11
❑ 507 Kevin Cheveldayoff .15 .07
❑ 508 Dennis Vaske .25 .11
❑ 509 Dave Chyzowski .25 .11
❑ 510 Travis Green 2.50 1.10
❑ 511 Dean Chynoweth .50 .23
❑ 512 Rob DiMaio .50 .23
❑ 513 Paul Guay .15 .07
❑ 514 Capital District Islanders TC .05 .02
❑ 515 Rick Knickle .50 .23
❑ 516 Curtis Hunt .15 .07
❑ 517 Bruce Racine .25 .11
❑ 518 Yves Heroux .15 .07
❑ 519 Joe Stefan .15 .07
❑ 520 Torrie Robertson .50 .23
❑ 521 Nick Beaulieu .15 .07
❑ 522 Dave Richter .25 .11
❑ 523 Jeff Waver .15 .07
❑ 524 Gordon Paddock .15 .07
❑ 525 Darryl Noren .15 .07
❑ 526 Byron Lomow .15 .07
❑ 527 Ivan Matulik .15 .07
❑ 528 Dan Woodley .15 .07
❑ 529 Dale Henry .15 .07
❑ 530 Soren True .15 .07
❑ 531 Stuart True .15 .07
❑ 532 Rob MacInnis .15 .07
❑ 533 Vern Smith .15 .07
❑ 534 Paul Laus 1.00 .45
❑ 535 Albany Choppers TC .05 .02
❑ 536 Robin Bawa .15 .07
❑ 537 Steven Fletcher .15 .07
❑ 538 Lonnie Loach .25 .11
❑ 539 Al Sims CO .25 .11
❑ 540 Colin Chin .15 .07
❑ 541 Bruce Boudreau P/CO .15 .07
❑ 542 Bob Lakso .15 .07
❑ 543 John Anderson .40 .18
❑ 544 Kevin Kaminski .40 .18
❑ 545 Bruce Major .15 .07
❑ 546 Stephane Brochu .15 .07
❑ 547 Peter Hankinson .15 .07
❑ 548 Carey Lucyk .15 .07
❑ 549 Tom Karalis .15 .07
❑ 550 Bob Jay .15 .07
❑ 551 Mike Butters .15 .07
❑ 552 Brian McKee .15 .07
❑ 553 Ray LeBlanc .50 .23
❑ 554 Tom Draper .40 .18
❑ 555 Steve Laurin .15 .07
❑ 556 Fort Wayne Komets TC .05 .02
❑ 557 Sergei Starikov .15 .07
❑ 558 Claude Vilgrain .40 .18
❑ 559 Jeff Sharples .25 .11
❑ 560 Bob Woods .15 .07
❑ 561 Perry Anderson .25 .11
❑ 562 Brennan Maley .15 .07
❑ 563 Mike Posma .15 .07
❑ 564 Tom McVie GM/CO .15 .07
❑ 565 Chris Palmer .15 .07
❑ 566 Bill Huard .40 .18
❑ 567 Marc Laniel .15 .07
❑ 568 Neil Brady .15 .07
❑ 569 Jason Simon .25 .11
❑ 570 Kevin Todd .50 .23
❑ 571 Jeff Madill .25 .11
❑ 572 Jeff Christian .15 .07
❑ 573 Todd Copeland .15 .07
❑ 574 Mike Bodnarchuk .15 .07
❑ 575 Chris Kiene .15 .07
❑ 576 Myles O'Connor .25 .11
❑ 577 Jamie Huscroft .40 .18
❑ 578 Mark Romaine .15 .07
❑ 579 Rollie Melanson .50 .23
❑ 580 Utica Devils Team .25 .11
❑ 581 Utica Devils TC .05 .02
❑ 582 Ron Handy .15 .07
❑ 583 Cam Plante .15 .07
❑ 584 Lee Giffin .25 .11
❑ 585 Jim Latos .15 .07
❑ 586 Stu Kulak .25 .11
❑ 587 Claude Julien .15 .07
❑ 588 Rick Barkovich .15 .07
❑ 589 Randy Exelby .25 .11
❑ 590 Mark Vichorek .15 .07
❑ 591 Darin Smith .15 .07
❑ 592 Mike Kelfer .15 .07
❑ 593 Andy Akervik .15 .07
❑ 594 Mike Hiltner .15 .07
❑ 595 Kevin Sullivan .15 .07
❑ 596 Troy Frederick .15 .07
❑ 597 Claudio Scremin .15 .07
❑ 598 Kurt Semandel .15 .07
❑ 599 Mike Colman .15 .07
❑ 600 Jeff Odgers .75 .35
❑ 601 Wade Flaherty .75 .35
❑ 602 Kansas City Blades TC .05 .02
❑ 603 Marc Bureau .50 .23
❑ 604 Darryl Olsen .15 .07
❑ 605 Rick Lessard .15 .07
❑ 606 Kevin Grant .15 .07
❑ 607 Rich Chernomaz .15 .07
❑ 608 Randy Bucyk .15 .07
❑ 609 Wayne Crowley .15 .07
❑ 610 Ken Sabourin .15 .07
❑ 611 Bob Francis CO .05 .02
❑ 612 Jamie Hislop CO .15 .07
❑ 613 Kevan Melrose .15 .07
❑ 614 Scott McCrady .15 .07
❑ 615 Corey Lyons .15 .07
❑ 616 Martin Simard .15 .07
❑ 617 C.J. Young .25 .11
❑ 618 Mark Osiecki .25 .11
❑ 619 Bryan Deasley .15 .07
❑ 620 Kerry Clark .15 .07
❑ 621 Paul Kruse .40 .18
❑ 622 Darren Banks .40 .18
❑ 623 Richard Zemlak .25 .11
❑ 624 Todd Harkins .15 .07
❑ 625 Warren Sharples .15 .07
❑ 626 Andrew McKim .40 .18
❑ 627 Steve Guenette .25 .11
❑ 628 Salt Lake City Golden Eagles TC .05 .02

## 1991-92 ProCards AHL/CHL/IHL

This 620-card standard-size set was produced by ProCards. Fronts feature a posed color photo enclosed by a white border. The player's name is in black within a gold bar at the top and the team name appears beneath in a

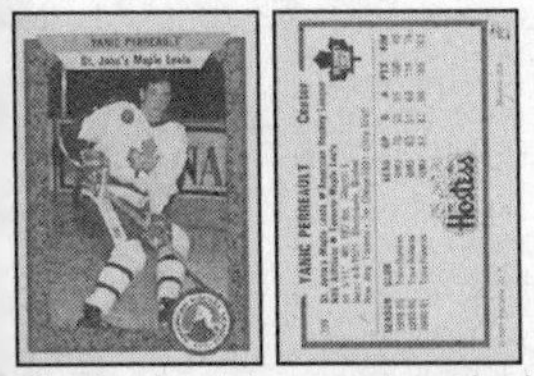

yellow bar. The photo appears in a red and black speckled "frame" enclosed by a small blue border. The respective league logo (American Hockey League, Colonial Hockey League, or International Hockey League) appears in the lower right corner. The horizontal backs carry biographical and statistical information on a pale yellow background enclosed with blue and white borders. The cards are numbered on the back and checklisted below according to teams as follows: Rochester Americans (1-24), Peoria Rivermen (25-47), Maine Mariners (48-69), Fredericton Canadiens (70-92), Springfield Indians (93-117), Adirondack Red Wings (118-142), Kalamazoo Wings (143-163), Moncton Hawks (164-189), Binghamton Rangers (190-214), Cape Breton Oilers (215-238), Fort Wayne Komets (239-262), Hershey Bears (263-287), Muskegon Lumberjacks (288-310), San Diego Gulls (311-334), St. John's Maple Leafs (335-359), New Haven Nighthawks (360-383), Phoenix Roadrunners (384-407), Utica Devils (408-428), Flint Bulldogs of the Colonial Hockey League (429-451), Capital District Islanders (452-476), Indianapolis Ice (477-504), Kansas City Blades (505-527), Halifax Citadels (528-546), Baltimore Skipjacks (547-573), Salt Lake City Golden Eagles (574-594), and Milwaukee Admirals (595-620). Although the team sets were originally sold with a suggested retail price of 4.00 per team set and packaged individually, they are listed below as one giant set.

| | MINT | NRMT |
|---|---|---|
| COMPLETE SET (620) | 100.00 | 45.00 |
| COMMON CARD (1-620) | .05 | .02 |

| | MINT | NRMT |
|---|---|---|
| ❑ 1 Bill Houlder | .35 | .16 |
| ❑ 2 Brian Curran | .25 | .11 |
| ❑ 3 Dan Frawley | .25 | .11 |
| ❑ 4 Darcy Loewen | .25 | .11 |
| ❑ 5 Jiri Sejba | .25 | .11 |
| ❑ 6 Lindy Ruff | .25 | .11 |
| ❑ 7 Chris Snell | .25 | .11 |
| ❑ 8 Bob Corkum | .35 | .16 |
| ❑ 9 Dave Baseggio | .15 | .07 |
| ❑ 10 Sean O'Donnell | .15 | .07 |
| ❑ 11 Brad Rubachuk | .15 | .07 |
| ❑ 12 Peter Ciavaglia | .25 | .11 |
| ❑ 13 Joel Savage | .15 | .07 |
| ❑ 14 Jason Winch | .15 | .07 |
| ❑ 15 Steve Ludzik | .25 | .11 |
| ❑ 16 Don McSween | .25 | .11 |
| ❑ 17 David DaVita | .15 | .07 |
| ❑ 18 Greg Brown | .25 | .11 |
| ❑ 19 David Littman | .25 | .11 |
| ❑ 20 Tom Draper | .25 | .11 |
| ❑ 21 Jody Gage | .35 | .16 |
| ❑ 22 Terry Martin | .20 | .09 |
| ❑ 23 Don Lever | .25 | .11 |
| ❑ 24 Rochester Checklist | .05 | .02 |
| ❑ 25 Jason Marshall | .25 | .11 |
| ❑ 26 Michel Mongeau | .25 | .11 |
| ❑ 27 Derek Frenette | .15 | .07 |
| ❑ 28 Kevin Miehm | .25 | .11 |
| ❑ 29 Guy Hebert | 4.00 | 1.80 |
| ❑ 30 Greg Poss | .15 | .07 |
| ❑ 31 Dave Mackey | .25 | .11 |
| ❑ 32 Dan Fowler | .15 | .07 |
| ❑ 33 Mark Bassen | .20 | .09 |
| ❑ 34 Yves Heroux | .25 | .11 |
| ❑ 35 Harold Snepsts | 1.00 | .45 |
| ❑ 36 Bruce Shoebottom | .20 | .09 |
| ❑ 37 Jaan Luik | .15 | .07 |
| ❑ 38 Alain Raymond | .15 | .07 |
| ❑ 39 Kyle Reeves | .15 | .07 |
| ❑ 40 Brian McKee | .15 | .07 |
| ❑ 41 Steve Tuttle | .25 | .11 |
| ❑ 42 Rob Tustian | .15 | .07 |
| ❑ 43 Richard Pion | .25 | .11 |
| ❑ 44 Joe Hawley | .15 | .07 |
| ❑ 45 Brian Pellerin | .15 | .07 |
| ❑ 46 Jason Ruff | .25 | .11 |
| ❑ 47 Rivermen Checklist | .05 | .02 |
| ❑ 48 Wes Walz | .25 | .11 |
| ❑ 49 Steve Bancroft | .15 | .07 |
| ❑ 50 John Blue | .25 | .11 |
| ❑ 51 Rick Allain | .15 | .07 |
| ❑ 52 Mike Walsh | .25 | .11 |
| ❑ 53 Dave Thomlinson | .25 | .11 |
| ❑ 54 Dennis Smith | .15 | .07 |
| ❑ 55 Jack Capuano | .25 | .11 |
| ❑ 56 Mike Rossetti | .15 | .07 |
| ❑ 57 Petr Prajsler | .25 | .11 |
| ❑ 58 Matt Glennon | .15 | .07 |
| ❑ 59 John Byce | .25 | .11 |
| ❑ 60 Howie Rosenblatt | .25 | .11 |
| ❑ 61 Brad Tiley | .15 | .07 |
| ❑ 62 Lou Crawford | .15 | .07 |
| ❑ 63 Matt Hervey | .25 | .11 |
| ❑ 64 Peter Douris | .25 | .11 |
| ❑ 65 Jeff Lazaro | .25 | .11 |
| ❑ 66 David Reid | .75 | .35 |
| ❑ 67 E.J. McGuire | .15 | .07 |
| ❑ 68 Frank Bathe | .20 | .09 |
| ❑ 69 Maine Checklist | .05 | .02 |
| ❑ 70 Paul DiPietro | .25 | .11 |
| ❑ 71 Darcy Simon | .15 | .07 |
| ❑ 72 Patrick Lebeau | .25 | .11 |
| ❑ 73 Gilbert Dionne | .35 | .16 |
| ❑ 74 John Ferguson | .25 | .11 |
| ❑ 75 Norman Desjardins | .15 | .07 |
| ❑ 76 Luc Gauthier | .20 | .09 |
| ❑ 77 Jean-Claude Bergeron | .35 | .16 |
| ❑ 78 Andre Racicot | .35 | .16 |
| ❑ 79 Steve Veilleux | .15 | .07 |
| ❑ 80 Patrice Brisebois | .50 | .23 |
| ❑ 81 Tom Sagissor | .15 | .07 |
| ❑ 82 Lindsay Vallis | .15 | .07 |
| ❑ 83 Steve Larouche | .25 | .11 |
| ❑ 84 Sean Hill | .50 | .23 |
| ❑ 85 Jesse Belanger | .50 | .23 |
| ❑ 86 Stephane J.G. Richer | .25 | .11 |
| ❑ 87 Marc Labelle | .15 | .07 |
| ❑ 88 Pierre Sevigny | .25 | .11 |
| ❑ 89 Eric Charron | .25 | .11 |
| ❑ 90 Ed Ronan | .25 | .11 |
| ❑ 91 Paulin Bordeleau | .25 | .11 |
| ❑ 92 Fredericton Checklist | .05 | .02 |
| ❑ 93 Daryl Reaugh | .35 | .16 |
| ❑ 94 Jergus Baca | .25 | .11 |
| ❑ 95 Karl Johnston | .15 | .07 |
| ❑ 96 Shawn Evans | .15 | .07 |
| ❑ 97 Scott Humeniuk | .15 | .07 |
| ❑ 98 Cam Brauer | .15 | .07 |
| ❑ 99 Scott Eichstadt | .15 | .07 |
| ❑ 100 Paul Cyr | .25 | .11 |
| ❑ 101 James Black | .25 | .11 |
| ❑ 102 Chris Govedaris | .25 | .11 |
| ❑ 103 Joe Day | .25 | .11 |
| ❑ 104 Chris Tancill | .25 | .11 |
| ❑ 105 Kerry Russell | .20 | .09 |
| ❑ 106 Denis Chalifoux | .15 | .07 |
| ❑ 107 Blair Atcheynum | .25 | .11 |
| ❑ 108 John Stevens | .15 | .07 |
| ❑ 109 Brian Chapman | .15 | .07 |
| ❑ 110 Chris Bright | .15 | .07 |
| ❑ 111 Jim Burke | .15 | .07 |
| ❑ 112 Scott Daniels | .25 | .11 |
| ❑ 113 Kelly Ens | .15 | .07 |
| ❑ 114 Mike Tomlak | .25 | .11 |
| ❑ 115 Mario Gosselin | .50 | .23 |
| ❑ 116 Jay Leach | .15 | .07 |
| ❑ 117 Springfield Checklist | .05 | .02 |
| ❑ 118 Allan Bester | .50 | .23 |
| ❑ 119 Daniel Shank | .25 | .11 |
| ❑ 120 Lonnie Loach | .25 | .11 |
| ❑ 121 Mark Reimer | .25 | .11 |
| ❑ 122 Kirk Tomlinson | .15 | .07 |
| ❑ 123 Stewart Malgunas | .15 | .07 |
| ❑ 124 Serge Anglehart | .15 | .07 |
| ❑ 125 Chris Luongo | .25 | .11 |
| ❑ 126 Keith Primeau | 3.00 | 1.35 |
| ❑ 127 Ken Quinney | .25 | .11 |
| ❑ 128 Dave Flanagan | .15 | .07 |
| ❑ 129 Pete Stauber | .15 | .07 |
| ❑ 130 Mike Sillinger | .25 | .11 |
| ❑ 131 Micah Aivazoff | .25 | .11 |
| ❑ 132 Gary Schuchuk | .25 | .11 |
| ❑ 133 Bill McDougall | .25 | .11 |
| ❑ 134 Sheldon Kennedy | .50 | .23 |
| ❑ 135 Derek Mayer | .15 | .07 |
| ❑ 136 Darin Bannister | .15 | .07 |
| ❑ 137 Guy Dupuis | .15 | .07 |
| ❑ 138 Gord Kruppke | .15 | .07 |
| ❑ 139 Jason York | .50 | .23 |
| ❑ 140 Barry Melrose | 1.00 | .45 |
| ❑ 141 Glenn Merkosky | .25 | .11 |
| ❑ 142 Adirondack Checklist | .05 | .02 |
| ❑ 143 Larry Dyck | .25 | .11 |
| ❑ 144 Roy Mitchell | .15 | .07 |
| ❑ 145 Greg Spenrath | .15 | .07 |
| ❑ 146 Steve Herniman | .15 | .07 |
| ❑ 147 Brad Berry | .25 | .11 |
| ❑ 148 Jim Nesich | .15 | .07 |
| ❑ 149 Tim Lenardon | .15 | .07 |
| ❑ 150 Steve Guenette | .25 | .11 |
| ❑ 151 Paul Jerrard | .15 | .07 |
| ❑ 152 Cal McGowan | .25 | .11 |
| ❑ 153 Scott Robinson | .15 | .07 |
| ❑ 154 Mitch Messier | .15 | .07 |
| ❑ 155 Tony Joseph | .15 | .07 |
| ❑ 156 Steve Maltais | .25 | .11 |
| ❑ 157 Steve Gotaas | .15 | .07 |
| ❑ 158 Doug Barrault | .25 | .11 |
| ❑ 159 Dave Moylan | .15 | .07 |
| ❑ 160 Mario Thyer | .25 | .11 |
| ❑ 161 Bob Hoffmeyer | .15 | .07 |
| ❑ 162 Wade Dawson | .15 | .07 |
| ❑ 163 Wings Checklist | .05 | .02 |
| ❑ 164 Rob Murray | .20 | .09 |
| ❑ 165 Chris Kiene | .15 | .07 |
| ❑ 166 Lee Davidson | .15 | .07 |
| ❑ 167 Rudy Poeschek | .35 | .16 |
| ❑ 168 Kent Paynter | .15 | .07 |
| ❑ 169 John LeBlanc | .20 | .09 |
| ❑ 170 Dallas Eakins | .15 | .07 |
| ❑ 171 Claude Julien | .15 | .07 |
| ❑ 172 Bob Joyce | .25 | .11 |
| ❑ 173 Derek Langille | .15 | .07 |
| ❑ 174 Rob Cowie | .25 | .11 |
| ❑ 175 Warren Rychel | .50 | .23 |
| ❑ 176 Tom Karalis | .15 | .07 |
| ❑ 177 Kris Draper | 1.00 | .45 |
| ❑ 178 Ken Gernander | .15 | .07 |
| ❑ 179 Tod Hartje | .25 | .11 |
| ❑ 180 Sean Gauthier | .15 | .07 |
| ❑ 181 Tyler Larter | .15 | .07 |
| ❑ 182 Scott Levins | .25 | .11 |
| ❑ 183 Jason Cirone | .15 | .07 |
| ❑ 184 Mark Kumpel | .25 | .11 |
| ❑ 185 Rick Tabaracci | 1.00 | .45 |
| ❑ 186 Luciano Borsato | .25 | .11 |
| ❑ 187 Dave Farrish | .25 | .11 |
| ❑ 188 Dave Prior | .15 | .07 |
| ❑ 189 Moncton Checklist | .05 | .02 |
| ❑ 190 Peter Fiorentino | .15 | .07 |
| ❑ 191 Glen Goodall | .15 | .07 |
| ❑ 192 John Mokosak | .15 | .07 |
| ❑ 193 Sam St.Laurent | .35 | .16 |
| ❑ 194 Daniel Lacroix | .50 | .23 |
| ❑ 195 Guy Larose | .25 | .11 |
| ❑ 196 Mike Hurlbut | .25 | .11 |
| ❑ 197 Peter Laviolette | .25 | .11 |
| ❑ 198 Eric Bennett | .15 | .07 |
| ❑ 199 Steven King | .25 | .11 |
| ❑ 200 Boris Rousson | .25 | .11 |
| ❑ 201 Jody Hull | .35 | .16 |
| ❑ 202 Shaun Sabol | .15 | .07 |
| ❑ 203 Joe Paterson | .15 | .07 |
| ❑ 204 Rob Zamuner | .75 | .35 |
| ❑ 205 Don Biggs | .25 | .11 |
| ❑ 206 Chris Cichocki | .20 | .09 |
| ❑ 207 Ross Fitzpatrick | .15 | .07 |
| ❑ 208 Mark LaForest | .25 | .11 |
| ❑ 209 Brian McReynolds | .20 | .09 |
| ❑ 210 Jeff Bloemberg | .25 | .11 |
| ❑ 211 Kord Cernich | .15 | .07 |
| ❑ 212 Ron Smith | .15 | .07 |
| ❑ 213 Al Hill | .25 | .11 |
| ❑ 214 Binghamton Checklist | .05 | .02 |
| ❑ 215 Francois Leroux | .35 | .16 |
| ❑ 216 Marc Laforge | .15 | .07 |
| ❑ 217 Max Middendorf | .20 | .09 |
| ❑ 218 Shjon Podein | .50 | .23 |
| ❑ 219 Jason Soules | .20 | .09 |
| ❑ 220 Collin Bauer | .15 | .07 |
| ❑ 221 Shaun Van Allen | .35 | .16 |
| ❑ 222 Eldon Reddick | .50 | .23 |
| ❑ 223 Evgeny Belosheiken | .25 | .11 |
| ❑ 224 David Haas | .15 | .07 |
| ❑ 225 Norm Foster | .25 | .11 |
| ❑ 226 Greg Hawgood | .50 | .23 |
| ❑ 227 Steven Rice | .35 | .16 |
| ❑ 228 Dan Currie | .25 | .11 |
| ❑ 229 Peter Soberlak | .15 | .07 |
| ❑ 230 Martin Rucinsky | 1.50 | .70 |
| ❑ 231 Tomas Kapusta | .25 | .11 |
| ❑ 232 Dean Antos | .15 | .07 |
| ❑ 233 Craig Fisher | .20 | .09 |
| ❑ 234 Tomas Srsen | .15 | .07 |
| ❑ 235 Don McAdam | .15 | .07 |
| ❑ 236 Norm Ferguson | .15 | .07 |
| ❑ 237 Coaching Staff | .05 | .02 |
| ❑ 238 Cape Breton Checklist | .05 | .02 |
| ❑ 239 Peter Hankinson | .15 | .07 |
| ❑ 240 Chris McRae | .15 | .07 |
| ❑ 241 Craig Martin | .25 | .11 |
| ❑ 242 Carey Lucyk | .15 | .07 |
| ❑ 243 Jean-Marc Richard | .15 | .07 |
| ❑ 244 Grant Richison | .15 | .07 |
| ❑ 245 Mark Turner | .15 | .07 |
| ❑ 246 Todd Flichel | .15 | .07 |
| ❑ 247 Scott Shaunessy | .15 | .07 |
| ❑ 248 Darin Smith | .15 | .07 |
| ❑ 249 Ian Boyce | .15 | .07 |
| ❑ 250 Colin Chin | .20 | .09 |
| ❑ 251 Bob Jones | .15 | .07 |
| ❑ 252 Bob Jay | .20 | .09 |
| ❑ 253 Kelly Hurd | .15 | .07 |
| ❑ 254 Scott Gruhl | .25 | .11 |
| ❑ 255 Kory Kocur | .20 | .09 |
| ❑ 256 Steven Fletcher | .15 | .07 |
| ❑ 257 Bob Lakso | .20 | .09 |
| ❑ 258 Dusty Imoo | .25 | .11 |
| ❑ 259 Mike O'Neill | .25 | .11 |
| ❑ 260 Bruce Boudreau | .25 | .11 |
| ❑ 261 Al Sims | .35 | .16 |
| ❑ 262 Komets Checklist | .05 | .02 |
| ❑ 263 Ray Letourneau | .15 | .07 |
| ❑ 264 Marc D'Amour | .25 | .11 |
| ❑ 265 Dominic Roussel | .75 | .35 |
| ❑ 266 Bill Armstrong (LW) | .20 | .09 |
| ❑ 267 Al Conroy | .25 | .11 |
| ❑ 268 Dale Kushner | .25 | .11 |
| ❑ 269 Toni Porkka | .15 | .07 |
| ❑ 270 Mike Stothers | .15 | .07 |
| ❑ 271 Darren Rumble | .25 | .11 |
| ❑ 272 Reid Simpson | .15 | .07 |
| ❑ 273 Claude Boivin | .25 | .11 |
| ❑ 274 Len Barrie | .25 | .11 |
| ❑ 275 Chris Jensen | .25 | .11 |
| ❑ 276 Pat Murray | .25 | .11 |
| ❑ 277 Eric Dandenault | .15 | .07 |
| ❑ 278 Rod Dallman | .15 | .07 |
| ❑ 279 Mark Freer | .25 | .11 |
| ❑ 280 Bill Armstrong (D) | .25 | .11 |
| ❑ 281 Tim Tookey | .25 | .11 |
| ❑ 282 Jamie Cooke | .15 | .07 |
| ❑ 283 Dave Fenyves | .25 | .11 |
| ❑ 284 Steve Morrow | .15 | .07 |
| ❑ 285 Martin Hostak | .25 | .11 |
| ❑ 286 Mike Eaves | .25 | .11 |
| ❑ 287 Hershey Checklist | .05 | .02 |
| ❑ 288 Dave Michayluk | .25 | .11 |
| ❑ 289 Glenn Mulvenna | .20 | .09 |
| ❑ 290 Jean Blouin | .15 | .07 |
| ❑ 291 Jock Callander | .25 | .11 |
| ❑ 292 Perry Ganchar | .15 | .07 |
| ❑ 293 Paul Laus | .75 | .35 |
| ❑ 294 Mark Major | .15 | .07 |
| ❑ 295 Bruce Racine | .25 | .11 |
| ❑ 296 Daniel Gauthier | .15 | .07 |
| ❑ 297 Mike Needham | .25 | .11 |
| ❑ 298 Jeff Daniels | .25 | .11 |
| ❑ 299 Sandy Smith | .15 | .07 |
| ❑ 300 Gilbert Delorme | .25 | .11 |
| ❑ 301 Rob Dopson | .25 | .11 |
| ❑ 302 Eric Brule | .15 | .07 |
| ❑ 303 Alain Morissette | .15 | .07 |
| ❑ 304 Paul Dyck | .15 | .07 |
| ❑ 305 Jason Smart | .15 | .07 |
| ❑ 306 Gord Dineen | .25 | .11 |
| ❑ 307 Todd Nelson | .25 | .11 |
| ❑ 308 Jamie Heward | .15 | .07 |
| ❑ 309 Paul Russell | .15 | .07 |
| ❑ 310 Lumberjack Checklist | .05 | .02 |
| ❑ 311 Soren True | .15 | .07 |
| ❑ 312 Murray Duval | .15 | .07 |
| ❑ 313 Dmitri Kvartalnov | .35 | .16 |
| ❑ 314 Larry Floyd | .15 | .07 |
| ❑ 315 Alan Legett | .15 | .07 |
| ❑ 316 Alan Hepple | .15 | .07 |
| ❑ 317 Ron Duguay | .50 | .23 |
| ❑ 318 Len Hachborn | .25 | .11 |
| ❑ 319 Steve Martinson | .25 | .11 |
| ❑ 320 Rick Knickle | .50 | .23 |
| ❑ 321 Darcy Norton | .15 | .07 |
| ❑ 322 Keith Gretzky | .75 | .35 |
| ❑ 323 Brian Straub | .15 | .07 |
| ❑ 324 Denny Lambert | .25 | .11 |
| ❑ 325 Jason Prosofsky | .25 | .11 |
| ❑ 326 Bruce Hoffort | .25 | .11 |
| ❑ 327 Sergei Starikov | .20 | .09 |
| ❑ 328 Dave Korol | .15 | .07 |
| ❑ 329 Robbie Nichols | .15 | .07 |
| ❑ 330 Kord Cernich | .15 | .07 |
| ❑ 331 Brent Sapergia | .25 | .11 |
| ❑ 332 Don Waddell | .15 | .07 |
| ❑ 333 Charlie Simmer | .50 | .23 |
| ❑ 334 San Diego Checklist | .05 | .02 |
| ❑ 335 Rob Mendel | .15 | .07 |
| ❑ 336 Curtis Hunt | .15 | .07 |
| ❑ 337 Jeff Serowik | .25 | .11 |
| ❑ 338 Bruce Bell | .25 | .11 |
| ❑ 339 Yanic Perreault | .75 | .35 |
| ❑ 340 Brad Aitken | .15 | .07 |
| ❑ 341 Keith Osborne | .15 | .07 |
| ❑ 342 Todd Hawkins | .15 | .07 |
| ❑ 343 Andrew McKim | .25 | .11 |
| ❑ 344 Kevin McClelland | .25 | .11 |
| ❑ 345 Mike Stevens | .25 | .11 |
| ❑ 346 Dave Tomlinson | .25 | .11 |
| ❑ 347 Kevin Maguire | .25 | .11 |
| ❑ 348 Mike MacWilliams | .15 | .07 |
| ❑ 349 Greg Walters | .15 | .07 |
| ❑ 350 Guy Lehoux | .15 | .07 |
| ❑ 351 Todd Gillingham | .15 | .07 |
| ❑ 352 Len Esau | .15 | .07 |
| ❑ 353 Greg Johnston | .25 | .11 |
| ❑ 354 Felix Potvin | 6.00 | 2.70 |
| ❑ 355 Damian Rhodes | 2.00 | .90 |
| ❑ 356 Joel Quenneville | .15 | .07 |
| ❑ 357 Marc Crawford | .75 | .35 |
| ❑ 358 Mike Eastwood | .25 | .11 |
| ❑ 359 St.Johns Checklist | .05 | .02 |
| ❑ 360 Lou Franceschetti | .25 | .11 |
| ❑ 361 John Murray Anderson | .15 | .07 |
| ❑ 362 Scott Schneider | .15 | .07 |
| ❑ 363 Jerome Bechard | .15 | .07 |
| ❑ 364 Mario Doyon | .20 | .09 |
| ❑ 365 Jeff Jackson | .25 | .11 |
| ❑ 366 John Tanner | .25 | .11 |
| ❑ 367 Al Tuer | .15 | .07 |
| ❑ 368 Paul Willett | .15 | .07 |
| ❑ 369 Darryl Williams | .15 | .07 |
| ❑ 370 George Maneluk | .25 | .11 |
| ❑ 371 Eric Ricard | .15 | .07 |
| ❑ 372 Trevor Stienburg | .15 | .07 |
| ❑ 373 Jerry Tarrant | .15 | .07 |
| ❑ 374 Michael McEwen | .25 | .11 |
| ❑ 375 Brian Dobbin | .25 | .11 |
| ❑ 376 David Latta | .15 | .07 |
| ❑ 377 Jim Sprott | .15 | .07 |
| ❑ 378 Trevor Pochipinski | .15 | .07 |
| ❑ 379 Stan Drulia | .25 | .11 |
| ❑ 380 Kent Hulst | .15 | .07 |
| ❑ 381 Brad Turner | .15 | .07 |
| ❑ 382 Doug Carpenter | .25 | .11 |
| ❑ 383 New Haven Checklist | .05 | .02 |
| ❑ 384 Bob Berg | .15 | .07 |
| ❑ 385 Steve Jaques | .15 | .07 |
| ❑ 386 Chris Norton | .15 | .07 |
| ❑ 387 Vern Smith | .15 | .07 |
| ❑ 388 Kevin MacDonald | .15 | .07 |
| ❑ 389 Ross Wilson | .15 | .07 |
| ❑ 390 Shawn McCosh | .15 | .07 |
| ❑ 391 Mike Vukonich | .15 | .07 |
| ❑ 392 Marc Saumier | .15 | .07 |
| ❑ 393 Mike Ruark | .15 | .07 |
| ❑ 394 Kris Miller | .15 | .07 |
| ❑ 395 Tim Breslin | .15 | .07 |
| ❑ 396 Paul Holden | .15 | .07 |
| ❑ 397 Jeff Rohlicek | .15 | .07 |
| ❑ 398 Kyosti Karjalainen | .25 | .11 |
| ❑ 399 David Goverde | .25 | .11 |
| ❑ 400 John Van Kessel | .15 | .07 |
| ❑ 401 Sean Whyte | .15 | .07 |
| ❑ 402 Brent Thompson | .25 | .11 |
| ❑ 403 Darryl Gilmour | .25 | .11 |
| ❑ 404 Scott Bjugstad | .20 | .09 |
| ❑ 405 Ralph Backstrom | .35 | .16 |
| ❑ 406 Rick Kozuback | .15 | .07 |
| ❑ 407 Roadrunner Checklist | .05 | .02 |
| ❑ 408 Brent Severyn | .35 | .16 |
| ❑ 409 Dean Malkoc | .25 | .11 |
| ❑ 410 Matt Ruchty | .15 | .07 |
| ❑ 411 Jarrod Skalde | .25 | .11 |
| ❑ 412 Brian Sullivan | .15 | .07 |
| ❑ 413 Ben Hankinson | .25 | .11 |
| ❑ 414 Bill Huard | .35 | .16 |
| ❑ 415 Jeff Christian | .15 | .07 |
| ❑ 416 Corey Schwab | .50 | .23 |
| ❑ 417 Kevin Dean | .15 | .07 |
| ❑ 418 Todd Copeland | .15 | .07 |
| ❑ 419 Mike Bodnarchuk | .15 | .07 |
| ❑ 420 Jason Miller | .15 | .07 |
| ❑ 421 Chad Erickson | .25 | .11 |
| ❑ 422 David Craievich | .15 | .07 |
| ❑ 423 Jim Dowd | .50 | .23 |
| ❑ 424 Jamie Huscroft | .35 | .16 |
| ❑ 425 Myles O'Connor | .25 | .11 |
| ❑ 426 Jon Morris | .25 | .11 |
| ❑ 427 Valeri Zelepukin | .50 | .23 |
| ❑ 428 Utica Checklist | .05 | .02 |
| ❑ 429 Brad Beck | .15 | .07 |
| ❑ 430 Brett MacDonald | .15 | .07 |
| ❑ 431 Jacques Mailhot | .15 | .07 |
| ❑ 432 Francois Ouellette | .15 | .07 |
| ❑ 433 Ron Kinghorn | .15 | .07 |
| ❑ 434 Dennis Miller | .15 | .07 |
| ❑ 435 Darren Miciak | .15 | .07 |
| ❑ 436 Tom Sasso | .15 | .07 |
| ❑ 437 Peter Corbett | .15 | .07 |
| ❑ 438 Brian Horan | .15 | .07 |
| ❑ 439 John Messuri | .15 | .07 |
| ❑ 440 E.J. Sauer | .15 | .07 |
| ❑ 441 Tom Mutch | .15 | .07 |
| ❑ 442 Jason Simon | .15 | .07 |
| ❑ 443 Steve Sullivan | .15 | .07 |
| ❑ 444 Scott Allen | .15 | .07 |
| ❑ 445 Stephane Brochu | .25 | .11 |
| ❑ 446 Ken Spangler | .25 | .11 |
| ❑ 447 Lee Odelein | .15 | .07 |
| ❑ 448 Antti Autere | .15 | .07 |
| ❑ 449 John Reid | .15 | .07 |
| ❑ 450 Skip Probst CO | .05 | .02 |
| ❑ 451 Flint Checklist | .05 | .02 |
| ❑ 452 Dean Ewen | .15 | .07 |
| ❑ 453 Brent Grieve | .35 | .16 |
| ❑ 454 Jim Culhane | .15 | .07 |
| ❑ 455 Joni Lehto | .15 | .07 |
| ❑ 456 Graeme Townshend | .25 | .11 |
| ❑ 457 Danny Lorenz | .25 | .11 |
| ❑ 458 Phil Huber | .15 | .07 |
| ❑ 459 Kevin Cheveldayoff | .20 | .09 |
| ❑ 460 Dennis Vaske | .35 | .16 |
| ❑ 461 Wayne Doucet | .15 | .07 |
| ❑ 462 Greg Parks | .20 | .09 |
| ❑ 463 Dean Chynoweth | .15 | .07 |
| ❑ 464 Lee Giffin | .25 | .11 |
| ❑ 465 Richard Kromm | .25 | .11 |
| ❑ 466 Derek Laxdal | .25 | .11 |
| ❑ 467 Travis Green | 1.50 | .70 |
| ❑ 468 Iain Fraser | .25 | .11 |
| ❑ 469 Rick Hayward | .25 | .11 |
| ❑ 470 Jeff Finley | .25 | .11 |
| ❑ 471 Dave Chyzowski | .20 | .09 |
| ❑ 472 Mark Fitzpatrick | 2.00 | .90 |
| ❑ 473 Hubie McDonough | .25 | .11 |
| ❑ 474 Sean LeBrun | .15 | .07 |
| ❑ 475 Chris Pryor | .15 | .07 |
| ❑ 476 Capital District CL | .05 | .02 |
| ❑ 477 Jeff Sirkka | .15 | .07 |
| ❑ 478 Owen Lessard | .15 | .07 |
| ❑ 479 Jim Playfair | .15 | .07 |
| ❑ 480 Dan Vincelette | .20 | .09 |
| ❑ 481 Tracey Egeland | .15 | .07 |
| ❑ 482 Shawn Byram | .15 | .07 |
| ❑ 483 Trevor Dam | .15 | .07 |
| ❑ 484 Martin Desjardins | .15 | .07 |
| ❑ 485 Milan Tichy | .25 | .11 |
| ❑ 486 Cam Russell | .35 | .16 |
| ❑ 487 Mike Speer | .15 | .07 |
| ❑ 488 Sean Williams | .15 | .07 |
| ❑ 489 Paul Gillis | .25 | .11 |
| ❑ 490 Brad Lauer | .25 | .11 |
| ❑ 491 Trent Yawney | .35 | .16 |
| ❑ 492 Craig Woodcroft | .25 | .11 |
| ❑ 493 Justin LaFayette | .15 | .07 |
| ❑ 494 Rob Conn | .25 | .11 |
| ❑ 495 Frantisek Kucera | .25 | .11 |
| ❑ 496 Mike Peluso | 1.00 | .45 |
| ❑ 497 Roch Belley | .25 | .11 |
| ❑ 498 Ryan McGill | .20 | .09 |
| ❑ 499 Kerry Toporowski | .25 | .11 |
| ❑ 500 Dominik Hasek | 10.00 | 4.50 |
| ❑ 501 Adam Bennett | .20 | .09 |
| ❑ 502 Ray LeBlanc | .50 | .23 |
| ❑ 503 John Marks | .20 | .09 |
| ❑ 504 Ice Checklist | .05 | .02 |
| ❑ 505 Mikhail Kravets | .20 | .09 |
| ❑ 506 Gary Emmons | .15 | .07 |
| ❑ 507 Ed Courtenay | .25 | .11 |
| ❑ 508 Claudio Scremin | .15 | .07 |
| ❑ 509 Jarmo Myllys | .50 | .23 |
| ❑ 510 Mike Coleman | .15 | .07 |
| ❑ 511 Kevin Evans | .25 | .11 |
| ❑ 512 Troy Frederick | .15 | .07 |
| ❑ 513 Ron Handy | .15 | .07 |
| ❑ 514 Murray Garbutt | .15 | .07 |
| ❑ 515 Gordon Frantti | .15 | .07 |
| ❑ 516 Dale Craigwell | .35 | .16 |
| ❑ 517 Wade Flaherty | .75 | .35 |
| ❑ 518 Dean Kolstad | .25 | .11 |
| ❑ 519 Rick Lessard | .25 | .11 |
| ❑ 520 Craig Coxe | .35 | .16 |
| ❑ 521 Jeff Madill | .25 | .11 |
| ❑ 522 Peter Lappin | .25 | .11 |
| ❑ 523 Duane Joyce | .15 | .07 |
| ❑ 524 Larry DePalma | .25 | .11 |
| ❑ 525 Pat MacLeod | .25 | .11 |
| ❑ 526 Andy Akervik | .15 | .07 |
| ❑ 527 Blades Checklist | .05 | .02 |

❑ 528 Mike Dagenais .15 .07
❑ 529 Gerald Bzdel .15 .07
❑ 530 Stephane Fiset 2.50 1.10
❑ 531 David Espe .15 .07
❑ 532 Patrick Lebrecque .35 .16
❑ 533 Niclas Andersson .25 .11
❑ 534 Jon Klemm .35 .16
❑ 535 Denis Chasse .50 .23
❑ 536 Stephane Charbonneau .15 .07
❑ 537 Ivan Matulik .15 .07
❑ 538 Serge Roberge .15 .07
❑ 539 Daniel Dore .15 .07
❑ 540 Sergei Kharin .25 .11
❑ 541 Jamie Baker .25 .11
❑ 542 Ken McRae .25 .11
❑ 543 David Marcinyshyn .20 .09
❑ 544 Clement Jodoin .15 .07
❑ 545 Dean Hopkins .15 .07
❑ 546 Checklist .05 .02
❑ 547 Jeff Greenlaw .20 .09
❑ 548 Byron Dafoe 1.50 .70
❑ 549 Jim Hrivnak .50 .23
❑ 550 Olaf Kolzig 1.50 .70
❑ 551 John Purves .20 .09
❑ 552 Bobby Reynolds .15 .07
❑ 553 Simon Wheeldon .20 .09
❑ 554 Jim Mathieson .15 .07
❑ 555 Trevor Halverson .25 .11
❑ 556 Steve Seftel .15 .07
❑ 557 Ken Lovsin .25 .11
❑ 558 Victor Gervais .15 .07
❑ 559 Steve Martell .25 .11
❑ 560 Chris Clarke .15 .07
❑ 561 Brent Hughes .25 .11
❑ 562 Jiri Vykoukal .15 .07
❑ 563 Tim Taylor .25 .11
❑ 564 Richie Walcott .15 .07
❑ 565 Harry Mews .15 .07
❑ 566 Craig Duncanson .25 .11
❑ 567 Todd Hlushko .25 .11
❑ 568 Mark Ferner .25 .11
❑ 569 Bobby Babcock .20 .09
❑ 570 Reggie Savage .25 .11
❑ 571 Rob Laird .15 .07
❑ 572 Barry Trotz .05 .02
❑ 573 Baltimore Checklist .05 .02
❑ 574 Kevan Melrose .15 .07
❑ 575 Kevin Grant .15 .07
❑ 576 Kevan Guy .25 .11
❑ 577 Darryl Olsen .15 .07
❑ 578 Kevin Worthman .15 .07
❑ 579 Darren Stolk .15 .07
❑ 580 Bryan Deasley .15 .07
❑ 581 Paul Kruse .25 .11
❑ 582 Darren Banks .25 .11
❑ 583 Corey Lyons .15 .07
❑ 584 Kenny Clark .15 .07
❑ 585 Todd Strueby .25 .11
❑ 586 Rich Chernomaz .15 .07
❑ 587 Tim Harris .15 .07
❑ 588 Shawn Heaphy .15 .07
❑ 589 Todd Harkins .25 .11
❑ 590 Richard Zemlak .25 .11
❑ 591 Warren Sharples .25 .11
❑ 592 Jason Muzzatti .75 .35
❑ 593 Dennis Holland .15 .07
❑ 594 Salt Lake City CL .05 .02
❑ 595 Shawn Antoski .35 .16
❑ 596 Peter Bakovic .15 .07
❑ 597 Robin Bawa .20 .09
❑ 598 Cam Brown .15 .07
❑ 599 Neil Eisenhut .25 .11
❑ 600 Jason Herter .20 .09
❑ 601 Ian Kidd .15 .07
❑ 602 Troy Neumeier .15 .07
❑ 603 Carl Valimont .15 .07
❑ 604 Phil Von Stefenelli .25 .11
❑ 605 Andrew McBain .25 .11
❑ 606 Eric Murano .25 .11
❑ 607 Rob Murphy .25 .11
❑ 608 Brian Blad .15 .07
❑ 609 Randy Boyd .15 .07
❑ 610 Don Gibson .15 .07
❑ 611 Paul Guay .25 .11
❑ 612 Jay Mazur .25 .11
❑ 613 Jeff Larmer .25 .11
❑ 614 Ladislav Tresl .25 .11
❑ 615 Dennis Snedden .15 .07
❑ 616 Corrie D'Alessio .25 .11
❑ 617 Bob Mason .25 .11
❑ 618 Jack McIlhargey .25 .11
❑ 619 Curt Fraser .25 .11
❑ 620 Admirals Checklist .05 .02

## 1999 Quebec Pee Wee Hockey World Championship Collection Souvenir

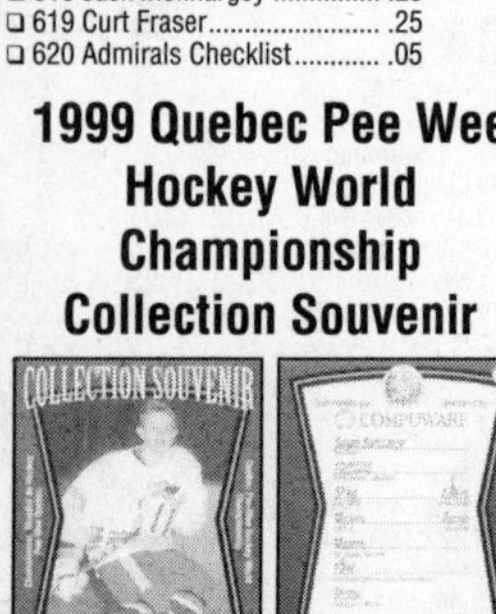
COLLECTION SOUVENIR
1999

Sponsored by Compuware, this set features color action photos of many current NHL superstars who played in the Quebec Pee Wee Hockey World Championships.

| | MINT | NRMT |
|---|---|---|
| COMPLETE SET (30) | 40.00 | 18.00 |
| COMMON CARD (1-30) | .50 | .23 |

❑ 1 Brad Park .50 .23
❑ 2 Guy Chouinard .50 .23
❑ 3 Manon Rheaume .75 .35
❑ 4 Patrick Roy 2.00 .90
❑ 5 Joe Juneau .50 .23
❑ 6 Sergei Samsonov 2.00 .90
❑ 7 Dainius Zubrus .50 .23
❑ 8 Robert Dome .50 .23
❑ 9 Daniel Tkaczuk 1.50 .70
❑ 10 Alex Tanguay 2.00 .90
❑ 11 Jean-Marc Pelletier .50 .23
❑ 12 Oleg Kvasha 1.00 .45
❑ 13 Steve Begin .50 .23
❑ 14 Daniel Corso 1.00 .45
❑ 15 Sacha Goc .50 .23
❑ 16 Marian Hossa 2.00 .90
❑ 17 Paul Mara 3.00 1.35
❑ 18 Jean Francois Damphousse 1.00 .45
❑ 19 Philippe Sauve 1.00 .45
❑ 20 Gregor Baumgartner .50 .23
❑ 21 Ladislav Nagy .50 .23
❑ 22 Vincent Lecavalier 5.00 2.20
❑ 23 David Legwand 4.00 1.80
❑ 24 Rico Fata 3.00 1.35
❑ 25 Mathieu Chouinard 2.00 .90
❑ 26 Eric Chouinard 2.00 .90
❑ 27 Mathieu Biron 2.00 .90
❑ 28 Simon Gagne 4.00 1.80
❑ 29 Mike Ribeiro 2.00 .90
❑ 30 Jonathan Girard 1.00 .45

## 1996 RHI Inaugural Edition

Inaugural Edition
1996
Vancouver
VooDoo
Arena: General Motors Place
800 Griffith Way
Vancouver, BC, Canada

This nineteen-card Roller Hockey International set features the logos of all the teams from the hip, new game on the front, with franchise information on the back.

| | MINT | NRMT |
|---|---|---|
| COMPLETE SET (19) | 3.00 | 1.35 |
| COMMON CARD (1-18) | .10 | .05 |

❑ 1 Los Angeles Blades .25 .11
❑ 2 Long Island Jaws .25 .11
❑ 3 Empire State Cobras .25 .11
❑ 4 Denver DareDevils .25 .11
❑ 5 Anaheim Bullfrogs .25 .11
❑ 6 Orlando Jackals .25 .11
❑ 7 Ottawa Loggers .25 .11
❑ 8 Oklahoma Coyotes .25 .11
❑ 9 Oakland Skates .25 .11
❑ 10 New Jersey Rockin Rollers .25 .11
❑ 11 Montreal Roadrunners .25 .11
❑ 12 Minnesota Arctic Blast .25 .11
❑ 13 Vancouver VooDoo .25 .11
❑ 14 St. Louis Vipers .25 .11
❑ 15 San Jose Rhinos .25 .11
❑ 16 San Diego Barracudas .25 .11
❑ 17 Sacramento River Rats .25 .11
❑ 18 Philadelphia Bulldogs .25 .11
❑ NNO Checklist .10 .05

## 1952-53 St. Lawrence Sales

— 78 —
Roger Bessette
Sherbrooke
GARDIEN DE BUTS

This 108-card black and white set put out by St. Lawrence Sales Agency featured members of the QSHL. The card backs are written in French. The cards measure approximately 1 15/16" by 2 15/16" and are numbered on the back. The key cards in the set are those of future (at that time) NHL greats Jean Beliveau and Jacques Plante. The complete set price includes both versions of card number 17.

| | EX-MT | VG-E |
|---|---|---|
| COMPLETE SET (108) | 1200.00 | 550.00 |
| COMMON CARD (1-107) | 8.00 | 3.60 |

❑ 1 Jacques Plante 350.00 160.00
❑ 2 Glen Harmon 8.00 3.60
❑ 3 Jimmy Moore 8.00 3.60
❑ 4 Gerard Desaulniers 8.00 3.60
❑ 5 Les Douglas 8.00 3.60
❑ 6 Fred Burchell 10.00 4.50
❑ 7 Ed Litzenberger 15.00 6.75
❑ 8 Rollie Rousseau 8.00 3.60
❑ 9 Roger Leger 8.00 3.60
❑ 10 Phil Samis 8.00 3.60
❑ 11 Paul Masnick 12.00 5.50
❑ 12 Walter Clune 8.00 3.60
❑ 13 Louis Denis 8.00 3.60
❑ 14 Gerry Plamondon 10.00 4.50
❑ 15 Cliff Malone 8.00 3.60
❑ 16 Pete Morin 12.00 5.50
❑ 17A Jack Schmidt 12.00 5.50
❑ 17B Aldo Guidolin 20.00 9.00
❑ 18 Paul Leclerc 8.00 3.60
❑ 19 Larry Kwong 10.00 4.50
❑ 20 Rosario Joanette 8.00 3.60
❑ 21 Tom Smelle 8.00 3.60
❑ 22 Gordie Haworth 10.00 4.50
❑ 23 Bruce Cline 10.00 4.50
❑ 24 Andre Corriveau 8.00 3.60
❑ 25 Jacques Deslauriers 8.00 3.60
❑ 26 Bingo Ernst 8.00 3.60
❑ 27 Jacques Chartrand 8.00 3.60
❑ 28 Phil Vitale 8.00 3.60
❑ 29 Renald Lacroix 8.00 3.60
❑ 30 J.P. Bisaillon 8.00 3.60
❑ 31 Jack Irvine 8.00 3.60
❑ 32 Georges Bougie 8.00 3.60
❑ 33 Paul Larivee 8.00 3.60
❑ 34 Carl Smelle 8.00 3.60
❑ 35 Walter Pawlyschyn 8.00 3.60
❑ 36 Jean Marois 8.00 3.60
❑ 37 Jack Gelineau 8.00 3.60
❑ 38 Danny Nixon 8.00 3.60
❑ 39 Jean Beliveau 400.00 180.00
❑ 40 Phil Renaud 8.00 3.60
❑ 41 Leon Bouchard 8.00 3.60
❑ 42 Dennis Smith 8.00 3.60
❑ 43 Joe Crozier 15.00 6.75
❑ 44 Al Bacari 8.00 3.60
❑ 45 Murdo MacKay 10.00 4.50
❑ 46 Gordie Hudson 8.00 3.60
❑ 47 Claude Robert 8.00 3.60
❑ 48 Yogi Kraiger 10.00 4.50
❑ 49 Ludger Tremblay 10.00 4.50
❑ 50 Pierre Brillant 8.00 3.60
❑ 51 Frank Mario 8.00 3.60
❑ 52 Copper Leyth 8.00 3.60
❑ 53 Herbie Carnegie 20.00 9.00
❑ 54 Punch Imlach 40.00 18.00
❑ 55 Howard Riopelle 8.00 3.60
❑ 56 Ken Laufman 8.00 3.60
❑ 57 Jackie Leclair 15.00 6.75
❑ 58 Bill Robinson 8.00 3.60
❑ 59 George Ford 8.00 3.60
❑ 60 Bill Johnson 8.00 3.60
❑ 61 Leo Gravelle 8.00 3.60
❑ 62 Jack Giesebrecht 8.00 3.60
❑ 63 John Arundel 8.00 3.60
❑ 64 Vic Gregg 8.00 3.60
❑ 65 Bep Guidolin 15.00 6.75
❑ 66 Al Kuntz 8.00 3.60
❑ 67 Emile Dagenais 8.00 3.60
❑ 68 Bill Richardson 8.00 3.60
❑ 69 Bob Robertson 8.00 3.60
❑ 70 Ray Fredericks 8.00 3.60
❑ 71 James O'Flaherty 8.00 3.60
❑ 72 Butch Stahan 8.00 3.60
❑ 73 Roger Roberge 8.00 3.60
❑ 74 Guy Labrie 8.00 3.60
❑ 75 Gilles Dube 8.00 3.60
❑ 76 Pete Wywrot 8.00 3.60
❑ 77 Tod Campeau 10.00 4.50
❑ 78 Roger Bessette 8.00 3.60
❑ 79 Martial Pruneau 8.00 3.60
❑ 80 Nils Tremblay 8.00 3.60
❑ 81 Jacques Locas 8.00 3.60
❑ 82 Rene Pepin 8.00 3.60
❑ 83 Bob Pepin 8.00 3.60
❑ 84 Tom McDougall 8.00 3.60
❑ 85 Peter Wright 8.00 3.60
❑ 86 Ronnie Matthews 8.00 3.60
❑ 87 Irene St-Hilaire 8.00 3.60
❑ 88 Dewar Thompson 8.00 3.60
❑ 89 Bob Dainville 8.00 3.60
❑ 90 Marcel Pelletier 8.00 3.60
❑ 91 Delphis Franche 8.00 3.60
❑ 92 Georges Roy 8.00 3.60
❑ 93 Andy McCallum 8.00 3.60
❑ 94 Lou Smrke 8.00 3.60
❑ 95 J.P. Lamirande 8.00 3.60
❑ 96 Normand Dussault 8.00 3.60
❑ 97 Stan Smrke 12.00 5.50
❑ 98 Jack Bownass 8.00 3.60
❑ 99 Billy Arcand 8.00 3.60
❑ 100 Lyall Wiseman 8.00 3.60
❑ 101 Jack Hamilton 8.00 3.60
❑ 102 Bob Leger 8.00 3.60
❑ 103 Larry Regan 12.00 5.50
❑ 104 Erwin Grosse 8.00 3.60
❑ 105 Roger Bedard 8.00 3.60
❑ 106 Ted Hodgson 8.00 3.60
❑ 107 Dave Gatherum 15.00 6.75

## 1989-90 7th Inn. Sketch OHL

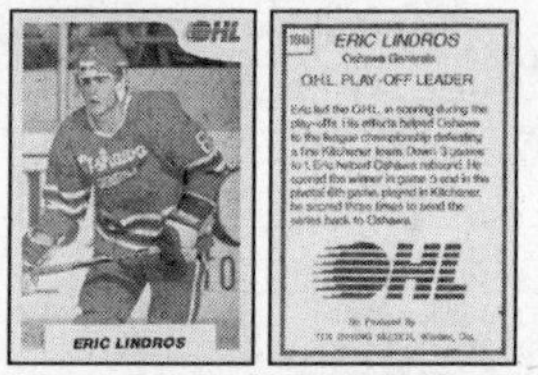
OHL
ERIC LINDROS
Oshawa Generals
OHL PLAY-OFF LEADER
OHL
ERIC LINDROS

This 200-card standard-size set was issued by 7th Inning Sketch featuring members of the Ontario Hockey League. The fronts of the cards have yellow borders which surround the player's photo and on the bottom of the front is the player's name. In the upper right hand corner, the team's name is featured. The backs of the cards feature statistical and biographical information. The set has been popular with collectors since it features early cards of Eric Lindros; most collectors consider card number 1 to be Lindros' regular card as opposed to the (Lindros) specials on cards 188, 195, and 196. The set was also issued on a limited basis (a numbered edition of 3000) as a factory set; however, the factory set only included 167 cards as 33 cards were dropped for unspecified reasons.

| | MINT | NRMT |
|---|---|---|
| COMPLETE SET (200) | 30.00 | 13.50 |
| COMPLETE FACT.SET (167) | 30.00 | 13.50 |
| COMMON CARD (1-200) | .05 | .02 |

❑ 1 Eric Lindros 4.00 1.80
(Beware counterfeits)
❑ 2 Jarrod Skalde .10 .05
❑ 3 Joe Busillo .10 .05
❑ 4 Dale Craigwell .35 .16
❑ 5 Clair Cornish .10 .05
❑ 6 Jean-Paul Davis .10 .05
❑ 7 Craig Donaldson .10 .05
❑ 8 Wade Simpson .10 .05
❑ 9 Mike Craig .25 .11
❑ 10 Mark Deazeley .10 .05
❑ 11 Scott Hollis .10 .05
❑ 12 Brian Grieve .10 .05
❑ 13 Dave Craievich .10 .05
❑ 14 Paul O'Hagan .10 .05
❑ 15 Matt Hoffman .10 .05
❑ 16 Trevor McIvor .10 .05
❑ 17 Cory Banika .10 .05
❑ 18 Kevin Butt .20 .09
❑ 19 Iain Fraser .10 .05
❑ 20 Bill Armstrong .20 .09
❑ 21 Scott Luik .10 .05
❑ 22 Brent Grieve .10 .05
❑ 23 Fred Brathwaite .25 .11
❑ 24 Paul Holden .10 .05
❑ 25 Trevor Dam .10 .05
❑ 26 Chris Taylor .10 .05
❑ 27 Mark Guy .10 .05
❑ 28 Louie DeBrusk .25 .11
❑ 29 John Battice .10 .05
❑ 30 Chris Crombie .10 .05
❑ 31 Sean Basilio .10 .05
❑ 32 Aaron Nagy .10 .05
❑ 33 Greg Ryan .10 .05
❑ 34 Steve Martell .10 .05
❑ 35 Scott MacKay .10 .05
❑ 36 Dennis Purdie .10 .05
❑ 37 Steve Boyd .10 .05
❑ 38 John Tanner .25 .11
❑ 39 David Anderson .10 .05
❑ 40 Rick Corriveau .10 .05
❑ 41 Todd Hlushko .30 .14
❑ 42 Doug Synish .10 .05
❑ 43 Dan LeBlanc .20 .09
❑ 44 Dave Noseworthy .10 .05
❑ 45 Karl Taylor .10 .05
❑ 46 Jeff Hodgen .10 .05
❑ 47 Mike Kelly .05 .02
Gary Agnew
❑ 48 Wayne Maxner .10 .05
❑ 49 Brett Seguin .10 .05
❑ 50 Greg Walters .10 .05
❑ 51 Chris Snell .10 .05
❑ 52 Troy Binnie .10 .05
❑ 53 Joni Lehto .10 .05
❑ 54 Steve Kluczkowski .10 .05
❑ 55 Ryan Kuwabara .20 .09
❑ 56 Chris Simon 1.50 .70
❑ 57 Jerrett DeFazio .20 .09
❑ 58 Rob Sangster .10 .05
❑ 59 Greg Clancy .10 .05
❑ 60 Peter Ambroziak .10 .05
❑ 61 Jeff Ricciardi .10 .05
❑ 62 John East .10 .05
❑ 63 Joey McTamney .10 .05
❑ 64 Dan Poirier .10 .05
❑ 65 Gairin Smith .10 .05
❑ 66 Wade Gibson .10 .05
❑ 67 Checklist Card .05 .02
❑ 68 Andrew Brodie .10 .05
❑ 69 Craig Wilson .10 .05
❑ 70 Peter McGlynn .10 .05
❑ 71 George Dourian .10 .05
❑ 72 Bob Berg .20 .09
❑ 73 Richard Fatrola .10 .05
❑ 74 Craig Fraser .10 .05
❑ 75 Brent Gretzky 1.00 .45
❑ 76 Jake Grimes .10 .05
❑ 77 Darren McCarty 1.00 .45
❑ 78 Ted Miskolczi .10 .05
❑ 79 Rob Pearson .25 .11
❑ 80 Gordon Pell .10 .05
❑ 81 John Porco .10 .05
❑ 82 Ken Rowbotham .10 .05
❑ 83 Scott Thornton .10 .05
❑ 84 Shawn Way .10 .05
❑ 85 Steve Bancroft .10 .05
❑ 86 Greg Bignell .10 .05
❑ 87 Scott Boston .10 .05
❑ 88 Scott Feasby .10 .05
❑ 89 Derek Morin .20 .09
❑ 90 Sean O'Reilly .20 .09
❑ 91 Jason Skelet .10 .05
❑ 92 Greg Dreveny .10 .05
❑ 93 Jeff Fife .10 .05
❑ 94 Rob Stopar .10 .05
❑ 95 Joe Desrosiers .05 .02
❑ 96 Danny Flynn .10 .05
❑ 97 Dr. R.L. Vaughan .05 .02
❑ 98 Troy Stephens .10 .05
❑ 99 Dan Brown .10 .05
❑ 100 Mike Ricci 1.00 .45
❑ 101 Brent Pope .10 .05
❑ 102 Mike Dagenais .20 .09
❑ 103 Scott Campbell .10 .05
❑ 104 Jamie Pegg .10 .05
❑ 105 Joe Hawley .10 .05
❑ 106 Jason Dawe .50 .23
❑ 107 Paul Mitton .10 .05
❑ 108 Mike Tomlinson .10 .05
❑ 109 Dave Lorentz .10 .05
❑ 110 Dale McTavish .10 .05
❑ 111 Willie McGarvey .10 .05
❑ 112 Don O'Neill .10 .05
❑ 113 Mark Myles .10 .05
❑ 114 Chris Longo .20 .09
❑ 115 Tom Hopkins .10 .05
❑ 116 Jassen Cullimore .10 .05
❑ 117 Geoff Ingram .10 .05
❑ 118 Twohey .05 .02
Bovair TR
❑ 119 Doug Searle .10 .05
❑ 120 Bryan Gendron .10 .05
❑ 121 Andrew Verner .20 .09
❑ 122 Todd Bocjun .20 .09
❑ 123 Dick Todd .10 .05
❑ 124 George Burnett .10 .05
❑ 125 Brad May 1.50 .70
❑ 126 David Benn .10 .05
❑ 127 Brian Mueggler .10 .05
❑ 128 Todd Coopman .10 .05
❑ 129 Geoff Rawson .10 .05
❑ 130 Keith Primeau 2.00 .90
❑ 131 Mark Lawrence .20 .09
❑ 132 Randy Hall .10 .05
❑ 133 Greg Suchan .10 .05
❑ 134 Ken Ruddick .10 .05
❑ 135 Jason Winch .20 .09
❑ 136 Paul Wolanski .10 .05
❑ 137 Dennis Scott .05 .02
❑ 138 Steve Udvari .10 .05
❑ 139 Roch Belley .20 .09
❑ 140 Don Pancoe .10 .05
❑ 141 Paul Bruneau .05 .02
❑ 142 Paul Laus .75 .35
❑ 143 Mike St. John .10 .05
❑ 144 John Johnson .10 .05
❑ 145 Greg Allen .10 .05
❑ 146 Don McConnell .10 .05
❑ 147 Andy Bezeau .10 .05
❑ 148 Jeff Walker .10 .05
❑ 149 John Spoltore .10 .05
❑ 150 Derek Switzer .20 .09
❑ 151 Tyler Ertel .10 .05
❑ 152 Shawn Antoski .25 .11
❑ 153 Jason Corrigan .10 .05
❑ 154 Derian Hatcher .75 .35
❑ 155 John Vary .10 .05
❑ 156 Jamie Caruso .10 .05
❑ 157 Trevor Halverson .10 .05
❑ 158 Robert Deschamps .10 .05
❑ 159 Jeff Gardiner .20 .09
❑ 160 Gary Miller .10 .05
❑ 161 Shayne Antoski .25 .11
❑ 162 John Van Kessel .10 .05
❑ 163 Colin Austin .10 .05
❑ 164 Tom Purcell .10 .05
❑ 165 Joel Morin .10 .05
❑ 166 Tim Favot .10 .05
❑ 167 Checklist Card .05 .02
❑ 168 Jason Beaton .10 .05
❑ 169 Chris Ottmann .10 .05
❑ 170 Mike Matuszek .10 .05
❑ 171 Rob Fournier .10 .05
❑ 172 Ron Bertrand .20 .09
❑ 173 Bert Templeton .10 .05
❑ 174 Casey Jones .05 .02
❑ 175 Robert Frayn .10 .05
❑ 176 Claude Noel .10 .05
❑ 177 Sean Basilio Award .10 .05
❑ 178 Chris Longo Rookie .10 .05
❑ 179 Cory Keenan AS .10 .05
❑ 180 Owen Nolan Award 1.50 .70
❑ 181 Steven Rice AS .25 .11
❑ 182 Shayne Stevenson .10 .05
Scorer
❑ 183 Mike Ricci Award .50 .23
❑ 184 Jason Firth Award .10 .05
❑ 185 John Slaney Award .10 .05
❑ 186 Iain Fraser Award .10 .05
❑ 187 Steven Rice Star .25 .11
❑ 188 Eric Lindros Scorer 3.00 1.35
❑ 189 Keith Primeau Scorer 1.00 .45
❑ 190 Mike Ricci Award .50 .23
❑ 191 Mike Torchia AS .25 .11
❑ 192 Mike Torchia Star .20 .09
❑ 193 Jarrod Skalde Champs .10 .05
❑ 194 Paul O'Hagan Award .10 .05
❑ 195 Eric Lindros 3.00 1.35
(Where in 1991)
❑ 196 Eric Lindros AS 3.00 1.35
❑ 197 Jeff Fife Award .10 .05
❑ 198 Iain Fraser MVP .10 .05
❑ 199 Bill Armstrong Winner .10 .05
❑ 200 Checklist Card .05 .02

## 1990 7th Inn. Sketch Memorial Cup

The 7th Inn. Sketch Memorial Cup Hockey set consists of 100 standard-size cards. The front features a borderless color posed photo of the player against an aqua blue background. The upper right corner of the picture is cut off and various hockey league logos are placed there. The back is printed in dark blue lettering on a yellow background and includes the card number, player information, the CHL logo, and the Coupe Memorial Cup logo. The set features players from the four semi-final teams in the 1990 Memorial Cup playoffs, Kamloops Blazers (1-25), Kitchener Rangers (26-49), Laval Titans (50-74), and Oshawa Generals (75-100). These cards were only issued as factory sets, with a numbered edition of 3000 sets. The set features cards of future NHL players Corey Hirsch, Eric Lindros, Martin Lapointe, Scott Niedermayer, and Darryl Sydor.

| | MINT | NRMT |
|---|---|---|
| COMPLETE SET (100) | 100.00 | 45.00 |
| COMMON CARD (1-100) | .25 | .11 |

- ❑ 1 Len Barrie .50 .23
- ❑ 2 Zac Boyer .50 .23
- ❑ 3 Dave Chyzowski .50 .23
- ❑ 4 Shea Esselmont .50 .23
- ❑ 5 Todd Esselmont .50 .23
- ❑ 6 Phil Huber .50 .23
- ❑ 7 Lance Johnson .50 .23
- ❑ 8 Paul Kruse 1.00 .45
- ❑ 9 Cal McGowan .50 .23
- ❑ 10 Mike Needham 1.00 .45
- ❑ 11 Brian Shantz .50 .23
- ❑ 12 Darryl Sydor 3.00 1.35
- ❑ 13 Jeff Watchorn .50 .23
- ❑ 14 Jarrett Bousquet .50 .23
- ❑ 15 Todd Harris .50 .23
- ❑ 16 Deen Malkoc .75 .35
- ❑ 17 Joey Mittelstadt .50 .23
- ❑ 18 Scott Niedermayer 4.00 1.80
- ❑ 19 Clayton Young .50 .23
- ❑ 20 Trevor Sim .50 .23
- ❑ 21 Murray Duval .50 .23
- ❑ 22 Steve Yule .50 .23
- ❑ 23 Craig Bonner .50 .23
- ❑ 24 Dale Masson .50 .23
- ❑ 25 Corey Hirsch 5.00 2.20
- ❑ 26 Joe McDonnell .50 .23
- ❑ 27 Rick Chambers .25 .11
- ❑ 28 John Finnie .50 .23
- ❑ 29 Randy Pearce .50 .23
- ❑ 30 Mark Montanari .50 .23
- ❑ 31 Mike Torchia .75 .35
- ❑ 32 Jason York 1.50 .70
- ❑ 33 Jason Firth .50 .23
- ❑ 34 Jamie Israel .50 .23
- ❑ 35 Richard Borgo .50 .23
- ❑ 36 John Uniac .50 .23
- ❑ 37 Steve Smith .50 .23
- ❑ 38 Steven Rice 1.00 .45
- ❑ 39 Gilbert Dionne 1.00 .45
- ❑ 40 Cory Keenan .50 .23
- ❑ 41 Rick Allain .50 .23
- ❑ 42 John Copley .50 .23
- ❑ 43 Gib Tucker .50 .23
- ❑ 44 Chris LiPuma .50 .23
- ❑ 45 Brad Barton .50 .23
- ❑ 46 Rival Fullum .50 .23
- ❑ 47 Joey St.Aubin .50 .23
- ❑ 48 Jack Williams .50 .23
- ❑ 49 Shayne Stevenson .50 .23
- ❑ 50 Pierre Creamer .50 .23
- ❑ 51 Carl Mantha .50 .23
- ❑ 52 Julian Cameron .50 .23
- ❑ 53 Sandy McCarthy 2.00 .90
- ❑ 54 Gino Odjick 2.00 .90
- ❑ 55 Eric Raymond .50 .23
- ❑ 56 Carl Boudreau .50 .23
- ❑ 57 Greg MacEachern .50 .23
- ❑ 58 Allen Kerr .50 .23
- ❑ 59 Patrice Brisebois 1.50 .70
- ❑ 60 Eric Bissonette .50 .23
- ❑ 61 Martin Lapointe 2.00 .90
- ❑ 62 Michel Gingras .50 .23
- ❑ 63 Sylvain Naud .50 .23
- ❑ 64 Pat Caron .50 .23
- ❑ 65 Regis Tremblay .50 .23
- ❑ 66 Francois Pelletier .50 .23
- ❑ 67 Jason Brousseau .50 .23
- ❑ 68 Eric Dubois .50 .23
- ❑ 69 Claude Boivin .50 .23
- ❑ 70 Denis Chalifoux .50 .23
- ❑ 71 Jim Bermingham .50 .23
- ❑ 72 Daniel Arsenault .50 .23
- ❑ 73 Normand Demers .50 .23
- ❑ 74 Serge Anglehart .50 .23
- ❑ 75 Rick Cornacchia .50 .23
- ❑ 76 Kevin Butt .75 .35
- ❑ 77 Fred Brathwaite 1.00 .45
- ❑ 78 Paul O'Hagan .50 .23
- ❑ 79 Craig Donaldson .50 .23
- ❑ 80 Jean-Paul Davis .50 .23
- ❑ 81 Brian Grieve .50 .23
- ❑ 82 Bill Armstrong .50 .23
- ❑ 83 Wade Simpson .50 .23
- ❑ 84 Dave Craievich .50 .23
- ❑ 85 Dale Craigwell 1.00 .45
- ❑ 86 Joe Busillo .50 .23
- ❑ 87 Cory Banika .50 .23
- ❑ 88 Eric Lindros 40.00 18.00
- ❑ 89 Iain Fraser 1.00 .45
- ❑ 90 Mike Craig 1.00 .45
- ❑ 91 Jarrod Skalde .50 .23
- ❑ 92 Brent Grieve 1.00 .45
- ❑ 93 Scott Luik .50 .23
- ❑ 94 Matt Hoffman .50 .23
- ❑ 95 Trevor McIvor .50 .23
- ❑ 96 Scott Hollis .50 .23
- ❑ 97 Mark Deazeley .50 .23
- ❑ 98 Clair Cornish .50 .23
- ❑ 99 Oshawa Wins 15.00 6.75 (Eric Lindros holding up Memorial Cup)
- ❑ 100 Checklist Card .25 .11

## 1990-91 7th Inn. Sketch OHL

The 7th Inning Sketch OHL Hockey set contains 400 standard-size cards. The front features a full color photo, enframed by different color borders. The player's position appears in a star at the lower left hand corner, with his name and "OHL" in the bar below the picture. The back has another color photo, with biographical information and career summary in a box running the length of the card. This set features a regular card (1) as well as a promo card of hockey star Eric Lindros. The promo version has the same front as Lindros' card number 1 but has an asterisk in the card number position on the card back. Players from the following teams are represented in this set: Oshawa Generals (1, 325-339, 341-345, 347-350), Belleville Bulls (2-10, 12-21, 23, 340, 346), Kingston Frontenacs (11, 51-75), Cornwall Royals (22, 24-50), Ottawa 67's (76-100, 230), Detroit Compuware Ambassadors (101-121, 123-125), North Bay Centennials (122, 301-324), London Knights (126-149), Sault Ste. Marie Greyhounds (150-173, 175-176), Windsor Spitfires (174, 177-200), Dukes of Hamilton (201-225), Kitchener Rangers (226-229, 231-250, 370), Niagara Falls Thunder (251-275), Owen Sound Platers (276-299), Peterborough Petes (351-369, 371-376), and Sudbury Wolves (377-400). First round picks (1991 NHL Draft) in this set include Eric Lindros (1), Alex Stojanov (7), Pat Peake (14), Glen Murray (18), and Trevor Halverson (21). First round picks (1992 NHL Draft rank indicated in parenthesis) in this set include Todd Warriner (4), Cory Stillman (6), Brandon Convery (8), Curtis Bowen (22), and Grant Marshall (23). A factory set, a numbered edition of 9000 sets, was produced and marketed separately.

| | MINT | NRMT |
|---|---|---|
| COMPLETE SET (400) | 18.00 | 8.00 |
| COMPLETE FACT.SET (400) | 20.00 | 9.00 |
| COMMON CARD (1-400) | .05 | .02 |

- ❑ 1 Eric Lindros 4.00 1.80
- ❑ 2 Greg Dreveny .10 .05
- ❑ 3 Belleville Checklist UER .05 .02
- ❑ 4 Richard Fatrola .10 .05
- ❑ 5 Craig Fraser .10 .05
- ❑ 6 Robert Frayn .10 .05
- ❑ 7 Brent Gretzky .50 .23
- ❑ 8 Jake Grimes .10 .05
- ❑ 9 Darren Hurley .10 .05
- ❑ 10 Rick Marshall .10 .05
- ❑ 11 Checklist UER .05 .02
- ❑ 12 Darren McCarty .75 .35
- ❑ 13 Derek Morin .10 .05
- ❑ 14 Sean O'Reilly .10 .05
- ❑ 15 Rob Pearson UER .35 .16 (Listed on Oshawa CL but reverse says Belleville Bulls)
- ❑ 16 John Porco .10 .05
- ❑ 17 Ken Rowbotham .10 .05
- ❑ 18 Ken Ruddick .10 .05
- ❑ 19 Jim Sonmez .10 .05
- ❑ 20 Brad Teichmann .10 .05
- ❑ 21 Chris Varga .10 .05
- ❑ 22 Checklist Card .05 .02
- ❑ 23 Larry Mavety CO .05 .02
- ❑ 24 Rival Fullum .15 .07
- ❑ 25 Nathan Lafayette .50 .23
- ❑ 26 Darren Bell .10 .05
- ❑ 27 Craig Brocklehurst .10 .05
- ❑ 28 Shawn Caplice .10 .05
- ❑ 29 Mike Cavanaugh .10 .05
- ❑ 30 Jason Cirone .15 .07
- ❑ 31 Chris Clancy .10 .05
- ❑ 32 Mark DeSantis .10 .05
- ❑ 33 Rob Dykeman .10 .05
- ❑ 34 Shayne Gaffar .10 .05
- ❑ 35 Ilpo Kauhanen .10 .05
- ❑ 36 Rob Kinghan .10 .05
- ❑ 37 Dave Lemay .10 .05
- ❑ 38 Guy Leveque .15 .07
- ❑ 39 Matt McGuffin .10 .05
- ❑ 40 Marcus Middleton .10 .05
- ❑ 41 Thomas Nemeth .15 .07
- ❑ 42 Rod Pasma .10 .05
- ❑ 43 Richard Raymond .10 .05
- ❑ 44 Jeff Reid .10 .05
- ❑ 45 Jerry Ribble .10 .05
- ❑ 46 Jean-Alain Schneider .10 .05
- ❑ 47 John Slaney .25 .11
- ❑ 48 Jeremy Stevenson .15 .07
- ❑ 49 Ryan VandenBussche .25 .11
- ❑ 50 Marc Crawford CO .75 .35
- ❑ 51 Tony Bella .10 .05
- ❑ 52 Drake Berehowsky .35 .16
- ❑ 53 Jason Chipman .10 .05
- ❑ 54 Tony Cimellaro .10 .05
- ❑ 55 Keli Corpse .15 .07
- ❑ 56 Mike Dawson .10 .05
- ❑ 57 Sean Gauthier UER .10 .05
- ❑ 58 Fred Goltz .10 .05
- ❑ 59 Gord Harris .10 .05
- ❑ 60 Tony Iob .20 .09
- ❑ 61 John Bernie .10 .05
- ❑ 62 Dale Junkin .10 .05
- ❑ 63 Nathan Lafayette .50 .23
- ❑ 64 Blake Martin .10 .05
- ❑ 65 Mark McCague .10 .05
- ❑ 66 Bob McKillop .10 .05
- ❑ 67 Justin Morrison .10 .05
- ❑ 68 Bill Robinson .10 .05
- ❑ 69 Joel Sandie .10 .05
- ❑ 70 Kevin King .10 .05
- ❑ 71 Dave Stewart .10 .05
- ❑ 72 Joel Washkurak .10 .05
- ❑ 73 Brock Woods .10 .05
- ❑ 74 Randy Hall CO .10 .05
- ❑ 75 John Vary .10 .05
- ❑ 76 Peter Ambroziak .10 .05
- ❑ 77 Troy Binnie .10 .05
- ❑ 78 Curt Bowen .35 .16
- ❑ 79 Andrew Brodie .10 .05
- ❑ 80 Ottawa Checklist .10 .05
- ❑ 81 Greg Clancy .10 .05
- ❑ 82 Jerrett DeFazio .10 .05
- ❑ 83 Kris Draper .75 .35
- ❑ 84 Wade Gibson .10 .05
- ❑ 85 Ryan Kuwabara .10 .05
- ❑ 86 Joni Lehto .10 .05
- ❑ 87 Donald MacPherson .10 .05
- ❑ 88 Grant Marshall .35 .16
- ❑ 89 Peter McGlynn .10 .05
- ❑ 90 Maurice O'Brien .10 .05
- ❑ 91 Jeff Ricciardi .15 .07
- ❑ 92 Brett Seguin .15 .07
- ❑ 93 Len DeVuono .10 .05
- ❑ 94 Gerry Skrypec .10 .05
- ❑ 95 Chris Snell .15 .07
- ❑ 96 Jason Snow .10 .05
- ❑ 97 Sean Spencer .10 .05
- ❑ 98 Brad Spry .10 .05
- ❑ 99 Matt Stone .10 .05
- ❑ 100 Brian Kilrea CO .10 .05
- ❑ 101 Kevin Butt .20 .09
- ❑ 102 Glen Craig .10 .05
- ❑ 103 Paul Doherty .10 .05
- ❑ 104 Mark Donahue .10 .05
- ❑ 105 Jeff Gardiner .10 .05
- ❑ 106 Trent Gleason .10 .05
- ❑ 107 Troy Gleason .10 .05
- ❑ 108 Mark Lawrence .25 .11
- ❑ 109 Trevor McIvor .10 .05
- ❑ 110 Paul Mitton .10 .05
- ❑ 111 David Myles .10 .05
- ❑ 112 Jeffery Nolan .10 .05
- ❑ 113 Rob Papineau .10 .05
- ❑ 114 Pat Peake .50 .23
- ❑ 115 Chris Phelps .10 .05
- ❑ 116 John Pinches .10 .05
- ❑ 117 James Shea .10 .05
- ❑ 118 James Sheehan .10 .05
- ❑ 119 John Stos .10 .05
- ❑ 120 Tom Sullivan .10 .05
- ❑ 121 John Wynne .10 .05
- ❑ 122 Robert Thorpe .10 .05
- ❑ 123 David Benn .10 .05
- ❑ 124 Andy Weidenbach CO UER .05 .02
- ❑ 125 Detroit Checklist .05 .02
- ❑ 126 David Anderson .10 .05
- ❑ 127 Sean Basilio .10 .05
- ❑ 128 Brent Brownlee .10 .05
- ❑ 129 Rick Corriveau .15 .07
- ❑ 130 Derrick Crane .10 .05
- ❑ 131 Chris Crombie .15 .07
- ❑ 132 Louie DeBrusk .25 .11
- ❑ 133 Mark Guy .10 .05
- ❑ 134 Brett Marrietti .10 .05
- ❑ 135 Steve Martell .10 .05
- ❑ 136 Scott McKay .10 .05
- ❑ 137 Aaron Nagy .20 .09
- ❑ 138 Brett Nicol .10 .05
- ❑ 139 Barry Potomski .35 .16
- ❑ 140 Dennis Purdie .15 .07
- ❑ 141 Kelly Reed .10 .05
- ❑ 142 Gregory Ryan .10 .05
- ❑ 143 Brad Smyth .10 .05
- ❑ 144 Nick Stajduhar .20 .09
- ❑ 145 John Tanner .20 .09
- ❑ 146 Chris Taylor .25 .11
- ❑ 147 Mark Visheau .10 .05
- ❑ 148 Gary Agnew CO .10 .05
- ❑ 149 London Checklist .10 .05
- ❑ 150 Sault Ste. Marie Checklist .10 .05
- ❑ 151 David Babcock .10 .05
- ❑ 152 Drew Bannister .35 .16
- ❑ 153 Bob Boughner .35 .16
- ❑ 154 Joe Busillo .10 .05
- ❑ 155 Mike DeCoff .10 .05
- ❑ 156 Jason Denomme .10 .05
- ❑ 157 Adam Foote .75 .35
- ❑ 158 Kevin Hodson 1.00 .45
- ❑ 159 Shaun Imber .10 .05
- ❑ 160 Ralph Intranuovo .25 .11
- ❑ 161 Kevin King .10 .05
- ❑ 162 Rick Kowalsky .10 .05
- ❑ 163 Chris Kraemer .10 .05
- ❑ 164 Dan Lambert .20 .09
- ❑ 165 Mike Lenarduzzi .20 .09
- ❑ 166 Tom MacDonald .10 .05
- ❑ 167 Mark Matier .10 .05
- ❑ 168 David Matsos .10 .05
- ❑ 169 Colin Miller .15 .07
- ❑ 170 Perry Pappas .10 .05
- ❑ 171 Jarrett Reid .20 .09
- ❑ 172 Kevin Reid .10 .05
- ❑ 173 Brad Tiley UER .15 .07
- ❑ 174 Windsor Checklist .05 .02
- ❑ 175 Wade Whitten .10 .05
- ❑ 176 Ted Nolan CO .50 .23
- ❑ 177 Sean Burns .10 .05
- ❑ 178 Jason Cirone .15 .07
- ❑ 179 John Copley .10 .05
- ❑ 180 Tyler Ertel .10 .05
- ❑ 181 Brian Forestell .10 .05
- ❑ 182 Rival Fullum .15 .07
- ❑ 183 Steve Gibson .10 .05
- ❑ 184 Leonard MacDonald .10 .05
- ❑ 185 Mike Speer .10 .05
- ❑ 186 Kevin MacKay .15 .07
- ❑ 187 Ryan Merritt .10 .05
- ❑ 188 Doug Minor .10 .05
- ❑ 189 Rick Morton .10 .05
- ❑ 190 Sean O'Hagan .10 .05
- ❑ 191 Mike Polano .10 .05
- ❑ 192 Cory Stillman .75 .35
- ❑ 193 Jason Stos .10 .05
- ❑ 194 Trevor Walsh .10 .05
- ❑ 195 Todd Warriner .75 .35
- ❑ 196 Jeff Wilson .10 .05
- ❑ 197 Jason York .35 .16
- ❑ 198 Jason Zohil .10 .05
- ❑ 199 Steve Smith .10 .05
- ❑ 200 Brad Smith CO .15 .07
- ❑ 201 Jeff Bes .25 .11
- ❑ 202 Mike Blum .10 .05
- ❑ 203 Sean Brown .10 .05
- ❑ 204 Darcy Cahill .10 .05
- ❑ 205 Dale Chokan .10 .05
- ❑ 206 Chris Code .10 .05
- ❑ 207 George Dourion .10 .05
- ❑ 208 Todd Gleason .10 .05
- ❑ 209 Hamilton Checklist UER .05 .02
- ❑ 210 Michael Hartwick .10 .05
- ❑ 211 Scott Jenkins .10 .05
- ❑ 212 Rob Leask .20 .09
- ❑ 213 Gordon Pell .10 .05
- ❑ 214 Michael Reier .10 .05
- ❑ 215 Kayle Short .10 .05
- ❑ 216 Jason Skellett .10 .05
- ❑ 217 Gairin Smith .10 .05
- ❑ 218 Jeff Smith .10 .05
- ❑ 219 Jason Soules .10 .05
- ❑ 220 Alex Stojanov .25 .11
- ❑ 221 Dan Tanevski .10 .05
- ❑ 222 Gary Taylor .10 .05
- ❑ 223 Brent Watson .10 .05
- ❑ 224 Steve Woods .10 .05
- ❑ 225 Jay Johnston CO UER .05 .02
- ❑ 226 Mike Allen .10 .05
- ❑ 227 Brad Barton .10 .05
- ❑ 228 Richard Borgo .10 .05
- ❑ 229 Justin Cullen .10 .05
- ❑ 230 Lenny DeVuono .10 .05
- ❑ 231 Norman Dezainde .10 .05
- ❑ 232 Jason Firth .15 .07
- ❑ 233 Derek Gauthier .10 .05
- ❑ 234 Jamie Israel .20 .09
- ❑ 235 Chris LiPuma .15 .07
- ❑ 236 Tony McCabe .10 .05
- ❑ 237 Paul McCallion .10 .05
- ❑ 238 Shayne McCosh .10 .05
- ❑ 239 Rod Saarinen .10 .05
- ❑ 240 Steve Smith .10 .05
- ❑ 241 Joey St.Aubin .10 .05
- ❑ 242 Rob Stopar .15 .07
- ❑ 243 Jason Zohil UER .10 .05
- ❑ 244 Mike Torchia .20 .09
- ❑ 245 Gib Tucker .10 .05
- ❑ 246 John Uniac .10 .05
- ❑ 247 Jack Williams .10 .05
- ❑ 248 Joe McDonnell CO .10 .05
- ❑ 249 Steven Rice .35 .16
- ❑ 250 Mike Polano .10 .05
- ❑ 251 Greg Allen .10 .05
- ❑ 252 Roch Belley .20 .09
- ❑ 253 Andy Bezeau .10 .05
- ❑ 254 Derek Booth .10 .05
- ❑ 255 Kevin Brown .15 .07
- ❑ 256 Mark Cardiff .10 .05
- ❑ 257 Jason Coles .10 .05
- ❑ 258 Todd Coopman .10 .05
- ❑ 259 Richard Girhiny .10 .05
- ❑ 260 Brian Holk .10 .05
- ❑ 261 John Johnson .10 .05
- ❑ 262 Dan Krisko .10 .05
- ❑ 263 Manny Legace .60 .25
- ❑ 264 Brad May .75 .35
- ❑ 265 Don McConnell .10 .05
- ❑ 266 Niagara Falls Checklist UER (Nigara& sic) .05 .02
- ❑ 267 Aaron Morrison .10 .05
- ❑ 268 Cory Pageau .10 .05
- ❑ 269 Geoff Rawson .10 .05
- ❑ 270 Todd Simon .15 .07
- ❑ 271 Steve Staios .25 .11
- ❑ 272 Jeff Walker .10 .05
- ❑ 273 Todd Wetzel .10 .05
- ❑ 274 Jason Winch .10 .05
- ❑ 275 Paul Wolanski .10 .05
- ❑ 276 Owen Sound Checklist .05 .02
- ❑ 277 Andrew Brunette .25 .11
- ❑ 278 Wyatt Buckland .10 .05
- ❑ 279 Jason Buetow .10 .05
- ❑ 280 Jason Castellan .10 .05
- ❑ 281 Trent Cull .10 .05
- ❑ 282 Robert Deschamps .10 .05
- ❑ 283 Chris Driscoll .10 .05
- ❑ 284 Bryan Drury .10 .05
- ❑ 285 Todd Hunter .10 .05
- ❑ 286 Troy Hutchinson .10 .05
- ❑ 287 Kirk Maltby .50 .23
- ❑ 288 Geordie Maynard .10 .05
- ❑ 289 Kevin McDougall .10 .05
- ❑ 290 Ted Miskolczi .10 .05
- ❑ 291 Steve Parson .10 .05
- ❑ 292 Jeff Perry .10 .05
- ❑ 293 Grayden Reid .20 .09
- ❑ 294 Mike Speer .10 .05
- ❑ 295 Mark Strohack .10 .05
- ❑ 296 Mark Vilneff .10 .05
- ❑ 297 Keith Whitmore .10 .05
- ❑ 298 Jim Brown .10 .05
- ❑ 299 Len McNamara CO .05 .02
- ❑ 300 David Branch COMM .25 .11
- ❑ 301 Shayne Antoski .25 .11
- ❑ 302 Jason Beaton .10 .05
- ❑ 303 Ron Bertrand .10 .05
- ❑ 304 Michael Burman .10 .05
- ❑ 305 Jamie Caruso .20 .09
- ❑ 306 Allan Cox .10 .05
- ❑ 307 Tim Favot .10 .05
- ❑ 308 Trevor Halverson .10 .05
- ❑ 309 Derian Hatcher .75 .35
- ❑ 310 Bill Lang .10 .05
- ❑ 311 Jason MacDonald .10 .05
- ❑ 312 Gary Miller .10 .05
- ❑ 313 Chris Ottmann .10 .05
- ❑ 314 Chad Penney .15 .07
- ❑ 315 Rick Pollard .10 .05
- ❑ 316 Bradley Shepard .10 .05
- ❑ 317 John Spoltore .15 .07
- ❑ 318 Derek Switzer .10 .05
- ❑ 319 Karl Taylor .10 .05
- ❑ 320 John Vary .10 .05
- ❑ 321 Kevin White .10 .05
- ❑ 322 Billy Wright .10 .05
- ❑ 323 Bert Templeton CO .15 .07
- ❑ 324 North Bay Checklist .05 .02
- ❑ 325 Oshawa Checklist UER .05 .02
- ❑ 326 Jan Benda .20 .09
- ❑ 327 Fred Brathwaite .25 .11
- ❑ 328 Markus Brunner .10 .05
- ❑ 329 Trevor Burgess .10 .05
- ❑ 330 Clair Cornish .10 .05
- ❑ 331 Mike Cote .10 .05
- ❑ 332 Dave Craievich .10 .05
- ❑ 333 Dale Craigwell .25 .11
- ❑ 334 Jean-Paul Davis .10 .05
- ❑ 335 Mark Deazeley .10 .05
- ❑ 336 Mike Fountain .20 .09
- ❑ 337 Brian Grieve .10 .05
- ❑ 338 Matt Hoffman .15 .07
- ❑ 339 Scott Hollis .15 .07
- ❑ 340 Scott Boston .10 .05
- ❑ 341 Scott Luik .10 .05
- ❑ 342 Craig Lutes .10 .05
- ❑ 343 William MacPherson .10 .05
- ❑ 344 Paul O'Hagan .20 .09
- ❑ 345 Wade Simpson .10 .05
- ❑ 346 Jarrod Skalde UER .25 .11 (Listed on Belleville CL but reverse says Oshawa Generals)
- ❑ 347 Troy Sweet .10 .05
- ❑ 348 Jason Weaver .15 .07
- ❑ 349 Rick Cornacchia CO .10 .05
- ❑ 350 The Trophy .20 .09
- ❑ 351 Greg Bailey .10 .05
- ❑ 352 Ryan Black .20 .09
- ❑ 353 Todd Bocjun UER .20 .09 (Reversed negative on card front)
- ❑ 354 Toby Burkitt .10 .05
- ❑ 355 Scott Campbell .10 .05
- ❑ 356 Jassen Cullimore .35 .16
- ❑ 357 Jason Dawe .50 .23
- ❑ 358 Dan Ferguson .10 .05
- ❑ 359 Bryan Gendron .10 .05
- ❑ 360 Michael Harding .10 .05
- ❑ 361 Joe Hawley .10 .05
- ❑ 362 Peterborough Checklist .05 .02

UER
❑ 363 Geordie Kinnear .10 .05
❑ 364 Chris Longo UER .15 .07
❑ 365 Dale McTavish .10 .05
❑ 366 Mark Myles .10 .05
❑ 367 Don O'Neill .10 .05
❑ 368 Jamie Pegg .10 .05
❑ 369 Brent Pope .10 .05
❑ 370 Kitchener Checklist .05 .02
UER
❑ 371 Doug Searle .10 .05
❑ 372 Troy Stephens .10 .05
❑ 373 Mike Tomlinson .15 .07
❑ 374 Brent Tully .25 .11
❑ 375 Andrew Verner .20 .09
❑ 376 Dick Todd CO .10 .05
❑ 377 John Tanner .20 .09
❑ 378 Adam Bennett .15 .07
❑ 379 Kyle Blacklock .10 .05
❑ 380 Terry Chitaroni .15 .07
❑ 381 Brandon Convery .50 .23
❑ 382 J.D. Eaton .10 .05
❑ 383 Derek Etches .10 .05
❑ 384 Rod Hinks .10 .05
❑ 385 Bill Kovacs .10 .05
❑ 386 Alain Laforge .10 .05
❑ 387 Jamie Matthews .20 .09
❑ 388 Glen Murray .50 .23
❑ 389 Dean Cull .10 .05
❑ 390 Sean O'Donnell .10 .05
❑ 391 Sudbury Checklist UER .05 .02
❑ 392 Mike Peca 1.00 .45
❑ 393 Shawn Rivers .20 .09
❑ 394 Dan Ryder .10 .05
❑ 395 Alastair Still .20 .09
❑ 396 Michael Yeo .10 .05
❑ 397 Barry Young .10 .05
❑ 398 Jason Young .15 .07
❑ 399 Ken MacKenzie CO .10 .05
❑ 400 Bob Berg UER .15 .07
(Missing draft eligibility information)
❑ NNO Eric Lindros promo 10.00 4.50

## 1990-91 7th Inn. Sketch QMJHL

This 268-card standard-size set was produced by 7th Inning Sketch featuring players from the Quebec Major Junior Hockey League. First round picks (1991 NHL Draft) in this set include Patrick Poulin (9), Martin Lapointe (10), and Philippe Boucher (13). The best known players in the set, however, are 1990 second-rounder Felix Potvin and 1991 first-rounder Martin Brodeur. A factory set, a numbered edition of 4,800, was produced and marketed separately.

| | MINT | NRMT |
|---|---|---|
| COMPLETE SET (268) | 15.00 | 6.75 |
| COMPLETE FACT.SET (268) | 15.00 | 6.75 |
| COMMON CARD (1-268) | .05 | .02 |

❑ 1 Patrick Poulin .25 .11
❑ 2 Steve Lupien .10 .05
❑ 3 Pierre Gagnon .10 .05
❑ 4 Eric Plante .10 .05
❑ 5 Stephane Desjardins .10 .05
❑ 6 Peter Valenta .10 .05
❑ 7 Alexander Legault .10 .05
❑ 8 Patrice Brisebois .50 .23
❑ 9 Martin Charrois .10 .05
❑ 10 Eric Dandenault .10 .05
❑ 11 Claude Jutras Jr. .10 .05
❑ 12 David Pekarek .10 .05
❑ 13 Denis Chasse .35 .16
❑ 14 Ian Laperriere .25 .11
❑ 15 Roger Larche .10 .05
❑ 16 Dave Paquet .15 .07
❑ 17 Pascal Lebrasseur .10 .05
❑ 18 Eric Meloche .10 .05
❑ 19 The Face Off .05 .02
❑ 20 Sylvain Rodrigue .10 .05
❑ 21 Dary Giarard .10 .05
❑ 22 Eric Rochette .10 .05
❑ 23 Steve Gosselin .10 .05
❑ 24 Martin Lavalle .10 .05
❑ 25 Martin Lapointe .75 .35
❑ 26 Eric Brule .15 .07
❑ 27 Richard Boivin .10 .05
❑ 28 Patrice Martineau .10 .05
❑ 29 Dave Tremblay .10 .05
❑ 30 Steve Larouche .10 .05
❑ 31 Danny Beauregard .10 .05
❑ 32 Francois Belanger .10 .05
❑ 33 Michel St.Jacques .15 .07
❑ 34 Patric Sissillan .10 .05
❑ 35 Felix Potvin 4.00 1.80
❑ 36 Sebastien Parent .10 .05
❑ 37 Eric Duchesne .15 .07
❑ 38 Gilles Bouchard .10 .05
❑ 39 Martin Gagne .10 .05
❑ 40 Stephane Charbonneau .10 .05
❑ 41 Martin Beaupre .10 .05
❑ 42 Daniel Paradis .15 .07
❑ 43 Joe Canale .15 .07
❑ 44 Georges Vezina Arena .10 .05
❑ 45 Francois Leblanc .10 .05
❑ 46 Martin Chaput .15 .07
❑ 47 Marc Beaucage .10 .05
❑ 48 Carl Mantha .10 .05
❑ 49 Jim Bermingham .10 .05
❑ 50 Philippe Boucher .35 .16
❑ 51 Denis Chalifoux .10 .05
❑ 52 Sylvain Naud .15 .07
❑ 53 Jean Roberge .10 .05
❑ 54 Sandy McCarthy .75 .35
❑ 55 Eric Dubois .10 .05
❑ 56 Jean Blouin .10 .05
❑ 57 Jason Brousseau .10 .05
❑ 58 Pierre Sandke .10 .05
❑ 59 Benoit Larose .10 .05
❑ 60 Yanick Frechette .10 .05
❑ 61 Pierre Calder .10 .05
❑ 62 Patric Grise .10 .05
❑ 63 Martin Balfeux .10 .05
❑ 64 Boris Rousson .25 .11
❑ 65 Martin Trudeli .10 .05
❑ 66 Carl Leblanc .10 .05
❑ 67 Martin Brochu .15 .07
❑ 68 Benoit Terrien .10 .05
❑ 69 QMJHL Action .10 .05
❑ 70 Pascal Vincent .10 .05
❑ 71 Christian Tardi .10 .05
❑ 72 Christian Campeau .10 .05
❑ 73 Eric Raymond .10 .05
❑ 74 John Kovacs .10 .05
❑ 75 Steve Areas .10 .05
❑ 76 Pascal Dufalt .10 .05
❑ 77 Greg MacEachern .10 .05
❑ 78 Remi Belliveau .10 .05
❑ 79 Jocelyn Langlois .10 .05
❑ 80 Carl Menard .10 .05
❑ 81 Sebastein Foneir .10 .05
❑ 82 Jean-Franco Gregoire .10 .05
❑ 83 Normand Demers .10 .05
❑ 84 Nicolas Lefebvre .10 .05
❑ 85 Dominic Maltais .15 .07
❑ 86 Mario Therrien .10 .05
❑ 87 Daniel Thibault .10 .05
❑ 88 Jean-Francois Labbe .40 .18
❑ 89 Alain Cote .15 .07
❑ 90 Eric Prillo .10 .05
❑ 91 Patrick Nadeau .10 .05
❑ 92 Claude Poner .10 .05
❑ 93 Stephanc Julier .10 .05
❑ 94 Patrice Rene .10 .05
❑ 95 Francis Coutineir .10 .05
❑ 96 Guy Lefebvre .10 .05
❑ 97 Carl Boudreau .15 .07
❑ 98 Jacques Parent .10 .05
❑ 99 Stephane Bouquet .10 .05
❑ 100 Yanic Perreault .50 .23
❑ 101 Yvan Bergeron .10 .05
❑ 102 Jean-Francois Rivard .10 .05
❑ 103 Daniel Laflamme .10 .05
❑ 104 Francois Bourdeau .10 .05
❑ 105 Yvan Charrois .10 .05
❑ 106 Patric Genest .10 .05
❑ 107 Herve Lapointe .10 .05
❑ 108 Jean-Francois Jomphe .50 .23
❑ 109 Marc Tardif .10 .05
❑ 110 Eric Cardinal .10 .05
❑ 111 Denis Cloutier .10 .05
❑ 112 QMJHL Action .10 .05
❑ 113 Alain Samscartier .05 .02
❑ 114 Marquis Mathieu .10 .05
❑ 115 Stephan Tartari .10 .05
❑ 116 QMJHL Action .10 .05
❑ 117 QMJHL Action .10 .05
❑ 118 Martin Ray .10 .05
❑ 119 David Boudreault .10 .05
❑ 120 Mario Durroulin .10 .05
❑ 121 Jean-Francis Dieard .10 .05
❑ 122 QMJHL Action .10 .05
❑ 123 QMJHL Action .10 .05
❑ 124 Mausime Gagne .10 .05
❑ 125 Stephane Guellet .10 .05
❑ 126 Steven Paiement .10 .05
❑ 127 Francois Olympique .10 .05
❑ 128 Eric Coci .10 .05
❑ 129 Simon Toupin .10 .05
❑ 130 Shane Doirrin .10 .05
❑ 131 Todd Sparks .10 .05
❑ 132 Bruno Lajeunesse .10 .05
❑ 133 Marcel Cousineau .75 .35
❑ 134 Claude-Charl Sauirol .10 .05
❑ 135 Eric Bellerose .15 .07
❑ 136 QMJHL Action .10 .05
❑ 137 QMJHL Action .10 .05
❑ 138 Martin Lepage .15 .07
❑ 139 Michael Langauer .10 .05
❑ 140 Fredric Boivin .10 .05
❑ 141 Steven Dion .10 .05
❑ 142 QMJHL Action .10 .05
❑ 143 QMJHL Action .10 .05
❑ 144 Dan Paolucci .10 .05
❑ 145 Bruno Villeneuve .15 .07
❑ 146 Checklist Card .15 .07
(Yanic Perreault)
❑ 147 Checklist Card .05 .02
❑ 148 Stefan Simoes .10 .05
❑ 149 Joel Blain .10 .05
❑ 150 Eric Lavigne .25 .11
❑ 151 Checklist Card .05 .02
❑ 152 Checklist Card .10 .05
(Patrick Poulin)
❑ 153 Robert Malanson .10 .05
❑ 154 Brian Rogger .10 .05
❑ 155 Checklist Card .05 .02
❑ 156 Checklist Card .05 .02
❑ 157 Francois Ouellette .15 .07
❑ 158 QMJHL Action .10 .05
❑ 159 Checklist Card 1.50 .70
(Felix Potvin)
❑ 160 Checklist Card .05 .02
❑ 161 Checklist Card .05 .02
❑ 162 Checklist Card .05 .02
❑ 163 QMJHL Action .10 .05
❑ 164 QMJHL Action .10 .05
❑ 165 Checklist Card .05 .02
❑ 166 Checklist Card .05 .02
❑ 167 QMJHL Action .10 .05
❑ 168 QMJHL Action .10 .05
❑ 169 Pierre Fillon .10 .05
❑ 170 Yanick Degrace .10 .05
❑ 171 Paul Daigneault .10 .05
❑ 172 Stacy Dellaire .10 .05
❑ 173 Steve Searles .10 .05
❑ 174 Todd Gillingham .10 .05
❑ 175 Yves Sarault .25 .11
❑ 176 Jason Downey .10 .05
❑ 177 Paul Brousseau .15 .07
❑ 178 Raymond Delarosbi .10 .05
❑ 179 Yvan Corbin .10 .05
❑ 180 Gaston Drapeau .10 .05
❑ 181 Celebration .10 .05
❑ 182 Reginald Brezeault .10 .05
❑ 183 Eric Lafrance .10 .05
❑ 184 Martin Lavalle .10 .05
❑ 185 Sebastein Lavallere .10 .05
❑ 186 Martin Lefebvre .10 .05
❑ 187 Richard Hamelin .10 .05
❑ 188 Eric Beauvois .10 .05
❑ 189 Hughes Mongeon .15 .07
❑ 190 Alaine Cole .10 .05
❑ 191 Eric Desrochers .10 .05
❑ 192 Eric Joyal .10 .05
❑ 193 Steve Dortigny .10 .05
❑ 194 Fredrick Lefebvre .10 .05
❑ 195 Patrick Hebert .10 .05
❑ 196 Johnny Lorenzo .10 .05
❑ 197 Sylvain Cornier .10 .05
❑ 198 QMJHL Action .10 .05
❑ 199 Dave Morissette .10 .05
❑ 200 Yanick Dupre .15 .07
❑ 201 Eric Marcoux .10 .05
❑ 202 Bruno Ducharme .10 .05
❑ 203 Martin Caron .10 .05
❑ 204 Yves Meunier .10 .05
❑ 205 Eric Bissonette .10 .05
❑ 206 Jason Underhill .10 .05
❑ 207 Dave Belliveau .10 .05
❑ 208 Steve Lapointe .10 .05
❑ 209 Dean Melanson .10 .05
❑ 210 Trevor Dehaime .10 .05
❑ 211 Jacques Leblanc .10 .05
❑ 212 Normand Pacquet .10 .05
❑ 213 Huges Laliberte .10 .05
❑ 214 Craig Prior .10 .05
❑ 215 Patrick Labrecque .50 .23
❑ 216 Patrick Cloutier .10 .05
❑ 217 Michael Bazinet .10 .05
❑ 218 Christian Proulx .15 .07
❑ 219 QMJHL Action .10 .05
❑ 220 Charles Poulin .20 .09
❑ 221 Christian Larivierre .10 .05
❑ 222 Martin Brodeur 6.00 2.70
❑ 223 Yanick Lemay .10 .05
❑ 224 Dennis Leblanc .10 .05
❑ 225 Francois Groleau .20 .09
❑ 226 Pierre Sevigny .25 .11
❑ 227 Pierre Allard .10 .05
❑ 228 Craig Martin .20 .09
❑ 229 Karl Dykhuis .35 .16
❑ 230 Etienne Lavoie .10 .05
❑ 231 Stan Malanson .10 .05
❑ 232 Dominic Rheaume .15 .07
❑ 233 Mario Nobili .20 .09
❑ 234 Martin Gendron .50 .23
❑ 235 Stephane Menard .10 .05
❑ 236 David St.Pierre .20 .09
❑ 237 Yan Arsenault .20 .09
❑ 238 Norman Flynn .05 .02
❑ 239 QMJHL Action .10 .05
❑ 240 David Chouinard .10 .05
❑ 241 Robert Guilliet .15 .07
❑ 242 Martin Lajeunesse .10 .05
❑ 243 Nichol Cloutier .10 .05
❑ 244 Joel Brouchard .10 .05
❑ 245 Donald Brashear .35 .16
❑ 246 Sebastein Tremblay .10 .05
❑ 247 Dominique Grandmaison .10 .05
❑ 248 Nicolas Lefebvre .15 .07
❑ 249 Joseph Napolitano .10 .05
❑ 250 Marc Savard .10 .05
❑ 251 Alain Gauthier .15 .07
❑ 252 Patrick Cole .10 .05
❑ 253 Richard Aimonette .10 .05
❑ 254 Martin Laitre .10 .05
❑ 255 Carl Lamonthe .10 .05
❑ 256 QMJHL Action .10 .05
❑ 257 Andre Durocher .10 .05
❑ 258 Jocelyn Martel .10 .05
❑ 259 Jeanot Ferland .10 .05
❑ 260 Claude Savoie .10 .05
❑ 262 Denis Beauchamp .10 .05
❑ 263 Jean-Francois Gagnon .10 .05
❑ 264 Andre Boulaine .10 .05
❑ 265 Paul-Emile Exantus .10 .05
❑ 266 Danny Nolet .10 .05
❑ 267 Jean Lebreau .10 .05
❑ 268 Claude Barthe .10 .05

## 1990-91 7th Inn. Sketch WHL

The 7th Inning Sketch WHL Hockey set contains 347 standard-size cards. The front features a full color photo, framed by different color borders. The player's position appears in a star at the lower left-hand corner, with his name and "WHL" in the bar below the picture. The back has another color photo, with biographical information and career summary in a box running the length of the card. Players from the following teams are represented in this set: Seattle Thunderbirds (1-22, 187), Medicine Hat Tigers (23-44), Swift Current Broncos (45-72) Saskatoon Blades (73-95), Tri-City Americans (96-120), Lethbridge Hurricanes (121-141), Moose Jaw Warriors (142-163), Regina Pats (164-186), Spokane Chiefs (188-213), Brandon Wheat Kings (214-236), Victoria Cougars (237-260), Prince Albert Raiders (261-283), Kamloops Blazers (284-309), and Portland Winter Hawks (310-333). First round picks (1991 NHL Draft) in this set include Pat Falloon (2), Scott Niedermayer (3), Richard Matvichuk (8), Tyler Wright (12), Brent Bilodeau (17), and Dean McAmmond (22). First round picks (1992 NHL Draft) in this set include Mike Rathje (3), David Cooper (11), Jason Bowen (15), Jason Smith (18), and David Wilkie (20). The best known player is 1991 third-rounder, Chris Osgood. A factory set, (a numbered edition of 6,000), was produced and marketed separately. Card number 120 was never issued.

| | MINT | NRMT |
|---|---|---|
| COMPLETE SET (347) | 18.00 | 8.00 |
| COMPLETE FACT.SET (347) | 20.00 | 9.00 |
| COMMON CARD (1-348) | .05 | .02 |

❑ 1 Brent Bilodeau .35 .16
❑ 2 Craig Chapman .10 .05
❑ 3 Jeff Jubenville .10 .05
❑ 4 Al Kinisky .10 .05
❑ 5 Kevin Malgunas .10 .05
❑ 6 Andy MacIntyre .10 .05
❑ 7 Darren McAusland .15 .07
❑ 8 Mike Seaton .10 .05
❑ 9 Turner Stevenson .50 .23
❑ 10 Lindsay Valis .15 .07
❑ 11 Dave Wilkie .25 .11
❑ 12 Jesse Wilson .10 .05
❑ 13 Dody Wood .20 .09
❑ 14 Bradley Zavisha .15 .07
❑ 15 Vince Boe .10 .05
❑ 16 Scott Davis .10 .05
❑ 17 Troy Hyatt .10 .05
❑ 18 Trevor Pennock .10 .05
❑ 19 Corey Schwab .35 .16
❑ 20 Scott Bellefontaine .15 .07
❑ 21 Travis Kelln .10 .05
❑ 22 Peter Anholt CO/GM .05 .02
❑ 23 Sonny Mignacca UER .20 .09
❑ 24 Chris Osgood 8.00 3.60
❑ 25 Murray Garbutt .10 .05
❑ 26 Kalvin Knibbs .10 .05
❑ 27 Jason Krywulak .10 .05
❑ 28 Jason Miller .10 .05
❑ 29 Rob Niedermayer 2.00 .90
❑ 30 Clayton Norris .10 .05
❑ 31 Jason Prosofsky .15 .07
❑ 32 Dana Rieder .10 .05
❑ 33 Kevin Riehl .10 .05
❑ 34 Tyler Romanchuk .10 .05
❑ 35 Dave Shute .10 .05
❑ 36 Lorne Toews .10 .05
❑ 37 Scott Townsend .10 .05
❑ 38 David Cooper .15 .07
❑ 39 Jon Duval .10 .05
❑ 40 Dan Kordic .35 .16
❑ 41 Mike Rathje .50 .23
❑ 42 Tim Bothwell CO .10 .05
❑ 43 Brent Thompson .25 .11
❑ 44 Jeff Knight .10 .05
❑ 45 Van Burgess .10 .05
❑ 46 Kimbi Daniels .15 .07
❑ 47 Curtis Friesen .10 .05
❑ 48 Todd Holt .15 .07
❑ 49 Blake Knox .10 .05
❑ 50 Trent McCleary .10 .05
❑ 51 Mark McFarlane .10 .05
❑ 52 Eddie Patterson .10 .05
❑ 53 Lloyd Pellitier .10 .05
❑ 54 Geoff Sanderson 2.50 1.10
❑ 55 Andrew Schneider .10 .05
❑ 56 Tyler Wright .25 .11
❑ 57 Joel Dyck .10 .05
❑ 58 Len MacAusland .10 .05
❑ 59 Evan Marble .10 .05
❑ 60 David Podlubny .10 .05
❑ 61 Kurt Seher .10 .05
❑ 62 Jason Smith .10 .05
❑ 63 Justin Burke .10 .05
❑ 64 Kelly Thiessen .10 .05
❑ 65 Todd Esselmont .10 .05
❑ 66 Graham James CO/GM .25 .11
❑ 67 Chris Herperger .15 .07
❑ 68 Mark McCoy .10 .05
❑ 69 Dean Malkoc .25 .11
❑ 70 Dennis Sproxton .10 .05
❑ 71 Centennial Civic Center .10 .05
❑ 72 Kimbi Daniels .15 .07
❑ 73 Shane Calder .10 .05
❑ 74 Mark Franks .15 .07
❑ 75 Greg Leahy .10 .05
❑ 76 Dean Rambo .10 .05
❑ 77 Scott Scissons .15 .07
❑ 78 David Struch .10 .05
❑ 79 Derek Tibbatts .10 .05
❑ 80 Shawn Yakimishyn .10 .05
❑ 81 Trent Coghill .10 .05
❑ 82 Robert Lelacheur .10 .05
❑ 83 Richard Matvichuk .75 .35
❑ 84 Mark Raiter .10 .05
❑ 85 Trevor Sherban .10 .05
❑ 86 Mark Wotton .25 .11
❑ 87 Cam Moon .10 .05
❑ 88 Trevor Robins .10 .05
❑ 89 Jeff Buchanan .10 .05
❑ 90 Ryan Strain .10 .05
❑ 91 Tim Cox .10 .05
❑ 92 Terry Ruskowski CO .15 .07
❑ 93 Saskatchewan Place .10 .05
❑ 94 Darin Bader .10 .05
❑ 95 Gaetan Blouin .10 .05
❑ 96 Rick Kozuback CO/GM .05 .02
❑ 97 Jason Bowen .10 .05
❑ 98 Fran Deferenza .10 .05
❑ 99 Terry Degner .15 .07
❑ 100 Devin Derksen .10 .05
❑ 101 Martin Svetlik .10 .05
❑ 102 Jeremy Warring .10 .05
❑ 103 Corey Jones .10 .05
❑ 104 Dean Tiltgen UER .10 .05
❑ 105 Ryan Fujita .20 .09
❑ 106 Jeff Fancy .10 .05
❑ 107 Terry Virtue .10 .05
❑ 108 Dennis Pinfold .10 .05
❑ 109 Kyle Reeves .15 .07
❑ 110 Steve McNutt UER .10 .05
❑ 111 Todd Klassen .15 .07
❑ 112 Darren Hastman .10 .05
❑ 113 Bill Lindsay .50 .23
❑ 114A Brian Sakic ERR .20 .09
(Misspelled Buan on card front)
❑ 114B Brian Sakic COR .20 .09
❑ 115 Dan Sherstenka .10 .05
❑ 116 Don Blishen .10 .05
❑ 117 Jason Marshall .20 .09
❑ 118 Dean Zayonce .10 .05
❑ 119 Brad Loring .10 .05
❑ 121 Darcy Austin UER .10 .05
❑ 122 Darcy Werenka .20 .09
❑ 123 Shane Peacock .15 .07
❑ 124 Rob Hartnell UER .10 .05
❑ 125 Brad Zimmer .10 .05
❑ 126 Allan Egeland .10 .05
❑ 127 Brad Rubachuk .10 .05
❑ 128 Jamie Pushor .50 .23
❑ 129 Jamie McLennan UER .75 .35
❑ 130 Lance Burns .10 .05
❑ 131 Ryan Smith .10 .05
❑ 132 Jason McBain .10 .05
❑ 133 Duane Maruschak UER .10 .05
❑ 134 Kevin St.Jacques .10 .05
❑ 135 Jason Sorochan .10 .05
❑ 136 Jason Widmer .20 .09
❑ 137 Bob Loucks CO .10 .05
❑ 138 Jason Ruff .15 .07
❑ 139 Pat Pylypuik .10 .05
❑ 140 Scott Adair .10 .05
❑ 141 Radek Sip .15 .07
❑ 142 Russ West .10 .05
❑ 143 Scott Thomas .15 .07
❑ 144 Kent Staniforth .10 .05
❑ 145 Travis Thiessen .10 .05
❑ 146 Mark Hussey .10 .05
❑ 147 Kevin Masters .10 .05
❑ 148 Todd Johnson .10 .05
❑ 149 Bob Loucks .10 .05
❑ 150A Rob Reimer ERR .15 .07
(Numbered 149 on back)
❑ 150B Rob Reimer COR .15 .07
❑ 151 Jeff Petruic .15 .07
❑ 152 Chris Schmidt .15 .07
❑ 153 Scott Barnstable .10 .05
❑ 154 Ian Layton .10 .05
❑ 155 Kevin Smyth .20 .09
❑ 156 Kim Deck .10 .05
❑ 157 Jason White .10 .05
❑ 158 Peter Cox .10 .05
❑ 159 Jeff Calvert UER .10 .05
❑ 160 Paul Dyck UER .15 .07
❑ 161 Derek Kletzel .10 .05
❑ 162 Jason Fitzsimmons UER .15 .07
❑ 163 Darcy Jerome .10 .05
❑ 164 Hal Christiansen .10 .05
❑ 165 Terry Hollinger .15 .07
❑ 166 Mike Risdale .15 .07
❑ 167 Jamie Heward .10 .05
❑ 168 Louis Dumont .10 .05
❑ 169 Cory Dosdall .10 .05
❑ 170 Terry Bendera .10 .05
❑ 171 Jamie Hayden .10 .05
❑ 172 Kelly Chotowetz .10 .05

❑ 173 Brad Scott .10 .05
❑ 174 Jeff Shantz .50 .23
❑ 175 Kelly Markwart .15 .07
❑ 176 Gary Pearce .10 .05
❑ 177 Kerry Biette .10 .05
❑ 178 Jamie Splett .10 .05
❑ 179 Frank Kovacs .10 .05
❑ 180 Greg Pankewicz .15 .07
❑ 181 Colin Ruck .10 .05
❑ 182 Brad Tippett CO .15 .07
❑ 183 Dusty Imoo .20 .09
❑ 184 Derek Eberle .10 .05
❑ 185 Heath Weenk .15 .07
❑ 186 Mike Sillinger .35 .16
❑ 187 Erin Thornton .10 .05
❑ 188 Mike Chrun .10 .05
❑ 189 Pat Falloon .75 .35
❑ 190 Bobby House UER .20 .09
❑ 191 Mike Jickling .10 .05
❑ 192 Trevor Tovall UER .15 .07
❑ 193 Steve Junker .15 .07
❑ 194 Shane Maitland .10 .05
❑ 195 Chris Lafreniere .10 .05
❑ 196 Frank Evans .10 .05
❑ 197 Jon Klemm .50 .23
❑ 198 Shawn Dietrich UER .15 .07
❑ 199 Dennis Saharchuk UER .15 .07
❑ 200 Mark Woolf .10 .05
❑ 201 Ray Whitney .35 .16
❑ 202 Scott Bailey .50 .23
❑ 203 Mark Ruark .10 .05
❑ 204 Brent Thurston .10 .05
❑ 205 Dan Faassen .10 .05
❑ 206 Kerry Toporowski .10 .05
❑ 207 Des Christopher .15 .07
❑ 208 Geoff Grandberg .10 .05
❑ 209 Bryan Maxwell CO .15 .07
❑ 210 Cam Danyluk .10 .05
❑ 211 Bram Vanderkracht .10 .05
❑ 212 Calvin Thudium .10 .05
❑ 213 Mark Szoke UER .15 .07
❑ 214 Kelly McCrimmon CO/GM .10 .05
❑ 215 Kevin Robertson UER .15 .07
❑ 216A Brian Purdy ERR .10 .05
(Misspelled Puroy on card front)
❑ 216B Brian Purdy COR .15 .07
❑ 217 Hardy Sauter .10 .05
❑ 218 Dwayne Gylywoychuk .10 .05
❑ 219 Bart Cote .10 .05
❑ 220 Merv Priest .10 .05
❑ 221 Jeff Hoad .10 .05
❑ 222 Glen Gulutzan .10 .05
❑ 223 Johan Skillgard .10 .05
❑ 224 Byron Penstock .10 .05
❑ 225A Mike Vandenberghe ERR .15 .07
(Misspelled Vandenberghe on card front)
❑ 225B Mike Vandenberghe COR .15 .07
❑ 226 Trevor Kidd 1.50 .70
❑ 227 Dan Kopec .10 .05
❑ 228 Greg Hutchings .10 .05
❑ 229 Chris Constant .10 .05
❑ 230 Glen Webster .10 .05
❑ 231 Rob Puchniak .10 .05
❑ 232 Calvin Flint .10 .05
❑ 233 Stuart Scantlebury .10 .05
❑ 234 Jason White .10 .05
❑ 235 Gary Audette .10 .05
❑ 236 Kevin Schmalz .10 .05
❑ 237 Dwayne Newman .10 .05
❑ 238 Chris Catellier .10 .05
❑ 239 Todd Harris .10 .05
❑ 240 Mike Shemko .10 .05
❑ 241 John Badduke .10 .05
❑ 242 Mark Cipriano .10 .05
❑ 243 Brad Bagu .10 .05
❑ 244 Ross Harris .10 .05
❑ 245 Dino Caputo .10 .05
❑ 246 Cam Bristow .10 .05
❑ 247 Jarret Zukiwsky UER .10 .05
❑ 248 Jason Knox .10 .05
❑ 249 Gerry St.Cyr .10 .05
❑ 250 Larry Woo .10 .05
❑ 251 Jason Peters .10 .05
❑ 252 Shane Stangby .10 .05
❑ 253 Dave McMillen .10 .05
❑ 254 Colin Gregor UER .10 .05
❑ 255 Steve Passmore .50 .23
❑ 256 Shayne Green UER .15 .07
❑ 257 Kevin Koopman .10 .05
❑ 258 Larry Watkins UER .10 .05
❑ 259 Scott Fukami UER .15 .07
❑ 260 Rick Hopper CO .05 .02
❑ 261 Laurie Billeck .10 .05
❑ 262 Rob Daum CO/GM UER .05 .02
❑ 263 Mark Stowe .10 .05
❑ 264 Curtis Regnier .20 .09
❑ 265 David Neilson .10 .05
❑ 266 Brian Pellerin .10 .05
❑ 267 Dean McAmmond .35 .16
❑ 268 Darren Van Impe .35 .16
❑ 269 Troy Neumeier .10 .05
❑ 270 Mike Langen .10 .05
❑ 271 Dan Kesa .25 .11
❑ 272 Travis Laycock .10 .05
❑ 273 Scott Allison .20 .09
❑ 274 Jeff Gorman .10 .05
❑ 275 Lee J. Leslie .15 .07
❑ 276 Jason Kwiatkowski .10 .05
❑ 277 Donevan Hextall UER .20 .09
❑ 278 Shane Zulyniak .10 .05
❑ 279 Darren Perkins .10 .05
❑ 280 Chad Seibel .10 .05
❑ 281 Jeff Nelson .20 .09
❑ 282 Troy Hjertas .10 .05
❑ 283 Jamie Linden .20 .09
❑ 284 Zac Boyer .20 .09
❑ 285 Jarret Bousquet .10 .05
❑ 286 Steven Yule .10 .05
❑ 287 Tommy Renney CO UER .25 .11
(Renny on back)
❑ 288 Lance Johnson .10 .05
❑ 289 Scott Niedermayer 1.50 .70
❑ 290 Ryan Harrison .10 .05
❑ 291 Ed Patterson .25 .11
❑ 292 Jeff Watchorn .10 .05
❑ 293 Cal McGowan .10 .05
❑ 294 Dale Masson .10 .05
❑ 295 Joey Mittelsteadt UER .10 .05
❑ 296 Scott Loucks .10 .05
❑ 297 Shea Esselmont .10 .05
❑ 298 Craig Bonner .10 .05
❑ 299 Mike Mathers .10 .05
❑ 300 Fred Hettle .10 .05
❑ 301 Craig Lyons .10 .05
❑ 302 Murray Duval .10 .05
❑ 303 Jamie Barnes .10 .05
❑ 304 Bryan Gourlie .10 .05
❑ 305 Chad Berezniuk .10 .05
❑ 306 Corey Hirsch 2.00 .90
❑ 307 Darryl Sydor .75 .35
❑ 308 Jarrett Deuling .15 .07
❑ 309 Cory Stock .10 .05
❑ 310 Chris Rowland .10 .05
❑ 311 Mike Ruark .10 .05
❑ 312 Steve Konowalchuk .75 .35
❑ 313 Jeff Sebastian .10 .05
❑ 314 Brandon Smith .10 .05
❑ 315 Greg Gatto .10 .05
❑ 316 Brad Harrison .10 .05
❑ 317 Brantt Myhres .25 .11
❑ 318 Jamie Black .15 .07
❑ 319 Colin Foley .10 .05
❑ 320 Cam Danyluk .10 .05
❑ 321 Dean Dorchak .10 .05
❑ 322 Ryan Slemko .10 .05
❑ 323 Kim Deck .10 .05
❑ 324 Kelly Harris .10 .05
❑ 325 Murray Bokenfohr .10 .05
❑ 326 Dean Intwert .10 .05
❑ 327 Dennis Saharchuk UER .10 .05
❑ 328 Shane Seiker UER .10 .05
❑ 329 Terry Virtue .10 .05
❑ 330 Josh Erdman .10 .05
❑ 331 Layne Roland .10 .05
❑ 332 Michel Michon .10 .05
❑ 333 Scott Mydan UER .10 .05
❑ 334 Brandon Wheat Kings .05 .02
❑ 335 Moose Jaw Warriors .05 .02
❑ 336 Swift Current Broncos .05 .02
❑ 337 Regina Pats UER .05 .02
❑ 338 Saskatoon Blades .05 .02
❑ 339 Medicine Hat Tigers .05 .02
❑ 340 The Goalmouth .05 .02
❑ 341 Portland Winter Hawks .05 .02
❑ 342 Kamloops Blazers UER .05 .02
❑ 343 Victoria Cougars .05 .02
❑ 344 Tri City Americans .05 .02
❑ 345 Spokane Chiefs .05 .02
❑ 346 Seattle Thunderbirds .05 .02
❑ 347 Lethbridge Hurricanes .05 .02
❑ 348 Prince Albert Raiders .05 .02

## 1991 7th Inn. Sketch CHL Award Winners

This 30-card boxed standard-size set features Canadian Hockey League Award Winners. Each box has on its back a checklist and the set serial number. The cards feature action color player photos with gray borders against a black card face. The player's specific achievement is printed in gray in the black margin at the top. His name and team appear in white at the bottom. The horizontal backs show a close-up player picture on one half of the card. A white panel of the same size takes up the rest of the card face and features the player's name, achievement, and sponsor logos. The picture and panel are outlined by a thin black line.

| | MINT | NRMT |
|---|---|---|
| COMPLETE SET (30) | 10.00 | 4.50 |
| COMMON CARD (1-30) | .20 | .09 |

❑ 1 Eric Lindros 2.50 1.10
❑ 2 Dale Craigwell .25 .11
❑ 3 Nathan Lafayette .35 .16
❑ 4 Chris Snell .25 .11
❑ 5 Cory Stillman .35 .16
❑ 6 Mike Torchia .25 .11
❑ 7 George Burnett .20 .09
❑ 8 Eric Lindros 2.50 1.10
❑ 9 Sherwood Bassin .20 .09
❑ 10 Eric Lindros 2.50 1.10
❑ 11 Scott Niedermayer .50 .23
❑ 12 Pat Falloon .35 .16
❑ 13 Scott Niedermayer .50 .23
❑ 14 Darryl Sydor .50 .23
❑ 15 Donevan Hextall .20 .09
❑ 16 Jamie McLennan .35 .16
❑ 17 Tom Renney .25 .11
❑ 18 Frank Evans .20 .09
❑ 19 Bob Brown .20 .09
❑ 20 Ray Whitney .25 .11
❑ 21 Phillippe Boucher .35 .16
❑ 22 Yanic Perreault .35 .16
❑ 23 Benoit Larose .20 .09
❑ 24 Patrice Brisebois .35 .16
❑ 25 Phillippe Boucher .35 .16
❑ 26 Felix Potvin 1.00 .45
❑ 27 Joe Canale .20 .09
❑ 28 Christian Lariviere .20 .09
❑ 29 Roland Janelle .20 .09
❑ 30 Yanic Perreault .35 .16

## 1991 7th Inn. Sketch Memorial Cup

The 1991 7th Inn. Sketch Memorial Cup Hockey set captures the four teams that participated in the Canadian junior hockey championship, with one team each from the OHL and WHL, and two from the QMJHL (the host league). The cards measure the standard size and feature on the fronts color action player photos enclosed by silver borders. The upper right and lower left corners are cut off to permit space for the CHL and '91 Memorial Cup logos respectively. The player's name in the bottom silver border rounds out the card face. The backs carry a second color player photo, with the card number, player's name, and biographical information in a box alongside the picture. The set is skip-numbered due to the fact that several cards were withdrawn from the set after only a few sets had been released. These 17 card numbers are 21, 36 (Rob Dykeman), 96 (Eric Lindros), 106 (Pat Peake), 107 (Steve Staios), 110 (Alex Stojanov), 111 (Glen Murray), 113 (Jason Dawe), 114 (Nathan Lafayette), 116 (Guy Leveque), 118 (Shayne Antoski), 119 (Eric Lindros), 120 (Dennis Purdie), 121 (Terry Chitaroni), and 124 (Jamie Matthews).

| | MINT | NRMT |
|---|---|---|
| COMPLETE SET (130) | 125.00 | 55.00 |
| COMPLETE SHORT SET (113) | 15.00 | 6.75 |
| COMMON CARD (1-130) | .15 | .07 |
| COMMON CARD SP | 2.50 | 1.10 |

❑ 1 Mike Lenarduzzi .25 .11
❑ 2 Kevin Hodson 1.50 .70
❑ 3 OHL Action .15 .07
Sault Ste. Marie vs. Oshawa
❑ 4 Bob Boughner .25 .11
❑ 5 Adam Foote .75 .35
❑ 6 Brad Tiley .15 .07
❑ 7 Brian Goudie .15 .07
❑ 8 Wade Whitten .15 .07
❑ 9 Jason Denomme .15 .07
❑ 10 David Matsos .15 .07
❑ 11 Rick Kowalsky .15 .07
❑ 12 Jarret Reid .15 .07
❑ 13 Perry Pappas .15 .07
❑ 14 Tom MacDonald .15 .07
❑ 15 Mike DeCoff .15 .07
❑ 16 Joe Busillo .15 .07
❑ 17 Denny Lambert .25 .11
❑ 18 Mark Matier .15 .07
❑ 19 Shaun Imber .15 .07
❑ 20 Ralph Intranuovo .25 .11
❑ 21 Not Known SP 2.50 1.10
❑ 22 Tony Iob .15 .07
❑ 23 Colin Miller .15 .07
❑ 24 Ted Nolan .25 .11
❑ 25 Sylvain Rodrigue .15 .07
❑ 26 Felix Potvin 4.00 1.80
❑ 27 Martin Lavallee .15 .07
❑ 28 Eric Brule .15 .07
❑ 29 Steve Larouche .15 .07
❑ 30 Michel St-Jacques .15 .07
❑ 31 Patrick Clement .15 .07
❑ 32 Patrick Bisaillon .15 .07
❑ 33A Checklist 62-131 SP 2.50 1.10
❑ 33B Checklist 62-131 .25 .11
(Withdrawn numbers omitted)
❑ 34 Gilles Bouchard .15 .07
❑ 35 Eric Rochette .15 .07
❑ 36 Rob Dykeman SP 2.50 1.10
❑ 37A Checklist 1-61 SP 2.50 1.10
❑ 37B Checklist 1-61 .25 .11
(Withdrawn numbers omitted)
❑ 38 Patrice Martineau .15 .07
❑ 39 Danny Beauregard .15 .07
❑ 40 Francois Belanger .15 .07
❑ 41 Sebastien Parent .25 .11
❑ 42 Martin Gagne .15 .07
❑ 43 Stephane Charbonneau .15 .07
❑ 44 Martin Beaupre .15 .07
❑ 45 Daniel Paradis .15 .07
❑ 46 Joe Canale .15 .07
❑ 47 OHL Action .15 .07
Sault Ste. Marie vs. Oshawa
❑ 48 Jubilation .15 .07
❑ 49 Steve Lupien .15 .07
❑ 50 Pierre Gagnon .15 .07
❑ 51 Alexandre Legault .15 .07
❑ 52 Martin Charrois .15 .07
❑ 53 Eric Dandenault .15 .07
❑ 54 Denis Chasse .25 .11
❑ 55 Guy Lehoux .15 .07
❑ 56 Ian Laperriere .50 .23
❑ 57 Hugo Proulx .15 .07
❑ 58 Dave Whittom .15 .07
❑ 59 Yanick Dupre UER .25 .11
❑ 60 Eric Plante .15 .07
❑ 61 Stephane Desjardins .35 .16
❑ 62 Patrice Brisebois .50 .23
❑ 63 Rene Corbet .75 .35
❑ 64 Marc Savard .15 .07
❑ 65 Claude Jutras Jr. .15 .07
❑ 66 David Pekarek .15 .07
❑ 67 Roger Larche UER .15 .07
(Name misspelled Larohe on front)
❑ 68 Dave Paquet .25 .11
❑ 69 Eric Meloche .15 .07
❑ 70 CHL Action .15 .07
Spokane vs. Lethbridge
❑ 71 Celebration .35 .16
Ed Chynoweth PRES
Jon Klemm
❑ 72 Felix Potvin MVP 2.00 .90
❑ 73 Scott Bailey .75 .35
❑ 74 Trevor Kidd .75 .35
❑ 75 Chris Lafreniere .15 .07
❑ 76 Frank Evans .15 .07
❑ 77 Jon Klemm .50 .23
❑ 78 Brent Thurston .15 .07
❑ 79 Jamie McLennan .50 .23
❑ 80 Steve Junker .15 .07
❑ 81 Mark Szoke .15 .07
❑ 82 Ray Whitney .35 .16
❑ 83 Geoff Grandberg .15 .07
❑ 84 Cam Danyluk .15 .07
❑ 85 Kerry Toporowski .15 .07
❑ 86 Trevor Tovell .15 .07
❑ 87 Pat Falloon .75 .35
❑ 88 Bram Vanderkracht .15 .07
❑ 89 Mike Jickling .15 .07
❑ 90 Murray Garbutt .15 .07
❑ 91 Calvin Thudium .15 .07
❑ 92 Mark Woolf .15 .07
❑ 93 Shane Maitland .15 .07
❑ 94 Bart Cote .15 .07
❑ 95 Bryan Maxwell .15 .07
❑ 96 Eric Lindros SP 40.00 18.00
❑ 97 Scott Niedermayer 1.00 .45
❑ 98 Patrick Poulin .25 .11
❑ 99 Brent Bilodeau .35 .16
❑ 100 Pat Falloon .75 .35
❑ 101 Darcy Werenka .25 .11
❑ 102 Martin Lapointe .75 .35
❑ 103 Philippe Boucher .50 .23
❑ 104 Jeff Nelson .25 .11
❑ 105 Rene Corbet .75 .35
❑ 106 Pat Peake SP 3.00 1.35
❑ 107 Steve Staios SP 2.50 1.10
❑ 108 Richard Matvichuk .50 .23
❑ 109 Dean McAmmond .35 .16
❑ 110 Alex Stojanov SP 2.50 1.10
❑ 111 Glen Murray SP 4.00 1.80
❑ 112 Tyler Wright .25 .11
❑ 113 Jason Dawe SP 3.00 1.35
❑ 114 Nathan Lafayette SP 2.50 1.10
❑ 115 Yanic Perreault .75 .35
❑ 116 Guy Leveque SP 2.50 1.10
❑ 117 Darren Van Impe .50 .23
❑ 118 Shawn Antoski SP 2.50 1.10
❑ 119 Eric Lindros SP 40.00 18.00
❑ 120 Dennis Purdie SP 2.50 1.10
❑ 121 Terry Chitaroni SP 2.50 1.10
❑ 122 Jamie Pushor .50 .23
❑ 123 Chris Osgood 4.00 1.80
❑ 124 Jamie Matthews SP 2.50 1.10
❑ 125 Yves Sarault .15 .07
❑ 126 Yanic Dupre UER .25 .11
❑ 127 Brad Zimmer .15 .07
❑ 128 Copps Coliseum .15 .07
❑ 129 Jason Widmer .25 .11
❑ 130 Marc Savard .15 .07

## 1991-92 7th Inn. Sketch OHL

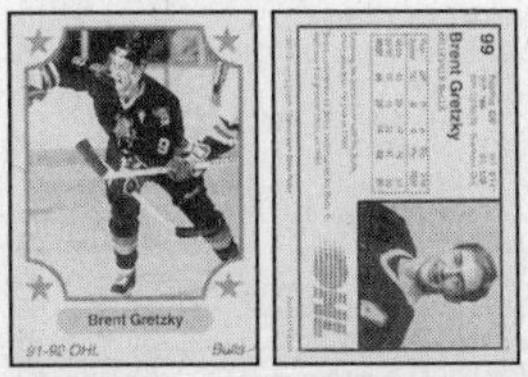

This 384-card standard-size set was issued by 7th Inning Sketch and features players of the Ontario Hockey League. The production run was limited to 9,000 factory sets, with each set individually numbered "X of 9,000." On a white card face, the fronts feature color action player photos enclosed by different color frames. The corners of the picture are cut out to permit space for gold stars. The player's name, the year and league, and the team name appear below the picture. In a horizontal format, the backs have biography, statistics, and player profile in French and English. The cards are numbered on the back and checklisted below according to teams as follows: Cornwall Royals (1-26), Detroit Ambassadors (27-50), North Bay Centennials (51-73), Kitchener Rangers (0/74-98), Belleville Bulls (99-122), Peterborough Petes(123-147), Oshawa Generals (148-172), Windsor Spitfires (173-196), Niagara Falls Thunder (197-221), Kingston Frontenacs (222-243), Sudbury Wolves (244-268), Owen Sound Platers (269-290), Ottawa 67's (291-312), Sault Ste. Marie Greyhounds (313-339), Guelph Storm (340-360), and London Knights (361-383). Cards numbered 98, 147, 293 and 360 were never produced.

| | MINT | NRMT |
|---|---|---|
| COMPLETE SET (384) | 15.00 | 6.75 |
| COMMON CARD (1-383) | .05 | .02 |

❑ 1 John Slaney .20 .09
❑ 2 Jason Meloche .10 .05
❑ 3 Mark DeSantis .10 .05
❑ 4 Richard Raymond .10 .05
❑ 5 Dave Lemay .10 .05
❑ 6 Matt McGuffin .10 .05
❑ 7 Sam Oliveira .10 .05
❑ 8 Jeremy Stevenson .15 .07
❑ 9 Todd Walker .10 .05
❑ 10 Jean-Alain Schneider .10 .05
❑ 11 Guy Leveque .15 .07
❑ 12 Shayne Gaffar .10 .05
❑ 13 Mike Prokopec .15 .07
❑ 14 Nathan LaFayette .20 .09
❑ 15 Larry Courville .25 .11
❑ 16 Chris Clancy .10 .05
❑ 17 Tom Nemeth .15 .07
❑ 18 Jeff Reid .10 .05
❑ 19 Ilpo Kauhanen .10 .05
❑ 20 Rob Dykeman .15 .07
❑ 21 Rival Fullum .15 .07
❑ 22 Ryan VandenBussche .15 .07
❑ 23 Gordon Pell .15 .07
❑ 24 Paul Andrea UER .10 .05
Team affiliation says Generals; should say Royals
❑ 25 John Lovell CO UER .05 .02
Team affiliation says Generals; should say Royals
❑ 26 Alan Letang .10 .05
❑ 27 Chris Phelps .10 .05
❑ 28 John Wynne .10 .05
❑ 29 Rob Kinghan .10 .05
❑ 30 Glen Craig .10 .05
❑ 31 Eric Cairns .25 .11
❑ 32 John Pinches .10 .05
❑ 33 Todd Harvey .50 .23
❑ 34 Craig Fraser .10 .05
❑ 35 Pat Peake .35 .16
❑ 36 Chris Skoryna .10 .05
❑ 37 Bob Wren .15 .07
❑ 38 Chris Varga .10 .05
❑ 39 David Benn .10 .05
❑ 40 Mark Lawrence .15 .07
❑ 41 Jeff Kostuch .10 .05
❑ 42 J.D. Eaton .10 .05
❑ 43 Derek Etches .10 .05
❑ 44 Jeff Gardiner .10 .05
❑ 45 James Shea .10 .05
❑ 46 Brad Teichmann .10 .05
❑ 47 Jim Rutherford CO .15 .07
❑ 48 Derek Wilkinson .15 .07
❑ 49 OHL Action .10 .05
❑ 50 OHL Action .10 .05
❑ 51 Sandy Allan .15 .07
❑ 52 Ron Bertrand .10 .05
❑ 53 Brad Brown .25 .11
❑ 54 Dennis Bonvie .15 .07
❑ 55 Bradley Shepard .10 .05
❑ 56 Allan Cox .10 .05
❑ 57 Jack Williams .15 .07
❑ 58 Chad Penney .15 .07
❑ 59 Jason Firth .10 .05
❑ 60 Bill Lang .10 .05
❑ 61 Ryan Merritt .10 .05
❑ 62 Michael Burman .10 .05
❑ 63 Billy Wright .10 .05
❑ 64 Dave Szabo .10 .05
❑ 65 James Sheehan .10 .05
❑ 66 John Spoltore .10 .05
❑ 67 Paul Rushforth .10 .05
❑ 68 Jeff Shevalier .20 .09
❑ 69 Robert Thorpe .10 .05
❑ 70 Drake Berehowsky .20 .09
❑ 71 Patrick Barton .10 .05
❑ 72 Bert Templeton CO .15 .07
❑ 73 Wade Gibson .10 .05
❑ 74 C.J. Denomme UER .10 .05
Name spelled C. Jay on back
❑ 75 Mike Torchia .25 .11
❑ 76 Mike Polano .10 .05
❑ 77 Tony McCabe .10 .05

❑ 78 Chris Kraemer .10 .05
❑ 79 Tim Spitzig .10 .05
❑ 80 Trevor Gallant .10 .05
❑ 81 Yvan Corbin .10 .05
❑ 82 Norman Dezainde .15 .07
❑ 83 Marc Robillard .10 .05
❑ 84 Derek Gauthier .10 .05
❑ 85 Gib Tucker .10 .05
❑ 86 Paul McCallion .10 .05
❑ 87 Eric Manlow .15 .07
❑ 88 Jamie Caruso .15 .07
❑ 89 Gary Miller .10 .05
❑ 90 Jason Stevenson .10 .05
❑ 91 Shayne McCosh .10 .05
❑ 92 Jason Gladney .10 .05
❑ 93 Brad Barton .10 .05
❑ 94 Chris LiPuma .20 .09
❑ 95 Justin Cullen .10 .05
❑ 96 Bill Smith SCOUT .05 .02
❑ 97 Joe McDonnell CO .05 .02
❑ 99 Brent Gretzky .25 .11
❑ 100 Gairin Smith .10 .05
❑ 101 Blair Scott .10 .05
❑ 102 Daniel Godbout .10 .05
❑ 103 Dan Preston .10 .05
❑ 104 Ian Keiller .10 .05
❑ 105 Rick Marshall .10 .05
❑ 106 Aaron Morrison .10 .05
❑ 107 Dominic Belanger .10 .05
❑ 108 Kevin Brown .15 .07
❑ 109 Tony Cimellaro .10 .05
❑ 110 Larry Mavety CO .05 .02
❑ 111 Jake Grimes .15 .07
❑ 112 Greg Dreveny .10 .05
❑ 113 Darren McCarty .75 .35
❑ 114 Doug Doull .10 .05
❑ 115 Scott Boston .15 .07
❑ 116 Dale Chokan .10 .05
❑ 117 Darren Hurley .10 .05
❑ 118 Brian Mielko UER .10 .05
Card misnumbered 61
❑ 119 Richard Gallace UER .10 .05
Card misnumbered 65
❑ 120 Shayne Antoski .25 .11
❑ 121 Greg Bailey .10 .05
❑ 122 Keith Redmond .10 .05
❑ 123 Dick Todd CO .15 .07
❑ 124 Scott Turner .10 .05
❑ 125 Colin Wilson .10 .05
❑ 126 Mike Tomlinson .10 .05
❑ 127 Dale McTavish .10 .05
❑ 120 Chris Longo .10 .05
❑ 129 Chad Lang .25 .11
❑ 130 Brent Tully .15 .07
❑ 131 Shawn Heins .10 .05
❑ 132 Geordie Kinnear .15 .07
❑ 133 Jeff Walker .10 .05
❑ 134 Chris Pronger 3.00 1.35
❑ 135 Chad Grills .10 .05
❑ 136 Michael Harding .10 .05
❑ 137 Matt St.Germain .10 .05
❑ 138 Don O'Neill .10 .05
❑ 139 Dave Roche .50 .23
❑ 140 Doug Searle .10 .05
❑ 141 Bryan Gendron .10 .05
❑ 142 Kelly Vipond .15 .07
❑ 143 Andrew Verner .20 .09
❑ 144 Ryan Black .15 .07
❑ 145 Jason Dawe .25 .11
❑ 146 Jassen Cullimore .25 .11
❑ 148 Jason Arnott 2.50 1.10
❑ 149 Jan Benda .15 .07
❑ 150 Todd Bradley .10 .05
❑ 151 Markus Brunner .15 .07
❑ 152 Jason Campeau .10 .05
❑ 153 Mark Deazeley .10 .05
❑ 154 Matt Hoffman .10 .05
❑ 155 Scott Hollis .10 .05
❑ 156 Neil Iserhoff .10 .05
❑ 157 Darryl Lafrance .10 .05
❑ 158 B.J. MacPherson .15 .07
❑ 159 Troy Sweet .10 .05
❑ 160 Jason Weaver .10 .05
❑ 161 Stephane Yelle .50 .23
❑ 162 Trevor Burgess .10 .05
❑ 163 Joe Cook .10 .05
❑ 164 Jean-Paul Davis .10 .05
❑ 165 Brian Grieve .10 .05
❑ 166 Rob Leask .20 .09
❑ 167 Wade Simpson .10 .05
❑ 168 Kevin Spero .10 .05
❑ 169 Fred Brathwaite .20 .09
❑ 170 Mike Fountain .20 .09
❑ 171 Rick Cornacchia .15 .07
❑ 172 Checklist 1-98 .05 .02
❑ 173 Todd Warriner .50 .23
❑ 174 Reuben Castella .10 .05
❑ 175 Cory Stillman .50 .23
❑ 176 Steve Gibson .10 .05
❑ 177 Trent Cull .10 .05
❑ 178 John Copley .10 .05
❑ 179 Craig Binns .10 .05
❑ 180 Ryan O'Neill .10 .05
❑ 181 Matthew Mullin .15 .07
❑ 182 Todd Hunter .10 .05
❑ 183 Jason Stos .10 .05
❑ 184 Robert Frayn .10 .05
❑ 185 Leonard MacDonald .10 .05
❑ 186 Tom Sullivan .10 .05
❑ 187 Steve Smith .10 .05
❑ 188 Bill Bowler .25 .11
❑ 189 James Allison .10 .05
❑ 190 Kevin MacKay .10 .05
❑ 191 David Myles .10 .05
❑ 192 Wayne Maxner GM CO .10 .05
❑ 193 Dave Prpich CO UER .05 .02
Windsor on front;
should say Spitfires
❑ 194 Brady Blain .10 .05
❑ 195 Eric Stamp UER .10 .05
Windsor on front;
should say Spitfires
❑ 196 OHL Action .10 .05
❑ 197 David Babcock .10 .05
❑ 198 Brad Love .10 .05
❑ 199 Dale Junkin .10 .05
❑ 200 Rick Corriveau .10 .05
❑ 201 Scott Campbell .10 .05
❑ 202 Jason Clarke .10 .05
❑ 203 George Burnett .10 .05
❑ 204 Ryan Tocher .10 .05
❑ 205 Dennis Maxwell .10 .05
❑ 206 Greg Scott .10 .05
❑ 207 Mark Tardiff .10 .05
❑ 208 Neil Fewster .10 .05
❑ 209 Jason Coles .10 .05
❑ 210 Randy Hall CO .05 .02
❑ 211 Todd Simon .15 .07
❑ 212 Ethan Moreau 1.00 .45
❑ 213 Todd Wetzel .10 .05
❑ 214 Tom Moores .10 .05
❑ 215 Geoff Rawson .10 .05
❑ 216 Dan Krisko .10 .05
❑ 217 Manny Legace .35 .16
❑ 218 Kevin Brown .15 .07
❑ 219 Steve Staios .20 .09
❑ 220 Checklist 99-196 .05 .02
❑ 221 Checklist 197-290 .05 .02
❑ 222 Tony Bella .10 .05
❑ 223 Shawn Caplice .10 .05
❑ 224 Keli Corpse .15 .07
❑ 225 Chris Gratton 2.00 .90
❑ 226 Geoff Harris .10 .05
❑ 227 Cory Johnson .10 .05
❑ 228 Kevin King .10 .05
❑ 229 Justin Morrison .15 .07
❑ 230 Alastair Still .10 .05
❑ 231 Chris Scharf .10 .05
❑ 232 Brian Stagg .10 .05
❑ 233 Mike Dawson .10 .05
❑ 234 Rod Pasma .10 .05
❑ 235 Craig Rivet .35 .16
❑ 236 Dave Stewart .10 .05
❑ 237 John Vary .10 .05
❑ 238 Jason Wadel .10 .05
❑ 239 Joel Yates .10 .05
❑ 240 Marc Lamothe .10 .05
❑ 241 Pete McGlynn .10 .05
❑ 242 OHL Action .10 .05
❑ 243 Checklist 291-383 .05 .02
❑ 244 Joel Sandie .10 .05
❑ 245 Glen Murray .25 .11
❑ 246 Derek Armstrong .10 .05
❑ 247 Michael Peca .50 .23
❑ 248 Barry Young .10 .05
❑ 249 Bernie John .10 .05
❑ 250 Terry Chitaroni .15 .07
❑ 251 Jason Young .10 .05
❑ 252 Rod Hinks .10 .05
❑ 253 Michael Yeo .10 .05
❑ 254 Kyle Blacklock .10 .05
❑ 255 Dan Ryder .15 .07
❑ 256 Doug Mason CO .05 .02
❑ 257 Jamie Rivers .50 .23
❑ 258 Brandon Convery .20 .09
❑ 259 Barrie Moore .10 .05
❑ 260 Shawn Rivers .15 .07
❑ 261 Jamie Matthews .20 .09
❑ 262 Tim Favot .10 .05
❑ 263 Bob MacIsaac .10 .05
❑ 264 Sean Gagnon .10 .05
❑ 265 Ken MacKenzie GM CO .05 .02
❑ 266 George Dourion .10 .05
❑ 267 Brian MacKenzie .10 .05
❑ 268 Jason Zohil .10 .05
❑ 269 Rick Tarasuk .10 .05
❑ 270 Jamie Storr 1.00 .45
❑ 271 Sean Basilio .15 .07
❑ 272 Rick Morton .10 .05
❑ 273 Jason Hughes .10 .05
❑ 274 Scott Walker .50 .23
❑ 275 Willie Skilliter .10 .05
❑ 276 Shawn Krueger .10 .05
❑ 277 Jason MacDonald .10 .05
❑ 278 Kirk Maltby .35 .16
❑ 279 Brock Woods .10 .05
❑ 280 Troy Hutchinson .10 .05
❑ 281 Geordie Maynard .10 .05
❑ 282 Luigi Calce .10 .05
❑ 283 Steven Parson .10 .05
❑ 284 Andrew Brunette .15 .07
❑ 285 Robert MacKenzie .10 .05
❑ 286 Jason Buetow .10 .05
❑ 287 Wyatt Buckland .10 .05
❑ 288 Jim Brown .10 .05
❑ 289 Gord Dickie .10 .05
❑ 290 Jeff Smith .10 .05
❑ 291 Peter Ambroziak .15 .07
❑ 292 Mark O'Donnell UER .10 .05
Name spelled
O'donnell on back
❑ 294 Grayden Reid .15 .07
❑ 295 Sean Spencer .10 .05
❑ 296 Gerry Skrypec .10 .05
❑ 297 Billy Hall .10 .05
❑ 298 Sean Gawley .10 .05
❑ 299 Grant Marshall .20 .09
❑ 300 Michael Johnson .10 .05
❑ 301 Brett Seguin .10 .05
❑ 302 Chris Coveny .10 .05
❑ 303 Ryan Kuwabara .15 .07
❑ 304 Jeff Ricciardi .10 .05
❑ 305 Curt Bowen .15 .07
❑ 306 Zbynek Kukacka .10 .05
❑ 307 Chris Gignac .10 .05
❑ 308 Steve Washburn .35 .16
❑ 309 Brian Kilrea CO .15 .07
❑ 310 Mike Lenarduzzi .15 .07
❑ 311 Matt Stone .10 .05
❑ 312 Ken Belanger .10 .05
❑ 313 Chris Simon .50 .23
❑ 314 Kiley Hill .10 .05
❑ 315 Chris Grenville .10 .05
❑ 316 Aaron Gavey .35 .16
❑ 317 Briane Thompson .10 .05
❑ 318 Ted Nolan CO .25 .11
❑ 319 Perry Pappas .10 .05
❑ 320 Kevin Hodson .75 .35
❑ 321 Colin Miller .10 .05
❑ 322 Tom MacDonald .10 .05
❑ 323 Shaun Imber .10 .05
❑ 324 Jarret Reid .10 .05
❑ 325 Tony Iob .10 .05
❑ 326 Mark Matier .10 .05
❑ 327 Drew Bannister .20 .09
❑ 328 Jason Denomme .10 .05
❑ 329 David Matsos .10 .05
❑ 330 Rick Kowalsky .10 .05
❑ 331 Tim Bacik .10 .05
❑ 332 Ralph Intranuovo .20 .09
❑ 333 Jonas Rudberg .10 .05
❑ 334 Jeff Toms .10 .05
❑ 335 Jason Julian .10 .05
❑ 336 Brian Goudie .10 .05
❑ 337 Gary Roach .10 .05
❑ 338 Brad Baber .10 .05
❑ 339 Todd Gleason UER .15 .07
Team affiliation says
Greyhounds; should
say Storm
❑ 340 Chris McMurtry .10 .05
❑ 341 Matt Turek .10 .05
❑ 342 Shane Johnson .10 .05
❑ 343 Grant Pritchett .10 .05
❑ 344 Mike Cote .10 .05
❑ 345 Duane Harmer .10 .05
❑ 346 Jeff Bes .15 .07
❑ 347A Wade Whitten .10 .05
❑ 347B Dan Tanevski UER .10 .05
(Should be number 360)
❑ 348 Bill Kovacs .15 .07
❑ 349 Kayle Short .10 .05
❑ 350 Sylvain Cloutier .20 .09
❑ 351 Brent Watson .10 .05
❑ 352 Brent Pope .10 .05
❑ 353 Craig Lutes .10 .05
❑ 354 Michael Hartwick .10 .05
❑ 355 Kevin Reid .10 .05
❑ 356 Toby Burkitt .10 .05
❑ 357 Todd Bertuzzi .75 .35
❑ 358 Angelo Amore .10 .05
❑ 359 Jeff Pawluk .10 .05
❑ 361 Gordon Ross .10 .05
❑ 362 Dennis Purdie .15 .07
❑ 363 Dave Gilmore .10 .05
❑ 364 Brent Brownlee .10 .05
❑ 365 Aaron Nagy .10 .05
❑ 366 Barry Potomski .25 .11
❑ 367 Steve Smillie .10 .05
❑ 368 Kelly Reed .20 .09
❑ 369 Gary Agnew CO .05 .02
❑ 370 Chris Taylor .15 .07
❑ 371 Brett Marietti .10 .05
❑ 372 Cory Evans .10 .05
❑ 373 Brian Stacey .10 .05
❑ 374 Chris Crombie .10 .05
❑ 375 Derrick Crane .10 .05
❑ 376 Scott McKay .15 .07
❑ 377 Gregory Ryan .10 .05
❑ 378 Mark Visheau .10 .05
❑ 379 Gerry Arcella .10 .05
❑ 380 Nick Stajduhar .15 .07
❑ 381 Jason Allison .75 .35
❑ 382 Sean O'Reilly .10 .05
❑ 383 Paul Wolanski .10 .05
❑ XXX Chris Schushack .15 .07
numbered 000

## 1991-92 7th Inn. Sketch QMJHL

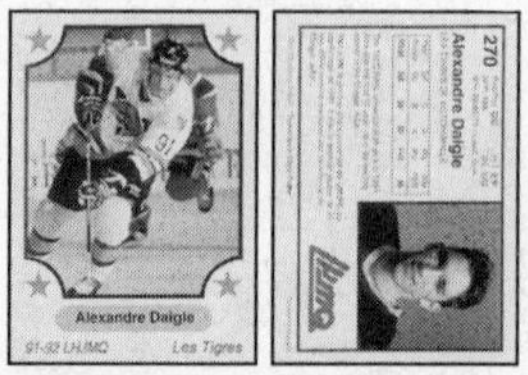

This 298-card standard-size set was issued by 7th Inning Sketch and features players of the Quebec Major Junior Hockey League. The production run was limited to 4,000 factory sets, with each set individually numbered "X of 4,000." On a white card face, the fronts feature color action player photos enclosed by different color frames. The corners of the picture are cut out to permit space for gold stars. The player's name, the year and league, and the team name appear below the picture. In a horizontal format, the backs have biography, statistics, and player profile in French and English. The cards are numbered on the back and checklisted below according to teams as follows: St. Hyacinthe Laser (1-28), Granby Bisons (29-52), Shawinigan Cataractes (53-77), Chicoutimi Sagueneens (78-101), Trois Rivieres Draveurs (102-125), Verdun College Francais (126-150), St. Jean Lynx (151-172), Beauport Harfangs (173-198), Hull Olympiques (199-223), Laval Titan (224-248), Victoriaville Tigres (249-273), and Drummondville Voltigeurs (274-298). Card number 256 was never produced.

| | MINT | NRMT |
|---|---|---|
| COMPLETE SET (297) | 15.00 | 6.75 |
| COMMON CARD (1-298) | .05 | .02 |

❑ 1 Martin Brodeur 4.00 1.80
❑ 2 Normand Paquet .10 .05
❑ 3 David Desnoyers .10 .05
❑ 4 Carlo Colombi .10 .05
❑ 5 Stephane Menard .10 .05
❑ 6 Sebastien Berube .10 .05
❑ 7 Marc Desgagne .10 .05
❑ 8 Mil Sukovic .10 .05
❑ 9 Patrick Belisle .10 .05
❑ 10 Patrick Poulin .25 .11
❑ 11 Martin Trudel .10 .05
❑ 12 Charles Poulin .15 .07
❑ 13 Etienne Thibault .10 .05
❑ 14 Pierre Allard .10 .05
❑ 15 Francois Gagnon .10 .05
❑ 16 Stephane Huard .10 .05
❑ 17 Yannik Lemay .10 .05
❑ 18 Dany Fortin .10 .05
❑ 19 Carl Menard .10 .05
❑ 20 Serge Labelle .10 .05
❑ 21 Dean Melanson .10 .05
❑ 22 Yves Meunier .10 .05
❑ 23 Pierre Petroni CO .05 .02
❑ 24 Mario Pouliot CO UER .05 .02
(Team affiliation says
Bisons; should say Laser)
❑ 25 Alain Cote UER .15 .07
(Team affiliation on
front says Bisons;
should say Lasers;
Back erroneously says
Kingston Frontenancs)
❑ 26 Hugues Laliberte .10 .05
❑ 27 Martin Gendron .25 .11
❑ 28 Stan Melanson .10 .05
❑ 29 Carl Leblanc .10 .05
❑ 30 Patrick Grise .10 .05
❑ 31 Yves Charron .10 .05
❑ 32 Hughes Mongeon .10 .05
❑ 33 Christian Tardif .10 .05
❑ 34 Patrick Tessier .10 .05
❑ 35 Christian Campeau .10 .05
❑ 36 Mario Therrien .10 .05
❑ 37 Martin Balleux .10 .05
❑ 38 Joel Brassard .10 .05
❑ 39 Sebastien Fortier .10 .05
❑ 40 Jocelyn Langlois .10 .05
❑ 41 Giuseppe Argentos .10 .05
❑ 42 Sylvain Brisson .10 .05
❑ 43 Philippe Boucher .35 .16
❑ 44 Martin Brochu .20 .09
❑ 45 Marc Rodgers .10 .05
❑ 46 Pascal Gagnon .10 .05
❑ 47 Benoit Therrien .10 .05
❑ 48 Robin Bouchard .10 .05
❑ 49 Michel Savoie .10 .05
❑ 50 Jean-Sebastien Boiteau .10 .05
❑ 51 Patrick Lamoureux .10 .05
❑ 52 Stephane Giard .10 .05
❑ 53 Maxime Jean .10 .05
❑ 54 Alain Cote .15 .07
❑ 55 Francois Groleau .15 .07
❑ 56 Richard Hamelin .15 .07
❑ 57 Eric Beauvis UER .15 .07
(Name misspelled
Beavis on back)
❑ 58 Steve Laplante .10 .05
❑ 59 Yves Meunier .10 .05
❑ 60 Steve Dontigny .10 .05
❑ 61 Simon Roy .10 .05
❑ 62 Jean-Francois Laroche .10 .05
❑ 63 Patrick Traverse .10 .05
❑ 64 Eric Joyal .10 .05
❑ 65 Jean-Francois .10 .05
Gregoire UER
(Name misspelled
Jean-Fracois on front)
❑ 66 Jocelyn Charbonneau .15 .07
❑ 67 Jean Imbeau .15 .07
❑ 68 Francois Bourdeau .10 .05
❑ 69 Alain Savage Jr. .10 .05
❑ 70 Johnny Lorenzo .10 .05
❑ 71 Patrick Lalime 1.00 .45
❑ 72 Patrick Melfi .10 .05
❑ 73 Marc Tardif .10 .05
❑ 74 Marc Savard .10 .05
❑ 75 Alain Sanscartier CO .05 .02
❑ 76 Pascal Lebrasseur .15 .07
❑ 77 Checklist 1-101 .05 .02
❑ 78 Dany Girard .10 .05
❑ 79 Eddy Gervais .10 .05
❑ 80 Dave Tremblay .10 .05
❑ 81 Dany Larochelle .10 .05
❑ 82 Michel St.Jacques .10 .05
❑ 83 Rodney Petawabano .10 .05
❑ 84 Eric Duchesne .10 .05
❑ 85 Patrick Clement .10 .05
❑ 86 Steve Gosselin .10 .05
❑ 87 Patrick Lacombe .10 .05
❑ 88 Patrice Martineau .10 .05
❑ 89 Danny Beauregard .10 .05
❑ 90 Martin Lamarche .10 .05
❑ 91 Sebastien Parent .10 .05
❑ 92 Christian Caron .10 .05
❑ 93 Sylvain Careau .10 .05
❑ 94 Martin Beaupre .10 .05
❑ 95 Daniel Paradis .10 .05
❑ 96 Sylvain Rodrigue .15 .07
❑ 97 Joe Canale CO .05 .02
❑ 98 Patrick Lampron .10 .05
❑ 99 Carl Blondin .10 .05
❑ 100 Carl Wiseman .10 .05
❑ 101 Hugo Hamelin .25 .11
❑ 102 Claude Poirier .10 .05
❑ 103 Charles Paquette .20 .09
❑ 104 Carl Fleury UER .15 .07
(Name spelled FLeury
on front)
❑ 105 Paolo Racicot .10 .05
❑ 106 Sebastien Moreau .10 .05
❑ 107 Pascal Trepanier .10 .05
❑ 108 Dominic Maltais .15 .07
❑ 109 Steve Ares .10 .05
❑ 110 Daniel Thibault .10 .05
❑ 111 Eric Messier .35 .16
❑ 112 Stephane Julien .10 .05
❑ 113 Dave Paquet .10 .05
❑ 114 Nicolas Turmel .10 .05
❑ 115 Pascal Rheaume .20 .09
❑ 116 Carl Boudreau .10 .05
❑ 117 Dave Boudreault .10 .05
❑ 118 Eric Bellerose .15 .07
❑ 119 Steve Searles .10 .05
❑ 120 Patrick Nadeau .15 .07
❑ 121 Stephan Viens .10 .05
❑ 122 Jean-Francois Labbe .35 .16
❑ 123 Jocelyn Thibault 3.00 1.35
❑ 124 Gaston Drapeau CO .05 .02
❑ 125 Checklist 102-198 .05 .02
❑ 126 Martin Lajeunesse .10 .05
❑ 127 Etienne Lavoie .10 .05
❑ 128 Dominic Rheaume .10 .05
❑ 129 Robert Guillet .10 .05
❑ 130 Francois Rivard .10 .05
❑ 131 Philippe DeRouville .35 .16
❑ 132 Andrej Dobrota .10 .05
❑ 133 Pierre Gendron .10 .05
❑ 134 Dave Chouinard .10 .05
❑ 135 Martin Tanguay .15 .07
❑ 136 Jacques Blouin .10 .05
❑ 137 Martin Larochelle .10 .05
❑ 138 Jean-Martin Morin .10 .05
❑ 139 Donald Brashear .25 .11
❑ 140 Stephane Paradis .10 .05
❑ 141 Jan Simcik .10 .05
❑ 142 Yan Arsenault .10 .05
❑ 143 Joel Bouchard .15 .07
❑ 144 Jean-Sebastien .10 .05
Lefebvre
❑ 145 David St. Pierre UER .15 .07
(Name misspelled
St-Pierre on front)
❑ 146 Mario Nobili .10 .05
❑ 147 Stacy Dallaire .10 .05
❑ 148 Carl Lamothe .15 .07
❑ 149 Andre Bouliane .10 .05
❑ 150 Simon Arial .10 .05
❑ 151 Stephane Madore .10 .05
❑ 152 Hughes Bouchard .10 .05
❑ 153 Steve Decaen .10 .05
❑ 154 Jason Downey .10 .05
❑ 155 Raymond Delarosbil .10 .05
❑ 156 Lino Salvo .10 .05
❑ 157 Reginald Brezeault .10 .05
❑ 158 Nathan Morin .10 .05
❑ 159 Samuel Groleau .15 .07
❑ 160 Patrick Carignan .10 .05
❑ 161 Stephane St-Amour .10 .05
❑ 162 Marquis Mathieu .10 .05
❑ 163 Yves Sarault .20 .09
❑ 164 Dave Belliveau .10 .05
❑ 165 Trevor Duhaime .10 .05
❑ 166 Eric O'Connor .10 .05
❑ 167 Christian Proulx .15 .07
❑ 168 Martin Lavallee .10 .05
❑ 169 Jean-Francois Gagnon .10 .05
❑ 170 Eric Lafrance .10 .05
❑ 171 Enrico Scardocchio .10 .05
❑ 172 David Bergeron .10 .05
❑ 173 Guillaume Morin .10 .05
❑ 174 Charlie Boucher .10 .05
❑ 175 Martin Rozon .10 .05
❑ 176 Brandon Piccarreto .10 .05
❑ 177 Simon Toupin .15 .07
❑ 178 Jamie Bird .10 .05
❑ 179 Herve Lapointe .10 .05
❑ 180 Ian MacIntyre .10 .05
❑ 181 Jean-Francois Rivard .10 .05
❑ 182 Alain Chainey CO .05 .02
❑ 183 Daniel Laflamme .10 .05
❑ 184 Patrice Paquin .10 .05
❑ 185 Patrick Deraspe .10 .05
❑ 186 Martin Roy .10 .05
❑ 187 Jeannot Ferland .10 .05
❑ 188 Patrick Genest .10 .05
❑ 189 Matthew Barnaby .75 .35
❑ 190 Jean-Guy Trudel .10 .05
❑ 191 Eric Moreau .10 .05
❑ 192 Eric Cool .15 .07
❑ 193 Alexandre Legault .10 .05
❑ 194 Gregg Pineo .10 .05
❑ 195 LHJMQ Action .10 .05
❑ 196 Radoslav Balaz .10 .05
❑ 197 Stefan Simoes .10 .05
❑ 198 LHJMQ Action .10 .05

❑ 199 Francois Paquette .10 .05
❑ 200 Paul Macdonald .10 .05
❑ 201 Shane Doiron .10 .05
❑ 202 Michal Longauer .10 .05
❑ 203 Joe Crowley .10 .05
❑ 204 Joey Deliva .10 .05
❑ 205 Pierre-Francois Lalonde .10 .05
❑ 206 Paul Brousseau .15 .07
❑ 207 Martin Lepage .10 .05
❑ 208 Yanick DeGrace .10 .05
❑ 209 Jim Campbell 1.50 .70
❑ 210 Sebastien Bordeleau .10 .05
❑ 211 Marc Legault .10 .05
❑ 212 Joel Blain .10 .05
❑ 213 Claude Jutras .10 .05
❑ 214 Eric Lavigne .15 .07
❑ 215 Todd Sparks .10 .05
❑ 216 Sylvain Lapointe .10 .05
❑ 217 Eric Lecompte .35 .16
❑ 218 Thierry Mayer .10 .05
❑ 219A Harold Hersh ERR .25 .11
(Jim Campbell photo on back)
❑ 219B Harold Hersh COR .10 .05
❑ 220 Frederic Boivin .10 .05
❑ 221 Steven Dion .10 .05
❑ 222 Alain Vigneault .35 .16
❑ 223 Checklist 199-298 .05 .02
❑ 224 Petr Valenta .10 .05
❑ 225 LHJMQ Action .10 .05
❑ 226 Jim Bermingham .10 .05
❑ 227 Yanick Dube .25 .11
❑ 228 Sandy McCarthy .35 .16
❑ 229 Dany Michaud .10 .05
❑ 230 Jason Brousseau .10 .05
❑ 231 Marc Beaucage .10 .05
❑ 232 Eric Cardinal .10 .05
❑ 233 Martin Chaput .10 .05
❑ 234 Jean Roberge .10 .05
❑ 235 Philip Gathercole .10 .05
❑ 236 Michael Gaul .10 .05
❑ 237 Yannick Frechette .10 .05
❑ 238 Sylvain Blouin .10 .05
❑ 239 David Pekarek .10 .05
❑ 240 John Kovacs .10 .05
❑ 241 Eric Raymond .10 .05
❑ 242 Emmanuel Fernandez .50 .23
❑ 243 Yan St. Pierre .10 .05
❑ 244 Brant Blackned .10 .05
❑ 245 Eric Veilleux .10 .05
❑ 246 Pascal Vincent .10 .05
❑ 247 Benoit Larose .10 .05
❑ 248 Olivier Guillaume .10 .05
❑ 249 Alain Gauthier .10 .05
❑ 250 Bruno Ducharme .10 .05
❑ 251 Patrick Charbonneau .10 .05
❑ 252 Daniel Germain .10 .05
❑ 253 Pascal Chiasson .10 .05
❑ 254 Marc Thibeault .10 .05
❑ 255 Martin Woods .10 .05
❑ 257 Dominic Grand'maison .10 .05
❑ 258 Carl Poirer .10 .05
❑ 259 Stephane Larocque .10 .05
❑ 260 Mario Dumoulin .10 .05
❑ 261 Yan Laterreur .10 .05
❑ 262 Claude Savoie .15 .07
❑ 263 Denis Beauchamp .10 .05
❑ 264 Patrick Bisaillon .10 .05
❑ 265 Pascal Bernier .10 .05
❑ 266 Nicolas Lefebvre .10 .05
❑ 267 LHJMQ Action .10 .05
❑ 268 Joseph Napolitano .10 .05
❑ 269 Sebastien Tremblay .10 .05
❑ 270 Alexandre Daigle 1.50 .70
❑ 271 Pierre Pillion .10 .05
❑ 272 Yves Lambert .10 .05
❑ 273 Pierre Aubry CO .05 .02
❑ 274 Yves Loubier .10 .05
❑ 275 Pierre Sandke UER .10 .05
(First name Peter on back)
❑ 276 Louis Bernard .10 .05
❑ 277 Alain Nasreddine .15 .07
❑ 278 Sylvain Ducharme .10 .05
❑ 279 Jeremy Caissie .10 .05
❑ 280 Eric Meloche .10 .05
❑ 281 Ian Laperriere .25 .11
❑ 282 Hugo Proulx .20 .09
❑ 283 Dave Whittom .10 .05
❑ 284 Yanick Dupre .15 .07
❑ 285 Eric Plante .10 .05
❑ 286 Stephane Desjardins .10 .05
❑ 287 Rene Corbet .50 .23
❑ 288 David Lessard .10 .05
❑ 289 Eric Marcoux .10 .05
❑ 290 Alexandre Duchesne .10 .05
❑ 291 Maxime Petitclerc UER .10 .05
(Name misspelled Peticlerc on front)
❑ 292 Pierre Gagnon .10 .05
❑ 293 Roger Larche UER .10 .05
(Name misspelled Larache on front)
❑ 294 Jean Hamel .10 .05
❑ 295 Alexandre Gaumond .10 .05
❑ 296 Paul-Emile Exentus .10 .05
❑ 297 LHJMQ Action .10 .05
❑ 298 LHJMQ Action .10 .05

## 1991-92 7th Inn. Sketch WHL

This 361-card standard-size set was issued by 7th Inning Sketch and features players of the

Western Hockey League. The production run was limited to 7,000 factory sets, with each set individually numbered "X of 7,000." On a white card face, the fronts feature color action player photos enclosed by different color frames. The corners of the picture are cut out to permit space for gold stars. The player's name, the year and league, and the team name appear below the picture. In a horizontal format, the backs have biography, statistics, and player profile in French and English. The cards are numbered on the back and checklisted below according to teams as follows: Spokane Chiefs (1-25), Portland Winter Hawks (26-49), Victoria Cougars (50-73), Kamloops Blazers (74-97), Saskatoon Blades (98-121), Seattle Thunderbirds (122-145), Tacoma Rockets (146-173), Swift Current Broncos (174-195), Brandon Wheat Kings (196-217), Regina Pats (218-242), Prince Albert Raiders (243-266), Moose Jaw Warriors (0/267-287), Tri-City Americans (288-311), Medicine Hat Tigers (312-335), and Lethbridge Hurricanes (336-360).

| | MINT | NRMT |
|---|---|---|
| COMPLETE SET (361) | 15.00 | 6.75 |
| COMMON CARD (1-360) | .05 | .02 |

❑ 1 Valeri Bure .50 .23
❑ 2 Hardy Sauter .10 .05
❑ 3 Bryan Maxwell CO .10 .05
❑ 4 Scott Bailey .40 .18
❑ 5 Mike Gray .10 .05
❑ 6 Mark Szoke .10 .05
❑ 7 Mike Jickling .10 .05
❑ 8 Frank Evans .10 .05
❑ 9 Steve Junker .20 .09
❑ 10 Greg Gatto .10 .05
❑ 11 Jared Bednar .10 .05
❑ 12 Justin Hocking .20 .09
❑ 13 Paxton Schulte .20 .09
❑ 14 Brad Toporowski .10 .05
❑ 15 Shane Maitland .10 .05
❑ 16 Aaron Boh .10 .05
❑ 17 Ryan Duthie .15 .07
❑ 18 Craig Reichert .15 .07
❑ 19 Danny Faassen .10 .05
❑ 20 Randy Toye .10 .05
❑ 21 Geoff Grandberg .10 .05
❑ 22 Jeremy Warring .10 .05
❑ 23 Tyler Romanchuck .10 .05
❑ 24 Jamie Linden .15 .07
❑ 25 1990-91 Champs .10 .05
❑ 26 Corey Jones .10 .05
❑ 27 Brandon Smith .10 .05
❑ 28 Mike Williamson .10 .05
❑ 29 Adam Murray .10 .05
❑ 30 Steve Konowalchuk .50 .23
❑ 31 Shawn Stone .10 .05
❑ 32 Adam Deadmarsh 1.50 .70
❑ 33 Rick Mearns .10 .05
❑ 34 Chris Rowland .10 .05
❑ 35 Brandon Coates .10 .05
❑ 36 Dave Cammock .10 .05
❑ 37 Colin Foley .10 .05
❑ 38 Dennis Saharchuk .10 .05
❑ 39 Jiri Beranek .10 .05
❑ 40 Chad Seibel .10 .05
❑ 41 Kelly Harris .10 .05
❑ 42 Layne Roland .10 .05
❑ 43 Cale Hulse .15 .07
❑ 44 Ken Hodge CO .10 .05
❑ 45 Peter Cox .10 .05
❑ 46 Joaquin Gage .20 .09
❑ 47 Brent Peterson CO .10 .05
❑ 48 Jason McBain .10 .05
❑ 49 John Badduke .10 .05
❑ 50 Rick Hopper .05 .02
❑ 51 Dave Hamilton .10 .05
❑ 52 Dwayne Newman .10 .05
❑ 53 Chris Catellier .10 .05
❑ 54 Fran Defrenza .10 .05
❑ 55 Randy Chadney .10 .05
❑ 56 David Hebky .10 .05
❑ 57 Craig Fletcher .10 .05
❑ 58 Kane Chaloner .10 .05
❑ 59 Ross Harris .10 .05
❑ 60 Mike Barrie .10 .05
❑ 61 Steve Lingren .10 .05
❑ 62 Shea Esselmont .10 .05
❑ 63 Matt Smith .10 .05
❑ 64 Gerry St.Cyr .15 .07
❑ 65 Andrew Laming .10 .05
❑ 66 Jeff Fancy .10 .05
❑ 67 Ryan Pellaers .10 .05
❑ 68 Steve Passmore .35 .16
❑ 69 Scott Fukami .10 .05
❑ 70 Darcy Mattersdorfer .10 .05
❑ 71 Chris Hawes .10 .05
❑ 72 The Goalies I .15 .07
❑ 73 Checklist 1-97 .05 .02
❑ 74 Riverside Coliseum .10 .05
❑ 75 Tom Renney .20 .09
❑ 76 Corey Hirsch 1.00 .45
❑ 77 Scott Ferguson .10 .05
❑ 78 Steve Yule .10 .05
❑ 79 Todd Johnson .10 .05
❑ 80 Jarrett Bousquet .10 .05
❑ 81 Mike Mathers .10 .05
❑ 82 Rod Stevens .10 .05
❑ 83 Lance Johnson .10 .05
❑ 84 Zac Boyer .10 .05
❑ 85 Craig Lyons .15 .07
❑ 86 Dale Masson .10 .05
❑ 87 Scott Loucks .15 .07
❑ 88 Darcy Tucker .25 .11
❑ 89 Shayne Green .15 .07
❑ 90 Michal Sup .10 .05
❑ 91 Craig Bonner .10 .05
❑ 92 Jeff Watchorn .10 .05
❑ 93 Jarrett Dueling .15 .07
❑ 94 Ed Patterson .20 .09
❑ 95 David Wilkie .30 .14
❑ 96 The Goalies III .15 .07
❑ 97 A Goal .10 .05
❑ 98 Andy MacIntyre .10 .05
❑ 99 Rhett Trombley .25 .11
❑ 100 Lorne Molleken CO .05 .02
❑ 101 Trevor Robins .10 .05
❑ 102 Jeff Buchanan .10 .05
❑ 103 Mark Raiter .10 .05
❑ 104 Bryce Goebel .10 .05
❑ 105 Paul Buczkowski .10 .05
❑ 106 James Startup .10 .05
❑ 107 Chad Rusnak .10 .05
❑ 108 Sean McFatridge .10 .05
❑ 109 Shane Calder .15 .07
❑ 110 Ryan Fujita .10 .05
❑ 111 Derek Tibbatts .10 .05
❑ 112 Glen Gulutzan .10 .05
❑ 113 Richard Matvichuk .50 .23
❑ 114 Chad Michalchuk .10 .05
❑ 115 Mark Wotton .25 .11
❑ 116 Mark Franks .10 .05
❑ 117 Norm Maracle .25 .11
❑ 118 Jason Becker .10 .05
❑ 119 Shawn Yakimishyn .10 .05
❑ 120 Ed Chynoweth PRES .15 .07
❑ 121 Checklist 98-195 .05 .02
❑ 122 Craig Chapman .10 .05
❑ 123 Jeff Jubenville .10 .05
❑ 124 George Zajankala .10 .05
❑ 125 Turner Stevenson .25 .11
❑ 126 Rob Tallas .50 .23
❑ 127 Ryan Brown .10 .05
❑ 128 Andrew Kemper .10 .05
❑ 129 Brendan Witt .50 .23
❑ 130 Troy Hyatt .10 .05
❑ 131 Mike Kennedy .25 .11
❑ 132 Jesse Wilson .10 .05
❑ 133 Kurt Seher .15 .07
❑ 134 Dody Wood .15 .07
❑ 135 Darren McAusland .10 .05
❑ 136 Jeff Sebastian .10 .05
❑ 137 Eric Bouchard .10 .05
❑ 138 Joel Dyck .10 .05
❑ 139 Blake Knox .10 .05
❑ 140 Peter Anholt CO .05 .02
❑ 141 Chris Wells .50 .23
❑ 142 Andrew Reimer .20 .09
❑ 143 Along the Boards .10 .05
❑ 144 Which Way Is Up .05 .02
❑ 145 Checklist 196-287 .05 .02
❑ 146 Tacoma Dome .10 .05
❑ 147 Opening Ceremonies .10 .05
❑ 148 Marcel Comeau CO .10 .05
❑ 149 Donn Clark CO .05 .02
❑ 150 John Varga .15 .07
❑ 151 Joey Young .10 .05
❑ 152 Laurie Billeck .10 .05
❑ 153 Jeff Calvert .10 .05
❑ 154 Tuomas Gronman .35 .16
❑ 155 Jason Knox .10 .05
❑ 156 Kevin Malgunas .10 .05
❑ 157 Dave McMillen .10 .05
❑ 158 Darryl Onofrychuk .10 .05
❑ 159 Mike Piersol .10 .05
❑ 160 Lasse Pirjeta .10 .05
❑ 161 Drew Schoneck .10 .05
❑ 162 Corey Stock .10 .05
❑ 163 Ryan Strain .10 .05
❑ 164 Michal Sykora .15 .07
❑ 165 Scott Thomas .15 .07
❑ 166 Toby Weishaar .10 .05
❑ 167 Jeff Whittle .15 .07
❑ 168 The Rockettes .10 .05
❑ 169 Allan Egeland .15 .07
❑ 170 Van Burgess .10 .05
❑ 171 Trever Fraser .10 .05
❑ 172 Jamie Black .15 .07
❑ 173 WHL Action .10 .05
❑ 174 Andy Schneider .15 .07
❑ 175 John McMulkin .10 .05
❑ 176 Rick Girard .15 .07
❑ 177 Shane Hnidy .10 .05
❑ 178 Jason Krywulak .15 .07
❑ 179 Jeremy Riehl .15 .07
❑ 180 Brent Bilodeau .25 .11
❑ 181 Mark McCoy .10 .05
❑ 182 Matt Young .10 .05
❑ 183 Dan Sherstenka .10 .05
❑ 184 Jarrod Daniel .10 .05
❑ 185 Lennie MacAusland .10 .05
❑ 186 Keith McCambridge .10 .05
❑ 187 Jason Horvath .10 .05
❑ 188 Kevin Koopman .10 .05
❑ 189 Chris Herperger .15 .07
❑ 190 Trent McCleary .25 .11
❑ 191 Tyler Wright .15 .07
❑ 192 Todd Holt .15 .07
❑ 193 Ashley Buckberger .15 .07
❑ 194 Bram Vanderkracht .10 .05
❑ 195 Ken Zilka .10 .05
❑ 196 Chris Osgood 3.00 1.35
❑ 197 Rob Puchniak .10 .05
❑ 198 Todd Dutiaume .10 .05
❑ 199 Mike Maneluk .20 .09
❑ 200 Shawn Dietrich .10 .05
❑ 201 Chris Johnston .10 .05
❑ 202 Brian Purdy .15 .07
❑ 203 Mike Chrun .10 .05
❑ 204 Dan Kopec .10 .05
❑ 205 Ryan Smith .15 .07
❑ 206 Marty Murray .50 .23
❑ 207 Merv Priest .10 .05
❑ 208 Bobby House .15 .07
❑ 209 Chris Constant .10 .05
❑ 210 Dwayne Gylywoychuk .10 .05
❑ 211 Stu Scantlebury .10 .05
❑ 212 Mark Kolesar .25 .11
❑ 213 Craig Geekie .10 .05
❑ 214 Terran Sandwith .10 .05
❑ 215 Jeff Hoad .10 .05
❑ 216 Kelly McCrimmon .10 .05
❑ 217 Carlos Bye .10 .05
❑ 218 Trevor Hanas .10 .05
❑ 219 Jeff Shantz .35 .16
❑ 220 Heath Weenk .10 .05
❑ 221 Nathan Dempsey .10 .05
❑ 222 Louis Dumont .10 .05
❑ 223 Garry Pearce .10 .05
❑ 224 Terry Bendera .10 .05
❑ 225 Hal Christiansen .10 .05
❑ 226 Jason Smith .30 .14
❑ 227 Kerry Biette .10 .05
❑ 228 Barry Becker .10 .05
❑ 229 Derek Eberle .10 .05
❑ 230 Ken Richardson .10 .05
❑ 231 Niklas Barklund .10 .05
❑ 232 Frank Kovacs .10 .05
❑ 233 Not Issued .05 .02
❑ 234 Not Issued .05 .02
❑ 235 Lloyd Pelletier .10 .05
❑ 236 Dale Vossen .05 .02
❑ 237 A.J. Kelham .10 .05
❑ 238 Mike Risdale .10 .05
❑ 239 Brad Bagu .10 .05
❑ 240 Niko Ovaska .10 .05
❑ 241 Brad Tippett CO .05 .02
❑ 242 The Goalies II .15 .07
❑ 243 Lee J. Leslie .15 .07
❑ 244 Darren Perkins .10 .05
❑ 245 Jason Kwiatkowski .15 .07
❑ 246 Jason Renard .10 .05
❑ 247 Dan Kesa .20 .09
❑ 248 Jason Klassen .10 .05
❑ 249 Nick Polychronopoulus .10 .05
❑ 250 David Neilson .10 .05
❑ 251 Merv Haney .10 .05
❑ 252 Troy Hjertaas .10 .05
❑ 253 Curt Regnier .20 .09
❑ 254 Dean McAmmond .25 .11
❑ 255 Travis Laycock .10 .05
❑ 256 Jeff Lank .10 .05
❑ 257 Barkley Swenson .10 .05
❑ 258 Darren Van Impe .25 .11
❑ 259 Ryan Pisiak .10 .05
❑ 260 Jeff Gorman .10 .05
❑ 261 Stan Matwijiw .15 .07
❑ 262 Mike Fedorko .10 .05
❑ 263 Mark Odnokon .05 .02
❑ 264 Shane Zulyniak .10 .05
❑ 265 Jeff Nelson .20 .09
❑ 266 Donevan Hextall .20 .09
❑ 267 Kevin Masters .10 .05
❑ 268 Chris Schmidt .10 .05
❑ 269 Jeff Budai .10 .05
❑ 270 Bill Hooson .10 .05
❑ 271 Fred Hettle .10 .05
❑ 272 Kent Staniforth .10 .05
❑ 273 Travis Stevenson .10 .05
❑ 274 David Jesiolowski .10 .05
❑ 275 Mike Babcock CO .05 .02
❑ 276 Scott Allison .10 .05
❑ 277 Travis Thiessen .10 .05
❑ 278 Marc Hussey .10 .05
❑ 279 Kevin Smyth .15 .07
❑ 280 Jason Fitzsimmons .15 .07
❑ 281 Jeff Petruic .10 .05
❑ 282 Russ West .10 .05
❑ 283 Derek Kletzel .15 .07
❑ 284 Jarret Zukiwsky .10 .05
❑ 285 Jason Carey .10 .05
❑ 286 Close Checking .10 .05
❑ 287 Checklist 288-360 .05 .02
❑ 288 Jason Bowen .15 .07
❑ 289 Dean Tiltgen .15 .07
❑ 290 Terry Degner .20 .09
❑ 291 Jodie Murphy .10 .05
❑ 292 Brian Sakic .15 .07
❑ 293 Jamie Barnes .10 .05
❑ 294 Darren Hastman .10 .05
❑ 295 Todd Klassen .15 .07
❑ 296 Mirsad Mujcin .10 .05
❑ 297 Trevor Sherban .10 .05
❑ 298 Chadden Cabana .10 .05
❑ 299 Adam Rettschlag .10 .05
❑ 300 Mark Toljanich .10 .05
❑ 301 Kory Mullin .10 .05
❑ 302 Byron Penstock .10 .05
❑ 303 Vladimir Vujtek .25 .11
❑ 304 Bill Lindsay .35 .16
❑ 305 Jeff Cej .10 .05
❑ 306 Mike Busniak CO .10 .05
❑ 307 Todd Harris .10 .05
❑ 308 Cory Dosdall .10 .05
❑ 309 Jason Smith .15 .07
❑ 310 Mark Dawkins .10 .05
❑ 311 Dan O'Rourke .10 .05
❑ 312 Darby Walker .10 .05
❑ 313 Olaf Kjenstadt .15 .07
❑ 314 Sonny Mignacca .25 .11
❑ 315 Jon Duval .10 .05
❑ 316 Lorne Toews .10 .05
❑ 317 Dana Rieder .10 .05
❑ 318 Clayton Norris .15 .07
❑ 319 David Cooper .20 .09
❑ 320 Larry Watkins .10 .05
❑ 321 Evan Marble .10 .05
❑ 322 Scott Lindsay .15 .07
❑ 323 Ryan Petz .10 .05
❑ 324 Jeramie Heistad .10 .05
❑ 325 Scott Townsend .10 .05
❑ 326 Stacy Roest .10 .05
❑ 327 Rob Niedermayer 1.50 .70
❑ 328 Tim Bothwell CO .15 .07
❑ 329 Kevin Riehl .20 .09
❑ 330 Mike Rathje .35 .16
❑ 331 Bryan McCabe .60 .25
❑ 332 MHT Tiger MASCOT .10 .05
❑ 333 Dean Intwert .10 .05
❑ 334 Mike Vandenberghe .10 .05
❑ 335 Cam Danyluk .10 .05
❑ 336 Darcy Austin .10 .05
❑ 337 Jason Knight .10 .05
❑ 338 Lee Sorochan .25 .11
❑ 339 Al Kinisky .10 .05
❑ 340 Rob Hartnell .10 .05
❑ 341 Radek Sip .10 .05
❑ 342 Jamie Pushor .35 .16
❑ 343 Shane Peacock .10 .05
❑ 344 Cadrin Smart .10 .05
❑ 345 Maurice Meagher .10 .05
❑ 346 Lance Burns .10 .05
❑ 347 Dominic Pittis .15 .07
❑ 348 Todd MacIsaac .10 .05
❑ 349 Brad Zimmer .10 .05
❑ 350 Jason Sorochan .10 .05
❑ 351 Darcy Werenka .20 .09
❑ 352 Kevin St.Jacques .15 .07
❑ 353 David Trofimenkoff .10 .05
❑ 354 Terry Hollinger .15 .07
❑ 355 Travis Munday .10 .05
❑ 356 Slade Stephenson .10 .05
❑ 357 Jason Widmer .20 .09
❑ 358 Brad Zavisha .15 .07
❑ 359 Bob Loucks CO .05 .02
❑ 360 Brantt Myhres .20 .09
❑ 0 Garfield Henderson .15 .07
Numbered 000

## 1995 Signature Rookies Club Promos

These five standard-size cards were sent to members of the Signature Rookies Club. The fronts feature the players photo occupying most of the right side of the card. The player's are identified underneath the photos. The cards are autographed just above the player's name while the sequential autograph number is under the player's name. The words Club Promo go vertically down the left side of the card while the Signature Rookies Hockey logo is in the lower left corner. The backs have a smaller duplication of the front photo on the left side while all relevant vital stats and biographical information are on the right side. The Signature Rookies authentic signature sticker is right above their logo on the back. Reports suggest that unsigned versions of these cards exist as well. These cards are marked PROMO, and are numbered One of 2,000. As these are rarely seen, no values have been tracked. It is fair to suggest, however, that they are worth considerably less than the signed versions.

| | MINT | NRMT |
|---|---|---|
| COMPLETE SET (5) | 50.00 | 22.00 |
| COMMON CARD (1-5) | 10.00 | 4.50 |

❑ 1 Sergei Luchinkin 10.00 4.50
❑ 2 Stefan Ustorf 10.00 4.50
❑ 3 Brad Brown 10.00 4.50
❑ 4 Yanick Dube 10.00 4.50
❑ 5 Vitali Yachmenev 15.00 6.75

## 1995 Signature Rookies

This 70-card standard-size set features a number of NHL draft picks from 1994 as well as several future draft prospects. With a suggested retail price of 5.00, each foil pack contained five regular cards, a mail-in offer or a chase card, and an autographed card. Each player signed 7,750 of their cards. The fronts

feature borderless color action player cut-outs on a colorful, computerized background. The player's name in gold-foil appears in a black bar at the bottom, while the production number "1 of 45,000" is printed in a gold-foil bar at the left. The backs carry a small color player photo, along with a short biography and player profile. 1,995 cases were produced; 1,000 cases were supposedly sold out of the country, with the remaining 995 cases available in the U.S. Several error cards exist in the set. Limited numbers of corrected versions exist for four of them, as noted below.

| | MINT | NRMT |
|---|---|---|
| COMPLETE SET (70) | 12.00 | 5.50 |
| COMMON CARD (1-70) | .10 | .05 |
| ❑ 1 Vaclav Varada | .25 | .11 |
| ❑ 2 Roman Vopat | .15 | .07 |
| ❑ 3 Yannick Dube | .20 | .09 |
| ❑ 4 Colin Cloutier | .15 | .07 |
| ❑ 5 Scott Cherrey | .15 | .07 |
| ❑ 6 Johan Finnstrom | .10 | .05 |
| ❑ 7 Fredrik Modin | .10 | .05 |
| ❑ 8 Stephane Roy | .15 | .07 |
| ❑ 9 Yevgeni Ryabchikov | .20 | .09 |
| ❑ 10 Jose Theodore | .75 | .35 |
| ❑ 11 Jason Holland | .20 | .09 |
| ❑ 12 Richard Park | .35 | .16 |
| ❑ 13 Jason Podollan | .35 | .16 |
| ❑ 14 Mattias Ohlund | .35 | .16 |
| ❑ 15 Chris Wells | .25 | .11 |
| ❑ 16 Hugh Hamilton | .10 | .05 |
| ❑ 17 Edvin Frylen | .10 | .05 |
| ❑ 18 Wade Belak | .20 | .09 |
| ❑ 19 Sebastien Bety | .10 | .05 |
| ❑ 20 Chris Dingman | .20 | .09 |
| ❑ 21 Peter Nylander | .15 | .07 |
| ❑ 22 Daymond Langkow | .75 | .35 |
| ❑ 23 Kelly Fairchild | .15 | .07 |
| ❑ 24 Norm Dezainde | .10 | .05 |
| ❑ 25 Nolan Baumgartner | .25 | .11 |
| ❑ 26 Deron Quint | .10 | .05 |
| ❑ 27 Sheldon Souray | .15 | .07 |
| ❑ 28 Stefan Ustorf | .10 | .05 |
| ❑ 29 Juha Vuorivirta | .15 | .07 |
| ❑ 30 Mark Seliger | .15 | .07 |
| ❑ 31 Ryan Smyth | .35 | .16 |
| ❑ 32 Dimitri Tabarin | .10 | .05 |
| ❑ 33 Nikolai Tsulygin | .20 | .09 |
| ❑ 34 Paul Vincent | .20 | .09 |
| ❑ 35 Rhett Warrener | .15 | .07 |
| ❑ 36 Jamie Rivers | .25 | .11 |
| ❑ 37 Rumun Ndur | .15 | .07 |
| ❑ 38 Phil Huber | .10 | .05 |
| ❑ 39 Radek Dvorak | .75 | .35 |
| ❑ 40 Mike Barrie | .10 | .05 |
| ❑ 41 Chris Hynnes | .10 | .05 |
| ❑ 42 Mike Dubinsky | .10 | .05 |
| ❑ 43 Steve Cheredaryk | .10 | .05 |
| ❑ 44 Jim Carey | 3.00 | 1.35 |
| ❑ 45A Dorian Anneck ERR | .15 | .07 |
| ❑ 45B Dorian Anneck COR | .15 | .07 |
| ❑ 46 Jorgen Jonsson | .15 | .07 |
| ❑ 47 Alyn McCauley | .30 | .14 |
| ❑ 48 Corey Nielson | .15 | .07 |
| ❑ 49 Daniel Tjarnqvist | .10 | .05 |
| ❑ 50 Vadim Yepanchintsev | .20 | .09 |
| ❑ 51 Sean Haggerty | .50 | .23 |
| ❑ 52A Milan Hejduk | .15 | .07 |
| ❑ 52B Milan Hejduk COR | .15 | .07 |
| ❑ 53 Adam Magarrell | .10 | .05 |
| ❑ 54 Dave Scatchard | .15 | .07 |
| ❑ 55 Sebastien Vallee | .15 | .07 |
| ❑ 56 Milos Guren | .20 | .09 |
| ❑ 57 Johan Davidsson | .15 | .07 |
| ❑ 58 Byron Briske | .10 | .05 |
| ❑ 59 Sylvain Blouin | .10 | .05 |
| ❑ 60 Bryan Berard UER (Name misspelled Brian on front) | 1.50 | .70 |
| ❑ 61 Tim Findlay | .10 | .05 |
| ❑ 62 Doug Bonner | .20 | .09 |
| ❑ 63 Curtis Brown | .15 | .07 |
| ❑ 64A Brad Symes ERR | .10 | .05 |
| ❑ 64B Brad Symes COR | .10 | .05 |
| ❑ 65 Andrew Taylor | .10 | .05 |
| ❑ 66 Brad Bombardir | .15 | .07 |
| ❑ 67 Joe Dziedzic | .15 | .07 |
| ❑ 68 Valentin Morozov | .40 | .18 |
| ❑ 69A Mark McArthur ERR | .20 | .09 |
| ❑ 69B Mark McArthur COR | .20 | .09 |
| ❑ 70 Checklist | .10 | .05 |

## 1995 Signature Rookies Cool Five

The five cards in this standard-size set were randomly inserted into packs. The left side of the front identifies the card as being 1 of 7,000, with the Cool Five logo in the lower left

corner. The remainder is devoted to a full-color player photo which bleeds to the corner. The back has a head-and-shoulders portrait on the left side along with his biography on the right side. Signatures from this 5-card set were randomly inserted throughout the packs.

| | MINT | NRMT |
|---|---|---|
| COMPLETE SET (5) | 25.00 | 11.00 |
| COMMON CARD (CF1-CF5) | 4.00 | 1.80 |
| ❑ CF1 Radek Bonk | 5.00 | 2.20 |
| ❑ CF2 Brad Park | 4.00 | 1.80 |
| ❑ CF3 Brian Leetch | 5.00 | 2.20 |
| ❑ CF4 Maurice Richard | 10.00 | 4.50 |
| ❑ CF5 Henri Richard | 5.00 | 2.20 |

## 1995 Signature Rookies Cool Five Signatures

The five cards in this standard-size set were randomly inserted into packs. The left side of the front identifies the set as 1 of 7,000 and the Cool Five logo is in the lower left corner. The card is autographed over the player's photo and the serial number of the autograph is on the bottom. The remainder of the card is devoted to a full-color player photo that bleeds to the corner. In the middle of the back is the Signature Rookies authentic signature logo. The remainder of the back features a head-and-shoulders player portrait on the left side along with his biography on the right side. The card is numbered in the upper right corner.

| | MINT | NRMT |
|---|---|---|
| COMPLETE SET (5) | 125.00 | 55.00 |
| COMMON AUTO. (CF1-CF5) | 20.00 | 9.00 |
| ❑ CF1 Radek Bonk | 30.00 | 13.50 |
| ❑ CF2 Brad Park | 20.00 | 9.00 |
| ❑ CF3 Brian Leetch | 30.00 | 13.50 |
| ❑ CF4 Maurice Richard | 50.00 | 22.00 |
| ❑ CF5 Henri Richard | 30.00 | 13.50 |

## 1995 Signature Rookies Future Flash

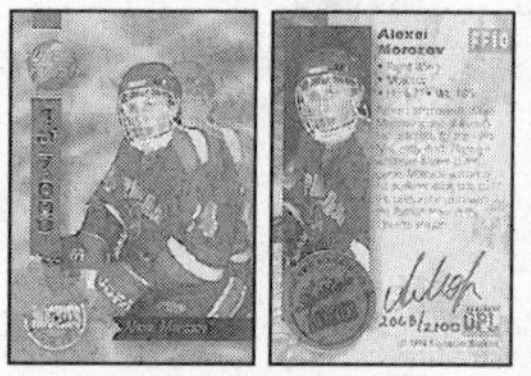

The ten cards in this standard-size set were randomly inserted into packs. The left side of the front identifies the card as being one of 7,000, with the Future Flash logo in the lower left corner. The remainder of the card is devoted to a full-color player photo with a multiple exposure effect that bleeds to the corner. The back has a head-and-shoulders player portrait on the left side along with his biography on the right side. The card is numbered in the upper right corner. Signatures from this 10-card set were randomly inserted throughout the packs.

| | MINT | NRMT |
|---|---|---|
| COMPLETE SET (10) | 30.00 | 13.50 |
| COMMON CARD (FF1-FF10) | 4.00 | 1.80 |
| ❑ FF1 Jeff Ambrosio | 4.00 | 1.80 |
| ❑ FF2 Brad Brown | 4.00 | 1.80 |
| ❑ FF3 Patrick Juhlin | 4.00 | 1.80 |
| ❑ FF4 Sergei Gorbachev | 4.00 | 1.80 |
| ❑ FF5 Vasili Kamenev | 4.00 | 1.80 |
| ❑ FF6 Oleg Orekhovski | 4.00 | 1.80 |
| ❑ FF7 Maxim Kuznetsov | 4.00 | 1.80 |
| ❑ FF8 Sergei Luchinkin | 4.00 | 1.80 |
| ❑ FF9 Scott Roche | 6.00 | 2.70 |
| ❑ FF10 Alexei Morozov | 6.00 | 2.70 |

## 1995 Signature Rookies Future Flash Signatures

The ten cards in this standard-size set were randomly inserted into packs. The left side of the front identifies the card as being 1 of 2,100, with the Future Flash logo in the lower left corner. The autograph is on the player's photo and is sequentially identified underneath the player's name. The remainder of the card is devoted to a full-color player photo with a multiple exposure effect that bleeds to the corner. The Signature Rookies Authentic Signature Logo is on the right side near the bottom. Other aspects of the back include a head-and-shoulders player portrait on the left side along with his biography on the right side. The cards are numbered in the upper right corner.

| | MINT | NRMT |
|---|---|---|
| COMPLETE SET (10) | 100.00 | 45.00 |
| COMMON AUTO (FF1-FF10) | 10.00 | 4.50 |
| ❑ FF1 Jeff Ambrosio | 10.00 | 4.50 |
| ❑ FF2 Brad Brown | 15.00 | 6.75 |
| ❑ FF3 Patrick Juhlin | 15.00 | 6.75 |
| ❑ FF4 Sergei Gorbachev | 10.00 | 4.50 |
| ❑ FF5 Vasili Kamenev | 10.00 | 4.50 |
| ❑ FF6 Oleg Orekhovski | 10.00 | 4.50 |
| ❑ FF7 Maxim Kuznetsov | 15.00 | 6.75 |
| ❑ FF8 Sergei Luchinkin | 10.00 | 4.50 |
| ❑ FF9 Scott Roche | 15.00 | 6.75 |
| ❑ FF10 Alexei Morozov | 25.00 | 11.00 |

## 1995 Signature Rookies Auto-Phonex

This 41-card set measures standard size. The fronts feature a color action player photo made to look as if breaking out of a blue background. The player's name is printed in a red diagonal stripe in the upper left corner. The backs carry a small close-up photo of the player with the team name, position, biographical information and statistics. The cards are numbered on the back. The production figures for this product were 499 16-box cases. Each 6-card pack consisted of five regular cards and one hand-signed phone card. All $3 phone cards were autographed and hand-numbered out of 3,000. Randomingly inserted throughout the packs were 1,000.00 cash cards of Bryan Berard and Wade Redden as well as 5.00 and 25.00 phone cards. Hot packs included five autographed cards and one autographed phone card.

| | MINT | NRMT |
|---|---|---|
| COMPLETE SET (41) | 12.00 | 5.50 |
| COMMON CARD (1-40) | .10 | .05 |
| ❑ 1 Mika Alatalo | .15 | .07 |
| ❑ 2 Chad Allan UER (Text reads four year veteran of pro hockey; should be junior hockey) | .10 | .05 |
| ❑ 3 Jonas Andersson-Junkka | .10 | .05 |
| ❑ 4 Serge Aubin | .10 | .05 |
| ❑ 5 David Belitski | .30 | .14 |
| ❑ 6 Aki-Petteri Berg | .75 | .35 |
| ❑ 7 Zac Bierk | .40 | .18 |
| ❑ 8 Lou Body | .10 | .05 |
| ❑ 9 Kevin Bolibruck | .10 | .05 |
| ❑ 10 Brian Boucher | .35 | .16 |
| ❑ 11 Jack Callahan | .10 | .05 |
| ❑ 12 Jake Deadmarsh | .10 | .05 |
| ❑ 13 Andy Delmore | .10 | .05 |
| ❑ 14 Shane Doan | .60 | .25 |
| ❑ 15 Dan Cleary | 1.50 | .70 |
| ❑ 16 Ian Gordon | .15 | .07 |
| ❑ 17 Jochen Hecht | .25 | .11 |
| ❑ 18 Martin Hohenberger | .20 | .09 |
| ❑ 19 Thomas Holmstrom | .50 | .23 |
| ❑ 20 Cory Keenan | .20 | .09 |
| ❑ 21 Shane Kenney | .10 | .05 |
| ❑ 22 Pavel Kriz | .10 | .05 |
| ❑ 23 Justin Kurtz | .10 | .05 |
| ❑ 24 Jan Labraaten | .20 | .09 |
| ❑ 25 Brad Larsen | .20 | .09 |
| ❑ 26 Donald MacLean | .15 | .07 |
| ❑ 27 Tavis MacMillan | .10 | .05 |
| ❑ 28 Mike Martin | .15 | .07 |
| ❑ 29 Bryan Berard | 2.50 | 1.10 |
| ❑ 30 Dimitri Nabokov | .75 | .35 |
| ❑ 31 Todd Norman | .10 | .05 |
| ❑ 32 Cory Peterson | .15 | .07 |
| ❑ 33 Johan Ramstedt | .10 | .05 |
| ❑ 34 Wade Redden | 1.00 | .45 |
| ❑ 35 Kevin Riehl | .10 | .05 |
| ❑ 36 David Roberts | .25 | .11 |
| ❑ 37 Terry Ryan | .50 | .23 |
| ❑ 38 Brian Scott | .10 | .05 |
| ❑ 39 Alexander Selivanov | 1.25 | .55 |
| ❑ 40 Peter Wallin | .10 | .05 |
| ❑ NNO Checklist | .10 | .05 |

## 1995 Signature Rookies Auto-Phonex Phone Cards

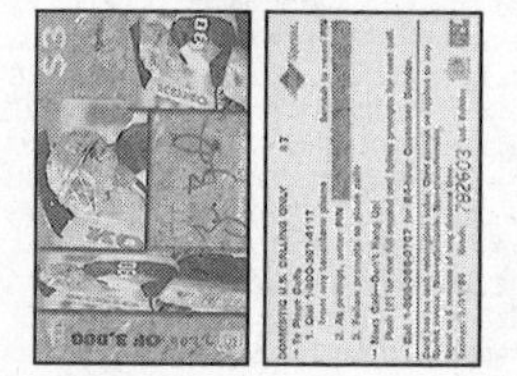

Inserted one per pack, this 39-phone card set features a number of top NHL prospects. Each phone card bears an authentic signature and is serially numbered on the front. Shane Doan, card 14, did not sign. The backs explain how to use the card. Values below are for unused $3 cards. Scratching the back to reveal the PIN number decreases the value by 50 percent. The higher value NNO phone cards listed at the bottom were random inserts at indeterminate odds.

| | MINT | NRMT |
|---|---|---|
| COMPLETE SET (40) | 275.00 | 125.00 |
| COMMON CARD (1-40) | 5.00 | 2.20 |
| ❑ 1 Mika Alatalo | 6.00 | 2.70 |
| ❑ 2 Chad Allan | 5.00 | 2.20 |
| ❑ 3 Jonas Andersson-Junkka | 5.00 | 2.20 |
| ❑ 4 Serge Aubin | 5.00 | 2.20 |
| ❑ 5 David Belitski | 8.00 | 3.60 |
| ❑ 6 Aki-Petteri Berg | 15.00 | 6.75 |
| ❑ 7 Zac Bierk | 10.00 | 4.50 |
| ❑ 8 Lou Body | 5.00 | 2.20 |
| ❑ 9 Kevin Bolibruck | 5.00 | 2.20 |
| ❑ 10 Brian Boucher | 8.00 | 3.60 |
| ❑ 11 Jack Callahan | 5.00 | 2.20 |
| ❑ 12 Jake Deadmarsh | 5.00 | 2.20 |
| ❑ 13 Andy Delmore | 5.00 | 2.20 |
| ❑ 15 Dan Cleary | 25.00 | 11.00 |
| ❑ 16 Ian Gordon | 6.00 | 2.70 |
| ❑ 17 Jochen Hecht | 7.00 | 3.10 |
| ❑ 18 Martin Hohenberger | 6.00 | 2.70 |
| ❑ 19 Thomas Holmstrom | 8.00 | 3.60 |
| ❑ 20 Cory Keenan | 7.00 | 3.10 |
| ❑ 21 Shane Kenney | 5.00 | 2.20 |
| ❑ 22 Pavel Kriz | 5.00 | 2.20 |
| ❑ 23 Justin Kurtz | 5.00 | 2.20 |
| ❑ 24 Jan Labraaten | 6.00 | 2.70 |
| ❑ 25 Brad Larsen | 7.00 | 3.10 |
| ❑ 26 Donald MacLean | 6.00 | 2.70 |
| ❑ 27 Tavis MacMillan | 5.00 | 2.20 |
| ❑ 28 Mike Martin | 6.00 | 2.70 |
| ❑ 29 Bryan Berard | 20.00 | 9.00 |
| ❑ 30 Dimitri Nabokov | 10.00 | 4.50 |
| ❑ 31 Todd Norman | 5.00 | 2.20 |
| ❑ 32 Cory Peterson | 6.00 | 2.70 |
| ❑ 33 Johan Ramstedt | 5.00 | 2.20 |
| ❑ 34 Wade Redden | 12.00 | 5.50 |
| ❑ 35 Kevin Riehl | 5.00 | 2.20 |
| ❑ 36 David Roberts | 8.00 | 3.60 |
| ❑ 37 Terry Ryan | 10.00 | 4.50 |
| ❑ 38 Brian Scott | 5.00 | 2.20 |
| ❑ 39 Alexander Selivanov | 12.00 | 5.50 |
| ❑ 40 Peter Wallin | 5.00 | 2.20 |
| ❑ NNO Terry Ryan $6 card | 10.00 | 4.50 |
| ❑ NNO Wade Redden $6 card | 10.00 | 4.50 |
| ❑ NNO Nolan Baumgartner $6 card | 10.00 | 4.50 |
| ❑ NNO Daymond Langkow $30 card | 20.00 | 9.00 |

## 1995 Signature Rookies Auto-Phonex Beyond 2000

Inserted one in every six packs, this set features five players who have a great shot at excelling well into the next century. The fronts feature the player's photo against a futuristic background. The player is identified on the upper right corner of the card with the words "Beyond 2000" in the lower left corner. The back has a player portrait along with his position, his '93-94 stats and a quote about that player's abilities. 5,000 sets were produced, and each player signed 200 cards. Signed versions are worth 5X to 10X basic cards.

| | MINT | NRMT |
|---|---|---|
| COMPLETE SET (5) | 25.00 | 11.00 |
| COMMON CARD (B1-B5) | 4.00 | 1.80 |
| ❑ B1 Jamie Rivers | 4.00 | 1.80 |
| ❑ B2 Terry Ryan | 5.00 | 2.20 |
| ❑ B3 Ryan Smyth | 5.00 | 2.20 |
| ❑ B4 Nolan Baumgartner | 4.00 | 1.80 |
| ❑ B5 Jose Theodore | 8.00 | 3.60 |

## 1995 Signature Rookies Auto-Phonex Jaromir Jagr

Inserted one in every 6 packs, this 5-card standard-size set showcases Jaromir Jagr. 5,000 sets were produced, and Jagr signed 500 of each card. The front features color photos picturing Jagr in action; the irregular fuchsia borders mimic the effect of water splattering on a surface. The back has a photo of Jagr along with biographical details and personal information located at the upper right corner.

| | MINT | NRMT |
|---|---|---|
| COMPLETE SET (5) | 20.00 | 9.00 |
| COMMON JAGR (JJ1-JJ5) | 4.00 | 1.80 |
| JAGR SIGNATURE (JJ1-JJ5) | 100.00 | 45.00 |
| ❑ JJ1 Jaromir Jagr (Skating--Full Figure) | 4.00 | 1.80 |
| ❑ JJ2 Jaromir Jagr (Faceoff) | 4.00 | 1.80 |
| ❑ JJ3 Jaromir Jagr (Battling S. Niedermayer) | 4.00 | 1.80 |
| ❑ JJ4 Jaromir Jagr (Battling M. Pivonka) | 4.00 | 1.80 |
| ❑ JJ5 Jaromir Jagr (Skating--Upper Torso) | 4.00 | 1.80 |

## 1995 Signature Rookies Auto-Phonex Prodigies

Inserted one in every six packs, this five-card standard-size set features five young guns. The front features the player showcased in action. The player's name is in red while the word "Prodigies" is printed in big, black bold letters against a yellow background on the bottom. The back features biographical information in the upper left corner. The rest of the reverse features a black-and-white player photo with his '93-94 stars and a quote about the player also placed on the bottom half. 5,000 sets were produced, and each player signed 200 of his cards. Signed versions are worth 5X to 8X basic cards.

| | MINT | NRMT |
|---|---|---|
| COMPLETE SET (5) | 30.00 | 13.50 |
| COMMON CARD (P1-P5) | 4.00 | 1.80 |
| ❑ P1 Bryan Berard UER (Name misspelled Brian) | 10.00 | 4.50 |
| ❑ P2 Daymond Langkow | 7.00 | 3.10 |
| ❑ P3 Dan Cleary | 6.00 | 2.70 |
| ❑ P4 Aki-Petteri Berg | 4.00 | 1.80 |
| ❑ P5 Wade Redden | 5.00 | 2.20 |

## 1995 Signature Rookies Miracle on Ice

This 50-card standard-size set features 20 players, two coaches, and special action shots. Just 299 cases were produced, and each six-card pack contained an autograph card. The

fronts display color action player photos that are edged on the left and bottom by a red, white and blue American flag design. Also the lower left corner of each card has a small oblique photo of the American team celebrating. The production run ("1 of 24,000"), a special "Miracle On Ice, 1980" emblem, and the player's name are gold foil-stamped on the front. On a ghosted red, white and blue flag design, the backs carry a color closeup photo, biography, and player profile.

| | MINT | NRMT |
|---|---|---|
| COMPLETE SET (50) | 9.00 | 4.00 |
| COMMON CARD (1-50) | .20 | .09 |

| | | |
|---|---|---|
| ❑ 1 Bill Baker | .20 | .09 |
| ❑ 2 Bill Baker | .20 | .09 |
| ❑ 3 Neal Broten | .75 | .35 |
| ❑ 4 Neal Broten | .75 | .35 |
| ❑ 5 Dave Christian | .50 | .23 |
| ❑ 6 Dave Christian | .50 | .23 |
| ❑ 7 Steve Christoff | .20 | .09 |
| ❑ 8 Steve Christoff | .20 | .09 |
| ❑ 9 Jim Craig | 1.00 | .45 |
| ❑ 10 Jim Craig | 1.00 | .45 |
| ❑ 11 Mike Eruzione | 1.00 | .45 |
| ❑ 12 Mike Eruzione | 1.00 | .45 |
| ❑ 13 John Harrington | .20 | .09 |
| ❑ 14 John Harrington | .20 | .09 |
| ❑ 15 Steve Janasak | .20 | .09 |
| ❑ 16 Steve Janasak | .20 | .09 |
| ❑ 17 Mark Johnson | .20 | .09 |
| ❑ 18 Mark Johnson | .20 | .09 |
| ❑ 19 Rob McClanahan | .20 | .09 |
| ❑ 20 Rob McClanahan | .20 | .09 |
| ❑ 21 Ken Morrow | .50 | .23 |
| ❑ 22 Ken Morrow | .50 | .23 |
| ❑ 23 Jack O'Callahan | .20 | .09 |
| ❑ 24 Jack O'Callahan | .20 | .09 |
| ❑ 25 Mark Pavelich | .20 | .09 |
| ❑ 26 Mark Pavelich | .20 | .09 |
| ❑ 27 Mike Ramsey | .25 | .11 |
| ❑ 28 Mike Ramsey | .25 | .11 |
| ❑ 29 Buzz Schneider | .20 | .09 |
| ❑ 30 Buzz Schneider | .20 | .09 |
| ❑ 31 Dave Silk | .20 | .09 |
| ❑ 32 Dave Silk | .20 | .09 |
| ❑ 33 Bob Suter | .20 | .09 |
| ❑ 34 Bob Suter | .20 | .09 |
| ❑ 35 Eric Strobel | .20 | .09 |
| ❑ 36 Eric Strobel | .20 | .09 |
| ❑ 37 Phil Verchota | .20 | .09 |
| ❑ 38 Phil Verchota | .20 | .09 |
| ❑ 39 Marc Wells | .20 | .09 |
| ❑ 40 Marc Wells | .20 | .09 |
| ❑ 41 Herb Brooks CO | .50 | .23 |
| ❑ 42 Herb Brooks CO | .50 | .23 |
| ❑ 43 Craig Patrick ACO | .50 | .23 |
| ❑ 44 Craig Patrick ACO | .50 | .23 |
| ❑ 45 Clinching The Gold | .50 | .23 |
| ❑ 46 Do You Believe In Miracles | .50 | .23 |
| ❑ 47 Eruzione Decides It | .50 | .23 |
| ❑ 48 Celebration | .50 | .23 |
| ❑ 49 A Dream Becomes Reality | .50 | .23 |
| ❑ 50 Checklist | .20 | .09 |

## 1995 Signature Rookies Miracle on Ice Signatures

This 43-card standard-size set features 20 players, two coaches, and special action shots. The cards are identical to the regular issue with the addition of authentic signatures inscribed across the fronts. Two thousand of each card were signed. Card numbers 41 and 45-50 were not issued in signed form. Cards are numbered out of 2,000 on front.

| | MINT | NRMT |
|---|---|---|
| COMPLETE SET (43) | 175.00 | 80.00 |
| COMMON CARD (1-40,42-44) | 4.00 | 1.80 |

*STARS: 15X TO 30X BASIC CARDS
*SEMISTARS: 10X TO 20X BASIC CARDS

## 1995 Signature Rookies Signatures

Inserted one per foil pack, this 69-card issue is a parallel set and features the same design as the regular issue. Each player signed 7,750 of his cards which are hand numbered. The fronts feature borderless color action player cut-outs on a colorful, computerized background. The player's name in gold-foil appears in a black bar at the bottom. The backs carry a small color player photo, along with a short biography and player profile. Because several players could not fulfill their signing committments in time for packaging, Signature Rookies inserted some redemption cards which specifically identified the player for whom the card could be redeemed. Once the redemption period expires, these cards will have limited market value.

| | MINT | NRMT |
|---|---|---|
| COMPLETE SET (69) | 250.00 | 110.00 |
| COMMON SIGNATURE (1-69) | 3.00 | 1.35 |

| | | |
|---|---|---|
| ❑ 1 Vaclav Varada | 6.00 | 2.70 |
| ❑ 2 Roman Vopat | 3.00 | 1.35 |
| ❑ 3 Yanick Dube | 3.00 | 1.35 |
| ❑ 4 Colin Cloutier | 3.00 | 1.35 |
| ❑ 5 Scott Cherrey | 3.00 | 1.35 |
| ❑ 6 Johan Finnstrom | 3.00 | 1.35 |
| ❑ 7 Fredrik Modin | 3.00 | 1.35 |
| ❑ 8 Stephane Roy | 3.00 | 1.35 |
| ❑ 9 Evgeni Ryabchikov | 3.00 | 1.35 |
| ❑ 10 Jose Theodore | 15.00 | 6.75 |
| ❑ 11 Jason Holland | 3.00 | 1.35 |
| ❑ 12 Richard Park | 6.00 | 2.70 |
| ❑ 13 Jason Podollan | 6.00 | 2.70 |
| ❑ 14 Mattias Ohlund | 15.00 | 6.75 |
| ❑ 15 Chris Wells | 6.00 | 2.70 |
| ❑ 16 Hugh Hamilton | 3.00 | 1.35 |
| ❑ 17 Edvin Frylen | 3.00 | 1.35 |
| ❑ 18 Wade Belak | 6.00 | 2.70 |
| ❑ 19 Sebastien Bety | 3.00 | 1.35 |
| ❑ 20 Chris Dingman | 4.00 | 1.80 |
| ❑ 21 Peter Nylander | 3.00 | 1.35 |
| ❑ 22 Daymond Langkow | 6.00 | 2.70 |
| ❑ 23 Kelly Fairchild | 3.00 | 1.35 |
| ❑ 24 Norm Dezainde | 3.00 | 1.35 |
| ❑ 25 Nolan Baumgartner | 6.00 | 2.70 |
| ❑ 26 Deron Quint | 3.00 | 1.35 |
| ❑ 27 Sheldon Souray | 3.00 | 1.35 |
| ❑ 28 Stefan Ustorf | 3.00 | 1.35 |
| ❑ 29 Juha Vuorvirta | 3.00 | 1.35 |
| ❑ 30 Marc Seliger | 3.00 | 1.35 |
| ❑ 31 Ryan Smyth | 8.00 | 3.60 |
| ❑ 32 Dimitri Tabarin | 3.00 | 1.35 |
| ❑ 33 Nikolai Tsulygin | 3.00 | 1.35 |
| ❑ 34 Paul Vincent | 3.00 | 1.35 |
| ❑ 35 Rhett Warrener | 3.00 | 1.35 |
| ❑ 36 Jamie Rivers | 8.00 | 3.60 |
| ❑ 37 Rumun Ndur | 4.00 | 1.80 |
| ❑ 38 Phil Huber | 3.00 | 1.35 |
| ❑ 39 Radek Dvorak | 8.00 | 3.60 |
| ❑ 40 Mike Barrie | 3.00 | 1.35 |
| ❑ 41 Chris Hynnes | 3.00 | 1.35 |
| ❑ 42 Mike Dubinsky | 3.00 | 1.35 |
| ❑ 43 Steve Cheredaryk | 3.00 | 1.35 |
| ❑ 44 Jim Carey | 6.00 | 2.70 |
| ❑ 45 Dorian Anneck | 3.00 | 1.35 |
| ❑ 46 Jorgen Jonsson | 3.00 | 1.35 |
| ❑ 47 Alyn McCauley | 8.00 | 3.60 |
| ❑ 48 Corey Nielson | 3.00 | 1.35 |
| ❑ 49 Daniel Tjarnqvist | 4.00 | 1.80 |
| ❑ 50 Vadim Epanchintsev | 5.00 | 2.20 |
| ❑ 51 Sean Haggerty | 5.00 | 2.20 |
| ❑ 52 Milan Hejduk | 15.00 | 6.75 |
| ❑ 53 Adam Magarrell | 3.00 | 1.35 |
| ❑ 54 Dave Scatchard | 3.00 | 1.35 |
| ❑ 55 Sebastien Vallee | 3.00 | 1.35 |
| ❑ 56 Milos Guren | 3.00 | 1.35 |
| ❑ 57 Johan Davidsson | 3.00 | 1.35 |
| ❑ 58 Byron Briske | 3.00 | 1.35 |
| ❑ 59 Sylvain Blouin | 3.00 | 1.35 |
| ❑ 60 Bryan Berard UER | 15.00 | 6.75 |
| ❑ 61 Tim Findlay | 3.00 | 1.35 |
| ❑ 62 Doug Bonner | 5.00 | 2.20 |
| ❑ 63 Curtis Brown | 3.00 | 1.35 |
| ❑ 64 Brad Symes | 3.00 | 1.35 |
| ❑ 65 Andrew Taylor | 3.00 | 1.35 |
| ❑ 66 Brad Bombardir | 3.00 | 1.35 |
| ❑ 67 Joe Dziedzic | 4.00 | 1.80 |
| ❑ 68 Valentin Morozhov | 10.00 | 4.50 |
| ❑ 69 Mark McArthur | 5.00 | 2.20 |

## 1994-95 Slapshot Promos

This eight-card set features a sampling of the 1994-95 Slapshot cards, which were issued in team set form. The designs are identical to the regular cards, although some cards carry the disclaimer "Promo". The Jamie Rivers card actually is his 1993-94 card. The cards are unnumbered and checklisted below in alphabetical order.

| | MINT | NRMT |
|---|---|---|
| COMPLETE SET (8) | 3.00 | 1.35 |
| COMMON CARD (1-8) | .05 | .02 |

| | | |
|---|---|---|
| ❑ 1 David Belitski | .50 | .23 |
| ❑ 2 Dan Graham | .10 | .05 |
| ❑ 3 Bill McGuigan | .20 | .09 |
| ❑ 4 Todd Norman | .50 | .23 |
| ❑ 5 Steve Rice | .20 | .09 |
| ❑ 6 Jamie Rivers | .50 | .23 |
| ❑ 7 Sudbury's World Juniors / Zdenek Nedved / Jason Bonsignore / Jamie Rivers / Rory Fitzpatrick | 1.00 | .45 |
| ❑ 8 Ad Card | .05 | .02 |

## 1995 Slapshot Memorial Cup

Produced by Slapshot Images Ltd., this 110-card standard-size set commemorates the 1995 Memorial Cup of the Canadian Hockey League. The set includes the champions of the three member leagues (Detroit/OHL; Hull/LMJHQ; Kamloops/WHL) as well as the host team (Brandon). On a simulated wood background, the fronts feature color action photos inside a jagged black or blue picture frame. The player's name is printed above the photo, while the team name is printed vertically running down the left edge. The backs have biography, a color headshot, and a player profile. The set is arranged according to teams as follows: Kamloops Blazers (1-25), Brandon Wheat Kings (26-50), Hull Olympiques (51-75), and Detroit Jr. Red Wings (76-100).

| | MINT | NRMT |
|---|---|---|
| COMPLETE SET (110) | 30.00 | 13.50 |
| COMMON CARD (1-107) | .20 | .09 |

| | | |
|---|---|---|
| ❑ 1 Rod Branch | .50 | .23 |
| ❑ 2 Jeff Oldenborger | .20 | .09 |
| ❑ 3 Jason Holland | .20 | .09 |
| ❑ 4 Nolan Baumgartner | 1.00 | .45 |
| ❑ 5 Keith McCambridge | .20 | .09 |
| ❑ 6 Ivan Vologjaninov | .50 | .23 |
| ❑ 7 Aaron Keller | .35 | .16 |
| ❑ 8 Greg Hart | .20 | .09 |
| ❑ 9 Jarome Iginla | 2.50 | 1.10 |
| ❑ 10 Ryan Huska | .20 | .09 |
| ❑ 11 Jeff Ainsworth | .20 | .09 |
| ❑ 12 Darcy Tucker | 1.00 | .45 |
| ❑ 13 Hnat Domenichelli | 1.00 | .45 |
| ❑ 14 Tyson Nash | .35 | .16 |
| ❑ 15 Shane Doan | 1.00 | .45 |
| ❑ 16 Jeff Antonovich | .20 | .09 |
| ❑ 17 Bonnie Kinney | .20 | .09 |
| ❑ 18 Ashley Buckberger | .50 | .23 |
| ❑ 19 Brad Lukowich | .20 | .09 |
| ❑ 20 Bob Westerby | .20 | .09 |
| ❑ 21 Jason Strudwick | .20 | .09 |
| ❑ 22 Bob Maudie | .20 | .09 |
| ❑ 23 Randy Petruk | .75 | .35 |
| ❑ 24 Shawn McNeil | .20 | .09 |
| ❑ 25 Don Hay CO | .50 | .23 |
| ❑ 26 Bryon Penstock | .50 | .23 |
| ❑ 27 Brian Elder | .35 | .16 |
| ❑ 28 Jeff Staples | .20 | .09 |
| ❑ 29 Scott Laluk | .20 | .09 |
| ❑ 30 Kevin Pozzo | .20 | .09 |
| ❑ 31 Wade Redden | 2.50 | 1.10 |
| ❑ 32 Justin Kurtz | .35 | .16 |
| ❑ 33 Sven Butenschon | .20 | .09 |
| ❑ 34 Bryan McCabe | 1.50 | .70 |
| ❑ 35 Kelly Smart | .20 | .09 |
| ❑ 36 Bobby Brown | .20 | .09 |
| ❑ 37 Mike Dubinsky | .20 | .09 |
| ❑ 38 Mike LeClerc | .20 | .09 |
| ❑ 39 Dean Kletzel | .20 | .09 |
| ❑ 40 Darren Ritchie | .75 | .35 |
| ❑ 41 Mark Dutiaume | .20 | .09 |
| ❑ 42 Ryan Robson | .20 | .09 |
| ❑ 43 Chris Dingman | .75 | .35 |
| ❑ 44 Darren Van Oene | .50 | .23 |
| ❑ 45 Colin Cloutier | .20 | .09 |
| ❑ 46 Darryl Stockham | .20 | .09 |
| ❑ 47 Peter Schaefer | .20 | .09 |
| ❑ 48 Marty Murray | 1.00 | .45 |
| ❑ 49 Alex Vasilevski | .50 | .23 |
| ❑ 50 Bob Lowes CO | .20 | .09 |
| ❑ 51 Michael Coveny | .20 | .09 |
| ❑ 52 Jan Nemecek | .35 | .16 |
| ❑ 53 Chris Hall | .20 | .09 |
| ❑ 54 Jason Groleau | .20 | .09 |
| ❑ 55 Alex Rodrigue | .20 | .09 |
| ❑ 56 Jamie Bird | .20 | .09 |
| ❑ 57 Harold Hersh | .35 | .16 |
| ❑ 58 Carl Prud'Homme | .20 | .09 |
| ❑ 59 Sean Farmer | .20 | .09 |
| ❑ 60 Carl Beaudoin | .20 | .09 |
| ❑ 61 Gordie Dwyer | .20 | .09 |
| ❑ 62 Richard Safarik | .20 | .09 |
| ❑ 63 Carl Charland | .20 | .09 |
| ❑ 64 Jean-Guy Trudel | .35 | .16 |
| ❑ 65 Francois Cloutier | .20 | .09 |
| ❑ 66 Roddie MacKenzie | .20 | .09 |
| ❑ 67 Colin White | .20 | .09 |
| ❑ 68 Martin Menard | .50 | .23 |
| ❑ 69 Sebastien Bordeleau | .75 | .35 |
| ❑ 70 Jonathan Delisle | .50 | .23 |
| ❑ 71 Peter Worrell | .20 | .09 |
| ❑ 72 Louis-Philippe Charbonneau | .50 | .23 |
| ❑ 73 Jose Theodore | 3.00 | 1.35 |
| ❑ 74 Neil Savary | .50 | .23 |
| ❑ 75 Michael McKay | .35 | .16 |
| ❑ 76 Darryl Foster | .50 | .23 |
| ❑ 77 Quade Lightbody | .20 | .09 |
| ❑ 78 Ryan MacDonald | .20 | .09 |
| ❑ 79 Mike Rucinski | .20 | .09 |
| ❑ 80 Murray Sheehan | .20 | .09 |
| ❑ 81 Matt Ball | .50 | .23 |
| ❑ 82 Gerry Lanigan | .20 | .09 |
| ❑ 83 Mike Morrone | .20 | .09 |
| ❑ 84 Tom Buckley | .20 | .09 |
| ❑ 85 Eric Manlow | .50 | .23 |
| ❑ 86 Bill McCauley | 1.00 | .45 |
| ❑ 87 Andrew Taylor | .20 | .09 |
| ❑ 88 Scott Blair | .20 | .09 |
| ❑ 89 Jeff Mitchell | .40 | .18 |
| ❑ 90 Jason Saal | .50 | .23 |
| ❑ 91 Jamie Allison | .35 | .16 |
| ❑ 92 Bryan Berard | 2.50 | 1.10 |
| ❑ 93 Dan Pawlaczyk | .20 | .09 |
| ❑ 94 Milan Kostolny | .20 | .09 |
| ❑ 95 Duane Harmer | .20 | .09 |
| ❑ 96 Shayne McCosh | .50 | .23 |
| ❑ 97 Sean Haggerty | 1.00 | .45 |
| ❑ 98 Nic Beaudoin | .20 | .09 |
| ❑ 99 Paul Maurice CO/GM | .35 | .16 |
| ❑ 100 Pete Deboer ACO | .20 | .09 |
| ❑ 101 Kamloops Checklist | .20 | .09 |
| ❑ 102 Brandon Checklist | .20 | .09 |
| ❑ 103 Hull Checklist | .20 | .09 |
| ❑ 104 Detroit Checklist | .20 | .09 |
| ❑ 105 OHL Champions / Detroit Jr. Red Wings | .20 | .09 |
| ❑ 106 WHL Champions / Kamloops Blazers | .20 | .09 |
| ❑ 107 LMJHQ Champions / Hull Olympiques | .20 | .09 |
| ❑ NNO OHL Playoff Summary | .20 | .09 |
| ❑ NNO LHJMQ Playoff Summary | .20 | .09 |
| ❑ NNO WHL Playoff Summary | .20 | .09 |

## 1995-96 Slapshot

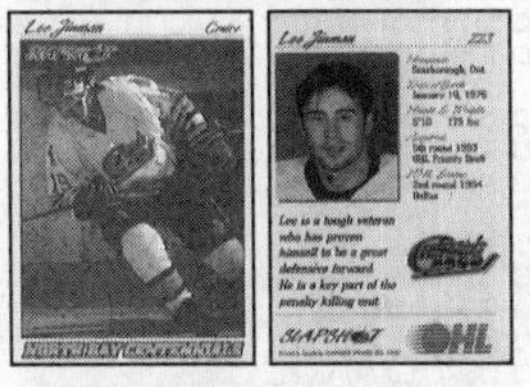

The 1995-96 Slapshot set features the players of the OHL and was issued in foil packs in one series totalling 440 cards. Randomly inserted into packs were promo cards and an autographed card of Zac Bierk. The set is notable for the inclusion of several top prospects, including Alexandre Volchkov, Boyd Devereaux, Joe Thornton, Daniel Cleary and Rico Fata.

| | MINT | NRMT |
|---|---|---|
| COMPLETE SET (440) | 70.00 | 32.00 |
| COMMON CARD (1-440) | .05 | .02 |

| | | |
|---|---|---|
| ❑ 1 Checklist | .05 | .02 |
| ❑ 2 Checklist | .05 | .02 |
| ❑ 3 Checklist | .05 | .02 |
| ❑ 4 Checklist | .05 | .02 |
| ❑ 5 Checklist | .05 | .02 |
| ❑ 6 Bert Templeton | .05 | .02 |
| ❑ 7 Chris George | .05 | .02 |
| ❑ 8 Chris Thompson | .25 | .11 |
| ❑ 9 Quade Lightbody | .05 | .02 |
| ❑ 10 Shane Delaronde | .05 | .02 |
| ❑ 11 Justin Robinson | .05 | .02 |
| ❑ 12 Shawn Frappier | .05 | .02 |
| ❑ 13 Lucio Nasato | .05 | .02 |
| ❑ 14 Jason Payne | .05 | .02 |
| ❑ 15 Jason Cannon | .05 | .02 |
| ❑ 16 Alexandre Volchkov | 2.00 | .90 |
| ❑ 17 Daniel Tkaczuk | 4.00 | 1.80 |
| ❑ 18 Gerry Lanigan | .05 | .02 |
| ❑ 19 Darrel Woodley | .05 | .02 |
| ❑ 20 Brian Barker | .05 | .02 |
| ❑ 21 Mauricio Alvarez | .05 | .02 |
| ❑ 22 Brock Boucher | .05 | .02 |
| ❑ 23 Jeff Cowan | .10 | .05 |
| ❑ 24 Jan Bulis | .50 | .23 |
| ❑ 25 Jeff Tetzlaff | .05 | .02 |
| ❑ 26 Caleb Ward | .15 | .07 |
| ❑ 27 Mike White | .05 | .02 |
| ❑ 28 Jeremy Miculinic | .05 | .02 |
| ❑ 29 Andrew Morrison | .05 | .02 |
| ❑ 30 Robert Dubois | .05 | .02 |
| ❑ 31 Kory Cooper | .25 | .11 |
| ❑ 32 Jason Gaggi | .25 | .11 |
| ❑ 33 Mike Van Volsen | .05 | .02 |
| ❑ 34 Paul McInness | .05 | .02 |
| ❑ 35 Harkie Stingh | .05 | .02 |
| ❑ 36 Robin Lacour | .05 | .02 |
| ❑ 37 Jamie Sokolsky | .05 | .02 |
| ❑ 38 Marc Dupuis | .05 | .02 |
| ❑ 39 Daniel Cleary | 4.00 | 1.80 |
| ❑ 40 David Peca | .05 | .02 |
| ❑ 41 Adam Robbins | .05 | .02 |
| ❑ 42 Steve Tracze | .05 | .02 |
| ❑ 43 James Boyd | .05 | .02 |
| ❑ 44 Jake Irsag | .05 | .02 |
| ❑ 45 Ryan Ready | .05 | .02 |
| ❑ 46 Walker McDonald | .05 | .02 |
| ❑ 47 Rob Guinn | .05 | .02 |
| ❑ 48 Rob Fitzgerald | .05 | .02 |
| ❑ 49 Joe Coombs | .05 | .02 |
| ❑ 50 Daniel Reja | .05 | .02 |
| ❑ 51 Joe Van Volsen | .10 | .05 |
| ❑ 52 Craig Mills | .50 | .23 |
| ❑ 53 Murray Hogg | .05 | .02 |
| ❑ 54 Andrei Shurupov | .50 | .23 |
| ❑ 55 Andrew Williamson | .05 | .02 |
| ❑ 56 Mike Minard | .25 | .11 |
| ❑ 57 Robert Esche | .75 | .35 |
| ❑ 58 Lee Jinman | .50 | .23 |
| ❑ 59 Corey Neilson | .20 | .09 |
| ❑ 60 Troy Smith | .05 | .02 |
| ❑ 61 Mike Rucinski | .20 | .09 |
| ❑ 62 Colin Beardsmore | .05 | .02 |
| ❑ 63 Dan Pawlacyzk | .05 | .02 |
| ❑ 64 Scott Blair | .05 | .02 |
| ❑ 65 Mike Morrone | .05 | .02 |
| ❑ 66 Matt Ball | .05 | .02 |
| ❑ 67 Steve Dumonski | .05 | .02 |
| ❑ 68 Murray Sheehan | .05 | .02 |
| ❑ 69 Sean Haggerty | 1.00 | .45 |
| ❑ 70 Andrew Taylor | .05 | .02 |
| ❑ 71 Steve Wasylko | .10 | .05 |
| ❑ 72 Jan Vodrazka | .05 | .02 |
| ❑ 73 Dan Preston | .05 | .02 |
| ❑ 74 Jesse Boulerice | .30 | .14 |
| ❑ 75 Bryan Berard | 2.00 | .90 |
| ❑ 76 Nicolas Beaudoin | .25 | .11 |
| ❑ 77 Tom Buckley | .10 | .05 |
| ❑ 78 Mark Cadotte | .20 | .09 |
| ❑ 79 Greg Stephan | .05 | .02 |
| ❑ 80 Peter DeBoer | .05 | .02 |
| ❑ 81 Regan Stocco | .05 | .02 |
| ❑ 82 Andy Adams | .25 | .11 |
| ❑ 83 Brett Thompson | .25 | .11 |
| ❑ 84 Darryl McArthur | .05 | .02 |
| ❑ 85 Ryan Risidore | .20 | .09 |
| ❑ 86 Joel Cort | .10 | .05 |
| ❑ 87 Chris Hajt | .50 | .23 |
| ❑ 88 Bryan McKinney | .05 | .02 |
| ❑ 89 Dwayne Hay | .50 | .23 |
| ❑ 90 Andrew Clark | .05 | .02 |
| ❑ 91 Ryan Robichaud | .05 | .02 |
| ❑ 92 Mike Vellinga | .05 | .02 |
| ❑ 93 Jamie Wright | .05 | .02 |
| ❑ 94 Herbert Vasilijevs | .05 | .02 |
| ❑ 95 Dan Cloutier | 1.00 | .45 |
| ❑ 96 Brian Wesenberg | .35 | .16 |
| ❑ 97 Michael Pittman | .05 | .02 |
| ❑ 98 Jeff Williams | .05 | .02 |
| ❑ 99 Todd Norman | .25 | .11 |
| ❑ 100 Brian Willsie | .05 | .02 |
| ❑ 101 Jason Jackman | .20 | .09 |
| ❑ 102 Mike Lankshear | .15 | .07 |
| ❑ 103 Andrew Long | .20 | .09 |
| ❑ 104 Nick Bootland | .10 | .05 |
| ❑ 105 E.J. McGuire | .05 | .02 |
| ❑ 106 Bujar Amidovski | .50 | .23 |
| ❑ 107 John Hultberg | .25 | .11 |
| ❑ 108 Eric Olsen | .05 | .02 |
| ❑ 109 Chris Allen | .40 | .18 |
| ❑ 110 Michael Tilson | .05 | .02 |
| ❑ 111 Jeff DaCosta | .05 | .02 |
| ❑ 112 Gord Walsh | .05 | .02 |
| ❑ 113 Matt Bradley | .05 | .02 |
| ❑ 114 Robert Mailloux | .05 | .02 |
| ❑ 115 Justin Davis | .05 | .02 |
| ❑ 116 Marc Moro | .25 | .11 |
| ❑ 117 Cail MacLean | .05 | .02 |
| ❑ 118 Jason Sands | .05 | .02 |
| ❑ 119 Matt Price | .05 | .02 |
| ❑ 120 Zdenek Skorepa | .10 | .05 |
| ❑ 121 Jason Morgan | .05 | .02 |
| ❑ 122 Mike Oliveira | .25 | .11 |
| ❑ 123 Colin Chaulk | .05 | .02 |
| ❑ 124 Dylan Taylor | .05 | .02 |
| ❑ 125 Kurt Johnston | .05 | .02 |
| ❑ 126 Bill Minkhorst | .05 | .02 |
| ❑ 127 Wes Swinson | .25 | .11 |
| ❑ 128 Adam Fleming | .05 | .02 |
| ❑ 129 Chris MacDonald | .05 | .02 |
| ❑ 130 Gary Agnew | .05 | .02 |
| ❑ 131 David Belitski | .50 | .23 |
| ❑ 132 Jarrett Rose | .05 | .02 |
| ❑ 133 Ryan Mougenel | .05 | .02 |
| ❑ 134 Rob Stanfield | .05 | .02 |
| ❑ 135 Duncan Fader | .05 | .02 |
| ❑ 136 Rob Maric | .05 | .02 |
| ❑ 137 Mark McMahon | .05 | .02 |
| ❑ 138 Serge Payer | .05 | .02 |
| ❑ 139 Paul Traynor | .05 | .02 |
| ❑ 140 Bogdan Rudenko | .05 | .02 |
| ❑ 141 Robert DeCiantis | .15 | .07 |
| ❑ 142 Andrew Dale | .25 | .11 |
| ❑ 143 Jeff Ambrosio | .10 | .05 |
| ❑ 144 Paul Doyle | .20 | .09 |
| ❑ 145 Bryan Duce | .05 | .02 |
| ❑ 146 Jason Byrnes | .05 | .02 |
| ❑ 147 Ryan Pepperall | .40 | .18 |
| ❑ 148 Wes Vander Wal | .05 | .02 |
| ❑ 149 Boyd Devereaux | 1.50 | .70 |
| ❑ 150 Keith Walsh | .05 | .02 |
| ❑ 151 Joe Birch | .05 | .02 |
| ❑ 152 Craig Nelson | .05 | .02 |
| ❑ 153 Brian Hayden | .05 | .02 |
| ❑ 154 Matt O'Dette | .05 | .02 |
| ❑ 155 Geoff Ward | .05 | .02 |
| ❑ 156 Frank Ivankovic | .25 | .11 |
| ❑ 157 Eoin McInerney | .25 | .11 |
| ❑ 158 Joel Dezainde | .05 | .02 |
| ❑ 159 Duncan Dalmad | .05 | .02 |
| ❑ 160 Brandon Sugden | .05 | .02 |
| ❑ 161 Jamie Wentzell | .05 | .02 |

| | | |
|---|---|---|
| ❑ 162 Ryan Burgoyne | .05 | .02 |
| ❑ 163 Todd Crane | .05 | .02 |
| ❑ 164 Chad Cavanagh | .05 | .02 |
| ❑ 165 Andrew Fagan | .05 | .02 |
| ❑ 166 Ryan Gardner | .05 | .02 |
| ❑ 167 Kevin Boyd | .05 | .02 |
| ❑ 168 Kevin Barry | .05 | .02 |
| ❑ 169 Richard Pitirri | .05 | .02 |
| ❑ 170 Adam Colagiacomo | 1.00 | .45 |
| ❑ 171 Jason Brooks | .05 | .02 |
| ❑ 172 Justin McPolin | .05 | .02 |
| ❑ 173 Travis Riggin | .05 | .02 |
| ❑ 174 Steve Lowe | .05 | .02 |
| ❑ 175 Todd St. Louis | .05 | .02 |
| ❑ 176 Kevin Slota | .05 | .02 |
| ❑ 177 Ryan McKie | .05 | .02 |
| ❑ 178 Corey Isen | .05 | .02 |
| ❑ 179 Sasha Cucuz | .05 | .02 |
| ❑ 180 Tom Barrett | .05 | .02 |
| ❑ 181 Ken Carroll | .05 | .02 |
| ❑ 182 Ryan Penney | .25 | .11 |
| ❑ 183 Jay McKee | .50 | .23 |
| ❑ 184 Ryan Taylor | .05 | .02 |
| ❑ 185 Jeff Paul | .05 | .02 |
| ❑ 186 Jason Ward | 2.00 | .90 |
| ❑ 187 Jesse Black | .10 | .05 |
| ❑ 188 Steve Nimigon | .20 | .09 |
| ❑ 189 Chris Haskett | .05 | .02 |
| ❑ 190 Geoff Peters | .40 | .18 |
| ❑ 191 Ryan Cirillo | .05 | .02 |
| ❑ 192 David Froh | .05 | .02 |
| ❑ 193 Jeff Johnstone | .05 | .02 |
| ❑ 194 Shane Nash | .20 | .09 |
| ❑ 195 Jason Robinson | .05 | .02 |
| ❑ 196 Rich Vrataric | .05 | .02 |
| ❑ 197 Colin Pepperall | .05 | .02 |
| ❑ 198 Craig Jalbert | .05 | .02 |
| ❑ 199 Andrew Williamson | .05 | .02 |
| ❑ 200 Greg Tymchuk | .05 | .02 |
| ❑ 201 Chester Gallant | .05 | .02 |
| ❑ 202 Mike Perna | .05 | .02 |
| ❑ 203 Adam Nitel | .05 | .02 |
| ❑ 204 Dave Burkholder | .05 | .02 |
| ❑ 205 Chris Johnstone | .05 | .02 |
| ❑ 206 Elliott Faust | .25 | .11 |
| ❑ 207 Scott Roche | .50 | .23 |
| ❑ 208 Kam White | .05 | .02 |
| ❑ 209 Scott Atkins | .05 | .02 |
| ❑ 210 Luc Belliveau | .05 | .02 |
| ❑ 211 Jamie Vossen | .05 | .02 |
| ❑ 212 Ryan MacDonald | .05 | .02 |
| ❑ 213 Jim Midgley | .05 | .02 |
| ❑ 214 Steven Carpenter | .05 | .02 |
| ❑ 215 Jake Martel | .05 | .02 |
| ❑ 216 Alex Matvichuk | .05 | .02 |
| ❑ 217 Trevor Gallant | .25 | .11 |
| ❑ 218 Ryan Gillis | .05 | .02 |
| ❑ 219 Kris Cantu | .05 | .02 |
| ❑ 220 Mark Provenzano | .05 | .02 |
| ❑ 221 Brian Whitley | .05 | .02 |
| ❑ 222 Dustin Virag | .05 | .02 |
| ❑ 223 Lee Jinman | .50 | .23 |
| ❑ 224 Peter McCague | .05 | .02 |
| ❑ 225 Herb Bonvie | .05 | .02 |
| ❑ 226 Philippe Poirier | .05 | .02 |
| ❑ 227 Greg Labanski | .05 | .02 |
| ❑ 228 Milan Kostolny | .05 | .02 |
| ❑ 229 Ryan Power | .05 | .02 |
| ❑ 230 Shane Parker | .05 | .02 |
| ❑ 231 Travis Scott | .35 | .16 |
| ❑ 232 Tyrone Garner | .25 | .11 |
| ❑ 233 Marty Wilford | .05 | .02 |
| ❑ 234 Ole Anderson | .05 | .02 |
| ❑ 235 Ryan Tocher | .05 | .02 |
| ❑ 236 Nathan Perrott | .05 | .02 |
| ❑ 237 Brandon Coalter | .05 | .02 |
| ❑ 238 John Tripp | .50 | .23 |
| ❑ 239 Jay LeGault | .10 | .05 |
| ❑ 240 Wayne Primeau | .75 | .35 |
| ❑ 241 Trevor Edgar | .05 | .02 |
| ❑ 242 Peter Hogan | .05 | .02 |
| ❑ 243 Warren Holmes | .05 | .02 |
| ❑ 244 Jason Metcalfe | .05 | .02 |
| ❑ 245 Mike Zanutto | .05 | .02 |
| ❑ 246 Jeff Ware | .40 | .18 |
| ❑ 247 Ian MacNeil | .05 | .02 |
| ❑ 248 Jan Snopek | .20 | .09 |
| ❑ 249 Kurt Walsh | .05 | .02 |
| ❑ 250 Marc Savard | .75 | .35 |
| ❑ 251 Darcy O'Shea | .05 | .02 |
| ❑ 252 Jason Sweitzer | .05 | .02 |
| ❑ 253 Ryan Lindsay | .05 | .02 |
| ❑ 254 Scott Seiling | .05 | .02 |
| ❑ 255 Stan Butler | .05 | .02 |
| ❑ 256 Tim Keyes | .25 | .11 |
| ❑ 257 Craig Hillier | .75 | .35 |
| ❑ 258 Craig Whynot | .05 | .02 |
| ❑ 259 David Bell | .05 | .02 |
| ❑ 260 Rich Bronila | .05 | .02 |
| ❑ 261 Roy Gray | .05 | .02 |
| ❑ 262 Nick Boynton | 1.50 | .70 |
| ❑ 263 Mike Sim | .50 | .23 |
| ❑ 264 B.J. Johnston | .05 | .02 |
| ❑ 265 Niall Maynard | .05 | .02 |
| ❑ 266 Dan Tudin | .05 | .02 |
| ❑ 267 Jure Kovacavic | .05 | .02 |
| ❑ 268 Ben Gustavson | .05 | .02 |
| ❑ 269 Steve Zaryk | .05 | .02 |
| ❑ 270 Darren Debrie | .05 | .02 |
| ❑ 271 Troy Stonier | .05 | .02 |
| ❑ 272 David Nemirovsky | .50 | .23 |
| ❑ 273 Joel Trottier | .25 | .11 |
| ❑ 274 Mike Lavell | .05 | .02 |
| ❑ 275 Brian Campbell | .05 | .02 |
| ❑ 276 Chris Despatis | .05 | .02 |
| ❑ 277 Sean Blanchard | .35 | .16 |
| ❑ 278 Alyn McCauley | 2.00 | .90 |
| ❑ 279 Chris Pittman | .20 | .09 |
| ❑ 280 Daryl Rivers | .05 | .02 |
| ❑ 281 Brent Johnston | .05 | .02 |
| ❑ 282 Shaun Gallant | .05 | .02 |
| ❑ 283 Shane Kenny | .05 | .02 |
| ❑ 284 Chris Biagini | .05 | .02 |
| ❑ 285 Jim Ensom | .10 | .05 |
| ❑ 286 Marek Babic | .05 | .02 |
| ❑ 287 Oleg Tsyrkunov | .05 | .02 |
| ❑ 288 Mike Loach | .05 | .02 |
| ❑ 289 Peter MacKeller | .05 | .02 |
| ❑ 290 Ryan Davis | .05 | .02 |
| ❑ 291 John Argiropoulos | .05 | .02 |
| ❑ 292 Jason Campbell | .05 | .02 |
| ❑ 293 Ryan Christie | .05 | .02 |
| ❑ 294 Dan Snyder | .05 | .02 |
| ❑ 295 Steve Gallace | .05 | .02 |
| ❑ 296 Scott Seiling | .05 | .02 |
| ❑ 297 Jeremy Rebek | .05 | .02 |
| ❑ 298 Adam Mair | .05 | .02 |
| ❑ 299 Matt Osborne | .05 | .02 |
| ❑ 300 Mike Gelati | .05 | .02 |
| ❑ 301 Wayne Primeau | .75 | .35 |
| ❑ 302 Chris Wismer | .05 | .02 |
| ❑ 303 Larry Paleczny | .05 | .02 |
| ❑ 304 Kurt Walsh | .05 | .02 |
| ❑ 305 John Lovell | .05 | .02 |
| ❑ 306 Allan Hitchen | .25 | .11 |
| ❑ 307 Zac Bierk | 1.00 | .45 |
| ❑ 308 Mike Martone | .05 | .02 |
| ❑ 309 Jonathan Murphy | .05 | .02 |
| ❑ 310 Adrian Murray | .05 | .02 |
| ❑ 311 Rob Giffin | .05 | .02 |
| ❑ 312 Corey Crocker | .40 | .18 |
| ❑ 313 Cameron Mann | 3.00 | 1.35 |
| ❑ 314 Ryan Pawluk | .05 | .02 |
| ❑ 315 Jason MacMillan | .05 | .02 |
| ❑ 316 Shawn Thornton | .05 | .02 |
| ❑ 317 Wade Dawe | .05 | .02 |
| ❑ 318 Eric Landry | .05 | .02 |
| ❑ 319 Steve Hogg | .05 | .02 |
| ❑ 320 Kevin Bolibruck | .05 | .02 |
| ❑ 321 Dave Duerden | .25 | .11 |
| ❑ 322 Mike Williams | .05 | .02 |
| ❑ 323 Andy Johnson | .05 | .02 |
| ❑ 324 Jaret Nixon | .05 | .02 |
| ❑ 325 Evgeny Korolev | .05 | .02 |
| ❑ 326 Matthew Lahey | .05 | .02 |
| ❑ 327 Ryan Schmidt | .05 | .02 |
| ❑ 328 Scott Barney | .75 | .35 |
| ❑ 329 Steve Jones | .05 | .02 |
| ❑ 330 Dave McQueen | .05 | .02 |
| ❑ 331 Jeff Salajko | .25 | .11 |
| ❑ 332 Patrick DesRochers | 2.50 | 1.10 |
| ❑ 333 Gerald Moriarty | .05 | .02 |
| ❑ 334 Allan Carr | .05 | .02 |
| ❑ 335 Tom Brown | .05 | .02 |
| ❑ 336 Andy Delmore | .40 | .18 |
| ❑ 337 Darren Mortier | .05 | .02 |
| ❑ 338 Aaron Brand | .40 | .18 |
| ❑ 339 Eric Boulton | .05 | .02 |
| ❑ 340 Jonathan Sim | .20 | .09 |
| ❑ 341 Trevor Letowski | .50 | .23 |
| ❑ 342 Michael Hanson | .05 | .02 |
| ❑ 343 Todd Miller | .05 | .02 |
| ❑ 344 Brendan Yarema | .05 | .02 |
| ❑ 345 Brad Simms | .05 | .02 |
| ❑ 346 David Nemirovsky | .50 | .23 |
| ❑ 347 Jeff Brown | .40 | .18 |
| ❑ 348 Andrew Proskurinicki | .05 | .02 |
| ❑ 349 Wes Mason | .40 | .18 |
| ❑ 350 Scott Corbett | .05 | .02 |
| ❑ 351 Dave Bourque | .05 | .02 |
| ❑ 352 Sean Brown | .50 | .23 |
| ❑ 353 Marcin Snita | .05 | .02 |
| ❑ 354 Rich Brown | .05 | .02 |
| ❑ 355 Mark Hunter | .05 | .02 |
| ❑ 356 Michal Podolka | .35 | .16 |
| ❑ 357 Dan Cloutier | 1.50 | .70 |
| ❑ 358 Cory Murphy | .05 | .02 |
| ❑ 359 Kevin Murnaghan | .05 | .02 |
| ❑ 360 Andre Payette | .05 | .02 |
| ❑ 361 Richard Uniacke | .20 | .09 |
| ❑ 362 Joe Seroski | .15 | .07 |
| ❑ 363 Joe Thornton | 8.00 | 3.60 |
| ❑ 364 Ben Schust | .05 | .02 |
| ❑ 365 Peter Cava | .05 | .02 |
| ❑ 366 Darryl Green | .05 | .02 |
| ❑ 367 Trevor Tokarczyk | .05 | .02 |
| ❑ 368 Jeff Gies | .05 | .02 |
| ❑ 369 Rico Fata | 4.00 | 1.80 |
| ❑ 370 Brian Secord | .05 | .02 |
| ❑ 371 Scott Cherrey | .15 | .07 |
| ❑ 372 Brian Stacey | .05 | .02 |
| ❑ 373 Lee Cole | .05 | .02 |
| ❑ 374 Richard Jackman | .50 | .23 |
| ❑ 375 Jason Doyle | .25 | .11 |
| ❑ 376 Brian Stewart | .10 | .05 |
| ❑ 377 Blaine Fitzpatrick | .05 | .02 |
| ❑ 378 Robert Mulick | .05 | .02 |
| ❑ 379 Andy Adams | .25 | .11 |
| ❑ 380 Joe Paterson | .05 | .02 |
| ❑ 381 Dave MacDonald | .25 | .11 |
| ❑ 382 Stephan Valiquette | .25 | .11 |
| ❑ 383 Tim Swartz | .05 | .02 |
| ❑ 384 Gregg Lalonde | .05 | .02 |
| ❑ 385 Tyson Flinn | .05 | .02 |
| ❑ 386 Ryan Sly | .05 | .02 |
| ❑ 387 Neal Martin | .05 | .02 |
| ❑ 388 Kevin Hansen | .05 | .02 |
| ❑ 389 Joe Lombardo | .05 | .02 |
| ❑ 390 Darryl Moxam | .05 | .02 |
| ❑ 391 Jeremy Adduono | .15 | .07 |
| ❑ 392 Ryan Shanahan | .05 | .02 |
| ❑ 393 Sean Venedam | .15 | .07 |
| ❑ 394 Andrew Dale | .25 | .11 |
| ❑ 395 Rob Butler | .05 | .02 |
| ❑ 396 Brian Scott | .05 | .02 |
| ❑ 397 Liam MacEachern | .05 | .02 |
| ❑ 398 Luc Gagne | .05 | .02 |
| ❑ 399 Richard Rochefort | .05 | .02 |
| ❑ 400 Noel Burkitt | .05 | .02 |
| ❑ 401 Simon Sherry | .05 | .02 |
| ❑ 402 Brad Domonsky | .05 | .02 |
| ❑ 403 Ron Newhook | .05 | .02 |
| ❑ 404 Serge Dunphy | .05 | .02 |
| ❑ 405 Todd Lalonde | .05 | .02 |
| ❑ 406 Ryan Gelinas | .25 | .11 |
| ❑ 407 Terry Joss | .20 | .09 |
| ❑ 408 Mike Martin | .20 | .09 |
| ❑ 409 Chris Van Dyk | .20 | .09 |
| ❑ 410 Denis Smith | .05 | .02 |
| ❑ 411 Glenn Crawford | .20 | .09 |
| ❑ 412 Robert Blain | .05 | .02 |
| ❑ 413 Matt Masterson | .05 | .02 |
| ❑ 414 Adam Young | .05 | .02 |
| ❑ 415 Matt Cooke | .40 | .18 |
| ❑ 416 Jeff Zehr | .75 | .35 |
| ❑ 417 Wes Ward | .20 | .09 |
| ❑ 418 Matt Elich | .35 | .16 |
| ❑ 419 Rob Shearer | .10 | .05 |
| ❑ 420 Dean Mando | .05 | .02 |
| ❑ 421 Chris Kerr | .05 | .02 |
| ❑ 422 Vladimir Kretchine | .05 | .02 |
| ❑ 423 Jeff Martin | .05 | .02 |
| ❑ 424 Valerojy Svoboda | .05 | .02 |
| ❑ 425 Dave Geris | .20 | .09 |
| ❑ 426 Ryan Pawluk | .05 | .02 |
| ❑ 427 Ryan Shaver | .05 | .02 |
| ❑ 428 Cameron Kincaid | .05 | .02 |
| ❑ 429 Tim Findlay | .20 | .09 |
| ❑ 430 Tim Bryan | .05 | .02 |
| ❑ 431 Alexandre Volchkov | 2.00 | .90 |
| ❑ 432 Boyd Devereaux | 2.00 | .90 |
| ❑ 433 Chris Allen | .40 | .18 |
| ❑ 434 Paul Doyle | .20 | .09 |
| ❑ 435 Wes Mason | .40 | .18 |
| ❑ 436 Chris Hajt | .40 | .18 |
| ❑ 437 Kurt Walsh | .05 | .02 |
| ❑ 438 Glenn Crawford | .20 | .09 |
| ❑ 439 Jeff Brown | .40 | .18 |
| ❑ 440 Geoff Peters | .50 | .23 |
| ❑ NNO Zac Bierk autograph | 25.00 | 11.00 |

## 1995-96 Slapshot Promos

This nine-card set was issued as inserts in the 95-96 Slapshot set. These cards were designed to be previews of the regular Slapshot issue. Since the cards are unnumbered we have sequenced them in alphabetical order.

| | MINT | NRMT |
|---|---|---|
| COMPLETE SET (9) | 18.00 | 8.00 |
| COMMON CARD (1-9) | .50 | .23 |
| ❑ 1 Zac Bierk | 3.00 | 1.35 |
| ❑ 2 Nick Boynton | 3.00 | 1.35 |
| ❑ 3 Adam Colagiacomo | 2.00 | .90 |
| ❑ 4 Sean Haggerty | 3.00 | 1.35 |
| ❑ 5 Cameron Mann | 5.00 | 2.20 |
| ❑ 6 Mike Martin | .50 | .23 |
| ❑ 7 Jay McKee | 1.00 | .45 |
| ❑ 8 Ryan Pepperall | 1.50 | .70 |
| ❑ 9 Scott Roche | 2.00 | .90 |

## 1991 Star Pics

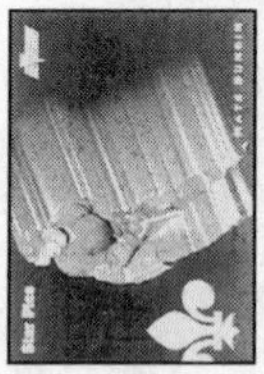

This 72 card standard-size set contained 18 1991 first round draft picks. The cards have glossy action color player photos, with a thin white border on a background picturing a hockey mask. The player's name appears in a white lettering below the picture. The backs ahve a biography, personal background and a mini-scouting report by Al Morganti, superimposed on a partially washed out color player photo. The print run was supposed to be 225, 000 individually numbered sets. Autographed cards were randomly inserted into the sets. The autograph cards are valued at 60X to 100X the prices below for flashback cards and 20X to 40X for the other cards.

| | MINT | NRMT |
|---|---|---|
| SEALED SET (72) | 4.00 | 1.80 |
| COMMON CARD (1-72) | .05 | .02 |
| ❑ 1 Draft Overview<br>Al Morganti | .05 | .02 |
| ❑ 2 Pat Falloon | .30 | .14 |
| ❑ 3 Jamie Pushor | .05 | .02 |
| ❑ 4 Jean Beliveau FLB<br>Hall of Fame | .25 | .11 |
| ❑ 5 Martin Lapointe | .05 | .02 |
| ❑ 6 Jamie Matthews | .05 | .02 |
| ❑ 7 Rod Gilbert FLB<br>Hall of Fame | .05 | .02 |
| ❑ 8 Niklas Sundblad | .05 | .02 |
| ❑ 9 Steve Konowalchuk | .05 | .02 |
| ❑ 10 Alex Delvecchio FLB<br>Hall of Fame | .05 | .02 |
| ❑ 11 Donevan Hextall | .05 | .02 |
| ❑ 12 Dody Wood | .05 | .02 |
| ❑ 13 Scott Niedermayer | .50 | .23 |
| ❑ 14 Trevor Halverson | .05 | .02 |
| ❑ 15 Terry Chitaroni | .05 | .02 |
| ❑ 16 Tyler Wright | .05 | .02 |
| ❑ 17 Andrei Lomakin UER | .05 | .02 |
| ❑ 18 Martin Hamrlik | .05 | .02 |
| ❑ 19 Dimitri Filimonov UER | .05 | .02 |
| ❑ 20 Ed Belfour FLB | .25 | .11 |
| ❑ 21 Andrew Verner | .05 | .02 |
| ❑ 22 Yanic Perreault | .05 | .02 |
| ❑ 23 Michael Nylander | .05 | .02 |
| ❑ 24 Scott Lachance | .05 | .02 |
| ❑ 25 Pavel Bure | 1.50 | .70 |
| ❑ 26 Mike Torchia | .05 | .02 |
| ❑ 27 Frank Mahovlich FLB<br>Hall of Fame | .05 | .02 |
| ❑ 28 Philippe Boucher | .05 | .02 |
| ❑ 29 Jiri Slegr | .05 | .02 |
| ❑ 30 Sergei Fedorov FLB | .75 | .35 |
| ❑ 31 Rene Corbet | .05 | .02 |
| ❑ 32 Jamie McLennan | .05 | .02 |
| ❑ 33 Shane Peacock | .05 | .02 |
| ❑ 34 Mario Nobili | .05 | .02 |
| ❑ 35 Peter Forsberg | 2.00 | .90 |
| ❑ 36 All-Rookie Team<br>Pat Falloon<br>Tyler Wright<br>Philippe Boucher<br>Andrew Verner<br>Scott Lachance | .05 | .02 |
| ❑ 37 Arturs Irbe | .30 | .14 |
| ❑ 38 Alexei Zhitnik | .05 | .02 |
| ❑ 39 Pat Peake | .05 | .02 |
| ❑ 40 Adam Oates FLB | .20 | .09 |
| ❑ 41 Markus Naslund | .05 | .02 |
| ❑ 42 Eric Lavigne | .05 | .02 |
| ❑ 43 Jeff Nelson | .05 | .02 |
| ❑ 44 Yanic Dupre UER | .05 | .02 |
| ❑ 45 Justin Morrison | .05 | .02 |
| ❑ 46 Alek Stojanov | .05 | .02 |
| ❑ 47 Marcel Cousineau | .05 | .02 |
| ❑ 48 Alexei Kovalev | .40 | .18 |
| ❑ 49 Andrei Trefilov | .05 | .02 |
| ❑ 50 Mats Sundin FLB | .25 | .11 |
| ❑ 51 Steve Staios | .05 | .02 |
| ❑ 52 Glenn Hall FLB | .25 | .11 |
| ❑ 53 Brent Bilodeau | .05 | .02 |
| ❑ 54 Darcy Werenka | .05 | .02 |
| ❑ 55 Chris Osgood | 1.00 | .45 |
| ❑ 56 Nathan Lafayette | .05 | .02 |
| ❑ 57 Richard Matvichuk | .05 | .02 |
| ❑ 58 Dimitri Mironov UER | .05 | .02 |
| ❑ 59 Jason Dawe | .05 | .02 |
| ❑ 60 Mike Ricci FLB | .05 | .02 |
| ❑ 61 Gerry Cheevers FLB | .25 | .11 |
| ❑ 62 Jim Campbell | .05 | .02 |
| ❑ 63 Francois Groleau | .05 | .02 |
| ❑ 64 Glen Murray | .05 | .02 |
| ❑ 65 Jason Young | .05 | .02 |
| ❑ 66 Dean McAmmond | .05 | .02 |
| ❑ 67 Guy Leveque | .05 | .02 |
| ❑ 68 Patrick Poulin | .05 | .02 |
| ❑ 69 Bobby House | .05 | .02 |
| ❑ 70 Jaromir Jagr FLB | 1.00 | .45 |
| ❑ 71 Jassen Cullimore | .05 | .02 |
| ❑ 72 Checklist Card | .05 | .02 |

## 1991 Ultimate Draft Promos

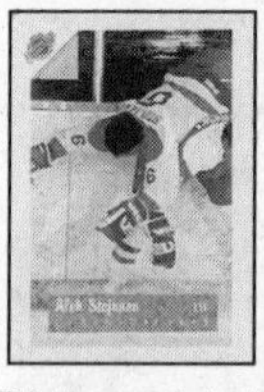

This three-card standard-size set was given out to dealers and collectors to promote the new Ultimate hockey draft picks cards. The front design is basically the same as the regular issue. The Torchia card displays a different player photo, while the Stojanov card is cropped differently. Also the promos have the team name below the player's name rather than city name as with their regular issue. The backs of the promos differ from those of the regular issue in that the photos on the back are more ghosted and the word "Sample" is stenciled over them. Also the player information on the Stojanov card back is arranged differently on the promo. The cards are unnumbered and checklisted below in alphabetical order.

| | MINT | NRMT |
|---|---|---|
| COMPLETE SET (3) | 1.00 | .45 |
| COMMON CARD (1-3) | .25 | .11 |
| ❑ 1 Pat Falloon | .50 | .23 |
| ❑ 2 Alex Stojanov | .25 | .11 |
| ❑ 3 Mike Torchia | .25 | .11 |

## 1991 Ultimate Draft

The 1991 Ultimate/Smokey's Draft Picks hockey set contains 90 standard-size cards. The front design has glossy, color action player photos, bordered in white. The upper left corner of the picture is cut off to allow space for a logo with the words "Sportscards Ultimate Hockey". The player's name, position, and team appear in white lettering in a blue-gray rectangle near the card bottom. The backs have biography, statistics, and player profile overlaying a player photo that is ghosted except for the head. The cards are numbered on the back. Cards 58-74 are a special subset of First Draft Picks (FDP) and cards 78-87 are a special subset of black-and-white photos (BW). Reportedly production quantities were as follows: 6,000 American set cases equalling 120,000 sets, 750 French set cases equalling 15,000 sets, 5,000 American ten-box wax cases, 1,500 French ten-box wax cases, and 500 autographed sets. Currently the French and English cards are valued equally. Autographed versions are worth 30X to 50X basic cards.

| | MINT | NRMT |
|---|---|---|
| COMPLETE SET (90) | 5.00 | 2.20 |
| COMMON CARD (1-90) | .05 | .02 |
| ❑ 1 Ultimate/Preview | .05 | .02 |
| ❑ 2 Pat Falloon | .20 | .09 |
| ❑ 3 Scott Niedermayer | .25 | .11 |
| ❑ 4 Scott Lachance | .05 | .02 |
| ❑ 5 Peter Forsberg | 1.00 | .45 |
| ❑ 6 Alek Stojanov | .05 | .02 |
| ❑ 7 Richard Matvichuk | .10 | .05 |
| ❑ 8 Patrick Poulin | .05 | .02 |
| ❑ 9 Martin Lapointe | .20 | .09 |
| ❑ 10 Tyler Wright | .05 | .02 |
| ❑ 11 Philippe Boucher | .05 | .02 |
| ❑ 12 Pat Peake | .10 | .05 |
| ❑ 13 Markus Naslund | .10 | .05 |
| ❑ 14 Brent Bilodeau | .05 | .02 |
| ❑ 15 Glen Murray | .10 | .05 |
| ❑ 16 Niklas Sundblad | .05 | .02 |
| ❑ 17 Trevor Halverson | .05 | .02 |
| ❑ 18 Dean McAmmond UER | .10 | .05 |
| ❑ 19 Jim Campbell | .50 | .23 |
| ❑ 20 Rene Corbet | .15 | .07 |
| ❑ 21 Eric Lavigne | .05 | .02 |
| ❑ 22 Steve Staios | .05 | .02 |
| ❑ 23 Jassen Cullimore | .05 | .02 |
| ❑ 24 Jamie Pushor | .15 | .07 |
| ❑ 25 Donevan Hextall | .05 | .02 |
| ❑ 26 Andrew Verner | .10 | .05 |
| ❑ 27 Jason Dawe | .10 | .05 |
| ❑ 28 Jeff Nelson | .05 | .02 |
| ❑ 29 Darcy Werenka | .05 | .02 |
| ❑ 30 Francois Groleau | .05 | .02 |
| ❑ 31 Guy Leveque | .05 | .02 |
| ❑ 32 Jamie Matthews | .05 | .02 |
| ❑ 33 Dody Wood | .05 | .02 |
| ❑ 34 Yanic Perreault | .10 | .05 |
| ❑ 35 Jamie McLennan UER | .10 | .05 |
| ❑ 36 Yanic Dupre | .05 | .02 |
| ❑ 37 1st Round Checklist | .05 | .02 |
| ❑ 38 Chris Osgood | .75 | .35 |
| ❑ 39 Fredrik Lindquist | .05 | .02 |
| ❑ 40 Jason Young | .05 | .02 |
| ❑ 41 Steve Konowalchuk | .20 | .09 |
| ❑ 42 Michael Nylander | .20 | .09 |
| ❑ 43 Shane Peacock | .05 | .02 |
| ❑ 44 Yves Sarault | .05 | .02 |
| ❑ 45 Marcel Cousineau | .15 | .07 |
| ❑ 46 Nathan Lafayette | .10 | .05 |
| ❑ 47 Bobby House | .05 | .02 |
| ❑ 48 Kerry Toporowski | .05 | .02 |
| ❑ 49 Terry Chitaroni | .05 | .02 |
| ❑ 50 Mike Torchia | .10 | .05 |
| ❑ 51 Mario Nobili | .05 | .02 |
| ❑ 52 Justin Morrison | .05 | .02 |
| ❑ 53 Grayden Reid | .05 | .02 |
| ❑ 54 Yanic Perreault<br>Underdog | .10 | .05 |
| ❑ 55 2nd Round Checklist | .05 | .02 |
| ❑ 56 Niedermayer& Falloon&<br>and Lachance | .25 | .11 |
| ❑ 57 The Goalies | .20 | .09 |
| ❑ 58 Pat Falloon FDP | .20 | .09 |
| ❑ 59 Scott Niedermayer FDP | .25 | .11 |
| ❑ 60 Scott Lachance FDP | .05 | .02 |
| ❑ 61 Peter Forsberg FDP | 1.00 | .45 |
| ❑ 62 Alek Stojanov FDP | .05 | .02 |
| ❑ 63 Richard Matvichuk FDP | .10 | .05 |
| ❑ 64 Patrick Poulin FDP | .05 | .02 |
| ❑ 65 Martin Lapointe FDP | .20 | .09 |
| ❑ 66 Tyler Wright FDP | .05 | .02 |
| ❑ 67 Philippe Boucher FDP | .05 | .02 |
| ❑ 68 Pat Peake FDP | .10 | .05 |
| ❑ 69 Markus Naslund FDP | .10 | .05 |
| ❑ 70 Brent Bilodeau FDP | .05 | .02 |

- ❑ 71 Glen Murray FDP .10 .05
- ❑ 72 Niklas Sundblad FDP .05 .02
- ❑ 73 Trevor Halverson FDP .05 .02
- ❑ 74 Dean McCammond FDP .10 .05
- ❑ 75 Award Winners .10 .05
  Philippe Boucher
  Jeff Nelson
  Scott Niedermayer
- ❑ 76 The Swedes .50 .23
  Markus Naslund
  Peter Forsberg
- ❑ 77 3rd and 4th Round .05 .02
  Checklist
- ❑ 78 Pat Falloon BW .20 .09
- ❑ 79 Scott Niedermayer BW .25 .11
- ❑ 80 Falloon/Niedermayer BW .15 .07
- ❑ 81 Scott Lachance BW .05 .02
- ❑ 82 Philippe Boucher BW .05 .02
- ❑ 83 Markus Naslund BW .10 .05
- ❑ 84 Glen Murray BW .10 .05
- ❑ 85 Niklas Sundblad BW .05 .02
- ❑ 86 Jason Dawe BW .10 .05
- ❑ 87 Yanic Perreault BW .10 .05
- ❑ 88 Offensive Threats .05 .02
  Yanic Dupre
  Mikael Nylander
- ❑ 89 Group Shot/Overview .05 .02
- ❑ 90 Face the Future/ .05 .02
  Ultimate

## 1995-96 Adirondack Red Wings

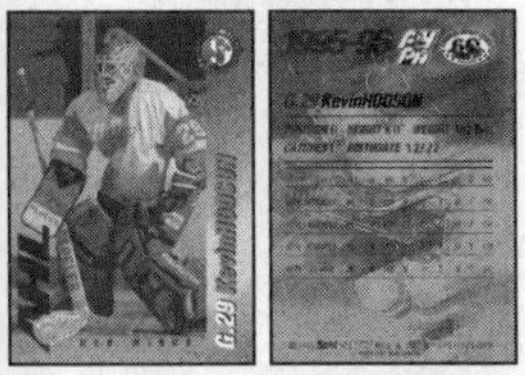

This 25-card set produced by Split Second features the Adirondack Red Wings of the AHL. The sets were available at games and by mail. The cards feature a glossy action photo along with team and manufacturer logos on the front. The backs include player stats. The cards are unnumbered and listed below in alphabetical order.

| | MINT | NRMT |
|---|---|---|
| COMPLETE SET (25) | 12.00 | 5.50 |
| COMMON CARD (1-25) | .10 | .05 |

- ❑ 1 Jeff Bloemberg .40 .18
- ❑ 2 Curtis Bowen .60 .25
- ❑ 3 Dave Chyzowski .40 .18
- ❑ 4 Sylvain Cloutier .40 .18
- ❑ 5 Ryan Duthie .40 .18
- ❑ 6 Anders Eriksson 1.00 .45
- ❑ 7 Yan Golubovski .60 .25
- ❑ 8 Ben Hankinson .40 .18
- ❑ 9 Kevin Hodson 1.50 .70
- ❑ 10 Scott Hollis .40 .18
- ❑ 11 Mike Knuble .60 .25
- ❑ 12 Jason MacDonald .40 .18
- ❑ 13 Mark Major .50 .23
- ❑ 14 Norm Maracle .75 .35
- ❑ 15 Kurt Miller .40 .18
- ❑ 16 Mike Needham .40 .18
- ❑ 17 Troy Neumeier .40 .18
- ❑ 18 Mark Ouimet .40 .18
- ❑ 19 Jamie Pushor .75 .35
- ❑ 20 Stacy Roest .40 .18
- ❑ 21 Brandon Smith .40 .18
- ❑ 22 Kerry Toporowski .40 .18
- ❑ 23 Wes Walz .40 .18
- ❑ 24 Aaron Ward .75 .35
- ❑ 25 Hockeye -- Mascot .10 .05

## 1995-96 AHCA

This 10-card set was produced by the American Hockey Coaches Association for the College Hockey Centennial and features black-and-white photos in a tan border. The backs carry information about the events pictured on the front, which all are key in the history of the development of hockey in the United States.

| | MINT | NRMT |
|---|---|---|
| COMPLETE SET (10) | 5.00 | 2.20 |
| COMMON CARD (1-10) | .50 | .23 |

- ❑ 1 The Pioneers .50 .23
- ❑ 2 The Inspiration 1.00 .45
  Hobey Baker
- ❑ 3 The Personalities .50 .23
  John Mariucci
- ❑ 4 The Champions .50 .23
  Michigan
- ❑ 5 The Colleges .50 .23
  Edward Jeremiah
- ❑ 6 The Coaches .50 .23
  Ron Mason
- ❑ 7 The Records .50 .23
  1970 Cornell squad
- ❑ 8 The Moments .50 .23
  Dean Talafous
- ❑ 9 The Traditions .50 .23
  1978 Boston University Champions
- ❑ 10 The Future 1.00 .45
  Cammi Granato

## 1995-96 Alaska Gold Kings

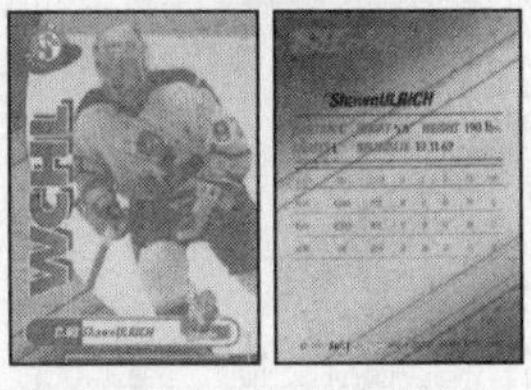

This 19-card set of the Alaska Gold Kings appears to be the first set produced for a club in the West Coast Hockey League. The set was manufactured and distributed by Jessen Associates. The fronts feature action color photos, complemented by the player's name, number and position, the team logo and the league name. The backs contain biographical and statistical data. The set is unnumbered, and listed in alphabetical order.

| | MINT | NRMT |
|---|---|---|
| COMPLETE SET (19) | 6.00 | 2.70 |
| COMMON CARD (1-19) | .10 | .05 |

- ❑ 1 Title Card .10 .05
- ❑ 2 Derby Bognar .40 .18
- ❑ 3 Geoff Bumstead .40 .18
- ❑ 4 Chris Cahill .40 .18
- ❑ 5 Warren Carter .40 .18
- ❑ 6 John Haddad .40 .18
- ❑ 7 Todd Henderson .50 .23
- ❑ 8 Wade Klippenstein .40 .18
- ❑ 9 Matt Koleski .40 .18
- ❑ 10 Donald Lester .40 .18
- ❑ 11 Derek Linnell .40 .18
- ❑ 12 Jamie Loewen .50 .23
- ❑ 13 Travis MacMillan .40 .18
- ❑ 14 Kirk Patton .40 .18
- ❑ 15 Guy Prince .40 .18
- ❑ 16 Rob Proffitt .40 .18
- ❑ 17 Ryan Reynard .40 .18
- ❑ 18 Wayne Sawchuk CO .10 .05
- ❑ 19 Shawn Ulrich .40 .18

## 1996-97 Alaska Gold Kings

This 14-card set of "Alaska's 1st Professional Hockey Team" features the Gold Kings of the West Coast Hockey Legue. The set was produced by Split Second, using unusually heavy card stock, and features grainy action photos on the front, along with the player's name and jersey number, and the team logo. The backs all include the team logo, as well as those of sponsors Coca-Cola of Fairbanks, Winchell's, Club Golf and Twisted Stitches. No player info is included. The cards are unnumbered, and are listed below alphabetically.

| | MINT | NRMT |
|---|---|---|
| COMPLETE SET (14) | 6.00 | 2.70 |
| COMMON CARD (1-14) | .10 | .05 |

- ❑ 1 Mark Costea .50 .23
- ❑ 2 Shane Fisher .50 .23
- ❑ 3 Colin Foley .50 .23
- ❑ 4 Chris French .75 .35
- ❑ 5 Yoshifumi Fujtsawa .50 .23
- ❑ 6 Todd Henderson .75 .35
- ❑ 7 Kelly Hrycun .50 .23
- ❑ 8 Shawn Lofroth .50 .23
- ❑ 9 Brad McCaughey CO .10 .05
- ❑ 10 Billy McGuigan .50 .23
- ❑ 11 Jay Murphy .50 .23
- ❑ 12 Sergei Olympiev .50 .23
- ❑ 13 Orion The Lion .10 .05
  Mascot
- ❑ 14 Shawn Ulrich .50 .23

## 1993-94 Amos Les Forestiers AAA Midget

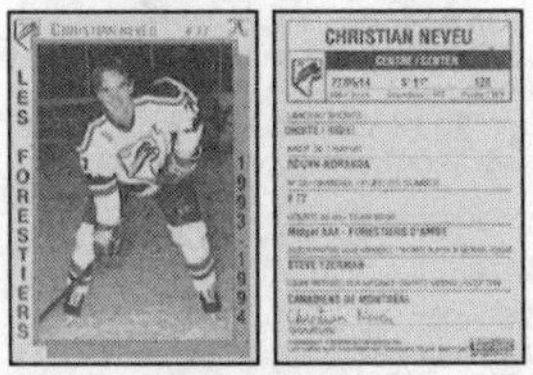

This 26-card standard-size set features Les Forestiers, a Midget AAA team in the province of Quebec. Les Forestiers is one of ten teams in the province from which the junior teams pick their players. The production run was reportedly 505 sets, including 60 autographed sets randomly placed in the lot. On a white card face, the fronts display posed color player photos framed by blue on the left and top and by magenta on the right and bottom. Player identification is printed in the top border, and the team name is printed in the left border. The backs present biographical and trivia information. The set includes 1995 NHL first rounder, Martin Biron.

| | MINT | NRMT |
|---|---|---|
| COMPLETE SET (26) | 12.00 | 5.50 |
| COMMON CARD (1-26) | .25 | .11 |

- ❑ 1 Jean-Francois Belley .50 .23
- ❑ 2 Carl Benoit .50 .23
- ❑ 3 Martin Biron 2.50 1.10
- ❑ 4 David Bolduc .50 .23
- ❑ 5 Martin Bradette .50 .23
- ❑ 6 Dave Fontaine .50 .23
- ❑ 7 Paul-Sebastien Gagnon .50 .23
- ❑ 8 Eric Germain .60 .25
- ❑ 9 Eric Houle .50 .23
- ❑ 10 Jacques Larrivee ACO .25 .11
- ❑ 11 Yannick Lavoie .50 .23
- ❑ 12 Mathieu Letourneau .50 .23
- ❑ 13 Vincent Levasseur .50 .23
- ❑ 14 Jonathan Levesque .50 .23
- ❑ 15 Eric Naud .75 .35
- ❑ 16 Christian Neveu .75 .35
- ❑ 17 Patrick Pelchat .50 .23
- ❑ 18 John Pyliotis .50 .23
- ❑ 19 Luc St-Germain .50 .23
- ❑ 20 Frederick Servant .50 .23
- ❑ 21 Philippe Tremblay .50 .23
- ❑ 22 Serge Trepanier CO .25 .11
- ❑ 23 Dany Villeneuve .50 .23
- ❑ 24 Les Veterans .60 .25
  Christian Neveu
  Mathieu Letourneau
- ❑ 25 Checklist .25 .11
- ❑ 26 Title card .25 .11

## 1996-97 Anchorage Aces

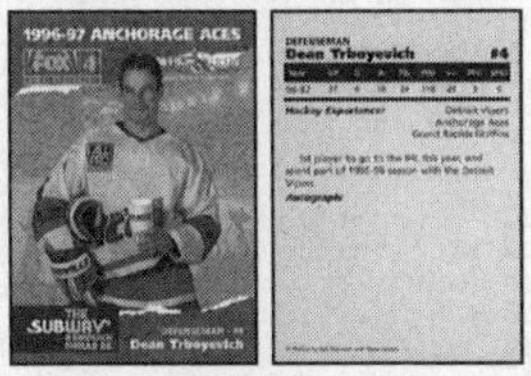

This 16-card set was produced as a promotional giveaway for the Anchorage Aces of the WCHL. The fronts feature posed photos with the players blatantly shilling for the Subway chain; that company's logo is prominently displayed in the lower left corner, along with those of the local FOX TV outlet and KWHL radio. The backs feature sketchy bio information. As the cards are unnumbered, they are listed below in alphabetical order.

| | MINT | NRMT |
|---|---|---|
| COMPLETE SET (16) | 6.00 | 2.70 |
| COMMON CARD (1-16) | .10 | .05 |

- ❑ 1 Alaska's Morning Show .10 .05
- ❑ 2 Derek Donald .50 .23
- ❑ 3 Kiddie Fox .50 .23
- ❑ 4 Dean Larson .50 .23
- ❑ 5 Steve MacSwain .50 .23
- ❑ 6 Mark The Hitman .50 .23
- ❑ 7 J.J. Michaels .50 .23
- ❑ 8 Black Mike .10 .05
- ❑ 9 Craig Mittleholt .50 .23
- ❑ 10 Chris Newans .50 .23
- ❑ 11 Frank Ouellette .50 .23
- ❑ 12 Chad Richard .50 .23
- ❑ 13 Sean Rowe .50 .23
- ❑ 14 Keith Street .50 .23
- ❑ 15 Dean Trboyevich .50 .23
- ❑ 16 Free Q-Zar Game Card .10 .05

## 1997-98 Anchorage Aces

| | MINT | NRMT |
|---|---|---|
| COMPLETE SET (25) | 5.00 | 2.20 |
| COMMON CARD (1-25) | .10 | .05 |

- ❑ 1 Title Card .10 .05
- ❑ 2 Walt Poddubny .30 .14
- ❑ 3 Kenny Huizenga .15 .07
- ❑ 4 Kord Cernich .25 .11
- ❑ 5 Bobby Cunningham .25 .11
- ❑ 6 Derek Donald .25 .11
- ❑ 7 Dallas Ferguson .25 .11
- ❑ 8 Derek Gauthier .25 .11
- ❑ 9 Jason Gibson .25 .11
- ❑ 10 Marc LaForge .25 .11
- ❑ 11 Dean Larson .25 .11
- ❑ 12 Dave Latta .25 .11
- ❑ 13 Steve MacSwain .25 .11
- ❑ 14 Chris Newans .25 .11
- ❑ 15 Hayden O'Rear .25 .11
- ❑ 16 Brian Renfrew .30 .14
- ❑ 17 Sean Rowe .25 .11
- ❑ 18 Jason Shmyr .25 .11
- ❑ 19 Keith Street .25 .11
- ❑ 20 Sergei Tkachenko .30 .14
- ❑ 21 George Wilcox .25 .11
- ❑ 22 Paul Williams .25 .11
- ❑ 23 Mascot .10 .05
- ❑ 24 Mascot .10 .05
- ❑ 25 Mascot .10 .05

## 1990-91 Arizona Icecats

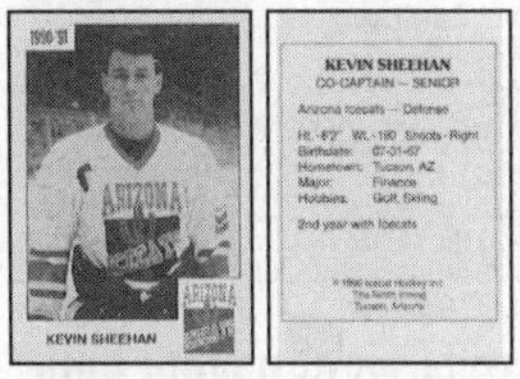

Produced by the Ninth Inning, this 16-card standard-size set features members of the Arizona Icecats. Production was reportedly limited to 2,150 sets, obtainable either at the Tucson Convention Center Ice Arena on game days or at the Ninth Inning (a card shop). The front features a posed color photo of the player, with thin black border on white card stock. The upper left and lower right hand corners of the picture are cut out, with the year and the team logo inserted in these spaces respectively. The back presents biographical information in a black box. Although the individual cards are unnumbered, they are checklisted below according to the numbering assigned to them on the checklist card.

| | MINT | NRMT |
|---|---|---|
| COMPLETE SET (16) | 8.00 | 3.60 |
| COMMON CARD (1-16) | .50 | .23 |

- ❑ 1 Leo Golembiewski CO .75 .35
- ❑ 2 Icecat Leaders 1.00 .45
  Kevin Sheehan
  John Allen
  Leo Golembiewski CO
  Kelly Walker
  John Wegener
- ❑ 3 John Allen .75 .35
- ❑ 4 Don Carlson .50 .23
- ❑ 5 Dan Divjak .75 .35
- ❑ 6 Frank DeMaio .50 .23
- ❑ 7 Jeremy Goltz .75 .35
- ❑ 8 Aaron Joffe .50 .23
- ❑ 9 Dan O'Day .50 .23
- ❑ 10 Dan Olberg .50 .23
- ❑ 11 Cory Oleson .75 .35
- ❑ 12 Kevin Sheehan .75 .35
- ❑ 13 Dean Sives .50 .23
- ❑ 14 Kelly Walker .75 .35
- ❑ 15 John Wegener .75 .35
- ❑ 16 Logo Card .50 .23
  (Checklist)

## 1991-92 Arizona Icecats

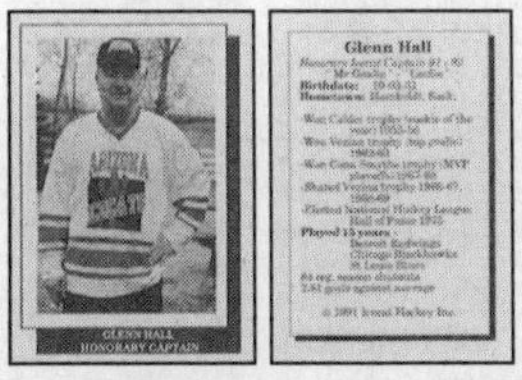

This 20-card standard-size set features members of the Arizona Icecats. The front features a posed color photo of the player, with thin blue border and a blue shadow-border on white card stock. The player's name appears in the bottom shadow- border. The back presents biographical information and statistics in a black shadow-bordered box. Though the individual cards are unnumbered, they are checklisted below according to the numbering assigned to them on the checklist card.

| | MINT | NRMT |
|---|---|---|
| COMPLETE SET (20) | 10.00 | 4.50 |
| COMMON CARD (1-20) | .25 | .11 |

- ❑ 1 Leo Golembiewski CO .25 .11
- ❑ 2 Don Carlson .50 .23
- ❑ 3 Kelly Walker .75 .35
- ❑ 4 Cory Oleson .75 .35
- ❑ 5 Drew Sibr .50 .23
- ❑ 6 Dan Divjak .75 .35
- ❑ 7 Jeremy Goltz .50 .23
- ❑ 8 Aaron Joffe .50 .23
- ❑ 9 Tommy Smith .50 .23
- ❑ 10 Dan Anderson .50 .23
- ❑ 11 Dean Sives .50 .23
- ❑ 12 Steve Hutchings .50 .23
- ❑ 13 Shane Fausel .50 .23
- ❑ 14 Greg Mitchell .50 .23
- ❑ 15 Ricky Pope .50 .23
- ❑ 16 Nate Soules .50 .23
- ❑ 17 Flavio Gentile .50 .23
- ❑ 18 Icecats Leaders .50 .23
  Leo Golembiewski CO
  Kelly Walker
  Cory Oleson
  Jeremy Goltz
  Dan Divjak
- ❑ 19 Glenn Hall 2.50 1.10
  Honorary Captain
- ❑ 20 Logo Card .25 .11
  (Checklist)

## 1992-93 Arizona Icecats

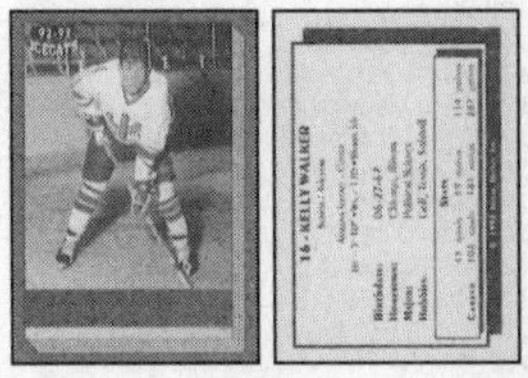

This 16-card standard-size set features the Arizona Icecats hockey team. The fronts display a posed color player photo with multiple blue drop borders. The player's name appears in a royal blue stripe across the bottom of the picture. The backs carry biographical information and statistics in a black shadow-bordered box. Though the individual cards are unnumbered, they are checklisted below according to the numbering assigned to them on the checklist card.

| | MINT | NRMT |
|---|---|---|
| COMPLETE SET (20) | 8.00 | 3.60 |
| COMMON CARD (1-20) | .25 | .11 |

- ❑ 1 Leo Golembiewski CO .25 .11
- ❑ 2 Kelly Walker .60 .25
- ❑ 3 Cory Oleson .60 .25
- ❑ 4 Tommy Smith .50 .23
- ❑ 5 John Allen .50 .23
- ❑ 6 Dan Anderson .50 .23
- ❑ 7 Aaron Joffe .50 .23
- ❑ 8 Dan Divjak .60 .25
- ❑ 9 Jeremy Goltz .50 .23
- ❑ 10 Steve Hutchings .50 .23
- ❑ 11 Greg Mitchell .50 .23
- ❑ 12 Ricky Pope .50 .23
- ❑ 13 Nate Soules .50 .23
- ❑ 14 Matt Glines .50 .23
- ❑ 15 Mark Thawley .50 .23
- ❑ 16 Andre Zafrani .50 .23
- ❑ 17 Chris Noga .50 .23
- ❑ 18 Jim Kolbe .25 .11
  Honorary Captain
- ❑ 19 Coach and Top Gun Line .75 .35
  Cory Oleson
  Leo Golembiewski CO
  Kelly Walker
  Tommy Smith
  John Allen
  Dan Anderson
- ❑ 20 Logo Card .25 .11
  (Checklist)

## 1991-92 Baltimore Skipjacks

Issued in a 3-card strips which are perforated. The set was a 10th anniversary set and was sponsored by Wendy's and Coca-Cola. The cards are numbered card "xx" of 15.

| | MINT | NRMT |
|---|---|---|
| COMPLETE SET (15) | 9.00 | 4.00 |
| COMMON CARD (1-15) | .50 | .23 |

- ❑ 1 Tim Taylor .75 .35
- ❑ 2 Brent Hughes .50 .23
- ❑ 3 Trevor Halverson .50 .23
- ❑ 4 Bobby Reynolds .50 .23
- ❑ 5 Ken Lovsin .50 .23
- ❑ 6 Olaf Kolzig 4.00 1.80
- ❑ 7 Reggie Savage .50 .23

□ 8 Jim Mathieson .50 .23
□ 9 Todd Hlushko .60 .25
□ 10 Mark Ferner .50 .23
□ 11 John Purves .50 .23
□ 12 Steve Seftel .50 .23
□ 13 Craig Duncanson .50 .23
□ 14 Simon Wheeldon .50 .23
□ 15 Bob Babcock .50 .23

## 1996-97 Barrie Colts

The set is unnumbered and checklisted below in alphabetical order.

| | MINT | NRMT |
|---|---|---|
| COMPLETE SET (30) | 10.00 | 4.50 |
| COMMON CARD (1-30) | .10 | .05 |

□ 1 Brian Barker .25 .11
□ 2 Brock Boucher .25 .11
□ 3 Casey Burnette .25 .11
□ 4 Michael Christian .25 .11
□ 5 Keith Delaney .25 .11
□ 6 Adam Deleeuw .25 .11
□ 7 Chris Feil .25 .11
□ 8 Brian Finley .40 .18
□ 9 Michael Henrich .25 .11
□ 10 John Hultberg .60 .25
□ 11 Richard Kazda .25 .11
□ 12 Darren Keily TR .10 .05
□ 13 Cody Leibel .25 .11
□ 14 Mihajlo Martinovich .25 .11
□ 15 Kevin McClelland ACO .10 .05
□ 16 Walker McDonald .25 .11
□ 17 Jeff McKercher .25 .11
□ 18 Luch Nasato .25 .11
□ 19 Ryan O'Keefe .25 .11
□ 20 Jason Pinizzotto .25 .11
□ 21 Ryan Shaver .25 .11
□ 22 Martin Skoula .40 .18
□ 23 Nick Smith .25 .11
□ 24 Brandon Sugden .25 .11
□ 25 Bert Templeton CO .25 .11
□ 26 Jeff Tetzlaff .25 .11
□ 27 Daniel Tkaczuk 3.00 1.35
□ 28 Charlie Horse(Mascot) .10 .05
□ 29 Barrie Colts Team Picture .30 .14
□ 30 Checklist .10 .05

## 1997-98 Barrie Colts

The set is unnumbered and checklisted below in alphabetical order.

| | MINT | NRMT |
|---|---|---|
| COMPLETE SET (27) | 10.00 | 4.50 |
| COMMON CARD (1-27) | .10 | .05 |

□ 1 Brian Barker .25 .11
□ 2 Brock Boucher .25 .11
□ 3 Jan Bulis .50 .23
□ 4 Casey Burnette .25 .11
□ 5 Jason Cannon .25 .11
□ 6 Keith Delaney .25 .11
□ 7 Chris George .25 .11
□ 8 Nick Grady .25 .11
□ 9 Mike Henrich .25 .11
□ 10 John Hultberg .60 .25
□ 11 Marcel Kars .25 .11
□ 12 Darren Keily .10 .05
□ 13 Gerry Lanigan .25 .11
□ 14 Kevin McClelland .10 .05
□ 15 Walker McDonald .25 .11
□ 16 Jeff McKercher .25 .11
□ 17 Brad Morgan .25 .11
□ 18 Luch Nasato .25 .11
□ 19 Corey Neilson .25 .11
□ 20 Nick Smith .25 .11
□ 21 Bert Templeton .25 .11
□ 22 Jeff Tetzlaff .25 .11
□ 23 Chris Thompson .25 .11
□ 24 Daniel Tkaczuk 3.00 1.35
□ 25 Alexandre Volchkov .50 .23
□ 26 Darrell Woodley .25 .11
□ 27 Charlie Horse(Mascot) .10 .05

## 1983-84 Belleville Bulls

This 30-card police set measures approximately 2 5/8" by 4 1/8" and was sponsored by the Board of Commissioners of Police and other local organizations. The fronts feature posed color player photos with white borders. The player's name and position

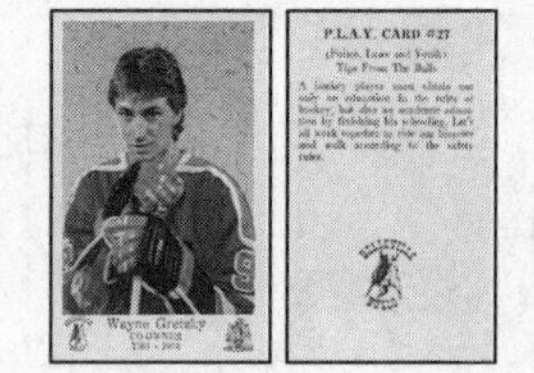

appear at the bottom. The backs carry P.L.A.Y. (Police, Laws and Youth) Card Tips from The Bulls which consist of a hockey term and relate it to everyday life.

| | MINT | NRMT |
|---|---|---|
| COMPLETE SET (30) | 60.00 | 27.00 |
| COMMON CARD (1-30) | .25 | .11 |

□ 1 Belleville Bulls Logo .50 .23
□ 2 Quinte Sports Centre .25 .11
□ 3 Dan Quinn 2.50 1.10
□ 4 Dave MacLean .50 .23
□ 5 Scott Gardiner .50 .23
□ 6 Mike Knuude .50 .23
□ 7 Brian Martin .50 .23
□ 8 R. Vaughan (Co-Owner) .25 .11
□ 9 John McDonald .50 .23
□ 10 Brian Small .50 .23
□ 11 Mike Savage .50 .23
□ 12 Dunc MacIntyre .50 .23
□ 13 Charlie Moore .50 .23
□ 14 Jim Andanoff .50 .23
□ 15 Mario Martini .50 .23
□ 16 Rick Adolfi .50 .23
□ 17 Mike Vellucci .50 .23
□ 18 Scott McMichel .50 .23
□ 19 Ali Butorac .50 .23
□ 20 Al Iafrate 8.00 3.60
□ 21 Rob Crocock .50 .23
□ 22 Craig Coxe 1.50 .70
□ 23 Grant Robertson .50 .23
□ 24 Craig Billington 4.00 1.80
□ 25 Darren Gani .50 .23
□ 26 Tim Bean .50 .23
□ 27 Wayne Gretzky 60.00 27.00
□ 28 Russ Soule TR .25 .11
□ 29 Larry Mavety CO/GM .25 .11
□ 30 Team Photo 2.00 .90

## 1984-85 Belleville Bulls

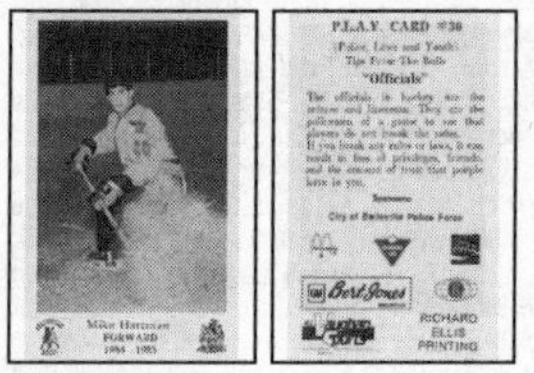

This 31-card police set measures approximately 2 5/8" by 4 1/8" and was sponsored by the City of Belleville Police Force and other local organizations. The fronts feature posed color player photos with white borders. The player's name, position, and the season (1984-85) appear at the bottom. The backs carry P.L.A.Y. (Police, Laws and Youth) Card Tips from The Bulls which explain a hockey term and relate it to everyday life.

| | MINT | NRMT |
|---|---|---|
| COMPLETE SET (31) | 15.00 | 6.75 |
| COMMON CARD (1-30) | .25 | .11 |

□ 1 Belleville Bulls 2.00 .90
(Team photo)
□ 2 R. Vaughan .25 .11
(Co-Owner)
□ 3 Larry Mavety CO/MG .25 .11
□ 4 Dunc MacIntyre .50 .23
□ 5 Belleville Bulls Logo .50 .23
□ 6 Mike Knuude .50 .23
□ 7 John Purves 1.00 .45
□ 8 Charlie Moore .50 .23
□ 9 Stan Drulia 1.00 .45
□ 10 Craig Billington 3.00 1.35
□ 11 Dave MacLean .50 .23
□ 12 Darren Moxam .50 .23
□ 13 Shane Doyle .50 .23
□ 14 Larry VanHerzele .50 .23
□ 15 Tim Bean .50 .23
□ 16 Kent Brimmer .50 .23
□ 17 Angelo Catenaro .50 .23
□ 18 Steve Linesman .50 .23
□ 19 Grant Robertson .50 .23
□ 20 John Reid .50 .23
□ 21 Dean Whyte .50 .23
□ 22 Darren Gani .50 .23
□ 23 Roger Robertson .50 .23
□ 24 Gary Callaghan .50 .23
□ 25 John Tamer .50 .23
□ 26 Todd Hawkins .50 .23
□ 27 Jim Andanoff .50 .23
□ 28 Chris Rutledge TR .25 .11
□ 29 Matt Taylor .50 .23
□ 30 Mike Hartman 1.00 .45
□ NNO Title Card .50 .23

## 1992-93 Binghamton Rangers

Issued by the team, these cards are printed on thin card stock. The cards are not numbered but numbers are assigned on the checklist card. The front is a full bleed photo with the player name appearing only on the back.

| | MINT | NRMT |
|---|---|---|
| COMPLETE SET (24) | 12.00 | 5.50 |
| COMMON CARD (1-24) | .25 | .11 |

□ 1 Team Card .50 .23
□ 2 Mike Hurlbut .50 .23
□ 3 Michael Stewart .50 .23
□ 4 Craig Duncanson .50 .23
□ 5 Rick Bennett .50 .23
□ 6 Dave Thomlinson .50 .23
□ 7 Mike Stevens .50 .23
□ 8 Rob Kenny .50 .23
□ 9 Chris Cichocki .50 .23
□ 10 Sergei Zubov 1.00 .45
□ 11 Don Biggs .50 .23
□ 12 Joby Messier .50 .23
□ 13 Steven King .50 .23
□ 14 Dave Archibald .50 .23
□ 15 Brian McReynolds .50 .23
□ 16 Dave Marcinyshyn .50 .23
□ 17 Jean-Yves Roy .60 .25
□ 18 Peter Fiorentino .50 .23
□ 19 Daniel Lacroix .50 .23
□ 20 Per Djoos .50 .23
□ 21 Boris Rousson .75 .35
□ 22 Corey Hirsch 2.00 .90
□ 23 Rockey Ranger .25 .11
Mascot
□ 24 Ranger Victory .25 .11

## 1994-95 Binghamton Rangers

This 22-card standard-size set was manufactured and distributed by Jessen Associates, Inc. for Classic. The fronts display color action player photos with a dark blue marbleized inner border and a black outer border. The player's name, jersey number, and position appear in the teal border on the right edge. Inside a black border on a marbleized background, the backs present biography, statistics, and sponsor logos. The cards are unnumbered and checklisted below in alphabetical order.

| | MINT | NRMT |
|---|---|---|
| COMPLETE SET (22) | 8.00 | 3.60 |
| COMMON CARD (1-22) | .40 | .18 |

□ 1 Eric Cairns .50 .23
□ 2 Craig Duncanson .40 .18
□ 3 Peter Fiorentino .40 .18
□ 4 Ken Gernander .50 .23
□ 5 Jim Hiller .40 .18
□ 6 Corey Hirsch 1.50 .70
□ 7 Rob Kenny .40 .18
□ 8 Andrei Kudinov .40 .18
□ 9 Darren Langdon .50 .23
□ 10 Scott Malone .40 .18
□ 11 Shawn McCosh .40 .18
□ 12 Mike McLaughlin .40 .18
□ 13 Joby Messier .50 .23
□ 14 Jeff Nielsen .40 .18
□ 15 Mattias Norstrom .75 .35
□ 16 Jamie Ram .60 .25
□ 17 Barry Richter .50 .23
□ 18 Jean-Yves Roy .50 .23
□ 19 Brad Rubachuk .40 .18
□ 20 Dave Smith .40 .18
□ 21 Dmitri Starostenko .40 .18
□ 22 Michael Stewart .40 .18
□ 23 Darcy Werenka .40 .18

## 1995-96 Binghamton Rangers

This 25-card set of the AHL Binghamton Rangers was manufactured and distributed by SplitSecond. The fronts feature color action player photos, while the backs carry player information. The cards are unnumbered and checklisted below in alphabetical order.

| | MINT | NRMT |
|---|---|---|
| COMPLETE SET (25) | 9.00 | 4.00 |
| COMMON CARD (1-25) | .10 | .05 |

□ 1 Sylvain Blouin .35 .16
□ 2 George Burnett CO .10 .05
□ 3 Mike Busniuk ACO .10 .05
□ 4 Eric Cairns .50 .23
□ 5 Chris Ferraro .75 .35
□ 6 Peter Ferraro 1.00 .45
□ 7 Maxim Galanov .35 .16
□ 8 Ken Gernander .50 .23
□ 9 Brad Jones .35 .16
□ 10 Pavel Komarov .35 .16
□ 11 Andrei Kudinov .35 .16
□ 12 Daniel Lacroix .50 .23
□ 13 Steve Larouche .50 .23
□ 14 Jon Hillebrandt .50 .23
□ 15 Scott Malone .35 .16
□ 16 Cal McGowan .35 .16
□ 17 Jeff Nielsen .35 .16
□ 18 Jamie Ram .50 .23
□ 19 Shawn Reid .35 .16
□ 20 Barry Richter .50 .23
□ 21 Andy Silverman .35 .16
□ 22 Lee Sorochan .50 .23
□ 23 Dmitri Starostenko .35 .16
□ 24 Ryan Vandenbussche .35 .16
□ 25 Rick Willis .35 .16

## 1996-97 Binghamton Rangers

This 24-card set features the Binghampton Rangers of the AHL. The cards were produced by SplitSecond and distributed by the team. The cards feature an action photo on the front, along with player name, number and team logo. The backs feature limited stats. The unnumbered cards are listed below alphabetically.

| | MINT | NRMT |
|---|---|---|
| COMPLETE SET (24) | 8.00 | 3.60 |
| COMMON CARD (1-24) | .10 | .05 |

□ 1 Micah Aivazoff .35 .16
□ 2 Sylvain Blouin .35 .16
□ 3 George Burnett CO .10 .05
□ 4 Mike Busniuk ACO .10 .05
□ 5 Ed Campbell .35 .16
□ 6 Dan Cloutier 1.00 .45
□ 7 Chris Ferraro .75 .35
□ 8 Peter Ferraro 1.00 .45
□ 9 Peter Fiorentino .35 .16
□ 10 Eric Flinton .35 .16
□ 11 Maxim Golanov .35 .16
□ 12 Ken Gernander .35 .16
□ 13 Mike Martin .35 .16
□ 14 Bob Maudie .35 .16
□ 15 Jeff Nielsen .35 .16
□ 16 Rocky Raccoon .10 .05
□ 17 Ken Shepard .35 .16
□ 18 Andy Silverman .35 .16
□ 19 Adam Smith .35 .16
□ 20 Lee Sorochan .50 .23
□ 21 Ryan VandenBussche .50 .23
□ 22 Vladimir Vorobiev .75 .35
□ 23 Rick Willis .35 .16
□ 24 AHL Hockey Card .10 .05

## 1992-93 Birmingham Bulls

The cards are larger than the standard size, and are numbered on the back. The set is sponsored by Fox-21, Coca-Cola and radio station WJOX-FM.

| | MINT | NRMT |
|---|---|---|
| COMPLETE SET (22) | 8.00 | 3.60 |
| COMMON CARD (1-22) | .10 | .05 |

□ 1 Logo Card .10 .05
□ 2 Jim Larkin .35 .16
□ 3 Brett Barnett .35 .16
□ 4 Joe Flanagan .35 .16
□ 5 Butch Kaebel .35 .16
□ 6 Scott Matusovich .35 .16
□ 7 Chuck Hughes .35 .16
□ 8 Dave Craievich .35 .16
□ 9 Alexander Havanov .35 .16
□ 10 Paul Marshall .35 .16
□ 11 Jim Peters .35 .16
□ 12 Chris Marshall .35 .16
□ 13 Jerome Bechard .35 .16
□ 14 Jean-Alain Schneider .35 .16
□ 15 Kevin Kerr .35 .16
□ 16 Rob Krauss .35 .16
□ 17 Greg Burke .35 .16
□ 18 Mark Romaine .35 .16
□ 19 Bruce Garber CO .10 .05
□ 20 Phil Roberto ACO .25 .11
□ 21 Dave Cavaliere TR .10 .05
□ 22 Birmingham Bulls CL .10 .05

## 1993-94 Birmingham Bulls

Sponsored by Coca-Cola, Fox 21 TV and WJOX AM 690, this 23-card set measures approximately 2 5/8" by 3 5/8" and features the

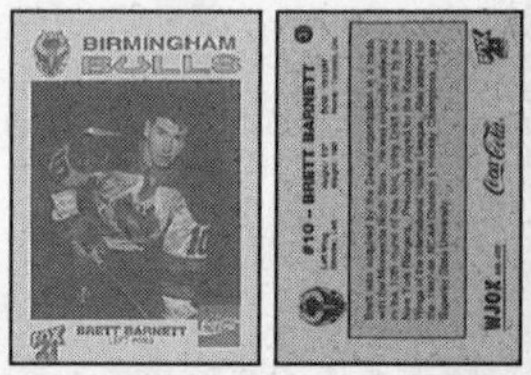

1993-94 Birmingham Bulls of the East Coast Hockey League. On a white card face, the fronts have posed color player photos. The team name and logo are printed above the photo, while the player's name, his position and sponsor logos appear below the picture. The horizontal backs carry player biography, profile and sponsor logos.

| | MINT | NRMT |
|---|---|---|
| COMPLETE SET (23) | 7.00 | 3.10 |
| COMMON CARD (1-22) | .10 | .05 |

□ 1 Logo Card .10 .05
□ 2 Jim Larkin .35 .16
□ 3 Brett Barnett .35 .16
□ 4 Joe Flanagan .35 .16
□ 5 Butch Kaebel .35 .16
□ 6 Scott Matusovich .35 .16
□ 7 Chuck E. Hughes .50 .23
□ 8 Dave Craievich .35 .16
□ 9 Alexander Havanov .35 .16
□ 10 Paul Marshall .35 .16
□ 11 Jim Peters .35 .16
□ 12 Chris Marshall .35 .16
□ 13 Jerome Bechard .35 .16
□ 14 Jean-Alain Schneider .35 .16
□ 15 Kevin Kerr .35 .16
□ 16 Rob Krauss .35 .16
□ 17 Greg Burke .35 .16
□ 18 Mark Romaine .50 .23
□ 19 Bruce Garber CO .10 .05
□ 20 Phil Roberto ACO .50 .23
□ 21 Dave Cavaliere TR .10 .05
□ 22 Tim Woodburn ANN .10 .05
□ NNO Title Card CL .10 .05

## 1994-95 Birmingham Bulls

Sponsored by Chevron, WBMG 45, and The New Mix 94.5 FM, this 22-card set measures approximately 2 3/4" by 3 3/4" and features the 1994-95 Birmingham Bulls of the ECHL. On a white card face, the fronts have posed color player photos. The team name appears alongside the left, while the player's name and position are printed below the photo. The team logo is superimposed at the lower left corner. The horizontal backs carry player biography, profile and stats, and sponsor logos. The cards are unnumbered and checklisted below in alphabetical order.

| | MINT | NRMT |
|---|---|---|
| COMPLETE SET (22) | 6.00 | 2.70 |
| COMMON CARD (1-22) | .10 | .05 |

□ 1 Greg Bailey .35 .16
□ 2 Norm Bazin .35 .16
□ 3 Jerome Bechard .35 .16
□ 4 Dave Boyd .35 .16
□ 5 David Craievich .35 .16
□ 6 Rob Donovan .35 .16
□ 7 Jon Duval .35 .16
□ 8 Sandy Galuppo .50 .23
□ 9 Todd Harris .35 .16
□ 10 Ian Hebert .35 .16
□ 11 Craig Johnson .35 .16
□ 12 John Joyce .35 .16
□ 13 Chris Kerber ANN .10 .05
□ 14 Olaf Kjenstad .50 .23
□ 15 Mike Krassner EQMG .10 .05
□ 16 Jim Larkin .35 .16
□ 17 Craig Lutes .35 .16
□ 18 Mark Michaud .35 .16
□ 19 Jean-Marc Plante .35 .16
□ 20 Phil Roberto CO .35 .16
□ 21 Brad Smyth .35 .16
□ 22 Title Card CL .10 .05

## 1995-96 Birmingham Bulls

This odd-sized (2 3/4" by 3 3/4") 29-card set features the Birmingham Bulls of the ECHL. The cards feature an action shot along with the team logo and player name on the front. The unnumbered backs contain player stats and sponsor logos. The set also contains a 6-card subset of WJOX DJs. The set was available

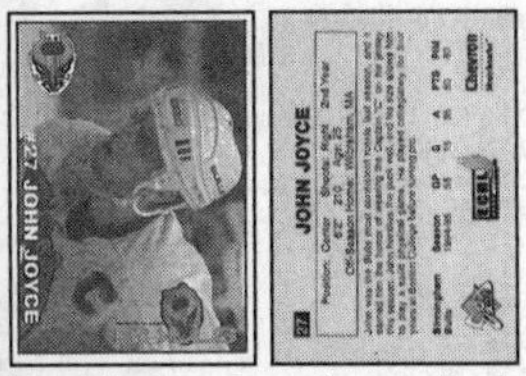

through the team; apparently, no mail order was available.

| | MINT | NRMT |
|---|---|---|
| COMPLETE SET (29) | 7.00 | 3.10 |
| COMMON CARD (1-29) | .10 | .05 |

| | MINT | NRMT |
|---|---|---|
| ❑ 1 Toro the Bull | .10 | .05 |
| ❑ 2 Phil Roberto CO | .25 | .11 |
| ❑ 3 Lance Brady | .35 | .16 |
| ❑ 4 Jeff Wells | .35 | .16 |
| ❑ 5 Brad Prefontaine | .35 | .16 |
| ❑ 6 Mark Raiter | .35 | .16 |
| ❑ 7 Rob Donovan | .35 | .16 |
| ❑ 8 Chris Grenville | .35 | .16 |
| ❑ 9 Colin Gregor | .35 | .16 |
| ❑ 10 Mike Latendresse | .50 | .23 |
| ❑ 11 John Morabito | .35 | .16 |
| ❑ 12 Brendan Creagh | .35 | .16 |
| ❑ 13 Chris Bergeron | .35 | .16 |
| ❑ 14 Jerome Bechard | .35 | .16 |
| ❑ 15 Craig Lutes | .35 | .16 |
| ❑ 16 Ian Hebert | .35 | .16 |
| ❑ 17 John Joyce | .35 | .16 |
| ❑ 18 Jeff Callinan | .35 | .16 |
| ❑ 19 Jason Dexter | .35 | .16 |
| ❑ 20 Olaf Kjenstad | .50 | .23 |
| ❑ 21 Chad Erickson | .50 | .23 |
| ❑ 22 Ray Pack EQMG | .10 | .05 |
| ❑ 23 Chris Kerber ANN | .10 | .05 |
| ❑ 24 M.Coulter/S.Griffi DJs | .10 | .05 |
| ❑ 25 Doug Laxton DJ | .10 | .05 |
| ❑ 26 Randy Armstrong DJ | .10 | .05 |
| ❑ 27 Lee Davis DJ | .10 | .05 |
| ❑ 28 Herb Winches DJ | .10 | .05 |
| ❑ 29 Ben Cook DJ | .10 | .05 |

## 1982-83 Brandon Wheat Kings

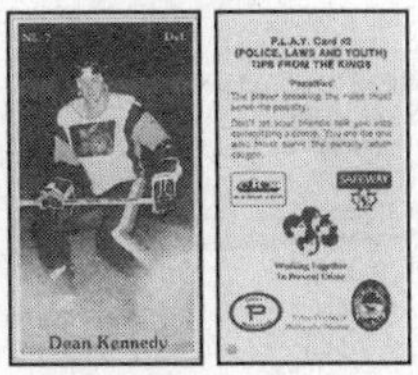

This 24-card set measures approximately 2 1/4" by 4" and features posed color player photos with thin yellow borders on a white card face. The player's name appears on the picture at the bottom. The backs carry P.L.A.Y. (Police, Laws and Youth) Tips From The Kings, which consist of a hockey term and relates it to a real life situation. Sponsor logos appear on the lower portion of the back.

| | MINT | EXC |
|---|---|---|
| COMPLETE SET (24) | 25.00 | 11.00 |
| COMMON CARD (1-24) | .25 | .11 |

| | MINT | EXC |
|---|---|---|
| ❑ 1 Wheat Kings Logo | .50 | .23 |
| ❑ 2 Kevin Pylypow | .75 | .35 |
| ❑ 3 Dean Kennedy | 2.00 | .90 |
| ❑ 4 Sonny Sodke | .75 | .35 |
| ❑ 5 Darren Schmidt | .75 | .35 |
| ❑ 6 Cam Plante | .75 | .35 |
| ❑ 7 Sid Cranston | .75 | .35 |
| ❑ 8 Bruce Thomson | .75 | .35 |
| ❑ 9 Dave McDowall CO | .50 | .23 |
| ❑ 10 Bill Vince | .75 | .35 |
| ❑ 11 Kelly Glowa | .75 | .35 |
| ❑ 12 Tom McMurchy | .75 | .35 |
| ❑ 13 Ed Palichuk | .75 | .35 |
| ❑ 14 Roy Caswell | .75 | .35 |
| ❑ 15 Allan Tarasuk | .75 | .35 |
| ❑ 16 Brent Jessiman | .75 | .35 |
| ❑ 17 Randy Slawson | .75 | .35 |
| ❑ 18 Gord Smith | .75 | .35 |
| ❑ 19 Mike Sturgeon | .75 | .35 |
| ❑ 20 Larry Bumstead | .75 | .35 |
| ❑ 21 Kirk Blomquist | .75 | .35 |
| ❑ 22 Ron Loustel | .75 | .35 |
| ❑ 23 Ron Hextall | 15.00 | 6.75 |
| ❑ 24 Brandon Police Logo | .25 | .11 |

## 1983-84 Brandon Wheat Kings

This 24-card set measures approximately 2 1/4" by 4" and features color posed action player photos with thin yellow borders on a white card face. The player's name is printed on the picture at the bottom. The backs carry P.L.A.Y. (Police, Laws and Youth) Tips From The Kings. Sponsor logos appear in the lower portion of the card.

| | MINT | NRMT |
|---|---|---|
| COMPLETE SET (24) | 25.00 | 11.00 |
| COMMON CARD (1-24) | .50 | .23 |

| | MINT | NRMT |
|---|---|---|
| ❑ 1 Brian Wells | .75 | .35 |
| ❑ 2 Jim Agnew | 1.00 | .45 |
| ❑ 3 Gord Paddock | .75 | .35 |
| ❑ 4 John Dzikowski | .75 | .35 |
| ❑ 5 Kelly Kozack | .75 | .35 |
| ❑ 6 Byron Lomow | .75 | .35 |
| ❑ 7 Pat Loyer | .75 | .35 |
| ❑ 8 Rob Ordman | .75 | .35 |
| ❑ 9 Brad Wells | .75 | .35 |
| ❑ 10 Dave Thomlinson | 1.00 | .45 |
| ❑ 11 Cam Plante | .75 | .35 |
| ❑ 12 Jay Palmer | .75 | .35 |
| ❑ 13 Boyd Lomow | .75 | .35 |
| ❑ 14 Brent Jessiman | .75 | .35 |
| ❑ 15 Paul More | .75 | .35 |
| ❑ 16 Stacy Prtt | .75 | .35 |
| ❑ 17 Brandon Wheat Kings Brandon City Police | .75 | .35 |
| ❑ 18 Jack Sangster CO | .50 | .23 |
| ❑ 19 Derek Laxdal | 1.00 | .45 |
| ❑ 20 Ray Ferraro | 5.00 | 2.20 |
| ❑ 21 Allan Tarasuk | .75 | .35 |
| ❑ 22 Randy Cameron | .75 | .35 |
| ❑ 23 Dave Curry | .75 | .35 |
| ❑ 24 Ron Hextall | 10.00 | 4.50 |

## 1984-85 Brandon Wheat Kings

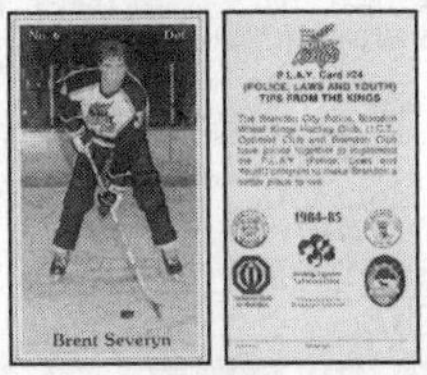

This 24-card set measures approximately 2 1/4" by 4" and features color posed action player photos with thin yellow borders on a white card face. The player's name is printed on the picture at the bottom. The backs carry P.L.A.Y. (Police, Laws and Youth) Tips From The Kings. Sponsor logos appear on the lower portion of the card.

| | MINT | NRMT |
|---|---|---|
| COMPLETE SET (24) | 12.00 | 5.50 |
| COMMON CARD (1-24) | .50 | .23 |

| | MINT | NRMT |
|---|---|---|
| ❑ 1 Garnet Kazuik | .50 | .23 |
| ❑ 2 Brent Mireau | .50 | .23 |
| ❑ 3 Byron Lomow | .50 | .23 |
| ❑ 4 Dean Shaw | .50 | .23 |
| ❑ 5 Dean Sexsmith | .50 | .23 |
| ❑ 6 Brad Mueller | .50 | .23 |
| ❑ 7 John Dzikowski | .50 | .23 |
| ❑ 8 Artie Feher | .50 | .23 |
| ❑ 9 Pat Loyer | .50 | .23 |
| ❑ 10 Murray Rice | .50 | .23 |
| ❑ 11 Derek Laxdal | .75 | .35 |
| ❑ 12 Perry Fafard | .50 | .23 |
| ❑ 13 Lee Trim | .50 | .23 |
| ❑ 14 Dan Hart | .50 | .23 |
| ❑ 15 Trent Ciprick | .50 | .23 |
| ❑ 16 Jeff Waver | .50 | .23 |
| ❑ 17 Brandon Wheat Kings Brandon City Police | 1.00 | .45 |
| ❑ 18 Jack Sangster CO | .25 | .11 |
| ❑ 19 Darwin McPherson | .50 | .23 |
| ❑ 20 Pokey Reddick | 2.00 | .90 |
| ❑ 21 Boyd Lomow | .50 | .23 |
| ❑ 22 Dave Thomlinson | .75 | .35 |
| ❑ 23 Paul More | .50 | .23 |
| ❑ 24 Brent Severyn | 1.00 | .45 |

## 1985-86 Brandon Wheat Kings

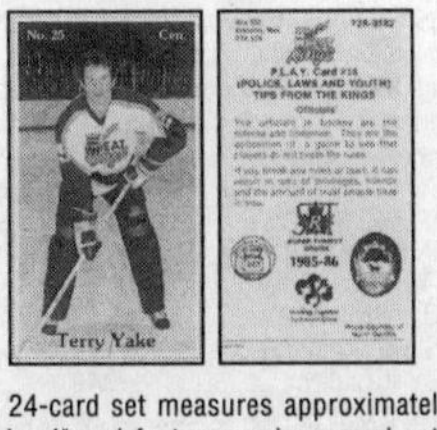

This 24-card set measures approximately 2 1/4" by 4" and features color posed action player photos with thin yellow borders on a white card face. The player's name is printed on the picture at the bottom. The backs carry P.L.A.Y. (Police, Laws and Youth) Tips From The Kings. Sponsor logos appear in the lower portion of the card.

| | MINT | NRMT |
|---|---|---|
| COMPLETE SET (24) | 10.00 | 4.50 |
| COMMON CARD (1-24) | .50 | .23 |

| | MINT | NRMT |
|---|---|---|
| ❑ 1 Kelly Hitchins | .50 | .23 |
| ❑ 2 Brent Mireau | .50 | .23 |
| ❑ 3 Byron Lomow | .50 | .23 |
| ❑ 4 Bob Heeney | .50 | .23 |
| ❑ 5 Dean Sexsmith | .50 | .23 |
| ❑ 6 Dave Curry | .50 | .23 |
| ❑ 7 John Dzikowski | .50 | .23 |
| ❑ 8 Artie Feher | .50 | .23 |
| ❑ 9 Kevin Mayo | .50 | .23 |
| ❑ 10 Murray Rice | .50 | .23 |
| ❑ 11 Derek Laxdal | 1.00 | .45 |
| ❑ 12 Al Cherniwchan | .50 | .23 |
| ❑ 13 Lee Trim | .50 | .23 |
| ❑ 14 Terry Yake | 1.00 | .45 |
| ❑ 15 Trent Ciprick | .50 | .23 |
| ❑ 16 Jeff Waver | .50 | .23 |
| ❑ 17 Team Photo | .75 | .35 |
| ❑ 18 Jack Sangster CO | .50 | .23 |
| ❑ 19 Mike Morin | .50 | .23 |
| ❑ 20 Jason Phillips | .50 | .23 |
| ❑ 21 Rod Williams | .50 | .23 |
| ❑ 22 Dave Thomlinson | 1.00 | .45 |
| ❑ 23 Shane Eirickson | .50 | .23 |
| ❑ 24 Randy Hoffart | .50 | .23 |

## 1988-89 Brandon Wheat Kings

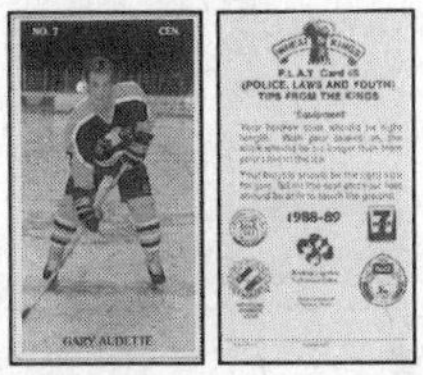

This 24-card set measures approximately 2 1/4" by 4" and features posed, color player photos with a thin yellow border stripe against a white card face. The backs carry P.L.A.Y. (Police, Laws and Youth) Tips from the Kings and sponsor logos.

| | MINT | NRMT |
|---|---|---|
| COMPLETE SET (24) | 14.00 | 6.25 |
| COMMON CARD (1-24) | .50 | .23 |

| | MINT | NRMT |
|---|---|---|
| ❑ 1 Kevin Cheveldayoff | .75 | .35 |
| ❑ 2 Bob Woods | .50 | .23 |
| ❑ 3 Dwayne Newman | .50 | .23 |
| ❑ 4 Mike Vandenberghe | .50 | .23 |
| ❑ 5 Brad Woods | .50 | .23 |
| ❑ 6 Gary Audette | .50 | .23 |
| ❑ 7 Mark Bassen | .50 | .23 |
| ❑ 8 Troy Frederick | .50 | .23 |
| ❑ 9 Troy Kennedy | .50 | .23 |
| ❑ 10 Barry Dreger | .50 | .23 |
| ❑ 11 Bill Whistle | .50 | .23 |
| ❑ 12 Jeff Odgers | 1.50 | .70 |
| ❑ 13 Sheldon Kowalchuk | .75 | .35 |
| ❑ 14 Chris Robertson | .50 | .23 |
| ❑ 15 Don Laurin | .50 | .23 |
| ❑ 16 Curtis Folkett | .50 | .23 |
| ❑ 17 Team Photo | 1.00 | .45 |
| ❑ 18 Kelly McCrimmon ACO | .50 | .23 |
| ❑ 19 Doug Sauter CO | .50 | .23 |
| ❑ 20 Kelly Hitchins | .50 | .23 |
| ❑ 21 Trevor Kidd | 5.00 | 2.20 |
| ❑ 22 Pryce Wood | .50 | .23 |
| ❑ 23 Cam Brown | .50 | .23 |
| ❑ 24 Greg Hutchings | .75 | .35 |

## 1989-90 Brandon Wheat Kings

This 24-card P.L.A.Y. (Police, Laws and Youth) set measures approximately 2 1/4" by 4". The fronts display color posed action photos inside of yellowish-orange borders. The player's name is printed in black across the bottom of the picture. In addition to sponsor logos, the backs carry "P.L.A.Y. Tips from the Kings" in the form of safety messages.

| | MINT | NRMT |
|---|---|---|
| COMPLETE SET (24) | 12.00 | 5.50 |
| COMMON CARD (1-24) | .25 | .11 |

| | MINT | NRMT |
|---|---|---|
| ❑ 1 Trevor Kidd | 3.00 | 1.35 |
| ❑ 2 Troy Frederick | .50 | .23 |
| ❑ 3 Kelly Thiessen | .75 | .35 |
| ❑ 4 Pryce Wood | .50 | .23 |
| ❑ 5 Mike Vandenberghe | .50 | .23 |
| ❑ 6 Chris Constant | .50 | .23 |
| ❑ 7 Hardy Sauter | .50 | .23 |
| ❑ 8 Cam Brown | .50 | .23 |
| ❑ 9 Bart Cote | .50 | .23 |
| ❑ 10 Jeff Hoad | .50 | .23 |
| ❑ 11 Kevin Robertson | .50 | .23 |
| ❑ 12 Dwayne Newman | .50 | .23 |
| ❑ 13 Calvin Flint | .50 | .23 |
| ❑ 14 Glen Webster | .50 | .23 |
| ❑ 15 Greg Hutchings | .75 | .35 |
| ❑ 16 Rob Puchniak | .50 | .23 |
| ❑ 17 Gary Audette | .50 | .23 |
| ❑ 18 Kevin Schmalz | .50 | .23 |
| ❑ 19 Dwayne Gylywoychuk | .50 | .23 |
| ❑ 20 Jeff Odgers | 1.00 | .45 |
| ❑ 21 Brian Purdy | .50 | .23 |
| ❑ 22 Merv Priest | .50 | .23 |
| ❑ 23 Doug Sauter CO | .25 | .11 |
| ❑ 24 Team Photo with Safety Mascots | 1.00 | .45 |

## 1990-91 Brandon Wheat Kings

This 24-card set measures approximately 2 1/4" by 4". The fronts feature posed color player photos with thin orange borders. The player's name appears on the picture at the bottom, while his uniform number and position are printed in the upper corners. On a white background, the backs carry P.L.A.Y. (Police, Laws and Youth) "Tips From The Kings". Sponsor logos and room for an autograph appear on the lower portion.

| | MINT | NRMT |
|---|---|---|
| COMPLETE SET (24) | 14.00 | 6.25 |
| COMMON CARD (1-24) | .25 | .11 |

| | MINT | NRMT |
|---|---|---|
| ❑ 1 Jeff Hoad | .50 | .23 |
| ❑ 2 Merv Priest | .50 | .23 |
| ❑ 3 Mike Vandenberghe | .50 | .23 |
| ❑ 4 Bart Cote | .50 | .23 |
| ❑ 5 Hardy Sauter | .50 | .23 |
| ❑ 6 Mark Johnston ACO | .25 | .11 |
| ❑ 7 Kelly McCrimmon CO | .25 | .11 |
| ❑ 8 Team Photo | .50 | .23 |
| ❑ 9 Kevin Robertson | .50 | .23 |
| ❑ 10 Glen Webster | .50 | .23 |
| ❑ 11 Greg Hutchings | .50 | .23 |
| ❑ 12 Dan Kopec | .50 | .23 |
| ❑ 13 Dwayne Gylywoychuk | .50 | .23 |
| ❑ 14 Brian Purdy | .50 | .23 |
| ❑ 15 Trevor Kidd | 4.00 | 1.80 |
| ❑ 16 Johan Skillgard | .50 | .23 |
| ❑ 17 Stu Scantlebury | .50 | .23 |
| ❑ 18 Byron Penstock | .50 | .23 |
| ❑ 19 Rob Puchniak | .50 | .23 |
| ❑ 20 Gary Audette | .50 | .23 |
| ❑ 21 Calvin Flint | .50 | .23 |
| ❑ 22 Jason White | .50 | .23 |
| ❑ 23 Chris Constant | .50 | .23 |
| ❑ 24 Glen Gulutzan | .50 | .23 |

## 1992-93 Brandon Wheat Kings

These 24 standard-size cards feature color player action shots on their fronts. Each picture is trimmed in white and has its corners blacked out, giving the impression of a mounted photograph. The player's uniform number and position are printed at the bottom, within the light mustard-colored border surrounding the picture. The player's name in white lettering appears near the bottom within an elongated mottled-green capsule. The white back carries the Wheat Kings name and logo at the top, with the player's name and biography just beneath, followed by a stat table, year of issue (1992-93), and P.L.A.Y. safety tips. The logos for the Brandon City Police, 7-Eleven stores, and the U.C.T. and Kinsmen organizations finish the card. The cards are unnumbered and checklisted below in alphabetical order.

| | MINT | NRMT |
|---|---|---|
| COMPLETE SET (24) | 10.00 | 4.50 |
| COMMON CARD (1-24) | .10 | .05 |

| | MINT | NRMT |
|---|---|---|
| ❑ 1 Aris Brimanis | .50 | .23 |
| ❑ 2 Colin Cloutier | .50 | .23 |
| ❑ 3 Chris Dingman | .50 | .23 |
| ❑ 4 Mike Dubinsky | .50 | .23 |
| ❑ 5 Todd Dutiaume | .35 | .16 |
| ❑ 6 Mark Franks | .35 | .16 |
| ❑ 7 Craig Geekie | .35 | .16 |
| ❑ 8 Dwayne Gylywoychuk | .35 | .16 |
| ❑ 9 Scott Hlady | .35 | .16 |
| ❑ 10 Jeff Hoad | .35 | .16 |
| ❑ 11 Bobby House | .35 | .16 |
| ❑ 12 Chris Johnston | .35 | .16 |
| ❑ 13 Mark Kolesar | .60 | .25 |
| ❑ 14 Scott Laluk | .35 | .16 |
| ❑ 15 Mike Maneluk | .50 | .23 |
| ❑ 16 Sean McFatridge | .35 | .16 |
| ❑ 17 Marty Murray | 2.00 | .90 |
| ❑ 18 Byron Penstock | .35 | .16 |
| ❑ 19 Darren Ritchie | .50 | .23 |
| ❑ 20 Trevor Robins | .35 | .16 |
| ❑ 21 Ryan Smith | .35 | .16 |
| ❑ 22 Jeff Staples | .35 | .16 |
| ❑ 23 Darcy Werenka | .50 | .23 |
| ❑ 24 Willie (Mascot) | .10 | .05 |

## 1983-84 Brantford Alexanders

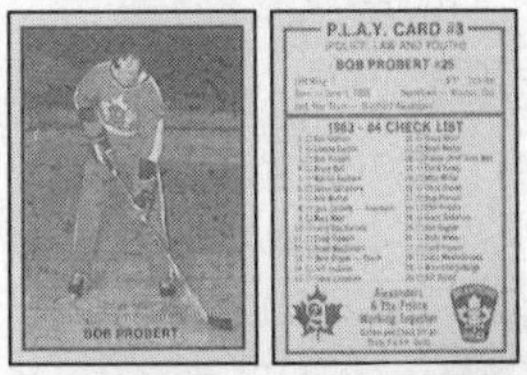

This 30-card set measures approximately 2 3/4" by 3 1/2". The fronts feature posed color player photos inside a thin black picture frame and white outer borders. The player's name appears on the picture at the bottom. On a white background, the backs carry the player's name, number, and a short biography in the upper portion; P.L.A.Y. (Police, Laws and Youth) "Tips From The Alexanders And The Brantford and Area Police" in the middle; and sponsor logos in the lower portion.

| | MINT | NRMT |
|---|---|---|
| COMPLETE SET (30) | 30.00 | 13.50 |
| COMMON CARD (1-30) | .50 | .23 |

| | MINT | NRMT |
|---|---|---|
| ❑ 1 Ken Gratton ACO | .50 | .23 |
| ❑ 2 Shayne Corson | 5.00 | 2.20 |
| ❑ 3 Bob Probert | 8.00 | 3.60 |
| ❑ 4 Bruce Bell | 1.50 | .70 |
| ❑ 5 Warren Bechard ACO | .50 | .23 |
| ❑ 6 Jason Lafreniere | 1.00 | .45 |
| ❑ 7 Rob Moffat | .75 | .35 |
| ❑ 8 Jack Calbeck PR | .50 | .23 |
| ❑ 9 Marc West | .75 | .35 |
| ❑ 10 Larry Van Herzele | .75 | .35 |
| ❑ 11 Doug Stewart | .75 | .35 |
| ❑ 12 Brian MacDonald | .75 | .35 |
| ❑ 13 Dave Draper CO/GM | .50 | .23 |
| ❑ 14 Jeff Jackson | 1.50 | .70 |
| ❑ 15 Steve Linseman | .75 | .35 |
| ❑ 16 Steve Short | .75 | .35 |
| ❑ 17 Allan Bester | 2.00 | .90 |
| ❑ 18 John Weir Chief of Police | .50 | .23 |
| ❑ 19 Chris Pusey | .75 | .35 |
| ❑ 20 Mike Millar | .75 | .35 |
| ❑ 21 Chris Glover | .75 | .35 |
| ❑ 22 Bob Pierson | .75 | .35 |
| ❑ 23 Phil Priddle | .75 | .35 |
| ❑ 24 Grant Anderson | .75 | .35 |
| ❑ 25 Ken Gagner | .75 | .35 |
| ❑ 26 Andy Alway TR | .50 | .23 |
| ❑ 27 Todd Francis | .75 | .35 |
| ❑ 28 John Meulenbroeks | .75 | .35 |
| ❑ 29 Mike Chettleburgh | .75 | .35 |
| ❑ 30 Bill Dynes TR | .50 | .23 |

## 1994-95 Brantford Smoke

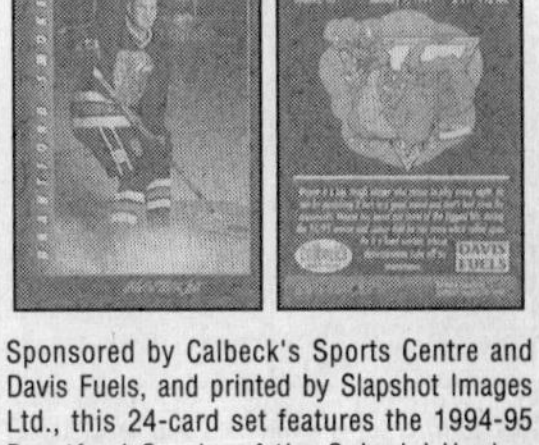

Sponsored by Calbeck's Sports Centre and Davis Fuels, and printed by Slapshot Images Ltd., this 24-card set features the 1994-95 Brantford Smoke of the Colonial Hockey League. On a black background, the fronts have posed color player photos with thin red borders. The player's name and position

appear at the top, while the team name is printed in a red fading bar alongside the left. On a black background, the backs carry player biography and profile, along with team and sponsor logos. Included in this set is a Slapshot ad card with a 1995 calendar on the back.

| | MINT | NRMT |
|---|---|---|
| COMPLETE SET (24) | 7.00 | 3.10 |
| COMMON CARD (1-23) | .10 | .05 |
| ❑ 1 Checklist | .10 | .05 |
| ❑ 2 Bob Delorimiere | .40 | .18 |
| ❑ 3 Todd Francis | .40 | .18 |
| ❑ 4 Pete Liptrott | .40 | .18 |
| ❑ 5 Lorne Knauft | .40 | .18 |
| ❑ 6 Paul Polillo | .40 | .18 |
| ❑ 7 Rob Arabski | .40 | .18 |
| ❑ 8 Derek Gauthier | .40 | .18 |
| ❑ 9 Joe Simon | .40 | .18 |
| ❑ 10 Brad Barton | .40 | .18 |
| ❑ 11 Terry Chitaroni | .50 | .23 |
| ❑ 12 Paul Mitton | .40 | .18 |
| ❑ 13 Wayne MacPhee | .40 | .18 |
| ❑ 14 Brian Blad | .50 | .23 |
| ❑ 15 John Laan | .40 | .18 |
| ❑ 16 Shane MacEachern | .40 | .18 |
| ❑ 17 Wayne Muir | .40 | .18 |
| ❑ 18 Ted Miskolczi | .35 | .16 |
| ❑ 19 Marc Delorme | .40 | .18 |
| ❑ 20 Mike Speer | .35 | .16 |
| ❑ 21 Bob Baird TR | .10 | .05 |
| Ken Crabb TR | | |
| ❑ 22 Ken Gratton CO | .10 | .05 |
| ❑ 23 Team Photo | .50 | .23 |
| ❑ NNO Ad Card | .10 | .05 |

## 1987-88 Brockville Braves

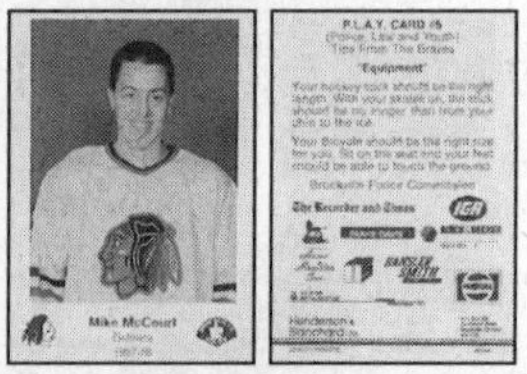

This 25-card set is printed on thin card stock, measures 2 5/8" by 3 5/8", and features posed color player photos with red studio backgrounds. The pictures are set on a white card face and show the player's name, position, and season in the white margin below the photo. The backs are white and carry public service messages in the form of P.L.A.Y. (Police, Law, and Youth) Tips From The Braves. Sponsor logos are shown on the back.

| | MINT | NRMT |
|---|---|---|
| COMPLETE SET (25) | 10.00 | 4.50 |
| COMMON CARD (1-25) | .25 | .11 |
| ❑ 1 Title Card | .25 | .11 |
| ❑ 2 Steve Harper TR | .25 | .11 |
| ❑ 3 Peter Kelly TR | .25 | .11 |
| ❑ 4 Mac MacLean CO/MG | .25 | .11 |
| ❑ 5 Mike McCourt | .50 | .23 |
| ❑ 6 Paul MacLean | .50 | .23 |
| ❑ 7 Mark Michaud | .50 | .23 |
| ❑ 8 Alain Marchessault | .50 | .23 |
| ❑ 9 Tom Roman | .50 | .23 |
| ❑ 10 Darren Burns | .50 | .23 |
| ❑ 11 Scott Halpenny | .50 | .23 |
| ❑ 12 Ray Gallagher | .50 | .23 |
| ❑ 13 Bob Lindsay | .50 | .23 |
| ❑ 14 Brett Harkins | 1.00 | .45 |
| ❑ 15 Dave Hyrsky | .50 | .23 |
| ❑ 16 Richard Marchessault | .50 | .23 |
| ❑ 17 Scott Boston | .50 | .23 |
| ❑ 18 Steve Hogg | .50 | .23 |
| ❑ 19 Chris Webster | .50 | .23 |
| ❑ 20 Stuart Birnie | .50 | .23 |
| ❑ 21 Brett Dunk | .50 | .23 |
| ❑ 22 Charles Cusson | .50 | .23 |
| ❑ 23 Pat Gooley | .50 | .23 |
| ❑ 24 Andy Rodman | .50 | .23 |
| ❑ 25 Peter Radlein | .50 | .23 |

## 1988-89 Brockville Braves

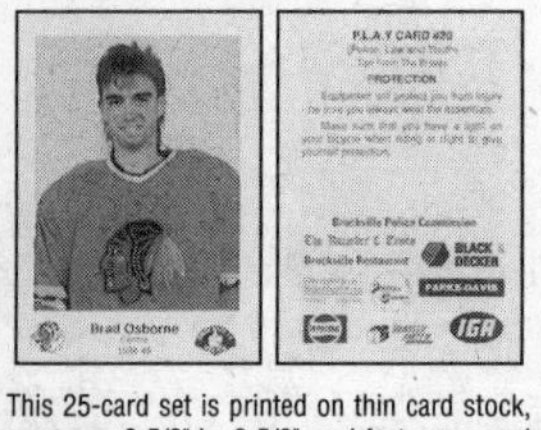

This 25-card set is printed on thin card stock, measures 2 5/8" by 3 5/8", and features posed color player photos with pale blue studio backgrounds. The pictures are set on a white card face and show the player's name, position, and season in the white margin below the photo. The backs are white and carry public service messages in the form of P.L.A.Y. (Police, Law, and Youth) Tips From The Braves. Sponsor logos are shown on the back.

| | MINT | NRMT |
|---|---|---|
| COMPLETE SET (25) | 10.00 | 4.50 |
| COMMON CARD (1-25) | .25 | .11 |
| ❑ 1 Ray Gallagher | .50 | .23 |
| ❑ 2 Peter Kelly TR | .25 | .11 |
| ❑ 3 Steve Harper TR | .25 | .11 |
| ❑ 4 Winston Jones ACO | .25 | .11 |
| ❑ 5 Mac MacLean CO/GM | .25 | .11 |
| ❑ 6 Kevin Doherty | .50 | .23 |
| ❑ 7 Stuart Birnie | .50 | .23 |
| ❑ 8 Charles Cusson | .50 | .23 |
| ❑ 9 Paul MacLean | .50 | .23 |
| ❑ 10 Bob Lindsay | .50 | .23 |
| ❑ 11 Darren Burns | .50 | .23 |
| ❑ 12 Rick Pracey | .50 | .23 |
| ❑ 13 Mike Malloy | .50 | .23 |
| ❑ 14 Dave Hyrsky | .50 | .23 |
| ❑ 15 Rob Percival | .50 | .23 |
| ❑ 16 Jarrett Eligh | .50 | .23 |
| ❑ 17 Pat Gooley | .50 | .23 |
| ❑ 18 Michael Bracco | .50 | .23 |
| ❑ 19 Ken Crook | .50 | .23 |
| ❑ 20 Brad Osborne | .50 | .23 |
| ❑ 21 Todd Reynolds | .50 | .23 |
| ❑ 22 Mike McCourt | .50 | .23 |
| ❑ 23 Chris Webster | .50 | .23 |
| ❑ 24 Kevin Lune | .50 | .23 |
| ❑ 25 Title Card | .50 | .23 |

## 1951-52 Buffalo Bison

| | MINT | NRMT |
|---|---|---|
| COMPLETE SET (19) | 75.00 | 34.00 |
| COMMON CARD (1-19) | 4.00 | 1.80 |
| ❑ 1 Team Photo | 4.00 | 1.80 |
| ❑ 2 Don Ashbee | 5.00 | 2.20 |
| ❑ 3 Frankie Christy | 4.00 | 1.80 |
| ❑ 4 Gerry Couture | 4.00 | 1.80 |
| ❑ 5 Lou Crowdis | 4.00 | 1.80 |
| ❑ 6 Harry Dick | 4.00 | 1.80 |
| ❑ 7 Lloyd Finkbeiner | 4.00 | 1.80 |
| ❑ 8 Ab Demarco | 4.00 | 1.80 |
| ❑ 9 Leroy Goldsworthy | 4.00 | 1.80 |
| ❑ 10 Les Hickey | 6.00 | 2.70 |
| ❑ 11 Vern Kaiser | 4.00 | 1.80 |
| ❑ 12 Sam Lavitt | 4.00 | 1.80 |
| ❑ 13 Stan Long | 4.00 | 1.80 |
| ❑ 14 Cal Mackay | 4.00 | 1.80 |
| ❑ 15 Ed Mazur | 4.00 | 1.80 |
| ❑ 16 Sid McNabney | 4.00 | 1.80 |
| ❑ 17 George Pargeter | 4.00 | 1.80 |
| ❑ 18 Gordie Pennell | 4.00 | 1.80 |
| ❑ 19 Grant Warwick | 4.00 | 1.80 |

## 1995 Buffalo Stampedes RHI

This standard size, team issued set, features color borderless fronts with players name and "1994 World Champions" in gold along the left side of the card. Backs are grey and black on a white background and feature biographical information along with 1994 statistics. Set came boxed and was available at home games. Cards are unnumbered and checklisted below by jersey number.

| | MINT | NRMT |
|---|---|---|
| COMPLETE SET (21) | 4.00 | 1.80 |
| COMMON CARD (1-21) | .10 | .05 |
| ❑ 14 John Hendry | .25 | .11 |
| ❑ 16 Tom Nemeth | .25 | .11 |
| ❑ 19 John Vechiarelli | .25 | .11 |
| ❑ 19 John Vechiarelli IA | .25 | .11 |
| ❑ 20 Len Soccio | .25 | .11 |
| ❑ 24 Chris Bergeron | .25 | .11 |
| ❑ 32 Mark Major | .25 | .11 |
| ❑ 34 Jason Cirone | .25 | .11 |
| ❑ 36 Nick Vitucci | .25 | .11 |
| ❑ 37 Dave Lemay | .25 | .11 |
| ❑ 43 John Blessman | .25 | .11 |
| ❑ 44 Jay Neal | .25 | .11 |
| ❑ 61 Craig Martin | .25 | .11 |
| ❑ 72 Rick Corriveau | .25 | .11 |
| ❑ 94 Alex Hicks | .25 | .11 |
| ❑ NNO1 Header Card | .10 | .05 |
| ❑ NNO2 Title Card | .10 | .05 |
| ❑ NNO3 Team Photo | .10 | .05 |
| ❑ NNO4 Terry Buchwald | .10 | .05 |
| ❑ NNO5 Stampede Cheerleaders | .10 | .05 |
| ❑ NNO6 Claude the Trumpeter | .10 | .05 |

## 1994-95 Cape Breton Oilers

This 23-card standard-size set was manufactured and distributed by Jessen Associates, Inc. for Classic. The fronts display color action player photos with a dark blue marbleized inner border and a black outer border. The player's name, jersey number, and position appear in the teal border on the right edge. Inside a black border on a marbleized background, the backs present biography,

statistics, and sponsor logos. The cards are unnumbered and checklisted below in alphabetical order.

| | MINT | NRMT |
|---|---|---|
| COMPLETE SET (23) | 10.00 | 4.50 |
| COMMON CARD (1-23) | .40 | .18 |
| ❑ 1 Scott Allison | .40 | .18 |
| ❑ 2 Martin Bakula | .40 | .18 |
| ❑ 3 Ladislav Benysek | .40 | .18 |
| ❑ 4 Dennis Bonvie | .40 | .18 |
| ❑ 5 Jozef Cierny | .40 | .18 |
| ❑ 6 Duane Dennis | .40 | .18 |
| ❑ 7 Greg DeVries | .75 | .35 |
| ❑ 8 Joaquin Gage | .75 | .35 |
| ❑ 9 Ian Herbers | .40 | .18 |
| ❑ 10 Ralph Intranuovo | .40 | .18 |
| ❑ 11 Claude Jutras | .40 | .18 |
| ❑ 12 Marc LaForge | .40 | .18 |
| ❑ 13 Todd Marchant | 1.00 | .45 |
| ❑ 14 Darcy Martini | .40 | .18 |
| ❑ 15 Roman Oksiuta | .50 | .23 |
| ❑ 16 David Oliver | .75 | .35 |
| ❑ 17 Steve Passmore | .75 | .35 |
| ❑ 18 Nick Stajduhar | .50 | .23 |
| ❑ 19 John Van Kessel | .40 | .18 |
| ❑ 20 David Vyborny | .40 | .18 |
| ❑ 21 Peter White | .40 | .18 |
| ❑ 22 Tyler Wright | .50 | .23 |
| ❑ 23 Brad Zavisha | .40 | .18 |

## 1998-99 Charlotte Checkers

| | MINT | NRMT |
|---|---|---|
| COMPLETE SET (24) | 4.00 | 1.80 |
| COMMON CARD (1-24) | .10 | .05 |
| ❑ 1 J.F. Aube | .20 | .09 |
| ❑ 2 Shannon Basaraba | .20 | .09 |
| ❑ 3 Doug Battaglia | .20 | .09 |
| ❑ 4 David Brosseau | .20 | .09 |
| ❑ 5 Tom Brown | .20 | .09 |
| ❑ 6 Pat Brownlee | .20 | .09 |
| ❑ 7 Brooke Chateau | .20 | .09 |
| ❑ 8 Jeff Heil | .20 | .09 |
| ❑ 9 Boyd Kane | .20 | .09 |
| ❑ 10 Kevin Kreutzer | .20 | .09 |
| ❑ 11 Darryl Noren | .20 | .09 |
| ❑ 12 Jason Norrie | .20 | .09 |
| ❑ 13 Nikolai Pronin | .20 | .09 |
| ❑ 14 Kurt Seher | .20 | .09 |
| ❑ 15 Bob Sheehan | .20 | .09 |
| ❑ 16 Ryan Sittler | .20 | .09 |
| ❑ 17 Martin Sychra | .20 | .09 |
| ❑ 18 Dean Zayonce | .20 | .09 |
| ❑ 19 Shawn Wheeler CO | .10 | .05 |
| ❑ 20 Chubby Checker | .10 | .05 |
| ❑ 21 The Captains | .10 | .05 |
| ❑ 22 Doug Battaglia | .20 | .09 |
| Pat Brownlee | | |
| ❑ 23 J.F. Aube | .20 | .09 |
| Bob Sheehan | | |
| ❑ 24 Checklist | .10 | .05 |

## 1984-85 Chicoutimi Sagueneens

This 24-card set sponsored by Mike's restaurants measures approximately 8 1/2" by 11" and features black-and-white player photos in a white-black-white-red frame. The complete set was issued in a protective folder. This folder is valued at $1. The card backs are blank. The cards are unnumbered and checklisted below in alphabetical order.

| | MINT | NRMT |
|---|---|---|
| COMPLETE SET (24) | 25.00 | 11.00 |
| COMMON CARD (1-24) | 1.00 | .45 |
| ❑ 1 Mario Barbe | 1.00 | .45 |
| ❑ 2 Mario Bazinet | 1.00 | .45 |
| ❑ 3 Daniel Bedard | 1.00 | .45 |
| Michel Boivin | | |
| Guy Byatt | | |
| Jean-Marc Couture | | |
| Patrice Gosselin | | |
| Jean-Yves Laberge | | |
| Germain Munger | | |
| Reginald Riverin | | |
| ❑ 4 Daniel Berthiaume | 3.00 | 1.35 |
| ❑ 5 Francis Breault | 1.50 | .70 |
| ❑ 6 Gregg Choules | 1.00 | .45 |
| ❑ 7 Christian Duperron | 1.00 | .45 |
| ❑ 8 Luc Dufour | 1.00 | .45 |
| ❑ 9 Luc Duval | 1.00 | .45 |
| ❑ 10 Patrick Emond | 1.00 | .45 |
| ❑ 11 Marc Fortier | 1.50 | .70 |
| ❑ 12 Steven Gauthier | 1.00 | .45 |
| ❑ 13 Yves Heroux | 1.50 | .70 |
| ❑ 14 Daniel Jomphe | 1.00 | .45 |
| ❑ 15 Gilles Laberge | 1.00 | .45 |
| ❑ 16 Claude Lajoie | 1.00 | .45 |
| ❑ 17 Serge Lauzon | 1.00 | .45 |
| ❑ 18 Roch Marinier | 1.50 | .70 |
| ❑ 19 Pierre Millier | 1.00 | .45 |
| ❑ 20 Marc Morin | 1.00 | .45 |
| ❑ 21 Scott Rettew | 1.00 | .45 |
| ❑ 22 Jean-Marc Richard | 1.00 | .45 |
| ❑ 23 Stephane Richer | 5.00 | 2.20 |
| ❑ 24 Pierre Sevigny | 1.00 | .45 |

## 1990-91 Cincinnati Cyclones

This 23-card set of the Cincinnati Cyclones of the ECHL was produced by 7th Inning Sketch. for distribution by the team. The cards are numbered 19-41 presumably because the company produced card sets for many ECHL teams this year.

| | MINT | NRMT |
|---|---|---|
| COMPLETE SET (23) | 7.00 | 3.10 |
| COMMON CARD (19-41) | .25 | .11 |
| ❑ 19 Steve McGrinder | .40 | .18 |
| ❑ 20 Steve Shaunessy | .40 | .18 |
| ❑ 21 Jay Rose | .40 | .18 |
| ❑ 22 Don Gagne | .40 | .18 |
| ❑ 23 Mike Williams | .40 | .18 |
| ❑ 24 Mike Chighisola | .40 | .18 |
| ❑ 25 Daryl Harpe | .40 | .18 |
| ❑ 26 Steve Cadieux | .40 | .18 |
| ❑ 27 Jeff Salzbrunn | .40 | .18 |
| ❑ 28 Rob Gador | .40 | .18 |
| ❑ 29 Chris Marshall | .40 | .18 |
| ❑ 30 Doug Melnyk | .40 | .18 |
| ❑ 31 Mark Turner | .40 | .18 |
| ❑ 32 Kevin Kerr | .40 | .18 |
| ❑ 33 Rob Krauss | .40 | .18 |
| ❑ 34 Mark Marentette | .40 | .18 |
| ❑ 35 Jamie Kompon | .40 | .18 |
| ❑ 36 Tom Neziol | .40 | .18 |
| ❑ 37 John Fletcher | .40 | .18 |
| ❑ 38 Dennis Desrosiers CO | .25 | .11 |
| ❑ 39 Todd Harrison TR | .25 | .11 |
| ❑ 40 Terry Ficorelli | .40 | .18 |
| ❑ 41 Craig Daly | .40 | .18 |

## 1991-92 Cincinnati Cyclones

The 1991-92 Cincinnati Cyclones of the East Coast Hockey League are represented in this 25-card set, which was sponsored by Cincinnati Bell Telephone and 19XIX Fox. The cards measure 2 3/8" by 3 1/2" and feature posed color action shots enclosed by a white border. The team logo and year appear across the top of the card face, with the team name in silver outlined in red. The white front bottom portion of the card carries player information, the 19XIX Fox logo, and the Cincinnati Bell Telephone logo. Horizontally oriented backs carry biography and statistics in a white box surrounded by a gray border. The cards are unnumbered and checklisted below in alphabetical order.

| | MINT | NRMT |
|---|---|---|
| COMPLETE SET (25) | 8.00 | 3.60 |
| COMMON CARD (1-25) | .10 | .05 |
| ❑ 1 Dan Beaudette | .50 | .23 |
| ❑ 2 Steve Benoit TR | .10 | .05 |
| ❑ 3 Steve Cadieux | .40 | .18 |
| ❑ 4 Craig Charron | .40 | .18 |
| ❑ 5 David Craievich | .40 | .18 |
| ❑ 6 Doug Dadswell | .50 | .23 |
| ❑ 7 Dennis Desrosiers CO | .10 | .05 |
| ❑ 8 Terry Ficorelli ANN | .10 | .05 |
| ❑ 9 Jeff Hogden | .40 | .18 |
| ❑ 10 Kevin Kerr | .40 | .18 |
| ❑ 11 Jaan Luik | .40 | .18 |
| ❑ 12 Scott Luik | .40 | .18 |
| ❑ 13 Chris Marshall | .40 | .18 |
| ❑ 14 Daryn McBride | .40 | .18 |
| ❑ 15 Doug Melnyk | .40 | .18 |
| ❑ 16 David Moore | .40 | .18 |
| ❑ 17 Tom Neziol | .40 | .18 |
| ❑ 18 Mark Romaine | .40 | .18 |
| ❑ 19 Jay Rose | .40 | .18 |
| ❑ 20 Martin St. Amour | .40 | .18 |
| ❑ 21 Kevin Scott | .40 | .18 |
| ❑ 22 Peter Schure | .40 | .18 |
| ❑ 23 Steve Shaunessy | .40 | .18 |
| ❑ 24 Blaine Stoughton CO | .50 | .23 |
| ❑ 25 Bobby Wallwork | .40 | .18 |

## 1996-97 Cincinnati Cyclones

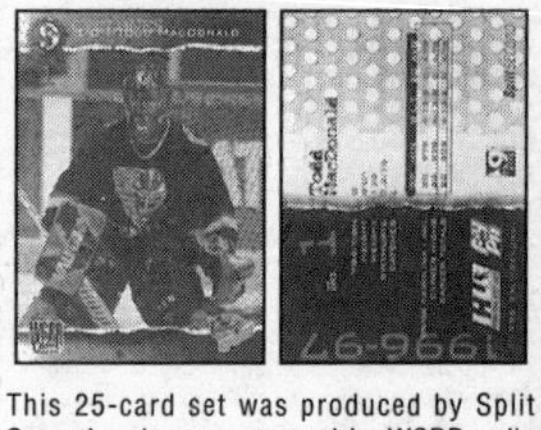

This 25-card set was produced by Split Second and was sponsored by WGRR radio and WCPD TV.. The unnumbered cards feature an action photo on the front, and stats package on the back. They are numbered below according to their sweater numbers, which are prominently featured on the backs.

| | MINT | NRMT |
|---|---|---|
| COMPLETE SET (25) | 7.00 | 3.10 |
| COMMON CARD | .10 | .05 |
| ❑ 1 Todd MacDonald | .50 | .23 |
| ❑ 3 Duane Joyce | .40 | .18 |
| ❑ 4 Ted Crowley | .40 | .18 |
| ❑ 5 Jeff Wells | .40 | .18 |
| ❑ 6 Myles O'Connor | .40 | .18 |
| ❑ 12 Todd Hawkins | .40 | .18 |
| ❑ 13 Paul Lawless | .40 | .18 |
| ❑ 17 Mike Casselman | .40 | .18 |
| ❑ 19 Scott Thomas | .40 | .18 |
| ❑ 22 Don Biggs | .40 | .18 |
| ❑ 24 Tony Horacek | .40 | .18 |
| ❑ 26 Marc Laniel | .40 | .18 |
| ❑ 27 Dave Marcinyshyn | .40 | .18 |
| ❑ 28 Scott Morrow | .40 | .18 |
| ❑ 29 Jeff Greenlaw | .40 | .18 |
| ❑ 31 Geoff Sarjeant | .50 | .23 |
| ❑ 33 Chris Cichocki | .40 | .18 |
| ❑ 37 Eric Dandenault | .40 | .18 |
| ❑ 44 Doug MacDonald | .40 | .18 |
| ❑ 51 Dale DeGray | .40 | .18 |
| ❑ NNO Al Hill ACO | .10 | .05 |
| ❑ NNO Mark Mills EQMG | .10 | .05 |
| ❑ NNO Nick Kenney TR | .10 | .05 |
| ❑ NNO Ron Smith CO | .10 | .05 |
| ❑ NNO Snowbird (Mascot) | .10 | .05 |

## 1998-99 Cincinnati Cyclones

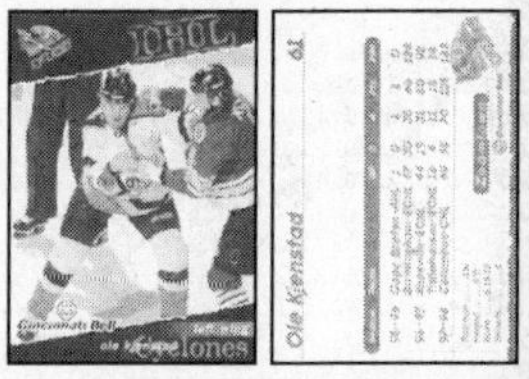

Card fronts feature full color photos along with team name and position. Backs feature 1997-98 statistics and biographical information. Cards are unnumbered and checklisted below in alphabetical order.

| | MINT | NRMT |
|---|---|---|
| COMPLETE SET (30) | 4.00 | 1.80 |
| COMMON CARD (1-30) | .10 | .05 |
| ❑ 1 Kaspars Ashtashenko | .15 | .07 |
| ❑ 2 Frederic Cassivi | .25 | .11 |
| ❑ 3 Phil Crowe | .15 | .07 |
| ❑ 4 Eric Dandenault | .15 | .07 |
| ❑ 5 Gilbert Dionne | .25 | .11 |
| ❑ 6 Todd Hawkins | .15 | .07 |
| ❑ 7 Jani Hurme | .25 | .11 |
| ❑ 8 Burt Henderson | .15 | .07 |
| ❑ 9 Chris Joseph | .25 | .11 |
| ❑ 10 Ole Kjenstad | .15 | .07 |
| ❑ 11 Fred Knipscheer | .15 | .07 |
| ❑ 12 Doug Macdonald | .15 | .07 |
| ❑ 13 Pat Macleod | .15 | .07 |
| ❑ 14 Scott Morrow | .15 | .07 |
| ❑ 15 Tom Nemeth | .15 | .07 |
| ❑ 16 Kirk Nielsen | .15 | .07 |
| ❑ 17 Ed Patterson | .15 | .07 |
| ❑ 18 Rastislav Pavlikovsky | .15 | .07 |
| ❑ 19 Jeff Shevalier | .15 | .07 |

| | | |
|---|---|---|
| ❑ 20 Todd Simon | .25 | .11 |
| ❑ 21 Geoff Smith | .15 | .07 |
| ❑ 22 Jeff Wells | .15 | .07 |
| ❑ 23 Snowbird Mascot | .10 | .05 |
| ❑ 24 Nick Kenney TR | .10 | .05 |
| ❑ 25 Mark Mills EQ | .10 | .05 |
| ❑ 26 Scott Macpherson ACO | .10 | .05 |
| ❑ 27 Chris Cichocki ACO | .10 | .05 |
| ❑ 28 Ron Smith CO | .10 | .05 |
| ❑ 29 Team Card | .10 | .05 |
| ❑ 30 Logo Card | .10 | .05 |

## 1992-93 Clarkson Knights

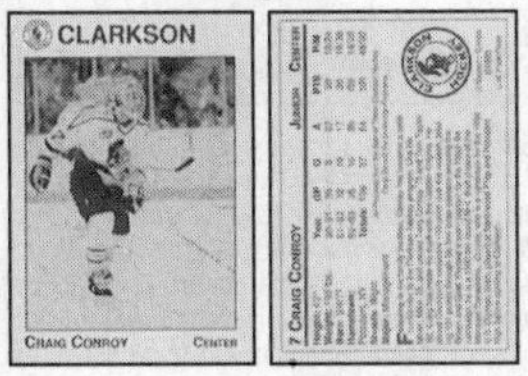


Issued in 1993 at the end of the hockey season, this 24-card standard-size set features the Clarkson Knights of the ECAC (Eastern Collegiate Athletic Conference). The cards feature on-ice player action and posed photos on the fronts. The pictures are on a white card face with the Clarkson hockey logo and name at the top and the player's name and position at the bottom. The horizontal backs carry biography, statistics for the 1991-92 and 1992-93 seasons, and career summary. The Clarkson hockey logo appears in the lower right. The cards are unnumbered and checklisted below in alphabetical order.

| | MINT | NRMT |
|---|---|---|
| COMPLETE SET (24) | 12.00 | 5.50 |
| COMMON CARD (1-24) | .50 | .23 |
| ❑ 1 Josh Bartell | .50 | .23 |
| ❑ 2 Hugo Belanger | .60 | .25 |
| ❑ 3 Craig Conroy | .75 | .35 |
| ❑ 4 Jason Currie | .50 | .23 |
| ❑ 5 Steve Dubinsky | .75 | .35 |
| ❑ 6 Shawn Fotheringham | .50 | .23 |
| ❑ 7 Dave Green | .50 | .23 |
| ❑ 8 Ed Henrich | .50 | .23 |
| ❑ 9 Chris Lipsett | .50 | .23 |
| ❑ 10 Todd Marchant | 2.00 | .90 |
| ❑ 11 Brian Mueller | .75 | .35 |
| ❑ 12 Kevin Murphy | .50 | .23 |
| ❑ 13 Martin d'Orsonnens | .60 | .25 |
| ❑ 14 Steve Palmer | .50 | .23 |
| ❑ 15 Patrice Robitaille | .50 | .23 |
| ❑ 16 Chris Rogles | .75 | .35 |
| ❑ 17 Jerry Rosenheck | .50 | .23 |
| ❑ 18 Chris de Ruiter | .50 | .23 |
| ❑ 19 Guy Sanderson | .50 | .23 |
| ❑ 20 David Seitz | .50 | .23 |
| ❑ 21 Mikko Tavi | .50 | .23 |
| ❑ 22 Patrick Theriault | .50 | .23 |
| ❑ 23 Marko Tuomainen | .75 | .35 |
| ❑ 24 Men's Hockey 1992-93 Martin d'Orsonnens Steve Dubinsky | .50 | .23 |

## 1951-52 Cleveland Barons

This set was issued as a photo pack. The cards are printed on thin card stock, and measure 9 X 6 inches. The last card, Joe Lund, may be from the previous year's set, as he did not play for Cleveland in 1951-52.

| | MINT | NRMT |
|---|---|---|
| COMPLETE SET (20) | 150.00 | 70.00 |
| COMMON CARD (1-20) | 5.00 | 2.20 |
| ❑ 1 Bun Cook CO | 10.00 | 4.50 |
| ❑ 2 Fred Shero | 20.00 | 9.00 |
| ❑ 3 Ed Reigle | 5.00 | 2.20 |
| ❑ 4 Ike Hildebrand | 5.00 | 2.20 |
| ❑ 5 Eddie Olson | 5.00 | 2.20 |
| ❑ 6 Jerry Reid | 5.00 | 2.20 |
| ❑ 7 Fred Thurier | 5.00 | 2.20 |
| ❑ 8 Steve Wochy | 5.00 | 2.20 |
| ❑ 9 Joe Carveth | 8.00 | 3.60 |
| ❑ 10 Tom Williams | 10.00 | 4.50 |
| ❑ 11 Johnny Bower | 50.00 | 22.00 |
| ❑ 12 Jack Gordon | 8.00 | 3.60 |
| ❑ 13 Ken Schultz | 5.00 | 2.20 |
| ❑ 14 Fern Perreault | 5.00 | 2.20 |
| ❑ 15 Ray Ceresino | 5.00 | 2.20 |
| ❑ 16 Bob Bailey | 5.00 | 2.20 |
| ❑ 17 Bob Chrystal | 8.00 | 3.60 |
| ❑ 18 Phil Samis | 5.00 | 2.20 |
| ❑ 19 Paul Gladu | 5.00 | 2.20 |
| ❑ 20 Joe Lund | 5.00 | 2.20 |

## 1960-61 Cleveland Barons

This 19-card set of oversized cards measures approximately 6 3/4" by 5 3/8". The set commemorates the Cleveland Barons 1959-60 season which ended with the team in fourth place after elimination in the Calder Cup Playoffs. The white-bordered fronts display action, black-and-white player photos. A facsimile autograph is printed near the bottom of the photo on all the cards except the team photo card. The backs are blank. Since the cards are unnumbered, they are checklisted below alphabetically.

| | NRMT | VG-E |
|---|---|---|
| COMPLETE SET (19) | 120.00 | 55.00 |
| COMMON CARD (1-19) | 5.00 | 2.20 |
| ❑ 1 Ron Attwell | 5.00 | 2.20 |
| ❑ 2 Les Binkley | 10.00 | 4.50 |
| ❑ 3 Bill Dineen | 8.00 | 3.60 |
| ❑ 4 John Ferguson | 20.00 | 9.00 |
| ❑ 5 Cal Gardner | 8.00 | 3.60 |
| ❑ 6 Fred Glover | 8.00 | 3.60 |
| ❑ 7 Jack Gordon | 8.00 | 3.60 |
| ❑ 8 Aldo Guidolin | 8.00 | 3.60 |
| ❑ 9 Greg Hicks | 5.00 | 2.20 |
| ❑ 10 Wayne Larkin | 5.00 | 2.20 |
| ❑ 11 Moe Mantha | 8.00 | 3.60 |
| ❑ 12 Gil Mayer | 5.00 | 2.20 |
| ❑ 13 Eddie Mazur | 5.00 | 2.20 |
| ❑ 14 Jim Mikol | 5.00 | 2.20 |
| ❑ 15 Bill Needham | 5.00 | 2.20 |
| ❑ 16 Cal Stearns | 5.00 | 2.20 |
| ❑ 17 Bill Sutherland | 8.00 | 3.60 |
| ❑ 18 Tom Williams | 8.00 | 3.60 |
| ❑ 19 Team Photo | 10.00 | 4.50 |

## 1992-93 Cleveland Lumberjacks

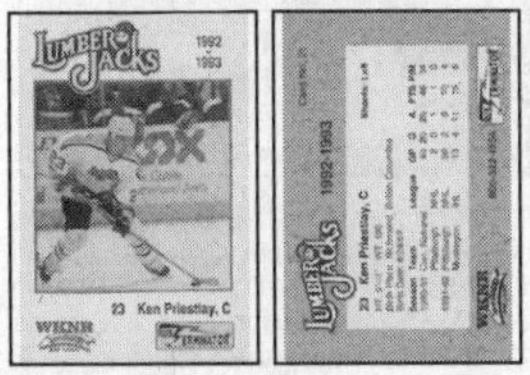

Issued to commemorate the Lumberjacks' first season in Cleveland, these 25 cards feature on their fronts red-trimmed and white-bordered color player action shots and measure 2 3/8" by 3 1/2". The player's name, uniform number and position appear beneath the photo in the lower white margin. The team logo and season are displayed in the margin above the photo. The logos for the two sponsors, WKNR radio and Rusterminator, rest at the bottom. The horizontal backs display the player's name, uniform number, position, biography and stats within the central white rectangle. In the wide gray border, the logos for the team and the sponsors round out the card.

| | MINT | NRMT |
|---|---|---|
| COMPLETE SET (25) | 10.00 | 4.50 |
| COMMON CARD (1-25) | .10 | .05 |
| ❑ 1 Title Card | .10 | .05 |
| ❑ 2 Larry Gordon GM | .10 | .05 |
| ❑ 3 Paul Laus | .75 | .35 |
| ❑ 4 Travis Thiessen | .50 | .23 |
| ❑ 5 Phil Russell CO | .50 | .23 |
| ❑ 6 Gilbert Delorme ACO | .50 | .23 |
| ❑ 7 Jamie Heward | .50 | .23 |
| ❑ 8 Greg Andrusak | .50 | .23 |
| ❑ 9 David Quinn | .50 | .23 |
| ❑ 10 Perry Ganchar | .50 | .23 |
| ❑ 11 George Zajankala UER (Birthplace misspelled Revelstroke on back) | .50 | .23 |
| ❑ 12 Todd Nelson | .50 | .23 |
| ❑ 13 Dave Michayluk | .50 | .23 |
| ❑ 14 Bruce Racine | .75 | .35 |
| ❑ 15 Rob Dopson | .75 | .35 |
| ❑ 16 Bert Godin TR | .10 | .05 |
| ❑ 17 Ed Patterson | .75 | .35 |
| ❑ 18 Justin Duberman | .50 | .23 |
| ❑ 19 Sandy Smith | .50 | .23 |
| ❑ 20 Jason Smart | .50 | .23 |
| ❑ 21 Ken Priestlay | .50 | .23 |
| ❑ 22 Daniel Gauthier | .50 | .23 |
| ❑ 23 Robert Melanson | .50 | .23 |
| ❑ 24 Mark Major | .50 | .23 |
| ❑ 25 Paul Dyck | .50 | .23 |

## 1993-94 Cleveland Lumberjacks

These 24 black-bordered cards feature the 1993-94 Cleveland Lumberjacks of the IHL (International Hockey League). The cards measure approximately 2 3/8" by 3 1/2" and display on their fronts color player action shots framed by red lines. The player's name, uniform number, and position are shown in white lettering in the black margin below the photo. The logos for sponsors WKNR SportsRadio and RusTerminator Electronic Rust Control rest at the bottom. The gray and white horizontal back carries the player's uniform number, name, position, biography, and statistics.

| | MINT | NRMT |
|---|---|---|
| COMPLETE SET (24) | 10.00 | 4.50 |
| COMMON CARD (1-24) | .25 | .11 |
| ❑ 1 Title Card | .25 | .11 |
| ❑ 2 Rick Paterson CO | .25 | .11 |
| ❑ 3 Gilbert Delorme ACO | .25 | .11 |
| ❑ 4 Paul Dyck | .50 | .23 |
| ❑ 5 Travis Thiessen | .50 | .23 |
| ❑ 6 Mike Dagenais | .50 | .23 |
| ❑ 7 Chris Tamer | .75 | .35 |
| ❑ 8 Greg Andrusak | .50 | .23 |
| ❑ 9 Todd Hawkins | .50 | .23 |
| ❑ 10 Jamie Black | .50 | .23 |
| ❑ 11 Justin Duberman | .60 | .25 |
| ❑ 13 Jock Callander UER (Misspelled Jack on front) | .60 | .25 |
| ❑ 14 Leonid Toropchenko | .50 | .23 |
| ❑ 15 Victor Gervais | .50 | .23 |
| ❑ 16 Perry Ganchar | .50 | .23 |
| ❑ 17 Ed Patterson | .75 | .35 |
| ❑ 18 Ladislav Karabin | .50 | .23 |
| ❑ 19 Dave Michayluk | .60 | .25 |
| ❑ 20 Jamie Heward | .50 | .23 |
| ❑ 21 Pat Neaton | .75 | .35 |
| ❑ 22 Rob Dopson | .75 | .35 |
| ❑ 23 Steve Bancroft | .50 | .23 |
| ❑ 24 Olie Sundstrom | .60 | .25 |

## 1993-94 Cleveland Lumberjacks Postcards

These 21 black-bordered cards feature the 1993-94 Cleveland Lumberjacks of the IHL (International Hockey League). The white-bordered postcards measure approximately 3 1/2" by 5 1/2" and display on their fronts color player action shots. The player's name, uniform number, position, and biography are shown in yellow lettering within a black rectangle beneath the picture. Sponsor logos for WMMS Radio and The Peak (a sports medicine and injury rehab facility) also appear on the front. The white horizontal back carries a tip on how to treat a minor muscle sprain. The cards are unnumbered and checklisted below in alphabetical order.

| | MINT | NRMT |
|---|---|---|
| COMPLETE SET (21) | 10.00 | 4.50 |
| COMMON CARD (1-21) | .25 | .11 |
| ❑ 1 Greg Andrusak | .50 | .23 |
| ❑ 2 Steve Bancroft | .50 | .23 |
| ❑ 3 Jamie Black | .50 | .23 |
| ❑ 4 Jock Callander | .60 | .25 |
| ❑ 5 Mike Dagenais | .50 | .23 |
| ❑ 6 Gilbert Delorme ACO | .25 | .11 |
| ❑ 7 Rob Dopson | .60 | .25 |
| ❑ 8 Justin Duberman | .60 | .25 |
| ❑ 9 Paul Dyck | .60 | .25 |
| ❑ 10 Perry Ganchar | .50 | .23 |
| ❑ 11 Todd Hawkins | .50 | .23 |
| ❑ 12 Jamie Heward | .50 | .23 |
| ❑ 13 Ladislav Karabin | .50 | .23 |
| ❑ 14 Dave Michayluk | .60 | .25 |
| ❑ 15 Pat Neaton | .75 | .35 |
| ❑ 16 Rick Paterson CO | .25 | .11 |
| ❑ 17 Ed Patterson | .75 | .35 |
| ❑ 18 Olie Sundstrom | .60 | .25 |
| ❑ 19 Chris Tamer | .75 | .35 |
| ❑ 20 Travis Thiessen | .50 | .23 |
| ❑ 21 Leonid Toropchenko | .50 | .23 |

## 1995-96 Cleveland Lumberjacks

This 24-card set of the Cleveland Lumberjacks was produced by SplitSecond for Collector's Edge. The set is sponsored by Huntington Banks and WKNR Radio. It features color player portraits on the fronts with player information and statistics on the backs. The cards are unnumbered and checklisted below in alphabetical order.

| | MINT | NRMT |
|---|---|---|
| COMPLETE SET (24) | 10.00 | 4.50 |
| COMMON CARD (1-24) | .10 | .05 |
| ❑ 1 Peter Allen | .35 | .16 |
| ❑ 2 Bill Armstrong | .35 | .16 |
| ❑ 3 Len Barrie | .35 | .16 |
| ❑ 4 Dave Baseggio | .35 | .16 |
| ❑ 5 Oleg Belov | .35 | .16 |
| ❑ 6 Drake Berehowsky | .35 | .16 |
| ❑ 7 Stefan Bergkvist | .50 | .23 |
| ❑ 8 Jock Callander | .35 | .16 |
| ❑ 9 Jeff Christian | .35 | .16 |
| ❑ 10 Philippe DeRouville | .50 | .23 |
| ❑ 11 Corey Foster | .35 | .16 |
| ❑ 12 Perry Ganchar ACO | .10 | .05 |
| ❑ 13 Victor Gervais | .35 | .16 |
| ❑ 14 Rick Hayward | .35 | .16 |
| ❑ 15 Patrick Lalime | 4.00 | 1.80 |
| ❑ 16 Brad Lauer | .35 | .16 |
| ❑ 17 Dave McLlwain | .50 | .23 |
| ❑ 18 Dave Michayluk | .35 | .16 |
| ❑ 19 Mark Osborne | .35 | .16 |
| ❑ 20 Rick Paterson CO | .10 | .05 |
| ❑ 21 Domenic Pittis | .35 | .16 |
| ❑ 22 Ryan Savoia | .35 | .16 |
| ❑ 23 Mike Stevens | .35 | .16 |
| ❑ 24 Title Card | .10 | .05 |

## 1996-97 Cleveland Lumberjacks

Cards are checklisted below in alphabetical order.

| | MINT | NRMT |
|---|---|---|
| COMPLETE SET (25) | 7.00 | 3.10 |
| COMMON CARD (1-25) | .25 | .11 |
| ❑ 1 Peter Allen | .25 | .11 |
| ❑ 2 Bill Armstrong | .25 | .11 |
| ❑ 3 Serge Aubin | .25 | .11 |
| ❑ 4 Brian Bonin | .25 | .11 |
| ❑ 5 Sven Butenschon | .25 | .11 |
| ❑ 6 Buzz Mascot | .25 | .11 |
| ❑ 7 Jock Callendar | .25 | .11 |
| ❑ 8 Jeff Christian | .25 | .11 |
| ❑ 9 Rusty Fitzgerald | .25 | .11 |
| ❑ 10 Corey Foster | .25 | .11 |
| ❑ 11 Rick Hayward | .25 | .11 |
| ❑ 12 Jan Hrdina | .25 | .11 |
| ❑ 13 Petr Klima | .60 | .25 |
| ❑ 14 Lane Lambert | .40 | .18 |
| ❑ 15 Brad Lauer | .50 | .23 |
| ❑ 16 Dave McLlwain | .25 | .11 |
| ❑ 17 Dave Michayluk | .25 | .11 |
| ❑ 18 Ian Moran | .25 | .11 |
| ❑ 19 Mark Osborne | .25 | .11 |
| ❑ 20 Jim Paek | .60 | .25 |
| ❑ 21 Richard Park | .60 | .25 |
| ❑ 22 Rick Paterson CO | .10 | .05 |
| ❑ 23 Ed Patterson | .25 | .11 |
| ❑ 24 Mike Tamburro | .25 | .11 |
| ❑ 25 Derek Wilkinson | .25 | .11 |

## 1967-68 Columbus Checkers

| | MINT | NRMT |
|---|---|---|
| COMPLETE SET (16) | 40.00 | 18.00 |
| COMMON CARD (1-16) | 2.00 | .90 |
| ❑ 1 Team Photo | 2.00 | .90 |
| ❑ 2 Moe Bartoli | 3.00 | 1.35 |
| ❑ 3 Bill Bond | 3.00 | 1.35 |
| ❑ 4 Serge Boudreault | 3.00 | 1.35 |
| ❑ 5 Gord Dibley | 3.00 | 1.35 |
| ❑ 6 Bert Fizzell | 3.00 | 1.35 |
| ❑ 7 Chuck Kelly | 3.00 | 1.35 |
| ❑ 8 Ted Leboda | 3.00 | 1.35 |
| ❑ 9 Nelson Leclair | 3.00 | 1.35 |
| ❑ 10 Rhiall Paquette | 3.00 | 1.35 |
| ❑ 11 Dick Proceviat | 3.00 | 1.35 |
| ❑ 12 Hartley Stakowski | 3.00 | 1.35 |
| ❑ 13 Ken Sutyla | 3.00 | 1.35 |
| ❑ 14 Nelson Tremblay | 3.00 | 1.35 |
| ❑ 15 Jack Turner | 3.00 | 1.35 |
| ❑ 16 Al White | 3.00 | 1.35 |

## 1969 Columbus Checkers

This 16-card set measures 4 x 7 1/4" and features a black and white photo on the front along with players name at the bottom. Backs are blank. Cards are unnumbered and checklisted below alphabetically.

| | MINT | NRMT |
|---|---|---|
| COMPLETE SET (16) | 70.00 | 32.00 |
| COMMON CARD | 5.00 | 2.20 |
| ❑ 1 John Bailey | 5.00 | 2.20 |
| ❑ 2 Moe Bartoli | 5.00 | 2.20 |
| ❑ 3 Kerry Bond | 5.00 | 2.20 |
| ❑ 4 Andre Daoust | 5.00 | 2.20 |
| ❑ 5 Bert Fizzell | 5.00 | 2.20 |
| ❑ 6 Marcel Goudreau | 5.00 | 2.20 |
| ❑ 7 Jim Graham | 5.00 | 2.20 |
| ❑ 8 Paul Jackson | 5.00 | 2.20 |
| ❑ 9 Ken Laidlaw | 5.00 | 2.20 |
| ❑ 10 Noel Lirette | 5.00 | 2.20 |
| ❑ 11 Gary Longman | 5.00 | 2.20 |
| ❑ 12 Garry Macmillan | 5.00 | 2.20 |
| ❑ 13 Gary Mork | 5.00 | 2.20 |
| ❑ 14 Matt Thorp | 5.00 | 2.20 |
| ❑ 15 Jack Turner | 5.00 | 2.20 |
| ❑ 16 Alton White | 5.00 | 2.20 |

## 1992-93 Cornell Big Red

The set is checklisted below in alphabetical order.

| | MINT | NRMT |
|---|---|---|
| COMPLETE SET (30) | 6.00 | 2.70 |
| COMMON CARD (1-30) | .10 | .05 |
| ❑ 1 Andrew Bandurski | .25 | .11 |
| ❑ 2 Etienne Belzile | .25 | .11 |
| ❑ 3 Geoff Bumstead | .25 | .11 |
| ❑ 4 Brad Chartrand | .25 | .11 |
| ❑ 5 Rick Davis | .25 | .11 |
| ❑ 6 John DeHart | .25 | .11 |
| ❑ 7 Andre Doll | .25 | .11 |
| ❑ 8 P.C. Drouin | .25 | .11 |
| ❑ 9 Dan Dufresne | .25 | .11 |
| ❑ 10 Blair Ettles | .25 | .11 |
| ❑ 11 Christian Felli | .25 | .11 |
| ❑ 12 Russ Hammond | .25 | .11 |
| ❑ 13 Shaun Hannah | .25 | .11 |
| ❑ 14 Steve Hayden | .25 | .11 |
| ❑ 15 Bill Holowatiuk | .25 | .11 |
| ❑ 16 Ryan Hughes | .25 | .11 |
| ❑ 17 Jake Karam | .25 | .11 |
| ❑ 18 Jiri Kloboucek | .25 | .11 |
| ❑ 19 Geoff Lopatka | .25 | .11 |
| ❑ 20 Joel McArter | .25 | .11 |
| ❑ 21 Tyler McManus | .25 | .11 |
| ❑ 22 Devon Nielsen | .25 | .11 |
| ❑ 23 Geoff Raynak | .25 | .11 |
| ❑ 24 Mike Sancimino | .25 | .11 |
| ❑ 25 Mark Scollan | .25 | .11 |
| ❑ 26 Tim Shean | .25 | .11 |
| ❑ 27 Greg Swenson | .25 | .11 |
| ❑ 28 Alex Vershinin | .25 | .11 |
| ❑ 29 Jason Vogel | .25 | .11 |
| ❑ 30 Mark Taylor ACO | .10 | .05 |

## 1993-94 Cornell Big Red

The set is checklisted below in alphabetical order.

| | MINT | NRMT |
|---|---|---|
| COMPLETE SET (30) | 6.00 | 2.70 |
| COMMON CARD (1-30) | .10 | .05 |
| ❑ 1 Vincent Auger | .25 | .11 |
| ❑ 2 Andrew Bandurski | .25 | .11 |
| ❑ 3 Geoff Bumstead | .25 | .11 |
| ❑ 4 Brad Chartrand | .25 | .11 |
| ❑ 5 Matt Cooney | .25 | .11 |
| ❑ 6 John DeHart | .25 | .11 |
| ❑ 7 Andre Doll | .25 | .11 |
| ❑ 8 Dan Dufresne | .25 | .11 |
| ❑ 9 Blair Ettles | .25 | .11 |
| ❑ 10 Christian Felli | .25 | .11 |
| ❑ 11 Tony Fergin | .25 | .11 |
| ❑ 12 Shaun Hannah | .25 | .11 |
| ❑ 13 Bill Holowatiuk | .25 | .11 |
| ❑ 14 Jake Karam | .25 | .11 |
| ❑ 15 Jason Kendall | .25 | .11 |
| ❑ 16 Jiri Kloboucek | .25 | .11 |
| ❑ 17 Geoff Lopatka | .25 | .11 |
| ❑ 18 Joel McArter | .25 | .11 |
| ❑ 19 Tyler McManus | .25 | .11 |
| ❑ 20 Jamie Papp | .25 | .11 |
| ❑ 21 Mike Sancimino | .25 | .11 |
| ❑ 22 Mark Scollan | .25 | .11 |
| ❑ 23 Tim Shean | .25 | .11 |
| ❑ 24 Eddy Skazyk | .25 | .11 |
| ❑ 25 Alex Vershinin | .25 | .11 |
| ❑ 26 Jason Weber | .25 | .11 |
| ❑ 27 Steve Wilson | .25 | .11 |
| ❑ 28 Chad Wilson | .25 | .11 |
| ❑ 29 Jason Zubkus | .25 | .11 |
| ❑ 30 Mark Taylor ACO | .10 | .05 |

## 1991-92 Cornwall Royals

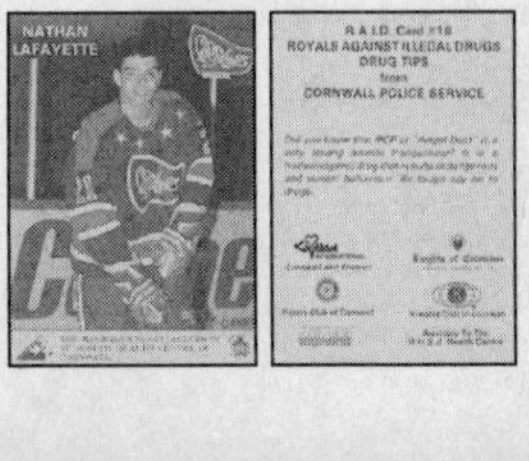

This 28-card set measures approximately 2 5/8" by 3 3/4". The fronts feature borderless posed color player photos. The player's name appears in the left upper corner, while the team logo is in the right upper corner. The Religious Hospitallers Of St. Joseph Health Centre Of Cornwall logo is printed in a white bar under the photo. On a white background, the backs carry "Royals Against Illegal Drug Tips from Cornwall Police Service" in the upper portion and sponsor logos below.

| | MINT | NRMT |
|---|---|---|
| COMPLETE SET (28) | 10.00 | 4.50 |
| COMMON CARD (1-28) | .10 | .05 |

| | | |
|---|---|---|
| ❑ 1 Jason Meloche | .35 | .16 |
| ❑ 2 Mark Desantis | .35 | .16 |
| ❑ 3 Richard Raymond | .35 | .16 |
| ❑ 4 Gord Pell | .35 | .16 |
| ❑ 5 Dave Lemay | .35 | .16 |
| ❑ 6 John Lovell CO | .10 | .05 |
| ❑ 7 Ryan Vandenbussche | .50 | .23 |
| ❑ 8 David Babcock | .35 | .16 |
| ❑ 9 Sam Oliveira | .35 | .16 |
| ❑ 10 Jeremy Stevenson | .35 | .16 |
| ❑ 11 Todd Walker | .35 | .16 |
| ❑ 12 Jean-Alain Schneider | .35 | .16 |
| ❑ 13 Ilpo Kauhanen | .35 | .16 |
| ❑ 14 Guy Leveque | .50 | .23 |
| ❑ 15 Shayne Gaffar | .35 | .16 |
| ❑ 16 Rival Fullum | .35 | .16 |
| ❑ 17 Mike Prokopec | .50 | .23 |
| ❑ 18 Nathan LaFayette | .75 | .35 |
| ❑ 19 Larry Courville | .75 | .35 |
| ❑ 20 Chris Clancy | .35 | .16 |
| ❑ 21 Tom Nemeth | .50 | .23 |
| ❑ 22 Jeff Reid | .35 | .16 |
| ❑ 23 Paul Andrea | .35 | .16 |
| ❑ 24 John Slaney | .75 | .35 |
| ❑ 25 Alan Letang | .35 | .16 |
| ❑ 26 Rob Dykeman | .35 | .16 |
| ❑ 27 Paul Fixter CO | .10 | .05 |
| Brian O'Leary CO | | |
| ❑ 28 Claude Shaver | .10 | .05 |
| Chief of Police | | |

## 1992-93 Dallas Freeze

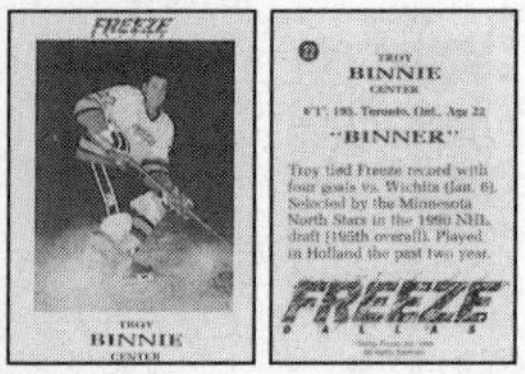

This 20-card standard-size set features the Dallas Freeze of the Central Hockey League. White-bordered color player photos adorn the fronts of these cards. The Freeze logo appears on both sides of the card. In the border beneath the photo are the player's name and position. The jersey number on the card back appears in white in a black circle at the top left. Brief biographical information and career summary fill out the back. The cards are unnumbered and checklisted below in alphabetical order.

| | MINT | NRMT |
|---|---|---|
| COMPLETE SET (20) | 8.00 | 3.60 |
| COMMON CARD (1-20) | .50 | .23 |

| | | |
|---|---|---|
| ❑ 1 Wayne Anchikoski | .50 | .23 |
| ❑ 2 Gary Audette | .50 | .23 |
| ❑ 3 Jeff Beaudin | .50 | .23 |
| ❑ 4 Troy Binnie | .50 | .23 |
| ❑ 5 Brian Bruininks | .50 | .23 |
| ❑ 6 Derek Crawford | .50 | .23 |
| ❑ 7 Dave Doucette | .50 | .23 |
| ❑ 8 Don Dwyer | .50 | .23 |
| ❑ 9 Joe Eagan | .50 | .23 |
| ❑ 10 Ron Flockhart CO | .75 | .35 |
| ❑ 11 Frank Lascala | .50 | .23 |
| ❑ 12 Robert Lewis | .50 | .23 |
| ❑ 13 Joey Mittelsteadt | .50 | .23 |
| ❑ 14 Rico Rossi | .50 | .23 |
| ❑ 15 Dean Shmyr | .50 | .23 |
| ❑ 16 Doug Sinclair | .50 | .23 |
| ❑ 17 Greg Smith | .50 | .23 |
| ❑ 18 Jason Taylor | .50 | .23 |
| ❑ 19 Mike Zanier | .75 | .35 |
| ❑ 20 Team Photo | .50 | .23 |

## 1993-94 Dallas Freeze

These oddly shaped round cards are approximately the size of a hockey puck. They came in a plastic container with the team logo on the front and were available from the team's booster club at home games.

| | MINT | NRMT |
|---|---|---|
| COMPLETE SET (18) | 6.00 | 2.70 |
| COMMON CARD (1-18) | .35 | .16 |

| | | |
|---|---|---|
| ❑ 1 Wayne Anchikoski | .50 | .23 |
| ❑ 2 Jeff Beaudin | .35 | .16 |
| ❑ 3 Troy Binnie | .35 | .16 |
| ❑ 4 Brian Bruininks | .35 | .16 |
| ❑ 5 Derek Crawford | .35 | .16 |
| ❑ 6 Dave Doucette | .50 | .23 |
| ❑ 7 Don Dwyer | .35 | .16 |
| ❑ 8 Mark Holick | .35 | .16 |
| ❑ 9 Randy Jaycock | .35 | .16 |
| ❑ 10 Frank LaScala | .35 | .16 |
| ❑ 11 Robert Lewis | .35 | .16 |
| ❑ 12 Joey McTamney | .35 | .16 |
| ❑ 13 Joey Mittelsteadt | .35 | .16 |
| ❑ 14 Dean Shmyr | .35 | .16 |
| ❑ 15 Greg Smith | .35 | .16 |
| ❑ 16 Jason Taylor | .35 | .16 |
| ❑ 17 Jason White | .35 | .16 |
| ❑ 18 Ron Flockhart CO | .50 | .23 |

## 1992-93 Dayton Bombers

Sponsored by WTVE 104.7, this 24-card standard-size set features the 1992-93 Dayton Bombers of the ECHL. Just 2,500 sets were produced, with 2,300 given away as a game-night promotion and the remaining 200 sold for 5.00 per pack. On a light apricot-color card face, the fronts feature color posed player photos on the ice with thin black, white and red borders. The player's name, number and position appear under the picture. Sponsor and team logos are printed under the photo and in the top right corner. The horizontal backs carry a short biography and information. The cards are unnumbered and checklisted below in alphabetical order.

| | MINT | NRMT |
|---|---|---|
| COMPLETE SET (24) | 7.00 | 3.10 |
| COMMON CARD (1-24) | .10 | .05 |

| | | |
|---|---|---|
| ❑ 1 John Beaulieu DJ | .10 | .05 |
| ❑ 2 Steve Bogoyevac | .35 | .16 |
| ❑ 3 Christopher DJ | .10 | .05 |
| ❑ 4 Darren Colbourne | .35 | .16 |
| ❑ 5 Derek Crawford | .35 | .16 |
| ❑ 6 Dan-O DJ | .10 | .05 |
| ❑ 7 Derek Donald | .35 | .16 |
| ❑ 8 Ray Edwards | .35 | .16 |
| ❑ 9 Doug Evans | .35 | .16 |
| ❑ 10 Sandy Galuppo | .50 | .23 |
| ❑ 11 Shayne Green | .35 | .16 |
| ❑ 12 Rod Houk | .35 | .16 |
| ❑ 13 Peter Kasowski | .35 | .16 |
| ❑ 14 Steve Kerrigan | .35 | .16 |
| ❑ 15 Frank Kovacs | .35 | .16 |
| ❑ 16 Darren Langdon | .50 | .23 |
| ❑ 17 Denis Larocque | .35 | .16 |
| ❑ 18 Darwin McPherson | .35 | .16 |
| ❑ 19 Tom Nemeth | .35 | .16 |
| ❑ 20 Claude Noel CO | .25 | .11 |
| ❑ 21 Tony Peters | .35 | .16 |
| ❑ 22 Marshall Phillips | .35 | .16 |
| ❑ 23 Mike Reier | .35 | .16 |
| ❑ 24 Steve Wilson | .35 | .16 |

## 1993-94 Dayton Bombers

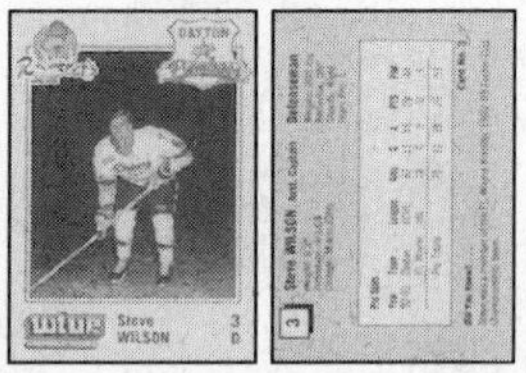

Sponsored by WTVE 104.7 radio station, this 28-card standard-size set features the 1993-94 Dayton Bombers of the ECHL. 2,500 sets were produced and given away as a game-night promotion. On a light blue card face, the fronts feature color posed player photos on the ice with thin black, white and red borders. The player's name, number and position appear under the photo. Sponsor and team logos are printed under the photo and in the top right and left corners. The horizontal backs carry a short player biography, stats and a notable fact about the player. Cards 19-28 feature radio disc jockeys.

| | MINT | NRMT |
|---|---|---|
| COMPLETE SET (28) | 7.00 | 3.10 |
| COMMON CARD (1-28) | .10 | .05 |

| | | |
|---|---|---|
| ❑ 1 Title Card CL | .10 | .05 |
| ❑ 2 Jeff Levy | .40 | .18 |
| ❑ 3 Steve Wilson | .40 | .18 |
| ❑ 4 Jason Downey | .40 | .18 |
| ❑ 5 Jim Peters | .40 | .18 |
| ❑ 6 Ondrej Kriz | .40 | .18 |
| ❑ 7 Steve Bogoyevac | .40 | .18 |
| ❑ 8 Jason Disiewich | .40 | .18 |
| ❑ 9 Marc Savard | .40 | .18 |
| ❑ 10 Dan O'Shea | .40 | .18 |
| ❑ 11 Tom Nemeth | .40 | .18 |
| ❑ 12 Guy Prince | .40 | .18 |
| ❑ 13 Ray Edwards | .40 | .18 |
| ❑ 14 Sergei Kharin | .40 | .18 |
| ❑ 15 Derek Donald | .40 | .18 |
| ❑ 16 Darwin McPherson | .40 | .18 |
| ❑ 17 Jeff Stolp | .40 | .18 |
| ❑ 18 Adam Bomber (Mascot) | .10 | .05 |
| ❑ 19 Kim | .10 | .05 |
| ❑ 20 Robby | .10 | .05 |
| ❑ 21 Lisa | .10 | .05 |
| ❑ 22 Marshall Phillips | .10 | .05 |
| ❑ 23 Dan-O | .10 | .05 |
| ❑ 24 John(B-Man) Beaulieu | .10 | .05 |
| ❑ 25 Christopher | .10 | .05 |
| ❑ 26 Steve Kerrigan | .40 | .18 |
| ❑ 27 Tony Peters | .40 | .18 |
| ❑ 28 Shaun Higgins | .10 | .05 |
| Major Dick Hale | | |

## 1994-95 Dayton Bombers

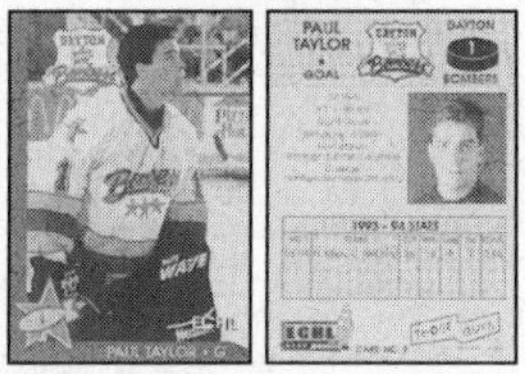

This 24-card standard-size set features the 1994-95 Dayton Bombers of the ECHL. 5,000 sets were produced, of which 1,500 were given away. The fronts feature color action player photos with a blue border on the bottom and on the left. The player's name and position appear under the photo. The team logo is printed in the upper right corner, while the player's number appears in the lower left corner. The backs carry a small black-and-white player portrait, along with biography and stats.

| | MINT | NRMT |
|---|---|---|
| COMPLETE SET (24) | 8.00 | 3.60 |
| COMMON CARD (1-24) | .10 | .05 |

| | | |
|---|---|---|
| ❑ 1 Title Card CL | .10 | .05 |
| ❑ 2 Paul Taylor | .35 | .16 |
| ❑ 3 Steve Wilson | .35 | .16 |
| ❑ 4 Jason Downey | .35 | .16 |
| ❑ 5 Craig Charron | .35 | .16 |
| ❑ 6 Jim Lessard | .35 | .16 |
| ❑ 7 Karson Kaebel | .35 | .16 |
| ❑ 8 Jamie Steer | .35 | .16 |
| ❑ 9 Rob Hartnell | .35 | .16 |
| ❑ 10 Mike Doers | .35 | .16 |
| ❑ 11 Sean Gagnon | .50 | .23 |
| ❑ 12 Kevin Brown | .35 | .16 |
| ❑ 13 John Brill | .35 | .16 |
| ❑ 14 Dean Fedorchuk | .35 | .16 |
| ❑ 15 Tony Gruba | .35 | .16 |
| ❑ 16 Steve Lingren | .35 | .16 |
| ❑ 17 Brandon Smith | .35 | .16 |
| ❑ 18 Jeff Stolp | .50 | .23 |
| ❑ 19 Mike Vandenberghe | .35 | .16 |
| ❑ 20 Jim Playfair | .35 | .16 |
| ❑ 21 Goal Celebration | .35 | .16 |
| ❑ 22 Jamie Steer | .35 | .16 |
| 1993-94 ECHL AS | | |
| ❑ 23 Steve Wilson | .35 | .16 |
| 1993-94 Best Defensive Player | | |
| ❑ 24 Jeff Stolp | .50 | .23 |
| 1993-94 Top Goaltender | | |

## 1995-96 Dayton Bombers

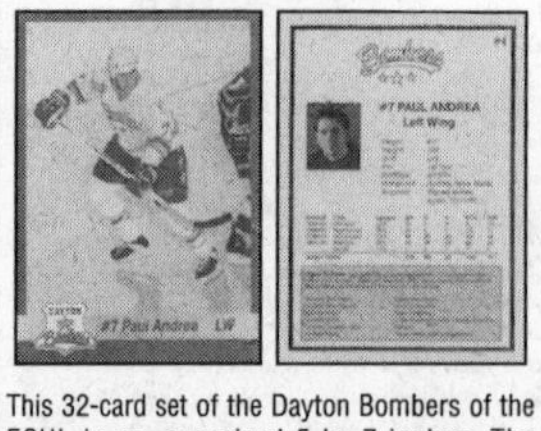

This 32-card set of the Dayton Bombers of the ECHL is an oversized 5 by 7 inches. The photo-cards featured a full color front action shot, and a black and white head shot on the back. The cards were limited in production to 500 copies each. One card was given away during each of 32 home games (3 games did not feature a card) inside the official game program. Purchase of a program was required to obtain a card.

| | MINT | NRMT |
|---|---|---|
| COMPLETE SET (32) | 25.00 | 11.00 |
| COMMON CARD (1-30) | .50 | .23 |

| | | |
|---|---|---|
| ❑ 1 Jim Playfair CO | .75 | .35 |
| ❑ 2 Sean Ortiz | .75 | .35 |
| ❑ 3 Derek Herlofsky | 1.00 | .45 |
| ❑ 4 Paul Andrea | .75 | .35 |
| ❑ 5 Nick Poole | .75 | .35 |
| ❑ 6 Steve Lingren | 1.00 | .45 |
| ❑ 7 Kevin Brown | .75 | .35 |
| ❑ 8 Jason Downey | .75 | .35 |
| ❑ 9 Sergei Kharin | 1.00 | .45 |
| ❑ 10 Matt McElwee | .75 | .35 |
| ❑ 11 Mike Naylor | .75 | .35 |
| ❑ 12 Ted Russell | .75 | .35 |
| ❑ 13 Colin Miller | 1.00 | .45 |
| ❑ 14 Brent Brekke | .75 | .35 |
| ❑ 15 John Brill | .75 | .35 |
| ❑ 16 Mike Murray | .75 | .35 |
| ❑ 17 Sean Gagnon | 1.00 | .45 |
| ❑ 18 Brian Renfrew | 1.00 | .45 |
| ❑ 19 Rob Peters | .75 | .35 |
| ❑ 20 Jeff Petruic | .75 | .35 |
| ❑ 21 Steve Roberts | .75 | .35 |
| ❑ 22 George Zajankala | .75 | .35 |
| ❑ 23 Adam Bomber | .50 | .23 |
| Mascot | | |
| ❑ 24 Steve Lingren | .75 | .35 |
| ECHL All-Star | | |
| ❑ 25 Jim Playfair CO | .75 | .35 |
| ECHL All-Star | | |
| ❑ 26 Jerry Buckley | 1.00 | .45 |
| ❑ 27 Jeremy Stasiuk | .75 | .35 |
| ❑ 28 Greg Burke | .75 | .35 |
| ❑ 29 Chris Johnston | .75 | .35 |
| ❑ 30 Dwayne Gylywoychuk | .75 | .35 |
| ❑ P1 Sean Gagnon | 1.50 | .70 |
| ❑ P2 Sergei Kharin | 1.50 | .70 |
| The Moscow Magician | | |

## 1996-97 Dayton Bombers

This 24-card set of the Dayton Bombers of the ECHL was issued as a promotional item within copies of the official game program. They were issued in 2-card strips, with the cards separated by a thin ad for sponsor WTUE radio. One strip was inserted during each of 12 home games over the course of the season. Purchase of the program was required to obtain the cards. The cards themselves were printed on thin stock, with color photos surrounded by a red border. The player's name, position and team and sponsor logos adorn the bottom. The backs were printed in black and white, with a mug shot, bio and statistical info. Production was limited to 500 copies of each strip.

| | MINT | NRMT |
|---|---|---|
| COMPLETE SET (24) | 25.00 | 11.00 |
| COMMON CARD (1-24) | 1.00 | .45 |

| | | |
|---|---|---|
| ❑ 1 Steve Roberts | 1.00 | .45 |
| ❑ 2 Chris Sullivan | 1.00 | .45 |
| ❑ 3 Steve Lingren | 1.50 | .70 |
| ❑ 4 Jordan Shields | 1.00 | .45 |
| ❑ 5 Ildar Yubin | 1.00 | .45 |
| ❑ 6 Dwight Parrish | 1.00 | .45 |
| ❑ 7 Brian Ridolfi | 1.00 | .45 |
| ❑ 8 Jordan Willis | 2.00 | .90 |
| ❑ 9 Dale Hooper | 1.00 | .45 |
| ❑ 10 Will Clarke | 1.00 | .45 |
| ❑ 11 Tavis Morrison | 1.00 | .45 |
| ❑ 12 Trent Schachle | 1.00 | .45 |
| ❑ 13 John Emmons | 1.00 | .45 |
| ❑ 14 Sam McKenney | 1.00 | .45 |
| ❑ 15 Bryan Richardson | 1.00 | .45 |
| ❑ 16 Ryan Gillis | 1.00 | .45 |
| ❑ 17 Marty Flichel | 1.50 | .70 |
| ❑ 18 Jason Downey | 1.00 | .45 |
| ❑ 19 Troy Christensen | 1.00 | .45 |
| ❑ 20 Derek Herlofsky | 2.00 | .90 |
| ❑ 21 Sal Manganaro | 1.00 | .45 |
| ❑ 22 Tom Nemeth | 1.00 | .45 |
| ❑ 23 Evgeny Ryabchikov | 2.00 | .90 |
| ❑ 24 Colin Miller | 1.50 | .70 |

## 1996-97 Denver University Pioneers

This 10-card set features color action photos on the front and a team schedule on the back.

| | MINT | NRMT |
|---|---|---|
| COMPLETE SET (10) | 2.00 | .90 |
| COMMON CARD (1-10) | .25 | .11 |

| | | |
|---|---|---|
| ❑ 1 Travis Smith | .25 | .11 |
| ❑ 2 Jim Mullin | .25 | .11 |
| ❑ 3 Mike Corbett | .25 | .11 |
| ❑ 4 Petri Gunther | .25 | .11 |
| ❑ 5 Garrett Buzan | .25 | .11 |
| ❑ 6 Antti Laaksonen | .25 | .11 |
| ❑ 7 Charlie Host | .25 | .11 |
| ❑ 8 Erik Andersson | .50 | .23 |
| ❑ 9 Warren Smith | .25 | .11 |
| ❑ 10 Anders Bjork | .25 | .11 |

## 1993-94 Detroit Jr. Red Wings

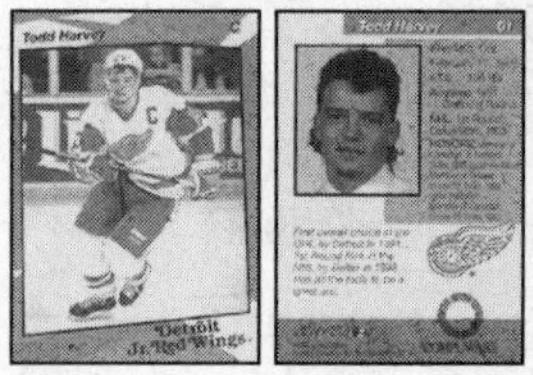

Sponsored by Compuware and printed by Slapshot Images Ltd., this standard size 26-card set features the 1993-94 Detroit Jr. Red Wings. On a geometrical red and white background, the fronts feature color action player photos with thin black borders. The player's name, position and team name, as well as the producer's logo, appear on the front. The backs carry a close-up color player portrait, and biographical information, along with team and sponsor's logos. The cards are numbered on the back. Included in this set is a Slapshot ad card with a 1994 calendar on the back.

| | MINT | NRMT |
|---|---|---|
| COMPLETE SET (26) | 10.00 | 4.50 |
| COMMON CARD (1-25) | .35 | .16 |

| | | |
|---|---|---|
| ❑ 1 Todd Harvey | 2.00 | .90 |
| ❑ 2 Jason Saal | .50 | .23 |
| ❑ 3 Aaron Ellis | .50 | .23 |
| ❑ 4 Chris Mailloux | .35 | .16 |
| ❑ 5 Robin Lacour | .35 | .16 |
| ❑ 6 Mike Rucinski | .35 | .16 |
| ❑ 7 Eric Cairns | .75 | .35 |
| ❑ 8 Matt Ball | .35 | .16 |
| ❑ 9 Dale Junkin | .35 | .16 |
| ❑ 10 Bill McCauley | .75 | .35 |
| ❑ 11 Jeremy Meehan | .35 | .16 |
| ❑ 12 Mike Harding | .35 | .16 |
| ❑ 13 Brad Cook | .35 | .16 |
| ❑ 14 Jeff Mitchell | .50 | .23 |
| ❑ 15 Jamie Allison | .50 | .23 |
| ❑ 16 Dan Pawlaczyk | .35 | .16 |
| ❑ 17 Kevin Brown | .50 | .23 |
| ❑ 18 Duane Harmer | .35 | .16 |
| ❑ 19 Gerry Skrypec | .35 | .16 |
| ❑ 20 Shayne McCosh | .50 | .23 |
| ❑ 21 Sean Haggerty | .75 | .35 |
| ❑ 22 Nic Beaudoin | .35 | .16 |
| ❑ 23 Paul Maurice CO | .50 | .23 |
| ❑ 24 Pete DeBoer ACO | .35 | .16 |
| ❑ 25 Bob Wren | .35 | .16 |
| ❑ NNO Slapshot Ad Card | .10 | .05 |

## 1994-95 Detroit Jr. Red Wings

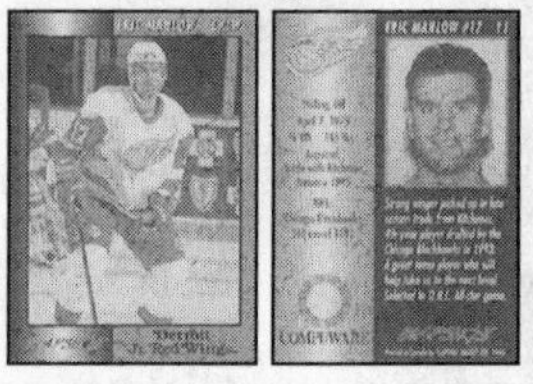

Sponsored by Compuware and printed by Slapshot Images Ltd., this 25-card set features the 1994-95 Detroit Jr. Red Wings. On a red and gray background, the fronts feature color action player photos with thin black borders. The player's name, position and team name, as well as the producer's logo, appear on the front. The backs carry a close-up color player portrait and biographical information, along with team and sponsor's logos.

| | MINT | NRMT |
|---|---|---|
| COMPLETE SET (25) | 12.00 | 5.50 |
| COMMON CARD (1-25) | .35 | .16 |

| | | |
|---|---|---|
| ❑ 1 Team Photo CL | .50 | .23 |
| ❑ 2 Darryl Foster | .35 | .16 |
| ❑ 3 Quade Lightbody | .35 | .16 |
| ❑ 4 Ryan MacDonald | .35 | .16 |
| ❑ 5 Mike Rucinski | .35 | .16 |
| ❑ 6 Murray Sheehan | .35 | .16 |
| ❑ 7 Matt Ball | .50 | .23 |
| ❑ 8 Gerry Lanigan | .35 | .16 |
| ❑ 9 Mike Morrone | .35 | .16 |
| ❑ 10 Tom Buckley | .35 | .16 |
| ❑ 11 Eric Manlow | .50 | .23 |
| ❑ 12 Bill McCauley | .60 | .25 |
| ❑ 13 Andrew Taylor | .35 | .16 |
| ❑ 14 Scott Blair | .35 | .16 |
| ❑ 15 Jeff Mitchell | .35 | .16 |
| ❑ 16 Jason Saal | .60 | .25 |
| ❑ 17 Jamie Allison | .60 | .25 |
| ❑ 18 Bryan Berard | 4.00 | 1.80 |
| ❑ 19 Dan Pawlaczyk | .35 | .16 |
| ❑ 20 Milan Kostolny | .35 | .16 |

❑ 21 Duane Harmer .35 .16
❑ 22 Shayne McCosh .50 .23
❑ 23 Sean Haggerty 1.00 .45
❑ 24 Nic Beaudoin .35 .16
❑ 25 Paul Maurice CO/GM .50 .23

## 1996-97 Detroit Vipers

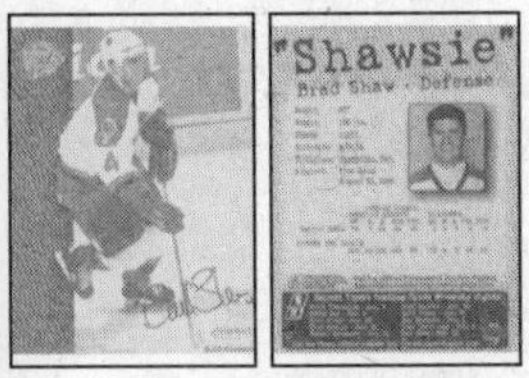


This odd-sized set commemorates the Detroit Vipers of the IHL. The set was produced by the club as a game-night premium. The cards were issued one per night at twenty different home games, beginning January 3, 1997 and ending April 13. The giveaway dates for each card can be found on the backs of the cards, along with a mugshot, player nickname and biographical data. The fronts feature an action photo, a reporduction of the player's autograph, and the logo of sponsor Ameritech.The unnumbered cards are listed below alphabetically. The set is noteworthy for the inclusion of 1997 draft pick Sergei Samsonov.

MINT NRMT
COMPLETE SET (20) 50.00 22.00
COMMON CARD (1-20) 2.00 .90

❑ 1 Darren Banks 2.00 .90
❑ 2 Peter Ciavaglia 2.00 .90
❑ 3 Yvon Corriveau 2.00 .90
❑ 4 Phil Crowe 2.00 .90
❑ 5 Mike Donnelly 2.00 .90
❑ 6 Stan Drulia 2.00 .90
❑ 7 Len Esau 2.00 .90
❑ 8 Ian Herbers 2.00 .90
❑ 9 Bobby Jay 2.00 .90
❑ 10 Dan Kesa 2.00 .90
❑ 11 Rich Parent 3.00 1.35
❑ 12 Jeff Parrott 2.00 .90
❑ 13 Wayne Presley 2.00 .90
❑ 14 Jeff Reese 3.00 1.35
❑ 15 Sergei Samsonov 20.00 9.00
❑ 16 Brad Shaw 2.00 .90
❑ 17 Todd Simon 2.00 .90
❑ 18 Patrice Tardif 2.00 .90
❑ 19 Phil Von Steffenelli 2.00 .90
❑ 20 Steve Walker 2.00 .90

## 1996-97 Detroit Whalers

This 25-card set was produced by the team and available for sale at games and by mail order for $5. The standard-size cards feature a color action photo with a seafoam green border. The backs contain a headshot, bio and stats.

MINT NRMT
COMPLETE SET (25) 8.00 3.60
COMMON CARD (1-25) .10 .05

❑ 1 Jessie Boulerice .50 .23
❑ 2 Mark Cadotte .50 .23
❑ 3 Chad Cavanagh .40 .18
❑ 4 Harold Druken 1.00 .45
❑ 5 Steve Dumonski .50 .23
❑ 6 Robert Esche .75 .35
❑ 7 Sergei Fedotov .50 .23
❑ 8 Randy Fitzgerald .40 .18
❑ 9 Eric Gooldy .40 .18
❑ 10 Kevin Holdridge .40 .18
❑ 11 John Paul Luciuk .40 .18
❑ 12 Mike Morrone .40 .18
❑ 13 Pat Parthenais .50 .23
❑ 14 Julian Smith .40 .18
❑ 15 Troy Smith .40 .18
❑ 16 Andrew Taylor .40 .18
❑ 17 Anthony Terzo .40 .18
❑ 18 Jan Vodrazka .40 .18
❑ 19 Steve Wasylko .50 .23
❑ 20 Nathan West .40 .18
❑ 21 Peter DeBoer CO .10 .05
❑ 22 Luc Rioux .40 .18
❑ 23 Slapshot (mascot) .10 .05
❑ 24 Checklist .10 .05
❑ 25 Discount Card .10 .05

## 1993-94 Drummondville Voltigeurs

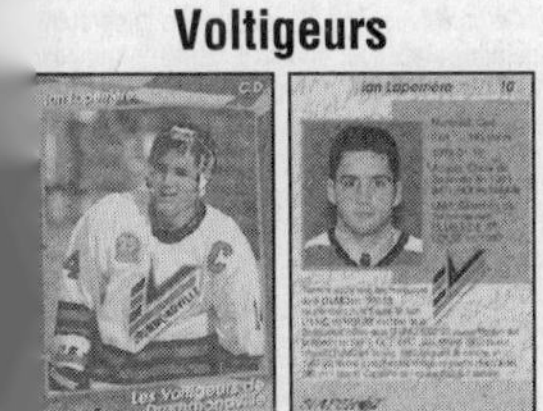


Printed by Slapshot Images Ltd., this standard size 28-card set features the 1993-94 Voltigeurs de Drummondville. On a geometrical purple and green background, the fronts feature color action player photos with thin grey borders. The player's name, position and team name, as well as the producer's logo, appear on the front. The backs carry a close-up color player portrait, and biographical information in French only, along with team logo. The cards are numbered on the back. Included in this set is a Slapshot ad card with a 1994 calendar on the back.

MINT NRMT
COMPLETE SET (28) 8.00 3.60
COMMON CARD (1-28) .10 .05

❑ 1 Title Card .10 .05
Checklist
❑ 2 Stephane Routhier .35 .16
❑ 3 Yannick Gagnon .50 .23
❑ 4 Sebastien Bety .50 .23
❑ 5 Martin Latulippe .35 .16
❑ 6 Nicolas Savage .35 .16
❑ 7 Sylvain Ducharme .35 .16
❑ 8 Yan St. Pierre .35 .16
❑ 9 Emmanuel Labranche .35 .16
❑ 10 Ian Laperriere .75 .35
❑ 11 Louis Bernard .35 .16
❑ 12 Stephane St. Amour .35 .16
❑ 13 Vincent Tremblay .35 .16
❑ 14 Denis Gauthier Jr. .35 .16
❑ 15 Eric Plante .35 .16
❑ 16 Christian Marcoux .35 .16
❑ 17 Patrice Charbonneau .35 .16
❑ 18 Raymond Delarosbil .35 .16
❑ 19 Patrick Livernoche .35 .16
❑ 20 Luc Decelles .35 .16
❑ 21 Francois Sasseville .35 .16
❑ 22 Steve Tardif .50 .23
❑ 23 Mathieu Sunderland .50 .23
❑ 24 Alexandre Duchesne .50 .23
❑ 25 Jean Hamel CO GM .10 .05
❑ 26 Mario Carrier ACO .10 .05
❑ 27 Me Andre Lepage TR .10 .05
❑ 28 Slapshot Ad Card .10 .05

## 1994-95 Dubuque Fighting Saints

This 29-card set measures the standard size. The fronts feature color action player photos with the player's name, jersey number, and team logo at the bottom. The team name runs down the left side of the front. The backs carry a black-and-white player portrait, the player's name, jersey number, biographical information, statistics, career summary, and team logo. The cards are unnumbered and checklisted below in alphabetical order.

MINT NRMT
COMPLETE SET (29) 7.00 3.10
COMMON CARD (1-29) .10 .05

❑ 1 Title Card .10 .05
Season schedule
❑ 2 Chris Addesa .35 .16
❑ 3 Matt Addesa .35 .16
❑ 4 Mark Allegrezza .25 .11
❑ 5 Todd Barclay .25 .11
❑ 6 Jay Boxer ACO .10 .05
❑ 7 Geoff Collard .25 .11
❑ 8 John Dwyer .25 .11
❑ 9 Jayme Filipowicz .25 .11
❑ 10 Zach Ham .25 .11
❑ 11 Mike Herrera .25 .11
❑ 12 Roger Holeczy .25 .11
❑ 13 Steve Holeczy .25 .11
❑ 14 John Hultberg .75 .35
❑ 15 Ryan Karasek .25 .11
❑ 16 Mike Kramer TR .10 .05
❑ 17 Chris Masters .25 .11
❑ 18 A.J. Melanson .25 .11
❑ 19 Mike Minichiello .25 .11
❑ 20 Berk Nelson .25 .11
❑ 21 Nik Patronas .25 .11
❑ 22 Andy Powers .25 .11
❑ 23 Matt Romaniski .25 .11
❑ 24 Tom Ryles .25 .11
❑ 25 John Sadowski .25 .11
❑ 26 Chris Showalter .25 .11
❑ 27 Dan Stepanek .25 .11
❑ 28 Trevor Tallackson .25 .11
❑ 29 Troy Ward GM/CO .10 .05

## 1994-95 Erie Panthers

Produced by CJ Sports, this 20-card standard-size set features the Erie Panthers of the East Coast Hockey League. The fronts display color action player photos with gray borders. The player's name, position, and sponsor's name are below. The team name and logo appear at the top. The backs are white, grey, and black with player biography and statistics.

MINT NRMT
COMPLETE SET (20) 6.00 2.70
COMMON CARD (1-20) .10 .05

❑ 1 Title Card .10 .05
❑ 2 Ron Hansis CO .10 .05
❑ 3 Barry Smith ACO .10 .05
❑ 4 Patrick Laughlin TR .10 .05
❑ 5 Larry Empey .35 .16
❑ 6 Vassili Demin .35 .16
❑ 7 Sergei Stas .35 .16
❑ 8 Brad Harrison .35 .16
❑ 9 Cam Brown .35 .16
❑ 10 Kevin McKinnon .35 .16
❑ 11 Andrei Kozlov .35 .16
❑ 12 Chris Tschupp .35 .16
❑ 13 Jason Smith .35 .16
❑ 14 Justin Peca .35 .16
❑ 15 Francis Ouellette .50 .23
❑ 16 Vern Guetens .50 .23
❑ 17 Scott Burfoot .50 .23
❑ 18 Vyacheslav Polikarkin .35 .16
❑ 19 Stephane Charbonneau .35 .16
❑ 20 Ian Decorby .35 .16

## 1991-92 Ferris State Bulldogs

This 30-card standard-size set features the 1991-92 Ferris State Bulldogs. The cards were available in the Ferris State University Pro Shop at the arena. The cards are unnumbered and checklisted below in alphabetical order.

MINT NRMT
COMPLETE SET (30) 8.00 3.60
COMMON CARD (1-30) .10 .05

❑ 1 Aaron Asp .50 .23
❑ 2 Seth Appert .30 .14
❑ 3 J.J. Bamberger .30 .14
❑ 4 Kevin Beals ACO .10 .05
❑ 5 Scot Bell .30 .14
❑ 6 Brad Burnham .30 .14
❑ 7 Dan Chaput .50 .23
❑ 8 Tim Christian .30 .14
❑ 9 Bob Daniels .30 .14
❑ 10 Colin Dodunski .30 .14
❑ 11 Mick Dolan .30 .14
❑ 12 John Duff .30 .14
❑ 13 Daryl Filipek .30 .14
❑ 14 John Gruden .50 .23
❑ 15 Luke Harvey .30 .14
❑ 16 Jeff Jestadt .30 .14
❑ 17 Dave Karpa .75 .35
❑ 18 Gary Kitching .30 .14
❑ 19 Mike Kolenda .30 .14
❑ 20 Craig Lisko .30 .14
❑ 21 Mike May .30 .14
❑ 22 Pat Mazzoli .30 .14
❑ 23 Robb McIntyre .30 .14
❑ 24 Kevin Moore .30 .14
❑ 25 Greg Paine .30 .14
❑ 26 Dwight Parrish .30 .14
❑ 27 Val Passarelli .30 .14
❑ 28 Keith Sergott .30 .14
❑ 29 Doug Smith .30 .14
❑ 30 The Bulldog (Mascot) .10 .05

## 1987-88 Flint Spirits

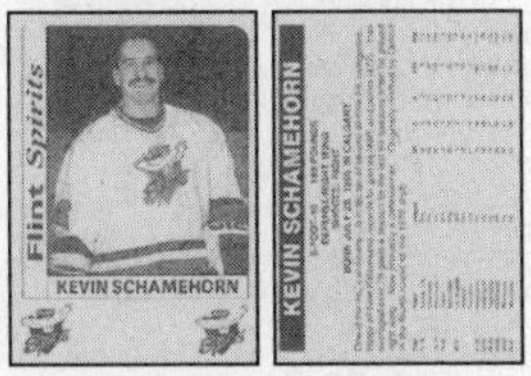


This 20-card standard-size set features white-bordered posed color player photos. The team name and the player's name edge the picture on the left and lower edges respectively. Team logos in the bottom border round out the front. The horizontal backs carry biography, player profile, and statistics.

MINT NRMT
COMPLETE SET (20) 10.00 4.50
COMMON CARD (1-20) .50 .23

❑ 1 Mario Chitaroni .50 .23
❑ 2 John Cullen 2.00 .90
❑ 3 Bob Fleming .50 .23
❑ 4 Keith Gretzky 1.50 .70
❑ 5 Todd Hawkins .50 .23
❑ 6 Mike Hoffman .50 .23
❑ 7 Curtis Hunt .50 .23
❑ 8 Dwaine Hutton .50 .23
❑ 9 Trent Kaese .50 .23
❑ 10 Tom Karalis .50 .23
❑ 11 Ray LeBlanc 1.00 .45
❑ 12 Darren Lowe .50 .23
❑ 13 Brett MacDonald .50 .23
❑ 14 Chris McSorley .75 .35
❑ 15 Mike Mersch .50 .23
❑ 16 Victor Posa .50 .23
❑ 17 Kevin Schamehorn .50 .23
❑ 18 Ron Stern .75 .35
❑ 19 Don Waddell .50 .23
❑ 20 Dan Woodley .50 .23

## 1988-89 Flint Spirits

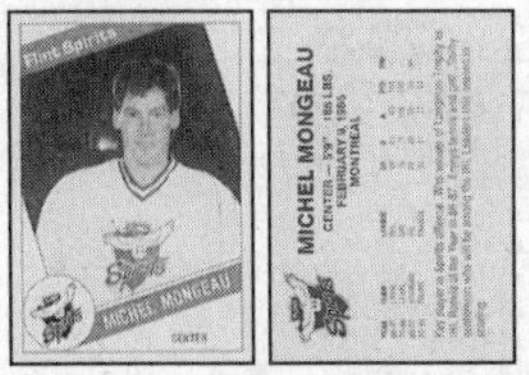


This 22-card standard-size features posed color player photos. The pictures are set at an angle on the card with green borders on the top and bottom. The player's name appears in the lower green border, while the team appears above. A thin blue line borders the front. The horizontal backs carry the player's name, biographical information, statistics, and career highlights. The cards are unnumbered and checklisted below in alphabetical order.

MINT NRMT
COMPLETE SET (22) 10.00 4.50
COMMON CARD (1-22) .50 .23

❑ 1 Dean Anderson .50 .23
❑ 2 Rob Bryden .50 .23
❑ 3 John Devereaux .50 .23
❑ 4 Stephane Giguere .50 .23
❑ 5 Steve Harrison .50 .23
❑ 6 Yves Heroux .75 .35
❑ 7 Mike Hoffman .50 .23
❑ 8 Peter Horachek .50 .23
❑ 9 Guy Jacob .50 .23
❑ 10 Bob Kennedy .50 .23
❑ 11 Gary Kruzich .50 .23
❑ 12 Lonnie Loach 1.00 .45
❑ 13 Brett MacDonald .50 .23
❑ 14 Mike MacWilliam .50 .23
❑ 15 Moe Mansi .50 .23
❑ 16 Mike Mersch .50 .23
❑ 17 Michel Mongeau 1.00 .45
❑ 18 Ken Spangler .50 .23
❑ 19 Three Amigos .75 .35
Steve Harrison
Mike Mersch
Mike Hoffman
❑ 20 Mark Vichorek .50 .23
❑ 21 Troy Vollhoffer .50 .23
❑ 22 Don Waddell GM .50 .23

## 1993-94 Flint Generals

This set of 20 cards features the Flint Generals of the Colonial Hockey League. It was produced for team distribution by Rising Star Sport Promotions. The fronts feature a posed photo, along with league logo and player information. The backs contain a smattering of biographical data and career numbers. The set is unnumbered.

MINT NRMT
COMPLETE SET (20) 7.00 3.10
COMMON CARD (1-20) .10 .05

❑ 1 Header Card .10 .05
❑ 2 Brent Stickney .35 .16
❑ 3 Brett Strot .35 .16
❑ 4 Brian Sakic .50 .23
❑ 5 Chris O'Rourke .35 .16
❑ 6 Dan Elsener .35 .16
❑ 7 Darcy Austin .35 .16
❑ 8 Dominic Niro .35 .16
❑ 9 Jim Duhart .35 .16
❑ 10 John Heasty .35 .16
❑ 11 Keith Whitmore .35 .16
❑ 12 Ken Spangler .35 .16
❑ 13 Kevin Kerr .35 .16
❑ 14 Larry Bernard .35 .16
❑ 15 Lorne Knauft .35 .16
❑ 16 Marc Vachon .35 .16
❑ 17 Mark Gowens .50 .23
❑ 18 Peter Horachek .35 .16
❑ 19 Stephane Brochu .35 .16
❑ 20 Todd Humphrey .50 .23

## 1994-95 Flint Generals

This 24-card set of the Flint Generals of the Colonial Hockey Leauge was produced by and distributed through the team. The set's familiar look comes from its homage to the lamentable 1991-92 Pro Set issue. The card backs also ape the design, although they are in black and white, containing another photo and player stats.

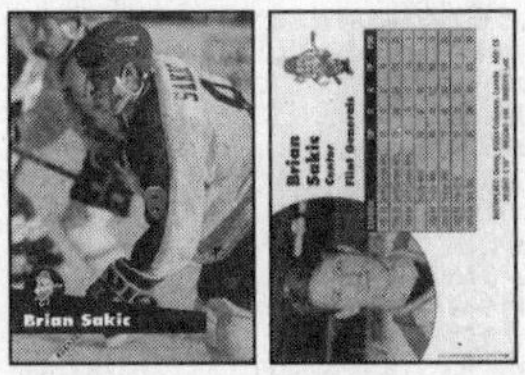


MINT NRMT
COMPLETE SET (24) 8.00 3.60
COMMON CARD (1-24) .35 .16

❑ 1 Kevin Barrett .35 .16
❑ 2 Larry Bernard .35 .16
❑ 3 Ken Blum .35 .16
❑ 4 Stephane Brochu .35 .16
❑ 5 Keith Carney .50 .23
❑ 6 Ryan Douglas .35 .16
❑ 7 Jim Duhart .35 .16
❑ 8 Ray Gallagher .35 .16
❑ 9 Mark Gowens .50 .23
❑ 10 Peter Horachek .35 .16
❑ 11 Todd Humphrey .35 .16
❑ 12 Fredrik Jax .50 .23
❑ 13 Doug Jones .35 .16
❑ 14 Kevin Kerr .35 .16
❑ 15 Petr Leska .35 .16
❑ 16 Stan Matwijiw .35 .16
❑ 17 Glen Mears .35 .16
❑ 18 Kyle Reeves .50 .23
❑ 19 Brian Sakic .50 .23
❑ 20 Stefan Simoes .35 .16
❑ 21 Ken Spangler .35 .16
❑ 22 Keith Whitmore .35 .16
❑ 23 Jeff Whittle .35 .16
❑ 24 Team Photo .35 .16

## 1995-96 Flint Generals

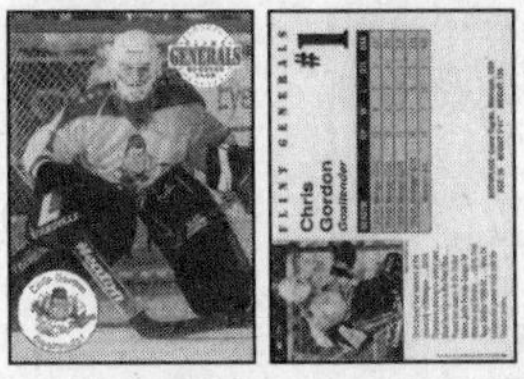

This 25-card set features the Flint Generals of the CHL. The set was produced by, and available only through, the team's booster club. The fronts feature an action photo and team and booster club logos. The back includes another photo, player stats and a brief bio.

MINT NRMT
COMPLETE SET (25) 9.00 4.00
COMMON CARD (1-25) .10 .05

❑ 1 Erin Whitten 2.50 1.10
❑ 2 Kevin Kerr .50 .23
❑ 3 Sverre Sears .35 .16
❑ 4 Scott Burfoot .50 .23
❑ 5 John Batten .35 .16
❑ 6 Chad Grills .35 .16
❑ 7 Lady Generals .25 .11
❑ 8 Gen.Rally -- Mascot .10 .05
❑ 9 Rob Nichols GM/CO .10 .05
❑ 10 Mikhail Nemirovsky .35 .16
❑ 11 Robin Bouchard .35 .16
❑ 12 Dominic Grandmaison .35 .16
❑ 13 Andrei Mezin .35 .16
❑ 14 Steve Beadle .35 .16
❑ 15 Darryl Lafrance .35 .16
❑ 16 Chris Gotziaman .35 .16
❑ 17 Gerry St. Cyr .35 .16
❑ 18 Derek Knorr .35 .16
❑ 19 Chris Gordon .50 .23
❑ 20 Brett MacDonald .35 .16
❑ 21 Brian Sakic .50 .23
❑ 22 Jamie Hearn .35 .16
❑ 23 Jeff Whittle .35 .16
❑ 24 Stephane Brochu .35 .16
❑ 25 Jim Duhart .35 .16

## 1998-99 Florida Everblades

MINT NRMT
COMPLETE SET (28) 4.00 1.80
COMMON CARD (1-28) .10 .05

❑ 1 Brett Bruininks .15 .07
❑ 2 Matt Brush .15 .07
❑ 3 Nick Checco .15 .07
❑ 4 Matt Demarski .15 .07

| | MINT | NRMT |
|---|---|---|
| ❑ 5 Sergei Fedotov | .20 | .09 |
| ❑ 6 Tim Ferguson | .15 | .07 |
| ❑ 7 Bob Ferguson CO | .10 | .05 |
| ❑ 8 Hugh Hamilton | .15 | .07 |
| ❑ 9 Mike Jickling | .15 | .07 |
| ❑ 10 Gary Koehler | .15 | .07 |
| ❑ 11 Greg Kuznik | .15 | .07 |
| ❑ 12 Dane Litke | .15 | .07 |
| ❑ 13 Marc Magliarditi | .15 | .07 |
| ❑ 14 Kevin McDonald | .15 | .07 |
| ❑ 15 Pat Mikesch | .15 | .07 |
| ❑ 16 P.K. O'Handley ACO | .10 | .05 |
| ❑ 17 Josh Penn EQ | .10 | .05 |
| ❑ 18 Randy Petruk | .15 | .07 |
| ❑ 19 Jason Prokepetz | .15 | .07 |
| ❑ 20 Dan Keimann | .15 | .07 |
| ❑ 21 Eric Ricard | .15 | .07 |
| ❑ 22 Eric Rud | .15 | .07 |
| ❑ 23 Steve Tardif | .15 | .07 |
| ❑ 24 Andrew Taylor | .15 | .07 |
| ❑ 25 Todd Wisocki | .15 | .07 |
| ❑ 26 Mascot | .10 | .05 |
| ❑ 27 Title Card | .10 | .05 |

## 1990-91 Fort Saskatchewan Traders

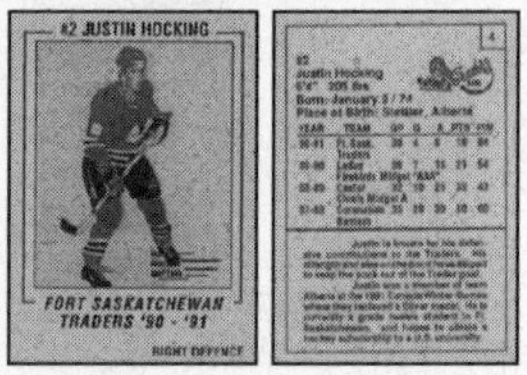

This sheet contains 24 standard-size cards. Each card contains a color action player photo with his jersey number and name at the top on a white background. Above this are listed the player's position with the team name and years. At the lower right are the words "Next Generation Sport Cards." Each photo is framed by a thin red line and white border. The cards are unnumbered and checklisted below in alphabetical order.

| | MINT | NRMT |
|---|---|---|
| COMPLETE SET (24) | 6.00 | 2.70 |
| COMMON CARD (1-24) | .35 | .16 |
| ❑ 1 Michael Buzak | .35 | .16 |
| ❑ 2 Wade Fennig | .35 | .16 |
| ❑ 3 Mark Goodkey | .35 | .16 |
| ❑ 4 Richard Groten | .35 | .16 |
| ❑ 5 Brett Gullion | .35 | .16 |
| ❑ 6 Keith Hill | .35 | .16 |
| ❑ 7 Justin Hocking | .75 | .35 |
| ❑ 8 Ian Kallay | .35 | .16 |
| ❑ 9 Scott Lindsay | .35 | .16 |
| ❑ 10 Faron Luchkow | .35 | .16 |
| ❑ 11 Wayne MacDonald | .35 | .16 |
| ❑ 12 Ted Oloriz | .35 | .16 |
| ❑ 13 Jason Plandowski | .35 | .16 |
| ❑ 14 Dory Reich | .35 | .16 |
| ❑ 15 Shawn Reich | .35 | .16 |
| ❑ 16 Darren Smith | .35 | .16 |
| ❑ 17 Mark Souch | .35 | .16 |
| ❑ 18 Bryan Stewart | .35 | .16 |
| ❑ 19 Paul Strand | .35 | .16 |
| ❑ 20 Tim Wiwchar | .35 | .16 |
| ❑ 21 Paul Wozney | .35 | .16 |
| ❑ 22 Allen Young | .35 | .16 |
| ❑ 23 Jason Yuzda | .35 | .16 |
| ❑ 24 Team Photo | .50 | .23 |

## 1992-93 Fort Worth Fire

Sponsored by Whataburger, this 18-card set was issued as a cut set and also as a sheet. The sheet was rimmed on the left and right sides by a row of coupons redeemable at Whataburger. Card strips featuring three player cards sandwiched between two coupons were also produced. The cards measure the standard size and feature posed, color player photos with either a peach or a white studio background on white card stock. The picture is set off-center on a white area framed by a thin black line and shadow-bordered. The player's name and uniform number are printed above the photo, while "Whataburger" is printed in burnt orange below. The backs carry biographical information and career highlights. The cards are unnumbered and checklisted below in alphabetical order.

| | MINT | NRMT |
|---|---|---|
| COMPLETE SET (18) | 8.00 | 3.60 |
| COMMON CARD (1-18) | .25 | .11 |
| ❑ 1 Ron Aubrey | .50 | .23 |
| ❑ 2 Roch Belley | .75 | .35 |
| ❑ 3 Jason Brousseau | .50 | .23 |
| ❑ 4 Eric Brule | .50 | .23 |
| ❑ 5 Todd Drevitch | .50 | .23 |
| ❑ 6 Trevor Duhaime | .50 | .23 |
| ❑ 7 Steve Harrison ACO | .25 | .11 |
| ❑ 8 Ernest Hornak | .50 | .23 |
| ❑ 9 Alex Kholomeyev | .75 | .35 |
| ❑ 10 Curt Krolak | .50 | .23 |
| ❑ 11 Ryan Leschasin | .50 | .23 |
| ❑ 12 Peter Mahovlich CO | 1.00 | .45 |
| ❑ 13 Mike McCormick | .50 | .23 |
| ❑ 14 Mike O'Hara | .50 | .23 |
| ❑ 15 Pat Penner | .50 | .23 |
| ❑ 16 Paolo Racicot | .50 | .23 |
| ❑ 17 Dan Rolfe | .50 | .23 |
| ❑ 18 Mike Sanderson | .50 | .23 |

## 1993-94 Fort Worth Fire

This 18-card set is similar in design to the Dallas Freeze issue of this year. the round cards are approximately the size of a hockey puck and came packaged in a plastic container with the team logo on the front. The sets were sold by the team's booster club at home games, and may have been made available through the mail.

| | MINT | NRMT |
|---|---|---|
| COMPLETE SET (18) | 6.00 | 2.70 |
| COMMON CARD (1-18) | .10 | .05 |
| ❑ 1 Ron Aubrey | .35 | .16 |
| ❑ 2 Derby Bognar | .35 | .16 |
| ❑ 3 Reggie Brezeault | .35 | .16 |
| ❑ 4 Jason Brousseau | .35 | .16 |
| ❑ 5 Ty Eigner | .50 | .23 |
| ❑ 6 Todd Huyber | .35 | .16 |
| ❑ 7 Chris Jensen | .50 | .23 |
| ❑ 8 Chad Johnson | .35 | .16 |
| ❑ 9 Ryan Leschasin | .35 | .16 |
| ❑ 10 Dominic Maltais | .50 | .23 |
| ❑ 11 Mike McCormick | .35 | .16 |
| ❑ 12 Patrick McGarry | .35 | .16 |
| ❑ 13 Mike O'Hara | .35 | .16 |
| ❑ 14 Sean Rowe | .35 | .16 |
| ❑ 15 Mike Sanderson | .35 | .16 |
| ❑ 16 Rob Striar | .35 | .16 |
| ❑ 17 Scott Zygulski | .35 | .16 |
| ❑ 18 Steve Harrison CO | .10 | .05 |

## 1995-96 Fort Worth Fire Team

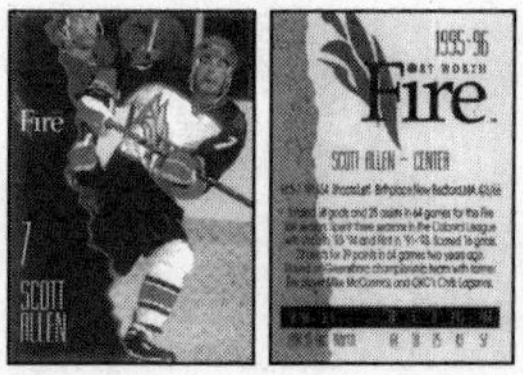

This 18-card team set features the Fort Worth Fire of the Central Hockey League. The set apparently was distributed by the booster club. In an unusual twist, the cards were not sold in team sets; instead, a 9-card assortment could be had for $3. Usually, it took three packs to assemble a complete set. The cards feature an action photo on the front, along with player bio and 1994-95 stats on the back.

| | MINT | NRMT |
|---|---|---|
| COMPLETE SET (18) | 6.00 | 2.70 |
| COMMON CARD (1-18) | .25 | .11 |
| ❑ 1 Team Photo | .35 | .16 |
| ❑ 2 Bill McDonald CO | .25 | .11 |
| ❑ 3 Phil Groeneveld | .35 | .16 |
| ❑ 4 Vern Ray | .35 | .16 |
| ❑ 5 Steve Dykstra | .50 | .23 |
| ❑ 6 Trevor Burgess | .35 | .16 |
| ❑ 7 Scott Allen | .35 | .16 |
| ❑ 8 Sean Whyte | .35 | .16 |
| ❑ 9 Troy Frederick | .35 | .16 |
| ❑ 10 Troy Stephens | .35 | .16 |
| ❑ 11 Jeff Massey | .35 | .16 |
| ❑ 12 Dwight Mullins | .35 | .16 |
| ❑ 13 Kyle Reeves | .50 | .23 |
| ❑ 14 Mike Gruttaduria | .35 | .16 |
| ❑ 15 Mark Hilton | .35 | .16 |
| ❑ 16 Brian Caruso | .35 | .16 |
| ❑ 17 Dennis Miller | .35 | .16 |
| ❑ 18 Steve Plouffe | .50 | .23 |

## 1996-97 Fort Worth Fire

This 18-card set features the CHL champion Fort Worth Fire. It was produced by the team and sold at the rink. The cards feature action photography surrounded by a condition sensitive black border. The player's name and number appear as well. The black and white back contains a player profile, but no numbering, hence the alphabetical listing below.

| | MINT | NRMT |
|---|---|---|
| COMPLETE SET (18) | 5.00 | 2.20 |
| COMMON CARD (1-18) | .10 | .05 |
| ❑ 1 Malcolm Cameron | .40 | .18 |
| ❑ 2 Steve Carter | .40 | .18 |
| ❑ 3 Mike Sanderson | .40 | .18 |
| ❑ 4 Stephane Larocque | .40 | .18 |
| ❑ 5 Murray Hogg | .40 | .18 |
| ❑ 6 Bob Delorimiere | .50 | .23 |
| ❑ 7 Steve Plouffe | .50 | .23 |
| ❑ 8 Glenn Painter | .40 | .18 |
| ❑ 9 Mark Strohack | .40 | .18 |
| ❑ 10 Brian Caruso | .40 | .18 |
| ❑ 11 Dwight Mullins | .40 | .18 |
| ❑ 12 Terry Menard | .40 | .18 |
| ❑ 13 Vern Ray | .40 | .18 |
| ❑ 14 Adam Robbins | .40 | .18 |
| ❑ 15 Mark O'Donnell | .40 | .18 |
| ❑ 16 Mike McCourt | .40 | .18 |
| ❑ 17 Ryan Black | .40 | .18 |
| ❑ 18 Bill McDonald CO | .10 | .05 |

## 1981-82 Fredericton Express

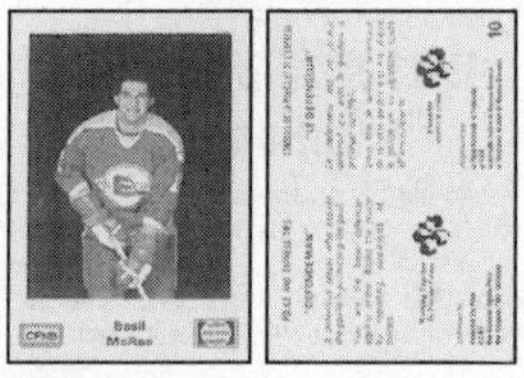

This 26-card set was issued by the team and endorsed by the Fredericton City Police, R.C.M.P., New Brunswick Highway Patrol, and New Brunswick Police Commission. The cards measure approximately 2 1/2" by 3 3/4" with a white border on the front. The fronts also carry a posed color player photo with the player's name printed below. The CFNB and Pepsi logos are printed in the lower left and right corners respectively. The horizontal backs are bilingual and carry a brief message relating to the game of hockey and a safety tip or public service announcement. The cards are numbered on the back.

| | MINT | NRMT |
|---|---|---|
| COMPLETE SET (26) | 18.00 | 8.00 |
| COMMON CARD (1-26) | .25 | .11 |
| ❑ 1 Team Photo | .50 | .23 |
| ❑ 2 B.J. MacDonald | .75 | .35 |
| ❑ 3 Sylvain Cote | .50 | .23 |
| ❑ 4 Michel Bolduc | .50 | .23 |
| ❑ 5 Gary Lupul | .50 | .23 |
| ❑ 6 Clint Malarchuk | 4.00 | 1.80 |
| ❑ 7 Tony Currie | .50 | .23 |
| ❑ 8 Tim Tookey | .50 | .23 |
| ❑ 9 Anders Eldebrink | .50 | .23 |
| ❑ 10 Basil McRae | 2.00 | .90 |
| ❑ 11 Kelly Elcombe | .50 | .23 |
| ❑ 12 Jacques Demers | 3.00 | 1.35 |
| ❑ 13 Frank Caprice | 1.00 | .45 |
| ❑ 14 Terry Johnson | .50 | .23 |
| ❑ 15 Grant Martin | .50 | .23 |
| ❑ 16 Andre Chartrain | .50 | .23 |
| ❑ 17 Marc Crawford | 3.00 | 1.35 |
| ❑ 18 Gaston Therrien | .50 | .23 |
| ❑ 19 Andy Schliebener | .50 | .23 |
| ❑ 20 Christian Tanguay | .50 | .23 |
| ❑ 21 Art Rutland | .50 | .23 |
| ❑ 22 Jean MarcGaulin | .50 | .23 |
| ❑ 23 Neil Belland | .50 | .23 |
| ❑ 24 Andre Cote | .50 | .23 |
| ❑ 25 Jim MacRae | .50 | .23 |
| ❑ 26 Scott Beckingham<br>Marty Flynn | .25 | .11 |

## 1982-83 Fredericton Express

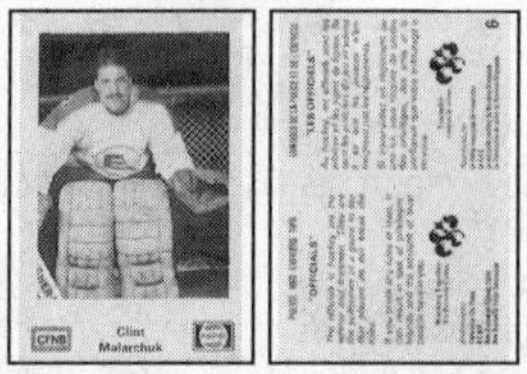

Sponsored by CFNB and Pepsi, this 26-card set measures approximately 2 1/2" by 3 3/4" and features posed, color player photos with white borders. The player's name and sponsor logos appear in the lower white margin. The horizontal backs carry Police and Express Tips relating to hockey skills and personal safety. The text is presented in both French and English. Sponsors are listed at the bottom.

| | MINT | EXC |
|---|---|---|
| COMPLETE SET (26) | 18.00 | 8.00 |
| COMMON CARD (1-26) | .25 | .11 |
| ❑ 1 Team Photo | 1.00 | .45 |
| ❑ 2 B.J. MacDonald | .75 | .35 |
| ❑ 3 Sylvain Cote | .50 | .23 |
| ❑ 4 Michel Bolduc | .50 | .23 |
| ❑ 5 Gary Lupul | .50 | .23 |
| ❑ 6 Clint Malarchuk | 3.00 | 1.35 |
| ❑ 7 Tony Currie | .50 | .23 |
| ❑ 8 Tim Tookey | .50 | .23 |
| ❑ 9 Anders Eldebrink | .50 | .23 |
| ❑ 10 Basil McRae | 2.00 | .90 |
| ❑ 11 Kelly Elcombe | .50 | .23 |
| ❑ 12 Jacques Demers | 2.50 | 1.10 |
| ❑ 13 Frank Caprice | 1.50 | .70 |
| ❑ 14 Terry Johnson | .50 | .23 |
| ❑ 15 Grant Martin | .50 | .23 |
| ❑ 16 Andre Chartrain | .50 | .23 |
| ❑ 17 Marc Crawford | 1.50 | .70 |
| ❑ 18 Gaston Therrien | .50 | .23 |
| ❑ 19 Andy Schliebener | .50 | .23 |
| ❑ 20 Christian Tanguay | .50 | .23 |
| ❑ 21 Art Rutland | .50 | .23 |
| ❑ 22 Jean-Marc Gaulin | .50 | .23 |
| ❑ 23 Neil Belland | .50 | .23 |
| ❑ 24 Andre Cote | .50 | .23 |
| ❑ 25 Jim MacRae | .50 | .23 |
| ❑ 26 Scott Beckingham TR<br>and Marty Flynn TR | .25 | .11 |

## 1983-84 Fredericton Express

This 27-card set measures 2 1/2" by 3 3/4" and features posed action color player photos with white borders. The player's name, position, and NHL affiliation appear below the picture in the white margin. The horizontal backs are white and carry Police and Express Tips in French and English.

| | MINT | NRMT |
|---|---|---|
| COMPLETE SET (27) | 14.00 | 6.25 |
| COMMON CARD (1-26) | .25 | .11 |
| ❑ 1 Team Photo | 1.00 | .45 |
| ❑ 2 Frank Caprice | 1.00 | .45 |
| ❑ 3 Michel Dufour | .50 | .23 |
| ❑ 4 Brian Ford | .50 | .23 |
| ❑ 5 Jean-Marc Lanthier | .50 | .23 |
| ❑ 6 Jim Dobson | .50 | .23 |
| ❑ 7 Mike Hough | 1.00 | .45 |
| ❑ 8 Rick Lapointe | .75 | .35 |
| ❑ 9 Michel Bolduc | .50 | .23 |
| ❑ 10 Christian Tanguay | .50 | .23 |
| ❑ 11 Tony Currie | .50 | .23 |
| ❑ 12 Moe Lemay | 1.00 | .45 |
| ❑ 13 Bruce Holloway | .50 | .23 |
| ❑ 14 Neil Belland | .50 | .23 |
| ❑ 15 Richard Turmel | .50 | .23 |
| ❑ 16 Claude Julien | .50 | .23 |
| ❑ 17 Andre Chartrain | .50 | .23 |
| ❑ 18 Grant Martin | .50 | .23 |
| ❑ 19 Rejean Vignola | .50 | .23 |
| ❑ 20 Andre Cote | .50 | .23 |
| ❑ 21 Jean-Marc Gaulin | .50 | .23 |
| ❑ 22 Andy Schliebener | .50 | .23 |
| ❑ 23 Stu Kulak | .75 | .35 |
| ❑ 24 Mike Eagles | 1.50 | .70 |
| ❑ 25 Earl Jessiman CO/GM | .25 | .11 |
| ❑ 26 Marty Flynn TR<br>Scott Beckingham TR | .25 | .11 |
| ❑ NNO Checklist | .50 | .23 |

## 1984-85 Fredericton Express

This 28-card set measures approximately 2 1/2" by 3 3/4" and features posed color player photos against a white card face. The player's name, biography, position, and NHL affiliation appear in black print below the picture. Sponsor logos are in the lower corners. The horizontal backs are white and carry Police and Express Tips in French and English.

| | MINT | NRMT |
|---|---|---|
| COMPLETE SET (28) | 12.00 | 5.50 |
| COMMON CARD (1-28) | .25 | .11 |
| ❑ 1 Dave Morrison | .50 | .23 |
| ❑ 2 Dave Shaw | 1.00 | .45 |
| ❑ 3 Bruce Holloway | .50 | .23 |
| ❑ 4 Roger Haegglund | .50 | .23 |
| ❑ 5 Neil Belland | .50 | .23 |
| ❑ 6 Gord Donnelly | 1.00 | .45 |
| ❑ 7 David Bruce | .50 | .23 |
| ❑ 8 Claude Julien | .50 | .23 |
| ❑ 9 Dan Wood | .50 | .23 |
| ❑ 10 Clint Malarchuk | 2.00 | .90 |
| ❑ 11 Jere Gillis | .50 | .23 |
| ❑ 12 Mike Hough | 1.00 | .45 |
| ❑ 13 Michel Bolduc | .50 | .23 |
| ❑ 14 Peter Loob | .50 | .23 |
| ❑ 15 Steve Driscoll | .50 | .23 |
| ❑ 16 Newell Brown | .50 | .23 |
| ❑ 17 Jim Dobson | .50 | .23 |
| ❑ 18 Wendell Young | 1.50 | .70 |
| ❑ 19 Mark Kumpel | .75 | .35 |
| ❑ 20 Mike Eagles | 1.00 | .45 |
| ❑ 21 Tom Thornbury | .50 | .23 |
| ❑ 22 Grant Martin | .50 | .23 |
| ❑ 23 Marc Crawford | 1.00 | .45 |
| ❑ 24 Andy Schliebener | .50 | .23 |
| ❑ 25 Earl Jessiman CO/GM | .25 | .11 |
| ❑ 26 Yvon Vautour | .50 | .23 |
| ❑ 27 Craig Coxe | .75 | .35 |
| ❑ 28 Blake Wesley | .50 | .23 |

## 1985-86 Fredericton Express

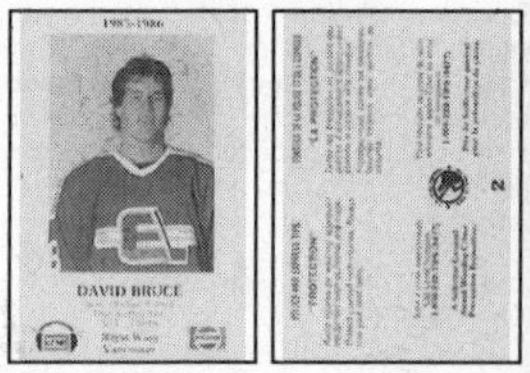

This 28-card set measures 2 1/2" by 3 3/4" and features posed color player photos against a white card face. The player's name, biography, position, and NHL affiliation appear in black print below the picture. Sponsor logos are in the lower corners. The horizontal backs are white and carry Police and Express Tips in French and English.

| | MINT | NRMT |
|---|---|---|
| COMPLETE SET (28) | 12.00 | 5.50 |
| COMMON CARD (1-28) | .25 | .11 |
| ❑ 1 Scott Tottle | .50 | .23 |
| ❑ 2 David Bruce | .50 | .23 |
| ❑ 3 Team Photo | 1.00 | .45 |
| ❑ 4 Marc Crawford | 1.00 | .45 |
| ❑ 5 Mike Stevens | .50 | .23 |
| ❑ 6 Gary Lupul | .50 | .23 |
| ❑ 7 Alain Lemieux | .75 | .35 |
| ❑ 8 Mike Hough | 1.00 | .45 |
| ❑ 9 Tony Currie | .50 | .23 |
| ❑ 10 Dunc MacIntyre | .50 | .23 |
| ❑ 11 Jere Gillis | .50 | .23 |
| ❑ 12 Wendell Young | 1.50 | .70 |
| ❑ 13 Jean-Marc Lanthier | .50 | .23 |
| ❑ 14 Ken Quinney | .75 | .35 |
| ❑ 15 Claude Julien | .50 | .23 |
| ❑ 16 Michel Petit | 1.00 | .45 |
| ❑ 17 Luc Guenette | .50 | .23 |
| ❑ 18 Andy Schliebener | .50 | .23 |
| ❑ 19 Mark Kirton | .50 | .23 |
| ❑ 20 Gord Donnelly | .75 | .35 |
| ❑ 21 Tom Karalis | .50 | .23 |
| ❑ 22 Daniel Poudrier | .50 | .23 |
| ❑ 23 Neil Belland | .50 | .23 |
| ❑ 24 Dale Dunbar | .50 | .23 |
| ❑ 25 Marty Flynn TR<br>Scott Beckingham TR | .25 | .11 |
| ❑ 26 Jean-Marc Gaulin | .50 | .23 |
| ❑ 27 Al MacAdam | .75 | .35 |
| ❑ 28 Andre Savard CO/GM | .50 | .23 |

## 1986-87 Fredericton Express

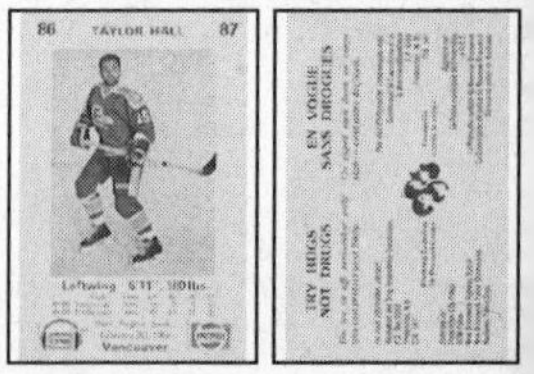

This 26-card set measures 2 1/2" by 3 3/4" and features posed color player photos against a white card face. The player's name, biography, position, statistics, and NHL affiliation appear in black print below the picture. Sponsor logos are in the lower corners. The horizontal backs are white and carry public service messages in French and English. The cards are unnumbered and checklisted below in alphabetical order.

| | MINT | NRMT |
|---|---|---|
| COMPLETE SET (26) | 9.00 | 4.00 |
| COMMON CARD (1-26) | .15 | .07 |
| ❑ 1 Jim Agnew | .50 | .23 |
| ❑ 2 Brian Bertuzzi | .35 | .16 |

□ 3 David Bruce .50 .23
□ 4 Frank Caprice .75 .35
□ 5 Marc Crawford .75 .35
□ 6 Steven Finn .75 .35
□ 7 Marty Flynn TR .15 .07
Scott Beckingham TR
□ 8 Jean-Marc Gaulin .35 .16
□ 9 Scott Gordon .50 .23
□ 10 Taylor Hall .35 .16
□ 11 Yves Heroux .50 .23
□ 12 Mike Hough .75 .35
□ 13 Tom Karalis .35 .16
□ 14 Mark Kirton .50 .23
□ 15 Jean-Marc Lanthier .35 .16
□ 16 Jean LeBlanc .35 .16
□ 17 Brett MacDonald .35 .16
□ 18 Duncan MacIntyre .35 .16
□ 19 Greg Malone .35 .16
□ 20 Terry Perkins .35 .16
□ 21 Daniel Poudrier .35 .16
□ 22 Jeff Rohlicek .35 .16
□ 23 Andre Savard CO .35 .16
□ 24 Mike Stevens .35 .16
□ 25 Trevor Stienburg .35 .16
□ 26 Team Photo .75 .35

## 1992-93 Fredericton Canadiens

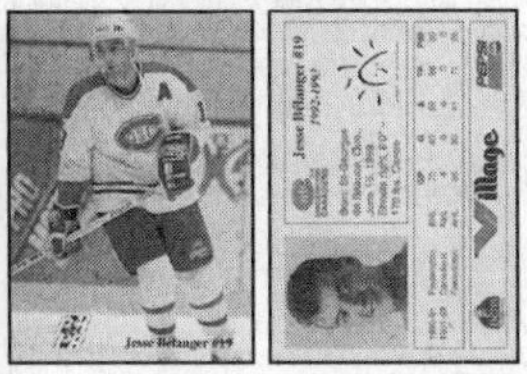

Printed on thin card stock, these 28 standard-size cards feature borderless color player action photos on the fronts. Each has the player's name and uniform number printed near the bottom and carries the Professional Hockey Player's Association logo. The white horizontal back displays a black-and-white posed player head shot in the upper left. The player's name, uniform number, and biography appear in a rectangle in the upper right, along with the Canadiens and Stay in School logos. A stat table is placed beneath, and the Pepsi, Village, and Ben's logos at the bottom round out the card. The cards are unnumbered and checklisted below in alphabetical order.

| | MINT | NRMT |
|---|---|---|
| COMPLETE SET (28) | 12.00 | 5.50 |
| COMMON CARD (1-27) | .10 | .05 |

□ 1 Jesse Belanger .75 .35
□ 2 Paulin Bordeleau CO .50 .23
□ 3 Donald Brashear .75 .35
□ 4 Patrik Carnback .50 .23
□ 5 Eric Charron .50 .23
□ 6 Frederic Chabot .75 .35
□ 7 Alain Cote .50 .23
□ 8 Paul DiPietro .75 .35
□ 9 Craig Ferguson .50 .23
□ 10 Gerry Fleming .50 .23
□ 11 Luc Gauthier .50 .23
□ 12 Robert Guillet .50 .23
□ 13 Patric Kjellberg .50 .23
□ 14 Les Kuntar .75 .35
□ 15 Ryan Kuwabara .50 .23
□ 16 Patrick Langlois TR .10 .05
□ 17 Steve Larouche .50 .23
□ 18 Jacques Parent TR .10 .05
□ 19 Charles Poulin .50 .23
□ 20 Oleg Petrov .50 .23
□ 21 Yves Sarault .50 .23
□ 22 Pierre Sevigny .50 .23
□ 23 Darcy Simon .50 .23
□ 24 Turner Stevenson .75 .35
□ 25 Tricolo (Mascot) .10 .05
□ 26 Lindsay Vallis .50 .23
□ 27 Steve Veilleux .50 .23
□ 28 Title card .25 .11

## 1993-94 Fredericton Canadiens

rinted on thin card stock, this 29-card tandard-size features 1993-94 Fredericton anadiens of the AHL. The fronts display color ction player photos framed by red borders. he player's name and number are printed in e border beneath the picture. The horizontal acks carry a black-and-white closeup photo, iography, statistics, and sponsor logos (Ben's Bakery, Village, and Pepsi). The cards are unnumbered and checklisted below in alphabetical order.

| | MINT | NRMT |
|---|---|---|
| COMPLETE SET (29) | 12.00 | 5.50 |
| COMMON CARD (1-29) | .10 | .05 |

□ 1 Brent Bilodeau .75 .35
□ 2 Paulin Bordeleau CO .25 .11
□ 3 Donald Brashear .60 .25
□ 4 Martin Brochu 1.00 .45
□ 5 Craig Darby .75 .35
□ 6 Kevin Darby .50 .23
□ 7 Mario Doyon .50 .23
□ 8 Craig Ferguson .50 .23
□ 9 Craig Fiander .50 .23
□ 10 Gerry Fleming .50 .23
□ 11 Luc Gauthier ACO .10 .05
□ 12 Robert Guillet .50 .23
□ 13 Les Kuntar .60 .25
□ 14 Ryan Kuwabara .50 .23
□ 15 Patrick Langlois .50 .23
□ 16 Marc Laniel .50 .23
□ 17 Christian Lariviere .50 .23
□ 18 Kevin O'Sullivan .50 .23
□ 19 Denis Ouellete .50 .23
□ 20 Jacques Parent THER .10 .05
□ 21 Oleg Petrov .60 .25
□ 22 Charles Poulin .50 .23
□ 23 Christian Proulx .50 .23
□ 24 Tony Prpic .50 .23
□ 25 Yves Sarault .50 .23
□ 26 Turner Stevenson .75 .35
□ 27 Tricolo (Mascot) .10 .05
□ 28 Lindsay Vallis .50 .23
□ 29 Title Card .10 .05

## 1994-95 Fredericton Canadiens

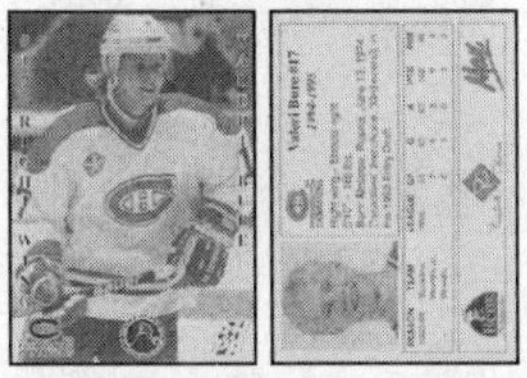

Printed on thin card stock, this 30-card standard-size set features the 1994-95 Fredericton Canadiens of the AHL. The fronts display borderless color action photos. The player's number and position, as well as his name, are printed vertically down the left and right sides respectively. The horizontal backs carry a black-and-white closeup photo, biography, statistics, and sponsor logos (Ben's Bakery, President's Choice, and Max). The cards are unnumbered and checklisted below in alphabetical order.

| | MINT | NRMT |
|---|---|---|
| COMPLETE SET (30) | 12.00 | 5.50 |
| COMMON CARD (1-30) | .10 | .05 |

□ 1 Louis Bernard .35 .16
□ 2 Brent Bilodeau .50 .23
□ 3 Paulin Bordeleau CO .35 .16
□ 4 Donald Brashear .50 .23
□ 5 Martin Brochu .75 .35
□ 6 Valeri Bure .75 .35
□ 7 Jim Campbell 1.50 .70
□ 8 Paul Chagnon .35 .16
□ 9 Craig Conroy .50 .23
□ 10 Craig Darby .50 .23
□ 11 Dion Darling .35 .16
□ 12 Craig Ferguson .35 .16
□ 13 Scott Fraser .50 .23
□ 14 Luc Gauthier ACO .10 .05
□ 15 Patrick Labrecque .50 .23
□ 16 Marc Lamothe .35 .16
□ 17 Patrick Langlois .35 .16
□ 18 Brad Layzelle .35 .16
□ 19 Derek Maguire .35 .16
□ 20 Chris Murray .60 .25
□ 21 Kevin O'Sullivan .35 .16
□ 22 Jacques Parent THER .10 .05
□ 23 Christian Proulx .35 .16
□ 24 Craig Rivet .60 .25
□ 25 Yves Sarault .35 .16
□ 26 Turner Stevenson .75 .35
□ 27 Martin Sychra .35 .16
□ 28 Tim Tisdale .35 .16
□ 29 Tricolo (Mascot) .10 .05
□ 30 David Wilkie .50 .23

## 1995-96 Fredericton Canadiens

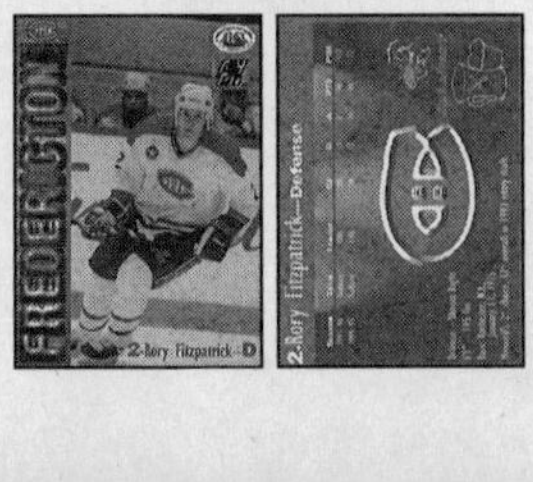

This 29-card set features color action player photos of the Fredericton Canadiens of the AHL. The backs carry biographical information and player statistics. The cards are unnumbered and checklisted below in alphabetical order.

| | MINT | NRMT |
|---|---|---|
| COMPLETE SET (29) | 9.00 | 4.00 |
| COMMON CARD (1-29) | .10 | .05 |

□ 1 Louis Bernard .25 .11
□ 2 Paulin Bordeleau CO .25 .11
□ 3 Sebastien Bordeleau .25 .11
□ 4 Martin Brochu .50 .23
□ 5 Jim Campbell 1.00 .45
□ 6 Paul Chagnon .10 .05
□ 7 Craig Conroy .50 .23
□ 8 Keli Corpse .25 .11
□ 9 Dion Darling .25 .11
□ 10 Rory Fitzpatrick .50 .23
□ 11 Scott Fraser .35 .16
□ 12 Gaston Gingras .35 .16
□ 13 David Grenier .25 .11
□ 14 Harold Hersh .35 .16
□ 15 Patrick Labrecque .50 .23
□ 16 Marc Lamothe .35 .16
□ 17 Patrick Langlois .10 .05
□ 18 Alan Letang .25 .11
□ 19 Alexei Lojkin .35 .16
□ 20 Xavier Majic .25 .11
□ 21 Chris Murray .50 .23
□ 22 Jacques Parent .10 .05
□ 23 Craig Rivet .50 .23
□ 24 Mario Roberge .35 .16
□ 25 Pierre Sevigny .35 .16
□ 26 Tricolo (Mascot) .10 .05
□ 27 Darcy Tucker .50 .23
□ 28 Adam Wiesel .25 .11
□ 29 Luc Gauthier ACO .10 .05

## 1977-78 Granby Vics

This odd-sized (3 1/2 X7") black and white set features the Granby Vics of the LMJHQ. The card fronts are in a horizontal format, with the left half of the card containing a player photo, and the right featuring a player bio and an ad from a local business. The backs are blank and the cards are unnumbered. They are presented below alphabetically.

| | MINT | NRMT |
|---|---|---|
| COMPLETE SET (20) | 18.00 | 8.00 |
| COMMON CARD | 1.00 | .45 |

□ 1 Mario Beauregard 1.00 .45
□ 2 Luc Breton 1.00 .45
□ 3 Daniel Caron 1.50 .70
□ 4 Mario Casavant 1.00 .45
□ 5 Marc Courtemanche 1.00 .45
□ 6 Yves Courtemanche 1.00 .45
□ 7 Sylvain d'Amour 1.00 .45
□ 8 Rene Delorme 1.00 .45
□ 9 Denis Dumas Jr. 1.00 .45
□ 10 Pierre Grondin 1.00 .45
□ 11 Andre Hebert 1.00 .45
□ 12 Marcel Lachance 1.00 .45
□ 13 Andre Lemieux 1.00 .45
□ 14 Pierre Lepage 1.00 .45
□ 15 Daniel Menard 1.00 .45
□ 16 Jacques Pomerleau 1.00 .45
□ 17 Mario Roy 1.00 .45
□ 18 Alain Tetrault 1.00 .45
□ 19 Paul Thibert 1.00 .45
□ 20 Luc Turgeon 1.00 .45

## 1996-97 Grand Rapids Griffins

This odd-sized set (2 3/4" by 4") was produced by Meijer Exhibit Graphic Design and sponsored by Kodak and Jim Hill Photography. The set was released in five series of five cards each (plus one title card per series) over the course of the club's inaugural season. As the cards are unnumbered, they are listed below in alphabetical order.

| | MINT | NRMT |
|---|---|---|
| COMPLETE SET (30) | 12.00 | 5.50 |
| COMMON CARD (1-25) | .25 | .11 |

□ 1 Kevyn Adams 1.00 .45
□ 2 Dave Allison CO .25 .11
□ 3 Danton Cole .50 .23
□ 4 Keli Corpse .50 .23
□ 5 Pavol Demitra 1.00 .45
□ 6 Griff .25 .11
Mascot
□ 7 Ben Hankinson .50 .23
□ 8 Stanislav Jasecko .50 .23
□ 10 Sean McCann .50 .23
□ 11 Cory Johnson .50 .23
□ 12 Jamie Linden .50 .23
□ 13 Don McSween .50 .23
□ 14 Tyler Moss .75 .35
□ 15 Jeff Nelson .50 .23
□ 16 Todd Nelson .50 .23
□ 17 Michel Picard .50 .23
□ 18 Bruce Ramsay .50 .23
□ 19 Pokey Reddick .75 .35
□ 20 Chad Remackel .50 .23
□ 21 Travis Richards .50 .23
□ 22 Matt Ruchty .50 .23
□ 23 Darcy Simon .50 .23
□ 24 1996 Inaugural Face-Off .25 .11
□ 25 1996/97 Inaugural Team .50 .23
□ 26 Van Andel Arena .25 .11
□ NNO Title card 1 .10 .05
□ NNO Title card 2 .10 .05
□ NNO Title card 3 .10 .05
□ NNO Title card 4 .10 .05
□ NNO Title card 5 .10 .05

## 1991-92 Greensboro Monarchs

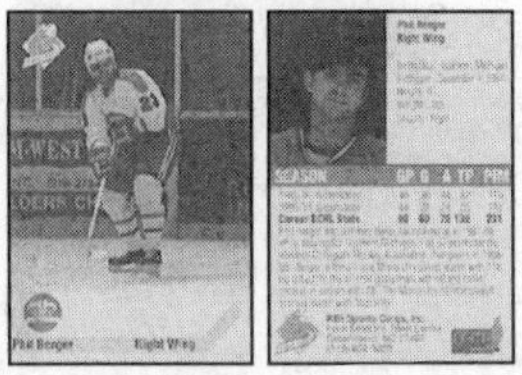

Sponsored by RBI Sports Cards Inc., this 19-card standard-size set features the Greensboro Monarchs of the East Coast Hockey League. The cards feature borderless, posed and action color player photos. The player's name and position appear on a mustard-colored hockey stick design at the bottom. The backs are subdivided by a red stripe and carry a close-up picture with biographical information above the stripe, and statistics and career highlights below it. The cards are unnumbered and checklisted below in alphabetical order.

| | MINT | NRMT |
|---|---|---|
| COMPLETE SET (19) | 8.00 | 3.60 |
| COMMON CARD (1-19) | .50 | .23 |

□ 1 Rob Bateman .60 .25
□ 2 Phil Berger .50 .23
□ 3 Mike Butters .50 .23
□ 4 John Devereaux .50 .23
□ 5 Eric Dubois .50 .23
□ 6 Todd Gordon .50 .23
□ 7 Chris Laganas .50 .23
□ 8 Eric LeMarque .50 .23
□ 9 Timo Makela .50 .23
□ 10 Greg Menges .50 .23
□ 11 Daryl Noren .50 .23
□ 12 Peter Sentner .50 .23
□ 13 Boyd Sutton .50 .23
□ 14 Nick Vitucci .60 .25
□ 15 Shawn Wheeler .50 .23
□ 16 Scott White .50 .23
□ 17 Chris Wolanin .50 .23
□ 18 Dean Zayonce .50 .23
□ 19 Team Photo .50 .23
(Photo of Jeff
Brubaker CO on back)

## 1992-93 Greensboro Monarchs

Sponsored by RBI Sports Cards Inc., this 19-card standard-size set features full-bleed, color, action player photos. The player's name and position appear in a blue and red stripe near the bottom. The backs display a close-up picture alongside biographical information. A red stripe below the photo divides the card in half and serves as a heading for statistics. A player profile appears below the statistics.

| | MINT | NRMT |
|---|---|---|
| COMPLETE SET (19) | 8.00 | 3.60 |
| COMMON CARD (1-19) | .50 | .23 |

□ 1 Team Photo .75 .35
□ 2 Chris Wolanin .50 .23
□ 3 Bill Horn .50 .23
□ 4 Brock Woods .50 .23
□ 5 Phil Berger .50 .23
□ 6 Dan Bylsma .50 .23
□ 7 Davis Payne .75 .35
□ 8 Wayne Muir .50 .23
□ 9 Andrei Iakovenko .50 .23
□ 10 Roger Larche .50 .23
□ 11 Jamie Nicolls .50 .23
□ 12 Darryl Noren .50 .23
□ 13 Todd Gordon .50 .23
□ 14 Claude Maillet .50 .23
□ 15 Dave Burke .50 .23
□ 16 Jamie Steer .60 .25
□ 17 Greg Capson .50 .23
□ 18 Chris Lappin .50 .23
□ 19 Greg Menges .50 .23

## 1993-94 Greensboro Monarchs

This 16-card set of the Greensboro Monarchs of the ECHL was produced by RBI Sportscards. It is similar in design to the Raleigh Icecaps issue from the same year. The cards feature an action photo on the front, while the backs include career stats.

| | MINT | NRMT |
|---|---|---|
| COMPLETE SET (16) | 5.00 | 2.20 |
| COMMON CARD (1-16) | .35 | .16 |

□ 1 Phil Berger .50 .23
□ 2 Trevor Burgess .35 .16
□ 3 Dan Bylsma .35 .16
□ 4 Greg Capson .35 .16
□ 5 Brendan Creagh .35 .16
□ 6 Dan Gravelle .35 .16
□ 7 Sebastien LaPlante .35 .16
□ 8 Savo Mitrovic .35 .16
□ 9 Tom Newman .35 .16
□ 10 Jamie Nicolls .35 .16
□ 11 Davis Payne .75 .35
□ 12 Stig Salomonsson .35 .16
□ 13 Sverre Sears .35 .16
□ 14 Chris Valicevic .35 .16
□ 15 John Young .35 .16
□ 16 Dean Zayonce .35 .16

## 1994-95 Greensboro Monarchs

This 20-card set of the Greensboro Monarchs of the ECHL was again produced by RBI Sportscards. This year's set mimics the design used by Pinnacle in 1993-94, although the photography lacks somewhat in the area of clarity. The backs are numbered, and contain stats for 1993-94. The sets apparently were not sold by the team; speculation suggests the booster club was in charge of distribution.

| | MINT | NRMT |
|---|---|---|
| COMPLETE SET (20) | 7.00 | 3.10 |
| COMMON CARD (1-20) | .10 | .05 |

□ 1 Dean Zayonce .35 .16
□ 2 Jeremy Stevenson .35 .16
□ 3 Glenn Stewart .35 .16
□ 4 Peter Skudra .50 .23
□ 5 Chad Seibel .35 .16
□ 6 Sverre Sears .35 .16
□ 7 Howie Rosenblatt .50 .23
□ 8 Hugo Proulx .35 .16
□ 9 Davis Payne .75 .35
□ 10 Ron Pasco .35 .16
□ 11 Monte -- Mascot .10 .05
□ 12 Scott McKay .35 .16
□ 13 Artur Kupacs .35 .16
□ 14 Bill Horn .35 .16
□ 15 Dwayne Gylywoychuk .35 .16
□ 16 Jeff Gabriel .35 .16
□ 17 Doug Evans .35 .16
□ 18 Mark DeSantis .35 .16
□ 19 Brendan Creagh .35 .16
□ 20 Phil Berger .35 .16

## 1993-94 Guelph Storm

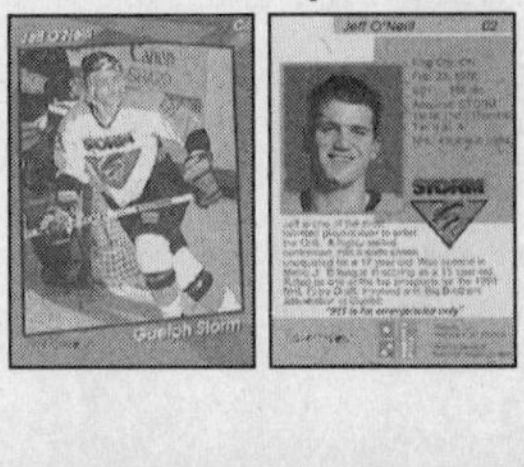

Sponsored by Domino's Pizza and printed by Slapshot Images Ltd., this standard size 31-card set features the 1993-94 Guelph Storm. On a geometrical blue and grey background, the fronts feature color action player photos with thin black borders. The player's name, position and team name, as well as the producer's logo, appear on the front. The backs carry a close-up color player portrait, and biographical information, along with team and sponsor's logos. Included in this set is a Slapshot ad card with a 1994 calendar on the back.

| | MINT | NRMT |
|---|---|---|
| COMPLETE SET (31) | 12.00 | 5.50 |
| COMMON CARD (1-30) | .10 | .05 |
| ❑ 1 Title Card | .10 | .05 |
| ❑ 2 Jeff O'Neill | 2.50 | 1.10 |
| ❑ 3 Mark McArthur | .50 | .23 |
| ❑ 4 Kayle Short | .35 | .16 |
| ❑ 5 Ryan Risidore | .50 | .23 |
| ❑ 6 Mike Rusk | .50 | .23 |
| ❑ 7 Regan Stocco | .35 | .16 |
| ❑ 8 Duane Harmer | .35 | .16 |
| ❑ 9 Sylvain Cloutier | .50 | .23 |
| ❑ 10 Eric Landry | .35 | .16 |
| ❑ 11 Jamie Wright | .35 | .16 |
| ❑ 12 Todd Norman | .75 | .35 |
| ❑ 13 Mike Pittman | .35 | .16 |
| ❑ 14 Ken Belanger | .35 | .16 |
| ❑ 15 Viktor Reuta | .35 | .16 |
| ❑ 16 Mike Prokopec | .50 | .23 |
| ❑ 17 Jeff Williams | .35 | .16 |
| ❑ 18 Chris Skoryna | .35 | .16 |
| ❑ 19 Stephane Lefebvre | .35 | .16 |
| ❑ 20 Jeff Cowan | .35 | .16 |
| ❑ 21 Murray Hogg | .35 | .16 |
| ❑ 22 Andy Adams | .35 | .16 |
| ❑ 23 Todd Bertuzzi | 2.00 | .90 |
| ❑ 24 Grant Pritchett | .35 | .16 |
| ❑ 25 Rumun Ndur | .75 | .35 |
| ❑ 26 Jeff O'Neill | 1.50 | .70 |
| ❑ 27 Paul Brydges ACO | .10 | .05 |
| ❑ 28 John Lovell CO | .10 | .05 |
| ❑ 29 Team Photo | .50 | .23 |
| Checklist | | |
| ❑ 30 Sponsor Card | .10 | .05 |
| Gurinder Saini | | |
| Domino's Pizza | | |
| ❑ NNO Slapshot Ad Card | .10 | .05 |

## 1994-95 Guelph Storm

Sponsored by Domino's Pizza and Burger King, and printed by Slaphot Images Inc., this 31-card standard-size set features the 1994-95 Guelph Storm. On a team color-coded background, the fronts have color action player photos with thin black borders. The player's name, position and team name, as well as the producer's logo, appear on the front. On a team color-coded background, the backs carry a close-up color player portrait, biographical information and profile, along with team and sponsor logos and a safety tip. Included in this set is a Slapshot ad card with a 1995 calendar on the back.

| | MINT | NRMT |
|---|---|---|
| COMPLETE SET (31) | 12.00 | 5.50 |
| COMMON CARD (1-30) | .10 | .05 |
| ❑ 1 Team Photo | .35 | .16 |
| Checklist | | |
| ❑ 2 Mark McArthur | .50 | .23 |
| ❑ 3 Andy Adams | .35 | .16 |
| ❑ 4 Bryan McKinney | .35 | .16 |
| ❑ 5 Ryan Risidore | .50 | .23 |
| ❑ 6 Joel Cort | .35 | .16 |
| ❑ 7 Chris Hajt | .75 | .35 |
| ❑ 8 Regan Stocco | .35 | .16 |
| ❑ 9 Dwayne Hay | 1.00 | .45 |
| ❑ 10 Andrew Clark | .35 | .16 |
| ❑ 11 Neil Fewster | .50 | .23 |
| ❑ 12 Jamie Wright | .50 | .23 |
| ❑ 13 Jason Jackman | .35 | .16 |
| ❑ 14 Pat Barton | .35 | .16 |
| ❑ 15 Tom Johnson | .35 | .16 |
| ❑ 16 Brian Wesenberg | .50 | .23 |
| ❑ 17 Mike Pittman | .35 | .16 |
| ❑ 18 Jeff Williams | .35 | .16 |
| ❑ 19 Todd Norman | .60 | .25 |
| ❑ 20 Mike Rusk | .50 | .23 |
| ❑ 21 David Lylyk | .35 | .16 |
| ❑ 22 Todd Bertuzzi | 1.50 | .70 |
| ❑ 23 Jeff Cowan | .35 | .16 |
| ❑ 24 Rumun Ndur | .60 | .25 |
| ❑ 25 Jeff O'Neill | 2.00 | .90 |
| ❑ 26 Andrew Long | .35 | .16 |
| ❑ 27 Craig Hartsburg CO | .50 | .23 |
| ❑ 28 Paul Brydges ACO | .10 | .05 |
| ❑ 29 Sponsor Card | .10 | .05 |
| Burger King | | |
| Coupon | | |
| ❑ 30 Sponsor Card | .10 | .05 |
| Domino's Pizza | | |
| Coupon | | |
| ❑ NNO Ad Card | .10 | .05 |

## 1995-96 Guelph Storm 5th Anniversary

This extremely attractive set was produced by Axiom Communications for distribution by the Storm at the club's pro shop. The set features strong action photography along with a dazzling desing element along the right border. The back features a color mug shot, personal information and logos of sponsors.

| | MINT | NRMT |
|---|---|---|
| COMPLETE SET (30) | 10.00 | 4.50 |
| COMMON CARD (1-30) | .10 | .05 |
| ❑ 1 Checklist | .35 | .16 |
| ❑ 2 Andrew Clark | .35 | .16 |
| ❑ 3 Dwayne Hay | .75 | .35 |
| ❑ 4 Jason Jackman | .35 | .16 |
| ❑ 5 Burger King Ad | .10 | .05 |
| ❑ 6 Nick Bootland | .35 | .16 |
| ❑ 7 Andrew Long | .35 | .16 |
| ❑ 8 Todd Norman | .50 | .23 |
| ❑ 9 Michael Pittman | .35 | .16 |
| ❑ 10 Herbert Vasilijevs | .50 | .23 |
| ❑ 11 Jeff Williams | .35 | .16 |
| ❑ 12 Joel Cort | .50 | .23 |
| ❑ 13 Chris Hajt | .50 | .23 |
| ❑ 14 Brian Willsie | .50 | .23 |
| ❑ 15 Brian Wesenberg | .75 | .35 |
| ❑ 16 Mike Lankshear | .35 | .16 |
| ❑ 17 Darryl McArthur | .35 | .16 |
| ❑ 18 Bryan McKinney | .35 | .16 |
| ❑ 19 Regan Stocco | .35 | .16 |
| ❑ 20 Ryan Risidore | .50 | .23 |
| ❑ 21 Mike Vellinga | .35 | .16 |
| ❑ 22 Dan Cloutier | 1.00 | .45 |
| ❑ 23 Bryan McMullen | .50 | .23 |
| ❑ 24 Brett Thompson | .50 | .23 |
| ❑ 25 Ryan Robichaud | .35 | .16 |
| ❑ 26 Kid's Club | .10 | .05 |
| ❑ 27 Jamie Wright | .50 | .23 |
| ❑ 28 Guelph Police | .10 | .05 |
| ❑ 29 Mike Galati | .35 | .16 |
| ❑ 30 Domino's Pizza Ad | .10 | .05 |

## 1996-97 Guelph Storm

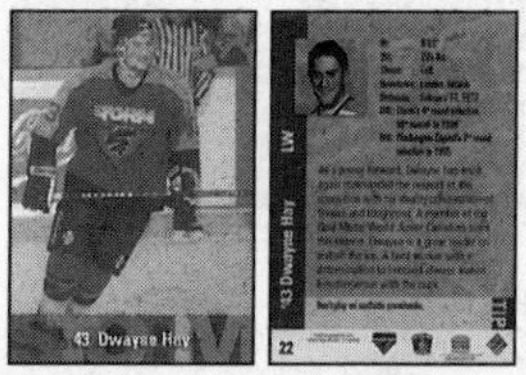

This 36-card set continues the tradition of high-quality sets from the Storm. The heavy-stock cards feature action photography on the front, alone with player name and number and team logo. The backs include a mug shot and personal information and a safety tip, but no playing stats. The set is noteworthy for the inclusion of Manny Malhotra, expected to be a high pick in 1998.

| | MINT | NRMT |
|---|---|---|
| COMPLETE SET (36) | 12.00 | 5.50 |
| COMMON CARD (1-36) | .10 | .05 |
| ❑ 1 Checklist | .10 | .05 |
| ❑ 2 Brett Thompson | .50 | .23 |
| ❑ 3 David MacDonald | .50 | .23 |
| ❑ 4 John Zubyck | .40 | .18 |
| ❑ 5 Denis Ivanov | .40 | .18 |
| ❑ 6 Joel Cort | .40 | .18 |
| ❑ 7 Chris Hajt | .50 | .23 |
| ❑ 8 Manny Malhotra | 2.00 | .90 |
| ❑ 9 Mike Dombkiewicz | .40 | .18 |
| ❑ 10 Ryan Robichaud | .40 | .18 |
| ❑ 11 Kent McDonell | .40 | .18 |
| ❑ 12 Joe Gerbe | .40 | .18 |
| ❑ 13 Mike Christian | .40 | .18 |
| ❑ 14 Brian Wesenberg | .50 | .23 |
| ❑ 15 Todd Norman | .50 | .23 |
| ❑ 16 Darryl McArthur | .40 | .18 |
| ❑ 17 Richard Irwin | .40 | .18 |
| ❑ 18 Brian Willsie | .50 | .23 |
| ❑ 19 Mike Vellinga | .40 | .18 |
| ❑ 20 Jason Jackman | .40 | .18 |
| ❑ 21 Chris Madden | .50 | .23 |
| ❑ 22 Dwayne Hay | .50 | .23 |
| ❑ 23 Joey Bartley | .40 | .18 |
| ❑ 24 Mike Lankshear | .50 | .23 |
| ❑ 25 Andrew Long | .40 | .18 |
| ❑ 26 Matt Bell | .40 | .18 |
| ❑ 27 Nick Bootland | .40 | .18 |
| ❑ 28 E.J. McGuire | .10 | .05 |
| ❑ 29 Rick Allain | .10 | .05 |
| ❑ 30 Burger King Ad | .10 | .05 |
| ❑ 31 Burger King Kid's Club | .10 | .05 |
| ❑ 32 Guelph Police | .50 | .23 |
| with Malhotra and Norman | | |
| ❑ 33 Domino's Pizza Ad | .10 | .05 |
| ❑ 34 Domino's Pizza Ad | .10 | .05 |
| ❑ 35 Chris Hajt/Dwayne Hay | .50 | .23 |
| ❑ 36 96-97 Team Picture | .50 | .23 |

## 1996-97 Guelph Storm Premier Collection

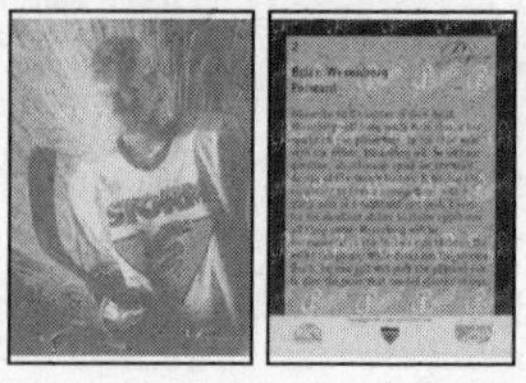

This odd-sized (4" X 6") collection was issued by the club along with game programs. The set is noteworthy for its outstanding photography and imaginative posing of the subjects; most appear out of hockey garb and in more expressive outfits and poses. The set also includes a card of top '98 prospect Manny Malhotra.

| | MINT | NRMT |
|---|---|---|
| COMPLETE SET (12) | 12.00 | 5.50 |
| COMMON CARD (1-12) | .75 | .35 |
| ❑ 1 Todd Norman | 1.00 | .45 |
| ❑ 2 Brian Wesenberg | 1.00 | .45 |
| ❑ 3 Mike Vellinga | .75 | .35 |
| ❑ 4 Brett Thompson | 1.00 | .45 |
| ❑ 5 Joel Cort | .75 | .35 |
| ❑ 6 Jason Jackman | .75 | .35 |
| ❑ 7 Brian Willsie | 1.00 | .45 |
| ❑ 8 Mike Lankshear | 1.00 | .45 |
| ❑ 9 Dwayne Hay | 1.00 | .45 |
| ❑ 10 Manny Malhotra | 5.00 | 2.20 |
| ❑ 11 Chris Hajt | 1.00 | .45 |
| ❑ 12 Nick Bootland | .75 | .35 |

## 1997-98 Guelph Storm

Card fronts feature a black and white action photo, with players name and number on the bottom. Card backs featuer biographical information and are numbered xx/34. Backs also featuer sponsor logos and safety tips.

| | MINT | NRMT |
|---|---|---|
| COMPLETE SET (34) | 12.00 | 5.50 |
| COMMON CARD (1-34) | .10 | .05 |
| ❑ 1 Header Card | .10 | .05 |
| ❑ 2 Chris Thompson | .30 | .14 |
| ❑ 3 Daniel Jacques | .30 | .14 |
| ❑ 4 Chris Madden | .50 | .23 |
| ❑ 5 Kevin Mitchell | .40 | .18 |
| ❑ 6 Joey Bartley | .40 | .18 |
| ❑ 7 Chris Hajt | .50 | .23 |
| ❑ 8 Manny Malhotra | 2.00 | .90 |
| ❑ 9 Mike Dombkiewicz | .40 | .18 |
| ❑ 10 Ian Forbes | .40 | .18 |
| ❑ 11 Joe Gerbe | .40 | .18 |
| ❑ 12 Mike Vellinga | .40 | .18 |
| ❑ 13 Lindsay Plunkett | .40 | .18 |
| ❑ 14 Kent McDonell | .40 | .18 |
| ❑ 15 Matt Lahey | .40 | .18 |
| ❑ 16 Bohuslav Subr | .30 | .14 |
| ❑ 17 Bob Crummer | .20 | .09 |
| ❑ 18 Andrew Long | .40 | .18 |
| ❑ 19 Brian Mcgrattan | .20 | .09 |
| ❑ 20 Darryl Mcarthur | .40 | .18 |
| ❑ 21 Brian Willsie | .50 | .23 |
| ❑ 22 John Zubyck | .40 | .18 |
| ❑ 23 Dusty Jamieson | .40 | .18 |
| ❑ 24 Eric Beaudoin | .40 | .18 |
| ❑ 25 Jason Jackman | .40 | .18 |
| ❑ 26 Nick Bootland | .40 | .18 |
| ❑ 27 George Burnett | .40 | .18 |
| ❑ 28 Rick Allain | .10 | .05 |
| ❑ 29 Spyke | .10 | .05 |
| ❑ 30 Guelph Police | .10 | .05 |
| ❑ 31 Burger King | .10 | .05 |
| ❑ 32 Burger King | .10 | .05 |
| ❑ 33 Domino's | .10 | .05 |
| ❑ 34 Domino's | .10 | .05 |

## 1989-90 Halifax Citadels

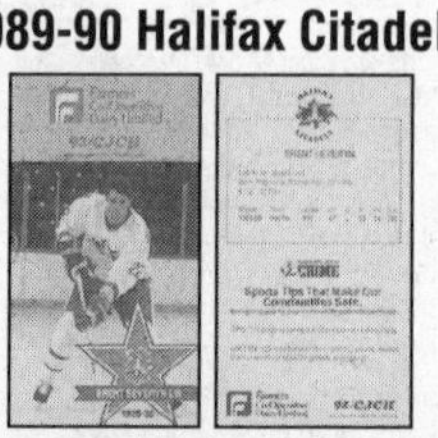

This 26-card set measures approximately 2" by 4 1/4". The fronts feature full-bleed posed action color photos, except at the top where a gray stripe displays the logos of the Farmers Co-Operative Dairy Limited and 92/CJCH. The team logo in the form of a red star appears in the lower right corner, with the player's name in a blue bar that is printed over the team logo. On a white background, the backs carry the player's name, biography, and stats in the upper portion, while "Sports Tips That Make Our Communities Safe" are in the lower portion. The cards are unnumbered and checklisted below in alphabetical order.

| | MINT | NRMT |
|---|---|---|
| COMPLETE SET (26) | 12.00 | 5.50 |
| COMMON CARD (1-26) | .25 | .11 |
| ❑ 1 Joel Baillargeon | .50 | .23 |
| ❑ 2 Jamie Baker | .75 | .35 |
| ❑ 3 Mario Brunetta | .75 | .35 |
| ❑ 4 Gerald Bzdel | .50 | .23 |
| ❑ 5 David Espe | .50 | .23 |
| ❑ 6 Bryan Fogarty | .75 | .35 |
| ❑ 7 Robbie Ftorek GM | .75 | .35 |
| ❑ 8 Scott Gordon | .75 | .35 |
| ❑ 9 Dean Hopkins | .50 | .23 |
| ❑ 10 Miroslav Ihnacak | .50 | .23 |
| ❑ 11 Claude Julien | .50 | .23 |
| ❑ 12 Kevin Kaminski | .50 | .23 |
| ❑ 13 Claude Lapointe | 1.00 | .45 |
| ❑ 14 Chris McQuaid EQ/MG | .25 | .11 |
| Brent Smith TR | | |
| ❑ 15 Max Middendorf | .50 | .23 |
| ❑ 16 Stephane Morin | .75 | .35 |
| ❑ 17 Dave Pichette | .50 | .23 |
| ❑ 18 Ken Quinney | .50 | .23 |
| ❑ 19 Jean-Marc Richard | .50 | .23 |
| ❑ 20 Jean Marc Routhier | .50 | .23 |
| ❑ 21 Jaroslav Sevcik | .50 | .23 |
| ❑ 22 Brent Severyn | .75 | .35 |
| ❑ 23 Greg Smyth | .50 | .23 |
| ❑ 24 Trevor Steinburg | .50 | .23 |
| ❑ 25 Mark Vermette | .50 | .23 |
| ❑ 26 Ladislav Tresl | .50 | .23 |

## 1990-91 Halifax Citadels

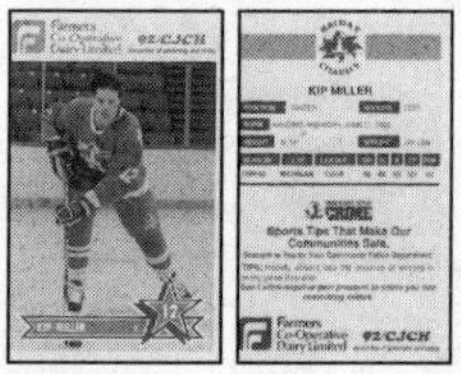

This 28-card set measures approximately 2 3/4" by 4 1/4" and features color, posed-action player photos with white borders. The Farmers Co-Operative Dairy Limited and the 92/CJCH logo appear in the top border. The player's name is printed on a red ribbon that intersects a red star design. The star contains the player's jersey number. The backs display the player's name, biographical information, and "Sports Tips That Make Our Communities Safe." The cards are unnumbered and checklisted below in alphabetical order.

| | MINT | NRMT |
|---|---|---|
| COMPLETE SET (28) | 12.00 | 5.50 |
| COMMON CARD (1-28) | .25 | .11 |
| ❑ 1 Jamie Baker | .50 | .23 |
| ❑ 2 Mike Bishop | .35 | .16 |
| ❑ 3 Gerald Bzdel | .35 | .16 |
| ❑ 4 Daniel Dore | .35 | .16 |
| ❑ 5 Mario Doyon | .35 | .16 |
| ❑ 6 Dave Espe | .35 | .16 |
| ❑ 7 Stephane Fiset | 3.00 | 1.35 |
| ❑ 8 Scott Gordon | .50 | .23 |
| ❑ 9 Stephane Guerard | .35 | .16 |
| ❑ 10 Dean Hopkins ACO | .25 | .11 |
| ❑ 11 Miroslav Ihnacak | .50 | .23 |
| ❑ 12 Jeff Jackson | .75 | .35 |
| ❑ 13 Clement Jodoin CO/MG | .25 | .11 |
| ❑ 14 Claude Lapointe | .50 | .23 |
| ❑ 15 Dave Latta | .35 | .16 |
| ❑ 16 Chris McQuaid EQ MG | .25 | .11 |
| ❑ 17 Kip Miller | .35 | .16 |
| ❑ 18 Stephane Morin | .50 | .23 |
| ❑ 19 Ken Quinney | .35 | .16 |
| ❑ 20 Jean-Marc Richard | .35 | .16 |
| ❑ 21 Serge Roberge | .35 | .16 |
| ❑ 22 Jaroslav Sevcik | .35 | .16 |
| ❑ 23 Brent Severyn | .75 | .35 |
| ❑ 24 Mike Shuman TR | .25 | .11 |
| ❑ 25 Greg Smyth | .35 | .16 |
| ❑ 26 Jim Sprott | .35 | .16 |
| ❑ 27 Trevor Stienburg | .35 | .16 |
| ❑ 28 Mark Vermette | .35 | .16 |

## 1961-62 Hamilton Redwings

| | MINT | NRMT |
|---|---|---|
| COMPLETE SET (21) | 75.00 | 34.00 |
| COMMON CARD (1-21) | 3.00 | 1.35 |
| ❑ 1 Bud Blom | 3.00 | 1.35 |
| ❑ 2 Eddie Bush | 4.00 | 1.80 |
| ❑ 3 Bob Dean | 3.00 | 1.35 |
| ❑ 4 John Gofton | 3.00 | 1.35 |
| ❑ 5 Bob Hamilton | 3.00 | 1.35 |
| ❑ 6 Bob Hamilton | 3.00 | 1.35 |
| ❑ 7 Ron Harris | 3.00 | 1.35 |
| ❑ 8 Earl Heiskala | 3.00 | 1.35 |
| ❑ 9 Paul Henderson | 10.00 | 4.50 |
| ❑ 10 Roger Lafreniere | 3.00 | 1.35 |
| ❑ 11 Lowell Macdonald | 6.00 | 2.70 |
| ❑ 12 Pit Martin | 5.00 | 2.20 |
| ❑ 13 Jim Mclellan | 3.00 | 1.35 |
| ❑ 14 Harvey Meisenheimer | 3.00 | 1.35 |
| ❑ 15 Howie Menard | 3.00 | 1.35 |
| ❑ 16 Wayne Rivers | 5.00 | 2.20 |
| ❑ 17 Jim Peters | 3.00 | 1.35 |
| ❑ 18 Bob Wall | 3.00 | 1.35 |
| ❑ 19 Jack Wildfong | 3.00 | 1.35 |
| ❑ 20 Terry Urkewicz | 3.00 | 1.35 |
| ❑ 21 Larry Zilliotto | 3.00 | 1.35 |

## 1975-76 Hamilton Fincups

This 18-card standard-size set features sepia-tone player portraits. The player's name and position are printed in the lower border, which is also sepia-tone. The team name is superimposed over the picture at the bottom center. The backs are blank and grayish in color. The cards are unnumbered and checklisted below in alphabetical order.

| | NRMT-MT | EXC |
|---|---|---|
| COMPLETE SET (18) | 20.00 | 9.00 |
| COMMON CARD (1-18) | 1.00 | .45 |
| ❑ 1 Jack Anderson | 1.00 | .45 |
| ❑ 2 Mike Clarke | 1.00 | .45 |
| ❑ 3 Greg Clause | 1.00 | .45 |
| ❑ 4 Joe Contini | 1.00 | .45 |
| ❑ 5 Mike Fedorko | 1.00 | .45 |
| ❑ 6 Paul Foley | 1.00 | .45 |
| ❑ 7 Greg Hickey | 1.00 | .45 |
| ❑ 8 Tony Horvath | 1.00 | .45 |
| ❑ 9 Mike Keating | 1.00 | .45 |
| ❑ 10 Archie King | 1.00 | .45 |
| ❑ 11 Ted Long | 1.00 | .45 |
| ❑ 12 Dale McCourt | 5.00 | 2.20 |
| ❑ 13 Dave Norris | 1.00 | .45 |
| ❑ 14 Greg Redquest | 1.00 | .45 |
| ❑ 15 Glen Richardson | 1.00 | .45 |
| ❑ 16 Ron Roscoe | 1.00 | .45 |
| ❑ 17 Ric Seiling | 2.50 | 1.10 |
| ❑ 18 Danny Shearer | 1.00 | .45 |

## 1992-93 Hamilton Canucks

Created by Diamond Memories Sportscards to commemorate the Canucks' inaugural season, these 30 standard-size cards feature black-bordered color player action photos on the fronts. The photos are offset toward the lower right, with the player's name and position in white lettering placed vertically on the left side, and the team name at the top, with "Hamilton" in white lettering and "Canucks" in yellow and red. The player's uniform number appears in black within a white-trimmed band that grades from yellow to red from left to right. The gray-bordered white horizontal back carries the player's name, uniform number, biography, and stat table. The Y95 Radio, Diamond Memories Sportscards, and Hamilton Canucks logos on the bottom round out the card. The cards are unnumbered and checklisted below in alphabetical order.

| | MINT | NRMT |
|---|---|---|
| COMPLETE SET (30) | 12.00 | 5.50 |
| COMMON CARD (1-30) | .10 | .05 |
| ❑ 1 Shawn Antoski | .75 | .35 |
| ❑ 2 Robin Bawa | .35 | .16 |
| ❑ 3 Jamie Carlson TR | .10 | .05 |
| ❑ 4 Jassen Cullimore | .50 | .23 |
| ❑ 5 Alain Deeks | .35 | .16 |
| ❑ 6 Neil Eisenhut | .35 | .16 |
| ❑ 7 Mike Fountain | .75 | .35 |
| ❑ 8 Troy Gamble | .75 | .35 |
| ❑ 9 Jason Herter | .35 | .16 |
| ❑ 10 Pat Hickey PR | .10 | .05 |
| ❑ 11 Dane Jackson | .35 | .16 |
| ❑ 12 Dan Kesa | .50 | .23 |
| ❑ 13 Jeff Lumby ANN | .10 | .05 |
| ❑ 14 Mario Marois UER | .50 | .23 |
| (Last name misspelled | | |
| Marios on front) | | |
| ❑ 15 Bob Mason | .75 | .35 |
| ❑ 16 Mike Maurice | .35 | .16 |
| ❑ 17 Jay Mazur | .35 | .16 |

| Card | MINT | NRMT |
|---|---|---|
| ❑ 18 Jack McIlhargey CO | .25 | .11 |
| ❑ 19 Sandy Moger | .75 | .35 |
| ❑ 20 Stephane Morin | .50 | .23 |
| ❑ 21 Eric Murano | .35 | .16 |
| ❑ 22 Troy Neumeier | .35 | .16 |
| ❑ 23 Matt Newsom GM | .10 | .05 |
| ❑ 24 Libor Polasek | .35 | .16 |
| ❑ 25 Phil von Stefenelli | .50 | .23 |
| ❑ 26 Doug Torrel | .35 | .16 |
| ❑ 27 Doug Tretiak TR | .10 | .05 |
| ❑ 28 Rick Vaive CO | .50 | .23 |
| ❑ 29 Opening Night<br>Puck-Drop<br>Mario Marois<br>Pat Hickey PR<br>AHL President | .35 | .16 |
| ❑ 30 Team Photo<br>(Checklist) | .75 | .35 |

## 1989-90 Hampton Roads Admirals

This 21-card set of the Hampton Roads Admirals of the ECHL features color photos on the front. The cards are unnumbered, and are listed below in alphabetical order.

| | MINT | NRMT |
|---|---|---|
| COMPLETE SET (21) | 9.00 | 4.00 |
| COMMON CARD (1-21) | .50 | .23 |
| ❑ 1 Mike Black | .50 | .23 |
| ❑ 2 John Brophy CO | .50 | .23 |
| ❑ 3 David Buckley | .50 | .23 |
| ❑ 4 Pat Cavanagh | .50 | .23 |
| ❑ 5 Mike Flanagan | .50 | .23 |
| ❑ 6 Frank Furlan | .50 | .23 |
| ❑ 7 Don Gagne | .50 | .23 |
| ❑ 8 Steve Greenberg | .50 | .23 |
| ❑ 9 Murray Hood | .50 | .23 |
| ❑ 10 Trevor Jobe | .50 | .23 |
| ❑ 11 Trevor Kruger | .50 | .23 |
| ❑ 12 Chris Lukey | .50 | .23 |
| ❑ 13 Brian Martin | .50 | .23 |
| ❑ 14 Dennis McEwen | .50 | .23 |
| ❑ 15 Bobby McGrath | .50 | .23 |
| ❑ 16 Darren Miciak | .50 | .23 |
| ❑ 17 Al Murphy | .50 | .23 |
| ❑ 18 Jody Praznik | .50 | .23 |
| ❑ 19 Alain Raymond | .50 | .23 |
| ❑ 20 Wayne Stripp | .50 | .23 |
| ❑ 21 Scott Taylor | .50 | .23 |

## 1990-91 Hampton Roads Admirals

This 20-card was issued by the Hampton Roads Admirals of the ECHL. They feature color action photography on the front, along with another photo and statistical information on the back. The numbering of the set is a mystery, as it clearly carries on from another issue. Interestingly, the previous year's Admirals set is unnumbered. The set, therefore, may be numbered consecutively with other ECHL issues from the same season.

| | MINT | NRMT |
|---|---|---|
| COMPLETE SET (20) | 7.00 | 3.10 |
| COMMON CARD (41-60) | .25 | .11 |
| ❑ 41 Scott King | .50 | .23 |
| ❑ 42 Greg Bignell | .35 | .16 |
| ❑ 43 David Buckley | .35 | .16 |
| ❑ 44 Jody Praznik | .35 | .16 |
| ❑ 45 John East | .35 | .16 |
| ❑ 46 Steve Greenberg | .35 | .16 |
| ❑ 47 Darcy Kaminski | .35 | .16 |
| ❑ 48 Glen Kehrer | .35 | .16 |
| ❑ 49 Murray Hood | .35 | .16 |
| ❑ 50 Dennis McEwen | .35 | .16 |
| ❑ 51 Billy Nolan | .35 | .16 |
| ❑ 52 Bill Thomas | .35 | .16 |
| ❑ 53 Pat Cavanagh | .35 | .16 |
| ❑ 54 Cory Banika | .35 | .16 |
| ❑ 55 Al Murphy | .35 | .16 |
| ❑ 56 Harry Mews | .35 | .16 |
| ❑ 57 Mark Bernard | .35 | .16 |
| ❑ 58 Brian Martin | .35 | .16 |
| ❑ 59 Curt Brackenbury ACO | .25 | .11 |
| ❑ 60 John Brophy CO | .35 | .16 |

## 1991-92 Hampton Roads Admirals

This 20-card set was produced by the team and available at the rink. The cards feature action photos on the front, with stats and bio on the back. This set, which features an early pro card of Olaf Kolzig, is unnumbered, and listed below alphabetically.

| | MINT | NRMT |
|---|---|---|
| COMPLETE SET (20) | 8.00 | 3.60 |
| COMMON CARD (1-20) | .10 | .05 |
| ❑ 1 Mark Bernard | .35 | .16 |
| ❑ 2 Mike Chighisola | .35 | .16 |
| ❑ 3 John East | .35 | .16 |
| ❑ 4 Victor Gervais | .35 | .16 |
| ❑ 5 Murray Hood | .35 | .16 |
| ❑ 6 Scott Johnson | .35 | .16 |
| ❑ 7 Olaf Kolzig | 2.00 | .90 |
| ❑ 8 Paul Krepelka | .35 | .16 |
| ❑ 9 Al MacIsaac | .35 | .16 |
| ❑ 10 Brian Martin | .35 | .16 |
| ❑ 11 Dennis McEwen | .35 | .16 |
| ❑ 12 Dave Morissette | .35 | .16 |
| ❑ 13 Billy Nolan | .35 | .16 |
| ❑ 14 Randy Pearce | .35 | .16 |
| ❑ 15 Steve Poapst | .50 | .23 |
| ❑ 16 Pete Siciliano | .35 | .16 |
| ❑ 17 Shawn Snesar | .35 | .16 |
| ❑ 18 Keith Whitmore | .35 | .16 |
| ❑ 19 John Brophy CO | .35 | .16 |
| ❑ 20 Darcy Kaminski ACO | .10 | .05 |

## 1992-93 Hampton Roads Admirals

This set is unnumbered and was sponsored by Ward's Corner Sporting Goods, Ogden Services, and radio station WCMS. The set is listed by the order of the player's jersey number, which is listed on the back.

| | MINT | NRMT |
|---|---|---|
| COMPLETE SET (20) | 8.00 | 3.60 |
| COMMON CARD (1-20) | .10 | .05 |
| ❑ 1 Shawn Snesar | .50 | .23 |
| ❑ 2 Paul Krepelka | .50 | .23 |
| ❑ 3 Claude Barthe | .50 | .23 |
| ❑ 4 Steve Poapst | .75 | .35 |
| ❑ 5 Kelly Sorenson | .50 | .23 |
| ❑ 6 Trevor Duhaime | .50 | .23 |
| ❑ 7 Steve Mirabile | .50 | .23 |
| ❑ 8 Kurt Kabat | .50 | .23 |
| ❑ 9 Victor Gervais | .60 | .25 |
| ❑ 10 Jason Rathbone | .50 | .23 |
| ❑ 11 Rod Taylor | .50 | .23 |
| ❑ 12 Al MacIsaac CO | .25 | .11 |
| ❑ 13 Brian Martin | .50 | .23 |
| ❑ 14 Dave Morisette | .50 | .23 |
| ❑ 15 Harry Mews | .50 | .23 |
| ❑ 16 Mark Bernard | .50 | .23 |
| ❑ 17 Nick Vitucci | .75 | .35 |
| ❑ 18 Steve Martell | .50 | .23 |
| ❑ 19 Chris Scarlata TR | .10 | .05 |
| ❑ 20 John Brophy CO | .50 | .23 |

## 1993-94 Hampton Roads Admirals

This set is unnumbered, and is listed by the player's jersey number, which is listed on the back. The set was sponsored by Ward's Corner Sporting Goods, Ogden Services and radio station WCMS. The set is nearly identical in design to the previous year's set.

| | MINT | NRMT |
|---|---|---|
| COMPLETE SET (20) | 8.00 | 3.60 |
| COMMON CARD (1-20) | .10 | .05 |
| ❑ 1 Mark Michaud | .50 | .23 |
| ❑ 2 Shawn Snesar | .50 | .23 |
| ❑ 3 Ron Pascucci | .50 | .23 |
| ❑ 4 Daniel Chaput | .50 | .23 |
| ❑ 5 Brian Goudie | .50 | .23 |
| ❑ 6 Darren Perkins | .50 | .23 |
| ❑ 7 Brendan Curley | .50 | .23 |
| ❑ 8 Dennis McEwen | .50 | .23 |
| ❑ 9 Victor Gervais | .60 | .25 |
| ❑ 10 Rod Taylor | .50 | .23 |
| ❑ 11 Kelly Sorenson | .50 | .23 |
| ❑ 12 Richie Walcott | .50 | .23 |
| ❑ 13 Kevin Malgunas | .50 | .23 |
| ❑ 14 Steven Perkovic | .50 | .23 |
| ❑ 15 Shawn Wheeler | .50 | .23 |
| ❑ 16 Jason MacIntyre | .50 | .23 |
| ❑ 17 Shamus Gregga | .50 | .23 |
| ❑ 18 John Brophy CO | .50 | .23 |
| ❑ 19 Al MacIsaac ACO | .10 | .05 |
| ❑ 20 Rick Burrill TR | .10 | .05 |

## 1994-95 Hampton Roads Admirals

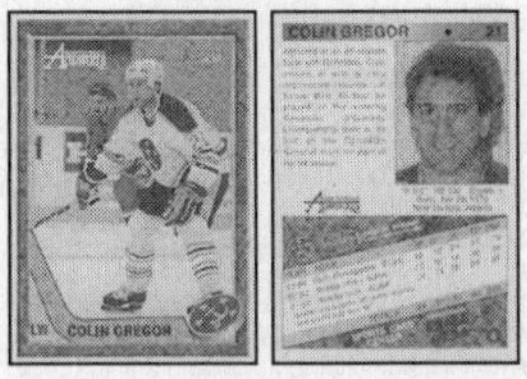


This 23-card set measures the standard size. On a white card face, the fronts feature color action player photos with a simulated blue marble frame and a thin yellow, inner border. The player's name appears inside a hockey stick on the bottom of the photo, with the team logo next to it. On a white background, the backs carry a small color player portrait, along with biography, profile, stats, and sponsor logos.

| | MINT | NRMT |
|---|---|---|
| COMPLETE SET (23) | 12.00 | 5.50 |
| COMMON CARD (1-23) | .10 | .05 |
| ❑ 1 John Brophy CO | .50 | .23 |
| ❑ 2 Al MacIsaac ACO | .10 | .05 |
| ❑ 3 Patrick Lalime | 5.00 | 2.20 |
| ❑ 4 Colin Gregor | .35 | .16 |
| ❑ 5 Ron Pascucci | .35 | .16 |
| ❑ 6 John Porco | .35 | .16 |
| ❑ 7 Trevor Halverson | .50 | .23 |
| ❑ 8 Rod Taylor | .35 | .16 |
| ❑ 9 Brian Goudie | .35 | .16 |
| ❑ 10 Chris Phelps | .35 | .16 |
| ❑ 11 Tom Menicci | .35 | .16 |
| ❑ 12 Anthony MacAulay | .35 | .16 |
| ❑ 13 Rick Kowalsky | .35 | .16 |
| ❑ 14 Dennis McEwen | .35 | .16 |
| ❑ 15 Kelly Sorenson | .35 | .16 |
| ❑ 16 Brendan Curley | .35 | .16 |
| ❑ 17 Jason MacIntyre | .35 | .16 |
| ❑ 18 Jim Brown | .35 | .16 |
| ❑ 19 Matt Mallgrave | .35 | .16 |
| ❑ 20 Ron Majic | .35 | .16 |
| ❑ 21 Corwin Saurdiff | .35 | .16 |
| ❑ 22 Rick Burrill TR | .10 | .05 |
| ❑ 23 Team Photo CL | .35 | .16 |
| ❑ NNO Logo Card | .10 | .05 |

## 1995-96 Hampton Roads Admirals

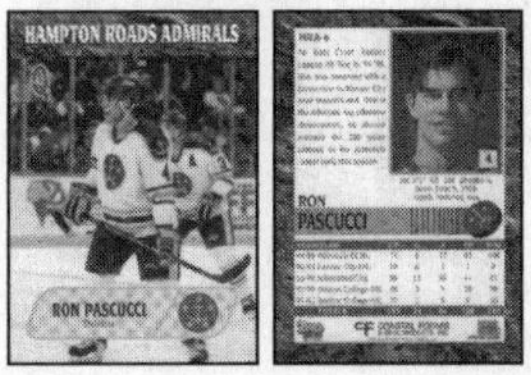


This 25-card set showcases the Hampton Roads Admirals of the ECHL. The set was produced by Q-Cards, and distributed by Ward's Corner Sporting Goods; it may also have been sold through the team at games. The set features action photography on the front and an expanded player information section on the numbered back.

| | MINT | NRMT |
|---|---|---|
| COMPLETE SET (25) | 8.00 | 3.60 |
| COMMON CARD (1-25) | .10 | .05 |
| ❑ 1 Team Photo | .35 | .16 |
| ❑ 2 John Brophy CO | .35 | .16 |
| ❑ 3 Al MacIsaac ACO | .10 | .05 |
| ❑ 4 Darryl Paquette | .50 | .23 |
| ❑ 5 Mark Bernard | .35 | .16 |
| ❑ 6 Ron Pascucci | .35 | .16 |
| ❑ 7 Dominic Maltais | .35 | .16 |
| ❑ 8 Jason MacIntyre | .35 | .16 |
| ❑ 9 Serge Aubin | .35 | .16 |
| ❑ 10 Rick Kowalsky | .25 | .11 |
| ❑ 11 Claude Fillion | .35 | .16 |
| ❑ 12 Rod Taylor | .35 | .16 |
| ❑ 13 Alexei Krivchenkov | .35 | .16 |
| ❑ 14 David St. Pierre | .35 | .16 |
| ❑ 15 Steve Richards | .35 | .16 |
| ❑ 16 Trevor Halverson | .50 | .23 |
| ❑ 17 Chris Phelps | .35 | .16 |
| ❑ 18 Jeff Kostuch | .35 | .16 |
| ❑ 19 Sean Selmser | .35 | .16 |
| ❑ 20 Aaron Downey | .35 | .16 |
| ❑ 21 Bob Woods | .35 | .16 |
| ❑ 22 Sergei Voronov | .35 | .16 |
| ❑ 23 Corwin Saurdiff | .35 | .16 |
| ❑ 24 Rick Burrell TR | .10 | .05 |
| ❑ 25 Gary Mansfield EQMG | .10 | .05 |

## 1996-97 Hampton Roads Admirals

This 25-card set of the Hampton Roads Admirals of the ECHL was produced by Blueline Communications, and sponsored by Kline Chevrolet and The Score, 1310 AM. The cards feature action photos on the front, along with the player name. The backs include statistical and biographical data.

| | MINT | NRMT |
|---|---|---|
| COMPLETE SET (25) | 8.00 | 3.60 |
| COMMON CARD (HRA1-HRA24) | .15 | .07 |
| ❑ HRA1 Darryl Paquette | .50 | .23 |
| ❑ HRA2 Mike Larkin | .40 | .18 |
| ❑ HRA3 Chris Phelps | .40 | .18 |
| ❑ HRA4 Alex Alexeev | .40 | .18 |
| ❑ HRA5 Joel Theriault | .40 | .18 |
| ❑ HRA6 Neal Martin | .40 | .18 |
| ❑ HRA7 Ryan Mulhern | .40 | .18 |
| ❑ HRA8 Darryl Shedden | .40 | .18 |
| ❑ HRA9 Victor Gervais | .40 | .18 |
| ❑ HRA10 Rod Taylor | .40 | .18 |
| ❑ HRA11 Andy Weidenbach | .40 | .18 |
| ❑ HRA12 Alain Savage | .40 | .18 |
| ❑ HRA13 Randy Pearce | .40 | .18 |
| ❑ HRA14 Chad Ackerman | .40 | .18 |
| ❑ HRA15 Alexei Krivchenkov | .40 | .18 |
| ❑ HRA16 Rick Kowalsky | .40 | .18 |
| ❑ HRA17 Dominic Maltais | .40 | .18 |
| ❑ HRA18 Joel Poirier | .40 | .18 |
| ❑ HRA19 Marc Seliger | .75 | .35 |
| ❑ HRA20 Aaron Downey | .40 | .18 |
| ❑ HRA21 John Brophy CO | .50 | .23 |
| ❑ HRA22 Al MacIsaac ACO | .15 | .07 |
| ❑ HRA23 G.Mansfield EQMG<br>K.Bender TR | .15 | .07 |
| ❑ HRA24 Salty (Mascot) | .15 | .07 |
| ❑ NNO Team Photo | .35 | .16 |

## 1992-93 Harvard Crimson

Cards are unnumbered and checklisted below in alphabetical order.

| | MINT | NRMT |
|---|---|---|
| COMPLETE SET (31) | 6.00 | 2.70 |
| COMPLETE SET (1-31) | .10 | .05 |
| ❑ 1 Brian Adams | .25 | .11 |
| ❑ 2 Chris Baird | .25 | .11 |
| ❑ 3 Lou Body | .25 | .11 |
| ❑ 4 Michel Breistroff | .25 | .11 |
| ❑ 5 Perry Cohagen | .25 | .11 |
| ❑ 6 Ben Coughlin | .25 | .11 |
| ❑ 7 Ted Drury | .25 | .11 |
| ❑ 8 Brian Farell | .25 | .11 |
| ❑ 9 Steven Flomenhoft | .25 | .11 |
| ❑ 10 Eric Grahling | .25 | .11 |
| ❑ 11 Cory Gustafson | .25 | .11 |
| ❑ 12 Kevin Hampe ACO | .10 | .05 |
| ❑ 13 Steve Hermsdorf | .25 | .11 |
| ❑ 14 Tom Holmes | .25 | .11 |
| ❑ 15 Aaron Israel | .25 | .11 |
| ❑ 16 Jason Karmanos | .25 | .11 |
| ❑ 17 Ian Kennish | .25 | .11 |
| ❑ 18 Brad Konik | .25 | .11 |
| ❑ 19 Bryan Lonsinger | .25 | .11 |
| ❑ 20 Derek Maguire | .25 | .11 |
| ❑ 21 Matt Mallgrave | .25 | .11 |
| ❑ 22 Geb Marett | .25 | .11 |
| ❑ 23 Steve Martins | .25 | .11 |
| ❑ 24 Sean McCann | .25 | .11 |
| ❑ 25 Peter McLaughlin | .25 | .11 |
| ❑ 26 Keith McLean | .25 | .11 |
| ❑ 27 Kirk Nielsen | .25 | .11 |
| ❑ 28 Jerry Pawloski ACO | .10 | .05 |
| ❑ 29 Ronn Tomassoni CO | .10 | .05 |
| ❑ 30 Tripp Tracy | .25 | .11 |
| ❑ 31 Header Card | .10 | .05 |

## 1993-94 Huntington Blizzard

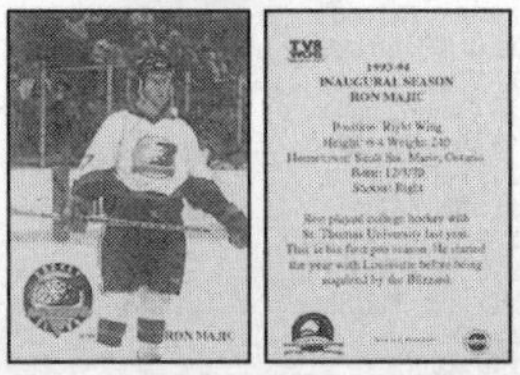


Sponsored by WCHS-TV8, this 27-card standard-size set commemorates the 1993-94 inaugural season of the Huntington Blizzard (ECHL). Just 2,500 sets were produced and each was hand-numbered "X of 2,500" on the title card. One thousand sets were given away on trading card night, with the rest being sold at the souvenir shops in the arena. The fronts feature borderless color action and posed player photos. The player's name and the team logo appear on the front. On a white background with black lettering, the backs carry player biography and profile. The cards are unnumbered and checklisted below in alphabetical order.

| | MINT | NRMT |
|---|---|---|
| COMPLETE SET (27) | 7.00 | 3.10 |
| COMMON CARD (1-27) | .10 | .05 |
| ❑ 1 Ray Alcindor | .35 | .16 |
| ❑ 2 Shayne Antoski | .35 | .16 |
| ❑ 3 Greg Bailey | .35 | .16 |
| ❑ 4 Jared Bednar | .35 | .16 |
| ❑ 5 Andy Borggaard | .35 | .16 |
| ❑ 6 Malcolm Cameron | .35 | .16 |
| ❑ 7 Dave Dimitri | .35 | .16 |
| ❑ 8 Mark Franks | .35 | .16 |
| ❑ 9 Ray Gallagher | .35 | .16 |
| ❑ 10 Murray Garbutt | .35 | .16 |
| ❑ 11 Brad Harrison | .35 | .16 |
| ❑ 12 Henry's Blizzard Babes | .50 | .23 |
| ❑ 13 Todd Huyber | .35 | .16 |
| ❑ 14 Klondike The Bear<br>(Mascot) | .10 | .05 |
| ❑ 15 Ron Majic | .35 | .16 |
| ❑ 16 Bob May | .35 | .16 |
| ❑ 17 Jim Mill | .35 | .16 |
| ❑ 18 Jim Mirabello ANN | .10 | .05 |
| ❑ 19 Dan Persigehl ANN | .10 | .05 |
| ❑ 20 Paul Pickard CO | .10 | .05 |
| ❑ 21 Scott Roberts<br>(TV anchorman) | .10 | .05 |
| ❑ 22 Greg Scott | .35 | .16 |
| ❑ 23 Geoff Simpson | .35 | .16 |
| ❑ 24 Doug Stromback | .35 | .16 |
| ❑ 25 Dave Weekley<br>(TV Sports Director) | .10 | .05 |
| ❑ 26 Misty Zambito | .50 | .23 |
| ❑ 27 Title Card | .10 | .05 |

## 1994-95 Huntington Blizzard

Sponsored by WSAZ Channel 3 and Oldies 93RVC radio, this 32-card standard-size set features the 1994-95 Huntington Blizzard of the ECHL. Approximately 3,000 sets were produced; 1,000 were given away on trading card night, while the others were sold at the souvenir shops in the arena. The fronts feature color action and posed player photos with gray bars below and above the photo. The player's name, his position and the league name appear under the photo, while the team logo is printed in the upper left corner. The backs carry a small black-and-white player portrait, along with player biography, stats and profile, and sponsor logos.

| | MINT | NRMT |
|---|---|---|
| COMPLETE SET (32) | 8.00 | 3.60 |
| COMMON CARD (1-32) | .10 | .05 |
| ❑ 1 Title Card CL | .35 | .16 |
| ❑ 2 Steve Barnes | .35 | .16 |
| ❑ 3 Jared Bednar | .35 | .16 |
| ❑ 4 Jim Bermingham | .35 | .16 |
| ❑ 5 Todd Brost | .50 | .23 |
| ❑ 6 Alan Brown | .35 | .16 |
| ❑ 7 Ray Edwards | .35 | .16 |
| ❑ 8 Trent Eigner | .35 | .16 |
| ❑ 9 Dan Fournel | .35 | .16 |
| ❑ 10 Mark Franks | .35 | .16 |
| ❑ 11 Gord Frantti | .35 | .16 |
| ❑ 12 Chris Gordon | .35 | .16 |
| ❑ 13 Kelly Harper | .35 | .16 |
| ❑ 14 J.C. Ihrig TR/EQMG | .10 | .05 |
| ❑ 15 Mitch Kean | .35 | .16 |
| ❑ 16 Jeff Levy | .50 | .23 |
| ❑ 17 Chris Morque | .35 | .16 |
| ❑ 18 Derek Schooley | .35 | .16 |
| ❑ 19 Jim Solly | .35 | .16 |
| ❑ 20 Mike Stone | .35 | .16 |
| ❑ 21 Jason Weinrich | .35 | .16 |
| ❑ 22 Mark Woolf | .35 | .16 |
| ❑ 23 Paul Pickard CO | .10 | .05 |
| ❑ 24 Klondike (Mascot) | .10 | .05 |
| ❑ 25 Blizzard Babes | .50 | .23 |
| ❑ 26 Jim Mirabello ANN | .10 | .05 |
| ❑ 27 Dan Persigehl ANN | .10 | .05 |
| ❑ 28 Jeff Crawford DJ<br>Van Man DJ | .10 | .05 |
| ❑ 29 Russell T. Hill DJ<br>Sarah Diamond DJ<br>Darrell Hicks DJ | .10 | .05 |
| ❑ 30 Jeff Ramsey DJ<br>Teresa Nichols DJ<br>Derek Scott DJ | .10 | .05 |
| ❑ 31 Melanie Shafer<br>Kevin Doran<br>(TV anchors) | .10 | .05 |
| ❑ 32 Title Card | .10 | .05 |

## 1981-82 Indianapolis Checkers

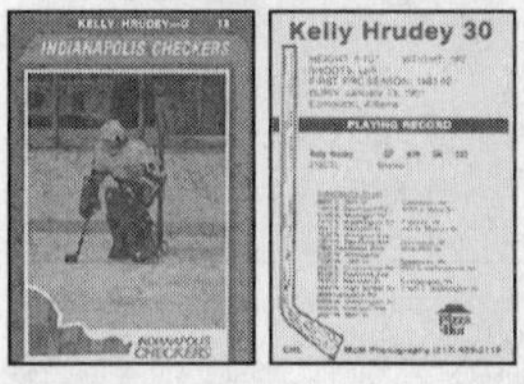


Sponsored by Pizza Hut, this 20-card standard-size set features the Indianapolis Checkers of the CHL. The cards were available singly at Pizza Hut restaurants and Checkers games on alternate weeks. On a blue background, the fronts have color action player photos with thin white borders. The team name appears above the photo in an orange border that extends down the right side. The player's name, position, and number are printed above the photo. On a white background, the backs carry player biography, statistics, and addresses of Indianapolis Pizza Huts. The cards are unnumbered and checklisted below in alphabetical order.

| | NRMT-MT | EXC |
|---|---|---|
| COMPLETE SET (20) | 25.00 | 11.00 |
| COMMON CARD (1-20) | 1.00 | .45 |
| ❑ 1 Bruce Andres | 1.00 | .45 |
| ❑ 2 Frank Beaton | 1.00 | .45 |
| ❑ 3 Kelly Davis | 1.00 | .45 |
| ❑ 4 Kevin Devine | 1.00 | .45 |
| ❑ 5 Glen Duncan | 1.00 | .45 |
| ❑ 6 Mats Hallin | 1.50 | .70 |
| ❑ 7 Neil Hawryliw | 1.00 | .45 |
| ❑ 8 Bob Holland | 1.00 | .45 |
| ❑ 9 Mike Hordy | 1.00 | .45 |
| ❑ 10 Kelly Hrudey | 12.00 | 5.50 |
| ❑ 11 Randy Johnston | 1.00 | .45 |
| ❑ 12 Red Laurence | 1.00 | .45 |
| ❑ 13 Tim Lockridge | 1.00 | .45 |
| ❑ 14 Garth MacGuigan | 1.00 | .45 |
| ❑ 15 John Marks | 1.50 | .70 |
| ❑ 16 Darcey Regier | 1.50 | .70 |
| ❑ 17 Charlie Skjodt | 1.00 | .45 |
| ❑ 18 Lorne Stamler | 1.00 | .45 |
| ❑ 19 Steve Stoyanovich | 1.00 | .45 |
| ❑ 20 Monty Trottier | 1.00 | .45 |

## 1982-83 Indianapolis Checkers

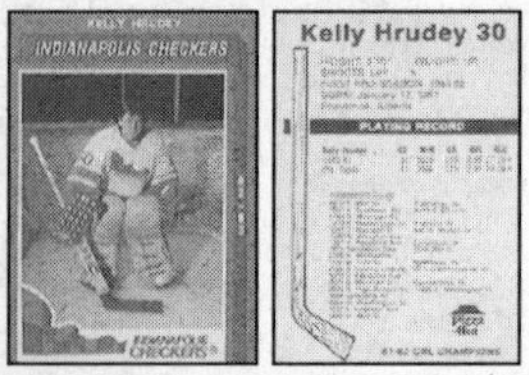


Sponsored by Pizza Hut, this 21-card standard-size set features the Indianapolis Checkers of the CHL. The cards were available singly at Pizza Hut restaurants and Checkers games on alternate weeks. On a red-orange background, the fronts have color action player photos with thin white borders. The team name appears above the photo in an orange border that extends down the right side. The player's name, position, and number are printed above the photo. On a white background, the backs carry player biography, statistics, and addresses of Indianapolis Pizza Huts. The cards are unnumbered and checklisted below in alphabetical order.

| | MINT | EXC |
|---|---|---|
| COMPLETE SET (21) | 25.00 | 11.00 |
| COMMON CARD (1-21) | 1.00 | .45 |
| ❑ 1 Kelly Davis | 1.00 | .45 |
| ❑ 2 Kevin Devine | 1.00 | .45 |
| ❑ 3 Gord Dineen | 2.00 | .90 |
| ❑ 4 Glen Duncan | 1.00 | .45 |
| ❑ 5 Greg Gilbert | 2.00 | .90 |
| ❑ 6 Mike Gredder | 1.00 | .45 |
| ❑ 7 Mats Hallin | 2.00 | .90 |
| ❑ 8 Dave Hanson | 1.00 | .45 |
| ❑ 9 Rob Holland | 1.00 | .45 |
| ❑ 10 Scott Howson | 1.00 | .45 |
| ❑ 11 Kelly Hrudey | 8.00 | 3.60 |
| ❑ 12 Randy Johnston | 1.00 | .45 |
| ❑ 13 Red Laurence | 1.00 | .45 |
| ❑ 14 Tim Lockridge | 1.00 | .45 |
| ❑ 15 Garth MacGuigan | 1.00 | .45 |
| ❑ 16 Darcey Regier | 1.50 | .70 |
| ❑ 17 Dan Revell | 1.00 | .45 |
| ❑ 18 Dave Simpson | 1.00 | .45 |
| ❑ 19 Lorne Stamler | 1.00 | .45 |
| ❑ 20 Steve Stoyanovich | 1.00 | .45 |
| ❑ 21 Monty Trottier | 1.00 | .45 |

## 1992-93 Indianapolis Ice

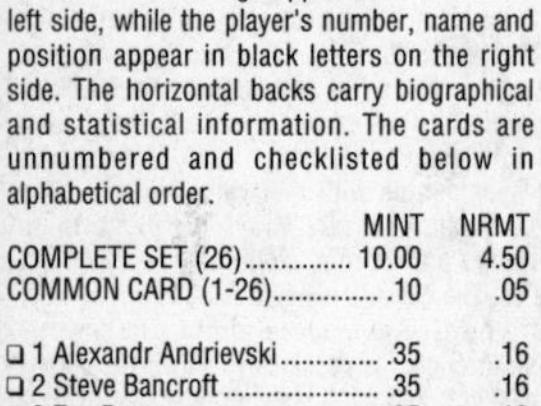


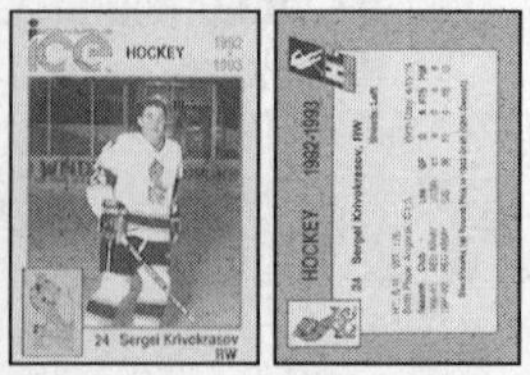

This 26-card set measures the standard size. On a light blue background, the fronts feature posed, color action photos with a thin red border. The team logo appears on the bottom left side, while the player's number, name and position appear in black letters on the right side. The horizontal backs carry biographical and statistical information. The cards are unnumbered and checklisted below in alphabetical order.

| | MINT | NRMT |
|---|---|---|
| COMPLETE SET (26) | 10.00 | 4.50 |
| COMMON CARD (1-26) | .10 | .05 |
| ❑ 1 Alexandr Andrievski | .35 | .16 |
| ❑ 2 Steve Bancroft | .35 | .16 |
| ❑ 3 Zac Boyer | .35 | .16 |
| ❑ 4 Rod Buskas | .50 | .23 |
| ❑ 5 Shawn Byram | .35 | .16 |
| ❑ 6 Joe Cleary | .35 | .16 |
| ❑ 7 Rob Conn | .35 | .16 |
| ❑ 8 Joe Crowley | .35 | .16 |
| ❑ 9 Trevor Dam | .35 | .16 |
| ❑ 10 Ivan Droppa | .35 | .16 |
| ❑ 11 Tracy Egeland | .35 | .16 |
| ❑ 12 Dave Hakstol | .35 | .16 |
| ❑ 13 Kevin Hodson | 2.00 | .90 |
| ❑ 14 Tony Horacek | .35 | .16 |
| ❑ 15 Tony Hrkac | .50 | .23 |
| ❑ 16 Sergei Krivokrasov | .75 | .35 |
| ❑ 17 Brad Lauer | .50 | .23 |
| ❑ 18 Ray LeBlanc | .50 | .23 |
| ❑ 19 Owen Lessard | .35 | .16 |
| ❑ 20 Jim Playfair ACO | .10 | .05 |
| John Marks CO | | |
| ❑ 21 Kevin St. Jacques | .35 | .16 |
| ❑ 22 Michael Speer | .35 | .16 |
| ❑ 23 Milan Tichy | .35 | .16 |
| ❑ 24 Kerry Toporowski | .35 | .16 |
| ❑ 25 Sean Williams | .35 | .16 |
| ❑ 26 Craig Woodcroft | .35 | .16 |

## 1994-95 Indianapolis Ice

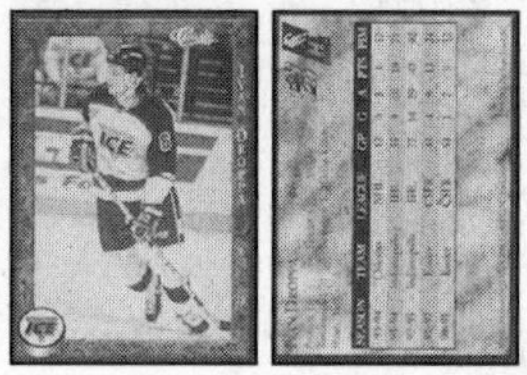

Manufactured and distributed by Jessen Associates, Inc. for Classic, this 26-card standard-size set features the 1994-95 Indianapolis Ice of the IHL. The fronts feature color action player photos with a marbleized purple frame and a thin black border around it. The player's name, number and position appear on the right next to the photo. Classic's logo is printed in the upper right corner, while the team logo is in the lower left corner. On a gray marbleized background, the horizontal backs carry player biography and stats. The cards are unnumbered and checklisted below in alphabetical order.

| | MINT | NRMT |
|---|---|---|
| COMPLETE SET (26) | 9.00 | 4.00 |
| COMMON CARD (1-26) | .35 | .16 |
| ❑ 1 Hugo Belanger | .35 | .16 |
| ❑ 2 Bruce Cassidy | .35 | .16 |
| ❑ 3 Rob Conn | .50 | .23 |
| ❑ 4 Ivan Droppa | .35 | .16 |
| ❑ 5 Steve Dubinsky | .50 | .23 |
| ❑ 6 Karl Dykhuis | .50 | .23 |
| ❑ 7 Craig Fisher | .35 | .16 |
| ❑ 8 Daniel Gauthier | .35 | .16 |
| ❑ 9 Tony Horacek | .35 | .16 |
| ❑ 10 Bobby House | .35 | .16 |
| ❑ 11 Bob Kellogg | .35 | .16 |
| ❑ 12 Sergei Klimovich | .35 | .16 |
| ❑ 13 Sergei Krivokrasov | .75 | .35 |
| ❑ 14 Andy MacIntyre | .35 | .16 |
| ❑ 15 Dean Malkoc | .50 | .23 |
| ❑ 16 Matt Oates | .35 | .16 |
| ❑ 17 Mike Pomichter | .35 | .16 |
| ❑ 18 Mike Prokopec | .35 | .16 |
| ❑ 19 Jeff Ricciardi | .35 | .16 |
| ❑ 20 Chris Rogles | .50 | .23 |
| ❑ 21 Bogdan Savenko | .35 | .16 |
| ❑ 22 Jeff Shantz | .75 | .35 |
| ❑ 23 Christian Soucy | .50 | .23 |
| ❑ 24 Duane Sutter CO | .50 | .23 |
| ❑ 25 Travis Thiessen | .35 | .16 |
| ❑ 26 Team Photo | .35 | .16 |

## 1995-96 Indianapolis Ice

This 23-card set was produced by SplitSecond for Collector's Edge. The cards featured the standard design element for that season, with the color schemes adapted for that of the team. As they are unnumbered, the cards are listed below alphabetically.

| | MINT | NRMT |
|---|---|---|
| COMPLETE SET (23) | 9.00 | 4.00 |
| COMMON CARD (1-23) | .35 | .16 |
| ❑ 1 Bill Armstrong | .35 | .16 |
| ❑ 2 James Black | .35 | .16 |
| ❑ 3 Jeff Buchanan | .35 | .16 |
| ❑ 4 Bruce Cassidy | .35 | .16 |
| ❑ 5 Ivan Droppa | .50 | .23 |
| ❑ 6 Steve Dubinsky | .35 | .16 |
| ❑ 7 Dmitri Filimonov | .35 | .16 |
| ❑ 8 Daniel Gauthier | .35 | .16 |
| ❑ 9 Ryan Huska | .35 | .16 |
| ❑ 10 Sergei Klimovich | .35 | .16 |
| ❑ 11 Eric Lecompte | .50 | .23 |
| ❑ 12 Andy MacIntyre | .35 | .16 |
| ❑ 13 Eric Manlow | .50 | .23 |
| ❑ 14 Steve McLaren | .35 | .16 |
| ❑ 15 Kip Miller | .35 | .16 |
| ❑ 16 Ethan Moreau | 1.50 | .70 |
| ❑ 17 Mike Prokopec | .50 | .23 |
| ❑ 18 Andre Racicot | .50 | .23 |
| ❑ 19 Jeff Serowik | .35 | .16 |
| ❑ 20 Christian Soucy | .60 | .25 |
| ❑ 21 Jimmy Waite | .60 | .25 |
| ❑ 22 Brad Werenka | .35 | .16 |
| ❑ 23 Bob Ferguson | .35 | .16 |

## 1989-90 Johnstown Chiefs

This 18-card set of the Johnstown Chiefs of the ECHL was produced by Big League Cards. The set is believed to have been issued by the team, but that is not a certainty. The set's numbering begins with 19, leading to speculation that a 1988-89 set exists as well. The fronts feature a posed photo, with the player seated beside a prominent logo of sponsor Sheetz convenience store; the backs offer limited biographical information.

| | MINT | NRMT |
|---|---|---|
| COMPLETE SET (18) | 10.00 | 4.50 |
| COMMON CARD (1-18) | .25 | .11 |
| ❑ 19 Rick Burchill | .50 | .23 |
| ❑ 20 Bob Goulet | .50 | .23 |
| ❑ 21 John Messuri | .50 | .23 |
| ❑ 22 Darren Servatius | .50 | .23 |
| ❑ 23 Rick Boyd | .50 | .23 |
| ❑ 24 Bob Kennedy | .50 | .23 |
| ❑ 25 Mike Rossetti | .50 | .23 |
| ❑ 26 Dan Williams | .50 | .23 |
| ❑ 27 Mark Bogoslowski | .50 | .23 |
| ❑ 28 Dean Hall | .50 | .23 |
| ❑ 29 Mitch Molloy | .50 | .23 |
| ❑ 30 Darren Schwartz | .50 | .23 |
| ❑ 31 Doug Weiss | .50 | .23 |
| ❑ 32 Marc Vachon | .50 | .23 |
| ❑ 33 Mike Jeffrey | .50 | .23 |
| ❑ 34 Frank Dell ANN | .25 | .11 |
| ❑ 35 Sean Finn | .50 | .23 |
| ❑ 36 Steve Carlson | 3.00 | 1.35 |

## 1991-92 Johnstown Chiefs

This 20-card set features the Johnstown Chiefs of the ECHL. The set was sponsored by Ponderosa Steakhouse and KB Card Company and likely was sold by the team at home games. The fronts feature a posed photo along with team and sponsor logos. The back has personal information and 1990-91 stats.

| | MINT | NRMT |
|---|---|---|
| COMPLETE SET (20) | 7.00 | 3.10 |
| COMMON CARD (1-20) | .10 | .05 |
| ❑ 1 Steve Carlson CO | 1.00 | .45 |
| ❑ 2 Dana Heinze TR | .10 | .05 |
| ❑ 3 John Fletcher | .35 | .16 |
| ❑ 4 Mark Krys | .35 | .16 |
| ❑ 5 Doug Sinclair | .35 | .16 |
| ❑ 6 Bruce Coles | .35 | .16 |
| ❑ 7 Doug Weiss | .35 | .16 |
| ❑ 8 Dave MacIntyre | .35 | .16 |
| ❑ 9 Bob Woods | .35 | .16 |
| ❑ 10 Mike Roberts | .35 | .16 |
| ❑ 11 Jeff Beaudin | .35 | .16 |
| ❑ 12 Brian Ferreira | .35 | .16 |
| ❑ 13 Christian Lariviere | .35 | .16 |
| ❑ 14 Ted Miskolczi | .35 | .16 |
| ❑ 15 Rob Hrytsak | .35 | .16 |
| ❑ 16 Mark Green | .35 | .16 |
| ❑ 17 Matt Glennon | .35 | .16 |
| ❑ 18 Mike Rossetti | .50 | .23 |
| ❑ 19 Stan Reddick | .50 | .23 |
| ❑ 20 Perry Florio | .35 | .16 |

## 1993-94 Johnstown Chiefs

This 22-card set features the Johnstown Chiefs of the ECHL. The set was sponsored by Ponderosa Steakhouse and KB Card Company and likely was sold by the team at home games. The fronts feature a posed photo along with team and sponsor logos. The back has personal information and 1992-93 stats.

| | MINT | NRMT |
|---|---|---|
| COMPLETE SET (22) | 7.00 | 3.10 |
| COMMON CARD (1-22) | .10 | .05 |
| ❑ 1 John Bradley | .40 | .18 |
| ❑ 2 Campbell Blair | .40 | .18 |
| ❑ 3 Francois Bourdeau | .40 | .18 |
| ❑ 4 Bob Woods | .40 | .18 |
| ❑ 5 Ted Dent | .40 | .18 |
| ❑ 6 Matt Hoffman | .40 | .18 |
| ❑ 7 Gord Christian | .40 | .18 |
| ❑ 8 Tim Hanus | .40 | .18 |
| ❑ 9 Phil Soukoroff | .40 | .18 |
| ❑ 10 Jason Jennings | .40 | .18 |
| ❑ 11 Dusty McLellan | .40 | .18 |
| ❑ 12 Dennis Purdie | .50 | .23 |
| ❑ 13 Chuck Wiegand | .40 | .18 |
| ❑ 14 Jamie Adams | .40 | .18 |
| ❑ 15 Jan Beran | .40 | .18 |
| ❑ 16 Rob Laurie | .50 | .23 |
| ❑ 17 Cory Banika | .40 | .18 |
| ❑ 18 Perry Florio | .40 | .18 |
| ❑ 19 Rob Leask | .40 | .18 |
| ❑ 20 Ed Johnstone CO | .25 | .11 |
| ❑ 21 John Daley GM | .10 | .05 |
| ❑ 22 Matt Koeck TR | .10 | .05 |
| ❑ NNO Header Card | .10 | .05 |

## 1994-95 Johnstown Chiefs

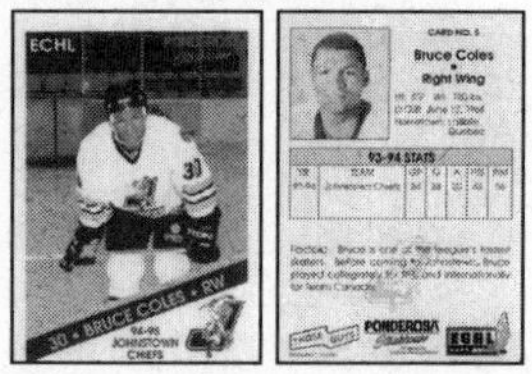


This 24-card set features the Johnstown Chiefs of the ECHL. The set was likely sold by the team at home games. The fronts feature a posed photo along with team and sponsor logos. The back has personal information and 1993-94 stats.

| | MINT | NRMT |
|---|---|---|
| COMPLETE SET (24) | 7.00 | 3.10 |
| COMMON CARD (1-24) | .10 | .05 |
| ❑ 1 Cover Card CL | .10 | .05 |
| ❑ 2 Jason Brousseau | .35 | .16 |
| ❑ 3 Brandon Christian | .35 | .16 |
| ❑ 4 Gord Christian | .35 | .16 |
| ❑ 5 Bruce Coles | .35 | .16 |
| ❑ 6 Ted Dent | .35 | .16 |
| ❑ 7 Martin D'Orsonnens | .35 | .16 |
| ❑ 8 Perry Florio | .35 | .16 |
| ❑ 9 Rod Hinks | .35 | .16 |
| ❑ 10 Matt Hoffman | .35 | .16 |
| ❑ 11 Aaron Israel | .35 | .16 |
| ❑ 12 Jason Jennings | .35 | .16 |
| ❑ 13 Rob Laurie | .35 | .16 |
| ❑ 14 Rob Leask | .35 | .16 |
| ❑ 15 Dennis Purdie | .50 | .23 |
| ❑ 16 Kevin Quinn | .35 | .16 |
| ❑ 17 Jason Richard | .35 | .16 |
| ❑ 18 Dan Sawyer | .35 | .16 |
| ❑ 19 Ben Wyzansky | .35 | .16 |
| ❑ 20 Matt Yingst | .35 | .16 |
| ❑ 21 Training Staff | .10 | .05 |
| ❑ 22 Ed Johnstone CO | .10 | .05 |
| ❑ 23 WMTZ-FM Personalities | .10 | .05 |
| ❑ 24 WMTZ-FM Personalities | .10 | .05 |

## 1977-78 Kalamazoo Wings

These standard size cards, sponsored by ISB bank, feature black and white photos with a white border. Backs feature players name, position, and card number.

| | MINT | NRMT |
|---|---|---|
| COMPLETE (15) | 10.00 | 4.50 |
| COMMON CARD | .75 | .35 |
| ❑ 1 George Klsons | .75 | .35 |
| ❑ 2 Ron Wilson | 2.00 | .90 |
| ❑ 3 Bob Lemieux | .75 | .35 |
| ❑ 4 Len Ircandia | .75 | .35 |
| ❑ 5 Ron Kennedy | .75 | .35 |
| ❑ 6 Daniel Poulin | .75 | .35 |
| ❑ 7 Terry Evans | .75 | .35 |
| ❑ 8 Yvon Douris | .75 | .35 |
| ❑ 9 Tom Milani | .75 | .35 |
| ❑ 10 Mike Wanchuk | .75 | .35 |
| ❑ 11 Steve Lee | .75 | .35 |
| ❑ 12 Yves Guilmette | .75 | .35 |
| ❑ 13 Al Genovy | .75 | .35 |
| ❑ 15 Jim Baxter | .75 | .35 |
| ❑ 18 Alvin White | .75 | .35 |

## 1984-85 Kamloops Blazers

This set features color action photos on the front along with team name, position, and number. Backs feature safety tips and sponsor logos. Cards are unnumbered and checklisted below in alphabetical order.

| | MINT | NRMT |
|---|---|---|
| COMPLETE SET (24) | 15.00 | 6.75 |
| COMMON CARD (1-24) | .20 | .09 |
| ❑ 1 Will Anderson | .75 | .35 |
| ❑ 2 Brian Benning | .75 | .35 |
| ❑ 3 Brian Bertuzzi | 1.00 | .45 |
| ❑ 4 Rob Brown | .75 | .35 |
| ❑ 5 Todd Carnelley | .75 | .35 |
| ❑ 6 Dean Clark | .75 | .35 |
| ❑ 7 Rob Dimaio | 1.00 | .45 |
| ❑ 8 Greg Evtuschevsi | .75 | .35 |
| ❑ 9 Mark Ferner | .75 | .35 |
| ❑ 10 Greg Hawgood | 1.00 | .45 |
| ❑ 11 Ken Hitchcock CO | 2.50 | 1.10 |
| ❑ 12 Mark Kachowski | .75 | .35 |
| ❑ 13 Bob Labrier ACO | .20 | .09 |
| ❑ 14 Pat Mangold | .75 | .35 |
| ❑ 15 Gord Mark | .75 | .35 |
| ❑ 16 Len Mark | .75 | .35 |
| ❑ 17 Rob McKinley | .75 | .35 |
| ❑ 18 Mike Nottingham | .75 | .35 |
| ❑ 19 Neil Pilon | .75 | .35 |
| ❑ 20 Rudy Poeschek | .75 | .35 |
| ❑ 21 Darryl Reaugh | .75 | .35 |
| ❑ 22 Ryan Stewart | .75 | .35 |
| ❑ 23 Mark Thietke | .75 | .35 |
| ❑ 24 Gord Walker | .75 | .35 |

## 1985-86 Kamloops Blazers

This standard size set features full color fronts along with sponsot logs and hockey tips on the backs. Cards are unnumbered and checklisted below in alphabetical order.

| | MINT | NRMT |
|---|---|---|
| COMPLETE SET (26) | 15.00 | 6.75 |
| COMMON CARD (1-26) | .20 | .09 |
| ❑ 1 Robin Bawa | .75 | .35 |
| ❑ 2 Craig Berube | .75 | .35 |
| ❑ 3 Pat Bingham | .75 | .35 |
| ❑ 4 Rob Brown | 1.00 | .45 |
| ❑ 5 Todd Carnelly | .75 | .35 |
| ❑ 6 Randy Hansch | .75 | .35 |
| ❑ 7 Greg Hawgood | 1.00 | .45 |
| ❑ 8 Ken Hitchcock CO | 2.50 | 1.10 |
| ❑ 9 Mark Kachowski | .75 | .35 |
| ❑ 10 Troy Kennedy | .75 | .35 |
| ❑ 11 R.T. Labrier ACO | .20 | .09 |
| ❑ 12 Dave Marcinyshyn | .75 | .35 |
| ❑ 13 Len Mark | .75 | .35 |
| ❑ 14 Rob McKinley | .75 | .35 |
| ❑ 15 Ken Morrison | .75 | .35 |
| ❑ 16 Pat Nogier | .75 | .35 |
| ❑ 17 Mike Nottingham | .75 | .35 |
| ❑ 18 Doug Pickell | .75 | .35 |
| ❑ 19 Rudy Poeschek | .75 | .35 |
| ❑ 20 Mike Ragot | .75 | .35 |
| ❑ 21 Don Schmidt | .75 | .35 |
| ❑ 22 Ron Shudra | .75 | .35 |
| ❑ 23 Peter Soberlak | .75 | .35 |
| ❑ 24 Lonnie Spink | .75 | .35 |
| ❑ 25 Chris Tarnowski | .75 | .35 |
| ❑ 26 Greg Wallace TR | .20 | .09 |

## 1986-87 Kamloops Blazers

This 24-card sheet was issued in nine four-card sheets. Six of the panels feature two cards and an advertisement, while the other three panels feature four cards per panel. The sheets are perforated vertically but not horizontally, which produces two-card stripes. If cut, the cards would measure the standard size. On a white card face, the fronts display posed action photos inside a bright blue border. The team logo and player information is presented in the wider bottom border. The backs carry "Tips from the Blazers," which consist of pointers about hockey and public service announcements. The cards are unnumbered and checklisted below in alphabetical order.

| | MINT | NRMT |
|---|---|---|
| COMPLETE SET (24) | 30.00 | 13.50 |
| COMMON CARD (1-24) | .75 | .35 |
| ❑ 1 Warren Babe | .75 | .35 |
| ❑ 2 Robin Bawa | .75 | .35 |
| ❑ 3 Rob Brown | 2.00 | .90 |
| ❑ 4 Dean Cook | .75 | .35 |
| ❑ 5 Scott Daniels | .75 | .35 |
| ❑ 6 Mario Desjardines | .75 | .35 |
| ❑ 7 Bill Harrington | .75 | .35 |
| ❑ 8 Greg Hawgood | 2.00 | .90 |
| ❑ 9 Serge Lajoie | .75 | .35 |
| ❑ 10 Dave Marcinyshyn | 1.00 | .45 |
| ❑ 11 Len Mark | .75 | .35 |
| ❑ 12 Rob McKinley | .75 | .35 |
| ❑ 13 Casey McMillan | .75 | .35 |
| ❑ 14 Darcy Norton | .75 | .35 |

❑ 15 Kelly Para .75 .35
❑ 16 Doug Pickell .75 .35
❑ 17 Rudy Poeschek 1.50 .70
❑ 18 Mark Recchi 15.00 6.75
❑ 19 Don Schmidt .75 .35
❑ 20 Ron Shudra .75 .35
❑ 21 Chris Tarnowski .75 .35
❑ 22 Steve Wienke .75 .35
❑ 23 Rich Wiest .75 .35
❑ 24 Team Photo 2.50 1.10

## 1987-88 Kamloops Blazers

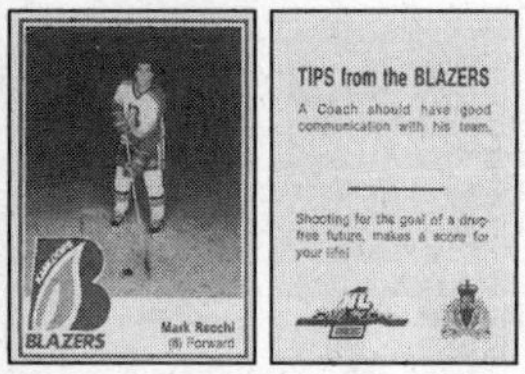

This 24-card set was issued in three-card perforated strips each consisting of two player cards and one advertisement or coupon card. (As listed below, two of these advertisement cards display team logos on the front). The strips measure 7 1/2" by 3 1/2", and if cut, the individual cards would measure the standard size. The features a color posed-action player photo with thin blue borders on a white card face. The player's name, jersey number, and position appear in the white bottom margin. The team logo overlaps the picture at the lower left. The backs carry Tips from the Blazers consisting of hockey tips and anti-drug messages. The cards are unnumbered and checklisted below in alphabetical order.

| | MINT | NRMT |
|---|---|---|
| COMPLETE SET (24) | 25.00 | 11.00 |
| COMMON CARD (1-24) | .50 | .23 |

❑ 1 Warren Babe .50 .23
❑ 2 Paul Checknita .50 .23
❑ 3 Dave Chyzowski 1.00 .45
❑ 4 Dean Cook .50 .23
❑ 5 Greg Davies .50 .23
❑ 6 Kim Deck .50 .23
❑ 7 Todd Decker .50 .23
❑ 8 Bill Harrington .50 .23
❑ 9 Phil Huber .50 .23
❑ 10 Steve Kloepzig .50 .23
❑ 11 Willie MacDonald .50 .23
❑ 12 Pat MacLeod 1.00 .45
❑ 13 Glenn Mulvenna .75 .35
❑ 14 Mike Needham 1.00 .45
❑ 15 Darcy Norton .50 .23
❑ 16 Devon Oleniuk .50 .23
❑ 17 Doug Pickell .50 .23
❑ 18 Garth Premak .50 .23
❑ 19 Mark Recchi 10.00 4.50
❑ 20 Don Schmidt .50 .23
❑ 21 Alec Sheflo .50 .23
❑ 22 Team Photo 2.00 .90
❑ 23 Logo Card .50 .23
❑ 24 Logo Card .50 .23

## 1988-89 Kamloops Blazers

his 36-card set was issued in three-card erforated strips that measure approximately 7 /2" by 3 1/2". After perforation, the individual ards measure approximately 2 1/2" by 3 1/2". ne of the cards on each three-card strip has e Kamloops logo in blue and orange on the ont and the back contains a coupon. The egular player cards have white borders with inner royal blue line surrounding a posed ayer photo. The Kamloops logo is uperimposed on the photo in the lower left orner with the player's name, team position, nd number printed in the lower right corner. he white backs carry "Tips from the Blazers" the form of public service announcements. he NL Radio station logo and the Royal anadian Mounted Police emblem round out e back. The cards are unnumbered and are ecklisted below in alphabetical order.

| | MINT | NRMT |
|---|---|---|
| OMPLETE SET (36) | 18.00 | 8.00 |
| OMMON CARD (1-24) | .50 | .23 |
| OMMON AD CARD (25-36) | .10 | .05 |

1 Cory Anderson .50 .23
2 Pat Bingham .50 .23
❑ 3 Ed Bertuzzi .50 .23
❑ 4 Zac Boyer .75 .35
❑ 5 Trevor Buchanan .50 .23
❑ 6 Dave Chyzowski .75 .35
❑ 7 Dean Cook .50 .23
❑ 8 Cory Crichton .50 .23
❑ 9 Kim Deck .50 .23
❑ 10 Ryan Harrison .50 .23
❑ 11 Brad Heschuk .50 .23
❑ 12 Corey Hirsch 4.00 1.80
❑ 13 Phil Huber .50 .23
❑ 14 Len Jorgenson .50 .23
❑ 15 Paul Kruse .75 .35
❑ 16 Dave Linford .50 .23
❑ 17 Pat MacLeod .75 .35
❑ 18 Darwin McClelland .50 .23
❑ 19 Cal McGowan .50 .23
❑ 20 Mike Needham .75 .35
❑ 21 Don Schmidt .50 .23
❑ 22 Brian Shantz .50 .23
❑ 23 Darryl Sydor 2.50 1.10
❑ 24 Steve Yule .50 .23
❑ 25 Hasty Market Ad .10 .05
❑ 26 McDonalds Ad .10 .05
❑ 27 Mr. Mike's Ad .10 .05
❑ 28 Yellow Submarine Ad .10 .05
❑ 29 Blazers Logo .10 .05
❑ 30 Blazers Logo .10 .05
❑ 31 Blazers Logo .10 .05
❑ 32 Blazers Logo .10 .05
❑ 33 Blazers Logo .10 .05
❑ 34 Blazers Logo .10 .05
❑ 35 Blazers Logo .10 .05
❑ 36 Blazers Logo .10 .05

## 1993-94 Kamloops Blazers

This 24-card set was issued on three-card perforated strips each consisting of two player cards and one advertisement or coupon card. The strips measure 7 1/2" by 3 1/2", and if cut, the individual cards would measure the standard size. The fronts feature a color posed-action player photo with thin blue borders on a white background. The player's name, number, and position appear in the top portion of the photo, while the team logo is printed at the bottom left corner. The backs carry "Tips from the Blazers" consisting of hockey and safety tips. Sponsor logos appear below. The cards are unnumbered and checklisted below in alphabetical order.

| | MINT | NRMT |
|---|---|---|
| COMPLETE SET (24) | 20.00 | 9.00 |
| COMMON CARD (1-24) | .50 | .23 |

❑ 1 Nolan Baumgartner 1.00 .45
❑ 2 Rod Branch .75 .35
❑ 3 Jarrett Deuling .50 .23
❑ 4 Shane Doan 2.00 .90
❑ 5 Hnat Domenichelli 2.00 .90
❑ 6 Scott Ferguson .50 .23
❑ 7 Greg Hart .50 .23
❑ 8 Jason Holland .50 .23
❑ 9 Ryan Huska .60 .25
❑ 10 Jarome Iginla 5.00 2.20
❑ 11 Mike Josephson .50 .23
❑ 12 Aaron Keller .50 .23
❑ 13 Mike Krooshoop .50 .23
❑ 14 Scott Loucks .60 .25
❑ 15 Brad Lukowich .50 .23
❑ 16 Bob Maudie .50 .23
❑ 17 Chris Murray .75 .35
❑ 18 Tyson Nash .50 .23
❑ 19 Steve Passmore .75 .35
❑ 20 Rod Stevens .50 .23
❑ 21 Jason Strudwick .60 .25
❑ 22 Darcy Tucker 1.00 .45
❑ 23 Bob Westerby .50 .23
❑ 24 David Wilkie .75 .35

## 1996-97 Kamloops Blazers

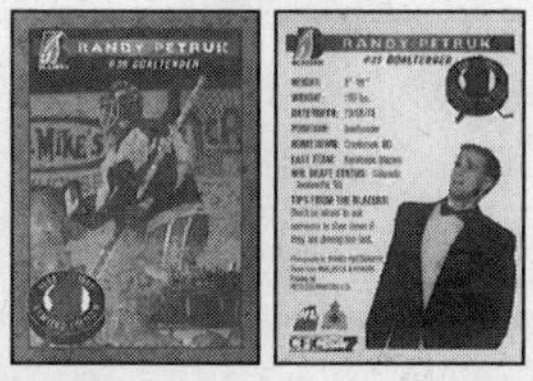

This 28-card set was distributed in 3-panel strips, each of which contained two player cards and one ad card for a local business. When separated the cards are standard size and feature color photos with player name, number and position at the top, while the bottom left corner is dominated by a flame-like element and an icon identifying the set as the '96-97 Limited Edition. The black and white backs include a photo of each player in a tux, along with a personal bio and safety tip. The cards are unnumbered and are listed below in alphabetical order.

| | MINT | NRMT |
|---|---|---|
| COMPLETE SET (28) | 12.00 | 5.50 |
| COMMON CARD (1-28) | .10 | .05 |

❑ 1 Jeff Ainsworth .50 .23
❑ 2 Steve Albrecht .50 .23
❑ 3 Nils Antons .50 .23
❑ 4 Ajay Baines .50 .23
❑ 5 Konrad Brand .50 .23
❑ 6 Wade Burt .50 .23
❑ 7 Jake Deadmarsh .75 .35
❑ 8 Ed Dempsey CO .25 .11
❑ 9 Digger .10 .05
Mascot
❑ 10 Micki DuPont .50 .23
❑ 11 Steve Gainey .75 .35
❑ 12 Jonathan Hobson .50 .23
❑ 13 Drew Kehler .50 .23
❑ 14 Donnie Kinney .50 .23
❑ 15 Alan Manness .50 .23
❑ 16 Shawn McNeil .50 .23
❑ 17 Randy Petruk 1.00 .45
❑ 18 Clayton Pool .75 .35
❑ 19 Gennady Razin .50 .23
❑ 20 Robyn Regehr .75 .35
❑ 21 Blair Rota .50 .23
❑ 22 Thomas Scantlebury .50 .23
❑ 23 Steve Shrum .50 .23
❑ 24 Rob Skrlac .50 .23
❑ 25 Darcy Smith .50 .23
❑ 26 Chris St. Croix .50 .23
❑ 27 Spike Wallace .25 .11
❑ 28 Darren Wright .50 .23

## 1990-91 Kansas City Blades

This 20-card standard-size set features posed, color player photos on a black card face. The pictures are bordered on three sides by a red design similar to a shadow border. Player information appears below the photo in the red border. The year and team name are printed at the upper left corner. The backs are white and carry the words "the jones store co.", the year, team logo, and the player's name and biography. One red star accents each corner.

| | MINT | NRMT |
|---|---|---|
| COMPLETE SET (20) | 10.00 | 4.50 |
| COMMON CARD (1-20) | .50 | .23 |

❑ 1 Claudio Scremin .50 .23
❑ 2 Jeff Odgers 1.00 .45
❑ 3 Wade Flaherty 1.00 .45
❑ 4 Rick Barkovich .50 .23
❑ 5 Ron Handy .50 .23
❑ 6 Kevin Sullivan .50 .23
❑ 7 Randy Exelby .60 .25
❑ 8 Darin Smith .50 .23
❑ 9 Stu Kulak .50 .23
❑ 10 Andrew Akervik .50 .23
❑ 11 Scott White .50 .23
❑ 12 Claude Julien .50 .23
❑ 13 Mike Hiltner .50 .23
❑ 14 Michael Colman .50 .23
❑ 15 Kurt Semandel .50 .23
❑ 16 Mike Kelfer .50 .23
❑ 17 Mark Karpen .50 .23
❑ 18 Lee Giffin .50 .23
❑ 19 Cam Plante .50 .23
❑ 20 Jim Latos .60 .25

## 1998-99 Kansas City Blades

| | MINT | NRMT |
|---|---|---|
| COMPLETE SET (30) | 4.00 | 1.80 |
| COMMON CARD (1-30) | .10 | .05 |

❑ 1 Title Card .10 .05
❑ 2 Brian Leitza .25 .11
❑ 3 Dan Ratushny .15 .07
❑ 4 Trevor Sherban .15 .07
❑ 5 Eric Rud .15 .07
❑ 6 Tuomas Gronman .25 .11
❑ 7 Eric Perrin .15 .07
❑ 8 Brendan Yarema .15 .07
❑ 9 Brian Bonin .15 .07
❑ 10 Pat Ferschweiler .15 .07
❑ 11 Dody Wood .15 .07
❑ 12 David Ling .15 .07
❑ 13 Rocky Weising .15 .07
❑ 14 Jean-Guy Trudel .15 .07
❑ 15 Vlastimil Kroupa .15 .07
❑ 16 Steven Low .15 .07
❑ 17 Ryan Mulhern .15 .07
❑ 18 Brent Bilodeau .15 .07
❑ 19 Grant Richison .15 .07
❑ 20 Dave Chyzowski .15 .07
❑ 21 David Vallieres .15 .07
❑ 22 Patrick Lalime .15 .07
❑ 23 Jean Sebastien Aubin .35 .16
❑ 24 Jason Cirone .20 .09
❑ 25 Paul MacLean CO .10 .05
❑ 26 Gary Emmons ACO .10 .05
❑ 27 John Doolan EQ .10 .05
❑ 28 Jeff Kreuser TR .10 .05
❑ 29 Scrapper Mascot .10 .05
❑ 30 Logo Card .10 .05

## 1984-85 Kelowna Wings

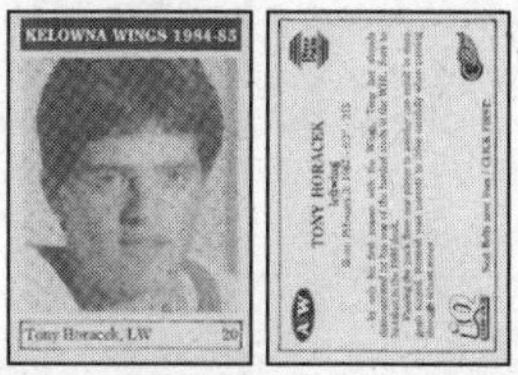

This 56-card safety standard-size set was sponsored by A and W, Pizza Patio, CKIQ (a radio station), and the Kelowna Wings. The cards feature black-and-white posed and action player photos. The words "Kelowna Wings 1984-85" are at the top of card numbers 2-22, while the words "Junior Hockey Grads" appear at the top of card numbers 1 and 23-56. The player's name, position, and the card number are at the bottom. The backs feature biographical and statistical information in red print. After a checklist card, the set is ordered by Kelowna players (2-22) and WHL graduates to the NHL (23-56). The cards are numbered on the front in the lower right corner.

| | MINT | NRMT |
|---|---|---|
| COMPLETE SET (56) | 60.00 | 27.00 |
| COMMON CARD (1-56) | .50 | .23 |

❑ 1 Checklist 1.50 .70
❑ 2 Darcy Wakaluk 1.50 .70
❑ 3 Stacey Nickel .50 .23
❑ 4 Jeff Sharples .75 .35
❑ 5 Greg Zuk .50 .23
❑ 6 Daryn Sivertson .50 .23
❑ 7 Randy Cameron .50 .23
❑ 8 Mark Fioretti .50 .23
❑ 9 Ron Viglasi .50 .23
❑ 10 Ian Herbers .50 .23
❑ 11 Mike Wegleitner .50 .23
❑ 12 Terry Zaporzan .50 .23
❑ 13 Dwaine Hutton .50 .23
❑ 14 Rod Williams .50 .23
❑ 15 Jeff Rohlicek .50 .23
❑ 16 Brent Gilchrist 1.50 .70
❑ 17 Rocky Dundas .50 .23
❑ 18 Grant Delcourt .50 .23
❑ 19 Cam Laroruk .50 .23
❑ 20 Tony Horacek .50 .23
❑ 21 Mark Wingerter .50 .23
❑ 22 Mick Vukota .75 .35
❑ 23 Danny Gare 1.50 .70
❑ 24 Rich Sutter 1.00 .45
❑ 25 Alfie Turcotte .50 .23
❑ 26 Bryan Trottier 8.00 3.60
❑ 27 Bill Derlago 1.00 .45
❑ 28 Stan Smyl 2.00 .90
❑ 29 Brent Sutter 2.00 .90
❑ 30 Mel Bridgman 1.00 .45
❑ 31 Paul Cyr .75 .35
❑ 32 Gary Lupul .50 .23
❑ 33 Ray Neufeld .75 .35
❑ 34 Brian Propp 2.50 1.10
❑ 35 Bob Nystrom 2.00 .90
❑ 36 Ryan Walter 1.00 .45
❑ 37 Russ Courtnall 3.00 1.35
❑ 38 Larry Playfair .50 .23
❑ 39 Ron Delorme .50 .23
❑ 40 Ron Sutter 1.00 .45
❑ 41 Bobby Clarke 8.00 3.60
❑ 42 Bob Bourne 1.00 .45
❑ 43 Cam Neely 15.00 6.75
❑ 44 Murray Craven 1.00 .45
❑ 45 Clark Gillies 2.50 1.10
❑ 46 Ron Flockhart .75 .35
❑ 47 Harold Snepsts 3.00 1.35
❑ 48 Duane Sutter 1.00 .45
❑ 49 Garth Butcher 1.00 .45
❑ 50 Bill Hajt .50 .23
❑ 51 Jim Benning .50 .23
❑ 52 Ray Allison .50 .23
❑ 53 Ken Wregget 3.00 1.35
❑ 54 Phil Russell .75 .35
❑ 55 Brad McCrimmon 1.50 .70
❑ 56 Dan Hodgson .50 .23

## 1996-97 Kentucky Thoroughblades

This set was sold at the Kentucky team store, and featured an SRP of $3.00. Set features color action photos on the front, with statistics and biographical information on the back.

| | MINT | NRMT |
|---|---|---|
| COMPLETE SET (26) | 6.00 | 2.70 |
| COMMON CARD (1-26) | .10 | .05 |

❑ 1 Ken Belanger .40 .18
❑ 2 Alexandre Boikov .25 .11
❑ 3 Jan Caloun .30 .14
❑ 4 Denis Chervyakov .25 .11
❑ 5 Jarrett Deuling .25 .11
❑ 6 Iain Fraser .25 .11
❑ 7 Dean Grillo .25 .11
❑ 8 Steve Guolla .50 .23
❑ 9 Sean Haggerty .25 .11
❑ 10 Jason Holland .25 .11
❑ 11 Lance Leslie .25 .11
❑ 12 Chris Lipuma .50 .23
❑ 13 Pat Mikesch .25 .11
❑ 14 Fredrik Oduya .25 .11
❑ 15 Jamie Ram .25 .11
❑ 16 Chris Tancill .40 .18
❑ 17 Jason Strudwick .25 .11
❑ 18 Steve Webb .25 .11
❑ 19 Jason Widmer .25 .11
❑ 20 Jim Wiley .25 .11
❑ 21 Alexei Yegorov .25 .11
❑ NNO Ad Card-In Your Face .10 .05
❑ NNO Ad Card-PHPA .10 .05
❑ NNO Lucky the Mascot .10 .05
❑ NNO Rupp Arena .10 .05
❑ NNO Team Photo .10 .05

## 1981-82 Kingston Canadians

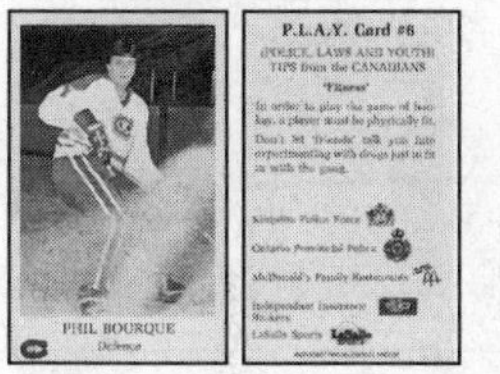

This 25-card set measures approximately 2 5/8" by 4" and features posed, color player photos on thin white card stock. The player's name, position, and the team logo are printed in black below the picture. The backs carry P.L.A.Y. (Police, Laws and Youth) Tips from the Canadians, which consist of public service messages. Sponsor logos are printed at the bottom.

| | NRMT-MT | EXC |
|---|---|---|
| COMPLETE SET (25) | 25.00 | 11.00 |
| COMMON CARD (1-25) | .50 | .23 |

❑ 1 Canadians Logo .50 .23
❑ 2 Scott MacLellan .50 .23
❑ 3 Dave Courtemanche .50 .23
❑ 4 Mark Reade .50 .23
❑ 5 Shawn Babcock .50 .23
❑ 6 Phil Bourque 2.00 .90
❑ 7 Ian MacInnis .50 .23
❑ 8 Neil Trineer .50 .23
❑ 9 Syl Grandmaitre .50 .23
❑ 10 Carmine Vani .75 .35
❑ 11 Chuck Brimmer .50 .23
❑ 12 Mike Linseman .50 .23
❑ 13 Steve Seguin .50 .23
❑ 14 Dan Wood .50 .23
❑ 15 Kirk Muller 15.00 6.75
❑ 16 Jim Aldred .50 .23
❑ 17 Rick Wilson 1.50 .70
❑ 18 Mike Siltala .50 .23
❑ 19 Howie Scruton .50 .23
❑ 20 Mike Stothers .75 .35
❑ 21 Dennis Smith .50 .23
❑ 22 Steve Richey .50 .23
❑ 23 Mike Moffat 1.50 .70
❑ 24 Jim Morrison CO/MG .50 .23
❑ 25 Randy Plumb .50 .23

## 1982-83 Kingston Canadians

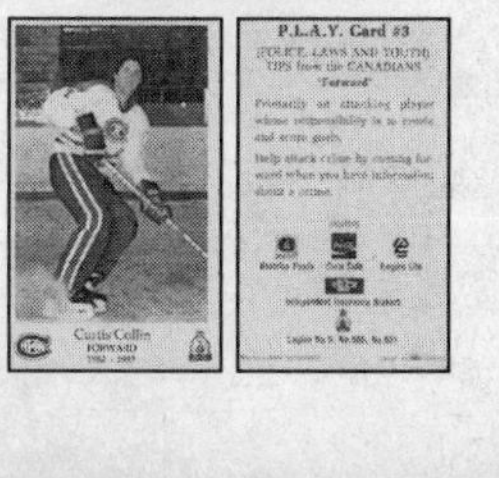

This 27-card set measures approximately 2 5/8" by 4 1/8" and features posed action, color player photos with white borders on thin card stock. The player's name, position, and year of issue appear below the picture between the team logo and the Kingston Police Force insignia. The backs carry hockey tips and public service messages in the form of P.L.A.Y. (Police, Laws and Youth) Tips from the Canadians. Sponsor logos appear on the lower portion of the card.

| | MINT | EXC |
|---|---|---|
| COMPLETE SET (27) | 12.00 | 5.50 |
| COMMON CARD (1-27) | .25 | .11 |
| ❑ 1 Jim Morrison MG | .25 | .11 |
| ❑ 2 Dennis Smith | .50 | .23 |
| ❑ 3 Curtis Collin | .50 | .23 |
| ❑ 4 Joel Brown | .50 | .23 |
| ❑ 5 Ron Handy | .50 | .23 |
| ❑ 6 Carmine Vani | .50 | .23 |
| ❑ 7 Al Andrews | .50 | .23 |
| ❑ 8 Mike Siltala | .50 | .23 |
| ❑ 9 Syl Grandmaitre | .50 | .23 |
| ❑ 10 Steve Seguin | .50 | .23 |
| ❑ 11 Brian Dobbin | .75 | .35 |
| ❑ 12 Mark Reade | .50 | .23 |
| ❑ 13 John Kemp | .50 | .23 |
| ❑ 14 Dan Mahon | .50 | .23 |
| ❑ 15 Keith Knight | .50 | .23 |
| ❑ 16 Ron Sanko | .50 | .23 |
| ❑ 17 John Landry | .50 | .23 |
| ❑ 18 Chris Brant | .50 | .23 |
| ❑ 19 Dave Simurda | .50 | .23 |
| ❑ 20 Mike Lafoy | .50 | .23 |
| ❑ 21 Scott MacLellan | .50 | .23 |
| ❑ 22 Brad Walcot | .50 | .23 |
| ❑ 23 Steve Richey | .50 | .23 |
| ❑ 24 Rod Graham CO | .25 | .11 |
| ❑ 25 Ben Levesque | .50 | .23 |
| ❑ 26 Canadians Logo | .50 | .23 |
| ❑ 27 International Hockey Hall of Fame | .50 | .23 |

## 1983-84 Kingston Canadians

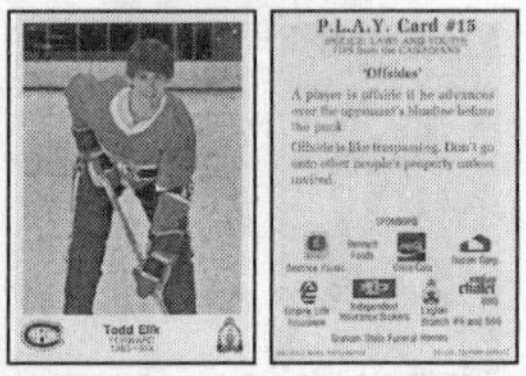

This 30-card set measures slightly larger than standard at 2 5/8" by 3 5/8" and features posed color player photos with white borders on thin card stock. The player's name, position, and year appears below the picture between the Canadians logo and the Kingston Police Force insignia. The backs carry public service messages in the form of P.L.A.Y. (Police, Laws and Youth) Tips from the Canadians. Sponsor logos fill out the lower portion.

| | MINT | NRMT |
|---|---|---|
| COMPLETE SET (30) | 12.00 | 5.50 |
| COMMON CARD (1-30) | .25 | .11 |
| ❑ 1 Kingston Police Crest (Checklist) | .50 | .23 |
| ❑ 2 Dennis Smith | .50 | .23 |
| ❑ 3 Ben Levesque | .50 | .23 |
| ❑ 4 Arie Moraal (Constable) | .25 | .11 |
| ❑ 5 Tom Allen | .50 | .23 |
| ❑ 6 Mike Plesh | .50 | .23 |
| ❑ 7 Roger Belanger | .50 | .23 |
| ❑ 8 Jeff Chychrun | 1.00 | .45 |
| ❑ 9 Mike King | .50 | .23 |
| ❑ 10 Scott Metcalfe | .75 | .35 |
| ❑ 11 David Lundmark | .50 | .23 |
| ❑ 12 Tim Salmon | .50 | .23 |
| ❑ 13 Ted Linesman | .50 | .23 |
| ❑ 14 Chris Clifford | .50 | .23 |
| ❑ 15 Todd Elik | 1.00 | .45 |
| ❑ 16 Kevin Conway | .50 | .23 |
| ❑ 17 Barry Burkholder | .50 | .23 |
| ❑ 18 Joel Brown | .50 | .23 |
| ❑ 19 Steve King | .50 | .23 |
| ❑ 20 Craig Kales | .50 | .23 |
| ❑ 21 John Humphries TR | .25 | .11 |
| ❑ 22 David James | .50 | .23 |
| ❑ 23 Dave Simurda | .50 | .23 |
| ❑ 24 Allen Bishop | .50 | .23 |
| ❑ 25 Jeff Hogg | .50 | .23 |
| ❑ 26 Rick Cornacchia CO | .75 | .35 |
| ❑ 27 Ken Slater Director of Player Personnel | .25 | .11 |
| ❑ 28 Bill Dextater (Constable) | .25 | .11 |
| ❑ 29 Canadians Crest | .50 | .23 |
| ❑ 30 International Hockey Hall of Fame logo | .50 | .23 |

## 1984-85 Kingston Canadians

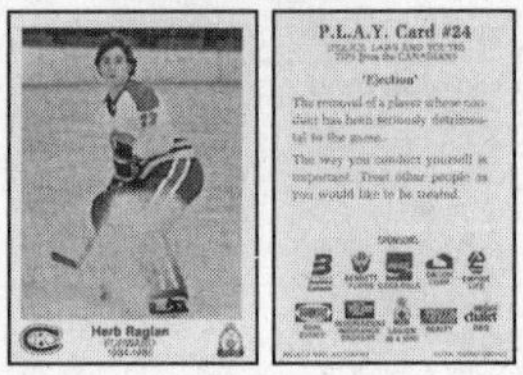

This 30-card set measures 2 5/8" by 3 5/8" and features color, posed action player photos with white borders. The player's name, position, and year appear at the bottom. The backs carry public service messages in the form of P.L.A.Y. (Police, Laws and Youth) Tips from the Canadians. Sponsor logos round out the lower portion of the back.

| | MINT | NRMT |
|---|---|---|
| COMPLETE SET (30) | 12.00 | 5.50 |
| COMMON CARD (1-30) | .25 | .11 |
| ❑ 1 Kingston Police Force Crest | .25 | .11 |
| ❑ 2 Rick Cornacchia CO | .50 | .23 |
| ❑ 3 Arie Moraal (Constable) | .25 | .11 |
| ❑ 4 Ken Slater Director of Player Personnel | .25 | .11 |
| ❑ 5 Kingston Canadians Crest | .50 | .23 |
| ❑ 6 Scott Metcalfe | .75 | .35 |
| ❑ 7 Chris Clifford | .50 | .23 |
| ❑ 8 Todd Elik | .75 | .35 |
| ❑ 9 Len Spratt | .50 | .23 |
| ❑ 10 Mike Plesh | .50 | .23 |
| ❑ 11 Marc Lyons | .50 | .23 |
| ❑ 12 Barry Burkholder | .50 | .23 |
| ❑ 13 Rick Fera | .50 | .23 |
| ❑ 14 David Hoover | .50 | .23 |
| ❑ 15 Andy Rivers | .50 | .23 |
| ❑ 16 Marc Laforge | .75 | .35 |
| ❑ 17 Peter Viscovich | .50 | .23 |
| ❑ 18 Jeff Chychrun | .75 | .35 |
| ❑ 19 Wayne Erskine | .50 | .23 |
| ❑ 20 Todd Clarke | .50 | .23 |
| ❑ 21 Darren Wright | .50 | .23 |
| ❑ 22 Tony Rocca | .50 | .23 |
| ❑ 23 Brian Verbeek | .50 | .23 |
| ❑ 24 Herb Raglan | .75 | .35 |
| ❑ 25 Daril Holmes | .50 | .23 |
| ❑ 26 Len Coyle TR | .25 | .11 |
| ❑ 27 Ted Linesman | .50 | .23 |
| ❑ 28 International Hockey Hall of Fame logo | .25 | .11 |
| ❑ 29 Troy MacNevin | .50 | .23 |
| ❑ 30 Peter Campbell TR | .25 | .11 |

## 1985-86 Kingston Canadians

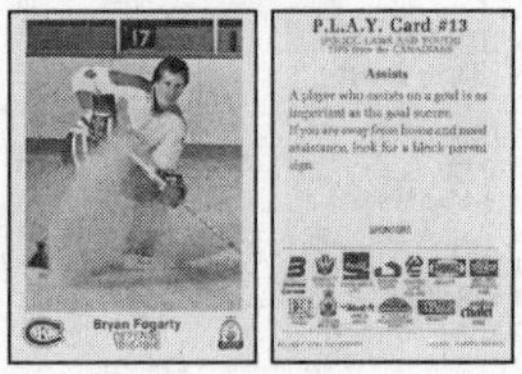

This 30-card set measures approximately 2 5/8" by 3 5/8" and features color, posed action player photos with white borders. The player's name and position appear at the bottom. The backs carry public service messages in the form of P.L.A.Y. (Police, Laws and Youth) Tips from the Canadians. Sponsor logos fill the lower portion of the back.

| | MINT | NRMT |
|---|---|---|
| COMPLETE SET (30) | 10.00 | 4.50 |
| COMMON CARD (1-30) | .25 | .11 |
| ❑ 1 Kingston Police Force Crest | .25 | .11 |
| ❑ 2 Dale Sandles ACO | .25 | .11 |
| ❑ 3 Arie Moraal (Constable) | .25 | .11 |
| ❑ 4 Fred O'Donnell GM/CO | .25 | .11 |
| ❑ 5 Kingston Canadian Crest | .50 | .23 |
| ❑ 6 Scott Metcalfe | .50 | .23 |
| ❑ 7 Chris Clifford | .50 | .23 |
| ❑ 8 Steve Seftel | .50 | .23 |
| ❑ 9 Andy Pearson | .50 | .23 |
| ❑ 10 Jeff Cornelius | .50 | .23 |
| ❑ 11 Marc Lyons | .50 | .23 |
| ❑ 12 Barry Burkholder | .50 | .23 |
| ❑ 13 Bryan Fogarty | .75 | .35 |
| ❑ 14 Jeff Sirkka | .50 | .23 |
| ❑ 15 Scott Pearson | 1.00 | .45 |
| ❑ 16 Marc Laforge | .50 | .23 |
| ❑ 17 Peter Viscovich | .50 | .23 |
| ❑ 18 Jeff Chychrun UER (Name misspelled Chycren) | .75 | .35 |
| ❑ 19 Wayne Erskine | .50 | .23 |
| ❑ 20 Todd Clarke | .50 | .23 |
| ❑ 21 Darren Wright | .50 | .23 |
| ❑ 22 Mike Maurice | .50 | .23 |
| ❑ 23 Brian Verbeek | .50 | .23 |
| ❑ 24 Mike Fiset | .50 | .23 |
| ❑ 25 Daril Holmes | .50 | .23 |
| ❑ 26 Len Coyle TR | .25 | .11 |
| ❑ 27 Ted Linesman | .50 | .23 |
| ❑ 28 International Hockey Hall of Fame | .25 | .11 |
| ❑ 29 Troy MacNevin | .50 | .23 |
| ❑ 30 Peter Campbell TR | .25 | .11 |

## 1986-87 Kingston Canadians

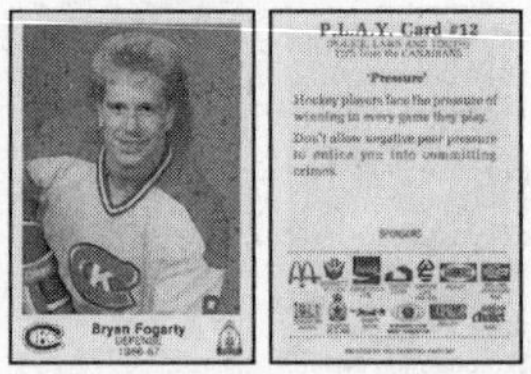

This 30-card set measures approximately 2 5/8" by 3 5/8" and features color, posed player portraits with blue studio backgrounds set on a white card face. The player's name, position, and year appear at the bottom. The backs carry public service messages in the form of P.L.A.Y. (Police, Laws and Youth) Tips from the Canadians. Sponsor logos fill the lower portion of the card.

| | MINT | NRMT |
|---|---|---|
| COMPLETE SET (30) | 8.00 | 3.60 |
| COMMON CARD (1-30) | .15 | .07 |
| ❑ 1 Kingston Canadians Crest | .35 | .16 |
| ❑ 2 Fred O'Donnell GM/CO | .15 | .07 |
| ❑ 3 Arie Moraal (Constable) | .15 | .07 |
| ❑ 4 Dale Sandles CO | .15 | .07 |
| ❑ 5 Kingston Police Force Crest | .15 | .07 |
| ❑ 6 Brian Tessier | .35 | .16 |
| ❑ 7 Franco Giammarco | .35 | .16 |
| ❑ 8 Peter Liptrott | .35 | .16 |
| ❑ 9 Chris Clifford | .35 | .16 |
| ❑ 10 Scott Metcalfe | .35 | .16 |
| ❑ 11 Scott Pearson | .50 | .23 |
| ❑ 12 Bryan Fogarty | .50 | .23 |
| ❑ 13 Daril Holmes | .35 | .16 |
| ❑ 14 Andy Rivers | .35 | .16 |
| ❑ 15 Troy MacNevin | .35 | .16 |
| ❑ 16 Marc Laforge | .35 | .16 |
| ❑ 17 Wayne Erskine | .35 | .16 |
| ❑ 18 Peter Viskovich | .35 | .16 |
| ❑ 19 Mike Maurice | .35 | .16 |
| ❑ 20 Steve Seftel | .35 | .16 |
| ❑ 21 Chad Badaway | .35 | .16 |
| ❑ 22 Marc Lyons | .35 | .16 |
| ❑ 23 Jeff Sirkka | .35 | .16 |
| ❑ 24 Mike Fiset | .35 | .16 |
| ❑ 25 John Battice | .35 | .16 |
| ❑ 26 Len Coyle TR | .15 | .07 |
| ❑ 27 Sloan Torti | .35 | .16 |
| ❑ 28 Alain Laforge | .35 | .16 |
| ❑ 29 Ted Linesman | .35 | .16 |
| ❑ 30 Peter Campbell TR | .15 | .07 |

## 1987-88 Kingston Canadians

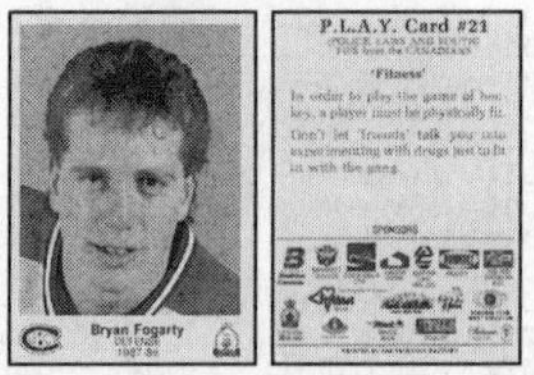

This 30-card P.L.A.Y. (Police, Laws and Youth) set measures approximately 2 3/4" by 3 5/8" and features color player portraits with blue studio backgrounds. The fronts are accented by white borders. The player's name, position, and the season year appear in the white border at the bottom. The backs carry public service messages in the form of "Tips From The Canadians."

| | MINT | NRMT |
|---|---|---|
| COMPLETE SET (30) | 12.00 | 5.50 |
| COMMON CARD (1-30) | .10 | .05 |
| ❑ 1 Arie Moraal (Constable) | .10 | .05 |
| ❑ 2 Gord Wood GM | .10 | .05 |
| ❑ 3 Kingston Canadians Kingston Police Crests | .25 | .11 |
| ❑ 4 Jacques Tremblay CO | .25 | .11 |
| ❑ 5 Rhonda Sheridan Public Relations | .10 | .05 |
| ❑ 6 Jeff Wilson | .50 | .23 |
| ❑ 7 Franco Giammarco | .50 | .23 |
| ❑ 8 Peter Liptrott | .50 | .23 |
| ❑ 9 David Weiss | .50 | .23 |
| ❑ 10 Joel Morin | .50 | .23 |
| ❑ 11 Mark Turner | .50 | .23 |
| ❑ 12 Jeff Sirkka | .50 | .23 |
| ❑ 13 James Henckle | .50 | .23 |
| ❑ 14 Mike Bodnarchuk | .50 | .23 |
| ❑ 15 Mike Cavanaugh | .50 | .23 |
| ❑ 16 Darcy Cahill | .50 | .23 |
| ❑ 17 Kevin Falesy | .50 | .23 |
| ❑ 18 Dean Pella | .50 | .23 |
| ❑ 19 Brad Gratton | .50 | .23 |
| ❑ 20 Steve Seftel | .50 | .23 |
| ❑ 21 Bryan Fogarty | .75 | .35 |
| ❑ 22 Scott Pearson | .75 | .35 |
| ❑ 23 Tyler Pella | .50 | .23 |
| ❑ 24 Mike Fiset | .50 | .23 |
| ❑ 25 John Battice | .50 | .23 |
| ❑ 26 Len Coyle TR | .10 | .05 |
| ❑ 27 Geoff Schneider | .50 | .23 |
| ❑ 28 Chris Lukey | .50 | .23 |
| ❑ 29 Trevor Smith | .50 | .23 |
| ❑ 30 Peter Campbell TR | .10 | .05 |

## 1993-94 Kingston Frontenacs

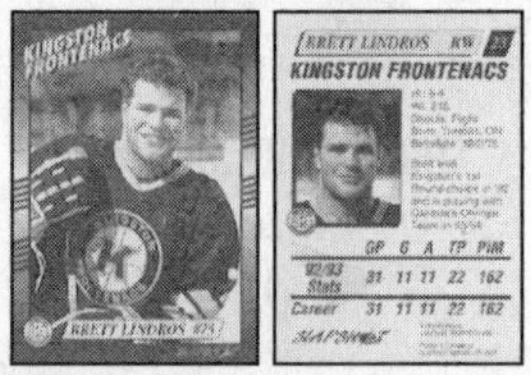

Printed by Slapshot Images Ltd., this standard size 25-card set features the 1993-94 Kingston Frontenacs. On a team color-coded background with black stripes, the fronts feature color action player photos with thin black borders. The team name is printed diagonally in the upper left corner of the photo, while the player's name and number appear in a yellow bar in the bottom edge of the photo. The team and producer's logos on the bottom round out the front. The white backs carry a close-up color player portrait, biography and statistics, along with team and sponsor's logos. Included in this set is a Slapshot ad card with a 1994 calendar on the back.

| | MINT | NRMT |
|---|---|---|
| COMPLETE SET (25) | 10.00 | 4.50 |
| COMMON CARD (1-24) | .10 | .05 |
| ❑ 1 Greg Lovell | .40 | .18 |
| ❑ 2 Marc Lamothe | .40 | .18 |
| ❑ 3 Tyler Moss | .50 | .23 |
| ❑ 4 Marc Moro | .50 | .23 |
| ❑ 5 Trevor Doyle | .50 | .23 |
| ❑ 6 Jeff Dacosta | .40 | .18 |
| ❑ 7 Gord Walsh | .50 | .23 |
| ❑ 8 Brian Scott | .40 | .18 |
| ❑ 9 Jason Disher | .40 | .18 |
| ❑ 10 Alexander Zhurik | .40 | .18 |
| ❑ 11 Ken Boone | .40 | .18 |
| ❑ 12 Cail MacLean | .40 | .18 |
| ❑ 13 Bill Maranduik | .40 | .18 |
| ❑ 14 Martin Sychra | .40 | .18 |
| ❑ 15 Duncan Fader | .40 | .18 |
| ❑ 16 David Ling | .50 | .23 |
| ❑ 17 Chad Kilger | 1.50 | .70 |
| ❑ 18 Greg Kraemer | .40 | .18 |
| ❑ 19 Trent Cull | .50 | .23 |
| ❑ 20 Steve Parson | .40 | .18 |
| ❑ 21 Craig Rivet | .75 | .35 |
| ❑ 22 Keli Corpse | .50 | .23 |
| ❑ 23 Brett Lindros | .75 | .35 |
| ❑ 24 David Allison CO Michael Allison ACO | .10 | .05 |
| ❑ NNO Slapshot Ad Card | .10 | .05 |

## 1982-83 Kitchener Rangers

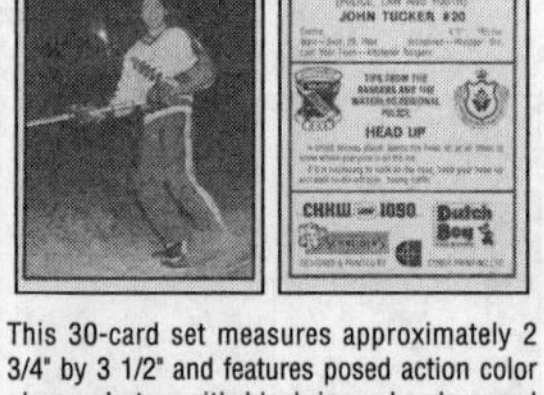

This 30-card set measures approximately 2 3/4" by 3 1/2" and features posed action color player photos with black inner borders and white outer borders. The backs are divided into three rectangular sections, each outlined by a thin black border. The upper section contains the player's name and biographical information. The middle section carries Tips from the Rangers and the Waterloo Regional Police. The bottom section contains sponsor logos.

| | MINT | EXC |
|---|---|---|
| COMPLETE SET (30) | 30.00 | 13.50 |
| COMMON CARD (1-30) | .25 | .11 |
| ❑ 1 Waterloo Regional Police Crest | .25 | .11 |
| ❑ 2 Harold Basse Chief of Police | .25 | .11 |
| ❑ 3 Sponsors' Card | .25 | .11 |
| ❑ 4 Joe Crozier GM/CO | .50 | .23 |
| ❑ 5 Checklist | .50 | .23 |
| ❑ 6 Kerry Kerch | .50 | .23 |
| ❑ 7 Tom St.James | .50 | .23 |
| ❑ 8 Wendell Young | 3.00 | 1.35 |
| ❑ 9 David Shaw | 2.00 | .90 |
| ❑ 10 Darryl Boudreau | .50 | .23 |
| ❑ 11 David Bruce | 1.00 | .45 |
| ❑ 12 Wayne Presley | 1.50 | .70 |
| ❑ 13 Garnet McKechney | .50 | .23 |
| ❑ 14 Kevin Petendra | .50 | .23 |
| ❑ 15 Brian Wilks | .50 | .23 |
| ❑ 16 Jim Quinn | .50 | .23 |
| ❑ 17 Al MacInnis | 15.00 | 6.75 |
| ❑ 18 Dave Nicholls | .50 | .23 |
| ❑ 19 Mike Eagles | 2.00 | .90 |
| ❑ 20 Mike Hough | 2.00 | .90 |
| ❑ 21 Greg Puhalski | .50 | .23 |
| ❑ 22 Darren Wright | .50 | .23 |
| ❑ 23 Todd Steffen | .50 | .23 |
| ❑ 24 John Tucker | 2.00 | .90 |
| ❑ 25 Kent Paynter | .50 | .23 |
| ❑ 26 Andy O'Brien | .50 | .23 |
| ❑ 27 Les Bradley TR | .25 | .11 |
| ❑ 28 Scott Biggs | .50 | .23 |
| ❑ 29 Chris Martin TR | .25 | .11 |
| ❑ 30 Dave Webster | .50 | .23 |

## 1983-84 Kitchener Rangers

The Kitchener Rangers of the OHL are featured in this 30-card P.L.A.Y. (Police, Law and Youth) set, which was sponsored by the Waterloo Regional Police in conjunction with several company sponsors. The cards measure approximately 2 3/4" by 3 1/2" and are printed on thin card stock. The fronts feature color photos with the players posed in action stances. The photos are framed by black and white borders, and a facsimile autograph is inscribed across the bottom of the picture. The backs have biography, safety tips, and sponsors' logos.

| | MINT | NRMT |
|---|---|---|
| COMPLETE SET (30) | 15.00 | 6.75 |
| COMMON CARD (1-30) | .25 | .11 |
| ❑ 1 Joe Mantione | 1.00 | .45 |
| ❑ 2 Jim Quinn | .50 | .23 |
| ❑ 3 Kitchener Rangers logo Checklist | .50 | .23 |
| ❑ 4 Rob MacInnis | .50 | .23 |
| ❑ 5 Louie Berardicurti | .50 | .23 |
| ❑ 6 Neil Sandilands | .50 | .23 |
| ❑ 7 Darren Wright | .50 | .23 |
| ❑ 8 Tom Barrett CO/GM | .25 | .11 |
| ❑ 9 Brian Wilks | .50 | .23 |
| ❑ 10 Garnet McKechney | .50 | .23 |
| ❑ 11 David Bruce | 1.00 | .45 |
| ❑ 12 Kent Paynter | .50 | .23 |
| ❑ 13 Sponsor's card P.L.A.Y. Rules | .25 | .11 |
| ❑ 14 Scott Kerr | .50 | .23 |
| ❑ 15 Greg Puhalski | .50 | .23 |
| ❑ 16 Wayne Presley | 1.00 | .45 |
| ❑ 17 Carmine Vani | .50 | .23 |
| ❑ 18 Shawn Burr | 2.00 | .90 |
| ❑ 19 Dave Latta | .75 | .35 |
| ❑ 20 John Tucker | 1.50 | .70 |
| ❑ 21 Mike Stevens | .50 | .23 |
| ❑ 22 Harold Basse Chief of Police | .25 | .11 |
| ❑ 23 Waterloo Regional Police | .25 | .11 |
| ❑ 24 Peter Bakovic | .50 | .23 |
| ❑ 25 Brian Ross | .50 | .23 |
| ❑ 26 Brad Balshin | .50 | .23 |
| ❑ 27 David Shaw | 1.50 | .70 |
| ❑ 28 Chris Trainer TR | .25 | .11 |
| ❑ 29 Les Bradley TR | .25 | .11 |
| ❑ 30 Ray LeBlanc | 1.50 | .70 |

## 1984-85 Kitchener Rangers

The Kitchener Rangers of the OHL are feature in this 30-card P.L.A.Y. (Police, Law an Youth) set, which was sponsored by th Waterloo Regional Police in conjunction wit several company sponsors. The card

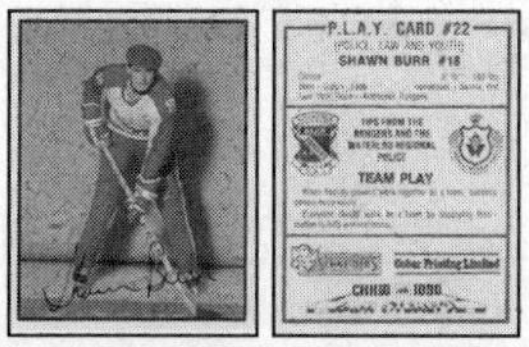


measure approximately 2 3/4" by 3 1/2" and are printed on thin card stock. The fronts feature color photos with the players posed in action stances. The photos are framed by black and white borders, and a facsimile autograph is inscribed across the bottom of the picture. The backs have biography, safety tips, and sponsors' logos.

| | MINT | NRMT |
|---|---|---|
| COMPLETE SET (30) | 10.00 | 4.50 |
| COMMON CARD (1-30) | .25 | .11 |
| ❑ 1 Waterloo Regional Police Crest | .25 | .11 |
| ❑ 2 Harold Basse Chief of Police | .25 | .11 |
| ❑ 3 Garnet McKechney | .50 | .23 |
| ❑ 4 Tom Barrett GM/CO | .25 | .11 |
| ❑ 5 Kitchener Rangers logo Checklist | .50 | .23 |
| ❑ 6 Mike Bishop | .50 | .23 |
| ❑ 7 Craig Wolanin | 1.00 | .45 |
| ❑ 8 Steve Marcolini | .50 | .23 |
| ❑ 9 Peter Langlois | .50 | .23 |
| ❑ 10 Dave Weiss | .50 | .23 |
| ❑ 11 Ken Alexander | .50 | .23 |
| ❑ 12 Ian Pound | .50 | .23 |
| ❑ 13 Doug Stromback | .50 | .23 |
| ❑ 14 Joel Brown | .50 | .23 |
| ❑ 15 Brian Wilks | .50 | .23 |
| ❑ 16 Robin Rubic | .50 | .23 |
| ❑ 17 Kent Paynter | .50 | .23 |
| ❑ 18 Jon Helinski | .50 | .23 |
| ❑ 19 Greg Puhalski | .50 | .23 |
| ❑ 20 Wayne Presley | 1.00 | .45 |
| ❑ 21 Dave McLlwain | 1.00 | .45 |
| ❑ 22 Shawn Burr | 1.00 | .45 |
| ❑ 23 Dave Latta | .60 | .25 |
| ❑ 24 John Keller | .50 | .23 |
| ❑ 25 Mike Stevens | .50 | .23 |
| ❑ 26 Sponsors' Card | .25 | .11 |
| ❑ 27 Richard Adolfi | .50 | .23 |
| ❑ 28 Grant Sanders | .50 | .23 |
| ❑ 29 Les Bradley TR | .25 | .11 |
| ❑ 30 Sponsors' Card | .25 | .11 |

## 1985-86 Kitchener Rangers

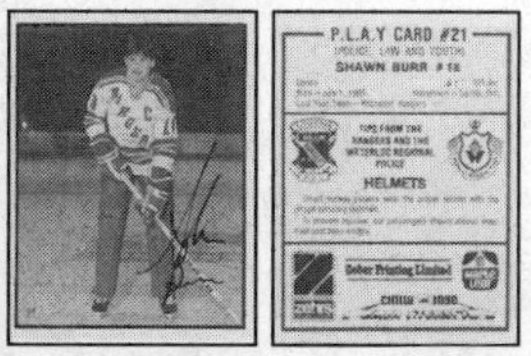


This 30-card set measures approximately 2 3/4" by 3 1/2" and is printed on thin card stock. The fronts feature posed, color player photos with thin black borders on a white card face. A facsimile autograph is inscribed across the picture. The backs carry the player's name, biographical information, and public service messages from the Rangers and the Waterloo Regional Police. The cards are numbered on the front and back.

| | MINT | NRMT |
|---|---|---|
| COMPLETE SET (30) | 10.00 | 4.50 |
| COMMON CARD (1-30) | .25 | .11 |
| ❑ 1 Waterloo Regional Police Crest | .25 | .11 |
| ❑ 2 Harold Basse Chief of Police | .25 | .11 |
| ❑ 3 Sponsors' Card | .25 | .11 |
| ❑ 4 Tom Barrett GM/CO | .25 | .11 |
| ❑ 5 Kitchener Rangers logo Checklist | .50 | .23 |
| ❑ 6 Dave Weiss | .50 | .23 |
| ❑ 7 Steve Marcolini | .50 | .23 |
| ❑ 8 Kevin Gant | .50 | .23 |
| ❑ 9 Ken Alexander | .50 | .23 |
| ❑ 10 Mike Volpe | .50 | .23 |
| ❑ 11 Ian Pound | .50 | .23 |
| ❑ 12 Brett MacDonald | .50 | .23 |
| ❑ 13 Scott Taylor | .50 | .23 |
| ❑ 14 Greg Hankkio | .50 | .23 |
| ❑ 15 Mike Morrison | .50 | .23 |
| ❑ 16 Mike Wolak | .50 | .23 |
| ❑ 17 Craig Booker | .50 | .23 |
| ❑ 18 Jeff Noble | .50 | .23 |
| ❑ 19 Shawn Tyers | .50 | .23 |
| ❑ 20 Peter Lisy | .50 | .23 |
| ❑ 21 Shawn Burr | 1.00 | .45 |
| ❑ 22 David Latta | .50 | .23 |
| ❑ 23 Ron Sanko | .50 | .23 |
| ❑ 24 Doug Jones | .50 | .23 |
| ❑ 25 Paul Penelton | .50 | .23 |
| ❑ 26 Blair MacPherson | .50 | .23 |
| ❑ 27 Richard Hawkins | .50 | .23 |
| ❑ 28 Brad Sparkes | .50 | .23 |
| ❑ 29 Ron Goodall | .50 | .23 |
| ❑ 30 Kevin Duguay TR | .25 | .11 |

## 1986-87 Kitchener Rangers

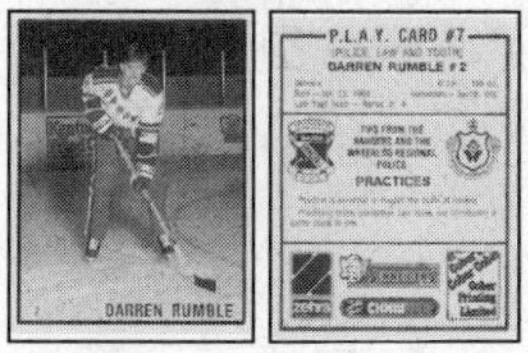


The Kitchener Rangers of the OHL are featured in this 30-card P.L.A.Y. (Police, Law and Youth) set, which was sponsored by the Waterloo Regional Police in conjunction with several corporate sponsors. The cards measure approximately 2 3/4" by 3 1/2" and are printed on thin card stock. The fronts feature color photos with the players posed in action stances. The photos are framed by black and white borders. The player's name appears in the lower right corner. The backs have biography, safety tips, and sponsors' logos. The cards are numbered on both sides.

| | MINT | NRMT |
|---|---|---|
| COMPLETE SET (30) | 8.00 | 3.60 |
| COMMON CARD (1-30) | .15 | .07 |
| ❑ 1 Waterloo Regional Police Crest | .15 | .07 |
| ❑ 2 Harold Basse Chief of Police | .15 | .07 |
| ❑ 3 Sponsor's Card | .15 | .07 |
| ❑ 4 Tom Barrett GM/CO | .15 | .07 |
| ❑ 5 Checklist | .35 | .16 |
| ❑ 6 Dave Weiss | .35 | .16 |
| ❑ 7 Darren Rumble | .50 | .23 |
| ❑ 8 Kevin Grant | .35 | .16 |
| ❑ 9 Len Fawcett | .35 | .16 |
| ❑ 10 Darren Beals | .35 | .16 |
| ❑ 11 Ed Kister | .35 | .16 |
| ❑ 12 Scott Taylor | .35 | .16 |
| ❑ 13 Darren Moxam | .35 | .16 |
| ❑ 14 Paul Epoch | .35 | .16 |
| ❑ 15 Richard Borgo | .35 | .16 |
| ❑ 16 Allan Lake | .35 | .16 |
| ❑ 17 Jeff Noble | .35 | .16 |
| ❑ 18 Mark Montanari | .35 | .16 |
| ❑ 19 Jim Hulton | .35 | .16 |
| ❑ 20 Kelly Cain | .35 | .16 |
| ❑ 21 Craig Booker | .35 | .16 |
| ❑ 22 David Latta | .50 | .23 |
| ❑ 23 Doug Jones | .35 | .16 |
| ❑ 24 Gary Callahan | .35 | .16 |
| ❑ 25 Bruno Lapensee | .35 | .16 |
| ❑ 26 Scott Montgomery TR | .15 | .07 |
| ❑ 27 Ron Goodall | .35 | .16 |
| ❑ 28 Discount Card | .15 | .07 |
| ❑ 29 Steve Ewing | .35 | .16 |
| ❑ 30 Joe McDonnell ACO | .25 | .11 |

## 1987-88 Kitchener Rangers

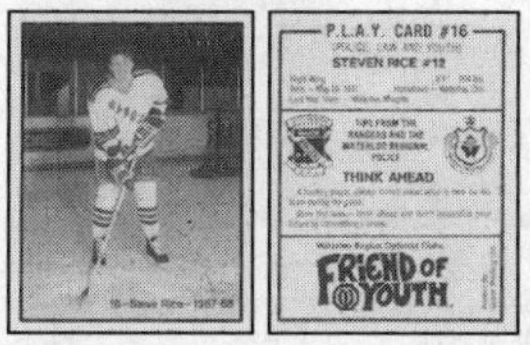


This 30-card set measures approximately 2 3/4" by 3 1/2" and was sponsored by Waterloo Region Optimist Clubs. The cards, which are printed on thin card stock, feature color posed action player photos with white borders. The card number, the player's name, and the season year appear in black print across the bottom of the photo. The backs are divided by thin black lines into three sections and carry player biography, tips from the Rangers and the Waterloo Regional Police, and the sponsor logo. The cards are numbered on both sides.

| | MINT | NRMT |
|---|---|---|
| COMPLETE SET (30) | 10.00 | 4.50 |
| COMMON CARD (1-30) | .10 | .05 |
| ❑ 1 Waterloo Regional Police Crest | .10 | .05 |
| ❑ 2 Harold Basse Chief of Police | .10 | .05 |
| ❑ 3 Children's Bonus Card | .10 | .05 |
| ❑ 4 Joe McDonnell GM/CO | .10 | .05 |
| ❑ 5 Kitchener Ranger logo Checklist | .50 | .23 |
| ❑ 6 Gus Morschauser | .75 | .35 |
| ❑ 7 Rick Allain | .50 | .23 |
| ❑ 8 Kevin Grant | .50 | .23 |
| ❑ 9 Rob Thiel | .50 | .23 |
| ❑ 10 Darren Beals | .50 | .23 |
| ❑ 11 Cory Keenan | .50 | .23 |
| ❑ 12 Rival Fullum | .50 | .23 |
| ❑ 13 Tony Crisp | .50 | .23 |
| ❑ 14 Tyler Ertel | .50 | .23 |
| ❑ 15 Richard Borgo | .50 | .23 |
| ❑ 16 Steven Rice | 1.00 | .45 |
| ❑ 17 Rob Sangster | .50 | .23 |
| ❑ 18 Jeff Noble | .50 | .23 |
| ❑ 19 Mark Montanari | .50 | .23 |
| ❑ 20 Jim Hulton | .50 | .23 |
| ❑ 21 Craig Booker | .50 | .23 |
| ❑ 22 Doug Jones | .50 | .23 |
| ❑ 23 Randy Pearce | .50 | .23 |
| ❑ 24 Darren Rumble | .75 | .35 |
| ❑ 25 Joe Ranger | .50 | .23 |
| ❑ 26 Optimist's Sponsor Card (A-K) | .10 | .05 |
| ❑ 27 Ron Goodall | .50 | .23 |
| ❑ 28 Allan Lake | .50 | .23 |
| ❑ 29 Scott Montgomery TR | .10 | .05 |
| ❑ 30 Optimist's Sponsor Card (L-W) | .10 | .05 |

## 1988-89 Kitchener Rangers

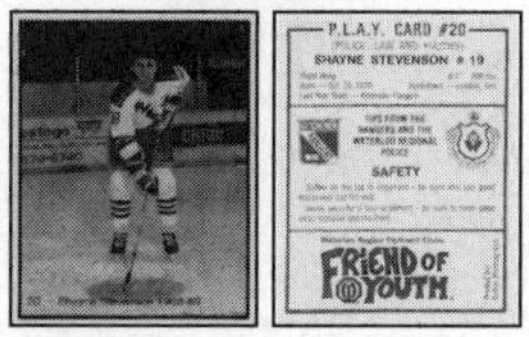


The Kitchener Rangers of the OHL are featured in this 30-card P.L.A.Y. (Police, Law and Youth) set, which was sponsored by the Waterloo Regional Police in conjunction with several area Optimist Clubs. The cards measure approximately 2 3/4" by 3 1/2" and are printed on thin card stock. The fronts feature color photos with the players posed in action stances. The photos are framed by black and white borders. The backs have biography, safety tips, and sponsors' logos. The cards are numbered on both sides.

| | MINT | NRMT |
|---|---|---|
| COMPLETE SET (30) | 10.00 | 4.50 |
| COMMON CARD (1-30) | .10 | .05 |
| ❑ 1 Waterloo Regional Police Crest | .10 | .05 |
| ❑ 2 Harold Basse Chief of Police | .10 | .05 |
| ❑ 3 Children's Bonus Card | .10 | .05 |
| ❑ 4 Joe McDonnell GM/CO | .10 | .05 |
| ❑ 5 Kitchener Rangers logo Checklist | .50 | .23 |
| ❑ 6 Mike Torchia | .75 | .35 |
| ❑ 7 Rick Allain | .50 | .23 |
| ❑ 8 John Uniac | .50 | .23 |
| ❑ 9 Rob Thiel | .50 | .23 |
| ❑ 10 Gus Morschauser | .75 | .35 |
| ❑ 11 Cory Keenan | .50 | .23 |
| ❑ 12 Rival Fullum | .50 | .23 |
| ❑ 13 Jason Firth | .50 | .23 |
| ❑ 14 Joey St. Aubin | .50 | .23 |
| ❑ 15 Richard Borgo | .50 | .23 |
| ❑ 16 Steven Rice | .75 | .35 |
| ❑ 17 Rob Sangster | .50 | .23 |
| ❑ 18 Gilbert Dionne | .75 | .35 |
| ❑ 19 Mark Montanari | .50 | .23 |
| ❑ 20 Shayne Stevenson | .50 | .23 |
| ❑ 21 Pierre Gagnon | .50 | .23 |
| ❑ 22 Kirk Tomlinson | .50 | .23 |
| ❑ 23 Randy Pearce | .50 | .23 |
| ❑ 24 Brad Barton | .50 | .23 |
| ❑ 25 Chris LiPuma | .50 | .23 |
| ❑ 26 Optimist's Sponsor's Card (A-K) | .10 | .05 |
| ❑ 27 Steve Herniman | .50 | .23 |
| ❑ 28 Darren Rumble | .50 | .23 |
| ❑ 29 Rick Chambers TR | .10 | .05 |
| ❑ 30 Optimist's Sponsor's Card (L-W) | .10 | .05 |

## 1989-90 Kitchener Rangers

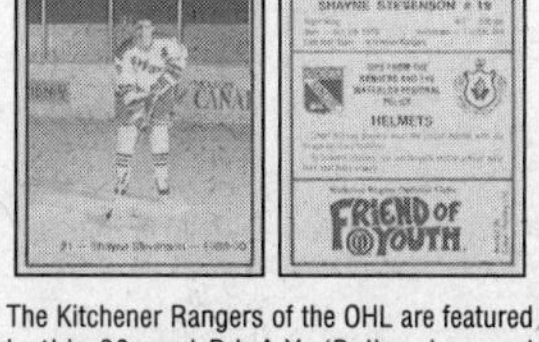


The Kitchener Rangers of the OHL are featured in this 30-card P.L.A.Y. (Police, Law and Youth) set, which was sponsored by the Waterloo Regional Police in conjunction with several area Optimist Clubs. The cards measure approximately 2 3/4" by 3 1/2" and are printed on thin card stock. The fronts feature posed color player photos inside a black picture frame and white outer borders. The backs have biography, safety tips, and sponsor logos. Most cards are numbered on both sides.

| | MINT | NRMT |
|---|---|---|
| COMPLETE SET (30) | 9.00 | 4.00 |
| COMMON CARD (1-30) | .10 | .05 |
| ❑ 1 Waterloo Regional Police Crest | .10 | .05 |
| ❑ 2 Harold Basse Chief of Police | .10 | .05 |
| ❑ 3 Children's Bonus Card | .10 | .05 |
| ❑ 4 Joe McDonnell GM/CO | .10 | .05 |
| ❑ 5 Kitchener Rangers Logo Checklist | .50 | .23 |
| ❑ 6 Mike Torchia | .75 | .35 |
| ❑ 7 Rick Allain | .50 | .23 |
| ❑ 8 John Uniac | .50 | .23 |
| ❑ 9 Jack Williams | .50 | .23 |
| ❑ 10 Dave Schill | .50 | .23 |
| ❑ 11 John Copley | .50 | .23 |
| ❑ 12 Cory Keenan | .50 | .23 |
| ❑ 13 Rival Fullum | .50 | .23 |
| ❑ 14 Jason Firth | .50 | .23 |
| ❑ 15 Joey St. Aubin | .50 | .23 |
| ❑ 16 Richard Borgo | .50 | .23 |
| ❑ 17 Steven Rice | .75 | .35 |
| ❑ 18 Rob Sangster | .50 | .23 |
| ❑ 19 Gilbert Dionne | .75 | .35 |
| ❑ 20 Jamie Israel | .50 | .23 |
| ❑ 21 Shayne Stevenson | .50 | .23 |
| ❑ 22 Gib Tucker | .50 | .23 |
| ❑ 23 Randy Pearce | .50 | .23 |
| ❑ 24 Brad Barton | .50 | .23 |
| ❑ 25 Chris Li Puma | .50 | .23 |
| ❑ 26 Optimist's Sponsors' Card (A-L) | .10 | .05 |
| ❑ 27 Kevin Falesy | .50 | .23 |
| ❑ 28 Steve Smith | .50 | .23 |
| ❑ 29 Rick Chambers TR | .10 | .05 |
| ❑ 30 Optimist's Sponsors' Card (M-W) | .10 | .05 |

## 1990-91 Kitchener Rangers

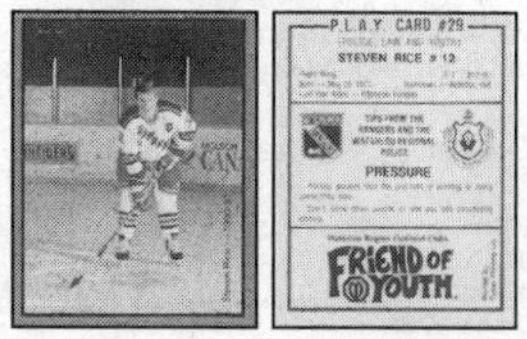


The Kitchener Rangers of the OHL are featured in this 30-card P.L.A.Y. (Police, Law and Youth) set, which was sponsored by the Waterloo Regional Police in conjunction with several area Optimist Clubs. The cards measure approximately 2 3/4" by 3 1/2" and are printed on thin card stock. The fronts feature color photos with the players posed in action stances. The photos are framed by black and red borders. The backs have biography, safety tips, and sponsors' logos. The cards are numbered on both sides.

| | MINT | NRMT |
|---|---|---|
| COMPLETE SET (30) | 8.00 | 3.60 |
| COMMON CARD (1-30) | .15 | .07 |
| ❑ 1 Waterloo Regional Police Crest | .10 | .05 |
| ❑ 2 Harold Basse Chief of Police | .10 | .05 |
| ❑ 3 Joe McDonnell GM/CO | .10 | .05 |
| ❑ 4 Rick Chambers TR | .10 | .05 |
| ❑ 5 Kitchener Rangers logo Checklist | .25 | .11 |
| ❑ 6 Mike Torchia | .50 | .23 |
| ❑ 7 Len DeVuono | .30 | .14 |
| ❑ 8 John Uniac | .30 | .14 |
| ❑ 9 Steve Smith | .30 | .14 |
| ❑ 10 Rob Stopar | .30 | .14 |
| ❑ 11 Tony McCabe | .30 | .14 |
| ❑ 12 Jason Firth | .30 | .14 |
| ❑ 13 Joey St. Aubin | .30 | .14 |
| ❑ 14 Richard Borgo | .30 | .14 |
| ❑ 15 Norm Dezainde | .30 | .14 |
| ❑ 16 Jeff Szeryk | .30 | .14 |
| ❑ 17 Derek Gauthier | .30 | .14 |
| ❑ 18 Jamie Israel | .30 | .14 |
| ❑ 19 Shayne McCosh | .30 | .14 |
| ❑ 20 Gib Tucker | .30 | .14 |
| ❑ 21 Paul McCallion | .30 | .14 |
| ❑ 22 Mike Allen | .30 | .14 |
| ❑ 23 Brad Barton | .30 | .14 |
| ❑ 24 Chris LiPuma | .40 | .18 |
| ❑ 25 Justin Cullen | .30 | .14 |
| ❑ 26 Optimist's Sponsor's Card (A-K) | .10 | .05 |
| ❑ 27 Rod Saarinen | .30 | .14 |
| ❑ 28 Jack Williams | .30 | .14 |
| ❑ 29 Steven Rice | .50 | .23 |
| ❑ 30 Optimist's Sponsor's Card (K-W) | .10 | .05 |

## 1993-94 Kitchener Rangers

Sponsored by Domino's Pizza and printed by Slapshot Images Ltd., this standard size 31-

card set features the Kitchener Rangers of the OHL. On a geometrical blue and red background, the fronts feature color action player photos with thin grey borders. The player's name, position and team name, as well as the producer's logo, appear on the front. The backs carry a close-up color player portrait, and biographical information, along with team and sponsor's logos.

| | MINT | NRMT |
|---|---|---|
| COMPLETE SET (31) | 9.00 | 4.00 |
| COMMON CARD (1-30) | .10 | .05 |
| ❑ 1 Eric Manlow Jason Gladney Tim Spitig Checklist | .50 | .23 |
| ❑ 2 David Belitski | .60 | .25 |
| ❑ 3 Darryl Whyte | .50 | .23 |
| ❑ 4 Greg McLean | .40 | .18 |
| ❑ 5 Jason Hughes | .40 | .18 |
| ❑ 6 Gord Dickie | .40 | .18 |
| ❑ 7 Travis Riggin | .40 | .18 |
| ❑ 8 Norm Dezainde | .40 | .18 |
| ❑ 9 Tim Spitzig | .40 | .18 |
| ❑ 10 Trevor Gallant | .40 | .18 |
| ❑ 11 Chris Pittman | .50 | .23 |
| ❑ 12 Ryan Pawluk UER (Name misspelled Pawluck on back) | .40 | .18 |
| ❑ 13 Jason Morgan | .40 | .18 |
| ❑ 14 James Boyd | .40 | .18 |
| ❑ 15 Todd Warriner | 1.00 | .45 |
| ❑ 16 Mark Donahue | .40 | .18 |
| ❑ 17 Peter Brearley | .40 | .18 |
| ❑ 18 Andrew Taylor | .40 | .18 |
| ❑ 19 Jason Gladney | .50 | .23 |
| ❑ 20 Wes Swinson | .50 | .23 |
| ❑ 21 Matt O'Dette | .40 | .18 |
| ❑ 22 Darren Schmidt | .40 | .18 |
| ❑ 23 Jason Johnson | .40 | .18 |
| ❑ 24 Eric Manlow | .60 | .25 |
| ❑ 25 Jeff Lillie | .40 | .18 |
| ❑ 26 Sergei Olympiev | .40 | .18 |
| ❑ 27 Joe McDonnell CO | .10 | .05 |
| ❑ 28 Rick Chambers TR | .10 | .05 |
| ❑ 29 Andrew Taylor Travis Riggin David Belitski Top Prospects | .40 | .18 |
| ❑ 30 Sponsor Card Domino's Pizza | .10 | .05 |
| ❑ NNO Slapshot Ad Card | .10 | .05 |

## 1994-95 Kitchener Rangers

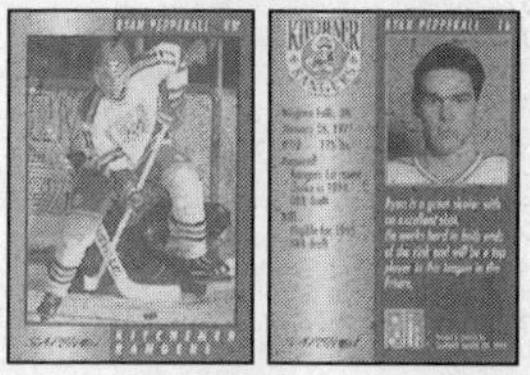


Sponsored by Domino's Pizza and printed by Slapshot Images Ltd., this 31-card set features the 1994-95 Kitchener Rangers. On a blue and red background, the fronts feature color action player photos with thin black borders. The player's name, position and team name, as well as the producer's logo, appear on the front. The backs carry a close-up color player portrait and biographical information, along with team and sponsor's logos. Included in this set is a Slapshot ad card with a 1995 calendar on the back.

| | MINT | NRMT |
|---|---|---|
| COMPLETE SET (31) | 9.00 | 4.00 |
| COMMON CARD (1-30) | .10 | .05 |
| ❑ 1 Checklist | .10 | .05 |
| ❑ 2 David Belitski | .75 | .35 |
| ❑ 3 Darryl Whyte | .50 | .23 |
| ❑ 4 Daniel Godbout | .35 | .16 |
| ❑ 5 Greg McLean | .35 | .16 |
| ❑ 6 Jason Hughes | .35 | .16 |
| ❑ 7 Jason Byrnes | .35 | .16 |
| ❑ 8 Paul Traynor | .35 | .16 |
| ❑ 9 Travis Riggin | .35 | .16 |
| ❑ 10 Tim Spitzig | .50 | .23 |
| ❑ 11 Trevor Gallant | .35 | .16 |
| ❑ 12 Chris Pittman | .50 | .23 |
| ❑ 13 Rick Emmett | .35 | .16 |
| ❑ 14 Jason Morgan | .35 | .16 |
| ❑ 15 Luch Nasato | .35 | .16 |
| ❑ 16 Ryan Pepperall | .75 | .35 |
| ❑ 17 Keith Welsh | .35 | .16 |

| | | |
|---|---|---|
| ❑ 18 Bill McGuigen | .35 | .16 |
| ❑ 19 Chris Brassard | .35 | .16 |
| ❑ 20 Andrew Taylor | .50 | .23 |
| ❑ 21 Rob Deciantis | .35 | .16 |
| ❑ 22 Wes Swinson | .50 | .23 |
| ❑ 23 Lucas Miller | .35 | .16 |
| ❑ 24 Sergei Olympiev | .35 | .16 |
| ❑ 25 Rob Maric | .35 | .16 |
| ❑ 26 Eric Manlow | .50 | .23 |
| ❑ 27 Geoff Ward CO | .10 | .05 |
| ❑ 28 Bob Ertel GM | .10 | .05 |
| ❑ 29 Rick Chambers TR<br>Dave Nicholls TR | .10 | .05 |
| ❑ 30 Sponsor Card<br>Domino's Pizza | .10 | .05 |
| ❑ NNO Ad Card | .10 | .05 |

## 1994-95 Kitchener Rangers Update

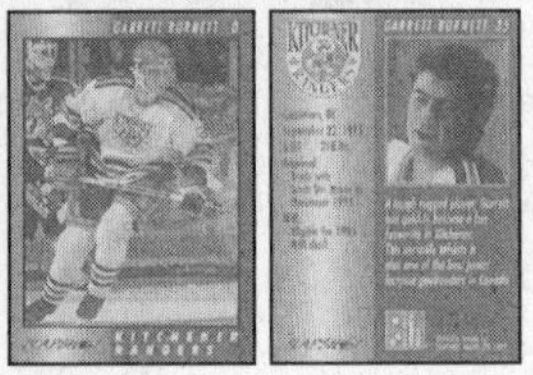

This update set has the same design as the 1994-95 Kitchener Rangers set and features players that were traded to the Rangers during the 1994-95 season. It was sold separately and also included a Slapshot ad card with a 1995 calendar on the back. The numbering is a continuation of the regular set.

| | MINT | NRMT |
|---|---|---|
| COMPLETE SET (7) | 2.00 | .90 |
| COMMON CARD (31-35) | .35 | .16 |
| ❑ 31 Brian Scott | .50 | .23 |
| ❑ 32 Robin LaCour | .35 | .16 |
| ❑ 33 Jim Ensom | .50 | .23 |
| ❑ 34 Dylan Seca | .35 | .16 |
| ❑ 35 Garrett Burnett | .35 | .16 |
| ❑ NNO Craig Bignell ACO<br>Mike Wright ACO | .35 | .16 |
| ❑ NNO Ad Card | .10 | .05 |

## 1996-97 Kitchener Rangers

| | MINT | NRMT |
|---|---|---|
| COMPLETE SET (30) | 10.00 | 4.50 |
| COMMON CARD (1-30) | .10 | .05 |
| ❑ 1 Jeff Ambrosio | .35 | .16 |
| ❑ 2 David Belitski | .35 | .16 |
| ❑ 3 Jason Byrnes | .35 | .16 |
| ❑ 4 Peter Bureaux | .35 | .16 |
| ❑ 5 Vratislav Cech | .35 | .16 |
| ❑ 6 Rob DeCiantis | .35 | .16 |
| ❑ 7 Shawn Degagne | .35 | .16 |
| ❑ 8 Boyd Devereaux | .75 | .35 |
| ❑ 9 Boyd Devereaux | .75 | .35 |
| ❑ 10 Bryan Duce | .35 | .16 |
| ❑ 11 Michal Dvorak | .35 | .16 |
| ❑ 12 Darcy Harris | .35 | .16 |
| ❑ 13 Bryan Hayton ACO | .10 | .05 |
| ❑ 14 Wes Jarvis | .35 | .16 |
| ❑ 15 Dan Lebold TR | .35 | .16 |
| ❑ 16 Adam Lewis | .35 | .16 |
| ❑ 17 Rob Marc | .35 | .16 |
| ❑ 18 Mark McMahon | .35 | .16 |
| ❑ 19 Ryan Milanovic | .35 | .16 |
| ❑ 20 Ryan Mougenel | .35 | .16 |
| ❑ 21 Serge Payer | .35 | .16 |
| ❑ 22 Ryan Pepperall | .35 | .16 |
| ❑ 23 Alan Rourke | .35 | .16 |
| ❑ 24 Rob Stanfield | .35 | .16 |
| ❑ 25 Paul Traynor | .35 | .16 |
| ❑ 26 Tim Verbeek | .35 | .16 |
| ❑ 27 Geoff Ward CO | .10 | .05 |
| ❑ 28 Keith Welsh | .35 | .16 |
| ❑ 29 Header Card | .10 | .05 |
| ❑ 30 Checklist | .10 | .05 |

## 1990-91 Knoxville Cherokees

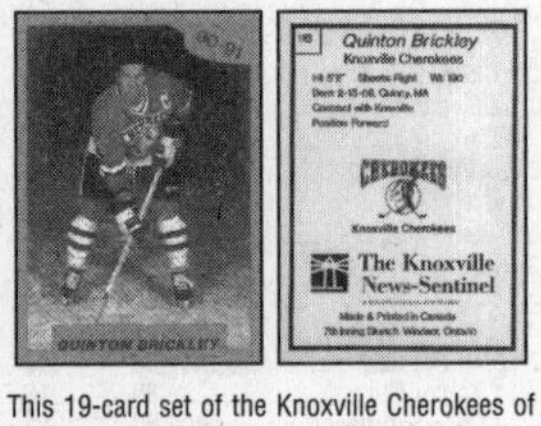

This 19-card set of the Knoxville Cherokees of the ECHL was produced by 7th Inning Sketch, and offered for sale by the team at home games. Interestingly, the set is numbered 101-119, suggesting it is the continuation of a larger (all ECHL?) set. The fronts feature a posed shot, while the backs offer limited player information and logos for the club and the Knoxville News-Sentinel.

| | MINT | NRMT |
|---|---|---|
| COMPLETE SET (19) | 9.00 | 4.00 |
| COMMON CARD (101-119) | .25 | .11 |
| ❑ 101 David Williams | .60 | .25 |
| ❑ 102 Paul Laus | .75 | .35 |
| ❑ 103 Don Jackson CO | .25 | .11 |
| ❑ 104 Steve Ryding | .50 | .23 |
| ❑ 105 Jeff Lindsay | .50 | .23 |
| ❑ 106 Daniel Gauthier | .50 | .23 |
| ❑ 107 Stan Drulia | .60 | .25 |
| ❑ 108 Mike Murray | .50 | .23 |
| ❑ 109 Tom Sasso | .50 | .23 |
| ❑ 110 Butch Kaebel | .50 | .23 |
| ❑ 111 Don McClennan | .50 | .23 |
| ❑ 112 Jamie Hanlon | .50 | .23 |
| ❑ 113 Troy Mick | .50 | .23 |
| ❑ 114 Brett Strot | .50 | .23 |
| ❑ 115 Dean Anderson | .50 | .23 |
| ❑ 116 Quinton Brickley | .50 | .23 |
| ❑ 117 Greg Batters | .50 | .23 |
| ❑ 118 Alex Daviault | .50 | .23 |
| ❑ 119 Mike Greenlay | .75 | .35 |

## 1991-92 Knoxville Cherokees

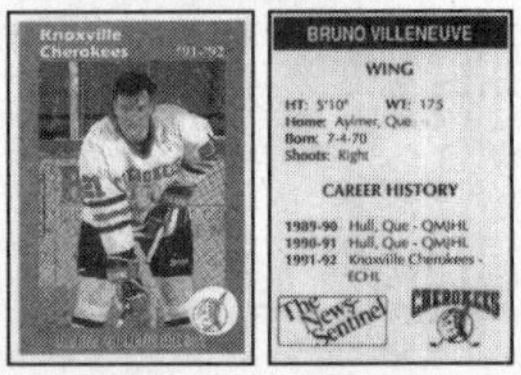

This 20-card set of the ECHL's Knoxville Cherokees was sponsored by the News-Sentinal, and offered for sale by the team at home games. The cards feature posed shots on the front; the unnumbered backs include vital statistics and a brief career history.

| | MINT | NRMT |
|---|---|---|
| COMPLETE SET (20) | 9.00 | 4.00 |
| COMMON CARD (1-20) | .10 | .05 |
| ❑ 1 Bill Nyrop CO | .50 | .23 |
| ❑ 2 Galen Head TR | .10 | .05 |
| ❑ 3 Mike Greenlay | .75 | .35 |
| ❑ 4 Karl Clauss | .75 | .35 |
| ❑ 5 Steve Ryding | .50 | .23 |
| ❑ 6 Mike Gober | .50 | .23 |
| ❑ 7 Chad Thompson | .50 | .23 |
| ❑ 8 Trevor Forsythe | .50 | .23 |
| ❑ 9 Greg Pankewicz | .50 | .23 |
| ❑ 10 David Shute | .50 | .23 |
| ❑ 11 Jamie Dabanovich | .50 | .23 |
| ❑ 12 Shawn Lillie | .50 | .23 |
| ❑ 13 Joel Gardner | .50 | .23 |
| ❑ 14 Roman Hubalek | .50 | .23 |
| ❑ 15 Bruno Villeneuve | .50 | .23 |
| ❑ 16 Troy Mick | .50 | .23 |
| ❑ 17 Dean McDonald | .50 | .23 |
| ❑ 18 Brett Lawrence | .50 | .23 |
| ❑ 19 Dean Anderson | .50 | .23 |
| ❑ 20 Robert Melanson | .50 | .23 |

## 1993-94 Knoxville Cherokees

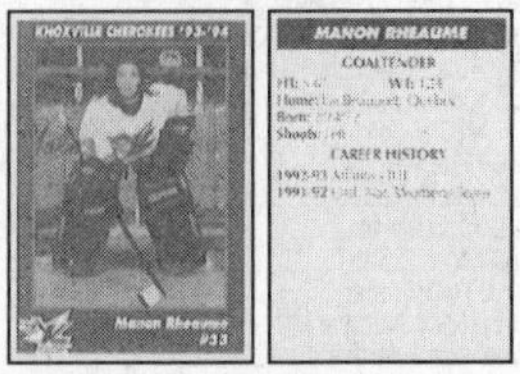

This 20-card standard-size set features the Knoxville Cherokees. On a black background with white borders, the fronts have color action and posed player photos with thin teal borders. The team name appears above the photo, while the player's name, position, and the team logo are under the photo. The white backs carry the player's name, position, biography, and career history. The cards are unnumbered and checklisted below in alphabetical order.

| | MINT | NRMT |
|---|---|---|
| COMPLETE SET (20) | 14.00 | 6.25 |
| COMMON CARD (1-20) | .25 | .11 |
| ❑ 1 Scott Boston | .40 | .18 |
| ❑ 2 Cory Cadden | .40 | .18 |
| ❑ 3 Tim Chase | .40 | .18 |
| ❑ 4 Steven Flomenhoft | .40 | .18 |
| ❑ 5 Scott Gordon | .50 | .23 |
| ❑ 6 Jon Larson | .40 | .18 |
| ❑ 7 Carl LeBlanc | .40 | .18 |
| ❑ 8 Kim Maier | .40 | .18 |
| ❑ 9 Wes McCauley | .40 | .18 |
| ❑ 10 Scott Metcalfe | .40 | .18 |
| ❑ 11 Mike Murray | .40 | .18 |
| ❑ 12 Hayden O'Rear | .40 | .18 |
| ❑ 13 Jeff Reid | .40 | .18 |
| ❑ 14 Manon Rheaume | 8.00 | 3.60 |
| ❑ 15 Marc Rodgers | .40 | .18 |
| ❑ 16 Doug Searle | .40 | .18 |
| ❑ 17 Barry Smith CO | .25 | .11 |
| ❑ 18 Martin Tanguay | .50 | .23 |
| ❑ 19 Nicholas Vachon | .50 | .23 |
| ❑ 20 Bruno Villeneuve | .40 | .18 |

## 1994-95 Knoxville Cherokees

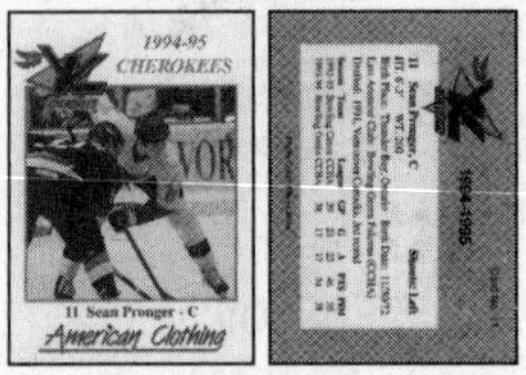

This 24-card set of the Knoxville Cherokees of the ECHL was issued by the team and available at home games.

| | MINT | NRMT |
|---|---|---|
| COMPLETE SET (24) | 7.00 | 3.10 |
| COMMON CARD (1-24) | .10 | .05 |
| ❑ 1 Checklist | .10 | .05 |
| ❑ 2 Barry Smith CO | .10 | .05 |
| ❑ 3 Aaron Fackler TR | .10 | .05 |
| ❑ 4 Andy Davis ANN | .10 | .05 |
| ❑ 5 Stephane Menard | .35 | .16 |
| ❑ 6 Doug Searle | .35 | .16 |
| ❑ 7 Hayden O'Rear | .35 | .16 |
| ❑ 8 Sean Brown | .35 | .16 |
| ❑ 9 Mike Murray | .35 | .16 |
| ❑ 10 Jon Jenkins | .35 | .16 |
| ❑ 11 Sean Pronger | .75 | .35 |
| ❑ 12 Steven Flomenhoft | .35 | .16 |
| ❑ 13 David Neilson | .35 | .16 |
| ❑ 14 Jack Callahan | .35 | .16 |
| ❑ 15 Carl LeBlanc | .35 | .16 |
| ❑ 16 Alain Deeks | .50 | .23 |
| ❑ 17 George Zajankala | .35 | .16 |
| ❑ 18 Chris Fess | .35 | .16 |
| ❑ 19 Michel Gaul | .35 | .16 |
| ❑ 20 Pat Murray | .35 | .16 |
| ❑ 21 Robb McIntyre | .35 | .16 |
| ❑ 22 Vaclav Nedomansky, Jr | .35 | .16 |
| ❑ 23 Cory Cadden | .35 | .16 |
| ❑ 24 Michael Burman | .35 | .16 |

## 1991-92 Lake Superior State Lakers

This 33-card standard-size set features the 1992 NCAA Champion Lake Superior State Lakers. The cards feature color, action player photos with gradated blue borders. The player's name and the Lakers logo appears below the picture. The backs carry black-and-white close-up photos along with biographical information, quick facts, and statistics. The cards are unnumbered and checklisted below in alphabetical order.

| | MINT | NRMT |
|---|---|---|
| COMPLETE SET (33) | 12.00 | 5.50 |
| COMMON CARD (1-33) | .35 | .16 |
| ❑ 1 Team Photo<br>1992 NCAA Champions | .50 | .23 |
| ❑ 2 Team Photo<br>1992 CCHA Champions | .50 | .23 |
| ❑ 3 Keith Aldridge | .35 | .16 |
| ❑ 4 Dan Angelelli | .35 | .16 |
| ❑ 5 Mark Astley | .50 | .23 |
| ❑ 6 Mike Bachusz | .35 | .16 |
| ❑ 7 Steven Barnes | .35 | .16 |
| ❑ 8 Clayton Beddoes | .50 | .23 |
| ❑ 9 David Gartshore | .35 | .16 |
| ❑ 10 Tim Hanley | .35 | .16 |
| ❑ 11 Matt Hansen | .35 | .16 |
| ❑ 12 John Hendry | .35 | .16 |
| ❑ 13 Dean Hulett | .35 | .16 |
| ❑ 14 Jeff Jackson | .50 | .23 |
| ❑ 15 Blaine Lacher | 1.00 | .45 |
| ❑ 16 Darrin Madeley | 1.00 | .45 |
| ❑ 17 Mike Matteucci | .35 | .16 |
| ❑ 18 Scott McCabe | .35 | .16 |
| ❑ 19 Kurt Miller | .35 | .16 |
| ❑ 20 Mike Morin | .35 | .16 |
| ❑ 21 Jay Ness | .35 | .16 |
| ❑ 22 Gino Pulente | .35 | .16 |
| ❑ 23 Brian Rolston | 1.50 | .70 |
| ❑ 24 Paul Sass | .35 | .16 |
| ❑ 25 Michael Smith | .35 | .16 |
| ❑ 26 Wayne Strachan | .35 | .16 |
| ❑ 27 Sean Tallaire | .50 | .23 |
| ❑ 28 Adam Thompson | .35 | .16 |
| ❑ 29 Jason Trzcinski | .35 | .16 |
| ❑ 30 Rob Valicevic | .35 | .16 |
| ❑ 31 Jason Welch | .35 | .16 |
| ❑ 32 Darren Wetherill | .35 | .16 |
| ❑ 33 Brad Willner | .35 | .16 |

## 1993-94 Las Vegas Thunder

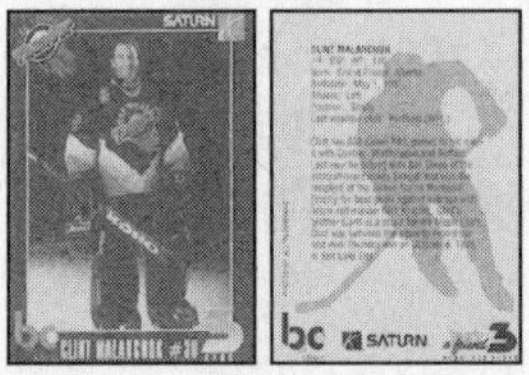

Sponsored by Saturn, bc and More, and KVBC (Channel 3), this 32-card standard-size set features the 1993-94 Las Vegas Thunder of the IHL. On a black card face, the fronts have posed color player photos with thin white borders. The player's name and number appear under the picture. The team and sponsor logos are printed in the four corners. The backs carry a player biography, profile and sponsor logos. The cards are unnumbered and checklisted below in alphabetical order. This set may also have been issued as a perforated sheet.

| | MINT | NRMT |
|---|---|---|
| COMPLETE SET (32) | 8.00 | 3.60 |
| COMMON CARD (1-32) | .10 | .05 |
| ❑ 1 Brent Ashton | .40 | .18 |
| ❑ 2 Boom Boom (Mascot) | .10 | .05 |
| ❑ 3 Bob Bourne CO | .40 | .18 |
| ❑ 4 Rod Buskas | .25 | .11 |
| ❑ 5 Lyndon Byers | .40 | .18 |
| ❑ 6 Rich Campbell TR | .10 | .05 |
| ❑ 7 Colin Cowherd ANN | .10 | .05 |
| ❑ 8 Butch Goring CO | .40 | .18 |
| ❑ 9 Steve Gotaas | .25 | .11 |
| ❑ 10 Marc Habscheid | .25 | .11 |
| ❑ 11 Brett Hauer | .25 | .11 |
| ❑ 12 Shawn Heaphy | .25 | .11 |
| ❑ 13 Scott Hollis | .25 | .11 |
| ❑ 14 Peter Ing | .40 | .18 |
| ❑ 15 Steve Jaques | .25 | .11 |
| ❑ 16 Bob Joyce | .25 | .11 |
| ❑ 17 Jim Kyte | .25 | .11 |
| ❑ 18 Patrice Lefebvre | .50 | .23 |
| ❑ 19 Clint Malarchuk | .50 | .23 |
| ❑ 20 Ken Quinney | .25 | .11 |
| ❑ 21 Jean-Marc Richard | .25 | .11 |
| ❑ 22 Todd Richards | .25 | .11 |
| ❑ 23 Marc Rodgers | .25 | .11 |
| ❑ 24 Jeff Sharples | .25 | .11 |
| ❑ 25 Randy Smith | .25 | .11 |
| ❑ 26 Greg Spenrath | .25 | .11 |
| ❑ 27 Bob Strumm GM | .10 | .05 |
| ❑ 28 Kirk Tomlinson | .25 | .11 |
| ❑ 29 Kerry Toporowski | .40 | .18 |
| ❑ 30 Mark Vermette | .25 | .11 |
| ❑ 31 Steve Wissman EQMG | .10 | .05 |
| ❑ 32 Title Card | .10 | .05 |

## 1994-95 Las Vegas Thunder

This 29-card standard-size set was manufactured and distributed by Jessen Associates, Inc. for Classic. The fronts display color action player photos with a teal marbleized inner border and a black outer border. The player's name, jersey number, and position appear in the teal border on the right edge. Inside a black border on a marbleized background, the backs present biography, statistics, and sponsor logos. The cards are unnumbered and checklisted below in alphabetical order.

| | MINT | NRMT |
|---|---|---|
| COMPLETE SET (29) | 12.00 | 5.50 |
| COMMON CARD (1-29) | .10 | .05 |
| ❑ 1 James Black | .35 | .16 |
| ❑ 2 Radek Bonk | 1.00 | .45 |
| ❑ 3 Boom Boom (Mascot) | .10 | .05 |
| ❑ 4 Rich Campbell<br>Athletic Therapist | .10 | .05 |
| ❑ 5 Frank Evans | .25 | .11 |
| ❑ 6 Marc Habscheid | .25 | .11 |
| ❑ 7 Alex Hicks | .50 | .23 |
| ❑ 8 Bob Joyce | .25 | .11 |
| ❑ 9 Jim Kyte | .25 | .11 |
| ❑ 10 Lark and Craig, DJs | .10 | .05 |
| ❑ 11 Patrice Lefebvre | .50 | .23 |
| ❑ 12 Darcy Loewen | .25 | .11 |
| ❑ 13 Sal Lombardi EQMG | .10 | .05 |
| ❑ 14 Clint Malarchuk | .50 | .23 |
| ❑ 15 Andrew McBain | .25 | .11 |
| ❑ 16 Chris McSorley CO | .25 | .11 |
| ❑ 17 David Neilson | .25 | .11 |
| ❑ 18 Jerry Olenyn | .25 | .11 |
| ❑ 19 Ken Quinney | .25 | .11 |
| ❑ 20 Pokey Reddick | .35 | .16 |
| ❑ 21 Jeff Reid | .25 | .11 |
| ❑ 22 Manon Rheaume | 5.00 | 2.20 |
| ❑ 23 Jean-Marc Richard | .25 | .11 |
| ❑ 24 Todd Richards | .25 | .11 |
| ❑ 25 Marc Rodgers | .25 | .11 |
| ❑ 26 Jeff Sharples | .25 | .11 |
| ❑ 27 Jarrod Skalde | .25 | .11 |
| ❑ 28 Bob Strumm GM/CO | .10 | .05 |
| ❑ 29 Kerry Toporowski | .25 | .11 |

## 1995-96 Las Vegas Thunder

This 26-card set of the Las Vegas Thunder of the IHL was produced by Split Second for Collector's Edge Ice. The set was available through the team at home games and by mail. The fronts feature action photography; the backs have player information. The cards are unnumbered, so are listed alphabetically. The set is notable for containing 1996 Anaheim first rounder Ruslan Salei, as well as bright NHL prospect Bill Bowler.

| | MINT | NRMT |
|---|---|---|
| COMPLETE SET (26) | 10.00 | 4.50 |
| COMMON CARD (1-26) | .10 | .05 |
| ❑ 1 Bill Bowler | .60 | .25 |
| ❑ 2 Peter Fiorentino | .35 | .16 |
| ❑ 3 Greg Hawgood | .50 | .23 |
| ❑ 4 Sasha Lakovic | .35 | .16 |
| ❑ 5 Patrice Lefebvre | .75 | .35 |
| ❑ 6 Darcy Loewen | .35 | .16 |
| ❑ 7 Gord Marx | .35 | .16 |
| ❑ 8 Blaine Moore | .35 | .16 |
| ❑ 9 Vaclav Nedomansky, Jr | .35 | .16 |
| ❑ 10 Pokey Reddick | .75 | .35 |
| ❑ 11 Jeff Ricciardi | .35 | .16 |
| ❑ 12 Jean-Marc Richard | .35 | .16 |
| ❑ 13 Marc Rodgers | .35 | .16 |
| ❑ 14 Chris Rogles | .75 | .35 |
| ❑ 15 Ken Quinney | .35 | .16 |
| ❑ 16 Ruslan Salei | .75 | .35 |
| ❑ 17 Jeff Sharples | .35 | .16 |
| ❑ 18 Daniel Shank | .60 | .25 |
| ❑ 19 Todd Simon | .35 | .16 |
| ❑ 20 Rhett Trombley | .50 | .23 |
| ❑ 21 Vladimir Tsyplakov | .75 | .35 |
| ❑ 22 Sergei Zholtok | .60 | .25 |
| ❑ 23 Chris McSorley CO | .10 | .05 |
| ❑ 24 Clint Malarchuk AGM | .35 | .16 |
| ❑ 25 Bob Strumm GM | .10 | .05 |
| ❑ 26 BoomBoom | .10 | .05 |

## 1996-97 Las Vegas Thunder

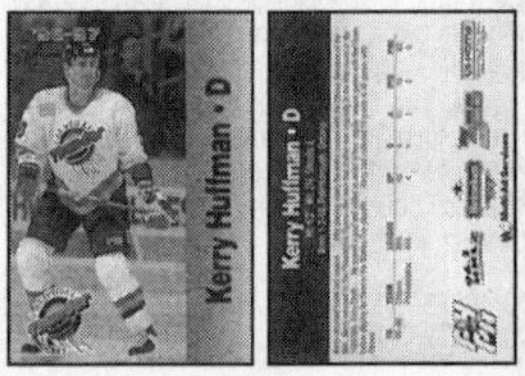

This 24-card set of the Las Vegas Thunder of the IHL was produced by Multi-Ad Services and sponsored by Heineken and U.S. Home, among others. The cards were sold by the team at the rink or through the mail. The fronts feature color action photos, with the player's name in a light teal bar along the right border. The backs feature statistical and biographical data. The cards are unnumbered, and are listed below alphabetically.

| | MINT | NRMT |
|---|---|---|
| COMPLETE SET (24) | 10.00 | 4.50 |
| COMMON CARD | .10 | .05 |
| ❑ 1 Egor Bashkatov | .50 | .23 |
| ❑ 2 Boom Boom(Mascot) | .25 | .11 |
| ❑ 3 Kevin Dahl | .50 | .23 |
| ❑ 4 Chris Dahlquist | .50 | .23 |
| ❑ 5 Pavol Demitra | .75 | .35 |
| ❑ 6 Parris Duffus | .75 | .35 |
| ❑ 7 Martin Gendron | .50 | .23 |
| ❑ 8 Brent Gretzky | .50 | .23 |
| ❑ 9 Kerry Huffman | .50 | .23 |
| ❑ 10 Igor Karpenko | .75 | .35 |
| ❑ 11 Don Larner | .50 | .23 |
| ❑ 12 Patrice Lefebvre | .75 | .35 |
| ❑ 13 Darcy Loewen | .50 | .23 |
| ❑ 14 Clint Malarchuk AGM | .25 | .11 |

❑ 15 Chris McSorley CO .25 .11
❑ 16 Blaine Moore .50 .23
❑ 17 Ken Quinney .50 .23
❑ 18 Jeff Serowik .50 .23
❑ 19 Jason Simon .50 .23
❑ 20 Bob Strumm GM .25 .11
❑ 21 Rhett Trombley .50 .23
❑ 22 Sergei Yerkovich .50 .23
❑ 23 Sergei Zholtok .75 .35
❑ 24 Logo Card .10 .05

## 1998-99 Las Vegas Thunder

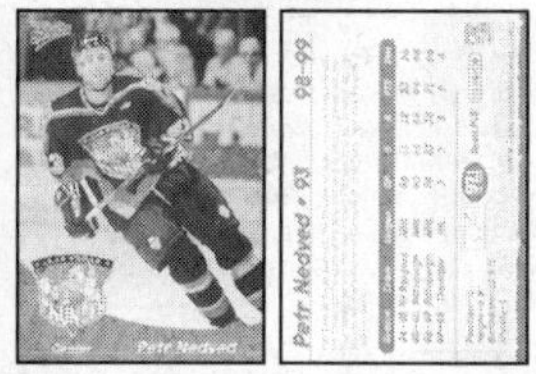

| | MINT | NRMT |
|---|---|---|
| COMPLETE SET (30) | 5.00 | 2.20 |
| COMMON CARD (1-30) | .10 | .05 |

❑ 1 Drew Bannister .10 .05
❑ 2 Sean Berens .10 .05
❑ 3 Dampy Brar .10 .05
❑ 4 Dean Ewen .10 .05
❑ 5 Petr Franek .10 .05
❑ 6 Brad Guzda .10 .05
❑ 7 Sami Helenius .10 .05
❑ 8 Bryan Helmer .10 .05
❑ 9 Scott Hollis .10 .05
❑ 10 Kevin Kaminski .10 .05
❑ 11 Patrice Lefebvre .10 .05
❑ 12 Jason McBain .10 .05
❑ 13 Taj Melson .10 .05
❑ 14 Brad Miller .10 .05
❑ 15 Nick Naumenko .10 .05
❑ 16 Petr Nedved 2.00 .90
❑ 17 Trevor Roenick .30 .14
❑ 18 Russ Romaniuk .10 .05
❑ 19 Konstantin Simchuk .10 .05
❑ 20 Andrei Srubko .10 .05
❑ 21 Stefan Ustorf .10 .05
❑ 22 Shawn Wansborough .10 .05
❑ 23 Mike Wilson .10 .05
❑ 24 Bob Strumm GM .10 .05
❑ 25 Bob Bourne CO .10 .05
❑ 26 Rod Buskas ACO .10 .05
❑ 27 Van Parfet TR .10 .05
❑ 28 Bubba Kennedy .10 .05
Richard Krouse EQ
❑ 29 BoomBoom Mascot .10 .05
❑ 30 Logo Card .10 .05

## 1988-89 Lethbridge Hurricanes

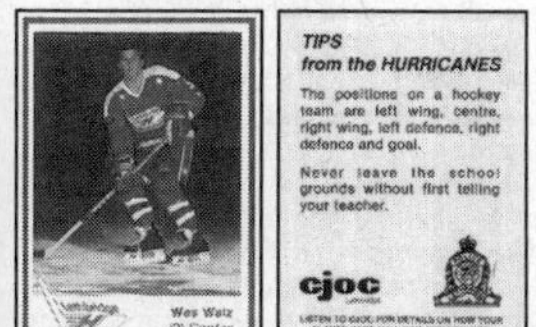


This 24-card set was issued in 12 strips of three perforated cards with the third card on each strip being an ad or coupon card. The strips measure approximately 7 1/2" by 3 1/2". The fronts feature color posed player photos with a heavy black line framing the edge of the card leaving white space between the line and the picture. The team name, player's name, jersey number, and position appear in the white margin at the bottom. The backs carry "Tips from the Hurricanes," which are hockey tips and public service messages. The cards are unnumbered and checklisted below in alphabetical order.

| | MINT | NRMT |
|---|---|---|
| COMPLETE SET (24) | 9.00 | 4.00 |
| COMMON CARD (1-24) | .35 | .16 |

❑ 1 Mark Bassen .50 .23
❑ 2 Pete Berthelsen .35 .16
❑ 3 Bryan Bosch .35 .16
❑ 4 Paul Checknita .35 .16
❑ 5 Kelly Ens .35 .16
❑ 6 Jeff Ferguson .35 .16
❑ 7 Scott Fukami .35 .16
❑ 8 Colin Gregor .35 .16
❑ 9 Mark Greig .75 .35
❑ 10 Rob Hale .35 .16
❑ 11 Ted Hutchings .35 .16
❑ 12 Dusty Imoo .50 .23
❑ 13 Ivan Jessey .35 .16
❑ 14 Mark Kuntz .35 .16
❑ 15 Corey Lyons .35 .16
❑ 16 Shane Mazutinec .35 .16
❑ 17 Casey McMillan .35 .16
❑ 18 Pat Pylypuik .35 .16
❑ 19 Brad Rubachuk .35 .16
❑ 20 Jason Ruff .35 .16
❑ 21 Chad Seibel .35 .16
❑ 22 Wes Walz .75 .35
❑ 23 Jim Wheatcroft .35 .16
❑ 24 Team Picture .50 .23

## 1989-90 Lethbridge Hurricanes

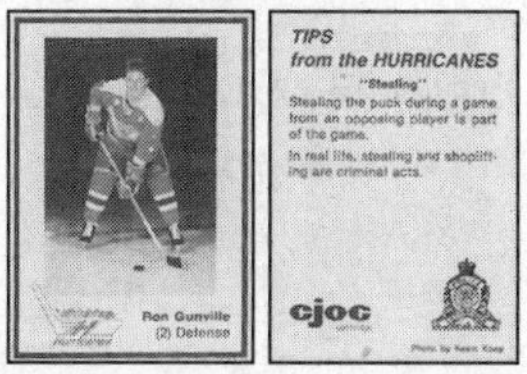


Showing signs of perforation, this 24-card set was issued in strips of several cards each. The cards measure the standard size when separated and feature posed, color player photos. The photos are set on a white card face with a heavy black line framing the edge of the card, leaving white space between the line and the picture. The player's name, jersey number, and position appear in the white margin at the bottom. The backs carry "Tips from the Hurricanes," which are hockey tips and public service messages. The cards are unnumbered and checklisted below in alphabetical order.

| | MINT | NRMT |
|---|---|---|
| COMPLETE SET (24) | 9.00 | 4.00 |
| COMMON CARD (1-24) | .25 | .11 |

❑ 1 Doug Barrault .50 .23
❑ 2 Peter Berthelsen .50 .23
❑ 3 Bryan Bosch .50 .23
❑ 4 Kelly Ens .50 .23
❑ 5 Mark Greig .75 .35
❑ 6 Ron Gunville .50 .23
❑ 7 Rob Hale .50 .23
❑ 8 Neil Hawryluk .50 .23
❑ 9 David Holzer .50 .23
❑ 10 Dusty Imoo .75 .35
❑ 11 Darcy Kaminski ACO .25 .11
❑ 12 Bob Loucks CO .25 .11
❑ 13 Corey Lyons .50 .23
❑ 14 Duane Maruschak .50 .23
❑ 15 Jamie McLennan 1.00 .45
❑ 16 Shane Peacock .50 .23
❑ 17 Pat Pylypuik .50 .23
❑ 18 Gary Reilly .50 .23
❑ 19 Brad Rubachuk .50 .23
❑ 20 Jason Ruff .50 .23
❑ 21 Kevin St. Jacques .50 .23
❑ 22 Wes Walz .75 .35
❑ 23 Darcy Werenka 1.00 .45
❑ 24 Brad Zimmer .50 .23

## 1993-94 Lethbridge Hurricanes

This 24-card set was issued on three-card perforated strips each consisting of two player cards and one advertisement or coupon card. The strips measure 7 1/2" by 3 1/2", and if cut, the individual cards would measure the standard size. The fronts of each card feature a color posed player photo with thin red borders on a white background. The player's name, number, and position and the team name appear under the photo. The backs carry 1992-93 season statistics, anti-drug messages, and sponsor logos. The cards are unnumbered and checklisted below in alphabetical order.

| | MINT | NRMT |
|---|---|---|
| COMPLETE SET (24) | 12.00 | 5.50 |
| COMMON CARD (1-24) | .10 | .05 |

❑ 1 Rob Daum CO .25 .11
❑ 2 Kirk DeWaele .50 .23
❑ 3 Derek Diener .50 .23
❑ 4 Scott Grieco .50 .23
❑ 5 David Jesiolowski .50 .23
❑ 6 Todd MacIsaac .50 .23
❑ 7 Stan Matwijiw .60 .25
❑ 8 Larry McMorran .50 .23
❑ 9 Brad Mehalko .50 .23
❑ 10 Shane Peacock .50 .23
❑ 11 Randy Perry .60 .25
❑ 12 Domenic Pittis .50 .23
❑ 12 Byron Ritchie .75 .35
❑ 14 Bryce Salvador .50 .23
❑ 15 Ryan Smith .50 .23
❑ 16 Lee Sorochan 1.00 .45
❑ 17 Mark Szoke .50 .23
❑ 18 Scott Townsend .50 .23
❑ 19 David Trofimenkoff .60 .25
❑ 20 Twister (Mascot) .10 .05
❑ 21 Ivan Vologjaninov .60 .25
❑ 22 Jason Widmer .75 .35
❑ 23 Derek Wood .50 .23
❑ 24 Aaron Zarowny .50 .23

## 1995-96 Lethbridge Hurricanes

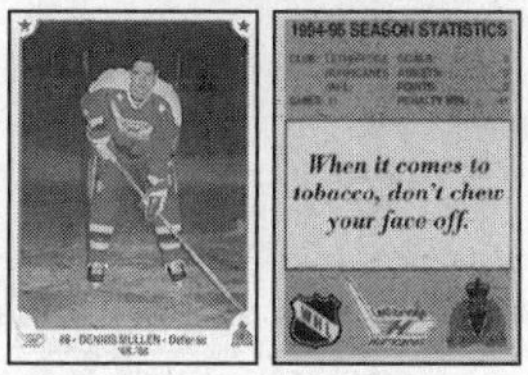


This 25-card set was issued on three-card perforated strips measuring approximately 7 1/2" by 3 1/2". Each strip consists of two player cards and one advertisement card. The cards include player jersey numbers on the front, but are checklisted below alphabetically.

| | MINT | NRMT |
|---|---|---|
| COMPLETE SET (25) | 10.00 | 4.50 |
| COMMON CARD (25) | .10 | .05 |

❑ 1 Mike Bayrack .35 .16
❑ 2 John Bradley .35 .16
❑ 3 Travis Brigley .60 .25
❑ 4 David Brumby .35 .16
❑ 5 Derek Diener .35 .16
❑ 6 Scott Grieco .35 .16
❑ 7 Lee Hamilton .35 .16
❑ 8 Trevor Hanas .35 .16
❑ 9 Ryan Hoople .35 .16
❑ 10 Mike Josephson .50 .23
❑ 11 Kirby Law .50 .23
❑ 12 Bryan Maxwell CO .10 .05
❑ 13 Doyle McMorris .35 .16
❑ 14 Brad Mehalko .75 .35
❑ 15 Dennis Mullen .35 .16
❑ 16 Jiri Novotny .35 .16
❑ 17 Mike O'Grady .35 .16
❑ 18 Randy Perry .35 .16
❑ 19 Byron Ritchie .75 .35
❑ 20 Bryce Salvador .35 .16
❑ 21 Darren Shakotto .35 .16
❑ 22 Mark Smith .35 .16
❑ 23 Dave Taylor .35 .16
❑ 24 Luc Theoret .60 .25
❑ 25 Windy Whiskers(Mascot) .10 .05

## 1996-97 Lethbridge Hurricanes

This 24-card set features color player photos with the club's nickname serving as a design element along the right border. The player's name and number, along with the team's anniversary logo also are featured. The backs include a color mug shot, player stats and bio information.The unnumbered cards are checklisted below alphabetically.

| | MINT | NRMT |
|---|---|---|
| COMPLETE SET (24) | 12.00 | 5.50 |
| COMMON CARD (1-24) | .25 | .11 |

❑ 1 Travis Brigley .75 .35
❑ 2 David Cameron .50 .23
❑ 3 Matt Demarski .50 .23
❑ 4 Paul Elliott .50 .23
❑ 5 Jason Hegberg .75 .35
❑ 6 Martin Hohenberger .75 .35
❑ 7 Ryan Hoople .75 .35
❑ 8 Mark Ivan .50 .23
❑ 9 Mike Josephson .50 .23
❑ 10 Kirby Law .60 .25
❑ 11 Mike O'Grady .50 .23
❑ 12 Dale Purinton .60 .25
❑ 13 Byron Ritchie 1.00 .45
❑ 14 Bryce Salvador .50 .23
❑ 15 Richard Seeley .50 .23
❑ 16 Cam Severson .50 .23
❑ 17 Darren Shakotto .50 .23
❑ 18 Wes Schneider .75 .35
❑ 19 Parry Shockey CO .25 .11
Bryan Maxwell GM
❑ 20 Mark Smith .50 .23
❑ 21 Dave Taylor .50 .23
❑ 22 Luc Theoret .75 .35
❑ 23 Evgeni Tsybouk .50 .23
❑ 24 Shane Yellowhorn .50 .23

## 1985-86 London Knights

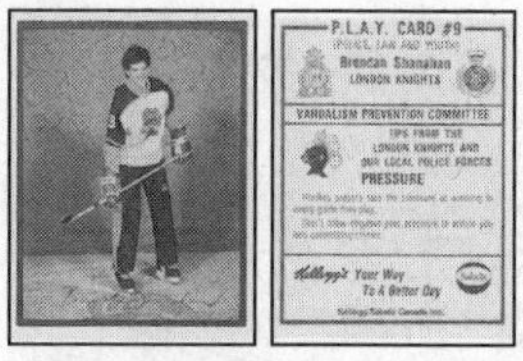


The London Knights of the OHL are featured in this 30-card P.L.A.Y. (Police, Law and Youth) set, which was sponsored by the London Crime Prevention Committee in conjunction with area businesses. The cards measure approximately 2 3/4" by 3 1/2" and are printed on thin card stock. The fronts feature color photos with the players posed in action stances. A facsimile autograph is inscribed at the bottom of the picture. The photos are framed by black and white borders. The backs have the player's name, safety tips, and sponsors' logos.

| | MINT | NRMT |
|---|---|---|
| COMPLETE SET (30) | 50.00 | 22.00 |
| COMMON CARD (1-30) | .25 | .11 |

❑ 1 LaVerne Shipley .25 .11
Chief of Police
❑ 2 Joe Ranger .50 .23
❑ 3 Kellogg's Ad .50 .23
Checklist
❑ 4 Don Boyd GM/CO .25 .11
❑ 5 Harry E. Sparling .25 .11
Superintendent
❑ 6 Murray Nystrom .50 .23
❑ 7 Bob Halkidis 1.00 .45
❑ 8 Morgan Watts .50 .23
❑ 9 Brendan Shanahan 40.00 18.00
❑ 10 Brian Dobbin .75 .35
❑ 11 Ed Kister .50 .23
❑ 12 Darin Smith .50 .23
❑ 13 Greg Puhalski .50 .23
❑ 14 Dave Haas .50 .23
❑ 15 Pete McLeod .50 .23
❑ 16 Frank Tremblay .50 .23
❑ 17 Matthew Smyth .50 .23
❑ 18 Glen Leslie .50 .23
❑ 19 Mike Zombo .50 .23
❑ 20 Jamie Groke .50 .23
❑ 21 Brad Schlegel .75 .35
❑ 22 Kelly Cain .50 .23
❑ 23 Tom Allen .50 .23
❑ 24 Rod Gerow .50 .23
❑ 25 Pat Vachon .50 .23
❑ 26 Paul Cook ACO .25 .11
❑ 27 Jeff Reese 1.50 .70
❑ 28 Fred Kean .25 .11
Dir. of PR/Marketing
❑ 29 Scott Cumming .50 .23
❑ 30 John Williams ACO .25 .11

## 1986-87 London Knights

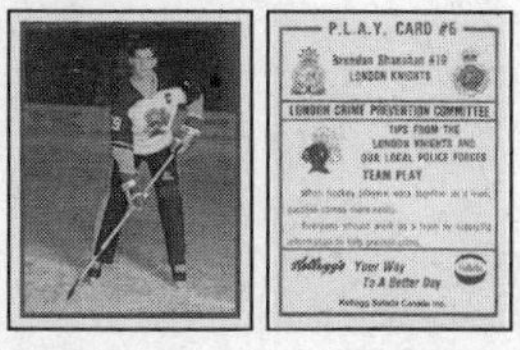


The London Knights of the OHL are featured in this 30-card P.L.A.Y. (Police, Law and Youth) set, which was sponsored by the London Crime Prevention Committee in conjunction with area businesses. The cards measure approximately 2 3/4" by 3 1/2" and are printed on thin card stock. The fronts feature color photos with the players posed in action stances. The photos are framed by black and white borders. The backs have biography, safety tips, and sponsors' logos.

| | MINT | NRMT |
|---|---|---|
| COMPLETE SET (30) | 35.00 | 16.00 |
| COMMON CARD (1-30) | .25 | .11 |

❑ 1 LaVerne Shipley .25 .11
Chief of Police
❑ 2 Tom Gosnell (Mayor) .25 .11
❑ 3 Kellogg's Ad .50 .23
Checklist
❑ 4 Wayne Maxner CO/GM .50 .23
❑ 5 Harry E. Sparling .25 .11
Superintendent
❑ 6 Brendan Shanahan 25.00 11.00
❑ 7 Pat Vachon .50 .23
❑ 8 Brad Schlegel .50 .23
❑ 9 Barry Earhart .50 .23
❑ 10 Jean Marc MacKenzie .50 .23
❑ 11 Jason Simon .50 .23
❑ 12 Jim Sprott .50 .23
❑ 13 Bill Long VP .25 .11
❑ 14 Murray Nystrom .50 .23
❑ 15 Shayne Stevenson .50 .23
❑ 16 Don Martin .50 .23
❑ 17 Ian Pound .50 .23
❑ 18 Peter Lisy .50 .23
❑ 19 Steve Marcolini .50 .23
❑ 20 Craig Majaury .50 .23
❑ 21 Trevor Dam .50 .23
❑ 22 Dave Akey .50 .23
❑ 23 Dennis McEwen .50 .23
❑ 24 Shane Whelan .50 .23
❑ 25 Greg Hankkio .50 .23
❑ 26 Pat Kelly TR .25 .11
❑ 27 Stephen Titus .50 .23
❑ 28 Fred Kean .25 .11
Director of PR
and Marketing
❑ 29 Chris Somers .50 .23
❑ 30 Gord Clark MD .25 .11

## 1993-94 London Knights

This standard size set was issued at home games during the 1993-94 season. Card fronts feature posed, color photos. Card backs feature statistics and biographical information. Cards are unnumbered and checklisted below alphabetically.

| | MINT | NRMT |
|---|---|---|
| COMPLETE SET (29) | 10.00 | 4.50 |
| COMMON CARD (1-29) | .10 | .05 |

❑ 1 Jason Allison 4.00 1.80
❑ 2 Ryan Appel .40 .18
❑ 3 Tim Bacik .40 .18
❑ 4 Ryan Black .25 .11
❑ 5 Chris Brassard .25 .11
❑ 6 Ryan Burgoyne .25 .11
❑ 7 Brodie Coffin .25 .11
❑ 8 Rob Frid .25 .11
❑ 9 David Gilmore .25 .11
❑ 10 Roy Gray .25 .11
❑ 11 John Guirestante .25 .11
❑ 12 Brent Holdsworth .25 .11
❑ 13 Don Margettie .25 .11
❑ 14 Dan Reja .25 .11
❑ 15 Daryl Rivers .25 .11
❑ 16 Gord Ross .25 .11
❑ 17 Kevin Slota .25 .11
❑ 18 Brian Stacey .25 .11
❑ 19 Nick Stajduhar .40 .18
❑ 20 Bill Tibbetts .25 .11
❑ 21 Ben Walker .25 .11
❑ 22 Jordan Willis .40 .18
❑ 23 Chris Zanutto .25 .11
❑ 24 Knights Top Picks .25 .11
Ryan Appel
Ben Walker
Den Reja
Roy Gray
❑ 25 Knights Future Stars 1.00 .45
Nick Stajduhar
Jason Allison
John Guirestante
Ryan Black
Jordan Willis
❑ 26 Gary Agnew CO .10 .05
❑ 27 Steve Stoyanovich ACO .10 .05
Tom Hedican CO
❑ 28 Murray Nystrom ACO .10 .05
❑ 29 Title Card .10 .05

## 1998-99 Long Beach Ice Dogs Promo

Given out to fans who attended a Long Beach Ice Dogs game during the 1998-99 season. Sponsored by Ice Breakers gum and licensed by the Ice Dogs and the IHL.

| | MINT | NRMT |
|---|---|---|
| COMPLETE SET (1) | 40.00 | 18.00 |
| COMMON CARD | 40.00 | 18.00 |

❑ NNO Patrik Stefan 40.00 18.00

## 1995-96 Louisiana Ice Gators

This 21-card set of the Louisiana Ice Gators of the ECHL features borderless color player photos with the player's name, position, and jersey number printed in a green bar across the bottom. The backs carry player information. The cards are unnumbered and

checklisted below in alphabetical order. This is the first of two sets released by the Ice Gators in 1995-96, their inaugural season.

| | MINT | NRMT |
|---|---|---|
| COMPLETE SET (21) | 9.00 | 4.00 |
| COMMON CARD (1-21) | .50 | .23 |
| ❑ 1 Bob Berg | .50 | .23 |
| ❑ 2 John Depourcq | .50 | .23 |
| ❑ 3 Wade Fournier | .50 | .23 |
| ❑ 4 Fred Goltz | .50 | .23 |
| ❑ 5 Ron Handy | .50 | .23 |
| ❑ 6 Mike Heany | .50 | .23 |
| ❑ 7 Dean Hulett | .50 | .23 |
| ❑ 8 Jim Latos | .50 | .23 |
| ❑ 9 George Maneluk | .75 | .35 |
| ❑ 10 Rob McCaig | .50 | .23 |
| ❑ 11 Jason McQuat | .50 | .23 |
| ❑ 12 Rod Pasma | .50 | .23 |
| ❑ 13 Sean Rowe | .50 | .23 |
| ❑ 14 Bryan Schoen | .75 | .35 |
| ❑ 15 Darryl Shedden | .50 | .23 |
| ❑ 16 Doug Shedden CO | .50 | .23 |
| ❑ 17 Fred Spoltore | .50 | .23 |
| ❑ 18 Chris Valicevic | .50 | .23 |
| ❑ 19 Rob Valicevic | .50 | .23 |
| ❑ 20 John Vary | .50 | .23 |
| ❑ 21 Marty Yewchuk | .50 | .23 |

## 1995-96 Louisiana Ice Gators Playoffs

This 21-card set features borderless color player photos with the player's name and jersey number printed in a black bar across the bottom. The backs carry player information. A note on the card back reveals no more than 2,500 sets were produced.The cards are unnumbered and checklisted below in alphabetical order.

| | MINT | NRMT |
|---|---|---|
| COMPLETE SET (21) | 9.00 | 4.00 |
| COMMON CARD (1-21) | .50 | .23 |
| ❑ 1 Bob Berg | .50 | .23 |
| ❑ 2 Aaron Boh | .50 | .23 |
| ❑ 3 Eric Cloutier | .50 | .23 |
| ❑ 4 John DePourcq | .50 | .23 |
| ❑ 5 Wade Fournier | .50 | .23 |
| ❑ 6 Ron Handy | .60 | .25 |
| ❑ 7 Mike Heaney | .50 | .23 |
| ❑ 8 Dean Hulett | .50 | .23 |
| ❑ 9 Jim Latos | .50 | .23 |
| ❑ 10 George Maneluk | .60 | .25 |
| ❑ 11 Rob McCaig | .60 | .25 |
| ❑ 12 Jason McQuat | .50 | .23 |
| ❑ 13 Chad Nelson | .50 | .23 |
| ❑ 14 Dan O'Rourke | .50 | .23 |
| ❑ 15 Rod Pasma | .50 | .23 |
| ❑ 16 Darryl Shedden | .50 | .23 |
| ❑ 17 Doug Shedden CO | .60 | .25 |
| ❑ 18 John Spoltore | .60 | .25 |
| ❑ 19 Chuck Thuss | .60 | .25 |
| ❑ 20 Rob Valicevic<br>Chris Valicevic | .50 | .23 |
| ❑ 21 John Vary | .50 | .23 |

## 1978-79 Louisville Gears

This 20-card set features black-and-white player posed photos. The team name and year appear in the top white border with the player's name printed in the bottom border. The player's position is listed on a puck at the bottom left of the photo. The backs are blank. The cards are unnumbered and checklisted below in alphabetical order.

| | NRMT-MT | EXC |
|---|---|---|
| COMPLETE SET (20) | 20.00 | 9.00 |
| COMMON CARD (1-20) | .50 | .23 |
| ❑ 1 Wren Blair OWN | 2.00 | .90 |
| ❑ 2 Marcel Comeau | 1.00 | .45 |
| ❑ 3 Dennis Desrosiers | 1.00 | .45 |
| ❑ 4 Jon Fontas | 1.00 | .45 |
| ❑ 5 Bob Froese | 4.00 | 1.80 |
| ❑ 6 Gunner Garrett TR | .50 | .23 |
| ❑ 7 Bob Gladney | 1.00 | .45 |
| ❑ 8 Warren Holmes | 1.00 | .45 |
| ❑ 9 Larry Hopkins | 1.00 | .45 |
| ❑ 10 Stu Irving | 1.00 | .45 |
| ❑ 11 Scott Jessee | 1.00 | .45 |
| ❑ 12 Lynn Jorgenson | 1.00 | .45 |
| ❑ 13 Doug Keans | 2.50 | 1.10 |
| ❑ 14 Claude Larochelle | 1.00 | .45 |
| ❑ 15 Paul McIntosh | 1.00 | .45 |
| ❑ 16 Don Perry CO | .50 | .23 |
| ❑ 17 Greg Steel | 1.00 | .45 |
| ❑ 18 Mark Suzor | 1.00 | .45 |
| ❑ 19 Mark Toffolo | 1.00 | .45 |
| ❑ 20 Dave Westner | 1.00 | .45 |

## 1996-97 Louisville Riverfrogs

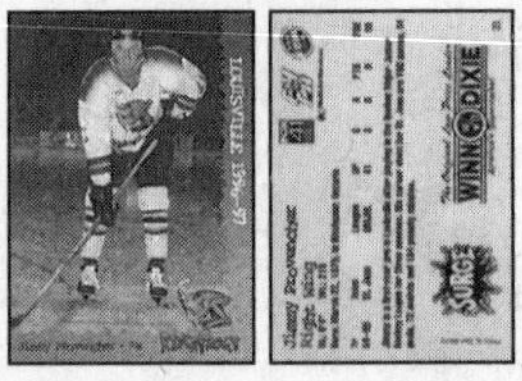

This 30-card set of the Louisville Riverfrogs of the ECHL was sponsored by Winn-Dixie, Surge and Fox 41. The cards feature action photography on the front, with '95-96 stats on the back. The cards were sold by the club at the rink and through the mail.

| | MINT | NRMT |
|---|---|---|
| COMPLETE SET (30) | 7.00 | 3.10 |
| COMMON CARD (1-30) | .10 | .05 |
| ❑ 1 Checklist | .10 | .05 |
| ❑ 2 Sandy Allan | .50 | .23 |
| ❑ 3 Gino Santerre | .25 | .11 |
| ❑ 4 Pete Liptrott | .25 | .11 |
| ❑ 5 Jason Hanchuk | .25 | .11 |
| ❑ 6 Adam Young | .25 | .11 |
| ❑ 7 Dan Reja | .25 | .11 |
| ❑ 8 Terry Lindgren | .25 | .11 |
| ❑ 9 Sheldon Gorski | .25 | .11 |
| ❑ 10 Jeff Kostuch | .25 | .11 |
| ❑ 11 Randy Stevens | .25 | .11 |
| ❑ 12 Chris Rowland | .25 | .11 |
| ❑ 13 Chris DeProfio | .25 | .11 |
| ❑ 14 Mike Sancimino | .25 | .11 |
| ❑ 15 Dean Seymour | .25 | .11 |
| ❑ 16 Stephane Madore | .25 | .11 |
| ❑ 17 Chet Cullic | .25 | .11 |
| ❑ 18 Tim Chase | .25 | .11 |
| ❑ 19 Jack Kowal | .25 | .11 |
| ❑ 20 Tom MacDonald | .25 | .11 |
| ❑ 21 Jimmy Provencher | .25 | .11 |
| ❑ 22 Lance Leslie | .50 | .23 |
| ❑ 23 Warren Young CO | .10 | .05 |
| ❑ 24 R.J. Romero TR | .10 | .05 |
| ❑ 25 Mark Shepherd EQMG | .10 | .05 |
| ❑ 26 David Wilson ANN | .10 | .05 |
| ❑ 27 Rowdy the Riverfrog | .10 | .05 |
| ❑ 28 Sandy Allan AS | .50 | .23 |
| ❑ 29 Warren Young CO<br>Brett Young | .10 | .05 |
| ❑ 30 Team Photo | .25 | .11 |

## 1997-98 Louisville Riverfrogs

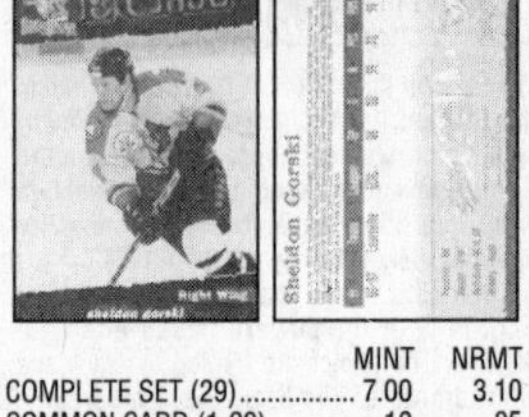

| | MINT | NRMT |
|---|---|---|
| COMPLETE SET (29) | 7.00 | 3.10 |
| COMMON CARD (1-29) | .10 | .05 |
| ❑ 1 Title Card | .10 | .05 |
| ❑ 2 Craig Nelson | .30 | .14 |
| ❑ 3 P.J. Lepler | .30 | .14 |
| ❑ 4 Jason Pain | .30 | .14 |
| ❑ 5 Terry Lindgren | .30 | .14 |
| ❑ 6 Michael Flynn | .30 | .14 |
| ❑ 7 Sheldon Gorski | .30 | .14 |
| ❑ 8 Jeff Kostuch | .30 | .14 |
| ❑ 9 Steve Ferranti | .30 | .14 |
| ❑ 10 Bob Gohde | .30 | .14 |
| ❑ 11 Marko Makinen | .30 | .14 |
| ❑ 12 Mike Sancimino | .30 | .14 |
| ❑ 13 Tobias Ablad | .30 | .14 |
| ❑ 14 Jeff Kikesch | .30 | .14 |
| ❑ 15 Stephane Madore | .30 | .14 |
| ❑ 16 Chris DeProfio | .30 | .14 |
| ❑ 17 Danny Reja | .30 | .14 |
| ❑ 18 Jack Kowal | .30 | .14 |
| ❑ 19 Dan Reimann | .30 | .14 |
| ❑ 20 Rob Frid | .30 | .14 |
| ❑ 21 Deiter Kochan | .30 | .14 |
| ❑ 22 Lance Leslie | .30 | .14 |
| ❑ 23 Warren Young | .30 | .14 |
| ❑ 24 R.J. Romeiro TR | .10 | .05 |
| ❑ 25 Mark Miller EQ | .10 | .05 |
| ❑ 26 Matt Gorsky BR | .10 | .05 |
| ❑ 27 Rowdy Mascot | .10 | .05 |
| ❑ 28 Sheldon Gorski | .30 | .14 |
| ❑ 29 Team Photo | .10 | .05 |

## 1995-96 Madison Monsters

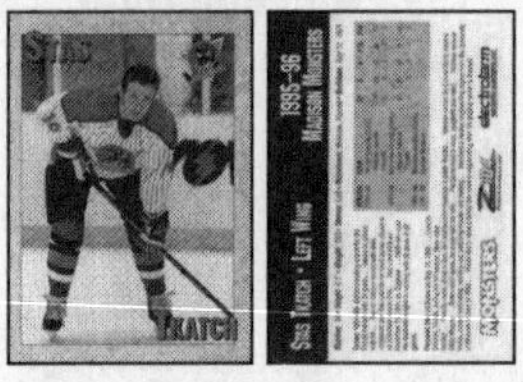

This 21-card set features the Madison Monsters of the Colonial Hockey League and was sponsored by Z-104 and Electrolarm. The cards, which apparently were a game night giveaway, feature a color shot on the front, along with the player name and team logo. The backs feature one of the most comprehensive player information packages ever seen on cardboard, including career stats and personal biography. The cards are unnumbered.

| | MINT | NRMT |
|---|---|---|
| COMPLETE SET (21) | 9.00 | 4.00 |
| COMMON CARD (1-21) | .10 | .05 |
| ❑ 1 Duane Derksen | .75 | .35 |
| ❑ 2 Brian Downey | .50 | .23 |
| ❑ 3 Dmitri Alekhin | .50 | .23 |
| ❑ 4 Monster -- Mascot | .10 | .05 |
| ❑ 5 Sean Wilmert | .50 | .23 |
| ❑ 6 Corey Grassel | .50 | .23 |
| ❑ 7 Dan Ruoho | .50 | .23 |
| ❑ 8 Billy Brown TR | .10 | .05 |
| ❑ 9 Kent Hawley | .50 | .23 |
| ❑ 10 Dan Laughlin | .50 | .23 |
| ❑ 11 Vyacheslav Polikarkin | .50 | .23 |
| ❑ 12 Todd Dvorak | .50 | .23 |
| ❑ 13 Brian Idalski | .50 | .23 |
| ❑ 14 Gunnar Kroseberg | .50 | .23 |
| ❑ 15 Brett Larson | .50 | .23 |
| ❑ 16 Paul Clatney | .50 | .23 |
| ❑ 17 Matt Loen | .50 | .23 |
| ❑ 18 Stanislav Tkach | .50 | .23 |
| ❑ 19 Glenn Painter | .50 | .23 |
| ❑ 20 Joe Bonvie | .50 | .23 |
| ❑ 21 Mark Johnson CO | .10 | .05 |

## 1992-93 Maine Black Bears

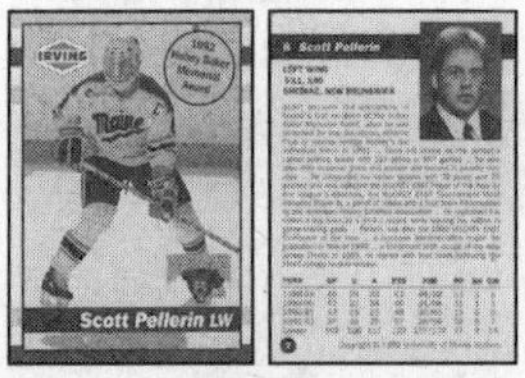

Featuring the Maine Black Bears, this 36-card standard-size set was issued as two series (1-16 and 17-36). The cards feature color, action player photos with light blue, dark blue, and white borders. A black stripe near the bottom carries the player's name and position in white print. The team logo is superimposed on the picture. The backs carry biographical information, career highlights, and statistics. This set includes one of the first cards of NHL superstar Paul Kariya.

| | MINT | NRMT |
|---|---|---|
| COMPLETE SET (36) | 40.00 | 18.00 |
| COMMON CARD (1-16) | .25 | .11 |
| COMMON CARD (17-36) | .25 | .11 |
| ❑ 1 Title Card | .25 | .11 |
| ❑ 2 Mike Dunham | 1.50 | .70 |
| ❑ 3 Andy Silverman | .50 | .23 |
| ❑ 4 Matt Martin | .75 | .35 |
| ❑ 5 Chris Imes | .50 | .23 |
| ❑ 6 Jason Weinrich | .50 | .23 |
| ❑ 7 Scott Pellerin | .50 | .23 |
| ❑ 8 Dan Murphy | .50 | .23 |
| ❑ 9 Dave LaCouture | .50 | .23 |
| ❑ 10 Patrice Tardif | .75 | .35 |
| ❑ 11 Eric Fenton | .50 | .23 |
| ❑ 12 Jim Montgomery | .75 | .35 |
| ❑ 13 Kent Salfi | .50 | .23 |
| ❑ 14 Jean-Yves Roy | .75 | .35 |
| ❑ 15 Garth Snow | 1.50 | .70 |
| ❑ 16 Cal Ingraham | .50 | .23 |
| ❑ 17 Title Card | .25 | .11 |
| ❑ 18 Mike Dunham | 1.50 | .70 |
| ❑ 19 Chris Imes | .50 | .23 |
| ❑ 20 Paul Kariya | 25.00 | 11.00 |
| ❑ 21 Mike Latendresse | .50 | .23 |
| ❑ 22 Dan Murphy | .50 | .23 |
| ❑ 23 Dave MacIsaac | .50 | .23 |
| ❑ 24 Dave LaCouture | .50 | .23 |
| ❑ 25 Chris Ferraro | 1.50 | .70 |
| ❑ 26 Peter Ferraro | 1.50 | .70 |
| ❑ 27 Jim Montgomery | .75 | .35 |
| ❑ 28 Brad Purdie | .50 | .23 |
| ❑ 29 Lee Saunders | .50 | .23 |
| ❑ 30 Justin Tomberlin | .50 | .23 |
| ❑ 31 Chuck Texeira | .50 | .23 |
| ❑ 32 Martin Mercier | .50 | .23 |
| ❑ 33 Garth Snow | 1.50 | .70 |
| ❑ 34 Cal Ingraham | .50 | .23 |
| ❑ 35 Greg Hirsch | .50 | .23 |
| ❑ 36 Jamie Thompson | .50 | .23 |

## 1993-94 Maine Black Bears

Measuring the standard size, this 26-card set features the Maine Black Bears. The fronts feature color action player photos with light blue, dark blue, and white borders. A black stripe near the bottom carries the player's name and position in white print. The team logo is superimposed on the picture. The backs carry biographical information, career highlights, and statistics along with a small black-and-white player headshot. The numbering continues where the previous year's numbering left off.

| | MINT | NRMT |
|---|---|---|
| COMPLETE SET (25) | 35.00 | 16.00 |
| COMMON CARD (37-61) | .50 | .23 |
| ❑ 37 Paul Kariya<br>Leo Wlasow<br>Title Card | 6.00 | 2.70 |
| ❑ 38 Andy Silverman | .50 | .23 |
| ❑ 39 Jason Weinrich | .50 | .23 |
| ❑ 40 Jason Mansoff | .50 | .23 |
| ❑ 41 Paul Kariya | 15.00 | 6.75 |
| ❑ 42 Mike Latendresse | .50 | .23 |
| ❑ 43 Barry Clukey | .50 | .23 |
| ❑ 44 Wayne Conlan | .50 | .23 |
| ❑ 45 Dave MacIsaac | .50 | .23 |
| ❑ 46 Patrice Tardif | .75 | .35 |
| ❑ 47 Brad Purdie | .50 | .23 |
| ❑ 48 Dan Shermerhorn | .50 | .23 |
| ❑ 49 Lee Saunders | .50 | .23 |
| ❑ 50 Justin Tomberlin | .50 | .23 |
| ❑ 51 Chuck Texeira | .50 | .23 |
| ❑ 52 Tim Lovell | .50 | .23 |
| ❑ 53 Cal Ingraham | .50 | .23 |
| ❑ 54 Leo Wlasow | .50 | .23 |
| ❑ 55 Blair Allison | .50 | .23 |
| ❑ 56 Blair Marsh | .50 | .23 |
| ❑ 57 Marcel Pineau | .50 | .23 |
| ❑ 58 Trevor Roenick | .75 | .35 |
| ❑ 59 Reg Cardinal | .50 | .23 |
| ❑ 60 Paul Kariya | 15.00 | 6.75 |
| ❑ 61 Jim Montgomery<br>Paul Kariya<br>Division I Champions | 6.00 | 2.70 |

## 1982-83 Medicine Hat Tigers

These 21 blank-backed cards measure approximately 3" by 4" and feature white-bordered, black-and-white posed studio head shots of the WHL Tigers on the left halves of the cards. The player's name, jersey number and biography, along with a space for an autograph, appear on the right half. The cards are unnumbered and checklisted below in alphabetical order.

| | MINT | EXC |
|---|---|---|
| COMPLETE SET (21) | 20.00 | 9.00 |
| COMMON CARD (1-21) | 1.00 | .45 |
| ❑ 1 Al Conroy | 1.50 | .70 |
| ❑ 2 Murray Craven | 3.00 | 1.35 |
| ❑ 3 Mark Frank | 1.00 | .45 |
| ❑ 4 Kevan Guy | 1.00 | .45 |
| ❑ 5 Jim Hougen | 1.00 | .45 |
| ❑ 6 Ken Jorgenson | 1.00 | .45 |
| ❑ 7 Matt Kabayama | 1.00 | .45 |
| ❑ 8 Brent Kisilivich | 1.00 | .45 |
| ❑ 9 Mark Lamb | 2.00 | .90 |
| ❑ 10 Mike Lay | 1.00 | .45 |
| ❑ 11 Dean McArthur | 1.00 | .45 |
| ❑ 12 Brent Meckling | 1.00 | .45 |
| ❑ 13 Shawn Nagurny | 1.00 | .45 |
| ❑ 14 Kodie Nelson | 1.00 | .45 |
| ❑ 15 Al Pedersen | 1.50 | .70 |
| ❑ 16 Todd Pederson | 1.00 | .45 |
| ❑ 17 Jay Reid | 1.00 | .45 |
| ❑ 18 Gord Shmyrko | 1.00 | .45 |
| ❑ 19 Brent Steblyk | 1.00 | .45 |
| ❑ 20 Rocky Trottier | 1.00 | .45 |
| ❑ 21 Dan Turner | 1.00 | .45 |

## 1983-84 Medicine Hat Tigers

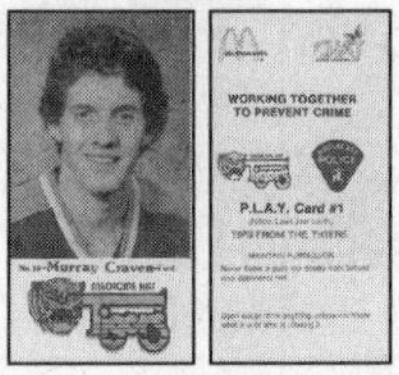

This 23-card P.L.A.Y. (Police, Laws and Youth) set measures approximately 2 3/4" by 5" and features color player portraits with a wide white bottom border. The border contains the player's jersey number and name. The team logo is also printed in this area. The backs carry sponsor logos and public service "Tips From The Tigers."

| | MINT | NRMT |
|---|---|---|
| COMPLETE SET (23) | 30.00 | 13.50 |
| COMMON CARD (1-23) | 1.00 | .45 |
| ❑ 1 Murray Craven | 3.00 | 1.35 |
| ❑ 2 Shane Churla | 5.00 | 2.20 |
| ❑ 3 Don Herczeg | 1.00 | .45 |
| ❑ 4 Gary Johnson | 1.00 | .45 |
| ❑ 5 Brent Kisilivich | 1.00 | .45 |
| ❑ 6 Blair MacGregor | 1.00 | .45 |
| ❑ 7 Terry Knight | 1.00 | .45 |
| ❑ 8 Mark Lamb | 2.00 | .90 |
| ❑ 9 Al Pedersen | 1.50 | .70 |
| ❑ 10 Trevor Semeniuk | 1.00 | .45 |
| ❑ 11 Dan Turner | 1.00 | .45 |
| ❑ 12 Brent Steblyk | 1.00 | .45 |
| ❑ 13 Rocky Trottier | 1.00 | .45 |
| ❑ 14 Kevan Guy | 1.50 | .70 |
| ❑ 15 Bobby Bassen | 3.00 | 1.35 |
| ❑ 16 Brent Meckling | 1.00 | .45 |
| ❑ 17 Matt Kabayama | 1.00 | .45 |
| ❑ 18 Gord Hynes | 1.50 | .70 |
| ❑ 19 Daryl Henry | 1.00 | .45 |
| ❑ 20 Jim Kambeitz | 1.00 | .45 |
| ❑ 21 Mike Lay | 1.50 | .70 |
| ❑ 22 Gord Shmyrko | 1.00 | .45 |
| ❑ 23 Al Conroy | 2.00 | .90 |

## 1985-86 Medicine Hat Tigers

This 24-card set measures approximately 2 1/4" by 4" and features posed, color player photos on white card stock. The player's name and the team logo are printed in the larger white margin at the bottom. The player's jersey number and position are printed on the picture in the upper corners. A thin red line encloses the picture, player's name, and logo. The backs display P.L.A.Y. (Police, Laws, and Youth) tips and sponsor logos.

| | MINT | NRMT |
|---|---|---|
| COMPLETE SET (24) | 20.00 | 9.00 |
| COMMON CARD (1-24) | .25 | .11 |
| ❑ 1 Mike Claringbull | .75 | .35 |
| ❑ 2 Doug Houda | 1.50 | .70 |
| ❑ 3 Mark Kuntz | .75 | .35 |
| ❑ 4 Guy Phillips | .75 | .35 |
| ❑ 5 Rob DiMaio | 2.00 | .90 |
| ❑ 6 Al Conroy | 1.00 | .45 |
| ❑ 7 Craig Berube | 2.00 | .90 |
| ❑ 8 Doug Sauter CO | .50 | .23 |
| ❑ 9 Dean Chynoweth | 1.00 | .45 |
| ❑ 10 Scott McCrady | .75 | .35 |
| ❑ 11 Neil Brady | .75 | .35 |
| ❑ 12 Dale Kushner | .75 | .35 |
| ❑ 13 Jeff Wenaas | .75 | .35 |
| ❑ 14 Wayne Hynes | .75 | .35 |
| ❑ 15 Troy Gamble | 2.00 | .90 |
| ❑ 16 Bryan Maxwell ACO | .50 | .23 |
| ❑ 17 Gord Hynes | 1.00 | .45 |
| ❑ 18 Wayne McBean | 1.00 | .45 |
| ❑ 19 Mark Pederson | 1.00 | .45 |
| ❑ 20 Darren Cota | .75 | .35 |
| ❑ 21 Randy Siska | .75 | .35 |
| ❑ 22 Dave Mackey | .75 | .35 |
| ❑ 23 Mark Fitzpatrick | 4.00 | 1.80 |
| ❑ 24 Doug Ball TR | .25 | .11 |

## 1995-96 Medicine Hat Tigers

This 21-card set features color player photos of the Medicine Hat Tigers of the WHL and was sponsored by Pizza Hut. The black front border is highly susceptible to dings, and thus

the set is considered condition sensitive. Although the cards feature player jersey numbers on the fronts, they are unnumbered, and thus the set is checklisted below in alphabetical order.

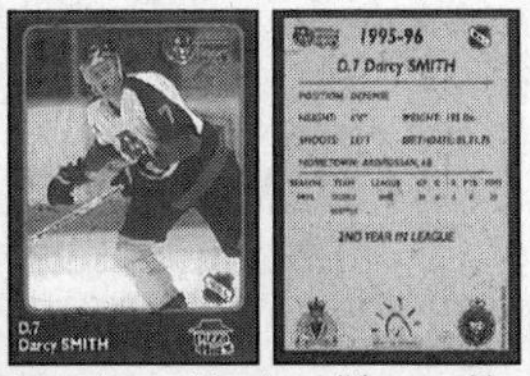

| | MINT | NRMT |
|---|---|---|
| COMPLETE SET (21) | 14.00 | 6.25 |
| COMMON CARD (1-21) | .10 | .05 |

| | | |
|---|---|---|
| 1 Johnathan Aitken | 1.50 | .70 |
| 2 Brady Austin | .50 | .23 |
| 3 Cal Benazic | .50 | .23 |
| 4 Scott Buhler | .75 | .35 |
| 5 Clint Cabana | .50 | .23 |
| 6 Mike Eley | .50 | .23 |
| 7 Josh Green | 2.00 | .90 |
| 8 Curtis Huppe | .50 | .23 |
| 9 Henry Kuster | .75 | .35 |
| 10 Aaron Millar | .50 | .23 |
| 11 Mark Polak | .50 | .23 |
| 12 Bryan Randall | .50 | .23 |
| 13 Chad Reich | .50 | .23 |
| 14 Kyle Ronan | .50 | .23 |
| 15 Rroary(Mascot) | .10 | .05 |
| 16 Blair St. Martin | .50 | .23 |
| 17 Paxton Schafer | 1.00 | .45 |
| 18 Derek Senkow | .50 | .23 |
| 19 Darcy Smith | .50 | .23 |
| 20 Rocky Thompson | .75 | .35 |
| 21 Trevor Wasyluk | 1.50 | .70 |

## 1996-97 Medicine Hat Tigers

This 25-card set features posed color player photos surrounded by an orange/yellow border. The player's name, number and position are listed along the left border, while the logos of the team and Canadian Tire can be found along the bottom. The top reads "Medicine Hat News Collector's Edition", leading to speculation that the set was issued as a premium either through the paper, or at a game night sponsored by the paper. The backs contain a large Canadian Tire logo, along with biographical info for the player. The cards are unnumbered, and are checklisted below in alphabetical order.

| | MINT | NRMT |
|---|---|---|
| COMPLETE SET (25) | 12.00 | 5.50 |
| COMMON CARD (1-25) | .25 | .11 |

| | | |
|---|---|---|
| 1 Berkeley Buchko | .40 | .18 |
| 2 Scott Buhler | .75 | .35 |
| 3 Jason Chimera | .50 | .23 |
| 4 Michael Dyck ACO | .25 | .11 |
| 5 Mike Eley | .40 | .18 |
| 6 Josh Green | 1.50 | .70 |
| 7 Derek Holland | .40 | .18 |
| 8 Curtis Huppe | .40 | .18 |
| 9 Henry Kuster | .60 | .25 |
| 10 Kurt Lackten CO | .25 | .11 |
| 11 Kevin McDonald | .40 | .18 |
| 12 Aaron Millar | .40 | .18 |
| 13 Doug Mosher GM | .25 | .11 |
| 14 Jaroslav Obsut | .75 | .35 |
| 15 Colin O'Hara | .40 | .18 |
| 16 Mark Polak | .40 | .18 |
| 17 Rroary(Mascot) | .25 | .11 |
| 18 Blair St. Martin | .40 | .18 |
| 19 Rob Sandrock | .40 | .18 |
| 20 Dustin Schwartz | .75 | .35 |
| 21 Lee Svangstu | .40 | .18 |
| 22 Jeff Temple | .40 | .18 |
| 23 Rocky Thompson | .75 | .35 |
| 24 Trevor Wasyluk | 1.00 | .45 |
| 25 Chad Wilchynski | .40 | .18 |

## 1993-94 Memphis River Kings

Round cards approximately the size of a hockey puck. They came in a plastic container with the team logo on the front.

| | MINT | NRMT |
|---|---|---|
| COMPLETE SET (18) | 4.00 | 1.80 |
| COMMON CARD (1-18) | .10 | .05 |

| | | |
|---|---|---|
| 1 Rocco Amonte | .25 | .11 |
| 2 Peter D'Amario | .25 | .11 |
| 3 Roydon Gunn | .25 | .11 |
| 4 Kyle Haviland | .25 | .11 |
| 5 Mike Jackson | .25 | .11 |
| 6 Scot Johnston | .25 | .11 |
| 7 Robert Kelley | .25 | .11 |
| 8 Mark McGinn | .25 | .11 |
| 9 Antoine Mindjimba | .25 | .11 |
| 10 David Moore | .25 | .11 |
| 11 Glenn Painter | .25 | .11 |
| 12 Scott Phillips | .25 | .11 |
| 13 Mike Roberts | .25 | .11 |
| 14 Andy Ross | .25 | .11 |
| 15 Steve Shaunessy | .25 | .11 |
| 16 Ken Venis | .25 | .11 |
| 17 Bobby Wallwork | .25 | .11 |
| 18 Randy Boyd CO | .10 | .05 |

## 1993-94 Michigan State

Produced by Phipps Sports Marketing, Inc., this 32-card standard-size set features the 1993-94 Michigan State Spartan hockey team. On a green background, the fronts have a mix of posed and action player photos in glossy color, within a thin silver border. The words "1993-94 MSU Spartan Hockey" are printed above the photo, while the player's name appears inside the photo. The player's position and number appear below, along with a large block-style "S" round out the front. Printed on a light green background with ghosted Spartan helmet logos and a dark green border, the horizontal backs carry a black-and-white player portrait, along with biography and personal information. The cards are unnumbered and checklisted below in alphabetical order.

| | MINT | NRMT |
|---|---|---|
| COMPLETE SET (32) | 15.00 | 6.75 |
| COMMON CARD (1-32) | .10 | .05 |

| | | |
|---|---|---|
| 1 Matt Albers | .35 | .16 |
| 2 Michael Burkett | .50 | .23 |
| 3 Mike Buzak | .35 | .16 |
| 4 Anson Carter | 3.00 | 1.35 |
| 5 Brian Clifford | .75 | .35 |
| 6 Brian Crane | .35 | .16 |
| 7 Steve Ferranti | .35 | .16 |
| 8 Ryan Fleming | .35 | .16 |
| 9 Steve Guolla | .50 | .23 |
| 10 Kelly Harper | .50 | .23 |
| 11 Eric Kruse | .35 | .16 |
| 12 Ron Mason CO | .35 | .16 |
| 13 Mike Mattis | .35 | .16 |
| 14 Rem Murray | 2.00 | .90 |
| 15 Steve Norton | .35 | .16 |
| 16 Nicolas Perreault | .50 | .23 |
| 17 Tom Ross | .50 | .23 |
| Spartan Great | | |
| 18 Chris Slater | .35 | .16 |
| 19 Chris Smith | .35 | .16 |
| 20 Bryan Smolinski | 4.00 | 1.80 |
| 21 Sparty (Mascot) | .10 | .05 |
| 22 Chris Sullivan | .35 | .16 |
| 23 Steve Suk | .35 | .16 |
| 24 Bart Turner | .35 | .16 |
| 25 Tony Tuzzolino | .35 | .16 |
| 26 Bart Vanstaalduinen | .35 | .16 |
| 27 Mike Ware | .35 | .16 |
| 28 John Weidenbach | .35 | .16 |
| 29 Josh Wiegand | .35 | .16 |
| 30 Scott Worden | .35 | .16 |
| 31 Munn Arena | .10 | .05 |
| 32 Title Card | .10 | .05 |

## 1990-91 Michigan Tech Huskies

This 31-card standard-size set was sponsored by The Daily Mining Gazette and showcases the Michigan Tech Huskies of the WCHA. Reportedly only 500 sets were produced. The cards are printed on thin cardboard stock. Borderless high gloss player photos grace the fronts, with the jersey number, team name, player name, and position given in a black stripe at the bottom of the card face. On a black and pale yellow background, each back has a black and white head shot, biography, statistics, and career summary. A "Huskies Hockey Quick Fact" completes the card back. The cards are unnumbered and checklisted below in alphabetical order.

| | MINT | NRMT |
|---|---|---|
| COMPLETE SET (31) | 15.00 | 6.75 |
| COMMON CARD (1-31) | .25 | .11 |

| | | |
|---|---|---|
| 1 Jim Bonner | .50 | .23 |
| 2 Newell Brown CO | .25 | .11 |
| 3 Dwight DeGiacomo | .50 | .23 |
| 4 Rod Ewacha | .50 | .23 |
| 5 Peter Grant | .25 | .11 |
| 6 Tim Hartnett | .50 | .23 |
| 7 Mike Hauswirth | .50 | .23 |
| 8 Kelly Hurd | .50 | .23 |
| 9 Kelly Hurd | .50 | .23 |
| Red Wings | | |
| 10 Layne Lebel | .50 | .23 |
| Jeff Hill | | |
| 11 Randy Lewis | .50 | .23 |
| 12 Jay Luknowsky | .50 | .23 |
| 13 Ken Martel CO | .25 | .11 |
| Mark Leach CO | | |
| 14 Darcy Martini | .50 | .23 |
| 15 Reid McDonald | .50 | .23 |
| 16 Hugh McEwen | .75 | .35 |
| Jim Storm | | |
| Kevin Manninen | | |
| 17 Don Osborne | .50 | .23 |
| 18 Greg Parnell | .50 | .23 |
| 19 Davis Payne | .60 | .23 |
| 20 Kirby Perrault | .50 | .23 |
| Darren Brkic | | |
| 21 Ken Plaquin | .50 | .23 |
| 22 Damian Rhodes | 2.50 | 1.10 |
| 23 Geoff Sarjeant | .75 | .35 |
| 24 Jamie Steer | .50 | .23 |
| 25 Rob Tustian | .50 | .23 |
| 26 Scott Vettraino | .75 | .35 |
| 27 Tim Watters | .60 | .25 |
| (black and white) | | |
| 28 John Young | .50 | .23 |
| 29 John Young | .50 | .23 |
| Kelly Hurd | | |
| 30 1991 MacInnes Cup | .50 | .23 |
| 31 1975 NCAA Champions | .50 | .23 |

## 1991-92 Michigan Tech Huskies

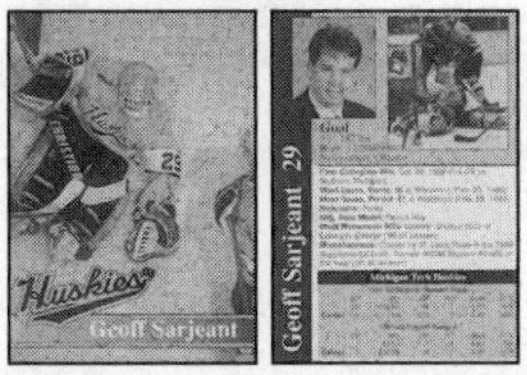

This 36-card standard-size set features the 1992-93 Michigan Tech Huskies. Reportedly approximately 2,000 sets were produced. The fronts features full-bleed color action player photos. A gray and yellow stripe at the bottom contains the player's name. The Huskies logo overlaps the picture and the stripe. The backs are divided into three sections. The upper section is bright yellow and displays a black-and-white head shot, an action shot, and biographical information. A white middle section carries a player profile. The lower yellow section contains statistics. The player's name and uniform number are printed vertically in a black stripe on the left edge. Some players have two cards, the second of which is distinguished by a subtitle. The cards are unnumbered and checklisted below in alphabetical order.

| | MINT | NRMT |
|---|---|---|
| COMPLETE SET (36) | 12.00 | 5.50 |
| COMMON CARD (1-36) | .10 | .05 |

| | | |
|---|---|---|
| 1 Jim Bonner | .35 | .16 |
| 2 Darren Brkic | .35 | .16 |
| 3 Rod Ewacha | .35 | .16 |
| 4 Tim Hartnett | .35 | .16 |
| 5 Mike Hauswirth | .35 | .16 |
| 6 Jeff Hill | .35 | .16 |
| 7 Layne LeBel | .35 | .16 |
| 8 Randy Lewis | .35 | .16 |
| 9 Randy Lewis | .35 | .16 |
| Hit Squad | | |
| 10 John MacInnes CO | .10 | .05 |
| 11 Darcy Martini | .50 | .23 |
| 12 Darcy Martini | .50 | .23 |
| Rink Blaster | | |
| 13 Reid McDonald | .35 | .16 |
| 14 Hugh McEwen | .35 | .16 |
| 15 Bob Olson ANN | .10 | .05 |
| 16 Don Osborne | .35 | .16 |
| 17 Greg Parnell | .35 | .16 |
| 18 Davis Payne | .35 | .16 |
| 19 Kirby Perrault | .35 | .16 |
| 20 Ken Plaquin | .35 | .16 |
| 21 Jamie Ram | .35 | .16 |
| 22 Geoff Sarjeant | .75 | .35 |
| 23 Geoff Sarjeant | .75 | .35 |
| WCHA Student-Athlete | | |
| 24 Jamie Steer | .35 | .16 |
| 25 Jamie Steer | .35 | .16 |
| Blade Runner | | |
| 26 Jim Storm | .50 | .23 |
| 27 Scott Vettraino | .35 | .16 |
| 28 John Young | .35 | .16 |
| 29 Credits (Team | .35 | .16 |
| huddling on ice) | | |
| 30 Freshman | .35 | .16 |
| Justin Peca | | |
| Liam Garvey | | |
| Randy Stevens | | |
| Brent Peterson | | |
| Travis Seale | | |
| 31 Great Lakes | .10 | .05 |
| Invitational | | |
| 32 Home Ice | .10 | .05 |
| MacInnes Student Ice Arena | | |
| 33 Team Photo | .50 | .23 |
| 34 NHL Draft | .50 | .23 |
| Darcy Martini | | |
| Davis Payne | | |
| Geoff Sarjeant | | |
| Ken Plaquin | | |
| Jim Storm | | |
| Jamie Ram | | |
| Jamie Steer | | |
| Jim Bonner | | |
| 35 Pep Band | .10 | .05 |
| 36 Michigan Tech Univ. | .10 | .05 |

## 1993-94 Michigan Tech Huskies

| | MINT | NRMT |
|---|---|---|
| COMPLETE SET (25) | 5.00 | 2.20 |
| COMMON CARD (1-25) | .10 | .05 |

| | | |
|---|---|---|
| 1 Pat Mikesch | .25 | .11 |
| 2 Eric Jensen | .25 | .11 |
| 3 Kyle Peterson | .25 | .11 |
| 4 Jay Storm | .25 | .11 |
| 5 Jason Hanchuk | .25 | .11 |
| 6 Mike Figliomeni | .25 | .11 |
| 7 Randy Stevens | .25 | .11 |
| 8 Brent Peterson | .25 | .11 |
| 9 Kirby Perrault | .25 | .11 |
| 10 Brian Hunter | .25 | .11 |
| 11 Travis Seale | .25 | .11 |
| 12 Jamie Ram | .50 | .23 |
| 13 Jeff Hill | .25 | .11 |
| 14 Justin Peca | .25 | .11 |
| 15 Layne LeBel | .25 | .11 |
| 16 Jeff Mikesch | .25 | .11 |
| 17 John Kisil | .25 | .11 |
| 18 Liam Garvey | .25 | .11 |
| 19 Kyle Ferguson | .25 | .11 |
| 20 Jason Wright | .40 | .18 |
| 21 Luciano Caravaggio | .25 | .11 |
| 22 Mitch Lane | .25 | .11 |
| 23 Randy Wakeham | .25 | .11 |
| 24 Martin Machacek | .25 | .11 |
| 25 Winter Carnival | .10 | .05 |

## 1991-92 Michigan Wolverines

These cards are unnumbered and checklisted below in alphabetical order.

| | MINT | NRMT |
|---|---|---|
| COMPLETE SET (25) | 10.00 | 4.50 |
| COMMON CARD (1-25) | .10 | .05 |

| | | |
|---|---|---|
| 1 Doug Evans | .25 | .11 |
| 2 Denny Felsner | .60 | .25 |
| 3 Anton Fedorov | .25 | .11 |
| 4 Chris Gordon | .25 | .11 |
| 5 David Harlock | .25 | .11 |
| 6 Mike Helber | .25 | .11 |
| 7 Tim Hogan | .25 | .11 |
| 8 Mike Knuble | .75 | .35 |
| 9 Ted Kramer | .25 | .11 |
| 10 Pat Neaton | .25 | .11 |
| 11 David Oliver | .25 | .11 |
| 12 David Roberts | .25 | .11 |
| 13 Marc Ouimet | .25 | .11 |
| 14 Ron Sacka | .25 | .11 |
| 15 Mark Sakala | .25 | .11 |
| 16 Steve Shields | 5.00 | 2.20 |
| 17 Alan Sinclair | .25 | .11 |
| 18 Cam Stewart | .25 | .11 |
| 19 Dan Stiver | .25 | .11 |
| 20 Mike Stone | .25 | .11 |
| 21 Chris Tamer | .60 | .25 |
| 22 Aaron Ward | .50 | .23 |
| 23 Rick Willis | .25 | .11 |
| 24 Brian Wiseman | .25 | .11 |
| 25 Team Card | .10 | .05 |

## 1993-94 Michigan Wolverines

Cards are unnumbered and checklisted below in alphabetical order.

| | MINT | NRMT |
|---|---|---|
| COMPLETE SET (28) | 10.00 | 4.50 |
| COMMON CARD (1-28) | .10 | .05 |

| | | |
|---|---|---|
| 1 John Arnold | .25 | .11 |
| 2 Jason Botterill | .50 | .23 |
| 3 Peter Bourke | .25 | .11 |
| 4 Drew Denzin | .25 | .11 |
| 5 Anton Fedorov | .25 | .11 |
| 6 Chris Frescoln | .25 | .11 |
| 7 Chris Gordon | .25 | .11 |
| 8 Steve Halko | .25 | .11 |
| 9 Kevin Hilton | .25 | .11 |
| 10 Tim Hogan | .25 | .11 |
| 11 Mike Knuble | .75 | .35 |
| 12 Mike Legg | .25 | .11 |
| 13 Al Loges | .25 | .11 |
| 14 Warren Luhning | .25 | .11 |
| 15 John Madden | .50 | .23 |
| 16 Brendan Morrison | .75 | .35 |
| 17 David Oliver | .25 | .11 |
| 18 Ron Sacka | .25 | .11 |
| 19 Mark Sakala | .25 | .11 |
| 20 Harold Schock | .25 | .11 |
| 21 Steve Shields | 5.00 | 2.20 |
| 22 Alan Sinclair | .25 | .11 |
| 23 Ryan Sittler | .75 | .35 |
| 24 Blake Sloan | .25 | .11 |
| 25 Mike Stone | .25 | .11 |
| 26 Rick Willis | .25 | .11 |
| 27 Brian Wiseman | .25 | .11 |
| 28 Team Photo | .10 | .05 |

## 1981-82 Milwaukee Admirals

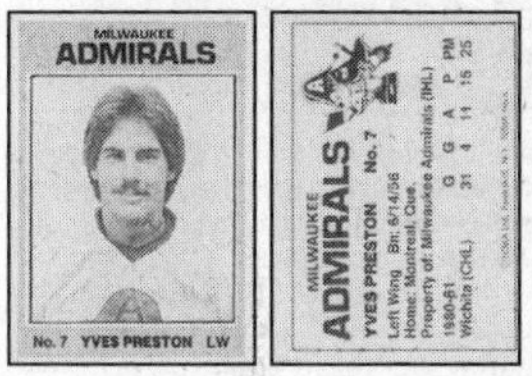

This 15-card standard-size set was produced by TCMA and features the members of the Milwaukee Admirals. The cards are made of thick card stock. On the front, a black-and-white player photo with thin black borders is framed in bright yellow. The team name appears in the yellow border above the photo, while the player's name, jersey number, and position appear below. The horizontal backs carry biography and statistics.

| | NRMT-MT | EXC |
|---|---|---|
| COMPLETE SET (15) | 12.00 | 5.50 |
| COMMON CARD (1-15) | .50 | .23 |

| | | |
|---|---|---|
| 1 Pat Rabbitt | 1.00 | .45 |
| 2 Real Paiement | 1.00 | .45 |
| 3 Fred Berry | 1.00 | .45 |
| 4 Blaine Peerless | 1.00 | .45 |
| 5 John Flesch | 1.00 | .45 |
| 6 Yves Preston | 1.00 | .45 |
| 7 Bruce McKay | 1.00 | .45 |
| 8 Dale Yakiwchuk | 1.00 | .45 |
| 9 Lorne Bokshowan | 1.00 | .45 |
| 10 Danny Lecours | 1.00 | .45 |
| 11 Sheldon Currie | 1.00 | .45 |
| 12 Doug Robb | 1.00 | .45 |
| 13 Rob Polman Tuin | 1.00 | .45 |
| 14 Bob Collyard | 1.00 | .45 |
| 15 Tim Ringler TR | .50 | .23 |

## 1994-95 Milwaukee Admirals

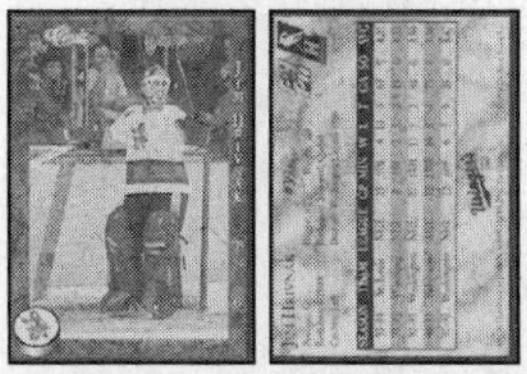

This 28-card standard-size set was manufactured and distributed by Jessen Associates, Inc. for Classic. The fronts depict color action player photos with a dark blue marbleized inner border and a black outer border. The player's name, jersey number, and position appear in the teal border on the right edge. Inside a black border on a marbleized background, the backs present biography, statistics, and sponsor logos. The cards are unnumbered and checklisted below in alphabetical order.

| | MINT | NRMT |
|---|---|---|
| COMPLETE SET (28) | 8.00 | 3.60 |
| COMMON CARD (1-28) | .10 | .05 |

| | | |
|---|---|---|
| 1 Doug Agnew TR | .10 | .05 |
| 2 Peter Bakovic ACO | .10 | .05 |
| 3 Matt Block | .25 | .11 |
| 4 Gino Cavallini | .35 | .16 |
| 5 Sylvain Couturier | .35 | .16 |
| 6 Brian Dobbin | .35 | .16 |
| 7 Shawn Evans | .25 | .11 |
| 8 Fabulous Fritz | .10 | .05 |
| 9 Chris Govedaris | .50 | .23 |
| 10 Jim Hrivnak | .75 | .35 |
| 11 Tony Hrkac | .50 | .23 |
| 12 Fabian Joseph | .35 | .16 |
| 13 Mark Laforest | .50 | .23 |

❑ 14 Don MacAdam ACO .10 .05
❑ 15 Dave Mackey .25 .11
❑ 16 Pat MacLeod .35 .16
❑ 17 Dave Marcinyshyn .25 .11
❑ 18 Bob Mason .50 .23
❑ 19 Mike McNeill .50 .23
❑ 20 Kent Paynter .25 .11
❑ 21 Ken Sabourin .25 .11
❑ 22 Trevor Sim .25 .11
❑ 23 Martin Simard .25 .11
❑ 24 Mike Tomlak .25 .11
❑ 25 Steve Tuttle .25 .11
❑ 26 Randy Velischek .35 .16
❑ 27 Brad Werenka .35 .16
❑ 28 Phil Wittliff CO .10 .05

## 1995-96 Milwaukee Admirals Bank One

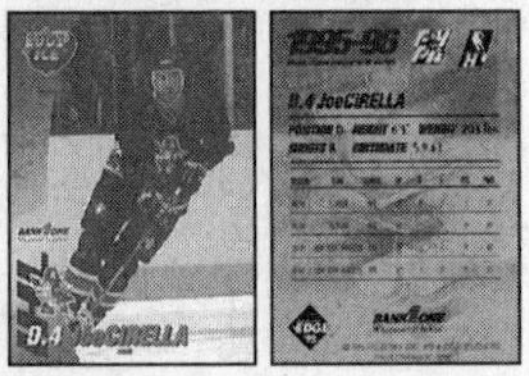

This high-quality 25-card set was produced for the team by Collector's Edge and sponsored by Bank One. The card fronts feature color action photography, along with the logos of the club, the bank and the manufacturer. The backs include limted stats. The last card in the set, entitled Dream Ride, features on the back the lyrics to the song of the same name, which apparently is near and dear to the hearts of Admirals fans everywhere. This marks what could be the first ever appropriation of song lyrics for the edification of card collectors. As they cards are unnumbered, they are listed below alphabetically.

| | MINT | NRMT |
|---|---|---|
| COMPLETE SET (25) | 6.00 | 2.70 |
| COMMON CARD (1-25) | .10 | .05 |

❑ 1 Shawn Anderson .25 .11
❑ 2 Jergus Baca .25 .11
❑ 3 Gino Cavallini .35 .16
❑ 4 Joe Cirella .25 .11
❑ 5 Sylvain Couturier .25 .11
❑ 6 Tom Draper .50 .23
❑ 7 Robert Guillet .25 .11
❑ 8 Tony Hrkac .35 .16
❑ 9 Fabian Joseph .35 .16
❑ 10 Mark LaForest .50 .23
❑ 11 Dave MacIsaac .25 .11
❑ 12 Mike McNeill .25 .11
❑ 13 Dave Mackey .25 .11
❑ 14 Kent Paynter .25 .11
❑ 15 Ken Sabourin .25 .11
❑ 16 Andrew Shier .25 .11
❑ 17 Tom Tilley .25 .11
❑ 18 Mike Tomlak .25 .11
❑ 19 Steve Tuttle .25 .11
❑ 20 Terry Yake .25 .11
❑ 21 Phil Wittliff CO .10 .05
❑ 22 Peter Bakovic ACO .10 .05
❑ 23 Rob Irsch ACO .10 .05
❑ 24 Doug Agnew TR .10 .05
❑ 25 Dream Ride .10 .05

## 1996-97 Milwaukee Admirals Bank One

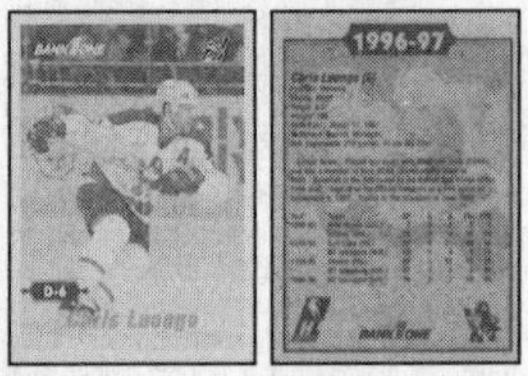

This odd-sized (2 1/2" X 4") 27-card set features the Milwaukee Admirals of the IHL. The cards were produced by the club and sponsored by Bank One as a promotional item. The cards feature action photography on the front surrounded by a thin white border. The logos of Bank One and the PHPA are in the top corners, while the player's name, position and uniform number are listed along the bottom. The backs contain career stats and biographical text. The cards are unnumbered, and are listed in alphabetical order.

| | MINT | NRMT |
|---|---|---|
| COMPLETE SET (27) | 8.00 | 3.60 |
| COMMON CARD | .10 | .05 |

❑ 1 Doug Agnew TR .10 .05
❑ 2 Peter Bakovic ACO .10 .05
❑ 3 Sylvain Couturier .30 .14
❑ 4 Larry DePalma .30 .14
❑ 5 Peter Douris .30 .14
❑ 6 Denny Felsner .30 .14
❑ 7 Eric Fenton .30 .14
❑ 8 Shannon Finn .30 .14
❑ 9 Tony Hrkac .50 .23
❑ 10 Fabian Joseph ACO .40 .18
❑ 11 Jacques Joubert .30 .14
❑ 12 Rick Knickle .60 .25
❑ 13 Brad Layzell .30 .14
❑ 14 Danny Lorenz .50 .23
❑ 15 Chris Luongo .30 .14
❑ 16 Dave Mackey .30 .14
❑ 17 Mike McNeill .30 .14
❑ 18 Michel Mongeau .50 .23
❑ 19 Kent Paynter .30 .14
❑ 20 Christian Proulx .30 .14
❑ 21 Patrice Robitaille .30 .14
❑ 22 Ken Sabourin .30 .14
❑ 23 Steve Strunk .30 .14
❑ 24 Tom Tilley .30 .14
❑ 25 Mike Tomlak .30 .14
❑ 26 Steve Tuttle .30 .14
❑ 27 Phil Wittliff CO .10 .05

## 1991-92 Minnesota Golden Gophers

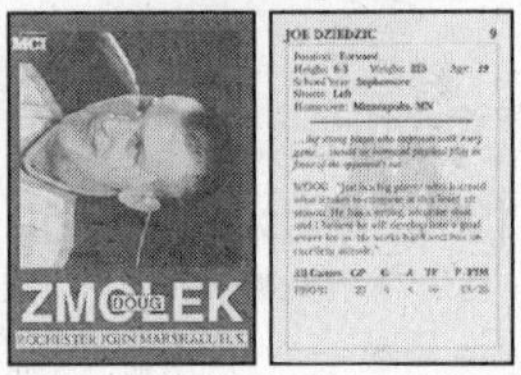

Sponsored by MCI, this 26-card standard-size set features the 1991-92 Minnesota Golden Gophers. On a maroon background, the horizontal and vertical fronts have color action player photos along with the player's name and the name of the high school he attended. The white backs carry the player's name, number, biography, and profile. The cards are unnumbered and checklisted below in alphabetical order.

| | MINT | NRMT |
|---|---|---|
| COMPLETE SET (26) | 10.00 | 4.50 |
| COMMON CARD (1-26) | .35 | .16 |

❑ 1 Scott Bell .35 .16
❑ 2 Tony Bianchi .35 .16
❑ 3 John Brill .35 .16
❑ 4 Jeff Callinan .35 .16
❑ 5 Joe Dziedzic .75 .35
❑ 6 Sean Fabian .35 .16
❑ 7 Jed Fiebelkorn .35 .16
❑ 8 Nick Gerebi .35 .16
❑ 9 Darby Hendrickson .75 .35
❑ 10 Craig Johnson .50 .23
❑ 11 Trent Klatt 1.50 .70
❑ 12 Cory Laylin .35 .16
❑ 13 Steve Magnusson .50 .23
❑ 14 Chris McAlpine .50 .23
❑ 15 Justin McHugh .35 .16
❑ 16 Eric Means .35 .16
❑ 17 Mike Muller .50 .23
❑ 18 Tom Newman .35 .16
❑ 19 Jeff Nielsen .35 .16
❑ 20 John O'Connell .35 .16
❑ 21 Larry Olimb .35 .16
❑ 22 Travis Richards .50 .23
❑ 23 Brandon Steege .35 .16
❑ 24 Jeff Stolp .35 .16
❑ 25 Todd Westlund .35 .16
❑ 26 Doug Zmolek .50 .23

## 1992-93 Minnesota Golden Gophers

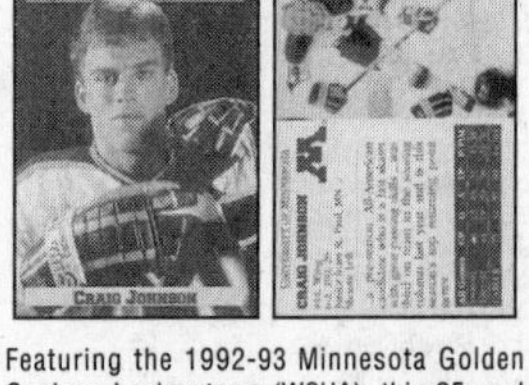

Featuring the 1992-93 Minnesota Golden Gophers hockey team (WCHA), this 25-card measures the standard-size. The fronts feature full-bleed, posed, color player photos. A gray bar at the top (or right edge) displays the school name, while the player's name is printed in maroon lettering in a yellow bar at the bottom. The horizontal backs carry biographical information, a player profile, and statistics, along with a photo of the player in action. The cards are unnumbered and checklisted below in alphabetical order.

| | MINT | NRMT |
|---|---|---|
| COMPLETE SET (25) | 10.00 | 4.50 |
| COMMON CARD (1-25) | .10 | .05 |

❑ 1 Scott Bell .35 .16
❑ 2 Jesse Bertogliat 1.00 .45
Brian Bonin
❑ 3 Tony Bianchi .35 .16
❑ 4 John Brill .50 .23
❑ 5 Jeff Callinan .35 .16
❑ 6 Bobby Dustin .50 .23
Dave Larson
❑ 7 Joe Dziedzic .75 .35
❑ 8 Jed Fiebelkorn .35 .16
❑ 9 Darby Hendrickson .50 .23
❑ 10 Craig Johnson .50 .23
❑ 11 Steve Magnusson .50 .23
❑ 12 Chris McAlpine .60 .25
❑ 13 Justin McHugh .35 .16
❑ 14 Eric Means .35 .16
❑ 15 Jeff Moen .35 .16
❑ 16 Tom Newman .35 .16
❑ 17 Jeff Nielsen .35 .16
❑ 18 Travis Richards .50 .23
❑ 19 Brandon Steege .35 .16
❑ 20 Matt Stelljes .50 .23
Ryan Alstead
❑ 21 Dan Trebil .10 .05
Greg Zwakman
❑ 22 Charlie Wasley .50 .23
Mike McAlpine
❑ 23 Todd Westlund .35 .16
❑ 24 Dan Woog .25 .11
Jim Hillman
❑ 25 Doug Woog CO .25 .11

## 1993-94 Minnesota Golden Gophers

This 30-card set measures the standard size. On a maroon background, the fronts feature posed, color action player photos and portraits with a thin yellow border. The player's name is printed in yellow letters with a maroon outline on the bottom of the photo. The words "Mariucci Arena Inaugural Season" are printed above the photo, while "1993-94 Minnesota Gopher Hockey" is printed below it. On a maroon background, the horizontal backs carry biographical information, a player profile, statistics, and a drawing of the team mascot, along with a black-and-white player portrait. The cards are unnumbered and checklisted below in alphabetical order.

| | MINT | NRMT |
|---|---|---|
| COMPLETE SET (30) | 9.00 | 4.00 |
| COMMON CARD (1-30) | .10 | .05 |

❑ 1 Brett Abrahamson .35 .16
❑ 2 Jesse Bertogliat .35 .16
❑ 3 Tony Bianchi .35 .16
❑ 4 Brian Bonin 1.00 .45
❑ 5 Andy Brink .50 .23
❑ 6 Jeff Callinan .35 .16
❑ 7 Nick Checco .50 .23
❑ 8 Bobby Dustin .35 .16
❑ 9 Joe Dziedzic .75 .35
❑ 10 Jed Fiebelkorn .35 .16
❑ 11 Brent Godbout .35 .16
❑ 12 Dan Hendrickson .50 .23
❑ 13 Jim Hillman .35 .16
❑ 14 John Hillman .35 .16
❑ 15 Brian LaFleur .35 .16
❑ 16 Dave Larson .35 .16
❑ 17 Steve Magnusson .35 .16
❑ 18 Chris McAlpine .50 .23
❑ 19 Mike McAlpine .35 .16
❑ 20 Justin McHugh .35 .16
❑ 21 Eric Means .35 .16
❑ 22 Jeff Moen .35 .16
❑ 23 Jeff Nielsen .35 .16
❑ 24 Brandon Steege .35 .16
❑ 25 Dan Trebil .35 .16
❑ 26 Charlie Wasley .50 .23
❑ 27 Dan Woog ACO .10 .05
❑ 28 Doug Woog CO .35 .16
❑ 29 Greg Zwakman .35 .16
❑ 30 Title Card .10 .05

## 1994-95 Minnesota Golden Gophers

This 31-card standard-size set was sponsored by SuperAmerica and Eveready. On a white card face with team color-coded stripes in the background, the fronts display water color portraits or action shots by artist M.L. Sahlberg. Inside a maroon border, the horizontal backs carry a black-and-white head shot, biography, player profile, and statistics. The cards are unnumbered and checklisted below in alphabetical order.

| | MINT | NRMT |
|---|---|---|
| COMPLETE SET (31) | 9.00 | 4.00 |
| COMMON CARD (1-31) | .10 | .05 |

❑ 1 Will Anderson .25 .11
❑ 2 Scott Bell .25 .11
❑ 3 Jesse Bertogliat .25 .11
❑ 4 Brian Bonin 1.00 .45
❑ 5 Andy Brink .35 .16
❑ 6 Aaron Broten 1.00 .45
Neal Broten
Paul Broten
❑ 7 Jeff Callinan .25 .11
❑ 8 Nick Checco .25 .11
❑ 9 Mike Crowley .25 .11
❑ 10 Steve DeBus .25 .11
❑ 11 Bobby Dustin .25 .11
❑ 12 Jed Fiebelkorn .35 .16
❑ 13 Brent Godbout .25 .11
❑ 14 Jason Godbout .25 .11
❑ 15 Casey Hankinson .25 .11
❑ 16 Dan Hendrickson .25 .11
❑ 17 Ryan Kraft .25 .11
❑ 18 Brian LaFleur .25 .11
❑ 19 Dave Larson .25 .11
❑ 20 Justin McHugh .25 .11
❑ 21 Jeff Moen .25 .11
❑ 22 Jay Moser .25 .11
❑ 23 Lou Nanne .50 .23
❑ 24 Joe Pankratz .35 .16
❑ 25 Jason Seils .25 .11
❑ 26 Brandon Steege .35 .16
❑ 27 Dan Trebil .25 .11
❑ 28 Charlie Wasley .25 .11
❑ 29 Dan Woog .10 .05
❑ 30 Doug Woog CO .10 .05
❑ 31 Greg Zwakman .25 .11

## 1995-96 Minnesota Golden Gophers

The set is unnumbered and checklisted in alphabetical order.

| | MINT | NRMT |
|---|---|---|
| COMPLETE SET (30) | 8.00 | 3.60 |
| COMMON CARD (1-30) | .10 | .05 |

❑ 1 Checklist .10 .05
❑ 2 Doug Woog CO .25 .11
❑ 3 Brett Abrahamson .25 .11
❑ 4 Mike Anderson .25 .11
❑ 5 Reggie Berg .25 .11
❑ 6 Jesse Bertogliat .25 .11
❑ 7 Brian Bonin .75 .35
❑ 8 Andy Brink .25 .11
❑ 9 Nick Checco .25 .11
❑ 10 Nick Crowley .25 .11
❑ 11 Steve Debus .25 .11
❑ 12 Bobby Dustin .25 .11
❑ 13 Jason Godbout .25 .11
❑ 14 Casey Hankinson .25 .11
❑ 15 Dan Hendrickson .25 .11
❑ 16 Clint Johnson .25 .11
❑ 17 Bill Kohn .25 .11
❑ 18 Ryan Kraft .25 .11
❑ 19 Brian LaFleur .25 .11
❑ 20 Dave Larson .25 .11
❑ 21 Jeff Moen .25 .11
❑ 22 Jay Moser .25 .11
❑ 23 Tom Nevers .25 .11
❑ 24 Erik Rasmussen 2.00 .90
❑ 25 Jason Seils .25 .11
❑ 26 Wyatt Smith .25 .11
❑ 27 Dan Trebil .25 .11
❑ 28 Charlie Wasley .25 .11
❑ 29 Dan Woog .10 .05
❑ 30 Greg Zwakman .25 .11

## 1996-97 Minnesota Golden Gophers Collect A Sport

| | MINT | NRMT |
|---|---|---|
| COMPLETE SET (27) | 15.00 | 6.75 |
| COMMON CARD (1-27) | .10 | .05 |

❑ 1 Checklist .10 .05
❑ 2 Doug Woog CO .10 .05
❑ 3 Brett Abrahmanson .75 .35
❑ 4 Mike Anderson .50 .23
❑ 5 Reggie Berg .50 .23
❑ 6 Nick Checco .50 .23
❑ 7 Ben Clymer .50 .23
❑ 8 Mike Crowley .75 .35
❑ 9 Eric Day .50 .23
❑ 10 Steve DeBus .50 .23
❑ 11 Brent Godbout .50 .23
❑ 12 Jason Godbout .50 .23
❑ 13 Casey Hankinson .50 .23
❑ 14 Dan Hendrickson .50 .23
❑ 15 Bill Kohn .50 .23
❑ 16 Ryan Kraft .50 .23
❑ 17 Brian LaFleur .50 .23
❑ 18 Mike Lyons .50 .23
❑ 19 Willy Marvin .50 .23
❑ 20 Cory Miller .50 .23
❑ 21 Nate Miller .50 .23
❑ 22 Rico Pagel .50 .23
❑ 23 Erik Rasmussen 2.50 1.10
❑ 24 Wyatt Smith .50 .23
❑ 25 Dave Spehar .50 .23
❑ 26 Ryan Trebil .50 .23
❑ 27 Dan Woog .50 .23

## 1985-86 Minnesota-Duluth

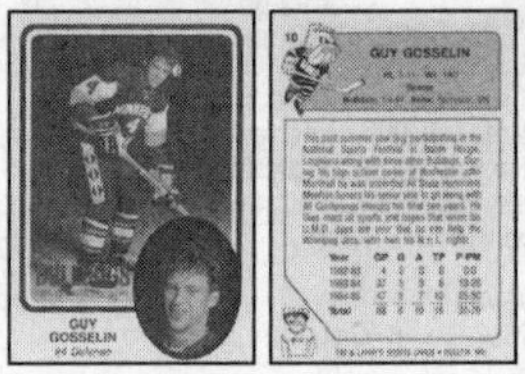

This 36-card standard-size set features color action player photos with rounded corners and black borders against a white card face. An oval inset at the lower right shows a head shot. The player's name is printed in black at the bottom. The backs carry biographical information, career highlights, and statistics. The cards are numbered on the back. It has been reported that this set may have been reprinted to take advantage of the popularity of Brett Hull.

| | MINT | NRMT |
|---|---|---|
| COMPLETE SET (36) | 30.00 | 13.50 |
| COMMON CARD (1-36) | .25 | .11 |

❑ 1 Skeeter Moore .50 .23
❑ 2 Terry Shold .35 .16
❑ 3 Mike DeAngelis .35 .16
❑ 4 Rob Pallin .35 .16
❑ 5 Norm Maciver 2.00 .90
❑ 6 Wayne Smith .35 .16
❑ 7 Dave Cowan .35 .16
❑ 8 Darin Illikainen .35 .16
❑ 9 Rick Hayko .35 .16
❑ 10 Guy Gosselin .50 .23
❑ 11 Paul Roff .35 .16
❑ 12 Jim Toninato .35 .16
❑ 13 Tom Hanson .35 .16
❑ 14 Mike Cortes .35 .16
❑ 15 Matt Christensen .35 .16
❑ 16 Bruce Fishback .35 .16
❑ 17 Mark Odnokon .35 .16
❑ 18 Brian Johnson .35 .16
❑ 19 Bob Alexander .35 .16
❑ 20 Tom Lorentz .35 .16
❑ 21 Roman Sindelar .35 .16
❑ 22 Jim Sprenger .35 .16
❑ 23 Dan Tousignant .35 .16
❑ 24 Sean Toomey .35 .16
❑ 25 Brian Durand .35 .16
❑ 26 John Hyduke .35 .16
❑ 27 Brian Nelson .35 .16
❑ 28 Brett Hull 20.00 9.00
❑ 29 Joe DeLisle .35 .16
❑ 30 Pat Janostin .35 .16
❑ 31 Ben Duffy .35 .16
❑ 32 Sean Krakiwsky .35 .16
❑ 33 Mike Sertich .35 .16
❑ 34 Coaching Staff .25 .11
Jim Knapp ACO
Glenn Kulyk ACO
Tim McDonald ACO
Mike Valesano ACO
Rick Menz EQUIP
Dale Hoganson EQUIP
Betty Fleissner TR
❑ 35 Cheerleaders .75 .35
❑ 36 Jay Jackson (Mascot) .25 .11
The Maroon Loon

## 1990 Hull Collection UMD

This 12-card standard-size set (The Brett Hul Collection), was issued by Universit Minnesota-Duluth in conjunction with Worl Class Marketing and Collect-A-Sport. Th cards have maroon and gold borders on th top and the bottom and are borderless on th side. The border colors are the school colo of University Minnesota-Duluth. Th horizontally formatted card back features hi amateur statistics along with variou biographical blurbs. Cards numbered 10 an 11 are in black and white while the rest of th set was issued with color photos. The set wa issued in a special white box with a photo o Brett Hull on the front as well. The sets ar numbered (out of 5,000) on the backs of th number 1 card.

| | MINT | NRMT |
|---|---|---|
| COMPLETE SET (12) | 15.00 | 6.75 |
| COMMON CARD (1-12) | 1.50 | .70 |
| ❑ 1 Hull Portrait | 3.00 | 1.35 |
| ❑ 2 Hull Behind the Net | 1.50 | .70 |
| ❑ 3 Hull Skating (8 in picture) | 1.50 | .70 |
| ❑ 4 Hull Shooting | 1.50 | .70 |
| ❑ 5 Hull Stick under right arm | 1.50 | .70 |
| ❑ 6 Hull Action stick at waist | 1.50 | .70 |
| ❑ 7 Hull in front of opponents bench | 1.50 | .70 |
| ❑ 8 Hull stickhandling | 1.50 | .70 |
| ❑ 9 Hull Against Providence | 1.50 | .70 |
| ❑ 10 Hull at the net (black and white; shown playing against the Russian Junior Red Army team in Leningrad) | 1.50 | .70 |
| ❑ 11 Hull Portrait (black and white) | 1.50 | .70 |
| ❑ 12 1985-86 UMD | 1.50 | .70 |

## 1993-94 Minnesota-Duluth

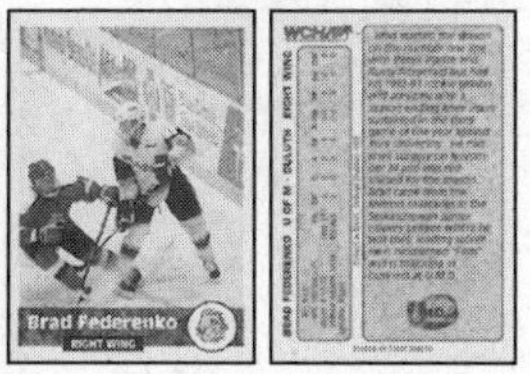

These 30 standard-size cards feature on their fronts white-bordered color player action shots. The player's name and position, along with the Minnesota Bulldog logo, appear within the brown stripe across the bottom of the photo. The back carries the player's name, position, biography, and statistics on the left. His career highlights appear on the right. The set was produced by Collect-A-Sport and features a card of Chris Marinucci, 1993-94 Hobey Baker winner. The cards are unnumbered and checklisted below in alphabetical order.

| | MINT | NRMT |
|---|---|---|
| COMPLETE SET (30) | 10.00 | 4.50 |
| COMMON CARD (1-30) | .10 | .05 |
| ❑ 1 Rod Aldoff | .35 | .16 |
| ❑ 2 Niklas Axelson | .35 | .16 |
| ❑ 3 David Buck | .35 | .16 |
| ❑ 4 Jerome Butler | .35 | .16 |
| ❑ 5 Brian Caruso | .50 | .23 |
| ❑ 6 Matt Christian Chet Culic | .50 | .23 |
| ❑ 7 Marc Christian | .35 | .16 |
| ❑ 8 Joe Ciccarello | .35 | .16 |
| ❑ 9 Kyle Erickson Adam Roy | .35 | .16 |
| ❑ 10 Brad Federenko | .50 | .23 |
| ❑ 11 Rusty Fitzgerald | .75 | .35 |
| ❑ 12 Jason Garatti | .35 | .16 |
| ❑ 13 Greg Hanson | .50 | .23 |
| ❑ 14 Don Jablonic | .35 | .16 |
| ❑ 15 Kraig Karakas | .35 | .16 |
| ❑ 16 Brett Larson | .50 | .23 |
| ❑ 17 Taras Lendzyk | .35 | .16 |
| ❑ 18 Derek Locker | .35 | .16 |
| ❑ 19 Chris Marinucci | 1.00 | .45 |
| ❑ 20 Todd Mickolajak Chris Snell | .50 | .23 |
| ❑ 21 Rod Miller | .35 | .16 |
| ❑ 22 Rick Mrozik | .50 | .23 |
| ❑ 23 Aaron Novak | .35 | .16 |
| ❑ 24 Corey Osmak | .35 | .16 |
| ❑ 25 Sergei Petrov | .35 | .16 |
| ❑ 26 Jeff Romfo | .35 | .16 |
| ❑ 27 Mike Sertich CO | .10 | .05 |
| ❑ 28 Chris Sittlow | .35 | .16 |
| ❑ 29 Joe Tamminen | .35 | .16 |
| ❑ 30 Title Card Roster | .25 | .11 |

## 1993-94 Minnesota-Duluth Commemorative

These four standard-size cards feature black-and-white fronts with color photos on the backs. The set was produced by Collect-A-Sport to commemorate the 1992-93 WCHA champs.

| | MINT | NRMT |
|---|---|---|
| COMPLETE SET (4) | 6.00 | 2.70 |
| COMMON CARD (1-4) | 1.00 | .45 |
| ❑ 1 Trophy Card (Chris Marinucci with trophy) | 2.00 | .90 |
| ❑ 2 Derek Plante | 3.00 | 1.35 |
| ❑ 3 Brett Hauer | 1.00 | .45 |
| ❑ 4 Jon Rohloff | 1.00 | .45 |

## 1983-84 Moncton Alpines

The Moncton Alpines are featured in this 28-card P.L.A.Y. (Police, Law and Youth) set, which was sponsored by the Moncton Police in conjunction with several company sponsors. The cards measure approximately 2 1/2" by 3 3/4" and are printed on thin card stock. The fronts feature color photos with the players posed in action stances. The photos are framed by white borders. The player's name and position are printed below the picture between Coke and Hostess logos. The backs have biography, statistics, and safety tips in English and French.

| | MINT | NRMT |
|---|---|---|
| COMPLETE SET (28) | 15.00 | 6.75 |
| COMMON CARD (1-27) | .25 | .11 |
| ❑ 1 Doug Messier CO | .50 | .23 |
| ❑ 2 Chris Smith | .50 | .23 |
| ❑ 3 Marco Baron | .75 | .35 |
| ❑ 4 Mike Zanier | .75 | .35 |
| ❑ 5 Dwayne Boettger | .50 | .23 |
| ❑ 6 Lowell Loveday | .50 | .23 |
| ❑ 7 Joe McDonnell | .50 | .23 |
| ❑ 8 Peter Dineen | .50 | .23 |
| ❑ 9 John Blum | .75 | .35 |
| ❑ 10 Steve Smith | 3.00 | 1.35 |
| ❑ 11 Reg Kerr | .75 | .35 |
| ❑ 12 Tom Rowe | .50 | .23 |
| ❑ 13 Ross Lambert | .50 | .23 |
| ❑ 14 Pat Conacher | 1.00 | .45 |
| ❑ 15 Paul Miller | .50 | .23 |
| ❑ 16 Bert Yachimel | .50 | .23 |
| ❑ 17 Tom Gorence | .75 | .35 |
| ❑ 18 Jeff Crawford | .50 | .23 |
| ❑ 19 Serge Boisvert | .75 | .35 |
| ❑ 20 Todd Strueby | .75 | .35 |
| ❑ 21 Todd Bidner | .50 | .23 |
| ❑ 22 Dean Dachyshyn | .50 | .23 |
| ❑ 23 Ray Cote | .50 | .23 |
| ❑ 24 Shawn Babcock | .50 | .23 |
| ❑ 25 Shawn Dineen | .50 | .23 |
| ❑ 26 Marc Habscheid | .75 | .35 |
| ❑ 27 Charlie Lavalee TR Kevin Ferris TR | .25 | .11 |
| ❑ NNO Checklist Card | .50 | .23 |

## 1984-85 Moncton Golden Flames

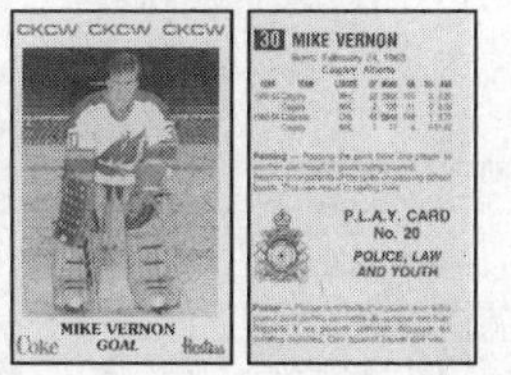

The Moncton Golden Flames are featured in this 26-card P.L.A.Y. (Police, Law and Youth) set, which was sponsored by the Moncton Police in conjunction with several company sponsors. The cards measure approximately 2 1/2" by 3 3/4" and are printed on thin card stock. The fronts feature color photos with the players posed in action stances. The photos are framed by white borders. The player's name and position are printed below the picture between Coke and Hostess logos. The backs have biography, statistics, and safety tips in English and French.

| | MINT | NRMT |
|---|---|---|
| COMPLETE SET (26) | 25.00 | 11.00 |
| COMMON CARD (1-26) | .25 | .11 |
| ❑ 1 Brian Patafie TR | .25 | .11 |
| ❑ 2 Mike Bianni TR | .25 | .11 |
| ❑ 3 Pierre Page CO | 1.00 | .45 |
| ❑ 4 Neil Sheehy | 1.00 | .45 |
| ❑ 5 George White | .50 | .23 |
| ❑ 6 Mark Lamb | 1.00 | .45 |
| ❑ 7 Dan Kane | .50 | .23 |
| ❑ 8 Dan Bolduc | 1.00 | .45 |
| ❑ 9 Lou Kiriakou | .50 | .23 |
| ❑ 10 Joel Otto | 4.00 | 1.80 |
| ❑ 11 Dale Degray | 1.00 | .45 |
| ❑ 12 Mike Clayton | .50 | .23 |
| ❑ 13 Mickey Volcan | .50 | .23 |
| ❑ 14 Ted Pearson | .50 | .23 |
| ❑ 15 Mario Simioni | .50 | .23 |
| ❑ 16 Keith Hanson | .50 | .23 |
| ❑ 17 Yves Courteau | .50 | .23 |
| ❑ 18 Dan Cormier | .50 | .23 |
| ❑ 19 Todd Hooey | .50 | .23 |
| ❑ 20 Mike Vernon | 12.00 | 5.50 |
| ❑ 21 Dave Meszaros | .50 | .23 |
| ❑ 22 Bruce Eakin | .50 | .23 |
| ❑ 23 Tony Stiles | .50 | .23 |
| ❑ 24 Ed Kastelic | 1.00 | .45 |
| ❑ 25 Pierre Rioux | .50 | .23 |
| ❑ 26 Gino Cavallini | 1.00 | .45 |

## 1985-86 Moncton Golden Flames

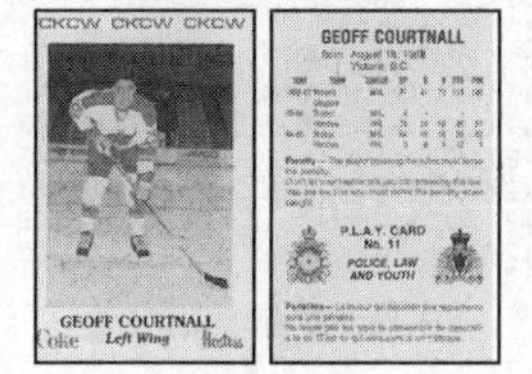

The Moncton Golden Flames are featured in this 28-card P.L.A.Y. (Police, Law and Youth) set, which was sponsored by the Moncton Police in conjunction with several company sponsors. The cards measure approximately 2 1/2" by 3 3/4" and are printed on thin card stock. The fronts feature color photos with the players posed in action stances. The photos are framed by white borders. The player's name and position are printed below the picture between Coke and Hostess logos. The backs have biography, statistics, and safety tips in English and French.

| | MINT | NRMT |
|---|---|---|
| COMPLETE SET (28) | 20.00 | 9.00 |
| COMMON CARD (1-28) | .25 | .11 |
| ❑ 1 Terry Crisp GM/CO | 1.50 | .70 |
| ❑ 2 Dan Bolduc ACO | .25 | .11 |
| ❑ 3 Terry Crisp GM/CO Dan Bolduc ACO | 1.00 | .45 |
| ❑ 4 Al Pedersen | .75 | .35 |
| ❑ 5 Dave Meszaros | .50 | .23 |
| ❑ 6 George White | .50 | .23 |
| ❑ 7 Mark Lamb | 1.00 | .45 |
| ❑ 8 Doug Kostynski | .50 | .23 |
| ❑ 9 Brian Bradley | 5.00 | 2.20 |
| ❑ 10 Rob Kivell | .50 | .23 |
| ❑ 11 Geoff Courtnall | 5.00 | 2.20 |
| ❑ 12 Tony Stiles | .50 | .23 |
| ❑ 13 Jim Buettgen | .50 | .23 |
| ❑ 14 Cleon Daskalakis | 1.00 | .45 |
| ❑ 15 Rick Kosti | .50 | .23 |
| ❑ 16 Kevan Guy | .75 | .35 |
| ❑ 17 John Blum | .75 | .35 |
| ❑ 18 Brian Patafie TR Mike Baiani Jamie Druet | .25 | .11 |
| ❑ 19 Greg Johnston | .75 | .35 |
| ❑ 20 Dale Degray | .50 | .23 |
| ❑ 21 John Meulenbroeks | .50 | .23 |
| ❑ 22 Dave Reid | 1.50 | .70 |
| ❑ 23 Jay Miller | 1.50 | .70 |
| ❑ 24 Yves Courteau | .50 | .23 |
| ❑ 25 Robin Bartel | .50 | .23 |
| ❑ 26 Benoit Doucet | .50 | .23 |
| ❑ 27 Pete Bakovic | .50 | .23 |
| ❑ 28 Team Photo | 2.00 | .90 |

## 1986-87 Moncton Golden Flames

The Moncton Golden Flames are featured in this 28-card P.L.A.Y. (Police, Law and Youth) set, which was sponsored by the Moncton Police in conjunction with several company sponsors. The cards measure approximately 2 1/2" by 3 3/4" and are printed on thin card stock. The fronts feature color photos with the players posed in action stances. The photos are framed by white borders. The player's name and position are printed below the picture between Coke and McDonald's logos. The backs have biography, statistics, and safety tips in English and French. This set includes first pro cards of Brett Hull, Gary Roberts, Bill Ranford, and Lyndon Byers.

| | MINT | NRMT |
|---|---|---|
| COMPLETE SET (28) | 60.00 | 27.00 |
| COMMON CARD (1-28) | .25 | .11 |
| ❑ 1 Terry Crisp CO/GM | 1.00 | .45 |
| ❑ 2 Danny Bolduc ACO | .25 | .11 |
| ❑ 3 Doug Dadswell | .50 | .23 |
| ❑ 4 Doug Kostynski | .50 | .23 |
| ❑ 5 Bill Ranford | 15.00 | 6.75 |
| ❑ 6 Brian Patafie TR | .25 | .11 |
| ❑ 7 Dave Pasin | .50 | .23 |
| ❑ 8 Darwin McCutcheon | .50 | .23 |
| ❑ 9 Team Photo | 2.00 | .90 |
| ❑ 10 Kevan Guy | .50 | .23 |
| ❑ 11 Kraig Nienhuis | .50 | .23 |
| ❑ 12 Gary Roberts | 8.00 | 3.60 |
| ❑ 13 Ken Sabourin | .75 | .35 |
| ❑ 14 Marc D'Amour | .75 | .35 |
| ❑ 15 Don Mercier | .50 | .23 |
| ❑ 16 Wade Campbell | .50 | .23 |
| ❑ 17 Mark Paterson | .50 | .23 |
| ❑ 18 Cleon Daskalakis | .75 | .35 |
| ❑ 19 Lyndon Byers | 1.00 | .45 |
| ❑ 20 Brett Hull | 40.00 | 18.00 |
| ❑ 21 Bob Sweeney | .75 | .35 |
| ❑ 22 Gord Hynes | .50 | .23 |
| ❑ 23 Peter Bakovic | .50 | .23 |
| ❑ 24 Dave Reid | 2.00 | .90 |
| ❑ 25 Mike Rucinski | .50 | .23 |
| ❑ 26 Ray Podloski | .50 | .23 |
| ❑ 27 Bob Bodak | .50 | .23 |
| ❑ 28 John Carter | .75 | .35 |

## 1987-88 Moncton Hawks

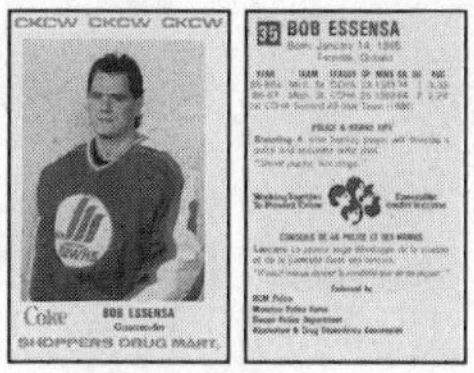

Sponsored by Coke, Shoppers Drug Mart, and CKCW, this 25-card set measures approximately 2 1/2" by 3 3/4" and features posed, color player photos with white studio backgrounds. The fronts have white borders with sponsor names printed in red above and below the picture. The player's name and position are printed in black just below the photo. The backs are white and carry biographical information, statistics, and "Police and Hawks Tips" in French and English. The cards are unnumbered and checklisted below in alphabetical order.

| | MINT | NRMT |
|---|---|---|
| COMPLETE SET (25) | 12.00 | 5.50 |
| COMMON CARD (1-25) | .25 | .11 |
| ❑ 1 Joel Baillargeon | .50 | .23 |
| ❑ 2 Rick Bowness CO | .50 | .23 |
| ❑ 3 Rick Carrano TR Wayne Flemming EQMG | .25 | .11 |
| ❑ 4 Bobby Dollas | .75 | .35 |
| ❑ 5 Peter Douris | .75 | .35 |
| ❑ 6 Iain Duncan | .50 | .23 |
| ❑ 7 Bob Essensa | 2.00 | .90 |
| ❑ 8 Todd Flichel | .50 | .23 |
| ❑ 9 Rob Fowler | .50 | .23 |
| ❑ 10 Randy Gilhen | .75 | .35 |
| ❑ 11 Matt Hervey | .50 | .23 |
| ❑ 12 Brent Hughes | .75 | .35 |
| ❑ 13 Jamie Husgen | .50 | .23 |
| ❑ 14 Mike Jeffrey | .50 | .23 |
| ❑ 15 Guy Larose | .75 | .35 |
| ❑ 16 Chris Levasseur | .50 | .23 |
| ❑ 17 Len Nielson | .50 | .23 |
| ❑ 18 Roger Ohman | .50 | .23 |
| ❑ 19 Dave Quigley | .50 | .23 |
| ❑ 20 Ron Pesetti | .50 | .23 |
| ❑ 21 Steve Penney | .75 | .35 |
| ❑ 22 Scott Schneider | .50 | .23 |
| ❑ 23 Ryan Stewart | .50 | .23 |
| ❑ 24 Gord Whitaker | .50 | .23 |
| ❑ 25 Team Photo | 1.00 | .45 |

## 1990-91 Moncton Hawks

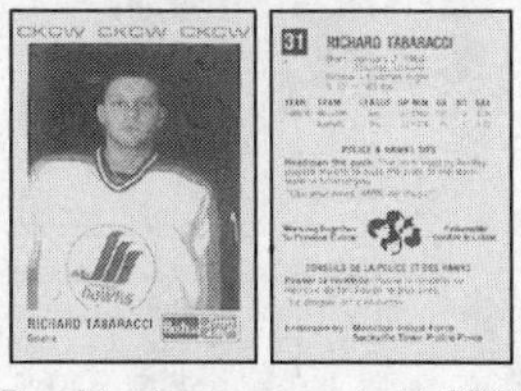

These 25 cards measure approximately 2 7/16" by 3 5/8" and feature on their fronts white-bordered posed-on-ice color shots of the '90-91 Moncton Hawks. The player's name and position appear at the lower left. The logos for the set's sponsors, Hostess, Frito Lay, and CKCW Radio, also appear on the front. The white back carries the player's name and uniform number at the top, followed below by biography, '89-90 statistics, and bilingual safety messages from the Hawks and Moncton Police. The cards are unnumbered and checklisted below in alphabetical order.

| | MINT | NRMT |
|---|---|---|
| COMPLETE SET (25) | 9.00 | 4.00 |
| COMMON CARD (1-25) | .10 | .05 |
| ❑ 1 Larry Bernard | .35 | .16 |
| ❑ 2 Lee Davidson | .35 | .16 |
| ❑ 3 Iain Duncan | .35 | .16 |
| ❑ 4 Craig Duncanson | .35 | .16 |
| ❑ 5 Dallas Eakins | .50 | .23 |
| ❑ 6 Dave Farrish CO/GM | .10 | .05 |
| ❑ 7 Wayne Flemming EQMG | .10 | .05 |
| ❑ 8 Todd Flichel | .35 | .16 |
| ❑ 9 Peter Hankinson | .35 | .16 |
| ❑ 10 Matt Hervey | .35 | .16 |
| ❑ 11 Brent Hughes | .50 | .23 |
| ❑ 12 Anthony Joseph | .35 | .16 |
| ❑ 13 Sergei Kharin | .35 | .16 |
| ❑ 14 Denis Larocque | .35 | .16 |
| ❑ 15 Guy Larose | .50 | .23 |
| ❑ 16 Scott Levins | .50 | .23 |
| ❑ 17 Bryan Marchment | 1.00 | .45 |
| ❑ 18 Chris Norton | .35 | .16 |
| ❑ 19 Mike O'Neill | .75 | .35 |
| ❑ 20 Grant Richison | .35 | .16 |
| ❑ 21 Scott Schneider | .35 | .16 |
| ❑ 22 Rob Snitzer TR | .10 | .05 |
| ❑ 23 Rick Tabaracci | 1.50 | .70 |
| ❑ 24 Simon Wheeldon | .35 | .16 |
| ❑ 25 Team Card | .50 | .23 |

## 1991-92 Moncton Hawks

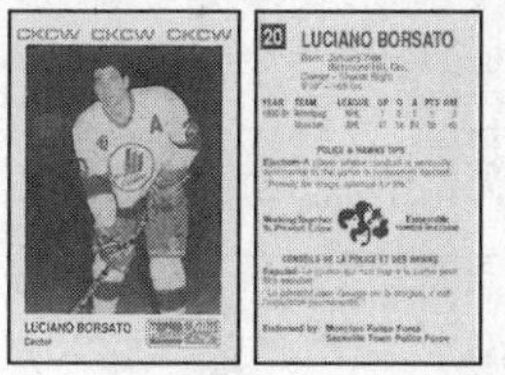

This 28-card set measures approximately 2 1/2" by 3 5/8" and was sponsored by the Moncton Police Force, the Sackville Police Force, and the Hostess/Frito Lay company. The fronts feature color photos with the players posed in action stances. The photos are framed by white borders. The player's name and position appear in the lower left corner, while the Hostess/Frito Lay logo is in the lower right corner. The backs carry biography, statistics, and safety tips in French and English. The cards are unnumbered and checklisted below in alphabetical order.

| | MINT | NRMT |
|---|---|---|
| COMPLETE SET (28) | 10.00 | 4.50 |
| COMMON CARD (1-28) | .10 | .05 |
| ❑ 1 Luciano Borsato | .35 | .16 |
| ❑ 2 Jason Cirone | .35 | .16 |
| ❑ 3 Rob Cowie | .35 | .16 |
| ❑ 4 Lee Davidson | .35 | .16 |
| ❑ 5 Kris Draper | .75 | .35 |
| ❑ 6 Dallas Eakins | .50 | .23 |
| ❑ 7 Dave Farrish GM/CO | .10 | .05 |
| ❑ 8 Wayne Flemming EQMG | .10 | .05 |
| ❑ 9 Sean Gauthier | .50 | .23 |
| ❑ 10 Ken Gernander | .35 | .16 |
| ❑ 11 Tod Hartje | .35 | .16 |
| ❑ 12 Bob Joyce | .50 | .23 |
| ❑ 13 Claude Julien | .35 | .16 |
| ❑ 14 Chris Kiene | .35 | .16 |
| ❑ 15 Mark Kumpel P/ACO | .35 | .16 |
| ❑ 16 Derek Langille | .35 | .16 |
| ❑ 17 Tyler Larter | .35 | .16 |
| ❑ 18 John LeBlanc | .35 | .16 |
| ❑ 19 Scott Levins | .35 | .16 |
| ❑ 20 Rob Murray | .35 | .16 |
| ❑ 21 Kent Paynter | .35 | .16 |
| ❑ 22 Rudy Poeschek | .50 | .23 |
| ❑ 23 Dave Prior CO | .10 | .05 |
| ❑ 24 Warren Rychel | .50 | .23 |
| ❑ 25 Rob Snitzer TR | .10 | .05 |
| ❑ 26 Rick Tabaracci | 1.50 | .70 |
| ❑ 27 The Hawk (Mascot) | .10 | .05 |
| ❑ 28 Darren Veitch | .50 | .23 |

## 1990-91 Montreal-Bourassa AAA

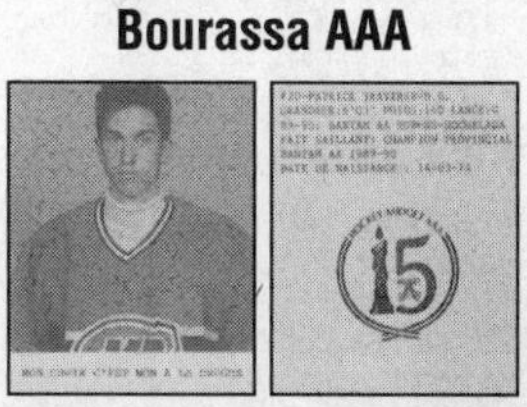

The 25 cards in this oversized set measure approximately 3" by 3 3/4" and feature players from the AAA Midget squad based in Bourassa, a suburb of Montreal. The cards feature a posed color photo on the front, with an anti-drug inscription written in French along the bottom. The crudely designed backs have biographical data, along with the logo celebrating the 15th anniversary of the club.

| | MINT | NRMT |
|---|---|---|
| COMPLETE SET (25) | 5.00 | 2.20 |
| COMMON CARD (1-25) | .10 | .05 |
| ❑ 1 Team Card | .10 | .05 |
| ❑ 2 Police Card | .10 | .05 |

| | MINT | NRMT |
|---|---|---|
| ❑ 3 Coach Card | .10 | .05 |
| ❑ 4 Coach Card | .10 | .05 |
| ❑ 5 Coach Card | .10 | .05 |
| ❑ 6 Peter Arvanitis | .25 | .11 |
| ❑ 7 Luc Bilodeau | .25 | .11 |
| ❑ 8 Luc Corriveau | .25 | .11 |
| ❑ 9 David Desnoyers | .25 | .11 |
| ❑ 10 Alexandre Duchesne | .25 | .11 |
| ❑ 11 Dominic Gagne | .25 | .11 |
| ❑ 12 Benoit Goyer | .25 | .11 |
| ❑ 13 Serge Kiopini | .25 | .11 |
| ❑ 14 Ted Laviolette | .25 | .11 |
| ❑ 15 Ian McIntyre | .25 | .11 |
| ❑ 16 Nathan Morin | .25 | .11 |
| ❑ 17 Valentino Passarelli | .25 | .11 |
| ❑ 18 Jean-Sebastien Perras | .25 | .11 |
| ❑ 19 Sylvain Pinel | .25 | .11 |
| ❑ 20 Sebastien Plouffe | .35 | .16 |
| ❑ 21 Simon Roy | .25 | .11 |
| ❑ 22 Erasmo Saltarelli | .35 | .16 |
| ❑ 23 Alain Savage | .25 | .11 |
| ❑ 24 Christian Sbrocca | .25 | .11 |
| ❑ 25 Patrick Traverse | .25 | .11 |

## 1955-56 Montreal Royals

Cards measure 5 1/4" x 4 1/2" and were issued by Hygrade Franks. Card fronts are black and white and card backs feauter an ad for Hygrade Franks that encourages purchasers to collect all six cards.

| | MINT | NRMT |
|---|---|---|
| COMPLETE SET (6) | 90.00 | 40.00 |
| COMMON CARD (1-6) | 10.00 | 4.50 |
| ❑ 1 Walter Cline | 10.00 | 4.50 |
| ❑ 2 Andre Corriveau | 10.00 | 4.50 |
| ❑ 3 Jacques Deslauriers | 10.00 | 4.50 |
| ❑ 4 Cec Hoekstra | 15.00 | 6.75 |
| ❑ 5 Gerry McNeil | 30.00 | 13.50 |
| ❑ 6 Guy Rousseau | 15.00 | 6.75 |

## 1993-94 Muskegon Fury

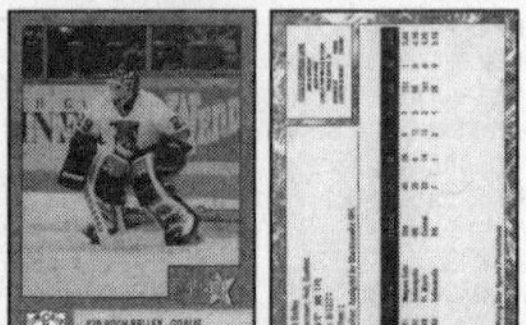

This 20-card set of the Muskegon Fury of the Colonial Hockey League was produced by Rising Star Sports Promotions. The cards feature action photography on the front inside a teal border, along with league logo and player name, number and position. the backs have complete stats but are unnumbered.

| | MINT | NRMT |
|---|---|---|
| COMPLETE SET (20) | 7.00 | 3.10 |
| COMMON CARD (1-20) | .10 | .05 |
| ❑ 1 Header Card | .10 | .05 |
| ❑ 2 Steve Ludzik CO | .35 | .16 |
| ❑ 3 Bob Jones | .35 | .16 |
| ❑ 4 Darrel Newman | .35 | .16 |
| ❑ 5 Brett Seguin | .35 | .16 |
| ❑ 6 Dan Woodley | .50 | .23 |
| ❑ 7 Jodi Murphy | .35 | .16 |
| ❑ 8 Mark Karpen | .35 | .16 |
| ❑ 9 Robert Melanson | .35 | .16 |
| ❑ 10 Paul Kelly | .35 | .16 |
| ❑ 11 Joey Simon | .35 | .16 |
| ❑ 12 Scott Feasby | .35 | .16 |
| ❑ 13 Scott Campbell | .35 | .16 |
| ❑ 14 Joe Hawley | .35 | .16 |
| ❑ 15 Justin Morrison | .35 | .16 |
| ❑ 16 Roch Belley | .75 | .35 |
| ❑ 17 Todd Charlesworth | .60 | .25 |
| ❑ 18 Kevin Barrett | .35 | .16 |
| ❑ 19 Mark Turner | .35 | .16 |
| ❑ 20 Steve Herniman | .35 | .16 |

## 1994-95 Muskegon Fury

This 18-card set of the Muskegon Fury of the CHL was produced by Rising Star Sports Promotions and sponsored by McDonald's. The cards feature and action photo inside a teal border. The logos of Rising Star and the CHL are prominently displayed alonsgside the player's name and position. Card backs contain complete career and personal stats, but are unnumbered. These cards are very similar in design to other Muskegon sets; check the stats on the back to determine the year of your set.

| | MINT | NRMT |
|---|---|---|
| COMPLETE SET (18) | 8.00 | 3.60 |
| COMMON CARD (1-18) | .10 | .05 |
| ❑ 1 Header Card | .10 | .05 |
| ❑ 2 Rich Parent | .75 | .35 |
| ❑ 3 Grant Block | .50 | .23 |
| ❑ 4 Justin Morrison | .50 | .23 |
| ❑ 5 Scott Feasby | .50 | .23 |
| ❑ 6 Scott Campbell | .50 | .23 |
| ❑ 7 Mark Vilneff | .50 | .23 |
| ❑ 8 Brett Seguin | .50 | .23 |
| ❑ 9 Todd Charlesworth | .50 | .23 |
| ❑ 10 Marc Saumier | .50 | .23 |
| ❑ 11 Norm Krumpschmid | .50 | .23 |
| ❑ 12 Darryl Gilmour | .75 | .35 |
| ❑ 13 Paul Kelly | .50 | .23 |
| ❑ 14 Steve Walker | .50 | .23 |
| ❑ 15 Wes McCauley | .50 | .23 |
| ❑ 16 Steve Herniman | .50 | .23 |
| ❑ 17 Andy Bezeau | .50 | .23 |
| ❑ 18 Jamie Black | .50 | .23 |

## 1995-96 Muskegon Fury

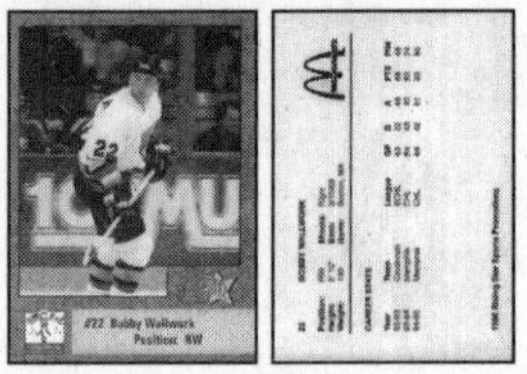

This 20-card set produced by Rising Star Promotions and sponsored by McDonald's features the Muskegon Fury of the Colonial Hockey League. The card fronts have a color action photo within a teal border. The league logo is in the lower left, with player name, number and position along the bottom. The back contains career information for each player. The cards are unnumbered. The design for this set is eerily similar to the previous two years: collectors should check the stats on the back to ascertain which year their set is from.

| | MINT | NRMT |
|---|---|---|
| COMPLETE SET (20) | 8.00 | 3.60 |
| COMMON CARD (1-20) | .10 | .05 |
| ❑ 1 Team Photo | .50 | .23 |
| ❑ 2 Mark Vilneff | .50 | .23 |
| ❑ 3 Kyle Haviland | .50 | .23 |
| ❑ 4 Brett Seguin | .50 | .23 |
| ❑ 5 Rick Girhiny | .50 | .23 |
| ❑ 6 Cory Johnson | .50 | .23 |
| ❑ 7 Paul Kelly | .50 | .23 |
| ❑ 8 Mark Turner | .50 | .23 |
| ❑ 9 Scott Feasby | .50 | .23 |
| ❑ 10 Stephen Webb | .50 | .23 |
| ❑ 11 Bobby Wallwork | .50 | .23 |
| ❑ 12 Richard Fatrola | .50 | .23 |
| ❑ 13 Steve Walker | .50 | .23 |
| ❑ 14 Robert Melanson | .50 | .23 |
| ❑ 15 Rich Parent | .75 | .35 |
| ❑ 16 Jamie Hearn | .50 | .23 |
| ❑ 17 Brian Greer | .50 | .23 |
| ❑ 18 Steve Herniman | .50 | .23 |
| ❑ 19 Terry Ficorelli ANN | .10 | .05 |
| ❑ 20 McDonald's Sponsor | .10 | .05 |

## 1989-90 Nashville Knights

This 23-card standard-size set was sponsored by Lee's Famous Recipe Country Chicken (a restaurant chain). The fronts feature color photos with the players in a variety of action and still poses. White borders enhance the front, and the player's name appears in the border below the picture. The corners of the picture are cut off to give the appearance of circular picture holders. The backs carry biography and advertisement information. The cards are unnumbered and checklisted below in alphabetical order.

| | MINT | NRMT |
|---|---|---|
| COMPLETE SET (23) | 7.00 | 3.10 |
| COMMON CARD (1-23) | .25 | .11 |
| ❑ 1 Pat Bingham | .35 | .16 |
| ❑ 2 Andre Brassard | .35 | .16 |
| ❑ 3 Mike Bukta | .35 | .16 |
| ❑ 4 Chris Cambio | .35 | .16 |
| ❑ 5 Chick-E-Lee (Mascot) | .25 | .11 |
| ❑ 6 Glen Engevik | .35 | .16 |
| ❑ 7 Matt Gallagher<br>Dir. Player Development<br>Scott Greer AGM | .25 | .11 |
| ❑ 8 Archie Henderson CO | .50 | .23 |
| ❑ 9 Billy Huard | .75 | .35 |
| ❑ 10 Craig Jenkins ANN<br>Dave Cavaliere TR | .25 | .11 |
| ❑ 11 Todd Jenkins | .35 | .16 |
| ❑ 12 Brock Kelly | .35 | .16 |
| ❑ 13 Paul Krayer | .35 | .16 |
| ❑ 14 Garth Lamb | .35 | .16 |
| ❑ 15 Rob Levasseur | .35 | .16 |
| ❑ 16 Dan O'Brien | .35 | .16 |
| ❑ 17 Bob Polk OWN<br>Ron Fuller OWN | .25 | .11 |
| ❑ 18 John Reid (In action) | .35 | .16 |
| ❑ 19 John Reid (Portrait) | .35 | .16 |
| ❑ 20 Jeff Salzbrunn | .35 | .16 |
| ❑ 21 Mike Schwalb | .50 | .23 |
| ❑ 22 Ron Servatius | .35 | .16 |
| ❑ 23 Jason Simon | .50 | .23 |

## 1991-92 Nashville Knights

This 24-card set of the Nashville Knights of the East Coast Hockey League was issued as a game premium. The set is unnumbered; the cards are listed by order of the player's jersey number, which is listed on the front of the card. It was sponsored by TV station WZTV, whose logo is garishly emblazoned across the card fronts.

| | MINT | NRMT |
|---|---|---|
| COMPLETE SET (24) | 7.00 | 3.10 |
| COMMON CARD (1-24) | .10 | .05 |
| ❑ 1 Header Card | .10 | .05 |
| ❑ 2 San Jose Sharks | .50 | .23 |
| ❑ 3 Chris Harvey | .35 | .16 |
| ❑ 4 Chris Grassie | .35 | .16 |
| ❑ 5 Daryll Mitchell | .50 | .23 |
| ❑ 6 Ron Majic | .35 | .16 |
| ❑ 7 Daniel Rolfe | .35 | .16 |
| ❑ 8 Mark Hilton | .35 | .16 |
| ❑ 9 Angelo Russo | .35 | .16 |
| ❑ 10 Jeff Jablonski | .35 | .16 |
| ❑ 11 Rob Dumas | .35 | .16 |
| ❑ 12 Chuck Wiegand | .35 | .16 |
| ❑ 13 Steve Chelios | .35 | .16 |
| ❑ 14 Kevin Sullivan | .35 | .16 |
| ❑ 15 Mike Hiltner | .35 | .16 |
| ❑ 16 Brock Kelly | .35 | .16 |
| ❑ 17 Paul Cohen | .35 | .16 |
| ❑ 18 Scott Taylor | .35 | .16 |
| ❑ 19 Mike DeCarle | .35 | .16 |
| ❑ 20 Jim Ritchie | .35 | .16 |
| ❑ 21 Michael Seaton | .35 | .16 |
| ❑ 22 Frank Anzalone CO | .25 | .11 |
| ❑ 23 Dave Cavaliere TR | .10 | .05 |
| ❑ 24 Mike Eruzione OWNER | .75 | .35 |

## 1992-93 Nashville Knights

This 25-card set of the Nashville Knights of the ECHL was sponsored by WZTV and issued as a game premium. The cards feature posed photos on the front and cursory stats on the back, along with card number.

| | MINT | NRMT |
|---|---|---|
| COMPLETE SET (25) | 8.00 | 3.60 |
| COMMON CARD (1-25) | .10 | .05 |
| ❑ 1 Header Card | .25 | .11 |
| ❑ 2 Nick Fotiu CO | .50 | .23 |
| ❑ 3 George Kozak ACO | .10 | .05 |
| ❑ 4 Tom Cole | .35 | .16 |
| ❑ 5 Scott Matusovich | .35 | .16 |
| ❑ 6 Chris Grassie | .35 | .16 |
| ❑ 7 Bob Creamer | .35 | .16 |
| ❑ 8 Ray DeSouza | .50 | .23 |
| ❑ 9 Stanislav Tkach | .35 | .16 |
| ❑ 10 Don Parsons | .35 | .16 |
| ❑ 11 Steve Sullivan | .35 | .16 |
| ❑ 12 Brian Ferreira | .35 | .16 |
| ❑ 13 Rob Dumas | .35 | .16 |
| ❑ 14 Michael Seaton | .35 | .16 |
| ❑ 15 Mike DeCarle | .35 | .16 |
| ❑ 16 Trevor Jobe | .35 | .16 |
| ❑ 17 Brian Horan | .35 | .16 |
| ❑ 18 Andrey Dylevsky | .35 | .16 |
| ❑ 19 Rob Pallante | .35 | .16 |
| ❑ 20 Bryan Krygier | .35 | .16 |
| ❑ 21 Troy Mick | .50 | .23 |
| ❑ 22 Darcy Kaminski | .35 | .16 |
| ❑ 23 Olie Sundstrom | .50 | .23 |
| ❑ 24 Dale King TR | .10 | .05 |
| ❑ 25 Kevin Krueger MED | .10 | .05 |

## 1989-90 New Haven Nighthawks

This black and white set which was issued on the 20th anniversary of the team. It commemorates the best players of the team's past. The set was sponsored by Casio. It is unnumbered and is listed alphabetically by player name.

| | MINT | NRMT |
|---|---|---|
| COMPLETE SET (15) | 12.00 | 5.50 |
| COMMON CARD (1-15) | .50 | .23 |
| ❑ 1 Ken Baumgartner | 2.00 | .90 |
| ❑ 2 John Bednarski | .50 | .23 |
| ❑ 3 Tom Colley | .50 | .23 |
| ❑ 4 Daryl Evans | .75 | .35 |
| ❑ 5 Ed Johnstone | .75 | .35 |
| ❑ 6 Alain Langlais | .50 | .23 |
| ❑ 7 Mark Lofthouse | .75 | .35 |
| ❑ 8 Hubie McDonough | 1.50 | .70 |
| ❑ 9 Bill Plager | 2.00 | .90 |
| ❑ 10 Ron Scott | .75 | .35 |
| ❑ 11 Bobby Sheehan | 1.00 | .45 |
| ❑ 12 Doug Soetaert | 1.50 | .70 |
| ❑ 13 Jim Wiemer | .75 | .35 |
| ❑ 14 Rick Dudley CO | 1.00 | .45 |
| ❑ 15 Parker McDonald GM/CO | .75 | .35 |

## 1990-91 Newmarket Saints

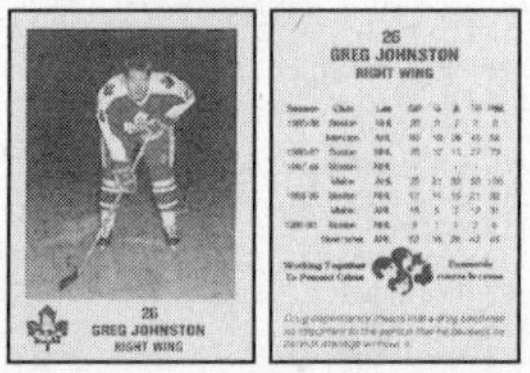

This 26-card set features the 1990-91 Newmarket Saints of the AHL (American Hockey League). Measuring approximately 2 1/2" by 3 3/4", the fronts feature on-ice color posed action shots. The pictures are framed by white borders; the team insignia and player information are printed in black in the bottom wider border. In addition to player information and season-by-season record, the backs carry a bilingual slogan ("Working Together To Prevent Crime" and "Ensemble contre le crime") and anti-drug or alcohol messages. The cards are unnumbered and checklisted below in alphabetical order.

| | MINT | NRMT |
|---|---|---|
| COMPLETE SET (26) | 9.00 | 4.00 |
| COMMON CARD (1-26) | .10 | .05 |
| ❑ 1 Frank Anzalone CO | .25 | .11 |
| ❑ 2 Tim Bean | .35 | .16 |
| ❑ 3 Brian Blad | .35 | .16 |
| ❑ 4 Bryan Cousineau<br>Deputy Chief | .10 | .05 |
| ❑ 5 Alan Hepple | .35 | .16 |
| ❑ 6 Donald Hillock<br>Chief of Police | .10 | .05 |
| ❑ 7 Robert Horyna | .35 | .16 |
| ❑ 8 Kent Hulst | .35 | .16 |
| ❑ 9 Mike Jackson | .35 | .16 |
| ❑ 10 Greg Johnston | .50 | .23 |
| ❑ 11 Eldred King<br>Chairman of Regional<br>Municipality | .10 | .05 |
| ❑ 12 Frank Kovacs<br>Police Sargeant | .10 | .05 |
| ❑ 13 Derek Langille | .35 | .16 |
| ❑ 14 Lanny<br>Police Dog | .10 | .05 |
| ❑ 15 Mike Millar | .35 | .16 |
| ❑ 16 Mike Moes | .35 | .16 |
| ❑ 17 Bill Purcell ACO | .10 | .05 |
| ❑ 18 Bobby Reynolds | .35 | .16 |
| ❑ 19 Damian Rhodes | 2.00 | .90 |
| ❑ 20 Bill Root | .50 | .23 |
| ❑ 21 Joe Sacco | .75 | .35 |
| ❑ 22 Darryl Shannon | .75 | .35 |
| ❑ 23 Doug Shedden | .75 | .35 |
| ❑ 24 Mike Stevens | .50 | .23 |
| ❑ 25 Darren Veitch | .50 | .23 |
| ❑ 26 Greg Walters | .35 | .16 |

## 1988-89 Niagara Falls Thunder

This 25-card set measures approximately 2 5/8" by 4 1/8" and was sponsored by the Niagara Falls Fire Department and area

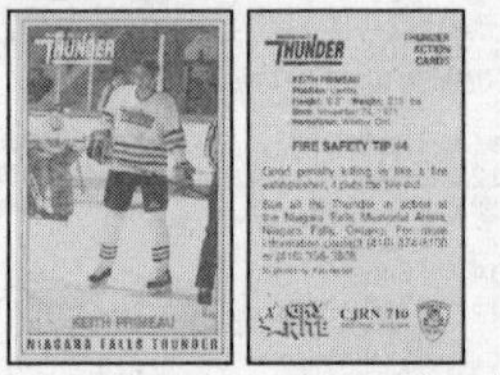

businesses. The cards are printed on thin card stock. The fronts have a white card face and feature color action player photos with two thin black lines forming a border. The player's name is printed in red on the picture at the bottom. The team name appears below the picture. The backs carry biography and fire safety tips.

| | MINT | NRMT |
|---|---|---|
| COMPLETE SET (25) | 25.00 | 11.00 |
| COMMON CARD (1-25) | .25 | .11 |
| ❑ 1 Title Card | .50 | .23 |
| ❑ 2 Brad May | 4.00 | 1.80 |
| ❑ 3 Paul Wolanski | .50 | .23 |
| ❑ 4 Keith Primeau | 10.00 | 4.50 |
| ❑ 5 Mark Lawrence | .75 | .35 |
| ❑ 6 Mike Rosati | .75 | .35 |
| ❑ 7 Dennis Vial | 1.00 | .45 |
| ❑ 8 Shawn McCosh | .50 | .23 |
| ❑ 9 Jason Soules | .50 | .23 |
| ❑ 10 Rob Fournier | .50 | .23 |
| ❑ 11 Scott Pearson | .75 | .35 |
| ❑ 12 Jamie Leach | .50 | .23 |
| ❑ 13 Colin Miller | .50 | .23 |
| ❑ 14 Bryan Fogarty | 1.00 | .45 |
| ❑ 15 Keith Osborne | .50 | .23 |
| ❑ 16 Stan Drulia | 1.00 | .45 |
| ❑ 17 Paul Laus | 2.00 | .90 |
| ❑ 18 Adrian Van Der Sloot | .50 | .23 |
| ❑ 19 Greg Allen | .50 | .23 |
| ❑ 20 Don Pancoe | .50 | .23 |
| ❑ 21 Alain LaForge | .50 | .23 |
| ❑ 22 Bill LaForge GM/CO | .25 | .11 |
| ❑ 23 Steve Locke | .50 | .23 |
| ❑ 24 Benny Rogano ACO | .25 | .11 |
| ❑ 25 Heavy Evason ACO | .25 | .11 |

## 1989-90 Niagara Falls Thunder

Sponsored by local Arby's and Pizza Pizza stores, these 25 cards measure approximately 2 5/8" by 4 1/8" and feature on their fronts white-bordered posed-on-ice color shots of the 1989-90 Niagara Falls Thunder. The player's name appears in red lettering within the white bottom margin. The white back carries the player's name and position at the top, followed by biography and 1989 statistics. The cards are unnumbered and checklisted below in alphabetical order.

| | MINT | NRMT |
|---|---|---|
| COMPLETE SET (25) | 15.00 | 6.75 |
| COMMON CARD (1-25) | .25 | .11 |
| ❑ 1 Greg Allen | .50 | .23 |
| ❑ 2 Roch Belley | .75 | .35 |
| ❑ 3 David Benn | .50 | .23 |
| ❑ 4 Andy Bezeau | .50 | .23 |
| ❑ 5 George Burnett CO | .50 | .23 |
| ❑ 6 Todd Coopman | .50 | .23 |
| ❑ 7 Randy Hall ACO | .25 | .11 |
| ❑ 8 John Johnson | .50 | .23 |
| ❑ 9 Paul Laus | 1.00 | .45 |
| ❑ 10 Mark Lawrence | .50 | .23 |
| ❑ 11 Brad May | 2.00 | .90 |
| ❑ 12 Don McConnell | .50 | .23 |
| ❑ 13 Brian Mueggler | .50 | .23 |
| ❑ 14 Don Pancoe | .50 | .23 |
| ❑ 15 Keith Primeau | 5.00 | 2.20 |
| ❑ 16 Geoff Rawson | .50 | .23 |
| ❑ 17 Ken Ruddick | .50 | .23 |
| ❑ 18 Greg Suchan | .50 | .23 |
| ❑ 19 Trainers<br>Paul Bruneau<br>Dennis Scott | .25 | .11 |
| ❑ 20 Steve Udvari | .50 | .23 |
| ❑ 21 Jeff Walker | .50 | .23 |
| ❑ 22 Jason Winch | .50 | .23 |
| ❑ 23 Paul Wolanski | .50 | .23 |
| ❑ 24 Title Card | .25 | .11 |
| ❑ 25 Checklist Card | .50 | .23 |

## 1993-94 Niagara Falls Thunder

Printed by Slapshot Images Ltd., this 29-card set features the 1993-94 Niagara Falls

Thunder. The cards measure standard size (2 1/2" by 3 1/2"). On a geometrical purple and green background, the fronts feature color action player photos with thin grey borders. The player's name, position and team name, as well as the producer's logo, appear on the front. The backs carry a close-up color player portrait, biography and statistics, along with team and sponsor's logos. The cards are numbered on the back. Included in this set is a Slapshot ad card with a 1994 calendar on the back.

| | MINT | NRMT |
|---|---|---|
| COMPLETE SET (29) | 12.00 | 5.50 |
| COMMON CARD (1-28) | .10 | .05 |
| ❑ 1 Title Card/Checklist | .10 | .05 |
| ❑ 2 Jimmy Hibbert | .35 | .16 |
| ❑ 3 Darryl Foster | .35 | .16 |
| ❑ 4 Gerry Skrypec | .35 | .16 |
| ❑ 5 Greg de Vries | .75 | .35 |
| ❑ 6 Tim Thompson | .35 | .16 |
| ❑ 7 Joel Yates | .35 | .16 |
| ❑ 8 Yianni Ioannou | .50 | .23 |
| ❑ 9 Steve Nimigon | .50 | .23 |
| ❑ 10 Jeff Johnstone | .35 | .16 |
| ❑ 11 Brandon Convery | .75 | .35 |
| ❑ 12 Dale Junkin | .35 | .16 |
| ❑ 13 Ethan Moreau | 2.00 | .90 |
| ❑ 14 Derek Grant | .35 | .16 |
| ❑ 15 Neil Fewster | .35 | .16 |
| ❑ 16 Jason Reesor | .35 | .16 |
| ❑ 17 Tom Moores | .35 | .16 |
| ❑ 18 Matthew Mayo | .35 | .16 |
| ❑ 19 Bogdan Savenko | .35 | .16 |
| ❑ 20 Corey Bricknell | .35 | .16 |
| ❑ 21 Derek Sylvester | .50 | .23 |
| ❑ 22 Anatoli Filatov | .35 | .16 |
| ❑ 23 Jason Bonsignore | .60 | .25 |
| ❑ 24 Mike Perna | .35 | .16 |
| ❑ 25 Manny Legace | .75 | .35 |
| ❑ 26 Randy Hall CO GM | .10 | .05 |
| ❑ 27 Chris Johnstone CO | .10 | .05 |
| ❑ 28 Jason Bonsignore<br>Ethan Moreau<br>Brandon Convery<br>Towering Prospects | 1.50 | .70 |
| ❑ NNO Slapshot Ad Card | .10 | .05 |

## 1982-83 North Bay Centennials

This 24-card set was printed on thick card stock. The fronts feature a mix of action poses and portraits bordered in white. The backs carry biographical information and sponsor logos, Aunt May's City Bakery (Northern) Limited and CFCH-600 Radio. The cards are unnumbered and checklisted below in alphabetical order.

| | MINT | EXC |
|---|---|---|
| COMPLETE SET (24) | 20.00 | 9.00 |
| COMMON CARD (1-24) | 1.00 | .45 |
| ❑ 1 Allen Bishop | 1.00 | .45 |
| ❑ 2 John Capel | 1.00 | .45 |
| ❑ 3 Rob Degagne | 1.00 | .45 |
| ❑ 4 Phil Drouillard | 1.00 | .45 |
| ❑ 5 Jeff Eatough | 1.00 | .45 |
| ❑ 6 Tony Gilliard | 1.00 | .45 |
| ❑ 7 Paul Gillis | 1.50 | .70 |
| ❑ 8 Pete Handley | 1.00 | .45 |
| ❑ 9 Mark Hatcher | 1.00 | .45 |
| ❑ 10 Tim Helmer | 1.00 | .45 |
| ❑ 11 Craig Kales | 1.00 | .45 |
| ❑ 12 Bob LaForest | 1.00 | .45 |
| ❑ 13 Mark LaForest | 2.00 | .90 |
| ❑ 14 Bill Maguire | 1.00 | .45 |
| ❑ 15 Andrew McBain | 1.50 | .70 |
| ❑ 16 Ron Meighan | 1.00 | .45 |
| ❑ 17 Rick Morocco | 1.00 | .45 |
| ❑ 18 Alain Raymond | 1.00 | .45 |
| ❑ 19 Joe Reekie | 2.00 | .90 |
| ❑ 20 Joel Smith | 1.00 | .45 |
| ❑ 21 Bert Templeton CO | 1.00 | .45 |
| ❑ 22 Kevin Vescio | 1.00 | .45 |
| ❑ 23 Peter Woodgate | 1.00 | .45 |
| ❑ 24 Don Young | 1.00 | .45 |

## 1983-84 North Bay Centennials

This 25-card set measures approximately 2 1/2" by 4" and is printed on thin card stock. The fronts carry color, posed action player photos with white borders. The player's name appears in a butterscotch-colored plaque that is superimposed over the picture. The backs carry biographical information and sponsor logos, Aunt May's City Bakery (Northern)

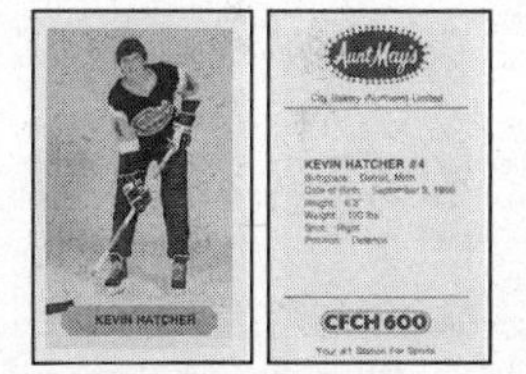

Limited and CFCH-600 Radio. The cards are unnumbered and checklisted below in alphabetical order.

| | MINT | NRMT |
|---|---|---|
| COMPLETE SET (25) | 20.00 | 9.00 |
| COMMON CARD (1-25) | .25 | .11 |
| ❑ 1 Sponsor's Card | .25 | .11 |
| ❑ 2 Peter Abric | .75 | .35 |
| ❑ 3 Richard Benoit | .75 | .35 |
| ❑ 4 Scott Birnie | .75 | .35 |
| ❑ 5 John Capel | .75 | .35 |
| ❑ 6 Curtis Collin | .75 | .35 |
| ❑ 7 Rob Degagne | .75 | .35 |
| ❑ 8 Kevin Hatcher | 5.00 | 2.20 |
| ❑ 9 Mark Hatcher | .75 | .35 |
| ❑ 10 Tim Helmer | .75 | .35 |
| ❑ 11 Jim Hunter | .75 | .35 |
| ❑ 12 Kevin Kerr | .75 | .35 |
| ❑ 13 Nick Kypreos | 1.50 | .70 |
| ❑ 14 Mike Larouche | .75 | .35 |
| ❑ 15 Greg Larsen | .75 | .35 |
| ❑ 16 Mark Lavarre | .75 | .35 |
| ❑ 17 Brett MacDonald | .75 | .35 |
| ❑ 18 Wayne Macphee | .75 | .35 |
| ❑ 19 Peter McGrath | .75 | .35 |
| ❑ 20 Rob Nichols | .75 | .35 |
| ❑ 21 Ron Sanko | .75 | .35 |
| ❑ 22 Kevin Vescio | .75 | .35 |
| ❑ 23 Mike Webber | .75 | .35 |
| ❑ 24 Peter Woodgate | .75 | .35 |
| ❑ 25 Bert Templeton CO/GM | .75 | .35 |

## 1993-94 North Bay Centennials

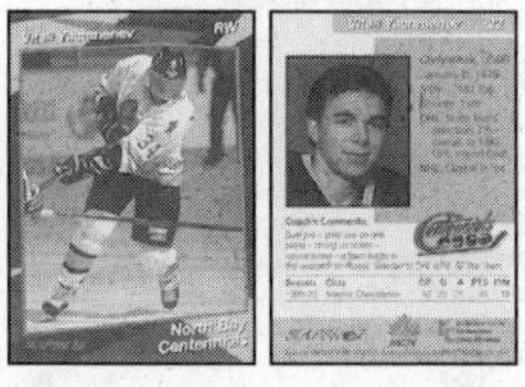

Co-sponsored by MCTV and Collectors Corner and printed by Slapshot Images Ltd., this standard size 26-card set features the 1993-94 North Bay Centennials. On a geometrical yellow and black background, the fronts feature color action player photos with thin grey borders. The player's name, position and team name, as well as the producer's logo, appear on the front. The team color-coded backs carry a close-up color player portrait, biography and statistics, along with team and sponsors' logos. The cards are numbered on the back. Included in this set is a Slapshot ad card with a 1994 calendar on the back.

| | MINT | NRMT |
|---|---|---|
| COMPLETE SET (26) | 10.00 | 4.50 |
| COMMON CARD (1-25) | .10 | .05 |
| ❑ 1 Brad Brown | .75 | .35 |
| ❑ 2 Sandy Allan | .75 | .35 |
| ❑ 3 Rob Lave | .35 | .16 |
| ❑ 4 Steve McLaren | .35 | .16 |
| ❑ 5 Andy Delmore | .60 | .25 |
| ❑ 6 Corey Neilson | .35 | .16 |
| ❑ 7 Jason Campeau | .35 | .16 |
| ❑ 8 Jim Ensom | .35 | .16 |
| ❑ 9 Bill Lang | .35 | .16 |
| ❑ 10 Ryan Gillis | .35 | .16 |
| ❑ 11 Michael Burman | .35 | .16 |
| ❑ 12 Stefan Rivard | .35 | .16 |
| ❑ 13 B.J. MacPherson | .35 | .16 |
| ❑ 14 Lee Jinman | .75 | .35 |
| ❑ 15 Scott Cherrey | .60 | .25 |
| ❑ 16 Damien Bloye | .35 | .16 |
| ❑ 17 Denis Gaudet | .35 | .16 |
| ❑ 18 Bob Thornton | .35 | .16 |
| ❑ 19 John Guirestante | .35 | .16 |
| ❑ 20 Jeff Shevalier | .75 | .35 |
| ❑ 21 Scott Roche | .75 | .35 |
| ❑ 22 Vitali Yachmenev | 1.50 | .70 |
| ❑ 23 Bert Templeton CO | .35 | .16 |
| ❑ 24 Rob Kirsch ACO | .10 | .05 |
| ❑ 25 Brad Brown<br>Vitali Yachmenev<br>Top Prospects | .50 | .23 |
| ❑ NNO Slapshot Ad Card | .10 | .05 |

## 1994-95 North Bay Centennials

Sponsored by MCTV, Guardian and Wingate Lottery, and printed by Slapshot Images Ltd., this 26-card set features the 1994-95 North

Bay Centennials. On a yellow and black background, the fronts feature color action player photos with thin gray borders. The player's name, position and team name, as well as the producer's logo, appear on the front. The team color-coded backs carry a close-up color player portrait, biography and statistics, along with team and sponsors' logos. Included in this set is a Slapshot ad card with a 1995 calendar on the back.

| | MINT | NRMT |
|---|---|---|
| COMPLETE SET (26) | 8.00 | 3.60 |
| COMMON CARD (1-25) | .10 | .05 |
| ❑ 1 Joel Gagnon | .50 | .23 |
| ❑ 2 Scott Roche | .75 | .35 |
| ❑ 3 Derek Lahnalampi | .35 | .16 |
| ❑ 4 Brad Brown | .50 | .23 |
| ❑ 5 Steve McLaren | .35 | .16 |
| ❑ 6 Kam White | .35 | .16 |
| ❑ 7 Corey Neilson | .35 | .16 |
| ❑ 8 Jason Campeau | .35 | .16 |
| ❑ 9 Stephen Carpenter | .35 | .16 |
| ❑ 10 Trevor Gallant | .50 | .23 |
| ❑ 11 Alex Matvichuk | .35 | .16 |
| ❑ 12 Ryan Gillis | .35 | .16 |
| ❑ 13 Kris Cantu | .35 | .16 |
| ❑ 14 Stefan Rivard | .35 | .16 |
| ❑ 15 Brian Whitley | .35 | .16 |
| ❑ 16 Dustin Virag | .35 | .16 |
| ❑ 17 Lee Jinman | .60 | .25 |
| ❑ 18 Scott Cherrey | .50 | .23 |
| ❑ 19 Damien Bloye | .35 | .16 |
| ❑ 20 Justin Robinson | .35 | .16 |
| ❑ 21 Kody Grigg | .35 | .16 |
| ❑ 22 John Guirestante | .35 | .16 |
| ❑ 23 Gary Roach | .35 | .16 |
| ❑ 24 Vitali Yachmenev | 1.00 | .45 |
| ❑ 25 Shane Parker CO/GM<br>Tom Hedican ACO | .10 | .05 |
| ❑ NNO Ad Card | .10 | .05 |

## 1992-93 North Dakota Fighting Sioux

Cards are unnumbered and checklisted below alphabetically.

| | MINT | NRMT |
|---|---|---|
| COMPLETE SET (27) | 9.00 | 4.00 |
| COMMON CARD (1-27) | .30 | .14 |
| ❑ 1 Akil Adams | .30 | .14 |
| ❑ 2 Darren Bear | .30 | .14 |
| ❑ 3 Sean Beswick | .30 | .14 |
| ❑ 4 Brad Bombardir | 1.00 | .45 |
| ❑ 5 Joby Bond | .30 | .14 |
| ❑ 6 Troy Davis | .30 | .14 |
| ❑ 7 Chris Gotziaman | .30 | .14 |
| ❑ 8 Dean Grillo | .30 | .14 |
| ❑ 9 Corey Howe | .30 | .14 |
| ❑ 10 Brett Hryniuk | .30 | .14 |
| ❑ 11 Greg Johnson | .50 | .23 |
| ❑ 12 Chad Johnson | .30 | .14 |
| ❑ 13 Cory Johnson | .30 | .14 |
| ❑ 14 Todd Jones | .30 | .14 |
| ❑ 15 Scott Kirton | .30 | .14 |
| ❑ 16 Page Klostreich | .30 | .14 |
| ❑ 17 Jon Larson | .30 | .14 |
| ❑ 18 Jeff Lembke | .30 | .14 |
| ❑ 19 John McCoy | .30 | .14 |
| ❑ 20 Kevin McKinnon | .30 | .14 |
| ❑ 21 Darcy Mitani | .30 | .14 |
| ❑ 22 Keith Murphy | .30 | .14 |
| ❑ 23 Nick Naumenko | .30 | .14 |
| ❑ 24 Jarrod Olson | .30 | .14 |
| ❑ 25 Lars Oxholm | .30 | .14 |
| ❑ 26 Kevin Powell | .30 | .14 |
| ❑ 27 Kevin Rappana | .30 | .14 |

## 1995-96 North Iowa Huskies

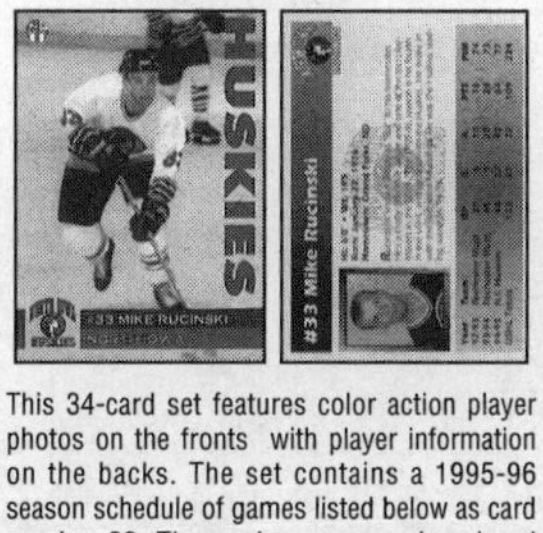

This 34-card set features color action player photos on the fronts with player information on the backs. The set contains a 1995-96 season schedule of games listed below as card number 33. The cards are unnumbered and checklisted below in alphabetical order.

| | MINT | NRMT |
|---|---|---|
| COMPLETE SET (34) | 9.00 | 4.00 |
| COMMON CARD (1-34) | .10 | .05 |
| ❑ 1 Dave Boehm | .35 | .16 |
| ❑ 2 Mike Cerniglia | .35 | .16 |
| ❑ 3 Lionel Crump | .35 | .16 |
| ❑ 4 Peter Cullen | .35 | .16 |
| ❑ 5 Nate Dicasmirro | .35 | .16 |
| ❑ 6 D.J. Drayna | .35 | .16 |
| ❑ 7 Andy Fermoyle | .35 | .16 |
| ❑ 8 Matt Fetterman | .35 | .16 |
| ❑ 9 Mike Fryar | .50 | .23 |
| ❑ 10 Shane Fukushima | .35 | .16 |
| ❑ 11 Bucky Gruber | .35 | .16 |
| ❑ 12 Jason Helgeson TR | .10 | .05 |
| ❑ 13 Mark Hicks ACO | .10 | .05 |
| ❑ 14 Huskies CL | .10 | .05 |
| ❑ 15 Furlin Husky (Mascot) | .10 | .05 |
| ❑ 16 Ryan James | .35 | .16 |
| ❑ 17 Tom Lund | .35 | .16 |
| ❑ 18 Kevin Mackey | .35 | .16 |
| ❑ 19 Erik Macy | .35 | .16 |
| ❑ 20 Josh Mizerek | .35 | .16 |
| ❑ 21 Joe Mussey ACO | .10 | .05 |
| ❑ 22 Gregg Naumenko | .50 | .23 |
| ❑ 23 Matt Noga | .35 | .16 |
| ❑ 24 P.K. O'Handley CO | .10 | .05 |
| ❑ 25 Mark Pannitto | .50 | .23 |
| ❑ 26 Matt Romaniski | .35 | .16 |
| ❑ 27 Mike Romano | .35 | .16 |
| ❑ 28 Mike Rucinski | .35 | .16 |
| ❑ 29 R.J. Schriefer | .35 | .16 |
| ❑ 30 Mike Skogland | .35 | .16 |
| ❑ 31 Matt Snesrud | .35 | .16 |
| ❑ 32 Team Media | .10 | .05 |
| ❑ 33 Season Schedule | .10 | .05 |
| ❑ 34 Title Card | .10 | .05 |

## 1992-93 Northern Michigan Wildcats

| | MINT | NRMT |
|---|---|---|
| COMPLETE SET (32) | 5.00 | 2.20 |
| COMMON CARD (1-32) | .10 | .05 |
| ❑ 1 Brian Barker | .25 | .11 |
| ❑ 2 Steve Carpenter | .25 | .11 |
| ❑ 3 Chad Dameworth | .25 | .11 |
| ❑ 4 Dustin Fahl | .25 | .11 |
| ❑ 5 Joe Frederick | .25 | .11 |
| ❑ 6 Bryan Ganz | .25 | .11 |
| ❑ 7 Scott Green | .25 | .11 |
| ❑ 8 Greg Hadden | .25 | .11 |
| ❑ 9 Steve Hamilton | .25 | .11 |
| ❑ 10 Mike Harding | .25 | .11 |
| ❑ 11 Jason Hehr | .25 | .11 |
| ❑ 12 Dave Huettl | .25 | .11 |
| ❑ 13 Troy Johnson | .25 | .11 |
| ❑ 14 Karson Kaebel | .25 | .11 |
| ❑ 15 Kory Karlander | .25 | .11 |
| ❑ 16 Rob Kruhlak | .25 | .11 |
| ❑ 17 Garett MacDonald | .25 | .11 |
| ❑ 18 Bill MacGillivray | .25 | .11 |
| ❑ 19 Don McCusker | .25 | .11 |
| ❑ 20 Brent Riplinger | .25 | .11 |
| ❑ 21 Dan Ruoho | .25 | .11 |
| ❑ 22 Corwin Saurdiff | .25 | .11 |
| ❑ 23 Kyuin Shim | .25 | .11 |
| ❑ 24 Geoff Simpson | .25 | .11 |
| ❑ 25 Scott Smith | .25 | .11 |
| ❑ 26 Paul Taylor | .25 | .11 |
| ❑ 27 Steve Woog | .25 | .11 |
| ❑ 28 Rick Comley CO | .10 | .05 |
| ❑ 29 Pat Ford ACO | .10 | .05 |
| ❑ 30 Morey Gare ACO | .10 | .05 |
| ❑ 31 Dave Shyiak | .25 | .11 |
| ❑ 32 Wildcat Willy | .10 | .05 |

## 1993-94 Northern Michigan Wildcats

| | MINT | NRMT |
|---|---|---|
| COMPLETE SET (32) | 5.00 | 2.20 |
| COMMON CARD (1-32) | .10 | .05 |
| ❑ 1 Brian Barker | .25 | .11 |
| ❑ 2 Keith Bartholomaus | .25 | .11 |
| ❑ 3 Steve Carpenter | .25 | .11 |
| ❑ 4 Darcy Dallas | .25 | .11 |
| ❑ 5 Chad Dameworth | .25 | .11 |
| ❑ 6 Bryan Ganz | .25 | .11 |
| ❑ 7 Justin George | .25 | .11 |
| ❑ 8 Scott Green | .25 | .11 |
| ❑ 9 Greg Hadden | .25 | .11 |
| ❑ 10 Steve Hamilton | .25 | .11 |
| ❑ 11 Patrick Hansson | .25 | .11 |
| ❑ 12 Mike Harding | .25 | .11 |
| ❑ 13 Jason Hehr | .25 | .11 |
| ❑ 14 Mike Hillock | .25 | .11 |
| ❑ 15 Trevor Janicki | .25 | .11 |
| ❑ 16 Karson Kaebel | .25 | .11 |
| ❑ 17 Kory Karlander | .25 | .11 |
| ❑ 18 Dieter Kochan | .25 | .11 |
| ❑ 19 Roger Lewis | .25 | .11 |
| ❑ 20 Garrett MacDonald | .25 | .11 |
| ❑ 21 Bill MacGillivray | .25 | .11 |
| ❑ 22 Don McCusker | .25 | .11 |
| ❑ 23 Brent Riplinger | .25 | .11 |
| ❑ 24 Dean Seymour | .25 | .11 |
| ❑ 25 Scott Smith | .25 | .11 |
| ❑ 26 Paul Taylor | .25 | .11 |
| ❑ 27 Shayne Tomlinson | .25 | .11 |
| ❑ 28 Jason Welch | .25 | .11 |
| ❑ 29 Steve Woog | .25 | .11 |
| ❑ 30 Pat Ford ACO | .10 | .05 |
| ❑ 31 Morey Gare ACO | .10 | .05 |
| ❑ 32 Rick Comley CO | .10 | .05 |

## 1977-78 Nova Scotia Voyageurs

Sponsored by the Farmers Twin Cities Co-op Dairy Ltd., this 24-card set measures approximately 2 1/8" by 4 1/2" and features the Nova Scotia Voyageurs of the American Hockey League. The fronts feature posed action player photos bordered in white. In the top border appears "Nova Scotia Voyageurs 1977-78," while the player's name, facsimile autograph, sponsor name and logo, and team logo are printed below the picture. The backs are blank. The cards are unnumbered and checklisted below in alphabetical order.

| | NRMT-MT | EXC |
|---|---|---|
| COMPLETE SET (24) | 25.00 | 11.00 |
| COMMON CARD (1-24) | .50 | .23 |
| ❑ 1 Bruce Baker | 1.00 | .45 |
| ❑ 2 Maurice Barrette | 1.00 | .45 |
| ❑ 3 Barry Borrett | 1.00 | .45 |
| ❑ 4 Tim Burke | 1.00 | .45 |
| ❑ 5 Jim Cahoon | 1.00 | .45 |
| ❑ 6 Norm Dupont | 1.50 | .70 |
| ❑ 7 Greg Fox | 1.50 | .70 |
| ❑ 8 Mike Hobin | 1.00 | .45 |
| ❑ 9 Bob Holland | 1.00 | .45 |
| ❑ 10 Don Howse | 1.00 | .45 |
| ❑ 11 Pat Hughes | 2.00 | .90 |
| ❑ 12 Chuck Luksa | 1.00 | .45 |
| ❑ 13 Dave Lumley | 2.00 | .90 |
| ❑ 14 Al MacNeil CO | 1.50 | .70 |
| ❑ 15 Gord McTavish | 1.00 | .45 |
| ❑ 16 Rick Meagher | 3.00 | 1.35 |
| ❑ 17 Mike Polich | 1.00 | .45 |
| ❑ 18 Moe Robinson | 1.00 | .45 |
| ❑ 19 Gaeton Rochette | 1.00 | .45 |
| ❑ 20 Pierre Roy | 1.00 | .45 |
| ❑ 21 Frank St.Marseille | 1.50 | .70 |
| ❑ 22 Derrick St.Marseille TR | .50 | .23 |
| ❑ 23 Rod Schutt | 1.00 | .45 |
| ❑ 24 Ron Wilson | 2.00 | .90 |

## 1983-84 Nova Scotia Voyageurs

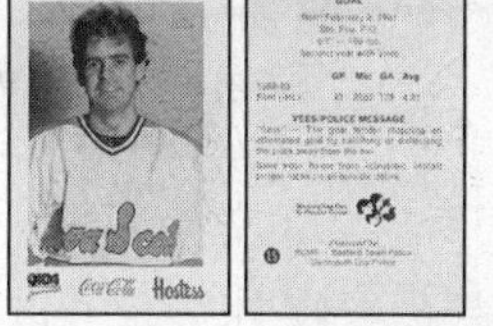

This 24-card police set features the Nova Scotia Oilers of the American Hockey League. The cards measure approximately 2 1/2" by 3 3/4" and were sponsored by Q104 (an FM radio station), Coca-Cola, and Hostess. The cards display posed color player photos on a white card face. The player's name and jersey number appear at the top. The three sponsors' logos are in the bottom white border. The backs are white and carry biography, statistics, and public service messages.

| | MINT | NRMT |
|---|---|---|
| COMPLETE SET (24) | 14.00 | 6.25 |
| COMMON CARD (1-24) | .25 | .11 |
| ❑ 1 Mark Holden | .75 | .35 |
| ❑ 2 Bill Kitchen | .50 | .23 |
| ❑ 3 Dave Allison | .50 | .23 |
| ❑ 4 Stephane Lefebvre | .50 | .23 |
| ❑ 5 Stan Hennigar | .50 | .23 |
| ❑ 6 Steve Marengere | .50 | .23 |
| ❑ 7 John Goodwin | .50 | .23 |
| ❑ 8 John Newberry | .50 | .23 |
| ❑ 9 Bill Riley | .75 | .35 |
| ❑ 10 Norman Baron | .75 | .35 |
| ❑ 11 Brian Skrudland | 3.00 | 1.35 |
| ❑ 12 Mike Lalor | 1.00 | .45 |
| ❑ 13 Blair Barnes | .50 | .23 |
| ❑ 14 Remi Gagne | .50 | .23 |
| ❑ 15 Steve Penney | 1.00 | .45 |
| ❑ 16 Michel Therrien | .50 | .23 |
| ❑ 17 Dave Stoyanovich | .50 | .23 |
| ❑ 18 Brian Patafie TR<br>Lou Christian TR | .25 | .11 |
| ❑ 19 Mike McPhee | 2.50 | 1.10 |
| ❑ 20 Wayne Thompson | .50 | .23 |
| ❑ 21 Ted Fauss | .50 | .23 |
| ❑ 22 Jeff Teal | .50 | .23 |
| ❑ 23 Larry Landon | .50 | .23 |
| ❑ 24 Greg Moffett | .50 | .23 |

## 1984-85 Nova Scotia Oilers

This 26-card police set features the Nova Scotia Oilers of the American Hockey League. The cards measure approximately 2 1/2" by 3 3/4" and were sponsored by Q104 (an FM radio station), Coca-Cola, Hostess, and the

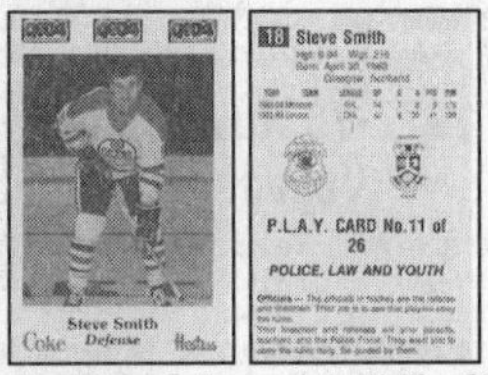


Bedford Town Police, and the Halifax City Police. The cards display posed color player photos on a white card face. The player's name and position appear at the bottom. The three sponsors' logos are across the top and in the bottom two corners. The backs are white and carry biography, statistics, and public service messages.

| | MINT | NRMT |
|---|---|---|
| COMPLETE SET (26) | 12.00 | 5.50 |
| COMMON CARD (1-26) | .25 | .11 |
| ❑ 1 Mark Holden | .75 | .35 |
| ❑ 2 Dave Allison | .50 | .23 |
| ❑ 3 Dwayne Boettger | .50 | .23 |
| ❑ 4 Lowell Loveday | .50 | .23 |
| ❑ 5 Rejean Cloutier | .50 | .23 |
| ❑ 6 Ray Cote | .50 | .23 |
| ❑ 7 Pat Conacher | 1.00 | .45 |
| ❑ 8 Ken Berry | .75 | .35 |
| ❑ 9 Steve Graves | .50 | .23 |
| ❑ 10 Todd Strueby | .75 | .35 |
| ❑ 11 Steve Smith | 2.00 | .90 |
| ❑ 12 Archie Henderson | .75 | .35 |
| ❑ 13 Dean Dachyshyn | .50 | .23 |
| ❑ 14 Marc Habscheid | 1.00 | .45 |
| ❑ 15 Larry Melnyk | .75 | .35 |
| ❑ 16 Raimo Summanen | .75 | .35 |
| ❑ 17 Jim Playfair | .50 | .23 |
| ❑ 18 Mike Zanier | .75 | .35 |
| ❑ 19 Ian Wood | .50 | .23 |
| ❑ 20 Dean Hopkins | .50 | .23 |
| ❑ 21 Norm Aubin | .50 | .23 |
| ❑ 22 Tony Currie | .50 | .23 |
| ❑ 23 Ross Lambert | .50 | .23 |
| ❑ 24 Terry Martin | .50 | .23 |
| ❑ 25 Ed Chadwick CO<br>Larry Kish CO<br>Bob Boucher CO | .75 | .35 |
| ❑ 26 Lou Christian TR<br>Kevin Farris TR | .25 | .11 |

## 1985-86 Nova Scotia Oilers

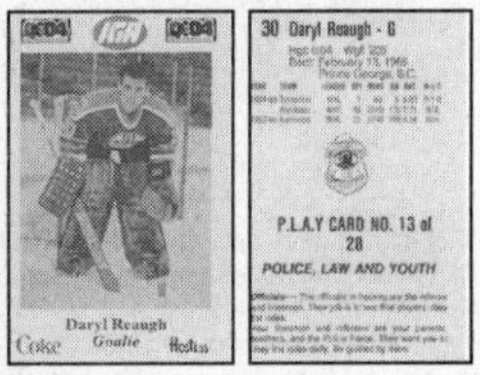


This 28-card police set features the Nova Scotia Oilers. The cards measure approximately 2 1/2" by 3 3/4" and were sponsored by Coca-Cola, Hostess, Q104 (an FM radio station), IGA foodstores, and the Halifax City Police. The fronts display color action photos on a white card face. The sponsor logos appear across the top and in the lower corners. The player's name and position is below the picture. The backs carry biographical information, statistics, and public service messages.

| | MINT | NRMT |
|---|---|---|
| COMPLETE SET (28) | 10.00 | 4.50 |
| COMMON CARD (1-28) | .25 | .11 |
| ❑ 1 Dean Hopkins | .50 | .23 |
| ❑ 2 Jeff Larmer | .50 | .23 |
| ❑ 3 Mike Moller | .50 | .23 |
| ❑ 4 Dean Dachyshyn | .50 | .23 |
| ❑ 5 Bruce Boudreau | .75 | .35 |
| ❑ 6 Ken Solheim | .50 | .23 |
| ❑ 7 Jeff Beukeboom | 1.00 | .45 |
| ❑ 8 Mark Lavarre | .50 | .23 |
| ❑ 9 John Ollson | .50 | .23 |
| ❑ 10 Lou Crawford | .50 | .23 |
| ❑ 11 Warren Skorodenski | .75 | .35 |
| ❑ 12 Dwayne Boettger | .50 | .23 |
| ❑ 13 Daryl Reaugh | .75 | .35 |
| ❑ 14 John Miner | .50 | .23 |
| ❑ 15 Jim Ralph | 1.50 | .70 |
| ❑ 16 Wayne Presley | .75 | .35 |
| ❑ 17 Steve Graves | .50 | .23 |
| ❑ 18 Tom McMurchy | .50 | .23 |
| ❑ 19 Darin Sceviour | .50 | .23 |
| ❑ 20 Kent Paynter | .50 | .23 |
| ❑ 21 Larry Kish GM/CO | .25 | .11 |
| ❑ 22 Jim Playfair | .50 | .23 |
| ❑ 23 Kevin Farris TR<br>Ralph Mosher TR | .25 | .11 |
| ❑ 24 Mickey Volcan | .50 | .23 |
| ❑ 25 Ron Low ACO | .75 | .35 |
| ❑ 26 Don Biggs | .50 | .23 |
| ❑ 27 Bruce Eakin | .50 | .23 |
| ❑ 28 Team Photo | 1.00 | .45 |

## 1992-93 Oklahoma City Blazers

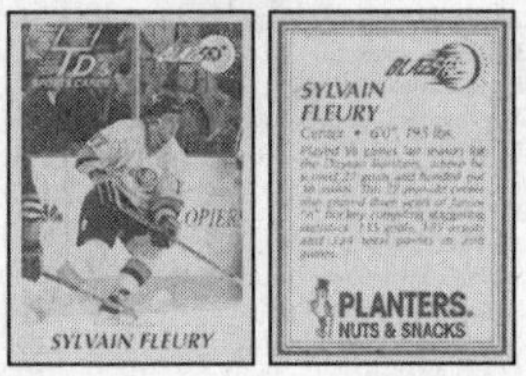


This 18-card standard-size set was sponsored by TD's Sports Cards (a Tulsa baseball card store) and Planters Nuts and Snacks. Ten thousand sets were produced. Randomly inserted thoughout the sets were 350 autographed cards of each player. The cards feature color action player photos with white borders. The player's name is superimposed on the photo at the bottom. The backs carry biography, career highlights, and the Planters logo. The cards are unnumbered and checklisted below in alphabetical order.

| | MINT | NRMT |
|---|---|---|
| COMPLETE SET (18) | 8.00 | 3.60 |
| COMMON CARD (1-18) | .25 | .11 |
| ❑ 1 Title Card | .25 | .11 |
| ❑ 2 Carl Boudreau | .50 | .23 |
| ❑ 3 Joe Burton | .50 | .23 |
| ❑ 4 Sylvain Fleury | .50 | .23 |
| ❑ 5 Brendan Garvey | .50 | .23 |
| ❑ 6 Guy Girouard | .50 | .23 |
| ❑ 7 Sean Gorman | .50 | .23 |
| ❑ 8 Jamie Hearn | .50 | .23 |
| ❑ 9 Craig Johnson | .50 | .23 |
| ❑ 10 Paul Krake | .75 | .35 |
| ❑ 11 Chris Laganas | .50 | .23 |
| ❑ 12 Daniel Larin | .50 | .23 |
| ❑ 13 Mark McGinn | .50 | .23 |
| ❑ 14 Alan Perry | .75 | .35 |
| ❑ 15 Steve Simoni | .50 | .23 |
| ❑ 16 Jim Solly | .50 | .23 |
| ❑ 17 Boyd Sutton | .50 | .23 |
| ❑ 18 Team Photo | .50 | .23 |

## 1993-94 Omaha Lancers

Printed by Pioneer Graphics, this 28-card set features the 1993-94 Omaha Lancers of the USHL (United States Hockey League). The set was available at hobby shops in the Omaha area and at AK-SAR-BEN arena where the Lancers play. The fronts feature posed action shots inside borders. The team name and player information appears in two stripes immediately below the picture. In addition to displaying various logos, the backs carry biography, player profile, and statistics. The cards are unnumbered and checklisted below in alphabetical order.

| | MINT | NRMT |
|---|---|---|
| COMPLETE SET (28) | 8.00 | 3.60 |
| COMMON CARD (1-28) | .10 | .05 |
| ❑ 1 Ryan Bencurik | .35 | .16 |
| ❑ 2 Jeff Borders | .35 | .16 |
| ❑ 3 Sean Bowman | .35 | .16 |
| ❑ 4 Doc Del Castillo ACO | .10 | .05 |
| ❑ 5 Jeff Edwards | .35 | .16 |
| ❑ 6 Tony Gasparini | .35 | .16 |
| ❑ 7 Mike Guentzel CO | .10 | .05 |
| ❑ 8 Scott Haig | .35 | .16 |
| ❑ 9 Ken Hemenway | .35 | .16 |
| ❑ 10 Bill Hubbard | .35 | .16 |
| ❑ 11 Klage Kaebel | .35 | .16 |
| ❑ 12 Rob Klasnick | .35 | .16 |
| ❑ 13 Tony Kolozsy | .35 | .16 |
| ❑ 14 Tom Kowal | .35 | .16 |
| ❑ 15 Charlie Lentz | .35 | .16 |
| ❑ 16 Justin Lyle | .35 | .16 |
| ❑ 17 Chris Marvel | .35 | .16 |
| ❑ 18 Mike Peluso | .35 | .16 |
| ❑ 19 Scott Pionk ACO | .10 | .05 |
| ❑ 20 Dan Riva | .35 | .16 |
| ❑ 21 Nathan Rocheleau | .35 | .16 |
| ❑ 22 Eric Runyan | .35 | .16 |
| ❑ 23 Joe Russo | .35 | .16 |
| ❑ 24 Brian Swanson | .35 | .16 |
| ❑ 25 Scott Swanson | .35 | .16 |
| ❑ 26 Justin Theel | .35 | .16 |
| ❑ 27 Jamie Thompson | .35 | .16 |
| ❑ 28 Brendan Walsh | .35 | .16 |

## 1980-81 Oshawa Generals

This 25-card P.L.A.Y. (Police, Laws and Youth) set measures approximately 2 5/8" by 4 1/8" and features color posed action player photos and is bordered by white borders accented by a thin red line. The player's name, position, and team are superimposed in white letters on the picture. The backs carry "Tips from the Generals" that include a hockey tip and its application to a life situation. The cards are numbered on the back and concludes with some former Generals' players (23-25).

| | NRMT-MT | EXC |
|---|---|---|
| COMPLETE SET (25) | 125.00 | 55.00 |
| COMMON CARD (1-25) | 2.00 | .90 |
| ❑ 1 Generals Logo | 2.00 | .90 |
| ❑ 2 Ray Flaherty | 2.00 | .90 |
| ❑ 3 Craig Kitchener | 2.00 | .90 |
| ❑ 4 Dan Revell | 2.00 | .90 |
| ❑ 5 Bob Kucheran | 2.00 | .90 |
| ❑ 6 Patrick Poulin | 2.00 | .90 |
| ❑ 7 Dave Andreychuk | 15.00 | 6.75 |
| ❑ 8 Barry Tabobondung | 2.00 | .90 |
| ❑ 9 Steve Konroyd | 4.00 | 1.80 |
| ❑ 10 Paul Edwards | 2.00 | .90 |
| ❑ 11 Dale Degray | 4.00 | 1.80 |
| ❑ 12 Joe Cirella | 4.00 | 1.80 |
| ❑ 13 Norm Schmidt | 2.00 | .90 |
| ❑ 14 Markus Lehto | 2.00 | .90 |
| ❑ 15 Mitch Lamoureux | 2.00 | .90 |
| ❑ 16 Tony Tanti | 4.00 | 1.80 |
| ❑ 17 Bill Laforge | 2.00 | .90 |
| ❑ 18 Greg Gravel | 2.00 | .90 |
| ❑ 19 Mike Lekun | 2.00 | .90 |
| ❑ 20 Chris Smith | 2.00 | .90 |
| ❑ 21 Peter Sidorkiewicz | 4.00 | 1.80 |
| ❑ 22 Greg Stefan | 4.00 | 1.80 |
| ❑ 23 Tom McCarthy | 4.00 | 1.80 |
| ❑ 24 Rick Lanz | 4.00 | 1.80 |
| ❑ 25 Bobby Orr | 80.00 | 36.00 |

## 1981-82 Oshawa Generals

This 25-card P.L.A.Y. (Police, Laws and Youth) set measures approximately 2 5/8" by 4 1/8" and features color posed action player photos. The backs carry "Tips from the Generals" that include a hockey tip and its application to a life situation.

| | NRMT-MT | EXC |
|---|---|---|
| COMPLETE SET (25) | 60.00 | 27.00 |
| COMMON CARD (1-25) | .50 | .23 |
| ❑ 1 Generals Logo | 1.00 | .45 |
| ❑ 2 Chris Smith | 1.50 | .70 |
| ❑ 3 Peter Sidorkiewicz | 4.00 | 1.80 |
| ❑ 4 Ali Butorac | 1.50 | .70 |
| ❑ 5 Dan Revell | 1.50 | .70 |
| ❑ 6 Mitch Lamoureux | 2.00 | .90 |
| ❑ 7 Norm Schmidt | 1.50 | .70 |
| ❑ 8 Paul Edwards | 1.50 | .70 |
| ❑ 9 Dan Nicholson | 1.50 | .70 |
| ❑ 10 John Hutchings | 1.50 | .70 |
| ❑ 11 Dave Gans | 1.50 | .70 |
| ❑ 12 Dave Andreychuk | 15.00 | 6.75 |
| ❑ 13 Mike Stern | 1.50 | .70 |
| ❑ 14 Dale Degray | 2.00 | .90 |
| ❑ 15 Mike Lekun | 1.50 | .70 |
| ❑ 16 Greg Gravel | 1.50 | .70 |
| ❑ 17 Dave MacLean | 1.50 | .70 |
| ❑ 18 Tony Tanti | 4.00 | 1.80 |
| ❑ 19 John MacLean | 20.00 | 9.00 |
| ❑ 20 Jim Uens | 1.50 | .70 |
| ❑ 21 Guy Jacob | 1.50 | .70 |
| ❑ 22 Jeff Steffan | 1.50 | .70 |
| ❑ 23 Paul Theriault | 1.50 | .70 |
| ❑ 24 Sherry Bassin | 1.50 | .70 |
| ❑ 25 Durham Regional<br>Police Logo | .50 | .23 |

## 1982-83 Oshawa Generals

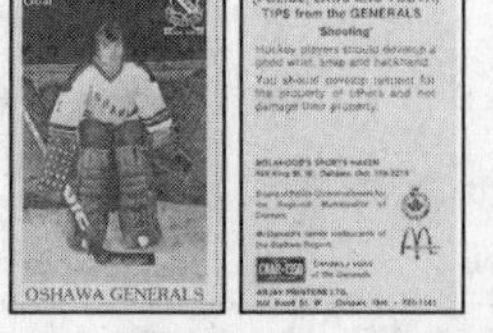

This 25-card set measures approximately 2 5/8" by 4 1/8" and features color, posed action player photos framed by thin red border lines that rest on a white card face. The player's name, position, and the team logo are superimposed across the top of the picture in white lettering. The team name appears below the photo in red. The backs carry P.L.A.Y. (Police, Laws and Youth) public service messages and hockey tips. Sponsor logos and name are printed on the lower portion of the card.

| | MINT | EXC |
|---|---|---|
| COMPLETE SET (25) | 35.00 | 16.00 |
| COMMON CARD (1-25) | .50 | .23 |
| ❑ 1 Generals Logo | 1.00 | .45 |
| ❑ 2 Jeff Hogg | 1.00 | .45 |
| ❑ 3 Peter Sidorkiewicz | 3.00 | 1.35 |
| ❑ 4 Dale Degray | 1.50 | .70 |
| ❑ 5 Joe Cirella | 2.50 | 1.10 |
| ❑ 6 Todd Smith | 1.00 | .45 |
| ❑ 7 Scott Brydges | 1.00 | .45 |
| ❑ 8 Jeff Steffen | 1.00 | .45 |
| ❑ 9 Don Biggs | 1.00 | .45 |
| ❑ 10 Todd Hooey | 1.00 | .45 |
| ❑ 11 Tony Tanti | 3.00 | 1.35 |
| ❑ 12 Danny Gratton | 1.00 | .45 |
| ❑ 13 Steve King | 1.00 | .45 |
| ❑ 14 Dan Defazio | 1.00 | .45 |
| ❑ 15 John MacLean | 8.00 | 3.60 |
| ❑ 16 Tim Burgess | 1.00 | .45 |
| ❑ 17 Mike Stern | 1.00 | .45 |
| ❑ 18 Dan Nicholson | 1.00 | .45 |
| ❑ 19 David Gans | 1.00 | .45 |
| ❑ 20 John Hutchings | 1.00 | .45 |
| ❑ 21 Norm Schmidt | 1.00 | .45 |
| ❑ 22 Todd Charlesworth | 1.00 | .45 |
| ❑ 23 Paul Theriault CO | .50 | .23 |
| ❑ 24 Sherry Bassin GM | 1.00 | .45 |
| ❑ 25 Durham Regional<br>Police Logo | .50 | .23 |

## 1983-84 Oshawa Generals

This 30-card P.L.A.Y. (Police, Laws and Youth) set measures approximately 2 5/8" by 4 1/8" and features color posed action player photos. The backs carry "Tips from the Generals" that include a hockey tip and its application to a life situation.

| | MINT | NRMT |
|---|---|---|
| COMPLETE SET (30) | 30.00 | 13.50 |
| COMMON CARD (1-30) | .25 | .11 |
| ❑ 1 Peter Sidorkiewicz | 3.00 | 1.35 |
| ❑ 2 Kirk McLean | 12.00 | 5.50 |
| ❑ 3 Todd Charlesworth | 1.00 | .45 |
| ❑ 4 Ian Ferguson | .75 | .35 |
| ❑ 5 John Hutchings | .75 | .35 |
| ❑ 6 Generals Logo | .75 | .35 |
| ❑ 7 Mark Haarmann | .75 | .35 |
| ❑ 8 Joel Curtis | .75 | .35 |
| ❑ 9 Dan Gratton | 1.00 | .45 |
| ❑ 10 Steve Hedington | .75 | .35 |
| ❑ 11 Scott Brydges | .75 | .35 |
| ❑ 12 CKAR Radio | .25 | .11 |
| ❑ 13 Brad Walcot | .75 | .35 |
| ❑ 14 Paul Theriault CO | .75 | .35 |
| ❑ 15 Jon Jenkins<br>Chief of Police | .25 | .11 |
| ❑ 16 Sherry Bassin GM | 1.00 | .45 |
| ❑ 17 Craig Morrison | .75 | .35 |
| ❑ 18 Bolahood's | .25 | .11 |
| ❑ 19 Bruce Melanson | .75 | .35 |
| ❑ 20 Mike Stern | .75 | .35 |
| ❑ 21 Gary McColgan | .75 | .35 |
| ❑ 22 Lee Giffin | 1.00 | .45 |
| ❑ 23 Brent Maki | .75 | .35 |
| ❑ 24 Ronald McDonald | .50 | .23 |
| ❑ 25 Jeff Steffen | .75 | .35 |
| ❑ 26 John Stevens | .75 | .35 |
| ❑ 27 David Gans | .75 | .35 |
| ❑ 28 Don Biggs | 1.00 | .45 |
| ❑ 29 Chip Crandall | .75 | .35 |
| ❑ 30 Durham Police Logo | .25 | .11 |

## 1989-90 Oshawa Generals

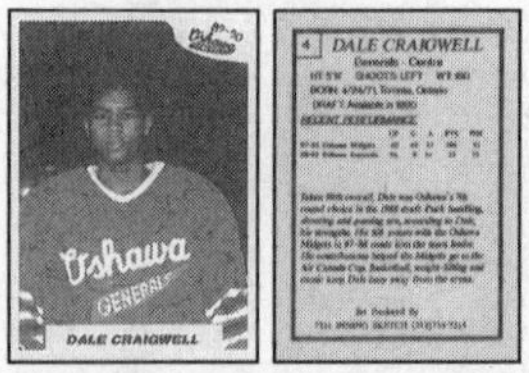


This set of the 1989-90 Oshawa Generals of the OHL was released by 7th Inning Sketch in advance of its full 1989-90 OHL issue. The cards, numbered 1-23, are the same as those found in the larger set. Card #1, featuring Eric Lindros, is susceptible to counterfeiting. Collectors should exercise caution when purchasing this card as a single.

| | MINT | NRMT |
|---|---|---|
| COMPLETE SET (23) | 12.00 | 5.50 |
| COMMON CARD (1-23) | .50 | .23 |
| ❑ 1 Eric Lindros | 5.00 | 2.20 |
| ❑ 2 Jarrod Skalde | .50 | .23 |
| ❑ 3 Joe Busillo | .50 | .23 |
| ❑ 4 Dale Craigwell | .75 | .35 |
| ❑ 5 Clair Cornish | .50 | .23 |
| ❑ 6 Jean-Paul Davis | .50 | .23 |
| ❑ 7 Craig Donaldson | .50 | .23 |
| ❑ 8 Wade Simpson | .50 | .23 |
| ❑ 9 Mike Craig | .50 | .23 |
| ❑ 10 Mark Deazeley | .50 | .23 |
| ❑ 11 Scott Hollis | .50 | .23 |
| ❑ 12 Brian Grieve | .50 | .23 |
| ❑ 13 Dave Craievich | .50 | .23 |
| ❑ 14 Paul O'Hagan | .50 | .23 |
| ❑ 15 Matt Hoffman | .50 | .23 |
| ❑ 16 Trevor McIvor | .50 | .23 |
| ❑ 17 Cory Banika | .50 | .23 |
| ❑ 18 Kevin Butt | .75 | .35 |
| ❑ 19 Iain Fraser | .50 | .23 |
| ❑ 20 Bill Armstrong | .50 | .23 |
| ❑ 21 Scott Luik | .50 | .23 |
| ❑ 22 Brent Grieve | .50 | .23 |
| ❑ 23 Fred Brathwaite | .75 | .35 |

## 1989-90 Oshawa Generals Police

These standard size cards feature color action photos on the front and drug tops and sponsor logos on the back. Cards were printed by Whitby Business Forms.

| | MINT | NRMT |
|---|---|---|
| COMPLETE SET (35) | 15.00 | 6.75 |
| COMMON CARD (1-35) | .50 | .23 |
| ❑ 1 Corey Banika | .50 | .23 |
| ❑ 2 David Craievich | .50 | .23 |
| ❑ 3 Scott Hollis | .50 | .23 |
| ❑ 4 Mike Decoff | .50 | .23 |
| ❑ 5 Joe Busillo | .50 | .23 |
| ❑ 6 Matt Hoffman | .50 | .23 |
| ❑ 7 Craig Donaldson | .50 | .23 |
| ❑ 8 Jason Denomme | .50 | .23 |
| ❑ 9 Brian Grieve | .50 | .23 |
| ❑ 10 Wade Simpson | .50 | .23 |
| ❑ 11 Dale Craigwell | .75 | .35 |
| ❑ 12 Mike Lenarduzzi | .50 | .23 |
| ❑ 13 Rick Cornacchia CO | .10 | .05 |
| ❑ 14 David Edwards | .50 | .23 |
| ❑ 15 Kevin Butt | .75 | .35 |
| ❑ 16 Team Photo | .20 | .09 |
| ❑ 17 Clair Cornish | .50 | .23 |
| ❑ 18 Jarrod Skalde | .50 | .23 |
| ❑ 19 Mark Deazeley | .50 | .23 |
| ❑ 20 Jean Paul Davis | .50 | .23 |
| ❑ 21 Todd Coopman | .10 | .05 |
| ❑ 22 Trevor McIvor | .10 | .05 |
| ❑ 23 Mike Craig | .50 | .23 |
| ❑ 24 Paul O'Hagan | .50 | .23 |
| ❑ 25 Iain Fraser | .50 | .23 |
| ❑ 26 Brent Grieve | .50 | .23 |
| ❑ 27 Lions International | .10 | .05 |
| ❑ 28 National Sports Centre | .10 | .05 |
| ❑ 29 Durham Regional Police | .10 | .05 |
| ❑ 30 Oshawa Generals | .10 | .05 |
| ❑ 31 Eric Lindros | 5.00 | 2.20 |
| ❑ 32 Bill Armstrong | .50 | .23 |
| ❑ 33 Chris Vanclief | .50 | .23 |
| ❑ 34 Scott Luik | .50 | .23 |
| ❑ 35 Fred Brathwaite | .75 | .35 |

## 1991-92 Oshawa Generals

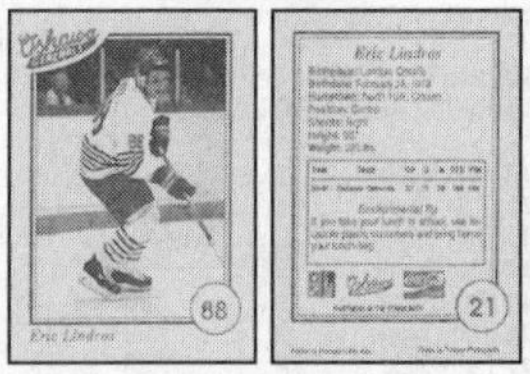


This 32-card standard-size set was sponsored by Coca-Cola and Domino's Pizza. The cards feature color action player photos framed by a royal blue double line. A white circle at the lower right corner carries the player's jersey number or the season year '91-'92. The upper left corner of the picture is cut off to permit space for the team name. The player's name is printed in red at the lower left corner. The backs display biographical information, statistics, environmental tips, and sponsor logos within a royal blue double line design like that on the front.

| | MINT | NRMT |
|---|---|---|
| COMPLETE SET (32) | 20.00 | 9.00 |
| COMMON CARD (1-32) | .10 | .05 |
| ❑ 1 Mike Fountain | .75 | .35 |
| ❑ 2 Brian Grieve | .35 | .16 |
| ❑ 3 Trevor Burgess | .35 | .16 |
| ❑ 4 Wade Simpson | .35 | .16 |
| ❑ 5 Ken Shepard | .35 | .16 |
| ❑ 6 Stephane Yelle | .75 | .35 |
| ❑ 7 Matt Hoffman | .35 | .16 |
| ❑ 8 Neil Iserhoff | .35 | .16 |
| ❑ 9 Rob Leask | .35 | .16 |
| ❑ 10 Kevin Spero | .35 | .16 |
| ❑ 11 Scott Hollis | .35 | .16 |
| ❑ 12 Sean Brown | .50 | .23 |
| ❑ 13 Todd Bradley | .35 | .16 |

❑ 14 Darryl LaFrance .35 .16
❑ 15 Markus Brunner .50 .23
❑ 16 B.J. MacPherson .35 .16
❑ 17 Jason Campeau .35 .16
❑ 18 Jason Weaver .35 .16
❑ 19 Jan Benda .50 .23
❑ 20 Jason Arnott 4.00 1.80
❑ 21 Eric Lindros 8.00 3.60
❑ 22 Wayne Daniels .10 .05
Dir. of Operations
❑ 23 Joe Cook .35 .16
❑ 24 Can't Beat the Real .10 .05
Thing (Coke Ad)
❑ 25 Experience the .10 .05
Domino's Effect
(Pizza Ad)
❑ 26 Mark Deazeley .35 .16
❑ 27 Jean-Paul Davis .35 .16
❑ 28 Brian Grieve .35 .16
❑ 29 Oshawa Generals 1.00 .45
Team Photo
❑ 30 Ian Young CO .10 .05
Larry Marson CO5
Rick Cornacchia CO
❑ 31 Sponsor Ads .10 .05
Checklist
❑ 32 Prosport's Action .10 .05

## 1991-92 Oshawa Generals Sheet

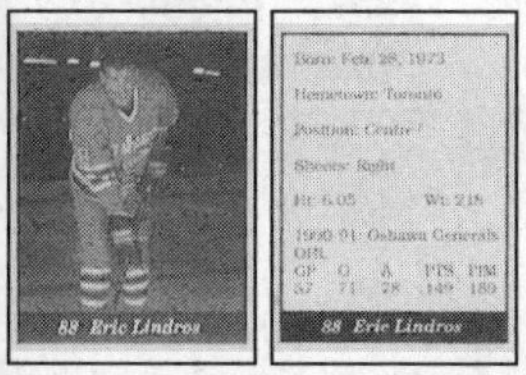


This 18" by 12" sheet was sponsored by the 8th Annual United Way Face-Off Breakfast. The front features posed, color player cards with the players' names printed in a black stripe that appears below each picture. The center of the sheet carries the words "8th Annual United Way Face-Off Breakfast" in sky blue print. The team name also appears in the center, along with the year, the individual sheet number, and the production run (5,000). The back displays the card backs which have biographical information and statistics. The card backs are white with black print. The players are checklisted below as they appear from left to right.

| | MINT | NRMT |
|---|---|---|
| COMPLETE SET (26) | 20.00 | 9.00 |
| COMMON CARD (1-26) | .35 | .16 |

❑ 1 Scott Hollis .35 .16
❑ 2 Jan Benda .50 .23
❑ 3 Joe Cook .35 .16
❑ 4 Wade Simpson .35 .16
❑ 5 B.J. MacPherson .35 .16
❑ 6 David Anderson .35 .16
❑ 7 Stephane Yelle .75 .35
❑ 8 Troy Sweet .35 .16
❑ 9 Matt Hoffman .35 .16
❑ 10 Trevor Burgess .35 .16
❑ 11 Jason Weaver .35 .16
❑ 12 Craig Lutes .35 .16
❑ 13 Darryl LaFrance .35 .16
❑ 14 Jason Arnott 4.00 1.80
❑ 15 Eric Lindros 8.00 3.60
❑ 16 Brian Grieve .35 .16
❑ 17 Mark Deazeley .35 .16
❑ 18 Mike Cote .35 .16
❑ 19 Markus Brunner .50 .23
❑ 20 Kevin Spero .35 .16
❑ 21 Todd Bradley .35 .16
❑ 22 Mike Fountain .75 .35
❑ 23 Fred Brathwaite .75 .35
❑ 24 Jean-Paul Davis .35 .16
❑ 25 Jason Campeau .35 .16
❑ 26 Neil Iserhoff .35 .16

## 1992-93 Oshawa Generals Sheet

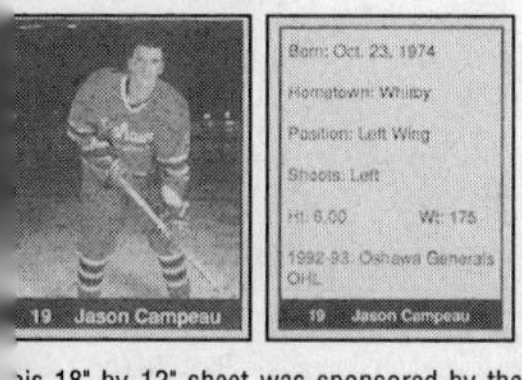


This 18" by 12" sheet was sponsored by the 9th Annual United Way Face-Off Breakfast. The front features posed, color player cards with the players' names printed in a black stripe that appears below each picture. The center of the sheet carries the words "9th Annual United Way Face-Off Breakfast" in black print. The team name also appears in the center, along with the year, the individual sheet number, and the production run (5,000). The back displays the card backs which have biographical information. The card backs are white with black print. The players are checklisted below as they appear from left to right.

| | MINT | NRMT |
|---|---|---|
| COMPLETE SET (26) | 15.00 | 6.75 |
| COMMON CARD (1-26) | .50 | .23 |

❑ 1 Wade Simpson .50 .23
❑ 2 Jamie Kress .50 .23
❑ 3 Sean Brown .50 .23
❑ 4 Jason Arnott 4.00 1.80
❑ 5 Mark Brooks .50 .23
❑ 6 Rob McQuat .50 .23
❑ 7 Joe Cook .50 .23
❑ 8 Chris Hall .50 .23
❑ 9 Jason McQuat .50 .23
❑ 10 Jason Julian .50 .23
❑ 11 Kevin Spero .50 .23
❑ 12 Steve Haight .50 .23
❑ 13 B.J. MacPherson .50 .23
❑ 14 Billy-Jay Johnston .50 .23
❑ 15 Stephane Soulliere .50 .23
❑ 16 Todd Bradley .50 .23
❑ 17 Darryl Lafrance .50 .23
❑ 18 Aaron Albright .50 .23
❑ 19 Trevor Burgess .50 .23
❑ 20 Scott Hollis .50 .23
❑ 21 Serge Dunphy .50 .23
❑ 22 Joel Gagnon .75 .35
❑ 23 Brian Kent .75 .35
❑ 24 Stephane Yelle 1.00 .45
❑ 25 Jason Campeau .50 .23
❑ 26 Neil Iserhoff .50 .23

## 1993-94 Oshawa Generals

Printed by Slapshot Images Ltd., this standard size 27-card set features the 1993-94 Oshawa Generals. Reportedly only 3,000 of these sets were produced; the title card also serves as a Certificate of Authenticity and has the number 3,000 printed in the lower right corner. On a geometrical team color-coded background, the fronts feature color action player photos with thin black borders. The player's name, position and team name, as well as the producer's logo, appear on the front. The backs carry a close-up color player portrait, biography and statistics, along with team and sponsor's logos. Included in this set is a Slapshot ad card with a 1994 calendar on the back.

| | MINT | NRMT |
|---|---|---|
| COMPLETE SET (27) | 9.00 | 4.00 |
| COMMON CARD (1-26) | .10 | .05 |

❑ 1 Title Card .10 .05
Checklist
❑ 2 Joel Gagnon .75 .35
❑ 3 Ken Shepard .50 .23
❑ 4 Jan Snopek .50 .23
❑ 5 David Froh .35 .16
❑ 6 Brandon Gray .35 .16
❑ 7 Damon Hardy .35 .16
❑ 8 Sean Brown .35 .16
❑ 9 Jeff Andrews .35 .16
❑ 10 Stephane Yelle .75 .35
❑ 11 Stephane Soulliere .35 .16
❑ 12 Andrew Power .35 .16
❑ 13 Todd Bradley .35 .16
❑ 14 Darryl Lafrance .50 .23
❑ 15 Darryl Moxam .35 .16
❑ 16 Robert Dubois .35 .16
❑ 17 Kevin Vaughan .35 .16
❑ 18 Rob McQuat .50 .23
❑ 19 B.J. Johnston .35 .16
❑ 20 Paul Doherty .35 .16
❑ 21 Eric Boulton .50 .23
❑ 22 Marc Savard 1.00 .45
❑ 23 Chris Hall .35 .16
❑ 24 Jason McQuat .35 .16
❑ 25 Ryan Lindsay .35 .16
❑ 26 Rick Cornacchia CO .10 .05
Wayne Daniels DIR
Brian Drumm ACO
❑ NNO Slapshot Ad Card .10 .05

## 1981-82 Ottawa 67's

This set was believed to contain 25 cards, but the existence of just 13 cards can be confirmed to date. Therefore, just these cards are checklisted below. The cards measure approximately 5 1/2" by 8 1/2" and feature black-and-white player portraits in white borders. A facsimile autograph and player's jersey number are printed in the wide bottom margin. The backs are blank. The cards are unnumbered and checklisted below in alphabetical order.

| | MINT | NRMT |
|---|---|---|
| COMPLETE SET (13) | 12.00 | 5.50 |
| COMMON CARD (1-13) | .50 | .23 |

❑ 1 Randy Boyd .75 .35
❑ 2 Adam Creighton 3.00 1.35
❑ 3 Bill Dowd .75 .35
❑ 4 Alan Hepple .75 .35
❑ 5 Mike James .75 .35
❑ 6 Moe Lemay 1.50 .70
❑ 7 Paul Louttit .75 .35
❑ 8 Don McLaren .75 .35
❑ 9 Brian Patafie TR .50 .23
❑ 10 Phil Patterson .75 .35
❑ 11 Jim Ralph 3.00 1.35
❑ 12 Doug Stewart .75 .35
❑ 13 Fraser Wood .75 .35

## 1982-83 Ottawa 67's

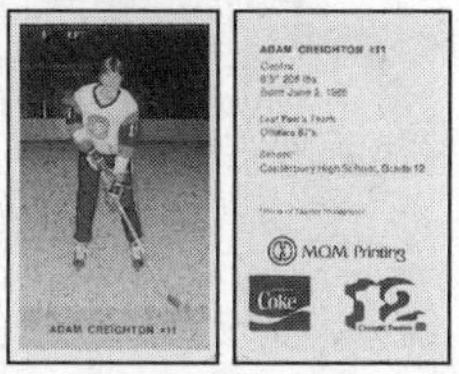

Sponsored by Coke and Channel 12, this 25-card set measures approximately 2 5/8" by 4 1/8" and features posed, color player photos with white borders. The player's name and jersey number are printed in black across the bottom of the picture. The backs carry biographical information, the team played for the previous year, and the player's school classification. Sponsor logos are printed at the bottom. The cards are unnumbered and checklisted below in alphabetical order.

| | MINT | EXC |
|---|---|---|
| COMPLETE SET (25) | 25.00 | 11.00 |
| COMMON CARD (1-25) | .50 | .23 |

❑ 1 Bruce Cassidy .75 .35
❑ 2 Greg Coram .75 .35
❑ 3 Adam Creighton 2.50 1.10
❑ 4 Bill Dowd .75 .35
❑ 5 Gord Hamilton ACO .50 .23
❑ 6 Scott Hammond .75 .35
❑ 7 Alan Hepple .75 .35
❑ 8 Alan Hepple .75 .35
❑ 9 Jim Jackson TR .50 .23
❑ 10 Mike James .75 .35
❑ 11 Brian Kilrea CO .75 .35
❑ 12 Paul Louttit .75 .35
❑ 13 Brian McKinnon .75 .35
❑ 14 Don McLaren .75 .35
❑ 15 John Ollson .75 .35
❑ 16 Darren Pang 3.00 1.35
❑ 17 Mark Paterson .75 .35
❑ 18 Phil Patterson .75 .35
❑ 19 Larry Power .75 .35
❑ 20 Gary Roberts 8.00 3.60
❑ 21 Brian Rome .75 .35
❑ 22 Darcy T. Roy .75 .35
❑ 23 Brad Shaw 2.50 1.10
❑ 24 Doug Stewart .75 .35
❑ 25 Jeff Vaive .75 .35

## 1983-84 Ottawa 67's

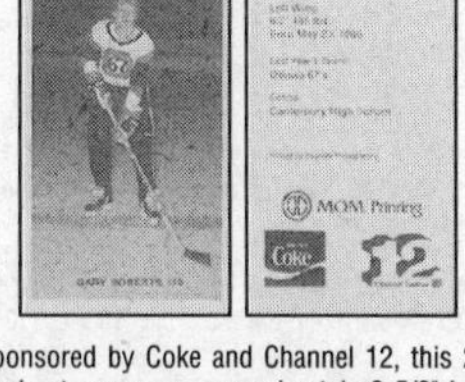

Sponsored by Coke and Channel 12, this 27-card set measures approximately 2 5/8" by 4 1/8". The fronts feature posed, color player photos with white borders. The player's name and jersey number are printed in black across the bottom of the picture. The backs carry biographical information, last year's team, and the school. Sponsor logos are printed at the bottom. The cards are unnumbered and checklisted below in alphabetical order.

| | MINT | NRMT |
|---|---|---|
| COMPLETE SET (27) | 18.00 | 8.00 |
| COMMON CARD (1-27) | .25 | .11 |

❑ 1 Richard Adolfi .50 .23
❑ 2 Bill Bennett .50 .23
❑ 3 Bruce Cassidy .75 .35
❑ 4 Todd Clarke .50 .23
❑ 5 Greg Coram .50 .23
❑ 6 Adam Creighton 2.00 .90
❑ 7 Bob Giffin .50 .23
❑ 8 Gord Hamilton ACO .25 .11
❑ 9 Gord Hamilton Jr. TR .25 .11
❑ 10 Scott Hammond .50 .23
❑ 11 John Hanna .50 .23
❑ 12 Tim Helmer .50 .23
❑ 13 Steve Hrynewich .50 .23
❑ 14 Jim Jackson TR .25 .11
❑ 15 Mike James .50 .23
❑ 16 Brian Kilrea CO/MG .50 .23
❑ 17 Larry MacAndrew TR .25 .11
❑ 18 Brian McKinnon .50 .23
❑ 19 Don McLaren .75 .35
❑ 20 Roy Myllari .50 .23
❑ 21 Darren Pang 2.00 .90
❑ 22 Mark Paterson .75 .35
❑ 23 Phil Patterson .50 .23
❑ 24 Gary Roberts 5.00 2.20
❑ 25 Darcy Roy .50 .23
❑ 26 Brad Shaw 2.00 .90
❑ 27 Steve Simoni .50 .23

## 1984-85 Ottawa 67's

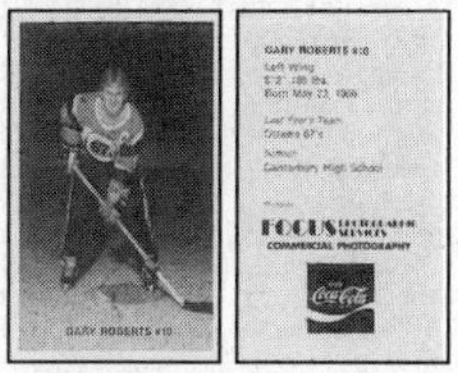

This 28-card set was sponsored by Coca-Cola and Focus Photographic Services Commercial Photography. The cards measure approximately 2 5/8" by 4 1/8" and feature color, full-length, posed player photos with white borders. The player's name and jersey number are superimposed on the bottom of the picture. The backs are white and carry biographical information, last year's team, and the player's high school. Sponsor logos are printed at the bottom. The cards are unnumbered and checklisted below in alphabetical order.

| | MINT | NRMT |
|---|---|---|
| COMPLETE SET (28) | 12.00 | 5.50 |
| COMMON CARD (1-28) | .25 | .11 |

❑ 1 Tom Allen .50 .23
❑ 2 Graydon Almstedt .50 .23
❑ 3 Bill Bennett .50 .23
❑ 4 Bruce Cassidy .50 .23
❑ 5 Greg Coram .50 .23
❑ 6 Bob Ellett CO .25 .11
❑ 7 Tony Geesink .50 .23
❑ 8 Bob Giffin .50 .23
❑ 9 John Hanna .50 .23
❑ 10 Tim Helmer .50 .23
❑ 11 Andy Helmuth .50 .23
❑ 12 Steve Hrynewich .50 .23
❑ 13 Rob Hudson .50 .23
❑ 14 Jim Jackson TR .25 .11
❑ 15 Steve Kayser .50 .23
❑ 16 Bill Kuchma .50 .23
❑ 17 Mike Larouche .50 .23
❑ 18 Tom Lawson MG .25 .11
❑ 19 Richard Lessard .50 .23
❑ 20 Gary Roberts 4.00 1.80
❑ 21 Jerry Scott .50 .23
❑ 22 John Shepherd PR .25 .11
❑ 23 Steve Simoni .50 .23
❑ 24 Greg Sliz .50 .23
❑ 25 Gord Thomas TR .25 .11
❑ 26 Chris Vickers .50 .23
❑ 27 Bert Weir .50 .23
❑ 28 Dennis Wigle .50 .23

## 1992 Ottawa 67's 25th Anniversary

Celebrating the 25th anniversary of the Ottawa 67's, this 24-card standard-size set features color posed and action player photos with purple borders. The player's name, position, and jersey number appear in a black vertical stripe on the left side of the card. The phrase "25th Anniversary" is printed at the bottom in large red and blue letters. The letters overlap the photo and a white bar at the bottom of the photo. The backs carry biographical information, a player profile, and statistics against a gradated sky blue background with yellow and black borders. The cards are unnumbered and checklisted below in alphabetical order.

| | MINT | NRMT |
|---|---|---|
| COMPLETE SET (24) | 12.00 | 5.50 |
| COMMON CARD (1-24) | .25 | .11 |

❑ 1 Ken Belanger .50 .23
❑ 2 Curt Bowen .75 .35
❑ 3 Rich Bronilla .50 .23
❑ 4 Mathew Burnett .50 .23
❑ 5 Shawn Caplice .50 .23
❑ 6 Mike Carr .50 .23
❑ 7 Chris Coveny .50 .23
❑ 8 Howard Darwin (Founder) .25 .11
❑ 9 Shean Donovan 1.00 .45
❑ 10 Mark Edmundson .50 .23
❑ 11 Billy Hall .50 .23
❑ 12 Mike Johnson .50 .23
❑ 13 Brian Kilrea GM/CO .50 .23
❑ 14 Grayson Lafoley .50 .23
❑ 15 Grant Marshall 1.00 .45
❑ 16 Cory Murphy .50 .23
❑ 17 Mike Peca 1.00 .45
❑ 18 Greg Ryan .50 .23
❑ 19 Jeff Salajko .50 .23
❑ 20 Gerry Skrypec .50 .23
❑ 21 Sean Spencer .50 .23
❑ 22 Steven Washburn 1.00 .45
❑ 23 Mark Yakabuski .50 .23
❑ 24 Title Card .25 .11

## 1993-94 Owen Sound Platers

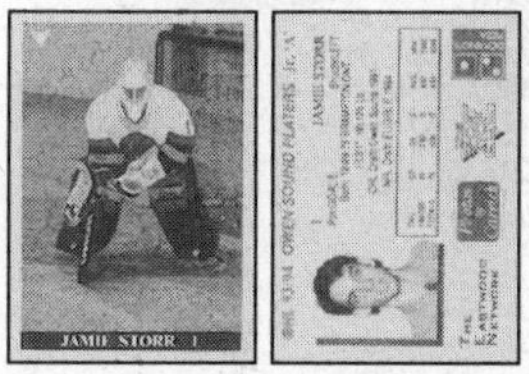


Sponsored by Domino's Pizza, The Eastwood Network, and The Sport Stop, this 36-card set measures the standard size. The fronts feature posed and action color player photos with white borders. The player's name and number appears in a black bar under the picture. The horizontal backs have a small black-and-white headshot in the top left corner, along with player biography, statistics, and sponsor logos. The cards are unnumbered and checklisted below in alphabetical order.

| | MINT | NRMT |
|---|---|---|
| COMPLETE SET (36) | 15.00 | 6.75 |
| COMMON CARD (1-36) | .10 | .05 |

❑ 1 Craig Binns .35 .16
❑ 2 Jim Brown .35 .16
❑ 3 Andrew Brunette .50 .23
❑ 4 Luigi Calce .35 .16
❑ 5 Jason Campbell .35 .16
❑ 6 Draft Veterans .35 .16
Rod Hinks
Jason MacDonald
Kevin Weekes
Marian Kacir
❑ 7 Paddy Flynn ACO .10 .05
❑ 8 Kirk Furey .35 .16
❑ 9 Jerry Harrigan CO .10 .05
❑ 10 Joe Harris .35 .16
❑ 11 Rod Hinks .35 .16
❑ 12 Marian Kacir .35 .16
❑ 13 Shane Kenny .35 .16
❑ 14 Jeff Kostuch .35 .16
❑ 15 Dave Lemay .35 .16
❑ 16 Jason MacDonald .50 .23
❑ 17 Rick Mancini TR .10 .05
❑ 18 Kirk Maltby .75 .35
❑ 19 Brian Medeiros .35 .16
❑ 20 Mike Morrone .35 .16
❑ 21 Ryan Mougenel .35 .16
❑ 22 Scott Penton .35 .16
❑ 23 Wayne Primeau .75 .35
❑ 24 Jeremy Rebek .35 .16
❑ 25 Rob Schweyer .35 .16
❑ 26 Willie Skilliter .35 .16
❑ 27 Jamie Storr 2.00 .90
❑ 28 Jamie Storr 2.00 .90
Pure Gold
❑ 29 Jamie Storr's Mask 1.50 .70
❑ 30 Jamie Storr 1.50 .70
Wayne Primeau
Sure Picks
❑ 31 Scott Walker .75 .35
❑ 32 Kevin Weekes .60 .25
❑ 33 Kevin Weekes' Mask .50 .23
❑ 34 Shayne Wright .35 .16
❑ 35 Title Card .10 .05
Domino's Ad Card
❑ 36 Title Card .10 .05
Eastwood Ad Card

## 1992-93 Peoria Rivermen Coke/Kroger

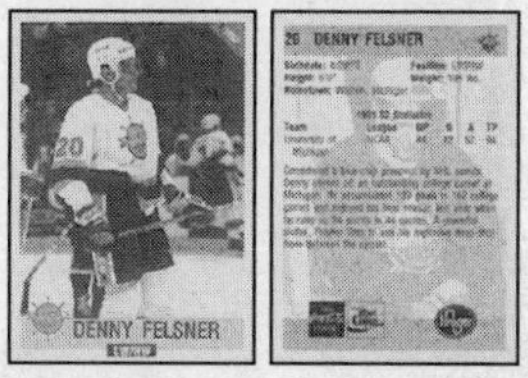


Sponsored by Coca-Cola and Kroger, this 30-

card set measures the standard size. The fronts feature color player photos with a white border. The team logo, the player's name, and position appear in a gray bar under the photo, while "1992" is printed in white letters on a blue triangle in the top right corner of the photo. The backs display biographical information, statistics, and sponsor logos against a light gray-in-gray player photo with a white border. Included in this set is a Coca-Cola coupon. The cards are unnumbered and checklisted below in alphabetical order.

| | MINT | NRMT |
|---|---|---|
| COMPLETE SET (30) | 9.00 | 4.00 |
| COMMON CARD (1-30) | .10 | .05 |
| ❑ 1 Jeff Batters | .35 | .16 |
| ❑ 2 Parris Duffus | .50 | .23 |
| ❑ 3 Greg Eberle TR | .10 | .05 |
| ❑ 4 John Faginkrantz MG | .10 | .05 |
| ❑ 5 Denny Felsner | .35 | .16 |
| ❑ 6 Derek Frenette | .35 | .16 |
| ❑ 7 Ron Handy | .35 | .16 |
| ❑ 8 Joe Hawley | .35 | .16 |
| ❑ 9 Terry Hollinger | .35 | .16 |
| ❑ 10 Ron Hoover | .35 | .16 |
| ❑ 11 Daniel LaPerriere | .50 | .23 |
| ❑ 12 Lee J. Leslie | .35 | .16 |
| ❑ 13 Dave Mackey | .35 | .16 |
| ❑ 14 Jason Marshall | .50 | .23 |
| ❑ 15 Brian McKee | .35 | .16 |
| ❑ 16 Rick Meagher CO | .35 | .16 |
| ❑ 17 Kevin Miehm | .35 | .16 |
| ❑ 18 Brian Pellerin ACO | .10 | .05 |
| ❑ 19 Mark Reeds | .35 | .16 |
| ❑ 20 Kyle Reeves | .35 | .16 |
| ❑ 21 Rob Robinson | .35 | .16 |
| ❑ 22 Jason Ruff | .35 | .16 |
| ❑ 23 Geoff Sarjeant | .75 | .35 |
| ❑ 24 Richard Pion | .35 | .16 |
| ❑ 25 Darren Veitch | .40 | .18 |
| ❑ 26 Doug Wickenheiser | .40 | .18 |
| ❑ 27 Shawn Wheeler | .35 | .16 |
| ❑ 28 Checklist | .10 | .05 |
| ❑ 29 Coca Cola Coupon | .10 | .05 |
| ❑ 30 Title Card | .10 | .05 |

## 1993-94 Peoria Rivermen

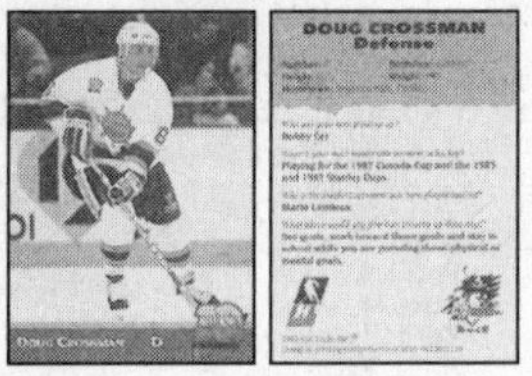

Produced by 1993 Hat Tricks, Inc., this 31-card D.A.R.E. (Drug Abuse Resistance Education) set measures approximately 2 3/8" by 3 1/4" and celebrates the tenth anniversary of the Peoria Rivermen (International Hockey League). The fronts feature full-bleed color action photos, except at the bottom where an orange stripe separates a thicker blue stripe carrying player information. The 10th anniversary logo in the lower right corner completes the front. In black print on a gray and white background, the backs present biography and additional information in a question-and-answer format. The cards are unnumbered and checklisted below in alphabetical order.

| | MINT | NRMT |
|---|---|---|
| COMPLETE SET (31) | 8.00 | 3.60 |
| COMMON CARD (1-31) | .10 | .05 |
| ❑ 1 Mark Bassen | .35 | .16 |
| ❑ 2 Jeff Batters | .35 | .16 |
| ❑ 3 Rene Chapdelaine | .35 | .16 |
| ❑ 4 Doug Crossman | .50 | .23 |
| ❑ 5 Parris Duffus | .50 | .23 |
| ❑ 6 Greg Eberle TR | .10 | .05 |
| ❑ 7 Doug Evans | .35 | .16 |
| ❑ 8 Kevin Evans | .35 | .16 |
| ❑ 9 John Faginkrantz EQMG | .10 | .05 |
| ❑ 10 Denny Felsner | .35 | .16 |
| ❑ 11 Derek Frenette | .35 | .16 |
| ❑ 12 Terry Hollinger | .35 | .16 |
| ❑ 13 Ron Hoover | .35 | .16 |
| ❑ 14 Butch Kaebel | .35 | .16 |
| ❑ 15 Nathan Lafayette | .50 | .23 |
| ❑ 16 Dan Laperriere | .50 | .23 |
| ❑ 17 Dave Mackey | .35 | .16 |
| ❑ 18 Paul MacLean CO | .35 | .16 |
| ❑ 19 Michel Mongeau | .50 | .23 |
| ❑ 20 Brian Pellerin | .35 | .16 |
| ❑ 21 Rick Pion | .35 | .16 |
| ❑ 22 Vitali Prokhorov | .35 | .16 |
| ❑ 23 Mark Reeds ACO | .10 | .05 |
| ❑ 24 John Roderick | .35 | .16 |
| ❑ 25 Geoff Sarjeant | .50 | .23 |
| ❑ 26 Steve Staios | .40 | .18 |
| ❑ 27 Darren Veitch | .40 | .18 |
| ❑ 28 Nick Vitucci | .50 | .23 |
| ❑ 29 Title card | .10 | .05 |
| ❑ 30 Checklist | .10 | .05 |
| ❑ 31 Alcohol Awareness | .10 | .05 |

## 1995-96 Peoria Rivermen

This standard-sized, 24-card set was produced by the Rivermen and offered for sale through the club at games and by mail. The cards are unnumbered and listed below in alphabetical order.

| | MINT | NRMT |
|---|---|---|
| COMPLETE SET (24) | 8.00 | 3.60 |
| COMMON CARD (1-24) | .35 | .16 |
| ❑ 1 Jon Casey | .75 | .35 |
| ❑ 2 Rene Chapdelaine | .35 | .16 |
| ❑ 3 Doug Evans | .35 | .16 |
| ❑ 4 Eric Fenton | .35 | .16 |
| ❑ 5 Shannon Finn | .35 | .16 |
| ❑ 6 Martin Hamrlik | .35 | .16 |
| ❑ 7 Ron Hoover | .35 | .16 |
| ❑ 8 Jacques Joubert | .35 | .16 |
| ❑ 9 Lee J. Leslie | .35 | .16 |
| ❑ 10 Dave MacIntyre | .35 | .16 |
| ❑ 11 Jason Miller | .35 | .16 |
| ❑ 12 Michel Mongeau | .50 | .23 |
| ❑ 13 Glenn Mulvenna | .35 | .16 |
| ❑ 14 Eric Murano | .35 | .16 |
| ❑ 15 Keith Osborne | .35 | .16 |
| ❑ 16 Greg Paslawski | .35 | .16 |
| ❑ 17 Jon Pratt | .35 | .16 |
| ❑ 18 Dan Ratushny | .35 | .16 |
| ❑ 19 Patrice Robitaille | .35 | .16 |
| ❑ 20 Paul Taylor | .35 | .16 |
| ❑ 21 Travis Thiessen | .35 | .16 |
| ❑ 22 Steve Thornton | .35 | .16 |
| ❑ 23 Kirk Tomlinson | .35 | .16 |
| ❑ 24 Steve Wilson | .35 | .16 |

## 1996-97 Peoria Rivermen

This 25-card set marks the debut of the Rivermen as a member club of the ECHL, but continues the tradition of fine sets. The cards feature action photos on the front, and full stats and bio on the reverse. The unnumbered cards are listed below in alphabetical order.

| | MINT | NRMT |
|---|---|---|
| COMPLETE SET (25) | 8.00 | 3.60 |
| COMMON CARD (1-25) | .10 | .05 |
| ❑ 1 Mike Barrie | .35 | .16 |
| ❑ 2 Doug Bonner | .50 | .23 |
| ❑ 3 Greg Eberle/John Krouse | .10 | .05 |
| ❑ 4 Brad Essex | .35 | .16 |
| ❑ 5 Doug Evans ASST CO | .10 | .05 |
| ❑ 6 Liam Garvey | .35 | .16 |
| ❑ 7 Trevor Hanas | .35 | .16 |
| ❑ 8 Jon Hillebrandt | .50 | .23 |
| ❑ 9 Dan Hodge | .35 | .16 |
| ❑ 10 Butch Kaebel | .35 | .16 |
| ❑ 11 Karson Kaebel | .35 | .16 |
| ❑ 12 Justin Krall | .35 | .16 |
| ❑ 13 Jeff Kungle | .35 | .16 |
| ❑ 14 Kevin Lune | .35 | .16 |
| ❑ 15 Darren Maloney | .35 | .16 |
| ❑ 16 Dustin McArthur | .35 | .16 |
| ❑ 17 Jon Pratt | .35 | .16 |
| ❑ 18 Brad Purdie | .35 | .16 |
| ❑ 19 Mark Reeds CO | .10 | .05 |
| ❑ 20 Jason Saal | .50 | .23 |
| ❑ 21 Jan Slavik | .35 | .16 |
| ❑ 22 Marc Terris | .35 | .16 |
| ❑ 23 Jean-Guy Trudel | .35 | .16 |
| ❑ 24 Paul Vincent | .35 | .16 |
| ❑ 25 Title Card | .10 | .05 |

## 1996-97 Peoria Rivermen Photo Album

This 24-card set was released in perforated album form as a game night promotional giveaway. The cards are unnumbered and therefore are listed below in alphabetical order.

| | MINT | NRMT |
|---|---|---|
| COMPLETE SET (24) | 10.00 | 4.50 |
| COMMON CARD (1-24) | .15 | .07 |
| ❑ 1 Mike Barrie | .50 | .23 |
| ❑ 2 Doug Bonner | .75 | .35 |
| ❑ 3 Greg Eberle TR | .15 | .07 |
| ❑ 4 Brad Essex | .50 | .23 |
| ❑ 5 Doug Evans ASST CO | .15 | .07 |
| ❑ 6 Liam Garvey | .50 | .23 |
| ❑ 7 Trevor Hanas | .50 | .23 |
| ❑ 8 Jon Hillebrandt | .75 | .35 |
| ❑ 9 Dan Hodge | .50 | .23 |
| ❑ 10 Butch Kaebel | .50 | .23 |
| ❑ 11 Karson Kaebel | .50 | .23 |
| ❑ 12 Justin Krall | .50 | .23 |
| ❑ 13 John Krouse EQUIP | .15 | .07 |
| ❑ 14 Jeff Kungle | .50 | .23 |
| ❑ 15 Kevin Lune | .50 | .23 |
| ❑ 16 Darren Maloney | .50 | .23 |
| ❑ 17 Dustin McArthur | .50 | .23 |
| ❑ 18 Jon Pratt | .50 | .23 |
| ❑ 19 Brad Purdie | .50 | .23 |
| ❑ 20 Jason Saal | .75 | .35 |
| ❑ 21 Jan Slavik | .50 | .23 |
| ❑ 22 Marc Terris | .50 | .23 |
| ❑ 23 Jean-Guy Trudel | .50 | .23 |
| ❑ 24 Paul Vincent | .50 | .23 |

## 1997-98 Peoria Rivermen

| | MINT | NRMT |
|---|---|---|
| COMPLETE SET (29) | 5.00 | 2.20 |
| COMMON CARD (1-29) | .10 | .05 |
| ❑ 1 Garru Gruber | .20 | .09 |
| ❑ 2 Derek Diener | .20 | .09 |
| ❑ 3 Samy Nasreddine | .20 | .09 |
| ❑ 4 Doug Evans | .20 | .09 |
| ❑ 5 Darren Maloney | .20 | .09 |
| ❑ 6 Joesph Craigen | .20 | .09 |
| ❑ 7 Rob Phillips | .20 | .09 |
| ❑ 8 Brian Clifford | .20 | .09 |
| ❑ 9 Darcy Smith | .20 | .09 |
| ❑ 10 Butch Kaebel | .20 | .09 |
| ❑ 11 Jean Guy Trudel | .20 | .09 |
| ❑ 12 Brad Essex | .20 | .09 |
| ❑ 13 Justin Krall | .20 | .09 |
| ❑ 14 John Dance | .20 | .09 |
| ❑ 15 Marc terris | .20 | .09 |
| ❑ 16 Trevor Hanas | .20 | .09 |
| ❑ 17 Dave Paradise | .20 | .09 |
| ❑ 18 David Vallieres | .20 | .09 |
| ❑ 19 Scott Roche | .30 | .14 |
| ❑ 20 Marcel Kuris | .30 | .14 |
| ❑ 21 Jon Pratt | .20 | .09 |
| ❑ 22 Rob Giffin | .20 | .09 |
| ❑ 23 Mark Reeds | .20 | .09 |
| ❑ 24 Greg Eberle | .20 | .09 |
| ❑ 25 John Krouse EQ | .10 | .05 |
| ❑ 26 Mascot | .10 | .05 |
| ❑ 27 Title Card | .10 | .05 |
| ❑ 28 Header Card | .10 | .05 |

## 1991-92 Peterborough Petes

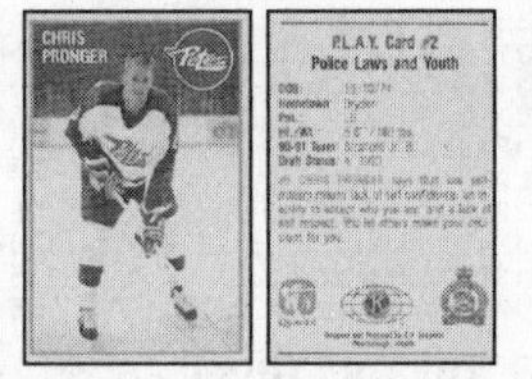

This 30-card P.L.A.Y. (Police, Laws and Youth) set measures approximately 2 1/2" by 3 3/4" and features posed, color player photos with bright blue and white borders. The player's name is printed on the picture in white letters in the upper left corner. The team logo appears in the upper right corner. The backs carry biographical information and public service messages.

| | MINT | NRMT |
|---|---|---|
| COMPLETE SET (30) | 18.00 | 8.00 |
| COMMON CARD (1-27) | .10 | .05 |
| ❑ 1 Jason Dawe | 1.00 | .45 |
| ❑ 2 Chris Pronger | 6.00 | 2.70 |
| ❑ 3 Scott Turner | .50 | .23 |
| ❑ 4 Chad Grills | .50 | .23 |
| ❑ 5 Brent Tully | .75 | .35 |
| ❑ 6 Mike Harding | .50 | .23 |
| ❑ 7 Chris Longo | .50 | .23 |
| ❑ 8 Slapshot (Mascot) | .10 | .05 |
| ❑ 9 Doug Searle | .50 | .23 |
| ❑ 10 Mike Tomlinson | .50 | .23 |
| ❑ 11 Bryan Gendron | .50 | .23 |
| ❑ 12 Andrew Verner | .75 | .35 |
| ❑ 13 Ryan Black | .60 | .25 |
| ❑ 14 Don O'Neill | .50 | .23 |
| ❑ 15 Jeff Twohey MG/CO | .10 | .05 |
| ❑ 16 Dale McTavish | .50 | .23 |
| ❑ 17 Jeff Walker | .50 | .23 |
| ❑ 18 Matt St. Germain | .50 | .23 |
| ❑ 19 Dave Roche | 1.00 | .45 |
| ❑ 20 Colin Wilson | .50 | .23 |
| ❑ 21 Jassen Cullimore | .75 | .35 |
| ❑ 22 Chad Lang | .75 | .35 |
| ❑ 23 Dick Todd MG/CO | .50 | .23 |
| ❑ 24 Geordie Kinnear | .50 | .23 |
| ❑ 25 Shawn Heins | .50 | .23 |
| ❑ 26 John Johnson | .50 | .23 |
| ❑ 27 Kelly Vipond | .50 | .23 |
| ❑ NNO Peterborough Police Crest | .10 | .05 |
| ❑ NNO Kiwanis Sponsor Card | .10 | .05 |
| ❑ NNO Quaker Sponsor Card | .10 | .05 |

## 1993-94 Peterborough Petes

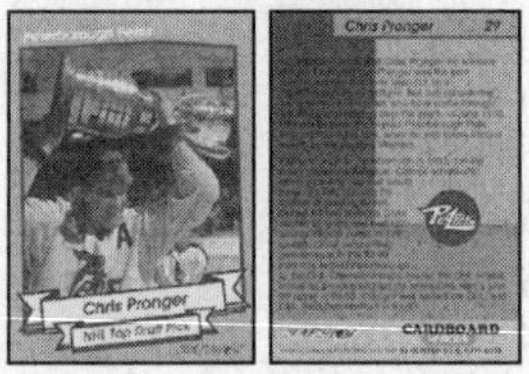

Sponsored by Cardboard Heroes and printed by Slapshot Images Ltd., this standard-size 31-card set features the 1993-94 Peterborough Petes. Only 3,000 of these sets have been produced; the first card also serves as a Certificate of Authenticity and has the individual set number printed in the upper left corner. On a grey background, the fronts feature color action player photos with thin maroon borders. The player's name, position and team name, as well as the producer's logo, appear on the front. The team color-coded backs carry a close-up color player portrait, and biographical information, along with team and sponsors' logos. Included in this set is a Slapshot ad card with a 1994 calendar on the back.

| | MINT | NRMT |
|---|---|---|
| COMPLETE SET (31) | 15.00 | 6.75 |
| COMMON CARD (1-30) | .10 | .05 |
| ❑ 1 1992-93 OHL Champions | .75 | .35 |
| ❑ 2 Jonathan Murphy | .50 | .23 |
| ❑ 3 Dave Roche | .75 | .35 |
| ❑ 4 Rob Giffin | .35 | .16 |
| ❑ 5 Mike Harding | .50 | .23 |
| ❑ 6 Tim Hill | .35 | .16 |
| ❑ 7 Darryl Moxam | .35 | .16 |
| ❑ 8 Pat Paone | .35 | .16 |
| ❑ 9 Brent Tully | .50 | .23 |
| ❑ 10 Zac Bierk | .75 | .35 |
| ❑ 11 Chad Grills | .35 | .16 |
| ❑ 12 Matt St. Germain | .35 | .16 |
| ❑ 13 Henrik Eppers | .50 | .23 |
| ❑ 14 Rick Emmett | .35 | .16 |
| ❑ 15 Chad Lang | .75 | .35 |
| ❑ 16 Cameron Mann | 3.00 | 1.35 |
| ❑ 17 Steve Hogg | .35 | .16 |
| ❑ 18 Mike Williams | .35 | .16 |
| ❑ 19 Ryan Nauss | .50 | .23 |
| ❑ 20 Jamie Langenbrunner | 2.00 | .90 |
| ❑ 21 Ryan Douglas | .50 | .23 |
| ❑ 22 Matt Johnson | .75 | .35 |
| ❑ 23 Kelvin Solari | .35 | .16 |
| ❑ 24 Dan Delmonte | .35 | .16 |
| ❑ 25 Quayde Lightbody | .35 | .16 |
| ❑ 26 Adrian Murray | .35 | .16 |
| ❑ 27 Jason Dawe | .75 | .35 |
| ❑ 28 Mike Harding | .50 | .23 |
| ❑ 29 Chris Pronger | 3.00 | 1.35 |
| ❑ 30 Sponsor Card<br>Cardboard Heroes<br>Greg Ball<br>Kevin Ball | .10 | .05 |
| ❑ NNO Slapshot Ad Card | .10 | .05 |

## 1992-93 Phoenix Roadrunners

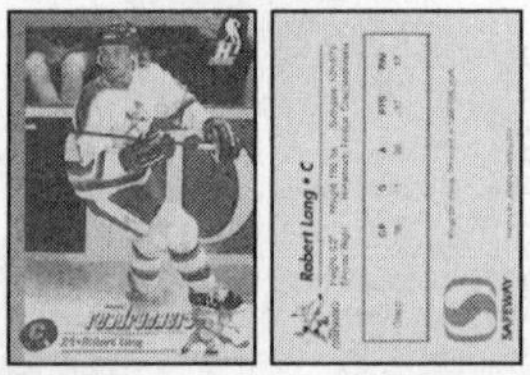

Sponsored by Safeway, this 28-card standard-size set features color action photos on the front edged by a blue border on the top and left margins, with full bleed on the bottom and right. The IHL logo is in the top right corner. The player's name and jersey number are printed in red at the bottom while the team name is printed in white immediately above. The team logo is in the lower right and the player's position is printed in red inside a hockey puck in the lower left. The horizontal backs have the team logo in the top left with biographical information beneath a red line. Statistics are presented in a red box and the red sponsor logo appears in the lower left. The cards are unnumbered and checklisted below in alphabetical order.

| | MINT | NRMT |
|---|---|---|
| COMPLETE SET (28) | 10.00 | 4.50 |
| COMMON CARD (1-28) | .10 | .05 |
| ❑ 1 Tim Bothwell CO | .35 | .16 |
| ❑ 2 Frank Breault | .35 | .16 |
| ❑ 3 Tim Breslin | .35 | .16 |
| ❑ 4 Rene Chapdelaine | .35 | .16 |
| ❑ 5 Sylvain Couturier | .50 | .23 |
| ❑ 6 Phil Crowe | .50 | .23 |
| ❑ 7 Darryl Gilmour | .50 | .23 |
| ❑ 8 David Goverde | .50 | .23 |
| ❑ 9 Ed Kastelic | .35 | .16 |
| ❑ 10 Rick Kozuback ACO | .10 | .05 |
| ❑ 11 Ted Kramer | .35 | .16 |
| ❑ 12 Robert Lang | .75 | .35 |
| ❑ 13 Guy Leveque | .35 | .16 |
| ❑ 14 Jim Maher | .35 | .16 |
| ❑ 15 Brad McCaughey | .35 | .16 |
| ❑ 16 Shawn McCosh | .35 | .16 |
| ❑ 17 John Mokosak | .35 | .16 |
| ❑ 18 Keith Redmond | .35 | .16 |
| ❑ 19 Mike Ruark | .35 | .16 |
| ❑ 20 Brandy Semchuk | .35 | .16 |
| ❑ 21 Dave Stewart | .35 | .16 |
| ❑ 22 Brad Tiley | .40 | .18 |
| ❑ 23 Dave Tretowicz | .35 | .16 |
| ❑ 24 Mike Vukonich | .35 | .16 |
| ❑ 25 Tim Watters | .50 | .23 |
| ❑ 26 Sean Whyte | .35 | .16 |
| ❑ 27 Darryl Williams | .35 | .16 |
| ❑ 28 Rocky Roadrunner (Mascot) | .10 | .05 |

## 1993-94 Phoenix Roadrunners

This 25-card set measures the standard size. On a black and white marbleized background, the fronts feature color action player photos with rounded corners and a thin blue border. The player's name, position, and number appear under the photo, along with the team logo. On a white background, the horizontal backs carry the player's name, number, biography, and statistics. The cards are unnumbered and checklisted below in alphabetical order.

| | MINT | NRMT |
|---|---|---|
| COMPLETE SET (25) | 9.00 | 4.00 |
| COMMON CARD (1-25) | .35 | .16 |
| ❑ 1 Tim Breslin | .35 | .16 |
| ❑ 2 Brian Chapman | .35 | .16 |
| ❑ 3 Stephane Charbonneau | .35 | .16 |
| ❑ 4 Dan Currie | .50 | .23 |
| ❑ 5 Rick Dudley CO | .50 | .23 |
| ❑ 6 Marc Fortier | .50 | .23 |
| ❑ 7 David Goverde | .50 | .23 |
| ❑ 8 Kevin Grant | .35 | .16 |
| ❑ 9 Mark Hardy P/CO | .35 | .16 |
| ❑ 10 Dean Hulett | .35 | .16 |
| ❑ 11 Pauli Jaks | .50 | .23 |
| ❑ 12 Bob Jay | .35 | .16 |
| ❑ 13 Rick Knickle | .75 | .35 |
| ❑ 14 Guy Leveque | .50 | .23 |
| ❑ 15 Eric Lavigne | .50 | .23 |
| ❑ 16 Dominic Lavoie | .35 | .16 |
| ❑ 17 Jim Maher | .35 | .16 |
| ❑ 18 Brian McReynolds | .35 | .16 |
| ❑ 19 Rob Murphy | .35 | .16 |
| ❑ 20 Keith Redmond | .35 | .16 |
| ❑ 21 Dave Stewart | .35 | .16 |
| ❑ 22 Dave Thomlinson | .35 | .16 |
| ❑ 23 Brad Tiley | .35 | .16 |
| ❑ 24 Jim Vesey | .35 | .16 |
| ❑ 25 Darryl Williams | .35 | .16 |

## 1995-96 Phoenix Roadrunners

This 24-card set was produced by Jesse Associates for Collector's Edge. The full colou cards were available as a free promotional iter at a game; they also were sold through th team's pro shop for $6. Approximately 8,00 sets were made. The cards are unnumbere and are checklisted below in alphabetica order.

| | MINT | NRM |
|---|---|---|
| COMPLETE SET (24) | 9.00 | 4.0 |
| COMMON CARD (1-24) | .10 | .0 |

| | | |
|---|---|---|
| □ 1 Ruslan Batyrshin | .35 | .16 |
| □ 2 Frederik Beaubien | .50 | .23 |
| □ 3 John Blue | .50 | .23 |
| □ 4 Mike Boback | .35 | .16 |
| □ 5 Kevin Brown | .50 | .23 |
| □ 6 Jim Burton | .35 | .16 |
| □ 7 Dan Bylsma | .35 | .16 |
| □ 8 Brian Chapman | .35 | .16 |
| □ 9 Rob Cowie | .35 | .16 |
| □ 10 Devin Edgerton | .35 | .16 |
| □ 11 Ken McRae | .35 | .16 |
| □ 12 Barry Potomski | .50 | .23 |
| □ 13 Daniel Rydmark | .35 | .16 |
| □ 14 Jeff Shevalier | .50 | .23 |
| □ 15 Gary Shuchuk | .35 | .16 |
| □ 16 Chris Snell | .35 | .16 |
| □ 17 Jamie Storr | 1.00 | .45 |
| □ 18 Dave Thomlinson | .35 | .16 |
| □ 19 Nicholas Vachon | .35 | .16 |
| □ 20 Jan Vopat | .75 | .35 |
| □ 21 Steve Wilson | .35 | .16 |
| □ 22 Training staff | .10 | .05 |
| □ 23 Rob Laird CO | .10 | .05 |
| □ 24 Rocky Roadrunner | .10 | .05 |

## 1993-94 Portland Pirates

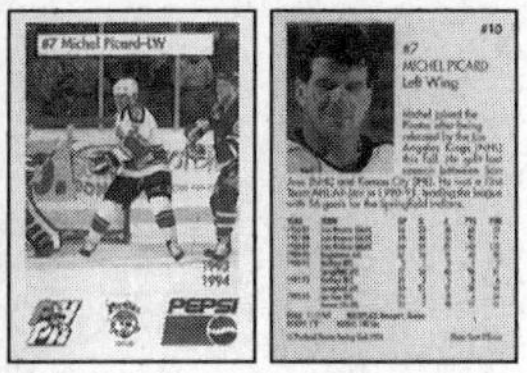

This 24-card set of the Portland Pirates of the American Hockey League was sponsored by Pepsi. The glossy cards were available at home games and through the mail. The glossy cards are numbered on the back.

| | MINT | NRMT |
|---|---|---|
| COMPLETE SET (24) | 10.00 | 4.50 |
| COMMON CARD (1-24) | .10 | .05 |
| □ 1 Randy Pearce | .40 | .18 |
| □ 2 Crackers Mascot | .10 | .05 |
| □ 3 Barry Trotz CO | .10 | .05 |
| □ 4 Paul Gardner ACO | .10 | .05 |
| □ 5 Chris Jensen | .25 | .11 |
| □ 6 Ken Klee | .40 | .18 |
| □ 7 Steve Poapst | .40 | .18 |
| □ 8 Jason Woolley | .75 | .35 |
| □ 9 Jim Mathieson | .40 | .18 |
| □ 10 Michel Picard | .40 | .18 |
| □ 11 Jeff Nelson | .40 | .18 |
| □ 12 Kent Hulst | .40 | .18 |
| □ 13 Eric Fenton | .40 | .18 |
| □ 14 Martin Jiranek | .40 | .18 |
| □ 15 Mike Boback | .40 | .18 |
| □ 16 Darren McAusland | .40 | .18 |
| □ 17 Chris Longo | .40 | .18 |
| □ 18 Kerry Clark | .40 | .18 |
| □ 19 Jeff Sirkka | .40 | .18 |
| □ 20 John Slaney | .50 | .23 |
| □ 21 Kevin Kaminski | .40 | .18 |
| □ 22 Byron Dafoe | 2.00 | .90 |
| □ 23 Olaf Kolzig | 2.00 | .90 |
| □ 24 Todd Nelson | .40 | .18 |
| □ NNO Header Card | .10 | .05 |

## 1994-95 Portland Pirates

This 23-card standard-size set was manufactured and distributed by Jessen Associates, Inc. for Classic. The fronts display color action player photos with a red marbleized inner border and a black outer border. The player's name, jersey number, and position appear in the teal border on the right edge. Inside a black border on a marbleized background, the backs present biography, statistics, and sponsor logos. The cards are unnumbered and checklisted below in alphabetical order.

| | MINT | NRMT |
|---|---|---|
| COMPLETE SET (23) | 12.00 | 5.50 |
| COMMON CARD (1-23) | .40 | .18 |
| □ 1 Norm Batherson | .40 | .18 |
| □ 2 Mike Boback | .40 | .18 |
| □ 3 Andrew Brunette | .50 | .23 |
| □ 4 Jim Carey | 3.50 | 1.55 |
| □ 5 Jason Christie | .40 | .18 |
| □ 6 Kerry Clark | .40 | .18 |
| □ 7 Brian Curran | .40 | .18 |
| □ 8 Martin Gendron | .75 | .35 |
| □ 9 Sergei Gonchar | 1.00 | .45 |
| □ 10 Kent Hulst | .40 | .18 |
| □ 11 Chris Jensen | .40 | .18 |
| □ 12 Kevin Kaminski | .50 | .23 |
| □ 13 Ken Klee | .40 | .18 |
| □ 14 Chris Longo | .40 | .18 |
| □ 15 Jim Mathieson | .40 | .18 |
| □ 16 Darren McAusland | .40 | .18 |
| □ 17 Jeff Nelson | .50 | .23 |
| □ 18 Todd Nelson | .40 | .18 |
| □ 19 Mike Parson | .40 | .18 |
| □ 20 Steve Poapst | .40 | .18 |
| □ 21 Andre Racicot | .50 | .23 |
| □ 22 Sergei Tertyshny | .50 | .23 |
| □ 23 Stefan Ustorf | .75 | .35 |

## 1995-96 Portland Pirates

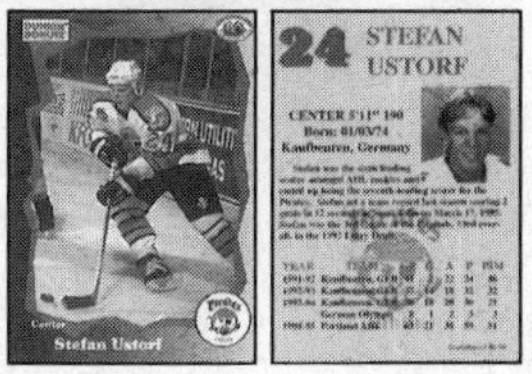

This 24-card set of the Portland Pirates was sponsored by Dunkin' Donuts and features color action player photos framed in red and shades of gray. The backs carry a small black-and-white player head photo with biographical information and player statistics. The cards are unnumbered and checklisted below in alphabetical order.

| | MINT | NRMT |
|---|---|---|
| COMPLETE SET (24) | 9.00 | 4.00 |
| COMMON CARD (1-24) | .10 | .05 |
| □ 1 Alexander Alexeev | .40 | .18 |
| □ 2 Jason Allison | .75 | .35 |
| □ 3 Norm Batherson | .40 | .18 |
| □ 4 Frank Bialowas | .40 | .18 |
| □ 5 Patrick Boileau | .40 | .18 |
| □ 6 Andrew Brunette | .75 | .35 |
| □ 7 Stephane Charbonneau | .40 | .18 |
| □ 8 Jason Christie | .40 | .18 |
| □ 9 Crackers (Mascot) | .10 | .05 |
| □ 10 Brian Curran | .25 | .11 |
| □ 11 Martin Gendron | .50 | .23 |
| □ 12 Kent Hulst | .40 | .18 |
| □ 13 Alexander Kharlamov | .75 | .35 |
| □ 14 Jim Mathieson | .40 | .18 |
| □ 15 Darren McAusland | .40 | .18 |
| □ 16 Jeff Nelson | .50 | .23 |
| □ 17 Darryl Paquette | .50 | .23 |
| □ 18 Rob Pearson | .40 | .18 |
| □ 19 Steve Poapst | .40 | .18 |
| □ 20 Joel Poirier | .40 | .18 |
| □ 21 Sergei Tertyshny | .40 | .18 |
| □ 22 Barry Trotz CO | .10 | .05 |
| □ 23 Ron Tugnutt | .75 | .35 |
| □ 24 Stefan Ustorf | .75 | .35 |

## 1996-97 Portland Pirates

This 25-card set was produced by Split Second. The set features action photos on the front and a statistical package on the reverse. The unnumbered cards feature the player's sweater number prominently on the back, and are numbered thusly below.

| | MINT | NRMT |
|---|---|---|
| COMPLETE SET (25) | 10.00 | 4.50 |
| COMMON CARD | .10 | .05 |
| □ 1 Robb Stauber | .50 | .23 |
| □ 3 Steve Poapst | .40 | .18 |
| □ 4 Stewart Malgunas | .40 | .18 |
| □ 5 Nolan Baumgartner | .75 | .35 |
| □ 6 Ron Pascucci | .40 | .18 |
| □ 7 Norm Batherson | .40 | .18 |
| □ 9 Marc Potvin | .40 | .18 |
| □ 10 Kent Hulst | .40 | .18 |
| □ 12 Brad Church | .75 | .35 |
| □ 14 Richard Zednik | .50 | .23 |
| □ 15 Jaroslav Svejkovsky | 1.50 | .70 |
| □ 16 Darren McAusland | .40 | .18 |
| □ 19 Andrew Brunette | .40 | .18 |
| □ 20 Miika Elomo | .75 | .35 |
| □ 21 Jason Christie | .40 | .18 |
| □ 22 Alexander Kharlamov | .50 | .23 |
| □ 24 Daniel Laperriere | .40 | .18 |
| □ 25 Benoit Gratton | .40 | .18 |
| □ 27 Patrick Boileau | .40 | .18 |
| □ 28 Trevor Halverson | .40 | .18 |
| □ 30 Martin Brochu | .50 | .23 |
| □ 33 Anson Carter | .75 | .35 |
| □ NNO Barry Trotz CO | .10 | .05 |
| □ NNO AHL Ad Card | .10 | .05 |
| □ NNO Paul Gardner ACO | .10 | .05 |

## 1986-87 Portland Winter Hawks

Sponsored by AM-PM Mini-Market, this 24-card set measures the standard size. The white-bordered fronts feature posed-on-ice color player photos. The player's name, number, and position appear in black lettering within the white margin beneath the picture, while the team name is printed vertically along the left border. The sponsor's logo appears at the upper right. The horizontal white back carries the player's name, uniform number, and position at the top, followed by biography, statistics, and "On And Off Ice Highlights." The cards are unnumbered and checklisted below in alphabetical order.

| | MINT | NRMT |
|---|---|---|
| COMPLETE SET (24) | 10.00 | 4.50 |
| COMMON CARD (1-24) | .50 | .23 |
| □ 1 Dave Archibald | .75 | .35 |
| □ 2 Bruce Basken | .50 | .23 |
| □ 3 Thomas Bjuhr | .50 | .23 |
| □ 4 Shaun Clouston | .50 | .23 |
| □ 5 Jeff Finley | .50 | .23 |
| □ 6 Bob Foglietta | .50 | .23 |
| □ 7 Brian Gerrits | .50 | .23 |
| □ 8 Darryl Gilmour | .75 | .35 |
| □ 9 Dennis Holland | .50 | .23 |
| □ 10 Steve Kloepzig | .50 | .23 |
| □ 11 Jim Latos | .50 | .23 |
| □ 12 Dave McLay | .50 | .23 |
| □ 13 Scott Melnyk | .50 | .23 |
| □ 14 Troy Mick | .50 | .23 |
| □ 15 Roy Mitchell | .50 | .23 |
| □ 16 Jamie Nicolls | .50 | .23 |
| □ 17 Trevor Pohl | .50 | .23 |
| □ 18 Troy Pohl | .50 | .23 |
| □ 19 Glen Seymour | .50 | .23 |
| □ 20 Jeff Sharples | .50 | .23 |
| □ 21 Jay Stark | .50 | .23 |
| □ 22 Jim Swan | .50 | .23 |
| □ 23 Glen Wesley | 1.50 | .70 |
| □ 24 Dan Woodley | .50 | .23 |

## 1987-88 Portland Winter Hawks

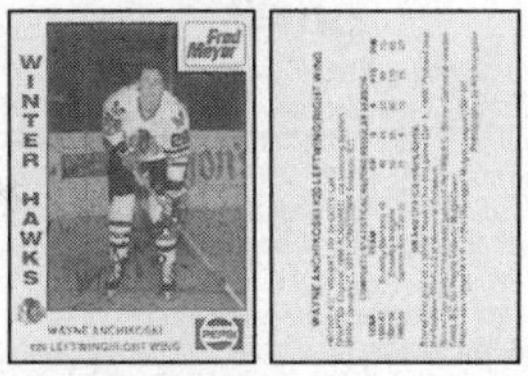

Sponsored by Fred Meyer and Pepsi, this 21-card standard-size set features the 1987-88 Portland Winter Hawks of the Western Hockey League. Inside white borders, the fronts feature posed color player photos shot on the ice at the stadium. The wider left border carries the team name, while the upper right corner of the picture has been cut off to allow space for the sponsor logo. Player information and the Pepsi logo are presented beneath the picture. The horizontal backs have biography, statistics, and a section titled "On and Off Ice Highlights." The cards are unnumbered and checklisted below in alphabetical order.

| | MINT | NRMT |
|---|---|---|
| COMPLETE SET (21) | 10.00 | 4.50 |
| COMMON CARD (1-21) | .10 | .05 |
| □ 1 Wayne Anchikoski | .50 | .23 |
| □ 2 Eric Badzgon | .50 | .23 |
| □ 3 Chad Biafore | .50 | .23 |
| □ 4 James(Hamish) Black | .50 | .23 |
| □ 5 Terry Black | .50 | .23 |
| □ 6 Shaun Clouston | .50 | .23 |
| □ 7 Byron Dafoe | 2.50 | 1.10 |
| □ 8 Brent Fleetwood | .50 | .23 |
| □ 9 Rob Flintoft | .50 | .23 |
| □ 10 Bryan Gourlie | .50 | .23 |
| □ 11 Mark Greyeyes | .50 | .23 |
| □ 12 Dennis Holland | .75 | .35 |
| □ 13 Kevin Jorgenson | .50 | .23 |
| □ 14 Greg Leahy | .50 | .23 |
| □ 15 Troy Mick | .50 | .23 |
| □ 16 Roy Mitchell | .50 | .23 |
| □ 17 Joey Mittelsteadt | .50 | .23 |
| □ 18 Mike Moore | .50 | .23 |
| □ 19 Scott Mydan | .50 | .23 |
| □ 20 Calvin Thudiun | .50 | .23 |
| □ 21 Pepsi Ad Card | .10 | .05 |

## 1988-89 Portland Winter Hawks

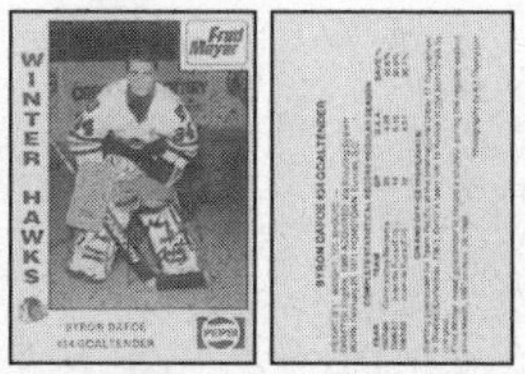

Sponsored by Pepsi and Fred Meyer, this 21-card set measures the standard size. On a white background, the fronts feature posed color player photos with a facsimile autograph in the bottom part of the picture. The player's name, number, and position appear under the picture, while the team name is printed alongside the left border. Sponsor logos complete the fronts. The horizontal backs carry player biography, statistics, and "On And Off Ice Highlights". The cards are unnumbered and checklisted below in alphabetical order.

| | MINT | NRMT |
|---|---|---|
| COMPLETE SET (21) | 9.00 | 4.00 |
| COMMON CARD (1-21) | .10 | .05 |
| □ 1 Wayne Anchikoski | .50 | .23 |
| □ 2 Eric Badzgon | .50 | .23 |
| □ 3 Chad Biafore | .50 | .23 |
| □ 4 James(Hamish) Black | .50 | .23 |
| □ 5 Terry Black | .50 | .23 |
| □ 6 Shaun Clouston | .50 | .23 |
| □ 7 Byron Dafoe | 1.00 | .45 |
| □ 8 Brent Fleetwood | .50 | .23 |
| □ 9 Rob Flintoft | .50 | .23 |
| □ 10 Bryan Gourlie | .50 | .23 |
| □ 11 Mark Greyeyes | .50 | .23 |
| □ 12 Dennis Holland | .50 | .23 |
| □ 13 Kevin Jorgenson | .50 | .23 |
| □ 14 Greg Leahy | .50 | .23 |
| □ 15 Troy Mick | .50 | .23 |
| □ 16 Roy Mitchell | .50 | .23 |
| □ 17 Joey Mittelsteadt | .50 | .23 |
| □ 18 Mike Moore | .50 | .23 |
| □ 19 Scott Mydan | .50 | .23 |
| □ 20 Calvin Thudiun | .50 | .23 |
| □ 21 Pepsi Coupon | .10 | .05 |

## 1989-90 Portland Winter Hawks

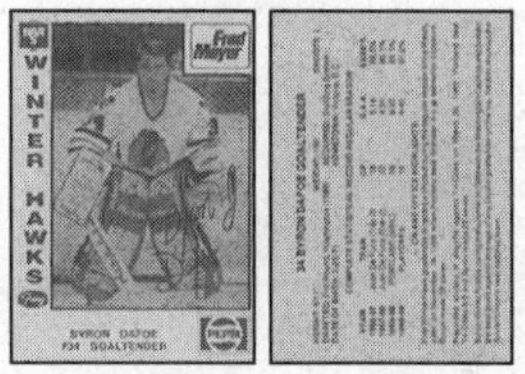

Sponsored by Pepsi and Fred Meyer, this 21-card set measures the standard size. The fronts feature posed color player photos inside a black picture frame and white outer borders. A facsimile autograph is inscribed across the picture. The player's name, number, and position appear under the photo, while the team name is printed alongside the left border. Sponsor logos complete the fronts. The horizontal backs carry player biography, statistics, and "On And Off Ice Highlights." The cards are unnumbered and checklisted below in alphabetical order.

| | MINT | NRMT |
|---|---|---|
| COMPLETE SET (21) | 9.00 | 4.00 |
| COMMON CARD (1-21) | .50 | .23 |
| □ 1 Jamie Black | .75 | .35 |
| □ 2 Vince Cocciolo | .50 | .23 |
| □ 3 Byron Dafoe | .75 | .35 |
| □ 4 Cam Danyluk | .50 | .23 |
| □ 5 Kim Deck | .50 | .23 |
| □ 6 Dean Dorchak | .50 | .23 |
| □ 7 Brent Fleetwood | .50 | .23 |
| □ 8 Rick Fry | .50 | .23 |
| □ 9 Bryan Gourlie | .50 | .23 |
| □ 10 Brad Harrison | .50 | .23 |
| □ 11 Judson Innes | .50 | .23 |
| □ 12 Dean Intwert | .50 | .23 |
| □ 13 Kevin Jorgenson | .50 | .23 |
| □ 14 Todd Kinniburgh | .50 | .23 |
| □ 15 Greg Leahy | .50 | .23 |
| □ 16 Jamie Linden | .50 | .23 |
| □ 17 Scott Mydan | .50 | .23 |
| □ 18 Mike Ruark | .50 | .23 |
| □ 19 Jeff Sebastian | .50 | .23 |
| □ 20 Brandon Smith | .50 | .23 |
| □ 21 Steve Young | .50 | .23 |

## 1984-85 Prince Albert Raiders Stickers

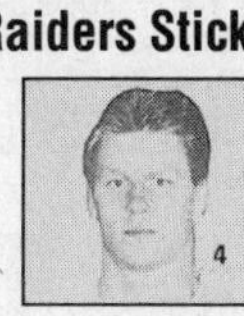

This set of 22 stickers was sponsored by Autotec Oil and Saskatchewan Ronald McDonald House. Each sticker measures 2" by 1 3/4" and could be pasted on a 17" by 11" poster printed in thin glossy paper. The stickers display a black-and-white head shot; the uniform number is also printed on the front. The stickers are unnumbered and checklisted below in alphabetical order.

| | MINT | NRMT |
|---|---|---|
| COMPLETE SET (22) | 20.00 | 9.00 |
| COMMON STICKER (1-22) | 1.00 | .45 |
| □ 1 Ken Baumgartner | 3.00 | 1.35 |
| □ 2 Brad Bennett | 1.00 | .45 |
| □ 3 Dean Braham | 1.00 | .45 |
| □ 4 Rod Dallman | 1.00 | .45 |
| □ 5 Neil Davey | 1.00 | .45 |
| □ 6 Pat Elynuik | 2.00 | .90 |
| □ 7 Collin Feser | 1.00 | .45 |
| □ 8 Dave Goertz | 1.00 | .45 |
| □ 9 Steve Gotaas | 1.00 | .45 |
| □ 10 Tony Grenier | 1.00 | .45 |
| □ 11 Roydon Gunn | 1.00 | .45 |
| □ 12 Doug Hobson | 1.00 | .45 |
| □ 13 Dan Hodgson | 1.00 | .45 |
| □ 14 Curtis Hunt | 1.00 | .45 |
| □ 15 Kim Issel | 1.00 | .45 |
| □ 16 Ward Komonosky | 1.00 | .45 |
| □ 17 David Manson | 1.00 | .45 |
| □ 18 Dale McFee | 1.00 | .45 |
| □ 19 Ken Morrison | 1.00 | .45 |
| □ 20 Dave Pasin | 1.00 | .45 |
| □ 21 Don Schmidt | 1.00 | .45 |
| □ 22 Emanuel Viveiros | 1.00 | .45 |

## 1990-91 Prince Albert Raiders

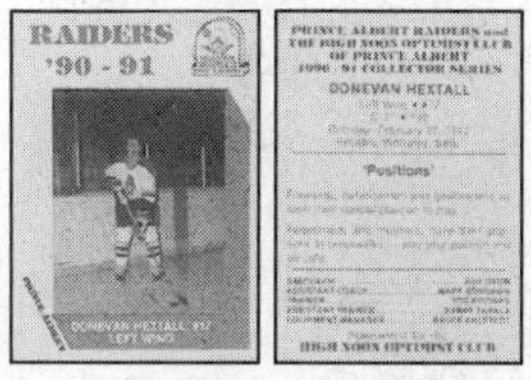

Sponsored by the High Noon Optimist Club, these 25 standard-size cards of the WHL's Prince Albert Raiders are printed on thin card stock and feature on their fronts color posed-on-ice player photos with white outer borders and yellow and green inner borders. The player's name, jersey number, and position appear in white lettering within the green inner border beneath the picture. The white back carries the player's name, position, jersey number, biography, safety message, and list of coaches and trainers. The cards are unnumbered and checklisted below in alphabetical order.

| | MINT | NRMT |
|---|---|---|
| COMPLETE SET (25) | 8.00 | 3.60 |
| COMMON CARD (1-25) | .10 | .05 |
| □ 1 Scott Allison | .35 | .16 |
| □ 2 Laurie Billeck | .35 | .16 |
| □ 3 Jeff Gorman | .35 | .16 |
| □ 4 Donevan Hextall | .50 | .23 |
| □ 5 Troy Hjertaas | .35 | .16 |
| □ 6 Dan Kesa | .50 | .23 |
| □ 7 Jason Kwiatkowski | .35 | .16 |
| □ 8 Travis Laycock | .35 | .16 |
| □ 9 Lee J. Leslie | .50 | .23 |
| □ 10 Jamie Linden | .35 | .16 |
| □ 11 Dean McAmmond | .75 | .35 |
| □ 12 Dave Neilson | .35 | .16 |
| □ 13 Jeff Nelson | .50 | .23 |
| □ 14 Troy Neumeier | .35 | .16 |
| □ 15 Pat Odnokon | .35 | .16 |
| □ 16 Brian Pellerin | .35 | .16 |
| □ 17 Darren Perkins | .35 | .16 |
| □ 18 Curt Regnier | .50 | .23 |
| □ 19 Chad Seibel | .35 | .16 |
| □ 20 Mark Stowe | .35 | .16 |
| □ 21 Darren Van Impe | .75 | .35 |
| □ 22 Shane Zulyniak | .35 | .16 |
| □ 23 Title Card | .10 | .05 |
| □ 24 Info Card (Strangers) | .10 | .05 |
| □ 25 Info Card (Vandalism) | .10 | .05 |

## 1991-92 Prince Albert Raiders

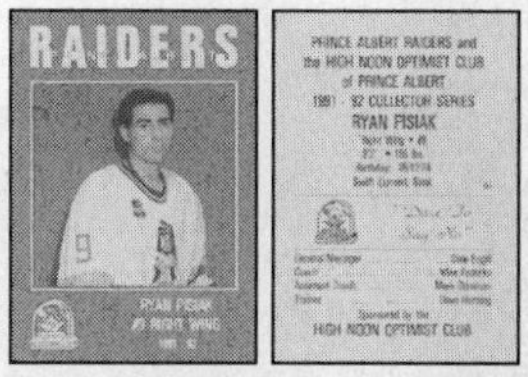

Sponsored by the High Noon Optimist Club, these 24 standard-size cards of the WHL's Prince Albert Raiders are printed on thin card stock and feature on their fronts color posed-on-ice player photos enclosed by green borders. The player's name, jersey number, and position appear in white lettering within the green border near the bottom. The white

back carries the player's name, position, jersey number, biography, safety message, and list of coaches and trainers. The cards are unnumbered and checklisted below in alphabetical order.

| | MINT | NRMT |
|---|---|---|
| COMPLETE SET (24) | 8.00 | 3.60 |
| COMMON CARD (1-24) | .10 | .05 |

| | | |
|---|---|---|
| ❑ 1 Mike Fedorko CO | .10 | .05 |
| ❑ 2 Jeff Gorman | .35 | .16 |
| ❑ 3 Merv Haney | .35 | .16 |
| ❑ 4 Donevan Hextall | .50 | .23 |
| ❑ 5 Troy Hjertaas | .35 | .16 |
| ❑ 6 Dan Kesa | .50 | .23 |
| ❑ 7 Jason Klassen | .35 | .16 |
| ❑ 8 Jason Kwiatkowski | .35 | .16 |
| ❑ 9 Jeff Lank | .35 | .16 |
| ❑ 10 Travis Laycock | .35 | .16 |
| ❑ 11 Lee J. Leslie | .35 | .16 |
| ❑ 12 Stan Matwijiw | .50 | .23 |
| ❑ 13 Dean McAmmond | .50 | .23 |
| ❑ 14 David Neilson | .35 | .16 |
| ❑ 15 Jeff Nelson | .35 | .16 |
| ❑ 16 Mark Odnokon ACO | .10 | .05 |
| ❑ 17 Darren Perkins | .35 | .16 |
| ❑ 18 Ryan Pisiak | .35 | .16 |
| ❑ 19 Nick Polychronopoulos | .35 | .16 |
| ❑ 20 Curt Regnier | .50 | .23 |
| ❑ 21 Jason Renard | .35 | .16 |
| ❑ 22 Barkley Swenson | .35 | .16 |
| ❑ 23 Darren Van Impe | .50 | .23 |
| ❑ 24 Shane Zulyniak | .35 | .16 |

## 1993-94 Prince Albert Raiders

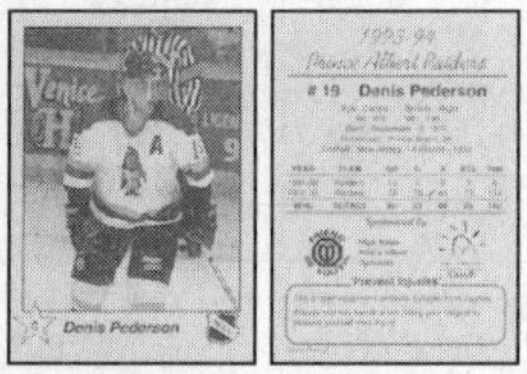

This 22-card standard-size set was sponsored by High Noon Prince Albert Optimists and "Stay in School Canada." On a white card face, the fronts feature color action player photos inside a black picture frame. The player's name appears in a yellow bar under the picture. The backs carry player biography, statistics, and hockey and safety tips. The cards are unnumbered and checklisted below in alphabetical order.

| | MINT | NRMT |
|---|---|---|
| COMPLETE SET (22) | 12.00 | 5.50 |
| COMMON CARD (1-22) | .35 | .16 |

| | | |
|---|---|---|
| ❑ 1 Ryan Bast | .35 | .16 |
| ❑ 2 Rodney Bowers | .35 | .16 |
| ❑ 3 Van Burgess | .35 | .16 |
| ❑ 4 Brad Church | 1.50 | .70 |
| ❑ 5 Joaquin Gage | .75 | .35 |
| ❑ 6 Jeff Gorman | .35 | .16 |
| ❑ 7 Merv Haney | .35 | .16 |
| ❑ 8 Greg Harvey | .35 | .16 |
| ❑ 9 Paul Healey | .50 | .23 |
| ❑ 10 Shane Hnidy | .35 | .16 |
| ❑ 11 Russell Hogue | .35 | .16 |
| ❑ 12 Jason Issel | .35 | .16 |
| ❑ 13 Steve Kelly | 2.00 | .90 |
| ❑ 14 Jeff Lank | .35 | .16 |
| ❑ 15 Mike McGhan | .35 | .16 |
| ❑ 16 Denis Pederson | 2.00 | .90 |
| ❑ 17 Mitch Shawara | .35 | .16 |
| ❑ 18 Shayne Toporowski | .50 | .23 |
| ❑ 19 David Van Drunen | .75 | .35 |
| ❑ 20 Dean Whitney | .35 | .16 |
| ❑ 21 Darren Wright | .35 | .16 |
| ❑ 22 Shane Zulyniak | .35 | .16 |

## 1994-95 Prince Albert Raiders

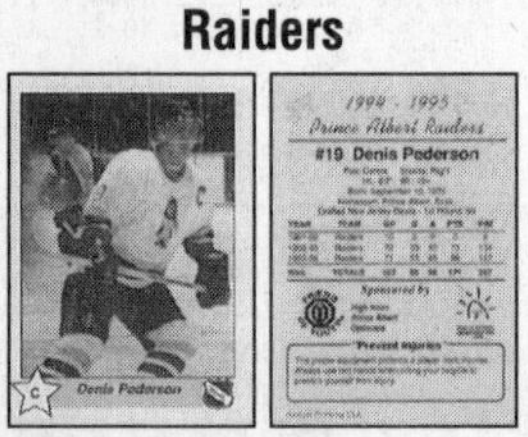

This 23-card set of the Prince Albert Raiders of the WHL was sponsored by the Prince Albert Optimists and "Stay in School Canada." The design mirrors that of the 1993-94 set. The set is noteworthy for the inclusion of several NHL first rounders, including Brad Church, Steve Kelly and Dennis Pederson. The cards are unnumbered, and are checklisted below alphabetically.

| | MINT | NRMT |
|---|---|---|
| COMPLETE SET (23) | 12.00 | 5.50 |
| COMMON CARD (1-23) | .35 | .16 |

| | | |
|---|---|---|
| ❑ 1 Sandy Allan | .50 | .23 |
| ❑ 2 Ryan Bast | .35 | .16 |
| ❑ 3 Brad Church | 2.00 | .90 |
| ❑ 4 Kris Fizzell | .35 | .16 |
| ❑ 5 Paul Healey | .35 | .16 |
| ❑ 6 Rob Hegberg | .35 | .16 |
| ❑ 7 Shane Hnidy | .35 | .16 |
| ❑ 8 Russell Hogue | .35 | .16 |
| ❑ 9 Craig Hordal | .50 | .23 |
| ❑ 10 Jason Issel | .35 | .16 |
| ❑ 11 Neil Johnston | .35 | .16 |
| ❑ 12 Steve Kelly | 1.50 | .70 |
| ❑ 13 Jeff Lank | .35 | .16 |
| ❑ 14 Mike McGhan | .35 | .16 |
| ❑ 15 Denis Pederson | 1.50 | .70 |
| ❑ 16 Sean Robertson | .35 | .16 |
| ❑ 17 Mitch Shawara | .35 | .16 |
| ❑ 18 Shayne Toporowski | .50 | .23 |
| ❑ 19 Kaleb Toth | .35 | .16 |
| ❑ 20 Dave Van Drunen | .75 | .35 |
| ❑ 21 Shane Willis | 1.00 | .45 |
| ❑ 22 Darren Wright | .35 | .16 |
| ❑ 23 Shane Zulyniak | .35 | .16 |

## 1995-96 Prince Albert Raiders

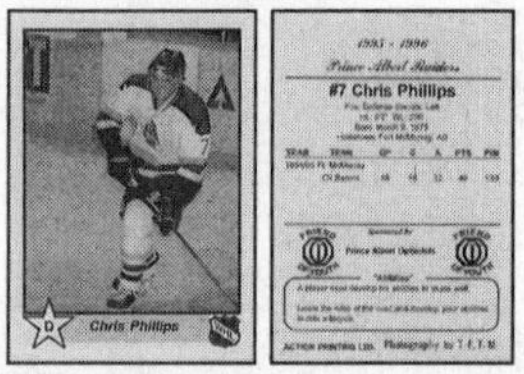

This 22-card set of the Prince Albert Raiders of the WHL was sponsored by the Prince Albert Optimists and features color action player photos in a thin back border on a white background. The player's name is printed in a yellow bar with his position in a white star below the picture. The backs carry player biography, statistics, and a hockey or safety tip. This set includes several first round selections, including 1996 first overall selection Chris Phillips. The cards are unnumbered and checklisted below in alphabetical order.

| | MINT | NRMT |
|---|---|---|
| COMPLETE SET (22) | 15.00 | 6.75 |
| COMMON CARD (1-22) | .35 | .16 |

| | | |
|---|---|---|
| ❑ 1 Rod Branch | .50 | .23 |
| ❑ 2 Curtis Brown | 1.00 | .45 |
| ❑ 3 Brad Church | 1.50 | .70 |
| ❑ 4 Kris Fizzell | .35 | .16 |
| ❑ 5 Dallas Flaman | .35 | .16 |
| ❑ 6 Don Halverson | .35 | .16 |
| ❑ 7 Shane Hnidy | .35 | .16 |
| ❑ 8 Russell Hogue | .35 | .16 |
| ❑ 9 Jason Issel | .35 | .16 |
| ❑ 10 Garnet Jacobson | .35 | .16 |
| ❑ 11 Kevin Kellett | .35 | .16 |
| ❑ 12 Steve Kelly | 2.50 | 1.10 |
| ❑ 13 Dylan Kemp | .35 | .16 |
| ❑ 14 Michael McGhan | .35 | .16 |
| ❑ 15 Marian Menhart | .35 | .16 |
| ❑ 16 Chris Phillips | 4.00 | 1.80 |
| ❑ 17 Blaine Russell | .50 | .23 |
| ❑ 18 Mitch Shawara | .35 | .16 |
| ❑ 19 Dave Van Drunen | .75 | .35 |
| ❑ 20 Roman Vopat | 1.00 | .45 |
| ❑ 21 Shane Willis | .75 | .35 |
| ❑ 22 Darren Wright | .35 | .16 |

## 1996-97 Prince Albert Raiders

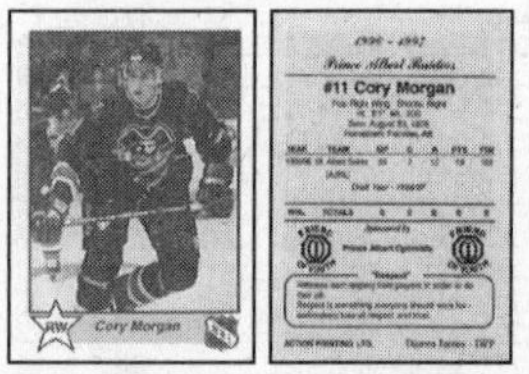

This 17-card set of the Prince Albert Raiders of the WHL was sponsored by the Prince Albert Optimists. The design mirrors that of the 1995-96 set. The number of cards below has led to speculation this may not be a complete checklist. Any additional information would be appreciated. The cards are unnumbered and thus are checklisted below in alphabetical order.

| | MINT | NRMT |
|---|---|---|
| COMPLETE SET (17) | 7.00 | 3.10 |
| COMMON CARD (1-17) | .40 | .18 |

| | | |
|---|---|---|
| ❑ 1 Trevor Baker | .40 | .18 |
| ❑ 2 Scott Botterill | .50 | .23 |
| ❑ 3 Craig Brunel | .40 | .18 |
| ❑ 4 Dallas Flaman | .40 | .18 |
| ❑ 5 Jeremy Goetzinger | .40 | .18 |
| ❑ 6 Don Halverson | .40 | .18 |
| ❑ 7 Russell Hogue | .40 | .18 |
| ❑ 8 Jason Issel | .50 | .23 |
| ❑ 9 Garnet Jacobson | .40 | .18 |
| ❑ 10 Kevin Kellett | .40 | .18 |
| ❑ 11 Evan Lindsay | 1.00 | .45 |
| ❑ 12 Marian Menhart | .50 | .23 |
| ❑ 13 Cory Morgan | .40 | .18 |
| ❑ 14 Derek Paget | .40 | .18 |
| ❑ 15 Harlan Pratt | .50 | .23 |
| ❑ 16 Dave Van Drunen | .75 | .35 |
| ❑ 17 Steve Wilejto | .40 | .18 |

## 1996-97 Prince Albert Raiders Optimists Club

Sponsored by the Prince Albert Optimists Clubs, this 23-card set features color player photos and jersey numbers on the front, and is checklisted below alphabetically.

| | MINT | NRMT |
|---|---|---|
| COMPLETE SET (23) | 12.00 | 5.50 |
| COMMON CARD (1-23) | .40 | .18 |

| | | |
|---|---|---|
| ❑ 1 Trevor Baker | .40 | .18 |
| ❑ 2 Scott Botterill | .60 | .25 |
| ❑ 3 Craig Brunel | .40 | .18 |
| ❑ 4 Marco Cefalo | .40 | .18 |
| ❑ 5 Dallas Flaman | .40 | .18 |
| ❑ 6 Jeremy Goetzinger | .40 | .18 |
| ❑ 7 Don Halverson | .40 | .18 |
| ❑ 8 Russell Hogue | .60 | .25 |
| ❑ 9 Jason Issel | .60 | .25 |
| ❑ 10 Garnet Jacobson | .40 | .18 |
| ❑ 11 Kevin Kellett | .40 | .18 |
| ❑ 12 Dylan Kemp | .40 | .18 |
| ❑ 13 Evan Lindsay | .75 | .35 |
| ❑ 14 Marian Menhart | .60 | .25 |
| ❑ 15 Cory Morgan | .40 | .18 |
| ❑ 16 Derek Paget | .40 | .18 |
| ❑ 17 Chris Phillips | 2.00 | .90 |
| ❑ 18 Harlan Pratt | .40 | .18 |
| ❑ 19 Blaine Russell | 1.00 | .45 |
| ❑ 20 Adam Stewart | .40 | .18 |
| ❑ 21 Dave Van Drunen | 1.00 | .45 |
| ❑ 22 Steve Wilejto | .40 | .18 |
| ❑ 23 Shane Willis | 1.00 | .45 |

## 1936-37 Providence Reds

Printed on thin card stock, this 10-card set measures approximately 2 1/4" by 3 1/2". The fronts feature black-and-white player photos bordered in white. The player's name and position are printed beneath the picture, along with the statement "A New 'Reds' Picture Every Amateur Hockey Night". Unlike the other nine cards, the name of the player on card 10 is not printed beneath his picture. From his facsimile autograph on the picture, his first name may be "Jacques," but his last name remains unidentified. The backs are blank. The cards are unnumbered and checklisted below in alphabetical order.

| | EX-MT | VG-E |
|---|---|---|
| COMPLETE SET (10) | 300.00 | 135.00 |
| COMMON CARD (1-10) | 25.00 | 11.00 |

| | | |
|---|---|---|
| ❑ 1 Bobby Bauer | 50.00 | 22.00 |
| ❑ 2 Paddy Byrne | 25.00 | 11.00 |
| ❑ 3 Woody(Porky) Dumart | 50.00 | 22.00 |
| ❑ 4 Jackie Keating | 25.00 | 11.00 |
| ❑ 5 Art Lesieur | 25.00 | 11.00 |
| ❑ 6 Bert McInenly | 25.00 | 11.00 |
| ❑ 7 Gus Rivers | 25.00 | 11.00 |
| ❑ 8 Milt Schmidt | 100.00 | 45.00 |
| ❑ 9 Jerry Shannon | 25.00 | 11.00 |
| ❑ 10 Player Unidentified | 25.00 | 11.00 |

## 1996-97 Providence Bruins

This 25-card set was produced by SplitSecond for sale by the club at the team shop. It was originally offered for sale for $5. The cards feature the standard SplitSecond design. The cards are listed below according to jersey number, which is displayed prominently on the card.

| | MINT | NRMT |
|---|---|---|
| COMPLETE SET (25) | 7.00 | 3.10 |
| COMMON CARD | .10 | .05 |

| | | |
|---|---|---|
| ❑ 2 Mark Cornforth | .40 | .18 |
| ❑ 3 Charles Paquette | .40 | .18 |
| ❑ 4 John Gruden | .40 | .18 |
| ❑ 6 Peter Laviolette | .40 | .18 |
| ❑ 8 Jean-Yves Roy | .40 | .18 |
| ❑ 9 Justin Gould | .40 | .18 |
| ❑ 10 David Emma | .40 | .18 |
| ❑ 11 Davis Payne | .40 | .18 |
| ❑ 13 Martin Simard | .40 | .18 |
| ❑ 14 Kirk Nielsen | .40 | .18 |
| ❑ 17 P.C. Drouin | .40 | .18 |
| ❑ 18 Jay Moser | .40 | .18 |
| ❑ 19 Bill McCauley | .40 | .18 |
| ❑ 21 Tim Sweeney LL | .40 | .18 |
| ❑ 22 Mitch Lamoureux | .40 | .18 |
| ❑ 23 Yevgeny Shaldybin | .40 | .18 |
| ❑ 25 Kevin Sawyer | .40 | .18 |
| ❑ 27 Brad Konik | .40 | .18 |
| ❑ 28 Milt Mastad | .40 | .18 |
| ❑ 29 Rob Tallas | .75 | .35 |
| ❑ 34 Bob Beers | .40 | .18 |
| ❑ 44 Brett Harkins | .40 | .18 |
| ❑ 49 Andre Roy | .40 | .18 |
| ❑ NNO Bob Francis CO | .10 | .05 |
| ❑ NNO AHL Hockey Card | .10 | .05 |

## 1950 Quebec Citadelles

These 20 blank-backed photos of the Quebec Citadelles measure 4" by 6" and feature cream-bordered sepiatones of the suited-up players posed on the ice. The players' facsimile autographs appear near the bottom of the pictures. The photos are unnumbered and checklisted below in alphabetical order. Blue-tinted variations of these cards exist. More difficult to locate, they command a premium of up to two times. This set includes the earliest known card-like element of all-time great, Jean Beliveau.

| | EX-MT | VG-E |
|---|---|---|
| COMPLETE SET (20) | 300.00 | 135.00 |
| COMMON CARD (1-20) | 8.00 | 3.60 |

| | | |
|---|---|---|
| ❑ 1 Neil Amadio | 10.00 | 4.50 |
| ❑ 2 Jean Beliveau | 200.00 | 90.00 |
| ❑ 3 Georges Bergeron CO | 8.00 | 3.60 |
| ❑ 4 Bruce Cline | 12.00 | 5.50 |
| ❑ 5 Norm Diviney | 8.00 | 3.60 |
| ❑ 6 Guy Gervais | 8.00 | 3.60 |
| ❑ 7 Bernard Guay | 8.00 | 3.60 |
| ❑ 8 Gord Haworth | 10.00 | 4.50 |
| ❑ 9 Camille Henry | 20.00 | 9.00 |
| ❑ 10 Gordie Hudson | 8.00 | 3.60 |
| ❑ 11 Claude Larochelle | 12.00 | 5.50 |
| ❑ 12 Bernie Lemonde | 8.00 | 3.60 |
| ❑ 13 Paul-Emile Legault | 8.00 | 3.60 |
| ❑ 14 Copper Leyte | 8.00 | 3.60 |
| ❑ 15 Rainer Makila | 10.00 | 4.50 |
| ❑ 16 Marcel Paille | 25.00 | 11.00 |
| ❑ 17 Jean-Marie Plante | 8.00 | 3.60 |
| ❑ 18 Claude Senechal | 8.00 | 3.60 |
| ❑ 19 Jean Tremblay | 20.00 | 9.00 |
| ❑ 20 Alphonses Gagnon CO | 8.00 | 3.60 |

## 1956-57 Quebec Aces

The set was also issued on a limited basis as a factory set in a black presentation box.This 15-card set measures approximately 5" by 7" and features black-and-white posed action player photos with a white border. The player's name is inscribed across the lower portion of the photo. On a white background, the backs carry the sponsor (Maurice Pollack Limitee) and team logos. The cards are unnumbered and checklisted below in alphabetical order.

| | EX-MT | VG-E |
|---|---|---|
| COMPLETE SET (16) | 120.00 | 55.00 |
| COMMON CARD (1-16) | 5.00 | 2.20 |

| | | |
|---|---|---|
| ❑ 1 Gene Achtynichuk | 5.00 | 2.20 |
| ❑ 2 Bob Beckett | 10.00 | 4.50 |
| ❑ 3 Marcel Bonin | 12.00 | 5.50 |
| ❑ 4 Joe Crozier | 15.00 | 6.75 |
| ❑ 5 Jacque Gagne | 5.00 | 2.20 |
| ❑ 6 Dick Garnelle | 5.00 | 2.20 |
| ❑ 7 Floyd Hillman | 10.00 | 4.50 |
| ❑ 8 Jean Paul Lamonde | 5.00 | 2.20 |
| ❑ 9 Jean-Marie Loisette | 5.00 | 2.20 |
| ❑ 10 Brent MacNab | 5.00 | 2.20 |
| ❑ 11 Al Millar | 5.00 | 2.20 |
| ❑ 12 Willie O'Ree | 25.00 | 11.00 |
| ❑ 13 Nick Tabuchie | 5.00 | 2.20 |
| ❑ 14 Skip Teal | 5.00 | 2.20 |
| ❑ 15 Orval Tessier | 12.00 | 5.50 |
| ❑ 16 Ludger Tremblay | 8.00 | 3.60 |

## 1962-63 Quebec Aces

This 21-card set features the Quebec Aces of the Quebec Senior Hockey League. The cards measure approximately 3 1/2" by 5 1/2" and have black and white posed action photos with white borders. The player's name is printed in black at the bottom. The backs are blank. The cards are unnumbered and checklisted below

in alphabetical order. The existence of a corrected version of the Bill Dineen card recently has been confirmed. The set is considered complete with either version.

| | NRMT | EXC |
|---|---|---|
| COMPLETE SET (21) | 100.00 | 45.00 |
| COMMON CARD (1-21) | 4.00 | 1.80 |

| | | |
|---|---|---|
| ❑ 1 Ronald Attwell | 4.00 | 1.80 |
| ❑ 2 Serge Aubry | 6.00 | 2.70 |
| ❑ 3 Guy Black | 4.00 | 1.80 |
| ❑ 4 Skippy Burchell | 4.00 | 1.80 |
| ❑ 5 Jean Marie Cossette | 4.00 | 1.80 |
| ❑ 6 Robert Courcy | 4.00 | 1.80 |
| ❑ 7A Bill Dineen ERR (Misspelled Dinenn) | 12.00 | 5.50 |
| ❑ 7B Bill Dineen COR | 15.00 | 6.75 |
| ❑ 8 Terry Gray | 10.00 | 4.50 |
| ❑ 9 Reggie Grigg | 4.00 | 1.80 |
| ❑ 10 John Hanna | 4.00 | 1.80 |
| ❑ 11 Michel Harvey | 4.00 | 1.80 |
| ❑ 12 Charlie Hodge | 25.00 | 11.00 |
| ❑ 13 Ed Hoekstra | 6.00 | 2.70 |
| ❑ 14 Michel Labadie | 4.00 | 1.80 |
| ❑ 15 Claude Labrosse | 4.00 | 1.80 |
| ❑ 16 Danny Lewicki | 8.00 | 3.60 |
| ❑ 17 Frank Martin | 4.00 | 1.80 |
| ❑ 18 Jim Morrison | 6.00 | 2.70 |
| ❑ 19 Guy Rousseau | 4.00 | 1.80 |
| ❑ 20 Dollard St. Laurent | 10.00 | 4.50 |
| ❑ 21 Bill Sutherland | 6.00 | 2.70 |

## 1963-64 Quebec Aces

This 23-card set features the Quebec Aces of the Quebec Senior Hockey League. The cards measure approximately 3 1/2" by 5 1/2" and have black and white posed action photos with white borders. The player's name is printed in black at the bottom. The backs are blank. The cards are unnumbered and checklisted below in alphabetical order.

| | NRMT | EXC |
|---|---|---|
| COMPLETE SET (23) | 150.00 | 70.00 |
| COMMON CARD (1-23) | 3.00 | 1.35 |

| | | |
|---|---|---|
| ❑ 1 Gilles Banville | 3.00 | 1.35 |
| ❑ 2 Don Blackburn | 3.00 | 1.35 |
| ❑ 3 Skippy Burchell | 3.00 | 1.35 |
| ❑ 4 Billy Carter | 3.00 | 1.35 |
| ❑ 5 Floyd Curry CO | 10.00 | 4.50 |
| ❑ 6 Bill Dineen | 10.00 | 4.50 |
| ❑ 7 Wayne Freitag | 3.00 | 1.35 |
| ❑ 8 Jean Gauthier | 3.00 | 1.35 |
| ❑ 9 Terry Gray | 5.00 | 2.20 |
| ❑ 10 John Hanna | 3.00 | 1.35 |
| ❑ 11 Doug Harvey | 30.00 | 13.50 |
| ❑ 12 Wayne Hicks | 3.00 | 1.35 |
| ❑ 13 Charlie Hodge (Standing before net) | 15.00 | 6.75 |
| ❑ 14 Charlie Hodge (Spread out before net in defensive posture) | 15.00 | 6.75 |
| ❑ 15 Ed Hoekstra | 5.00 | 2.20 |
| ❑ 16 Frank Martin | 3.00 | 1.35 |
| ❑ 17 Rene LaCasse | 3.00 | 1.35 |
| ❑ 18 Cleland Mortson | 3.00 | 1.35 |
| ❑ 19 Gerry O'Drowski | 5.00 | 2.20 |
| ❑ 20 Rino Robazzo | 5.00 | 2.20 |
| ❑ 21 Leon Rochefort | 3.00 | 1.35 |
| ❑ 22 Cliff Pennington | 5.00 | 2.20 |
| ❑ 23 Lorne Worsley | 35.00 | 16.00 |

## 1963-64 Quebec Aces QSHL

This 22-card set features the Quebec Aces of the Quebec Senior Hockey League. The cards measure approximately 3 1/2" by 5 1/2" and have black and white posed action photos with white borders. The player's name is printed in black at the bottom. The backs are blank. The cards are unnumbered and checklisted below in alphabetical order.

| | NRMT | VG-E |
|---|---|---|
| COMPLETE SET (22) | 125.00 | 55.00 |
| COMMON CARD (1-22) | 3.00 | 1.35 |

| | | |
|---|---|---|
| ❑ 1 Don Blackburn | 3.00 | 1.35 |
| ❑ 2 Skippy Burchell | 3.00 | 1.35 |

❑ 3 Billy Carter 3.00 1.35
❑ 4 Floyd Curry CO 10.00 4.50
❑ 5 Bill Dineen 10.00 4.50
❑ 6 Wayne Freitag 3.00 1.35
❑ 7 Jean Gauthier 3.00 1.35
❑ 8 Terry Gray 5.00 2.20
❑ 9 John Hanna 3.00 1.35
❑ 10 Doug Harvey 25.00 11.00
❑ 11 Wayne Hicks 3.00 1.35
❑ 12 Charlie Hodge 15.00 6.75
(Standing before net)
❑ 13 Charlie Hodge 15.00 6.75
(Spread out before net
in defensive posture)
❑ 14 Ed Hoekstra 5.00 2.20
❑ 15 Frank Martin 3.00 1.35
❑ 16 Jim Morrison 5.00 2.20
❑ 17 Cleland Mortson 3.00 1.35
❑ 18 Gerry O'Drowski 3.00 1.35
❑ 19 Rino Robazza 5.00 2.20
❑ 20 Leon Rochefort 3.00 1.35
❑ 21 Bill Sutherland 6.00 2.70
❑ 22 Lorne Worsley 25.00 11.00

## 1964-65 Quebec Aces

This 19-card set features the Quebec Aces of the Quebec Senior Hockey League. The cards measure approximately 3 1/2" by 5 1/2". The fronts have posed black-and-white player photos with white borders. The player's name is printed in black at the bottom. The backs are blank. The cards are unnumbered and checklisted below in alphabetical order.

| | NRMT | EXC |
|---|---|---|
| COMPLETE SET (19) | 125.00 | 55.00 |
| COMMON CARD (1-19) | 3.00 | 1.35 |

❑ 1 Gilles Banville 3.00 1.35
❑ 2 Red Berenson 10.00 4.50
❑ 3 Don Blackburn 3.00 1.35
❑ 4 Jean Guy Gendron 8.00 3.60
❑ 5 Bernard Geoffrion 30.00 13.50
❑ 6 Terry Gray 8.00 3.60
❑ 7 John Hanna 3.00 1.35
❑ 8 Doug Harvey 25.00 11.00
❑ 9 Wayne Hicks 3.00 1.35
❑ 10 Edward Hoekstra 5.00 2.20
❑ 11 Rene Lacasse 3.00 1.35
❑ 12 Raymond Larose 3.00 1.35
❑ 13 Jimmy Morrison 5.00 2.20
❑ 14 Cleland Mortson 3.00 1.35
❑ 15 Leon Rochefort 8.00 3.60
❑ 16 Guy Rousseau 3.00 1.35
❑ 17 Bill Sutherland 4.00 1.80
❑ 18 Brian Watson 4.00 1.80
❑ 19 Lorne Worsley 25.00 11.00

## 1965-66 Quebec Aces

This 19-card set measures 3 1/2" by 5 1/2". The fronts feature white-bordered posed action shots. The player's name is printed in the wider white border at the bottom. The backs are blank. The cards are unnumbered and checklisted below in alphabetical order.

| | NRMT-MT | EXC |
|---|---|---|
| COMPLETE SET (19) | 75.00 | 34.00 |
| COMMON CARD (1-19) | 3.00 | 1.35 |

❑ 1 Gilles Banville 3.00 1.35
❑ 2 Gary Bauman 3.00 1.35
❑ 3 Don Blackburn 3.00 1.35
❑ 4 Jean-Guy Gendron 5.00 2.20
❑ 5 Bernard Geoffrion CO 25.00 11.00
❑ 6 Terry Gray 5.00 2.20
❑ 7 John Hanna 3.00 1.35
❑ 8 Wayne Hicks 3.00 1.35
❑ 9 Ed Hoekstra 5.00 2.20
❑ 10 Don Johns 3.00 1.35
❑ 11 Gordon Labossiere 5.00 2.20
❑ 12 Yvon Lacoste 3.00 1.35
❑ 13 Jimmy Morrison 5.00 2.20
❑ 14 Cleland Mortson 3.00 1.35
❑ 15 Simon Nolet 8.00 3.60
❑ 16 Noel Price 5.00 2.20
❑ 17 Rino Robazzo 5.00 2.20
❑ 18 Leon Rochefort 5.00 2.20
❑ 19 Bill Sutherland 4.00 1.80

## 1980-81 Quebec Remparts

This 22-card set measures approximately 2" by 3" and features posed color player photos. The cards were issued as part of a contest. The pictures are full-bleed except for a white bottom border that contains the team logo, player's name, and jersey number. The backs are blank. The collector who obtained the entire set and turned it in became eligible to enter a contest in which the grand prize was a trip to Disneyworld. The cards are unnumbered and checklisted below in alphabetical order.

| | NRMT-MT | EXC |
|---|---|---|
| COMPLETE SET (22) | 15.00 | 6.75 |
| COMMON CARD (1-22) | .50 | .23 |

❑ 1 Marc Bertrand .75 .35
❑ 2 Jacques Chouinard .75 .35
❑ 3 Roger Cote .75 .35
❑ 4 Gaston Drapeau CO .50 .23
❑ 5 Claude Drouin .75 .35
❑ 6 Gaetan Duchesne 2.00 .90
❑ 7 Scott Fraser .75 .35
❑ 8 Jean-Marc Lanthier .75 .35
❑ 9 Jean Paul Lariviere .75 .35
❑ 10 Andre Larocque .75 .35
❑ 11 Roberto Lavoie .75 .35
❑ 12 Marc Lemay .75 .35
❑ 13 Stephane Lessard .75 .35
❑ 14 Paul Levesque .75 .35
❑ 15 Richard Linteau .75 .35
❑ 16 Patrice Masse .75 .35
❑ 17 David Pretty .75 .35
❑ 18 Guy Riel .75 .35
❑ 19 Daniel Rioux .75 .35
❑ 20 Roberto Romano 1.50 .70
❑ 21 Michel Therrien 1.50 .70
❑ 22 Gilles Tremblay 1.50 .70

## 1998-99 Quebec Remparts

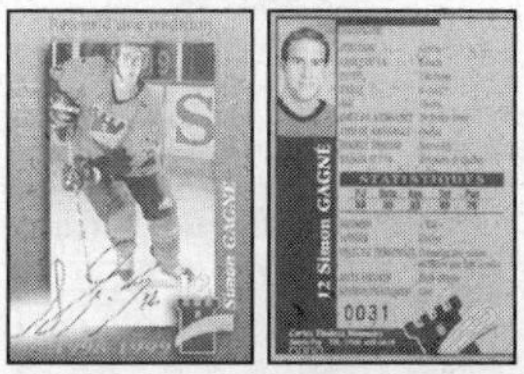

Produced by Cartes Timbres Monnaies in conjunction with the Quebec Ramparts. Set was limited to only 100 serial #'d sets and the entire set is signed (except for Joey Fetta who was traded). Set is unnumbered and checklisted below in alphabetical order.

| | MINT | NRMT |
|---|---|---|
| COMPLETE SET (25) | 100.00 | 45.00 |
| COMMON CARD (1-25) | 3.00 | 1.35 |

❑ 1 David Archambault 3.00 1.35
❑ 2 David Bernier 3.00 1.35
❑ 3 Nicholas Bilotto 3.00 1.35
❑ 4 Tommy Bolduc 3.00 1.35
❑ 5 Eric Chouinard 15.00 6.75
❑ 6 Ray Dalton 3.00 1.35
❑ 7 Joey Fetta 3.00 1.35
❑ 8 Simon Gagne 30.00 13.50
❑ 9 Martin Grenier 3.00 1.35
❑ 10 Eric Laplante 8.00 3.60
❑ 11 Jeff Leblanc 3.00 1.35
❑ 12 Pierre Loiselle 8.00 3.60
❑ 13 Jerome Marois 3.00 1.35
❑ 14 Andre Martineau 3.00 1.35
❑ 15 Martin Moise 3.00 1.35
❑ 16 Alexandre Morel 3.00 1.35
❑ 17 Maxime Ouellet 20.00 9.00
❑ 18 Sylvain Plamondon 3.00 1.35
❑ 19 Wesley Scanzano 3.00 1.35
❑ 20 Simon Tremblay 3.00 1.35
❑ 21 Dmitri Tolkunov 3.00 1.35
❑ 22 Antoine Vermette 3.00 1.35
❑ 23 Jonathan Wilhelmy 3.00 1.35
❑ 24 Travis Zachary 3.00 1.35
❑ 25 Title Card 3.00 1.35

## 1992-93 Quebec Int. Pee-Wees Gold

This three-card insert standard-size set features color player photos with metallic-gold borders on white card stock. The player's name is printed in the border at the top, while

the card title is printed below the picture. The backs carry a player profile against a metallic-gold background with white borders. Two of the cards are numbered, while one is not. The listing below reflects this numbering.

| | MINT | NRMT |
|---|---|---|
| COMPLETE SET (3) | 12.00 | 5.50 |
| COMMON CARD (1-3) | 1.00 | .45 |

❑ 1 Brad Park 2.00 .90
❑ 2 Manon Rheaume 10.00 4.50
❑ NNO Guy Chouinard 1.00 .45

## 1992-93 Raleigh Icecaps

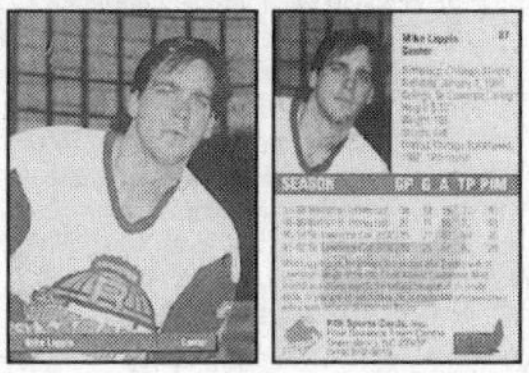

This 38-card standard-size set features the Raleigh Icecaps of the ECHL. Inside a blue-and-white border design, the fronts feature on-ice posed color player photos with rounded corners. The player's name and position appear under the photo, while the words "1992-93 Raleigh IceCaps" are printed above the photo. The backs carry biography, stats, and a player profile. The cards were issued in two separate series. The first series cards, produced by Sportsprint (Atlanta, GA), are unnumbered and checklisted below in alphabetical order, whereas the second series cards, produced by RBI Sports Cards Inc. (Greensboro, North Carolina), are numbered on the back.

| | MINT | NRMT |
|---|---|---|
| COMPLETE SET (38) | 15.00 | 6.75 |
| COMMON CARD (1-19) | .10 | .05 |
| COMMON CARD (20-38) | .35 | .16 |

❑ 1 Cappy Bear (Mascot) .10 .05
❑ 2 Sean Cowan .50 .23
❑ 3 Joel Gardner .50 .23
❑ 4 Bill Kovacs .50 .23
❑ 5 Alan Leggett .50 .23
❑ 6 Kirby Lindal .50 .23
❑ 7 Derek Linnell .50 .23
❑ 8 Jim Mill .50 .23
❑ 9 Kris Miller .50 .23
❑ 10 Todd Person .50 .23
❑ 11 Chic Pojar .50 .23
❑ 12 Jim Powers .50 .23
❑ 13 Stan(Smokey) Reddick .75 .35
❑ 14 Doug Roberts .50 .23
❑ 15 Jeff Robison .50 .23
❑ 16 Jeff Tomlinson .50 .23
❑ 17 Brian Tulik .50 .23
❑ 18 Bruno Villeneuve .50 .23
❑ 19 Lyle Wildgoose .50 .23
❑ 20 Team Photo DP .35 .16
❑ 21 Bruno Villeneuve .50 .23
❑ 22 Jeff Robison .50 .23
❑ 23 Jim Powers .50 .23
❑ 24 Derek Linnell .50 .23
❑ 25 Chris Marshall .50 .23
❑ 26 Kris Miller .50 .23
❑ 27 Joel Gardner .50 .23
❑ 28 Stan(Smokey) Reddick .75 .35
❑ 29 Jim Mill .50 .23
❑ 30 Alan Leggett .50 .23
❑ 31 Brian Tulik .50 .23
❑ 32 Kirby Lindal .50 .23
❑ 33 Sean Cowan .50 .23
❑ 34 Lyle Wildgoose .50 .23
❑ 35 Todd Person .50 .23
❑ 36 Chic Pojar .50 .23
❑ 37 Mike Lappin .50 .23
❑ 38 Doug Bacon .50 .23

## 1993-94 Raleigh Icecaps

Produced by RBI Sports Cards, this 20-card standard-size set features the Raleigh Icecaps of the ECHL. On a white card face, the fronts feature color action player photos inside purple borders. The player's name appears under the photo. On white card stock with blue lettering, the backs carry player biography, stats, and player profile.

| | MINT | NRMT |
|---|---|---|
| COMPLETE SET (20) | 7.00 | 3.10 |
| COMMON CARD (1-20) | .25 | .11 |

❑ 1 Ralph Barahona .40 .18
❑ 2 Rick Barkovich .40 .18
❑ 3 Matt Delguidice .50 .23
❑ 4 Martin D'Orsonnens .40 .18
❑ 5 Jamie Erb .40 .18
❑ 6 Chad Erickson .50 .23
❑ 7 Donevan Hextall .50 .23
❑ 8 Shaun Kane .40 .18
❑ 9 Al Leggett .40 .18
❑ 10 Derek Linnell .40 .18
❑ 11 Joe McCarthy .40 .18
❑ 12 Chris Nelson .40 .18
❑ 13 Barry Nieckar .40 .18
❑ 14 Jim Powers .40 .18
❑ 15 Stan Reddick .50 .23
❑ 16 Kevin Riehl .40 .18
❑ 17 Jeff Robison .40 .18
❑ 18 David Shute .40 .18
❑ 19 Lyle Wildgoose .40 .18
❑ 20 Kurt Kleinendorst CO .25 .11

## 1994-95 Raleigh Icecaps

Produced by RBI Sports Cards, this 19-card standard-size set features the Raleigh Icecaps of the ECHL. Just 1,000 sets were produced. On a black card face, the fronts feature color action and posed player photos inside a white frame. The player's name appears under the photo, while the team name is printed above the photo. On a black background, the backs carry player biography, stats, and player profile. There are several production errors in this set. Card number 12 was not produced. Card numbers 9 and 18 were mistakenly duplicated and explains the absence of card numbers 10 and 19.

| | MINT | NRMT |
|---|---|---|
| COMPLETE SET (19) | 6.00 | 2.70 |
| COMMON CARD (1-20) | .25 | .11 |

❑ 1 John Blessman .40 .18
❑ 2 Rick Barkovich CO .25 .11
❑ 3 Alexsandr Chunchukov .40 .18
❑ 4 Frank Cirone .40 .18
❑ 5 Brett Duncan .40 .18
❑ 6 Anton Fedorov .40 .18
❑ 7 Todd Hunter .40 .18
❑ 8 Rodrigo Lavinsh .40 .18
❑ 9 Derek Linnell .40 .18
❑ 10 Eric Long UER .40 .18
(Card misnumbered
9 on back)
❑ 11 Scott MacNair .40 .18
❑ 13 Brad Mullahy .40 .18
❑ 14 Lenny Pereira .40 .18
❑ 15 Jimmy Powers .40 .18
❑ 16 Chic Pojar .40 .18
❑ 17 Kevin Riehl .40 .18
❑ 18 Todd Reirden .40 .18
❑ 19 Justin Tomberlin UER .50 .23
(Card misnumbered
18 on back)
❑ 20 Lyle Wildgoose .40 .18

## 1989-90 Rayside-Balfour Jr. Canadians

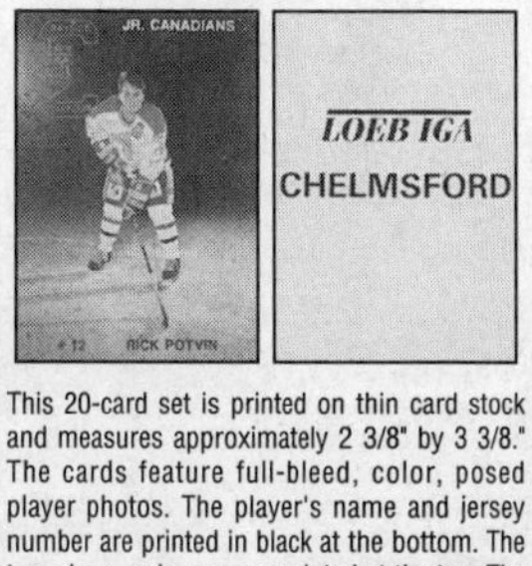
JR. CANADIANS
RICK POTVIN
LOEB IGA
CHELMSFORD

This 20-card set is printed on thin card stock and measures approximately 2 3/8" by 3 3/8." The cards feature full-bleed, color, posed player photos. The player's name and jersey number are printed in black at the bottom. The team logo and name are printed at the top. The backs are white and carry sponsor information. The cards are unnumbered and checklisted below in alphabetical order.

| | MINT | NRMT |
|---|---|---|
| COMPLETE SET (20) | 8.00 | 3.60 |
| COMMON CARD (1-20) | .50 | .23 |

❑ 1 Team Photo 1.00 .45
❑ 2 Dave Barrett .50 .23
❑ 3 Dan Baston .50 .23
❑ 4 Rick Chartrand .50 .23
❑ 5 Simon Chartrand .50 .23
❑ 6 Ron Clark .50 .23
❑ 7 Brian Dickinson .50 .23
❑ 8 Trevor Duncan .50 .23
❑ 9 Don Gauthier .50 .23
❑ 10 Shawn Hawkins .50 .23
❑ 11 Roy Hildebrandt .50 .23
❑ 12 Al Laginski .50 .23
❑ 13 Eric Lanteigne .50 .23
❑ 14 Mike Leblanc .50 .23
❑ 15 Kevin MacDonald .50 .23
❑ 16 Mike Mooney .50 .23
❑ 17 Rick Potvin .50 .23
❑ 18 Rick Poulin .50 .23
❑ 19 Steve Prior .50 .23
❑ 20 Scott Sutton .50 .23

## 1990-91 Rayside-Balfour Jr. Canadians

JR. CANADIANS
North West Lumber
DENIS GOSSELIN

This 23-card set is printed on thin card stock and measures approximately 2 3/8" by 3 1/4." The cards feature full-bleed, color, posed player photos. The player's name and jersey number are printed in black at the bottom. The team logo and name are printed at the top. The backs are white and carry sponsor information. The cards are unnumbered and checklisted below in alphabetical order.

| | MINT | NRMT |
|---|---|---|
| COMPLETE SET (23) | 7.00 | 3.10 |
| COMMON CARD (1-23) | .10 | .05 |

❑ 1 Dan Baston .40 .18
❑ 2 Jon Boeve .40 .18
❑ 3 Jordan Boyle .40 .18
❑ 4 Serge Coulombe .40 .18
❑ 5 Mike Dore .40 .18
❑ 6 Denis Gosselin .40 .18
❑ 7 Mike Gratton .40 .18
❑ 8 Jason Hall .40 .18
❑ 9 Grant Healey .40 .18
❑ 10 Marc Lafreniere .40 .18
❑ 11 Alain Leclair .40 .18
❑ 12 Mike Longo .40 .18
❑ 13 Troy Mallette 1.00 .45
1985-86 rookie photo
❑ 14 Matthew Mooney .40 .18
❑ 15 Virgil Nose .40 .18
❑ 16 Trevor Oystrick .40 .18
❑ 17 Steve Proceviat .40 .18
❑ 18 Chris Puskas .40 .18
❑ 19 Yvon Quenneville .40 .18
❑ 20 Michael Sullivan .50 .23
❑ 21 Trevor Tremblay .40 .18
❑ 22 Sean Van Amburg .40 .18
❑ 23 Title Card .10 .05

## 1991-92 Rayside-Balfour Jr. Canadians

JR. CANADIANS
STEELCRAFT
MANUFACTURING
&
HEAT TREATING
phone 705-560-7794
FAX 705-566-5247

This 23-card set measures approximately 2 3/8" by 3 5/16" and is printed on thin card stock. The fronts feature color, full-bleed, posed action player photos. The player's name and jersey number are printed in black at the bottom. The team logo appears in either red or white at the upper left corner. The backs are white with black print and carry advertisements from local businesses. The cards are unnumbered and checklisted below in alphabetical order.

| | MINT | NRMT |
|---|---|---|
| COMPLETE SET (23) | 8.00 | 3.60 |
| COMMON CARD (1-23) | .10 | .05 |

❑ 1 Dan Baston .50 .23
❑ 2 Don Cucksey .50 .23
❑ 3 Dean Cull .50 .23
❑ 4 Mike Dore .50 .23
❑ 5 Denis Gosselin .50 .23
❑ 6 Jason Hall .50 .23
❑ 7 Grant Healey .50 .23

❑ 8 Marc Lafreniere .50 .23
❑ 9 Mike Longo .50 .23
❑ 10 Scott Maclellan .50 .23
❑ 11 Matt Mooney .50 .23
❑ 12 Rob Moxness .50 .23
❑ 13 Virgil Nose .50 .23
❑ 14 Trent Oystrick .50 .23
❑ 15 Jon Stewart .50 .23
❑ 16 Jon Stos .50 .23
❑ 17 Dave Sutton .50 .23
❑ 18 Scott Sutton .50 .23
❑ 19 Trevor Tremblay .50 .23
❑ 20 Jaak Valiots .50 .23
❑ 21 Sean Van Amburg .50 .23
❑ 22 Jason Young .10 .05
Stickboy
❑ 23 Title Card .10 .05

## 1993-94 Red Deer Rebels

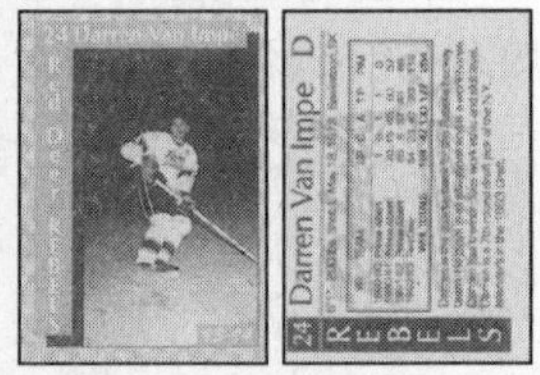

This 30-card set measures the standard size. The fronts feature posed action on-ice player photos with hatched borders. The player's name and number are printed in white letters inside a silver bar above the picture, while the team name appears alongside the left short side. The horizontal backs carry a short player biography, statistics, and a player profile. The cards are unnumbered and checklisted below in alphabetical order.

| | MINT | NRMT |
|---|---|---|
| COMPLETE SET (30) | 10.00 | 4.50 |
| COMMON CARD (1-30) | .10 | .05 |

❑ 1 Peter Anholt CO .10 .05
❑ 2 Byron Briske .75 .35
❑ 3 Curtis Cardinal .35 .16
❑ 4 Jason Clague .50 .23
❑ 5 Dale Donaldson .35 .16
❑ 6 Dave Greenway .35 .16
❑ 7 Scott Grimwood TR .10 .05
❑ 8 Sean Halifax .35 .16
❑ 9 Chris Kibermanis .35 .16
❑ 10 Pete LeBoutillier .35 .16
❑ 11 Pete LeBoutillier .35 .16
In Action
❑ 12 Terry Lindgren .50 .23
❑ 13 Chris Maillet .35 .16
❑ 14 Eddy Marchant .35 .16
❑ 15 Mike McBain .75 .35
❑ 16 Mike Moller ACO .10 .05
❑ 17 Andy Nowicki ACO .10 .05
❑ 18 Berkley Pennock .35 .16
❑ 19 Tyler Quiring .50 .23
❑ 20 Craig Reichert .50 .23
❑ 21 Ken Richardson .35 .16
❑ 22 Sean Selmser .35 .16
❑ 23 Vaclav Slansky .35 .16
❑ 24 Mark Toljanich .35 .16
❑ 25 Darren Van Impe .75 .35
❑ 26 Pete Vandermeer .35 .16
❑ 27 Chris Wickenheiser .50 .23
❑ 28 Brad Zimmer .35 .16
❑ 29 Jonathan Zukiwsky .50 .23
❑ 30 The Centrum .10 .05

## 1995-96 Red Deer Rebels

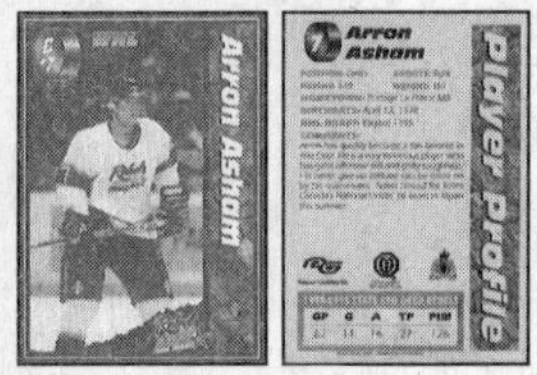


This 24-card set of the Red Deer Rebels of the WHL features extremely blurry color player photos in gray and black borders. The backs carry a player profile. The cards are unnumbered and checklisted below in alphabetical order.

| | MINT | NRMT |
|---|---|---|
| COMPLETE SET (24) | 8.00 | 3.60 |
| COMMON CARD (1-24) | .10 | .05 |

❑ 1 Arron Asham .35 .16
❑ 2 Bryan Boorman .25 .11
❑ 3 Aleksei Boudaev .50 .23
❑ 4 Mike Broda .25 .11
❑ 5 Mike Brown .75 .35
❑ 6 Jay Henderson .25 .11
❑ 7 David Hruska .25 .11
❑ 8 Chris Kibermanis .25 .11
❑ 9 Brad Leeb .25 .11
❑ 10 Terry Lindgren .35 .16
❑ 11 Mike McBain .75 .35
❑ 12 Brent McDonald .25 .11
❑ 13 Ken McKay .25 .11
❑ 14 Harlan Pratt .25 .11
❑ 15 Greg Schmidt .25 .11
❑ 16 Pete Vandermeer .25 .11
❑ 17 Jesse Wallin .75 .35
❑ 18 Lance Ward .75 .35
❑ 19 Mike Whitney .35 .16
❑ 20 Chris Wickenheiser .75 .35
❑ 21 B.J. Young .25 .11
❑ 22 Jonathan Zukiwsky .50 .23
❑ 23 Drug Awareness Team .10 .05
❑ 24 Team Picture .25 .11

## 1981-82 Regina Pats

This 25-card set measures approximately 2 5/8" by 4 1/8" and is printed on thin card stock. The fronts feature color, posed action player photos with white borders accented by a thin red line. The player's jersey number, name, and position appear in black print across the bottom of the picture. The backs carry P.L.A.Y. (Police, Laws and Youth) public service messages and sponsor logos. The cards are unnumbered and checklisted below in alphabetical order.

| | NRMT-MT | EXC |
|---|---|---|
| COMPLETE SET (25) | 25.00 | 11.00 |
| COMMON CARD (1-25) | .50 | .23 |

❑ 1 Pats Logo 1.00 .45
❑ 2 Garth Butcher 3.00 1.35
❑ 3 Lyndon Byers 3.00 1.35
❑ 4 Jock Callander 2.00 .90
❑ 5 Marc Centrone 1.00 .45
❑ 6 Dave Goertz 1.00 .45
❑ 7 Evans Dobni 1.00 .45
❑ 8 Dale Derkatch 1.00 .45
❑ 9 Jeff Crawford 1.00 .45
❑ 10 Jim Clarke 1.00 .45
❑ 11 Jayson Meyer 1.00 .45
❑ 12 Gary Leeman 3.00 1.35
❑ 13 Bruce Holloway 1.00 .45
❑ 14 Ken Heppner 1.00 .45
❑ 15 Taylor Hall 1.00 .45
❑ 16 Wally Schreiber 1.50 .70
❑ 17 Kevin Pylypow 1.00 .45
❑ 18 Ray Plamondon 1.00 .45
❑ 19 Brent Pascal 1.00 .45
❑ 20 Dave Michayluk 1.50 .70
❑ 21 Barry Trotz 1.00 .45
❑ 22 Al Tuer 1.50 .70
❑ 23 Tony Vogel 1.00 .45
❑ 24 Martin Wood 1.00 .45
❑ 25 Regina Police Logo .50 .23

## 1982-83 Regina Pats

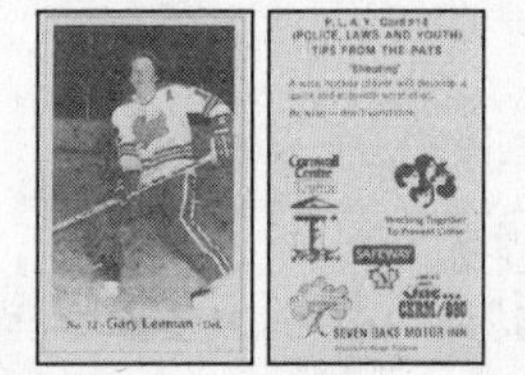

This 25-card set measures approximately 2 5/8" by 4 1/8" and features color, posed action player photos on white card stock. The pictures are framed by a thin red line. The player's name, jersey number, and position are printed in black on the photo. The backs carry P.L.A.Y. (Police, Laws, and Youth) public service and hockey tips. Sponsor logos are printed on the lower portion of the card back.

| | MINT | EXC |
|---|---|---|
| COMPLETE SET (25) | 15.00 | 6.75 |
| COMMON CARD (1-25) | .50 | .23 |

❑ 1 Regina Pats and .50 .23
Police Logo
❑ 2 Todd Lumbard .75 .35
❑ 3 Jamie Reeve .75 .35
❑ 4 Dave Goertz .75 .35
❑ 5 John Miner .75 .35
❑ 6 Doug Trapp .75 .35
❑ 7 R.J. Dundas .75 .35
❑ 8 Stu Grimson 2.00 .90
❑ 9 Al Tuer .75 .35
❑ 10 Rick Herbert .75 .35
❑ 11 Tony Vogel .75 .35
❑ 12 John Bekkers .75 .35
❑ 13 Dale Derkatch .75 .35
❑ 14 Gary Leeman 2.00 .90
❑ 15 Nevin Markwart 1.00 .45
❑ 16 Kurt Wickenheiser .75 .35
❑ 17 Jeff Frank .75 .35
❑ 18 Marc Centrone .75 .35
❑ 19 Taylor Hall .75 .35
❑ 20 Lyndon Byers 2.00 .90
❑ 21 Jayson Meyer .75 .35
❑ 22 Jeff Crawford .75 .35
❑ 23 Don Boyd CO .50 .23
❑ 24 Barry Trapp ACO .50 .23
❑ 25 K-9 Big Blue (Mascot) .50 .23

## 1983-84 Regina Pats

This 25-card set measures approximately 2 5/8" by 4 1/8" and features color, posed action player photos with white borders accented by a thin red line. The player's name is superimposed at the bottom of the picture. The backs carry P.L.A.Y. (Police, Laws and Youth) public service messages in the form of "Tips From The Pats." Sponsor logos appear on the lower portion of the card.

| | MINT | NRMT |
|---|---|---|
| COMPLETE SET (25) | 15.00 | 6.75 |
| COMMON CARD (1-25) | .25 | .11 |

❑ 1 Title Card .75 .35
❑ 2 Todd Lumbard .75 .35
❑ 3 Jamie Reeve .75 .35
❑ 4 Dave Goertz .75 .35
❑ 5 John Miner .75 .35
❑ 6 Doug Trapp .75 .35
❑ 7 R.J. Dundas .75 .35
❑ 8 Stu Grimson 2.50 1.10
❑ 9 Al Tuer .75 .35
❑ 10 Rick Herbert .75 .35
❑ 11 Tony Vogel .75 .35
❑ 12 John Bekkers .75 .35
❑ 13 Dale Derkatch .75 .35
❑ 14 Gary Leeman 1.50 .70
❑ 15 Nevin Markwart 1.00 .45
❑ 16 Kurt Wickenheiser .75 .35
❑ 17 Jeff Frank .75 .35
❑ 18 Marc Centrone .75 .35
❑ 19 Taylor Hall .75 .35
❑ 20 Lyndon Byers 1.50 .70
❑ 21 Jayson Meyer .75 .35
❑ 22 Jeff Crawford .75 .35
❑ 23 Don Boyd CO .50 .23
❑ 24 Barry Trapp ACO .50 .23
❑ 25 K-9 Big Blue (Mascot) .25 .11

## 1986-87 Regina Pats

Produced by Royal Studios, this 30-card set measures the standard size. The fronts feature color posed action player photos with red and white borders. The player's name and number are printed in red in the bottom white margin along with the team name and year, which are printed in black. The backs carry biographical information, statistics, and player profile within a box formed by a thin black line. The cards are unnumbered and checklisted below in alphabetical order.

| | MINT | NRMT |
|---|---|---|
| COMPLETE SET (30) | 14.00 | 6.25 |
| COMMON CARD (1-30) | .25 | .11 |

❑ 1 Troy Bakogeorge .50 .23
❑ 2 Grant Chorney .50 .23
❑ 3 Gary Dickie .50 .23
❑ 4 Milan Dragicevic .50 .23
❑ 5 Mike Dyck .50 .23
❑ 6 Craig Endean .50 .23
❑ 7 Mike Gibson .50 .23
❑ 8 Erin Ginnell .50 .23
❑ 9 Brad Hornung .50 .23
❑ 10 Mark Janssens 1.00 .45
❑ 11 K-9 (Mascot) .25 .11
❑ 12 Trent Kachur .50 .23
❑ 13 Craig Kalawsky .50 .23
❑ 14 Dan Logan .50 .23
❑ 15 Jim Mathieson .50 .23
❑ 16 Darin McInnes .50 .23
❑ 17 Darrin McKechnie .50 .23
❑ 18 Rob McKinley .50 .23
❑ 19 Brad Miller .50 .23
❑ 20 Stacy Nickel .50 .23
❑ 21 Cregg Nicol .50 .23
❑ 22 Len Nielsen .50 .23
❑ 23 Darren Parsons .50 .23
❑ 24 Doug Sauter .50 .23
❑ 25 Ray Savard .50 .23
❑ 26 Dennis Sobchuk .75 .35
❑ 27 Chris Tarnowski .50 .23
❑ 28 Mike Van Slooten .50 .23
❑ 29 Brian Wilkie .50 .23
❑ 30 Rod Williams .50 .23

## 1987-88 Regina Pats

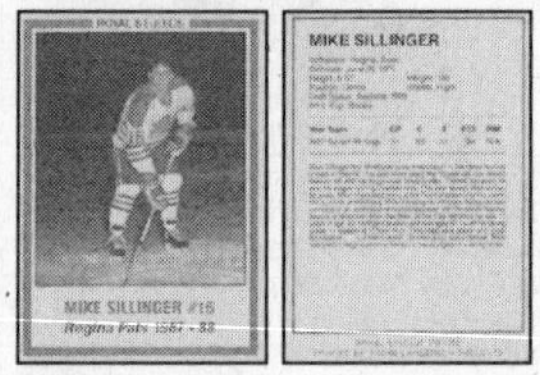

Produced by Royal Studios, this 28-card standard-size set features color, posed action player photos with red and white borders. The player's name is printed in red in the bottom white margin along with the team name and year, which are printed in black. The backs carry biographical information, statistics, and player profile within a box formed by a thin black line. The cards are unnumbered and checklisted below in alphabetical order.

| | MINT | NRMT |
|---|---|---|
| COMPLETE SET (28) | 12.00 | 5.50 |
| COMMON CARD (1-28) | .25 | .11 |

❑ 1 Kevin Clemens .50 .23
❑ 2 Gary Dickie .50 .23
❑ 3 Milan Dragicevic .50 .23
❑ 4 Mike Dyck .50 .23
❑ 5 Craig Endean .50 .23
❑ 6 Kevin Gallant PR .25 .11
❑ 7 Jamie Heward .50 .23
❑ 8 Rod Houk .50 .23
❑ 9 Mark Janssens 1.00 .45
❑ 10 Trent Kachur .50 .23
❑ 11 Craig Kalawsky .50 .23
❑ 12 K-9 (Mascot) .25 .11
❑ 13 Frank Kovacs .50 .23
❑ 14 Darren Kwiatkowski .50 .23
❑ 15 Brian Leibel .50 .23
❑ 16 Tim Logan .50 .23
❑ 17 Jim Mathieson .50 .23
❑ 18 Darrin McKechnie .50 .23
❑ 19 Rob McKinley .50 .23
❑ 20 Brad Miller .50 .23
❑ 21 Cregg Nicol .50 .23
❑ 22 Doug Sauter CO .25 .11
❑ 23 Dan Sexton .50 .23
❑ 24 Mike Sillinger 1.00 .45
❑ 25 Dennis Sobchuk .75 .35
❑ 26 Stanley Szumlak TR .25 .11
❑ 27 Mike Van Slooten .50 .23
❑ 28 Team Photo .75 .35

## 1988-89 Regina Pats

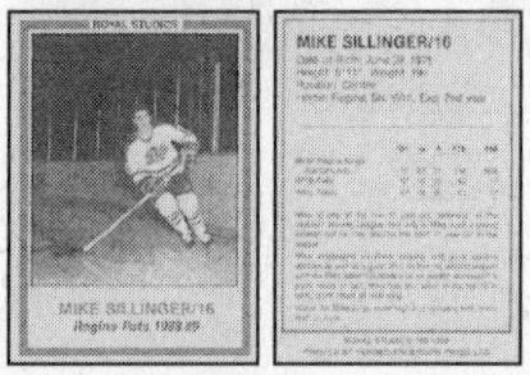

This 24-card standard-size set features color, posed action player photos with red and white borders. The player's name is printed in red in the bottom white margin along with the team name and year, which are printed in black. The backs carry biographical information, statistics, and a player profile within a box formed by a thin black line. The cards are unnumbered and checklisted below in alphabetical order.

| | MINT | NRMT |
|---|---|---|
| COMPLETE SET (24) | 12.00 | 5.50 |
| COMMON CARD (1-24) | .25 | .11 |

❑ 1 Shane Bogden .50 .23
❑ 2 Cam Brauer .50 .23
❑ 3 Scott Daniels .75 .35
❑ 4 Gary Dickie .50 .23
❑ 5 Mike Dyck .50 .23
❑ 6 Dave Gerse .50 .23
❑ 7 Kevin Haller 1.00 .45
❑ 8 Jamie Heward .50 .23
❑ 9 Terry Hollinger .75 .35
❑ 10 Rod Houk .50 .23
❑ 11 Frank Kovacs .50 .23
❑ 12 Brian Leibel .50 .23
❑ 13 Bernie Lynch CO .50 .23
❑ 14 Kelly Markwart .50 .23
❑ 15 Jim Mathieson .50 .23
❑ 16 Brad Miller .50 .23
❑ 17 Dwayne Monteith TR .25 .11
❑ 18 Curtis Nykyforuk .50 .23
❑ 19 Darren Parsons .50 .23
❑ 20 Cory Paterson .50 .23
❑ 21 Jeff Sebastian .50 .23
❑ 22 Mike Sillinger .75 .35
❑ 23 Chad Silver .50 .23
❑ 24 Jamie Splett .50 .23

## 1989-90 Regina Pats

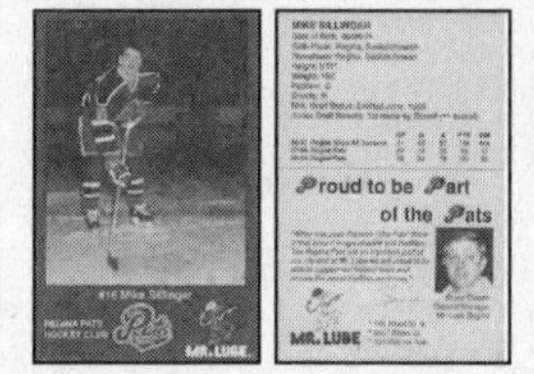

Sponsored by Mr. Lube, this 19-card set measures approximately 4" by 6" and is printed on thin card stock. The fronts feature black-and-white posed action photos with royal blue borders. The player's jersey number and name are printed in white in the bottom margin along with the team and sponsor logo. The backs are white and carry biographical information and a message from Bruce Olesen, general manager of Mr. Lube. The cards are unnumbered and checklisted below in alphabetical order.

| | MINT | NRMT |
|---|---|---|
| COMPLETE SET (19) | 8.00 | 3.60 |
| COMMON CARD (1-19) | .50 | .23 |

❑ 1 Kelly Chotowetz .50 .23
❑ 2 Hal Christiansen .50 .23
❑ 3 Scott Daniels 1.00 .45
❑ 4 Wade Fennig .50 .23
❑ 5 Jason Glickman .50 .23
❑ 6 Jamie Heward .50 .23
❑ 7 Terry Hollinger .50 .23
❑ 8 Frank Kovacs .50 .23
❑ 9 Kelly Markwart .50 .23
❑ 10 Jim Mathieson .50 .23
❑ 11 Cam McLellan .50 .23
❑ 12 Troy Mick .50 .23
❑ 13 Greg Pankewicz .50 .23
❑ 14 Cory Paterson .50 .23
❑ 15 Garry Pearce .50 .23
❑ 16 Mike Risdale .50 .23
❑ 17 Colin Ruck .50 .23
❑ 18 Mike Sillinger .75 .35
❑ 19 Jamie Splett .50 .23

## 1996-97 Regina Pats

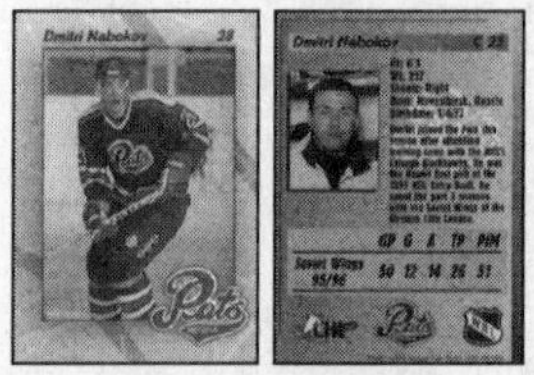

This 25-card set features the Regina Pats of the WHL. The cards were produced by the team and offered for sale for $7 at the team shop. The fronts feature a color action photo superimposed over a cutaway rink shot. The player's name and number appear at the top, with the team logo in the bottom right. The back includes a color mug shot, stats, and league and team logos. The set includes several prominent prospects, including NHL first rounders Josh Holden, Dmitri Nabokov and Derek Morris, along with top 1998 prospect Brad Stuart.

| | MINT | NRMT |
|---|---|---|
| COMPLETE SET (25) | 12.00 | 5.50 |
| COMMON CARD (1-25) | .25 | .11 |

❑ 1 Josh Holden 2.00 .90
❑ 2 Curtis Tipler .50 .23
❑ 3 Shane Lanigan .40 .18
❑ 4 Brad Stuart 1.00 .45
❑ 5 David Maruca .40 .18
❑ 6 Perry Johnson .40 .18
❑ 7 Chad Mercier .50 .23
❑ 8 Kyle Calder .40 .18
❑ 9 Josh Dobbyn .40 .18
❑ 10 Aaron Mori .50 .23
❑ 11 Gerad Adams .40 .18
❑ 12 Boyd Kane .50 .23
❑ 13 Lars Pattersen .50 .23
❑ 14 Dean Arsene .40 .18
❑ 15 Andy Adams .50 .23
❑ 16 Derek Morris 1.00 .45
❑ 17 Kyle Freadrich .40 .18
❑ 18 Bryan Randall .40 .18
❑ 19 Clint Orr .40 .18
❑ 20 Brett Lysak .40 .18
❑ 21 Joey Bouvier .40 .18
❑ 22 Cody Jensen .40 .18
❑ 23 Rich Preston CO .25 .11
❑ 24 Team Photo .50 .23
❑ 25 Dmitri Nabokov 2.00 .90

## 1993-94 Rensselaer Engineers

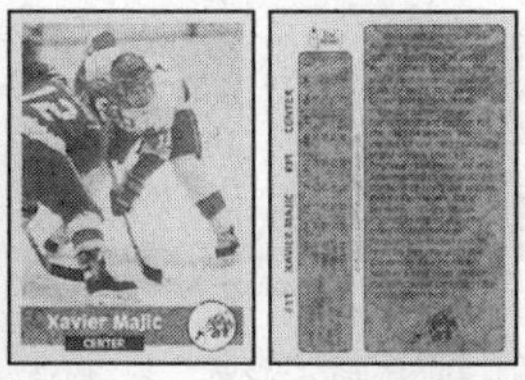


This 31-card set of the RPI Engineers was produced by Collect-A-Sport. Reportedly, production was limited to 2,000 sets, all of which were offered for sale at the arena on game nights.

| | MINT | NRMT |
|---|---|---|
| COMPLETE SET (31) | 7.00 | 3.10 |
| COMMON CARD (1-31) | .10 | .05 |

| | | |
|---|---|---|
| ❑ 1 Kelly Askew | .25 | .11 |
| ❑ 2 Adam Bartell | .35 | .16 |
| ❑ 3 Kobie Boykins | .25 | .11 |
| ❑ 4 Jeff Brick | .25 | .11 |
| ❑ 5 Tim Carvel | .25 | .11 |
| ❑ 6 Wayne Clarke | .35 | .16 |
| ❑ 7 Cam Cuthbert | .25 | .11 |
| ❑ 8 Steve Duncan ACO | .10 | .05 |
| ❑ 9 Dan Fridgen ACO | .10 | .05 |
| ❑ 10 Jeff Gabriel | .25 | .11 |
| ❑ 11 Craig Hamelin | .25 | .11 |
| ❑ 12 Chris Kiley | .25 | .11 |
| ❑ 13 Ken Kwasniewski | .25 | .11 |
| ❑ 14 Brad Layzell | .40 | .18 |
| ❑ 15 Neil Little | .50 | .23 |
| ❑ 16 Xavier Majic | .50 | .23 |
| ❑ 17 Jeff Matthews | .25 | .11 |
| ❑ 18 Chris Maye | .25 | .11 |
| ❑ 19 Jeff O'Connor | .25 | .11 |
| ❑ 20 Ron Pasco | .25 | .11 |
| ❑ 21 Eric Perardi | .25 | .11 |
| ❑ 22 Jon Pirrong | .25 | .11 |
| ❑ 23 Buddy Powers CO | .10 | .05 |
| ❑ 24 Tim Regan | .25 | .11 |
| ❑ 25 Bryan Richardson | .25 | .11 |
| ❑ 26 Patrick Rochon | .25 | .11 |
| ❑ 27 Mike Rolanti | .25 | .11 |
| ❑ 28 Tim Spadafore | .35 | .16 |
| ❑ 29 Mike Tamburro | .25 | .11 |
| ❑ 30 1993-94 Team | .50 | .23 |
| ❑ 31 Checklist | .10 | .05 |

## 1984-85 Richelieu Riverains

his 19-card set of the Richelieu Riverains of he Quebec Midget AAA league measures pproximately 4" by 5 1/2". The fronts feature lack-and-white posed player portraits with a acsimile autograph and jersey number on the ft. The backs are blank. The cards are nnumbered and checklisted below in phabetical order.

| | MINT | NRMT |
|---|---|---|
| OMPLETE SET (19) | 12.00 | 5.50 |
| OMMON CARD (1-19) | .75 | .35 |

| | | |
|---|---|---|
| 1 Miguel Baldris | .75 | .35 |
| 2 Nicolas Beaulieu | .75 | .35 |
| 3 Martin Cote | .75 | .35 |
| 4 Sylvain Coutourier | 1.00 | .45 |
| 5 Dominic Edmond | .75 | .35 |
| 6 Yues Gaucher | .75 | .35 |
| 7 Eric Gobel | .75 | .35 |
| 8 Carl Lemieux | .75 | .35 |
| 9 Michel Levesque | .75 | .35 |
| 10 Brad Loi | .75 | .35 |
| 11 Eric Primeau | .75 | .35 |
| 12 Stephane Quintal | 2.50 | 1.10 |
| 13 Jean-Michel Ray | .75 | .35 |
| 14 Serge Richard | .75 | .35 |
| 15 Stephane Robinson | .75 | .35 |
| 16 Danny Rochefort | .75 | .35 |
| 17 Martin Savaria | .75 | .35 |
| 18 Sylvain Senecal | .75 | .35 |
| 19 Eric Sharron | .75 | .35 |

## 1990-91 Richmond Renegades

oduced by 7th Inning Sketch and sponsored Richmond Comix and Cardz Inc., this 18-rd standard-size set features posed color ayer photos with red borders. The player's me appears at the bottom. The year is inted diagonally in the upper right corner.

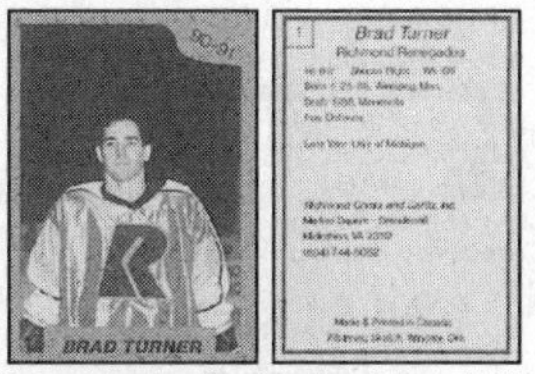


The red border dips into the picture at this point to provide a background for the year. The backs carry biographical information within a black box.

| | MINT | NRMT |
|---|---|---|
| COMPLETE SET (18) | 8.00 | 3.60 |
| COMMON CARD (1-18) | .50 | .23 |

| | | |
|---|---|---|
| ❑ 1 Brad Turner | .50 | .23 |
| ❑ 2 Victor Posa | .50 | .23 |
| ❑ 3 Antti Autere | .50 | .23 |
| ❑ 4 Phil Huber | .50 | .23 |
| ❑ 5 Steve Spott | .50 | .23 |
| ❑ 6 Kelly Mills | .50 | .23 |
| ❑ 7 Paul Cain | .50 | .23 |
| ❑ 8 Shawn Lillie | .50 | .23 |
| ❑ 9 Kirby Lindal | .50 | .23 |
| ❑ 10 Dave Aiken | .50 | .23 |
| ❑ 11 Terry McCutcheon | .50 | .23 |
| ❑ 12 Jordan Fois | .50 | .23 |
| ❑ 13 Brad Beck | .50 | .23 |
| ❑ 14 Doug Pickell | .50 | .23 |
| ❑ 15 Frank Lascala | .50 | .23 |
| ❑ 16 John Haley | .50 | .23 |
| ❑ 17 Peter Harris | .50 | .23 |
| ❑ 18 Chris McSorley CO | 1.00 | .45 |

## 1991-92 Richmond Renegades

Sponsored by "Bleacher Bums" Sports Cards Inc. and Domino's Pizza, this 20-card set was issued as a trifold sheet, one 12 1/2" by 7" team photo and two sheets with ten standard-size player cards per sheet. The fronts feature color action player photos accented by a border design that shades from orange at the top to black at the bottom. The player's name and position appear below the picture as do sponsor names. The team name appears above the picture. Inside a thin black border, the backs have the team name and logo on an orange panel with biography and sponsor logos below.

| | MINT | NRMT |
|---|---|---|
| COMPLETE SET (20) | 9.00 | 4.00 |
| COMMON CARD (1-20) | .25 | .11 |

| | | |
|---|---|---|
| ❑ 1 Rob Vanderydt | .50 | .23 |
| ❑ 2 Larry Rooney | .35 | .16 |
| ❑ 3 Brendan Flynn | .35 | .16 |
| ❑ 4 Scott Drevitch | .35 | .16 |
| ❑ 5 Joni Lehto | .35 | .16 |
| ❑ 6 Todd Drevitch | .35 | .16 |
| ❑ 7 Paul Rutherford | .35 | .16 |
| ❑ 8 Dave Aiken | .35 | .16 |
| ❑ 9 Pat Bingham | .35 | .16 |
| ❑ 10 Trevor Jobe | .35 | .16 |
| ❑ 11 Bob Berg | .35 | .16 |
| ❑ 12 Mark Kuntz | .35 | .16 |
| ❑ 13 Joe Capprini | .35 | .16 |
| ❑ 14 Trevor Converse | .35 | .16 |
| ❑ 15 Steve Scheifele | .35 | .16 |
| ❑ 16 Jon Gustafson | .50 | .23 |
| ❑ 17 Marco Fuster | .35 | .16 |
| ❑ 18 Guy Gadowsky | .35 | .16 |
| ❑ 19 Dave Allison CO | .25 | .11 |
| ❑ 20 Jamie McLennan | 1.00 | .45 |
| ❑ NNO Large Team Photo | 2.00 | .90 |

## 1992-93 Richmond Renegades

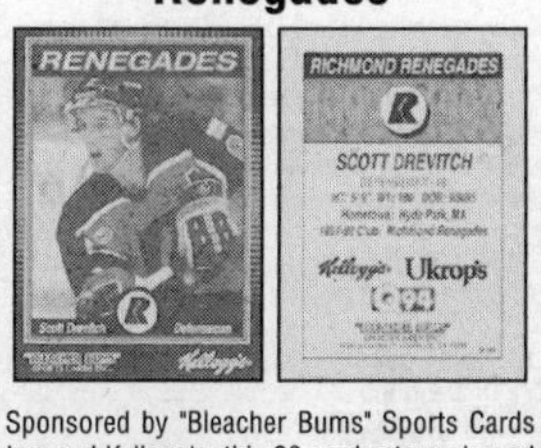


Sponsored by "Bleacher Bums" Sports Cards Inc. and Kellogg's, this 20-card set was issued as a trifold sheet, one 12 1/2" by 7" team photo and two sheets with ten standard-size player cards per sheet. The fronts feature color action player photos accented by a black and orange border design. The picture itself is rimmed by an orange and white frame. Outside the frame is an orange design with varying sizes of stripes against a black background. The player's name and position appear below the picture as do sponsor names. The team name appears above the picture. The backs carry a player biography and sponsor logos. The cards are unnumbered and checklisted below in alphabetical order.

| | MINT | NRMT |
|---|---|---|
| COMPLETE SET (20) | 8.00 | 3.60 |
| COMMON CARD (1-20) | .10 | .05 |

| | | |
|---|---|---|
| ❑ 1 Will Averill | .35 | .16 |
| ❑ 2 Frank Bialowas | .50 | .23 |
| ❑ 3 Scott Drevitch | .35 | .16 |
| ❑ 4 Brendan Flynn | .35 | .16 |
| ❑ 5 Guy Gadowsky ACO | .10 | .05 |
| ❑ 6 Jon Gustafson | .50 | .23 |
| ❑ 7 Phil Huber | .35 | .16 |
| ❑ 8 Mike James | .35 | .16 |
| ❑ 9 Jeffery Kampersal | .35 | .16 |
| ❑ 10 Mark Kuntz | .35 | .16 |
| ❑ 11 Sean LeBrun | .35 | .16 |
| ❑ 12 Kevin Malgunas | .35 | .16 |
| ❑ 13 Jim McGeough | .50 | .23 |
| ❑ 14 Ed Sabo | .35 | .16 |
| ❑ 15 Jeff Saterdalen | .35 | .16 |
| ❑ 16 Alan Schuler | .35 | .16 |
| ❑ 17 Martin Smith | .35 | .16 |
| ❑ 18 Roy Sommer CO | .10 | .05 |
| ❑ 19 Jeff Torrey | .35 | .16 |
| ❑ 20 Ben Wyzansky | .35 | .16 |
| ❑ NNO Large Team Photo | 2.50 | 1.10 |

## 1993-94 Richmond Renegades

Sponsored by "Bleacher Bum" Collectibles, Inc., radio station XL102, and Kellogg's, this 20-card set features the 1993-94 Richmond Renegades. The standard-size cards are printed on thin card stock. On a team color-coded background, the fronts feature color action player photos with purple borders, along with the player's name, position and team name. The white backs carry a short player biography and team and sponsors' logos.

| | MINT | NRMT |
|---|---|---|
| COMPLETE SET (20) | 7.00 | 3.10 |
| COMMON CARD (1-20) | .25 | .11 |

| | | |
|---|---|---|
| ❑ 1 Ken Weiss | .35 | .16 |
| ❑ 2 Guy Phillips | .35 | .16 |
| ❑ 3 Alexander Zhdan | .35 | .16 |
| ❑ 4 Alan Schuler | .35 | .16 |
| ❑ 5 John Craighead | .35 | .16 |
| ❑ 6 Colin Gregor | .35 | .16 |
| ❑ 7 Rob MacInnis | .35 | .16 |
| ❑ 8 Devin Derksen | .50 | .23 |
| ❑ 9 Jason Renard | .35 | .16 |
| ❑ 10 Peter Allen | .35 | .16 |
| ❑ 11 Roy Sommer CO | .25 | .11 |
| ❑ 12 Milan Hnilicka | .75 | .35 |
| ❑ 13 Oleg Santurian | .35 | .16 |
| ❑ 14 Brendan Flynn | .35 | .16 |
| ❑ 15 Ken Blum | .35 | .16 |
| ❑ 16 Steve Bogoyevac | .35 | .16 |
| ❑ 17 Eric Germain | .35 | .16 |
| ❑ 18 Chris Foy | .35 | .16 |
| ❑ 19 Darren Colbourne | .35 | .16 |
| ❑ 20 Jon Gustafson | .50 | .23 |

## 1994-95 Richmond Renegades

This 20-card set produced by Bleacher Bums and sponsored by Q-94 features the Richmond Renegades of the ECHL. The sets were available through the team. The fronts feature dynamic action shots over a blurred background, while the backs include player stats. The cards are unnumbered and are listed below as they came out of the team bag. Reportedly, production was significantly shorter for this set than the previous two Richmond issues.

| | MINT | NRMT |
|---|---|---|
| COMPLETE SET (20) | 7.00 | 3.10 |
| COMMON CARD (1-20) | .25 | .11 |

| | | |
|---|---|---|
| ❑ 1 Andrew Shier | .35 | .16 |
| ❑ 2 Shane Henry | .35 | .16 |
| ❑ 3 Shawn Snesar | .35 | .16 |
| ❑ 4 Steve Bogoyevac | .35 | .16 |
| ❑ 5 Chris Foy | .35 | .16 |
| ❑ 6 Scott Gruhl | .50 | .23 |
| ❑ 7 Blaine Moore | .35 | .16 |
| ❑ 8 Don Lester | .35 | .16 |
| ❑ 9 Kurt Mallett | .35 | .16 |
| ❑ 10 Garett MacDonald | .35 | .16 |
| ❑ 11 Jay Murphy | .35 | .16 |
| ❑ 12 Darren Wetherill | .35 | .16 |
| ❑ 13 Grant Sjervin | .35 | .16 |
| ❑ 14 Jan Benda | .75 | .35 |
| ❑ 15 Lou Body | .35 | .16 |
| ❑ 16 Mike Taylor | .35 | .16 |
| ❑ 17 Sean O'Brien | .35 | .16 |
| ❑ 18 Chris Tucker | .35 | .16 |
| ❑ 19 Jason Currie | .35 | .16 |
| ❑ 20 Roy Sommer CO | .25 | .11 |

## 1995-96 Richmond Renegades

This 25-card set of the Richmond Renegades of the ECHL was produced by Bleacher Bum and was supported by a wealth of sponsors. The cards were originally issued in a strip, thus single cards will have perforated edges. The cards feature a dynamic front design including an action photo and the Riley Cup Championship logo in the bottom right. The backs contain career stats. The cards are unnumbered, and are ordered as they appeared on the strips.

| | MINT | NRMT |
|---|---|---|
| COMPLETE SET (25) | 8.00 | 3.60 |
| COMMON CARD (1-25) | .10 | .05 |

| | | |
|---|---|---|
| ❑ 1 Greg Hadden | .35 | .16 |
| ❑ 2 Mike Taylor | .35 | .16 |
| ❑ 3 Jay Murphy | .35 | .16 |
| ❑ 4 Todd Sparks | .35 | .16 |
| ❑ 5 Lou Body | .35 | .16 |
| ❑ 6 Sandy Allan | .75 | .35 |
| ❑ 7 Darren Wetherill | .35 | .16 |
| ❑ 8 Brian Goudie | .35 | .16 |
| ❑ 9 Brendan Flynn | .60 | .25 |
| ❑ 10 Kurt Mallett | .35 | .16 |
| ❑ 11 Dmitri Pankov | .35 | .16 |
| ❑ 12 Steve Carpenter | .35 | .16 |
| ❑ 13 Jason Mallon | .35 | .16 |
| ❑ 14 Scott Gruhl | .75 | .35 |
| ❑ 15 Trevor Senn | .35 | .16 |
| ❑ 16 Garett MacDonald | .35 | .16 |
| ❑ 17 Martin Roy | .35 | .16 |
| ❑ 18 Michael Burman | .35 | .16 |
| ❑ 19 Grant Sjervin | .35 | .16 |
| ❑ 20 Mike Morin | .35 | .16 |
| ❑ 21 Andy Davis ANN | .10 | .05 |
| ❑ 22 The Gade -- Mascot | .10 | .05 |
| ❑ 23 Rob Jones TR | .10 | .05 |
| ❑ 24 Roy Sommer CO | .10 | .05 |
| ❑ 25 C.Laughlin GM H.Feuerstein CEO | .10 | .05 |

## 1996-97 Richmond Renegades

Cards feature full color fronts with statistical information and a profile photo on the back. Cards are unnumbered and checklisted below in alphabetical order.

| | MINT | NRMT |
|---|---|---|
| COMPLETE SET (25) | 8.00 | 3.60 |
| COMMON CARD (1-25) | .10 | .05 |

| | | |
|---|---|---|
| ❑ 1 Scott Burfoot | .35 | .16 |
| ❑ 2 Taylor Clarke | .35 | .16 |
| ❑ 3 David Dartsch | .35 | .16 |
| ❑ 4 Freezer | .10 | .05 |
| ❑ 5 Gade | .10 | .05 |
| ❑ 6 Matt Garzone | .35 | .16 |
| ❑ 7 Brian Goudie | .35 | .16 |
| ❑ 8 Scott Gruhl CO | .75 | .35 |
| ❑ 9 Garry Gulash | .35 | .16 |
| ❑ 10 Mike Harding | .35 | .16 |
| ❑ 11 Tommy Holmes | .35 | .16 |
| ❑ 12 Rod Langway ACO | .10 | .05 |
| ❑ 13 Paul Lepler | .35 | .16 |
| ❑ 14 Jay McNeill | .35 | .16 |
| ❑ 15 Craig Paterson | .35 | .16 |
| ❑ 16 Chris Pittman | .35 | .16 |
| ❑ 17 Mike Rucinski | .35 | .16 |
| ❑ 18 Brian Secord | .35 | .16 |
| ❑ 19 Trevor Senn | .35 | .16 |
| ❑ 20 Grant Sjerven | .35 | .16 |
| ❑ 21 Andrew Shier | .35 | .16 |
| ❑ 22 Mike Taylor | .35 | .16 |
| ❑ 23 Tripp Tracy | .35 | .16 |
| ❑ 24 Jason Wright | .35 | .16 |
| ❑ 25 Title Card | .10 | .05 |

## 1996-97 Rimouski Oceanic

This 28-card set was the first of two this season to feature the Oceanic of the QMJHL. The cards featured a color action photo and jersey number on the front, with a head shot and statistical data on the back. It was sold through the team and at convenience stores in the region. The set is unnumbered, and listed in alphabetical order. The most noteworthy player in the set is Vincent Lecavalier, a forward looked upon as an early favorite for the top pick in the 1998 NHL Entry Draft. Less than 3,000 of these sets were produced.

| | MINT | NRMT |
|---|---|---|
| COMPLETE SET (28) | 12.00 | 5.50 |
| COMMON CARD (1-28) | .25 | .11 |

| | | |
|---|---|---|
| ❑ 1 Jonathan Beaulieu | .40 | .18 |
| ❑ 2 Martin Bedard | .40 | .18 |
| ❑ 3 Eric Belzile | .40 | .18 |
| ❑ 4 Denis Boily | .40 | .18 |
| ❑ 5 Dave Bolduc | .40 | .18 |
| ❑ 6 Yan Bouchard | .50 | .23 |
| ❑ 7 Nicolas Chabot | .75 | .35 |
| ❑ 8 Eryc Collin | .40 | .18 |
| ❑ 9 Eric Drouin | .40 | .18 |
| ❑ 10 Yannick Dupont | .40 | .18 |
| ❑ 11 Frederic Girard | .40 | .18 |
| ❑ 12 Jimmy Grondin | .40 | .18 |
| ❑ 13 Bobby Lebel CO | .25 | .11 |
| ❑ 14 Vincent Lecavalier | 10.00 | 4.50 |
| ❑ 15 Frederic Levac | .40 | .18 |
| ❑ 16 Francois Levesque | .40 | .18 |
| ❑ 17 Philippe Lord | .40 | .18 |
| ❑ 18 Dave Malenfant | .40 | .18 |
| ❑ 19 Eric Normandin | .75 | .35 |
| ❑ 20 Mathieu Normandin | .40 | .18 |
| ❑ 21 Philippe Plante | .40 | .18 |
| ❑ 22 Martin Poitras | .50 | .23 |
| ❑ 23 Saison 1996-1997 | .25 | .11 |
| ❑ 24 Philippe Sauve | .40 | .18 |
| ❑ 25 Sebastien Simard | .40 | .18 |
| ❑ 26 David St-Onge | .40 | .18 |
| ❑ 27 Mathieu Sunderland | .50 | .23 |
| ❑ 28 Gaston Therrien CO | .25 | .11 |

## 1996-97 Rimouski Oceanic Update

This 10-card set was produced as a companion set to the basic Rimouski series issued earlier in the season. The design for both series is identical. The players featured in the update were late arrivals due to trades. Less than 1200 of these sets were produced. The cards are unnumbered and thus are listed in alphabetical order.

| | MINT | NRMT |
|---|---|---|
| COMPLETE SET (10) | 4.00 | 1.80 |
| COMMON CARD (1-10) | .25 | .11 |

| | | |
|---|---|---|
| ❑ 1 Eric Belanger (LW) | .50 | .23 |
| ❑ 2 Eric Belanger (C) | .75 | .35 |
| ❑ 3 Philippe Grondin | .50 | .23 |
| ❑ 4 Jason Lehoux | .50 | .23 |
| ❑ 5 Jonathan Levesque | .50 | .23 |
| ❑ 6 Louki (Mascot) | .25 | .11 |
| ❑ 7 Guillaume Rodrigue | .50 | .23 |
| ❑ 8 Joe Rullier | .50 | .23 |
| ❑ 9 Russell Smith | .50 | .23 |
| ❑ 10 Derrick Walser | .50 | .23 |

## 1996-97 Rimouski Oceanic Quebec Provincial Police

Cardfronts feature color photos, along with players jersey number and the Rimouski logo. Card backs feature statistical information and all text is in French. Each card also bears a serial number. Cards are unnumbered and checklisted below alphabetically.

| | MINT | NRMT |
|---|---|---|
| COMPLETE SET (26) | 20.00 | 9.00 |
| COMMON CARD | .10 | .05 |
| ❑ 1 Jonathan Beaulieu | .40 | .18 |
| ❑ 2 Martin Bedard | .40 | .18 |
| ❑ 3 Eric Belzile | .40 | .18 |
| ❑ 4 Maxime Blouin | .40 | .18 |
| ❑ 5 Denis Boily | .40 | .18 |
| ❑ 6 Yan Bouchard | .40 | .18 |
| ❑ 7 Nicolas Chabot | .40 | .18 |
| ❑ 8 Eryc Collin | .40 | .18 |
| ❑ 9 Eric Drouin | .40 | .18 |
| ❑ 10 Yannick Dupont | .40 | .18 |
| ❑ 11 Frederic Girard | .40 | .18 |
| ❑ 12 Jimmy Grondin | .40 | .18 |
| ❑ 13 Vincent Lecavalier | 12.00 | 5.50 |
| ❑ 14 Frederic Levac | .40 | .18 |
| ❑ 15 Francois Levesque | .40 | .18 |
| ❑ 16 Philipe Lord | .40 | .18 |
| ❑ 17 Dave Malenfant | .40 | .18 |
| ❑ 18 Eric Normandin | .75 | .35 |
| ❑ 19 Mathieu Normandin | .40 | .18 |
| ❑ 20 Philippe Plante | .40 | .18 |
| ❑ 21 Martin Poitras | .50 | .23 |
| ❑ 22 Philippe Sauve | .50 | .23 |
| ❑ 23 Nicola Spaccucci | .40 | .18 |
| ❑ 24 David St-Onge | .40 | .18 |
| ❑ 25 Sebastien Tremblay | .40 | .18 |
| ❑ 26 Title Card | .10 | .05 |

## 1997-98 Rimouski Oceanic

| | MINT | NRMT |
|---|---|---|
| COMPLETE SET (25) | 12.00 | 5.50 |
| COMMON CARD (1-25) | .10 | .05 |
| ❑ 4 Vincent Lecavalier | 8.00 | 3.60 |
| ❑ 7 Joe Rullier | .40 | .18 |
| ❑ 9 Jonathan Beaulieu | .40 | .18 |
| ❑ 10 David Bilodeau | .25 | .11 |
| ❑ 11 Jimmy Grondin | .40 | .18 |
| ❑ 14 Dave Malenfant | .40 | .18 |
| ❑ 17 Kevin Bolduc | .40 | .18 |
| ❑ 19 Eric Normandin | .75 | .35 |
| ❑ 20 Francois Drainville | .40 | .18 |
| ❑ 21 Eric Belanger | 1.00 | .45 |
| ❑ 22 Eric Drouin | .40 | .18 |
| ❑ 24 Julien Desrosiers | .40 | .18 |
| ❑ 25 David St-Onge | .40 | .18 |
| ❑ 27 Phillippe Grondin | .40 | .18 |
| ❑ 33 Phillippe Sauve | .40 | .18 |
| ❑ 35 Jean-Marc Pelletier | .40 | .18 |
| ❑ 36 Jonathan St-Louis | .40 | .18 |
| ❑ 39 Brad Richards | .25 | .11 |
| ❑ 44 Guillaume Couture | .40 | .18 |
| ❑ 45 Chad Gagnon | .25 | .11 |
| ❑ 55 Casey Leggett | .25 | .11 |
| ❑ 79 Denis Boily | .40 | .18 |
| ❑ 91 Derrick Walser | .40 | .18 |
| ❑ 98 Adam Borzecki | .25 | .11 |
| ❑ NNO Team Card | .10 | .05 |

## 1988-89 Riverains Du Richelieu

Cards measure approximately 3" x 4" with card fronts featuring color posed photos. Card backs have players name and number along with safety tips in French.

| | MINT | NRMT |
|---|---|---|
| COMPLETE SET (30) | 15.00 | 6.75 |
| COMMON CARD (1-30) | .20 | .09 |
| ❑ 1 Header Card | .20 | .09 |
| ❑ 2 Marc Beaurivage | .50 | .23 |
| ❑ 3 Denis Benoit | .50 | .23 |
| ❑ 4 Jonathan Black | .50 | .23 |
| ❑ 5 Richard Boisvert | .50 | .23 |
| ❑ 6 Hugues Bouchard | .50 | .23 |
| ❑ 7 Francois Bourdeau | .50 | .23 |
| ❑ 8 Guy Caplette | .50 | .23 |
| ❑ 9 Bertrand Cournoyer | .50 | .23 |
| ❑ 10 Yves Cournoyer | .50 | .23 |
| ❑ 11 Michel Deguise | .50 | .23 |
| ❑ 12 Patrick Grise | .50 | .23 |
| ❑ 13 Robert Guillet | .50 | .23 |
| ❑ 14 Jimmy Lachance | .50 | .23 |
| ❑ 15 Roger Laporte | .50 | .23 |
| ❑ 16 Frederic Lefebvre | .50 | .23 |
| ❑ 17 Frederic Maltais | .50 | .23 |
| ❑ 18 Andre Kid Millette | .50 | .23 |
| ❑ 19 Joseph Napolitano | .50 | .23 |
| ❑ 20 Remy Patoine | .50 | .23 |
| ❑ 21 Jean Plamondon | .50 | .23 |
| ❑ 22 Steve Plasse | .50 | .23 |
| ❑ 23 Jean Francois Poirier | .50 | .23 |
| ❑ 24 Jacques Provencal | .50 | .23 |
| ❑ 25 Alain Rancourt | .50 | .23 |
| ❑ 26 Francois St.Germain | .50 | .23 |
| ❑ 27 Frederic Savard | .50 | .23 |
| ❑ 28 Martin Tanguay | .50 | .23 |
| ❑ 29 Richard Valois | .50 | .23 |
| ❑ 30 Stephane Valois | .50 | .23 |

## 1993-94 Roanoke Express

Sponsored by Advance Auto Parts, First Virginia Bank, radio station J93.5 FM and WJPR TV 27, this 25-card standard-size set commemorates the inaugural season of the Roanoke Express. The fronts feature borderless color action player photos. The team logo appears on the bottom left with the player's name, position and number in two red bars next to it. The horizontal backs carry player biography, profile, and stats along with sponsor logos. The cards are unnumbered and checklisted below in alphabetical order.

| | MINT | NRMT |
|---|---|---|
| COMPLETE SET (25) | 7.00 | 3.10 |
| COMMON CARD (1-25) | .10 | .05 |
| ❑ 1 Frank Anzalone CO | .25 | .11 |
| ❑ 2 Will Averill | .35 | .16 |
| ❑ 3 Claude Barthe | .35 | .16 |
| ❑ 4 Lev Berdichevsky | .35 | .16 |
| ❑ 5 Hughes Bouchard | .35 | .16 |
| ❑ 6 Reggie Brezeault | .35 | .16 |
| ❑ 7 Ilja Dubkov | .35 | .16 |
| ❑ 8 Pat Ferschweiler | .35 | .16 |
| ❑ 9 Kyle Galloway | .35 | .16 |
| ❑ 10 Jeff Jestadt | .35 | .16 |
| ❑ 11 Roger Larche | .35 | .16 |
| ❑ 12 Dana McGuane TR | .10 | .05 |
| ❑ 13 Jim Mill | .35 | .16 |
| ❑ 14 Dave Morissette | .35 | .16 |
| ❑ 15 Chris Potter | .35 | .16 |
| ❑ 16 Dan Ryder | .35 | .16 |
| ❑ 17 Gairin Smith | .35 | .16 |
| ❑ 18 Michael Smith | .35 | .16 |
| ❑ 19 Tony Szabo | .35 | .16 |
| ❑ 20 Stephen Tepper | .35 | .16 |
| ❑ 21 Oleg Yashin | .35 | .16 |
| ❑ 22 Team Photo | .35 | .16 |
| ❑ 23 Dave Morissette<br>First Franchise Goal | .10 | .05 |
| ❑ 24 Sponsor Card<br>Advance Auto Parts | .10 | .05 |
| ❑ 25 Sponsor Card<br>First Virginia Bank | .10 | .05 |

## 1994-95 Roanoke Express

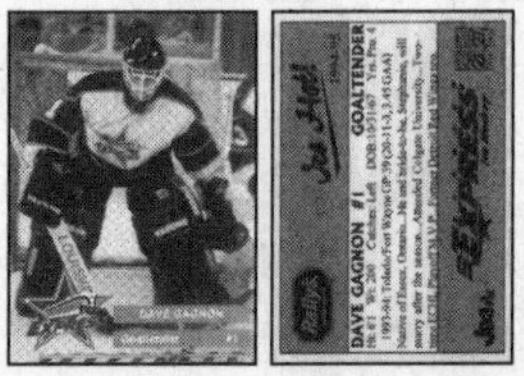

This 24-card set features the Roanoke Express of the ECHL. The cards -- which were printed on extremely thin paper -- were available through the team, and possibly offered as a game night promotion. The fronts feature a blurry action photo, with team logo and player name and position. The unnumbered backs include stats and the logos of several sponsors.

| | MINT | NRMT |
|---|---|---|
| COMPLETE SET (24) | 7.00 | 3.10 |
| COMMON CARD (1-24) | .10 | .05 |
| ❑ 1 Team Photo | .35 | .16 |
| ❑ 2 Dave Gagnon | .50 | .23 |
| ❑ 3 Chris Potter | .35 | .16 |
| ❑ 4 Dave Stewart | .35 | .16 |
| ❑ 5 Michael Smith | .35 | .16 |
| ❑ 6 Jon Larson | .35 | .16 |
| ❑ 7 Carl Fleury | .35 | .16 |
| ❑ 8 Jeff Jestadt | .35 | .16 |
| ❑ 9 Marty Schriner | .35 | .16 |
| ❑ 10 Rouslan Toujikov | .35 | .16 |
| ❑ 11 Jason Clarke | .35 | .16 |
| ❑ 12 Stephane Desjardins | .35 | .16 |
| ❑ 13 Robin Bouchard | .35 | .16 |
| ❑ 14 Oleg Yashin | .35 | .16 |
| ❑ 15 Ilja Dubkov | .50 | .23 |
| ❑ 16 Derek Laxdal | .50 | .23 |
| ❑ 17 Mark Luger | .35 | .16 |
| ❑ 18 Pat Ferschweiler | .35 | .16 |
| ❑ 19 Dan Ryder | .35 | .16 |
| ❑ 20 Frank Anzalone CO | .25 | .11 |
| ❑ 21 Dana McGuane TR | .10 | .05 |
| ❑ 22 Loco -- Mascot | .10 | .05 |
| ❑ 23 Board of Directors | .10 | .05 |
| ❑ 24 Fan Card | .10 | .05 |

## 1995-96 Roanoke Express

This 25-card set of the Roanoke Express of the ECHL was a team-produced issue, and available only through the club. The fronts feature sharp, pseudo-action shots with the player's name in a red border along the left, and position and number in a green border along the top. A gold foil Express logo graces the lower right corner. The full color backs include two more photos, as well as team stats. The cards are unnumbered.

| | MINT | NRMT |
|---|---|---|
| COMPLETE SET (25) | 7.00 | 3.10 |
| COMMON CARD (1-25) | .10 | .05 |
| ❑ 1 Jeff Jestadt | .35 | .16 |
| ❑ 2 Dave Stewart | .35 | .16 |
| ❑ 3 Matt DelGuidice | .50 | .23 |
| ❑ 4 Dave Holum | .35 | .16 |
| ❑ 5 Mike Stacchi | .35 | .16 |
| ❑ 6 Paul Croteau | .35 | .16 |
| ❑ 7 Marty Schriner | .35 | .16 |
| ❑ 8 L.P. Charbonneau | .35 | .16 |
| ❑ 9 Michael Smith | .35 | .16 |
| ❑ 10 Ilja Dubkov | .50 | .23 |
| ❑ 11 Tim Christian | .35 | .16 |
| ❑ 12 Brian Gallentine | .35 | .16 |
| ❑ 13 Jeff Jablonski | .35 | .16 |
| ❑ 14 Daniel Berthiaume | .50 | .23 |
| ❑ 15 Duane Harmer | .35 | .16 |
| ❑ 16 Jason Clarke | .35 | .16 |
| ❑ 17 Tim Hanley | .35 | .16 |
| ❑ 18 Jon Larson | .35 | .16 |
| ❑ 19 Nick Jones | .35 | .16 |
| ❑ 20 Chris Potter | .35 | .16 |
| ❑ 21 Craig Herr | .35 | .16 |
| ❑ 22 Frank Anzalone CO | .25 | .11 |
| ❑ 23 Chris Pollack TR | .10 | .05 |
| ❑ 24 Loco -- Mascot | .10 | .05 |
| ❑ 25 Team Photo | .10 | .05 |

## 1996-97 Roanoke Express

This 24-card set of the Roanoke Express of the ECHL was team issued. The cards feature action photography on the front, along with a comprehensive stats package on the reverse. The cards prominently feature the player's jersey number on the back, and are listed below thusly.

| | MINT | NRMT |
|---|---|---|
| COMPLETE SET (24) | 7.00 | 3.10 |
| COMMON CARD | .10 | .05 |
| ❑ 1 Dave Gagnon | .50 | .23 |
| ❑ 2 Dave Stewart | .35 | .16 |
| ❑ 3 Eric Landry | .35 | .16 |
| ❑ 5 Michael Smith | .35 | .16 |
| ❑ 7 Jeff Loder | .35 | .16 |
| ❑ 8 Duane Harmer | .35 | .16 |
| ❑ 10 Bobby Brown | .35 | .16 |
| ❑ 11 J.F. Tremblay | .35 | .16 |
| ❑ 12 Ryan Equale | .35 | .16 |
| ❑ 14 Doug Searle | .35 | .16 |
| ❑ 15 Jeff Jablonski | .35 | .16 |
| ❑ 17 Jeff Cowan | .35 | .16 |
| ❑ 18 Sean Brown | .35 | .16 |
| ❑ 21 Ilya Dubkov | .35 | .16 |
| ❑ 22 Matt O'Dette | .35 | .16 |
| ❑ 23 Chris Lipsett | .35 | .16 |
| ❑ 24 Tim Christian | .35 | .16 |
| ❑ 35 Larry Moberg | .50 | .23 |
| ❑ NNO Loco the Railyard Dog | .10 | .05 |
| ❑ NNO Elmer the Engine | .10 | .05 |
| ❑ NNO Mike Holden TR | .10 | .05 |
| ❑ NNO Team Photo | .35 | .16 |
| ❑ NNO Checklist | .10 | .05 |
| ❑ NNO Frank Anzalone CO | .10 | .05 |

## 1963-64 Rochester Amerks

Printed on thin paper stock, this set of twenty photos, was issued in two series and measures approximately 4" by 6". This set features borderless black-and-white posed or action shots of the AHL (American Hockey League) Amerks. The white back carries the player's name, age, height, weight, and statistics from previous years in the minors. The cards are unnumbered and checklisted below in alphabetical order.

| | NRMT | VG-E |
|---|---|---|
| COMPLETE SET (20) | 200.00 | 90.00 |
| COMMON CARD (1-20) | 5.00 | 2.20 |
| ❑ 1 Lou Angotti | 8.00 | 3.60 |
| ❑ 2 Al Arbour | 20.00 | 9.00 |
| ❑ 3 Norm Armstrong | 5.00 | 2.20 |
| ❑ 4 Ed Babiuk | 5.00 | 2.20 |
| ❑ 5 Wally Boyer | 8.00 | 3.60 |
| ❑ 6 Arnie Brown | 8.00 | 3.60 |
| ❑ 7 Gerry Cheevers UER<br>(Misspelled Jerry<br>on card back) | 50.00 | 22.00 |
| ❑ 8 Don Cherry | 60.00 | 27.00 |
| ❑ 9 Mike Corbett | 5.00 | 2.20 |
| ❑ 10 Joe Crozier CO | 5.00 | 2.20 |
| ❑ 11 Jack Curran TR | 5.00 | 2.20 |
| ❑ 12 Les Duff | 5.00 | 2.20 |
| ❑ 13 Gerry Ehman | 5.00 | 2.20 |
| ❑ 14 Dick Gamble | 8.00 | 3.60 |
| ❑ 15 Larry Hillman | 5.00 | 2.20 |
| ❑ 16 Bronco Horvath | 15.00 | 6.75 |
| ❑ 17 Eddie Lawson | 5.00 | 2.20 |
| ❑ 18 Jim Pappin | 8.00 | 3.60 |
| ❑ 19 Darryl Sly | 5.00 | 2.20 |
| ❑ 20 Stan Smrke | 6.00 | 2.70 |

## 1971-72 Rochester Americans

Cards measure 5" x 7" and feature black and white glossy photos on the front, along with a facsimile autograph. Backs are blank. Cards are unnumbered and checklisted below alphabetically.

| | MINT | NRMT |
|---|---|---|
| COMPLETE SET (18) | 15.00 | 6.75 |
| COMMON CARD (1-18) | 1.00 | .45 |
| ❑ 1 Red Armstrong | 1.00 | .45 |
| ❑ 2 Guy Burrowes | 1.00 | .45 |
| ❑ 3 Gaye Cooley | 1.00 | .45 |
| ❑ 4 Bob Craig | 1.00 | .45 |
| ❑ 5 Bob Ellett | 1.00 | .45 |
| ❑ 6 Ron Fogal | 1.00 | .45 |
| ❑ 7 Rod Graham | 1.00 | .45 |
| ❑ 8 Dave Hrechosky | 1.00 | .45 |
| ❑ 9 Herman Karp | 1.00 | .45 |
| ❑ 10 Bob Kelly | 2.00 | .90 |
| ❑ 11 Larry McKillop | 1.00 | .45 |
| ❑ 12 Bob Malcolm | 1.00 | .45 |
| ❑ 13 Barry Merrell | 1.00 | .45 |
| ❑ 14 Wayne Morusyk | 1.00 | .45 |
| ❑ 15 Rick Pagnutti | 1.00 | .45 |
| ❑ 16 Gerry Sillers | 1.00 | .45 |
| ❑ 17 Gene Sobchuk | 1.00 | .45 |
| ❑ 18 Lynn Zimmerman | 1.00 | .45 |

## 1977-78 Rochester Americans

Cards measure 11" x 17" and feature black and white front photos with a facsimile autograph. Front also features players name, position, biographical information, and statistics. Cards are unnumberd and checklisted below in alphabetical order.

| | MINT | NRMT |
|---|---|---|
| COMPLETE SET (24) | 8.00 | 3.60 |
| COMMON CARD (1-24) | .10 | .05 |
| ❑ 1 Team Photo | .10 | .05 |
| ❑ 2 Duane Rupp | .50 | .23 |
| ❑ 3 Nate Angelo TR | .10 | .05 |
| ❑ 4 Earl Anderson | .50 | .23 |
| ❑ 5 Bill Bennett | .50 | .23 |
| ❑ 6 Daryl Drader | .50 | .23 |
| ❑ 7 Rene Drolet | .50 | .23 |
| ❑ 8 Rene Drolet | .50 | .23 |
| ❑ 9 Darryl Edestrand | .50 | .23 |
| ❑ 10 Ron Garwasiuk | .50 | .23 |
| ❑ 11 Rod Graham | .50 | .23 |
| ❑ 12 Rod Graham | .50 | .23 |
| ❑ 13 Doug Halward | .75 | .35 |
| ❑ 14 Bjorn Johansson | .50 | .23 |
| ❑ 15 Steve Langdon | .50 | .23 |
| ❑ 16 Ray Maluta | .50 | .23 |
| ❑ 17 Brian McGregor | .50 | .23 |
| ❑ 18 Clayton Pachal | .50 | .23 |
| ❑ 19 Dave Parro | .50 | .23 |
| ❑ 20 Jim Pettie | .50 | .23 |
| ❑ 21 Sean Shanahan | .50 | .23 |
| ❑ 22 Al Sims | .50 | .23 |
| ❑ 23 Barry Smith | .50 | .23 |

## 1991-92 Rochester Americans Dunkin' Donuts

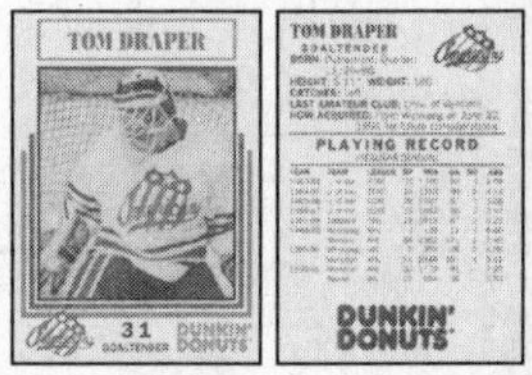


Sponsored by Dunkin' Donuts, this 20-card set measures the standard size. It was issued in four perforated strips, each consisting of four player cards and a Dunkin' Donuts coupon. On white card stock, the fronts feature color action player photos. Blue and red border stripes edge the picture on the bottom and half way on each side. The player's name is printed in a red-lined box above the picture, while logos and additional player information appear beneath it. In black print on a white background, the backs carry biography, statistics, and sponsor logo. The cards are unnumbered and checklisted below in alphabetical order.

| | MINT | NRMT |
|---|---|---|
| COMPLETE SET (20) | 8.00 | 3.60 |
| COMMON CARD (1-16) | .50 | .23 |
| DUNKIN' DONUT COUPON (17-20) | .05 | .02 |
| ❑ 1 Greg Brown | .50 | .23 |
| ❑ 2 Peter Ciavaglia | .75 | .35 |
| ❑ 3 Bob Corkum | .75 | .35 |
| ❑ 4 Brian Curran | .50 | .23 |
| ❑ 5 David DiVita | .50 | .23 |
| ❑ 6 Tom Draper | .75 | .35 |
| ❑ 7 Jody Gage | .75 | .35 |
| ❑ 8 Dan Frawley | .50 | .23 |
| ❑ 9 Dave Littman | .75 | .35 |
| ❑ 10 Darcy Loewen | .50 | .23 |
| ❑ 11 Don McSween | .75 | .35 |
| ❑ 12 Brad Rubachuk | .50 | .23 |
| ❑ 13 Lindy Ruff | .75 | .35 |
| ❑ 14 Joel Savage | .50 | .23 |
| ❑ 15 Jiri Sejba | .50 | .23 |
| ❑ 16 Chris Snell | .50 | .23 |
| ❑ 17 Coupon Dunkin' Donuts | .05 | .02 |
| ❑ 18 Coupon Dunkin' Donuts | .05 | .02 |
| ❑ 19 Coupon Dunkin' Donuts | .05 | .02 |
| ❑ 20 Coupon Dunkin' Donuts | .05 | .02 |

## 1991-92 Rochester Americans Kodak

The 1991-92 Rochester American Team Phot and Trading Card Set was co-sponsored b Kodak and Wegmons Photo Center. It consist of three 11 1/4" by 9 1/2" sheets joine together and tri-folded. The first sheet display a team photo of the players dressed in stre clothes. The second and third sheets consis of 15 cards each arranged in three rows of fiv cards. The last four slots of the third she display sponsor coupons. After perforatio the cards would measure approximately 2 1/ by 3 1/8". The player photos on the fronts hav rounded corners and are poses shot from th waist up against a studio background. Tea color-coded (red and blue) stripes edge th pictures on the bottom and each side. Th player's name, position, and the team logo a above the picture, while sponsor logos and th uniform number are below it. In red and blu print, the backs carry biography and statistic The cards are checklisted below as they a arranged in the album, with coaches presente

first and then the players in alphabetical order.

| | MINT | NRMT |
|---|---|---|
| COMPLETE SET (26) | 12.00 | 5.50 |
| COMMON CARD (1-26) | .25 | .11 |
| ❑ 1 Don Lever CO | .25 | .11 |
| ❑ 2 Terry Martin ACO | .25 | .11 |
| ❑ 3 Ian Boyce | .50 | .23 |
| ❑ 4 John Bradley | .50 | .23 |
| ❑ 5 Greg Brown | .50 | .23 |
| ❑ 6 Keith Carney | .50 | .23 |
| ❑ 7 Peter Ciavaglia | .50 | .23 |
| ❑ 8 Bob Corkum | .75 | .35 |
| ❑ 9 Brian Curran | .50 | .23 |
| ❑ 10 David DiVita | .50 | .23 |
| ❑ 11 Lou Franceschetti | .50 | .23 |
| ❑ 12 Dan Frawley | .50 | .23 |
| ❑ 13 Jody Gage | .75 | .35 |
| ❑ 14 Kevin Haller | .75 | .35 |
| ❑ 15 Dave Littman | .60 | .25 |
| ❑ 16 Darcy Loewen | .50 | .23 |
| ❑ 17 Steve Ludzik | .50 | .23 |
| ❑ 18 Don McSween | .50 | .23 |
| ❑ 19 Brad Miller | .50 | .23 |
| ❑ 20 Sean O'Donnell | .50 | .23 |
| ❑ 21 Brad Rubachuk | .50 | .23 |
| ❑ 22 Lindy Ruff | .50 | .23 |
| ❑ 23 Joel Savage | .50 | .23 |
| ❑ 24 Jiri Sejba | .50 | .23 |
| ❑ 25 Chris Snell | .50 | .23 |
| ❑ 26 Jason Winch | .50 | .23 |

## 1991-92 Rochester Americans Postcards

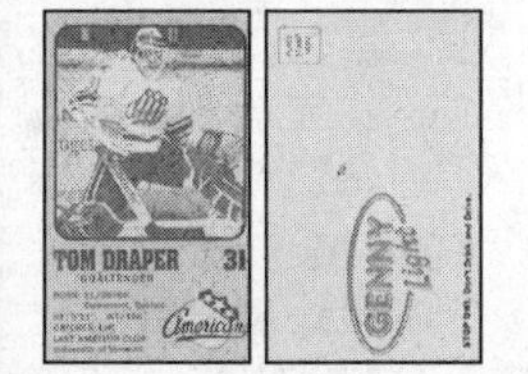


Sponsored by Genny Light, this 21-card set measures approximately 3 1/2" by 5 1/2" and features the 1991-92 Rochester Americans of the American Hockey League. The fronts have black-and-white action player photos with rounded corners and black borders. The player's name, uniform number, position, biography and last amateur club appear beneath the photo, along with the team logo. The backs are in postcard format and carry the sponsor's logo along with the words "STOP DWI. Don't Drink and Drive". The cards are unnumbered and checklisted below in alphabetical order.

| | MINT | NRMT |
|---|---|---|
| COMPLETE SET (21) | 10.00 | 4.50 |
| COMMON CARD (1-21) | .25 | .11 |
| ❑ 1 Dave Baseggio | .50 | .23 |
| ❑ 2 John Bradley | .50 | .23 |
| ❑ 3 Greg Brown | .50 | .23 |
| ❑ 4 Keith Carney | .50 | .23 |
| ❑ 5 Peter Ciavaglia | .50 | .23 |
| ❑ 6 Bob Corkum | .75 | .35 |
| ❑ 7 David DiVita | .50 | .23 |
| ❑ 8 Tom Draper | .75 | .35 |
| ❑ 9 Lou Franceschetti | .50 | .23 |
| ❑ 10 Dan Frawley | .50 | .23 |
| ❑ 11 Bill Houlder | .75 | .35 |
| ❑ 12 Don Lever CO | .25 | .11 |
| ❑ 13 David Littman | .75 | .35 |
| ❑ 14 Terry Martin ACO | .25 | .11 |
| ❑ 15 Don McSween | .50 | .23 |
| ❑ 16 Sean O'Donnell | .50 | .23 |
| ❑ 17 Lindy Ruff | .50 | .23 |
| ❑ 18 Joel Savage | .50 | .23 |
| ❑ 19 Jiri Sejba | .50 | .23 |
| ❑ 20 Chris Snell | .50 | .23 |
| ❑ 21 Ed Zawatsky | .50 | .23 |

## 1992-93 Rochester Americans Dunkin' Donuts

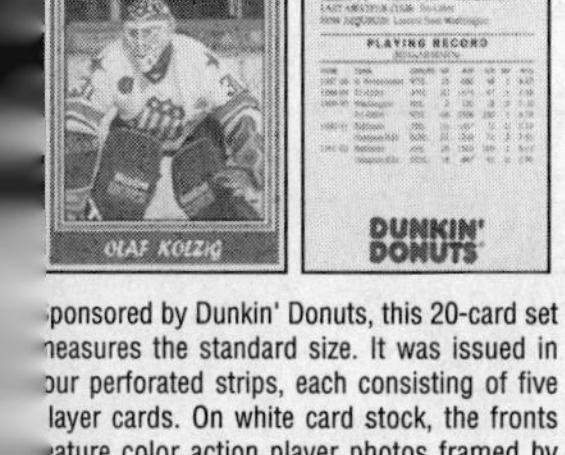


ponsored by Dunkin' Donuts, this 20-card set neasures the standard size. It was issued in our perforated strips, each consisting of five layer cards. On white card stock, the fronts eature color action player photos framed by eam color-coded (red and blue) border tripes. Logos, jersey number, and position re printed above the picture, while the layer's name is printed on the wider blue stripe beneath the picture. In black print on a white background, the backs carry biography, statistics, and sponsor logo. The cards are unnumbered and checklisted below in alphabetical order.

| | MINT | NRMT |
|---|---|---|
| COMPLETE SET (20) | 10.00 | 4.50 |
| COMMON CARD (1-20) | .50 | .23 |
| ❑ 1 Peter Ambroziak | .50 | .23 |
| ❑ 2 Greg Brown | .50 | .23 |
| ❑ 3 Peter Ciavaglia | .60 | .25 |
| ❑ 4 Jozef Cierny | .50 | .23 |
| ❑ 5 David DiVita | .50 | .23 |
| ❑ 6 Dan Frawley | .50 | .23 |
| ❑ 7 Jody Gage | .75 | .35 |
| ❑ 8 Andrei Jakovenko | .50 | .23 |
| ❑ 9 Olaf Kolzig | 1.50 | .70 |
| ❑ 10 Doug Macdonald | .50 | .23 |
| ❑ 11 Mike McLaughlin | .50 | .23 |
| ❑ 12 Sean O'Donnell | .50 | .23 |
| ❑ 13 Bill Pye | .50 | .23 |
| ❑ 14 Brad Rubachuk | .50 | .23 |
| ❑ 15 Bruce Shoebottom | .50 | .23 |
| ❑ 16 Todd Simon | .50 | .23 |
| ❑ 17 Jeff Sirkka | .50 | .23 |
| ❑ 18 Chris Snell | .50 | .23 |
| ❑ 19 Scott Thomas | .50 | .23 |
| ❑ 20 Jason Young | .50 | .23 |

## 1992-93 Rochester Americans Kodak

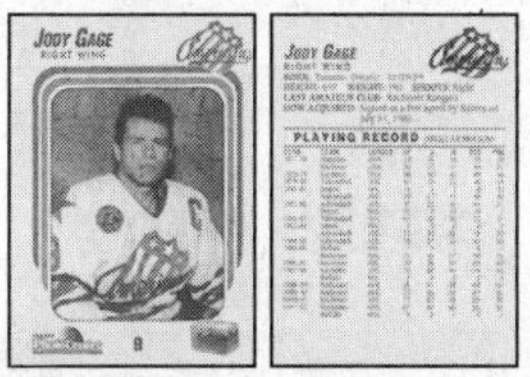


The 1992-93 Rochester American Team Photo and Trading Card Set was co-sponsored by Kodak and Wegmons Photo Center. It consists of three 11 1/4" by 9 1/2" sheets joined together and tri-folded. The first sheet displays a team photo of the players in uniform. The second and third sheets consist of 15 cards each arranged in three rows of five cards. (The last four slots of the third sheet display sponsor coupons.) After perforation, the cards would measure approximately 2 1/4" by 3 1/8". The player photos on the fronts have rounded corners and are poses shot from the waist up against a studio background. Team color-coded (red and blue) stripes edge the pictures on the top and each side. The player's name, position, and the team logo are above the picture, while sponsor logos and the uniform number are below it. In red and blue print, the backs carry biography and statistics. The cards are checklisted below as they are arranged in the album, with coaches presented first and then the players in alphabetical order.

| | MINT | NRMT |
|---|---|---|
| COMPLETE SET (26) | 9.00 | 4.00 |
| COMMON CARD (1-26) | .10 | .05 |
| ❑ 1 John Van Boxmeer CO | .35 | .16 |
| ❑ 2 Terry Martin ACO | .10 | .05 |
| ❑ 3 Peter Ambroziak | .35 | .16 |
| ❑ 4 Greg Brown | .35 | .16 |
| ❑ 5 Peter Ciavaglia | .35 | .16 |
| ❑ 6 Jozef Cierny | .35 | .16 |
| ❑ 7 David DiVita | .35 | .16 |
| ❑ 8 Dan Frawley | .35 | .16 |
| ❑ 9 Jody Gage | .60 | .25 |
| ❑ 10 The Moose (mascot) | .10 | .05 |
| ❑ 11 Tony Iob | .35 | .16 |
| ❑ 12 Olaf Kolzig | 1.25 | .55 |
| ❑ 13 Doug MacDonald | .35 | .16 |
| ❑ 14 Mike McLaughlin | .35 | .16 |
| ❑ 15 Sean O'Donnell | .35 | .16 |
| ❑ 16 Brad Pascall | .35 | .16 |
| ❑ 17 Bill Pye | .50 | .23 |
| ❑ 18 Brad Rubachuk | .35 | .16 |
| ❑ 19 Joel Savage | .35 | .16 |
| ❑ 20 Bruce Shoebottom | .35 | .16 |
| ❑ 21 Todd Simon | .35 | .16 |
| ❑ 22 Jeff Sirkka | .35 | .16 |
| ❑ 23 Chris Snell | .35 | .16 |
| ❑ 24 Scott Thomas | .35 | .16 |
| ❑ 25 Jason Winch | .35 | .16 |
| ❑ 26 Jason Young | .35 | .16 |

## 1993-94 Rochester Americans Kodak

This 25-card set of the Rochester Americans of the AHL was sponsored by Kodak and distributed by the team's booster club. The set was issued in sheet form, with each card measuring 2 1/2" by 3 1/4". The card fronts carry a posed phot, player name and position and logos of the club and sponsors. The backs are unnumbered, but carry comprehensive stats.

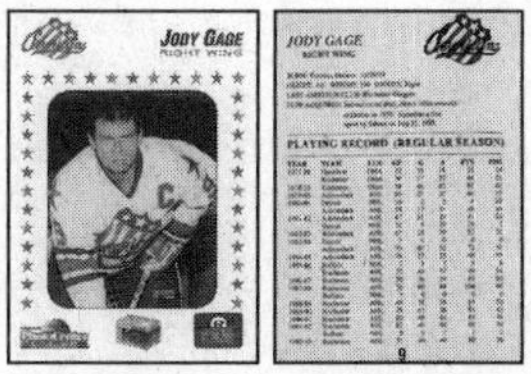


| | MINT | NRMT |
|---|---|---|
| COMPLETE SET (25) | 15.00 | 6.75 |
| COMMON CARD (1-25) | .25 | .11 |
| ❑ 1 John Van Boxmeer CO | .50 | .23 |
| ❑ 2 Terry Martin ACO | .25 | .11 |
| ❑ 3 Peter Ambroziak | .60 | .25 |
| ❑ 4 Mike Bavis | .60 | .25 |
| ❑ 5 James Black | .60 | .25 |
| ❑ 6 Derek Booth | .60 | .25 |
| ❑ 7 Philippe Boucher | 1.00 | .45 |
| ❑ 8 David Cooper | .60 | .25 |
| ❑ 9 Todd Flichel | .60 | .25 |
| ❑ 10 Jody Gage | 1.00 | .45 |
| ❑ 11 Viktor Gordiouk | .75 | .35 |
| ❑ 12 Bill Horn | .60 | .25 |
| ❑ 13 Markus Ketterer | 1.00 | .45 |
| ❑ 14 Mark Krys | .60 | .25 |
| ❑ 15 Doug MacDonald | .60 | .25 |
| ❑ 16 Dean Melanson | .60 | .25 |
| ❑ 17 Moose -- Mascot | .25 | .11 |
| ❑ 18 Sean O'Donnell | .60 | .25 |
| ❑ 19 Brad Pascall | .60 | .25 |
| ❑ 20 Sergei Petrenko | .60 | .25 |
| ❑ 21 Brad Rubachuk | .60 | .25 |
| ❑ 22 Todd Simon | .60 | .25 |
| ❑ 23 Scott Thomas | .60 | .25 |
| ❑ 24 Mikhail Volkov | .60 | .25 |
| ❑ 25 Jason Young | .60 | .25 |

## 1995-96 Rochester Americans Split Second

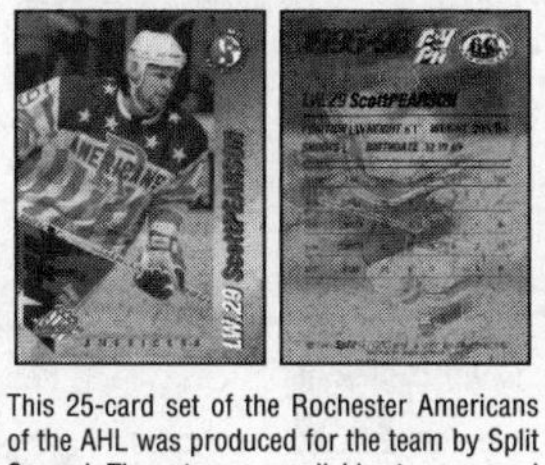

This 25-card set of the Rochester Americans of the AHL was produced for the team by Split Second. The sets were available at games and by mail through the club. The set features a blurry action photo on the front and complete stats on the back. Unnumbered, the cards are presented in alphabetical order.

| | MINT | NRMT |
|---|---|---|
| COMPLETE SET (25) | 12.00 | 5.50 |
| COMMON CARD (1-25) | .25 | .11 |
| ❑ 1 Craig Charron | .50 | .23 |
| ❑ 2 David Cooper | .50 | .23 |
| ❑ 3 Dan Frawley | .50 | .23 |
| ❑ 4 Jody Gage | .75 | .35 |
| ❑ 5 Terry Hollinger | .50 | .23 |
| ❑ 6 Dane Jackson | .50 | .23 |
| ❑ 7 Ladislav Karabin | .50 | .23 |
| ❑ 8 Sergei Klimentiev | .60 | .25 |
| ❑ 9 Jamie Leach | .50 | .23 |
| ❑ 10 Jay Mazur | .50 | .23 |
| ❑ 11 Dean Melanson | .50 | .23 |
| ❑ 12 Scott Metcalfe | .50 | .23 |
| ❑ 13 Barrie Moore | .60 | .25 |
| ❑ 14 Scott Nichol | .50 | .23 |
| ❑ 15 Roman Ndur | .60 | .25 |
| ❑ 16 Scott Pearson | .50 | .23 |
| ❑ 17 Serge Roberge | .50 | .23 |
| ❑ 18 Steve Shields | 1.50 | .70 |
| ❑ 19 Robb Stauber | .75 | .35 |
| ❑ 20 Mikhail Volkov | .50 | .23 |
| ❑ 21 Dixon Ward | .50 | .23 |
| ❑ 22 Bob Westerby | .50 | .23 |
| ❑ 23 Mike Wilson | .75 | .35 |
| ❑ 24 Shayne Wright | .50 | .23 |
| ❑ 25 John Tortorella CO | .25 | .11 |

## 1994-95 St. John Flames

This 26-card standard-size set was manufactured and distributed by Jessen Associates, Inc. for Classic. The fronts display color action player photos with a red marbleized inner border and a black outer border. The player's name, jersey number, and position appear in the teal border on the right edge. Inside a black border on a marbleized background, the backs present biography, statistics, and sponsor logos. The cards are unnumbered and checklisted below in alphabetical order.

| | MINT | NRMT |
|---|---|---|
| COMPLETE SET (26) | 8.00 | 3.60 |
| COMMON CARD (1-26) | .10 | .05 |
| ❑ 1 Joel Bouchard | .60 | .25 |
| ❑ 2 Rick Carriere ACO | .10 | .05 |
| ❑ 3 Ryan Duthie | .25 | .11 |
| ❑ 4 Neil Eisenhut | .35 | .16 |
| ❑ 5 Leonard Esau | .25 | .11 |
| ❑ 6 Bob Francis CO | .10 | .05 |
| ❑ 7 Mark Greig | .35 | .16 |
| ❑ 8 Francois Groleau | .25 | .11 |
| ❑ 9 Sami Helenius | .25 | .11 |
| ❑ 10 Todd Hlushko | .35 | .16 |
| ❑ 11 Dale Kushner | .25 | .11 |
| ❑ 12 Bobby Marshall | .25 | .11 |
| ❑ 13 Scott Morrow | .25 | .11 |
| ❑ 14 Michael Murray | .25 | .11 |
| ❑ 15 Jason Muzzatti | .75 | .35 |
| ❑ 16 Barry Nieckar | .35 | .16 |
| ❑ 17 Nicolas Perreault | .25 | .11 |
| ❑ 18 Jeff Perry | .25 | .11 |
| ❑ 19 Dwayne Roloson | .50 | .23 |
| ❑ 20 Todd Simpson | .25 | .11 |
| ❑ 21 Harbour Station | .10 | .05 |
| ❑ 22 Cory Stillman | 1.00 | .45 |
| ❑ 23 David Struch | .25 | .11 |
| ❑ 24 Niklas Sundblad | .35 | .16 |
| ❑ 25 Andrei Trefilov | .50 | .23 |
| ❑ 26 Vesa Viitakoski | .35 | .16 |

## 1995-96 St. John Flames

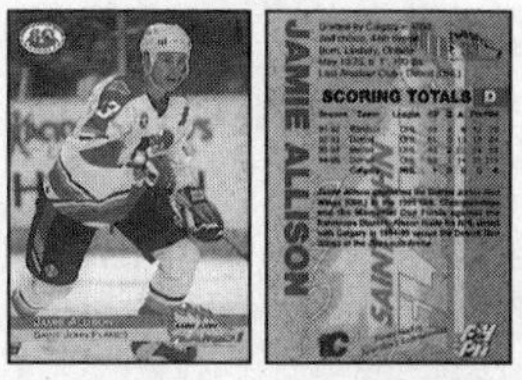


This 25-card set features borderless color action player photos of the St. John Flames of the AHL. The backs carry player information and statistics. The cards are unnumbered and checklisted below in alphabetical order.

| | MINT | NRMT |
|---|---|---|
| COMPLETE SET (25) | 8.00 | 3.60 |
| COMMON CARD (1-25) | .10 | .05 |
| ❑ 1 Jamie Allison | .25 | .11 |
| ❑ 2 Paul Baxter CO | .25 | .11 |
| ❑ 3 Joel Bouchard | .50 | .23 |
| ❑ 4 Tom Coolen CO | .10 | .05 |
| ❑ 5 Brett Duncan | .25 | .11 |
| ❑ 6 Ian Gordon | .35 | .16 |
| ❑ 7 Sami Helenius | .50 | .23 |
| ❑ 8 Todd Hlushko | .35 | .16 |
| ❑ 9 Marc Hussey | .25 | .11 |
| ❑ 10 Ladislav Kohn | .50 | .23 |
| ❑ 11 Frank Kovacs | .25 | .11 |
| ❑ 12 David Ling | .35 | .16 |
| ❑ 13 Jesper Mattsson | .50 | .23 |
| ❑ 14 Keith McCambridge | .25 | .11 |
| ❑ 15 Marty Murray | .75 | .35 |
| ❑ 16 Michael Murray | .25 | .11 |
| ❑ 17 David Neilson | .25 | .11 |
| ❑ 18 Jeff Perry | .25 | .11 |
| ❑ 19 Darren Ritchie | .25 | .11 |
| ❑ 20 Dwayne Roloson | .75 | .35 |
| ❑ 21 Todd Simpson | .25 | .11 |
| ❑ 22 Jarrod Skalde | .25 | .11 |
| ❑ 23 David Struch | .25 | .11 |
| ❑ 24 Niklas Sundblad | .35 | .16 |
| ❑ 25 Vesa Viitakoski | .50 | .23 |

## 1992-93 St. John's Maple Leafs

Measuring approximately 2 1/2" by 3 3/4", this 25-card set features the St. John's Maple Leafs of the American Hockey League. The fronts display color action player photos framed by white borders. In the wider bottom border, the player's name, uniform number, position, and logos are printed in black. On a white background inside a thin blue border, the backs present biographical and statistical information. The team logo in blue is printed at the upper left corner. The cards are unnumbered and checklisted below in alphabetical order.

| | MINT | NRMT |
|---|---|---|
| COMPLETE SET (25) | 12.00 | 5.50 |
| COMMON CARD (1-25) | .10 | .05 |
| ❑ 1 Patrik Augusta | .35 | .16 |
| ❑ 2 Drake Berehowsky | .35 | .16 |
| ❑ 3 Robert Cimetta | .35 | .16 |
| ❑ 4 Marc Crawford CO | .75 | .35 |
| ❑ 5 Ted Crowley | .35 | .16 |
| ❑ 6 Mike Eastwood | .50 | .23 |
| ❑ 7 Todd Hawkins | .35 | .16 |
| ❑ 8 Curtis Hunt | .35 | .16 |
| ❑ 9 Eric Lacroix | 1.00 | .45 |
| ❑ 10 Guy Lehoux | .35 | .16 |
| ❑ 11 Kent Manderville | .50 | .23 |
| ❑ 12 Kevin McClelland | .35 | .16 |
| ❑ 13 Ken McRae | .35 | .16 |
| ❑ 14 Brad Miller | .35 | .16 |
| ❑ 15 Yanic Perreault | .75 | .35 |
| ❑ 16 Rudy Poeschek | .50 | .23 |
| ❑ 17 Joel Quenneville ACO | .25 | .11 |
| ❑ 18 Damian Rhodes | 1.50 | .70 |
| ❑ 19 Joe Sacco | .50 | .23 |
| ❑ 20 Jeff Serowik | .35 | .16 |
| ❑ 21 Scott Sharples | .35 | .16 |
| ❑ 22 Dave Tomlinson | .35 | .16 |
| ❑ 23 Nick Wohlers | .35 | .16 |
| ❑ 24 Team Photo | 1.00 | .45 |
| ❑ 25 Buddy (Mascot) | .10 | .05 |

## 1993-94 St. John's Maple Leafs

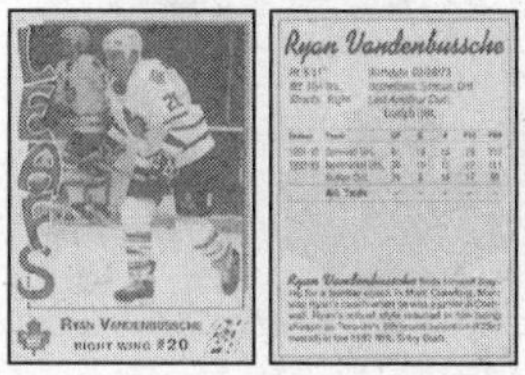


This 25-card standard-size set features the St. John's Maple Leafs of the American Hockey League. The fronts feature color action player photos with white borders and a gray shadow border. The team name "Leafs" in blue lettering edges the left side of the picture. Player information and logos appear in the lower white margin. The backs carry biography, statistics, and player profile. The cards are unnumbered and checklisted below in alphabetical order.

| | MINT | NRMT |
|---|---|---|
| COMPLETE SET (25) | 9.00 | 4.00 |
| COMMON CARD (1-25) | .10 | .05 |
| ❑ 1 Patrik Augusta | .35 | .16 |
| ❑ 2 Frank Bialowas | .35 | .16 |
| ❑ 3 Buddy (Mascot) | .10 | .05 |
| ❑ 4 Rich Chernomaz | .35 | .16 |
| ❑ 5 Terry Chitaroni | .35 | .16 |
| ❑ 6 Marcel Cousineau | 1.00 | .45 |
| ❑ 7 Marc Crawford CO | .50 | .23 |
| ❑ 8 Todd Gillingham | .35 | .16 |
| ❑ 9 Chris Govedaris | .35 | .16 |
| ❑ 10 Paul Holden | .35 | .16 |
| ❑ 11 Curtis Hunt | .35 | .16 |
| ❑ 12 Alexei Kudashov | .35 | .16 |
| ❑ 13 Eric Lacroix | .75 | .35 |
| ❑ 14 Guy Lehoux | .35 | .16 |
| ❑ 15 Matt Mallgrave | .35 | .16 |
| ❑ 16 Grant Marshall | .35 | .16 |
| ❑ 17 Ken McRae | .35 | .16 |
| ❑ 18 Yanic Perreault | .75 | .35 |
| ❑ 19 Bruce Racine | .60 | .25 |
| ❑ 20 Damian Rhodes | 1.50 | .70 |
| ❑ 21 Chris Snell | .35 | .16 |
| ❑ 22 Dan Stiver | .35 | .16 |
| ❑ 23 Andy Sullivan | .35 | .16 |
| ❑ 24 Ryan Vandenbussche | .50 | .23 |
| ❑ 25 Steffon Walby | .35 | .16 |

## 1994-95 St. John's Maple Leafs

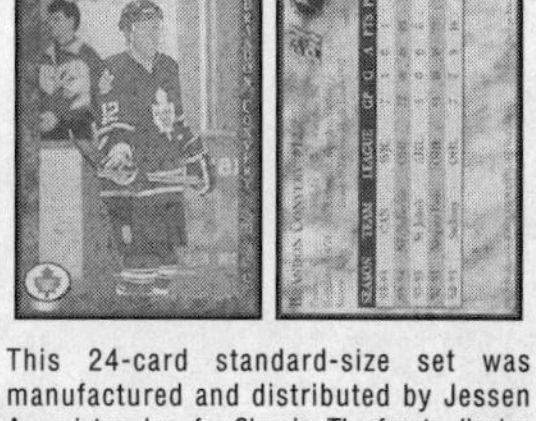

This 24-card standard-size set was manufactured and distributed by Jessen Associates, Inc. for Classic. The fronts display color action player photos with a dark blue marbleized inner border and a black outer border. The player's name, jersey number, and position appear in the teal border on the right edge. Inside a black border on a marbleized background, the backs present biography,

statistics, and sponsor logos. The cards are unnumbered and checklisted below in alphabetical order.

| | MINT | NRMT |
|---|---|---|
| COMPLETE SET (24) | 9.00 | 4.00 |
| COMMON CARD (1-24) | .25 | .11 |
| □ 1 Patrik Augusta | .25 | .11 |
| □ 2 Ken Belanger | .25 | .11 |
| □ 3 Frank Bialowis | .35 | .16 |
| □ 4 Rich Chernomaz | .25 | .11 |
| □ 5 Brandon Convery | .50 | .23 |
| □ 6 Marcel Cousineau | .75 | .35 |
| □ 7 Trent Cull | .25 | .11 |
| □ 8 Nathan Dempsey | .35 | .16 |
| □ 9 Kelly Fairchild | .35 | .16 |
| □ 10 Janne Gronvall | .50 | .23 |
| □ 11 David Harlock | .25 | .11 |
| □ 12 Darby Hendrickson | .50 | .23 |
| □ 13 Marc Hussey | .25 | .11 |
| □ 14 Kenny Jonsson | 2.00 | .90 |
| □ 15 Mark Kolesar | .35 | .16 |
| □ 16 Alexei Kudashov | .25 | .11 |
| □ 17 Guy Lehoux | .25 | .11 |
| □ 18 Guy Leveque | .25 | .11 |
| □ 19 Matt Martin | .50 | .23 |
| □ 20 Robb McIntyre | .25 | .11 |
| □ 21 Bruce Racine | .50 | .23 |
| □ 22 Ryan Vandenbussche | .35 | .16 |
| □ 23 Steffon Walby | .25 | .11 |
| □ 24 Todd Warriner | .75 | .35 |

## 1995-96 St. John's Maple Leafs

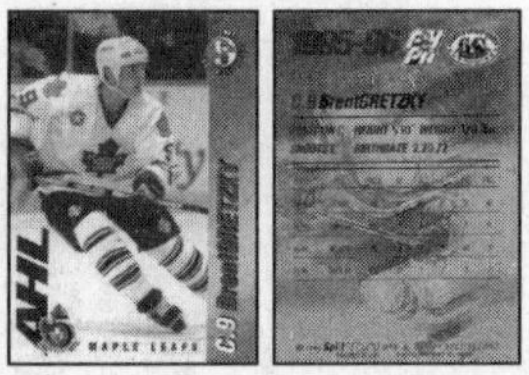

This 25-card set of the St. John's Maple Leafs of the AHL was produced by Split Second for distribution by the team at home games and via mail order. The set features the standard Split Second design elements, and a number of decent prospects including Todd Warriner, Brandon Convery and Jason Saal.

| | MINT | NRMT |
|---|---|---|
| COMPLETE SET (25) | 10.00 | 4.50 |
| COMMON CARD (1-25) | .10 | .05 |
| □ 1 Team Photo | .35 | .16 |
| □ 2 Ken Belanger | .35 | .16 |
| □ 3 Rob Butz | .35 | .16 |
| □ 4 Brandon Convery | .50 | .23 |
| □ 5 Marcel Cousineau | .75 | .35 |
| □ 6 Trent Cull | .35 | .16 |
| □ 7 Nathan Dempsey | .50 | .23 |
| □ 8 Kelly Fairchild | .50 | .23 |
| □ 9 Brent Gretzky | .75 | .35 |
| □ 10 Janne Gronvall | .35 | .16 |
| □ 11 David Harlock | .35 | .16 |
| □ 12 Jamie Heward | .35 | .16 |
| □ 13 Mark Kolesar | .60 | .25 |
| □ 14 Guy Lehoux | .35 | .16 |
| □ 15 Kent Manderville | .50 | .23 |
| □ 16 Kory Mullin | .35 | .16 |
| □ 17 Jason Saal | .50 | .23 |
| □ 18 Shayne Toporowski | .35 | .16 |
| □ 19 Paul Vincent | .35 | .16 |
| □ 20 Steffon Walby | .35 | .16 |
| □ 21 Mike Ware | .35 | .16 |
| □ 22 Todd Warriner | 1.00 | .45 |
| □ 23 Tom Watt CO | .10 | .05 |
| □ 24 Mike Foligno CO | .25 | .11 |
| □ 25 Buddy -- Mascot | .10 | .05 |

## 1996-97 St. John's Maple Leafs

This standard size set features color action photos on the front and backs are loaded with biographical information. The players name and position are featured in a triangle in the lower right corner of the card front. Cards are unnumbered and checklisted below in alphabetical order.

| | MINT | NRMT |
|---|---|---|
| COMPLETE SET (25) | 10.00 | 4.50 |
| COMMON CARD (1-25) | .10 | .05 |
| □ 1 Don Beaupre | .50 | .23 |
| □ 2 Jared Bednar | .35 | .16 |
| □ 3 Aaron Brand | .40 | .18 |
| □ 4 Rich Brown | .35 | .16 |
| □ 5 Buddy | .10 | .05 |
| □ 6 Greg Bullock | .35 | .16 |
| □ 7 Rob Butz | .35 | .16 |
| □ 8 Shawn Carter | .35 | .16 |
| □ 9 Jason Cipolla | .35 | .16 |
| □ 10 Brandon Convery | .50 | .23 |
| □ 11 David Cooper | .35 | .16 |
| □ 12 John Craighead | .35 | .16 |
| □ 13 Trent Cull | .35 | .16 |
| □ 14 Nathan Dempsey | .50 | .23 |
| □ 15 Mark Deyell | .35 | .16 |
| □ 16 Jamie Heward | .35 | .16 |
| □ 17 Mark Hunter | .35 | .16 |
| □ 18 Mark Kolesar | .35 | .16 |
| □ 19 Guy Lehoux | .35 | .16 |
| □ 20 Randy Mercer | .35 | .16 |
| □ 21 Jason Saal | .35 | .16 |
| □ 22 Greg Smyth | .35 | .16 |
| □ 23 Shayne Toporowski | .35 | .16 |
| □ 24 Yannick Tremblay | .50 | .23 |
| □ 25 Brian Wiseman | .40 | .18 |

## 1997-98 St. John's Maple Leafs

| | MINT | NRMT |
|---|---|---|
| COMPLETE SET (25) | 10.00 | 4.50 |
| COMMON CARD (1-25) | .10 | .05 |
| □ 1 Kevyn Adams | .35 | .16 |
| □ 2 Lonny Bohonos | .75 | .35 |
| □ 3 Aaron Brand | .40 | .18 |
| □ 4 Rich Brown ACO | .10 | .05 |
| □ 5 Buddy | .10 | .05 |
| □ 6 Shawn Carter | .35 | .16 |
| □ 7 David Cooper | .35 | .16 |
| □ 8 Marcel Cousineau | .75 | .35 |
| □ 9 Nathan Dempsey | .50 | .23 |
| □ 10 Mark Deyell | .35 | .16 |
| □ 11 Todd Gillingham | .35 | .16 |
| □ 12 Per Gustafsson | .50 | .23 |
| □ 13 Mike Kennedy | .35 | .16 |
| □ 14 Francis Larivee | .35 | .16 |
| □ 15 Al MacAdam CO | .10 | .05 |
| □ 16 Daniil Markov | .60 | .25 |
| □ 17 Zdenek Markov | .35 | .16 |
| □ 18 Clayton Norris | .35 | .16 |
| □ 19 Warren Norris | .35 | .16 |
| □ 20 Ryan Pepperall | .35 | .16 |
| □ 21 Jason Podoll | .35 | .16 |
| □ 22 D.J. Smith | .50 | .23 |
| □ 23 Greg Smyth | .35 | .16 |
| □ 24 Shawn Thornton | .35 | .16 |
| □ 25 Jeff Ware | .60 | .25 |

## 1988-89 Salt Lake City Golden Eagles

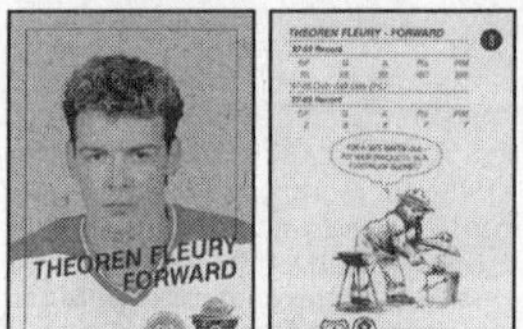


Commemorating the 20th anniversary of the Salt Lake City Golden Eagles, this 24-card standard-size set features color close-up shots against a light blue background. The player's name and position are printed diagonally in black across the front. The set was sponsored by the USDA Forest Service and Utah State Lands and Forestry agency. The backs are white with black print and include player statistics and a fire prevention cartoon starring Smokey the Bear. Card number 10 was never issued.

| | MINT | NRMT |
|---|---|---|
| COMPLETE SET (24) | 20.00 | 9.00 |
| COMMON CARD (1-24) | .50 | .23 |
| □ 1 Rick Barkovich | .50 | .23 |
| □ 2 Michael Dark | .50 | .23 |
| □ 3 Terry Perkins | .50 | .23 |
| □ 4 Peter Lappin | .50 | .23 |
| □ 5 Wayne Cowley | .50 | .23 |
| □ 6 Rich Chernomaz | .75 | .35 |
| □ 7 Steve Smith | .50 | .23 |
| □ 8 Theoren Fleury | 10.00 | 4.50 |
| □ 9 Dave Reierson | .50 | .23 |
| □ 11 Martin Simard | .50 | .23 |
| □ 12 Stu Grimson | 2.00 | .90 |
| □ 13 Darwin McCutcheon | .50 | .23 |
| □ 14 Doug Clarke | .50 | .23 |
| □ 15 Doug Pickell | .50 | .23 |
| □ 16 Randy Bucyk | .50 | .23 |
| □ 17 Jim Johannson | .50 | .23 |
| □ 18 Rick Lessard | .50 | .23 |
| □ 19 Ken Sabourin | .50 | .23 |
| □ 20 Chris Biotti | .50 | .23 |
| □ 21 Jeff Wenaas | .50 | .23 |
| □ 22 Mark Holmes | .50 | .23 |
| □ 23 Bob Bodak | .50 | .23 |
| □ 24 Marc Bureau | 1.00 | .45 |
| □ NNO Cover Card (Smokey the Bear) | .50 | .23 |

## 1992-93 San Diego Gulls

This 24-card standard-size set features full-bleed, color player photos. The player's name is superimposed on the picture in red lettering. The player's position appears in a black circle in the lower left corner. The horizontal backs carry biographical information, statistics, and a player profile. The cards are unnumbered and checklisted below in alphabetical order.

| | MINT | NRMT |
|---|---|---|
| COMPLETE SET (24) | 9.00 | 4.00 |
| COMMON CARD (1-24) | .35 | .16 |
| □ 1 John Anderson | .50 | .23 |
| □ 2 Perry Anderson | .35 | .16 |
| □ 3 Scott Arniel | .50 | .23 |
| □ 4 Michael Brewer | .35 | .16 |
| □ 5 Dale DeGray | .35 | .16 |
| □ 6 Gord Dineen | .35 | .16 |
| □ 7 Rick Dudley CO | .35 | .16 |
| □ 8 Larry Floyd | .35 | .16 |
| □ 9 Keith Gretzky | .75 | .35 |
| □ 10 Peter Hankinson | .35 | .16 |
| □ 11 Bill Houlder | .50 | .23 |
| □ 12 Andrei Iakovenko | .35 | .16 |
| □ 13 Rick Knickle | .50 | .23 |
| □ 14 Denny Lambert | .35 | .16 |
| □ 15 Mitch Lamoureux | .35 | .16 |
| □ 16 Clint Malarchuk | .75 | .35 |
| □ 17 Steve Martinson | .35 | .16 |
| □ 18 Hubie McDonough | .35 | .16 |
| □ 19 Don McSween | .35 | .16 |
| □ 20 Mitch Molloy | .35 | .16 |
| □ 21 Robbie Nichols | .35 | .16 |
| □ 22 Lindy Ruff | .35 | .16 |
| □ 23 Daniel Shank | .50 | .23 |
| □ 24 Sergei Starikov | .35 | .16 |

## 1994-95 Sarnia Sting

Sponsored by Big V Drug Stores and Pizza Hut and printed by Slapshot Images Ltd., this 31-card set commemorates the Sting's inaugural year. On a black and silver background, the fronts feature color action player photos with thin grey borders. The player's name, position and team name, as well as the producer's logo, also appear on the front. The team color-coded backs carry a close-up player portrait and biographical information, along with team and sponsor logos. Included in this set is a Slapshot ad card with a 1995 calendar on the back.

| | MINT | NRMT |
|---|---|---|
| COMPLETE SET (31) | 10.00 | 4.50 |
| COMMON CARD (1-30) | .10 | .05 |
| □ 1 Checklist | .10 | .05 |
| □ 2 Ken Carroll | .50 | .23 |
| □ 3 Scott Hay | .50 | .23 |
| □ 4 Kam White | .35 | .16 |
| □ 5 Joe Doyle | .35 | .16 |
| □ 6 Tom Brown | .50 | .23 |
| □ 7 Jeremy Miculinic | .35 | .16 |
| □ 8 Darren Mortier | .35 | .16 |
| □ 9 Aaron Brand | .50 | .23 |
| □ 10 Chris George | .35 | .16 |
| □ 11 Stephane Soulliere | .35 | .16 |
| □ 12 Paul McInnes | .35 | .16 |
| □ 13 Trevor Letowski | .75 | .35 |
| □ 14 Dustin McArthur | .35 | .16 |
| □ 15 Rob Massa | .35 | .16 |
| □ 16 Brendan Yarema | .35 | .16 |
| □ 17 Dan DelMonte | .50 | .23 |
| □ 18 B.J. Johnston | .35 | .16 |
| □ 19 Wes Mason | .50 | .23 |
| □ 20 Rob Guinn | .35 | .16 |
| □ 21 Jeff Brown | .60 | .25 |
| □ 22 Dennis Maxwell | .35 | .16 |
| □ 23 Damon Hardy | .35 | .16 |
| □ 24 Alan Letang | .35 | .16 |
| □ 25 Matt Hogan | .35 | .16 |
| □ 26 Sasha Cucuz | .35 | .16 |
| □ 27 Rich Brown CO | .10 | .05 |
| □ 28 Gord Hamilton TR | .10 | .05 |
| □ 29 Dino Ciccarelli / Shawn Burr | .75 | .35 |
| □ 30 Buzz (Mascot) | .10 | .05 |
| □ NNO Ad Card | .10 | .05 |

## 1996-97 Sarnia Sting

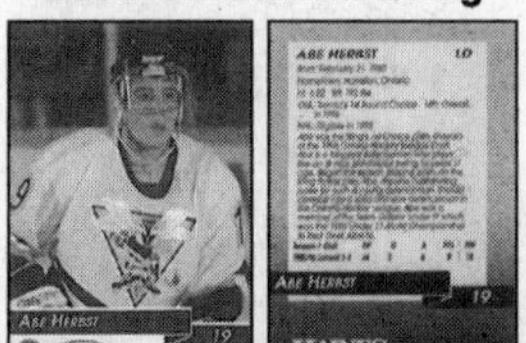


This attractive 31-card set was produced by Haines Printing for the Sting and was distributed by the club at the rink. The cards feature action photography on the front, with the player's name and number, and the insignia of the sponsor, Bayview Chrysler, along the bottom. The backs feature comprehensive personal and statistical information. The set is noteworthy for the inclusion of Patrick DesRochers, expected to be a high pick in '98, and a special card of captain Trevor Letowski as a member of the Canadian National Junior team.

| | MINT | NRMT |
|---|---|---|
| COMPLETE SET (31) | 10.00 | 4.50 |
| COMMON CARD (1-31) | .10 | .05 |
| □ 1 Bill Abercrombie ACO | .10 | .05 |
| □ 2 Louie Blackbird | .50 | .23 |
| □ 3 Bryan Blair | .35 | .16 |
| □ 4 Dave Bourque | .35 | .16 |
| □ 5 Joe Canale CO | .35 | .16 |
| □ 6 Scott Corbett | .35 | .16 |
| □ 7 Andy Delmore | .50 | .23 |
| □ 8 Patrick DesRochers | 1.50 | .70 |
| □ 9 Michael Hanson | .35 | .16 |
| □ 10 Abe Herbst | .50 | .23 |
| □ 11 Shane Kenny | .50 | .23 |
| □ 12 Darryl Knight | .35 | .16 |
| □ 13 Trevor Letowski | .75 | .35 |
| □ 14 Trevor Letowski Team Canada | 1.00 | .45 |
| □ 15 Wes Mason | .75 | .35 |
| □ 16 Darren Mortier | .35 | .16 |
| □ 17 Kevin Mota | .35 | .16 |
| □ 18 Eoin McInerney | .50 | .23 |
| □ 19 Lucas Nehrling | .50 | .23 |
| □ 20 Dan Pawlaczyk | .35 | .16 |
| □ 21 Andrew Proskurnicki | .35 | .16 |
| □ 22 Richard Rochefort | .35 | .16 |
| □ 23 Bogdan Rudenko | .35 | .16 |
| □ 24 Jon Sim | .50 | .23 |
| □ 25 Brad Simms | .35 | .16 |
| □ 26 Marcin Snita | .35 | .16 |
| □ 27 Casey Wolak | .35 | .16 |
| □ 28 Season Line-Up | .10 | .05 |
| □ 29 Title Card | .10 | .05 |
| □ 30 Team Logo | .10 | .05 |
| □ 31 Calendar Card | .10 | .05 |

## 1981-82 Saskatoon Blades

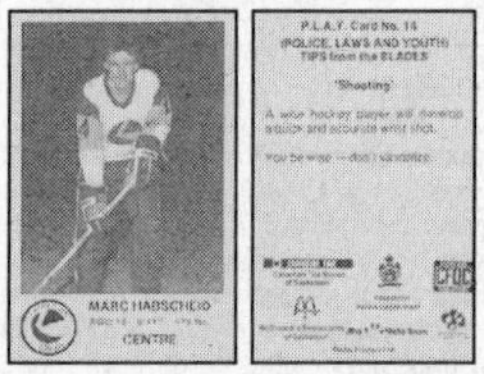


This 25-card P.L.A.Y. (Police, Laws and Youth) set was sponsored by the Saskatoon Police Department and area businesses. The cards measure approximately 2 1/2" by 3 3/4" and are printed on thin card stock. The fronts feature white-bordered color photos with the player's posed in action stances. The player's name, biographical information, and position appear in the bottom white margin. The team logo appears in the lower left corner. The backs carry public service messages in the form of "Tips from the Blades." Sponsor logos appear at the bottom.

| | NRMT-MT | EXC |
|---|---|---|
| COMPLETE SET (25) | 15.00 | 6.75 |
| COMMON CARD (1-25) | .50 | .23 |
| □ 1 Blades Team Photo | 2.00 | .90 |
| □ 2 Daryl Stanley | .75 | .35 |
| □ 3 Leroy Gorski | .75 | .35 |
| □ 4 Donn Clark | .75 | .35 |
| □ 5 Brad Duggan | .75 | .35 |
| □ 6 Dave Chartier | .75 | .35 |
| □ 7 Dave Brown | 1.50 | .70 |
| □ 8 Adam Thompson | .75 | .35 |
| □ 9 Bruce Eakin | .75 | .35 |
| □ 10 Brian Skrudland | 4.00 | 1.80 |
| □ 11 Roger Kortko | .75 | .35 |
| □ 12 Ron Dreger | .75 | .35 |
| □ 13 Daryl Lubiniecki | .75 | .35 |
| □ 14 Marc Habscheid | 1.00 | .45 |
| □ 15 Saskatoon Police Logo | .50 | .23 |
| □ 16 Todd Strueby | .75 | .35 |
| □ 17 Craig Hurley | .75 | .35 |
| □ 18 Bill Hlynsky | .75 | .35 |
| □ 19 Lane Lambert | 1.00 | .45 |
| □ 20 Mike Bloski | .75 | .35 |
| □ 21 Bruce Gordon | .75 | .35 |
| □ 22 Perry Ganchar | .75 | .35 |
| □ 23 Ron Loustel | .75 | .35 |
| □ 24 Blades Logo | .50 | .23 |
| □ 25 Checklist Card | .50 | .23 |

## 1983-84 Saskatoon Blades

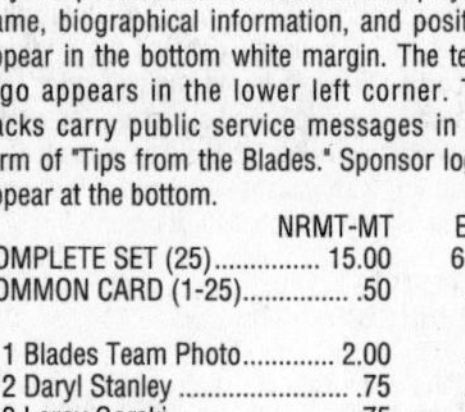


This set contains 24 P.L.A.Y. (Police, Law and Youth) cards and features the Saskatoon Blades of the Western Hockey League. The cards measure approximately 2 7/16" by 3 3/4". The fronts feature a color posed action shot with white borders. The team logo appears in the lower left corner, with player information to the right in black lettering. The backs have sponsors' logos at the bottom and "Tips from the Blades," which consist of definitions of hockey terms paralleled by public service or anti-crime messages.

| | MINT | NRMT |
|---|---|---|
| COMPLETE SET (24) | 30.00 | 13.50 |
| COMMON CARD (1-24) | .50 | .23 |
| □ 1 Team Photo | 1.00 | .45 |
| □ 2 Trent Yawney | 1.50 | .70 |
| □ 3 Grant Jennings | 1.50 | .70 |
| □ 4 Duncan MacPherson | .75 | .35 |
| □ 5 Greg Holtby | .75 | .35 |
| □ 6 Dan Leier | .75 | .35 |
| □ 7 Dwaine Hutton | .75 | .35 |
| □ 8 Wendel Clark | 15.00 | 6.75 |
| □ 9 Kerry Laviolette | .75 | .35 |
| □ 10 Dave Chartier | .75 | .35 |
| □ 11 Dale Henry | .75 | .35 |
| □ 12 Randy Smith | .75 | .35 |
| □ 13 Kevin Kowalchuk | .75 | .35 |
| □ 14 Todd McLellan | .75 | .35 |
| □ 15 Title Card Saskatoon Police | .50 | .23 |
| □ 16 Larry Korchinkski | .75 | .35 |
| □ 17 Curtis Chamberlin | .75 | .35 |
| □ 18 Greg Lebsack | .75 | .35 |
| □ 19 Ron Dreger | .75 | .35 |
| □ 20 Doug Kyle | .75 | .35 |
| □ 21 Rick Smith | .75 | .35 |
| □ 22 Joey Kocur | 4.00 | 1.80 |
| □ 23 Allan Larochelle | .75 | .35 |
| □ 24 Mark Thietke | .75 | .35 |

## 1984-85 Saskatoon Blades Stickers

This set of 20 stickers was sponsored by Autotec Oil and Saskatchewan Ronald McDonald House. Each sticker measures approximately 2" by 1 3/4" and could be pasted on a 17" by 11" poster printed in thin glossy paper. The stickers display a black-and-white head shot; the uniform number is also printed on the front. The stickers are unnumbered and checklisted below in alphabetical order.

| | MINT | NRMT |
|---|---|---|
| COMPLETE SET (20) | 25.00 | 11.00 |
| COMMON CARD (1-20) | 1.00 | .45 |
| □ 1 Jack Bowkus | 1.00 | .45 |
| □ 2 Curtis Chamberlain | 1.00 | .45 |
| □ 3 Wendel Clark | 10.00 | 4.50 |
| □ 4 Ron Dreger | 1.00 | .45 |
| □ 5 Randy Hoffart | 1.00 | .45 |
| □ 6 Mark Holick | 1.00 | .45 |
| □ 7 Greg Holtby | 1.00 | .45 |
| □ 8 Grant Jennings | 1.50 | .70 |
| □ 9 Kevin Kowalchuk | 1.00 | .45 |
| □ 10 Bryan Larkin | 1.00 | .45 |
| □ 11 James Latos | 1.00 | .45 |
| □ 12 Duncan MacPherson | 1.00 | .45 |
| □ 13 Rod Matechuk | 1.00 | .45 |
| □ 14 Todd McLellan | 1.00 | .45 |
| □ 15 Darren Moren | 1.00 | .45 |
| □ 16 Mike Morin | 1.00 | .45 |
| □ 17 Devon Oleniuk | 1.00 | .45 |
| □ 18 Grant Tkachuk | 1.00 | .45 |
| □ 19 Troy Vollhoffer | 1.00 | .45 |
| □ 20 Trent Yawney | 1.50 | .70 |

## 1988-89 Saskatoon Blades

This standard size set features posed color photos on the front, and safety tips and logos on the back. Cards are numbered as seen below.

| | MINT | NRMT |
|---|---|---|
| COMPLETE SET (25) | 10.00 | 4.50 |
| COMMON CARD (1-25) | .20 | .09 |
| □ 1 Joe Penkala | .50 | .23 |
| □ 2 Saskatoon Police Emblem | .20 | .09 |
| □ 3 Marcel Comeau | .50 | .23 |
| □ 4 Dean Kuntz | .50 | .23 |
| □ 5 Mike Greenlay | .50 | .23 |
| □ 6 Jody Praznik | .50 | .23 |
| □ 7 Ken Sutton | .50 | .23 |
| □ 8 Sawn Snesar | .50 | .23 |
| □ 9 Shane Langager | .50 | .23 |
| □ 10 Dean Holdien | .50 | .23 |
| □ 11 Rob Lelacheur | .50 | .23 |
| □ 12 David Struch | .50 | .23 |
| □ 13 Collin Bauer | .50 | .23 |
| □ 14 Kevin Yellowaga | .50 | .23 |

❑ 15 Drew Sawtell .50 .23
❑ 16 Brian Gerrits .50 .23
❑ 17 Kirk Roworth .50 .23
❑ 18 Tracey Katelnikoff .50 .23
❑ 19 Scott Scissons .75 .35
❑ 20 Jason Smart .50 .23
❑ 21 Jason Christie .50 .23
❑ 22 Daren Bader .50 .23
❑ 23 Kevin Kaminski .50 .23
❑ 24 Kory Kocur .50 .23
❑ 25 Darwin McPherson .50 .23

## 1989-90 Saskatoon Blades

| | MINT | NRMT |
|---|---|---|
| COMPLETE SET (25) | 10.00 | 4.50 |
| COMMON CARD (1-25) | .50 | .23 |

❑ 1 Terry Ruskowski .50 .23
❑ 2 Cam Moon .50 .23
❑ 3 Damon Kustra .50 .23
❑ 4 Trevor Robins .50 .23
❑ 5 Mark Raiter .50 .23
❑ 6 Mark Wotton .75 .35
❑ 7 Shawn Snesar .50 .23
❑ 8 Trevor Sherban .50 .23
❑ 9 Shane Langager .50 .23
❑ 10 Dean Holdien .50 .23
❑ 11 Rob Lelacheur .50 .23
❑ 12 David Struch .50 .23
❑ 13 Derek Tibbatts .50 .23
❑ 14 Drew Sawtell .50 .23
❑ 15 Richard Matvichuk .75 .35
❑ 16 Trent Coghill .50 .23
❑ 17 Jeff Buchanan .50 .23
❑ 18 Grant Chorney .50 .23
❑ 19 Shawn Yakimishyn .50 .23
❑ 20 Scott Scissons .50 .23
❑ 21 Jason Smart .50 .23
❑ 22 Jason Christie .50 .23
❑ 23 Darin Bader .50 .23
❑ 24 Dean Rambo .50 .23
❑ 25 Collin Bauer .50 .23

## 1990-91 Saskatoon Blades

This 27-card P.L.A.Y. (Police, Laws and Youth) set was sponsored by the Saskatoon Police Department and area businesses. The cards measure approximately 2 1/2" by 3 3/4" and are printed on thin card stock. On a blue card face, the fronts feature white-bordered posed action color photos. The player's name, position, and biographical information appear in the bottom blue margin. The yellow and blue team logo apppears in the lower right corner. The backs carry public service messages. Biographical player information and sponsor logos are printed at the bottom.

| | MINT | NRMT |
|---|---|---|
| COMPLETE SET (27) | 12.00 | 5.50 |
| COMMON CARD (1-27) | .50 | .23 |

❑ 1 Terry Ruskowski CO .60 .25
❑ 2 Trevor Robins .50 .23
❑ 3 Cam Moon .50 .23
❑ 4 Jeff Buchanan .50 .23
❑ 5 Mark Raiter .50 .23
❑ 6 Trevor Sherban .50 .23
❑ 7 Jason Knox .50 .23
❑ 8 Dean Rambo .50 .23
❑ 9 Rob LeLacheur .50 .23
❑ 10 David Struch .50 .23
❑ 11 Greg Leahy .50 .23
❑ 12 Derek Tibbatts .50 .23
❑ 13 Shane Calder .50 .23
❑ 14 Richard Matvichuk 1.00 .45
❑ 15 Trent Coghill .50 .23
❑ 16 Mark Wotton 1.00 .45
❑ 17 Kelly Markwart .50 .23
❑ 18 Mark Franks .50 .23
❑ 19 Scott Scissons .50 .23
❑ 20 Tim Cox .50 .23
❑ 21 Gaetan Blouin .50 .23
❑ 22 Darin Bader .50 .23
❑ 23 Shawn Yakimishyn .50 .23
❑ 24 Ryan Strain .50 .23
❑ 25 Jason Peters .50 .23
❑ 26 Team Card .50 .23
❑ 27 Title Card .50 .23

## 1991-92 Saskatoon Blades

This 25-card P.L.A.Y. (Police, Laws and Youth) set was issued as a sheet measuring approximately 12 1/2" by 17 1/2", with five rows of five cards each. If cut, the individual

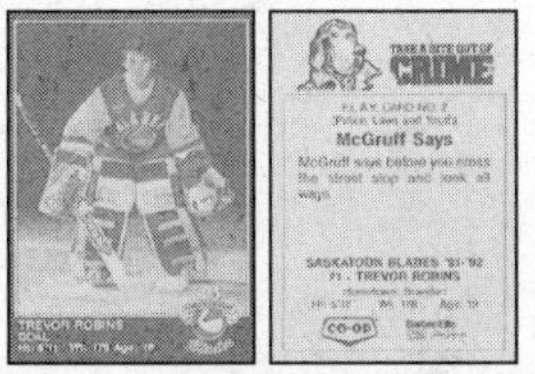

cards would measure the standard size. On a black card face, the fronts feature posed color player photos with thin white borders. The player's name and biography along with the team's 25th anniversary logo appear below the picture. The backs carry a safety tip, biography, and sponsor logos. The cards are numbered on the back.

| | MINT | NRMT |
|---|---|---|
| COMPLETE SET (25) | 12.00 | 5.50 |
| COMMON CARD (1-24) | .10 | .05 |

❑ 1 Lorne Molleken CO .25 .11
❑ 2 Trevor Robins .50 .23
❑ 3 Norm Maracle .75 .35
❑ 4 Jeff Buchanan .50 .23
❑ 5 Mark Raiter .50 .23
❑ 6 Bryce Goebel .50 .23
❑ 7 Rhett Trombley .75 .35
❑ 8 Chad Rusnak .50 .23
❑ 9 Jason Knight .50 .23
❑ 10 David Struch .50 .23
❑ 11 Shane Calder .50 .23
❑ 12 Derek Tibbatts .50 .23
❑ 13 Glen Gulutzan .50 .23
❑ 14 Richard Matvichuk 1.00 .45
❑ 15 Chad Michalchuk .50 .23
❑ 16 Mark Wotton .75 .35
❑ 17 Mark Franks .50 .23
❑ 18 Andy MacIntyre .50 .23
❑ 19 Ryan Fujita .50 .23
❑ 20 Sean McFatridge .50 .23
❑ 21 Jason Becker .50 .23
❑ 22 Shawn Yakimishyn .50 .23
❑ 23 James Startup .50 .23
❑ 24 Paul Buczkowski .50 .23
❑ NNO McGruff .10 .05

## 1993-94 Saskatoon Blades

Sponsored by Coca-Cola, this is an oversized 24-card set measuring approximately 8 1/2" by 5 1/2". The borderless fronts feature posed color player photos on the ice surrounded by a Coca-Cola advertising display. The player's name and number in black letters appear in the lower left corner. The words "Best on Ice - Blades and Coca-Cola" are printed over the top of the photo in red, white, and blue. The backs are blank. The cards are unnumbered and checklisted below in alphabetical order.

| | MINT | NRMT |
|---|---|---|
| COMPLETE SET (24) | 14.00 | 6.25 |
| COMMON CARD (1-24) | .50 | .23 |

❑ 1 Chad Allan .75 .35
❑ 2 Frank Banham .75 .35
❑ 3 Frank Banham .75 .35
Mark Deyell
Ivan Salon
❑ 4 Wade Belak 1.50 .70
❑ 5 Paul Buczkowski .50 .23
❑ 6 Shane Calder .60 .25
❑ 7 Mark Deyell 1.00 .45
❑ 8 Jason Duda .50 .23
❑ 9 Trevor Ethier .50 .23
❑ 10 Mike Gray .50 .23
❑ 11 Trevor Hanas .50 .23
❑ 12 Devon Hanson .50 .23
❑ 13 Andrew Kemper .50 .23
❑ 14 Kirby Law .50 .23
❑ 15 Andy Macintyre .50 .23
❑ 16 Norm Maracle .75 .35
❑ 17 Ivan Salon .50 .23
❑ 18 Todd Simpson .50 .23
❑ 19 Derek Tibbatts .50 .23
❑ 20 Derek Tibbatts .50 .23
Clarke Wilm
Andy Macintyre
❑ 21 Rhett Warrener 1.00 .45
❑ 22 Clarke Wilm .50 .23
❑ 23 Mark Wotton .75 .35
❑ 24 Team Photo .50 .23

## 1995-96 Saskatoon Blades

The 27 oversized (2 1/2" by 4 1/2") cards set

feature the Saskatoon Blades of the WHL. Apparently, the cards were issued as a promotional giveaway at PW Pharmacies in Saskatoon. The front displays a color action photo, along with the player's name and number and the Blades logo. A Carlton cards logo appears in the upper right. The backs contain biographical information as well as the logos of all participating sponsors. Complete cards also included a coupon for savings on various products at PW. The cards are worth 50 percent of the value below without the coupon. The cards are unnumbered and thus are checklisted below in alphabetical order.

| | MINT | NRMT |
|---|---|---|
| COMPLETE SET (27) | 14.00 | 6.25 |
| COMMON CARD (1-27) | .10 | .05 |

❑ 1 Chad Allan .75 .35
❑ 2 Frank Banham .75 .35
❑ 3 Dennis Bassett .75 .35
❑ 4 Wade Belak 1.00 .45
❑ 5 Ryan Bonni .75 .35
❑ 6 Paul Buczkowski .50 .23
❑ 7 Don Clark CO .50 .23
❑ 8 Mattieu Cusson .50 .23
❑ 9 Mark Deyell 1.00 .45
❑ 10 Pavel Kriz .75 .35
❑ 11 Jeromie Kufflick .50 .23
❑ 12 Laird Laluk .50 .23
❑ 13 Erik Leefe .50 .23
❑ 14 Richard Peacock .75 .35
❑ 15 Greg Phillips .50 .23
❑ 16 Garrett Prosofsky .60 .25
❑ 17 Nathan Rempel .50 .23
❑ 18 Cory Sarich 1.00 .45
❑ 19 Jeremy Schaefer .50 .23
❑ 20 Mark Smith .50 .23
❑ 21 Martin Sonnenberg .50 .23
❑ 22 Randy Weinberger .50 .23
❑ 23 Clark Wilm .50 .23
❑ 24 Team Logo CL .10 .05
❑ 25 Crime Stoppers Logo .10 .05
❑ 26 Celebration 30 Years .10 .05
❑ 27 Assistant Coaches .10 .05
Chartier
Engele
Federke

## 1996-97 Saskatoon Blades

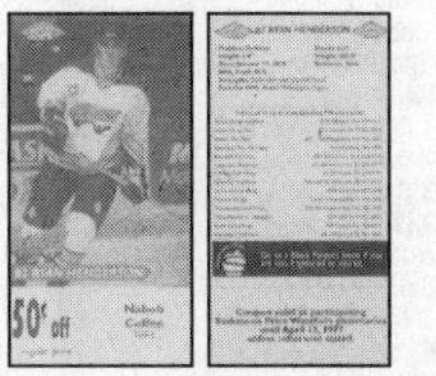

This set of the Saskatoon Blades features 28 oversized (2 1/2" X 4 1/2") cards. The fronts display color photos, with the player's name, jersey number and Blades logo inscribed along the bottom. The backs feature biographical data, a safety tip, and the locations of every PW Pharmacy in Saskatoon. PW sponsored the set as a promotional giveaway at local stores. Interestingly, the backs exhort fans to collect all 27 cards, but the set contains 28. The cards come attached to money-saving coupons from PW; if the coupon is removed, the value is 50 percent that listed below. The unnumbered cards are checklisted below alphabetically.

| | MINT | NRMT |
|---|---|---|
| COMPLETE SET (28) | 12.00 | 5.50 |
| COMMON CARD (1-28) | .25 | .11 |

❑ 1 Stewart Bacharuk .40 .18
❑ 2 Jon Barkman .40 .18
❑ 3 Justin Bekkering .40 .18
❑ 4 Derek Bjornson .40 .18
❑ 5 Ryan Bonni 1.00 .45
❑ 6 Christian Chartier .40 .18
❑ 7 Matt Cockell .75 .35
❑ 8 Mathieu Cusson .40 .18
❑ 9 Jared Dumba .60 .25
❑ 10 Ryan Gaucher .40 .18
❑ 11 Ryan Henderson .40 .18
❑ 12 Ryan Johnston .40 .18
❑ 13 Vladislav Klochkov .40 .18
❑ 14 Laird Laluk .40 .18
❑ 15 Tyler Love .75 .35
❑ 16 Sheldon Nedielski .40 .18
❑ 17 Greg Phillips .40 .18
❑ 18 Garrett Prosofsky .75 .35
❑ 19 Nathan Rempel .40 .18
❑ 20 Cory Sarich 1.00 .45
❑ 21 Brian Skrudland .75 .35
❑ 22 Martin Sonnenberg .40 .18
❑ 23 Lyle Steenbergen .40 .18
❑ 24 Rhett Warrener .75 .35
❑ 25 Kyle Werner .40 .18
❑ 26 Team Logo CL .25 .11
❑ 27 Action/Goal .25 .11
❑ 28 Team(Reebok) .25 .11

## 1980-81 Sault Ste. Marie Greyhounds

Sponsored by Blue Bird Bakery Limited and Coke, this 25-card set captures the 1980-81 Soo Greyhounds of the OHL. The cards measure approximately 2 1/2" by 4" and feature posed, color player photos. Of interest to collectors are the first cards of current NHL stars John Vanbiesbrouck and Ron Francis.

| | NRMT-MT | EXC |
|---|---|---|
| COMPLETE SET (25) | 80.00 | 36.00 |
| COMMON CARD (1-25) | .50 | .23 |

❑ 1 Ken Porteous .75 .35
❑ 2 Brian Petterle .75 .35
❑ 3 Gord Dineen 1.00 .45
❑ 4 Tony Cella .75 .35
❑ 5 Doug Shedden 1.50 .70
❑ 6 Terry Tait .75 .35
❑ 7 Greyhounds Logo .50 .23
❑ 8 Steve Smith .75 .35
❑ 9 Huey Larkin .75 .35
❑ 10 Steve Gatzos .75 .35
❑ 11 Tim Zwijack .75 .35
❑ 12 Vic Morin .75 .35
❑ 13 John Vanbiesbrouck 30.00 13.50
❑ 14 Ron Francis 25.00 11.00
❑ 15 Tony Butorac .75 .35
❑ 16 John Goodwin .75 .35
❑ 17 Ron Handy .75 .35
❑ 18 Jim Pavese 1.00 .45
❑ 19 Sault Ste. Marie .50 .23
Police Logo
❑ 20 Rick Morocco .75 .35
❑ 21 Ken Latta .75 .35
❑ 22 Kirk Rueter .75 .35
❑ 23 OMJHL Logo .50 .23
❑ 24 Terry Crisp 2.50 1.10
❑ 25 Marc D'Amour 1.00 .45

## 1981-82 Sault Ste. Marie Greyhounds

Sponsored by Blue Bird Bakery Limited, Coke, 920 CKCY radio, and Canadian Tire, this 28-card set measures approximately 2 1/8" by 4 1/8" and features posed, color player photos with white borders. The player's name is printed in white on the picture, above the player's head. His position and the team name are printed in fuchsia at the bottom. The backs display biographical information, statistics, and sponsor logos. The cards are unnumbered and checklisted below in alphabetical order. This set contains early cards of Rick Tocchet, John Vanbiesbrouck and Ron Francis.

| | NRMT-MT | EXC |
|---|---|---|
| COMPLETE SET (28) | 65.00 | 29.00 |
| COMMON CARD (1-28) | .50 | .23 |

❑ 1 Jim Aldred .75 .35
❑ 2 Dave Andreoli .75 .35
❑ 3 Richard Beaulne .75 .35
❑ 4 Bruce Bell .75 .35
❑ 5 Chuck Brimmer .75 .35
❑ 6 Tony Cella .75 .35
❑ 7 Kevin Conway .75 .35
❑ 8 Terry Crisp CO 2.00 .90
❑ 9 Marc D'Amour 1.00 .45
❑ 10 Gord Dineen 1.00 .45
❑ 11 Chris Felix 1.00 .45
❑ 12 Ron Francis 20.00 9.00
❑ 13 Steve Graves .75 .35
❑ 14 Wayne Groulx .75 .35
❑ 15 Huey Larkin .75 .35
❑ 16 Ken Latta .75 .35
❑ 17 Mike Lococo .75 .35
❑ 18 Jim Pavese 1.00 .45
❑ 19 Dirk Rueter .75 .35
❑ 20 Steve Smith .75 .35
❑ 21 Terry Tait .75 .35
❑ 22 Rick Tocchet 15.00 6.75
❑ 23 John Vanbiesbrouck 20.00 9.00
❑ 24 Harry Wolfe ANN .50 .23
❑ 25 J.D. Yari .50 .23
❑ 26 Bluebird Bakery .50 .23
Limited Logo
❑ 27 Canadian Tire Logo .50 .23
❑ 28 Coca-Cola Ad .50 .23

## 1982-83 Sault Ste. Marie Greyhounds

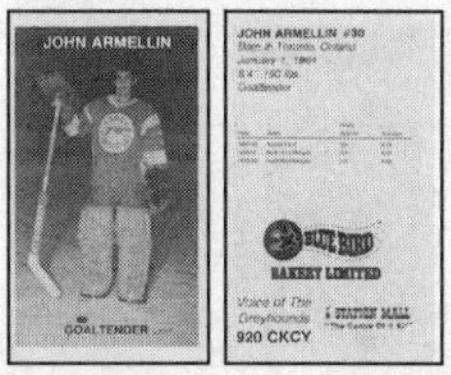

Sponsored by Blue Bird Bakery Limited and 920 CKCY radio station, this 25-card set measures approximately 2 1/2" by 4" and feature color, posed player photos with white borders. The player's name is superimposed on the photo in white lettering. His position is in black at the bottom. The backs carry biographical information, statistics, and sponsor logos. The cards are unnumbered and checklisted below in alphabetical order.

| | MINT | EXC |
|---|---|---|
| COMPLETE SET (25) | 40.00 | 18.00 |
| COMMON CARD (1-25) | .25 | .11 |

❑ 1 Jim Aldred .75 .35
❑ 2 John Armelin .75 .35
❑ 3 Richard Beaulne .75 .35
❑ 4 Jeff Beukeboom 2.00 .90
❑ 5 Tony Cella .75 .35
❑ 6 Kevin Conway .75 .35
❑ 7 Terry Crisp 1.50 .70
❑ 8 Chris Felix .75 .35
❑ 9 Steve Graves .75 .35
❑ 10 Gus Greco .75 .35
❑ 11 Wayne Groulx .75 .35
❑ 12 Sam Haidy .75 .35
❑ 13 Tim Hoover .75 .35
❑ 14 Pat Lahey .75 .35
❑ 15 Huey Larkin .75 .35
❑ 16 Mike Lococo .75 .35
❑ 17 Mike Neill .75 .35
❑ 18 Ken Sabourin .75 .35
❑ 19 Steve Smith .75 .35
❑ 20 Terry Tait .75 .35
❑ 21 Rick Tocchet 10.00 4.50
❑ 22 John Vanbiesbrouck 20.00 9.00
❑ 23 Harry Wolfe ANN .50 .23
❑ 24 Station Mall Sponsor .25 .11
❑ 25 Bluebird Bakery Ltd. .25 .11

## 1983-84 Sault Ste. Marie Greyhounds

Sponsored by 920 CKCY radio, Coke, and IGA, the cards in this 25-card set measure approximately 2 1/2" by 4" and feature color, posed player photos with white borders. The player's name appears in an orange bar at the bottom of the picture. The backs carry biographical information, statistics, and sponsor logos. The cards are unnumbered and checklisted below in alphabetical order.

| | MINT | NRMT |
|---|---|---|
| COMPLETE SET (25) | 20.00 | 9.00 |
| COMMON CARD (1-25) | .50 | .23 |

❑ 1 Jeff Beukeboom 2.00 .90
❑ 2 Graeme Bonar .75 .35
❑ 3 Chris Brant .75 .35
❑ 4 John English .75 .35
❑ 5 Chris Felix 1.00 .45
❑ 6 Rick Fera .75 .35
❑ 7 Marc Fournier .75 .35
❑ 8 Steve Graves .75 .35
❑ 9 Gus Greco .75 .35
❑ 10 Wayne Groulx .75 .35
❑ 11 Sam Haidy .75 .35
❑ 12 Tim Hoover .75 .35
❑ 13 Jerry Iuliano .75 .35
❑ 14 Pat Lahey .75 .35
❑ 15 Mike Lococo .75 .35
❑ 16 Jean-Marc MacKenzie .75 .35
❑ 17 Mike Oliverio .75 .35
❑ 18 Brit Peer .75 .35
❑ 19 Joey Rampton .75 .35
❑ 20 Ken Sabourin 1.00 .45
❑ 21 Jim Samec .75 .35
❑ 22 Rick Tocchet 8.00 3.60
❑ 23 Harry Wolfe ANN .50 .23
❑ 24 IGA Sponsor Card .50 .23
❑ 25 Coke Sponsor Card .50 .23

## 1984-85 Sault Ste. Marie Greyhounds

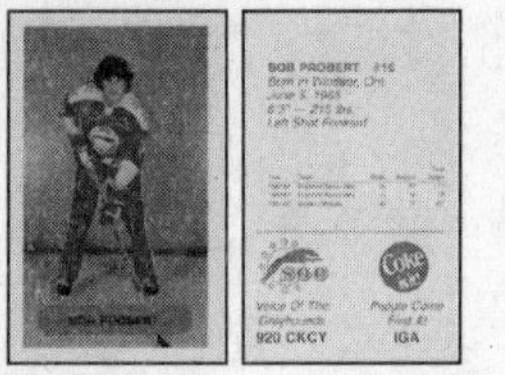

Sponsored by 920 CKCY radio, Coke, and IGA, this 25-card set measures approximately 2 1/2" by 4" and features white-bordered, posed, color photos of the players on ice with a blue studio background. The player's name appears on a bright red plaque near the bottom. The backs carry biographical information, statistics, and sponsor logos. The cards are unnumbered and checklisted below in alphabetical order.

| | MINT | NRMT |
|---|---|---|
| COMPLETE SET (25) | 15.00 | 6.75 |
| COMMON CARD (1-25) | .50 | .23 |
| ❑ 1 Marty Abrams | .50 | .23 |
| ❑ 2 Jeff Beukeboom | 1.50 | .70 |
| ❑ 3 Graeme Bonar | .50 | .23 |
| ❑ 4 Chris Brant | .50 | .23 |
| ❑ 5 Terry Crisp CO | 1.00 | .45 |
| ❑ 6 Chris Felix | .75 | .35 |
| ❑ 7 Scott Green | .50 | .23 |
| ❑ 8 Wayne Groulx | .50 | .23 |
| ❑ 9 Steve Hollett | .50 | .23 |
| ❑ 10 Tim Hoover | .50 | .23 |
| ❑ 11 Derek King | 2.50 | 1.10 |
| ❑ 12 Tyler Larter | .50 | .23 |
| ❑ 13 Jean-Marc MacKenzie | .50 | .23 |
| ❑ 14 Scott Mosey | .50 | .23 |
| ❑ 15 Mike Oliverio | .50 | .23 |
| ❑ 16 Brit Peer | .50 | .23 |
| ❑ 17 Wayne Presley | 1.00 | .45 |
| ❑ 18 Bob Probert | 6.00 | 2.70 |
| ❑ 19 Brian Rome | .50 | .23 |
| ❑ 20 Ken Sabourin | .75 | .35 |
| ❑ 21 Rob Veccia | .50 | .23 |
| ❑ 22 Harry Wolfe ANN | .25 | .11 |
| ❑ 23 Rob Zettler | 1.50 | .70 |
| ❑ 24 IGA Ad | .25 | .11 |
| ❑ 25 Coca-Cola Ad | .25 | .11 |

## 1987-88 Sault Ste. Marie Greyhounds

Printed on thin card stock, this 35-card set features players from the 1987-88 season of the Sault Ste. Marie Greyhounds and also past Greyhounds players who have gone on to NHL fame, such as Wayne Gretzky. The fronts feature white-bordered posed-on-ice color player photos. The player's name appears in white lettering near the top; his position and the team name appear in blue lettering near the bottom. The white back carries a hockey tip and a safety tip. Multiple sponsor logos at the bottom round out the back.

| | MINT | NRMT |
|---|---|---|
| COMPLETE SET (35) | 110.00 | 50.00 |
| COMMON CARD (1-35) | .25 | .11 |
| ❑ 1 Barry King | .25 | .11 |
| Chief of Police | | |
| ❑ 2 Dan Currie | .75 | .35 |
| ❑ 3 Mike Glover | .75 | .35 |
| ❑ 4 Tyler Larter | .75 | .35 |
| ❑ 5 Bob Jones | .75 | .35 |
| ❑ 6 Lyndon Slewidge | .25 | .11 |
| National Anthem Singer | | |
| ❑ 7 Brad Jones | .75 | .35 |
| ❑ 8 Ron Francis | 7.00 | 3.10 |
| ❑ 9 Dale Turnbull | .75 | .35 |
| ❑ 10 Don McConnell | .75 | .35 |
| ❑ 11 Chris Felix | .75 | .35 |
| ❑ 12 Steve Udvari | .75 | .35 |
| ❑ 13 Shawn Simpson | 1.00 | .45 |
| ❑ 14 Rob Zettler | 1.00 | .45 |
| ❑ 15 Phil Esposito | 10.00 | 4.50 |
| Co-owner | | |
| ❑ 16 John Vanbiesbrouck | 15.00 | 6.75 |
| ❑ 17 Mike Oliverio | .75 | .35 |
| ❑ 18 Colin Ford | .75 | .35 |
| ❑ 19 Steve Herniman | .75 | .35 |
| ❑ 20 Troy Mallette | 1.00 | .45 |
| ❑ 21 Craig Hartsburg | 2.00 | .90 |
| ❑ 22 Don Boyd CO/GM | .25 | .11 |
| ❑ 23 Peter Fiorentino | .75 | .35 |
| ❑ 24 Jeff Columbus | .75 | .35 |
| ❑ 25 Brad Stepan | .75 | .35 |
| ❑ 26 Rick Tocchet | 5.00 | 2.20 |
| ❑ 27 Shane Sargant | .75 | .35 |
| ❑ 28 Wayne Muir | .75 | .35 |
| ❑ 29 Wayne Gretzky | 100.00 | 45.00 |
| ❑ 30 Gary Luther | .75 | .35 |
| ❑ 31 Harry Wolfe ANN | .25 | .11 |
| ❑ 32 Rod Thacker | .75 | .35 |
| ❑ 33 Coaches Card | .25 | .11 |
| Terry Tait | | |
| Ted Nolan | | |
| Mark Pavoni | | |
| ❑ 34 Brian Hoard | .75 | .35 |
| ❑ 35 Glen Johnston | .75 | .35 |

## 1989-90 Sault Ste. Marie Greyhounds

This 30-card P.L.A.Y. (Police, Law and Youth) set measures 2 3/4" by 3 1/2". The fronts feature posed on-ice player photos with black and white borders. The player's name and number appear on the bottom. The backs carry sponsor logos at the bottom and "Tips from the Hounds."

| | MINT | NRMT |
|---|---|---|
| COMPLETE SET (30) | 15.00 | 6.75 |
| COMMON CARD (1-30) | .25 | .11 |
| ❑ 1 Barry King CL | .25 | .11 |
| Chief of Police | | |
| ❑ 2 Sault Ste. Marie | .25 | .11 |
| Police Logo | | |
| ❑ 3 Ted Nolan CO | 1.00 | .45 |
| ❑ 4 Team Logo | .50 | .23 |
| ❑ 5 Sherry Bassin GM | .50 | .23 |
| ❑ 6 Jim Ritchie | .50 | .23 |
| ❑ 7 Bob Boughner | .75 | .35 |
| ❑ 8 Denny Lambert | .75 | .35 |
| ❑ 9 Doug Minor | .50 | .23 |
| ❑ 10 Rick Pracey | .50 | .23 |
| ❑ 11 Colin Miller | .50 | .23 |
| ❑ 12 Kevin King | .50 | .23 |
| ❑ 13 Ron Francis | 5.00 | 2.20 |
| ❑ 14 Rick Kowalsky | .50 | .23 |
| ❑ 15 Adam Foote | 1.00 | .45 |
| ❑ 16 Wade Whitten | .50 | .23 |
| ❑ 17 Dale Turnbull | .50 | .23 |
| ❑ 18 Bob Jones | .50 | .23 |
| ❑ 19 David Carrie | .50 | .23 |
| ❑ 20 Brad Tiley | .75 | .35 |
| ❑ 21 Wayne Muir | .50 | .23 |
| ❑ 22 Dave Babcock | .50 | .23 |
| ❑ 23 David Matsos | .50 | .23 |
| ❑ 24 Dan Ferguson | .50 | .23 |
| ❑ 25 Jeff Szeryk | .50 | .23 |
| ❑ 26 Mike Zuke ACO | .25 | .11 |
| ❑ 27 Dave Doucette | .50 | .23 |
| ❑ 28 John Campbell | .25 | .11 |
| Constable | | |
| ❑ 29 Graeme Harvey | .50 | .23 |
| ❑ 30 John Fuselli ACO | .25 | .11 |

## 1993-94 Sault Ste. Marie Greyhounds

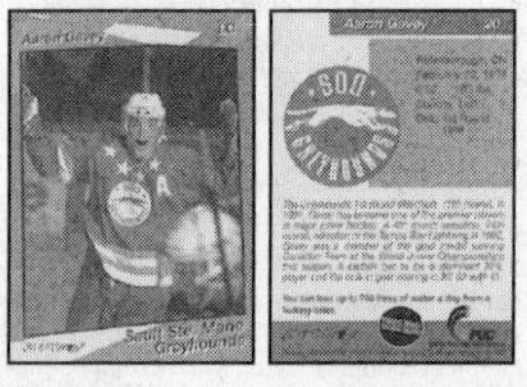

Sponsored by Pino's Food Trunk Road and Sault Ste. Marie Public Utilities Commission, and printed by Slapshot Images Ltd., this standard-size 30-card set features the 1993-94 Sault Ste. Marie Greyhounds. On a geometrical team color-coded background, the fronts feature color action player photos with thin black borders. The player's name, position and team name, as well as the producer's logo, also appear on the front. The team color-coded backs carry biographical player information, along with team and sponsors' logos. A fire safety message also appears on the back.

| | MINT | NRMT |
|---|---|---|
| COMPLETE SET (30) | 10.00 | 4.50 |
| COMMON CARD (1-30) | .10 | .05 |
| ❑ 1 Andrea Carpano | .35 | .16 |
| ❑ 2 Ryan Douglas | .35 | .16 |
| ❑ 3 Dan Cloutier | 1.50 | .70 |
| ❑ 4 Oliver Pastinsky | .35 | .16 |
| ❑ 5 Scott King | .35 | .16 |
| ❑ 6 Drew Bannister | .75 | .35 |
| ❑ 7 Sean Gagnon | .50 | .23 |
| ❑ 8 Andre Payette | .35 | .16 |
| ❑ 9 Peter MacKellar | .35 | .16 |
| UER Name spelled | | |
| Mackellar on front | | |
| ❑ 10 Richard Uniacke | .50 | .23 |
| ❑ 11 Steve Zoryk | .35 | .16 |
| ❑ 12 Brad Baber | .35 | .16 |
| ❑ 13 Gary Roach | .50 | .23 |
| ❑ 14 Jeff Gies | .35 | .16 |
| ❑ 15 Tom MacDonald | .35 | .16 |
| ❑ 16 Rhett Trombley | .50 | .23 |
| ❑ 17 Joe Van Volsen | .35 | .16 |
| ❑ 18 Andrew Clark | .35 | .16 |
| ❑ 19 Briane Thompson | .35 | .16 |
| ❑ 20 Aaron Gavey | 1.00 | .45 |
| ❑ 21 Wade Gibson | .50 | .23 |
| ❑ 22 Chad Grills | .35 | .16 |
| ❑ 23 Jeff Toms | .50 | .23 |
| ❑ 24 Steve Sullivan | .75 | .35 |
| ❑ 25 Jeremy Stevenson | .50 | .23 |
| ❑ 26 Corey Moylan | .35 | .16 |
| ❑ 27 Steve Spina | .35 | .16 |
| ❑ 28 Dave Mayville GM | .10 | .05 |
| ❑ 29 Ted Nolan CO | .75 | .35 |
| ❑ 30 Dan Flynn ACO | .10 | .05 |
| Mike Zuke ACO | | |

## 1993-94 Sault Ste. Marie Greyhounds Memorial Cup

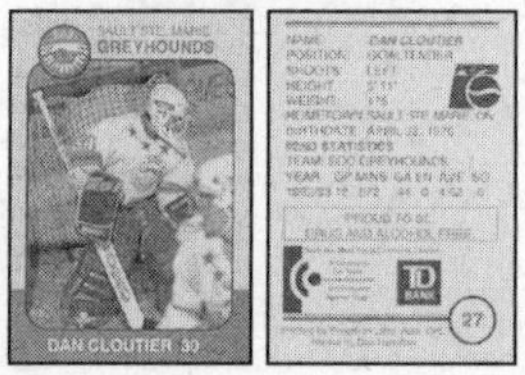

This 32-card standard-size set was printed by Precision Litho. The fronts feature color action player photos with rounded corners and gray-and-red team color-coded borders. The team name and logo are printed above the photos, while the player's name and number appear below. The backs present biography, 1992-93 statistics, an anti-drug or alcohol slogan, and sponsor logos.

| | MINT | NRMT |
|---|---|---|
| COMPLETE SET (32) | 15.00 | 6.75 |
| COMMON CARD (1-32) | .10 | .05 |
| ❑ 1 Memorial Cup | 1.00 | .45 |
| ❑ 2 Dan Tanevski | .35 | .16 |
| ❑ 3 Mark Matier | .35 | .16 |
| ❑ 4 Oliver Pastinsky | .35 | .16 |
| ❑ 5 Peter MacKellar | .35 | .16 |
| ❑ 6 Drew Bannister | .75 | .35 |
| ❑ 7 Sean Gagnon | .50 | .23 |
| ❑ 8 Joe Clarke | .35 | .16 |
| ❑ 9 Chad Penney | .50 | .23 |
| ❑ 10 Neal Martin | .35 | .16 |
| ❑ 11 Perry Pappas | .35 | .16 |
| ❑ 12 David Matsos | .50 | .23 |
| ❑ 13 Rick Kowalsky | .50 | .23 |
| ❑ 14 Gary Roach | .50 | .23 |
| ❑ 15 Jarret Reid | .50 | .23 |
| ❑ 16 Steve Sullivan | .75 | .35 |
| ❑ 17 Tom MacDonald | .35 | .16 |
| ❑ 18 Jodie Murphy | .35 | .16 |
| ❑ 19 Ralph Intranuovo | .50 | .23 |
| ❑ 20 Brad Baber | .35 | .16 |
| ❑ 21 Briane Thompson | .35 | .16 |
| ❑ 22 Aaron Gavey | 1.00 | .45 |
| ❑ 23 Wade Gibson | .35 | .16 |
| ❑ 24 Kiley Hill | .35 | .16 |
| ❑ 25 Jeff Toms | .50 | .23 |
| ❑ 26 Joe Van Volsen | .35 | .16 |
| ❑ 27 Dan Cloutier | 1.50 | .70 |
| ❑ 28 Kevin Hodson | 2.00 | .90 |
| ❑ 29 David Mayville DIR | .10 | .05 |
| Sherry Bassin GM | | |
| ❑ 30 Ted Nolan CO | .50 | .23 |
| Danny Flynn ACO | | |
| ❑ 31 Executive Staff | .10 | .05 |
| ❑ 32 Mike Zuke ACO | .10 | .05 |
| Forrest Varcoe TR | | |
| John Mayne TR | | |
| Maurice Sicard TR | | |

## 1995-96 Sault Ste. Marie Greyhounds

This 30-card set was produced by the Greyhounds for distribution at the rink, by mail, and through the team's webpage. The cards feature action photography on the front, with player name, number and bio superimposed over a Hounds logo on the back. The cards are unnumbered and are listed below alphabetically. The set is noteworthy for including the first cards ever of several outstanding prospects, including Joe Thornton, Rico Fata and Richard Jackman.

| | MINT | NRMT |
|---|---|---|
| COMPLETE SET (30) | 30.00 | 13.50 |
| COMMON CARD | .10 | .05 |
| ❑ 1 Peter Cava | .25 | .11 |
| ❑ 2 Scott Cherrey | .25 | .11 |
| ❑ 3 Dan Cloutier | .75 | .35 |
| ❑ 4 Lee Cole | .25 | .11 |
| ❑ 5 Jason Doyle | .50 | .23 |
| ❑ 6 Rico Fata | 5.00 | 2.20 |
| ❑ 7 Blaine Fitzpatrick | .25 | .11 |
| ❑ 8 Jeff Gies | .25 | .11 |
| ❑ 9 Richard Jackman | 1.50 | .70 |
| ❑ 10 Steve Lowe | .25 | .11 |
| ❑ 11 Dave Mayville | .10 | .05 |
| Director of Operations | | |
| ❑ 12 Robert Mulick | .25 | .11 |
| ❑ 13 Kevin Murnaghan | .25 | .11 |
| ❑ 14 Cory Murphy | .25 | .11 |
| ❑ 15 Joe Paterson CO | .10 | .05 |
| ❑ 16 Andre Payette | .25 | .11 |
| ❑ 17 Michal Podolka | .75 | .35 |
| ❑ 18 Ben Schust | .25 | .11 |
| ❑ 19 Brian Stacey | .25 | .11 |
| ❑ 20 Brian Stewart | .25 | .11 |
| ❑ 21 Joe Thornton | 15.00 | 6.75 |
| ❑ 22 Trevor Tokarczyk | .25 | .11 |
| ❑ 23 Richard Uniacke | .75 | .35 |
| ❑ 24 Joe Van Volsen | .25 | .11 |
| ❑ 25 Jamie Wentzell | .25 | .11 |
| ❑ 26 M.Zuke/B.Jones | .10 | .05 |
| Asst. Coaches | | |
| ❑ 27 Greyhounds Executive Staff | .10 | .05 |
| ❑ 28 Greyhounds | .25 | .11 |
| Toronto Bank and Trust | | |
| ❑ 29 Greyhounds | .25 | .11 |
| Toronto School of Business | | |
| ❑ 30 Greyhounds Team Photo | .10 | .05 |

## 1996-97 Sault Ste. Marie Greyhounds

This 30-card set may stand as the top junior issue of the year. The cards feature color action photography, along with the player's name and number. The backs feature comprehensive stats, but are unnumbered, hence the alphabetical listing below. The set is noteworthy for the inclusion of two cards of Joe Thornton, the top pick in the '97 NHL draft. The second card features him as a member of the Canadian National Junior Team.

| | MINT | NRMT |
|---|---|---|
| COMPLETE SET (30) | 25.00 | 11.00 |
| COMMON CARD (1-30) | .10 | .05 |
| ❑ 1 Wes Booker | .25 | .11 |
| ❑ 2 Bill Browne | .25 | .11 |
| ❑ 3 Peter Cava | .25 | .11 |
| ❑ 4 Justin Davis | .25 | .11 |
| ❑ 5 J.J. Dickie | .25 | .11 |
| ❑ 6 Oak Hewer | .50 | .23 |
| ❑ 7 Richard Jackman | 1.00 | .45 |
| ❑ 8 Richard Jackman | 1.00 | .45 |
| Team Canada 1997 | | |
| ❑ 9 Matt Lahey | .25 | .11 |
| ❑ 10 David Mayville | .10 | .05 |
| Director of Operations | | |
| ❑ 11 Jake McCracken | 1.00 | .45 |
| ❑ 12 Marc Moro | .50 | .23 |
| ❑ 13 Robert Mulick | .25 | .11 |
| ❑ 14 Joe Paterson CO | .10 | .05 |
| ❑ 15 Daniel Passero | .25 | .11 |
| ❑ 16 Nathan Perrott | .25 | .11 |
| ❑ 17 Michael Podolka | .50 | .23 |
| ❑ 18 Nick Robinson | .25 | .11 |
| ❑ 19 Ben Schust | .25 | .11 |
| ❑ 20 Joe Seroski | .50 | .23 |
| ❑ 21 Chad Spurr | .25 | .11 |
| ❑ 22 Brian Stewart | .25 | .11 |
| ❑ 23 Joe Thornton | 5.00 | 2.20 |
| ❑ 24 Joe Thornton | 5.00 | 2.20 |
| Team Canada 1997 | | |
| ❑ 25 Trevor Tokarczyk | .25 | .11 |
| ❑ 26 Richard Uniacke | .25 | .11 |
| ❑ 27 David Wight | .25 | .11 |
| ❑ 28 Chad Woollard | .25 | .11 |
| ❑ 29 Mike Zuke ACO | .10 | .05 |
| B.Jones ACO | | |
| ❑ 30 Team Photo | .50 | .23 |

## 1996-97 Sault Ste. Marie Greyhounds Autographed

Along with the regular version of the team set, the Hounds also offered a completely signed version for $15. This set includes two signed cards from 1997 top pick Joe Thornton as well as a pair from 1996 first rounder Richard Jackman, among other solid prospects. The cards do not bear any authenticating marks, so it is possible that an autographed set could be compiled individually.

| | MINT | NRMT |
|---|---|---|
| COMPLETE SET (28) | 80.00 | 36.00 |
| COMMON CARD | 1.00 | .45 |
| ❑ 1 Wes Booker | 1.00 | .45 |
| ❑ 2 Bill Browne | 1.00 | .45 |
| ❑ 3 Peter Cava | 1.00 | .45 |
| ❑ 4 Justin Davis | 1.00 | .45 |
| ❑ 5 J.J. Dickie | 1.00 | .45 |
| ❑ 6 Oak Hewer | 1.00 | .45 |
| ❑ 7 Richard Jackman | 5.00 | 2.20 |
| ❑ 8 Richard Jackman | 5.00 | 2.20 |
| Team Canada 1997 | | |
| ❑ 9 Matt Lahey | 1.00 | .45 |
| ❑ 11 Jake McCracken | 4.00 | 1.80 |
| ❑ 12 Marc Moro | 3.00 | 1.35 |
| ❑ 13 Robert Mulick | 1.00 | .45 |
| ❑ 14 Joe Paterson CO | 1.00 | .45 |
| ❑ 15 Daniel Passero | 1.00 | .45 |
| ❑ 16 Nathan Perrott | 1.00 | .45 |
| ❑ 17 Michael Podolka | 4.00 | 1.80 |
| ❑ 18 Nick Robinson | 1.00 | .45 |
| ❑ 19 Ben Schust | 1.00 | .45 |
| ❑ 20 Joe Seroski | 2.00 | .90 |
| ❑ 21 Chad Spurr | 1.00 | .45 |
| ❑ 22 Brian Stewart | 1.00 | .45 |
| ❑ 23 Joe Thornton | 20.00 | 9.00 |
| ❑ 24 Joe Thornton | 20.00 | 9.00 |
| Team Canada 1997 | | |
| ❑ 25 Trevor Tokarczyk | 1.00 | .45 |
| ❑ 26 Richard Uniacke | 2.00 | .90 |
| ❑ 27 David Wight | 1.00 | .45 |
| ❑ 28 Chad Woollard | 1.00 | .45 |

## 1969-70 Seattle Totems WHL

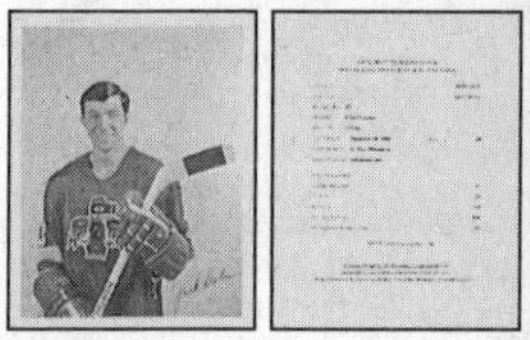

A White Front Stores exclusive at stores in Aurora, Tacoma, Burien, and Bellevue, this set of 20 team photos measures approximately 8" by 10". The set features members of the Seattle Totems of the Western Hockey League. Printed on thin paper, the front features a posed color player photo with a studio background. The pictures have white borders, and the player's signature is inscribed in the lower right corner. In black print on white, the backs present biography and statistics from the past season.

| | NRMT-MT | EXC |
|---|---|---|
| COMPLETE SET (20) | 200.00 | 90.00 |
| COMMON CARD (1-20) | 5.00 | 2.20 |
| ❑ 1 Don Head | 15.00 | 6.75 |
| ❑ 2 Chuck Holmes | 10.00 | 4.50 |
| ❑ 3 Bob Courcy | 10.00 | 4.50 |
| ❑ 4 Marc Boileau | 15.00 | 6.75 |
| ❑ 5 Gerry Leonard | 15.00 | 6.75 |
| ❑ 6 Art Stratton | 10.00 | 4.50 |
| ❑ 7 Gary Kilpatrick | 10.00 | 4.50 |
| ❑ 8 Don Ward | 10.00 | 4.50 |
| ❑ 9 Jack Michie | 10.00 | 4.50 |
| ❑ 10 Ronald Ingram | 10.00 | 4.50 |
| ❑ 11 John Hanna | 10.00 | 4.50 |
| ❑ 12 Ray Larose | 10.00 | 4.50 |
| ❑ 13 Jack Dale | 10.00 | 4.50 |
| ❑ 14 Tom McVie | 20.00 | 9.00 |
| ❑ 15 Gerry Meehan | 20.00 | 9.00 |
| ❑ 16 Chris Worthy | 10.00 | 4.50 |
| ❑ 17 Bobby Schmautz | 15.00 | 6.75 |
| ❑ 18 Dwight Carruthers | 10.00 | 4.50 |
| ❑ 19 Pat Dunn TR | 5.00 | 2.20 |
| ❑ 20 Bill MacFarland CO | 10.00 | 4.50 |

## 1993-94 Seattle Thunderbirds

This 30-card standard-size set features the 1993-94 Seattle Thunderbirds of the Western Hockey League (WHL). On a white card face, the fronts display posed color player photos. The pictures are edged by a row of blue stars on the left and by "Thunderbirds" in green print on the right. At the top left corner appears the team logo, while the player's name and position are printed in black beneath the

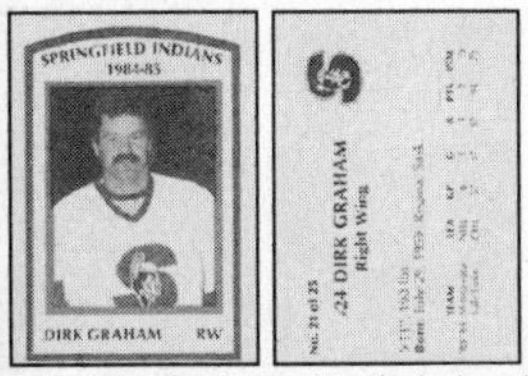


photo. In black print on white, the horizontal backs present biography and a player profile.

| | MINT | NRMT |
|---|---|---|
| COMPLETE SET (30) | 12.00 | 5.50 |
| COMMON CARD (1-30) | .10 | .05 |
| ❑ 1 Mike Barrie | .35 | .16 |
| ❑ 2 Doug Bonner | 1.00 | .45 |
| ❑ 3 Davie Carson | .35 | .16 |
| ❑ 4 Jeff Dewar | .35 | .16 |
| ❑ 5 Brett Duncan | .35 | .16 |
| ❑ 6 Shawn Gervais | .50 | .23 |
| ❑ 7 Chris Herperger | .75 | .35 |
| ❑ 8 Troy Hyatt | .35 | .16 |
| ❑ 9 Curt Kamp TR | .10 | .05 |
| ❑ 10 Olaf Kjenstadt | .50 | .23 |
| ❑ 11 Walt Kyle CO | .10 | .05 |
| ❑ 12 Milt Mastad | .50 | .23 |
| ❑ 13 Larry McMorran | .35 | .16 |
| ❑ 14 Jim McTaggart ACO | .10 | .05 |
| ❑ 15 Regan Mueller | .35 | .16 |
| ❑ 16 Kevin Mylander | .35 | .16 |
| ❑ 17 Drew Palmer | .50 | .23 |
| ❑ 18 Jeff Peddigrew | .35 | .16 |
| ❑ 19 Darryl Plandowski ACO | .10 | .05 |
| ❑ 20 Deron Quint | 1.25 | .55 |
| ❑ 21 Darrell Sandback | .35 | .16 |
| ❑ 22 Chris Schmidt | .35 | .16 |
| ❑ 23 Lloyd Shaw | .35 | .16 |
| ❑ 24 Alexandre Matvichuk | .50 | .23 |
| ❑ 25 Darcy Smith | .35 | .16 |
| ❑ 26 Rob Tallas | 1.00 | .45 |
| ❑ 27 Paul Vincent | .50 | .23 |
| ❑ 28 Chris Wells | 1.00 | .45 |
| ❑ 29 Brendan Witt | 1.50 | .70 |
| ❑ 30 Team photo | .50 | .23 |

## 1995-96 Seattle Thunderbirds

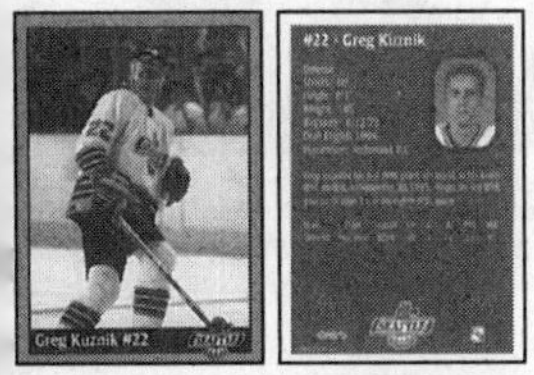


This 32-card set was produced and sold by the club. The fronts feature action photography, while the backs include a headshot, stats and bio. The set is noteworthy for including the first appearance of Patrick Marleau, the second player selected in the 1997 Entry Draft. The cards are unnumbered and are listed below in alphabetical order.

| | MINT | NRMT |
|---|---|---|
| COMPLETE SET (32) | 12.00 | 5.50 |
| COMMON CARD (1-32) | .10 | .05 |
| ❑ 1 Perry Andrusiak ACO | .10 | .05 |
| ❑ 2 Shane Belter | .40 | .18 |
| ❑ 3 Rick Berry | .40 | .18 |
| ❑ 4 Jeff Blair | .50 | .23 |
| ❑ 5 Doug Bonner | .75 | .35 |
| ❑ 6 Kevin Borris | .40 | .18 |
| ❑ 7 Torrey DiRoberto | .50 | .23 |
| ❑ 8 Michal Divisek | .40 | .18 |
| ❑ 9 Paul Ferone | .40 | .18 |
| ❑ 10 Shawn Gervais | .40 | .18 |
| ❑ 11 Jan Hrdina | .40 | .18 |
| ❑ 12 Curt Kamp TR | .10 | .05 |
| ❑ 13 Greg Kuznik | .40 | .18 |
| ❑ 14 Blair Manning | .40 | .18 |
| ❑ 15 Patrick Marleau | 5.00 | 2.20 |
| ❑ 16 Jim McTaggart ASST CO | .10 | .05 |
| ❑ 17 Tony Mohagen | .40 | .18 |
| ❑ 18 Don Nachbaur CO | .10 | .05 |
| ❑ 19 Jason Norrie | .40 | .18 |
| ❑ 20 Drew Palmer | .40 | .18 |
| ❑ 21 Tyler Perry | .40 | .18 |
| ❑ 22 Jame Pollock | .40 | .18 |
| ❑ 23 Kevin Popp | .40 | .18 |
| ❑ 24 Jeremy Reich | .75 | .35 |
| ❑ 25 Cody Rudkowsky | .40 | .18 |
| ❑ 26 Chris Schmidt | .40 | .18 |
| ❑ 27 Lloyd Shaw | .40 | .18 |
| ❑ 28 Chris Thompson | .40 | .18 |
| ❑ 29 Dan Tompkins | .40 | .18 |
| ❑ 30 Cool Bird (Mascot) | .10 | .05 |
| ❑ 32 Seattle Key Arena | .10 | .05 |
| ❑ NNO Title Card | .10 | .05 |

## 1996-97 Seattle Thunderbirds

This 28-card set was produced by S&H Ltd. The cards were available through the team at the rink or through the mail. The cards feature action photos on the front, and statistical analysis on the backs. The player's sweater number is displayed in the lower right hand corner. As the cards themselves are unnumbered, they are listed below according to the sweater number. The set is noteworthy for the inclusion of Patrick Marleau, the second overall pick in the 1997 NHL Entry Draft.

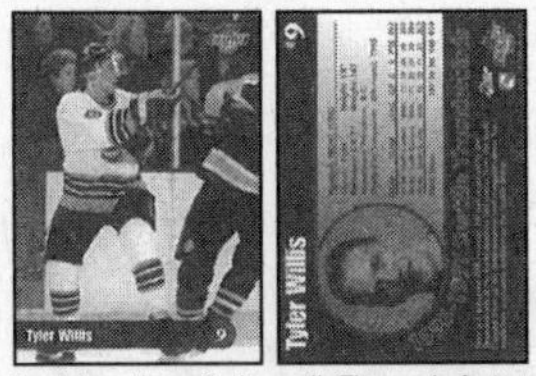


| | MINT | NRMT |
|---|---|---|
| COMPLETE SET (28) | 10.00 | 4.50 |
| COMMON CARD | .10 | .05 |
| ❑ 1 Jeff Blair | .50 | .23 |
| ❑ 3 Rod LeRoux | .25 | .11 |
| ❑ 4 Nathan Forster | .25 | .11 |
| ❑ 5 Brad Swanson | .25 | .11 |
| ❑ 6 Rick Berry | .25 | .11 |
| ❑ 7 Paul Ferone | .25 | .11 |
| ❑ 8 Jame Pollock | .25 | .11 |
| ❑ 9 Tyler Willis | .25 | .11 |
| ❑ 11 Chris Thompson | .25 | .11 |
| ❑ 12 Patrick Marleau | 3.00 | 1.35 |
| ❑ 13 Jouni Kuokkanen | .25 | .11 |
| ❑ 14 Martin Cerven | .25 | .11 |
| ❑ 15 Jeremy Reich | .75 | .35 |
| ❑ 16 Bret DeCecco | .25 | .11 |
| ❑ 17 Tony Mohagen | .25 | .11 |
| ❑ 18 Torrey DiRoberto | .25 | .11 |
| ❑ 19 Nick Szadkowski | .25 | .11 |
| ❑ 21 Brian Ballman | .25 | .11 |
| ❑ 22 Greg Kuznik | .25 | .11 |
| ❑ 23 Randy Perry | .25 | .11 |
| ❑ 24 Shawn Skolney | .25 | .11 |
| ❑ 30 Cody Rudkowsky | .50 | .23 |
| ❑ 31 Kris Cantu | .25 | .11 |
| ❑ 32 Shane Belter | .25 | .11 |
| ❑ NNO Cool Bird MASCOT | .10 | .05 |
| ❑ NNO Thunderbirds Through the Years | .10 | .05 |
| ❑ NNO Don Nachbaur CO | .10 | .05 |
| ❑ NNO Rob Sumner ACO | .10 | .05 |

## 1986-87 Sherbrooke Canadiens

This 30-card set of the Sherbrooke Canadiens of the AHL was produced by Graphique Estrie, Inc. The cards feature action photos on the front, surrounded by a white border. The team logo, player name and sweater name appear along the bottom, along with the position in French. The back includes stats and biographical data, along with a helpful tip for kids, all of which is in French as well. The unnumbered cards are listed below in alphabetical order.

| | MINT | NRMT |
|---|---|---|
| COMPLETE SET (30) | 9.00 | 4.00 |
| COMMON CARD (1-30) | .10 | .05 |
| ❑ 1 Entraineurs 1986-87 | .10 | .05 |
| ❑ 2 Soigneurs 1986-87 | .10 | .05 |
| ❑ 3 Coupe Stanley 1986 | .50 | .23 |
| ❑ 4 Joel Baillargeon | .40 | .18 |
| ❑ 5 Daniel Berthiaume | .50 | .23 |
| ❑ 6 Serge Boisvert | .40 | .18 |
| ❑ 7 Graeme Bonar | .40 | .18 |
| ❑ 8 Randy Bucyk | .40 | .18 |
| ❑ 9 Bill Campbell | .40 | .18 |
| ❑ 10 Jose Charbonneau | .40 | .18 |
| ❑ 11 Rejean Cloutier | .40 | .18 |
| ❑ 12 Bobby Dollas | .40 | .18 |
| ❑ 13 Peter Douris | .40 | .18 |
| ❑ 14 Steven Fletcher | .40 | .18 |
| ❑ 15 Perry Ganchar | .40 | .18 |
| ❑ 16 Luc Gauthier | .40 | .18 |
| ❑ 17 Randy Gilhen | .40 | .18 |
| ❑ 18 Scott Harlow | .40 | .18 |
| ❑ 19 Rick Hayward | .40 | .18 |
| ❑ 20 Kevin Houle | .40 | .18 |
| ❑ 21 Rick Knickle | .50 | .23 |
| ❑ 22 Vincent Riendeau | .50 | .23 |
| ❑ 23 Guy Rouleau | .40 | .18 |
| ❑ 24 Scott Sandelin | .40 | .18 |
| ❑ 25 Karel Svoboda | .40 | .18 |
| ❑ 26 Peter Taglianetti | .40 | .18 |
| ❑ 27 Gilles Thibaudeau | .40 | .18 |
| ❑ 28 Ernie Vargas | .40 | .18 |
| ❑ 29 Andre Villeneuve | .40 | .18 |
| ❑ 30 Brian Williams | .40 | .18 |

## 1974-75 Sioux City Musketeers

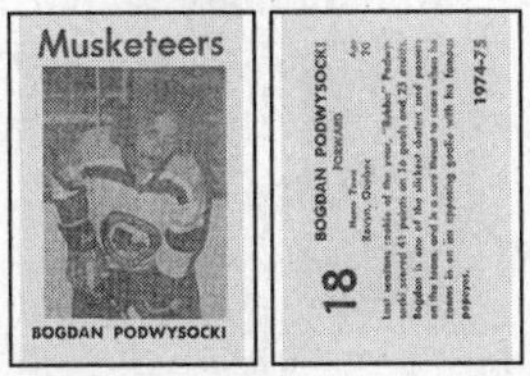


This 20-card set is printed on yellow stock. According to the producer, the cards were intended to be standard size but actually came out a little larger. The fronts feature bordered, posed player photos that have a dark green tint to them. In dark green lettering, the team name is printed above the picture while the player's name is printed below it. Green and gold were the Musketeers' team colors. The horizontal backs have the uniform number, brief biographical information, and player profile. The set year in the lower right corner rounds out the back. The cards are unnumbered and checklisted below in alphabetical order. Reportedly only 250 sets were made and they were originally sold at home games for 2.50.

| | NRMT-MT | EXC |
|---|---|---|
| COMPLETE SET (20) | 15.00 | 6.75 |
| COMMON CARD (1-20) | 1.00 | .45 |
| ❑ 1 Steve Boyle | 1.00 | .45 |
| ❑ 2 Dave Davies | 1.00 | .45 |
| ❑ 3 Steve Desloges | 1.00 | .45 |
| ❑ 4 Greg Gilbert | 1.00 | .45 |
| ❑ 5 Barry Head | 1.00 | .45 |
| ❑ 6 Steve Heathwood | 1.00 | .45 |
| ❑ 7 Dave Kartio | 1.00 | .45 |
| ❑ 8 Ralph Kloiber | 1.00 | .45 |
| ❑ 9 Pete Maxwell | 1.00 | .45 |
| ❑ 10 Randy McDonald | 1.00 | .45 |
| ❑ 11 Terry Mulroy | 1.00 | .45 |
| ❑ 12 Sam Nelligan | 1.00 | .45 |
| ❑ 13 Julian Nixon | 1.00 | .45 |
| ❑ 14 Mike Noel | 1.00 | .45 |
| ❑ 15 Jim Peck | 1.00 | .45 |
| ❑ 16 Bogdan Podwysocki | 2.00 | .90 |
| ❑ 17 John Saville P/CO | 1.00 | .45 |
| ❑ 18 Alex Shibicky Jr. | 2.00 | .90 |
| ❑ 19 Bob Thomerson | 1.00 | .45 |
| ❑ 20 Jim White | 6.00 | 2.70 |

## 1995-96 South Carolina Stingrays

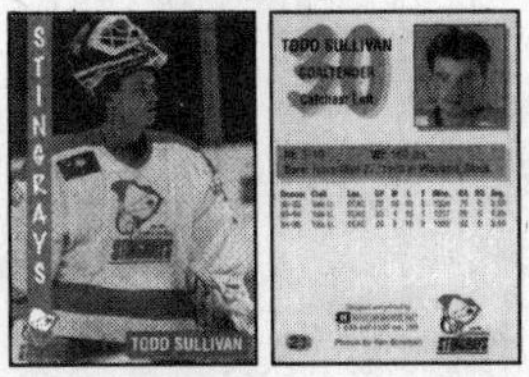


This 24-card set of the South Carolina Stingrays of the ECHL was produced for the team by Multi-Ad Services. The set was distributed through the team as well. The fronts feature a blurry action photo, along with team and player name. The numbered backs include a portrait and stats.

| | MINT | NRMT |
|---|---|---|
| COMPLETE SET (24) | 7.00 | 3.10 |
| COMMON CARD (1-24) | .10 | .05 |
| ❑ 1 Rick Vaive CO | .50 | .23 |
| ❑ 2 Dan Wiebe ACO | .10 | .05 |
| ❑ 3 Joseph Cramp TR | .10 | .05 |
| ❑ 4 Aaron Fackler EQMG | .10 | .05 |
| ❑ 5 Mikhail Volkov | .40 | .18 |
| ❑ 6 Jason Cipolla | .40 | .18 |
| ❑ 7 Mike Ross | .40 | .18 |
| ❑ 8 Rob Concannon | .40 | .18 |
| ❑ 9 Dan Fournel | .40 | .18 |
| ❑ 10 Mark Bavis | .40 | .18 |
| ❑ 11 Darren Ritchie | .40 | .18 |
| ❑ 12 Mike Barrie | .40 | .18 |
| ❑ 13 Marc Tardif | .40 | .18 |
| ❑ 14 Chris Foy | .40 | .18 |
| ❑ 15 Scott Boston | .50 | .23 |
| ❑ 16 Carl LeBlanc | .40 | .18 |
| ❑ 17 Brett Marietti | .40 | .18 |
| ❑ 18 Jared Bednar | .40 | .18 |
| ❑ 19 Paul Rushforth | .40 | .18 |
| ❑ 20 Kevin Knopp | .40 | .18 |
| ❑ 21 Todd Sullivan | .50 | .23 |
| ❑ 22 Justin Duberman | .40 | .18 |
| ❑ 23 Sean Gauthier | .50 | .23 |
| ❑ 24 Mark Rupnow | .40 | .18 |
| ❑ NNO Header Card | .10 | .05 |

## 1996-97 South Carolina Stingrays

This 27-card set features the South Carolina Stingrays of the ECHL, and was produced by the team, in conjunction with Marvin Foy Marketing, Inc. The cards feature action photography on the front, complemented by a pair of Stingrays logos on the left side, and the player's name along the lower right border. The back contains two more photos, as well as statistical and biographical data. The set is noteworthy for the rare inclusion of a card depicting a fight in progress (Dan Fournel). The cards boldly feature the player's sweater number on the back of the card, precipitating their numbering thusly below.

| | MINT | NRMT |
|---|---|---|
| COMPLETE SET (27) | 6.00 | 2.70 |
| COMMON CARD | .10 | .05 |
| ❑ 9 Mike Ross | .25 | .11 |
| ❑ 10 Marc Genest | .25 | .11 |
| ❑ 11 Dan Fournel | .50 | .23 |
| ❑ 12 David Mayes | .25 | .11 |
| ❑ 14 David Seitz | .25 | .11 |
| ❑ 15 Jeff Romfo | .25 | .11 |
| ❑ 16 Kyle Ferguson | .25 | .11 |
| ❑ 17 Marc Tardif | .25 | .11 |
| ❑ 18 Steve Parson | .25 | .11 |
| ❑ 19 Doug Wood | .25 | .11 |
| ❑ 20 Scott Boston | .25 | .11 |
| ❑ 21 Rob Concannon | .25 | .11 |
| ❑ 22 Rob Butler | .25 | .11 |
| ❑ 24 Brett Marietti | .25 | .11 |
| ❑ 25 Jared Bednar | .25 | .11 |
| ❑ 27 Ed Courtenay | .25 | .11 |
| ❑ 28 Kevin Knopp | .25 | .11 |
| ❑ 29 Jay Moser | .25 | .11 |
| ❑ 30 Corey Cadden | .25 | .11 |
| ❑ 31 Jason Fitzsimmons | .35 | .16 |
| ❑ 33 Chris Hynnes | .25 | .11 |
| ❑ 35 Taras Lendzyk | .25 | .11 |
| ❑ NNO Aaron Fackler EQMG | .10 | .05 |
| ❑ NNO Rick Adduono ACO | .10 | .05 |
| ❑ NNO Rick Vaive CO | .25 | .11 |
| ❑ NNO Randy Page ANN | .10 | .05 |
| ❑ NNO Kenny Snider TR | .10 | .05 |

## 1989-90 Spokane Chiefs

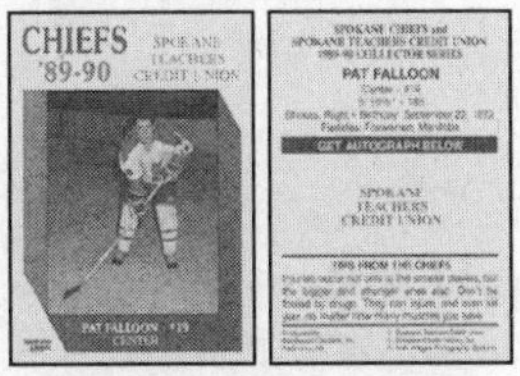


Sponsored by the Spokane Teachers Credit Union, this 20-card standard-size set of the 1989-90 Spokane Chiefs features color posed-on-ice player photos on its fronts. The photos are bordered in team colors (red, white, and blue). The player's name, uniform number, and position appear within the blue border below the picture. The white back carries the player's name, position, and uniform number near the top, followed below by biography, a space for an autograph, and an antidrug message from the Chiefs. The cards are unnumbered and checklisted below in alphabetical order. Reportedly only 3,600 sets were made.

| | MINT | NRMT |
|---|---|---|
| COMPLETE SET (20) | 12.00 | 5.50 |
| COMMON CARD (1-20) | .50 | .23 |
| ❑ 1 Mike Chrun | .50 | .23 |
| ❑ 2 John Colvin | .50 | .23 |
| ❑ 3 Shawn Dietrich | .50 | .23 |
| ❑ 4 Milan Dragicevic | .50 | .23 |
| ❑ 5 Frank Evans | .50 | .23 |
| ❑ 6 Pat Falloon | 2.00 | .90 |
| ❑ 7 Scott Farrell | .50 | .23 |
| ❑ 8 Jeff Ferguson | .50 | .23 |
| ❑ 9 Travis Green | 3.00 | 1.35 |
| ❑ 10 Mike Hawes | .50 | .23 |
| ❑ 11 Bobby House | .75 | .35 |
| ❑ 12 Mike Jickling | .50 | .23 |
| ❑ 13 Steve Junker | .75 | .35 |
| ❑ 14 Jon Klemm | 1.00 | .45 |
| ❑ 15 Chris Rowland | .50 | .23 |
| ❑ 16 Dennis Saharchuk | .50 | .23 |
| ❑ 17 Kerry Toporowski | .75 | .35 |
| ❑ 18 Trevor Tovell | .50 | .23 |
| ❑ 19 Bram Vanderkracht | .50 | .23 |
| ❑ 20 Ray Whitney | 1.00 | .45 |

## 1995-96 Spokane Chiefs

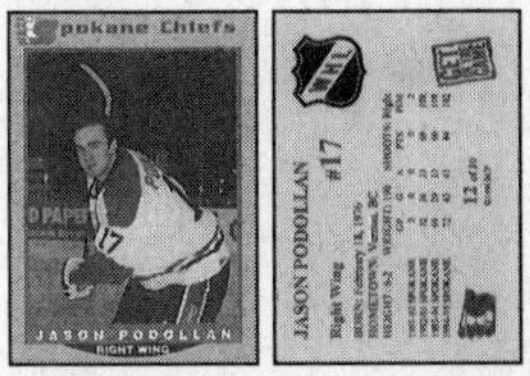


This 30-card set features color player photos in a thin red border on a silver background. The backs carry player information.

| | MINT | NRMT |
|---|---|---|
| COMPLETE SET (30) | 10.00 | 4.50 |
| COMMON CARD (1-30) | .10 | .05 |
| ❑ 1 David Lemanowicz | .50 | .23 |
| ❑ 2 Scott Fletcher | .35 | .16 |
| ❑ 3 Hugh Hamilton | .50 | .23 |
| ❑ 4 Chris Lane | .35 | .16 |
| ❑ 5 Dmitri Leonov | .35 | .16 |
| ❑ 6 Darren Sinclair | .35 | .16 |
| ❑ 7 Ty Jones | 1.00 | .45 |
| ❑ 8 Kris Graf | .35 | .16 |
| ❑ 9 Trent Whitfield | .75 | .35 |
| ❑ 10 Martin Cerven | .50 | .23 |
| ❑ 11 Randy Favaro | .35 | .16 |
| ❑ 12 Jason Podollan | 1.50 | .70 |
| ❑ 13 Joel Boschman | .35 | .16 |
| ❑ 14 Jared Hope | .35 | .16 |
| ❑ 15 Greg Leeb | .35 | .16 |
| ❑ 16 John Cirjak | .35 | .16 |
| ❑ 17 Mike Haley | .35 | .16 |
| ❑ 18 Ryan Berry | .35 | .16 |
| ❑ 19 Sean Gillam | .35 | .16 |
| ❑ 20 Derek Schutz | .35 | .16 |
| ❑ 21 Joe Cardarelli | .35 | .16 |
| ❑ 22 Adam Magarrell | .35 | .16 |
| ❑ 23 Jay Bertsch | .35 | .16 |
| ❑ 24 John Shockey | .35 | .16 |
| ❑ 25 Mike Babcock CO | .35 | .16 |
| ❑ 26 Parry Shockey ACO | .10 | .05 |
| ❑ 27 T.D. Forss EQMG | .10 | .05 |
| ❑ 28 Ted Schott AEQMG | .10 | .05 |
| ❑ 29 Dan Mitchell | .10 | .05 |
| ❑ 30 Aren Miller | .50 | .23 |

## 1983-84 Springfield Indians

Produced by Card Collectors Closet (Springfield, MA), this 25-card standard-size set features black-and-white player portraits on a white card face. The team name and year are printed in black at the top. The player's name and position appear at the bottom. The pictures are framed by a royal blue border while a red border encloses the photo and text. The backs carry the producer's advertisement.

| | MINT | NRMT |
|---|---|---|
| COMPLETE SET (25) | 12.00 | 5.50 |
| COMMON CARD (1-25) | .50 | .23 |
| ❑ 1 Gil Hudon | .75 | .35 |
| ❑ 2 Jim Ralph | 1.50 | .70 |
| ❑ 3 Todd Bergen | .75 | .35 |
| ❑ 4 Len Hachborn | .75 | .35 |
| ❑ 5 John Ollson | .50 | .23 |
| ❑ 6 Steve Tsujiura | .50 | .23 |
| ❑ 7 Gordie Williams | .50 | .23 |
| ❑ 8 Dave Brown | 1.00 | .45 |
| ❑ 9 Dan Frawley | .50 | .23 |
| ❑ 10 Tom McMurchy | .50 | .23 |
| ❑ 11 Dave Michayluk | .75 | .35 |
| ❑ 12 Bob Mormina | .50 | .23 |
| ❑ 13 Perry Pelensky | .50 | .23 |
| ❑ 14 Andy Brickley | .75 | .35 |
| ❑ 15 Ross Fitzpatrick | .50 | .23 |
| ❑ 16 Florent Robidoux | .50 | .23 |
| ❑ 17 Jeff Smith | .50 | .23 |
| ❑ 18 Rod Willard | .50 | .23 |
| ❑ 19 Darrell Anholt | .50 | .23 |
| ❑ 20 Steve Blyth | .50 | .23 |
| ❑ 21 Don Dietrich | .50 | .23 |
| ❑ 22 Steve Smith | .50 | .23 |
| ❑ 23 Daryl Stanley | .75 | .35 |
| ❑ 24 Taras Zytynsky | .50 | .23 |
| ❑ 25 Doug Sauter CO | .50 | .23 |

## 1984-85 Springfield Indians

Produced by Card Collectors Closet (Springfield, MA), this 25-card standard-size

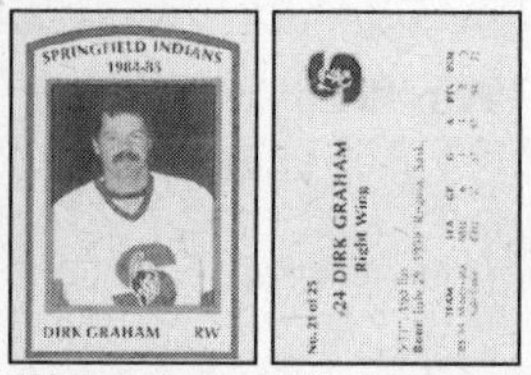


set features black-and-white player portraits on a white card face. The team name and year are printed in black at the top. The player's name and position appear at the bottom. The pictures are framed by a royal blue border while a red border encloses the photo and the text. On a white background, the horizontal backs carry the player's name, number, position, short biography, and statistics. The cards are numbered on the back as "x of 25."

| | MINT | NRMT |
|---|---|---|
| COMPLETE SET (25) | 12.00 | 5.50 |
| COMMON CARD (1-25) | .50 | .23 |
| ❑ 1 Mike Sands | .75 | .35 |
| ❑ 2 Lorne Molleken | .50 | .23 |
| ❑ 3 Todd Lumbard | .50 | .23 |
| ❑ 4 Randy Velischek | .75 | .35 |
| ❑ 5 David Jensen | .75 | .35 |
| ❑ 6 Ken Leiter | .50 | .23 |
| ❑ 7 Vern Smith | .50 | .23 |
| ❑ 8 Alan Kerr | .75 | .35 |
| ❑ 9 Scott Howson | .50 | .23 |
| ❑ 10 Tim Coulis | .50 | .23 |
| ❑ 11 Terry Tait | .50 | .23 |
| ❑ 12 Tim Trimper | .50 | .23 |
| ❑ 13 Rob Flockhart | .75 | .35 |
| ❑ 14 Ron Handy | .50 | .23 |
| ❑ 15 Jiri Poner | .50 | .23 |
| ❑ 16 Chris Pryor | .50 | .23 |
| ❑ 17 Dale Henry | .50 | .23 |
| ❑ 18 Mark Hamway | .50 | .23 |
| ❑ 19 Monty Trottier | .50 | .23 |
| ❑ 20 Miroslav Maly | .50 | .23 |
| ❑ 21 Dirk Graham | 3.00 | 1.35 |
| ❑ 22 Roger Kortko | .50 | .23 |
| ❑ 23 Bob Bodak | .50 | .23 |
| ❑ 24 Lorne Henning CO | .75 | .35 |
| ❑ 25 Checklist Card | .50 | .23 |

## 1996-97 Springfield Falcons

This 21-card set was produced by Split Second. These unnumbered cards feature an action photo on the front with a stats package on the reverse. The cards were available through the club at the rink or by mail order.

| | MINT | NRMT |
|---|---|---|
| COMPLETE SET (21) | 8.00 | 3.60 |
| COMMON CARD | .35 | .16 |
| ❑ 3 Brent Thompson | .35 | .16 |
| ❑ 4 Deron Quint | .75 | .35 |
| ❑ 5 Steve Cheredaryk | .35 | .16 |
| ❑ 10 Kent Manderville | .35 | .16 |
| ❑ 11 Hnat Domenichelli | .75 | .35 |
| ❑ 12 Steve Martins | .35 | .16 |
| ❑ 14 Tom Buckley | .35 | .16 |
| ❑ 15 Juha Ylonen | .50 | .23 |
| ❑ 16 Chris Longo | .35 | .16 |
| ❑ 17 Rhett Gordon | .35 | .16 |
| ❑ 19 Tavis Hansen | .35 | .16 |
| ❑ 20 Steve Halko | .35 | .16 |
| ❑ 22 Scott Levins | .35 | .16 |
| ❑ 23 Rob Murray | .35 | .16 |
| ❑ 25 Jason McBain | .35 | .16 |
| ❑ 27 Jeff Daniels | .35 | .16 |
| ❑ 28 Ryan Risidore | .50 | .23 |
| ❑ 30 Manny Legace | .75 | .35 |
| ❑ 33 Reggie Savage | .35 | .16 |
| ❑ 34 Nolan Pratt | .35 | .16 |
| ❑ 35 Scott Langkow | .50 | .23 |
| ❑ 44 Kevin Brown | .35 | .16 |
| ❑ NNO AHL Ad Card | .10 | .05 |

## 1961-62 Sudbury Wolves

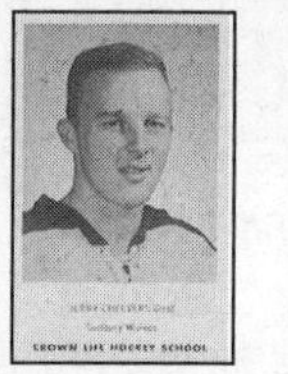

This 18-card set measures approximately 4" by 6 1/8" and features black-and-white player portraits with white borders. The player's name and position, the team name and the words "Crown Life Hockey School" appear under the photo. The backs are blank. The cards are unnumbered and checklisted below in alphabetical order.

| | NRMT | VG-E |
|---|---|---|
| COMPLETE SET (18) | 100.00 | 45.00 |
| COMMON CARD (1-18) | 4.00 | 1.80 |
| ❑ 1 Norm Armstrong | 4.00 | 1.80 |
| ❑ 2 Ed Babiuk | 4.00 | 1.80 |
| ❑ 3 Vern Buffey | 4.00 | 1.80 |
| ❑ 4 Murph Chamberlain CO | 4.00 | 1.80 |
| ❑ 5 Gerry Cheevers UER (misspelled Jerry) | 50.00 | 22.00 |
| ❑ 6 Wally Chevrier | 4.00 | 1.80 |
| ❑ 7 Marc Dufour | 5.00 | 2.20 |
| ❑ 8 Edgar Ehrenverth | 4.00 | 1.80 |
| ❑ 9 Bill Friday | 6.00 | 2.70 |
| ❑ 10 Jim Johnson | 4.00 | 1.80 |
| ❑ 11 Chico Kozurok | 4.00 | 1.80 |
| ❑ 12 Gord LaBossiere | 6.00 | 2.70 |
| ❑ 13 Dunc McCallum | 6.00 | 2.70 |
| ❑ 14 Dave McComb | 4.00 | 1.80 |
| ❑ 15 Mike McMahon | 4.00 | 1.80 |
| ❑ 16 Joe Spence | 4.00 | 1.80 |
| ❑ 17 Ted Taylor | 4.00 | 1.80 |
| ❑ 18 Bob Woytowich | 6.00 | 2.70 |

## 1962-63 Sudbury Wolves

These 22 blank-backed cards measure approximately 4" by 6" and feature white-bordered, posed black-and-white studio head shots of Wolves players (Eastern Professional Hockey League). The player's name and postion appear above the team name within the broad white bottom border. The imprint, "Crown Life Hockey School," rounds out the card at the bottom. The cards are unnumbered and checklisted below in alphabetical order.

| | NRMT | VG-E |
|---|---|---|
| COMPLETE SET (22) | 75.00 | 34.00 |
| COMMON CARD (1-22) | 1.50 | .70 |
| ❑ 1 Paul Andrea | 5.00 | 2.20 |
| ❑ 2 Norm Armstrong | 3.00 | 1.35 |
| ❑ 3 Ed Babiuk | 3.00 | 1.35 |
| ❑ 4 Hub Beaudry ANN | 1.50 | .70 |
| ❑ 5 Vern Buffey REF | 3.00 | 1.35 |
| ❑ 6 Murph Chamberlain CO | 3.00 | 1.35 |
| ❑ 7 Gerry Cheevers UER (Misspelled Jerry on card front) | 30.00 | 13.50 |
| ❑ 8 Wally Chevrier | 3.00 | 1.35 |
| ❑ 9 Marc Dufour | 4.00 | 1.80 |
| ❑ 10 Edgar Ehrenverth | 3.00 | 1.35 |
| ❑ 11 Bill Friday REF | 5.00 | 2.20 |
| ❑ 12 Jim Johnson | 3.00 | 1.35 |
| ❑ 13 Chico Kozurok TR | 1.50 | .70 |
| ❑ 14 Gord Labossiere | 4.00 | 1.80 |
| ❑ 15 Dunc McCallum | 8.00 | 3.60 |
| ❑ 16 Dave McComb | 3.00 | 1.35 |
| ❑ 17 Hugh McLean REF | 3.00 | 1.35 |
| ❑ 18 Mike McMahon | 3.00 | 1.35 |
| ❑ 19 Dave Richardson | 3.00 | 1.35 |
| ❑ 20 Joe Spence ANN | 1.50 | .70 |
| ❑ 21 Ted Taylor | 3.00 | 1.35 |
| ❑ 22 Bob Woytowich | 8.00 | 3.60 |

## 1984-85 Sudbury Wolves

This 16-card set measures approximately 3 1/2" by 6" and features color, action player photos accented by a hockey stick graphic design in white, green, gray, and red. The player's name and sponsor logos are printed on the design. A discount coupon for 2.50 off any children's admission to a game is attached at the bottom and can be torn along perforations. The card measures approximately 5 1/4" tall when the coupon is removed. The backs carry biographical information and sponsor logos. The cards are numbered on the front near the right edge.

| | MINT | NRMT |
|---|---|---|
| COMPLETE SET (16) | 14.00 | 6.25 |
| COMMON CARD (1-16) | .50 | .23 |
| ❑ 1 Andy Spruce CO | .50 | .23 |
| ❑ 2 Sean Evoy | .75 | .35 |
| ❑ 3 Mario Martini | .75 | .35 |
| ❑ 4 Brent Daugherty | .75 | .35 |
| ❑ 5 Mario Chitaroni | 1.00 | .45 |
| ❑ 6 Dan Chiasson | .75 | .35 |
| ❑ 7 Jeff Brown | 4.00 | 1.80 |
| ❑ 8 Todd Sepkowski | .75 | .35 |
| ❑ 9 Brad Belland | .75 | .35 |
| ❑ 10 Glenn Greenough | .75 | .35 |
| ❑ 11 John Landry | .75 | .35 |
| ❑ 12 Max Middendorf | .75 | .35 |
| ❑ 13 David Moylan | .75 | .35 |
| ❑ 14 Jamie Nadjiwan | .75 | .35 |
| ❑ 15 Warren Rychel | 2.00 | .90 |
| ❑ 16 Ed Smith | .75 | .35 |

## 1985-86 Sudbury Wolves

This 26-card set measures approximately 2 3/4" by 4" and features color, posed player photos with white borders. A facsimile autograph is inscribed across the bottom of the picture. The backs carry biographical information, P.L.A.Y. (Police, Laws and Youth) public service messages in English and French, and sponsor logos.

| | MINT | NRMT |
|---|---|---|
| COMPLETE SET (26) | 12.00 | 5.50 |
| COMMON CARD (1-26) | .25 | .11 |
| ❑ 1 Sudbury Regional Police Crest | .25 | .11 |
| ❑ 2 Sponsors' Card | .25 | .11 |
| ❑ 3 Sudbury Wolves logo Checklist | 1.00 | .45 |
| ❑ 4 R. Zanibbi Chief of Police | .25 | .11 |
| ❑ 5 Wayne Maxner CO | .50 | .23 |
| ❑ 6 Sean Evoy | .50 | .23 |
| ❑ 7 Todd Lalonde | .50 | .23 |
| ❑ 8 Costa Papista | .50 | .23 |
| ❑ 9 Robin Rubic | .50 | .23 |
| ❑ 10 Dave Moylan | .50 | .23 |
| ❑ 11 Brent Daugherty | .50 | .23 |
| ❑ 12 Glenn Greenough | .50 | .23 |
| ❑ 13 Mario Chitaroni | .75 | .35 |
| ❑ 14 Ken McRae | .75 | .35 |
| ❑ 15 Mike Hudson | 1.00 | .45 |
| ❑ 16 Andy Paquette | .50 | .23 |
| ❑ 17 Ed Lemaire | .50 | .23 |
| ❑ 18 Mark Turner | .50 | .23 |
| ❑ 19 Craig Duncanson | .50 | .23 |
| ❑ 20 Jeff Brown | 2.00 | .90 |
| ❑ 21 Team Photo | 1.00 | .45 |
| ❑ 22 Max Middendorf | .75 | .35 |
| ❑ 23 Keith Van Rooyen | .50 | .23 |
| ❑ 24 Brad Walcot | .50 | .23 |
| ❑ 25 Rob Wilson | .50 | .23 |
| ❑ 26 Bill White | .50 | .23 |

## 1986-87 Sudbury Wolves

Cards measure approximately 3" x 4" and feature color action photos and a facsimile autograph on the front.The card backs feature biographical information along with P.L.A.Y. public service messages.

| | MINT | NRMT |
|---|---|---|
| COMPLETE SET (28) | 12.00 | 5.50 |
| COMMON CARD (1-28) | .25 | .11 |
| ❑ 1 Ted Mielczarek | .50 | .23 |
| ❑ 2 Todd Lalonde | .50 | .23 |
| ❑ 3 Costa Papista | .50 | .23 |
| ❑ 4 Justin Corbeil | .50 | .23 |
| ❑ 5 Dave Moylan | .50 | .23 |
| ❑ 6 Brent Daugherty | .50 | .23 |
| ❑ 8 Mario Chitaroni | .75 | .35 |
| ❑ 9 Jim Way | .50 | .23 |
| ❑ 10 Dean Jalbert | .50 | .23 |
| ❑ 11 Joe Dragon | .50 | .23 |
| ❑ 12 Ken Mcrae | .50 | .23 |
| ❑ 14 Steve Hedington | .50 | .23 |
| ❑ 15 Mike Hudson | .75 | .35 |
| ❑ 16 Pierre Gagnon | .50 | .23 |
| ❑ 17 Peter Hughes | .50 | .23 |
| ❑ 18 Mark Turner | .50 | .23 |
| ❑ 19 Sudbury Police Logo | .25 | .11 |
| ❑ 20 Wayne Doucet | .50 | .23 |
| ❑ 21 Paul Dipietro | .60 | .25 |
| ❑ 22 Max Middendorf | .75 | .35 |
| ❑ 23 Phil Paquette | .50 | .23 |
| ❑ 25 Rob Wilson | .50 | .23 |
| ❑ 26 Checklist | .25 | .11 |
| ❑ 27 Chief of Police | .25 | .11 |
| ❑ 28 Claud D'Amour | .30 | .14 |
| ❑ 29 Guy Blanchard | .50 | .23 |
| ❑ 30 Joe Desrosiers | .50 | .23 |
| ❑ 31 Jake Disschops | .50 | .23 |
| ❑ 33 Bill White | .50 | .23 |

## 1987-88 Sudbury Wolves

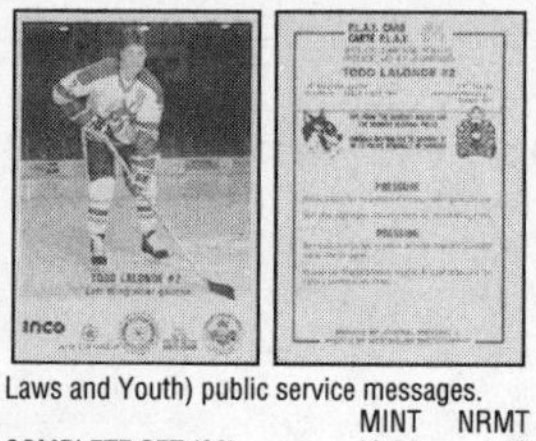

This 26-card set measures approximately 3" by 4 1/8" and features color, posed action player photos with white borders. The player's name, jersey number, and position are superimposed on the photo at the bottom. Sponsor logos in the white bottom border are INCO, Air Canada, Rotary International, Pure Spring Ginger Ale, and the Sudbury chapter of the United Steel Workers of America. The backs carry biographical information and P.L.A.Y. (Police, Laws and Youth) public service messages.

| | MINT | NRMT |
|---|---|---|
| COMPLETE SET (26) | 10.00 | 4.50 |
| COMMON CARD (1-26) | .10 | .05 |
| ❑ 1 Checklist Card | .25 | .11 |
| ❑ 2 Ted Mielczarek | .50 | .23 |
| ❑ 3 Dan Gatenby | .50 | .23 |
| ❑ 4 Todd Lalonde | .50 | .23 |
| ❑ 5 Justin Corbeil | .50 | .23 |
| ❑ 6 Jordan Fois | .50 | .23 |
| ❑ 7 Rodney Lapointe | .50 | .23 |
| ❑ 8 Dave Akey | .50 | .23 |
| ❑ 9 Jim Smith | .50 | .23 |
| ❑ 10 Fred Pennell | .50 | .23 |
| ❑ 11 Joey Simon | .50 | .23 |
| ❑ 12 Luciano Fagioli | .50 | .23 |
| ❑ 13 Robb Graham | .50 | .23 |
| ❑ 14 John Uniac | .50 | .23 |
| ❑ 15 Dave Carrie | .50 | .23 |
| ❑ 16 Pierre Gagnon | .50 | .23 |
| ❑ 17 Peter Hughes | .50 | .23 |
| ❑ 18 Scott McCullough | .50 | .23 |
| ❑ 19 Dean Guitard | .50 | .23 |
| ❑ 20 Pat Holley | .50 | .23 |
| ❑ 21 Chad Badaway | .50 | .23 |
| ❑ 22 Paul DiPietro | .75 | .35 |
| ❑ 23 Derek Thompson | .50 | .23 |
| ❑ 24 Scott Luce | .50 | .23 |
| ❑ 25 Rob Wilson | .50 | .23 |
| ❑ 26 R. Zanibbi Chief of Police | .10 | .05 |

## 1988-89 Sudbury Wolves

This 26-card set measures approximately 3" by 4 1/8" and features color, posed action player photos with white borders. The player's name, jersey number, and position are superimposed on the photo at the bottom. Sponsor logos in the white bottom border are INCO, Loeb, IGA, Air Canada, Air Ontario, Rotary International, Pizza Hut, and the Sudbury chapter of the United Steel Workers of America. The backs carry biographical information and P.L.A.Y. (Police, Law and Youth) public service messages.

| | MINT | NRMT |
|---|---|---|
| COMPLETE SET (26) | 10.00 | 4.50 |
| COMMON CARD (1-26) | .25 | .11 |
| ❑ 1 Checklist | .25 | .11 |
| ❑ 2 David Goverde | .75 | .35 |
| ❑ 3 Ted Mielczarek | .50 | .23 |
| ❑ 4 Adam Bennett | .75 | .35 |
| ❑ 5 Kevin Grant | .50 | .23 |
| ❑ 6 Jordan Fois | .50 | .23 |
| ❑ 7 Sean O'Donnell | .50 | .23 |
| ❑ 8 Kevin Meisner | .50 | .23 |
| ❑ 9 Jim Smith | .50 | .23 |
| ❑ 10 Red Pennell | .50 | .23 |
| ❑ 11 Tyler Pella | .50 | .23 |
| ❑ 12 Dean Pella | .50 | .23 |
| ❑ 13 Darren Bell | .50 | .23 |
| ❑ 14 Derek Thompson | .50 | .23 |
| ❑ 15 Terry Chitaroni | .50 | .23 |
| ❑ 16 Sean Stansfield | .50 | .23 |
| ❑ 17 Alastair Still | .50 | .23 |
| ❑ 18 Jim Sonmez | .50 | .23 |
| ❑ 19 Shannon Bolton | .50 | .23 |
| ❑ 20 Andy Paquette | .50 | .23 |
| ❑ 21 Mark Turner | .50 | .23 |
| ❑ 22 Paul DiPietro | .75 | .35 |
| ❑ 23 Robert Knesaurek | .50 | .23 |
| ❑ 24 Todd Lalonde | .50 | .23 |
| ❑ 25 Scott Herniman | .50 | .23 |
| ❑ 26 R. Zanibbi Chief of Police | .25 | .11 |

## 1989-90 Sudbury Wolves

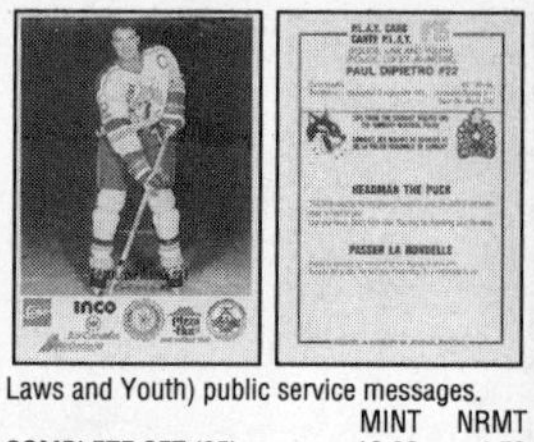

This 25-card set measures approximately 3" by 4 1/8" and features color, posed action player photos with white borders. The player's name, jersey number, and position are superimposed on the photo at the bottom. Sponsor logos in the white bottom border are Coke, INCO, Air Canada, Air Ontario, Rotary International, Pizza Hut, and the Sudbury chapter of the United Steel Workers of America. The backs carry biographical information and P.L.A.Y. (Police, Laws and Youth) public service messages.

| | MINT | NRMT |
|---|---|---|
| COMPLETE SET (25) | 10.00 | 4.50 |
| COMMON CARD (1-25) | .25 | .11 |
| ❑ 1 Checklist NNO | .25 | .11 |
| ❑ 2 Alastair Still | .50 | .23 |
| ❑ 3 Bill Kovacs | .50 | .23 |
| ❑ 4 Darren Bell | .50 | .23 |
| ❑ 5 Scott Mahoney | .50 | .23 |
| ❑ 6 Glen Murray | 1.00 | .45 |
| ❑ 7 Alain Laforge | .50 | .23 |
| ❑ 8 Jamie Matthews | .75 | .35 |
| ❑ 9 Jon Boeve | .50 | .23 |
| ❑ 10 Adam Bennett | .75 | .35 |
| ❑ 11 Derek Etches | .50 | .23 |
| ❑ 12 Marcus Middleton | .50 | .23 |
| ❑ 13 Jim Sonmez | .50 | .23 |
| ❑ 14 Leonard MacDonald | .50 | .23 |
| ❑ 15 Paul DiPietro | .75 | .35 |
| ❑ 16 Neil Ethier | .50 | .23 |
| ❑ 17 Sean O'Donnell | .50 | .23 |
| ❑ 18 Andy MacVicar | .50 | .23 |
| ❑ 19 David Goverde | .75 | .35 |
| ❑ 20 Jason Young | .50 | .23 |
| ❑ 21 Wade Bartley | .50 | .23 |
| ❑ 22 Barry Young | .50 | .23 |
| ❑ 23 R. Zanibbi Chief of Police | .25 | .11 |
| ❑ 24 Terry Chitaroni | .50 | .23 |
| ❑ 25 Rob Knesaurek | .50 | .23 |

## 1990-91 Sudbury Wolves

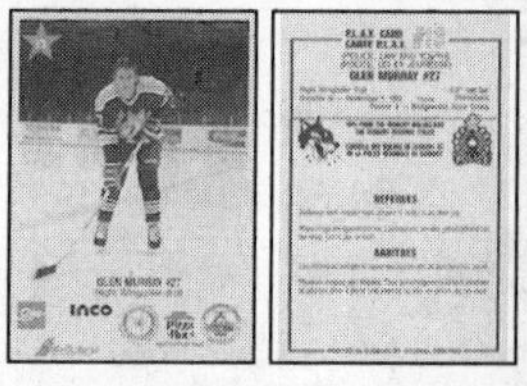

This 25-card P.L.A.Y. (Police, Law and Youth) set measures approximately 3" by 4 1/8" and features color posed action player photos with white borders. The player's name and position is superimposed on the picture at the bottom. Sponsor logos in the white bottom border are Coke, INCO, Air Ontario, Rotary International, Pizza Hut, and the Sudbury chapter of the United Steel Workers of America. The backs carry biographical information and Tips From The Sudbury Wolves and the Sudbury Regional Police. For the most part, the cards are numbered on both sides after the player's jersey number (except for card number 7 and 18).

| | MINT | NRMT |
|---|---|---|
| COMPLETE SET (25) | 10.00 | 4.50 |
| COMMON CARD (1-25) | .10 | .05 |
| ❑ 1 Darryl Paquette | .60 | .25 |
| ❑ 2 Adam Bennett | .50 | .23 |
| ❑ 3 Barry Young | .50 | .23 |
| ❑ 4 Jon Boeve | .50 | .23 |
| ❑ 5 Kyle Blacklock | .50 | .23 |
| ❑ 6 Sean O'Donnell | .50 | .23 |
| ❑ 7 Dan Ryder | .60 | .25 |
| ❑ 8 Wade Bartley | .50 | .23 |
| ❑ 9 Jamie Matthews | .60 | .25 |
| ❑ 10 Rod Hinks | .50 | .23 |
| ❑ 11 Derek Etches | .50 | .23 |
| ❑ 12 Brandon Convery | .75 | .35 |
| ❑ 13 Glen Murray | .75 | .35 |
| ❑ 14 Bill Kovacs | .50 | .23 |
| ❑ 15 Terry Chitaroni | .50 | .23 |
| ❑ 16 Jason Young | .50 | .23 |
| ❑ 17 Alastair Still | .50 | .23 |
| ❑ 18 Shawn Rivers | .50 | .23 |
| ❑ 19 Alain Laforge | .50 | .23 |
| ❑ 20 J.D. Eaton | .50 | .23 |
| ❑ 21 Mike Peca | 1.50 | .70 |
| ❑ 22 Howler (Mascot) | .10 | .05 |
| ❑ 23 Mike Yeo | .50 | .23 |
| ❑ 24 L'il Rookie Checklist | .10 | .05 |
| ❑ 25 R. Zanibbi Chief of Police | .10 | .05 |

## 1991-92 Sudbury Wolves

This 25-card set measures approximately 3" by 4 1/8" and features color, posed action player photos with white borders. The player's name, jersey number, and position are superimposed on the photo at the bottom. Sponsor logos in the white bottom border are Coke, INCO, Air Ontario, The Westbury, Pizza Hut, and the Sudbury chapter of the United Steel Workers

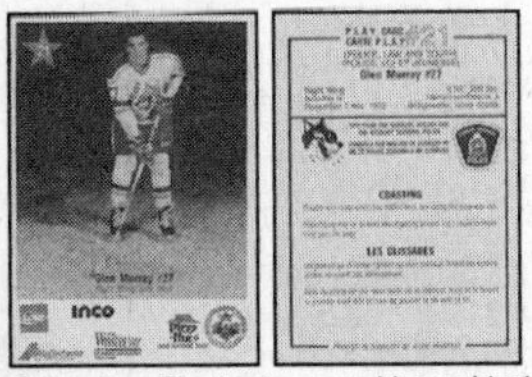

of America. The backs carry biographical information and P.L.A.Y. (Police, Laws and Youth) public service messages. The cards are numbered on the front in a star and on the back.

| | MINT | NRMT |
|---|---|---|
| COMPLETE SET (25) | 10.00 | 4.50 |
| COMMON CARD (1-25) | .10 | .05 |
| ❑ 1 R. Zanibbi<br>Chief of Police | .10 | .05 |
| ❑ 2 Howler (Mascot) | .10 | .05 |
| ❑ 3 Team Photo | .50 | .23 |
| ❑ 4 Kyle Blacklock | .35 | .16 |
| ❑ 5 Sean Gagnon | .50 | .23 |
| ❑ 6 Bernie John | .35 | .16 |
| ❑ 7 Bob MacIsaac | .35 | .16 |
| ❑ 8 Jamie Rivers | .75 | .35 |
| ❑ 9 Shawn Rivers | .35 | .16 |
| ❑ 10 Joel Sandie | .35 | .16 |
| ❑ 11 Barry Young | .35 | .16 |
| ❑ 12 George Dourian | .35 | .16 |
| ❑ 13 Dan Ryder | .60 | .25 |
| ❑ 14 Derek Armstrong | .35 | .16 |
| ❑ 15 Terry Chitaroni | .35 | .16 |
| ❑ 16 Brandon Convery | .75 | .35 |
| ❑ 17 Tim Favot | .35 | .16 |
| ❑ 18 Rod Hinks | .35 | .16 |
| ❑ 19 Jamie Matthews | .50 | .23 |
| ❑ 20 Barrie Moore | .50 | .23 |
| ❑ 21 Glen Murray | .75 | .35 |
| ❑ 22 Michael Peca | 1.00 | .45 |
| ❑ 23 Michael Yeo | .35 | .16 |
| ❑ 24 Jason Young | .35 | .16 |
| ❑ 25 Jason Zohil | .35 | .16 |

## 1992-93 Sudbury Wolves

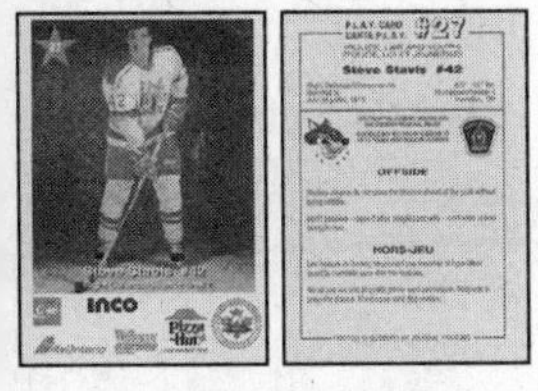

These 27 oversized bilingual cards measure approximately 3" by 4 3/16" and feature on their fronts white-bordered color posed-on-ice player photos. The player's name, jersey number, and position are displayed on each card in white lettering at the bottom of the photo. Beneath the photo, on the broad white bottom margin, appear the logos for Coke, Air Ontario, The Westbury Hotel, INCO, Pizza Hut, and the Sudbury local of the United Steel Workers of America. The white back carries the player's name, jersey number, and biography near the top. The Wolves' and Sudbury Regional Police logos along with a P.L.A.Y. (Police, Law and Youth) safety tip appear beneath. The cards are numbered on both sides.

| | MINT | NRMT |
|---|---|---|
| COMPLETE SET (27) | 14.00 | 6.25 |
| COMMON CARD (1-27) | .10 | .05 |
| ❑ 1 Howler and Lil Rookie<br>(Toy mascot and<br>police car) | .10 | .05 |
| ❑ 2 Sudbury Regional Police<br>Chief R. Zanibbi | .10 | .05 |
| ❑ 3 Bob MacIsaac | .50 | .23 |
| ❑ 4 Joel Sandie | .50 | .23 |
| ❑ 5 Rory Fitzpatrick | .75 | .35 |
| ❑ 6 Mike Wilson | .75 | .35 |
| ❑ 7 Shawn Frappier | .50 | .23 |
| ❑ 8 Bernie John | .50 | .23 |
| ❑ 9 Jamie Rivers | 1.00 | .45 |
| ❑ 10 Jamie Matthews | .60 | .25 |
| ❑ 11 Zdenek Nedved | 1.50 | .70 |
| ❑ 12 Ryan Shanahan | .50 | .23 |
| ❑ 13 Corey Crane | .50 | .23 |
| ❑ 14 Matt Kiereck | .50 | .23 |
| ❑ 15 Rick Bodkin | .50 | .23 |
| ❑ 16 Derek Armstrong | .50 | .23 |
| ❑ 17 Barrie Moore | .50 | .23 |
| ❑ 18 Rod Hinks | .50 | .23 |
| ❑ 19 Kayle Short | .50 | .23 |
| ❑ 20 Michael Yeo | .50 | .23 |
| ❑ 21 Gary Coupal | .50 | .23 |
| ❑ 22 Dennis Maxwell | .50 | .23 |
| ❑ 23 Steve Potvin | .50 | .23 |
| ❑ 24 Joel Poirier | .50 | .23 |
| ❑ 25 Greg Dreveny | .50 | .23 |
| ❑ 26 Mark Gowan | .50 | .23 |
| ❑ 27 Steve Staios | .75 | .35 |

## 1993-94 Sudbury Wolves

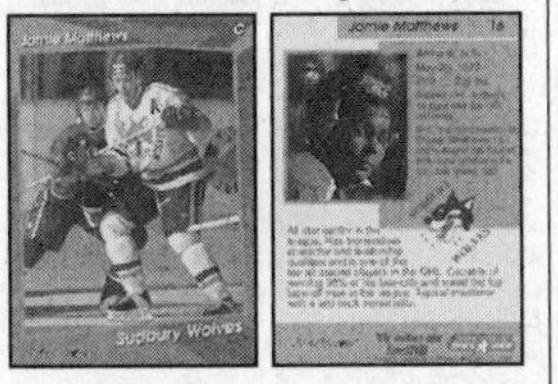

Sponsored by The Sudbury Star, CoverStory, and Sudbury Sports North, and printed by Slapshot Images Ltd., this standard-size 25-card set features the 1993-94 Sudbury Wolves. On a geometrical team color-coded background, the fronts feature color action player photos with thin grey borders. The player's name, position and team name, as well as the producer's logo, also appear on the front. The backs carry a close-up player portrait and biographical information, along with team and sponsors' logos. Included in this set is a Slapshot ad card with a 1994 calendar on the back.

| | MINT | NRMT |
|---|---|---|
| COMPLETE SET (25) | 10.00 | 4.50 |
| COMMON CARD (1-24) | .35 | .16 |
| ❑ 1 Shawn Silver | .40 | .18 |
| ❑ 2 Jeff Melnechuk | .40 | .18 |
| ❑ 3 Jay McKee | .75 | .35 |
| ❑ 4 Chris McMurtry | .40 | .18 |
| ❑ 5 Rory Fitzpatrick | .50 | .23 |
| ❑ 6 Mike Wilson | .75 | .35 |
| ❑ 7 Shawn Frappier | .40 | .18 |
| ❑ 8 Jamie Rivers | .75 | .35 |
| ❑ 9 Zdenek Nedved | 1.00 | .45 |
| ❑ 10 Ryan Shanahan | .50 | .23 |
| ❑ 11 Sean Venedam | .50 | .23 |
| ❑ 12 Andrew Dale | .40 | .18 |
| ❑ 13 Mark Giannetti | .40 | .18 |
| ❑ 14 Rick Bodkin | .50 | .23 |
| ❑ 15 Barrie Moore | .50 | .23 |
| ❑ 16 Jamie Matthews | .50 | .23 |
| ❑ 17 Gary Coupal | .40 | .18 |
| ❑ 18 Ilya Lysenko | .40 | .18 |
| ❑ 19 Simon Sherry | .40 | .18 |
| ❑ 20 Steve Potvin | .40 | .18 |
| ❑ 21 Joel Poirier | .50 | .23 |
| ❑ 22 Mike Yeo | .40 | .18 |
| ❑ 23 Bob MacIsaac | .40 | .18 |
| ❑ 24 Paul DiPietro | .50 | .23 |
| ❑ NNO Slapshot Ad Card | .10 | .05 |

## 1993-94 Sudbury Wolves Police

| | MINT | NRMT |
|---|---|---|
| COMPLETE SET (26) | 10.00 | 4.50 |
| COMMON CARD (1-26) | .20 | .09 |
| ❑ 1 Chief of Police | .20 | .09 |
| ❑ 2 The Howler | .20 | .09 |
| ❑ 3 Jay McKee | .75 | .35 |
| ❑ 4 Chris McMurtry | .40 | .18 |
| ❑ 5 Rory Fitzpatrick | .50 | .23 |
| ❑ 6 Mike Wilson | .75 | .35 |
| ❑ 7 Shawn Frappier | .40 | .18 |
| ❑ 8 Jamie Rivers | .75 | .35 |
| ❑ 9 Jamie Matthews | .50 | .23 |
| ❑ 10 Zdenek Nedved | .75 | .35 |
| ❑ 11 Ryan Shanahan | .50 | .23 |
| ❑ 12 Andrew Dale | .40 | .18 |
| ❑ 13 Mark Giannetti | .40 | .18 |
| ❑ 14 Rick Bodkin | .50 | .23 |
| ❑ 15 Barrie Moore | .50 | .23 |
| ❑ 16 Gary Coupal | .40 | .18 |
| ❑ 17 Ilya Lysenko | .40 | .18 |
| ❑ 18 Simon Sherry | .40 | .18 |
| ❑ 19 Steve Potvin | .40 | .18 |
| ❑ 20 Joel Poirier | .50 | .23 |
| ❑ 21 Shawn Silver | .40 | .18 |
| ❑ 22 Micheal Yeo | .40 | .18 |
| ❑ 23 Jeff Melnechuk | .40 | .18 |
| ❑ 24 Sean Venedam | .50 | .23 |
| ❑ 25 Bob Macisaac | .40 | .18 |
| ❑ 26 Sudbury Police | .20 | .09 |

## 1994-95 Sudbury Wolves

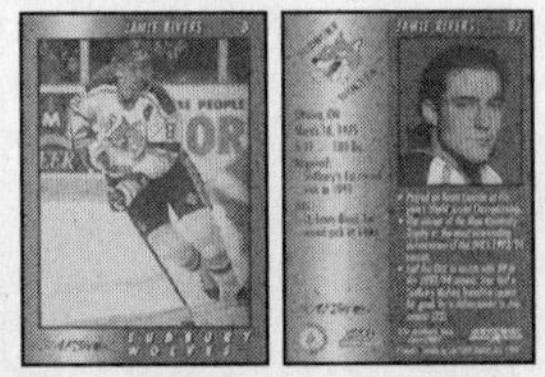

Sponsored by The Sudbury Star CoverStory, Sudbury Sports North and Nick's Sports Cards, and printed by Slapshot Images Ltd., this set features the 1994-95 Sudbury Wolves. On a silver and blue background, the fronts feature color action player photos with thin black borders. The player's name, position and team name, as well as the producer's logo, also appear on the front. The team color-coded backs carry a close-up player portrait and biographical information, along with team and sponsor logos. Included in this set is a Slapshot ad card with a 1995 calendar on the back.

| | MINT | NRMT |
|---|---|---|
| COMPLETE SET (26) | 10.00 | 4.50 |
| COMMON CARD (1-25) | .10 | .05 |
| ❑ 1 Checklist | .10 | .05 |
| ❑ 2 Dave MacDonald | .50 | .23 |
| ❑ 3 Rory Fitzpatrick | .50 | .23 |
| ❑ 4 Mike Wilson | .60 | .25 |
| ❑ 5 Neal Martin | .35 | .16 |
| ❑ 6 Shawn Frappier | .35 | .16 |
| ❑ 7 Jamie Rivers | .75 | .35 |
| ❑ 8 Zdenek Nedved | .75 | .35 |
| ❑ 9 Ryan Shanahan | .35 | .16 |
| ❑ 10 Sean Venedam | .35 | .16 |
| ❑ 11 Andrew Dale | .35 | .16 |
| ❑ 12 Rick Bodkin | .35 | .16 |
| ❑ 13 Luc Gagne | .35 | .16 |
| ❑ 14 Barrie Moore | .50 | .23 |
| ❑ 15 Richard Rochefort | .35 | .16 |
| ❑ 16 Krystof Secemski | .35 | .16 |
| ❑ 17 Jason Bonsignore | .75 | .35 |
| ❑ 18 Liam MacEachern | .35 | .16 |
| ❑ 19 Simon Sherry | .35 | .16 |
| ❑ 20 Ethan Moreau | 1.50 | .70 |
| ❑ 21 Matt Mullin | .50 | .23 |
| ❑ 22 Aaron Starnyski | .35 | .16 |
| ❑ 23 Ron Newhook | .35 | .16 |
| ❑ 24 Glenn Merkosky CO/GM<br>Todd Lalonde ACO/MG | .10 | .05 |
| ❑ 25 Dan Lebold TR<br>Jason Allen ATR | .10 | .05 |
| ❑ NNO Ad Card | .10 | .05 |

## 1994-95 Sudbury Wolves Police

Card fronts feature a posed color photo surrounded by a white border. The card number is located in a star in the upper left corner. Card backs contain hockey and safety tips in French and English.

| | MINT | NRMT |
|---|---|---|
| COMPLETE SET (27) | 10.00 | 4.50 |
| COMMON CARD (1-27) | .10 | .05 |
| ❑ 1 Chief of Police | .10 | .05 |
| ❑ 2 The Howler | .10 | .05 |
| ❑ 3 Rick Bodkin | .35 | .16 |
| ❑ 4 Gary Coupal | .50 | .23 |
| ❑ 5 Andrew Dale | .35 | .16 |
| ❑ 6 Luc Gagne | .35 | .16 |
| ❑ 7 Chester Gallant | .10 | .05 |
| ❑ 8 Kiley Hill | .35 | .16 |
| ❑ 9 Liam MacEachern | .35 | .16 |
| ❑ 10 Barrie Moore | .50 | .23 |
| ❑ 11 Zdenek Nedved | .75 | .35 |
| ❑ 12 Ron Newhook | .35 | .16 |
| ❑ 13 Richard Rochefort | .35 | .16 |
| ❑ 14 Krysztof Secemski | .35 | .16 |
| ❑ 15 Ryan Shanahan | .35 | .16 |
| ❑ 16 Simon Sherry | .35 | .16 |
| ❑ 17 Sean Venedam | .35 | .16 |
| ❑ 18 Rory Fitzpatrick | .50 | .23 |
| ❑ 19 Shawn Frappier | .35 | .16 |
| ❑ 20 Gregg Lalonde | .50 | .23 |
| ❑ 21 Neal Martin | .35 | .16 |
| ❑ 22 Jay McKee | .35 | .16 |
| ❑ 23 Jamie Rivers | .75 | .35 |
| ❑ 24 Mike Wilson | .60 | .25 |
| ❑ 25 Dave Macdonald | .50 | .23 |
| ❑ 26 Matt Mullin | .50 | .23 |
| ❑ 27 Steve Valiquette | .35 | .16 |

## 1995-96 Sudbury Wolves

This 25-card set was one of two produced to commemorate the '95-96 Wolves. This one was released by the team, in conjunction with sponsors Four Star Sports and Belanger's. The set is standard size with an action photo on the front, while the backs contain a player bio.

| | MINT | NRMT |
|---|---|---|
| COMPLETE SET (25) | 8.00 | 3.60 |
| COMMON CARD (1-25) | .10 | .05 |
| ❑ 1 Sean Venedam | .50 | .23 |
| ❑ 2 Brad Domonsky | .35 | .16 |
| ❑ 3 Joe Lombardo | .35 | .16 |
| ❑ 4 Tyson Flinn | .35 | .16 |
| ❑ 5 Luc Gagne | .35 | .16 |
| ❑ 6 Ryan Shanahan | .35 | .16 |
| ❑ 7 Simon Sherry | .35 | .16 |
| ❑ 8 Kevin Hansen | .35 | .16 |
| ❑ 9 Gregg Lalonde | .35 | .16 |
| ❑ 10 Liam MacEachern | .35 | .16 |
| ❑ 11 Jeremy Adduono | .50 | .23 |
| ❑ 12 Ron Newhook | .35 | .16 |
| ❑ 13 Noel Burkitt | .35 | .16 |
| ❑ 14 Neal Martin | .35 | .16 |
| ❑ 15 Tim Swartz | .35 | .16 |
| ❑ 16 Rob Butler | .35 | .16 |
| ❑ 17 Darryl Moxam | .35 | .16 |
| ❑ 18 Steve Valiquette | .50 | .23 |
| ❑ 19 Ryan Sly | .35 | .16 |
| ❑ 20 Dave MacDonald | .50 | .23 |
| ❑ 21 Andrew Dale | .35 | .16 |
| ❑ 22 Belanger's All-Star Team | .10 | .05 |
| ❑ 23 Four Star Sports | .10 | .05 |
| ❑ 24 Richard Rochefort | .35 | .16 |
| ❑ 25 Title Card | .10 | .05 |

## 1995-96 Sudbury Wolves Police

This 24-card P.L.A.Y. set measures approximately 3" by 4 1/8" and features color posed player photos augmented by a white border. The player's name and position is superimposed on the photo along the bottom. Just below that is an array of sponsor logos, including Coke, Air Ontario and The Westbury Hotel. The backs carry biographical data and Tips from the Wolves and local police, written in both of Canada's official languages. The cards are numbered on both sides.

| | MINT | NRMT |
|---|---|---|
| COMPLETE SET (24) | 8.00 | 3.60 |
| COMMON CARD (1-24) | .10 | .05 |
| ❑ 1 Chief Alex McCauley | .10 | .05 |
| ❑ 2 The Howler<br>Mascot | .10 | .05 |
| ❑ 3 Jeremy Adduono | .50 | .23 |
| ❑ 4 Noel Burkitt | .40 | .18 |
| ❑ 5 Rob Butler | .40 | .18 |
| ❑ 6 Andrew Dale | .40 | .18 |
| ❑ 7 Brad Domonsky | .40 | .18 |
| ❑ 8 Tyson Flinn | .40 | .18 |
| ❑ 9 Luc Gagne | .40 | .18 |
| ❑ 10 Kevin Hansen | .40 | .18 |
| ❑ 11 Gregg Lalonde | .40 | .18 |
| ❑ 12 Joe Lombardo | .40 | .18 |
| ❑ 13 Dave MacDonald | .50 | .23 |
| ❑ 14 Liam MacEachern | .40 | .18 |
| ❑ 15 Neal Martin | .40 | .18 |
| ❑ 16 Darryl Moxam | .40 | .18 |
| ❑ 17 Ron Newhook | .40 | .18 |
| ❑ 18 Richard Rochefort | .40 | .18 |
| ❑ 19 Ryan Shanahan | .40 | .18 |
| ❑ 20 Simon Sherry | .40 | .18 |
| ❑ 21 Ryan Sly | .40 | .18 |
| ❑ 22 Shawn Sobush | .40 | .18 |
| ❑ 23 Steve Valiquette | .50 | .23 |
| ❑ 24 Sean Venedam | .50 | .23 |

## 1996-97 Sudbury Wolves

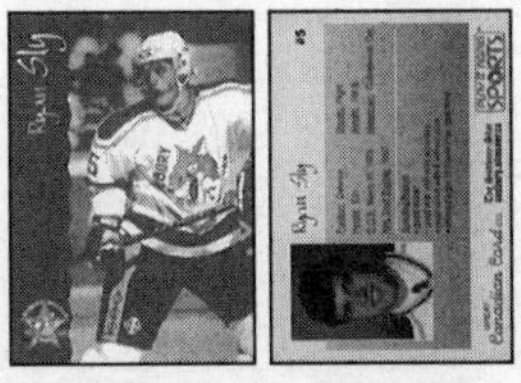

One of two sets issued to commemorate the Wolves' 25th anniversary season, this 27-card standard sized issue was produced by the team and sponsored by Play It Again Sports, The Great Canadian Card. Co. and the Sudbury Star. The cards were produced by the team and sold through arena concessions. The card feature action photography on the front complimented by a black border containing the player's name and the team logo on the left. The backs contain biographical data, including a scouting report on the positive aspects of each player's game.

| | MINT | NRMT |
|---|---|---|
| COMPLETE SET (27) | 9.00 | 4.00 |
| COMMON CARD (1-27) | .10 | .05 |
| ❑ 1 Title card | .25 | .11 |
| ❑ 2 Jeremy Adduono | .50 | .23 |
| ❑ 3 Louie Blackbird | .40 | .18 |
| ❑ 4 Tom Brown | .50 | .23 |
| ❑ 5 Peter Campbell | .40 | .18 |
| ❑ 6 Brad Domonsky | .40 | .18 |
| ❑ 7 Jason Gaggi | .50 | .23 |
| ❑ 8 Luc Gagne | .40 | .18 |
| ❑ 9 Kevin Hansen | .40 | .18 |
| ❑ 10 Jason Hurlbut | .40 | .18 |
| ❑ 11 Konstantin Kalmikov | .75 | .35 |
| ❑ 12 Robin LaCour | .40 | .18 |
| ❑ 13 Paul Mara | 1.00 | .45 |
| ❑ 14 Norm Milley | .75 | .35 |
| ❑ 15 Gerald Moriarty | .40 | .18 |
| ❑ 16 Scott Page | .40 | .18 |
| ❑ 17 Steve Reid | .40 | .18 |
| ❑ 18 Richard Rochefort | .40 | .18 |
| ❑ 19 Brian Scott | .40 | .18 |
| ❑ 20 Chris Shanahan | .40 | .18 |
| ❑ 21 Ryan Sly | .40 | .18 |
| ❑ 22 Jonas Soling | .40 | .18 |
| ❑ 23 Steve Valiquette | .50 | .23 |
| ❑ 24 Sean Venedam | .50 | .23 |
| ❑ 25 Great Canadian Card Co. | .10 | .05 |
| ❑ 26 LaSalle Court Plaza | .10 | .05 |
| ❑ 27 Derek Chartrand | .25 | .11 |

## 1996-97 Sudbury Wolves Police

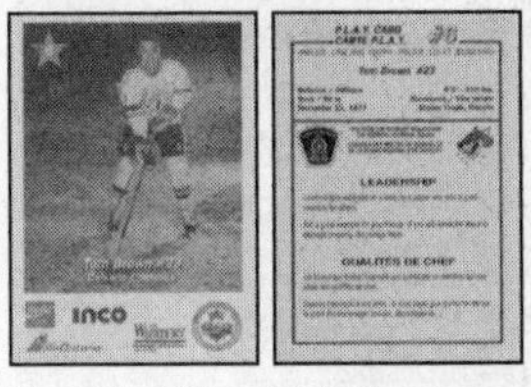

This oversized (3" by 4 3/16"), 26-card set was issued in conjunction with the Sudbury Police Department. The card fronts feature a posed color photo surrounded by a white border. The player's name, number and position are along the bottomm, with the card number is displayed in a star in the upper left corner. The lower portion of the card is filled with sponsor logos, including Coke, Air Ontario and INCO. The sparse card backs feature stats and a player tip in both French and English.

| | MINT | NRMT |
|---|---|---|
| COMPLETE SET (26) | 10.00 | 4.50 |
| COMMON CARD (1-26) | .10 | .05 |
| ❑ 1 Chief Alex McCauley | .10 | .05 |
| ❑ 2 The Howler<br>Mascot | .10 | .05 |
| ❑ 3 Sudbury Wolves<br>25th Anniversary Card | .10 | .05 |
| ❑ 4 Jeremy Adduono | .60 | .25 |
| ❑ 5 Louie Blackbird | .40 | .18 |
| ❑ 6 Tom Brown | .60 | .25 |
| ❑ 7 Peter Campbell | .40 | .18 |
| ❑ 8 Brad Domonsky | .40 | .18 |
| ❑ 9 Tyson Flinn | .40 | .18 |
| ❑ 10 Jason Gaggi | .60 | .25 |
| ❑ 11 Luc Gagne | .40 | .18 |
| ❑ 12 Kevin Hansen | .40 | .18 |
| ❑ 13 Konstantin Kalmikov | 1.00 | .45 |
| ❑ 14 Robin Lacour | .40 | .18 |
| ❑ 15 Joe Lombardo | .40 | .18 |
| ❑ 16 Paul Mara | 1.25 | .55 |
| ❑ 17 Norm Milley | 1.00 | .45 |
| ❑ 18 Scott Page | .40 | .18 |
| ❑ 19 Richard Rochefort | .40 | .18 |
| ❑ 20 Brian Scott | .40 | .18 |
| ❑ 21 Chris Shanahan | .40 | .18 |
| ❑ 22 Ryan Sly | .40 | .18 |
| ❑ 23 Jonas Soling | .40 | .18 |
| ❑ 24 Tim Swartz | .40 | .18 |
| ❑ 25 Steve Valiquette | .60 | .25 |
| ❑ 26 Sean Venedam | .60 | .25 |

## 1997-98 Sudbury Wolves Police

Card fronts feature a posed color photo surrounded by a white border. The card number is located in a star in the upper left corner. Card backs contain hockey and safety tips in French and English.

| | MINT | NRMT |
|---|---|---|
| COMPLETE SET (25) | 10.00 | 4.50 |
| COMMON CARD (1-25) | .10 | .05 |
| ❑ 1 Chief of Police | .10 | .05 |
| ❑ 2 Jeremy Adduono | .35 | .16 |
| ❑ 3 Ryan Barnes | .40 | .18 |
| ❑ 4 Peter Campbell | .35 | .16 |
| ❑ 5 Konstantin Kalmikov | .35 | .16 |
| ❑ 6 Tom Watt | .35 | .16 |
| ❑ 7 Norm Milley | .75 | .35 |
| ❑ 8 Scott Page | .35 | .16 |
| ❑ 9 Jonas Soling | .35 | .16 |
| ❑ 10 Mike Fisher | .35 | .16 |
| ❑ 11 Taylor Pyatt | .75 | .35 |
| ❑ 12 Derek Mackenzie | .50 | .23 |
| ❑ 13 Nevin Patterson | .35 | .16 |
| ❑ 14 Jason Sands | .35 | .16 |
| ❑ 15 Colin Scotland | .35 | .16 |
| ❑ 16 Paul Mara | 1.50 | .70 |
| ❑ 17 David Cornacchia | .35 | .16 |
| ❑ 18 Ryan Mckie | .35 | .16 |
| ❑ 19 Michael Tilson | .35 | .16 |
| ❑ 20 Brad Morgan | .35 | .16 |
| ❑ 21 Matthew Hodges | .35 | .16 |
| ❑ 22 Brad Simms | .35 | .16 |
| ❑ 23 Steve Valiquette | .40 | .18 |
| ❑ 24 Andrew Raycroft | .35 | .16 |
| ❑ 25 The Howler | .10 | .05 |

## 1995-96 Swift Current Broncos

This 20-card set features color player photos on a blue-and-green background. The backs carry player information. The cards are unnumbered and checklisted below in alphabetical order.

| | MINT | NRMT |
|---|---|---|
| COMPLETE SET (20) | 8.00 | 3.60 |
| COMMON CARD (1-20) | .25 | .11 |

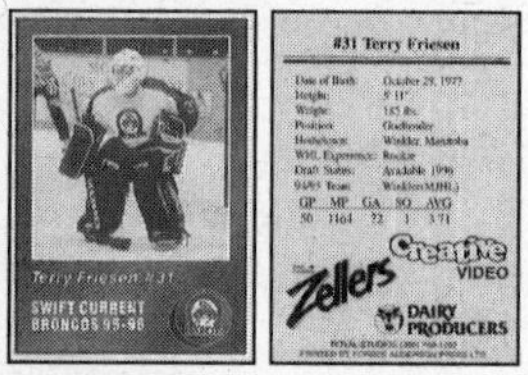

❑ 1 Derek Arbez .25 .11
❑ 2 Chad Beagle .25 .11
❑ 3 Kurt Drummond .25 .11
❑ 4 Terry Friesen 1.00 .45
❑ 5 Ryan Geremia .35 .16
❑ 6 Jeff Henkelman .35 .16
❑ 7 Jeff Kirwan .35 .16
❑ 8 Brad Larsen .75 .35
❑ 9 Aaron MacDonald 1.00 .45
❑ 10 Craig Millar .35 .16
❑ 11 Jaroslav Obsut .35 .16
❑ 12 Colin O'Hara .35 .16
❑ 13 Jeff Schaeffer .35 .16
❑ 14 Brent Sopel .35 .16
❑ 15 Josh St. Louis .35 .16
❑ 16 Chris Szysky .35 .16
❑ 17 Jesse Rezansoff .35 .16
❑ 18 Jeremy Rondeau .35 .16
❑ 19 Sergei Varlamov .35 .16
❑ 20 Tyler Willis .35 .16

## 1996-97 Swift Current Broncos

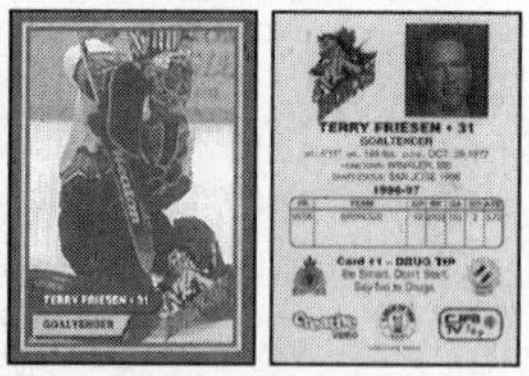

This 24-card set was produced by the club for distribution at the rink and by mail. The cards feature an action photograph surrounded by a blue, white and green borders. The black and white backs feature a mug shot, team logo, personal stats and bio and a drug tip.

| | MINT | NRMT |
|---|---|---|
| COMPLETE SET (24) | 8.00 | 3.60 |
| COMMON CARD (1-24) | .35 | .16 |

❑ 1 Terry Friesen .75 .35
❑ 2 Lindsey Materi .50 .23
❑ 3 Kevin Mackie .35 .16
❑ 4 Jeff Henkelman .35 .16
❑ 5 Michal Rozsival .35 .16
❑ 6 Brent Sopel .35 .16
❑ 7 Lawrence Nycholat .35 .16
❑ 8 Chad Beagle .35 .16
❑ 9 Jeff Schaeffer .35 .16
❑ 10 Tyler Shybunka .35 .16
❑ 11 Josh St. Louis .35 .16
❑ 12 Chris Szysky .35 .16
❑ 13 Tyler Perry .35 .16
❑ 14 Dreu Volk .35 .16
❑ 15 Nathan Strueby .35 .16
❑ 16 Kurt Drummond .35 .16
❑ 17 Brad Larsen .75 .35
❑ 18 Ryan Tobler .35 .16
❑ 19 Jeremy Rondeau .35 .16
❑ 20 Jeff Kirwan .35 .16
❑ 21 Brett Allan .35 .16
❑ 22 Andrew Milne .35 .16
❑ 23 Sergei Varlamov .35 .16
❑ 24 Derek Arbez .35 .16

## 1996-97 Syracuse Crunch

This 25-card set was produced by Split Second and sponsored by Y94 radio and Healthsource. The set features action photos on the front, and statistical information on the back. The cards were sold by the club at the rink or through the mail. The unnumbered cards are listed below according to their sweater numbers, which are displayed prominently in the upper left hand corner of each card back.

| | MINT | NRMT |
|---|---|---|
| COMPLETE SET (25) | 8.00 | 3.60 |
| COMMON CARD | .10 | .05 |

❑ 1 Mike Fountain .50 .23
❑ 4 Mark Wotton .40 .18
❑ 5 Mark Krys .40 .18
❑ 9 Robb Gordon .50 .23
❑ 10 Darren Sinclair .40 .18
❑ 11 Ian McIntyre .40 .18
❑ 14 John Badduke .40 .18
❑ 16 Doug Ast .40 .18
❑ 17 Brian Loney .40 .18
❑ 18 Tyson Nash .40 .18
❑ 19 Lonny Bohonos .75 .35
❑ 21 Dave Scatchard .40 .18
❑ 23 Chad Allan .40 .18
❑ 25 Bogdan Savenko .40 .18
❑ 26 John Namestnikov .40 .18
❑ 27 Bert Robertsson .40 .18
❑ 28 Chris McAllister .50 .23
❑ 30 Frederic Cassivi .50 .23
❑ 35 Larry Courville .50 .23
❑ 37 Rick Girard .40 .18
❑ 38 Rod Stevens .40 .18
❑ 44 Brent Tully .40 .18
❑ NNO Crunchman (Mascot) .10 .05
❑ NNO Jack McIlhargey CO .10 .05
❑ NNO AHL Ad Card .10 .05

## 1992-93 Tacoma Rockets

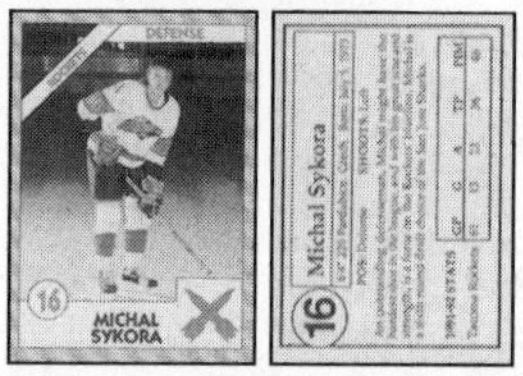

This 30-card standard-size set features hatch-bordered, posed-on-ice color player photos. In a white field under the photo are the player's name, and in the right corner, the team logo of crossed red rockets. The uniform number appears in turquoise to the lower left in a circle that straddles the picture and the white field. The team name appears in a diagonal across the top left corner of the photo and the player's position is in blue letters across the top. The horizontal backs have the encircled player number in the top left with the player's name and biography boxed just to the right. The center portion of the card contains a player profile with 1991-92 stats presented in a box. The cards are unnumbered and checklisted below in alphabetical order.

| | MINT | NRMT |
|---|---|---|
| COMPLETE SET (30) | 10.00 | 4.50 |
| COMMON CARD (1-30) | .10 | .05 |

❑ 1 Alexander Alexeev .50 .23
❑ 2 Jamie Black .50 .23
❑ 3 Jamie Butt .50 .23
❑ 4 Jeff Calvert .40 .18
❑ 5 Don Clark ACO .10 .05
❑ 6 Marcel Comeau CO .40 .18
❑ 7 Duane Crouse TR .10 .05
❑ 8 Allan Egeland .50 .23
❑ 9 Marty Flichel .50 .23
❑ 10 Trever Fraser .40 .18
❑ 11 Jason Kwiatkowski .50 .23
❑ 12 Todd MacDonald .50 .23
❑ 13 Dave McMillen .40 .18
❑ 14 Tony Pechthalt TR .10 .05
❑ 15 Ryan Phillips .40 .18
❑ 16 Mike Piersol .40 .18
❑ 17 Dennis Pinfold .40 .18
❑ 18 Kevin Powell .40 .18
❑ 19 Tyler Prosofsky .50 .23
❑ 20 Stu Scantlebury .40 .18
❑ 21 Drew Schoneck .40 .18
❑ 22 Adam Smith .40 .18
❑ 23 Corey Stock .40 .18
❑ 24 Barkley Swenson .40 .18
❑ 25 Michal Sykora .50 .23
❑ 26 Dallas Thompson .40 .18
❑ 27 John Varga .50 .23
❑ 28 Toby Weishaar .40 .18
❑ 29 Michal Sykora IA .50 .23
❑ 30 Cover Card (Team Logo) .25 .11

## 1993-94 Tacoma Rockets

This 30-card standard-size set features the 1993-94 Tacoma Rockets. The set is printed on thin card stock. The fronts have hatch-bordered color action player photos, with the player's name and position printed in white letters in a dark turquoise shadowed border above the photo. The team name also appears in a dark turquoise shadowed bar to the left of the photo. Printed on a ghosted grey team logo background, the horizontal backs carry player biography and statistics. The cards are unnumbered and checklisted below in alphabetical order.

| | MINT | NRMT |
|---|---|---|
| COMPLETE SET (30) | 12.00 | 5.50 |
| COMMON CARD (1-30) | .10 | .05 |

❑ 1 Alexander Alexeev .50 .23
❑ 2 Jamie Butt .50 .23
❑ 3 Trevor Cairns .40 .18
❑ 4 Jeff Calvert .40 .18
❑ 5 Marcel Comeau CO .40 .18
❑ 6 Jason Deleurme .40 .18
❑ 7 Allan Egeland .50 .23
❑ 8 Marty Flichel .40 .18
❑ 9 Trever Fraser .40 .18
❑ 10 Michal Grosek .75 .35
❑ 11 Lada Hampeis .40 .18
❑ 12 Tavis Hansen .50 .23
❑ 13 Burt Henderson .40 .18
❑ 14 Jeff Jubenville .40 .18
❑ 15 Todd MacDonald .50 .23
❑ 16 Kyle McLaren 1.50 .70
❑ 17 Kory Mullin .40 .18
❑ 18 Steve Oviatt TR .10 .05
❑ 19 Ryan Phillips .40 .18
❑ 20 Mike Piersol .40 .18
❑ 21 Dennis Pinfold .40 .18
❑ 22 Tyler Prosofsky .50 .23
❑ 23 Jamie Reeve ACO .10 .05
❑ 24 Adam Smith .40 .18
❑ 25 Corey Stock .40 .18
❑ 26 Dallas Thompson .40 .18
❑ 27 John Varga .50 .23
❑ 28 Team Photo .50 .23
❑ 29 The Tacoma Dome .10 .05
❑ 30 The Tacoma Rockets .40 .18
In Action
Marty Flichel

## 1995-96 Tallahassee Tiger Sharks

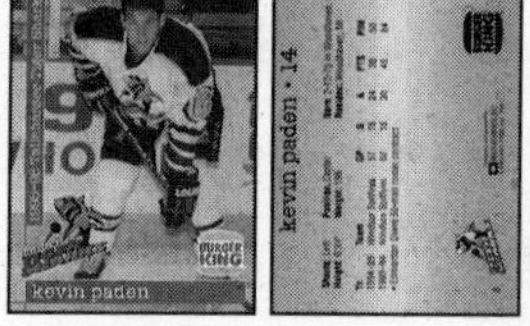

This 27-card set of the Tallahasse Tiger Sharks of the ECHL was sponsored by Burger King and features color action player photos. The backs carry player information.

| | MINT | NRMT |
|---|---|---|
| COMPLETE SET (27) | 7.00 | 3.10 |
| COMMON CARD (1-27) | .10 | .05 |

❑ 1 Rodrigo Lavinsh .40 .18
❑ 2 John Engfer .40 .18
❑ 3 Rod Aldoff .40 .18
❑ 4 Aaron Kriss .40 .18
❑ 5 Ron Pasco .40 .18
❑ 6 Mark Deazley .50 .23
❑ 7 Sean O'Brien .50 .23
❑ 8 Kevin Paden .40 .18
❑ 9 Darren Schwartz .40 .18
❑ 10 Jim Paradise .40 .18
❑ 11 John Uniac .40 .18
❑ 12 Cal Ingraham .40 .18
❑ 13 Matt Osiecki .40 .18
❑ 14 Greg Geldart .40 .18
❑ 15 Alexander Savchenkov .40 .18
❑ 16 Casey Hungle .40 .18
❑ 17 Mark Richards .50 .23
❑ 18 Bob Bell .50 .23
❑ 19 Frenzy (Mascot) .10 .05
❑ 20 Jim Mirabello ANN .10 .05
❑ 21 Mark Richards .50 .23
Bob Bell
❑ 22 Terry Christensen CO .10 .05
❑ 23 Jack Capuano ACO .10 .05
❑ 24 Jerry Hilker TR .10 .05
❑ 25 Walter Edwards VP/GM .10 .05
❑ 26 Tony Mancuso AGM .10 .05
❑ 27 John Summers ANN .10 .05

## 1993-94 Thunder Bay Senators

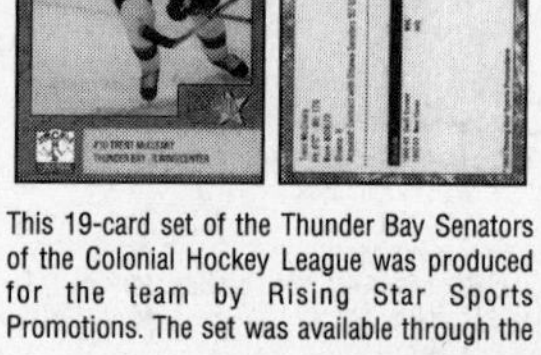

This 19-card set of the Thunder Bay Senators of the Colonial Hockey League was produced for the team by Rising Star Sports Promotions. The set was available through the club, and may have been offered as a game night premium. The set features the standard RSSP design on the front and player stats on the back. The cards are unnumbered.

| | MINT | NRMT |
|---|---|---|
| COMPLETE SET (19) | 7.00 | 3.10 |
| COMMON CARD (1-19) | .40 | .18 |

❑ 1 Jean-Francois Labbe 1.00 .45
❑ 2 Jamie Hayden .40 .18
❑ 3 Llew NcWana .40 .18
❑ 4 Chris Hynnes .40 .18
❑ 5 Trent McCleary 1.00 .45
❑ 6 Richard Borgo .40 .18
❑ 7 Bryan Wells .40 .18
❑ 8 Don Osborne .40 .18
❑ 9 Todd Howarth .40 .18
❑ 10 Bruce Ramsay .40 .18
❑ 11 Brian Downey .40 .18
❑ 12 Barry McKinley .40 .18
❑ 13 Ron Talakowki .40 .18
❑ 14 Tom Warden .40 .18
❑ 15 Mel Angelstad .40 .18
❑ 16 Tommi Hietala .40 .18
❑ 17 Vern Ray .40 .18
❑ 18 Gerry St. Cyr .40 .18
❑ 19 Terry Menard .40 .18

## 1994-95 Thunder Bay Senators

This 20-card set of the Thunder Bay Senators of the CHL was produced for the team by Rising Star Sports Promotions. The cards were available through the team and may have been issued as a game night giveaway. The cards feature the standard RSSP design on the front, with player stats on the back. The cards are unnumbered.

| | MINT | NRMT |
|---|---|---|
| COMPLETE SET (20) | 7.00 | 3.10 |
| COMMON CARD (1-20) | .40 | .18 |

❑ 1 Todd Howarth .40 .18
❑ 2 Darren Perkins .40 .18
❑ 3 Derek Scanlan .40 .18
❑ 4 Pat Szturm .50 .23
❑ 5 Barry McKinley .40 .18
❑ 6 Jake Grimes .40 .18
❑ 7 Alain Cote .40 .18
❑ 8 Rival Fullum .40 .18
❑ 9 Terry Menard .50 .23
❑ 10 Mike McCourt .40 .18
❑ 11 Mel Angelstad .40 .18
❑ 12 Jason Firth .40 .18
❑ 13 Llew NcWana .40 .18
❑ 14 Lance Leslie .40 .18
❑ 15 Neal Purdon .40 .18
❑ 16 Steve Parson .40 .18
❑ 17 Chris Rowland .40 .18
❑ 18 Bruce Ramsay .40 .18
❑ 19 Don Osborne .40 .18
❑ 20 Jean Blouin .40 .18

## 1995-96 Thunder Bay Senators

This 20-card set of the Thunder Bay Senators of the Colonial Hockey League was produced by Rising Star Sports Promotions. The cards were only available through Shoppers Drug Mart stores in Thunder Bay, making hobby acquisition difficult. The cards feature a blurry action photo on the front, an complete stats on the back, along with the Shoppers logos. The cards are unnumbered and listed below alphabetically.

| | MINT | NRMT |
|---|---|---|
| COMPLETE SET (20) | 10.00 | 4.50 |
| COMMON CARD (1-20) | .50 | .23 |

❑ 1 Team Photo .50 .23
❑ 2 Mel Angelstad .50 .23
❑ 3 Omer Belisle .50 .23
❑ 4 Frederic Cassivi .75 .35
❑ 5 Brandon Christian .50 .23
❑ 6 Jason Disher .50 .23
❑ 7 Jason Firth .50 .23
❑ 8 Rival Fullum .50 .23
❑ 9 Todd Howarth .50 .23
❑ 10 Chris Hynnes .50 .23
❑ 11 Barry McKinley .50 .23
❑ 12 Terry Menard .50 .23
❑ 13 Derek Nicolson .50 .23
❑ 14 Llew NcWana .50 .23
❑ 15 Steve Parson .50 .23
❑ 16 Darren Perkins .50 .23
❑ 17 Dan Poirier .50 .23
❑ 18 Neal Purdon .50 .23
❑ 19 Bruce Ramsay .50 .23
❑ 20 Pat Szturm .75 .35

## 1992-93 Toledo Storm

This 25-card set features the Toledo Storm of the ECHL. The set features action photography -- which often suffers from the poor quality -- on the front, with stats and bio on the back. The cards were offered for sale by the club at the rink on game nights.

| | MINT | NRMT |
|---|---|---|
| COMPLETE SET (25) | 7.00 | 3.10 |
| COMMON CARD (1-25) | .10 | .05 |

❑ 1 Checklist .10 .05
❑ 2 Chris McSorley CO .10 .05
❑ 3 Scott Luhrmann EQMG .10 .05
❑ 4 Barry Soskin GM .10 .05
❑ 5 Tim Mouser PR .10 .05
❑ 6 Jeff Gibbons PR .10 .05
❑ 7 Claude Scott .10 .05
The Happy Trumpeter
❑ 8 Scott King .50 .23
❑ 9 Andy Suhy .35 .16
❑ 10 Pat Pylypuik .35 .16
❑ 11 Alex Roberts .35 .16
❑ 12 Mark Deazley .35 .16
❑ 13 John Johnson .35 .16
❑ 14 Jeff Rohlicek .35 .16
❑ 15 Dan Wiebe .35 .16
❑ 16 Jeff Jablonski .35 .16
❑ 17 Greg Puhalski .35 .16
❑ 18 Bruce MacDonald .35 .16
❑ 19 Iain Duncan .35 .16
❑ 20 Rick Judson .35 .16
❑ 21 Alex Hicks .75 .35
❑ 22 Barry Potomski .50 .23
❑ 23 Derek Booth .35 .16
❑ 24 Rick Corriveau .35 .16
❑ 25 Mark Richards .35 .16

## 1993-94 Toledo Storm

This 29-card standard-size set features the 1992-93 Riley Cup Champions Toledo Storm of the ECHL (East Coast Hockey League). Inside a white and a thin red border, the fronts feature color action player photos with the player's name and position in a red border at the bottom of the card. The team logo also appears at the bottom. The horizontal backs carry the player's name, number and position, biographical information, statistics, career highlights, and team logo.

| | MINT | NRMT |
|---|---|---|
| COMPLETE SET (29) | 9.00 | 4.00 |
| COMMON CARD (1-29) | .10 | .05 |

❑ 1 Checklist Card .10 .05
❑ 2 Chris McSorley CO .25 .11
❑ 3 Barry Soskin PRES .10 .05
❑ 4 Tim Mouser MG .10 .05
❑ 5 Jeff Gibbons ANN .10 .05
❑ 6 Scott Luhrmann TR .10 .05
❑ 7 Nick Vitucci .25 .11
❑ 8 Andy Suhy .25 .11
❑ 9 Pat Pylypuik .25 .11
❑ 10 Chris Belanger .25 .11
❑ 11 Mike Markovich .25 .11
❑ 12 Darren Perkins .25 .11
❑ 13 Dennis Snedden .25 .11
❑ 14 Mark Deazley .35 .16
❑ 15 Mark McCreary .25 .11
❑ 16 Jeff Rohlicek .25 .11
❑ 17 Chris Bergeron .25 .11
❑ 18 John Hendry .25 .11
❑ 19 Greg Puhalski .25 .11
❑ 20 Bruce MacDonald .25 .11
❑ 21 Marc Lyons .25 .11
❑ 22 Rick Judson .25 .11
❑ 23 Alex Hicks .50 .23
❑ 24 Barry Potomski .50 .23
❑ 25 Rick Corriveau .35 .16
❑ 26 Kyle Reeves .35 .16
❑ 27 Erin Whitten 3.00 1.35
❑ 28 Brian Schoen .25 .11
❑ 29 Riley Cup Champions .25 .11

## 1994-95 Toledo Storm

This 24-card standard-size set features the 1993-94 Riley Cup Champion Storm of the

ECHL. The borderless fronts have color action player photos with the player's name, number and position across the bottom. The words "Toledo Hockey" are printed vertically down the right edge, while the team logo appears in the upper left corner. The horizontal backs carry a small, black-and-white player photo, along with biography, player profile, and stats. The cards are unnumbered and checklisted below in alphabetical order.

| | MINT | NRMT |
|---|---|---|
| COMPLETE SET (24) | 7.00 | 3.10 |
| COMMON CARD (1-24) | .10 | .05 |
| ❑ 1 Dave Bankoske | .35 | .16 |
| ❑ 2 Wyatt Buckland | .35 | .16 |
| ❑ 3 Rick Corriveau | .35 | .16 |
| ❑ 4 Norm Dezainde | .50 | .23 |
| ❑ 5 Iain Duncan | .35 | .16 |
| ❑ 6 Jeff Gibbons | .35 | .16 |
| ❑ 7 Alain Harvey | .50 | .23 |
| ❑ 8 John Hendry | .35 | .16 |
| ❑ 9 Ed Henrich | .35 | .16 |
| ❑ 10 Rick Judson | .35 | .16 |
| ❑ 11 Mike Latendresse | .35 | .16 |
| ❑ 12 Scott Luhrmann TR | .10 | .05 |
| ❑ 13 B.J. MacPherson | .35 | .16 |
| ❑ 14 Jim Maher | .35 | .16 |
| ❑ 15 Jay Neal | .35 | .16 |
| ❑ 16 Marquis Mathieu | .35 | .16 |
| ❑ 17 Shawn Penn | .35 | .16 |
| ❑ 18 Darren Perkins | .35 | .16 |
| ❑ 19 Greg Puhalski CO | .10 | .05 |
| ❑ 20 Barry Soskin PR/GM | .10 | .05 |
| ❑ 21 Gerry St. Cyr | .35 | .16 |
| ❑ 22 Rhett Trombley | .50 | .23 |
| ❑ 23 Nick Vitucci | .50 | .23 |
| ❑ 24 1993-94 Riley Cup Champions | .50 | .23 |

## 1995-96 Toledo Storm

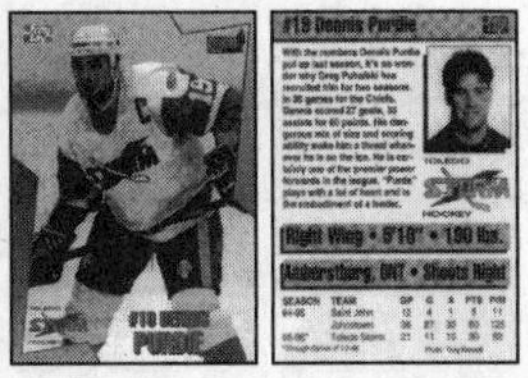

This 26-card set of the Toledo Storm of the ECHL was sponsored by Frito-Lay and available through the team and its booster club. The fronts feature an action photo along with team, league and sponsor logos. The unnumbered backs contain player analysis and stats.

| | MINT | NRMT |
|---|---|---|
| COMPLETE SET (26) | 7.00 | 3.10 |
| COMMON CARD (1-26) | .10 | .05 |
| ❑ 1 Rob Laurie | .35 | .16 |
| ❑ 2 Nicolas Perreault | .50 | .23 |
| ❑ 3 Brandon Carper | .35 | .16 |
| ❑ 4 Paul Koch | .35 | .16 |
| ❑ 5 Glen Mears | .35 | .16 |
| ❑ 6 Dan Carter | .35 | .16 |
| ❑ 7 Patrick Gladu | .35 | .16 |
| ❑ 8 Todd Wetzel | .35 | .16 |
| ❑ 9 B.J. MacPherson | .35 | .16 |
| ❑ 10 Mark Stitt | .35 | .16 |
| ❑ 11 Dennis Purdie | .50 | .23 |
| ❑ 12 Rick Judson | .35 | .16 |
| ❑ 13 Mike Whitton | .35 | .16 |
| ❑ 14 Norm Dezainde | .35 | .16 |
| ❑ 15 Jason Gladney | .35 | .16 |
| ❑ 16 Wade Bartley | .35 | .16 |
| ❑ 17 Jason Smart | .35 | .16 |
| ❑ 18 Mike Kolenda | .35 | .16 |
| ❑ 19 Shawn Penn | .35 | .16 |
| ❑ 20 David Goverde | .50 | .23 |
| ❑ 21 Barry Soskin OWN | .10 | .05 |
| ❑ 22 Greg Puhalski CO | .10 | .05 |
| ❑ 23 Chuck Imburgia DIR | .10 | .05 |
| ❑ 24 Scott Luhrmann EQMG | .10 | .05 |
| ❑ 25 Mark Kelly ANN | .10 | .05 |
| ❑ 26 Sponsor Card | .10 | .05 |

## 1996-97 Toledo Storm

This 23-card set was produced by Split Second. The unnumbered cards feature an action photo on the front, with a brief statistical package on the back. The club offered them for sale at games and through the mail.

| | MINT | NRMT |
|---|---|---|
| COMPLETE SET (23) | 7.00 | 3.10 |
| COMMON CARD | .10 | .05 |

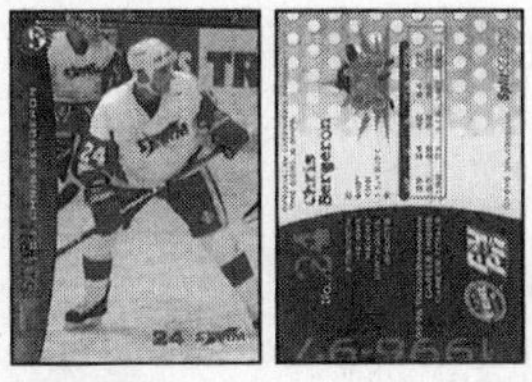

| | | |
|---|---|---|
| ❑ 1 Ryan Bach | .50 | .23 |
| ❑ 5 Paul Koch | .35 | .16 |
| ❑ 6 Ryan Bast | .35 | .16 |
| ❑ 11 Brian Clifford | .35 | .16 |
| ❑ 14 Mike Sullivan | .35 | .16 |
| ❑ 17 Alex Matvichuk | .35 | .16 |
| ❑ 18 Arturs Kupaks | .35 | .16 |
| ❑ 19 Dennis Purdie | .35 | .16 |
| ❑ 20 Rick Judson | .35 | .16 |
| ❑ 22 Norm Dezainde | .35 | .16 |
| ❑ 23 Jason Gladney | .35 | .16 |
| ❑ 24 Chris Bergeron | .35 | .16 |
| ❑ 25 Mike Whitton | .35 | .16 |
| ❑ 27 Mike Kolenda | .35 | .16 |
| ❑ 28 Dan Pawlaczyk | .35 | .16 |
| ❑ 29 Jeremy Mylymok | .35 | .16 |
| ❑ 32 Don Larner | .35 | .16 |
| ❑ 33 Rob Thorpe | .35 | .16 |
| ❑ 35 David Goverde | .50 | .23 |
| ❑ NNO Barry Soskin PRES | .10 | .05 |
| ❑ NNO Scott Luhrmann TR | .10 | .05 |
| ❑ NNO Mark Kelly (Broadcaster) | .10 | .05 |
| ❑ NNO Greg Puhalski CO | .10 | .05 |

## 1994-95 Tri-City Americans

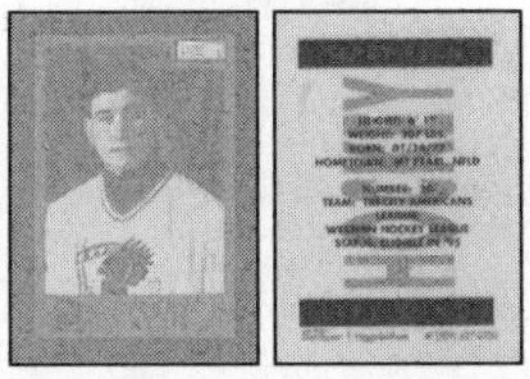

This unusual series was produced by Summit. Four of the cards (#4-7) are standard size, while the other four are slightly oversized, suggesting that they may have been released at different times, or in two separate series. The larger four cards also have a slightly darker blue border around the posed studio shot. All of the cards appear to be laminated, or made strictly from a plastic-type material. The checklist below may be incomplete. Additional information from the readership would be appreciated.

| | MINT | NRMT |
|---|---|---|
| COMPLETE SET (8) | 12.00 | 5.50 |
| COMMON CARD (1-8) | .50 | .23 |
| ❑ 1 Dorian Anneck | 1.00 | .45 |
| ❑ 2 Brent Ascroft | .50 | .23 |
| ❑ 3 Brian Boucher | 3.00 | 1.35 |
| ❑ 4 Rob Butz | .50 | .23 |
| ❑ 5 Chad Cabana | .75 | .35 |
| ❑ 6 Daymond Langkow | 4.00 | 1.80 |
| ❑ 7 Ryan Marsh | .50 | .23 |
| ❑ 8 Terry Ryan | 3.00 | 1.35 |

## 1995-96 Tri-City Americans

This 31-card set was produced by S&H Ltd. The cards feature action photos on the front, with a mugshot and bio on the back. Unnumbered, the cards are listed below in alphabetical order. The set is noteworthy for the inclusion of three first round selections from the 1995 Entry Draft: Daymond Langkow (TB), Terry Ryan (MTL) and Brian Boucher (PHI).

| | MINT | NRMT |
|---|---|---|
| COMPLETE SET (31) | 14.00 | 6.25 |
| COMMON CARD (1-31) | .10 | .05 |
| ❑ 1 Chris Anderson | .35 | .16 |
| ❑ 2 Dorian Anneck | .50 | .23 |
| ❑ 3 Brent Ascroft | .35 | .16 |
| ❑ 4 Aaron Baker | .50 | .23 |
| ❑ 5 Alexandre Boikov | .35 | .16 |
| ❑ 6 Brian Boucher | 1.50 | .70 |
| ❑ 7 Byron Briske | .50 | .23 |
| ❑ 8 Bob Brown GM | .10 | .05 |
| ❑ 9 Jerry Fredericksen TR | .10 | .05 |
| ❑ 10 Dan Focht | .75 | .35 |
| ❑ 11 Dylan Gyori | .35 | .16 |
| ❑ 12 Mark Hurley | .35 | .16 |
| ❑ 13 Mike Hurley | .35 | .16 |
| ❑ 14 Zenith Komarniski | .50 | .23 |
| ❑ 15 Daymond Langkow | 1.50 | .70 |
| ❑ 16 Jody Lapeyre | .35 | .16 |
| ❑ 17 Bob Loucks CO | .10 | .05 |
| ❑ 18 Scott McCallum | .35 | .16 |
| ❑ 19 Boyd Olson | .35 | .16 |
| ❑ 20 Warren Renden ACO | .10 | .05 |
| ❑ 21 Terry Ryan | 1.00 | .45 |
| ❑ 22 Eric Schneider | .35 | .16 |
| ❑ 23 Dan Smith | .35 | .16 |
| ❑ 24 Craig Stahl | .35 | .16 |
| ❑ 25 Jaroslav Svejkovsky | 1.50 | .70 |
| ❑ 26 Jeremy Thompson | .35 | .16 |
| ❑ 27 Gary Toor | .35 | .16 |
| ❑ 28 Tom Zavediuk | .35 | .16 |
| ❑ 29 Eddie the Eagle (Mascot) | .10 | .05 |
| ❑ 30 B.Boucher/D.Langkow/T.Ryan | .50 | .23 |
| ❑ 31 Logo Card | .10 | .05 |

## 1966-67 Tulsa Oilers

| | MINT | NRMT |
|---|---|---|
| COMPLETE SET (12) | 25.00 | 11.00 |
| COMMON CARD (1-12) | 2.00 | .90 |
| ❑ 1 Ken Campbell | 2.00 | .90 |
| ❑ 2 Adrew Champagne | 2.00 | .90 |
| ❑ 3 Doug Dunville | 2.00 | .90 |
| ❑ 4 Will Flett | 3.00 | 1.35 |
| ❑ 5 Nick Harbaruk | 2.00 | .90 |
| ❑ 6 Lowell Macdonald | 5.00 | 2.20 |
| ❑ 7 Jim McKenny | 3.00 | 1.35 |
| ❑ 8 Al Millar | 2.00 | .90 |
| ❑ 9 Marc Reaume | 3.00 | 1.35 |
| ❑ 10 Harry Shaw | 2.00 | .90 |
| ❑ 11 Gary Venneruzzo | 3.00 | 1.35 |
| ❑ 12 Ron Ward | 2.00 | .90 |

## 1961-62 Union Oil WHL

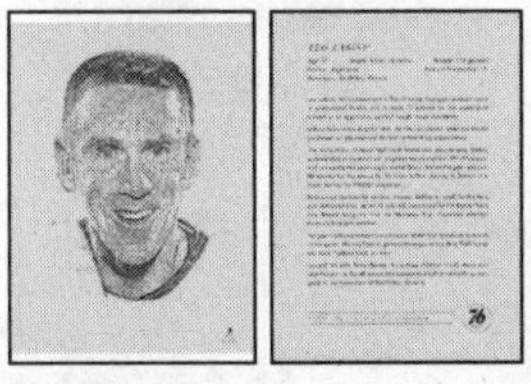

This 12-drawing set features players from the Los Angeles Blades (1-8) and the San Francisco Seals (9-12) of the Western Hockey League. The black-and-white drawings by artist Sam Patrick measure approximately 6" by 8" and are printed on textured white paper. The back of each drawing carries the player's career highlights and biographical information. The Union Oil name and logo at the bottom round out the backs. The cards are unnumbered and listed below alphabetically within teams. Reportedly only eight cards were issued to the public, making four of the cards extremely scarce.

| | NRMT | VG-E |
|---|---|---|
| COMPLETE SET (12) | 100.00 | 45.00 |
| COMMON BLADES (1-8) | 6.00 | 2.70 |
| COMMON SEALS (9-12) | 6.00 | 2.70 |
| ❑ 1 Jack Bownass | 6.00 | 2.70 |
| ❑ 2 Ed Diachuk | 6.00 | 2.70 |
| ❑ 3 Leo LaBine | 10.00 | 4.50 |
| ❑ 4 Willie O'Ree | 40.00 | 18.00 |
| ❑ 5 Bruce Carmichael | 6.00 | 2.70 |
| ❑ 6 Gordon Haworth | 8.00 | 3.60 |
| ❑ 7 Fleming Mackell | 10.00 | 4.50 |
| ❑ 8 Robert Solinger | 6.00 | 2.70 |
| ❑ 9 Gary Edmundson | 6.00 | 2.70 |
| ❑ 10 Al Nicholson | 6.00 | 2.70 |
| ❑ 11 Orland Kurtenbach | 15.00 | 6.75 |
| ❑ 12 Tom Thurlby | 6.00 | 2.70 |

## 1998-99 Val d'Or Foreurs

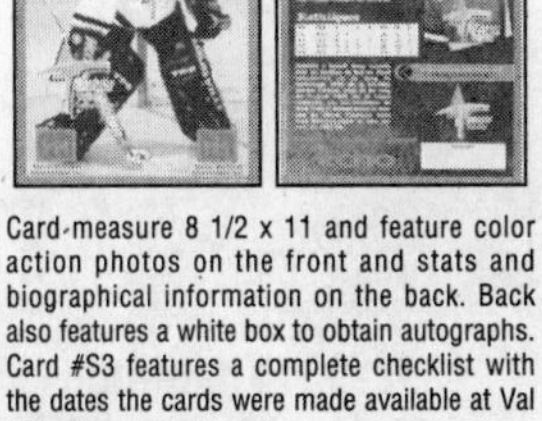

Card measure 8 1/2 x 11 and feature color action photos on the front and stats and biographical information on the back. Back also features a white box to obtain autographs. Card #S3 features a complete checklist with the dates the cards were made available at Val d'Or Foreurs games.

| | MINT | NRMT |
|---|---|---|
| COMPLETE SET (29) | 15.00 | 6.75 |
| COMMON CARD (1-26) | .50 | .23 |
| ❑ 1 Christian Daigle | .50 | .23 |
| ❑ 2 Benoit Dusablon | .50 | .23 |
| ❑ 3 Guillaume Lamoureux | .50 | .23 |
| ❑ 4 Danny Groulx | .50 | .23 |
| ❑ 5 Alain Charbonneau | .50 | .23 |
| ❑ 6 Jonathan Fauteux | .50 | .23 |
| ❑ 7 Didier Tremblay | .50 | .23 |
| ❑ 8 Dynamit | .10 | .05 |
| ❑ 9 Roberto Luongo | 2.50 | 1.10 |
| ❑ 10 Nick Greenough | .50 | .23 |
| ❑ 11 Lucio DeMartinis | .50 | .23 |
| ❑ 12 Gaston Therien | .50 | .23 |
| ❑ 13 Francois Hardy | .50 | .23 |
| ❑ 14 David St.Germain | .50 | .23 |
| ❑ 15 Sebastien Laprise | .50 | .23 |
| ❑ 16 Luc Girard | .75 | .35 |
| ❑ 17 Simon Gamache | .50 | .23 |
| ❑ 18 Steve Morency | .50 | .23 |
| ❑ 19 Seneque Hyacinthe | .50 | .23 |
| ❑ 20 Dave Verville | .50 | .23 |
| ❑ 21 Alexandre Page | .50 | .23 |
| ❑ 22 Denis Boily | .50 | .23 |
| ❑ 23 Dwight Wolfe | .50 | .23 |
| ❑ 24 Jerome Petit | .75 | .35 |
| ❑ 25 Eric Dubois | .75 | .35 |
| ❑ 26 Jonathan Charron | .50 | .23 |
| ❑ S1 Anthony Quessy | .50 | .23 |
| ❑ S2 Mathieau Lendick | .40 | .18 |
| ❑ S3 Philippe Ouellette | .75 | .35 |

## 1995 Vancouver VooDoo RHI

This 25-card set from Slapshot Images features the Vancouver VooDoo of Roller Hockey International. The cards feature color player photos in a thin gray frame on a black background with a purple zig-zag stripe down the left. The backs carry player information.

| | MINT | NRMT |
|---|---|---|
| COMPLETE SET (25) | 7.00 | 3.10 |
| COMMON CARD (1-25) | .10 | .05 |
| ❑ 1 Title Card CL | .10 | .05 |
| ❑ 2 Dave "Tiger" Williams | .50 | .23 |
| ❑ 3 James Jenson | .50 | .23 |
| ❑ 4 Laurie Billeck | .35 | .16 |
| ❑ 5 Doug McCarthy | .35 | .16 |
| ❑ 6 Jason Knox | .35 | .16 |
| ❑ 7 Brent Thurston | .35 | .16 |
| ❑ 8 Dave Cairns CO | .10 | .05 |
| ❑ 9 Jason Jennings | .35 | .16 |
| ❑ 10 Shayne Green | .35 | .16 |
| ❑ 11 Rob Dumas | .35 | .16 |
| ❑ 12 Ivan Matulik | .35 | .16 |
| ❑ 13 Rob Stewart | .35 | .16 |
| ❑ 14 Doug Ast | .35 | .16 |
| ❑ 15 Chris Morrison | .35 | .16 |
| ❑ 17 Ryan Harrison | .35 | .16 |
| ❑ 17 Kevin Hoffman | .35 | .16 |
| ❑ 18 Ken Kinney | .50 | .23 |
| ❑ 19 Merv Priest | .35 | .16 |
| ❑ 20 Steve Brown | .35 | .16 |
| ❑ 21 Ryan Harrison 1994 All Star Card | .35 | .16 |
| ❑ 22 VooDoo Dolls | .35 | .16 |
| ❑ 23 1995 Season Schedules | .10 | .05 |
| ❑ 24 VooDoo Merchandise Card | .10 | .05 |
| ❑ 25 Titan (Mascot) | .10 | .05 |

## 1981-82 Victoria Cougars

This 16-card set was sponsored by the West Coast Savings Credit Union and Saanich Police Department Community Services. The cards measure approximately 3" by 5" and feature posed, color player photos with white borders. The player's name, position, and biographical information appear at the bottom. The backs carry public service messages that relate a hockey term to a life situation. The cards are unnumbered and checklisted below in alphabetical order.

| | NRMT-MT | EXC |
|---|---|---|
| COMPLETE SET (16) | 18.00 | 8.00 |
| COMMON CARD (1-16) | .75 | .35 |
| ❑ 1 Bob Bales | .75 | .35 |
| ❑ 2 Greg Barber | .75 | .35 |
| ❑ 3 Ray Benik | .75 | .35 |
| ❑ 4 Rich Chernomaz | 1.00 | .45 |
| ❑ 5 Daryl Coldwell | .75 | .35 |
| ❑ 6 Geoff Courtnall | 10.00 | 4.50 |
| ❑ 7 Paul Cyr | 2.00 | .90 |
| ❑ 8 Wade Jenson | .75 | .35 |
| ❑ 9 Stu Kulak | 1.50 | .70 |
| ❑ 10 Peter Martin | .75 | .35 |
| ❑ 11 John Mokosak | .75 | .35 |
| ❑ 12 Mark Morrison | .75 | .35 |
| ❑ 13 Bryant Seaton | .75 | .35 |
| ❑ 14 Jack Shupe | .75 | .35 |
| ❑ 15 Eric Thurston | .75 | .35 |
| ❑ 16 Randy Wickware | .75 | .35 |

## 1982-83 Victoria Cougars

Featuring current and past players, this 23-card set was sponsored by the West Coast Savings Credit Union, GFAX 1070 Radio, and the Greater Victoria Police Departments. The cards measure approximately 3" by 5" and feature color player portraits with red and blue borders on a white card face. The player's name, position, and biographical information appear at the bottom. Past player cards have the words "Graduation Series" stamped in the lower right corner of the picture (card numbers 7, 8, 13, 20-21). The backs carry a brief player profile and public service messages. The cards are unnumbered and checklisted below in alphabetical order. There has been a report of a twenty-fourth card picturing Doug Hannesson; this card has yet to be confirmed and the set is considered complete without it.

| | MINT | EXC |
|---|---|---|
| COMPLETE SET (23) | 40.00 | 18.00 |
| COMMON CARD (1-23) | .75 | .35 |
| ❑ 1 Steve Bayliss | .75 | .35 |
| ❑ 2 Ray Benik | .75 | .35 |
| ❑ 3 Rich Chernomaz | 1.00 | .45 |
| ❑ 4 Geoff Courtnall | 5.00 | 2.20 |
| ❑ 5 Russ Courtnall | 8.00 | 3.60 |
| ❑ 6 Paul Cyr | 1.50 | .70 |
| ❑ 7 Curt Fraser | 2.00 | .90 |
| ❑ 8 Grant Fuhr | 25.00 | 11.00 |
| ❑ 9 Shawn Green | .75 | .35 |
| ❑ 10 Fabian Joseph | 1.00 | .45 |
| ❑ 11 Stu Kulak | 1.00 | .45 |
| ❑ 12 Brenn Leach | .75 | .35 |
| ❑ 13 Gary Lupul | .75 | .35 |
| ❑ 14 Jack MacKeigan | .75 | .35 |
| ❑ 15 Dave Mackey | 1.00 | .45 |
| ❑ 16 Mark McLeary | .75 | .35 |
| ❑ 17 Dan Moberg | .75 | .35 |
| ❑ 18 John Mokosak | .75 | .35 |
| ❑ 19 Mark Morrison | .75 | .35 |
| ❑ 20 Brad Palmer | 1.00 | .45 |
| ❑ 21 Barry Pederson | 3.00 | 1.35 |
| ❑ 22 Eric Thurston | .75 | .35 |
| ❑ 23 Ron Viglasi | .75 | .35 |

## 1983-84 Victoria Cougars

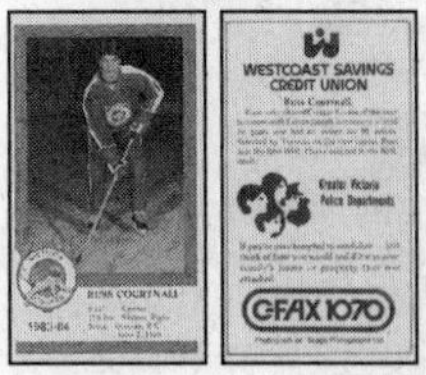

Featuring current and past players, this 24-card set was sponsored by the West Coast Savings Credit Union, GFAX 1070 Radio, and the Greater Victoria Police Departments. The cards measure approximately 3" by 5" and feature color player portraits with red and blue borders on a white card face. The player's name, position, and biographical information appear at the bottom. Past player cards have the words "Graduation Series" stamped in the lower right corner of the picture (card number 2 and 20). The cards are unnumbered and checklisted below in alphabetical order.

| | MINT | NRMT |
|---|---|---|
| COMPLETE SET (24) | 18.00 | 8.00 |
| COMMON CARD (1-24) | .75 | .35 |
| ❑ 1 Misko Antisin | 1.00 | .45 |
| ❑ 2 Murray Bannerman | 2.00 | .90 |

❑ 3 Steve Baylis .75 .35
❑ 4 Paul Bifano .75 .35
❑ 5 Russ Courtnall 6.00 2.70
❑ 6 Greg Davies .75 .35
❑ 7 Dean Drozdiak .75 .35
❑ 8 Jim Gunn .75 .35
❑ 9 Richard Hajdu .75 .35
❑ 10 Randy Hansch 1.00 .45
❑ 11 Matt Hervey .75 .35
❑ 12 Fabian Joseph 1.00 .45
❑ 13 Rob Kivell .75 .35
❑ 14 Brenn Leach .75 .35
❑ 15 Jack Mackeigan .75 .35
❑ 16 Dave Mackey .75 .35
❑ 17 Tom Martin .75 .35
❑ 18 Darren Moren .75 .35
❑ 19 Adam Morrison .75 .35
❑ 20 Gord Roberts .75 .35
❑ 21 Dan Sexton .75 .35
❑ 22 Randy Siska .75 .35
❑ 23 Eric Thurston .75 .35
❑ 24 Simon Wheeldon .75 .35

## 1984-85 Victoria Cougars

Featuring current and past players, this 24-card set was sponsored by the West Coast Savings Credit Union, GFAX 1070 Radio, and the Greater Victoria Police Departments. The cards measure approximately 3" by 5" and feature color player portraits with red and blue borders on a white card face. The player's name, position, and biographical information appear at the bottom. Past player cards have the words "Graduation Series" stamped in the lower right corner of the picture (card numbers 6 and 20). The backs carry a brief player profile and public service messages. The cards are unnumbered and checklisted below in alphabetical order.

| | MINT | NRMT |
|---|---|---|
| COMPLETE SET (24) | 15.00 | 6.75 |
| COMMON CARD (1-24) | .50 | .23 |

❑ 1 Misko Antisin .75 .35
❑ 2 Greg Batters .50 .23
❑ 3 Mel Bridgman 1.50 .70
❑ 4 Chris Calverly .50 .23
❑ 5 Darin Choquette .50 .23
❑ 6 Geoff Courtnall 3.00 1.35
❑ 7 Russ Courtnall 4.00 1.80
❑ 8 Rick Davidson .50 .23
❑ 9 Bill Gregoire .50 .23
❑ 10 Richard Hajdu .75 .35
❑ 11 Randy Hansch .75 .35
❑ 12 Rob Kivell .50 .23
❑ 13 Brad Melin .50 .23
❑ 14 Jim Mentis .50 .23
❑ 15 Adam Morrison .50 .23
❑ 16 Mark Morrison .50 .23
❑ 17 Kodie Nelson .50 .23
❑ 18 Ken Priestlay .75 .35
❑ 19 Bruce Pritchard .50 .23
❑ 20 Torrie Robertson 1.00 .45
❑ 21 Trevor Semeniuk .50 .23
❑ 22 Dan Sexton .50 .23
❑ 23 Randy Siska .50 .23
❑ 24 Chris Tarnowski .50 .23

## 1989-90 Victoria Cougars

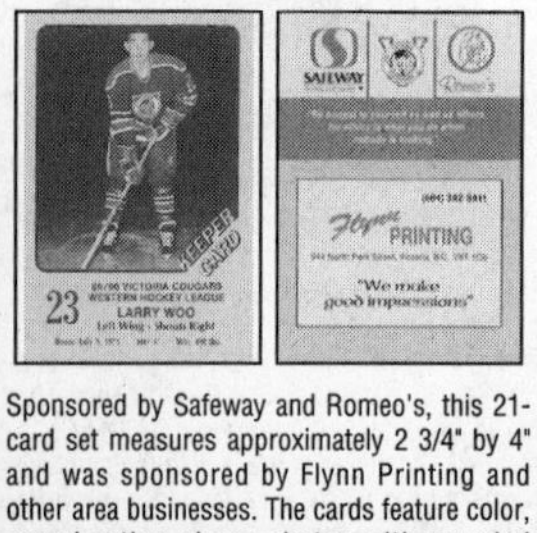

Sponsored by Safeway and Romeo's, this 21-card set measures approximately 2 3/4" by 4" and was sponsored by Flynn Printing and other area businesses. The cards feature color, posed action player photos with rounded corners on a yellow card face. The lower right corner of the picture is cut off and the words "Keeper Card" are written diagonally. The player's name, position, and biographical information appear below the picture. The backs carry sponsor logos in red and black print. A public service message appears in a wide red stripe near the middle of the card. The cards are unnumbered and checklisted below in alphabetical order.

| | MINT | NRMT |
|---|---|---|
| COMPLETE SET (21) | 8.00 | 3.60 |
| COMMON CARD (1-21) | .50 | .23 |

❑ 1 John Badduke .50 .23
❑ 2 Terry Bendera .50 .23
❑ 3 Trevor Buchanan .50 .23
❑ 4 Jaret Burgoyne .50 .23
❑ 5 Dino Caputo .50 .23
❑ 6 Chris Catellier .50 .23
❑ 7 Mark Cipriano .50 .23
❑ 8 Milan Drag .50 .23
❑ 9 Dean Dyer .50 .23
❑ 10 Shayne Green .50 .23
❑ 11 Ryan Harrison .50 .23
❑ 12 Corey Jones .50 .23
❑ 13 Terry Klapstein .50 .23
❑ 14 Jason Knox .50 .23
❑ 15 Curtis Nykyforuk .50 .23
❑ 16 Jason Peters .50 .23
❑ 17 Blair Scott .50 .23
❑ 18 Mike Seaton .50 .23
❑ 19 Rob Sumner .50 .23
❑ 20 Larry Woo .50 .23
❑ 21 Jarret Zukiwsky .50 .23

## 1993-94 Waterloo Black Hawks

This 27-card standard-size set features the Waterloo Black Hawks of the USHL (United States Hockey League). The fronts feature color action player photos, with the team name and logo in a red border above the photo, and the player's name, number, and position beneath it. The horizontal backs carry a black-and-white player portrait, the player's name and number, biographical information, statistics, a career summary, and the team logo. The cards are unnumbered and checklisted below in alphabetical order.

| | MINT | NRMT |
|---|---|---|
| COMPLETE SET (27) | 6.00 | 2.70 |
| COMMON CARD (1-27) | .10 | .05 |

❑ 1 Brent Bessey .25 .11
❑ 2 Jason Blake .25 .11
❑ 3 Scott Brand GM .10 .05
❑ 4 Eric Brown .25 .11
❑ 5 Rod Butler .25 .11
❑ 6 Chris Coakley .25 .11
❑ 7 Austin Crawford .25 .11
❑ 8 Doug Dietz ACO .10 .05
❑ 9 Jon Garver .25 .11
❑ 10 Brian Folden .25 .11
❑ 11 Bobby Hayes .25 .11
❑ 12 Jake Jacoby .25 .11
❑ 13 Terry Jarkowsky .25 .11
❑ 14 Jeff Kozakowski UER .25 .11
(Misspelled
Kozakowskl on front)
❑ 15 Josh Lampman .25 .11
❑ 16 Marty Laurila .25 .11
❑ 17 Steve McCall ANN .10 .05
❑ 18 Bill McNelis .25 .11
❑ 19 Rich Metro .25 .11
❑ 20 Scott Mikesch CO .10 .05
❑ 21 Barry Soskin PR .10 .05
❑ 22 Ben Stadey .25 .11
❑ 23 Ed Stanek .25 .11
❑ 24 Todd Steinmetz .25 .11
❑ 25 Scott Swanjord .35 .16
❑ 26 Miles Van Tassel .25 .11
❑ 27 Supporting Staff .10 .05
Dave Christians
Mike Christians
Bill Eggers

## 1992-93 Western Michigan

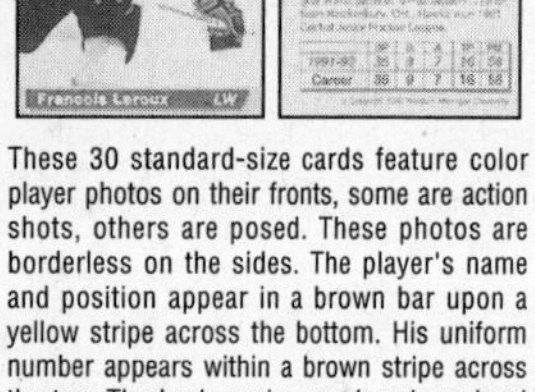

These 30 standard-size cards feature color player photos on their fronts, some are action shots, others are posed. These photos are borderless on the sides. The player's name and position appear in a brown bar upon a yellow stripe across the bottom. His uniform number appears within a brown stripe across the top. The back carries a color player head shot at the upper left. A brief player biography appears alongside on the right. Below are his career highlights and, within a yellow panel, 1991-92 and career statistics. Aside from the players' uniform numbers appearing on the front and back, the cards are unnumbered and checklisted below in alphabetical order.

| | MINT | NRMT |
|---|---|---|
| COMPLETE SET (30) | 10.00 | 4.50 |
| COMMON CARD (1-30) | .10 | .05 |

❑ 1 Chris Belanger .50 .23
❑ 2 Joe Bonnett .40 .18
❑ 3 Brent Brekke .50 .23
❑ 4 Chris Brooks .40 .18
❑ 5 Craig Brown .40 .18
❑ 6 Jeremy Brown .40 .18
❑ 7 Tom Carriere .40 .18
❑ 8 Scott Chartier .50 .23
❑ 9 Ryan D'Arcy .40 .18
❑ 10 Pat Ferschweiler .40 .18
❑ 11 Brian Gallentine .40 .18
❑ 12 Jim Holman .40 .18
❑ 13 Derek Innanen .40 .18
❑ 14 Jason Jennings .50 .23
❑ 15 Mikhail Lapin .50 .23
❑ 16 Francois Leroux .75 .35
❑ 17 Jamal Mayers .50 .23
❑ 18 Kevin McCaffrey ACO .10 .05
❑ 19 Dave Mitchell .40 .18
❑ 20 Brian Renfrew .40 .18
❑ 21 Mike Schafer ACO .10 .05
❑ 22 Derek Schooley .40 .18
❑ 23 Neil Smith .50 .23
WMU Hall of Fame
❑ 24 Colin Ward .40 .18
❑ 25 Dave Weaver .40 .18
❑ 26 Mike Whitton .40 .18
❑ 27 Bill Wilkinson CO .10 .05
❑ 28 Peter Wilkinson .40 .18
❑ 29 Byron Witkowski .40 .18
❑ 30 Lawson Arena .10 .05

## 1993-94 Western Michigan

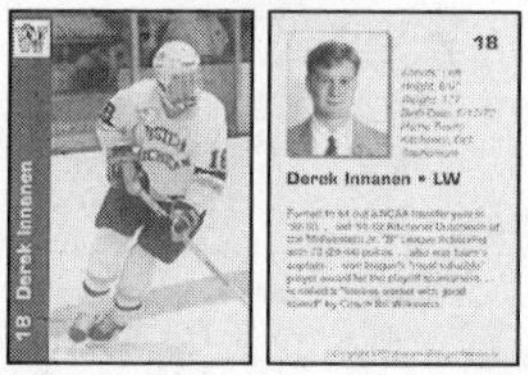

These 30 standard-size cards feature color player photos on their fronts, some are action shots, others are posed. These photos are borderless on three sides. The player's name and uniform number appear vertically in the brown left margin. The back carries a black-and-white player head shot at the upper left. A brief player biography appears alongside on the right. Below are his career highlights and 1992-93 statistics. Aside from the players' uniform numbers appearing on the front and back, the cards are unnumbered and checklisted below in alphabetical order.

| | MINT | NRMT |
|---|---|---|
| COMPLETE SET (30) | 8.00 | 3.60 |
| COMMON CARD (1-30) | .10 | .05 |

❑ 1 David Agnew .40 .18
❑ 2 Brent Brekke .50 .23
❑ 3 Chris Brooks .40 .18
❑ 4 Craig Brown .40 .18
❑ 5 Jeremy Brown .40 .18
❑ 6 Justin Cardwell .40 .18
❑ 7 Tom Carriere .40 .18
❑ 8 Tony Code .40 .18
❑ 9 Matt Cressman .40 .18
❑ 10 Jim Culhane ACO .10 .05
❑ 11 Ryan D'Arcy .40 .18
❑ 12 Brian Gallentine .40 .18
❑ 13 Matt Greene .40 .18
❑ 14 Rob Hodge .40 .18
WMU Hall of Fame
❑ 15 Jim Holman .40 .18
❑ 16 Derek Innanen .40 .18
❑ 17 Mark Jodoin .40 .18
❑ 18 Brendan Kenny .40 .18
❑ 19 Misha Lapin .50 .23
❑ 20 Darren Maloney .40 .18
❑ 21 Jamal Mayers .50 .23
❑ 22 Dave Mitchell .40 .18
❑ 23 Brian Renfrew .40 .18
❑ 24 Mike Schafer ACO .10 .05
❑ 25 Derek Schooley .40 .18
❑ 26 Colin Ward .40 .18
❑ 27 Mike Whitton .40 .18
❑ 28 Bill Wilkinson CO .10 .05
❑ 29 Peter Wilkinson .40 .18
❑ 30 Shawn Zimmerman .40 .18

## 1992-93 Wheeling Thunderbirds

This 24-card standard-size set features color, posed action player photos. The pictures are set on a gray card face with a red banner

above the photo that contains the year and the manufacturer name (Those Guys Productions). The player's name, position, and team name are printed below the picture. The horizontal backs have white borders and are divided into three sections by a gray, white, and gray stripe design. The upper gray area contains the player's name and biographical information. The middle white section holds statistics from the previous season. The lower gray section carries promotional information.

| | MINT | NRMT |
|---|---|---|
| COMPLETE SET (24) | 7.00 | 3.10 |
| COMMON CARD (1-24) | .10 | .05 |

❑ 1 Title Card .10 .05
❑ 2 Claude Barthe .40 .18
❑ 3 Joel Blain .40 .18
❑ 4 Derek DeCosty .40 .18
❑ 5 Marc Deschamps .40 .18
❑ 6 Tom Dion .40 .18
❑ 7 Devin Edgerton .40 .18
❑ 8 Pete Heine .40 .18
❑ 9 Kim Maier .40 .18
❑ 10 Mike Millham .50 .23
❑ 11 Cory Paterson .40 .18
❑ 12 Trevor Pochipinski .40 .18
❑ 13 Tim Roberts .40 .18
❑ 14 Mark Rodgers .40 .18
❑ 15 Darren Schwartz .40 .18
❑ 16 Trevor Senn .40 .18
❑ 17 Tim Tisdale .40 .18
❑ 18 John Uniac .50 .23
❑ 19 Denny Magruder MG .10 .05
❑ 20 Chuck Greenwood .10 .05
Jim Smith (Producers)
❑ 21 Larry Kish VP/MG .10 .05
❑ 22 Doug Sauter CO .10 .05
❑ 23 T-Bird (Mascot) .10 .05
❑ 24 Doug Bacon .40 .18

## 1993-94 Wheeling Thunderbirds

Minor league expert Ralph Slate reports that these cards were distributed in three different manners: Cards 1-21 were the standard team set, available all season long at home games. Cards PC1-PC4 were handed out as premiums at games. Cards UD1-UD10 comprise a late-season update set which was sold separately. The three are combined here for cataloguing purposes, but may be found on the market as separate entities.

| | MINT | NRMT |
|---|---|---|
| COMPLETE SET (21) | 14.00 | 6.25 |
| COMMON CARD (1-21) | .10 | .05 |
| COMMON CARD (PC1-PC4) | 1.00 | .45 |
| COMMON CARD (UD1-UD10) | .10 | .05 |

❑ 1 Header Card CL .10 .05
❑ 2 Darren Schwartz .40 .18
❑ 3 Cory Paterson .40 .18
❑ 4 Derek DeCosty .40 .18
❑ 5 Jim Bermingham .40 .18
❑ 6 Brock Woods .40 .18
❑ 7 Tim Roberts .40 .18
❑ 8 Eric Raymond .40 .18
❑ 9 Brett Abel .40 .18
❑ 10 Sebastien Fortier .40 .18
❑ 11 John Johnson .40 .18
❑ 12 Brent Pope .40 .18
❑ 13 Marquis Mathieu .40 .18
❑ 14 Terry Virtue .40 .18
❑ 15 Vadim Slivchenko .50 .23
❑ 16 Clayton Gainer .40 .18
❑ 17 Sylvain LaPointe .40 .18
❑ 18 Doug Sauter CO .10 .05
❑ 19 Larry Kish VP GM .10 .05
❑ 20 Denny Magruder GM .10 .05
❑ 21 Bill Cordery ASST TR .10 .05
❑ PC1 Wheeling Thunderbirds 1.00 .45
❑ PC2 Darren Schwartz 1.00 .45
❑ PC3 Tim Tisdale 1.00 .45
❑ PC4 Cory Paterson 1.00 .45
❑ UD1 Update Checklist .10 .05
❑ UD2 Tim Tisdale .50 .23
❑ UD3 John Van Kessel .50 .23
❑ UD4 Rival Fullum .75 .35
❑ UD5 Steve Gibson .75 .35
❑ UD6 Dave Goucher .10 .05
Director of Communication
❑ UD7 Gary Zearott .10 .05
Photographer
❑ UD8 Darren Schwartz .10 .05
T-Bird Leader
❑ UD9 Vadim Slivchenko .75 .35
T-Bird Leader
❑ UD10 Brock Woods .50 .23
T-Bird Leader

## 1994-95 Wheeling Thunderbirds

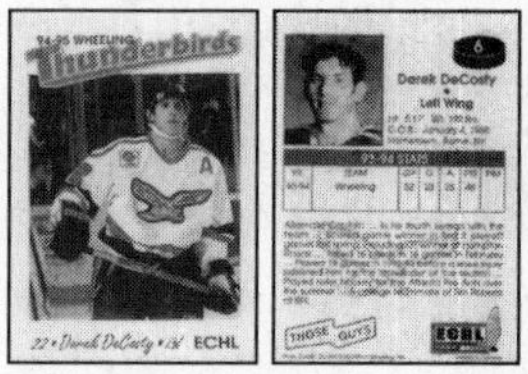

This small, 12-card set of the Wheeling Thunderbirds of the ECHL was produced by Those Guys for the team. The set was available through the club at games. The stylish fronts featured a player photo, name, number and position, along with team logo. The numbered backs contain a small portrait and player stats.

| | MINT | NRMT |
|---|---|---|
| COMPLETE SET (12) | 5.00 | 2.20 |
| COMMON CARD (1-12) | .25 | .11 |

❑ 1 Checklist .25 .11
❑ 2 Tim Tisdale .50 .23
❑ 3 Brock Woods .50 .23
❑ 4 Vadim Slivchenko .50 .23
❑ 5 Tim Roberts .50 .23
❑ 6 Derek DeCosty .50 .23
❑ 7 Steve Gibson .50 .23
❑ 8 Xavier Majic .60 .25
❑ 9 Peter Marek .50 .23
❑ 10 Greg Louder .50 .23
❑ 11 Gairin Smith .50 .23
❑ 12 Darren McAusland .50 .23
❑ 13 Brent Pope .25 .11
❑ 14 Dominic Fafard .25 .11
❑ 15 Pat Barton .25 .11
❑ 16 Patrick Labrecque .25 .11
❑ 17 Lorne Toews .25 .11
❑ 18 Scott Matusovich .25 .11
❑ 19 Louis Bernard .25 .11
❑ 20 Doug Sutter .25 .11
❑ 21 Scott Allegrino TR .25 .11
❑ 22 Bill Cordery .25 .11
❑ 23 Mark Landini .25 .11

## 1996-97 Wheeling Nailers

This 23-card set of the Wheeling Nailers of the ECHL was produced by Split Second. The cards feature action photography on the front, along with the player's name and number and the team logo. The backs have a brief stats package, along with a larger interpretation of the player's number. As these cards are unnumbered otherwise, they are listed alphabetically below.

| | MINT | NRMT |
|---|---|---|
| COMPLETE SET (23) | 7.00 | 3.10 |
| COMMON CARD | .10 | .05 |

❑ 1 John Tanner .50 .23
❑ 2 Frederic Barbeau .40 .18
❑ 4 Greg McLean .40 .18
❑ 8 Keli Corpse .40 .18
❑ 9 Don Chase .40 .18
❑ 10 Eric Royal .40 .18
❑ 11 Ian McIntyre .40 .18
❑ 14 John Varga .40 .18
❑ 15 John Badduke .40 .18
❑ 17 Brad Symes .40 .18
❑ 18 Perry Pappas .40 .18
❑ 20 Greg Callahan .40 .18
❑ 21 Jason Clark .40 .18
❑ 22 Chad Dameworth .40 .18
❑ 25 Martin LePage .40 .18
❑ 28 John Blessman .40 .18
❑ 33 Ryan Haggerty .50 .23
❑ 35 Mike Minard .50 .23
❑ 36 Rob Trumbley .40 .18
❑ 44 Francis Bouillon .40 .18
❑ NNO Scotty Allegrino TR .10 .05
❑ NNO Spike(Mascot) .10 .05
❑ NNO Tom McVie CO .40 .18

## 1999 Wichita Thunder

Cards feature full color fronts with name and position on the lower front of the card. Backs feature statistical and biographical information. Cards are unnumbered and checklisted below in alphabetical order.

| | MINT | NRMT |
|---|---|---|
| COMPLETE SET (25) | 5.00 | 2.20 |
| COMMON CARD (1-25) | .10 | .05 |

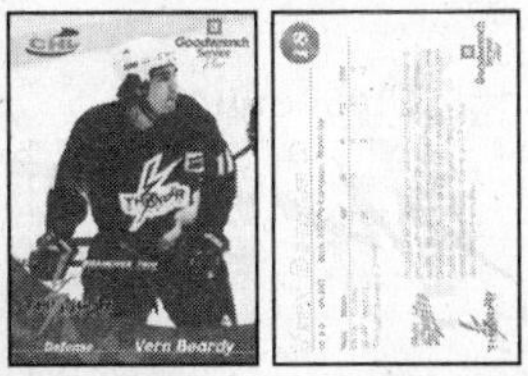

| | | |
|---|---|---|
| ❑ 1 Vern Beardy | .20 | .09 |
| ❑ 2 Travis Clayton | .20 | .09 |
| ❑ 3 Chris Dashney | .20 | .09 |
| ❑ 4 Mike Donaghue | .20 | .09 |
| ❑ 5 Jason Duda | .20 | .09 |
| ❑ 6 Rhett Dudley | .20 | .09 |
| ❑ 7 Trevor Folk | .20 | .09 |
| ❑ 8 Todd Howarth | .20 | .09 |
| ❑ 9 John Kachur | .20 | .09 |
| ❑ 10 Mark Karpen | .20 | .09 |
| ❑ 11 Lance Leslie | .25 | .11 |
| ❑ 12 Brad Link | .25 | .11 |
| ❑ 13 Mark Macera | .20 | .09 |
| ❑ 14 Walker McDonald | .20 | .09 |
| ❑ 15 Jim McGeoug | .20 | .09 |
| ❑ 16 Thomas Migdal | .20 | .09 |
| ❑ 17 Aaron novak | .20 | .09 |
| ❑ 18 Sean O'Reiley | .20 | .09 |
| ❑ 19 Kevin Powell | .20 | .09 |
| ❑ 20 Greg Smith | .25 | .11 |
| ❑ 21 Travis Tipler | .20 | .09 |
| ❑ 22 Troy Yarosh | .20 | .09 |
| ❑ 23 Bryan Wells | .10 | .05 |
| ❑ 24 Title Card | .10 | .05 |
| ❑ 25 Dealer Logo Card | .10 | .05 |

## 1989-90 Windsor Spitfires

This 22-card standard-size set features members of the 1989-90 Windsor Spitfires of the Ontario Hockey league (OHL). The fronts feature posed shots of the players in front of their lockers. The backs carry biography, date of birth, personal interests, and a "last year" feature. The cards are unnumbered and checklisted below in alphabetical order.

| | MINT | NRMT |
|---|---|---|
| COMPLETE SET (22) | 8.00 | 3.60 |
| COMMON CARD (1-22) | .50 | .23 |
| ❑ 1 Sean Burns | .50 | .23 |
| ❑ 2 Glen Craig | .50 | .23 |
| ❑ 3 Brian Forestell | .50 | .23 |
| ❑ 4 Chris Fraser | .50 | .23 |
| ❑ 5 Trent Gleason | .50 | .23 |
| ❑ 6 Jon Hartley | .50 | .23 |
| ❑ 7 Ron Jones | .50 | .23 |
| ❑ 8 Bob Leeming | .50 | .23 |
| ❑ 9 Kevin MacKay | .50 | .23 |
| ❑ 10 Kevin McDougall | .50 | .23 |
| ❑ 11 Ryan Merritt | .50 | .23 |
| ❑ 12 David Myles | .50 | .23 |
| ❑ 13 Sean O'Hagan | .50 | .23 |
| ❑ 14 Mike Polano | .50 | .23 |
| ❑ 15 Jason Snow | .50 | .23 |
| ❑ 16 Brad Smith CO | .50 | .23 |
| ❑ 17 Jason Stos | .50 | .23 |
| ❑ 18 Jon Stos | .50 | .23 |
| ❑ 19 Jamie Vargo | .50 | .23 |
| ❑ 20 Trevor Walsh | .50 | .23 |
| ❑ 21 K.J. White | .50 | .23 |
| ❑ 22 Jason Zohl | .50 | .23 |

## 1992-93 Windsor Spitfires

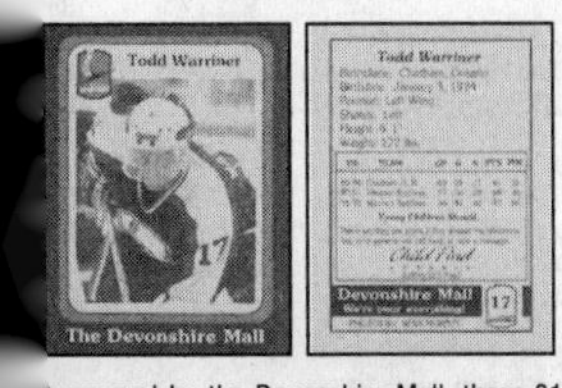

Sponsored by the Devonshire Mall, these 31 cards measure approximately 2 5/8" by 3 5/8" and feature on their fronts posed-on-ice color shots of the 1992-93 Windsor Spitfires bordered in red, white, and blue. The player's name and the Spitfires logo appear in the white area above the photo. The white back is framed by a black line and carries the player's name at the top, followed below by biography, statistics, and a safety message for children.

| | MINT | NRMT |
|---|---|---|
| COMPLETE SET (31) | 12.00 | 5.50 |
| COMMON CARD (1-31) | .10 | .05 |
| ❑ 1 Team Card/Checklist | .25 | .11 |
| ❑ 2 Mike Martin | .50 | .23 |
| ❑ 3 Luke Clowes | .40 | .18 |
| ❑ 4 Jason Haelzle | .40 | .18 |
| ❑ 5 Adam Graves | 3.00 | 1.35 |
| ❑ 6 Craig Lutes | .40 | .18 |
| ❑ 7 David Pluck | .40 | .18 |
| ❑ 8 Colin Wilson | .40 | .18 |
| ❑ 9 Bill Bowler | .75 | .35 |
| ❑ 10 Ryan O'Neill | .40 | .18 |
| ❑ 11 Adam Young | .40 | .18 |
| ❑ 12 Gerrard Masse | .40 | .18 |
| ❑ 13 Daryl Lavoie | .40 | .18 |
| ❑ 14 Peter Allison | .40 | .18 |
| ❑ 15 Ernie Godden RET | .50 | .23 |
| ❑ 16 Brady Blain | .40 | .18 |
| ❑ 17 Todd Warriner | 1.50 | .70 |
| ❑ 18 Rick Marshall | .40 | .18 |
| ❑ 19 Craig Johnson | .40 | .18 |
| ❑ 20 Kelly Vipond | .40 | .18 |
| ❑ 21 Devy Bear MASCOT | .10 | .05 |
| ❑ 22 Stephen Webb | .40 | .18 |
| ❑ 23 Scott Miller RET | .40 | .18 |
| ❑ 24 Dennis Purdie | .40 | .18 |
| ❑ 25 Steve Gibson | .40 | .18 |
| ❑ 26 Mike Hartwick | .40 | .18 |
| ❑ 27 Shawn Heins | .40 | .18 |
| ❑ 28 David Benn | .40 | .18 |
| ❑ 29 Matt Mullin | .50 | .23 |
| ❑ 30 David Mitchell | .40 | .18 |
| ❑ 31 The Dynamic Duo<br>Todd Warriner<br>Cory Stillman | 1.00 | .45 |

## 1993-94 Windsor Spitfires

Co-sponsored by Pizza Hut and radio station CKLW AM 800, and printed by Slapshot Images Ltd., this 27-card standard-size set features the 1993-94 Windsor Spitfires. On a geometrical team color-coded background, the fronts feature color action player photos with thin grey borders. The player's name, position and team name, as well as the producer's logo, also appear on the front. The backs carry a close-up color player portrait and biographical information, along with team and sponsors' logos. The cards are numbered on the back. Included in this set is a Slapshot ad card with a 1994 calendar on the back.

| | MINT | NRMT |
|---|---|---|
| COMPLETE SET (27) | 12.00 | 5.50 |
| COMMON CARD (1-26) | .10 | .05 |
| ❑ 1 Ed Jovanovski | 4.00 | 1.80 |
| ❑ 2 Shawn Silver | .40 | .18 |
| ❑ 3 Travis Scott | .75 | .35 |
| ❑ 4 Mike Martin | .50 | .23 |
| ❑ 5 Daryl Lavoie | .40 | .18 |
| ❑ 6 Craig Lutes | .40 | .18 |
| ❑ 7 David Pluck | .40 | .18 |
| ❑ 8 Bill Bowler | .75 | .35 |
| ❑ 9 David Green | .40 | .18 |
| ❑ 10 Adam Young | .40 | .18 |
| ❑ 11 Mike Loach | .40 | .18 |
| ❑ 12 Brady Blain | .40 | .18 |
| ❑ 13 Shayne McCosh | .40 | .18 |
| ❑ 14 Rob Shearer | .50 | .23 |
| ❑ 15 Joel Poirier | .40 | .18 |
| ❑ 16 Cory Evans | .40 | .18 |
| ❑ 17 Vladimir Kretchine | .40 | .18 |
| ❑ 18 Dave Roche | 1.00 | .45 |
| ❑ 19 Ryan Stewart | .40 | .18 |
| ❑ 20 Dave Geris | .50 | .23 |
| ❑ 21 Dan West | .40 | .18 |
| ❑ 22 Luke Clowes | .40 | .18 |
| ❑ 23 John Cooper | .40 | .18 |
| ❑ 24 Akil Adams | .40 | .18 |
| ❑ 25 Sponsor Card<br>Pizza Hut | .10 | .05 |
| ❑ 26 Sponsor Card<br>Steve Bell<br>Radio station AM 800 | .10 | .05 |
| ❑ NNO Slapshot Ad Card | .10 | .05 |

## 1994-95 Windsor Spitfires

Sponsored by Pizza Hut, Mr. Lube, CKLW AM 800, and printed by Slapshot Images Ltd., this 29-card set features the 1994-95 Windsor Spitfires. On a red and blue background, the fronts feature color player action photos with thin black borders. The player's name, position and team name, as well as the producer's logo, also appear on the front. The backs carry

a close-up color player portrait and biographical information, along with team and sponsor logos. Included in this set is a Slapshot ad card with a 1995 calendar on the back.

| | MINT | NRMT |
|---|---|---|
| COMPLETE SET (29) | 12.00 | 5.50 |
| COMMON CARD (1-28) | .10 | .05 |
| ❑ 1 Checklist | .10 | .05 |
| ❑ 2 Jamie Storr | 2.00 | .90 |
| ❑ 3 Travis Scott | .50 | .23 |
| ❑ 4 Paul Beazley | .40 | .18 |
| ❑ 5 Mike Martin | .50 | .23 |
| ❑ 6 Chris Van Dyk | .40 | .18 |
| ❑ 7 Denis Smith | .75 | .35 |
| ❑ 8 Glenn Crawford | .50 | .23 |
| ❑ 9 David Pluck | .40 | .18 |
| ❑ 10 Bill Bowler | .50 | .23 |
| ❑ 11 David Green | .40 | .18 |
| ❑ 12 Adam Young | .40 | .18 |
| ❑ 13 Wes Ward | .40 | .18 |
| ❑ 14 Ed Jovanovski | 3.00 | 1.35 |
| ❑ 15 Kevin Paden | .40 | .18 |
| ❑ 16 Rob Shearer | .50 | .23 |
| ❑ 17 Joel Poirier | .40 | .18 |
| ❑ 18 Cory Evans | .40 | .18 |
| ❑ 19 Vladimir Kretchine | .40 | .18 |
| ❑ 20 David Roche | .75 | .35 |
| ❑ 21 Rick Emmett | .40 | .18 |
| ❑ 22 David Geris | .50 | .23 |
| ❑ 23 Caleb Ward | .40 | .18 |
| ❑ 24 Luke Clowes | .40 | .18 |
| ❑ 25 John Cooper | .40 | .18 |
| ❑ 26 Tim Findlay | .50 | .23 |
| ❑ 27 Sponsor Card<br>Pizza Hut | .10 | .05 |
| ❑ 28 Sponsor Card<br>Steve Bell<br>Radio station AM 800 | .10 | .05 |
| ❑ NNO Ad Card | .10 | .05 |

## 1996-97 Fife Flyers

| | MINT | NRMT |
|---|---|---|
| COMPLETE SET (20) | 12.00 | 5.50 |
| COMMON CARD (1-20) | .50 | .23 |
| ❑ 1 Gavin Fleming | .75 | .35 |
| ❑ 2 John Reid | .75 | .35 |
| ❑ 3 Russ Parent | .75 | .35 |
| ❑ 4 Derek King | .75 | .35 |
| ❑ 5 Colin Grubb | .75 | .35 |
| ❑ 6 Colin Hamilton | .75 | .35 |
| ❑ 7 Andy Finlay | .75 | .35 |
| ❑ 8 Richard Dingwall | .75 | .35 |
| ❑ 9 Andy Samuel | .75 | .35 |
| ❑ 10 Wayne Maxwell | .75 | .35 |
| ❑ 11 Craig Wilson | .75 | .35 |
| ❑ 12 Daryl Venters | .75 | .35 |
| ❑ 13 Gordon Latto | .75 | .35 |
| ❑ 14 Ruichard Danskin | .75 | .35 |
| ❑ 15 Martin McKay | .75 | .35 |
| ❑ 16 Kyle Horne | .75 | .35 |
| ❑ 17 Mark Morrison CO | .50 | .23 |
| ❑ 18 Frank Morris | .75 | .35 |
| ❑ 19 Steven King | .75 | .35 |
| ❑ 20 Lee Mercer | .75 | .35 |

## 1997-98 Fife Flyers

| | MINT | NRMT |
|---|---|---|
| COMPLETE SET (20) | 12.00 | 5.50 |
| COMMON CARD (1-20) | .50 | .23 |
| ❑ 1 Team Photo | .50 | .23 |
| ❑ 2 Bernie McCrone | .75 | .35 |
| ❑ 3 Wayne Maxwell | .75 | .35 |
| ❑ 4 Derek King | .75 | .35 |
| ❑ 5 Mark Slater | .75 | .35 |
| ❑ 6 Bill Moody | .75 | .35 |
| ❑ 7 Lee Cowmedow | .75 | .35 |
| ❑ 8 Richard Charles | .75 | .35 |
| ❑ 9 Andy Finlay | .75 | .35 |
| ❑ 10 Daryl Venters | .75 | .35 |
| ❑ 11 Steven King | .75 | .35 |
| ❑ 12 Andy Samuel | .75 | .35 |
| ❑ 13 Gordon Latto | .75 | .35 |
| ❑ 14 Mark Morrison CO | .50 | .23 |
| ❑ 15 John Haig | .75 | .35 |
| ❑ 16 Lee Mercer | .75 | .35 |
| ❑ 17 Gary Wishart | .75 | .35 |
| ❑ 18 Colin Hamilton | .75 | .35 |
| ❑ 19 Frank Morris | .75 | .35 |
| ❑ 20 David Smith | .75 | .35 |

## 1993-94 Finnish Jyvas Hyva Stickers

This 349-sticker set features the players of Finland's SM-Liiga. The odd-sized stickers (1 X 1 1/2") were inserted as premiums with candy products. Interestingly, the set appears to skip the following numbers: 30,60,90,120, 50,180,210,240,270,300,330. There are no spaces for these cards in the binder produced to store the set. Collectors with further information as to the existence of the missing stickers are encouraged to contact Beckett Publications. The set is noteworthy for early apperances of Saku Koivu and Janne Niinimaa.

| | MINT | NRMT |
|---|---|---|
| COMPLETE SET | 60.00 | 27.00 |
| COMMON STICKER | .10 | .05 |
| ❑ 1 HIFK Team Photo | .10 | .05 |
| ❑ 2 HIFK Team Photo | .10 | .05 |
| ❑ 3 HIFK Team Photo | .10 | .05 |
| ❑ 4 HIFK Team Photo | .10 | .05 |
| ❑ 5 HIFK Team Photo | .10 | .05 |
| ❑ 6 HIFK Team Photo | .10 | .05 |
| ❑ 7 HIFK Team Photo | .10 | .05 |
| ❑ 8 HIFK Team Photo | .10 | .05 |
| ❑ 9 HIFK Team Photo | .10 | .05 |
| ❑ 10 HIFK Team Photo | .10 | .05 |
| ❑ 11 HIFK Team Photo | .10 | .05 |
| ❑ 12 HIFK Team Photo | .10 | .05 |
| ❑ 13 Harri Rindell CO | .15 | .07 |
| ❑ 14 Sakari Lindfors | .50 | .23 |
| ❑ 15 Simo Saarinen | .15 | .07 |
| ❑ 16 Pertti Lehtonen | .15 | .07 |
| ❑ 17 Jari Laukkanen | .15 | .07 |
| ❑ 18 Valeri Krykov | .15 | .07 |
| ❑ 19 Iiro Jarvi | .25 | .11 |
| ❑ 20 Jari Munck | .15 | .07 |
| ❑ 21 Pasi Sormunen | .15 | .07 |
| ❑ 22 Pekka Peltola | .15 | .07 |
| ❑ 23 Teppo Kivela | .15 | .07 |
| ❑ 24 Pekka Tuomisto | .15 | .07 |
| ❑ 25 Kai Tervonen | .15 | .07 |
| ❑ 26 Dan Lambert | .30 | .14 |
| ❑ 27 Marco Poulsen | .15 | .07 |
| ❑ 28 Ville Peltonen | 1.00 | .45 |
| ❑ 29 Kim Ahlroos | .15 | .07 |
| ❑ 31 HPK Team Photo | .10 | .05 |
| ❑ 32 HPK Team Photo | .10 | .05 |
| ❑ 33 HPK Team Photo | .10 | .05 |
| ❑ 34 HPK Team Photo | .10 | .05 |
| ❑ 35 HPK Team Photo | .10 | .05 |
| ❑ 36 HPK Team Photo | .10 | .05 |
| ❑ 37 HPK Team Photo | .10 | .05 |
| ❑ 38 HPK Team Photo | .10 | .05 |
| ❑ 39 HPK Team Photo | .10 | .05 |
| ❑ 40 HPK Team Photo | .10 | .05 |
| ❑ 41 HPK Team Photo | .10 | .05 |
| ❑ 42 HPK Team Photo | .10 | .05 |
| ❑ 43 Pentti Matikainen | .15 | .07 |
| ❑ 44 Kari Rosenberg | .25 | .11 |
| ❑ 45 Mikko Myllykoski | .15 | .07 |
| ❑ 46 Janne Laukkanen | 1.00 | .45 |
| ❑ 47 Jarkko Nikander | .25 | .11 |
| ❑ 48 Tomas Kapusta | .20 | .09 |
| ❑ 49 Mika Lartama | .15 | .07 |
| ❑ 50 Niko Marttila | .15 | .07 |
| ❑ 51 Jari Haapamaki | .15 | .07 |
| ❑ 52 Tommi Varjonen | .15 | .07 |
| ❑ 53 Toni Virta | .15 | .07 |
| ❑ 54 Marko Palo | .25 | .11 |
| ❑ 55 Marko Allen | .15 | .07 |
| ❑ 56 Miikka Ruokonen | .15 | .07 |
| ❑ 57 Jani Hassinen | .15 | .07 |
| ❑ 58 Pasi Kivila | .15 | .07 |
| ❑ 59 Markku Piikkila | .15 | .07 |
| ❑ 61 Ilves Team Photo | .10 | .05 |
| ❑ 62 Ilves Team Photo | .10 | .05 |
| ❑ 63 Ilves Team Photo | .10 | .05 |
| ❑ 64 Ilves Team Photo | .10 | .05 |
| ❑ 65 Ilves Team Photo | .10 | .05 |
| ❑ 66 Ilves Team Photo | .10 | .05 |
| ❑ 67 Ilves Team Photo | .10 | .05 |
| ❑ 68 Ilves Team Photo | .10 | .05 |
| ❑ 69 Ilves Team Photo | .10 | .05 |
| ❑ 70 Ilves Team Photo | .10 | .05 |
| ❑ 71 Ilves Team Photo | .10 | .05 |
| ❑ 72 Ilves Team Photo | .10 | .05 |
| ❑ 73 Jukka Jalonen CO | .15 | .07 |
| ❑ 74 Jukka Tammi | .50 | .23 |
| ❑ 75 Jani Nikko | .35 | .16 |
| ❑ 76 Hannu Henriksson | .15 | .07 |
| ❑ 77 Juha Jarvenpaa | .20 | .09 |
| ❑ 78 Hannu Mattila | .15 | .07 |
| ❑ 79 Timo Peltomaa | .25 | .11 |
| ❑ 80 Jukka Ollila | .15 | .07 |
| ❑ 81 Juha-Matti Marijarvi | .15 | .07 |
| ❑ 82 Mikko Louvi | .25 | .11 |
| ❑ 83 Jarno Peltonen | .15 | .07 |
| ❑ 84 Pasi Maattanen | .15 | .07 |
| ❑ 85 Juha Lampinen | .15 | .07 |
| ❑ 86 Allan Measures | .15 | .07 |
| ❑ 87 Janne Seva | .15 | .07 |
| ❑ 88 Risto Jalo | .20 | .09 |
| ❑ 89 Esa Tommila | .15 | .07 |
| ❑ 91 Jokerit Team Photo | .10 | .05 |
| ❑ 92 Jokerit Team Photo | .10 | .05 |
| ❑ 93 Jokerit Team Photo | .10 | .05 |
| ❑ 94 Jokerit Team Photo | .10 | .05 |
| ❑ 95 Jokerit Team Photo | .10 | .05 |
| ❑ 96 Jokerit Team Photo | .10 | .05 |
| ❑ 97 Jokerit Team Photo | .10 | .05 |
| ❑ 98 Jokerit Team Photo | .10 | .05 |
| ❑ 99 Jokerit Team Photo | .10 | .05 |
| ❑ 100 Jokerit Team Photo | .10 | .05 |
| ❑ 101 Jokerit Team Photo | .10 | .05 |
| ❑ 102 Jokerit Team Photo | .10 | .05 |
| ❑ 103 Alpo Suhonen CO | .25 | .11 |
| ❑ 104 Ari Sulander | .75 | .35 |
| ❑ 105 Kari Martikainen | .25 | .11 |
| ❑ 106 Erik Hamalainen | .35 | .16 |
| ❑ 107 Juha Jokiharju | .20 | .09 |
| ❑ 108 Otakar Janecky | .35 | .16 |
| ❑ 109 Petri Varis | .75 | .35 |
| ❑ 110 Waltteri Immonen | .20 | .09 |
| ❑ 111 Mika Stromberg | .35 | .16 |
| ❑ 112 Keijo Sailynoja | .20 | .09 |
| ❑ 113 Timo Saarikoski | .15 | .07 |
| ❑ 114 Juha Ylonen | .50 | .23 |
| ❑ 115 Ari Salo | .15 | .07 |
| ❑ 116 Heikki Riihijarvi | .15 | .07 |
| ❑ 117 Timo Norppa | .15 | .07 |
| ❑ 118 Jali Wahlsten | .15 | .07 |
| ❑ 119 Rami Koivisto | .15 | .07 |
| ❑ 121 JYP HT Team Photo | .10 | .05 |
| ❑ 122 JYP HT Team Photo | .10 | .05 |
| ❑ 123 JYP HT Team Photo | .10 | .05 |
| ❑ 124 JYP HT Team Photo | .10 | .05 |
| ❑ 125 JYP HT Team Photo | .10 | .05 |
| ❑ 126 JYP HT Team Photo | .10 | .05 |
| ❑ 127 JYP HT Team Photo | .10 | .05 |
| ❑ 128 JYP HT Team Photo | .10 | .05 |
| ❑ 129 JYP HT Team Photo | .10 | .05 |
| ❑ 130 JYP HT Team Photo | .10 | .05 |
| ❑ 131 JYP HT Team Photo | .10 | .05 |
| ❑ 132 JYP HT Team Photo | .10 | .05 |
| ❑ 133 Kari Savolainen CO | .15 | .07 |
| ❑ 134 Ari-Pekka Siekkinen | .25 | .11 |
| ❑ 135 Harri Laurila | .15 | .07 |
| ❑ 136 Markku Heikkinen | .15 | .07 |
| ❑ 137 Jari Lindroos | .25 | .11 |
| ❑ 138 Lasse Nieminen | .15 | .07 |
| ❑ 139 Risto Kurkinen | .15 | .07 |
| ❑ 140 Jarmo Jokilahti | .15 | .07 |
| ❑ 141 Veli-Pekka Hard | .15 | .07 |
| ❑ 142 Joni Lius | .15 | .07 |
| ❑ 143 Jyrki Jokinen | .15 | .07 |
| ❑ 144 Mika Arvaja | .15 | .07 |
| ❑ 145 Vesa Ponto | .15 | .07 |
| ❑ 146 Jarmo Rantanen | .15 | .07 |
| ❑ 147 Mika Paananen | .15 | .07 |
| ❑ 148 Marko Virtanen | .25 | .11 |
| ❑ 149 Marko Ek | .15 | .07 |
| ❑ 151 Kalpa Team Photo | .10 | .05 |
| ❑ 152 Kalpa Team Photo | .10 | .05 |
| ❑ 153 Kalpa Team Photo | .10 | .05 |
| ❑ 154 Kalpa Team Photo | .10 | .05 |
| ❑ 155 Kalpa Team Photo | .10 | .05 |
| ❑ 156 Kalpa Team Photo | .10 | .05 |
| ❑ 157 Kalpa Team Photo | .10 | .05 |
| ❑ 158 Kalpa Team Photo | .10 | .05 |
| ❑ 159 Kalpa Team Photo | .10 | .05 |
| ❑ 160 Kalpa Team Photo | .10 | .05 |
| ❑ 161 Kalpa Team Photo | .10 | .05 |
| ❑ 162 Kalpa Team Photo | .10 | .05 |
| ❑ 163 Hannu Kapanen | .15 | .07 |
| ❑ 164 Pasi Kuivalainen | .20 | .09 |
| ❑ 165 Kimmo Timonen | .35 | .16 |
| ❑ 166 Vesa Salo | .15 | .07 |
| ❑ 167 Jani Rautio | .15 | .07 |
| ❑ 168 Pekka Tirkkonen | .20 | .09 |
| ❑ 169 Dimitri Zinine | .15 | .07 |
| ❑ 170 Antti Tuomenoksa | .15 | .07 |
| ❑ 171 Jari Jarvinen | .15 | .07 |
| ❑ 172 Tuomas Kalliomaki | .15 | .07 |
| ❑ 173 Tommi Miettinen | .25 | .11 |
| ❑ 174 Sami Kapanen | 1.50 | .70 |
| ❑ 175 Vesa Ruotsalainen | .15 | .07 |
| ❑ 176 Mikko Tavi | .15 | .07 |
| ❑ 177 Sami Mettovaara | .15 | .07 |
| ❑ 178 Veli-Pekka Pekkarinen | .15 | .07 |
| ❑ 179 Arto Sirvio | .15 | .07 |
| ❑ 181 Kiekko-Espoo Team Photo | .10 | .05 |
| ❑ 182 Kiekko-Espoo Team Photo | .10 | .05 |
| ❑ 183 Kiekko-Espoo Team Photo | .10 | .05 |
| ❑ 184 Kiekko-Espoo Team Photo | .10 | .05 |
| ❑ 185 Kiekko-Espoo Team Photo | .10 | .05 |
| ❑ 186 Kiekko-Espoo Team Photo | .10 | .05 |
| ❑ 187 Kiekko-Espoo Team Photo | .10 | .05 |
| ❑ 188 Kiekko-Espoo Team Photo | .10 | .05 |
| ❑ 189 Kiekko-Espoo Team Photo | .10 | .05 |
| ❑ 190 Kiekko-Espoo Team Photo | .10 | .05 |
| ❑ 191 Kiekko-Espoo Team Photo | .10 | .05 |
| ❑ 192 Kiekko-Espoo Team Photo | .10 | .05 |
| ❑ 193 Martti Merra | .15 | .07 |
| ❑ 194 Timo Maki | .15 | .07 |
| ❑ 195 Sami Nuutinen | .15 | .07 |
| ❑ 196 Teemu Sillanpaa | .15 | .07 |
| ❑ 197 Tero Lehtera | .25 | .11 |
| ❑ 198 Jan Langbacka | .15 | .07 |
| ❑ 199 Jukka Tiilikainen | .15 | .07 |
| ❑ 200 Petri Pulkkinen | .15 | .07 |
| ❑ 201 Robert Salo | .15 | .07 |
| ❑ 202 Petro Koivunen | .25 | .11 |
| ❑ 203 Juha Ikonen | .15 | .07 |
| ❑ 204 Mikko Lempiainen | .15 | .07 |
| ❑ 205 Marko Halonen | .15 | .07 |
| ❑ 206 Jimi Helin | .15 | .07 |
| ❑ 207 Timo Hirvonen | .15 | .07 |
| ❑ 208 Mikko Halonen | .15 | .07 |
| ❑ 209 Kimmo Maki-Kokkila | .15 | .07 |
| ❑ 211 Lukko Team Photo | .10 | .05 |
| ❑ 212 Lukko Team Photo | .10 | .05 |
| ❑ 213 Lukko Team Photo | .10 | .05 |
| ❑ 214 Lukko Team Photo | .10 | .05 |
| ❑ 215 Lukko Team Photo | .10 | .05 |
| ❑ 216 Lukko Team Photo | .10 | .05 |
| ❑ 217 Lukko Team Photo | .10 | .05 |
| ❑ 218 Lukko Team Photo | .10 | .05 |
| ❑ 219 Lukko Team Photo | .10 | .05 |
| ❑ 220 Lukko Team Photo | .10 | .05 |
| ❑ 221 Lukko Team Photo | .10 | .05 |
| ❑ 222 Lukko Team Photo | .10 | .05 |
| ❑ 223 Vaclav Sykora | .15 | .07 |
| ❑ 224 Jarmo Myllys | .75 | .35 |
| ❑ 225 Kari-Pekka Friman | .15 | .07 |
| ❑ 226 Timo Kulonen | .15 | .07 |
| ❑ 227 Pasi Saarela | .15 | .07 |

❑ 228 Kalle Sahlstedt .25 .11
❑ 229 Kimmo Rintanen .35 .16
❑ 230 Jarmo Kuusisto .15 .07
❑ 231 Tuomas Gronman .35 .16
❑ 232 Tero Arkiomaa .15 .07
❑ 233 Petr Korinek .25 .11
❑ 234 Mika Alatalo .35 .16
❑ 235 Marko Tuulola .15 .07
❑ 236 Pasi Huura .20 .09
❑ 237 Tommi Pullola .15 .07
❑ 238 Mika Valila .15 .07
❑ 239 Jari Torkki .15 .07
❑ 241 Reipas Lahti Team Photo .10 .05
❑ 242 Reipas Lahti Team Photo .10 .05
❑ 243 Reipas Lahti Team Photo .10 .05
❑ 244 Reipas Lahti Team Photo .10 .05
❑ 245 Reipas Lahti Team Photo .10 .05
❑ 246 Reipas Lahti Team Photo .10 .05
❑ 247 Reipas Lahti Team Photo .10 .05
❑ 248 Reipas Lahti Team Photo .10 .05
❑ 249 Reipas Lahti Team Photo .10 .05
❑ 250 Reipas Lahti Team Photo .10 .05
❑ 251 Reipas Lahti Team Photo .10 .05
❑ 252 Reipas Lahti Team Photo .10 .05
❑ 253 Kari Makinen CO .15 .07
❑ 254 Oldrich Svoboda .15 .07
❑ 255 Timo Kahelin .15 .07
❑ 256 Pasi Ruponen .15 .07
❑ 257 Tommy Kiviaho .15 .07
❑ 258 Jari Multanen .15 .07
❑ 259 Erkki Makela .15 .07
❑ 260 Jari Parviainen .15 .07
❑ 261 Petri Koski .15 .07
❑ 262 Jouni Vauhkonen .35 .16
❑ 263 Toni Koivunen .15 .07
❑ 264 Sami Wikstrom .15 .07
❑ 265 Jarkko Hamalainen .15 .07
❑ 266 Sami Helenius .15 .07
❑ 267 Sami Lekkerimaki .15 .07
❑ 268 Jari Kauppila .15 .07
❑ 269 Jani Uski .15 .07
❑ 271 Tappara Team Photo .10 .05
❑ 272 Tappara Team Photo .10 .05
❑ 273 Tappara Team Photo .10 .05
❑ 274 Tappara Team Photo .10 .05
❑ 275 Tappara Team Photo .10 .05
❑ 276 Tappara Team Photo .10 .05
❑ 277 Tappara Team Photo .10 .05
❑ 278 Tappara Team Photo .10 .05
❑ 279 Tappara Team Photo .10 .05
❑ 280 Tappara Team Photo .10 .05
❑ 281 Tappara Team Photo .10 .05
❑ 282 Tappara Team Photo .10 .05
❑ 283 Boris Majorov .15 .07
❑ 284 Timo Hankela .15 .07
❑ 285 Timo Jutila .35 .16
❑ 286 Samuli Rautio .15 .07
❑ 287 Ari Haanpaa .20 .09
❑ 288 Mikko Peltola .15 .07
❑ 289 Pauli Jarvinen .15 .07
❑ 290 Pekka Laksola .15 .07
❑ 291 Janne Gronvall .35 .16
❑ 292 Kari Heikkinen .15 .07
❑ 293 Tommi Pohja .15 .07
❑ 294 Petri Aaltonen .15 .07
❑ 295 Petri Kalteva .15 .07
❑ 296 Tommi Haapsaari .15 .07
❑ 297 Teemu Numminen .15 .07
❑ 298 Pasi Forsberg .15 .07
❑ 299 Veli-Pekka Kautonen .15 .07
❑ 301 TPS Team Photo .10 .05
❑ 302 TPS Team Photo .10 .05
❑ 303 TPS Team Photo .10 .05
❑ 304 TPS Team Photo .10 .05
❑ 305 TPS Team Photo .10 .05
❑ 306 TPS Team Photo .10 .05
❑ 307 TPS Team Photo .10 .05
❑ 308 TPS Team Photo .10 .05
❑ 309 TPS Team Photo .10 .05
❑ 310 TPS Team Photo .10 .05
❑ 311 TPS Team Photo .10 .05
❑ 312 TPS Team Photo .10 .05
❑ 313 Vladimir Jursinov CO .15 .07
❑ 314 Jouni Rokama .25 .11
❑ 315 Hannu Virta .40 .18
❑ 316 Erik Kakko .15 .07
❑ 317 Jukka Vilander .15 .07
❑ 318 Esa Keskinen .75 .35
❑ 319 Ari Vuori .15 .07
❑ 320 Jouko Narvanmaa .15 .07
❑ 321 Marko Kiprusoff .35 .16
❑ 322 Jere Lehtinen 2.00 .90
❑ 323 Saku Koivu 12.00 5.50
❑ 324 Marko Jantunen .35 .16
❑ 325 Kari Harila .15 .07
❑ 326 Alexander Smirnov .15 .07
❑ 327 Toni Sihvonen .15 .07
❑ 328 Harri Sillgren .15 .07
❑ 329 Kai Nurminen .75 .35
❑ 331 Assat Team Photo .10 .05
❑ 332 Assat Team Photo .10 .05
❑ 333 Assat Team Photo .10 .05
❑ 334 Assat Team Photo .10 .05
❑ 335 Assat Team Photo .10 .05
❑ 336 Assat Team Photo .10 .05
❑ 337 Assat Team Photo .10 .05
❑ 338 Assat Team Photo .10 .05
❑ 339 Assat Team Photo .10 .05
❑ 340 Assat Team Photo .10 .05
❑ 341 Assat Team Photo .10 .05
❑ 342 Assat Team Photo .10 .05
❑ 343 Veli-Pekka Ketola CO .25 .11
❑ 344 Kari Takko .35 .16
❑ 345 Olli Kaski .15 .07
❑ 346 Karri Kivi .20 .09
❑ 347 Arto Heiskanen .15 .07
❑ 348 Janne Virtanen .15 .07
❑ 349 Mikael Kotkaniemi .15 .07
❑ 350 Stanislav Meciar .15 .07
❑ 351 Jarno Miikkulainen .15 .07
❑ 352 Jokke Heinanen .15 .07
❑ 353 Vjatseslav Fandul .25 .11
❑ 354 Ari Saarinen .15 .07
❑ 355 Jouni Vento .15 .07
❑ 356 Arto Javanainen .15 .07
❑ 357 Jari Korpisalo .35 .16
❑ 358 Rauli Raitanen .15 .07
❑ 359 Jari Levonen .15 .07
❑ NNO Binder 10.00 4.50

## 1993-94 Finnish SISU

Manufactured by Leaf in Turku, Finland, the 396 standard-size cards comprising this first series of players from the Finnish Hockey League feature on-ice color player photos on their fronts. The photos are bordered in a gray lithic, and each carries the player's name, uniform number, and team logo near the bottom. The gray lithic design continues on the horizontal back, which carries the player's team name in a yellow stripe across the top, followed below by his name, position, biography, and statistics. With a few exceptions, all text is in Finnish. Cards 301-396 differ from the others in that the design is orange lithic instead of gray, and some have horizontal fronts. The cards are numbered on the front. Cards 1-300 are organized by team as follows: Jokerit (1-26), TPS (27-55), Tappara (56-80), HIFK (81-106), Ilves (107-133), JyP HT (134-158), KalPa (159-180), Lukko (181-205), Assat (206-231), HPK (232-253), Kiekko-Espoo (254-277), and Reipas Lahti (278-300). These are followed by subsets of Game Action Cards (301-344), Playoff Cards (345-359), League Leaders (360-365), All Stars (366-371), Award Winners (372-380), and NHL Draft (388-396).

| | MINT | NRMT |
|---|---|---|
| COMPLETE SET (396) | 50.00 | 22.00 |
| COMMON CARD (1-396) | .10 | .05 |

❑ 1 Jokerit Team Card .25 .11
❑ 2 Alpo Suhonen .25 .11
❑ 3 Ari Sulander .50 .23
❑ 4 Marko Rantanen .15 .07
❑ 5 Ari Salo .10 .05
❑ 6 Kalle Koskinen .15 .07
❑ 7 Sebastian Sulku .10 .05
❑ 8 Waltteri Immonen .15 .07
❑ 9 Mika Stromberg .25 .11
❑ 10 Heikki Riihijarvi .10 .05
❑ 11 Kari Martikainen .15 .07
❑ 12 Erik Hamalainen .25 .11
❑ 13 Juha Jokiharju .15 .07
❑ 14 Timo Norppa .10 .05
❑ 15 Rami Koivisto .10 .05
❑ 16 Antti Tormanen 1.00 .45
❑ 17 Keijo Sailynoja .15 .07
❑ 18 Jere Keskinen .10 .05
❑ 19 Jali Wahlsten .10 .05
❑ 20 Mikko Kontilla .10 .05
❑ 21 Juha Ylonen .35 .16
❑ 22 Jussi Vielonen .10 .05
❑ 23 Petri Varis .50 .23
❑ 24 Juha Lind .75 .35
❑ 25 Timo Saarikoski .10 .05
❑ 26 Otakar Janecky .25 .11
❑ 27 TPS Team Card .15 .07
❑ 28 Vladimir Jursinov CO .10 .05
❑ 29 Jouni Rokama .15 .07
❑ 30 Kimmo Lecklin .10 .05
❑ 31 Jouko Narvanmaa .10 .05
❑ 32 Petteri Nummelin .15 .07
❑ 33 Erik Kakko .10 .05
❑ 34 Tom Koivisto .10 .05
❑ 35 Marko Kiprusoff .25 .11
❑ 36 Kari Harila .10 .05
❑ 37 Hannu Virta .30 .14
❑ 38 Aki-Petteri Berg 2.00 .90
❑ 39 Aleksander Smirnov .10 .05
❑ 40 Esa Keskinen .50 .23
❑ 41 Saku Koivu 10.00 4.50
❑ 42 Jukka Vilander .10 .05
❑ 43 Antti Aalto .50 .23
❑ 44 Mika Karapuu .10 .05
❑ 45 Toni Sihvonen .10 .05
❑ 46 Pavel Torgajev .35 .16
❑ 47 Jere Lehtinen 1.50 .70
❑ 48 Kai Nurminen .50 .23
❑ 49 Harri Sillgren .10 .05
❑ 50 Niko Mikkola .10 .05
❑ 51 Ari Vuori .10 .05
❑ 52 Lasse Pirjeta .10 .05
❑ 53 Reijo Mikkolainen .10 .05
❑ 54 Marko Jantunen .25 .11
❑ 55 Mikko Virolainen .10 .05
❑ 56 Tappara Team Card .15 .07
❑ 57 Boris Majorov CO .10 .05
❑ 58 Jaromir Sindel .25 .11
❑ 59 Timo Hankela .10 .05
❑ 60 Teemu Kivinen .10 .05
❑ 61 Petri Kalteva .10 .05
❑ 62 Jari Harjumaki .10 .05
❑ 63 Timo Jutila .25 .11
❑ 64 Janne Gronvall .25 .11
❑ 65 Jari Gronstrand .20 .09
❑ 66 Pekka Laksola .10 .05
❑ 67 Tommi Haapsaari .10 .05
❑ 68 Veli-Pekka Kautonen .10 .05
❑ 69 Mikko Peltola .10 .05
❑ 70 Kari Heikkinen .10 .05
❑ 71 Teemu Numminen .10 .05
❑ 72 Jiri Kucera .15 .07
❑ 73 Pauli Jarvinen .10 .05
❑ 74 Pasi Forsberg .10 .05
❑ 75 Tero Toivola .10 .05
❑ 76 Ari Haanpaa .15 .07
❑ 77 Tommi Pohja .10 .05
❑ 78 Samuli Rautio .10 .05
❑ 79 Markus Oijennus .10 .05
❑ 80 Petri Aaltonen .10 .05
❑ 81 HIFK Team Card .15 .07
❑ 82 Harri Rindell CO .10 .05
❑ 83 Sakari Lindfors .35 .16
❑ 84 Mikael Granlund .10 .05
❑ 85 Kimmo Hyttinen .10 .05
❑ 86 Jere Karalahti .50 .23
❑ 87 Dan Lambert .20 .09
❑ 88 Simo Saarinen .10 .05
❑ 89 Pasi Sormunen .10 .05
❑ 90 Tommi Hamalainen .10 .05
❑ 91 Pertti Lehtonen .10 .05
❑ 92 Jari Munck .10 .05
❑ 93 Kai Tervonen .10 .05
❑ 94 Kim Ahlroos .10 .05
❑ 95 Teppo Kivela .10 .05
❑ 96 Darren Boyko .15 .07
❑ 97 Pekka Peltola .10 .05
❑ 98 Marco Poulsen .10 .05
❑ 99 Valeri Krykov .10 .05
❑ 100 Jari Laukkanen .10 .05
❑ 101 Ville Peltonen 1.00 .45
❑ 102 Pekka Tuomisto .10 .05
❑ 103 Miro Haapaniemi .10 .05
❑ 104 Mika Kortelainen .10 .05
❑ 105 Marko Ojanen .10 .05
❑ 106 Iiro Jarvi .15 .07
❑ 107 Ilves Tampere Team Card .15 .07
❑ 108 Jukka Jalonen CO .10 .05
❑ 109 Jukka Tammi .35 .16
❑ 110 Mika Manninen .15 .07
❑ 111 Jani Nikko .25 .11
❑ 112 Jukka Ollila .10 .05
❑ 113 Juha Lampinen .10 .05
❑ 114 Hannu Henriksson .10 .05
❑ 115 Sami Lehtonen .10 .05
❑ 116 Mikko Niemi .10 .05
❑ 117 Juha-Matti Marijarvi .10 .05
❑ 118 Jarkko Glad .10 .05
❑ 119 Allan Measures .10 .05
❑ 120 Mikko Luovi .15 .07
❑ 121 Risto Jalo .15 .07
❑ 122 Juha Jarvenpaa .15 .07
❑ 123 Jarno Peltonen .10 .05
❑ 124 Matti Kaipainen .10 .05
❑ 125 Timo Peltomaa .15 .07
❑ 126 Esa Tommila .10 .05
❑ 127 Hannu Mattila .10 .05
❑ 128 Jari Neuvonen .10 .05
❑ 129 Pasi Maattanen .10 .05
❑ 130 Juha Hautamaa .10 .05
❑ 131 Janne Seva .10 .05
❑ 132 Sami Ahlberg .10 .05
❑ 133 Jari Virtanen .10 .05
❑ 134 JyP HT Team Card .15 .07
❑ 135 Kari Savolainen CO .10 .05
❑ 136 Ari-Pekka Siekkinen .15 .07
❑ 137 Marko Leinonen .10 .05
❑ 138 Jan Latvala .10 .05
❑ 139 Markku Heikkinen .10 .05
❑ 140 Jarmo Jokilahti .10 .05
❑ 141 Veli-Pekka Hard .10 .05
❑ 142 Kalle Koskinen .10 .05
❑ 143 Vesa Ponto .10 .05
❑ 144 Petri Kujala .10 .05
❑ 145 Jarmo Rantanen .10 .05
❑ 146 Harri Laurila .10 .05
❑ 147 Lasse Nieminen .10 .05
❑ 148 Mika Paananen .10 .05
❑ 149 Mika Arvaja .10 .05
❑ 150 Marko Virtanen .15 .07
❑ 151 Marko Ek .10 .05
❑ 152 Joni Lius .10 .05
❑ 153 Teemu Kohvakka .10 .05
❑ 154 Jari Lindroos .15 .07
❑ 155 Marko Kupari .10 .05
❑ 156 Markku Ikonen .10 .05
❑ 157 Jyrki Jokinen .10 .05
❑ 158 Risto Kurkinen .10 .05
❑ 159 KalPa Team Card .15 .07
❑ 160 Hannu Kapanen CO .10 .05
❑ 161 Pasi Kuivalainen .15 .07
❑ 162 Kimmo Kapanen .10 .05
❑ 163 Kimmo Timonen .25 .11
❑ 164 Jari Jarvinen .10 .05
❑ 165 Mikko Tavi .10 .05
❑ 166 Jermu Pisto .10 .05
❑ 167 Antti Tuomenoksa .10 .05
❑ 168 Vesa Ruotsalainen .10 .05
❑ 169 Vesa Salo .10 .05
❑ 170 Veli-Pekka Pekkarinen .10 .05
❑ 171 Tuomas Kalliomaki .10 .05
❑ 172 Dimitri Zinine .10 .05
❑ 173 Jani Rautio .10 .05
❑ 174 Janne Kekalainen .10 .05
❑ 175 Arto Sirvio .10 .05
❑ 176 Sami Mettovaara .10 .05
❑ 177 Sami Simonen .10 .05
❑ 178 Pekka Tirkkonen .15 .07
❑ 179 Sami Kapanen 1.00 .45
❑ 180 Jussi Tarvainen .10 .05
❑ 181 Lukko Team Card .15 .07
❑ 182 Vaclav Sykora .10 .05
❑ 183 Jarmo Myllys .50 .23
❑ 184 Kimmo Vesa .10 .05
❑ 185 Mika Yli-Maenpaa .20 .09
❑ 186 Jarmo Kuusisto .10 .05
❑ 187 Marko Tuulola .10 .05
❑ 188 Tuomas Gronman .25 .11
❑ 189 Timo Kulonen .10 .05
❑ 190 Kari-Pekka Friman .10 .05
❑ 191 Pasi Huura .15 .07
❑ 192 Harri Suvanto .10 .05
❑ 193 Kamil Kastak .10 .05
❑ 194 Jari Torkki .10 .05
❑ 195 Kalle Sahlstedt .15 .07
❑ 196 Tommi Pullola .10 .05
❑ 197 Mika Valila .10 .05
❑ 198 Tero Arkiomaa .10 .05
❑ 199 Pasi Saarela .10 .05
❑ 200 Matti Forss .10 .05
❑ 201 Jussi Kiuru .10 .05
❑ 202 Mika Alatalo .25 .11
❑ 203 Kimmo Rintanen .25 .11
❑ 204 Petri Latti .10 .05
❑ 205 Petr Korinek .20 .09
❑ 206 Assat Team Card .15 .07
❑ 207 Veli-Pekka Ketola CO .15 .07
❑ 208 Kari Takko .25 .11
❑ 209 Timo Jarvinen .10 .05
❑ 210 Marko Sten .10 .05
❑ 211 Pasi Peltonen .10 .05
❑ 212 Olli Kaski .15 .07
❑ 213 Jarno Miikkulainen .10 .05
❑ 214 Jouni Vento .10 .05
❑ 215 Karri Kivi .15 .07
❑ 216 Stanislav Meciar .10 .05
❑ 217 Nemo Nokkosmaki .10 .05
❑ 218 Arto Javanainen .10 .05
❑ 219 Janne Virtanen .10 .05
❑ 220 Vjatseslav Fandul .15 .07
❑ 221 Jari Levonen .10 .05
❑ 222 Jarno Levonen .10 .05
❑ 223 Jari Korpisalo .25 .11
❑ 224 Jokke Heinanen .10 .05
❑ 225 Harri Lonnberg .10 .05
❑ 226 Ari Saarinen .10 .05
❑ 227 Kari Syvasalmi .10 .05
❑ 228 Jarno Makela .10 .05
❑ 229 Rauli Raitanen .10 .05
❑ 230 Arto Heiskanen .10 .05
❑ 231 Mikael Kotkaniemi .10 .05
❑ 232 HPK Team Card .15 .07
❑ 233 Pentti Matikainen .10 .05
❑ 234 Kari Rosenberg .15 .07
❑ 235 Petri Vilen .10 .05
❑ 236 Marko Allen .10 .05
❑ 237 Mikko Myllykoski .10 .05
❑ 238 Kim Vahanen .10 .05
❑ 239 Janne Laukkanen .75 .35
❑ 240 Jari Haapamaki .10 .05
❑ 241 Niko Marttila .10 .05
❑ 242 Esa Sateri .10 .05
❑ 243 Toni Virta .10 .05
❑ 244 Marko Palo .15 .07
❑ 245 Markku Piikkila .10 .05
❑ 246 Jani Hassinen .10 .05
❑ 247 Jarkko Nikander .15 .07
❑ 248 Pasi Kivila .10 .05
❑ 249 Mika Lartama .10 .05
❑ 250 Tomas Kapusta .15 .07
❑ 251 Tommi Varjonen .10 .05
❑ 252 Teemu Tamminen .10 .05
❑ 253 Jukka Seppo .15 .07
❑ 254 Kiekko-Espoo Team Card .15 .07
❑ 255 Martti Merra .10 .05
❑ 256 Scott Brower .15 .07
❑ 257 Timo Maki .10 .05
❑ 258 Petri Pulkkinen .10 .05
❑ 259 Robert Salo .10 .05
❑ 260 Sami Nuutinen .10 .05
❑ 261 Teemu Sillanpaa .10 .05
❑ 262 Marko Halonen .10 .05
❑ 263 Jimi Helin .10 .05
❑ 264 Kari Haakana .10 .05
❑ 265 Jukka Tiilikainen .10 .05
❑ 266 Jan Langbacka .10 .05
❑ 267 Jarmo Muukkonen .10 .05
❑ 268 Timo Hirvonen .15 .07
❑ 269 Pasi Heinisto .10 .05
❑ 270 Kimmo Maki-Kokkila .10 .05
❑ 271 Mikko Lempiainen .10 .05
❑ 272 Tero Lehtera .15 .07
❑ 273 Hannu Jarvenpaa .15 .07
❑ 274 Riku Kuusisto .10 .05
❑ 275 Mikko Halonen .10 .05
❑ 276 Markku Takala .10 .05
❑ 277 Petro Koivunen .15 .07
❑ 278 Reipas Lahti Team Card .15 .07
❑ 279 Kari Makinen CO .10 .05
❑ 280 Oldrich Svoboda .10 .05
❑ 281 Pekka Ilmivalta .10 .05
❑ 282 Matti Vuorio .10 .05
❑ 283 Jari Parviainen .10 .05
❑ 284 Timo Kahelin .10 .05
❑ 285 Ville Skinnari .10 .05
❑ 286 Petri Koski .10 .05
❑ 287 Jarkko Hamalainen .10 .05
❑ 288 Pasi Ruponen .10 .05
❑ 289 Oldrich Valek .10 .05
❑ 290 Juha Nurminen .10 .05
❑ 291 Erkki Laine .10 .05
❑ 292 Sami Lekkerimaki .10 .05
❑ 293 Tommy Kiviaho .10 .05
❑ 294 Jyrki Poikolainen .10 .05
❑ 295 Sami Wikstrom .10 .05
❑ 296 Jonni Vauhkonen .25 .11
❑ 297 Erkki Laine .10 .05
❑ 298 Jani Uski .10 .05
❑ 299 Jari Multanen .10 .05
❑ 300 Toni Koivunen .10 .05
❑ 301 Runkosarjan .10 .05
❑ 302 Runkosarjan .10 .05
❑ 303 Runkosarjan .10 .05
❑ 304 Runkosarjan .10 .05
❑ 305 Runkosarjan .10 .05
❑ 306 Runkosarjan .10 .05
❑ 307 Runkosarjan .10 .05
❑ 308 Runkosarjan .10 .05
❑ 309 Runkosarjan .10 .05
❑ 310 Runkosarjan .10 .05
❑ 311 Runkosarjan .10 .05
❑ 312 Runkosarjan .10 .05
❑ 313 Runkosarjan .10 .05
❑ 314 Runkosarjan .10 .05
❑ 315 Runkosarjan .10 .05
❑ 316 Runkosarjan .10 .05
❑ 317 Runkosarjan .10 .05
❑ 318 Runkosarjan .10 .05
❑ 319 Runkosarjan .10 .05
❑ 320 Runkosarjan .10 .05
❑ 321 Runkosarjan .10 .05
❑ 322 Runkosarjan .10 .05
❑ 323 Runkosarjan .10 .05
❑ 324 Runkosarjan .10 .05
❑ 325 Runkosarjan .10 .05
❑ 326 Runkosarjan .10 .05
❑ 327 Runkosarjan .10 .05
❑ 328 Runkosarjan .10 .05
❑ 329 Runkosarjan .10 .05
❑ 330 Runkosarjan .10 .05
❑ 331 Runkosarjan .10 .05
❑ 332 Runkosarjan .10 .05
❑ 333 Runkosarjan .10 .05
❑ 334 Runkosarjan .10 .05
❑ 335 Runkosarjan .10 .05
❑ 336 Runkosarjan .10 .05
❑ 337 Runkosarjan .10 .05
❑ 338 Runkosarjan .10 .05
❑ 339 Runkosarjan .10 .05
❑ 340 Runkosarjan .10 .05
❑ 341 Runkosarjan .10 .05
❑ 342 Runkosarjan .10 .05
❑ 343 Runkosarjan .10 .05
❑ 344 Runkosarjan .10 .05
❑ 345 Paikallisottelut .10 .05
(HIFK/Jokerit/K-Espoo)
❑ 346 Paikallisottelut .10 .05
(Lukko/TPS/Assat)
❑ 347 Paikallisottelut .10 .05
(HPK/Ilves/Tappara)
❑ 348 Paikallisottelut .10 .05
(JyP HT/KalPa/Reipas)
❑ 349 Puolivaliera .10 .05
(HPK/Lukko)
❑ 350 Puolivaliera .10 .05
(Jokerit/Assat)
❑ 351 Puolivaliera .10 .05
(Jokerit/Assat)
❑ 352 Puolivaliera .10 .05
(TPS/Ilves)
❑ 353 Valiera .10 .05
(HPK/JyP HT)
❑ 354 Valiera .10 .05
(TPS/Assat)
❑ 355 Pronssiottelu .10 .05
❑ 356 1.Finaali .10 .05
(TPS 9, HPK 3)
❑ 357 2. Finaali .10 .05
❑ 358 3.Finaali .10 .05
(TPS 3, HPK 2)
❑ 360 Esa Keskinen LL .25 .11
❑ 361 Tomas Kapusta LL .10 .05
❑ 362 Erik Hamalainen LL .20 .09
❑ 363 Brian Tutt LL .10 .05
❑ 364 Otakar Janecky LL .20 .09
❑ 365 Ville Peltonen LL .75 .35
❑ 366 Petr Briza AS .35 .16
❑ 367 Janne Laukkanen AS .50 .23
❑ 368 Timo Jutila AS .25 .11
❑ 369 Juha Riihijarvi AS .25 .11
❑ 370 Esa Keskinen AS .35 .16
❑ 371 Jarkko Varvio AS .15 .07
❑ 372 Esa Keskinen AW .35 .16
❑ 373 Vladimir Jursinov AW .10 .05
❑ 374 Erik Hamalainen AW .20 .09
❑ 375 Timo Lehkonen AW .15 .07
❑ 376 German Titov AW .25 .11
❑ 377 Raimo Summanen AW .20 .09
❑ 378 Mikko Haapakoski AW .10 .05
❑ 379 Marko Palo AW .10 .05
❑ 380 Seppo Makela AW .10 .05
❑ 381 TPS, Turku Team Card .10 .05
❑ 382 HPK Hameenlinna .10 .05
❑ 383 JyP HT Jyvaskyla .10 .05
❑ 384 Juha Riihijarvi MVP .15 .07
❑ 385 Jukka Virtanen .15 .07
❑ 386 Kari Jalonen .15 .07
❑ 387 Matti Forss .10 .05
❑ 388 Arto Javanainen .10 .05
❑ 389 Saku Koivu NHLD 10.00 4.50
❑ 390 Janne Niinimaa NHLD 5.00 2.20
❑ 391 Ville Peltonen NHLD .75 .35
❑ 392 Jonni Vauhkonen NHLD .15 .07
❑ 392 Jonni Vauhkonen NHLD .25 .11
❑ 393 Petri Varis NHLD .50 .23
❑ 394 Antti Aalto NHLD .50 .23
❑ 395 Jere Karalahti NHLD .35 .16
❑ 396 Kimmo Timonen NHLD .25 .11

## 1994 Finnish Jaa Kiekko

This 360-card set was issued in Finland by Semic in conjunction with the 1994 World Championships. The set includes players from the traditional hockey powers, as well as Great

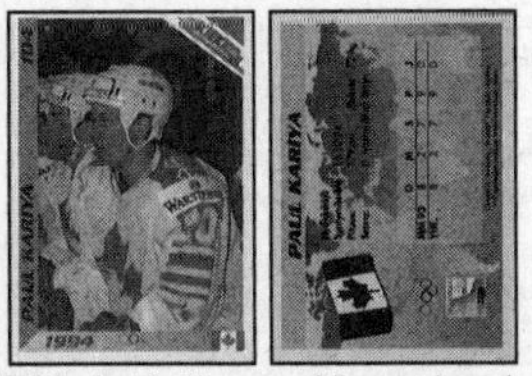


Britain, Austria, Norway and France, shown in action for their countries. A number of NHL players who had participated in previous Canada Cups or World Championships are also pictured. The cards were distributed in 5-card packets. A binder also was available to house the collection.

| | MINT | NRMT |
|---|---|---|
| COMPLETE SET (360) | 135.00 | 60.00 |
| COMMON CARD (1-360) | .10 | .05 |

| | | |
|---|---|---|
| ❑ 1 Jarmo Myllys | .25 | .11 |
| ❑ 2 Pasi Kuivalainen | .10 | .05 |
| ❑ 3 Jukka Tammi | .20 | .09 |
| ❑ 4 Markus Ketterer | .25 | .11 |
| ❑ 5 Timo Jutila | .15 | .07 |
| ❑ 6 Mikko Haapakoski | .10 | .05 |
| ❑ 7 Marko Tuulola | .10 | .05 |
| ❑ 8 Jyrki Lumme | .35 | .16 |
| ❑ 9 Kari Harila | .10 | .05 |
| ❑ 10 Teppo Numminen | .35 | .16 |
| ❑ 11 Pasi Sormunen | .10 | .05 |
| ❑ 12 Petteri Nummelin | .10 | .05 |
| ❑ 13 Harri Laurila | .10 | .05 |
| ❑ 14 Mika Stromberg | .15 | .07 |
| ❑ 15 Ville Siren | .15 | .07 |
| ❑ 16 Pekka Laksola | .10 | .05 |
| ❑ 17 Janne Laukkanen | .20 | .09 |
| ❑ 18 Marko Kiprusoff | .15 | .07 |
| ❑ 19 Waltteri Immonen | .15 | .07 |
| ❑ 20 Teemu Selanne | 4.00 | 1.80 |
| ❑ 21 Mika Alatalo | .15 | .07 |
| ❑ 22 Vesa Viitakoski | .15 | .07 |
| ❑ 23 Tero Arkiomaa | .10 | .05 |
| ❑ 24 Jari Kurri | .75 | .35 |
| ❑ 25 Pekka Tirkkonen | .10 | .05 |
| ❑ 26 Jarmo Kekalainen | .15 | .07 |
| ❑ 27 Saku Koivu | 4.00 | 1.80 |
| ❑ 28 Antti Tormanen | .20 | .09 |
| ❑ 29 Jere Lehtinen | .50 | .23 |
| ❑ 30 Raimo Helminen | .15 | .07 |
| ❑ 31 Mikko Makela | .15 | .07 |
| ❑ 32 Marko Jantunen | .15 | .07 |
| ❑ 33 Ville Peltonen | .35 | .16 |
| ❑ 34 Esa Tikkanen | .50 | .23 |
| ❑ 35 Janne Ojanen | .15 | .07 |
| ❑ 36 Mika Nieminen | .20 | .09 |
| ❑ 37 Marko Palo | .10 | .05 |
| ❑ 38 Rauli Raitanen | .10 | .05 |
| ❑ 39 Sami Kapanen | .35 | .16 |
| ❑ 40 Juha Riihijarvi | .15 | .07 |
| ❑ 41 Esa Keskinen | .15 | .07 |
| ❑ 42 Jari Korpisalo | .15 | .07 |
| ❑ 43 Christian Ruuttu | .15 | .07 |
| ❑ 44 Jarkko Varvio | .15 | .07 |
| ❑ 45 Sami Wahlsten | .10 | .05 |
| ❑ 46 Petri Varis | .25 | .11 |
| ❑ 47 Timo Saarikoski | .10 | .05 |
| ❑ 48 Timo Norppa | .10 | .05 |
| ❑ 49 Marko Virtanen | .10 | .05 |
| ❑ 50 Pauli Jarvinen | .10 | .05 |
| ❑ 51 Hakan Algotsson | .20 | .09 |
| ❑ 52 Tommy Soderstrom | .50 | .23 |
| ❑ 53 Rolf Ridderwall | .15 | .07 |
| ❑ 54 Tomas Jonsson | .15 | .07 |
| ❑ 55 Christian Due-Boje | .10 | .05 |
| ❑ 56 Peter Popovic | .15 | .07 |
| ❑ 57 Fredrik Stillman | .10 | .05 |
| ❑ 58 Magnus Svensson | .20 | .09 |
| ❑ 59 Fredrik Nilsson | .10 | .05 |
| ❑ 60 Tommy Albelin | .15 | .07 |
| ❑ 61 Joacim Esbjors | .10 | .05 |
| ❑ 62 Roger Johansson | .15 | .07 |
| ❑ 63 Stefan Nilsson | .10 | .05 |
| ❑ 64 Hakan Loob | .35 | .16 |
| ❑ 65 Peter Ottosson | .10 | .05 |
| ❑ 66 Daniel Rydmark | .10 | .05 |
| ❑ 67 Mikael Renberg | 1.50 | .70 |
| ❑ 68 Patrik Juhlin | .20 | .09 |
| ❑ 69 Thomas Rundqvist | .15 | .07 |
| ❑ 70 Andreas Johansson | .15 | .07 |
| ❑ 71 Stefan Ornskog | .15 | .07 |
| ❑ 72 Nillas Eriksson | .10 | .05 |
| ❑ 73 Jonas Bergqvist | .25 | .11 |
| ❑ 74 Mats Sundin | 1.00 | .45 |
| ❑ 75 Peter Forsberg | 8.00 | 3.60 |
| ❑ 76 Stefan Elvenes | .10 | .05 |
| ❑ 77 Tomas Forslund | .15 | .07 |
| ❑ 78 Patric Kjellberg | .15 | .07 |
| ❑ 79 Bill Ranford | .50 | .23 |
| ❑ 80 Corey Hirsch | .75 | .35 |
| ❑ 81 Larry Murphy | .50 | .23 |
| ❑ 82 Mark Tinordi | .15 | .07 |
| ❑ 83 Scott Stevens | .35 | .16 |
| ❑ 84 Al MacInnis | .50 | .23 |
| ❑ 85 Steve Smith | .25 | .11 |
| ❑ 86 Paul Coffey | 1.50 | .70 |
| ❑ 87 Eric Desjardins | .25 | .11 |
| ❑ 88 Eric Lindros | 8.00 | 3.60 |
| ❑ 89 Dale Hawerchuk | .50 | .23 |
| ❑ 90 Steve Larmer | .35 | .16 |
| ❑ 91 Brent Sutter | .20 | .09 |
| ❑ 92 Luc Robitaille | .75 | .35 |
| ❑ 93 Shayne Corson | .35 | .16 |
| ❑ 94 Mark Messier | 2.50 | 1.10 |
| ❑ 95 Rick Tocchet | .50 | .23 |
| ❑ 96 Theoren Fleury | 1.00 | .45 |
| ❑ 97 Dirk Graham | .25 | .11 |
| ❑ 98 Russ Courtnall | .25 | .11 |
| ❑ 99 Wayne Gretzky | 10.00 | 4.50 |
| ❑ 100 Brendan Shanahan | 3.00 | 1.35 |
| ❑ 101 Mark Recchi | .75 | .35 |
| ❑ 102 David Harlock | .15 | .07 |
| ❑ 103 Craig Woodcroft | .15 | .07 |
| ❑ 104 Paul Kariya | 8.00 | 3.60 |
| ❑ 105 Jason Marshall | .15 | .07 |
| ❑ 106 Brett Lindros | .35 | .16 |
| ❑ 107 Mike Richter | 2.00 | .90 |
| ❑ 108 Mike Dunham | .25 | .11 |
| ❑ 109 Craig Wolanin | .15 | .07 |
| ❑ 110 Jim Johnson | .15 | .07 |
| ❑ 111 Chris Chelios | 1.50 | .70 |
| ❑ 112 Eric Weinrich | .15 | .07 |
| ❑ 113 Brian Leetch | 1.50 | .70 |
| ❑ 114 Kevin Hatcher | .25 | .11 |
| ❑ 115 Ed Olczyk | .15 | .07 |
| ❑ 116 Kevin Miller | .20 | .09 |
| ❑ 117 Doug Brown | .15 | .07 |
| ❑ 118 Joe Mullen | .25 | .11 |
| ❑ 119 Craig Janney | .25 | .11 |
| ❑ 120 Pat LaFontaine | .75 | .35 |
| ❑ 121 Gary Suter | .25 | .11 |
| ❑ 122 Jeremy Roenick | 1.50 | .70 |
| ❑ 123 Brett Hull | 2.50 | 1.10 |
| ❑ 124 Joel Otto | .25 | .11 |
| ❑ 125 Mike Modano | 1.00 | .45 |
| ❑ 126 Tony Granato | .25 | .11 |
| ❑ 127 Dave Christian | .20 | .09 |
| ❑ 128 Brian Mullen | .15 | .07 |
| ❑ 129 Chris Ferraro | .20 | .09 |
| ❑ 130 John Lilley | .15 | .07 |
| ❑ 131 Jeff Lazaro | .15 | .07 |
| ❑ 132 Peter Ferraro | .35 | .16 |
| ❑ 133 Brian Rolston | .25 | .11 |
| ❑ 134 David Roberts | .15 | .07 |
| ❑ 135 Nikolai Khabibulin | 1.00 | .45 |
| ❑ 136 Andrei Trefilov | .25 | .11 |
| ❑ 137 Vladimir Malakhov | .25 | .11 |
| ❑ 138 Alexander Karpovtsev | .20 | .09 |
| ❑ 139 Alexander Kmirnov | .10 | .05 |
| ❑ 140 Sergei Zubov | .35 | .16 |
| ❑ 141 Sergei Seljanin | .10 | .05 |
| ❑ 142 Sergei Shendelev | .10 | .05 |
| ❑ 143 Alexei Kasatonov | .20 | .09 |
| ❑ 144 Sergei Sorokin | .10 | .05 |
| ❑ 145 Vjatseslav Bykov | .25 | .11 |
| ❑ 146 Sergei Fedorov | 4.00 | 1.80 |
| ❑ 147 Alexei Yashin | .50 | .23 |
| ❑ 148 Vjatseslav Butsajev | .15 | .07 |
| ❑ 149 Konstantin Astrahantsev | .10 | .05 |
| ❑ 150 Alexei Zhamnov | .50 | .23 |
| ❑ 151 Dimitri Frolov | .10 | .05 |
| ❑ 152 Slava Kozlov | .50 | .23 |
| ❑ 153 Sergei Pushkov | .10 | .05 |
| ❑ 154 Andrei Khomutov | .25 | .11 |
| ❑ 155 Sergei Makarov | .35 | .16 |
| ❑ 156 Igor Larionov | .50 | .23 |
| ❑ 157 Valeri Kamenski | .75 | .35 |
| ❑ 158 Alexander Semak | .15 | .07 |
| ❑ 159 Alexei Gusarov | .15 | .07 |
| ❑ 160 Andrei Lomakin | .15 | .07 |
| ❑ 161 Igor Korolev | .15 | .07 |
| ❑ 162 Ravil Haidarov | .10 | .05 |
| ❑ 163 Dominik Hasek | 4.00 | 1.80 |
| ❑ 164 Oldrich Svoboda | .10 | .05 |
| ❑ 165 Petr Briza | .35 | .16 |
| ❑ 166 Leo Gudas | .10 | .05 |
| ❑ 167 Kamil Prachar | .10 | .05 |
| ❑ 168 Richard Smehlik | .20 | .09 |
| ❑ 169 Frantisek Kucera | .15 | .07 |
| ❑ 170 Drahomir Kadlec | .15 | .07 |
| ❑ 171 Jan Vopat | .25 | .11 |
| ❑ 172 Frantisek Prochazka | .10 | .05 |
| ❑ 173 Antonin Stavjana | .10 | .05 |
| ❑ 174 Bedrich Scerban | .10 | .05 |
| ❑ 175 Kamil Kastak | .10 | .05 |
| ❑ 176 Josef Beranek | .25 | .11 |
| ❑ 177 Martin Rucinsky | .50 | .23 |
| ❑ 178 Michal Pivonka | .25 | .11 |
| ❑ 179 Tomas Jelinek | .10 | .05 |
| ❑ 180 Richard Zemlicka | .15 | .07 |
| ❑ 181 Robert Kron | .20 | .09 |
| ❑ 182 Jiri Slegr | .25 | .11 |
| ❑ 183 Jaromir Jagr | 7.00 | 3.10 |
| ❑ 184 Robert Reichel | .35 | .16 |
| ❑ 185 David Vyborny | .15 | .07 |
| ❑ 186 Robert Lang | .15 | .07 |
| ❑ 187 Petr Rosol | .10 | .05 |
| ❑ 188 Otakar Janecky | .10 | .05 |
| ❑ 189 Martin Hostak | .10 | .05 |
| ❑ 190 Jiri Kucera | .15 | .07 |
| ❑ 191 Eduard Hartmann | .25 | .11 |
| ❑ 192 Lubomir Sekeras | .10 | .05 |
| ❑ 193 Marian Smerciak | .10 | .05 |
| ❑ 194 Jan Varholik | .10 | .05 |
| ❑ 195 Lubomir Rybovic | .10 | .05 |
| ❑ 196 Miroslav Marcinko | .10 | .05 |
| ❑ 197 Stanislav Medrik | .10 | .05 |
| ❑ 198 Zdeno Ciger | .20 | .09 |
| ❑ 199 Jergus Baca | .15 | .07 |
| ❑ 200 Peter Stastny | .50 | .23 |
| ❑ 201 Peter Veselovsky | .10 | .05 |
| ❑ 202 Anton Stastny | .20 | .09 |
| ❑ 203 Lubomir Kolnik | .15 | .07 |
| ❑ 204 Roman Kontsek | .10 | .05 |
| ❑ 205 Rene Pucher | .10 | .05 |
| ❑ 206 Slavomir Ilvasky | .10 | .05 |
| ❑ 207 Zigmund Palffy | 2.50 | 1.10 |
| ❑ 208 Vlastimil Plavucha | .10 | .05 |
| ❑ 209 Dusan Pohorelec | .10 | .05 |
| ❑ 210 Robert Petrovicky | .15 | .07 |
| ❑ 211 Michel Valliere | .10 | .05 |
| ❑ 212 Petri Ylonen | .25 | .11 |
| ❑ 213 Jean-Philippe Lemoine | .10 | .05 |
| ❑ 214 Christophe Moyon | .10 | .05 |
| ❑ 215 Denis Perez | .10 | .05 |
| ❑ 216 Bruno Saunier | .10 | .05 |
| ❑ 217 Stephane Botteri | .10 | .05 |
| ❑ 218 Michel Breistroff | .10 | .05 |
| ❑ 219 Geralf Guennelon | .10 | .05 |
| ❑ 220 Serge Poudrier | .10 | .05 |
| ❑ 221 Benjamin Agnel | .10 | .05 |
| ❑ 222 Stephane Arcangeloni | .10 | .05 |
| ❑ 223 Pierrick Maia | .10 | .05 |
| ❑ 224 Antoine Richer | .10 | .05 |
| ❑ 225 Christoph Ville | .10 | .05 |
| ❑ 226 Michael Babin | .10 | .05 |
| ❑ 227 Lionel Orsolini | .10 | .05 |
| ❑ 228 Stephane Barin | .10 | .05 |
| ❑ 229 Arnaud Briand | .10 | .05 |
| ❑ 230 Franck Pajonkowski | .20 | .09 |
| ❑ 231 Claus Dalpiaz | .20 | .09 |
| ❑ 232 Brian Stankiewicz | .10 | .05 |
| ❑ 233 Rob Doyle | .10 | .05 |
| ❑ 234 Michael Guntner | .10 | .05 |
| ❑ 235 Martin Krainz | .10 | .05 |
| ❑ 236 Michael Shea | .10 | .05 |
| ❑ 237 Martin Ulrich | .10 | .05 |
| ❑ 238 Erich Solderer | .10 | .05 |
| ❑ 239 Wayne Groulx | .10 | .05 |
| ❑ 240 Andreas Pusnik | .10 | .05 |
| ❑ 241 Dieter Kalt | .10 | .05 |
| ❑ 242 Gerhard Pusnik | .10 | .05 |
| ❑ 243 Werner Kerth | .10 | .05 |
| ❑ 244 Richard Nasheim | .10 | .05 |
| ❑ 245 Arno Maier | .10 | .05 |
| ❑ 246 Mario Schaden | .10 | .05 |
| ❑ 247 Reinhard Lampert | .10 | .05 |
| ❑ 248 Karl Heinzle | .10 | .05 |
| ❑ 249 Wolfgang Kromp | .10 | .05 |
| ❑ 250 Marty Dallman | .10 | .05 |
| ❑ 251 Jim Marthinsen | .20 | .09 |
| ❑ 252 Rob Schistad | .10 | .05 |
| ❑ 253 Tom Cato Andersen | .10 | .05 |
| ❑ 254 Anders Myrvold | .20 | .09 |
| ❑ 255 Svein Enok Norstebo | .10 | .05 |
| ❑ 256 Tommy Jakobsen | .10 | .05 |
| ❑ 257 Pal Kristiansen | .10 | .05 |
| ❑ 258 Petter Salsten | .10 | .05 |
| ❑ 259 Ole Eskild Dahlstrom | .10 | .05 |
| ❑ 260 Morten Finstad | .10 | .05 |
| ❑ 261 Espen Knutsen | .25 | .11 |
| ❑ 262 Erik Kristiansen | .10 | .05 |
| ❑ 263 Geir Hoff | .10 | .05 |
| ❑ 264 Roy Johansen | .10 | .05 |
| ❑ 265 Trond Magnussen | .10 | .05 |
| ❑ 266 Marius Rath | .10 | .05 |
| ❑ 267 Vegar Barlie | .10 | .05 |
| ❑ 268 Arne Billkvam | .10 | .05 |
| ❑ 269 Tom Johansen | .10 | .05 |
| ❑ 270 Petter Thoresen | .10 | .05 |
| ❑ 271 Klaus Merk | .25 | .11 |
| ❑ 272 Josef Heiss | .20 | .09 |
| ❑ 273 Rikhard Amann | .10 | .05 |
| ❑ 274 Torsten Kienass | .15 | .07 |
| ❑ 275 Mirco Ludemann | .15 | .07 |
| ❑ 276 Jason Meyer | .10 | .05 |
| ❑ 277 Uli Hiemer | .15 | .07 |
| ❑ 278 Karsten Mende | .10 | .05 |
| ❑ 279 Andreas Niederberger | .10 | .05 |
| ❑ 280 Thomas Brandl | .10 | .05 |
| ❑ 281 Benoit Doucet | .15 | .07 |
| ❑ 282 Robert Hock | .10 | .05 |
| ❑ 283 Georg Franz | .10 | .05 |
| ❑ 284 Ernst Kopf, Jr. | .10 | .05 |
| ❑ 285 Reemt Pyka | .15 | .07 |
| ❑ 286 Jurgen Rumrich | .15 | .07 |
| ❑ 287 Dieter Hegen | .15 | .07 |
| ❑ 288 Raimund Hilger | .15 | .07 |
| ❑ 289 Thomas Schinko | .10 | .05 |
| ❑ 290 Leo Stefan | .10 | .05 |
| ❑ 291 David Delfino | .20 | .09 |
| ❑ 292 Elmar Parth | .10 | .05 |
| ❑ 293 Luigi Da Corte | .10 | .05 |
| ❑ 294 Phil De Gaetano | .10 | .05 |
| ❑ 295 Ralph Di Fiore | .10 | .05 |
| ❑ 296 Giorgio Comploi | .10 | .05 |
| ❑ 297 Alexander Thaler | .10 | .05 |
| ❑ 298 Giovanni Marchetti | .10 | .05 |
| ❑ 299 Gaetano Orlando | .15 | .07 |
| ❑ 300 Frank Di Muzio | .10 | .05 |
| ❑ 301 Giuseppe Foglietta | .10 | .05 |
| ❑ 302 Stefano Figliuzzi | .10 | .05 |
| ❑ 303 John Vecchiarelli | .10 | .05 |
| ❑ 304 Maurizio Mansi | .10 | .05 |
| ❑ 305 Santino Pellegrino | .10 | .05 |
| ❑ 306 Lino De Toni | .10 | .05 |
| ❑ 307 Mario Chitarroni | .10 | .05 |
| ❑ 308 Bruno Zarillo | .10 | .05 |
| ❑ 309 Armando Chelodi | .10 | .05 |
| ❑ 310 Carmine Vani | .10 | .05 |
| ❑ 311 Martin McKay | .10 | .05 |
| ❑ 312 Scott O'Connor | .10 | .05 |
| ❑ 313 John McCrone | .10 | .05 |
| ❑ 314 Stephen Cooper | .10 | .05 |
| ❑ 315 Mike O'Connor | .10 | .05 |
| ❑ 316 Chris Kelland | .10 | .05 |
| ❑ 317 Graham Waghorn | .10 | .05 |
| ❑ 318 Nicky Chinn | .10 | .05 |
| ❑ 319 Damian Smith | .10 | .05 |
| ❑ 320 Tim Cranston | .10 | .05 |
| ❑ 321 Scott Morrisson | .10 | .05 |
| ❑ 322 Antony Johnson | .10 | .05 |
| ❑ 323 Tony Hand | .15 | .07 |
| ❑ 324 Kevin Conway | .10 | .05 |
| ❑ 325 Rick Fera | .10 | .05 |
| ❑ 326 Doug McEwen | .10 | .05 |
| ❑ 327 Scott Neil | .10 | .05 |
| ❑ 328 John Iredale | .10 | .05 |
| ❑ 329 Iain Robertson | .10 | .05 |
| ❑ 330 Ian Cooper | .10 | .05 |
| ❑ 331 Bill Ranford DT | .50 | .23 |
| ❑ 332 Jarmo Myllys DT | .25 | .11 |
| ❑ 333 Dominik Hasek DT | 4.00 | 1.80 |
| ❑ 334 Tommy Soderstrom DT | .50 | .23 |
| ❑ 335 Teppo Numminen DT | .25 | .11 |
| ❑ 336 Mihail Tatarinov DT | .15 | .07 |
| ❑ 337 Paul Coffey DT | 1.50 | .70 |
| ❑ 338 Chris Chelios DT | 1.50 | .70 |
| ❑ 339 Brian Leetch DT | 1.50 | .70 |
| ❑ 340 Al MacInnis DT | .50 | .23 |
| ❑ 341 Vladimir Malakhov DT | .25 | .11 |
| ❑ 342 Kevin Hatcher DT | .25 | .11 |
| ❑ 343 Jiri Slegr DT | .15 | .07 |
| ❑ 344 Wayne Gretzky DT | 12.00 | 5.50 |
| ❑ 345 Teemu Selanne DT | 5.00 | 2.20 |
| ❑ 346 Jari Kurri DT | .75 | .35 |
| ❑ 347 Brett Hull DT | 2.50 | 1.10 |
| ❑ 348 Sergei Fedorov DT | 4.00 | 1.80 |
| ❑ 349 Esa Tikkanen DT | .50 | .23 |
| ❑ 350 Mark Messier DT | 2.50 | 1.10 |
| ❑ 351 Jaromir Jagr DT | 6.00 | 2.70 |
| ❑ 352 Jeremy Roenick DT | 1.50 | .70 |
| ❑ 353 Luc Robitaille DT | .75 | .35 |
| ❑ 354 Tomas Sandstrom DT | .25 | .11 |
| ❑ 355 Peter Forsberg DT | 8.00 | 3.60 |
| ❑ 356 Alexei Zhamnov DT | .50 | .23 |
| ❑ 357 Theoren Fleury DT | .75 | .35 |
| ❑ 358 Rick Tocchet DT | .50 | .23 |
| ❑ 359 Pat LaFontaine DT | .75 | .35 |
| ❑ 360 Eric Lindros DT | 8.00 | 3.60 |
| ❑ NNO Album | 10.00 | 4.50 |

## 1994-95 Finnish SISU

Manufactured by Leaf in Turku, Finland, this set consists of 400 standard-size cards and features Finnish Hockey League players. The cards were sold in eight-card foil packs. The fronts have a border along the bottom with color action player photos. The player's name in white letters appears in a team color-coded bar under the photo, with the team logo at the lower left corner. The team color-coded backs carry a color closeup photo, a short biography and stats. With a few exceptions, all text is in Finnish. The Canada Bowl Super Chase Card was inserted in first series foil packs. The Saku Koivu Super Chase Card was randomly inserted in second series foil packs at a rate of one in 192 packs. Several notable NHLers, including Teemu Selanne, Jari Kurri and Esa Tikkanen returned to Finland during the 1994 NHL lockout and thus appear in the second series.

| | MINT | NRMT |
|---|---|---|
| COMPLETE SET (400) | 80.00 | 36.00 |
| COMPLETE SERIES 1 (200) | 30.00 | 13.50 |
| COMPLETE SERIES 2 (200) | 50.00 | 22.00 |
| COMMON CARD (1-400) | .10 | .05 |

| | | |
|---|---|---|
| ❑ 1 Pasi Kuivolainen | .20 | .09 |
| ❑ 2 Jere Karalahti | .50 | .23 |
| ❑ 3 Markku Heikkinen | .10 | .05 |
| ❑ 4 Marko Allen | .10 | .05 |
| ❑ 5 Jarmo Kuusisto | .10 | .05 |
| ❑ 6 Marko Tuulola | .10 | .05 |
| ❑ 7 Marko Kiprusoff | .50 | .23 |
| ❑ 8 Vesa Ponto | .10 | .05 |
| ❑ 9 Tero Lehtera | .20 | .09 |
| ❑ 10 Darren Boyko | .15 | .07 |
| ❑ 11 Kari Heikkinen | .10 | .05 |
| ❑ 12 Niko Marttila | .10 | .05 |
| ❑ 13 Jari Torkki | .10 | .05 |
| ❑ 14 Jiri Kucera | .20 | .09 |
| ❑ 15 Jari Levonen | .10 | .05 |
| ❑ 16 Juha Ikonen | .10 | .05 |
| ❑ 17 Joni Lius | .10 | .05 |
| ❑ 18 Pekka Tuomisto | .10 | .05 |
| ❑ 19 Petri Kokku | .10 | .05 |
| ❑ 20 Jere Lehtinen | 2.00 | .90 |
| ❑ 21 Janne Kekalainen | .10 | .05 |
| ❑ 22 Ari Haanpaa | .10 | .05 |
| ❑ 23 Hannu Jarvenpaa | .20 | .09 |
| ❑ 24 Waltteri Immonen | .20 | .09 |
| ❑ 25 Jari Lindroos | .20 | .09 |
| ❑ 26 Jan Langbacka | .10 | .05 |
| ❑ 27 Kari Takko | .50 | .23 |
| ❑ 28 Pasi Maattanen | .10 | .05 |
| ❑ 29 Jan Latvala | .10 | .05 |
| ❑ 30 Arto Heiskanen | .10 | .05 |
| ❑ 31 Iiro Jarvi | .25 | .11 |
| ❑ 32 Igor Boldin | .10 | .05 |
| ❑ 33 Sami Simonen | .10 | .05 |
| ❑ 34 Kari Rosenberg | .20 | .09 |
| ❑ 35 Sakari Lindfors | .50 | .23 |
| ❑ 36 Veli-Pekka Hard | .15 | .07 |
| ❑ 37 Jari Halme | .25 | .11 |
| ❑ 38 Jukka Tammi | .50 | .23 |
| ❑ 39 Kalle Koskinen | .15 | .07 |
| ❑ 40 Pekka Tirkkonen | .15 | .07 |
| ❑ 41 Ari Sulander | .50 | .23 |
| ❑ 42 Joni Hassinen | .10 | .05 |
| ❑ 43 Timo Peltomaa | .15 | .07 |
| ❑ 44 Sami Mettovaara | .10 | .05 |
| ❑ 45 Mika Yli-Maenpaa | .25 | .11 |
| ❑ 46 Toni Virta | .10 | .05 |
| ❑ 47 Kimmo Lecklin | .20 | .09 |
| ❑ 48 Rauli Raitanen | .10 | .05 |
| ❑ 49 Juha Lind | .75 | .35 |
| ❑ 50 Ari-Pekka Siekkinen | .20 | .09 |
| ❑ 51 Kim Ahlroos | .10 | .05 |
| ❑ 52 Jarkko Nikander | .15 | .07 |
| ❑ 53 Jouni Vento | .10 | .05 |
| ❑ 54 Juha Lampinen | .10 | .05 |
| ❑ 55 Kalle Sahlstedt | .15 | .07 |
| ❑ 56 Teemu Sillanpaa | .10 | .05 |
| ❑ 57 Lasse Nieminen | .10 | .05 |
| ❑ 58 Janne Niinimaa | 4.00 | 1.80 |
| ❑ 59 Timo Jutila | .20 | .09 |
| ❑ 60 Tommi Haapsaari | .10 | .05 |
| ❑ 61 Allan Measures | .10 | .05 |
| ❑ 62 Petteri Nummelin | .15 | .07 |
| ❑ 63 Antti Tormanen | .50 | .23 |
| ❑ 64 Pekka Laksola | .10 | .05 |
| ❑ 65 Esa Sateri | .10 | .05 |
| ❑ 66 Petro Koivunen | .15 | .07 |
| ❑ 67 Janne Virtanen | .10 | .05 |
| ❑ 68 Pekka Peltola | .10 | .05 |
| ❑ 69 Matti Kaipainen | .10 | .05 |
| ❑ 70 Semi Pekki | .10 | .05 |
| ❑ 71 Jussi Tarvainen | .10 | .05 |
| ❑ 72 Jari Virtanen | .10 | .05 |
| ❑ 73 Kimmo Salminen | .10 | .05 |
| ❑ 74 Tommi Varjonen | .10 | .05 |
| ❑ 75 Pauli Jarvinen | .10 | .05 |
| ❑ 76 Hannu Mattila | .10 | .05 |
| ❑ 77 Aleksander Smirnov | .10 | .05 |
| ❑ 78 Arto Kulmala | .10 | .05 |
| ❑ 79 Roland Carlsson | .10 | .05 |
| ❑ 80 Jarma Miikkulainen | .10 | .05 |
| ❑ 81 Jarmo Muukkonen | .10 | .05 |
| ❑ 82 Mika Paananen | .10 | .05 |
| ❑ 83 Pasi Kivila | .10 | .05 |
| ❑ 84 Jari Laukkanen | .10 | .05 |
| ❑ 85 Tero Arkiomaa | .10 | .05 |
| ❑ 86 Tommi Miettinen | .20 | .09 |
| ❑ 87 Juha Jarvenpaa | .10 | .05 |
| ❑ 88 Niko Mikkola | .10 | .05 |
| ❑ 89 Antti Tuomenoksa | .10 | .05 |
| ❑ 90 Ilkka Sinisalo | .25 | .11 |
| ❑ 91 Otakar Janecky | .20 | .09 |
| ❑ 92 Arto Sirvio | .10 | .05 |
| ❑ 93 Robert Salo | .10 | .05 |
| ❑ 94 Ari Saarinen | .10 | .05 |
| ❑ 95 Kari Martikainen | .10 | .05 |
| ❑ 96 Miro Haapaniemi | .10 | .05 |
| ❑ 97 Fredrik Norrena | .20 | .09 |
| ❑ 98 Erik Hamalainen | .20 | .09 |
| ❑ 99 Simo Saarinen | .10 | .05 |
| ❑ 100 Harri Suvanto | .10 | .05 |
| ❑ 101 Kai Nurminen | .50 | .23 |
| ❑ 102 Rami Koivisto | .10 | .05 |
| ❑ 103 Pasi Peltonen | .10 | .05 |
| ❑ 104 Kari-Pekka Friman | .10 | .05 |
| ❑ 105 Mika Kortelainen | .20 | .09 |
| ❑ 106 Timo Hirvanen | .10 | .05 |
| ❑ 107 Jari Haapamaki | .10 | .05 |
| ❑ 108 Mika Manninen | .10 | .05 |
| ❑ 109 Ari Vuori | .10 | .05 |
| ❑ 110 Markku Ikonen | .10 | .05 |
| ❑ 111 Mikko Konttila | .10 | .05 |
| ❑ 112 Harri Sillgren | .10 | .05 |
| ❑ 113 Mikko Teui | .10 | .05 |
| ❑ 114 Markus Oijennus | .10 | .05 |
| ❑ 115 Kimmo Hyttinen | .10 | .05 |
| ❑ 116 Jokke Heinanen | .10 | .05 |
| ❑ 117 Sami Ahlberg | .10 | .05 |
| ❑ 118 Mika Rautio | .20 | .09 |
| ❑ 119 Ari Salo | .20 | .09 |
| ❑ 120 Juha Hautamaa | .10 | .05 |
| ❑ 121 Kari Haakana | .10 | .05 |
| ❑ 122 Sami Nuutinen | .10 | .05 |
| ❑ 123 Lasse Pirjeta | .10 | .05 |
| ❑ 124 Koijo Sailynoja | .20 | .09 |
| ❑ 125 Mikael Kotkaniemi | .10 | .05 |
| ❑ 126 Samuli Rautio | .10 | .05 |
| ❑ 127 Veli-Pekka Pekkarinen | .10 | .05 |
| ❑ 128 Hannu Henriksson | .10 | .05 |
| ❑ 129 Antti Aalto | .75 | .35 |
| ❑ 130 Jyrki Jokinen | .10 | .05 |
| ❑ 131 Marko Ek | .15 | .07 |
| ❑ 132 Marko Ojanen | .10 | .05 |
| ❑ 133 Mika Arvaja | .10 | .05 |
| ❑ 134 Karri Kivi | .10 | .05 |
| ❑ 135 Timo Saarikoski | .10 | .05 |
| ❑ 136 Toni Sihvonen | .10 | .05 |
| ❑ 137 Mika Laaksonen | .10 | .05 |
| ❑ 138 HIFK Helsinki Team Card | .20 | .09 |
| ❑ 139 HPK Team Card | .20 | .09 |
| ❑ 140 Ilves Team Card | .10 | .05 |
| ❑ 141 Jokerit Team Card | .25 | .11 |
| ❑ 142 JyP HT Team Card | .10 | .05 |
| ❑ 143 KalPa Team Card | .10 | .05 |
| ❑ 144 Kiekko-Espoo Team Card | .10 | .05 |
| ❑ 145 Lukko Team Card | .20 | .09 |
| ❑ 146 Tappara Team Card | .20 | .09 |
| ❑ 147 TPS Turku Team Card | .20 | .09 |
| ❑ 148 TuTo Turku Team Card | .10 | .05 |
| ❑ 149 Assat Team Card | .10 | .05 |
| ❑ 150 Petteri Nummelin CL | .20 | .09 |
| ❑ 151 Kari Takko CL | .25 | .11 |

❑ 152 Vladimir Jursinov CL .10 .05
❑ 153 Juha Lind CL .35 .16
❑ 154 Marko Jantunen LL .20 .09
❑ 155 Jere Lehtinen LL 1.00 .45
❑ 156 Esa Keskinen LL .25 .11
❑ 157 Jere Lehtinen LL 1.00 .45
❑ 158 Timo Peltomaa LL .25 .11
❑ 159 Janne Gronval LL .25 .11
❑ 160 Jarmo Myllys AS .50 .23
❑ 161 Markko Kiprusoff AS .50 .23
❑ 162 Timo Jutila AS .20 .09
❑ 163 Sami Kapanen AS .35 .16
❑ 164 Esa Keskinen AS .25 .11
❑ 165 Mika Alatalo AS .50 .23
❑ 166 Ville Peltonen .50 .23
HIFK
❑ 167 Igor Boldin .10 .05
HPK
❑ 168 Sami Lehtonen .10 .05
Ilves
❑ 169 Juha Jokiharju .10 .05
Jokerit
❑ 170 Harri Laurila .10 .05
JyP HT
❑ 171 Pekka Tirkkonen .15 .07
KalPa
❑ 172 Mikko Halonen .10 .05
Kiekko-Espoo
❑ 173 Tero Arkiomaa .10 .05
Lukko
❑ 174 Jonni Vauhkonen .25 .11
Reipas
❑ 175 Janne Gronvall .35 .16
Tappara
❑ 176 Marko Jantunen .10 .05
TPS
❑ 177 Jouni Vento .20 .09
Assat
❑ 178 HIFK .10 .05
Season Statistics
❑ 179 HPK .10 .05
Season Statistics
❑ 180 Ilves Tampere .10 .05
❑ 181 JyP HT .10 .05
❑ 182 Jokerit .10 .05
Season Statistics
❑ 183 KalPa .10 .05
Season Statistics
❑ 184 Kiekko-Espoo .10 .05
Season Statistics
❑ 185 Lukko .10 .05
Season Statistics
❑ 186 Tappara .10 .05
Team Performance
❑ 187 TPS .10 .05
Season Statistics
❑ 188 Reipas .10 .05
Season Statistics
❑ 189 Assat .10 .05
Season Statistics
❑ 190 Jokerit .50 .23
Finnish Champions
❑ 191 Lukko .10 .05
2nd Place National
❑ 192 TPS .50 .23
European Champions 1994
❑ 193 TPS .50 .23
European Cup Champions
❑ 194 Playoffs .10 .05
❑ 195 Playoffs .10 .05
❑ 196 Playoffs .10 .05
❑ 197 Finals Game 1 .10 .05
❑ 198 Finals Game 2 .10 .05
❑ 199 Finals Game 3 .10 .05
❑ 200 Finals Game 4 .10 .05
❑ 201 Jouni Rokama .20 .09
❑ 202 Sami Leinonen .10 .05
❑ 203 Jani Nikko .35 .16
❑ 204 Arto Vuoti .10 .05
❑ 205 Petr Pavlas .10 .05
❑ 206 Reijo Mikkolainen .10 .05
❑ 207 Jari Kurri 3.00 1.35
❑ 208 Janne Ojanen .50 .23
❑ 209 Sami Kapanen .75 .35
❑ 210 Teppo Kivela .10 .05
❑ 211 Saku Koivu 8.00 3.60
❑ 212 Pekka Virta .10 .05
❑ 213 Risto Jalo .20 .09
❑ 214 Sergei Prjakhin .25 .11
❑ 215 Aleksander Barkov .10 .05
❑ 216 Ville Peltonen .75 .35
❑ 217 Jari Korpisalo .20 .09
❑ 218 Jari Liikkanen .10 .05
❑ 219 Timo Lehkonen .20 .09
❑ 220 Juha Ylonen .50 .23
❑ 221 Harri Lonnberg .10 .05
❑ 222 Teemu Vuorinen .10 .05
❑ 223 Pertti Lehtonen .10 .05
❑ 224 Tommi Pullola .15 .07
❑ 225 Tomas Kapusta .20 .09
❑ 226 Joonas Jaaskelainen .10 .05
❑ 227 Jukka Tiilikainen .10 .05
❑ 228 Jarno Kultanen .10 .05
❑ 229 Kimmo Kapanen .25 .11
❑ 230 Jari Kauppila .10 .05
❑ 231 Jarkko Glad .10 .05
❑ 232 Nemo Nokkosmaki .10 .05
❑ 233 Petri Matikainen .10 .05
❑ 234 Christian Ruutu .50 .23
❑ 235 Martti Jarventie .20 .09
❑ 236 Sami Salo .10 .05
❑ 237 Timo Kulonen .10 .05
❑ 238 Pasi Sormunen .10 .05
❑ 239 Timo Nurmberg .10 .05
❑ 240 Jari Hirsimaki .10 .05
❑ 241 Tommi Hamalainen .10 .05
❑ 242 Vesa Salo .25 .11
❑ 243 Juha Nurminen .10 .05
❑ 244 Petr Korinek .10 .05
❑ 245 Kimmo Vesa .20 .09
❑ 246 Jukka Seppo .10 .05
❑ 247 Jarno Makela .10 .05
❑ 248 Petri Varis .75 .35
❑ 249 Marko Virtanen .10 .05
❑ 250 Risto Siltanen .25 .11
❑ 251 Juha Jarvenpaa .10 .05
❑ 252 Raimo Summanen .25 .11
❑ 253 Markus Hatinen .10 .05
❑ 254 Kimmo Nurro .10 .05
❑ 255 Timo Salonen .10 .05
❑ 256 Jari Munck .10 .05
❑ 257 Kimmo Rintanen .50 .23
❑ 258 Jarno Levonen .10 .05
❑ 259 Jarno Peltonen .10 .05
❑ 260 Valeri Krykov .10 .05
❑ 261 Kai Rautio .10 .05
❑ 262 Timo Blomqvist .25 .11
❑ 263 Teemu Selanne 10.00 4.50
❑ 264 Juha Virtanen .10 .05
❑ 265 Veli-Pekka Kautonen .10 .05
❑ 266 Mikko Koivunoro .10 .05
❑ 267 Mikko Luovi .25 .11
❑ 268 Jaroslav Otevrel .15 .07
❑ 269 Erik Kakko .10 .05
❑ 270 Peter Ahola .20 .09
❑ 271 Miikka Kemppi .10 .05
❑ 272 Toni Makiaho .10 .05
❑ 273 Pekka Poikolainen .10 .05
❑ 274 Tuomo Norppa .10 .05
❑ 275 Sebastian Sulku .10 .05
❑ 276 Esa Tikkanen 1.50 .70
❑ 277 Pasi Saarela .10 .05
❑ 278 Ilpo Kauhanen .50 .23
❑ 279 Mika Alatalo .75 .35
❑ 280 Jukka Suomalainen .10 .05
❑ 281 Tony Arima .10 .05
❑ 282 Mika Puhakka .10 .05
❑ 283 Jussi Kiuru .10 .05
❑ 284 Jarkko Isotalo .10 .05
❑ 285 Esa Tommila .10 .05
❑ 286 Jouni Loponen .10 .05
❑ 287 Jermu Pisto .10 .05
❑ 288 Pasi Heinisto .10 .05
❑ 289 Toni Porkka .10 .05
❑ 290 Juha Vuorivirta .50 .23
❑ 291 Vesa Karjalainen .10 .05
❑ 292 Tom Koivisto .10 .05
❑ 293 Markku Hurme .10 .05
❑ 294 Mika Kannisto .10 .05
❑ 295 Marko Rantanen .20 .09
❑ 296 Petri Kalteva .10 .05
❑ 297 Pasi Huura .15 .07
❑ 298 Miikka Ruokonen .10 .05
❑ 299 Tuomo Raty .10 .05
❑ 300 Vadim Shaidullin .10 .05
❑ 301 Juha Riihijarvi .20 .09
❑ 302 Brad Turner .10 .05
❑ 303 Marko Toivola .10 .05
❑ 304 Kimmo Timonen .75 .35
❑ 305 Kai Nurminen .50 .23
❑ 306 Vesa Lehtonen .10 .05
❑ 307 Mika Niittymaki .10 .05
❑ 308 Sami Wahlsten .10 .05
❑ 309 Pavel Torgajev .25 .11
❑ 310 Pasi Kemppainen .10 .05
❑ 311 Markku Kallio .10 .05
❑ 312 Timo Maki .20 .09
❑ 313 Mika Stromberg .50 .23
❑ 314 Tuomas Gronman .35 .16
❑ 315 Tommi Rajamaki .35 .16
❑ 316 Juri Kuznetsov .20 .09
❑ 317 Mikko Myllykoski .10 .05
❑ 318 Brian Tutt .10 .05
❑ 319 Teemu Numminen .20 .09
❑ 320 Juha Jokiharju .10 .05
❑ 321 Mika Lehtinen .10 .05
❑ 322 Jari Pulliainen .10 .05
❑ 323 Kimmo Maki-Kokkila .10 .05
❑ 324 Mikko Peltola .10 .05
❑ 325 Risto Kurkinen .10 .05
❑ 326 Harri Laurila .10 .05
❑ 327 Vjatcheslav Fandul .10 .05
❑ 328 Niklas Hede .10 .05
❑ 329 Boris Rousson .50 .23
❑ 330 Jukka Ollila .25 .11
❑ 331 Jouni Tuominen .10 .05
❑ 332 Marko Harkonen .20 .09
❑ 333 Petri Engman .20 .09
❑ 334 Mikko Halonen .10 .05
❑ 335 Aki-Petteri Berg 1.50 .70
❑ 336 Kristian Fagerstrom .10 .05
❑ 337 Jiri Veber .10 .05
❑ 338 Tommy Kiviaho .10 .05
❑ 339 Konstantin Astrahantsev .10 .05
❑ 340 Jukka Makitalo .20 .09
❑ 341 Timo Nykopp .10 .05
❑ 342 Sami Lehtonen .10 .05
❑ 343 Joni Lehto .20 .09
❑ 344 Jouko Myrra .10 .05
❑ 345 Mikko Makela .50 .23
❑ 346 Marco Poulsen .10 .05
❑ 347 Janne Seva .10 .05
❑ 348 Shawn McEachern 1.00 .45
❑ 349 Jarkko Varvio .20 .09
❑ 350 Mikko Konttila .10 .05
❑ 351 Veli-Pekka Ahonen .10 .05
❑ 352 Michael Nylander 1.00 .45
❑ 353 Kristian Taubert .10 .05
❑ 354 Ismo Kuoppala .10 .05
❑ 355 Kimmo Hyttinen .10 .05
❑ 356 Petri Latti .10 .05
❑ 357 Ted Donato .75 .35
❑ 358 Jari Harjumaki .10 .05
❑ 359 Teppo Numminen .50 .23
❑ 360 Jyrki Lumme .50 .23
❑ 361 German Titov .50 .23
❑ 362 Kari Eloranta .25 .11
❑ 363 Raimo Helminen .25 .11
❑ 364 Marko Jantunen .25 .11
❑ 365 Olli Kaski .10 .05
❑ 366 Jarmo Kekalainen .20 .09
❑ 367 Esa Keskinen .25 .11
❑ 368 Jarmo Makitalo .10 .05
❑ 369 Mika Nieminen .25 .11
❑ 370 Marko Palo .10 .05
❑ 371 Ville Siren .25 .11
❑ 372 Kari Suoraniemi .10 .05
❑ 373 Otakar Janecky PM .25 .11
❑ 374 Jari Lindroos PM .15 .07
❑ 375 Teppo Kivela PM .10 .05
❑ 376 Petri Varis PM .50 .23
❑ 377 Pekka Laksola PM .10 .05
❑ 378 Jari Korpisalo PM .20 .09
❑ 379 Iiro Jarvi PM .25 .11
❑ 380 Timo Saarikoski PM .10 .05
❑ 381 Rauli Raitanen PM .10 .05
❑ 382 Juha Riihijarvi PM .20 .09
❑ 383 Juha Jokiharju PM .10 .05
❑ 384 Vesa Salo PM .10 .05
❑ 385 Mika Nieminen CL .25 .11
❑ 386 Marko Jantunen CL .10 .05
❑ 387 Jere Lehtinen CL .75 .35
❑ 388 Ari Sulander CL .25 .11
❑ 389 Hannu Kapanen CO .10 .05
❑ 390 Hannu Savolainen CO .10 .05
❑ 391 Heikki Vesala CO .10 .05
❑ 392 Hannu Aravirta CO .10 .05
❑ 393 Kari Savolainen CO .10 .05
❑ 394 Anatoli Bogdanov CO .10 .05
❑ 395 Harri Rindell CO .10 .05
❑ 396 Vaclav Sykora CO .10 .05
❑ 397 Boris Majorov CO .10 .05
❑ 398 Vladimir Jursinov CO .10 .05
❑ 399 Seppo Suoraniemi CO .10 .05
❑ 400 Veli-Pekka Ketola CO .25 .11
❑ NNO Canada Bowl 25.00 11.00
Super Chase Card
❑ NNO2 Saku Koivu 75.00 34.00
Super Chase Card

## 1994-95 Finnish SISU Fire On Ice

This 20-card set highlights players who had multiple games of three or more points during the 1993-94 Finnish season. The cards were randomly inserted in first series packs. The full bleed fronts feature a cutout photo of the player superimposed over stylized background photo of fireworks. The gold foil Leaf logo is embossed in the top left corner, while the words Fire On Ice, in English, appear in the lower right corner. The card backs gives the dates, opponenents and offensive totals for the multi-point games over a light blue background.

MINT NRMT
COMPLETE SET (20) 50.00 22.00
COMMON CARD (1-20) 2.00 .90

❑ 1 Tero Arkiomoa 2.00 .90
❑ 2 Igor Boldin 2.00 .90
❑ 3 Vjatseslav Fandul 2.00 .90
❑ 4 Otakar Janecky 3.00 1.35
❑ 5 Marko Jantunen 3.00 1.35
❑ 6 Timo Jutila 2.00 .90
❑ 7 Pauli Jarvinen 2.00 .90
❑ 8 Sami Kapanen 5.00 2.20
❑ 9 Tomas Kapusta 2.00 .90
❑ 10 Esa Keskinen 3.00 1.35
❑ 11 Saku Koivu 15.00 6.75
❑ 12 Petro Koivunen 2.00 .90
❑ 13 Petr Korinek 2.00 .90
❑ 14 Jari Karpisolo 2.00 .90
❑ 15 Risto Kurkinen 2.00 .90
❑ 16 Tero Lehtera 3.00 1.35
❑ 17 Juha Nurminen 2.00 .90
❑ 18 Kai Nurminen 3.00 1.35
❑ 19 Janne Ojanen 3.00 1.35
❑ 20 Jari Torkki 2.00 .90

## 1994-95 Finnish SISU Guest Specials

Randomly inserted at a rate of one in thirteen series two foil packs, this 12-card standard-size set focuses on NHL stars who signed on to play in the Finnish league during the 1994 NHL lockout. The cards feature a cutout photo of the player, surrounded by ghosted images of the same photo, on a royal blue background. The top and bottom of the card have a bronze foil border; the top bears the set title, while the bottom has the player name and the Leaf logo. The backs contain a profile phot, a map showing the path the player travelled to get to Finland, and personal commentary.

MINT NRMT
COMPLETE SET (12) 70.00 32.00
COMMON CARD (1-12) 3.00 1.35

❑ 1 Ted Donato 5.00 2.20
❑ 2 Jari Kurri 8.00 3.60
❑ 3 Jyrki Lumme 3.00 1.35
❑ 4 Shawn McEachern 5.00 2.20
❑ 5 Mikko Makela 3.00 1.35
❑ 6 Teppo Numminen 3.00 1.35
❑ 7 Michael Nylander 5.00 2.20
❑ 8 Christian Ruuttu 3.00 1.35
❑ 9 Teemu Selanne 40.00 18.00
❑ 10 Esa Tikkanen 6.00 2.70
❑ 11 German Titov 4.00 1.80
❑ 12 Jarkko Varvio 3.00 1.35

## 1994-95 Finnish SISU Horoscopes

Randomly inserted at a rate of one in four second series foil packs, this 20-card standard-size set describes the players' personalities according to the astrological signs they were born under.

MINT NRMT
COMPLETE SET (20) 25.00 11.00
COMMON CARD (1-20) 1.00 .45

❑ 1 Juha Lind 2.00 .90
❑ 2 Jukka Seppo 1.50 .70
❑ 3 Antti Tuomenoksa 1.00 .45
❑ 4 Tuomas Gronman 2.00 .90
❑ 5 Peter Ahola 2.00 .90
❑ 6 Ville Peltonen 3.00 1.35
❑ 7 Timo Saarikoski 1.00 .45
❑ 8 Timo Peltomaa 1.50 .70
❑ 9 Jari Levonen 1.00 .45
❑ 10 Teppo Kivela 1.00 .45
❑ 11 Valeri Krykov 1.00 .45
❑ 12 Juha Riihijarvi 2.00 .90
❑ 13 Kai Nurminen 3.00 1.35
❑ 14 Mikko Luovi 1.00 .45
❑ 15 Raimo Summanen 1.50 .70
❑ 16 Tommy Kiviaho 1.00 .45
❑ 17 Hannu Jarvenpaa 2.00 .90
❑ 18 Marko Virtanen 1.00 .45
❑ 19 Sami Lehtonen 1.00 .45
❑ 20 Mika Alatalo 2.00 .90

## 1994-95 Finnish SISU Junior

These standard size cards feature ten of Finland's brightest young stars as they appeared as youth hockey players. The cards were randomly inserted into series I packs. The fronts feature a sepia-toned photograph of the player as a boy, with his name and current team along the lower right border. The leaf logo is embossed in gold foil in the top left corner, while the word Junior is embossed in silver foil along the bottom. The card's number, out of ten, rests directly above the card title. The backs feature a current color photo of the player, along with personal recollections of junior days, written in Finnish.

MINT NRMT
COMPLETE SET (10) 30.00 13.50
COMMON CARD (1-10) 2.00 .90

❑ 1 Saku Koivu 15.00 6.75
❑ 2 Jekke Heimanen 2.00 .90
❑ 3 Tommi Miettinen 3.00 1.35
❑ 4 Jere Karalahti 4.00 1.80
❑ 5 Kalle Koskinen 2.00 .90
❑ 6 Kari Rosenberg 2.00 .90
❑ 7 Mika Manninen 2.00 .90
❑ 8 Jussi Tarvainen 2.00 .90
❑ 9 Mika Stromberg 4.00 1.80
❑ 10 Kalle Sahlstedt 2.00 .90

## 1994-95 Finnish SISU Magic Numbers

This ten-card standard-size set was randomly inserted at a rate of one in eight second series foil packs. The fronts display a shot of the player from the back, so as to display his sweater number. His name and number appear in the top left and right corners, respectively, while the title, spelled MA6IC NUM3ER5 appears in red foil along the bottom. The card back explains why that number is significant to the player (in Finnish) over a ghosted reprise of the front photo.

MINT NRMT
COMPLETE SET (10) 15.00 6.75
COMMON CARD (1-10) 1.50 .70

❑ 1 Pasi Kuivalainen 1.50 .70
❑ 2 Petteri Nummelin 1.50 .70
❑ 3 Jarmo Kuusisto 1.50 .70
❑ 4 Janne Ojanen 2.00 .90
❑ 5 Sami Kapanen 5.00 2.20
❑ 6 Pekka Virta 1.50 .70
❑ 7 Antti Tormanen 2.00 .90
❑ 8 Jari Korpisalo 1.50 .70
❑ 9 Kimmo Salminen 1.50 .70
❑ 10 Jukka Tammi 3.00 1.35

## 1994-95 Finnish SISU NHL Draft

Randomly inserted at a rate of one in twenty foil second series packs, this eight-card standard-size set spotlights seven Finns who were drafted by NHL teams in 1994. The fronts display a color shot of the player, with the words NHL Draft embossed on a gold foil shield at the bottom. Card backs carry information about the player, including who drafted him and when.

MINT NRMT
COMPLETE SET (8) 25.00 11.00
COMMON CARD (1-8) 2.00 .90

❑ 1 Title Card 2.00 .90
❑ 2 Marko Kiprusoff 4.00 1.80
❑ 3 Jussi Tarvainen 3.00 1.35
❑ 4 Arto Kuki 3.00 1.35
❑ 5 Tommi Rajamaki 5.00 2.20
❑ 6 Tero Lehtera 4.00 1.80
❑ 7 Tommi Miettinen 5.00 2.20
❑ 8 Antti Tormanen 4.00 1.80

## 1994-95 Finnish SISU NIL Phenoms

These standard size cards feature ten goaltenders who posted multiple shutouts during the 1993-94 Finnish campaign. The cards show the netminder cutout photo of the netminder over a brown backdrop. The old foil Leaf logo is embossed in the top right corner, with the word "Nolla" printed seven times down the right side. The player's name appears in silver foil along the bottom.

MINT NRMT
COMPLETE SET (10) 50.00 22.00
COMMON CARD (1-10) 5.00 2.20

❑ 1 Mika Manninen 5.00 2.20
❑ 2 Kari Takko 7.50 3.40
❑ 3 Ari Sulander 7.50 3.40
❑ 4 Jouni Rokama 5.00 2.20
❑ 5 Kari Rosenberg 5.00 2.20
❑ 6 Mika Rautio 5.00 2.20
❑ 7 Ari-Pekka Siekkinen 5.00 2.20
❑ 8 Allain Roy 7.50 3.40
❑ 9 Pasi Kuivalainen 5.00 2.20
❑ 10 Sakari Lindfors 7.50 3.40

## 1994-95 Finnish SISU Specials

These ten standard sized cards were random inserts in Leaf first series packs and showcase winners of the player of the month award, among other titles. The cards feature full bleed action photography with the players name and club in the top left corner and his accomplishment, in English, along the bottom left. The word SISU, in stylized silver foil script, dominates the bottom of the card front.

MINT NRMT
COMPLETE SET (10) 40.00 18.00
COMMON CARD (1-10) 2.00 .90

❑ 1 Mika Alatalo 4.00 1.80
❑ 2 Jari Korpisalo 2.00 .90
❑ 3 Petteri Nummelin 3.00 1.35
❑ 4 Janne Ojanen 3.00 1.35
❑ 5 Sami Kapanen 6.00 2.70
❑ 6 Kari Takko 4.00 1.80
❑ 7 Esa Keskinen 3.00 1.35
❑ 8 Ari Sulander 5.00 2.20
❑ 9 Jarmo Myllys 5.00 2.20
❑ 10 Saku Koivu 20.00 9.00

## 1995 Finnish Karjala World Championship Labels

This unusual set is comprised of 24 odd-sized (2 1/2 by 2 1/2") labels that were issued on the front of Karjala beer bottles in Finland to commemorate that country's first World Championship. Each label features an action photo of the player superimposed over the gold medal, with his name underneath. The Finnish national team logo is in the upper left corner, and World Champions, 1995 (in Finnish) is in the right. The labels are blank backed. As they are unnumbered, the labels are listed below in alphabetical order.

MINT NRMT
COMPLETE SET (24) 40.00 18.00
COMMON LABEL 1.00 .45

❑ 1 Erik Hamalainen 1.00 .45
❑ 2 Raimo Helminen 1.00 .45
❑ 3 Timo Jutila 1.50 .70
❑ 4 Sami Kapanen 2.00 .90
❑ 5 Esa Keskinen 1.00 .45

□ 6 Marko Kiprusoff 1.00 .45
□ 7 Saku Koivu 10.00 4.50
□ 8 Tero Lehtera 1.00 .45
□ 9 Jere Lehtinen 3.00 1.35
□ 10 Curt Lindstrom 1.00 .45
□ 11 Jarmo Myllys 2.00 .90
□ 12 Mika Nieminen 1.00 .45
□ 13 Janne Niinimaa 5.00 2.20
□ 14 Petteri Nummelin 1.00 .45
□ 15 Janne Ojanen 1.00 .45
□ 16 Marko Palo 1.00 .45
□ 17 Ville Peltonen 1.50 .70
□ 18 Mika Stromberg 1.00 .45
□ 19 Ari Sulander 2.00 .90
□ 20 Raimo Summanen 1.00 .45
□ 21 Jukka Tammi 2.00 .90
□ 22 Antti Tormanen 1.50 .70
□ 23 Hannu Virta 1.50 .70
□ 24 Juha Ylonen 1.50 .70

## 1995 Finnish Semic World Championships

This 240 standard-size card set features players from Finland and other countries who have taken part in international competition. The fronts feature a color action photo depicting the player in the uniform of his national team surrounded by a gold border. The Semic logo rests in the top right corner, while a black bar along the bottom contains the card number, player name and national flag. The card backs picture a rink, along with a national flag, biographical information in Finnish, and stats from international competition. Subsets include All Stars, Maalivahti Extra and Future Stars.

| | MINT | NRMT |
|---|---|---|
| COMPLETE SET (240) | 100.00 | 45.00 |
| COMMON CARD (1-240) | .10 | .05 |

□ 1 Pasi Kuivalainen .10 .05
□ 2 Marko Kiprusoff .20 .09
□ 3 Tuomas Gronman .15 .07
□ 4 Erik Hamalainen .10 .05
□ 5 Timo Jutila .15 .07
□ 6 Pasi Sormunen .10 .05
□ 7 Waltteri Immonen .15 .07
□ 8 Janne Ojanen .15 .07
□ 9 Esa Keskinen .15 .07
□ 10 Kimmo Timonen .15 .07
□ 11 Saku Koivu 4.00 1.80
□ 12 Janne Laukkanen .25 .11
□ 13 Marko Palo .10 .05
□ 14 Raimo Helminen .15 .07
□ 15 Mika Alatalo .15 .07
□ 16 Ville Peltonen .50 .23
□ 17 Jari Kurri .75 .35
□ 18 Jari Korpisalo .15 .07
□ 19 Kimmo Rintanen .15 .07
□ 20 Jere Lehtinen .75 .35
□ 21 Kalle Sahlstedt .15 .07
□ 22 Christian Ruuttu .15 .07
□ 23 Hannu Virta .15 .07
□ 24 Sami Kapanen .50 .23
□ 25 Marko Tuulola .10 .05
□ 26 Mika Stromberg .20 .09
□ 27 Tero Lehtera .20 .09
□ 28 Petri Varis .25 .11
□ 29 Mikko Peltola .10 .05
□ 30 Jukka Tammi .20 .09
□ 31 Tero Arkiomaa .10 .05
□ 32 Olli Kaski .10 .05
□ 33 Pekka Laksola .10 .05
□ 34 Mika Valila .10 .05
□ 35 Jarmo Myllys .35 .16
□ 36 Harri Laurila .10 .05
□ 37 Teppo Numminen .35 .16
□ 38 Jyrki Lumme .20 .09
□ 39 Petteri Nummelin .10 .05
□ 40 Mika Nieminen .15 .07
□ 41 Teemu Selanne 3.00 1.35
□ 42 Mikko Makela .15 .07
□ 43 Esa Tikkanen .40 .18
□ 44 Jarkko Varvio .15 .07
□ 45 Vesa Viitakoski .15 .07
□ 46 Juha Riihijarvi .15 .07
□ 47 Markus Ketterer .25 .11
□ 48 Mikko Haapakoski .10 .05
□ 49 Antti Tormanen .20 .09
□ 50 Timo Peltomaa .10 .05
□ 51 Rauli Raitanen .10 .05
□ 52 Roger Nordstrom .10 .05
□ 53 Tommy Salo .50 .23
□ 54 Tommy Soderstrom .50 .23
□ 55 Magnus Svensson .15 .07
□ 56 Fredrik Stillman .10 .05
□ 57 Nicklas Lidstrom .50 .23
□ 58 Roger Johansson .10 .05
□ 59 Kenny Jonsson .50 .23
□ 60 Peter Andersson .10 .05
□ 61 Tommy Sjodin .15 .07
□ 62 Mats Sundin 1.00 .45
□ 63 Jonas Bergqvist .15 .07
□ 64 Peter Forsberg 6.00 2.70
□ 65 Roger Hansson .10 .05
□ 66 Jorgen Jonsson .10 .05
□ 67 Charles Berglund .10 .05
□ 68 Mikael Johansson .10 .05
□ 69 Tomas Forslund .15 .07
□ 70 Anders Dackell .25 .11
□ 71 Stefan Ornskog .10 .05
□ 72 Mikael Andersson .15 .07
□ 73 Jan Larsson .10 .05
□ 74 Patrik Carnback .15 .07
□ 75 Hakan Loob .35 .16
□ 76 Patrik Juhlin .25 .11
□ 77 Bill Ranford .50 .23
□ 78 Ed Belfour 2.00 .90
□ 79 Rob Blake .25 .11
□ 80 Yves Racine .15 .07
□ 81 Steve Smith .15 .07
□ 82 Paul Coffey 1.00 .45
□ 83 Larry Murphy .50 .23
□ 84 Mark Tinordi .15 .07
□ 85 Al MacInnis .50 .23
□ 86 Paul Kariya 6.00 2.70
□ 87 Joe Sakic 5.00 2.20
□ 88 Brendan Shanahan 3.00 1.35
□ 89 Luc Robitaille .75 .35
□ 90 Rod Brind'Amour .75 .35
□ 91 Shayne Corson .25 .11
□ 92 Mike Ricci .35 .16
□ 93 Mario Lemieux ERR 8.00 3.60
Name Misspelled Lemiux
□ 94 Eric Lindros 6.00 2.70
□ 95 Russ Courtnall .25 .11
□ 96 Theoren Fleury 1.00 .45
□ 97 Mark Messier 2.50 1.10
□ 98 Rick Tocchet .40 .18
□ 99 Wayne Gretzky 10.00 4.50
□ 100 Steve Larmer .35 .16
□ 101 Brett Lindros .25 .11
□ 102 John Vanbiesbrouck 5.00 2.20
□ 103 Craig Wolanin .15 .07
□ 104 Chris Chelios 1.00 .45
□ 105 Brian Leetch .75 .35
□ 106 Kevin Hatcher .20 .09
□ 107 Craig Janney .25 .11
□ 108 Tim Sweeney .15 .07
□ 109 Shawn Chambers .15 .07
□ 110 Scott Young .15 .07
□ 111 John Lilley .15 .07
□ 112 Joe Sacco .15 .07
□ 113 Brett Hull 2.50 1.10
□ 114 Pat LaFontaine .75 .35
□ 115 Joel Otto .25 .11
□ 116 Mike Modano .75 .35
□ 117 Tony Granato .20 .09
□ 118 Jeremy Roenick 1.50 .70
□ 119 Jeff Lazaro .15 .07
□ 120 Brian Mullen .15 .07
□ 121 Mihail Shtalenkov .50 .23
□ 122 Valeri Ivannikov .10 .05
□ 123 Andrei Nikolishin .25 .11
□ 124 Ilya Byakin .15 .07
□ 125 Alexander Smirnov .10 .05
□ 126 Dmitri Yushkevitch .15 .07
□ 127 Sergei Shendelev .10 .05
□ 128 Alexei Zhitnik .20 .09
□ 129 Igor Ulanov .15 .07
□ 130 Dmitri Frolov .10 .05
□ 131 Valeri Kamensky .50 .23
□ 132 Igor Fedulov .10 .05
□ 133 Andrei Kovalenko .35 .16
□ 134 Valeri Bure .50 .23
□ 135 Sergei Berezin 1.00 .45
□ 136 Alexei Yashin .50 .23
□ 137 Vyatcheslav Kozlov .35 .16
□ 138 Vyatcheslav Bykov .35 .16
□ 139 Andrei Khomutov .25 .11
□ 140 Petr Briza .35 .16
□ 141 Dominik Hasek 3.00 1.35
□ 142 Roman Turek 1.00 .45
□ 143 Jan Vopat .25 .11
□ 144 Drahomir Kadlec .20 .09
□ 145 Petr Pavlas .10 .05
□ 146 Frantisek Kucera .20 .09
□ 147 Jiri Veber .10 .05
□ 148 David Vyborny .15 .07
□ 149 Radek Toupal .15 .07
□ 150 Jiri Kucera .15 .07
□ 151 Richard Zemlicka .15 .07
□ 152 Martin Rucinsky .35 .16
□ 153 Jiri Dolezal .20 .09
□ 154 Josef Beranek .15 .07
□ 155 Martin Prochazka .50 .23
□ 156 Tomas Srsen .15 .07
□ 157 David Bruk .10 .05
□ 158 Jaromir Jagr 6.00 2.70
□ 159 Jan Caloun .20 .09
□ 160 Martin Straka .25 .11
□ 161 Roman Horak .10 .05
□ 162 Frantisek Musil .15 .07
□ 163 Peter Hrbek .10 .05
□ 164 Jan Alino .10 .05
□ 165 Joseph Heiss .20 .09
□ 166 Peter Gulda .10 .05
□ 167 Jayson Meyer .10 .05
□ 168 Ernst Kopf .10 .05
□ 169 Raimund Hilger .10 .05
□ 170 Richard Bohm .10 .05
□ 171 Michael Rosati .15 .07
□ 172 Michael DeAngelis .10 .05
□ 173 Anthony Circelli .10 .05
□ 174 Gaetano Orlando .10 .05
□ 175 Lucio Topatigh .10 .05
□ 176 Martin Pavlu .10 .05
□ 177 Jim Marthinsen .20 .09
□ 178 Petter Salsten .10 .05
□ 179 Tommy Jacobson .10 .05
□ 180 Morten Finsted .10 .05
□ 181 Tom Andersen .10 .05
□ 182 Manus Rath .10 .05
□ 183 Michael Puschacher .15 .07
□ 184 James Burton .10 .05
□ 185 Michael Shea .10 .05
□ 186 Dieter Kalt .10 .05
□ 187 Manfred Muhr .10 .05
□ 188 Andreas Pusnik .10 .05
□ 189 Renato Tosio .10 .05
□ 190 Doug Honneger .10 .05
□ 191 Felix Hollenstein .10 .05
□ 192 Jorg Eberle .10 .05
□ 193 Gil Montandon .10 .05
□ 194 Roberto Triuizi .10 .05
□ 195 Petri Ylonen .25 .11
□ 196 Bruno Maynort .10 .05
□ 197 Michel LeBlanc .10 .05
□ 198 Benoit Laborte .10 .05
□ 199 Christophe Ville .10 .05
□ 200 Antoine Richer .10 .05
□ 201 Bill Ranford AS .50 .23
□ 202 Timo Jutila AS .15 .07
□ 203 Magnus Svensson AS .15 .07
□ 204 Jari Kurri AS .75 .35
□ 205 Saku Koivu AS 4.00 1.80
□ 206 Paul Kariya AS 6.00 2.70
□ 207 Jarmo Myllys ME .25 .11
□ 208 Bill Ranford ME .50 .23
□ 209 Roger Nordstrom ME .10 .05
□ 210 Guy Hebert ME .50 .23
□ 211 Mihail Shtalenkov ME .50 .23
□ 212 Tommy Soderstrom ME .50 .23
□ 213 Petr Briza ME .35 .16
□ 214 Dominik Hasek ME 3.00 1.35
□ 215 Tom Barrasso ME .35 .16
□ 216 Jukka Tammi ME .20 .09
□ 217 John Vanbiesbrouck ME 5.00 2.20
□ 218 Mike Richter ME 2.00 .90
□ 219 Saku Koivu Special 4.00 1.80
□ 220 Saku Koivu Special 4.00 1.80
□ 221 Saku Koivu Special 4.00 1.80
□ 222 Saku Koivu Special 4.00 1.80
□ 223 Saku Koivu Special 4.00 1.80
□ 224 Saku Koivu Special 4.00 1.80
□ 225 Tuomas Gronman FS .15 .07
□ 226 Jani Nikko FS .10 .05
□ 227 Janne Niinimaa FS 2.50 1.10
□ 228 Jukka Tiilikainen FS .10 .05
□ 229 Kimmo Rintanen FS .15 .07
□ 230 Ville Peltonen FS .50 .23
□ 231 Sami Kapanen FS .50 .23
□ 232 Jere Lehtinen FS .75 .35
□ 233 Kimmo Timonen FS .15 .07
□ 234 Jonni Vauhkonen FS .15 .07
□ 235 Juha Lind FS .50 .23
□ 236 Tommi Miettinen FS .15 .07
□ 237 Jere Karalahti FS .25 .11
□ 238 Antti Aalto FS .40 .18
□ 239 Teemu Kohvakka FS .10 .05
□ 240 Niko Mikkola FS .10 .05

## 1995-96 Finnish Beckett Ad Cards

This eight-card set features color action player photos on a perforated sheet which measures approximately 3" by 9". The top half of the sheet contains the photo while the bottom half is a form to subscribe to the Finnish Beckett Hockey Monthly magazine. The backs are blank. Although these look like cards, they actually were meant to be folded in half and used as a protective covering for trading cards which were dispensed through vending machines in Finland during the 1995-96 season. The cards were not manufactured by Beckett, but by Semic, the company which produced the Finnish and Swedish versions of Beckett Hockey Monthly.

| | MINT | NRMT |
|---|---|---|
| COMPLETE SET (8) | 25.00 | 11.00 |
| COMMON CARD (1-8) | 2.00 | .90 |

□ 1 Saku Koivu 10.00 4.50
□ 2 Jere Lehtinen 5.00 2.20
□ 3 Ville Peltonen 3.00 1.35
□ 4 Erik Hamalainen 2.00 .90
□ 5 Sami Kapanen 6.00 2.70
□ 6 Marko Kiprusoff 3.00 1.35
□ 7 Mika Stromberg 2.00 .90
□ 8 Marko Palo 2.00 .90

## 1995-96 Finnish Jaa Kiekko Lehti Ad Cards

This eight-card set features color action photos on a perforated sheet which measures approximately 3" by 9". The top half of the sheet contains the photo of a popular Finnish national team member, while the bottom half is a form to subscribe to Jaa Kiekko Lehti, the leading hockey magazine in that country. The backs are blank. Although these look like cards when separated, they actually were meant to be folded in half and used as a protective barrier for trading cards which were dispensed through vending machines in Finland during the 1995-96 season. The cards were produced by Semic, and were numbered out of 8 on the front.

| | MINT | NRMT |
|---|---|---|
| COMPLETE SET (8) | 35.00 | 16.00 |
| COMMON CARD (1-8) | 2.00 | .90 |

□ 1 Jarmo Myllys 3.00 1.35
□ 2 Jari Kurri 4.00 1.80
□ 3 Saku Koivu 10.00 4.50
□ 4 Teemu Selanne 15.00 6.75
□ 5 Esa Tikkanen 3.00 1.35
□ 6 Christian Ruuttu 2.00 .90
□ 7 Mika Nieminen 2.00 .90
□ 8 Timo Jutila 2.00 .90

## 1995-96 Finnish SISU

This 400-card set features the players of Finland's top hockey circuit, the SM-Liiga. The cards were distributed in two series of 200 cards each, and in packs of eight cards. The fronts feature a full-bleed photo with the player's name ghosted along the bottom. The Saku Koivu Super Chase card was randomly inserted in series 1 packs at a rate of 1:600. The Koivu Super Bonus and Niinimaa Super Chase cards were found in series 2 packs at a rate of 1:480. The latter Koivu card could be redeemed to Leaf in Finland for an exclusive Koivu SISU Specials jumbo card. Little is known about this card, so it is not priced below.

| | MINT | NRMT |
|---|---|---|
| COMPLETE SET (400) | 60.00 | 27.00 |
| COMPLETE SERIES 1 (200) | 35.00 | 16.00 |
| COMPLETE SERIES 2 (200) | 25.00 | 11.00 |
| COMMON CARD (1-400) | .10 | .05 |

□ 1 HIFK, Team Card .10 .05
□ 2 Kimmo Kapanen .10 .05
□ 3 Juri Kuznetsov .20 .09
□ 4 Simo Saarinen .15 .07
□ 5 Roland Carlsson .10 .05
□ 6 Veli-Pekka Fagerstrom .10 .05
□ 7 Kristian Fagerstrom .10 .05
□ 8 Mika Kortelainen .15 .07
□ 9 Jari Laukkanen .10 .05
□ 10 Juha Nurminen .10 .05
□ 11 Markku Hurme .10 .05
□ 12 Sami Kapanen 2.00 .90
□ 13 Darren Boyko .20 .09
□ 14 Marko Ojanen .10 .05
□ 15 HPK, Team Card .10 .05
□ 16 Kari Rosenberg .25 .11
□ 17 Petri Engman .10 .05
□ 18 Niko Marttila .10 .05
□ 19 Jari Haapamaki .10 .05
□ 20 Marko Allen .10 .05
□ 21 Erik Kakko .10 .05
□ 22 Mikko Myllykoski .10 .05
□ 23 Jani Hassinen .10 .05
□ 24 Risto Jalo .25 .11
□ 25 Juha Jarvenpaa .20 .09
□ 26 Jari Kauppila .10 .05
□ 27 Toni Makiaho .10 .05
□ 28 Ilves, Team Card .10 .05
□ 29 Mika Manninen .35 .16
□ 30 Hannu Henriksson .10 .05
□ 31 Petri Kokko .10 .05
□ 32 Martti Jarventie .10 .05
□ 33 Allan Measures .10 .05
□ 34 Pasi Huura .10 .05
□ 35 Janne Seva .10 .05
□ 36 Tommy Kiviaho .10 .05
□ 37 Reijo Mikkolainen .10 .05
□ 38 Hannu Mattila .10 .05
□ 39 Jari Virtanen .10 .05
□ 40 Sami Ahlberg .10 .05
□ 41 Juha Hautamaa .10 .05
□ 42 Jokerit, Team Card .10 .05
□ 43 Ari Sulander .50 .23
□ 44 Santeri Immonen .15 .07
□ 45 Pasi Sormunen .10 .05
□ 46 Waltteri Immonen .15 .07
□ 47 Mika Stromberg .25 .11
□ 48 Kari Martikainen .10 .05
□ 49 Tommi Sova .35 .16
□ 50 Juha Lind .75 .35
□ 51 Niko Halttunen .10 .05
□ 52 Keijo Sailynoja .25 .11
□ 53 Otakar Janecky .25 .11
□ 54 Timo Saarikoski .10 .05
□ 55 JYP HT, Team Card .10 .05
□ 56 Ari-Pekka Siekkinen .25 .11
□ 57 Vesa Ponto .20 .09
□ 58 Kalle Koskinen .10 .05
□ 59 Jouni Loponen .10 .05
□ 60 Miska Kangasniemi .25 .11
□ 61 Mika Paananen .10 .05
□ 62 Markku Ikonen .10 .05
□ 63 Kimmo Salminen .10 .05
□ 64 Joni Lius .10 .05
□ 65 Lasse Nieminen .10 .05
□ 66 Janne Kurjenniemi .10 .05
□ 67 Marko Virtanen .10 .05
□ 68 KalPa, Team Card .10 .05
□ 69 Jarkko Kortesoja .10 .05
□ 70 Petri Matikainen .10 .05
□ 71 Mika Laaksonen .10 .05
□ 72 Kai Rautio .10 .05
□ 73 Jarno Kultanen .10 .05
□ 74 Miikka Ruokonen .10 .05
□ 75 Jussi Tarvainen .10 .05
□ 76 Mikko Honkonen .10 .05
□ 77 Sami Simonen .10 .05
□ 78 Petr Korinek .15 .07
□ 79 Veli-Pekka Pekkarinen .10 .05
□ 80 Pekka Tirkkonen .15 .07
□ 81 Kiekko-Espoo, Team Card .10 .05
□ 82 Iiro Itamies .25 .11
□ 83 Tommi Nyyssonen .10 .05
□ 84 Robert Salo .10 .05
□ 85 Sami Nuutinen .10 .05
□ 86 Timo Blomqvist .20 .09
□ 87 Ismo Kuoppala .10 .05
□ 88 Mikko Koivunoro .10 .05
□ 89 Petro Koivunen .25 .11
□ 90 Jarmo Muukkonen .10 .05
□ 91 Sergei Prjahin .15 .07
□ 92 Teemu Riihijarvi .75 .35
□ 93 Juha Ikonen .10 .05
□ 94 Lukko, Team Card .10 .05
□ 95 Boris Rousson .50 .23
□ 96 Vesa Salo .35 .16
□ 97 Toni Porkka .10 .05
□ 98 Mika Yli-Maenpaa .25 .11
□ 99 Juha Riihijarvi .25 .11
□ 100 Petri Latti .10 .05
□ 101 Veli-Pekka Ahonen .10 .05
□ 102 Mikko Peltola .10 .05
□ 103 Kalle Sahlstedt .25 .11
□ 104 Jari Torkki .15 .07
□ 105 Jussi Kiuru .10 .05
□ 106 Sakari Palsola .10 .05
□ 107 Tappara, Team Card .10 .05
□ 108 Ilpo Kauhanen .50 .23
□ 109 Sami Lehtonen .10 .05
□ 110 Pasi Petrilainen .10 .05
□ 111 Pekka Laksola .10 .05
□ 112 Tommi Haapsaari .10 .05
□ 113 Ville Nieminen .10 .05
□ 114 Arto Kulmala .10 .05
□ 115 Valeri Krykov .10 .05
□ 116 Timo Nurmberg .10 .05
□ 117 Aleksander Barkov .10 .05
□ 118 Miikka Kemppi .10 .05
□ 119 Marko Toivola .10 .05
□ 120 Juha Vuorivirta .35 .16
□ 121 TPS, Team Card .10 .05
□ 122 Miikka Kiprusoff 1.00 .45
□ 123 Kimmo Timonen .35 .16
□ 124 Sami Salo .10 .05
□ 125 Kari Harila .10 .05
□ 126 Tuomas Gronman .25 .11
□ 127 Vjatsheslav Fandul .10 .05
□ 128 Mika Alatalo .50 .23
□ 129 Jukka Tiilikainen .10 .05
□ 130 Kimmo Rintanen .35 .16
□ 131 Hannes Hyvonen .10 .05
□ 132 Simo Rouvali .10 .05
□ 133 Harri Sillgren .20 .09
□ 134 Harri Suvanto .10 .05
□ 135 TuTo, Team Card .10 .05
□ 136 Markus Korhonen .10 .05
□ 137 Sebastian Sulku .10 .05
□ 138 Jukka Suomalainen .10 .05
□ 139 Timo Kulonen .10 .05
□ 140 Risto Siltanen .25 .11
□ 141 Sami Leinonen .10 .05
□ 142 Juha Virtanen .10 .05
□ 143 Jari Hirsimaki .10 .05
□ 144 Jouni Tuominen .10 .05
□ 145 Vesa Karjalainen .10 .05
□ 146 Pekka Virta .10 .05
□ 147 Jouko Myrra .10 .05
□ 148 Assat, Team Card .10 .05
□ 149 Kari Takko .50 .23
□ 150 Timo Nykopp .10 .05
□ 151 Harri Laurila .10 .05
□ 152 Jarno Miikkulainen .10 .05
□ 153 Pasi Peltonen .10 .05
□ 154 Jari Korpisalo .15 .07
□ 155 Teppo Kivela .10 .05
□ 156 Jari Levonen .10 .05
□ 157 Janne Virtanen .10 .05
□ 158 Jarno Makela .10 .05
□ 159 Mikael Kotkaniemi .10 .05
□ 160 Ari Saarinen .10 .05
□ 161 Boris Rousson AS .50 .23
□ 162 Joni Lehto AS .15 .07
□ 163 Marko Kiprusoff AS .35 .16
□ 164 Jere Lehtinen AS 1.50 .70
□ 165 Saku Koivu AS 10.00 4.50
□ 166 Kai Nurminen AS .50 .23
□ 167 Ari Sulander AS .50 .23
□ 168 Mika Stromberg AS .25 .11
□ 169 All Stars/Kuusisto .15 .07
□ 170 All Stars/Arkiomaa .15 .07
□ 171 Otakar Janecky AS .25 .11
□ 172 Ville Peltonen AS 1.00 .45
□ 173 Milestones/Arima .10 .05
□ 174 Milestones/Boyko .15 .07
□ 175 Milestones/Friman .10 .05
□ 176 Milestones/Heiskanen .10 .05
□ 177 Milestones/Henriksson .10 .05
□ 178 Milestones/Hamalainen .10 .05
□ 179 Milestones/Jalo .10 .05
□ 180 Timo Jutila AS .20 .09
□ 181 Milestones/Jarvenpaa .10 .05

| | | |
|---|---|---|
| ❑ 182 Milestones/Kuusisto | .15 | .07 |
| ❑ 183 Milestones/Laksola | .10 | .05 |
| ❑ 184 Milestones/Laurila | .10 | .05 |
| ❑ 185 Milestones/Lehtonen | .10 | .05 |
| ❑ 186 Milestones/Lindroos | .15 | .07 |
| ❑ 187 Milestones/Mikkolainen | .10 | .05 |
| ❑ 188 Milestones/Tommila | .10 | .05 |
| ❑ 189 Milestones/Torkki | .10 | .05 |
| ❑ 190 Milestones/Tuomenoksa | .10 | .05 |
| ❑ 191 Milestones/Vuori | .10 | .05 |
| ❑ 192 TPS, SM-kultaa | .10 | .05 |
| ❑ 193 Jokerit, SM-hopeaa | .25 | .11 |
| ❑ 194 Assat, SM-pronssia | .10 | .05 |
| ❑ 195 Jokerit, EM-kultaa | .25 | .11 |
| ❑ 196 TPS, EM-pronssia | .10 | .05 |
| ❑ 197 Kai Nurminen CL | .35 | .16 |
| ❑ 198 Checklist 51-100, Kautonen | .10 | .05 |
| ❑ 199 Koivu Checklist | 5.00 | 2.20 |
| ❑ 200 Kiprusoff Checklist | .25 | .11 |
| ❑ 201 HIFK, Fan Card | .10 | .05 |
| ❑ 202 Sakari Lindfors | .50 | .23 |
| ❑ 203 Lauri Puolanne | .10 | .05 |
| ❑ 204 Pertti Lehtonen | .10 | .05 |
| ❑ 205 Peter Ahola | .15 | .07 |
| ❑ 206 Jere Karalahti | .35 | .16 |
| ❑ 207 Kimmo Maki-Kokkila | .10 | .05 |
| ❑ 208 Tom Laaksonen | .10 | .05 |
| ❑ 209 Tero Hamalainen | .10 | .05 |
| ❑ 210 Miro Haapaniemi | .10 | .05 |
| ❑ 211 Toni Sihvonen | .10 | .05 |
| ❑ 212 Sami Laine | .10 | .05 |
| ❑ 213 Iiro Jarvi | .25 | .11 |
| ❑ 214 Pekka Tuomisto | .10 | .05 |
| ❑ 215 HPK, Fan Card | .10 | .05 |
| ❑ 216 Mika Pietila | .25 | .11 |
| ❑ 217 Tom Koivisto | .10 | .05 |
| ❑ 218 Tommi Hamalainen | .10 | .05 |
| ❑ 219 Kai Rautio | .10 | .05 |
| ❑ 220 Jani Nikko | .25 | .11 |
| ❑ 221 Mika Kannisto | .10 | .05 |
| ❑ 222 Jason Miller | .10 | .05 |
| ❑ 223 Niklas Hede | .10 | .05 |
| ❑ 224 Tony Virta | .10 | .05 |
| ❑ 225 Aleksander Andrijevski | .15 | .07 |
| ❑ 226 Mika Puhakka | .10 | .05 |
| ❑ 227 Timo Peltomaa | .15 | .07 |
| ❑ 228 Toni Saarinen | .10 | .05 |
| ❑ 229 Ilves, Fan Card | .10 | .05 |
| ❑ 230 Vesa Toskala | 1.00 | .45 |
| ❑ 231 Pekka Kangasalusta | .10 | .05 |
| ❑ 232 Juha Lampinen | .10 | .05 |
| ❑ 233 Pasi Saarinen | .10 | .05 |
| ❑ 234 Teemu Vuorinen | .10 | .05 |
| ❑ 235 Jarno Peltonen | .10 | .05 |
| ❑ 236 Matti Kaipainen | .10 | .05 |
| ❑ 237 Semi Pekki | .10 | .05 |
| ❑ 238 Sami Karjalainen | .10 | .05 |
| ❑ 239 Juoni Lahtinen | .10 | .05 |
| ❑ 240 Pasi Maatanen | .10 | .05 |
| ❑ 241 Petri Murtovaara | .10 | .05 |
| ❑ 242 Tomi Hirvonen | .10 | .05 |
| ❑ 243 Mikko Eloranta | .10 | .05 |
| ❑ 244 Mika Arvaja | .10 | .05 |
| ❑ 245 Juha Jarvenpaa | .25 | .11 |
| ❑ 246 Jokerit, Fan Card | .10 | .05 |
| ❑ 247 Marko Rantanen | .20 | .09 |
| ❑ 248 Marko Tuulola | .10 | .05 |
| ❑ 249 Jani-Matti Loikala | .10 | .05 |
| ❑ 250 Antti-Jussi Niemi | .75 | .35 |
| ❑ 251 Janne Niinimaa | 5.00 | 2.20 |
| ❑ 252 Jari Lindroos | .15 | .07 |
| ❑ 253 Paso Saarela | .10 | .05 |
| ❑ 254 Juha Ylonen | .35 | .16 |
| ❑ 255 Mika Asikainen | .25 | .11 |
| ❑ 256 Eero Somervuori | .75 | .35 |
| ❑ 257 Tero Lehtera | .15 | .07 |
| ❑ 258 Jukka Penttinen | .10 | .05 |
| ❑ 259 Petri Varis | .75 | .35 |
| ❑ 260 JyP HT, Fan Card | .10 | .05 |
| ❑ 261 Marko Leinonen | .10 | .05 |
| ❑ 262 Jan Latvala | .10 | .05 |
| ❑ 263 Jukka Laamanen | .10 | .05 |
| ❑ 264 Pekka Poikolainen | .10 | .05 |
| ❑ 265 Thomas Sjogren | .20 | .09 |
| ❑ 266 Pasi Kangas | .25 | .11 |
| ❑ 267 Tini Koivunen | .10 | .05 |
| ❑ 268 Lasse Jamsen | .10 | .05 |
| ❑ 269 Petri Kujala | .10 | .05 |
| ❑ 270 Mikko Inkinen | .10 | .05 |
| ❑ 271 Kalpa, Fan Card | .10 | .05 |
| ❑ 272 Pasi Kuivalainen | .50 | .23 |
| ❑ 273 Pasi Kolehmainen | .10 | .05 |
| ❑ 274 Reijo Ruotsalainen | .25 | .11 |
| ❑ 275 Jarkko Glad | .10 | .05 |
| ❑ 276 Ivan Vlzek | .10 | .05 |
| ❑ 277 Jarmo Levonen | .10 | .05 |
| ❑ 278 Janne Kekalainen | .10 | .05 |
| ❑ 279 Veli-Pekka Nutikka | .75 | .35 |
| ❑ 280 Mikko Konttila | .25 | .11 |
| ❑ 281 Janne Virtanen | .10 | .05 |
| ❑ 282 Pasi Kemppainen | .10 | .05 |
| ❑ 283 Kiekko-Espoo, Fan Card | .10 | .05 |
| ❑ 284 Mika Rautio | .25 | .11 |
| ❑ 285 Kari Haakana | .10 | .05 |
| ❑ 286 Teemu Sillanpaa | .10 | .05 |
| ❑ 287 Timo Nykopp | .10 | .05 |
| ❑ 288 Miikka Teimonen | .10 | .05 |
| ❑ 289 Tero Tiainen | .10 | .05 |
| ❑ 290 Joonas Jaaskelainen | .10 | .05 |
| ❑ 291 Lubomir Kolnik | .35 | .16 |
| ❑ 292 Arto Sirvio | .10 | .05 |
| ❑ 293 Iikka Sinisalo | .25 | .11 |
| ❑ 294 Timo Hirvonen | .10 | .05 |
| ❑ 295 Arto Kuki | .10 | .05 |
| ❑ 296 Timo Norppa | .10 | .05 |
| ❑ 297 Lukko, Fan Card | .10 | .05 |
| ❑ 298 Timo Kauharren | .10 | .05 |
| ❑ 299 Joni Lehto | .15 | .07 |
| ❑ 300 Jarno Miikkulainen | .10 | .05 |
| ❑ 301 Kimmo Lotvonen | .10 | .05 |
| ❑ 302 Robert Nordmark | .15 | .07 |
| ❑ 303 Riku Kallioniemi | .10 | .05 |
| ❑ 304 Matti Raunio | .10 | .05 |
| ❑ 305 Tommi Turunen | .10 | .05 |
| ❑ 306 Jarkko Varvio | .15 | .07 |
| ❑ 307 Tero Arkiomaa | .15 | .07 |
| ❑ 308 Harri Lonnberg | .25 | .11 |
| ❑ 309 Mikko Luovi | .20 | .09 |
| ❑ 310 Tappara, Fan Card | .10 | .05 |
| ❑ 311 Jussi Markkanen | .10 | .05 |
| ❑ 312 Timo Jutila | .15 | .07 |
| ❑ 313 Jukka Ollila | .20 | .09 |
| ❑ 314 Antti Rahkonen | .10 | .05 |
| ❑ 315 Derek Mayer | .20 | .09 |
| ❑ 316 Petri Kalteva | .10 | .05 |
| ❑ 317 Jarkko Nikander | .10 | .05 |
| ❑ 318 Pauli Jarvinen | .10 | .05 |
| ❑ 319 Mikko Helisten | .10 | .05 |
| ❑ 320 Ari Haanpaa | .10 | .05 |
| ❑ 321 Markus Oijennus | .10 | .05 |
| ❑ 322 Janne Ojanen | .35 | .16 |
| ❑ 323 TPS, Fan Card | .10 | .05 |
| ❑ 324 Fredrik Norrena | .35 | .16 |
| ❑ 325 Mika Lehtinen | .10 | .05 |
| ❑ 326 Karlis Skrastins | .10 | .05 |
| ❑ 327 Marru Laapas | .10 | .05 |
| ❑ 328 Antti Aalto | .75 | .35 |
| ❑ 329 Teemu Numminen | .10 | .05 |
| ❑ 330 Tommi Miettinen | .10 | .05 |
| ❑ 331 Lasse Pirjeta | .10 | .05 |
| ❑ 332 Miikka Rousu | .10 | .05 |
| ❑ 333 Marko Makinen | .10 | .05 |
| ❑ 334 Mikko Markkanen | .10 | .05 |
| ❑ 335 Tomi Kallio | .35 | .16 |
| ❑ 336 Miika Elomo | 1.50 | .70 |
| ❑ 337 Sami Mettovaara | .10 | .05 |
| ❑ 338 TuTo, Fan Card | .10 | .05 |
| ❑ 339 Jukka Tammi | .50 | .23 |
| ❑ 340 Kari-Pekka Friman | .10 | .05 |
| ❑ 341 Veli-Pekka Hard | .10 | .05 |
| ❑ 342 Antti Tirkkonen | .10 | .05 |
| ❑ 343 Jukka Seppo | .10 | .05 |
| ❑ 344 Kim Ahlroos | .10 | .05 |
| ❑ 345 Marto Poulsen | .10 | .05 |
| ❑ 346 Juha Kuusisaari | .10 | .05 |
| ❑ 347 Mikko Laaksonen | .10 | .05 |
| ❑ 348 Tuomas Jalava | .10 | .05 |
| ❑ 349 Tommi Pullola | .35 | .16 |
| ❑ 350 Tuomas Kalliomaki | .10 | .05 |
| ❑ 351 Assat, Fan Card | .10 | .05 |
| ❑ 352 Karri Kivi | .20 | .09 |
| ❑ 353 Olli Kaski | .10 | .05 |
| ❑ 354 Jouni Vento | .10 | .05 |
| ❑ 355 Tommi Rajamaki | .25 | .11 |
| ❑ 356 Jokke Heinanen | .10 | .05 |
| ❑ 357 Tomas Kapusta | .15 | .07 |
| ❑ 358 Jaroslav Otevrel | .20 | .09 |
| ❑ 359 Timo Salonen | .10 | .05 |
| ❑ 360 Pekka Virta | .10 | .05 |
| ❑ 361 Vesa Goman | .10 | .05 |
| ❑ 362 Pekka Peltola | .10 | .05 |
| ❑ 363 Rauli Raitanen | .10 | .05 |
| ❑ 364 Pasi Tuominen | .10 | .05 |
| ❑ 365 Kari Syvasalmi | .10 | .05 |
| ❑ 366 Timo Hakanen | .10 | .05 |
| ❑ 367 Foreigners/Andrijevski | .10 | .05 |
| ❑ 368 Foreigners/Barkov | .10 | .05 |
| ❑ 369 Foreigners/Boyko | .15 | .07 |
| ❑ 370 Foreigners/Fandul | .10 | .05 |
| ❑ 371 Foreigners/Janecky | .15 | .07 |
| ❑ 372 Foreigners/Kapusta | .10 | .05 |
| ❑ 373 Foreigners/Kolnik | .20 | .09 |
| ❑ 374 Foreigners/Korinek | .10 | .05 |
| ❑ 375 Foreigners/Mayer | .15 | .07 |
| ❑ 376 Foreigners/Measures | .10 | .05 |
| ❑ 377 Foreigners/Miller | .10 | .05 |
| ❑ 378 Foreigners/Nordmark | .10 | .05 |
| ❑ 379 Foreigners/Otevrel | .15 | .07 |
| ❑ 380 Foreigners/Prjahin | .20 | .09 |
| ❑ 381 Foreigners/Rousson | .50 | .23 |
| ❑ 382 Foreigners/Sjogren | .10 | .05 |
| ❑ 383 Foreigners/Skrastins | .10 | .05 |
| ❑ 384 Foreigners/Vlzek | .10 | .05 |
| ❑ 385 Vladimir Jursinov CO | .10 | .05 |
| ❑ 386 Hannu Aravirta CO | .10 | .05 |
| ❑ 387 Veli-Pekka Ketola CO | .25 | .11 |
| ❑ 388 Vaclav Sykora CO | .10 | .05 |
| ❑ 389 Hannu Kapanen CO | .10 | .05 |
| ❑ 390 Kari Savolainen CO | .10 | .05 |
| ❑ 391 Harri Rindell CO | .10 | .05 |
| ❑ 392 Anatoli Bogdanov | .10 | .05 |
| ❑ 393 Sakari Pietilla | .10 | .05 |
| ❑ 394 Jukka Rautakorpi | .10 | .05 |
| ❑ 395 Harri Jalava | .10 | .05 |
| ❑ 396 Vladimir Jursinov Jr. | .10 | .05 |
| ❑ 397 Jere Lehtinen CL | .75 | .35 |
| ❑ 398 Checklist 251-300 | .10 | .05 |
| ❑ 399 Checklist 301-350 | .10 | .05 |
| ❑ 400 Koivu Checklist | 5.00 | 2.20 |
| ❑ NNO Saku Koivu Super Chase | 100.00 | 45.00 |
| ❑ NNO Saku Koivu Super Bonus | 75.00 | 34.00 |
| ❑ NNO Janne Niinimaa Super Chase | 50.00 | 22.00 |

## 1995-96 Finnish SISU Double Trouble

This eight-card set features action shots of the top two players from the teams of the SM-Liiga. The cards were randomly inserted at a rate of 1:17 series 2 packs.

| | MINT | NRMT |
|---|---|---|
| COMPLETE SET (8) | 35.00 | 16.00 |
| COMMON CARD (1-8) | 5.00 | 2.20 |
| ❑ 1 Tuomas Gronman / Kimmo Timonen | 5.00 | 2.20 |
| ❑ 2 Waltteri Immonen / Mika Stromberg | 5.00 | 2.20 |
| ❑ 3 Olli Kaski / Karri Kivi | 5.00 | 2.20 |
| ❑ 4 Joni Lehto / Robert Nordmark | 5.00 | 2.20 |
| ❑ 5 Peter Ahola / Pertti Lehtonen | 5.00 | 2.20 |
| ❑ 6 Timo Blomqvist / Sami Nuutinen | 5.00 | 2.20 |
| ❑ 7 Reijo Ruotsalainen / Ivan Vizek | 5.00 | 2.20 |
| ❑ 8 Timo Jutila / Pekka Laksola | 5.00 | 2.20 |

## 1995-96 Finnish SISU Drafted Dozen

Randomly inserted at a rate of 1:19 series 2 packs, this set depicts a dozen players from the SM-Liiga who were selected in the NHL Entry Draft.

| | MINT | NRMT |
|---|---|---|
| COMPLETE SET (12) | 50.00 | 22.00 |
| COMMON CARD (1-12) | 4.00 | 1.80 |
| ❑ 1 Aki-Petteri Berg | 6.00 | 2.70 |
| ❑ 2 Teemu Riihijarvi | 6.00 | 2.70 |
| ❑ 3 Miika Elomo | 7.00 | 3.10 |
| ❑ 4 Marko Makinen | 4.00 | 1.80 |
| ❑ 5 Tomi Kallio | 5.00 | 2.20 |
| ❑ 6 Sami Kapanen | 8.00 | 3.60 |
| ❑ 7 Vesa Toskala | 5.00 | 2.20 |
| ❑ 8 Miikka Kiprusoff | 5.00 | 2.20 |
| ❑ 9 Timo Hakanen | 4.00 | 1.80 |
| ❑ 10 Juha Vuorivirta | 5.00 | 2.20 |
| ❑ 11 Tomi Hirvonen | 4.00 | 1.80 |
| ❑ 12 Mikko Markkanen | 4.00 | 1.80 |

## 1995-96 Finnish SISU Ghost Goalies

This 10-card set focuses on the top netminders of the SM-Liiga. The cards were randomly inserted at a rate of 1:24 series 1 packs.

| | MINT | NRMT |
|---|---|---|
| COMPLETE SET (10) | 65.00 | 29.00 |
| COMMON CARD (1-10) | 6.00 | 2.70 |
| ❑ 1 Sakari Lindfors | 10.00 | 4.50 |
| ❑ 2 Boris Rousson | 8.00 | 3.60 |
| ❑ 3 Ari Sulander | 10.00 | 4.50 |
| ❑ 4 Kari Takko | 8.00 | 3.60 |
| ❑ 5 Fredrik Norrena | 6.00 | 2.70 |
| ❑ 6 Kari Rosenberg | 6.00 | 2.70 |
| ❑ 7 Ari-Pekka Siekkinen | 6.00 | 2.70 |
| ❑ 8 Jukka Tammi | 8.00 | 3.60 |
| ❑ 9 Pasi Kuivalainen | 6.00 | 2.70 |
| ❑ 10 Ilpo Kauhanen | 6.00 | 2.70 |

## 1995-96 Finnish SISU Gold Cards

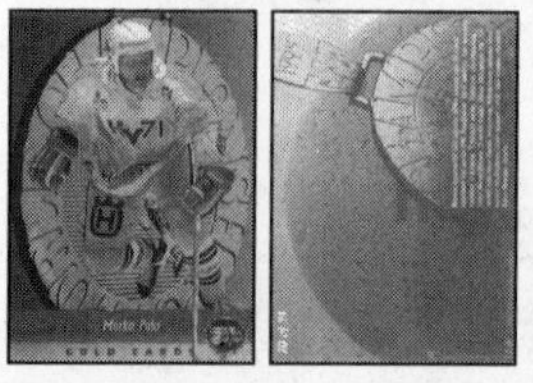

This 24-card set celebrates the players who earned Finland's first major title by winning the 1995 World Championship. The cards were distributed over both series in a scattered (ie, not 1-12 and 13-24) fashion. The cards were randomly inserted at a rate of 1:10 series 1 packs and 1:9 series 2 packs.

| | MINT | NRMT |
|---|---|---|
| COMPLETE SET (24) | 100.00 | 45.00 |
| COMMON CARD (1-24) | 3.00 | 1.35 |
| ❑ 1 Title Card | 5.00 | 2.20 |
| ❑ 2 Jarmo Myllys | 8.00 | 3.60 |
| ❑ 3 Ari Sulander | 6.00 | 2.70 |
| ❑ 4 Jukka Tammi | 5.00 | 2.20 |
| ❑ 5 Erik Hamalainen | 3.00 | 1.35 |
| ❑ 6 Timo Jutila | 3.00 | 1.35 |
| ❑ 7 Marko Kiprusoff | 4.00 | 1.80 |
| ❑ 8 Janne Niinimaa | 15.00 | 6.75 |
| ❑ 9 Petteri Nummelin | 3.00 | 1.35 |
| ❑ 10 Mika Stromberg | 3.00 | 1.35 |
| ❑ 11 Hannu Virta | 3.00 | 1.35 |
| ❑ 12 Raimo Helminen | 3.00 | 1.35 |
| ❑ 13 Sami Kapanen | 6.00 | 2.70 |
| ❑ 14 Esa Keskinen | 4.00 | 1.80 |
| ❑ 15 Saku Koivu | 25.00 | 11.00 |
| ❑ 16 Tero Lehtera | 3.00 | 1.35 |
| ❑ 17 Jere Lehtinen | 6.00 | 2.70 |
| ❑ 18 Mika Nieminen | 4.00 | 1.80 |
| ❑ 19 Janne Ojanen | 4.00 | 1.80 |
| ❑ 20 Marko Palo | 3.00 | 1.35 |
| ❑ 21 Ville Peltonen | 4.00 | 1.80 |
| ❑ 22 Raimo Summanen | 3.00 | 1.35 |
| ❑ 23 Antti Tormanen | 3.00 | 1.35 |
| ❑ 24 Juha Ylonen | 3.00 | 1.35 |

## 1995-96 Finnish SISU Painkillers

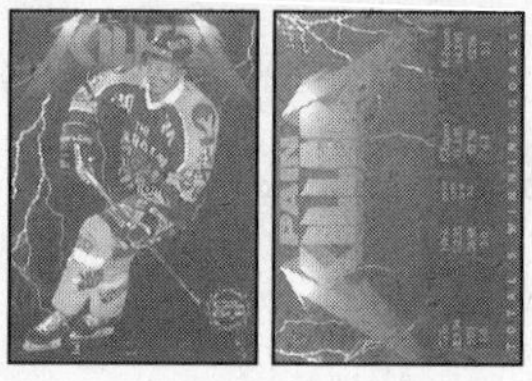

Randomly inserted in series 1 packs at a rate of 1:15, these eight cards highlight some of the dominant snipers of the SM-Liiga.

| | MINT | NRMT |
|---|---|---|
| COMPLETE SET (8) | 20.00 | 9.00 |
| COMMON CARD (1-8) | 2.00 | .90 |
| ❑ 1 Jokke Heinanen | 2.00 | .90 |
| ❑ 2 Mika Alatalo | 3.00 | 1.35 |
| ❑ 3 Joni Lehto | 2.00 | .90 |
| ❑ 4 Harri Lonnberg | 2.00 | .90 |
| ❑ 5 Ville Peltonen | 5.00 | 2.20 |
| ❑ 6 Harri Sillgren | 2.00 | .90 |
| ❑ 7 Petri Varis | 5.00 | 2.20 |
| ❑ 8 Marko Virtanen | 3.00 | 1.35 |

## 1995-96 Finnish SISU Specials

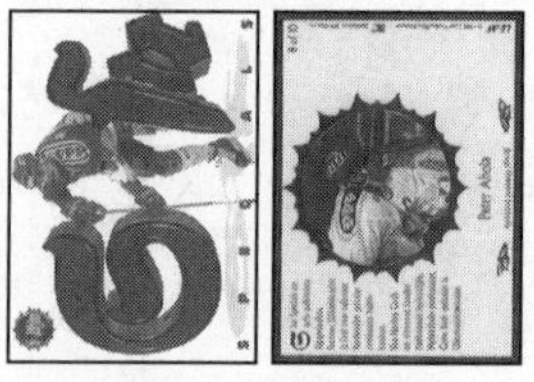

Randomly inserted at a rate of 1:24 series 1 packs, these cards picture some of the most popular players in the SM-Liiga, including several NHLers who played there during the 1994 lockout.

| | MINT | NRMT |
|---|---|---|
| COMPLETE SET (10) | 60.00 | 27.00 |
| COMMON CARD (1-10) | 3.00 | 1.35 |
| ❑ 1 Petri Varis | 6.00 | 2.70 |
| ❑ 2 Boris Rousson | 5.00 | 2.20 |
| ❑ 3 Saku Koivu | 25.00 | 11.00 |
| ❑ 4 Jari Kurri | 10.00 | 4.50 |
| ❑ 5 Jarmo Kuusisto | 3.00 | 1.35 |
| ❑ 6 Janne Ojanen | 4.00 | 1.80 |
| ❑ 7 Jere Lehtinen | 6.00 | 2.70 |
| ❑ 8 Peter Ahola | 4.00 | 1.80 |
| ❑ 9 Jukka Seppo | 3.00 | 1.35 |
| ❑ 10 Michael Nylander | 5.00 | 2.20 |

## 1995-96 Finnish SISU Spotlights

This eight-card series shines the -- yes -- spotlight on some of the most offensively gifted players in the SM-Liiga. The cards were randomly inserted in series 2 packs at a rate of 1:8.

| | MINT | NRMT |
|---|---|---|
| COMPLETE SET (8) | 20.00 | 9.00 |
| COMMON CARD (1-8) | 2.00 | .90 |
| ❑ 1 Otakar Janecky | 4.00 | 1.80 |
| ❑ 2 Jari Korpisalo | 3.00 | 1.35 |
| ❑ 3 Juha Riihijarvi | 4.00 | 1.80 |
| ❑ 4 Iiro Jarvi | 3.00 | 1.35 |
| ❑ 5 Thomas Sjogren | 2.00 | .90 |
| ❑ 6 Risto Jalo | 3.00 | 1.35 |
| ❑ 7 Jari Hirsimaki | 2.00 | .90 |
| ❑ 8 Juha Hautamaa | 2.00 | .90 |

## 1995-96 Finnish SISU Limited

This 108-card set is the first super-premium issue released in Europe. The cards are printed on 24-point stock and picture the elite athletes of the Finnish SM-Liiga. Production was announced as 7,500 individually numbered boxes. Each box contained 18, 5-card "packs". Thes packs were actually boxes themselves, and pictured either Saku Koivu, Teemu Selanne or Esa Tikkanen. The card fronts have a color photo of the player over his ghosted close-up in the background. The back contains another photo as well as a brief bio in Finnish and the Leaf trademark. Several NHLers who played here during the 1994 lockout are featured, including Selanne, Jari Kurri, and 1996 Calder candidate Koivu. One Koivu Line super chase card was randomly inserted in every 219 packs. These cards were individually numbered out of 720.

| | MINT | NRMT |
|---|---|---|
| COMPLETE SET (108) | 75.00 | 34.00 |
| COMMON CARD (1-108) | .20 | .09 |
| ❑ 1 Fredrik Norrena | .75 | .35 |
| ❑ 2 Hannu Virta | .50 | .23 |
| ❑ 3 Petteri Nummelin | .35 | .16 |
| ❑ 4 Tuomas Gronman | .50 | .23 |
| ❑ 5 Marko Kiprusoff | .75 | .35 |
| ❑ 6 Saku Koivu | 15.00 | 6.75 |
| ❑ 7 Raimo Summanen | .35 | .16 |
| ❑ 8 Esa Keskinen | .50 | .23 |
| ❑ 9 Jere Lehtinen | 2.50 | 1.10 |
| ❑ 10 Ari Sulander | 1.00 | .45 |
| ❑ 11 Waltteri Immonen | .35 | .16 |
| ❑ 12 Mika Stromberg | .50 | .23 |
| ❑ 13 Janne Niinimaa | 8.00 | 3.60 |
| ❑ 14 Otakar Janecky | .50 | .23 |
| ❑ 15 Teemu Selanne | 15.00 | 6.75 |
| ❑ 16 Jari Kurri | 4.00 | 1.80 |
| ❑ 17 Antti Tormanen | .75 | .35 |
| ❑ 18 Petri Varis | 1.00 | .45 |
| ❑ 19 Kari Takko | 1.00 | .45 |
| ❑ 20 Olli Kaski | .20 | .09 |
| ❑ 21 Rauli Raitanen | .20 | .09 |
| ❑ 22 Jari Korpisalo | .35 | .16 |
| ❑ 23 Teppo Kivela | .20 | .09 |
| ❑ 24 Jokke Heinanen | .20 | .09 |
| ❑ 25 Arto Javanainen | .20 | .09 |
| ❑ 26 Jari Levonen | .20 | .09 |
| ❑ 27 Arto Heiskanen | .20 | .09 |
| ❑ 28 Jarmo Myllys | 1.00 | .45 |
| ❑ 29 Boris Rousson | 1.00 | .45 |
| ❑ 30 Jarmo Kuusisto | .20 | .09 |
| ❑ 31 Joni Lehto | .35 | .16 |
| ❑ 32 Robert Nordmark | .35 | .16 |
| ❑ 33 Tero Arkiomaa | .35 | .16 |
| ❑ 34 Jari Torkki | .35 | .16 |
| ❑ 35 Juha Riihijarvi | .50 | .23 |
| ❑ 36 Matti Forss | .20 | .09 |
| ❑ 37 Sakari Lindfors | 1.00 | .45 |
| ❑ 38 Pertti Lehtonen | .20 | .09 |
| ❑ 39 Simo Saarinen | .35 | .16 |
| ❑ 40 Esa Tikkanen | 2.50 | 1.10 |
| ❑ 41 Ville Peltonen | 1.50 | .70 |
| ❑ 42 Christian Ruuttu | .75 | .35 |
| ❑ 43 Mika Kortelainen | .35 | .16 |
| ❑ 44 Darren Boyko | .50 | .23 |
| ❑ 45 Iiro Jarvi | .50 | .23 |
| ❑ 46 Ari-Pekka Siekkinen | .50 | .23 |
| ❑ 47 Harri Laurila | .20 | .09 |
| ❑ 48 Jouni Loponen | .20 | .09 |
| ❑ 49 Joni Lius | .20 | .09 |
| ❑ 50 Jari Lindroos | .35 | .16 |
| ❑ 51 Risto Kurkinen | .20 | .09 |
| ❑ 52 Thomas Sjogren | .35 | .16 |
| ❑ 53 Marko Virtanen | .20 | .09 |
| ❑ 54 Michael Nylander | 1.00 | .45 |
| ❑ 55 Mika Rautio | .50 | .23 |
| ❑ 56 Sami Nuutinen | .20 | .09 |
| ❑ 57 Peter Ahola | .35 | .16 |
| ❑ 58 Timo Blomqvist | .50 | .23 |
| ❑ 59 Ikka Sinisalo | .50 | .23 |
| ❑ 60 Petro Koivunen | .50 | .23 |
| ❑ 61 Sergei Prjahin | .35 | .16 |
| ❑ 62 Tero Lehtera | .35 | .16 |
| ❑ 63 Mariusz Czerkawski | 1.50 | .70 |
| ❑ 64 Pasi Kuivalainen | 1.00 | .45 |
| ❑ 65 Kimmo Timonen | .75 | .35 |
| ❑ 66 Reijo Ruotsalainen | .50 | .23 |
| ❑ 67 Vesa Salo | .75 | .35 |
| ❑ 68 Petr Korinek | .35 | .16 |
| ❑ 69 Marko Jantunen | .50 | .23 |
| ❑ 70 Pekka Tirkkonen | .35 | .16 |
| ❑ 71 Janne Kekalainen | .20 | .09 |
| ❑ 72 Sami Kapanen | 3.00 | 1.35 |
| ❑ 73 Timo Jutila | .35 | .16 |

| | | |
|---|---|---|
| ❑ 74 Pekka Laksola | .20 | .09 |
| ❑ 75 Janne Gronvall | .50 | .23 |
| ❑ 76 Jiri Kucera | .35 | .16 |
| ❑ 77 Janne Ojanen | .75 | .35 |
| ❑ 78 Pauli Jarvinen | .20 | .09 |
| ❑ 79 Ari Haanpaa | .20 | .09 |
| ❑ 80 Aleksander Barkov | .20 | .09 |
| ❑ 81 Theoren Fleury | 4.00 | 1.80 |
| ❑ 82 Kari Rosenberg | .50 | .23 |
| ❑ 83 Janne Laukkanen | .75 | .35 |
| ❑ 84 Jani Nikko | .50 | .23 |
| ❑ 85 Mika Lartama | .20 | .09 |
| ❑ 86 Kai Nurminen | 1.00 | .45 |
| ❑ 87 Tomas Kapusta | .35 | .16 |
| ❑ 88 Marko Palo | .35 | .16 |
| ❑ 89 Jarkko Varvio | .35 | .16 |
| ❑ 90 Risto Jalo | .50 | .23 |
| ❑ 91 Jukka Tammi | 1.00 | .45 |
| ❑ 92 Risto Siltanen | .50 | .23 |
| ❑ 93 Teppo Numminen | 1.00 | .45 |
| ❑ 94 Marco Poulsen | .20 | .09 |
| ❑ 95 Jukka Seppo | .20 | .09 |
| ❑ 96 Vesa Karjalainen | .20 | .09 |
| ❑ 97 Ted Donato | 1.50 | .70 |
| ❑ 98 Juha Virtanen | .20 | .09 |
| ❑ 99 Jari Hirsimaki | .20 | .09 |
| ❑ 100 Vesa Toskala | 2.00 | .90 |
| ❑ 101 Jyrki Lumme | 1.50 | .70 |
| ❑ 102 Hannu Henriksson | .20 | .09 |
| ❑ 103 Allan Measures | .20 | .09 |
| ❑ 104 Timo Peltomaa | .35 | .16 |
| ❑ 105 Juha Hautamaa | .20 | .09 |
| ❑ 106 Mikko Makela | .50 | .23 |
| ❑ 107 Juha Jarvenpaa | .50 | .23 |
| ❑ 108 Semi Pekki | .20 | .09 |
| ❑ NNO Koivu Line Super Chase | 75.00 | 34.00 |

## 1995-96 Finnish SISU Limited Leaf Gallery

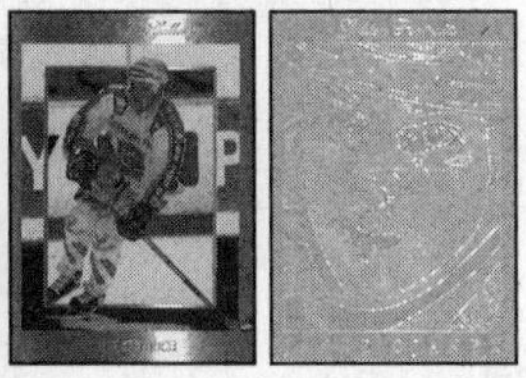

The nine cards in this set were randomly inserted at a rate of 1 in 6 packs of SISU Limited. The fronts feature a dynamic action photo surrounded by a refractive holofoil border. The cards are numbered of 9 on the front. The backs display a gold-foil etched protrait of the player.

| | MINT | NRMT |
|---|---|---|
| COMPLETE SET (9) | 60.00 | 27.00 |
| COMMON CARD (1-9) | 5.00 | 2.20 |
| ❑ 1 Jyrki Lumme | 10.00 | 4.50 |
| ❑ 2 Janne Laukkanen | 7.50 | 3.40 |
| ❑ 3 Michael Nylander | 10.00 | 4.50 |
| ❑ 4 Janne Ojanen | 5.00 | 2.20 |
| ❑ 5 Peter Ahola | 5.00 | 2.20 |
| ❑ 6 Kari Takko | 10.00 | 4.50 |
| ❑ 7 Hannu Virta | 5.00 | 2.20 |
| ❑ 8 Juha Lind | 10.00 | 4.50 |
| ❑ 9 Sakari Lindfors | 10.00 | 4.50 |

## 1995-96 Finnish SISU Limited Signed and Sealed

The nine cards in this set were randomly inserted at a rate of 1 in 9 SISU Limited packs. The set features a number of current and former NHLers. The cards feature an action photo printed on a silver foil background. The player's "signature" is embossed in gold foil across the bottom of the photo. The backs feature another photo and are numbered out of 9.

| | MINT | NRMT |
|---|---|---|
| COMPLETE SET (9) | 100.00 | 45.00 |
| COMMON CARD (1-9) | 5.00 | 2.20 |
| ❑ 1 Sami Kapanen | 12.00 | 5.50 |
| ❑ 2 Christian Ruuttu | 5.00 | 2.20 |
| ❑ 3 Teemu Selanne | 40.00 | 18.00 |
| ❑ 4 Aki Berg | 8.00 | 3.60 |
| ❑ 5 Joni Lehto | 5.00 | 2.20 |
| ❑ 6 Teppo Numminen | 7.00 | 3.10 |
| ❑ 7 Jari Kurri | 15.00 | 6.75 |
| ❑ 8 Esa Tikkanen | 10.00 | 4.50 |
| ❑ 9 Theoren Fleury | 15.00 | 6.75 |

## 1996-97 Finnish SISU Redline

This set featuring players of Finland's SM-Liiga is complete at 200 cards; although a second series was intended, it was not produced as a result of disappointing sales for the first series. The cards themselves were quite attractive, with a color action photo surrounded by a thin border, a stylized rendition of the player's name, and the team name along the bottom. The back included a large head shot, with player bio and '95-96 stats. The Super Chase and Super Bonus cards were randomly inserted at the rate of 1:240 packs. If found, they could be exchanged by mail with Leaf for one of five Silver Signature goalie cards that were limited to 400 copies. We have no further information on these Silver Signature cards.

| | MINT | NRMT |
|---|---|---|
| COMPLETE SET (200) | 25.00 | 11.00 |
| COMMON CARD (1-200) | .10 | .05 |
| ❑ 1 Checklist (1-50) | .10 | .05 |
| ❑ 2 Sakari Lindfors | .50 | .23 |
| ❑ 3 Peter Ahola | .15 | .07 |
| ❑ 4 Jere Karalahti | .35 | .16 |
| ❑ 5 Pertti Lehtonen | .10 | .05 |
| ❑ 6 Lauri Puolanne | .10 | .05 |
| ❑ 7 Sami Laine | .10 | .05 |
| ❑ 8 Tommy Kiviaho | .10 | .05 |
| ❑ 9 Markku Hurme | .10 | .05 |
| ❑ 10 Jari Laukkanen | .10 | .05 |
| ❑ 11 Tero Nyman | .10 | .05 |
| ❑ 12 Toni Sihvonen | .10 | .05 |
| ❑ 13 Mika Kortelainen | .15 | .07 |
| ❑ 14 Tero Hamalainen | .10 | .05 |
| ❑ 15 Mika Pietila | .25 | .11 |
| ❑ 16 Erik Kakko | .10 | .05 |
| ❑ 17 Tom Koivisto | .10 | .05 |
| ❑ 18 Jani Nikko | .25 | .11 |
| ❑ 19 Risto Jalo | .25 | .11 |
| ❑ 20 Aleksander Andrievski | .15 | .07 |
| ❑ 21 Jari Kauppila | .10 | .05 |
| ❑ 22 Jarkko Savijoki | .10 | .05 |
| ❑ 23 Toni Makiaho | .10 | .05 |
| ❑ 24 Mika Kannisto | .10 | .05 |
| ❑ 25 Mika Puhakka | .10 | .05 |
| ❑ 26 Toni Saarinen | .10 | .05 |
| ❑ 27 Vesa Toskala | 1.00 | .45 |
| ❑ 28 Teemu Vuorinen | .10 | .05 |
| ❑ 29 Petri Kokko | .10 | .05 |
| ❑ 30 Pekka Kangasalusta | .10 | .05 |
| ❑ 31 Tommi Kahiluoto | .10 | .05 |
| ❑ 32 Jarno Peltonen | .10 | .05 |
| ❑ 33 Mika Arvaja | .10 | .05 |
| ❑ 34 Matti Kaipainen | .10 | .05 |
| ❑ 35 Hannu Mattila | .10 | .05 |
| ❑ 36 Tomi Hirvonen | .10 | .05 |
| ❑ 37 Jouni Lahtinen | .10 | .05 |
| ❑ 38 Jari Suorsa | .10 | .05 |
| ❑ 39 Juha Jarvenpaa | .20 | .09 |
| ❑ 40 Semi Pekki | .10 | .05 |
| ❑ 41 Ari Sulander | .50 | .23 |
| ❑ 42 Mika Stromberg | .25 | .11 |
| ❑ 43 Marko Tuulola | .10 | .05 |
| ❑ 44 Pasi Sormunen | .10 | .05 |
| ❑ 45 Waltteri Immonen | .15 | .07 |
| ❑ 46 Jukka Penttinen | .10 | .05 |
| ❑ 47 Petri Varis | .75 | .35 |
| ❑ 48 Keijo Sailynoja | .25 | .11 |
| ❑ 49 Tero Lehtera | .15 | .07 |
| ❑ 50 Checklist (51-100) | .10 | .05 |
| ❑ 51 Jari Lindroos | .15 | .07 |
| ❑ 52 Ismo Kuoppala | .10 | .05 |
| ❑ 53 Juha Ylonen | .25 | .11 |
| ❑ 54 Pasi Saarela | .15 | .07 |
| ❑ 55 Marko Leinonen | .10 | .05 |
| ❑ 56 Kalle Koskinen | .10 | .05 |
| ❑ 57 J-P Laamanen | .10 | .05 |
| ❑ 58 Jouni Loponen | .10 | .05 |
| ❑ 59 Pekka Poikolainen | .10 | .05 |
| ❑ 60 Jan Latvala | .10 | .05 |
| ❑ 61 Timo Ahmaoja | .10 | .05 |
| ❑ 62 Mika Paananen | .10 | .05 |
| ❑ 63 Kimmo Salminen | .10 | .05 |
| ❑ 64 Lasse Jamsen | .10 | .05 |
| ❑ 65 Thomas Sjogren | .20 | .09 |
| ❑ 66 Juha Viinikainen | .10 | .05 |
| ❑ 67 Mikko Inkinen | .10 | .05 |
| ❑ 68 Toni Koivunen | .10 | .05 |
| ❑ 69 Pasi Kuivalainen | .35 | .16 |
| ❑ 70 Tommi Kovanen | .10 | .05 |
| ❑ 71 Jermu Pisto | .10 | .05 |
| ❑ 72 Ivan Vlzek | .10 | .05 |
| ❑ 73 Mika Laaksonen | .10 | .05 |
| ❑ 74 Miikka Ruokonen | .10 | .05 |
| ❑ 75 Sami Simonen | .10 | .05 |
| ❑ 76 Mikko Honkonen | .10 | .05 |
| ❑ 77 Veli-Pekka Nutikka | .75 | .35 |
| ❑ 78 Arto Sirvio | .10 | .05 |
| ❑ 79 Janne Kekalainen | .10 | .05 |
| ❑ 80 Jarno Levonen | .10 | .05 |
| ❑ 81 Jussi Tarvainen | .10 | .05 |
| ❑ 82 Iiro Itamies | .25 | .11 |
| ❑ 83 Tommi Nyyssonen | .10 | .05 |
| ❑ 84 Kari Haakana | .10 | .05 |
| ❑ 85 Jarmo Muukkonen | .10 | .05 |
| ❑ 86 Tero Nissinen | .10 | .05 |
| ❑ 87 Tero Tiainen | .10 | .05 |
| ❑ 88 Joonas Jaaskelainen | .10 | .05 |
| ❑ 89 Juha Ikonen | .10 | .05 |
| ❑ 90 Timo Norppa | .10 | .05 |
| ❑ 91 Teemu Riihijarvi | .75 | .35 |
| ❑ 92 Mikko Koivunoro | .10 | .05 |
| ❑ 93 Sergei Prjahin | .15 | .07 |
| ❑ 94 Timo Hirvonen | .10 | .05 |
| ❑ 95 Boris Rousson | .50 | .23 |
| ❑ 96 Kimmo Lotvonen | .10 | .05 |
| ❑ 97 Riku Kallioniemi | .10 | .05 |
| ❑ 98 Martti Jarventie | .10 | .05 |
| ❑ 99 Mikko Luovi | .20 | .09 |
| ❑ 100 Checklist (101-150) | .10 | .05 |
| ❑ 101 Kalle Sahlstedt | .25 | .11 |
| ❑ 102 Sakari Palsola | .10 | .05 |
| ❑ 103 Tommi Turunen | .10 | .05 |
| ❑ 104 Petri Latti | .10 | .05 |
| ❑ 105 Jonni Vauhkonen | .15 | .07 |
| ❑ 106 Veli-Pekka Ahonen | .10 | .05 |
| ❑ 107 Jari Torkki | .15 | .07 |
| ❑ 108 Jarkko Varvio | .15 | .07 |
| ❑ 109 Matti Viitakoski | .10 | .05 |
| ❑ 110 Mikko Myllykoski | .10 | .05 |
| ❑ 111 Petri Peronmaa | .10 | .05 |
| ❑ 112 Vesa Ruotsalainen | .10 | .05 |
| ❑ 113 Timo Lohko | .10 | .05 |
| ❑ 114 Simo Liukka | .10 | .05 |
| ❑ 115 Juha-Pekka Rinkinen | .10 | .05 |
| ❑ 116 Timo Makinen | .10 | .05 |
| ❑ 117 Marko Ek | .15 | .07 |
| ❑ 118 Matti Nevalainen | .10 | .05 |
| ❑ 119 Ari Santanen | .10 | .05 |
| ❑ 120 Jonas Hemming | .10 | .05 |
| ❑ 121 Mika Karapuu | .10 | .05 |
| ❑ 122 Ilpo Kauhanen | .50 | .23 |
| ❑ 123 Sami-Ville Salomaa | .10 | .05 |
| ❑ 124 Antti Rahkonen | .10 | .05 |
| ❑ 125 Harri Laurilla | .10 | .05 |
| ❑ 126 Sami Lehtonen | .10 | .05 |
| ❑ 127 Pasi Petrilainen | .10 | .05 |
| ❑ 128 Arto Kulmala | .10 | .05 |
| ❑ 129 Jarkko Nikander | .10 | .05 |
| ❑ 130 Timo Nurmberg | .10 | .05 |
| ❑ 131 Tuomas Reijonen | .10 | .05 |
| ❑ 132 Aleksander Barkov | .10 | .05 |
| ❑ 133 Mika Niittymaki | .10 | .05 |
| ❑ 134 Valeri Krykov | .10 | .05 |
| ❑ 135 Fredrik Norrena | .35 | .16 |
| ❑ 136 Mika Lehtinen | .10 | .05 |
| ❑ 137 Sami Salo | .10 | .05 |
| ❑ 138 Riku-Petteri Lehtonen | .10 | .05 |
| ❑ 139 Mikko Sokka | .10 | .05 |
| ❑ 140 Manu Laapas | .10 | .05 |
| ❑ 141 Hannes Hyvonen | .10 | .05 |
| ❑ 142 Miikka Rousu | .10 | .05 |
| ❑ 143 Simo Rouvali | .10 | .05 |
| ❑ 144 Tommi Miettinen | .10 | .05 |
| ❑ 145 Kimmo Rintanen | .35 | .16 |
| ❑ 146 Tomi Kallio | .35 | .16 |
| ❑ 147 Antti Aalto | .75 | .35 |
| ❑ 148 Miika Elomo | 1.00 | .45 |
| ❑ 149 Kari Takko | .50 | .23 |
| ❑ 150 Checklist (151-200) | .10 | .05 |
| ❑ 151 Tommi Rajamaki | .25 | .11 |
| ❑ 152 Pasi Peltonen | .10 | .05 |
| ❑ 153 Karri Kivi | .20 | .09 |
| ❑ 154 Jokke Heinanen | .10 | .05 |
| ❑ 155 Teppo Kivela | .10 | .05 |
| ❑ 156 Vesa Goman | .10 | .05 |
| ❑ 157 Pekka Virta | .10 | .05 |
| ❑ 158 Pasi Tuominen | .10 | .05 |
| ❑ 159 Timo Hakanen | .10 | .05 |
| ❑ 160 Jari Levonen | .10 | .05 |
| ❑ 161 Jari Korpisalo | .15 | .07 |
| ❑ 162 Timo Salonen | .10 | .05 |
| ❑ 163 Jokerit | .25 | .11 |
| ❑ 164 Jokerit | .10 | .05 |
| ❑ 165 Jokerit | .10 | .05 |
| ❑ 166 Jokerit | .10 | .05 |
| ❑ 167 Jokerit | .10 | .05 |
| ❑ 168 Jokerit | .10 | .05 |
| ❑ 169 Jokerit | .10 | .05 |
| ❑ 170 Jokerit | .10 | .05 |
| ❑ 171 Jokerit | .10 | .05 |
| ❑ 172 Jokerit | .10 | .05 |
| ❑ 173 Jokerit | .10 | .05 |
| ❑ 174 Jokerit | .10 | .05 |
| ❑ 175 Ari Sulander | .50 | .23 |
| ❑ 176 Joni Lehto | .15 | .07 |
| ❑ 177 Timo Jutila | .15 | .07 |
| ❑ 178 Mikko Peltola | .10 | .05 |
| ❑ 179 Juha Riihijarvi | .25 | .11 |
| ❑ 180 Petri Varis | .75 | .35 |
| ❑ 181 Boris Rousson | .50 | .23 |
| ❑ 182 Kimmo Timonen | .35 | .16 |
| ❑ 183 Mika Stromberg | .25 | .11 |
| ❑ 184 Jari Korpisalo | .15 | .07 |
| ❑ 185 Otakar Janecky | .25 | .11 |
| ❑ 186 Juha Lind | .50 | .23 |
| ❑ 187 Aarne Honkavaara | .50 | .23 |
| ❑ 188 Esko Niemi | .10 | .05 |
| ❑ 189 Raimo Kilpio | .10 | .05 |
| ❑ 190 Jarmo Wasama | .10 | .05 |
| ❑ 191 Lalli Partinen | .10 | .05 |
| ❑ 192 Urpo Ylonen | .25 | .11 |
| ❑ 193 Ilpo Koskela | .50 | .23 |
| ❑ 194 Jorma Vehmanen | .10 | .05 |
| ❑ 195 Pekka Marjamaki | .10 | .05 |
| ❑ 196 Veli-Pekka Ketola | .25 | .11 |
| ❑ 197 Matti Murto | .10 | .05 |
| ❑ 198 Juhani Tamminen | .25 | .11 |
| ❑ 199 Matti Hagman | .20 | .09 |
| ❑ 200 Mask CL | 1.00 | .45 |
| ❑ NNO Kari Takko-Super Bonus | 25.00 | 11.00 |
| ❑ NNO J.Riihijarvi-Golden Helmet | 25.00 | 11.00 |

## 1996-97 Finnish SISU Redline At The Gala

This set of inserts showcases the 1995-96 award winners from the SM-Liiga. The cards were randomly inserted at a rate of 1:6 packs. The card fronts display the players in the tuxedos accepting the awards, while the backs show the player in action.

| | MINT | NRMT |
|---|---|---|
| COMPLETE SET (8) | 30.00 | 13.50 |
| COMMON CARD (1-8) | 2.00 | .90 |
| ❑ 1 Petri Varis | 10.00 | 4.50 |
| ❑ 2 Juha Riihijarvi | 5.00 | 2.20 |
| ❑ 3 Waltteri Immonen | 2.00 | .90 |
| ❑ 4 Jani Hurme | 10.00 | 4.50 |
| ❑ 5 Pasi Kuivalainen | 5.00 | 2.20 |
| ❑ 6 Mika Stromberg | 2.00 | .90 |
| ❑ 7 Sakari Pietila | 2.00 | .90 |
| ❑ 8 Ari Sulander | 5.00 | 2.20 |

## 1996-97 Finnish SISU Redline Keeping It Green

This most difficult of the SISU inserts (1:60) features four top netminders in a set promoting environmental awareness, as well as keeping the light behind their nets from turning red.

| | MINT | NRMT |
|---|---|---|
| COMPLETE SET (4) | 100.00 | 45.00 |
| COMMON CARD (1-4) | 25.00 | 11.00 |
| ❑ 1 Ari Sulander | 25.00 | 11.00 |
| ❑ 2 Jani Hurme | 40.00 | 18.00 |
| ❑ 3 Boris Rousson | 25.00 | 11.00 |
| ❑ 4 Mika Pietila | 25.00 | 11.00 |

## 1996-97 Finnish SISU Redline Mighty Adversaries

This 9-card set with a two-front format was inserted at a rate of 1:8 packs. Each side featured either a forward or a goalie, with the ghosted image of the counterpart's face in the background. Each side also had text addressing their adversarial relationship.

| | MINT | NRMT |
|---|---|---|
| COMPLETE SET (9) | 40.00 | 18.00 |
| COMMON CARD (1-9) | 5.00 | 2.20 |
| ❑ 1 K.Takko/K.Rintanen | 5.00 | 2.20 |
| ❑ 2 B.Rousson/P.Saarela | 5.00 | 2.20 |
| ❑ 3 I.Kauhanen/A.Andrijevski | 5.00 | 2.20 |
| ❑ 4 A.Sulander/M.Kortelainen | 5.00 | 2.20 |
| ❑ 5 P.Kuivalainen/T.Sjogren | 5.00 | 2.20 |
| ❑ 6 V.Toskala/J.Ojanen | 5.00 | 2.20 |
| ❑ 7 F.Norrena/O.Janecky | 5.00 | 2.20 |
| ❑ 8 S.Lindfors/J.Korpisalo | 5.00 | 2.20 |
| ❑ 9 A.Siekkinen/J.Lindroos | 5.00 | 2.20 |

## 1996-97 Finnish SISU Redline Rookie Energy

This 9-card set features the top rookies from the SM-Liiga's 95-96 campaign. The cards were randomly inserted into packs at a rate of 1:6. The card fronts feature an image of the player over a colored sky highlighted by lightning bolts. The backs include a head shot as well as some text relating the player's fine season

| | MINT | NRMT |
|---|---|---|
| COMPLETE SET (9) | 60.00 | 27.00 |
| COMMON CARD (1-9) | 5.00 | 2.20 |
| ❑ 1 Jani Hurme | 20.00 | 9.00 |
| ❑ 2 Mikko Eloranta | 5.00 | 2.20 |
| ❑ 3 Sami Salo | 5.00 | 2.20 |
| ❑ 4 Tero Hamalainen | 5.00 | 2.20 |
| ❑ 5 Miika Elomo | 10.00 | 4.50 |
| ❑ 6 Mika Pietila | 8.00 | 3.60 |
| ❑ 7 Arto Kuki | 5.00 | 2.20 |
| ❑ 8 Vesa Toskala | 10.00 | 4.50 |
| ❑ 9 Miikka Rousu | 5.00 | 2.20 |

## 1996-97 Finnish SISU Redline Sledgehammers

These 9 cards were randomly inserted into packs at a rate of 1:6. The cards are essentially double-fronted, with both sides picturing the player in action, superimposed over a Sledgehammer logo.

| | MINT | NRMT |
|---|---|---|
| COMPLETE SET (9) | 25.00 | 11.00 |
| COMMON CARD (1-9) | 3.00 | 1.35 |
| ❑ 1 Hannu Henriksson | 3.00 | 1.35 |
| ❑ 2 Robert Nordmark | 3.00 | 1.35 |
| ❑ 3 Pasi Sormunen | 3.00 | 1.35 |
| ❑ 4 Tuomas Gronman | 3.00 | 1.35 |
| ❑ 5 Derek Mayer | 3.00 | 1.35 |
| ❑ 6 Toni Porkka | 3.00 | 1.35 |
| ❑ 7 Timo Peltomaa | 3.00 | 1.35 |
| ❑ 8 Iiro Jarvi | 3.00 | 1.35 |
| ❑ 9 Joni Lehto | 3.00 | 1.35 |

## 1994-95 French National Team

These standard-size cards were made available to fans at venues where the national team was appearing in France. The cards feature simulated action photography, surrounded by red, white and blue borders. The player's name is at the top of the card, while the words "Equipe de France 94-95" line the bottom. Card backs contain a color headshot, and international statistics. The cards are unnumbered and checklisted below in alphabetical order.

| | MINT | NRMT |
|---|---|---|
| COMPLETE SET (35) | 15.00 | 6.75 |
| COMMON CARD (1-35) | .50 | .23 |
| ❑ 1 Benjamin Agnel | .50 | .23 |
| ❑ 2 Richard Aimonetto | .50 | .23 |
| ❑ 3 Stephane Arcangeloni | .50 | .23 |
| ❑ 4 Mickael Babin | .50 | .23 |
| ❑ 5 Alain Beaule | .50 | .23 |
| ❑ 6 J. Francois Bonnard | .50 | .23 |
| ❑ 7 Arnaud Briand | .50 | .23 |
| ❑ 8 Karl DeWolf | .50 | .23 |
| ❑ 9 Serge Djelloul | .50 | .23 |
| ❑ 10 Roger Dube | .50 | .23 |
| ❑ 11 Patrick Dunn | .50 | .23 |
| ❑ 12 J. Christophe Filippin | .50 | .23 |
| ❑ 13 Michel Galarneau | .50 | .23 |
| ❑ 14 Gerald Guennelon | .50 | .23 |
| ❑ 15 Eric Lemarque | .50 | .23 |
| ❑ 16 J. Philippe Lemoine | .50 | .23 |
| ❑ 17 Fabrice LHenry | .75 | .35 |
| ❑ 18 Pierrick Maia | .50 | .23 |
| ❑ 19 Antoine Mindjimba | .75 | .35 |
| ❑ 20 Christophe Moyon | .50 | .23 |
| ❑ 21 Lionel Orsolini | .50 | .23 |
| ❑ 22 Franck Pajonkowski | .75 | .35 |
| ❑ 23 Denis Perez | .50 | .23 |
| ❑ 24 Eric Pinard | .50 | .23 |
| ❑ 25 Serge Poudrier | .75 | .35 |
| ❑ 26 Christian Pouget | .50 | .23 |
| ❑ 27 Pierre Pousse | .50 | .23 |
| ❑ 28 Antoine Richer | .50 | .23 |
| ❑ 29 Franck Saunier | .50 | .23 |
| ❑ 30 J. Marc Soghomonian | .50 | .23 |
| ❑ 31 Juhani Tamminen | .50 | .23 |
| ❑ 32 Michel Valliere | .75 | .35 |
| ❑ 33 Andre Vittenberg | .50 | .23 |
| ❑ 34 Steven Woodburn | .50 | .23 |
| ❑ 35 Petri Ylonen | 1.00 | .45 |

## 1994-95 German DEL Eishockey

This 440-card set of the German hockey league was produced (apparently) by International Hockey Archives. The cards feature an action photo on the front, with player and team name along the borders. The back contain a space for autographing, as well as another photo and player bio in German. The set includes NHL prospects Florian Keller and Jochen Hecht, as well as several ex-NHL players.

| | MINT | NRMT |
|---|---|---|
| COMPLETE SET (440) | 45.00 | 20.00 |
| COMMON CARD (1-440) | .10 | .05 |
| ❑ 1 Int'l Hockey Association | .10 | .05 |
| ❑ 2 DEL 1994/95 | .10 | .05 |
| ❑ 3 Season 1994-95 | .10 | .05 |
| ❑ 4 Augsburger Panther Team Card | .10 | .05 |
| ❑ 5 Gunnar Leidborg | .10 | .05 |
| ❑ 6 Gary Prior | .15 | .07 |
| ❑ 7 Scott Campbell | .10 | .05 |
| ❑ 8 Dieter Medicus | .10 | .05 |
| ❑ 9 Duanne Moeser | .10 | .05 |
| ❑ 10 Daniel Naud | .10 | .05 |
| ❑ 11 Andy Romer | .10 | .05 |
| ❑ 12 Thomas Groger | .10 | .05 |
| ❑ 13 Sven Zywitza | .10 | .05 |
| ❑ 14 Fritz Meyer | .10 | .05 |
| ❑ 15 Christian Curth | .10 | .05 |
| ❑ 16 Toni Krinner | .10 | .05 |
| ❑ 17 Patrik Pysz | .20 | .09 |
| ❑ 18 Heinrich Romer | .10 | .05 |

❑ 19 Ales Polcar .20 .09
❑ 20 Philip Kukuk .10 .05
❑ 21 Dietrich Adam .10 .05
❑ 22 Tim Schnobrich .10 .05
❑ 23 Tim Ferguson .10 .05
❑ 24 Robert Heidt .10 .05
❑ 25 Alfred Burkhard .10 .05
❑ 26 Charly Fliegauf .10 .05
❑ 27 Robert Paclik .10 .05
❑ 28 Stefan Mayer .10 .05
❑ 29 Reinhard Haider .10 .05
❑ 30 Dennis Schrapp .10 .05
❑ 31 Eisbaren Berlin Team Card .10 .05
❑ 32 Walter Jaroslav .10 .05
❑ 33 Klaus Schroder .10 .05
❑ 34 Andre Dietsch .10 .05
❑ 35 Juri Stumpf .10 .05
❑ 36 Torsten Deutscher .10 .05
❑ 37 Frank Kannewurf .10 .05
❑ 38 Thomas Graul .10 .05
❑ 39 Sven Felski .10 .05
❑ 40 Moritz Schmidt .10 .05
❑ 41 Marco Swibenko .10 .05
❑ 42 Holger Mix .10 .05
❑ 43 Jiri Dopita .20 .09
❑ 44 Dirk Perschau .10 .05
❑ 45 Guido Hiller .10 .05
❑ 46 Daniel Held .10 .05
❑ 47 Richard Zemlicka .20 .09
❑ 48 Jan Schertz .10 .05
❑ 49 Mike Losch .10 .05
❑ 50 Patrick Solf .10 .05
❑ 51 Rupert Meister .10 .05
❑ 52 BSC Preussen Team Card .10 .05
❑ 53 Billy Flynn .20 .09
❑ 54 Tony Tanti .35 .16
❑ 55 Jochen Molling .10 .05
❑ 56 Andreas Schubert .10 .05
❑ 57 Stefan Steinecker .10 .05
❑ 58 Josef Lehner .10 .05
❑ 59 Tom O'Regan .20 .09
❑ 60 Gaetan Malo .10 .05
❑ 61 Michael Komma .10 .05
❑ 62 Marco Schinko .10 .05
❑ 63 Marco Rentzsch .10 .05
❑ 64 Georg Holzmann .10 .05
❑ 65 Mark Kosturik .10 .05
❑ 66 Jurgen Rumrich .10 .05
❑ 67 John Chabot .25 .11
❑ 68 Harald Windler .10 .05
❑ 69 Mark Teevens .10 .05
❑ 70 Klaus Merk .75 .35
❑ 71 Stephan Sinner .10 .05
❑ 72 Mark Gronau .10 .05
❑ 73 Bruce Hardy .10 .05
❑ 74 Fabian Brannstrom .10 .05
❑ 75 Daniel Poudrier .20 .09
❑ 76 Dusseldorfer EG Team Card .10 .05
❑ 77 Hans Zach .10 .05
❑ 78 Helmut DeRaaf .25 .11
❑ 79 Markus Kehle .10 .05
❑ 80 Christian Schmitz .10 .05
❑ 81 Lorenz Funk .10 .05
❑ 82 Chris Valentine .25 .11
❑ 83 Rafael Jedamzik .10 .05
❑ 84 Torsten Kienass .50 .23
❑ 85 Christopher Kreutzer .10 .05
❑ 86 Benoit Doucet .25 .11
❑ 87 Bernd Kuhnhauser .10 .05
❑ 88 Andreas Niederberger .10 .05
❑ 89 Rick Amann .10 .05
❑ 90 Thorsten Van Leyen .10 .05
❑ 91 Bruce Eakin .15 .07
❑ 92 Pierre Rioux .10 .05
❑ 93 Andreas Brockmann .15 .07
❑ 94 Uli Hiemer .25 .11
❑ 95 Bernd Truntschka .25 .11
❑ 96 Wolfgang Kummer .10 .05
❑ 97 Carsten Gossmann .10 .05
❑ 98 Ernst Kopf .20 .09
❑ 99 Robert Sterflinger .10 .05
❑ 100 Kevin LaVallee .20 .09
❑ 101 Rainer Zerwesz .10 .05
❑ 102 Frankfurt Lions Team Card .10 .05
❑ 103 Pjotr Vorobjev .15 .07
❑ 104 Peter Obresa .10 .05
❑ 105 Vladimir Quapp .10 .05
❑ 106 Florian Storf .10 .05
❑ 107 Alexander Wedl .10 .05
❑ 108 Olaf Scholz .10 .05
❑ 109 Ilya Vorobjev .10 .05
❑ 110 Ladislav Strompf .10 .05
❑ 111 Udo Dohler .10 .05
❑ 112 Alexander Wunsch .10 .05
❑ 113 Jiri Lala .20 .09
❑ 114 Andrej Jaufmann .10 .05
❑ 115 Thomas Muhlbauer .10 .05
❑ 116 Markus Kempf .10 .05
❑ 117 Igor Schultz .10 .05
❑ 118 Martin Schultz .10 .05
❑ 119 Michael Raubal .10 .05
❑ 120 Rudi Gorgenlander .10 .05
❑ 121 Jurgen Schaal .10 .05
❑ 122 Patrick Vozar .10 .05
❑ 123 Rochus Schneider .10 .05
❑ 124 Toni Raubal .10 .05
❑ 125 Stefan Koniger .10 .05
❑ 126 EC Hannover Team Card .10 .05
❑ 127 Hartmut Nickel .10 .05
❑ 128 Joachim Lempio .10 .05
❑ 129 Torsten Hanusch .10 .05
❑ 130 Thomas Jungwirth .10 .05
❑ 131 David Reierson .10 .05
❑ 132 Friedhelm Bogelsack .10 .05
❑ 133 Thomas Werner .10 .05
❑ 134 Dirk Rohrbach .10 .05
❑ 135 Harald Kuhnke .10 .05
❑ 136 Florian Funk .10 .05
❑ 137 Mark Maroste .10 .05
❑ 138 Anton Maidl .10 .05
❑ 139 Rene Reuter .10 .05
❑ 140 Rene Ledock .10 .05
❑ 141 Marco Herbst .10 .05
❑ 142 Milos Vanik .10 .05
❑ 143 Gunther Preuss .10 .05
❑ 144 Troy Tumbach .10 .05
❑ 145 Marc Wittbrock .10 .05
❑ 146 Roger Mede .10 .05
❑ 147 Craig Topolnisky .10 .05
❑ 148 Josef Schlickenrieder .10 .05
❑ 149 Marcus Bleicher .10 .05
❑ 150 EC Kassel Team Card .10 .05
❑ 151 Ross Yates .10 .05
❑ 152 Josef Kontny .10 .05
❑ 153 Milan Mokros .10 .05
❑ 154 Alexander Engel .10 .05
❑ 155 Greg Johnston .25 .11
❑ 156 Jedrzej Kasperczyk .10 .05
❑ 157 Dave Morrison .10 .05
❑ 158 Jaro Mucha .10 .05
❑ 159 Mike Millar .20 .09
❑ 160 Ireneusz Pacula .10 .05
❑ 161 Vitalij Grossmann .10 .05
❑ 162 Murray McIntosh .10 .05
❑ 163 Manfred Ahne .10 .05
❑ 164 Peter Kwasigroch .10 .05
❑ 165 Georg Guttler .10 .05
❑ 166 Falk Ozellis .10 .05
❑ 167 Mario Naster .10 .05
❑ 168 Sergej Wikulow .10 .05
❑ 169 Gerhard Hegen .10 .05
❑ 170 Brian Hannon .10 .05
❑ 171 Tino Boos .10 .05
❑ 172 Kaufbeurer Adler Team Card .10 .05
❑ 173 Peter Kathan .10 .05
❑ 174 Kenneth Karpuk .10 .05
❑ 175 Michael Olbrich .10 .05
❑ 176 Drahomir Kadlec .20 .09
❑ 177 Christian Seeberger .10 .05
❑ 178 Elmar Boiger .10 .05
❑ 179 Oto Hascak .25 .11
❑ 180 Thorsten Rau .10 .05
❑ 181 Tomas Martinec .10 .05
❑ 182 Norbert Zabel .10 .05
❑ 183 Daniel Kunce .10 .05
❑ 184 Hans-Jorg Mayer .20 .09
❑ 185 Manfred Jorde .10 .05
❑ 186 Roland Timoschuk .10 .05
❑ 187 Jim Hoffmann .10 .05
❑ 188 Andreas Volland .10 .05
❑ 189 Rolf Hammer .10 .05
❑ 190 Manuel Hess .10 .05
❑ 191 Timo Gschwill .10 .05
❑ 192 Marc Pethke .10 .05
❑ 193 Axel Kammerer .10 .05
❑ 194 Jurgen Simon .10 .05
❑ 195 Patrick Lange .10 .05
❑ 196 Ronny Martin .10 .05
❑ 197 Kolner EC Team Card .10 .05
❑ 198 Vladimir Vassiliev .10 .05
❑ 199 Bernd Haake .10 .05
❑ 200 Joseph Heiss 1.00 .45
❑ 201 Jorg Mayr .20 .09
❑ 202 Thomas Brandl .25 .11
❑ 203 Stephan Mann .10 .05
❑ 204 Tonny Reddo .10 .05
❑ 205 Mirco Ludemann .25 .11
❑ 206 Leo Stefan .25 .11
❑ 207 Andreas Pokorny .10 .05
❑ 208 Peter Draisaitl .35 .16
❑ 209 Ralf Dobrzynski .10 .05
❑ 210 Andreas Lupzig .20 .09
❑ 211 Karsten Mende .10 .05
❑ 212 Frank Hohenadl .10 .05
❑ 213 Marco Heinrichs .10 .05
❑ 214 Michael Rumrich .10 .05
❑ 215 Martin Ondrejka .10 .05
❑ 216 Herbert Hohenberger .25 .11
❑ 217 Thorsten Sendt .10 .05
❑ 218 Thorsten Koslowski .10 .05
❑ 219 Olaf Grundmann .10 .05
❑ 220 Franz Demmel .10 .05
❑ 221 Sergej Berezin 5.00 2.20
❑ 222 Krefelder EV Team Card .10 .05
❑ 223 Michael Zettel .10 .05
❑ 224 Frank Brunsing .10 .05
❑ 225 Karel Lang .10 .05
❑ 226 Markus Kranwinkel .10 .05
❑ 227 Earl Spry .10 .05
❑ 228 Andre Grein .10 .05
❑ 229 Greg Evtushevski .15 .07
❑ 230 Herberts Vasiljevs .10 .05
❑ 231 Ken Petrash .10 .05
❑ 232 Greg Thomson .10 .05
❑ 233 Reemt Pyka .35 .16
❑ 234 Brad Bergen .10 .05
❑ 235 Chris Lindberg .25 .11
❑ 236 Markus Kranwinkel .10 .05
❑ 237 Martin Gebel .10 .05
❑ 238 Francois Sills .10 .05
❑ 239 Klaus Micheller .10 .05
❑ 240 Peter Ihnacak .25 .11
❑ 241 Marek Stebnicki .10 .05
❑ 242 Johnny Walker .10 .05
❑ 243 Gunter Oswald .10 .05
❑ 244 James Hanlon .10 .05
❑ 245 Rene Bielke .10 .05
❑ 246 EV Landshut Team Card .10 .05
❑ 247 Bernhard Johnston .10 .05
❑ 248 Mark Stuckey .10 .05
❑ 249 Michael Bresagk .10 .05
❑ 250 Bernd Wagner .10 .05
❑ 251 Eduard Uvria .10 .05
❑ 252 Mike Smazal .10 .05
❑ 253 Jacek Plachta .10 .05
❑ 254 Georg Franz .10 .05
❑ 255 Stephan Retzer .10 .05
❑ 256 Henri Marcoux .10 .05
❑ 257 Andreas Loth .10 .05
❑ 258 Mike Bullard .50 .23
❑ 259 Markus Berwanger .10 .05
❑ 260 Petr Briza 1.50 .70
❑ 261 Wally Schreiber .50 .23
❑ 262 Peter Gulda .10 .05
❑ 263 Ralf Hantschke .10 .05
❑ 264 Steve McNeil .10 .05
❑ 265 Christian Kunast .10 .05
❑ 266 Jorg Hendrick .10 .05
❑ 267 Helmut Steiger .10 .05
❑ 268 Udo Kiessling .35 .16
❑ 269 Mike Lay .25 .11
❑ 270 Adler Mannheim Team Card .10 .05
❑ 271 Lance Nethery .25 .11
❑ 272 Marcus Kuhl .10 .05
❑ 273 Joachim Appel .10 .05
❑ 274 Harold Kreis .10 .05
❑ 275 Mike Heidt .25 .11
❑ 276 Mario Gehrig .10 .05
❑ 277 Pavel Gross .25 .11
❑ 278 Steffen Michel .10 .05
❑ 279 Daniel Korber .10 .05
❑ 280 Robert Cimetta .25 .11
❑ 281 Dale Krentz .25 .11
❑ 282 Jochen Hecht 4.00 1.80
❑ 283 Till Feser .10 .05
❑ 284 Lars Bruggemann .10 .05
❑ 285 Toni Plattner .10 .05
❑ 286 Alexander Schuster .10 .05
❑ 287 Dieter Willmann .10 .05
❑ 288 Markus Flemming .10 .05
❑ 289 Rick Goldmann .10 .05
❑ 290 Damian Adamus .10 .05
❑ 291 Frederik Ledlin .10 .05
❑ 292 David Musial .10 .05
❑ 293 Michael Gabler .10 .05
❑ 294 Sven Valenti .10 .05
❑ 295 Maddogs Munchen Team Card .10 .05
❑ 296 Robert Murdoch .25 .11
❑ 297 Alexander Genze .10 .05
❑ 298 Greg Muller .10 .05
❑ 299 Mike Schmidt .10 .05
❑ 300 Zdenek Travnicek .10 .05
❑ 301 Christian Lukes .10 .05
❑ 302 Gordon Sherven .25 .11
❑ 303 Anthony Vogel .10 .05
❑ 304 Michael Hreuss .10 .05
❑ 305 Dale Derkatch .25 .11
❑ 306 Sergej Schendelew .25 .11
❑ 307 Christian Brittig .10 .05
❑ 308 Harald Waibel .10 .05
❑ 309 Rainer Lutz .10 .05
❑ 310 Ewald Steiger .10 .05
❑ 311 Didi Hegen .50 .23
❑ 312 Ralf Reisinger .10 .05
❑ 313 Henrik Holscher .10 .05
❑ 314 Karl Friesen .50 .23
❑ 315 Christian Frutel .10 .05
❑ 316 Tobias Abstreiter .10 .05
❑ 317 Christopher Sandner .10 .05
❑ 318 Harald Birk .10 .05
❑ 319 Chris Strausse .10 .05
❑ 320 EHC 80 Nurnberg Team Card .10 .05
❑ 321 Josef Golonka .25 .11
❑ 322 Christian Gerum .10 .05
❑ 323 Paul Geddes .10 .05
❑ 324 Ian Young .10 .05
❑ 325 Stefan Steinbock .10 .05
❑ 326 Doug Irwin .10 .05
❑ 327 Christian Flugge .10 .05
❑ 328 Klaus Birk .10 .05
❑ 329 Jurgen Lechl .10 .05
❑ 330 Thomas Popiesch .10 .05
❑ 331 Miroslav Maly .10 .05
❑ 332 Stephan Eder .10 .05
❑ 333 Arno Brux .10 .05
❑ 334 Jiri Dolezal .25 .11
❑ 335 Reiner Vorderbruggen .10 .05
❑ 336 Thomas Sterflinger .10 .05
❑ 337 Bernhard Engelbrecht .10 .05
❑ 338 Michael Weinfurther .10 .05
❑ 339 Sepp Wassermann .10 .05
❑ 340 Stephan Bauer .10 .05
❑ 341 Otto Sykora .10 .05
❑ 342 Ratingen Die Lowen Team Card .10 .05
❑ 343 Bill Lochead .25 .11
❑ 344 Pavel Mann .10 .05
❑ 345 Christian Kohmann .10 .05
❑ 346 Sven Prusa .10 .05
❑ 347 Otto Keresztes .10 .05
❑ 348 Frank Kovacs .10 .05
❑ 349 Jiri Smicek .10 .05
❑ 350 Richard Brodnicke .10 .05
❑ 351 Andrej Fuchs .10 .05
❑ 352 Oliver Kasper .10 .05
❑ 353 Michael Kratz .10 .05
❑ 354 Klaus Striemitzer .10 .05
❑ 355 Oliver Schwarz .10 .05
❑ 356 Boris Fuchs .10 .05
❑ 357 Christian Althoff .10 .05
❑ 358 Waldemar Novosjolov .10 .05
❑ 359 Thomas Imdahl .10 .05
❑ 360 Helmut Elters .10 .05
❑ 361 Andrej Hanisz .10 .05
❑ 362 Peter Lutter .10 .05
❑ 363 Martem Janov .10 .05
❑ 364 Mark Bassen .10 .05
❑ 365 Udo Schmid .10 .05
❑ 366 Mark Bassen .10 .05
❑ 367 Rosenheim Star Bulls Team Card .10 .05
❑ 368 Ernst Hofner .10 .05
❑ 369 Ludek Bukac .20 .09
❑ 370 Markus Wieland .10 .05
❑ 371 Andreas Schneider .10 .05
❑ 372 Raphael Kruger .10 .05
❑ 373 Michael Tattner .10 .05
❑ 374 Rick Boehm .10 .05
❑ 375 Robert Hock .10 .05
❑ 376 Joachim Reil .10 .05
❑ 377 Radek Toupal .20 .09
❑ 378 Martin Reichel .20 .09
❑ 379 Ron Fischer .10 .05
❑ 380 Raimund Hilger .25 .11
❑ 381 Petr Hrbek .25 .11
❑ 382 Oliver Hausler .10 .05
❑ 383 Christian Gegenfurther .10 .05
❑ 384 Marc Seliger .50 .23
❑ 385 Venci Sebek .10 .05
❑ 386 Florian Keller 2.50 1.10
❑ 387 Heinrich Schiffl .10 .05
❑ 388 Michael Pohl .10 .05
❑ 389 Fuchse Sachsen Team Card .10 .05
❑ 390 Jiri Kochta .10 .05
❑ 391 Boris Capla .10 .05
❑ 392 Matthias Kliemann .10 .05
❑ 393 Josef Rednicek .10 .05
❑ 394 Branjo Heisig .10 .05
❑ 395 Jens Schwabe .75 .35
❑ 396 Frank Peschke .10 .05
❑ 397 Thomas Schubert .10 .05
❑ 398 Torsten Eisebitt .10 .05
❑ 399 Marcel Lichnovsky .10 .05
❑ 400 Jari Gronstrand .35 .16
❑ 401 Thomas Knobloch .10 .05
❑ 402 Falk Herzig .10 .05
❑ 403 Thomas Wagner .10 .05
❑ 404 Jan Tabor .25 .11
❑ 405 Sebastian Klenner .10 .05
❑ 406 Peter Hofmann .10 .05
❑ 407 Terry Cambell .10 .05
❑ 408 Antonio Fonso .10 .05
❑ 409 Thomas Bresagk .10 .05
❑ 410 Peter Franke .10 .05
❑ 411 Andreas Ott .10 .05
❑ 412 Michael Flemming .10 .05
❑ 413 Janusz Janikowski .10 .05
❑ 414 Schwenningen Wild Wings Team Card .10 .05
❑ 415 Miroslav Berek .10 .05
❑ 416 Bob Burns .10 .05
❑ 417 Thomas Gaus .10 .05
❑ 418 Richard Trojan .10 .05
❑ 419 Ilmar Toman .10 .05
❑ 420 Alan Young .10 .05
❑ 421 Michael Pastika .10 .05
❑ 422 Thomas Schadler .10 .05
❑ 423 Andrei Kovalev .25 .11
❑ 424 Alexander Horn .10 .05
❑ 425 Petr Kopta .10 .05
❑ 426 Robert Brezina .10 .05
❑ 427 Wayne Hynes .10 .05
❑ 428 Frantisek Frosch .10 .05
❑ 429 Carsten Solbach .10 .05
❑ 430 George Fritz .10 .05
❑ 431 Mike Bader .10 .05
❑ 432 Thomas Deiter .10 .05
❑ 433 Daniel Nowak .10 .05
❑ 434 Peter Heinold .10 .05
❑ 435 Matthias Hoppe .10 .05
❑ 436 Grant Martin .10 .05
❑ 437 Roger Bruns .10 .05
❑ 438 Andreas Renz .10 .05
❑ 439 Karsten Schulz .10 .05
❑ 440 Alfie Turcotte .15 .07

## 1995-96 German DEL Eishockey

This 450-card set features the players of Germany's top hockey division, the DEL. The cards measure the standard size, and were issued in six-card packs for 2.5 marks. The card fronts feature action photography with the player name, position and team logo along the bottom. The back includes another photo along with stats. The set is highlighted by the inclusion of several NHLers who played in the DEL during the 1994 lockout including Pavel Bure, Jeremy Roenick and Brendan Shanahan. The hologram chase card was randomly inserted in 1:375 packs. A collector's album to house the cards was available through a wrapper offer for 45 marks.

| | MINT | NRMT |
|---|---|---|
| COMPLETE SET (450) | 90.00 | 40.00 |
| COMMON CARD (1-450) | .10 | .05 |

❑ 1 Gary Prior .15 .07
❑ 2 Rupert Meister .10 .05
❑ 3 Dennis Schrapp .10 .05
❑ 4 Scott Campbell .10 .05
❑ 5 Fritz Meyer .10 .05
❑ 6 Rob Mendel .10 .05
❑ 7 Ken Collins .15 .07
❑ 8 Stefan Mayer .10 .05
❑ 9 Torsten Fendt .10 .05
❑ 10 Andrei Skopintsev .35 .16
❑ 11 Bob Wilkie .10 .05
❑ 12 Duanne Moeser .10 .05
❑ 13 M. Nagler .10 .05
❑ 14 Sven Zywitza .10 .05
❑ 15 Marc Habscheid .25 .11
❑ 16 Daniel Held .10 .05
❑ 17 Heinrich Romer .10 .05
❑ 18 R. Laycock .10 .05
❑ 19 R. Francz .10 .05
❑ 20 Tim Ferguson .10 .05
❑ 21 Robert Heidt .15 .07
❑ 22 E. Dylla .10 .05
❑ 23 Harald Birk .10 .05
❑ 24 Rochus Schneider .10 .05
❑ 25 Billy Flynn .10 .05
❑ 26 Andre Dietsch .10 .05
❑ 27 Udo Dohler .10 .05
❑ 28 Juri Stumpf .10 .05
❑ 29 Torsten Deutscher .10 .05
❑ 30 Frank Kannewurf .10 .05
❑ 31 Thomas Graul .10 .05
❑ 32 Dirk Perschau .10 .05
❑ 33 Patrick Solf .10 .05
❑ 34 Daniel Poudrier .10 .05
❑ 35 B. Kaminski .10 .05
❑ 36 C. Hadraschek .10 .05
❑ 37 Sven Felski .10 .05
❑ 38 Marco Swibenko .10 .05
❑ 39 Holger Mix .10 .05
❑ 40 Mark Maroste .10 .05
❑ 41 Troy Tumbach .10 .05
❑ 42 Jan Schertz .10 .05
❑ 43 Mike Losch .10 .05
❑ 44 A. Naumann .15 .07
❑ 45 M. Garthe .10 .05
❑ 46 I. Dorochin .10 .05
❑ 47 T. Mitew .10 .05
❑ 48 C. Lundmark .10 .05
❑ 49 Chris Panek .10 .05
❑ 50 Klaus Merk .75 .35
❑ 51 Mark Gronau .10 .05
❑ 52 Stefan Steinecker .10 .05
❑ 53 Josef Lehner .10 .05
❑ 54 Tom O'Regan .15 .07
❑ 55 Fredrik Stillmann .10 .05
❑ 56 Marco Rentzsch .10 .05
❑ 57 Stephan Sinner .10 .05
❑ 58 Andreas Schubert .15 .07
❑ 59 Tony Tanti .35 .16
❑ 60 Gaeten Malo .10 .05
❑ 61 Michael Komma .10 .05
❑ 62 Thomas Schinko .10 .05
❑ 63 Georg Holzmann .10 .05
❑ 64 Mark Kosturik .10 .05
❑ 65 Christian Brittig .10 .05
❑ 66 Jurgen Rumrich .10 .05
❑ 67 John Chabot .25 .11
❑ 68 Andreas Dimbat .10 .05
❑ 69 Ulrich Liebsch .10 .05
❑ 70 Mark Teevens .20 .09
❑ 71 Fabian Brannstom .10 .05
❑ 72 D. Meyer .10 .05
❑ 73 L. Hoffmann .10 .05
❑ 74 Hardy Nilsson CO .10 .05
❑ 75 Marcus Karlsson .10 .05
❑ 76 Helmut deRaaf .25 .11
❑ 77 Kai Fischer .75 .35
❑ 78 Carsten Gossmann .10 .05
❑ 79 Torsten Kienass .25 .11
❑ 80 Christopher Kreutzer .10 .05
❑ 81 Brad Bergen .10 .05
❑ 82 Andreas Niederberger .15 .07
❑ 83 Rick Amann .10 .05
❑ 84 Uli Hiemer .20 .09
❑ 85 Sergei Sorokin .15 .07
❑ 86 Robert Sterflinger .10 .05
❑ 87 Lorenz Funk .10 .05
❑ 88 Chris Valentine .15 .07
❑ 89 Gord Sherven .15 .07
❑ 90 Boris Lingemann .10 .05
❑ 91 Benoit Doucet .25 .11
❑ 92 Bernd Kuhnhauser .10 .05
❑ 93 Bruce Eakin .15 .07
❑ 94 Dieter Hegen .50 .23
❑ 95 Andreas Brockmann .10 .05
❑ 96 Bernd Truntschka .25 .11
❑ 97 Wolfgang Kummer .10 .05
❑ 98 Mikko Makela .25 .11
❑ 99 Nikolaus Mondt .10 .05
❑ 100 Piotr Vorobjew .15 .07
❑ 101 Peter Obresa .10 .05
❑ 102 Thierry Mayer .10 .05
❑ 103 Marc Seliger .35 .16
❑ 104 Florian Storf .10 .05
❑ 105 Ladislav Strompf .10 .05
❑ 106 Greg Thompson .10 .05
❑ 107 Sergei Schendelev .10 .05
❑ 108 M. Duris .10 .05
❑ 109 R. Gorgenlander .10 .05
❑ 110 A. Raubal .10 .05
❑ 111 Stephan Ziesche .15 .07
❑ 112 Petr Kopta .10 .05
❑ 113 Thomas Popiesch .10 .05
❑ 114 Francois Sills .10 .05
❑ 115 Jiri Lala .15 .07
❑ 116 Robert Reichel 1.50 .70
❑ 117 Markus Kempf .10 .05
❑ 118 Igor Schultz .10 .05
❑ 119 Martin Schultz .10 .05
❑ 120 Brian Hannon .10 .05
❑ 121 Jurgen Schaal .10 .05
❑ 122 Patrick Vozar .10 .05
❑ 123 Ron Kennedy .10 .05
❑ 124 Friedhelm Bogelsack .15 .07
❑ 125 Marco Herbst .10 .05
❑ 126 Josef Schlickenrieder .10 .05
❑ 127 Torsten Hanusch .10 .05

❑ 128 Thomas Jungwirth .10 .05
❑ 129 David Reierson .10 .05
❑ 130 Christian Curth .10 .05
❑ 131 Anton Maidl .10 .05
❑ 132 Marc Wittbrock .10 .05
❑ 133 Brad Schlegel .25 .11
❑ 134 Thomas Werner .10 .05
❑ 135 Dirk Rohrbach .10 .05
❑ 136 Bruce Hardy .10 .05
❑ 137 Harald Kuhnke .10 .05
❑ 138 Florian Funk .10 .05
❑ 139 Rene Reuter .10 .05
❑ 140 Milos Vanik .10 .05
❑ 141 Gunther Preuss .10 .05
❑ 142 Kevin LaVallee .20 .09
❑ 143 Marcus Bleicher .10 .05
❑ 144 Anton Krinner .10 .05
❑ 145 Harald Waibel .10 .05
❑ 146 Hans Zach .10 .05
❑ 147 Josef Kontny .10 .05
❑ 148 Gerhard Hegen .10 .05
❑ 149 Milan Mokros .10 .05
❑ 150 Venci Sebek .10 .05
❑ 151 Alexander Engel .10 .05
❑ 152 Alexander Wedl .10 .05
❑ 153 Jaro Mucha .10 .05
❑ 154 Murray McIntosh .10 .05
❑ 155 Georg Guttler .10 .05
❑ 156 Greg Johnston .20 .09
❑ 157 Jederzej Kaspercyk .10 .05
❑ 158 Dave Morrison .10 .05
❑ 159 Mike Millar .20 .09
❑ 160 Ireneusz Pacula .10 .05
❑ 161 Vitalij Grossmann .10 .05
❑ 162 I. Varitsky .10 .05
❑ 163 Peter Kwasigroch .10 .05
❑ 164 Branjo Heisig .10 .05
❑ 165 Greg Evtushevski .15 .07
❑ 166 Falk Ozellis .10 .05
❑ 167 Tino Boos .10 .05
❑ 168 J. Tolvanen .10 .05
❑ 169 Dieter Medicus .10 .05
❑ 170 Michael Olbrich .10 .05
❑ 171 Marc Pethke .10 .05
❑ 172 Drahomir Kadlec .20 .09
❑ 173 Christian Seeberger .10 .05
❑ 174 G. Kunce .10 .05
❑ 175 Daniel Kunce .10 .05
❑ 176 Timo Gschwill .10 .05
❑ 177 M. Eltner .10 .05
❑ 178 Jurgen Simon .10 .05
❑ 179 A. Herbst .10 .05
❑ 180 Elmar Boiger .10 .05
❑ 181 Otto Hascak .25 .11
❑ 182 Tim Schnobrich .10 .05
❑ 183 Anthony Vogel .10 .05
❑ 184 Tomas Martinec .10 .05
❑ 185 Hans-Jorg Mayer .15 .07
❑ 186 Roland Timoschuk .10 .05
❑ 187 Jim Hoffmann .10 .05
❑ 188 Andreas Volland .10 .05
❑ 189 Rolf Hammer .10 .05
❑ 190 Manuel Hess .10 .05
❑ 191 Dale Derkatch .15 .07
❑ 192 S. Schwele .10 .05
❑ 193 Bob Murdoch .25 .11
❑ 194 Bernd Haake .10 .05
❑ 195 Joseph Heiss 1.00 .45
❑ 196 Olaf Grundmann .10 .05
❑ 197 Alexander Genze .10 .05
❑ 198 A. von Trzcinski .10 .05
❑ 199 Jorg Mayr .15 .07
❑ 200 Mirco Ludemann .25 .11
❑ 201 Andreas Pokorny .10 .05
❑ 202 Jayson Meyer .10 .05
❑ 203 Karsten Mende .10 .05
❑ 204 Herbert Hohenberger .15 .07
❑ 205 Thomas Brandt .10 .05
❑ 206 Stefan Mann .10 .05
❑ 207 Luciano Borsato .25 .11
❑ 208 Leo Stefan .25 .11
❑ 209 Peter Draisaitl .35 .16
❑ 210 Andreas Lupzig .25 .11
❑ 211 Ralf Reisinger .10 .05
❑ 212 Rainer Zerwesz .10 .05
❑ 213 Michael Rumrich .10 .05
❑ 214 Martin Ondrejka .10 .05
❑ 215 Tobias Abstreiter .10 .05
❑ 216 Franz Demmel .10 .05
❑ 217 Sergei Berezin 5.00 2.20
❑ 218 Miroslav Berek CO .10 .05
❑ 219 Karel Lang .10 .05
❑ 220 Rene Bieike .10 .05
❑ 221 Markus Krawinkel .10 .05
❑ 222 Kenneth Karpuk .10 .05
❑ 223 Klaus Micheller .10 .05
❑ 224 Earl Spry .10 .05
❑ 225 Andreas Ott .10 .05
❑ 226 Petri Limatainen .10 .05
❑ 227 Andre Grein .10 .05
❑ 228 Ken Petrash .10 .05
❑ 229 James Hanlon .10 .05
❑ 230 Reemt Pyka .25 .11
❑ 231 Thomas Imdahl .10 .05
❑ 232 Chris Lindberg .25 .11
❑ 233 J. Luknovsky .10 .05
❑ 234 Peter Ihnacak .25 .11
❑ 235 Marek Stebnicki .10 .05
❑ 236 Johnny Walker .10 .05
❑ 237 Arno Brux .10 .05
❑ 238 R. Busch .10 .05
❑ 239 Mark Bassen .10 .05
❑ 240 Martin Gebel .10 .05
❑ 241 Bernhard Johnston .10 .05
❑ 242 Petr Briza 1.00 .45
❑ 243 Christian Kunast .10 .05
❑ 244 Michael Bresagk .10 .05
❑ 245 Eduard Uvria .10 .05
❑ 246 Michael Heidt .10 .05
❑ 247 Peter Gulda .10 .05
❑ 248 Udo Kiessling .25 .11
❑ 249 Dieter Bloem .10 .05
❑ 250 Tony Vogl .10 .05
❑ 251 Jacek Plachta .10 .05
❑ 252 Georg Franz .10 .05
❑ 253 Stephan Retzer .10 .05
❑ 254 Henri Marcoux .10 .05
❑ 255 Andreas Loth .10 .05
❑ 256 Mike Bullard .35 .16
❑ 257 Jose Charbonneau .25 .11
❑ 258 Wally Schreiber .25 .11
❑ 259 Jorg Handrick .10 .05
❑ 260 Holger Steiger .10 .05
❑ 261 Marco Sturm 3.00 1.35
❑ 262 Lance Nethery .15 .07
❑ 263 Marcus Kuhl .10 .05
❑ 264 Joachim Appel .10 .05
❑ 265 Markus Flemming .15 .07
❑ 266 Harold Kreis .10 .05
❑ 267 Paul Stanton .25 .11
❑ 268 Christian Lukes .10 .05
❑ 269 Steffen Michel .10 .05
❑ 270 Stephane J.G. Richer .15 .07
❑ 271 Jorg Hanft .10 .05
❑ 272 Erich Goldmann .10 .05
❑ 273 Mario Gehrig .10 .05
❑ 274 Pavel Gross .10 .05
❑ 275 Daniel Korber .10 .05
❑ 276 Rob Cimetta .25 .11
❑ 277 Jochen Hecht 3.00 1.35
❑ 278 Till Feser .10 .05
❑ 279 Alexander Serikow 3.00 1.35
❑ 280 Patrik Pysz .20 .09
❑ 281 Darian Adamus .10 .05
❑ 282 David Musial .10 .05
❑ 283 Michael Hreus .10 .05
❑ 284 Chris Strausse .10 .05
❑ 285 Sven Valenti .10 .05
❑ 286 Sebastien Thivierge .10 .05
❑ 287 Jan Eysselt CO .10 .05
❑ 288 R. Neubauer .10 .05
❑ 289 Roman Turek 5.00 2.20
❑ 290 Stefan Lahn .10 .05
❑ 291 Christian Gerum .10 .05
❑ 292 Heiko Smazal .10 .05
❑ 293 Miroslav Maly .10 .05
❑ 294 Thomas Sterflinger .10 .05
❑ 295 M. Weinfurter .10 .05
❑ 296 Stephan Bauer .10 .05
❑ 297 Lars Bruggemann .10 .05
❑ 298 Markus Kehle .10 .05
❑ 299 Paul Geddes .10 .05
❑ 300 Ian Young .10 .05
❑ 301 Stefan Steinbock .10 .05
❑ 302 Jurgen Lechl .10 .05
❑ 303 M. Goerlitz .10 .05
❑ 304 Jiri Dolozal .25 .11
❑ 305 Henrik Holscher .10 .05
❑ 306 Sepp Wassermann .10 .05
❑ 307 Otto Sykora .10 .05
❑ 308 Bil Lochead .15 .07
❑ 309 Patrick Lange .10 .05
❑ 310 Ian Wood .10 .05
❑ 311 H. Thorn .10 .05
❑ 312 Doug Irwin .10 .05
❑ 313 Christian Schmitz .10 .05
❑ 314 Alexander Wunsch .10 .05
❑ 315 Cory Holden .10 .05
❑ 316 J. Bartman .10 .05
❑ 317 Peter Lutter .10 .05
❑ 318 Pavel Mann .10 .05
❑ 319 Greg Muller .10 .05
❑ 320 Christian Kohmann .10 .05
❑ 321 Paul Beraldo .15 .07
❑ 322 Thomas Groger .10 .05
❑ 323 Andrej Fuchs .10 .05
❑ 324 Klaus Birk .10 .05
❑ 325 D. Rich .10 .05
❑ 326 Boris Fuchs .10 .05
❑ 327 Thomas Muhlbauer .10 .05
❑ 328 Axel Kammerer .10 .05
❑ 329 Jeff Lazaro .15 .07
❑ 330 Olaf Scholz .10 .05
❑ 331 Bobby Reynolds .10 .05
❑ 332 Jaroslav Sevcik .25 .11
❑ 333 P.M. Arnholt .10 .05
❑ 334 G. Stranka .10 .05
❑ 335 Vincent Riendeau .35 .16
❑ 336 Michael Schmidt .10 .05
❑ 337 T. Gobel .10 .05
❑ 338 Vladimir Fedosov .10 .05
❑ 339 R. Jadamzik .10 .05
❑ 340 Frank Hohendahl .10 .05
❑ 341 A. Raubal .10 .05
❑ 342 C. Schonmoser .10 .05
❑ 343 A. Ludwig .10 .05
❑ 344 K. Ostler .10 .05
❑ 345 Markus Berwanger .10 .05
❑ 346 M. Holzer .10 .05
❑ 347 J. Feller .10 .05
❑ 348 H. Domke .10 .05
❑ 349 A. Maurer .10 .05
❑ 350 A. Gebauer .10 .05
❑ 351 Guntar Oswald .10 .05
❑ 352 H. Buchwieser .10 .05
❑ 353 B. Stewart .10 .05
❑ 354 Christopher Sandner .10 .05
❑ 355 J. Haglsperger .10 .05
❑ 356 Robert Hock .10 .05
❑ 357 Mark Jooris .10 .05
❑ 358 Ernst Hofner .10 .05
❑ 359 Gary Clark CO .10 .05
❑ 360 Karl Friesen .75 .35
❑ 361 Klaus Dalpiaz .25 .11
❑ 362 Markus Wieland .10 .05
❑ 363 Chris Clarke .10 .05
❑ 364 Markus Pottinger .10 .05
❑ 365 Raphael Kruger .10 .05
❑ 366 Ron Fischer .10 .05
❑ 367 Christian Gegenfurter .10 .05
❑ 368 Heinrich Schiffl .10 .05
❑ 369 Andreas Schneider .10 .05
❑ 370 V. Mitterfellner .10 .05
❑ 371 Richard Bohm .10 .05
❑ 372 Dale Krentz .25 .11
❑ 373 T. Schraven .10 .05
❑ 374 Florian Keller 2.00 .90
❑ 375 Doug Derraugh .10 .05
❑ 376 Martin Reichel .15 .07
❑ 377 M. Draxler .10 .05
❑ 378 Raimund Hilger .20 .09
❑ 379 Michael Pohl .10 .05
❑ 380 M. Kropf .10 .05
❑ 381 Joel Savage .15 .07
❑ 382 J. Eckmaier .10 .05
❑ 383 R.R. Burns .10 .05
❑ 384 Gunnar Leidborg .10 .05
❑ 385 Carsten Solbach .10 .05
❑ 386 Matthias Hoppe .10 .05
❑ 387 Gord Hynes .15 .07
❑ 388 Thomas Gaus .10 .05
❑ 389 Zdenek Travnicek .10 .05
❑ 390 Richard Trojan .10 .05
❑ 391 Frantisek Frosch .10 .05
❑ 392 Daniel Nowak .10 .05
❑ 393 Andreas Renz .10 .05
❑ 394 Alan Young .10 .05
❑ 395 Robert Brezina .10 .05
❑ 396 Wayne Hynes .10 .05
❑ 397 George Fritz .10 .05
❑ 398 Mike Bader .10 .05
❑ 399 Grant Martin .10 .05
❑ 400 Karsten Schulz .10 .05
❑ 401 Mike Lay .10 .05
❑ 402 Jackson Penney .15 .07
❑ 403 Rich Chernomaz .15 .07
❑ 404 Mark MacKay .15 .07
❑ 405 Sana Hassan .10 .05
❑ 406 Jiri Kochta .10 .05
❑ 407 Thomas Bresagk .10 .05
❑ 408 Peter Franke .10 .05
❑ 409 Jochen Molling .10 .05
❑ 410 Frantisek Prochazka .10 .05
❑ 411 Josef Reznicek .10 .05
❑ 412 Thomas Schubert .10 .05
❑ 413 Ronny Martin .10 .05
❑ 414 Marcel Lichnovsky .10 .05
❑ 415 Matthias Kliemann .10 .05
❑ 416 Ronny Reddo .10 .05
❑ 417 Frank Peschke .10 .05
❑ 418 Torsten Eisebitt .10 .05
❑ 419 Janusz Janikowski .10 .05
❑ 420 Thomas Knobloch .10 .05
❑ 421 Falk Herzig .10 .05
❑ 422 Thomas Wagner .10 .05
❑ 423 Jan Tabor .15 .07
❑ 424 J. Pohling .10 .05
❑ 425 Pavel Vit .10 .05
❑ 426 Vadim Kulabuchov .10 .05
❑ 427 D. Cup Meister 1995 .25 .11
❑ 428 Kingston/Kuhnhauser/Genze .25 .11
❑ 429 Heiss/Lupzig .50 .23
❑ 430 Brandl/Mann .25 .11
❑ 431 Doucet/Nowak .25 .11
❑ 432 Meyer/Pyka .25 .11
❑ 433 Hegen/Kunce .25 .11
❑ 434 Rumrich/Ludemann .25 .11
❑ 435 Benda/Kosturik .25 .11
❑ 436 Kienass/Brockmann/Hanft .15 .07
❑ 437 Draisaitl/Simon/Schneider .25 .11
❑ 438 Andreas Niederberger .25 .11
❑ 439 Martin Reichel .15 .07
❑ 440 Klaus Merk 1.00 .45
❑ 441 Glenn Anderson 2.50 1.10
❑ 442 Pavel Bure 25.00 11.00
❑ 443 Vincent Damphousse 4.00 1.80
❑ 444 Uwe Krupp 1.00 .45
❑ 445 Robert Reichel 1.50 .70
❑ 446 Jeremy Roenick 10.00 4.50
❑ 447 Brendan Shanahan 25.00 11.00
❑ 448 Jozef Stumpel 1.50 .70
❑ 449 Doug Weight 5.00 2.20
❑ 450 Scott Young .75 .35
❑ NNO Hologram Karte 15.00 6.75

## 1996-97 German DEL Eishockey

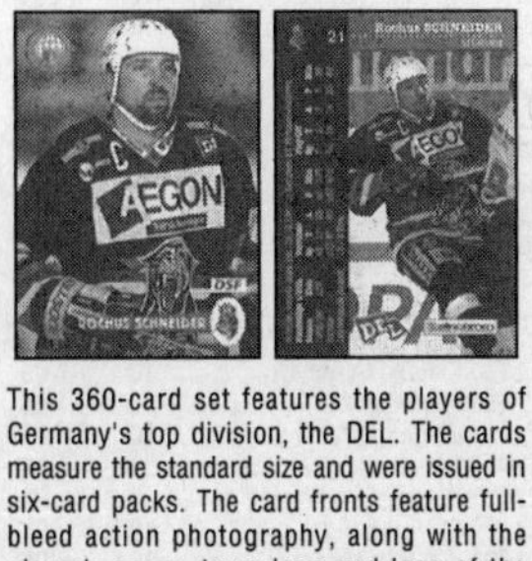

This 360-card set features the players of Germany's top division, the DEL. The cards measure the standard size and were issued in six-card packs. The card fronts feature full-bleed action photography, along with the player's name, team logo and logo of the manufacturer. The back includes another photo, affiliated logos, and stats for the '95-96 season, along with career totals and, in some cases, NHL totals. In a few instances, no stats are provided in the case of those players making their debuts in the DEL.

| | MINT | NRMT |
|---|---|---|
| COMPLETE SET (360) | 60.00 | 27.50 |
| COMMON CARD (1-360) | .10 | .05 |

❑ 1 Gary Prior CO .10 .05
❑ 2 Bruno Campese .10 .05
❑ 3 Leonardo Conti .10 .05
❑ 4 Scott Campbell .10 .05
❑ 5 Robert Mendel .10 .05
❑ 6 Serge Poudrier .10 .05
❑ 7 Torsten Fendt .10 .05
❑ 8 Shawn Rivers .10 .05
❑ 9 Stefan Mayer .10 .05
❑ 10 Michael Bakos .10 .05
❑ 11 Tommy Jakobsen .10 .05
❑ 12 Duanne Moeser .10 .05
❑ 13 Tero Arkiomaa .10 .05
❑ 14 Sven Zywitza .10 .05
❑ 15 Craig Streu .10 .05
❑ 16 Terry Campbell .10 .05
❑ 17 Timothy Ferguson .10 .05
❑ 18 Yves Heroux .10 .05
❑ 19 Max Boldt .10 .05
❑ 20 Andre Faust .10 .05
❑ 21 Rochus Schneider .10 .05
❑ 22 Ron Kennedy CO .10 .05
❑ 23 Barry Lewis ACO .10 .05
❑ 24 Mario Brunetta .10 .05
❑ 25 Udo Dohler .10 .05
❑ 26 Dirk Perschau .10 .05
❑ 27 Darren Durdle .10 .05
❑ 28 Greg Andrusak .10 .05
❑ 29 Leif Carlsson .10 .05
❑ 30 Derek Mayer .10 .05
❑ 31 Rob Leask .10 .05
❑ 32 Chad Biafore .10 .05
❑ 33 Thomas Steen .10 .05
❑ 34 Lorenz Funk .10 .05
❑ 35 Florian Funk .10 .05
❑ 36 Sven Felski .10 .05
❑ 37 Peter Lee .10 .05
❑ 38 Andrew McKim .10 .05
❑ 39 Andrej Lomakin .10 .05
❑ 40 Pelle Svensson .10 .05
❑ 41 Jan Schertz .10 .05
❑ 42 Kraig Nienhuis .10 .05
❑ 43 Niklas Hede .10 .05
❑ 44 Mario Chitarroni .10 .05
❑ 45 Chris Govedaris .10 .05
❑ 46 Pentti Matikainen CO .10 .05
❑ 47 Jukka Tammi .10 .05
❑ 48 Rupert Meister .10 .05
❑ 49 Florian Storf .10 .05
❑ 50 Greg Thomson .10 .05
❑ 51 Toni Porkka .10 .05
❑ 52 Sergej Schendelev .10 .05
❑ 53 Kai Rautio .10 .05
❑ 54 Rudi Gorgenlander .10 .05
❑ 55 Petr Kopta .10 .05
❑ 56 Tony Virta .10 .05
❑ 57 Ilja Vorobjev .10 .05
❑ 58 Thomas Popiesch .10 .05
❑ 59 Francois Sills .10 .05
❑ 60 Iiro Jarvi .10 .05
❑ 61 Jurgen Schaal .10 .05
❑ 62 Pavel Vit .10 .05
❑ 63 Timo Peltomaa .10 .05
❑ 64 Igor Schultz .10 .05
❑ 65 Dave Archibald .10 .05
❑ 66 Joni Lehto .10 .05
❑ 67 Brad Jones .10 .05
❑ 68 Miroslav Berek CO .10 .05
❑ 69 Karel Lang .10 .05
❑ 70 Peter Franke .10 .05
❑ 71 Markus Krawinkel .10 .05
❑ 72 Zdenek Travnicek .10 .05
❑ 73 Martin Gebel .10 .05
❑ 74 Klaus Micheller .10 .05
❑ 75 Earl Spry .10 .05
❑ 76 Frantisek Frosch .10 .05
❑ 77 Petri Liimatainen .10 .05
❑ 78 Andre Grein .10 .05
❑ 79 Ken Petrash .10 .05
❑ 80 James Hanlon .10 .05
❑ 81 Andrej Kovalev .10 .05
❑ 82 Reemt Pyka .10 .05
❑ 83 Chris Lindberg .10 .05
❑ 84 Jay Luknowsky .10 .05
❑ 85 Peter Ihnacak .10 .05
❑ 86 Marek Stebnicki .10 .05
❑ 87 Johnny Walker .10 .05
❑ 88 Danton Cole .10 .05
❑ 89 Michael Hreus .10 .05
❑ 90 Damian Adamus .10 .05
❑ 91 Bill Lochead CO .10 .05
❑ 92 Joakim Persson .10 .05
❑ 93 Ian Wood .10 .05
❑ 94 Pierre Jonsson .10 .05
❑ 95 Juha Lampinen .10 .05
❑ 96 Christian Schmitz .10 .05
❑ 97 Cory Holden .10 .05
❑ 98 Peter Lutter .10 .05
❑ 99 Dieter Bloem .10 .05
❑ 100 Maurizio Catenacci .10 .05
❑ 101 Andrej Fuchs .10 .05
❑ 102 Mark Montanari .10 .05
❑ 103 Boris Fuchs .10 .05
❑ 104 Andreas Salomonsson .10 .05
❑ 105 Robert Reynolds .10 .05
❑ 106 Axel Kammerer .10 .05
❑ 107 Jeffrey Lazaro .10 .05
❑ 108 Olaf Scholz .10 .05
❑ 109 Tony Cimellaro .10 .05
❑ 110 Kenneth Hodge .10 .05
❑ 111 Gregory Burke .10 .05
❑ 112 Tom Coolen CO .10 .05
❑ 113 Marc Pethke .10 .05
❑ 114 Christian Kunast .10 .05
❑ 115 Drahomir Kadlec .10 .05
❑ 116 Florian Kuhn .10 .05
❑ 117 Erich Goldmann .10 .05
❑ 118 Jurgen Simon .10 .05
❑ 119 Jeff Winstanley .10 .05
❑ 120 Stefano Figliuzzi .10 .05
❑ 121 Maurice Mansi .10 .05
❑ 122 Agostino Casale .10 .05
❑ 123 Hans-Jorg Mayer .10 .05
❑ 124 Dino Felicetti .10 .05
❑ 125 Roland Timoschuk .10 .05
❑ 126 Jim Hoffmann .10 .05
❑ 127 John Porco .10 .05
❑ 128 Rolf Hammer .10 .05
❑ 129 Manuel Hess .10 .05
❑ 130 Andy Rymsha .10 .05
❑ 131 Wolfgang Kummer .10 .05
❑ 132 Trevor Burgess .10 .05
❑ 133 Daniel Kunce .10 .05
❑ 134 Timo Sutinen CO .10 .05
❑ 135 Petr Briza .10 .05
❑ 136 Markus Nachtmann .10 .05
❑ 137 Markus Wieland .10 .05
❑ 138 Mike Heidt .10 .05
❑ 139 Peter Gulda .10 .05
❑ 140 Jacek Plachta .10 .05
❑ 141 Georg Franz .10 .05
❑ 142 Stephan Retzer .10 .05
❑ 143 Henry Marcoux .10 .05
❑ 144 Mike Bullard .10 .05
❑ 145 Jose Charbonneau .10 .05
❑ 146 Wally Schreiber .10 .05
❑ 147 Jorg Handrick .10 .05
❑ 148 Helmut Steiger .10 .05
❑ 149 Marco Sturm .10 .05
❑ 150 Jonas Johnsson .10 .05
❑ 151 Vesa Salo .10 .05
❑ 152 Gino Cavallini .10 .05
❑ 153 Lars Hurtig .10 .05
❑ 154 Olli Kaski .10 .05
❑ 155 007 Charly .10 .05
❑ 156 Lance Nethery CO .10 .05
❑ 157 Ross Yates ACO .10 .05
❑ 158 Joachim Appel .10 .05
❑ 159 Mike Rosati .10 .05
❑ 160 Harold Kreis .10 .05
❑ 161 Paul Stanton .10 .05
❑ 162 Christian Lukes .10 .05
❑ 163 Robert Nardella .10 .05
❑ 164 Alexander Erdmann .10 .05
❑ 165 Stephane J.G. Richer .10 .05
❑ 166 Martin Ulrich .10 .05
❑ 167 Mike Pellegrims .10 .05
❑ 168 Mario Gehrig .10 .05
❑ 169 Pavel Gross .10 .05
❑ 170 Dave Tomlinson .10 .05
❑ 171 Daniel Korber .10 .05
❑ 172 Francois Guay .10 .05
❑ 173 Jochen Hecht .10 .05
❑ 174 Florian Keller .10 .05
❑ 175 Till Feser .10 .05
❑ 176 Alexander Serikow .10 .05
❑ 177 Christian Pouget .10 .05
❑ 178 Dieter Kalt .10 .05
❑ 179 Paul Beraldo .10 .05
❑ 180 Steven Thornton .10 .05
❑ 181 Robert Cimetta .10 .05
❑ 182 Gary Clark CO .10 .05
❑ 183 Bjorn Leonhardt .10 .05
❑ 184 Claus Dalpiaz .10 .05
❑ 185 Jesper Duus .10 .05
❑ 186 Manuel Hiemer .10 .05
❑ 187 Markus Pottinger .10 .05
❑ 188 Chris Bartolone .10 .05
❑ 189 Christian Gegenfurther .10 .05
❑ 190 Heinrich Schiffl .10 .05
❑ 191 Per Lundell .10 .05
❑ 192 Joel Savage .10 .05
❑ 193 Josef Muller .10 .05
❑ 194 Jari Torkki .10 .05
❑ 195 James Hiller .10 .05
❑ 196 Doug Derraugh .10 .05
❑ 197 Pekka Tirkkonen .10 .05
❑ 198 Martin Reichel .10 .05
❑ 199 Raimond Hilger .10 .05
❑ 200 Michael Schneidawind .10 .05
❑ 201 Scott Beattie .10 .05
❑ 202 Paris Proft .10 .05
❑ 203 Kevin Gaudet CO .10 .05
❑ 204 Wayne Cowley .10 .05
❑ 205 Marco Herbst .10 .05
❑ 206 Andreas Schubert .10 .05
❑ 207 Stephan Sinner .10 .05
❑ 208 Heinrich Synowietz .10 .05
❑ 209 Paul Synowietz .10 .05
❑ 210 Dimitri Frolov .10 .05
❑ 211 Andrej Saposhnikov .10 .05
❑ 212 Jedrzej Kasperczyk .10 .05
❑ 213 Joseph West .10 .05
❑ 214 Fabian Ahrens .10 .05
❑ 215 Maurice Lemay .10 .05
❑ 216 Mark Kosturik .10 .05
❑ 217 Mark Jooris .10 .05
❑ 218 Len Soccio .10 .05
❑ 219 Mark Mahon .10 .05
❑ 220 Frank LaScala .10 .05
❑ 221 Jari Pasanen .10 .05
❑ 222 Ralph Vos .10 .05
❑ 223 Anthony Cirelli .10 .05

❑ 224 Emilio Iovio .10 .05
❑ 225 Gerhard Brunner CO .10 .05
❑ 226 Pavel Cagas .10 .05
❑ 227 Jonas Eriksson .10 .05
❑ 228 Alexander Engel .10 .05
❑ 229 Gregory Johnston .10 .05
❑ 230 Alexander Wedl .10 .05
❑ 231 Jouni Vento .10 .05
❑ 232 Roger Ohman .10 .05
❑ 233 David Morrison .10 .05
❑ 234 Bruce Eakin .10 .05
❑ 235 Michael Millar .10 .05
❑ 236 Roger Hansson .10 .05
❑ 237 Peter Kwasigroch .10 .05
❑ 238 Branjo Heisig .10 .05
❑ 239 Jukka Seppo .10 .05
❑ 240 Greg Evtushevski .10 .05
❑ 241 Falk Ozellis .10 .05
❑ 242 Daniel Larin .10 .05
❑ 243 Tino Boos .10 .05
❑ 244 Toni Krinner .10 .05
❑ 245 Milan Mokros .10 .05
❑ 246 Peter Ustorf CO .10 .05
❑ 247 Klaus Merk .10 .05
❑ 248 David Berge .10 .05
❑ 249 Georg Holzmann .10 .05
❑ 250 Tom O'Regan .10 .05
❑ 251 Jochen Molling .10 .05
❑ 252 Joseph Lehner .10 .05
❑ 253 Marco Rentzsch .10 .05
❑ 254 Pekka Laksola .10 .05
❑ 255 Petri Matikainen .10 .05
❑ 256 Tony Tanti .10 .05
❑ 257 Gaetan Malo .10 .05
❑ 258 Thomas Schinko .10 .05
❑ 259 Vitali Karamnov .10 .05
❑ 260 Gunther Oswald .10 .05
❑ 261 Christian Brittig .10 .05
❑ 262 Jurgen Rumrich .10 .05
❑ 263 John Chabot .10 .05
❑ 264 Andreas Dimbat .10 .05
❑ 265 Mark Teevens .10 .05
❑ 266 Veli-Pekka Kautonen .10 .05
❑ 267 Jarno-Sakari Peltonen .10 .05
❑ 268 Hardy Nilsson CO .10 .05
❑ 269 Martin Karlsson ACO .10 .05
❑ 270 Ake Lilljebjorn .10 .05
❑ 271 Kai Fischer .10 .05
❑ 272 Brad Bergen .10 .05
❑ 273 Andreas Niederberger .10 .05
❑ 274 Sergej Sorokin .10 .05
❑ 275 Robert Sterflinger .10 .05
❑ 276 Peter Andersson .10 .05
❑ 277 Viktor Gordiouk .10 .05
❑ 278 Gordon Sherven .10 .05
❑ 279 Benoit Doucet .10 .05
❑ 280 Bernd Kuhnhauser .10 .05
❑ 281 Dieter Hegen .10 .05
❑ 282 Andreas Brockmann .10 .05
❑ 283 Ernst Kopf .10 .05
❑ 284 Alexej Kudashov .10 .05
❑ 285 Bernd Truntschka .10 .05
❑ 286 Mikko Makela .10 .05
❑ 287 Nikolaus Mondt .10 .05
❑ 288 Boris Lingemann .10 .05
❑ 289 Thomas Brandl .10 .05
❑ 290 Leo Stefan .10 .05
❑ 291 Bob Burns CO .10 .05
❑ 292 Carsten Solbach .10 .05
❑ 293 Matthias Hoppe .10 .05
❑ 294 Sascha Goc .10 .05
❑ 295 Gordon Hynes .10 .05
❑ 296 Thomas Gaus .10 .05
❑ 297 Brian Tutt .10 .05
❑ 298 Richard Trojan .10 .05
❑ 299 Daniel Nowak .10 .05
❑ 300 Andreas Renz .10 .05
❑ 301 Sana Hassan .10 .05
❑ 302 Alan Young .10 .05
❑ 303 Mike Bader .10 .05
❑ 304 Robert Brezina .10 .05
❑ 305 Wayne Hynes .10 .05
❑ 306 Mark Bassen .10 .05
❑ 307 Andrew Clark .10 .05
❑ 308 Grant Martin .10 .05
❑ 309 Michael Lay .10 .05
❑ 310 Jackson Penney .10 .05
❑ 311 Rich Chernomaz .10 .05
❑ 312 Mark MacKay .10 .05
❑ 313 Vladimir Fedosov .10 .05
❑ 314 Emanuel Viveiros .10 .05
❑ 315 Jan Eysselt CO .10 .05
❑ 316 Michel Valliere .10 .05
❑ 317 Stefan Lahn .10 .05
❑ 318 Christian Gerum .10 .05
❑ 319 Heiko Smazal .10 .05
❑ 320 Christian Curth .10 .05
❑ 321 Miroslav Maly .10 .05
❑ 322 Torsten Kienass .10 .05
❑ 323 Thomas Sterflinger .10 .05
❑ 324 Lars Bruggemann .10 .05
❑ 325 Paul Geddes .10 .05
❑ 326 Rolan Ramoser .10 .05
❑ 327 Martin Jiranek .10 .05
❑ 328 Stefan Steinbock .10 .05
❑ 329 Martin Ekrt .10 .05
❑ 330 Jurgen Lechl .10 .05
❑ 331 Dion Del Monte .10 .05
❑ 332 Markus Welz .10 .05
❑ 333 Henrik Holscher .10 .05
❑ 334 Otto Sykora .10 .05
❑ 335 Milos Vanik .10 .05
❑ 336 Robert Murdoch CO .10 .05
❑ 337 Bernd Haake ACO .10 .05
❑ 338 Joseph Heiss .10 .05
❑ 339 Olaf Grundmann .10 .05
❑ 340 Alexander Genze .10 .05
❑ 341 Jorg Mayr .10 .05
❑ 342 Mirco Ludemann .10 .05
❑ 343 Jayson Meyer .10 .05
❑ 344 Karsten Mende .10 .05
❑ 345 Herbert Hohenberger .10 .05
❑ 346 Joe Cirella .10 .05
❑ 347 Petter Nilsson .10 .05
❑ 348 Jim Montgomery .10 .05
❑ 349 Stefan Mann .10 .05
❑ 350 Luciano Borsato .10 .05
❑ 351 Dwayne Norris .10 .05
❑ 352 Bruno Zarrillo .10 .05
❑ 353 Peter Draisaitl .10 .05
❑ 354 Joe Busillo .10 .05
❑ 355 Andreas Lupzig .10 .05
❑ 356 Rainer Zerwesz .10 .05
❑ 357 Thomas Forslund .10 .05
❑ 358 Tobias Abstreiter .10 .05
❑ 359 Patrick Carnback .10 .05
❑ 360 Franz Demmel .10 .05

## 1998-99 German DEL Eishockey

| | MINT | NRMT |
|---|---|---|
| COMPLETE SET (341) | 40.00 | 18.00 |
| COMMON CARD (1-341) | .10 | .05 |

❑ 1 Burke Murphy .10 .05
❑ 2 Marc Seliger .25 .11
❑ 3 Jason Clark .10 .05
❑ 4 Mike McNeill .10 .05
❑ 5 Norm Matherson .10 .05
❑ 6 Jeff Sebastien .10 .05
❑ 7 Phil Huber .10 .05
❑ 8 Todd Wtzel .10 .05
❑ 9 Jesper Morin .10 .05
❑ 10 Marc Pethke .10 .05
❑ 11 Jacek Plachta .10 .05
❑ 12 Marcus Adolfson .10 .05
❑ 13 Christian Schmitz .10 .05
❑ 14 Bob Marshall .10 .05
❑ 15 Peter Lutter .10 .05
❑ 16 Stefan Mayer .10 .05
❑ 17 Daniel Korber .10 .05
❑ 18 Carsten Gosdeck .10 .05
❑ 19 Jiri Kochta .10 .05
❑ 20 Petri Liimatainen .10 .05
❑ 21 Thomas Brandl .10 .05
❑ 22 Andrej Kovalev .25 .11
❑ 23 Johnny Walker .10 .05
❑ 24 Neil Eisenhut .25 .11
❑ 25 Karel Lang .10 .05
❑ 26 Marek Stebnicki .10 .05
❑ 27 Chris Bartolone .10 .05
❑ 28 John Van Kessel .10 .05
❑ 29 Lars Bruggemann .10 .05
❑ 30 Jason Meyer .10 .05
❑ 31 Reemt Pyka .10 .05
❑ 32 Mark Pederson .10 .05
❑ 33 Veli-Pekka Kautonen .10 .05
❑ 34 Tommie Hartogs .10 .05
❑ 35 Frantisek Frosch .10 .05
❑ 36 Leo van den Thillart .10 .05
❑ 37 Vitali Karamnov .25 .11
❑ 38 Stephane Barin .10 .05
❑ 39 Roger Nordstrom .10 .05
❑ 40 Robert Ouellet .10 .05
❑ 41 Doug Mason .10 .05
❑ 42 Francois Guay .10 .05
❑ 43 Greg Johnston .25 .11
❑ 44 Greg Evtushevski .10 .05
❑ 45 Shane Peacock .10 .05
❑ 46 Chris Rogles .35 .16
❑ 47 Gunter Oswald .10 .05
❑ 48 Jukka Seppo .10 .05
❑ 49 Jurgen Rumrich .10 .05
❑ 50 Roger Hansson .10 .05
❑ 51 Stephane Robitaille .10 .05
❑ 52 Orjan Lindmark .10 .05
❑ 53 Jeff MacLeod .10 .05
❑ 54 Alexander Wedl .10 .05
❑ 55 Jochen Molling .10 .05
❑ 56 Paul Cohen .10 .05
❑ 57 Daniel Kreutzer .10 .05
❑ 58 Nikolaus Mondt .10 .05
❑ 59 John Lilley .25 .11
❑ 60 Roland Ramoser .10 .05
❑ 61 Thomas Dolak .10 .05
❑ 62 Tino Boos .10 .05
❑ 63 Tobias Abstreiter .10 .05
❑ 64 Hans Zach .10 .05
❑ 65 Peter Brize .10 .05
❑ 66 Wally Schreiber .25 .11
❑ 67 Chris Luongo .25 .11
❑ 68 Dean Evason .25 .11
❑ 69 David Bruce .25 .11
❑ 70 Peter Douris .25 .11
❑ 71 Jason Herter .25 .11
❑ 72 Jorg Hendrick .10 .05
❑ 73 Rob Murphy .25 .11
❑ 74 Mike Casselmann .10 .05
❑ 75 Steve Junker .10 .05
❑ 76 Zbynek Kukacka .10 .05
❑ 77 Mark Krys .10 .05
❑ 78 Markus Wieland .10 .05
❑ 79 Evan Marble .10 .05
❑ 80 Jari Korpisalo .10 .05
❑ 81 Peter Gulda .10 .05
❑ 82 Bob Joyce .25 .11
❑ 83 Johan Rosen .10 .05
❑ 84 Christian Kunast .10 .05
❑ 85 Olli Kaski .10 .05
❑ 86 Chris Valentine .25 .11
❑ 87 Corey Millen .25 .11
❑ 88 Tomas Forslund .25 .11
❑ 89 Bruno Zarrillo .10 .05
❑ 90 Igor Alexandrov .10 .05
❑ 91 Bob Halkidis .25 .11
❑ 92 Petri Varis .35 .16
❑ 93 Joseph Heiss .25 .11
❑ 94 Greg Brown .25 .11
❑ 95 Dwayne Norris .25 .11
❑ 96 Mirko Ludemann .10 .05
❑ 97 John Miner .10 .05
❑ 98 Boris Rousson .35 .16
❑ 99 Craig Woodcroft .10 .05
❑ 100 Jorg Mayr .10 .05
❑ 101 Steve Wilson .10 .05
❑ 102 Rainer Zerwesz .10 .05
❑ 103 Brian McReynolds .10 .05
❑ 104 Andreas Lupzig .10 .05
❑ 105 Giuseppe Busillo .10 .05
❑ 106 Jeff Ricciardi .10 .05
❑ 107 Mike Hartman .25 .11
❑ 108 Timo Lahtinen .10 .05
❑ 109 Stephane Morin .50 .23
❑ 110 Paul Broten .25 .11
❑ 111 Robert Guillet .10 .05
❑ 112 Clayton Beddoes .25 .11
❑ 113 Robert Cimetta .25 .11
❑ 114 Dave MacIntyre .10 .05
❑ 115 Johan Norgren .10 .05
❑ 116 Todd Nelson .10 .05
❑ 117 Guy Phillips .10 .05
❑ 118 Craig Martin .25 .11
❑ 119 Parris Duffus .25 .11
❑ 120 Christian Brittig .10 .05
❑ 121 Thomas Schinko .10 .05
❑ 122 Mario Gehrig .10 .05
❑ 123 Fredrik Ytfeldt .10 .05
❑ 124 Lawrence Rucchin .10 .05
❑ 125 Heinz Ehlers .10 .05
❑ 126 Heinrich Schiffl .10 .05
❑ 127 Sylvain Couturier .25 .11
❑ 128 Hakan Galiamoutsas .10 .05
❑ 129 David Berge .10 .05
❑ 130 Marc Savard .10 .05
❑ 131 Dale McCourt .25 .11
❑ 132 Jukka Tammi .35 .16
❑ 133 Chris Snell .25 .11
❑ 134 John Chabot .25 .11
❑ 135 Len Barrie .25 .11
❑ 136 Lija Vorobjev .10 .05
❑ 137 Steve Palmer .10 .05
❑ 138 Fabrice Lhenry .10 .05
❑ 139 Rob Doyle .10 .05
❑ 140 Victor Gervais .10 .05
❑ 141 Jose Charbonneau .25 .11
❑ 142 Thorsten Apel .10 .05
❑ 143 Michael Bresagk .10 .05
❑ 144 Rick Hayward .25 .11
❑ 145 Phil von Steffenelli .25 .11
❑ 146 Martin Williams .10 .05
❑ 147 Toni Porkka .10 .05
❑ 148 Jean-Marc Richard .10 .05
❑ 149 Douglas Kirton .10 .05
❑ 150 Joel Savage .25 .11
❑ 151 Ralf Hantschke .10 .05
❑ 152 Ken Quinney .25 .11
❑ 153 Marcus Bleicher .10 .05
❑ 154 Bob Manno .25 .11
❑ 155 Rob Cowie .10 .05
❑ 156 Mike Bullard .35 .16
❑ 157 Maren Valenti .10 .05
❑ 158 Sven Felski .10 .05
❑ 159 Andrew McKim .25 .11
❑ 160 Derek Mayer .25 .11
❑ 161 Niklas Hede .10 .05
❑ 162 Thomas Steen .35 .16
❑ 163 Mario Brunetta .25 .11
❑ 164 Marc Fortier .25 .11
❑ 165 Thomas Rhodin .10 .05
❑ 166 Nico Pyka .10 .05
❑ 167 Chris Govedaris .25 .11
❑ 168 Lorenz Funk .10 .05
❑ 169 Florian Funk .10 .05
❑ 170 Yvon Corriveau .25 .11
❑ 171 Mikael Wahlberg .10 .05
❑ 172 Darren Durdle .10 .05
❑ 173 Pelle Svensson .10 .05
❑ 174 Greg Andrusak .25 .11
❑ 175 Leif Carlsson .10 .05
❑ 176 Andreas Brockmann .10 .05
❑ 177 Robert Leask .10 .05
❑ 178 Mario Chitaroni .10 .05
❑ 179 Chad Biafore .10 .05
❑ 180 Peter John Lee .10 .05
❑ 181 Len Soccio .10 .05
❑ 182 Jason Lafreniere .25 .11
❑ 183 Joe West .10 .05
❑ 184 Brent Tully .10 .05
❑ 185 Mark Kosturik .10 .05
❑ 186 David Haas .10 .05
❑ 187 Darcy Martini .10 .05
❑ 188 Gary Leeman .35 .16
❑ 189 Lee Davidson .10 .05
❑ 190 Scott Metcalfe .25 .11
❑ 191 Tom Pederson .10 .05
❑ 192 Francois Gravel .10 .05
❑ 193 Bjorn Leonhardt .10 .05
❑ 194 Mike Johnson .10 .05
❑ 195 Claudio Scremin .10 .05
❑ 196 Mike Ware .10 .05
❑ 197 Jurgen Trattner .10 .05
❑ 198 Dan Currie .25 .11
❑ 199 Patrick Curcio .10 .05
❑ 200 Patrick Senger .10 .05
❑ 201 Frank Di Muzio .10 .05
❑ 202 Kevin Gaudet .10 .05
❑ 203 Mark MacKay .10 .05
❑ 204 Claude Vilgrain .25 .11
❑ 205 Rich Chernomaz .10 .05
❑ 206 Daniel Laperriere .25 .11
❑ 207 Wayne Hynes .10 .05
❑ 208 Todd Harkins .10 .05
❑ 209 Scott McCrory .25 .11
❑ 210 Andrew Rymsha .25 .11
❑ 211 Daniel Nowak .10 .05
❑ 212 Andy Schneider .25 .11
❑ 213 David Marcinshyn .25 .11
❑ 214 Marc Laniel .10 .05
❑ 215 Guy Lehoux .10 .05
❑ 216 Matthias Vater .10 .05
❑ 217 Jens Stramkowski .10 .05
❑ 218 Alexander Dexheimer .10 .05
❑ 219 Mark Bassen .10 .05
❑ 220 Steffen Karg .10 .05
❑ 221 Randy Perry .10 .05
❑ 222 Robert Schistad .10 .05
❑ 223 Andreas Renz .10 .05
❑ 224 Matthias Hoppe .10 .05
❑ 225 Ron Ivany .10 .05
❑ 226 Phillippe Bozon .25 .11
❑ 227 Dave Tomlinson .25 .11
❑ 228 Stephane Richer .10 .05
❑ 229 Paul Stanton .25 .11
❑ 230 Pavel Gross .10 .05
❑ 231 Christian Pouget .10 .05
❑ 232 Jackson Penney .10 .05
❑ 233 Gordon Hynes .25 .11
❑ 234 Jason Young .10 .05
❑ 235 Alexander Serikow 1.00 .45
❑ 236 Mike Stevens .10 .05
❑ 237 Mike Pellegrims .10 .05
❑ 238 Reid Simonton .10 .05
❑ 239 Christian Lukes .10 .05
❑ 240 Ron Pasco .10 .05
❑ 241 Mike Hudson .25 .11
❑ 242 Denis Perez .10 .05
❑ 243 Svan Rampf .10 .05
❑ 244 Danny Lorenz .25 .11
❑ 245 Brian Tutt .10 .05
❑ 246 Jan Alston .10 .05
❑ 247 Lance Nethery .10 .05
❑ 248 Sergio Momesso .25 .11
❑ 249 Andrej Mezin .25 .11
❑ 250 Jarno Peltonen .10 .05
❑ 251 Martin Reichel .10 .05
❑ 252 Sergej Stas .10 .05
❑ 253 Martin Jiranek .10 .05
❑ 254 Jason Miller .10 .05
❑ 255 Jozef Cierny .25 .11
❑ 256 Liam Garvey .10 .05
❑ 257 Kevin Grant .10 .05
❑ 258 Chris Strausse .10 .05
❑ 259 Heiko Smazal .10 .05
❑ 260 Vadim Shakhraichuk .10 .05
❑ 261 Leszek Laszkiewicz .10 .05
❑ 262 Sven Valenti .10 .05
❑ 263 Michel Valliere .10 .05
❑ 264 Per Lundell .10 .05
❑ 265 Dimitri Dudik .10 .05
❑ 266 Daniel Kunce .10 .05
❑ 267 Ivan Droppa .10 .05
❑ 268 Peter Ihnacak .25 .11
❑ 269 Harald Birk .10 .05
❑ 270 Bradley Bergen .10 .05
❑ 271 Pierre Rioux .10 .05
❑ 272 Jim Camazzola .10 .05
❑ 273 Klaus Merk .25 .11
❑ 274 Rick Girard .10 .05
❑ 275 Andre Faust .10 .05
❑ 276 Hakan Ahlund .10 .05
❑ 277 Kyosti Karjalainen .25 .11
❑ 278 Leonardo Conti .10 .05
❑ 279 Leo Gudas .10 .05
❑ 280 Mathias Ahxner .10 .05
❑ 281 Francois Groleau .10 .05
❑ 282 Michael Bakos .10 .05
❑ 283 Alan Reader .10 .05
❑ 284 Nordin Harfaoui .10 .05
❑ 285 Dale Craigwell .25 .11
❑ 286 Dimitri Gromling .10 .05
❑ 287 Duanne Moeser .10 .05
❑ 288 Tommy Jakobsen .10 .05
❑ 289 Patrik Degerstedt .10 .05
❑ 290 Greg Bullock .10 .05
❑ 291 Gunnar Leidborg .10 .05
❑ 292 Dieter Hegen .10 .05
❑ 293 Derek Cormier .10 .05
❑ 294 Jim Hiller .10 .05
❑ 295 Gordon Sherven .25 .11
❑ 296 Eric Murana .10 .05
❑ 297 Robert Muller .10 .05
❑ 298 Klaus Kathan .10 .05
❑ 299 Raimond Hilger .10 .05
❑ 300 Christian Due-Boje .10 .05
❑ 301 Jesper Duus .10 .05
❑ 302 Michael Pohl .10 .05
❑ 303 Bernd Kuhnhauser .10 .05
❑ 304 Frank Hohenadl .10 .05
❑ 305 Alexander Jansen .10 .05
❑ 306 Teemu Sillanpaa .10 .05
❑ 307 Hans Abranamsson .10 .05
❑ 308 Claus Dalpiaz .25 .11
❑ 309 Kari Haakana .10 .05
❑ 310 Christian Gegenfurtner .10 .05
❑ 311 Peter Ottosson .10 .05
❑ 312 Wolfgang Kummer .10 .05
❑ 313 Beppi Eckmaier .10 .05
❑ 314 Gerhard Brunner .10 .05
❑ 315 Mirko Ludemann .25 .11
❑ 316 Sven Felski .10 .05
❑ 317 Reemt Pyka .10 .05
❑ 318 Jorg Mayr .10 .05
❑ 319 Michael Bresagk .10 .05
❑ 320 Andraes Lupzig .10 .05
❑ 321 Jurgen Rumrich .10 .05
❑ 322 Josef Lehner .10 .05
❑ 323 Peter Draisaitl .10 .05
❑ 324 Leo Stefan .10 .05
❑ 325 Joseph Heiss .25 .11
❑ 326 Klaus Kathan .10 .05
❑ 327 Klaus Merk .25 .11
❑ 328 Peter Gulda .10 .05
❑ 329 Daniel Nowak .10 .05
❑ 330 Bradley Bergen .10 .05
❑ 331 Thomas Dolak .10 .05
❑ 332 Martin Reichel .10 .05
❑ 333 Alexander Serikow 1.00 .45
❑ 334 Harold Birk .10 .05
❑ 335 Michael Bakos .10 .05
❑ 336 Mario Gehrig .10 .05
❑ 337 Mark Mackay .10 .05
❑ 338 Dieter Hegen .10 .05
❑ 339 Hans Zach .10 .05
❑ 340 Erich Kuhnackl .10 .05
❑ 341 Ernst Hofner .10 .05

## 1994-95 Guildford Flames

| | MINT | NRMT |
|---|---|---|
| COMPLETE SET (25) | 6.00 | 2.70 |
| COMMON CARD (1-25) | .30 | .14 |

❑ 1 Ben Challice .30 .14
❑ 2 Wayne Trunchion .30 .14
❑ 3 Terry Kurtenbach .30 .14
❑ 4 Fred Perlini .30 .14
❑ 5 Andy Sparks .30 .14
❑ 6 Rob Friesen .30 .14
❑ 7 Drew Chapman .30 .14
❑ 8 Kevin Parish .30 .14
❑ 9 John Noctor .30 .14
❑ 10 Ron Charbonneau GM .30 .14
❑ 11 Peter Morley .30 .14
❑ 12 Andy Allan .30 .14
❑ 13 Ryan Campbell .30 .14
❑ 14 Ronnie Evans-Harvey .30 .14
❑ 15 Paul Thompson .30 .14
❑ 16 Bill Rawles .30 .14
❑ 17 Nicky Landoli .30 .14
❑ 18 Elliott Andrews .30 .14
❑ 19 Dean Russell-Samways .30 .14
❑ 20 Home Kit .30 .14
❑ 21 Away Kit .30 .14
❑ 22 5 Imports .30 .14
❑ 23 3 Letters .30 .14
❑ 24 Spectrum .30 .14
❑ 25 Checklist .30 .14

## 1995-96 Guildford Flames

| | MINT | NRMT |
|---|---|---|
| COMPLETE SET (30) | 6.00 | 2.70 |
| COMMON CARD (1-30) | .30 | .14 |

❑ 1 Dave Gregory .30 .14
❑ 2 Wayne Trunchion .30 .14
❑ 3 Andy Allan .30 .14
❑ 4 Terru Kurtenbach .30 .14
❑ 5 Ryan Campbell .30 .14
❑ 6 Fred Perlini .30 .14
❑ 7 Ronnie Evans-Harvey .30 .14
❑ 8 Andy Sparks .30 .14
❑ 9 Paul Thompson .30 .14
❑ 10 Nick Rothwell .30 .14
❑ 11 Drew Chapman .30 .14
❑ 12 Troy Kennedy .30 .14
❑ 13 Barrie Aisbitt .30 .14
❑ 14 Elliott Andrews .30 .14
❑ 15 Darrin Zinger .30 .14
❑ 16 Dean Russell-Samways .30 .14
❑ 17 Dave Graham .30 .14
❑ 18 Ivan Brown .30 .14
❑ 19 Home Kit .30 .14
❑ 20 Away Kit .30 .14
❑ 21 Spectrum .30 .14
❑ 22 Checklist .30 .14
❑ 23 Home Action .30 .14
❑ 24 Away Action .30 .14
❑ 25 P.C. Jim Bennett .30 .14
❑ 26 Terry Kurtenbach GOLD .30 .14
❑ 27 Paul Thompson GOLD .30 .14
❑ 28 Fred Perlini GOLD .30 .14
❑ 29 Future GOLD .30 .14
❑ 30 Celebration GOLD .30 .14

## 1996-97 Guildford Flames

| | MINT | NRMT |
|---|---|---|
| COMPLETE SET (30) | 6.00 | 2.70 |
| COMMON CARD (1-30) | .30 | .14 |

❑ 1 John Wolfe .30 .14
❑ 2 Rob Lamey .30 .14
❑ 3 Wayne Crawford .30 .14
❑ 4 Terry Kurtenbach .30 .14
❑ 5 Ryan Campbell .30 .14
❑ 6 Fred Parlini .30 .14
❑ 7 Paul Thompson .30 .14
❑ 8 Mike Bettens .30 .14
❑ 9 Mark Finney .30 .14
❑ 10 Ryan Ferster .30 .14
❑ 11 Nick Cross .30 .14

| | | |
|---|---|---|
| ❑ 12 Damian Smith | .30 | .14 |
| ❑ 13 Mikw Mowbray | .30 | .14 |
| ❑ 14 Elliott Andrews | .30 | .14 |
| ❑ 15 Darrin Zinger | .30 | .14 |
| ❑ 16 Brad Kirkwood | .30 | .14 |
| ❑ 17 Derek DeCosty | .30 | .14 |
| ❑ 18 Mark Hazelhurst | .30 | .14 |
| ❑ 19 Lee Saunders | .30 | .14 |
| ❑ 20 Barrie Aisbitt | .30 | .14 |
| ❑ 21 Paul McCallion | .30 | .14 |
| ❑ 22 Valeri Vasie | .30 | .14 |
| ❑ 23 Goalies | .30 | .14 |
| ❑ 24 Capt. , Ast.Capt. | .30 | .14 |
| ❑ 25 Celebration | .30 | .14 |
| ❑ 26 Pep Talk | .30 | .14 |
| ❑ 27 Home Kit | .30 | .14 |
| ❑ 28 Away Kit | .30 | .14 |
| ❑ 29 Spectrum | .30 | .14 |
| ❑ 30 Training Staff | .30 | .14 |

## 1997-98 Guildford Flames

| | MINT | NRMT |
|---|---|---|
| COMPLETE SET (30) | 6.00 | 2.70 |
| COMMON CARD (1-30) | .30 | .14 |
| ❑ 1 Peter Morley | .30 | .14 |
| ❑ 2 Rob Larney | .30 | .14 |
| ❑ 3 Andrew Hannah | .30 | .14 |
| ❑ 4 Joe Johnson | .30 | .14 |
| ❑ 5 Terry Kurtenbach | .30 | .14 |
| ❑ 6 Ryan Campbell | .30 | .14 |
| ❑ 7 Scott Adair | .30 | .14 |
| ❑ 8 Paul Thompson | .30 | .14 |
| ❑ 9 Ricky Plant | .30 | .14 |
| ❑ 10 Pete Kasowski | .30 | .14 |
| ❑ 11 Andrew Einhorn | .30 | .14 |
| ❑ 12 Bobby Brown | .30 | .14 |
| ❑ 13 Anthony Page | .30 | .14 |
| ❑ 14 Nick Rothwell | .30 | .14 |
| ❑ 15 Mike Harding | .30 | .14 |
| ❑ 16 Darrin Zinger | .30 | .14 |
| ❑ 17 Jamie Organ | .30 | .14 |
| ❑ 18 Barcley Pearce | .30 | .14 |
| ❑ 19 Simon Smith | .30 | .14 |
| ❑ 20 Russ Plant | .30 | .14 |
| ❑ 21 Stan Marple CO | .30 | .14 |
| ❑ 22 Home Kit | .30 | .14 |
| ❑ 23 Away Kit | .30 | .14 |
| ❑ 24 Dressing Room | .30 | .14 |
| ❑ 25 Capt. , Ast. Capt. | .30 | .14 |
| ❑ 26 Celebration | .30 | .14 |
| ❑ 27 Checklist | .30 | .14 |
| ❑ 28 Spectrum | .30 | .14 |
| ❑ 29 Sizzler | .30 | .14 |
| ❑ 30 Training Staff | .30 | .14 |

## 1993-94 Humberside Hawks Postcards

| | MINT | NRMT |
|---|---|---|
| COMPLETE SET (18) | 5.00 | 2.20 |
| COMMON CARD | .30 | .14 |
| ❑ 1 Kenny Johnson | .30 | .14 |
| ❑ 2 Gavin De Jonge | .30 | .14 |
| ❑ 3 Chris Hobson | .30 | .14 |
| ❑ 4 Mike Bishop | .30 | .14 |
| ❑ 6 Paul Simpson | .30 | .14 |
| ❑ 7 Stewart Carvil | .30 | .14 |
| ❑ 8 Shaun Johnson | .30 | .14 |
| ❑ 9 Arren Burn | .30 | .14 |
| ❑ 10 Stephon Johnson | .30 | .14 |
| ❑ 12 Anthony Johnson | .30 | .14 |
| ❑ 15 Anthony Payne | .30 | .14 |
| ❑ 16 Andy Giles | .30 | .14 |
| ❑ 17 Mike O'Conner | .30 | .14 |
| ❑ 19 Andy Steel | .30 | .14 |
| ❑ 20 Frank Killen | .30 | .14 |
| ❑ 21 Dan Dorian | .30 | .14 |
| ❑ 23 Alexander Koulikov | .30 | .14 |
| ❑ NNO Peter Johnson CO | .30 | .14 |

## 1994-95 Humberside Hawks Postcards

| | MINT | NRMT |
|---|---|---|
| COMPLETE SET (20) | 5.00 | 2.20 |
| COMMON CARD (1-20) | .30 | .14 |
| ❑ 2 Malcolm Bell | .30 | .14 |
| ❑ 4 Mike Bishop | .30 | .14 |
| ❑ 5 Scott Young | .30 | .14 |
| ❑ 6 Paul Simpson | .30 | .14 |
| ❑ 8 Shaun Johnson | .30 | .14 |
| ❑ 9 Wayne Anchikoski | .30 | .14 |
| ❑ 10 Stephon Johnson | .30 | .14 |
| ❑ 12 Anthony Johnson | .30 | .14 |
| ❑ 14 Tony Saxby | .30 | .14 |
| ❑ 15 Darcy Cahill | .30 | .14 |
| ❑ 16 Chris Hobson | .30 | .14 |
| ❑ 17 Danny Parkin | .30 | .14 |
| ❑ 19 Scott Morrison | .30 | .14 |
| ❑ 20 Danny Thompson | .30 | .14 |
| ❑ 21 Paul cast | .30 | .14 |
| ❑ 22 Andy Port | .30 | .14 |
| ❑ 23 Dominik Love | .30 | .14 |
| ❑ NNO Gavin De Jonge | .30 | .14 |
| ❑ NNO David Standling | .30 | .14 |
| ❑ NNO Peter Johnson CO | .30 | .14 |

## 1997-98 Kingston Hawks Stickers

| | MINT | NRMT |
|---|---|---|
| COMPLETE SET (20) | 6.00 | 2.70 |
| COMMON CARD (1-20) | .30 | .14 |
| ❑ 1 Keith Milhench CO | .30 | .14 |
| ❑ 2 Bobby McEwen ACO | .30 | .14 |
| ❑ 3 Malcolm Bell | .30 | .14 |
| ❑ 4 Michael Knights | .30 | .14 |
| ❑ 5 Paul Simpson | .30 | .14 |
| ❑ 6 Kelly Reid | .30 | .14 |
| ❑ 7 Dominic Love | .30 | .14 |
| ❑ 8 Phil Brook | .30 | .14 |
| ❑ 9 Anthony Payne | .30 | .14 |
| ❑ 10 Chris Hobson | .30 | .14 |
| ❑ 11 Steve Smillie | .30 | .14 |
| ❑ 12 Andy Steel | .30 | .14 |
| ❑ 13 Ashlye Tait | .30 | .14 |
| ❑ 14 Slave Koulikov | .30 | .14 |
| ❑ 15 Norman Pinnington | .30 | .14 |
| ❑ 16 Tony McAleavy | .30 | .14 |
| ❑ 17 Pasi Raitinen | .30 | .14 |
| ❑ 18 The Kingston Kid | .30 | .14 |
| ❑ 19 Ian Defty | .30 | .14 |
| ❑ 20 Michael Tasker | .30 | .14 |

## 1979 Panini Stickers

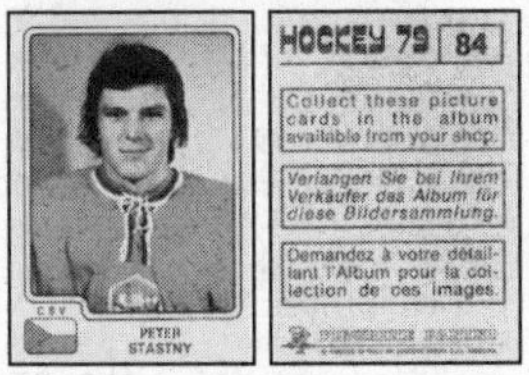


This "global" hockey set was produced by Figurine Panini and printed in Italy. Each sticker measures approximately 1 15/16" by 2 3/4". The set also has an album available. This set is complete with 400 numbered small cards featuring hockey players from all over the world. The numbering within the cards in the set is organized by topical subgroups, i.e., Referee Signals (1-19), Action Pairs (20-39), National Team Logos (40-47), Four Part Photo (48-51), Canadian Players (52-69), Four Part Photo (70-73), Czech Players (74-91), Four Part Photo (92-95), FDR Players (96-113), Four Part Photo (114-117), Poland Players (118-135), Four Part Photo (136-139), USSR Players (140-157), Four Part Photo (158-161), Finland Players (162-179), Four Part Photo (180-183), Sweden Players (184-201), Four Part Photo (202-205), USA Players (206-223), Action Pairs (225-238), National Team Logos (239-246), DDR (247-255), Switzerland (256-264), Hungary (265-273), Netherlands (274-282), Japan (283-291), Norway (292-300), Austria (301-309), Romania (310-318), Action Pairs (320-328), National Team Logos (329-336), Belgium (337-344), Bulgaria (345-352), China (353-360), Denmark (361-368), Spain (369-376), France (377-384), Italy (385-392), and Yugoslavia (393-400).

| | NRMT | VG-E |
|---|---|---|
| COMPLETE SET (400) | 100.00 | 45.00 |
| COMMON STICKER (1-400) | .20 | .09 |
| ❑ 1 Goal Disallowed | .40 | .18 |
| ❑ 2 Butt-Ending | .20 | .09 |
| ❑ 3 Slow Whistle | .20 | .09 |
| ❑ 4 Hooking | .20 | .09 |
| ❑ 5 Charging | .20 | .09 |
| ❑ 6 Misconduct Penalty | .20 | .09 |
| ❑ 7 Holding | .20 | .09 |
| ❑ 8 High-Sticking | .20 | .09 |
| ❑ 9 Tripping | .20 | .09 |
| ❑ 10 Cross-Checking | .20 | .09 |
| ❑ 11 Elbowing | .20 | .09 |
| ❑ 12 Icing (I) | .20 | .09 |
| ❑ 13 Icing (II) | .20 | .09 |
| ❑ 14 Boarding | .20 | .09 |
| ❑ 15 Kneeing | .20 | .09 |
| ❑ 16 Slashing | .20 | .09 |
| ❑ 17 Excessive Roughness | .20 | .09 |
| ❑ 18 Spearing | .20 | .09 |
| ❑ 19 Interference | .20 | .09 |
| ❑ 20 Poster | .20 | .09 |
| ❑ 21 Czech.-USSR 6-4 | .50 | .23 |
| ❑ 22 Czech.-USSR 6-4 | .50 | .23 |
| ❑ 23 USSR-Czech. 3-1 | .50 | .23 |
| ❑ 24 USSR-Czech. 3-1 | .50 | .23 |
| ❑ 25 USSR-Czech. 3-1 | .50 | .23 |
| ❑ 26 USSR-Czech. 3-1 | .50 | .23 |
| ❑ 27 Can-Sweden 3-2 | .50 | .23 |
| ❑ 28 Can-Sweden 3-2 | .50 | .23 |
| ❑ 29 USSR-Canada 5-1 | .75 | .35 |
| ❑ 30 USSR-Canada 5-1 | .75 | .35 |
| ❑ 31 Czech.-Canada 3-2 | .50 | .23 |
| ❑ 32 Czech.-Canada 3-2 | .50 | .23 |
| ❑ 33 USSR-Sweden 7-1 | .50 | .23 |
| ❑ 34 USSR-Sweden 7-1 | .50 | .23 |
| ❑ 35 USA-Finland 4-3 | .50 | .23 |
| ❑ 36 USA-Finland 4-3 | .50 | .23 |
| ❑ 37 Finland-DDR 7-2 | .20 | .09 |
| ❑ 38 DDR-BRD 0-0 | .20 | .09 |
| ❑ 39 DDR-BRD 0-0 | .20 | .09 |
| ❑ 40 Czechoslovakia | .20 | .09 |
| ❑ 41 Poland | .20 | .09 |
| ❑ 42 USSR | 1.25 | .55 |
| ❑ 43 USA | 1.25 | .55 |
| ❑ 44 Canada | 2.00 | .90 |
| ❑ 45 Deutschland-BRD | .20 | .09 |
| ❑ 46 Finland | .20 | .09 |
| ❑ 47 Sweden | .50 | .23 |
| ❑ 48 Canada Team Picture (upper left) | 1.00 | .45 |
| ❑ 49 Canada Team Picture (upper right) | 1.00 | .45 |
| ❑ 50 Canada Team Picture (lower left) | 1.00 | .45 |
| ❑ 51 Canada Team Picture (lower right) | 1.00 | .45 |
| ❑ 52 Denis Herron | 1.50 | .70 |
| ❑ 53 Dan Bouchard | 1.50 | .70 |
| ❑ 54 Rick Hampton | .50 | .23 |
| ❑ 55 Robert Picard | .50 | .23 |
| ❑ 56 Brad Maxwell | .50 | .23 |
| ❑ 57 David Shand | .50 | .23 |
| ❑ 58 Dennis Kearns | .50 | .23 |
| ❑ 59 Tom Lysiak | .75 | .35 |
| ❑ 60 Dennis Maruk | 1.50 | .70 |
| ❑ 61 Marcel Dionne | 6.00 | 2.70 |
| ❑ 62 Guy Charron | .75 | .35 |
| ❑ 63 Glen Sharpley | .50 | .23 |
| ❑ 64 Jean Pronovost | .75 | .35 |
| ❑ 65 Don Lever | .50 | .23 |
| ❑ 66 Bob MacMillan | .75 | .35 |
| ❑ 67 Wilf Paiement | .75 | .35 |
| ❑ 68 Pat Hickey | .75 | .35 |
| ❑ 69 Mike Murphy | .50 | .23 |
| ❑ 70 Czechoslovakia Team Picture (upper left) | .50 | .23 |
| ❑ 71 Czechoslovakia Team Picture (upper right) | .50 | .23 |
| ❑ 72 Czechoslovakia Team Picture (lower left) | .50 | .23 |
| ❑ 73 Czechoslovakia Team Picture (lower right) | .50 | .23 |
| ❑ 74 Jiri Holecek | .75 | .35 |
| ❑ 75 Jiri Crha | 1.00 | .45 |
| ❑ 76 Jiri Bubla | .75 | .35 |
| ❑ 77 Milan Kajki | .20 | .09 |
| ❑ 78 Miroslav Dvorak | .50 | .23 |
| ❑ 79 Milan Chalupa | .50 | .23 |
| ❑ 80 Frantisek Kaberle | .40 | .18 |
| ❑ 81 Jan Zajicek | .20 | .09 |
| ❑ 82 Jiri Novak | .20 | .09 |
| ❑ 83 Ivan Hlinka | .50 | .23 |
| ❑ 84 Peter Stastny | 8.00 | 3.60 |
| ❑ 85 Milan Novy | .50 | .23 |
| ❑ 86 Vladimir Martinec | .20 | .09 |
| ❑ 87 Jaroslav Pouzar | .50 | .23 |
| ❑ 88 Pavel Richter | .20 | .09 |
| ❑ 89 Bohuslav Ebermann | .20 | .09 |
| ❑ 90 Marian Stastny | 1.00 | .45 |
| ❑ 91 Frantisek Cernick | .40 | .18 |
| ❑ 92 FDR Team Picture (upper left) | .20 | .09 |
| ❑ 93 FDR Team Picture (upper right) | .20 | .09 |
| ❑ 94 FDR Team Picture (lower left) | .20 | .09 |
| ❑ 95 FDR Team Picture (lower right) | .20 | .09 |
| ❑ 96 Erich Weishaupt | .20 | .09 |
| ❑ 97 Bernhard Engelbrecht | .20 | .09 |
| ❑ 98 Ignaz Berndaner | .20 | .09 |
| ❑ 99 Robert Murray | .20 | .09 |
| ❑ 100 Udo Kiessling | .50 | .23 |
| ❑ 101 Klaus Auhuber | .20 | .09 |
| ❑ 102 Horst Kretschmer | .20 | .09 |
| ❑ 103 Erich Kuhnhackl | .50 | .23 |
| ❑ 104 Martin Wild | .20 | .09 |
| ❑ 105 Lorenz Funk | .20 | .09 |
| ❑ 106 M. Hinterstocker | .20 | .09 |
| ❑ 107 Alois Schloder | .20 | .09 |
| ❑ 108 Rainer Philipp | .20 | .09 |
| ❑ 109 H. Hinterstocker | .20 | .09 |
| ❑ 110 Franz Reindl | .20 | .09 |
| ❑ 111 Walter Koberle | .50 | .23 |
| ❑ 112 Johann Zach | .20 | .09 |
| ❑ 113 Marcus Kuhl | .20 | .09 |
| ❑ 114 Poland Team Picture (upper left) | .20 | .09 |
| ❑ 115 Poland Team Picture (upper right) | .20 | .09 |
| ❑ 116 Poland Team Picture (lower left) | .20 | .09 |
| ❑ 117 Poland Team Picture (lower right) | .20 | .09 |
| ❑ 118 Henryk Wojtynek | .20 | .09 |
| ❑ 119 T. Slowakiewicz | .20 | .09 |
| ❑ 120 Henryk Janiszewski | .20 | .09 |
| ❑ 121 Henryk Gruth | .20 | .09 |
| ❑ 122 Andr. Slowakiewicz | .20 | .09 |
| ❑ 123 Andrzej Eskrzycki | .20 | .09 |
| ❑ 124 Jerzy Potz | .50 | .23 |
| ❑ 125 Marek Marcinczak | .20 | .09 |
| ❑ 126 Jozef Batkiewicz | .20 | .09 |
| ❑ 127 Stefan Chowaniec | .20 | .09 |
| ❑ 128 Andrzej Malysiak | .20 | .09 |
| ❑ 129 Walenty Zietara | .20 | .09 |
| ❑ 130 Henryk Pytel | .20 | .09 |
| ❑ 131 Andrezei Zabawa | .20 | .09 |
| ❑ 133 Tadeusz Oboj | .20 | .09 |
| ❑ 134 Jan Piecko | .20 | .09 |
| ❑ 135 Leszek Tokarz | .20 | .09 |
| ❑ 136 USSR Team Picture (upper left) | .75 | .35 |
| ❑ 137 USSR Team Picture (upper right) | .75 | .35 |
| ❑ 138 USSR Team Picture (lower left) | .75 | .35 |
| ❑ 139 USSR Team Picture (lower right) | .75 | .35 |
| ❑ 140 Vladislav Tretiak | 10.00 | 4.50 |
| ❑ 141 Viacheslav Fetisov | 5.00 | 2.20 |
| ❑ 142 Vladimir Lutchenko | 1.00 | .45 |
| ❑ 143 Vasilij Pervukhin | .75 | .35 |
| ❑ 144 Valeri Vasiliev | 2.00 | .90 |
| ❑ 145 Gennady Tsygankov | 1.00 | .45 |
| ❑ 146 Juri Fedorov | .40 | .18 |
| ❑ 147 Vladimir Petrov | 3.00 | 1.35 |
| ❑ 148 Vladimir Golikov | .40 | .18 |
| ❑ 149 Victor Zhluktov | .50 | .23 |
| ❑ 150 Boris Mikhailov | 3.00 | 1.35 |
| ❑ 151 Valeri Kharlamov | 6.00 | 2.70 |
| ❑ 152 Helmut Balderis | 1.00 | .45 |
| ❑ 153 Sergej Kapustin | .75 | .35 |
| ❑ 154 Alexander Golikov | .40 | .18 |
| ❑ 155 Alexander Maltsev | 3.00 | 1.35 |
| ❑ 156 Yuri Lebedev | .75 | .35 |
| ❑ 157 Sergei Makarov | 5.00 | 2.20 |
| ❑ 158 Finland Team Picture (upper left) | .20 | .09 |
| ❑ 159 Finland Team Picture (upper right) | .20 | .09 |
| ❑ 160 Finland Team Picture (lower left) | .20 | .09 |
| ❑ 161 Finland Team Picture (lower right) | .20 | .09 |
| ❑ 162 Urpo Ylonen | .50 | .23 |
| ❑ 163 Antero Kivela | .20 | .09 |
| ❑ 164 Pekka Rautakallio | 1.00 | .45 |
| ❑ 165 Timo Nummelin | .20 | .09 |
| ❑ 166 Risto Siltanen | 1.00 | .45 |
| ❑ 167 Pekka Marjamaki | .20 | .09 |
| ❑ 168 Tapio Levo | .40 | .18 |
| ❑ 169 Lasse Litma | .20 | .09 |
| ❑ 170 Esa Peitonen | .20 | .09 |
| ❑ 171 Martti Jarkko | .20 | .09 |
| ❑ 172 Matti Hagman | .50 | .23 |
| ❑ 173 Seppo Repo | .40 | .18 |
| ❑ 174 Pertti Korvulahti | .20 | .09 |
| ❑ 175 Seppo Ahokainen | .20 | .09 |
| ❑ 176 Juhani Tamminen | .40 | .18 |
| ❑ 177 Jukko Provari | .20 | .09 |
| ❑ 178 Mikko Leinonen | .75 | .35 |
| ❑ 179 Matti Rautiainen | .20 | .09 |
| ❑ 180 Sweden Team Picture (upper left) | .50 | .23 |
| ❑ 181 Sweden Team Picture (upper right) | .50 | .23 |
| ❑ 182 Sweden Team Picture (lower left) | .50 | .23 |
| ❑ 183 Sweden Team Picture (lower right) | .50 | .23 |
| ❑ 184 Goran Hogasta | .40 | .18 |
| ❑ 185 Hardy Astrom | 1.50 | .70 |
| ❑ 186 Stig Ostling | .40 | .18 |
| ❑ 187 Ulf Weinstock | .20 | .09 |
| ❑ 188 Mats Waltin | .20 | .09 |
| ❑ 189 Stig Salming | .50 | .23 |
| ❑ 190 Lars Zetterstrom | .20 | .09 |
| ❑ 191 Lars Lindgren | .50 | .23 |
| ❑ 192 Leif Holmgren | .20 | .09 |
| ❑ 193 Roland Ericksson | .20 | .09 |
| ❑ 194 Rolf Edberg | .20 | .09 |
| ❑ 195 Per-Olov Brasar | .50 | .23 |
| ❑ 196 Mats Ahlberg | .20 | .09 |
| ❑ 197 Bengt Lundholm | .50 | .23 |
| ❑ 198 Lars Gunnar Lundberg | .20 | .09 |
| ❑ 199 Nils-Olov Olsson | .20 | .09 |
| ❑ 200 Kent-Erik Anderson | .75 | .35 |
| ❑ 201 Thomas Gradin | 1.50 | .70 |
| ❑ 202 USA Team Picture (upper left) | .75 | .35 |
| ❑ 203 USA Team Picture (upper right) | .75 | .35 |
| ❑ 204 USA Team Picture (lower left) | .75 | .35 |
| ❑ 205 USA Team Picture (lower right) | .75 | .35 |
| ❑ 206 Peter Lopresti | .75 | .35 |
| ❑ 207 Jim Warden | .50 | .23 |
| ❑ 208 Dick Lamby | .50 | .23 |
| ❑ 209 Craig Norwich | .50 | .23 |
| ❑ 210 Glen Patrick | .50 | .23 |
| ❑ 211 Patrick Westrum | .50 | .23 |
| ❑ 212 Don Jackson | .50 | .23 |
| ❑ 213 Mark Johnson | 1.00 | .45 |
| ❑ 214 Curt Bennett | .50 | .23 |
| ❑ 215 Dave Debol | .50 | .23 |
| ❑ 216 Bob Collyard | .50 | .23 |
| ❑ 217 Mike Fidler | .50 | .23 |
| ❑ 218 Tom Younghans | .50 | .23 |
| ❑ 219 Harvey Bennett | .50 | .23 |
| ❑ 220 Steve Jensen | .75 | .35 |
| ❑ 221 Jim Warner | .50 | .23 |
| ❑ 222 Mike Eaves | .50 | .23 |
| ❑ 223 William Gilligan | .50 | .23 |
| ❑ 224 Poster | .50 | .23 |
| ❑ 225 Poland-Rom. 8-6 | .20 | .09 |
| ❑ 226 Poland-Rom. 8-6 | .20 | .09 |
| ❑ 227 Poland-Rom. 8-6 | .20 | .09 |
| ❑ 228 Poland-Rom. 8-6 | .20 | .09 |
| ❑ 229 Poland-Hun. 7-2 | .20 | .09 |
| ❑ 230 Poland-Hun. 7-2 | .20 | .09 |
| ❑ 231 Japan-Yug. 6-1 | .20 | .09 |
| ❑ 232 Japan-Yug. 6-1 | .20 | .09 |
| ❑ 233 Italy-Yug. 6-1 | .20 | .09 |
| ❑ 234 Italy-Yug. 6-1 | .20 | .09 |
| ❑ 235 Rom.-Italy 5-5 | .20 | .09 |
| ❑ 236 Rom.-Italy 5-5 | .20 | .09 |
| ❑ 237 Poland | .20 | .09 |
| ❑ 238 Poland | .20 | .09 |
| ❑ 239 Deutschland-DDR | .20 | .09 |
| ❑ 240 Hungary | .20 | .09 |
| ❑ 241 Netherland | .20 | .09 |
| ❑ 242 Romania | .20 | .09 |
| ❑ 243 Switzerland | .20 | .09 |
| ❑ 244 Japan | .20 | .09 |
| ❑ 245 Norway | .20 | .09 |
| ❑ 246 Austria | .20 | .09 |
| ❑ 247 DDR | .20 | .09 |
| ❑ 248 DDR | .20 | .09 |
| ❑ 249 Herzig and Kraske | .20 | .09 |
| ❑ 250 Simon and Peters | .20 | .09 |
| ❑ 251 Frenzel and Lempio | .20 | .09 |
| ❑ 252 Fengler and Slapke | .20 | .09 |
| ❑ 253 Patschinski and Bielas 1 | .20 | .09 |
| ❑ 254 Peters and Scholz | .20 | .09 |
| ❑ 255 Bogelsack and Stasche | .20 | .09 |
| ❑ 256 Switzerland | .20 | .09 |
| ❑ 257 Switzerland | .20 | .09 |
| ❑ 258 Grubauer and Anken | .20 | .09 |
| ❑ 259 Zenhausern and Meyer | .20 | .09 |
| ❑ 260 Kolliker and Locher | .20 | .09 |
| ❑ 261 Mattli and Conte | .20 | .09 |
| ❑ 262 Holzer and Dellsberger | .20 | .09 |
| ❑ 263 Horisberger and Rossetti | .20 | .09 |
| ❑ 264 Berger and Schmid | .20 | .09 |
| ❑ 265 Hungary | .20 | .09 |
| ❑ 266 Hungary | .20 | .09 |
| ❑ 267 Balagh and Farkas | .20 | .09 |
| ❑ 268 Kovacs and Hajzer | .20 | .09 |
| ❑ 269 Flora and Kereszty | .20 | .09 |
| ❑ 270 Palla and Meszoly | .20 | .09 |
| ❑ 271 Menyhart and Havran | .20 | .09 |
| ❑ 272 Poth and Muhr | .20 | .09 |
| ❑ 273 Buzas and Pek | .20 | .09 |
| ❑ 274 Netherlands | .20 | .09 |
| ❑ 275 Netherlands | .20 | .09 |
| ❑ 276 Van Bilsen and Krikke | .20 | .09 |
| ❑ 277 Van Soldt and Peternousek | .20 | .09 |
| ❑ 278 Kolijn and Van Den Broek | .20 | .09 |
| ❑ 279 Van Wieren and Toren | .20 | .09 |
| ❑ 280 Van Onlangs and Schaffer | .20 | .09 |
| ❑ 281 Janssen and Van Der Griendt | .20 | .09 |
| ❑ 282 De Heer and Koopmans | .20 | .09 |
| ❑ 283 Japan | .20 | .09 |
| ❑ 284 Japan | .20 | .09 |
| ❑ 285 Iwamoto and Misaw | .20 | .09 |
| ❑ 286 Ito and Tonozaki | .20 | .09 |
| ❑ 287 Hori and Nakayama | .20 | .09 |
| ❑ 288 Tanaka and Kyoya | .20 | .09 |
| ❑ 289 Kawamura and Hoshino | .20 | .09 |
| ❑ 290 Misawa and Sakurai | .20 | .09 |
| ❑ 291 Honma and Hanzawa | .20 | .09 |
| ❑ 292 Norway | .20 | .09 |
| ❑ 293 Norway | .20 | .09 |
| ❑ 294 Walberg and Goldstein | .20 | .09 |
| ❑ 295 Martinsen and Molberg | .20 | .09 |
| ❑ 296 Nilsen and Erevik | .20 | .09 |
| ❑ 297 Lien and Roymark | .20 | .09 |
| ❑ 298 Eriksen and Ovstedal | .20 | .09 |
| ❑ 299 Johansen and Haraldsen | .20 | .09 |
| ❑ 300 Stethereng and Throrkildsen | .20 | .09 |
| ❑ 301 Austria | .20 | .09 |
| ❑ 302 Austria | .20 | .09 |
| ❑ 303 Schilcherl and Prohaska | .20 | .09 |
| ❑ 304 Hyytaienen and Russ | .20 | .09 |
| ❑ 305 Staribacher and Schneider | .20 | .09 |
| ❑ 306 Kotnauer and Pok | .20 | .09 |
| ❑ 307 Sadjina and Konig | .20 | .09 |
| ❑ 308 Mortl and Pepeunig | .20 | .09 |
| ❑ 309 Schilchner and Haiszan | .20 | .09 |
| ❑ 310 Romania | .20 | .09 |
| ❑ 311 Romania | .20 | .09 |
| ❑ 312 Hutan and Netedu | .20 | .09 |
| ❑ 313 Antal and Gall | .20 | .09 |
| ❑ 314 Lustinian and Lonita | .20 | .09 |
| ❑ 315 Hutanu and Halauca | .20 | .09 |
| ❑ 316 Tureanu and Axinte | .20 | .09 |
| ❑ 317 Nagy and Costea | .20 | .09 |
| ❑ 318 Nistor and Olenici | .20 | .09 |
| ❑ 319 Poster | .20 | .09 |
| ❑ 320 Den.-Net 3-3 | .20 | .09 |
| ❑ 321 Den.-Net 3-3 | .20 | .09 |
| ❑ 322 Net.-Spain 19-0 | .20 | .09 |

❑ 323 Net.-Spain 19-0 .20 .09
❑ 324 Aus.-Den 7-4 .20 .09
❑ 325 Aus.-Den 7-4 .20 .09
❑ 326 Net.-Bul. 8-0 .20 .09
❑ 327 China-Den. 3-2 .20 .09
❑ 328 China-France 8-4 .20 .09
❑ 329 Bulgaria .20 .09
❑ 330 France .20 .09
❑ 331 Italy .20 .09
❑ 332 Yugoslavia .20 .09
❑ 333 Belgium .20 .09
❑ 334 China .20 .09
❑ 335 Denmark .20 .09
❑ 336 Spain .20 .09
❑ 337 Belgium .20 .09
❑ 338 Belgium .20 .09
❑ 339 Smeets and Lauwers .20 .09
❑ 340 Adriaensen and Zwikel .20 .09
❑ 341 Cuvelier and Sarazin .20 .09
❑ 342 Vermeulen and Voskertian .20 .09
❑ 343 Verschraegen and Arnould .20 .09
❑ 344 Lejeune and Langh .20 .09
❑ 345 Bulgaria .20 .09
❑ 346 Bulgaria .20 .09
❑ 347 Iliev and Lazarov .20 .09
❑ 348 Iliev and Krastinov .20 .09
❑ 349 Hristov and Petrov .20 .09
❑ 350 Atanasov and Nenov .20 .09
❑ 351 Todorov and Stoilov .20 .09
❑ 352 Guerasimov and Batchvarov .20 .09
❑ 353 China .20 .09
❑ 354 China .20 .09
❑ 355 Ting Wen and Yung Ke .20 .09
❑ 356 Ke and Shao Tang .20 .09
❑ 357 Ta Chun and Ung Sheng .20 .09
❑ 358 Hsi Kiang and Chang Shun .20 .09
❑ 359 Cheng Hsin and Te Hsi .20 .09
❑ 360 Shu Ching and Sheng Wen .20 .09
❑ 361 Denmark .20 .09
❑ 362 Denmark .20 .09
❑ 363 Hansen and Holten Moller .20 .09
❑ 364 Andersen and Pedersen .20 .09
❑ 365 Henriksen and Hviid .20 .09
❑ 366 Nielsen and Thomsen .20 .09
❑ 367 Nielsen and Kahl .20 .09
❑ 368 Jensen and Gjerding .20 .09
❑ 369 Spain .20 .09
❑ 370 Spain .20 .09
❑ 371 Estrada and Lizarraga .20 .09
❑ 372 Gonzalez and Munitiz .20 .09
❑ 373 Marin and Aguado .20 .09
❑ 374 Raventos and Encinas .20 .09
❑ 375 Capillas and Sarazirar .20 .09
❑ 376 Labayen and Plaza .20 .09
❑ 377 France .20 .09
❑ 378 France .20 .09
❑ 379 Maric and Del Monaco .20 .09
❑ 380 Oprandi and Combe .20 .09
❑ 381 Allard and Le Blond .20 .09
❑ 382 Vassieux and Rey .20 .09
❑ 383 Galiay and Le Blond .20 .09
❑ 384 Vinard and Smaniotto .20 .09
❑ 385 Italy .20 .09
❑ 386 Italy .20 .09
❑ 387 Tigliani and Gasser .20 .09
❑ 388 Kostner and Pasqualotto .20 .09
❑ 389 Lacedelli and Polloni .20 .09
❑ 390 Insam and De Toni .20 .09
❑ 391 Strohmaier and Kasslatter .20 .09
❑ 392 De Marchi and Pugliese .20 .09
❑ 393 Yugoslavia .20 .09
❑ 394 Yugoslavia .20 .09
❑ 395 Zbontar and Scap .20 .09
❑ 396 Kumar and Kosir .20 .09
❑ 397 Kavec and Smolej .20 .09
❑ 398 Kafner and Lepsa .20 .09
❑ 399 Poljansek and Kosir .20 .09
❑ 400 Klemenc and Jan .20 .09
❑ xx Sticker Album 20.00 9.00

## 1983 Russian National Team

This 23-card set presents Russian hockey players. The cards were packaged in a cardboard sleeve that displays a photo of the 1983 Russian national team. The cards measure approximately 5 1/2" by 7" and feature full-bleed head and shoulders shots of

the players dressed in civilian clothing. On the left portion, the backs carry three action shots in a filmstrip format while the right portion has player information in Russian. The cards are unnumbered and checklisted below in alphabetical order.

| | MINT | NRMT |
|---|---|---|
| COMPLETE SET (23) | 75.00 | 34.00 |
| COMMON CARD (1-23) | 2.50 | 1.10 |

❑ 1 Sergei Babinov 2.50 1.10
❑ 2 Helmut Balderis 3.50 1.55
❑ 3 Zinetula Bilyaletinov 2.50 1.10
❑ 4 Vyacheslav Bykov 5.00 2.20
❑ 5 Vyacheslav Fetisov 10.00 4.50
❑ 6 Irek Gimaev 2.50 1.10
❑ 7 Sergei Kapustin 2.50 1.10
❑ 8 Alexei Kasatonov 6.00 2.70
❑ 9 Andrei Khomotov 5.00 2.20
❑ 10 Vladimir Krutov 10.00 4.50
❑ 11 Igor Larionov 10.00 4.50
❑ 12 Sergei Makarov 10.00 4.50
❑ 13 Alexander Maltsev 5.00 2.20
❑ 14 Vasily Pervukhin 2.50 1.10
❑ 15 Sergei Shepelev 2.50 1.10
❑ 16 Alexander Skvorstsov 2.50 1.10
❑ 17 Sergei Starikov 3.50 1.55
❑ 18 Viktor Tikhonov CO 5.00 2.20
❑ 19 Vladislav Tretiak 12.00 5.50
❑ 20 Mikhael Vasiliev 2.50 1.10
❑ 21 Vladimir Yurzinov CO 2.50 1.10
❑ 22 Viktor Zhluktov 2.50 1.10
❑ 23 Vladimir Zubkov 2.50 1.10

## 1987 Russian National Team

This 24-card set presents Russian hockey players and is subtitled "The USSR 1987 National Hockey Team." The cards were printed in the USSR, released by Panorama Publishers (USSR), and distributed in North America by Tri-Globe International, Inc. The production run was reportedly 25,000 sets. The cards were packaged in a cardboard sleeve that displays a team photo from the world championships. The cards measure approximately 4 1/8" by 5 13/16" and feature full-bleed head and shoulders shots of the players dressed in coat and tie. The player's autograph and uniform number are printed on the lower portion of the picture in gold lettering. The backs are in Russian and present player profile and statistics. The cards are unnumbered and checklisted below in alphabetical order.

| | MINT | NRMT |
|---|---|---|
| COMPLETE SET (24) | 30.00 | 13.50 |
| COMMON CARD (1-24) | 1.00 | .45 |

❑ 1 Sergei Ageikin 1.00 .45
❑ 2 Evgeny Belosheikin 1.50 .70
❑ 3 Zinetula Belyaletdinov 1.00 .45
❑ 4 Viacheslav Bykov 2.00 .90
❑ 5 Viacheslav Fetisov 5.00 2.20
❑ 6 Alexei Gusarov 1.50 .70
❑ 7 Valeri Kamensky 3.00 1.35
❑ 8 Alexei Kasatonov 2.00 .90
❑ 9 Yuri Khmylev 1.50 .70
❑ 10 Andrei Khomutov 2.00 .90
❑ 11 Vladimir Konstantinov 3.00 1.35
❑ 12 Vladimir Krutov 3.00 1.35
❑ 13 Igor Larionov 5.00 2.20
❑ 14 Sergei Makarov 5.00 2.20
❑ 15 Sergei Mylnikov 1.50 .70
❑ 16 Vasili Pervukhin 1.00 .45
❑ 17 Sergei Starikov 1.00 .45
❑ 18 Igor Stelnov 1.00 .45
❑ 19 Sergei Svetlov 1.00 .45
❑ 20 Viktor Tikhonov CO 2.00 .90
❑ 21 Viktor Tjumenev 1.00 .45
❑ 22 Michael Varnakov 1.00 .45
❑ 23 Sergei Yashin 1.00 .45
❑ 24 Vladimir Yursinov CO 1.00 .45

## 1989 Russian National Team

This set of 24 postcards was released by Plakat Publishers, USSR. The cards measure approximately 4 1/8" by 5 13/16" and features some of the best Russian players of modern years. The set features 22 player cards and two coach cards. The cards were packaged in a cardboard sleeve that displays an action photo of Valeri Kamensky. Reportedly 100,000 sets were printed but most were sold in the USSR and fewer sets made it to the U.S. and Canada. The fronts have head and shoulder shots of Russian Team players in coat and tie (street clothes) with a superimposed facsimile autograph while the backs contain biographical information in Russian. An unauthorized reprint of the set was issued in 1991, but the size was reduced to 2 1/2" by 3 1/2". The players in the reprint set who had since played in the NHL were given English biographies on labels added to the back. The cards are listed below alphabetically since they are unnumbered.

| | MINT | NRMT |
|---|---|---|
| COMPLETE SET (24) | 25.00 | 11.00 |
| COMMON CARD (1-24) | .50 | .23 |

❑ 1 Ilya Byakin .75 .35
❑ 2 Viachaslav Bykov 1.00 .45
❑ 3 Alexandr Chernik .50 .23
❑ 4 Igor Dmitriev CO .50 .23
❑ 5 Sergei Fedorov 8.00 3.60
❑ 6 Viacheslav Fetisov 2.50 1.10
❑ 7 Alexei Gusarov .75 .35
❑ 8 Arturs Irbe 4.00 1.80
❑ 9 Valeri Kamensky 2.00 .90
❑ 10 Alexei Kasatonov 1.50 .70
❑ 11 Svatoslav Khalizov .50 .23
❑ 12 Yuri Khmylev .75 .35
❑ 13 Andrei Khomutov 1.00 .45
❑ 14 Vladimir Konstantinov 2.00 .90
❑ 15 Vladimir Krutov 1.50 .70
❑ 16 Dimitri Kvartalnov 1.00 .45
❑ 17 Igor Larionov 3.00 1.35
❑ 18 Sergei Makarov 2.50 1.10
❑ 19 Vladimir Mishkin 1.00 .45
❑ 20 Sergei Mylnikov 1.00 .45
❑ 21 Sergei Nemchinov 1.00 .45
❑ 22 Valeri Shirjaev .50 .23
❑ 23 Viktor Tikhonov CO 1.00 .45
❑ 24 Sergei Yashin .50 .23

## 1991 Russian Stars in NHL

This 11-card standard-size set was reportedly printed in Leningrad by Ivan Fiodorov Press as a special limited edition; it is claimed that there were only 50,000 sets issued. The cards essentially feature Russian players in the NHL. The front has a full-color player photo, bordered on the two sides by hockey sticks (with hockey gloves below). A red banner is draped across the top of the picture, with the player's name in between USSR (sickle and hammer) and USA (US flag) emblems. In contrast to the dark purple background, the bottom is light purple and presents the message "Sports Unites Hearts" in English and Russian. The horizontally-oriented back provide player information in two colored panels (English and Russian) and has a head shot of the player as well.

| | MINT | NRMT |
|---|---|---|
| COMPLETE SET (11) | 8.00 | 3.60 |
| COMMON CARD (1-11) | .25 | .11 |

❑ 1 Sergei Fedorov 4.00 1.80
❑ 2 Viachelsav Fetisov .75 .35
❑ 3 Alexei Gusarov .25 .11
❑ 4 Alexei Kasatonov .50 .23
❑ 5 Vladimir Konstantinov .75 .35
❑ 6 Igor Larionov 1.00 .45
❑ 7 Sergei Makarov 1.00 .45
❑ 8 Alexander Mogilny 1.50 .70
❑ 9 Mikhail Tatarinov .25 .11
❑ 10 Vladislav Tretiak 2.00 .90
❑ 11 Team Photo .35 .16
USSR National Team

## 1991-92 Russian Stars Red Ace

This 17-card standard-size set, featuring Russian stars in the NHL, was produced by Red Ace. The cards were packaged in a box, on which it is claimed that the production run was limited to 50,000 sets. The fronts feature borderless action shots with the player's name. Printed on white cover stock, the horizontal backs feature a close-up photograph as well as biographical and statistical information in Russian and English. The cards are unnumbered and checklisted below in alphabetical order.

| | MINT | NRMT |
|---|---|---|
| COMPLETE SET (17) | 10.00 | 4.50 |
| COMMON CARD (1-17) | .25 | .11 |

❑ 1 Pavel Bure 3.00 1.35
❑ 2 Evgeny Davydov .25 .11
❑ 3 Sergei Fedorov 3.00 1.35
❑ 4 Viacheslav Fetisov .75 .35
❑ 5 Alexei Gusarov .25 .11
❑ 6 Valeri Kamensky .75 .35
❑ 7 Alexei Kasatonov .50 .23
❑ 8 Ravil Khaidarov .25 .11
❑ 9 Vladimir Konstantinov .75 .35
❑ 10 Igor Kravchuk .35 .16
❑ 11 Igor Larionov .75 .35
❑ 12 Andrei Lomakin .25 .11
❑ 13 Sergei Makarov .75 .35
❑ 14 Alexander Mogilny 1.25 .55
❑ 15 Sergei Nemchinov .35 .16
❑ 16 Anatoli Semenov .35 .16
❑ 17 Mikhail Tatarinov .25 .11

## 1991-92 Russian Tri-Globe Bure

This standard-size five-card set was produced by Tri-Globe as part of the "The Magnificent Five" series. These sets spotlight five Russian hockey stars currently playing in the NHL, with set 2 featuring Pavel Bure. It is claimed that 5,000 numbered display boxes were produced, each containing 40 sets (ten for each player). Printed in Russia on heavy laminated textured stock, card fronts feature full-color action shots in various formats and accented predominantly in green. In a horizontal format, the green backs carry another full-color photo and career statistics printed in English and French. The card number appears in a circle at the top right along with the sponsor's logo. Each set includes a checklist on the back of a Sergei Fedorov promo card.

| | MINT | NRMT |
|---|---|---|
| COMPLETE SET (6) | 7.00 | 3.10 |
| COMMON CARD (6-10) | 1.50 | .70 |

❑ 6 Pavel Bure 1.50 .70
One of the World's Best
❑ 7 Pavel Bure 1.50 .70
A World Champion
❑ 8 Pavel Bure 1.50 .70
A World Class Forward
❑ 9 Pavel Bure 1.50 .70
Champion of the USSR
❑ 10 Pavel Bure 1.50 .70
A European Champion
❑ NNO Sergei Fedorov .50 .23
Checklist

## 1991-92 Russian Tri-Globe Fedorov

This five-card set honoring Sergei Fedorov is the product of a joint venture between Tri-Globe International, Inc. and Ivan Fiodorov Press. The cards measure approximately 2 1/2" by 3 3/4" and are printed on a grainy cardboard stock. The fronts feature color action game shots. The first card has the player's name printed in a green stripe to the right of the picture. In a yellow stripe below the picture, card numbers 2-5 have a caption and a drawing of a leopard, elk, bear, and lion respectively. The backs of all the cards have smaller color action shots and career summary in English and Russian. The cards are numbered on the back. Dealers who purchased 50 or more sets received a promotion poster, which uses the same player photo as on card number 1. According to Tri-Globe, 600 uncut, numbered sheets were printed, producing the equivalent of 3,000 sets, as well as 1,000 uncut, numbered five-card strips. Moreover, 100,000 five-card sets were reportedly produced.

| | MINT | NRMT |
|---|---|---|
| COMPLETE SET (5) | 6.00 | 2.70 |
| COMMON CARD (1-5) | 1.25 | .55 |

❑ 1 Sergei Fedorov 1.25 .55
❑ 2 Sergei Fedorov 1.25 .55
Some men are faster
❑ 3 Sergei Fedorov 1.25 .55
Some men are tougher
❑ 4 Sergei Fedorov 1.25 .55
Some men are stronger
❑ 5 Sergei Fedorov 1.25 .55
Some men are better

## 1991-92 Russian Tri-Globe Irbe

This standard-size five-card set was produced by Tri-Globe as part of the "The Magnificent Five" series. These sets spotlight five Russian hockey stars currently playing in the NHL, with set four featuring Arturs Irbe. It is claimed that 5,000 numbered display boxes were produced, each containing 40 sets (ten for each player). Printed in Russia on heavy laminated textured stock, card fronts feature full-color action shots in various formats and accented predominantly in yellowish orange. In a horizontal format, the yellowish orange backs carry another full-color photo and career statistics printed in English and French. The card number appears in a circle at the top right along with the sponsor's logo. Each set includes a checklist on the back of a Sergei Fedorov promo card.

| | MINT | NRMT |
|---|---|---|
| COMPLETE SET (6) | 4.00 | 1.80 |
| COMMON CARD (16-20) | .75 | .35 |

❑ 16 Arturs Irbe .75 .35
One of the World's Best
❑ 17 Arturs Irbe .75 .35
A European Champion
❑ 18 Arturs Irbe .75 .35
A World Class Goaltender
❑ 19 Arturs Irbe .75 .35
A World Champion
❑ 20 Arturs Irbe .75 .35
There are only few of them
❑ NNO Sergei Fedorov .50 .23
Checklist

## 1991-92 Russian Tri-Globe Kamensky

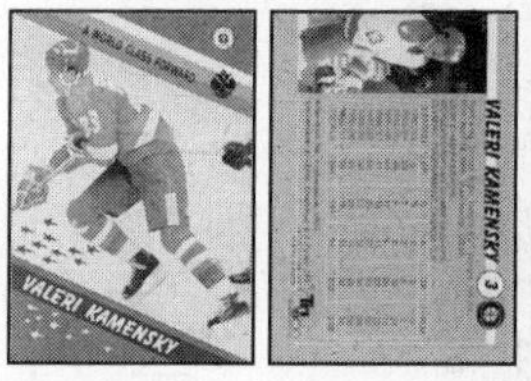


This standard-size five-card set was produced by Tri-Globe as part of the "The Magnificent Five" series. These sets spotlight five Russian hockey stars currently playing in the NHL, with set 1 featuring Valeri Kamensky. It is claimed that 5,000 numbered display boxes were produced, each containing 40 sets (ten for each player). Printed in Russia on heavy laminated textured stock, card fronts feature full-color action shots in various formats and accented predominantly in purple. In a horizontal format, the lavender backs carry another full-color photo and career statistics printed in English and French. The card number appears in a circle at the top right along with the sponsor's logo. Each set includes a checklist on the back of a Sergei Fedorov promo card.

| | MINT | NRMT |
|---|---|---|
| COMPLETE SET (6) | 4.00 | 1.80 |
| COMMON CARD (1-5) | .75 | .35 |

❑ 1 Valeri Kamensky .75 .35
One of the World's Best
❑ 2 Valeri Kamensky .75 .35
A World Champion
❑ 3 Valeri Kamensky .75 .35
A World Class Forward
❑ 4 Valeri Kamensky .75 .35
Champion of the USSR
❑ 5 Valeri Kamensky .75 .35
There are only few of them
❑ NNO Sergei Fedorov .50 .23
Checklist

## 1991-92 Russian Tri-Globe Semenov

This standard-size five-card set was produced by Tri-Globe as part of the "The Magnificent

Five" series. These sets spotlight five Russian hockey stars currently playing in the NHL, with set three featuring Anatoli Semenov. It is claimed that 5,000 numbered display boxes were produced, each containing 40 sets (ten for each player). Printed in Russia on heavy laminated textured stock, card fronts feature full-color action shots in various formats and accented predominantly in aqua. In a horizontal format, the aqua backs carry another full-color photo and career statistics printed in English and French. The card number appears in a circle at the top right along with the sponsor's logo. Each set includes a checklist on the back of a Sergei Fedorov promo card.

| | MINT | NRMT |
|---|---|---|
| COMPLETE SET (6) | 1.50 | .70 |
| COMMON CARD (11-15) | .25 | .11 |
| ❑ 11 Anatoli Semenov One of the World's Best | .25 | .11 |
| ❑ 12 Anatoli Semenov An Olympic Champion | .25 | .11 |
| ❑ 13 Anatoli Semenov A World Class Forward | .25 | .11 |
| ❑ 14 Anatoli Semenov Champion of the USSR | .25 | .11 |
| ❑ 15 Anatoli Semenov There are only few of them | .25 | .11 |
| ❑ NNO Sergei Fedorov Checklist | .50 | .23 |

## 1992 Russian Stars Red Ace

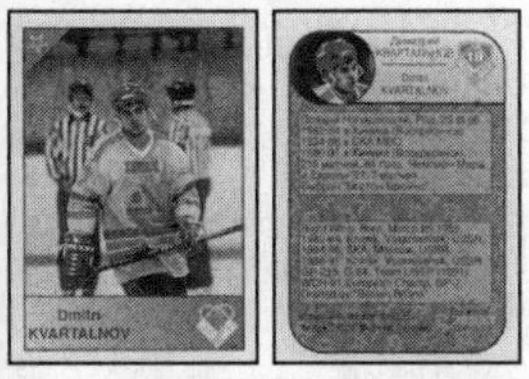

The 1992 Red Ace Russian Hockey Stars boxed set was co-sponsored by the World of Hockey Magazine and World Sport. The cards were sold in a light blue box with production limited supposedly to 25,000 sets. The cards are printed on thin card stock and measure approximately 2 1/2" by 3 3/8". The light blue bordered fronts feature color action player photos. The player's name appears on a light green diagonal stripe in an upper corner, accented with a red triangle containing a white star. The Red Ace logo is printed in a lower corner of the picture. The white backs display a small head shot next to the player's name on a green bar. In a pale pink panel below is the player's biography and career highlights in Russian and English. The cards are numbered on the back.

| | MINT | NRMT |
|---|---|---|
| COMPLETE SET (36) | 12.00 | 5.50 |
| COMMON CARD (1-36) | .25 | .11 |
| ❑ 1 Darius Kasparaitis | .50 | .23 |
| ❑ 2 Alexei Zhamnov | 1.00 | .45 |
| ❑ 3 Dmitri Khristich | .50 | .23 |
| ❑ 4 Andrei Trefilov | .50 | .23 |
| ❑ 5 Vitali Prokhorov | .25 | .11 |
| ❑ 6 Dmitri Filimonov | .25 | .11 |
| ❑ 7 Valeri Zelepukin | .35 | .16 |
| ❑ 8 Alexei Kovalev | 1.00 | .45 |
| ❑ 9 Dmitri Kvartalnov | .35 | .16 |
| ❑ 10 Igor Korolev | .25 | .11 |
| ❑ 11 Nikolai Borschevsky | .35 | .16 |
| ❑ 12 Igor Boldin | .25 | .11 |
| ❑ 13 Arturs Irbe | 1.00 | .45 |
| ❑ 14 Viacheslav Butsayev | .35 | .16 |
| ❑ 15 Boris Mironov | .50 | .23 |
| ❑ 16 Sergei Bautin | .25 | .11 |
| ❑ 17 Alexander Kharlamov | .50 | .23 |
| ❑ 18 Viacheslav Kozlov | 1.00 | .45 |
| ❑ 19 Mikhail Shtalenkov | .50 | .23 |
| ❑ 20 Roman Oksyuta | .35 | .16 |
| ❑ 21 Sandis Ozolinsh | 1.50 | .70 |
| ❑ 22 Dmitri Mironov | .50 | .23 |
| ❑ 23 Sergei Brylin | .25 | .11 |
| ❑ 24 Vladimir Grachev | .25 | .11 |
| ❑ 25 Dmitri Starostenko | .25 | .11 |
| ❑ 26 Andrei Nazarov | .35 | .16 |
| ❑ 27 Alexei Yashin | 1.50 | .70 |
| ❑ 28 Vladimir Malakhov | .50 | .23 |
| ❑ 29 Ravil Jakubov | .25 | .11 |
| ❑ 30 Sergei Klimovich | .25 | .11 |
| ❑ 31 Artur Oktjabrev | .25 | .11 |
| ❑ 32 Lev Berdichevski | .25 | .11 |
| ❑ 33 Ian Kaminski | .35 | .16 |
| ❑ 34 Andrei Kovalenko | .50 | .23 |
| ❑ 35 Dmitri Yushkevich | .35 | .16 |
| ❑ 36 Checklist | .25 | .11 |

## 1992 Tri-Globe From Russia With Puck

Twelve Russian hockey stars who are currently playing in the NHL are featured in this 24-card boxed standard-size set, with two cards devoted to each player. The production run was reportedly 50,000 sets. The fronts of all cards display color action player photos. On the player's first card (i.e., an odd-numbered card), his name appears at the top in a silver stripe, and red, white, and blue stripes accent the picture on three sides. On his second card (i.e., an even-numbered card), black-and-white speckled stripes edge the picture above and below. The back of the player's first card carries a second color action photo and biographical information, while the back of his second card has a close-up color photo and career statistics. All text is in French and English.

| | MINT | NRMT |
|---|---|---|
| COMPLETE SET (24) | 8.00 | 3.60 |
| COMMON CARD (1-24) | .25 | .11 |
| ❑ 1 Igor Larionov | .50 | .23 |
| ❑ 2 Igor Larionov | .50 | .23 |
| ❑ 3 Andrei Lomakin | .25 | .11 |
| ❑ 4 Andrei Lomakin | .25 | .11 |
| ❑ 5 Pavel Bure | 2.00 | .90 |
| ❑ 6 Pavel Bure | 2.00 | .90 |
| ❑ 7 Alexei Zhamnov | .75 | .35 |
| ❑ 8 Alexei Zhamnov | .75 | .35 |
| ❑ 9 Sergei Krivokrasov | .25 | .11 |
| ❑ 10 Sergei Krivokrasov | .25 | .11 |
| ❑ 11 Valeri Kamensky | .35 | .16 |
| ❑ 12 Valeri Kamensky | .35 | .16 |
| ❑ 13 Viacheslav Kozlov | .50 | .23 |
| ❑ 14 Viacheslav Kozlov | .50 | .23 |
| ❑ 15 Valeri Zelepukin | .25 | .11 |
| ❑ 16 Valeri Zelepukin | .25 | .11 |
| ❑ 17 Igor Kravchuk | .25 | .11 |
| ❑ 18 Igor Kravchuk | .25 | .11 |
| ❑ 19 Vladimir Malakhov | .35 | .16 |
| ❑ 20 Vladimir Malakhov | .35 | .16 |
| ❑ 21 Boris Mironov | .50 | .23 |
| ❑ 22 Boris Mironov | .50 | .23 |
| ❑ 23 Arturs Irbe | .75 | .35 |
| ❑ 24 Arturs Irbe | .75 | .35 |

## 1992-93 Russian Stars Red Ace

This 37-card, standard-size set features action color player photos bordered in white. The player's name and the Red Ace logo appear in a gradated violet stripe at the bottom. A red triangle at the upper left corner of the picture carries a white star outline. In a red box with rounded corners, the back provides biography in Cyrillic (Russian) and English. The top portion of the back has a yellow background and displays a close-up photo in a circular format and the player's name in Russian and English. The cards are numbered on the back essentially alphabetically.

| | MINT | NRMT |
|---|---|---|
| COMPLETE SET (37) | 10.00 | 4.50 |
| COMMON CARD (1-36) | .25 | .11 |
| ❑ 1 Alexander Barkov | .25 | .11 |
| ❑ 2 Sergei Bautin | .25 | .11 |
| ❑ 3 Igor Boldin | .25 | .11 |
| ❑ 4 Nikolai Borchevsky | .35 | .16 |
| ❑ 5 Sergei Brylin | .25 | .11 |
| ❑ 6 Viacheslav Butsayev | .25 | .11 |
| ❑ 7 Alexander Cherbajev | .35 | .16 |
| ❑ 8 Evgeny Garanin | .25 | .11 |
| ❑ 9 Sergei Gonchar | .35 | .16 |
| ❑ 10 Alexander Karpovtsev | .35 | .16 |
| ❑ 11 Darius Kasparaitis | .50 | .23 |
| ❑ 12 Alexander Kharlamov | .50 | .23 |
| ❑ 13 Yuri Khmylev | .35 | .16 |
| ❑ 14 Sergei Klimovich | .25 | .11 |
| ❑ 15 Igor Korolev | .25 | .11 |
| ❑ 16 Andrei Kovalenko | .50 | .23 |
| ❑ 17 Alexei Kovalev UER (Back photo is Igor Korolev) | 1.00 | .45 |
| ❑ 18 Dmitri Kvartalnov | .35 | .16 |
| ❑ 19 Vladimir Malakhov | .35 | .16 |
| ❑ 20 Maxim Mikhailovsky | .25 | .11 |
| ❑ 21 Boris Mironov | .50 | .23 |
| ❑ 22 Dmitri Mironov | .50 | .23 |
| ❑ 23 Andrei Nazarov | .35 | .16 |
| ❑ 24 Roman Oksyuta | .35 | .16 |
| ❑ 25 Artur Oktyabrev | .25 | .11 |
| ❑ 26 Sergei Petrenko | .25 | .11 |
| ❑ 27 Oleg Petrov | .25 | .11 |
| ❑ 28 Andrei Potaichuk | .25 | .11 |
| ❑ 29 Vitali Prokhorov | .25 | .11 |
| ❑ 30 Alexander Semak | .35 | .16 |
| ❑ 31 Dmitri Starostenko | .25 | .11 |
| ❑ 32 Ravil Yakubov | .25 | .11 |
| ❑ 33 Alexei Yashin | 1.50 | .70 |
| ❑ 34 Dmitri Yushkevich | .25 | .11 |
| ❑ 35 Alexei Zhamnov | 1.00 | .45 |
| ❑ 36 Alexei Zhitnik | .50 | .23 |
| ❑ NNO Checklist Card | .25 | .11 |

## 1993-94 Sheffield Steelers

| | MINT | NRMT |
|---|---|---|
| COMPLETE SET (19) | 6.00 | 2.70 |
| COMMON CARD (1-19) | .15 | .07 |
| ❑ 1 Andy Havenhand | .30 | .14 |
| ❑ 2 Alan Hague | .30 | .14 |
| ❑ 3 Tim Cranston | .30 | .14 |
| ❑ 4 Neil Abel | .30 | .14 |
| ❑ 5 Scott Neil | .30 | .14 |
| ❑ 6 Steve Nemeth | .30 | .14 |
| ❑ 7 Tommy Plommer | .30 | .14 |
| ❑ 8 Ivan Matulik | .30 | .14 |
| ❑ 9 Danny Boome | .30 | .14 |
| ❑ 10 Mark Wright | .30 | .14 |
| ❑ 11 Chris Kelland | .30 | .14 |
| ❑ 12 Les Millie | .30 | .14 |
| ❑ 13 Selmar Odeline | .30 | .14 |
| ❑ 14 Ron Shudra | .30 | .14 |
| ❑ 15 Martin McKay | .30 | .14 |
| ❑ 16 Dampier w/Tuyl | .30 | .14 |
| ❑ 17 Netminders | .30 | .14 |
| ❑ 18 Team Photo | .15 | .07 |
| ❑ 19 Sheffield Scimitars | .30 | .14 |

## 1994-95 Sheffield Steelers

| | MINT | NRMT |
|---|---|---|
| COMPLETE SET (25) | 6.00 | 2.70 |
| COMMON CARD (1-25) | .15 | .07 |
| ❑ 1 Alex Dampier MGR | .30 | .14 |
| ❑ 2 Clyde Tuyl CO | .30 | .14 |
| ❑ 3 Paul Jackson | .30 | .14 |
| ❑ 4 Scott Neil | .30 | .14 |
| ❑ 5 Team Photo | .15 | .07 |
| ❑ 6 Ron Handy | .30 | .14 |
| ❑ 7 Patrick O'Conner | .30 | .14 |
| ❑ 8 Dean Smith | .30 | .14 |
| ❑ 9 Mike O'Conner | .30 | .14 |
| ❑ 10 Backroom Staff | .30 | .14 |
| ❑ 11 Tim Cranston | .30 | .14 |
| ❑ 12 Les Millie | .30 | .14 |
| ❑ 13 Alan Hague | .30 | .14 |
| ❑ 14 Perry Doyle | .30 | .14 |
| ❑ 15 Ron Shudra | .30 | .14 |
| ❑ 16 Mark Wright | .30 | .14 |
| ❑ 17 Tommy Plommer | .30 | .14 |
| ❑ 18 Scott Heaton | .30 | .14 |
| ❑ 19 Neil Abel | .30 | .14 |
| ❑ 20 Steeler Dan | .30 | .14 |
| ❑ 21 Rob Wilson | .30 | .14 |
| ❑ 22 Chris Kelland | .30 | .14 |
| ❑ 23 Andy Havenhand | .30 | .14 |
| ❑ 24 Martin McKay | .30 | .14 |
| ❑ 25 Steve Nemeth | .30 | .14 |

## 1995-96 Sheffield Steelers

| | MINT | NRMT |
|---|---|---|
| COMPLETE SET (24) | 6.00 | 2.70 |
| COMMON CARD (1-24) | .15 | .07 |
| ❑ 1 Martin McKay | .30 | .14 |
| ❑ 2 Ron Shudra | .30 | .14 |
| ❑ 3 Ken Priestlay | .30 | .14 |
| ❑ 4 Steve Nemeth | .30 | .14 |
| ❑ 5 Tommy Plommer | .30 | .14 |
| ❑ 6 Nicky Chinn | .30 | .14 |
| ❑ 7 Tony Hand | .30 | .14 |
| ❑ 8 Mike O'Conner | .30 | .14 |
| ❑ 9 Mark Wright | .30 | .14 |
| ❑ 10 Chris Kelland | .30 | .14 |
| ❑ 11 Andre Malo | .30 | .14 |
| ❑ 12 Les Millie | .30 | .14 |
| ❑ 13 Sheffield Arena | .30 | .14 |
| ❑ 14 Team Photo | .15 | .07 |
| ❑ 15 Scott Heaton | .30 | .14 |
| ❑ 16 Tim Cranston | .30 | .14 |
| ❑ 17 Neil Abel | .30 | .14 |
| ❑ 18 Scott Neil | .30 | .14 |
| ❑ 19 Perry Doyle | .30 | .14 |
| ❑ 20 Backroom Staff | .30 | .14 |
| ❑ 21 Alex Dampier MGR | .30 | .14 |
| ❑ 22 Clyde Tuyl CO | .30 | .14 |
| ❑ 23 The Silverware | .30 | .14 |
| ❑ 24 Steeler Foggy Dan | .30 | .14 |

## 1997-98 Sheffield Steelers

| | MINT | NRMT |
|---|---|---|
| COMPLETE SET (25) | 6.00 | 2.70 |
| COMMON CARD (1-25) | .15 | .07 |
| ❑ 1 James Hibbert | .30 | .14 |
| ❑ 2 Tim Cranston | .30 | .14 |
| ❑ 3 Rob Wilson | .30 | .14 |
| ❑ 4 Ken Priestlay | .30 | .14 |
| ❑ 5 Tommy Plommer | .30 | .14 |
| ❑ 6 Frank Kovacs | .30 | .14 |
| ❑ 7 Nicky Chinn | .30 | .14 |
| ❑ 8 David Longstaff | .30 | .14 |
| ❑ 9 Tony Hand | .30 | .14 |
| ❑ 10 Dion Del Monte | .30 | .14 |
| ❑ 11 Scott Allison | .30 | .14 |
| ❑ 12 Chris Kelland | .30 | .14 |
| ❑ 13 Sheffield Arena | .30 | .14 |
| ❑ 14 Team Photo | .15 | .07 |
| ❑ 15 Andre Malo | .30 | .14 |
| ❑ 16 Jamie Van Der Horst | .30 | .14 |
| ❑ 17 Andre Malo | .30 | .14 |
| ❑ 18 Mike Ware | .30 | .14 |
| ❑ 19 Ron Shudra | .30 | .14 |
| ❑ 20 Ed Courtenay | .30 | .14 |
| ❑ 21 Piero Greco | .30 | .14 |
| ❑ 22 Corey Beaulieu | .30 | .14 |
| ❑ 23 Steeler Foggy Dan | .30 | .14 |
| ❑ 24 Alex Dampier MGR | .30 | .14 |
| ❑ 25 Clyde Tuyl CO | .30 | .14 |

## 1995-96 Slovakian APS National Team

This set of 28-cards features the 1996 Slovakian national team. The cards were sold in team set form at home games. The cards feature an action photo complemented by national and federation logos. The card backs reprise the front photo along with international statistics. The set is notable for the inclusion of sniper Peter Bondra, among other NHLers.

| | MINT | NRMT |
|---|---|---|
| COMPLETE SET (28) | 20.00 | 9.00 |
| COMMON CARD (1-28) | .25 | .11 |
| ❑ 1 Dr. Jan Mitosinka CO | .25 | .11 |
| ❑ 2 Dusan Pasek CO | .35 | .16 |
| ❑ 3 Julius Supler CO | .25 | .11 |
| ❑ 4 Jan Selvek | .25 | .11 |
| ❑ 5 Jaromir Dragan | 1.00 | .45 |
| ❑ 6 Eduard Hartmann | .50 | .23 |
| ❑ 7 Roman Cunderlik | .25 | .11 |
| ❑ 8 Stanislav Jasecko | .25 | .11 |
| ❑ 9 Lubomir Sekeras | .25 | .11 |
| ❑ 10 Stanislav Medrik | .25 | .11 |
| ❑ 11 Jan Varholik | .25 | .11 |
| ❑ 12 Marian Smerciak | .25 | .11 |
| ❑ 13 Robert Svehla | 1.00 | .45 |
| ❑ 14 Slavomir Vorobel | .50 | .23 |
| ❑ 15 Vlastimil Plavucha | .50 | .23 |
| ❑ 16 Oto Hascak | .50 | .23 |
| ❑ 17 Peter Bondra | 5.00 | 2.20 |
| ❑ 18 Rene Pucher | .25 | .11 |
| ❑ 19 Miroslav Satan | 2.00 | .90 |
| ❑ 20 Branislav Janos | .25 | .11 |
| ❑ 21 Lubomir Kolnik | 1.00 | .45 |
| ❑ 22 Peter Stastny | 2.00 | .90 |
| ❑ 23 Zdeno Ciger | 1.00 | .45 |
| ❑ 24 Zigmund Palffy | 8.00 | 3.60 |
| ❑ 25 Josef Dano | .25 | .11 |
| ❑ 26 Robert Petrovicky | .50 | .23 |
| ❑ 27 Dusan Pohorelec | .25 | .11 |
| ❑ 28 Jozef Stumpel | 2.00 | .90 |

## 1995 Slovakia-Quebec Pee-Wee Tournament

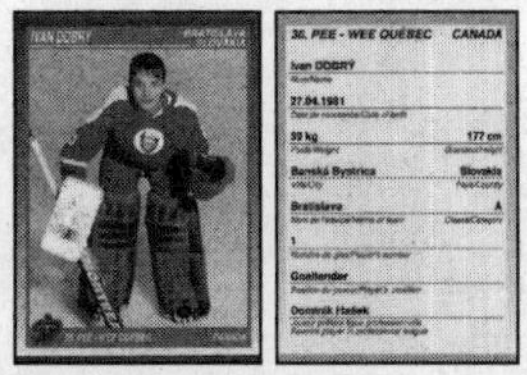

This 29-card set features the group of youngsters who represented Slovakia at the 1995 Quebec Pee Wee Tournament. The cards were sold at the tournament to help finance the team's trip. The cards have color player photos with red inside and faded purple outside borders. The backs carry player information. The cards are unnumbered and checklisted below in alphabetical order.

| | MINT | NRMT |
|---|---|---|
| COMPLETE SET (29) | 6.00 | 2.70 |
| COMMON CARD (1-29) | .25 | .11 |
| ❑ 1 Josef Balej | .25 | .11 |
| ❑ 2 Patrik Behan | .25 | .11 |
| ❑ 3 Michal Bela | .25 | .11 |
| ❑ 4 Ivan Dobry | .25 | .11 |
| ❑ 5 Milan Dornic CO | .25 | .11 |
| ❑ 6 Vladimir Dubek | .25 | .11 |
| ❑ 7 Ladislav Gero CO | .25 | .11 |
| ❑ 8 Marian Hutyra | .25 | .11 |
| ❑ 9 Peter Hutyra | .25 | .11 |
| ❑ 10 Dr. Leopold Karafiat MG | .25 | .11 |
| ❑ 11 Miroslav Karafiat CO | .25 | .11 |
| ❑ 12 Vladimir Kulich | .25 | .11 |
| ❑ 13 Marek Laco | .25 | .11 |
| ❑ 14 Michal Loksa | .25 | .11 |
| ❑ 15 Igor Martak | .25 | .11 |
| ❑ 16 Branislav Medzihorsky | .25 | .11 |
| ❑ 17 Miroslav Micuda | .25 | .11 |
| ❑ 18 Tomas Mihalik | .25 | .11 |
| ❑ 19 Stanislav Mistrik | .25 | .11 |
| ❑ 20 Andrej Mrena | .25 | .11 |
| ❑ 21 Marian Nemeth | .25 | .11 |
| ❑ 22 Vladimir Polacek | .25 | .11 |
| ❑ 23 Rastislav Sendrey | .25 | .11 |
| ❑ 24 Norbert Skorvaga | .25 | .11 |
| ❑ 25 Tomas Surovy | .25 | .11 |
| ❑ 26 Michal Turcer | .25 | .11 |
| ❑ 27 Sponsor Card | .25 | .11 |
| ❑ 28 Team Card | .25 | .11 |
| ❑ 29 Title Card | .25 | .11 |

## 1996 Slovakia-Quebec Pee-Wee Tournament

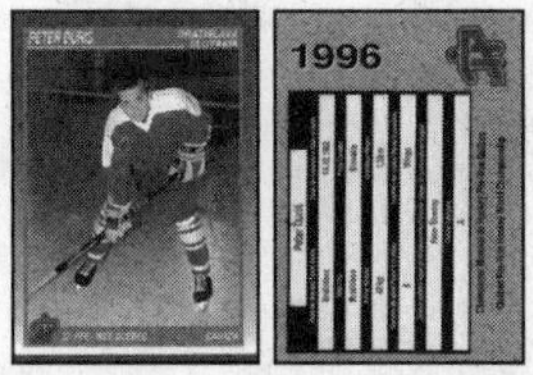

This 30-card set features color player photos with red inside and faded purple outside borders. The backs carry player information. The cards are unnumbered and checklisted below in alphabetical order.

| | MINT | NRMT |
|---|---|---|
| COMPLETE SET (30) | 10.00 | 4.50 |
| COMMON CARD (1-30) | .40 | .18 |
| ❑ 1 Jozei Balej | .40 | .18 |
| ❑ 2 Michal Baranka | .40 | .18 |
| ❑ 3 Jan Behan CO | .40 | .18 |
| ❑ 4 Martin Bonda | .40 | .18 |
| ❑ 5 Robert Cerny | .40 | .18 |
| ❑ 6 Peter Duris | .40 | .18 |
| ❑ 7 Jan Frkan | .40 | .18 |
| ❑ 8 Milan Fujerik CO | .40 | .18 |
| ❑ 9 Michal Gunis | .40 | .18 |
| ❑ 10 Stefan Hlusek | .40 | .18 |
| ❑ 11 Peter Holecko | .40 | .18 |
| ❑ 12 Dr. Leopold Karafial GM | .40 | .18 |
| ❑ 13 Lukas Krejci | .40 | .18 |
| ❑ 14 Miroslav Kristin | .40 | .18 |
| ❑ 15 Andrej Kucko | .40 | .18 |
| ❑ 16 Roman Kyndl | .40 | .18 |
| ❑ 17 Michal Macho | .40 | .18 |
| ❑ 18 Tomas Mikus | .75 | .35 |
| ❑ 19 Juraj Nemcak | .75 | .35 |
| ❑ 20 Viliam Ondrejik | .40 | .18 |
| ❑ 21 Miroslav Pistek | .40 | .18 |
| ❑ 22 Marek Pollak | .75 | .35 |
| ❑ 23 Tomas Psenka | .40 | .18 |
| ❑ 24 Milan Sitar CO | .40 | .18 |
| ❑ 25 Frantisek Skladany | .40 | .18 |
| ❑ 26 Peter Steklac | .40 | .18 |
| ❑ 27 Richard Svrbik | .40 | .18 |
| ❑ 28 Michal Sykora | .40 | .18 |
| ❑ 29 Martin Wala | .40 | .18 |
| ❑ 30 Team Picture | .40 | .18 |

## 1995-96 Solihull Barons

| | MINT | NRMT |
|---|---|---|
| COMPLETE SET (13) | 4.00 | 1.80 |
| COMMON CARD (1-13) | .30 | .14 |
| ❑ 1 Jamie Van Der Horst | .30 | .14 |
| ❑ 2 Nick Henry | .30 | .14 |
| ❑ 3 Gareth Roddis | .30 | .14 |
| ❑ 4 Jake Armstrong | .30 | .14 |
| ❑ 5 Andy Havenhand | .30 | .14 |
| ❑ 6 Paul Frankum | .30 | .14 |
| ❑ 7 David Wilkie | .30 | .14 |
| ❑ 8 Phil Lee | .30 | .14 |
| ❑ 9 Dan Pracher | .30 | .14 |
| ❑ 10 Alan Hague | .30 | .14 |
| ❑ 11 Justin George | .30 | .14 |
| ❑ 12 Liam Young | .30 | .14 |
| ❑ 13 Stephen Doyle | .30 | .14 |

## 1964 Swedish Coralli ISHockey

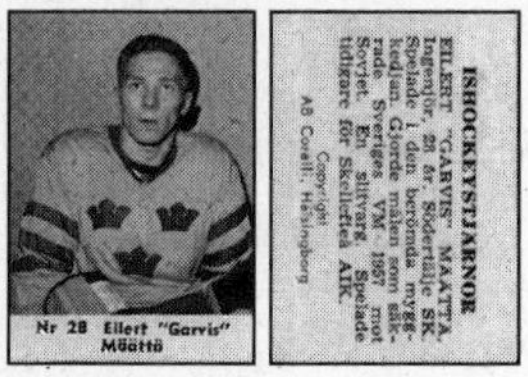


These tiny cards (1 7/8" by 1 1/4") feature players from the Swedish national team, Tre Kroner, as well as many club teams. The cards apparently were distributed as premiums in chocolate bars. According to reports, such sets existed in Sweden as far back as 1955. The card fronts have a posed player photo, name and card number. The backs offer a brief biography in Swedish. An album to hold these cards is believed to exist; this, however, has not been confirmed.

| | NRMT | EX |
|---|---|---|
| COMPLETE SET (165) | 300.00 | 135.00 |
| COMMON CARD (1-165) | 2.00 | .90 |

| | | |
|---|---|---|
| ❑ 1 Sven Johansson | 3.00 | 1.35 |
| ❑ 2 Ove Malmberg | 2.00 | .90 |
| ❑ 3 Bjorn Larsson | 2.00 | .90 |
| ❑ 4 Ulf Sterner | 2.00 | .90 |
| ❑ 5 Bertil Karlsson | 2.00 | .90 |
| ❑ 6 Leif Holmqvist | 10.00 | 4.50 |
| ❑ 7 Uno Ohrlund | 2.00 | .90 |
| ❑ 8 Mats Lonn | 2.00 | .90 |
| ❑ 9 Bjorn Palmqvist | 2.00 | .90 |
| ❑ 10 Nils Johansson | 2.00 | .90 |
| ❑ 11 Anders Andersson | 2.00 | .90 |
| ❑ 12 Lennart Haggroth | 4.00 | 1.80 |
| ❑ 13 Hans Svedberg | 2.00 | .90 |
| ❑ 14 Ronald Pettersson | 2.00 | .90 |
| ❑ 15 Lars Eric Lundvall | 2.00 | .90 |
| ❑ 16 Gert Blome | 2.00 | .90 |
| ❑ 17 Bo Englund | 2.00 | .90 |
| ❑ 18 Folke Bengtsson | 2.00 | .90 |
| ❑ 19 Nils Nilsson | 2.00 | .90 |
| ❑ 20 Lennart Johansson | 2.00 | .90 |
| ❑ 21 Lennart Svedberg | 5.00 | 2.20 |
| ❑ 22 Lars Ake Sivertsson | 2.00 | .90 |
| ❑ 23 Hakan Wickberg | 2.00 | .90 |
| ❑ 24 Tord Lundstrom | 2.00 | .90 |
| ❑ 25 Ove Andersson | 2.00 | .90 |
| ❑ 26 Bert Ola Nordlander | 3.00 | 1.35 |
| ❑ 27 Jan Erik Nilsson | 2.00 | .90 |
| ❑ 28 Eilert Maatta | 2.00 | .90 |
| ❑ 29 Roland Stoltz | 2.00 | .90 |
| ❑ 30 Kurt Thulin | 2.00 | .90 |
| ❑ 31 Ove Andersson | 2.00 | .90 |
| ❑ 32 Ingemar Johansson | 2.00 | .90 |
| ❑ 33 Rune Lind | 2.00 | .90 |
| ❑ 34 Bert-Ola Nordlander | 3.00 | 1.35 |
| ❑ 35 Hans Eriksson | 2.00 | .90 |
| ❑ 36 Antik Johansson | 2.00 | .90 |
| ❑ 37 Bo Hansson | 2.00 | .90 |
| ❑ 38 Jan Back | 2.00 | .90 |
| ❑ 39 Lennart Soderberg | 2.00 | .90 |
| ❑ 40 Benny Soderling | 2.00 | .90 |
| ❑ 41 Anders Parmstrom | 2.00 | .90 |
| ❑ 42 Lennart Selinder | 2.00 | .90 |
| ❑ 43 Bjorn Larsson | 2.00 | .90 |
| ❑ 44 Jorma Salmi | 2.00 | .90 |
| ❑ 45 Berndt Arvidsson | 2.00 | .90 |
| ❑ 46 P.A. Karlstrom | 2.00 | .90 |
| ❑ 47 Lars Erik Sjoberg | 10.00 | 4.50 |
| ❑ 48 Vilgot Larsson | 2.00 | .90 |
| ❑ 49 Gunnar Andersson | 2.00 | .90 |
| ❑ 50 Roland Bond | 2.00 | .90 |
| ❑ 51 Goran Lysen | 2.00 | .90 |
| ❑ 52 Bosse Englund | 2.00 | .90 |
| ❑ 53 Stig Pavels | 2.00 | .90 |
| ❑ 54 Bengt Bornstrom | 2.00 | .90 |
| ❑ 55 Nisse Nilsson | 2.00 | .90 |
| ❑ 56 Lennart Lange | 2.00 | .90 |
| ❑ 57 Des Moroney | 2.00 | .90 |
| ❑ 58 Folke Bengtsson | 2.00 | .90 |
| ❑ 59 Olle Sjogren | 2.00 | .90 |
| ❑ 60 Knut Knutsson | 2.00 | .90 |
| ❑ 61 Kjell Svensson | 2.00 | .90 |
| ❑ 62 Rickard Fagerlund | 5.00 | 2.20 |
| ❑ 63 Arne Loong | 2.00 | .90 |
| ❑ 64 Stig Carlsson | 2.00 | .90 |
| ❑ 65 Lars Hagg | 2.00 | .90 |
| ❑ 66 Olle Stenar | 2.00 | .90 |
| ❑ 67 Einar Granath | 2.00 | .90 |
| ❑ 68 Leif Andersson | 2.00 | .90 |
| ❑ 69 Hans Soderstrom | 2.00 | .90 |
| ❑ 70 Kalle Lilja | 2.00 | .90 |
| ❑ 71 Soren Maatta | 2.00 | .90 |
| ❑ 72 Sven Bystrom | 2.00 | .90 |
| ❑ 73 Hans Karlsson | 2.00 | .90 |
| ❑ 74 Stig Goran Johansson | 3.00 | 1.35 |
| ❑ 75 Jan Allinger | 2.00 | .90 |
| ❑ 76 Kjell Larsson | 2.00 | .90 |
| ❑ 77 Hakan Wickberg | 2.00 | .90 |
| ❑ 78 Tord Lundstrom | 2.00 | .90 |
| ❑ 79 Lennart Svedberg | 5.00 | 2.20 |
| ❑ 80 Jan Erik Lyck | 2.00 | .90 |
| ❑ 81 Hans Eriksson | 2.00 | .90 |
| ❑ 82 Kjell Jonsson | 2.00 | .90 |
| ❑ 83 Lars Hedenstrom | 2.00 | .90 |
| ❑ 84 Lars Ake Sivertsson | 2.00 | .90 |
| ❑ 85 Lennart Johansson | 2.00 | .90 |
| ❑ 86 Hans Sjoberg | 2.00 | .90 |
| ❑ 87 Hans Dahllof | 2.00 | .90 |
| ❑ 88 Leif Jansson | 2.00 | .90 |
| ❑ 89 Lars Byling | 2.00 | .90 |
| ❑ 90 Bertil Lindstrom | 2.00 | .90 |
| ❑ 91 Arne Eriksson | 2.00 | .90 |
| ❑ 92 Gert Blomer | 2.00 | .90 |
| ❑ 93 Kjell Adrian | 2.00 | .90 |
| ❑ 94 Jan Olsen | 2.00 | .90 |
| ❑ 95 Benny Karlsson | 2.00 | .90 |
| ❑ 96 Tommy Carlsson | 2.00 | .90 |
| ❑ 97 Ulf Sterner | 2.00 | .90 |
| ❑ 98 Kjell-Ove Gustafsson | 2.00 | .90 |
| ❑ 99 Lars Erik Lundvall | 2.00 | .90 |
| ❑ 100 Kjell-Ronny Pettersson | 2.00 | .90 |
| ❑ 101 Ronald Pettersson | 2.00 | .90 |
| ❑ 102 Kjell Jonsson | 2.00 | .90 |
| ❑ 103 Gote Hansson | 2.00 | .90 |
| ❑ 104 Rolf Eklof | 2.00 | .90 |
| ❑ 105 Eine Olsson | 2.00 | .90 |
| ❑ 106 Hans-Erik Fernstrom | 2.00 | .90 |
| ❑ 107 Leif Holmqvist | 2.00 | .90 |
| ❑ 108 Bo Zetterberg | 2.00 | .90 |
| ❑ 109 Ake Zattlin | 2.00 | .90 |
| ❑ 110 Bengt-Olov Andreasson | 2.00 | .90 |
| ❑ 111 Borje Mohlander | 2.00 | .90 |
| ❑ 112 Sture Sundin | 2.00 | .90 |
| ❑ 113 Bertil Karlsson | 2.00 | .90 |
| ❑ 114 Lars Molander | 2.00 | .90 |
| ❑ 115 Benno Persson | 2.00 | .90 |
| ❑ 116 Gert Nystrom | 2.00 | .90 |
| ❑ 117 Sune Bohlin | 2.00 | .90 |
| ❑ 118 Olle Westlund | 2.00 | .90 |
| ❑ 119 Goran Wallin | 2.00 | .90 |
| ❑ 120 Ingemar Persson | 2.00 | .90 |
| ❑ 121 Tommy Bjorkman | 2.00 | .90 |
| ❑ 122 Eddie Wingren | 2.00 | .90 |
| ❑ 123 Lars Bjorn | 2.00 | .90 |
| ❑ 124 Roland Stoltz | 2.00 | .90 |
| ❑ 125 Sven Johansson | 3.00 | 1.35 |
| ❑ 126 Leif Skold | 2.00 | .90 |
| ❑ 127 Hans Mild | 2.00 | .90 |
| ❑ 128 Kurt Thulin | 2.00 | .90 |
| ❑ 129 Ake Rydberg | 2.00 | .90 |
| ❑ 130 Ove Malmberg | 2.00 | .90 |
| ❑ 131 Lars Lundqvist | 2.00 | .90 |
| ❑ 132 Kurt Svensson | 2.00 | .90 |
| ❑ 133 Gosta Westerlund | 2.00 | .90 |
| ❑ 134 Lars Andersson | 2.00 | .90 |
| ❑ 135 Ulf Rydin | 2.00 | .90 |
| ❑ 136 Lennart Haggroth | 4.00 | 1.80 |
| ❑ 137 Jan Hedberg | 2.00 | .90 |
| ❑ 138 Karl Soren Hedlund | 2.00 | .90 |
| ❑ 139 Hans Svedberg | 2.00 | .90 |
| ❑ 140 Sture Hoverberg | 2.00 | .90 |
| ❑ 141 Anders Ronnblom | 2.00 | .90 |
| ❑ 142 Ulf Eriksson | 2.00 | .90 |
| ❑ 143 Anders Andersson | 2.00 | .90 |
| ❑ 144 Henrik Hedlund | 2.00 | .90 |
| ❑ 145 Per Lundstrom | 2.00 | .90 |
| ❑ 146 Hakan Nygren | 2.00 | .90 |
| ❑ 147 Bo Berglund | 4.00 | 1.80 |
| ❑ 148 Lars Ake Warning | 2.00 | .90 |
| ❑ 149 Sven-Olov Johansson | 2.00 | .90 |
| ❑ 150 Ove Stenlund | 2.00 | .90 |
| ❑ 151 Ivar Larsson | 2.00 | .90 |
| ❑ 152 Nils Johansson | 2.00 | .90 |
| ❑ 153 Sten Olsen | 2.00 | .90 |
| ❑ 154 Lars Gidlund | 2.00 | .90 |
| ❑ 155 Tor Haarstad | 2.00 | .90 |
| ❑ 156 K-O Barrefjord | 2.00 | .90 |
| ❑ 157 Bjorn Palmqvist | 2.00 | .90 |
| ❑ 158 Soren Lindstrom | 2.00 | .90 |
| ❑ 159 Henna Svensson | 2.00 | .90 |
| ❑ 160 Lars Hagstrom | 2.00 | .90 |
| ❑ 161 Ake Eklof | 2.00 | .90 |
| ❑ 162 Ulf Lundstrom | 2.00 | .90 |
| ❑ 163 Ronny Nordstrom | 2.00 | .90 |
| ❑ 164 Paul Stahl | 2.00 | .90 |
| ❑ 165 Kenneth Sahlen | 3.00 | 1.35 |

## 1965 Swedish Coralli ISHockey

These tiny (1 7/8" by 1 1/4") feature players from the Swedish National Team, Tre Kroner, as well as many club teams. The cards apparently were issued as premiums with chocolate bars. The card fronts have a posed player photo, name and card number. The backs offer a brief biography in Swedish.

| | MINT | NRMT |
|---|---|---|
| COMPLETE SET (214) | 250.00 | 110.00 |
| COMMON CARD (1-214) | 1.50 | .70 |

| | | |
|---|---|---|
| ❑ 1 Sven Johansson | 2.50 | 1.10 |
| ❑ 2 Ove Malmberg | 1.50 | .70 |
| ❑ 3 Bjorn Larsson | 1.50 | .70 |
| ❑ 4 Ulf Sterner | 1.50 | .70 |
| ❑ 5 Bertil Karlsson | 2.00 | .90 |
| ❑ 6 Leif Holmqvist | 8.00 | 3.60 |
| ❑ 7 Uno Ohrlund | 1.50 | .70 |
| ❑ 8 Mats Lonn | 1.50 | .70 |
| ❑ 9 Bjorn Palmqvist | 1.50 | .70 |
| ❑ 10 Nils Johansson | 1.50 | .70 |
| ❑ 11 Ander Andersson | 1.50 | .70 |
| ❑ 12 Lennart Haggroth | 3.00 | 1.35 |
| ❑ 13 Hans Svedberg | 1.50 | .70 |
| ❑ 14 Ronald Pettersson | 1.50 | .70 |
| ❑ 15 Lars Eric Lundvall | 1.50 | .70 |
| ❑ 16 Gert Blome | 1.50 | .70 |
| ❑ 17 Bo Englund | 1.50 | .70 |
| ❑ 18 Folke Bengtsson | 1.50 | .70 |
| ❑ 19 Nils Nilsson | 1.50 | .70 |
| ❑ 20 Lennart Johansson | 1.50 | .70 |
| ❑ 21 Lennart Svedberg | 3.50 | 1.55 |
| ❑ 22 Lars Ake Sivertsson | 1.50 | .70 |
| ❑ 23 Hakan Wickberg | 1.50 | .70 |
| ❑ 24 Tord Lundstrom | 1.50 | .70 |
| ❑ 25 Ove Andersson | 1.50 | .70 |
| ❑ 26 Bert Ola Nordlander | 2.50 | 1.10 |
| ❑ 27 Jan Erik Nilsson | 1.50 | .70 |
| ❑ 28 Eilert Maatta | 1.50 | .70 |
| ❑ 29 Roland Stoltz | 1.50 | .70 |
| ❑ 30 Kurt Thulin | 1.50 | .70 |
| ❑ 31A Ove Andersson | 1.50 | .70 |
| ❑ 31B Leif Holmquist | 8.00 | 3.60 |
| ❑ 32 Ingemar Johansson | 2.00 | .90 |
| ❑ 33 Rune Lind | 1.50 | .70 |
| ❑ 34 Bert-Ola Nordlander | 2.50 | 1.10 |
| ❑ 35 Hans Eriksson | 1.50 | .70 |
| ❑ 36 Antik Johansson | 1.50 | .70 |
| ❑ 37 Bo Hansson | 1.50 | .70 |
| ❑ 38A Jan Back | 1.50 | .70 |
| ❑ 38B Hans-Ake Carlsson | 1.50 | .70 |
| ❑ 39 Lennart Soderberg | 1.50 | .70 |
| ❑ 40 Benny Soderling | 1.50 | .70 |
| ❑ 41 Anders Parmstrom | 1.50 | .70 |
| ❑ 42 Lennart Selinder | 1.50 | .70 |
| ❑ 43 Bjorn Larsson | 1.50 | .70 |
| ❑ 44A Jorma Salmi | 1.50 | .70 |
| ❑ 44B Ove Hedberg | 1.50 | .70 |
| ❑ 45 Berndt Arvidsson | 1.50 | .70 |
| ❑ 46 P.A. Carlstrom | 1.50 | .70 |
| ❑ 47 Lars Erik Sjoberg | 8.00 | 3.60 |
| ❑ 48A Vilgot Larsson | 1.50 | .70 |
| ❑ 48B Kjell Fihnn | 1.50 | .70 |
| ❑ 49 Gunnar Andersson | 1.50 | .70 |
| ❑ 50 Roland Bond | 1.50 | .70 |
| ❑ 51 Goran Lysen | 1.50 | .70 |
| ❑ 52 Bosse Englund | 1.50 | .70 |
| ❑ 53 Stig Pavels | 1.50 | .70 |
| ❑ 54 Bengt Bornstrom | 1.50 | .70 |
| ❑ 55 Nisse Nilsson | 1.50 | .70 |
| ❑ 56 Lennart Lange | 1.50 | .70 |
| ❑ 57A Des Moroney | 1.50 | .70 |
| ❑ 57B Tommy Abrahamsson | 8.00 | 3.60 |
| ❑ 58 Folke Bengtsson | 1.50 | .70 |
| ❑ 59 Olle Sjogren | 1.50 | .70 |
| ❑ 60 Knut Knutsson | 1.50 | .70 |
| ❑ 61 Kjell Svensson | 1.50 | .70 |
| ❑ 62 Rickard Fagerlund | 3.50 | 1.55 |
| ❑ 63A Arne Loong | 1.50 | .70 |
| ❑ 63B Eilert Maatta | 1.50 | .70 |
| ❑ 64 Stig Carlsson | 1.50 | .70 |
| ❑ 65 Lars Hagg | 1.50 | .70 |
| ❑ 66 Olle Stenar | 1.50 | .70 |
| ❑ 67 Einar Andersson | 1.50 | .70 |
| ❑ 68 Leif Andersson | 1.50 | .70 |
| ❑ 69A Hans Soderstrom | 1.50 | .70 |
| ❑ 69B Percy Lind | 1.50 | .70 |
| ❑ 70A Kalle Lilja | 1.50 | .70 |
| ❑ 70B Gonnar Tallberg | 1.50 | .70 |
| ❑ 71 Soren Maatta | 1.50 | .70 |
| ❑ 72 Sven Bystrom | 1.50 | .70 |
| ❑ 73 Hans Carlsson | 1.50 | .70 |
| ❑ 74 Stig Goran Johansson | 2.50 | 1.10 |
| ❑ 75A Jan Allinger | 1.50 | .70 |
| ❑ 75B Thomas Warming | 1.50 | .70 |
| ❑ 76 Kjell Larsson | 1.50 | .70 |
| ❑ 77 Hakan Wickberg | 1.50 | .70 |
| ❑ 78 Tord Lundstrom | 1.50 | .70 |
| ❑ 79 Lennart Svedberg | 4.00 | 1.80 |
| ❑ 80 Jan Erik Lyck | 1.50 | .70 |
| ❑ 81A Hans Eriksson | 1.50 | .70 |
| ❑ 81B Stefan Carlsson | 1.50 | .70 |
| ❑ 82 Kjell Jonsson | 1.50 | .70 |
| ❑ 83 Lars Hedenstrom | 1.50 | .70 |
| ❑ 84 Lars Ake Sivertsson | 1.50 | .70 |
| ❑ 85 Lennart Johansson | 1.50 | .70 |
| ❑ 86 Hans Sjoberg | 1.50 | .70 |
| ❑ 87 Hans Dahllof | 1.50 | .70 |
| ❑ 88A Leif Jansson | 1.50 | .70 |
| ❑ 88B Hans Lindberg | 1.50 | .70 |
| ❑ 89 Lars Bylund | 1.50 | .70 |
| ❑ 90A Bertil Lindstrom | 1.50 | .70 |
| ❑ 90B Sten Edqvist | 1.50 | .70 |
| ❑ 91 Arne Ericsson | 1.50 | .70 |
| ❑ 92 Gert Blomer | 1.50 | .70 |
| ❑ 93 Kjell Adrian | 1.50 | .70 |
| ❑ 94 Jan Olsen | 1.50 | .70 |
| ❑ 95 Benny Karlsson | 1.50 | .70 |
| ❑ 96A Tommy Carlsson | 1.50 | .70 |
| ❑ 96B Jorma Salmi | 1.50 | .70 |
| ❑ 97 Ulf Sterner | 1.50 | .70 |
| ❑ 98 Kjell-Ove Gustafsson | 1.50 | .70 |
| ❑ 99 Lars Erik Lundvall | 1.50 | .70 |
| ❑ 100 Kjell-Ronny Pettersson | 2.00 | .90 |
| ❑ 101 Ronald Pettersson | 1.50 | .70 |
| ❑ 102 Kjell Jonsson | 1.50 | .70 |
| ❑ 103 Gote Hansson | 1.50 | .70 |
| ❑ 104A Rolf Eklof | 1.50 | .70 |
| ❑ 104B Ove Sterner | 1.50 | .70 |
| ❑ 105 Eine Olsson | 1.50 | .70 |
| ❑ 106 Hans-Erik Fernstrom | 1.50 | .70 |
| ❑ 107A Leif Holmkvist | 1.50 | .70 |
| ❑ 107B Per-Olov Hardin | 1.50 | .70 |
| ❑ 108 Bo Zetterberg | 1.50 | .70 |
| ❑ 109 Ake Zettlin | 1.50 | .70 |
| ❑ 110 Bengt-Olov Andreasson | 1.50 | .70 |
| ❑ 111 Borje Molander | 1.50 | .70 |
| ❑ 112 Sture Sundin | 1.50 | .70 |
| ❑ 113 Bertil Karlsson | 2.00 | .90 |
| ❑ 114 Lars Molander | 1.50 | .70 |
| ❑ 115 Benno Persson | 1.50 | .70 |
| ❑ 116A Gert Nystrom | 1.50 | .70 |
| ❑ 116B Rolf Larsson | 1.50 | .70 |
| ❑ 117A Sune Bohlin | 1.50 | .70 |
| ❑ 117B Ronny Francis | 1.50 | .70 |
| ❑ 118 Olle Westlund | 1.50 | .70 |
| ❑ 119 Goran Wallin | 1.50 | .70 |
| ❑ 120 Ingemar Persson | 1.50 | .70 |
| ❑ 121 Tommy Bjorkman | 1.50 | .70 |
| ❑ 122 Eddie Wingren | 1.50 | .70 |
| ❑ 123 Lars Bjorn | 1.50 | .70 |
| ❑ 124 Roland Stoltz | 1.50 | .70 |
| ❑ 125 Sven Johansson | 2.50 | 1.10 |
| ❑ 126A Leif Skold | 1.50 | .70 |
| ❑ 126B Arne Loong | 1.50 | .70 |
| ❑ 127 Hans Mild | 1.50 | .70 |
| ❑ 128 Kurt Thulin | 1.50 | .70 |
| ❑ 129 Ake Rydberg | 1.50 | .70 |
| ❑ 130 Ove Malmberg | 1.50 | .70 |
| ❑ 131 Lars Lundqvist | 1.50 | .70 |
| ❑ 132 Kurt Svensson | 1.50 | .70 |
| ❑ 133 Gosta Westerlund | 1.50 | .70 |
| ❑ 134 Lars Andersson | 1.50 | .70 |
| ❑ 135 Ulf Rydin | 1.50 | .70 |
| ❑ 136 Lennart Haggroth | 3.00 | 1.35 |
| ❑ 137 Jan Hedberg | 1.50 | .70 |
| ❑ 138A Karl Soren Hedlund | 1.50 | .70 |
| ❑ 138B Anders Carlberg | 1.50 | .70 |
| ❑ 139 Hans Svedberg | 1.50 | .70 |
| ❑ 140 Sture Hofverberg | 1.50 | .70 |
| ❑ 141 Anders Ronnblom | 1.50 | .70 |
| ❑ 142 Ulf Eriksson | 1.50 | .70 |
| ❑ 143 Anders Andersson | 1.50 | .70 |
| ❑ 144 Henrik Hedlund | 1.50 | .70 |
| ❑ 145A Per Lundstrom | 1.50 | .70 |
| ❑ 145B Roger Boman | 1.50 | .70 |
| ❑ 146A Hakan Nugren | 1.50 | .70 |
| ❑ 146B Bo Astrom | 1.50 | .70 |
| ❑ 147 Bo Berglund | 3.00 | 1.35 |
| ❑ 148 Lars Ake Warning | 1.50 | .70 |
| ❑ 149 Sven-Olov Johansson | 1.50 | .70 |
| ❑ 150 Ove Stenlund | 1.50 | .70 |
| ❑ 151 Ivar Larsson | 1.50 | .70 |
| ❑ 152 Nicke Johansson | 1.50 | .70 |
| ❑ 153 Sten Olsen | 1.50 | .70 |
| ❑ 154 Lars Gidlund | 1.50 | .70 |
| ❑ 155 Tor Haarstad | 1.50 | .70 |
| ❑ 156A K-O Barrefjord | 1.50 | .70 |
| ❑ 156B Hakan Nygren | 1.50 | .70 |
| ❑ 157 Bjorn Palmqvist | 1.50 | .70 |
| ❑ 158 Soren Lindstrom | 1.50 | .70 |
| ❑ 159 Henry Svensson | 1.50 | .70 |
| ❑ 160 Lars Hagstrom | 1.50 | .70 |
| ❑ 161 Ake Eklof | 1.50 | .70 |
| ❑ 162 Ulf Lundstrom | 1.50 | .70 |
| ❑ 163 Ronny Nordstrom | 1.50 | .70 |
| ❑ 164 Paul Stahl | 1.50 | .70 |
| ❑ 165 Kenneth Sahlen | 2.50 | 1.10 |
| ❑ 166 Anders Hedlund | 1.50 | .70 |
| ❑ 167 Ingemar Caris | 1.50 | .70 |
| ❑ 168 Arne Carlsson | 1.50 | .70 |
| ❑ 169 Gote Bostram | 1.50 | .70 |
| ❑ 170 Roger Olsson | 1.50 | .70 |
| ❑ 171 Ole Jacobson | 1.50 | .70 |
| ❑ 172 Curt Edenvik | 1.50 | .70 |
| ❑ 173 Goran Svensson | 1.50 | .70 |
| ❑ 174 Eje Lindstrom | 1.50 | .70 |
| ❑ 175 Curt Larsson | 5.00 | 2.20 |
| ❑ 176 unknown | 1.50 | .70 |
| ❑ 177 Anders Nordin | 1.50 | .70 |
| ❑ 178 Ulf Torstensson | 1.50 | .70 |
| ❑ 179 Kent Lindgren | 1.50 | .70 |
| ❑ 180 Kent Sjalin | 1.50 | .70 |
| ❑ 181 Lars Goran Nilsson | 1.50 | .70 |
| ❑ 182 Heimo Kockare | 1.50 | .70 |
| ❑ 183 Lars Sattare | 1.50 | .70 |
| ❑ 184 unknown | 1.50 | .70 |
| ❑ 185 Kjell Savstrom | 1.50 | .70 |
| ❑ 186 Carl-Goran Oberg | 1.50 | .70 |
| ❑ 187 Bjorn Larsson | 1.50 | .70 |
| ❑ 188 Leif Eriksson | 1.50 | .70 |
| ❑ 189 Dag Olsson | 1.50 | .70 |
| ❑ 190 Lars Lohman | 1.50 | .70 |
| ❑ 191 unknown | 1.50 | .70 |
| ❑ 192 unknown | 1.50 | .70 |
| ❑ 193 unknown | 1.50 | .70 |
| ❑ 194 unknown | 1.50 | .70 |
| ❑ 195 unknown | 1.50 | .70 |
| ❑ 196 unknown | 1.50 | .70 |
| ❑ 197 unknown | 1.50 | .70 |
| ❑ 198 unknown | 1.50 | .70 |
| ❑ 199 unknown | 1.50 | .70 |
| ❑ 200 Hans Aleblad | 1.50 | .70 |
| ❑ 201 Karl Soren Hedlund | 1.50 | .70 |
| ❑ 202 Clarence Carlsson | 1.50 | .70 |
| ❑ 203 Bjorn Johansson | 1.50 | .70 |
| ❑ 204 Kent Persson | 1.50 | .70 |
| ❑ 205 Goran Thelin | 1.50 | .70 |
| ❑ 206 Leif Ohrlund | 1.50 | .70 |
| ❑ 207 Mats Davidsson | 1.50 | .70 |
| ❑ 208 Leif Artursson | 1.50 | .70 |
| ❑ 209 Karl Gunnar Backman | 1.50 | .70 |
| ❑ 210 Hans Mellinger | 1.50 | .70 |
| ❑ 211 Hans Inge Lund | 1.50 | .70 |
| ❑ 212 Kent Jansson | 1.50 | .70 |
| ❑ 213 Anders Ronnkvist | 1.50 | .70 |
| ❑ 214 Bo Olofsson | 1.50 | .70 |

## 1967-68 Swedish Hockey

This 300-card set features the skaters from the Swedish first and second division teams from the 1967-68 season, as well as the national team, Tre Kronor. The cards measure 2" by 3 1/8" and feature posed color photos on the front. The national team cards have the words Tre Kronor and the three crown logo across the top. The backs have the card number, player stats and an invitation to purchase a collectors album, all in Swedish. The album for the set includes numerous pages of text and photos about Swedish hockey, and is valued at $35. Although short on widely recognizable names, the set does include early -- if not first -- cards of Inge Hammarstrom and Christer Abrahamssom.

| | MINT | NRMT |
|---|---|---|
| COMPLETE SET (300) | 125.00 | 55.00 |
| COMMON CARD (1-300) | .50 | .23 |

| | | |
|---|---|---|
| ❑ 1 Christer Abrahamsson | 4.00 | 1.80 |
| ❑ 2 Tommy Abrahamsson | 2.00 | .90 |
| ❑ 3 Folke Bengtsson | .50 | .23 |
| ❑ 4 Arne Carlsson | .50 | .23 |
| ❑ 5 Bengt-Ake Gustavsson | .50 | .23 |
| ❑ 6 Anders Hagstrom | .50 | .23 |
| ❑ 7 Inge Hammarstrom | 5.00 | 2.20 |
| ❑ 8 Leif Henriksson | .50 | .23 |
| ❑ 9 Leif Holmqvist | 2.00 | .90 |
| ❑ 10 Per-Arne Hubinette | .50 | .23 |
| ❑ 11 Mats Hysing | .50 | .23 |
| ❑ 12 Nils Johansson | .50 | .23 |
| ❑ 13 Stig-Goran Johansson | .50 | .23 |
| ❑ 14 Hans Lindberg | .50 | .23 |
| ❑ 15 Tord Lundstrom | .50 | .23 |
| ❑ 16 Lars-Goran Nilsson | .50 | .23 |
| ❑ 17 Anders Nordin | .50 | .23 |
| ❑ 18 Bert-Ola Nordlander | .50 | .23 |
| ❑ 19 Roger Olsson | .50 | .23 |
| ❑ 20 Bjorn Palmquist | .50 | .23 |
| ❑ 21 Kjell Sundstrom | .50 | .23 |
| ❑ 22 Lennart Svedberg | 1.00 | .45 |
| ❑ 23 Hakan Wickberg | .50 | .23 |
| ❑ 24 Carl-Goran Oberg | .50 | .23 |
| ❑ 25 Lasse Ohman | .50 | .23 |
| ❑ 26 Curt Edenvik | .50 | .23 |
| ❑ 27 Hans Eriksson | .50 | .23 |
| ❑ 28 Rolf Hallgren | .50 | .23 |
| ❑ 29 Bo Hansson | .50 | .23 |
| ❑ 30 Ove Hedberg | .50 | .23 |
| ❑ 31 Kjell Hedman | 1.00 | .45 |
| ❑ 32 Leif Holmqvist | 2.00 | .90 |
| ❑ 33 Anders Johansson | .50 | .23 |
| ❑ 34 Bengt Larsson | .50 | .23 |
| ❑ 35 Bjorn Larsson | .50 | .23 |
| ❑ 36 Rune Lindh | .50 | .23 |
| ❑ 37 Borje Molander | .50 | .23 |
| ❑ 38 Kjell Nilsson | .50 | .23 |
| ❑ 39 Bert-Ola Nordlander | .50 | .23 |
| ❑ 40 Anders Parmstrom | .50 | .23 |
| ❑ 41 Lennart Sellinder | .50 | .23 |
| ❑ 42 Kjell Savstrom | .50 | .23 |
| ❑ 43 Lars Bylund | .50 | .23 |
| ❑ 44 Hans Dahllof | 1.00 | .45 |
| ❑ 45 Lennart Gustafsson | .50 | .23 |
| ❑ 46 Lars Hedenstrom | .50 | .23 |
| ❑ 47 Lennart Johansson | .50 | .23 |
| ❑ 48 Kjell Johnsson | .50 | .23 |
| ❑ 49 Stefan Karlsson | .50 | .23 |
| ❑ 50 Nisse Larsson | .50 | .23 |
| ❑ 51 Lennart Lind | .50 | .23 |
| ❑ 52 Hans Lindberg | .50 | .23 |
| ❑ 53 Tord Lundstrom | .50 | .23 |
| ❑ 54 Jan-Erik Lyck | .50 | .23 |
| ❑ 55 Lars-Goran Nilsson | .50 | .23 |
| ❑ 56 Anders Sahlin | 1.00 | .45 |
| ❑ 57 Lars-Ake Sivertsson | .50 | .23 |
| ❑ 58 Hans Sjoberg | .50 | .23 |
| ❑ 59 Hakan Wickberg | .50 | .23 |
| ❑ 60 Tommy Bjorkman | 1.00 | .45 |
| ❑ 61 Lasse Bjorn | .50 | .23 |
| ❑ 62 Thomas Carlsson | .50 | .23 |
| ❑ 63 Roland Einarsson | 1.00 | .45 |
| ❑ 64 Kjell Keijser | .50 | .23 |
| ❑ 65 Stig Larsson | .50 | .23 |
| ❑ 66 Kent Lindgren | .50 | .23 |
| ❑ 67 Tommie Lindgren | .50 | .23 |
| ❑ 68 Lars-Ake Lundell | .50 | .23 |
| ❑ 69 Per Lundstrom | .50 | .23 |
| ❑ 70 Bjorn Palmquist | .50 | .23 |
| ❑ 71 Ulf Rydin | .50 | .23 |
| ❑ 72 Lars-Eric Sjoberg | 4.00 | 1.80 |
| ❑ 73 Lars Starck | .50 | .23 |
| ❑ 74 Roland Stoltz | .50 | .23 |
| ❑ 75 Henry Svensson | .50 | .23 |
| ❑ 76 Kurt Thulin | .50 | .23 |
| ❑ 77 Gosta Westerlund | .50 | .23 |
| ❑ 78 Eddie Wingren | .50 | .23 |
| ❑ 79 Carl-Goran Oberg | .50 | .23 |
| ❑ 80 Anders Andersson | .50 | .23 |
| ❑ 81 Hasse Andersson | .50 | .23 |
| ❑ 82 Hakan Andersson | .50 | .23 |
| ❑ 83 Anders Asplund | .50 | .23 |
| ❑ 84 Hans Bergqvist | .50 | .23 |
| ❑ 85 Hans Bostrom | .50 | .23 |
| ❑ 86 Kjell Eriksson | 1.00 | .45 |
| ❑ 87 Conny Evensson | 1.00 | .45 |
| ❑ 88 Bjorn Fagerlund | 1.00 | .45 |
| ❑ 89 Ingemar Magnusson | .50 | .23 |
| ❑ 90 Hans-Ake Nilsson | .50 | .23 |
| ❑ 91 Rune Nilsson | .50 | .23 |
| ❑ 92 Kent Olsson | .50 | .23 |
| ❑ 93 Lars Stalberg | .50 | .23 |

❑ 94 Christer Sundquist .50 .23
❑ 95 Christer Abrahamsson 4.00 1.80
❑ 96 Tommy Abrahamsson 2.00 .90
❑ 97 Bosse Andersson .50 .23
❑ 98 Gunnar Andersson .50 .23
❑ 99 Lars Andersson .50 .23
❑ 100 Folke Bengtsson .50 .23
❑ 101 Roland Bond .50 .23
❑ 102 Kjell Fihnn .50 .23
❑ 103 Jan-Olof Kroon .50 .23
❑ 104 Lennart Lange .50 .23
❑ 105 Sture Leksell 1.00 .45
❑ 106 Goran Lysen .50 .23
❑ 107 Ulf Martensson .50 .23
❑ 108 Nisse Nilsson .50 .23
❑ 109 Dag Ohlsson .50 .23
❑ 110 Olle Sioren .50 .23
❑ 111 Ake Sunesson .50 .23
❑ 112 Dan Soderstrom .50 .23
❑ 113 Goran Winge .50 .23
❑ 114 Mats Ahlberg .50 .23
❑ 115 Olle Ost .50 .23
❑ 116 Gunnar Backman 1.00 .45
❑ 117 Lage Edin .50 .23
❑ 118 Ake Eklof .50 .23
❑ 119 Torbjorn Hubinette .50 .23
❑ 120 Nils Johansson .50 .23
❑ 121 Ulf Kroon .50 .23
❑ 122 Ivar Larsson 1.00 .45
❑ 123 Christer Nilsson .50 .23
❑ 124 Anders Nordin .50 .23
❑ 125 Hakan Nygren .50 .23
❑ 126 Sten Olsen .50 .23
❑ 127 Paul Stahl .50 .23
❑ 128 Gunnar Safsten .50 .23
❑ 129 Ulf Torstensson .50 .23
❑ 130 Ulf Wigren .50 .23
❑ 131 Lars Ohman .50 .23
❑ 132 Tore Ohman .50 .23
❑ 133 Bengt Andersson .50 .23
❑ 134 Nils Carlsson .50 .23
❑ 135 Kjell Eklind .50 .23
❑ 136 Allan Fernstrom .50 .23
❑ 137 Bengt Gustavsson .50 .23
❑ 138 Bengt-Ake Gustavsson 1.00 .45
❑ 139 Gote Hansson .50 .23
❑ 140 Per-Arne Hubinette .50 .23
❑ 141 Sven-Ake Jakobsson .50 .23
❑ 142 Goran Johansson 1.00 .45
❑ 143 Mats Lind .50 .23
❑ 144 Mats Lonn .50 .23
❑ 145 Ulf Nises .50 .23
❑ 146 Bo Olsson .50 .23
❑ 147 Lennart Svedberg 1.00 .45
❑ 148 Evert Tysk .50 .23
❑ 149 Stig Ostling .50 .23
❑ 150 Ulf Berglund .50 .23
❑ 151 Clarence Carlsson .50 .23
❑ 152 Arne Ekenberg .50 .23
❑ 153 Kenneth Ekman .50 .23
❑ 154 Tom Haugh 1.00 .45
❑ 155 Rolf Joelsson .50 .23
❑ 156 Bjorn Johanesson .50 .23
❑ 157 Arne Johansson .50 .23
❑ 158 Bengt-Goran Karlsson .50 .23
❑ 159 Kjell Larsson .50 .23
❑ 160 Lasse Larsson .50 .23
❑ 161 Barry Murman .50 .23
❑ 162 Klas Goran Nilsson .50 .23
❑ 163 Rolf Norell .50 .23
❑ 164 Lennart Skordaker .50 .23
❑ 165 Ulf Sterner 1.00 .45
❑ 166 Arne Wickstrom .50 .23
❑ 167 Bengt-Olov Andreasson 1.00 .45
❑ 168 Leif Eriksson .50 .23
❑ 169 Ove Evaldson .50 .23
❑ 170 Hans-Erik Fernstrom .50 .23
❑ 171 Kenneth Hillgren .50 .23
❑ 172 Per-Olof Hardin .50 .23
❑ 173 Bertil Karlsson .50 .23
❑ 174 Torsten Karlsson .50 .23
❑ 175 Rolf Larsson .50 .23
❑ 176 William Lofqvist 2.00 .90
❑ 177 Lars Mollander .50 .23
❑ 178 Gert Nystrom .50 .23
❑ 179 Olle Westlund .50 .23
❑ 180 Bo Zetterberg .50 .23
❑ 181 Leif Andersson .50 .23
❑ 182 Borje Burlin .50 .23
❑ 183 Hans Carlsson .50 .23
❑ 184 Stig Carlsson .50 .23
❑ 185 Einar Granath .50 .23
❑ 186 Kjell-Ake Hedstrom .50 .23
❑ 187 Mats Hysing .50 .23
❑ 188 Stig-Goran Johansson .50 .23
❑ 189 Curt Larsson 2.50 1.10
❑ 190 Eilert Maatta .50 .23
❑ 191 Soren Maatta .50 .23
❑ 192 Nils-Olof Schilstrom .50 .23
❑ 193 Jan Schullstrom .50 .23
❑ 194 Kjell Svensson 1.00 .45
❑ 195 Gunnar Tallberg .50 .23
❑ 196 Dick Yderstrom .50 .23
❑ 197 Sten Andersson 1.00 .45
❑ 198 Lars Arne Bergkvist .50 .23
❑ 199 Anders Edstrom .50 .23
❑ 200 Lars Bertil Eriksson .50 .23
❑ 201 Charles Gustavsson .50 .23
❑ 202 Ake Johansson .50 .23
❑ 203 Lars Karestal .50 .23
❑ 204 Rolf Karlsson .50 .23
❑ 205 Erik Lindahl .50 .23
❑ 206 Freddy Lindfors 1.00 .45
❑ 207 Lennart Lindkvist .50 .23
❑ 208 Kjell Rune Milton .50 .23
❑ 209 Olle Nilsater .50 .23
❑ 210 Birger Nordlund .50 .23
❑ 211 Inge Tornlund .50 .23
❑ 212 Jan Roger Oberg .50 .23
❑ 213 Kjell Sture Oberg .50 .23
❑ 214 Tommy Andersson .50 .23
❑ 215 Soren Bostrom .50 .23
❑ 216 Anders Bryner .50 .23
❑ 217 Anders Claesson 1.00 .45
❑ 218 Svante Granholm .50 .23
❑ 219 Inge Hammarstrom 5.00 2.20
❑ 220 Borje Holmstrom .50 .23
❑ 221 Jan Johansson .50 .23
❑ 222 Antero Jonasson .50 .23
❑ 223 Ove Jonsson .50 .23
❑ 224 Lennart Lind 1.00 .45
❑ 225 Jan-Erik Nilsson .50 .23
❑ 226 Kurt Olofsson .50 .23
❑ 227 Gosta Sjokvist .50 .23
❑ 228 Jan Stolpe .50 .23
❑ 229 Kjell Westerlund .50 .23
❑ 230 Olle Ahman .50 .23
❑ 231 Jan-Ivar Bergqvist .50 .23
❑ 232 Lars-Ake Brannlund 1.00 .45
❑ 233 Hans Bohlmark .50 .23
❑ 234 Jan Christriansson .50 .23
❑ 235 Bengt Eriksson .50 .23
❑ 236 Arne Grenemo .50 .23
❑ 237 Lars-Olof Henriksson .50 .23
❑ 238 Kurt Jakobsson .50 .23
❑ 239 Leif Jakobsson .50 .23
❑ 240 Lars-Goran Johansson .50 .23
❑ 241 Kimo Kivela .50 .23
❑ 242 Borje Maatta .50 .23
❑ 243 Anders Rapp .50 .23
❑ 244 Tommy Sahlsten .50 .23
❑ 245 Stig-Olof Zetterbrg .50 .23
❑ 246 Lennart Abrahamsson .50 .23
❑ 247 John Andersson .50 .23
❑ 248 Ove Andersson 1.00 .45
❑ 249 Kjell-olov Barrefjord .50 .23
❑ 250 Ulf Barrefjord .50 .23
❑ 251 Kent Bjork .50 .23
❑ 252 Lars Dahlgren .50 .23
❑ 253 Karl-Ove Eriksson .50 .23
❑ 254 Osten Folkesson .50 .23
❑ 255 Anders Hagstrom .50 .23
❑ 256 Eric Jarvholm .50 .23
❑ 257 Ulf Larsson .50 .23
❑ 258 Bengt Lovgren .50 .23
❑ 259 Roger Nilsson .50 .23
❑ 260 Bengt Persson 1.00 .45
❑ 261 Kjell Sundstrom .50 .23
❑ 262 Roger Osterlund .50 .23
❑ 263 Hans Aleblad 1.00 .45
❑ 264 Ake Bolander .50 .23
❑ 265 Karl-Gunnar Backman .50 .23
❑ 266 Mats Davidsson .50 .23
❑ 267 Bosse Englund .50 .23
❑ 268 Tommy Eriksson .50 .23
❑ 269 Karl-Soren Hedlund .50 .23
❑ 270 Don Hughes .50 .23
❑ 271 Krister Lindgren .50 .23
❑ 272 Hans Mellinger .50 .23
❑ 273 Des Moroney .50 .23
❑ 274 Bo Olofsson .50 .23
❑ 275 Hakan Olsson .50 .23
❑ 276 Kent Persson .50 .23
❑ 277 Ove Stenlund .50 .23
❑ 278 Goran Thelin .50 .23
❑ 279 Ove Thelin .50 .23
❑ 280 Leif Ohrlund .50 .23
❑ 281 Uno Ohrlund .50 .23
❑ 282 Jan Ostling .50 .23
❑ 283 Gert Blome .50 .23
❑ 284 Ingemar Caris 1.00 .45
❑ 285 Arne Carlsson .50 .23
❑ 286 Kjell-Ove Gustafsson .50 .23
❑ 287 Henric Hedlund .50 .23
❑ 288 Leif Henriksson .50 .23
❑ 289 Kjell Jonsson .50 .23
❑ 290 Berny Karlsson .50 .23
❑ 291 Goran Lindberg .50 .23
❑ 292 Bernt Lundqvist .50 .23
❑ 293 Lars Eric Lundvall .50 .23
❑ 294 Carl-Fredrik Montan .50 .23
❑ 295 Eine Ohlsson 1.00 .45
❑ 296 Jan Olsen .50 .23
❑ 297 Roger Olsson .50 .23
❑ 298 Kjell-Ronnie Pettersson 1.00 .45
❑ 299 Ronald Pettersson .50 .23
❑ 300 Roland Sarnholm .50 .23

## 1969-70 Swedish World Championships

This 200-card set was released in Sweden to commemorate the 1970 World Championships held in Bern and Geneva, Switzerland. The cards measure approximately 2 3/4" by 3 3/4" and feature color action photos of players from the eight teams who competed in the previous year's tourney. The cards were distributed in 5-card, clear plastic packages. The key cards in the set are two of HOFer Ken Dryden as a member of Team Canada. The cards precede his RC by two years. An album was available to store the cards; it is valued at $30.

| | MINT | NRMT |
|---|---|---|
| COMPLETE SET (200) | 300.00 | 135.00 |
| COMMON CARD (1-200) | .50 | .23 |

❑ 1 Vladimir Dzurila 8.00 3.60
❑ 2 Jozef Golonka 1.00 .45
❑ 3 Jiri Holik .75 .35
❑ 4 Vaclav Nedomansky 2.50 1.10
❑ 5 Vaclav Nedomansky 2.50 1.10
❑ 6 Jaroslav Holik 1.00 .45
❑ 7 Jozef Golonka 1.00 .45
❑ 8 Vaclav Nedomansky 2.50 1.10
❑ 9 Vladimir Bednar .50 .23
❑ 10 Jan Havel .50 .23
❑ 11 Jan Hrbaty .50 .23
❑ 12 Jan Suchy .75 .35
❑ 13 Lasse Oksanen .50 .23
❑ 14 Urpo Ylonen 1.00 .45
❑ 15 Michael Curran 1.50 .70
❑ 16 Gary Begg 1.00 .45
❑ 17 Carl Lackey 1.00 .45
❑ 18 Terry O'Malley 1.50 .70
❑ 19 Gary Gamucci 1.00 .45
❑ 20 Seppo Lindstrom .50 .23
❑ 21 Vladimir Lucenko 1.50 .70
Yevgeny Misjakov
Vitalij Davidov
Alexandr Ragulin
Vladimir Petrov
Igor Romisjevsky
Victor Putjkov
Valerij Charlamov
Vladimir Jursinov
Anatolij Firsov
❑ 22 Victor Putjkov .75 .35
❑ 23 Alexandr Ragulin 2.00 .90
❑ 24 Gerry Pinder 2.50 1.10
❑ 25 Fran Huck 1.00 .45
❑ 26 Ken Dryden 80.00 36.00
❑ 27 Viktor Zinger .75 .35
❑ 28 Vladimir Petrov 5.00 2.20
❑ 29 Igor Romisjevsky 1.00 .45
Viktor Zinger
❑ 30 Valerij Charlamov 10.00 4.50
❑ 31 Alexandr Ragulin 2.00 .90
❑ 32 Ab Demarco 2.00 .90
❑ 33 Morris Mott 1.50 .70
❑ 34 Fran Huck 1.00 .45
❑ 35 Vjatjeslav Starsinov 1.50 .70
❑ 36 Lars-Goran Nilsson 1.00 .45
Roger Bourbonnais
❑ 37 Stig-Goran Johansson 1.00 .45
❑ 38 Leif "Honken" Holmqvist 2.00 .90
❑ 39 Hakan Nygren .50 .23
❑ 40 Tord Lundstrom .50 .23
❑ 41 Ulf Sterner .50 .23
❑ 42 Lars-Erik Sjoberg 3.00 1.35
❑ 43 Kjell-Rune Milton .50 .23
❑ 44 Leif "Honken" Holmqvist 2.00 .90
❑ 45 Stefan Karlsson .50 .23
❑ 46 Lennart Svedberg 1.00 .45
❑ 47 Tord Lundstrom .50 .23
❑ 48 Ulf Sterner .50 .23
❑ 49 unknown .50 .23
❑ 50 Lennart Svedberg 1.00 .45
❑ 51 Sverige (12 st) .50 .23
❑ 52 Bert-Ola Nordlander .75 .35
❑ 53 Leif "Honken" Holmqvist 2.00 .90
❑ 54 Lars-Erik Sjoberg 3.00 1.35
❑ 55 Lars-Erik Sjoberg 3.00 1.35
❑ 56 Nils Johansson .50 .23
❑ 57 Ulf Sterner .50 .23
❑ 58 Ulf Sterner .50 .23
Leif Henriksson
❑ 59 Tord Lundstrom .50 .23
❑ 60 Mats Hysing .50 .23
Nils Johansson
❑ 61 Lars-Goran Nilsson .50 .23
❑ 62 Hakan Nygren .50 .23
❑ 63 Gerry Pinder 2.50 1.10
Anatolij Firsov
❑ 64 Evgenij Misjakov 1.00 .45
❑ 65 Vjatjeslav Starsinov 1.50 .70
❑ 66 Alexandr Ragulin 2.00 .90
❑ 67 Alexandr Maltsev 5.00 2.20
❑ 68 Anatolij Firsov 4.00 1.80
❑ 69 Vladimir Lucenko 1.50 .70
❑ 70 Vladimir Petrov 5.00 2.20
❑ 71 Vladimir Petrov 5.00 2.20
❑ 72 Vjatjeslav Starsinov 1.50 .70
❑ 73 Vladimir Vikulov 1.00 .45
❑ 74 Vitaly Davidov 1.00 .45
❑ 75 Evgenij Zimin .75 .35
❑ 76 Vladimir Bednar 2.50 1.10
Vladimir Dzurila
❑ 77 Jan Suchy .75 .35
❑ 78 Jaroslav Holik 1.00 .45
❑ 79 Josef Horesovsky .50 .23
❑ 80 Jozef Golonka 1.00 .45
❑ 81 Richard Farda .50 .23
❑ 82 Frantisek Pospisil 1.00 .45
Oldrich Machac
❑ 83 Ilpo Koskela .50 .23
❑ 84 Juhani Jylha .50 .23
❑ 85 Esa Peltonen .50 .23
❑ 86 Lasse Oksanen .50 .23
❑ 87 Juhani Wahlsten .50 .23
❑ 88 Juha Rantasila .50 .23
❑ 89 Bob Paradise 1.00 .45
❑ 90 Bob Paradise 1.00 .45
❑ 91 Tim Sheehy 1.00 .45
❑ 92 Michael Curran 1.50 .70
❑ 93 Ken Dryden 80.00 36.00
❑ 94 Morris Mott 1.50 .70
❑ 95 Fran Huck 1.00 .45
❑ 96 unknown .50 .23
❑ 97 unknown .50 .23
❑ 98 unknown .50 .23
❑ 99 unknown .50 .23
❑ 100 unknown .50 .23
❑ 101 Arne Carlsson .50 .23
❑ 102 Nils Johansson .50 .23
❑ 103 Leif Holmqvist 2.00 .90
❑ 104 Leif Henriksson .50 .23
❑ 105 Lennart Svedberg 1.00 .45
❑ 106 Hakan Wickberg .50 .23
❑ 107 Gennar Backman .50 .23
❑ 108 Roger Olsson .50 .23
❑ 109 Kjell-Rune Milton .50 .23
❑ 110 Mats Hysing .50 .23
❑ 111 Lars-Erik Sjoberg 3.00 1.35
❑ 112 Anders Hedberg 10.00 4.50
❑ 113 Bjorn Palmqvist .50 .23
❑ 114 Tord Lundstrom .50 .23
❑ 115 Ulf Sterner .50 .23
❑ 116 Stig-Goran Johansson 1.00 .45
❑ 117 Lars-Goran Nilsson .50 .23
❑ 118 Stefan Karlsson .50 .23
❑ 119 Anders Nordin .50 .23
❑ 120 Hans Lindberg .50 .23
❑ 121 Vitalij Davidov 1.00 .45
Vjatjeslav Starsinov
Victor Polupanov
Alexandr Jakusjev
Alexandr Maltsev
Anatolij Firsov
❑ 122 Vitaly Davidov 1.00 .45
❑ 123 Alexandr Jakusjev 5.00 2.20
Valtonen O. Rantasila
❑ 124 Alexandr Maltsev 5.00 2.20
❑ 125 Valerij Charlamov 10.00 4.50
❑ 126 Alexandr Ragulin 2.00 .90
❑ 127 Igor Romisjevskij .50 .23
❑ 128 Boris Michailov 5.00 2.20
❑ 129 Vyatcheslav Starsinov 1.00 .45
Victor Polupanov
Alexander Ragulin
Vladimir Lucenko
❑ 130 Victor Konovalenko .50 .23
❑ 131 Alexandr Jakusjev 4.00 1.80
Vitaly Davidov
Boris Michailov
Vladislav Tretjak
Alexandr Maltsev
Evgenij Paladjev
❑ 132 Vladimir Lucenko 3.00 1.35
Vladimir Petrov
Anatolij Firsov
Valerij Nikitin
Igor Romisjevskij
Vladimir Vikulov
Alexandr Jakusjev
❑ 133 Alexandr Maltsev 5.00 2.20
❑ 134 Valerij Nikitin .50 .23
❑ 135 Vladimir Vikulov 1.00 .45
❑ 136 Vjatjeslav Starsinov 1.50 .70
❑ 137 Evgenij Paladjev .50 .23
❑ 138 Vladimir Shapovalov .50 .23
❑ 139 Anatolij Firsov 4.00 1.80
❑ 140 Victor Polupanov .50 .23
❑ 141 Jaroslav Jirik .50 .23
❑ 142 Miroslav Lacky 1.00 .45
❑ 143 Jan Suchy .75 .35
❑ 144 Lubomir Ujvary .50 .23
❑ 145 Vladimir Bednar .50 .23
❑ 146 Richard Farda .50 .23
❑ 147 Josef Cernyh .75 .35
❑ 148 Vaclav Nedomansky 2.50 1.10
❑ 149 Jaroslav Holik 1.50 .70
❑ 150 Jiri Holik .75 .35
❑ 151 Julius Haas .75 .35
Vladislav Martinec
❑ 152 Vaclav Nedomansky 2.50 1.10
❑ 153 Josef Horesovsky .50 .23
❑ 154 Oldrich Machac .50 .23
❑ 155 Tommy Abrahamsson 1.00 .45
Jiri Kochta
❑ 156 Vladimir Dzurila 4.00 1.80
Jan Suchy
Vladimir Bednar
❑ 157 Jorma Valtonen 1.00 .45
❑ 158 Veli-Pekka Ketola 2.00 .90
❑ 159 Matti Murto .50 .23
Lauri Mononen
❑ 160 Heikki Riihiranta 1.00 .45
❑ 161 Pekka Leimu .50 .23
❑ 162 Lasse Oksanen .50 .23
❑ 163 Jorma Valtonen .50 .23
Vaino Kolkka
Pekka Marjamaki
❑ 164 Urpo Ylonen 1.00 .45
❑ 165 Matti Keinonen .50 .23
❑ 166 Juha Rantasila 1.50 .70
Anatolij Firsov
❑ 167 Jorma Vehmanen .50 .23
❑ 168 Matti Murto .50 .23
❑ 169 Peter Slapke .50 .23
❑ 170 Claus Hirche .50 .23
❑ 171 Frank Braun .50 .23
❑ 172 Rolf Bielas .50 .23
❑ 173 Reinhard Kargar .50 .23
Hiller
Ziesche
Frank Braun
❑ 174 Rolf Beilas .50 .23
Frank Braun
Claus Hirche
Jim Kolbe
❑ 175 Wilfried Rohrbach .50 .23
Hartmut Nickel
❑ 176 Wolfgang Plotka .50 .23
Bernd Karrenbauer
Wilfried Rohrbach
Rainer Patschinski
❑ 177 John Mayasich .50 .23
James Branch
❑ 178 Larry Skime 1.00 .45
❑ 179 Paul Coppo 1.00 .45
❑ 180 Larry Pleau 1.00 .45
❑ 181 Bruce Riutta 1.00 .45
Ron Nasland
John Lothrop
❑ 182 Jerry Lackey 1.00 .45
Larry Skime
Tim Sheehy
Larry Stordahl
❑ 183 Bob Paradise 1.50 .70
Michael Curran
Carl Lackey
❑ 184 Paul Coppo 1.00 .45
Peter Markle
❑ 185 Roger Bourbonnais 1.50 .70
❑ 186 Ted Hargreaves 1.50 .70
❑ 187 Fran Huck 1.00 .45
❑ 188 Wayne Stephenson 5.00 2.20
❑ 189 Morris Mott 1.50 .70
❑ 190 Gerry Pinder 2.50 1.10
❑ 191 Gary Begg 1.00 .45
❑ 192 unknown .50 .23
❑ 193 Felix Goralczyk .50 .23
❑ 194 Andrzej Tkacz .50 .23
❑ 195 Jan Modzelewski .50 .23
❑ 196 Marian Kajzerek .50 .23
❑ 197 Josef Stefaniak .50 .23
❑ 198 Walery Kosyl .50 .23
❑ 199 Jan Modzelewski .50 .23
❑ 200 Pajerski .50 .23
Felix Goralczyk
Chachowski
Polen

## 1969-70 Swedish Hockey Stickers

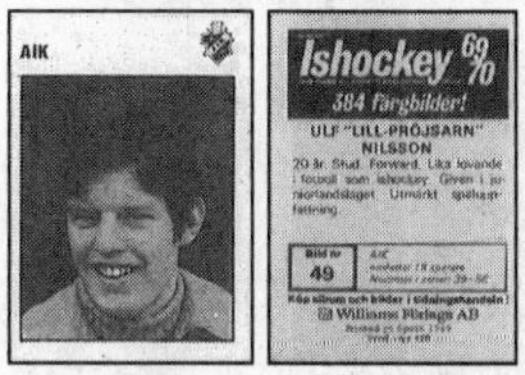

This 384-sticker set was released in Sweden by Williams Forlags AB to commemorate the players and nations competing in the World Championships, as well as club teams from Sweden. The stickers measured 1 7/8" by 2 1/2" and featured a small portrait on the front, along with team name and emblem. The backs gave the player's name, vital stats (in Swedish) and sticker number. Early (first?) appearances by many legends make this set notable: look for Valeri Kharlamov, Alexander Yakushev and Ulf Nilsson. An album was available which not only housed the set, but offered stories, photos and stats to wrap up the previous season. This album is valued at $50.

| | MINT | NRMT |
|---|---|---|
| COMPLETE SET (384) | 400.00 | 180.00 |
| COMMON CARD (1-384) | .75 | .35 |

❑ 1 Valerij Charlamov 15.00 6.75
❑ 2 Vitalij Davydov 1.50 .70
❑ 3 Anatolij Firsov 6.00 2.70
❑ 4 Alexander Jakusjev 8.00 3.60
❑ 5 Vladimir Jursinov 2.00 .90
❑ 6 Victor Kuzkin .75 .35
❑ 7 Vladimir Lutjenko 2.00 .90
❑ 8 Alexander Maltsev 8.00 3.60
❑ 9 Boris Michailov 8.00 3.60
❑ 10 Jevgenij Misjakov 3.00 1.35
❑ 11 Vladimir Petrov 8.00 3.60
❑ 12 Jevgenij Poladjev .75 .35
❑ 13 Victor Putjkov 1.00 .45
❑ 14 Alexander Ragulin 3.00 1.35
❑ 15 Igor Romisjevskij .75 .35
❑ 16 Vjatjeslav Starsjinov 2.50 1.10
❑ 17 Vladimir Vikulov 1.50 .70
❑ 18 Jevgenij Zimin 1.50 .70
❑ 19 Victor Zinger 1.00 .45
❑ 20 Josef Augusta .75 .35
❑ 21 Vladimir Bednar .75 .35
❑ 22 Josef Cerny 1.00 .45
❑ 23 Vladimir Dzurilla 10.00 4.50
❑ 24 Richard Farda .75 .35
❑ 25 Josef Golonka 1.50 .70
❑ 26 Jan Havel .75 .35
❑ 27 Jaroslav Holik 1.50 .70
❑ 28 Jiri Holik 1.00 .45
❑ 29 Josef Horesovsky .75 .35
❑ 30 Jan Hrbaty .75 .35
❑ 31 Jaroslav Jirik .75 .35
❑ 32 Jan Klapac .75 .35
❑ 33 Miroslav Lacky 1.50 .70
❑ 34 Oldrich Machac .75 .35
❑ 35 Vaclav Nedomansky 4.00 1.80
❑ 36 Frantisek Pospisil 2.00 .90
❑ 37 Frantisek Sevcik 1.00 .45
❑ 38 Jan Suchy 1.00 .45
❑ 39 Ake Carlsson .75 .35
❑ 40 Curt Edenvik .75 .35
❑ 41 Hans Eriksson .75 .35
❑ 42 Bo Hansson .75 .35
❑ 43 Ove Hedberg .75 .35
❑ 44 Kjell Hedman 1.50 .70
❑ 45 Leif Holmqvist 3.00 1.35
❑ 46 Anders Johansson .75 .35
❑ 47 Bjorn Larsson .75 .35

❑ 48 Borje Molander .75 .35
❑ 49 Ulf Nilsson 20.00 9.00
❑ 50 Bert-Ola Nordlander 1.00 .45
❑ 51 Bo Olofsson .75 .35
❑ 52 Anders Parmstrom .75 .35
❑ 53 Lennart Selinder .75 .35
❑ 54 Hans Stromberg .75 .35
❑ 55 Kjell Savstrom .75 .35
❑ 56 Lars-Ake Warning .75 .35
❑ 57 Lars Bylund .75 .35
❑ 58 Inge Hammarstrom 5.00 2.20
❑ 59 Hans Dahllof 1.50 .70
❑ 60 Lars Hedenstrom .75 .35
❑ 61 Kjell Johnsson .75 .35
❑ 62 Lennart Johansson .75 .35
❑ 63 Bertil Karlsson .75 .35
❑ 64 Stefan Karlsson .75 .35
❑ 65 Lennart Lind .75 .35
❑ 66 Hans Lindberg .75 .35
❑ 67 Tord Lundstrom .75 .35
❑ 68 Jan-Erik Lyck .75 .35
❑ 69 William Lovqvist 2.00 .90
❑ 70 Lars-Goran Nilsson .75 .35
❑ 71 Stig Salming 1.00 .45
❑ 72 Lars-Ake Sivertsson .75 .35
❑ 73 Lars-Goran Tano .75 .35
❑ 74 Hakan Wickberg .75 .35
❑ 75 Rolf Berglund .75 .35
❑ 76 Lars Alserydh 1.50 .70
❑ 77 Tage Blom .75 .35
❑ 78 Alf Granstrom .75 .35
❑ 79 Lennart Haggroth 1.50 .70
❑ 80 Bertil Karlsson .75 .35
❑ 81 Sven-Bertil Lindstrom .75 .35
❑ 82 Anders Lundberg .75 .35
❑ 83 Goran Lundmark 1.50 .70
❑ 84 Sven-Erik Lundqvist .75 .35
❑ 85 Hans Lundstrom .75 .35
❑ 86 Kjell Lang .75 .35
❑ 87 Borje Lofstedt .75 .35
❑ 88 Olle Nilsson .75 .35
❑ 89 Jan-Olof Nordin .75 .35
❑ 90 Kjell Rehnstrom .75 .35
❑ 91 Peder Rehnstrom .75 .35
❑ 92 Leif Tjernstrom .75 .35
❑ 93 Kjell-Arne Wikstrom .75 .35
❑ 94 Anders Andren .75 .35
❑ 95 Thomas Carlsson .75 .35
❑ 96 Roland Einarsson 2.00 .90
❑ 97 Lars Granlund .75 .35
❑ 98 Stig Larsson .75 .35
❑ 99 Lars-Ake Lundell .75 .35
❑ 100 Per Lundstrom .75 .35
❑ 101 Bjorn Palmquist .75 .35
❑ 102 Ulf Rydin .75 .35
❑ 103 Christer Sehlstedt 1.50 .70
❑ 104 Lars Starck .75 .35
❑ 105 Roland Stoltz .75 .35
❑ 106 Billy Sundstrom .75 .35
❑ 107 Henry Svensson .75 .35
❑ 108 Ove Svensson .75 .35
❑ 109 Ulf Torstensson .75 .35
❑ 110 Christer Abrahamsson 5.00 2.20
❑ 111 Tommy Abrahamsson 2.00 .90
❑ 112 Gunnar Andersson .75 .35
❑ 113 Folke Bengtsson .75 .35
❑ 114 Kjell Brus .75 .35
❑ 115 Ake Danielsson .75 .35
❑ 116 Bo Englund .75 .35
❑ 117 Lennart Gustavsson .75 .35
❑ 118 Hans Jax .75 .35
❑ 119 Jan-Olov Kroon .75 .35
❑ 120 Roger Lindqvist .75 .35
❑ 121 Gunnar Mars 1.50 .70
❑ 122 Ulf Martensson .75 .35
❑ 123 Nisse Nilsson .75 .35
❑ 124 Lars-Erik Sjoberg 5.00 2.20
❑ 125 Olle Sjogren .75 .35
❑ 126 Dan Soderstrom .75 .35
❑ 127 Mats Ahlberg .75 .35
❑ 128 Gunnar Backman 2.00 .90
❑ 129 Ulf Croon .75 .35
❑ 130 Lage Edin .75 .35
❑ 131 Ake Eklof .75 .35
❑ 132 Anders Hedberg 20.00 9.00
❑ 133 Torbjorn Hubinette .75 .35
❑ 134 Nils Johansson .75 .35
❑ 135 Ivar Larsson 2.00 .90
❑ 136 Christer Nilsson .75 .35
❑ 137 Lennart Norberg .75 .35
❑ 138 Anders Nordin .75 .35
❑ 139 Hakan Nygren .75 .35
❑ 140 Sten Olsen .75 .35
❑ 141 Anders Schahlin .75 .35
❑ 142 Gunnar Safsten .75 .35
❑ 143 Ulf Wigren .75 .35
❑ 144 Lars Ohman .75 .35
❑ 145 Tore Ohman .75 .35
❑ 146 Nils Carlsson .75 .35
❑ 147 Kjell Eklund .75 .35
❑ 148 Bengt Gustavsson .75 .35
❑ 149 Bengt-Ake Gustavsson 2.00 .90
❑ 150 Gote Hansson .75 .35
❑ 151 Hans Hansson .75 .35
❑ 152 Per-Arne Hubinette .75 .35
❑ 153 Sven-Ake Jakobsson .75 .35
❑ 154 Goran Johansson 1.50 .70
❑ 155 Mats Lind .75 .35
❑ 156 Mats Lonn .75 .35
❑ 157 Borje Marcus .75 .35
❑ 158 Lars Mjoberg .75 .35
❑ 159 Ulf Nises .75 .35
❑ 160 Bo Olsson .75 .35
❑ 161 Erling Sundblad .75 .35
❑ 162 Lennart Svedberg 2.00 .90
❑ 163 Evert Tysk .75 .35
❑ 164 Stig Ostling .75 .35
❑ 165 Magnus Andersson .75 .35
❑ 166 Erling Bergmark .75 .35
❑ 167 Kenneth Hellman .75 .35
❑ 168 Bjorn Johansson .75 .35
❑ 169 Ulf Johansson .75 .35
❑ 170 Berny Karlsson .75 .35
❑ 171 Nils-Erik Karlsson .75 .35
❑ 172 Rolf Larsson .75 .35
❑ 173 Tore Larsson .75 .35
❑ 174 Roland Lestander 1.50 .70
❑ 175 Lennart Lindgren .75 .35
❑ 176 Finn Lundstrom .75 .35
❑ 177 Kenneth Manberg .75 .35
❑ 178 Lars Molander .75 .35
❑ 179 Lennart Rudby .75 .35
❑ 180 Sven-Ake Rudby .75 .35
❑ 181 Curt Svensson .75 .35
❑ 182 Sverker Torstensson .75 .35
❑ 183 Gunnar Backman 2.00 .90
❑ 184 Arne Carlsson .75 .35
❑ 185 Leif Henriksson .75 .35
❑ 186 Leif Holmqvist 3.00 1.35
❑ 187 Mats Hysing .75 .35
❑ 188 Nils Johansson .75 .35
❑ 189 Stig-Goran Johansson 1.50 .70
❑ 190 Stefan Karlsson .75 .35
❑ 191 Tord Lundstrom .75 .35
❑ 192 Kjell-Rune Milton .75 .35
❑ 193 Lars-Goran Nilsson .75 .35
❑ 194 Bert-Ola Nordlander 1.00 .45
❑ 195 Hakan Nygren .75 .35
❑ 196 Roger Olsson .75 .35
❑ 197 Bjorn Palmquist .75 .35
❑ 198 Lars-Erik Sjoberg 4.00 1.80
❑ 199 Ulf Sterner .75 .35
❑ 200 Lennart Svedberg 1.50 .70
❑ 201 Dick Yderstrom .75 .35
❑ 202 Lennart Abrahamsson .75 .35
❑ 203 Anders Bengtsson 1.50 .70
❑ 204 Agne Bylund .75 .35
❑ 205 Jan Edlund .75 .35
❑ 206 Goran Hedberg .75 .35
❑ 207 Christer Johansson .75 .35
❑ 208 Rolf Jager .75 .35
❑ 209 Per-Erik Kall .75 .35
❑ 210 Anders Norberg .75 .35
❑ 211 Janne Pettersson 1.50 .70
❑ 212 Bo Sjostrom .75 .35
❑ 213 Dick Sjostrom .75 .35
❑ 214 Lasse Sjostrom .75 .35
❑ 215 Ulf Stecksen .75 .35
❑ 216 Lennart Strohm .75 .35
❑ 217 Kurt Tillander .75 .35
❑ 218 Roger Osterlund .75 .35
❑ 219 Hans-Ake Andersson .75 .35
❑ 220 Hans Bejbom .75 .35
❑ 221 Carl-Axel Berglund .75 .35
❑ 222 Goran Borell .75 .35
❑ 223 Bjarne Brostrom .75 .35
❑ 224 Per Backman .75 .35
❑ 225 Kennet Calen .75 .35
❑ 226 Lennart Carlsson .75 .35
❑ 227 Mats Davidasson .75 .35
❑ 228 Curt Ferding .75 .35
❑ 229 Lars-Olof Granstrom .75 .35
❑ 230 Rolf Hansson .75 .35
❑ 231 Rune Holmgren .75 .35
❑ 232 Rune Norrstrom .75 .35
❑ 233 Bert-Ake Olsson .75 .35
❑ 234 Olle Olsson .75 .35
❑ 235 Jan Svedman .75 .35
❑ 236 Walter Winsth .75 .35
❑ 237 Goran Akerlund .75 .35
❑ 238 Borje Burlin .75 .35
❑ 239 Hans Carlsson .75 .35
❑ 240 Stig Carlsson .75 .35
❑ 241 Gunnar Granberg .75 .35
❑ 242 Allan Helenefors .75 .35
❑ 243 Mats Hysing .75 .35
❑ 244 Bertil Jacobsson .75 .35
❑ 245 Stig-Goran Johansson 1.50 .70
❑ 246 Curt Larsson 2.50 1.10
❑ 247 Eilert Maatta .75 .35
❑ 248 Soren Maatta .75 .35
❑ 249 Tommy Bergman .75 .35
❑ 250 Nils-Olof Schilstrom .75 .35
❑ 251 Jan Schullstrom .75 .35
❑ 252 Kjell Svensson 1.50 .70
❑ 253 Gunnar Tallberg .75 .35
❑ 254 Borje Ulweback .75 .35
❑ 255 Dick Yderstrom .75 .35
❑ 256 Tommy Andersson .75 .35
❑ 257 Bulla Berggren .75 .35
❑ 258 Anders Bryner .75 .35
❑ 259 Anders Claesson 1.50 .70
❑ 260 Jan Johansson .75 .35
❑ 261 Ove Jonsson .75 .35
❑ 262 Lennart Lind .75 .35
❑ 263 Arne Lundstrom .75 .35
❑ 264 Ake Lundstrom .75 .35
❑ 265 Jan-Erik Nilsson .75 .35
❑ 266 Lennart Norberg .75 .35
❑ 267 Sten-Olov Olsson .75 .35
❑ 268 Hakan Pettersson .75 .35
❑ 269 Stefan Pettersson .75 .35
❑ 270 Gosta Sjokvist .75 .35
❑ 271 Jan Stolpe .75 .35
❑ 272 Ake Soderberg .75 .35
❑ 273 Kjell Westerlund .75 .35
❑ 274 Olle Ahman .75 .35
❑ 275 Krister Andersson 1.50 .70
❑ 276 Bert Danielsson .75 .35
❑ 277 Gert Danielsson .75 .35
❑ 278 Bengt Eriksson .75 .35
❑ 279 Lars-Anders Gustavsson .75 .35
❑ 280 Curt Jacobsson .75 .35
❑ 281 Leif Jacobsson .75 .35
❑ 282 Lars-Erik Jakobsson .75 .35
❑ 283 Lars-Goran Johansson .75 .35
❑ 284 Des Moroney .75 .35
❑ 285 Borje Maatta .75 .35
❑ 286 Lars-Ake Nordin .75 .35
❑ 287 Kenneth Pedersen .75 .35
❑ 288 Anders Rapp .75 .35
❑ 289 Benny Runesson .75 .35
❑ 290 Jonny Ryman .75 .35
❑ 291 Ake Ryman .75 .35
❑ 292 Goran Ahstrom 1.50 .70
❑ 293 John Andersson .75 .35
❑ 294 Kjell-Olov Barrefjord .75 .35
❑ 295 Ulf Barrefjord .75 .35
❑ 296 Kent Bjork .75 .35
❑ 297 Lars Dahlgren .75 .35
❑ 298 Karl-Olof Eriksson .75 .35
❑ 299 Osten Folkesson .75 .35
❑ 300 Anders Hagstrom .75 .35
❑ 301 Eric Jarvholm .75 .35
❑ 302 Ulf Larsson .75 .35
❑ 303 Bo Leong 1.50 .70
❑ 304 Bengt Lofgren .75 .35
❑ 305 Roger Nilsson .75 .35
❑ 306 Bengt Persson 1.50 .70
❑ 307 Ulf Stromsoe .75 .35
❑ 308 Kjell Sundstrom .75 .35
❑ 309 Leif Andersson .75 .35
❑ 310 Bernt Augustsson .75 .35
❑ 311 Kjell Augustsson .75 .35
❑ 312 Tommy Eriksson 2.00 .90
❑ 313 Lars-Olof Feltendahl .75 .35
❑ 314 Karl-Soren Hedlund .75 .35
❑ 315 Penti Hyytiainen .75 .35
❑ 316 Arne Johansson .75 .35
❑ 317 Bengt-Goran Karlsson .75 .35
❑ 318 Curt Lundmark 2.00 .90
❑ 319 Hakan Olsson 1.50 .70
❑ 320 Kent Persson .75 .35
❑ 321 Ove Stenlund .75 .35
❑ 322 Goran Thelin .75 .35
❑ 323 Ove Thelin .75 .35
❑ 324 Bo Astrom .75 .35
❑ 325 Hasse Mellinger .75 .35
❑ 326 Uno Ohrlund .75 .35
❑ 327 Jan Ostling .75 .35
❑ 328 Kjell Andersson .75 .35
❑ 329 Ronny Andersson 2.00 .90
❑ 330 Gert Blome .75 .35
❑ 331 Ingemar Caris 2.00 .90
❑ 332 Arne Carlsson .75 .35
❑ 333 Svante Granholm .75 .35
❑ 334 Henric Hedlund .75 .35
❑ 335 Leif Henriksson .75 .35
❑ 336 Anders Johansson .75 .35
❑ 337 Kjell Jonsson .75 .35
❑ 338 Bjorn Lindberg .75 .35
❑ 339 Goran Lindberg .75 .35
❑ 340 Carl-Fredrik Montan .75 .35
❑ 341 Leif Nilsson .75 .35
❑ 342 Kurt Olofsson .75 .35
❑ 343 Jan Olsen .75 .35
❑ 344 Roger Olsson .75 .35
❑ 345 Kjell-Ronnie Petterson .75 .35
❑ 346 Ulf Sterner .75 .35
❑ 347 Rickie Bayes 2.50 1.10
❑ 348 Gary Begg 1.50 .70
❑ 349 Roger Bourbonnais 2.00 .90
❑ 350 Jack Bownass 2.00 .90
❑ 351 Terry Caffery 2.50 1.10
❑ 352 Steve Carlyle 2.50 1.10
❑ 353 Ab Demarco 3.00 1.35
❑ 354 Ted Hargreaves 2.00 .90
❑ 355 Bill Heindl 2.50 1.10
❑ 356 Fran Huck 1.50 .70
❑ 357 Steve King 2.50 1.10
❑ 358 Chuck Lefley 4.00 1.80
❑ 359 Morris Mott 2.50 1.10
❑ 360 Terry O'Malley 2.00 .90
❑ 361 Kevin O'Shea 2.50 1.10
❑ 362 Gerry Pinder 4.00 1.80
❑ 363 Steve Rexe 3.00 1.35
❑ 364 Ken Stephenson 2.50 1.10
❑ 365 Wayne Stephenson 8.00 3.60
❑ 366 Matti Harju .75 .35
❑ 367 Esa Isaksson .75 .35
❑ 368 Kari Johansson .75 .35
❑ 369 Juhani Jylha .75 .35
❑ 370 Matti Keinonen .75 .35
❑ 371 Veli-Pekka Ketola 3.00 1.35
❑ 372 Lasse Kiili 1.50 .70
❑ 373 Ilpo Koskela .75 .35
❑ 374 Pekka Leimu .75 .35
❑ 375 Seppo Lindstrom .75 .35
❑ 376 Pekka Marjamaki .75 .35
❑ 377 Lauri Mononen .75 .35
❑ 378 Lasse Oksanen .75 .35
❑ 379 Lalli Partanen .75 .35
❑ 380 Esa Peltonen .75 .35
❑ 381 Jorma Peltonen .75 .35
❑ 382 Juhani Rantasila .75 .35
❑ 383 Juhani Wahlsten .75 .35
❑ 384 Urpo Ylonen 2.50 1.10

## 1970-71 Swedish Hockey Stickers

This set of 384 stickers was issued by Williams Forlags AB and printed by Panini in Italy. The stickers, which measure approximately 2 1/2" by 1 3/4", feature teams from the Swedish first and second divisions, as well as national team members from Tre

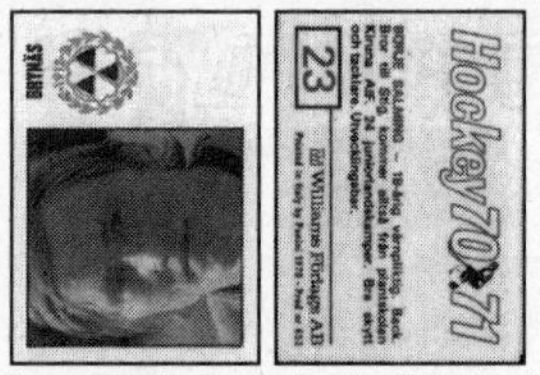

Kroner, Russia, Czechoslovakia, Finland and East Germany. The card fronts feature a small player portrait along with the team emblem. The backs give player name, a brief bio and card number. The set includes many well known international stars, most prominently the first appearance of HOFer Borje Salming. An album to house the stickers was available as well; it also included text and photos to give a brief history of the teams involved. It is valued at approximately $40.

| | MINT | NRMT |
|---|---|---|
| COMPLETE SET (384) | 400.00 | 180.00 |
| COMMON STICKER (1-384) | .75 | .35 |

❑ 1 Leif (Honken) Holmqvist 2.50 1.10
❑ 2 Kjell Hedman 1.50 .70
❑ 3 Lars Danielsson .75 .35
❑ 4 Ake Fagerstrom .75 .35
❑ 5 Per-Arne Hubinette .75 .35
❑ 6 Hakan Lindgren .75 .35
❑ 7 Bert-Ola Nordlander 1.00 .45
❑ 8 Rolf (Rattan) Edberg .75 .35
❑ 9 Bo Hansson .75 .35
❑ 10 Jan-Olov Kroon .75 .35
❑ 11 Ulf Nilsson 10.00 4.50
❑ 12 Bosse Olofsson .75 .35
❑ 13 Lennart Selinder .75 .35
❑ 14 Hans Stromberg .75 .35
❑ 15 Kjell Savstrom .75 .35
❑ 16 Lars-Ake Warning .75 .35
❑ 17 Lars-Goran Nilsson 1.50 .70
Alexander Yakushev
❑ 18 William Lofqvist 1.50 .70
❑ 19 Hans Dahllof 1.50 .70
❑ 20 Lars Bylund .75 .35
❑ 21 Lars Hedenstrom .75 .35
❑ 22 Kjell Johnsson .75 .35
❑ 23 Borje Salming 20.00 9.00
❑ 24 Stig Salming .75 .35
❑ 25 Stif Ostling .75 .35
❑ 26 Inge Hammarstrom 5.00 2.20
❑ 27 Lennart Johansson .75 .35
❑ 28 Stefan Karlsson .75 .35
❑ 29 Lennart Lind .75 .35
❑ 30 Hans (Virus) Lindberg .75 .35
❑ 31 Tord Lundstrom .75 .35
❑ 32 Jan-Erik Lyck .75 .35
❑ 33 Lars-Goran Nilsson .75 .35
❑ 34 Lars-Ake Sivertsson .75 .35
❑ 35 Hakan Wickberg .75 .35
❑ 36 puzzle .75 .35
❑ 37 puzzle .75 .35
❑ 38 puzzle .75 .35
❑ 39 puzzle .75 .35
❑ 40 puzzle .75 .35
❑ 41 puzzle .75 .35
❑ 42 puzzle 1.00 .45
❑ 43 puzzle 1.00 .45
❑ 44 puzzle .75 .35
❑ 45 puzzle .75 .35
❑ 46 puzzle 1.00 .45
❑ 47 puzzle 1.00 .45
❑ 48 Roland Einarsson 1.50 .70
❑ 49 Ake Eklof .75 .35
❑ 50 Christer Ahlstrand .75 .35
❑ 51 Thomas Carlsson .75 .35
❑ 52 Anders Rylin .75 .35
❑ 53 Billy Sundstrom .75 .35
❑ 54 Folke Bengtsson .75 .35
❑ 55 Stig Larsson .75 .35
❑ 56 Lars-Ake Lundell .75 .35
❑ 57 Per Lundstrom .75 .35
❑ 58 Bjorn Palmqvist .75 .35
❑ 59 Ulf Rydin .75 .35
❑ 60 Ove Svensson .75 .35
❑ 61 Jan Zabrodsky .75 .35
❑ 62 Leif Holmqvist PUZ 2.00 .90
❑ 63 Leif Holmqvist PUZ 2.00 .90
❑ 64 Leif Holmqvist PUZ 2.00 .90
❑ 65 Leif Holmqvist PUZ 2.00 .90
❑ 66 Christer Abrahamsson 3.00 1.35
❑ 67 Christer Sterner 1.50 .70
❑ 68 Thommy Abrahamsson 1.50 .70
❑ 69 Karl-Gustaf Alander .75 .35
❑ 70 Gunnar Andersson .75 .35
❑ 71 Roland Bond .75 .35
❑ 72 Ake Danielsson .75 .35
❑ 73 Per-Olov Brasar 3.00 1.35
❑ 74 Kjell Brus .75 .35
❑ 75 Hans Jax .75 .35
❑ 76 Dan Labraaten 3.00 1.35
❑ 77 Roger Lindqvist .75 .35
❑ 78 Ulf Martensson .75 .35
❑ 79 Olle Sjogren .75 .35
❑ 80 Ingemar Snis .75 .35
❑ 81 Dan Soderstrom .75 .35
❑ 82 Mats Ahlberg .75 .35
❑ 83 Gunnar Backman 1.50 .70
❑ 84 Ivar Larsson 1.50 .70
❑ 85 Lage Edin .75 .35
❑ 86 Kjell-Rune Milton .75 .35
❑ 87 Ulf Torstensson .75 .35
❑ 88 Ulf Wigren .75 .35
❑ 89 Ulf Croon .75 .35
❑ 90 Hakan Dahllof .75 .35
❑ 91 Anders Hedberg 10.00 4.50
❑ 92 Torbjorn Hubinette .75 .35
❑ 93 Christer Nilsson .75 .35
❑ 94 Lennart Norberg .75 .35
❑ 95 Anders Nordin .75 .35
❑ 96 Hakan Nygren .75 .35
❑ 97 Per-Olof Uusitalo .75 .35
❑ 98 Lars Ohman .75 .35
❑ 99 Tore Ohman .75 .35
❑ 100 V. Dzurilla PUZ 1.50 .70
❑ 101 V. Dzurilla PUZ 1.50 .70
❑ 102 V. Dzurilla PUZ 1.50 .70
❑ 103 V. Dzurilla PUZ 1.50 .70
❑ 104 V. Dzurilla PUZ 1.50 .70
❑ 105 V. Dzurilla PUZ 1.50 .70
❑ 106 V. Dzurilla PUZ 1.50 .70
❑ 107 V. Dzurilla PUZ 1.50 .70
❑ 108 V. Dzurilla PUZ 1.50 .70
❑ 109 V. Dzurilla PUZ 1.50 .70
❑ 110 V. Dzurilla PUZ 1.50 .70
❑ 111 V. Dzurilla PUZ 1.50 .70
❑ 112 Bengt-Ake Gustavsson 1.50 .70
❑ 113 Lars Gustavsson 1.50 .70
❑ 114 Tommy Andersson .75 .35
❑ 115 Hans-Olov Ernlund .75 .35
❑ 116 Lars Mjoberg .75 .35
❑ 117 Gote Hansson .75 .35
❑ 118 L. Svedberg PUZ 1.00 .45
❑ 119 B. Mikhailov PUZ 3.00 1.35
❑ 120 L. Holmqvist PUZ 2.00 .90
❑ 121 Hans Hansson .75 .35
❑ 122 Sven-Ake Jakobsson .75 .35
❑ 123 Mats Lind .75 .35
❑ 124 Mats Lonn .75 .35
❑ 125 Borje Marcus .75 .35
❑ 126 Ulf Nises .75 .35
❑ 127 Borje Skoog .75 .35
❑ 128 Erling Sundblad .75 .35
❑ 129 Kent Sundkvist .75 .35
❑ 130 Curt Larsson 2.00 .90
❑ 131 Torbjorn Hellsing 1.50 .70
❑ 132 Tommie Bergman 4.00 1.80
❑ 133 Arne Carlsson .75 .35
❑ 134 Allan Helenefors .75 .35
❑ 135 Eilert Maatta .75 .35
❑ 136 Jan Schullstrom .75 .35
❑ 137 Hans Carlsson .75 .35
❑ 138 Tommy Carlsson .75 .35
❑ 139 Gunnar Granberg .75 .35
❑ 140 Mats Hysing .75 .35
❑ 141 Bertil Jacobsson .75 .35
❑ 142 Stig-Goran Johansson .75 .35
❑ 143 Soren Maatta .75 .35
❑ 144 Nils-Olov Schilstrom .75 .35
❑ 145 Dick Yderstrom .75 .35
❑ 146 Carl-Goran Oberg .75 .35
❑ 147 Lennart Svedberg 1.00 .45
❑ 148 Anders Claesson 1.50 .70
❑ 149 Kent Othberg 1.50 .70
❑ 150 Jan Johansson .75 .35
❑ 151 Jan-Erik Nilsson .75 .35
❑ 152 Stefan Pettersson .75 .35
❑ 153 Lennart Svedberg 1.50 .70
❑ 154 Bo Berggren .75 .35
❑ 155 Arne Lundstrom .75 .35
❑ 156 Finn Lundstrom .75 .35
❑ 157 I. Romisjevskij PUZ .75 .35
❑ 158 I. Romisjevskij PUZ 1.00 .45
❑ 159 Ake Lundstrom .75 .35
❑ 160 V. Tretiak PUZ 8.00 3.60
❑ 161 V. Tretiak PUZ 8.00 3.60
❑ 162 Lennart Norberg .75 .35
❑ 163 Hakan Pettersson .75 .35
❑ 164 Ake Soderberg 1.00 .45
❑ 165 Olle Ahman .75 .35
❑ 166 puzzle .75 .35
❑ 167 puzzle .75 .35
❑ 168 puzzle .75 .35
❑ 169 puzzle .75 .35
❑ 170 puzzle .75 .35
❑ 171 puzzle .75 .35
❑ 172 puzzle .75 .35
❑ 173 puzzle .75 .35
❑ 174 puzzle .75 .35
❑ 175 puzzle .75 .35
❑ 176 puzzle .75 .35
❑ 177 puzzle .75 .35
❑ 178 Christer Andersson 1.50 .70
❑ 179 Goran Astrom 1.50 .70
❑ 180 Kenneth Ekman .75 .35
❑ 181 Lars Erik Jakobsson .75 .35
❑ 182 Des Moroney .75 .35
❑ 183 Borje Maatta .75 .35
❑ 184 Kenneth Pedersen .75 .35
❑ 185 Anders Rapp .75 .35
❑ 186 Sven Crabo .75 .35
❑ 187 Lars Anders Gustavsson .75 .35
❑ 188 Kurt Jacobsson .75 .35
❑ 189 Leif Jacobsson .75 .35
❑ 190 Lars Goran Johansson .75 .35
❑ 191 Bernt Karlsson .75 .35
❑ 192 Benny Runesson .75 .35
❑ 193 Jonny Ryman .75 .35
❑ 194 Ake Ryman .75 .35
❑ 195 Christer Grahn 1.50 .70
❑ 196 Ronny Sandstrom .75 .35
❑ 197 John Andersson .75 .35
❑ 198 Karl-Olof Eriksson .75 .35
❑ 199 Anders Hagstrom .75 .35
❑ 200 Rof Jager .75 .35
❑ 201 Erik Jarvholm .75 .35
❑ 202 Lars Nordin .75 .35
❑ 203 Ulf Barrefjord .75 .35
❑ 204 Lars Dahlgren .75 .35

❑ 205 Ulf Ingvarsson .75 .35
❑ 206 Ulf Larsson .75 .35
❑ 207 Jan Lundqvist .75 .35
❑ 208 Ulf Lundstrom .75 .35
❑ 209 Bengt Lovgren .75 .35
❑ 210 Lars SJostrom .75 .35
❑ 211 Kjell Sundstrom .75 .35
❑ 212 Ulf Stromsoe .75 .35
❑ 213 Hakan Olsson 1.50 .70
❑ 214 Leif Andersson .75 .35
❑ 215 Tommy Eriksson 1.50 .70
❑ 216 Karl-Soren Hedlund .75 .35
❑ 217 Curt Lundmark 1.50 .70
❑ 218 Ove Nystrom .75 .35
❑ 219 Gote Gustavsson .75 .35
❑ 220 Hans Hjelm .75 .35
❑ 221 Pennti Hyytiainen .75 .35
❑ 222 Arne Johansson .75 .35
❑ 223 Bengt-Goran Karlsson .75 .35
❑ 224 Kent Persson .75 .35
❑ 225 Ove Stenlund .75 .35
❑ 226 Goran Thelin .75 .35
❑ 227 Ove Thelin .75 .35
❑ 228 Bo Astrom .75 .35
❑ 229 Jan Ostling .75 .35
❑ 230 V. Tretiak action 15.00 6.75
❑ 231 V. Konovalenko PUZ .75 .35
❑ 232 V. Konovalenko PUZ .75 .35
❑ 233 V. Konovalenko PUZ .75 .35
❑ 234 V. Konovalenko PUZ .75 .35
❑ 235 V. Konovalenko PUZ .75 .35
❑ 236 V. Konovalenko PUZ .75 .35
❑ 237 V. Konovalenko PUZ .75 .35
❑ 238 V. Konovalenko PUZ .75 .35
❑ 239 V. Konovalenko PUZ .75 .35
❑ 240 V. Konovalenko PUZ .75 .35
❑ 241 V. Konovalenko PUZ .75 .35
❑ 242 V. Konovalenko PUZ .75 .35
❑ 243 Ingemar Caris 1.50 .70
❑ 244 Ronny Andersson 1.50 .70
❑ 245 Gert Blome .75 .35
❑ 246 Anders Johansson .75 .35
❑ 247 Goran Lindberg .75 .35
❑ 248 Jan Olsen .75 .35
❑ 249 Lars-Erik Sjoberg 4.00 1.80
❑ 250 Kjell Andersson .75 .35
❑ 251 Svante Granholm .75 .35
❑ 252 Henrik Hedlund .75 .35
❑ 253 Leif Henriksson .75 .35
❑ 254 Bjorn Lindberg .75 .35
❑ 255 Billy Lindstrom .75 .35
❑ 256 Carl-Fredrik Montan .75 .35
❑ 257 Leif Nilsson .75 .35
❑ 258 Kurt Olofsson .75 .35
❑ 259 Roger Olsson .75 .35
❑ 260 Kjell-Ronnie Pettersson .75 .35
❑ 261 Soviet team PUZ .75 .35
❑ 262 Soviet team PUZ .75 .35
❑ 263 Soviet team PUZ .75 .35
❑ 264 Soviet team PUZ .75 .35
❑ 265 Soviet team PUZ .75 .35
❑ 266 Soviet team PUZ .75 .35
❑ 267 Soviet team PUZ .75 .35
❑ 268 Soviet team PUZ .75 .35
❑ 269 Soviet team PUZ .75 .35
❑ 270 Soviet team PUZ .75 .35
❑ 271 Soviet team PUZ .75 .35
❑ 272 Soviet team PUZ .75 .35
❑ 273 Leif Holmqvist 2.00 .90
❑ 274 Gunnar Backman 1.50 .70
❑ 275 Christer Abrahamsson 3.00 1.35
❑ 276 Thommy Abrahamsson 1.50 .70
❑ 277 Arne Carlsson .75 .35
❑ 278 Nils Johansson .75 .35
❑ 279 Ljell-Rune Milton .75 .35
❑ 280 Lars-Erik Sjoberg 4.00 1.80
❑ 281 Lennart Svedberg 1.50 .70
❑ 282 Anders Hedberg 10.00 4.50
❑ 283 Stig-Goran Johansson .75 .35
❑ 284 Stefan Karlsson .75 .35
❑ 285 Hans Lindberg .75 .35
❑ 286 Tord Lundstrom .75 .35
❑ 287 Lars-Goran Nilsson .75 .35
❑ 288 Anders Nordin .75 .35
❑ 289 Roger Olsson .75 .35
❑ 290 Bjorn Palmqvist .75 .35
❑ 291 Ulf Sterner .75 .35
❑ 292 Hakan Wickberg .75 .35
❑ 293 Urpo Ylonen 2.00 .90
❑ 294 Jorma Valtonen 1.50 .70
❑ 295 Ilpo Koskela .75 .35
❑ 296 Seppo Lindstrom .75 .35
❑ 297 Pekka Marjamaki .75 .35
❑ 298 Lalli Partinen .75 .35
❑ 299 Juha Rantasila .75 .35
❑ 300 Heikki Riihiranta 2.00 .90
❑ 301 Pekka Keimu .75 .35
❑ 302 Matti Keinonen .75 .35
❑ 303 Veli-Pekka Ketola 3.00 1.35
❑ 304 Vaino Kolkka .75 .35
❑ 305 Harri Linnonmaa .75 .35
❑ 306 Lauri Mononen .75 .35
❑ 307 Matti Murto 1.50 .70
❑ 308 Lasse Oksanen .75 .35
❑ 309 Esa Peltonen .75 .35
❑ 310 Jorma Peltonen .75 .35
❑ 311 Juhani Tamminen 1.50 .70
❑ 312 Jorma Vehmanen 1.50 .70
❑ 313 Viktor Konovalenko 1.50 .70
❑ 314 Vladislav Tretjak 30.00 13.50
❑ 315 Vitalij Davidov 1.50 .70
❑ 316 Vladimir Lutjenko 1.50 .70
❑ 317 Jevgenij Paladjev .75 .35
❑ 318 Alexander Ragulin 3.00 1.35
❑ 319 Igor Romisjevski 1.00 .45
❑ 320 Valerij Vasiljev 5.00 2.20
❑ 321 Valerij Nikitin 1.00 .45
❑ 322 Valerij Charlamov 15.00 6.75
❑ 323 Anatolij Firsov 8.00 3.60
❑ 324 Alexander Jakusjev 8.00 3.60
❑ 325 Alexander Maltsev 8.00 3.60
❑ 326 Boris Michailov 8.00 3.60
❑ 327 Jevgenij Misjakov 2.50 1.10
❑ 328 Vladimir Petrov 5.00 2.20
❑ 329 Viktor Polupanov .75 .35
❑ 330 Vladimir Sjadrin 3.00 1.35
❑ 331 Vjatjeslav Starsinov 2.50 1.10
❑ 332 Vladimir Vikulov 1.00 .45
❑ 333 puzzle .75 .35
❑ 334 puzzle .75 .35
❑ 335 puzzle .75 .35
❑ 336 puzzle .75 .35
❑ 337 puzzle .75 .35
❑ 338 puzzle .75 .35
❑ 339 puzzle .75 .35
❑ 340 puzzle .75 .35
❑ 341 puzzle .75 .35
❑ 342 puzzle .75 .35
❑ 343 puzzle .75 .35
❑ 344 puzzle .75 .35
❑ 345 Vladimir Dzurilla 5.00 2.20
❑ 346 Miroslav Lacky 1.50 .70
❑ 347 Vladimir Bednar .75 .35
❑ 348 Josef Horesovsky .75 .35
❑ 349 Oldrich Machac .75 .35
❑ 350 Frantisek Pospisil 1.50 .70
❑ 351 Jan Suchy 1.00 .45
❑ 352 Lubomir Ujvary .75 .35
❑ 353 Josef Cerny 1.00 .45
❑ 354 Richard Farda .75 .35
❑ 355 Julius Haas .75 .35
❑ 356 Ivan Hlinka 1.50 .70
❑ 357 Jaroslav Holik 1.00 .45
❑ 358 Jiri Holik 1.00 .45
❑ 359 Jan Hrbaty .75 .35
❑ 360 Jiri Kochta .75 .35
❑ 361 Vladislav Martinec .75 .35
❑ 362 Vaclav Nedomansky 3.00 1.35
❑ 363 Stanislav Pryl .75 .35
❑ 364 Frantisek Sevcik .75 .35
❑ 365 Klaus Hirche 1.50 .70
❑ 366 Diter Purschel 1.50 .70
❑ 367 Frank Braun .75 .35
❑ 368 Dieter Dewitz .75 .35
❑ 369 Bernd Karrenbauer .75 .35
❑ 370 Helmut Novy .75 .35
❑ 371 Dietmar Peters .75 .35
❑ 372 Wolfgang Plotka .75 .35
❑ 373 Peter Slapke .75 .35
❑ 374 Rolf Bielas .75 .35
❑ 375 Lothar Fuchs .75 .35
❑ 376 Bernd Hiller .75 .35
❑ 377 Reinhard Karger .75 .35
❑ 378 Hartmut Nickel .75 .35
❑ 379 Rudiger Noack .75 .35
❑ 380 Rainer Patschinski .75 .35
❑ 381 Peter Prusa .75 .35
❑ 382 Wilfried Rohrbach .75 .35
❑ 383 Dieter Rohl .75 .35
❑ 384 Joachim Ziesche .75 .35

## 1971-72 Swedish Hockey Stickers

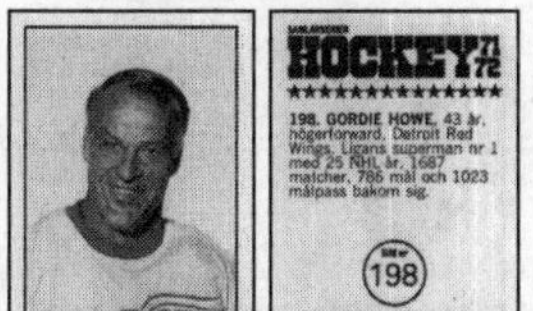

This set of 400 stickers was printed by Panini and released in Sweden by Williams Forlags AB. The stickers -- which measure approximately 2 1/2" by 1 3/4" -- feature players from Sweden's top league, as well as from several national teams and NHL clubs. The fronts offer a simple player portrait; the backs contain sticker number and a brief player bio in Swedish. An album to house the set can be found; it is valued approximately at $40. Key stars in this loaded set include Bobby Orr, Gordie Howe and Vladislav Tretiak.

| | MINT | NRMT |
|---|---|---|
| COMPLETE SET (400) | 400.00 | 180.00 |
| COMMON STICKER (1-400) | .50 | .23 |

❑ 1 Christer Abrahamsson 2.00 .90
❑ 2 Leif Holmqvist 1.00 .45
❑ 3 William Lofqvist 1.00 .45
❑ 4 Thommy Abrahamsson 1.00 .45
❑ 5 Gunnar Andersson .50 .23
❑ 6 Thommie Bergman 3.00 1.35
❑ 7 Arne Carlsson .50 .23
❑ 8 Kjell-Rune Milton .50 .23
❑ 9 Bert-Ola Nordlander 1.00 .45
❑ 10 Lennart Svedberg 1.00 .45
❑ 11 Lars-Erik Sjoberg 2.00 .90
❑ 12 Stig Ostling .50 .23
❑ 13 Inge Hammarstrom 3.00 1.35
❑ 14 Anders Hedberg 7.50 3.40
❑ 15 Stig-Goran Johansson 1.00 .45
❑ 16 Stefan Karlsson .50 .23
❑ 17 Dan Labraaten 2.00 .90
❑ 18 Hans Lindberg .50 .23
❑ 19 Tord Lundstrom .50 .23
❑ 20 Lars-Goran Nilsson .50 .23
❑ 21 Hakan Nygren .50 .23
❑ 22 Bjorn Plamqvist .50 .23
❑ 23 Hakan Pettersson .50 .23
❑ 24 Ulf Sterner .50 .23
❑ 25 Hakan Wickberg .50 .23
❑ 26 Viktor Konovalenko .75 .35
❑ 27 Vladislav Tretjak 20.00 9.00
❑ 28 Gennadij Tsigankov .75 .35
❑ 29 Vitali Davidov .50 .23
❑ 30 Victor Kuskin .50 .23
❑ 31 Vladimir Lutjenko 1.00 .45
❑ 32 Alexander Ragulin 2.50 1.10
❑ 33 Igor Romisjevskij .75 .35
❑ 34 Valerij Charlamov 10.00 4.50
❑ 35 Anatolij Firsov 5.00 2.20
❑ 36 Alexander Maltsev 5.00 2.20
❑ 37 Boris Michailov 5.00 2.20
❑ 38 Jevgenij Misjakov 2.00 .90
❑ 39 Vladmir Petrov 5.00 2.20
❑ 40 Vjatjeslav Starshinov 2.00 .90
❑ 41 Vladimir Vikulov .75 .35
❑ 42 Evgenij Zimin 1.50 .70
❑ 43 Jiri Holecek 1.00 .45
❑ 44 Josef Horesovsky .50 .23
❑ 45 Oldrich Machac .50 .23
❑ 46 Frantisek Pancharek .50 .23
❑ 47 Frantisek Pospisil .75 .35
❑ 48 Jan Suchy .75 .35
❑ 49 Josef Cerny .75 .35
❑ 50 Richard Farda .50 .23
❑ 51 Jan Havel .50 .23
❑ 52 Ivan Hlinka 1.00 .45
❑ 53 Jiri Holik .75 .35
❑ 54 Jiri Kochta .50 .23
❑ 55 Vladimir Martinec .75 .35
❑ 56 Vaclav Nedomansky 2.00 .90
❑ 57 Eduard Novak .50 .23
❑ 58 Bohuslav Stastny 1.00 .45
❑ 59 Jorma Valtonen 1.00 .45
❑ 60 Urpo Ylonen 1.00 .45
❑ 61 Ilpo Koskela .50 .23
❑ 62 Seppo Lindstrom .50 .23
❑ 63 Hannu Luojola .50 .23
❑ 64 Pekka Marjamaki .50 .23
❑ 65 Esa Isaksson .50 .23
❑ 66 Veli-Pekka Ketola 2.00 .90
❑ 67 Harri Linnonmaa .50 .23
❑ 68 Erkki Mononen .50 .23
❑ 69 Lauri Mononen .50 .23
❑ 70 Matti Murto 1.00 .45
❑ 71 Lasse Oksanen .50 .23
❑ 72 Esa Peltonen .50 .23
❑ 73 Juhanni Tamminen 1.00 .45
❑ 74 Jorma Vehmanen .50 .23
❑ 75 Leif Holmqvist 1.00 .45
❑ 76 Bert Jattne 1.00 .45
❑ 77 Lars Danielsson .50 .23
❑ 78 Ake Fagerstrom .50 .23
❑ 79 Per-Arne Hubinette .50 .23
❑ 80 Hakan Lindgren .50 .23
❑ 81 Bert-Ola Nordlander 1.00 .45
❑ 82 Lennart Pettersson .50 .23
❑ 83 Rolf Edberg .50 .23
❑ 84 Bo Hansson .50 .23
❑ 85 Jan-Olov Kroon .50 .23
❑ 86 Gunnar Lindkvist .50 .23
❑ 87 Christer Lundberg .50 .23
❑ 88 Ulf Nilsson 8.00 3.60
❑ 89 Bo Olofsson .50 .23
❑ 90 Jan Olsson .50 .23
❑ 91 Lennart Selinder .50 .23
❑ 92 Soren Sjogren .50 .23
❑ 93 Hans Stromberg .50 .23
❑ 94 Jan Ostling .50 .23
❑ 95 Kjell Helling 1.00 .45
❑ 96 William Lofqvist 1.00 .45
❑ 97 Lars Bylund .50 .23
❑ 98 Kjell Johnsson .50 .23
❑ 99 Par Malmstrom .50 .23
❑ 100 Borje Salming 10.00 4.50
❑ 101 Stig Salming .50 .23
❑ 102 Stig Ostling .50 .23
❑ 103 Inge Hammarstrom 3.00 1.35
❑ 104 Lennart Johansson .50 .23
❑ 105 Stefan Karlsson .50 .23
❑ 106 Lennart Lind .50 .23
❑ 107 Hans Lindberg .50 .23
❑ 108 Tord Lundstrom .50 .23
❑ 109 Jan-Erik Lyck .50 .23
❑ 110 Lars-Goran Nilsson .50 .23
❑ 111 Leif Olsson .50 .23
❑ 112 Lars-Ake Sivertsson .50 .23
❑ 113 Hakan Wickberg .50 .23
❑ 114 Lars Oberg .50 .23
❑ 115 Roland Einarsson 1.00 .45
❑ 116 Peder Nilsson 1.00 .45
❑ 117 Kent Olsson 1.00 .45
❑ 118 Thomas Carlsson .50 .23
❑ 119 Lars-Ake Lundell .50 .23
❑ 120 Jorgen Palm .50 .23
❑ 121 Anders Rylin .50 .23
❑ 122 Billy Sundstrom .50 .23
❑ 123 Kent Soderlund .50 .23
❑ 124 Folke Bengtsson .50 .23
❑ 125 Ake Eklof .50 .23
❑ 126 Stig Larsson .50 .23
❑ 127 Sven-Bertil Lindstrom .50 .23
❑ 128 Thomas Palm .50 .23
❑ 129 Bjorn Palmqvist .50 .23
❑ 130 Ulf Rydin .50 .23
❑ 131 Ove Svensson .50 .23
❑ 132 Per-Allan Wikstrom .50 .23
❑ 133 Anders Andren .50 .23
❑ 134 Per Lundstrom .50 .23
❑ 135 Lennart Andersson 1.00 .45
❑ 136 Kent Bodin 1.00 .45
❑ 137 Bjorn Fagerlund 1.00 .45
❑ 138 Ake Carlsson .50 .23
❑ 139 Nils Johansson .50 .23
❑ 140 Lars-Goran Nilsson .50 .23
❑ 141 Kent Olsson 1.00 .45
❑ 142 Hans-Ake Rosendahl .50 .23
❑ 143 Karl-Johan Sundqvist .50 .23
❑ 144 Benny Andersson .50 .23
❑ 145 Hasse Andersson .50 .23
❑ 146 Kent-Erik Andersson .50 .23
❑ 147 Berndt Augustsson .50 .23
❑ 148 Kjell Augustsson .50 .23
❑ 149 Per-Ole Backman .50 .23
❑ 150 Conny Evensson 1.00 .45
❑ 151 Sten Johansson .50 .23
❑ 152 Leif Labraaten .50 .23
❑ 153 Sven-Ove Olsson .50 .23
❑ 154 Ulf Sterner .50 .23
❑ 155 Christer Abrahamsson 2.00 .90
❑ 156 Krister Sterner 1.00 .45
❑ 157 Thommy Abrahamsson 1.00 .45
❑ 158 Karl-Gustaf Alander .50 .23
❑ 159 Gunnar Andersson .50 .23
❑ 160 Roland Bond .50 .23
❑ 161 Ake Danielsson .50 .23
❑ 162 Ulf Weinstock .50 .23
❑ 163 Per-Olov Brasar 2.00 .90
❑ 164 Kjell Brus .50 .23
❑ 165 Hans Jax .50 .23
❑ 166 Dan Labraaten 2.00 .90
❑ 167 Roger Lindqvist .50 .23
❑ 168 Ulf Martensson 1.00 .45
❑ 169 Stig Nordin .50 .23
❑ 170 Olle Sjogren .50 .23
❑ 171 Ingemar Snis .50 .23
❑ 172 Dan Soderstrom .50 .23
❑ 173 Bo Theander .75 .35
❑ 174 Mats Ahlberg .50 .23
❑ 175 Gunnar Backman .50 .23
❑ 176 Ivar Larsson 1.00 .45
❑ 177 Sture Andersson .50 .23
❑ 178 Lage Edin .50 .23
❑ 179 Kjell-Rune Milton .50 .23
❑ 180 Per-Olof Uusitalo .50 .23
❑ 181 Ulf Wigren .50 .23
❑ 182 Hakan Dahlof .50 .23
❑ 183 Anders Hedberg 8.00 3.60
❑ 184 Torbjorn Hubinette .50 .23
❑ 185 Assar Lundgren .50 .23
❑ 186 Per Lundqvist .50 .23
❑ 187 Christer Nilsson .50 .23
❑ 188 Kenneth Nordenberg .50 .23
❑ 189 Anders Nordin .50 .23
❑ 190 Hakan Nygren .50 .23
❑ 191 Ulf Thors .50 .23
❑ 192 Ulf Torstensson .50 .23
❑ 193 Lars Ohman .50 .23
❑ 194 Tore Ohman .50 .23
❑ 195 Tony Esposito 25.00 11.00
❑ 196 Bobby Orr 80.00 36.00
❑ 197 Jean Beliveau 25.00 11.00
❑ 198 Gordie Howe 60.00 27.00
❑ 199 Phil Esposito 25.00 11.00
❑ 200 Bobby Hull 40.00 18.00
❑ 201 Bengt-Ake Gustavsson 1.00 .45
❑ 202 Lars Gustavsson 1.00 .45
❑ 203 Tommy Andersson .50 .23
❑ 204 Hans-Olov Ernlund .50 .23
❑ 205 Tord Johansson .50 .23
❑ 206 Lars Mjoberg .50 .23
❑ 207 Per-Erik Olsson .50 .23
❑ 208 Tord Svensson .50 .23
❑ 209 Jan Danielsson .50 .23
❑ 210 Tommy Eriksson 1.00 .45
❑ 211 Gote Hansson .50 .23
❑ 212 Hans Hansson .50 .23
❑ 213 Sven-Ake Jacobsson .50 .23
❑ 214 Mats Lonn .50 .23
❑ 215 Borje Marcus .50 .23
❑ 216 Lars Munther .50 .23
❑ 217 Ulf Nises .50 .23
❑ 218 Anders Rosen .50 .23
❑ 219 Borje Skogs .50 .23
❑ 220 Kent Sundkvist .50 .23
❑ 221 Mikael Collin 1.00 .45
❑ 222 Bjorn Jansson 1.00 .45
❑ 223 Curt Larsson 1.00 .45
❑ 224 Thommie Bergman 3.00 1.35
❑ 225 Arne Carlsson .50 .23
❑ 226 Christer Karlsson .50 .23
❑ 227 Eilert Maatta .50 .23
❑ 228 Jan Schullstrom .50 .23
❑ 229 Borje (Poppen) Burlin .50 .23
❑ 230 Hans Carlsson .50 .23
❑ 231 Tommy Carlsson .50 .23
❑ 232 Mats Hysing .50 .23
❑ 233 Bertil Jacobsson .50 .23
❑ 234 Stig-Goran Johansson 1.00 .45
❑ 235 Dan Landegren .50 .23
❑ 236 Kjell Landstrom .50 .23
❑ 237 Soren Maatta .50 .23
❑ 238 Nils-Olov Schilstrom .50 .23
❑ 239 Dick Yderstrom .50 .23
❑ 240 Carl Goran Oberg .50 .23
❑ 241 Anders Claesson 1.00 .45
❑ 242 Kent Othberg 1.00 .45
❑ 243 Jan Johansson .50 .23
❑ 244 Jan-Erik Nilsson .50 .23
❑ 245 Stefan Pettersson .50 .23
❑ 246 Tord Salomonsson .50 .23
❑ 247 Lennart Svedberg 1.00 .45
❑ 248 Bo Berggren .50 .23
❑ 249 Bjorn Broman .50 .23
❑ 250 Lennart Broman .50 .23
❑ 251 Ove Larsson .50 .23
❑ 252 Rolf Larsson .50 .23
❑ 253 Orjan Lindstrom .50 .23
❑ 254 Arne Lundstrom .50 .23
❑ 255 Fhinn Lundstrom .50 .23
❑ 256 Ake Lundstrom .50 .23
❑ 257 Lennart Norberg .50 .23
❑ 258 Hakan Pettersson .50 .23
❑ 259 Ake Soderberg .50 .23
❑ 260 Olle Ahman .50 .23
❑ 261 Christer Andersson 1.00 .45
❑ 262 Bengt Gustavsson .50 .23
❑ 263 Goran Astrom .50 .23
❑ 264 Anders Brostrom .50 .23
❑ 265 Kenneth Ekman .50 .23
❑ 266 Soren Gunnarsson .50 .23
❑ 267 Lars-Erik Jacobsson .50 .23
❑ 268 Des Moroney .50 .23
❑ 269 Borje Maatta .50 .23
❑ 270 Tommy Pettersson .50 .23
❑ 271 Bengt Alm .50 .23
❑ 272 Sven Crabo .50 .23
❑ 273 Bengt Eriksson .50 .23
❑ 274 Kurt Jakobsson .50 .23
❑ 275 Leif Jakobsson .50 .23
❑ 276 Lars-Goran Johansson .50 .23
❑ 277 Bert Karlsson .50 .23
❑ 278 Benny Runesson .50 .23
❑ 279 Ake Ryman .50 .23
❑ 280 Jan Roger Strand .50 .23
❑ 281 Christer Grahn .75 .35
❑ 282 Ronny Sandstrom .50 .23
❑ 283 John Andersson .50 .23
❑ 284 Karl-Olov Eriksson .50 .23
❑ 285 Anders Hagstrom .50 .23
❑ 286 Ulf Ingvarsson .50 .23
❑ 287 Rolf Jager .50 .23
❑ 288 Erik Jarvholm .50 .23
❑ 289 Bo Westling .50 .23
❑ 290 Ulf Barrefjord .50 .23
❑ 291 Kent Bjork .50 .23
❑ 292 Lars Dahlgren .50 .23
❑ 293 Ulf Larsson .50 .23
❑ 294 Jan Lundqvist .50 .23
❑ 295 Ulf Lundstrom .50 .23
❑ 296 Bengt Lovgren .50 .23
❑ 297 Leif Martensson .50 .23
❑ 298 Lars-Ake Nordin .50 .23
❑ 299 Lars Sjostrom .50 .23
❑ 300 Kjell Sundstrom .50 .23
❑ 301 Ronny Andersson 1.00 .45
❑ 302 Ingemar Caris 1.00 .45
❑ 303 Anders Johansson .50 .23
❑ 304 Hakan Norstrom .50 .23
❑ 305 Jan Olsen .50 .23
❑ 306 Lars-Erik Sjoberg 1.00 .45
❑ 307 Bengt Sjoholm .50 .23
❑ 308 Kjell Andersson .50 .23
❑ 309 Svante Granholm .50 .23
❑ 310 Kjell-Ove Gustavsson .50 .23
❑ 311 Henrik Hedlund .50 .23
❑ 312 Leif Henriksson .50 .23
❑ 313 Lars-Erik Johansson .50 .23
❑ 314 Bjorn Lindberg .50 .23
❑ 315 Evert Lindstrom .50 .23
❑ 316 Willy Lindstrom 2.00 .90
❑ 317 Leif Nilsson .50 .23
❑ 318 Kurt Olofsson .50 .23
❑ 319 Roger Olsson .50 .23
❑ 320 Kjell-Ronnie Pettersson .50 .23
❑ 321 Kenneth Holmstedt 1.00 .45
❑ 322 Lars-Erik Larsson .50 .23
❑ 323 Lennart Eriksson .50 .23
❑ 324 Lennart Gustavsson .50 .23
❑ 325 Jan-Ake Karlsson .50 .23
❑ 326 Rolf Karlsson .50 .23
❑ 327 Bengt Lundberg .50 .23
❑ 328 Anders Thelander .50 .23
❑ 329 Kent Bengtsson .50 .23
❑ 330 Gunnar Backman 1.00 .45
❑ 331 Stefan Canderyd .50 .23
❑ 332 Curt Edenvik .50 .23
❑ 333 Per Edenvik .50 .23
❑ 334 Weine Gullberg .50 .23
❑ 335 Nils-Arne Hedqvist .50 .23
❑ 336 Bengt-Ake Karlsson .50 .23
❑ 337 Christer Kihlstrom .50 .23
❑ 338 Stig-Olof Persson .50 .23
❑ 339 Christer Sjoberg .50 .23
❑ 340 Roddy Skyllqvist .50 .23
❑ 341 Lars Blomqvist 1.00 .45
❑ 342 Bjorn Forsberg 1.00 .45
❑ 343 Anders Hedlund .50 .23
❑ 344 Lennart Johansson .50 .23
❑ 345 Martin Kruger .50 .23
❑ 346 Harry Namd .50 .23
❑ 347 Lennart Strohm .50 .23
❑ 348 Peter Bejemark .50 .23
❑ 349 Bertil Bond .50 .23
❑ 350 Nils Carlsson .50 .23
❑ 351 Ulf Pilo .50 .23
❑ 352 Claes-Ove Fjallby .50 .23
❑ 353 Lars Granlund .50 .23
❑ 354 Kjell Keijser .50 .23
❑ 355 Lennart Lange .50 .23
❑ 356 Bo Mellbin .50 .23
❑ 357 Lars Starck .50 .23
❑ 358 Leif Svensson .50 .23
❑ 359 Kjell Ahlen .50 .23
❑ 360 Henry Svensson .50 .23
❑ 361 Sven-Allan Ellstrom 1.00 .45
❑ 362 Tommy Eriksson 1.00 .45
❑ 363 Walter Winsth 1.00 .45
❑ 364 Hans-Ake Andersson .50 .23
❑ 365 Jan Andersson .50 .23
❑ 366 Hans Bejbom .50 .23

| | | |
|---|---|---|
| ❑ 367 Goran Borell | .50 | .23 |
| ❑ 368 Bo Schilstrom | .50 | .23 |
| ❑ 369 Bjarne Brostrom | .50 | .23 |
| ❑ 370 Kenneth Calen | .50 | .23 |
| ❑ 371 Lennart Carlsson | .50 | .23 |
| ❑ 372 Mats Davidsson | .50 | .23 |
| ❑ 373 Rolf Hansson | .50 | .23 |
| ❑ 374 Rune Norrstrom | .50 | .23 |
| ❑ 375 Gunther Rauch | .50 | .23 |
| ❑ 376 Jan Vestberg | .50 | .23 |
| ❑ 377 Bengt Wistling | .50 | .23 |
| ❑ 378 Kent Zetterberg | .50 | .23 |
| ❑ 379 Goran Akerlund | .50 | .23 |
| ❑ 380 Uno Ohrlund | .50 | .23 |
| ❑ 381 Goran Hogosta | 1.50 | .70 |
| ❑ 382 Juha Raninen | 1.00 | .45 |
| ❑ 383 Bert Backman | .50 | .23 |
| ❑ 384 Christer Collin | .50 | .23 |
| ❑ 385 Dag Olsson | .50 | .23 |
| ❑ 386 Bjorn Resare | .50 | .23 |
| ❑ 387 Lars Thoreus | .50 | .23 |
| ❑ 388 Stig Andersson | .50 | .23 |
| ❑ 389 Borje Engblom | .50 | .23 |
| ❑ 390 Christer Englund | .50 | .23 |
| ❑ 391 Bo Eriksson | .50 | .23 |
| ❑ 392 Mats Eriksson | .50 | .23 |
| ❑ 393 Roland Riksson | .50 | .23 |
| ❑ 394 Olle Henriksson | .50 | .23 |
| ❑ 395 Yngve Hindrikes | .50 | .23 |
| ❑ 396 Kjell Jansson | .50 | .23 |
| ❑ 397 Jan Johansson | .50 | .23 |
| ❑ 398 Jan Karlsson | .50 | .23 |
| ❑ 399 Agne Norberg | .50 | .23 |
| ❑ 400 Christian Reuthie | .50 | .23 |

## 1972-73 Swedish Hockey Stickers

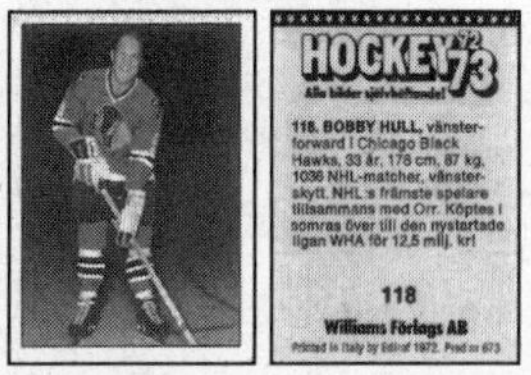


This 300-sticker set was issued in Sweden by Williams Forlags AB for the 1972-73 season. While the majority of the set is taken up by players from the Swedish Elitserien, there also are stickers featuring stars from Russia, Czechoslovakia, Finland and the NHL. Key stickers include pre-NHL appearances from Anders Hedberg, Borje Salming and Ulf Nilsson. NHL stars such as Bobby Orr, Ken Dryden and Bobby Hull also are featured, along with Soviet greats such as Tretiak and Kharlamov. The card fronts feature a posed color photo, while the backs have the sticker number and player information in Swedish. A book to hold the stickers was available at the time for 3.5 kroner, or about fifty cents. It is filled with stories about the teams, league schedules and photos, along with spaces for the stickers. It is valued now at $25. The prices below are for unused stickers; because it was the habit then to put them in the album, relatively few remain in their original state.

| | MINT | NRMT |
|---|---|---|
| COMPLETE SET (300) | 250.00 | 110.00 |
| COMMON CARD (1-300) | .50 | .23 |
| ❑ 1 Christer Abrahamsson | 1.50 | .70 |
| ❑ 2 Leif Holmqvist | 1.00 | .45 |
| ❑ 3 Thommy Abrahamsson | 1.00 | .45 |
| ❑ 4 Thommie Bergman | 2.00 | .90 |
| ❑ 5 Bjorn Johansson | .50 | .23 |
| ❑ 6 Kjell Rune Milton | .50 | .23 |
| ❑ 7 Borje Salming | 10.00 | 4.50 |
| ❑ 8 Lars-Erik Sjoberg | 1.50 | .70 |
| ❑ 9 Karl Johan Sundqvist | .50 | .23 |
| ❑ 10 Stig Ostling | .50 | .23 |
| ❑ 11 Inge Hammarstrom | 2.00 | .90 |
| ❑ 12 Anders Hedberg | 5.00 | 2.20 |
| ❑ 13 Atig-Goran Johansson | .50 | .23 |
| ❑ 14 Stefan Karlsson | .50 | .23 |
| ❑ 15 Hans Lindberg | .50 | .23 |
| ❑ 16 Mats Lindh | .50 | .23 |
| ❑ 17 Tord Lundstrom | .50 | .23 |
| ❑ 18 Lars-Goran Nilsson | .50 | .23 |
| ❑ 19 Bjorn Palmqvist | .50 | .23 |
| ❑ 20 Hakan Wickberg | .50 | .23 |
| ❑ 21 Jiri Holecek | 1.00 | .45 |
| ❑ 22 Josef Horesovsky | .50 | .23 |
| ❑ 23 Frantisek Pospisil | .75 | .35 |
| ❑ 24 Jaroslav Holik | .50 | .23 |
| ❑ 25 Jiri Holik | .75 | .35 |
| ❑ 26 Vaclav Nedomansky | 1.50 | .70 |
| ❑ 27 Vladislav Tretjak | 20.00 | 9.00 |
| ❑ 28 Gennadij Tsigankov | .75 | .35 |
| ❑ 29 Igor Romisjevskij | .75 | .35 |
| ❑ 30 Valeri Kharlamov | 10.00 | 4.50 |
| ❑ 31 Alexander Maltsev | 5.00 | 2.20 |
| ❑ 32 Vladimir Vikulov | .75 | .35 |
| ❑ 33 Jorma Valtonen | .75 | .35 |
| ❑ 34 Pekka Marjamaki | .50 | .23 |
| ❑ 35 Matti Keinonen | .50 | .23 |
| ❑ 36 Veli-Pekka Ketola | 1.50 | .70 |
| ❑ 37 Lauri Mononen | .50 | .23 |
| ❑ 38 Lasse Oksanen | .50 | .23 |
| ❑ 39 Krister Sterner | 1.00 | .45 |
| ❑ 40 Sten Ake Bark | .50 | .23 |
| ❑ 41 Jan-Erik Silfverberg | .50 | .23 |
| ❑ 42 Steffan Andersson | .50 | .23 |
| ❑ 43 Roland Eriksson | .50 | .23 |
| ❑ 44 Gunnar Johansson | .50 | .23 |
| ❑ 45 Jiri Holecek | 1.00 | .45 |
| ❑ 46 Thommie Bergman | 2.00 | .90 |
| ❑ 47 Josef Horesovsky | .50 | .23 |
| ❑ 48 Vladimir Vikulov | .75 | .35 |
| ❑ 49 Alexander Maltsev | 5.00 | 2.20 |
| ❑ 50 Valeri Kharlamov | 10.00 | 4.50 |
| ❑ 51 Leif Holmqvist | 1.00 | .45 |
| ❑ 52 Lars Danielsson | .50 | .23 |
| ❑ 53 Ake Fagerstrom | .50 | .23 |
| ❑ 54 Per Arne Hubinette | .50 | .23 |
| ❑ 55 Hakan Lindgren | .50 | .23 |
| ❑ 56 Bert-Ola Nordlander | .50 | .23 |
| ❑ 57 Bo Olofsson | .50 | .23 |
| ❑ 58 Soren Sjogren | .50 | .23 |
| ❑ 59 Jan Olsson | .50 | .23 |
| ❑ 60 Lennart Selinder | .50 | .23 |
| ❑ 61 Jan Olof Kroon | .50 | .23 |
| ❑ 62 Rolf Edberg | .50 | .23 |
| ❑ 63 Ulf Nilsson | 5.00 | 2.20 |
| ❑ 64 Leif Holmgren | .50 | .23 |
| ❑ 65 Jan Ostling | .50 | .23 |
| ❑ 66 Christer Grahn | 1.00 | .45 |
| ❑ 67 Karl-Olov Grahn | 1.00 | .45 |
| ❑ 68 Anders Hagstrom | .50 | .23 |
| ❑ 69 Erik Jarvholm | .50 | .23 |
| ❑ 70 Bo Westling | .50 | .23 |
| ❑ 71 Ulf Ingvarsson | .50 | .23 |
| ❑ 72 Bengt Lovgren | .50 | .23 |
| ❑ 73 Kjell Sundstrom | .50 | .23 |
| ❑ 74 Kent Bjork | .50 | .23 |
| ❑ 75 Ulf Lundstrom | .50 | .23 |
| ❑ 76 Mats Lundmark | .50 | .23 |
| ❑ 77 Ulf Barrefjord | .50 | .23 |
| ❑ 78 Lars Dahlgren | .50 | .23 |
| ❑ 79 Olle Nilsson | .50 | .23 |
| ❑ 80 Roger Nilsson | .50 | .23 |
| ❑ 81 Willie Lofqvist | 1.00 | .45 |
| ❑ 82 Jan-Erik Silfverberg | .50 | .23 |
| ❑ 83 Kjell Johnsson | .50 | .23 |
| ❑ 84 Jan Olof Svensson | .50 | .23 |
| ❑ 85 Stig Salming | .50 | .23 |
| ❑ 86 Borje Salming | 10.00 | 4.50 |
| ❑ 87 Stig Ostling | .50 | .23 |
| ❑ 88 Tord Lundstrom | .50 | .23 |
| ❑ 89 Inge Hammarstrom | 2.00 | .90 |
| ❑ 90 Lars-Goran Nilsson | .50 | .23 |
| ❑ 91 Hans Lindberg | .50 | .23 |
| ❑ 92 Hakan Wickberg | .50 | .23 |
| ❑ 93 Jan Erik Lyck | .50 | .23 |
| ❑ 94 Stefan Karlsson | .50 | .23 |
| ❑ 95 Lars Oberg | .50 | .23 |
| ❑ 96 Roland Einarsson | 1.00 | .45 |
| ❑ 97 Billy Sundstrom | .50 | .23 |
| ❑ 98 Anders Rylin | .50 | .23 |
| ❑ 99 Tomas Carlsson | .50 | .23 |
| ❑ 100 Ulf Ojerklint | .50 | .23 |
| ❑ 101 L-A Gustavsson | 1.00 | .45 |
| ❑ 102 Jorgen Palm | .50 | .23 |
| ❑ 103 Lars-Ake Lundell | .50 | .23 |
| ❑ 104 Ake Eklof | .50 | .23 |
| ❑ 105 B-A Karlsson | .50 | .23 |
| ❑ 106 Bjorn Palmqvist | .50 | .23 |
| ❑ 107 P-A Wickstrom | .50 | .23 |
| ❑ 108 Seppo Lindstrom | .50 | .23 |
| ❑ 109 Totte Bengtsson | .50 | .23 |
| ❑ 110 Stig Larsson | .50 | .23 |
| ❑ 111 Ken Dryden | 40.00 | 18.00 |
| ❑ 112 Jacques Laperriere | 3.00 | 1.35 |
| ❑ 113 Bobby Orr | 60.00 | 27.00 |
| ❑ 114 Brad Park | 5.00 | 2.20 |
| ❑ 115 Phil Esposito | 20.00 | 9.00 |
| ❑ 116 Rod Gilbert | 5.00 | 2.20 |
| ❑ 117 Vic Hadfield | 3.00 | 1.35 |
| ❑ 118 Bobby Hull | 25.00 | 11.00 |
| ❑ 119 Frank Mahovlich | 10.00 | 4.50 |
| ❑ 120 Jean Ratelle | 5.00 | 2.20 |
| ❑ 121 Lennart Andersson | 1.00 | .45 |
| ❑ 122 Karl Johan Sundqvist | .50 | .23 |
| ❑ 123 Nicke Johansson | .50 | .23 |
| ❑ 124 Lars Goran Nilsson | .50 | .23 |
| ❑ 125 Ake Carlsson | .50 | .23 |
| ❑ 126 Hans Ake Rosendahl | .50 | .23 |
| ❑ 127 Sten Ake Bark | .50 | .23 |
| ❑ 128 Par Backman | .50 | .23 |
| ❑ 129 Leif Labraaten | .50 | .23 |
| ❑ 130 Berndt Augustsson | .50 | .23 |
| ❑ 131 Uffe Sterner | .50 | .23 |
| ❑ 132 Benny Andersson | .50 | .23 |
| ❑ 133 Conny Evensson | 1.00 | .45 |
| ❑ 134 Kjell Augustsson | .50 | .23 |
| ❑ 135 Hans Andersson | .50 | .23 |
| ❑ 136 Kenneth Holmstedt | 1.00 | .45 |
| ❑ 137 Lennart Gustavsson | .50 | .23 |
| ❑ 138 Lennart Eriksson | .50 | .23 |
| ❑ 139 Rolf Carlsson | .50 | .23 |
| ❑ 140 Bengt Lundberg | .50 | .23 |
| ❑ 141 Jan-Ake Karlsson | .50 | .23 |
| ❑ 142 Curt Edenvik | .50 | .23 |
| ❑ 143 Per Edenvik | .50 | .23 |
| ❑ 144 Weine Gullberg | .50 | .23 |
| ❑ 145 Gunnar Backman | 1.00 | .45 |
| ❑ 146 Roddy Skyllqvist | .50 | .23 |
| ❑ 147 Stefan Canderyd | .50 | .23 |
| ❑ 148 Christer Kihlstrom | .50 | .23 |
| ❑ 149 Nils Arne Hedqvist | .50 | .23 |
| ❑ 150 Stig-Olof Persson | .50 | .23 |
| ❑ 151 Christer Abrahamsson | 1.50 | .70 |
| ❑ 152 Thommy Abrahamsson | 1.00 | .45 |
| ❑ 153 Roland Bond | .50 | .23 |
| ❑ 154 Gunnar Andersson | .50 | .23 |
| ❑ 155 Ulf Weinstock | .50 | .23 |
| ❑ 156 Ake Danielsson | .50 | .23 |
| ❑ 157 Peter Gudmundsson | .50 | .23 |
| ❑ 158 Olle Sjogren | .50 | .23 |
| ❑ 159 Hans Jax | .50 | .23 |
| ❑ 160 Mats Ahlberg | .50 | .23 |
| ❑ 161 Dan Labraaten | 1.50 | .70 |
| ❑ 162 Ulf Martensson | .50 | .23 |
| ❑ 163 Kjell Brus | .50 | .23 |
| ❑ 164 Dan Soderstrom | .50 | .23 |
| ❑ 165 Per Olof Brasar | 1.50 | .70 |
| ❑ 166 Ivar Larsson | 1.00 | .45 |
| ❑ 167 Sture Andersson | .50 | .23 |
| ❑ 168 Lage Edin | .50 | .23 |
| ❑ 169 Kjell Rune Milton | .50 | .23 |
| ❑ 170 Ulf Wigren | .50 | .23 |
| ❑ 171 Hakan Dahllof | .50 | .23 |
| ❑ 172 Anders Hedberg | 5.00 | 2.20 |
| ❑ 173 Assar Lundgren | .50 | .23 |
| ❑ 174 Christer Nilsson | .50 | .23 |
| ❑ 175 Anders Nordin | .50 | .23 |
| ❑ 176 Hakan Nygren | .50 | .23 |
| ❑ 177 Ulf Thors | .50 | .23 |
| ❑ 178 Ulf Torstensson | .50 | .23 |
| ❑ 179 Lasse Ohman | .50 | .23 |
| ❑ 180 Tore Ohman | .50 | .23 |
| ❑ 181 Bengt Ake Gustafsson | .75 | .35 |
| ❑ 182 Tommy Andersson | .50 | .23 |
| ❑ 183 Hans Olof Ernlund | .50 | .23 |
| ❑ 184 Tord Johansson | .50 | .23 |
| ❑ 185 Tord Svensson | .50 | .23 |
| ❑ 186 Jan Danielsson | .50 | .23 |
| ❑ 187 Tommy Eriksson | 1.00 | .45 |
| ❑ 188 Gote Hansson | .50 | .23 |
| ❑ 189 Hans Hansson | .50 | .23 |
| ❑ 190 Sven Ake Jacobsson | .50 | .23 |
| ❑ 191 Mats Lonn | .50 | .23 |
| ❑ 192 Lars Mjoberg | .50 | .23 |
| ❑ 193 Lars Munther | .50 | .23 |
| ❑ 194 Ulf Nises | .50 | .23 |
| ❑ 195 Borje Skogs | .50 | .23 |
| ❑ 196 Roland Lestander | .50 | .23 |
| ❑ 197 Bosse Andersson | .50 | .23 |
| ❑ 198 Hakan Dahlin | .50 | .23 |
| ❑ 199 Martin Johansson | .50 | .23 |
| ❑ 200 Anders Lindberg | .50 | .23 |
| ❑ 201 Lars Fredrik Nystrom | .50 | .23 |
| ❑ 202 Hans Gunnar Skarin | .50 | .23 |
| ❑ 203 Jerry Aberg | .50 | .23 |
| ❑ 204 Anders Almqvist | .50 | .23 |
| ❑ 205 Christer Johansson | .50 | .23 |
| ❑ 206 Per Johansson | .50 | .23 |
| ❑ 207 Martin Karlsson | .50 | .23 |
| ❑ 208 Lars Gunnar Lundberg | .50 | .23 |
| ❑ 209 Hardy Nilsson | .50 | .23 |
| ❑ 210 Kjell Arne Wikstrom | .50 | .23 |
| ❑ 211 Mikael Collin | 1.00 | .45 |
| ❑ 212 Curt Larsson | 1.00 | .45 |
| ❑ 213 Arne Carlsson | .50 | .23 |
| ❑ 214 Bjorn Johansson | .50 | .23 |
| ❑ 215 Nils-Olaf Schilstrom | .50 | .23 |
| ❑ 216 Jan Schullstrom | .50 | .23 |
| ❑ 217 Borje Burlin | .50 | .23 |
| ❑ 218 Hans Carlsson | .50 | .23 |
| ❑ 219 Mats Hysing | .50 | .23 |
| ❑ 220 Bertil Jacobsson | .50 | .23 |
| ❑ 221 Stisse Johansson | .50 | .23 |
| ❑ 222 Dan Landegren | .50 | .23 |
| ❑ 223 Kjell Landstrom | .50 | .23 |
| ❑ 224 Dick Yderstrom | .50 | .23 |
| ❑ 225 Carl Goran Oberg | .50 | .23 |
| ❑ 226 Christer Sehlstedt | .50 | .23 |
| ❑ 227 Tommie Lindgren | .50 | .23 |
| ❑ 228 Jan Erik Nilsson | .50 | .23 |
| ❑ 229 Stefan Pettersson | .50 | .23 |
| ❑ 230 Tord Nansen | .50 | .23 |
| ❑ 231 Bo Berggren | .50 | .23 |
| ❑ 232 Bjorn Broman | .50 | .23 |
| ❑ 233 Ove Larsson | .50 | .23 |
| ❑ 234 Kent Lindgren | .50 | .23 |
| ❑ 235 Orjan Lindstrom | .50 | .23 |
| ❑ 236 Lennart Norberg | .50 | .23 |
| ❑ 237 Arne Lundstrom | .50 | .23 |
| ❑ 238 Hakan Pettersson | .50 | .23 |
| ❑ 239 Ake Soderberg | .50 | .23 |
| ❑ 240 Olle Ahman | .50 | .23 |
| ❑ 241 Christer Andersson | 1.00 | .45 |
| ❑ 242 Anders Brostrom | .50 | .23 |
| ❑ 243 Kenneth Ekman | .50 | .23 |
| ❑ 244 Soren Gunnarsson | .50 | .23 |
| ❑ 245 Borje Maatta | .50 | .23 |
| ❑ 246 Tommy Pettersson | .50 | .23 |
| ❑ 247 Kurt Jakobsson | .50 | .23 |
| ❑ 248 Leif Jakobsson | .50 | .23 |
| ❑ 249 Lars Goran Johansson | .50 | .23 |
| ❑ 250 Bengt Goran Karlsson | .50 | .23 |
| ❑ 251 Berndt Karlsson | .50 | .23 |
| ❑ 252 Tadeusz Niedomyst | .50 | .23 |
| ❑ 253 Benny Runesson | .50 | .23 |
| ❑ 254 Ake Ryman | .50 | .23 |
| ❑ 255 Jan Roger Strand | .50 | .23 |
| ❑ 256 Goran Hogosta | 1.00 | .45 |
| ❑ 257 Bert Backman | .50 | .23 |
| ❑ 258 Christer Collin | .50 | .23 |
| ❑ 259 Bo Eriksson | .50 | .23 |
| ❑ 260 Hakan Norstrom | .50 | .23 |
| ❑ 261 Lars Thoreus | .50 | .23 |
| ❑ 262 Stig Andersson | .50 | .23 |
| ❑ 263 Mats Eriksson | .50 | .23 |
| ❑ 264 Roland Eriksson | .50 | .23 |
| ❑ 265 Kjell Fhinn | .50 | .23 |
| ❑ 266 Olle Henriksson | .50 | .23 |
| ❑ 267 Yngve Hindrikes | .50 | .23 |
| ❑ 268 Jan Karlsson | .50 | .23 |
| ❑ 269 Kjell Jansson | .50 | .23 |
| ❑ 270 Ingemar Snis | .50 | .23 |
| ❑ 271 Christer Stahl | .50 | .23 |
| ❑ 272 Leif Andersson | .50 | .23 |
| ❑ 273 Tommy Eriksson | 1.00 | .45 |
| ❑ 274 Christer Holmstrom | .50 | .23 |
| ❑ 275 Curt Lundmark | 1.50 | .70 |
| ❑ 276 Dennis Pettersson | .50 | .23 |
| ❑ 277 Ove Thelin | .50 | .23 |
| ❑ 278 Bo Wahlberg | .50 | .23 |
| ❑ 279 Gote Gustavsson | .50 | .23 |
| ❑ 280 Christer Lindgren | .50 | .23 |
| ❑ 281 Kent Persson | .50 | .23 |
| ❑ 282 Par Marts | .50 | .23 |
| ❑ 283 Ove Stenlund | .50 | .23 |
| ❑ 284 Bo Olsson | .50 | .23 |
| ❑ 285 Bo Astrom | .50 | .23 |
| ❑ 286 Ronny Andersson | 1.00 | .45 |
| ❑ 287 Roger Bergman | .50 | .23 |
| ❑ 288 Thommie Bergman | 2.00 | .90 |
| ❑ 289 Anders Johansson | .50 | .23 |
| ❑ 290 Jan Olsen | .50 | .23 |
| ❑ 291 Lars Erik Sjoberg | 2.00 | .90 |
| ❑ 292 Kjell Andersson | .50 | .23 |
| ❑ 293 Svante Granholm | .50 | .23 |
| ❑ 294 Henric Hedlund | .50 | .23 |
| ❑ 295 Leif Henriksson | .50 | .23 |
| ❑ 296 Mats Lindh | .50 | .23 |
| ❑ 297 Evert Lindstrom | .50 | .23 |
| ❑ 298 Willy Lindstrom | 1.50 | .70 |
| ❑ 299 Roger Olsson | .50 | .23 |
| ❑ 300 Kjell Ronnie Pettersson | .50 | .23 |

## 1972-73 Swedish Semic World Championship

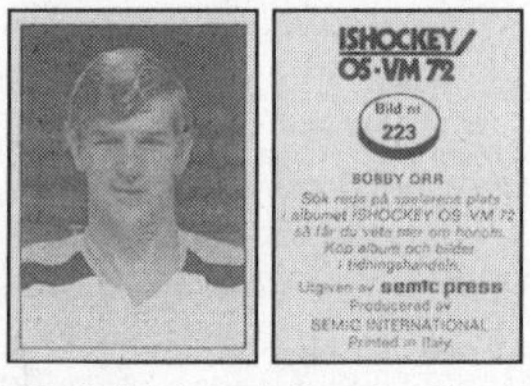


Printed in Italy by Semic Press, the 233 cards comprising this set measure 1 7/8" by 2 1/2" and feature posed color player photos on their white-bordered fronts. The white back carries the player's name and text in Swedish. The cards are numbered on the back and arranged by national teams as follows: Soviet Union (1-20), Czechoslovakia (21-41), Sweden (42-70), Finland (71-92), Germany (93-117), United States (118-137), France (138-162), and Canada (163-233).

| | NRMT-MT | EXC |
|---|---|---|
| COMPLETE SET (233) | 300.00 | 135.00 |
| COMMON STICKER (1-233) | .50 | .23 |
| ❑ 1 Viktor Konovalenko | .75 | .35 |
| ❑ 2 Vitalij Davydov | .75 | .35 |
| ❑ 3 Vladimir Lutjenko | .75 | .35 |
| ❑ 4 Viktor Kuskin | .75 | .35 |
| ❑ 5 Alexander Ragulin | 1.50 | .70 |
| ❑ 6 Igor Romitjevskij | .75 | .35 |
| ❑ 7 Gennadij Tsigankov | .75 | .35 |
| ❑ 8 Vjatsjeslav Starsjinov | 1.50 | .70 |
| ❑ 9 Evgenij Zimin | 1.00 | .45 |
| ❑ 10 Alexander Maltsev | 5.00 | 2.20 |
| ❑ 11 Anatolij Firsov | 2.50 | 1.10 |
| ❑ 12 Evgenij Misjakov | .75 | .35 |
| ❑ 13 Boris Michailov | 4.00 | 1.80 |
| ❑ 14 Juri Ljapkin | 1.00 | .45 |
| ❑ 15 Alexander Martinyk | .75 | .35 |
| ❑ 16 Vladimir Petrov | 4.00 | 1.80 |
| ❑ 17 Valeri Kharlamov | 10.00 | 4.50 |
| ❑ 18 Vladimir Vikulov | .75 | .35 |
| ❑ 19 Vladimir Sjadrin | 1.00 | .45 |
| ❑ 20 Vladislav Tretiak | 20.00 | 9.00 |
| ❑ 21 Marcel Sakac | .50 | .23 |
| ❑ 22 Jiri Holecek | 1.00 | .45 |
| ❑ 23 Josef Horesovsky | .50 | .23 |
| ❑ 24 Oldrich Machac | .50 | .23 |
| ❑ 25 Rudolf Tajcnar | .50 | .23 |
| ❑ 26 Frantisek Panchartek | .50 | .23 |
| ❑ 27 Frantisek Pospisil | .75 | .35 |
| ❑ 28 Jiri Kochta | .50 | .23 |
| ❑ 29 Jan Havel | .50 | .23 |
| ❑ 30 Vladimir Martinec | .50 | .23 |
| ❑ 31 Richard Farda | .50 | .23 |
| ❑ 32 Bohuslav Stastny | .75 | .35 |
| ❑ 33 Vaclav Nedomansky | 1.50 | .70 |
| ❑ 34 Josef Cerny | .50 | .23 |
| ❑ 35 Bedrich Brunchk | .50 | .23 |
| ❑ 36 Jan Suchy | .50 | .23 |
| ❑ 37 Eduard Novak | .50 | .23 |
| ❑ 38 Jiri Bubla | 1.50 | .70 |
| ❑ 39 Jiri Holik | .75 | .35 |
| ❑ 40 Ivan Hlinka | .75 | .35 |
| ❑ 41 Vladimir Bednar | .50 | .23 |
| ❑ 42 Leif Holmqvist | 1.00 | .45 |
| ❑ 43 Christer Abrahamsson | 1.50 | .70 |
| ❑ 44 Christer Andersson | 1.00 | .45 |
| ❑ 45 Lars-Erik Sjoberg | 1.50 | .70 |
| ❑ 46 Lennart Svedberg | 1.00 | .45 |
| ❑ 47 Stig-Goran Johansson | .50 | .23 |
| ❑ 48 Bert-Ola Nordlander | .50 | .23 |
| ❑ 49 Thommy Abrahamsson | 1.00 | .45 |
| ❑ 50 Arne Carlsson | .50 | .23 |
| ❑ 51 Stefan Karlsson | .50 | .23 |
| ❑ 52 Hakan Wickberg | .50 | .23 |
| ❑ 53 Hakan Nygren | .50 | .23 |
| ❑ 54 Lars-Goran Nilsson | .50 | .23 |
| ❑ 55 Thommie Bergman | 2.00 | .90 |
| ❑ 56 Ulf Sterner | .75 | .35 |
| ❑ 57 Hans Lindberg | .50 | .23 |
| ❑ 58 Tord Lundstrom | .50 | .23 |
| ❑ 59 Gunnar Andersson | .50 | .23 |
| ❑ 60 Bjorn Palmqvist | .50 | .23 |
| ❑ 61 Inge Hammarstrom | 2.00 | .90 |
| ❑ 62 Kjell-Rune Milton | .50 | .23 |
| ❑ 63 Kjell Brus | .50 | .23 |
| ❑ 64 Kenneth Ekman | .50 | .23 |
| ❑ 65 Bengt-Goran Karlsson | .50 | .23 |
| ❑ 66 Hakan Pettersson | .50 | .23 |
| ❑ 67 Dan Labraaten | 1.50 | .70 |
| ❑ 68 Dan Soderstrom | .50 | .23 |
| ❑ 69 Anders Hedberg | 5.00 | 2.20 |
| ❑ 70 Ake Soderberg | .50 | .23 |
| ❑ 71 Urpo Ylonen | .50 | .23 |
| ❑ 72 Ilpo Koskela | .50 | .23 |
| ❑ 73 Seppo Lindstrom | .50 | .23 |
| ❑ 74 Hannu Luojola | .50 | .23 |
| ❑ 75 Pekka Marjamaki | .50 | .23 |
| ❑ 76 Jouko Oystila | .50 | .23 |
| ❑ 77 Heikki Jarn | .50 | .23 |
| ❑ 78 Esa Isaksson | .50 | .23 |
| ❑ 79 Veli-Pekka Ketola | 1.50 | .70 |
| ❑ 80 Harri Linnonmaa | .50 | .23 |
| ❑ 81 Erkki Mononen | .50 | .23 |
| ❑ 82 Lauri Mononen | .50 | .23 |
| ❑ 83 Matti Murto | .50 | .23 |
| ❑ 84 Lasse Oksanen | .50 | .23 |
| ❑ 85 Esa Peltonen | .50 | .23 |
| ❑ 86 Seppo Repo | .50 | .23 |
| ❑ 87 Tommi Salmelainen | .50 | .23 |
| ❑ 88 Juhani Tamminen | .50 | .23 |
| ❑ 89 Jorma Vehmanen | .50 | .23 |
| ❑ 90 Jorma Valtonen | .75 | .35 |
| ❑ 91 Matti Keinonen | .50 | .23 |
| ❑ 92 Juha Rantasila | .50 | .23 |
| ❑ 93 Toni Kehle | .50 | .23 |
| ❑ 94 Josef Schramm | .50 | .23 |
| ❑ 95 Walter Stadler | .50 | .23 |
| ❑ 96 Josef Volk | .50 | .23 |
| ❑ 97 Hans Schichtl | .50 | .23 |
| ❑ 98 Erwin Riedmeier | .50 | .23 |
| ❑ 99 Werner Modes | .50 | .23 |
| ❑ 100 Johann Eimannsberger | .50 | .23 |
| ❑ 101 Karlheinz Egger | .50 | .23 |
| ❑ 102 Lorenz Funk | .50 | .23 |
| ❑ 103 Klaus Ego | .50 | .23 |
| ❑ 104 Anton Hofherr | .50 | .23 |
| ❑ 105 Otto Schneitberger | .50 | .23 |
| ❑ 106 Heinz Weisenbach | .50 | .23 |
| ❑ 107 Alois Schloder | .50 | .23 |
| ❑ 108 Gustav Hanig | .50 | .23 |
| ❑ 109 Rainer Philipp | .50 | .23 |
| ❑ 110 Bernd Kuhn | .50 | .23 |
| ❑ 111 Paul Langner | .50 | .23 |
| ❑ 112 Franz Hofherr | .50 | .23 |
| ❑ 113 Reinhold Bauer | .50 | .23 |
| ❑ 114 Johann Rotkirch | .50 | .23 |
| ❑ 115 Walter Koberle | .50 | .23 |
| ❑ 116 Rainer Makatsch | .50 | .23 |
| ❑ 117 Carl Wetzel | .75 | .35 |
| ❑ 118 Mike Curran | .75 | .35 |
| ❑ 119 Jim McElmury | .75 | .35 |
| ❑ 120 Bruce Riutta | .75 | .35 |
| ❑ 121 Tom Mellor | .75 | .35 |
| ❑ 122 Don Ross | .75 | .35 |
| ❑ 123 Gary Gambucci | .75 | .35 |
| ❑ 124 Keith Christiansen | .75 | .35 |
| ❑ 125 Len Lilyholm | .75 | .35 |
| ❑ 126 Henry Boucha | 1.50 | .70 |
| ❑ 127 Craig Falkman | .75 | .35 |
| ❑ 128 Tim Sheehy | .75 | .35 |
| ❑ 129 Kevin Ahearn | .75 | .35 |
| ❑ 130 Craig Patrick | 2.00 | .90 |
| ❑ 131 Pete Fichuk | .75 | .35 |
| ❑ 132 George Konik | .75 | .35 |
| ❑ 133 Dick McGlynn | .75 | .35 |
| ❑ 134 Dick Toomey | .75 | .35 |
| ❑ 135 Paul Schilling | .75 | .35 |
| ❑ 136 Bob Lindberg | .75 | .35 |
| ❑ 137 Dick Tomasoni | .75 | .35 |
| ❑ 138 Nando Mathieu | .50 | .23 |
| ❑ 139 Francis Reinhard | .50 | .23 |
| ❑ 140 Gaston Furrer | .50 | .23 |
| ❑ 141 Bruno Wittwer | .50 | .23 |
| ❑ 142 Andre Berra | .50 | .23 |
| ❑ 143 Hans Keller | .50 | .23 |
| ❑ 144 Peter Luthi | .50 | .23 |
| ❑ 145 Peter Aeschlimann | .50 | .23 |
| ❑ 146 Werner Kuenzi | .50 | .23 |
| ❑ 147 Tony Neininger | .50 | .23 |
| ❑ 148 Jacques Pousaz | .50 | .23 |
| ❑ 149 Roger Chappot | .50 | .23 |
| ❑ 150 Charly Henzen | .50 | .23 |
| ❑ 151 Paul Probst | .50 | .23 |
| ❑ 152 Guy Dubois | .50 | .23 |
| ❑ 153 Rene Sgualdo | .50 | .23 |
| ❑ 154 Rene Hueguenin | .50 | .23 |
| ❑ 155 Gaston Pelletier | .50 | .23 |
| ❑ 156 Beat Kaufmann | .50 | .23 |
| ❑ 157 Alfio Molina | .50 | .23 |
| ❑ 158 Gerald Rigolet | .50 | .23 |
| ❑ 159 Harald Jones | .50 | .23 |
| ❑ 160 Gilbert Mathieu | .50 | .23 |
| ❑ 161 Michel Turler | .50 | .23 |
| ❑ 162 Reto Taillens | .50 | .23 |
| ❑ 163 Norm Ullman | 3.00 | 1.35 |
| ❑ 164 Dave Keon | 4.00 | 1.80 |
| ❑ 165 Roger Crozier | 2.00 | .90 |
| ❑ 166 Ron Ellis | 1.50 | .70 |
| ❑ 167 Paul Henderson | 3.00 | 1.35 |
| ❑ 168 Jim Dorey | 1.00 | .45 |
| ❑ 169 Jacques Plante | 15.00 | 6.75 |
| ❑ 170 Jean-Guy Gendron | 1.00 | .45 |

| | | |
|---|---|---|
| □ 171 Gary Smith | 2.00 | .90 |
| □ 172 Dennis Hextall | 1.00 | .45 |
| □ 173 Norm Ferguson | 1.00 | .45 |
| □ 174 Simon Nolet | 1.00 | .45 |
| □ 175 Bernie Parent | 6.00 | 2.70 |
| □ 176 Ted Hampson | 1.00 | .45 |
| □ 177 Earl Ingarfield | 1.00 | .45 |
| □ 178 Larry Hillman | 1.00 | .45 |
| □ 179 Gary Dornhoefer | 1.50 | .70 |
| □ 180 Gary Croteau | 1.00 | .45 |
| □ 181 Carol Vadnais | 1.00 | .45 |
| □ 182 Jim Roberts | 1.00 | .45 |
| □ 183 Red Berenson | 1.50 | .70 |
| □ 184 Phil Esposito | 15.00 | 6.75 |
| □ 185 John McKenzie | 1.50 | .70 |
| □ 186 Barclay Plager | 1.50 | .70 |
| □ 187 Glenn Hall | 8.00 | 3.60 |
| □ 188 Gerry Cheevers | 7.00 | 3.10 |
| □ 189 Jim McKenny | 1.00 | .45 |
| □ 190 Gordie Howe | 40.00 | 18.00 |
| □ 191 Garry Unger | 1.50 | .70 |
| □ 192 Roy Edwards | 2.00 | .90 |
| □ 193 Alex Delvecchio | 3.00 | 1.35 |
| □ 194 Brad Park | 4.00 | 1.80 |
| □ 195 Frank Mahovlich | 8.00 | 3.60 |
| □ 196 Phil Goyette | 1.00 | .45 |
| □ 197 Don Marshall | 1.00 | .45 |
| □ 198 Henri Richard | 8.00 | 3.60 |
| □ 199 Claude Larose | 1.00 | .45 |
| □ 200 Bobby Rousseau | 1.00 | .45 |
| □ 201 Lorne Worsley | 8.00 | 3.60 |
| □ 202 Gilles Marotte | 1.00 | .45 |
| □ 203 Bob Pulford | 2.00 | .90 |
| □ 204 Yvan Cournoyer | 3.00 | 1.35 |
| □ 205 Eddie Joyal | 1.00 | .45 |
| □ 206 Ross Lonsberry | 1.00 | .45 |
| □ 207 Jean Beliveau | 15.00 | 6.75 |
| □ 208 Jacques Lemaire | 3.00 | 1.35 |
| □ 209 Orland Kurtenbach | 1.50 | .70 |
| □ 210 Andre Boudrias | 1.00 | .45 |
| □ 211 Jim Neilson | 1.00 | .45 |
| □ 212 Walter Tkaczuk | 1.00 | .45 |
| □ 213 Ed Giacomin | 8.00 | 3.60 |
| □ 214 Jean Ratelle | 4.00 | 1.80 |
| □ 215 Les Binkley | 2.00 | .90 |
| □ 216 Jean Pronovost | 1.00 | .45 |
| □ 217 Bryan Watson | 1.00 | .45 |
| □ 218 Dean Prentice | 1.00 | .45 |
| □ 219 Jean-Paul Parise | 1.00 | .45 |
| □ 220 Bill Goldsworthy | 1.50 | .70 |
| □ 221 Wayne Maki | 1.00 | .45 |
| □ 222 Dale Tallon | 1.50 | .70 |
| □ 223 Bobby Orr | 50.00 | 22.00 |
| □ 224 Pit Martin | 1.00 | .45 |
| □ 225 Jacques Laperriere | 2.00 | .90 |
| □ 226 Bill Flett | 1.00 | .45 |
| □ 227 Stan Mikita | 8.00 | 3.60 |
| □ 228 Bobby Hull | 20.00 | 9.00 |
| □ 229 Larry Pleau | 1.00 | .45 |
| □ 230 Keith Magnuson | 1.50 | .70 |
| □ 231 Tony Esposito | 10.00 | 4.50 |
| □ 232 Rogatien Vachon | 4.00 | 1.80 |
| □ 233 Mickey Redmond | 3.00 | 1.35 |

## 1973-74 Swedish Hockey Stickers

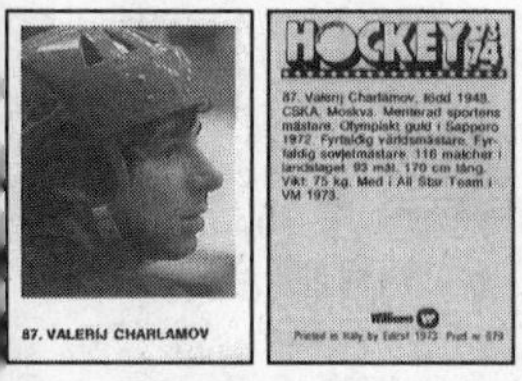


This 243-sticker set was produced in Sweden by Williams Forlags AB. It features players from the top Swedish league, as well as several Russian teams. The set includes such legendary figures as Valeri Kharlamov, Vladislav Tretiak and a rare card of notorious head coach Vselvolod Bobrov. The fronts feature a color player photo, while the backs have sticker number and information in Swedish. There was an album available to store the set; it currently retails for around $20.

| | MINT | NRMT |
|---|---|---|
| COMPLETE SET (243) | 175.00 | 80.00 |
| COMMON CARD (1-243) | .50 | .23 |
| □ 1 Christer Abrahamsson | 1.50 | .70 |
| □ 2 William Lofqvist | 1.00 | .45 |
| □ 3 Arne Karlsson | .50 | .23 |
| □ 4 Lars-Erik Sjoberg | 2.00 | .90 |
| □ 5 Bjorn Johansson | .50 | .23 |
| □ 6 Thommy Abrahamsson | 1.00 | .45 |
| □ 7 Borje Salming | 10.00 | 4.50 |
| □ 8 Karl Johan Sundqvist | .50 | .23 |
| □ 9 Ulf Sterner | .50 | .23 |
| □ 10 Ulf Nilsson | 5.00 | 2.20 |
| □ 11 Kjell-Arne Wickstrom | .50 | .23 |
| □ 12 Inge Hammarstrom | 3.00 | 1.35 |
| □ 13 Hakan Wickberg | .50 | .23 |
| □ 14 Tord Lundstrom | .50 | .23 |
| □ 15 Dan Soderstrom | .50 | .23 |
| □ 16 Mats Ahlberg | 1.00 | .45 |
| □ 17 Anders Hedberg | 5.00 | 2.20 |
| □ 18 Dick Yderstrom | .75 | .35 |
| □ 19 Stefan Karlsson | .50 | .23 |
| □ 20 Roland Bond | .50 | .23 |
| □ 21 Kjell-Rune Milton | .50 | .23 |
| □ 22 Willy Lindstrom | 1.50 | .70 |
| □ 23 Kurt Carlsson | .75 | .35 |
| □ 24 Mats Walltin | .50 | .23 |
| □ 25 Roland Eriksson | .50 | .23 |
| □ 26 Martin Karlsson | .50 | .23 |
| □ 27 Jiri Holecek | 1.00 | .45 |
| □ 28 Josef Horesovsky | .50 | .23 |
| □ 29 Oldrich Machac | .50 | .23 |
| □ 30 Vladimir Martinec | 1.00 | .45 |
| □ 31 Vaclav Nedomansky | 1.50 | .70 |
| □ 32 Jiri Kochta | .50 | .23 |
| □ 33 Jorma Valtonen | 1.00 | .45 |
| □ 34 Heikki Riihiranta | 1.00 | .45 |
| □ 35 Lauri Mononen | .50 | .23 |
| □ 36 Timo Turunen | .50 | .23 |
| □ 37 Matti Keinonen | .50 | .23 |
| □ 38 Seppo Repo | .50 | .23 |
| □ 39 Christer Abrahamsson | 1.50 | .70 |
| □ 40 Lars Stenvall | .50 | .23 |
| □ 41 Per Karlsson | .50 | .23 |
| □ 42 Roland Bond | .50 | .23 |
| □ 43 Thommy Abrahamsson | 1.00 | .45 |
| □ 44 Ulf Weinstock | .50 | .23 |
| □ 45 Gunnar Andersson | .50 | .23 |
| □ 46 Hans Eriksson | .50 | .23 |
| □ 47 Peter Gudmundsson | .50 | .23 |
| □ 48 Mats Ahlberg | 1.00 | .45 |
| □ 49 Per-Olov Brasar | 1.50 | .70 |
| □ 50 Roger Lindqvist | .50 | .23 |
| □ 51 Dan Soderstrom | .50 | .23 |
| □ 52 Ulf Martensson | .50 | .23 |
| □ 53 Kjell Brus | .50 | .23 |
| □ 54 Hans Jax | .50 | .23 |
| □ 55 Dan Labraaten | 1.50 | .70 |
| □ 56 Nils-Olov Olsson | .50 | .23 |
| □ 57 Stig Nordin | .50 | .23 |
| □ 58 Bo Theander | .50 | .23 |
| □ 59 Curt Larsson | 1.00 | .45 |
| □ 60 Mikael Collin | 1.00 | .45 |
| □ 61 Arne Carlsson | .50 | .23 |
| □ 62 Leif Svensson | .50 | .23 |
| □ 63 Sverker Torstensson | .50 | .23 |
| □ 64 Bjorn Johansson | .50 | .23 |
| □ 65 Stisse Johansson | .50 | .23 |
| □ 66 Carl-Goran Oberg | .50 | .23 |
| □ 67 Mats Hysing | .50 | .23 |
| □ 68 Mats Walltin | .50 | .23 |
| □ 69 Hans Carlsson | .50 | .23 |
| □ 70 Nils-Olov Schilstrom | .50 | .23 |
| □ 71 Kjell-Arne Wickstrom | .50 | .23 |
| □ 72 Jan Schullstrom | .50 | .23 |
| □ 73 Borje Burlin | .50 | .23 |
| □ 74 Dick Yderstrom | .75 | .35 |
| □ 75 Dan Landegren | .50 | .23 |
| □ 76 Kjell Landstrom | .50 | .23 |
| □ 77 Vladislav Tretjak | 20.00 | 9.00 |
| □ 78 Alexander Sidelnikov | 2.00 | .90 |
| □ 79 Alexander Ragulin | 2.50 | 1.10 |
| □ 80 Vladimir Luttjenko | 2.00 | .90 |
| □ 81 Gennadij Tsygankov | 1.50 | .70 |
| □ 82 Alexander Gusev | 1.00 | .45 |
| □ 83 Jevgenij Poladiev | .75 | .35 |
| □ 84 Jurij Liapkin | 1.50 | .70 |
| □ 85 Valerij Vasiljev | 3.00 | 1.35 |
| □ 86 Boris Michailov | 5.00 | 2.20 |
| □ 87 Valeri Kharlamov | 10.00 | 4.50 |
| □ 88 Vladimir Petrov | 5.00 | 2.20 |
| □ 89 Alexander Maltsev | 5.00 | 2.20 |
| □ 90 Vladimir Sjadrin | 2.50 | 1.10 |
| □ 91 Alexander Jakusjev | 5.00 | 2.20 |
| □ 92 Alexander Martynjuk | .75 | .35 |
| □ 93 Vjateslav Anissin | 1.00 | .45 |
| □ 94 Jurij Lebedev | 2.00 | .90 |
| □ 95 Alexander Bodunov | 1.00 | .45 |
| □ 96 Alexander Voltjkov | 2.00 | .90 |
| □ 97 Vsevolod Bobrov | 4.00 | 1.80 |
| □ 98 Konstantin Loktev | .50 | .23 |
| □ 99 Anatolij Firsov | 3.00 | 1.35 |
| □ 100 Viktor Kuzkin | 1.00 | .45 |
| □ 101 Jurij Blochin | .50 | .23 |
| □ 102 Vladimir Vikulov | 1.00 | .45 |
| □ 103 Jurij Blinov | 1.00 | .45 |
| □ 104 Jevgenij Misjakov | 2.00 | .90 |
| □ 105 Vladimir Trunov | .50 | .23 |
| □ 106 Sergej Glazov | .50 | .23 |
| □ 107 Vladimir Popov | 1.50 | .70 |
| □ 108 Viktor Zinger | 1.00 | .45 |
| □ 109 Viktor Krivolapov | .75 | .35 |
| □ 110 Jevgenij Kazatjkin | .50 | .23 |
| □ 111 Viktor Korotkov | 1.50 | .70 |
| □ 112 Valentin Markov | .50 | .23 |
| □ 113 Alexander Sapjolkin | .50 | .23 |
| □ 114 Leonid Borzov | .50 | .23 |
| □ 115 Gennadij Krylov | .50 | .23 |
| □ 116 Konstantin Klimov | .50 | .23 |
| □ 117 Jevgenij Zimin | 1.00 | .45 |
| □ 118 Vladimir Gurejev | .50 | .23 |
| □ 119 Viktor Jaroslavtsev | .50 | .23 |
| □ 120 Alexander Pasjkov | .75 | .35 |
| □ 121 Vladimir Polupanov | 1.00 | .45 |
| □ 122 Vitalij Davydov | 1.50 | .70 |
| □ 123 Michail Alexeenko | .50 | .23 |
| □ 124 Alexander Filippov | 1.00 | .45 |
| □ 125 Valerij Nazarov | .50 | .23 |
| □ 126 Vladimir Orlov | .50 | .23 |
| □ 127 Stanislav Sjtjegolev | .50 | .23 |
| □ 128 Anatolij Bjelonozjkin | .50 | .23 |
| □ 129 Vladimir Devjatov | .50 | .23 |
| □ 130 Jevgenij Kotlov | .50 | .23 |
| □ 131 Anatolij Motovilov | .50 | .23 |
| □ 132 Jurij Reps | .50 | .23 |
| □ 133 Igor Samotjernov | .50 | .23 |
| □ 134 Alexander Sevidov | .50 | .23 |
| □ 135 Viktor Sjilov | .50 | .23 |
| □ 136 Jurij Tjitjurin | .75 | .35 |
| □ 137 Sune Odling | .50 | .23 |
| □ 138 Lars-Erik Sjoberg | 2.00 | .90 |
| □ 139 Bengt Sjoholm | .50 | .23 |
| □ 140 Leif Henriksson | .50 | .23 |
| □ 141 Henric Hedlund | .50 | .23 |
| □ 142 Roger Olsson | .50 | .23 |
| □ 143 Kjell-Rune Milton | .50 | .23 |
| □ 144 Kjell-Ronnie Pettersson | .50 | .23 |
| □ 145 Svante Granholm | .50 | .23 |
| □ 146 Kjell Andersson | .50 | .23 |
| □ 147 Lars-Erik Esbjorn | .50 | .23 |
| □ 148 Bjorn Lindberg | .50 | .23 |
| □ 149 Willy Lindstrom | 1.50 | .70 |
| □ 150 Evert Lindstrom | .50 | .23 |
| □ 151 Lars-Erik Johansson | .50 | .23 |
| □ 152 Krister Sterner | .75 | .35 |
| □ 153 Mats Lindh | .50 | .23 |
| □ 154 Roger Bergman | .50 | .23 |
| □ 155 Willie Lofqvist | 1.00 | .45 |
| □ 156 Jan Olov Svensson | .50 | .23 |
| □ 157 Jan Erik Silfverberg | .50 | .23 |
| □ 158 Stig Ostling | 1.00 | .45 |
| □ 159 Kjell Johansson | .50 | .23 |
| □ 160 Borje Salming | 10.00 | 4.50 |
| □ 161 Stig Salming | 1.00 | .45 |
| □ 162 Tord Lundstrom | .50 | .23 |
| □ 163 Hakan Wickberg | .50 | .23 |
| □ 164 Inge Hammarstrom | 3.00 | 1.35 |
| □ 165 Lars Goran Nilsson | .50 | .23 |
| □ 166 Jan Erik Lyck | .50 | .23 |
| □ 167 Stefan Karlsson | .50 | .23 |
| □ 168 Lennart Lind | 1.00 | .45 |
| □ 169 Hans Ake Persson | .50 | .23 |
| □ 170 Lars Oberg | .50 | .23 |
| □ 171 Lars Erik Eriksson | .50 | .23 |
| □ 172 Bjorn Fagerlund | .75 | .35 |
| □ 173 Nicke Johansson | .50 | .23 |
| □ 174 Lars Goran Nilsson | .50 | .23 |
| □ 175 Hans Erik Jansson | .50 | .23 |
| □ 176 Per Backman | .50 | .23 |
| □ 177 Jorgen Palm | .50 | .23 |
| □ 178 Conny Evensson | .75 | .35 |
| □ 179 Ulf Sterner | .50 | .23 |
| □ 180 Sven Ake Rudby | .50 | .23 |
| □ 181 Lennart Andersson | .75 | .35 |
| □ 182 Kent Erik Andersson | .50 | .23 |
| □ 183 Hans Ake Rosendahl | .50 | .23 |
| □ 184 Karl Johan Sundqvist | .50 | .23 |
| □ 185 Hasse Andersson | .50 | .23 |
| □ 186 Benny Andersson | .50 | .23 |
| □ 187 Gunnar Johansson | .50 | .23 |
| □ 188 Sten Ake Bark | .50 | .23 |
| □ 189 Lasse Zetterstrom | .50 | .23 |
| □ 190 Leif Holmqvist | 1.00 | .45 |
| □ 191 Bert Jattne | 1.00 | .45 |
| □ 192 Lars Danielsson | 1.00 | .45 |
| □ 193 Hakan Lindgren | .50 | .23 |
| □ 194 Ake Fagerstrom | .50 | .23 |
| □ 195 Bert-Ola Nordlander | .75 | .35 |
| □ 196 Leif Holmgren | .50 | .23 |
| □ 197 Soren Sjogren | .50 | .23 |
| □ 198 Hans Lindberg | .50 | .23 |
| □ 199 Jan-Olov Kroon | .50 | .23 |
| □ 200 Rolf Edberg | .50 | .23 |
| □ 201 Lennart Selinder | 1.00 | .45 |
| □ 202 Ulf Nilsson | 5.00 | 2.20 |
| □ 203 Jan Olsson | .50 | .23 |
| □ 204 Jan Ostling | .50 | .23 |
| □ 205 Christer Lundberg | .50 | .23 |
| □ 206 Christer Englund | .50 | .23 |
| □ 207 Bo Olofsson | .50 | .23 |
| □ 208 Roland Einarsson | 1.00 | .45 |
| □ 209 Ake Danielsson | .50 | .23 |
| □ 210 Billy Sundstrom | .50 | .23 |
| □ 211 Thomas Carlsson | .50 | .23 |
| □ 212 Stig Larsson | .50 | .23 |
| □ 213 Lars Ake Gustavsson | 1.00 | .45 |
| □ 214 Bjorn Palmqvist | .50 | .23 |
| □ 215 Anders Hedberg | 5.00 | 2.20 |
| □ 216 Anders Rylin | .50 | .23 |
| □ 217 Sven Bertil Lindstrom | .50 | .23 |
| □ 218 Kjell Nilsson | .50 | .23 |
| □ 219 Claes Goran Wallin | .50 | .23 |
| □ 220 Ake Eklof | .50 | .23 |
| □ 221 Peder Nilsson | .75 | .35 |
| □ 222 Lars Ake Lundell | .50 | .23 |
| □ 223 Bengt Ake Karlsson | .50 | .23 |
| □ 224 Ove Svensson | .50 | .23 |
| □ 225 Soren Johansson | .50 | .23 |
| □ 226 Christer Sehlstedt | .75 | .35 |
| □ 227 Lage Edin | .50 | .23 |
| □ 228 Tommy Andersson | .50 | .23 |
| □ 229 Janerik Nilsson | .50 | .23 |
| □ 230 Tommie Lindgren | .50 | .23 |
| □ 231 Bo Bergman | .50 | .23 |
| □ 232 Lennart Norberg | .50 | .23 |
| □ 233 Olle Ahman | .50 | .23 |
| □ 234 Arne Lundstrom | .75 | .35 |
| □ 235 Kent Lindgren | .50 | .23 |
| □ 236 Orjan Lindstrom | .50 | .23 |
| □ 237 Kent Othberg | .75 | .35 |
| □ 238 Finn Lundstrom | .50 | .23 |
| □ 239 Ake Soderberg | .50 | .23 |
| □ 240 Jan Kock | .50 | .23 |
| □ 241 Ove Larsson | .50 | .23 |
| □ 242 Hakan Pettersson | .50 | .23 |
| □ 243 Stefan Pettersson | .50 | .23 |

## 1973-74 Swedish World Championship Stickers

The 243 stickers in this set measure approximately 2" by 3" and feature color photos in a white border of players from several European national teams, as well as club teams from Sweden and the USSR. The stickers were designed to be put into a book that measures approximately 8 3/4" by 11 7/8". The book not only holds the stickers, but has plenty of text describing team and league histories, rules, etc, all written in Swedish. The original retail price on the book was about fifty cents. It now is valued at around $30.

| | MINT | NRMT |
|---|---|---|
| COMPLETE SET (243) | 175.00 | 80.00 |
| COMMON STICKER (1-243) | .50 | .23 |
| □ 1 Christer Abrahamsson | 1.50 | .70 |
| □ 2 William Lofqvist | 1.00 | .45 |
| □ 3 Arne Karlsson | .50 | .23 |
| □ 4 Lars-Erik Sjoberg | 2.00 | .90 |
| □ 5 Bjorn Johansson | .50 | .23 |
| □ 6 Thommy Abrahamsson | 1.00 | .45 |
| □ 7 Borje Salming | 10.00 | 4.50 |
| □ 8 Karl Johan Sundqvist | .50 | .23 |
| □ 9 Ulf Sterner | .50 | .23 |
| □ 10 Ulf Nilsson | 5.00 | 2.20 |
| □ 11 Kjell-Arne Wickstrom | .50 | .23 |
| □ 12 Inge Hammarstrom | 3.00 | 1.35 |
| □ 13 Hakan Wickberg | .50 | .23 |
| □ 14 Tord Lundstrom | .50 | .23 |
| □ 15 Dan Soderstrom | .50 | .23 |
| □ 16 Mats Ahlberg | .50 | .23 |
| □ 17 Anders Hedberg | 5.00 | 2.20 |
| □ 18 Dick Yderstrom | .75 | .35 |
| □ 19 Stefan Karlsson | .50 | .23 |
| □ 20 Roland Bond | .50 | .23 |
| □ 21 Kjell-Rune Milton | .50 | .23 |
| □ 22 Willy Lindstrom | 2.00 | .90 |
| □ 23 Kurt Carlsson | .75 | .35 |
| □ 24 Mats Walltin | .50 | .23 |
| □ 25 Roland Eriksson | .50 | .23 |
| □ 26 Martin Karlsson | .50 | .23 |
| □ 27 Jiri Holecek | 1.00 | .45 |
| □ 28 Josef Horesovsky | .50 | .23 |
| □ 29 Oldrich Machac | .50 | .23 |
| □ 30 Vladimir Martinec | 1.00 | .45 |
| □ 31 Vaclav Nedomansky | 1.50 | .70 |
| □ 32 Jiri Kochta | .50 | .23 |
| □ 33 Jorma Valtonen | 1.00 | .45 |
| □ 34 Heikki Riihiranta | 1.00 | .45 |
| □ 35 Lauri Mononen | .50 | .23 |
| □ 36 Timo Turunen | .50 | .23 |
| □ 37 Matti Keinonen | .50 | .23 |
| □ 38 Seppo Repo | .50 | .23 |
| □ 39 Christer Abrahamsson | 1.50 | .70 |
| □ 40 Lars Stenvall | .50 | .23 |
| □ 41 Per Karlsson | .50 | .23 |
| □ 42 Roland Bond | .50 | .23 |
| □ 43 Thommy Abrahamsson | 1.00 | .45 |
| □ 44 Ulf Weinstock | .50 | .23 |
| □ 45 Gunnar Andersson | .50 | .23 |
| □ 46 Hans Eriksson | .50 | .23 |
| □ 47 Peter Gudmundsson | .50 | .23 |
| □ 48 Mats Ahlberg | .50 | .23 |
| □ 49 Per-Olov Brasar | 1.50 | .70 |
| □ 50 Roger Linqvist | .50 | .23 |
| □ 51 Dan Soderstrom | .50 | .23 |
| □ 52 Ulf Martensson | .50 | .23 |
| □ 53 Kjell Brus | .50 | .23 |
| □ 54 Hans Jax | .50 | .23 |
| □ 55 Dan Labraaten | 1.50 | .70 |
| □ 56 Nils-Olov Olsson | .50 | .23 |
| □ 57 Stig Nordin | .50 | .23 |
| □ 58 Bo Theander | .50 | .23 |
| □ 59 Curt Larsson | 1.00 | .45 |
| □ 60 Mikael Collin | 1.00 | .45 |
| □ 61 Arne Carlsson | .50 | .23 |
| □ 62 Leif Svensson | .50 | .23 |
| □ 63 Sverker Torstensson | .50 | .23 |
| □ 64 Bjorn Johansson | .50 | .23 |
| □ 65 Stisse Johansson | .50 | .23 |
| □ 66 Carl-Goran Oberg | .50 | .23 |
| □ 67 Mats Hysing | .50 | .23 |
| □ 68 Mats Walltin | .50 | .23 |
| □ 69 Hans Carlsson | .50 | .23 |
| □ 70 Nils-Olov Schilstrom | .50 | .23 |
| □ 71 Kjell-Arne Wickstrom | .50 | .23 |
| □ 72 Jan Schullstrom | .50 | .23 |
| □ 73 Borje Burlin | .50 | .23 |
| □ 74 Dick Yderstrom | .75 | .35 |
| □ 75 Dan Landegren | .50 | .23 |
| □ 76 Kjell Landstrom | .50 | .23 |
| □ 77 Vladislav Tretjak | 20.00 | 9.00 |
| □ 78 Alexander Sidelnikov | 2.00 | .90 |
| □ 79 Alexander Ragulin | 2.50 | 1.10 |
| □ 80 Vladimir Luttjenko | 2.00 | .90 |
| □ 81 Gennadij Tsygankov | 1.50 | .70 |
| □ 82 Alexander Gusev | 1.00 | .45 |
| □ 83 Jevgenij Poladiev | .75 | .35 |
| □ 84 Jurij Liapkin | 1.50 | .70 |
| □ 85 Valerij Vasiljev | 4.00 | 1.80 |
| □ 86 Boris Michailov | 5.00 | 2.20 |
| □ 87 Valerij Charlamov | 10.00 | 4.50 |
| □ 88 Vladimir Petrov | 5.00 | 2.20 |
| □ 89 Alexander Maltsev | 5.00 | 2.20 |
| □ 90 Vladimir Sjadrin | 2.50 | 1.10 |
| □ 91 Alexander Jakusjev | 5.00 | 2.20 |
| □ 92 Alexander Martynjuk | .75 | .35 |
| □ 93 Vjateslav Anissin | 1.00 | .45 |
| □ 94 Jurij Lebedev | 2.00 | .90 |
| □ 95 Alexander Bodunov | 1.00 | .45 |
| □ 96 Alexander Voltjkov | 2.00 | .90 |
| □ 97 Vsevolod Bobrov | 4.00 | 1.80 |
| □ 98 Konstantin Loktev | .50 | .23 |
| □ 99 Anatolij Firsov | 3.00 | 1.35 |
| □ 100 Viktor Duzkin | .50 | .23 |
| □ 101 Jurij Blochin | .50 | .23 |
| □ 102 Vladimir Vikulov | 1.00 | .45 |
| □ 103 Jurij Blinov | 1.00 | .45 |
| □ 104 Jevgenij Misjakov | 2.00 | .90 |
| □ 105 Vladimir Trunov | .50 | .23 |
| □ 106 Sergej Glazov | .50 | .23 |
| □ 107 Vladimir Popov | 1.50 | .70 |
| □ 108 Viktor Zinger | 1.00 | .45 |
| □ 109 Viktor Krivolapov | .75 | .35 |
| □ 110 Jevgenij Kazatjkin | .50 | .23 |
| □ 111 Viktor Korotkov | 1.50 | .70 |
| □ 112 Valentin Markov | .50 | .23 |
| □ 113 Alexander Sapjolkin | .50 | .23 |
| □ 114 Leonid Borzov | .50 | .23 |
| □ 115 Gennadij Krylov | .50 | .23 |
| □ 116 Konstantin Klimov | .50 | .23 |
| □ 117 Jevgenij Zimin | 1.00 | .45 |
| □ 118 Vladimir Gurejev | .50 | .23 |
| □ 119 Viktor Jaroslavtsev | .50 | .23 |
| □ 120 Alexander Pasjkov | .75 | .35 |
| □ 121 Vladimir Polupanov | 1.00 | .45 |
| □ 122 Vitalij Davydov | 1.50 | .70 |
| □ 123 Michail Alexeenko | .50 | .23 |
| □ 124 Alexander Filippov | 1.00 | .45 |
| □ 125 Valerij Nazarov | .50 | .23 |
| □ 126 Vladimir Orlov | .50 | .23 |
| □ 127 Stanislav Sjtjegolev | .50 | .23 |
| □ 128 Anatolij Bjelonozjkin | .50 | .23 |
| □ 129 Vladimir Devjatov | .50 | .23 |
| □ 130 Jevgenij Kotlov | .50 | .23 |
| □ 131 Anatolij Motovilov | .50 | .23 |
| □ 132 Jurij Reps | .50 | .23 |
| □ 133 Igor Samotijernov | .50 | .23 |
| □ 134 Alexander Sevidov | .50 | .23 |
| □ 135 Viktor Sjilov | .50 | .23 |
| □ 136 Jurij Tjitjurin | .75 | .35 |
| □ 137 Sune Odling | .50 | .23 |
| □ 138 Lars-Erik Sjoberg | 2.00 | .90 |
| □ 139 Bengt Sjoholm | .50 | .23 |
| □ 140 Leif Henriksson | .50 | .23 |
| □ 141 Henric Hedlund | .50 | .23 |
| □ 142 Roger Olsson | .50 | .23 |
| □ 143 Kjell-Rune Milton | .50 | .23 |
| □ 144 Kjell-Ronnie Pettersson | .50 | .23 |
| □ 145 Svante Granholm | .50 | .23 |
| □ 146 Kjell Andersson | .50 | .23 |
| □ 147 Lars-Erik Esbjorn | .50 | .23 |
| □ 148 Bjorn Lindberg | .50 | .23 |
| □ 149 Willy Lindstrom | 1.50 | .70 |
| □ 150 Evert Lindstrom | .50 | .23 |
| □ 151 Lars-Erik Johansson | .50 | .23 |
| □ 152 Krister Sterner | .75 | .35 |
| □ 153 Mats Lindh | .50 | .23 |
| □ 154 Roger Bergman | .50 | .23 |
| □ 155 Willem Lofqvist | 1.00 | .45 |
| □ 156 Jan Olov Svensson | .50 | .23 |
| □ 157 Jan Erik Silfverberg | .50 | .23 |
| □ 158 Stig Ostling | 1.00 | .45 |
| □ 159 Kjell Johansson | .50 | .23 |
| □ 160 Borje Salming | 10.00 | 4.50 |
| □ 161 Stig Salming | 1.00 | .45 |
| □ 162 Tord Lundstrom | .50 | .23 |
| □ 163 Hakan Wickberg | .50 | .23 |
| □ 164 Inge Hammarstrom | 3.00 | 1.35 |
| □ 165 Lars Goran Nilsson | .50 | .23 |
| □ 166 Jan Erik Lyck | .50 | .23 |
| □ 167 Stefan Karlsson | .50 | .23 |
| □ 168 Lennart Lind | 1.00 | .45 |
| □ 169 Hans Ake Persson | .50 | .23 |
| □ 170 Lars Oberg | .50 | .23 |
| □ 171 Lars Erik Eriksson | .50 | .23 |
| □ 172 Bjorn Fagerlund | .75 | .35 |
| □ 173 Nicke Johansson | .50 | .23 |
| □ 174 Lars Goran Nilsson | .50 | .23 |
| □ 175 Hans Erik Jansson | .50 | .23 |
| □ 176 Per Backman | .50 | .23 |
| □ 177 Jorgen Palm | .50 | .23 |
| □ 178 Conny Evensson | .75 | .35 |
| □ 179 Ulf Sterner | .50 | .23 |
| □ 180 Sven Ake Rudby | .50 | .23 |
| □ 181 Lennart Andersson | .75 | .35 |
| □ 182 Kent Erik Andersson | .50 | .23 |
| □ 183 Hans Ake Rosendahl | .50 | .23 |
| □ 184 Karl Johan Sundqvist | .50 | .23 |
| □ 185 Hasse Andersson | .50 | .23 |
| □ 186 Benny Andersson | .50 | .23 |
| □ 187 Gunnar Johansson | .50 | .23 |
| □ 188 Sten Ake Bark | .50 | .23 |
| □ 189 Lasse Zetterstrom | .50 | .23 |
| □ 190 Leif Holmqvist | 1.00 | .45 |
| □ 191 Bert Jattne | 1.00 | .45 |
| □ 192 Lars Danielsson | 1.00 | .45 |
| □ 193 Hakan Lindgren | .50 | .23 |
| □ 194 Ake Fagerstrom | .50 | .23 |
| □ 195 Bert-Ola Nordlander | .75 | .35 |
| □ 196 Leif Holmgren | .50 | .23 |
| □ 197 Soren Sjogren | .50 | .23 |
| □ 198 Hans Lindberg | .50 | .23 |
| □ 199 Jan-Olov Kroon | .50 | .23 |
| □ 200 Rolf Edberg | .50 | .23 |
| □ 201 Lennart Selinder | 1.00 | .45 |
| □ 202 Ulf Nilsson | 5.00 | 2.20 |
| □ 203 Jan Olsson | .50 | .23 |
| □ 204 Jan Ostling | .50 | .23 |
| □ 205 Christer Lundberg | .50 | .23 |
| □ 206 Christer Englund | .50 | .23 |
| □ 207 Bo Olofsson | .50 | .23 |
| □ 208 Roland Einarsson | 1.00 | .45 |
| □ 209 Ake Danielsson | .50 | .23 |
| □ 210 Billy Sundstrom | .50 | .23 |
| □ 211 Thomas Carlsson | .50 | .23 |
| □ 212 Stig Larsson | .50 | .23 |
| □ 213 Lars Ake Gustavsson | 1.00 | .45 |
| □ 214 Bjorn Palmqvist | .50 | .23 |
| □ 215 Anders Hedberg | 5.00 | 2.20 |
| □ 216 Anders Rylin | .50 | .23 |
| □ 217 Sven Bertil Lindstrom | .50 | .23 |
| □ 218 Kjell Nilsson | .50 | .23 |
| □ 219 Claes Goran Wallin | .50 | .23 |

- ❑ 220 Ake Eklof .50 .23
- ❑ 221 Peder Nilsson .75 .35
- ❑ 222 Lars Ake Lundell .50 .23
- ❑ 223 Bengt Ake Karlsson .50 .23
- ❑ 224 Ove Svensson .50 .23
- ❑ 225 Soren Johansson .50 .23
- ❑ 226 Christer Sehlstedt .75 .35
- ❑ 227 Lage Edin .50 .23
- ❑ 228 Tommy Andersson .50 .23
- ❑ 229 Jan Erik Nilsson .50 .23
- ❑ 230 Tommie Lindgren .50 .23
- ❑ 231 Bo Bergman .50 .23
- ❑ 232 Lennart Norberg .50 .23
- ❑ 233 Olle Ahman .50 .23
- ❑ 234 Arne Lundstrom .75 .35
- ❑ 235 Kent Lindgren .50 .23
- ❑ 236 Orjan Lindstrom .50 .23
- ❑ 237 Kent Othberg .75 .35
- ❑ 238 Finn Lundstrom .50 .23
- ❑ 239 Ake Soderberg .50 .23
- ❑ 240 Jan Kock .50 .23
- ❑ 241 Ove Larsson .50 .23
- ❑ 242 Hakan Pettersson .50 .23
- ❑ 243 Stefan Pettersson .50 .23

## 1974-75 Swedish Semic World Championship Stickers

This 100-sticker set featuring World Championship players was produced by Semic of Sweden. The stickers measure approximately 2" by 3", and were designed to be placed in a special collector's album, now valued at $25. Because of the small size of this set in comparison to similar Semic issues, there is some thought this may not be a complete checklist. That, however, cannot be confirmed.

| | MINT | NRMT |
|---|---|---|
| COMPLETE SET (100) | 75.00 | 34.00 |
| COMMON STICKER (1-100) | .50 | .23 |

- ❑ 1 Christer Abrahamsson 1.50 .70
- ❑ 2 William Lofqvist 1.00 .45
- ❑ 3 Arne Carlsson .50 .23
- ❑ 4 Lars-Erik Sjoberg 2.00 .90
- ❑ 5 Bjorn Johansson .50 .23
- ❑ 6 Tommy Abrahamsson 1.00 .45
- ❑ 7 Karl-Johan Sundqvist .50 .23
- ❑ 8 Ulf Nilsson 4.00 1.80
- ❑ 9 Hakan Wickberg .50 .23
- ❑ 10 Dan Soderstrom .50 .23
- ❑ 11 Mats Ahlberg .75 .35
- ❑ 12 Anders Hedberg 4.00 1.80
- ❑ 13 Dick Yderstrom .50 .23
- ❑ 14 Stefan Karlsson .50 .23
- ❑ 15 Roland Bond .50 .23
- ❑ 16 Kjell-Rune Milton .50 .23
- ❑ 17 Willy Lindstrom 1.00 .45
- ❑ 18 Mats Waltin .50 .23
- ❑ 19 Lars-Goran Nilsson .50 .23
- ❑ 20 Bjorn Palmquist .50 .23
- ❑ 21 Stig-Goran Johansson .50 .23
- ❑ 22 Bo Berggren .50 .23
- ❑ 23 Dan Labraaten 1.50 .70
- ❑ 24 Curt Larsson .75 .35
- ❑ 25 Mats Lindh .50 .23
- ❑ 26 Vladislav Tretiak 15.00 6.75
- ❑ 27 Alexander Ragulin 1.00 .45
- ❑ 28 Vladimir Luttjenko 1.00 .45
- ❑ 29 Gennadij Tsygankov 1.00 .45
- ❑ 30 Alexander Gusev 1.00 .45
- ❑ 31 Jevgenij Poladiev .50 .23
- ❑ 32 Jurij Ljapkin 1.00 .45
- ❑ 33 Boris Michailov 4.00 1.80
- ❑ 34 Valeri Kharlamov 6.00 2.70
- ❑ 35 Vladimir Petrov 4.00 1.80
- ❑ 36 Alexander Maltsev 4.00 1.80
- ❑ 37 Vladimir Sjadrin .75 .35
- ❑ 38 Alexander Jakusjev 4.00 1.80
- ❑ 39 Alexander Martynjuk .75 .35
- ❑ 40 Jurij Lebedev 1.50 .70
- ❑ 41 Alexander Bodunov 1.00 .45
- ❑ 42 Anatolij Firsov 1.50 .70
- ❑ 43 Vitalij Davydov .75 .35
- ❑ 44 Vjateslav Starsjinov .75 .35
- ❑ 45 Viktor Kuzkin .50 .23
- ❑ 46 Igor Romitjevskij .50 .23
- ❑ 47 Jevgenij Zimin .75 .35
- ❑ 48 Jevgenij Misjakov 1.00 .45
- ❑ 49 Vladimir Vikulov .75 .35
- ❑ 50 Viktor Konovalenko 1.00 .45
- ❑ 51 Jiri Holecek 1.00 .45
- ❑ 52 Frantisek Pospisil .75 .35
- ❑ 53 Jiri Bubla 1.00 .45
- ❑ 54 Josef Horesovsky .50 .23
- ❑ 55 Oldrich Machac .50 .23
- ❑ 56 Vladimir Martinec .50 .23
- ❑ 57 Vaclav Nedomansky 1.50 .70
- ❑ 58 Jiri Kochta .50 .23
- ❑ 59 Milan Novy 1.00 .45
- ❑ 60 Jaroslav Holik .75 .35
- ❑ 61 Jiri Holik 1.00 .45
- ❑ 62 Jiri Klapac .50 .23
- ❑ 63 Richard Farda .75 .35
- ❑ 64 Bohuslav Stastny .75 .35
- ❑ 65 Jiri Novak .50 .23
- ❑ 66 Ivan Hlinka .75 .35
- ❑ 67 Jan Suchy .75 .35
- ❑ 68 Vladimir Bednar .50 .23
- ❑ 69 Rudolf Tajcnar .50 .23
- ❑ 70 Josef Cerny .50 .23
- ❑ 71 Jan Havel .75 .35
- ❑ 72 Marcel Sakac .50 .23
- ❑ 73 Frantisek Pancharek .50 .23
- ❑ 74 Bedrich Brunchk .50 .23
- ❑ 75 Edvard Novak .50 .23
- ❑ 76 Jorma Valtonen 1.00 .45
- ❑ 77 Seppo Lindstrom .50 .23
- ❑ 78 Pekka Marjamaki .50 .23
- ❑ 79 Pekka Rautakallio 1.50 .70
- ❑ 80 Heikki Riihiranta 1.00 .45
- ❑ 81 Seppo Suoraniemi .50 .23
- ❑ 82 Jouko Oystila .50 .23
- ❑ 83 Veli-Pekka Ketola 1.50 .70
- ❑ 84 Henry Leppa .50 .23
- ❑ 85 Harri Linnonmaa .50 .23
- ❑ 86 Matti Murto .50 .23
- ❑ 87 Lasse Oksanen .50 .23
- ❑ 88 Esa Peltonen .50 .23
- ❑ 89 Seppo Repo .50 .23
- ❑ 90 Raimo Suoniemi .50 .23
- ❑ 91 Timo Sutinen .50 .23
- ❑ 92 Juhani Tamminen 1.00 .45
- ❑ 93 Leo Seppanen .50 .23
- ❑ 94 Hannu Haapalainen .50 .23
- ❑ 95 Pertti Valkeapaa .50 .23
- ❑ 96 Sakari Ahlberg .50 .23
- ❑ 97 Antti Leppanen .50 .23
- ❑ 98 Kalevi Numminen .50 .23
- ❑ 99 Lauri Mononen .50 .23
- ❑ 100 Ilpo Koskela .75 .35

## 1974-75 Swedish Hockey Stickers

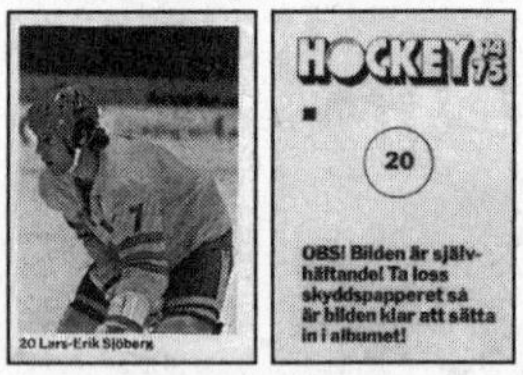


This set of 324 stickers commemorates the competitors on the 1974-75 World Championship, along with players from club teams across Europe. The stickers -- which measure approximately 3" by 2" -- feature action photography on the front, with player name and card number along the bottom. The backs have the set logo, a reprise of the card number and encouragement in Swedish to build the entire set. The last six cards are unidentified at the moment.

| | MINT | NRMT |
|---|---|---|
| COMPLETE SET (324) | 175.00 | 80.00 |
| COMMON STICKER (1-324) | .50 | .23 |

- ❑ 1 Vladislav Tretiak 15.00 6.75
- ❑ 2 Gennadij Tsigannkov 1.00 .45
- ❑ 3 Valerij Vasiljev 3.00 1.35
- ❑ 4 Alexander Gusev 1.00 .45
- ❑ 5 Valeri Kharlamov 6.00 2.70
- ❑ 6 Vladimir Petrov 4.00 1.80
- ❑ 7 Boris Michailov 4.00 1.80
- ❑ 8 Alexander Maltsev 4.00 1.80
- ❑ 9 Alexander Jakusjev 4.00 1.80
- ❑ 10 Jiri Chra 3.00 1.35
- ❑ 11 Jiri Bubla 1.00 .45
- ❑ 12 Milan Kuzela .50 .23
- ❑ 13 Oldrich Machac .50 .23
- ❑ 14 Ivan Hlinka .50 .23
- ❑ 15 Vaclav Nedomansky 1.50 .70
- ❑ 16 Boshulav Stastny 1.50 .70
- ❑ 17 Vladimir Martinec .50 .23
- ❑ 18 Richard Farda .50 .23
- ❑ 19 Curt Larsson .75 .35
- ❑ 20 Lars-Erik Sjoberg 2.00 .90
- ❑ 21 Thommy Abrahamsson 1.00 .45
- ❑ 22 Kjell-Rune Milton .50 .23
- ❑ 23 Anders Hedberg 4.00 1.80
- ❑ 24 Mats Ahlberg .75 .35
- ❑ 25 Dan Soderstrom .50 .23
- ❑ 26 Ulf Nilsson 4.00 1.80
- ❑ 27 Per-Olof Brassar 1.50 .70
- ❑ 28 Stig Wetzell .50 .23
- ❑ 29 Juha Rantasila .50 .23
- ❑ 30 Heikki Riihiranta 1.00 .45
- ❑ 31 Timo Saari .50 .23
- ❑ 32 Seppo Repo .50 .23
- ❑ 33 Esa Peltonen .50 .23
- ❑ 34 Juhani Tamminen 1.00 .45
- ❑ 35 Matti Murto .50 .23
- ❑ 36 Harri Linnonmaa .50 .23
- ❑ 37 Gennadij Lapsjenkov 1.00 .45
- ❑ 38 Pjotr Zjulin .50 .23
- ❑ 39 Vladimir Merinov .50 .23
- ❑ 40 Sergej Tyznych 2.00 .90
- ❑ 41 Valerij Kostin .50 .23
- ❑ 42 Valerij Nikitin 1.00 .45
- ❑ 43 Sergej Gusev 1.00 .45
- ❑ 44 Valentin Kozin .50 .23
- ❑ 45 Viktor Liksiutkin .50 .23
- ❑ 46 Alexander Golikov 1.00 .45
- ❑ 47 Viktor Zjutjok 1.00 .45
- ❑ 48 Anatolij Frolov 1.50 .70
- ❑ 49 Vladimir Golikov 2.00 .90
- ❑ 50 Nikolaj Epstein .50 .23
- ❑ 51 Alexander Kasjajev .50 .23
- ❑ 52 Alexander Sidelnikov 2.00 .90
- ❑ 53 Valerij Kuzmin 1.00 .45
- ❑ 54 Viktor Kuznetsov 1.00 .45
- ❑ 55 Jurij Terechin .75 .35
- ❑ 56 Jurij Tjitjurin .75 .35
- ❑ 57 Jurij Sjatavalov .75 .35
- ❑ 58 Vjatjeslav Anissin .75 .35
- ❑ 59 Alexander Bodunov 1.00 .45
- ❑ 60 Jurij Lebedev 1.50 .70
- ❑ 61 Igor Dmitriev 4.00 1.80
- ❑ 62 Konstantin Klimov .75 .35
- ❑ 63 Sergej Kapustin .75 .35
- ❑ 64 Vladimir Repnjov .75 .35
- ❑ 65 Jevgenij Kucharzj .75 .35
- ❑ 66 Boris Kulagin 2.00 .90
- ❑ 67 Viktor Afonin .50 .23
- ❑ 68 Juris Liberts .75 .35
- ❑ 69 Igor Kobzev .75 .35
- ❑ 70 Valerij Odintsov .75 .35
- ❑ 71 Vjatjeslav Nazarov 1.00 .45
- ❑ 72 Andris Hendelis .75 .35
- ❑ 73 Alexander Sokolovskij .75 .35
- ❑ 74 Michail Denisov .75 .35
- ❑ 75 Helmut Balderis 4.00 1.80
- ❑ 76 Vladimir Sorokin .50 .23
- ❑ 77 Vladimir Sernjajev .50 .23
- ❑ 78 Viktor Verizjnikov .50 .23
- ❑ 79 Vladimir Markov .50 .23
- ❑ 80 Viktor Tichonov 5.00 2.20
- ❑ 81 Edgar Rosenberg .50 .23
- ❑ 82 Alexander Kotomkin .50 .23
- ❑ 83 Vladimir Astafjev 1.00 .45
- ❑ 84 Alexander Kulikov .50 .23
- ❑ 85 Sergej Mosjkarov .50 .23
- ❑ 86 Vjatjeslav Usjmakov .50 .23
- ❑ 87 Jurij Fjodorov 1.00 .45
- ❑ 88 Victor Dobrochotov .50 .23
- ❑ 89 Vitalij Krajov .50 .23
- ❑ 90 Alexej Masjin .50 .23
- ❑ 91 Vladimir Orlov .50 .23
- ❑ 92 Vladimir Smagin .50 .23
- ❑ 93 Alexander Usov .50 .23
- ❑ 94 Alexander Fedotov 1.00 .45
- ❑ 95 Alexander Prilepskij .50 .23
- ❑ 96 Alexander Rogov .50 .23
- ❑ 97 Seppo Ahokainen .50 .23
- ❑ 98 Lasse Oksanen .50 .23
- ❑ 99 Jorma Peltonen 1.00 .45
- ❑ 100 Henry Leppa .50 .23
- ❑ 101 Seppo Suoraniemi .50 .23
- ❑ 102 Timi Sutinen .50 .23
- ❑ 103 Jorma Valtonen 1.00 .45
- ❑ 104 Antti Leppanen .50 .23
- ❑ 105 Pekka Marjamaki .50 .23
- ❑ 106 Juoko Oystila .50 .23
- ❑ 107 Seppo Lindstrom .50 .23
- ❑ 108 Veli-Pekka Ketola 1.50 .70
- ❑ 109 Jiri Holecek 1.00 .45
- ❑ 110 Jiri Kochta .50 .23
- ❑ 111 Josef Horesovsky .50 .23
- ❑ 112 Jaroslav Sima .50 .23
- ❑ 113 Frantisek Vorlicek .50 .23
- ❑ 114 Vladimir Kostka .50 .23
- ❑ 115 Jaroslav Holik .75 .35
- ❑ 116 Jiri Holik 1.00 .45
- ❑ 117 Jan Suchy .75 .35
- ❑ 118 Josef Augusta, .50 .23
- ❑ 119 Miroslav Dvorak 1.00 .45
- ❑ 120 Jan Hrbaty .50 .23
- ❑ 121 AIK .50 .23
- ❑ 122 If Bjorkloven .50 .23
- ❑ 123 Brynas IF .50 .23
- ❑ 124 Djurgardens IF .50 .23
- ❑ 125 Farjestads BK .50 .23
- ❑ 126 IF Karlskoga .50 .23
- ❑ 127 Leksands IF .50 .23
- ❑ 128 MoDo .50 .23
- ❑ 129 Mora IK .50 .23
- ❑ 130 Skelleftea AIK .50 .23
- ❑ 131 Sodertalje SK .50 .23
- ❑ 132 Timra IK .50 .23
- ❑ 133 Tingsryds AIF .50 .23
- ❑ 134 V. Frolunda IF .50 .23
- ❑ 135 Vasteras IK .50 .23
- ❑ 136 Orebro IK .50 .23
- ❑ 137 Christer Abrahamsson 1.50 .70
- ❑ 138 Christer Andersson .50 .23
- ❑ 139 Mikael Collin 1.00 .45
- ❑ 140 Bjorn Fagerlund .50 .23
- ❑ 141 Christer Grahn 1.00 .45
- ❑ 142 Kenneth Holmstedt .50 .23
- ❑ 143 Goran Hogosta 1.00 .45
- ❑ 144 Bert Jattne .50 .23
- ❑ 145 Curt Larsson .75 .35
- ❑ 146 Ivar Larsson .50 .23
- ❑ 147 Wille Lofqvist 1.00 .45
- ❑ 148 Peder Nilsson .50 .23
- ❑ 149 Christer Sehlstedt .50 .23
- ❑ 150 Krister Sterner .75 .35
- ❑ 151 Christer Stahl .50 .23
- ❑ 152 Sune Odling .50 .23
- ❑ 153 Thommy Abrahamsson 1.00 .45
- ❑ 154 Gunnar Andersson .50 .23
- ❑ 155 Jan Andersson .50 .23
- ❑ 156 Leif Andersson .50 .23
- ❑ 157 Sture Andersson .50 .23
- ❑ 158 Tommy Andersson .50 .23
- ❑ 159 Sten Ake Bark .50 .23
- ❑ 160 Roger Bergman .50 .23
- ❑ 161 Roland Bond .50 .23
- ❑ 162 Arne Carlsson .50 .23
- ❑ 163 Thomas Carlsson .50 .23
- ❑ 164 Lasse Danielsson .50 .23
- ❑ 165 Ake Danielsson .50 .23
- ❑ 166 Kenneth Ekman .50 .23
- ❑ 167 Lars Erik Esbjors .50 .23
- ❑ 168 Soren Gunnarsson .50 .23
- ❑ 169 Mats Hysing .50 .23
- ❑ 170 Bjorn Johansson .50 .23
- ❑ 171 Martin Johansson .50 .23
- ❑ 172 Jan Kock .50 .23
- ❑ 173 Hakan Lindgren .50 .23
- ❑ 174 Larsake Lundell .50 .23
- ❑ 175 Mats Lundmark .50 .23
- ❑ 176 Kjell-Rune Milton .50 .23
- ❑ 177 Jan Erik Nilsson .50 .23
- ❑ 178 Lars Goran Nilsson .50 .23
- ❑ 179 Hakan Nygren .50 .23
- ❑ 180 Jan Olsson .50 .23
- ❑ 181 Jorgen Palm .50 .23
- ❑ 182 Dennis Pettersson .50 .23
- ❑ 183 Stefan Pettersson .50 .23
- ❑ 184 Anders Rylin .50 .23
- ❑ 185 Stig Salming .75 .35
- ❑ 186 Nils-Olof Schilstrom .50 .23
- ❑ 187 Jan Erik Silfverberg .50 .23
- ❑ 188 Lars Erik Sjoberg 3.00 1.35
- ❑ 189 Karl-Johan Sundqvist .50 .23
- ❑ 190 Jan-Olof Svensson .50 .23
- ❑ 191 Leif Svensson .50 .23
- ❑ 192 Tord Svensson .50 .23
- ❑ 193 Sverker Torstensson .50 .23
- ❑ 194 Mats Waltin .50 .23
- ❑ 195 Ulf Weinstock .50 .23
- ❑ 196 Jan Ove Wiberg .50 .23
- ❑ 197 Lars Zetterstrom .50 .23
- ❑ 198 Stig Ostling .75 .35
- ❑ 199 Hans Andersson .50 .23
- ❑ 200 Kent-Erik Andersson .50 .23
- ❑ 201 Kjell Andersson .50 .23
- ❑ 202 Ulf Barrefjord .50 .23
- ❑ 203 Kent Bengtsson .50 .23
- ❑ 204 Bo Berggren .50 .23
- ❑ 205 Kjell Brus .50 .23
- ❑ 206 Per-Olof Brassar 1.50 .70
- ❑ 207 Borje Burlin .50 .23
- ❑ 208 Per Backman .50 .23
- ❑ 209 Stefan Canderyd .50 .23
- ❑ 210 Hans Carlsson .50 .23
- ❑ 211 Hakan Dahlov .50 .23
- ❑ 212 Rolf Edberg .50 .23
- ❑ 213 Ake Eklof .50 .23
- ❑ 214 Roland Eriksson .50 .23
- ❑ 215 Conny Evensson 1.00 .45
- ❑ 216 Svante Granholm .50 .23
- ❑ 217 Peter Gudmundsson .50 .23
- ❑ 218 Hans Hansson .50 .23
- ❑ 219 Anders Hedberg 4.00 1.80
- ❑ 220 Henric Hedlund .50 .23
- ❑ 221 Nils Arne Hedqvist .50 .23
- ❑ 222 Leif Henriksson .50 .23
- ❑ 223 Leif Holmgren .50 .23
- ❑ 224 Sven-Ake Jacobsson .50 .23
- ❑ 225 Hans Jax .50 .23
- ❑ 226 Christer Johansson .50 .23
- ❑ 227 Gunnar Johansson .50 .23
- ❑ 228 Lars Erik Johansson .50 .23
- ❑ 229 Stig-Goran Johansson .50 .23
- ❑ 230 Soren Johansson .50 .23
- ❑ 231 Bengt Goran Karlsson .50 .23
- ❑ 232 Bengt-Ake Karlsson .50 .23
- ❑ 233 Martin Karlsson .50 .23
- ❑ 234 Stefan Karlsson .50 .23
- ❑ 235 Jan-Olov Kroon .50 .23
- ❑ 236 Dan Labraaten 1.50 .70
- ❑ 237 Dan Landegren .50 .23
- ❑ 238 Kjell Landstrom .50 .23
- ❑ 239 Ove Larsson .50 .23
- ❑ 240 Stig Larsson .50 .23
- ❑ 241 Hans Lindberg .50 .23
- ❑ 242 Mats Lindh .50 .23
- ❑ 243 Willy Lindstrom 1.00 .45
- ❑ 244 Orjan Lindstrom .50 .23
- ❑ 245 Christer Lundberg .50 .23
- ❑ 246 Lars-Gunnar Lundberg .50 .23
- ❑ 247 Per Lundqvist .50 .23
- ❑ 248 Arne Lundstrom 1.00 .45
- ❑ 249 Fhinn Lundstrom .50 .23
- ❑ 250 Bengt Lovgren .50 .23
- ❑ 251 Ulf Martensson .50 .23
- ❑ 252 Par Marts .50 .23
- ❑ 253 Tadeusz Niedomysl .50 .23
- ❑ 254 Hardy Nilsson .50 .23
- ❑ 255 Lars Goran Nilsson .50 .23
- ❑ 256 Ulf Nilsson 4.00 1.80
- ❑ 257 Anders Nordin .50 .23
- ❑ 258 Nils-Olof Olsson .50 .23
- ❑ 259 Bjorn Palmqvist .50 .23
- ❑ 260 Kent Persson .50 .23
- ❑ 261 Hakan Pettersson .50 .23
- ❑ 262 Sven-Ake Rudby .50 .23
- ❑ 263 Benny Runesson .50 .23
- ❑ 264 Jan Roger Strand .50 .23
- ❑ 265 Ake Soderberg 1.00 .45
- ❑ 266 Dan Soderstrom .50 .23
- ❑ 267 Ulf Torstensson .50 .23
- ❑ 268 Claes Goran Wallin .50 .23
- ❑ 269 Hakan Wickberg .50 .23
- ❑ 270 Kjell Arne Wickstrom .50 .23
- ❑ 271 Per Allan Wickstrom .50 .23
- ❑ 272 Dick Yderstrom .50 .23
- ❑ 273 Mats Ahlberg .75 .35
- ❑ 274 Olle Ahman .50 .23
- ❑ 275 Lars Oberg .50 .23
- ❑ 276 Jan Ostling .50 .23
- ❑ 277 Akning .50 .23
- ❑ 278 Akning .50 .23
- ❑ 279 Akning .50 .23
- ❑ 280 Skott .50 .23
- ❑ 281 Skott .50 .23
- ❑ 282 Skott .50 .23
- ❑ 283 Puckforing .50 .23
- ❑ 284 Tekning .50 .23
- ❑ 285 Malvaktsspel 1.00 .45
- ❑ 286 Malvaktsspel 1.00 .45
- ❑ 287 Forsvarsspel .50 .23
- ❑ 288 Forsvarsspel .50 .23
- ❑ 289 Forsvarsspel .50 .23
- ❑ 290 Forsvarsspel .50 .23
- ❑ 291 Forsvarsspel .50 .23
- ❑ 292 Forsvarsspel .50 .23
- ❑ 293 Forsvarsspel .50 .23
- ❑ 294 Forsvarsspel .50 .23
- ❑ 295 Forsvarsspel .50 .23
- ❑ 296 Forsvarsspel .50 .23
- ❑ 297 Forsvarsspel .50 .23
- ❑ 298 Forsvarsspel .50 .23
- ❑ 299 Forsvarsspel .50 .23
- ❑ 300 Forsvarsspel .50 .23
- ❑ 301 Forsvarsspel .50 .23
- ❑ 302 Forsvarsspel .50 .23
- ❑ 303 Anfallsspel .50 .23
- ❑ 304 Anfallsspel .50 .23
- ❑ 305 Anfallsspel .50 .23
- ❑ 306 Anfallsspel .50 .23
- ❑ 307 Anfallsspel .50 .23
- ❑ 308 Anfallsspel .50 .23
- ❑ 309 Anfallsspel .50 .23
- ❑ 310 Anfallsspel .50 .23
- ❑ 311 Anfallsspel .50 .23
- ❑ 312 Anfallsspel .50 .23
- ❑ 313 Inge Hammarstrom 2.00 .90
- ❑ 314 Borje Salming 6.00 2.70
- ❑ 315 Thommie Bergman 2.50 1.10
- ❑ 316 Leif Holmqvist 1.00 .45
- ❑ 317 Ulf Sterner .50 .23
- ❑ 318 Tord Lundstrom .50 .23
- ❑ 319 player unknown .50 .23
- ❑ 320 player unknown .50 .23
- ❑ 321 player unknown .50 .23
- ❑ 322 player unknown .50 .23
- ❑ 323 player unknown .50 .23
- ❑ 324 player unknown .50 .23

## 1981 Swedish Semic Hockey VM Stickers

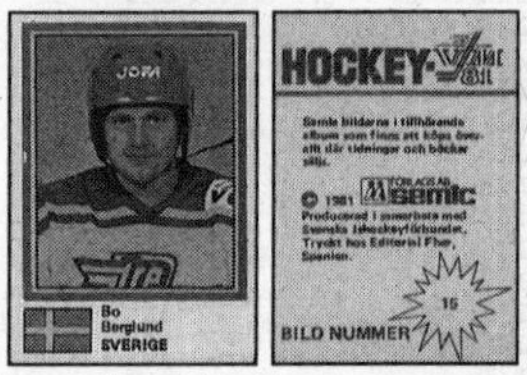


This 144-sticker set was released in conjunction with the 1981 World Championships. The stickers, which measure 3" by 2 1/8", feature a color photo on the front along with the player name, country and national flag. The backs contain the card number and a remainder to place the stickers in the special set album (which retails now in the $25 range). The set is notable for the inclusion of Glenn Anderson in his RC year, as well as Mats Naslund and Neal Broten prior to their RCs. The set also features members of the American "Miracle On Ice" Olympic team; in some cases, these are the only "legitimate" card-like elements of players such as Mike Eruzione, Buzz Schneider, etc.

| | MINT | NRMT |
|---|---|---|
| COMPLETE SET (144) | 75.00 | 34.00 |
| COMMON CARD (1-144) | .25 | .11 |

- ❑ 1 Goran Hogosta .50 .23
- ❑ 2 Tomas Jonsson .50 .23
- ❑ 3 Ulf Weinstock .25 .11
- ❑ 4 Goran Nilsson .25 .11
- ❑ 5 Jan Eriksson .25 .11
- ❑ 6 Tommy Samuelsson .25 .11
- ❑ 7 Mats Waltin .25 .11
- ❑ 8 Peter Helander .25 .11
- ❑ 9 Per Lundqvist .25 .11
- ❑ 10 Conny Silfverberg .25 .11
- ❑ 11 Mats Naslund 5.00 2.20
- ❑ 12 Lennart Norberg .25 .11
- ❑ 13 Bengt Lundholm 1.00 .45
- ❑ 14 Leif Holmgren .25 .11
- ❑ 15 Bo Berglund 1.00 .45
- ❑ 16 Dan Soderstrom .25 .11
- ❑ 17 Lars Molin .75 .35
- ❑ 18 Tore Oqvist .25 .11
- ❑ 19 Ari Hellgren .25 .11
- ❑ 20 Hannu Lassila .25 .11
- ❑ 21 Kari Eloranta 1.00 .45
- ❑ 22 Lasse Litma .25 .11
- ❑ 23 Seppo Suoraniemi .25 .11
- ❑ 24 Tapio Levo .50 .23
- ❑ 25 Timo Nummelin .25 .11
- ❑ 26 Reijo Routsalainen 1.00 .45
- ❑ 27 Markku Kiimalainen .25 .11
- ❑ 28 Mikko Leinonen .75 .35
- ❑ 29 Reijo Leppanen .25 .11
- ❑ 30 Hannu Koskinen .25 .11
- ❑ 31 Timo Susi .25 .11
- ❑ 32 Jukka Porvari .25 .11
- ❑ 33 Arto Javanainen .25 .11
- ❑ 34 Juhanni Tamminen 1.00 .45
- ❑ 35 Pertti Koivulahti .25 .11
- ❑ 36 Antero Lehtonen .25 .11
- ❑ 37 Vladislav Tretiak 10.00 4.50
- ❑ 38 Vladimir Mysjkin 1.50 .70
- ❑ 39 Vjatjeslav Fetisov 4.00 1.80
- ❑ 40 Vladimir Luttjenko .75 .35

❑ 41 Sergei Babinov .50 .23
❑ 42 Vasilij Pervuchin .75 .35
❑ 43 Sergej Starikov .75 .35
❑ 44 Zinetula Biljaletdinov .75 .35
❑ 45 Vladimir Krutov 4.00 1.80
❑ 46 Alexander Maltsev 3.00 1.35
❑ 47 Jurij Lebedev .75 .35
❑ 48 Viktor Tiumenev .50 .23
❑ 49 Nikolaj Drozdetskij .25 .11
❑ 50 Valeri Kharlamov 6.00 2.70
❑ 51 Sergej Makarov 4.00 1.80
❑ 52 Vladimir Golikov .75 .35
❑ 53 Alexander Skvortsov .50 .23
❑ 54 Michail Varnakov .75 .35
❑ 55 Jiri Kralik .50 .23
❑ 56 Jaromir Sindel 1.50 .70
❑ 57 Miroslav Dvorak .75 .35
❑ 58 Frantisek Kaberle .50 .23
❑ 59 Arnold Kadlec .50 .23
❑ 60 Jan Neliba .25 .11
❑ 61 Radoslav Svoboda .25 .11
❑ 62 Jaroslav Iycka .25 .11
❑ 63 Milan Novy 1.00 .45
❑ 64 Jaroslav Pouzar 1.00 .45
❑ 65 Miroslav Frycer 1.50 .70
❑ 66 Karel Holy .25 .11
❑ 67 Ladislav Svozil .25 .11
❑ 68 Marian Bezak .25 .11
❑ 69 Jindrich Kokrment .25 .11
❑ 70 Jiri Lala .75 .35
❑ 71 Ludos Penicka .25 .11
❑ 72 Ivan Hlinka .75 .35
❑ 73 Wayne Stephenson 2.00 .90
❑ 74 Ron Paterson .75 .35
❑ 75 Warren Anderson .75 .35
❑ 76 Brad Pirie .75 .35
❑ 77 Randy Gregg 1.50 .70
❑ 78 Tim Watters 1.00 .45
❑ 79 Joe Grant .75 .35
❑ 80 Don Spring .75 .35
❑ 81 Ron Davidson .75 .35
❑ 82 Glenn Anderson 8.00 3.60
❑ 83 Kevin Maxwell .75 .35
❑ 84 Jim Nill 1.00 .45
❑ 85 John Devaney .75 .35
❑ 86 Paul MacLean 1.50 .70
❑ 87 Dan D'Alvise .75 .35
❑ 88 Ken Berry .75 .35
❑ 89 David Hindmarch .75 .35
❑ 90 Kevin Primeau .75 .35
❑ 91 Steve Janaszak 1.50 .70
❑ 92 Bob Suter 1.00 .45
❑ 93 Ken Morrow 2.00 .90
❑ 94 Mike Ramsey 2.00 .90
❑ 95 Bill Baker 1.00 .45
❑ 96 Dave Christian 2.00 .90
❑ 97 Les Auge .75 .35
❑ 98 Dave Silk 1.50 .70
❑ 99 Neal Broten 5.00 2.20
❑ 100 Mark Johnson 2.00 .90
❑ 101 Steve Christoff 1.00 .45
❑ 102 Mark Pavelich 1.50 .70
❑ 103 Eric Strobel 1.00 .45
❑ 104 Mike Eruzione 10.00 4.50
❑ 105 Rob McClanahan 1.50 .70
❑ 106 Buzz Schneider 1.50 .70
❑ 107 Phil Verchota 1.00 .45
❑ 108 John Harrington 1.00 .45
❑ 109 Leif Holmqvist 1.00 .45
❑ 110 Kjell Svensson .75 .35
❑ 111 Roland Stoltz .25 .11
❑ 112 Bert-Ola Nordlander .25 .11
❑ 113 Nils Johansson .25 .11
❑ 114 Lennart Svedberg .50 .23
❑ 115 Ulf Sterner .25 .11
❑ 116 Hakan Wickberg .25 .11
❑ 117 Tord Lundstrom .25 .11
❑ 118 Carl-Goran Oberg .25 .11
❑ 119 Eilert Maatta .25 .11
❑ 120 Lars-Goran Nilsson .25 .11
❑ 121 Nils Nilsson .25 .11
❑ 122 Hans Oberg .25 .11
❑ 123 Lars-Erik Lundvall .25 .11
❑ 124 Sven Tumba Johansson .50 .23
❑ 125 Lars Bjorn .25 .11
❑ 126 Ronald Pettersson .25 .11
❑ 127 World Championships 1981 .25 .11
❑ 128 Sweden .25 .11
❑ 129 Finland .25 .11
❑ 130 Soviet Union .25 .11
❑ 131 CSSR .25 .11
❑ 132 Canada .75 .35
❑ 133 U.S.A. .75 .35
❑ 134 West Germany .25 .11
❑ 135 Holland .25 .11
❑ 136 Referee's Signs .25 .11
❑ 137 Referee's Signs .25 .11
❑ 138 Referee's Signs .25 .11
❑ 139 Referee's Signs .25 .11
❑ 140 Referee's Signs .25 .11
❑ 141 Referee's Signs .25 .11
❑ 142 Referee's Signs .25 .11
❑ 143 Referee's Signs .25 .11
❑ 144 Referee's Signs .25 .11

## 1982 Swedish Semic Hockey VM Stickers

This 162-sticker set was released in 1982 to commemorate the World Championships held in Helsinki and Tampere, Finland. The stickers measure 3" by 2 1/8" and feature color photos along with the player's name and emblem (national or NHL) on the front. The backs have the sticker number, along with text in both

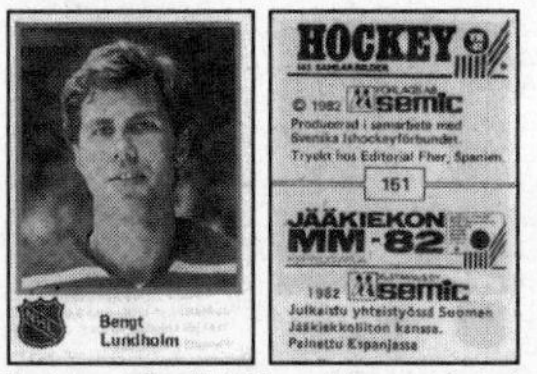


Finnish and Swedish. The set does not include any North American-born NHLers, but does have several prominent Swedish NHL stars, including Hakan Loob, Mats Naslund, and Kent Nilsson.

| | MINT | NRMT |
|---|---|---|
| COMPLETE SET (162) | 60.00 | 27.00 |
| COMMON STICKER (1-162) | .25 | .11 |

❑ 1 Peter Lindmark 1.00 .45
❑ 2 Gote Walitalo .25 .11
❑ 3 Gunnar Leidborg .25 .11
❑ 4 Goran Lindblom .25 .11
❑ 5 Thomas Eriksson .25 .11
❑ 6 Mats Waltin .25 .11
❑ 7 Jan Eriksson .25 .11
❑ 8 Mats Thelin .50 .23
❑ 9 Peter Helander .25 .11
❑ 10 Tommy Samuelsson .25 .11
❑ 11 Bo Ericsson .25 .11
❑ 12 Peter Andersson .50 .23
❑ 13 Mats Naslund 4.00 1.80
❑ 14 Ulf Isaksson .25 .11
❑ 15 Patrik Sundstrom 2.00 .90
❑ 16 Peter Sundstrom 1.50 .70
❑ 17 Thomas Rundqvist .75 .35
❑ 18 Mats Ulander .25 .11
❑ 19 Tommy Morth .25 .11
❑ 20 Ove Olsson .25 .11
❑ 21 Rolf Edberg .25 .11
❑ 22 Hakan Loob 4.00 1.80
❑ 23 Leif Holmgren 1.00 .45
❑ 24 Jan Erixon 1.50 .70
❑ 25 Harald Luckner .25 .11
❑ 26 Hannu Kamppuri 1.00 .45
❑ 27 Hannu Issila .50 .23
❑ 28 Kari Heikkila .25 .11
❑ 29 Timo Nummelin .25 .11
❑ 30 Pertti Lehtonen .25 .11
❑ 31 Raimo Hirvonen .25 .11
❑ 32 Seppo Suoraniemi .25 .11
❑ 33 Juha Huikari .25 .11
❑ 34 Hannu Helander .25 .11
❑ 35 Lasse Litma .25 .11
❑ 36 Hakan Hjerpe .25 .11
❑ 37 Kari Jalonen .50 .23
❑ 38 Arto Javanainen .50 .23
❑ 39 Jari Lindgren .25 .11
❑ 40 Markku Kiimalainen .25 .11
❑ 41 Jarmo Makitalo .25 .11
❑ 42 Jorma Sevon .25 .11
❑ 43 Erkki Laine .25 .11
❑ 44 Hannu Koskinen .25 .11
❑ 45 Reijo Leppanen .25 .11
❑ 46 Pekka Arbelius .25 .11
❑ 47 Markku Hakulinen .25 .11
❑ 48 Timo Susi .25 .11
❑ 49 Esa Peltonen .25 .11
❑ 50 Juhani Tamminen 1.00 .45
❑ 51 Vladislav Tretiak 8.00 3.60
❑ 52 Vladimir Mysjkin .75 .35
❑ 53 Vjatjeslav Fetisov 3.00 1.35
❑ 54 Sergej Babinov .50 .23
❑ 55 Vasilij Pervuchin .50 .23
❑ 56 Valerij Vasiljev .75 .35
❑ 57 Aleksej Kasatonov 2.00 .90
❑ 58 Zinetula Biljaletdinov .75 .35
❑ 59 Sergej Starikov .75 .35
❑ 60 Sergej Makarov 3.00 1.35
❑ 61 Sergej Sjepelev .75 .35
❑ 62 Vladimir Krutov 3.00 1.35
❑ 63 Nikolaj Drozdetskij .75 .35
❑ 64 Viktor Zjluktov .50 .23
❑ 65 Viktor Sjalimov .50 .23
❑ 66 Vladimir Golikov .50 .23
❑ 67 Aleksandr Maltsev 2.50 1.10
❑ 68 Andrej Chomutov 2.00 .90
❑ 69 Sergej Svetlov .50 .23
❑ 70 Helmut Balderis .75 .35
❑ 71 Sergej Kapustin .50 .23
❑ 72 Vladimir Zubkov .35 .16
❑ 73 Aleksandr Kozjevnikov .35 .16
❑ 74 Jurij Lebedev .35 .16
❑ 75 Nikolaj Makarov .35 .16
❑ 76 Jiri Kralik .35 .16
❑ 77 Karel Lang .25 .11
❑ 78 Jaromir Sindel 1.00 .45
❑ 79 Miroslav Horava .50 .23
❑ 80 Milan Chalupa .50 .23
❑ 81 Stanislav Hajdusek .25 .11
❑ 82 Arnold Kadlec .35 .16
❑ 83 Miroslav Dvorak .35 .16
❑ 84 Jan Neliba .25 .11
❑ 85 Petr Misek .25 .11
❑ 86 Eduard Uvira .25 .11
❑ 87 Milan Novy .50 .23
❑ 88 Frantisek Cerny .50 .23
❑ 89 Jiri Lala .50 .23
❑ 90 Jindrich Kokrment .25 .11
❑ 91 Frantisek Cernik .50 .23
❑ 92 Darius Rusnak .25 .11
❑ 93 Dusan Pasek .50 .23
❑ 94 Lubomir Penicka .25 .11
❑ 95 Jaroslav Korbela .25 .11
❑ 96 Peter Ihnacak 1.00 .45
❑ 97 Jaroslav Hrdina .25 .11
❑ 98 Igor Liba .50 .23
❑ 99 Peter Slania .25 .11
❑ 100 Vincent Lukac .25 .11
❑ 101 Erich Weishaupt .50 .23
❑ 102 Bernhard Engelbrecht .50 .23
❑ 103 Robert Murray .35 .16
❑ 104 Peter Gailer .25 .11
❑ 105 Udo Kiessling .50 .23
❑ 106 Harold Kreis .35 .16
❑ 107 Joachim Reil .25 .11
❑ 108 Harald Krull .25 .11
❑ 109 Ulrich Egen .25 .11
❑ 110 Marcus Kuhl .25 .11
❑ 111 Peter Schiller .25 .11
❑ 112 Erich Kuhnhackl .50 .23
❑ 113 Holger Meitinger .25 .11
❑ 114 Ernst Hofner .25 .11
❑ 115 Vladimir Vacatko .25 .11
❑ 116 Manfred Wolf .25 .11
❑ 117 Johann Morz .25 .11
❑ 118 Franz Reindl .25 .11
❑ 119 Helmut Steiger .25 .11
❑ 120 Georg Holzmann .25 .11
❑ 121 Roy Roedger .25 .11
❑ 122 Jim Corsi .75 .35
❑ 123 Nick Sanza .25 .11
❑ 124 Guido Tenisi .25 .11
❑ 125 Erwin Kostner .25 .11
❑ 126 Mike Amodeo .50 .23
❑ 127 John Bellio .25 .11
❑ 128 Dave Tomassoni .25 .11
❑ 129 Daniel Pupillo .25 .11
❑ 130 Giulio Francella .25 .11
❑ 131 Fabio Polloni .25 .11
❑ 132 Adolf Insam .25 .11
❑ 133 Patrick Dell'Jannone .25 .11
❑ 134 Rick Bragnalo .25 .11
❑ 135 Michael Mair .25 .11
❑ 136 Alberto DiFazio .25 .11
❑ 137 Cary Farelli .25 .11
❑ 138 Tom Milani .25 .11
❑ 139 Martin Pavlu .25 .11
❑ 140 Bob De Piero .25 .11
❑ 141 Grant Goegan .25 .11
❑ 142 Jerry Ciarcia .25 .11
❑ 143 Borje Salming 2.50 1.10
❑ 144 Lars Lindgren .50 .23
❑ 145 Ulf Nilsson 2.00 .90
❑ 146 Bengt-Ake Gustavsson 1.50 .70
❑ 147 Kent Nilsson 4.00 1.80
❑ 148 Thomas Gradin 3.00 1.35
❑ 149 Lars Molin .75 .35
❑ 150 Thomas Steen 3.00 1.35
❑ 151 Bengt Lundholm .75 .35
❑ 152 Jorgen Pettersson .75 .35
❑ 153 Jukka Porvari .50 .23
❑ 154 Tapio Levo .50 .23
❑ 155 Reijo Ruotsalainen .75 .35
❑ 156 Matti Hagman .75 .35
❑ 157 Risto Siltanen .75 .35
❑ 158 Ilkka Sinisalo .75 .35
❑ 159 Markus Mattsson .75 .35
❑ 160 Mikko Leinonen .50 .23
❑ 161 Pekka Rautakallio .75 .35
❑ 162 Veli-Pekka Ketola .75 .35

## 1983-84 Swedish Semic Elitserien

Card fronts feature action photos from players in the Swedish Elite League. Many players have cards in this set that predate their rookie cards.

| | MINT | NRMT |
|---|---|---|
| COMPLETE SET (243) | 60.00 | 27.00 |
| COMMON STICKER (1-243) | .25 | .11 |

❑ 1 Gunnar Leidborg .50 .23
❑ 2 Peter Aslin 1.00 .45
❑ 3 Mats Thelin .75 .35
❑ 4 Jan Eriksson .25 .11
❑ 5 Hans Cederholm .25 .11
❑ 6 Bo Ericsson .25 .11
❑ 7 Bjorn Hellman .25 .11
❑ 8 Tomas Nord .25 .11
❑ 9 Anders Wallin .25 .11
❑ 10 Mats Alba .25 .11
❑ 11 Ronny Jansson .25 .11
❑ 12 Roger Lindstrom .25 .11
❑ 13 Mats Hessel .25 .11
❑ 14 Peter Gradin .25 .11
❑ 15 Mats Ulander .25 .11
❑ 16 Per-Erik Eklund 3.00 1.35
❑ 17 Ulf Isaksson .25 .11
❑ 18 Rolf Eriksson .25 .11
❑ 19 Michael Wikstrom .25 .11
❑ 20 Leif Holmgren .25 .11
❑ 21 Per Martinelle .25 .11
❑ 22 Tommy Lehmann .75 .35
❑ 23 Hans Norberg .25 .11
❑ 24 Jan Ericsson .25 .11
❑ 25 Per Backman .25 .11
❑ 26 Gote Walitalo .25 .11
❑ 27 Jakob Gustavsson .25 .11
❑ 28 Staffan Andersson .25 .11
❑ 29 Torbjorn Andersson .25 .11
❑ 30 Anders Bostrom .25 .11
❑ 31 Jan Lindholm .25 .11
❑ 32 Ulf Nilsson 6.00 2.70
❑ 33 Par Sjolander .25 .11
❑ 34 Lennart Dahlberg .25 .11
❑ 35 Rolf Berglund .25 .11
❑ 36 Patrik Aberg .25 .11
❑ 37 Tom Eklund .25 .11
❑ 38 Stefan Nilsson .25 .11
❑ 39 Matti Pauna .25 .11
❑ 40 Jan Lundstrom .25 .11
❑ 41 Mikael Andersson 3.00 1.35
❑ 42 Hans Edlund .25 .11
❑ 43 Jon Lundstrom .25 .11
❑ 44 Tony Lundgren .25 .11
❑ 45 Ulf Wikgren .25 .11
❑ 46 Tomas Hedin .25 .11
❑ 47 Lars-Gunnar Pettersson .25 .11
❑ 48 Peter Edstrom .25 .11
❑ 49 Tore Okvist .25 .11
❑ 50 Tommy Sandlin .75 .35
❑ 51 Lars Eriksson .25 .11
❑ 52 Ake Lilljebjorn .50 .23
❑ 53 Anders Backstrom .25 .11
❑ 54 Goran Grundstrom .25 .11
❑ 55 Jan Kock .25 .11
❑ 56 Gunnar Persson .25 .11
❑ 57 Torbjorn Mattsson .25 .11
❑ 58 Stig Ostling .25 .11
❑ 59 Hans Johansson .25 .11
❑ 60 Robert Nordmark 1.00 .45
❑ 61 Mikael Sandstrom .25 .11
❑ 62 Anders Carlsson .25 .11
❑ 63 Christer Andersson .25 .11
❑ 64 Per Hedenstrom .25 .11
❑ 65 Bjorn Akerblom .25 .11
❑ 66 Conny Silfverberg .25 .11
❑ 67 Jonny Stridh .25 .11
❑ 68 Goran Sjoberg .25 .11
❑ 69 Kenneth Andersson .25 .11
❑ 70 Fredrik Lundstrom .25 .11
❑ 71 Henrik Cedergren .25 .11
❑ 72 Tomas Sandstrom 5.00 2.20
❑ 73 Anders Huss .25 .11
❑ 74 Stig Salming .50 .23
❑ 75 Rolf Ridderwall 1.00 .45
❑ 76 Bo Larsson .25 .11
❑ 77 Mikael Westling .25 .11
❑ 78 Tord Nansen .25 .11
❑ 79 Tommy Albelin 2.00 .90
❑ 80 Orvar Stambert .25 .11
❑ 81 Karl-Erik Lilja .25 .11
❑ 82 Mats Waltin .25 .11
❑ 83 Stefan Perlstrom .25 .11
❑ 84 Michael Thelven 1.00 .45
❑ 85 Stefan Jansson .25 .11
❑ 86 Jens Ohling .25 .11
❑ 87 Peter Nilsson .25 .11
❑ 88 Hakan Eriksson .25 .11
❑ 89 Jorgen Holmberg .25 .11
❑ 90 Tommy Morth .25 .11
❑ 91 Jan Claesson .25 .11
❑ 92 Per Goransson .25 .11
❑ 93 Martin Linse .25 .11
❑ 94 Bjorn Carlsson .25 .11
❑ 95 Hakan Sodergren .25 .11
❑ 96 Anders Johnsson .25 .11
❑ 97 Jan Viktorsson .50 .23
❑ 98 Jeff Hallegard .25 .11
❑ 99 Leif Boork .25 .11
❑ 100 Hakan Hermansson .25 .11
❑ 101 Thomas Blom .25 .11
❑ 102 Christer Dalgard .25 .11
❑ 103 Tommy Samuelsson .25 .11
❑ 104 Lars-Goran Nilsson .25 .11
❑ 105 Peter Andersson 1.00 .45
❑ 106 Mats Lusth .25 .11
❑ 107 Tommy Moller .25 .11
❑ 108 Leif Carlsson .25 .11
❑ 109 Urban Larsson .25 .11
❑ 110 Hakan Nordin .25 .11
❑ 111 Harald Luckner .25 .11
❑ 112 Thomas Rundqvist 1.50 .70
❑ 113 Kjell Dahlin 2.00 .90
❑ 114 Robin Eriksson .25 .11
❑ 115 Jan Ingman .25 .11
❑ 116 Stefan Persson .25 .11
❑ 117 Peter Berndtsson .25 .11
❑ 118 Anders Eriksson .25 .11
❑ 119 Claes-Henrik Silfver .25 .11
❑ 120 Magnus Roupe 1.00 .45
❑ 121 Jan Wickberg .25 .11
❑ 122 Dan Mohlin .25 .11
❑ 123 Kent Olsson .25 .11
❑ 124 Stefan Lunner .25 .11
❑ 125 Niklas Holmberg .25 .11
❑ 126 Anders Alverud .25 .11
❑ 127 Stefan Svensson .25 .11
❑ 128 Lars Karlsson .25 .11
❑ 129 Ulf Weinstock .25 .11
❑ 130 Kjell Samuelsson 4.00 1.80
❑ 131 Magnus Svensson 1.00 .45
❑ 132 Ove Pettersson .25 .11
❑ 133 Hans Eriksson .25 .11
❑ 134 Ulf Samuelsson 5.00 2.20
❑ 135 Roland Eriksson .25 .11
❑ 136 Kjell Bond .25 .11
❑ 137 Per Nordlinder .25 .11
❑ 138 Ivan Hansen .25 .11
❑ 139 Sivert Andersson .25 .11
❑ 140 Jonas Bergkvist 1.00 .45
❑ 141 Per-Olof Carlsson .25 .11
❑ 142 Dan Labraaten 1.50 .70
❑ 143 Ulf Skoglund .25 .11
❑ 144 Ove Olsson .25 .11
❑ 145 Mikael Leek .25 .11
❑ 146 Mats Loov .25 .11
❑ 147 Lennart Ahlberg .25 .11
❑ 148 Hardy Astrom 4.00 1.80
❑ 149 Anders Bergman .25 .11
❑ 150 Per Forsberg .25 .11
❑ 151 Sture Andersson .25 .11
❑ 152 Mikael Good .25 .11
❑ 153 Jan Nyman .25 .11
❑ 154 Roger Eliasson .25 .11
❑ 155 Jan Karlsson .25 .11
❑ 156 Lennart Jonsson .25 .11
❑ 157 Robert Frestadius .25 .11
❑ 158 Juha Tuohimaa .25 .11
❑ 159 Jerry Lundberg .25 .11
❑ 160 Tommy Sjalin .25 .11
❑ 161 Ulf Norberg .25 .11
❑ 162 Michael Hjalm .25 .11
❑ 163 Per Nilsson .25 .11
❑ 164 Lars Nyberg .25 .11
❑ 165 Ulf Odmark .25 .11
❑ 166 Ingemar Strom .25 .11
❑ 167 Erik Holmberg .25 .11
❑ 168 Lars Bystrom .25 .11
❑ 169 Lars Hellstrom .25 .11
❑ 170 Henry Saleva .25 .11
❑ 171 Hardy Nilsson .25 .11
❑ 172 Mats Abrahamsson .25 .11
❑ 173 Ulf Nilsson 6.00 2.70
❑ 174 Jens Johansson .25 .11
❑ 175 Lars Marklund .25 .11
❑ 176 Robert Ohman .25 .11
❑ 177 Goran Lindblom .25 .11
❑ 178 Ola Stenlund .25 .11
❑ 179 Ulf Agren .25 .11
❑ 180 Thomas Ahlen .25 .11
❑ 181 Tomas Jonsson 2.00 .90
❑ 182 Mikael Granstedt .25 .11
❑ 183 Mats Lundstrom .25 .11
❑ 184 Per Andersson .25 .11
❑ 185 Johnny Forsman .25 .11
❑ 186 Lars Nystrom .25 .11
❑ 187 Niklas Mannberg .25 .11
❑ 188 Peter Lundmark 1.50 .70
❑ 189 Claes Lindblom .25 .11
❑ 190 Leif Hedlund .25 .11
❑ 191 Roland Stoltz .25 .11
❑ 192 Martin Pettersson .25 .11
❑ 193 Jorgen Marklund .25 .11
❑ 194 Mats Lundstrom .25 .11
❑ 195 Tommy Andersson .25 .11
❑ 196 Ake Andersson .25 .11
❑ 197 Lars Fernqvist .25 .11
❑ 198 Anders Eldebrink 1.00 .45
❑ 199 Ulf Borg .25 .11
❑ 200 Mats Kihlstrom .75 .35
❑ 201 Bo Andersson .25 .11
❑ 202 Peter Ekroth .25 .11
❑ 203 Jukka Hirsimaki .25 .11
❑ 204 Stefan Jonsson .25 .11
❑ 205 Peter Loob .50 .23
❑ 206 Tomas Jernberg .25 .11
❑ 207 Dan Hermansson .25 .11
❑ 208 Glenn Johansson .25 .11
❑ 209 Leif R. Carlsson .25 .11
❑ 210 Johan Mellstrom .25 .11
❑ 211 Tomas Gustavsson .25 .11
❑ 212 Olof Johansson .25 .11
❑ 213 Peter Wallin .25 .11
❑ 214 Hans Sarkijarvi .25 .11
❑ 215 Reine Karlsson .25 .11
❑ 216 Conny Jansson .25 .11
❑ 217 Jarmo Makitalo .25 .11
❑ 218 Mikael Johansson .25 .11
❑ 219 Timo Lahtinen .25 .11
❑ 220 Goran Nilsson .25 .11
❑ 221 Joakim Hokegard .25 .11
❑ 222 Peter Pettersson .25 .11
❑ 223 Goran Nilsson .25 .11
❑ 224 Jan Carlsson .25 .11
❑ 225 Soren Johansson .25 .11
❑ 226 Thomas Lundin .25 .11
❑ 227 Calle Johansson 2.00 .90
❑ 228 Anders Brostrom .25 .11
❑ 229 Stefan Larsson .25 .11
❑ 230 Thomas Karrbrandt .25 .11
❑ 231 Roger Hagglund .25 .11
❑ 232 Christer Kellgren .25 .11
❑ 233 Kent Eriksson .25 .11
❑ 234 Mikael Andersson 3.00 1.35
❑ 235 Ove Karlsson .25 .11
❑ 236 Peter Elander .25 .11
❑ 237 Hans Jonsson .25 .11
❑ 238 Hasse Sjoo .25 .11
❑ 239 Ulf Labraaten .25 .11
❑ 240 Jens Hellgren .25 .11
❑ 241 Roger Ahsberg .25 .11
❑ 242 Kurt Carlsson .25 .11
❑ 243 Peter Gustavsson .25 .11

## 1984-85 Swedish Semic Elitserien

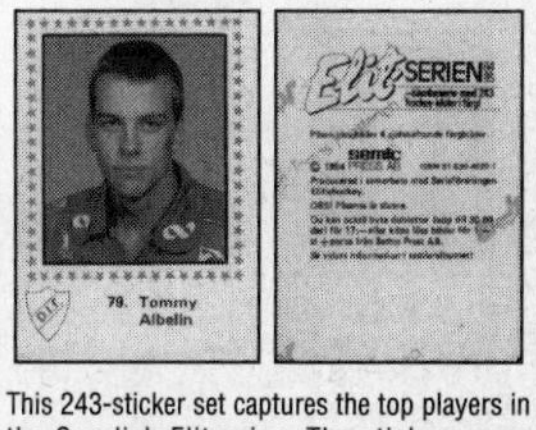


This 243-sticker set captures the top players in the Swedish Elitserien. The stickers were produced by Semic Press AB, and measure approximately 3" by 2 1/4". The fronts display a color portrait along with player name, card number and team emblem. The backs have ordering information for the set album (valued at $10) and more stickers.

| | MINT | NRMT |
|---|---|---|
| COMPLETE SET (243) | 40.00 | 18.00 |
| COMMON CARD (1-243) | .25 | .11 |
| ❑ 1 Gunnar Leidborg | .50 | .23 |
| ❑ 2 Thomas Ostlund | 2.00 | .90 |
| ❑ 3 Jan Eriksson | .25 | .11 |
| ❑ 4 Tomas Nord | .25 | .11 |
| ❑ 5 Bjorn Hellman | .25 | .11 |
| ❑ 6 Hans Cederholm | .25 | .11 |
| ❑ 7 Mats Alba | .25 | .11 |
| ❑ 8 Roger Hellgren | .25 | .11 |
| ❑ 9 Peter Zetterholm | .25 | .11 |
| ❑ 10 Tony Bartelsson | .25 | .11 |
| ❑ 11 Roger Lindstrom | .25 | .11 |
| ❑ 12 Mats Hessel | .25 | .11 |
| ❑ 13 Peter Gradin | .25 | .11 |
| ❑ 14 Per-Erik Eklund | 2.00 | .90 |
| ❑ 15 Ulf Isaksson | .25 | .11 |
| ❑ 16 Harri Tiala | .25 | .11 |
| ❑ 17 Michael Wikstrom | .25 | .11 |
| ❑ 18 Per Backe | .25 | .11 |
| ❑ 19 Per Martinelle | .25 | .11 |
| ❑ 20 Tommy Lehmann | .50 | .23 |
| ❑ 21 Hans Norberg | .25 | .11 |
| ❑ 22 Odd Nilsson | .25 | .11 |
| ❑ 23 Henrik Cedergren | .25 | .11 |
| ❑ 24 Stefan Sandin | .25 | .11 |
| ❑ 25 Per Backman | .25 | .11 |
| ❑ 26 Gote Walitalo | .25 | .11 |
| ❑ 27 Jakob Gustavsson | .25 | .11 |
| ❑ 28 Torbjorn Andersson | .25 | .11 |
| ❑ 29 Anders Bostrom | .25 | .11 |
| ❑ 30 Jan Lindholm | .25 | .11 |
| ❑ 31 Lars Karlsson | .25 | .11 |
| ❑ 32 Rolf Berglund | .25 | .11 |
| ❑ 33 Lennart Dahlberg | .25 | .11 |
| ❑ 34 Patric Aberg | .25 | .11 |
| ❑ 35 Ulf Nilsson | 4.00 | 1.80 |
| ❑ 36 Mats Jacobsson | .25 | .11 |
| ❑ 37 Michael Hjalm | .25 | .11 |
| ❑ 38 Stefan Nilsson | .25 | .11 |
| ❑ 39 Matti Pauna | .25 | .11 |
| ❑ 40 Jan Lundstrom | .25 | .11 |
| ❑ 41 Mikael Andersson | 2.00 | .90 |
| ❑ 42 Hans Edlund | .25 | .11 |
| ❑ 43 Jon Lundstrom | .25 | .11 |
| ❑ 44 Tony Lundgren | .25 | .11 |
| ❑ 45 Ulf Wikgren | .25 | .11 |
| ❑ 46 Thomas Hedin | .25 | .11 |
| ❑ 47 Lars-Gunnar Pettersson | .25 | .11 |
| ❑ 48 Peter Edstrom | .25 | .11 |
| ❑ 49 Tommy Sandlin | .50 | .23 |
| ❑ 50 Lars Eriksson | .25 | .11 |
| ❑ 51 Ake Lilljebjorn | .50 | .23 |
| ❑ 52 Mats Kihlstrom | .50 | .23 |
| ❑ 53 Anders Backstrom | .25 | .11 |
| ❑ 54 Lars Ivarsson | 1.00 | .45 |
| ❑ 55 Jan Kock | .25 | .11 |
| ❑ 56 Gunnar Persson | .25 | .11 |
| ❑ 57 Torbjorn Mattsson | .25 | .11 |
| ❑ 58 Per Jarnberg | .25 | .11 |
| ❑ 59 Hans Johansson | .25 | .11 |
| ❑ 60 Anders Huss | .25 | .11 |
| ❑ 61 Per Nilsson | .25 | .11 |
| ❑ 62 Owe Eriksson | .25 | .11 |
| ❑ 63 Christer Andersson | .25 | .11 |
| ❑ 64 Per Hedenstrom | .25 | .11 |
| ❑ 65 Jan Larsson | .25 | .11 |
| ❑ 66 Conny Silfverberg | .25 | .11 |
| ❑ 67 Jonny Stridh | .25 | .11 |
| ❑ 68 Erik Holmberg | .25 | .11 |
| ❑ 69 Kenneth Andersson | .25 | .11 |
| ❑ 70 Fredrik Lundstrom | .25 | .11 |
| ❑ 71 Peter Eriksson | .25 | .11 |
| ❑ 72 Peter Eriksson | .25 | .11 |
| ❑ 73 Stig Salming | .50 | .23 |
| ❑ 74 Rolf Ridderwall | 1.00 | .45 |
| ❑ 75 Mats Ytter | .25 | .11 |
| ❑ 76 Michael Thelven | .75 | .35 |
| ❑ 77 Stefan Perlstrom | .25 | .11 |
| ❑ 78 Tord Nansen | .25 | .11 |
| ❑ 79 Tommy Albelin | 2.00 | .90 |
| ❑ 80 Orvar Stambert | .25 | .11 |
| ❑ 81 Karl-Erik Lilja | .25 | .11 |
| ❑ 82 Kristian Henriksson | .25 | .11 |
| ❑ 83 Arto Blomsten | .75 | .35 |
| ❑ 84 Anders Johnsson | .25 | .11 |
| ❑ 85 Pontus Molander | .25 | .11 |
| ❑ 86 Jens Ohling | .25 | .11 |
| ❑ 87 Peter Nilsson | .25 | .11 |
| ❑ 88 Hakan Sodergren | .25 | .11 |
| ❑ 89 Jorgen Holmberg | .25 | .11 |
| ❑ 90 Tommy Morth | .25 | .11 |
| ❑ 91 Jan Claesson | .25 | .11 |
| ❑ 92 Per Goransson | .25 | .11 |
| ❑ 93 Jan Viktorsson | .50 | .23 |
| ❑ 94 Bjorn Carlsson | .25 | .11 |
| ❑ 95 Erik Ahlstrom | .25 | .11 |
| ❑ 96 Peter Schank | .25 | .11 |
| ❑ 97 Ake Eksell | .25 | .11 |
| ❑ 98 Gunnar Svensson | .25 | .11 |
| ❑ 99 Peter Lindmark | .25 | .11 |
| ❑ 100 Christer Dalgard | .25 | .11 |
| ❑ 101 Hakan Nordin | .25 | .11 |
| ❑ 102 Fredrik Olausson | 3.00 | 1.35 |
| ❑ 103 Tommy Samuelsson | .25 | .11 |
| ❑ 104 Anders Svensson | .25 | .11 |
| ❑ 105 Peter Andersson | .75 | .35 |
| ❑ 106 Mats Lusth | .25 | .11 |
| ❑ 107 Tommy Moller | .25 | .11 |
| ❑ 108 Leif Carlsson | .25 | .11 |
| ❑ 109 Kent-Erik Andersson | .25 | .11 |
| ❑ 110 Erkki Laine | .25 | .11 |
| ❑ 111 Harald Luckner | .25 | .11 |
| ❑ 112 Staffan Lundh | .25 | .11 |
| ❑ 113 Kjell Dahlin | 2.00 | .90 |
| ❑ 114 Dan Mohlin | .25 | .11 |
| ❑ 115 Jan Ingman | .25 | .11 |
| ❑ 116 Stefan Persson | 1.00 | .45 |
| ❑ 117 Peter Berndtsson | .25 | .11 |
| ❑ 118 Lars Karlsson | .25 | .11 |
| ❑ 119 Claes-Henrik Silfver | .25 | .11 |
| ❑ 120 Magnus Roupe | .75 | .35 |
| ❑ 121 Conny Evensson | .75 | .35 |
| ❑ 122 Bo Larsson | .25 | .11 |
| ❑ 123 Hans-Goran Elo | .25 | .11 |
| ❑ 124 Carsten Bokstrom | .25 | .11 |
| ❑ 125 Claes Norstrom | .25 | .11 |
| ❑ 126 Alf Tornqvist | .25 | .11 |
| ❑ 127 Bruno Ohlzon | .25 | .11 |
| ❑ 128 Peter Lindgren | .25 | .11 |
| ❑ 129 Christian Due-Boije | .50 | .23 |
| ❑ 130 Tony Landeskog | .25 | .11 |
| ❑ 131 Tomas Lunden | .25 | .11 |
| ❑ 132 Lars Lindskog | .25 | .11 |
| ❑ 133 Anders Karlsson | .25 | .11 |
| ❑ 134 Morgan Craas | .25 | .11 |
| ❑ 135 Ulf Andersson | .25 | .11 |
| ❑ 136 Timo Salomaa | .25 | .11 |
| ❑ 137 Ulf Radbjer | .25 | .11 |
| ❑ 138 Hans Segerberg | .25 | .11 |
| ❑ 139 Roger Melin | .25 | .11 |
| ❑ 140 Rolf Edberg | .25 | .11 |
| ❑ 141 Lasse Bjork | .25 | .11 |
| ❑ 142 Robin Eriksson | .25 | .11 |
| ❑ 143 Thomas Jagenstedt | .25 | .11 |
| ❑ 144 Jan Lindberg | .25 | .11 |
| ❑ 145 Bjorn Berggren | .25 | .11 |
| ❑ 146 Tommy Nilsson | .25 | .11 |
| ❑ 147 Stefan Lunner | .25 | .11 |
| ❑ 148 Niklas Holmberg | .25 | .11 |
| ❑ 149 Anders Alverud | .25 | .11 |
| ❑ 150 Stefan Svensson | .25 | .11 |
| ❑ 151 Jussi Lepisto | .25 | .11 |
| ❑ 152 Kjell Samuelsson | 4.00 | 1.80 |
| ❑ 153 Magnus Svensson | .75 | .35 |
| ❑ 154 Ove Pettersson | .25 | .11 |
| ❑ 155 Stefan Nilsson | .25 | .11 |
| ❑ 156 Jens Christiansson | .25 | .11 |
| ❑ 157 Orjan Lindmark | .25 | .11 |
| ❑ 158 Tomas Gustafsson | .25 | .11 |
| ❑ 159 Jan Segersten | .25 | .11 |
| ❑ 160 Jonas Bergqvist | 1.00 | .45 |
| ❑ 161 Per-Olof Carlsson | .25 | .11 |
| ❑ 162 Hannu Oksanen | .25 | .11 |
| ❑ 163 Dan Labraaten | 1.50 | .70 |
| ❑ 164 Ulf Skoglund | .25 | .11 |
| ❑ 165 Ove Olsson | .25 | .11 |
| ❑ 166 Mats Loov | .25 | .11 |
| ❑ 167 Hakan Olsson | .25 | .11 |
| ❑ 168 Carl-Erik Larsson | .25 | .11 |
| ❑ 169 Dan Soderstrom | .25 | .11 |
| ❑ 170 Mats Blomqvist | .25 | .11 |
| ❑ 171 Robert Skoog | .25 | .11 |
| ❑ 172 Lars Lindgren | .25 | .11 |
| ❑ 173 Robert Nordmark | .75 | .35 |
| ❑ 174 Kjell-Ake Johansson | .25 | .11 |
| ❑ 175 Kari Heikkila | .25 | .11 |
| ❑ 176 Torbjorn Wirf | .25 | .11 |
| ❑ 177 Lars Modig | .25 | .11 |
| ❑ 178 Bo Eriksson | .25 | .11 |
| ❑ 179 Roger Ohman | .75 | .35 |
| ❑ 180 Mats Ohman | .25 | .11 |
| ❑ 181 Matti Ruisma | .25 | .11 |
| ❑ 182 Erik Stalnacke | .25 | .11 |
| ❑ 183 Jari Lindgren | .25 | .11 |
| ❑ 184 Jens Hellgren | .25 | .11 |
| ❑ 185 Lars-Goran Niemi | .25 | .11 |
| ❑ 186 Tore Okvist | .25 | .11 |
| ❑ 187 Ingemar Mikko | .25 | .11 |
| ❑ 188 Roger Mikko | .25 | .11 |
| ❑ 189 Rolf Karlsson | .25 | .11 |
| ❑ 190 Petter Antti | .25 | .11 |
| ❑ 191 Johan Stromvall | .25 | .11 |
| ❑ 192 Tomas Backstrom | .25 | .11 |
| ❑ 193 Jan Nilsson | .25 | .11 |
| ❑ 194 Freddy Lindfors | .25 | .11 |
| ❑ 195 Mats Abrahamsson | .25 | .11 |
| ❑ 196 Ulf Nilsson | 4.00 | 1.80 |
| ❑ 197 Goran Lindblom | .25 | .11 |
| ❑ 198 Thomas Ahlen | .25 | .11 |
| ❑ 199 Jens Johansson | .25 | .11 |
| ❑ 200 Lars Marklund | .25 | .11 |
| ❑ 201 Ola Stenlund | .25 | .11 |
| ❑ 202 Ulf Lindblom | .25 | .11 |
| ❑ 203 Olle Haggstrom | .25 | .11 |
| ❑ 204 Ulf Agren | .25 | .11 |
| ❑ 205 Mikael Granstedt | .25 | .11 |
| ❑ 206 Hans Nilsson | .25 | .11 |
| ❑ 207 Per Andersson | .25 | .11 |
| ❑ 208 Jonny Forsman | .25 | .11 |
| ❑ 209 Lars Nystrom | .25 | .11 |
| ❑ 210 Niklas Mannberg | .25 | .11 |
| ❑ 211 Peter Lundmark | 1.00 | .45 |
| ❑ 212 Claes Lindblom | .25 | .11 |
| ❑ 213 Leif Hedlund | .25 | .11 |
| ❑ 214 Roland Stoltz | .25 | .11 |
| ❑ 215 Martin Pettersson | .25 | .11 |
| ❑ 216 Jorgen Marklund | .25 | .11 |
| ❑ 217 Mats Lundstrom | .25 | .11 |
| ❑ 218 Tommy Andersson | .25 | .11 |
| ❑ 219 Mats Astrom | 3.00 | 1.35 |
| ❑ 220 Sam Lindstahl | .75 | .35 |
| ❑ 221 Jari Luoma | .25 | .11 |
| ❑ 222 Anders Eldebrink | .75 | .35 |
| ❑ 223 Ulf Borg | .25 | .11 |
| ❑ 224 Bo Ericson | .25 | .11 |
| ❑ 225 Tomas Jernberg | .25 | .11 |
| ❑ 226 Peter Ekroth | .25 | .11 |
| ❑ 227 Stefan Jonsson | .25 | .11 |
| ❑ 228 Niklas Gallstedt | .25 | .11 |
| ❑ 229 Jonas Heed | .25 | .11 |
| ❑ 230 Jarmo Makitalo | .25 | .11 |
| ❑ 231 Thom Eklund | .25 | .11 |
| ❑ 232 Dan Hermansson | .25 | .11 |
| ❑ 233 Glenn Johansson | .25 | .11 |
| ❑ 234 Leif R. Carlsson | .25 | .11 |
| ❑ 235 Johan Mellstrom | .25 | .11 |
| ❑ 236 Niclas Lindgren | .25 | .11 |
| ❑ 237 Peter Wallin | .25 | .11 |
| ❑ 238 Hans Sarkijarvi | .25 | .11 |
| ❑ 239 Anders Carlsson | .25 | .11 |
| ❑ 240 Reine Karlsson | .25 | .11 |
| ❑ 241 Conny Jansson | .25 | .11 |
| ❑ 242 Stefan Karlsson | .25 | .11 |
| ❑ 243 Timo Lahtinen | .25 | .11 |

## 1985-86 Swedish Panini Stickers

This set of 240 stickers was produced by Panini Italy for distribution in Sweden. The stickers feature the top players of the Swedish elite league and were packaged five per pack. The 2 1/2" by 2" stickers feature a player portrait on the front. An album for housing the stickers also was available; it now trades in the $10 range. North American collectors may not rave about the player selection, but some of Sweden's best are represented including Peter Lindmark, Tomas Rundqvist and Anders Eldebrink.

| | MINT | NRMT |
|---|---|---|
| COMPLETE SET (240) | 60.00 | 27.00 |
| COMMON CARD (1-240) | .25 | .11 |
| ❑ 1 AIK Team Emblem | .25 | .11 |
| ❑ 2 Per Backman | .25 | .11 |
| ❑ 3 Tomas Ostlund | 2.00 | .90 |
| ❑ 4 Gunnar Leidborg | .25 | .11 |
| ❑ 5 Jari Munck | .25 | .11 |
| ❑ 6 Jan Eriksson | .25 | .11 |
| ❑ 7 Hans Cederholm | .25 | .11 |
| ❑ 8 Bjorn Hellman | .25 | .11 |
| ❑ 9 Tomas Ahlen | .25 | .11 |
| ❑ 10 Roger Hellgren | .25 | .11 |
| ❑ 11 Mats Alba | .25 | .11 |
| ❑ 12 Roger Lindstrom | .25 | .11 |
| ❑ 13 Team Picture Left | .25 | .11 |
| ❑ 14 Team Picture Right | .25 | .11 |
| ❑ 15 Mats Hessel | .25 | .11 |
| ❑ 16 Peter Gradin | .25 | .11 |
| ❑ 17 Thomas Bjuhr | .25 | .11 |
| ❑ 18 Per Martinelle | .25 | .11 |
| ❑ 19 Tommy Lehman | .50 | .23 |
| ❑ 20 Thomas Jagenstedt | .25 | .11 |
| ❑ 21 Hans Segerberg | .25 | .11 |
| ❑ 22 Odd Nilsson | .25 | .11 |
| ❑ 23 Bjorkloven Team Picture | .25 | .11 |
| ❑ 24 Bjorkloven Team Picture | .25 | .11 |
| ❑ 25 Jakob Gustavsson | .25 | .11 |
| ❑ 26 Gote Walitalo | .25 | .11 |
| ❑ 27 Torbjorn Andersson | .25 | .11 |
| ❑ 28 Jan Lindholm | .25 | .11 |
| ❑ 29 Lars Karlsson | .25 | .11 |
| ❑ 30 Calle Johansson | 3.00 | 1.35 |
| ❑ 31 Ulf Nilsson | 3.00 | 1.35 |
| ❑ 32 Rolf Berglund | .25 | .11 |
| ❑ 33 Matti Pauna | .25 | .11 |
| ❑ 34 Mikael Andersson | 2.00 | .90 |
| ❑ 35 Tommy Sandlin | .25 | .11 |
| ❑ 36 Team Emblem | .25 | .11 |
| ❑ 37 Hans Edlund | .25 | .11 |
| ❑ 38 Ulf Dahlen | 4.00 | 1.80 |
| ❑ 39 Mikael Hjalm | .25 | .11 |
| ❑ 40 Jon Lundstrom | .25 | .11 |
| ❑ 41 Lars-Gunnar Pettersson | .25 | .11 |
| ❑ 42 Peter Edstrom | .25 | .11 |
| ❑ 43 Tore Oqvist | .25 | .11 |
| ❑ 44 Par Edlund | .25 | .11 |
| ❑ 45 Brynas Team Emblem | .25 | .11 |
| ❑ 46 Stig Salming | .25 | .11 |
| ❑ 47 Lars Eriksson | .25 | .11 |
| ❑ 48 Ake Lilljebjorn | .25 | .11 |
| ❑ 49 Anders Backstrom | .25 | .11 |
| ❑ 50 Lars Ivarsson | .25 | .11 |
| ❑ 51 Mats Kihlstrom | .25 | .11 |
| ❑ 52 Jan Ove Mettavainio | .25 | .11 |
| ❑ 53 Gunnar Persson | .25 | .11 |
| ❑ 54 Torbjorn Mattsson | .25 | .11 |
| ❑ 55 Christer Andersson | .25 | .11 |
| ❑ 56 Per Hedenstrom | .25 | .11 |
| ❑ 57 Team Picture L | .25 | .11 |
| ❑ 58 Team Picture R | .25 | .11 |
| ❑ 59 Per Nilsson | .25 | .11 |
| ❑ 60 Conny Silfverberg | .25 | .11 |
| ❑ 61 Jonny Stridh | .25 | .11 |
| ❑ 62 Owe Eriksson | .25 | .11 |
| ❑ 63 Kenneth Andersson | .25 | .11 |
| ❑ 64 Erik Holmberg | .25 | .11 |
| ❑ 65 Joakim Pehrson | .25 | .11 |
| ❑ 66 Anders Huss | .50 | .23 |
| ❑ 67 Djurgarden Team Picture L | .25 | .11 |
| ❑ 68 Djurgarden Team Picture R | .25 | .11 |
| ❑ 69 Rolf Ridderwall | 1.00 | .45 |
| ❑ 70 Mats Ytter | .50 | .23 |
| ❑ 71 Orvar Stambert | .25 | .11 |
| ❑ 72 Karl-Erik Lilja | .25 | .11 |
| ❑ 73 Arto Blomsten | .50 | .23 |
| ❑ 74 Stefan Perlstrom | .25 | .11 |
| ❑ 75 Peter Lindgren | .25 | .11 |
| ❑ 76 Tommy Albelin | .75 | .35 |
| ❑ 77 Jens Ohling | .25 | .11 |
| ❑ 78 Peter Nilsson | .25 | .11 |
| ❑ 79 Gunnar Svenson | .25 | .11 |
| ❑ 80 Team Emblem | .25 | .11 |
| ❑ 81 Jorgen Holmberg | .25 | .11 |
| ❑ 82 Tommy Morth | .25 | .11 |
| ❑ 83 Bjorn Carlsson | .25 | .11 |
| ❑ 84 Hakan Sodergren | .50 | .23 |
| ❑ 85 Anders Johnson | .25 | .11 |
| ❑ 86 Mikael Johansson | .25 | .11 |
| ❑ 87 Jan Viktorsson | .25 | .11 |
| ❑ 88 Erik Ahlstrom | .25 | .11 |
| ❑ 89 Farjestad Team Emblem | .25 | .11 |
| ❑ 90 Conny Evensson | .50 | .23 |
| ❑ 91 Peter Lindmark | 1.50 | .70 |
| ❑ 92 Christer Dalgard | .25 | .11 |
| ❑ 93 Tommy Samuelsson | .25 | .11 |
| ❑ 94 Peter Andersson | .75 | .35 |
| ❑ 95 Mats Lusth | .25 | .11 |
| ❑ 96 Leif Karlsson | .25 | .11 |
| ❑ 97 Fredrik Olausson | 1.00 | .45 |
| ❑ 98 Hakan Nordin | .25 | .11 |
| ❑ 99 Harald Luckner | .25 | .11 |
| ❑ 100 Tomas Rundqvist | .50 | .23 |
| ❑ 101 Team Picture L | .25 | .11 |
| ❑ 102 Team Picture R | .25 | .11 |
| ❑ 103 Jan Ingman | .25 | .11 |
| ❑ 104 Erkki Laine | .25 | .11 |
| ❑ 105 Stefan Persson | 1.00 | .45 |
| ❑ 106 Claes-Henrik Silfver | .25 | .11 |
| ❑ 107 Magnus Roupe | .75 | .35 |
| ❑ 108 Mikael Holmberg | .25 | .11 |
| ❑ 109 Kent-Erik Andersson | .25 | .11 |
| ❑ 110 Staffan Lundh | .25 | .11 |
| ❑ 111 Kjell Dahlin Upper | .50 | .23 |
| ❑ 112 Kjell Dahlin Lower | .50 | .23 |
| ❑ 113 Kjell Samuelsson U | 1.00 | .45 |
| ❑ 114 Kjell Samuelsson L | 1.00 | .45 |
| ❑ 115 Peter Lindmark U | .50 | .23 |
| ❑ 116 Peter Lindmark L | .50 | .23 |
| ❑ 117 Pelle Lindberg U | 10.00 | 4.50 |
| ❑ 118 Pelle Lindberg L | 10.00 | 4.50 |
| ❑ 119 Per-Erik Eklund U | .75 | .35 |
| ❑ 120 Per-Erik Eklund L | .75 | .35 |
| ❑ 121 Anders Eldebrink L | .35 | .16 |
| ❑ 122 Anders Eldebrink R | .35 | .16 |
| ❑ 123 Michael Thelven U | .35 | .16 |
| ❑ 124 Michael Thelvin L | .35 | .16 |
| ❑ 125 Dan Labraaten L | .50 | .23 |
| ❑ 126 Dan Labraaten R | .50 | .23 |
| ❑ 127 Ove Olsson L | .25 | .11 |
| ❑ 128 Ove Olsson R | .25 | .11 |
| ❑ 129 Kent-E Andersson L | .25 | .11 |
| ❑ 130 Kent-E Andersson R | .25 | .11 |
| ❑ 131 Leksand Team Emblem | .25 | .11 |
| ❑ 132 Dan Soderstrom | .25 | .11 |
| ❑ 133 Stefan Lunner | .25 | .11 |
| ❑ 134 Peter Aslin | 1.00 | .45 |
| ❑ 135 Jussi Lepisto | .25 | .11 |
| ❑ 136 Magnus Svensson | .75 | .35 |
| ❑ 137 Owe Pettersson | .25 | .11 |
| ❑ 138 Stefan Nilsson | .25 | .11 |
| ❑ 139 Orjan Lindmark | .25 | .11 |
| ❑ 140 Tomas Nord | .25 | .11 |
| ❑ 141 Robert Burakovsky | .50 | .23 |
| ❑ 142 Jan Segersten | .25 | .11 |
| ❑ 143 Team Picture L | .25 | .11 |
| ❑ 144 Team Picture R | .25 | .11 |
| ❑ 145 Jonas Bergkvist | .75 | .35 |
| ❑ 146 Per-Olof Carlsson | .25 | .11 |
| ❑ 147 Dan Labraaten | 1.00 | .45 |
| ❑ 148 Ulf Skoglund | .25 | .11 |
| ❑ 149 Ove Olsson | .25 | .11 |
| ❑ 150 Heinz Ehlers | .25 | .11 |
| ❑ 151 Mats Loov | .25 | .11 |
| ❑ 152 Jarmo Makitalo | .25 | .11 |
| ❑ 153 Lulea Team Picture L | .25 | .11 |
| ❑ 154 Lulea Team Picture R | .25 | .11 |
| ❑ 155 Mats Blomqvist | .25 | .11 |
| ❑ 156 Robert Skoog | .25 | .11 |
| ❑ 157 Lars Modig | .25 | .11 |
| ❑ 158 Kjell-A Johansson | .25 | .11 |
| ❑ 159 Bo Eriksson | .25 | .11 |
| ❑ 160 Robert Nordmark | .50 | .23 |
| ❑ 161 Kari Heikkila | .25 | .11 |
| ❑ 162 Lars Lindgren | .25 | .11 |
| ❑ 163 Roger Mikko | .25 | .11 |
| ❑ 164 Kari Jaako | .25 | .11 |
| ❑ 165 Hans Lindberg | .25 | .11 |
| ❑ 166 Team Emblem | .25 | .11 |
| ❑ 167 Petter Antti | .25 | .11 |
| ❑ 168 Johan Stromvall | .25 | .11 |
| ❑ 169 Juha Nurmi | .25 | .11 |
| ❑ 170 Erik Stalnacke | .25 | .11 |
| ❑ 171 Lars Hurtig | .25 | .11 |
| ❑ 172 Jari Lindgren | .25 | .11 |
| ❑ 173 Jens Hellgren | .25 | .11 |
| ❑ 174 Hans Norberg | .25 | .11 |
| ❑ 175 HV 71 Team Emblem | .25 | .11 |
| ❑ 176 Curt Lundmark | .75 | .35 |
| ❑ 177 Kenneth Johansson | .25 | .11 |
| ❑ 178 Tomas Javeblad | .25 | .11 |
| ❑ 179 Nils-G Svensson | .25 | .11 |
| ❑ 180 Bert-Roland Naslund | .25 | .11 |
| ❑ 181 Kevan Beaton | .25 | .11 |
| ❑ 182 Jan Hedell | .25 | .11 |
| ❑ 183 Fredrik Stillman | .35 | .16 |
| ❑ 184 Kari Eloranta | .75 | .35 |
| ❑ 185 Klas Heed | .25 | .11 |
| ❑ 186 Hans Sallin | .25 | .11 |
| ❑ 187 Team Picture L | .25 | .11 |
| ❑ 188 Team Picture R | .25 | .11 |
| ❑ 189 Ove Tornberg | .25 | .11 |
| ❑ 190 Thomas Ljungberg | .25 | .11 |
| ❑ 191 Bengt Kinell | .25 | .11 |
| ❑ 192 Roland Eriksson | .25 | .11 |
| ❑ 193 Uno Johansson | .25 | .11 |
| ❑ 194 Ivan Hansen | .25 | .11 |
| ❑ 195 Thomas Lindster | .25 | .11 |
| ❑ 196 Per Martinsson | .25 | .11 |
| ❑ 197 MoDo Team Picture L | .25 | .11 |
| ❑ 198 MoDo Team Picture R | .25 | .11 |
| ❑ 199 Anders Bergman | .25 | .11 |
| ❑ 200 Goran Arnmark | .25 | .11 |
| ❑ 201 Thomas Olofsson | .25 | .11 |
| ❑ 202 Jorgen Palm | .25 | .11 |
| ❑ 203 Ulf Agren | .25 | .11 |
| ❑ 204 Roger Eliasson | .25 | .11 |
| ❑ 205 Juha Tuohimaa | .25 | .11 |
| ❑ 206 Jan Karlsson | .25 | .11 |
| ❑ 207 Lennart Jonsson | .25 | .11 |
| ❑ 208 Ulf Norberg | .25 | .11 |
| ❑ 209 Hakan Nygren | .25 | .11 |
| ❑ 210 Team Emblem | .25 | .11 |
| ❑ 211 Hakan Hjarpe | .25 | .11 |
| ❑ 212 Anders Wikberg | .25 | .11 |
| ❑ 213 P-A Alexandersson | .25 | .11 |
| ❑ 214 Ingemar Strom | .25 | .11 |
| ❑ 215 Tommy Eriksson | .25 | .11 |
| ❑ 216 Lars Molin | .50 | .23 |
| ❑ 217 Lars Bystrom | .25 | .11 |
| ❑ 218 Pekka Arbelius | .25 | .11 |
| ❑ 219 Sodertalje Team Emblem | .25 | .11 |
| ❑ 220 Kjell Larsson | .25 | .11 |
| ❑ 221 Sam Lindstal | .25 | .11 |
| ❑ 222 Hardy Astrom | 1.00 | .45 |
| ❑ 223 Anders Eldebrink | .75 | .35 |
| ❑ 224 Niklas Gallstedt | .25 | .11 |
| ❑ 225 Jonas Heed | .25 | .11 |
| ❑ 226 Peter Ekroth | .25 | .11 |
| ❑ 227 Bo Eriksson | .25 | .11 |
| ❑ 228 Stefan Jonsson | .25 | .11 |
| ❑ 229 Thom Eklund | .25 | .11 |
| ❑ 230 Glenn Johansson | .25 | .11 |
| ❑ 231 Team Picture L | .25 | .11 |
| ❑ 232 Team Picture R | .25 | .11 |
| ❑ 233 Leif Carlsson | .25 | .11 |
| ❑ 234 Jan Claesson | .25 | .11 |
| ❑ 235 Niclas Lindgren | .25 | .11 |
| ❑ 236 Peter Wallin | .25 | .11 |
| ❑ 237 Hans Sarkijarvi | .25 | .11 |
| ❑ 238 Reine Karlsson | .25 | .11 |
| ❑ 239 Conny Jansson | .25 | .11 |
| ❑ 240 Anders Carlsson | .25 | .11 |

## 1986-87 Swedish Panini Stickers

This 270-sticker set features the top players in Sweden for the '86-87 season. The stickers -- which measure approximately 2 1/2" by 2" -- were produced by Panini in Italy. The fronts feature a portrait along with name and team logo. The backs are numbered and include information about completing the set and the available album (valued at $10).The set is short on recognizable names, but does include early apperances by Ulf Dahlen and Calle Johansson, among others.

| | MINT | NRMT |
|---|---|---|
| COMPLETE SET (270) | 45.00 | 20.00 |
| COMMON CARD (1-270) | .25 | .11 |
| ❑ 1 Bjorkloven Team Emblem | .25 | .11 |
| ❑ 2 Hans Lindberg | .25 | .11 |
| ❑ 3 Gote Walitalo | .25 | .11 |
| ❑ 4 Jakob Gustavsson | .25 | .11 |
| ❑ 5 Torbjorn Andersson | .25 | .11 |
| ❑ 6 Lars Karlsson | .25 | .11 |
| ❑ 7 Calle Johansson | 3.00 | 1.35 |
| ❑ 8 Rolf Berglund | .25 | .11 |
| ❑ 9 Patrik Aberg | .25 | .11 |
| ❑ 10 Niclas Holmgren | .25 | .11 |
| ❑ 11 Roger Hagglund | .25 | .11 |
| ❑ 12 Team Picture Left | .25 | .11 |
| ❑ 13 Team Picture Right | .25 | .11 |
| ❑ 14 Peter Andersson | .75 | .35 |
| ❑ 15 Tore Oqvist | .25 | .11 |
| ❑ 16 Johan Tornqvist | .25 | .11 |
| ❑ 17 Par Edlund | .25 | .11 |
| ❑ 18 Stefan Nilsson | .25 | .11 |
| ❑ 19 Matti Pauna | .25 | .11 |
| ❑ 20 Lars-Gunnar Pettersson | .25 | .11 |
| ❑ 21 Mikael Hjalm | .25 | .11 |
| ❑ 22 Hans Edlund | .25 | .11 |
| ❑ 23 Peter Sundstrom | 1.00 | .45 |
| ❑ 24 Jon Lundstrom | .25 | .11 |
| ❑ 25 Peter Edstrom | .25 | .11 |
| ❑ 26 Mikael Andersson | 2.50 | 1.10 |
| ❑ 27 Ulf Dahlen | 3.00 | 1.35 |
| ❑ 28 Brynas Team Emblem | .25 | .11 |
| ❑ 29 Stig Salming | .25 | .11 |
| ❑ 30 Ake Lilljebjorn | .25 | .11 |
| ❑ 31 Lars Eriksson | .25 | .11 |
| ❑ 32 Christer Lundqvist | .25 | .11 |
| ❑ 33 Lars Ivarsson | .25 | .11 |
| ❑ 34 Torbjorn Mattsson | .25 | .11 |
| ❑ 35 Gunnar Persson | .25 | .11 |
| ❑ 36 Anders Backstrom | .25 | .11 |
| ❑ 37 Team Picture L | .25 | .11 |
| ❑ 38 Team Picture R | .25 | .11 |
| ❑ 39 Jan Ove Mettavainio | .25 | .11 |

❑ 40 Par Djoos .50 .23
❑ 41 Tommy Sjodin 1.50 .70
❑ 42 Conny Silfverberg .25 .11
❑ 43 Christer Andersson .25 .11
❑ 44 Kenneth Andersson .25 .11
❑ 45 Lars Andersson .25 .11
❑ 46 Anders Huss .25 .11
❑ 47 Joakim Pehrson .25 .11
❑ 48 Jonny Stridh .25 .11
❑ 49 Patrik Eriksson .25 .11
❑ 50 Anders Ivarsson .25 .11
❑ 51 Mikael Lindholm .25 .11
❑ 52 Jan Larsson .25 .11
❑ 53 Peter Eriksson .25 .11
❑ 54 Jan Gronberg .25 .11
❑ 55 Djurgarden Team Emblem .25 .11
❑ 56 Leif Boork .25 .11
❑ 57 Rolf Ridderwall 1.00 .45
❑ 58 Hans-Goran Elo .25 .11
❑ 59 Tommy Albelin 1.00 .45
❑ 60 Orvar Stambert .25 .11
❑ 61 Tomas Eriksson .25 .11
❑ 62 Stefan Perlstrom .25 .11
❑ 63 Arto Blomsten .50 .23
❑ 64 Christian Due-Boije .50 .23
❑ 65 Kalle Lilja .25 .11
❑ 66 Team Picture L .25 .11
❑ 67 Team Picture R .25 .11
❑ 68 Stefan Jansson .25 .11
❑ 69 Hakan Sodergren .25 .11
❑ 70 Jens Ohling .25 .11
❑ 71 Peter Nilsson .25 .11
❑ 72 Tommy Morth .25 .11
❑ 73 Bjorn Carlsson .25 .11
❑ 74 Per Goransson .25 .11
❑ 75 Pontus Molander .25 .11
❑ 76 Jeff Hallegard .25 .11
❑ 77 Tomaz Eriksson .25 .11
❑ 78 Mikael Johansson .25 .11
❑ 79 Anders Johnson .25 .11
❑ 80 Jan Viktorsson .25 .11
❑ 81 Johan Garpenlov 3.00 1.35
❑ 82 Farjestad Team Emblem .25 .11
❑ 83 Conny Evensson .50 .23
❑ 84 Peter Lindmark 1.00 .45
❑ 85 Christer Dalgard .25 .11
❑ 86 Tommy Samuelsson .25 .11
❑ 87 Mats Lusth .25 .11
❑ 88 Peter Andersson .25 .11
❑ 89 Hakan Nordin .25 .11
❑ 90 Leif Carlsson .25 .11
❑ 91 Team Picture L .25 .11
❑ 92 Team Picture R .25 .11
❑ 93 Patrik Lundback .25 .11
❑ 94 Anders Berglund .25 .11
❑ 95 Roger Johansson .25 .11
❑ 96 Thomas Rundqvist .50 .23
❑ 97 Harald Luckner .25 .11
❑ 98 Erkki Laine .25 .11
❑ 99 Jan Ingman .25 .11
❑ 100 Staffan Lund .25 .11
❑ 101 Claes-Henrik Silfver .25 .11
❑ 102 Magnus Roupe .50 .23
❑ 103 Stefan Persson 1.00 .45
❑ 104 Daniel Rydmark .25 .11
❑ 105 Bo Svanberg .25 .11
❑ 106 Mikael Holmberg .25 .11
❑ 107 Tomas Tallberg .25 .11
❑ 108 Kjell Augustsson .25 .11
❑ 109 HV 71 Team Emblem .25 .11
❑ 110 Curt Lundmark .50 .23
❑ 111 Thomas Javeblad .25 .11
❑ 112 Kenneth Johansson .25 .11
❑ 113 Kari Eloranta .75 .35
❑ 114 Jan Hedell .25 .11
❑ 115 Arto Routanen .25 .11
❑ 116 Klas Heed .25 .11
❑ 117 Bert-Roland Naslund .25 .11
❑ 118 Nils-Gunnar Svensson .25 .11
❑ 119 Fredrik Stillman .25 .11
❑ 120 Team Picture L .25 .11
❑ 121 Team Picture R .25 .11
❑ 122 Nicklas Carlsson .25 .11
❑ 123 Ivan Hansen .25 .11
❑ 124 Thomas Ljungberg .25 .11
❑ 125 Peter Eriksson .25 .11
❑ 126 Hans Wallin .25 .11
❑ 127 Ove Thornberg .25 .11
❑ 128 Per Martinsson .25 .11
❑ 129 Mats Loov .25 .11
❑ 130 Stefan Nilsson .25 .11
❑ 131 Peter Eriksson .25 .11
❑ 132 Thomas Lindster .25 .11
❑ 133 Boo Peterzen .25 .11
❑ 134 Stefan Falk .25 .11
❑ 135 Torgny Karlsson .25 .11
❑ 136 Leksand Team Emblem .25 .11
❑ 137 Kalle Alander .25 .11
❑ 138 Peter Aslin .75 .35
❑ 139 Bengt-Ake Pers .25 .11
❑ 140 Magnus Svensson .50 .23
❑ 141 Ove Pettersson .25 .11
❑ 142 Stefan Nilsson .25 .11
❑ 143 Jens Christiansson .25 .11
❑ 144 Leif Eriksson .25 .11
❑ 145 Team Picture L .25 .11
❑ 146 Team Picture R .25 .11
❑ 147 Orjan Lindmark .25 .11
❑ 148 Thomas Nord .25 .11
❑ 149 Peter Imhauser .25 .11
❑ 150 Dan Labraaten 1.00 .45
❑ 151 Ulf Skoglund .25 .11
❑ 152 Jarmo Makitalo .25 .11
❑ 153 Per-Olof Carlsson .25 .11
❑ 154 Ove Olsson .25 .11
❑ 155 Heinz Ehlers .25 .11
❑ 156 Jonas Bergqvist .50 .23
❑ 157 Robert Burakovsky .50 .23
❑ 158 Carl-Erik Larsson .25 .11
❑ 159 Cenneth Soderlund .25 .11
❑ 160 Ola Sundberg .25 .11
❑ 161 Ronny Reichenberg .25 .11
❑ 162 Hans Jax .25 .11
❑ 163 Lulea Team Emblem .25 .11
❑ 164 Freddy Lindfors .25 .11
❑ 165 Mats Blomqvist .25 .11
❑ 166 Robert Skoog .25 .11
❑ 167 Robert Nordmark .50 .23
❑ 168 Lars Lindgren .25 .11
❑ 169 Lars Modig .25 .11
❑ 170 Bo Eriksson .25 .11
❑ 171 Kjell-Ake Johansson .25 .11
❑ 172 Roger Akerstrom .25 .11
❑ 173 Juha Tuohimaa .25 .11
❑ 174 Team Picture L .25 .11
❑ 175 Team Picture R .25 .11
❑ 176 Mats Ohman .25 .11
❑ 177 Erik Stalnacke .25 .11
❑ 178 Juha Nurmi .25 .11
❑ 179 Lars-Goran Niemi .25 .11
❑ 180 Hans Norberg .25 .11
❑ 181 Jari Lindgren .25 .11
❑ 182 Roger Mikko .25 .11
❑ 183 Lars Hurtig .25 .11
❑ 184 Johan Stromvall .25 .11
❑ 185 Jens Hellgren .25 .11
❑ 186 Kari Jaako .25 .11
❑ 187 Stefan Nilsson .25 .11
❑ 188 Ulf Taavola .25 .11
❑ 189 Tomas Edstrom .25 .11
❑ 190 MoDo Team Emblem .25 .11
❑ 191 Hakan Nygren .25 .11
❑ 192 Anders Bergman .25 .11
❑ 193 Fredrik Andersson .25 .11
❑ 194 Robert Frestadius .25 .11
❑ 195 Jouko Narvanmaa .25 .11
❑ 196 Jan Asplund .25 .11
❑ 197 Ulf Agren .25 .11
❑ 198 Jorgen Palm .25 .11
❑ 199 Team Picture L .25 .11
❑ 200 Team Picture R .25 .11
❑ 201 Per Forsberg .25 .11
❑ 202 Jens Johansson .25 .11
❑ 203 Hans Lodin .25 .11
❑ 204 Lars Molin .25 .11
❑ 205 Per-Arne Alexandersson .25 .11
❑ 206 Pecka Arbelius .25 .11
❑ 207 Per Nilsson .25 .11
❑ 208 Anders Wikberg .25 .11
❑ 209 Lars Bystrom .25 .11
❑ 210 Ulf Odmark .25 .11
❑ 211 Robert Tedenby .25 .11
❑ 212 Kent Lantz .25 .11
❑ 213 Ulf Sandstrom .25 .11
❑ 214 Mikael Pettersson .25 .11
❑ 215 Peter Smedberg .25 .11
❑ 216 Mikael Stahl .25 .11
❑ 217 Skelleftea Team Emblem .25 .11
❑ 218 Christer Abrahamsson 1.00 .45
❑ 219 Mats Abrahamsson .25 .11
❑ 220 Ulf Nilsson 2.50 1.10
❑ 221 Goran Lindblom .25 .11
❑ 222 Lars Marklund .25 .11
❑ 223 Ola Stenlund .25 .11
❑ 224 Serge Roy .50 .23
❑ 225 Mikael Lindman .25 .11
❑ 226 Robert Larsson .25 .11
❑ 227 Stefan Svensson .25 .11
❑ 228 Team Picture L .25 .11
❑ 229 Team Picture R .25 .11
❑ 230 Roland Stoltz .25 .11
❑ 231 Martin Pettersson .25 .11
❑ 232 Jonny Forsman .25 .11
❑ 233 Tomas Hedin .25 .11
❑ 234 Mikael Granstedt .25 .11
❑ 235 Randy Heath .25 .11
❑ 236 Peter Lundmark .75 .35
❑ 237 Niklas Mannberg .25 .11
❑ 238 Claes Lindblom .50 .23
❑ 239 Mats Lundmark .25 .11
❑ 240 Jorgen Marklund .25 .11
❑ 241 Daniel Pettersson .25 .11
❑ 242 Mats Lundstrom .25 .11
❑ 243 Hans Hjalmar .25 .11
❑ 244 Sodertalje Team Emblem .25 .11
❑ 245 Dan Hober .25 .11
❑ 246 Sam Lindstahl .25 .11
❑ 247 Reino Sundberg .25 .11
❑ 248 Anders Eldebrink .50 .23
❑ 249 Mats Kihlstrom .25 .11
❑ 250 Ulf Borg .25 .11
❑ 251 Bo Ericsson .25 .11
❑ 252 Peter Ekroth .25 .11
❑ 253 Team Picture L .25 .11
❑ 254 Team Picture R .25 .11
❑ 255 Jonas Heed .25 .11
❑ 256 Stefan Jonsson .25 .11
❑ 257 Hans Pettersson .25 .11
❑ 258 Hans Sarkijarvi .25 .11
❑ 259 Thom Eklund .25 .11
❑ 260 Glenn Johansson .25 .11
❑ 261 Peter Loob .25 .11
❑ 262 Niklas Lindgren .25 .11
❑ 263 Conny Jansson .25 .11
❑ 264 Tomas Jernberg .25 .11
❑ 265 Reine Karlsson .25 .11
❑ 266 Anders Frykbo .25 .11
❑ 267 Jan Loob .25 .11
❑ 268 Peter Larsson .25 .11
❑ 269 Erik Holmberg .25 .11
❑ 270 Jorgen Winborg .25 .11

## 1987-88 Swedish Panini Stickers

This 270-sticker set features the top players from the Elitserien. The stickers -- which measure approximately 2 1/2" by 2" -- wer produced by Panini in Italy. The fronts feature a portrait along with player name and team logo. The backs are numbered and contain information about completing the set and acquiring a collector's album (valued now at about $10).

| | MINT | NRMT |
|---|---|---|
| COMPLETE SET (270) | 40.00 | 18.00 |
| COMMON STICKER (1-270) | .25 | .11 |

❑ 1 AIK Team Emblem .25 .11
❑ 2 AIK Team Picture Left .25 .11
❑ 3 AIK Team Picture Right .25 .11
❑ 4 Lars-Gunnar Jansson .25 .11
❑ 5 Ake Liljebjorn .25 .11
❑ 6 Thomas Ostlund 1.00 .45
❑ 7 Jan Eriksson .25 .11
❑ 8 Hans Cederholm .25 .11
❑ 9 Rickard Franzen .35 .16
❑ 10 Thomas Ahlen .25 .11
❑ 11 Mats Thelin .50 .23
❑ 12 Bjorn Hellman .25 .11
❑ 13 Peter Gradin .50 .23
❑ 14 Bjorn Carlsson .25 .11
❑ 15 Anders Gozzi .25 .11
❑ 16 Per Martinelle .25 .11
❑ 17 Bo Berglund .50 .23
❑ 18 Thomas Gradin 1.00 .45
❑ 19 Hans Segerberg .25 .11
❑ 20 Odd Nilsson .25 .11
❑ 21 Mats Hessel .25 .11
❑ 22 IF Bjorkloven Team Emblem .25 .11
❑ 23 IF Bjorkloven .25 .11
Team Picture Left
❑ 24 IF Bjorkloven .25 .11
Team Picture Right
❑ 25 Rolf Jager .25 .11
❑ 26 Gote Walitalo .25 .11
❑ 27 Staffan Andersson .25 .11
❑ 28 Torbjorn Andersson .25 .11
❑ 29 Lars Karlsson .25 .11
❑ 30 Roger Hagglund .25 .11
❑ 31 Rolf Berglund .25 .11
❑ 32 Peter Andersson .25 .11
❑ 33 Age Ellingsen .25 .11
❑ 34 Matti Pauna .25 .11
❑ 35 Tore Oqvist .25 .11
❑ 36 Mikael Andersson 1.50 .70
❑ 37 Hans Edlund .25 .11
❑ 38 Johan Tornqvist .25 .11
❑ 39 Peter Edstrom .25 .11
❑ 40 Par Edlund .25 .11
❑ 41 Erik Kristiansen .25 .11
❑ 42 Ulf Andersson .25 .11
❑ 43 Brynas IF Team Emblem .25 .11
❑ 44 Brynas IF Team Picture Left .25 .11
❑ 45 Brynas IF Team Picture Right .25 .11
❑ 46 Tord Lundstrom .25 .11
❑ 47 Lars Eriksson .25 .11
❑ 48 Michael Sundlov .75 .35
❑ 49 Lars Ivarsson .25 .11
❑ 50 Par Djoos .50 .23
❑ 51 Jan Ove Mettavainio .25 .11
❑ 52 Anders Backstrom .25 .11
❑ 53 Gunnar Persson .25 .11
❑ 54 Christer Andersson .25 .11
❑ 55 Conny Silfverberg .25 .11
❑ 56 Jonny Stridh .25 .11
❑ 57 Kyosti Karjalainen .50 .23
❑ 58 Willy Lindstrom .75 .35
❑ 59 Joakim Pehrson .25 .11
❑ 60 Patrik Erickson .25 .11
❑ 61 Anders Huss .25 .11
❑ 62 Peter Eriksson .25 .11
❑ 63 Jan Larsson .25 .11
❑ 64 Djurgardens IF Team Emblem .25 .11
❑ 65 Djurgardens IF .25 .11
Team Picture Left
❑ 66 Djurgardens IF .25 .11
Team Picture Right
❑ 67 Ingvar Karlsson .25 .11
❑ 68 Rolf Ridderwall .75 .35
❑ 69 Hans-Goran Elo .25 .11
❑ 70 Orvar Stambert .25 .11
❑ 71 Kalle Lilja .25 .11
❑ 72 Arto Blomsten .50 .23
❑ 73 Stefan Jansson .25 .11
❑ 74 Tomas Eriksson .25 .11
❑ 75 Christian Due-Boije .50 .23
❑ 76 Jens Ohling .25 .11
❑ 77 Pontus Molander .25 .11
❑ 78 Tommy Morth .25 .11
❑ 79 Johan Garpenlov 2.00 .90
❑ 80 Hakan Sodergren .25 .11
❑ 81 Anders Johnson .25 .11
❑ 82 Mikael Johansson .25 .11
❑ 83 Jan Viktorsson .35 .16
❑ 84 Peter Nilsson .25 .11
❑ 85 Farjestads BK Team Emblem .25 .11
❑ 86 Farjestads BK .25 .11
Team Picture Left
❑ 87 Farjestads BK .25 .11
Team Picture Right
❑ 88 Per Backman .25 .11
❑ 89 Peter Lindmark .75 .35
❑ 90 Christer Dalgard .25 .11
❑ 91 Tommy Samuelsson .25 .11
❑ 92 Peter Andersson .25 .11
❑ 93 Mats Lusth .25 .11
❑ 94 Leif Carlsson .25 .11
❑ 95 Jesper Duus .25 .11
❑ 96 Hakan Nordin .25 .11
❑ 97 Thomas Rundqvist .50 .23
❑ 98 Staffan Lund .25 .11
❑ 99 Harald Luckner .25 .11
❑ 100 Erkki Laine .25 .11
❑ 101 Stefan Persson .75 .35
❑ 102 Bo Svanberg .25 .11
❑ 103 Claes-Henrik Silfver .25 .11
❑ 104 Mikael Holmberg .25 .11
❑ 105 Roger Johansson .25 .11
❑ 106 HV 71 Team Emblem .25 .11
❑ 107 HV 71 Team Picture Left .25 .11
❑ 108 HV 71 Team Picture Right .25 .11
❑ 109 Curt Lundmark .50 .23
❑ 110 Kenneth Johansson .25 .11
❑ 111 Boo Peterzen .25 .11
❑ 112 Arto Routanen .25 .11
❑ 113 Jan Hedell .25 .11
❑ 114 Fredrik Stillman .25 .11
❑ 115 Reijo Ruotsalainen 1.00 .45
❑ 116 Bert-Roland Naslund .25 .11
❑ 117 Peter Eriksson .25 .11
❑ 118 Hans Wallin .25 .11
❑ 119 Peter Berndtsson .25 .11
❑ 120 Mats Loov .25 .11
❑ 121 Thomas Lindster .25 .11
❑ 122 Peter Eriksson .25 .11
❑ 123 Hasse Sjoo .25 .11
❑ 124 Stefan Nilsson .25 .11
❑ 125 Stefan Falk .25 .11
❑ 126 Ove Thornberg .25 .11
❑ 127 Wash Out .25 .11
❑ 128 Butt-Ending .25 .11
❑ 129 Fordrojd Signal .25 .11
❑ 130 Hakning .25 .11
❑ 131 Charging .25 .11
❑ 132 Olampligt Upptradande .25 .11
❑ 133 Fasthallning .25 .11
❑ 134 Hog Klubba .25 .11
❑ 135 Tripping .25 .11
❑ 136 Cross Checking .25 .11
❑ 137 Armbagstackling .25 .11
❑ 138 Icing .25 .11
❑ 139 Icing .25 .11
❑ 140 Boarding .25 .11
❑ 141 Slashing .25 .11
❑ 142 Roughing .25 .11
❑ 143 Spearing .25 .11
❑ 144 Interference .25 .11
❑ 145 Leksands IF Team Emblem .25 .11
❑ 146 Leksands IF Team Picture Left .25 .11
❑ 147 Leksands IF .25 .11
Team Picture Right
❑ 148 Christer Abrahamsson .75 .35
❑ 149 Peter Aslin .50 .23
❑ 150 Bengt-Ake Pers .25 .11
❑ 151 Magnus Svensson .50 .23
❑ 152 Stefan Nilsson .25 .11
❑ 153 Orjan Lindmark .25 .11
❑ 154 Thomas Nord .25 .11
❑ 155 Peter Imhauser .25 .11
❑ 156 Stefan Larsson .25 .11
❑ 157 Robert Burakovsky .50 .23
❑ 158 Jonas Bergqvist .50 .23
❑ 159 Heinz Ehlers .25 .11
❑ 160 Ivan Hansen .25 .11
❑ 161 Jarmo Makitalo .25 .11
❑ 162 Dan Labraaten .75 .35
❑ 163 Per-Olof Carlsson .25 .11
❑ 164 Carl-Erik Larsson .25 .11
❑ 165 Ulf Skoglund .25 .11
❑ 166 Lulea Hockey Team Emblem .25 .11
❑ 167 Lulea Hockey .25 .11
Team Picture Left
❑ 168 Lulea Hockey .25 .11
Team Picture Right
❑ 169 Freddy Lindfors .25 .11
❑ 170 Tomas Javeblad .25 .11
❑ 171 Robert Skoog .25 .11
❑ 172 Juha Tuohimaa .25 .11
❑ 173 Bo Eriksson .25 .11
❑ 174 Roger Akerstrom .25 .11
❑ 175 Lars Lindgren .25 .11
❑ 176 Lars Modig .25 .11
❑ 177 Erik Stalnacke .25 .11
❑ 178 Johan Stromvall .25 .11
❑ 179 Juha Nurmi .25 .11
❑ 180 Lars-Goran Niemi .25 .11
❑ 181 Jari Lindgren .25 .11
❑ 182 Lars-Gunnar Pettersson .25 .11
❑ 183 Hans Norberg .25 .11
❑ 184 Kari Jaako .25 .11
❑ 185 Lars Hurtig .25 .11
❑ 186 Jens Hellgren .25 .11
❑ 187 MoDo Hockey Team Emblem .25 .11
❑ 188 MoDo Hockey .25 .11
Team Picture Left
❑ 189 MoDo Hockey .25 .11
Team Picture Right
❑ 190 Anders Nordin .25 .11
❑ 191 Anders Bergman .25 .11
❑ 192 Fredrik Andersson .25 .11
❑ 193 Hans Lodin .25 .11
❑ 194 Jens Johansson .25 .11
❑ 195 Juouko Narvanmaa .25 .11
❑ 196 Robert Frestadius .25 .11
❑ 197 Per Forsberg .25 .11
❑ 198 Mikael Hjalm .25 .11
❑ 199 Ulf Sandstrom .25 .11
❑ 200 Ulf Odmark .25 .11
❑ 201 Per Nilsson .25 .11
❑ 202 Anders Wikberg .25 .11
❑ 203 Lars Molin .50 .23
❑ 204 Per-Arne Alexandersson .25 .11
❑ 205 Lars Bystrom .25 .11
❑ 206 Mikael Stahl .25 .11
❑ 207 Ove Pettersson .25 .11
❑ 208 Skelleftea Hockey Team .25 .11
Emblem
❑ 209 Skelleftea Hockey Team .25 .11
Picture Left
❑ 210 Skelleftea Hockey Team .25 .11
Picture Right
❑ 211 Tommie Bergman .75 .35
❑ 212 Ulf Nilsson 2.00 .90
❑ 213 Sam Lindstahl .25 .11
❑ 214 Lars Marklund .25 .11
❑ 215 Goran Lindblom .25 .11
❑ 216 Ola Stenlund .25 .11
❑ 217 Stefan Svensson .25 .11
❑ 218 Kari Suoraniemi .25 .11
❑ 219 Hans Hjalmar .25 .11
❑ 220 Mikael Granstedt .25 .11
❑ 221 Mats Lundstrom .25 .11
❑ 222 Jonny Forsman .25 .11
❑ 223 Kari Jalonen .50 .23
❑ 224 Claes Lindblom .50 .23
❑ 225 Tomas Hedin .25 .11
❑ 226 Martin Pettersson .25 .11
❑ 227 Jorgen Marklund .25 .11
❑ 228 Niklas Mannberg .25 .11
❑ 229 Sodertalje SK Team Emblem .25 .11
❑ 230 Sodertalje SK .25 .11
Team Picture Left
❑ 231 Sodertalje SK .25 .11
Team Picture Right
❑ 232 John Pettersson .25 .11
❑ 233 Reino Sundberg .25 .11
❑ 234 Jari Luoma .25 .11
❑ 235 Anders Eldebrink .50 .23
❑ 236 Mats Kihlstrom .25 .11
❑ 237 Jonas Heed .25 .11
❑ 238 Bo Ericsson .35 .16
❑ 239 Ulf Borg .25 .11
❑ 240 Stefan Jonsson .25 .11
❑ 241 Mats Hallin .25 .11
❑ 242 Glenn Johansson .25 .11
❑ 243 Thomas Ljungberg .25 .11
❑ 244 Hans Sarkijarvi .25 .11
❑ 245 Thom Eklund .25 .11
❑ 246 Peter Larsson .25 .11
❑ 247 Conny Jansson .25 .11
❑ 248 Niklas Lindgren .25 .11
❑ 249 Reine Karlsson .25 .11
❑ 250 Vasby IK Team Emblem .25 .11
❑ 251 Vasby IK Team Picture Left .25 .11
❑ 252 Vasby IK Team Picture Right .25 .11
❑ 253 Anders Jacobsen .25 .11
❑ 254 Jorgen Larsson .25 .11
❑ 255 Stefan Sohlin .25 .11
❑ 256 Torbjorn Mattsson .25 .11
❑ 257 Hakan Persson .25 .11
❑ 258 Kenneth Lindqvist .25 .11
❑ 259 Jens Mackegard .25 .11
❑ 260 Jens Mackegard .25 .11
❑ 261 Mats Edholm .25 .11
❑ 262 Mats Poppler .25 .11
❑ 263 Claes Gustafsson .25 .11
❑ 264 Per Bergman .25 .11
❑ 265 Peter Wallen .25 .11
❑ 266 Hans-Rickard Andersson .25 .11
❑ 267 Arto Heinola .25 .11
❑ 268 Mats Lindberg .25 .11
❑ 269 Urban Jakobsson .25 .11
❑ 270 Stefan Sandin .25 .11

## 1989 Swedish Semic World Championship Stickers

This 200-sticker set captures some of the players who have represented their country at the World Championships. The stickers, which came in packs of five, measure 3" by 2 1/8" and feature color photos, along with player name, card number and national flag. The backs contain an ad for Pepsi. The NHL players are pictured in their team sweaters, including stars such as Wayne Gretzky and Patrick Roy. An album to house the set also was available; it retails for about $10.

| | MINT | NRMT |
|---|---|---|
| COMPLETE SET (200) | 90.00 | 40.00 |
| COMMON STICKER (1-200) | .10 | .05 |

❑ 1 Sweden National Emblem .10 .05
❑ 2 Tommy Sandlin .25 .11
❑ 3 Peter Lindmark .25 .11
❑ 4 Rolf Ridderwall .25 .11
❑ 5 Tomas Jonsson .25 .11
❑ 6 Tommy Albelin .25 .11
❑ 7 Mats Kihlstrom .10 .05
❑ 8 Tommy Samuelsson .10 .05
❑ 9 Anders Eldebrink .15 .07
❑ 10 Fredrik Olausson .25 .11

❑ 11 Peter Andersson .15 .07
❑ 12 Thomas Eriksson .10 .05
❑ 13 Thom Eklund .10 .05
❑ 14 Bo Berglund .15 .07
❑ 15 Thomas Steen .35 .16
❑ 16 Ulf Sandstrom .10 .05
❑ 17 Jonas Bergkvist .25 .11
❑ 18 Thomas Rundqvist .15 .07
❑ 19 Per-Erik Eklund .50 .23
❑ 20 Bengt-Ake Gustavsson .15 .07
❑ 21 Patrik Sundstrom .35 .16
❑ 22 Mikael Johansson .15 .07
❑ 23 Hakan Sodergren .10 .05
❑ 24 Kent Nilsson .50 .23
❑ 25 Lars-Gunnar Pettersson .10 .05
❑ 26 Finland National Emblem .10 .05
❑ 27 Pentti Matikainen .25 .11
❑ 28 Jukka Tammi .25 .11
❑ 29 Sakari Lindfors .25 .11
❑ 30 Reijo Ruotsalainen .25 .11
❑ 31 Kari Eloranata .25 .11
❑ 32 Timo Blomqvist .25 .11
❑ 33 Simo Saarinen .10 .05
❑ 34 Hannu Virta .25 .11
❑ 35 Jouko Narvanmaa .10 .05
❑ 36 Jarmo Kuusisto .10 .05
❑ 37 Kari Suoraniemi .10 .05
❑ 38 Reijo Mikkolainen .10 .05
❑ 39 Raimo Helminen .25 .11
❑ 40 Raimo Summanen .25 .11
❑ 41 Mikko Makela .25 .11
❑ 42 Kari Jalonen .10 .05
❑ 43 Kari Laitinen .10 .05
❑ 44 Petri Skriko .35 .16
❑ 45 Erkki Laine .10 .05
❑ 46 Pauli Jarvinen .10 .05
❑ 47 Jukka Vilander .10 .05
❑ 48 Esa Keskinen .35 .16
❑ 49 Ari Vuori .10 .05
❑ 50 Mika Nieminen .35 .16
❑ 51 Canada National Emblem .25 .11
❑ 52 Dave King .25 .11
❑ 53 Grant Fuhr 1.00 .45
❑ 54 Patrick Roy 15.00 6.75
❑ 55 Ron Hextall 1.00 .45
❑ 56 Al MacInnis .75 .35
❑ 57 Ray Bourque 2.00 .90
❑ 58 Scott Stevens .50 .23
❑ 59 Paul Coffey 2.00 .90
❑ 60 Zarley Zalapski .35 .16
❑ 61 James Patrick .35 .16
❑ 62 Kevin Lowe .35 .16
❑ 63 Brad McCrimmon .35 .16
❑ 64 Mario Lemieux 15.00 6.75
❑ 65 Wayne Gretzky 20.00 9.00
❑ 66 Denis Savard .75 .35
❑ 67 Dale Hawerchuk 1.00 .45
❑ 68 Luc Robitaille 1.00 .45
❑ 69 Mark Messier 4.00 1.80
❑ 70 Michel Goulet .50 .23
❑ 71 Cam Neely 2.00 .90
❑ 72 Steve Yzerman 10.00 4.50
❑ 73 Bernie Nicholls .75 .35
❑ 74 Joe Nieuwendyk 1.00 .45
❑ 75 Mike Gartner 1.00 .45
❑ 76 Soviet Union National Emblem .25 .11
❑ 77 Viktor Tichonov .20 .09
❑ 78 Jevgenij Belosjejkin .50 .23
❑ 79 Sergei Mylnikov .35 .16
❑ 80 Sergei Golosjumov .25 .11
❑ 81 Aleksej Kasatonov .50 .23
❑ 82 Aleksej Gusarov .25 .11
❑ 83 Andrej Smirnov .15 .07
❑ 84 Valerij Sjirjajev .15 .07
❑ 85 Igor Stelnov .15 .07
❑ 86 Vladimir Konstantinov 1.00 .45
❑ 87 Vjatjeslav Fetisov 1.00 .45
❑ 88 Sergei Jasjin .15 .07
❑ 89 Vladimir Krutov .75 .35
❑ 90 Igor Larionov 1.50 .70
❑ 91 Valerij Kamenskij 1.50 .70
❑ 92 Vjatjeslav Bykov .50 .23
❑ 93 Andrej Chomutov .50 .23
❑ 94 Yuri Khmylev .50 .23
❑ 95 Sergei Nemchinov .50 .23
❑ 96 Sergei Makarov 1.00 .45
❑ 97 Igor Jesmantovitj .15 .07
❑ 98 Andrej Lomakin .20 .09
❑ 99 Anatolij Semjonov .25 .11
❑ 100 Aleksandr Tjernych .15 .07
❑ 101 West Germany National Emblem .10 .05
❑ 102 Xaver Unsinn .25 .11
❑ 103 Karl Friesen .25 .11
❑ 104 Josef Schlickenrieder .10 .05
❑ 105 Matthias Hoppe .10 .05
❑ 106 Andreas Niederberger .10 .05
❑ 107 Udo Kiessling .15 .07
❑ 108 Uli Hiemer .15 .07
❑ 109 Harold Kreis .15 .07
❑ 110 Manfred Schuster .10 .05
❑ 111 Jorg Hanft .10 .05
❑ 112 Ron Fischer .10 .05
❑ 113 Michael Heidt .15 .07
❑ 114 Dieter Hegen .15 .07
❑ 115 Gerd Truntschka .15 .07
❑ 116 Helmut Steiger .10 .05
❑ 117 Georg Franz .10 .05
❑ 118 Georg Holzmann .10 .05
❑ 119 Peter Obresa .10 .05
❑ 120 Bernd Truntschka .15 .07
❑ 121 Manfred Wolf .10 .05
❑ 122 Roy Roedger .10 .05
❑ 123 Axel Kammerer .10 .05
❑ 124 Peter Draisaitl .20 .09
❑ 125 Daniel Held .10 .05
❑ 126 Poland National Emblem .10 .05
❑ 127 Leszek Lejczyk .20 .09
❑ 128 Jerzy Mruk .20 .09
❑ 129 Andrezej Hanisz .10 .05
❑ 130 Dariusz Wieczorek .10 .05
❑ 131 Jacek Zamojski .10 .05
❑ 132 Marek Cholewa .10 .05
❑ 133 Henryk Gruth .10 .05
❑ 134 Robert Szopinski .10 .05
❑ 135 Jerzy Potz .10 .05
❑ 136 Andrzej Swiatek .10 .05
❑ 137 Ludvik Czapka .10 .05
❑ 138 Piotr Zdunek .10 .05
❑ 139 Jedrzej Kasperczyk .10 .05
❑ 140 Krzysztof Podsiadlo .10 .05
❑ 141 Miroslaw Copija .10 .05
❑ 142 Krzysztof Bujar .10 .05
❑ 143 Janusz Adamiec .10 .05
❑ 144 Jacek Solinski .10 .05
❑ 145 Roman Steblecki .10 .05
❑ 146 Adam Fraszko .10 .05
❑ 147 Leszek Minge .10 .05
❑ 148 Piotr Kwasigroch .10 .05
❑ 149 Ireneusz Pacula .10 .05
❑ 150 1989 World Championship Emblem .10 .05
❑ 151 USA National Emblem .25 .11
❑ 152 Art Berglund .10 .05
❑ 153 Tom Barrasso .50 .23
❑ 154 John Vanbiesbrouck 4.00 1.80
❑ 155 Gary Suter .50 .23
❑ 156 Phil Housley .35 .16
❑ 157 Chris Chelios 2.00 .90
❑ 158 Mike Ramsey .25 .11
❑ 159 Rod Langway .25 .11
❑ 160 Mark Howe .35 .16
❑ 161 Brian Leetch 2.00 .90
❑ 162 Al Iafrate .35 .16
❑ 163 Jimmy Carson .15 .07
❑ 164 Pat LaFontaine 1.00 .45
❑ 165 Neal Broten .50 .23
❑ 166 Dave Christian .35 .16
❑ 167 Brett Hull 4.00 1.80
❑ 168 Bob Carpenter .25 .11
❑ 169 Ed Olczyk .25 .11
❑ 170 Joe Mullen .35 .16
❑ 171 Bob Brooke .15 .07
❑ 172 Brian Lawton .15 .07
❑ 173 Craig Janney .50 .23
❑ 174 Mark Johnson .25 .11
❑ 175 Chris Nilan .25 .11
❑ 176 CSSR National Emblem .10 .05
❑ 177 Pavel Wohl .25 .11
❑ 178 Dominik Hasek 7.50 3.40
❑ 179 Jaromir Sindel .25 .11
❑ 180 Petr Briza 1.00 .45
❑ 181 Antonin Stavjana .25 .11
❑ 182 Bedrich Scerban .20 .09
❑ 183 Petr Slanina .10 .05
❑ 184 Frantisek Kucera .20 .09
❑ 185 Jergus Baca .15 .07
❑ 186 Leo Gudas .15 .07
❑ 187 Drahomir Kadlec .15 .07
❑ 188 Mojmir Bozik .10 .05
❑ 189 Petr Vlk .10 .05
❑ 190 Vladimir Ruzicka .25 .11
❑ 191 Otakar Janecky .25 .11
❑ 192 Jan Vodila .10 .05
❑ 193 Jiri Dolezal .10 .05
❑ 194 Rostislav Vlach .10 .05
❑ 195 Jiri Kucera .20 .09
❑ 196 Jiri Sejba .15 .07
❑ 197 Oldrich Valek .10 .05
❑ 198 Jiri Lala .15 .07
❑ 199 Robert Kron .25 .11
❑ 200 Petr Rosol .15 .07

## 1989-90 Swedish Semic Elitserien Stickers

This 285-sticker set captures the excitement of the Elitserien in thrilling posed color photos. The 3" by 2 1/8" sticker fronts are complemented by player name, sticker number and team emblem. the backs contain an ad for Pripp's Energy drink. The set is notable for the first "card" appearances of Mats Sundin and Nicklas Lidstrom.

| | MINT | NRMT |
|---|---|---|
| COMPLETE SET (285) | 35.00 | 16.00 |
| COMMON STICKER (1-285) | .10 | .05 |

❑ 1 AIK .10 .05
❑ 2 Ake Lilljebjorn .25 .11
❑ 3 Thomas Ostlund .35 .16
❑ 4 Mats Thelin .25 .11
❑ 5 Thomas Ahlen .10 .05
❑ 6 Petri Liimatainen .10 .05
❑ 7 Roger Ohman .10 .05
❑ 8 Rikard Franzen .15 .07
❑ 9 Stefan Claesson .10 .05
❑ 10 Tommy Hedlund .10 .05
❑ 11 Stefan Jansson .10 .05
❑ 12 Peter Gradin .10 .05
❑ 13 Thomas Gradin .50 .23
❑ 14 Bo Berglund .10 .05
❑ 15 Heinz Ehlers .10 .05
❑ 16 Robert Burakovsky .25 .11
❑ 17 Alexander Kozjevnikov .10 .05
❑ 18 Peter Hammarstrom .10 .05
❑ 19 Anders Gozzi .15 .07
❑ 20 Thomas Bjuhr .10 .05
❑ 21 Patric Englund .10 .05
❑ 22 Odd Nilsson .10 .05
❑ 23 Mats Lindberg .10 .05
❑ 24 Peter Johansson .10 .05
❑ 25 Patric Kjellberg .15 .07
❑ 26 Brynas IF .10 .05
❑ 27 Lars Eriksson .25 .11
❑ 28 Michael Sundlov .25 .11
❑ 29 Par Djoos .15 .07
❑ 30 Tommy Sjodin .25 .11
❑ 31 Nikolaj Davydkin .10 .05
❑ 32 Niklas Gallstedt .10 .05
❑ 33 Mikael Lindman .10 .05
❑ 34 Jan-Erik Stormqvist .10 .05
❑ 35 Tommy Melkersson .10 .05
❑ 36 Mikael Enander .10 .05
❑ 37 Anders Huss .10 .05
❑ 38 Anders Carlsson .10 .05
❑ 39 Willy Lindstrom .35 .16
❑ 40 Kyosti Karjalainen .15 .07
❑ 41 Jan Larsson .10 .05
❑ 42 Patrik Erickson .10 .05
❑ 43 Joakim Pehrson .10 .05
❑ 44 Johan Brummer .10 .05
❑ 45 Peter Eriksson .10 .05
❑ 46 Peter Gustafsson .10 .05
❑ 47 Tomas Olund .10 .05
❑ 48 Magnus Asberg .10 .05
❑ 49 Djurgardens IF .10 .05
❑ 50 Rolf Ridderwall .35 .16
❑ 51 Tommy Soderstrom 2.50 1.10
❑ 52 Thomas Eriksson .10 .05
❑ 53 Arto Blomsten .25 .11
❑ 54 Orvar Stambert .10 .05
❑ 55 Christian Due-Boje .15 .07
❑ 56 Kenneth Kennholt .15 .07
❑ 57 Mats Waltin .10 .05
❑ 58 Karl-Erik Lilja .10 .05
❑ 59 Marcus Ragnarsson 1.00 .45
❑ 60 Hakan Sodergren .10 .05
❑ 61 Mikael Johansson .10 .05
❑ 62 Jens Ohling .15 .07
❑ 63 Jan Viktorsson .15 .07
❑ 64 Peter Nilsson .10 .05
❑ 65 Charles Berglund .10 .05
❑ 66 Kent Johansson .10 .05
❑ 67 Johan Garpenlov .50 .23
❑ 68 Ola Andersson .10 .05
❑ 69 Anders Johnson .10 .05
❑ 70 Bengt Akerblom .10 .05
❑ 71 Ola Josefsson .10 .05
❑ 72 Mats Sundin 10.00 4.50
❑ 73 Farjestads BK .10 .05
❑ 74 Anders Bergman .25 .11
❑ 75 Jorgen Ryden .25 .11
❑ 76 Tommy Samuelsson .10 .05
❑ 77 Fredrik Olausson .50 .23
❑ 78 Peter Hasselblad .10 .05
❑ 79 Jesper Duus .10 .05
❑ 80 Anders Berglund .10 .05
❑ 81 Mattias Andersson .10 .05
❑ 82 Mattias Olsson .10 .05
❑ 83 Greger Artursson .10 .05
❑ 84 Jacob Karlsson .10 .05
❑ 85 Thomas Rundqvist .25 .11
❑ 86 Staffan Lundh .10 .05
❑ 87 Jan Ingman .10 .05
❑ 88 Kjell Dahlin .25 .11
❑ 89 Bengt-Ake Gustafsson .50 .23
❑ 90 Magnus Roupe .25 .11
❑ 91 Hakan Loob 1.00 .45
❑ 92 Mikael Holmberg .10 .05
❑ 93 Daniel Rydmark .25 .11
❑ 94 Lars Karlsson .10 .05
❑ 95 Peter Ottosson .10 .05
❑ 96 HV 71 .10 .05
❑ 97 Kenneth Johansson .25 .11
❑ 98 Claes Heljemo .25 .11
❑ 99 Lars Ivarsson .10 .05
❑ 100 Arto Ruotanen .10 .05
❑ 101 Fredrik Stillman .25 .11
❑ 102 Klas Heed .10 .05
❑ 103 Nils-Gunnar Svensson .10 .05
❑ 104 Per Gustafsson .10 .05
❑ 105 Tommy Fritz .10 .05
❑ 106 Mats Nilsson .10 .05
❑ 107 Hasse Sjoo .10 .05
❑ 108 Mats Loov .10 .05
❑ 109 Ove Thornberg .10 .05
❑ 110 Eddy Ericsson .10 .05
❑ 111 Ivan Avdejev .10 .05
❑ 112 Stefan Persson .35 .16
❑ 113 Rick Erdall .10 .05
❑ 114 Stefan Nilsson .10 .05
❑ 115 Stefan Ornskog .15 .07
❑ 116 Patrik Ross .10 .05
❑ 117 Stefan Falk .10 .05
❑ 118 Claes Roupe .10 .05
❑ 119 Peter Ekelund .10 .05
❑ 120 Leksands IF .10 .05
❑ 121 Peter Aslin .35 .16
❑ 122 Olow Sundstrom .25 .11
❑ 123 Jonas Leven .10 .05
❑ 124 Tomas Jonsson .35 .16
❑ 125 Magnus Svensson .25 .11
❑ 126 Ricard Persson .35 .16
❑ 127 Per Lundell .10 .05
❑ 128 Tomas Nord .10 .05
❑ 129 Peter Wallin .10 .05
❑ 130 Orjan Lindmark .10 .05
❑ 131 Henric Bjorkman .10 .05
❑ 132 Anders Pettersson .10 .05
❑ 133 Per-Olof Carlsson .10 .05
❑ 134 Tomas Forslund .35 .16
❑ 135 Niklas Eriksson .10 .05
❑ 136 Richard Kromm .25 .11
❑ 137 Jarmo Makitalo .10 .05
❑ 138 Peter Lundmark .35 .16
❑ 139 Ronny Reichenberg .10 .05
❑ 140 Cenneth Soderlund .10 .05
❑ 141 Jens Nielsen .10 .05
❑ 142 Marcus Thuresson .10 .05
❑ 143 Anders Broms .10 .05
❑ 144 Joakim Backlund .10 .05
❑ 145 Lulea HF .10 .05
❑ 146 Robert Skoog .25 .11
❑ 147 Tomas Javeblad .25 .11
❑ 148 Lars Modig .10 .05
❑ 149 Jan-Ove Mettavainio .10 .05
❑ 150 Osmo Soutokorva .10 .05
❑ 151 Torbjorn Lindberg .10 .05
❑ 152 Timo Jutila .35 .16
❑ 153 Roger Akerstrom .15 .07
❑ 154 Per Ljusterdang .10 .05
❑ 155 Tomas Lilja .10 .05
❑ 156 Johan Stromvall .10 .05
❑ 157 Lars-Gunnar Pettersson .10 .05
❑ 158 Lars Hurtig .10 .05
❑ 159 Morgan Samuelsson .10 .05
❑ 160 Stefan Nilsson .10 .05
❑ 161 Vesa Kangas .10 .05
❑ 162 Kari Jaako .10 .05
❑ 163 Juha Nurmi .10 .05
❑ 164 Jens Hellgren .10 .05
❑ 165 Tomas Berglund .10 .05
❑ 166 Lars Edstrom .10 .05
❑ 167 Petter Antti .10 .05
❑ 168 MoDo HK .10 .05
❑ 169 Fredrik Andersson .25 .11
❑ 170 Goran Arnmark .25 .11
❑ 171 Timo Blomqvist .25 .11
❑ 172 Hakan Stromqvist .10 .05
❑ 173 Robert Frestadius .10 .05
❑ 174 Lars Jansson .10 .05
❑ 175 Hans Lodin .10 .05
❑ 176 Ove Pettersson .10 .05
❑ 177 Tony Olofsson .10 .05
❑ 178 Jorgen Eriksson .10 .05
❑ 179 Ulf Sandstrom .10 .05
❑ 180 Michael Hjalm .10 .05
❑ 181 Urban Nordin .10 .05
❑ 182 Lars Bystrom .10 .05
❑ 183 Jens Ohman .10 .05
❑ 184 Ulf Odmark .10 .05
❑ 185 Mikael Stahl .10 .05
❑ 186 Per Nilsson .10 .05
❑ 187 Ingemar Strom .10 .05
❑ 188 Kent Lantz .10 .05
❑ 189 Kent Norberg .10 .05
❑ 190 Patrik Soderholm .10 .05
❑ 191 Skelleftea HC .10 .05
❑ 192 Sam Lindstahl .25 .11
❑ 193 Dick Andersson .25 .11
❑ 194 Kari Suoraniemi .10 .05
❑ 195 Robert Larsson .10 .05
❑ 196 Kari Yli-Maenpaa .25 .11
❑ 197 Ola Stenlund .10 .05
❑ 198 Tony Barthelson .10 .05
❑ 199 Lars Marklund .10 .05
❑ 200 Glenn Hedman .10 .05
❑ 201 Dick Burlin .10 .05
❑ 202 Michael Granstedt .10 .05
❑ 203 Pekka Jarvela .10 .05
❑ 204 Hans Hjalmar .10 .05
❑ 205 Mats Lundstrom .10 .05
❑ 206 Martin Pettersson .10 .05
❑ 207 Johnny Forsman .10 .05
❑ 208 Daniel Pettersson .10 .05
❑ 209 Niklas Mannberg .10 .05
❑ 210 Niklas Brannstrom .10 .05
❑ 211 Jan Johansson .10 .05
❑ 212 Jorgen Wannstrom .10 .05
❑ 213 Leif Johansson .10 .05
❑ 214 Par Mikaelsson .10 .05
❑ 215 Fredrik Andersson .10 .05
❑ 216 Sodertalje SK .10 .05
❑ 217 Reino Sundberg .25 .11
❑ 218 Jari Luoma .25 .11
❑ 219 Anders Eldebrink .25 .11
❑ 220 Mats Kilstrom .10 .05
❑ 221 Jonas Heed .10 .05
❑ 222 Hans Pettersson .10 .05
❑ 223 Jan Bergman .10 .05
❑ 224 Thomas Carlsson .10 .05
❑ 225 Stefan Jonsson .10 .05
❑ 226 Thom Eklund .10 .05
❑ 227 Ola Rosander .10 .05
❑ 228 Bjorn Carlsson .10 .05
❑ 229 Thomas Sjogren .25 .11
❑ 230 Thomas Ljungbergh .10 .05
❑ 231 Stefan Olsson .10 .05
❑ 232 Reine Landgren .10 .05
❑ 233 Anders Frykbo .10 .05
❑ 234 Conny Jansson .10 .05
❑ 235 Peter Larsson .10 .05
❑ 236 Tomaz Eriksson .10 .05
❑ 237 Erik Holmberg .10 .05
❑ 238 Patrik Lindh .10 .05
❑ 239 Vasteras IK .10 .05
❑ 240 Mats Ytter .25 .11
❑ 241 Par Hellenberg .25 .11
❑ 242 Jan Eriksson .10 .05
❑ 243 Peter Popovic .25 .11
❑ 244 Tore Lindgren .10 .05
❑ 245 Leif Rohlin .35 .16
❑ 246 Henrik Andersson .10 .05
❑ 247 Nicklas Lidstrom 4.00 1.80
❑ 248 Jan Karlsson .10 .05
❑ 249 Peter Jacobsson .10 .05
❑ 250 Patrik Juhlin 1.00 .45
❑ 251 Goran Sjoberg .10 .05
❑ 252 Fredrik Nilsson .10 .05
❑ 253 Stefan Hellkvist .10 .05
❑ 254 Tomas Strandberg .10 .05
❑ 255 Anders Berglund .10 .05
❑ 256 Claes Lindblom .10 .05
❑ 257 Magnus Wallin .10 .05
❑ 258 Bjorn Akerblom .10 .05
❑ 259 Joakim Lundholm .10 .05
❑ 260 Jorgen Holmberg .10 .05
❑ 261 Ronny Hansen .10 .05
❑ 262 Misjat Fachrutdinov .15 .07
❑ 263 Vastra Frolunda HC .10 .05
❑ 264 Hakan Algotsson .35 .16
❑ 265 Per Lundbergh .25 .11
❑ 266 Jan Karlsson .10 .05
❑ 267 Joacim Esbjors .15 .07
❑ 268 Leif Carlsson .10 .05
❑ 269 Stefan Axelsson .25 .11
❑ 270 Peter Ekroth .10 .05
❑ 271 Jorgen Palm .10 .05
❑ 272 Hakan Nordin .10 .05
❑ 273 Stefan Larsson .10 .05
❑ 274 Mikael Andersson .50 .23
❑ 275 Terho Koskela .10 .05
❑ 276 Patrik Carnback .35 .16
❑ 277 Serge Boisvert .25 .11
❑ 278 Arto Sirvio .10 .05
❑ 279 Peter Berndtsson .10 .05
❑ 280 Jorgen Pettersson .10 .05
❑ 281 Niklas Andersson .25 .11
❑ 282 Peter Gustavsson .10 .05
❑ 283 Paul Andersson .10 .05
❑ 284 Mats Graesen .10 .05
❑ 285 Kent Orrgren .10 .05

## 1990-91 Swedish Semic Elitserien Stickers

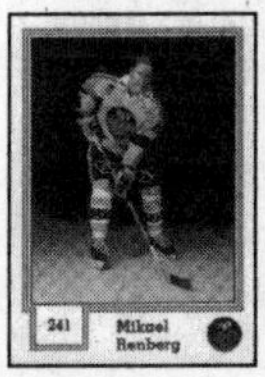


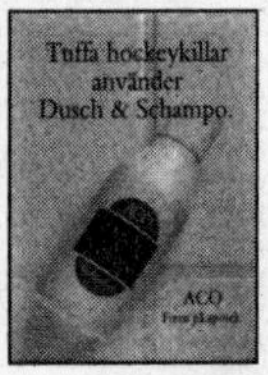


This 294-sticker set features the players of the Swedish Elitserien. The stickers measure 3" by 2 1/8" and utilize posed color player photos on the front, along with sticker number, name and club emblem. The backs feature consumer ads. The set includes the first "card" of players such as Mikael Renberg and Markus Naslund.

| | MINT | NRMT |
|---|---|---|
| COMPLETE SET (294) | 40.00 | 18.00 |
| COMMON STICKER (1-294) | .10 | .05 |

❑ 1 MoDo Hockey Team Team Emblem .10 .05
❑ 2 MoDo Hockey Team Picture .10 .05
❑ 3 Fredrik Andersson .25 .11
❑ 4 Goran Arnmark .25 .11
❑ 5 Ari Salo .10 .05
❑ 6 Anders Berglund .10 .05
❑ 7 Lars Jansson .10 .05
❑ 8 Hans Lodin .10 .05
❑ 9 Ove Pettersson .10 .05
❑ 10 Jorgen Eriksson .10 .05
❑ 11 Tony Olofsson .10 .05
❑ 12 Tomas Nanzen .10 .05
❑ 13 Michael Hjalm .10 .05
❑ 14 Erik Holmberg .10 .05
❑ 15 Urban Nordin .10 .05
❑ 16 Kent Lantz .10 .05
❑ 17 Lars Bystrom .10 .05
❑ 18 Jens Ohman .10 .05
❑ 19 Ulf Odmark .10 .05
❑ 20 Mikael Stahl .10 .05
❑ 21 Ingemar Strom .10 .05
❑ 22 Tommy Pettersson .10 .05
❑ 23 Marcus Naslund 1.00 .45
❑ 24 Per Wallin .15 .07
❑ 25 Vastra Frolunda HC Team Emblem .10 .05
❑ 26 Vastra Frolunda HC Team Picture .10 .05
❑ 27 Ake Lilljebjorn .25 .11
❑ 28 Hakan Algotsson .35 .16
❑ 29 Leif Carlsson .10 .05
❑ 30 Jonas Heed .10 .05
❑ 31 Hakan Nordin .10 .05
❑ 32 Joacim Esbjors .15 .07
❑ 33 Stefan Axelsson .35 .16
❑ 34 Stefan Larsson .15 .07
❑ 35 Jorgen Palm .10 .05
❑ 36 Oscar Ackerstrom .10 .05
❑ 37 Patrik Carnback .25 .11
❑ 38 Mats Lundstrom .10 .05
❑ 39 Niklas Andersson .25 .11
❑ 40 Serge Boisvert .20 .09
❑ 41 Arto Sirvio .10 .05
❑ 42 Terho Koskela .10 .05

❑ 43 Kari Jaako .10 .05
❑ 44 Peter Berndtsson .10 .05
❑ 45 Mikael Andersson .25 .11
❑ 46 Par Edlund .10 .05
❑ 47 Jonas Andersson .10 .05
❑ 48 Johan Witehall .10 .05
❑ 49 Sodertalje SK .10 .05
Team Emblem
❑ 50 Sodertalje SK .10 .05
Team Picture
❑ 51 Reino Sundberg .25 .11
❑ 52 Jari Luoma .25 .11
❑ 53 Mats Kilstrom .10 .05
❑ 54 Stefan Jonsson .10 .05
❑ 55 Peter Ekroth .10 .05
❑ 56 Mats Waltin .10 .05
❑ 57 Jan Bergman .10 .05
❑ 58 Hans Pettersson .10 .05
❑ 59 Stefan Nyman .10 .05
❑ 60 Conny Jansson .10 .05
❑ 61 Thom Eklund .10 .05
❑ 62 Otakar Hascak .20 .09
❑ 63 Morgan Samuelsson .15 .07
❑ 64 Reine Landgren .10 .05
❑ 65 Bjorn Carlsson .10 .05
❑ 66 Ola Andersson .10 .05
❑ 67 Tomaz Eriksson .10 .05
❑ 68 Bert-Olav Karlsson .10 .05
❑ 69 Ola Rosander .10 .05
❑ 70 Stefan Olsson .10 .05
❑ 71 Scott Moore .10 .05
❑ 72 Anders Frykbo .10 .05
❑ 73 AIK .10 .05
Team Emblem
❑ 74 AIK .10 .05
Team Picture
❑ 75 Thomas Ostlund .35 .16
❑ 76 Sam Lindstahl .25 .11
❑ 77 Borje Salming 1.50 .70
❑ 78 Mats Thelin .25 .11
❑ 79 Petter Salsten .10 .05
❑ 80 Petri Liimatainen .10 .05
❑ 81 Rikard Franzen .15 .07
❑ 82 Stefan Claesson .10 .05
❑ 83 Torbjorn Mattsson .10 .05
❑ 84 Daniel Jardemyre .10 .05
❑ 85 Robert Burakovsky .20 .09
❑ 86 Peter Gradin .10 .05
❑ 87 Thomas Bjuhr .10 .05
❑ 88 Heinz Ehlers .10 .05
❑ 89 Tommy Lehmann .20 .09
❑ 90 Peter Hammarstrom .10 .05
❑ 91 Patric Kjellberg .25 .11
❑ 92 Patric Englund .10 .05
❑ 93 Mats Lindberg .10 .05
❑ 94 Peter Johansson .10 .05
❑ 95 Kristian Gahn .20 .09
❑ 96 Niklas Sundblad .25 .11
❑ 97 Erik Andersson .10 .05
❑ 98 HV 71 .10 .05
Team Emblem
❑ 99 HV 71 .10 .05
Team Picture
❑ 100 Peter Aslin .25 .11
❑ 101 Kenneth Johansson .25 .11
❑ 102 Arto Ruotanen .10 .05
❑ 103 Fredrik Stillman .15 .07
❑ 104 Lars Ivarsson .10 .05
❑ 105 Klas Heed .10 .05
❑ 106 Per Gustafsson .50 .23
❑ 107 Mathias Svedberg .10 .05
❑ 108 Tommy Fritz .10 .05
❑ 109 Mats Nilsson .10 .05
❑ 110 Peter Eriksson .10 .05
❑ 111 Risto Kurkinen .10 .05
❑ 112 Thomas Ljungbergh .10 .05
❑ 113 Ove Thornberg .10 .05
❑ 114 Mats Loov .10 .05
❑ 115 Eddy Ericsson .10 .05
❑ 116 Stefan Ornskog .25 .11
❑ 117 Patrik Ross .10 .05
❑ 118 Stefan Persson .25 .11
❑ 119 Dennis Strom .10 .05
❑ 120 Peter Ekelund .10 .05
❑ 121 Jonas Jonsson .10 .05
❑ 122 Torbjorn Persson .10 .05
❑ 123 Malmo IF .10 .05
Team Emblem
❑ 124 Malmo IF .10 .05
Team Picture
❑ 125 Peter Lindmark .25 .11
❑ 126 Roger Nordstrom .25 .11
❑ 127 Timo Blomqvist .25 .11
❑ 128 Peter Andersson .25 .11
❑ 129 Mats Lusth .10 .05
❑ 130 Johan Salle .10 .05
❑ 131 Roger Ohman .15 .07
❑ 132 Anders Svensson .10 .05
❑ 133 Peter Imhauser .10 .05
❑ 134 Johan Norgren .10 .05
❑ 135 Raimo Helminen .25 .11
❑ 136 Peter Sundstrom .25 .11
❑ 137 Mats Hallin .10 .05
❑ 138 Matti Pauna .10 .05
❑ 139 Patrik Gustavsson .10 .05
❑ 140 Hakan Ahlund .10 .05
❑ 141 Daniel Rydmark .15 .07
❑ 142 Lennart Hermansson .10 .05
❑ 143 Carl-Erik Larsson .10 .05
❑ 144 Rick Erdall .10 .05
❑ 145 Bo Svanberg .10 .05
❑ 146 Fredrik Johansson .10 .05
❑ 147 Jens Hemstrom .10 .05
❑ 148 Vasteras IK .10 .05
Team Emblem
❑ 149 Vasteras IK .10 .05
Team Picture
❑ 150 Mats Ytter .25 .11
❑ 151 Par Hellenberg .25 .11
❑ 152 Nicklas Lidstrom 3.00 1.35
❑ 153 Leif Rohlin .35 .16
❑ 154 Peter Popovic .35 .16
❑ 155 Jan Karlsson .10 .05
❑ 156 Henrik Andersson .10 .05
❑ 157 Tore Lindgren .10 .05
❑ 158 Peter Jacobsson .10 .05
❑ 159 Pierre Ivarsson .10 .05
❑ 160 Jan Eriksson .10 .05
❑ 161 Goran Sjoberg .10 .05
❑ 162 Misjat Fachrutdinov .15 .07
❑ 163 Anders Berglund .10 .05
❑ 164 Claes Lindblom .10 .05
❑ 165 Jorgen Holmberg .10 .05
❑ 166 Stefan Hellkvist .10 .05
❑ 167 Tomas Strandberg .10 .05
❑ 168 Bjorn Akerblom .10 .05
❑ 169 Ronny Hansen .10 .05
❑ 170 Fredrik Nilsson .15 .07
❑ 171 Patrik Juhlin .50 .23
❑ 172 Henrik Nilsson .10 .05
❑ 173 Brynas IF .10 .05
Team Emblem
❑ 174 Brynas IF .10 .05
Team Picture
❑ 175 Michael Sundlov .25 .11
❑ 176 Lars Eriksson .25 .11
❑ 177 Tommy Sjodin .25 .11
❑ 178 Brad Berry .10 .05
❑ 179 Niklas Gallstedt .10 .05
❑ 180 Mikael Lindman .10 .05
❑ 181 Urban Molander .10 .05
❑ 182 Jan-Erik Stormqvist .10 .05
❑ 183 Stefan Klockare .20 .09
❑ 184 Tommy Melkersson .10 .05
❑ 185 Anders Carlsson .10 .05
❑ 186 Patrik Erickson .10 .05
❑ 187 Anders Huss .10 .05
❑ 188 Jan Larsson .10 .05
❑ 189 Peter Larsson .10 .05
❑ 190 Anders Gozzi .15 .07
❑ 191 Joakim Pehrson .15 .07
❑ 192 Peter Gustafsson .10 .05
❑ 193 Peter Eriksson .10 .05
❑ 194 Johan Brummer .10 .05
❑ 195 Tomas Olund .10 .05
❑ 196 Kenneth Andersson .10 .05
❑ 197 Leksands IF .10 .05
Team Emblem
❑ 198 Leksands IF .10 .05
Team Picture
❑ 199 Olow Sundstrom .25 .11
❑ 200 Lars-Erik Lord .25 .11
❑ 201 Jonas Leven .10 .05
❑ 202 Tomas Jonsson .25 .11
❑ 203 Ricard Persson .25 .11
❑ 204 Per Lundell .10 .05
❑ 205 Tomas Nord .10 .05
❑ 206 Mattias Andersson .10 .05
❑ 207 Henric Bjorkman .10 .05
❑ 208 Orjan Lindmark .25 .11
❑ 209 Tomas Forslund .25 .11
❑ 210 Niklas Eriksson .10 .05
❑ 211 Peter Lundmark .15 .07
❑ 212 Per-Olof Carlsson .10 .05
❑ 213 Marcus Thuresson .10 .05
❑ 214 Jens Nielsen .10 .05
❑ 215 Cenneth Soderlund .10 .05
❑ 216 Markus Akerblom .15 .07
❑ 217 Ronny Reichenberg .10 .05
❑ 218 Fredrik Olsson .10 .05
❑ 219 Niklas Hillblom .10 .05
❑ 220 Magnus Gustafsson .10 .05
❑ 221 Fredrik Jax .15 .07
❑ 222 Lulea HF .10 .05
Team Emblem
❑ 223 Lulea HF .10 .05
Team Picture
❑ 224 Robert Skoog .25 .11
❑ 225 Tomas Javeblad .25 .11
❑ 226 Timo Jutila .25 .11
❑ 227 Per Ljusterang .10 .05
❑ 228 Lars Modig .10 .05
❑ 229 Torbjorn Lindberg .10 .05
❑ 230 Tomas Lilja .10 .05
❑ 231 Osmo Soutukorva .10 .05
❑ 232 Jan-Ove Mettavainio .10 .05
❑ 233 Roger Akerstrom .10 .05
❑ 234 Johan Stromvall .10 .05
❑ 235 Ulf Sandstrom .10 .05
❑ 236 Lars-Gunnar Pettersson .10 .05
❑ 237 Pauli Jarvinen .10 .05
❑ 238 Lars Hurtig .10 .05
❑ 239 Tomas Berglund .10 .05
❑ 240 Stefan Nilsson .10 .05
❑ 241 Mikael Renberg 10.00 4.50
❑ 242 Hans Hjalmar .10 .05
❑ 243 Jens Hellgren .10 .05
❑ 244 Lars Edstrom .10 .05
❑ 245 Robert Nordberg .25 .11
❑ 246 Farjestads BK .10 .05
Team Emblem
❑ 247 Farjestads BK .10 .05
Team Picture
❑ 248 Anders Bergman .25 .11
❑ 249 Jorgen Ryden .25 .11
❑ 250 Patrik Haltia .35 .16
❑ 251 Tommy Samuelsson .10 .05
❑ 252 Jim Leavins .10 .05
❑ 253 Peter Hasselblad .10 .05
❑ 254 Jesper Duus .10 .05
❑ 255 Mattias Olsson .10 .05
❑ 256 Greger Artursson .10 .05
❑ 257 Jacob Karlsson .10 .05
❑ 258 Thomas Rhodin .10 .05
❑ 259 Bengt-Ake Gustafsson .35 .16
❑ 260 Hakan Loob 1.00 .45
❑ 261 Thomas Rundqvist .25 .11
❑ 262 Kjell Dahlin .25 .11
❑ 263 Magnus Roupe .25 .11
❑ 264 Jan Ingman .10 .05
❑ 265 Lars Karlsson .10 .05
❑ 266 Mikael Holmberg .10 .05
❑ 267 Staffan Lundh .10 .05
❑ 268 Peter Ottosson .10 .05
❑ 269 Jonas Hoglund .50 .23
❑ 270 Clas Eriksson .10 .05
❑ 271 Djurgardens IF .10 .05
Team Emblem
❑ 272 Djurgardens IF .10 .05
Team Picture
❑ 273 Tommy Soderstrom 1.50 .70
❑ 274 Joakim Persson .50 .23
❑ 275 Thomas Eriksson .10 .05
❑ 276 Arto Blomsten .25 .11
❑ 277 Kenneth Kennholt .15 .07
❑ 278 Christian Due-Boje .20 .09
❑ 279 Orvar Stambert .10 .05
❑ 280 Per Nygards .10 .05
❑ 281 Marcus Ragnarsson .75 .35
❑ 282 Thomas Johansson .10 .05
❑ 283 Ronnie Pettersson .10 .05
❑ 284 Charles Berglund .10 .05
❑ 285 Jan Viktorsson .20 .09
❑ 286 Jens Ohling .15 .07
❑ 287 Ola Josefsson .10 .05
❑ 288 Peter Nilsson .10 .05
❑ 289 Andres Johnson .10 .05
❑ 290 Hakan Sodergren .10 .05
❑ 291 Stefan Gustavson .10 .05
❑ 292 Magnus Jansson .10 .05
❑ 293 Mikael Johansson .10 .05
❑ 294 Johan Lindstedt .10 .05

## 1991-92 Swedish Semic World Championship Stickers

These hockey stickers, which measure approximately 2 1/8" by 2 7/8", were sold five to a packet. Also an album was available to display all 250 stickers. The fronts display color posed player shots framed by a red inner border studded with yellow miniature stars and a white outer border. The team flag, the player's name, and the sticker number appear in the white border below the picture. The backs are blank. The stickers are grouped according to country. Teemu Selanne appears in his Rookie Card year.

| | MINT | NRMT |
|---|---|---|
| COMPLETE SET (250) | 90.00 | 40.00 |
| COMMON CARD (1-250) | .10 | .05 |

❑ 1 Finnish Emblem .10 .05
❑ 2 Markus Ketterer .50 .23
❑ 3 Sakari Lindfors .25 .11
❑ 4 Jukka Tammi .25 .11
❑ 5 Timo Jutila .15 .07
❑ 6 Hannu Virta .15 .07
❑ 7 Simo Saarinen .10 .05
❑ 8 Jukka Marttila .10 .05
❑ 9 Ville Siren .15 .07
❑ 10 Pasi Huura .15 .07
❑ 11 Unknown .10 .05
❑ 12 Arto Ruotanen .10 .05
❑ 13 Ari Haanpaa .10 .05
❑ 14 Pauli Jarvinen .10 .05
❑ 15 Teppo Kivela .10 .05
❑ 16 Risto Kurkinen .10 .05
❑ 17 Mika Nieminen .15 .07
❑ 18 Jari Kurri .75 .35
❑ 19 Esa Keskinen .25 .11
❑ 20 Raimo Summanen .10 .05
❑ 21 Teemu Selanne 8.00 3.60
❑ 22 Jari Torkki .10 .05
❑ 23 Hannu Jarvenpaa .15 .07
❑ 24 Raimo Helminen .15 .07
❑ 25 Timo Peltomaa .15 .07
❑ 26 Swedish Emblem .10 .05
❑ 27 Peter Lindmark .25 .11
❑ 28 Rolf Ridderwall .15 .07
❑ 29 Tommy Soderstrom .50 .23
❑ 30 Thomas Eriksson .15 .07
❑ 31 Nicklas Lidstrom .50 .23
❑ 32 Tomas Jonsson .15 .07
❑ 33 Tommy Samuelsson .10 .05
❑ 34 Fredrik Stillman .15 .07
❑ 35 Peter Andersson .15 .07
❑ 36 Peter Andersson .15 .07
❑ 37 Kenneth Kennholt .15 .07
❑ 38 Hakan Loob .25 .11
❑ 39 Thomas Rundqvist .15 .07
❑ 40 Hakan Ahlund .10 .05
❑ 41 Jan Viktorsson .10 .05
❑ 42 Charles Berglund .15 .07
❑ 43 Mikael Johansson .10 .05
❑ 44 Robert Burakovsky .10 .05
❑ 45 Bengt-Ake Gustafsson .15 .07
❑ 46 Patrik Carnback .10 .05
❑ 47 Patrik Erickson .10 .05
❑ 48 Anders Carlsson .10 .05
❑ 49 Mats Naslund .35 .16
❑ 50 Kent Nilsson .35 .16
❑ 51 Canadian Emblem 1.00 .45
❑ 52 Patrick Roy 12.00 5.50
❑ 53 Ed Belfour 1.50 .70
❑ 54 Daniel Berthiaume .15 .07
❑ 55 Ray Bourque 1.50 .70
❑ 56 Scott Stevens .20 .09
❑ 57 Al MacInnis .35 .16
❑ 58 Paul Coffey 1.50 .70
❑ 59 Paul Cavallini .15 .07
❑ 60 Zarley Zalapski .15 .07
❑ 61 Steve Duchesne .15 .07
❑ 62 Dave Ellett .15 .07
❑ 63 Mark Messier 3.00 1.35
❑ 64 Wayne Gretzky 15.00 6.75
❑ 65 Steve Yzerman 5.00 2.20
❑ 66 Pierre Turgeon .75 .35
❑ 67 Bernie Nicholls .20 .09
❑ 68 Cam Neely 1.00 .45
❑ 69 Joe Nieuwendyk .35 .16
❑ 70 Luc Robitaille .75 .35
❑ 71 Kevin Dineen .15 .07
❑ 72 John Cullen .15 .07
❑ 73 Steve Larmer .20 .09
❑ 74 Mark Recchi .75 .35
❑ 75 Joe Sakic 5.00 2.20
❑ 76 Soviet Emblem .50 .23
❑ 77 Arturs Irbe .50 .23
❑ 78 Alexei Marin .10 .05
❑ 79 Mikhail Shtalenkov .25 .11
❑ 80 Vladimir Malakhov .25 .11
❑ 81 Vladimir Konstantinov .50 .23
❑ 82 Igor Kravchuk .15 .07
❑ 83 Ilya Byakin .15 .07
❑ 84 Dimitri Mironov .20 .09
❑ 85 Vladimir Turikov .10 .05
❑ 86 Vjatjeslav Uvajev .10 .05
❑ 87 Vladimir Fedosov .10 .05
❑ 88 Valeri Kamensky .50 .23
❑ 89 Pavel Bure 4.00 1.80
❑ 90 Vyacheslav Butsayev .15 .07
❑ 91 Igor Maslennikov .10 .05
❑ 92 Evgeny Davydov .15 .07
❑ 93 Andrei Kovalev .10 .05
❑ 94 Alexander Semak .15 .07
❑ 95 Alexei Zhamnov .35 .16
❑ 96 Sergei Nemchinov .15 .07
❑ 97 Viktor Gordijuk .10 .05
❑ 98 Vyacheslav Kozlov .75 .35
❑ 99 Andrei Khomotov .50 .23
❑ 100 Vyacheslav Bykov .35 .16
❑ 101 Czech Emblem .10 .05
❑ 102 Petr Brisa .25 .11
❑ 103 Dominik Hasek 3.00 1.35
❑ 104 Eduard Hartmann .15 .07
❑ 105 Bedrich Scerban .15 .07
❑ 106 Jiri Slegr .20 .09
❑ 107 Josef Reznicek .10 .05
❑ 108 Petr Pavlas .10 .05
❑ 109 Peter Slanina .10 .05
❑ 110 Martin Maskarinec .10 .05
❑ 111 Antonin Stavjana .15 .07
❑ 112 Stanislav Medrik .10 .05
❑ 113 Dusan Pasek .20 .09
❑ 114 Jiri Lala .15 .07
❑ 115 Darius Rusnak .10 .05
❑ 116 Oto Hascak .15 .07
❑ 117 Radek Toupal .15 .07
❑ 118 Pavel Pycha .10 .05
❑ 119 Lubomir Kolnik .10 .05
❑ 120 Libor Dolana .10 .05
❑ 121 Ladislav Lubina .15 .07
❑ 122 Tomas Jelinek .10 .05
❑ 123 Petr Vlk .10 .05
❑ 124 Vladimir Petrovka .10 .05
❑ 125 Richard Zemlicka .15 .07
❑ 126 U.S.A. Emblem .50 .23
❑ 127 John Vanbiesbrouck 5.00 2.20
❑ 128 Mike Richter 2.00 .90
❑ 129 Chris Terreri .25 .11
❑ 130 Chris Chelios 1.50 .70
❑ 131 Brian Leetch 1.00 .45
❑ 132 Gary Suter .20 .09
❑ 133 Phil Housley .25 .11
❑ 134 Mark Howe .15 .07
❑ 135 Al Iafrate .25 .11
❑ 136 Kevin Hatcher .25 .11
❑ 137 Mathieu Schneider .25 .11
❑ 138 Pat LaFontaine .75 .35
❑ 139 Darren Turcotte .15 .07
❑ 140 Neal Broten .20 .09
❑ 141 Mike Modano 1.00 .45
❑ 142 Dave Christian .15 .07
❑ 143 Craig Janney .35 .16
❑ 144 Brett Hull 3.00 1.35
❑ 145 Kevin Stevens .35 .16
❑ 146 Joe Mullen .25 .11
❑ 147 Tony Granato .20 .09
❑ 148 Ed Olczyk .15 .07
❑ 149 Jeremy Roenick 2.00 .90
❑ 150 Jimmy Carson .15 .07
❑ 151 West German Emblem .10 .05
❑ 152 Helmut De Raaf .10 .05
❑ 153 Josef Heiss .20 .09
❑ 154 Karl Friesen .20 .09
❑ 155 Uli Hiemer .15 .07
❑ 156 Harold Kreis .10 .05
❑ 157 Udo Kiessling .15 .07
❑ 158 Michael Schmidt .10 .05
❑ 159 Michael Heidt .15 .07
❑ 160 Andreas Pokorny .10 .05
❑ 161 Bernd Wagner .10 .05
❑ 162 Uwe Krupp .25 .11
❑ 163 Gerd Truntschka .15 .07
❑ 164 Bernd Truntschka .15 .07
❑ 165 Thomas Brandl .10 .05
❑ 166 Peter Draisaitl .10 .05
❑ 167 Andreas Brockmann .10 .05
❑ 168 Ulrich Liebsch .10 .05
❑ 169 Ralf Hantschke .10 .05
❑ 170 Thomas Schinko .10 .05
❑ 171 Anton Krinner .10 .05
❑ 172 Thomas Werner .10 .05
❑ 173 Dieter Hegen .15 .07
❑ 174 Helmut Steiger .10 .05
❑ 175 Georg Franz .10 .05
❑ 176 Swiss Emblem .10 .05
❑ 177 Renato Tosio .10 .05
❑ 178 Reto Pavoni .15 .07
❑ 179 Dino Stecher .10 .05
❑ 180 Sven Leuenberger .10 .05
❑ 181 Rick Tschumi .10 .05
❑ 182 Patrice Brasey .10 .05
❑ 183 Didier Massy .10 .05
❑ 184 Sandro Bertaggia .10 .05
❑ 185 Samuel Balmer .10 .05
❑ 186 Martin Rauch .10 .05
❑ 187 Marc Leuenberger .10 .05
❑ 188 Jorg Eberle .10 .05
❑ 189 Fredy Luthi .10 .05
❑ 190 Andy Ton .10 .05
❑ 191 Raymond Walder .10 .05
❑ 192 Manuele Celio .10 .05
❑ 193 Roman Wager .10 .05
❑ 194 Felix Hollenstein .10 .05
❑ 195 Andre Rotheli .10 .05
❑ 196 Christian Weber .10 .05
❑ 197 Peter Jaks .10 .05
❑ 198 Gil Montandon .10 .05
❑ 199 Oliver Hoffmann .10 .05
❑ 200 Thomas Vrabec .10 .05
❑ 201 Teppo Numminen .20 .09
❑ 202 Jyrki Lumme .15 .07
❑ 203 Esa Tikkanen .35 .16
❑ 204 Petri Skriko .15 .07
❑ 205 Christian Ruutu .20 .09
❑ 206 Ilkka Sinisalo .20 .09
❑ 207 Calle Johansson .20 .09
❑ 208 Tomas Sandstrom .20 .09
❑ 209 Thomas Steen .20 .09
❑ 210 Per-Erik Eklund .20 .09
❑ 211 Mats Sundin 1.50 .70
❑ 212 Johan Garpenlov .20 .09
❑ 213 Vyacheslav Fetisov .50 .23
❑ 214 Alexei Kasatonov .35 .16
❑ 215 Mikhail Tatarinov .10 .05
❑ 216 Sergei Makarov .50 .23
❑ 217 Igor Larionov .50 .23
❑ 218 Alexander Mogilny 1.50 .70
❑ 219 Sergei Fedorov 4.00 1.80
❑ 220 Petr Klima .15 .07
❑ 221 David Volek .20 .09
❑ 222 Michal Pivonka .25 .11
❑ 223 Robert Reichel .25 .11
❑ 224 Robert Holik .20 .09
❑ 225 Jaromir Jagr 7.00 3.10
❑ 226 Urpo Ylonen .10 .05
❑ 227 Ilpo Koskela .10 .05
❑ 228 Pekka Rautakallio .10 .05
❑ 229 Lasse Oksanen .10 .05
❑ 230 Veli-Pekka Ketola .20 .09
❑ 231 Leif Holmqvist .15 .07
❑ 232 Lennart Svedberg .15 .07
❑ 233 Sven Tumba Johansson .10 .05
❑ 234 Ulf Sterner .10 .05
❑ 235 Anders Hedberg .25 .11
❑ 236 Ken Dryden 3.00 1.35
❑ 237 Bobby Orr 8.00 3.60
❑ 238 Gordie Howe 4.00 1.80
❑ 239 Bobby Hull 2.00 .90
❑ 240 Phil Esposito 1.50 .70
❑ 241 Vladislav Tretiak 3.00 1.35
❑ 242 Alexander Ragulin .25 .11
❑ 243 Anatoli Firsov .25 .11
❑ 244 Valeri Kharlamov 1.00 .45
❑ 245 Alexander Maltsev .50 .23
❑ 246 Jiri Holecek .20 .09
❑ 247 Jan Suchy .10 .05
❑ 248 Jozef Golonka .10 .05
❑ 249 Vaclav Nedomansky .20 .09
❑ 250 Ivan Hlinka .20 .09

## 1991-92 Swedish Semic Elitserien Stickers

This 360-sticker series captures the players of the Swedish Elitserien. The sticker, which measure 3" by 2 1/8", have posed color photos on the front, along with player name, team emblem and sticker number. The backs note

the set's sponsor "Cloetta" -- a Swedish confectioner. The set includes early appearances by Mats Sundin, Peter Forsberg and Mikael Renberg. An album was available to house the sticker collection; it is valued at $10.

| | MINT | NRMT |
|---|---|---|
| COMPLETE SET (360) | 50.00 | 22.00 |
| COMMON STICKER (1-360) | .10 | .05 |

❑ 1 AIK .10 .05
Team Emblem
❑ 2 Thomas Ostlund .25 .11
❑ 3 Sam Lindstahl .25 .11
❑ 4 Borje Salming .75 .35
❑ 5 Petri Liimatainen .10 .05
❑ 6 Mats Thelin .15 .07
❑ 7 Rikard Franzen .15 .07
❑ 8 Petter Sahlsten .10 .05
❑ 9 Daniel Jardemyr .10 .05
❑ 10 Thomas Nilsson .10 .05
❑ 11 Niclas Havelid .10 .05
❑ 12 Mattias Norstrom .25 .11
❑ 13 Peter Gradin .10 .05
❑ 14 Peter Hammarstrom .10 .05
❑ 15 Patrik Ericksson .15 .07
❑ 16 Thomas Bjuhr .10 .05
❑ 17 Thomas Strandberg .10 .05
❑ 18 Tommy Lehmann .20 .09
❑ 19 Mats Lindberg .10 .05
❑ 20 Patric Kjellberg .20 .09
❑ 21 Michael Nylander 1.50 .70
❑ 22 Patric Englund .10 .05
❑ 23 Niclas Sundblad .50 .23
❑ 24 Kristian Gahn .25 .11
❑ 25 Erik Andersson .10 .05
❑ 26 Bjorn Ahlstrom .10 .05
❑ 27 Brynas .10 .05
Team Emblem
❑ 28 Michael Sundlov .25 .11
❑ 29 Lars Eriksson .25 .11
❑ 30 Lars Karlsson .10 .05
❑ 31 Tommy Sjodin .20 .09
❑ 32 Nikolaj Davydkin .10 .05
❑ 33 Niklas Gallstedt .10 .05
❑ 34 Mikael Lindman .10 .05
❑ 35 Tommy Melkersson .10 .05
❑ 36 Mikael Enander .10 .05
❑ 37 Urban Molander .10 .05
❑ 38 Stefan Klockare .15 .07
❑ 39 Anders Huss .15 .07
❑ 40 Mikael Lindholm .10 .05
❑ 41 Jan Larsson .10 .05
❑ 42 Anders Gozzi .15 .07
❑ 43 Peter Larsson .10 .05
❑ 44 Thomas Tallberg .15 .07
❑ 45 Peter Gustafsson .10 .05
❑ 46 Joakim Persson .75 .35
❑ 47 Peter Eriksson .10 .05
❑ 48 Ove Mohlin .15 .07
❑ 49 Jonas Johnson .10 .05
❑ 50 Johan Schillgard .10 .05
❑ 51 Andreas Dackell .25 .11
❑ 52 Tom Bissett .15 .07
❑ 53 Djurgarden .10 .05
Team Emblem
❑ 54 Tommy Soderstrom .75 .35
❑ 55 Joakim Persson .75 .35
❑ 56 Petter Ronnqvist .25 .11
❑ 57 Thomas Eriksson .10 .05
❑ 58 Kenneth Kennholt .15 .07
❑ 59 Arto Blomsten .20 .09
❑ 60 Orvar Stambert .10 .05
❑ 61 Christian Due-Boje .15 .07
❑ 62 Marcus Ragnarsson 1.50 .70
❑ 63 Per Nygards .10 .05
❑ 64 Thomas Johansson .10 .05
❑ 65 Mikael Johansson .10 .05
❑ 66 Charles Berglund .15 .07
❑ 67 Jan Viktorsson .15 .07
❑ 68 Ola Josefsson .10 .05
❑ 69 Jens Ohling .15 .07
❑ 70 Magnus Jansson .10 .05
❑ 71 Peter Nilsson .10 .05
❑ 72 Fredrik Lindquist .25 .11
❑ 73 Mariusz Czerkawski 1.50 .70
❑ 74 Johan Lindstedt .10 .05
❑ 75 Stefan Ketola .25 .11
❑ 76 Erik Huusko .15 .07
❑ 77 Anders Huusko .15 .07
❑ 78 Farjestad .10 .05
Team Emblem
❑ 79 Anders Bergman .25 .11
❑ 80 Jorgen Ryden .25 .11
❑ 81 Patrik Haltia .35 .16
❑ 82 Tommy Samuelsson .10 .05
❑ 83 Per Lundell .10 .05
❑ 84 Leif Carlsson .10 .05
❑ 85 Jesper Duus .10 .05
❑ 86 Mattias Olsson .10 .05
❑ 87 Thomas Rhodin .10 .05
❑ 88 Jacob Karlsson .10 .05
❑ 89 Greger Artursson .10 .05
❑ 90 Thomas Rundqvist .15 .07
❑ 91 Bengt-Ake Gustafsson .25 .11
❑ 92 Hakan Loob 1.00 .45
❑ 93 Lars Karlsson .10 .05
❑ 94 Magnus Roupe .20 .09
❑ 95 Kjell Dahlin .25 .11
❑ 96 Staffan Lundh .10 .05
❑ 97 Peter Ottosson .10 .05
❑ 98 Niklas Brannstrom .10 .05
❑ 99 Jonas Hoglund .15 .07
❑ 100 Clas Eriksson .15 .07
❑ 101 Andreas Johansson .15 .07
❑ 102 Mathias Johansson .10 .05
❑ 103 HV 71 .10 .05
Team Emblem
❑ 104 Peter Aslin .35 .16
❑ 105 Boo Ahl .50 .23
❑ 106 Stefan Magnusson .10 .05
❑ 107 Fredrik Stillman .20 .09
❑ 108 Lars Ivarsson .10 .05
❑ 109 Klas Heed .10 .05
❑ 110 Arto Ruotanen .10 .05
❑ 111 Per Gustafsson .10 .05
❑ 112 Tommy Fritz .10 .05
❑ 113 Mathias Svedberg .10 .05
❑ 114 Kristian Pedersen .10 .05
❑ 115 Peter Eriksson .10 .05
❑ 116 Risto Kurkinen .10 .05
❑ 117 Ove Thornberg .10 .05
❑ 118 Stefan Ornskog .25 .11
❑ 119 Thomas Ljungberg .10 .05
❑ 120 Patrik Ross .10 .05
❑ 121 Eddy Ericsson .10 .05
❑ 122 Dennis Strom .10 .05
❑ 123 Torbjorn Persson .10 .05
❑ 124 Jonas Jonsson .10 .05
❑ 125 Peter Ekelund .10 .05
❑ 126 Stefan Falk .25 .11
❑ 127 Ronny Nilsson .10 .05
❑ 128 Leksand .10 .05
Team Emblem
❑ 129 Olow Sundstrom .25 .11
❑ 130 Jonas Leven .25 .11
❑ 131 Tomas Jonsson .25 .11
❑ 132 Ricard Persson .25 .11
❑ 133 Magnus Svensson .35 .16
❑ 134 Mattias Andersson .10 .05
❑ 135 Henric Bjorkman .10 .05
❑ 136 Orjan Lindmark .10 .05
❑ 137 Orjan Nilsson .10 .05
❑ 138 Tomas Ring .10 .05
❑ 139 Roger Johansson .10 .05
❑ 140 Marcus Thuresson .10 .05
❑ 141 Per-Olof Carlsson .10 .05
❑ 142 Jens Nielsen .10 .05
❑ 143 Cenneth Soderlund .10 .05
❑ 144 Markus Akerblom .20 .09
❑ 145 Fredrik Jax .20 .09
❑ 146 Reine Rauhala .15 .07
❑ 147 Niklas Eriksson .10 .05
❑ 148 Martin Wiita .10 .05
❑ 149 Jonas Bergqvist .20 .09
❑ 150 Hannu Jarvenpaa .25 .11
❑ 151 Lulea .10 .05
Team Emblem
❑ 152 Robert Skoog .25 .11
❑ 153 Erik Granqvist .25 .11
❑ 154 Timo Jutila .25 .11
❑ 155 Tomas Lilja .10 .05
❑ 156 Lars Modig .10 .05
❑ 157 Per Ljusterang .10 .05
❑ 158 Jari Gronstrand .10 .05
❑ 159 Torbjorn Lindberg .10 .05
❑ 160 Patrik Hoglund .20 .09
❑ 161 Petter Nilsson .10 .05
❑ 162 Daniel Behm .10 .05
❑ 163 Johan Stromvall .10 .05
❑ 164 Pauli Jarvinen .10 .05
❑ 165 Lars Edstrom .10 .05
❑ 166 Lars-Gunnar Pettersson .10 .05
❑ 167 Stefan Nilsson .10 .05
❑ 168 Lars Hurtig .10 .05
❑ 169 Tomas Berglund .10 .05
❑ 170 Robert Nordberg .25 .11
❑ 171 Mikael Renberg 5.00 2.20
❑ 172 Ulf Sandstrom .10 .05
❑ 173 Jens Hellgren .10 .05
❑ 174 Mikael Engstrom .10 .05
❑ 175 Malmo .10 .05
Team Emblem
❑ 176 Peter Lindmark .35 .16
❑ 177 Roger Nordstrom .35 .16
❑ 178 Johan Mansson .10 .05
❑ 179 Timo Blomqvist .35 .16
❑ 180 Peter Andersson .25 .11
❑ 181 Mats Lusth .10 .05
❑ 182 Roger Ohman .10 .05
❑ 183 Johan Salle .10 .05
❑ 184 Anders Svensson .10 .05
❑ 185 Johan Norgren .10 .05
❑ 186 Raimo Helminen .35 .16
❑ 187 Mats Hallin .25 .11
❑ 188 Mats Naslund 1.00 .45
❑ 189 Robert Burakovsky .25 .11
❑ 190 Hakan Ahlund .10 .05
❑ 191 Peter Sundstrom .35 .16
❑ 192 Daniel Rydmark .20 .09
❑ 193 Matti Pauna .10 .05
❑ 194 Roger Hansson .10 .05
❑ 195 Patrik Gustavsson .10 .05
❑ 196 Rick Erdall .10 .05
❑ 197 Bo Svanberg .10 .05
❑ 198 Jesper Mattsson 1.00 .45
❑ 199 Jonas Hakansson .10 .05
❑ 200 MoDo .10 .05
Team Emblem
❑ 201 Fredrik Andersson .25 .11
❑ 202 Goran Arnmark .25 .11
❑ 203 Miroslav Horava .25 .11
❑ 204 Hans Lodin .10 .05
❑ 205 lars Jansson .10 .05
❑ 206 Jorgen Eriksson .10 .05
❑ 207 Anders Berglund .10 .05
❑ 208 Osmo Soutokorva .10 .05
❑ 209 Tomas Nanzen .10 .05
❑ 210 Hans Jonsson .10 .05
❑ 211 Fredrik Bergqvist .10 .05
❑ 212 Erik Holmberg .10 .05
❑ 213 Peter Forsberg 10.00 4.50
❑ 214 Markus Naslund 1.50 .70
❑ 215 Magnus Wernblom .10 .05
❑ 216 Lars Bystrom .10 .05
❑ 217 Kent Lantz .10 .05
❑ 218 Per Wallin .20 .09
❑ 219 Lennart Henriksson .10 .05
❑ 220 Ingemar Strom .10 .05
❑ 221 Ulf Odmark .10 .05
❑ 222 Jens Ohman .10 .05
❑ 223 Tommy Pettersson .10 .05
❑ 224 Andreas Salomonsson .15 .07
❑ 225 Sodertalje .10 .05
Team Emblem
❑ 226 Reino Sundberg .25 .11
❑ 227 Stefan Dernestal .25 .11
❑ 228 Mats Kihlstrom .10 .05
❑ 229 Stefan Jonsson .10 .05
❑ 230 Jan Bergman .10 .05
❑ 231 Peter Ekroth .10 .05
❑ 232 Stefan Nyman .10 .05
❑ 233 Thomas Carlsson .10 .05
❑ 234 Stefan Claesson .10 .05
❑ 235 Oto Hascak .20 .09
❑ 236 Morgan Samuelsson .10 .05
❑ 237 Tomaz Eriksson .10 .05
❑ 238 Thom Eklund .10 .05
❑ 239 Conny Jansson .10 .05
❑ 240 Bjorn Carlsson .10 .05
❑ 241 Scott Moore .10 .05
❑ 242 Reine Landgren .10 .05
❑ 243 Ola Rosander .10 .05
❑ 244 Stefan Olsson .10 .05
❑ 245 Anders Frykbo .10 .05
❑ 246 Ola Andersson .10 .05
❑ 247 Joe Tracy .10 .05
❑ 248 Christer Ljungberg .10 .05
❑ 249 Patrik Nyberg .10 .05
❑ 250 Joakim Skold .10 .05
❑ 251 Vasteras .10 .05
Team Emblem
❑ 252 Mats Ytter .25 .11
❑ 253 Par Hellenberg .25 .11
❑ 254 Tommy Salo 2.00 .90
❑ 255 Nicklas Lidstrom 1.50 .70
❑ 256 Robert Nordmark .25 .11
❑ 257 Leif Rohlin .35 .16
❑ 258 Roger Akerstrom .15 .07
❑ 259 Peter Popovic .25 .11
❑ 260 Jan Karlsson .10 .05
❑ 261 Tore Lindgren .10 .05
❑ 262 Peter Jacobsson .10 .05
❑ 263 Pierre Ivarsson .10 .05
❑ 264 Misjat Fachrutdinov .10 .05
❑ 265 Paul Andersson .10 .05
❑ 266 Patrik Juhlin .50 .23
❑ 267 Henrik Nilsson .10 .05
❑ 268 Anders Berglund .10 .05
❑ 269 Claes Lindblom .10 .05
❑ 270 Jorgen Holmberg .10 .05
❑ 271 Stefan Hellkvist .10 .05
❑ 272 Fredrik Nilsson .25 .11
❑ 273 Johan Brummer .10 .05
❑ 274 Micael Karlberg .10 .05
❑ 275 Niclas Lundberg .10 .05
❑ 276 Vastra Frolunda .10 .05
Team Emblem
❑ 277 Ake Lilljebjorn .25 .11
❑ 278 Hakan Algotsson .35 .16
❑ 279 Hakan Nordin .10 .05
❑ 280 Jonas Heed .10 .05
❑ 281 Joacim Esbjors .15 .07
❑ 282 Stefan Larsson .10 .05
❑ 283 Stefan Axelsson .25 .11
❑ 284 Oscar Ackestrom .10 .05
❑ 285 Jerk Hogstrom .10 .05
❑ 286 Patric Aberg .10 .05
❑ 287 Patrok Carnback .25 .11
❑ 288 Serge Boisvert .25 .11
❑ 289 Mats Lundstrom .10 .05
❑ 290 Mikael Andersson .50 .23
❑ 291 Kari Jaako .10 .05
❑ 292 Terho Koskela .10 .05
❑ 293 Lars Dahlstrom .10 .05
❑ 294 Jerry Persson .10 .05
❑ 295 Peter Berndtsson .10 .05
❑ 296 Thomas Sjogren .15 .07
❑ 297 Par Edlund .10 .05
❑ 298 Christian Lechtaler .10 .05
❑ 299 Jonas Esbjors .15 .07
❑ 300 Dennis Fredriksson .10 .05
❑ 301 Mats Hjalmarsson .10 .05
❑ 302 Leif Holmgren CO .10 .05
❑ 303 Tommy Sandlin CO .10 .05
❑ 304 Lars Falk CO .10 .05
❑ 305 Harald Luckner CO .10 .05
❑ 306 Lars-Erik Lundstrom CO .10 .05
❑ 307 Staffan Tholson CO .10 .05
❑ 308 Freddy Lindfors CO .10 .05
❑ 309 Timo Lahtinen CO .10 .05
❑ 310 Jan-Ake Andersson CO .10 .05
❑ 311 Claes-Goran Wallin CO .10 .05
❑ 312 Mikael Lundstrom CO .10 .05
❑ 313 Leif Boork CO .10 .05
❑ 314 Thomas Rundqvist .25 .11
❑ 315 Hakan Loob 1.00 .45
❑ 316 Tommy Soderstrom .75 .35
❑ 317 Niklas Andersson .10 .05
❑ 318 Hakan Loob 1.00 .45
❑ 319 Tomas Sandstrom .50 .23
❑ 320 Rolf Ridderwall .25 .11
❑ 321 Thomas Eriksson .10 .05
❑ 322 Nicklas Lidstrom 1.50 .70
❑ 323 Mats Sundin 4.00 1.80
❑ 324 Thomas Rundqvist .25 .11
❑ 325 Hakan Loob 1.00 .45
❑ 326 Marcus Karlsson .10 .05
❑ 327 Anders Eriksson .10 .05
❑ 328 Mats Lindgren 1.00 .45
❑ 329 Mikael Hakansson .25 .11
❑ 330 Mathias Johansson .10 .05
❑ 331 Niclas Sundstrom 2.00 .90
❑ 332 Jesper Mattsson 1.00 .45
❑ 333 Anders Soderberg .50 .23
❑ 334 Swedish IHF Emblem .10 .05
❑ 335 1991 World Champions .10 .05
❑ 336 Rolf Ridderwall .25 .11
❑ 337 Peter Lindmark .35 .16
❑ 338 Tommy Soderstrom .75 .35
❑ 339 Kjell Samuelsson .10 .05
❑ 340 Calle Johansson .50 .23
❑ 341 Nicklas Lidstrom 1.50 .70
❑ 342 Tomas Jonsson .25 .11
❑ 343 Peter Andersson .25 .11
❑ 344 Kenneth Kennholt .15 .07
❑ 345 Fredrik Stillman .20 .09
❑ 346 Thomas Rundqvist .25 .11
❑ 347 Hakan Loob 1.00 .45
❑ 348 Bengt-Ake Gustafsson .25 .11
❑ 349 Mats Naslund 1.00 .45
❑ 350 Mikael Johansson .10 .05
❑ 351 Charles Berglund .15 .07
❑ 352 Jan Viktorsson .15 .07
❑ 353 Johan Garpenlov .10 .05
❑ 354 Anders Carlsson .10 .05
❑ 355 Patrik Ericksson .15 .07
❑ 356 Jonas Bergqvist .20 .09
❑ 357 Mats Sundin 4.00 1.80
❑ 358 Per-Erik Eklund .10 .05
❑ 359 Conny Svensson .10 .05
❑ 360 Curt Lundmark .10 .05

## 1992-93 Swedish Semic Elitserien Stickers

This 356-sticker set covers the Swedish Elitserien. The stickers, which measure 3" by 2 1/8", feature posed color photos and player name on the front. The back has card number, and a cartoon ad for Buster, a sports magazine for Swedish boys. The set is highlighted by the pre-NHL appearances of Peter Forsberg, Mikael Renberg and Tommy Salo, as well as former greats such as Borje Salming and Hakan Loob.

| | MINT | NRMT |
|---|---|---|
| COMPLETE SET (356) | 75.00 | 34.00 |
| COMMON CARD (1-356) | .10 | .05 |

❑ 1 AIK .10 .05
Team Picture
❑ 2 AIK .10 .05
Team Picture
❑ 3 Brynas .10 .05
Team Picture
❑ 4 Brynas .10 .05
Team Picture
❑ 5 Djurgarden .10 .05
Team Picture
❑ 6 Djurgarden .10 .05
Team Picture
❑ 7 Farjestad .10 .05
Team Picture
❑ 8 Farjestad .10 .05
Team Picture
❑ 9 HV 71 .10 .05
Team Picture
❑ 10 HV 71 .10 .05
Team Picture
❑ 11 Leksand .10 .05
Team Picture
❑ 12 Leksand .10 .05
Team Picture
❑ 13 Lulea .10 .05
Team Picture
❑ 14 Lulea .10 .05
Team Picture
❑ 15 Malmo .10 .05
Team Picture
❑ 16 Malmo .10 .05
Team Picture
❑ 17 MoDo .10 .05
Team Picture
❑ 18 MoDo .10 .05
Team Picture
❑ 19 Rogle .10 .05
Team Picture
❑ 20 Rogle .10 .05
Team Picture
❑ 21 Vasteras .10 .05
Team Picture
❑ 22 Vasteras .10 .05
Team Picture
❑ 23 Vastra Frolunda .10 .05
Team Picture
❑ 24 Vastra Frolunda .10 .05
Team Picture
❑ 25 AIK .10 .05
Team Emblem
❑ 26 Rolf Ridderwall .25 .11
❑ 27 Sam Lindstahl .20 .09
❑ 28 Ronnie Karlsson .10 .05
❑ 29 Mats Thelin .15 .07
❑ 30 Mattias Norstrom .75 .35
❑ 31 Dick Tarnstrom .35 .16
❑ 32 Petri Liimatainen .10 .05
❑ 33 Rikard Franzen .15 .07
❑ 34 Daniel Jardemyr .10 .05
❑ 35 Niclas Havelid .15 .07
❑ 36 Borje Salming 2.00 .90
❑ 37 Thomas Bjuhr .10 .05
❑ 38 Peter Hammarstrom .10 .05
❑ 39 Thomas Strandberg .10 .05
❑ 40 Mats Lindberg .10 .05
❑ 41 Anders Bjork .10 .05
❑ 42 Anders Johnson .10 .05
❑ 43 Patrik Erickson .15 .07
❑ 44 Torbjorn Ohrlund .10 .05
❑ 45 Bjorn Ahlstrom .10 .05
❑ 46 Niclas Sundblad .15 .07
❑ 47 Patric Englund .10 .05
❑ 48 Kristian Gahn .10 .05
❑ 49 Morgan Samuelsson .15 .07
❑ 50 Brynas .10 .05
Team Emblem
❑ 51 Michael Sundlov .25 .11
❑ 52 Lars Karlsson .25 .11
❑ 53 Bedrich Scerban .15 .07
❑ 54 Mikael Lindman .10 .05
❑ 55 Tommy Melkersson .10 .05
❑ 56 Stefan Klockare .15 .07
❑ 57 Mikael Enander .15 .07
❑ 58 Roger Karlsson .10 .05
❑ 59 Niklas Gallstedt .10 .05
❑ 60 Christer Olsson .50 .23
❑ 61 Anders Carlsson .10 .05
❑ 62 Thomas Tallberg .15 .07
❑ 63 Tom Bissett .15 .07
❑ 64 Andreas Dackell .50 .23
❑ 65 Mikael Wahlberg .10 .05
❑ 66 Jan Larsson .10 .05
❑ 67 Anders Gozzi .10 .05
❑ 68 Ove Molin .10 .05
❑ 69 Anders Huss .15 .07
❑ 70 Peter Gustafsson .10 .05
❑ 71 Jonas Johnson .10 .05
❑ 72 Peter Larsson .10 .05
❑ 73 Mikael Lindholm .10 .05
❑ 74 Djurgarden .10 .05
Team Emblem
❑ 75 Thomas Ostlund .35 .16
❑ 76 Petter Ronnquist .20 .09
❑ 77 Christian Due-Boje .15 .07
❑ 78 Arto Blomsten .15 .07
❑ 79 Kenneth Kennholt .20 .09
❑ 80 Marcus Ragnarsson 1.00 .45
❑ 81 Thomas Johansson .10 .05
❑ 82 Joakim Lundberg .10 .05
❑ 83 Thomas Eriksson .10 .05
❑ 84 Bjorn Nord .15 .07
❑ 85 Mikael Magnusson .10 .05
❑ 86 Charles Berglund .10 .05
❑ 87 Erik Huusko .15 .07
❑ 88 Anders Huusko .10 .05
❑ 89 Tony Skopac .10 .05
❑ 90 Jens Ohling .20 .09
❑ 91 Peter Nilsson .10 .05
❑ 92 Magnus Jansson .10 .05
❑ 93 Kent Nilsson .75 .35
❑ 94 Mikael Hakansson .10 .05
❑ 95 Ola Josefsson .10 .05
❑ 96 Jerry Friman .10 .05
❑ 97 Fredrik Lindquist .35 .16
❑ 98 Mathias Hallback .10 .05
❑ 99 Jan Viktorsson .10 .05
❑ 100 Farjestad .10 .05
Team Emblem
❑ 101 Anders Bergman .25 .11
❑ 102 Jonas Eriksson .20 .09
❑ 103 Patrik Haltia .25 .11
❑ 104 Tommy Samuelsson .10 .05
❑ 105 Jesper Duus .10 .05
❑ 106 Leif Carlsson .10 .05
❑ 107 Per Lundell .10 .05
❑ 108 Jacob Karlsson .10 .05
❑ 109 Thomas Rhodin .10 .05
❑ 110 Mattias Olsson .10 .05
❑ 111 Hakan Loob 1.00 .45
❑ 112 Thomas Rundqvist .10 .05
❑ 113 Andreas Johansson .35 .16
❑ 114 Staffan Lundh .10 .05
❑ 115 Jonas Hoglund .50 .23
❑ 116 Bengt-Ake Gustafsson .35 .16
❑ 117 Mattias Johansson .10 .05
❑ 118 Clas Eriksson .10 .05
❑ 119 Peter Ottosson .10 .05
❑ 120 Niklas Brannstrom .10 .05
❑ 121 Lars Karlsson .25 .11
❑ 122 Peter Hagstrom .10 .05
❑ 123 Kjell Dahlin .35 .16
❑ 124 HV 71 .10 .05
Team Emblem
❑ 125 Peter Aslin .25 .11
❑ 126 Boo Ahl .50 .23
❑ 127 Antonin Stavjana .20 .09
❑ 128 Klas Heed .10 .05
❑ 129 Tommy Fritz .10 .05
❑ 130 Kristian Pedersen .10 .05
❑ 131 Per Gustafsson .75 .35
❑ 132 Mathias Svedberg .10 .05
❑ 133 Niclas Rahm .10 .05
❑ 134 Martin Danielsson .10 .05
❑ 135 Fredrik Stillman .10 .05
❑ 136 Lars Ivarsson .10 .05
❑ 137 Ove Thornberg .10 .05
❑ 138 Peter Ekelund .10 .05

| | | |
|---|---|---|
| ❑ 139 Eddy Eriksson | .10 | .05 |
| ❑ 140 Stefan Ornskog | .20 | .09 |
| ❑ 141 Patrik Ross | .10 | .05 |
| ❑ 142 Torbjorn Persson | .10 | .05 |
| ❑ 143 Kamil Kastak | .20 | .09 |
| ❑ 144 Dennis Strom | .10 | .05 |
| ❑ 145 Peter Eriksson | .10 | .05 |
| ❑ 146 Magnus Axelsson | .20 | .09 |
| ❑ 147 Stefan Falk | .20 | .09 |
| ❑ 148 Thomas Ljungberg | .10 | .05 |
| ❑ 149 Leksand Team Emblem | .10 | .05 |
| ❑ 150 Ake Lilljebjorn | .25 | .11 |
| ❑ 151 Jonas Leven | .25 | .11 |
| ❑ 152 Johan Hedberg | .35 | .16 |
| ❑ 153 Tomas Jonsson | .35 | .16 |
| ❑ 154 Henric Bjorkman | .10 | .05 |
| ❑ 155 Mattias Andersson | .10 | .05 |
| ❑ 156 Rickard Persson | .35 | .16 |
| ❑ 157 Orjan Nilsson | .10 | .05 |
| ❑ 158 Magnus Svensson | .25 | .11 |
| ❑ 159 Orjan Lindmark | .10 | .05 |
| ❑ 160 Jan Huokko | .10 | .05 |
| ❑ 161 Reine Rauhala | .10 | .05 |
| ❑ 162 Emil Skoglund | .10 | .05 |
| ❑ 163 Jens Nielsen | .10 | .05 |
| ❑ 164 Marcus Thuresson | .10 | .05 |
| ❑ 165 Niklas Eriksson | .10 | .05 |
| ❑ 166 Tomas Srsen | .15 | .07 |
| ❑ 167 Jonas Bergqvist | .25 | .11 |
| ❑ 168 Per-Olof Carlsson | .10 | .05 |
| ❑ 169 Markus Akerblom | .10 | .05 |
| ❑ 170 Greg Parks | .15 | .07 |
| ❑ 171 Mattias Loof | .10 | .05 |
| ❑ 172 Cenneth Soderlund | .10 | .05 |
| ❑ 173 Jarmo Makitalo | .10 | .05 |
| ❑ 174 Lulea Team Emblem | .10 | .05 |
| ❑ 175 Robert Skoog | .20 | .09 |
| ❑ 176 Erik Grankvist | .20 | .09 |
| ❑ 177 Lars Modig | .10 | .05 |
| ❑ 178 Patrik Hoglund | .10 | .05 |
| ❑ 179 Niklas Bjornfot | .10 | .05 |
| ❑ 180 Torbjorn Lindberg | .10 | .05 |
| ❑ 181 Ville Siren | .25 | .11 |
| ❑ 182 Petter Nilsson | .10 | .05 |
| ❑ 183 Joakim Gunler | .10 | .05 |
| ❑ 184 Tomas Lilja | .10 | .05 |
| ❑ 185 Stefan Jonsson | .10 | .05 |
| ❑ 186 Stefan Nilsson | .20 | .09 |
| ❑ 187 Johan Stromvall | .10 | .05 |
| ❑ 188 Robert Nordberg | .15 | .07 |
| ❑ 189 Tomas Berglund | .15 | .07 |
| ❑ 190 Mikael Renberg | 5.00 | 2.20 |
| ❑ 191 Lars-Gunnar Pettersson | .10 | .05 |
| ❑ 192 Lars Edstrom | .10 | .05 |
| ❑ 193 Kyosti Karjalainen | .20 | .09 |
| ❑ 194 Lars Hurtig | .10 | .05 |
| ❑ 195 Fredrik Oberg | .10 | .05 |
| ❑ 196 Mikael Engstrom | .10 | .05 |
| ❑ 197 Mika Nieminen | .50 | .23 |
| ❑ 198 Malmo Team Emblem | .10 | .05 |
| ❑ 199 Peter Lindmark | .35 | .16 |
| ❑ 200 Roger Nordstrom | .25 | .11 |
| ❑ 201 Johan Mansson | .10 | .05 |
| ❑ 202 Anders Svensson | .10 | .05 |
| ❑ 203 Timo Blomqvist | .35 | .16 |
| ❑ 204 Johan Norgren | .10 | .05 |
| ❑ 205 Mats Lusth | .10 | .05 |
| ❑ 206 Peter Hasselblad | .10 | .05 |
| ❑ 207 Robert Svehla | 1.00 | .45 |
| ❑ 208 Johan Salle | .10 | .05 |
| ❑ 209 Roger Ohman | .10 | .05 |
| ❑ 210 Raimo Helminen | .35 | .16 |
| ❑ 211 Roger Hansson | .20 | .09 |
| ❑ 212 Per Rosenqvist | .10 | .05 |
| ❑ 213 Bo Svanberg | .10 | .05 |
| ❑ 214 Daniel Rydmark | .20 | .09 |
| ❑ 215 Patrik Sylvegard | .10 | .05 |
| ❑ 216 Jonas Hakansson | .10 | .05 |
| ❑ 217 Jesper Mattsson | 1.00 | .45 |
| ❑ 218 Hakan Ahlund | .10 | .05 |
| ❑ 219 Peter Sundstrom | .35 | .16 |
| ❑ 220 Mats Naslund | 2.00 | .90 |
| ❑ 221 Robert Burakovsky | .15 | .07 |
| ❑ 222 MoDo Team Emblem | .10 | .05 |
| ❑ 223 Fredrik Andersson | .20 | .09 |
| ❑ 224 Anders Nasstrom | .20 | .09 |
| ❑ 225 Anders Berglund | .10 | .05 |
| ❑ 226 Miroslav Horava | .15 | .07 |
| ❑ 227 Hans Lodin | .10 | .05 |
| ❑ 228 Lars Jansson | .10 | .05 |
| ❑ 229 Jorgen Eriksson | .10 | .05 |
| ❑ 230 Anders Eriksson | 2.00 | .90 |
| ❑ 231 Hans Jonsson | .10 | .05 |
| ❑ 232 Tomas Nanzen | .10 | .05 |
| ❑ 233 Mattias Timander | .75 | .35 |
| ❑ 234 Fredrik Bergqvist | .10 | .05 |
| ❑ 235 Magnus Wernblom | .20 | .09 |
| ❑ 236 Martin Hostak | .15 | .07 |
| ❑ 237 Mikael Pettersson | .10 | .05 |
| ❑ 238 Lennart Hermansson | .10 | .05 |
| ❑ 239 Tommy Lehmann | .20 | .09 |
| ❑ 240 Markus Naslund | 1.00 | .45 |
| ❑ 241 Ulf Odmark | .10 | .05 |
| ❑ 242 Peter Forsberg | 15.00 | 6.75 |
| ❑ 243 Andreas Salomonsson | .10 | .05 |
| ❑ 244 Niklas Sundstrom | 4.00 | 1.80 |
| ❑ 245 Lars Bystrom | .10 | .05 |
| ❑ 246 Erik Holmberg | .10 | .05 |
| ❑ 247 Henrik Gradin | .10 | .05 |
| ❑ 248 Rogle Team Emblem | .10 | .05 |
| ❑ 249 Kenneth Johansson | .25 | .11 |
| ❑ 250 Billy Nilsson | .25 | .11 |
| ❑ 251 Orjan Jacobsson | .10 | .05 |
| ❑ 252 Daniel Johansson | .50 | .23 |
| ❑ 253 Kenny Jonsson | 2.00 | .90 |
| ❑ 254 Kari Eloranta | .25 | .11 |
| ❑ 255 Kari Suoraniemi | .10 | .05 |
| ❑ 256 Hakan Persson | .10 | .05 |
| ❑ 257 Rikard Gronborg | .10 | .05 |
| ❑ 258 Stefan Nilsson | .10 | .05 |
| ❑ 259 Per Ljusterang | .10 | .05 |
| ❑ 260 Igor Stelnov | .10 | .05 |
| ❑ 261 Peter Lundmark | .25 | .11 |
| ❑ 262 Heinz Ehlers | .10 | .05 |
| ❑ 263 Michael Hjalm | .10 | .05 |
| ❑ 264 Jan Ericson | .10 | .05 |
| ❑ 265 Pelle Svensson | .10 | .05 |
| ❑ 266 Mats Loov | .15 | .07 |
| ❑ 267 Stefan Elvenes | .15 | .07 |
| ❑ 268 Roger Elvenes | .20 | .09 |
| ❑ 269 Peter Wennberg | .10 | .05 |
| ❑ 270 Per Wallin | .35 | .16 |
| ❑ 271 Torgny Lowgren | .10 | .05 |
| ❑ 272 Jorgen Jonsson | .10 | .05 |
| ❑ 273 Vasteras Team Emblem | .10 | .05 |
| ❑ 274 Mats Ytter | .25 | .11 |
| ❑ 275 Tommy Salo | 2.50 | 1.10 |
| ❑ 276 Erik Bergstrom | .10 | .05 |
| ❑ 277 Pierre Ivarsson | .10 | .05 |
| ❑ 278 Peter Popovic | .20 | .09 |
| ❑ 279 Sergei Fokin | .10 | .05 |
| ❑ 280 Edvin Frylen | .25 | .11 |
| ❑ 281 Leif Rohlin | .35 | .16 |
| ❑ 282 Peter Karlsson | .10 | .05 |
| ❑ 283 Peter Jacobsson | .10 | .05 |
| ❑ 284 Roger Akerstrom | .15 | .07 |
| ❑ 285 Robert Nordmark | .20 | .09 |
| ❑ 286 Patrik Juhlin | .75 | .35 |
| ❑ 287 Mishat Fahrutdinov | .15 | .07 |
| ❑ 288 Henrik Nilsson | .10 | .05 |
| ❑ 289 Mikael Pettersson | .10 | .05 |
| ❑ 290 Fredrik Nilsson | .15 | .07 |
| ❑ 291 Stefan Hellkvist | .10 | .05 |
| ❑ 292 Henrik Pettersson | .10 | .05 |
| ❑ 293 Micael Karlberg | .10 | .05 |
| ❑ 294 Anders Berglund | .10 | .05 |
| ❑ 295 Claes Lindblom | .15 | .07 |
| ❑ 296 Johan Brummer | .10 | .05 |
| ❑ 297 Patrik Ulin | .10 | .05 |
| ❑ 298 Paul Andersson | .10 | .05 |
| ❑ 299 Vastra Frolunda Team Emblem | .10 | .05 |
| ❑ 300 Hakan Algotsson | .35 | .16 |
| ❑ 301 Mikael Sandberg | .25 | .11 |
| ❑ 302 Patric Aberg | .10 | .05 |
| ❑ 303 Joacim Esbjors | .15 | .07 |
| ❑ 304 Oscar Ackestrom | .10 | .05 |
| ❑ 305 Jonas Heed | .10 | .05 |
| ❑ 306 Stefan Axelsson | .25 | .11 |
| ❑ 307 Ronnie Sundin | .35 | .16 |
| ❑ 308 Stefan Larsson | .10 | .05 |
| ❑ 309 Jonathan Hagrenius | .10 | .05 |
| ❑ 310 Serge Boisvert | .15 | .07 |
| ❑ 311 Jerry Persson | .10 | .05 |
| ❑ 312 Trond Magnussen | .10 | .05 |
| ❑ 313 Terho Koskela | .10 | .05 |
| ❑ 314 Peter Derndtsson | .10 | .05 |
| ❑ 315 Mikael Persson | .10 | .05 |
| ❑ 316 Mats Hjalmarsson | .10 | .05 |
| ❑ 317 Henrik Lundin | .10 | .05 |
| ❑ 318 Jonas Esbjors | .10 | .05 |
| ❑ 319 Daniel Alfredsson | 5.00 | 2.20 |
| ❑ 320 Stefan Ketola | .10 | .05 |
| ❑ 321 Lars Dahlstrom | .10 | .05 |
| ❑ 322 Par Edlund | .10 | .05 |
| ❑ 323 Thomas Sjogren | .15 | .07 |
| ❑ 324 Leif Holmgren CO | .10 | .05 |
| ❑ 325 Tommy Sandlin CO | .10 | .05 |
| ❑ 326 Lars Falk CO | .10 | .05 |
| ❑ 327 Harald Luckner CO | .10 | .05 |
| ❑ 328 Lars-Erik Lundstrom CO | .10 | .05 |
| ❑ 329 Wayne Fleming CO | .10 | .05 |
| ❑ 330 Freddy Lindfors CO | .10 | .05 |
| ❑ 331 Timo Lahtinen CO | .10 | .05 |
| ❑ 332 Kent Forsberg CO | .25 | .11 |
| ❑ 333 Christer Abrahamsson CO | .25 | .11 |
| ❑ 334 Mikael Lundstrom CO | .10 | .05 |
| ❑ 335 Leif Boork CO | .10 | .05 |
| ❑ 336 Tommy Sjodin | .25 | .11 |
| ❑ 337 Hakan Loob | 1.00 | .45 |
| ❑ 338 Michael Nylander | 1.00 | .45 |
| ❑ 339 Michael Nylander | 1.00 | .45 |
| ❑ 340 Hakan Loob | 1.00 | .45 |
| ❑ 341 Calle Johansson | .50 | .23 |
| ❑ 342 Tommy Sandlin CO | .10 | .05 |
| ❑ 343 Tommy Soderstrom | 1.00 | .45 |
| ❑ 344 Tommy Sjodin | .25 | .11 |
| ❑ 345 Peter Andersson | .15 | .07 |
| ❑ 346 Hakan Loob | 1.00 | .45 |
| ❑ 347 Peter Forsberg | 15.00 | 6.75 |
| ❑ 348 Mats Sundin | 5.00 | 2.20 |
| ❑ 349 Jonas Forsberg | .35 | .16 |
| ❑ 350 Stefan Bjork | .15 | .07 |
| ❑ 351 Edvin Frylen | .25 | .11 |
| ❑ 352 Mikael Tjallden | .15 | .07 |
| ❑ 353 Johan Davidsson | .75 | .35 |
| ❑ 354 Markus Eriksson | .15 | .07 |
| ❑ 355 Fredrik Lindh | .15 | .07 |
| ❑ 356 Peter Nylander | .15 | .07 |

## 1993 Swedish Semic World Championships Stickers

This 1993 issue of 288-stickers was issued in Sweden to commemorate the 1993 World Championships. The stickers measure 3" by 2 1/8" and feature players from ten nations, mostly in action shots in their national team garb. The NHL players (#169-208) are shown in the club team sweaters. The backs bear the sticker number, as well as player information in Swedish. An album to hold the stickers is valued at about $10.

| | MINT | NRMT |
|---|---|---|
| COMPLETE SET (288) | 75.00 | 34.00 |
| COMMON CARD (1-288) | .10 | .05 |
| ❑ 1 Peter Aslin | .25 | .11 |
| ❑ 2 Hakan Algotsson | .25 | .11 |
| ❑ 3 Kenneth Kennholt | .10 | .05 |
| ❑ 4 Arto Blomsten | .15 | .07 |
| ❑ 5 Tomas Jonsson | .20 | .09 |
| ❑ 6 Fredrik Stillman | .10 | .05 |
| ❑ 7 Stefan Larsson | .10 | .05 |
| ❑ 8 Peter Popovic | .20 | .09 |
| ❑ 9 Hakan Loob | .35 | .16 |
| ❑ 10 Thomas Rundqvist | .10 | .05 |
| ❑ 11 Patrik Juhlin | .35 | .16 |
| ❑ 12 Mikael Renberg | 1.50 | .70 |
| ❑ 13 Peter Forsberg | 8.00 | 3.60 |
| ❑ 14 Markus Naslund | .50 | .23 |
| ❑ 15 Bengt-Ake Gustafsson | .25 | .11 |
| ❑ 16 Jan Larsson | .10 | .05 |
| ❑ 17 Fredrik Nilsson | .20 | .09 |
| ❑ 18 Roger Hansson | .10 | .05 |
| ❑ 19 Tommy Soderstrom | .35 | .16 |
| ❑ 20 Anders Eldebrink | .15 | .07 |
| ❑ 21 Ulf Samuelsson | .35 | .16 |
| ❑ 22 Kjell Samuelsson | .25 | .11 |
| ❑ 23 Nicklas Lidstrom | .75 | .35 |
| ❑ 24 Tommy Sjodin | .15 | .07 |
| ❑ 25 Calle Johansson | .25 | .11 |
| ❑ 26 Fredrik Olausson | .25 | .11 |
| ❑ 27 Peter Andersson | .15 | .07 |
| ❑ 28 Tommy Albelin | .15 | .07 |
| ❑ 29 Roger Johansson | .15 | .07 |
| ❑ 30 Par Djoos | .15 | .07 |
| ❑ 31 Mikael Johansson | .10 | .05 |
| ❑ 32 Tomas Sandstrom | .35 | .16 |
| ❑ 33 Mats Sundin | 1.50 | .70 |
| ❑ 34 Ulf Dahlen | .25 | .11 |
| ❑ 35 Jan Erixon | .15 | .07 |
| ❑ 36 Thomas Steen | .25 | .11 |
| ❑ 37 Mikael Andersson | .15 | .07 |
| ❑ 38 Johan Garpenlov | .25 | .11 |
| ❑ 39 Per-Erik Eklund | .25 | .11 |
| ❑ 40 Michael Nylander | .50 | .23 |
| ❑ 41 Tomas Forslund | .20 | .09 |
| ❑ 42 Patric Kjellberg | .20 | .09 |
| ❑ 43 Patrik Carnback | .20 | .09 |
| ❑ 44 Niclas Andersson | .20 | .09 |
| ❑ 45 Markus Ketterer | .25 | .11 |
| ❑ 46 Sakari Lindfors | .25 | .11 |
| ❑ 47 Jarmo Myllys | .25 | .11 |
| ❑ 48 Peter Ahola | .15 | .07 |
| ❑ 49 Mikko Haapakoski | .10 | .05 |
| ❑ 50 Kai Harila | .10 | .05 |
| ❑ 51 Pasi Huura | .15 | .07 |
| ❑ 52 Waltteri Immonen | .15 | .07 |
| ❑ 53 Timo Jutila | .20 | .09 |
| ❑ 54 Janne Laukkanen | .25 | .11 |
| ❑ 55 Harri Laurila | .10 | .05 |
| ❑ 56 Jyrki Lumme | .25 | .11 |
| ❑ 57 Teppo Numminen | .25 | .11 |
| ❑ 58 Sami Nuutinen | .10 | .05 |
| ❑ 59 Ville Siren | .15 | .07 |
| ❑ 60 Pasi Sormunen | .10 | .05 |
| ❑ 61 Mika Stromberg | .15 | .07 |
| ❑ 62 Mika Alatalo | .20 | .09 |
| ❑ 63 Raimo Helminen | .20 | .09 |
| ❑ 64 Pauli Jarvinen | .10 | .05 |
| ❑ 65 Jarmo Kekalainen | .15 | .07 |
| ❑ 66 Jari Korpisalo | .15 | .07 |
| ❑ 67 Jari Kurri | .75 | .35 |
| ❑ 68 Mikko Makela | .25 | .11 |
| ❑ 69 Mika Nieminen | .20 | .09 |
| ❑ 70 Timo Norppa | .10 | .05 |
| ❑ 71 Janne Ojanen | .20 | .09 |
| ❑ 72 Timo Peltomaa | .20 | .09 |
| ❑ 73 Rauli Raitanen | .10 | .05 |
| ❑ 74 Juha Riihijarvi | .25 | .11 |
| ❑ 75 Christian Ruuttu | .25 | .11 |
| ❑ 76 Timo Saarikoski | .10 | .05 |
| ❑ 77 Teemu Selanne | 5.00 | 2.20 |
| ❑ 78 Jukka Seppo | .15 | .07 |
| ❑ 79 Petri Skriko | .25 | .11 |
| ❑ 80 Esa Tikkanen | .50 | .23 |
| ❑ 81 Pekka Tuomisto | .10 | .05 |
| ❑ 82 Petri Varis | .25 | .11 |
| ❑ 83 Jarkko Varvio | .15 | .07 |
| ❑ 84 Vesa Viitakoski | .15 | .07 |
| ❑ 85 Marko Virtanen | .10 | .05 |
| ❑ 86 Jali Wahlsten | .10 | .05 |
| ❑ 87 Sami Wahlsten | .10 | .05 |
| ❑ 88 Pentti Matikainen | .10 | .05 |
| ❑ 89 Petr Briza | .25 | .11 |
| ❑ 90 Roman Turek | 1.00 | .45 |
| ❑ 91 Milos Holan | .20 | .09 |
| ❑ 92 Drahomir Kadlec | .15 | .07 |
| ❑ 93 Bedrick Scerban | .15 | .07 |
| ❑ 94 Frantisek Prochazka | .10 | .05 |
| ❑ 95 Richard Zemlicka | .15 | .07 |
| ❑ 96 Roman Turek | .75 | .35 |
| ❑ 97 Lubos Rob | .10 | .05 |
| ❑ 98 Jiri Kucera | .15 | .07 |
| ❑ 99 Tomas Kapusta | .10 | .05 |
| ❑ 100 Roman Rysanek | .10 | .05 |
| ❑ 101 Roman Hamrlik | .75 | .35 |
| ❑ 102 Robert Svehla | .75 | .35 |
| ❑ 103 Tomas Jelinek | .15 | .07 |
| ❑ 104 Petr Klima | .20 | .09 |
| ❑ 105 Josef Beranek | .20 | .09 |
| ❑ 106 Robert Petrovicky | .15 | .07 |
| ❑ 107 Kamil Kastak | .15 | .07 |
| ❑ 108 David Volek | .15 | .07 |
| ❑ 109 Renato Tosio | .20 | .09 |
| ❑ 110 Patrick Schopf | .10 | .05 |
| ❑ 111 Samuel Balmer | .10 | .05 |
| ❑ 112 Andreas Beutler | .10 | .05 |
| ❑ 113 Patrice Brasey | .10 | .05 |
| ❑ 114 Rick Tschumi | .10 | .05 |
| ❑ 115 Sven Leuenberger | .10 | .05 |
| ❑ 116 Sandro Bertaggia | .10 | .05 |
| ❑ 117 Patrick Howald | .10 | .05 |
| ❑ 118 Andy Ton | .10 | .05 |
| ❑ 119 Keith Fair | .10 | .05 |
| ❑ 120 Mario Brodmann | .10 | .05 |
| ❑ 121 Fredy Luhti | .10 | .05 |
| ❑ 122 Jorg Eberle | .15 | .07 |
| ❑ 123 Roman Wager | .10 | .05 |
| ❑ 124 Manuele Celio | .10 | .05 |
| ❑ 125 Christian Weber | .10 | .05 |
| ❑ 126 Roger Thony | .10 | .05 |
| ❑ 127 Felix Hollenstein | .10 | .05 |
| ❑ 128 Gil Montandon | .10 | .05 |
| ❑ 129 Nikolai Khabibulin | .75 | .35 |
| ❑ 130 Alexei Cherviakov | .10 | .05 |
| ❑ 131 Ilja Biakin | .15 | .07 |
| ❑ 132 Dmitri Filimonov | .15 | .07 |
| ❑ 133 Alexander Karpovtsev | .25 | .11 |
| ❑ 134 Sergei Sorokin | .15 | .07 |
| ❑ 135 Andrei Sapozhnikov | .10 | .05 |
| ❑ 136 Alexei Yashin | .75 | .35 |
| ❑ 137 Alexander Cherbayev | .20 | .09 |
| ❑ 138 Konstantin Astrakhantsev | .15 | .07 |
| ❑ 139 Sergei Petrenko | .15 | .07 |
| ❑ 140 Viktor Kozlov | .25 | .11 |
| ❑ 141 Roman Oksyuta | .20 | .09 |
| ❑ 142 Vladimir Malakhov | .25 | .11 |
| ❑ 143 Andrei Lomakin | .15 | .07 |
| ❑ 144 Dmitri Yushkevich | .20 | .09 |
| ❑ 145 Igor Korolev | .20 | .09 |
| ❑ 146 Darius Kasparaitis | .50 | .23 |
| ❑ 147 Vyacheslav Bykov | .25 | .11 |
| ❑ 148 Andrei Khomutov | .25 | .11 |
| ❑ 149 Helmut De Raaf | .20 | .09 |
| ❑ 150 Klaus Merk | .35 | .16 |
| ❑ 151 Michael Heidt | .35 | .16 |
| ❑ 152 Michael Schmidt | .10 | .05 |
| ❑ 153 Uli Hiemer | .15 | .07 |
| ❑ 154 Andreas Niederberger | .10 | .05 |
| ❑ 155 Rick Amann | .10 | .05 |
| ❑ 156 Andreas Brockmann | .10 | .05 |
| ❑ 157 Gerd Truntschka | .15 | .07 |
| ❑ 158 Dieter Hegen | .15 | .07 |
| ❑ 159 Stefan Ustorf | .25 | .11 |
| ❑ 160 Georg Holzmann | .10 | .05 |
| ❑ 161 Ernst Kopf Jr. | .10 | .05 |
| ❑ 162 Bernd Truntschka | .15 | .07 |
| ❑ 163 Raimund Hilger | .15 | .07 |
| ❑ 164 Wolfgang Kummer | .10 | .05 |
| ❑ 165 Georg Franz | .10 | .05 |
| ❑ 166 Thomas Brandl | .10 | .05 |
| ❑ 167 Michael Rumrich | .10 | .05 |
| ❑ 168 Uwe Krupp | .25 | .11 |
| ❑ 169 Tom Barrasso | .50 | .23 |
| ❑ 170 Mike Richter | 1.50 | .70 |
| ❑ 171 Brian Leetch | 1.00 | .45 |
| ❑ 172 Chris Chelios | 1.00 | .45 |
| ❑ 173 Al Iafrate | .25 | .11 |
| ❑ 174 Phil Housley | .25 | .11 |
| ❑ 175 Kevin Hatcher | .25 | .11 |
| ❑ 176 Gary Suter | .25 | .11 |
| ❑ 177 Mathieu Schneider | .25 | .11 |
| ❑ 178 Joe Mullen | .25 | .11 |
| ❑ 179 Kevin Stevens | .25 | .11 |
| ❑ 180 Jeremy Roenick | 2.00 | .90 |
| ❑ 181 Tony Granato | .25 | .11 |
| ❑ 182 Mike Modano | .75 | .35 |
| ❑ 183 Pat LaFontaine | .75 | .35 |
| ❑ 184 Ed Olczyk | .15 | .07 |
| ❑ 185 Brett Hull | 3.00 | 1.35 |
| ❑ 186 Craig Janney | .25 | .11 |
| ❑ 187 Jimmy Carson | .15 | .07 |
| ❑ 188 Tony Amonte | .50 | .23 |
| ❑ 189 Patrick Roy | 12.00 | 5.50 |
| ❑ 190 Kirk McLean | .50 | .23 |
| ❑ 191 Larry Murphy | .25 | .11 |
| ❑ 192 Ray Bourque | 1.00 | .45 |
| ❑ 193 Al MacInnis | .35 | .16 |
| ❑ 194 Steve Duchesne | .25 | .11 |
| ❑ 195 Eric Desjardins | .25 | .11 |
| ❑ 196 Scott Stevens | .25 | .11 |
| ❑ 197 Paul Coffey | 1.00 | .45 |
| ❑ 198 Mario Lemieux | 12.00 | 5.50 |
| ❑ 199 Wayne Gretzky | 15.00 | 6.75 |
| ❑ 200 Rick Tocchet | .50 | .23 |
| ❑ 201 Eric Lindros | 10.00 | 4.50 |
| ❑ 202 Mark Messier | 3.00 | 1.35 |
| ❑ 203 Steve Yzerman | 6.00 | 2.70 |
| ❑ 204 Luc Robitaille | .75 | .35 |
| ❑ 205 Mark Recchi | .75 | .35 |
| ❑ 206 Joe Sakic | 6.00 | 2.70 |
| ❑ 207 Owen Nolan | .50 | .23 |
| ❑ 208 Gary Roberts | .50 | .23 |
| ❑ 209 David Delfino | .25 | .11 |
| ❑ 210 Mike Rosati | .25 | .11 |
| ❑ 211 Robert Oberrauch | .10 | .05 |
| ❑ 212 Jim Camazzola | .10 | .05 |
| ❑ 213 Bill Stewart | .10 | .05 |
| ❑ 214 Mike DeAngelis | .10 | .05 |
| ❑ 215 Anthony Circelli | .10 | .05 |
| ❑ 216 Georg Comploy | .10 | .05 |
| ❑ 217 Frank DiMuzio | .10 | .05 |
| ❑ 218 Gates Orlando | .15 | .07 |
| ❑ 219 John Vecchiarelli | .10 | .05 |
| ❑ 220 Joe Foglietta | .10 | .05 |
| ❑ 221 Lucio Topatigh | .10 | .05 |
| ❑ 222 Carmine Vani | .15 | .07 |
| ❑ 223 Lino DeToni | .10 | .05 |
| ❑ 224 Mario Chitarroni | .10 | .05 |
| ❑ 225 Bruno Zarrillo | .10 | .05 |
| ❑ 226 Maurizio Mansi | .10 | .05 |
| ❑ 227 Stefan Figliuzzi | .10 | .05 |
| ❑ 228 Santino Pellegrino | .10 | .05 |
| ❑ 229 Jim Marthinsen | .25 | .11 |
| ❑ 230 Rob Schistad | .25 | .11 |
| ❑ 231 Petter Salsten | .10 | .05 |
| ❑ 232 Cato Tom Andersen | .10 | .05 |
| ❑ 233 Tommy Jakobsen | .10 | .05 |
| ❑ 234 Svein E Norstebo | .10 | .05 |
| ❑ 235 Jon Magne Karlstad | .10 | .05 |
| ❑ 236 Kim Sogaard | .10 | .05 |
| ❑ 237 Geir Hoff | .10 | .05 |
| ❑ 238 Erik Kristiansen | .10 | .05 |
| ❑ 239 Petter Thoresen | .10 | .05 |
| ❑ 240 Ole Eskild Dahlstrom | .10 | .05 |
| ❑ 241 Espen Knutsen | .35 | .16 |
| ❑ 242 Oystein Olsen | .10 | .05 |
| ❑ 243 Roy Johansen | .10 | .05 |
| ❑ 244 Trond Magnussen | .10 | .05 |
| ❑ 245 Arne Billkvam | .10 | .05 |
| ❑ 246 Marius Rath | .10 | .05 |
| ❑ 247 Tom Erik Olsen | .10 | .05 |
| ❑ 248 Morten Finstad | .10 | .05 |
| ❑ 249 Petri Ylonen | .25 | .11 |
| ❑ 250 Michel Valliere | .25 | .11 |
| ❑ 251 Stephane Botteri | .10 | .05 |
| ❑ 252 Serge Poudrier | .15 | .07 |
| ❑ 253 Eric Durand | .10 | .05 |
| ❑ 254 Jean-Philippe Lemoine | .15 | .07 |
| ❑ 255 Denis Perez | .15 | .07 |
| ❑ 256 Sebastien Marquet | .10 | .05 |
| ❑ 257 Michael Babin | .10 | .05 |
| ❑ 258 Stephane Barin | .10 | .05 |
| ❑ 259 Arnaud Briand | .10 | .05 |
| ❑ 260 Yves Crettenand | .10 | .05 |
| ❑ 261 Laurent Deschaume | .10 | .05 |
| ❑ 262 Roger Dube | .10 | .05 |
| ❑ 263 Patrick Dunn | .10 | .05 |
| ❑ 264 Franck Pajonkowski | .15 | .07 |
| ❑ 265 Pierre Pousse | .10 | .05 |
| ❑ 266 Antoine Richer | .10 | .05 |
| ❑ 267 Christophe Ville | .10 | .05 |
| ❑ 268 Philippe Bozon | .15 | .07 |
| ❑ 269 Brian Stankiewicz | .10 | .05 |
| ❑ 270 Claus Dalpiaz | .25 | .11 |
| ❑ 271 Michael Shea | .25 | .11 |
| ❑ 272 Robin Doyle | .10 | .05 |
| ❑ 273 Martin Ulrich | .10 | .05 |
| ❑ 274 Martin Krainz | .10 | .05 |
| ❑ 275 Erich Solderer | .10 | .05 |
| ❑ 276 Michael Guntner | .10 | .05 |
| ❑ 277 Friedrich Ganster | .10 | .05 |
| ❑ 278 Wayne Groulx | .10 | .05 |
| ❑ 279 Dieter Kalt | .10 | .05 |
| ❑ 280 Werner Kerth | .10 | .05 |
| ❑ 281 Arno Maier | .10 | .05 |
| ❑ 282 Richard Nasheim | .10 | .05 |
| ❑ 283 Christian Perthaler | .10 | .05 |
| ❑ 284 Andreas Puschnik | .10 | .05 |
| ❑ 285 Gerhard Puschnig | .10 | .05 |
| ❑ 286 Walter Putnik | .10 | .05 |
| ❑ 287 Reinhard Lampert | .10 | .05 |
| ❑ 288 Mario Schaden | .10 | .05 |

## 1993-94 Swedish Semic Elitserien

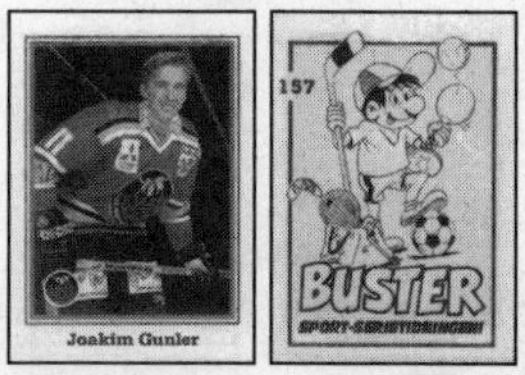


This 320-sticker set was the collectible to own for fans of the Elitserien. This comprehensive issue had a posed player photo and name on the front, with card number and a cartoon ad for the whimsical boy's sports magazine, "Buster" on the back.

| | MINT | NRMT |
|---|---|---|
| COMPLETE SET (320) | 75.00 | 34.00 |
| COMMON CARD (1-320) | .10 | .05 |
| ❑ 1 Bjorkloven Team Emblem | .10 | .05 |

❑ 2 Patrik Hofbauer .10 .05
❑ 3 Jorgen Wikstrom .10 .05
❑ 4 Mattias Hedlund .10 .05
❑ 5 Yuri Kuznetsov .20 .09
❑ 6 Ulf Odling .10 .05
❑ 7 Jorgen Eriksson .10 .05
❑ 8 Jorgen Hermansson .10 .05
❑ 9 Peter Andersson .10 .05
❑ 10 Joakim Lindgren .10 .05
❑ 11 Glenn Hedman .10 .05
❑ 12 Roger Kyro .10 .05
❑ 13 Niklas Norberg .10 .05
❑ 14 Alexander Belyavsky .15 .07
❑ 15 Anders Nejdsater .10 .05
❑ 16 Stefan Olofsson .10 .05
❑ 17 Mikael Andersson .25 .11
❑ 18 Ulf Andersson .10 .05
❑ 19 Patrik Sundstrom .25 .11
❑ 20 Hakan Hermansson .10 .05
❑ 21 Micael Karlberg .10 .05
❑ 22 Peder Bejegard .10 .05
❑ 23 Johan Boman .10 .05
❑ 24 Joakim Lindgren .10 .05
❑ 25 Brynas Team Emblem .10 .05
❑ 26 Michael Sundlov .20 .09
❑ 27 Lars Karlsson .20 .09
❑ 28 Bedrich Scerban .10 .05
❑ 29 Mikael Lindman .10 .05
❑ 30 Johan Tornberg .10 .05
❑ 31 Tommy Melkersson .10 .05
❑ 32 Stefan Klockare .15 .07
❑ 33 Mikael Enander .10 .05
❑ 34 Mikael Wiklander .10 .05
❑ 35 Christer Olsson .35 .16
❑ 36 Thomas Tallberg .15 .07
❑ 37 Andreas Dackell .50 .23
❑ 38 Mikael Wahlberg .10 .05
❑ 39 Anders Gozzi .10 .05
❑ 40 Niklas Gallstedt .10 .05
❑ 41 Per-Johan Johansson .10 .05
❑ 42 Joakim Persson .25 .11
❑ 43 Branislav Janos .10 .05
❑ 44 Ove Molin .10 .05
❑ 45 Anders Huss .10 .05
❑ 46 Jonas Johnson .10 .05
❑ 47 Peter Larsson .10 .05
❑ 48 Anders Carlsson .10 .05
❑ 49 Djurgarden Team Emblem .10 .05
❑ 50 Thomas Ostlund .25 .11
❑ 51 Petter Ronnquist .15 .07
❑ 52 Christian Due-Boje .15 .07
❑ 53 Marcus Ragnarsson .75 .35
❑ 54 Joakim Musakka .10 .05
❑ 55 Thomas Johansson .10 .05
❑ 56 Thomas Eriksson .10 .05
❑ 57 Bjorn Nord .15 .07
❑ 58 Mikael Magnusson .10 .05
❑ 59 Robert Nordmark .15 .07
❑ 60 Charles Berglund .10 .05
❑ 61 Erik Huusko .15 .07
❑ 62 Anders Huusko .10 .05
❑ 63 Jens Ohling .15 .07
❑ 64 Peter Nilsson .10 .05
❑ 65 Magnus Jansson .10 .05
❑ 66 Mikael Hakansson .10 .05
❑ 67 Ola Josefsson .10 .05
❑ 68 Jerry Friman .10 .05
❑ 69 Mariusz Czerkawski 1.00 .45
❑ 70 Fredrik Lindquist .20 .09
❑ 71 Mattias Hallback .10 .05
❑ 72 Patrik Erickson .10 .05
❑ 73 Farjestad Team Emblem .10 .05
❑ 74 Anders Bergman .25 .11
❑ 75 Jonas Eriksson .20 .09
❑ 76 Tommy Samuelsson .10 .05
❑ 77 Jesper Duus .10 .05
❑ 78 Leif Carlsson .10 .05
❑ 79 Per Lundell .10 .05
❑ 80 Brian Tutt .15 .07
❑ 81 Jacob Karlsson .10 .05
❑ 82 Thomas Rhodin .10 .05
❑ 83 Mattias Olsson .10 .05
❑ 84 Hakan Loob .75 .35
❑ 85 Andreas Johansson .25 .11
❑ 86 Magnus Arvedsson .10 .05
❑ 87 Anders Oberg .10 .05
❑ 88 Mattias Johansson .10 .05
❑ 89 Mats Lindgren 1.00 .45
❑ 90 Clas Eriksson .10 .05
❑ 91 Patrik Degerstedt .10 .05
❑ 92 Peter Ottosson .10 .05
❑ 93 Niklas Brannstrom .10 .05
❑ 94 Lars Karlsson .20 .09
❑ 95 Kjell Dahlin .25 .11
❑ 96 Jonas Hoglund .25 .11
❑ 97 HV 71 Team Emblem .10 .05
❑ 98 Peter Aslin .25 .11
❑ 99 Boo Ahl .25 .11
❑ 100 Antonin Stavjana .20 .09
❑ 101 Kenneth Kennholt .15 .07
❑ 102 Hans Abrahamsson .10 .05
❑ 103 Andreas Schultz .10 .05
❑ 104 Per Gustafsson .50 .23
❑ 105 Mathias Svedberg .10 .05
❑ 106 Niklas Rahm .10 .05
❑ 107 Fredrik Stillman .10 .05
❑ 108 Owe Thornberg .10 .05
❑ 109 Thomas Gustavsson .10 .05
❑ 110 Stefan Ornskog .15 .07
❑ 111 Peter Hammarstrom .10 .05
❑ 112 Torbjorn Persson .10 .05
❑ 113 John Byce .15 .07
❑ 114 Peter Eriksson .10 .05
❑ 115 Magnus Axelsson .15 .07
❑ 116 Stefan Falk .15 .07
❑ 117 Patric Kjellberg .20 .09
❑ 118 Johan Davidsson .50 .23
❑ 119 Thomas Ljungberg .10 .05
❑ 120 Patrik Ross .10 .05
❑ 121 Leksand Team Emblem .10 .05
❑ 122 Johan Hedberg .25 .11
❑ 123 Ake Lilljebjorn .15 .07
❑ 124 Tomas Jonsson .25 .11
❑ 125 Stefan Bergkvist .15 .07
❑ 126 Henric Bjorkman .10 .05
❑ 127 Hans Lodin .10 .05
❑ 128 Magnus Svensson .15 .07
❑ 129 Orjan Lindmark .10 .05
❑ 130 Jan Huokko .10 .05
❑ 131 Roger Johansson .10 .05
❑ 132 Per Widmark .10 .05
❑ 133 Marcus Thuresson .10 .05
❑ 134 Niklas Eriksson .10 .05
❑ 135 Peter Ciavaglia .15 .07
❑ 136 Jonas Bergkvist .25 .11
❑ 137 Martin Wiita .10 .05
❑ 138 Markus Akerblom .10 .05
❑ 139 Greg Parks .15 .07
❑ 140 Mattias Loof .10 .05
❑ 141 Andreas Karlsson .10 .05
❑ 142 Markus Eriksson .10 .05
❑ 143 Tomas Forslund .25 .11
❑ 144 Jarmo Makitalo .10 .05
❑ 145 Lulea Team Emblem .10 .05
❑ 146 Robert Skoog .15 .07
❑ 147 Erik Grankvist .20 .09
❑ 148 Lars Modig .10 .05
❑ 149 Patrik Hoglund .10 .05
❑ 150 Niklas Bjornfot .10 .05
❑ 151 Torbjorn Lindberg .10 .05
❑ 152 Ville Siren .20 .09
❑ 153 Petter Nilsson .10 .05
❑ 154 Tomas Lilja .10 .05
❑ 155 Stefan Jonsson .10 .05
❑ 156 Stefan Nilsson .10 .05
❑ 157 Joakim Gunler .10 .05
❑ 158 Johan Stromvall .10 .05
❑ 159 Kyosti Karjalainen .20 .09
❑ 160 Robert Nordberg .10 .05
❑ 161 Tomas Berglund .10 .05
❑ 162 Lars-Gunnar Pettersson .10 .05
❑ 163 Lars Edstrom .10 .05
❑ 164 Lars Hurtig .10 .05
❑ 165 Fredrik Oberg .10 .05
❑ 166 Mikael Engstrom .10 .05
❑ 167 Johan Rosen .10 .05
❑ 168 Mika Nieminen .25 .11
❑ 169 Malmo Team Emblem .10 .05
❑ 170 Peter Lindmark .25 .11
❑ 171 Roger Nordstrom .15 .07
❑ 172 Daniel Granqvist .15 .07
❑ 173 Johan Norgren .10 .05
❑ 174 Johan Salle .10 .05
❑ 175 Petri Liimatainen .10 .05
❑ 176 Peter Hasselblad .10 .05
❑ 177 Robert Svehla .75 .35
❑ 178 Ricard Persson .25 .11
❑ 179 Roger Ohman .10 .05
❑ 180 Raimo Helminen .25 .11
❑ 181 Marcus Magnertoft .10 .05
❑ 182 Mattias Bosson .10 .05
❑ 183 Roger Hansson .10 .05
❑ 184 Bo Svanberg .10 .05
❑ 185 Daniel Rydmark .20 .09
❑ 186 Patrik Sylvegard .10 .05
❑ 187 Jens Hemstrom .10 .05
❑ 188 Jesper Mattsson .75 .35
❑ 189 Hakan Ahlund .10 .05
❑ 190 Peter Sundstrom .25 .11
❑ 191 Mats Naslund 1.50 .70
❑ 192 Mikko Makela .20 .09
❑ 193 MoDo Team Emblem .10 .05
❑ 194 Henrik Arvsell .10 .05
❑ 195 Fredrik Andersson .15 .07
❑ 196 Anders Berglund .10 .05
❑ 197 Mattias Timander .50 .23
❑ 198 Miroslav Horava .15 .07
❑ 199 Lars Jansson .10 .05
❑ 200 Anders Eriksson 1.50 .70
❑ 201 Hans Jonsson .10 .05
❑ 202 Tomas Nanzen .10 .05
❑ 203 Fredrik Bergqvist .10 .05
❑ 204 Magnus Wernblom .15 .07
❑ 205 Anders Soderberg .50 .23
❑ 206 Martin Hostak .15 .07
❑ 207 Lennart Hermansson .10 .05
❑ 208 Ulf Odmark .10 .05
❑ 209 Peter Forsberg 10.00 4.50
❑ 210 Per Svartvadet .50 .23
❑ 211 Andreas Salomonsson .10 .05
❑ 212 Niklas Sundstrom 3.00 1.35
❑ 213 Lars Bystrom .10 .05
❑ 214 Mats Lundstrom .10 .05
❑ 215 Erik Holmberg .10 .05
❑ 216 Henrik Gradin .10 .05
❑ 217 Rogle Team Emblem .10 .05
❑ 218 Kenneth Johansson .20 .09
❑ 219 Magnus Swardh .10 .05
❑ 220 Daniel Johansson .35 .16
❑ 221 Kari Suoraniemi .10 .05
❑ 222 Pierre Johnsson .10 .05
❑ 223 Kenny Jonsson 1.50 .70
❑ 224 Per Ljusterang .10 .05
❑ 225 Arto Ruotanen .10 .05
❑ 226 Daniel Tjarnquist .35 .16
❑ 227 Kari Eloranta .10 .05
❑ 228 Per Wallin .25 .11
❑ 229 Peter Lundmark .15 .07
❑ 230 Roger Elvenes .15 .07
❑ 231 Michael Hjalm .10 .05
❑ 232 Mattias Olivestedt .10 .05
❑ 233 Jan Ericsson .10 .05
❑ 234 Tomas Srsen .10 .05
❑ 235 Pelle Svensson .10 .05
❑ 236 Jorgen Jonsson .10 .05
❑ 237 Stefan Elvenes .15 .07
❑ 238 Fredrik Moller .10 .05
❑ 239 Tord Elvenes .10 .05
❑ 240 Mats Loov .10 .05
❑ 241 Vasteras Team Emblem .10 .05
❑ 242 Mats Ytter .20 .09
❑ 243 Tommy Salo 1.50 .70
❑ 244 Sergei Fokin .10 .05
❑ 245 Edvin Frylen .20 .09
❑ 246 Leif Rohlin .25 .11
❑ 247 Peter Karlsson .10 .05
❑ 248 Peter Jacobsson .10 .05
❑ 249 Thomas Carlsson .10 .05
❑ 250 Lars Ivarsson .10 .05
❑ 251 Roger Akerstrom .15 .07
❑ 252 Patrik Juhlin .35 .16
❑ 253 Alexei Salomatin .15 .07
❑ 254 Mishat Fahrutdinov .15 .07
❑ 255 Henrik Nilsson .10 .05
❑ 256 Mikael Pettersson .10 .05
❑ 257 Stefan Hellkvist .10 .05
❑ 258 Jens Nielsen .10 .05
❑ 259 Hans Huczkowski .10 .05
❑ 260 Claes Lindblom .10 .05
❑ 261 Johan Brummer .10 .05
❑ 262 Dejan Kostic .10 .05
❑ 263 Paul Andersson .10 .05
❑ 264 Henrik Nordfeldt .10 .05
❑ 265 Vastra Frolunda Team Emblem .10 .05
❑ 266 Hakan Algotsson .25 .11
❑ 267 Mikael Sandberg .20 .09
❑ 268 Stefan Nyman .10 .05
❑ 269 Joacim Esbjors .15 .07
❑ 270 Oscar Ackestrom .10 .05
❑ 271 Vladimir Kramskoy .10 .05
❑ 272 Richard Sohrman .10 .05
❑ 273 Stefan Axelsson .15 .07
❑ 274 Ronnie Sundin .25 .11
❑ 275 Stefan Larsson .10 .05
❑ 276 Thomas Sjogren .10 .05
❑ 277 Serge Boisvert .15 .07
❑ 278 Jerry Persson .10 .05
❑ 279 Terho Koskela .10 .05
❑ 280 Peter Strom .10 .05
❑ 281 Peter Berndtsson .10 .05
❑ 282 Henrik Lundin .10 .05
❑ 283 Jonas Esbjors .10 .05
❑ 284 Daniel Alfredsson 4.00 1.80
❑ 285 Stefan Ketola .10 .05
❑ 286 Lars Dahlstrom .10 .05
❑ 287 Par Edlund .10 .05
❑ 288 Oto Hascak .15 .07
❑ 289 Lars-Gunnar Jansson CO .10 .05
❑ 290 Tommy Sandlin CO .10 .05
❑ 291 Tommy Boustedt CO .10 .05
❑ 292 Jorgen Palm CO .10 .05
❑ 293 Hakan Nygren CO .10 .05
❑ 294 Wayne Fleming CO .10 .05
❑ 295 Sakari Pietila CO .10 .05
❑ 296 Timo Lahtinen CO .10 .05
❑ 297 Kent Forsberg CO .20 .09
❑ 298 Christer Abrahamsson CO .25 .11
❑ 299 Mikael Lundstrom CO .10 .05
❑ 300 Leif Boork CO .10 .05
❑ 301 Peter Forsberg 10.00 4.50
❑ 302 Peter Forsberg 10.00 4.50
❑ 303 Hakan Loob .75 .35
❑ 304 Kenny Jonsson 1.50 .70
❑ 305 Peter Forsberg 10.00 4.50
❑ 306 Mats Sundin 4.00 1.80
❑ 307 Micheal Sundlov AS .20 .09
❑ 308 Roger Akerstrom AS .15 .07
❑ 309 Fredrik Stillman AS .10 .05
❑ 310 Mikael Renberg AS 4.00 1.80
❑ 311 Peter Forsberg AS 10.00 4.50
❑ 312 Ulf Dahlen AS .35 .16
❑ 313 Pal Grotnes FS .20 .09
❑ 314 Daniel Tjarnquist FS .35 .16
❑ 315 Henrik Rehnberg FS .15 .07
❑ 316 Mattias Ohlund FS 1.00 .45
❑ 317 Jan Labraaten FS .25 .11
❑ 318 Patrik Wallenberg FS .20 .09
❑ 319 Niklas Wallin FS .20 .09
❑ 320 Tobias Thermell FS .20 .09

## 1995 Swedish Globe World Championships

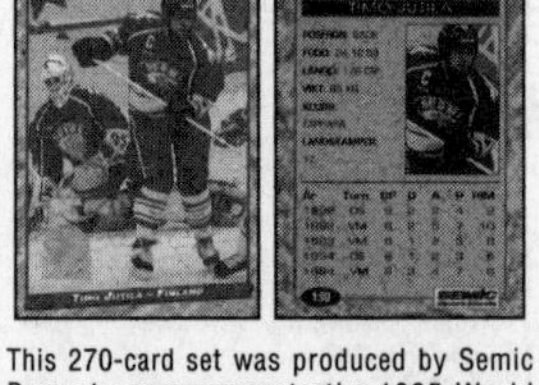

This 270-card set was produced by Semic Press to commemorate the 1995 World Championships, which were held in Stockholm. The players pictured have represented their countries at some point in international competition, and thus are shown wearing their national team garb. Card fronts feature a variegated yellow-orange border, with the Globe and World Championships logo (VM '95) along the top. Player name and country are listed in a blue bar and in Swedish text, along the bottom. A silver foil Globe '95 icon is set in the lower left corner. Card backs include a small reprise of the front photo, along with personal information, including all statistics from major international tournaments. No card number 85 is in the set - Mike Gartner was misnumbered 86. An NNO two-sided card of Peter Forsberg and Mats Sundin was randomly inserted in packs. It is believed that there are less than 2,000 of these cards in circulation. A special binder was released to store the set; it is valued at $5.

| | MINT | NRMT |
|---|---|---|
| COMPLETE SET (270) | 100.00 | 45.00 |
| COMMON CARD (1-270) | .10 | .05 |

❑ 1 Tommy Soderstrom .50 .23
❑ 2 Roger Nordstrom .10 .05
❑ 3 Tommy Salo .50 .23
❑ 4 Hakan Algotsson .20 .09
❑ 5 Thomas Ostlund .20 .09
❑ 6 Johan Hedberg .20 .09
❑ 7 Ulf Samuelsson .15 .07
❑ 8 Calle Johansson .20 .09
❑ 9 Nicklas Lidstrom .50 .23
❑ 10 Tommy Albelin .15 .07
❑ 11 Peter Andersson .10 .05
❑ 12 Magnus Svensson .15 .07
❑ 13 Mats Sundin 1.50 .70
❑ 14 Tomas Jonsson .15 .07
❑ 15 Kenny Jonsson .35 .16
❑ 16 Tommy Sjodin .15 .07
❑ 17 Fredrik Stillman .10 .05
❑ 18 Marcus Ragnarsson .25 .11
❑ 19 Peter Popovic .15 .07
❑ 20 Arto Blomsten .10 .05
❑ 21 Peter Forsberg 5.00 2.20
❑ 22 Roger Johansson .10 .05
❑ 23 Leif Rohlin .15 .07
❑ 24 Bjorn Nord .10 .05
❑ 25 Stefan Larsson .10 .05
❑ 26 Fredrik Olausson .15 .07
❑ 27 Kjell Samuelsson .15 .07
❑ 28 Tomas Sandstrom .25 .11
❑ 29 Mikael Renberg 1.00 .45
❑ 30 Mikael Johansson .10 .05
❑ 31 Patrik Juhlin .15 .07
❑ 32 Roger Hansson .10 .05
❑ 33 Daniel Rydmark .15 .07
❑ 34 Jonas Bergqvist .15 .07
❑ 35 Michael Nylander .25 .11
❑ 36 Johan Garpenlov .15 .07
❑ 37 Charles Berglund .10 .05
❑ 38 Jorgen Jonsson .10 .05
❑ 39 Stefan Ornskog .10 .05
❑ 40 Thomas Steen .15 .07
❑ 41 Patrik Carnback .15 .07
❑ 42 Mikael Andersson .15 .07
❑ 43 Markus Naslund .25 .11
❑ 44 Andreas Dackell .10 .05
❑ 45 Erik Huusko .10 .05
❑ 46 Tomas Forslund .15 .07
❑ 47 Daniel Alfredsson 1.00 .45
❑ 48 Ulf Dahlen .25 .11
❑ 49 Anders Huusko .10 .05
❑ 50 Tomas Holmstrom .50 .23
❑ 51 Niklas Andersson .10 .05
❑ 52 Hakan Loob .35 .16
❑ 53 Per-Erik Eklund .15 .07
❑ 54 Patrik Erickson .10 .05
❑ 55 Jonas Forsberg .25 .11
❑ 56 Daniel Johansson .15 .07
❑ 57 Mattias Ohlund .50 .23
❑ 58 Anders Eriksson .50 .23
❑ 59 Fredrik Modin .35 .16
❑ 60 Niklas Sundstrom .50 .23
❑ 61 Jesper Mattson .50 .23
❑ 62 Johan Davidsson .35 .16
❑ 63 Mats Lindgren .50 .23
❑ 64 Leif Holmqvist .15 .07
❑ 65 Pelle Lindbergh 2.00 .90
❑ 66 Lennart Svedberg .10 .05
❑ 67 Borje Salming .25 .11
❑ 68 Sven Tumba Johansson .10 .05
❑ 69 Ulf Sterner .10 .05
❑ 70 Anders Hedberg .25 .11
❑ 71 Kent Nilsson .25 .11
❑ 72 Mats Naslund .25 .11
❑ 73 Patrick Roy 8.00 3.60
❑ 74 Ed Belfour 1.50 .70
❑ 75 Bill Ranford .50 .23
❑ 76 Paul Coffey 1.50 .70
❑ 77 Ray Bourque 1.50 .70
❑ 78 Steve Smith .15 .07
❑ 79 Al MacInnis .35 .16
❑ 80 Mark Tinordi .15 .07
❑ 81 Scott Stevens .35 .16
❑ 82 Rob Blake .25 .11
❑ 83 Theo Fleury 1.25 .55
❑ 84 Mark Messier 2.00 .90
❑ 85 Mike Gartner UER .50 .23
card numbered #86
❑ 86 Brendan Shanahan 3.00 1.35
❑ 87 Mario Lemieux 8.00 3.60
❑ 88 Eric Lindros 6.00 2.70
❑ 89 Steve Yzerman 5.00 2.20
❑ 90 Adam Oates .75 .35
❑ 91 Paul Kariya 6.00 2.70
❑ 92 Rick Tocchet .40 .18
❑ 93 Doug Gilmour 1.25 .55
❑ 94 Luc Robitaille .75 .35
❑ 95 Jason Arnott .75 .35
❑ 96 Adam Graves .35 .16
❑ 97 Petr Nedved .50 .23
❑ 98 Mark Recchi .75 .35
❑ 99 Wayne Gretzky 10.00 4.50
❑ 100 Mike Richter 1.50 .70
❑ 101 John Vanbiesbrouck 2.50 1.10
❑ 102 Tom Barrasso .35 .16
❑ 103 Brian Leetch .75 .35
❑ 104 Gary Suter .15 .07
❑ 105 Kevin Hatcher .15 .07
❑ 106 Phil Housley .25 .11
❑ 107 Chris Chelios 1.50 .70
❑ 108 Eric Weinrich .15 .07
❑ 109 Derian Hatcher .15 .07
❑ 110 Craig Wolanin .15 .07
❑ 111 Mike Modano .75 .35
❑ 112 Joe Mullen .25 .11
❑ 113 Joel Otto .25 .11
❑ 114 Doug Brown .15 .07
❑ 115 Brett Hull 2.00 .90
❑ 116 Pat LaFontaine .75 .35
❑ 117 Jeremy Roenick 1.50 .70
❑ 118 Craig Janney .25 .11
❑ 119 Kevin Miller .15 .07
❑ 120 Tony Granato .20 .09
❑ 121 Tony Amonte .50 .23
❑ 122 Kevin Stevens .50 .23
❑ 123 Darren Turcotte .15 .07
❑ 124 Scott Young .15 .07
❑ 125 Doug Weight .75 .35
❑ 126 Phil Bourque .15 .07
❑ 127 Markus Ketterer .25 .11
❑ 128 Jarmo Myllys .35 .16
❑ 129 Jyrki Lumme .15 .07
❑ 130 Timo Jutila .15 .07
❑ 131 Marko Kiprusoff .15 .07
❑ 132 Hannu Virta .15 .07
❑ 133 Teppo Numminen .35 .16
❑ 134 Janne Laukkanen .25 .11
❑ 135 Mika Nieminen .15 .07
❑ 136 Janne Ojanen .15 .07
❑ 137 Jari Kurri .50 .23
❑ 138 Esa Tikkanen .25 .11
❑ 139 Saku Koivu 3.00 1.35
❑ 140 Teemu Selanne 3.00 1.35
❑ 141 Raimo Helminen .15 .07
❑ 142 Mikko Makela .15 .07
❑ 143 Christian Ruuttu .15 .07
❑ 144 Esa Keskinen .15 .07
❑ 145 Dominik Hasek 3.00 1.35
❑ 146 Petr Briza .35 .16
❑ 147 Richard Smehlik .15 .07
❑ 148 Leo Gudas .10 .05
❑ 149 Roman Hamrlik .50 .23
❑ 150 Antonin Stavjana .15 .07
❑ 151 Jiri Slegr .15 .07
❑ 152 Jiri Vykoukal .15 .07
❑ 153 Tomas Jelinek .15 .07
❑ 154 Richard Zemlicka .15 .07
❑ 155 Robert Lang .15 .07
❑ 156 Michal Pivonka .35 .16
❑ 157 Jaromir Jagr 5.00 2.20
❑ 158 Josef Beranek .15 .07
❑ 159 Robert Reichel .25 .11
❑ 160 Petr Hrbek .10 .05
❑ 161 Jiri Kucera .15 .07
❑ 162 Kamil Kastak .10 .05
❑ 163 Andrei Trefilov .25 .11
❑ 164 Mikhail Shtalenkov .25 .11
❑ 165 Sergei Zubov .35 .16
❑ 166 Vladimir Malakhov .25 .11
❑ 167 Igor Kravchuk .15 .07
❑ 168 Alexei Gusarov .15 .07
❑ 169 Alexei Zhitnik .15 .07
❑ 170 Alexander Smirnov .10 .05
❑ 171 Dmitri Yushkevich .15 .07
❑ 172 Alexei Yashin .50 .23
❑ 173 Alexei Zhamnov .35 .16
❑ 174 Pavel Bure 3.00 1.35
❑ 175 Sergei Fedorov 3.00 1.35
❑ 176 Andrei Kovalenko .35 .16
❑ 177 Alexei Kovalev .35 .16
❑ 178 Andrei Khomutov .25 .11
❑ 179 Valeri Kamensky .50 .23
❑ 180 Viacheslav Bykov .20 .09
❑ 181 Claus Dalpiaz .15 .07
❑ 182 Michael Puschacher .15 .07
❑ 183 Ken Strong .10 .05
❑ 184 Martin Ulrich .10 .05
❑ 185 Andreas Puschnik .10 .05
❑ 186 Herbert Hohenberger .10 .05
❑ 187 Marty Dallmann .10 .05
❑ 188 James Burton .10 .05
❑ 189 Michael Shea .10 .05
❑ 190 Jim Marthinsen .20 .09
❑ 191 Orjan Lovdal .10 .05
❑ 192 Cato Tom Andersen .10 .05
❑ 193 Geir Hoff .10 .05
❑ 194 Tommy Jakobsen .10 .05
❑ 195 Marius Rath .10 .05
❑ 196 Trond Magnussen .10 .05
❑ 197 Svein Enok Norstebo .10 .05
❑ 198 Espen Knutsen .25 .11
❑ 199 Petri Ylonen .25 .11
❑ 200 Michel Valliere .10 .05
❑ 201 Franck Pajonkowski .15 .07
❑ 202 Pierrick Maia .10 .05
❑ 203 Christophe Ville .10 .05
❑ 204 Serge Poudrier .10 .05
❑ 205 Philippe Bozon .15 .07
❑ 206 Gerald Guennelon .10 .05
❑ 207 Antoine Richer .10 .05
❑ 208 Reto Pavoni .15 .07
❑ 209 Renato Tosio .15 .07
❑ 210 Jorg Eberle .10 .05
❑ 211 Fredy Luthi .10 .05
❑ 212 Christian Weber .10 .05
❑ 213 Sandro Bertaggia .10 .05
❑ 214 Patrick Howald .10 .05

❑ 215 Gil Montandon .10 .05
❑ 216 Rick Tschumi .10 .05
❑ 217 Klaus Merk .20 .09
❑ 218 Josef Heiss .20 .09
❑ 219 Rick Amann .10 .05
❑ 220 Michael Rumrich .10 .05
❑ 221 Thomas Brandl .10 .05
❑ 222 Andreas Niederberger .10 .05
❑ 223 Leo Stefan .10 .05
❑ 224 Stefan Ustorf .15 .07
❑ 225 Dieter Hegen .15 .07
❑ 226 Michael Rosati .15 .07
❑ 227 Bruno Campese .15 .07
❑ 228 Roberto Oberrauch .10 .05
❑ 229 Anthony Circelli .10 .05
❑ 230 Bill Stewart .10 .05
❑ 231 Bruno Zarillo .10 .05
❑ 232 Gaetano Orlando .10 .05
❑ 233 Stefan Figliuzzi .10 .05
❑ 234 Jimmy Carnazzola .10 .05
❑ 235 Vladislav Tretiak 2.00 .90
❑ 236 Viacheslav Fetisov .25 .11
❑ 237 Alexei Kasatonov .25 .11
❑ 238 Sergei Makarov .35 .16
❑ 239 Igor Larionov .50 .23
❑ 240 Vladimir Krutov .35 .16
❑ 241 Valeri Kharlamov .35 .16
❑ 242 Vladimir Petrov .15 .07
❑ 243 Boris Mikhailov .25 .11
❑ 244 Sweden .25 .11
Olympic Gold 94
(Team photo)
❑ 245 Sweden .25 .11
Olympic Gold 94
(Hakan Loob)
❑ 246 Sweden .25 .11
Olympic Gold 94
(Celebration)
❑ 247 Canada .75 .35
World Champions 94
(Team photo)
❑ 248 Canada .25 .11
World Champions 94
(Steve Thomas)
❑ 249 Canada .50 .23
World Champions 94
(Luc Robitaille)
❑ 250 Manon Rheaume 4.00 1.80
❑ 251 Sundin and Andersson .50 .23
❑ 252 Brolin and Knutsen .15 .07
❑ 253 Peter Forsberg 5.00 2.20
Special
❑ 254 Peter Forsberg 5.00 2.20
Special
❑ 255 Peter Forsberg 5.00 2.20
Special
❑ 256 Mats Sundin 1.50 .70
Special
❑ 257 Mats Sundin 1.50 .70
Special
❑ 258 Mats Sundin 1.50 .70
Special
❑ 259 Mikael Renberg 1.00 .45
Special
❑ 260 Mikael Renberg 1.00 .45
Special
❑ 261 Mikael Renberg 1.00 .45
Special
❑ 262 Eric Lindros 6.00 2.70
Special
❑ 263 Eric Lindros 6.00 2.70
Special
❑ 264 Eric Lindros 6.00 2.70
Special
❑ 265 Wayne Gretzky 12.00 5.50
Special
❑ 266 Wayne Gretzky 12.00 5.50
Special
❑ 267 Wayne Gretzky 12.00 5.50
Special
❑ 268 Checklist 1-90 1.50 .70
(Renberg)
❑ 269 Checklist 91-180 1.00 .45
(Sundin)
❑ 270 Checklist 181-270 4.00 1.80
(Forsberg)
❑ XX Binder 5.00 2.20
❑ NNO Peter Forsberg 75.00 34.00
Mats Sundin

## 1994-95 Swedish Leaf Elit

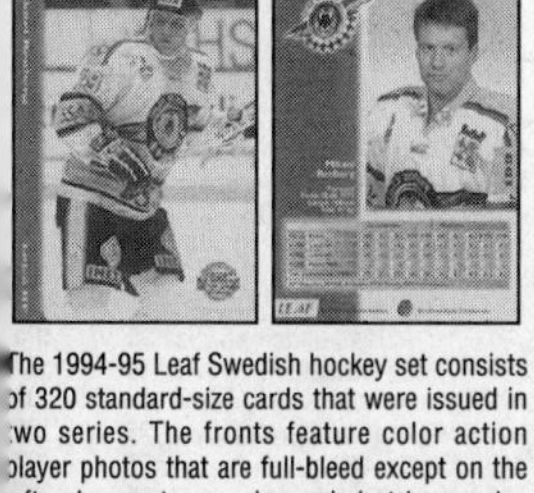

The 1994-95 Leaf Swedish hockey set consists of 320 standard-size cards that were issued in two series. The fronts feature color action player photos that are full-bleed except on the left, where a team color-coded stripe carries the player's name and his team's name. Leaf's logo in gold-foil appears in one of the corners. The team color-coded backs carry a color player close-up with a short biography, career stats and the team logo. Each series closes with team cards (135-158, 307-318) and checklists (159-160, 319-320).

| | MINT | NRMT |
|---|---|---|
| COMPLETE SET (320) | 80.00 | 36.00 |
| COMPLETE SERIES 1 (1-160) | 30.00 | 13.50 |
| COMPLETE SERIES 2 (161-320) | 50.00 | 22.00 |
| COMMON CARD (1-320) | .15 | .07 |

❑ 1 Thomas Tallberg .15 .07
❑ 2 Hakan Algotsson .25 .11
❑ 3 Mikael Magnusson .15 .07
❑ 4 Per Lundell .15 .07
❑ 5 Kenneth Kennholt .20 .09
❑ 6 Jan Huokko .15 .07
❑ 7 Petter Nilsson .15 .07
❑ 8 Johan Norgren .15 .07
❑ 9 Anders Berglund .20 .09
❑ 10 Kari Eloranta .20 .09
❑ 11 Sam Lindstahl .20 .09
❑ 12 Johan Rosen .15 .07
❑ 13 Jonas Johnsson .15 .07
❑ 14 Erik Huusko .20 .09
❑ 15 Thomas Rhodin .15 .07
❑ 16 Patric Kjellberg .25 .11
❑ 17 Fredrik Andersson .20 .09
❑ 18 Stefan Nilsson .15 .07
❑ 19 Petri Liimatainen .15 .07
❑ 20 Lars Jansson .15 .07
❑ 21 Per Wallin .25 .11
❑ 22 Mika Nieminen .25 .11
❑ 23 Lars Ivarsson .15 .07
❑ 24 Ronnie Sundin .50 .23
❑ 25 Bedrich Scerban .15 .07
❑ 26 Anders Huusko .15 .07
❑ 27 Erik Grankvist .20 .09
❑ 28 Stefan Ornskog .20 .09
❑ 29 Marcus Thuresson .15 .07
❑ 30 Johan Stromvall .15 .07
❑ 31 Peter Hasselblad .15 .07
❑ 32 Anders Eriksson 1.50 .70
❑ 33 Roger Elvenes .20 .09
❑ 34 Stefan Larsson .15 .07
❑ 35 Alexei Salomatin .15 .07
❑ 36 Niclas Havelid .15 .07
❑ 37 Mikael Lindman .15 .07
❑ 38 Jens Ohling .15 .07
❑ 39 Hakan Loob .75 .35
❑ 40 Johan Hedberg .25 .11
❑ 41 Niklas Eriksson .15 .07
❑ 42 Robert Nordberg .15 .07
❑ 43 Robert Svehla .75 .35
❑ 44 Hans Jonsson .15 .07
❑ 45 Thomas Srsen .15 .07
❑ 46 Thomas Sjogren .15 .07
❑ 47 Mishat Fahrutdinov .15 .07
❑ 48 Thomas Strandberg .15 .07
❑ 49 Andreas Dackell .75 .35
❑ 50 Peter Nilsson .15 .07
❑ 51 Andreas Johansson .75 .35
❑ 52 Stefan Falk .15 .07
❑ 53 Marcus Akerblom .15 .07
❑ 54 Peter Aslin .25 .11
❑ 55 Ricard Persson .35 .16
❑ 56 Tomas Nanzen .15 .07
❑ 57 Per-Johan Svensson .15 .07
❑ 58 Terho Koskela .15 .07
❑ 59 Henrik Nilsson .15 .07
❑ 60 Mats Lindberg .15 .07
❑ 61 Anders Huss .15 .07
❑ 62 Magnus Jansson .15 .07
❑ 63 Mats Lindgren 1.00 .45
❑ 64 Thomas Ljungberg .15 .07
❑ 65 Tomas Forslund .25 .11
❑ 66 Thomas Ostlund .35 .16
❑ 67 Raimo Helminen .25 .11
❑ 68 Magnus Wernblom .15 .07
❑ 69 Jorgen Jonsson .15 .07
❑ 70 Peter Berndtsson .15 .07
❑ 71 Stefan Hellkvist .15 .07
❑ 72 Tommy Lehmann .20 .09
❑ 73 Stefan Klockare .15 .07
❑ 74 Ola Josefsson .15 .07
❑ 75 Peter Lindmark .25 .11
❑ 76 Owe Thornberg .15 .07
❑ 77 Jarmo Makitalo .15 .07
❑ 78 Tomas Berglund .15 .07
❑ 79 Bo Svanberg .15 .07
❑ 80 Lennart Hermansson .15 .07
❑ 81 Stefan Elvenes .15 .07
❑ 82 Daniel Alfredsson 5.00 2.20
❑ 83 Claes Lindblom .15 .07
❑ 84 Bjorn Ahlstrom .15 .07
❑ 85 Ove Molin .15 .07
❑ 86 Fredrik Lindquist .25 .11
❑ 87 Clas Eriksson .15 .07
❑ 88 Peter Hammarstrom .15 .07
❑ 89 Magnus Swardh .15 .07
❑ 90 Lars Hurtig .15 .07
❑ 91 Daniel Rydmark .25 .11
❑ 92 Lars Bystrom .15 .07
❑ 93 Mats Loov .15 .07
❑ 94 Lars Dahlstrom .15 .07
❑ 95 Johan Brummer .15 .07
❑ 96 Patric Englund .15 .07
❑ 97 Christer Olsson .50 .23
❑ 98 Patrik Erickson .15 .07
❑ 99 Peter Ottosson .15 .07
❑ 100 Tomas Jonsson .25 .11
❑ 101 Lars Modig .15 .07
❑ 102 Ake Lilljebjorn .15 .07
❑ 103 Patrik Sylvegard .15 .07
❑ 104 Daniel Johansson .50 .23
❑ 105 Edvin Frylen .25 .11
❑ 106 Par Edlund .15 .07
❑ 107 Paul Andersson .15 .07
❑ 108 Rikard Franzen .15 .07
❑ 109 Christian Due-Boje .25 .11
❑ 110 Tommy Samuelsson .15 .07
❑ 111 Mathias Svedberg .15 .07
❑ 112 Hans Lodin .15 .07
❑ 113 Jonas Eriksson .25 .11
❑ 114 Mikael Engstrom .15 .07
❑ 115 Hakan Ahlund .15 .07
❑ 116 Kari Suoraniemi .15 .07
❑ 117 Peter Jacobsson .15 .07
❑ 118 Kristian Gahn .20 .09
❑ 119 Tommy Melkersson .15 .07
❑ 120 Oscar Ackestrom .15 .07
❑ 121 Thomas Johansson .15 .07
❑ 122 Jesper Duus .15 .07
❑ 123 Hans Abrahamsson .15 .07
❑ 124 Orjan Lindmark .15 .07
❑ 125 Torbjorn Lindberg .15 .07
❑ 126 Michael Sundlov .25 .11
❑ 127 Peter Sundstrom .25 .11
❑ 128 Pierre Johnsson .15 .07
❑ 129 Thomas Carlsson .15 .07
❑ 130 Stefan Axelsson .15 .07
❑ 131 Robert Nordmark .20 .09
❑ 132 Torbjorn Persson .15 .07
❑ 133 Bjorn Nord .15 .07
❑ 134 Mats Ytter .25 .11
❑ 135 AIK .15 .07
Team Statistics
❑ 136 Brynas IF .15 .07
Team Statistics
❑ 137 Djurgardens IF .15 .07
Team Statistics
❑ 138 Vastra Frolunda .15 .07
Team Statistics
❑ 139 Farjestad BK .15 .07
Team Statistics
❑ 140 HV-71 .15 .07
Team Statistics
❑ 141 Leksand IF .15 .07
Team Statistics
❑ 142 Lulea HF .15 .07
Team Statistics
❑ 143 Malmo IF .15 .07
Team Statistics
❑ 144 MoDo Hockey .15 .07
Team Statistics
❑ 145 Rogle BK .15 .07
Team Statistics
❑ 146 Varsteras IK .15 .07
Team Statistics
❑ 147 AIK Logo .25 .11
❑ 148 Brynas IF Logo .20 .09
❑ 149 Djurgardens IF .25 .11
❑ 150 Vastra Frolunda Logo .20 .09
❑ 151 Farjestads BK .20 .09
❑ 152 HV-71 Logo .20 .09
❑ 153 Leksands IF Logo .20 .09
❑ 154 Lulea HF .20 .09
❑ 155 Malmo IF .20 .09
❑ 156 MoDo Hockey .25 .11
❑ 157 Rogle BK .20 .09
❑ 158 Vasteras IK .20 .09
❑ 159 Checklist 1-80 .15 .07
❑ 160 Checklist 81-160 .15 .07
❑ 161 Kenneth Johansson .25 .11
❑ 162 Stefan Jonsson .15 .07
❑ 163 Mikael Wahlberg .15 .07
❑ 164 Per Djoos .25 .11
❑ 165 Andreas Schultz .15 .07
❑ 166 Sacha Molin .15 .07
❑ 167 Marcus Ramen .15 .07
❑ 168 Jergus Baca .25 .11
❑ 169 Erik Bergstrom .25 .11
❑ 170 Jonas Forsberg .35 .16
❑ 171 Olli Kaski .15 .07
❑ 172 Morgan Samuelsson .15 .07
❑ 173 Anders Burstrom .15 .07
❑ 174 Stanislav Meciar .15 .07
❑ 175 Leif Rohlin .35 .16
❑ 176 Lars Edstrom .15 .07
❑ 177 Esa Keskinen .25 .11
❑ 178 Daniel Casselstahl .15 .07
❑ 179 Mattias Timander .75 .35
❑ 180 Peter Nordstrom .15 .07
❑ 181 Patric Aberg .15 .07
❑ 182 Mikael Enander .15 .07
❑ 183 Charles Berglund .25 .11
❑ 184 Jonas Andersson-Junkka .35 .16
❑ 185 Sergei Fokin .15 .07
❑ 186 Boo Ahl .35 .16
❑ 187 Jiri Kucera .25 .11
❑ 188 Roger Nordstrom .15 .07
❑ 189 Peter Forsberg 20.00 9.00
❑ 190 Arto Ruotanen .15 .07
❑ 191 Mikael Wiklander .15 .07
❑ 192 Joakim Persson .25 .11
❑ 193 Peter Larsson .15 .07
❑ 194 Per Eklund .35 .16
❑ 195 Joacim Esbjors .15 .07
❑ 196 Magnus Arvedsson .15 .07
❑ 197 Marko Palo .15 .07
❑ 198 Mikael Holmberg .15 .07
❑ 199 Mikael Renberg 5.00 2.20
❑ 200 Tero Lehtera .35 .16
❑ 201 Fredrik Lindh .15 .07
❑ 202 Joham Finnstrom .15 .07
❑ 203 Peter Popovic .25 .11
❑ 204 Tony Barthelson .15 .07
❑ 205 Stefan Polla .15 .07
❑ 206 Jonas Esbjors .15 .07
❑ 207 Roger Hansson .15 .07
❑ 208 Mikael Hakansson .15 .07
❑ 209 Daniel Tjarnqvist .35 .16
❑ 210 Anders Carlsson .25 .11
❑ 211 Dick Tarnstrom .50 .23
❑ 212 Johan Tornberg .15 .07
❑ 213 Joakim Lundberg .15 .07
❑ 214 Marko Jantunen .35 .16
❑ 215 Patrik Haltia .25 .11
❑ 216 Fredrik Stillman .15 .07
❑ 217 Andy Schneider .15 .07
❑ 218 Thomas Holmstrom 1.00 .45
❑ 219 Jens Hemstrom .15 .07
❑ 220 Anders Soderberg .50 .23
❑ 221 Peter Lundmark .15 .07
❑ 222 Patrik Juhlin .50 .23
❑ 223 Anders Gozzi .15 .07
❑ 224 Marcus Ragnarsson .75 .35
❑ 225 Mattias Olsson .15 .07
❑ 226 Andreas Karlsson .15 .07
❑ 227 Tomas Lilja .15 .07
❑ 228 Stefan Ohman .15 .07
❑ 229 Jarmo Kekalainen .25 .11
❑ 230 Tony Skopac .15 .07
❑ 231 Lars Karlsson .25 .11
❑ 232 Mats Sundin 5.00 2.20
❑ 233 Peter Strom .15 .07
❑ 234 Mattias Johansson .15 .07
❑ 235 Johan Lindbom .15 .07
❑ 236 Mats Lusth .15 .07
❑ 237 Marcus Magnertoft .15 .07
❑ 238 Martin Hostak .15 .07
❑ 239 Mikael Pettersson .15 .07
❑ 240 Johan Akerman .15 .07
❑ 241 Mathias Hallback .15 .07
❑ 242 Johan Davidsson .50 .23
❑ 243 Per-Erik Eklund .35 .16
❑ 244 Johan Salle .15 .07
❑ 245 Per Svartvadet .50 .23
❑ 246 Ville Siren .25 .11
❑ 247 Mattias Loof .15 .07
❑ 248 Per-Johan Axelsson .35 .16
❑ 249 Peter Gerhardsson .15 .07
❑ 250 Jonas Bergqvist .25 .11
❑ 251 Per-Johan Johansson .35 .16
❑ 252 Mattias Bosson .15 .07
❑ 253 Andreas Olsson .15 .07
❑ 254 Patrik Zetterberg .15 .07
❑ 255 Michael Johansson .15 .07
❑ 256 Stefan Gustavson .15 .07
❑ 257 Jerry Persson .15 .07
❑ 258 Stefan Nilsson .15 .07
❑ 259 Roger Johansson .15 .07
❑ 260 Jarmo Myllys .50 .23
❑ 261 Kyosti Karjalainen .25 .11
❑ 262 Thomas Eriksson .15 .07
❑ 263 Michael Hjalm .15 .07
❑ 264 Espen Knutsen .50 .23
❑ 265 Andreas Salomonsson .15 .07
❑ 266 Patrik Hoglund .15 .07
❑ 267 Peter Andersson .15 .07
❑ 268 Brett Hauer .25 .11
❑ 269 Stefan Ketola .15 .07
❑ 270 Patrik Carnback .25 .11
❑ 271 Petter Ronnqvist .20 .09
❑ 272 Roger Ohman .15 .07
❑ 273 Fredrik Modin .75 .35
❑ 274 Alexander Beliavski .15 .07
❑ 275 Niklas Brannstrom .15 .07
❑ 276 Per Gustafsson .50 .23
❑ 277 Nicklas Nordquist .15 .07
❑ 278 Roger Akerstrom .15 .07
❑ 279 Jiri Vykoukal .25 .11
❑ 280 Jesper Mattsson .75 .35
❑ 281 Henrik Nordfeldt .15 .07
❑ 282 Joakim Musakka .15 .07
❑ 283 Anders Johnson .15 .07
❑ 284 Niklas Sundstrom 4.00 1.80
❑ 285 Nicklas Lidstrom 3.00 1.35
❑ 286 Tomas Sandstrom .75 .35
❑ 287 Jens Nielsen .15 .07
❑ 288 Mattias Ohlund 1.00 .45
❑ 289 Markus Eriksson .15 .07
❑ 290 Mikael Sandberg .25 .11
❑ 291 Sergeij Pushkov .15 .07
❑ 292 Jonas Hoglund .75 .35
❑ 293 Peter Ekelund .15 .07
❑ 294 Fredrik Bergqvist .15 .07
❑ 295 Torgny Bendelin .15 .07
❑ 296 Tommy Sandlin CO .15 .07
❑ 297 Tommy Boustedt CO .15 .07
❑ 298 Conny Evensson CO .15 .07
❑ 299 Sune Bergman CO .15 .07
❑ 300 Wayne Fleming CO .15 .07
❑ 301 Lars Bergstrom CO .15 .07
❑ 302 Hannu Jortikka CO .15 .07
❑ 303 Leif Boork CO .15 .07
❑ 304 Christer Abrahamsson CO .25 .11
❑ 305 Randy Edmonds CO .15 .07
❑ 306 Ulf Labraaten CO .15 .07
❑ 307 AIK .25 .11
❑ 308 Brynas IF .25 .11
❑ 309 Djurgardens IF .25 .11
❑ 310 Farjestads BK .25 .11
❑ 311 HV 71 .25 .11
❑ 312 Leksands IF .25 .11
❑ 313 Lulea HF .25 .11
❑ 314 Malmo IF .25 .11
❑ 315 MoDo .25 .11
❑ 316 Rogle BK .25 .11
❑ 317 Vasteras IK .25 .11
❑ 318 Vastra Frolunda .25 .11
❑ 319 Checklist 161-240 .15 .07
❑ 320 Checklist 241-320 .15 .07
❑ NNO1 Malmo IF SuperChase 25.00 11.00
❑ NNO2 M.Lindgren SuperChase 35.00 16.00

## 1994-95 Swedish Leaf Elit Clean Sweepers

This 10-card standard size set highlights 10 of

the top goalies in the Swedish Elitserien. The cards were randomly inserted into series one packs. The fronts have a color photo with the player's name in yellow on a red background at the bottom. The word "Cleansweepers" is at the top in gold-foil as are the words "Elit Set" in the bottom right corner. The backs have player information in green with a blue background. The cards are numbered "X of 10."

| | MINT | NRMT |
|---|---|---|
| COMPLETE SET (10) | 50.00 | 22.00 |
| COMMON CARD (1-10) | 5.00 | 2.20 |

❑ 1 Peter Lindmark 6.00 2.70
❑ 2 Michael Sundlov 6.00 2.70
❑ 3 Thomas Ostlund 6.00 2.70
❑ 4 Jonas Eriksson 5.00 2.20
❑ 5 Peter Aslin 5.00 2.20
❑ 6 Ake Lilljebjorn 5.00 2.20
❑ 7 Johan Hedberg 5.00 2.20
❑ 8 Henrik Arvsell 5.00 2.20
❑ 9 Frederik Andersson 5.00 2.20
❑ 10 Hakan Algotsson 6.00 2.70

## 1994-95 Swedish Leaf Elit Foreign Affairs

Featuring foreign-born players competing in the Elitserien, this ten-card set was inserted in foil packs. The fronts feature a color player cutout superimposed over his country's flag. The words "Foreign Affairs" in foil letters are printed on the bottom, while the player's name and his team's name appear vertically on the right. The backs carry player profile. All information is printed in Swedish.

| | MINT | NRMT |
|---|---|---|
| COMPLETE SET (10) | 30.00 | 13.50 |
| COMMON CARD (1-10) | 3.00 | 1.35 |

❑ 1 Espen Knutsen 5.00 2.20
❑ 2 Esa Keskinen 4.00 1.80
❑ 3 Marko Jantunen 4.00 1.80
❑ 4 Jarmo Myllys 4.00 1.80
❑ 5 Jiri Kucera 3.00 1.35
❑ 6 Jiri Vykoukal 3.00 1.35
❑ 7 Jarmo Kekalainen 3.00 1.35
❑ 8 Olli Kaski 3.00 1.35
❑ 9 Jergus Baca 3.00 1.35
❑ 10 Tero Lehtera 3.00 1.35

## 1994-95 Swedish Leaf Elit Gold Cards

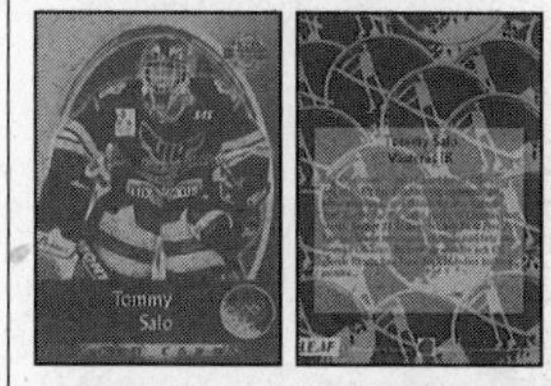

This 24-card standard size set commemorates the members of Sweden's 1994 Olympic gold medal team. The cards were randomly inserted into series one packs. The fronts have a full-color photo ghosted over an image of the gold medal with the player's name at the bottom. The words "Gold Cards" are at the bottom in gold-foil as are the words "Elit Set" in the top right corner. The backs have the player's name and information with a stick figure playing hockey numerous times being the background. The cards are numbered "X of 24."

| | MINT | NRMT |
|---|---|---|
| COMPLETE SET (24) | 125.00 | 55.00 |
| COMMON CARD (1-24) | 3.00 | 1.35 |

❑ 1 Title Card 10.00 4.50
❑ 2 Andreas Dackell 5.00 2.20
❑ 3 Charles Berglund 3.00 1.35
❑ 4 Christian Due-Boje 4.00 1.80
❑ 5 Daniel Rydmark 4.00 1.80
❑ 6 Fredrik Stillman 4.00 1.80
❑ 7 Hakan Algotsson 5.00 2.20

❑ 8 Hakan Loob 10.00 4.50
❑ 9 Jonas Bergqvist 5.00 2.20
❑ 10 Jorgen Jonsson 3.00 1.35
❑ 11 Kenny Jonsson 6.00 2.70
❑ 12 Leif Rohlin 4.00 1.80
❑ 13 Magnus Svensson 5.00 2.20
❑ 14 Mats Naslund 10.00 4.50
❑ 15 Michael Sundlov 5.00 2.20
❑ 16 Niklas Eriksson 3.00 1.35
❑ 17 Patric Kjellberg 3.00 1.35
❑ 18 Patrick Juhlin 4.00 1.80
❑ 19 Peter Forsberg 50.00 22.00
❑ 20 Roger Hansson 3.00 1.35
❑ 21 Roger Johansson 3.00 1.35
❑ 22 Stefan Ornskog 3.00 1.35
❑ 23 Tomas Jonsson 5.00 2.20
❑ 24 Tommy Salo 10.00 4.50

## 1994-95 Swedish Leaf Elit Guest Special

Featuring players who joined the Elitserien during the 1994 NHL lockout, this eight card set was inserted in second-series foil packs. The fronts feature a color player action shot. The words "Guest Special" appear in a foil bar above the photo, while the player's name is printed in a foil bar below. The horizontal backs carry a color player cut-out superimposed over a drawing of the world.

| | MINT | NRMT |
|---|---|---|
| COMPLETE SET (8) | 80.00 | 36.00 |
| COMMON CARD (1-8) | 5.00 | 2.20 |

❑ 1 Mats Sundin 15.00 6.75
❑ 2 Tomas Sandstrom 6.00 2.70
❑ 3 Peter Forsberg 40.00 18.00
❑ 4 Nicklas Lidstrom 10.00 4.50
❑ 5 Mikael Renberg 15.00 6.75
❑ 6 Roger Johansson 5.00 2.20
❑ 7 Peter Popovic 5.00 2.20
❑ 8 Patrick Juhlin 5.00 2.20

## 1994-95 Swedish Leaf Elit NHL Draft

This ten-card standard-size set featuring players drafted by NHL teams in 1994 was inserted in second-series foil packs. The fronts feature a color player action shot. The year 1994 is separated by the NHL draft logo. The backs contain information in Swedish about the player's selection in the 1994 NHL draft.

| | MINT | NRMT |
|---|---|---|
| COMPLETE SET (10) | 55.00 | 25.00 |
| COMMON CARD (1-10) | 4.00 | 1.80 |

❑ 1 Mattias Ohlund 10.00 4.50
❑ 2 Johan Davidsson 6.00 2.70
❑ 3 Fredrik Modin 6.00 2.70
❑ 4 Johan Finnstrom 4.00 1.80
❑ 5 Edvin Frylen 4.00 1.80
❑ 6 Daniel Alfredsson 15.00 6.75
❑ 7 Patrik Haltia 6.00 2.70
❑ 8 Peter Strom 4.00 1.80
❑ 9 Thomas Holmstrom 10.00 4.50
❑ 10 Dick Tarnstrom 5.00 2.20

## 1994-95 Swedish Leaf Elit Playmakers

This six-card standard size set shines the spotlight on five of the top goal scorers in the Swedish Elitserien. The cards were randomly inserted into series one packs. The fronts have a full-color photo with an orange and black background. The words "Play Makers" are on the left side and the words "Elit Set" is in the bottom right corner in gold-foil. The backs have "Play Makers" at the top in silver with an orange background. The player's name and number of assists he had in each of the previous three seasons with a black background. Card #1 is different in that it is a title card and has a picture of all five players in the set. The cards are numbered "X of 6."

| | MINT | NRMT |
|---|---|---|
| COMPLETE SET (6) | 18.00 | 8.00 |
| COMMON CARD (1-6) | 3.00 | 1.35 |

❑ 1 Title Card 5.00 2.20
❑ 2 Stefan Nilsson 3.00 1.35
❑ 3 Mika Nieminen 4.00 1.80
❑ 4 Raimo Helminen 3.00 1.35
❑ 5 Peter Larsson 3.00 1.35
❑ 6 Hakan Loob 6.00 2.70

## 1994-95 Swedish Leaf Elit Rookie Rockets

Inserted in second-series foil packs, this 10-card set features rookies in the Swedish league. Borderless horizontal fronts feature a color player cut-out along with "Rookie" in big foil letters. The player's name and his team's name appears in a red bar on the bottom. The horizontal back carry another color player cut-out along with player profile.

| | MINT | NRMT |
|---|---|---|
| COMPLETE SET (10) | 35.00 | 16.00 |
| COMMON CARD (1-10) | 3.00 | 1.35 |

❑ 1 Fredrik Modin 5.00 2.20
❑ 2 Jonas Andersson-Junkka 3.00 1.35
❑ 3 Thomas Holmstrom 6.00 2.70
❑ 4 Mattias Ohlund 6.00 2.70
❑ 5 Per Eklund 4.00 1.80
❑ 6 Daniel Tjarnqvist 4.00 1.80
❑ 7 Joakim Persson 4.00 1.80
❑ 8 Patrik Haltia 4.00 1.80
❑ 9 Andreas Karlsson 3.00 1.35
❑ 10 Stefan Nilsson 3.00 1.35

## 1994-95 Swedish Leaf Elit Studio Signatures

This 12-card standard-size set was inserted in second-series foil packs. The fronts feature borderless color studio photos. The player's facsimile autograph in foil letters appears at the bottom. The backs carry a drawing of the player in close-up.

| | MINT | NRMT |
|---|---|---|
| COMPLETE SET (12) | 35.00 | 16.00 |
| COMMON CARD (1-12) | 3.00 | 1.35 |

❑ 1 Rikard Franzen 3.00 1.35
❑ 2 Anders Huss 3.00 1.35
❑ 3 Jens Ohling 5.00 2.20
❑ 4 Tommy Samuelsson 3.00 1.35
❑ 5 Fredrik Stillman 5.00 2.20
❑ 6 Jonas Bergqvist 5.00 2.20
❑ 7 Johan Stromvall 3.00 1.35
❑ 8 Roger Nordstrom 5.00 2.20
❑ 9 Lars Bystrom 3.00 1.35
❑ 10 Roger Elvenes 3.00 1.35
❑ 11 Leif Rohlin 5.00 2.20
❑ 12 Tero Koskela 3.00 1.35

## 1994-95 Swedish Leaf Elit Top Guns

This 10-card standard size set consists of some of the top goal scorers in the Swedish Elitserien. The cards were randomly inserted into series one packs. The fronts have a full-color photo with a background that looks like fire works. In one of the top corners the words "Top Gun" are in gold-foil as are the words "Elit Set" in the bottom right corner. The backs have "Top Gun" in red at the top as if it were underneath rippling water. At the bottom is the number of goals they scored each of the previous three seasons. The cards are numbered "X of 10."

| | MINT | NRMT |
|---|---|---|
| COMPLETE SET (10) | 50.00 | 22.00 |
| COMMON CARD (1-10) | 5.00 | 2.20 |

❑ 1 Thomas Srsen 5.00 2.20
❑ 2 Hakan Loob 10.00 4.50
❑ 3 Lars Hurtig 5.00 2.20
❑ 4 Stefan Elvenes 5.00 2.20
❑ 5 Jorgen Jonsson 5.00 2.20
❑ 6 Robert Svehla 7.00 3.10
❑ 7 Daniel Rydmark 5.00 2.20
❑ 8 Owe Thornberg 5.00 2.20
❑ 9 Patric Kjellberg 5.00 2.20
❑ 10 Mats Loov 5.00 2.20

## 1995-96 Swedish Leaf Elit

The 1995-96 Leaf Elit set was issued in two series (150 and 160 cards, respectively) and featured the players of Sweden's top league, the Elitserien. The cards feature a beautiful full-bleed design, with the player's name ghosted along the bottom. The set was distributed in 8-card packs. The NNO Per-Erik (Pelle) Eklund card was randomly inserted in series 1 packs, while the HV71 card, commemorating the team's 1994-95 championship, could be found in series 2 packs.

| | MINT | NRMT |
|---|---|---|
| COMPLETE SET (310) | 50.00 | 22.00 |
| COMPLETE SERIES 1 (150) | 25.00 | 11.00 |
| COMPLETE SERIES 2 (160) | 25.00 | 11.00 |
| COMMON CARD (1-310) | .15 | .07 |

❑ 1 Hakan Loob .75 .35
❑ 2 AIK .25 .11
❑ 3 AIK, Season Stats .15 .07
❑ 4 Joakim Persson .25 .11
❑ 5 Niclas Havelid .15 .07
❑ 6 Tony Barthelson .15 .07
❑ 7 Patric Aberg .15 .07
❑ 8 Johan Akerman .15 .07
❑ 9 Dick Tarnstrom .25 .11
❑ 10 Stefan Gustavson .15 .07
❑ 11 Anders Gozzi .15 .07
❑ 12 Morgan Samuelsson .25 .11
❑ 13 Brynas IF .15 .07
❑ 14 Brynas, Season Stats .15 .07
❑ 15 Michael Sundlov .25 .11
❑ 16 Stefan Klockare .25 .11
❑ 17 Bedrich Scerban .15 .07
❑ 18 Andreas Dackell .25 .11
❑ 19 Fredrik Modin .75 .35
❑ 20 Ove Molin .15 .07
❑ 21 Mikael Wahlberg .15 .07
❑ 22 Thomas Tallberg .15 .07
❑ 23 Peter Larsson .15 .07
❑ 24 Stefan Ketola .25 .11
❑ 25 Djurgardens IF .25 .11
❑ 26 Djurgarden, Season Stats .15 .07
❑ 27 Jonas Forsberg .35 .16
❑ 28 Christian Due-Boje .25 .11
❑ 29 Mikael Magnusson .15 .07
❑ 30 Thomas Johansson .15 .07
❑ 31 Joakim Musakka .15 .07
❑ 32 Erik Hussko .25 .11
❑ 33 Jens Ohling .25 .11
❑ 34 Per Eklund .25 .11
❑ 35 Espen Knutsen .50 .23
❑ 36 Patrik Erickson .15 .07
❑ 37 Farjestads BK .15 .07
❑ 38 Farjestad, Season Stats .15 .07
❑ 39 Patrik Haltia .25 .11
❑ 40 Sergei Fokin .15 .07
❑ 41 Thomas Rhodin .15 .07
❑ 42 Stefan Nilsson .15 .07
❑ 43 Magnus Arvedsson .15 .07
❑ 44 Mattias Johansson .15 .07
❑ 45 Clas Eriksson .15 .07
❑ 46 Peter Ottosson .15 .07
❑ 47 HV 71 .15 .07
❑ 48 HV 71, Season Stats .15 .07
❑ 49 Boo Ahl .35 .16
❑ 50 Kenneth Kennholt .15 .07
❑ 51 Hans Abrahamsson .15 .07
❑ 52 Peter Hammarstrom .15 .07
❑ 53 Johan Davidsson .50 .23
❑ 54 Stefan Falk .15 .07
❑ 55 Johan Lindbom .15 .07
❑ 56 Esa Keskinen .25 .11
❑ 57 Stefan Ornskog .25 .11
❑ 58 Peter Ekelund .15 .07
❑ 59 Leksands IF .15 .07
❑ 60 Leksand, Season Stats .15 .07
❑ 61 Johan Hedberg .25 .11
❑ 62 Tomas Jonsson .25 .11
❑ 63 Hans Lodin .15 .07
❑ 64 Orjan Lindmark .15 .07
❑ 65 Jan Huokko .15 .07
❑ 66 Markus Eriksson .15 .07
❑ 67 Andreas Karlsson .15 .07
❑ 68 Mikael Holmberg .15 .07
❑ 69 Jonas Bergqvist .25 .11
❑ 70 Niklas Eriksson .15 .07
❑ 71 Per-Erik Eklund .35 .16
❑ 72 Lulea HF .15 .07
❑ 73 Lulea, Season Stats .15 .07
❑ 74 Jarmo Myllys .50 .23
❑ 75 Mattias Ohlund .75 .35
❑ 76 Lars Modig .15 .07
❑ 77 Torbjorn Lindberg .15 .07
❑ 78 Roger Akerstrom .15 .07
❑ 79 Stefan Jonsson .15 .07
❑ 80 Johan Rosen .15 .07
❑ 81 Tomas Berglund .15 .07
❑ 82 Robert Nordberg .15 .07
❑ 83 Jiri Kucera .25 .11
❑ 84 Tomas Holmstrom .75 .35
❑ 85 Malmo IF .15 .07
❑ 86 Malmo, Season Stats .15 .07
❑ 87 Peter Andersson .15 .07
❑ 88 Roger Ohman .15 .07
❑ 89 Marcus Magnertoft .15 .07
❑ 90 Patrik Sylvegard .15 .07
❑ 91 Hakan Ahlund .15 .07
❑ 92 Jesper Mattsson .75 .35
❑ 93 Roger Hansson .15 .07
❑ 94 Mattias Bosson .15 .07
❑ 95 Bo Svanberg .15 .07
❑ 96 Raimo Halminen .25 .11
❑ 97 MoDo Hockey .25 .11
❑ 98 MoDo, Season Stats .15 .07
❑ 99 Petter Ronnqvist .25 .11
❑ 100 Lars Jansson .15 .07
❑ 101 Mattias Timander .75 .35
❑ 102 Hans Jonsson .15 .07
❑ 103 Anders Soderberg .35 .16
❑ 104 Martin Hostak .15 .07
❑ 105 Kyosti Karjalainen .25 .11
❑ 106 Mikael Hakanson .15 .07
❑ 107 Per Svartvadet .35 .16
❑ 108 Andreas Salomonsson .15 .07
❑ 109 Lars Bystrom .15 .07
❑ 110 Magnus Wernblom .15 .07
❑ 111 Rogle BK .15 .07
❑ 112 Rogle, Season Stats .15 .07
❑ 113 Magnus Swardh .25 .11
❑ 114 Arto Ruotanen .15 .07
❑ 115 Johan Finnstrom .25 .11
❑ 116 Daniel Tjarnqvist .50 .23
❑ 117 Pierre Johnsson .15 .07
❑ 118 Per Wallin .35 .16
❑ 119 Michael Johansson .15 .07
❑ 120 Per-Johan Svensson .15 .07
❑ 121 Roger Elvenes .15 .07
❑ 122 Mats Loov .15 .07
❑ 123 Michael Hjalm .25 .11
❑ 124 Vasteras IK .15 .07
❑ 125 Vasteras, Season Stats .15 .07
❑ 126 Mats Ytter .25 .11
❑ 127 Erik Bergstrom .25 .11
❑ 128 Lars Ivarsson .15 .07
❑ 129 Mishat Fahrutdinov .15 .07
❑ 130 Claes Lindblom .15 .07
❑ 131 Paul Andersson .15 .07
❑ 132 Henrik Nordfeldt .15 .07
❑ 133 Alexei Salomatin .25 .11
❑ 134 Mikael Pettersson .15 .07
❑ 135 Vastra Frolunda HC .15 .07
❑ 136 Frolunda, Season Stats .15 .07
❑ 137 Hakan Algotsson .25 .11
❑ 138 Jonas Andersson-Junkka .35 .16
❑ 139 Stefan Larsson .15 .07
❑ 140 Par Djoos .25 .11
❑ 141 Ronnie Sundin .25 .11
❑ 142 Par Edlund .25 .11
❑ 143 Peter Berndtsson .15 .07
❑ 144 Joacim Esbjors .15 .07
❑ 145 Alexander Beliavski .15 .07
❑ 146 Jonas Esbjors .15 .07
❑ 147 Marko Jantunen .25 .11
❑ 148 Peter Strom .15 .07
❑ 149 Checklist 1-75 .15 .07
❑ 150 Checklist 76-150 .15 .07
❑ 151 AIK .25 .11
❑ 152 AIK, Captains .15 .07
❑ 153 Mikael Nilsson .15 .07
❑ 154 Juha Jokiharju .25 .11
❑ 155 Stefan Andersson .15 .07
❑ 156 Thomas Strandberg .15 .07
❑ 157 Mats Lindberg .15 .07
❑ 158 Peter Gerhardsson .15 .07
❑ 159 Tommy Lehmann .25 .11
❑ 160 Tommy Hedlund .15 .07
❑ 161 Peter Wallin .25 .11
❑ 162 Bjorn Ahlstrom .15 .07
❑ 163 Erik Hamalainen .25 .11
❑ 164 Patric Englund .15 .07
❑ 165 Rikard Franzen .15 .07
❑ 166 Brynas IF .15 .07
❑ 167 Brynas, Captains .15 .07
❑ 168 Lars Karlsson .15 .07
❑ 169 Jonas Lofstrom .15 .07
❑ 170 Stefan Polla .15 .07
❑ 171 Mikael Lind .15 .07
❑ 172 Brian Rafalski .25 .11
❑ 173 Roger Kyro .15 .07
❑ 174 Per-Johan Johansson .15 .07
❑ 175 Greg Parks .15 .07
❑ 176 Per Lofstrom .15 .07
❑ 177 Jonas Johnson .15 .07
❑ 178 Mikael Lindman .15 .07
❑ 179 Mikael Wiklander .15 .07
❑ 180 Tommy Melkersson .15 .07
❑ 181 Djurgardens IF .25 .11
❑ 182 Djurgarden, Captains .15 .07
❑ 183 Thomas Ostlund .50 .23
❑ 184 Patrik Hofbauer .15 .07
❑ 185 Magnus Jansson .15 .07
❑ 186 Niklas Falk .15 .07
❑ 187 Ola Josefsson .15 .07
❑ 188 Joakim Lundberg .15 .07
❑ 189 Fredrik Lindquist .25 .11
❑ 190 Patrik Kjellberg .25 .11
❑ 191 Jan Viktorsson .25 .11
❑ 192 Bjorn Nord .15 .07
❑ 193 Tommy Jacobsen .15 .07
❑ 194 Anders Huusko .15 .07
❑ 195 Kristofer Ottosson .15 .07
❑ 196 Vastra Frolunda HC .15 .07
❑ 197 Frolunda, Captains .15 .07
❑ 198 Mikael Sandberg .15 .07
❑ 199 Jerry Persson .15 .07
❑ 200 Peter Hogardh .15 .07
❑ 201 Stefan Axelsson .50 .23
❑ 202 Lars Edstrom .15 .07
❑ 203 Lars-Goran Wiklander .25 .11
❑ 204 Per-Johan Axelsson .50 .23
❑ 205 Henrik Nilsson .15 .07
❑ 206 Petteri Nummelin .25 .11
❑ 207 Christian Ruuttu .50 .23
❑ 208 Oscar Ackestrom .15 .07
❑ 209 Farjestads BK .15 .07
❑ 210 Farjestad, Captains .15 .07
❑ 211 Markus Ketterer .50 .23
❑ 212 Bjorn Eriksson .15 .07
❑ 213 Jonas Hoglund .75 .35
❑ 214 Peter Nordstrom .15 .07
❑ 215 Jorgen Jonsson .15 .07
❑ 216 Greger Artursson .15 .07
❑ 217 Jesper Duus .15 .07
❑ 218 Roger Johansson .15 .07
❑ 219 Leif Carlsson .15 .07
❑ 220 Per Lundell .15 .07
❑ 221 Vitali Prokhorov .25 .11
❑ 222 HV 71 .15 .07
❑ 223 HV 71, Captains .15 .07
❑ 224 Kenneth Johansson .15 .07
❑ 225 Thomas Gustavsson .15 .07
❑ 226 Marcus Thuresson .15 .07
❑ 227 Vesa Salo .25 .11
❑ 228 Kai Nurminen .50 .23
❑ 229 Johan Brummer .15 .07
❑ 230 Daniel Johansson .25 .11
❑ 231 Per Gustafsson .50 .23
❑ 232 Niklas Rahm .15 .07
❑ 233 Leksands IF .15 .07
❑ 234 Leksand, Captains .15 .07
❑ 235 Per-Ragnar Bergkvist .25 .11
❑ 236 Anders Carlsson .15 .07
❑ 237 Micael Karlberg .15 .07
❑ 238 Torgny Lowgren .15 .07
❑ 239 Stefan Hellkvist .15 .07
❑ 240 Markus Akerblom .15 .07
❑ 241 Joakim Lidgren .15 .07
❑ 242 Tomas Forslund .25 .11
❑ 243 Torbjorn Johansson .15 .07
❑ 244 Nicklas Nordquist .15 .07
❑ 245 Lulea HF .15 .07
❑ 246 Lulea, Captains .15 .07
❑ 247 Erik Grankvist .15 .07
❑ 248 Mikael Lindholm .15 .07
❑ 249 Johan Stromvall .15 .07
❑ 250 Anders Burstrom .15 .07
❑ 251 Lars Hurtig .15 .07
❑ 252 Stefan Nilsson .15 .07
❑ 253 Jan Mertzig .25 .11
❑ 254 Petter Nilsson .15 .07
❑ 255 Malmo IF .15 .07
❑ 256 Malmo IF, Captains .15 .07
❑ 257 Peter Lindmark .35 .16
❑ 258 Roger Nordstrom .25 .11
❑ 259 Andreas Lilja .15 .07
❑ 260 Brian McReynolds .15 .07
❑ 261 Ilja Byakin .25 .11
❑ 262 Robert Burakovsky .15 .07
❑ 263 Mikael Burakovsky .15 .07
❑ 264 Stefan Elvenes .25 .11
❑ 265 Johan Salle .15 .07
❑ 266 Kim Johnsson .15 .07
❑ 267 Peter Hasselblad .15 .07
❑ 268 Marko Palo .15 .07
❑ 269 MoDo Hockey .25 .11
❑ 270 MoDo, Captains .25 .11
❑ 271 Fredrik Andersson .15 .07
❑ 272 Frantisek Kaberle .15 .07
❑ 273 Samuel Pahlsson .25 .11
❑ 274 Jan Larsson .15 .07
❑ 275 Per-Anton Lundstrom .25 .11
❑ 276 Tomas Nansen .15 .07
❑ 277 Marcus Karlsson .15 .07
❑ 278 Jan-Axel Alavaara .25 .11
❑ 279 Kristian Gahn .35 .16
❑ 280 Rogle BK .15 .07
❑ 281 Rogle, Captains .15 .07
❑ 282 Patrik Backlund .15 .07
❑ 283 Peter Lundmark .15 .07
❑ 284 Anders Berglund .15 .07
❑ 285 Harijs Vitolins .15 .07

| | | |
|---|---|---|
| ❑ 286 Jens Nielsen | .15 | .07 |
| ❑ 287 Greg Brown | .25 | .11 |
| ❑ 288 Bjorn Linden | .15 | .07 |
| ❑ 289 Vasteras IK | .15 | .07 |
| ❑ 290 Vasteras, Captains | .15 | .07 |
| ❑ 291 Jacob Karlsson | .15 | .07 |
| ❑ 292 Patrik Zetterberg | .15 | .07 |
| ❑ 293 Mattias Loof | .15 | .07 |
| ❑ 294 Johan Tornberg | .15 | .07 |
| ❑ 295 Andrei Korolev | .15 | .07 |
| ❑ 296 Mattias Olsson | .15 | .07 |
| ❑ 297 Roger Rosen | .15 | .07 |
| ❑ 298 Andrei Lulin | .15 | .07 |
| ❑ 299 Edvin Fylen | .25 | .11 |
| ❑ 300 Mats Lusth | .15 | .07 |
| ❑ 301 Fredrik Oberg | .15 | .07 |
| ❑ 302 Jarmo Myllys AS | .35 | .16 |
| ❑ 303 Tomas Jonsson AS | .25 | .11 |
| ❑ 304 All Stars Andersson | .25 | .11 |
| ❑ 305 Hakan Loob AS | .50 | .23 |
| ❑ 306 Esa Keskinen AS | .25 | .11 |
| ❑ 307 Christian Ruuttu AS | .35 | .16 |
| ❑ 308 Checklist 151-230 | .15 | .07 |
| ❑ 309 Checklist 231-310 | .15 | .07 |
| ❑ 310 Checklist Insert Cards | .15 | .07 |
| ❑ NNO HV71, Svenska Mastare | 25.00 | 11.00 |
| ❑ NNO Per-Erik Eklund | 25.00 | 11.00 |

## 1995-96 Swedish Leaf Elit Champs

Randomly inserted in series 1 packs at a rate of 1:11, this 15-card set celebrates members of Sweden's championship team. The cards are individually serially numbered on the back. It is believed that 1,000 of each were produced.

| | MINT | NRMT |
|---|---|---|
| COMPLETE SET (15) | 50.00 | 22.00 |
| COMMON CARD (1-15) | 3.00 | 1.35 |
| ❑ 1 Tomas Jonsson | 4.00 | 1.80 |
| ❑ 2 Patrik Kjellberg | 4.00 | 1.80 |
| ❑ 3 Hakan Loob | 10.00 | 4.50 |
| ❑ 4 Peter Lindmark | 5.00 | 2.20 |
| ❑ 5 Anders Carlsson | 3.00 | 1.35 |
| ❑ 6 Raimo Helminen | 4.00 | 1.80 |
| ❑ 7 Esa Keskinen | 4.00 | 1.80 |
| ❑ 8 Jan Larsson | 3.00 | 1.35 |
| ❑ 9 Roger Johansson | 3.00 | 1.35 |
| ❑ 10 Andreas Dackell | 8.00 | 3.60 |
| ❑ 11 Stefan Ornskog | 3.00 | 1.35 |
| ❑ 12 Michael Sundlov | 5.00 | 2.20 |
| ❑ 13 Per-Erik Eklund | 5.00 | 2.20 |
| ❑ 14 Kenneth Kennholt | 3.00 | 1.35 |
| ❑ 15 Jan Viktorsson | 3.00 | 1.35 |

## 1995-96 Swedish Leaf Elit Face to Face

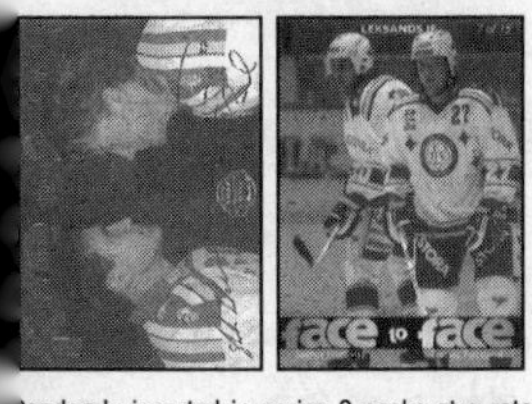

Randomly inserted in series 2 packs at a rate of 1:5, this 15-card set features the top two talents on each of the Elitserien teams.

| | MINT | NRMT |
|---|---|---|
| COMPLETE SET (15) | 35.00 | 16.00 |
| COMMON CARD (1-15) | 2.00 | .90 |
| ❑ 1 M.Samuelsson/T.Strandberg | 2.00 | .90 |
| ❑ 2 B.Scerban/G.Parks | 2.00 | .90 |
| ❑ 3 E.Huusko/A.Hussko | 2.00 | .90 |
| ❑ 4 S.Larsson/M.Jantunen | 2.00 | .90 |
| ❑ 5 H.Loob/R.Johansson | 5.00 | 2.20 |
| ❑ 6 K.Kennholt/P.Gustafsson | 3.00 | 1.35 |
| ❑ 7 S.Hillkvist/T.Forslund | 2.00 | .90 |
| ❑ 8 T.Holmstrom/R.Akerstrom | 5.00 | 2.20 |
| ❑ 9 S.Elvenes/R.Burakovsky | 3.00 | 1.35 |
| ❑ 10 M.Hostak/M.Timander | 4.00 | 1.80 |
| ❑ 11 M.Loov/M.Hjalm | 2.00 | .90 |
| ❑ 12 A.Salomatin/F.Oberg | 2.00 | .90 |
| ❑ 13 P.Erickson/E.Knutsen | 4.00 | 1.80 |
| ❑ 14 P.Andersson/P.Hasselblad | 2.00 | .90 |
| ❑ 15 T.Jonsson/M.Akerblom | 3.00 | 1.35 |

## 1995-96 Swedish Leaf Elit Goldies

Randomly inserted in series 1 packs at a rate of 1:14, this 10-card set captures some of the top young scorers in Sweden.

| | MINT | NRMT |
|---|---|---|
| COMPLETE SET (10) | 35.00 | 16.00 |
| COMMON CARD (1-10) | 4.00 | 1.80 |
| ❑ 1 Morgan Samuelsson | 4.00 | 1.80 |
| ❑ 2 Ove Molin | 4.00 | 1.80 |
| ❑ 3 Fredrik Lindquist | 5.00 | 2.20 |
| ❑ 4 Peter Strom | 4.00 | 1.80 |
| ❑ 5 Mattias Johansson | 4.00 | 1.80 |
| ❑ 6 Stefan Ornskog | 4.00 | 1.80 |
| ❑ 7 Niklas Eriksson | 4.00 | 1.80 |
| ❑ 8 Johan Rosen | 4.00 | 1.80 |
| ❑ 9 Roger Ohman | 4.00 | 1.80 |
| ❑ 10 Anders Soderberg | 6.00 | 2.70 |

## 1995-96 Swedish Leaf Elit Mega

The fifteen cards in this set were randomly inserted at a rate of 1:20 series 1 packs.

| | MINT | NRMT |
|---|---|---|
| COMPLETE SET (15) | 80.00 | 36.00 |
| COMMON CARD (1-15) | 5.00 | 2.20 |
| ❑ 1 Michael Sundlov | 6.00 | 2.70 |
| ❑ 2 Jonas Bergqvist | 6.00 | 2.70 |
| ❑ 3 Marko Jantunen | 5.00 | 2.20 |
| ❑ 4 Thomas Ostlund | 6.00 | 2.70 |
| ❑ 5 Tomas Jonsson | 5.00 | 2.20 |
| ❑ 6 Esa Keskinen | 5.00 | 2.20 |
| ❑ 7 Roger Nordstrom | 5.00 | 2.20 |
| ❑ 8 Mattias Ohlund | 10.00 | 4.50 |
| ❑ 9 Hakan Loob | 12.00 | 5.50 |
| ❑ 10 Raimo Helminen | 5.00 | 2.20 |
| ❑ 11 Per-Erik Eklund | 8.00 | 3.60 |
| ❑ 12 Jarmo Myllys | 8.00 | 3.60 |
| ❑ 13 Rikard Franzen | 5.00 | 2.20 |
| ❑ 14 Christer Olsson | 6.00 | 2.70 |
| ❑ 15 Per Gustafsson | 6.00 | 2.70 |

## 1995-96 Swedish Leaf Elit Rookies

Randomly inserted in series one packs at a rate of 1:6, this nine card set reveals Leaf's picks as the top frosh in the Elitserien.

| | MINT | NRMT |
|---|---|---|
| COMPLETE SET (9) | 30.00 | 13.50 |
| COMMON CARD (1-9) | 3.00 | 1.35 |
| ❑ 1 Peter Wallin | 5.00 | 2.20 |
| ❑ 2 Jan-Axel Alavaara | 5.00 | 2.20 |
| ❑ 3 Niklas Falk | 5.00 | 2.20 |
| ❑ 4 Lars-Goran Wiklander | 5.00 | 2.20 |
| ❑ 5 Torbjorn Johansson | 3.00 | 1.35 |
| ❑ 6 Jan Mertzig | 3.00 | 1.35 |
| ❑ 7 Mikael Burakovsky | 3.00 | 1.35 |
| ❑ 8 Marcus Karlsson | 3.00 | 1.35 |
| ❑ 9 Roger Rosen | 3.00 | 1.35 |

## 1995-96 Swedish Leaf Elit Spidermen

The stingiest netminders in Sweden are the focus of this 14-card set. The cards were randomly inserted at the rate of 1:8 series one packs.

| | MINT | NRMT |
|---|---|---|
| COMPLETE SET (14) | 70.00 | 32.00 |
| COMMON CARD (1-14) | 5.00 | 2.20 |
| ❑ 1 Joakim Persson | 5.00 | 2.20 |
| ❑ 2 Michael Sundlov | 6.00 | 2.70 |
| ❑ 3 Thomas Ostlund | 6.00 | 2.70 |
| ❑ 4 Hakan Algotsson | 5.00 | 2.20 |
| ❑ 5 Patrik Haltia | 5.00 | 2.20 |
| ❑ 6 Boo Ahl | 6.00 | 2.70 |
| ❑ 7 Johan Hedberg | 5.00 | 2.20 |
| ❑ 8 Jarmo Myllys | 10.00 | 4.50 |
| ❑ 9 Jonas Forsberg | 6.00 | 2.70 |
| ❑ 10 Petter Ronnqvist | 5.00 | 2.20 |
| ❑ 11 Magnus Swardh | 5.00 | 2.20 |
| ❑ 12 Mats Ytter | 5.00 | 2.20 |
| ❑ 13 Mikael Sandberg | 5.00 | 2.20 |
| ❑ 14 Roger Nordstrom | 5.00 | 2.20 |

## 1995-96 Swedish Upper Deck Elit

The 1995-96 Upper Deck Swedish Elit set was issued in one series totalling 260 cards. The set was issued in 10-card packs and features players from the Swedish Elitserien and was endorsed by its Players Association (SICO). The highlight is the subset Where Are They Now? (234-248) which showcases a number of former Swedish stars now in the NHL.

| | MINT | NRMT |
|---|---|---|
| COMPLETE SET (260) | 50.00 | 22.00 |

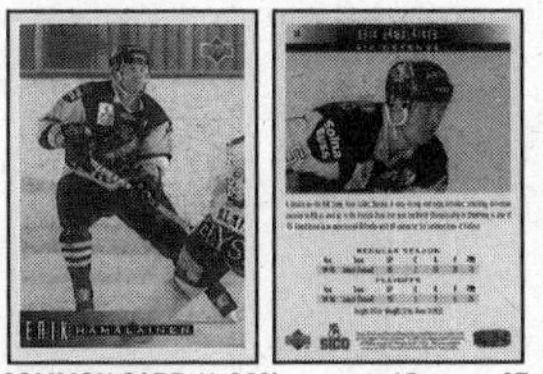

| | | |
|---|---|---|
| COMMON CARD (1-260) | .15 | .07 |
| ❑ 1 Joakim Persson | .25 | .11 |
| ❑ 2 Erik Hamalainen | .25 | .11 |
| ❑ 3 Dick Tarnstrom | .25 | .11 |
| ❑ 4 Rikard Franzen | .15 | .07 |
| ❑ 5 Niclas Havelid | .15 | .07 |
| ❑ 6 Tony Barthelson | .15 | .07 |
| ❑ 7 Tommy Hedlund | .15 | .07 |
| ❑ 8 Patric Aberg | .15 | .07 |
| ❑ 9 Stefan Gustavson | .15 | .07 |
| ❑ 10 Anders Gozzi | .15 | .07 |
| ❑ 11 David Engblom | .15 | .07 |
| ❑ 12 Stefan Andersson | .15 | .07 |
| ❑ 13 Tomas Strandberg | .15 | .07 |
| ❑ 14 Mats Lindberg | .15 | .07 |
| ❑ 15 Tommy Lehmann | .25 | .11 |
| ❑ 16 Bjorn Ahlstrom | .15 | .07 |
| ❑ 17 Patric Englund | .15 | .07 |
| ❑ 18 Morgan Samuelsson | .25 | .11 |
| ❑ 19 Michael Sundlov | .25 | .11 |
| ❑ 20 Bedrich Scerban | .15 | .07 |
| ❑ 21 Mikael Lindman | .15 | .07 |
| ❑ 22 Mikael Wiklander | .15 | .07 |
| ❑ 23 Tommy Melkersson | .15 | .07 |
| ❑ 24 Stefan Klockare | .25 | .11 |
| ❑ 25 Per Lofstrom | .15 | .07 |
| ❑ 26 Jonas Johnson | .15 | .07 |
| ❑ 27 Roger Kyro | .15 | .07 |
| ❑ 28 Jonas Lofstrom | .15 | .07 |
| ❑ 29 Stefan Ketola | .25 | .11 |
| ❑ 30 Mikael Wahlberg | .15 | .07 |
| ❑ 31 Stefan Polla | .15 | .07 |
| ❑ 32 Greg Parks | .15 | .07 |
| ❑ 33 Ove Molin | .15 | .07 |
| ❑ 34 Peter Larsson | .15 | .07 |
| ❑ 35 Fredrik Modin | .75 | .35 |
| ❑ 36 Andreas Dackell | .75 | .35 |
| ❑ 37 Thomas Ostlund | .50 | .23 |
| ❑ 38 Tommy Jakobsen | .15 | .07 |
| ❑ 39 Christian Due-Boje | .25 | .11 |
| ❑ 40 Thomas Johansson | .15 | .07 |
| ❑ 41 Joakim Lundberg | .15 | .07 |
| ❑ 42 Bjorn Nord | .15 | .07 |
| ❑ 43 Mikael Magnusson | .15 | .07 |
| ❑ 44 Erik Huusko | .25 | .11 |
| ❑ 45 Anders Huusko | .15 | .07 |
| ❑ 46 Kristofer Ottosson | .15 | .07 |
| ❑ 47 Magnus Jansson | .15 | .07 |
| ❑ 48 Nichlas Falk | .25 | .11 |
| ❑ 49 Ola Josefsson | .15 | .07 |
| ❑ 50 Per Eklund | .25 | .11 |
| ❑ 51 Espen Knutsen | .50 | .23 |
| ❑ 52 Jens Ohling | .15 | .07 |
| ❑ 53 Patric Kjellberg | .25 | .11 |
| ❑ 54 Patrik Erickson | .15 | .07 |
| ❑ 55 Jan Viktorsson | .25 | .11 |
| ❑ 56 Markus Ketterer | .50 | .23 |
| ❑ 57 Jesper Duus | .15 | .07 |
| ❑ 58 Sergei Fokin | .15 | .07 |
| ❑ 59 Per Lundell | .15 | .07 |
| ❑ 60 Thomas Rhodin | .15 | .07 |
| ❑ 61 Henrik Rehnberg | .15 | .07 |
| ❑ 62 Roger Johansson | .15 | .07 |
| ❑ 63 Leif Carlsson | .15 | .07 |
| ❑ 64 Hakan Loob | .75 | .35 |
| ❑ 65 Stefan Nilsson | .15 | .07 |
| ❑ 66 Vitali Prokhorov | .25 | .11 |
| ❑ 67 Magnus Arvedsson | .15 | .07 |
| ❑ 68 Jonas Hoglund | .75 | .35 |
| ❑ 69 Mathias Johansson | .15 | .07 |
| ❑ 70 Patrik Wallenberg | .15 | .07 |
| ❑ 71 Clas Eriksson | .15 | .07 |
| ❑ 72 Jorgen Jonsson | .15 | .07 |
| ❑ 73 Peter Nordstrom | .15 | .07 |
| ❑ 74 Peter Ottosson | .15 | .07 |
| ❑ 75 Boo Ahl | .35 | .16 |
| ❑ 76 Per Gustafsson | .50 | .23 |
| ❑ 77 Niklas Rahm | .15 | .07 |
| ❑ 78 Hans Abrahamsson | .15 | .07 |
| ❑ 79 Kenneth Kennholt | .15 | .07 |
| ❑ 80 Daniel Johansson | .25 | .11 |
| ❑ 81 Vesa Salo | .25 | .11 |
| ❑ 82 Thomas Gustavsson | .15 | .07 |
| ❑ 83 Stefan Ornskog | .25 | .11 |
| ❑ 84 Stefan Falk | .15 | .07 |
| ❑ 85 Peter Hammarstrom | .15 | .07 |
| ❑ 86 Johan Davidsson | .50 | .23 |
| ❑ 87 Peter Ekelund | .15 | .07 |
| ❑ 88 Johan Lindbom | .15 | .07 |
| ❑ 89 Esa Keskinen | .25 | .11 |
| ❑ 90 Kai Nurminen | .50 | .23 |
| ❑ 91 Magnus Eliasson | .15 | .07 |
| ❑ 92 Marcus Thuresson | .15 | .07 |
| ❑ 93 Johan Brummer | .15 | .07 |
| ❑ 94 Johan Hedberg | .25 | .11 |
| ❑ 95 Tomas Jonsson | .25 | .11 |
| ❑ 96 Torbjorn Johansson | .15 | .07 |
| ❑ 97 Hans Lodin | .15 | .07 |
| ❑ 98 Orjan Lindmark | .15 | .07 |
| ❑ 99 Jan Huokko | .15 | .07 |
| ❑ 100 Joakim Lidgren | .15 | .07 |
| ❑ 101 Per-Erik Eklund | .35 | .16 |
| ❑ 102 Anders Carlsson | .15 | .07 |
| ❑ 103 Niklas Eriksson | .15 | .07 |
| ❑ 104 Micael Karlberg | .15 | .07 |
| ❑ 105 Jonas Bergqvist | .25 | .11 |
| ❑ 106 Torgny Lowgren | .15 | .07 |
| ❑ 107 Stefan Hellkvist | .15 | .07 |
| ❑ 108 Markus Akerblom | .15 | .07 |
| ❑ 109 Mikael Holmberg | .15 | .07 |
| ❑ 110 Andreas Karlsson | .15 | .07 |
| ❑ 111 Markus Akerblom | .15 | .07 |
| ❑ 112 Tomas Forslund | .25 | .11 |
| ❑ 113 Jarmo Myllys | .50 | .23 |
| ❑ 114 Lars Modig | .15 | .07 |
| ❑ 115 Patrik Hoglund | .15 | .07 |
| ❑ 116 Torbjorn Lindberg | .15 | .07 |
| ❑ 117 Jan Mertzig | .25 | .11 |
| ❑ 118 Petter Nilsson | .15 | .07 |
| ❑ 119 Mattias Ohlund | .75 | .35 |
| ❑ 120 Roger Akerstrom | .15 | .07 |
| ❑ 121 Stefan Jonsson | .15 | .07 |
| ❑ 122 Stefan Nilsson | .15 | .07 |
| ❑ 123 Tomas Holmstrom | .75 | .35 |
| ❑ 124 Mikael Lindholm | .15 | .07 |
| ❑ 125 Johan Stromvall | .15 | .07 |
| ❑ 126 Jiri Kucera | .25 | .11 |
| ❑ 127 Joakim Backlund | .15 | .07 |
| ❑ 128 Robert Nordberg | .15 | .07 |
| ❑ 129 Tomas Berglund | .15 | .07 |
| ❑ 130 Fredrik Johansson | .15 | .07 |
| ❑ 131 Lars Hurtig | .15 | .07 |
| ❑ 132 Johan Rosen | .15 | .07 |
| ❑ 133 Roger Nordstrom | .25 | .11 |
| ❑ 134 Kim Johnsson | .15 | .07 |
| ❑ 135 Peter Hasselblad | .15 | .07 |
| ❑ 136 Ilya Byakin | .25 | .11 |
| ❑ 137 Johan Salle | .15 | .07 |
| ❑ 138 Peter Andersson | .15 | .07 |
| ❑ 139 Roger Ohman | .15 | .07 |
| ❑ 140 Marko Palo | .15 | .07 |
| ❑ 141 Raimo Helminen | .25 | .11 |
| ❑ 142 Mattias Bosson | .15 | .07 |
| ❑ 143 Markus Magnertoft | .15 | .07 |
| ❑ 144 Roger Hansson | .15 | .07 |
| ❑ 145 Bo Svanberg | .15 | .07 |
| ❑ 146 Patrik Sylvegard | .15 | .07 |
| ❑ 147 Brian McReynolds | .15 | .07 |
| ❑ 148 Hakan Ahlund | .15 | .07 |
| ❑ 149 Robert Burakovsky | .15 | .07 |
| ❑ 150 Stefan Elvenes | .25 | .11 |
| ❑ 151 Patrik Boij | .15 | .07 |
| ❑ 152 Petter Ronnquist | .25 | .11 |
| ❑ 153 Mattias Timander | .75 | .35 |
| ❑ 154 Lars Jansson | .15 | .07 |
| ❑ 155 Frantisek Kaberle | .15 | .07 |
| ❑ 156 Hans Jonsson | .15 | .07 |
| ❑ 157 Tomas Nansen | .15 | .07 |
| ❑ 158 Marcus Karlsson | .15 | .07 |
| ❑ 159 Kristian Gahn | .35 | .16 |
| ❑ 160 Magnus Wernblom | .15 | .07 |
| ❑ 161 Anders Soderberg | .35 | .16 |
| ❑ 162 Martin Hostak | .15 | .07 |
| ❑ 163 Kyosti Karjalainen | .25 | .11 |
| ❑ 164 Mikael Hakanson | .15 | .07 |
| ❑ 165 Jan Larsson | .15 | .07 |
| ❑ 166 Per Svartvadet | .35 | .16 |
| ❑ 167 Andreas Salomonsson | .15 | .07 |
| ❑ 168 Samuel Pahlsson | .25 | .11 |
| ❑ 169 Lars Bystrom | .15 | .07 |
| ❑ 170 Magnus Swardh | .25 | .11 |
| ❑ 171 Anders Berglund | .15 | .07 |
| ❑ 172 Pierre Johnsson | .15 | .07 |
| ❑ 173 Johan Finnstrom | .25 | .11 |
| ❑ 174 Arto Ruotanen | .15 | .07 |
| ❑ 175 Daniel Tjarnqvist | .50 | .23 |
| ❑ 176 Greg Brown | .25 | .11 |
| ❑ 177 Per Wallin | .35 | .16 |
| ❑ 178 Peter Lundmark | .15 | .07 |
| ❑ 179 Roger Elvenes | .15 | .07 |
| ❑ 180 Michael Hjalm | .25 | .11 |
| ❑ 181 Jens Hemstrom | .15 | .07 |
| ❑ 182 Pelle Svensson | .15 | .07 |
| ❑ 183 Harijs Vitolins | .15 | .07 |
| ❑ 184 Jens Nielsen | .15 | .07 |
| ❑ 185 Mats Loov | .15 | .07 |
| ❑ 186 Mats Ytter | .25 | .11 |
| ❑ 187 Lars Ivarsson | .15 | .07 |
| ❑ 188 Edvin Frylen | .25 | .11 |
| ❑ 189 Andrei Lyulin | .15 | .07 |
| ❑ 190 Johan Tornberg | .15 | .07 |
| ❑ 191 Mattias Olsson | .15 | .07 |
| ❑ 192 Mats Lusth | .15 | .07 |
| ❑ 193 Fredrik Oberg | .15 | .07 |
| ❑ 194 Alexei Salomatin | .25 | .11 |
| ❑ 195 Mishat Fahrutdinov | .15 | .07 |
| ❑ 196 Mikael Pettersson | .15 | .07 |
| ❑ 197 Andrei Korolev | .15 | .07 |
| ❑ 198 Mattias Loof | .15 | .07 |
| ❑ 199 Claes Lindblom | .15 | .07 |
| ❑ 200 Paul Andersson | .15 | .07 |
| ❑ 201 Roger Rosen | .15 | .07 |
| ❑ 202 Hakan Algotsson | .25 | .11 |
| ❑ 203 Par Djoos | .25 | .11 |
| ❑ 204 Mikael Sandberg | .15 | .07 |
| ❑ 205 Joacim Esbjors | .15 | .07 |
| ❑ 206 Stefan Axelsson | .50 | .23 |
| ❑ 207 Ronnie Sundin | .25 | .11 |
| ❑ 208 Stefan Larsson | .15 | .07 |
| ❑ 209 Petteri Nummelin | .25 | .11 |
| ❑ 210 Christian Ruuttu | .50 | .23 |
| ❑ 211 Marko Jantunen | .25 | .11 |
| ❑ 212 Peter Strom | .15 | .07 |
| ❑ 213 Peter Berndtsson | .15 | .07 |
| ❑ 214 Lars Edstrom | .15 | .07 |
| ❑ 215 Peter Hogardh | .15 | .07 |
| ❑ 216 Par Edlund | .15 | .07 |
| ❑ 217 Lars-Goran Wiklander | .25 | .11 |
| ❑ 218 Henrik Nilsson | .15 | .07 |
| ❑ 219 Rikard Franzen | .15 | .07 |
| ❑ 220 Fredrik Modin | .75 | .35 |
| ❑ 221 Anders Soderberg | .35 | .16 |
| ❑ 222 Per Eklund | .25 | .11 |
| ❑ 223 Hakan Loob | .75 | .35 |
| ❑ 224 Markus Ketterer | .50 | .23 |
| ❑ 225 Esa Keskinen | .25 | .11 |
| ❑ 226 Per Gustafsson | .50 | .23 |
| ❑ 227 Tomas Jonsson | .25 | .11 |
| ❑ 228 Per-Erik Eklund | .35 | .16 |
| ❑ 229 Mattias Ohlund | .75 | .35 |
| ❑ 230 Jarmo Myllys | .50 | .23 |
| ❑ 231 Peter Andersson | .15 | .07 |
| ❑ 232 Raimo Helminen | .25 | .11 |
| ❑ 233 Christian Ruuttu | .50 | .23 |
| ❑ 234 Peter Forsberg | 10.00 | 4.50 |
| ❑ 235 Mikael Renberg | 2.00 | .90 |
| ❑ 236 Mats Sundin | 2.00 | .90 |
| ❑ 237 Michael Nylander | .50 | .23 |
| ❑ 238 Tommy Soderstrom | .75 | .35 |
| ❑ 239 Nicklas Lidstrom | 1.25 | .55 |
| ❑ 240 Kenny Jonsson | .75 | .35 |
| ❑ 241 Patrik Carnback | .25 | .11 |
| ❑ 242 Johan Garpenlov | .50 | .23 |
| ❑ 243 Magnus Svensson | .35 | .16 |
| ❑ 244 Patrik Juhlin | .35 | .16 |
| ❑ 245 Markus Naslund | .75 | .35 |
| ❑ 246 Tommy Salo | 1.00 | .45 |
| ❑ 247 Fredrik Olausson | .50 | .23 |
| ❑ 248 Tommy Albelin | .25 | .11 |
| ❑ 249 Rikard Franzen | .15 | .07 |
| ❑ 250 Jonas Johnson | .15 | .07 |
| ❑ 251 Thomas Ostlund | .50 | .23 |
| ❑ 252 Hakan Loob | .75 | .35 |
| ❑ 253 Per Gustafsson | .50 | .23 |
| ❑ 254 Per-Erik Eklund | .35 | .16 |
| ❑ 255 Tomas Jonsson | .25 | .11 |
| ❑ 256 Mattias Ohlund | .75 | .35 |
| ❑ 257 Peter Andersson | .15 | .07 |
| ❑ 258 Christian Ruuttu | .50 | .23 |
| ❑ 259 Checklist | .15 | .07 |
| ❑ 260 Checklist | .15 | .07 |

## 1995-96 Swedish Upper Deck Elit 1st Division Stars

This 20-card insert series, which was included in packs at indeterminate odds (estimated at 1:8) features players from the Swedish First Division, a league one step below the Elitserien.

| | MINT | NRMT |
|---|---|---|
| COMPLETE SET (20) | 20.00 | 9.00 |
| COMMON CARD (DS1-DS20) | 1.00 | .45 |
| ❑ DS1 Anders Huss | 1.00 | .45 |
| ❑ DS2 Igor Vlasov | 1.00 | .45 |
| ❑ DS3 Ulf Sandstrom | 1.00 | .45 |
| ❑ DS4 Hans Huczkowski | 1.00 | .45 |
| ❑ DS5 Johan Ramstedt | 2.00 | .90 |
| ❑ DS6 Anders Eldebrink | 2.00 | .90 |
| ❑ DS7 Niklas Brannstrom | 1.00 | .45 |
| ❑ DS8 Peter Nilsson | 1.00 | .45 |
| ❑ DS9 Sam Lindstahl | 1.00 | .45 |
| ❑ DS10 Tony Skopac | 1.00 | .45 |
| ❑ DS11 Jonas Eriksson | 1.00 | .45 |
| ❑ DS12 Anders Lonn | 1.00 | .45 |
| ❑ DS13 Peter Hagstrom | 1.00 | .45 |
| ❑ DS14 Magnus Roupe | 2.00 | .90 |
| ❑ DS15 Peter Pettersson | 1.00 | .45 |
| ❑ DS16 Peter Eriksson | 1.00 | .45 |
| ❑ DS17 Fredrik Bergqvist | 1.00 | .45 |
| ❑ DS18 Larry Pilut | 1.00 | .45 |
| ❑ DS19 Peter Olsson | 1.00 | .45 |
| ❑ DS20 Staffan Lundh | 1.00 | .45 |

## 1995-96 Swedish Upper Deck Elit Ticket to North America

This 20-card set was randomly inserted in packs at indeterminate odds (estimated at 1:10) and features athletes whose strong play has led to them being selected in the draft and may earn them a shot at the NHL.

| | MINT | NRMT |
|---|---|---|
| COMPLETE SET (20) | 75.00 | 34.00 |
| COMMON CARD (NA1-NA20) | 3.00 | 1.35 |
| ❑ NA1 Joakim Persson | 4.00 | 1.80 |
| ❑ NA2 Dick Tarnstrom | 5.00 | 2.20 |
| ❑ NA3 Andreas Dackell | 5.00 | 2.20 |
| ❑ NA4 Fredrik Modin | 6.00 | 2.70 |
| ❑ NA5 Per Eklund | 3.00 | 1.35 |
| ❑ NA6 Espen Knutsen | 6.00 | 2.70 |
| ❑ NA7 Fredrik Lindquist | 4.00 | 1.80 |
| ❑ NA8 Jonas Hoglund | 6.00 | 2.70 |
| ❑ NA9 Jorgen Jonsson | 3.00 | 1.35 |
| ❑ NA10 Johan Davidsson | 5.00 | 2.20 |
| ❑ NA11 Per Gustafsson | 4.00 | 1.80 |
| ❑ NA12 Johan Lindbom | 3.00 | 1.35 |
| ❑ NA13 Markus Akerblom | 3.00 | 1.35 |
| ❑ NA14 Jan Huokko | 3.00 | 1.35 |
| ❑ NA15 Tomas Holmstrom | 10.00 | 4.50 |
| ❑ NA16 Mattias Ohlund | 10.00 | 4.50 |
| ❑ NA17 Johan Rosen | 3.00 | 1.35 |
| ❑ NA18 Frantisek Kaberle | 3.00 | 1.35 |
| ❑ NA19 Mattias Timander | 6.00 | 2.70 |
| ❑ NA20 Magnus Wernblom | 3.00 | 1.35 |

## 1996 Swedish Semic Wien

The 1996 Semic Wien set was issued in one series totalling 240 cards to commemorate the 1996 World Championships held in Vienna. The set features players who have competed for their countries in various tournaments, wearing their national team colors. Many top NHLers are featured, including Wayne Gretzky, Eric Lindros and Ray Bourque. The cards were distributed in ten-card packs. There was a type of partial parallel set available as well. This set -- called the Coca-Cola Dream Team -- came in four-card packs and was distributed with the purchase of gas at petrol stations in Sweden. The complete checklist is not known, but Forsberg has been confirmed. These cards are similar in appearance to the regular cards, but have a silver foil icon of the mascot from the Vienna WC in the upper corner. These cards command a premium of 100 percent.

| | MINT | NRMT |
|---|---|---|
| COMPLETE SET (240) | 60.00 | 27.00 |
| COMMON CARD (1-240) | .10 | .05 |

| | | |
|---|---|---|
| ❑ 1 Jarmo Myllys | .25 | .11 |
| ❑ 2 Marko Kiprusoff | .15 | .07 |
| ❑ 3 Petteri Nummelin | .10 | .05 |
| ❑ 4 Erik Hamalainen | .10 | .05 |
| ❑ 5 Timo Jutila | .15 | .07 |
| ❑ 6 Janne Ninimaa | 1.50 | .70 |
| ❑ 7 Raimo Summanen | .15 | .07 |
| ❑ 8 Janne Ojanen | .15 | .07 |
| ❑ 9 Esa Keskinen | .15 | .07 |
| ❑ 10 Ari Sulander | .25 | .11 |
| ❑ 11 Saku Koivu | 3.00 | 1.35 |
| ❑ 12 Jukka Tammi | .25 | .11 |
| ❑ 13 Marko Palo | .10 | .05 |
| ❑ 14 Raimo Helminen | .15 | .07 |
| ❑ 15 Antti Tormanen | .15 | .07 |
| ❑ 16 Ville Peltonen | .35 | .16 |
| ❑ 17 Tero Lehtera | .15 | .07 |
| ❑ 18 Mika Stromberg | .15 | .07 |
| ❑ 19 Sami Kapanen | .35 | .16 |
| ❑ 20 Jere Lehtinen | .50 | .23 |
| ❑ 21 Juha Ylonen | .15 | .07 |
| ❑ 22 Mika Nieminen | .15 | .07 |
| ❑ 23 Hannu Virta | .15 | .07 |
| ❑ 24 Jari Kurri | .50 | .23 |
| ❑ 25 Christian Ruuttu | .15 | .07 |
| ❑ 26 Jyrki Lumme | .15 | .07 |
| ❑ 27 Teppo Numminen | .25 | .11 |
| ❑ 28 Esa Tikkanen | .25 | .11 |
| ❑ 29 Janne Laukkanen | .20 | .09 |
| ❑ 30 Aki-Petteri Berg | .35 | .16 |
| ❑ 31 Teemu Selanne | 3.00 | 1.35 |
| ❑ 32 Markus Ketterer | .25 | .11 |
| ❑ 33 Joni Lehto | .10 | .05 |
| ❑ 34 Juha Riihijarvi | .15 | .07 |
| ❑ 35 Sakari Lindfors | .50 | .23 |
| ❑ 36 Kai Nurminen | .25 | .11 |
| ❑ 37 Huey, Dewey, Louie | 2.00 | .90 |
| ❑ 38 Tommy Soderstrom | .35 | .16 |
| ❑ 39 Tommy Salo | .75 | .35 |
| ❑ 40 Thomas Ostlund | .20 | .09 |
| ❑ 41 Boo Ahl | .20 | .09 |
| ❑ 42 Calle Johansson | .20 | .09 |
| ❑ 43 Tommy Albelin | .15 | .07 |
| ❑ 44 Ulf Samuelsson | .15 | .07 |
| ❑ 45 Nicklas Lidstrom | .50 | .23 |
| ❑ 46 Magnus Svensson | .15 | .07 |
| ❑ 47 Tomas Jonsson | .15 | .07 |
| ❑ 48 Tommy Sjodin | .15 | .07 |
| ❑ 49 Marcus Ragnarsson | .25 | .11 |
| ❑ 50 Christer Olsson | .20 | .09 |
| ❑ 51 Rikard Franzen | .10 | .05 |
| ❑ 52 Mattias Ohlund | .35 | .16 |
| ❑ 53 Kenny Jonsson | .50 | .23 |
| ❑ 54 Roger Johansson | .10 | .05 |
| ❑ 55 Anders Eriksson | .50 | .23 |
| ❑ 56 Mats Sundin | .75 | .35 |
| ❑ 57 Peter Forsberg | 5.00 | 2.20 |
| ❑ 58 Mikael Renberg | .75 | .35 |
| ❑ 59 Tomas Sandstrom | .20 | .09 |
| ❑ 60 Ulf Dahlen | .15 | .07 |
| ❑ 61 Michael Nylander | .15 | .07 |
| ❑ 62 Patrik Juhlin | .15 | .07 |
| ❑ 63 Patrik Carnback | .15 | .07 |
| ❑ 64 Andreas Johansson | .20 | .09 |
| ❑ 65 Mikael Johansson | .10 | .05 |
| ❑ 66 Per-Erik Eklund | .15 | .07 |
| ❑ 67 Tomas Forslund | .15 | .07 |
| ❑ 68 Andreas Dackell | .20 | .09 |
| ❑ 69 Per Eklund | .15 | .07 |
| ❑ 70 Tomas Holmstrom | .50 | .23 |
| ❑ 71 Jonas Bergqvist | .15 | .07 |
| ❑ 72 Daniel Alfredsson | 1.00 | .45 |
| ❑ 73 Fredrik Modin | .35 | .16 |
| ❑ 74 Magic Moment | 1.00 | .45 |
| ❑ 75 Ed Belfour | 1.50 | .70 |
| ❑ 76 Bill Ranford | .50 | .23 |
| ❑ 77 Sean Burke | .35 | .16 |
| ❑ 78 Ray Bourque | 1.50 | .70 |
| ❑ 79 Paul Coffey | 1.50 | .70 |
| ❑ 80 Scott Stevens | .35 | .16 |
| ❑ 81 Al MacInnis | .35 | .16 |
| ❑ 82 Larry Murphy | .25 | .11 |
| ❑ 83 Eric Desjardins | .35 | .16 |
| ❑ 84 Steve Duchesne | .20 | .09 |
| ❑ 85 Mario Lemieux | 8.00 | 3.60 |
| ❑ 86 Mark Messier | 2.00 | .90 |
| ❑ 87 Theoren Fleury | .75 | .35 |
| ❑ 88 Eric Lindros | 6.00 | 2.70 |
| ❑ 89 Rick Tocchet | .25 | .11 |
| ❑ 90 Brendan Shanahan | 3.00 | 1.35 |
| ❑ 91 Claude Lemieux | .50 | .23 |
| ❑ 92 Joe Juneau | .50 | .23 |
| ❑ 93 Luc Robitaille | .75 | .35 |
| ❑ 94 Paul Kariya | 6.00 | 2.70 |
| ❑ 95 Joe Sakic | 4.00 | 1.80 |
| ❑ 96 Mark Recchi | .50 | .23 |
| ❑ 97 Jason Arnott | .50 | .23 |
| ❑ 98 Rod Brind'Amour | .50 | .23 |
| ❑ 99 Wayne Gretzky | 10.00 | 4.50 |
| ❑ 100 Adam Oates | .75 | .35 |
| ❑ 101 Steve Yzerman | 5.00 | 2.20 |
| ❑ 102 Roman Turek | .50 | .23 |
| ❑ 103 Dominik Hasek | 3.00 | 1.35 |
| ❑ 104 Petr Briza | .25 | .11 |
| ❑ 105 Antonin Stavjana | .15 | .07 |
| ❑ 106 Frantisek Kaberle | .15 | .07 |
| ❑ 107 Jiri Vykoukal | .15 | .07 |
| ❑ 108 Jan Vopat | .20 | .09 |
| ❑ 109 Libor Prochazka | .10 | .05 |
| ❑ 110 Petr Kuchyna | .15 | .07 |
| ❑ 111 Frantisek Musil | .15 | .07 |
| ❑ 112 Leo Gudas | .10 | .05 |
| ❑ 113 Jiri Slegr | .15 | .07 |
| ❑ 114 Pavel Patera | .25 | .11 |
| ❑ 115 Otakar Vejvoda | .25 | .11 |
| ❑ 116 Martin Prochazka | .35 | .16 |
| ❑ 117 Jiri Kucera | .10 | .05 |
| ❑ 118 Pavel Janku | .20 | .09 |
| ❑ 119 Roman Meluzin | .10 | .05 |
| ❑ 120 Richard Zemlicka | .10 | .05 |
| ❑ 121 Martin Hostak | .15 | .07 |
| ❑ 122 Jiri Dopita | .10 | .05 |
| ❑ 123 Radek Belohlav | .20 | .09 |
| ❑ 124 Roman Horak | .10 | .05 |
| ❑ 125 Jaromir Jagr | 5.00 | 2.20 |
| ❑ 126 Michal Pivonka | .25 | .11 |
| ❑ 127 Josef Beranek | .15 | .07 |
| ❑ 128 Robert Reichel | .25 | .11 |
| ❑ 129 Nikolai Khabibulin | 1.00 | .45 |
| ❑ 130 Sergei Abramov | .20 | .09 |
| ❑ 131 Yevgeny Tarasov | .10 | .05 |
| ❑ 132 Igor Kravchuk | .15 | .07 |
| ❑ 133 Dmitri Mironov | .25 | .11 |
| ❑ 134 Alexei Zhitnik | .15 | .07 |
| ❑ 135 Vladimir Malakhov | .20 | .09 |
| ❑ 136 Sergei Zubov | .25 | .11 |
| ❑ 137 Dimitri Yushkevich | .15 | .07 |
| ❑ 138 Ilya Byakin | .15 | .07 |
| ❑ 139 Alexander Smirnov | .10 | .05 |
| ❑ 140 Andrei Skopintsev | .15 | .07 |
| ❑ 141 Sergei Fedorov | 3.00 | 1.35 |
| ❑ 142 Pavel Bure | 3.00 | 1.35 |
| ❑ 143 Alexei Zhamnov | .35 | .16 |
| ❑ 144 Andrei Kovalenko | .25 | .11 |
| ❑ 145 Igor Korolev | .15 | .07 |
| ❑ 146 Slava Kozlov | .35 | .16 |
| ❑ 147 Viktor Kozlov | .15 | .07 |
| ❑ 148 Alexei Yashin | .50 | .23 |
| ❑ 149 Valeri Kamensky | .50 | .23 |
| ❑ 150 Stanislav Romanov | .10 | .05 |
| ❑ 151 Viacheslav Bykov | .20 | .09 |
| ❑ 152 Andrei Khomutov | .25 | .11 |
| ❑ 153 Sergei Berezin | .75 | .35 |
| ❑ 154 German Titov | .15 | .07 |
| ❑ 155 Dmitri Denisov | .10 | .05 |
| ❑ 156 John Vanbiesbrouck | 2.50 | 1.10 |
| ❑ 157 Jim Carey | .75 | .35 |
| ❑ 158 Mike Richter | 1.50 | .70 |
| ❑ 159 Chris Chelios | 1.50 | .70 |
| ❑ 160 Brian Leetch | 1.50 | .70 |
| ❑ 161 Phil Housley | .15 | .07 |
| ❑ 162 Gary Suter | .20 | .09 |
| ❑ 163 Kevin Hatcher | .20 | .09 |
| ❑ 164 Brett Hull | 2.00 | .90 |
| ❑ 165 Pat LaFontaine | .75 | .35 |
| ❑ 166 Mike Modano | .75 | .35 |
| ❑ 167 Jeremy Roenick | 1.50 | .70 |
| ❑ 168 Keith Tkachuk | 2.00 | .90 |
| ❑ 169 Joe Mullen | .20 | .09 |
| ❑ 170 Craig Janney | .25 | .11 |
| ❑ 171 Joel Otto | .20 | .09 |
| ❑ 172 Doug Weight | .75 | .35 |
| ❑ 173 Scott Young | .15 | .07 |
| ❑ 174 Michael Rosati | .15 | .07 |
| ❑ 175 Bruno Campese | .15 | .07 |
| ❑ 176 Robert Oberrauch | .10 | .05 |
| ❑ 177 Robert Nardella | .10 | .05 |
| ❑ 178 Stefano Figfuzzi | .10 | .05 |
| ❑ 179 Maurizio Mansi | .10 | .05 |
| ❑ 180 Gaetano Orlando | .10 | .05 |
| ❑ 181 Mario Chitarroni | .10 | .05 |
| ❑ 182 Martin Pavlu | .10 | .05 |
| ❑ 183 Petri Ylonen | .20 | .09 |
| ❑ 184 Michel Valliere | .10 | .05 |
| ❑ 185 Serge Poudrier | .10 | .05 |
| ❑ 186 Denis Perez | .10 | .05 |
| ❑ 187 Antoine Richer | .10 | .05 |
| ❑ 188 Philippe Bozon | .15 | .07 |
| ❑ 189 Christian Pouget | .10 | .05 |
| ❑ 190 Franck Pajonkowski | .15 | .07 |
| ❑ 191 Stephane Barin | .10 | .05 |
| ❑ 192 Klaus Merk | .20 | .09 |
| ❑ 193 Marc Seliger | .15 | .07 |
| ❑ 194 Mirco Ludermann | .10 | .05 |
| ❑ 195 Jayson Meyer | .10 | .05 |
| ❑ 196 Benoit Doucet | .15 | .07 |
| ❑ 197 Thomas Brandl | .10 | .05 |
| ❑ 198 Dieter Hegen | .15 | .07 |
| ❑ 199 Martin Reichel | .10 | .05 |
| ❑ 200 Leo Stefan | .10 | .05 |
| ❑ 201 Robert Schistad | .10 | .05 |
| ❑ 202 Jim Marthinsen | .20 | .09 |
| ❑ 203 Tommy Jakobsen | .10 | .05 |
| ❑ 204 Petter Salsten | .10 | .05 |
| ❑ 205 Svein Norstebo | .10 | .05 |
| ❑ 206 Espen Knutsen | .25 | .11 |
| ❑ 207 Trond Magnussen | .10 | .05 |
| ❑ 208 Henrik Aaby | .10 | .05 |
| ❑ 209 Marius Rath | .10 | .05 |
| ❑ 210 Claus Dalpiaz | .15 | .07 |
| ❑ 211 Michael Puschacher | .15 | .07 |
| ❑ 212 Robin Doyle | .10 | .05 |
| ❑ 213 James Burton | .10 | .05 |
| ❑ 214 Herbert Hohenberger | .10 | .05 |
| ❑ 215 Andreas Pusnik | .10 | .05 |
| ❑ 216 Richard Nasheim | .10 | .05 |
| ❑ 217 Deiter Kalt | .10 | .05 |
| ❑ 218 Werner Kerth | .10 | .05 |
| ❑ 219 Eduard Hartmann | .15 | .07 |
| ❑ 220 Jaromir Dragan | .25 | .11 |
| ❑ 221 Robert Svehla | .35 | .16 |
| ❑ 222 Lubomir Sekeras | .10 | .05 |
| ❑ 223 Marian Smerciak | .10 | .05 |
| ❑ 224 Jergus Baca | .15 | .07 |
| ❑ 225 Stanslav Medrik | .10 | .05 |
| ❑ 226 Miroslav Marcinko | .10 | .05 |
| ❑ 227 Peter Stastny | .35 | .16 |
| ❑ 228 Peter Bondra | 1.50 | .70 |
| ❑ 229 Zdeno Ciger | .25 | .11 |
| ❑ 230 Jozef Stumpel | .35 | .16 |
| ❑ 231 Miroslav Satan | .35 | .16 |
| ❑ 232 Lubomir Kolnik | .20 | .09 |
| ❑ 233 Robert Petrovicky | .15 | .07 |
| ❑ 234 Zigmund Palffy | 2.00 | .90 |
| ❑ 235 Oto Hascak | .15 | .07 |
| ❑ 236 Jozef Dano | .10 | .05 |
| ❑ 237 Checklist | .25 | .11 |
| ❑ 238 Checklist | .25 | .11 |
| ❑ 239 Checklist | .25 | .11 |
| ❑ 240 Checklist | .25 | .11 |
| ❑ NNO Renberg/Koivu Super Chase | 75.00 | 34.00 |

## 1996 Swedish Semic Wien Hockey Legends

Randomly inserted in packs at a rate of one in 6, this 18-card set recalls some of the best to lace 'em up on either side of the pond. The card front features a period action photo, with the Hockey Legends logo above in gold foil. The backs display another vintage photo, along with career notes and international play totals. The cards are numbered with an HL prefix.

| | MINT | NRMT |
|---|---|---|
| COMPLETE SET (18) | 50.00 | 22.00 |
| COMMON CARD (HL1-HL18) | 2.00 | .90 |

| | | |
|---|---|---|
| ❑ HL1 Ken Dryden | 10.00 | 4.50 |
| ❑ HL2 Guy Lafleur | 6.00 | 2.70 |
| ❑ HL3 Mike Bossy | 5.00 | 2.20 |
| ❑ HL4 Valeri Vasiliev | 2.00 | .90 |
| ❑ HL5 Anatoli Firsov | 2.00 | .90 |
| ❑ HL6 Alexander Maltsev | 3.00 | 1.35 |
| ❑ HL7 Tony Esposito | 5.00 | 2.20 |
| ❑ HL8 Rod Langway | 2.00 | .90 |
| ❑ HL9 Bryan Trottier | 3.00 | 1.35 |
| ❑ HL10 Lennart Haggroth | 2.00 | .90 |
| ❑ HL11 Ulf Nilsson | 3.00 | 1.35 |
| ❑ HL12 Lars-Gunnar Lundberg | 2.00 | .90 |
| ❑ HL13 Veli-Pekka Ketola | 2.00 | .90 |
| ❑ HL14 Lasse Oksanen | 2.00 | .90 |
| ❑ HL15 Pekka Rautakallio | 2.00 | .90 |
| ❑ HL16 Jiri Holocek | 3.00 | 1.35 |
| ❑ HL17 Jan Suchy | 2.00 | .90 |
| ❑ HL18 Vaclav Nedomansky | 3.00 | 1.35 |

## 1996 Swedish Semic Wien Nordic Stars

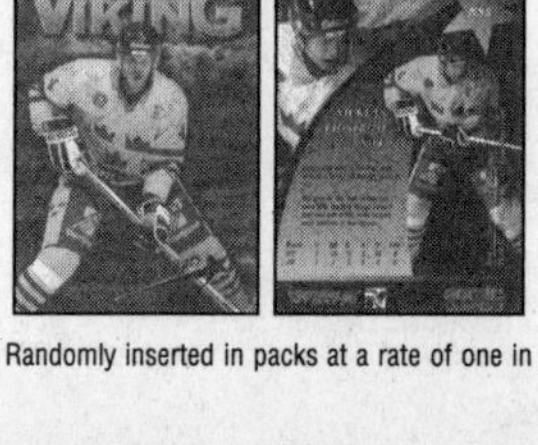

Randomly inserted in packs at a rate of one in 48, this 6-card set heaps praise on Scandinavia's best. Card fronts utilize an action photo over a stylized background with an apt description of the player prominently featured. The backs display international totals, wiht a brief bio in English. The cards are numbered with an NS prefix.

| | MINT | NRMT |
|---|---|---|
| COMPLETE SET (6) | 80.00 | 36.00 |
| COMMON CARD (NS1-NS6) | 8.00 | 3.60 |

| | | |
|---|---|---|
| ❑ NS1 Peter Forsberg | 40.00 | 18.00 |
| ❑ NS2 Teemu Selanne | 25.00 | 11.00 |
| ❑ NS3 Mats Sundin | 15.00 | 6.75 |
| ❑ NS4 Jari Kurri | 10.00 | 4.50 |
| ❑ NS5 Nicklas Lidstrom | 8.00 | 3.60 |
| ❑ NS6 Esa Tikkanen | 8.00 | 3.60 |

## 1996 Swedish Semic Wien Super Goalies

Randomly inserted in packs at a rate of one in 12, this 9-card set captures the last line of defense of some elite hockey nations. The fronts have an action photo over a ghosted, maskless image. The back has another photo and a brief bio in English. The cards are numbered with an SG prefix out of 9. The key card is a rare shot of Patrick Roy from a Team Canada training camp session.

| | MINT | NRMT |
|---|---|---|
| COMPLETE SET (9) | 75.00 | 34.00 |
| COMMON CARD (SG1-SG9) | 4.00 | 1.80 |

| | | |
|---|---|---|
| ❑ SG1 Dominik Hasek | 15.00 | 6.75 |
| ❑ SG2 Ed Belfour | 10.00 | 4.50 |
| ❑ SG3 Jarmo Myllys | 4.00 | 1.80 |
| ❑ SG4 Tommy Soderstrom | 4.00 | 1.80 |
| ❑ SG5 Jim Carey | 10.00 | 4.50 |
| ❑ SG6 Roman Turek | 8.00 | 3.60 |
| ❑ SG7 Patrick Roy | 30.00 | 13.50 |
| ❑ SG8 Markus Ketterer | 4.00 | 1.80 |
| ❑ SG9 Tommy Salo | 8.00 | 3.60 |

## 1996 Swedish Semic Wien 1995 All Stars

Randomly inserted in packs at a rate of one in 20, this 6-card , double-sided set acknowledges the first and second team all-stars from, as you guessed, the 1995 WC. Both sides share similar designs; the player on the side with the gold foil stars across the top was the first team selection.

| | MINT | NRMT |
|---|---|---|
| COMPLETE SET (6) | 30.00 | 13.50 |
| COMMON CARD (AS1-AS6) | 4.00 | 1.80 |

| | | |
|---|---|---|
| ❑ AS1 Roman Turek<br>Jarmo Myllys | 5.00 | 2.20 |
| ❑ AS2 Timo Jutila<br>Christer Olsson | 4.00 | 1.80 |
| ❑ AS3 Tommy Sjodin<br>Marko Kiprusoff | 4.00 | 1.80 |
| ❑ AS4 Jere Lehtinen<br>Sergei Berezin | 8.00 | 3.60 |
| ❑ AS5 Saku Koivu<br>Pelle Eklund | 15.00 | 6.75 |
| ❑ AS6 Ville Peltonen<br>Andrew McKim | 4.00 | 1.80 |

## 1996 Swedish Semic Wien Coca-Cola Dream Team

This 12-card set was created as a promotion to tie in with both the World Championships and the Semic Wien set. The cards were issued three to a pack at participating Shell gas stations in Sweden with the purchase of a Coca-Cola product. The cards mirror their counterparts in the regular Semic Wien set, save for the numbering and the silver Dream Team icon on the upper corner of each.

| | MINT | NRMT |
|---|---|---|
| COMPLETE SET (12) | 30.00 | 13.50 |
| COMMON CARD (1-12) | .50 | .23 |

| | | |
|---|---|---|
| ❑ 1 Tommy Soderstrom | 1.50 | .70 |
| ❑ 2 Boo Ahl | 1.00 | .45 |
| ❑ 3 Tomas Jonsson | .75 | .35 |
| ❑ 4 Rikard Franzen | .50 | .23 |
| ❑ 5 Mattias Ohlund | 1.50 | .70 |
| ❑ 6 Roger Johansson | .50 | .23 |
| ❑ 7 Mats Sundin | 4.00 | 1.80 |
| ❑ 8 Peter Forsberg | 25.00 | 11.00 |
| ❑ 9 Mikael Renberg | 4.00 | 1.80 |
| ❑ 10 Per-Erik Eklund | .75 | .35 |
| ❑ 11 Andreas Dackell | 1.00 | .45 |
| ❑ 12 Jonas Bergqvist | .75 | .35 |

## 1998 UD Choice SHL

| | MINT | NRMT |
|---|---|---|
| COMPLETE SET (225) | 60.00 | 27.00 |
| COMMON CARD (1-225) | .10 | .05 |

| | | |
|---|---|---|
| ❑ 1 Jonas Forsberg | .25 | .11 |
| ❑ 2 Rikard Franzen | .10 | .05 |
| ❑ 3 Mathias Svedberg | .10 | .05 |
| ❑ 4 Dick Tarnstrom | .25 | .11 |
| ❑ 5 Jan Sandstrom | .10 | .05 |
| ❑ 6 Johan Silfwerplatz | .10 | .05 |
| ❑ 7 Henrik Tallinder | .25 | .11 |
| ❑ 8 Stefan Gustavson | .10 | .05 |
| ❑ 9 Kristian Gahn | .25 | .11 |
| ❑ 10 Bjorn Ahlstrom | .10 | .05 |
| ❑ 11 Peter Hammarstrom | .10 | .05 |
| ❑ 12 Anders Gozzi | .10 | .05 |
| ❑ 13 Fredrik Krekula | .10 | .05 |
| ❑ 14 Erik Norback | .10 | .05 |
| ❑ 15 Niklas Anger | .35 | .16 |
| ❑ 16 Mats Lindberg | .10 | .05 |
| ❑ 17 Jorgen Wikstrom | .10 | .05 |
| ❑ 18 Per-Anton Lundstrom | .25 | .11 |
| ❑ 19 Mattias Hedlund | .10 | .05 |
| ❑ 20 Jorgen Hermansson | .10 | .05 |
| ❑ 21 Fredrik Bergquist | .10 | .05 |
| ❑ 22 Joakim Lidgren | .10 | .05 |
| ❑ 23 Robert Karlsson | .10 | .05 |
| ❑ 24 Christian Lechtaler | .10 | .05 |
| ❑ 25 Aleksandrs Beljavskis | .10 | .05 |
| ❑ 26 Jens Ohman | .10 | .05 |
| ❑ 27 Stefan Ohman | .10 | .05 |
| ❑ 28 Martin Wiita | .10 | .05 |
| ❑ 29 Johan Ramstedt | .10 | .05 |
| ❑ 30 Per Ledin | .10 | .05 |
| ❑ 31 Jukka Penttinen | .10 | .05 |
| ❑ 32 Aleksandrs Semjonovs | .10 | .05 |
| ❑ 33 Johan Holmqvist | .10 | .05 |
| ❑ 34 Tommy Melkersson | .10 | .05 |
| ❑ 35 Marko Tuulola | .10 | .05 |
| ❑ 36 Johan Hansson | .10 | .05 |
| ❑ 37 Par Djoos | .10 | .05 |
| ❑ 38 Per Lofstrom | .10 | .05 |
| ❑ 39 Niclas Wallin | .25 | .11 |
| ❑ 40 Roger Kyro | .10 | .05 |
| ❑ 41 Ove Molin | .10 | .05 |
| ❑ 42 Stefan Lundqvist | .10 | .05 |
| ❑ 43 Peter Nylander | .10 | .05 |
| ❑ 44 Jan Larsson | .10 | .05 |
| ❑ 45 Teppo Kivela | .10 | .05 |
| ❑ 46 Tom Bissett | .10 | .05 |
| ❑ 47 Anders Huss | .10 | .05 |
| ❑ 48 Mikko Luovi | .25 | .11 |
| ❑ 49 Tommy Soderstrom | .75 | .35 |
| ❑ 50 Bjorn Nord | .10 | .05 |
| ❑ 51 Ronnie Pettersson | .10 | .05 |
| ❑ 52 Thomas Johansson | .10 | .05 |
| ❑ 53 Daniel Tjarnqvist | .25 | .11 |
| ❑ 54 Anders Myrvold | .25 | .11 |
| ❑ 55 Mikael Magnusson | .10 | .05 |
| ❑ 56 Mikael Johansson | .10 | .05 |
| ❑ 57 Nichlas Falk | .25 | .11 |
| ❑ 58 Mikael Hakanson | .10 | .05 |
| ❑ 59 Charles Berglund | .25 | .11 |
| ❑ 60 Lars-Goran Wiklander | .10 | .05 |
| ❑ 61 Per Eklund | .10 | .05 |
| ❑ 62 Jan Viktorsson | .10 | .05 |
| ❑ 63 Patrik Erickson | .10 | .05 |
| ❑ 64 Espen Knutsen | .25 | .11 |
| ❑ 65 Jimmie Olvestad | .75 | .35 |
| ❑ 66 Mikael Sandberg | .10 | .05 |
| ❑ 67 Christer Olsson | .10 | .05 |
| ❑ 68 Petter Nilsson | .10 | .05 |
| ❑ 69 Magnus Johansson | .10 | .05 |
| ❑ 70 Ronnie Sundin | .25 | .11 |
| ❑ 71 Radek Hamr | .10 | .05 |
| ❑ 72 Stefan Larsson | .10 | .05 |
| ❑ 73 Mattias Nilimaa | .10 | .05 |
| ❑ 74 Linus Fagemo | .10 | .05 |
| ❑ 75 Marko Jantunen | .10 | .05 |
| ❑ 76 Patrik Carnback | .10 | .05 |
| ❑ 77 Peter Berndtsson | .10 | .05 |
| ❑ 78 Mikael Samuelsson | .10 | .05 |
| ❑ 79 Peter Strom | .10 | .05 |
| ❑ 80 Par Edlund | .10 | .05 |
| ❑ 81 Henrik Nilsson | .50 | .23 |
| ❑ 82 Jonas Johnson | .10 | .05 |
| ❑ 83 Kimmo Lecklin | .10 | .05 |
| ❑ 84 Roger Johansson | .10 | .05 |

| | | |
|---|---|---|
| ❑ 85 Sergei Fokin | .10 | .05 |
| ❑ 86 Greger Artursson | .10 | .05 |
| ❑ 87 Jonas Elofsson | .35 | .16 |
| ❑ 88 Peter Jakobsson | .10 | .05 |
| ❑ 89 Dimitri Erofeev | .10 | .05 |
| ❑ 90 Patrik Zetterberg | .10 | .05 |
| ❑ 91 Niklas Sjokvist | .10 | .05 |
| ❑ 92 Trond Magnussen | .10 | .05 |
| ❑ 93 Peter Hagstrom | .10 | .05 |
| ❑ 94 Pelle Prestberg | .10 | .05 |
| ❑ 95 Mathias Johansson | .10 | .05 |
| ❑ 96 Michael Holmqvist | .50 | .23 |
| ❑ 97 Clas Eriksson | .10 | .05 |
| ❑ 98 Kristian Huselius | .35 | .16 |
| ❑ 99 Jorgen Jonsson | .10 | .05 |
| ❑ 100 Kari Takko | .25 | .11 |
| ❑ 101 David Petrasek | .10 | .05 |
| ❑ 102 Daniel Johansson | .50 | .23 |
| ❑ 103 Per Gustafsson | .10 | .05 |
| ❑ 104 Fredrik Stillman | .10 | .05 |
| ❑ 105 Nicklas Rahm | .10 | .05 |
| ❑ 106 Mikael Lindman | .10 | .05 |
| ❑ 107 Jerry Persson | .10 | .05 |
| ❑ 108 Esa Keskinen | .10 | .05 |
| ❑ 109 Peter Ekelund | .10 | .05 |
| ❑ 110 Antti Tormanen | .10 | .05 |
| ❑ 111 Marcus Kristoffersson | .10 | .05 |
| ❑ 112 Anders Huusko | .10 | .05 |
| ❑ 113 Erik Huusko | .10 | .05 |
| ❑ 114 Johan Lindbom | .10 | .05 |
| ❑ 115 Jarkko Varvio | .10 | .05 |
| ❑ 116 Ulf Dahlen | .25 | .11 |
| ❑ 117 Johan Hedberg | .25 | .11 |
| ❑ 118 Jan Huokko | .10 | .05 |
| ❑ 119 Torbjorn Johansson | .10 | .05 |
| ❑ 120 Hans Lodin | .10 | .05 |
| ❑ 121 Nicklas Nordqvist | .10 | .05 |
| ❑ 122 Stefan Bergqvist | .10 | .05 |
| ❑ 123 Magnus Svensson | .10 | .05 |
| ❑ 124 Andreas Karlsson | .10 | .05 |
| ❑ 125 Per-Erik Eklund | .25 | .11 |
| ❑ 126 Anders Carlsson | .10 | .05 |
| ❑ 127 Niklas Erikkson | .10 | .05 |
| ❑ 128 Stefan Hellkvist | .10 | .05 |
| ❑ 129 Jens Nielsen | .10 | .05 |
| ❑ 130 Anders Lonn | .10 | .05 |
| ❑ 131 Markus Akerblom | .10 | .05 |
| ❑ 132 Mikael Karlberg | .10 | .05 |
| ❑ 133 Jarmo Myllys | .25 | .11 |
| ❑ 134 Stefan Jonsson | .10 | .05 |
| ❑ 135 Osmo Soutokorva | .10 | .05 |
| ❑ 136 Johan Finnstrom | .10 | .05 |
| ❑ 137 Roger Akerstrom | .25 | .11 |
| ❑ 138 Igor Matushkin | .10 | .05 |
| ❑ 139 Jonas Ronnkvist | .10 | .05 |
| ❑ 140 Thomas Sjogren | .10 | .05 |
| ❑ 141 Tomas Berglund | .10 | .05 |
| ❑ 142 Mikael Lovgren | .10 | .05 |
| ❑ 143 Anders Burstrom | .10 | .05 |
| ❑ 144 Jorgen Bemstrom | .10 | .05 |
| ❑ 145 Martin Hostak | .10 | .05 |
| ❑ 146 Bert-Olav Karlsson | .10 | .05 |
| ❑ 147 Lars Edstrom | .10 | .05 |
| ❑ 148 Jiri Kucera | .10 | .05 |
| ❑ 149 Andrew Verner | .25 | .11 |
| ❑ 150 Kim Johnsson | .10 | .05 |
| ❑ 151 Kari Harila | .10 | .05 |
| ❑ 152 Niclas Havelid | .50 | .23 |
| ❑ 153 Jesper Damgaard | .10 | .05 |
| ❑ 154 Johan Tornberg | .10 | .05 |
| ❑ 155 Mats Lusth | .10 | .05 |
| ❑ 156 Jan Hammar | .10 | .05 |
| ❑ 157 Marcus Magnertoft | .10 | .05 |
| ❑ 158 Marcus Thuresson | .25 | .11 |
| ❑ 159 Magnus Nilsson | .10 | .05 |
| ❑ 160 Mikael Lindholm | .25 | .11 |
| ❑ 161 Patrik Sylvegard | .10 | .05 |
| ❑ 162 Juha Riihijarvi | .25 | .11 |
| ❑ 163 Jesper Mattsson | .25 | .11 |
| ❑ 164 Niklas Sundblad | .10 | .05 |
| ❑ 165 Toivo Suursoo | .10 | .05 |
| ❑ 166 Petter Ronnquist | .10 | .05 |
| ❑ 167 Pierre Hedin | .50 | .23 |
| ❑ 168 Per Hallberg | .10 | .05 |
| ❑ 169 Jan-Axel Alavaara | .10 | .05 |
| ❑ 170 Hans Jonsson | .10 | .05 |
| ❑ 171 Lars Jansson | .10 | .05 |
| ❑ 172 Frantisek Kaberle | .25 | .11 |
| ❑ 173 Andreas Salomonsson | .10 | .05 |
| ❑ 174 Magnus Wernblom | .25 | .11 |
| ❑ 175 Mikael Pettersson | .10 | .05 |
| ❑ 176 Per Svartvadet | .50 | .23 |
| ❑ 177 Daniel Sedin | 5.00 | 2.20 |
| ❑ 178 Henrik Sedin | 4.00 | 1.80 |
| ❑ 179 Jan Alinc | .10 | .05 |
| ❑ 180 Samuel Pahlsson | .50 | .23 |
| ❑ 181 Anders Soderberg | .35 | .16 |
| ❑ 182 Magnus Eriksson | .10 | .05 |
| ❑ 183 Andrei Lulin | .10 | .05 |
| ❑ 184 Jakob Karlsson | .25 | .11 |
| ❑ 185 Patrik Hoglund | .10 | .05 |
| ❑ 186 Joakim Lundberg | .10 | .05 |
| ❑ 187 Arto Blomsten | .10 | .05 |
| ❑ 188 Mattias Loof | .10 | .05 |
| ❑ 189 Mikael Pettersson | .10 | .05 |
| ❑ 190 Joakim Backlund | .10 | .05 |
| ❑ 191 Daniel Rydmark | .10 | .05 |
| ❑ 192 Johan Molin | .10 | .05 |
| ❑ 193 Paul Andersson-Everberg | .10 | .05 |
| ❑ 194 Henrik Nordfeldt | .10 | .05 |
| ❑ 195 Jonas Olsson | .10 | .05 |
| ❑ 196 Fredrik Oberg | .10 | .05 |
| ❑ 197 Roger Rosen | .10 | .05 |
| ❑ 198 Roland Stoltz | .10 | .05 |
| ❑ 199 Lars Bjorn | .10 | .05 |
| ❑ 200 Ulf Sterner | .10 | .05 |
| ❑ 201 Leif Holmqvist | .25 | .11 |
| ❑ 202 Hans Mild | .10 | .05 |
| ❑ 203 Bert-Ola Nordlander | .10 | .05 |
| ❑ 204 Eilert Maatta | .10 | .05 |
| ❑ 205 Ronald Pettersson | .10 | .05 |
| ❑ 206 Tord Lundstrom | .10 | .05 |
| ❑ 207 Lennart Svedberg | .25 | .11 |
| ❑ 208 Roland Stoltz | .10 | .05 |
| ❑ 209 Eilert Maatta | .10 | .05 |
| ❑ 210 Lennart Svedberg | .25 | .11 |
| ❑ 211 Tord Lundstrom | .10 | .05 |
| ❑ 212 Leif Holmqvist | .25 | .11 |
| ❑ 213 Magnus Nilsson | .35 | .16 |
| ❑ 214 Mikael Holmqvist | .35 | .16 |
| ❑ 215 Mattias Karlin | .50 | .23 |
| ❑ 216 Pierre Hedin | .50 | .23 |
| ❑ 217 Henrik Petre | .35 | .16 |
| ❑ 218 Johan Forsander | .25 | .11 |
| ❑ 219 Daniel Sedin | 5.00 | 2.20 |
| ❑ 220 Henrik Sedin | 4.00 | 1.80 |
| ❑ 221 Markus Nilsson | 1.00 | .45 |
| ❑ 222 Checklist | .10 | .05 |
| ❑ 223 Checklist | .10 | .05 |
| ❑ 224 Checklist | .10 | .05 |
| ❑ 225 Checklist | .10 | .05 |
| ❑ GJ1 D.Sedin/H.Sedin | 250.00 | 110.00 |
| ❑ GJA1 D.Sedin/H.Sedin | 800.00 | 350.00 |

## 1998 UD Choice SHL Day in the Life

| | MINT | NRMT |
|---|---|---|
| COMPLETE SET (10) | 20.00 | 9.00 |
| COMMON CARD (1-100 | 2.00 | .90 |
| ❑ 1 Rikard Franzen | 2.00 | .90 |
| ❑ 2 Par Djoos | 2.00 | .90 |
| ❑ 3 Tommy Soderstrom | 5.00 | 2.20 |
| ❑ 4 Pelle Prestberg | 2.00 | .90 |
| ❑ 5 Esa Keskinen | 2.00 | .90 |
| ❑ 6 Johan Hedberg | 3.00 | 1.35 |
| ❑ 7 Jarmo Myllys | 3.00 | 1.35 |
| ❑ 8 Marcus Thuresson | 2.00 | .90 |
| ❑ 9 Samuel Pahlson | 2.00 | .90 |
| ❑ 10 Christer Olsson | 2.00 | .90 |

## 1993-94 Swiss HNL

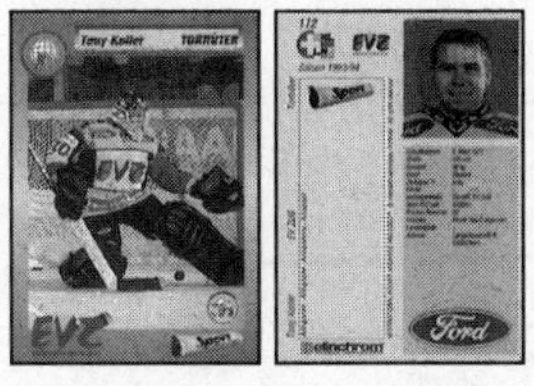

This large set, released by Jurg Ochsner and sponsored by Ford and Sport newspaper, appears to include everyone who performed in the Swiss National League in 1992-93. The set is highlighted by bright, team-color coordinated design elements and sharp photography, as well as the presence of several ex-NHLers. The set appears to use three languages on the card fronts, varying as to the main language in the team's home locale. All coaches cards below are marked TR (the abbreviation for the French "traineur"). A limited number of factory sets were available; each was serially numbered out of 3,000 and registered to the person making the purchase. A collectible binder to hold the set is valued at $5.

| | MINT | NRMT |
|---|---|---|
| COMPLETE SET (510) | 60.00 | 27.00 |
| COMMON CARD (1-510) | .15 | .07 |
| ❑ 1 Title Card | .15 | .07 |
| ❑ 2 Title Card | .15 | .07 |
| ❑ 3 Title Card | .15 | .07 |
| ❑ 4 EHC-Kloten | .15 | .07 |
| ❑ 5 EHC-Kloten | .15 | .07 |
| ❑ 6 Conny Evensson TR | .20 | .09 |
| ❑ 7 Ernst Bruderer ATR | .15 | .07 |
| ❑ 8 Reto Pavoni | .75 | .35 |
| ❑ 9 Claudio Bayer | .50 | .23 |
| ❑ 10 Martin Bruderer | .15 | .07 |
| ❑ 11 Anders Eldebrink | .25 | .11 |
| ❑ 12 Marco Kloti | .15 | .07 |
| ❑ 13 Marco Knecht | .15 | .07 |
| ❑ 14 Martin Kout | .15 | .07 |
| ❑ 15 Fausto Mazzoleni | .15 | .07 |
| ❑ 16 Daniel Sigg | .15 | .07 |
| ❑ 17 Daniel Weber | .15 | .07 |
| ❑ 18 Manuele Celio | .15 | .07 |
| ❑ 19 Patric Della Rossa | .35 | .16 |
| ❑ 20 Michael Diener | .15 | .07 |
| ❑ 21 Bruno Erni | .15 | .07 |
| ❑ 22 Oliver Hoffmann | .15 | .07 |
| ❑ 23 Felix Hollenstein | .25 | .11 |
| ❑ 24 Mikael Johansson | .35 | .16 |
| ❑ 25 Daniel Knecht | .15 | .07 |
| ❑ 26 Roger Meier | .15 | .07 |
| ❑ 27 Sacha Ochsner | .35 | .16 |
| ❑ 28 Peter Schlagenhauf | .15 | .07 |
| ❑ 29 Roman Wager | .35 | .16 |
| ❑ 30 HC Fribourg-Gotteron | .15 | .07 |
| ❑ 31 HC Fribourg-Gotteron | .15 | .07 |
| ❑ 32 Paul-Andre Cadieux TR | .15 | .07 |
| ❑ 33 Francois Huppe ATR | .15 | .07 |
| ❑ 34 Dino Stecher | .50 | .23 |
| ❑ 35 Marc Gygli | .50 | .23 |
| ❑ 36 Patrice Brasey | .15 | .07 |
| ❑ 37 Fredy Bobillier | .15 | .07 |
| ❑ 38 Antoine Descloux | .15 | .07 |
| ❑ 39 Christian Hofstetter | .15 | .07 |
| ❑ 40 Doug Honegger | .15 | .07 |
| ❑ 41 Olivier Keller | .15 | .07 |
| ❑ 42 David Leibzig | .15 | .07 |
| ❑ 43 Didier Princi | .15 | .07 |
| ❑ 44 Joel Aeschlimann | .15 | .07 |
| ❑ 45 Christophe Brown | .15 | .07 |
| ❑ 46 Slava Bykov | 1.00 | .45 |
| ❑ 47 Stefan Grogg | .15 | .07 |
| ❑ 48 Andrej Khomutov | 1.00 | .45 |
| ❑ 49 Marc Leuenberger | .15 | .07 |
| ❑ 50 Bruno Maurer | .15 | .07 |
| ❑ 51 Frank Monnier | .15 | .07 |
| ❑ 52 Alain Reymond | .15 | .07 |
| ❑ 53 Mario Rottaris | .15 | .07 |
| ❑ 54 Pascal Schaller | .15 | .07 |
| ❑ 55 Chad Silver | .15 | .07 |
| ❑ 56 SC Bern | .15 | .07 |
| ❑ 57 SC Bern | .15 | .07 |
| ❑ 58 Hannu Jortikka | .15 | .07 |
| ❑ 59 Jim Koleff | .15 | .07 |
| ❑ 60 Renato Tosio | .50 | .23 |
| ❑ 61 Roland Meyer | .50 | .23 |
| ❑ 62 Raoul Baumgartner | .15 | .07 |
| ❑ 63 Andreas Beutler | .15 | .07 |
| ❑ 64 Martin Brich | .15 | .07 |
| ❑ 65 Mikko Haapakoski | .15 | .07 |
| ❑ 66 Martin Rauch | .15 | .07 |
| ❑ 67 Jorg Reber | .15 | .07 |
| ❑ 68 Daniel Rutschi | .15 | .07 |
| ❑ 69 Gaetan Voisard | .25 | .11 |
| ❑ 70 Peter Bartschi | .15 | .07 |
| ❑ 71 Michael Buhler | .15 | .07 |
| ❑ 72 Rene Friedli | .15 | .07 |
| ❑ 73 Regis Fuchs | .15 | .07 |
| ❑ 74 Gregor Horak | .15 | .07 |
| ❑ 75 Michael Meier | .15 | .07 |
| ❑ 76 Gil Montandon | .15 | .07 |
| ❑ 77 Dan Quinn | .75 | .35 |
| ❑ 78 Harry Rogenmoser | .15 | .07 |
| ❑ 79 Roberto Triulzi | .15 | .07 |
| ❑ 80 Thomas C. Vrabec | .15 | .07 |
| ❑ 81 HC Lugano | .15 | .07 |
| ❑ 82 HC Lugano | .15 | .07 |
| ❑ 83 John Slettvoll TR | .15 | .07 |
| ❑ 84 Bruno Rogger ATR | .15 | .07 |
| ❑ 85 Lars Weibel | 1.00 | .45 |
| ❑ 86 Christophe Wahl | .50 | .23 |
| ❑ 87 Samuel Balmer | .15 | .07 |
| ❑ 88 Sandro Bertaggia | .50 | .23 |
| ❑ 89 Per Djoos | .25 | .11 |
| ❑ 90 Claudio Ghillioni | .15 | .07 |
| ❑ 91 Davide Jelmini | .15 | .07 |
| ❑ 92 Sven Leuenberger | .15 | .07 |
| ❑ 93 Ruedi Niderost | .15 | .07 |
| ❑ 94 Patrick Sutter | .15 | .07 |
| ❑ 95 Jean-Jacques Aeschlimann | .25 | .11 |
| ❑ 96 Jorg Eberle | .35 | .16 |
| ❑ 97 Ruben Fontana | .15 | .07 |
| ❑ 98 Axel Heim | .15 | .07 |
| ❑ 99 Christian Hofstetter | .15 | .07 |
| ❑ 100 Patrick Howald | .25 | .11 |
| ❑ 101 Marcel Jenni | .15 | .07 |
| ❑ 102 Andreas Keller | .15 | .07 |
| ❑ 103 Jan Larsson | .15 | .07 |
| ❑ 104 Andre Rotheli | .15 | .07 |
| ❑ 105 Matthias Schenkel | .15 | .07 |
| ❑ 106 Raymond Walder | .15 | .07 |
| ❑ 107 EV Zug | .15 | .07 |
| ❑ 108 EV Zug | .15 | .07 |
| ❑ 109 Bjorn Kinding | .15 | .07 |
| ❑ 110 Sean Simpson | .15 | .07 |
| ❑ 111 Patrick Schopf | .50 | .23 |
| ❑ 112 Tony Koller | .50 | .23 |
| ❑ 113 Jakub Horak | .15 | .07 |
| ❑ 114 Dino Kessler | .25 | .11 |
| ❑ 115 Andre Kunzi | .15 | .07 |
| ❑ 116 Thomas Kunzi | .15 | .07 |
| ❑ 117 Andreas Ritsch | .15 | .07 |
| ❑ 118 Bill Schafhauser | .15 | .07 |
| ❑ 119 Pat Schafhauser | .15 | .07 |
| ❑ 120 Misko Antisin | .25 | .11 |
| ❑ 121 Mario Brodmann | .15 | .07 |
| ❑ 122 Tom Fergus | .75 | .35 |
| ❑ 123 Andreas Fischer | .15 | .07 |
| ❑ 124 Patrick Fischer | .15 | .07 |
| ❑ 125 Daniel Giger | .15 | .07 |
| ❑ 126 Daniel Meier | .15 | .07 |
| ❑ 127 Colin Muler | .15 | .07 |
| ❑ 128 P. Neuenschwander | .15 | .07 |
| ❑ 129 Daniel Schaltegger | .15 | .07 |
| ❑ 130 Franz Steffen | .15 | .07 |
| ❑ 131 Ken Yaremchuk | .50 | .23 |
| ❑ 132 HC Ambri-Piotta | .15 | .07 |
| ❑ 133 HC Ambri-Piotta | .15 | .07 |
| ❑ 134 Perry Pearn TR | .25 | .11 |
| ❑ 135 Dale McCourt ATR | .25 | .11 |
| ❑ 136 Markus Bachschmied | .50 | .23 |
| ❑ 137 Marco Baron | .50 | .23 |
| ❑ 138 Mark Astley | .25 | .11 |
| ❑ 139 Brenno Celio | .15 | .07 |
| ❑ 140 Filippo Celio | .15 | .07 |
| ❑ 141 Ivan Gazzaroli | .15 | .07 |
| ❑ 142 Tiziano Gianini | .35 | .16 |
| ❑ 143 Blair Muller | .15 | .07 |
| ❑ 144 Luigi Riva | .15 | .07 |
| ❑ 145 Rick Tschumi | .15 | .07 |
| ❑ 146 Nicola Celio | .35 | .16 |
| ❑ 147 Keith Fair | .15 | .07 |
| ❑ 148 Igor Fedulov | .15 | .07 |
| ❑ 149 Mathias Holzer | .15 | .07 |
| ❑ 150 Peter Jaks | .15 | .07 |
| ❑ 151 Vincent Lechenne | .15 | .07 |
| ❑ 152 Juri Leonov | .15 | .07 |
| ❑ 153 Petr Malkov | .15 | .07 |
| ❑ 154 Markus Studer | .15 | .07 |
| ❑ 155 Stafano Togni | .15 | .07 |
| ❑ 156 Luca Vigano | .15 | .07 |
| ❑ 157 Theo Wittmann | .15 | .07 |
| ❑ 158 Zurcher SC | .15 | .07 |
| ❑ 159 Zurcher SC | .15 | .07 |
| ❑ 160 Arno Del Curto TR | .15 | .07 |
| ❑ 161 Ueli Hofmann ATR | .15 | .07 |
| ❑ 162 Daniel Riesen | .50 | .23 |
| ❑ 163 Rolf Simmen | .50 | .23 |
| ❑ 164 Marco Bayer | .25 | .11 |
| ❑ 165 Jiri Faic | .15 | .07 |
| ❑ 166 Yvan Griga | .15 | .07 |
| ❑ 167 Noel Guyaz | .15 | .07 |
| ❑ 168 Edgar Salis | .15 | .07 |
| ❑ 169 Christian Sigrist | .15 | .07 |
| ❑ 170 Bruno Vollmer | .15 | .07 |
| ❑ 171 Andreas Zehnder | .15 | .07 |
| ❑ 172 Matthias Baechler | .15 | .07 |
| ❑ 173 Vjeran Ivankovic | .15 | .07 |
| ❑ 174 Peter Kobel | .15 | .07 |
| ❑ 175 Ronnie Leuthold | .15 | .07 |
| ❑ 176 Claudio Micheli | .15 | .07 |
| ❑ 177 Patrizio Morger | .15 | .07 |
| ❑ 178 Sergei Priakhin | .35 | .16 |
| ❑ 179 Roger Thony | .15 | .07 |
| ❑ 180 Andy Ton | .15 | .07 |
| ❑ 181 Christian Weber | .15 | .07 |
| ❑ 182 Vladimir Yeremin | .15 | .07 |
| ❑ 183 Michel Zeiter | .15 | .07 |
| ❑ 184 EHC Biel-Bienne | .15 | .07 |
| ❑ 185 EHC Biel-Bienne | .15 | .07 |
| ❑ 186 Jakob Kolliker TR | .15 | .07 |
| ❑ 187 B. Lautenschlager ATR | .15 | .07 |
| ❑ 188 Oliver Anken | .50 | .23 |
| ❑ 189 Christian Cretin | .50 | .23 |
| ❑ 190 Beat Cattaruzza | .15 | .07 |
| ❑ 191 Jean-Michel Clavien | .15 | .07 |
| ❑ 192 Sven Dick | .15 | .07 |
| ❑ 193 Daniel Dubois | .15 | .07 |
| ❑ 194 Leo Gudas | .25 | .11 |
| ❑ 195 Bjorn Schneider | .15 | .07 |
| ❑ 196 Martin Steinegger | .15 | .07 |
| ❑ 197 Gaetan Boucher | .15 | .07 |
| ❑ 198 Thomas Burillo | .15 | .07 |
| ❑ 199 Reynlad De Ritz | .15 | .07 |
| ❑ 200 Patrick Glanzmann | .15 | .07 |
| ❑ 201 Freddy Luthi | .15 | .07 |
| ❑ 202 Beat Nuspliger | .15 | .07 |
| ❑ 203 Cyrill Pasche | .15 | .07 |
| ❑ 204 Robert Yannick | .15 | .07 |
| ❑ 205 Andre Rufener | .15 | .07 |
| ❑ 206 Bernhard Schuemperli | .25 | .11 |
| ❑ 207 Marc Weber | .25 | .11 |
| ❑ 208 Ramil Yuldashev | .15 | .07 |
| ❑ 209 HC Davos | .15 | .07 |
| ❑ 210 HC Davos | .15 | .07 |
| ❑ 211 Mats Waltin TR | .15 | .07 |
| ❑ 212 Marcus Theus ATR | .15 | .07 |
| ❑ 213 Nando Wieser | .50 | .23 |
| ❑ 214 Marino Buriola | .50 | .23 |
| ❑ 215 Thomi Derungs | .15 | .07 |
| ❑ 216 Egli Andy | .15 | .07 |
| ❑ 217 Beat Equilino | .15 | .07 |
| ❑ 218 Marc Gianola | .15 | .07 |
| ❑ 219 Andrea Haller | .15 | .07 |
| ❑ 220 Massy Didier | .15 | .07 |
| ❑ 221 Roland Ruedi | .15 | .07 |
| ❑ 222 Roger Sigg | .15 | .07 |
| ❑ 223 Mica Blaha | .25 | .11 |
| ❑ 224 Gian Marco Crameri | .15 | .07 |
| ❑ 225 Remo Gross | .15 | .07 |
| ❑ 226 Martin Hanggi | .15 | .07 |
| ❑ 227 Markus Morf | .15 | .07 |
| ❑ 228 Rene Muller | .15 | .07 |
| ❑ 229 Andi Naser | .15 | .07 |
| ❑ 230 Oliver Roth | .15 | .07 |
| ❑ 231 Rato Schneider | .15 | .07 |
| ❑ 232 Serge Soguel | .15 | .07 |
| ❑ 233 Gilles Thibaudeau | .50 | .23 |
| ❑ 234 Steve Tsujiura | .25 | .11 |
| ❑ 235 EHC Olten | .15 | .07 |
| ❑ 236 EHC Olten | .15 | .07 |
| ❑ 237 Dick Decloe TR | .15 | .07 |
| ❑ 238 Beat Aebischer | .50 | .23 |
| ❑ 239 Sascha Friedli | .50 | .23 |
| ❑ 240 Matthias Aregger | .15 | .07 |
| ❑ 241 Eric Bourquin | .15 | .07 |
| ❑ 242 Fabian Gull | .15 | .07 |
| ❑ 243 Urs Hirschi | .15 | .07 |
| ❑ 244 Alessandro Reinhart | .15 | .07 |
| ❑ 245 Christian Schuster | .15 | .07 |
| ❑ 246 Christian Silling | .15 | .07 |
| ❑ 247 Richard Stucki | .15 | .07 |
| ❑ 248 Adrian Bachofner | .15 | .07 |
| ❑ 249 Markus Butler | .15 | .07 |
| ❑ 250 Ralph Donghi | .15 | .07 |
| ❑ 251 Guido Egli | .15 | .07 |
| ❑ 252 Paul Gagne | .50 | .23 |
| ❑ 253 Thomas Loosli | .15 | .07 |
| ❑ 254 Steve Metzger | .15 | .07 |
| ❑ 255 Viktor Muller | .15 | .07 |
| ❑ 256 Mike Richard | .15 | .07 |
| ❑ 257 Kevin Schlapfer | .15 | .07 |
| ❑ 258 Peter Trummer | .15 | .07 |
| ❑ 259 Andre Von Rohr | .15 | .07 |
| ❑ 260 HC Ajoie | .15 | .07 |
| ❑ 261 HC Ajoie | .15 | .07 |
| ❑ 262 Michael McNamara TR | .15 | .07 |
| ❑ 263 Claude Fugere ATR | .15 | .07 |
| ❑ 264 Nicola Fraschina | .50 | .23 |
| ❑ 265 Didier Tosi | .50 | .23 |
| ❑ 266 Dave Baechler | .15 | .07 |
| ❑ 267 Sandro Capaul | .15 | .07 |
| ❑ 268 Romain Fleury | .15 | .07 |
| ❑ 269 Carl Lapointe | .15 | .07 |
| ❑ 270 John Miner | .15 | .07 |
| ❑ 271 Daniel Rohrbach | .15 | .07 |
| ❑ 272 Ralph Tanner | .15 | .07 |
| ❑ 273 Yann Voillat | .15 | .07 |
| ❑ 274 Mauro Bornet | .15 | .07 |
| ❑ 275 Kalle Furer | .15 | .07 |
| ❑ 276 Thomas Griga | .15 | .07 |
| ❑ 277 Patrice Heiz | .15 | .07 |
| ❑ 278 Willy Kohler | .15 | .07 |
| ❑ 279 Daniel Lamminger | .15 | .07 |
| ❑ 280 Francois Marquis | .15 | .07 |
| ❑ 281 Marco Mozzini | .15 | .07 |
| ❑ 282 Giovanni Pestrin | .15 | .07 |
| ❑ 283 Ken Priestlay | .35 | .16 |
| ❑ 284 Frederic Rothen | .15 | .07 |
| ❑ 285 EHC Chur | .15 | .07 |
| ❑ 286 EHC Chur | .15 | .07 |
| ❑ 287 Bengt Ericsson TR | .15 | .07 |
| ❑ 288 Roberto Lavoie TR | .15 | .07 |
| ❑ 289 Peter Martin | .50 | .23 |
| ❑ 290 Thomas Liesch | .50 | .23 |
| ❑ 291 Marco Capaul | .15 | .07 |
| ❑ 292 Marco Gazzola | .15 | .07 |
| ❑ 293 B. Habisreutinger | .15 | .07 |
| ❑ 294 Markus Knobel | .15 | .07 |
| ❑ 295 Thomas Locher | .15 | .07 |
| ❑ 296 Roger Schnoz | .15 | .07 |
| ❑ 297 Roland Simonet | .15 | .07 |
| ❑ 298 Ivo Stoffel | .15 | .07 |
| ❑ 299 Rene Ackermann | .15 | .07 |
| ❑ 300 Patrice Bosch | .15 | .07 |
| ❑ 301 Derungs Harry | .15 | .07 |
| ❑ 302 Marco Ferrari | .15 | .07 |
| ❑ 303 Miguel Fondado | .15 | .07 |
| ❑ 304 Claudio Kalser | .15 | .07 |
| ❑ 305 Claudio Krattli | .15 | .07 |
| ❑ 306 Zbysek Kurylowski | .15 | .07 |
| ❑ 307 Andrei Kwartalnov | .15 | .07 |
| ❑ 308 Albert Malgin | .15 | .07 |
| ❑ 309 Wayne Manley | .15 | .07 |
| ❑ 310 Signorell Riccardo | .15 | .07 |
| ❑ 311 HC Martigny | .15 | .07 |
| ❑ 312 HC Martigny | .15 | .07 |
| ❑ 313 Bob Mongrain | .15 | .07 |
| ❑ 314 Thierry Audrey | .50 | .23 |
| ❑ 315 Florian Garnier | .50 | .23 |
| ❑ 316 Thierry Evequoz | .15 | .07 |
| ❑ 317 Alexandre Formaz | .15 | .07 |
| ❑ 318 Tom Jaeggi | .15 | .07 |
| ❑ 319 Adrian Jezzone | .15 | .07 |
| ❑ 320 Jaques Mauron | .15 | .07 |
| ❑ 321 Patrick Neukom | .15 | .07 |
| ❑ 322 Brian Rueger | .15 | .07 |
| ❑ 323 Bruno Steck | .15 | .07 |
| ❑ 324 Steve Aebersold | .15 | .07 |
| ❑ 325 Nicolas Baumann | .15 | .07 |
| ❑ 326 Alain Bernard | .15 | .07 |
| ❑ 327 Jean-Daniel Bonito | .15 | .07 |
| ❑ 328 Olivier Ecoeur | .15 | .07 |
| ❑ 329 Kelly Glowa | .15 | .07 |
| ❑ 330 Thomas Heldner | .15 | .07 |
| ❑ 331 Thierry Moret | .15 | .07 |
| ❑ 332 Stefan Nussberger | .15 | .07 |
| ❑ 333 Petr Rosol | .25 | .11 |
| ❑ 334 Gabriel Taccoz | .15 | .07 |
| ❑ 335 SC Herisau | .15 | .07 |
| ❑ 336 SC Herisau | .15 | .07 |
| ❑ 337 Mike McParland TR | .15 | .07 |
| ❑ 338 Mark McGregor ATR | .15 | .07 |
| ❑ 339 Stephan Mor | .50 | .23 |
| ❑ 340 Stefan Allenspach | .50 | .23 |
| ❑ 341 Urs Balzarek | .15 | .07 |
| ❑ 342 Sascha Bleiker | .15 | .07 |
| ❑ 343 Damian Freitag | .15 | .07 |
| ❑ 344 Karl Knopf | .15 | .07 |
| ❑ 345 Andy Krapf | .15 | .07 |
| ❑ 346 Andreas Maag | .15 | .07 |
| ❑ 347 Paul Summermatter | .15 | .07 |
| ❑ 348 Markus Wetter | .15 | .07 |
| ❑ 349 Marco Beer | .15 | .07 |
| ❑ 350 Bernhard Blochliger | .15 | .07 |
| ❑ 351 Libor Dolana | .15 | .07 |
| ❑ 352 Philipp Egli | .15 | .07 |
| ❑ 353 Marco Fischer | .15 | .07 |
| ❑ 354 Reto Germann | .15 | .07 |
| ❑ 355 Urs Hartmann | .15 | .07 |
| ❑ 356 Markus Keller | .15 | .07 |
| ❑ 357 Trevor Meier | .15 | .07 |
| ❑ 358 Roger Nater | .15 | .07 |
| ❑ 359 Petr Vlk | .25 | .11 |
| ❑ 360 Gerd Zenhausern | .15 | .07 |
| ❑ 361 SC Rapperswil-Jona | .15 | .07 |
| ❑ 362 SC Rapperswil-Jona | .15 | .07 |
| ❑ 363 Pekka Rautakallio TR | .50 | .23 |
| ❑ 364 Ueli Scheidegger ATR | .15 | .07 |
| ❑ 365 Marius Boesch | .15 | .07 |
| ❑ 366 Michael Habig | .35 | .16 |
| ❑ 367 Armin Berchtold | .15 | .07 |
| ❑ 368 Daniel Bunzli | .15 | .07 |
| ❑ 369 Erich Frey | .15 | .07 |
| ❑ 370 Patrick Gotz | .15 | .07 |
| ❑ 371 Marc Haueter | .15 | .07 |
| ❑ 372 Christian Langer | .15 | .07 |
| ❑ 373 Markus Naef | .15 | .07 |
| ❑ 374 Daniel Aeschbacher | .15 | .07 |
| ❑ 375 Ray Allison | .15 | .07 |
| ❑ 376 Tom Bissett | .25 | .11 |
| ❑ 377 Warren Bruetsch | .15 | .07 |
| ❑ 378 Turi Camenzind | .15 | .07 |
| ❑ 379 Jean-Noel Honegger | .15 | .07 |
| ❑ 380 Roman Kessler | .15 | .07 |
| ❑ 381 Hans Kossman | .15 | .07 |

❑ 382 Marco Seeholzer .15 .07
❑ 383 Laurent Stehlin .15 .07
❑ 384 Marco Werder .15 .07
❑ 385 EHC Bulach .15 .07
❑ 386 EHC Bulach .15 .07
❑ 387 Lars-Erik Lundstrom TR .15 .07
❑ 388 Urs Liljequist ATR .15 .07
❑ 389 Ronnie Rueger .50 .23
❑ 390 Carlo Buriola .50 .23
❑ 391 Rolf Bunter .15 .07
❑ 392 David Erny .15 .07
❑ 393 Urs Gull .15 .07
❑ 394 Thomas Jaggli .15 .07
❑ 395 Stefan Meier .15 .07
❑ 396 Marco Schellenberg .15 .07
❑ 397 Marcel Schonhaar .15 .07
❑ 398 Robin Bauer .15 .07
❑ 399 Daniele Celio .15 .07
❑ 400 Peter Ekelund .15 .07
❑ 401 Urs Luthi .15 .07
❑ 402 Don McLaren .35 .16
❑ 403 Kim Pedersen .15 .07
❑ 404 Matthias Pittet .15 .07
❑ 405 Ercan Sahin .15 .07
❑ 406 Thomas Studer .15 .07
❑ 407 Markus Suter .15 .07
❑ 408 Martin Caretta .15 .07
❑ 409 Mike Tschumi .15 .07
❑ 410 Lausanne HC .15 .07
❑ 411 Lausanne HC .15 .07
❑ 412 Jean Lussier TR .15 .07
❑ 413 Beat Kindler .25 .11
❑ 414 Michel Pilet .15 .07
❑ 415 Urs Burkart .15 .07
❑ 416 Jean Gagnon .15 .07
❑ 417 Nicolas Goumaz .15 .07
❑ 418 Fabian Guignard .15 .07
❑ 419 Benedict Sapin .15 .07
❑ 420 Raymond Wyssen .15 .07
❑ 421 Laurent Bucher .15 .07
❑ 422 Olivier Chenuz .15 .07
❑ 423 Alain Comte .15 .07
❑ 424 Martin Desjardins .15 .07
❑ 425 Gaby Epiney .15 .07
❑ 426 Stephane Gasser .15 .07
❑ 427 Nicolas Gauch .15 .07
❑ 428 Gilles Guyaz .15 .07
❑ 429 Dan Hodgson .50 .23
❑ 430 Maxime Lapointe .15 .07
❑ 431 Laurent Pasquini .15 .07
❑ 432 Gilles Prince .15 .07
❑ 433 Yannick Theler .15 .07
❑ 434 HC Thurgau .15 .07
❑ 435 HC Thurgau .15 .07
❑ 436 Anders Sorensen TR .15 .07
❑ 437 Max Baumann .15 .07
❑ 438 Martin Studer .50 .23
❑ 439 Thomas Berger .50 .23
❑ 440 Andy Gasser .15 .07
❑ 441 Patrick Henry .15 .07
❑ 442 Reto Muller .15 .07
❑ 443 Ralph Ott .15 .07
❑ 444 Mike Posma .15 .07
❑ 445 Hadrian Rosenberg .15 .07
❑ 446 Marcel Stocker .15 .07
❑ 447 Robert Wiesmann .15 .07
❑ 448 Gianni Dalla Vecchia .15 .07
❑ 449 Dan Daoust .50 .23
❑ 450 Matthias Keller .15 .07
❑ 451 Roger Keller .15 .07
❑ 452 Peter Kostli .15 .07
❑ 453 Bernhard Lauber .15 .07
❑ 454 Benjamin Mueller .15 .07
❑ 455 Silvio Schai .15 .07
❑ 456 Rolf Schrepfer .15 .07
❑ 457 Robert Slehofer .15 .07
❑ 458 Thomas Steger .15 .07
❑ 459 Cuno Weisser .15 .07
❑ 460 Grasshoppers-Club Zurich .15 .07
❑ 461 Grasshoppers-Club Zurich .15 .07
❑ 462 Esa Siren TR .15 .07
❑ 463 Bruno Aegerter ATR .15 .07
❑ 464 Marcel Kohli .50 .23
❑ 465 Olivier Leuenberger .50 .23
❑ 466 Giorgio Giacomelli .15 .07
❑ 467 Roman Honegger .15 .07
❑ 468 Sandro Just .15 .07
❑ 469 Mats Lusth .15 .07
❑ 470 Marcel Wick .15 .07
❑ 471 Lukas Zehnder .15 .07
❑ 472 Rolf Ziegler .15 .07
❑ 473 Jerry Zuurmond .15 .07
❑ 474 Alain Ayer .15 .07
❑ 475 Leo Cadisch .15 .07
❑ 476 Pascal Fah .15 .07
❑ 477 Roman Furrer .15 .07
❑ 478 Marco Hagmann .15 .07
❑ 479 Peter Hofmann .15 .07
❑ 480 Adrian Hotz .15 .07
❑ 481 Patrick Looser .15 .07
❑ 482 Oliver Muffler .15 .07
❑ 483 Keith Osborne .25 .11
❑ 484 Thierry Paterlini .15 .07
❑ 485 Markus Schellenberg .15 .07
❑ 486 HC La Chaux-de-Fonds .15 .07
❑ 487 HC LaChaux-de-Fonds .15 .07
❑ 488 Ricardo Fuhrer TR .15 .07
❑ 489 Jean-Luc Schnegg .35 .16
❑ 490 Thierry Loup .35 .16
❑ 491 Thierry Baume .15 .07
❑ 492 Jean-Luc Christen .15 .07
❑ 493 Thierry Murisier .15 .07
❑ 494 Danny Ott .15 .07
❑ 495 Guido Pfosi .15 .07
❑ 496 Rene Raess .15 .07
❑ 497 Valeri Shirajev .35 .16
❑ 498 Frank Vuillemin .15 .07
❑ 499 Marco Dick .15 .07
❑ 500 Michael Ferrari .15 .07
❑ 501 Olivier Gazzaroli .15 .07
❑ 502 Sandy Jeannin .15 .07
❑ 503 Lane Lambert .35 .16
❑ 504 Guido Laczko .15 .07
❑ 505 Boris Leimgruber .15 .07
❑ 506 Claude Luthi .15 .07
❑ 507 Patrick Oppliger .15 .07
❑ 508 Jean-Luc Rod .15 .07
❑ 509 Gabriel Rohrbach .15 .07
❑ 510 Yvan Zimmermann .15 .07

## 1995-96 Swiss HNL

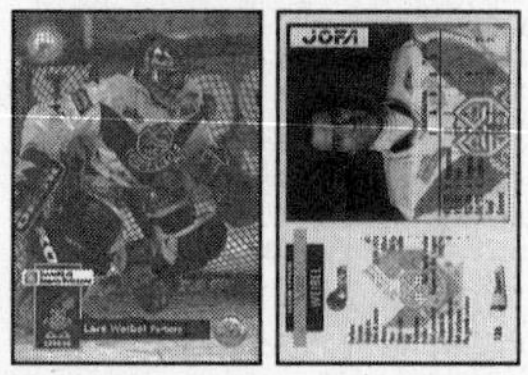

This very large set, released by Jurg Ochsner and sponsored by the Swiss Bank Society appears to include everyone who performed in the Swiss national hockey league in 1994-95. They were distributed in 6-card packs for 2 francs. The set is highlighted by marvelous color action photography, a subset of six NNO referee cards, and the inclusion of six NHLers who played in Switzerland during the NHL lockout including Doug Gilmour and Chris Chelios. Of interest is the usage of three languages (French, German and Italian) on the card fronts, which varies by the main language in the team's home locale. Note: the TR suffix in this case is the direct translation of coach (traineur). A collector's album also was available by mail. It is valued at $5.00.

| | MINT | NRMT |
|---|---|---|
| COMPLETE SET (545) | 70.00 | 32.00 |
| COMMON CARD (1-545) | .10 | .05 |

❑ 1 Kloten .10 .05
❑ 2 Kloten .10 .05
❑ 3 Alpo Suhonen CO .15 .07
❑ 4 Ernst Bruderer ACO .10 .05
❑ 5 Matthias Muller .35 .16
❑ 6 Reto Pavoni .50 .23
❑ 7 Marco Bayer .10 .05
❑ 8 Martin Bruderer .10 .05
❑ 9 Marco Kloti .10 .05
❑ 10 Michael Kress .10 .05
❑ 11 Marc Ochsner .10 .05
❑ 12 Bjorn Schneider .10 .05
❑ 13 Daniel Sigg .10 .05
❑ 14 Daniel Weber .10 .05
❑ 15 Charles Berglund .10 .05
❑ 16 Manuele Celio .10 .05
❑ 17 Patrik Della Rossa .20 .09
❑ 18 Michael Diener .10 .05
❑ 19 Bruno Erni .10 .05
❑ 20 Oliver Hoffmann .10 .05
❑ 21 Felix Hollenstein .15 .07
❑ 22 Mathias Holzer .10 .05
❑ 23 Mikael Johansson .10 .05
❑ 24 Roger Meier .10 .05
❑ 25 Sacha Oscsner .10 .05
❑ 26 Frederic Rothen .10 .05
❑ 27 Roman Wager .10 .05
❑ 28 ZSC .10 .05
❑ 29 ZSC .10 .05
❑ 30 Larry Huras CO .10 .05
❑ 31 Ted Snell ACO .10 .05
❑ 32 Thomas Papp .35 .16
❑ 33 Dino Stecher .35 .16
❑ 34 Patrick Hager .10 .05
❑ 35 Martin Kout .10 .05
❑ 36 Didier Princi .10 .05
❑ 37 Edgar Salis .10 .05
❑ 38 Bruno Steck .10 .05
❑ 39 Nicholas Steiger .10 .05
❑ 40 Andreas Zehnder .10 .05
❑ 41 Mario Brodmann .10 .05
❑ 42 Marc Fortier .20 .09
❑ 43 Nicholas Gauch .10 .05
❑ 44 Vjeran Ivankovic .10 .05
❑ 45 Sandy Jeannin .10 .05
❑ 46 Patrick Lebeau .25 .11
❑ 47 Phillipp Luber .10 .05
❑ 48 Don McLaren .20 .09
❑ 49 Claudio Micheli .10 .05
❑ 50 Patrizio Morger .10 .05
❑ 51 Marco Seeholzer .10 .05
❑ 52 Bruno Vollmer .10 .05
❑ 53 Michel Zeiter .10 .05
❑ 54 Fribourg .10 .05
❑ 55 Fribourg .10 .05
❑ 56 Kjell Larsson CO .10 .05
❑ 57 Ueli Hofmann ACO .10 .05
❑ 58 David Aebischer .35 .16
❑ 59 Thomas Berger .35 .16
❑ 60 Steve Meuwly .20 .09
❑ 61 Johan Bertholet .10 .05
❑ 62 Fredy Bobillier .10 .05
❑ 63 Patrice Brasey .10 .05
❑ 64 Antoine Descloux .10 .05
❑ 65 Andy Egli .10 .05
❑ 66 Christian Hofstetter .10 .05
❑ 67 Olivier Keller .10 .05
❑ 68 Andrej Lomakin .25 .11
❑ 69 Mark Streit .10 .05
❑ 70 Christophe Brown .10 .05
❑ 71 Slava Bykov .50 .23
❑ 72 Matthias Bachler .10 .05
❑ 73 Axel Heim .10 .05
❑ 74 Andrei Khomutov .50 .23
❑ 75 Marc Leuenberger .10 .05
❑ 76 Alfred Luthi .10 .05
❑ 77 Daniel Meier .10 .05
❑ 78 Mario Rottaris .10 .05
❑ 79 Pascal Schaller .10 .05
❑ 80 Sacha Schneider .10 .05
❑ 81 Joel Aeschlimann .10 .05
❑ 82 Bern .10 .05
❑ 83 Bern .10 .05
❑ 84 Brian Lefley CO .10 .05
❑ 85 Ueli Schwarz ACO .10 .05
❑ 86 Reto Schurch .35 .16
❑ 87 Renato Tosio .35 .16
❑ 88 Mikko Haapakoski .10 .05
❑ 89 Christian Langer .10 .05
❑ 90 Sven Leuenberger .10 .05
❑ 91 Phillippe Portner .10 .05
❑ 92 Martin Rauch .10 .05
❑ 93 Pascal Sommer .10 .05
❑ 94 Martin Steinegger .10 .05
❑ 95 Gaeton Voisard .15 .07
❑ 96 Rene Friedli .10 .05
❑ 97 Regis Fuchs .10 .05
❑ 98 Patrick Howald .10 .05
❑ 99 Andy Keller .10 .05
❑ 100 Vincent Lechenne .10 .05
❑ 101 Lars Leuenberger .10 .05
❑ 102 Trevor Meier .10 .05
❑ 103 Gilles Montandon .15 .07
❑ 104 Philippe Muller .10 .05
❑ 105 Gaetano Orlando .20 .09
❑ 106 Roberto Triulzi .10 .05
❑ 107 Thomas Vrabec .20 .09
❑ 108 Davos .10 .05
❑ 109 Davos .10 .05
❑ 110 Mats Waltin CO .10 .05
❑ 111 Evgeni Popichin ACO .10 .05
❑ 112 Ivo Kleeb .35 .16
❑ 113 Nando Wiesser .35 .16
❑ 114 Samuel Balmer .10 .05
❑ 115 Martin Brich .10 .05
❑ 116 Beat Equilino .10 .05
❑ 117 Ivan Gazzaroli .10 .05
❑ 118 Marc Gianola .10 .05
❑ 119 Andrea Haeller .10 .05
❑ 120 Doug Honegger .10 .05
❑ 121 Andrej Kovalev .15 .07
❑ 122 Jan Alston .10 .05
❑ 123 Gian-Marco Crameri .10 .05
❑ 124 Dan Hodgson .20 .09
❑ 125 Rene Muller .10 .05
❑ 126 Andy Naser .10 .05
❑ 127 Oliver Roth .10 .05
❑ 128 Ivo Ruthemann .10 .05
❑ 129 Reto Stirnimann .10 .05
❑ 130 Reto Von Arx .10 .05
❑ 131 Christian Weber .10 .05
❑ 132 Lugano .10 .05
❑ 133 Lugano .10 .05
❑ 134 John Slettvoll CO .10 .05
❑ 135 Nicola Fraschina .35 .16
❑ 136 Lars Weibel .75 .35
❑ 137 Sandro Bertaggia .20 .09
❑ 138 Francesco Bizzozero .10 .05
❑ 139 Michel Kamber .10 .05
❑ 140 Ruedi Niderost .10 .05
❑ 141 Pat Schafhauser .10 .05
❑ 142 Tommy Sjodin .20 .09
❑ 143 Patrick Sutter .10 .05
❑ 144 Rick Tschumi .10 .05
❑ 145 J. Jacques Aeschlimann .10 .05
❑ 146 Markus Butler .10 .05
❑ 147 Jorg Eberle .20 .09
❑ 148 Keith Fair .10 .05
❑ 149 Marcel Jenni .10 .05
❑ 150 Stephan Lebeau .25 .11
❑ 151 Patrick Looser .10 .05
❑ 152 Stefano Togni .10 .05
❑ 153 Andy Ton .10 .05
❑ 154 Remo Walder .10 .05
❑ 155 EVZ .10 .05
❑ 156 EVZ .10 .05
❑ 157 Jim Koleff CO .10 .05
❑ 158 Bob Lesley ACO .10 .05
❑ 159 Sacha Friedli .35 .16
❑ 160 Patrick Schopf .35 .16
❑ 161 Livio Fazio .10 .05
❑ 162 Stefan Grauwiler .10 .05
❑ 163 Dino Kessler .10 .05
❑ 164 Andre Kunzi .10 .05
❑ 165 Thomas Kunzi .10 .05
❑ 166 Fausto Mazzoleni .10 .05
❑ 167 John Miner .10 .05
❑ 168 Bill Schafhauser .10 .05
❑ 169 Steve Aebersold .10 .05
❑ 170 Misko Antisin .10 .05
❑ 171 Patrick Fischer .10 .05
❑ 172 Daniel Giger .10 .05
❑ 173 Mathias Keller .10 .05
❑ 174 Marco Koppel .10 .05
❑ 175 Colin Muller .10 .05
❑ 176 Philipp Neuenschwander .10 .05
❑ 177 Andre Rotheli .10 .05
❑ 178 Chad Silver .10 .05
❑ 179 Franz Steffen .10 .05
❑ 180 Ken Yaremchuk .25 .11
❑ 181 Ambri Piotta .10 .05
❑ 182 Ambri Piotta .10 .05
❑ 183 Alexander Jakushev TR .35 .16
❑ 184 Petr Malkov ACO .10 .05
❑ 185 Markus Bachschmied .35 .16
❑ 186 Paolo Della Bella .35 .16
❑ 187 Pauli Jaks .50 .23
❑ 188 Brenno Celio .10 .05
❑ 189 Tiziano Gianini .20 .09
❑ 190 Fabian Gull .10 .05
❑ 191 Noel Guyaz .10 .05
❑ 192 Jakub Horak .10 .05
❑ 193 Alessandro Reinhart .10 .05
❑ 194 Luigi Riva .10 .05
❑ 195 Gianni Sanese .10 .05
❑ 196 Oskar Szczepaniec .10 .05
❑ 197 Mattia Baldi .10 .05
❑ 198 Nicola Celio .20 .09
❑ 199 Dmitri Denisov .10 .05
❑ 200 Gaby Epiney .10 .05
❑ 201 John Fritsche .10 .05
❑ 202 Patrick Glansmann .10 .05
❑ 203 Thomas Heldner .10 .05
❑ 204 Paolo Imperatori .10 .05
❑ 205 Peter Jaks .10 .05
❑ 206 Dimitri Kvartalnov .50 .23
❑ 207 Omar Tognini .10 .05
❑ 208 Nicola Pini .10 .05
❑ 209 Luca Vigano .10 .05
❑ 210 Theo Wittmann .10 .05
❑ 211 Rapperswil .10 .05
❑ 212 Rapperswil .10 .05
❑ 213 Pekka Rautakallio CO .25 .11
❑ 214 Ueli Scheidegger ACO .10 .05
❑ 215 Claudio Bayer .35 .16
❑ 216 Christian Cretin .35 .16
❑ 217 Daniel Bunzli .10 .05
❑ 218 Marco Capaul .10 .05
❑ 219 Roland Kradolfer .10 .05
❑ 220 Blair Muller .10 .05
❑ 221 Andreas Ritsch .10 .05
❑ 222 Daniel Rutschi .10 .05
❑ 223 Roger Sigg .10 .05
❑ 224 Adrian Bachofner .10 .05
❑ 225 Arthur Camenzind .10 .05
❑ 226 Christian Hofstetter .10 .05
❑ 227 Michael Meier .10 .05
❑ 228 Mike Richard .20 .09
❑ 229 Harry Rogenmoser .10 .05
❑ 230 Andy Rufener .10 .05
❑ 231 Sergio Soguel .10 .05
❑ 232 Gilles Thibaudeau .25 .11
❑ 233 Roger Thony .10 .05
❑ 234 Marc Weber .10 .05
❑ 235 Marco Werder .10 .05
❑ 236 Lausanne HC .10 .05
❑ 237 Jean Lussier CO .10 .05
❑ 238 Thierry Andrey .35 .16
❑ 239 Beat Kindler .35 .16
❑ 240 Jean Gagnon .10 .05
❑ 241 Fabian Guignard .10 .05
❑ 242 Philippe Marquis .10 .05
❑ 243 Stephan Schneider .10 .05
❑ 244 Roland Simonet .10 .05
❑ 245 Ivo Stoffel .10 .05
❑ 246 Marcel Wick .10 .05
❑ 247 Raymond Wyssen .10 .05
❑ 248 Martin Desjardins .10 .05
❑ 249 Maxime Lapointe .10 .05
❑ 250 Bruno Maurer .10 .05
❑ 251 Frank Monnier .10 .05
❑ 252 Cyrill Pasche .10 .05
❑ 253 Laurent Pasquini .10 .05
❑ 254 Alain Reymond .10 .05
❑ 255 Yannick Robert .10 .05
❑ 256 Kevin Schlapfer .10 .05
❑ 257 Gabriel Taccoz .10 .05
❑ 258 Claude Verret .10 .05
❑ 259 Gerd Zenhausern .10 .05
❑ 260 Biel .10 .05
❑ 261 Biel .10 .05
❑ 262 Barry Jenkins CO .10 .05
❑ 263 Sacha Devaux .35 .16
❑ 264 Christoph Wahl .35 .16
❑ 265 Beat Cattaruzza .10 .05
❑ 266 Sven Dick .10 .05
❑ 267 Claudio Ghillioni .10 .05
❑ 268 Stefan Lutz .10 .05
❑ 269 Guido Pfosi .10 .05
❑ 270 Sven Schmid .10 .05
❑ 271 Daniel Schneider .10 .05
❑ 272 Frank Aeschlimann .10 .05
❑ 273 Thomas Burillo .10 .05
❑ 274 Stefan Choffat .10 .05
❑ 275 Reynald DeRitz .10 .05
❑ 276 Marco Dick .10 .05
❑ 277 Ralph Donghi .10 .05
❑ 278 Stefan Groff .10 .05
❑ 279 Andrei Kvartalnov .10 .05
❑ 280 Albert Malgin .10 .05
❑ 281 Oliver Muller .10 .05
❑ 282 Michael Riesen 5.00 2.20
❑ 283 Bernhard Schumperli .15 .07
❑ 284 Mike Tschumi .10 .05
❑ 285 Grasshopper .10 .05
❑ 286 Grasshopper .10 .05
❑ 287 Bruno Aegerter CO .10 .05
❑ 288 Matti Alatalo ACO .10 .05
❑ 289 Marcel Kohli .35 .16
❑ 290 Stephan Morf .35 .16
❑ 291 Michel Faeh .10 .05
❑ 292 Marc Haueter .10 .05
❑ 293 Roman Honegger .10 .05
❑ 294 Arne Ramholt .10 .05
❑ 295 Hannu Virta .20 .09
❑ 296 Rolf Ziegler .10 .05
❑ 297 Jerry Zuurmond .10 .05
❑ 298 Alain Ayer .10 .05
❑ 299 Andre Baumann .10 .05
❑ 300 Warren Bruetsch .10 .05
❑ 301 Pascal Faeh .10 .05
❑ 302 Roman Furrer .10 .05
❑ 303 Marco Hagmann .10 .05
❑ 304 Dominik Jenny .10 .05
❑ 305 Mikka Mieminen .10 .05
❑ 306 Fabio Obrist .10 .05
❑ 307 Thierry Paterlini .10 .05
❑ 308 Marco Schellenberg .10 .05
❑ 309 Mathias Schenkel .10 .05
❑ 310 Peter Schlagenhauf .10 .05
❑ 311 Markus Studer .10 .05
❑ 312 Thomas Ziegler .10 .05
❑ 313 Thurgau .10 .05
❑ 314 Thurgau .10 .05
❑ 315 Mike McParland CO .10 .05
❑ 316 Fritz Lanz ACO .10 .05
❑ 317 Roger Hugentobler .35 .16
❑ 318 Peter Martin .35 .16
❑ 319 Dominik Schmid .20 .09
❑ 320 Andrea Baumgartner .10 .05
❑ 321 Nicolas Goumaz .10 .05
❑ 322 Martin Granicher .10 .05
❑ 323 Ralph Ott .10 .05
❑ 324 Henry Patrick .10 .05
❑ 325 Mike Posma .10 .05
❑ 326 Marcel Schmid .10 .05
❑ 327 Robert Wiesmann .10 .05
❑ 328 Dan Daoust .20 .09
❑ 329 Slaven Imhof .10 .05
❑ 330 Roger Keller .10 .05
❑ 331 Martin Knopfli .10 .05
❑ 332 Guido Laczko .10 .05
❑ 333 Bernhard Lauber .10 .05
❑ 334 Gery Othman .10 .05
❑ 335 Rolf Schrepfer .10 .05
❑ 336 Thomas Seitz .10 .05
❑ 337 Robert Slehofer .10 .05
❑ 338 Rene Stussi .10 .05
❑ 339 Cuno Weisser .10 .05
❑ 340 Benjamin Winkler .10 .05
❑ 341 Langnau .10 .05
❑ 342 Langnau .10 .05
❑ 343 Paul Andre Cadieux CO .10 .05
❑ 344 Jakob Kolliker ACO .10 .05
❑ 345 Thomas Dreier .35 .16
❑ 346 Toni Koller .35 .16
❑ 347 Daniel Aegerter .10 .05
❑ 348 Raoul Baumgartner .10 .05
❑ 349 Andreas Beutler .10 .05
❑ 350 Urs Hirschi .10 .05
❑ 351 Stefan Probst .10 .05
❑ 352 Raphael Schneider .10 .05
❑ 353 Pascal Stoller .10 .05
❑ 354 Rolf Badertscher .10 .05
❑ 355 Peter Bartschi .10 .05
❑ 356 Beat Friedrich .10 .05
❑ 357 Walter Gerber .10 .05
❑ 358 Kelly Glowa .10 .05
❑ 359 Alan Hirschi .10 .05
❑ 360 Markus Hirschi .10 .05
❑ 361 Gregor Horak .10 .05
❑ 362 Lane Lambert .20 .09
❑ 363 Beat Nuspliger .10 .05
❑ 364 Stefan Tschiemer .10 .05
❑ 365 Chaux De Fonds .10 .05
❑ 366 Chaux De Fonds .10 .05
❑ 367 Riccardo Fuhrer CO .10 .05
❑ 368 Roland Meyer .35 .16
❑ 369 Jean-Luc Schnegg .35 .16
❑ 370 Eric Bourquin .10 .05
❑ 371 Daniel Dubois .10 .05
❑ 372 Andres Egger .10 .05
❑ 373 Daniel Elsener .10 .05
❑ 374 Thierry Murisier .10 .05
❑ 375 Daniel Ott .10 .05
❑ 376 Jorg Reber .10 .05
❑ 377 Valeri Chiriaev .10 .05
❑ 378 Michele Bizzozero .10 .05
❑ 379 Philippe Bozon .20 .09
❑ 380 Jean-Marc Brunner .10 .05
❑ 381 Florian Chappot .10 .05
❑ 382 Gilles Dubois .10 .05
❑ 383 Willy Kohler .10 .05
❑ 384 Boris Leimgruber .10 .05
❑ 385 Patrick Oppliger .10 .05
❑ 386 Benoit Pont .10 .05
❑ 387 Laurent Stehlin .10 .05
❑ 388 Olivier Wuthrich .10 .05
❑ 389 Herisau .10 .05
❑ 390 Herisau .10 .05
❑ 391 Mark McGregor CO .10 .05
❑ 392 Reto Roveda ACO .10 .05
❑ 393 Michael Habig .35 .16
❑ 394 Ronald Rueger .35 .16
❑ 395 Urs Balzarek .10 .05
❑ 396 Thomas Derungs .10 .05
❑ 397 Damian Freitag .10 .05
❑ 398 Roland Habisreutinger .10 .05
❑ 399 Marco Knecht .10 .05
❑ 400 Kari Knopf .10 .05
❑ 401 Andy Maag .10 .05
❑ 402 Krister Cantoni .10 .05
❑ 403 Rico Enzler .10 .05
❑ 404 John Fust .10 .05
❑ 405 Remo Gastaldo .10 .05
❑ 406 Reto German .10 .05
❑ 407 Frank Guay .10 .05
❑ 408 Daniel Knecht .10 .05
❑ 409 Andy Krapf .10 .05
❑ 410 Roger Nater .10 .05
❑ 411 Marco Tanner .10 .05
❑ 412 Claude Vilgrain .25 .11
❑ 413 Chur .10 .05
❑ 414 Chur .10 .05

| | | |
|---|---|---|
| ❑ 415 Juri Voshakov CO | .10 | .05 |
| ❑ 416 Thomas Liesch | .35 | .16 |
| ❑ 417 Reto Zuccolini | .35 | .16 |
| ❑ 418 Sacha Bleiker | .10 | .05 |
| ❑ 419 Patrick Fischer | .10 | .05 |
| ❑ 420 Bruno Habisreutinger | .10 | .05 |
| ❑ 421 Jurg Hardegger | .10 | .05 |
| ❑ 422 Dominic Meier | .10 | .05 |
| ❑ 423 Loris Papa | .10 | .05 |
| ❑ 424 Robert Papp | .10 | .05 |
| ❑ 425 Valery Belov | .10 | .05 |
| ❑ 426 Valery Chorny | .10 | .05 |
| ❑ 427 Miguel Fondado | .10 | .05 |
| ❑ 428 Oliver Gazzaroli | .10 | .05 |
| ❑ 429 Claudio Krattli | .10 | .05 |
| ❑ 430 Claudio Peer | .10 | .05 |
| ❑ 431 Michael Putzi | .10 | .05 |
| ❑ 432 Roger Rieder | .10 | .05 |
| ❑ 433 Riccardo Signorell | .10 | .05 |
| ❑ 434 Peter Thoma | .10 | .05 |
| ❑ 435 Patrick Werthan | .10 | .05 |
| ❑ 436 Olten | .10 | .05 |
| ❑ 437 Olten | .10 | .05 |
| ❑ 438 Milan Mrukvia ACO | .10 | .05 |
| ❑ 439 Beat Aebischer | .35 | .16 |
| ❑ 440 Thierry Loup | .35 | .16 |
| ❑ 441 Ralph Gugelmann | .10 | .05 |
| ❑ 442 Roland Ruedi | .10 | .05 |
| ❑ 443 Andre Schneeberger | .10 | .05 |
| ❑ 444 Richard Stucki | .10 | .05 |
| ❑ 445 Thomas Studer | .10 | .05 |
| ❑ 446 Ville Siren | .20 | .09 |
| ❑ 447 Pius Weber | .10 | .05 |
| ❑ 448 Rene Ackermann | .10 | .05 |
| ❑ 449 Lars Aebi | .10 | .05 |
| ❑ 450 Andreas Fischer | .10 | .05 |
| ❑ 451 Marcel Franzi | .10 | .05 |
| ❑ 452 Paul Gagne | .20 | .09 |
| ❑ 453 Stephane Gasser | .10 | .05 |
| ❑ 454 Pirmin Keller | .10 | .05 |
| ❑ 455 Claude Luthi | .10 | .05 |
| ❑ 456 Patrick Siegwart | .10 | .05 |
| ❑ 457 Patrik Traber | .10 | .05 |
| ❑ 458 Andre Van Rohr | .10 | .05 |
| ❑ 459 HCM | .10 | .05 |
| ❑ 460 Kent Ruhnke CO | .10 | .05 |
| ❑ 461 Patrick Grand | .35 | .16 |
| ❑ 462 Didier Tosi | .35 | .16 |
| ❑ 463 Pascal Avanthay | .10 | .05 |
| ❑ 464 Bernard Bauer | .10 | .05 |
| ❑ 465 Ayocholos Escher | .10 | .05 |
| ❑ 466 Thierry Evequoz | .10 | .05 |
| ❑ 467 David Jelmini | .10 | .05 |
| ❑ 468 Xavier Kappeler | .10 | .05 |
| ❑ 469 Patrik Neukom | .10 | .05 |
| ❑ 470 Pierr-Alain Ancay | .10 | .05 |
| ❑ 471 Florian Andenmatten | .10 | .05 |
| ❑ 472 J-Daniel Bonito | .10 | .05 |
| ❑ 473 Alain Darbellay | .10 | .05 |
| ❑ 474 Olivier Ecoeur | .10 | .05 |
| ❑ 475 Igor Fedulov | .10 | .05 |
| ❑ 476 Nicolas Gastaldo | .10 | .05 |
| ❑ 477 Thierry Moret | .10 | .05 |
| ❑ 478 Stephan Nussberger | .10 | .05 |
| ❑ 479 Achim Pleschberger | .10 | .05 |
| ❑ 480 Petr Rosol | .20 | .09 |
| ❑ 481 Fabrizio Silietti | .10 | .05 |
| ❑ 482 Yannick Theler | .10 | .05 |
| ❑ 483 Geneve | .10 | .05 |
| ❑ 484 Geneve | .10 | .05 |
| ❑ 485 Francois Huppe CO | .10 | .05 |
| ❑ 486 Gary Shennan ACO | .10 | .05 |
| ❑ 487 Jean-Philippe Challande | .35 | .16 |
| ❑ 488 Jerome Hagmann | .35 | .16 |
| ❑ 489 Claude Cienciala | .10 | .05 |
| ❑ 490 Chris Felix | .20 | .09 |
| ❑ 491 Romain Fleury | .10 | .05 |
| ❑ 492 Daniel Herlea | .10 | .05 |
| ❑ 493 Camille Meylan | .10 | .05 |
| ❑ 494 Toni Nelli | .10 | .05 |
| ❑ 495 Christian Serena | .10 | .05 |
| ❑ 496 David Leibzig | .10 | .05 |
| ❑ 497 Antoine Cloux | .10 | .05 |
| ❑ 498 Nicolas Corthay | .10 | .05 |
| ❑ 499 Marc Hinni | .10 | .05 |
| ❑ 500 Olivier Honsberger | .10 | .05 |
| ❑ 501 Gael Kertudo | .10 | .05 |
| ❑ 502 Jorg Ledermann | .10 | .05 |
| ❑ 503 Andrew McKim | .25 | .11 |
| ❑ 504 Benjamin Muller | .10 | .05 |
| ❑ 505 Martin Stastny | .10 | .05 |
| ❑ 506 Michel Wicky | .10 | .05 |
| ❑ 507 Schwiezer (Nat'l Team) | .25 | .11 |
| ❑ 508 C. Weber/J. Eberle | .50 | .23 |
| ❑ 509 J.J Aeschlimann/T.Vrabac | .35 | .16 |
| ❑ 510 S.Bertaggia/L.Weibel | .50 | .23 |
| ❑ 511 Lars Weibel | .75 | .35 |
| ❑ 512 Tommy Sjodin | .25 | .11 |
| ❑ 513 Andrei Khomutov | .75 | .35 |
| ❑ 514 Lars Weibel | .75 | .35 |
| ❑ 515 Anders Eldebrink | .25 | .11 |
| ❑ 516 Ken Yaremchuk | .35 | .16 |
| ❑ 517 Reto Pavoni | .50 | .23 |
| ❑ 518 Dino Kessler | .15 | .07 |
| ❑ 519 Fausto Mazzoleni | .15 | .07 |
| ❑ 520 Andy Ton | .15 | .07 |
| ❑ 521 Dan Hodgson | .35 | .16 |
| ❑ 522 Roman Wager | .15 | .07 |
| ❑ 523 Reto Pavoni | .50 | .23 |
| ❑ 524 Reijo Ruotsalainen | .35 | .16 |
| ❑ 525 Tommy Sjodin | .25 | .11 |
| ❑ 526 Andrei Kvartalnov | .15 | .07 |
| ❑ 527 Mikael Johansson | .15 | .07 |
| ❑ 528 Ken Yaremchuk | .35 | .16 |
| ❑ 529 Reto Pavoni | .50 | .23 |
| ❑ 530 Dino Kessler | .15 | .07 |
| ❑ 531 Marco Bayer | .15 | .07 |
| ❑ 532 Misko Antisin | .15 | .07 |
| ❑ 533 Sacha Ochsner | .15 | .07 |
| ❑ 534 Roman Wager | .15 | .07 |
| ❑ 535 Reto Pavoni | .50 | .23 |
| ❑ 536 Reijo Ruotsalainen | .35 | .16 |
| ❑ 537 Andreas Eldebrink | .20 | .09 |
| ❑ 538 Ken Yaremchuk | .35 | .16 |
| ❑ 539 Mikael Johansson | .15 | .07 |
| ❑ 540 Tom Fergus | .50 | .23 |
| ❑ 541 Dan Quinn | .50 | .23 |
| ❑ 542 Valeri Kamenski | 4.00 | 1.80 |
| ❑ 543 Phil Housley | 2.00 | .90 |
| ❑ 544 Chris Chelios | 15.00 | 6.75 |
| ❑ 545 Doug Gilmour | 15.00 | 6.75 |
| ❑ NNO Beat Eichmann | .10 | .05 |
| ❑ NNO Reto Bertolotti | .10 | .05 |
| ❑ NNO Roland Stalder | .10 | .05 |
| ❑ NNO Danny Kurmann | .10 | .05 |

## 1993 Hockey American

This 12-piece set was issued by Cincinnati-based Kenner Toy Company. It was the first line for the National Hockey League. The statues feature top hockey stars in action poses and are accompanied by two cards of each player. The regular card front has either a posed or action color shot. The back has biographical and statistical information. The front feature either a posed or action color shot. The back features a paragraph about the accomplishments of that player. The Grant Fuhr piece was the only one not included in the Candian set.

| | MINT | NRMT |
|---|---|---|
| COMP.SET (12) | 500.00 | 375.00 |
| ❑ Ed Belfour | 120.00 | 90.00 |
| ❑ Ray Bourque | 20.00 | 15.00 |
| ❑ Grant Fuhr | 140.00 | 105.00 |
| ❑ Brett Hull | 12.00 | 9.00 |
| ❑ Jaromir Jagr | 30.00 | 22.00 |
| ❑ Pat LaFontaine | 70.00 | 52.50 |
| ❑ Mario Lemieux | 30.00 | 22.00 |
| ❑ Eric Lindros | 35.00 | 26.00 |
| ❑ Mark Messier | 30.00 | 22.00 |
| ❑ Jeremy Roenick | 20.00 | 15.00 |
| ❑ Patrick Roy | 90.00 | 70.00 |
| ❑ Steve Yzerman | 20.00 | 15.00 |

## 1993 Hockey Canadian

This 11-piece set was issued by Cincinnati-based Kenner Toy Company. It was the first line for the National Hockey League. The statues feature top hockey stars in action poses and are accompanied by two cards of each player. The regular card front has either a posed or action color shot. The back has biographical and statistical information. The front feature either a posed or action color shot. The back features a paragraph about the accomplishments of that player. The Grant Fuhr piece was the only one not included in the Candian set that was contained in the American set.

| | MINT | NRMT |
|---|---|---|
| COMP.SET (11) | 250.00 | 190.00 |
| ❑ Ed Belfour | 60.00 | 45.00 |
| ❑ Ray Bourque | 18.00 | 13.50 |
| ❑ Brett Hull | 12.00 | 9.00 |
| ❑ Jaromir Jagr | 25.00 | 19.00 |
| ❑ Pat LaFontaine | 40.00 | 30.00 |
| ❑ Mario Lemieux | 18.00 | 13.50 |
| ❑ Eric Lindros | 30.00 | 22.00 |
| ❑ Mark Messier | 25.00 | 19.00 |
| ❑ Jeremy Roenick | 18.00 | 13.50 |
| ❑ Patrick Roy | 70.00 | 52.50 |
| ❑ Steve Yzerman | 18.00 | 13.50 |

## 1994 Hockey American

This 20-piece set was issued by Cincinnati-based Kenner Toy Company. The statues feature top hockey stars in action poses and are accompanied by a card of each player. The regular card front has either a posed or action color shot. The back has biographical and statistical information. The front feature either a posed or action color shot. The back features a paragraph about the accomplishments of that player. Notable first pieces in this set include Tom Barrasso, Arturs Irbe and Mike Richter.

| | MINT | NRMT |
|---|---|---|
| COMP.SET (20) | 350.00 | 160.00 |
| ❑ Tom Barrasso FP | 30.00 | 13.50 |
| ❑ Ray Bourque | 24.00 | 11.00 |
| ❑ Pavel Bure FP | 18.00 | 8.00 |
| ❑ Sergei Fedorov FP | 15.00 | 6.75 |
| ❑ Doug Gilmour FP | 12.00 | 5.50 |
| ❑ Brett Hull | 12.00 | 5.50 |
| ❑ Arturs Irbe FP | 30.00 | 13.50 |
| ❑ Jaromir Jagr | 20.00 | 9.00 |
| ❑ Pat LaFontaine | 14.00 | 6.25 |
| ❑ Brian Leetch FP | 18.00 | 8.00 |
| ❑ Mario Lemieux | 18.00 | 8.00 |
| ❑ Eric Lindros | 25.00 | 11.00 |
| ❑ Mark Messier | 50.00 | 22.00 |
| ❑ Alexander Mogilny FP | 15.00 | 6.75 |
| ❑ Adam Oates FP | 15.00 | 6.75 |
| ❑ Mike Richter FP | 25.00 | 11.00 |
| ❑ Luc Robitaille FP | 25.00 | 11.00 |
| ❑ Jeremy Roenick | 20.00 | 9.00 |
| ❑ Teemu Selanne FP | 20.00 | 9.00 |
| ❑ Steve Yzerman | 15.00 | 6.75 |

## 1994 Hockey Canadian

This 13-piece set was issued by Cincinnati-based Kenner Toy Company. The statues feature top hockey stars in action poses and are accompanied by a card of each player. The regular card front has either a posed or action color shot. The back has biographical and statistical information. The front feature either a posed or action color shot. The back features a paragraph about the accomplishments of that player. Notable first pieces in this set include Mike Richter. The Grant Fuhr piece was a particular hot item that was only included in the Canadian release.

| | MINT | NRMT |
|---|---|---|
| COMP.SET (13) | 225.00 | 100.00 |
| ❑ Pavel Bure FP | 15.00 | 6.75 |
| ❑ Sergei Fedorov FP | 15.00 | 6.75 |
| ❑ Grant Fuhr | 75.00 | 34.00 |
| ❑ Doug Gilmour FP | 12.00 | 5.50 |
| ❑ Brian Leetch FP | 20.00 | 9.00 |
| ❑ Mario Lemieux | 12.00 | 5.50 |
| ❑ Eric Lindros | 15.00 | 6.75 |
| ❑ Alexander Mogilny FP | 12.00 | 5.50 |
| ❑ Adam Oates FP | 12.00 | 5.50 |
| ❑ Mike Richter FP | 25.00 | 11.00 |
| ❑ Luc Robitaille FP | 18.00 | 8.00 |
| ❑ Teemu Selanne FP | 18.00 | 8.00 |
| ❑ Steve Yzerman | 14.00 | 6.25 |

## 1995 Hockey American

This 19-piece set was issued by Cincinnati-based Kenner Toy Company. The statues feature top hockey stars in action poses and are accompanied by a card of each player. The regular card front has either a posed or action color shot. The back has biographical and statistical information. The front feature either a posed or action color shot. The back features a paragraph about the accomplishments of that player. Notable first pieces in this set include Martin Brodeur, Dominik Hasek and Felix Potvin.

| | MINT | NRMT |
|---|---|---|
| COMP.SET (19) | 200.00 | 90.00 |
| ❑ Rob Blake FP | 12.00 | 5.50 |
| ❑ Martin Brodeur FP | 30.00 | 13.50 |
| ❑ Pavel Bure | 15.00 | 6.75 |
| ❑ Chris Chelios FP | 10.00 | 4.50 |
| ❑ Bob Corkum FP | 10.00 | 4.50 |
| ❑ Sergei Fedorov | 10.00 | 4.50 |
| ❑ Theo Fleury FP | 12.00 | 5.50 |
| ❑ Adam Graves FP | 12.00 | 5.50 |
| ❑ Dominik Hasek FP | 35.00 | 16.00 |
| ❑ Brett Hull | 12.00 | 5.50 |
| ❑ Mike Modano FP | 15.00 | 6.75 |
| ❑ Kirk Muller FP | 10.00 | 4.50 |
| ❑ Cam Neely FP | 12.00 | 5.50 |
| ❑ Sandis Ozolinsh FP | 12.00 | 5.50 |
| ❑ Felix Potvin FP | 25.00 | 11.00 |
| ❑ Luc Robitaille | 12.00 | 5.50 |
| ❑ Brendan Shanahan FP | 14.00 | 6.25 |
| ❑ Scott Stevens FP | 10.00 | 4.50 |
| ❑ Pierre Turgeon FP | 10.00 | 4.50 |

## 1995 Hockey Canadian

This 13-piece set was issued by Cincinnati-based Kenner Toy Company. The statues feature top hockey stars in action poses and are accompanied by a card of each player. The regular card front has either a posed or action color shot. The back has biographical and statistical information. The front feature either a posed or action color shot. The back features a paragraph about the accomplishments of that player. Notable first pieces in this set include Martin Brodeur, Dominik Hasek and Felix Potvin.

| | MINT | NRMT |
|---|---|---|
| COMP.SET (13) | 175.00 | 80.00 |
| ❑ Tom Barrasso | 25.00 | 11.00 |
| ❑ Rob Blake FP | 12.00 | 5.50 |
| ❑ Martin Brodeur FP | 25.00 | 11.00 |
| ❑ Chris Chelios FP | 10.00 | 4.50 |
| ❑ Theo Fleury FP | 12.00 | 5.50 |
| ❑ Adam Graves FP | 10.00 | 4.50 |
| ❑ Dominik Hasek FP | 30.00 | 13.50 |
| ❑ Arturs Irbe | 25.00 | 11.00 |
| ❑ Mike Modano FP | 12.00 | 5.50 |
| ❑ Cam Neely FP | 12.00 | 5.50 |
| ❑ Felix Potvin FP | 25.00 | 11.00 |
| ❑ Brendan Shanahan FP | 14.00 | 6.25 |
| ❑ Scott Stevens FP | 10.00 | 4.50 |

## 1996 Hockey American

This 22-piece set was issued by Cincinnati-based Kenner Toy Company. The statues feature top hockey stars in action poses and are accompanied by a card of each player. The regular card front has either a posed or action color shot. The back has biographical and statistical information. The front feature either a posed or action color shot. The back features a paragraph about the accomplishments of that player. Notable first pieces in this set include Jim Carey, Paul Kariya and Joe Sakic. The Tom Barrasso and Pat LaFontaine Hill's special pieces are not included in the complete set price.

| | MINT | NRMT |
|---|---|---|
| COMP.SET (22) | 275.00 | 125.00 |
| ❑ Tom Barrasso | 18.00 | 8.00 |
| Hills Special | | |
| ❑ Brian Bradley FP | 12.00 | 5.50 |
| ❑ Jim Carey FP | 20.00 | 9.00 |
| ❑ Paul Coffey FP | 14.00 | 6.25 |
| ❑ Sergei Fedorov | 12.00 | 5.50 |
| ❑ Ron Francis FP | 12.00 | 5.50 |
| ❑ Dominik Hasek | 30.00 | 13.50 |
| ❑ Paul Kariya FP | 20.00 | 9.00 |
| ❑ Pat LaFontaine | 18.00 | 8.00 |
| Hills Special | | |
| ❑ John LeClair FP | 15.00 | 6.75 |
| ❑ Brian Leetch | 12.00 | 5.50 |
| ❑ Eric Lindros | 18.00 | 8.00 |
| ❑ Al MacInnis FP | 12.00 | 5.50 |
| ❑ Scott Mellanby FP | 14.00 | 6.25 |
| ❑ Mark Messier | 15.00 | 6.75 |
| ❑ Mike Modano | 14.00 | 6.25 |
| ❑ Adam Oates | 12.00 | 5.50 |
| ❑ Mikael Renberg FP | 12.00 | 5.50 |
| ❑ Stephane Richer FP | 10.00 | 4.50 |
| ❑ Jeremy Roenick | 14.00 | 6.25 |
| ❑ Patrick Roy | 50.00 | 22.00 |
| ❑ Joe Sakic FP | 20.00 | 9.00 |
| ❑ Brendan Shanahan | 14.00 | 6.25 |
| ❑ Mats Sundin FP | 14.00 | 6.25 |

## 1996 Hockey Canadian

This 15-piece set was issued by Cincinnati-based Kenner Toy Company. The statues feature top hockey stars in action poses and are accompanied by a card of each player. The regular card front has either a posed or action color shot. The back has biographical and statistical information. The front feature either a posed or action color shot. The back features a paragraph about the accomplishments of that player. Notable first pieces in this set include Jim Carey, Paul Kariya and Joe Sakic.

| | MINT | NRMT |
|---|---|---|
| COMP.SET (15) | 225.00 | 100.00 |
| ❑ Brian Bradley FP | 12.00 | 5.50 |
| ❑ Jim Carey FP | 20.00 | 9.00 |
| ❑ Sergei Fedorov | 12.00 | 5.50 |
| ❑ Ron Francis FP | 12.00 | 5.50 |
| ❑ Paul Kariya FP | 20.00 | 9.00 |
| ❑ John LeClair FP | 15.00 | 6.75 |
| ❑ Brian Leetch | 12.00 | 5.50 |
| ❑ Eric Lindros | 18.00 | 8.00 |
| ❑ Al MacInnis FP | 12.00 | 5.50 |
| ❑ Scott Mellanby FP | 12.00 | 5.50 |
| ❑ Mark Messier | 15.00 | 6.75 |
| ❑ Mikael Renberg FP | 15.00 | 6.75 |
| ❑ Patrick Roy | 50.00 | 22.00 |
| ❑ Joe Sakic FP | 20.00 | 9.00 |
| ❑ Mats Sundin FP | 14.00 | 6.25 |

## 1997 Hockey American

This 21-piece set was issued by Cincinnati-based Kenner Toy Company. The statues feature top hockey stars in action poses and are accompanied by a card of each player. The regular card front has either a posed or action color shot. The back has biographical and statistical information. The front feature either a posed or action color shot. The pieces were distributed in two assortments. The Paul Coffey BOSCOV and Patrick LaLime Pittsburgh Store specials are not included in the complete set price.

| | MINT | NRMT |
|---|---|---|
| COMP.SET (19) | 200.00 | 90.00 |
| ❑ Daniel Alfredsson FP | 10.00 | 4.50 |
| ❑ Jason Arnott FP | 10.00 | 4.50 |
| ❑ Peter Bondra FP | 15.00 | 6.75 |
| ❑ Martin Brodeur | 20.00 | 9.00 |
| ❑ Paul Coffey | 18.00 | 8.00 |
| BOSCOV Special | | |
| ❑ Chris Chelios | 10.00 | 4.50 |
| ❑ Peter Forsberg FP | 18.00 | 8.00 |
| ❑ Wayne Gretzky FP | 30.00 | 13.50 |
| ❑ Ron Hextall FP | 15.00 | 6.75 |
| ❑ Jaromir Jagr | 15.00 | 6.75 |
| ❑ Patrick LaLime | 20.00 | 9.00 |
| Pittsburgh Special | | |
| ❑ Eric Lindros | 15.00 | 6.75 |
| ❑ Mark Messier | 15.00 | 6.75 |
| ❑ Chris Osgood FP | 15.00 | 6.75 |
| ❑ Sandis Ozolinsh | 10.00 | 4.50 |
| ❑ Zigmund Palffy FP | 10.00 | 4.50 |
| ❑ Darren Puppa FP | 20.00 | 9.00 |
| ❑ Mark Recchi FP | 12.00 | 5.50 |
| ❑ Teemu Selanne | 12.00 | 5.50 |
| ❑ Keith Tkachuk FP | 12.00 | 5.50 |
| ❑ John Vanbiesbrouck FP | 15.00 | 6.75 |

## 1997 Hockey Canadian

| | MINT | NRMT |
|---|---|---|
| ❑ Daniel Alfredsson FP | 10.00 | 4.50 |
| ❑ Jason Arnott FP | 10.00 | 4.50 |
| ❑ Peter Bondra FP | 15.00 | 6.75 |
| ❑ Martin Brodeur | 20.00 | 9.00 |
| ❑ Chris Chelios | 10.00 | 4.50 |
| ❑ Peter Forsberg FP | 18.00 | 8.00 |
| ❑ Wayne Gretzky FP | 30.00 | 13.50 |
| ❑ Ron Hextall FP | 12.00 | 5.50 |
| ❑ Jaromir Jagr | 15.00 | 6.75 |
| ❑ Eric Lindros | 15.00 | 6.75 |
| ❑ Mark Messier | 15.00 | 6.75 |
| ❑ Chris Osgood FP | 15.00 | 6.75 |
| ❑ Sandis Ozolinsh | 10.00 | 4.50 |
| ❑ Zigmund Palffy FP | 10.00 | 4.50 |

| | MINT | NRMT |
|---|---|---|
| ❑ Darren Puppa FP | 20.00 | 9.00 |
| ❑ Mark Recchi FP | 12.00 | 5.50 |
| ❑ Teemu Selanne | 12.00 | 5.50 |
| ❑ Keith Tkachuk FP | 12.00 | 5.50 |
| ❑ J.Vanbiesbrouck FP | 15.00 | 6.75 |

## 1997 Hockey One on One

This seven combo figure set was produced in two assortments and had a suggested retail price of $19.99. The package features either one goalie and one player shooting with a net or two non-goalie players in a face-off action pose. Players are attached to a new base, which is designed to look like ice.

| | MINT | NRMT |
|---|---|---|
| COMP.SET (7) | 225.00 | 100.00 |
| ❑ Wayne Gretzky | 90.00 | 40.00 |
| Dominik Hasek | | |
| ❑ Jaromir Jagr | 30.00 | 13.50 |
| Patrick Roy | | |
| ❑ Eric Lindros | 30.00 | 13.50 |
| Paul Kariya | | |
| ❑ Owen Nolan | 30.00 | 13.50 |
| Chris Osgood | | |
| ❑ Jeremy Roenick | 30.00 | 13.50 |
| Steve Yzerman | | |
| ❑ Joe Sakic | 30.00 | 13.50 |
| Mike Richter | | |
| ❑ Mats Sundin | 30.00 | 13.50 |
| Ray Bourque | | |

## 1998 Hockey

The 1998 version was produced by the Cincinnati based Kenner Corporation. This set features 23 pieces that were available in three different assortments. Key first pieces include Tony Amonte, Brian Berard, Jim Campbell, Vincent Damphousse, Kirk McLean, Rob Neidermayer, Joe Thornton and Alexei Yashin. Prices below refer to in-package pieces.

| | MINT | NRMT |
|---|---|---|
| COMPLETE SET (23) | 250.00 | 110.00 |
| ❑ Tony Amonte FP | 15.00 | 6.75 |
| ❑ Ed Belfour | 15.00 | 6.75 |
| ❑ Brian Berard FP | 15.00 | 6.75 |
| ❑ Peter Bondra EXT | 12.00 | 5.50 |
| ❑ Martin Brodeur | 20.00 | 9.00 |
| ❑ Jim Campbell FP | 12.00 | 5.50 |
| ❑ Vincent Damphousse FP | 12.00 | 5.50 |
| ❑ Theo Fleury EXT | 12.00 | 5.50 |
| ❑ Grant Fuhr EXT | 15.00 | 6.75 |
| ❑ Doug Gilmour EXT | 12.00 | 5.50 |
| ❑ Wayne Gretzky | 20.00 | 9.00 |
| ❑ Wayne Gretzky Cup | 25.00 | 11.00 |
| ❑ Dominik Hasek | 18.00 | 8.00 |
| ❑ Jaromir Jagr | 12.00 | 5.50 |
| ❑ Paul Kariya | 12.00 | 5.50 |
| ❑ Trevor Kidd EXT | 15.00 | 6.75 |
| ❑ N.Khabibulin FP EXT | 15.00 | 6.75 |
| ❑ Olaf Kolzig FP EXT | 15.00 | 6.75 |

| | MINT | NRMT |
|---|---|---|
| ❑ Brian Leetch | 12.00 | 5.50 |
| ❑ Eric Lindros | 12.00 | 5.50 |
| ❑ Kirk McLean FP | 20.00 | 9.00 |
| ❑ Mark Messier | 10.00 | 4.50 |
| ❑ Rob Neidermayer FP | 12.00 | 5.50 |
| ❑ Chris Osgood | 14.00 | 6.25 |
| ❑ Felix Potvin | 15.00 | 6.75 |
| ❑ Darin Puppa FP EXT | 15.00 | 6.75 |
| ❑ Jeremy Roenick | 15.00 | 6.75 |
| ❑ Patrick Roy | 20.00 | 9.00 |
| ❑ Joe Sakic | | |
| ❑ B.Shanahan EXT | 18.00 | 8.00 |
| ❑ Joe Thornton FP | 15.00 | 6.75 |
| ❑ J.Vanbiesbrouck EXT | 15.00 | 6.75 |
| ❑ Alexei Yashin FP | 15.00 | 6.75 |
| ❑ Steve Yzerman Cup | 25.00 | 11.00 |

## 1998 Hockey 12" Figures

| | MINT | NRMT |
|---|---|---|
| COMPLETE SET (3) | 80.00 | 36.00 |
| ❑ Wayne Gretzky | 40.00 | 18.00 |
| ❑ Mario Lemieux | 30.00 | 13.50 |
| ❑ Bobby Orr | 30.00 | 13.50 |

## 1998 Hockey Classic Doubles

Released for the first year by Kenner, this 5-piece set focuses on some of the better teammates from the NHL. The pieces were distributed in one assortment. The prices below refer to in-package pieces.

| | MINT | NRMT |
|---|---|---|
| COMPLETE SET (5) | 110.00 | 50.00 |
| ❑ M.Brodeur/S.Stevens | 25.00 | 11.00 |
| ❑ S.Fedorov/M.Vernon | 25.00 | 11.00 |
| ❑ W.Gretzky/M.Messier | 35.00 | 16.00 |
| ❑ J.Jagr/T.Barrasso | 25.00 | 11.00 |
| ❑ P.Roy/J.LeClair | 25.00 | 11.00 |

## 1998 Hockey One on One

Released for the second year by Kenner, this six-piece set features top players from the NHL matched up against each other on "ice". The pieces were distributed in two assortments. Prices below refer to in-package pieces.

| | MINT | NRMT |
|---|---|---|
| COMPLETE SET (6) | 125.00 | 55.00 |
| ❑ W.Gretzky/P.Bure | 30.00 | 13.50 |
| ❑ E.Lindros/A.Moog | 25.00 | 11.00 |
| ❑ M.Messier/S.Ozolinsh | 25.00 | 11.00 |
| ❑ M.Modano/M.Vernon | 20.00 | 9.00 |
| ❑ B.Shanahan/Hackett | 20.00 | 9.00 |
| ❑ K.Tkachuk/J.LeClair | 25.00 | 11.00 |

## 1999 Hockey

| | MINT | NRMT |
|---|---|---|
| COMPLETE SET (17) | | |
| ❑ Mike Dunham FP | | |
| ❑ Peter Forsberg | | |
| ❑ Wayne Gretzky | | |
| ❑ Jeff Hackett FP | | |
| ❑ Dominik Hasek | | |
| ❑ Jaromir Jagr | | |
| ❑ Curtis Joseph FP | | |
| ❑ Paul Kariya | | |
| ❑ Nicolai Khabibulin | | |
| ❑ Olaf Kolzig | | |
| ❑ Nicklas Lidstrom FP | | |
| ❑ Eric Lindros | | |
| ❑ Mike Modano | | |

| | MINT | NRMT |
|---|---|---|
| ❑ Keith Primeau FP | | |
| ❑ Chris Pronger FP | | |
| ❑ Sergei Samsonov FP | | |
| ❑ Steve Yzerman | | |

## 1999 Hockey 12" Figures

| | MINT | NRMT |
|---|---|---|
| COMPLETE SET (6) | | |
| ❑ Wayne Gretzky | | |
| ❑ Dominik Hasek | | |
| ❑ Jaromir Jagr | | |
| ❑ Mark Messier | | |
| ❑ Chris Osgood | | |
| ❑ Patrick Roy | | |

## 1999 Hockey Classic Doubles

| | MINT | NRMT |
|---|---|---|
| COMPLETE SET (4) | | |
| ❑ G.Fuhr/W.Gretzky | | |
| ❑ M.Messier/M.Richter | | |
| ❑ J.Sakic/P.Roy | | |
| ❑ S.Yzerman/C.Osgood | | |

## 1999 Hockey One on One

| | MINT | NRMT |
|---|---|---|
| ❑ B.Hull/W.Gretzky | | |
| ❑ C.Joseph/C.Chelios | | |
| ❑ O.Kolzig/A.Yashin | | |

## Kenner Club Pieces

❑ Mario Lemieux SEPT

## 1995 Timeless Legends

| | | |
|---|---|---|
| ❑ Gordie Howe | 12.00 | 5.50 |
| ❑ Bobby Hull | 12.00 | 5.50 |

## 1997 Timeless Legends

| | | |
|---|---|---|
| ❑ Tony Esposito | 12.00 | 5.50 |
| ❑ Maurice Richard | 12.00 | 5.50 |

## 1998 Timeless Legends

| | | |
|---|---|---|
| ❑ Mike Bossy | 12.00 | 5.50 |
| ❑ Marcel Dionne | 12.00 | 5.50 |
| ❑ Mike Eruzione | 12.00 | 5.50 |
| ❑ Glenn Hall | 12.00 | 5.50 |
| ❑ Mario Lemieux | 18.00 | 8.00 |

## 1996 Canadian Timeless Legends

| | MINT | NRMT |
|---|---|---|
| COMP.SET (6) | 100.00 | 45.00 |
| ❑ Jean Beliveau | 20.00 | 9.00 |
| ❑ Phil Esposito | 20.00 | 9.00 |
| ❑ Tony Esposito | 20.00 | 9.00 |
| ❑ Gordie Howe | 20.00 | 9.00 |
| ❑ Bobby Hull | 20.00 | 9.00 |
| ❑ Maurice Richard | 20.00 | 9.00 |

## 1997 Canadian Timeless Legends

This set of six figures was produced in one assortment.

| | MINT | NRMT |
|---|---|---|
| COMP.SET (6) | 100.00 | 45.00 |

| | | |
|---|---|---|
| ❑ Jean Beliveau | 20.00 | 9.00 |
| ❑ Mike Bossy | 20.00 | 9.00 |
| ❑ Marcel Dionne | 20.00 | 9.00 |
| ❑ Phil Esposito | 20.00 | 9.00 |
| ❑ Glenn Hall | 20.00 | 9.00 |
| ❑ Bernie Parent | 20.00 | 9.00 |

## 1998 Canadian Timeless Legends

Released for the third year by Kenner, this set features some of the best players from Canada. This five-piece set was released in one assortment. Prices below refer to in-package pieces.

| | MINT | NRMT |
|---|---|---|
| COMPLETE SET (4) | 55.00 | 25.00 |
| ❑ Mike Bossy | 15.00 | 6.75 |
| ❑ Bobby Clarke | 15.00 | 6.75 |
| ❑ Marcel Dionne | 15.00 | 6.75 |
| ❑ Glenn Hall | 15.00 | 6.75 |

## Convention/Show Pieces

❑ W.Gretzky 99 East-NOV

## 1996 Headliners Hockey

This series of figures was produced by Corinthian Marketing. Each figures stands 3 1/4" tall. Also in the blister package the pieces comes in is a "Headliners Collector's Catalog." The figures were primarily sold through mass market retail outlets at a suggested retail price of $3.99. The values listed below refer to unopened packages. The figures are unnumbered and checklisted below in alphabetical order. The set price does not include the White's Special pieces.

| | MINT | NRMT |
|---|---|---|
| COMP.SET (21) | 200.00 | 90.00 |
| ❑ Ray Bourque | 5.00 | 2.20 |
| ❑ Martin Brodeur | 8.00 | 3.60 |
| ❑ Pavel Bure | 5.00 | 2.20 |
| ❑ Chris Chelios | 5.00 | 2.20 |
| ❑ Sergei Fedorov | 5.00 | 2.20 |
| ❑ Wayne Gretzky | 12.00 | 5.50 |
| ❑ Wayne Gretzky | 20.00 | 9.00 |
| White's Special | | |
| ❑ Jaromir Jagr | 8.00 | 3.60 |
| ❑ Jaromir Jagr | 20.00 | 9.00 |
| White's Exclusive | | |
| ❑ Jari Kurri | 5.00 | 2.20 |
| ❑ Brian Leetch | 5.00 | 2.20 |
| ❑ Claude Lemieux | 5.00 | 2.20 |
| ❑ Mario Lemieux | 8.00 | 3.60 |
| ❑ Mario Lemieux | 20.00 | 9.00 |
| White's Special | | |
| ❑ Eric Lindros | 8.00 | 3.60 |
| ❑ Eric Lindros | 20.00 | 9.00 |
| White's Special | | |
| ❑ Mark Messier | 5.00 | 2.20 |
| ❑ Jeremy Roenick | 5.00 | 2.20 |
| ❑ Jeremy Roenick | 15.00 | 6.75 |
| White's Special | | |
| ❑ Patrick Roy | 12.00 | 5.50 |
| ❑ Patrick Roy | 20.00 | 9.00 |
| White's Exclusive | | |
| ❑ Joe Sakic | 5.00 | 2.20 |
| ❑ Teemu Selanne | 5.00 | 2.20 |
| ❑ Brendan Shanahan | 5.00 | 2.20 |
| ❑ Mats Sundin | 5.00 | 2.20 |
| ❑ Keith Tkachuk | 5.00 | 2.20 |

| | | |
|---|---|---|
| ❑ John Vanbiesbrouck | 5.00 | 2.20 |

## 1997 Headliners Hockey

Produced by Corinthian Marketing, this 30-figure set was fully licensed by both the NHLPA and the NHL.

| | MINT | NRMT |
|---|---|---|
| COMP.SET (30) | 150.00 | 70.00 |
| ❑ Martin Brodeur | 8.00 | 3.60 |
| ❑ Pavel Bure | 5.00 | 2.20 |
| ❑ Chris Chelios | 5.00 | 2.20 |
| ❑ Paul Coffey FP | 6.00 | 2.70 |
| ❑ Sergei Fedorov | 5.00 | 2.20 |
| ❑ Peter Forsberg FP | 6.00 | 2.70 |
| ❑ Grant Fuhr FP | 6.00 | 2.70 |
| ❑ Wayne Gretzky | 6.00 | 2.70 |
| ❑ Brett Hull FP | 8.00 | 3.60 |
| ❑ Jaromir Jagr | 6.00 | 2.70 |
| ❑ Paul Kariya FP | 6.00 | 2.70 |
| ❑ Jari Kurri | 5.00 | 2.20 |
| ❑ Pat Lafontaine FP | 5.00 | 2.20 |
| ❑ Brian Leetch | 5.00 | 2.20 |
| ❑ Claude Lemieux | 5.00 | 2.20 |
| ❑ Mario Lemieux | 6.00 | 2.70 |
| ❑ Eric Lindros | 6.00 | 2.70 |
| ❑ Mark Messier | 5.00 | 2.20 |
| ❑ Felix Potvin FP | 15.00 | 6.75 |
| ❑ Mike Richter FP | 5.00 | 2.20 |
| ❑ Jeremy Roenick | 5.00 | 2.20 |
| ❑ Patrick Roy | 8.00 | 3.60 |
| ❑ Joe Sakic | 5.00 | 2.20 |
| ❑ Teemu Selanne | 5.00 | 2.20 |
| ❑ Brendan Shanahan | 5.00 | 2.20 |
| ❑ Mats Sundin | 5.00 | 2.20 |
| ❑ Keith Tkachuk | 5.00 | 2.20 |
| ❑ Pierre Turgeon FP | 5.00 | 2.20 |
| ❑ John Vanbiesbrouck | 5.00 | 2.20 |
| ❑ Steve Yzerman FP | 5.00 | 2.20 |

## 1998 Headliners Hockey In the Crease

| | MINT | NRMT |
|---|---|---|
| COMP.SET (5) | 60.00 | 27.00 |
| ❑ Martin Brodeur | 15.00 | 6.75 |
| ❑ Grant Fuhr | 15.00 | 6.75 |
| ❑ Mike Richter | 15.00 | 6.75 |
| ❑ Patrick Roy | 15.00 | 6.75 |
| ❑ John Vanbiesbrouck | 15.00 | 6.75 |

## 1998 Headliners Hockey XL

| | MINT | NRMT |
|---|---|---|
| COMPLETE SET (8) | 60.00 | 27.00 |
| ❑ Chris Chelios | 8.00 | 3.60 |
| ❑ Brett Hull | 8.00 | 3.60 |
| ❑ Jaromir Jagr | 10.00 | 4.50 |
| ❑ Paul Kariya | 10.00 | 4.50 |
| ❑ Eric Lindros | 10.00 | 4.50 |
| ❑ Mike Richter | 8.00 | 3.60 |
| ❑ Patrick Roy | 10.00 | 4.50 |
| ❑ John Vanbiesbrouck | 8.00 | 3.60 |

# Vintage Autographs Price Guide

**Sid Abel (1969)**
3 X 5 10.00
8 X 10 Photo 20.00
Single Signed Puck 25.00

**Syl Apps Sr. (1961) d.1998**
3 X 5 75.00
8 X 10 Photo 150.00
Single Signed Puck 225.00

**George Armstrong (1975)**
3 X 5 20.00
8 X 10 Photo 75.00
Single Signed Puck 50.00

**Ace Bailey (1975) d. 1992**
3 X 5 50.00
8 X 10 Photo 200.00
Single Signed Puck 300.00

**Bill Barber (1990)**
3 X 5 5.00
8 X 10 Photo 20.00
Single Signed Puck 20.00

**Marty Barry (1965) d. 1969**
3 X 5 75.00

**Andy Bathgate (1978)**
3 X 5 10.00
8 X 10 Photo 20.00
Single Signed Puck 20.00

**Bobby Bauer (1996) d. 1964**
3 X 5 100.00

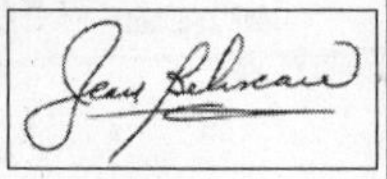

**Jean Beliveau (1972)**
3 X 5 10.00
8 X 10 Photo 20.00
Single Signed Puck 25.00

**Clint Benedict (1956) d. 1976**
3 X 5 100.00

**Doug Bentley (1964) d. 1972**
3 X 5 100.00

**Max Bentley (1966) d. 1984**
3 X 5 100.00

**Toe Blake (1966) d. 1995**
3 X 5 50.00
8 X 10 Photo 125.00

**Leo Boivin (1986)**
3 X 5 5.00
8 X 10 Photo 30.00
Single Signed Puck 30.00

**Mike Bossy (1991)**
3 X 5 10.00
8 X 10 Photo 25.00
Single Signed Puck 25.00

**Butch Bouchard (1966)**
3 X 5 20.00
8 X 10 Photo 25.00
Single Signed Puck 30.00

**Frank Boucher (1958) d. 1977**
3 X 5 100.00

**George Boucher (1960) d. 1960**
3 X 5 50.00
8 X 10 Photo 150.00

**Johnny Bower (1976)**
3 X 5 5.00
8 X 10 Photo 15.00
Single Signed Puck 20.00

**Frank Brimsek (1966)**
3 X 5 30.00
8 X 10 Photo 50.00
Single Signed Puck 75.00

**Punch Broadbent (1962) d. 1971**
3 X 5 100.00

**Turk Broda (1967) d. 1972**
3 X 5 200.00

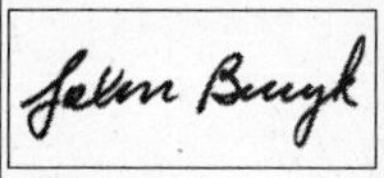

**John Bucyk (1981)**
3 X 5 10.00
8 X 10 Photo 20.00
Single Signed Puck 25.00

**Billy Burch (1974) d. 1950**
3 X 5 100.00
8 X 10 Photo 250.00

**Harry Cameron (1962) d. 1953**
3 X 5 100.00
8 X 10 Photo 300.00

**Gerry Cheevers (1985)**
3 X 5 10.00
8 X 10 Photo 20.00
Single Signed Puck 25.00

**King Clancy (1958) d. 1986**
3 X 5 100.00

**Dit Clapper (1947) d. 1978**
3 X 5 75.00

**Bobby Clarke (1987)**
3 X 5 6.00
8 X 10 Photo 35.00
Single Signed Puck 35.00

**Sprague Cleghorn (1958) d. 1956**
3 X 5 250.00

**Neil Colville (1967) d. 1987**
3 X 5 70.00

**Charlie Conacher (1961) d. 1967**
3 X 5 75.00
8 X 10 Photo 200.00

**Bill Cook (1952) d. 1986**
3 X 5 75.00

**Art Coulter (1974)**
3 X 5 30.00
8 X 10 Photo 35.00

**Yvan Cournoyer (1982)**
3 X 5 10.00
8 X 10 Photo 20.00
Single Signed Puck 20.00

**Bill Cowley (1968) d. 1993**
3 X 5 40.00
8 X 10 Photo 100.00

**Rusty Crawford (1962) d. 1971**
3 X 5 150.00

**Hap Day (1961) d. 1990**
3 X 5 70.00
8 X 10 Photo 125.00

**Alex Delvecchio (1977)**
3 X 5 10.00
8 X 10 Photo 20.00
Single Signed Puck 20.00

**Cy Denneny (1959) d. 1970**
3 X 5 200.00

**Marcel Dionne (1992)**
3 X 5 5.00
8 X 10 Photo 20.00
Single Signed Puck 20.00

**Gordie Drillon (1975) d. 1986**
3 X 5 70.00

**Ken Dryden**
3 x 5 25.00
8 x 10 Photo 130.00
Single signed puck 150.00

**Woody Dumart (1992)**
3 X 5 5.00
8 X 10 Photo 20.00
Single Signed Puck 25.00

**Bill Durnan (1964) d. 1972**
3 X 5 200.00

**Red Dutton (1958) d. 1987**
3 X 5 50.00

**Babe Dye (1970) d. 1962**
3 X 5 125.00

**Phil Esposito (1984)**
3 X 5 15.00
8 X 10 Photo 25.00
Single Signed Puck 30.00

**Tony Esposito (1988)**
3 X 5 15.00
8 X 10 Photo 25.00
Single Signed Puck 30.00

**Fern Flaman (1990)**
3 X 5 5.00
8 X 10 Photo 15.00
Single Signed Puck 20.00

**Frank Foyston (1958) d. 1966**
3 X 5 50.00
8 X 10 Photo 150.00

**Frank Frederickson (1958) d. 1979**
3 X 5 65.00

**Bill Gadsby (1970)**
3 X 5 5.00
8 X 10 Photo 20.00
Single Signed Puck 20.00

**Bob Gainey (1992)**
3 X 5 5.00
8 X 10 Photo 25.00
Single Signed Puck 25.00

**Herb Gardiner (1958) d. 1972**
3 X 5 75.00

**Boom Boom Geoffrion (1972)**
3 X 5 10.00
8 X 10 Photo 15.00
Single Signed Puck 25.00

**Eddie Giacomin (1987)**
3 X 5 10.00
8 X 10 Photo 25.00
Single Signed Puck 25.00

**Rod Gilbert (1982)**
3 X 5 5.00
8 X 10 Photo 20.00
Single Signed Puck 25.00

**Ebbie Goodfellow (1963) d. 1985**
3 X 5 70.00

**George Hainsworth (1961) d. 1950**
3 X 5 300.00

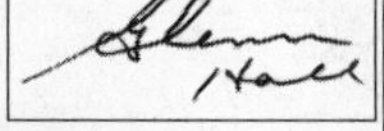

**Glenn Hall (1975)**
3 X 5 10.00
8 X 10 Photo 20.00
Single Signed Puck 25.00

**Doug Harvey (1973) d. 1989**
3 X 5 125.00
8 X 10 Photo 250.00
Single Signed Puck 300.00

**George Hay (1958) d. 1975**
3 X 5 70.00

**Bryan Hextall (1969) d. 1984**
3 X 5 40.00
8 X 10 Photo 60.00

**Tim Horton (1977) d. 1974**
3 X 5 150.00
8 X 10 Photo 400.00

**Gordie Howe (1972)**
3 X 5 30.00
8 X 10 Photo 50.00

Single Signed Puck 60.00

**Syd Howe (1965) d. 1976**
3 X 5 125.00

**Harry Howell (1979)**
3 X 5 5.00
8 X 10 Photo 20.00
Single Signed Puck 20.00

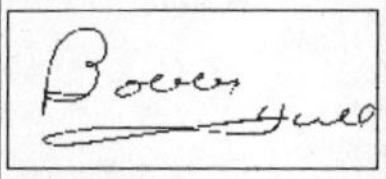

**Bobby Hull (1983)**
3 X 5 10.00
8 X 10 Photo 30.00
Single Signed Puck 35.00

**Dick Irvin (1958) d. 1957**
3 X 5 75.00
8 X 10 Photo 200.00

**Busher Jackson (1971) d. 1966**
3 X 5 125.00

**Ching Johnson (1958) d. 1979**
3 X 5 100.00

**Tom Johnson (1970)**
3 X 5 8.00
8 X 10 Photo 20.00
Single Signed Puck 25.00

**Aurel Joliat (1947) d. 1986**
3 X 5 175.00

**Duke Keats (1958) d. 1972**
3 X 5 75.00

**Red Kelly (1969)**
3 X 5 10.00
8 X 10 Photo 20.00
Single Signed Puck 20.00

**Teeder Kennedy (1966)**
3 X 5 10.00
8 X 10 Photo 20.00
Single Signed Puck 25.00

**Dave Keon (1986)**
3 X 5 10.00
8 X 10 Photo 25.00
Single Signed Puck 25.00

**Elmer Lach (1966)**
3 X 5 10.00
8 X 10 Photo 20.00
Single Signed Puck 25.00

**Guy Lafleur (1988)**
3 X 5 10.00
8 X 10 Photo 25.00
Single Signed Puck 25.00

**Jacques Laperriere (1987)**
3 X 5 5.00
8 X 10 Photo 20.00
Single Signed Puck 20.00

**Guy Lapointe (1993)**
3 X 5 5.00
8 X 10 Photo 20.00
Single Signed Puck 20.00

**Edgar Laprade (1993)**
3 X 5 10.00
8 X 10 Photo 25.00
Single Signed Puck 30.00

**Jacques Lemaire (1984)**
3 X 5 5.00
8 X 10 Photo 25.00
Single Signed Puck 25.00

**Mario Lemieux**
3 X 5 15.00
8 X 10 Photo 80.00
Single Signed Puck 100.00

**Ted Lindsay (1966)**
3 X 5 5.00
8 X 10 Photo 15.00
Single Signed Puck 20.00

**Harry Lumley (1980) d. 1998**
3 X 5 8.00
8 X 10 Photo 30.00
Single Signed Puck 40.00

**Mickey MacKay (1952) d. 1940**
3 X 5 100.00
8 X 10 Photo 300.00

**Frank Mahovlich (1981)**
3 X 5 5.00
8 X 10 Photo 20.00
Single Signed Puck 20.00

**Sylvia Mantha (1960) d. 1974**
3 X 5 100.00

**Lanny McDonald (1992)**
3 X 5 5.00
8 X 10 Photo 20.00
Single Signed Puck 20.00

**George McNamara (1958) d. 1952**
3 X 5 150.00

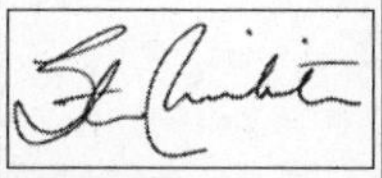

**Stan Mikita (1983)**
3 X 5 10.00
8 X 10 Photo 25.00
Single Signed Puck 30.00

**Dickie Moore (1974)**
3 X 5 5.00
8 X 10 Photo 20.00
Single Signed Puck 20.00

**Howie Morenz (1945) d. 1937**
3 X 5 800.00

**Bill Mosienko (1965) d. 1994**
3 X 5 20.00
8 X 10 Photo 40.00
Single Signed Puck 150.00

**Frank Nighbor (1947) d. 1966**
3 X 5 125.00

**Reg Noble (1962) d. 1962**
3 X 5 75.00

**Buddy O'Connor (1988) d. 1977**
3 X 5 50.00

**Harry Oliver (1967) d. 1985**
3 X 5 60.00
8 X 10 Photo 150.00

**Bert Olmstead (1985)**
3 X 5 5.00
8 X 10 Photo 40.00
Single Signed Puck 60.00

**Bobby Orr (1979)**
3 X 5 20.00
8 X 10 Photo 75.00
Single Signed Puck 75.00

**Bernie Parent (1984)**
3 X 5 10.00
8 X 10 Photo 25.00
Single Signed Puck 60.00

**Brad Park (1988)**
3 X 5 5.00
8 X 10 Photo 20.00
Single Signed Puck 20.00

**Gil Perreault (1990)**
3 X 5 5.00
8 X 10 Photo 20.00
Single Signed Puck 25.00

**Pierre Pilote (1975)**
3 X 5 5.00
8 X 10 Photo 20.00
Single Signed Puck 20.00

**Jacques Plante (1978) d. 1986**
3 X 5 150.00
8 X 10 Photo 400.00

**Denis Potvin (1991)**
3 X 5 5.00
8 X 10 Photo 25.00
Single Signed Puck 25.00

**Joe Primeau (1963) d. 1989**
3 X 5 100.00

**Marcel Pronovost (1978)**
3 X 5 5.00
8 X 10 Photo 20.00
Single Signed Puck 25.00

**Bob Pulford (1991)**
3 X 5 5.00
8 X 10 Photo 25.00
Single Signed Puck 25.00

**Harry Pulford (1945) d. 1940**
3 X 5 150.00
8 X 10 Photo 350.00

**Bill Quackenbush (1976)**
3 X 5 10.00
8 X 10 Photo 40.00

**Jean Ratelle (1985)**
3 X 5 5.00
8 X 10 Photo 60.00
Single Signed Puck 60.00

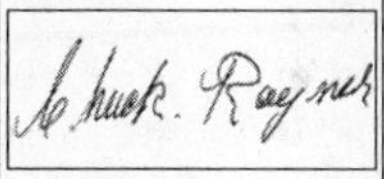

**Chuck Rayner (1973)**
3 X 5 5.00
8 X 10 Photo 20.00
Single Signed Puck 20.00

**Ken Reardon (1966)**
3 X 5 10.00
8 X 10 Photo 25.00
Single Signed Puck 30.00

**Henri Richard (1979)**
3 X 5 10.00
8 X 10 Photo 20.00
Single Signed Puck 25.00

**Maurice Richard (1961)**
3 X 5 10.00
8 X 10 Photo 30.00
Single Signed Puck 40.00

**Gordon Roberts (1971) d. 1966**
3 X 5 50.00
8 X 10 Photo 150.00

**Art Ross (1945) d. 1964**
3 X 5 125.00

**Blair Russell (1965) d. 1961**
3 X 5 75.00
8 X 10 Photo 200.00

**Ernie Russell (1965) d. 1963**
3 X 5 60.00
8 X 10 Photo 150.00

**Jack Ruttan (1962) d. 1973**
3 X 5 100.00

**Serge Savard (1986)**
3 X 5 5.00
8 X 10 Photo 20.00
Single Signed Puck 25.00

**Terry Sawchuk (1971) d. 1970**
3 X 5 300.00

**Milt Schmidt (1961)**
3 X 5 5.00
8 X 10 Photo 20.00
Single Signed Puck 25.00

**Sweeney Schriner (1962) d. 1990**
3 X 5 75.00

**Dave Schultz**
3 X 5 5.00
8 X 10 Photo 25.00
Single Signed Puck 25.00

**Earl Seibert (1963) d. 1990**
3 X 5 60.00

**Eddie Shore (1947) d. 1985**
3 X 5 100.00

**Steve Shutt (1993)**
3 X 5 5.00
8 X 10 Photo 20.00
Single Signed Puck 20.00

**Joe Simpson (1962) d. 1973**
3 X 5 100.00

**Darryl Sittler (1989)**
3 X 5 5.00
8 X 10 Photo 20.00
Single Signed Puck 25.00

**Al Smith (1962) d. 1953**
3 X 5 100.00
8 X 10 Photo 300.00

**Billy Smith (1993)**
3 X 5 5.00
8 X 10 Photo 20.00
Single Signed Puck 20.00

**Clint Smith (1991)**
3 X 5 5.00
8 X 10 Photo 20.00
Single Signed Puck 25.00

**Hooley Smith (1972) d. 1963**
3 X 5 125.00

**Allan Stanley (1981)**
3 X 5 10.00
8 X 10 Photo 20.00
Single Signed Puck 25.00

**Jack Stewart (1964) d. 1983**
3 X 5 75.00

**Nels Stewart (1962) d. 1957**
3 X 5 225.00

**Tiny Thompson (1959) d. 1981**
3 X 5 100.00

**Vladislav Tretiak (1989)**
3 X 5 15.00
8 X 10 Photo 30.00
Single Signed Puck 35.00

**Bryan Trottier**
3 X 5 8.00
8 X 10 Photo 25.00
Single Signed Puck 25.00

**Norm Ullman (1982)**
3 X 5 10.00
8 X 10 Photo 20.00
Single Signed Puck 25.00

**Harry Watson (1994)**
3 X 5 10.00
8 X 10 Photo 20.00
Single Signed Puck 25.00

**Cooney Weiland (1971) d. 1965**
3 X 5 80.00

**Phat Wilson (1962) d. 1970**
3 X 5 200.00

**Gump Worsley (1980)**
3 X 5 10.00
8 X 10 Photo 20.00
Single Signed Puck 25.00

# Modern Autographs Price Guide

**Jason Allison**
8 X 10 Photo 15.00
Authentic Jersey 200.00
Replica Jersey 100.00
Signed Card 5.00
Signed Puck 20.00

**Tony Amonte**
8 X 10 Photo 20.00
Authentic Jersey 200.00
Replica Jersey 100.00
Signed Card 10.00
Signed Puck 20.00

**Dave Andreychuk**
8 X 10 Photo 15.00
Authentic Jersey 200.00
Replica Jersey 100.00
Signed Card 5.00
Signed Puck 20.00

**Tom Barrasso**
8 X 10 Photo 30.00
Authentic Jersey 275.00
Mini Mask 75.00
Replica Jersey 150.00
Signed Card 12.00
Signed Puck 30.00

**Ed Belfour**
8 X 10 Photo 30.00
Authentic Jersey 250.00
Mini Mask 60.00
Replica Jersey 125.00
Signed Card 10.00
Signed Puck 30.00

**Bryan Berard**
8 X 10 Photo 15.00
Authentic Jersey 200.00
Replica Jersey 100.00
Signed Card 6.00
Signed Puck 20.00

**Peter Bondra**
8 X 10 Photo 25.00
Authentic Jersey 200.00
Replica Jersey 100.00
Signed Card 10.00
Signed Puck 25.00

**Ray Bourque**
8 X 10 Photo 25.00
Authentic Jersey 275.00
Replica Jersey 150.00
Signed Card 15.00
Signed Puck 30.00

**Rod Brind'Amour**
8 X 10 Photo 20.00
Authentic Jersey 200.00
Replica Jersey 100.00
Signed Card 6.00
Signed Puck 20.00

**Martin Brodeur**
8 X 10 Photo 25.00
Authentic Jersey 275.00
Mini Mask 75.00
Replica Jersey 150.00
Signed Card 15.00
Signed Puck 30.00

**Pavel Bure**
8 X 10 Photo 35.00
Authentic Jersey 275.00
Mini Helmet 75.00
Replica Jersey 150.00
Signed Card 15.00
Signed Puck 35.00

**Chris Chelios**
8 X 10 Photo 25.00
Authentic Jersey 250.00
Replica Jersey 150.00
Signed Card 15.00
Signed Puck 30.00

**Dino Ciccarelli**
8 X 10 Photo 25.00
Authentic Jersey 200.00
Replica Jersey 100.00
Signed Card 6.00
Signed Puck 25.00

**Wendel Clark**
8 X 10 Photo 20.00
Authentic Jersey 200.00
Replica Jersey 100.00
Signed Card 6.00
Signed Puck 25.00

**Paul Coffey**
8 X 10 Photo 25.00
Authentic Jersey 250.00
Replica Jersey 150.00
Signed Card 15.00
Signed Puck 25.00

**Byron Dafoe**
8 X 10 Photo 20.00
Authentic Jersey 200.00
Mini Mask 50.00
Replica Jersey 100.00
Signed Card 5.00
Signed Puck 20.00

**Vincent Damphousse**
8 X 10 Photo 15.00
Authentic Jersey 200.00
Replica Jersey 100.00
Signed Card 5.00
Signed Puck 20.00

**Eric Daze**
8 X 10 Photo 15.00
Authentic Jersey 200.00
Replica Jersey 100.00
Signed Card 5.00
Signed Puck 15.00

**Tie Domi**
8 X 10 Photo 15.00
Authentic Jersey 200.00
Replica Jersey 100.00
Signed Card 5.00
Signed Puck 20.00

**Sergei Fedorov**
8 X 10 Photo 50.00
Authentic Jersey 350.00
Mini Helmet 100.00
Replica Jersey 150.00
Signed Card 20.00
Signed Puck 50.00

**Theo Fleury**
8 X 10 Photo 30.00
Authentic Jersey 250.00
Replica Jersey 125.00
Signed Card 10.00
Signed Puck 30.00

**Peter Forsberg**
8 X 10 Photo 40.00
Authentic Jersey 350.00
Mini Helmet 100.00
Replica Jersey 150.00
Signed Card 20.00
Signed Puck 40.00

**Ron Francis**
8 X 10 Photo 25.00
Authentic Jersey 250.00
Replica Jersey 100.00
Signed Card 6.00
Signed Puck 25.00

**Grant Fuhr**
8 X 10 Photo 25.00
Authentic Jersey 250.00
Mini Mask 75.00
Replica Jersey 125.00
Signed Card 10.00
Signed Puck 25.00

**Mike Gartner**
8 X 10 Photo 40.00
Authentic Jersey 300.00
Replica Jersey 125.00
Signed Card 6.00
Signed Puck 40.00

**Doug Gilmour**
8 X 10 Photo 20.00
Authentic Jersey 250.00
Replica Jersey 125.00
Signed Card 10.00
Signed Puck 25.00

**Adam Graves**
8 X 10 Photo 25.00
Authentic Jersey 225.00
Replica Jersey 125.00
Signed Card 6.00
Signed Puck 25.00

**Wayne Gretzky**
8 X 10 Photo 100.00
Authentic Jersey 500.00
Mini Helmet 150.00
Replica Jersey 200.00
Signed Card 30.00
Signed Puck 100.00

**Dominik Hasek**
8 X 10 Photo 60.00
Authentic Jersey 300.00
Mini Mask 100.00
Replica Jersey 150.00
Signed Card 15.00
Signed Puck 60.00

**Guy Hebert**
8 X 10 Photo 15.00
Authentic Jersey 200.00
Mini Mask 50.00
Replica Jersey 100.00
Signed Card 5.00
Signed Puck 20.00

**Ron Hextall**
8 X 10 Photo 25.00
Authentic Jersey 250.00
Mini Mask 50.00
Replica Jersey 100.00
Signed Card 8.00
Signed Puck 20.00

**Brett Hull**
8 X 10 Photo 35.00
Authentic Jersey 300.00
Mini Helmet 80.00
Replica Jersey 150.00
Signed Card 15.00
Signed Puck 35.00

**Arturs Irbe**
8 x 10 Photo 20.00
Authentic Jersey 225.00
Replica Jersey 125.00
Signed Card 6.00
Signed Puck 25.00

**Jaromir Jagr**
8 X 10 Photo 50.00
Authentic Jersey 350.00
Mini Helmet 100.00
Replica Jersey 175.00
Signed Card 20.00
Signed Puck 50.00

**Curtis Joseph**
8 X 10 Photo 25.00
Authentic Jersey 250.00
Mini Mask 75.00
Replica Jersey 125.00
Signed Card 10.00
Signed Puck 25.00

**Paul Kariya**
8 X 10 Photo 60.00
Authentic Jersey 350.00
Mini Helmet 100.00
Replica Jersey 200.00
Signed Card 20.00
Signed Puck 60.00

**Nikolai Khabibulin**
8 X 10 Photo 25.00
Authentic Jersey 250.00
Mini Mask 50.00
Replica Jersey 100.00
Signed Card 8.00
Signed Puck 25.00

**Saku Koivu**
8 X 10 Photo 20.00
Authentic Jersey 225.00
Replica Jersey 100.00
Signed Card 10.00
Signed Puck 25.00

**Olaf Kolzig**
8 X 10 Photo 20.00
Authentic Jersey 225.00
Mini Mask 60.00
Replica Jersey 100.00
Signed Card 10.00
Signed Puck 25.00

**Jari Kurri**
8 X 10 Photo 30.00
Authentic Jersey 250.00
Replica Jersey 125.00
Signed Card 10.00
Signed Puck 30.00

**Pat LaFontaine**
8 X 10 Photo 20.00
Authentic Jersey 225.00
Replica Jersey 100.00
Signed Card 10.00
Signed Puck 25.00

**Vincent Lecavalier**
8 x 10 Photo 25.00
Authentic Jersey 250.00
Replica Jersey 150.00
Signed Card 10.00
Signed Puck 25.00

**John LeClair**
8 X 10 Photo 30.00
Authentic Jersey 300.00
Replica Jersey 175.00
Signed Card 15.00
Signed Puck 30.00

**Brian Leetch**
8 X 10 Photo 40.00
Authentic Jersey 300.00
Mini Helmet 80.00
Replica Jersey 150.00
Signed Card 15.00
Signed Puck 40.00

**Nicklas Lidstrom**
8 X 10 Photo 30.00
Authentic Jersey 250.00
Replica Jersey 100.00
Signed Card 6.00
Signed Puck 30.00

**Eric Lindros**
8 X 10 Photo 50.00
Authentic Jersey 350.00
Mini Helmet 100.00
Replica Jersey 175.00
Signed Card 20.00
Signed Puck 50.00

**Al MacInnis**
8 X 10 Photo 20.00
Authentic Jersey 200.00
Replica Jersey 100.00
Signed Card 8.00
Signed Puck 25.00

**Patrick Marleau**
8 X 10 Photo 25.00
Authentic Jersey 250.00
Replica Jersey 150.00
Signed Card 10.00
Signed Puck 30.00

**Mark Messier**
8 X 10 Photo 60.00
Authentic Jersey 400.00
Mini Helmet 150.00
Replica Jersey 250.00
Signed Card 25.00
Signed Puck 75.00

**Mike Modano**
8 X 10 Photo 30.00
Authentic Jersey 275.00
Replica Jersey 150.00
Signed Card 15.00
Signed Puck 30.00

**Alexander Mogilny**
8 X 10 Photo 25.00
Authentic Jersey 225.00
Replica Jersey 125.00
Signed Card 10.00
Signed Puck 25.00

**Joe Mullen**
8 X 10 Photo 15.00
Authentic Jersey 200.00
Replica Jersey 100.00
Signed Card 5.00
Signed Puck 15.00

**Joe Nieuwendyk**
8 X 10 Photo 25.00
Authentic Jersey 200.00
Replica Jersey 100.00
Signed Card 8.00
Signed Puck 25.00

**Owen Nolan**
8 X 10 Photo 15.00
Authentic Jersey 200.00
Replica Jersey 100.00
Signed Card 6.00
Signed Puck 20.00

**Adam Oates**
8 X 10 Photo 15.00
Authentic Jersey 200.00
Replica Jersey 100.00
Signed Card 6.00
Signed Puck 20.00

**Chris Osgood**
8 X 10 Photo 30.00
Authentic Jersey 275.00
Mini Mask 75.00
Replica Jersey 125.00
Signed Card 10.00
Signed Puck 30.00

**Sandis Ozolinsh**
8 X 10 Photo 15.00
Authentic Jersey 200.00
Replica Jersey 100.00
Signed Card 6.00
Signed Puck 20.00

**Zigmund Palffy**
8 X 10 Photo 25.00
Authentic Jersey 250.00
Replica Jersey 150.00
Signed Card 10.00
Signed Puck 25.00

**Felix Potvin**
8 X 10 Photo 20.00
Authentic Jersey 250.00
Mini Mask 75.00
Replica Jersey 125.00
Signed Card 10.00
Signed Puck 25.00

**Keith Primeau**
8 x 10 Photo 20.00
Authentic Jersey 225.00
Replica Jersey 125.00
Signed Card 6.00
Signed Puck 25.00

**Mark Recchi**
8 X 10 Photo 20.00
Authentic Jersey 200.00
Replica Jersey 100.00
Signed Card 6.00
Signed Puck 25.00

**Robert Reichel**
8 X 10 Photo 15.00
Authentic Jersey 200.00
Replica Jersey 100.00
Signed Card 5.00
Signed Puck 15.00

**Mikael Renberg**
8 X 10 Photo 15.00
Authentic Jersey 200.00
Replica Jersey 100.00
Signed Card 6.00
Signed Puck 20.00

**Manon Rheaume**
8 X 10 Photo 20.00
Authentic Jersey 250.00
Mini Mask 60.00
Replica Jersey 125.00
Signed Card 8.00
Signed Puck 20.00

**Mike Richter**
8 X 10 Photo 40.00
Authentic Jersey 300.00
Mini Mask 100.00
Replica Jersey 150.00
Signed Card 15.00
Signed Puck 40.00

**Luc Robitaille**
8 X 10 Photo 20.00
Authentic Jersey 225.00
Replica Jersey 125.00
Signed Card 8.00
Signed Puck 25.00

**Jeremy Roenick**
8 X 10 Photo 25.00
Authentic Jersey 250.00
Replica Jersey 150.00
Signed Card 10.00
Signed Puck 30.00

**Patrick Roy**
8 X 10 Photo 50.00
Authentic Jersey 350.00
Mini Mask 100.00
Replica Jersey 200.00
Signed Card 20.00
Signed Puck 60.00

**Joe Sakic**
8 X 10 Photo 40.00
Authentic Jersey 350.00
Mini Helmet 80.00
Replica Jersey 150.00
Signed Card 15.00
Signed Puck 40.00

**Sergei Samsonov**
8 X 10 Photo 30.00
Authentic Jersey 250.00
Replica Jersey 150.00
Signed Card 15.00
Signed Puck 30.00

**Teemu Selanne**
8 X 10 Photo 30.00
Authentic Jersey 300.00
Mini Helmet 80.00
Replica Jersey 150.00
Signed Card 15.00
Signed Puck 40.00

**Brendan Shanahan**
8 X 10 Photo 50.00
Authentic Jersey 325.00
Replica Jersey 125.00
Signed Card 12.00
Signed Puck 50.00

**Scott Stevens**
8 X 10 Photo 20.00
Authentic Jersey 200.00
Replica Jersey 100.00
Signed Card 8.00
Signed Puck 20.00

**Jozef Stumpel**
8 X 10 Photo 15.00
Authentic Jersey 200.00
Replica Jersey 100.00
Signed Card 5.00
Signed Puck 15.00

**Mats Sundin**
8 X 10 Photo 25.00
Authentic Jersey 250.00
Replica Jersey 125.00
Signed Card 6.00
Signed Puck 30.00

**Jocelyn Thibault**
8 X 10 Photo 15.00
Authentic Jersey 200.00
Mini Mask 50.00
Replica Jersey 125.00
Signed Card 5.00
Signed Puck 20.00

**Joe Thornton**
8 x 10 Photo 25.00
Authentic Jersey 250.00
Replica Jersey 150.00
Signed Card 10.00
Signed Puck 25.00

**Keith Tkachuk**
8 X 10 Photo 25.00
Authentic Jersey 250.00
Replica Jersey 150.00
Signed Card 8.00
Signed Puck 30.00

**Rick Tocchet**
8 X 10 Photo 20.00
Authentic Jersey 200.00
Replica Jersey 100.00
Signed Card 6.00
Signed Puck 20.00

**Pierre Turgeon**
8 X 10 Photo 20.00
Authentic Jersey 200.00
Replica Jersey 100.00
Signed Card 6.00
Signed Puck 25.00

**John Vanbiesbrouck**
8 X 10 Photo 35.00
Authentic Jersey 300.00
Mini Mask 75.00
Replica Jersey 175.00
Signed Card 15.00
Signed Puck 35.00

**Mike Vernon**
8 X 10 Photo 20.00
Authentic Jersey 250.00
Mini Mask 75.00
Replica Jersey 150.00
Signed Card 15.00
Signed Puck 25.00

**Doug Weight**
8 X 10 Photo 20.00
Authentic Jersey 200.00
Replica Jersey 100.00
Signed Card 6.00
Signed Puck 25.00

**Alexei Yashin**
8 X 10 Photo 30.00
Authentic Jersey 250.00
Replica Jersey 100.00
Signed Card 6.00
Signed Puck 30.00

**Steve Yzerman**
8 X 10 Photo 60.00
Authentic Jersey 375.00
Mini Helmet 100.00
Replica Jersey 200.00
Signed Card 20.00
Signed Puck 60.00

All Prices In U.S. Funds

# Hockey Memorabilia Price Guide

## NHL All-Star Programs

| | | Nr-Mt | Ex-Mt |
|---|---|---|---|
| 1 | 1947-48 at Toronto | 300.00 | 200.00 |
| 2 | 1948-49 at Chicago | 225.00 | 150.00 |
| 3 | 1949-50 at Toronto | 200.00 | 125.00 |
| 4 | 1950-51 at Detroit | 225.00 | 150.00 |
| 5 | 1951-52 at Toronto | 175.00 | 100.00 |
| 6 | 1952-53 at Detroit | 175.00 | 100.00 |
| 7 | 1953-54 at Montreal | 150.00 | 90.00 |
| 8 | 1954-55 at Detroit | 125.00 | 75.00 |
| 9 | 1955-56 at Detroit | 125.00 | 75.00 |
| 10 | 1956-57 at Montreal | 125.00 | 75.00 |
| 11 | 1957-58 at Montreal | 125.00 | 75.00 |
| 12 | 1958-59 at Montreal | 100.00 | 60.00 |
| 13 | 1959-60 at Montreal | 100.00 | 60.00 |
| 14 | 1960-61 at Montreal | 100.00 | 60.00 |
| 15 | 1961-62 at Chicago | 125.00 | 75.00 |
| 16 | 1962-63 at Toronto | 100.00 | 60.00 |
| 17 | 1963-64 at Toronto | 100.00 | 60.00 |

| | | Nr-Mt | Ex-Mt |
|---|---|---|---|
| 18 | 1964-65 at Toronto | 100.00 | 60.00 |
| 19 | 1965-66 at Toronto | 100.00 | 60.00 |
| 20 | 1966-67 at Montreal | 100.00 | 60.00 |
| 21 | 1967-68 at Toronto | 100.00 | 60.00 |
| 22 | 1968-69 at Montreal | 75.00 | 50.00 |
| 23 | 1969-70 at St. Louis | 75.00 | 50.00 |
| 24 | 1970-71 at Boston | 90.00 | 60.00 |
| 25 | 1971-72 at Minnesota | 60.00 | 40.00 |
| 26 | 1972-73 at New York | 50.00 | 30.00 |
| 27 | 1973-74 at Chicago | 50.00 | 30.00 |
| 28 | 1974-75 at Montreal | 50.00 | 30.00 |
| 29 | 1975-76 at Philadelphia | 50.00 | 30.00 |
| 30 | 1976-77 at Vancouver | 40.00 | 25.00 |
| 31 | 1977-78 at Buffalo | 40.00 | 25.00 |
| 32 | 1978-79 at New York | 40.00 | 25.00 |
| 33 | 1979-80 at Detroit | 50.00 | 30.00 |
| 34 | 1980-81-1991-92 | 35.00 | 20.00 |
| 35 | 1992-93-PRESENT | 10.00 | 6.00 |

## NHL All-Star Ticket Stubs

$15.00

Complete tickets are valued 2 to 5 times that of a stub.

| | | Nr-Mt | Ex-Mt |
|---|---|---|---|
| 1 | 1947-48 at Toronto | 250.00 | 150.00 |
| 2 | 1948-49 at Chicago | 175.00 | 100.00 |
| 3 | 1949-50 at Toronto | 150.00 | 90.00 |
| 4 | 1950-51 at Detroit | 150.00 | 90.00 |
| 5 | 1951-52 at Toronto | 125.00 | 75.00 |
| 6 | 1952-53 at Detroit | 125.00 | 75.00 |
| 7 | 1953-54 at Montreal | 100.00 | 60.00 |
| 8 | 1954-55 at Detroit | 75.00 | 50.00 |
| 9 | 1955-56 at Detroit | 75.00 | 50.00 |
| 10 | 1956-57 at Montreal | 75.00 | 50.00 |
| 11 | 1957-58 at Montreal | 75.00 | 50.00 |
| 12 | 1958-59 at Montreal | 60.00 | 35.00 |
| 13 | 1959-60 at Montreal | 60.00 | 35.00 |
| 14 | 1960-61 at Montreal | 60.00 | 35.00 |
| 15 | 1961-62 at Chicago | 75.00 | 50.00 |
| 16 | 1962-63 at Toronto | 60.00 | 35.00 |
| 17 | 1963-64 at Toronto | 60.00 | 35.00 |
| 18 | 1964-65 at Toronto | 60.00 | 35.00 |
| 19 | 1965-66 at Toronto | 60.00 | 35.00 |
| 20 | 1966-67 at Montreal | 50.00 | 30.00 |
| 21 | 1967-68 at Toronto | 50.00 | 30.00 |
| 22 | 1968-69 at Montreal | 50.00 | 30.00 |
| 23 | 1969-70 at St. Louis | 40.00 | 25.00 |
| 24 | 1970-71 at Boston | 60.00 | 35.00 |
| 25 | 1971-72 at Minnesota | 50.00 | 30.00 |
| 26 | 1972-73 at New York | 40.00 | 25.00 |
| 27 | 1973-74 at Chicago | 40.00 | 25.00 |
| 28 | 1974-75 at Montreal | 40.00 | 25.00 |
| 29 | 1975-76 at Philadelphia | 40.00 | 25.00 |
| 30 | 1976-77 at Vancouver | 35.00 | 20.00 |
| 31 | 1977-78 at Buffalo | 35.00 | 20.00 |
| 32 | 1978-79 at New York | 35.00 | 20.00 |
| 33 | 1979-80 at Detroit | 40.00 | 25.00 |
| 34 | 1980-81-Present | 30.00 | 20.00 |

## WHA All-Star Programs

| | | Nr-Mt | Ex-Mt |
|---|---|---|---|
| 1 | 1972-73 at Quebec City | 125.00 | 75.00 |
| 2 | 1973-74 at Saint Paul | 100.00 | 60.00 |
| 3 | 1974-75 at Edmonton | 60.00 | 35.00 |
| 4 | 1975-76 at Cleveland | 35.00 | 20.00 |
| 5 | 1976-77 at Hartford | 40.00 | 25.00 |
| 6 | 1977-78 at Quebec City | 35.00 | 20.00 |
| 7 | 1978-79 at Edmonton | 35.00 | 20.00 |

## WHA All-Star Ticket Stubs

Complete tickets are valued 2 to 5 times that of a stub.

| | | Nr-Mt | Ex-Mt |
|---|---|---|---|
| 1 | 1972-73 at Quebec City | 100.00 | 60.00 |
| 2 | 1973-74 at Saint Paul | 75.00 | 50.00 |
| 3 | 1974-75 at Edmonton | 50.00 | 30.00 |
| 4 | 1975-76 at Cleveland | 30.00 | 18.00 |
| 5 | 1976-77 at Hartford | 35.00 | 20.00 |
| 6 | 1977-78 at Quebec City | 30.00 | 18.00 |
| 7 | 1978-79 at Edmonton | 30.00 | 18.00 |

## Sports Illustrated Hockey Covers

| | |
|---|---|
| 2/10/75 Rogie Vachon | 6.00 |
| 11/17/75 Hockey Violence | 5.00 |
| 2/23/76 Bobby Clarke | 10.00 |
| 5/24/76 Larry Robinson | 8.00 |
| 2/7/77 Guy Lafleur | 10.00 |
| 5/9/77 Brad Park | 8.00 |
| 12/12/77 Bryan Trottier | 8.00 |
| 5/29/78 K.Dryden/L.Robinson | 10.00 |
| 4/16/79 Denis Potvin | 8.00 |
| 1/21/80 Gordie Howe | 12.00 |
| 3/3/80 USA Hockey Team | 40.00 |

| | |
|---|---|
| 3/10/80 Jim Craig | 10.00 |
| 12/22/80* USA Hockey Team SOY | 20.00 |
| 2/23/81 Bobby Carpenter | 5.00 |
| 10/12/81 Wayne Gretzky (FC) | 35.00 |
| 2/15/82 Wayne Gretzky | 20.00 |
| 12/27/82* Wayne Gretzky SOY | 25.00 |
| 5/23/83 Billy Smith | 6.00 |
| 5/14/84 Mike Bossy | 6.00 |
| 2/18/85 Wayne Gretzky | 15.00 |
| 6/2/86 Montreal Canadiens | 8.00 |
| 6/1/87 Wayne Gretzky | 12.00 |
| 5/30/88 Wayne Gretzky | 12.00 |
| 8/22/88 W.Gretzky/M.Johnson | 15.00 |
| 2/6/89 Mario Lemieux (FC) | 15.00 |

| | |
|---|---|
| 10/9/89 V.Fetisov/S.Starikov | 6.00 |
| 12/18/89 Montana/Magic/Gretzky | 15.00 |
| 4/23/90 Tomas Sandstrom | 3.00 |
| 3/18/91 Brett Hull | 6.00 |
| 6/8/92 Mario Lemieux | 8.00 |
| 4/19/93 Mario Lemieux | 8.00 |
| 6/14/93 M.Schneider/T.Sandstrom | 3.00 |
| 6/13/94 Mark Messier | 5.00 |
| 6/20/94 Richter/Bure/Ewing | 4.00 |
| 6/20/94 Mike Richter (NY only) | 10.00 |
| 6/5/95 Sergei Fedorov (Can.only) | 10.00 |
| 10/9/95 Eric Lindros (Can.only) | 12.00 |
| 11/27/95 Mike Keenan (Can.only) | 6.00 |
| 3/11/96 Gretzky/N.O'Donnell | 4.00 |
| 6/17/96 Patrick Roy (Colo.only) | 10.00 |
| 10/7/96 NHL PV:Gretzky/Messier | 6.00 |

# UDA, Cereal Box and Highland Mint Price Guide

## UDA

### UDA Wayne Gretzky Cards/Blowups

| | |
|---|---|
| 10-card Heroes set framed/2800 (NC) | 225.00 |
| '92-93 UD #25 2-card set/500 (NC) | 100.00 |
| '92-93 #1 blowup card/500 (NC) | 100.00 |
| '93-94 UD 2-card set/500 (NC) | 100.00 |
| Howe Selects #G5 blowup card/500 (NC) | 100.00 |
| '93-94 UD blowup/500 (NC) | 100.00 |
| '95 UD #1 2-card set/1000 (NC) | 90.00 |
| '95 Parkhurst 802 Commem.card/500 (NC) | 100.00 |
| '95 SP #54 2-card set/1000 (NC) | 90.00 |
| '95 SP 2500 Point blowup card/500 (NC) | 100.00 |
| '95 UD 'Freeze Frame' 5x7 card blowup/500 | 110.00 |
| '96 SP sample 2-card set/500 (NC) | 100.00 |
| '96 SP 2-card set/500 (NC) | 100.00 |
| '96 CC #170 2-card set/500 (NC) | 90.00 |

### UDA Wayne Gretzky Jerseys

| | |
|---|---|
| Kings white jersey framed | 700.00 |
| Kings white jersey unframed | 600.00 |
| 802 Commem. Kings jersey framed/1000* | 1000.00 |
| 802 Commem. Kings jersey unframed/1000* | 800.00 |
| Blues white jersey unframed (NC) | 600.00 |
| Blues blue jersey unframed (NC) | 600.00 |
| Great One Edmonton white jersey/499 | 800.00 |
| Rangers Starter white jersey unframed | 600.00 |
| Rangers Starter 3rd jersey unframed | 650.00 |
| Edmonton blue jersey unframed | 600.00 |

### UDA Wayne Gretzky Photos

| | |
|---|---|
| 8x10 Kings photo unframed | 100.00 |
| 16x20 Kings horiz.photo framed/300* (NC) | 225.00 |
| 8x10 Kings photo framed | 150.00 |
| 16x20 Kings horiz.photo unframed/300* (NC) | 150.00 |
| 16x20 Kings vert.photo framed/300* (NC) | 225.00 |
| 16x20 Kings vert.photo unframed/300* (NC) | 150.00 |
| 16x20 Kings ice spray photo unframed/1000* | 175.00 |
| 16x20 Kings ice spray photo framed/1000* | 250.00 |
| 16x20 photo 802 Goal unframed/802* (NC) | 200.00 |
| 16x20 photo 802 Goal framed/802* (NC) | 300.00 |
| 16x20 Oilers photo 'Flying' framed | 275.00 |
| 16x20 Oilers photo 'Flying' unframed | 175.00 |
| Great One Photo Collection w/Letter/499 | 650.00 |
| 8x10 photo w/helmet unframed | 100.00 |
| 8x10 Rangers photo unframed/250 | 100.00 |
| 8x10 Rangers photo profile/200 | 90.00 |
| 16x20 photo Stanley Cup framed/99 | 250.00 |
| 16x20 Rangers photo framed/250 | 250.00 |
| 8x10 Rangers photo (3rd jersey)/250 | 90.00 |
| 8x10 photo w/letter/199 | 110.00 |
| 8x10 photo 802 Goal unframed | 100.00 |
| 8x10 photo St. Louis First Game unframed | 100.00 |

### UDA Wayne Gretzky Other

| | |
|---|---|
| '97 All-Star puck | 160.00 |
| Campbell Conf. AS UD sheet/500 (NC) | 100.00 |
| Kings white helmet (NC) | 200.00 |
| First Kings litho w/o ticket framed/500 (NC) | 175.00 |

| | |
|---|---|
| Kings puck | 120.00 |
| Easton 'Silver Tip' Hockey Stick | 300.00 |
| First Kings litho with ticket framed/500 (NC) | 250.00 |
| Pair of Easton gloves/350 (NC) | 400.00 |
| 'Best Ever' Gretzky/Howe puck set w/display | 225.00 |
| Kings white helmet w/display (NC) | 250.00 |
| Salvino Kings figurine/1400 (NC) | 400.00 |
| 801/802 Gretzky/Howe puck set w/display (NC) | 250.00 |
| Woody Woodpecker cel framed/250* (NC) | 700.00 |
| Woody Woodpecker cel unframed/250* (NC) | 600.00 |
| Puck and blowup card framed (NC) | 200.00 |
| Blues puck | 125.00 |
| Rangers puck | 125.00 |
| Great One Easton blade and puck/499 | 325.00 |
| Mini shadow box w/puck and 5x7/99 | 400.00 |
| Rangers white helmet | 225.00 |

### UDA Los Angeles Kings

| | |
|---|---|
| Luc Robitaille '92-93 card blowup/500 | 30.00 |
| Tony Granato puck | 25.00 |
| Tony Granato 8x10 photo unframed | 30.00 |
| Marty McSorley puck (NC) | 25.00 |
| Marty McSorley 8x10 photo unframed (NC) | 30.00 |
| Tomas Sandstrom puck | 20.00 |
| Tomas Sandstrom 8x10 photo unframed | 25.00 |
| Rob Blake puck | 25.00 |
| Rob Blake 8x10 photo unframed | 30.00 |
| Paul Coffey puck | 35.00 |
| Paul Coffey 8x10 photo unframed | 40.00 |
| Kelly Hrudey puck (NC) | 25.00 |
| Kelly Hrudey 8x10 photo unframed | 30.00 |
| Jari Kurri puck | 30.00 |
| Jari Kurri 8x10 photo unframed | 35.00 |
| Luc Robitaille 8x10 photo unframed (NC) | 35.00 |

### UDA Misc Hockey

| | |
|---|---|
| Mike Bossy puck (NC) | 30.00 |
| Cam Neely 8x10 Photo Unframed (NC) | 50.00 |
| Ray Bourque 16x20 Photo Unframed (NC) | 65.00 |
| Patrick Roy Montreal puck (NC) | 100.00 |
| Patrick Roy '93 AS UD sheet/400 (NC) | 80.00 |
| Patrick Roy ad reprint framed/250 (NC) | 125.00 |

## Cereal Boxes

### Kellogg's Corn Flakes Hockey

| | |
|---|---|
| 1992 Wendel Clark (Can.) | 20.00 |
| 1993 Montreal Canadians (Can.) | 25.00 |
| 1996 Wendel Clark (Can.) | 15.00 |
| 1996 Gordie Howe (Can.) | 20.00 |
| 1996 Mario Lemieux (Can.) | 25.00 |
| 1996 Maurice Richard (Can.) | 20.00 |
| 1997 Felix Potvin (Can.; reg or Honey Nut) | 20.00 |

### Kellogg's Frosted Flakes Hockey

| | |
|---|---|
| 1992 Jaromir Jagr/Mario Lemieux | 35.00 |
| 1993 Wayne Gretzky | 40.00 |
| 1993 Montreal Canadians | 25.00 |
| 1993 L.A. Kings | 35.00 |

| | |
|---|---|
| 1994 Brett Hull (Can.) | 20.00 |
| 1994 Brett Hull w/Tony the Tiger (Can.) | 20.00 |
| 1996 N.Y. Rangers champs | 30.00 |
| 1996 Brett Hull (Can.) | 20.00 |
| 1997 Felix Potvin (Can.) | 20.00 |

### Kellogg's Raisin Bran Various Sports

| | |
|---|---|
| NHL: 1996 Brett Hull (Can.) | 15.00 |
| NHL: 1996 Mario Lemieux (Can.) | 20.00 |
| NHL: 1997 Curtis Joseph (Can.) | 15.00 |

### Post Canadian Hockey

| | |
|---|---|
| 1995 Doug Gilmour (Sugar Crisps) | 15.00 |
| 1996 Doug Gilmour (Honeycomb) | 15.00 |
| 1996 Wayne Gretzky (Honeycomb) | 20.00 |
| 1996 Wayne Gretzky (Sugar Crisp) | 20.00 |
| 1997 Chris Chelios (Sugar Crisp) | 12.00 |
| 1997 Vincent Damphousse (Shreddies) | 12.00 |
| 1997 Theo Fleury (Shreddies) | 12.00 |
| 1997 Doug Gilmour (Shreddies) | 12.00 |
| 1997 Paul Kariya (Honeycomb) | 15.00 |
| 1997 Joe Sakic (Alpha-Bits) | 15.00 |
| 1997 Brendan Shanahan (Fruity Pebbles) | 15.00 |

### Wheaties Other Sports

| | |
|---|---|
| NHL: 1991 Pittsburgh Penguins Champs R | 25.00 |
| NHL: 1992 Jaromir Jagr/Mario Lemieux no logo R | 40.00 |
| NHL: 1992 Jaromir Jagr/Mario Lemieux logo R | 50.00 |
| NHL: 1992 Pittsburgh Penguins Champs R | 25.00 |

### Miscellaneous Cereal Canadian Hockey

| | |
|---|---|
| 1992 Wayne Gretzky (Pro Stars) | 25.00 |
| 1996 Mario Lemieux (Corn Pops) | 20.00 |
| 1996 Mario Lemieux (Mini-Wheats) | 20.00 |
| 1996 Lanny McDonald (Mini-Wheats) | 15.00 |

## Highland Mint

### Hockey Mint-Cards Topps

| | | |
|---|---|---|
| COMMON BRONZE MINT-CARD | 35.00 | 50.00 |
| COMMON SILVER MINT-CARD | 200.00 | 250.00 |
| Ray Bourque 80/S/128 | 200.00 | 250.00 |
| Ray Bourque 80/B/634 | 50.00 | 65.00 |
| Pavel Bure 92/S/414 | 175.00 | 225.00 |
| Pavel Bure 92/B/1519 | 35.00 | 50.00 |
| Sergei Fedorov 91/S/208 | 200.00 | 250.00 |
| Sergei Fedorov 91/B/914 | 45.00 | 60.00 |
| Doug Gilmour 85/S/101 | 200.00 | 250.00 |
| Doug Gilmour 85/B/461 | 35.00 | 50.00 |
| Wayne Gretzky 79/S/1000 | 375.00 | 500.00 |
| Wayne Gretzky 79/B/5000 | 100.00 | 140.00 |
| Bobby Hull 95/S/500 | 175.00 | 225.00 |
| Bobby Hull 95/B/2500 | 35.00 | 50.00 |
| Brett Hull 88/S/500 | 175.00 | 225.00 |
| Brett Hull 88/B/1202 | 35.00 | 50.00 |
| Mario Lemieux 85/S/999 | 250.00 | 325.00 |
| Mario Lemieux 85/B/3557 | 45.00 | 60.00 |
| Eric Lindros 92/S/694 | 200.00 | 250.00 |
| Eric Lindros 92/B/2668 | 45.00 | 60.00 |
| Mark Messier 84/S/280 | 175.00 | 225.00 |

| | | |
|---|---|---|
| Mark Messier 84/B/1034 | 35.00 | 50.00 |
| Felix Potvin 92/S/210 | 175.00 | 225.00 |
| Felix Potvin 92/B/902 | 35.00 | 50.00 |
| Patrick Roy 86/S/500 | 200.00 | 250.00 |
| Patrick Roy 86/B/1986 | 50.00 | 65.00 |
| Teemu Selanne 92/S/131 | 175.00 | 225.00 |
| Teemu Selanne 92/B/537 | 35.00 | 50.00 |
| Steve Yzerman 84/S/233 | 175.00 | 225.00 |
| Steve Yzerman 84/B/926 | 55.00 | 75.00 |

### Hockey Mint-Cards Pinnacle/Score

| | | |
|---|---|---|
| COMMON BRONZE MINT-CARD | 35.00 | 50.00 |
| COMMON SILVER MINT-CARD | 175.00 | 225.00 |
| Martin Brodeur 95/S/250 | 175.00 | 225.00 |
| Martin Brodeur 95/B/1500 | 45.00 | 60.00 |
| Alexander Daigle 94/S/250 | 175.00 | 225.00 |
| Alexander Daigle 94/B/1500 | 35.00 | 50.00 |
| Jaromir Jagr 94/S/500 | 175.00 | 225.00 |
| Jaromir Jagr 94/B/2500 | 45.00 | 60.00 |
| Paul Kariya 94/S/250 | 175.00 | 225.00 |
| Paul Kariya 94/B/1500 | 45.00 | 60.00 |
| Pat LaFontaine 93/S/250 | 175.00 | 225.00 |
| Pat LaFontaine 93/B/1500 | 35.00 | 50.00 |
| Cam Neely 95/S/250 | 175.00 | 225.00 |
| Cam Neely 95/B/1500 | 35.00 | 50.00 |
| Jeremy Roenick 94/S/500 | 175.00 | 225.00 |
| Jeremy Roenick 94/B/2500 | 35.00 | 50.00 |

### Hockey Legends Mint-Cards

| | | |
|---|---|---|
| Gordie Howe 95/S/1000 | 175.00 | 225.00 |
| Gordie Howe 95/B/5000 | 35.00 | 50.00 |
| Bobby Orr 95/S/1000 | 175.00 | 225.00 |
| Bobby Orr 95/B/5000 | 35.00 | 50.00 |

### Hockey Sandblast Mint-Cards

| | | |
|---|---|---|
| Mario Lemieux 96/S/250 | 200.00 | 250.00 |
| Mario Lemieux 96/B/1500 | 50.00 | 65.00 |

### Hockey Mint-Coins

| | | |
|---|---|---|
| COMMON BRONZE MINT-COIN | 8.00 | 12.00 |
| COMMON SILVER MINT-COIN | 14.00 | 20.00 |
| Ray Bourque S/5000 | 15.00 | 20.00 |
| Pavel Bure S/5000 | 15.00 | 20.00 |
| Sergei Fedorov S/5000 | 20.00 | 25.00 |
| Brett Hull S/5000 | 15.00 | 20.00 |
| Jaromir Jagr S/5000 | 20.00 | 25.00 |
| Mario Lemieux Gold Sig./1000 | 45.00 | 60.00 |
| Mario Lemieux S/5000 | 20.00 | 25.00 |
| Mario Lemieux B/25000 | 9.00 | 12.00 |
| Eric Lindros Gold Sig./1000 | 45.00 | 60.00 |
| Eric Lindros S/5000 | 20.00 | 25.00 |
| Bobby Orr S/5000 | 20.00 | 25.00 |
| B.Orr/R.Bourque S/500 | 35.00 | 50.00 |
| Chris Osgood S/5000 | 15.00 | 20.00 |
| Patrick Roy S/5000 | 20.00 | 25.00 |
| Teemu Selanne S/5000 | 15.00 | 20.00 |
| John Vanbiesbrouck S/5000 | 20.00 | 25.00 |
| Steve Yzerman S/5000 | 15.00 | 20.00 |

### Hockey Magnum Series Medallions

| | | |
|---|---|---|
| Colorado Avalanche S/250 | 150.00 | 200.00 |
| Colorado Avalanche B/1000 | 45.00 | 60.00 |

# Legend

| | |
|---|---|
| 7ECreCar | 7-Eleven Credit Cards |
| 7EDis | 7-Eleven Discs |
| 7thInnSCHLAW | 7th Inn. Sketch CHL Award Winners |
| 7thInnSMC | 7th Inn. Sketch Memorial Cup |
| 7thInnSOHL | 7th Inn. Sketch OHL |
| 7thInnSQMJHL | 7th Inn. Sketch QMJHL |
| 7thInnSWHL | 7th Inn. Sketch WHL |
| ActPacBHP | Action Packed Badge of Honor Promos |
| ActPacBPP | Action Packed Big Picture Promos |
| ActPacHOFI | Action Packed HOF Induction |
| ActPacPro | Action Packed Prototypes |
| AdiRedW | Adirondack Red Wings |
| AHC | AHCA |
| AirCanSJHL | Air Canada SJHL |
| AirCanSJHLAS | Air Canada SJHL All-Stars |
| AlaGolKin | Alaska Gold Kings |
| AlbIntTC | Alberta International Team Canada |
| AllWorMLP | All World Mario Lemieux Promos |
| AmeLicSPC | American Licorice Sour Punch Caps |
| AmoLesFAM | Amos Les Forestiers AAA Midget |
| AncAce | Anchorage Aces |
| AreDraPic | Arena Draft Picks |
| AriIce | Arizona Icecats |
| AurSty | Pacific Aurora Styrotechs |
| AusNatTea | Austrian National Team |
| AvaPin | Avalanche Pins |
| BalSki | Baltimore Skipjacks |
| BAPLetL | Be A Player Lethal Lines |
| BAPUpCP | Be A Player Up Close and Personal |
| BarCol | Barrie Colts |
| BayBobO | BayBank Bobby Orr |
| Baz | Bazooka |
| Be A PPA | Be A Player |
| Be A PPAA | Be A Player Autographs |
| Be A PPAAF | Be A Player Autograph Gold |
| Be A PPAD | Be A Player Autographs Die-Cuts |
| Be A PPAGUSC | Be A Player All-Star Game Used Stick Cards |
| Be A PPAJ | Be A Player All-Star Game Used Jersey Cards |
| Be A PPALGH | Be A Player All-Star Legend Gordie Howe |
| Be A PPAM | Be A Player All-Star Milestones |
| Be A PPAPD | Be A Player Autographs Prismatic Die-Cuts |
| Be A PPGUJA | Be A Player Playoff Game Used Jersey Cards Autographed |
| Be A PPPGUJC | Be A Player Playoff Game Used Jersey Cards |
| Be A PPPH | Be A Player Playoff Highlights |
| Be A PPPL | Be A Player Playoff Legend Mario Lemieux |
| Be A PPPPUJC | Be A Player Playoff Practice Used Jersey Cards |
| Be A PPSE | Be A Player Spring Expo |
| Be A PPTBASG | Be A Player Tampa Bay All Star Game |
| Be APG | Be A Player Gold |
| BeAP99A | Be A Player 99 All-Stars |
| BeAPAut | Be A Player Autographs |
| BeAPAutSil | Be A Player Autographs Silver |
| BeAPBisITB | Be A Player Biscuit In The Basket |
| BeAPGreGM | Be A Player Gretzky's Great Memories |
| BeAPla | Be A Player |
| BeAPlaAut | Be A Player Autographs |
| BeAPlaPOT | Be A Player One Timers |
| BeAPlaSTP | Be A Player Stacking the Pads |
| BeAPlaTAN | Be A Player Take A Number |
| BeAPLemDC | Be A Player Lemieux Die Cut |
| BeAPLH | Be A Player Link to History |
| BeAPLHAut | Be A Player Link to History Autographs |
| BeAPLHAutSil | Be A Player Link to History Autographs Silver |
| BeAPLinDC | Be A Player Lindros Die Cut |
| BeAPMesDC | Be A Player Messier Die Cut |
| BeAPSig | Be A Player Signature Cards |
| BeAPSig | Be A Player Signatures |
| BeAPSigDC | Be A Player Signatures Die Cuts |
| BeAPStaTP | Be A Player Stacking the Pads |
| BeeAutA | Beehive Authentic Autographs |
| BeeGro1P | Beehive Group I Photos |
| BeeGro2P | Beehive Group II Photos |
| BeeGro3P | Beehive Group III Photos |
| BelBul | Belleville Bulls |
| BinRan | Binghamton Rangers |
| BirBul | Birmingham Bulls |
| BirSouSta | Birmingham South Stars |
| Bla | Blackhawks |
| BlaBor | Blackhawks Borderless |
| BlaBorP | Blackhawks Borderless Postcards |
| BlaBorPos | Blackhawks Borderless Postcards |
| BlaBroBac | Blackhawks Brown Background |
| BlaCok | Blackhawks Coke |
| BlaLeg | Blackhawks Legends |
| BlaWhiBor | Blackhawks White Border |
| Ble23KMR | Bleachers 23K Manon Rheaume |
| BluKod | Blues Kodak |
| BluPos | Blues Postcards |
| BluTeaIss | Blues Team Issue |
| BluTeaPho | Blues Team Photos |
| BluUDBB | Blues Upper Deck Best of the Blues |
| BluWhiBor | Blues White Border |
| Bow | Bowman |
| BowAllFoi | Bowman All Foil |
| BowBes | Bowman's Best |
| BowBesA | Bowman's Best Autographs |
| BowBesAAR | Bowman's Best Autographs Atomic Refractors |
| BowBesAR | Bowman's Best Atomic Refractors |
| BowBesAR | Bowman's Best Autographs Refractors |
| BowBesMIF | Bowman's Best Mirror Image Fusion |
| BowBesMIFAR | Bowman's Best Mirror Image Fusion Atomic Refractors |
| BowBesMIFR | Bowman's Best Mirror Image Fusion Refractors |
| BowBesP | Bowman's Best Performers |
| BowBesPAR | Bowman's Best Performers Atomic Refractors |
| BowBesPR | Bowman's Best Performers Refractors |
| BowBesR | Bowman's Best Refractors |
| BowBesRef | Bowman's Best Refractors |
| BowBesSBB | Bowman's Best Scotty Bowman's Best |
| BowBesSBBAR | Bowman's Best Scotty Bowman's Best Atomic Refractors |
| BowBesSBBR | Bowman's Best Scotty Bowman's Best Refractors |
| BowCHL | Bowman CHL |
| BowCHLAu | Bowman CHL Autographs |
| BowCHLAuB | Bowman CHL Certified Autographs Blue |
| BowCHLAuG | Bowman CHL Certified Autographs Gold |
| BowCHLAuS | Bowman CHL Certified Autographs Silver |
| BowCHLBB | Bowman CHL Bowman's Best |
| BowCHLBowBesAR | Bowman CHL Bowman's Best Atomic Refractors |
| BowCHLBowBesR | Bowman CHL Bowman's Best Refractor |
| BowCHLGA | Bowman CHL Golden Anniversary |
| BowCHLOI | Bowman CHL OPC International |
| BowCHLOPC | Bowman CHL OPC |
| BowCHLSC | Bowman CHL Scout's Choice |
| BowChrC | Bowman Chrome CHL |
| BowChrCGA | Bowman Chrome CHL Golden Anniversary |
| BowChrCGAR | Bowman Chrome CHL Golden Anniversary Refractors |
| BowChrCOI | Bowman Chrome CHL OPC International |
| BowChrCOIR | Bowman Chrome CHL OPC International Refractors |
| BowChrCR | Bowman Chrome CHL Refractors |
| BowDraPro | Bowman Draft Prospects |
| BowHatTri | Bowman Hat Tricks |
| BowTif | Bowman Tiffany |
| BraAle | Brantford Alexanders |
| BraSmo | Brantford Smoke |
| BraWheK | Brandon Wheat Kings |
| BriColJHL | British Columbia JHL |
| BroBra | Brockville Braves |
| BruGarMS | Bruins Garden Magazine Supplement |
| BruPho | Bruins Photos |
| BruPos | Bruins Postcards |
| BruSpoA | Bruins Sports Action |
| BruSpoAL | Bruins Sports Action Legends |
| BruSpoAU | Bruins Sports Action Update |
| BruTeaIss | Bruins Team Issue |
| BufBis | Buffalo Bison |
| BufStaRHI | Buffalo Stampedes RHI |
| C144ChaCig | C144 Champ's Cigarettes |
| C55 | C55 |
| C55SweCP | Sweet Caporal Postcards |
| C56 | C56 |
| C57 | C57 |
| CanaIGA | Canadiens IGA |
| CanaKra | Canadiens Kraft |
| CanaMol | Canadiens Molson |
| CanaPanTS | Canadiens Panini Team Stickers |
| CanaPin | Canadiens Pins |
| CanaPla | Canadiens Placemats |
| CanaPos | Canadiens Postcards |
| CanaPosBW | Canadiens Postcards BW |
| CanaPosC | Canadiens Postcards Color |
| CanaPro | Canadiens Provigo |
| CanaProF | Canadiens Provigo Figurines |
| CanaShe | Canadiens Sheets |
| CanaSte | Canadiens Steinberg |
| CanaSteG | Canadiens Steinberg Glasses |
| CanaVacS | Canadiens Vachon Stickers |
| CanCanDC | Canucks Canada Dry Cans |
| CanGamNHLP | Canada Games NHL POGS |
| CanGreWLP | Canadiens Great West Life Prints |
| CanNatJ | Canadian National Juniors |
| Canu | Canucks |
| CanuAutC | Canucks Autograph Cards |
| CanuBuiDA | Canucks Building the Dream Art |
| CanuMoh | Canucks Mohawk |
| CanuMol | Canucks Molson |
| CanuNal | Canucks Nalley's |
| CanuPanTS | Canucks Panini Team Stickers |
| CanuPos | Canucks Postcards |
| CanuProI | Canucks Program Inserts |
| CanuRoaTA | Canucks Road Trip Art |
| CanuRoyB | Canucks Royal Bank |
| CanuSheOil | Canucks Shell Oil |
| CanuSilD | Canucks Silverwood Dairies |
| CanuTeaI | Canucks Team Issue |
| CanuTeaI8 | Canucks Team Issue 8x10 |
| Cap | Capitals |
| CapBor | Capitals Borderless |
| CapBreO | Cape Breton Oilers |
| CapJun5 | Capitals Junior 5x7 |
| CapKod | Capitals Kodak |
| CapPizH | Capitals Pizza Hut |
| CapPol | Capitals Police |
| CapPos | Capitals Postcards |
| CapSmo | Capitals Smokey |
| CapTeaIss | Capitals Team Issue |
| CapWhiB | Capitals White Borders |
| CarHur | Carolina Hurricanes |
| CenHocL | Central Hockey League |
| ChaChe | Charlotte Checkers |
| ChaPos | Champion Postcards |
| ChePho | Chex Photos |
| ChiSag | Chicoutimi Sagueneens |
| CinCyc | Cincinnati Cyclones |
| Cla | Classic |
| Cla95DP | Classic Draft Prospects |
| ClaAllAme | Classic All-Americans |
| ClaAllRT | Classic All-Rookie Team |
| ClaAut | Classic Autographs |
| ClaCanML | Clark Candy Mario Lemieux |
| ClaCHLAS | Classic CHL All-Stars |
| ClaCHLP | Classic CHL Previews |
| ClaCla94 | Classic Class of '94 |
| ClaCraNum | Classic Crash Numbered |
| ClaDraD | Classic Draft Day |
| ClaDraGol | Classic Draft Gold |
| ClaEnf | Classic Enforcers |
| ClaEnfP | Classic Enforcers Promo |
| ClaGol | Classic Gold |
| ClaGolP | Classic Gold Promo |
| ClaIceBre | Classic Ice Breakers |
| ClaIceBreDC | Classic Ice Breakers Die Cuts |
| ClaKni | Clarkson Knights |
| ClaLPs | Classic LPs |
| ClaManRCP | Classic Manon Rheaume C3 Presidential |
| ClaManRP | Classic Manon Rheaume Promo |
| ClaPic | Classic Picks |
| ClaPre | Classic Previews |
| ClaPriPGH | Classic Printer's Proofs Gold |
| ClaPriPH | Classic Printer's Proofs |
| ClaPromo | Classic Promos |
| ClaProP | Classic Pro Prospects |
| ClaProPBC | Classic Pro Prospects BCs |
| ClaProPIA | Classic Pro Prospects Ice Ambassadors |
| ClaProPIH | Classic Pro Prospects International Heroes |
| ClaProPLP | Classic Pro Prospects LPs |
| ClaProPPro | Classic Pro Prospects Promo |
| ClaProPProt | Classic Pro Prospects Prototype |
| ClaProPProt | Classic Pro Prospects Prototypes |
| ClaProPro | Classic Pro Prospects |
| ClaROYS | Classic ROY Sweepstakes |
| ClaSilH | Classic Silver |
| ClaTeaCan | Classic Team Canada |
| ClaTopTen | Classic Top Ten |
| ClaTri | Classic Tri-Cards |
| ClaWomOH | Classic Women of Hockey |
| CleBar | Cleveland Barons |
| CleCruWHA | Cleveland Crusaders WHA |
| CleLum | Cleveland Lumberjacks |
| CleLumPos | Cleveland Lumberjacks Postcards |
| Coc | Coca-Cola |
| CocBoo | Coca-Cola Booklets |
| CocCap | Coca-Cola Caps |
| CokMilGP | Coke/Mac's Milk Gretzky POGs |
| ColChe | Columbus Checkers |
| ColCho | Collector's Choice |
| ColChoBlo | Collector's Choice Blow-Ups |
| ColChoBloBi | Collector's Choice Blow-ups Bi-Way |
| ColChoCTG | Collector's Choice Crash the Game |
| ColChoCTGE | Collector's Choice Crash the Game Exchange |
| ColChoCTGEG | Collector's Choice Crash the Game Exchange Gold |
| ColChoCTGG | Collector's Choice Crash the Game Gold |
| ColChoCTGGB | Collector's Choice Crash the Game Gold Bonus |
| ColChoCTGGR | Collector's Choice Crash the Game Gold Redeemed |
| ColChoCTGSB | Collector's Choice Crash the Game Silver Bonus |
| ColChoCTGSR | Collector's Choice Crash the Game Silver Redeemed |
| ColChoMM | Collectors Choice Magic Men |
| ColChoMVP | Collector's Choice MVP |
| ColChoMVPG | Collector's Choice MVP Gold |
| ColChoPC | Collector's Choice Player's Club |
| ColChoPCP | Collector's Choice Player's Club Platinum |
| ColChoSta | Collector's Choice Star Quest |
| ColChoSti | Collector's Choice Stick'Ums |
| ColChoWD | Collectors Choice World Domination |
| ColEdgI | Collector's Edge Ice |
| ColEdgIC | Collector's Edge Ice Crucibles |
| ColEdgILL | Collector's Edge Ice Livin' Large |
| ColEdgIP | Collector's Edge Ice Promos |
| ColEdgIQ | Collector's Edge Ice QuantumMotion |
| ColEdgITW | Collector's Edge Ice The Wall |
| ColHea | Colgate Heads |
| ColSta | Colgate Stamps |
| CorBigRed | Cornell Big Red |
| CorRoy | Cornwall Royals |
| CreFal | Crescent Falcon-Tigers |
| CreSel | Crescent Selkirks |
| CroRoyCCAJG | Crown Royale Cramer's Choice Awards Jumbos Gold |
| CroRoyCCAJG | Crown Royale Cramer's Choice Awards Jumbos Green |
| CroRoyCCAJLB | Crown Royale Cramer's Choice Awards Jumbos Light Blue |
| CroRoyCCAJP | Crown Royale Cramer's Choice Awards Jumbos Purple |
| CroRoyCCAJR | Crown Royale Cramer's Choice Awards Jumbos Red |
| CruCleWHAL | Crusaders Cleveland WHA Linnett |
| CzeAPSE | Czech APS Extraliga |
| DadCoo | Dad's Cookies |
| DalFre | Dallas Freeze |
| DayBom | Dayton Bombers |
| DenUniPio | Denver University Pioneers |
| DetJrRW | Detroit Jr. Red Wings |
| DetVip | Detroit Vipers |
| DetWha | Detroit Whalers |
| Dev | Devils |
| DevCar | Devils Caretta |

|  |  |
|---|---|
| DevPol | Devils Police |
| DevPos | Devils Postcards |
| DevPowP | Devils Power Play |
| DevTeaC | Devils Teams Carvel |
| DiaMatS | Diamond Matchbooks Silver |
| DiaMatT2 | Diamond Matchbooks Tan 2 |
| DiaMatT3 | Diamond Matchbooks Tan 3 |
| DiaMatT4 | Diamond Matchbooks Tan 4 |
| DiaMatT5 | Diamond Matchbooks Tan 5 |
| DiaMatT6 | Diamond Matchbooks Tan 6 |
| DiaMatTl | Diamond Matchbooks Tan I |
| DisMigDM | Disney Mighty Ducks Movie |
| Don | Donruss |
| DonBetPip | Donruss Between the Pipes |
| DonBetTP | Donruss Between The Pipes |
| DonCanl | Donruss Canadian Ice |
| DonCanIDS | Donruss Canadian Ice Dominion Series |
| DonCanIGPP | Donruss Canadian Ice Gold Press Proofs |
| DonCanILG | Donruss Canadian Ice Les Gardiens |
| DonCanILGP | Donruss Canadian Ice Les Gardiens Promos |
| DonCanIMLS | Donruss Canadian Ice Mario Lemieux Scrapbook |
| DonCanINP | Donruss Canadian Ice National Pride |
| DonCanIOC | Donruss Canadian Ice O Canada |
| DonCanIPS | Donruss Canadian Ice Provincial Series |
| DonCanIRPP | Donruss Canadian Ice Red Press Proofs |
| DonCanISCS | Donruss Canadian Ice Stanley Cup Scrapbook |
| DonCanWJT | Donruss Canadian World Junior Team |
| DonDom | Donruss Dominators |
| DonEli | Donruss Elite |
| DonEliAsp | Donruss Elite Aspirations |
| DonEliBttF | Donruss Elite Back to the Future |
| DonEliBttFA | Donruss Elite Back to the Future Autographs |
| DonEliC | Donruss Elite Craftsmen |
| DonEliCE | Donruss Elite Cutting Edge |
| DonEliDCS | Donruss Elite Die Cut Stars |
| DonEliDCU | Donruss Elite Die Cut Uncut |
| DonEliHTH | Donruss Elite Hart to Hart |
| DonEliIns | Donruss Elite |
| DonEliIns | Donruss Elite Inserts |
| DonEliInsG | Donruss Elite Inserts Gold |
| DonEliLLS | Donruss Elite Lemieux/Lindros Series |
| DonEliMC | Donruss Elite Master Craftsmen |
| DonEliP | Donruss Elite Perspective |
| DonEliPN | Donruss Elite Prime Numbers |
| DonEliPNDC | Donruss Elite Prime Numbers Die-Cuts |
| DonEliPW | Donruss Elite Painted Warriors |
| DonEliR | Donruss Elite Rookies |
| DonEliS | Donruss Elite Status |
| DonEliWJ | Donruss Elite World Juniors |
| DonGoTS | Donruss Go Top Shelf |
| DonHitLis | Donruss Hit List |
| DonIceKin | Donruss Ice Kings |
| DonIceMas | Donruss Ice Masters |
| DonIgn | Donruss Igniters |
| DonLim | Donruss Limited |
| DonLimExp | Donruss Limited Exposure |
| DonLimFOTG | Donruss Limited Fabric of the Game |
| DonLin2L | Donruss Line 2 Line |
| DonLin2LDC | Donruss Line 2 Line Die Cut |
| DonMar | Donruss Marksmen |
| DonMasM | Donruss Masked Marvels |
| DonMed | Donruss Medalist |
| DonPre | Donruss Preferred |
| DonPreCG | Donruss Preferred Color Guard |
| DonPreCGP | Donruss Preferred Color Guard Promos |
| DonPreCttC | Donruss Preferred Cut to the Chase |
| DonPreDWT | Donruss Preferred Tin Packs Double Wide |
| DonPreLotT | Donruss Preferred Line of the Times |
| DonPrePM | Donruss Preferred Precious Metals |
| DonPrePro | Donruss Press Proofs |
| DonPreProG | Donruss Press Proofs Gold |
| DonPreProS | Donruss Press Proofs Silver |
| DonPreT | Donruss Preferred Tin Packs |
| DonPreTB | Donruss Preferred Tin Boxes |
| DonPreTBC | Donruss Preferred Tin Boxes Canadian |
| DonPreTPC | Donruss Preferred Tin Packs Canadian |
| DonPreTPG | Donruss Preferred Tin Packs Gold |
| DonPri | Donruss Priority |
| DonPriDD | Donruss Priority Direct Deposit |
| DonPriODI | Donruss Priority Postcards Opening Day Issues |
| DonPriP | Donruss Priority Postcards |
| DonPriPG | Donruss Priority Postmaster General |
| DonPriPGP | Donruss Priority Postmaster Generals Promos |
| DonPriS | Donruss Priority Stamps |
| DonPriSB | Donruss Priority Stamps Bronze |
| DonPriSG | Donruss Priority Stamps Gold |
| DonPriSoA | Donruss Priority Stamp of Approval |
| DonPriSS | Donruss Priority Stamps Silver |
| DonProPoi | Donruss Pro Pointers |
| DonRatR | Donruss Rated Rookies |
| DonRatRoo | Donruss Rated Rookies |
| DonRedAle | Donruss Red Alert |
| DonRooTea | Donruss Rookie Team |
| DonSpeP | Donruss Special Print |
| DonTeaC | Donruss Team Canada |
| DonTeaUSA | Donruss Team USA |
| DruVol | Drummondville Voltigeurs |
| DubFigS | Dubuque Fighting Saints |
| Duc | Ducks |
| DucCarJr | Ducks Carl's Jr. |
| DucMilCap | Ducks Milk Caps |
| DurAllT | Duracell All-Cherry Team |
| DurL'EB | Duracell L'Equipe Beliveau |
| DurPan | Durivage Panini |
| DurSco | Durivage Score |
| EASpo | EA Sports |
| ElProDis | El Producto Discs |
| Emo | Emotion |
| EmoGen | Emotion generatioNext |
| EmoNteP | Emotion Ntense Power |
| EmoSam | Emotion Sample |
| EmoXce | Emotion Xcel |
| EmoXci | Emotion Xcited |
| EnoMarM | Enor Mark Messier |
| EriPan | Erie Panthers |
| Ess | Esso |
| EssAllSta | Esso All-Stars |
| EssOlyHH | Esso Olympic Hockey Heroes |
| EssOlyHHF | Esso Olympic Hockey Heroes French |
| EssPowPla | Esso Power Players |
| ExhCan | Exhibits Canadian |
| FanPhiE | Fanfest Phil Esposito |
| FerStaB | Ferris State Bulldogs |
| FifFly | Fife Flyers |
| FigSaiPos | Fighting Saints Postcards WHA |
| FigSaiWHA | Fighting Saints WHA |
| Fin | Finest |
| FinBowB | Finest Bowman's Best |
| FinBowBR | Finest Bowman's Best Refractors |
| FinCen | Finest Centurion |
| FinCenR | Finest Centurion Refractors |
| FinDivFCC | Finest Division's Finest Clear Cut |
| FinDouMF | Finest Double Sided Mystery Finest |
| FinDouSMFR | Finest Double Sided Mystery Finest Refractors |
| FinFutF | Finest Futures Finest |
| FinFutFR | Finest Futures Finest Refractors |
| FinnBecAC | Finnish Beckett Ad Cards |
| FinnJaaK | Finnish Jaa Kiekko |
| FinnJaaKLAC | Finnish Jaa Kiekko Lehti Ad Cards |
| FinnJyvHS | Finnish Jyvas Hyva Stickers |
| FinnKarWCL | Finnish Karjala World Championship Labels |
| FinNo P | Finest No Protectors |
| FinNo PR | Finest No Protectors Refractors |
| FinnSemWC | Finnish Semic World Championships |
| FinnSIS | Finnish SISU |
| FinnSISDD | Finnish SISU Drafted Dozen |
| FinnSISDT | Finnish SISU Double Trouble |
| FinnSISFI | Finnish SISU Fire On Ice |
| FinnSISGC | Finnish SISU Gold Cards |
| FinnSISGG | Finnish SISU Ghost Goalies |
| FinnSISGS | Finnish SISU Guest Specials |
| FinnSISH | Finnish SISU Horoscopes |
| FinnSISJ | Finnish SISU Junior |
| FinnSISL | Finnish SISU Limited |
| FinnSISLLG | Finnish SISU Limited Leaf Gallery |
| FinnSISLSS | Finnish SISU Limited Signed and Sealed |
| FinnSISMN | Finnish SISU Magic Numbers |
| FinnSISND | Finnish SISU NHL Draft |
| FinnSISNP | Finnish SISU NIL Phenoms |
| FinnSISP | Finnish SISU Painkillers |
| FinnSISR | Finnish SISU Redline |
| FinnSISRATG | Finnish SISU Redline At The Gala |
| FinnSISRKIG | Finnish SISU Redline Keeping It Green |
| FinnSISRMA | Finnish SISU Redline Mighty Adversaries |
| FinnSISRRE | Finnish SISU Redline Rookie Energy |
| FinnSISRS | Finnish SISU Redline Sledgehammers |
| FinnSISS | Finnish SISU Specials |
| FinnSISSpe | Finnish SISU Specials |
| FinnSISSpo | Finnish SISU Spotlights |
| FinOve | Finest Oversize |
| FinOveR | Finest Oversize Refractors |
| FinPro | Finest Promos |
| FinRedL | Finest Red Lighters |
| FinRedLR | Finest Red Lighters Refractors |
| FinRef | Finest Refractors |
| FinRinL | Finest Ring Leaders |
| FinSupTW | Finest Super Team Winners |
| Fla | Flair |
| FlaBluI | Flair Blue Ice |
| FlaCenIS | Flair Center Ice Spotlight |
| FlaCenS | Flair Center Spotlight |
| FlaHotG | Flair Hot Gloves |
| FlaHotN | Flair Hot Numbers |
| Flam | Flames |
| FlamDol | Flames Dollars |
| FlamIGA | Flames IGA |
| FlamIGA | Flames IGA/McGavin's |
| FlamPanTS | Flames Panini Team Stickers |
| FlamPos | Flames Postcards |
| FlamRedR | Flames Red Rooster |
| FlamRedRP | Flames Red Rooster Police |
| FlaNowAT | Flair Now And Then |
| FlaScoP | Flair Scoring Power |
| FlaTeal | Flames Team Issue |
| Fle | Fleer |
| FleArtRos | Fleer Art Ross |
| FleCalCan | Fleer Calder Candidates |
| FleFraFut | Fleer Franchise Futures |
| FleHea | Fleer Headliners |
| FleHocT | Fleury Hockey Tips |
| FleMetPP | Fleer Metal Promo Panel |
| FleNet | Fleer Netminders |
| FleNor | Fleer Norris |
| FlePCC | Fleer Picks Captain's Choice |
| FlePea | Fleer Pearson |
| FlePic | Fleer Picks |
| FlePicDL | Fleer Picks Dream Lines |
| FlePicF5 | Fleer Picks Fabulous 50 |
| FlePicFF | Fleer Picks Fantasy Force |
| FlePicJE | Fleer Picks Jagged Edge |
| FleProShe | Fleer Promo Sheet |
| FleRooS | Fleer Rookie Sensations |
| FleRooSen | Fleer Rookie Sensations |
| FleSlaA | Fleer Slapshot Artists |
| FleVez | Fleer Vezina |
| FliGen | Flint Generals |
| FliSpi | Flint Spirits |
| FloEve | Florida Everblades |
| FlyCanDC | Flyers Canada Dry Cans |
| FlyJCP | Flyers J.C. Penney |
| FlyLin | Flyers Linnett |
| FlyMigM | Flyers Mighty Milk |
| FlyPos | Flyers Postcards |
| FlyUppDS | Flyers Upper Deck Sheets |
| FooSanMC | Highland Mint Sandblast Mint-Cards |
| ForSasTra | Fort Saskatchewan Traders |
| ForWorF | Fort Worth Fire |
| ForWorFT | Fort Worth Fire Team |
| FreCan | Fredericton Canadiens |
| FreExp | Fredericton Express |
| FreNatT | French National Team |
| FriLay | Frito Lay |
| FriLayS | Frito-Lay Stickers |
| FroFlaMas | Frosted Flakes Masks |
| FutTre76CC | Future Trends '76 Canada Cup |
| FutTreC72 | Future Trends Canada '72 |
| FutTreC72P | Future Trends Canada '72 Promos |
| FutTrePS | Future Trends Promo Sheet |
| GenMil | General Mills |
| GerDELE | German DEL Eishockey |
| Gil | Gillette |
| GraRapG | Grand Rapids Griffins |
| GraVic | Granby Vics |
| GreMon | Greensboro Monarchs |
| GueSto | Guelph Storm |
| GueSto5A | Guelph Storm 5th Anniversary |
| GueStoPC | Guelph Storm Premier Collection |
| GuiFla | Guildford Flames |
| HalCit | Halifax Citadels |
| HalFC | Hall of Fame Cards |
| HalFL | Hall of Fame Legends |
| HalFP | Hall of Fame Postcards |
| HalFT | Hall of Fame Tickets |
| HaloFM | Hall of Fame Medallions |
| HamCan | Hamilton Canucks |
| HamFin | Hamilton Fincups |
| HamRed | Hamilton Redwings |
| HamRoaA | Hampton Roads Admirals |
| HarCri | Harvard Crimson |
| HerSta | Heroes Stand-Ups |
| Hig5Pre | High-5 Previews |
| HigLinGG | High Liner Greatest Goalies |
| HigLinSC | High Liner Stanley Cup |
| HigMinHLMC | Highland Mint Legends Mint-Cards |
| HigMinHMC | Highland Mint Mint-Coins |
| HigMinMagSM | Highland Mint Magnum Series Medallions |
| HocGreC | Hockey Greats Coins |
| HocGreCG | Hockey Greats Coins Gold |
| HocWit | Hockey Wit |
| HolCre | Holland Creameries |
| HulColUMD | Hull Collection UMD |
| HumDum1 | Humpty Dumpty I |
| HumDum2 | Humpty Dumpty II |
| HumHawP | Humberside Hawks Postcards |
| HunBli | Huntington Blizzard |
| Ima | Images |
| ImaAut | Images Autographs |
| ImaCleE | Images Clear Excitement |
| ImaGol | Images Gold |
| ImaPlaPDC | Images Platinum Premier Draft Choice |
| ImaPlaPl | Images Platinum Players |
| ImaPlaPr | Images Platinum Prospects |
| ImpSti | Imperial Stickers |
| ImpStiDCS | Imperial Stickers Die Cut Superstars |
| IndChe | Indianapolis Checkers |
| IndIce | Indianapolis Ice |
| Isl | Islanders |
| IslCheBA | Islanders Chemical Bank Alumni |
| IslIsIN | Islanders Islander News |
| IslIsINT | Islanders Islander News Trottier |
| IslPos | Islander Postcards |
| IslPowP | Islanders Power Play |
| IslTeaIss | Islanders Team Issue |
| IslTrans | Islanders Transparencies |
| JelSpo | Jello Spoons |
| Jet | Jets |
| JetBor | Jets Borderless |
| JetIGA | Jets IGA |
| JetPanTS | Jets Panini Team Stickers |
| JetPol | Jets Police |
| JetPos | Jets Postcards |
| JetReaC | Jets Readers Club |
| JetRuf | Jets Ruffles |
| JetSaf | Jets Safeway |
| JetSilD | Jets Silverwood Dairy |
| JetTeaIss | Jets Team Issue |
| JofKoh | Jofa/Koho |
| JohChi | Johnstown Chiefs |
| JunBluT | Juniors Blue Tint |
| KalWin | Kalamazoo Wings |
| KamBla | Kamloops Blazers |
| KanCitB | Kansas City Blades |
| KanCitBla | Kansas City Blades |
| Kat | Katch |
| KatGol | Katch Gold |
| KatMas | Katch Masks |
| KatSil | Katch Silver |

|  |  |
|---|---|
| KelAccD | Kellogg's Accordion Discs |
| KelDon | Kellogg's Donruss |
| KelIroT | Kellogg's Iron-On Transfers |
| KelPos | Kellogg's Posters |
| KelTro | Kellogg's Trophies |
| KelWin | Kelowna Wings |
| KenStaLA | Kenner Starting Lineup American |
| KenStaLC | Kenner Starting Lineup Canadian |
| KenTho | Kentucky Thoroughblades |
| Kin20tATI | Kings 20th Anniversary Team Issue |
| KinCan | Kingston Canadians |
| KinCarN | Kings Card Night |
| KinFro | Kingston Frontenacs |
| KinHaw | Kingston Hawks Stickers |
| KinLA TC | Kings LA Times Coins |
| KinPowP | Kings Power Play |
| KinSmo | Kings Smokey |
| KinSmoG8 | Kings Smokey Gretzky 8x10 |
| KinTeal4 | Kings Team Issue 4x6 |
| KinUppDST | Kings Upper Deck Season Ticket |
| KitRan | Kitchener Rangers |
| KitRanU | Kitchener Rangers Update |
| KnoChe | Knoxville Cherokees |
| Koll | Kollectorfest |
| Kra | Kraft |
| KraAllSS | Kraft All-Stars Stickers |
| KraDra | Kraft Drawings |
| KraGoaM | Kraft Goalie Masks |
| KraRec | Kraft Recipes |
| KraUppD | Kraft Upper Deck |
| LakSupSL | Lake Superior State Lakers |
| LaPat | La Patrie |
| LasVegT | Las Vegas Thunder |
| LasVegThu | Las Vegas Thunder |
| LavDaiLSJ | Laval Dairy Lac St. Jean |
| LavDaiQSHL | Laval Dairy QSHL |
| LavDaiS | Laval Dairy Subset |
| Lea | Leaf |
| LeaBanSea | Leaf Banner Season |
| LeaCreP | Leaf Crease Patrol |
| LeaFirOI | Leaf Fire On Ice |
| LeaFirOIce | Leaf Fire On Ice |
| LeaFirOnIce | Leaf Fire On Ice |
| LeaFraMat | Leaf Fractal Matrix |
| LeaFraMDC | Leaf Fractal Matrix Die Cuts |
| LeaFreFra | Leaf Freeze Frame |
| LeaFrePhe | Leaf Freshman Phenoms |
| LeaGolAS | Leaf Gold All-Stars |
| LeaGolR | Leaf Gold Rookies |
| LeaGolS | Leaf Gold Stars |
| LeaHatTA | Leaf Hat Trick Artists |
| LeaInt | Leaf International |
| LeaIntUI | Leaf International Universal Ice |
| LeaLeaAL | Leaf Leather And Laces |
| LeaLeaALP | Leaf Leather And Laces Promos |
| LeaLemB | Leaf Lemieux's Best |
| LeaLim | Leaf Limited |
| LeaLimBTB | Leaf Limited Bash The Boards |
| LeaLimBTBLE | Leaf Limited Bash The Boards Limited Edition |
| LeaLimBTBP | Leaf Limited Bash the Boards Promos |
| LeaLimG | Leaf Limited Gold |
| LeaLimI | Leaf Limited Inserts |
| LeaLimR | Leaf Limited Rookies |
| LeaLimRG | Leaf Limited Rookies Gold |
| LeaLimRP | Leaf Limited Rookie Phenoms |
| LeaLimSG | Leaf Limited Stars of the Game |
| LeaLimSS | Leaf Limited Stick Side |
| LeaLimStu | Leaf Limited Stubble |
| LeaLimWJC | Leaf Limited World Juniors Canada |
| LeaLimWJUSA | Leaf Limited World Juniors USA |
| LeaLinCol | Leaf Lindros Collection |
| LeaMarLem | Leaf Mario Lemieux |
| LeaPaiWar | Leaf Painted Warriors |
| LeaPhe | Leaf Phenoms |
| LeaPipDre | Leaf Pipe Dreams |
| LeaPre | Leaf Preferred |
| LeaPreMM | Leaf Preferred Masked Marauders |
| LeaPreP | Leaf Press Proofs |
| LeaPrePP | Leaf Preferred Press Proofs |
| LeaPreSG | Leaf Preferred Steel Gold |
| LeaPreSP | Leaf Preferred Steel Power |
| LeaPreSte | Leaf Preferred Steel |
| LeaPreVP | Leaf Preferred Vanity Plates |
| LeaPreVPG | Leaf Preferred Vanity Plates Gold |
| LeaRoaCup | Leaf Road To The Cup |
| LeaShuDow | Leaf Shut Down |
| LeaStuR | Leaf Studio Rookies |
| LeaStuS | Leaf Studio Signature |
| LeaSwe | Leaf Sweaters Away |
| LeaSwe( | Leaf Sweaters Home |
| LeaTheBO. | Leaf The Best Of ... |
| LetActR | Letraset Action Replays |
| LetHur | Lethbridge Hurricanes |
| LigHeaP | Lightning Health Plan |
| LigKasK | Lightning Kash n'Karry |
| LigPhoA | Lightning Photo Album |
| LigPos | Lightning Postcards |
| LigSealR | Lightning Season in Review |
| LigShe | Lightning Sheraton |
| LigTeal | Lightning Team Issue |
| LipSou | Lipton Soup |
| LonBeaIDP | Long Beach Ice Dogs Promo |
| LonKni | London Knights |
| LouGea | Louisville Gears |
| LouIceG | Louisiana Ice Gators |
| LouIceGP | Louisiana Ice Gators Playoffs |
| LouRiv | Louisville Riverfrogs |
| LouRivF | Louisville Riverfrogs |
| LunGoaG | Lunchables Goalie Greats |
| LunGoaGS | Lunchables Goalie Greats Squares |
| MacMil | Mac's Milk |
| MadMon | Madison Monsters |
| MaiBlaB | Maine Black Bears |
| MapLeaG | Maple Leafs Gangsters |
| MapLeaGP | Maple Leaf Gardens Postcards |
| MapLeaK | Maple Leafs Kodak |
| MapLeaP | Maple Leafs Police |
| MapLeaP | Maple Leafs Postcards |
| MapLeaPLA | Maple Leafs PLAY |
| MapLeaPO | Maple Leafs Postcards Oversized |
| MapLeaPuP | Maple Leafs Pin-up Posters |
| MapLeaPTS | Maple Leafs Panini Team Stickers |
| MapLeaWB | Maple Leafs White Border |
| MapLeaWBG | Maple Leafs White Border Glossy |
| MapLeaWBM | Maple Leafs White Border Matte |
| MarSanDW | Mariners San Diego WHA |
| MatMinRec | Mattel Mini-Records |
| McD | McDonald's |
| McDGamFil | McDonald's Game Film |
| McDGreM | McDonald's Gretzky's Moments |
| McDGreT | McDonald's Gretzky's Teammates |
| McDIroO | McDonald's Iron-Ons |
| McDPin | McDonald's Pinnacle |
| McDSti | McDonald's Stickers |
| McDUppD | McDonald's Upper Deck |
| MedHatT | Medicine Hat Tigers |
| MemRivK | Memphis River Kings |
| Met | Metal |
| MetHM | Metal Heavy Metal |
| MetIS | Metal International Steel |
| MetIW | Metal Iron Warriors |
| MetUni | Metal Universe |
| MetUniAP | Metal Universe Armor Plate |
| MetUniAPSP | Metal Universe Armor Plate Super Power |
| MetUniCS | Metal Universe Cool Steel |
| MetUniCSSP | Metal Universe Cool Steel Super Power |
| MetUniIC | Metal Universe Ice Carvings |
| MetUniICSP | Metal Universe Ice Carvings Super Power |
| MetUniLW | Metal Universe Lethal Weapons |
| MetUniLWSP | Metal Universe Lethal Weapons Super Power |
| MetWin | Metal Winners |
| MicSta | Michigan State |
| MicTecH | Michigan Tech Huskies |
| MicTecHus | Michigan Tech Huskies |
| MicWol | Michigan Wolverines |
| MilAdm | Milwaukee Admirals |
| MilAdmBO | Milwaukee Admirals Bank One |
| MinDul | Minnesota-Duluth |
| MinDulCom | Minnesota-Duluth Commemorative |
| MinGolG | Minnesota Golden Gophers |
| MinGolGCAS | Minnesota Golden Gophers Collect A Sport |
| MonAAA | Montreal-Bourassa AAA |
| MonAlp | Moncton Alpines |
| MonGolF | Moncton Golden Flames |
| MonHaw | Moncton Hawks |
| MonRoy | Montreal Royals |
| MPSPhoSJHL | MPS Photographics SJHL |
| MusFur | Muskegon Fury |
| NasKni | Nashville Knights |
| NatOttWHA | Nationals Ottawa WHA |
| NeiGre | Neilson's Gretzky |
| NewHavN | New Haven Nighthawks |
| NewSai | Newmarket Saints |
| NHLAcePC | NHL Aces Playing Cards |
| NHLActSta | NHL Action Stamps |
| NHLActStaU | NHL Action Stamps Update |
| NHLCooT | NHL Cool Trade |
| NHLKeyTAG | NHL Key Tags |
| NHLProSTA | NHL Pro Stamps |
| NiaFalT | Niagara Falls Thunder |
| NoFeaAdCa | No Fear Ad Cards |
| NorBayC | North Bay Centennials |
| Nord | Nordiques |
| NorDakFS | North Dakota Fighting Sioux |
| NordBurK | Nordiques Burger King |
| NordGenF | Nordiques General Foods |
| NordMarA | Nordiques Marie Antoinette |
| NordMcD | Nordiques McDonald's |
| NordPanTS | Nordiques Panini Team Stickers |
| NordPet | Nordiques Petro-Canada |
| NordPla | Nordiques Placemats |
| NordPol | Nordiques Police |
| NordPos | Nordiques Postcards |
| NordPro | Nordiques Provigo |
| NordTeal | Nordiques Team Issue |
| NordYumY | Nordiques Yum-Yum |
| NorIowH | North Iowa Huskies |
| NorMicW | Northern Michigan Wildcats |
| NorPet | Nordiques Petro-Canada |
| NorSta7E | North Stars 7-Eleven |
| NorStaA | North Stars ADA |
| NorStaADA | North Stars ADA |
| NorStaAP | North Stars Action Posters |
| NorStaCD | North Stars Cloverleaf Dairy |
| NorStaGP | North Stars Glossy Photos |
| NorStaP | North Stars Postcards |
| NorStaPos | North Stars Postcards |
| NovScoO | Nova Scotia Oilers |
| NovScoV | Nova Scotia Voyageurs |
| O'KeeMapL | O'Keefe Maple Leafs |
| O-PChr | OPC Chrome |
| O-PChrBFtP | OPC Chrome Blast From the Past |
| O-PChrBFtPR | OPC Chrome Blast From the Past Refractors |
| O-PChrBM | OPC Chrome Board Members |
| O-PChrBMR | OPC Chrome Board Members Refractors |
| O-PChrR | OPC Chrome Refractors |
| O-PChrSB | OPC Chrome Season's Best |
| O-PChrSBR | OPC Chrome Season's Best Refractors |
| OilDol | Oilers Dollars |
| OilIGA | Oilers IGA |
| OilMcD | Oilers McDonald's |
| OilPanTS | Oilers Panini Team Stickers |
| OilPos | Oilers Postcards |
| OilRedR | Oilers Red Rooster |
| OilTeal | Oilers Team Issue |
| OilTenAnn | Oilers Tenth Anniversary |
| OilWesEM | Oilers West Edmonton Mall |
| OklCitB | Oklahoma City Blazers |
| OldTim | Old Timers |
| OmaLan | Omaha Lancers |
| OPC | O-Pee-Chee |
| OPC | OPC/Topps |
| OPC25AI | O-Pee-Chee 25th Anniv. Inserts |
| OPCBoxB | O-Pee-Chee Box Bottoms |
| OPCCanHF | O-Pee-Chee Canadiens Hockey Fest |
| OPCCanP | O-Pee-Chee Canadiens Panel |
| OPCDec | O-Pee-Chee Deckle |
| OPCFinIns | O-Pee-Chee Finest Inserts |
| OPCFou | O-Pee-Chee Four-in-One |
| OPCIns | O-Pee-Chee Inserts |
| OPCMin | O-Pee-Chee Minis |
| OPCNHL | O-Pee-Chee NHL |
| OPCPlaC | O-Pee-Chee Player Crests |
| OPCPos | O-Pee-Chee Posters |
| OPCPre | OPC Premier |
| OPCPreBG | OPC Premier Black Gold |
| OPCPreF | OPC Premier Finest |
| OPCPreG | OPC Premier Gold |
| OPCPreSE | OPC Premier Special Effects |
| OPCPreSP | OPC Premier Star Performers |
| OPCPreTC | OPC Premier Team Canada |
| OPCPreTR | OPC Premier Top Rookies |
| OPCPucSti | O-Pee-Chee Puck Stickers |
| OPCRedA | O-Pee-Chee Red Army |
| OPCRin | O-Pee-Chee Rings |
| OPCSta | O-Pee-Chee Stamps |
| OPCSti | O-Pee-Chee Stickers |
| OPCStiBC | O-Pee-Chee Sticker Back Cards |
| OPCSup | O-Pee-Chee Super |
| OPCTBoo | O-Pee-Chee/Topps Booklets |
| OPCTeaBoo | O-Pee-Chee Team Booklets |
| OPCTeaC | O-Pee-Chee Team Canada |
| OPCTeaL | O-Pee-Chee Team Logos |
| OPCTeaLog | O-Pee-Chee Team Logos |
| OPCTroW | O-Pee-Chee Trophy Winners |
| OPCV3011 | O-Pee-Chee V301-1 |
| OPCV3012 | O-Pee-Chee V301-2 |
| OPCV304A | O-Pee-Chee V304A |
| OPCV304B | O-Pee-Chee V304B |
| OPCV304C | O-Pee-Chee V304C |
| OPCV304D | O-Pee-Chee V304D |
| OPCV304E | O-Pee-Chee V304E |
| OPCWHA | O-Pee-Chee WHA |
| OPCWHAP | O-Pee-Chee WHA Posters |
| OshGen | Oshawa Generals |
| OshGenP | Oshawa Generals Police |
| OshGenS | Oshawa Generals Sheet |
| Ott67 | Ottawa 67's |
| Ott672A | Ottawa 67's 25th Anniversary |
| OweSouPla | Owen Sound Platers |
| Pac | Pacific |
| PacAur | Pacific Aurora |
| PacAurALC | Pacific Aurora Atomic Laser Cuts |
| PacAurC | Pacific Aurora Cubes |
| PacAurCC | Pacific Aurora Canvas Creations |
| PacAurCF | Pacific Aurora Championship Fever |
| PacAurCFC | Pacific Aurora Championship Fever Copper |
| PacAurCFIB | Pacific Aurora Championship Fever Ice Blue |
| PacAurCFPB | Pacific Aurora Championship Fever Platinum Blue |
| PacAurCFR | Pacific Aurora Championship Fever Red |
| PacAurCFS | Pacific Aurora Championship Fever Silver |
| PacAurCP | Pacific Aurora Complete Players |
| PacAurCPP | Pacific Aurora Complete Players Parallel |
| PacAurFL | Pacific Aurora Front Line Copper |
| PacAurFLIB | Pacific Aurora Front Line Ice Blue |
| PacAurFLR | Pacific Aurora Front Line Red |
| PacAurGU | Pacific Aurora Glove Unlimited |
| PacAurMAC | Pacific Aurora Man Advantage Cel-Fusions |
| PacAurNC | Pacific Aurora NHL Command |
| PacAurPD | Pacific Aurora Premiere Date |
| PacAurT | Pacific Aurora Toronto |
| PacCarSup | Pacific Card-Supials |
| PacCarSupM | Pacific Card-Supials Minis |
| PacCop | Pacific Copper |
| PacCra | Pacific Cramer's Choice Awards |
| PacCraCA | Pacific Cramer's Choice Awards |
| PacCraChoAwa | Pacific Cramer's Choice Awards |
| PacCroR | Crown Royale |
| PacCroRBoSDC | Crown Royale Blades of Steel Die-Cuts |
| PacCroRCCA | Crown Royale Cramer's Choice Awards Jumbos |
| PacCroRCCAJ | Crown Royale Cramer's Choice Awards Jumbos Dark Blue |
| PacCroRCCJ | Crown Royale Cramer's Choice Jumbos |
| PacCroRCCJG | Crown Royale Cramer's Choice Jumbos Gold |
| PacCroRCCJS | Crown Royale Cramer's Choice Jumbos Signed |
| PacCroREG | Crown Royale Emerald Green |
| PacCroRFODC | Crown Royale Freeze Out Die-Cuts |

| | |
|---|---|
| PacCroRHTDC | Crown Royale Hat Tricks Die-Cuts |
| PacCroRIB | Crown Royale Ice Blue |
| PacCroRLCDC | Crown Royale Lamplighters Cel-Fusion Die-Cuts |
| PacCroRLL | Crown Royale Living Legends |
| PacCroRLS | Crown Royale Limited Series |
| PacCroRMP | Crown Royale Master Performers |
| PacCroRPotG | Crown Royale Pillars of the Game |
| PacCroRPP | Crown Royale Pivotal Players |
| PacCroRRC | Crown Royale Rookie Class |
| PacCroRS | Crown Royale Silver |
| PacDyn | Pacific Dynagon |
| PacDynBKS | Pacific Dynagon Best Kept Secrets |
| PacDynC | Pacific Dynagon Copper |
| PacDynDD | Pacific Dynagon Dynamic Duos |
| PacDynDG | Pacific Dynagon Dark Gray |
| PacDynEG | Pacific Dynagon Emerald Green |
| PacDynI | Pacific Dynagon Ice |
| PacDynI | Pacific Dynagon Ice Inserts |
| PacDynIAR | Pacific Dynagon Ice Adrenaline Rush |
| PacDynIARB | Pacific Dynagon Ice Adrenaline Rush Bronze |
| PacDynIARIB | Pacific Dynagon Ice Adrenaline Rush Ice Blue |
| PacDynIARR | Pacific Dynagon Ice Adrenaline Rush Red |
| PacDynIARS | Pacific Dynagon Ice Adrenaline Rush Silver |
| PacDynIB | Pacific Dynagon Ice Blue |
| PacDynIFT | Pacific Dynagon Ice Forward Thinking |
| PacDynIIB | Pacific Dynagon Ice Blue |
| PacDynIIW | Pacific Dynagon Ice Watchmen |
| PacDynIM | Pacific Dynagon Ice Montreal |
| PacDynIPP | Pacific Dynagon Ice Preeminent Players |
| PacDynIR | Pacific Dynagon Ice Red |
| PacDynIR | Pacific Dynagon Ice Rookies |
| PacDynITC | Pacific Dynagon Ice Team Checklists |
| PacDynKotN | Pacific Dynagon Kings of the NHL |
| PacDynR | Pacific Dynagon Red |
| PacDynSil | Pacific Dynagon Silver |
| PacDynSto | Pacific Dynagon Stonewallers |
| PacDynTan | Pacific Dynagon Tandems |
| PacEmeGre | Pacific Emerald Green |
| PacEO P | Pacific Omega EO Portraits |
| PacGol | Pacific Gold |
| PacGolCD | Pacific Gold Crown Die-Cuts |
| PacGolCroDC | Pacific Gold Crown Die-Cuts |
| PacHomaA | Pacific Home and Away |
| PacIceB | Pacific Ice Blue |
| PacIn tCN | Pacific In the Cage Net-Fusions |
| PacInTheCLC | Pacific In The Cage Laser Cuts |
| PacInv | Pacific Invincible |
| PacInvAZ | Pacific Invincible Attack Zone |
| PacInvC | Pacific Invincible Copper |
| PacInvEG | Pacific Invincible Emerald Green |
| PacInvFP | Pacific Invincible Feature Performers |
| PacInvIB | Pacific Invincible Ice Blue |
| PacInvNRB | Pacific Invincible NHL Regime Bonus |
| PacInvOTG | Pacific Invincible Off The Glass |
| PacInvR | Pacific Invincible Red |
| PacInvS | Pacific Invincible Silver |
| PacOme | Pacific Omega |
| PacOmeC | Pacific Omega Copper |
| PacOmeCS | Pacific Omega Championship Spotlight |
| PacOmeCSG | Pacific Omega Championship Spotlight Gold |
| PacOmeCSG | Pacific Omega Championship Spotlight Green |
| PacOmeCSR | Pacific Omega Championship Spotlight Red |
| PacOmeDG | Pacific Omega Dark Gray |
| PacOmeEG | Pacific Omega Emerald Green |
| PacOmeEP1o1 | Pacific Omega EO Portraits 1 of 1 |
| PacOmeFtF | Pacific Omega Face to Face |
| PacOmeG | Pacific Omega Gold |
| PacOmeGFDCC | Pacific Omega Game Face Die-Cut Cel-Fusions |
| PacOmeH | Pacific Omega |
| PacOmeIB | Pacific Omega Ice Blue |
| PacOmeNSZ | Pacific Omega No Scoring Zone |
| PacOmeO | Pacific Omega Online |
| PacOmeODI | Pacific Omega Opening Day Issue |
| PacOmeP | Pacific Omega Prism |
| PacOmePI | Pacific Omega Planet Ice |
| PacOmePIB | Pacific Omega Planet Ice Parallel |
| PacOmeR | Pacific Omega Red |
| PacOmeSE | Pacific Omega Spring Expo |
| PacOmeSil | Pacific Omega Silks |
| PacOmeSLC | Pacific Omega Stick Handle Laser Cuts |
| PacOmeTL | Pacific Omega Team Leaders |
| PacPar | Pacific Paramount |
| PacParBNDC | Pacific Paramount Big Numbers Die-Cuts |
| PacParC | Pacific Paramount Copper |
| PacParCG | Pacific Paramount Canadian Greats |
| PacParDG | Pacific Paramount Dark Grey |
| PacParEG | Pacific Paramount Emerald Green |
| PacParGSL | Pacific Paramount Glove Side Laser Cuts |
| PacParGSLC | Pacific Paramount Glove Side Laser Cuts |
| PacParH | Pacific Paramount Holo-Electric |
| PacParHoFB | Pacific Paramount Hall of Fame Bound |
| PacParHoFBPP | Pacific Paramount Hall of Fame Bound Pacific Proofs |
| PacParIB | Pacific Paramount Ice Blue |
| PacParIG | Pacific Paramount Ice Galaxy |
| PacParIGG | Pacific Paramount Ice Galaxy Gold |
| PacParIGS | Pacific Paramount Ice Galaxy Silver |
| PacParP | Pacific Paramount Photoengravings |
| PacParRed | Pacific Paramount Red |
| PacParS | Pacific Paramount Silver |
| PacParSDDC | Pacific Paramount Special Delivery Die-Cuts |
| PacParSil | Pacific Paramount Silver |
| PacParTCD | Pacific Paramount Team Checklists Die-Cuts |
| PacPasAP | Pacific Past and Present |
| PacPreD | Pacific Premiere Date |
| PacRed | Pacific Red |

| | |
|---|---|
| PacRev | Revolution |
| PacRev1AGD | Revolution 1998 All-Star Game Die-Cuts |
| PacRevADC | Revolution All-Star Die Cuts |
| PacRevC | Revolution Copper |
| PacRevCTL | Revolution Chalk Talk Laser-Cuts |
| PacRevE | Revolution Emerald |
| PacRevIB | Revolution Ice Blue |
| PacRevIS | Revolution Ice Shadow |
| PacRevNI | Revolution NHL Icons |
| PacRevNID | Revolution NHL Icons Die-Cuts |
| PacRevR | Revolution Red |
| PacRevRtSD | Revolution Return to Sender Die-Cuts |
| PacRevS | Revolution Showstoppers |
| PacRevS | Revolution Silver |
| PacRevTCL | Revolution Team Checklist Laser Cuts |
| PacSil | Pacific Silver |
| PacSlaSDC | Pacific Slap Shots Die-Cuts |
| PacTeaC | Pacific Team Checklists |
| PacTeaCCC | Pacific Team Checklist Cel Cards |
| PacTeaL | Pacific Team Leaders |
| PacTim | Pacific Timelines |
| PacTitI | Pacific Titanium Ice |
| PacTroW | Pacific Trophy Winners |
| PanPop | Panthers Pop-ups |
| PanSti | Panini Stickers |
| PanStiFre | Panini Stickers French |
| PanTeaI | Panthers Team Issue |
| Par | Parkhurst |
| Par66 | Parkhurst '66-67 |
| Par66Coi | Parkhurst '66-67 Coins |
| Par66P | Parkhurst '66-67 Promos |
| ParAreTS | Parkhurst Arena Tour Sheets |
| ParBeeP | Parkhurst Beehive Promos |
| ParCalC | Parkhurst Calder Candidates |
| ParCalCG | Parkhurst Calder Candidates Gold |
| ParCheP | Parkhurst Cherry Picks |
| ParChePH | Parkhurst Cherry's Playoff Heroes |
| ParChePS | Parkhurst Cherry Picks Sheet |
| ParCraG | Parkhurst Crash The Game |
| ParEasWesS | Parkhurst East/West Stars |
| ParEmeI | Parkhurst Emerald Ice |
| ParFirO | Parkhurst First Overall |
| ParFre | Parkhurst French |
| ParGol | Parkhurst Gold |
| ParInt | Parkhurst International |
| ParIntAS | Parkhurst International All-Stars |
| ParIntCCGS1 Series 1 | Parkhurst International Crown Collection Gold |
| ParIntCCGS2 Series 2 | Parkhurst International Crown Collection Gold |
| ParIntCCSS1 Series 1 | Parkhurst International Crown Collection Silver |
| ParIntCCSS2 Series 2 | Parkhurst International Crown Collection Silver |
| ParIntEI | Parkhurst International Emerald Ice |
| ParIntGP | Parkhurst International Goal Patrol |
| ParIntNHLAS | Parkhurst International NHL All-Stars |
| ParIntPTP | Parkhurst International Parkie's Trophy Picks |
| ParIntTW | Parkhurst International Trophy Winners |
| ParMisL | Parkhurst Missing Link |
| ParMisLA | Parkhurst Missing Link Autographs |
| ParMisLFS | Parkhurst Missing Link Future Stars |
| ParMisLP | Parkhurst Missing Link Pop-Ups |
| ParParR | Parkhurst Parkie Reprints |
| ParParRCI | Parkhurst Parkie Reprints Case Inserts |
| ParParS | Parkhurst Parkie Sheets |
| ParPHC | Parkhurst PHC |
| ParPHCF | Parkhurst PHC French |
| ParPre | Parkhurst Previews |
| ParProS | Parkhurst Promo Sheets |
| ParQuaO | Parkhurst Quaker Oats |
| ParSE | Parkhurst SE |
| ParSEES | Parkhurst SE Euro-Stars |
| ParSEG | Parkhurst SE Gold |
| ParSEV | Parkhurst SE Vintage |
| ParTalB | Parkhurst Tall Boys |
| ParTalBA | Parkhurst Tall Boys Autographs |
| ParTalBFS | Parkhurst Tall Boys Future Stars |
| ParTalBG | Parkhurst Tall Boys Greats |
| ParTalBM | Parkhurst Tall Boys Mail-Ins |
| ParUSACG | Parkhurst USA/Canada Gold |
| ParVin | Parkhurst Vintage |
| PenCok | Penguins Coke |
| PenCokC | Penguins Coke/Clark |
| PenCokE | Penguins Coke/Elby's |
| PenFoo | Penguins Foodland |
| PenFooCS | Penguins Foodland Coupon Stickers |
| PenHeiP | Penguins Heinz Photos |
| PenKod | Penguins Kodak |
| PenMask | Penguins Masks |
| PenPos | Penguins Postcards |
| PenPucB | Penguins Puck Bucks |
| PenSti | Penguins Stickers |
| PenTeaIP | Penguins Team Issue Photos |
| PenTri | Penguins Tribune-Review |
| PeoRiv | Peoria Rivermen |
| PeoRivC | Peoria Rivermen Coke/Kroger |
| PeoRivPA | Peoria Rivermen Photo Album |
| PepCap | Pepsi-Cola Caps |
| PetPet | Peterborough Petes |
| PhoRoa | Phoenix Roadrunners |
| PhoRoaWP | Phoenix Roadrunners WHA Pins |
| Pin | Pinnacle |
| Pin1HS | Pinnacle I Hobby Samples |
| Pin1S | Pinnacle I Samples |
| Pin2HS | Pinnacle II Hobby Samples |

| | |
|---|---|
| PinAllS | Pinnacle All-Stars |
| PinAllSC | Pinnacle All-Stars Canadian |
| PinAmePP | Pinnacle American Promo Panel |
| PinArtP | Pinnacle Artist's Proofs |
| PinB | Pinnacle B |
| PinBee | Beehive |
| PinBeeGOA | Beehive Golden Originals Autographs |
| PinBeeGP | Beehive Golden Portraits |
| PinBeeGT | Beehive Gold Team |
| PinBeeT | Beehive Team |
| PinBFre | Pinnacle B French |
| PinBoo | Pinnacle Boomers |
| PinByTN | Pinnacle By The Numbers |
| PinByTNP | Pinnacle By The Numbers Premium |
| PinCan | Pinnacle Canadian |
| PinCanPP | Pinnacle Canadian Promo Panels |
| PinCap | Pinnacle Captains |
| PinCapC | Pinnacle Captains Canadian |
| PinCBCHNiC | Pinnacle CBC Hockey Night in Canada |
| PinCer | Pinnacle Certified |
| PinCerGT | Pinnacle Certified Gold Team |
| PinCerMB | Pinnacle Certified Mirror Blue |
| PinCerMG | Pinnacle Certified Mirror Gold |
| PinCerMR | Pinnacle Certified Mirror Red |
| PinCerR | Pinnacle Certified Red |
| PinCerRR | Pinnacle Certified Rookie Redemption |
| PinCerRRG | Pinnacle Certified Rookie Redemption Gold |
| PinCerRRMG | Pinnacle Certified Rookie Redemption Mirror Gold |
| PinCerSS | Pinnacle Certified Summit Silver |
| PinCerT | Pinnacle Certified Team |
| PinCleS | Pinnacle Clear Shots |
| PinDaiED | Pinnacle Daigle Entry Draft |
| PinEpiGE | Pinnacle Epix Game Emerald |
| PinEpiGO | Pinnacle Epix Game Orange |
| PinEpiGP | Pinnacle Epix Game Purple |
| PinEpiME | Pinnacle Epix Moment Emerald |
| PinEpiMO | Pinnacle Epix Moment Orange |
| PinEpiMP | Pinnacle Epix Moment Purple |
| PinEpiPE | Pinnacle Epix Play Emerald |
| PinEpiPO | Pinnacle Epix Play Orange |
| PinEpiPP | Pinnacle Epix Play Purple |
| PinEpiSE | Pinnacle Epix Season Emerald |
| PinEpiSO | Pinnacle Epix Season Orange |
| PinEpiSP | Pinnacle Epix Season Purple |
| PinEriL | Pinnacle Eric Lindros |
| PinExp | Pinnacle Expansion |
| PinFan | Pinnacle Fantasy |
| PinFirS | Pinnacle First Strike |
| PinFoi | Pinnacle Foil |
| PinFre | Pinnacle French |
| PinFulC | Pinnacle Full Contact |
| PinGam | Pinnacle Gamers |
| PinGloG | Pinnacle Global Gold |
| PinGoaG | Pinnacle Goaltending Greats |
| PinHocMC | Highland Mint Mint-Cards Pinnacle/Score |
| PinIns | Pinnacle Inside |
| PinInsC | Pinnacle Inside Cans |
| PinInsCC | Pinnacle Inside Coach's Collection |
| PinInsCG | Pinnacle Inside Cans Gold |
| PinInsEC | Pinnacle Inside Executive Collection |
| PinInsSto | Pinnacle Inside Stoppers |
| PinInsSUG | Pinnacle Inside Stand Up Guys |
| PinInsT | Pinnacle Inside Track |
| PinMarMG | Pinnacle Mario's Moments Gold |
| PinMarMom | Pinnacle Mario's Moments |
| PinMas | Pinnacle Masks |
| PinMasDC | Pinnacle Masks Die Cuts |
| PinMasJ | Pinnacle Masks Jumbos |
| PinMasPro | Pinnacle Masks Promos |
| PinMcD | McDonald's |
| PinMin | Pinnacle Mint |
| PinMinB | Pinnacle Mint Bronze |
| PinMinCBP | Pinnacle Mint Coins Brass Proofs |
| PinMinCGPP | Pinnacle Mint Coins Gold Plated Proofs |
| PinMinCNSP | Pinnacle Mint Coins Nickel Silver Proofs |
| PinMinCoiB | Pinnacle Mint Coins Brass |
| PinMinCoiGP | Pinnacle Mint Coins Gold Plated |
| PinMinCoiN | Pinnacle Mint Coins Nickel |
| PinMinCoiN | Pinnacle Mint Coins Nickel Silver |
| PinMinCoiS | Pinnacle Mint Coins Silver |
| PinMinCoiSG | Pinnacle Mint Coins Solid Gold |
| PinMinCoiSS | Pinnacle Mint Coins Solid Silver |
| PinMinG | Pinnacle Mint Gold |
| PinMinGolTea | Pinnacle Mint Gold Team |
| PinMinMC | Pinnacle Mint Minternational Coins |
| PinMinMin | Pinnacle Mint Minternational |
| PinMinS | Pinnacle Mint Silver |
| PinMinSilTea | Pinnacle Mint Silver Team |
| PinNifFif | Pinnacle Nifty Fifty |
| PinNorLig | Pinnacle Northern Lights |
| PinPow | Pinnacle Power |
| PinPowPac | Pinnacle Power Pack |
| PinPrePBB | Pinnacle Press Plates Back Black |
| PinPrePBC | Pinnacle Press Plates Back Cyan |
| PinPrePBM | Pinnacle Press Plates Back Magenta |
| PinPrePBY | Pinnacle Press Plates Back Yellow |
| PinPrePFC | Pinnacle Press Plates Front Cyan |
| PinPrePFM | Pinnacle Press Plates Front Magenta |
| PinPrePFY | Pinnacle Press Plates Front Yellow |
| PinPrePla | Pinnacle Press Plates Front Black |
| PinPreS | Pinnacle Premium Stock |
| PinRepMas | Pinnacle Replica Masks |
| PinRinC | Pinnacle Rink Collection |
| PinRoa2 | Pinnacle Roaring 20s |
| PinRooTP | Pinnacle Rookie Team Pinnacle |

| | |
|---|---|
| PinSupR | Pinnacle Super Rookies |
| PinSupRC | Pinnacle Super Rookies Canadian |
| PinTea2 | Pinnacle Team 2000 |
| PinTea2 | Pinnacle Team 2001 |
| PinTea2C | Pinnacle Team 2001 Canadian |
| PinTea2F | Pinnacle Team 2000 French |
| PinTeaP | Pinnacle Team Pinnacle |
| PinTeaPC | Pinnacle Team Pinnacle Canadian |
| PinTeaPDP | Pinnacle Team Pinnacle Dufex Parallel |
| PinTeaPF | Pinnacle Team Pinnacle French |
| PinTeaPM | Pinnacle Team Pinnacle Mirror |
| PinTeaPP | Pinnacle Team Pinnacle Parallel |
| PinTeaPPM | Pinnacle Team Pinnacle Parallel Mirror |
| PinTin | Pinnacle Tins |
| PinTotCMPG | Pinnacle Totally Certified Mirror Platinum Gold |
| PinTotCPB | Pinnacle Totally Certified Platinum Blue |
| PinTotCPG | Pinnacle Totally Certified Platinum Gold |
| PinTotCPR | Pinnacle Totally Certified Platinum Red |
| PinTro | Pinnacle Trophies |
| PinWorEdi | Pinnacle World Edition |
| PlaOneoOne | Playoff One on One |
| Pop | Popsicle |
| PorPir | Portland Pirates |
| PorWinH | Portland Winter Hawks |
| PosActT | Post Action Transfers |
| PosCer | Post Cereal |
| PosCerBB | Post Cereal Box Backs |
| PosCerM | Post Cereal Marbles |
| PosCerS | Post Cereal Shooters |
| PosFliB | Post Flip Books |
| PosPin | Post Pinnacle |
| PosSta | Post Standups |
| PosUppD | Post Upper Deck |
| Pow | PowerPlay |
| PowGam | PowerPlay Gamebreakers |
| PowGloG | PowerPlay Global Greats |
| PowNet | PowerPlay Netminders |
| PowPoiL | PowerPlay Point Leaders |
| PowRisS | PowerPlay Rising Stars |
| PowRooS | PowerPlay Rookie Standouts |
| PowSecYS | PowerPlay Second Year Stars |
| PowSlaA | PowerPlay Slapshot Artists |
| PriAlbR | Prince Albert Raiders |
| PriAlbROC | Prince Albert Raiders Optimists Club |
| PriAlbRS | Prince Albert Raiders Stickers |
| ProAHL | ProCards AHL |
| ProAHLCHL | ProCards AHL/CHL/IHL |
| ProAHLIHL | ProCards AHL/IHL |
| ProAll | Pro-Sport All-Stars |
| ProBru | Providence Bruins |
| ProIHL | ProCards IHL |
| ProMag | Pro Magnets |
| ProSet | Pro Set |
| ProSetAW | Pro Set Award Winners |
| ProSetCC | Pro Set CC |
| ProSetCCF | Pro Set CC French |
| ProSetFre | Pro Set French |
| ProSetGaz | Pro Set Gazette |
| ProSetGTL | Pro Set Gold Team Leaders |
| ProSetHI | Pro Set HOF Induction |
| ProSetNHLAS | Pro Set NHL Awards Special |
| ProSetNHLSA | Pro Set NHL Sponsor Awards |
| ProSetON | Pro Set Opening Night |
| ProSetPC | Pro Set Puck Candy |
| ProSetPCP | Pro Set Puck Candy Promos |
| ProSetPla | Pro Set Platinum |
| ProSetPlaHOF75 | Pro Set Platinum HOF 75th |
| ProSetPlaPC | Pro Set Platinum PC |
| ProSetPM | Pro Set Player of the Month |
| ProSetPOTM | Pro Set Player of the Month |
| ProSetPre | Pro Set Preview |
| ProSetRGL | Pro Set Rookie Goal Leaders |
| ProSetRR | Pro Set Rink Rat |
| ProSetSLM | Pro Set St. Louis Midwest |
| ProvRed | Providence Reds |
| PufSti | Puffy Stickers |
| QuaOatP | Quaker Oats Photos |
| QuaOatWHA | Quaker Oats WHA |
| QueAce | Quebec Aces |
| QueAceQ | Quebec Aces QSHL |
| QueCit | Quebec Citadelles |
| QueIntP | Quebec Int. Pee-Wees |
| QueIntPWG | Quebec Int. Pee-Wees Gold |
| QuePeeWHWCCS | Quebec Pee Wee Hockey World Championship Collection Souvenir |
| QueRem | Quebec Remparts |
| RalIce | Raleigh Icecaps |
| RanMarMB | Rangers Marine Midland Bank |
| RanPowP | Rangers Power Play |
| RayJrC | Rayside-Balfour Jr. Canadians |
| RedDeeR | Red Deer Rebels |
| RedWinCitTum | Red Wings Citgo Tumblers |
| RedWinDNFP | Red Wings Detroit News/Free Press |
| RedWinLC | Red Wings Little Caesars |
| RedWinM | Red Wings Marathon |
| RedWinMP | Red Wings McCarthy Postcards |
| RedWinOld | Red Wings Oldtimers |
| RedWinP | Red Wings Postcards |
| RedWinTI | Red Wings Team Issue |
| RegPat | Regina Pats |
| RenEng | Rensselaer Engineers |
| RetHoc | Upper Deck Retro |
| RevThrPA | Revolution Three Pronged Attack |
| RevThrPA | Revolution Three Pronged Attack Parallel |
| RHIInaE | RHI Inaugural Edition |
| RicRen | Richmond Renegades |

| | |
|---|---|
| RicRiv | Richelieu Riverains |
| RimOce | Rimouski Oceanic |
| RimOceQPP | Rimouski Oceanic Quebec Provincial Police |
| RimOceU | Rimouski Oceanic Update |
| RivDu R | Riverains Du Richelieu |
| RoaExp | Roanoke Express |
| RoaPhoWHA | Roadrunners Phoenix WHA |
| Roc | Rockies |
| RocAme | Rochester Americans |
| RocCokCan | Rockies Coke Cans |
| RochAme | Rochester Amerks |
| RochAmeDD | Rochester Americans Dunkin' Donuts |
| RochAmeKod | Rochester Americans Kodak |
| RochAmePos | Rochester Americans Postcards |
| RochAmeSS | Rochester Americans Split Second |
| RocPos | Rockies Postcards |
| RocPucBuc | Rockies Puck Bucks |
| RoyDesH | Royal Desserts Hockey |
| RusNatT | Russian National Team |
| RusStaNHL | Russian Stars in NHL |
| RusStaRA | Russian Stars Red Ace |
| RusTriBur | Russian Tri-Globe Bure |
| RusTriFed | Russian Tri-Globe Fedorov |
| RusTriIrb | Russian Tri-Globe Irbe |
| RusTriKam | Russian Tri-Globe Kamensky |
| RusTriSem | Russian Tri-Globe Semenov |
| SabBel | Sabres Bells |
| SabBluS | Sabres Blue Shield |
| SabBluSS | Sabres Blue Shield Small |
| SabBluSSma | Sabres Blue Shield Small |
| SabCam | Sabres Campbell's |
| SabGla | Sabres Glasses |
| SabJubF | Sabres Jubilee Foods |
| SabLimETI | Sabres Limited Edition Team Issue |
| SabMilP | Sabres Milk Panels |
| SabNoc | Sabres Noco |
| SabPepC | Sabres Pepsi/Campbell's |
| SabPepPB | Sabres Pepsi Pinback Buttons |
| SabPos | Sabres Postcards |
| SabWonBH | Sabres Wonder Bread/Hostess |
| SalLakCGE | Salt Lake City Golden Eagles |
| SanDieG | San Diego Gulls |
| SanDieMW | San Diego Mariners WHA |
| SarProSta | Sargent Promotions Stamps |
| SarSti | Sarnia Sting |
| SasBla | Saskatoon Blades |
| SasBlaS | Saskatoon Blades Stickers |
| SauSteMG | Sault Ste. Marie Greyhounds |
| SauSteMGA | Sault Ste. Marie Greyhounds Autographed |
| SauSteMGM | Sault Ste. Marie Greyhounds Memorial Cup |
| Sco | Score |
| Sco90PC | Score 90 Plus Club |
| ScoAme | Score American |
| ScoArtPro | Score Artist's Proofs |
| ScoAva | Score Avalanche |
| ScoAvaPla | Score Avalanche Platinum |
| ScoAvaPre | Score Avalanche Premier |
| ScoBla | Maple Leafs Score Black's |
| ScoBlaIce | Score Black Ice |
| ScoBlaIceAP | Score Black Ice Artist's Proofs |
| ScoBlu | Score Blues |
| ScoBluPla | Score Blues Platinum |
| ScoBluPre | Score Blues Premier |
| ScoBobO | Score Bobby Orr |
| ScoBorBat | Score Border Battle |
| ScoBru | Score Bruins |
| ScoBruPla | Score Bruins Platinum |
| ScoBruPre | Score Bruins Premier |
| ScoCan | Score Canadian |
| ScoCan | Score Canadiens |
| ScoCanO | Score Canadian Olympians |
| ScoCanPla | Score Canadiens Platinum |
| ScoCanPla | Score Canucks Platinum |
| ScoCanPre | Score Canadiens Premier |
| ScoCanPre | Score Canucks Premier |
| ScoCanPS | Score Canadian Promo Sheets |
| ScoCanu | Score Canucks |
| ScoChel | Score Check It |
| ScoCheIt | Score Check It |
| ScoDeaCAP | Score Dealer's Choice Artist's Proofs |
| ScoDev | Score Devils |
| ScoDevPla | Score Devils Platinum |
| ScoDevPre | Score Devils Premier |
| ScoDreTea | Score Dream Team |
| ScoDynDC | Score Dynamic Duos Canadian |
| ScoDynDUS | Score Dynamic Duos U.S. |
| ScoEriL | Score Eric Lindros |
| ScoFan | Score Fanfest |
| ScoFly | Score Flyers |
| ScoFlyPla | Score Flyers Platinum |
| ScoFlyPre | Score Flyers Premier |
| ScoFra | Score Franchise |
| ScoGol | Score Gold |
| ScoGolB | Score Golden Blades |
| ScoGolBla | Score Golden Blades |
| ScoHobS | Score Hobby Samples |
| ScoHotC | Score Hot Cards |
| ScoHotRS | Score Hottest/Rising Stars |
| ScoIntS | Score International Stars |
| ScoIntSC | Score International Stars Canadian |
| ScoKel | Score Kellogg's |
| ScoLam | Score Lamplighters |
| ScoMapL | Score Maple Leafs |
| ScoMapLPla | Score Maple Leafs Platinum |
| ScoMapLPre | Score Maple Leafs Premier |
| ScoMigDPla | Score Mighty Ducks Platinum |

| | |
|---|---|
| ScoMigDPre | Score Mighty Ducks Premier |
| ScoMigDuc | Score Mighty Ducks |
| ScoNat | Score National |
| ScoNatCWC | Score National Candy Wholesalers Convention |
| ScoNetW | Score Net Worth |
| ScoPen | Score Penguins |
| ScoPenPla | Score Penguins Platinum |
| ScoPenPre | Score Penguins Premier |
| ScoPlaTS | Score Platinum Team Sets |
| ScoPro | Score Promos |
| ScoProP | Score Promo Panel |
| ScoRan | Score Rangers |
| ScoRanPla | Score Rangers Platinum |
| ScoRanPre | Score Rangers Premier |
| ScoRedW | Score Red Wings |
| ScoRedWPla | Score Red Wings Platinum |
| ScoRedWPre | Score Red Wings Premier |
| ScoRoo | Score Rookie/Traded |
| ScoSab | Score Sabres |
| ScoSabPla | Score Sabres Platinum |
| ScoSabPre | Score Sabres Premier |
| ScoSam | Score Samples |
| ScoSha | Score Sharpshooters |
| ScoShaCan | Score Sharpshooters Canadian |
| ScoSpeAP | Score Special Artist's Proofs |
| ScoSudDea | Score Sudden Death |
| ScoSup | Score Superstitions |
| ScoTeaC | Score Team Canada |
| ScoTopRR | Score Top Rookie Redemption |
| ScoUSAG | Score USA Greats |
| ScoYouS | Score Young Superstars |
| SeaPat | Seasons Patches |
| SeaThu | Seattle Thunderbirds |
| SeaTotW | Seattle Totems WHL |
| Sel | Select |
| SelCer | Select Certified |
| SelCerAP | Select Certified Artist's Proofs |
| SelCerBlu | Select Certified Blue |
| SelCerCor | Select Certified Cornerstones |
| SelCerDS | Select Certified Double Strike |
| SelCerDSG | Select Certified Double Strike Gold |
| SelCerFre | Select Certified Freezers |
| SelCerFut | Select Certified Future |
| SelCerGT | Select Certified Gold Team |
| SelCerMB | Select Certified Mirror Blue |
| SelCerMG | Select Certified Mirror Gold |
| SelCerMR | Select Certified Mirror Red |
| SelCerP | Select Certified Promos |
| SelCerRed | Select Certified Red |
| SelFirLin | Select First Line |
| SelGol | Select Gold |
| SelPro | Select Promos |
| SelYouExp | Select Youth Explosion |
| Sen | Senators |
| SenBelM | Senators Bell Mobility |
| SenKraS | Senators Kraft Sheets |
| SenPizH | Senators Pizza Hut |
| ShaFleAS | Sharks Fleer All-Star Sheet |
| ShaLosAW | Sharks Los Angeles WHA |
| ShaSanJSA | Sharks San Jose Sports Action |
| SheCan | Sherbrooke Canadiens |
| SheSte | Sheffield Steelers |
| ShiCoi | Shirriff Coins |
| ShiCoi | Shirriff/Salada Coins |
| ShiMetC | Shirriff Metal Coins |
| SigRoo | Signature Rookies |
| SigRooA | Signature Rookies Auto-Phonex |
| SigRooAB2 | Signature Rookies Auto-Phonex Beyond 2000 |
| SigRooAJJ | Signature Rookies Auto-Phonex Jaromir Jagr |
| SigRooAP | Signature Rookies Auto-Phonex Prodigies |
| SigRooAPC | Signature Rookies Auto-Phonex Phone Cards |
| SigRooCF | Signature Rookies Cool Five |
| SigRooCFS | Signature Rookies Cool Five Signatures |
| SigRooCP | Signature Rookies Club Promos |
| SigRooFF | Signature Rookies Future Flash |
| SigRooFFS | Signature Rookies Future Flash Signatures |
| SigRooMI | Signature Rookies MIracle on Ice |
| SigRooSig | Signature Rookies Signatures |
| SigRooSMIS | Signature Rookies Miracle on Ice Signatures |
| SioCitM | Sioux City Musketeers |
| SkyImp | SkyBox Impact |
| SkyImpB | SkyBox Impact BladeRunners |
| SkyImpCI | SkyBox Impact Countdown to Impact |
| SkyImpD | SkyBox Impact Deflectors |
| SkyImpIQ | SkyBox Impact Ice Quake |
| SkyImpNHLF | SkyBox Impact NHL on Fox |
| SkyImpPP | SkyBox Impact Promo Panel |
| SkyImpVer | SkyBox Impact VersaTeam |
| SkyImpZH | SkyBox Impact Zero Heroes |
| Sla | Slapshot |
| SlaMemC | Slapshot Memorial Cup |
| SlaPro | Slapshot Promos |
| SloAPSNT | Slovakian APS National Team |
| SloPeeWT | Slovakia-Quebec Pee-Wee Tournament |
| SluCupWHA | 7-Eleven Slurpee Cups WHA |
| SolBar | Solihull Barons |
| SouCarS | South Carolina Stingrays |
| SP | SP |
| SP Aut | SP Authentic |
| SP AutA | SP Authentic Authentics |
| SP AutI | SP Authentic Icons |
| SP AutPS | SP Authentic Power Shift |
| SP AutSM | SP Authentic Stat Masters |
| SP AutSotTG | SP Authentic Sign of the Times Gold |
| SP AutSS | SP Authentic Snapshots |
| SPAut | SP Authentic |

| | |
|---|---|
| SPAutAut | SP Authentic Authentics |
| SPAutID | SP Authentic Icons Die-Cuts |
| SPAutIE | SP Authentic Icons Embossed |
| SPAutMoaL | SP Authentic Mark of a Legend |
| SPAutSotT | SP Authentic Sign of the Times |
| SPAutTra | SP Authentic Tradition |
| SPCleWin | SP Clearcut Winner |
| SPDieCut | SP Die Cuts |
| SPGamFil | SP Game Film |
| SPHol | SP Holoviews |
| SPHolCol | SP Holoview Collection |
| SPHolSpFX | SP Holoviews Special FX |
| SPInsInf | SP Inside Info |
| SPInsInfG | SP Inside Info Gold |
| Spo | Sportscasters |
| SpoChi | Spokane Chiefs |
| SpoFla | Sport-Flash |
| SPPre | SP Premier |
| SPPreDC | SP Premier Die-Cuts |
| SprFal | Springfield Falcons |
| SprInd | Springfield Indians |
| SPSPxFor | SP SPx Force |
| SPSPxForAut | SP SPx Force Autographs |
| SPStaEto | SP Stars/Etoiles |
| SPStaEtoG | SP Stars/Etoiles Gold |
| SPx | SPx |
| SPxBro | SPx Bronze |
| SPxDim | SPx Dimension |
| SPxDuo | SPx DuoView |
| SPxDuoAut | SPx DuoView Autographs |
| SPxFin | SPx Finite |
| SPxFinR | SPx Finite Radiance |
| SPxFinS | SPx Finite Spectrum |
| SPxGol | SPx Gold |
| SPxGraF | SPx Grand Finale |
| SPxHolH | SPx Holoview Heroes |
| SPxSil | SPx Silver |
| SPxSte | SPx Steel |
| SPXTopP | SPx Top Prospects |
| SPXTopPF | SPx Top Prospects Radiance |
| SPXTopPHH | SPx Top Prospects Highlight Heroes |
| SPXTopPLI | SPx Top Prospects Lasting Impressions |
| SPXTopPPS | SPx Top Prospects Premier Stars |
| SPXTopPR | SPx Top Prospects Spectrum |
| SPXTopPWM | SPx Top Prospects Winning Materials |
| SPXTopPYotGO | SPx Top Prospects Year of the Great One |
| SSASotT | SP Authentic Sign of the Times |
| St.JohF | St. John Flames |
| St.JohML | St. John's Maple Leafs |
| St.LawS | St. Lawrence Sales |
| StaClu | Stadium Club |
| StaCluAS | Stadium Club All-Stars |
| StaCluDD | Stadium Club Dynasty and Destiny |
| StaCluDDMO | Stadium Club Dynasty and Destiny Members Only |
| StaCluEN | Stadium Club Extreme North |
| StaCluFDI | Stadium Club First Day Issue |
| StaCluFDIO | Stadium Club First Day Issue OPC |
| StaCluFea | Stadium Club Fearless |
| StaCluFI | Stadium Club Finest Inserts |
| StaCluFIMO | Stadium Club Finest Inserts Members Only |
| StaCluFin | Stadium Club Finest |
| StaCluGTSC | Stadium Club Generation TSC |
| StaCluM | Stadium Club Metalists |
| StaCluMasP | Stadium Club Master Photos |
| StaCluMasPW | Stadium Club Master Photos Winners |
| StaCluMO | Stadium Club Members Only |
| StaCluMOMS | Stadium Club Members Only Master Set |
| StaCluMPT | Stadium Club Master Photo Test |
| StaCluNem | Stadium Club Nemeses |
| StaCluO | Stadium Club OPC |
| StaCluPS | Stadium Club Power Streak |
| StaCluST | Stadium Club Super Teams |
| StaCluSTWC | Stadium Club Super Team Winner Cards |
| StaCluTUSA | Stadium Club Team USA |
| StaHoc | Stars HockeyKaps |
| StaPicH | Star Pics |
| StaPinS | Stars Pinnacle Sheet |
| StaPos | Stars Postcards |
| StaScoS | Stars Score Sheet |
| StiKah | Stingers Kahn's |
| Stu | Studio |
| StuHarH | Studio Hard Hats |
| StuPor | Studio Portraits |
| StuPrePG | Studio Press Proofs Gold |
| StuPrePS | Studio Press Proofs Silver |
| StuSil | Studio Silhouettes |
| StuSil8 | Studio Silhouettes 8 x 10 |
| SudWol | Sudbury Wolves |
| SudWolP | Sudbury Wolves Police |
| Sum | Summit |
| SumArtP | Summit Artist's Proofs |
| SumGM | Summit GM's Choice |
| SumHigV | Summit High Voltage |
| SumHigVM | Summit High Voltage Mirage |
| SumIce | Summit Ice |
| SumInTheCre | Summit In The Crease |
| SumInTheCrePS | Summit In The Crease Premium Stock |
| SumMadH | Summit Mad Hatters |
| SumMet | Summit Metal |
| SumPreS | Summit Premium Stock |
| SumUnt | Summit Untouchables |
| SweCap | Sweet Caporal |
| SweCorl | Swedish Coralli ISHockey |
| SweGloWC | Swedish Globe World Championships |
| SweHoc | Swedish Hockey |
| SweHocS | Swedish Hockey Stickers |
| SweLeaE | Swedish Leaf Elit |
| SweLeaEC | Swedish Leaf Elit Champs |
| SweLeaECS | Swedish Leaf Elit Clean Sweepers |
| SweLeaEFA | Swedish Leaf Elit Foreign Affairs |
| SweLeaEFF | Swedish Leaf Elit Face to Face |
| SweLeaEG | Swedish Leaf Elit Goldies |
| SweLeaEGC | Swedish Leaf Elit Gold Cards |
| SweLeaEGS | Swedish Leaf Elit Guest Special |
| SweLeaEM | Swedish Leaf Elit Mega |
| SweLeaENHLD | Swedish Leaf Elit NHL Draft |
| SweLeaEP | Swedish Leaf Elit Playmakers |
| SweLeaER | Swedish Leaf Elit Rookies |
| SweLeaERR | Swedish Leaf Elit Rookie Rockets |
| SweLeaES | Swedish Leaf Elit Spidermen |
| SweLeaESS | Swedish Leaf Elit Studio Signatures |
| SweLeaETG | Swedish Leaf Elit Top Guns |
| SwePanS | Swedish Panini Stickers |
| SweSemCDT | Swedish Semic Wien Coca-Cola Dream Team |
| SweSemE | Swedish Semic Elitserien |
| SweSemE | Swedish Semic Elitserien Stickers |
| SweSemHVS | Swedish Semic Hockey VM Stickers |
| SweSemHVS | Swedish Semic World Championship Stickers |
| SweSemW | Swedish Semic Wien |
| SweSemWAS | Swedish Semic Wien 1995 All Stars |
| SweSemWC | Swedish Semic World Championship |
| SweSemWCS | Swedish Semic World Championship Stickers |
| SweSemWCS | Swedish Semic World Championships Stickers |
| SweSemWHL | Swedish Semic Wien Hockey Legends |
| SweSemWNS | Swedish Semic Wien Nordic Stars |
| SweSemWSG | Swedish Semic Wien Super Goalies |
| SweUppDE | Swedish Upper Deck Elit |
| SweUppDE1DS | Swedish Upper Deck Elit 1st Division Stars |
| SweUppDETNA | Swedish Upper Deck Elit Ticket to North America |
| SweWorC | Swedish World Championships |
| SweWorCS | Swedish World Championship Stickers |
| SwiCurB | Swift Current Broncos |
| SwiHNL | Swiss HNL |
| SyrCru | Syracuse Crunch |
| TacRoc | Tacoma Rockets |
| TalTigS | Tallahassee Tiger Sharks |
| TCMA | TCMA |
| TeaCanLWHA | Team Canada L'Equipe WHA |
| TeaOut | Team Out |
| ThuBayS | Thunder Bay Senators |
| TitGuyL | Titrex Guy Lafleur |
| TitGuyLI | Titrex Guy Lafleur Insert |
| TolSto | Toledo Storm |
| Top | Topps |
| TopAut | Topps Autographs |
| TopBlaFTP | Topps Blast From The Past |
| TopBlaFTPA | Topps Blast From The Past Autographs |
| TopBlaLGR' | Topps Gold Label Goal Race '99 Black |
| TopBoaM | Topps Board Members |
| TopBowPS | Topps/Bowman Preview Sheet |
| TopBoxB | Topps Box Bottoms |
| TopCanG | Topps Canadian Gold |
| TopCanWJ | Topps Canadian World Juniors |
| TopFinB | Topps Finest Bronze |
| TopFinI | Topps Finest Inserts |
| TopGloI | Topps Glossy Inserts |
| TopGloS | Topps/O-Pee-Chee Glossy Square |
| TopGol | Topps Gold |
| TopGolLC1 | Topps Gold Label Class 1 |
| TopGolLC1B | Topps Gold Label Class 1 Black |
| TopGolLC1BOoO | Topps Gold Label Class 1 Black One of One |
| TopGolLC1OoO | Topps Gold Label Class 1 One of One |
| TopGolLC1R | Topps Gold Label Class 1 Red |
| TopGolLC1ROoO | Topps Gold Label Class 1 Red One of One |
| TopGolLC2 | Topps Gold Label Class 2 |
| TopGolLC2B | Topps Gold Label Class 2 Black |
| TopGolLC2BOoO | Topps Gold Label Class 2 Black One of One |
| TopGolLC2OoO | Topps Gold Label Class 2 One of One |
| TopGolLC2R | Topps Gold Label Class 2 Red |
| TopGolLC2ROoO | Topps Gold Label Class 2 Red One of One |
| TopGolLC3 | Topps Gold Label Class 3 |
| TopGolLC3B | Topps Gold Label Class 3 Black |
| TopGolLC3BOoO | Topps Gold Label Class 3 Black One of One |
| TopGolLC3OoO | Topps Gold Label Class 3 One of One |
| TopGolLC3R | Topps Gold Label Class 3 Red |
| TopGolLC3ROoO | Topps Gold Label Class 3 Red One of One |
| TopGolLGR' | Topps Gold Label Goal Race '99 |
| TopGolLGR'BOoO | Topps Gold Label Goal Race '99 Black One of One |
| TopGolLGR'OoO | Topps Gold Label Goal Race '99 One of One |
| TopGolLGR'ROoO | Topps Gold Label Goal Race '99 Red One of One |
| TopHidGem | Topps Hidden Gems |
| TopHocBuc | Topps Hockey Bucks |
| TopHocMC | Highland Mint Mint-Cards Topps |
| TopHomGC | Topps Home Grown Canada |
| TopHomGUSA | Topps Home Grown USA |
| TopIceA2 | Topps Ice Age 2000 |
| TopLocL | Topps Local Legends |
| TopMarMPB | Topps Marquee Men Power Boosters |
| TopMysF | Topps Mystery Finest |
| TopMysFB | Topps Mystery Finest Bronze |
| TopMysFBR | Topps Mystery Finest Bronze Refractors |
| TopMysFG | Topps Mystery Finest Gold |
| TopMysFGR | Topps Mystery Finest Gold Refractors |
| TopMysFR | Topps Mystery Finest Refractors |
| TopMysFS | Topps Mystery Finest Silver |
| TopMysFSR | Topps Mystery Finest Silver Refractors |
| TopNewG | Topps New To The Game |
| TopNHLP | Topps Picks |
| TopO-P | Topps O-Pee-Chee |
| TopOPCGlo | Topps/O-Pee-Chee Glossy |
| TopOPCI | Topps OPC Inserts |
| TopPic5C | Topps Picks 500 Club |
| TopPicFT | Topps Picks Fantasy Team |
| TopPicID | Topps Picks Ice D |
| TopPicOI | Topps Picks OPC Inserts |
| TopPicRS | Topps Picks Rookie Stars |
| TopPicTS | Topps Picks Top Shelf |
| TopPowL | Topps Power Lines |
| TopPre | Topps/OPC Premier |
| TopPreBG | Topps Premier Black Gold |
| TopPreF | Topps Premier Finest |
| TopPreG | Topps/OPC Premier Gold |
| TopPreGTG | Topps/OPC Premier The Go To Guy |
| TopPrePS | Topps Premier Promo Sheet |
| TopPreSE | Topps/OPC Premier Special Effects |
| TopPreTUSA | Topps Premier Team USA |
| TopPro | Topps Profiles |
| TopRedLGR' | Topps Gold Label Goal Race '99 Red |
| TopRinL | Topps Rink Leaders |
| TopSeaB | Topps Season's Best |
| TopSta | Topps Stamps |
| TopStiIns | Topps Sticker Inserts |
| TopStiS | Topps/OPC Sticker Stamps |
| TopSupSki | Topps SuperSkills |
| TopSupSkiPla | Topps SuperSkills Platinum |
| TopSupSkiSR | Topps SuperSkills Super Rookies |
| TopTeal | Topps Team Inserts |
| TopTeaP | Topps Team Posters |
| TopTeaSL | Topps Team Scoring Leaders |
| TopTif | Topps Tiffany |
| TopUSAT | Topps USA Test |
| TopYouS | Topps Young Stars |
| TorSta | Toronto Star |
| TorSun | Toronto Sun |
| TriAme | Tri-City Americans |
| TriFroRWP | Tri-Globe From Russia With Puck |
| TriPos | Triumph Postcards |
| TulOil | Tulsa Oilers |
| UC | UD Choice |
| UCMBH | UD Choice Mini Bobbing Head |
| UCSB | UD Choice StarQuest Blue |
| UCSG | UD Choice StarQuest Gold |
| UCSG | UD Choice StarQuest Green |
| UCSR | UD Choice StarQuest Red |
| UD ChoDYOTC | UD Choice Draw Your Own Trading Card |
| UD ChoPCR | UD Choice Prime Choice Reserve |
| UD ChoR | UD Choice Reserve |
| UD ChoS | UD Choice SHL |
| UD ChoSDitL | UD Choice SHL Day in the Life |
| UD3 | UD3 |
| UD3DieC | UD3 Die Cuts |
| UDAWayGC | UDA Commemorative Cards |
| UDCP | UD Choice Preview |
| Ult | Ultra |
| UltAdaO | Ultra Adam Oates |
| UltAllRoo | Ultra All-Rookies |
| UltAllRooGM | Ultra All-Rookie Gold Medallion |
| UltAllS | Ultra All-Stars |
| UltAwaW | Ultra Award Winners |
| UltCleTheIce | Ultra Clear the Ice |
| UltCreCra | Ultra Crease Crashers |
| UltDra | Ultimate Draft |
| UltDraP | Ultimate Draft Promos |
| UltExtAtt | Ultra Extra Attackers |
| UltGloGre | Ultra Global Greats |
| UltGolM | Ultra Gold Medallion |
| UltHigSpe | Ultra High Speed |
| UltImp | Ultra Imports |
| UltJerR | Ultra Jeremy Roenick |
| UltMr.Mom | Ultra Mr. Momentum |
| UltOriS | Ultimate Original Six |
| UltOriSBB | Ultimate Original Six Box Bottoms |
| UltOriSF | Ultimate Original Six French |
| UltPow | Ultra Power |
| UltPowBL | Ultra Power Blue Line |
| UltPowRL | Ultra Power Red Line |
| UltPreP | Ultra Premier Pivots |
| UltPrePadMen | Ultra Premier Pad Men |
| UltPrePadMenGM | Ultra Premier Pad Men Gold Medallion |
| UltPrePiv | Ultra Premier Pivots |
| UltPrePivGM | Ultra Premier Pivots Gold Medallion |
| UltPrePM | Ultra Premier Pad Men |
| UltPro | Ultra Prospects |
| UltProS | Ultra Promo Sheet |
| UltRedLS | Ultra Red Light Specials |
| UltRedLSGM | Ultra Red Light Specials Gold Medallion |
| UltRisS | Ultra Rising Stars |
| UltRisSGM | Ultra Rising Stars Gold Medallion |
| UltRoo | Ultra Rookies |
| UltScoK | Ultra Scoring Kings |
| UltSerFed | Ultra Sergei Fedorov |
| UltSpeM | Ultra Speed Merchants |
| UltUltHP | Ultra Ultraview Hot Pack |
| UltUltV | Ultra Ultraview |
| UltWavF | Ultra Wave of the Future |
| UniOilW | Union Oil WHL |
| UppAllSGP | Upper Deck All-Star Game Predictors |
| UppDec | Upper Deck |
| UppDecACH | Upper Deck Ameri/Can Holograms |
| UppDecAGPRW | Upper Deck All-Star Game Predictors Redemption Winner |
| UppDecART | Upper Deck All-Rookie Team |
| UppDecAW | Upper Deck Award Winners |
| UppDecAWH | Upper Deck Award Winner Holograms |
| UppDecAWT | Upper Deck All-World Team |

| Code | Description |
|---|---|
| UppDecB | Upper Deck Blow-Ups |
| UppDecBB | Upper Deck Box Bottoms |
| UppDecBD | Upper Deck Black Diamond |
| UppDecBDDD | Upper Deck Black Diamond Double Diamond |
| UppDecBDG | Upper Deck Black Diamond Gold |
| UppDecBDPC | Upper Deck Black Diamond Premium Cut |
| UppDecBDPCDD | Upper Deck Black Diamond Premium Cut Double Diamond |
| UppDecBDPCM | Upper Deck Black Diamond Premium Cut Quadruple Diamond Verticals |
| UppDecBDPCQD | Upper Deck Black Diamond Premium Cut Quadruple Diamond Horizontal |
| UppDecBDPCTD | Upper Deck Black Diamond Premium Cut Triple Diamond |
| UppDecBDQD | Upper Deck Black Diamond Quadruple Diamond |
| UppDecBDRFTC | Upper Deck Black Diamond Run for the Cup |
| UppDecBDTD | Upper Deck Black Diamond Triple Diamond |
| UppDecBDYotGO | Upper Deck Black Diamond Year of the Great One |
| UppDecBHH | Upper Deck Brett Hull Heroes |
| UppDecBHHF | Upper Deck Brett Hull Heroes French |
| UppDecCC | Upper Deck Calder Candidates |
| UppDecCtAG | Upper Deck Crash the All-Star Game |
| UppDecCWJC | Upper Deck Czech World Juniors |
| UppDecDD | Upper Deck Black Diamond Double Diamond |
| UppDecDV | Upper Deck Diamond Vision |
| UppDecDVDM | Upper Deck Diamond Vision Defining Moments |
| UppDecDVSM | Upper Deck Diamond Vision Signature Moves |
| UppDecE | Upper Deck Exclusive |
| UppDecE1o1 | Upper Deck Exclusive 1 of 1 |
| UppDecEIeIce | Upper Deck Electric Ice |
| UppDecEIeIceG | Upper Deck Electric Ice Gold |
| UppDecER | Upper Deck Euro-Rookies |
| UppDecERT | Upper Deck Euro-Rookie Team |
| UppDecES | Upper Deck Euro-Stars |
| UppDecESF | Upper Deck Euro-Stars French |
| UppDecF | Upper Deck French |
| UppDecFF | Upper Deck Fantastic Finishers |
| UppDecFF | Upper Deck Fantastic Finishers Quantum 3 |
| UppDecFFQ1 | Upper Deck Fantastic Finishers Quantum 1 |
| UppDecFFQ2 | Upper Deck Fantastic Finishers Quantum 2 |
| UppDecFH | Upper Deck Future Heroes |
| UppDecFIT | Upper Deck Frozen In Time |
| UppDecFITQ1 | Upper Deck Frozen In Time Quantum 1 |
| UppDecFITQ2 | Upper Deck Frozen In Time Quantum 2 |
| UppDecFITQ3 | Upper Deck Frozen In Time Quantum 3 |
| UppDecFreFra | Upper Deck Freeze Frame |
| UppDecFreFraJ | Upper Deck Freeze Frame Jumbo |
| UppDecG24KG | Upper Deck Gretzky 24K Gold |
| UppDecGBB | Upper Deck Gretzky Box Bottom |
| UppDecGDM | Upper Deck Game Dated Moments |
| UppDecGGO | Upper Deck Gretzky's Great Ones |
| UppDecGHH | Upper Deck Gordie Howe Heroes |
| UppDecGHS | Upper Deck Gordie Howe Selects |
| UppDecGJ | Upper Deck Game Jerseys |
| UppDecGN | Upper Deck Generation Next |
| UppDecGNQ1 | Upper Deck Generation Next Quantum 1 |
| UppDecGNQ2 | Upper Deck Generation Next Quantum 2 |
| UppDecGNQ3 | Upper Deck Generation Next Quantum 3 |
| UppDecGR | Upper Deck Gold Reserve |
| UppDecGreCol | Upper Deck Gretzky Collection |
| UppDecGreColJ | Upper Deck Gretzky Collection Jumbo |
| UppDecGS | Upper Deck Gretzky Sheet |
| UppDecHH | Upper Deck Hart Hopefuls Bronze |
| UppDecHHG | Upper Deck Hart Hopefuls Gold |
| UppDecHHS | Upper Deck Hart Hopefuls Silver |
| UppDecHol | Upper Deck Holograms |
| UppDecHT | Upper Deck Hat Tricks |
| UppDecIC | Upper Deck Ice Champions |
| UppDecIC2 | Upper Deck Ice Champions 2 |
| UppDecIce | Upper Deck Ice |
| UppDecIceDF | Upper Deck Ice Dynasty Foundation |
| UppDecIceP | Upper Deck Ice Parallel |
| UppDecIcePar | Upper Deck Ice Parallel |
| UppDecIceSCF | Upper Deck Ice Stanley Cup Foundation |
| UppDecIG | Upper Deck Ice Gallery |
| UppDecILL | Upper Deck Ice Lethal Lines |
| UppDecILL2 | Upper Deck Ice Lethal Lines 2 |
| UppDecIPS | Upper Deck Ice Power Shift |
| UppDecLAS | Upper Deck Locker All-Stars |
| UppDecLSH | Upper Deck Lord Stanley Heroes |
| UppDecLSH | Upper Deck Lord Stanley's Heroes Quarterfinals |
| UppDecLSHF | Upper Deck Lord Stanley's Heroes Finals |
| UppDecLSHQ1 | Upper Deck Lord Stanley Heroes Quantum 1 |
| UppDecLSHQ2 | Upper Deck Lord Stanley Heroes Quantum 2 |
| UppDecLSHQ3 | Upper Deck Lord Stanley Heroes Quantum 3 |
| UppDecLSHS | Upper Deck Lord Stanley's Heroes Semifinals |
| UppDecM | Upper Deck MVP |
| UppDecM1 | Upper Deck Black Diamond Myriad 1 |
| UppDecM2 | Upper Deck Black Diamond Myriad 2 |
| UppDecM2CN | Upper Deck MVP 21st Century NHL |
| UppDecM9S | Upper Deck MVP 90's Snapshots |
| UppDecMD | Upper Deck MVP Dynamics |
| UppDecMDR | Upper Deck MVP Draft Report |
| UppDECMGS | Upper Deck MVP Game Souvenirs |
| UppDecMGS | Upper Deck MVP Game-Used Souvenirs |
| UppDecMGS | Upper Deck MVP Gold Script |
| UppDecMGUSA | Upper Deck MVP Game Used Souvenirs Autographed |
| UppDecMHoG | Upper Deck MVP Hands of Gold |
| UppDecMLL | Upper Deck MVP Last Line |
| UppDecMLO | Upper Deck MVP Legendary One |
| UppDecMOH | Upper Deck MVP OT Heroes |
| UppDecMP | Upper Deck MVP ProSign |
| UppDecMPG | Upper Deck MVP Power Game |
| UppDecMPS | Upper Deck MVP Pro Sign |
| UppDecMS | Upper Deck MVP Snipers |
| UppDecMSF | Upper Deck MVP Special Forces |
| UppDecMSS | Upper Deck MVP Silver Script |
| UppDecMSS | Upper Deck MVP Super Script |
| UppDecMT | Upper Deck MVP Talent |
| UppDecNB | Upper Deck NHL's Best |
| UppDecNBAP | Upper Deck NHLPA/Be A Player |
| UppDecNHLAS | Upper Deck NHL All-Stars |
| UppDecNL | Upper Deck Next In Line |
| UppDecNR | Upper Deck NHLPA/Roots |
| UppDecP | Upper Deck Profiles |
| UppDecP | Upper Deck Promos |
| UppDecPC | Upper Deck Predictor Canadian |
| UppDecPCEG | Upper Deck Predictor Candian Exchange Gold |
| UppDecPCES | Upper Deck Predictor Canadian Exchange Silver |
| UppDecPH | Upper Deck Predictor Hobby |
| UppDecPHE | Upper Deck Predictor Hobby Exchange |
| UppDecPHEG | Upper Deck Predictor Hobby Exchange Gold |
| UppDecPHES | Upper Deck Predictor Hobby Exchange Silver |
| UppDecPHG | Upper Deck Predictor Hobby Gold |
| UppDecPOE | Upper Deck Program of Excellence |
| UppDecPP | Upper Deck Power Performers |
| UppDecPQ1 | Upper Deck Profiles Quantum 1 |
| UppDecPQ2 | Upper Deck Profiles Quantum 2 |
| UppDecPQ3 | Upper Deck Profiles Quantum 3 |
| UppDecPR | Upper Deck Predictor Retail |
| UppDecPRE | Upper Deck Predictor Retail Exchange |
| UppDecPreGSE | Upper Deck Predictor Gold/Silver Exchange |
| UppDecPreH | Upper Deck Predictor Hobby |
| UppDecPreR | Upper Deck Predictor Retail |
| UppDecPreRG | Upper Deck Predictor Retail Gold |
| UppDecQD | Upper Deck Black Diamond Quadruple Diamond |
| UppDecRDR | Upper Deck Retro Distant Replay |
| UppDecRDRI | Upper Deck Retro Distant Replay II |
| UppDecREG | Upper Deck Retro Epic Gretzky |
| UppDecREGI | Upper Deck Retro Epic Gretzky II |
| UppDecRG | Upper Deck Retro Generation |
| UppDecRG | Upper Deck Retro Gold |
| UppDecRGI | Upper Deck Retro Generation II |
| UppDecRII | Upper Deck Retro Inkredible II |
| UppDecRIL1 | Upper Deck Retro Inkredible |
| UppDecRM | Upper Deck Retro Momento |
| UppDecRP | Upper Deck Retro Platinum |
| UppDecRTotC | Upper Deck Retro Turn of the Century |
| UppDecSG | Upper Deck Smooth Grooves |
| UppDecShe | Upper Deck Sheets |
| UppDecSilSka | Upper Deck Silver Skates |
| UppDecSilSkaG | Upper Deck Silver Skates Gold |
| UppDecSP | Upper Deck SP |
| UppDecSpeE | Upper Deck Special Edition |
| UppDecSpeEdiG | Upper Deck Special Edition Gold |
| UppDecSPI | Upper Deck SP Inserts |
| UppDecSPIDC | Upper Deck SP Inserts Die Cuts |
| UppDecSS | Upper Deck Superstar Showdown |
| UppDecSSM | Upper Deck Sixth Sense Masters |
| UppDecSSW | Upper Deck Sixth Sense Wizards |
| UppDecTD | Upper Deck Black Diamond Triple Diamond |
| UppDecTS | Upper Deck The Specialists |
| UppDecTSL2 | Upper Deck The Specialists Level 2 |
| UppDecTSS | Upper Deck Three Star Selects |
| UppDecWFG | Upper Deck Black Diamond Winning Formula Gold |
| UppDecWFP | Upper Deck Black Diamond Winning Formula Platinum |
| UppDecWGGJA | Upper Deck Wayne Gretzky Game Jersey Autographs |
| UppDecWGH | Upper Deck Wayne Gretzky Heroes |
| UppDecWJA | Upper Deck World Junior Alumni |
| UppDecWJG | Upper Deck World Junior Grads |
| UppDecYotGO | Upper Deck Year of the Great One |
| UppDecYotGOQ1 | Upper Deck Year of the Great One Quantum 1 |
| UppDecYotGOQ2 | Upper Deck Year of the Great One Quantum 2 |
| UppDecYotGOQ3 | Upper Deck Year of the Great One Quantum 3 |
| UppDWO | Upper Deck Willie O'Ree Commemorative Card |
| USAOlyTMP | USA Olympic Team Mini Pics |
| USSOlyTMP | USSR Olympic Team Mini Pics |
| V1281PauC | V128-1 Paulin's Candy |
| V1282PauC | V128-2 Paulins Candy |
| V129 | V129 |
| V130MapC | V130 Maple Crispette |
| V1451 | V145-1 |
| V1452 | V145-2 |
| V252CanG | V252 Canadian Gum |
| V288HamG | V288 Hamilton Gum |
| V356WorG | V356 Worldwide Gum |
| V3572IceKP | V357-2 Ice Kings Premiums |
| V357IceK | V357 Ice Kings |
| Vac | Vachon |
| Vald'OF | Val d'Or Foreurs |
| VanVooRHI | Vancouver VooDoo RHI |
| VicCou | Victoria Cougars |
| WatBlaH | Waterloo Black Hawks |
| WesMic | Western Michigan |
| WhaBobS | Whalers Bob's Stores |
| WhaCok | Whalers Coke |
| WhaDai | Whalers Dairymart |
| WhaJr7E | Whalers Jr. 7-Eleven |
| WhaJunBK | Whalers Jr. Burger King/Pepsi |
| WhaJunGR | Whalers Junior Ground Round |
| WhaJunHC | Whalers Junior Hartford Courant |
| WhaJunM | Whalers Junior Milk |
| WhaJunT | Whalers Junior Thomas' |
| WhaJunW | Whalers Junior Wendy's |
| WhaNewEWHA | Whalers New England WHA |
| WheNai | Wheeling Nailers |
| WheThu | Wheeling Thunderbirds |
| WicThu | Wichita Thunder |
| WinSpi | Windsor Spitfires |
| WonBreL | Wonder Bread Labels |
| WonBrePP | Wonder Bread Premium Photos |
| YorActOct | York Action Octagons |
| YorIroOTra | York Iron-On Transfers |
| YorPreP | York Premium Photos |
| YorWhiB | York White Backs |
| YorYelB | York Yellow Backs |
| ZelMasH | Zellers Masters of Hockey |
| ZelMasoH | Zellers Masters of Hockey Signed |
| ZelMasoHS | Zellers Masters of Hockey Signed |
| Zen | Zenith |
| Zen5x7 | Zenith 5 x 7 |
| ZenArtP | Zenith Artist's Proofs |
| ZenAss | Zenith Assailants |
| ZenChaS | Zenith Champion Salute |
| ZenChaSD | Zenith Champion Salute Diamond |
| ZenChaTC | Zenith Chasing The Cup |
| ZenGifG | Zenith Gifted Grinders |
| ZenGolImp | Zenith 5 x 7 Gold Impulse |
| ZenRooR | Zenith Rookie Reign |
| ZenRooRC | Zenith Rookie Roll Call |
| ZenSilImp | Zenith 5 x 7 Silver Impulse |
| ZenZGol | Zenith Z-Gold |
| ZenZSil | Zenith Z-Silver |
| ZenZT | Zenith Z-Team |
| ZenZT5x7 | Zenith Z-Team 5 x 7 |
| ZenZTG | Zenith Z-Team Gold |

# Hockey Alphabetical Index

This alphabetical index presents all the cards issued for any particular player (or person) included in the card sets listed in the Beckett Hockey Card Price Guide. It will prove to be an invaluable tool for seasoned and novice collectors alike. Although this book was carefully compiled and proofread, it is inevitable that errors, misspellings, and inconsistencies may occur. This is especially true when considering the foreign cards linked into this index, and all the various "interpretive" spellings that entails. Also, with team or group-type card photos, we have tried to identify and link at least the main figures on the card. If you should come across a card where we have not identified all persons on the card of if there are any errors that come to your attention, please send them to the author. These corrections will be incorporated into future editions of the hockey alphabetical checklist.

## How to Use the Alphabetical Checklist

The alphabetical checklist has been designed to be user friendly. The set code abbreviations used throughout are easily identified and memorized. The format adopted for card identification is explained below. However, the large number of card sets contained in this volume require that the reader first become familiar with how the abbreviations are organized. PLEASE READ THE FOLLOWING SECTION CAREFULLY BEFORE ATTEMPTING TO USE THE CHECKLIST.

The cards are listed alphabetically by the player's current last name. Where appropriate, widely used nicknames (e.g. Dave "Tiger" Williams) are listed before the players' first name (which will be in parentheses). Different players with otherwise identical names are sometimes distinguished by additional information (e.g. Bill McCreary and Bill REF McCreary). The codes following the players' names are indented and give the card sets and card numbers in the sets in which the players appeared. The set codes are designed so that each code is distinctive for a particular card set.

The set code for each set name is done in a simple to use formula throughout the alphabetical checklist. The abbreviations are in a 3-3-1-1-1-1

pattern. What this means is that each set in the book has been abbreviated to the first three letters of the first name of the set, the first three letters of the second name of the set, and the first letter of each name after that. Here is an example:

Dufour, Luc
  83BruTeal-4
  84NorPos-7

The first card is a 1983-84 Bruins Team Issue card #4. The first three letters of the first name (Bruins), the first three letters of the second name (Team) and the first letter of the third name (Issue) were used to create this abbreviation. The second card is a 1984-85 Nordiques Postcard #7. Again the first three letters of the first and second name of the set (Nordiques Postcards) are used to give us the NorPos part of the abbreviation. In all cases, the year of issue is abbreviated to simply read as a single year. Therefore, a 1984-85 Topps listing would read 84Top.

Depending on the particular card set, the set code abbreviations consist of from three to five distinctive elements:
  a) Year of issue (listed in ascending chronological order);
  b) Manufacturer or sponsor;
  c) Insert name (where applicable)
  d) Number on card
  e) Individual card descriptive prefixes or suffixes.

When two or more different manufacturers issued cards for a player in the same year, the cards are listed alphabetically according to the maker's name (e.g. 1992-93 OPC precedes 1992-93 Parkhurst).

The card number typically corresponds to the particular number on the card itself; in some instances, the card number also involves letter prefixes. For the most part, cards in unnumbered sets are usually entered alphabetically according to the players's last name and assigned a number arbitrarily. In a few instances unnumbered cards are simply identified as if their card number were "NNO."

**Aaby, Henrik**
☐ 96SweSemW-208
**Aalto, Antti**
☐ 93Cla-35
☐ 93FinnSIS-43
☐ 93FinnSIS-394
☐ 94Fin-122
☐ 94FinnSIS-129
☐ 94FinRef-122
☐ 94FinnSupTW-122
☐ 94ParSE-SE227
☐ 94ParSEG-SE227
☐ 94SP-161
☐ 94SPDieCut-161
☐ 94UppDec-511
☐ 94UppDecEIeIce-511
☐ 95FinnSemWC-238
☐ 95FinnSIS-328
☐ 96FinnSISR-147
☐ 98PacOmeH-9
☐ 98PacOmeODI-9
☐ 98PacOmeR-9
☐ 98UC-9
☐ 98UD ChoPCR-9
☐ 98UD ChoR-9
☐ 98UppDec-1
☐ 98UppDecE-1
☐ 98UppDecE1o1-1
☐ 98UppDecGR-1
**Aaltonen, Petri**
☐ 93FinnJyvHS-294
☐ 93FinnSIS-80
**Abbott, Reggie**
☐ 48ExhCan-1
**Abbott, Timothy**
☐ 89ProAHL-311
**Abel, Brett**
☐ 93WheThu-9
**Abel, Gerry**
☐ 76OldTim-1
☐ 81RedWinOld-9
**Abel, Neil**
☐ 93SheSte-4
☐ 94SheSte-19
☐ 97SheSte-17
**Abel, Sid**
☐ 34BeeGro1P-86
☐ 390PCV3011-68
☐ 44BeeGro2P-149
☐ 48ExhCan-43
☐ 51Par-64
☐ 52RoyDesH-4
☐ 60Par-23
☐ 60ShiCoi-60
☐ 61ShiCoi-61
☐ 62Par-34
☐ 64Top-93
☐ 65Top-41
☐ 66Top-42
☐ 76OldTim-2
☐ 83HalFP-A1
☐ 85HalFC-2
☐ 91UltOriS-66
☐ 91UltOriSF-66
☐ 92HalFL-12
☐ 94ParTalB-65
**Abel, Taffy (Clarence)**
☐ 33V252CanG-1
☐ 34DiaMatS-1
**Aberg, Jerry**
☐ 72SweHocS-203
**Aberg, Patric**
☐ 83SweSemE-36
☐ 84SweSemE-34
☐ 86SwePanS-9
☐ 91SweSemE-286
☐ 92SweSemE-302
☐ 94SweLeaE-181
☐ 95SweLeaE-7
☐ 95SweUppDE-8
**Abid, Ramzi**
☐ 98BowBes-141
☐ 98BowBesAR-141
☐ 98BowBesR-141
☐ 98BowCHL-110
☐ 98BowCHL-121
☐ 98BowCHLAuB-A18
☐ 98BowCHLAuG-A18
☐ 98BowCHLAuS-A18
☐ 98BowCHLGA-110
☐ 98BowCHLGA-121
☐ 98BowCHLOI-110
☐ 98BowCHLOI-121
☐ 98BowChrC-110
☐ 98BowChrC-121
☐ 98BowChrCGA-110
☐ 98BowChrCGA-121
☐ 98BowChrCGAR-110
☐ 98BowChrCGAR-121
☐ 98BowChrCOI-110
☐ 98BowChrCOI-121
☐ 98BowChrCOIR-110
☐ 98BowChrCOIR-121
☐ 98BowChrCR-110
☐ 98BowChrCR-121
☐ 98O-PChr-221
☐ 98O-PChrR-221
☐ 98Top-221
☐ 98TopO-P-221
**Ablad, Tobias**
☐ 97LouRivF-13
**Abrahamson, Brett**
☐ 93MinGolG-1
☐ 95MinGolG-3
**Abrahamsson, Christer**

☐ 67SweHocS-1
☐ 67SweHoc-95
☐ 69SweHocS-110
☐ 70SweHocS-66
☐ 70SweHocS-275
☐ 71SweHocS-1
☐ 71SweHocS-155
☐ 72SweHocS-1
☐ 72SweSemWC-43
☐ 73SweHocS-1
☐ 73SweHocS-39
☐ 73SweWorCS-1
☐ 73SweWorCS-39
☐ 74SweHocS-137
☐ 74SweSemHVS-1
☐ 750PCWHA-28
☐ 760PCWHA-67
☐ 760PCWHA-110
☐ 86SwePanS-218
☐ 87SwePanS-148
☐ 92SweSemE-333
☐ 93SweSemE-298
☐ 94SweLeaE-304
**Abrahamsson, Hans**
☐ 93SweSemE-102
☐ 94SweLeaE-123
☐ 95SweLeaE-51
☐ 95SweUppDE-78
☐ 98GerDELE-307
**Abrahamsson, Lennart**
☐ 67SweHoc-246
☐ 69SweHocS-202
**Abrahamsson, Mats**
☐ 83SweSemE-172
☐ 84SweSemE-195
☐ 86SwePanS-219
**Abrahamsson, Tommy**
☐ 65SweCorI-57B
☐ 67SweHoc-2
☐ 67SweHoc-96
☐ 69SweHocS-111
☐ 69SweWorC-155
☐ 70SweHocS-68
☐ 70SweHocS-276
☐ 71SweHocS-4
☐ 71SweHocS-157
☐ 72SweHocS-3
☐ 72SweHocS-152
☐ 72SweSemWC-49
☐ 73SweHocS-6
☐ 73SweHocS-43
☐ 73SweWorCS-6
☐ 73SweWorCS-43
☐ 74SweHocS-21
☐ 74SweHocS-153
☐ 74SweSemHVS-6
☐ 750PCWHA-127
☐ 760PCWHA-79
**Abrahamson, Brett**
☐ 96MinGolGCAS-3
**Abramov, Sergei**
☐ 96SweSemW-130
**Abrams, Marty**
☐ 84SauSiteMG-1
**Abric, Peter**
☐ 83NorBayC-2
**Abstreiter, Tobias**
☐ 94GerDELE-316
☐ 95GerDELE-215
☐ 96GerDELE-358
☐ 98GerDELE-61
**Achtynichuk, Gene**
☐ 56QueAce-1
**Ackerman, Chad**
☐ 96HamRoaA-HRA14
**Ackestrom, Oscar**
☐ 90SweSemE-36
☐ 91SweSemE-284
☐ 92SweSemE-304
☐ 93SweSemE-270
☐ 94SweLeaE-120
☐ 95SweLeaE-208
**Acton, Keith**
☐ 80CanaPos-1
☐ 80PepCap-41
☐ 81CanaPos-2
☐ 810PC-181
☐ 82CanaPos-1
☐ 82CanaSte-1
☐ 820PC-179
☐ 820PC-180
☐ 820PCSti-42
☐ 820PCSti-43
☐ 82PosCer-10
☐ 83NorStaPos-1
☐ 830PC-184
☐ 84NorSta7E-6
☐ 84NorStaPos-1
☐ 840PC-93
☐ 85NorSta7E-10
☐ 85NorStaPos-1
☐ 850PC-82
☐ 850PCSti-38
☐ 85Top-82
☐ 860PC-172
☐ 86Top-172
☐ 87NorStaPos-1
☐ 87OilTeal-23
☐ 88OilTenAnn-77
☐ 89FlyPos-1
☐ 890PC-254
☐ 89NorStaPos-1
☐ 90Bow-113

☐ 90BowTif-113
☐ 90FlyPos-1
☐ 900PC-180
☐ 900PC-355
☐ 90ProSet-497
☐ 90Sco-301A
☐ 90ScoCan-301A
☐ 90Top-180
☐ 90Top-355
☐ 90TopTif-355
☐ 90UppDec-445
☐ 90UppDecF-445
☐ 91Bow-244
☐ 91FlyJCP-1
☐ 910PC-77
☐ 91PanSti-237
☐ 91ScoAme-133
☐ 91ScoCan-133
☐ 91StaClu-247
☐ 91Top-77
☐ 92Bow-184
☐ 92FlyJCP-1
☐ 92FlyUppDS-4
☐ 92FlyUppDS-25
☐ 92FlyUppDS-35
☐ 920PC-368
☐ 92Pin-363
☐ 92PinFre-363
☐ 92Sco-341
☐ 92ScoCan-341
☐ 92StaClu-223
☐ 92Top-199
☐ 92TopGol-199G
☐ 92Ult-368
☐ 93Lea-420
☐ 930PCPre-407
☐ 930PCPreG-407
☐ 93PanSti-50
☐ 93Sco-301
☐ 93ScoCan-301
☐ 93StaCluFDI-205
☐ 93StaCluFDIO-205
☐ 93StaCluO-205
☐ 93TopPre-407
☐ 93TopPreG-407
**Adair, Scott**
☐ 907thInnSWHL-140
☐ 97GuiFla-7
**Adam, Dietrich**
☐ 94GerDELE-21
**Adam, Richard**
☐ 95CzeAPSE-204
**Adam, Russ**
☐ 82MapLeaP-1
**Adamcik, Dusan**
☐ 95CzeAPSE-240
**Adamiec, Janusz**
☐ 89SweSemWCS-143
**Adams, Akil**
☐ 92NorDakFS-1
☐ 93WinSpi-24
**Adams, Andy**
☐ 93GueSto-22
☐ 94GueSto-3
☐ 95Sla-82
☐ 95Sla-379
☐ 96RegPat-15
**Adams, Brandon**
☐ 92DisMigDM-1
**Adams, Brian**
☐ 92HarCri-1
**Adams, Charles F**
☐ 83HalFP-D1
☐ 85HalFC-47
**Adams, Gerad**
☐ 96RegPat-11
**Adams, Greg A**
☐ 82WhaJunHC-1
☐ 85DevPos-1
☐ 86CapKod-1
☐ 86CapPol-1
☐ 86DevPol-1
☐ 860PC-10
☐ 860PCBoxB-A
☐ 860PCSti-196
☐ 86Top-10
☐ 86TopBoxB-A
☐ 87CanuSheOil-1
☐ 87CapKod-22
☐ 87CapTealss-1
☐ 870PC-135
☐ 87PanSti-84
☐ 87PanSti-185
☐ 87Top-135
☐ 88CanuMoh-1
☐ 88OilTenAnn-85
☐ 880PC-162
☐ 880PCSti-66
☐ 88PanSti-136
☐ 88Top-162
☐ 89CanuMoh-1
☐ 890PC-178
☐ 89PanSti-154
☐ 89Top-178
☐ 90Bow-59
☐ 90BowTif-59
☐ 90CanuMoh-1
☐ 900PC-106
☐ 90PanSti-303
☐ 90ProSet-291
☐ 90Sco-240
☐ 90ScoCan-240
☐ 90Top-106
☐ 90TopTif-106

☐ 90UppDec-342
☐ 90UppDecF-342
☐ 91Bow-311
☐ 91CanuAutC-1
☐ 91CanuMol-1
☐ 91CanuPanTS-1
☐ 91CanuTeal8-1
☐ 910PC-340
☐ 91PanSti-39
☐ 91Par-183
☐ 91ParFre-183
☐ 91Pin-218
☐ 91PinFre-218
☐ 91ProSet-243
☐ 91ProSetFre-243
☐ 91ProSetPla-125
☐ 91ScoAme-44
☐ 91ScoCan-44
☐ 91StaClu-52
☐ 91Top-340
☐ 91UppDec-426
☐ 91UppDecF-426
☐ 92Bow-333
☐ 92CanuRoaTA-1
☐ 920PC-365
☐ 92Par-195
☐ 92ParEmel-195
☐ 92Pin-28
☐ 92PinFre-28
☐ 92Sco-146
☐ 92ScoCan-146
☐ 92StaClu-232
☐ 92Top-507
☐ 92TopGol-507G
☐ 92UppDec-192
☐ 93Don-350
☐ 93Lea-219
☐ 93PanSti-173
☐ 93Par-480
☐ 93ParEmel-480
☐ 93Pin-247
☐ 93PinCan-247
☐ 93Pow-247
☐ 93Sco-196
☐ 93ScoCan-196
☐ 93Ult-19
☐ 93UppDec-77
☐ 93UppDecSP-161
☐ 94CanGamNHLP-96
☐ 94CanuProI-1
☐ 94Don-101
☐ 94Fla-187
☐ 94Lea-222
☐ 940PCPre-414
☐ 940PCPreSE-414
☐ 94ParSE-SE185
☐ 94ParSEG-SE185
☐ 94Pin-240
☐ 94PinArtP-240
☐ 94PinRinC-240
☐ 94StaCluFDI-156
☐ 94StaCluMOMS-156
☐ 94StaCluSTWC-156
☐ 94TopPre-414
☐ 94TopPreSE-414
☐ 94Ult-380
☐ 94UppDec-211
☐ 94UppDecEIeIce-211
☐ 95BeAPla-22
☐ 95BeAPSig-S22
☐ 95BeAPSigDC-S22
☐ 95CanGamNHLP-91
☐ 95ColCho-286
☐ 95ColChoPC-286
☐ 95ColChoPCP-286
☐ 95Don-158
☐ 95Lea-112
☐ 95Met-37
☐ 95ParInt-327
☐ 95ParIntEI-327
☐ 95Sco-89
☐ 95ScoBlaIce-89
☐ 95ScoBlaIceAP-89
☐ 95StaScoS-89
☐ 95Ult-227
☐ 95UppDec-26
☐ 95UppDecEIeIce-26
☐ 95UppDecEIceIceG-26
☐ 95UppDecSpeC-SE113
☐ 95UppDecSpeEdiG-SE113
☐ 96Don-82
☐ 96DonPrePro-82
☐ 96Lea-103
☐ 96LeaPreP-103
☐ 96Pin-194
☐ 96PinArtP-194
☐ 96PinFoi-194
☐ 96PinPreS-194
☐ 96PinRinC-194
☐ 96Sco-39
☐ 96ScoArtPro-39
☐ 96ScoDeaCAP-39
☐ 96ScoGolB-39
☐ 96ScoSpeAP-39
☐ 96StaScoS-39
☐ 96Sum-95
☐ 96SumArtP-95
☐ 96SumIce-95
☐ 96SumMet-95
☐ 96SumPreS-95
☐ 96UppDecBD-23
☐ 96UppDecBDG-23

☐ 96UppDecIce-14
☐ 96UppDecIcePar-14
☐ 97Be A PPAD-164
☐ 97Be A PPAPD-164
☐ 97BeAPla-164
☐ 97BeAPlaAut-164
☐ 97ColCho-71
☐ 97PacInvNRB-59
☐ 97PacOme-66
☐ 97PacOmeC-66
☐ 97PacOmeDG-66
☐ 97PacOmeEG-66
☐ 97PacOmeG-66
☐ 97PacOmeIB-66
☐ 97UppDec-265
☐ 98Pac-171
☐ 98PacIceB-171
☐ 98PacRed-171
☐ 98UppDec-344
☐ 98UppDecE-344
☐ 98UppDecE1o1-344
☐ 98UppDecGR-344
☐ 99Pac-315
☐ 99PacCop-315
☐ 99PacIceB-315
☐ 99PacPreD-315
**Adams, Greg C.**
☐ 860PC-253
☐ 870PC-139
☐ 87Top-139
☐ 880PC-199
☐ 88Top-199
☐ 900PC-518
**Adams, Jack**
☐ 23V1451-24
☐ 24C144ChaCig-1
☐ 24V1452-53
☐ 34BeeGro1P-133
☐ 36V356WorG-99
☐ 40OPCV3012-104
☐ 83HalFP-J1
☐ 85HalFC-182
☐ 92HalFL-21
**Adams, Jamie**
☐ 93JohChi-14
☐ 94CenHocL-1
**Adams, John**
☐ 74CapWhiB-1
**Adams, Kevyn**
☐ 93DonTeaUSA-1
☐ 93Pin-488
☐ 93PinCan-488
☐ 93UppDec-568
☐ 96GraRapG-1
☐ 97Pin-22
☐ 97PinArtP-22
☐ 97PinPrePBB-22
☐ 97PinPrePBC-22
☐ 97PinPrePBM-22
☐ 97PinPrePBY-22
☐ 97PinPrePFC-22
☐ 97PinPrePFM-22
☐ 97PinPrePFY-22
☐ 97PinPrePLa-22
☐ 97PinRinC-22
☐ 97Sco-60
☐ 97ScoArtPro-60
☐ 97ScoGolBla-60
☐ 97ScoMapL-15
☐ 97ScoMapLPla-15
☐ 97ScoMapLPre-15
☐ 97St.JohML-1
**Adams, Weston W**
☐ 83HalFP-I1
☐ 85HalFC-122
**Adamson, Ian**
☐ 91AirCanSJHL-E37
☐ 92MPSPhoSJHL-114
**Adamus, Damian**
☐ 94GerDELE-290
☐ 95GerDELE-281
☐ 96GerDELE-90
**Addesa, Chris**
☐ 94DubFigS-2
**Addesa, Matt**
☐ 94DubFigS-3
**Adduono, Jeremy**
☐ 95Sla-391
☐ 95SudWol-11
☐ 96SudWol-2
☐ 96SudWol-4
☐ 97SudWolP-2
☐ 98BowCHL-29
☐ 98BowCHLGA-29
☐ 98BowCHLOI-29
☐ 98BowChrC-29
☐ 98BowChrCGA-29
☐ 98BowChrCGAR-29
☐ 98BowChrCOI-29
☐ 98BowChrCOIR-29
☐ 98BowChrCR-29
**Adlys, Bernie**
☐ 91AirCanSJHL-D17
☐ 91AirCanSJHL-E34
**Adolfi, Richard (Rick)**
☐ 83BeiBul-16
☐ 830tt67-1
☐ 84KitRan-27
**Adolfsson, Marcus**
☐ 98GerDELE-12
**Adrian, Kjell**
☐ 65SweCorI-93
**Aeschlimann, Jean-Jacques**
☐ 93SwiHNL-95

☐ 95SwiHNL-509
**Aeschlimann, Joel**
☐ 93SwiHNL-44
☐ 95SwiHNL-81
**Aeschlimann, Peter**
☐ 72SweSemWC-145
**Affleck, Bruce**
☐ 74NHLActSta-55
☐ 760PCNHL-305
☐ 770PCNHL-376
☐ 780PC-279
**Afinogenov, Maxim**
☐ 97UppDecBD-43
☐ 97UppDecBDDD-43
☐ 97UppDecBDQD-43
☐ 97UppDecBDTD-43
☐ 98SPXTopP-76
☐ 98SPXTopPF-76
☐ 98SPXTopPR-76
☐ 98UC-282
☐ 98UD ChoPCR-282
☐ 98UD ChoR-282
☐ 98UppDecBD-108
☐ 98UppDecBDD-108
☐ 98UppDecQD-108
☐ 98UppDecTD-108
**Afonin, Viktor**
☐ 74SweHocS-67
**Ageikin, Sergei**
☐ 87RusNatT-1
**Agnel, Benjamin**
☐ 94FinnJaaK-221
☐ 94FreNatT-1
**Agnew, David**
☐ 93WesMic-1
**Agnew, Gary**
☐ 907thInnSOHL-148
☐ 917thInnSOHL-369
☐ 93LonKni-26
**Agnew, Jim**
☐ 83BraWheK-2
☐ 86FreExp-1
☐ 89ProIHL-185
☐ 90CanuMoh-2
☐ 91CanuPanTS-2
☐ 92WhaDai-1
**Agren, Ulf**
☐ 83SweSemE-179
☐ 84SweSemE-204
☐ 85SwePanS-203
☐ 86SwePanS-197
**Ahearn, Kevin**
☐ 72SweSemWC-129
**Ahearn, T. Franklin**
☐ 83HalFP-E1
**Ahearne, Bunny (JF)**
☐ 83HalFP-J2
☐ 85HalFC-183
**Ahenakew, Jason**
☐ 91AirCanSJHL-E10
☐ 92MPSPhoSJHL-27
**Ahern, Fred**
☐ 760PCNHL-298
☐ 770PCNHL-280
☐ 780PC-386
**Ahl, Boo**
☐ 91SweSemE-105
☐ 92SweSemE-126
☐ 93SweSemE-99
☐ 94SweLeaE-186
☐ 95SweLeaE-6
☐ 95SweUppDE-75
☐ 96SweSemCDT-2
☐ 96SweSemW-41
**Ahlberg, Lennart**
☐ 83SweSemE-147
**Ahlberg, Mats**
☐ 67SweHoc-114
☐ 69SweHocS-127
☐ 70SweHocS-82
☐ 71SweHocS-174
☐ 72SweHocS-160
☐ 73SweHocS-48
☐ 73SweWorCS-16
☐ 73SweWorCS-48
☐ 74SweHocS-24
☐ 74SweHocS-273
☐ 74SweSemHVS-11
☐ 79PanSti-196
**Ahlberg, Sakari**
☐ 74SweSemHVS-96
**Ahlberg, Sami**
☐ 93FinnSIS-132
☐ 94FinnSIS-117
☐ 95FinnSIS-40
**Ahlen, Kjell**
☐ 71SweHocS-359
**Ahlen, Tomas**
☐ 83SweSemE-180
☐ 84SweSemE-198
☐ 85SwePanS-9
☐ 87SwePanS-10
☐ 89SweSemE-5
**Ahlroos, Kim**
☐ 91FinnJyvHS-29
☐ 93FinnSIS-94
☐ 93FinnSIS-51
☐ 95FinnSIS-344
**Ahlstrand, Christer**
☐ 70SweHocS-50
**Ahlstrom, Bjorn**
☐ 91SweSemE-26

☐ 92SweSemE-45
☐ 94SweLeaE-84
☐ 95SweLeaE-162
☐ 95SweUppDE-16
**Ahlstrom, Erik**
☐ 84SweSemE-95
☐ 85SwePanS-88
**Ahlund, Hakan**
☐ 90SweSemE-140
☐ 91SweSemE-190
☐ 91SweSemWCS-40
☐ 92SweSemE-218
☐ 93SweSemE-189
☐ 94SweLeaE-115
☐ 95SweLeaE-91
☐ 95SweUppDE-148
☐ 98GerDELE-276
**Ahman, Olle**
☐ 67SweHoc-230
☐ 69SweHocS-274
☐ 70SweHocS-165
☐ 71SweHocS-260
☐ 72SweHocS-240
☐ 73SweHocS-233
☐ 73SweWorCS-233
☐ 74SweHocS-274
**Ahmaoja, Timo**
☐ 96FinnSISR-61
☐ 97UppDecBD-102
☐ 97UppDecBDDD-102
☐ 97UppDecBDQD-102
☐ 97UppDecBDTD-102
☐ 98UC-280
☐ 98UD ChoPCR-280
☐ 98UD ChoR-280
**Ahne, Manfred**
☐ 94GerDELE-163
**Ahokainen, Seppo**
☐ 74SweHocS-97
☐ 79PanSti-175
**Ahola, Peter**
☐ 91Par-65
☐ 91ParFre-65
☐ 91Pin-312
☐ 91PinFre-312
☐ 91ProSet-540
☐ 91ProSetFre-540
☐ 91ProSetPla-257
☐ 91UppDec-543
☐ 91UppDecF-543
☐ 92Bow-353
☐ 920PC-268
☐ 92Pin-243
☐ 92PinFre-243
☐ 92ProSet-73
☐ 92Sco-310
☐ 92ScoCan-310
☐ 92StaClu-192
☐ 92Top-73
☐ 92TopGol-73G
☐ 92Ult-78
☐ 92Ult-376
☐ 92UppDec-41
☐ 92UppDec-526
☐ 92UppDecERT-ERT4
☐ 92UppDecES-E5
☐ 93SweSemWCS-48
☐ 94FinnSIS-270
☐ 94FinnSISH-5
☐ 95FinnSIS-205
☐ 95FinnSISDT-5
☐ 95FinnSISL-5
☐ 95FinnSISLLG-5
☐ 95FinnSISSpe-8
☐ 96FinnSISR-3
**Ahonen, Veli-Pekka**
☐ 94FinnSIS-351
☐ 95FinnSIS-101
☐ 96FinnSISR-106
**Ahrens, Chris**
☐ 74NHLActSta-143
☐ 740PCNHL-346
☐ 750PCNHL-371
**Ahrens, Fabian**
☐ 96GerDELE-214
**Ahrgren, Johan**
☐ 92BriColJHL-39
**Ahsberg, Roger**
☐ 83SweSemE-241
**Ahstrom, Goran**
☐ 69SweHocS-292
**Ahxner, Mathias**
☐ 98GerDELE-280
**Aiken, Dave**
☐ 90RicRen-10
☐ 91RicRen-8
**Aimonette, Richard**
☐ 907thInnSQMJHL-253
☐ 94FreNatT-2
**Ainsworth, Jeff**
☐ 95SlaMemC-11
☐ 96KamBla-1
**Aisbitt, Barrie**
☐ 95GuiFla-13
☐ 96GuiFla-20
**Aitken, Brad**
☐ 88ProIHL-43
☐ 89ProHL-155
☐ 90ProAHLIHL-388
☐ 91ProAHLCHL-340
**Aitken, Johnathan**
☐ 95BowDraPro-P1
☐ 95Cla-56
☐ 95MedHatT-1
**Aitkenhead, Andy**

❑ 35DiaMatTI-1
**Aivazoff, Micah**
❑ 89ProAHL-6
❑ 90ProAHLIHL-417
❑ 91ProAHLCHL-131
❑ 93Don-421
❑ 93OPCPre-345
❑ 93OPCPreG-345
❑ 93Par-253
❑ 93ParEmel-253
❑ 93StaClu-263
❑ 93StaCluFDI-263
❑ 93StaCluO-263
❑ 93TopPre-345
❑ 93TopPreG-345
❑ 93Ult-303
❑ 93UppDec-432
❑ 94BeAPSig-173
❑ 94ClaProP-72
❑ 94OPCPre-104
❑ 94OPCPreSE-104
❑ 94TopPre-104
❑ 94TopPreSE-104
❑ 96BinRan-1
**Akerblom, Bengt**
❑ 89SweSemE-70
**Akerblom, Bjorn**
❑ 83SweSemE-65
❑ 89SweSemE-258
❑ 90SweSemE-168
**Akerblom, Markus**
❑ 90SweSemE-216
❑ 91SweSemE-144
❑ 92SweSemE-169
❑ 93SweSemE-138
❑ 94SweLeaE-53
❑ 95SweLeaE-240
❑ 95SweLeaEFF-15
❑ 95SweUppDE-108
❑ 95SweUppDE-111
❑ 95SweUppDETNA-NA13
**Akerlund, Goran**
❑ 69SweHocS-237
❑ 71SweHocS-379
**Akerman, Johan**
❑ 94SweLeaE-240
❑ 95SweLeaE-8
**Akerstrom, Roger**
❑ 86SwePanS-172
❑ 87SwePanS-174
❑ 89SweSemE-153
❑ 90SweSemE-233
❑ 91SweSemE-258
❑ 92SweSemE-284
❑ 93SweSemE-251
❑ 93SweSemE-308
❑ 94SweLeaE-278
❑ 95SweLeaE-78
❑ 95SweLeaEFF-8
❑ 95SweUppDE-120
**Akervik, Andrew (Andy)**
❑ 88ProIHL-24
❑ 90KanCitBla-10
❑ 90ProAHLIHL-593
❑ 91ProAHLCHL-526
**Akey, Dave**
❑ 86LonKni-22
❑ 87SudWol-8
**Akulinin, Igor**
❑ 90OPC-491
**Alain, Gabriel**
❑ 52JunBluT-71
**Alander, Karl-Gustaf**
❑ 70SweHocS-69
❑ 71SweHocS-158
❑ 86SwePanS-137
**Alatalo, Mika**
❑ 93FinnJyvHS-234
❑ 93FinnSIS-202
❑ 93SweSemWCS-62
❑ 94ClaTri-T76
❑ 94FinnJaaK-21
❑ 94FinnSIS-165
❑ 94FinnSIS-279
❑ 94FinnSISH-20
❑ 94FinnSISS-1
❑ 95FinnSemWC-15
❑ 95FinnSIS-128
❑ 95FinnSISP-2
❑ 95SigRooA-1
❑ 95SigRooAPC-1
**Alavaara, Jan-Axel**
❑ 95SweLeaE-278
❑ 95SweLeaER-2
**Alba, Mats**
❑ 83SweSemE-10
❑ 84SweSemE-7
❑ 85SwePanS-11
**Albelin, Tommy**
❑ 83SweSemE-79
❑ 84SweSemE-79
❑ 85SwePanS-76
❑ 86SwePanS-59
❑ 87NordGenF-1
❑ 88NordGenF-1
❑ 88NordTeal-1
❑ 88OPC-210
❑ 88OPCSti-184
❑ 88PanSti-348
❑ 89DevCar-1
❑ 89OPC-241
❑ 89PanSti-257
❑ 89SweSemWCS-6
❑ 90Dev-1
❑ 90OPC-323
❑ 90PanSti-76
❑ 90ProSet-162
❑ 90Sco-378
❑ 90ScoCan-378
❑ 90Top-323
❑ 90TopTif-323
❑ 90UppDec-88
❑ 90UppDecF-88
❑ 91ScoCan-393
❑ 93SweSemWCS-28
❑ 94FinnJaaK-60
❑ 94OPCPre-251
❑ 94OPCPreSE-251
❑ 94Pin-508
❑ 94PinArtP-508
❑ 94PinRinC-508
❑ 94TopPre-251
❑ 94TopPreSE-251
❑ 95ParInt-126
❑ 95ParIntEl-126
❑ 95SweGloWC-10
❑ 95SweUppDE-248
❑ 96BeAPAut-161
❑ 96BeAPAutSil-161
❑ 96BeAPla-161
❑ 96SweSemW-43
❑ 97PacInvNRB-26
❑ 97UppDec-237
**Albers, Matt**
❑ 93MicSta-1
**Albert, Marv**
❑ 91ProSetPla-291
**Albrecht, Steve**
❑ 96KamBla-2
**Albright, Aaron**
❑ 92OshGenS-18
**Albright, Clint**
❑ 44BeeGro2P-295
**Alcindor, Ray**
❑ 93HunBli-1
**Aldcorn, Gary**
❑ 44BeeGro2P-370
❑ 57Par-T24
❑ 58Par-18
❑ 60Par-33
❑ 60ShiCoi-53
❑ 94ParMisL-122
**Aldoff, Rod**
❑ 93MinDul-1
❑ 95TalTigS-3
**Aldred, Jim**
❑ 81KinCan-16
❑ 81SauSteMG-1
❑ 82SauSteMG-1
**Aldridge, Keith**
❑ 91LakSupSL-3
**Aleblad, Hans**
❑ 65SweCorl-200
❑ 67SweHoc-263
**Alekhin, Dmitri**
❑ 95MadMon-3
**Alexander, Bob**
❑ 85MinDul-19
**Alexander, Claire**
❑ 74MapLeaP-1
❑ 75MapLeaP-1
❑ 76MapLeaP-1
❑ 76OPCNHL-321
**Alexander, Ken**
❑ 84KitRan-11
❑ 85KitRan-9
**Alexandersson, Per-Arne**
❑ 85SwePanS-213
❑ 86SwePanS-205
❑ 87SwePanS-204
**Alexandrov, Boris**
❑ 92FutTre76CC-150
**Alexandrov, Igor**
❑ 92UppDec-611
❑ 98GerDELE-90
**Alexeenko, Mikhail**
❑ 73SweHocS-123
❑ 73SweWorCS-123
**Alexeyev, Alexander**
❑ 92Cla-54
❑ 92TacRoc-1
❑ 93TacRoc-1
❑ 95PorPir-1
❑ 96ClaGol-54
❑ 96HamRoaA-HRA4
**Alfredsson, Daniel**
❑ 92SweSemE-319
❑ 93SweSemE-284
❑ 94SweLeaE-82
❑ 94SweLeaENHLD-6
❑ 95BAPLetL-LL6
❑ 95BeAPla-171
❑ 95BeAPSig-S171
❑ 95BeAPSigDC-S171
❑ 95Bow-110
❑ 95BowAllFoi-110
❑ 95BowBes-BB16
❑ 95BowBesRef-BB16
❑ 95ColCho-406
❑ 95Don-299
❑ 95DonEli-25
❑ 95DonEliDCS-25
❑ 95DonEliDCU-25
❑ 95DonEliR-3
❑ 95DonRatRoo-14
❑ 95Fin-116
❑ 95FinRef-116
❑ 95LeaLim-25
❑ 95LeaLimRP-2
❑ 95Met-169
❑ 95ParInt-257
❑ 95ParInt-507
❑ 95ParIntCCGS2-15
❑ 95ParIntCCSS2-15
❑ 95ParIntEl-257
❑ 95ParIntEl-507
❑ 95ParIntPTP-PP38
❑ 95SelCer-122
❑ 95SelCerMG-122
❑ 95Sen-1
❑ 95SkyImp-214
❑ 95SP-100
❑ 95SPHol-FX15
❑ 95SPHolSpFX-FX15
❑ 95StaClu-206
❑ 95StaCluMOMS-206
❑ 95Sum-182
❑ 95SumArtP-182
❑ 95SumIce-182
❑ 95SweGloWC-47
❑ 95Top-369
❑ 95TopOPCI-369
❑ 95TopSupSkiSR-SR12
❑ 95Ult-329
❑ 95UltHigSpe-1
❑ 95UppDec-504
❑ 95UppDecEleIce-504
❑ 95UppDecEleIceG-504
❑ 95UppDecNHLAS-AS12
❑ 95UppDecPHE-H23
❑ 95UppDecPreH-H23
❑ 95Zen-149
❑ 95ZenRooRC-10
❑ 96BeAPBisITB-23
❑ 96ColCho-177
❑ 96ColCho-344
❑ 96ColChoBloBi-6
❑ 96ColChoCTG-C13A
❑ 96ColChoCTG-C13B
❑ 96ColChoCTG-C13C
❑ 96ColChoCTGE-CR13
❑ 96ColChoCTGEG-CR13
❑ 96ColChoCTGG-C13A
❑ 96ColChoCTGG-C13B
❑ 96ColChoCTGG-C13C
❑ 96ColChoMVP-UD39
❑ 96ColChoMVPG-UD39
❑ 96DonCanI-34
❑ 96DonCanIGPP-34
❑ 96DonCanIRPP-34
❑ 96DonEli-100
❑ 96DonEliAsp-2
❑ 96DonEliDCS-100
❑ 96DonRatR-10
❑ 96Fla-63
❑ 96FlaBluI-63
❑ 96Fle-73
❑ 96Fle-136
❑ 96FlePic-78
❑ 96FlePicDL-3
❑ 96FlePicF5-1
❑ 96FlePicJE-1
❑ 96FleRooSen-1
❑ 96KraUppD-45
❑ 96Lea-210
❑ 96LeaLim-73
❑ 96LeaLimG-73
❑ 96LeaPre-48
❑ 96LeaPreP-210
❑ 96LeaPrePP-48
❑ 96LeaPreSG-35
❑ 96LeaPreSte-35
❑ 96LeaSwe-14
❑ 96LeaSwe(-14
❑ 96MetUni-103
❑ 96NHLACEPC-1
❑ 96Pin-205
❑ 96PinArtP-205
❑ 96PinByTN-10
❑ 96PinByTNP-10
❑ 96PinFoi-205
❑ 96PinMcD-9
❑ 96PinMin-10
❑ 96PinMinB-10
❑ 96PinMinCoiB-10
❑ 96PinMinCoiGP-10
❑ 96PinMinCoiN-10
❑ 96PinMinCoiS-10
❑ 96PinMinCoiSG-10
❑ 96PinMinG-10
❑ 96PinMinS-10
❑ 96PinPreS-205
❑ 96PinRinC-205
❑ 96PinTro-4
❑ 96PlaOneoOne-341
❑ 96Sco-240
❑ 96ScoArtPro-240
❑ 96ScoDeaCAP-240
❑ 96ScoGolB-240
❑ 96ScoSpeAP-240
❑ 96SelCer-47
❑ 96SelCerAP-47
❑ 96SelCerBlu-47
❑ 96SelCerMB-47
❑ 96SelCerMG-47
❑ 96SelCerMR-47
❑ 96SelCerRed-47
❑ 96SenPizH-1
❑ 96SkyImp-86
❑ 96SkyImp-164
❑ 96SkyImpNHLF-1
❑ 96SP-107
❑ 96SPGamFil-GF20
❑ 96SPHolCol-HC9
❑ 96SPx-32
❑ 96SPx-GF1
❑ 96SPxGol-32
❑ 96StaCluMO-38
❑ 96Sum-167
❑ 96SumArtP-167
❑ 96SumHigV-4
❑ 96SumHigVM-4
❑ 96SumIce-167
❑ 96SumMet-167
❑ 96SumPreS-167
❑ 96SweSemW-72
❑ 96TeaOut-42
❑ 96TopPicRS-RS1
❑ 96Ult-113
❑ 96UltGolM-114
❑ 96UppDec-113
❑ 96UppDecBD-141
❑ 96UppDecBDG-141
❑ 96UppDecGN-X6
❑ 96UppDecIce-95
❑ 96UppDecIcePar-95
❑ 96UppDecSS-SS18A
❑ 96Zen-103
❑ 96ZenArtP-103
❑ 96ZenZT-13
❑ 97ColCho-172
❑ 97ColChoSta-SQ51
❑ 97ColChoSti-S11
❑ 97Don-17
❑ 97DonCanI-112
❑ 97DonCanIDS-112
❑ 97DonCanIPS-112
❑ 97DonEli-104
❑ 97DonEliAsp-104
❑ 97DonEliS-104
❑ 97DonLim-22
❑ 97DonLim-186
❑ 97DonLimExp-22
❑ 97DonLimExp-186
❑ 97DonLimFOTG-46
❑ 97DonPre-90
❑ 97DonPreCttC-90
❑ 97DonPreProG-17
❑ 97DonPreProS-17
❑ 97DonPri-113
❑ 97DonPriDD-27
❑ 97DonPriSoA-113
❑ 97EssOlyHH-44
❑ 97EssOlyHHF-44
❑ 97Kat-97
❑ 97KatGol-97
❑ 97KatSil-97
❑ 97Lea-145
❑ 97LeaFraMat-145
❑ 97LeaFraMDC-145
❑ 97LeaInt-145
❑ 97LeaIntUI-145
❑ 97Pac-58
❑ 97PacCop-58
❑ 97PacCroR-89
❑ 97PacCroREG-89
❑ 97PacCroRIB-89
❑ 97PacCroRS-89
❑ 97PacDyn-83
❑ 97PacDynC-83
❑ 97PacDynDG-83
❑ 97PacDynEG-83
❑ 97PacDynIB-83
❑ 97PacDynR-83
❑ 97PacDynSil-83
❑ 97PacDynTan-71
❑ 97PacEmeGre-58
❑ 97PacIceB-58
❑ 97PacInv-92
❑ 97PacInvC-92
❑ 97PacInvEG-92
❑ 97PacInvIB-92
❑ 97PacInvR-92
❑ 97PacInvS-92
❑ 97PacOme-152
❑ 97PacOmeC-152
❑ 97PacOmeDG-152
❑ 97PacOmeEG-152
❑ 97PacOmeG-152
❑ 97PacOmeIB-152
❑ 97PacPar-122
❑ 97PacParC-122
❑ 97PacParDG-122
❑ 97PacParEG-122
❑ 97PacParIB-122
❑ 97PacParRed-122
❑ 97PacParSil-122
❑ 97PacRed-58
❑ 97PacRev-92
❑ 97PacRevC-92
❑ 97PacRevE-92
❑ 97PacRevIB-92
❑ 97PacRevR-92
❑ 97PacRevS-92
❑ 97PacRevTCL-17
❑ 97PacSil-58
❑ 97Pin-155
❑ 97PinBee-48
❑ 97PinBeeGP-48
❑ 97PinCer-114
❑ 97PinCerMB-114
❑ 97PinCerMG-114
❑ 97PinCerMR-114
❑ 97PinCerR-114
❑ 97PinIns-26
❑ 97PinInsCC-26
❑ 97PinInsEC-26
❑ 97PinPrePBB-155
❑ 97PinPrePBM-155
❑ 97PinPrePBY-155
❑ 97PinPrePFC-155
❑ 97PinPrePFM-155
❑ 97PinPrePFY-155
❑ 97PinPrePla-155
❑ 97PinTotCMPG-114
❑ 97PinTotCPB-114
❑ 97PinTotCPG-114
❑ 97PinTotCPR-114
❑ 97Sco-131
❑ 97ScoArtPro-131
❑ 97ScoGolBla-131
❑ 97SP AutI-I30
❑ 97SPAut-106
❑ 97SPAutID-I30
❑ 97SPAutIE-I30
❑ 97SPx-34
❑ 97SPxBro-34
❑ 97SPxGol-34
❑ 97SPxGraF-34
❑ 97SPxSil-34
❑ 97SPxSte-34
❑ 97Stu-94
❑ 97StuPrePG-94
❑ 97StuPrePS-94
❑ 97UppDec-112
❑ 97UppDecBD-73
❑ 97UppDecBDDD-73
❑ 97UppDecBDQD-73
❑ 97UppDecBDTD-73
❑ 97UppDecGDM-112
❑ 97UppDecIce-11
❑ 97UppDecIceP-11
❑ 97UppDecILL-L4A
❑ 97UppDecILL2-L4A
❑ 97UppDecIPS-11
❑ 97UppDecSSM-SS27
❑ 97UppDecSSW-SS27
❑ 97UppDecTSS-14A
❑ 97Zen-43
❑ 97Zen5x7-25
❑ 97ZenGolImp-25
❑ 97ZenSilImp-25
❑ 97ZenZGol-43
❑ 97ZenZSil-43
❑ 98Be A PPA-98
❑ 98Be A PPAA-98
❑ 98Be A PPAAF-98
❑ 98Be A PPTBASG-98
❑ 98Be APG-98
❑ 98BowBes-16
❑ 98BowBesAR-16
❑ 98BowBesR-16
❑ 98Fin-13
❑ 98FinCen-C19
❑ 98FinCenR-C19
❑ 98FinNo P-13
❑ 98FinNo PR-13
❑ 98FinRef-13
❑ 98O-PChr-130
❑ 98O-PChrR-130
❑ 98Pac-305
❑ 98PacAur-128
❑ 98PacAurCF-32
❑ 98PacAurCFC-32
❑ 98PacAurCFIB-32
❑ 98PacAurCFR-32
❑ 98PacAurCFS-32
❑ 98PacAurFL-6
❑ 98PacAurFLIB-6
❑ 98PacAurFLR-6
❑ 98PacCroR-92
❑ 98PacCroRLS-92
❑ 98PacDynI-126
❑ 98PacDynIIB-126
❑ 98PacDynIR-126
❑ 98PacIceB-305
❑ 98PacOmeH-163
❑ 98PacOmeODI-163
❑ 98PacOmeR-163
❑ 98PacPar-160
❑ 98PacParC-160
❑ 98PacParEG-160
❑ 98PacParH-160
❑ 98PacParIB-160
❑ 98PacParS-160
❑ 98PacRed-305
❑ 98PacRev-98
❑ 98PacRevIS-98
❑ 98PacRevR-98
❑ 98SP Aut-60
❑ 98SP AutSotTG-DA
❑ 98SSASotT-DA
❑ 98Top-130
❑ 98TopGolLC1-69
❑ 98TopGolLC1B-69
❑ 98TopGolLC1BOoO-69
❑ 98TopGolLC1OoO-69
❑ 98TopGolLC1R-69
❑ 98TopGolLC1ROoO-69
❑ 98TopGolLC2-69
❑ 98TopGolLC2B-69
❑ 98TopGolLC2BOoO-69
❑ 98TopGolLC2OoO-69
❑ 98TopGolLC2R-69
❑ 98TopGolLC2ROoO-69
❑ 98TopGolLC3-69
❑ 98TopGolLC3B-69
❑ 98TopGolLC3BOoO-69
❑ 98TopGolLC3OoO-69
❑ 98TopGolLC3R-69
❑ 98TopGolLC3ROoO-69
❑ 98TopO-P-130
❑ 98UC-144
❑ 98UD ChoPCR-144
❑ 98UD ChoR-144
❑ 98UppDec-327
❑ 98UppDecBD-61
❑ 98UppDecDD-61
❑ 98UppDecE-327
❑ 98UppDecE1o1-327
❑ 98UppDecGR-327
❑ 98UppDecM-141
❑ 98UppDecMGS-141
❑ 98UppDecMSS-141
❑ 98UppDecMSS-141
❑ 98UppDecQD-61
❑ 98UppDecTD-61
❑ 99Pac-283
❑ 99PacCop-283
❑ 99PacGol-283
❑ 99PacIceB-283
❑ 99PacPreD-283
❑ 99SP AutPS-60
❑ 99UppDecM-140
❑ 99UppDecMGS-140
❑ 99UppDecMSS-140
❑ 99UppDecMSS-140
**Algotsson, Hakan**
❑ 89SweSemE-264
❑ 90SweSemE-28
❑ 91SweSemE-278
❑ 92SweSemE-300
❑ 93SweSemE-266
❑ 93SweSemWCS-2
❑ 94FinnJaaK-51
❑ 94SweLeaE-2
❑ 94SweLeaEGC-10
❑ 94SweLeaEGC-7
❑ 95SweGloWC-4
❑ 95SweLeaE-137
❑ 95SweLeaES-4
❑ 95SweUppDE-202
**Alino, Jan**
❑ 94CzeAPSE-224
❑ 95CzeAPSE-171
❑ 95FinnSemWC-164
**Allain, Rick**
❑ 87KitRan-7
❑ 88KitRan-7
❑ 89KitRan-7
❑ 907thInnSMC-41
❑ 90ProAHLIHL-139
❑ 91ProAHLCHL-51
❑ 96GueSto-29
❑ 97GueSto-28
**Allaire, Francois**
❑ 87CanaPos-9
❑ 87CanaVacS-9
❑ 88CanaPos-1
❑ 89CanaPos-1
❑ 90CanaPos-1
❑ 91CanaPos-1
**Allan, Andy**
❑ 94GuiFla-12
❑ 95GuiFla-3
**Allan, Brett**
❑ 98BowCHL-122
❑ 98BowCHLAuB-A26
❑ 98BowCHLAuG-A26
❑ 98BowCHLAuS-A26
❑ 98BowCHLGA-122
❑ 98BowCHLOI-122
❑ 98BowChrC-122
❑ 98BowChrCGA-122
❑ 98BowChrCGAR-122
❑ 98BowChrCOI-122
❑ 98BowChrCOIR-122
❑ 98BowChrCR-122
**Allan, Chad**
❑ 93SasBla-1
❑ 94Fin-147
❑ 94FinRef-147
❑ 94FinSupTW-147
❑ 94UppDec-499
❑ 95DonCanWJ-4
❑ 95DonEliWJ-3
❑ 95SasBla-1
❑ 95SigRooA-2
❑ 95SigRooAPC-2
❑ 95TopCanWJ-17CJ
❑ 95UppDec-532
❑ 96SyrCru-23
**Allan, Richard**
❑ 71TorSun-18
**Allan, Sandy**
❑ 917thInnSOHL-51
❑ 92Cla-19
❑ 93NorBayC-2
❑ 94PriAlbR-1
❑ 95RicRen-6
❑ 96ClaGol-19
❑ 96LouRiv-2
❑ 96LouRiv-28
**Allan, Sir Montagu**
❑ 83HalFP-I2
❑ 85HalFC-123
**Allard, Pierre**
❑ 907thInnSQMJHL-227
❑ 917thInnSQMJHL-14
**Allegrezza, Mark**
❑ 94DubFigS-4
**Allegrino, Scott**
❑ 94WheThu-21
**Allen, Bryan**
❑ 97UppDec-401
❑ 98BowCHL-25
❑ 98BowCHL-133
❑ 98BowCHLAuB-A12
❑ 98BowCHLAuG-A12
❑ 98BowCHLAuS-A12
❑ 98BowCHLGA-25
❑ 98BowCHLGA-133
❑ 98BowCHLOI-25
❑ 98BowCHLOI-133
❑ 98BowCHLSC-SC1
❑ 98BowChrC-25
❑ 98BowChrC-133
❑ 98BowChrCGA-25
❑ 98BowChrCGA-133
❑ 98BowChrCGAR-25
❑ 98BowChrCGAR-133
❑ 98BowChrCOI-25
❑ 98BowChrCOI-133
❑ 98BowChrCOIR-25
❑ 98BowChrCOIR-133
❑ 98BowChrCR-25
❑ 98BowChrCR-133
❑ 98FinFutF-F5
❑ 98FinFutFR-F5
❑ 98O-PChr-226
❑ 98O-PChrR-226
❑ 98Top-226
❑ 98TopO-P-226
**Allen, Chad**
❑ 94UppDecEleIce-499
❑ 95UppDecEleIce-532
❑ 95UppDecEleIceG-532
**Allen, Chris**
❑ 95BowDraPro-P2
❑ 95Sla-109
❑ 95Sla-433
❑ 96ColEdgSS&D-2
❑ 99UppDecM-91
❑ 99UppDecMGS-91
❑ 99UppDecMSS-91
❑ 99UppDecMSS-91
**Allen, George**
❑ 34BeeGro1P-38
❑ 37OPCV304E-157
❑ 39OPCV3011-79
❑ 45QuaOatP-61
**Allen, Greg**
❑ 88NiaFalT-19
❑ 897thInnSOHL-145
❑ 89NiaFalT-1
❑ 907thInnSOHL-251
**Allen, John**
❑ 90ArIce-2
❑ 90ArIce-3
❑ 92ArIce-5
**Allen, Keith**
❑ 54Par-47
❑ 92FlyUppDS-44
**Allen, Marko**
❑ 93FinnJyvHS-55
❑ 93FinnSIS-236
❑ 94FinnSIS-4
❑ 95FinnSIS-20
**Allen, Mike**
❑ 907thInnSOHL-226
❑ 90KitRan-22
**Allen, Peter**
❑ 93RicRen-10
❑ 96CleLum-1
❑ 96CleLum-1
**Allen, Scott**
❑ 91ProAHLCHL-444
❑ 94CenHocL-19
❑ 95ForWorFT-7
**Allen, Shaun Van**
❑ 93StaCluFDI-361
❑ 95ColChoPC-173
❑ 95ColChoPCP-173
**Allen, Tom**
❑ 83KinCan-5
❑ 84Ott67-1
❑ 85LonKni-23
**Allen, Viv**
❑ 34BeeGro1P-211
**Allinger, Jan**
❑ 65SweCorl-75A
**Allison, Blair**
❑ 91AirCanSJHL-E3
❑ 92MPSPhoSJHL-4
❑ 93MaiBlaB-55
**Allison, Dave (David)**
❑ 83NovScoV-3
❑ 84NovScoO-2
❑ 88ProIHL-9
❑ 91RicRen-19
❑ 93KinFro-24
❑ 96GraRapG-2
**Allison, Jamie**
❑ 917thInnSOHL-189
❑ 93DetJrRW-15
❑ 94DetJrRW-17
❑ 94UppDec-464
❑ 94UppDecEleIce-464
❑ 95ColEdgI-75
❑ 95SlaMemC-91
❑ 95St.JohF-1
❑ 97Don-131
❑ 97DonPreProG-131
❑ 97DonPreProS-131
❑ 97Pac-315
❑ 97PacCop-315
❑ 97PacEmeGre-315
❑ 97PacIceB-315
❑ 97PacRed-315
❑ 97PacSil-315
**Allison, Jason**
❑ 917thInnSOHL-381
❑ 93Cla-13
❑ 93DonTeaC-1

93LonKni-1
93LonKni-25
93Pin-466
93PinCan-466
93UppDec-537
94BeAPla-R155
94Cla-110
94ClaCHLAS-C1
94ClaDraGol-110
94ClaPic-CP14
94ClaPre-HK1
94ClaROYS-R1
94ClaTri-T73
94Fin-55
94Fin-154
94FinRef-55
94FinRef-154
94FinSupTW-55
94FinSupTW-154
94Fla-195
94Fle-231
94Lea-511
94LeaGolR-13
94LeaLim-98
94OPCPre-467
94OPCPreSE-467
94ParSE-SE194
94ParSE-SE208
94ParSEG-SE194
94ParSEG-SE208
94Pin-247
94Pin-474
94Pin-530
94PinArtP-247
94PinArtP-474
94PinArtP-530
94PinRinC-247
94PinRinC-474
94PinRinC-530
94PinRooTP-7
94Sco-206
94Sco-231
94ScoGol-206
94ScoGol-231
94ScoPla-206
94ScoPla-231
94ScoPlaTS-231
94Sel-193
94SelGol-193
94SelYouExp-YE8
94SP-151
94SPDieCut-151
94StaClu-118
94StaCluFDI-118
94StaCluMOMS-118
94StaCluSTWC-118
94TopPre-467
94TopPreSE-467
94Ult-386
94UppDec-242
94UppDec-535
94UppDecEIeIce-242
94UppDecEIeIce-535
94UppDecPC-C4
94UppDecPCEG-C4
94UppDecPCES-C4
94UppDecSPI-SP174
94UppDecSPIDC-SP174
95Cap-1
95Don-75
95DonCanWJT-12
95Emo-185
95Lea-103
95LeaLim-5
95ParInt-494
95ParIntEl-494
95PlaOneoOne-106
95PorPir-2
95ProMag-31
95Sco-128
95ScoBlaIce-128
95ScoBlaIceAP-128
95TopCanWJ-4CJ
95UppDec-59
95UppDecEIeIce-59
95UppDecEIeIceG-59
96BeAPAut-36
96BeAPAutSil-36
96BeAPla-36
96NHLProSTA-31
96SP-168
96Zen-125
96ZenArtP-125
97ColCho-16
97DonPri-122
97DonPriSoA-122
97PacCroR-6
97PacCroREG-6
97PacCroRIB-6
97PacCroRS-6
97PacDyn-6
97PacDynC-6
97PacDynDG-6
97PacDynEG-6
97PacDynIB-6
97PacDynR-6
97PacDynSil-6
97PacDynTan-29
97PacInv-6
97PacInvC-6
97PacInvEG-6
97PacInvIB-6
97PacInvR-6
97PacInvS-6
97PacOme-10

97PacOmeC-10
97PacOmeDG-10
97PacOmeEG-10
97PacOmeG-10
97PacOmeIB-10
97PacRev-6
97PacRevC-6
97PacRevE-6
97PacRevIB-6
97PacRevR-6
97PacRevS-6
97Pin-147
97PinIns-147
97PinPrePBB-147
97PinPrePBC-147
97PinPrePBM-147
97PinPrePBY-147
97PinPrePFC-147
97PinPrePFM-147
97PinPrePFY-147
97PinPrePla-147
97Sco-233
97ScoBru-7
97ScoBruPla-7
97ScoBruPre-7
97SPAut-10
97UppDec-8
97UppDecBD-32
97UppDecBDDD-32
97UppDecBDQD-32
97UppDecBDTD-32
97Zen-80
97Zen5x7-28
97ZenGolImp-28
97ZenSilImp-28
97ZenZGol-80
97ZenZSil-80
98Be A PPA-156
98Be A PPAA-156
98Be A PPAAF-156
98Be A PPSE-156
98Be APG-156
98BowBes-51
98BowBesAR-51
98BowBesR-51
98Fin-141
98FinCen-C8
98FinCenR-C8
98FinNo P-141
98FinNo PR-141
98FinRedL-R13
98FinRedLR-R13
98FinRef-141
98O-PChr-125
98O-PChrR-125
98O-PChrSB-SB27
98O-PChrSBR-SB27
98Pac-41
98PacAur-7
98PacCroR-6
98PacCroRLS-6
98PacDynI-7
98PacDynIIB-7
98PacDynIR-7
98PacIceB-41
98PacOmeH-10
98PacOmeODI-10
98PacOmeR-10
98PacPar-8
98PacParC-8
98PacParEG-8
98PacParH-8
98PacParIB-8
98PacParS-8
98PacRed-41
98PacRev-6
98PacRevIS-6
98PacRevR-6
98SP Aut-6
98SP AutSotTG-JA
98SPxFin-6
98SPxFinR-6
98SPxFinS-6
98SSASotT-JA
98Top-125
98TopAut-A1
98TopGolLC1-50
98TopGolLC1B-50
98TopGolLC1Boo0-50
98TopGolLC1Ooo0-50
98TopGolLC1R-50
98TopGolLC1Roo0-50
98TopGolLC2-50
98TopGolLC2B-50
98TopGolLC2Boo0-50
98TopGolLC2Ooo0-50
98TopGolLC2R-50
98TopGolLC2Roo0-50
98TopGolLC3-50
98TopGolLC3B-50
98TopGolLC3Boo0-50
98TopGolLC3Ooo0-50
98TopGolLC3R-50
98TopGolLC3Roo0-50
98TopIceA2-16
98TopO-P-125
98TopSeaB-SB27
98UC-14
98UD ChoPCR-14
98UD ChoR-14
98UppDec-41
98UppDecBD-6
98UppDecDD-6
98UppDecE-41
98UppDecE1o1-41

98UppDecFF-FF26
98UppDecFF26
98UppDecFFQ1-FF26
98UppDecFFQ2-FF26
98UppDecGR-41
98UppDecM-13
98UppDecMGS-13
98UppDecMP-JA
98UppDecMSS-13
98UppDecMSS-13
98UppDecQD-6
98UppDecTD-6
99Pac-17
99PacAur-9
99PacAurPD-9
99PacCop-17
99PacGol-17
99PacIceB-17
99PacPreD-17
99SP AutPS-6
99UppDecM-15
99UppDecMGS-15
99UppDecMSS-15
99UppDecMSS-15
**Allison, Mike**
81OPC-221
81Top-E94
82PosCer-13
86MapLeaP-1
87MapLeaPLA-18
88KinSmo-1
88PanSti-73
89KinSmo-4
89OPC-141
89Top-141
90OPC-417
**Allison, Peter**
92WinSpi-14
**Allison, Ray**
80OPC-155
80Top-126
83FlyJCP-1
83OPC-259
84KelWin-52
89ProAHL-338
94CapBreO-1
97SheSte-11
**Allison, Scott**
90thInnSWHL-273
90PriAlbR-1
90Sco-424
90ScoCan-424
91thInnSWHL-276
94CapBreO-1
97SheSte-11
**Alm, Bengt**
71SweHocS-271
**Almqvist, Anders**
72SweHocS-204
**Almstedt, Graydon**
84Ott67-2
**Alserydh, Lars**
69SweHocS-76
**Alstead, Ryan**
92MinGolG-20
**Alston, Jan**
98GerDELE-246
**Althoff, Christian**
94GerDELE-357
**Altrichter, Martin**
94CzeAPSE-250
95CzeAPSE-125
96CzeAPSE-288
**Alvarez, Mauricio**
95Sla-21
**Alverud, Anders**
83SweSemE-126
84SweSemE-149
**Amadio, Dave**
68OPC-157
68ShiCoi-59
70OPC-33
70Top-33
**Amadio, Leo**
52JunBluT-75
**Amadio, Neil**
50QueCit-1
**Amann, Rick**
93SweSemWCS-155
94FinnJaaK-273
94GerDELE-89
95GerDELE-83
95SweGloWC-219
**Ambrosio, Jeff (Jeffrey)**
94ParSE-SE266
94ParSEG-SE266
95SigRooFF-FF1
95SigRooFFS-FF1
95Sla-143
96KitRan-1
**Ambroziak, Peter**
89thInnSOHL-60
90thInnSOHL-74
91thInnSOHL-291
92RochAmeDD-1
92RochAmeKod-3
93RochAmeKod-3
**Amidovski, Bujar**
95Sla-106
98BowCHL-32
98BowCHLGA-32
98BowCHLOI-32
98BowCHLSC-SC4
98BowChrCGA-32
98BowChrCGAR-32

98BowChrCOI-32
98BowChrCOIR-32
98BowChrCR-32
98O-PChr-239
98O-PChrR-239
98Top-239
98TopO-P-239
**Amodeo, Dominic**
92AlbIntTC-1
**Amodeo, Mike**
72NatOttWHA-1
72OPC-291
78JetPos-1
79JetPos-1
79OPC-268
82SweSemHVS-126
**Amonte, Tony**
91OPC-26
91OPCPre-11
91Par-114
91Par-443
91ParFre-114
91ParFre-443
91Pin-301
91Pin-390
91PinFre-301
91PinFre-390
91ProSet-550
91ProSetPre-550
91ProSetPla-262
91ScoAme-398
91ScoCan-288
91Top-26
91UppDec-440
91UppDec-450
91UppDecF-440
91UppDecF-450
92Bow-389
92OPC-155
92OPC-255
92OPC25AI-24
92PanSti-270
92PanSti-T
92PanStiFre-270
92PanStiFre-T
92Par-107
92Par-235
92ParEmel-107
92ParEmel-235
92Pin-55
92PinFre-55
92PinTea2-4
92PinTea2F-4
92ProSet-118
92ProSetRGL-1
92Sco-389
92Sco-415
92Sco-506
92ScoCan-389
92ScoCan-415
92ScoCan-506
92ScoYouS-2
92SeaPat-27
92StaClu-32
92StaClu-250
92Top-6
92Top-229
92TopGol-6G
92TopGol-229G
92Ult-133
92UltRoo-1
92UppDec-13
92UppDec-138
92UppDec-359
92UppDec-453
92UppDec-635
92UppDecART-AR1
92UppDecART-AR7
93Don-217
93Don-411
93Lea-17
93OPCPre-70
93OPCPreG-70
93PanSti-90
93Pin-6
93Pin1S-1
93PinCan-6
93PinTea2-19
93PinTea2C-19
93Pow-156
93Sco-215
93ScoCan-215
93StaClu-226
93StaClu-458
93StaCluFDI-226
93StaCluFDI-458
93StaCluFDIO-226
93StaCluO-226
93StaCluO-458
93SweSemWCS-188
93TopPre-70
93TopPreG-70
93Ult-202
93UppDec-64
93UppDecLAS-51
93UppDecSP-97
94BeAPla-R17
94BeAPSig-97
94CanGamNHLP-65
94Don-107
94Fle-37
94HocWit-2
94Lea-2
94OPCPre-5
94OPCPreSE-5

94ParSE-SE36
94ParSEG-SE36
94ParVin-V56
94Pin-16
94PinArtP-16
94PinRinC-16
94PosCerBB-1
94Sco-92
94ScoGol-92
94ScoPla-92
94ScoPlaTS-92
94Sel-115
94SelGol-115
94SP-26
94SPDieCut-26
94TopPre-5
94TopPreSE-5
94Ult-273
94UppDec-4
94UppDecEIeIce-4
94UppDecNBAP-1
94UppDecSPI-SP105
94UppDecSPIDC-SP105
95ColCho-206
95ColChoPC-206
95ColChoPCP-206
95Don-121
95Lea-17
95ParInt-311
95ParIntEl-311
95PlaOneoOne-235
95Sco-133
95ScoBlaIce-133
95ScoBlaIceAP-133
95SP-28
95StaCluMOMS-117
95Sum-165
95SumArtP-165
95SumIce-165
95SweGloWC-121
95Top-79
95TopOPCI-79
95TopPowL-4PL
95Ult-216
95UppDec-18
95UppDecEIeIce-18
95UppDecEIeIceG-18
95UppDecSpeE-SE18
95UppDecSpeEdiG-SE18
96BeAPAut-66
96BeAPAutSil-66
96BeAPla-66
96ColCho-49
96Don-80
96DonPrePro-80
96Fla-14
96FlaBlul-14
96Lea-92
96LeaPreP-92
96MetUni-24
96Pin-54
96PinArtP-54
96PinFoi-54
96PinPreS-54
96Sco-169
96ScoArtPro-169
96ScoDeaCAP-169
96ScoGolB-169
96ScoSpeAP-169
96SkyImp-16
96SP-32
96SPHolCol-HC18
96TopNHLP-133
96TopPicOI-133
96Ult-28
96UltGolM-28
96UppDec-32
96UppDecBD-173
96UppDecBDG-173
96UppDecIce-13
96UppDecIcePar-13
97ColCho-44
97ColChoCTG-C10A
97ColChoCTG-C10B
97ColChoCTG-C10C
97ColChoCTGE-CR10
97ColChoSta-SQ65
97Don-102
97DonCanI-34
97DonCanIDS-34
97DonCanIS-34
97DonEli-97
97DonEliS-97
97DonLim-105
97DonLimExp-105
97DonPre-64
97DonPreCttC-64
97DonPreProG-102
97DonPreProS-102
97DonPri-151
97DonPriSoA-151
97Kat-31
97KatGol-31
97KatSil-31
97Lea-139
97LeaFraMat-139
97LeaFraMDC-139
97LeaInt-139
97LeaIntUI-139
97Pac-264
97PacCop-264
97PacCroR-27

97PacCroREG-27
97PacCroRIB-27
97PacCroRS-27
97PacDyn-24
97PacDynC-24
97PacDynDG-24
97PacDynEG-24
97PacDynR-24
97PacDynIB-24
97PacDynSil-24
97PacDynTan-33
97PacEmeGre-264
97PacIceB-264
97PacInv-27
97PacInvC-27
97PacInvEG-27
97PacInvIB-27
97PacInvR-27
97PacInvS-27
97PacOme-46
97PacOmeC-46
97PacOmeDG-46
97PacOmeEG-46
97PacOmeIB-46
97PacPar-40
97PacParC-40
97PacParDG-40
97PacParEG-40
97PacParIB-40
97PacParRed-40
97PacParSil-40
97PacRed-264
97PacRev-27
97PacRevC-27
97PacRevE-27
97PacRevIB-27
97PacRevR-27
97PacRevS-27
97PacSil-264
97Pin-148
97PinCer-68
97PinCerMB-68
97PinCerMG-68
97PinCerMR-68
97PinCerR-68
97PinIns-53
97PinInsCC-53
97PinInsEC-53
97PinPrePBB-148
97PinPrePBC-148
97PinPrePBM-148
97PinPrePBY-148
97PinPrePFC-148
97PinPrePFM-148
97PinPrePFY-148
97PinPrePla-148
97PinTotCMPG-68
97PinTotCPB-68
97PinTotCPG-68
97PinTotCPR-68
97Sco-114
97ScoArtPro-114
97ScoGolBla-114
97SP AutI-I29
97SPAut-29
97SPAutID-I29
97SPAutIE-I29
97SPAutSotT-TA
97SPx-8
97SPxBro-8
97SPxGol-8
97SPxGraF-8
97SPxSil-8
97SPxSte-8
97Stu-99
97StuPreG-99
97StuPreS-99
97UppDec-208
97UppDec-245
97UppDecBD-101
97UppDecBDDD-101
97UppDecBDQD-101
97UppDecBDTD-101
97UppDecCtaG-1
97UppDecCtAG-AR1
97UppDecDV-19
97UppDecDVSM-19
97UppDecGDM-245
97UppDecGJ-GJ6
97UppDecIce-63
97UppDecIceP-63
97UppDecIPS-63
97UppDecSG-SG10
97UppDecSSM-SS18
97UppDecSSW-SS18
97UppDecTS-23
97UppDecTSL2-23
97UppDecTSS-9A
97Zen-78
97ZenZGol-78
97ZenZSil-78
98Be A PPA-28
98Be A PPAA-28
98Be A PPAAF-28
98Be A PPPGUJC-G22
98Be A PPPPUJC-P11
98Be A PPTBASG-28
98Be APG-28
98BowBes-77
98BowBesAR-77
98BowBesR-77
98Fin-29
98FinNo P-29
98FinNo PR-29

98FinRef-29
98O-PChr-204
98O-PChrR-204
98Pac-142
98PacAur-38
98PacCroR-27
98PacCroRLS-27
98PacDynI-38
98PacDynIIB-38
98PacDynIR-38
98PacIceB-142
98PacOmeH-48
98PacOmeR-48
98PacOmeODI-48
98PacOmeR-48
98PacPar-43
98PacParC-43
98PacParEG-43
98PacParH-43
98PacParIB-43
98PacParS-43
98PacRed-142
98PacRev-28
98PacRevADC-1
98PacRevIS-28
98PacRevR-28
98PacRevS-7
98SP Aut-17
98SPxFin-18
98SPxFin-106
98SPxFinR-18
98SPxFinR-106
98SPxFinS-18
98SPxFinS-106
98SPXTopP-9
98SPXTopPP-9
98SPXTopPPS-PS20
98SPXTopPR-9
98Top-204
98TopBlaLGR'-GR9
98TopGolLC1-33
98TopGolLC1B-33
98TopGolLC1BOo0-33
98TopGolLC1Oo0-33
98TopGolLC1R-33
98TopGolLC1ROo0-33
98TopGolLC2-33
98TopGolLC2B-33
98TopGolLC2BOo0-33
98TopGolLC2Oo0-33
98TopGolLC2R-33
98TopGolLC2ROo0-33
98TopGolLC3-33
98TopGolLC3B-33
98TopGolLC3BOo0-33
98TopGolLC3Oo0-33
98TopGolLC3R-33
98TopGolLC3ROo0-33
98TopGolLGR'-GR9
98TopGolLGR'BOo0-GR9
98TopGolLGR'Oo0-GR9
98TopGolLGR'ROo0-GR9
98TopO-P-204
98TopRedLGR'-GR9
98UC-17
98UCSB-SQ26
98UCSG-SQ26
98UCSG-SQ26
98UCSR-SQ26
98UD ChoPCR-51
98UD ChoR-51
98UDCP-51
98UppDec-243
98UppDecBD-20
98UppDecDD-20
98UppDecE-243
98UppDecE1o1-243
98UppDecFF-FF16
98UppDecFF-FF16
98UppDecFFQ1-FF16
98UppDecFFQ2-FF16
98UppDecGR-243
98UppDecM-45
98UppDecMGS-45
98UppDecMSS-45
98UppDecMSS-45
98UppDecQD-20
98UppDecTD-20
99Pac-84
99PacAur-30
99PacAurPD-30
99PacCop-84
99PacGol-84
99PacIceB-84
99PacPreD-84
99RetHoc-17
99SP AutPS-17
99UppDecM-46
99UppDecMGS-46
99UppDecMSS-46
99UppDecMSS-46
99UppDecRG-17
99UppDecRII-TA
99UppDecRIL1-TA
99UppDecRP-17
**Amore, Angelo**
91thInnSOHL-358
**Anchikoski, Wayne**
87PorWinH-1
88PorWinH-1
91BriColJHL-156
91BriColJHL-167
91BriColJHL-NNO
92DalFre-1
93DalFre-1
94CenHocL-2

94HumHawP-9

**Ancicka, Martin**
94CzeAPSE-55

**Andanoff, Jim**
83BelBul-14
84BelBul-27

**Andersen, Cato Tom**
93SweSemWCS-232
94FinnJaaK-253
95FinnSemWC-181
95SweGloWC-192

**Anderson, Chris**
95TriAme-1

**Anderson, Cory**
88KamBla-1

**Anderson, Dan**
91Arilce-10
92Arilce-6

**Anderson, David**
897thInnSOHL-39
907thInnSOHL-126
91OshGenS-6

**Anderson, Dean**
88FliSpi-1
89ProAHL-105
90KnoChe-115
90ProAHLIHL-166
91KnoChe-19

**Anderson, Earl**
77OPCNHL-114
77RocAme-4
77Top-114

**Anderson, Ernie**
23V1281PauC-66

**Anderson, Evan**
91AirCanSJHL-A45
91AirCanSJHLAS-28
91AirCanSJHLAS-48

**Anderson, Glenn**
80PepCap-21
81OilRedR-9
81OPC-108
81OPCSti-217
81SweSemHVS-82
82OilRedR-9
82OPC-100
82OPCSti-99
82OPCSti-100
82PosCer-6
83Ess-1
83OilMcD-24
83OPC-24
83OPCSti-92
83OPCSti-93
83OPCSti-158
83PufSti-2
83Vac-21
84TEDis-13
84OilRedR-9
84OilTeal-1
84OPC-238
84OPCSti-247
84OPCSti-248
85OilRedR-9
85OPC-168
85OPCSti-227
86KraDra-1
86OilRedR-9
86OilTeal-9
86OPC-80
86OPCSti-78
86Top-80
87OilTeal-9
87OPC-199
87OPCMin-1
87OPCSti-95
87PanSti-265
88FriLayS-26
88OilTeal-1
88OilTenAnn-9
88OPC-189
88OPCSti-229
88PanSti-57
88Top-189
89Kra-10
89OilTeal-1
89OPC-226
89OPC-303
89OPCSti-218
89PanSti-77
90Bow-195
90BowTif-195
90OilIGA-1
90OPC-145
90PanSti-227
90ProSet-81
90Sco-114
90ScoCan-114
90ScoHotRS-54
90Top-145
90TopTif-145
90UppDec-284
90UppDecF-284
91Bow-116
91MapLeaP-1
91OilPanTS-1
91OPC-124
91OPCPre-10
91PanSti-109
91Par-177
91ParFre-177
91Pin-12
91PinFre-12
91ProSet-75
91ProSetFre-75

91ScoAme-47
91ScoCan-47
91ScoCan-611
91ScoRoo-61T
91StaClu-116
91Top-124
91UppDec-250
91UppDecF-250
92Bow-104
92MapLeaK-1
92OPC-134
92PanSti-76
92PanStiFre-76
92Par-178
92ParEmel-178
92Pin-355
92PinFre-355
92ProSet-185
92Sco-241
92ScoCan-241
92StaClu-124
92Top-162
92TopGol-162G
92Ult-207
93Don-340
93Don-460
93Lea-41
93OPCPre-104
93OPCPreG-104
93PanSti-225
93Par-201
93ParEmel-201
93Pin-398
93PinCan-398
93Pow-237
93Sco-180
93Sco-449
93ScoBla-3
93ScoCan-180
93ScoCan-449
93StaClu-168
93StaCluFDI-168
93StaCluFDIO-168
93StaCluO-168
93TopPre-104
93TopPreG-104
93Ult-9
94Don-254
94HocWit-50
94Lea-14
94OPCPre-270
94OPCPreSE-270
94TopPre-270
94TopPreSE-270
94Ult-135
95ColCho-46
95ColChoPC-46
95ColChoPCP-46
95GerDELE-441
96Pin-171
96PinArtP-171
96PinFoi-171
96PinPreS-171
96PinRinC-171

**Anderson, Grant**
83BraAle-24

**Anderson, Jack**
75HamFin-1

**Anderson, Jimmy**
74CapWhiB-2
74OPCNHL-118
74Top-118

**Anderson, John**
78MapLeaP-1
79MapLeaP-1
80MapLeaP-1
80OPC-79
80PepCap-81
80Top-79
81MapLeaP-1
81OPC-313
81OPCSti-107
82MapLeaP-2
82OPC-315
82OPCSti-73
82OPCSti-74
82PosCer-18
83Ess-2
83MapLeaP-1
83OPC-325
83OPCSti-30
83OPCSti-31
83PufSti-4
83Vac-81
84TEDis-44
84KelAccD-5A
84MapLeaP-1
84OPC-295
84OPCSti-18
84Top-136
85NordGenF-1
85NordPla-6
85NordPro-1
85OPC-20
85OPCSti-10
85Top-20
86NordMcD-1
86OPC-13
86OPCSti-54
86Top-13
86WhaJunT-1
87OPC-45
87OPCSti-204
87PanSti-45
87Top-45

87WhaJunBK-1
88OPC-190
88OPCSti-270
88PanSti-239
88Top-190
88WhaJunGR-1
89OPC-124
89Top-124
90ProAHLIHL-543
92SanDieG-1

**Anderson, Mike**
95MinGolG-4
96MinGolGCAS-4

**Anderson, Ole**
95Sla-234

**Anderson, Perry**
85DevPos-2
86DevPol-2
88DevCar-1
89ProAHL-216
90ProAHLIHL-561
91OPC-501
91Par-164
91ParFre-164
91ProSetFre-481
91ScoCan-649
91ScoRoo-99T
91ShaSanJSA-1
91Top-501
92OPC-38
92SanDieG-2
92StaClu-89
92Top-286
92TopGol-286G

**Anderson, Ron**
69OPC-14
70ColSta-48
70EssPowPla-84
70SarProSta-18
71OPC-163
71SarProSta-1a
71SarProSta-1b
72OPC-298
74CapWhiB-3
74NHLActSta-312
74OPCNHL-314

**Anderson, Russ**
77PenPucB-7
78OPC-156
78Top-156
79OPC-264
79Top-264
82WhaJunHC-2
84KinSmo-1

**Anderson, Shawn**
86SabBluS-1
86SabBluSSma-1
87SabWonBH-2
88ProAHL-261
89SabCam-1
90ProSet-513
91Bow-147
91StaClu-358
92CapKod-1
94Lea-346
95MilAdmBO-1

**Anderson, Tommy**
34BeeGro1P-212
35DiaMatT2-1
35DiaMatT3-1
39OPCV3011-61

**Anderson, Vern**
91AirCanSJHL-C13

**Anderson, Warren**
81SweSemHVS-75

**Anderson, Will**
84KamBla-1
94MinGolG-1

**Andersson, Ake**
83SweSemE-196

**Andersson, Anders**
64SweCorl-11
64SweCorl-143
65SweCorl-11
65SweCorl-143
67SweHoc-80

**Andersson, Benny**
67SweHoc-133
71SweHocS-144
72SweHocS-131
72SweHocS-132
73SweHocS-186
73SweWorCS-186

**Andersson, Bosse**
67SweHoc-97
72SweHocS-197
83SweSemE-201

**Andersson, Christer**
70SweHocS-178
71SweHocS-261
72SweHocS-241
72SweSemWC-44
74SweHocS-138
83SweSemE-63
84SweSemE-63
85SwePanS-43
87SwePanS-54

**Andersson, Dick**
89SweSemE-193

**Andersson, Einar**
65SweCorl-67

**Andersson, Erik**
90SweSemE-97

91SweSemE-25
96DenUniPio-8

**Andersson, Fredrik**
86SwePanS-193
87SwePanS-192
89SweSemE-169
89SweSemE-215
90SweSemE-3
91SweSemE-201
92SweSemE-223
93SweSemE-195
94SweLeaE-17
94SweLeaECS-9
94SweLeaE-271

**Andersson, Gunnar**
64SweCorl-49
65SweCorl-49
67SweHoc-49
69SweHocS-112
70SweHocS-70
71SweHoc-5
71SweHocS-159
72SweHocS-154
72SweSemWC-59
73SweHocS-45
73SweWorCS-45
74SweHocS-154

**Andersson, Hakan**
67SweHoc-81
67SweHoc-82
69SweHocS-219
71SweHocS-145
71SweHocS-364
73SweHocS-185

**Andersson, Hans**
72SweHocS-135
73SweWorCS-185
74SweHocS-199

**Andersson, Hans-Rickard**
87SwePanS-266

**Andersson, Henrik**
89SweSemE-246
90SweSemE-156

**Andersson, Jan**
71SweHocS-365
74SweHocS-155

**Andersson, John**
67SweHoc-247
69SweHocS-293
70SweHocS-197
71SweHocS-283

**Andersson, Jonas**
90SweSemE-74

**Andersson, Kenneth**
83SweSemE-69
84SweSemE-69
85SwePanS-63
86SwePanS-44
90SweSemE-196

**Andersson, Kent Erik**
71SweHocS-146
73SweHocS-182
74SweHocS-200
78NorStaCD-4
78OPC-17
78Top-17
79NorStaPos-1
79PanSti-200
80NorStaPos-1
80OPC-383
81NorStaPos-1
81OPC-158
81Top-W102
82OPC-218
82PosCer-9
84SweSemE-109
85SwePanS-109
85SwePanS-129
85SwePanS-130

**Andersson, Kjell**
69SweHocS-328
70SweHocS-250
71SweHocS-308
72SweHocS-292
73SweHocS-146
74SweHocS-201

**Andersson, Krister**
69SweHocS-275

**Andersson, Lars**
65SweCorl-134
67SweHoc-99
86SwePanS-45

**Andersson, Leif**
64SweCorl-68
65SweCorl-68
67SweHoc-181
69SweHocS-309
70SweHocS-214
72SweHocS-272
73SweHocS-181
73SweWorCS-181

**Andersson, Lennart**
71SweHocS-135
72SweHocS-121
73SweHocS-181
73SweWorCS-181

**Andersson, Magnus**
88SweHocS-165

**Andersson, Mattias**
89SweSemE-81
90SweSemE-206
91SweSemE-134
95SweSemE-155

**Andersson, Mikael**

83SweSemE-41
83SweSemE-234
84SweSemE-41
85SabBluS-1
85SabBluSS-1
85SwePanS-34
86SwePanS-26
87SabBluS-1
87SabWonBH-1
87SwePanS-36
88ProAHL-264
88SabBluS-1
88SabWonBH-1
89SweSemE-274
89WhaJunM-1
90OPC-35
90PanSti-47
90ProSet-98
90SweSemE-45
90Top-35
90TopTif-35
90WhaJr7E-1
91Bow-11
91OPC-197
91Par-63
91ParFre-63
91ProSet-394
91ProSetFre-394
91ProSetPla-180
91StaClu-39
91SweSemE-290
91Top-197
91UppDec-238
91UppDecF-238
91WhaJr7E-1
92Bow-158
92LigShe-1
92OPC-214
92OPCPre-55
92PanSti-258
92PanStiFre-258
92Par-169
92ParEmel-169
92Pin-384
92PinFre-384
92ProSet-65
92Sco-215
92ScoCan-215
92StaClu-348
92Top-151
92TopGol-151G
92UppDec-103
93Don-322
93Lea-285
93LigSealR-1
93OPCPre-150
93OPCPreG-150
93PanSti-216
93Par-198
93ParEmel-198
93Pin-329
93PinCan-329
93Pow-440
93Sco-427
93ScoCan-427
93StaClu-97
93StaClu-427
93StaCluFDI-97
93StaCluFDI-427
93StaCluFDIO-97
93StaCluO-97
93StaCluO-427
93SweSemE-17
93SweSemWCS-37
93TopPre-150
93TopPreG-150
93Ult-421
94CanGamNHLP-220
94Don-14
94EASpo-130
94Lea-347
94LigPhoA-1
94LigPos-1
94OPCPre-287
94OPCPreSE-287
94Par-226
94ParGol-226
94Pin-451
94PinArtP-451
94PinRinC-451
94StaClu-75
94StaCluFDI-75
94StaCluMOMS-75
94StaCluSTWC-75
94TopPre-287
94TopPreSE-287
94Ult-370
94UppDec-297
94UppDecEleIce-297
95ColCho-182
95ColChoPC-182
95ColChoPCP-182
95FinnSemWC-72
95LigTeal-1
95ParInt-196
95ParIntEl-196
95SweGloWC-42
95Top-123
95TopOPCI-123
96BeAPAut-65
96BeAPAutSil-65
96BeAPla-65
96UppDec-155
97PacInvNRB-182

98Pac-395
98PacIceB-395
98PacRed-395

**Andersson, Niklas**
89SweSemE-281
90SweSemE-39
91ProAHLCHL-533
91SweSemE-317
91UppDec-29
91UppDecF-29
93ClaProPro-120
93Sco-460
93ScoCan-460
93SweSemWCS-44
93UppDec-239
95Bow-126
95BowAllFoi-126
95ParInt-398
95ParIntEl-398
95SweGloWC-51
96BeAPAut-98
96BeAPAutSil-98
96BeAPla-98
96ColCho-165
96ColEdgFL-2
96Don-214
96DonEli-89
96DonEliDCS-89
96DonPrePro-214
96IslPos-1
96Sco-248
96ScoArtPro-248
96ScoDeaCAP-248
96ScoGolB-248
96ScoSpeAP-248
96SelCer-57
96SelCerAP-57
96SelCerBlu-57
96SelCerMB-57
96SelCerMG-57
96SelCerMR-57
96SelCerRed-57
96SkyImp-165
96Sum-172
96SumArtP-172
96SumIce-172
96SumMet-172
96SumPreS-172
96UppDec-292
97ColCho-156
97Pac-144
97PacCop-144
97PacEmeGre-144
97PacIceB-144
97PacRed-144
97PacSil-144

**Andersson, Ola**
89SweSemE-68
90SweSemE-66
91SweSemE-246

**Andersson, Ove**
64SweCorl-25
64SweCorl-31
65SweCorl-25
65SweCorl-31A
67SweHoc-248

**Andersson, Paul**
89SweSemE-283
91SweSemE-265
92SweSemE-298
93SweSemE-263
94SweLeaE-107
95SweLeaE-131
95SweUppDE-200

**Andersson, Per**
83SweSemE-184
84SweSemE-207

**Andersson, Peter**
82SweSemHVS-12
83SweSemE-105
84SweSemE-105
85SwePanS-94
86SwePanS-14
86SwePanS-88
87SwePanS-32
87SwePanS-92
89SweSemWCS-11
90SweSemE-128
91SweSemE-180
91SweSemE-343
91SweSemWCS-35
91SweSemWCS-36
92SweSemE-345
92UppDec-481
93SweSemE-9
93SweSemWCS-27
93UppDec-71
94OPCPre-212
94OPCPreSE-212
94Par-88
94ParGol-88
94SweLeaE-267
94TopPre-212
94TopPreSE-212
95FinnSemWC-60
95SweGloWC-11
95SweLeaE-87
95SweLeaE-304
95SweLeaEFF-14
95SweUppDE-138
95SweUppDE-231
95SweUppDE-257
96GerDELE-276

**Andersson, Ronny**
69SweHocS-329

70SweHocS-244
71SweHocS-301
72SweHocS-286

**Andersson, Sivert**
83SweSemE-139

**Andersson, Staffan**
83SweSemE-28
87SwePanS-27

**Andersson, Stefan**
72SweHocS-42
95SweLeaE-155
95SweUppDE-12

**Andersson, Sten**
67SweHoc-197

**Andersson, Stig**
71SweHocS-388
72SweHocS-262

**Andersson, Sture**
71SweHocS-177
72SweHocS-167
74SweHocS-157
83SweSemE-151

**Andersson, Tommy**
67SweHoc-214
69SweHocS-256
70SweHocS-114
71SweHocS-203
72SweHocS-182
73SweHocS-228
73SweWorCS-228
74SweHocS-158
83SweSemE-195
84SweSemE-218

**Andersson, Torbjorn**
83SweSemE-29
84SweSemE-28
85SwePanS-27
86SwePanS-5
87SwePanS-28

**Andersson, Ulf**
84SweSemE-135
87SwePanS-42
93SweSemE-18

**Andersson-Junkka, Jonas**
94ParSE-SE238
94ParSEG-SE238
94SweLeaE-184
94SweLeaERR-2
95SigRooA-3
95SigRooAPC-3
95SweLeaE-138

**Andrea, Paul**
62SudWol-1
68ShiCoi-142
70EssPowPla-87
70OPC-77
70Top-77
917thInnSOHL-24
91CorRoy-23
95DayBom-4

**Andreasson, Bengt-Olov**
65SweCorl-110
67SweHoc-167

**Andren, Anders**
69SweHocS-94
71SweHocS-133

**Andreoli, Dave**
81SauSteMG-2

**Andres, Bruce**
81IndChe-1

**Andrews, Al**
82KinCan-7

**Andrews, Elliott**
94GuiFla-18
95GuiFla-14
96GuiFla-14

**Andrews, Jeff**
93OshGen-9

**Andrews, Lloyd**
23V1451-21
24C144ChaCig-2
24V1452-59

**Andreychuk, Dave**
800shGen-7
810shGen-12
83CanNatJ-1
84OPC-17
84OPC-353
84OPCSti-209
84OPCSti-210
84SabBluS-1
84Top-13
85OPC-143
85OPCSti-187
85SabBluS-2
85SabBluSS-2
85Top-143
86OPC-16
86OPCSti-49
86SabBluS-2
86SabBluSSma-2
86Top-16
87OPC-3
87OPCSti-147
87PanSti-27
87SabBluS-2
87SabWonBH-3
87Top-3
88OPC-163
88OPCBoxB-M
88OPCSti-261
88PanSti-223
88SabBluS-2
88SabWonBH-2
88Top-163

❑ 97PacSil-300
**Armstrong, George**
❑ 44BeeGro2P-373A
❑ 44BeeGro2P-373B
❑ 44BeeGro2P-373C
❑ 45QuaOatP-2
❑ 52Par-51
❑ 53Par-11
❑ 54Par-24
❑ 55Par-4
❑ 55ParQuaO-4
❑ 57Par-T1
❑ 58Par-7
❑ 58Par-11
❑ 58Par-48
❑ 59Par-7
❑ 60Par-17
❑ 60ShiCoi-9
❑ 60YorPreP-1
❑ 61Par-17
❑ 61ShiCoi-51
❑ 61YorYelB-37
❑ 62Par-13
❑ 62ShiMetC-10
❑ 62YorIroOTra-17
❑ 63ChePho-1
❑ 63Par-13
❑ 63Par-73
❑ 63TorSta-1
❑ 63YorWhiB-16
❑ 64BeeGro3P-151
❑ 64Top-69
❑ 65Coc-96
❑ 65MapLeaWB-1
❑ 65Top-19
❑ 66Top-84
❑ 66TopUSAT-17
❑ 67PosFliB-9
❑ 67Top-83
❑ 67YorActOct-3
❑ 67YorActOct-4
❑ 68ShiCoi-159
❑ 69MapLeaWBG-1
❑ 70OPC-113
❑ 70Top-113
❑ 83HalFP-N1
❑ 85HalFC-197
❑ 92ParParR-PR17
❑ 93ParParR-PR38
❑ 94ParMisL-125
❑ 94ParTalB-122
❑ 95Par66-116
❑ 95Par66Coi-116
**Armstrong, Jack**
❑ 52JunBluT-91
**Armstrong, Jake**
❑ 95SolBar-4
**Armstrong, Murray**
❑ 34BeeGro1P-299
❑ 37OPCV304E-146
❑ 39OPCV3011-19
**Armstrong, Neil P**
❑ 91ProSetHI-5
**Armstrong, Norm**
❑ 61SudWol-1
❑ 62SudWol-2
❑ 63RochAme-3
**Armstrong, Red**
❑ 71RocAme-1
**Armstrong, Tim**
❑ 88ProAHL-233
❑ 89ProAHL-114
**Arnason, Chuck**
❑ 72CanaPos-1
❑ 74NHLActSta-224
❑ 74OPCNHL-385
❑ 74PenPos-2
❑ 75OPCNHL-57
❑ 75Top-57
❑ 76OPCNHL-92
❑ 76RocCokCan-2
❑ 76RocPucBuc-2
❑ 76Top-92
❑ 77OPCNHL-379
❑ 78OPC-389
**Arnholt, P.M.**
❑ 95GerDELE-333
**Arniel, Scott**
❑ 81JetPos-1
❑ 82Jet-1
❑ 82PosCer-21
❑ 83Jet-1
❑ 83OPC-379
❑ 83PufSti-2
❑ 83Vac-121
❑ 847EDis-55
❑ 84JetPol-1
❑ 84OPC-333
❑ 84OPCSti-286
❑ 85JetPol-1
❑ 86OPC-194
❑ 86SabBluS-3
❑ 86SabBluSSma-3
❑ 86Top-194
❑ 87OPC-137
❑ 87SabBluS-3
❑ 87SabWonBH-4
❑ 87Top-137
❑ 88OPC-90
❑ 88OPCSti-258
❑ 88PanSti-224
❑ 88SabBluS-3
❑ 88SabWonBH-3
❑ 88Top-90
❑ 89OPC-187
❑ 89PanSti-213
❑ 89SabBluS-2
❑ 89SabCam-3
❑ 89Top-187
❑ 90Bow-243
❑ 90BowTif-243
❑ 90JetIGA-1
❑ 90OPC-324
❑ 90OPCPre-1
❑ 90PanSti-30
❑ 90ProSet-18A
❑ 90ProSet-18B
❑ 90ProSet-557
❑ 90Sco-251
❑ 90ScoCan-251
❑ 90ScoRoo-68T
❑ 90Top-324
❑ 90TopTif-324
❑ 90UppDec-397
❑ 90UppDecF-397
❑ 91Bow-206
❑ 91JetPanTS-1
❑ 91OPC-137
❑ 91PanSti-74
❑ 91ScoCan-256
❑ 91StaClu-30
❑ 91Top-137
❑ 92SanDieG-3
❑ 95ColEdgI-129
**Arnmark, Goran**
❑ 85SwePanS-200
❑ 89SweSemE-170
❑ 90SweSemE-4
❑ 91SweSemE-202
**Arnold, John**
❑ 93MicWol-1
**Arnost, Tomas**
❑ 94CzeAPSE-258
❑ 95CzeAPSE-155
**Arnott, Jason**
❑ 917thInnSOHL-148
❑ 91OshGen-20
❑ 91OshGenS-14
❑ 92OshGenS-4
❑ 93Cla-7
❑ 93ClaTopTen-DP7
❑ 93Don-120
❑ 93DonRatR-12
❑ 93DonSpeP-H
❑ 93Kra-67
❑ 93Lea-382
❑ 93LeaFrePhe-7
❑ 93Par-261
❑ 93ParCalC-C6
❑ 93ParCalCG-C6
❑ 93ParEasWesS-W8
❑ 93ParEmeI-261
❑ 93Pin-441
❑ 93PinCan-441
❑ 93PinSupR-7
❑ 93PinSupRC-7
❑ 93Pow-337
❑ 93PowRooS-1
❑ 93Sco-594
❑ 93ScoCan-594
❑ 93ScoDynDC-7
❑ 93ScoGol-594
❑ 93StaClu-345
❑ 93StaCluFDI-345
❑ 93StaCluO-345
❑ 93Ult-312
❑ 93UltWavF-1
❑ 93UppDec-423
❑ 93UppDecSilSka-R9
❑ 93UppDecSilSkaG-R9
❑ 93UppDecSP-48
❑ 94BeAPla-R34
❑ 94BeAPla-R93
❑ 94BeAPla-R134
❑ 94BeAPSig-110
❑ 94CanGamNHLP-97
❑ 94Cla-TC1
❑ 94ClaAllRT-AR2
❑ 94ClaProP-11
❑ 94ClaProP-NNO
❑ 94ClaProPProt-NNO
❑ 94Don-25
❑ 94DonEliIns-1
❑ 94Fin-21
❑ 94FinRef-21
❑ 94FinSupTW-21
❑ 94Fla-56
❑ 94FlaCenS-1
❑ 94Fle-68
❑ 94FleFraFut-1
❑ 94Kra-15
❑ 94Lea-133
❑ 94LeaGolR-2
❑ 94LeaGolS-10
❑ 94LeaLim-66
❑ 94LeaLimI-8
❑ 94McDUppD-McD37
❑ 94OPCFinIns-10
❑ 94OPCPre-193
❑ 94OPCPre-530
❑ 94OPCPreSE-193
❑ 94OPCPreSE-530
❑ 94Par-271
❑ 94ParCratGB-8
❑ 94ParCratGG-8
❑ 94ParCratGR-8
❑ 94ParGol-271
❑ 94ParSE-SE59
❑ 94ParSEG-SE59
❑ 94ParVin-V84
❑ 94Pin-124
❑ 94Pin-463
❑ 94PinArtP-124
❑ 94PinArtP-463
❑ 94PinNorLig-NL14
❑ 94PinRinC-124
❑ 94PinRinC-463
❑ 94PosCerBB-2
❑ 94Sco-254
❑ 94ScoFra-TF8
❑ 94ScoGol-254
❑ 94ScoHobS-254
❑ 94ScoPla-254
❑ 94ScoPlaTS-254
❑ 94Sel-87
❑ 94SelGol-87
❑ 94SP-40
❑ 94SPDieCut-40
❑ 94StaClu-7
❑ 94StaClu-115
❑ 94StaCluFDI-7
❑ 94StaCluFDI-115
❑ 94StaCluMO-49
❑ 94StaCluMOMS-7
❑ 94StaCluMOMS-115
❑ 94StaCluSTWC-7
❑ 94StaCluSTWC-115
❑ 94TopPre-193
❑ 94TopPre-530
❑ 94TopPreSE-193
❑ 94TopPreSE-530
❑ 94Ult-68
❑ 94UltAllRoo-1
❑ 94UltPow-2
❑ 94UltPreP-1
❑ 94UppDec-305
❑ 94UppDecEleIce-305
❑ 94UppDecIG-IG2
❑ 94UppDecNBAP-19
❑ 94UppDecSPI-SP26
❑ 94UppDecSPIDC-SP26
❑ 95CanGamNHLP-106
❑ 95ColCho-41
❑ 95ColChoCTG-C19
❑ 95ColChoCTG-C19B
❑ 95ColChoCTG-C19C
❑ 95ColChoCTGGB-C19
❑ 95ColChoCTGGR-C19
❑ 95ColChoCTGSB-C19
❑ 95ColChoCTGSR-C19
❑ 95ColChoPC-41
❑ 95ColChoPCP-41
❑ 95Don-44
❑ 95DonEli-101
❑ 95DonEliDCS-101
❑ 95DonEliDCU-101
❑ 95Emo-61
❑ 95Fin-139
❑ 95FinRef-139
❑ 95ImpSti-44
❑ 95ImpStiDCS-13
❑ 95Kra-2
❑ 95Lea-119
❑ 95LeaLim-22
❑ 95McDPin-MCD-14
❑ 95Met-52
❑ 95MetIW-1
❑ 95NHLAcePC-6D
❑ 95ParInt-73
❑ 95ParIntEI-73
❑ 95Pin-16
❑ 95PinArtP-16
❑ 95PinFan-22
❑ 95PinFulC-8
❑ 95PinRinC-16
❑ 95PlaOneoOne-37
❑ 95PosUppD-13
❑ 95ProMag-81
❑ 95Sco-8
❑ 95ScoBlaIce-8
❑ 95ScoBlaIceAP-8
❑ 95ScoGolBla-20
❑ 95ScoPro-8
❑ 95SelCer-9
❑ 95SelCerDS-8
❑ 95SelCerDSG-8
❑ 95SelCerMG-9
❑ 95SkyImp-59
❑ 95SkyImp-237
❑ 95SP-51
❑ 95SPHol-FX8
❑ 95SPHolSpFX-FX8
❑ 95StaClu-171
❑ 95StaCluMO-31
❑ 95StaCluMOMS-171
❑ 95StaCluMPT-1
❑ 95Sum-18
❑ 95SumArtP-18
❑ 95SumIce-18
❑ 95SumMadH-6
❑ 95SweGloWC-95
❑ 95Top-17
❑ 95Top-340
❑ 95TopCanG-3CG
❑ 95TopMarMPB-17
❑ 95TopOPCI-17
❑ 95TopOPCI-340
❑ 95TopSupSki-67
❑ 95TopSupSkiPla-67
❑ 95TopYouS-YS10
❑ 95Ult-52
❑ 95UltCreCra-1
❑ 95UltGolM-52
❑ 95UltHigSpe-2
❑ 95UltRisS-1
❑ 95UltRisSGM-1
❑ 95UppDec-29
❑ 95UppDecEleIce-29
❑ 95UppDecEleIceG-29
❑ 95UppDecSpeE-SE119
❑ 95UppDecSpeEdiG-SE119
❑ 95Zen-23
❑ 95ZenGifG-15
❑ 96BeAPBisITB-21
❑ 96BeAPLH-5B
❑ 96BeAPLHAut-5B
❑ 96BeAPLHAutSil-5B
❑ 96ColCho-92
❑ 96ColCho-317
❑ 96ColChoBloBi-3
❑ 96ColChoCTG-C23A
❑ 96ColChoCTG-C23B
❑ 96ColChoCTG-C23C
❑ 96ColChoCTGE-CR23
❑ 96ColChoCTGEG-CR23
❑ 96ColChoCTGG-C23A
❑ 96ColChoCTGG-C23B
❑ 96ColChoCTGG-C23C
❑ 96Don-143
❑ 96DonCanI-68
❑ 96DonCanIGPP-68
❑ 96DonCanIRPP-68
❑ 96DonDom-5
❑ 96DonEli-46
❑ 96DonEli-150
❑ 96DonEliDCS-46
❑ 96DonEliDCS-150
❑ 96DonPrePro-143
❑ 96Fla-32
❑ 96FlaBluI-32
❑ 96Fle-36
❑ 96FlePic-58
❑ 96Lea-179
❑ 96LeaLim-43
❑ 96LeaLimG-43
❑ 96LeaPre-20
❑ 96LeaPreP-179
❑ 96LeaPrePP-20
❑ 96LeaPreSG-19
❑ 96LeaPreSte-19
❑ 96MetUni-52
❑ 96NHLACEPC-2
❑ 96NHLProSTA-81
❑ 96OilPos-7
❑ 96Pin-118
❑ 96PinArtP-118
❑ 96PinFoi-118
❑ 96PinPreS-118
❑ 96PinRinC-118
❑ 96Sco-55
❑ 96ScoArtPro-55
❑ 96ScoDeaCAP-55
❑ 96ScoGolB-55
❑ 96ScoSpeAP-55
❑ 96SelCer-38
❑ 96SelCerAP-38
❑ 96SelCerBlu-38
❑ 96SelCerMB-38
❑ 96SelCerMG-38
❑ 96SelCerMR-38
❑ 96SelCerRed-38
❑ 96SkyImp-41
❑ 96SP-55
❑ 96SPHolCol-HC4
❑ 96Sum-103
❑ 96SumArtP-103
❑ 96SumIce-103
❑ 96SumMet-103
❑ 96SumPreS-103
❑ 96SweSemW-97
❑ 96TeaOut-22
❑ 96Ult-57
❑ 96UltGolM-57
❑ 96UppDec-57
❑ 96UppDecBD-97
❑ 96UppDecBDG-97
❑ 96UppDecGN-X12
❑ 96UppDecIce-20
❑ 96UppDecIceDF-S9
❑ 96UppDecIcePar-20
❑ 96UppDecIceSCF-S9
❑ 96UppDecPP-P6
❑ 96UppDecSS-SS19B
❑ 96Zen-65
❑ 96ZenArtP-65
❑ 96ZenAss-3
❑ 97ColCho-95
❑ 97ColChoSta-SQ7
❑ 97Don-145
❑ 97DonCanI-117
❑ 97DonCanIDS-117
❑ 97DonCanINP-12
❑ 97DonCanIPS-117
❑ 97DonEli-95
❑ 97DonEliAsp-95
❑ 97DonEliS-95
❑ 97DonLim-27
❑ 97DonLim-79
❑ 97DonLimExp-27
❑ 97DonLimExp-79
❑ 97DonPre-31
❑ 97DonPreCttC-31
❑ 97DonPreProG-145
❑ 97DonPreProS-145
❑ 97DonPri-97
❑ 97DonPriDD-30
❑ 97DonPriSoA-97
❑ 97Kat-55
❑ 97KatGol-55
❑ 97KatSil-55
❑ 97Lea-61
❑ 97LeaFraMat-61
❑ 97LeaFraMDC-61
❑ 97LeaInt-61
❑ 97LeaIntUI-61
❑ 97Pac-79
❑ 97PacCop-79
❑ 97PacCroR-52
❑ 97PacCroREG-52
❑ 97PacCroRIB-52
❑ 97PacCroRS-52
❑ 97PacEmeGre-79
❑ 97PacIceB-79
❑ 97PacInv-54
❑ 97PacInvC-54
❑ 97PacInvEG-54
❑ 97PacInvIB-54
❑ 97PacInvR-54
❑ 97PacInvS-54
❑ 97PacOme-125
❑ 97PacOmeC-125
❑ 97PacOmeDG-125
❑ 97PacOmeEG-125
❑ 97PacOmeG-125
❑ 97PacOmeIB-125
❑ 97PacPar-72
❑ 97PacParC-72
❑ 97PacParDG-72
❑ 97PacParEG-72
❑ 97PacParIB-72
❑ 97PacParRed-72
❑ 97PacParSil-72
❑ 97PacRed-79
❑ 97PacSil-79
❑ 97Pin-61
❑ 97PinArtP-61
❑ 97PinCer-124
❑ 97PinCerMB-124
❑ 97PinCerMG-124
❑ 97PinCerMR-124
❑ 97PinCerR-124
❑ 97PinIns-55
❑ 97PinInsCC-55
❑ 97PinInsEC-55
❑ 97PinPrePBB-61
❑ 97PinPrePBC-61
❑ 97PinPrePBM-61
❑ 97PinPrePBY-61
❑ 97PinPrePFC-61
❑ 97PinPrePFM-61
❑ 97PinPrePFY-61
❑ 97PinPrePla-61
❑ 97PinRinC-61
❑ 97PinTotCMPG-124
❑ 97PinTotCPB-124
❑ 97PinTotCPG-124
❑ 97PinTotCPR-124
❑ 97PosPin-6
❑ 97Sco-136
❑ 97ScoArtPro-136
❑ 97ScoGolBla-136
❑ 97SPAut-59
❑ 97SPx-18
❑ 97SPxBro-18
❑ 97SPxGol-18
❑ 97SPxGraF-18
❑ 97SPxSil-18
❑ 97SPxSte-18
❑ 97Stu-35
❑ 97StuPor-29
❑ 97StuPrePG-35
❑ 97StuPrePS-35
❑ 97UppDec-66
❑ 97UppDecBD-117
❑ 97UppDecBDDD-117
❑ 97UppDecBDQD-117
❑ 97UppDecBDTD-117
❑ 97UppDecTSS-17A
❑ 98Be A PPA-78
❑ 98Be A PPAA-78
❑ 98Be A PPAAF-78
❑ 98Be A PPTBASG-78
❑ 98Be APG-78
❑ 98O-PChr-199
❑ 98O-PChrR-199
❑ 98Pac-261
❑ 98PacAur-107
❑ 98PacCroR-77
❑ 98PacCroRLS-77
❑ 98PacDynI-107
❑ 98PacDynIIB-107
❑ 98PacDynIR-107
❑ 98PacIceB-261
❑ 98PacOmeH-135
❑ 98PacOmeODI-135
❑ 98PacOmeR-135
❑ 98PacPar-131
❑ 98PacParC-131
❑ 98PacParEG-131
❑ 98PacParH-131
❑ 98PacParIB-131
❑ 98PacParS-131
❑ 98PacRed-261
❑ 98PacRev-82
❑ 98PacRevIS-82
❑ 98PacRevR-82
❑ 98Top-199
❑ 98TopO-P-199
❑ 98UC-118
❑ 98UD ChoPCR-118
❑ 98UD ChoR-118
❑ 98UppDec-120
❑ 98UppDecE-120
❑ 98UppDecE1o1-120
❑ 98UppDecGR-120
❑ 98UppDecM-122
❑ 98UppDecMGS-122
❑ 98UppDecMP-JAR
❑ 98UppDecMSS-122
❑ 98UppDecMSS-122
❑ 99Pac-234
❑ 99PacAur-83
❑ 99PacAurPD-83
❑ 99PacCop-234
❑ 99PacGol-234
❑ 99PacIceB-234
❑ 99PacPreD-234
❑ 99UppDecM-120
❑ 99UppDecMGS-120
❑ 99UppDecMSS-120
❑ 99UppDecMSS-120
**Arsenault, Daniel**
❑ 907thInnSMC-72
**Arsenault, Yan**
❑ 907thInnSQMJHL-237
❑ 917thInnSQMJHL-142
**Arsene, Dean**
❑ 96RegPat-14
**Arthur, Fred**
❑ 82OPC-245
❑ 82PosCer-14
**Artursson, Greger**
❑ 89SweSemE-83
❑ 90SweSemE-256
❑ 91SweSemE-89
❑ 95SweLeaE-216
**Artursson, Leif**
❑ 65SweCorI-208
**Arundel, John**
❑ 51LavDaiS-99
❑ 52St.LawS-63
**Arvaja, Mika**
❑ 93FinnJyvHS-144
❑ 93FinnSIS-149
❑ 94FinnSIS-133
❑ 95FinnSIS-244
❑ 96FinnSISR-33
**Arvanitis, Peter**
❑ 90MonAAA-6
❑ 92BriColJHL-57
**Arvedson, Magnus**
❑ 93SweSemE-86
❑ 94SweLeaE-196
❑ 95SweLeaE-43
❑ 95SweUppDE-67
❑ 97Be A PPAD-225
❑ 97Be A PPAPD-225
❑ 97BeAPla-225
❑ 97BeAPlaAut-225
❑ 97PacOme-153
❑ 97PacOmeC-153
❑ 97PacOmeDG-153
❑ 97PacOmeEG-153
❑ 97PacOmeG-153
❑ 97PacOmeIB-153
❑ 97Pin-16
❑ 97PinArtP-16
❑ 97PinPrePBB-16
❑ 97PinPrePBC-16
❑ 97PinPrePBM-16
❑ 97PinPrePBY-16
❑ 97PinPrePFC-16
❑ 97PinPrePFM-16
❑ 97PinPrePFY-16
❑ 97PinPrePla-16
❑ 97PinRinC-16
❑ 97Sco-70
❑ 97ScoArtPro-70
❑ 97ScoGolBla-70
❑ 97UppDec-324
❑ 97UppDecIce-37
❑ 97UppDecIceP-37
❑ 97UppDecIPS-37
❑ 97ZenRooR-5
❑ 98Pac-306
❑ 98PacIceB-306
❑ 98PacPar-161
❑ 98PacParC-161
❑ 98PacParEG-161
❑ 98PacParH-161
❑ 98PacParIB-161
❑ 98PacParS-161
❑ 98PacRed-306
❑ 98UppDec-138
❑ 98UppDecE-138
❑ 98UppDecE1o1-138
❑ 98UppDecGR-138
❑ 98UppDecM-142
❑ 98UppDecMGS-142
❑ 98UppDecMSS-142
❑ 98UppDecMSS-142
❑ 99Pac-284
❑ 99PacAur-98
❑ 99PacAurPD-98
❑ 99PacCop-284
❑ 99PacGol-284
❑ 99PacIceB-284
❑ 99PacPreD-284
**Arvidsson, Berndt**
❑ 65SweCorI-45
**Arvsell, Henrik**
❑ 93SweSemE-194
❑ 94SweLeaECS-8
**Asberg, Magnus**
❑ 89SweSemE-48
**Ascroft, Brent**
❑ 94TriAme-2
❑ 95TriAme-3
**Asham, Arron**
❑ 95RedDeeR-1
❑ 95UppDec-509
❑ 95UppDecEleIce-509
❑ 95UppDecEleIceG-509
❑ 97BowCHL-107
❑ 97BowCHLOPC-107
❑ 99UppDecM-105
❑ 99UppDecMGS-105
❑ 99UppDecMSS-105
❑ 99UppDecMSS-105
**Ashbee, Barry**
❑ 65Coc-16
❑ 70EssPowPla-202
❑ 70FlyPos-1
❑ 71LetActR-21
❑ 71OPC-104
❑ 71TorSun-188
❑ 72OPC-206
❑ 73FlyLin-1
**Ashbee, Don**
❑ 51BufBis-2
**Ashby, Don**
❑ 75MapLeaP-2
❑ 75MapLeaP-3
❑ 76MapLeaP-2
❑ 77OPCNHL-365
❑ 78OPC-351
❑ 88OilTenAnn-112
**Ashley, John G**
❑ 83HalFP-O2
❑ 85HalFC-213
**Ashtashenko, Kaspars**
❑ 98CinCyc-1
**Ashton, Brent**
❑ 79CanuRoyB-1
❑ 80CanuSilD-1
❑ 80CanuTeal-1
❑ 80PepCap-101
❑ 81RocPos-1
❑ 82OPC-135
❑ 82OPCSti-227
❑ 82PosCer-11
❑ 83NorStaPos-2
❑ 83OPC-225
❑ 84NordPos-1
❑ 85NordGenF-2
❑ 85NordMcD-1
❑ 85NordPla-1
❑ 85NordPla-6
❑ 85NordPro-2
❑ 85NordTeal-1
❑ 85OPC-170
❑ 85OPCSti-153
❑ 86KraDra-2
❑ 86NordGenF-1
❑ 86NordMcD-2
❑ 86OPC-181
❑ 86OPCSti-25
❑ 86Top-181
❑ 87OPC-100
❑ 87OPCSti-108
❑ 87PanSti-244
❑ 87RedWinLC-1
❑ 87Top-100
❑ 88JetPol-1
❑ 88OPC-128
❑ 88OPCSti-250
❑ 88PanSti-40
❑ 88Top-128
❑ 89JetSaf-1
❑ 89Kra-46
❑ 89OPC-181
❑ 89OPCSti-138
❑ 89PanSti-164
❑ 89Top-181
❑ 90Bow-130
❑ 90BowTif-130
❑ 90JetIGA-2
❑ 90OPC-24
❑ 90PanSti-321
❑ 90ProSet-323
❑ 90Sco-31A
❑ 90Sco-31B
❑ 90ScoCan-31A
❑ 90ScoCan-31B
❑ 90Top-24
❑ 90TopTif-24
❑ 90UppDec-220
❑ 90UppDecF-220
❑ 91Bow-211
❑ 91BruSpoA-1
❑ 91JetPanTS-2
❑ 91OPC-240
❑ 91PanSti-70
❑ 91Pin-280
❑ 91PinFre-280
❑ 91ProSet-272
❑ 91ProSet-352
❑ 91ProSetFre-272
❑ 91ProSetFre-352
❑ 91ProSetPla-155
❑ 91ScoAme-78
❑ 91ScoCan-78
❑ 91ScoRoo-22T
❑ 91StaClu-90
❑ 91Top-240
❑ 91UppDec-303
❑ 91UppDecF-303
❑ 92Bow-357
❑ 92Par-258
❑ 92ParEmel-258
❑ 92Sco-164
❑ 92ScoCan-164
❑ 92StaClu-146
❑ 92Top-191
❑ 92TopGol-191G

92Ult-1
93LasVegThu-1
93Sco-434
93ScoCan-434
93StaClu-51
93StaCluFDI-51
93StaCluFDIO-51
93StaCluO-51

**Asikainen, Mika**
95FinnSIS-255

**Askew, Kelly**
93RenEng-1

**Askey, Tom**
98Pac-67
98PacIceB-67
98PacRed-67
98UppDec-36
98UppDecE-36
98UppDecE1o1-36
98UppDecGR-36

**Aslin, Peter**
83SweSemE-2
85SwePanS-134
86SwePanS-138
87SwePanS-149
89SweSemE-121
90SweSemE-100
91SweSemE-104
92SweSemE-125
93SweSemE-98
93SweSemWCS-1
94SweLeaE-54
94SweLeaECS-5

**Asp, Aaron**
91FerStaB-1

**Asplund, Anders**
67SweHoc-83

**Asplund, Jan**
86SwePanS-196

**Asselstine, Ron**
90ProSet-681

**Asseltine, Jack**
23V1281PauC-25

**Ast, Doug**
91BriColJHL-135
92BriColJHL-24
95VanVooRHI-14
96SyrCru-16

**Astafjev, Vladimir**
74SweHocS-83

**Astley, Mark**
91LakSupSL-5
92AlbIntTC-2
93Don-44
93OPCPre-342
93OPCPreG-342
93Par-295
93ParEmel-295
93StaClu-311
93StaCluO-311
93SwiHNL-138
93TopPre-342
93TopPreG-342
93UppDec-494
94ScoTeaC-CT13
95ColEdgI-62
95Ima-68
95ImaGoI-68
95Ult-209

**Astrahantsev, Konstantin**
93SweSemWCS-138
94FinnJaaK-149
94FinnSIS-339

**Astrom, Bo**
65SweCorI-146B
69SweHocS-324
70SweHocS-228
72SweHocS-285

**Astrom, Goran**
70SweHocS-179
71SweHocS-263

**Astrom, Hardy**
79PanSti-185
79Roc-1
80OPC-269
83SweSemE-148
84SweSemE-219
84SwePanS-222

**Atcheynum, Blair**
89ProAHL-288
90ProAHLIHL-178
91ProAHLHCL-107
97Be A PPAD-210
97Be A PPAPD-210
97BeAPla-210
97BeAPlaAut-210
97PacRev-116
97PacRevC-116
97PacRevE-116
97PacRevIB-116
97PacRevR-116
97PacRevS-116
98Pac-361
98PacIceB-361
98PacPar-120
98PacParC-120
98PacParEG-120
98PacParH-120
98PacParIB-120
98PacParS-120
98PacRed-361
98UppDec-300
98UppDecE-300
98UppDecE1o1-300
98UppDecGR-300

99Pac-351
99PacCop-351
99PacGol-351
99PacIceB-351
99PacPreD-351

**Atchinson, A.**
12C57-4

**Atkins, Scott**
95Sla-209

**Atkinson, Steve**
70EssPowPla-86
71OPC-162
71SabPos-2
72OPC-40
72SarProSta-40
72Top-47
73OPC-245
74CapWhiB-4
74NHLActSta-311
74OPCNHL-192
74Top-192

**Attersley, Bob**
52JunBluT-84

**Attwell, Ron**
60CleBar-1
62QueAce-1

**Aube, J.F.**
98ChaChe-1
98ChaChe-23

**Aubin, Jean-Sebastien**
98KanCitB-23
98PacOmeH-192
98PacOmeODI-192
98PacOmeR-192
98PacRev-115
98PacRevIS-115
98PacRevR-115
98SP Aut-105
98UppDec-350
98UppDecE1o1-350
98UppDecGR-350

**Aubin, Norm (Normand)**
82MapLeaP-3
82OPC-316
82PosCer-18
84NovScoO-21

**Aubin, Serge**
95HamRoaA-9
95SigRooA-4
95SigRooAPC-4
96CleLum-3

**Aubrey, Ron**
92ForWorF-1
93ForWorF-1
94CenHocL-55

**Aubry, Pierre**
81NordPos-1
82NordPos-1
82OPC-277
83NordPos-1
83OPC-289
917thInnSQMJHL-273

**Aubry, Serge**
62QueAce-2
72NordPos-2
73NordTeal-2
75OPCWHA-3
75StiKah-1
76NordPos-1
88NordTeal-2
89Nord-1

**Aucoin, Adrian**
92AlbIntTC-3
92UppDec-584
93AlbIntTC-1
93OPCPreTC-3
93Pow-478
93Ult-458
93UppDec-251
94ClaProPIA-IA1
94ClaProPIH-LP11
94ScoTeaC-CT14
95UppDec-56
95UppDecEIeIce-56
95UppDecEIeIceG-56
96BeAPAut-79
96BeAPAutSiI-79
96BeAPla-79
96CanuPos-6
97PacInvNRB-198
97ScoCanPla-14
97ScoCanPre-14
97ScoCanu-14
98BowBes-36
98BowBesAR-36
98BowBesR-36
98PacOmeH-234
98PacOmeODI-234
98PacOmeR-234
99Pac-419
99PacCop-419
99PacGol-419
99PacIceB-419
99PacPreD-419

**Audet, Gerard**
51LavDaiLSJ-23

**Audet, Philippe**
95Cla-44
97BowCHL-52
97BowCHLOPC-52

**Audette, Donald**
89ProAHL-265
90ProAHLIHL-289
90SabBluS-2
90SabCam-2
90ScoBlaIce-101
90UppDecF-519
91OPC-273
91Par-11
91ParFre-11
91Pin-330
91PinFre-330
91ProSet-524
91ProSetFre-524
91ProSetPla-249
91SabBluS-2
91SabPepC-2
91ScoAme-389
91ScoCan-279
91Top-273
91UppDec-585
91UppDecF-585
92Bow-288
92OPC-117
92PanSti-U
92PanStiFre-U
92Par-11
92Par-231
92ParEmel-18
92ParEmel-231
92Pin-38
92PinFre-38
92ProSet-18
92ProSetRGL-3
92SabBluS-2
92SabJubF-11
92Sco-393
92ScoCan-393
92ScoSha-19
92ScoShaCan-19
92SeaPat-43
92StaClu-112
92Top-12
92Top-206
92TopGol-12G
92TopGol-206G
92UltRoo-2
92UppDec-2
92UppDec-306
93Don-32
93Lea-272
93OPCPre-61
93OPCPreG-61
93PanSti-103
93Par-26
93ParEmel-26
93Pin-274
93PinCan-274
93Pow-295
93Sco-77
93ScoCan-77
93StaClu-213
93StaCluFDI-213
93StaCluFDIO-213
93StaCluO-213
93TopPre-61
93TopPreG-61
93Ult-273
93UppDec-5
94BeAPSig-31
94CanGamNHLP-48
94Don-305
94Fla-15
94Fle-19
94Lea-64
94OPCPre-289
94OPCPreSE-289
94Par-23
94ParGol-23
94Pin-244
94PinArtP-244
94PinRinC-244
94Sco-157
94ScoGol-157
94ScoPla-157
94ScoPlaTS-157
94Sel-26
94SelGoI-26
94StaClu-87
94StaCluFDI-87
94StaCluMOMS-87
94TopPre-289
94TopPreSE-289
94Ult-19
94UppDec-30
94UppDecEIeIce-30
94UppDecSPI-SP97
94UppDecSPIDC-SP97
95ColCho-217
95ColChoPC-217
95ColChoPCP-217
95Don-141
95DonEli-49
95DonEliDCS-49
95DonEliDCU-49
95Emo-12
95Fin-71
95FinRef-71
95Lea-274

95LeaLim-12
95Met-12
95ParInt-292
95ParIntEI-292
95Pin-104
95PinArtP-104
95PinRinC-104
95PlaOneoOne-11
95ProMag-106
95Sco-101
95ScoBlaIce-101
95ScoBlaIceAP-101
95SkyImp-14
95StaClu-54
95StaCluMOMS-54
95Top-214
95TopOPCI-214
95TopSupSki-3
95TopSupSkiPla-3
95Ult-15
95UltGoIM-15
95UppDec-2
95UppDecEIeIce-2
95UppDecEIeIceG-2
95UppDecSpeE-SE9
95UppDecSpeEdiG-SE9
96BeAPAut-73
96BeAPAutSiI-73
96BeAPla-73
96MetUni-12
96NHLProSTA-106
96Pin-59
96PinArtP-59
96PinFoi-59
96PinPreS-59
96PinRinC-59
96Sco-233
96ScoArtPro-233
96ScoDeaCAP-233
96ScoGoIB-233
96ScoSpeAP-233
96Ult-13
96UltGoIM-13
96UppDec-13
96UppDecBD-30
96UppDecBDG-30
97ColCho-28
97ColChoCTG-C12A
97ColChoCTG-C12B
97ColChoCTG-C12C
97ColChoCTGE-CR12
97Don-44
97DonLim-118
97DonLimExp-118
97DonPreProG-44
97DonPreProS-44
97DonPri-126
97DonPriSoA-126
97Lea-99
97LeaFraMat-99
97LeaFraMDC-99
97LeaInt-99
97LeaIntUI-99
97Pac-184
97PacCop-184
97PacEmeEre-184
97PacIceB-184
97PacRed-184
97PacSiI-184
97Pin-102
97PinIns-105
97PinPrePBB-102
97PinPrePBC-102
97PinPrePBM-102
97PinPrePBY-102
97PinPrePFC-102
97PinPrePFM-102
97PinPrePFY-102
97PinPrePla-102
97Sco-179
97ScoSab-4
97ScoSabPla-4
97ScoSabPre-4
97UppDec-20
98Pac-103
98PacIceB-103
98PacRed-103
98UC-28
98UD ChoPCR-28
98UD ChoR-28
98UppDecE-227
98UppDecE101-227
98UppDecGR-227
98UppDecM-96
98UppDecMGS-96
98UppDecMSS-96
98UppDecMSS-96
99Pac-186
99PacAur-67
99PacAurPD-67
99PacCop-186
99PacGol-186
99PacIceB-186
99PacPreD-186
99UppDecM-95
99UppDecMGS-95
99UppDecMPS-DA
99UppDecMSS-95

**Audette, Gary**
88BraWheK-3
89BraWheK-17
907thInnSWHL-235
90BraWheK-20

91BriColJHL-20
92DalFre-2

**Auge, Les**
81SweSemHVS-97

**Auger, Dominic**
98BowCHL-112
98BowCHLGA-112
98BowCHLOI-112
98BowChrC-112
98BowChrCGA-112
98BowChrCGAR-112
98BowChrCOI-112
98BowChrCOIR-112
98BowChrCR-112

**Auger, Vincent**
93CorBigRed-1

**Augusta, Josef**
69SweHocS-20
74SweHocS-118
92FutTre76CC-136
94CzeAPSE-276
95CzeAPSE-98

**Augusta, Patrik**
92St.JohML-1
93ClaProPro-36
93St.JohML-1
94St.JohML-1
95ColEdgI-148

**Augusta, Pavel**
94CzeAPSE-231
95CzeAPSE-25
96CzeAPSE-146

**Augustsson, Bernt**
69SweHocS-310
71SweHocS-147
72SweHocS-130

**Augustsson, Kjell**
69SweHocS-311
71SweHocS-148
72SweHocS-134
86SwePanS-108

**Auhuber, Klaus**
79PanSti-101

**Aurie, Larry**
330PCV304B-51
33V129-19
33V252CanG-2
33V288HamG-44
33V357IceK-59
34BeeGro1P-87
34SweCap-36
360PCV304D-131

**Austin, Brady**
95MedHatT-2

**Austin, Colin**
897thInnSOHL-163

**Austin, Darcy**
907thInnSWHL-121
917thInnSWHL-336
93FliGen-7

**Austman, J.**
24HolCre-10

**Autere, Antti**
90RicRen-3
91ProAHLCHL-448

**Avalanche, Colorado**
97HigMinMagSM-1
97HigMinMagSM-2

**Avdejev, Ivan**
89SweSemE-111

**Averill, Will**
92RicRen-1
93RoaExp-2

**Avery, Sean**
98BowCHL-35
98BowCHLGA-35
98BowCHLOI-35
98BowChrC-35
98BowChrCGA-35
98BowChrCGAR-35
98BowChrCOI-35
98BowChrCOIR-35
98BowChrCR-35

**Awrey, Don**
65Coc-17
65Top-99
67Top-37
68OPC-3
68OPC-43
68ShiCoi-3
68Top-3
68Top-43
69OPC-203
70BruPos-20
70BruTeaIss-10
70DadCoo-2
70EssPowPla-71
70OPC-4
70SarProSta-2
70Top-4
71BruTeaIss-18
71LetActR-8
71OPC-3
71SarProSta-13
71TorSun-2
72OPC-170
72SarProSta-23
73BluWhiBor-2
73OPC-240
74NHLActSta-337
74NHLActStaU-22
74OPCNHL-80
74Top-98
75CanaPos-1

750PCNHL-344
760PCNHL-311
770PCNHL-137
77Top-137
78OPC-383
91FutTreC72-17
94ParTalB-19
95Par66-12
95Par66Coi-12

**Axelson, Niklas**
93MinDul-2

**Axelsson, Magnus**
92SweSemE-146
93SweSemE-115

**Axelsson, Per Johan**
94ParSE-SE240
94ParSEG-SE240
94SweLeaE-248
95SweLeaE-204
97Be A PPAD-238
97Be A PPAPD-238
97BeAPla-238
97BeAPlaAut-238
97Kat-7
97KatGol-7
97KatSiI-7
97PacOme-11
97PacOmeC-11
97PacOmeDG-11
97PacOmeEG-11
97PacOmeG-11
97PacOmeIB-11
97UppDec-220
98Pac-69
98PacIceB-69
98PacPar-9
98PacParC-9
98PacParEG-9
98PacParH-9
98PacParIB-9
98PacParS-9
98PacRed-69
99Pac-18
99PacCop-18
99PacGol-18
99PacIceB-18
99PacPreD-18

**Axelsson, Stefan**
89SweSemE-269
90SweSemE-33
91SweSemE-283
92SweSemE-306
93SweSemE-273
94SweLeaE-130
95SweLeaE-201
95SweUppDE-206

**Ayers, Vernon**
330PCV304B-65
33V357IceK-51

**Ayres, Vern**
35DiaMatT2-2
35DiaMatT3-2
35DiaMatT1-2

**Babando, Pete**
44BeeGro2P-2
44BeeGro2P-76
44BeeGro2P-151
51Par-51
52Par-16

**Babcock, Bobby (Bob)**
89ProAHL-84
90ProAHLIHL-209
91BalSki-15
91ProAHLCHL-569
92OPCPre-56

**Babcock, David**
89SauSteMG-22

**Babcock, Mike**
917thInnSWHL-275
95SpoChi-25

**Babcock, Shawn**
81KinCan-5
83MonAlp-24

**Babe, Warren**
86KamBla-1
87KamBla-1
87NorStaPos-3
88ProIHL-36
90ProAHLIHL-101

**Baber, Brad**
917thInnSOHL-338
93SauSteMG-12
93SauSteMGM-20

**Babic, Marek**
95Sla-286

**Babin, Michael**
93SweSemWCS-257
94FinnJaaK-226
94FreNatT-4

**Babinov, Sergei**
81SweSemHVS-41
82SweSemHVS-54
83RusNatT-1

**Babiuk, Ed**
61SudWol-2
62SudWol-3
63RochAme-4

**Baby, John**
780PC-366
79OPC-357

**Babych, Dave**
80JetPos-1

80PepCap-121
81JetPos-2
810PC-358
81OPCSti-137
81PosSta-26
81Top-1
82Jet-2
820PC-375
820PC-376
820PCSti-207
82PosCer-21
83Ess-3
83Jet-2
830PC-380
830PCSti-163
830PCSti-285
830PCSti-286
83PufSti-1
83Vac-122
847EDis-56
84JetPol-2
84KelAccD-4
840PC-334
840PCSti-287
84Top-150
850PC-10
850PCSti-249
85Top-10
860PC-73
860PCSti-50
86Top-73
86WhaJunT-2
870PC-5
870PCSti-208
87PanSti-40
87Top-5
87WhaJunBK-2
880PC-164
880PCSti-267
88PanSti-236
88Top-164
88WhaJunGR-2
890PC-46
890PCSti-265
89PanSti-225
89Top-46
89WhaJunM-2
90Bow-256
90BowTif-256
90Kra-1
900PC-328
90PanSti-40
90ProSet-99
90Sco-172
90ScoCan-172
90Top-328
90TopTif-328
90UppDec-194
90UppDecF-194
90WhaJr7C-2
91CanuAutC-3
91CanuTeaI8-3
91Par-187
91ParFre-187
91Pin-270
91PinFre-270
91ProSet-503
91ProSetFre-503
91ScoCan-584
91ScoRoo-34T
92Bow-119
92CanuRoaTA-3
920PC-213
92PanSti-35
92PanStiFre-35
92Par-424
92ParEmel-424
92Pin-201
92PinFre-201
92ProSet-200
92Sco-212
92ScoCan-212
92StaClu-120
92Top-138
92TopGol-138G
92Ult-218
930PCPre-428
930PCPreG-428
93Par-481
93ParEmel-481
93Pow-456
93TopPre-428
93TopPreG-428
93UppDec-376
94CanuPro-3
94Lea-430
940PCPre-256
940PCPreSE-256
94Pin-353
94PinArtP-353
94PinRinC-353
94TopPre-256
94TopPreSE-256
95BeAPla-94
95BeAPSig-S94
95BeAPSigDC-S94
95CanuBuiDA-18
95Ult-315
96CanuPos-44
97Be A PPAD-49
97Be A PPAPD-49
97BeAPla-49
97BeAPlaAut-49
97PacInvNRB-199
97ScoCanPla-20

97ScoCanPre-20
97ScoCanu-20
99RetHoc-58
99UppDecRG-58
99UppDecRP-58
**Babych, Wayne**
78BluPos-1
790PC-142
79Top-142
800PC-281
810PC-290
810PCSti-130
81Top-W114
820PC-299
820PCSti-201
82PosCer-17
830PC-310
840PC-181
85NordPre-3
850PC-108
850PCSti-103
85Top-108
860PC-213
86WhaJunT-3
92BluUDBB-10
**Baca, Jergus**
89SweSemWCS-185
900PCPre-2
90ScoRoo-101T
910PC-131
91ProAHLCHL-94
91Top-131
91UppDec-425
91UppDecF-425
92Top-64
92TopGol-64G
94FinnJaaK-199
94SweLeaE-168
94SweLeaEFA-9
95MilAdmBO-2
96CzeAPSE-270
96SweSemW-224
**Baccari, Al**
51LavDaiS-10
52St.LawS-44
**Bach, Ryan**
91AirCanSJHL-B28
96TolSto-1
**Bacharuk, Stewart**
96SasBla-1
**Bachusz, Mike**
91LakSupSL-6
**Bacik, Tim**
917thInnSOHL-331
93LonKni-3
**Back, Jan**
64SweCorl-38
65SweCorl-38A
**Backe, Per**
84SweSemE-18
**Backlund, Joakim**
89SweSemE-144
95SweUppDE-127
**Backlund, Patrik**
95SweLeaE-282
**Backman, Bert**
71SweHocS-383
72SweHocS-257
**Backman, Gunnar**
65SweCorl-209
67SweHoc-116
67SweHoc-265
69SweHocS-128
69SweHocS-183
69SweWorC-107
70SweHocS-83
70SweHocS-274
71SweHocS-175
71SweHocS-330
72SweHocS-145
**Backman, Per**
69SweHocS-224
71SweHocS-149
72SweHocS-128
73SweHocS-176
73SweWorCS-176
74SweHocS-208
83SweSemE-25
84SweSemE-25
85SwePanS-2
87SwePanS-88
**Backstrom, Anders**
83SweSemE-53
84SweSemE-53
85SwePanS-49
86SwePanS-36
87SwePanS-52
**Backstrom, Ralph**
44BeeGro2P-220
58Par-16
59Par-29
60Par-41
60Par-56
60ShiCoi-31
60YorPreP-2
61Par-39
61ShiCoi-114
61YorYelB-24
62Par-44
62ShiMetC-26
62YorIroOTra-16
63ChePho-2
63Par-24
63Par-83
63YorWhiB-27

64BeeGro3P-97
64CanaPos-1
64CocCap-59
64Top-78
65CanaSteG-1
65Coc-59
65Top-73
66CanalGA-2
66Top-75
66TopUSAT-6
67CanalGA-6
67PosFliB-11
67Top-67
67YorActOct-14
67YorActOct-27
67YorActOct-34
68CanalGA-6
68CanaPosBW-1
680PC-60
68PosCerM-1
68ShiCoi-82
68Top-60
69CanaPos-1
690PC-166
70CanaPin-21
70ColSta-21
700PC-54
70Top-54
71Baz-22
710PC-108
71Top-108
71TorSun-105
720PC-131
72Top-133
740PCWHA-47
74TeaCanLWHA-1
750PCWHA-23
760PCWHA-124
90ProAHLIHL-367
91ProAHLCHL-405
91UltOriS-7
91UltOriSF-7
92ParParR-PR18
930PCCanHF-33
94ParMisL-77
94ParTalB-73
95Par66-64
95Par66Col-64
**Backstrom, Tomas**
84SweSemE-192
**Bacon, Doug**
92Rallce-38
92WheThu-24
**Badal, Ales**
94CzeAPSE-129
**Badaway, Chad**
86KinCan-21
87SudWol-21
**Badduke, John**
89VicCou-1
907thInnSWHL-241
917thInnSWHL-49
94ClaEnf-E4
96SyrCru-14
96WheNai-15
**Bader, Darin**
88SasBla-22
89SasBla-23
907thInnSWHL-94
90SasBla-22
**Bader, Mike**
94GerDELE-431
95GerDELE-398
96GerDELE-303
**Badzgon, Eric**
87PorWinH-2
88PorWinH-2
**Bagu, Brad**
907thInnSWHL-243
917thInnSWHL-94
92MPSPhoSJHL-48
**Bailey, Ace**
32OKeeMapL-6
330PCV304A-13
33V129-3
33V252CanG-3
33V288HamG-11
33V357IceK-22
55Par-30
55ParQuaO-30
70BruPos-5
73RedWinTI-1
83HalFP-N2
85HalFC-198
91ProSet-335
91ProSetFre-335
92HalFL-32
94ParTalB-G1
94ParTalBG-1
**Bailey, Bob**
44BeeGro2P-374
51CleBar-16
54Par-28
57Top-19
**Bailey, Christina**
94ClaWomOH-W38
**Bailey, Garnet**
70BruTealss-1
70EssPowPla-64
700PC-10
70SarProSta-13
70Top-10
71BruTealss-10
71TorSun-3

720PC-191
72SarProSta-28
73RedWinMP-1
74NHLActSta-251
740PCNHL-332
750PCNHL-284
750PCNHL-330
75Top-284
75Top-330
760PCNHL-304
770PCNHL-196
77Top-196
780PC-276
**Bailey, Greg**
907thInnSOHL-351
917thInnSOHL-121
93HunBli-3
94BirBul-1
**Bailey, John**
69ColChe-1
**Bailey, Reid**
82PosCer-14
**Bailey, Scott**
907thInnSWHL-202
917thInnSWHL-73
917thInnSWHL-4
95Bow-158
95BowAllFoi-158
95ColEdgI-58
95ParInt-524
95ParIntEI-524
96PinPreS-215
96Zen-143
96ZenArtP-143
**Baillargeon, Joel**
86SheCan-4
87MonHaw-1
88NordGenF-2
88NordTeal-4
88ProAHL-101
89HalCit-1
89ProAHL-178
**Bain, Dan**
83HalFP-B1
85HalFC-227
94HalFT-3
**Baines, Ajay**
96KamBla-4
**Baird, Chris**
92HarCri-2
**Baird, Ken**
750PCWHA-37
770PCWHA-46
**Baird, Mark**
91AirCanSJHL-B11
**Baker, Aaron**
95TriAme-4
**Baker, Bill**
80CanaPos-1
81SweSemHVS-95
82PosCer-17
830PC-240
95SigRooMI-1
95SigRooMI-2
95SigRooSMIS-1
95SigRooSMIS-2
**Baker, Bruce**
77NovScoV-1
**Baker, Darin**
88ProIHL-38
**Baker, Hobey**
83HalFP-B2
85HalFC-17
92HalFL-6*
95AHC-2
**Baker, Jamie**
89HalCit-2
90HalCit-1
90ProAHLIHL-449
91Bow-136
91Pin-348
91PinFre-348
91ProAHLCHL-541
92Bow-436
920PC-41
92Par-353
92ParEmel-353
92Sen-1
92StaClu-136
92Top-506
92TopGol-506G
92Ult-360
92UppDec-130
92UppDec-464
93Lea-134
930PCPre-22
930PCPreG-22
93PanSti-113
93Par-459
93ParEmel-459
93Pin-378
93PinCan-378
93Sco-57
93ScoCan-57
93ScoCan-546
93ScoGol-546
93StaClu-461
93StaCluFDI-461
93StaCluO-461
93TopPre-22
93TopPreG-22
93TopPrePS-22
93Ult-6

94EASpo-93
94Lea-421
94Pin-502
94PinArtP-502
94PinRinC-502
94StaClu-249
94StaCluFDI-249
94StaCluMOMS-249
94StaCluSTWC-249
94UppDec-439
94UppDecEleIce-439
95CanGamNHLP-232
95PlaOneoOne-301
96BeAPAut-17
96BeAPAutSil-17
96BeAPla-17
96PlaOneoOne-402
96Sum-74
96SumArtP-74
96SumIce-74
96SumMet-74
96SumPreS-74
97PacInvNRB-190
97ScoMapL-19
97ScoMapLPla-19
97ScoMapLPre-19
**Baker, Steve**
800PC-346
810PC-231
**Baker, Trevor**
96PriAlbR-1
96PriAlbROC-1
**Bakogeorge, Troy**
86RegPat-1
**Bakos, Michael**
96GerDELE-10
98GerDELE-282
98GerDELE-335
**Bakovic, Pete (Peter)**
83KitRan-24
85MonGolF-27
86MonGolF-23
89ProIHL-168
90ProAHLIHL-326
91ProAHLCHL-596
94MilAdm-2
95MilAdmBO-22
96MilAdmBO-2
**Bakula, Martin**
94CapBreO-2
94ClaProP-158
96CzeAPSE-102
**Bal, Jag**
91BriColJHL-144
92BriColJHL-37
**Balaz, Radoslav**
917thInnSQMJHL-196
**Balazs, David**
94CzeAPSE-227
95CzeAPSE-162
96CzeAPSE-184
**Balcombe, Darren**
92MPSPhoSJHL-59
**Balderis, Helmut**
74SweHocS-75
79PanSti-152
82SweSemHVS-70
83RusNatT-2
92FutTre76CC-130
**Baldris, Miguel**
84RicRiv-1
**Baldwin, Doug**
44BeeGro2P-3
**Balej, Josef**
95SloPeeWT-1
96SloPeeWT-1
**Bales, Bob**
81VicCou-1
**Bales, Mike**
92Cla-73
93Cla-126
95ParInt-419
95ParIntEI-419
95Sen-3
96ClaGol-73
**Balfeux, Martin**
917thInnSQMJHL-63
**Balfour, Earl**
44BeeGro2P-77
44BeeGro2P-375
54Par-25
58Top-37
59Top-50
60ShiCoi-68
61Top-3
61Top-21
**Balfour, Murray**
44BeeGro2P-78
59Top-33
60ShiCoi-65
60Top-12
60TopSta-1
61ShiCoi-30
61Top-33
62Top-36
63Top-35
64BeeGro3P-1
64CocCap-9
64Top-90
94ParTalB-17
**Balkovec, Maco**
92BriColJHL-236
**Ball, Matt**
93DetJrRW-8

94DetJrRW-7
95Sla-66
95SlaMemC-81
**Ball, Terry**
72FigSaiPos-3
**Ballard, Harold**
78MapLeaP-24
79MapLeaP-2
80MapLeaP-2
81MapLeaP-2
81MapLeaP-26
83HalFP-E2
85HalFC-63
85MapLeaP-1
86MapLeaP-2
87MapLeaPLA-4
88MapLeaPLA-13
**Balleux, Martin**
917thInnSQMJHL-37
**Ballman, Brian**
96SeaThu-21
**Balmer, Samuel**
91SweSemWCS-185
93SweSemWCS-111
93SwiHNL-87
95SwiHNL-114
**Balmockhnyk, Maxim**
97UppDecBD-47
97UppDecBDDD-47
97UppDecBDQD-47
97UppDecBDTD-47
98UC-283
98UD ChoPCR-283
98UD ChoR-283
**Balog, Tyson**
91AirCanSJHL-A3
92MPSPhoSJHL-143
**Balon, Dave**
44BeeGro2P-221
44BeeGro2P-296A
44BeeGro2P-296B
60ShiCoi-94
62Top-56
62TopHocBuc-1
63ChePho-3
63Par-38
63Par-97
63YorWhiB-33
64BeeGro3P-98
64CocCap-69
64Top-37
64TorSta-1
65Top-72
66Top-74
660PC-169
68ShiCoi-107
690PC-191
70ColSta-33
70EssPowPla-192
700PC-61
70SarProSta-119
70Top-61
710PC-229
71SarProSta-125
71TorSun-168
72CanuRoyB-1
720PC-162
72SarProSta-220
72Top-117
94ParTalB-68
95Par66-62
95Par66Col-62
**Balshin, Brad**
83KitRan-26
**Baltimore, Bryon**
750PCWHA-9
880IlTenAnn-138
**Bamberger, J.J.**
91FerStaB-3
**Bancroft, Steve**
897thInnSOHL-85
90ProAHLIHL-159
91ProAHLCHL-49
92IndIce-2
93ClaProPro-48
93CleLum-3
93CleLumPos-2
**Bandurski, Andrew**
92CorBigRed-1
93CorBigRed-2
**Banham, Frank**
93SasBla-2
93SasBla-3
95SasBla-2
97Don-203
97DonPreProG-203
97DonPreProS-203
98Pac-43
98PacIceB-43
98PacRed-43
**Banika, Cory**
897thInnSOHL-17
89OshGen-17
89OshGenP-1
907thInnSMC-87
90HamRoaA-54
93JohChi-17
**Bankoske, Dave**
94TolSto-1
**Banks, Darren**
90ProAHLIHL-622
91ProAHLCHL-582
920PCPre-118
93Par-286
93ParEmel-286

96DetVip-1
**Bannerman, Murray**
80BlaWhiBor-1
81BlaBorPos-1
810PC-68
820PC-61
83BlaBorPos-1
830PC-97
830PCSti-113
830PCSti-164
83VicCou-2
840PC-32
840PCSti-32
840PCSti-135
84Top-27
850PC-27
850PCSti-27
85Top-27
86BlaCok-1
860PC-180
86Top-180
87BlaCok-1
87PanSti-221
**Bannister, Darin**
90ProAHLIHL-298
91ProAHLCHL-136
**Bannister, Drew**
907thInnSOHL-152
917thInnSOHL-327
93DonTeaC-3
93Pin-460
93PinCan-460
93SauSteMG-6
93SauSteMGM-6
94Cla-64
94ClaDraGol-64
95Bow-104
95BowAllFoi-104
95ColEdgI-49
95ParInt-467
95ParIntEI-467
96BeAPAut-219
96BeAPAutSil-219
96BeAPla-219
96BeAPla-P219
97ColCho-94
98LasVegT-1
**Banville, Gilles**
63QueAce-1
64QueAce-1
65QueAce-1
**Barahona, Ralph**
90ProAHLIHL-132
91UppDec-496
91UppDecF-496
**Baranka, Michal**
96SloPeeWT-2
**Barbe, Mario**
84ChiSag-1
89ProAHL-84
89ProAHL-132
90ProAHLIHL-228
**Barbeau, Frederic**
96WheNai-2
**Barber, Bill**
73FlyLin-2
730PC-81
73Top-81
74LipSou-31
74NHLActSta-205
740PCNHL-8
74Top-8
75FlyCanDC-1
750PCNHL-226
75Top-226
760PCNHL-178
760PCNHL-215
760PCNHL-391
76Top-178
76Top-215
76TopGlol-12
770PCNHL-227
77Top-227
780PC-69
780PC-176
78Top-69
78Top-176
790PC-140
79Top-140
800PC-200
80Top-200
810PC-238
810PC-247
810PC-253
810PCSti-155
810PCSti-174
81Top-2
81Top-59
81Top-E123
82McDSti-11
820PC-244
820PC-246
820PC-247
820PCSti-110
82PosCer-14
83FlyJCP-2
830PC-260
830PCSti-5
830PCSti-194
83PufSti-9
840PC-156
85FlyPos-1

86FlyPos-1
90Sco-356
90ScoCan-356
92FlyUppDS-44
92FutTre76CC-169
92Par-469
92ParEmel-469
94HocWit-13
**Barber, Don**
90Bow-179
90BowTif-179
90JetIGA-3
900PC-53
90PanSti-259
90ProSet-558
90Sco-284
90ScoCan-284
90ScoRoo-14T
90Top-53
90TopTif-53
90UppDec-28
90UppDecF-28
91NordPet-2
91ProSet-464
91ProSetFre-464
**Barber, Greg**
81VicCou-1
**Barclay, Todd**
94DubFigS-5
**Baril, Tony**
24CreSel-3
**Barilko, Bill**
44BeeGro2P-376
45QuaOatP-4A
45QuaOatP-4B
45QuaOatP-4C
48ExhCan-28
51Par-52
91ProSet-340
91ProSetFre-340
93ParParR-PR35
**Barin, Stephane**
93SweSemWCS-258
94FinnJaaK-228
96SweSemW-191
98GerDELE-8
**Bark, Sten Ake**
72SweHocS-40
72SweHocS-127
73SweHocS-188
73SweWorCS-188
74SweHocS-159
**Barker, Brian**
92NorMicW-1
93NorMicW-1
95Sla-20
**Barker, Eldon**
92MPSPhoSJHL-93
**Barker, Randy**
92BriColJHL-223
**Barkley, Doug**
44BeeGro2P-152A
44BeeGro2P-152B
62YorIroOTra-24
63Par-60
63YorWhiB-46
64BeeGro3P-61
64CocCap-41
64Top-9
65Coc-41
65Top-43
76OldTim-3
94ParTalB-49
**Barklund, Niklas**
917thInnSWHL-231
**Barkman, Jon**
96SasBla-2
**Barkov, Alexander**
92RusStaRA-1
94FinnSIS-215
95FinnSIS-117
95FinnSIS-368
95FinnSISL-80
96FinnSISR-132
**Barkovich, Rick**
88ProIHL-22
88SalLakCGE-1
89ProIHL-193
90KanCitBla-4
90ProAHLIHL-588
93Rallce-2
94Rallce-2
**Barlie, Vegar**
94FinnJaaK-267
**Barlow, Bob**
690PC-196
700PC-45
70SarProSta-93
70Top-45
74PhoRoaWP-1
**Barlow, Hugh**
52JunBluT-33
**Barnaby, Matthew**
917thInnSQMJHL-189
92Par-483
92ParEmel-483
93Don-42
93Lea-362
930PCPre-346
930PCPreG-346
93Par-296
93ParEmel-296
93Pin-216
93PinCan-216
93StaClu-321

93StaCluFDI-321
93StaCluO-321
93TopPre-346
93TopPreG-346
93Ult-13
93UppDec-439
93UppDecSP-13
94ClaProP-179
94Don-289
94Lea-285
95Don-383
95UppDec-341
95UppDecEleIce-341
95UppDecEleIceG-341
96BeAPAut-147
96BeAPAutSil-147
96BeAPla-147
96ColCho-33
96Don-152
96DonPrePro-152
96Sco-188
96ScoArtPro-188
96ScoDeaCAP-188
96ScoGolB-188
96ScoSpeAP-188
97ColCho-27
97Don-170
97DonCanI-84
97DonCanIDS-84
97DonCanIPS-84
97DonLim-68
97DonLimExp-68
97DonPreProG-170
97DonPreProS-170
97Kat-13
97KatGol-13
97KatSil-13
97Pac-210
97PacCop-210
97PacEmeGre-210
97PacIceB-210
97PacPar-17
97PacParC-17
97PacParDG-17
97PacParEG-17
97PacParIB-17
97PacParRed-17
97PacParSil-17
97PacRed-210
97PacRev-12
97PacRevC-12
97PacRevE-12
97PacRevIB-12
97PacRevR-12
97PacRevS-12
97PacSil-210
97Pin-108
97PinIns-176
97PinPrePBB-108
97PinPrePBC-108
97PinPrePBM-108
97PinPrePBY-108
97PinPrePFC-108
97PinPrePFM-108
97PinPrePFY-108
97PinPrePla-108
97Sco-216
97ScoSab-5
97ScoSabPla-5
97ScoSabPre-5
97UppDec-16
97UppDec-393
98Be A PPA-14
98Be A PPAA-14
98Be A PPAAF-14
98Be A PPTBASG-14
98Be APG-14
980-PChr-213
980-PChrR-213
98Pac-36
98PacAur-15
98PacCroR-11
98PacCroRLS-11
98PacDynI-16
98PacDynIIB-16
98PacDynIR-16
98PacIceB-36
98PacOmeH-20
98PacOmeODI-20
98PacOmeR-20
98PacPar-17
98PacParC-17
98PacParEG-17
98PacParH-17
98PacParIB-17
98PacParS-17
98PacRed-36
98PacRev-12
98PacRevIS-12
98PacRevR-12
98RevThrPA-1
98RevThrPA-1
98SP AutSotTG-MB
98SPxFin-11
98SPxFinR-11
98SPxFinS-11
98SSASotT-MB
98Top-213
98TopO-P-213
98UppDec-228
98UppDecE-228
98UppDecE1o1-228
98UppDecGR-228
98UppDecM-22
98UppDecMGS-22
98UppDecMSS-22
98UppDecMSS-22
99Pac-333
99PacAur-114
99PacAurPD-114
99PacCop-333
99PacGol-333
99PacIceB-333
99PacPreD-333
99UppDecM-171
99UppDecMGS-171
99UppDecMSS-171
99UppDecMSS-171

**Barnes, Blair**
83NovScoV-13

**Barnes, Brian**
91BriColJHL-102
92BriColJHL-121

**Barnes, Jamie**
97SudWolP-3

**Barnes, Norm**
800PC-308
810PCSti-67

**Barnes, Ryan**
98UppDec-345
95UppDecEleIce-345
95UppDecEleIceG-345
95UppDecSpeE-SE33
95UppDecSpeEdiG-SE33

**Barnes, Steven**
91LakSupSL-7
94HunBil-2

**Barnes, Stu**
89JetSaf-2
90AlbIntTC-10
90Sco-391
90ScoCan-391
91JetIGA-1
91OPCPre-109
91Par-419
91ParFre-419
91Pin-319
91PinFre-319
91ProSet-566
91ProSetFre-566
91ProSetPla-273
91ScoCan-630
91ScoRoo-80T
91UppDec-53
91UppDecF-53
92Bow-26
92OPC-39
92Sco-319
92ScoCan-319
92StaClu-285
92Top-210
92TopGol-210G
92UppDec-426
93Don-377
93Don-432
93JetRuf-1
93Lea-350
93OPCPre-351
93OPCPreG-351
93Par-226
93ParEmel-226
93Pin-426
93PinCan-426
93Pow-345
93Sco-380
93ScoCan-380
93ScoCan-644
93ScoGol-644
93TopPre-351
93TopPreG-351
93UppDec-94
94CanGamNHLP-104
94Don-306
94Fin-66
94FinRef-66
94FinSupTW-66
94Fle-76
94Lea-73
94OPCPre-458
94PanPop-4
94ParSE-SE66
94ParSEG-SE66
94Pin-47
94PinArtP-47
94PinRinC-47
94Sco-138
94ScoGol-138
94ScoPla-138
94ScoPlaTS-138
94SP-43
94SPDieCut-43
94StaClu-261
94StaCluFDI-261
94StaCluMOMS-261
94StaCluSTWC-261
94TopPre-458
94TopPreSE-458
94Ult-138
94UppDec-493
94UppDecEleIce-493
95BeAPla-127
95BeAPSig-S127
95BeAPSigDC-S127
95CanGamNHLP-115
95ColCho-209
95ColChoPC-209
95Don-132
95Emo-68
95Fin-68
95FinRef-68
95ImpSti-48
95Lea-36
95Met-58
95ParInt-86
95ParIntEl-86
95Pin-40
95PinArtP-40
95PinRinC-40
95PlaOneoOne-152
95Sco-22
95ScoBlaIce-22
95ScoBlaIceAP-22
95SkyImp-66
95StaClu-73
95StaCluMOMS-73
95Sum-47
95SumArtP-47
95SumIce-47
95Top-110
95TopOPCI-110
95TopSupSki-38
95TopSupSkiPla-38
95Ult-59
95UltGolM-59
95UppDec-345
95UppDecEleIce-345
95UppDecEleIceG-345
95UppDecSpeE-SE33
95UppDecSpeEdiG-SE33
96ColCho-110
96Don-68
96DonPrePro-68
96Lea-30
96LeaPreP-30
96Pin-135
96PinArtP-135
96PinFoi-135
96PinPreS-135
96PinRinC-135
96Sco-180
96ScoArtPro-180
96ScoDeaCAP-180
96ScoGolB-180
96ScoSpeAP-180
96Sum-131
96SumArtP-131
96SumIce-131
96SumMet-131
96SumPreS-131
96UppDec-64
97ColCho-212
97Par-175
97PacCop-175
97PacEmeGre-175
97PacIceB-175
97PacOme-181
97PacOmeDG-181
97PacOmeEG-181
97PacOmeIB-181
97PacRed-175
97PacRev-110
97PacRevC-110
97PacRevE-110
97PacRevIB-110
97PacRevR-110
97PacRevS-110
97PacSil-175
97Sco-237
97ScoPen-9
97ScoPenPla-9
97ScoPenPre-9
98Be A PPA-114
98Be A PPAA-114
98Be A PPAAF-114
98Be A PPTBASG-114
98Be APG-114
98Fin-131
98FinNo P-131
98FinNo PR-131
98FinRef-131
980-PChr-98
980-PChrR-98
98Pac-348
98PacAur-151
98PacIceB-348
98PacOmeH-193
98PacOmeR-193
98PacPar-189
98PacParC-189
98PacParEG-189
98PacParH-189
98PacParIB-189
98PacParS-189
98PacRed-348
98PacRev-116
98PacRevIS-116
98PacRevR-116
98SPxFin-69
98SPxFinR-69
98SPxFinS-69
98Top-98
98TopGolLC1-52
98TopGolLC1B-52
98TopGolLC10oO-52
98TopGolLC1R-52
98TopGolLC1ROoO-52
98TopGolLC2-52
98TopGolLC2B-52
98TopGolLC2BOoO-52
98TopGolLC2OoO-52
98TopGolLC2R-52
98TopGolLC2ROoO-52
98TopGolLC3-52
98TopGolLC3B-52
98TopGolLC3OoO-52
98TopGolLC3OoO-52
98TopGolLC3R-52
98TopGolLC3ROoO-52
98TopO-P-98
98UC-167
98UD ChoPCR-167
98UD ChoR-167
98UppDec-347
98UppDecE-347
98UppDecE1o1-347
98UppDecGR-347
98UppDecM-167
98UppDecMGS-167
98UppDecMSS-167
99Pac-33
99PacCop-33
99PacGol-33
99PacIceB-33
99PacPreD-33

**Barnett, Brett**
89ProlHL-92
90ProAHLIHL-107
92BirBul-3
93BirBul-3

**Barney, Scott**
95Sla-328
96UppDec-379
96UppDecBD-14
96UppDecBDG-14
97BowCHL-150
97BowCHLAu-30
97BowCHLBB-14
97BowCHLBowBesAR-14
97BowCHLBowBesR-14
97BowCHLOPC-150
97ColCho-310
98BowCHL-39
98BowCHLGA-39
98BowCHLOI-39
98BowChrC-39
98BowChrCGA-39
98BowChrCGAR-39
98BowChrCOI-39
98BowChrCOIR-39
98BowChrCR-39

**Barnstable, Scott**
907thInnSWHL-153

**Baron, Marco**
83MonAlp-3
880ilTenAnn-156
93SwiHNL-137

**Baron, Murray**
89ProAHL-334
90FlyPos-2
90ProAHLIHL-35
90Sco-399
90ScoCan-399
90UppDec-275
90UppDecF-275
91BluPos-1
91OPC-373
91Pin-204
91PinFre-204
91ProSet-472
91ScoAme-183
91ScoCan-183
91ScoCan-616
91ScoYouS-27
91StaClu-334
91Top-373
91UppDec-497
91UppDecF-497
92Bow-409
92Pin-144
92PinFre-144
92Sco-176
92ScoCan-176
92StaClu-194
92Top-354
92TopGol-354G
93Sco-294
93ScoCan-294
93Ult-407
94StaClu-168
94StaCluFDI-168
94StaCluMOMS-168
94StaCluSTWC-168
95BeAPla-158
95BeAPSigDC-S158
96CanaPos-1
96UppDec-143
96UppDec-198

**Baron, Norman**
83NovScoV-10

**Barr, Dave**
860PC-237
87RedWinLC-2
88RedWinLC-1
890PC-13
890PCSti-250
89PanSti-60
89RedWinLC-1
89Top-13
90Bow-231
90BowTif-231
900PC-308
90ProSet-65
90Top-308
90TopTif-308
90UppDec-257
90UppDecF-257
91Bow-49
910PC-147
910PCPre-54
91ProSet-65
91ProSetFre-65
91ScoAme-187
91ScoCan-187
91ScoCan-597
91ScoRoo-47T
91StaClu-141
91Top-147
92Sco-315
92ScoCan-315
92StaClu-291
92Top-197
92TopGol-197G

**Barr, Don**
92BriColJHL-4
92BriColJHL-18

**Barrasso, Tom**
847EDis-3
840PC-18
840PC-212
840PC-215
840PC-227
840PC-228
84SabBluS-2
84Top-14
84Top-158
84ParEmel-157
84PenFoo-24
857ECreCar-2
850PC-105
850PC-263
850PCSti-55
850PCSti-114
850PCSti-189
85SabBluS-3
85SabBluSS-3
85Top-105
85TopStiIns-12
860PC-91
860PCSti-45
86SabBluS-4
86SabBluSSma-4
86Top-91
870PC-78
870PCSti-148
87PanSti-22
87SabBluS-4
87SabWonBH-5
87Top-78
88FriLayS-19
880PC-107
880PCMin-1
880PCSti-259
88PanSti-219
88Top-107
890PC-36
890PCSti-235
89PanSti-312
89PenFoo-15
89SweSemWCS-153
89Top-36
90Bow-209
90BowTif-209
900PC-65
90PanSti-134
90PenFoo-5
90ProSet-227
90ProSetPM-P1
90Sco-121
90ScoCan-121
90Top-65
90TopTif-65
90UppDec-121
90UppDecF-121
91Bow-80
91Bow-419
91PenFoo-22
91Pin-20
91PinFre-20
91ProSet-186
91ProSetFre-186
91ProSetPC-22
91ProSetPlaPC-PC3
91ScoCan-225
91StaClu-155
91Top-402
91UppDec-116
91UppDecF-116
92Bow-250
92Kra-25
920PC-340
92PanSti-219
92PanStiFre-219
92Par-134
92PenCokC-1
92PenFoo-5
92Pin-298
92PinFre-298
92ProSet-145
92Sco-70
92ScoCan-70
92SeaPat-36
92StaClu-416
92Top-503
92TopGol-503G
92Ult-162
92UppDec-243
93Don-260
93HigLinGG-6
93Kra-50
93Lea-196
93LeaGolAS-5
93LeaPaiWar-9
930PCPre-175
930PCPre-204
930PCPre-446
930PCPre-501
930PCPreBG-9
930PCPreG-175
930PCPreG-204
930PCPreG-446
930PCPreG-501
93PanSti-88
93PanSti-141
93Par-157
93ParEmel-157
93PenFoo-24
93PenSti-1
93Pin-3
93Pin1S-2
93PinCan-3
93PinTeaP-7
93PinTeaPC-7
93Pow-187
93PowNet-1
93Sco-225
93ScoCan-225
93ScoCan-483
93ScoDreTea-1
93StaClu-79
93StaCluFDI-79
93StaCluFDIO-79
93StaCluMasP-12
93StaCluMasPW-12
93StaCluO-79
93SweSemWCS-169
93TopPre-175
93TopPre-204
93TopPre-446
93TopPre-501
93TopPreBG-11
93TopPreG-175
93TopPreG-204
93TopPreG-446
93TopPreG-501
93Ult-26
93UppDec-45
93UppDecSP-120
94CanGamNHLP-291
94Don-208
94EASpo-108
94FinRinL-19
94Fla-133
94HocWit-25
94KenStaLA-1
94Kra-31
94Lea-103
940PCPre-84
940PCPre-206
940PCPre-311
940PCPreSE-84
940PCPreSE-206
940PCPreSE-311
94Par-182
94ParGol-182
94PenFoo-22
94Pin-20
94PinArtP-20
94PinRinC-20
94Sco-31
94ScoGol-31
94ScoPla-31
94ScoPlaTS-31
94Sel-88
94SelGol-88
94StaCluDD-1
94StaCluDDMO-1
94TopPre-84
94TopPre-206
94TopPre-311
94TopPreSE-84
94TopPreSE-206
94TopPreSE-311
94Ult-162
94UppDec-70
94UppDecEleIce-70
95BeAPla-124
95BeAPSig-S124
95BeAPSigDC-S124
95Bow-47
95BowAllFoi-47
95CanGamNHLP-221
95ColCho-53
95ColChoPC-53
95ColChoPCP-53
95Don-291
95Fin-129
95FinnSemWC-215
95FinRef-129
95KenStaLC-1
95Kra-35
95Met-115
95ParInt-435
95ParIntEl-435
95PenFoo-10
95Pin-97
95PinArtP-97
95PinRinC-97
95Sco-152
95ScoBlaIce-152
95ScoBlaIceAP-152
95SelCer-95
95SelCerMG-95
95SP-119
95StaClu-158
95StaCluM-M6
95StaCluMOMS-158
95Sum-88
95SumArtP-88
95SumIce-88
95SweGloWC-102
95Top-262
95TopOPCI-262
95TopSupSki-79
95TopSupSkiPla-79
95Ult-364
95UppDec-115
95UppDecEleIce-115
95UppDecEleIceG-115
95UppDecSpeE-SE68
95UppDecSpeEdiG-SE68
95Zen-97
96ColCho-213
96Don-67
96DonCanI-70
96DonCanIGPP-70
96DonCanIRPP-70
96DonEli-63
96DonEliDCS-63
96DonPrePro-67
96Fle-84
96Lea-26
96LeaPre-46
96LeaPreP-26
96LeaPreSG-27
96LeaPreSte-27
96MetUni-124
96PenTri-5
96Pin-95
96PinArtP-95
96PinFoi-95
96PinPreS-95
96PinRinC-95
96Sco-124
96ScoArtPro-124
96ScoDeaCAP-124
96ScoGolB-124
96ScoNetW-12
96ScoSpeAP-124
96ScoSudDea-10
96SkyImp-99
96Sum-93
96SumArtP-93
96SumIce-93
96SumMet-93
96SumPreS-93
96Ult-138
96UltGolM-138
96UppDec-132
96Zen-98
96ZenArtP-98
97DonPri-139
97DonPriPG-17
97DonPriPGP-17
97DonPriSoA-139
97Kat-115
97KatGol-115
97KatSil-115
97PacCroR-108
97PacCroREG-108
97PacCroRFODC-16
97PacCroRIB-108
97PacCroRS-108
97PacInvNRB-157
97PacOme-182
97PacOmeC-182
97PacOmeDG-182
97PacOmeEG-182
97PacOmeG-182
97PacPar-147
97PacParDG-147
97PacParEG-147
97PacParGSL-17
97PacParIB-147
97PacParRed-147
97PacParSil-147
97PacRev-111
97PacRevC-111
97PacRevE-111
97PacRevIB-111
97PacRevR-111
97PacRevRtSD-16

❑ 97PacRevS-111
❑ 97Pin-76
❑ 97PinArtP-76
❑ 97PinInsSUG-1A/B
❑ 97PinInsSUG-1C/D
❑ 97PinPrePBB-76
❑ 97PinPrePBC-76
❑ 97PinPrePBM-76
❑ 97PinPrePBY-76
❑ 97PinPrePFC-76
❑ 97PinPrePFM-76
❑ 97PinPrePFY-76
❑ 97PinPrePla-76
❑ 97PinRinC-76
❑ 97Sco-17
❑ 97ScoArtPro-17
❑ 97ScoGolBla-17
❑ 97ScoPen-1
❑ 97ScoPenPla-1
❑ 97ScoPenPre-1
❑ 97Zen-77
❑ 97ZenZGol-77
❑ 97ZenZSil-77
❑ 98BowBes-56
❑ 98BowBesAR-56
❑ 98BowBesR-56
❑ 98Fin-142
❑ 98FinNo P-142
❑ 98FinNo PR-142
❑ 98FinRef-142
❑ 980-PChr-209
❑ 980-PChrR-209
❑ 980-PChrSB-SB6
❑ 980-PChrSBR-SB6
❑ 98Pac-35
❑ 98PacAur-152
❑ 98PacAurCF-39
❑ 98PacAurCFC-39
❑ 98PacAurCFIB-39
❑ 98PacAurCFR-39
❑ 98PacAurCFS-39
❑ 98PacCroR-108
❑ 98PacCroRLS-108
❑ 98PacDynI-148
❑ 98PacDynIIB-148
❑ 98PacDynIR-148
❑ 98PacGolCD-28
❑ 98PacIceB-35
❑ 98PacOmeH-194
❑ 98PacOmeODI-194
❑ 98PacOmeR-194
❑ 98PacPar-190
❑ 98PacParC-190
❑ 98PacParEG-190
❑ 98PacParGSLC-16
❑ 98PacParH-190
❑ 98PacParIB-190
❑ 98PacParS-190
❑ 98PacRed-35
❑ 98PacRev-117
❑ 98PacRevIS-117
❑ 98PacRevR-117
❑ 98SPxFin-70
❑ 98SPxFinR-70
❑ 98SPxFinS-70
❑ 98Top-209
❑ 98TopGolLC1-78
❑ 98TopGolLC1B-78
❑ 98TopGolLC1BOoO-78
❑ 98TopGolLC1OoO-78
❑ 98TopGolLC1R-78
❑ 98TopGolLC1ROoO-78
❑ 98TopGolLC2-78
❑ 98TopGolLC2B-78
❑ 98TopGolLC2BOoO-78
❑ 98TopGolLC2OoO-78
❑ 98TopGolLC2R-78
❑ 98TopGolLC2ROoO-78
❑ 98TopGolLC3-78
❑ 98TopGolLC3B-78
❑ 98TopGolLC3BOoO-78
❑ 98TopGolLC3OoO-78
❑ 98TopGolLC3R-78
❑ 98TopGolLC3ROoO-78
❑ 98TopO-P-209
❑ 98TopSeaB-SB6
❑ 98UC-165
❑ 98UC-250
❑ 98UD ChoPCR-165
❑ 98UD ChoPCR-250
❑ 98UD ChoR-165
❑ 98UD ChoR-250
❑ 98UppDec-162
❑ 98UppDecE-162
❑ 98UppDecE1o1-162
❑ 98UppDecGR-162
❑ 98UppDecM-164
❑ 98UppDecMGS-164
❑ 98UppDecMSS-164
❑ 98UppDecMSS-164
❑ 99Pac-334
❑ 99PacAur-115
❑ 99PacAurPD-115
❑ 99PacCop-334
❑ 99PacGol-334
❑ 99PacIceB-334
❑ 99PacIn tCN-16
❑ 99PacPreD-334
❑ 99UppDecM-168
❑ 99UppDecMGS-168
❑ 99UppDecMLL-LL8
❑ 99UppDecMSS-168
❑ 99UppDecMSS-168
**Barrault, Doug**
❑ 89LetHur-1
❑ 91ProAHLCHL-158
❑ 93ClaProPro-61
❑ 93Pow-88
❑ 93Sco-457
❑ 93ScoCan-457
❑ 94Ult-294
**Barrefjord, Kjell-Olov**
❑ 64SweCorI-156
❑ 65SweCorI-156A
❑ 67SweHoc-249
❑ 69SweHocS-294
**Barrefjord, Ulf**
❑ 67SweHoc-250
❑ 69SweHocS-295
❑ 70SweHocS-203
❑ 71SweHocS-290
❑ 72SweHocS-77
❑ 74SweHocS-202
**Barrett, Dave**
❑ 89RayJrC-2
**Barrett, Fred**
❑ 70EssPowPla-165
❑ 71OPC-128
❑ 71TorSun-126
❑ 73NorStaP-1
❑ 73OPC-264
❑ 74NHLActSta-135
❑ 74OPCNHL-234
❑ 74Top-234
❑ 75OPCNHL-124
❑ 75Top-124
❑ 76OPCNHL-249
❑ 76Top-249
❑ 77OPCNHL-291
❑ 78NorStaCD-2
❑ 78OPC-185
❑ 78Top-185
❑ 79NorStaPos-2
❑ 80NorStaPos-2
❑ 80OPC-253
❑ 80Top-253
❑ 81NorStaPos-2
❑ 82NorStaPos-1
❑ 82PosCer-9
**Barrett, John**
❑ 82OPC-80
❑ 82PosCer-5
❑ 83OPC-117
❑ 84OPC-49
❑ 86CapKod-2
❑ 86CapPol-2
❑ 87CapKod-6
❑ 87CapTealss-2
**Barrett, Kevin**
❑ 93MusFur-18
❑ 94FliGen-1
**Barrett, Tom**
❑ 83KitRan-8
❑ 84KitRan-4
❑ 85KitRan-4
❑ 86KitRan-4
❑ 95Sla-180
**Barrette, Maurice**
❑ 77NovScoV-2
**Barrie, Doug**
❑ 70EssPowPla-76
❑ 71OPC-22
❑ 71SabPos-3
❑ 71SarProSta-28
❑ 71Top-22
❑ 71TorSun-23
❑ 75OPCWHA-117
❑ 76OPCWHA-119
**Barrie, Len**
❑ 907thInnSMC-1
❑ 90ProAHLIHL-49
❑ 91ProAHLCHL-274
❑ 91UppDec-459
❑ 91UppDecF-459
❑ 93ClaProPro-53
❑ 93Par-351
❑ 93ParEmel-351
❑ 94Fle-161
❑ 94Lea-491
❑ 94PenFoo-4
❑ 95CleLum-3
❑ 95Top-66
❑ 95TopOPCI-66
❑ 98GerDELE-135
**Barrie, Mike**
❑ 917thInnSWHL-60
❑ 93SeaThu-1
❑ 95SigRoo-40
❑ 95SigRooSig-40
❑ 95SouCarS-12
❑ 96PeoRiv-1
❑ 96PeoRivPA-1
**Barry, Kevin**
❑ 95Sla-168
**Barry, Marty**
❑ 33V129-38
❑ 33V357IceK-27
❑ 34BeeGro1P-88
❑ 34BeeGro1P-134
❑ 34DiaMatS-2
❑ 35OPCV304C-81
❑ 36ChaPos-1
❑ 36V356WorG-4
❑ 39OPCV3011-57
❑ 83HalFP-O3
❑ 85HalFC-214
**Barry, Ray**
❑ 44BeeGro2P-3
❑ 51Par-32
**Barta, Libor**
❑ 95CzeAPSE-200
❑ 96CzeAPSE-143
**Bartanus, Karol**
❑ 97BowCHL-59
❑ 97BowCHL-130
❑ 97BowCHLAu-10
❑ 97BowCHLOPC-59
❑ 97BowCHLOPC-130
❑ 98BowCHL-98
❑ 98BowCHLGA-98
❑ 98BowCHLOI-98
❑ 98BowCHLSC-SC11
❑ 98BowChrC-98
❑ 98BowChrCGA-98
❑ 98BowChrCGAR-98
❑ 98BowChrCOI-98
❑ 98BowChrCOIR-98
❑ 98BowChrCR-98
**Bartecko, Lubos**
❑ 98PacOmeH-208
❑ 98PacOmeODI-208
❑ 98PacOmeR-208
❑ 99Pac-352
❑ 99PacCop-352
❑ 99PacGol-352
❑ 99PacIceB-352
❑ 99PacPreD-352
❑ 99UppDecM-187
❑ 99UppDecMGS-187
❑ 99UppDecMSS-187
❑ 99UppDecMSS-187
**Bartel, Robin**
❑ 85MonGolF-25
**Bartell, Adam**
❑ 93RenEng-2
**Bartell, Josh**
❑ 92ClaKni-1
**Bartelsson, Tony**
❑ 84SweSemE-10
**Barth, Todd**
❑ 92MPSPhoSJHL-112
**Barthe, Claude**
❑ 907thInnSQMJHL-268
❑ 92HamRoaA-3
❑ 92WheThu-2
❑ 93RoaExp-3
**Barthelson, Tony**
❑ 89SweSemE-198
❑ 94SweLeaE-204
❑ 95SweLeaE-6
❑ 95SweUppDE-6
**Bartholomaus, Keith**
❑ 93NorMicW-2
**Bartlett, Jim**
❑ 58Top-26
❑ 59Top-51
❑ 60ShiCoi-113
**Bartley, Joey**
❑ 96GueSto-23
❑ 97GueSto-6
**Bartley, Wade**
❑ 89SudWol-21
❑ 90SudWol-8
❑ 95TolSto-16
**Bartmann, J.**
❑ 95GerDELE-316
**Bartoli, Moe**
❑ 67ColChe-2
❑ 69ColChe-2
**Bartolone, Chris**
❑ 96GerDELE-188
❑ 98GerDELE-27
**Barton, Brad**
❑ 88KitRan-24
❑ 89KitRan-24
❑ 907thInnSMC-45
❑ 907thInnSOHL-227
❑ 90KitRan-23
❑ 917thInnSOHL-93
❑ 94BraSmo-10
**Barton, Pat**
❑ 94WheThu-15
**Barton, Patrick**
❑ 917thInnSOHL-71
❑ 94GueSto-14
**Barus, Miroslav**
❑ 94CzeAPSE-247
❑ 95CzeAPSE-12
❑ 96CzeAPSE-262
**Basalgin, Andrei**
❑ 91OPCIns-49R
**Basanta, Mark**
❑ 91BriColJHL-41
❑ 92BriColJHL-122
❑ 92BriColJHL-221
**Basaraba, Shannon**
❑ 98ChaChe-2
**Baseggio, Dave**
❑ 89ProAHL-277
❑ 90ProAHLIHL-270
❑ 91ProAHLCHL-9
❑ 91RochAmePos-1
❑ 96CleLum-4
**Bashkatov, Egor**
❑ 96LasVegThu-1
**Basilio, Sean**
❑ 897thInnSOHL-31
❑ 897thInnSOHL-177
❑ 907thInnSOHL-127
❑ 917thInnSOHL-271
**Basken, Bruce**
❑ 86PorWinH-2
**Basque, Claude**
❑ 51LavDaiLSJ-48
**Basse, Harold**
❑ 82KitRan-2
❑ 83KitRan-22
❑ 84KitRan-2
❑ 85KitRan-2
❑ 86KitRan-2
❑ 87KitRan-2
❑ 88KitRan-2
❑ 89KitRan-2
❑ 90KitRan-2
**Bassen, Bobby (Bob)**
❑ 83MedHatT-15
❑ 89BlaCok-12
❑ 89ProIHL-53
❑ 90BluKod-1
❑ 90ProSet-520
❑ 91BluPos-2
❑ 91Bow-379
❑ 91OPC-51
❑ 91PanSti-29
❑ 91Par-379
❑ 91ParFre-379
❑ 91ProSet-221
❑ 91ProSetFre-221
❑ 91ScoAme-179
❑ 91ScoCan-179
❑ 91StaClu-367
❑ 91Top-51
❑ 91UppDec-319
❑ 91UppDecF-319
❑ 92Bow-378
❑ 92OPC-139
❑ 92Pin-203
❑ 92PinFre-203
❑ 92Sco-132
❑ 92ScoCan-132
❑ 92StaClu-176
❑ 92Top-454
❑ 92TopGol-454G
❑ 92Ult-182
❑ 92UppDec-181
❑ 93Don-476
❑ 93PanSti-163
❑ 93Par-445
❑ 93ParEmel-445
❑ 93Pin-169
❑ 93PinCan-169
❑ 93Sco-279
❑ 93ScoCan-279
❑ 93Ult-408
❑ 93UppDec-2
❑ 94Don-257
❑ 94NordBurK-2
❑ 94Par-184
❑ 94ParGol-184
❑ 94Pin-327
❑ 94PinArtP-327
❑ 94PinRinC-327
❑ 94UppDec-481
❑ 94UppDecEleIce-481
❑ 95CanGamNHLP-83
❑ 95Emo-44
❑ 95PlaOneoOne-245
❑ 95Sco-216
❑ 95ScoBlaIce-216
❑ 95ScoBlaIceAP-216
❑ 95SkyImp-43
❑ 96BeAPAut-89
❑ 96BeAPAutSil-89
❑ 96BeAPla-89
❑ 96BeAPla-P89
❑ 96Sco-218
❑ 96ScoArtPro-218
❑ 96ScoDeaCAP-218
❑ 96ScoGolB-218
❑ 96ScoSpeAP-218
❑ 96StaPos-2
❑ 96Sum-122
❑ 96SumArtP-122
❑ 96SumIce-122
❑ 96SumMet-122
❑ 96SumPreS-122
**Bassen, Hank**
❑ 44BeeGro2P-153
❑ 61ShiCoi-80
❑ 62Par-19
❑ 64BeeGro3P-62
❑ 65Coc-54
❑ 65Top-106
❑ 66Top-107
**Bassen, Mark**
❑ 88BraWheK-7
❑ 88LetHur-1
❑ 89ProAHL-355
❑ 90ProAHLIHL-43
❑ 91ProAHLCHL-33
❑ 92AlbIntTC-4
❑ 93PeoRiv-1
❑ 94GerDELE-364
❑ 94GerDELE-366
❑ 95GerDELE-239
❑ 96GerDELE-306
❑ 98GerDELE-219
**Bassett, Dennis**
❑ 95SasBla-3
**Bassin, Sherwood (Sherry)**
❑ 81OshGen-24
❑ 82OshGen-24
❑ 83OshGen-16
❑ 89SauSteMG-5
❑ 917thInnSCHLAW-9
❑ 93SauSteMGM-29
**Bast, Ryan**
❑ 93PriAlbR-1
❑ 94PriAlbR-2
❑ 96TolSto-6
❑ 99UppDecM-153
❑ 99UppDecMGS-153
❑ 99UppDecMSS-153
❑ 99UppDecMSS-153
**Bastien, Baz**
❑ 45QuaOatP-5
**Bastien, Morris**
❑ 36V356WorG-131
**Baston, Dan**
❑ 89RayJrC-3
❑ 90RayJrC-1
❑ 91RayJrC-1
**Bateman, Rob**
❑ 91GreMon-1
**Bates, Shawn**
❑ 97DonPre-156
❑ 97DonPreCttC-156
❑ 97PacDyn-NNO
❑ 97PacDynC-NNO
❑ 97PacDynDG-NNO
❑ 97PacDynEG-NNO
❑ 97PacDynIB-NNO
❑ 97PacDynR-NNO
❑ 97PacDynSil-NNO
❑ 97ScoBru-1
❑ 97ScoBruPla-1
❑ 97ScoBruPre-1
❑ 98UC-18
❑ 98UD ChoPCR-18
❑ 98UD ChoR-18
❑ 99Pac-19
❑ 99PacCop-19
❑ 99PacGol-19
❑ 99PacIceB-19
❑ 99PacPreD-19
❑ 99UppDecM-18
❑ 99UppDecMGS-18
❑ 99UppDecMSS-18
❑ 99UppDecMSS-18
**Bathe, Frank**
❑ 80OPC-389
❑ 83FlyJCP-3
❑ 91ProAHLCHL-68
**Batherson, Norm**
❑ 94ClaProP-157
❑ 94PorPir-1
❑ 95PorPir-3
❑ 96PorPir-7
❑ 98GerDELE-5
**Bathgate, Andy**
❑ 44BeeGro2P-297A
❑ 44BeeGro2P-297B
❑ 44BeeGro2P-377
❑ 53Par-56
❑ 54Top-11
❑ 57Top-60
❑ 58Top-21
❑ 59Top-34
❑ 60ShiCoi-89
❑ 60Top-45
❑ 60TopSta-2
❑ 61ShiCoi-88
❑ 61Top-22
❑ 61Top-53
❑ 62ShiMetC-48
❑ 62Top-52
❑ 62TopHocBuc-2
❑ 63Top-52
❑ 63TorSta-2
❑ 64BeeGro3P-63A
❑ 64BeeGro3P-63B
❑ 64BeeGro3P-152
❑ 64CocCap-95
❑ 64CocCap-96
❑ 64Top-86
❑ 64TorSta-2
❑ 65Coc-51
❑ 65Top-48
❑ 66Top-44
❑ 68OPC-104
❑ 68ShiCoi-139
❑ 68Top-104
❑ 70EssPowPla-224
❑ 70OPC-207
❑ 70SarProSta-173
❑ 81TCMA-8
❑ 83HalFP-O4
❑ 85HalFC-215
❑ 91UltOriS-18
❑ 91UltOriS-74
❑ 91UltOriSF-18
❑ 91UltOriSF-74
❑ 92ParParR-PR22
❑ 93ZelMasH-1
❑ 93ZelMasoHS-1
❑ 94HalFT-9
❑ 94ParMisL-90
❑ 94ParMisL-173
❑ 94ParTalB-124
❑ 94ParTalB-174
❑ 95Par66-44
❑ 95Par66Coi-44
❑ 97PinBee-62
❑ 97PinBeeGOA-62
❑ 97PinBeeGP-62
**Bathgate, Frank**
❑ 51LavDaiS-89
**Batkiewicz, Jozef**
❑ 79PanSti-126
**Battaglia, Bates**
❑ 98BowBesMIF-F1
❑ 98BowBesMIFAR-F1
❑ 98BowBesMIFR-F1
❑ 98SP AutSotTG-BB
❑ 98SPxFin-17
❑ 98SPxFin-137
❑ 98SPxFinR-17
❑ 98SPxFinR-137
❑ 98SPxFinS-17
❑ 98SPxFinS-137
❑ 98SSASotT-BB
❑ 98UC-38
❑ 98UD ChoPCR-38
❑ 98UD ChoR-38
❑ 98UD3-17
❑ 98UD3-77
❑ 98UD3-137
❑ 98UD3DieC-17
❑ 98UD3DieC-77
❑ 98UD3DieC-137
❑ 98UppDec-62
❑ 98UppDecE-62
❑ 98UppDecE1o1-62
❑ 98UppDecGR-62
❑ 99Pac-67
❑ 99PacCop-67
❑ 99PacGol-67
❑ 99PacIceB-67
❑ 99PacPreD-67
❑ 99UppDecM-43
❑ 99UppDecMGS-43
❑ 99UppDecMSS-43
❑ 99UppDecMSS-43
**Battaglia, Doug**
❑ 98ChaChe-3
❑ 98ChaChe-22
**Battaglia, Jon**
❑ 97PacOme-38
❑ 97PacOmeC-38
❑ 97PacOmeDG-38
❑ 97PacOmeEG-38
❑ 97PacOmeG-38
❑ 97PacOmeIB-38
**Batten, John**
❑ 95FliGen-5
**Batters, Greg**
❑ 84VicCou-2
❑ 90KnoChe-117
**Batters, Jeff**
❑ 92PeoRivC-1
❑ 93PeoRiv-2
**Battersby, Brooke**
❑ 91AirCanSJHL-E1
❑ 92MPSPhoSJHL-10
**Battice, John**
❑ 86KinCan-25
❑ 87KinCan-25
❑ 897thInnSOHL-29
**Batyrshin, Ruslan**
❑ 95PhoRoa-1
**Bauer, Bobby**
❑ 34BeeGro1P-1
❑ 36ProvRed-1
❑ 39OPCV3011-99
❑ 91BruSpoAL-36
**Bauer, Collin**
❑ 88SasBla-13
❑ 89SasBla-25
❑ 90ProAHLIHL-238
❑ 91ProAHLCHL-220
**Bauer, Lubomir**
❑ 96CzeAPSE-73
**Bauer, Reinhold**
❑ 72SweSemWC-113
**Bauer, Stephan**
❑ 94GerDELE-340
❑ 95GerDELE-296
**Bauman, Gary**
❑ 65QueAce-2
❑ 68OPC-145
**Baumgartner, Gregor**
❑ 97BowCHL-151
❑ 97BowCHLAu-31
❑ 97BowCHLOPC-151
❑ 99QuePeeWHWCCS-20
**Baumgartner, Ken**
❑ 84PriAlbRS-1
❑ 88KinSmo-2
❑ 88ProAHL-192
❑ 89NewHavN-1
❑ 90OPC-414
❑ 90ProSet-178
❑ 90Sco-265
❑ 90ScoCan-265
❑ 90UppDec-439
❑ 90UppDecF-439
❑ 91OPC-316
❑ 91Pin-239
❑ 91PinFre-239
❑ 91ProSet-432
❑ 91ProSetFre-432
❑ 91ScoAme-148
❑ 91ScoCan-148
❑ 91Top-316
❑ 91UppDec-402
❑ 91UppDecF-402
❑ 92MapLeaK-4
❑ 92PanSti-85
❑ 92PanStiFre-85
❑ 92Par-413
❑ 92ParEmel-413
❑ 92Sco-35
❑ 92ScoCan-35
❑ 92StaClu-103
❑ 92Top-217
❑ 92TopGol-217G
❑ 92Ult-416
❑ 93Par-207
❑ 93ParEmel-207
❑ 93Pow-448
❑ 93ScoBla-17
❑ 93Ult-429
❑ 93UppDecNR-29
❑ 94BeAPla-R140
❑ 94BeAPla-R166
❑ 94BeAPSig-149
❑ 94Don-288
❑ 94MapLeaG-2
❑ 94MapLeaK-2
❑ 94MapLeaPP-19
❑ 94StaClu-98
❑ 94StaCluFDI-98
❑ 94StaCluMOMS-98
❑ 94StaCluSTWC-98
❑ 94Ult-212
❑ 95ParInt-476
❑ 95ParIntEl-476
❑ 95PlaOneoOne-201
❑ 95PlaOneoOne-314
❑ 96BeAPAut-32
❑ 96BeAPAutSil-32
❑ 96BeAPla-32
❑ 96Don-9
❑ 96DonPrePro-9
❑ 96Duc-12
❑ 96PlaOneoOne-393
❑ 96Sco-206
❑ 96ScoArtPro-206
❑ 96ScoDeaCAP-206
❑ 96ScoGolB-206
❑ 96ScoSpeAP-206
❑ 97PacInvNRB-1
❑ 97ScoBru-15
❑ 97ScoBruPla-15
❑ 97ScoBruPre-15
❑ 98Be A PPA-160
❑ 98Be A PPAA-160
❑ 98Be A PPAAF-160
❑ 98Be A PPSE-160
❑ 98Be APG-160
❑ 980-PChr-201
❑ 980-PChrR-201
❑ 98Pac-70
❑ 98PacIceB-70
❑ 98PacRed-70
❑ 98Top-201
❑ 98TopO-P-201
**Baumgartner, Nolan**
❑ 93KamBla-1
❑ 94Cla-9
❑ 94ClaCHLP-CP6
❑ 94ClaDraGol-9
❑ 94Fin-148
❑ 94FinRef-148
❑ 94FinSupTW-148
❑ 94LeaLimWJC-1
❑ 94Pin-525
❑ 94PinArtP-525
❑ 94PinRinC-525
❑ 94UppDec-505
❑ 94UppDecEleIce-505
❑ 95ClaCHLAS-AS1
❑ 95ClaIceBre-BK20
❑ 95DonCanWJT-3
❑ 95DonEliWJ-4
❑ 95ParInt-491
❑ 95ParIntEl-491
❑ 95SigRoo-25
❑ 95SigRooAB2-B4
❑ 95SigRooSig-25
❑ 95SlaMemC-4
❑ 95SP-174
❑ 95TopCanWJ-11CJ
❑ 95UppDec-353
❑ 95UppDecEleIce-353
❑ 95UppDecEleIceG-353
❑ 96ClaIceBreDC-BK20
❑ 96Don-235
❑ 96DonPrePro-235
❑ 96Fle-121
❑ 96FlePic-168
❑ 96LeaGolR-6
❑ 96MetUni-169
❑ 96Pin-245
❑ 96PinArtP-245
❑ 96PinFoi-245
❑ 96PinPreS-245
❑ 96PinRinC-245
❑ 96PorPir-5
❑ 96Sco-251
❑ 96ScoArtPro-251
❑ 96ScoDeaCAP-251
❑ 96ScoGolB-251
❑ 96ScoSpeAP-251
❑ 96SkyImp-144
❑ 96Sum-173
❑ 96SumArtP-173
❑ 96SumIce-173
❑ 96SumMet-173
❑ 96SumPreS-173
❑ 98UppDec-387
❑ 98UppDecE-387
❑ 98UppDecE1o1-387
❑ 98UppDecGR-387
❑ 99Pac-450
❑ 99PacCop-450
❑ 99PacGol-450
❑ 99PacIceB-450
❑ 99PacPreD-450
**Baun, Bobby (Bob)**
❑ 44BeeGro2P-378
❑ 57Par-T20
❑ 58Par-15
❑ 59Par-21
❑ 60Par-11

☐ 60ShiCoi-7
☐ 60YorPreP-3
☐ 61Par-11
☐ 61ShiCoi-50
☐ 61YorYelB-1
☐ 62Par-3
☐ 62ShiMetC-19
☐ 63ChePho-4
☐ 63MapLeaWB-1
☐ 63MapLeaWB-2
☐ 63Par-18
☐ 63Par-78
☐ 63TorSta-3
☐ 63YorWhiB-7
☐ 64BeeGro3P-153A
☐ 64BeeGro3P-153B
☐ 64CocCap-104
☐ 64Top-57
☐ 64TorSta-3
☐ 65Coc-103
☐ 65MapLeaWB-2
☐ 65Top-13
☐ 66Top-83
☐ 68OPC-24
☐ 68ShiCoi-46
☐ 68Top-24
☐ 69OPC-57
☐ 69OPCFou-1
☐ 69Top-57
☐ 70ColSta-66
☐ 70DadCoo-3
☐ 70EssPowPla-32
☐ 70OPC-223
☐ 70SarProSta-64
☐ 70Top-24
☐ 71FriLay-6
☐ 71LetActR-9
☐ 71MapLeaP-1
☐ 71OPC-196
☐ 71SarProSta-196
☐ 71TorSun-254
☐ 72MapLeaP-1
☐ 72OPC-66
☐ 72SarProSta-199
☐ 72Top-134
☐ 91Kra-28
☐ 91Kra-78
☐ 91UltOriS-30
☐ 91UltOriS-93
☐ 91UltOriSF-30
☐ 91UltOriSF-93
☐ 92ParParR-PR12
☐ 94ParMisL-123
☐ 94ParTalR-120
☐ 95Par66-117
☐ 95Par66Coi-117

**Baustad, Colin**
☐ 94CenHocL-91

**Bautin, Sergei**
☐ 920PCPre-84
☐ 92Par-435
☐ 92ParEmel-435
☐ 92RusStaRA-16
☐ 92RusStaRA-2
☐ 92Ult-440
☐ 92UppDec-337
☐ 92UppDec-499
☐ 93Don-378
☐ 93JetRuf-2
☐ 93Lea-242
☐ 930PCPre-332
☐ 930PCPreG-332
☐ 93Pin-197
☐ 93PinCan-197
☐ 93Pow-268
☐ 93Sco-351
☐ 93ScoCan-351
☐ 93TopPre-332
☐ 93TopPreG-332
☐ 93Ult-10
☐ 93UppDec-514

**Bavis, Mark**
☐ 93Cla-60
☐ 94ClaAut-NNO
☐ 95SouCarS-10

**Bavis, Mike**
☐ 93RochAmeKod-4
☐ 94ClaProP-66

**Bawa, Robin**
☐ 85KamBla-1
☐ 86KamBla-2
☐ 88ProAHL-27
☐ 89ProAHL-99
☐ 90ProAHLIHL-536
☐ 91ProAHLCHL-597
☐ 92HamCan-2
☐ 93StaClu-445
☐ 93StaCluFDI-445
☐ 93StaCluO-445
☐ 95ColEdgI-187

**Bawlf, Nick**
☐ 10C56-18

**Baxter, Jim**
☐ 77KalWin-15

**Baxter, Paul**
☐ 76NordMarA-1
☐ 76NordPos-2
☐ 79OPC-372
☐ 820PC-238
☐ 82PosCer-15
☐ 83PenHeiP-1
☐ 83Vac-1
☐ 85FlamRedRP-1
☐ 86FlamRedR-1
☐ 90FlamIGA-1

☐ 91FlamIGA-27
☐ 93BlaCok-28
☐ 95St.JohF-2

**Bayes, Rickie**
☐ 69SweHocS-347

**Bayliss, Steve**
☐ 82VicCou-1
☐ 83VicCou-3

**Bayrack, Mike**
☐ 95LetHur-1

**Bazin, Norm**
☐ 94BirBul-2

**Bazinet, Mario**
☐ 84ChiSag-2

**Bazinet, Michael**
☐ 907thInnSQMJHL-217

**Beadle, Steve**
☐ 90ProAHLIHL-37
☐ 95FliGen-14

**Beagan, Beth**
☐ 94ClaWomOH-W36

**Beagle, Chad**
☐ 95SwiCurB-2

**Beals, Darren**
☐ 86KitRan-10
☐ 87KitRan-10
☐ 88ProAHL-85

**Beals, Kevin**
☐ 91FerStaB-4

**Beamin, Ryan**
☐ 92BriColJHL-92

**Bean, Tim**
☐ 83BelBul-26
☐ 84BelBul-15
☐ 89ProAHL-116
☐ 90NewSai-2
☐ 90ProAHLIHL-163

**Bear, Darren**
☐ 92NorDakFS-2

**Bear, Robby**
☐ 91AirCanSJHL-D24

**Bear, Smokey the**
☐ 88CapSmo-24

**Beardsmore, Colin**
☐ 95Sla-62

**Beardy, Vern**
☐ 99WicThu-1

**Beaton, Frank**
☐ 81IndChe-2

**Beaton, Jason**
☐ 897thInnSOHL-168
☐ 907thInnSOHL-302

**Beaton, Kevan**
☐ 85SwePanS-181

**Beattie, Donald**
☐ 52JunBluT-56

**Beattie, Red**
☐ 28V1282PauC-46
☐ 33V129-35
☐ 33V357IceK-29
☐ 34BeeGro1P-2
☐ 34DiaMatS-3
☐ 38BruGarMS-1

**Beattie, Scott**
☐ 91AirCanSJHL-B25
☐ 96GerDELE-201

**Beaubien, Frederick**
☐ 95ColEdgI-181
☐ 95PhoRoa-2

**Beaucage, Marc**
☐ 907thInnSQMJHL-47
☐ 917thInnSQMJHL-231

**Beauchamp, Denis**
☐ 907thInnSQMJHL-262
☐ 917thInnSQMJHL-263
☐ 94CenHocL-37

**Beauchemin, Francois**
☐ 98BowCHL-92
☐ 98BowCHLL-153
☐ 98BowCHLAuB-A13
☐ 98BowCHLAuG-A13
☐ 98BowCHLAuS-A13
☐ 98BowCHLGA-92
☐ 98BowCHLGA-153
☐ 98BowCHLOI-92
☐ 98BowCHLOI-153
☐ 98BowChrC-92
☐ 98BowChrCGA-92
☐ 98BowChrCGA-153
☐ 98BowChrCGAR-92
☐ 98BowChrCGAR-153
☐ 98BowChrCOI-92
☐ 98BowChrCOI-153
☐ 98BowChrCOIR-92
☐ 98BowChrCOIR-153
☐ 98BowChrCR-92
☐ 98BowChrCR-153

**Beauchesne, Serge**
☐ 92BriColJHL-197

**Beaudette, Dan**
☐ 91CinCyc-1

**Beaudin, Jeff**
☐ 91JohChi-11
☐ 92DalFre-3
☐ 93DalFre-2
☐ 94CenHocL-3

**Beaudin, Norm**
☐ 70OPC-48
☐ 70Top-48
☐ 72OPC-290
☐ 72SluCupWHA-9
☐ 74OPCWHA-11

**Beaudoin, Carl**

☐ 95SlaMemC-60

**Beaudoin, Eric**
☐ 97GueSto-24

**Beaudoin, Nic**
☐ 93DetJrRW-22
☐ 94DetJrRW-24

**Beaudoin, Roger**
☐ 51LavDailSJ-46

**Beaudoin, Serge**
☐ 75RoaPhoWHA-5
☐ 76RoaPhoWHA-1

**Beaufait, Mark**
☐ 93ClaProPo-24
☐ 93Pin-206
☐ 93PinCan-206
☐ 93Pow-498
☐ 93StaCluTUSA-1
☐ 93TopPreTUSA-6
☐ 93Ult-478

**Beaule, Alain**
☐ 94FreNatT-5

**Beaulieu, Corey**
☐ 89ProAHL-286
☐ 97SheSte-22

**Beaulieu, Jonathan**
☐ 96RimOce-1
☐ 96RimOceQPP-1
☐ 97RimOce-9

**Beaulieu, Nick**
☐ 84RicRiv-2
☐ 88ProAHL-83
☐ 89ProIHL-109
☐ 90ProAHLIHL-521

**Beaulne, Richard**
☐ 81SauSteMG-3
☐ 83SauSteMG-3

**Beaupre, Claude**
☐ 52JunBluT-166

**Beaupre, Don**
☐ 80NorStaPos-3
☐ 81NorStaPos-3
☐ 810PC-159
☐ 810PCSti-89
☐ 810PCSti-146
☐ 81Top-W103
☐ 82NorStaPos-2
☐ 820PC-163
☐ 820PCSti-193
☐ 83NorStaPos-3
☐ 830PC-166
☐ 830PCSti-122
☐ 84NorStaPos-2
☐ 840PC-94
☐ 84Top-70
☐ 85IslIsINT-23
☐ 85NorSta7E-4
☐ 85NorStaPos-2
☐ 850PC-142
☐ 85Top-142
☐ 86NorSta7E-5
☐ 860PC-89
☐ 86Top-89
☐ 87NorStaPos-4
☐ 870PC-132
☐ 870PCSti-51
☐ 87PanSti-289
☐ 87Top-132
☐ 880PC-42
☐ 880PCSti-196
☐ 88PanSti-84
☐ 88Top-42
☐ 89CapKod-33
☐ 89CapTealss-1
☐ 90Bow-72
☐ 90BowTif-72
☐ 90CapKod-1
☐ 90CapPos-1
☐ 90CapSmo-1
☐ 900PC-253
☐ 900PCBoxB-O
☐ 90PanSti-158
☐ 90ProSet-307
☐ 90Sco-215
☐ 90ScoCan-215
☐ 90Top-253
☐ 90TopBoxB-O
☐ 90TopTif-253
☐ 90UppDec-217
☐ 90UppDecF-217
☐ 91Bow-304
☐ 91CapJun5-1
☐ 91CapKod-1
☐ 910PC-505
☐ 91PanSti-201
☐ 91Par-416
☐ 91ParFre-416
☐ 91Pin-148
☐ 91PinFre-148
☐ 91ProSet-257
☐ 91ProSet-601
☐ 91ProSetFre-257
☐ 91ProSetFre-601
☐ 91ProSetPla-139
☐ 91ScoAme-185
☐ 91ScoCan-185
☐ 91StaClu-246
☐ 91Top-505
☐ 91UppDec-197
☐ 91UppDecF-197
☐ 92Bow-222
☐ 92Bow-297
☐ 92CapKod-2

☐ 92Kra-26
☐ 92McDUppD-15
☐ 920PC-28
☐ 92PanSti-159
☐ 92PanStiFre-159
☐ 92Par-197
☐ 92ParEmel-197
☐ 92Pin-48
☐ 92Pin-268
☐ 92PinFre-48
☐ 92PinFre-268
☐ 92ProSet-206
☐ 92Sco-320
☐ 92ScoCan-320
☐ 92SeaPat-49
☐ 92StaClu-270
☐ 92Top-195
☐ 92TopGol-195G
☐ 92Ult-229
☐ 92UppDec-23
☐ 92UppDec-310
☐ 930PCPre-304
☐ 930PCPreG-304
☐ 93PanSti-33
☐ 93Par-225
☐ 93ParEmel-225
☐ 93Pin-292
☐ 93PinCan-292
☐ 93Pow-463
☐ 93Sco-58
☐ 93ScoCan-58
☐ 93StaClu-71
☐ 93StaCluFDI-71
☐ 93StaCluFDIO-71
☐ 93StaCluO-71
☐ 93TopPre-304
☐ 93TopPreG-304
☐ 93Ult-28
☐ 93UppDec-123
☐ 94CanGamNHLP-298
☐ 94EASpo-156
☐ 94Fle-141
☐ 94Kra-32
☐ 94Pin-355
☐ 94PinArtP-355
☐ 94PinRinC-355
☐ 94Sel-12
☐ 94SelGol-12
☐ 94SenBelM-2
☐ 94SP-82
☐ 94SPDieCut-82
☐ 94Ult-387
☐ 94UppDec-389
☐ 94UppDecEleIce-389
☐ 94UppDecSPI-SP143
☐ 94UppDecSPIDC-SP143
☐ 95BeAPla-96
☐ 95BeAPSig-S96
☐ 95BeAPSigDC-S96
☐ 95CanGamNHLP-200
☐ 95ColCho-11
☐ 95ColChoPC-11
☐ 95ColChoPCP-11
☐ 95Don-246
☐ 95Emo-121
☐ 95Kra-40
☐ 95Lea-52
☐ 95Met-102
☐ 95ParInt-152
☐ 95ParIntEl-152
☐ 95Pin-87
☐ 95PinArtP-87
☐ 95PinRinC-87
☐ 95PlaOneoOne-177
☐ 95Sco-246
☐ 95ScoBlaIce-246
☐ 95ScoBlaIceAP-246
☐ 95SelCer-104
☐ 95SelCerMG-104
☐ 95SkyImp-116
☐ 95StaClu-44
☐ 95StaCluMOMS-44
☐ 95Sum-35
☐ 95SumArtP-35
☐ 95SumIce-35
☐ 95Top-142
☐ 95TopOPCI-142
☐ 95Ult-109
☐ 95UltGolM-109
☐ 95UppDec-402
☐ 95UppDecEleIce-402
☐ 95UppDecEleIceG-402
☐ 95UppDecSpeE-SE61
☐ 95UppDecSpeEdiG-SE61
☐ 96ColCho-264
☐ 96PlaOneoOne-381
☐ 96St.JohML-1

**Beaupre, Martin**
☐ 907thInnSQMJHL-41
☐ 917thInnSMC-93
☐ 917thInnSQMJHL-94

**Beauregard, Danny**
☐ 907thInnSQMJHL-31
☐ 917thInnSMC-39
☐ 917thInnSQMJHL-89

**Beauregard, Mario**
☐ 77GraVic-1

**Beauregard, Stephane**
☐ 88ProAHL-183
☐ 89ProIHL-139
☐ 90JetIGA-4
☐ 900PC-223
☐ 90ProSet-648
☐ 90Sco-282
☐ 90ScoCan-282

☐ 90Top-223
☐ 90TopTif-223
☐ 90UppDec-415
☐ 90UppDecF-415
☐ 91JetIGA-2
☐ 91JetPanTS-3
☐ 91Par-426
☐ 91ParFre-426
☐ 91ScoCan-638
☐ 92Bow-405
☐ 92FlyJCP-2
☐ 92FlyUppDS-21
☐ 920PCPre-88
☐ 92Sco-402
☐ 92ScoCan-402
☐ 92StaClu-304
☐ 92Top-62
☐ 92TopGol-62G
☐ 92Ult-369
☐ 92UppDec-536
☐ 93JetRuf-3
☐ 93Ult-451
☐ 95ColEdgI-188
☐ 96ColEdgFL-26

**Beaurivage, Marc**
☐ 88RivDu R-2

**Beausoleil, Luc**
☐ 94CenHocL-92

**Beauvis, Eric**
☐ 907thInnSQMJHL-188
☐ 917thInnSQMJHL-57

**Beazley, Paul**
☐ 94WinSpi-4

**Bechard, Jerome**
☐ 90ProAHLHL-356
☐ 91ProAHLCHL-363
☐ 92BirBul-13
☐ 93BirBul-13
☐ 94BirBul-13
☐ 94ClaProP-229
☐ 95BirBul-14

**Beck, Barry**
☐ 77RocCokCan-2
☐ 78OPC-121
☐ 78Top-121
☐ 79OPC-35
☐ 79Top-35
☐ 80OPC-90
☐ 80Top-90
☐ 81OPC-220
☐ 81OPCSti-168
☐ 81PosSta-14
☐ 81Top-3
☐ 81Top-E124
☐ 82McDSti-27
☐ 82OPC-219
☐ 82OPC-220
☐ 82OPCSti-135
☐ 82PosCer-13
☐ 83OPC-241
☐ 83OPCSti-210
☐ 83PufSti-20
☐ 84KelAccD-5A
☐ 84KelAccD-5B
☐ 84OPC-140
☐ 84OPCSti-100
☐ 84Top-105
☐ 857ECreCar-13
☐ 85OPC-138
☐ 85OPCSti-82
☐ 85Top-138
☐ 89KinSmo-9

**Beck, Brad**
☐ 88ProIHL-19
☐ 90RicRen-13
☐ 91ProAHLCHL-429

**Beck, Rob**
☐ 91AirCanSJHL-A40
☐ 91AirCanSJHLAS-13
☐ 92MPSPhoSJHL-22

**Becker, Barry**
☐ 917thInnSWHL-228

**Becker, Jason**
☐ 917thInnSWHL-118
☐ 91SasBla-21

**Becker, Troy**
☐ 91BriColJHL-10

**Beckett, Bob**
☐ 56QueAce-2
☐ 94ParMisL-13

**Bedard, Daniel**
☐ 84ChiSag-3

**Bedard, Gamill**
☐ 52JunBluT-41

**Bedard, Jim**
☐ 44BeeGro2P-79
☐ 78OPC-243
☐ 78Top-243
☐ 79OPC-62
☐ 79Top-62

**Bedard, Martin**
☐ 96RimOce-2
☐ 96RimOceQPP-2

**Bedard, Roger**
☐ 51LavDaiS-115
☐ 52St.LawS-105

**Beddoes, Clayton**
☐ 91LakSupSL-8
☐ 94Cla-50
☐ 94ClaDraGol-50
☐ 95Bow-102

☐ 95BowAllFoi-102
☐ 95ColEdgI-59
☐ 95ParInt-286
☐ 95ParIntEl-286
☐ 98GerDELE-112

**Bednar, Jared**
☐ 917thInnSWHL-11
☐ 93HunBli-4
☐ 94HunBli-3
☐ 95SouCarS-18
☐ 96SouCarS-25
☐ 96St.JohML-2

**Bednar, Jaroslav**
☐ 95CzeAPSE-145

**Bednar, Vladimir**
☐ 69SweHocS-21
☐ 69SweWorC-9
☐ 69SweWorC-76
☐ 69SweWorC-145
☐ 69SweWorC-156
☐ 70SweHocS-247
☐ 72SweSemWC-41
☐ 74SweSemHVS-68

**Bednarski, John**
☐ 76OPCNHL-231
☐ 76Top-231
☐ 88OilTenAnn-125
☐ 89NewHavN-2

**Beech, Kris**
☐ 98SP Aut-123
☐ 98SP AutSotTG-KB
☐ 98SSASotT-KB
☐ 98UppDec-400
☐ 98UppDecE-400
☐ 98UppDecE1o1-400
☐ 98UppDecGR-400
☐ 99SP AutPS-123

**Beers, Bob**
☐ 89ProAHL-68
☐ 90Bow-34
☐ 90BowTif-34
☐ 90BruSpoA-1
☐ 900PC-113
☐ 90ProAHLIHL-140
☐ 90Sco-385
☐ 90ScoCan-385
☐ 90Top-113
☐ 90TopTif-113
☐ 90UppDec-125
☐ 90UppDecF-125
☐ 91BruSpoA-2
☐ 91Pin-326
☐ 91PinFre-326
☐ 91ProSet-520
☐ 91ProSetFre-520
☐ 91UppDec-490
☐ 91UppDecF-490
☐ 92LigShe-2
☐ 92Par-401
☐ 92ParEmel-401
☐ 92Ult-407
☐ 92Don-426
☐ 930PCPre-44
☐ 930PCPreG-44
☐ 93PanSti-217
☐ 93Pin-186
☐ 93PinCan-186
☐ 93Pow-227
☐ 93Pow-338
☐ 93Sco-369
☐ 93Sco-575
☐ 93ScoCan-369
☐ 93ScoCan-575
☐ 93ScoGol-575
☐ 93TopPre-44
☐ 93TopPreG-44
☐ 93Ult-18
☐ 94EASpo-127
☐ 94Lea-43
☐ 94Lea-537
☐ 940PCPre-41
☐ 940PCPreSE-41
☐ 94Pin-419
☐ 94PinArtP-419
☐ 94PinRinC-419
☐ 94Sco-7
☐ 94ScoGol-7
☐ 94ScoHobS-7
☐ 94ScoPla-7
☐ 94ScoPlaTS-7
☐ 94StaCluST-8
☐ 94TopPre-41
☐ 94TopPreSE-41
☐ 94Ult-69
☐ 95ColCho-107
☐ 95ColChoPC-107
☐ 95ColChoPCP-107
☐ 95UppDecEleIce-412
☐ 95UppDecEleIceG-412
☐ 96ProBru-34
☐ 97PacInvNRB-9

**Beers, Ed**
☐ 830PC-76
☐ 830PCSti-141
☐ 83Vac-2
☐ 840PC-219
☐ 840PC-354
☐ 840PCSti-243
☐ 84Top-24
☐ 85FlamRedRP-2
☐ 850PC-144
☐ 850PCSti-214
☐ 85Top-144
☐ 860PC-238

**Begg, Gary**

☐ 69SweHocS-348
☐ 69SweWorC-16
☐ 69SweWorC-191

**Begin, Steve**
☐ 97BowCHL-58
☐ 97BowCHLOPC-58
☐ 97PacPar-25
☐ 97PacParC-25
☐ 97PacParDG-25
☐ 97PacParEG-25
☐ 97PacParIB-25
☐ 97PacParRed-25
☐ 97PacParSil-25
☐ 98UC-267
☐ 98UD ChoPCR-267
☐ 98UD ChoR-267
☐ 98UppDec-49
☐ 98UppDecE-49
☐ 98UppDecE1o1-49
☐ 98UppDecGR-49
☐ 99QuePeeWHWCCS-13

**Behan, Patrik**
☐ 95SloPeeWT-2

**Behm, Daniel**
☐ 91SweSemC-162

**Behrend, Marc**
☐ 84JetPol-3

**Bejbom, Hans**
☐ 69SweHocS-220

**Bejegard, Peder**
☐ 93SweSemC-22

**Bejemark, Peter**
☐ 71SweHocS-348

**Bekkering, Justin**
☐ 96SasBla-3

**Bekkers, John**
☐ 82RegPar-12
☐ 83RegPar-12

**Bela, Michal**
☐ 95SloPeeWT-3

**Belak, Wade**
☐ 93SasBla-4
☐ 94Cla-11
☐ 94ClaDraGol-11
☐ 95Ima-20
☐ 95ImaGol-20
☐ 95SasBla-4
☐ 95SigRoo-18
☐ 95SigRooSig-18
☐ 97Don-222
☐ 97DonPreProG-222
☐ 97DonPrePros-222
☐ 97UppDec-186
☐ 98Pac-156
☐ 98PacIceB-156
☐ 98PacOme-66
☐ 98PacOmeODI-66
☐ 98PacOmeR-66
☐ 98PacRed-156
☐ 98PxFin-25
☐ 98PxFinR-25
☐ 98PxFinS-25
☐ 98UppDec-252
☐ 98UppDecE-252
☐ 98UppDecE1o1-252
☐ 98UppDecGR-252
☐ 99UppDecM-33
☐ 99UppDecMGS-33
☐ 99UppDecMSS-33

**Belanger, Chris**
☐ 92WesMic-1
☐ 93TolSto-10
☐ 94ClaProP-246

**Belanger, Dominic**
☐ 917thInnSOHL-107

**Belanger, Eric**
☐ 97BowCHL-73
☐ 97RimOce-21

**Belanger, Eric (C)**
☐ 96RimOceU-2
☐ 97BowCHLOPC-25

**Belanger, Eric (LW)**
☐ 96RimOceU-1

**Belanger, Francois**
☐ 907thInnSQMJHL-32
☐ 917thInnSMC-40

**Belanger, Hugo**
☐ 92ClaKro-2
☐ 94ClaProP-147
☐ 94IndIce-1

**Belanger, Jesse**
☐ 90ProAHLIHL-71
☐ 91ProAHLCHL-85
☐ 92FreCan-1
☐ 92Par-488
☐ 92ParEmel-488
☐ 93ClaProPBC-BC11
☐ 93ClaProPro-115
☐ 93Don-123
☐ 93Lea-278
☐ 930PCPre-451
☐ 930PCPreG-451
☐ 93Par-346
☐ 93ParCalC-C15
☐ 93ParCalCG-C15
☐ 93ParEmel-346
☐ 93Pow-89
☐ 93PowRooS-2
☐ 93Sco-454
☐ 93Sco-585
☐ 93ScoCan-454
☐ 93ScoCan-585
☐ 93ScoGol-585

❑ 93TopPre-451
❑ 93TopPreG-451
❑ 93Ult-320
❑ 94CanGamNHLP-368
❑ 94Don-321
❑ 94Fla-63
❑ 94Fle-77
❑ 94Lea-145
❑ 94LeaLim-19
❑ 94OPCFinIns-12
❑ 94OPCPre-197
❑ 94OPCPre-544
❑ 94OPCPreSE-197
❑ 94OPCPreSE-545
❑ 94PanPop-5
❑ 94Par-86
❑ 94Par-284
❑ 94ParGol-86
❑ 94ParGol-284
❑ 94ParVin-V31
❑ 94Pin-122
❑ 94PinArtP-122
❑ 94PinRinC-122
❑ 94Sco-257
❑ 94ScoGol-257
❑ 94ScoPla-257
❑ 94ScoPlaTS-257
❑ 94StaClu-63
❑ 94StaCluFDI-63
❑ 94StaCluMOMS-63
❑ 94StaCluSTWC-63
❑ 94TopPre-197
❑ 94TopPre-544
❑ 94TopPreSE-197
❑ 94TopPreSE-545
❑ 94Ult-79
❑ 94UppDec-72
❑ 94UppDecEleIce-72
❑ 94UppDecSPI-SP119
❑ 94UppDecSPIDC-SP119
❑ 95BeAPla-143
❑ 95BeAPSig-S143
❑ 95BeAPSigDC-S143
❑ 95CanGamNHLP-114
❑ 95ColCho-66
❑ 95ColChoPC-66
❑ 95ColChoPCP-66
❑ 95Don-204
❑ 95Emo-69
❑ 95Kra-59
❑ 95Lea-62
❑ 95ParInt-87
❑ 95ParIntEl-87
❑ 95Pin-18
❑ 95PinArtP-18
❑ 95PinRinC-18
❑ 95PlaOneoOne-40
❑ 95PlaOneoOne-153
❑ 95Sco-155
❑ 95ScoBlaIce-155
❑ 95ScoBlaIceAP-155
❑ 95SkyImp-67
❑ 95StaClu-133
❑ 95StaCluMOMS-133
❑ 95Sum-20
❑ 95SumArtP-20
❑ 95SumIce-20
❑ 95Top-159
❑ 95TopOPCI-159
❑ 95Ult-60
❑ 95UltGolM-60
❑ 95UppDec-209
❑ 95UppDecEleIce-209
❑ 95UppDecEleIceG-209
❑ 96Don-70
❑ 96DonPrePro-70
❑ 96PlaOneoOne-339
❑ 96Sco-222
❑ 96ScoArtPro-222
❑ 96ScoDeaCAP-222
❑ 96ScoGolB-222
❑ 96ScoSpeAP-222

**Belanger, Ken**

❑ 917thInnSOHL-312
❑ 92Ott672A-1
❑ 93GueSto-14
❑ 94St.JohML-2
❑ 95St.JohML-2
❑ 96KenTho-1
❑ 97Be A PPAD-145
❑ 97Be A PPAPD-145
❑ 97BeAPla-145
❑ 97BeAPlaAut-145
❑ 97Pac-351
❑ 97PacCop-351
❑ 97PacEmeGre-351
❑ 97PacIceB-351
❑ 97PacRed-351
❑ 97PacSil-351
❑ 97UppDec-190
❑ 98PacOmeH-11
❑ 98PacOmeODI-11
❑ 98PacOmeR-11

**Belanger, Roger**

❑ 83KinCan-7

**Belanger, Yves**

❑ 76OPCNHL-168
❑ 76Top-168
❑ 77OPCNHL-367
❑ 78OPC-44
❑ 78Top-44

**Belecki, Brent**

❑ 98BowCHL-41
❑ 98BowCHL-162
❑ 98BowCHLGA-41
❑ 98BowCHLGA-162
❑ 98BowCHLOI-41
❑ 98BowCHLOI-162
❑ 98BowChrC-41
❑ 98BowChrC-162
❑ 98BowChrCGA-41
❑ 98BowChrCGA-162
❑ 98BowChrCGAR-41
❑ 98BowChrCGAR-162
❑ 98BowChrCOI-41
❑ 98BowChrCOI-162
❑ 98BowChrCOIR-41
❑ 98BowChrCOIR-162
❑ 98BowChrCR-41
❑ 98BowChrCR-162

**Belfour, Ed**

❑ 88BlaCok-1
❑ 88ProIHL-95
❑ 90BlaCok-16
❑ 90Bow-7
❑ 90BowTif-7
❑ 90ProSet-598
❑ 90ScoRoo-103T
❑ 90UppDec-55
❑ 90UppDecF-55
❑ 91BlaCok-1
❑ 91Bow-390
❑ 91Gil-18
❑ 91OPC-4
❑ 91OPC-20
❑ 91OPC-263
❑ 91OPC-271
❑ 91OPC-288
❑ 91OPC-425
❑ 91OPC-430
❑ 91OPC-518
❑ 91OPC-519
❑ 91OPCPre-19
❑ 91PanSti-9
❑ 91PanSti-337
❑ 91Par-30
❑ 91Par-218
❑ 91ParFre-30
❑ 91ParFre-218
❑ 91Pin-127
❑ 91Pin-388
❑ 91Pin-400
❑ 91PinFre-127
❑ 91PinFre-388
❑ 91PinFre-400
❑ 91ProSet-43
❑ 91ProSet-321
❑ 91ProSet-600
❑ 91ProSetFre-43
❑ 91ProSetFre-321
❑ 91ProSetFre-600
❑ 91ProSetNHLAS-AC1
❑ 91ProSetNHLSA-AC19
❑ 91ProSetPla-26
❑ 91ScoAme-290
❑ 91ScoAme-348
❑ 91ScoAme-410
❑ 91ScoAme-411
❑ 91ScoAme-430
❑ 91ScoAme-431
❑ 91ScoAme-433
❑ 91ScoCan-300
❑ 91ScoCan-301
❑ 91ScoCan-320
❑ 91ScoCan-321
❑ 91ScoCan-323
❑ 91ScoCan-378
❑ 91ScoCan-510
❑ 91ScoFan-6
❑ 91ScoHotC-9
❑ 91ScoNat-6
❑ 91ScoNatCWC-6
❑ 91ScoYouS-32
❑ 91StaClu-333
❑ 91StaPicH-20
❑ 91SweSemWCS-53
❑ 91Top-4
❑ 91Top-20
❑ 91Top-263
❑ 91Top-271
❑ 91Top-288
❑ 91Top-425
❑ 91Top-518
❑ 91Top-519
❑ 91TopBowPS-5
❑ 91UppDec-39
❑ 91UppDec-81
❑ 91UppDec-164
❑ 91UppDec-625
❑ 91UppDecAWH-AW2
❑ 91UppDecAWH-AW4
❑ 91UppDecAWH-AW7
❑ 91UppDecF-39
❑ 91UppDecF-81
❑ 91UppDecF-164
❑ 91UppDecF-625
❑ 92Bow-90
❑ 92Bow-199
❑ 92Hig5Pre-P6
❑ 92Hig5Pre-*P6
❑ 92Kra-36
❑ 92McDUppD-1
❑ 92OPC-81
❑ 92PanSti-3
❑ 92PanSti-284
❑ 92PanStiFre-3
❑ 92PanStiFre-284
❑ 92Par-28
❑ 92Par-461
❑ 92ParEmel-28
❑ 92ParEmel-461
❑ 92Pin-118
❑ 92Pin-265
❑ 92PinFre-118
❑ 92PinFre-265
❑ 92PinTeaP-1
❑ 92PinTeaPF-1
❑ 92ProSet-33
❑ 92Sco-178
❑ 92ScoCan-178
❑ 92ScoYouS-25
❑ 92SeaPat-3
❑ 92StaClu-243
❑ 92StaClu-333
❑ 92Top-22
❑ 92TopGol-22G
❑ 92Ult-32
❑ 92UltAllS-9
❑ 92UppDec-203
❑ 93BlaCok-14
❑ 93Don-64
❑ 93HigLinGG-2
❑ 93KenStaLA-1
❑ 93KenStaLC-1
❑ 93Kra-1
❑ 93Lea-62
❑ 93Lea-175
❑ 93LeaGolAS-10
❑ 93LeaPaiWar-6
❑ 93McDUppD-H6
❑ 93OPCPre-60
❑ 93OPCPre-95
❑ 93OPCPreBG-16
❑ 93OPCPreG-60
❑ 93OPCPreG-95
❑ 93PanSti-140
❑ 93PanSti-155
❑ 93Par-44
❑ 93ParEmel-44
❑ 93Pin-224
❑ 93Pin-227
❑ 93Pin-255
❑ 93PinAllS-42
❑ 93PinAllSC-42
❑ 93PinCan-224
❑ 93PinCan-227
❑ 93PinCan-255
❑ 93PinTeaP-1
❑ 93PinTeaPC-1
❑ 93Pow-46
❑ 93PowNet-2
❑ 93Sco-70
❑ 93Sco-485
❑ 93ScoCan-70
❑ 93ScoCan-485
❑ 93SeaPat-1
❑ 93StaClu-99
❑ 93StaClu-144
❑ 93StaClu-150
❑ 93StaCluAS-1
❑ 93StaCluFDI-99
❑ 93StaCluFDI-144
❑ 93StaCluFDI-150
❑ 93StaCluFDIO-99
❑ 93StaCluFDIO-144
❑ 93StaCluFDIO-150
❑ 93StaCluO-99
❑ 93StaCluO-144
❑ 93StaCluO-150
❑ 93TopPre-60
❑ 93TopPre-95
❑ 93TopPreBG-14
❑ 93TopPreG-60
❑ 93TopPreG-95
❑ 93Ult-22
❑ 93UltAllS-10
❑ 93UltAwaW-1
❑ 93UppDec-247
❑ 93UppDecAW-AW3
❑ 93UppDecLAS-19
❑ 93UppDecSP-27
❑ 94CanGamNHLP-276
❑ 94Don-275
❑ 94DonDom-7
❑ 94DonIceMas-1
❑ 94DonMasM-1
❑ 94EASpo-30
❑ 94EASpo-187
❑ 94Fin-51
❑ 94FinDivFCC-11
❑ 94FinRef-51
❑ 94FinSupTW-51
❑ 94Fla-31
❑ 94Fle-38
❑ 94FleNet-1
❑ 94HocWit-18
❑ 94Kra-33
❑ 94KraGoaM-1
❑ 94Lea-296
❑ 94LeaCreP-2
❑ 94LeaGolS-7
❑ 94LeaLim-3
❑ 94OPCPre-285
❑ 94OPCPreSE-285
❑ 94Par-41
❑ 94ParGol-41
❑ 94ParSEV-14
❑ 94Pin-42
❑ 94PinArtP-42
❑ 94PinGoaG-GT4
❑ 94PinRinC-42
❑ 94Sco-149
❑ 94ScoGol-149
❑ 94ScoPla-149
❑ 94ScoPlaTS-149
❑ 94Sel-53
❑ 94SelGol-53
❑ 94SP-24
❑ 94SPDieCut-24
❑ 94StaClu-155
❑ 94StaClu-180
❑ 94StaCluFDI-155
❑ 94StaCluFDI-180
❑ 94StaCluMOMS-155
❑ 94StaCluMOMS-180
❑ 94StaCluST-5
❑ 94StaCluSTWC-155
❑ 94StaCluSTWC-180
❑ 94TopPre-285
❑ 94TopPreSE-285
❑ 94Ult-39
❑ 94UppDec-290
❑ 94UppDecEleIce-290
❑ 94UppDecPH-H27
❑ 94UppDecPHEG-H27
❑ 94UppDecPHES-H27
❑ 94UppDecPHG-H27
❑ 94UppDecSPI-SP15
❑ 94UppDecSPIDC-SP15
❑ 95BeAPla-194
❑ 95BeAPSig-S194
❑ 95BeAPSigDC-S194
❑ 95Bow-53
❑ 95BowAllFoi-53
❑ 95CanGamNHLP-20
❑ 95CanGamNHLP-71
❑ 95ColCho-109
❑ 95ColCho-387
❑ 95ColChoPC-109
❑ 95ColChoPC-387
❑ 95ColChoPCP-109
❑ 95ColChoPCP-387
❑ 95Don-108
❑ 95DonBetTP-10
❑ 95DonDom-8
❑ 95DonEli-20
❑ 95DonEliDCS-20
❑ 95DonEliDCU-20
❑ 95DonEliPW-4
❑ 95DonEliPW-P4
❑ 95Emo-27
❑ 95Fin-108
❑ 95FinnSemWC-78
❑ 95FinRef-108
❑ 95ImpSti-23
❑ 95Kra-25
❑ 95Kra-52
❑ 95Lea-329
❑ 95LeaLim-15
❑ 95LeaLimSS-8
❑ 95McDPin-MCD-29
❑ 95Met-23
❑ 95MetIW-2
❑ 95NHLAcePC-5C
❑ 95NHLCooT-14
❑ 95NHLCooT-RP14
❑ 95ParInt-41
❑ 95ParIntEl-41
❑ 95ParIntGP-6
❑ 95ParIntNHLAS-6
❑ 95Pin-153
❑ 95PinArtP-153
❑ 95PinFirS-7
❑ 95PinRinC-153
❑ 95PlaOneoOne-21
❑ 95ProMag-6
❑ 95Sco-87
❑ 95Sco-318
❑ 95ScoBlaIce-87
❑ 95ScoBlaIce-318
❑ 95ScoBlaIceAP-87
❑ 95ScoBlaIceAP-318
❑ 95SelCer-93
❑ 95SelCerMG-93
❑ 95SkyImp-27
❑ 95SkyImpD-9
❑ 95SP-27
❑ 95StaClu-55
❑ 95StaCluM-M5
❑ 95StaCluMO-35
❑ 95StaCluMOMS-55
❑ 95Sum-120
❑ 95SumArtP-120
❑ 95SumIce-120
❑ 95SumInTheCre-4
❑ 95SweGloWC-74
❑ 95Top-130
❑ 95Top-378
❑ 95TopHomGC-HGC24
❑ 95TopMarMPB-378
❑ 95TopOPCI-130
❑ 95TopOPCI-378
❑ 95TopPro-PF16
❑ 95TopSupSki-90
❑ 95TopSupSkiPla-90
❑ 95Ult-30
❑ 95Ult-365
❑ 95UltGolM-30
❑ 95UltPrePadMen-1
❑ 95UltPrePadMenGM-1
❑ 95UppDec-216
❑ 95UppDec-455
❑ 95UppDecEleIce-216
❑ 95UppDecEleIce-455
❑ 95UppDecEleIceG-216
❑ 95UppDecEleIceG-455
❑ 95UppDecPHE-H18
❑ 95UppDecSpeE-SE19
❑ 95UppDecSpeEdiG-SE19
❑ 95UppPreHV-H18
❑ 95Zen-95
❑ 96ColCho-55
❑ 96Don-62
❑ 96DonBetPip-6
❑ 96DonCanI-113
❑ 96DonCanIGPP-113
❑ 96DonCanIOC-6
❑ 96DonCanIRPP-113
❑ 96DonEli-93
❑ 96DonEliDCS-91
❑ 96DonEliPW-7
❑ 96DonEliPW-P7
❑ 96DonPrePro-62
❑ 96Fla-83
❑ 96FlaBluI-83
❑ 96FlaHotG-1
❑ 96Fle-15
❑ 96FlePicDL-8
❑ 96FleVez-1
❑ 96HocGreC-1
❑ 96HocGreCG-1
❑ 96KraUppD-15
❑ 96Lea-199
❑ 96LeaLim-53
❑ 96LeaLimG-53
❑ 96LeaLimStu-6
❑ 96LeaPre-30
❑ 96LeaPreMM-12
❑ 96LeaPreP-199
❑ 96LeaPrePP-30
❑ 96LeaPreVP-14
❑ 96LeaPreVPG-14
❑ 96LeaShuDow-4
❑ 96MetUni-25
❑ 96MetUniAP-1
❑ 96MetUniAPSP-1
❑ 96NHLProSTA-6
❑ 96Pin-94
❑ 96PinArtP-94
❑ 96PinFan-FC20
❑ 96PinFoi-94
❑ 96PinMcD-37
❑ 96PinPreS-94
❑ 96PinRinC-94
❑ 96PlaOneoOne-394
❑ 96Sco-123
❑ 96ScoArtPro-123
❑ 96ScoDeaCAP-123
❑ 96ScoGolB-123
❑ 96ScoNetW-5
❑ 96ScoSpeAP-123
❑ 96ScoSudDea-4
❑ 96SelCer-11
❑ 96SelCerAP-11
❑ 96SelCerBlu-11
❑ 96SelCerFre-6
❑ 96SelCerMB-11
❑ 96SelCerMG-11
❑ 96SelCerMR-11
❑ 96SelCerRed-11
❑ 96SkyImp-17
❑ 96SkyImpZH-1
❑ 96SP-28
❑ 96SPGamFil-GF11
❑ 96StaCluMO-6
❑ 96Sum-97
❑ 96SumArtP-97
❑ 96SumIce-97
❑ 96SumInTheCre-3
❑ 96SumInTheCrePS-3
❑ 96SumMet-97
❑ 96SumPreS-97
❑ 96SweSemW-75
❑ 96SweSemWSG-SG2
❑ 96TeaOut-70
❑ 96TopNHLP-179
❑ 96TopPicOI-179
❑ 96Ult-29
❑ 96UltGolM-29
❑ 96UppDec-234
❑ 96UppDecBD-34
❑ 96UppDecBDG-34
❑ 96UppDecGN-X18
❑ 96UppDecIce-11
❑ 96UppDecIcePar-11
❑ 96UppDecSS-SS22A
❑ 96Zen-25
❑ 96ZenArtP-25
❑ 97Be A PPAD-249
❑ 97Be A PPAPD-249
❑ 97BeAPla-249
❑ 97BeAPlaAut-249
❑ 97BeAPlaSTP-5
❑ 97BeAPlaTAN-3
❑ 97ColCho-216
❑ 97ColChoSta-SQ36
❑ 97ColChoSti-S20
❑ 97Don-164
❑ 97DonCanI-26
❑ 97DonCanIDS-26
❑ 97DonCanINP-22
❑ 97DonCanIPS-26
❑ 97DonEli-102
❑ 97DonEliAsp-102
❑ 97DonEliS-102
❑ 97DonLim-28
❑ 97DonLim-164
❑ 97DonLimExp-28
❑ 97DonLimExp-164
❑ 97DonLimFOTG-33
❑ 97DonPre-54
❑ 97DonPreCG-16
❑ 97DonPreCGP-16
❑ 97DonPreCttC-54
❑ 97DonPreProG-164
❑ 97DonPreProS-164
❑ 97DonPri-71
❑ 97DonPriPG-7
❑ 97DonPriPGP-7
❑ 97DonPriSoA-71
❑ 97Kat-43
❑ 97KatGol-43
❑ 97KatSil-43
❑ 97Lea-87
❑ 97LeaFraMat-87
❑ 97LeaFraMDC-87
❑ 97LeaInt-87
❑ 97LeaIntUI-87
❑ 97Pac-20
❑ 97PacCop-20
❑ 97PacCroR-39
❑ 97PacCroREG-39
❑ 97PacCroRFODC-6
❑ 97PacCroRIB-39
❑ 97PacCroRS-39
❑ 97PacEmeGre-20
❑ 97PacIceB-20
❑ 97PacInTheCLC-19
❑ 97PacInv-123
❑ 97PacInvC-123
❑ 97PacInvEG-123
❑ 97PacInvIB-123
❑ 97PacInvNRB-174
❑ 97PacInvR-123
❑ 97PacInvS-123
❑ 97PacOme-67
❑ 97PacOmeC-67
❑ 97PacOmeDG-67
❑ 97PacOmeEG-67
❑ 97PacOmeG-67
❑ 97PacOmeIB-67
❑ 97PacOmeNSZ-3
❑ 97PacOmeTL-6
❑ 97PacPar-56
❑ 97PacParC-56
❑ 97PacParDG-56
❑ 97PacParEG-56
❑ 97PacParGSL-6
❑ 97PacParIB-56
❑ 97PacParRed-56
❑ 97PacParSil-56
❑ 97PacRed-20
❑ 97PacRev-40
❑ 97PacRev1AGD-9
❑ 97PacRevC-40
❑ 97PacRevE-40
❑ 97PacRevIB-40
❑ 97PacRevR-40
❑ 97PacRevRtSD-6
❑ 97PacRevS-40
❑ 97PacSil-20
❑ 97Pin-51
❑ 97PinArtP-51
❑ 97PinBee-10
❑ 97PinBeeGP-10
❑ 97PinCer-9
❑ 97PinCerMB-9
❑ 97PinCerMG-9
❑ 97PinCerMR-9
❑ 97PinCerR-9
❑ 97PinIns-74
❑ 97PinInsCC-74
❑ 97PinInsEC-74
❑ 97PinInsSto-24
❑ 97PinPrePBB-51
❑ 97PinPrePBC-51
❑ 97PinPrePBM-51
❑ 97PinPrePBY-51
❑ 97PinPrePFC-51
❑ 97PinPrePFM-51
❑ 97PinPrePFY-51
❑ 97PinPrePla-51
❑ 97PinRinC-51
❑ 97PinTotCMPG-9
❑ 97PinTotCPB-9
❑ 97PinTotCPG-9
❑ 97PinTotCPR-9
❑ 97Sco-20
❑ 97ScoArtPro-20
❑ 97ScoGolBla-20
❑ 97ScoNetW-18
❑ 97SP AutI-I13
❑ 97SPAut-44
❑ 97SPAutID-I13
❑ 97SPAutIE-I13
❑ 97Stu-58
❑ 97StuPrePG-58
❑ 97StuPrePS-58
❑ 97UppDec-259
❑ 97UppDecBD-134
❑ 97UppDecBDDD-134
❑ 97UppDecBDQD-134
❑ 97UppDecBDTD-134
❑ 97Zen-49
❑ 97Zen5x7-10
❑ 97ZenChaTC-10
❑ 97ZenGolImp-10
❑ 97ZenSilImp-10
❑ 97ZenZGol-49
❑ 97ZenZSil-49
❑ 98Be A PPA-190
❑ 98Be A PPAA-190
❑ 98Be A PPAAF-190
❑ 98Be A PPAGUSC-S22
❑ 98Be A PPAJ-AS24
❑ 98Be A PPPGUJC-G19
❑ 98Be A PPPPUJC-P6
❑ 98Be A PPSE-190
❑ 98Be APG-190
❑ 98BowBes-34
❑ 98BowBesAR-34
❑ 98BowBesR-34
❑ 98Fin-3
❑ 98FinNo P-3
❑ 98FinNo PR-3
❑ 98FinRef-3
❑ 98LunGoaG-1
❑ 98LunGoaGS-1
❑ 98McD-21
❑ 98O-PChr-123
❑ 98O-PChrR-123
❑ 98O-PChrSB-SB3
❑ 98O-PChrSBR-SB3
❑ 98Pac-20
❑ 98PacAur-53
❑ 98PacAurC-14
❑ 98PacAurCFC-14
❑ 98PacAurCFIB-14
❑ 98PacAurCFR-14
❑ 98PacAurCFS-14
❑ 98PacCroR-37
❑ 98PacCroRLS-37
❑ 98PacCroRPotG-9
❑ 98PacDynI-53
❑ 98PacDynIIB-53
❑ 98PacDynIIW-3
❑ 98PacDynIR-53
❑ 98PacGolCD-11
❑ 98PacIceB-20
❑ 98PacOmeH-68
❑ 98PacOmeO-11
❑ 98PacOmeODI-68
❑ 98PacOmePI-7
❑ 98PacOmePIB-7
❑ 98PacOmeR-68
❑ 98PacPar-62
❑ 98PacParC-62
❑ 98PacParEG-62
❑ 98PacParGSLC-7
❑ 98PacParH-62
❑ 98PacParIB-62
❑ 98PacParS-62
❑ 98PacRed-20
❑ 98PacRev-40
❑ 98PacRevADC-2
❑ 98PacRevIS-40
❑ 98PacRevR-40
❑ 98PacRevS-13
❑ 98PacTim-6
❑ 98RevThrPA-13
❑ 98RevThrPA-13
❑ 98SP Aut-26
❑ 98SPxFin-29
❑ 98SPxFinR-29
❑ 98SPxFinS-29
❑ 98SPXTopP-20
❑ 98SPXTopPF-20
❑ 98SPXTopPR-20
❑ 98Top-123
❑ 98TopGolLC1-24
❑ 98TopGolLC1B-24
❑ 98TopGolLC1BOoO-24
❑ 98TopGolLC1OoO-24
❑ 98TopGolLC1R-24
❑ 98TopGolLC1ROoO-24
❑ 98TopGolLC2-24
❑ 98TopGolLC2B-24
❑ 98TopGolLC2BOoO-24
❑ 98TopGolLC2OoO-24
❑ 98TopGolLC2R-24
❑ 98TopGolLC2ROoO-24
❑ 98TopGolLC3-24
❑ 98TopGolLC3B-24
❑ 98TopGolLC3BOoO-24
❑ 98TopGolLC3OoO-24
❑ 98TopGolLC3R-24
❑ 98TopGolLC3ROoO-24
❑ 98TopO-P-123
❑ 98TopSeaB-SB3
❑ 98UC-63
❑ 98UC-249
❑ 98UCMBH-BH26
❑ 98UCSB-SQ17
❑ 98UCSG-SQ17
❑ 98UCSG-SQ17
❑ 98UCSR-SQ17
❑ 98UD ChoPCR-63
❑ 98UD ChoPCR-249
❑ 98UD ChoR-63
❑ 98UD ChoR-249
❑ 98UD3-45
❑ 98UD3-105
❑ 98UD3-165
❑ 98UD3DieC-45
❑ 98UD3DieC-105
❑ 98UD3DieC-165
❑ 98UDCP-63
❑ 98UppDec-80
❑ 98UppDecBD-26
❑ 98UppDecDD-26
❑ 98UppDecE-80
❑ 98UppDecE1o1-80
❑ 98UppDecFIT-FT26
❑ 98UppDecFITQ1-FT26
❑ 98UppDecFITQ2-FT26
❑ 98UppDecFITQ3-FT26
❑ 98UppDecGJ-GJ7
❑ 98UppDecGR-80
❑ 98UppDecLSH-LS23
❑ 98UppDecLSHQ1-LS23
❑ 98UppDecLSHQ2-LS23
❑ 98UppDecLSHQ3-LS23
❑ 98UppDecM-60
❑ 98UppDecMGS-60
❑ 98UppDecMSS-60

□ 98UppDecMSS-60
□ 98UppDecQD-26
□ 98UppDecTD-26
□ 98UppDecWFG-WF9
□ 98UppDecWFP-WF9
□ 99AurSty-7
□ 99Pac-117
□ 99PacAur-43
□ 99PacAurCF-10
□ 99PacAurCFC-10
□ 99PacAurCFPB-10
□ 99PacAurGU-7
□ 99PacAurPD-43
□ 99PacCop-117
□ 99PacGol-117
□ 99PacGolCD-13
□ 99PacIceB-117
□ 99PacIn tCN-6
□ 99PacPasAP-9
□ 99PacPreD-117
□ 99RetHoc-26
□ 99SP AutPS-26
□ 99UppDecM-62
□ 99UppDecMLL-LL5
□ 99UppDecMSS-62
□ 99UppDecMSS-62
□ 99UppDecRG-26
□ 99UppDecRP-26

**Belhumeur, Michel**
□ 720PC-273
□ 74CapWhiB-5
□ 740PCNHL-153
□ 74Top-153
□ 750PCNHL-232
□ 75Top-232
□ 760PCNHL-296

**Beliavski, Alexander**
□ 93SweSemE-14
□ 94SweLeaE-274
□ 95SweLeaE-145

**Belisle, Omar**
□ 95ThuBayS-3

**Belisle, Patrick**
□ 917thInnSQMJHL-9

**Belitski, David**
□ 93KitRan-2
□ 93KitRan-29
□ 94KitRan-2
□ 94ParSE-SE251
□ 94ParSEG-SE251
□ 94SlaPro-1
□ 95Cla-87
□ 95SigRooA-5
□ 95SigRooAPC-5
□ 95Sla-131
□ 96KitRan-2

**Beliveau, Jean**
□ 44BeeGro2P-222
□ 45QuaOatP-62
□ 48ExhCan-2
□ 48ExhCan-3
□ 50QueCit-2
□ 51LavDaiQSHL-1
□ 52St.LawS-39
□ 53Par-27
□ 54Par-3
□ 55Par-44
□ 55Par-74
□ 55Par-77
□ 55ParQuaO-44
□ 55ParQuaO-74
□ 55ParQuaO-77
□ 57Par-M3
□ 58Par-34
□ 59Par-6
□ 60Par-49
□ 60Par-59
□ 60ShiCoi-30
□ 60YorPreP-4
□ 61Par-45
□ 61ShiCoi-102
□ 61YorYelB-10
□ 62Par-39
□ 62ShiMetC-32
□ 62YorIrooTra-8
□ 63ChePho-5A
□ 63ChePho-5B
□ 63Par-30
□ 63Par-89
□ 63TorSta-4
□ 63YorWhiB-26
□ 64BeeGro3P-99
□ 64CanaPos-2
□ 64CocCap-58
□ 64Top-33
□ 64TorSta-4
□ 65CanaSteG-2
□ 65Coc-58
□ 65Top-6
□ 66Top-73
□ 66Top-127
□ 66TopUSAT-31
□ 67CanalGA-4
□ 67GenMil-1
□ 67PosFliB-7
□ 67PosFliB-8
□ 67Top-74
□ 67YorActOct-3
□ 67YorActOct-23
□ 67YorActOct-25
□ 67YorActOct-28
□ 68CanalGA-4
□ 68CanaPosBW-2

□ 680PC-166
□ 680PCPucSti-7
□ 68PosCerM-2
□ 68ShiCoi-80
□ 68Top-61
□ 69CanaPosC-2
□ 690PC-10
□ 690PC-220
□ 690PCFou-5
□ 690PCSta-1
□ 69Top-10
□ 70CanaPin-1
□ 70DadCoo-4
□ 70EssPowPla-4
□ 700PC-55
□ 700PCDec-21
□ 70SarProSta-108
□ 70Top-55
□ 70TopStiS-1
□ 710PC-263
□ 71SweHocS-197
□ 72SweSemWC-207
□ 73CanaPos-1
□ 81TCMA-11
□ 83CanaPos-1
□ 83HalFP-C1
□ 85HalFC-31
□ 88EssAllSta-1
□ 91StaPicH-4
□ 92ParParR-PR30
□ 92SpoFla-4
□ 930PCCanHF-14
□ 930PCCanHF-27
□ 930PCCanHF-44
□ 930PCCanHF-59
□ 930PCCanP-1
□ 94HocWit-23
□ 94ParMisL-64
□ 94ParMisL-138
□ 94ParMisL-149
□ 94ParMisL-150
□ 94ParMisL-156
□ 94ParMisL-157
□ 94ParMisL-172
□ 94ParMisLA-5
□ 94ParTalB-85
□ 94ParTalB-142
□ 94ParTalB-146
□ 94ParTalB-159
□ 94ParTalB-172
□ 94ZelMasH-1
□ 94ZelMasH-NNO
□ 94ZelMasoHS-1
□ 95Par66-73
□ 95Par66-PR125
□ 95Par66Coi-73
□ 95Par66P-4
□ 96DurL'EB-JB21
□ 96DurL'EB-JB22
□ 99RetHoc-85
□ 99UppDecCL-6
□ 99UppDecCLCLC-6
□ 99UppDecES-13
□ 99UppDecRG-G5A
□ 99UppDecRG-85
□ 99UppDecRGI-G5A
□ 99UppDecRIL1-JOB
□ 99UppDecRP-85

**Bell, Bob**
□ 91BriColJHL-118
□ 95TalTigS-18

**Bell, Bruce**
□ 81SauSteMG-4
□ 83BraAle-4
□ 84NordPos-2
□ 850PC-231
□ 850PCSti-142
□ 87PanSti-308
□ 89ProAHL-135
□ 90ProAHLIHL-234
□ 91ProAHLCHL-338
□ 94CenHocL-20

**Bell, Darren**
□ 88SudWol-13
□ 89SudWol-14
□ 907thInnSOHL-26

**Bell, David**
□ 95Sla-259

**Bell, Gordon**
□ 45QuaOatP-6

**Bell, Malcolm**
□ 94HumHawP-2
□ 97KinHaw-3

**Bell, Mark**
□ 98BowBes-138
□ 98BowBesAR-138
□ 98BowBesR-138
□ 98BowCHL-36
□ 98BowCHL-123
□ 98BowCHLAuB-A8
□ 98BowCHLAuG-A8
□ 98BowCHLAuS-A8
□ 98BowCHLGA-36
□ 98BowCHLGA-123
□ 98BowCHLOI-36
□ 98BowCHLOI-123
□ 98BowChrC-36
□ 98BowChrC-123
□ 98BowChrCGA-36
□ 98BowChrCGA-123
□ 98BowChrCGAR-36
□ 98BowChrCGAR-123
□ 98BowChrCOI-36
□ 98BowChrCOI-123
□ 98BowChrCOIR-36

□ 98BowChrCOIR-123
□ 98BowChrCR-36
□ 98BowChrCR-123
□ 98FinFutF-F7
□ 98FinFutFR-F7
□ 980-PChr-222
□ 980-PChrR-222
□ 98Top-222
□ 98TopO-P-222

**Bell, Matt**
□ 96GueSto-26

**Bell, Scott**
□ 91FerStaB-5
□ 91MinGolG-1
□ 92MinGolG-1
□ 94MinGolG-2

**Bell, Tim**
□ 92BriColJHL-11

**Bella, Tony**
□ 907thInnSOHL-51
□ 917thInnSOHL-222

**Belland, Brad**
□ 84SudWol-9

**Belland, Neil**
□ 81FreExp-23
□ 82FreExp-23
□ 83FreExp-14
□ 84Canu-1
□ 84FreExp-5
□ 85FreExp-23

**Bellefeuille, Blake**
□ 95Cla-7

**Bellefontaine, Scott**
□ 907thInnSWHL-20
□ 91AirCanSJHL-C41
□ 91AirCanSJHLAS-42
□ 91AirCanSJHLAS-45

**Bellemore, Bob**
□ 88DevCar-2
□ 89DevCar-2

**Bellerose, Eric**
□ 907thInnSQMJHL-135
□ 917thInnSQMJHL-118
□ 92AlbIntTC-5

**Belley, Jean-Francois**
□ 93AmoLesFAM-1

**Belley, Roch**
□ 897thInnSOHL-139
□ 89NiaFalT-2
□ 907thInnSOHL-252
□ 91ProAHLCHL-497
□ 92ForWorF-2
□ 93MusFur-16

**Bellio, John**
□ 82SweSemHVS-127

**Belliveau, Dave**
□ 907thInnSQMJHL-207
□ 917thInnSQMJHL-164

**Belliveau, Luc**
□ 95Sla-210

**Belliveau, Remi**
□ 907thInnSQMJHL-78

**Bellows, Brian**
□ 82NorStaPos-3
□ 83NorStaPos-4
□ 830PC-165
□ 830PC-167
□ 830PCSti-142
□ 83PufSti-17
□ 847EDis-26
□ 84NorSta7E-4
□ 84NorStaPos-3
□ 840PC-95
□ 840PC-359
□ 840PCSti-44
□ 840PCSti-45
□ 84Top-71
□ 857ECreCar-9
□ 85NorSta7E-9
□ 85NorStaPos-3
□ 850PC-50
□ 850PCSti-41
□ 85Top-50
□ 85TopBoxB-A
□ 86NorSta7E-12
□ 860PC-75
□ 860PCSti-167
□ 86Top-75
□ 87NorStaPos-5
□ 870PC-94
□ 870PCSti-53
□ 87PanSti-296
□ 87Top-94
□ 88FriLayS-5
□ 88NorStaADA-1
□ 880PC-95
□ 880PCSti-203
□ 88PanSti-89
□ 88Top-95
□ 890PC-177
□ 890PCSti-200
□ 89PanSti-105
□ 89Top-177
□ 90Bow-182
□ 90BowTif-182
□ 90Kra-2
□ 900PC-70
□ 900PC-200
□ 900PCPre-3
□ 90PanSti-257
□ 90ProSet-130A
□ 90ProSet-130B
□ 90Sco-7
□ 90Sco-322

□ 90ScoCan-7
□ 90ScoCan-322
□ 90ScoHotRS-3
□ 90Top-70
□ 90Top-200
□ 90TopTeaSL-15
□ 90TopTif-70
□ 90TopTif-200
□ 90UppDec-126
□ 90UppDec-308
□ 90UppDecF-126
□ 90UppDecF-308
□ 91Bow-129
□ 91Kra-38
□ 910PC-44
□ 910PC-110
□ 91PanSti-108
□ 91Par-79
□ 91Pin-129
□ 91PinFre-129
□ 91ProSet-109
□ 91ProSetFre-109
□ 91ProSetPC-13
□ 91ProSetPla-59
□ 91ProSetPla-143
□ 91ScoAme-160
□ 91ScoCan-160
□ 91StaClu-87
□ 91Top-110
□ 91UppDec-236
□ 91UppDecF-236
□ 92Bow-200
□ 92Bow-260
□ 92CanaPos-1
□ 92McdUppD-2
□ 920PC-384
□ 920PCPre-75
□ 92PanSti-88
□ 92PanStiFre-88
□ 92Par-87
□ 92ParEmel-87
□ 92Pin-325
□ 92PinFre-325
□ 92Sco-335
□ 92ScoCan-335
□ 92StaClu-293
□ 92Top-240
□ 92TopGol-240G
□ 92Ult-100
□ 92Ult-324
□ 92UppDec-172
□ 92UppDec-471
□ 92UppDec-636
□ 92UppDecGHS-G1
□ 93CanaMol-1
□ 93CanaPos-1
□ 93Don-170
□ 93Lea-76
□ 930PCCanHF-60
□ 930PCPre-202
□ 930PCPreG-202
□ 93PanSti-15
□ 93Par-371
□ 93ParEmel-371
□ 93Pin-22
□ 93PinCan-22
□ 93Pow-124
□ 93Sco-4
□ 93ScoCan-4
□ 93ScoDynDC-6
□ 93ScoSam-4
□ 93StaClu-156
□ 93StaCluFDI-156
□ 93StaCluO-156
□ 93TopPre-202
□ 93TopPreG-202
□ 93Ult-4
□ 93UppDec-390
□ 93UppDecF-390
□ 94CanaPos-1
□ 94CanGamNHLP-132
□ 94Don-203
□ 94EASpo-71
□ 94Fin-105
□ 94FinRef-105
□ 94FinSupTW-105
□ 94Fla-84
□ 94Fle-101
□ 94HocWit-11
□ 94Lea-301
□ 940PCPre-219
□ 940PCPreSE-219
□ 94Par-112
□ 94ParGol-112
□ 94Pin-290
□ 94PinArtP-290
□ 94PinRinC-290
□ 94Sco-73
□ 94ScoGol-73
□ 94ScoPla-73
□ 94ScoPlaTS-73
□ 94Sel-91
□ 94SelGol-91
□ 94TopPre-219
□ 94TopPreSE-219
□ 94Ult-105
□ 94UppDec-309
□ 94UppDecElcIce-309
□ 94UppDecSPI-SP130
□ 94UppDecSPIDC-SP130
□ 95BeAPla-32
□ 95BeAPSig-S32
□ 95BeAPSigDC-S32

□ 95CanGamNHLP-253
□ 95ColCho-84
□ 95ColChoPC-84
□ 95ColChoPCP-84
□ 95Don-341
□ 95ImpSti-115
□ 95LigTeal-2
□ 95ParInt-466
□ 95ParIntEI-466
□ 95PlaOneoOne-91
□ 95Sco-231
□ 95ScoBlaIce-231
□ 95ScoBlaIceAP-231
□ 95Sum-11
□ 95SumArtP-11
□ 95SumIce-11
□ 95Top-253
□ 95TopOPCI-253
□ 95Ult-307
□ 95UppDec-404
□ 95UppDecElcIce-404
□ 95UppDecElcIceG-404
□ 96Don-64
□ 96DonPrePro-64
□ 96Duc-13
□ 96Lea-10
□ 96LeaPreP-10
□ 96Sco-221
□ 96ScoArtPro-221
□ 96ScoDeaCAP-221
□ 96ScoGolB-221
□ 96ScoSpeAP-221
□ 96UppDecBD-104
□ 96UppDecBDG-104
□ 97Pac-70
□ 97PacCop-70
□ 97PacDyn-1
□ 97PacDynC-1
□ 97PacDynDG-1
□ 97PacDynEG-1
□ 97PacDynIB-1
□ 97PacDynR-1
□ 97PacDynSil-1
□ 97PacDynTan-29
□ 97PacEmeGre-70
□ 97PacIceB-70
□ 97PacInv-1
□ 97PacInvC-1
□ 97PacInvEG-1
□ 97PacInvIB-1
□ 97PacInvR-1
□ 97PacInvS-1
□ 97PacRed-70
□ 97PacSil-70
□ 97PinIns-140
□ 98Be A PPA-145
□ 98Be A PPAA-145
□ 98Be A PPAAF-145
□ 98Be A PPTBASG-145
□ 98Be APG-145
□ 980-PChr-133
□ 980-PChrR-133
□ 98Pac-23
□ 98PacAur-193
□ 98PacOmeH-243
□ 98PacOmeODI-243
□ 98PacOmeR-243
□ 98PacPar-241
□ 98PacParEG-241
□ 98PacParH-241
□ 98PacParIB-241
□ 98PacParS-241
□ 98PacRed-23
□ 98Top-133
□ 98TopO-P-133
□ 98UppDec-204
□ 98UppDecE-204
□ 98UppDecE1o1-204
□ 98UppDecGR-204
□ 98UppDecM-213
□ 98UppDecMGS-213
□ 98UppDecMP-BB
□ 98UppDecMSS-213
□ 98UppDecMSS-213
□ 99Pac-435
□ 99PacCop-435
□ 99PacGol-435
□ 99PacIceB-435
□ 99PacPreD-435

**Belohlav, Radek**
□ 94CzeAPSE-110
□ 95CzeAPSE-64
□ 96CzeAPSE-255
□ 96CzeAPSE-343
□ 96SweSemW-123

**Belosheikin, Evgeny**
□ 87RusNatT-2
□ 89SweSemWCS-78
□ 91ProAHLCHL-223

**Belov, Oleg**
□ 93UppDec-274
□ 95CleLum-5

**Belov, Valerij**
□ 96CzeAPSE-115

**Belter, Shane**
□ 95SeaThu-2
□ 96SeaThu-32

**Belushi, James**
□ 91ProSetPla-300

**Belzile, Eric**
□ 96RimOce-3
□ 96RimOceQPP-3

**Belzile, Etienne**
□ 78BluPos-3

□ 92CorBigRed-2

**Benak, Jaroslav**
□ 94CzeAPSE-168

**Benaquez, Fernand**
□ 51LavDaiSJ-17

**Benard, Leo**
□ 23CreSel-2
□ 23V1281PauC-10
□ 24CreSel-11

**Benazic, Cal**
□ 92BriColJHL-185
□ 95MedHatT-3

**Bencurik, Ryan**
□ 93OmaLan-1

**Benda, Jan**
□ 907thInnSOHL-326
□ 917thInnSOHL-149
□ 91OshGen-19
□ 91OshGenS-2
□ 94RicRen-14
□ 95GerDELE-435
□ 96CzeAPSE-140

**Bendelin, Torgny**
□ 94SweLeaE-295

**Bendera, Terry**
□ 89VicCou-2
□ 907thInnSWHL-170
□ 917thInnSWHL-224

**Benedict, Clint**
□ 12C57-3
□ 23V1451-7
□ 24C144ChaCig-3
□ 24V130MapC-2
□ 24V1452-32
□ 83HalFP-H1
□ 85HalFC-107
□ 94HalFT-6

**Benes, Stanislav**
□ 94CzeAPSE-141
□ 95CzeAPSE-250

**Bengtsson, Anders**
□ 69SweHocS-203

**Bengtsson, Folke**
□ 64SweCorl-18
□ 64SweCorl-58
□ 65SweCorl-18
□ 65SweCorl-58

**Bengtsson, Kent**
□ 67SweHoc-3
□ 67SweHoc-100
□ 69SweHocS-113
□ 70SweHocS-54
□ 71SweHocS-124

**Bengtsson, Kent**
□ 71SweHocS-329
□ 74SweHocS-203

**Bengtsson, Totte**
□ 72SweHocS-109

**Benic, Geoff**
□ 88ProIHL-12

**Benik, Ray**
□ 81VicCou-3
□ 82VicCou-2

**Benn, David**
□ 897thInnSOHL-126
□ 89NiaFalT-3
□ 907thInnSOHL-123
□ 917thInnSOHL-39
□ 92WinSpi-28

**Bennett, Adam**
□ 88SudWol-4
□ 89SudWol-10
□ 907thInnSOHL-378
□ 90SudWol-2
□ 91ProAHLCHL-501
□ 93Par-334
□ 93ParEmel-334
□ 93UppDec-237
□ 94Lea-389
□ 94Par-77
□ 94ParGol-77
□ 94UppDec-202
□ 94UppDecElcIce-202

**Bennett, Bill**
□ 77RocAme-5
□ 83Ott67-2
□ 84Ott67-3

**Bennett, Brad**
□ 84PriAlbRS-2
□ 90AlbIntTC-11

**Bennett, Curt**
□ 72Flam-1
□ 730PC-149
□ 73Top-152
□ 74NHLActSta-4
□ 740PCNHL-33
□ 74Top-33
□ 750PCNHL-8
□ 75Top-8
□ 760PCNHL-202
□ 760PCNHL-379
□ 76Top-202
□ 770PCNHL-97
□ 77Top-97
□ 78BluPos-2
□ 780PC-31
□ 78Top-31
□ 79FlamPos-1
□ 79FlaTeal-1
□ 790PC-344
□ 79PanSti-214

**Bennett, Eric**
□ 91ProAHLCHL-198

**Bennett, Harvey**
□ 770PCNHL-282
□ 78BluPos-3

□ 780PC-163
□ 78Top-163
□ 79PanSti-219

**Bennett, Jim**
□ 95GuiFla-25

**Bennett, Rick**
□ 900PC-252
□ 90ProAHLIHL-21
□ 90Sco-400
□ 90ScoCan-400
□ 90Top-252
□ 90TopTif-252
□ 90UppDec-540
□ 90UppDecF-540
□ 92BinRan-5

**Benning, Brian**
□ 84KamBla-2
□ 87BluKod-1
□ 87BluTealss-1
□ 870PC-122
□ 870PCMin-1
□ 870PCSti-124
□ 87Top-122
□ 88BluKod-2
□ 88BluTealss-1
□ 880PC-174
□ 880PCSti-18
□ 88PanSti-101
□ 88Top-174
□ 89KinSmo-21
□ 890PC-86
□ 890PCSti-24
□ 89PanSti-124
□ 89Top-86
□ 90KinSmo-7
□ 900PC-365
□ 90ProSet-114
□ 90Sco-306A
□ 90ScoCan-306A
□ 90Top-365
□ 90TopTif-365
□ 910PC-359
□ 91Pin-402
□ 91PinFre-402
□ 91ProSet-398
□ 91ProSetFre-398
□ 91ProSetPla-182
□ 91ScoAme-186
□ 91ScoCan-186
□ 91Top-359
□ 91UppDec-415
□ 91UppDecF-415
□ 92Bow-39
□ 92FlyJCP-3
□ 92FlyUppDS-2
□ 920PC-68
□ 92Par-125
□ 92Par-284
□ 92ParEmel-125
□ 92ParEmel-284
□ 92Pin-45
□ 92PinFre-45
□ 92ProSet-135
□ 92Sco-133
□ 92ScoCan-133
□ 92StaClu-91
□ 92Top-250
□ 92TopGol-250G
□ 92Ult-151
□ 92UppDec-301
□ 93Don-129
□ 93Lea-328
□ 93Par-343
□ 93ParEmel-343
□ 93Pin-341
□ 93Pin2HS-341
□ 93PinCan-341
□ 93Pow-90
□ 93Sco-64
□ 93ScoCan-64
□ 93ScoCan-512
□ 93ScoGol-512
□ 93Ult-3
□ 93Ult-321
□ 93UppDec-496
□ 94CanGamNHLP-111
□ 94Lea-379
□ 940PCPre-389
□ 940PCPreSE-389
□ 94ParSE-SE65
□ 94ParSEG-SE65
□ 94Pin-414
□ 94PinArtP-414
□ 94PinRinC-414
□ 94StaClu-157
□ 94StaCluFDI-157
□ 94StaCluMOMS-157
□ 94StaCluSTWC-157
□ 94TopPre-389
□ 94TopPreSE-389
□ 94UppDec-217
□ 94UppDecElcIce-217

**Benning, Jim**
□ 81MapLeaP-4
□ 82MapLeaP-4
□ 820PC-317
□ 820PCSti-64
□ 82PosCer-18
□ 83MapLeaP-2
□ 830PC-326
□ 83Vac-82
□ 84KelWin-51
□ 84MapLeaP-2
□ 840PC-296

- 84OPCSti-21
- 85MapLeaP-2
- 850PC-250
- 850PCSti-16
- 870PC-260
- 870PCSti-197
- 88CanuMoh-2
- 880PCSti-58
- 89CanuMoh-2
- 900PC-455
- 90ProAHLIHL-329
- 90ProSet-292
- 92ProSet-181

**Benny OO, Mascot**
- 89JetSaf-28
- 90JetIGA-34
- 95JetTealss-2

**Benoit, Carl**
- 93AmoLesFAM-2

**Benoit, Denis**
- 88RivDu R-3

**Benoit, Joe**
- 34BeeGro1P-135
- 400PCV3012-121
- 45QuaOatP-63

**Benoit, Richard**
- 83NorBayC-3

**Benson, Bill**
- 34BeeGro1P-215
- 400PCV3012-135

**Benson, Bobbie (R.J.)**
- 23V1281PauC-65
- 24HolCre-6

**Bentley, Doug**
- 34BeeGro1P-39
- 44BeeGro2P-80
- 48ExhCan-49
- 51Par-48
- 83HalFP-F1
- 85HalFC-77
- 94ParMisLP-P11

**Bentley, Max**
- 34BeeGro1P-40
- 400PCV3012-131
- 44BeeGro2P-298
- 44BeeGro2P-379
- 45QuaOatP-7A
- 45QuaOatP-7B
- 45QuaOatP-7C
- 48ExhCan-42
- 51Par-81
- 52Par-95
- 53Par-55
- 83HalFP-C2
- 85HalFC-32
- 99UppDecCL-49
- 99UppDecCLCLC-49

**Benysek, Ladislav**
- 94CapBreO-3
- 96CzeAPSE-271

**Beraldo, Paul**
- 88ProAHL-149
- 89ProAHL-55
- 95GerDELE-321
- 96GerDELE-179

**Beran, Jan**
- 93JohChi-15

**Beran, Karel**
- 95CzeAPSE-203

**Beranek, Jiri**
- 917thInnSWHL-39
- 94CzeAPSE-157
- 95CzeAPSE-87
- 96CzeAPSE-90

**Beranek, Josef**
- 910ilIGA-1
- 910ilTeal-1
- 910PCPre-149
- 91Par-47
- 91ParFre-47
- 91Pin-303
- 91PinFre-303
- 91ProSet-534
- 91ProSetFre-534
- 91ProSetPla-255
- 91UppDec-17
- 91UppDecF-17
- 91UppDecF-595
- 92Bow-100
- 92FlyUppDS-31
- 92FlyUppDS-32
- 920ilIGA-2
- 920PC-178
- 92PanSti-l
- 92PanStiFre-l
- 92Par-360
- 92ParEmel-360
- 92Pin-208
- 92PinFre-208
- 92Sco-105
- 92ScoCan-105
- 92StaClu-214
- 92Top-177
- 92TopGol-177G
- 92Ult-56
- 92UppDec-196
- 92UppDecES-E11
- 93ClaProPro-81
- 93Don-247
- 93Lea-103
- 930PCPre-467
- 930PCPreG-467

- 93Par-153
- 93ParEmel-153
- 93Pin-424
- 93PinCan-424
- 93Pow-177
- 93Sco-439
- 93ScoCan-439
- 93StaClu-69
- 93StaCluFDI-69
- 93StaCluFDIO-69
- 93StaClu0-69
- 93SweSemWCS-105
- 93TopPre-467
- 93TopPreG-467
- 93Ult-17
- 93UppDec-15
- 93UppDecSP-113
- 94CanGamNHLP-355
- 94CzeAPSE-243
- 94Don-13
- 94FinnJaaK-176
- 94Fle-221
- 94Lea-31
- 940PCPre-141
- 940PCPreSE-141
- 94Par-166
- 94ParGol-166
- 94Pin-148
- 94PinArtP-148
- 94PinRinC-148
- 94Sco-77
- 94ScoGol-77
- 94ScoPla-77
- 94ScoPlaTS-77
- 94TopPre-141
- 94TopPreSE-141
- 94Ult-153
- 94UppDec-117
- 94UppDecElcIce-117
- 94UppDecSPI-SP56
- 94UppDecSPIDC-SP56
- 95ColCho-312
- 95ColChoPC-312
- 95ColChoPCP-312
- 95CzeAPSE-148
- 95Don-356
- 95Emo-176
- 95FinnSemWC-154
- 95Lea-232
- 95ParInt-208
- 95ParIntEl-208
- 95Pin-140
- 95PinArtP-140
- 95PinRinC-140
- 95Sco-118
- 95ScoBlaIce-118
- 95ScoBlaIceAP-118
- 95SweGloWC-158
- 95Top-149
- 95TopOPCI-149
- 95UppDec-67
- 95UppDecElcIce-67
- 95UppDecElcIceG-67
- 96CzeAPSE-165
- 96SweSemW-127
- 97PacInvNRB-158
- 98Be A PPA-203
- 98Be A PPAA-203
- 98Be A PPAAF-203
- 98Be A PPSE-203
- 98Be APG-203
- 98PacOmeH-90
- 98PacOmeODI-90
- 98PacOmeR-90
- 99Pac-152
- 99PacCop-152
- 99PacGol-152
- 99PacIceB-152
- 99PacPreD-152

**Berard, Bryan**
- 94DetJrRW-18
- 94Fin-114
- 94FinRef-114
- 94FinSupTW-114
- 94LeaLimWJUSA-1
- 94ParSE-SE250
- 94ParSEG-SE250
- 94Sel-149
- 94SelGol-149
- 94SP-174
- 94SPDieCut-174
- 94UppDec-522
- 94UppDecElcIce-522
- 95Cla-1
- 95Cla-84
- 95Cla-99
- 95ClaCHLAS-AS8
- 95ClaIceBre-BK1
- 95DonEliWJ-25
- 95Ima-1
- 95ImaCleE-CE1
- 95ImaGol-1
- 95ImaPlaPDC-PD1
- 95SigRoo-60
- 95SigRooA-29
- 95SigRooAPC-29
- 95SigRooSig-60
- 95Sla-75
- 95SlaMemC-92
- 96CalIceBreDC-BK1
- 96ColCho-359
- 96DonCanI-131
- 96DonCanIGPP-131
- 96DonCanIRPP-131

- 96DonEli-147
- 96DonEliAsp-23
- 96DonEliDCS-147
- 96Fla-114
- 96FiaBluI-114
- 96LeaLimR-3
- 96LeaLimRG-3
- 96LeaPre-129
- 96LeaPrePP-129
- 96MetUni-170
- 96SelCer-114
- 96SelCerAP-114
- 96SelCerBlu-114
- 96SelCerMB-114
- 96SelCerMG-114
- 96SelCerMR-114
- 96SelCerRed-114
- 96SP-182
- 96SPSPxFor-4
- 96Ult-188
- 96UltGoIM-99
- 96UltRoo-1
- 96UppDec-294
- 96UppDecBD-161
- 96UppDecBDG-161
- 96UppDecGN-X23
- 96UppDecGol-69
- 96UppDecIcePar-93
- 96Zen-126
- 96ZenArtP-126
- 97Be A PPAD-18
- 97Be A PPAPD-18
- 97BeAPla-18
- 97BeAPlaAut-18
- 97BeAPlaTAN-9
- 97ColCho-155
- 97ColChoSta-SQ1
- 97Don-163
- 97DonCanI-92
- 97DonCanIDS-92
- 97DonCanIPS-92
- 97DonEli-29
- 97DonEli-124
- 97DonEliAsp-29
- 97DonEliAsp-124
- 97DonEliC-26
- 97DonEliMC-26
- 97DonEliS-29
- 97DonEliS-124
- 97DonLim-70
- 97DonLim-181
- 97DonLim-182
- 97DonLimExp-70
- 97DonLimExp-181
- 97DonLimExp-182
- 97DonLimFOTG-31
- 97DonPre-79
- 97DonPre-186
- 97DonPreCttC-79
- 97DonPreCttC-186
- 97DonPreProG-163
- 97DonPreProS-163
- 97DonPri-54
- 97DonPri-194
- 97DonPriODI-20
- 97DonPriP-25
- 97DonPriS-25
- 97DonPriSB-25
- 97DonPriSG-25
- 97DonPriSoA-54
- 97DonPriSoA-194
- 97DonPriSS-25
- 97Kat-85
- 97KatGol-85
- 97KatSil-85
- 97Lea-30
- 97Lea-183
- 97LeaBanSea-18
- 97LeaFraMat-30
- 97LeaFraMat-183
- 97LeaFraMDC-30
- 97LeaFraMDC-183
- 97LeaInt-30
- 97LeaIntUI-30
- 97McD-10
- 97Pac-222
- 97PacCop-222
- 97PacCroR-78
- 97PacCroRBoSDC-13
- 97PacCroREG-78
- 97PacCroRIB-78
- 97PacCroRS-78
- 97PacDyn-72
- 97PacDynBKS-107
- 97PacDynC-72
- 97PacDynDD-9A
- 97PacDynDG-72
- 97PacDynEG-72
- 97PacDynIB-72
- 97PacDynR-72
- 97PacDynSil-72
- 97PacDynTan-11
- 97PacEmeGre-222
- 97PacIceB-222
- 97PacInv-80
- 97PacInvAZ-12
- 97PacInvC-80
- 97PacInvEG-80
- 97PacInvIB-80
- 97PacInvR-80
- 97PacInvS-80
- 97PacOme-136
- 97PacOmeC-136

- 97PacOmeDG-136
- 97PacOmeEG-136
- 97PacOmeG-136
- 97PacOmeIB-136
- 97PacPar-106
- 97PacParC-106
- 97PacParDG-106
- 97PacParEG-106
- 97PacParIB-106
- 97PacParRed-106
- 97PacParSil-106
- 97PacRed-222
- 97PacRev-80
- 97PacRevC-80
- 97PacRevE-80
- 97PacRevIB-80
- 97PacRevR-80
- 97PacRevS-80
- 97PacSil-222
- 97Pin-145
- 97PinBee-8
- 97PinBeeGP-8
- 97PinCer-40
- 97PinCerMB-40
- 97PinCerMG-40
- 97PinCerMR-40
- 97PinCerR-40
- 97PinIns-80
- 97PinInsCC-80
- 97PinInsEC-80
- 97PinPrePBB-145
- 97PinPrePBC-145
- 97PinPrePBM-145
- 97PinPrePBY-145
- 97PinPrePFC-145
- 97PinPrePFM-145
- 97PinPrePla-145
- 97PinTotCMPG-40
- 97PinTotCPB-40
- 97PinTotCPG-40
- 97PinTotCPR-40
- 97Sco-137
- 97Sco-267
- 97ScoArtPro-137
- 97ScoChel-137
- 97ScoGolBla-137
- 97SPAut-92
- 97SPAutSotT-BB
- 97SPAutTra-T4
- 97SPx-29
- 97SPxBro-29
- 97SPxDim-SPX8
- 97SPxGol-29
- 97SPxGraF-29
- 97SPxSil-29
- 97SPxSte-29
- 97Stu-27
- 97StuHarH-4
- 97StuPor-24
- 97StuPrePG-27
- 97StuPrePS-27
- 97UppDec-98
- 97UppDecBD-12
- 97UppDecBDDD-12
- 97UppDecBDPC-PC16
- 97UppDecBDPCDD-PC16
- 97UppDecBDPCM-PC16
- 97UppDecBDPCTD-PC16
- 97UppDecBDQD-12
- 97UppDecBDTD-12
- 97UppDecGDM-98
- 97UppDecIce-54
- 97UppDecIceP-54
- 97UppDecIPS-54
- 97UppDecSG-SG34
- 97UppDecSSM-SS28
- 97UppDecSSW-SS28
- 97UppDecTS-29
- 97UppDecTSL2-29
- 97UppDecTSS-4A
- 97Zen-53
- 97Zen5x7-32
- 97ZenGolImp-32
- 97ZenSilImp-32
- 97ZenZGol-53
- 97ZenZSil-53
- 98Be A PPA-85
- 98Be A PPAA-85
- 98Be A PPAAF-85
- 98Be A PPTBASG-85
- 98Be APG-85
- 98Bow-80
- 98BowBesAR-80
- 98BowBesR-80
- 98Fin-107
- 98FinCen-C2
- 98FinCenR-C2
- 98FinNo P-107
- 98FinNo PR-107
- 98FinRef-107
- 980-PChr-198
- 980-PChrR-198
- 98Pac-275
- 98PacCroR-82
- 98PacCroRLS-82
- 98PacDynIIB-113
- 98PacIceB-275
- 98PacOmeH-225
- 98PacOmeODI-225
- 98PacOmeR-225

- 98PacPar-140
- 98PacParC-140
- 98PacParEG-140
- 98PacParH-140
- 98PacParIB-140
- 98PacParS-140
- 98PacRed-275
- 98SP Aut-53
- 98SPxFin-51
- 98SPxFinR-51
- 98SPxFinS-51
- 98Top-198
- 98TopO-P-198
- 98UC-123
- 98UD ChoPCR-123
- 98UD ChoR-123
- 98UDCP-123
- 98UppDec-21
- 98UppDec-127
- 98UppDecBD-54
- 98UppDecDD-54
- 98UppDecE-21
- 98UppDecE-127
- 98UppDecE101-21
- 98UppDecE101-127
- 98UppDecGR-21
- 98UppDecGR-127
- 98UppDecLSH-LS19
- 98UppDecLSHQ1-LS19
- 98UppDecLSHQ2-LS19
- 98UppDecLSHQ3-LS19
- 98UppDecM-200
- 98UppDecMGS-200
- 98UppDecMSS-200
- 98UppDecMSS-200
- 98UppDecPos-0
- 98UppDecQD-54
- 98UppDecTD-54
- 99Pac-401
- 99PacCop-401
- 99PacGol-401
- 99PacIceB-401
- 99PacPreD-401
- 99SP AutPS-53
- 99UppDecM-401
- 99UppDecMGS-201
- 99UppDecMSS-201
- 99UppDecMSS-201
- 99UppDecRG-G1C
- 99UppDecRGI-G1C

**Berardicurti, Louie**
- 83KitRan-5

**Berdichevsky, Lev**
- 910PCIns-50R
- 92RusStaRA-32
- 93RoaExp-4

**Berehowsky, Drake**
- 907thInnSOHL-52
- 90Sco-434
- 90ScoCan-434
- 90UppDec-361
- 90UppDecF-361
- 917thInnSOHL-70
- 91MapLeaPTS-1
- 910PC-70
- 91ScoAme-385
- 91ScoCan-275
- 91Top-70
- 92HumDum2-1
- 92MapLeaK-5
- 920PCPre-131
- 92Pin-231
- 92PinFre-231
- 92St.JohML-2
- 92Ult-417
- 92UppDec-415
- 93ClaProPro-59
- 93Don-336
- 930PCPre-69
- 930PCPreG-69
- 93Par-199
- 93ParEmel-199
- 93Pow-239
- 93Sco-355
- 93ScoBla-14
- 93ScoCan-355
- 93StaClu-331
- 93StaCluFDI-331
- 93StaClu0-331
- 93TopPre-69
- 93TopPreG-69
- 93Ult-90
- 94BeAPSig-55
- 94Lea-410
- 94MapLeaK-3
- 94ParSE-SE177
- 94ParSEG-SE177
- 94UppDec-458
- 94UppDecElcIce-458
- 95CanGamNHLP-218
- 95CleLum-6
- 980-PChr-137
- 980-PChrR-137
- 98Top-137
- 98TopO-P-137
- 99Pac-217
- 99PacCop-217
- 99PacGol-217
- 99PacIceB-217
- 99PacPreD-217

**Berek, Miroslav**
- 94GerDELE-415
- 96GerDELE-218
- 96GerDELE-68

**Berens, Sean**

- 98LasVegT-2

**Berenson, Red**
- 44BeeGro2P-223A
- 44BeeGro2P-223B
- 62ShiMetC-42
- 63ChePho-6
- 63Par-26
- 63Par-85
- 63YorWhiB-36
- 64BeeGro3P-100
- 64QueAce-2
- 64Top-61
- 64TorSta-5
- 65Top-9
- 66Top-92
- 66TopUSAT-10
- 67Top-24
- 680PC-114
- 68ShiCoi-150
- 68Top-114
- 690PC-20
- 690PCFou-16
- 690PCSta-2
- 69Top-20
- 70ColSta-24
- 70DadCoo-5
- 70EssPowPla-240
- 700PC-103
- 700PCDec-25
- 70SarProSta-177
- 70Top-103
- 70TopStiS-2
- 710PC-91
- 710PCPos-10
- 71SarProSta-51
- 71Top-91
- 71TorSun-84
- 720PC-123
- 720PCPlaC-7
- 720PCTeaC-2
- 72SarProSta-73
- 72SweSemWC-183
- 72Top-95
- 730PC-10
- 73RedWinTI-2
- 73Top-174
- 74LipSou-25
- 74NHLActSta-104
- 74NHLActStaU-30
- 740PCNHL-19
- 74Top-19
- 750PCNHL-22
- 75Top-22
- 760PCNHL-236
- 76Top-236
- 770PCNHL-107
- 77Top-107
- 78BluPos-4
- 780PC-218
- 78Top-218
- 91FutTreC72-48
- 92BluUDBB-11
- 94ParTalB-80
- 95Par66-92
- 95Par66Coi-92

**Berenzweig, Bubba (Andrew)**
- 94Cla95DP-DP1
- 94Sel-151
- 94SelGol-151

**Berezan, Perry**
- 85FlamRedRP-3
- 86FlamRedR-2
- 87FlamRedRP-1
- 89PanSti-110
- 900PC-357
- 90ProSet-459
- 90Sco-379
- 90ScoCan-379
- 90Top-357
- 90TopTif-357
- 910PC-485
- 91Par-381
- 91ParFre-381
- 91Pin-287
- 91PinFre-287
- 91ProSet-487
- 91ProSetFre-487
- 91ScoCan-527
- 91ScoRoo-94T
- 91ShaSanJSA-2
- 91StaClu-227
- 91Top-485
- 92Bow-105
- 920PC-182
- 92Pin-148
- 92PinFre-148
- 92Sco-169
- 92ScoCan-169
- 92StaClu-441
- 92Top-342
- 92TopGol-342G
- 92UppDec-451

**Berezin, Sergei**
- 94Cla-67
- 94ClaDraGol-67
- 94GerDELE-221
- 95FinnSemWC-135
- 95GerDELE-217
- 96BeAPLH-3A
- 96BeAPLHAut-3A
- 96BeAPLHAutSil-3A
- 96ColCho-350
- 96DonCanI-119
- 96DonCanIGPP-119

- 96DonCanIRPP-119
- 96DonEli-138
- 96DonEliAsp-17
- 96DonEliDCS-138
- 96Fla-124
- 96FiaBluI-124
- 96HocGreC-21
- 96HocGreCG-21
- 96LeaLimR-7
- 96LeaLimRG-7
- 96LeaPre-123
- 96LeaPrePG-123
- 96MapLeaAPLH-2
- 96MetUni-171
- 96SelCer-98
- 96SelCerAP-98
- 96SelCerBlu-98
- 96SelCerMB-98
- 96SelCerMG-98
- 96SelCerMR-98
- 96SelCerRed-98
- 96SP-188
- 96SPSPxFor-4
- 96SweSemW-153
- 96SweSemWAS-AS4
- 96Ult-161
- 96UltGolM-161
- 96UltRoo-2
- 96UppDec-346
- 96UppDecB-94
- 96UppDecBDG-94
- 96UppDecGN-X31
- 96UppDecIce-103
- 96UppDecIcePar-103
- 96Zen-127
- 96ZenArtP-127
- 97ColCho-247
- 97ColChoSta-SQ48
- 97Don-165
- 97DonEli-55
- 97DonEliAsp-55
- 97DonEliS-55
- 97DonLim-8
- 97DonLim-13
- 97DonLim-154
- 97DonLimExp-8
- 97DonLimExp-13
- 97DonLimExp-154
- 97DonLimFOTG-57
- 97DonPre-77
- 97DonPreCttC-77
- 97DonPreProG-165
- 97DonPreProS-165
- 97DonPri-28
- 97DonPriSoA-28
- 97Lea-66
- 97LeaBanSea-21
- 97LeaFraMat-66
- 97LeaFraMDC-66
- 97LeaInt-66
- 97LeaIntUI-66
- 97Pac-36
- 97PacCop-36
- 97PacCroR-128
- 97PacCroREG-128
- 97PacCroRIB-128
- 97PacCroRS-128
- 97PacDyn-120
- 97PacDyn-144
- 97PacDynBKS-91
- 97PacDynC-120
- 97PacDynDG-120
- 97PacDynDG-144
- 97PacDynEG-120
- 97PacDynEG-144
- 97PacDynIB-120
- 97PacDynIB-144
- 97PacDynR-144
- 97PacDynSil-120
- 97PacDynSil-144
- 97PacDynTan-10
- 97PacDynTan-27
- 97PacEmeGre-36
- 97PacIceB-36
- 97PacInv-135
- 97PacInvC-135
- 97PacInvEG-135
- 97PacInvFP-32
- 97PacInvIB-135
- 97PacInvNRB-191
- 97PacInvOTG-19
- 97PacInvR-135
- 97PacInvS-135
- 97PacOme-217
- 97PacOmeC-217
- 97PacOmeDG-217
- 97PacOmeEG-217
- 97PacOmeG-217
- 97PacOmeIB-217
- 97PacPar-178
- 97PacParC-178
- 97PacParDG-178
- 97PacParEG-178
- 97PacParIB-178
- 97PacParRed-178
- 97PacParSil-178
- 97PacRed-36
- 97PacSil-36
- 97PacSlaSDC-10C
- 97Pin-162
- 97PinCer-127
- 97PinCerMB-127
- 97PinCerMG-127

❑ 97PinCerMR-127
❑ 97PinCerR-127
❑ 97PinIns-120
❑ 97PinPrePBB-162
❑ 97PinPrePBC-162
❑ 97PinPrePBM-162
❑ 97PinPrePBY-162
❑ 97PinPrePFC-162
❑ 97PinPrePFM-162
❑ 97PinPrePFY-162
❑ 97PinPrePla-162
❑ 97PinTotCMPG-127
❑ 97PinTotCPB-127
❑ 97PinTotCPG-127
❑ 97PinTotCPR-127
❑ 97PosPin-15
❑ 97Sco-145
❑ 97ScoArtPro-145
❑ 97ScoGolBla-145
❑ 97ScoMapL-6
❑ 97ScoMapLPla-6
❑ 97ScoMapLPre-6
❑ 97SPAut-153
❑ 97SPAutSotT-SB
❑ 97Stu-104
❑ 97StuHarH-14
❑ 97StuPrePG-104
❑ 97StuPrePS-104
❑ 97UppDec-161
❑ 97UppDecIce-4
❑ 97UppDecIceP-4
❑ 97UppDecIPS-4
❑ 97UppDecSG-SG51
❑ 97UppDecTSS-19A
❑ 98Be A PPA-285
❑ 98Be A PPAA-285
❑ 98Be A PPAAF-285
❑ 98Be A PPSE-285
❑ 98Be APG-285
❑ 98O-PChr-55
❑ 98O-PChrR-55
❑ 98Pac-410
❑ 98PacAur-179
❑ 98PacCroR-128
❑ 98PacCroRLS-128
❑ 98PacDynI-177
❑ 98PacDynIIB-177
❑ 98PacDynIR-177
❑ 98PacIceB-410
❑ 98PacPar-224
❑ 98PacParC-224
❑ 98PacParEG-224
❑ 98PacParH-224
❑ 98PacParIB-224
❑ 98PacParS-224
❑ 98PacRed-410
❑ 98Top-55
❑ 98TopO-P-55
❑ 98UC-201
❑ 98UD ChoPCR-201
❑ 98UD ChoR-201
❑ 98UDCP-201
❑ 98UppDec-186
❑ 98UppDecE-186
❑ 98UppDecE1o1-186
❑ 98UppDecGR-186
❑ 99Pac-402
❑ 99PacAur-134
❑ 99PacAurPD-134
❑ 99PacCop-402
❑ 99PacGol-402
❑ 99PacGolCD-33
❑ 99PacIceB-402
❑ 99PacPreD-402
❑ 99RetHoc-73
❑ 99UppDecM-199
❑ 99UppDecMGS-199
❑ 99UppDecMSS-199
❑ 99UppDecMSS-199
❑ 99UppDecRG-73
❑ 99UppDecRP-73
**Berezniuk, Chad**
❑ 907thInnSWHL-305
**Berg, Aki Petteri**
❑ 93FinnSIS-38
❑ 94Cla95DP-DP2
❑ 94FinnSIS-335
❑ 95Bow-146
❑ 95BowAllFoi-146
❑ 95Cla-3
❑ 95ClaIceBre-BK3
❑ 95ColCho-337
❑ 95ColCho-410
❑ 95ColChoPC-337
❑ 95ColChoPCP-337
❑ 95Don-325
❑ 95Fin-138
❑ 95FinnSISDD-1
❑ 95FinnSISLSS-4
❑ 95FinRef-138
❑ 95LeaLim-20
❑ 95Met-170
❑ 95ParInt-253
❑ 95ParInt-510
❑ 95ParIntEl-253
❑ 95ParIntEl-510
❑ 95SelCer-127
❑ 95SelCerMG-127
❑ 95SigRooA-6
❑ 95SigRooAP-P4
❑ 95SigRooAPC-6
❑ 95SkyImp-203
❑ 95SP-69
❑ 95StaClu-201
❑ 95StaCluMOMS-201
❑ 95Sum-175
❑ 95SumArtP-175
❑ 95SumIce-175
❑ 95Top-267
❑ 95TopOPCI-267
❑ 95TopSupSkiSR-SR6
❑ 95Ult-330
❑ 95UppDec-267
❑ 95UppDecEleIce-267
❑ 95UppDecEleIceG-267
❑ 95UppDecPHE-H25
❑ 95UppDecPreH-H25
❑ 95Zen-146
❑ 95ZenRooRC-6
❑ 96ClaIceBreDC-BK3
❑ 96ColCho-128
❑ 96ColEdgFL-27
❑ 96DonEli-108
❑ 96DonEliDCS-108
❑ 96MetUni-72
❑ 96Sco-264
❑ 96ScoArtPro-264
❑ 96ScoDeaCAP-264
❑ 96ScoGolB-264
❑ 96ScoSpeAP-264
❑ 96Sum-164
❑ 96SumArtP-164
❑ 96SumIce-164
❑ 96SumMet-164
❑ 96SumPreS-164
❑ 96SweSemW-30
❑ 97Be A PPAD-155
❑ 97Be A PPAPD-155
❑ 97BeAPla-155
❑ 97BeAPlaAut-155
❑ 97ColCho-121
❑ 97Don-129
❑ 97DonLim-85
❑ 97DonLimExp-85
❑ 97DonPre-112
❑ 97DonPreCttC-112
❑ 97DonPreProG-129
❑ 97DonPreProS-129
❑ 97Kat-67
❑ 97KatGol-67
❑ 97KatSil-67
❑ 97PacDynBKS-44
**Berg, Bill**
❑ 88ProAHL-305
❑ 89ProAHL-232
❑ 91Bow-216
❑ 91OPC-122
❑ 91ProSet-145
❑ 91ProSetFre-145
❑ 91ScoCan-541
❑ 91StaClu-385
❑ 91Top-122
❑ 92MapLeaK-6
❑ 93Lea-287
❑ 93Par-472
❑ 93ParEmel-472
❑ 93ScoBla-15
❑ 94BeAPSig-57
❑ 94MapLeaG-3
❑ 94MapLeaK-4
❑ 94MapLeaPP-9
❑ 94OPCPre-136
❑ 94OPCPreSE-136
❑ 94ParSE-SE181
❑ 94ParSEG-SE181
❑ 94Pin-57
❑ 94PinArtP-57
❑ 94PinRinC-57
❑ 94TopPre-136
❑ 94TopPreSE-136
❑ 96BeAPAut-84
❑ 96BeAPAutSil-84
❑ 96BeAPla-84
❑ 97ScoRan-9
❑ 97ScoRanPla-9
❑ 97ScoRanPre-9
**Berg, Bob**
❑ 897thInnSOHL-72
❑ 907thInnSOHL-400
❑ 90ProAHLIHL-432
❑ 91ProAHLCHL-384
❑ 91RicRen-11
❑ 94CenHocL-109
❑ 95LouIceG-1
❑ 95LouIceGP-1
**Berg, Reg**
❑ 95DonEliWJ-32
❑ 95MinGolG-5
❑ 95UppDec-567
❑ 95UppDecEleIce-567
❑ 95UppDecEleIceG-567
❑ 96MinGolGCAS-5
**Berge, David**
❑ 96GerDELE-248
❑ 96GerDELE-129
**Bergen, Brad**
❑ 94GerDELE-234
❑ 95GerDELE-81
❑ 96GerDELE-272
❑ 98GerDELE-270
❑ 98GerDELE-330
**Bergen, Todd**
❑ 83SprInd-3
**Berger, Mike**
❑ 87NorStaPos-6
❑ 88ProIHL-31
❑ 89ProAHL-285
❑ 92-TulOil-1
❑ 94CenHocL-93
**Berger, Phil**
❑ 91GreMon-2
❑ 92GreMon-5
❑ 93GreMon-1
❑ 94GreMon-20
**Berger, Stanislav**
❑ 94CzeAPSE-284
❑ 95CzeAPSE-268
**Bergeron, Chris**
❑ 93TolSto-17
❑ 95BirBul-13
❑ 95BufStaRHI-24
❑ 96TolSto-24
**Bergeron, David**
❑ 917thInnSQMJHL-172
**Bergeron, Gerard**
❑ 52JunBluT-37
**Bergeron, Germain**
❑ 51LavDaiLSJ-44
**Bergeron, J.C.**
❑ 89ProAHL-181
❑ 90CanaPos-2
❑ 90OPCPre-4
❑ 90ProSet-614
❑ 90UppDec-408
❑ 90UppDecF-408
❑ 91Bow-335
❑ 91CanaPanTS-1
❑ 91ProAHLCHL-77
❑ 92LigShe-3
❑ 93PanSti-220
❑ 94LigPhoA-2
❑ 95Don-241
❑ 95LigTeal-3
❑ 95ParInt-465
❑ 95ParIntEl-465
❑ 95Top-174
❑ 95TopOPCI-174
**Bergeron, Martin**
❑ 90ProAHLIHL-17
**Bergeron, Michel**
❑ 76OPCNHL-71
❑ 76OPCNHL-385
❑ 76Top-71
❑ 77OPCNHL-159
❑ 77Top-159
❑ 78OPC-273
❑ 80NordPos-1
❑ 81NordPos-2
❑ 82NordPos-2
❑ 83NordPos-2
❑ 84NordPos-3
❑ 85NordGenF-3
❑ 85NordPro-4
❑ 85NordTeal-2
❑ 86NordGenF-2
❑ 89Nord-2
❑ 89NordGenF-1
**Bergeron, Remi**
❑ 98BowCHL-102
❑ 98BowCHLGA-102
❑ 98BowCHLOI-102
❑ 98BowChrC-102
❑ 98BowChrCGA-102
❑ 98BowChrCGAR-102
❑ 98BowChrCOI-102
❑ 98BowChrCOIR-102
❑ 98BowChrCR-102
**Bergeron, Yvan**
❑ 907thInnSQMJHL-101
**Bergeron, Yves**
❑ 72NordPos-3
❑ 73NordTeal-3
**Bergevin, Marc**
❑ 86BlaCok-2
❑ 87BlaCok-2
❑ 89OPC-249
❑ 89ProAHL-251
❑ 91ProSet-397
❑ 91ProSetFre-397
❑ 91ProSetPla-176
❑ 91WhaJr7E-2
❑ 92DurPan-30
❑ 92LigShe-4
❑ 92Pin-385
❑ 92PinFre-385
❑ 92Sco-404
❑ 92ScoCan-404
❑ 92StaClu-174
❑ 92Top-61
❑ 92TopGol-61G
❑ 92Ult-200
❑ 93LigSealR-2
❑ 93OPCPre-373
❑ 93OPCPreG-373
❑ 93Pin-304
❑ 93PinCan-304
❑ 93PinCap-22
❑ 93PinCapC-22
❑ 93Sco-363
❑ 93ScoCan-363
❑ 93StaClu-154
❑ 93StaCluFDI-154
❑ 93StaCluFDIO-154
❑ 93StaCluO-154
❑ 93TopPre-373
❑ 93TopPreG-373
❑ 94BeAPSig-10
❑ 94Lea-384
❑ 94LigPhoA-3
❑ 94OPCPre-507
❑ 94OPCPreSE-507
❑ 94Pin-183
❑ 94PinArtP-183
❑ 94PinRinC-183
❑ 94StaClu-101
❑ 94StaCluFDI-101
❑ 94StaCluMOMS-101
❑ 94StaCluSTWC-101
❑ 94TopPre-507
❑ 94TopPreSE-507
❑ 96BeAPAut-85
❑ 96BeAPAutSil-85
❑ 96BeAPla-85
❑ 97PacInvNRB-166
❑ 97ScoBlu-19
❑ 97ScoBluPla-19
❑ 97ScoBluPre-19
❑ 97UppDec-351
**Berggren, Bjorn**
❑ 84SweSemE-145
**Berggren, Bulla**
❑ 69SweHocS-257
❑ 70SweHocS-154
❑ 71SweHocS-248
❑ 72SweHocS-231
❑ 74SweHocS-204
❑ 74SweSemHVS-22
**Bergin, Tony**
❑ 91AirCanSJHL-E36
❑ 92MPSPhoSJHL-109
**Bergkvist, Lars-Arne**
❑ 67SweHoc-198
**Bergkvist, Per Ragnar**
❑ 95SweLeaE-235
❑ 95UppDec-564
❑ 95UppDecEleIce-564
❑ 95UppDecEleIceG-564
**Bergland, Tim**
❑ 88ProAHL-26
❑ 89CapKod-11
❑ 89ProAHL-95
❑ 90CapKod-2
❑ 90CapPos-2
❑ 90CapSmo-2
❑ 90OPC-507
❑ 90ProSet-550
❑ 91Bow-297
❑ 91CapJun5-2
❑ 91CapKod-2
❑ 91OPC-34
❑ 91Par-409
❑ 91ParFre-409
❑ 91ProSet-507
❑ 91ProSetFre-507
❑ 91StaClu-351
❑ 91Top-34
❑ 92LigShe-5
❑ 92StaClu-127
❑ 92Top-244
❑ 92TopGol-244G
**Berglund, Anders**
❑ 86SwePanS-94
❑ 89SweSemE-80
❑ 89SweSemE-255
❑ 90SweSemE-6
❑ 90SweSemE-163
❑ 91SweSemE-207
❑ 91SweSemE-268
❑ 92SweSemE-225
❑ 92SweSemE-294
❑ 93SweSemE-196
❑ 94SweLeaE-9
❑ 95SweLeaE-284
❑ 95SweUppDE-171
**Berglund, Art**
❑ 89SweSemWCS-152
**Berglund, Bo**
❑ 64SweCorI-147
❑ 65SweCorI-147
❑ 81SweSemHVS-15
❑ 83Vac-61
❑ 84OPC-276
❑ 85NorStaPos-4
❑ 87SwePanS-17
❑ 89SweSemE-14
❑ 89SweSemWCS-14
**Berglund, Carl-Axel**
❑ 69SweHocS-221
**Berglund, Charles**
❑ 89SweSemE-65
❑ 90SweSemE-284
❑ 91SweSemE-66
❑ 91SweSemE-351
❑ 91SweSemWCS-42
❑ 92SweSemE-86
❑ 93SweSemE-60
❑ 94SweLeaE-183
❑ 94SweLeaEGC-3
❑ 95FinnSemWC-67
❑ 95SweGloWC-37
❑ 95SwiHNL-15
**Berglund, Rolf**
❑ 69SweHocS-75
❑ 83SweSemE-35
❑ 84SweSemE-32
❑ 85SwePanS-32
❑ 86SwePanS-8
❑ 87SwePanS-31
**Berglund, Tomas**
❑ 89SweSemE-165
❑ 90SweSemE-239
❑ 91SweSemE-169
❑ 92SweSemE-189
❑ 93SweSemE-161
❑ 94SweLeaE-78
❑ 94SweLeaE-81
❑ 95SweUppDE-129
**Berglund, Ulf**
❑ 67SweHoc-150
**Bergman, Anders**
❑ 83SweSemE-149
❑ 85SwePanS-199
❑ 86SwePanS-192
❑ 87SwePanS-191
❑ 89SweSemE-79
❑ 90SweSemE-248
❑ 91SweSemE-79
❑ 92SweSemE-101
❑ 93SweSemE-74
**Bergman, Bo**
❑ 73SweHocS-231
❑ 73SweWorCS-231
**Bergman, Gary**
❑ 64BeeGro3P-64
❑ 64CocCap-51
❑ 64Top-8
❑ 65Coc-53
❑ 65Top-107
❑ 66Top-47
❑ 66TopUSAT-47
❑ 67Top-47
❑ 68OPC-25
❑ 68ShiCoi-34
❑ 68Top-25
❑ 69OPC-58
❑ 69Top-58
❑ 70ColSta-73
❑ 70DadCoo-6
❑ 70EssPowPla-128
❑ 70OPC-154
❑ 70RedWinM-1
❑ 70SarProSta-49
❑ 71LetActR-19
❑ 71OPC-119
❑ 71SarProSta-54
❑ 71Top-119
❑ 71TorSun-85
❑ 72OPC-164
❑ 72OPCPlaC-8
❑ 72OPCTeaC-3
❑ 72SarProSta-79
❑ 72Top-49
❑ 73MacMil-1
❑ 73NorStaP-2
❑ 73OPC-65
❑ 73RedWinTI-3
❑ 73Top-65
❑ 74NHLActSta-136
❑ 74NHLActStaU-9
❑ 75OPCNHL-236A
❑ 75OPCNHL-236B
❑ 75Top-236
❑ 76Top-159
❑ 81RedWinOld-3
❑ 91FutTreC72-87
❑ 91UltOriS-67
❑ 91UltOriSF-67
❑ 94ParTalB-57
❑ 95Par66-41
❑ 95Par66Coi-41
**Bergman, Jan**
❑ 89SweSemE-223
❑ 90SweSemE-57
❑ 91SweSemE-230
**Bergman, Per**
❑ 87SwePanS-264
**Bergman, Roger**
❑ 72SweHocS-287
❑ 73SweHocS-154
❑ 73SweWorCS-154
❑ 74SweHocS-160
**Bergman, Thommie**
❑ 69SweHocS-95
❑ 70SweHocS-132
❑ 71SweHocS-6
❑ 71SweHocS-224
❑ 72SweHocS-4
❑ 72SweHocS-46
❑ 72SweHocS-288
❑ 72SweSemWC-55
❑ 73OPC-204
❑ 73RedWinMP-2
❑ 73RedWinTI-4
❑ 74NHLActSta-108
❑ 74OPCNHL-365
❑ 74SweHocS-315
❑ 75OPCWHA-29
❑ 76OPCWHA-51
❑ 79OPC-148
❑ 79RedWinP-1
❑ 79Top-148
❑ 87SwePanS-211
**Bergmark, Erling**
❑ 69SweHocS-166
**Bergqvist, Fredrik**
❑ 91SweSemE-211
❑ 92SweSemE-234
❑ 93SweSemE-203
❑ 94SweLeaE-294
❑ 95SweUppDE1DS-DS17
**Bergqvist, Hans**
❑ 67SweHoc-84
**Bergqvist, Jan-Ivar**
❑ 67SweHoc-231
**Bergqvist, Jonas**
❑ 83SweSemE-140
❑ 84SweSemE-160
❑ 85SwePanS-145
❑ 86SwePanS-166
❑ 87SwePanS-158
❑ 89SweSemWCS-17
❑ 91SweSemE-149
❑ 91SweSemE-356
❑ 92SweSemE-167
❑ 93SweSemE-136
❑ 94FinnJaaK-73
❑ 94SweLeaE-250
❑ 94SweLeaEGC-9
❑ 94SweLeaESS-6
❑ 95FinnSemWC-63
❑ 95SweGloWC-34
❑ 95SweLeaE-69
❑ 95SweLeaEM-2
❑ 95SweUppDE-105
❑ 96SweSemCDT-12
❑ 96SweSemW-71
**Bergqvist, Stefan**
❑ 93SweSemE-125
❑ 94Cla-28
❑ 94ClaDraGol-28
❑ 95Cla-88
❑ 95CleLum-7
❑ 96UppDec-323
**Bergstrom, Erik**
❑ 92SweSemE-276
❑ 94SweLeaE-169
❑ 95SweLeaE-127
**Berlinquette, Louis**
❑ 23V1281PauC-32
❑ 24C144ChaCig-4
❑ 24V130MapC-30
❑ 24V1452-41
**Bermingham, Jim**
❑ 907thInnSMC-71
❑ 907thInnSQMJHL-49
❑ 917thInnSQMJHL-226
❑ 93WheThu-5
❑ 94HunBli-4
**Bernard, Larry**
❑ 89ProAHL-32
❑ 90MonHaw-1
❑ 90ProAHLIHL-245
❑ 93FliGen-14
❑ 94FliGen-2
**Bernard, Louis**
❑ 917thInnSQMJHL-276
❑ 93DruVol-11
❑ 94FreCan-1
❑ 94WheThu-19
❑ 95FreCan-1
**Bernard, Mark**
❑ 90HamRoaA-57
❑ 91HamRoaA-1
❑ 92HamRoaA-16
❑ 95HamRoaA-5
**Berndaner, Ignaz**
❑ 79PanSti-98
**Berndtsson, Peter**
❑ 83SweSemE-117
❑ 84SweSemE-117
❑ 87SwePanS-119
❑ 89SweSemE-279
❑ 90SweSemE-44
❑ 91SweSemE-295
❑ 93SweSemE-281
❑ 94SweLeaE-70
❑ 95SweLeaE-143
❑ 95SweUppDE-213
**Bernhardt, Tim**
❑ 85MapLeaP-3
❑ 85OPC-166
❑ 85OPCSti-9
❑ 86MapLeaP-3
❑ 88ProAHL-244
❑ 89ProAHL-110
**Bernie, John**
❑ 907thInnSOHL-61
**Bernier, Art**
❑ 10C55SweCP-37
❑ 10C56-25
❑ 11C55-37
❑ 12C57-6
**Bernier, David**
❑ 98QueRem-2
**Bernier, Jean**
❑ 76NordPos-3
❑ 77OPCWHA-2
**Bernier, Pascal**
❑ 917thInnSQMJHL-265
**Bernier, Serge**
❑ 70EssPowPla-214
❑ 71Baz-24
❑ 71OPC-19
❑ 71SarProSta-155
❑ 71Top-19
❑ 71TorSun-189
❑ 72FlyMigM-1
❑ 72OPC-152
❑ 72SarProSta-97
❑ 72Top-36
❑ 74OPCWHA-5
❑ 74TeaCanLWHA-2
❑ 75OPCWHA-60
❑ 75OPCWHA-70
❑ 76NordMarA-2
❑ 76NordPos-4
❑ 76OPCWHA-109
❑ 77OPCWHA-60
❑ 79OPC-47
❑ 79Top-47
❑ 80NordPos-2
❑ 80OPC-309
❑ 80PepCap-61
**Berra, Andre**
❑ 72SweSemWC-142
**Berry, Bob**
❑ 70EssPowPla-158
❑ 71OPC-76
❑ 71Top-76
❑ 71TorSun-106
❑ 72OPC-9
❑ 72SarProSta-98
❑ 72Top-21
❑ 73OPC-175
❑ 73Top-172
❑ 74NHLActSta-120
❑ 74OPCNHL-18
❑ 74Top-18
❑ 75OPCNHL-196
❑ 75Top-196
❑ 75Top-320
❑ 76OPCNHL-300
❑ 77OPCNHL-268
❑ 81CanaPos-3
❑ 82CanaPos-2
❑ 83CanaPos-2
❑ 86PenKod-1
❑ 93Kra-28
**Berry, Brad**
❑ 86JetBor-1
❑ 87Jet-1
❑ 89JetSaf-3
❑ 90SweSemE-178
❑ 91ProAHLCHL-147
❑ 92Par-312
❑ 92ParEmel-312
❑ 94StaHoc-2
❑ 96SeaThu-6
**Berry, Brent**
❑ 92BriColJHL-156
**Berry, Doug**
❑ 79Roc-2
**Berry, Fred**
❑ 81MilAdm-3
**Berry, Ken**
❑ 81SweSemHVS-88
❑ 84NovScoO-8
❑ 88CanuMoh-3
❑ 88OilTenAnn-67
**Berry, Rick**
❑ 95SeaThu-3
**Berry, Ryan**
❑ 95SpoChi-18
**Bertaggia, Sandro**
❑ 91SweSemWCS-184
❑ 93SweSemWCS-116
❑ 93SwiHNL-88
❑ 95SweGloWC-213
❑ 95SwiHNL-137
❑ 95SwiHNL-510
**Berthelsen, Peter**
❑ 88LetHur-2
❑ 89LetHur-2
**Berthiaume, Daniel**
❑ 84ChiSag-4
❑ 86SheCan-5
❑ 87Jet-2
❑ 87OPC-217
❑ 87OPCMin-3
❑ 87OPCSti-249
❑ 87PanSti-356
❑ 88OPC-142
❑ 88OPCSti-149
❑ 88PanSti-148
❑ 88Top-142
❑ 89JetSaf-4
❑ 89OPC-296
❑ 90KinSmo-19
❑ 90OPC-180
❑ 90OPC-247
❑ 90OPCPre-5
❑ 90ProSet-454
❑ 90ScoRoo-73T
❑ 90Top-180
❑ 90Top-247
❑ 90TopTif-247
❑ 90UppDec-381
❑ 90UppDec-412
❑ 90UppDecF-381
❑ 90UppDecF-412
❑ 91Bow-190
❑ 91BruSpoA-3
❑ 91OPC-313
❑ 91Pin-165
❑ 91PinFre-165
❑ 91ScoAme-132
❑ 91ScoCan-132
❑ 91StaClu-290
❑ 91SweSemWCS-54
❑ 91Top-313
❑ 91UppDec-150
❑ 91UppDecF-150
❑ 92Bow-140
❑ 92Par-359
❑ 92ParEmel-359
❑ 92Sen-2
❑ 92StaClu-101
❑ 92Top-505
❑ 92TopGol-505G
❑ 92Ult-361
❑ 93Ult-54
❑ 95RoaExp-14
**Bertogliat, Jesse**
❑ 92MinGolG-2
❑ 93MinGolG-2
❑ 94MinGolG-3
❑ 95MinGolG-6
**Bertrand, Marc**
❑ 80QueRem-1
**Bertrand, Ron**
❑ 897thInnSOHL-172
❑ 907thInnSOHL-303
❑ 917thInnSOHL-52
**Bertsch, Jay**
❑ 95SpoChi-23

**Bertuzzi, Brian**
❑ 84KamBla-3
❑ 86FreExp-2
**Bertuzzi, Ed**
❑ 88KamBla-3
**Bertuzzi, Todd**
❑ 917thInnSOHL-357
❑ 93Cla-14
❑ 93GueSto-23
❑ 94Cla-103
❑ 94ClaDraGol-103
❑ 94ClaTri-T40
❑ 94GueSto-22
❑ 95BeAPla-168
❑ 95BeAPSig-S168
❑ 95BeAPSigDC-S168
❑ 95Bow-156
❑ 95BowAllFoi-156
❑ 95BowBes-BB30
❑ 95BowBesRef-BB30
❑ 95Cla-85
❑ 95Don-346
❑ 95DonEli-57
❑ 95DonEliDCS-57
❑ 95DonEliDCU-57
❑ 95DonEliR-4
❑ 95DonRatRoo-2
❑ 95Emo-103
❑ 95EmoGen-8
❑ 95Fin-146
❑ 95FinRef-146
❑ 95Ima-37
❑ 95ImaGol-37
❑ 95LeaLim-19
❑ 95LeaLimRP-10
❑ 95Met-171
❑ 95ParInt-264
❑ 95ParIntEl-264
❑ 95ParIntPTP-PP44
❑ 95SelCer-123
❑ 95SelCerMG-123
❑ 95SkyImp-208
❑ 95SP-88
❑ 95StaClu-204
❑ 95StaCluMOMS-204
❑ 95Sum-193
❑ 95SumArtP-193
❑ 95SumIce-193
❑ 95Top-339
❑ 95TopOPCI-339
❑ 95TopSupSkiSR-SR7
❑ 95Ult-331
❑ 95UltHigSpe-3
❑ 95UppDecSpeE-SE53
❑ 95UppDecSpeEdiG-SE53
❑ 95Zen-140
❑ 95ZenRooRC-9
❑ 96ColCho-164
❑ 96ColCho-323
❑ 96ColCho-338
❑ 96DonCanI-28
❑ 96DonCanIGPP-28
❑ 96DonCanIRPP-28
❑ 96DonEli-18
❑ 96DonEliAsp-4
❑ 96DonEliDCS-18
❑ 96DonRatR-9
❑ 96Fle-63
❑ 96FleRooSen-2
❑ 96IsIPos-3
❑ 96Lea-205
❑ 96LeaLim-19
❑ 96LeaLimG-19
❑ 96LeaLimStu-9
❑ 96LeaPre-93
❑ 96LeaPreP-205
❑ 96LeaPrePP-93
❑ 96LeaPreSG-20
❑ 96LeaPreSte-20
❑ 96MetUni-91
❑ 96Pin-208
❑ 96PinArtP-208
❑ 96PinFoi-208
❑ 96PinPreS-208
❑ 96PinRinC-208
❑ 96Sco-244
❑ 96ScoArtPro-244
❑ 96ScoDeaCAP-244
❑ 96ScoGolB-244
❑ 96ScoSpeAP-244
❑ 96SelCer-80
❑ 96SelCerAP-80
❑ 96SelCerBlu-80
❑ 96SelCerMB-80
❑ 96SelCerMG-80
❑ 96SelCerMR-80
❑ 96SelCerRed-80
❑ 96SkyImp-74
❑ 96SkyImp-166
❑ 96SkyImpNHLF-2
❑ 96SP-96
❑ 96SPx-30
❑ 96SPxGol-30
❑ 96Sum-154
❑ 96SumArtP-154
❑ 96SumIce-154
❑ 96SumMet-154
❑ 96SumPreS-154
❑ 96TopNHLP-121
❑ 96TopPicOI-121
❑ 96TopPicRS-RS10
❑ 96Ult-99
❑ 96UltGolM-100
❑ 96UppDec-291
❑ 96UppDecBD-84
❑ 96UppDecBDG-84
❑ 96UppDecGN-X14
❑ 96UppDecPP-P7
❑ 96Zen-81
❑ 96ZenArtP-81
❑ 96ZenAss-6
❑ 97Be A PPAD-168
❑ 97Be A PPAPD-168
❑ 97BeAPla-168
❑ 97BeAPlaAut-168
❑ 97ColCho-154
❑ 97Don-12
❑ 97DonLim-30
❑ 97DonLimExp-30
❑ 97DonPreProG-12
❑ 97DonPreProS-12
❑ 97DonPri-155
❑ 97DonPriSoA-155
❑ 97Lea-134
❑ 97LeaFraMat-134
❑ 97LeaFraMDC-134
❑ 97LeaInt-134
❑ 97LeaIntUI-134
❑ 97PacInvNRB-115
❑ 97PacPar-107
❑ 97PacParC-107
❑ 97PacParDG-107
❑ 97PacParEG-107
❑ 97PacParIB-107
❑ 97PacParRed-107
❑ 97PacParSil-107
❑ 97SPAut-96
❑ 97UppDec-103
❑ 98Be A PPA-292
❑ 98Be A PPAA-292
❑ 98Be A PPAAF-292
❑ 98Be A PPSE-292
❑ 98Be APG-292
❑ 98Pac-424
❑ 98PacAur-186
❑ 98PacDynI-185
❑ 98PacDynIIB-185
❑ 98PacDynIR-185
❑ 98PacIceB-424
❑ 98PacPar-232
❑ 98PacParC-232
❑ 98PacParEG-232
❑ 98PacParH-232
❑ 98PacParIB-232
❑ 98PacParS-232
❑ 98PacRed-424
❑ 98SPxFin-85
❑ 98SPxFinR-85
❑ 98SPxFinS-85
❑ 98UC-212
❑ 98UD ChoPCR-212
❑ 98UD ChoR-212
❑ 98UppDec-194
❑ 98UppDecE-194
❑ 98UppDecE1o1-194
❑ 98UppDecGR-194
❑ 99Pac-420
❑ 99PacCop-420
❑ 99PacGol-420
❑ 99PacIceB-420
❑ 99PacPreD-420
**Berube, Craig**
❑ 85KamBla-2
❑ 85MedHatT-7
❑ 89FlyPos-2
❑ 90FlyPos-3
❑ 90OPC-448
❑ 90ProSet-498
❑ 90UppDec-450
❑ 90UppDecF-450
❑ 91MapLeaP-2
❑ 91OPCPre-47
❑ 91Par-246
❑ 91ParFre-246
❑ 91ProSet-495
❑ 91ProSetFre-495
❑ 91ScoCan-578
❑ 91ScoRoo-28T
❑ 92FlamIGA-2
❑ 92OPC-147
❑ 92Sco-258
❑ 92ScoCan-258
❑ 92StaClu-458
❑ 92Top-208
❑ 92TopGol-208G
❑ 93Lea-314
❑ 94BeAPSig-64
❑ 94Lea-343
❑ 94OPCPre-433
❑ 94OPCPreSE-433
❑ 94Pin-515
❑ 94PinArtP-515
❑ 94PinRinC-515
❑ 94TopPre-433
❑ 94TopPreSE-433
❑ 95Cap-2
❑ 96BeAPAut-115
❑ 96BeAPAutSil-115
❑ 96BeAPla-115
❑ 97PacDynBKS-99
❑ 98Be A PPA-298
❑ 98Be A PPAA-298
❑ 98Be A PPAAF-298
❑ 98Be A PPSE-298
❑ 98Be APG-298
❑ 98Pac-437
❑ 98PacIceB-437
❑ 98PacOmeH-244
❑ 98PacOmeODI-244
❑ 98PacOmeR-244
❑ 98PacRed-437
**Berube, Sebastien**
❑ 917thInnSQMJHL-6
**Berwanger, Markus**
❑ 94GerDELE-259
❑ 95GerDELE-345
**Bes, Jeff**
❑ 907thInnSOHL-201
❑ 917thInnSOHL-346
❑ 93UppDec-255
❑ 94ClaProP-144
**Bessette, Marcel**
❑ 51LavDaiQSHL-68
**Bessette, Roger**
❑ 51LavDaiQSHL-48
❑ 52St.LawS-78
**Bessey, Brent**
❑ 93WatBlaH-1
**Bester, Allan**
❑ 83BraAle-17
❑ 84MapLeaP-3
❑ 84OPC-297
❑ 84OPCSti-20
❑ 87MapLeaP-1
❑ 87MapLeaPLA-12
❑ 87MapLeaPO-1
❑ 87OPC-236
❑ 87OPCSti-162
❑ 87PanSti-323
❑ 88MapLeaPLA-11
❑ 88PanSti-116
❑ 89OPC-271
❑ 89OPCSti-169
❑ 89PanSti-139
❑ 90Bow-154
❑ 90BowTif-154
❑ 90OPC-32
❑ 90ProSet-275A
❑ 90ProSet-275B
❑ 90Sco-27
❑ 90ScoCan-27
❑ 90Top-32
❑ 90TopTif-32
❑ 90UppDec-241
❑ 90UppDecF-241
❑ 91MapLeaPTS-2
❑ 91ProAHLCHL-118
❑ 95ColEdgI-170
**Beswick, Sean**
❑ 92NorDakFS-3
**Bets, Maxim**
❑ 93Cla-15
❑ 93Pin-502
❑ 93PinCan-502
❑ 94Cla-92
❑ 94ClaDraGol-92
❑ 94Don-33
❑ 94Par-10
❑ 94ParGol-10
❑ 94ParVin-V37
❑ 94Pin-483
❑ 94PinArtP-483
❑ 94PinRinC-483
❑ 94PinRooTP-6
❑ 94Sco-232
❑ 94ScoGol-232
❑ 94ScoPla-232
❑ 94ScoPlaTS-232
❑ 94UppDec-353
❑ 94UppDecElelce-353
❑ 94UppDecSPI-SP1
❑ 94UppDecSPIDC-SP1
**Bettens, Mike**
❑ 96GuiFla-8
**Bettiol, Frank**
❑ 52JunBluT-53
**Betts, Blair**
❑ 97UppDec-407
❑ 98BowCHL-124
❑ 98BowCHLAuB-A32
❑ 98BowCHLAuG-A32
❑ 98BowCHLAuS-A32
❑ 98BowCHLGA-124
❑ 98BowCHLOI-124
❑ 98BowChrC-124
❑ 98BowChrCGA-124
❑ 98BowChrCGAR-124
❑ 98BowChrCOI-124
❑ 98BowChrCOIR-124
❑ 98BowChrCR-124
**Bety, Sebastien**
❑ 93DruVol-4
❑ 95SigRoo-19
❑ 95SigRooSig-19
**Beukeboom, Jeff**
❑ 82SauSteMG-4
❑ 83SauSteMG-1
❑ 84SauSteMG-2
❑ 85NovScoO-7
❑ 86OilRedR-6
❑ 86OilTeal-6
❑ 87OilTeal-6
❑ 88OilTeal-2
❑ 88OilTenAnn-17
❑ 88PanSti-56
❑ 89OilTeal-2
❑ 90OilIGA-2
❑ 90OPC-471
❑ 90ProSet-439
❑ 91Bow-110
❑ 91OilPanTS-2
❑ 91OilTeal-2
❑ 91OPC-284
❑ 91Par-341
❑ 91ParFre-341
❑ 91Pin-229
❑ 91PinFre-229
❑ 91ProSet-444
❑ 91ProSetFre-444
❑ 91ProSetPla-206
❑ 91ScoCan-253
❑ 91StaClu-350
❑ 91Top-284
❑ 91UppDec-394
❑ 91UppDecF-394
❑ 92Bow-347
❑ 92OPC-237
❑ 92Pin-112
❑ 92PinFre-112
❑ 92Sco-137
❑ 92ScoCan-137
❑ 92StaClu-129
❑ 92Top-57
❑ 92TopGol-57G
❑ 92Ult-351
❑ 92UppDec-161
❑ 93OPCPre-54
❑ 93OPCPreG-54
❑ 93Pin-309
❑ 93PinCan-309
❑ 93Pow-389
❑ 93Sco-94
❑ 93ScoCan-94
❑ 93StaClu-7
❑ 93StaCluFDI-7
❑ 93StaCluFDIO-7
❑ 93StaCluO-7
❑ 93TopPre-54
❑ 93TopPreG-54
❑ 94BeAPSig-107
❑ 94FinRinL-9
❑ 94Fla-110
❑ 94Fle-131
❑ 94Lea-528
❑ 94OPCPre-138
❑ 94OPCPreSE-138
❑ 94Par-148
❑ 94ParGol-148
❑ 94Pin-195
❑ 94PinArtP-195
❑ 94PinRinC-195
❑ 94Sco-66
❑ 94ScoGol-66
❑ 94ScoPla-66
❑ 94ScoPlaTS-66
❑ 94TopPre-138
❑ 94TopPreSE-138
❑ 94Ult-136
❑ 94UppDec-339
❑ 94UppDecElelce-339
❑ 95CanGamNHLP-185
❑ 95ColCho-317
❑ 95ColChoPC-317
❑ 95ColChoPCP-317
❑ 95ParInt-410
❑ 95ParIntEl-410
❑ 95Pin-112
❑ 95PinArtP-112
❑ 95PinRinC-112
❑ 95Top-63
❑ 95TopOPCI-63
❑ 95UppDec-203
❑ 95UppDecElelce-203
❑ 95UppDecElelceG-203
❑ 96BeAPAut-158
❑ 96BeAPAutSil-158
❑ 96BeAPla-158
❑ 96DonEli-87
❑ 96DonEliDCS-87
❑ 96Sum-71
❑ 96SumArtP-71
❑ 96SumIce-71
❑ 96SumMet-71
❑ 96SumPreS-71
❑ 96UppDec-105
❑ 97Pac-57
❑ 97PacCop-57
❑ 97PacEmeGre-57
❑ 97PacIceB-57
❑ 97PacRed-57
❑ 97PacSil-57
❑ 97ScoRan-20
❑ 97ScoRanPla-20
❑ 97ScoRanPre-20
❑ 97UppDec-314
❑ 98Be A PPA-242
❑ 98Be A PPAA-242
❑ 98Be A PPAAF-242
❑ 98Be A PPSE-242
❑ 98Be APG-242
❑ 98O-PChr-87
❑ 98O-PChrR-87
❑ 98Pac-290
❑ 98PacIceB-290
❑ 98PacRed-290
❑ 98Top-87
❑ 98TopO-P-87
❑ 98UC-136
❑ 98UD ChoPCR-136
❑ 98UD ChoR-136
❑ 98UppDec-326
❑ 98UppDecE-326
❑ 98UppDecE1o1-326
❑ 98UppDecGR-326
**Beuselinck, Derek**
❑ 91AirCanSJHL-E44
**Beutler, Andreas**
❑ 93SweSemWCS-112
❑ 93SwiHNL-63
❑ 95SwiHNL-349
**Beveridge, Bill**
❑ 33OPCV304B-54
❑ 33V129-25
❑ 33V357IceK-60
❑ 34BeeGro1P-189
❑ 35DiaMatTI-3
❑ 36V356WorG-82
❑ 37OPCV304E-161
**Beverley, Nick**
❑ 72OPC-281
❑ 73OPC-239
❑ 75OPCNHL-279
❑ 75Top-279
❑ 76OPCNHL-41
❑ 76Top-41
❑ 77OPCNHL-198
❑ 77Top-198
❑ 78OPC-111
❑ 78Top-111
❑ 79Roc-3
**Bezak, Marian**
❑ 81SweSemHVS-68
**Bezeau, Andy**
❑ 897thInnSOHL-147
❑ 89NiaFalT-4
❑ 907thInnSOHL-253
❑ 94MusFur-17
❑ 95ColEdgI-125
**Biafore, Chad**
❑ 87PorWinH-3
❑ 88PorWinH-3
❑ 96GerDELE-32
❑ 98GerDELE-179
**Biagini, Chris**
❑ 95Sla-284
**Bialowas, Dwight**
❑ 74OPCNHL-372
❑ 75OPCNHL-106
❑ 75Top-106
❑ 76OPCNHL-198
❑ 76Top-198
❑ 77OPCNHL-271
**Bialowas, Frank**
❑ 92RicRen-2
❑ 93St.JohML-2
❑ 94Par-237
❑ 94ParGol-237
❑ 94St.JohML-3
❑ 95PorPir-4
**Bianchi, Tony**
❑ 91MinGolG-2
❑ 92MinGolG-3
❑ 93MinGolG-3
**Bianchin, Wayne**
❑ 74NHLActSta-219
❑ 77OPCNHL-188
❑ 77PenPucB-14
❑ 77Top-188
❑ 78OPC-103
❑ 78Top-103
❑ 79OPC-290
❑ 88OilTenAnn-107
**Bianni, Mike**
❑ 84MonGolF-2
**Bibeault, Paul**
❑ 34BeeGro1P-136
**Bicanek, Radim**
❑ 93Cla-36
❑ 93UppDec-262
❑ 94Cla-111
❑ 94ClaDraGol-111
❑ 94ClaTri-T46
❑ 94SenBelM-3
❑ 95Cla-83
❑ 95Don-15
❑ 95Ima-43
❑ 95ImaGol-43
❑ 95Lea-69
❑ 95Pin-217
❑ 95PinArtP-217
❑ 95PinRinC-217
❑ 95Sco-306
❑ 95ScoBlaIce-306
❑ 95ScoBlaIceAP-306
❑ 97PacDynBKS-64
**Bickell, J.P.**
❑ 83HalFP-J3
❑ 85HalFC-184
**Bidner, Todd**
❑ 83MonAlp-21
**Biegl, Radovan**
❑ 94CzeAPSE-24
**Bielas, Rolf**
❑ 69SweWorC-172
❑ 69SweWorC-174
❑ 70SweHocS-374
**Bielke, Rene**
❑ 94GerDELE-245
❑ 95GerDELE-220
**Bierk, Zac**
❑ 93PetPet-10
❑ 95SigRooA-7
❑ 95SigRooAPC-7
❑ 95Sla-307
❑ 95Sla-NNO
❑ 95Sla-NNO
❑ 97BowCHL-19
❑ 97BowCHLOPC-19
❑ 98Pac-396
❑ 98PacIceB-396
❑ 98PacOmeH-224
❑ 98PacOmeODI-224
❑ 98PacOmeR-224
❑ 98PacRed-396
❑ 98SPxFin-79
❑ 98SPxFin-148
❑ 98SPxFinR-79
❑ 98SPxFinR-148
❑ 98SPxFinS-79
❑ 98SPxFinS-148
❑ 98UppDec-181
❑ 98UppDecE-181
❑ 98UppDecE1o1-181
❑ 98UppDecGR-181
**Biette, Kerry**
❑ 907thInnSWHL-177
❑ 917thInnSWHL-227
**Bifano, Paul**
❑ 83VicCou-4
**Biggs, Don**
❑ 82OshGen-9
❑ 83OshGen-28
❑ 85NovScoO-26
❑ 88ProAHL-137
❑ 89ProAHL-331
❑ 91ProAHLCHL-205
❑ 92BinRan-11
❑ 94ClaProP-83
❑ 95ColEdgI-110
❑ 96CinCyc-22
**Biggs, Kenneth**
❑ 51LavDaiQSHL-40
**Biggs, Scott**
❑ 82KitRan-28
**Bignell, Greg**
❑ 897thInnSOHL-86
❑ 90HamRoaA-42
**Biles, C.**
❑ 28V1282PauC-59
**Billeck, Laurie**
❑ 907thInnSWHL-261
❑ 90PriAlbR-2
❑ 917thInnSWHL-152
❑ 95VanVooRHI-4
**Billington, Craig**
❑ 83BelBul-24
❑ 84BelBul-10
❑ 85DevPos-3
❑ 87PanSti-72
❑ 88ProAHL-333
❑ 89ProAHL-224
❑ 90AlbIntTC-1
❑ 91Par-320
❑ 91ParFre-320
❑ 91ProSetPla-197
❑ 91UppDec-559
❑ 91UppDecF-559
❑ 92Bow-102
❑ 92OPC-372
❑ 92Par-330
❑ 92ParEmel-330
❑ 92Sco-228
❑ 92ScoCan-228
❑ 92StaClu-343
❑ 92Top-48
❑ 92TopGol-48G
❑ 92Ult-334
❑ 92UppDec-315
❑ 93Don-226
❑ 93Lea-354
❑ 93OPCPre-374
❑ 93OPCPreG-374
❑ 93Par-138
❑ 93ParEmel-138
❑ 93Pin-352
❑ 93PinAllS-1
❑ 93PinAllSC-1
❑ 93PinCan-352
❑ 93Pow-169
❑ 93Sco-207
❑ 93Sco-521
❑ 93ScoCan-207
❑ 93ScoCan-521
❑ 93ScoGol-521
❑ 93SenKraS-2
❑ 93StaCluAS-7
❑ 93TopPre-374
❑ 93TopPreG-374
❑ 93Ult-378
❑ 93UppDec-424
❑ 93UppDecSP-105
❑ 94CanGamNHLP-289
❑ 94Don-209
❑ 94Fla-119
❑ 94Kra-34
❑ 94Lea-84
❑ 94OPCPre-482
❑ 94OPCPreSE-482
❑ 94Par-158
❑ 94ParGol-158
❑ 94Pin-320
❑ 94PinArtP-320
❑ 94PinRinC-320
❑ 94Sco-167
❑ 94ScoGol-167
❑ 94ScoPla-167
❑ 94ScoPlaTS-167
❑ 94Sel-49
❑ 94SelGol-49
❑ 94SenBelM-4
❑ 94TopPre-482
❑ 94TopPreSE-482
❑ 94Ult-145
❑ 94UppDec-370
❑ 94UppDecElelce-370
❑ 94UppDecSPI-SP53
❑ 94UppDecSPIDC-SP53
❑ 95BeAPla-151
❑ 95BeAPSig-S151
❑ 95BeAPSigDC-S151
❑ 95Don-381
❑ 95ParInt-285
❑ 95ParIntEl-285
❑ 95UppDec-112
❑ 95UppDecElelce-112
❑ 95UppDecElelceG-112
❑ 96Sco-231
❑ 96ScoArtPro-231
❑ 96ScoDeaCAP-231
❑ 96ScoGolB-231
❑ 96ScoSpeAP-231
❑ 97Be A PPAD-138
❑ 97Be A PPAPD-138
❑ 97BeAPla-138
❑ 97BeAPlaAut-138
❑ 97PacDynBKS-23
❑ 97PacOme-54
❑ 97PacOmeC-54
❑ 97PacOmeDG-54
❑ 97PacOmeEG-54
❑ 97PacOmeG-54
❑ 97PacOmeIB-54
❑ 97Sco-19
❑ 97ScoArtPro-19
❑ 97ScoAva-2
❑ 97ScoAvaPla-2
❑ 97ScoAvaPre-2
❑ 97ScoGolBla-19
❑ 98Be A PPA-185
❑ 98Be A PPAA-185
❑ 98Be A PPAAF-185
❑ 98Be A PPSE-185
❑ 98Be APG-185
❑ 98Pac-157
❑ 98PacIceB-157
❑ 98PacPar-52
❑ 98PacParC-52
❑ 98PacParEG-52
❑ 98PacParH-52
❑ 98PacParIB-52
❑ 98PacParS-52
❑ 98PacRed-157
❑ 99Pac-100
❑ 99PacCop-100
❑ 99PacGol-100
❑ 99PacIceB-100
❑ 99PacPreD-100
**Billkvam, Arne**
❑ 93SweSemWCS-245
❑ 94FinnJaaK-268
**Bilodeau, Brent**
❑ 907thInnSWHL-1
❑ 917thInnSMC-99
❑ 917thInnSWHL-180
❑ 91AreDraPic-13
❑ 91Cla-14
❑ 91StaPicH-53
❑ 91UltDra-14
❑ 91UltDra-70
❑ 91UppDec-694
❑ 91UppDecCWJC-81
❑ 91UppDecF-694
❑ 93FreCan-1
❑ 94ClaProP-58
❑ 94FreCan-2
❑ 98KanCitB-18
**Bilodeau, David**
❑ 97RimOce-10
**Bilodeau, Luc**
❑ 90MonAAA-7
**Bilotto, Nicholas**
❑ 98QueRem-3
**Bilous, Jason**
❑ 91BriColJHL-136
**Bilsen, Van**
❑ 79PanSti-276
**Bilyaletinov, Zinetula**
❑ 81SweSemHVS-44
❑ 82SweSemHVS-58
❑ 83RusNatT-3
❑ 87RusNatT-3
❑ 93JetRuf-5
**Bingham, Pat**
❑ 85KamBla-3
❑ 88KamBla-2
❑ 89NasKni-1
❑ 91RicRen-9
**Binkley, Les**
❑ 52JunBluT-174
❑ 60CleBar-2
❑ 68OPC-100
❑ 68ShiCoi-140
❑ 68Top-100
❑ 69OPC-110
❑ 69OPCFou-2
❑ 69OPCSta-3
❑ 69Top-110
❑ 70ColSta-75
❑ 70DadCoo-7
❑ 70EssPowPla-234
❑ 70OPC-200
❑ 70OPCDec-10
❑ 70SarProSta-175
❑ 71OPC-192
❑ 71PenPos-2
❑ 71SarProSta-166
❑ 71TorSun-211
❑ 72NatOttWHA-2
❑ 72OPC-300
❑ 72SweSemWC-215
**Binnie, Troy**
❑ 897thInnSOHL-52
❑ 907thInnSOHL-77
❑ 92DalFre-4
❑ 93DalFre-3

□ 94CenHocL-4
**Binns, Craig**
□ 917thInnSOHL-179
□ 93OweSouPla-1
**Bionda, Jack**
□ 44BeeGro2P-380
□ 57BruTealss-2
□ 57Top-2
□ 94ParMisL-14
**Biotti, Chris**
□ 88SalLakCGE-20
□ 89ProIHL-202
**Birch, Joe**
□ 95Sla-151
**Bird, Jamie**
□ 917thInnSQMJHL-178
□ 95SlaMemC-56
**Birk, Harald**
□ 94GerDELE-318
□ 95GerDELE-23
□ 98GerDELE-269
□ 98GerDELE-334
**Birk, Klaus**
□ 94GerDELE-328
□ 95GerDELE-324
**Birnie, Scott**
□ 83NorBayC-4
**Birnie, Stuart**
□ 87BroBra-20
□ 88BroBra-7
**Biron, Martin**
□ 93AmoLesFAM-3
□ 95Cla-16
□ 95ClaIceBre-BK13
□ 95ParInt-295
□ 95ParIntEl-295
□ 96ClaIceBreDC-BK13
□ 96DonCanILG-9
□ 96Fle-122
□ 96Lea-213
□ 96LeaPreP-213
□ 96Pin-224
□ 96PinArtP-224
□ 96PinFoi-224
□ 96PinPreS-224
□ 96PinRinC-224
□ 96SkyImp-145
□ 96Sum-179
□ 96SumArtP-179
□ 96SumIce-179
□ 96SumMet-179
□ 96SumPreS-179
□ 96UppDecIce-118
□ 99Pac-34
□ 99PacCop-34
□ 99PacGol-34
□ 99PacIceB-34
□ 99PacPreD-34
□ 99UppDecM-25
□ 99UppDecMGS-25
□ 99UppDecMSS-25
□ 99UppDecMSS-25
**Biron, Mathieu**
□ 98BowCHL-154
□ 98BowCHLAuB-A21
□ 98BowCHLAuG-A21
□ 98BowCHLAuS-A21
□ 98BowCHLGA-154
□ 98BowCHLOI-154
□ 98BowChrC-154
□ 98BowChrCGA-154
□ 98BowChrCGAR-154
□ 98BowChrCOI-154
□ 98BowChrCOIR-154
□ 98BowChrCR-154
□ 98O-PChr-238
□ 98O-PChrR-238
□ 98Top-238
□ 98TopO-P-238
□ 99QuePeeWHWCCS-27
**Bisaillon, J.P.**
□ 51LavDaiQSHL-71
□ 52St.LawS-30
**Bisaillon, Patrick**
□ 917thInnSMC-32
□ 917thInnSQMJHL-264
**Bishop, Allen**
□ 82NorBayC-1
□ 83KinCan-24
**Bishop, Mike**
□ 84KitRan-6
□ 90HalCit-2
□ 90ProAHLIHL-465
□ 93HumHawP-4
□ 94HumHawP-4
**Bissett, Tom**
□ 90ProAHLIHL-480
□ 91SweSemE-52
□ 92SweSemE-63
□ 93SwiHNL-376
**Bisson, Steve**
□ 88ProAHL-283
□ 89ProIHL-130
**Bissonette, Eric**
□ 907thInnSMC-60
□ 907thInnSQMJHL-205
**Bjelonozkjin, Anatoli**
□ 73SweHocS-128
□ 73SweWorCS-128
**Bjork, Anders**
□ 92SweSemE-41
□ 96DenUniPio-10
**Bjork, Kent**
□ 67SweHoc-251
□ 69SweHocS-296
□ 71SweHocS-291
□ 72SweHocS-74
**Bjork, Lasse**
□ 84SweSemE-141
**Bjork, Stefan**
□ 92SweSemE-350
**Bjorkman, Henric**
□ 89SweSemE-131
□ 90SweSemE-207
□ 91SweSemE-135
□ 92SweSemE-154
□ 93SweSemE-126
**Bjorkman, Tommy**
□ 65SweCorI-121
□ 67SweHoc-60
**Bjorn, Lars**
□ 64SweCorI-123
□ 65SweCorI-123
□ 67SweHoc-61
□ 81SweSemHVS-125
**Bjornfot, Niklas**
□ 92SweSemE-179
□ 93SweSemE-150
**Bjornson, Derek**
□ 96SasBla-4
**Bjugstad, Scott**
□ 84NorStaPos-4
□ 85NorSta7E-2
□ 85NorStaPos-5
□ 86NorSta7E-4
□ 86OPC-23
□ 86OPCSti-168
□ 86Top-23
□ 87NorStaPos-7
□ 88PanSti-90
□ 88ProIHL-30
□ 89ProAHL-15
□ 90ProSet-455
□ 91ProAHLCHL-404
**Bjuhr, Thomas**
□ 85SwePanS-17
□ 86PorWinH-3
□ 89SweSemE-20
□ 90SweSemE-87
□ 91SweSemE-16
□ 92SweSemE-37
**Black, Clint**
□ 91BriColJHL-133
□ 92BriColJHL-27
**Black, Guy**
□ 62QueAce-3
**Black, James**
□ 87PorWinH-4
□ 88PorWinH-4
□ 89PorWinH-1
□ 89ProAHL-292
□ 90ProAHLIHL-191
□ 91ProAHLCHL-101
□ 91UppDec-580
□ 91UppDecF-580
□ 91WhaJr7E-3
□ 92Bow-252
□ 92OPC-388
□ 92StaClu-303
□ 92Top-232
□ 92TopGol-232G
□ 92UppDec-323
□ 93Don-85
□ 93RochAmeKod-5
□ 93UppDec-517
□ 94LasVegThu-1
□ 95IndIce-2
□ 96ColEdgFL-48
□ 97Be A PPAD-186
□ 97Be A PPAPD-186
□ 97BeAPla-186
□ 97BeAPlaAut-186
□ 97PacDynBKS-19
□ 98TopO-P-195
□ 99Pac-436
□ 99PacCop-436
□ 99PacGol-436
□ 99PacIceB-436
□ 99PacPreD-436
**Black, Jamie**
□ 907thInnSWHL-318
□ 917thInnSWHL-172
□ 92TacRoc-2
□ 93CleLum-10
□ 93CleLumPos-3
□ 94ClaProP-122
□ 94MusFur-18
**Black, Jesse**
□ 95Sla-187
**Black, Jonathan**
□ 88RivDu R-4
**Black, Mike**
□ 89HamRoaA-1
**Black, Ryan**
□ 907thInnSOHL-352
□ 917thInnSOHL-144
□ 91PetPet-13
□ 93LonKni-4
□ 96ForWorF-17
**Black, Stephen**
□ 44BeeGro2P-154
**Black, Terry**
□ 87PorWinH-5
□ 88PorWinH-5
**Blackbird, Louie**
□ 96SarSti-2
□ 96SudWol-3
□ 96SudWolP-5
**Blackburn, Bob**
□ 69OPC-113
□ 70EssPowPla-220
**Blackburn, Don**
□ 63QueAce-2
□ 63QueAceQ-1
□ 64QueAce-3
□ 65QueAce-3
□ 68ShiCoi-130
**Blackburn, Joe**
□ 98SPXTopP-89
□ 98SPXTopPF-89
□ 98SPXTopPR-89
□ 98UppDecBD-119
□ 98UppDecDD-119
□ 98UppDecQD-119
□ 98UppDecTD-119
**Blacklock, Kyle**
□ 907thInnSOHL-379
□ 90SudWol-5
□ 917thInnSOHL-254
□ 91SudWol-4
**Blackned, Brant**
□ 917thInnSQMJHL-244
**Blad, Brian**
□ 88ProAHL-235
□ 89ProAHL-107
□ 90NewSai-3
□ 90ProAHLIHL-164
□ 91ProAHLCHL-608
□ 94BraSmo-14
**Bladon, Tom**
□ 73FlyLin-3
□ 74NHLActSta-209
□ 74OPCNHL-396
□ 75FlyCanDC-2
□ 75OPCNHL-74
□ 75Top-74
□ 76OPCNHL-164
□ 76Top-164
□ 77OPCNHL-131
□ 77Top-131A
□ 77Top-131B
□ 78OPC-152
□ 78Top-152
□ 79OPC-204
□ 79Top-204
□ 80OPC-135
□ 80Top-135
□ 88OilTenAnn-108
**Blaha, Jan**
□ 94CzeAPSE-60
**Blaha, Michael**
□ 91UppDec-669
□ 91UppDecCWJC-30
□ 91UppDecF-669
□ 93SwiHNL-223
**Blaha, Pavel**
□ 94CzeAPSE-255
**Blain, Brady**
□ 917thInnSOHL-194
□ 92WinSpi-16
□ 93WinSpi-12
**Blain, Jacques**
□ 72NordPos-4
□ 73NordTeal-4
**Blain, Joel**
□ 907thInnSQMJHL-149
□ 917thInnSQMJHL-212
□ 92WheThu-3
**Blain, Robert**
□ 95Sla-412
**Blair, Andy**
□ 32O'KeeMapL-5
□ 33OPCV304B-70
□ 33V129-11
□ 33V288HamG-9
□ 33V357IceK-4
□ 34BeeGro1P-300
□ 35DiaMatT4-1
□ 36V356WorG-56
**Blair, Bryan**
□ 96SarSti-3
**Blair, Campbell**
□ 93JohChi-2
**Blair, Danny**
□ 52JunBluT-50
**Blair, Darcy**
□ 91AirCanSJHL-E30
**Blair, Jeff**
□ 95SeaThu-4
□ 96SeaThu-1
**Blair, Scott**
□ 94DetJrRW-14
□ 95Sla-64
□ 95SlaMemC-88
**Blair, Wren**
□ 78LouGea-1
**Blaisdell, Mike**
□ 82OPC-81
□ 82PosCer-5
□ 83OPC-242
□ 86PenKod-2
□ 88ProAHL-225
**Blake, Jason**
□ 93WatBlaH-2
**Blake, Rob**
□ 90Bow-142
□ 90BowTif-142
□ 90KinSmo-3
□ 90OPCPre-6
□ 90ProSet-611
□ 90Sco-421
□ 90ScoCan-421
□ 90UppDec-45
□ 90UppDecF-45
□ 91Bow-182
□ 91Gil-6
□ 91OPC-6
□ 91OPC-112
□ 91OPCPre-44
□ 91PanSti-86
□ 91PanSti-339
□ 91Par-293
□ 91ParFre-293
□ 91Pin-201
□ 91Pin-382
□ 91PinFre-201
□ 91PinFre-382
□ 91ProSet-92
□ 91ProSetFre-92
□ 91ProSetPla-51
□ 91ProSetPlaPC-PC8
□ 91ScoAme-27
□ 91ScoAme-349
□ 91ScoCan-27
□ 91ScoCan-379
□ 91ScoKel-22
□ 91ScoYouS-8
□ 91StaClu-348
□ 91Top-6
□ 91Top-112
□ 91UppDec-43
□ 91UppDec-148
□ 91UppDecF-43
□ 91UppDecF-148
□ 92Bow-367
□ 92OPC-243
□ 92PanSti-71
□ 92PanStiFre-71
□ 92Par-302
□ 92ParEmel-302
□ 92Pin-32
□ 92PinFre-32
□ 92PinTea2-16
□ 92PinTea2F-16
□ 92ProSet-67
□ 92Sco-177
□ 92ScoCan-177
□ 92ScoYouS-38
□ 92StaClu-23
□ 92Top-211
□ 92TopGol-211G
□ 92Ult-79
□ 92UppDec-140
□ 93Don-158
□ 93Lea-172
□ 93OPCPre-56
□ 93OPCPreG-56
□ 93PanSti-209
□ 93Par-94
□ 93ParEmel-94
□ 93Pin-46
□ 93PinCan-46
□ 93Pow-113
□ 93Sco-236
□ 93ScoCan-236
□ 93StaClu-246
□ 93StaCluFDI-246
□ 93StaCluFDIO-246
□ 93StaCluO-246
□ 93TopPre-56
□ 93TopPreG-56
□ 93Ult-24
□ 93UppDec-317
□ 93UppDecNR-20
□ 93UppDecSP-68
□ 94BeAP99A-G3
□ 94BeAPla-R40
□ 94CanGamNHLP-129
□ 94EASpo-61
□ 94Fin-45
□ 94FinRef-45
□ 94FinSupTW-45
□ 94Fla-77
□ 94Fle-93
□ 94FleFraFut-2
□ 94Lea-12
□ 94LeaGolS-12
□ 94LeaLim-32
□ 94McDUppD-McD17
□ 94OPCPre-498
□ 94OPCPreSE-498
□ 94Par-105
□ 94ParGol-105
□ 94ParVin-V85
□ 94Pin-9
□ 94PinArtP-9
□ 94PinBoo-BR10
□ 94PinRinC-9
□ 94Sco-47
□ 94ScoGol-47
□ 94ScoPla-47
□ 94ScoPlaTS-47
□ 94Sel-98
□ 94SelGol-98
□ 94SP-53
□ 94SPDieCut-53
□ 94StaClu-135
□ 94StaCluFDI-135
□ 94StaCluMO-8
□ 94StaCluMOMS-135
□ 94StaCluST-11
□ 94StaCluSTWC-135
□ 94TopPre-498
□ 94TopPreSE-498
□ 94Ult-96
□ 94UppDec-488
□ 94UppDec-564
□ 94UppDecEleIce-488
□ 94UppDecEleIce-564
□ 94UppDecPC-C32
□ 94UppDecPCEG-C32
□ 94UppDecSPI-SP35
□ 94UppDecSPIDC-SP35
□ 95BeAPla-113
□ 95BeAPSig-S113
□ 95BeAPSigDC-S113
□ 95CanGamNHLP-138
□ 95ColCho-160
□ 95ColChoPC-160
□ 95ColChoPCP-160
□ 95Don-22
□ 95Emo-80
□ 95FinnSemWC-79
□ 95ImpSti-58
□ 95KenStaLA-1
□ 95KenStaLC-2
□ 95Lea-148
□ 95LeaLim-71
□ 95Met-69
□ 95ParInt-106
□ 95ParIntEl-106
□ 95Pin-198
□ 95PinArtP-198
□ 95PinRinC-198
□ 95PlaOneoOne-48
□ 95PosUppD-24
□ 95ProMag-66
□ 95Sco-11
□ 95ScoBlaIce-11
□ 95ScoBlaIceAP-11
□ 95ScoChelt-9
□ 95SelCer-74
□ 95SelCerMG-74
□ 95SkyImp-78
□ 95StaClu-56
□ 95StaCluMOMS-56
□ 95Sum-86
□ 95SumArtP-86
□ 95SumIce-86
□ 95SweGloWC-82
□ 95Top-307
□ 95TopOPCI-307
□ 95Ult-73
□ 95UltGolM-73
□ 95UppDec-478
□ 95UppDecEleIce-478
□ 95UppDecEleIceG-478
□ 95UppDecSpeE-SE42
□ 95UppDecSpeEdiG-SE42
□ 95Zen-28
□ 96Don-100
□ 96DonCanI-42
□ 96DonCanIGPP-42
□ 96DonCanIRPP-42
□ 96DonEli-48
□ 96DonEliDCS-48
□ 96DonPrePro-100
□ 96Fla-45
□ 96FlaBluI-45
□ 96KraUppD-33
□ 96Lea-177
□ 96LeaPreP-177
□ 96MetUni-73
□ 96NHLProSTA-66
□ 96Sco-130
□ 96ScoArtPro-130
□ 96ScoDeaCAP-130
□ 96ScoGolB-130
□ 96ScoSpeAP-130
□ 96SP-74
□ 96TeaOut-79
□ 96TopNHLP-159
□ 96TopPicOI-159
□ 96Ult-77
□ 96UltGolM-78
□ 96UppDec-278
□ 96UppDecBD-144
□ 96UppDecBDG-144
□ 96UppDecGN-X35
□ 96UppDecIce-29
□ 96UppDecIcePar-29
□ 97ColCho-125
□ 97ColChoSti-S4
□ 97ColChoWD-W13
□ 97DonCanI-57
□ 97DonCanIDS-57
□ 97DonCanIPS-57
□ 97DonPri-49
□ 97DonPriSoA-49
□ 97EssOlyHH-16
□ 97EssOlyHHF-16
□ 97Kat-68
□ 97KatGol-68
□ 97KatSil-68
□ 97Pac-193
□ 97PacCop-193
□ 97PacCroR-62
□ 97PacCroREG-62
□ 97PacCroRIB-62
□ 97PacCroRS-62
□ 97PacDyn-58
□ 97PacDynC-58
□ 97PacDynDG-58
□ 97PacDynEG-58
□ 97PacDynIB-58
□ 97PacDynR-58
□ 97PacDynSil-58
□ 97PacDynTan-45
□ 97PacEmeGre-193
□ 97PacIceB-193
□ 97PacInv-65
□ 97PacInvC-65
□ 97PacInvEG-65
□ 97PacInvIB-65
□ 97PacInvR-65
□ 97PacInvS-65
□ 97PacOme-106
□ 97PacOmeC-106
□ 97PacOmeDG-106
□ 97PacOmeEG-106
□ 97PacOmeG-106
□ 97PacOmeIB-106
□ 97PacPar-87
□ 97PacParC-87
□ 97PacParDG-87
□ 97PacParEG-87
□ 97PacParIB-87
□ 97PacParRed-87
□ 97PacParSil-87
□ 97PacRed-193
□ 97PacSil-193
□ 97PacTeaCCC-12
□ 97Pin-64
□ 97PinArtP-64
□ 97PinCer-77
□ 97PinCerMB-77
□ 97PinCerMG-77
□ 97PinCerMR-77
□ 97PinCerR-77
□ 97PinIns-71
□ 97PinInsCC-71
□ 97PinInsEC-71
□ 97PinPrePBB-64
□ 97PinPrePBC-64
□ 97PinPrePBM-64
□ 97PinPrePBY-64
□ 97PinPrePFC-64
□ 97PinPrePFM-64
□ 97PinPrePFY-64
□ 97PinPrePla-64
□ 97PinRinC-64
□ 97PinTotCMPG-77
□ 97PinTotCPB-77
□ 97PinTotCPG-77
□ 97PinTotCPR-77
□ 97Sco-148
□ 97ScoArtPro-148
□ 97ScoGolBla-148
□ 97SPAut-72
□ 97SPx-23
□ 97SPxBro-23
□ 97SPxGol-23
□ 97SPxGraF-23
□ 97SPxSil-23
□ 97SPxSte-23
□ 97UppDecBD-103
□ 97UppDecBDDD-103
□ 97UppDecBDQD-103
□ 97UppDecBDTD-103
□ 98Be A PPA-212
□ 98Be A PPAA-212
□ 98Be A PPAAF-212
□ 98Be A PPSE-212
□ 98Be APG-212
□ 98BowBes-9
□ 98BowBesAR-9
□ 98BowBesR-9
□ 98Fin-7
□ 98FinNo P-7
□ 98FinNo PR-7
□ 98FinRef-7
□ 98KinLA TC-1
□ 98KinPowP-LAK1
□ 98McDGreT-T11
□ 98O-PChr-63
□ 98O-PChrBM-B11
□ 98O-PChrBMR-B11
□ 98O-PChrR-63
□ 98Pac-4
□ 98PacAur-85
□ 98PacAurCF-23
□ 98PacAurCFC-23
□ 98PacAurCFIB-23
□ 98PacAurCFR-23
□ 98PacAurCFS-23
□ 98PacCroR-62
□ 98PacCroRLS-62
□ 98PacDynI-86
□ 98PacDynIB-86
□ 98PacDynIR-86
□ 98PacDynITC-12
□ 98PacIceB-4
□ 98PacOmeH-109
□ 98PacOmeODI-109
□ 98PacOmeR-109
□ 98PacPar-102
□ 98PacParC-102
□ 98PacParEG-102
□ 98PacParH-102
□ 98PacParIB-102
□ 98PacParS-102
□ 98PacParTCD-12
□ 98PacRed-4
□ 98PacRev-65
□ 98PacRevIS-65
□ 98PacRevR-65
□ 98SP Aut-39
□ 98SP AutA-6
□ 98SP AutA-7
□ 98SP AutSotTG-RB
□ 98SPxFin-42
□ 98SPxFin-108
□ 98SPxFinR-42
□ 98SPxFinR-108
□ 98SPxFinS-42
□ 98SPxFinS-108
□ 98SPXTopP-30
□ 98SPXTopPF-30
□ 98SPXTopPR-30
□ 98SSASotT-RB
□ 98Top-63
□ 98TopBoaM-B11
□ 98TopGolLC1-96
□ 98TopGolLC1B-96
□ 98TopGolLC1BOoO-96
□ 98TopGolLC1OoO-96
□ 98TopGolLC1R-96
□ 98TopGolLC1ROoO-96
□ 98TopGolLC2-96
□ 98TopGolLC2B-96
□ 98TopGolLC2BOoO-96
□ 98TopGolLC2OoO-96
□ 98TopGolLC2R-96
□ 98TopGolLC2ROoO-96
□ 98TopGolLC3-96
□ 98TopGolLC3B-96
□ 98TopGolLC3BOoO-96
□ 98TopGolLC3OoO-96
□ 98TopGolLC3R-96
□ 98TopGolLC3ROoO-96
□ 98TopO-P-63
□ 98UC-95
□ 98UC-227
□ 98UC-234
□ 98UCMBH-BH20
□ 98UD ChoPCR-95
□ 98UD ChoPCR-227
□ 98UD ChoPCR-234
□ 98UD ChoR-95
□ 98UD ChoR-227
□ 98UD ChoR-234
□ 98UDCP-95
□ 98UppDec-285
□ 98UppDecBD-41
□ 98UppDecDD-41
□ 98UppDecE-285
□ 98UppDecE1o1-285
□ 98UppDecFIT-FT7
□ 98UppDecFITQ1-FT7
□ 98UppDecFITQ2-FT7
□ 98UppDecFITQ3-FT7
□ 98UppDecGR-285
□ 98UppDecM-94
□ 98UppDecMGS-94
□ 98UppDecMSS-94
□ 98UppDecMSS-94
□ 98UppDecQD-41
□ 98UppDecTD-41
□ 99Pac-187
□ 99PacAur-68
□ 99PacAurPD-68
□ 99PacCop-187
□ 99PacGol-187
□ 99PacIceB-187
□ 99PacPreD-187
□ 99RetHoc-38
□ 99SP AutPS-39
□ 99UppDecM-92
□ 99UppDecMGS-92
□ 99UppDecMSS-92
□ 99UppDecMSS-92
□ 99UppDecRG-38
□ 99UppDecRP-38
**Blake, Toe**
□ 34BeeGro1P-137
□ 37OPCV304E-160
□ 38QuaOatP-2
□ 40OPCV3012-101
□ 45QuaOatP-64A
□ 45QuaOatP-64B
□ 45QuaOatP-64C
□ 48ExhCan-4
□ 51LavDaiQSHL-76
□ 55Par-67
□ 55ParQuaO-67
□ 57Par-M16
□ 58Par-9
□ 59Par-27
□ 60ShiCoi-40
□ 61ShiCoi-101
□ 61YorYelB-22
□ 62ShiMetC-31
□ 63ChePho-7
□ 63Par-34
□ 63Par-93
□ 64CanaPos-3
□ 64Top-43
□ 65Top-1
□ 66Top-1
□ 67CanaIGA-NNO
□ 83HalFP-G1
□ 85HalFC-92
□ 91ProSet-337
□ 91ProSetFre-337
□ 93OPCCanHF-5
□ 93OPCCanHF-59
□ 93OPCCanHF-65
□ 93ParParR-PR47
□ 94ParMisL-84
□ 94ParTaIB-87
**Blanchard, Guy**
□ 86SudWol-29
**Blanchard, Sean**
□ 95Sla-277
□ 97BowCHL-13
□ 97BowCHLOPC-13
□ 98BowCHL-24
□ 98BowCHLGA-24
□ 98BowCHLOI-24
□ 98BowChrC-24
□ 98BowChrCGA-24
□ 98BowChrCGAR-24
□ 98BowChrCOI-24
□ 98BowChrCOIR-24
□ 98BowChrCR-24

- 98UC-264
- 98UD ChoPCR-264
- 98UD ChoR-264

**Blasko, Daniel (Dan)**
- 91BriColJHL-19
- 92BriColJHL-81

**Blazek, Ladislav**
- 94CzeAPSE-2
- 95CzeAPSE-102
- 96CzeAPSE-265

**Blazek, Roman**
- 94CzeAPSE-264
- 95CzeAPSE-141

**Blazek, Tomas**
- 93Par-517
- 93ParEmel-517
- 94CzeAPSE-41
- 94SP-156
- 94SPDieCut-156

**Bleicher, Marcus**
- 94GerDELE-149
- 95GerDELE-143
- 98GerDELE-153

**Blessman, John**
- 88ProAHL-343
- 94Rallce-1
- 95BufStaRHI-43
- 96WheNai-28

**Blight, Rick**
- 75CanuRoyB-1
- 76CanuRoyB-1
- 76OPCNHL-238
- 76Top-238
- 77CanCanDC-1
- 77CanuRoyB-1
- 77OPCNHL-259
- 77Top-259
- 78CanuRoyB-1
- 78OPC-7
- 78Top-7
- 79CanuRoyB-2
- 79OPC-395
- 80OPC-372

**Blinco, Russ**
- 34BeeGro1P-190
- 34SweCap-15
- 350PCV304C-75
- 360PCV304D-127
- 36V356WorG-30
- 370PCV304E-169

**Blinov, Yuri**
- 73SweHocS-103
- 73SweWorCS-103
- 91FutTreC72-34

**Blishen, Don**
- 907thInnSWHL-116

**Blochin, Juri**
- 73SweHocS-101
- 73SweWorCS-101

**Block, Grant**
- 94MusFur-3

**Block, Ken**
- 73QuaOatWHA-37

**Block, Matt**
- 94MilAdm-3

**Bloem, Dieter**
- 95GerDELE-249
- 96GerDELE-99

**Bloemberg, Jeff**
- 89ProIHL-38
- 89RanMarMB-38
- 90OPC-483
- 90ProAHLIHL-10
- 90UppDec-370
- 90UppDecF-370
- 91ProAHLCHL-210
- 95AdiRedW-1

**Blom, Bud**
- 61HamRed-1

**Blom, Tage**
- 69SweHocS-77

**Blom, Thomas**
- 83SweSemE-101

**Blomer, Gert**
- 64SweCorl-16
- 64SweCorl-92
- 65SweCorl-16
- 65SweCorl-92
- 67SweHoc-283
- 69SweHocS-330
- 70SweHocS-245

**Blomquist, Kirk**
- 82BraWheK-21

**Blomqvist, Lars**
- 71SweHocS-341

**Blomqvist, Mats**
- 84SweSemE-170
- 85SwePanS-155
- 86SwePanS-155

**Blomqvist, Timo**
- 81Cap-1
- 82Cap-1
- 86DevPol-3
- 89SweSemE-171
- 89SweSemWCS-32
- 90SweSemE-127
- 91SweSemE-179
- 92SweSemE-203
- 94FinnSIS-262
- 95FinnSIS-86
- 95FinnSISDT-6
- 95FinnSISL-58

**Blomsten, Arto**
- 84SweSemE-83
- 85SwePanS-73

- 86SwePanS-63
- 87SwePanS-72
- 89SweSemE-53
- 90SweSemE-276
- 91SweSemE-59
- 92SweSemE-78
- 92UppDec-369
- 92UppDec-376
- 93Don-506
- 93JetRuf-6
- 93OPCPre-453
- 93OPCPreG-453
- 93Par-232
- 93ParEmel-232
- 93SweSemWCS-4
- 93TopPre-453
- 93TopPreG-453
- 93UppDec-505
- 93UppDecSP-174
- 94Lea-125
- 95ParInt-373
- 95ParIntEl-373
- 95SweWoGlWC-20

**Blondin, Carl**
- 917thInnSQMJHL-99

**Bloom, Mike**
- 74CapWhiB-6
- 74NHLActSta-318
- 740PCNHL-376
- 750PCNHL-376
- 760PCNHL-56
- 76Top-56
- 770PCNHL-375

**Bloski, Jeff**
- 91AirCanSJHL-E28

**Bloski, Mike**
- 81SasBla-20

**Blouin, Gaetan**
- 907thInnSWHL-95
- 90SasBla-21

**Blouin, Jacques**
- 917thInnSQMJHL-136

**Blouin, Jean**
- 907thInnSQMJHL-56
- 91ProAHLCHL-290
- 94ThuBayS-20

**Blouin, Maxime**
- 96RimOceQPP-4

**Blouin, Sylvain**
- 917thInnSQMJHL-238
- 95BinRan-1
- 95SigRoo-59
- 95SigRooSig-59
- 96BinRan-2

**Bloye, Damien**
- 93NorBayC-16
- 94NorBayC-19

**Blue, John**
- 90ProAHLIHL-103
- 91ProAHLCHL-50
- 92Par-245
- 92ParChaP-CP19
- 92ParEmel-245
- 930PCPre-209
- 930PCPreG-209
- 93Pin-335
- 93PinCan-335
- 93Pow-287
- 93Sco-399
- 93ScoCan-399
- 93StaClu-334
- 93StaCluFDI-334
- 93StaCluO-334
- 93TopPre-209
- 93TopPreG-209
- 93UppDec-74
- 94CanGamNHLP-271
- 95PhoRoa-3

**Blum, John**
- 83MonAlp-9
- 85MonGolF-17
- 86CapKod-3
- 880ilTenAnn-106
- 88ProAHL-25
- 89ProAHL-73
- 90ProAHLIHL-128

**Blum, Ken**
- 93RicRen-15
- 94FliGen-3

**Blum, Mike**
- 907thInnSOHL-202

**Blyth, Steve**
- 83SprInd-20

**Boake, Peter**
- 91AirCanSJHL-B8

**Boback, Mike**
- 92Cla-83
- 93PorPir-15
- 94ClaProP-46
- 94PorPir-2
- 95PhoRoa-4
- 96ClaGol-83

**Bobrov, Vsevolod**
- 73SweHocS-97
- 73SweWorCS-97
- 91FutTreC72-10

**Bobyck, Brent**
- 90ProAHLIHL-59

**Bocjun, Todd**
- 897thInnSOHL-122
- 907thInnSOHL-353

**Bodak, Bob**
- 84SprInd-23
- 86MonGolF-27
- 88SalLakCGE-23

- 89ProAHL-295
- 90ProAHLIHL-3

**Boddy, Gregg**
- 72CanuRoyB-2
- 72SarProSta-223
- 730PC-235
- 74CanuRoyB-1
- 74NHLActSta-286
- 740PCNHL-349
- 75CanuRoyB-2
- 750PCNHL-285
- 75Top-285

**Bodger, Doug**
- 85OPC-38
- 85OPCSti-99
- 85Top-38
- 860PC-24
- 860PCSti-232
- 86PenKod-3
- 86Top-24
- 870PC-125
- 87PanSti-141
- 87PenKod-1
- 87PenMask-1
- 87Top-125
- 880PC-96
- 880PCSti-234
- 88PanSti-332
- 88SabBluS-4
- 88SabWonBH-4
- 88Top-96
- 890PC-154
- 890PCSti-257
- 89PanSti-209
- 89SabBluS-3
- 89SabCam-4
- 89Top-154
- 90Bow-245
- 90BowTif-245
- 900PC-282
- 90PanSti-33
- 90ProSet-19
- 90SabBluS-3
- 90SabCam-3
- 90Sco-211
- 90ScoCan-211
- 90Top-282
- 90TopTif-282
- 90UppDec-50
- 90UppDecF-50
- 91Bow-21
- 910PC-207
- 91PanSti-307
- 91Par-15
- 91ParFre-15
- 91Pin-8
- 91PinFre-8
- 91ProSet-19
- 91ProSetFre-19
- 91ProSetPC-3
- 91ProSetPla-12
- 91SabBluS-3
- 91SabPepC-3
- 91ScoAme-297
- 91ScoCan-517
- 91StaClu-114
- 91Top-207
- 91UppDec-477
- 91UppDecF-477
- 92Bow-13
- 920PC-146
- 92PanSti-249
- 92PanStiFre-245
- 92Par-253
- 92ParEmel-253
- 92Pin-97
- 92PinFre-97
- 92SabBluS-3
- 92SabJubF-2
- 92Sco-226
- 92ScoCan-226
- 92StaClu-147
- 92Top-247
- 92TopGol-247G
- 92Ult-258
- 92UppDec-207
- 93Don-33
- 93Lea-19
- 930PCPre-29
- 930PCPreG-29
- 93PanSti-109
- 93Pin-82
- 93PinCan-82
- 93Pow-26
- 93SabLimETI-1
- 93Sco-21
- 93ScoCan-21
- 93StaClu-354
- 93StaCluFDI-354
- 93StaCluO-354
- 93TopPre-29
- 93TopPreG-29
- 93Ult-31
- 93UppDec-187
- 94BeAPSig-39
- 94CanGamNHLP-49
- 94EASpo-13
- 94Fla-16
- 94Lea-357
- 94Pin-357
- 94PinArtP-357
- 94PinRinC-357
- 94Sco-198
- 94ScoGol-198
- 94ScoPla-198

- 94ScoPlaTS-198
- 94StaClu-148
- 94StaCluFDI-148
- 94StaCluMOMS-148
- 94StaCluSTWC-148
- 94Ult-20
- 94UppDec-494
- 94UppDecElElce-494
- 95ColCho-77
- 95ColChoPC-77
- 95ColChoPCP-77
- 95Don-226
- 95ParInt-454
- 95ParIntEl-454
- 95Sco-171
- 95ScoBlaIce-171
- 95ScoBlaIceAP-171
- 95SP-134
- 95UppDec-165
- 95UppDecElElce-165
- 95UppDecElElceG-165
- 96BeAPAut-208
- 96BeAPAutSil-208
- 96BeAPla-208
- 96FlePic-164
- 97PacInvNRB-175
- 97ShaFleAS-1

**Bodin, Kent**
- 71SweHocS-136

**Bodkin, Rick**
- 92SudWol-15
- 93SudWol-14
- 93SudWolP-14
- 94SudWol-12
- 94SudWolP-3

**Bodnar, Gus**
- 44BeeGro2P-4
- 44BeeGro2P-81
- 45QuaOatP-8
- 51Par-40
- 52Par-37
- 53Par-75
- 54Par-62
- 91UltOriS-31
- 91UltOriSF-31

**Bodnarchuk, Mike**
- 87KinCan-14
- 90ProAHLIHL-574
- 91ProAHLCHL-419

**Bodunov, Alexander**
- 73SweHocS-95
- 73SweWorCS-95
- 74SweHocS-59
- 74SweSemHVS-41
- 91FutTreC72-32

**Body, Lou**
- 92HarCri-3
- 94RicRen-15
- 95RicRen-5
- 95SigRooA-8
- 95SigRooAPC-8

**Boe, Vince**
- 907thInnSWHL-15

**Boehm, Dave**
- 95NorlowH-1

**Boehm, Rick**
- 94GerDELE-374

**Boesch, Garth**
- 44BeeGro2P-381
- 45QuaOatP-9A
- 45QuaOatP-9B
- 45QuaOatP-9C

**Boettger, Dwayne**
- 83MonAlp-5
- 84NovScoO-3
- 85NovScoO-12

**Boeve, Jon**
- 89SudWol-9
- 90RayJrC-2
- 90SudWol-4

**Bogas, Chris**
- 95DonEliWJ-26

**Bogdanov, Anatoli**
- 95FinnSIS-392

**Bogden, Shane**
- 88RegPat-1

**Bogelsack, Friedhelm**
- 94GerDELE-132
- 95GerDELE-124

**Bognar, Derby**
- 93ForWorF-2
- 95AlaGolKin-2

**Bogoslowski, Mark**
- 89JohChi-27

**Bogoyevac, Steve**
- 92DayBom-2
- 93DayBom-7
- 93RicRen-16
- 94RicRen-4

**Boh, Aaron**
- 917thInnSWHL-16
- 95LouIceGP-2

**Bohacek, Jan**
- 94CzeAPSE-72
- 95CzeAPSE-180
- 96CzeAPSE-124

**Bohlin, Sune**
- 65SweCorl-117A

**Bohlmark, Hans**
- 67SweHoc-233

**Bohm, Richard**
- 95FinnSemWC-170

**Bohm, Richard**
- 95GerDELE-371

**Bohonos, Lonny**
- 95Bow-93

- 95BowAllFoi-93
- 95ColEdgI-87
- 95Ima-69
- 95ImaGol-69
- 96SyrCru-19
- 97Be A PPAD-148
- 97BeAPla-148
- 97BeAPlaAut-148
- 97Don-15
- 97DonPreProG-15
- 97DonPreProS-15
- 97Pac-310
- 97PacCop-310
- 97PacEmeGre-310
- 97PacIceB-310
- 97PacRed-310
- 97PacSil-310
- 97Sco-78
- 97ScoArtPro-78
- 97ScoCanPla-9
- 97ScoCanPre-9
- 97ScoCanu-9
- 97ScoGolBla-78
- 97St.JohML-2
- 97UppDec-172
- 99Pac-403
- 99PacCop-403
- 99PacGol-403
- 99PacIceB-403
- 99PacPreD-403

**Bohun, Bryce**
- 91AirCanSJHL-A6
- 91AirCanSJHLAS-14

**Boiger, Elmar**
- 94GerDELE-178
- 95GerDELE-180

**Boij, Patrik**
- 95SweUppDE-151

**Boikov, Alexandre**
- 95TriAme-5
- 96KenTho-2

**Boileau, Claude**
- 52JunBluT-136

**Boileau, Marc**
- 52JunBluT-116
- 62Par-29
- 69SeaTotW-4
- 740PCNHL-49
- 74Top-49

**Boileau, Patrick**
- 95ColEdgI-51
- 95PorPir-5
- 96PorPir-27

**Boily, Denis**
- 96RimOce-4
- 96RimOceQPP-5
- 97RimOce-79
- 98Vald'OF-22

**Boimistruck, Fred**
- 81MapLeaP-4
- 82MapLeaP-5
- 820PC-318
- 82PosCer-18

**Boisvert, Andre**
- 51LavDaiLSJ-18

**Boisvert, Gilles**
- 52SarProSta-51

**Boisvert, Richard**
- 88RivDu R-5

**Boisvert, Serge**
- 82MapLeaP-6
- 83MonAlp-19
- 85CanaPla-5
- 85CanaPla-7
- 85CanaPos-1
- 85CanaPos-2
- 86SheCan-6
- 89SweSemE-277
- 90SweSemE-40
- 91SweSemE-288
- 92SweSemE-310
- 93SweSemE-277

**Boiteau, Jean-Sebastien**
- 917thInnSQMJHL-50

**Boivin, Claude**
- 907thInnSMC-69
- 90ProAHLIHL-48
- 91ProAHLCHL-273
- 91ProSetPla-264
- 91UppDec-475
- 91UppDecF-475
- 92FlyJCP-5
- 92FlyUppDS-9
- 92ProSet-130
- 92Sco-352
- 92ScoCan-352
- 92StaClu-16
- 92Top-427
- 92TopGol-427G
- 92UppDec-57
- 93Par-146
- 93ParEmel-146
- 94ParGol-159
- 94SenBelM-5
- 94UppDec-146
- 94UppDecElElce-146

**Boivin, Frederic**
- 907thInnSQMJHL-140
- 917thInnSQMJHL-220

**Boivin, Leo**
- 44BeeGro2P-5
- 44BeeGro2P-382
- 45QuaOatP-11

- 52Par-34
- 53Par-6
- 54Par-26
- 55BruPho-3
- 57BruTealss-3
- 57Top-18
- 58Top-20
- 59Top-26
- 60ShiCoi-107
- 60Top-62
- 60TopSta-3
- 61ShiCoi-141
- 61Top-7
- 62Top-5
- 62TopHocBuc-3
- 63Top-5
- 63TorSta-5
- 64BeeGro3P-2
- 64BeeGro3P-65
- 64CocCap-15
- 64Top-50
- 64TorSta-6
- 65Coc-13
- 65Top-32
- 66Top-50
- 680PC-101
- 68ShiCoi-141
- 68Top-101
- 690PC-122
- 690PCFou-5
- 69Top-122
- 700PC-42
- 700PCDec-15
- 70Top-42
- 85HalFC-252
- 91BruSpoAL-2
- 91BruSpoAL-35
- 94ParMisL-11
- 94ParTalB-9
- 95Par66-48
- 95Par66Coi-48

**Boivin, Michel**
- 84ChiSag-3

**Boivin, Richard**
- 907thInnSQMJHL-27

**Boivin, Robbie**
- 92QueIntP-29

**Bokenfohr, Murray**
- 907thInnSWHL-325

**Bokshowan, Lorne**
- 81MilAdm-9

**Bokstrom, Carsten**
- 84SweSemE-124

**Boland, Mike**
- 72NatOttWHA-3

**Bolander, Ake**
- 67SweHoc-264

**Boldin, Igor**
- 92RussStaRA-12
- 92RussStaRA-3
- 94FinnSIS-32
- 94FinnSIS-167
- 94FinnSISFI-2

**Boldirev, Ivan**
- 71TorSun-4
- 720PC-41
- 72SarProSta-51
- 72Top-146
- 730PC-68
- 73Top-68
- 74NHLActSta-84
- 740PCNHL-16
- 74Top-16
- 750PCNHL-12
- 75Top-12
- 760PCNHL-251
- 76Top-251
- 770PCNHL-61
- 77Top-61
- 780PC-135
- 78Top-135
- 79FlaTeal-2
- 790PC-127
- 79Top-127
- 80CanuSilD-2
- 80CanuTeal-9
- 800PC-52
- 80PepCap-102
- 80Top-52
- 81CanuSilD-2
- 81CanuTeal-1
- 810PC-329
- 82Canu-1
- 820PC-338
- 820PCSti-241
- 82PosCer-19
- 830PC-118
- 830PCSti-132
- 840PC-50
- 840PCSti-39
- 84Top-38
- 850PC-92
- 850PCSti-34
- 85Top-92

**Boldt, Max**
- 96GerDELE-19

**Bolduc, Alex**
- 36V356WorG-119

**Bolduc, Danny (Dan)**
- 790PC-173
- 79RedWinP-2
- 79Top-173
- 84MonGolF-8
- 85MonGolF-2
- 86MonGolF-2

**Bolduc, David**
- 93AmoLesFAM-4
- 96RimOce-5

**Bolduc, Kevin**
- 97RimOce-17

**Bolduc, Michel**
- 81FreExp-4
- 82FreExp-4
- 83FreExp-9
- 84FreExp-13

**Bolduc, Tommy**
- 98QueRem-4

**Bolibruck, Kevin**
- 95Cla-94
- 95SigRooA-9
- 95SigRooAPC-9
- 95Sla-320
- 97BowCHL-14
- 97BowCHLOPC-14

**Boll, Buzz**
- 33V129-4
- 34BeeGro1P-301
- 350PCV304C-90
- 360PCV304D-119
- 36V356WorG-40
- 370PCV304E-140
- 380QuaOatP-3
- 390PCV3011-21

**Bolonchuk, Larry**
- 72CanuRoyB-3
- 760PCNHL-322
- 780PC-387

**Bolton, Hugh**
- 44BeeGro2P-383
- 45QuaOatP-10
- 51Par-79
- 55Par-14
- 55Par-69
- 55ParQuaO-14
- 55ParQuaO-69
- 57Par-T13
- 94ParMisL-124

**Bolton, Shannon**
- 88SudWol-19

**Boman, Johan**
- 93SweSemE-23

**Boman, Roger**
- 65SweCorl-145B

**Bombardir, Brad**
- 91UppDecCWJC-55
- 92NorDakFS-4
- 95Ima-51
- 95ImaGol-51
- 95SigRoo-66
- 95SigRooSig-66
- 96ColEdgFL-1
- 97Be A PPAD-214
- 97Be A PPAPD-214
- 97BeAPla-214
- 97BeAPlaAut-214
- 97PacOme-126
- 97PacOmeC-126
- 97PacOmeDG-126
- 97PacOmeEG-126
- 97PacOmeG-126
- 97PacOmeIB-126

**Bonar, Dan**
- 820PC-150

**Bonar, Graeme**
- 83SauSteMG-2
- 84SauSteMG-3
- 86SheCan-7
- 88ProIHL-15

**Bond, Bertil**
- 71SweHocS-349

**Bond, Bill**
- 67ColChe-3

**Bond, Joby**
- 92NorDakFS-5

**Bond, Kerry**
- 83SweSemE-136

**Bond, Kjell**
- 83SweSemE-136

**Bond, Roland**
- 64SweCorl-50
- 65SweCorl-50
- 67SweHoc-101
- 70SweHocS-71
- 71SweHocS-160
- 72SweHocS-153
- 73SweHocS-20
- 73SweHocS-42
- 73SweWorCS-42
- 74SweHocS-161
- 74SweSemHVS-15

**Bonda, Martin**
- 96SloPeeWT-4

**Bondra, Peter**
- 90CapKod-3
- 90CapPos-3
- 90CapSmo-3
- 900PCPre-7
- 90ProSet-645
- 90ScoRoo-71T
- 90UppDec-536
- 90UppDecF-536
- 91Bow-299
- 91CapJun-3
- 91CapKod-3
- 910PC-362
- 91Par-188
- 91ParFre-188
- 91Pin-87
- 91PinFre-87

94Fin-117
94FinRef-117
94FinSupTW-117
94LeaLimWJUSA-3
94Sco-209
94ScoGol-209
94ScoPla-209
94SlaPro-7
94SP-173
94SPDieCut-173
94SudWol-17
94UppDec-523
94UppDecIeIce-523
95BeAPla-179
95BeAPSig-S179
95BeAPSigDC-S179
95Bow-101
95BowAllFoi-101
95Cla-97
95ClaIceBre-BK17
95Don-249
95DonProPoi-3
95EmoGen-3
95Ima-45
95ImaAut-45A
95ImaGol-45
95Lea-229
95LeaLim-59
95LeaStuR-12
95Met-172
95ParInt-80
95ParIntEI-80
95Pin-207
95PinArtP-207
95PinRinC-207
95PlaOneoOne-256
95ProMag-82
95Sco-308
95ScoBIaIce-308
95ScoBIaIceAP-308
95SelCer-113
95SelCerMG-113
95SkyImp-196
95StaClu-191
95StaCluMOMS-191
95TopSupSkiSR-SR2
95Ult-332
95UppDec-266
95UppDecIeIce-266
95UppDecIeIceG-266
95Zen-136
96CIaIceBreDC-BK17
96Fle-123
96NHLProSTA-82
96SkyImp-146
96UppDec-62
98O-PChr-129
98O-PChrR-129
98Pac-64
98PacIceB-64
98PacRed-64
98Top-129
98TopO-P-129
98UppDec-180
98UppDecE-180
98UppDecE1o1-180
98UppDecGR-180

**Bonvie, Dennis**
917thInnSOHL-54
94CapBreO-4
95Lea-306
95UppDec-393
95UppDecIeIce-393
95UppDecIeIceG-393
97UppDec-277

**Bonvie, Herb**
95Sla-225

**Bonvie, Joe**
95MadMon-20

**Booker, Craig**
85KitRan-17
86KitRan-21
87KitRan-21

**Booker, Wes**
96SauSteMG-1
96SauSteMGA-1

**Boome, Danny**
93SheSte-9

**Boomer, Ron**
52JunBIuT-180

**Boon, Dickie**
60Top-17
60TopSta-4
83HalFP-H2
85HalFC-108

**Boone, Ken**
93KinFro-11

**Boork, Leif**
83SweSemE-99
86SwePanS-56
91SweSemE-313
92SweSemE-335
93SweSemE-300

**Boorman, Bryan**
95RedDeeR-2

**Boos, Tino**
94GerDELE-171
95GerDELE-167
96GerDELE-243
98GerDELE-62

**Booth, Derek**
907thInnSOHL-254
92TolSto-23
93RochAmeKod-6

**Boothman, George**

34BeeGro1P-302

**Bootland, Nick**
95GueSto5A-6
95Sla-104
96GueSto-27
96GueStoPC-12
97GueSto-26

**Bordeleau, Chris**
69CanaPosC-3
70EssPowPla-251
70SarProSta-185
71LetActR-24
710PC-51
71SarProSta-187
71Top-51
71TorSun-234
72SluCupWHA-2
730PCWHAP-17
73QuaOatWHA-15
750PCWHA-116
76NordPos-5
760PCWHA-49

**Bordeleau, J.P.**
730PC-258
74NHLActSta-83
740PCNHL-69
740PCNHL-309
74Top-69
750PCNHL-368
760PCNHL-208
76Top-208
770PCNHL-156
77Top-156
78Top-101
790PC-212
79Top-212
80BIaWhiBor-2
800PC-339

**Bordeleau, Paulin**
73CanuRoyB-1
74CanuRoyB-2
74NHLActSta-283
75CanuRoyB-3
750PCNHL-151
75Top-151
76NordMarA-3
76NordPos-6
760PCWHA-98
770PCWHA-32
90ProAHLIHL-74
91ProAHLCHL-91
92FreCan-2
93FreCan-2
94FreCan-3
95FreCan-2

**Bordeleau, Sebastien**
917thInnSQMJHL-210
95ColEdgI-38
95FreCan-3
95SlaMemC-69
96CanaPos-2
96UppDec-193
97Be A PPAD-211
97Be A PPAPD-211
97BeAPla-211
97BeAPlaAut-211
97CanaPos-1
97DonLim-195
97DonLimExp-195
97Pac-194
97PacCop-194
97PacEmeGre-194
97PacIceB-194
97PacRed-194
97PacSil-194
97ScoCan-14
97ScoCanPla-14
97UppDec-87
98ScoCanPre-14
98UppDec-298
98UppDecE-298
98UppDecE1o1-298
98UppDecGR-298
98UppDecM-115
98UppDecMGS-115
98UppDecMSS-115
98UppDecMSS-115
99Pac-218
99PacCop-218
99PacGol-218
99PacIceB-218
99PacPreD-218
99UppDecM-113
99UppDecMGS-113
99UppDecMSS-113
99UppDecMSS-113

**Borders, Jeff**
93OmaLan-2

**Borell, Goran**
69SweHocS-222
71SweHocS-367

**Borg, Ulf**
83SweSemE-199
84SweSemE-223
86SwePanS-250
87SwePanS-239

**Borggaard, Andy**
93HunBli-5

**Borgo, Richard**
86KitRan-15
87KitRan-15
88KitRan-15

89KitRan-16
907thInnSMC-35
907thInnSOHL-228
90KitRan-14
93ClaProPro-103
93ThuBayS-6

**Borgqvist, Robert**
95ColCho-348
95ColChoPC-348
95ColChoPCP-348

**Borland, Bill**
23V1281PauC-1
24CreSel-14
28V1282PauC-77

**Bornstrom, Bengt**
65SweCorl-54

**Borrett, Barry**
77NovScoV-3

**Borris, Kevin**
95SeaThu-6

**Borsato, Luciano**
89ProAHL-35
91JetIGA-3
91MonHaw-1
91Par-425
91ParFre-425
91Pin-353
91PinFre-353
91ProAHLCHL-186
91ProSetPla-275
91UppDec-599
91UppDecFre-599
92Bow-52
920PC-149
92PanSti-E
92PanStiFre-E
92Par-439
92ParEmel-439
92Pin-218
92PinFre-218
92ProSetGTL-15
92ProSetRGL-8
92Sco-256
92ScoCan-256
92StaClu-81
92Top-239
92TopGol-239G
92Ult-239
92UppDec-77
93JetRuf-7
930PCPre-234
930PCPreG-234
93PanSti-195
93Par-501
93ParEmel-501
93Pow-471
93Sco-401
93ScoCan-401
93StaClu-317
93StaCluFDI-317
93StaCluO-317
93TopPre-234
93TopPreG-234
93Ult-452
940PCPre-148
940PCPreSE-148
94ParSE-SE200
94ParSEG-SE200
94TopPre-148
94TopPreSE-148
95GerDELE-207
96GerDELE-350

**Borschevsky, Nikolai**
92Cla-52
92MapLeaK-7
920PCPre-100
92Par-186
92Par-216
92ParEmel-186
92ParEmel-216
92Pin-397
92PinFre-397
92RusStaRA-11
92RusStaRA-4
92Ult-418
92UltImp-1
92UppDec-572
93Don-332
93Lea-137
930PCPre-107
930PCPreG-107
93PanSti-224
93Par-203
93ParEmel-203
93Pin-12
93PinCan-12
93Pow-240
93Sco-41
93ScoBla-18
93ScoCan-41
93ScoIntS-12
93ScoIntSC-12
93StaClu-375
93StaCluFDI-375
93StaCluO-375
93TopPre-107
94CanGamNHLP-230
94EASpo-137
94Lea-279
94MapLeaG-4
94MapLeaK-5

94MapLeaPP-6
94Par-231
94ParGol-231
94Pin-160
94PinArtP-160
94PinRinC-160
94Sco-30
94ScoGol-30
94ScoPla-30
94ScoPlaTS-30
94StaClu-209
94StaCluFDI-209
94StaCluMOMS-209
94StaCluSTWC-209
94Ult-375
94UppDec-405
94UppDecIeIce-405
95ColCho-300
95ColChoPC-300
95ColChoPCP-300
95UppDec-173
95UppDecIeIce-173
95UppDecIeIce-490
95UppDecIeIceG-173
95UppDecIeIceG-490
96ClaGol-52

**Borys, Cory**
91AirCanSJHL-D35

**Borzecki, Adam**
97RimOce-98
98BowCHL-120
98BowCHLGA-120
98BowCHLOI-120
98BowChrC-120
98BowChrCGA-120
98BowChrCGAR-120
98BowChrCOI-120
98BowChrCOIR-120
98BowChrCR-120

**Borzov, Leonid**
73SweHocS-114
73SweWorCS-114

**Bosch, Bryan**
88LetHur-3
89LetHur-3

**Boscher, Richard**
91AirCanSJHL-B1
92MPSPhoSJHL-130

**Boschman, Joel**
95SpoChi-13

**Boschman, Laurie**
79MapLeaP-3
80MapLeaP-3
80MapLeaP-4
800PC-179
80PepCap-82
80Top-179
81MapLeaP-5
810PC-314
810PCSti-103
820ilRedR-14
83Jet-3
830PC-381
83Vac-123
847EDis-57
84JetPol-4
840PC-335
840PCSti-288
84Top-151
85JetPol-2
85JetSilD-1
850PC-251
850PCSti-254
86JetBor-2
86KraDra-3
860PC-184
860PCSti-111
86Top-184
87Jet-3
870PC-222
87PanSti-368
88JetPol-2
880ilTenAnn-94
880PC-200
880PCSti-139
89JetSaf-5
890PCSti-147
89PanSti-169
89Dev-1
900PC-39
900PCPre-39
90PanSti-320
90ProSet-324
90ProSet-476
90ScoRoo-63T
90Top-39
90TopTif-39
90UppDec-103
90UppDecF-103
91Bow-282
910PC-202
91PanSti-215
91Par-316
91ParFre-316
91ProSet-426
91ProSetPre-426
91ScoCan-436
91StaClu-202
91Top-202
91UppDec-279
91UppDecF-279
92Par-122
92ParEmel-122
92Pin-375

92PinFre-375
92Sco-374
92Sco-513
92ScoCan-374
92ScoCan-513
92StaClu-310
92Top-246
92TopGol-246G
93Sco-289
93ScoCan-289
93StaClu-3
93StaCluFDI-3
93StaCluFDIO-3
93StaCluO-3

**Bosson, Mattias**
93SweSemE-182
94SweLeaE-252
95SweLeaE-94
95SweUppDE-142

**Bossy, Mike**
780PC-1
780PC-63
780PC-67
780PC-115
78Top-1
78Top-63
78Top-67
78Top-115
79IslTrans-1
790PC-1
790PC-5
790PC-7
790PC-161
790PC-230
79Top-1
79Top-5
79Top-7
79Top-161
79Top-230
800PC-25
800PC-204
800PCSup-12
80Top-25
80Top-204
810PC-198
810PC-208
810PC-219
810PC-382
810PC-386
810PC-388
810PC-390
810PCSti-150
810PCSti-158
810PCSti-253
81PosSta-6
81Top-4
81Top-57
81Top-E125
82McDSti-6
82McDSti-21
820PC-2
820PC-197
820PC-199
820PCSti-50
820PCSti-51
820PCSti-165
82PosCer-12
83IslTealss-1
830PC-1
830PC-3
830PC-197
830PC-205
830PC-210
830PCSti-10
830PCSti-78
830PCSti-176
830PCSti-306
830PCSti-321
83PufSti-19
84IslIsIsIN-2
84IslIsIsIN-35
84KelAccD-1
840PC-122
840PC-209
840PC-362
840PC-376
840PCSti-82
840PCSti-83
840PCSti-235
84Top-91
84Top-155
857ECreCar-12
85IslIsIsIN-2
85IslIsIsIN-32
85IslIsIsINT-32
850PC-110
850PCSti-66
850PCSti-118
85Top-130
85TopStiIns-9
860PC-90
860PCBoxB-B
860PCSti-117
860PCSti-194
860PCSti-217
86Top-90
86TopBoxB-B
86TopStiIns-4
870PC-105
870PCSti-244
87PanSti-97

87ProAll-6
87Top-105
88EssAllSta-2
90ProSet-650
91ProSetHI-1
91UppDec-45
920PC-391
920PC25AI-11
92Pin-245
92PinFre-245
93Cla-116
93Cla-AU1
93IslCheBA-2
95ZelMasoH-1
96SweSemWHL-HL3
99RetHoc-96
99UppDecCL-20
99UppDecCLCLC-20
99UppDecES-12
99UppDecJotC-JC2
99UppDecRG-96
99UppDecRII-MB
99UppDecRIL1-MB
99UppDecRP-96

**Boston, Scott**
87BroBra-17
897thInnSOHL-87
907thInnSOHL-340
917thInnSOHL-115
93KnoChe-1
95SouCarS-15
96SouCarS-20

**Bostrom, Anders**
83SweSemE-30
84SweSemE-29

**Bostrom, Gote**
65SweCorl-169

**Bostrom, Hans**
67SweHoc-85

**Bostrom, Helge**
33V252CanG-4

**Bostrom, Soren**
67SweHoc-215

**Bothwell, Tim**
840PC-182
850PC-161
850PCSti-49
85Top-161
87BluKod-2
870PCSti-26
87Top-29
88BluKod-6
88ProIHL-68
89ProAHL-23
907thInnSWHL-42
917thInnSWHL-328
92PhoRoa-1

**Botteri, Stephane**
93SweSemWCS-251
94FinnJaaK-217

**Botterill, Jason**
93DonTeaC-4
93MicWol-2
93Pin-467
93PinCan-467
93UppDec-534
94Fin-144
94FinRef-144
94FinSupTW-144
94Sco-202
94ScoGol-202
94ScoPla-202
94SP-143
94SPDieCut-143
95DonCanWJT-18
95DonEliWJ-10
95SP-175
95TopCanWJ-14CJ
98McD-25
98Pac-172
98PacIceB-172
98PacRed-172
98UppDec-260
98UppDecE-260
98UppDecE1o1-260
98UppDecGR-260

**Botterill, Scott**
96PriAlbR-2
96PriAlbROC-2

**Boucha, Henry**
72SarProSta-84
72SweSemWC-126
73NorStaAP-1
730PC-33
73RedWinMP-3
73Top-33
74LipSou-32
74NHLActSta-141
740PCNHL-38
74Top-38
750PCWHA-79
760PCNHL-209
76RocPucBuc-3
76Top-209

**Bouchard, Butch**
34BeeGro1P-98
44BeeGro2P-225
45QuaOatP-65A
45QuaOatP-65B
45QuaOatP-65C
48ExhCan-5
51Par-3
52Par-13
53Par-32

54Par-6
54Par-69
55Par-46
55Par-71
55ParQuaO-46
83HalFP-M1
85HalFC-228
91UltOriS-8
91UltOriSF-8

**Bouchard, Dan**
72Flam-2
720PC-203
72SarProSta-14
730PC-45
73Top-45
74LipSou-44
74NHLActSta-6
740PCNHL-15
74Top-15
750PCNHL-268
75Top-268
760PCNHL-111
76Top-111
770PCNHL-37
77Top-37
780PC-169
78Top-169
79FlamPos-2
79FlaTeaI-3
790PC-28
79Top-28
80FlamPos-1
80NordPos-3
800PC-68
80PepCap-1
80Top-68
81NordPos-3
810PC-270
810PCSti-73
810PCSti-84
82McDSti-1
82NordPos-3
820PC-278
820PCSti-27
83NordPos-3
830PC-290
830PCSti-245
83PufSti-18
83Vac-62
84NordPos-4
840PC-277
840PCSti-172
840PCSti-173
84Top-128
85JetPol-3
850PC-246
850PCSti-143
92NorPet-2

**Bouchard, Eddie**
23V1451-37
24C144ChaCig-5
24V1452-19

**Bouchard, Emile**
930PCCanHF-2

**Bouchard, Eric**
917thInnSWHL-137

**Bouchard, Gilles**
907thInnSQMJHL-38
917thInnSMC-34

**Bouchard, Hughes**
88RivDu R-6
917thInnSQMJHL-152
93RoaExp-5

**Bouchard, Joel**
907thInnSQMJHL-143
917thInnSQMJHL-143
93DonTeaC-5
93Pin-461
93PinCan-461
93UppDec-541
94St.JohF-1
95St.JohF-3
96UppDecIce-8
96UppDecIcePar-8
97Be A PPAD-129
97Be A PPAPD-129
97BeAPla-129
97BeAPlaAut-129
97Pac-338
97PacCop-338
97PacEmeGre-338
97PacIceB-338
97PacRed-338
97PacSil-338

**Bouchard, Leon**
51LavDaiS-25
52St.LawS-41

**Bouchard, Pierre**
69CanaPosC-4
71Baz-20
71CanaPos-1
710PC-2
71SarProSta-12
71TorSun-147
72CanaPos-2
72CanGreWLP-1
720PC-165
72SarProSta-116
73CanaPos-2
730PC-261
74CanaPos-1
74NHLActSta-159
740PCNHL-178
740PCNHL-254

- 74Top-178
- 74Top-254
- 75CanaPos-2
- 750PCNHL-304
- 75Top-304
- 76CanaPos-1
- 760PCNHL-177
- 76Top-177
- 77CanaPos-1
- 770PCNHL-20
- 77Top-20
- 780PC-116
- 78Top-116
- 790PC-289
- 800PC-373

**Bouchard, Robin**
- 917thInnSQMJHL-48
- 94RoaExp-13
- 95FliGen-11

**Bouchard, Yannick**
- 96RimOce-6
- 96RimOceQPP-6

**Boucher, Billy**
- 23V1451-16
- 24C144ChaCig-6
- 24V130MapC-11
- 24V1452-46

**Boucher, Bob**
- 24C144ChaCig-7

**Boucher, Brian**
- 94Sel-155
- 94SelGol-155
- 94TriAme-3
- 95DonEliWJ-23
- 95SigRooA-10
- 95SigRooAPC-10
- 95TriAme-6
- 95TriAme-30
- 96UppDecIce-148
- 97BowCHL-81
- 97BowCHLOPC-81

**Boucher, Brock**
- 95Sla-22

**Boucher, Buck (George)**
- 23V1451-6
- 24V1452-2
- 83HalFP-L1
- 85HalFC-229

**Boucher, Charlie**
- 917thInnSQMJHL-174

**Boucher, Denis**
- 52JunBluT-135

**Boucher, Frank (Francois)**
- 34BeeGro1P-261
- 34DiaMatS-4
- 35DiaMatT2-3
- 35DiaMatT2-4
- 35DiaMatT3-3
- 36V356WorG-16
- 60Top-29
- 60TopSta-5
- 83HalFP-G2
- 85HalFC-93

**Boucher, Gaetan**
- 91ProSetPla-298
- 93SwiHNL-197

**Boucher, Philippe**
- 907thInnSQMJHL-50
- 917thInnSCHLAW-21
- 917thInnSCHLAW-25
- 917thInnSMC-103
- 917thInnSQMJHL-43
- 91AreDraPic-10
- 91Cla-11
- 91StaPicH-28
- 91StaPicH-36
- 91UltDra-11
- 91UltDra-67
- 91UltDra-75
- 91UltDra-82
- 91UppDec-68
- 91UppDecF-68
- 920PCPre-72
- 92Par-16
- 92ParEmel-16
- 92UppDec-484
- 93ClaProPro-68
- 93DurSco-24
- 93Par-24
- 93ParCalC-C11
- 93ParCalCG-C11
- 93ParEmel-24
- 93Pin-213
- 93PinCan-213
- 93Pow-296
- 93RochAmeKod-7
- 93Sco-455
- 93ScoCan-455
- 93Ult-70
- 93UltAllRoo-1
- 93UppDec-82
- 93UppDecSP-14
- 94Lea-539
- 940PCPre-374
- 940PCPreSE-371
- 94ParSE-SE16
- 94ParSEG-SE16
- 94StaClu-64
- 94StaCluFDI-64
- 94StaCluMOMS-64
- 94StaCluSTWC-64
- 94TopPre-371
- 94TopPreSE-371
- 94UppDec-71
- 94UppDecEleIce-71

- 95Top-136
- 95TopOPCI-136
- 96BeAPAut-74
- 96BeAPAutSil-74
- 96BeAPla-74
- 97PacInvNRB-92
- 98UppDecM-99
- 98UppDecMGS-99
- 98UppDecMSS-99
- 98UppDecMSS-99

**Boucher, Scott**
- 92BriColJHL-167

**Boucher, Tyler**
- 91BriColJHL-90
- 91BriColJHL-159
- 92BriColJHL-119

**Boudaev, Aleksei**
- 95RedDeeR-3

**Boudreau, Bruce**
- 78MapLeaP-2
- 780PC-280
- 790PC-354
- 85NovScoO-5
- 88ProAHL-302
- 89ProIHL-108
- 90ProAHLIHL-541
- 91ProAHLCHL-260

**Boudreau, Carl**
- 907thInnSMC-56
- 907thInnSQMJHL-97
- 917thInnSQMJHL-116
- 920IkICitB-2

**Boudreau, Darryl**
- 82KitRan-10

**Boudreau, Rene**
- 36V356WorG-117

**Boudreault, David (Dave)**
- 907thInnSQMJHL-119
- 917thInnSQMJHL-117

**Boudreault, Serge**
- 67ColChe-4

**Boudrias, Andre**
- 680PC-53
- 68ShiCoi-64
- 68Top-53
- 690PC-16
- 69Top-16
- 70CanuRoyB-1
- 70DadCoo-8
- 70EssPowPla-43
- 700PC-121
- 70SarProSta-219
- 70Top-121
- 71Baz-16
- 71CanuRoyB-16
- 710PC-12
- 71SarProSta-215
- 71Top-12
- 71TorSun-276
- 72CanuNal-1
- 72CanuRoyB-4
- 720PC-93
- 72SarProSta-214
- 72SweSemWC-210
- 72Top-158
- 73CanuRoyB-2
- 730PC-19
- 73Top-19
- 74CanuRoyB-3
- 74LipSou-14
- 74NHLActSta-277
- 740PCNHL-117
- 740PCNHL-191
- 74Top-117
- 74Top-191
- 75CanuRoyB-4
- 750PCNHL-60
- 750PCNHL-329
- 75Top-60
- 75Top-329
- 76NordMarA-4
- 76NordPos-7
- 760PCWHA-87

**Bouge, Art**
- 81RedWinOld-20

**Boughner, Bob**
- 89SauSteMG-7
- 907thInnSOHL-153
- 917thInnSMC-4
- 96BeAPAut-178
- 96BeAPAutSil-178
- 96BeAPla-178
- 97PacDynBKS-9
- 99Pac-219
- 99PacCop-219
- 99PacGol-219
- 99PacIceB-219
- 99PacPreD-219
- 99RetHoc-43
- 99UppDecRG-43
- 99UppDecRP-43

**Bougie, Georges**
- 51LavDaiQSHL-77
- 52St.LawS-32

**Bouillon, Francis**
- 96WheNai-44

**Boulerice, Jesse**
- 95Sla-74
- 96DetWha-1
- 97UppDecBD-98
- 97UppDecBDDD-98
- 97UppDecBDQD-98
- 97UppDecBDTD-98
- 98UC-305
- 98UD ChoPCR-305

- 98UD ChoR-305

**Bouliane, Andre**
- 907thInnSQMJHL-264
- 917thInnSQMJHL-149

**Boulin, Vladislav**
- 94Fla-125
- 94Lea-456
- 940PCPre-434
- 940PCPreSE-434
- 94ParSE-SE125
- 94ParSEG-SE125
- 94TopPre-434
- 94TopPreSE-434
- 94Ult-342
- 94UppDec-266
- 94UppDecEleIce-266

**Boulton, Eric**
- 93OshGen-21
- 95Sla-339

**Bouquet, Stephane**
- 907thInnSQMJHL-99

**Bourassa, Bertrand**
- 51LavDaiQSHL-81

**Bourbonnais, Rick**
- 770PCNHL-312

**Bourbonnais, Roger**
- 69SweHocS-349
- 69SweWorC-185

**Bourdeau, Francois**
- 88RivDu R-7
- 907thInnSQMJHL-104
- 917thInnSQMJHL-68
- 93JohChi-3
- 94CenHocL-21

**Bourdon, Armand**
- 51LavDaiLSJ-9

**Bourgeault, Leo**
- 33OPCV304A-28

**Bourgeois, Charlie**
- 81FlamPos-1
- 85FlamRedRP-4
- 860PC-239
- 860PCSti-178
- 87BluKod-3
- 87PanSti-309
- 88ProAHL-62

**Bourgeois, Shawn**
- 91BriColJHL-15
- 92BriColJHL-202

**Bourke, Peter**
- 93MicWol-3

**Bourne, Bob**
- 750PCNHL-163
- 75Top-163
- 770PCNHL-93
- 77Top-93
- 780PC-69
- 780PC-126
- 78Top-69
- 78Top-126
- 79IslTrans-2
- 790PC-56
- 79Top-56
- 800PC-276
- 810PC-201
- 810PCSti-163
- 81Top-E87
- 820PC-198
- 820PCSti-53
- 82PosCer-12
- 83IslTealss-2
- 830PC-4
- 830PCSti-80
- 830PCSti-174
- 84IslIsIsIN-3
- 84KelWin-42
- 840PC-123
- 840PCSti-89
- 84Top-92
- 85IslIsIsIN-3
- 850PC-97
- 850PCSti-67
- 85Top-97
- 86Kin20tATI-1
- 860PC-14
- 860PCSti-208
- 86Top-14
- 87KinTeal4-1
- 870PC-167
- 87Top-167
- 880PC-101
- 880PCMin-2
- 880PCSti-213
- 88PanSti-399
- 88Top-101
- 93LasVegThu-3
- 93LasVegT-25

**Bourque, Claude**
- 34BeeGro1P-139
- 39OPCV3011-28

**Bourque, Dave**
- 95Sla-351
- 96SarSti-4

**Bourque, Phil**
- 81KinCan-6
- 83PenTealP-1
- 890PC-19
- 89PanSti-317
- 89PenCokE-1
- 89PenFoo-5
- 89Top-19
- 90Bow-205
- 90BowTif-205
- 900PC-41
- 90PanSti-129

- 90PenFoo-1
- 90ProSet-228A
- 90ProSet-228B
- 90Sco-234
- 90ScoCan-234
- 90Top-41
- 90TopTif-41
- 90UppDec-31
- 90UppDecF-31
- 91Bow-94
- 910PC-33
- 91PanSti-272
- 91Par-136
- 91ParFre-136
- 91PenCokE-29
- 91PenFoo-15
- 91Pin-227
- 91PinFre-227
- 91ProSet-189
- 91ProSetFre-189
- 91ScoAme-69
- 91ScoCan-69
- 91StaClu-168
- 91Top-33
- 91UppDec-398
- 91UppDecF-398
- 92Bow-293
- 920PCPre-73
- 92PanSti-225
- 92PanStiFre-225
- 92Pin-353
- 92PinFre-353
- 92Sco-223
- 92ScoCan-223
- 92StaClu-282
- 92Top-442
- 92TopGol-442G
- 92Ult-352
- 92UppDec-141
- 92UppDec-452
- 93Pin-331
- 93PinCan-331
- 93Sco-308
- 93ScoCan-308
- 94Pin-112
- 94PinArtP-112
- 94PinRinC-112
- 94SenBelM-7
- 95ColCho-86
- 95ColChoPC-86
- 95ColChoPCP-86
- 95SweGloWC-126

**Bourque, Raymond (Ray)**
- 800PC-2
- 800PC-140
- 80Top-2
- 80Top-140
- 810PC-1
- 810PC-17
- 810PCSti-49
- 81PosSta-1
- 81Top-5
- 81Top-E126
- 82McDSti-28
- 820PC-7
- 820PC-24
- 820PCSti-86
- 820PCSti-87
- 820PCSti-166
- 82PosCer-1
- 830PC-45
- 830PCSti-46
- 830PCSti-47
- 830PCSti-173
- 83PufSti-11
- 847EDis-1
- 840PC-1
- 840PC-211
- 840PCSti-143
- 840PCSti-183
- 84Top-1
- 84Top-157
- 857ECreCar-1
- 850PC-40
- 850PCBoxB-B
- 850PCSti-115
- 850PCSti-157
- 85Top-40
- 85TopBoxB-B
- 85TopStiIns-5
- 860PC-1
- 860PCSti-34
- 860PCSti-119
- 86Top-1
- 86TopStiIns-11
- 870PC-87
- 870PCBoxB-F
- 870PCMin-4
- 870PCSti-116
- 870PCSti-140
- 870PCSti-178
- 87PanSti-6
- 87PanSti-381
- 87Top-87
- 87TopBoxB-F
- 87TopStiIns-1
- 88BruPos-1
- 88BruSpoA-24
- 88EssAllSta-3
- 88FriLayS-16
- 880PC-73
- 880PCBoxB-I
- 880PCMin-3

- 880PCSti-23
- 880PCSti-117
- 880PCSti-208
- 88PanSti-405
- 88TopBoxB-I
- 88TopStiIns-5
- 89BruSpoA-1
- 89BruSpoAU-1
- 89BruSpoAU-12
- 89Kra-52
- 89KraAllSS-4
- 890PC-110
- 890PCSti-32
- 890PCSti-72
- 890PCSti-162
- 890PCSti-210
- 89PanSti-187
- 89PanSti-201
- 89SweSemWCS-57
- 89Top-110
- 89TopStiIns-7
- 90Bow-31
- 90BowTif-31
- 90BruSpoA-2
- 90Kra-3
- 90Kra-80
- 900PC-43
- 900PC-165
- 900PC-196
- 900PC-475
- 900PCBoxB-I
- 900PCPre-9
- 90PanSti-17
- 90PanSti-322
- 90ProSet-1B
- 90ProSet-1C
- 90ProSet-357
- 90ProSet-384
- 90Sco-200
- 90Sco-313
- 90Sco-363
- 90Sco-368
- 90ScoCan-200
- 90ScoCan-313
- 90ScoCan-363
- 90ScoHotRS-35
- 90ScoPro-200
- 90Top-43
- 90Top-165
- 90Top-196
- 90Top-475
- 90TopBoxB-I
- 90TopTif-43
- 90TopTif-196
- 90UppDec-64
- 90UppDec-204
- 90UppDec-320
- 90UppDec-489
- 90UppDecF-64
- 90UppDecF-204
- 90UppDecF-320
- 90UppDecF-489
- 91Bow-356
- 91BruSpoA-4
- 91BruSpoA-24
- 91BruSpoA-3
- 91Gil-26
- 91Kra-57
- 91McDUppD-10
- 91McDUppD-H3
- 910PC-66
- 910PC-170
- 910PC-261
- 910PC-517
- 910PCPre-119
- 910PCPre-192
- 91PanSti-171
- 91PanSti-335
- 91Par-9
- 91Par-221
- 91Par-469
- 91Par-472
- 91ParFre-9
- 91ParFre-221
- 91ParFre-469
- 91ParFre-472
- 91Pin-15
- 91Pin-368
- 91PinB-B2
- 91PinBFre-B2
- 91PinFre-15
- 91PinFre-368
- 91ProSet-9
- 91ProSet-296
- 91ProSet-322
- 91ProSet-567
- 91ProSetFre-9
- 91ProSetFre-296
- 91ProSetFre-322
- 91ProSetFre-567
- 91ProSetNHLAS-AC7
- 91ProSetPC-1
- 91ProSetPla-2
- 91ProSetPla-278
- 91ScoAme-50
- 91ScoAme-344
- 91ScoAme-415
- 91ScoAme-429
- 91ScoCan-50
- 91ScoCan-331
- 91ScoCan-374
- 91ScoFan-3
- 91ScoNat-3

- 91ScoNatCWC-3
- 91StaClu-233
- 91SweSemWCS-55
- 91Top-66
- 91Top-261
- 91Top-517
- 91TopBowPS-4
- 91TopTeaSL-19
- 91UppDec-255
- 91UppDec-633
- 91UppDecAWH-AW5A
- 91UppDecAWH-AW5B
- 91UppDecF-255
- 91UppDecF-633
- 92Bow-3
- 92Bow-223
- 92BruPos-1
- 92DurPan-31
- 92Hig5Pre-P5
- 92HumDum1-1
- 92Kra-37
- 92McDUppD-H5
- 920PC-126
- 920PC-348
- 92PanSti-144
- 92PanSti-279
- 92PanStiFre-144
- 92PanStiFre-279
- 92Par-1
- 92Par-464
- 92ParEmel-1
- 92ParEmel-464
- 92Pin-2
- 92PinFre-2
- 92PinTeaP-2
- 92PinTeaPF-2
- 92ProSet-4
- 92ProSet-261
- 92Sco-100
- 92Sco-419
- 92Sco-447
- 92Sco-490
- 92Sco-520
- 92ScoCan-100
- 92ScoCan-419
- 92ScoCan-447
- 92ScoCan-490
- 92ScoCan-520
- 92SeaPat-17
- 92StaClu-249
- 92StaClu-267
- 92Top-221
- 92Top-262
- 92TopGol-221G
- 92TopGol-262G
- 92Ult-2
- 92UltAllS-2
- 92UltAwaW-8
- 92UppDec-265
- 92UppDec-626
- 93Don-24
- 93DurSco-26
- 93KenStaLA-2
- 93KenStaLC-2
- 93Kra-29
- 93Lea-215
- 93LeaGolAS-7
- 93McDUppD-H4
- 930PCPre-93
- 930PCPre-350
- 930PCPre-383
- 930PCPreBG-21
- 930PCPreG-93
- 930PCPreG-350
- 930PCPreG-383
- 93PanSti-10
- 93Par-14
- 93ParEmel-14
- 93Pin-250
- 93PinAllS-21
- 93PinAllS-48
- 93PinAllSC-21
- 93PinAllSC-48
- 93PinCan-250
- 93PinCap-2
- 93PinCapC-2
- 93PinTeaP-8
- 93PinTeaPC-8
- 93Pow-16
- 93PowSlaA-2
- 93Sco-29
- 93ScoCan-29
- 93ScoDreTea-7
- 93ScoFra-1
- 93StaClu-160
- 93StaCluAS-2
- 93StaCluFDI-160
- 93StaCluFDIO-160
- 93StaCluFin-12
- 93StaCluMasP-3
- 93StaCluMasPW-3
- 93StaCluO-160
- 93SweSemWCS-192
- 93TopPre-93
- 93TopPre-350
- 93TopPre-383
- 93TopPreBG-15
- 93TopPreG-93
- 93TopPreG-383
- 93TopPrePS-602
- 93Ult-1
- 93UltAllS-2
- 93UppDec-116
- 93UppDecLAS-39

- 93UppDecNL-NL4
- 93UppDecSP-7
- 94BeAPla-R32
- 94BeAPSig-32
- 94CanGamNHLP-42
- 94CanGamNHLP-263
- 94Don-68
- 94DonDom-2
- 94EASpo-7
- 94EASpo-185
- 94Fin-35
- 94FinBowB-B1
- 94FinBowBR-B1
- 94FinDivFCC-2
- 94FinRef-35
- 94FinSupTW-35
- 94Fla-3
- 94Fle-9
- 94HocWit-77
- 94KenStaLA-2
- 94Kra-57
- 94Kra-67
- 94Lea-77
- 94LeaGolS-6
- 94LeaLim-84
- 94McDUppD-McD5
- 940PCPre-36
- 940PCPre-420
- 940PCPre-454
- 940PCPre-490
- 940PCPreSE-36
- 940PCPreSE-420
- 940PCPreSE-454
- 940PCPreSE-490
- 94Par-13
- 94Par-304
- 94ParCratGB-2
- 94ParCratGG-2
- 94ParCratGR-2
- 94ParGol-13
- 94ParGol-304
- 94ParSEV-18
- 94Pin-190
- 94PinArtP-190
- 94PinBoo-BR7
- 94PinRinC-190
- 94PinTeaP-TP3
- 94PinTeaPDP-TP3
- 94PosCerBB-3
- 94Sco-180
- 94Sco90PC-21
- 94ScoDreTea-DT3
- 94ScoGol-180
- 94ScoPla-180
- 94ScoPlaTS-180
- 94Sel-18
- 94SelFirLin-2
- 94SelGol-18
- 94SP-6
- 94SPDieCut-6
- 94SPPre-20
- 94SPPreDC-20
- 94StaClu-77
- 94StaCluFDI-77
- 94StaCluFDI-267
- 94StaCluFIMO-8
- 94StaCluMO-25
- 94StaCluMOMS-77
- 94StaCluMOMS-267
- 94StaCluSTWC-77
- 94StaCluSTWC-267
- 94TopFinB-20
- 94TopPre-36
- 94TopPre-420
- 94TopPre-454
- 94TopPre-490
- 94TopPreSE-36
- 94TopPreSE-420
- 94TopPreSE-454
- 94TopPreSE-490
- 94Ult-10
- 94UltAllS-1
- 94UltAwaW-1
- 94UppDec-296
- 94UppDecEleIce-296
- 94UppDecPC-C26
- 94UppDecPCEG-C26
- 94UppDecPR-R14
- 94UppDecPRE-R14
- 94UppDecPRERG-R14
- 94UppDecSPI-SP4
- 94UppDecSPIDC-SP4
- 95Bow-2
- 95BowAllFoi-2
- 95CanGamNHLP-4
- 95CanGamNHLP-18
- 95CanGamNHLP-36
- 95ColCho-216
- 95ColCho-385
- 95ColChoCTG-C24
- 95ColChoCTG-C24B
- 95ColChoCTG-C24C
- 95ColChoCTGGB-C24
- 95ColChoCTGGR-C24
- 95ColChoCTGSB-C24
- 95ColChoCTGSR-C24
- 95ColChoPC-216
- 95ColChoPC-385
- 95ColChoPCP-216
- 95ColChoPCP-385
- 95Don-127
- 95DonDom-3
- 95DonEli-9

❑ 83RegPat-23
❑ 85LonKni-4
❑ 87SauSteMG-22
**Boyd, James**
❑ 93KitRan-14
❑ 95Sla-43
**Boyd, Jim**
❑ 75RoaPhoWHA-14
**Boyd, Kevin**
❑ 95Sla-167
**Boyd, Randy**
❑ 81Ott67-1
❑ 83OPC-283
❑ 83PenHeiP-3
❑ 83PenTealP-3
❑ 87CanuSheOil-3
❑ 88CanuMoh-4
❑ 91ProAHLCHL-609
**Boyd, Rick**
❑ 88ProIHL-2
❑ 89JohChi-23
**Boyd, Stephanie**
❑ 94ClaWomOH-W33
**Boyd, Steve**
❑ 897thInnSOHL-37
**Boyd, Yank (Irwin)**
❑ 34BeeGro1P-4
**Boyer, Wally**
❑ 63RochAme-5
❑ 64BeeGro3P-31
❑ 64BeeGro3P-155
❑ 66Top-55
❑ 68OPC-105
❑ 68ShiCoi-146
❑ 68Top-105
❑ 69OPC-118
❑ 69Top-118
❑ 70DadCoo-9
❑ 70EssPowPla-230
❑ 70OPC-203
❑ 70SarProSta-171
❑ 71TorSun-212
❑ 72OPC-308
**Boyer, Zac**
❑ 88KamBla-4
❑ 907thInnSMC-2
❑ 907thInnSWHL-284
❑ 917thInnSWHL-84
❑ 92IndIce-3
❑ 94ClaProP-114
**Boykins, Kobie**
❑ 93RenEng-3
**Boyko, Darren**
❑ 93FinnSIS-96
❑ 94FinnSIS-10
❑ 95FinnSIS-13
❑ 95FinnSIS-174
❑ 95FinnSIS-369
❑ 95FinnSISL-44
**Boyko, Rob**
❑ 95Cla-82
**Boyle, Dan**
❑ 99Pac-185
❑ 99PacCop-185
❑ 99PacGol-185
❑ 99PacIceB-185
❑ 99PacPreD-185
**Boyle, Jordan**
❑ 90RayJrC-3
**Boyle, Steve**
❑ 74SioCitM-1
**Boynton, Nick**
❑ 95Cla-92
❑ 95Sla-262
❑ 95Sla-NNO
❑ 96UppDec-373
❑ 96UppDecBD-22
❑ 96UppDecBDG-22
❑ 97BowCHL-15
❑ 97BowCHL-154
❑ 97BowCHLAu-34
❑ 97BowCHLBB-6
❑ 97BowCHLBowBesAR-6
❑ 97BowCHLBowBesR-6
❑ 97BowCHLOPC-15
❑ 97BowCHLOPC-154
❑ 97ColCho-309
❑ 98BowCHL-27
❑ 98BowCHLGA-27
❑ 98BowCHLOI-27
❑ 98BowChrC-27
❑ 98BowChrCGA-27
❑ 98BowChrCGAR-27
❑ 98BowChrCOI-27
❑ 98BowChrCOIR-27
❑ 98BowChrCR-27
**Bozek, Darwin**
❑ 89ProAHL-11
**Bozek, Roman**
❑ 94CzeAPSE-112
❑ 95CzeAPSE-70
**Bozek, Steve**
❑ 82OPC-151
❑ 82OPCSti-233
❑ 82PosCer-8
❑ 83OPC-77
❑ 83Vac-3
❑ 84OPC-220
❑ 85FlamRedRP-5
❑ 86FlamRedR-3
❑ 87FlamRedRP-2
❑ 87OPC-216
❑ 88CanuMoh-5
❑ 89CanuMoh-3
❑ 89OPCSti-67
❑ 90Bow-64
❑ 90BowTif-64
❑ 90CanuMoh-3
❑ 90OPC-76
❑ 90PanSti-301
❑ 90ProSet-293
❑ 90ScoRoo-89T
❑ 90Top-76
❑ 90TopTif-76
❑ 91Bow-325
❑ 91CanuPanTS-3
❑ 91OPC-397
❑ 91PanSti-48
❑ 91Pin-61
❑ 91PinFre-61
❑ 91ProSet-486
❑ 91ProSetFre-486
❑ 91ScoCan-252
❑ 91ScoCan-556
❑ 91ScoRoo-6T
❑ 91ShaSanJSA-3
❑ 91StaClu-28
❑ 91Top-397
❑ 92Sco-37
❑ 92ScoCan-37
**Bozik, Mojmir**
❑ 89SweSemWCS-188
**Bozon, Philippe**
❑ 91Par-375
❑ 91ParFre-375
❑ 92OPC-257
❑ 92OPCPre-25
❑ 92Par-159
❑ 92Par-452
❑ 92ParEmel-159
❑ 92ParEmel-452
❑ 92StaClu-8
❑ 92Top-433
❑ 92TopGol-433G
❑ 92Ult-392
❑ 92UppDec-283
❑ 93OPCPre-68
❑ 93OPCPreG-68
❑ 93Par-179
❑ 93ParEmel-179
❑ 93StaClu-214
❑ 93StaCluFDI-214
❑ 93StaCluFDIO-214
❑ 93StaCluO-214
❑ 93SweSemWCS-268
❑ 93TopPre-68
❑ 93TopPreG-68
❑ 93Ult-210
❑ 93UppDec-113
❑ 93UppDecSP-134
❑ 94Don-261
❑ 94Lea-321
❑ 94ParSE-SE153
❑ 94ParSEG-SE153
❑ 94StaClu-233
❑ 94StaCluFDI-233
❑ 94StaCluMOMS-233
❑ 94StaCluSTWC-233
❑ 95SweGloWC-205
❑ 95SwiHNL-379
❑ 96SweSemW-188
❑ 98GerDELE-226
**Brabec, Jaroslav**
❑ 94CzeAPSE-105
❑ 95CzeAPSE-71
❑ 95CzeAPSE-266
**Brabenec, Kamil**
❑ 96CzeAPSE-261
**Bracco, Jon**
❑ 92MPSPhoSJHL-102
**Bracco, Michael**
❑ 88BroBra-18
**Brackenbury, Curt**
❑ 76NordMarA-5
❑ 76NordPos-8
❑ 76OPCWHA-4
❑ 79OPC-308
❑ 80PepCap-22
❑ 81OilRedR-15
❑ 81OPC-109
❑ 88OilTenAnn-10
❑ 90HamRoaA-59
**Bradette, Martin**
❑ 93AmoLesFAM-5
**Bradford, Brent**
❑ 92BriColJHL-63
**Bradley, Brian**
❑ 85MonGolF-9
❑ 86FlamRedR-4
❑ 88CanuMoh-6
❑ 89CanuMoh-4
❑ 89OPC-287
❑ 89OPC-315
❑ 89OPCSti-63
❑ 89PanSti-152
❑ 90Bow-58
❑ 90BowTif-58
❑ 90CanuMol-1
❑ 90OPC-59
❑ 90OPC-115
❑ 90PanSti-302
❑ 90ProSet-294
❑ 90Sco-198
❑ 90ScoCan-198
❑ 90Top-59
❑ 90Top-115
❑ 90TopTif-59
❑ 90TopTif-115
❑ 90UppDec-79
❑ 90UppDecF-79
❑ 91Bow-159
❑ 91CanuPanTS-4
❑ 91MapLeaP-3
❑ 91OPC-234
❑ 91OPCPre-185
❑ 91OPCPre-190
❑ 91PanSti-93
❑ 91Par-171
❑ 91ParFre-171
❑ 91Pin-90
❑ 91PinFre-90
❑ 91ProSet-489
❑ 91ProSetFre-489
❑ 91ProSetPla-231
❑ 91ScoCan-255
❑ 91StaClu-257
❑ 91Top-234
❑ 92Bow-283
❑ 92LigShe-6
❑ 92OPC-27
❑ 92Par-174
❑ 92ParEmel-174
❑ 92Pin-387
❑ 92PinCanPP-2
❑ 92PinFre-387
❑ 92ProSet-174
❑ 92Sco-259
❑ 92ScoCan-259
❑ 92StaClu-163
❑ 92Top-291
❑ 92TopGol-291G
❑ 92Ult-408
❑ 92UppDec-544
❑ 93Don-324
❑ 93Kra-2
❑ 93Lea-209
❑ 93LigKasK-1
❑ 93LigSealR-3
❑ 93McDUppD-1
❑ 93OPCPre-117
❑ 93OPCPreG-117
❑ 93PanSti-S
❑ 93Par-465
❑ 93ParEmel-465
❑ 93Pin-60
❑ 93PinAllS-33
❑ 93PinAllSC-33
❑ 93PinCan-60
❑ 93Pow-228
❑ 93Sco-230
❑ 93ScoCan-230
❑ 93ScoFra-20
❑ 93StaClu-212
❑ 93StaCluAS-11
❑ 93StaCluFDI-212
❑ 93StaCluFDIO-212
❑ 93StaCluO-212
❑ 93TopPre-117
❑ 93TopPreG-117
❑ 93Ult-36
❑ 93UppDec-121
❑ 93UppDec-305
❑ 93UppDecLAS-20
❑ 93UppDecSP-148
❑ 94CanGamNHLP-221
❑ 94Don-40
❑ 94EASpo-129
❑ 94Fla-170
❑ 94Fle-203
❑ 94Lea-42
❑ 94LigPhoA-4
❑ 94LigPos-2
❑ 94OPCPre-247
❑ 94OPCPreSE-247
❑ 94Par-221
❑ 94ParGol-221
❑ 94ParVin-V71
❑ 94Pin-278
❑ 94PinArtP-278
❑ 94PinRinC-278
❑ 94Sco-179
❑ 94ScoGol-179
❑ 94ScoPla-179
❑ 94ScoPlaTS-179
❑ 94Sel-43
❑ 94SelGol-43
❑ 94SP-114
❑ 94SPDieCut-114
❑ 94StaCluMO-41
❑ 94TopPre-247
❑ 94TopPreSE-247
❑ 94Ult-202
❑ 94UppDec-118
❑ 94UppDecEleIce-118
❑ 94UppDecSPI-SP74
❑ 94UppDecSPIDC-SP74
❑ 95BeAPla-117
❑ 95BeAPSig-S117
❑ 95BeAPSigDC-S117
❑ 95CanGamNHLP-246
❑ 95ColCho-128
❑ 95ColChoPC-128
❑ 95ColChoPCP-128
❑ 95Don-139
❑ 95DonEli-82
❑ 95DonEliDCS-82
❑ 95DonEliDCU-82
❑ 95Emo-162
❑ 95Fin-143
❑ 95FinRef-143
❑ 95ImpSti-113
❑ 95Kra-69
❑ 95Lea-159
❑ 95LigTeal-4
❑ 95Met-135
❑ 95NHLAcePC-4C
❑ 95ParInt-190
❑ 95ParIntEl-190
❑ 95PlaOneoOne-197
❑ 95ProMag-71
❑ 95Sco-232
❑ 95ScoBlaIce-232
❑ 95ScoBlaIceAP-232
❑ 95SelCer-83
❑ 95SelCerMG-83
❑ 95SkyImp-153
❑ 95StaClu-39
❑ 95StaCluMOMS-39
❑ 95Sum-146
❑ 95SumArtP-146
❑ 95SumIce-146
❑ 95Top-148
❑ 95TopOPCI-148
❑ 95TopSupSki-59
❑ 95TopSupSkiPla-59
❑ 95Ult-308
❑ 95UppDec-83
❑ 95UppDecEleIce-83
❑ 95UppDecEleIceG-83
❑ 95UppDecSpeE-SE166
❑ 95UppDecSpeEdiG-SE166
❑ 96ColCho-250
❑ 96Don-116
❑ 96DonPrePro-116
❑ 96Fle-103
❑ 96Lea-58
❑ 96LeaLim-76
❑ 96LeaLimG-76
❑ 96LeaPre-18
❑ 96LeaPreP-58
❑ 96LeaPrePP-18
❑ 96MetUni-142
❑ 96NHLProSTA-71
❑ 96Pin-17
❑ 96PinArtP-17
❑ 96PinFoi-17
❑ 96PinPreS-17
❑ 96PinRinC-17
❑ 96Sco-45
❑ 96ScoArtPro-45
❑ 96ScoDeaCAP-45
❑ 96ScoGolB-45
❑ 96ScoSpeAP-45
❑ 96SkyImp-120
❑ 96SkyImpB-1
❑ 96SP-149
❑ 96Sum-18
❑ 96SumArtP-18
❑ 96SumIce-18
❑ 96SumMet-18
❑ 96SumPreS-18
❑ 96TopNHLP-71
❑ 96TopPicOI-71
❑ 96Ult-155
❑ 96UltGolM-155
❑ 96Zen-59
❑ 96ZenArtP-59
❑ 97Kat-133
❑ 97KatGol-133
❑ 97KatSil-133
❑ 97Pac-64
❑ 97PacCop-64
❑ 97PacEmeGre-64
❑ 97PacIceB-64
❑ 97PacRed-64
❑ 97PacSil-64
**Bradley, John**
❑ 91RochAmeKod-4
❑ 91RochAmePos-2
❑ 93JohChi-1
❑ 95LetHur-2
**Bradley, Les**
❑ 82KitRan-27
❑ 83KitRan-29
❑ 84KitRan-29
**Bradley, Matt**
❑ 95BowDraPro-P3
❑ 95Sla-113
❑ 98BowCHL-28
❑ 98BowCHLGA-28
❑ 98BowCHLOI-28
❑ 98BowChrC-28
❑ 98BowChrCGA-28
❑ 98BowChrCGAR-28
❑ 98BowChrCOI-28
❑ 98BowChrCOIR-28
❑ 98BowChrCR-28
❑ 98UC-274
❑ 98UD ChoPCR-274
❑ 98UD ChoR-274
**Bradley, Todd**
❑ 917thInnSOHL-150
❑ 91OshGen-13
❑ 91OshGenS-21
❑ 92OshGenS-16
❑ 93OshGen-13
**Brady, Fred**
❑ 52JunBluT-60
**Brady, Lance**
❑ 95BirBul-3
**Brady, Neil**
❑ 85MedHatT-11
❑ 88ProAHL-337
❑ 89DevCar-3
❑ 90Bow-88
❑ 90BowTif-88
❑ 90ProAHLIHL-568
❑ 92OPCPre-82
❑ 92Par-124
❑ 92ParEmel-124
❑ 92Sen-3
❑ 93OPCPre-17
❑ 93OPCPreG-17
❑ 93PanSti-119
❑ 93Sco-293
❑ 93ScoCan-293
❑ 93StaClu-199
❑ 93StaCluFDI-199
❑ 93StaCluFDIO-199
❑ 93StaCluO-199
❑ 93TopPre-17
❑ 93TopPreG-17
❑ 93UppDec-81
**Bragnalo, Rick**
❑ 77OPCNHL-296
❑ 78OPC-308
❑ 82SweSemHVS-134
**Braham, Dean**
❑ 84PriAlbRS-3
**Branch, David**
❑ 907thInnSOHL-300
**Branch, James**
❑ 69SweWorC-177
**Branch, Rod**
❑ 93KamBla-2
❑ 95PriAlbR-1
❑ 95SlaMemC-1
**Brancik, Richard**
❑ 94CzeAPSE-21
❑ 95CzeAPSE-118
**Brand, Aaron**
❑ 94SarSti-9
❑ 95Cla-96
❑ 95Sla-338
❑ 96St.JohML-3
❑ 97St.JohML-3
**Brand, Konrad**
❑ 96KamBla-5
**Brander, Christoph**
❑ 95AusNatTea-1
**Brandl, Thomas**
❑ 91SweSemWCS-165
❑ 93SweSemWCS-166
❑ 94FinnJaaK-280
❑ 94GerDELE-202
❑ 95GerDELE-205
❑ 95GerDELE-430
❑ 95SweGloWC-221
❑ 96GerDELE-289
❑ 96SweSemW-197
❑ 98GerDELE-71
**Brandon, Howard**
❑ 23CreSel-4
❑ 23V1281PauC-7
❑ 24CreSel-1
**Brannare, Stefan**
❑ 92BriColJHL-154
**Brannlund, Lars-Ake**
❑ 67SweHoc-232
**Brannstrom, Fabian**
❑ 94GerDELE-74
❑ 95GerDELE-71
**Brannstrom, Niklas**
❑ 89SweSemE-210
❑ 91SweSemE-98
❑ 92SweSemE-120
❑ 93SweSemE-93
❑ 94SweLeaE-275
❑ 95SweUppDE1DS-DS7
**Brant, Chris**
❑ 82KinCan-18
❑ 83SauSteMG-3
❑ 84SauSteMG-4
❑ 88ProAHL-59
**Brar, Dampy**
❑ 98LasVegT-3
**Brasar, Per Olov**
❑ 70SweHocS-73
❑ 71SweHocS-163
❑ 72SweHocS-165
❑ 73SweHocS-49
❑ 73SweWorCS-49
❑ 74SweHocS-27
❑ 74SweHocS-206
❑ 78NorStaCD-2
❑ 78OPC-99
❑ 78Top-99
❑ 79OPC-192
❑ 79PanSti-195
❑ 79Top-192
❑ 80CanuSilD-3
❑ 80CanuTeal-3
❑ 80OPC-291
❑ 80PepCap-103
❑ 81CanuSilD-15
❑ 81CanuTeal-2
❑ 81OPC-330
❑ 81OPCSti-244
**Brasey, Patrice**
❑ 91SweSemWCS-182
❑ 93SweSemWCS-113
❑ 93SwiHNL-36
❑ 95SwiHNL-63
**Brashear, Donald**
❑ 907thInnSQMJHL-245
❑ 917thInnSQMJHL-139
❑ 92FreCan-3
❑ 93FreCan-3
❑ 94CanaPos-2
❑ 94ClaEnf-E1
❑ 94ClaProP-146
❑ 94Don-146
❑ 94FreCan-4
❑ 94Lea-227
❑ 94Ult-310
❑ 95CanaPos-1
❑ 95UppDec-411
❑ 95UppDecEleIce-411
❑ 95UppDecEleIceG-411
❑ 96BeAPAut-181
❑ 96BeAPAutSil-181
❑ 96BeAPla-181
❑ 96CanuPos-8
❑ 97PacInvNRB-200
❑ 97PacOme-227
❑ 97PacOmeC-227
❑ 97PacOmeDG-227
❑ 97PacOmeEG-227
❑ 97PacOmeG-227
❑ 97PacOmeIB-227
❑ 97PacRev-138
❑ 97PacRevC-138
❑ 97PacRevE-138
❑ 97PacRevIB-138
❑ 97PacRevR-138
❑ 97PacRevS-138
❑ 97ScoCanPla-17
❑ 97ScoCanPre-17
❑ 97ScoCanu-17
❑ 97UppDec-376
❑ 98Be A PPA-143
❑ 98Be A PPAA-143
❑ 98Be A PPAAF-143
❑ 98Be A PPTBASG-143
❑ 98Be APG-143
❑ 98Pac-425
❑ 98PacAur-187
❑ 98PacCroR-133
❑ 98PacCroRLS-133
❑ 98PacDynI-186
❑ 98PacDynIIB-186
❑ 98PacDynIR-186
❑ 98PacIceB-425
❑ 98PacPar-233
❑ 98PacParC-233
❑ 98PacParEG-233
❑ 98PacParH-233
❑ 98PacParIB-233
❑ 98PacParS-233
❑ 98PacRed-425
❑ 98RevThrPA-10
❑ 98RevThrPA-10
❑ 99Pac-421
❑ 99PacCop-421
❑ 99PacGol-421
❑ 99PacIceB-421
❑ 99PacPreD-421
**Brassard, Andre**
❑ 89NasKni-2
**Brassard, Chris**
❑ 93LonKni-5
❑ 94KitRan-19
**Brassard, Joel**
❑ 917thInnSQMJHL-38
**Bratash, Oleg**
❑ 90OPC-525
**Brathwaite, Fred**
❑ 897thInnSOHL-23
❑ 89OshGen-23
❑ 89OshGenP-35
❑ 907thInnSMC-77
❑ 907thInnSOHL-327
❑ 917thInnSOHL-169
❑ 91OshGenS-23
❑ 93Don-119
❑ 93Pow-339
❑ 93Sco-618
❑ 93ScoCan-618
❑ 93ScoGol-618
❑ 93Ult-313
❑ 93UppDec-435
❑ 94Don-320
❑ 94Lea-26
❑ 94Ult-289
❑ 95ColEdgI-31
❑ 99Pac-51
❑ 99PacCop-51
❑ 99PacGol-51
❑ 99PacIceB-51
❑ 99PacPreD-51
**Brauer, Cam**
❑ 88RegPat-2
❑ 90ProAHLIHL-173
❑ 91ProAHLCHL-98
**Braun, Frank**
❑ 69SweWorC-171
❑ 69SweWorC-173
❑ 69SweWorC-174
❑ 70SweHocS-367
**Brazda, Radomir**
❑ 94CzeAPSE-256
❑ 96CzeAPSE-145
**Brearley, Peter**
❑ 93KitRan-17
**Breault, Francois (Frank)**
❑ 84ChiSag-5
❑ 88ProAHL-216
❑ 89ProAHL-2
❑ 90KinSmo-13
❑ 90ProSet-612
❑ 91OPC-496
❑ 91ProSet-541
❑ 91ProSetFre-541
❑ 91Top-496
❑ 92PhoRoa-2
**Breen, George**
❑ 95Cla-70
❑ 95ClaAut-1
**Breistroff, Michel**
❑ 92HarCri-4
❑ 94FinnJaaK-218
**Breitenbach, Ken**
❑ 77OPCNHL-279
**Brekke, Brent**
❑ 92WesMic-3
❑ 93WesMic-2
❑ 95DayBom-14
**Brennan, Doug**
❑ 33V357IceK-45
❑ 34BeeGro1P-262
❑ 34DiaMatS-5
**Brennan, Lester**
❑ 36V356WorG-106
**Brennan, Michael**
❑ 91AirCanSJHL-B50
**Brennan, Rich**
❑ 91UppDecCWJC-76
❑ 97Be A PPAD-236
❑ 97Be A PPAPD-236
❑ 97BeAPla-236
❑ 97BeAPlaAut-236
❑ 98Pac-377
❑ 98PacIceB-377
❑ 98PacRed-377
**Brenneman, John**
❑ 64BeeGro3P-156
❑ 64CocCap-27
❑ 65MapLeaWB-4
❑ 68OPC-83
❑ 68ShiCoi-110
❑ 68Top-83
**Brent, Steven (Steve)**
❑ 91AirCanSJHL-D42
❑ 92MPSPhoSJHL-6
**Bresagk, Michael**
❑ 94GerDELE-249
❑ 95GerDELE-244
❑ 98GerDELE-143
❑ 98GerDELE-319
**Bresagk, Thomas**
❑ 94GerDELE-409
❑ 95GerDELE-407
**Breslin, Tim**
❑ 91ProAHLCHL-395
❑ 92PhoRoa-3
❑ 93PhoRoa-1
**Breton, Luc**
❑ 77GraVic-2
**Brewer, Carl**
❑ 44BeeGro2P-385
❑ 59Par-3
❑ 60Par-18
❑ 60ShiCoi-3
❑ 60YorPreP-7
❑ 61Par-18
❑ 61ShiCoi-45
❑ 61YorYelB-13
❑ 62Par-8
❑ 62ShiMetC-5
❑ 62ShiMetC-51
❑ 62YorIroOTra-5
❑ 63MapLeaWB-3
❑ 63MapLeaWB-4
❑ 63Par-8
❑ 63Par-68
❑ 63TorSta-7
❑ 63YorWhiB-17
❑ 64BeeGro3P-157
❑ 64CocCap-92
❑ 64Top-75
❑ 64TorSta-7
❑ 65Top-78
❑ 69OPC-59
❑ 69OPCFou-7
❑ 69Top-59
❑ 70OPC-243
❑ 71BluPos-3
❑ 71OPC-222
❑ 71TorSun-235
❑ 72SluCupWHA-3
❑ 79MapLeaP-5
❑ 92ParParR-PR13
❑ 94ParMisLFS-FS1
❑ 94ParTalB-114
**Brewer, Eric**
❑ 97BowCHL-153
❑ 97BowCHLAu-33
❑ 97BowCHLBB-8
❑ 97BowCHLBowBesAR-8
❑ 97BowCHLBowBesR-8
❑ 97BowCHLOPC-153
❑ 97UppDecBD-90
❑ 97UppDecBDDD-90
❑ 97UppDecBDQD-90
❑ 97UppDecBDTD-90
❑ 98Be A PPA-235
❑ 98Be A PPAA-235
❑ 98Be A PPAAF-235
❑ 98Be A PPSE-235
❑ 98Be APG-235
❑ 98BowBes-115
❑ 98BowBesAR-115
❑ 98BowBesMIF-F17
❑ 98BowBesMIFAR-F17
❑ 98BowBesMIFR-F17
❑ 98BowBesR-115
❑ 98PacDynI-114
❑ 98PacDynIIB-114
❑ 98PacDynIR-114
❑ 98PacOmeH-153
❑ 98PacOmeODI-153
❑ 98PacOmeR-153
❑ 98SP Aut-102
❑ 98SP AutSS-SS21
❑ 98SPXTopP-37

❑ 98SPXTopPF-37
❑ 98SPXTopPR-37
❑ 98TopGolLC1-68
❑ 98TopGolLC1B-68
❑ 98TopGolLC1BOoO-68
❑ 98TopGolLC1OoO-68
❑ 98TopGolLC1R-68
❑ 98TopGolLC1ROoO-68
❑ 98TopGolLC2-68
❑ 98TopGolLC2B-68
❑ 98TopGolLC2BOoO-68
❑ 98TopGolLC2OoO-68
❑ 98TopGolLC2R-68
❑ 98TopGolLC2ROoO-68
❑ 98TopGolLC3-68
❑ 98TopGolLC3B-68
❑ 98TopGolLC3BOoO-68
❑ 98TopGolLC3OoO-68
❑ 98TopGolLC3R-68
❑ 98TopGolLC3ROoO-68
❑ 98UC-256
❑ 98UD ChoPCR-256
❑ 98UD ChoR-256
❑ 98UppDec-417
❑ 98UppDecBD-52
❑ 98UppDecDD-52
❑ 98UppDecE-417
❑ 98UppDecE1o1-417
❑ 98UppDecGJ-GJ12
❑ 98UppDecGN-GN18
❑ 98UppDecGNQ1-GN18
❑ 98UppDecGNQ2-GN18
❑ 98UppDecGNQ3-GN18
❑ 98UppDecGR-417
❑ 98UppDecM-124
❑ 98UppDecM1-M29
❑ 98UppDecM2-M29
❑ 98UppDecMGS-124
❑ 98UppDecMP-EB
❑ 98UppDecMSS-124
❑ 98UppDecMSS-124
❑ 98UppDecP-P5
❑ 98UppDecPQ1-P5
❑ 98UppDecPQ2-P5
❑ 98UppDecPQ3-P5
❑ 98UppDecQD-52
❑ 98UppDecTD-52
❑ 99Pac-251
❑ 99PacCop-251
❑ 99PacGol-251
❑ 99PacIceB-251
❑ 99PacPreD-251
❑ 99SP AutPS-102
❑ 99UppDecM-126
❑ 99UppDecMGS-126
❑ 99UppDecMSS-126
❑ 99UppDecMSS-126

**Brewer, Mike (Michael)**
❑ 92AlbIntTC-6
❑ 92SanDieG-4

**Brezeault, Reginald**
❑ 907thInnSQMJHL-182
❑ 917thInnSQMJHL-157
❑ 93ForWorF-3
❑ 93RoaExp-6

**Brezgunov, Vadim**
❑ 91OPCIns-11R

**Brezina, Robert**
❑ 94GerDELE-426
❑ 95GerDELE-395
❑ 96GerDELE-304

**Briand, Arnaud**
❑ 93SweSemWCS-259
❑ 94FinnJaaK-229
❑ 94FreNatT-7

**Brick, Jeff**
❑ 93RenEng-4

**Bricker, Harry**
❑ 89ProAHL-357
❑ 90ProAHLIHL-52

**Brickley, Andy**
❑ 83PenCok-2
❑ 83SprInd-14
❑ 84PenHeiP-2
❑ 86DevPol-4
❑ 87PanSti-86
❑ 88BruPos-2
❑ 89BruSpoA-2
❑ 89OPC-29
❑ 89PanSti-194
❑ 89Top-29
❑ 90Bow-27
❑ 90BowTif-27
❑ 90BruSpoA-3
❑ 90OPC-88
❑ 90PanSti-16
❑ 90ProSet-406
❑ 90Top-88
❑ 90TopTif-88
❑ 90UppDec-84
❑ 90UppDecF-84
❑ 92Bow-17
❑ 92Sco-296
❑ 92ScoCan-296
❑ 92StaClu-208
❑ 92Top-109
❑ 92TopGol-109G

**Brickley, Quintan**
❑ 90KnoChe-116

**Bricknell, Corey**
❑ 93NiaFalT-20

**Bridgman, Mel**
❑ 75FlyCanDC-3
❑ 76OPCNHL-26
❑ 76Top-26
❑ 77OPCNHL-121
❑ 77Top-121
❑ 78OPC-26
❑ 78Top-26
❑ 79OPC-201
❑ 79Top-201
❑ 80OPC-189
❑ 80Top-189
❑ 81FlamPos-2
❑ 81OPC-248
❑ 82FlamDol-1
❑ 82OPC-39
❑ 82OPC-40
❑ 82OPCSti-213
❑ 82PosCer-3
❑ 83OPC-226
❑ 83OPCSti-265
❑ 847EDis-31
❑ 84DevPos-18
❑ 84KelWin-30
❑ 84OPC-109
❑ 84OPC-361
❑ 84OPCSti-71
❑ 84Top-84
❑ 84VicCou-3
❑ 857ECreCar-11
❑ 85OPC-42
❑ 85OPCSti-57
❑ 85Top-42
❑ 86DevPol-5
❑ 86OPC-136
❑ 86OPCSti-203
❑ 86Top-136
❑ 87OPC-17
❑ 87PanSti-249
❑ 87RedWinLC-3
❑ 87Top-17

**Briere, Daniel**
❑ 94ParSE-SE261
❑ 94ParSEG-SE261
❑ 95BowDraPro-P4
❑ 95Cla-58
❑ 95ClaCHLAS-AS17
❑ 96UppDecIce-120
❑ 97BowCHL-50
❑ 97BowCHLOPC-50
❑ 98BowBes-108
❑ 98BowBesAR-108
❑ 98BowBesP-BP8
❑ 98BowBesPAR-BP8
❑ 98BowBesPR-BP8
❑ 98BowBesR-108
❑ 98McD-27
❑ 98O-PChr-149
❑ 98O-PChrR-149
❑ 98PacCroRRC-7
❑ 98PacOmeH-182
❑ 98PacOmeODI-182
❑ 98PacOmeR-182
❑ 98PacRev-109
❑ 98PacRevIS-109
❑ 98PacRevR-109
❑ 98SP Aut-104
❑ 98SPxFin-143
❑ 98SPxFinR-143
❑ 98SPxFinS-143
❑ 98SPXTopP-48
❑ 98SPXTopPF-48
❑ 98SPXTopPR-48
❑ 98Top-149
❑ 98TopO-P-149
❑ 98UC-163
❑ 98UD ChoPCR-163
❑ 98UD ChoR-163
❑ 98UDCP-163
❑ 98UppDec-7
❑ 98UppDecBD-67
❑ 98UppDecDD-67
❑ 98UppDecE-7
❑ 98UppDecE1o1-7
❑ 98UppDecGN-GN19
❑ 98UppDecGNQ1-GN19
❑ 98UppDecGNQ2-GN19
❑ 98UppDecGNQ3-GN19
❑ 98UppDecGR-7
❑ 98UppDecM-157
❑ 98UppDecMGS-157
❑ 98UppDecMSS-157
❑ 98UppDecMSS-157
❑ 98UppDecQD-67
❑ 98UppDecTD-67
❑ 99SP AutPS-104
❑ 99UppDecM-162
❑ 99UppDecMGS-162
❑ 99UppDecMSS-162
❑ 99UppDecMSS-162

**Briffey, Shean**
❑ 92QueIntP-39

**Bright, Chris**
❑ 90ProAHLIHL-188
❑ 91ProAHLCHL-110
❑ 94ClaProP-245

**Brigley, Travis**
❑ 95LetHur-3
❑ 96LetHur-1
❑ 97BowCHL-110
❑ 97BowCHLOPC-110

**Brill, John**
❑ 91MinGolG-3
❑ 92MinGolG-4
❑ 94ClaProP-232
❑ 94DayBom-13
❑ 95DayBom-15

**Brillant, Pierre**
❑ 51LavDaiS-13
❑ 52St.LawS-50

**Brimanis, Aris**
❑ 92BraWheK-1
❑ 94ClaProP-138
❑ 94Don-65
❑ 94Lea-123
❑ 95Ima-76
❑ 95ImaAut-76A
❑ 95ImaGol-76

**Brimmer, Chuck**
❑ 81KinCan-11
❑ 81SauSteMG-5

**Brimmer, Kent**
❑ 84BelBul-16

**Brimsek, Frank**
❑ 34BeeGro1P-5A
❑ 34BeeGro1P-5B
❑ 39OPCV3011-97
❑ 44BeeGro2P-6
❑ 44BeeGro2P-82
❑ 83HalFP-I3
❑ 85HalFC-124
❑ 91BruSpoAL-4
❑ 94ParTalBG-7

**Brind'Amour, Rod**
❑ 89BluKod-19
❑ 90BluKod-2
❑ 90Bow-23
❑ 90BowTif-23
❑ 90OPC-332
❑ 90PanSti-266
❑ 90PanSti-343
❑ 90ProSet-259
❑ 90Sco-131
❑ 90Sco-328
❑ 90ScoCan-131
❑ 90ScoCan-328
❑ 90ScoHotRS-98
❑ 90ScoYouS-31
❑ 90Top-332
❑ 90TopTif-332
❑ 90UppDec-36
❑ 90UppDec-347
❑ 90UppDecF-36
❑ 90UppDecF-347
❑ 91Bow-374
❑ 91FlyJCP-2
❑ 91OPC-490
❑ 91OPCPre-94
❑ 91PanSti-30
❑ 91Par-124
❑ 91ParFre-124
❑ 91Pin-9
❑ 91PinFre-9
❑ 91ProSet-211
❑ 91ProSet-453
❑ 91ProSetFre-211
❑ 91ProSetFre-453
❑ 91ProSetPC-20
❑ 91ProSetPla-90
❑ 91ScoAme-85
❑ 91ScoCan-85
❑ 91ScoCan-618
❑ 91ScoRoo-68T
❑ 91StaClu-184
❑ 91Top-490
❑ 91UppDec-189
❑ 91UppDec-547
❑ 91UppDecF-189
❑ 91UppDecF-547
❑ 92Bow-224
❑ 92Bow-268
❑ 92FlyJCP-4
❑ 92FlyUppDS-5
❑ 92FlyUppDS-27
❑ 92HumDum1-2
❑ 92McDUppD-16
❑ 92OPC-49
❑ 92OPCPreSP-9
❑ 92PanSti-187
❑ 92PanStiFre-187
❑ 92Par-126
❑ 92ParEmel-126
❑ 92Pin-26
❑ 92PinFre-26
❑ 92PinTea2-18
❑ 92PinTea2F-18
❑ 92ProSet-132
❑ 92Sco-324
❑ 92ScoCan-324
❑ 92ScoYouS-26
❑ 92SeaPat-39
❑ 92StaClu-202
❑ 92Top-90
❑ 92TopGol-90G
❑ 92Ult-152
❑ 92UppDec-15
❑ 92UppDec-264
❑ 93Don-248
❑ 93Lea-26
❑ 93OPCPre-115
❑ 93OPCPreG-115
❑ 93PanSti-47
❑ 93Par-152
❑ 93ParEmel-152
❑ 93Pin-170
❑ 93PinCan-170
❑ 93PinTea2-11
❑ 93PinTea2C-11
❑ 93Pow-178
❑ 93Sco-45
❑ 93ScoCan-45
❑ 93StaClu-78
❑ 93StaCluFDI-78
❑ 93StaCluFDIO-78
❑ 93StaCluO-78
❑ 93TopPre-115
❑ 93TopPreG-115
❑ 93Ult-74
❑ 93UppDec-361
❑ 93UppDecSP-114
❑ 94BeAPSig-175
❑ 94CanGamNHLP-373
❑ 94Don-80
❑ 94EASpo-100
❑ 94Fin-85
❑ 94FinRef-85
❑ 94FinSupTW-85
❑ 94Fla-126
❑ 94Fle-150
❑ 94HocWit-59
❑ 94Lea-150
❑ 94LeaLim-78
❑ 94OPCPre-17
❑ 94OPCPreSE-17
❑ 94Par-167
❑ 94ParGol-167
❑ 94ParSEV-25
❑ 94Pin-273
❑ 94PinArtP-273
❑ 94PinRinC-273
❑ 94Sco-132
❑ 94Sco90PC-13
❑ 94ScoGol-132
❑ 94ScoPla-132
❑ 94ScoPlaTS-132
❑ 94Sel-119
❑ 94SelGol-119
❑ 94SP-86
❑ 94SPDieCut-86
❑ 94TopPre-17
❑ 94TopPreSE-17
❑ 94Ult-155
❑ 94UppDec-111
❑ 94UppDecEleIce-111
❑ 94UppDecSPI-SP57
❑ 94UppDecSPIDC-SP57
❑ 95CanGamNHLP-202
❑ 95ColCho-29
❑ 95ColChoPC-29
❑ 95ColChoPCP-29
❑ 95Don-188
❑ 95DonEli-91
❑ 95DonEliDCS-91
❑ 95DonEliDCU-91
❑ 95Emo-129
❑ 95Fin-44
❑ 95FinnSemWC-90
❑ 95FinRef-44
❑ 95ImpSti-94
❑ 95Lea-154
❑ 95LeaLim-69
❑ 95Met-108
❑ 95ParInt-158
❑ 95ParIntEl-158
❑ 95Pin-109
❑ 95PinArtP-109
❑ 95PinRinC-109
❑ 95PlaOneoOne-291
❑ 95ProMag-51
❑ 95Sco-244
❑ 95ScoBlaIce-244
❑ 95ScoBlaIceAP-244
❑ 95SelCer-59
❑ 95SelCerMG-59
❑ 95SkyImp-123
❑ 95SP-110
❑ 95StaClu-36
❑ 95StaCluMOMS-36
❑ 95Sum-79
❑ 95SumArtP-79
❑ 95SumIce-79
❑ 95Top-39
❑ 95TopOPCI-39
❑ 95Ult-115
❑ 95UltCreCra-2
❑ 95UltGolM-115
❑ 95UppDec-324
❑ 95UppDecEleIce-324
❑ 95UppDecEleIceG-324
❑ 95UppDecSpeE-SE64
❑ 95UppDecSpeEdiG-SE64
❑ 95Zen-68
❑ 96BeAPAut-21
❑ 96BeAPAutSil-21
❑ 96BeAPla-21
❑ 96ColCho-192
❑ 96Don-155
❑ 96DonEli-93
❑ 96DonEliDCS-93
❑ 96DonPrePro-155
❑ 96Fle-78
❑ 96FlePic-54
❑ 96FlyPos-2
❑ 96Lea-41
❑ 96LeaPre-64
❑ 96LeaPreP-41
❑ 96LeaPrePP-64
❑ 96MetUni-109
❑ 96NHLACEPC-4
❑ 96NHLProSTA-51
❑ 96Pin-123
❑ 96PinArtP-123
❑ 96PinFoi-123
❑ 96PinPreS-123
❑ 96PinRinC-123
❑ 96Sco-102
❑ 96ScoArtPro-102
❑ 96ScoDeaCAP-102
❑ 96ScoGolB-102
❑ 96ScoSpeAP-102
❑ 96SkyImp-92
❑ 96Sum-123
❑ 96SumArtP-123
❑ 96SumIce-123
❑ 96SumMet-123
❑ 96SumPreS-123
❑ 96SweSemW-98
❑ 96Ult-121
❑ 96UltGolM-122
❑ 96UppDec-121
❑ 96UppDecBD-117
❑ 96UppDecBDG-117
❑ 96UppDecIce-48
❑ 96UppDecIcePar-48
❑ 96UppDecPP-P26
❑ 97ColCho-192
❑ 97ColChoWD-W8
❑ 97Don-157
❑ 97DonCanI-113
❑ 97DonCanIDS-113
❑ 97DonCanIPS-113
❑ 97DonLim-82
❑ 97DonLimExp-82
❑ 97DonPre-67
❑ 97DonPreCttC-67
❑ 97DonPreProG-157
❑ 97DonPreProS-157
❑ 97DonPri-33
❑ 97DonPriSoA-33
❑ 97EssOlyHH-11
❑ 97EssOlyHHF-11
❑ 97Lea-125
❑ 97LeaFraMat-125
❑ 97LeaFraMDC-125
❑ 97LeaInt-125
❑ 97LeaIntUI-125
❑ 97Pac-31
❑ 97PacCop-31
❑ 97PacCroR-95
❑ 97PacCroREG-95
❑ 97PacCroRIB-95
❑ 97PacCroRS-95
❑ 97PacDyn-88
❑ 97PacDynBKS-68
❑ 97PacDynC-88
❑ 97PacDynDG-88
❑ 97PacDynEG-88
❑ 97PacDynIB-88
❑ 97PacDynR-88
❑ 97PacDynSil-88
❑ 97PacDynTan-20
❑ 97PacEmeGre-31
❑ 97PacIceB-31
❑ 97PacInv-98
❑ 97PacInvC-98
❑ 97PacInvEG-98
❑ 97PacInvIB-98
❑ 97PacInvNRB-139
❑ 97PacInvR-98
❑ 97PacInvS-98
❑ 97PacOme-160
❑ 97PacOmeC-160
❑ 97PacOmeDG-160
❑ 97PacOmeEG-160
❑ 97PacOmeG-160
❑ 97PacOmeIB-160
❑ 97PacOmeTL-15
❑ 97PacPar-130
❑ 97PacParC-130
❑ 97PacParDG-130
❑ 97PacParEG-130
❑ 97PacParIB-130
❑ 97PacParRed-130
❑ 97PacParSil-130
❑ 97PacRed-31
❑ 97PacRev-97
❑ 97PacRevC-97
❑ 97PacRevE-97
❑ 97PacRevIB-97
❑ 97PacRevR-97
❑ 97PacRevS-97
❑ 97PacSil-31
❑ 97PacSlaSDC-6A
❑ 97Pin-111
❑ 97PinCer-93
❑ 97PinCerMB-93
❑ 97PinCerMG-93
❑ 97PinCerMR-93
❑ 97PinCerR-93
❑ 97PinIns-92
❑ 97PinPrePBB-111
❑ 97PinPrePBC-111
❑ 97PinPrePBM-111
❑ 97PinPrePBY-111
❑ 97PinPrePFC-111
❑ 97PinPrePFM-111
❑ 97PinPrePFY-111
❑ 97PinPrePla-111
❑ 97PinTotCMPG-93
❑ 97PinTotCPB-93
❑ 97PinTotCPG-93
❑ 97PinTotCPR-93
❑ 97Sco-127
❑ 97ScoArtPro-127
❑ 97ScoChel-16
❑ 97ScoFly-5
❑ 97ScoFlyPla-5
❑ 97ScoFlyPre-5
❑ 97ScoGolBla-127
❑ 97SPAut-115
❑ 97UppDec-121
❑ 97UppDecBD-61
❑ 97UppDecBDDD-61
❑ 97UppDecBDQD-61
❑ 97UppDecBDTD-61
❑ 97UppDecGDM-121
❑ 97UppDecTSS-17C
❑ 97Zen-74
❑ 97Zen5x7-49
❑ 97ZenGolImp-49
❑ 97ZenSilImp-49
❑ 97ZenZGol-74
❑ 97ZenZSil-74
❑ 98Be A PPA-251
❑ 98Be A PPAA-251
❑ 98Be A PPAAF-251
❑ 98Be A PPSE-251
❑ 98Be APG-251
❑ 98BowBes-67
❑ 98BowBesAR-67
❑ 98BowBesR-67
❑ 98Fin-17
❑ 98FinNo P-17
❑ 98FinNo PR-17
❑ 98FinRef-17
❑ 98JelSpo-1
❑ 98O-PChr-116
❑ 98O-PChrR-116
❑ 98Pac-17
❑ 98PacAur-135
❑ 98PacCroR-97
❑ 98PacCroRLS-97
❑ 98PacDynI-133
❑ 98PacDynIIB-133
❑ 98PacDynIR-133
❑ 98PacIceB-17
❑ 98PacOmeH-172
❑ 98PacOmeODI-172
❑ 98PacOmeR-172
❑ 98PacPar-169
❑ 98PacParC-169
❑ 98PacParEG-169
❑ 98PacParH-169
❑ 98PacParIB-169
❑ 98PacParS-169
❑ 98PacRed-17
❑ 98PacRev-103
❑ 98PacRevIS-103
❑ 98PacRevR-103
❑ 98SP Aut-64
❑ 98SPxFin-62
❑ 98SPxFinR-62
❑ 98SPxFinS-62
❑ 98Top-116
❑ 98TopGolLC1-99
❑ 98TopGolLC1B-99
❑ 98TopGolLC1BOoO-99
❑ 98TopGolLC1OoO-99
❑ 98TopGolLC1R-99
❑ 98TopGolLC1ROoO-99
❑ 98TopGolLC2-99
❑ 98TopGolLC2B-99
❑ 98TopGolLC2BOoO-99
❑ 98TopGolLC2OoO-99
❑ 98TopGolLC2R-99
❑ 98TopGolLC2ROoO-99
❑ 98TopGolLC3-99
❑ 98TopGolLC3B-99
❑ 98TopGolLC3BOoO-99
❑ 98TopGolLC3OoO-99
❑ 98TopGolLC3R-99
❑ 98TopGolLC3ROoO-99
❑ 98TopO-P-116
❑ 98UC-149
❑ 98UD ChoPCR-149
❑ 98UD ChoR-149
❑ 98UppDec-334
❑ 98UppDecBD-65
❑ 98UppDecDD-65
❑ 98UppDecE-334
❑ 98UppDecE1o1-334
❑ 98UppDecGR-334
❑ 98UppDecM-155
❑ 98UppDecMGS-155
❑ 98UppDecMSS-155
❑ 98UppDecMSS-155
❑ 98UppDecQD-65
❑ 98UppDecTD-65
❑ 99Pac-299
❑ 99PacAur-103
❑ 99PacAurPD-103
❑ 99PacCop-299
❑ 99PacGol-299
❑ 99PacIceB-299
❑ 99PacPreD-299
❑ 99SP AutPS-64
❑ 99UppDecM-149
❑ 99UppDecMGS-149
❑ 99UppDecMPS-RBR
❑ 99UppDecMSS-149
❑ 99UppDecMSS-149

**Brink, Andy**
❑ 93DonTeaUSA-3
❑ 93MinGolG-5
❑ 93Pin-490
❑ 93PinCan-490
❑ 94MinGolG-5
❑ 95MinGolG-8

**Brisebois, Patrice**
❑ 907thInnSMC-59
❑ 907thInnSQMJHL-8
❑ 90UppDec-454
❑ 90UppDecF-454
❑ 917thInnSCHLAW-24
❑ 917thInnSMC-62
❑ 91CanaPos-2
❑ 91Par-309
❑ 91ParFre-309
❑ 91ProAHLCHL-80
❑ 91ScoAme-382
❑ 91ScoCan-272
❑ 91UppDec-442
❑ 91UppDecF-442
❑ 92Bow-435
❑ 92CanaPos-2
❑ 92DurPan-32
❑ 92OPC-239
❑ 92PanSti-155
❑ 92PanStiFre-155
❑ 92Par-320
❑ 92ParEmel-320
❑ 92Pin-153
❑ 92PinFre-153
❑ 92Sco-388
❑ 92ScoCan-388
❑ 92StaClu-238
❑ 92Top-189
❑ 92TopGol-189G
❑ 92Ult-325
❑ 92UppDec-277
❑ 93CanaPos-2
❑ 93Don-171
❑ 93DurSco-7
❑ 93Lea-191
❑ 93OPCCanHF-49
❑ 93OPCPre-59
❑ 93OPCPreG-59
❑ 93Par-105
❑ 93ParEmel-105
❑ 93Pin-253
❑ 93PinCan-253
❑ 93Pow-125
❑ 93Sco-163
❑ 93ScoCan-163
❑ 93StaClu-27
❑ 93StaCluFDI-27
❑ 93StaCluFDIO-27
❑ 93StaCluO-27
❑ 93TopPre-59
❑ 93TopPreG-59
❑ 93Ult-52
❑ 93UppDec-318
❑ 94CanaPos-3
❑ 94Don-250
❑ 94Fla-85
❑ 94Fle-102
❑ 94Lea-325
❑ 94Par-116
❑ 94ParGol-116
❑ 94Pin-191
❑ 94PinArtP-191
❑ 94PinRinC-191
❑ 94Ult-106
❑ 94UppDec-193
❑ 94UppDecEleIce-193
❑ 95BeAPla-44
❑ 95BeAPSig-S44
❑ 95BeAPSigDC-S44
❑ 95CanaPos-2
❑ 95CanaShe-10
❑ 95CanGamNHLP-152
❑ 95ColCho-61
❑ 95ColChoPC-61
❑ 95ColChoPCP-61
❑ 95ParInt-380
❑ 95ParIntEl-380
❑ 95PlaOneoOne-272
❑ 95Sco-148
❑ 95ScoBlaIce-148
❑ 95ScoBlaIceAP-148
❑ 95SP-77
❑ 95Top-199
❑ 95TopOPCI-199
❑ 95Ult-254
❑ 95UppDec-6
❑ 95UppDecEleIce-6
❑ 95UppDecEleIceG-6
❑ 96CanaPos-3
❑ 96CanaShe-1
❑ 96ColCho-142
❑ 96FlePic-160
❑ 96UppDec-88
❑ 97CanaPos-2
❑ 97ScoCan-20
❑ 97ScoCanPla-20
❑ 97UppDec-295
❑ 98Be A PPA-216
❑ 98Be A PPAA-216
❑ 98Be A PPAAF-216
❑ 98Be A PPSE-216
❑ 98Be APG-216
❑ 98O-PChr-80
❑ 98O-PChrR-80
❑ 98ScoCanPre-20
❑ 98Top-80
❑ 98TopO-P-80
❑ 98UppDec-293
❑ 98UppDecE-293
❑ 98UppDecE1o1-293
❑ 98UppDecGR-293

**Briske, Byron**
❑ 93RedDeeR-2
❑ 95SigRoo-58
❑ 95SigRooSig-58
❑ 95TriAme-7

**Brisson, Sylvain**
❑ 917thInnSQMJHL-42

**Brisson, Therese**
❑ 94ClaWomOH-W4
❑ 97ColCho-286

**Bristow, Cam**
❑ 907thInnSWHL-246
❑ 91AirCanSJHL-D41
❑ 92MPSPhoSJHL-49

**Brittig, Christian**
❑ 94GerDELE-307
❑ 95GerDELE-65
❑ 96GerDELE-261
❑ 98GerDELE-120
**Briza, Petr**
❑ 89SweSemWCS-180
❑ 91SweSemWCS-102
❑ 93FinnSIS-366
❑ 93SweSemWCS-89
❑ 94FinnJaaK-165
❑ 94GerDELE-260
❑ 95FinnSemWC-140
❑ 95FinnSemWC-213
❑ 95GerDELE-242
❑ 95SweGloWC-146
❑ 96GerDELE-135
❑ 96SweSemW-104
❑ 98GerDELE-65
**Brkic, Darren**
❑ 90MicTecHus-20
❑ 91MicTecHus-2
**Brklaicich, Steve**
❑ 51LavDaiS-61
**Broadbelt, Dave**
❑ 52JunBluT-163
**Broadbent, Punch**
❑ 12C57-2
❑ 23V1451-9
❑ 24C144ChaCig-8
❑ 24V130MapC-18
❑ 24V1452-39
❑ 83HalFP-A2
❑ 85HalFC-3
**Brochu, Martin**
❑ 907thInnSQMJHL-67
❑ 917thInnSQMJHL-44
❑ 93FreCan-4
❑ 94ClaProP-94
❑ 94FreCan-5
❑ 95ColEdgI-39
❑ 95ColEdgIQ-IR11
❑ 95FreCan-4
❑ 96PorPir-30
**Brochu, Stephane**
❑ 90ProAHLIHL-546
❑ 91ProAHLCHL-445
❑ 93FliGen-19
❑ 94FliGen-4
❑ 95FliGen-24
**Brocklehurst, Craig**
❑ 907thInnSOHL-27
**Brockmann, Andreas**
❑ 91SweSemWCS-167
❑ 93SweSemWCS-156
❑ 94GerDELE-93
❑ 95GerDELE-95
❑ 95GerDELE-436
❑ 96GerDELE-282
❑ 98GerDELE-176
**Broda, Mike**
❑ 95RedDeeR-4
**Broda, Turk**
❑ 34BeeGro1P-303
❑ 36OPCV304D-97
❑ 37OPCV304E-133
❑ 38QuaOatP-4
❑ 39OPCV3011-2
❑ 40OPCV3012-108
❑ 40OPCV3012-130
❑ 44BeeGro2P-386
❑ 45QuaOatP-12A
❑ 45QuaOatP-12B
❑ 45QuaOatP-12C
❑ 48ExhCan-29
❑ 51Par-75
❑ 55Par-23
❑ 55ParQuaO-23
❑ 64BeeGro3P-158
❑ 83HalFP-G3
❑ 85HalFC-94
❑ 91Kra-37
❑ 92ParParR-PR6
❑ 94ParMisLP-P6
**Broden, Connie**
❑ 94ParMisL-82
**Broderick, Ken**
❑ 69OPC-197
❑ 75OPCNHL-340
❑ 76OPCWHA-44
❑ 77OPCWHA-4
**Broderick, Len**
❑ 57Par-M21
❑ 57Par-M23
**Brodeur, Martin**
❑ 907thInnSQMJHL-222
❑ 90Sco-439
❑ 90ScoCan-439
❑ 917thInnSQMJHL-1
❑ 92OPC-59
❑ 92Sco-480
❑ 92ScoCan-480
❑ 92StaClu-233
❑ 92Top-513
❑ 92TopGol-513G
❑ 92UppDec-408
❑ 93Don-195
❑ 93DonRatR-10
❑ 93DurSco-5
❑ 93Lea-345
❑ 93OPCPre-401
❑ 93OPCPreG-401
❑ 93Par-380
❑ 93ParEmeI-380
❑ 93Pow-374
❑ 93Sco-648
❑ 93ScoCan-648
❑ 93ScoGol-648
❑ 93StaClu-352
❑ 93StaCluFDI-352
❑ 93StaCluO-352
❑ 93TopPre-401
❑ 93TopPreG-401
❑ 93Ult-357
❑ 93UltWavF-2
❑ 93UppDec-334
❑ 94BeAPla-R58
❑ 94BeAPla-R130
❑ 94BeAPSig-3
❑ 94CanGamNHLP-284
❑ 94CanGamNHLP-326
❑ 94ClaAllRT-AR1
❑ 94ClaProP-12
❑ 94Don-24
❑ 94DonEliIns-2
❑ 94DonMasM-2
❑ 94Fin-71
❑ 94FinRef-71
❑ 94FinSupTW-71
❑ 94Fla-92
❑ 94Fle-111
❑ 94FleNet-2
❑ 94Kra-35
❑ 94Kra-58
❑ 94Lea-56
❑ 94LeaCreP-9
❑ 94LeaGolR-1
❑ 94LeaGolS-8
❑ 94LeaLim-70
❑ 94LeaLimI-13
❑ 94McDUppD-McD35
❑ 94OPCFinIns-14
❑ 94OPCPre-83
❑ 94OPCPre-190
❑ 94OPCPre-380
❑ 94OPCPre-470
❑ 94OPCPreSE-83
❑ 94OPCPreSE-190
❑ 94OPCPreSE-380
❑ 94OPCPreSE-470
❑ 94Par-126
❑ 94Par-278
❑ 94ParGol-126
❑ 94ParGol-278
❑ 94ParSEV-8
❑ 94Pin-145
❑ 94Pin-462
❑ 94PinArtP-145
❑ 94PinArtP-462
❑ 94PinGoaG-GT7
❑ 94PinRinC-145
❑ 94PinRinC-462
❑ 94PosCerBB-4
❑ 94Sel-78
❑ 94SelGol-78
❑ 94SP-63
❑ 94SPDieCut-63
❑ 94StaClu-119
❑ 94StaClu-186
❑ 94StaClu-264
❑ 94StaCluFDI-119
❑ 94StaCluFDI-186
❑ 94StaCluFDI-264
❑ 94StaCluMO-46
❑ 94StaCluMOMS-119
❑ 94StaCluMOMS-186
❑ 94StaCluMOMS-264
❑ 94StaCluST-13
❑ 94StaCluSTWC-119
❑ 94StaCluSTWC-186
❑ 94StaCluSTWC-264
❑ 94TopFinB-12
❑ 94TopPre-83
❑ 94TopPre-190
❑ 94TopPre-380
❑ 94TopPre-470
❑ 94TopPreSE-83
❑ 94TopPreSE-190
❑ 94TopPreSE-380
❑ 94TopPreSE-470
❑ 94Ult-115
❑ 94UltAllRoo-2
❑ 94UltAwaW-2
❑ 94UppDec-96
❑ 94UppDecEleIce-96
❑ 94UppDecIG-IG11
❑ 94UppDecPH-H12
❑ 94UppDecPH-H29
❑ 94UppDecPHEG-H12
❑ 94UppDecPHEG-H29
❑ 94UppDecPHES-H12
❑ 94UppDecPHES-H29
❑ 94UppDecPHG-H12
❑ 94UppDecPHG-H29
❑ 94UppDecSPI-SP43
❑ 94UppDecSPIDC-SP43
❑ 95Bow-70
❑ 95BowAllFoi-70
❑ 95BowBes-BB8
❑ 95BowBesRef-BB8
❑ 95CanGamNHLP-167
❑ 95ColCho-204
❑ 95ColChoPC-204
❑ 95ColChoPCP-204
❑ 95ColEdgILL-L11
❑ 95Don-149
❑ 95DonBetTP-5
❑ 95DonDom-4
❑ 95DonEli-13
❑ 95DonEliDCS-43
❑ 95DonEliDCU-43
❑ 95DonEliPW-3
❑ 95Emo-94
❑ 95EmoXci-18
❑ 95Fin-45
❑ 95Fin-178
❑ 95FinRef-45
❑ 95FinRef-178
❑ 95ImpSti-70
❑ 95ImpStiDCS-16
❑ 95KenStaLA-2
❑ 95KenStaLC-3
❑ 95Kra-21
❑ 95Lea-66
❑ 95LeaLim-18
❑ 95LeaLimSS-2
❑ 95LeaRoaCup-2
❑ 95McDPin-MCD-27
❑ 95Met-81
❑ 95NHLAcePC-9C
❑ 95NHLCooT-18
❑ 95NHLCooT-RP18
❑ 95ParInt-122
❑ 95ParInt-NNO3
❑ 95ParIntCCGS1-11
❑ 95ParIntCCSS1-11
❑ 95ParIntEI-122
❑ 95ParIntGP-1
❑ 95ParIntNHLAS-6
❑ 95ParIntPTP-PP32
❑ 95PinCleS-1
❑ 95PinFan-19
❑ 95PinMas-2
❑ 95PinRoa2-3
❑ 95PlaOneoOne-57
❑ 95PlaOneoOne-275
❑ 95PosUppD-2
❑ 95ProMag-36
❑ 95Sco-25
❑ 95Sco-323
❑ 95ScoBlaIce-25
❑ 95ScoBlaIce-323
❑ 95ScoBlaIceAP-25
❑ 95ScoBlaIceAP-323
❑ 95ScoPro-25
❑ 95SelCer-24
❑ 95SelCerGT-9
❑ 95SelCerMG-24
❑ 95SkyImp-90
❑ 95SkyImpD-11
❑ 95SP-79
❑ 95SPHol-FX12
❑ 95SPHolSpFX-FX12
❑ 95SPStaEto-E18
❑ 95SPStaEtoG-E18
❑ 95StaClu-15
❑ 95StaCluGTSC-GT5
❑ 95StaCluMOMS-85
❑ 95StaCluNem-N6
❑ 95Sum-27
❑ 95SumArtP-27
❑ 95SumGM-2
❑ 95SumIce-27
❑ 95SumInTheCre-1
❑ 95Top-9
❑ 95Top-325
❑ 95TopMarMPB-9
❑ 95TopMysF-M21
❑ 95TopMysFR-M21
❑ 95TopOPCI-9
❑ 95TopOPCI-325
❑ 95TopPro-PF6
❑ 95TopSupSki-80
❑ 95TopSupSkiPla-80
❑ 95TopYouS-YS2
❑ 95Ult-86
❑ 95Ult-186
❑ 95Ult-366
❑ 95UltGolM-86
❑ 95UltGolM-186
❑ 95UltHigSpe-5
❑ 95UltPrePadMen-2
❑ 95UltPrePadMenGM-2
❑ 95UppDec-211
❑ 95UppDecAGPRW-29
❑ 95UppDecEleIce-211
❑ 95UppDecEleIceG-211
❑ 95UppDecFreFra-F14
❑ 95UppDecFreFraJ-F14
❑ 95UppDecNHLAS-AS6
❑ 95UppDecPHE-H5
❑ 95UppDecPHE-H11
❑ 95UppDecPRE-R57
❑ 95UppDecPreR-R57
❑ 95UppDecSpeE-SE135
❑ 95UppDecSpeEdiG-SE135
❑ 95UppPreHV-H5
❑ 95UppPreHV-H11
❑ 95UppPreRP-R57
❑ 95Zen-12
❑ 95ZenZT-2
❑ 95ZenZT-S2
❑ 96BeAPStaTP-5
❑ 96ColCho-144
❑ 96ColCho-306
❑ 96ColCho-322
❑ 96ColChoMVP-UD21
❑ 96ColChoMVPG-UD21
❑ 96ColChoSti-S24
❑ 96Dev-30
❑ 96Don-148
❑ 96DonBetPip-2
❑ 96DonCanI-46
❑ 96DonCanIGPP-46
❑ 96DonCanILG-4
❑ 96DonCanIRPP-46
❑ 96DonDom-1
❑ 96DonEli-16
❑ 96DonEliDCS-16
❑ 96DonEliPW-8
❑ 96DonEliPW-P8
❑ 96DonPrePro-148
❑ 96DurL'EB-JB6
❑ 96Fla-52
❑ 96FlaBluI-52
❑ 96FlaHotG-2
❑ 96Fle-58
❑ 96Fle-145
❑ 96Fle-146
❑ 96FlePicDL-3
❑ 96FlePicF5-4
❑ 96FlePicFF-8
❑ 96KraUppD-14
❑ 96Lea-6
❑ 96LeaLim-87
❑ 96LeaLimG-87
❑ 96LeaLimStu-11
❑ 96LeaPre-81
❑ 96LeaPreMM-2
❑ 96LeaPreP-6
❑ 96LeaPrePP-81
❑ 96LeaPreSG-2
❑ 96LeaPreSte-2
❑ 96LeaShuDow-6
❑ 96LeaSwe-6
❑ 96LeaSwe(-6
❑ 96MetUni-86
❑ 96MetUniAP-2
❑ 96MetUniAPSP-2
❑ 96MetUniIC-1
❑ 96MetUniICSP-1
❑ 96NHLACEPC-5
❑ 96NHLProSTA-36
❑ 96Pin-92
❑ 96PinArtP-92
❑ 96PinFoi-92
❑ 96PinMas-4
❑ 96PinMasDC-4
❑ 96PinMcD-33
❑ 96PinMin-23
❑ 96PinMinB-23
❑ 96PinMinCoiB-23
❑ 96PinMinCoiGP-23
❑ 96PinMinCoiN-23
❑ 96PinMinCoiS-23
❑ 96PinMinCoiSG-23
❑ 96PinMinG-23
❑ 96PinMinS-23
❑ 96PinPreS-92
❑ 96PinRinC-92
❑ 96PinTeaP-9
❑ 96PlaOneoOne-440
❑ 96Sco-10
❑ 96ScoArtPro-10
❑ 96ScoDeaCAP-10
❑ 96ScoGolB-10
❑ 96ScoNetW-2
❑ 96ScoSam-10
❑ 96ScoSpeAP-10
❑ 96ScoSudDea-1
❑ 96SelCer-6
❑ 96SelCerAP-6
❑ 96SelCerBlu-6
❑ 96SelCerFre-1
❑ 96SelCerMB-6
❑ 96SelCerMG-6
❑ 96SelCerMR-6
❑ 96SelCerRed-6
❑ 96SkyImp-68
❑ 96SP-86
❑ 96SPSPxFor-3
❑ 96SPSPxFor-5
❑ 96SPSPxForAut-3
❑ 96SPx-25
❑ 96SPxGol-25
❑ 96StaCluMO-29
❑ 96Sum-114
❑ 96SumArtP-114
❑ 96SumIce-114
❑ 96SumInTheCre-8
❑ 96SumInTheCrePS-8
❑ 96SumMet-114
❑ 96SumPreS-114
❑ 96SumUnt-16
❑ 96TeaOut-61
❑ 96TopNHLP-27
❑ 96TopPicFT-FT3
❑ 96TopPicID-ID6
❑ 96TopPicOI-27
❑ 96Ult-93
❑ 96UltGolM-94
❑ 96UppDec-91
❑ 96UppDecBD-134
❑ 96UppDecBDG-134
❑ 96UppDecGN-X18
❑ 96UppDecHH-HH10
❑ 96UppDecHHG-HH10
❑ 96UppDecHHS-HH10
❑ 96UppDecIce-92
❑ 96UppDecIcePar-92
❑ 96UppDecLSH-LS5
❑ 96UppDecLSHF-LS5
❑ 96UppDecLSHS-LS5
❑ 96UppDecSS-SS12A
❑ 96Zen-2
❑ 96ZenArtP-2
❑ 96ZenChaS-15
❑ 96ZenChaS-P15
❑ 96ZenChaSD-15
❑ 97Be A PPAD-2
❑ 97Be A PPAPD-2
❑ 97BeAPla-2
❑ 97BeAPlaAut-2
❑ 97BeAPlaSTP-11
❑ 97ColCho-141
❑ 97ColChoSta-SQ50
❑ 97ColChoSti-S3
❑ 97ColChoWD-W20
❑ 97Don-126
❑ 97DonBetTP-2
❑ 97DonCanI-42
❑ 97DonCanIDS-42
❑ 97DonCanILG-3
❑ 97DonCanILGP-3
❑ 97DonCanIPS-42
❑ 97DonCanISCS-24
❑ 97DonEli-8
❑ 97DonEli-137
❑ 97DonEliAsp-8
❑ 97DonEliAsp-137
❑ 97DonEliBttF-7
❑ 97DonEliBttFA-7
❑ 97DonEliC-8
❑ 97DonEliIns-10
❑ 97DonEliMC-8
❑ 97DonEliS-8
❑ 97DonEliS-137
❑ 97DonLim-74
❑ 97DonLim-127
❑ 97DonLim-149
❑ 97DonLim-150
❑ 97DonLimExp-74
❑ 97DonLimExp-127
❑ 97DonLimExp-149
❑ 97DonLimExp-150
❑ 97DonLimFOTG-2
❑ 97DonPre-16
❑ 97DonPre-185
❑ 97DonPreCG-2
❑ 97DonPreCGP-2
❑ 97DonPreCttC-16
❑ 97DonPreCttC-185
❑ 97DonPreDWT-9
❑ 97DonPrePM-6
❑ 97DonPreProG-126
❑ 97DonPreProS-126
❑ 97DonPreT-10
❑ 97DonPreTB-10
❑ 97DonPreTBC-10
❑ 97DonPreTPC-10
❑ 97DonPreTPG-10
❑ 97DonPri-7
❑ 97DonPri-196
❑ 97DonPriODI-7
❑ 97DonPriP-24
❑ 97DonPriPG-10
❑ 97DonPriPGP-10
❑ 97DonPriS-24
❑ 97DonPriSB-24
❑ 97DonPriSG-24
❑ 97DonPriSoA-7
❑ 97DonPriSoA-196
❑ 97DonPriSS-24
❑ 97Kat-79
❑ 97KatGol-79
❑ 97KatSil-79
❑ 97Lea-7
❑ 97Lea-174
❑ 97Lea-P6
❑ 97LeaFraMat-7
❑ 97LeaFraMat-174
❑ 97LeaFraMDC-7
❑ 97LeaFraMDC-174
❑ 97LeaInt-7
❑ 97LeaIntUI-7
❑ 97LeaPipDre-6
❑ 97McD-25
❑ 97Pac-30
❑ 97PacCarSup-10
❑ 97PacCarSupM-10
❑ 97PacCop-30
❑ 97PacCroR-73
❑ 97PacCroREG-73
❑ 97PacCroRFODC-11
❑ 97PacCroRIB-73
❑ 97PacCroRS-73
❑ 97PacDyn-68
❑ 97PacDynBKS-52
❑ 97PacDynBKS-106
❑ 97PacDynC-68
❑ 97PacDynDG-68
❑ 97PacDynEG-68
❑ 97PacDynIB-68
❑ 97PacDynR-68
❑ 97PacDynSil-68
❑ 97PacDynSto-12
❑ 97PacDynTan-12
❑ 97PacEmeGre-30
❑ 97PacGolCroDC-14
❑ 97PacIceB-30
❑ 97PacInTheCLC-12
❑ 97PacInv-76
❑ 97PacInvC-76
❑ 97PacInvEG-76
❑ 97PacInvFP-19
❑ 97PacInvIB-76
❑ 97PacInvNRB-108
❑ 97PacInvR-76
❑ 97PacInvS-76
❑ 97PacOme-127
❑ 97PacOmeC-127
❑ 97PacOmeDG-127
❑ 97PacOmeEG-127
❑ 97PacOmeG-127
❑ 97PacOmeIB-127
❑ 97PacOmeNSZ-7
❑ 97PacOmeSil-7
❑ 97PacOmeTL-13
❑ 97PacPar-101
❑ 97PacParBNDC-12
❑ 97PacParC-101
❑ 97PacParCG-9
❑ 97PacParDG-101
❑ 97PacParEG-101
❑ 97PacParGSL-11
❑ 97PacParIB-101
❑ 97PacParRed-101
❑ 97PacParSil-101
❑ 97PacRed-30
❑ 97PacRev-75
❑ 97PacRev1AGD-13
❑ 97PacRevC-75
❑ 97PacRevE-75
❑ 97PacRevIB-75
❑ 97PacRevNID-6
❑ 97PacRevR-75
❑ 97PacRevRtSD-11
❑ 97PacRevS-75
❑ 97PacRevTCL-14
❑ 97PacSil-30
❑ 97PacTeaCCC-14
❑ 97Pin-43
❑ 97PinArtP-43
❑ 97PinBee-45
❑ 97PinBeeGP-45
❑ 97PinBeeGT-6
❑ 97PinBeeT-6
❑ 97PinCer-3
❑ 97PinCerGT-1
❑ 97PinCerMB-3
❑ 97PinCerMG-3
❑ 97PinCerMR-3
❑ 97PinCerR-3
❑ 97PinCerT-1
❑ 97PinEpiGO-8
❑ 97PinEpiGP-8
❑ 97PinEpiME-8
❑ 97PinEpiMO-8
❑ 97PinEpiMP-8
❑ 97PinEpiPE-8
❑ 97PinEpiPO-8
❑ 97PinEpiPP-8
❑ 97PinEpiSE-8
❑ 97PinEpiSO-8
❑ 97PinEpiSP-8
❑ 97PinHocMC-1
❑ 97PinHocMC-2
❑ 97PinIns-7
❑ 97PinInsC-17
❑ 97PinInsCC-7
❑ 97PinInsCG-17
❑ 97PinInsEC-7
❑ 97PinInsSto-4
❑ 97PinInsSUG-2A/B
❑ 97PinInsSUG-2C/D
❑ 97PinInsT-6
❑ 97PinMas-3
❑ 97PinMasDC-3
❑ 97PinMasJ-3
❑ 97PinMasPro-3
❑ 97PinMin-16
❑ 97PinMinB-16
❑ 97PinMinCBP-16
❑ 97PinMinCGPP-16
❑ 97PinMinCNSP-16
❑ 97PinMinCoiB-16
❑ 97PinMinCoiGP-16
❑ 97PinMinCoiN-16
❑ 97PinMinCoiSG-16
❑ 97PinMinCoiSS-16
❑ 97PinMinGolTea-16
❑ 97PinMinSilTea-16
❑ 97PinPowPac-7
❑ 97PinPrePBB-43
❑ 97PinPrePBC-43
❑ 97PinPrePBM-43
❑ 97PinPrePBY-43
❑ 97PinPrePFC-43
❑ 97PinPrePFM-43
❑ 97PinPrePFY-43
❑ 97PinPrePla-43
❑ 97PinRepMas-1
❑ 97PinRinC-43
❑ 97PinTeaP-1
❑ 97PinTeaPM-1
❑ 97PinTeaPP-1
❑ 97PinTeaPPM-1
❑ 97PinTin-1
❑ 97PinTotCMPG-3
❑ 97PinTotCPB-3
❑ 97PinTotCPG-3
❑ 97PinTotCPR-3
❑ 97PosPin-8
❑ 97Sco-30
❑ 97Sco-269
❑ 97ScoArtPro-30
❑ 97ScoDev-16
❑ 97ScoDevPla-16
❑ 97ScoDevPre-16
❑ 97ScoGolBla-30
❑ 97ScoNetW-14
❑ 97SP AutI-I14
❑ 97SPAut-87
❑ 97SPAutID-I14
❑ 97SPAutIE-I14
❑ 97SPAutSotT-MB
❑ 97SPx-27
❑ 97SPxBro-27
❑ 97SPxDuo-3
❑ 97SPxDuoAut-3
❑ 97SPxGol-27
❑ 97SPxGraF-27
❑ 97SPxSil-27
❑ 97SPxSte-27
❑ 97Stu-20
❑ 97StuPor-20
❑ 97StuPor-NNO
❑ 97StuPrePG-20
❑ 97StuPrePS-20
❑ 97StuSil-4
❑ 97StuSil8-4
❑ 97UppDec-300
❑ 97UppDecBD-122
❑ 97UppDecBDDD-122
❑ 97UppDecBDPC-PC24
❑ 97UppDecBDPCDD-PC24
❑ 97UppDecBDPCM-PC24
❑ 97UppDecBDPCQD-PC24
❑ 97UppDecBDPCTD-PC24
❑ 97UppDecBDQD-122
❑ 97UppDecBDTD-122
❑ 97UppDecDV-5
❑ 97UppDecDVSM-5
❑ 97UppDecGDM-300
❑ 97UppDecIC-IC7
❑ 97UppDecIC2-IC7
❑ 97UppDecIce-7
❑ 97UppDecIceP-7
❑ 97UppDecIPS-7
❑ 97UppDecSG-SG4
❑ 97UppDecTS-30
❑ 97UppDecTSL2-30
❑ 97UppDecTSS-10A
❑ 97Zen-21
❑ 97Zen5x7-5
❑ 97ZenChaTC-11
❑ 97ZenGolImp-5
❑ 97ZenSilImp-5
❑ 97ZenZGol-21
❑ 97ZenZSil-21
❑ 97ZenZT-8
❑ 97ZenZT5x7-8
❑ 97ZenZTG-8
❑ 98Be A PPA-79
❑ 98Be A PPAA-79
❑ 98Be A PPAAF-79
❑ 98Be A PPAGUSC-S8
❑ 98Be A PPAJ-AS8
❑ 98Be A PPGUJA-G9
❑ 98Be A PPPGUJC-G9
❑ 98Be A PPPH-H4
❑ 98Be A PPPUJC-P19
❑ 98Be A PPTBASG-79
❑ 98Be APG-79
❑ 98BowBes-8
❑ 98BowBesAR-8
❑ 98BowBesMIF-F19
❑ 98BowBesMIFAR-F19
❑ 98BowBesMIFR-F19
❑ 98BowBesR-8
❑ 98BowBesSBB-SB2
❑ 98BowBesSBBAR-SB2
❑ 98BowBesSBBR-SB2
❑ 98CroRoyCCAJG-7
❑ 98CroRoyCCAJG-7
❑ 98CroRoyCCAJLB-7
❑ 98CroRoyCCAJP-7
❑ 98CroRoyCCAJR-7
❑ 98Fin-35
❑ 98FinCen-C11
❑ 98FinCenR-C11
❑ 98FinDouMF-M21
❑ 98FinDouMF-M22
❑ 98FinDouMF-M23
❑ 98FinDouMF-M24
❑ 98FinDouSMFR-M21
❑ 98FinDouSMFR-M22
❑ 98FinDouSMFR-M23
❑ 98FinDouSMFR-M24
❑ 98FinNo P-35
❑ 98FinNo PR-35
❑ 98FinOve-3
❑ 98FinOveR-3
❑ 98FinRef-35
❑ 98LunGoaG-2
❑ 98LunGoaGS-2
❑ 98McD-17
❑ 98O-PChr-20
❑ 98O-PChrR-20
❑ 98O-PChrSB-SB2
❑ 98O-PChrSBR-SB2
❑ 98Pac-30
❑ 98PacAur-108
❑ 98PacAurALC-12
❑ 98PacAurC-11
❑ 98PacAurCF-26
❑ 98PacAurCF-NNO
❑ 98PacAurCFC-26
❑ 98PacAurCFC-NNO
❑ 98PacAurCFIB-26
❑ 98PacAurCFR-26
❑ 98PacAurCFS-26
❑ 98PacAurNC-7
❑ 98PacCraCA-6
❑ 98PacCroR-78
❑ 98PacCroRCCA-7
❑ 98PacCroRCCAJ-7
❑ 98PacCroRLL-7
❑ 98PacCroRLS-78
❑ 98PacCroRMP-13
❑ 98PacCroRPotG-16
❑ 98PacCroRPP-14
❑ 98PacDynI-108
❑ 98PacDynI-12
❑ 98PacDynIIB-108

98PacDynIIW-5
98PacDynIPP-7
98PacDynIR-108
98PacDynITC-15
98PacEO P-13
98PacGolCD-18
98PacIceB-30
98PacOmeCS-6
98PacOmeCSG-6
98PacOmeCSR-6
98PacOmeEP101-13
98PacOmeFtF-1
98PacOmeH-136
98PacOmeO-19
98PacOmeODI-136
98PacOmeP-12
98PacOmePI-19
98PacOmePIB-19
98PacOmeR-136
98PacPar-132
98PacPar-NNO
98PacParC-132
98PacParEG-132
98PacParGSLC-10
98PacParH-132
98PacParH-NNO
98PacParHoFB-6
98PacParHoFBPP-6
98PacParB-132
98PacParIG-6
98PacParIGG-6
98PacParIGS-6
98PacParS-132
98PacParTCD-15
98PacRed-30
98PacRev-83
98PacRevADC-5
98PacRevIS-83
98PacRevNI-7
98PacRevR-83
98PacRevS-21
98PacTeaC-15
98PacTitl-12
98PacTroW-1
98PinEpiGE-8
98RevThrPA-15
98RevThrPA-15
98SP Aut-48
98SP AutSM-S13
98SP AutSS-SS13
98SPxFin-46
98SPxFin-105
98SPxFin-161
98SPxFin-176
98SPxFinR-46
98SPxFinR-105
98SPxFinR-161
98SPxFinR-176
98SPxFinS-46
98SPxFinS-105
98SPxFinS-161
98SPxFinS-176
98SPXTopP-35
98SPXTopPF-35
98SPXTopPHH-H17
98SPXTopPLI-L21
98SPXTopPPS-PS5
98SPXTopPR-35
98Top-20
98TopGolLC1-10
98TopGolLC1B-10
98TopGolLC1BOo0-10
98TopGolLC1Oo0-10
98TopGolLC1R-10
98TopGolLC1ROo0-10
98TopGolLC2-10
98TopGolLC2B-10
98TopGolLC2Oo0-10
98TopGolLC2O0o0-10
98TopGolLC2R-10
98TopGolLC2ROo0-10
98TopGolLC3-10
98TopGolLC3B-10
98TopGolLC3BOo0-10
98TopGolLC3Oo0-10
98TopGolLC3O0o0-10
98TopGolLC3R-10
98TopGolLC3ROo0-10
98TopLocL-L6
98TopMysFB-M12
98TopMysFBR-M12
98TopMysFG-M12
98TopMysFGR-M12
98TopMysFS-M12
98TopMysFSR-M12
98TopO-P-20
98TopSeaB-SB2
98UC-116
98UC-245
98UCMBH-BH7
98UCSB-SQ23
98UCSG-SQ23
98UCSR-SQ23
98UD ChoPCR-116
98UD ChoPCR-245
98UD ChoR-116
98UD ChoR-245
98UD3-36
98UD3-96
98UD3DieC-36
98UD3DieC-96
98UD3DieC-156
98UppDec-118

98UppDecBD-50
98UppDecBD-50
98UppDecE-118
98UppDecE1o1-118
98UppDecFIT-FT4
98UppDecFITQ1-FT4
98UppDecFITQ2-FT4
98UppDecFITQ3-FT4
98UppDecGJ-GJ6
98UppDecGR-118
98UppDecLSH-LS5
98UppDecLSHQ1-LS5
98UppDecLSHQ2-LS5
98UppDecLSHQ3-LS5
98UppDecM-117
98UppDecM1-M21
98UppDecM2-M21
98UppDecMGS-117
98UppDecMSF-F9
98UppDecMSS-117
98UppDecMSS-117
98UppDecP-P6
98UppDecPQ1-P6
98UppDecPQ2-P6
98UppDecPQ3-P6
98UppDecQD-50
98UppDecTD-50
98UppDecWFP-WF15
98UppDecWFP-WF15
99AurSty-12
99DevPowP-NJD3
99Pac-235
99PacAur-84
99PacAurCF-15
99PacAurCFC-15
99PacAurCFPB-15
99PacAurGU-11
99PacAurPD-84
99PacCop-235
99PacGol-235
99PacGolCD-21
99PacHomaA-15
99PacIceB-235
99PacIn tCN-10
99PacPasAP-15
99PacPreD-235
99PacTeaL-16
99RetHoc-45
99SP AutPS-48
99UppDecCL-64
99UppDecCLCLC-64
99UppDecM-115
99UppDecMGS-115
99UppDecMSS-115
99UppDecMSS-115
99UppDecMT-MVP9
99UppDecRDR-DR2
99UppDecRDRI-DR2
99UppDecRG-45
99UppDecRP-45
99UppDecRTotC-TC2

**Brodeur, Richard**
73NordTeal-5
75OPCWHA-44
76NordMarA-6
76NordPos-9
76OPCWHA-12
77OPCWHA-38
79OPC-176
79Top-176
80CanuSIlD-4
80CanuTeal-4
80PepCap-104
81CanuSIlD-10
81CanuTeal-3
810PC-331
82Canu-2
82McDSti-2
820PC-339
820PC-340
820PCSti-7
820PCSti-247
82PosCer-19
83Canu-1
83Ess-4
830PC-346
830PCSti-276
830PCSti-277
83PufSti-1
83Vac-101
847EDis-48
84Canu-2
84KelAccD-1
840PC-314
840PCSti-277
85Canu-1
850PC-180
86Canu-1
86KraDra-4
860PC-246
860PCSti-98
87CanuSheOil-4
870PC-257
870PCSti-189
87PanSti-340
88ProAHL-53

**Brodie, Andrew**
897thInnSOHL-68
907thInnSOHL-79

**Brodmann, Mario**
93SweSemWCS-120
93SwiHNL-121
95SwiHNL-41

**Brodnicke, Richard**
94GerDELE-350

**Broman, Bjorn**
71SweHocS-249
72SweHocS-232

**Broman, Lennart**
71SweHocS-250

**Bromley, Gary**
74NHLActSta-41
740PCNHL-7
74Top-7
750PCNHL-368
770PCWHA-45
78CanuRoyB-2
79CanuRoyB-3
790PC-167
79Top-167
80CanuSIlD-5
80CanuTeal-5
800PC-330

**Broms, Anders**
89SweSemE-143

**Bronilla, Rich**
92Ott672A-3
95Sla-260

**Brook, Phil**
97KinHaw-8

**Brookbank, Leigh**
91AirCanSJHL-B30
92MPSPhoSJHL-157

**Brooke, Bob**
850PC-202
86NorSta7E-11
86OPC-48
860PCSti-219
86Top-48
87NorStaPos-8
870PC-64
87Top-64
88NorStaADA-2
880PC-61
88PanSti-91
88Top-61
890PC-215
89SweSemWCS-171
90Bow-79
90BowTif-79
900PC-105
90Top-105
90TopTif-105

**Brooks, Chris**
92WesMic-4
93WesMic-3

**Brooks, Gordy**
74CapWhiB-7
74NHLActSta-316

**Brooks, Herb**
80USAOlyTMP-15
87NorStaPos-9
95SigRooMI-41
95SigRooMI-42
95SigRooSMIS-41
95SigRooSMIS-42

**Brooks, Jason**
95Sla-171

**Brooks, Mark**
920shGenS-5

**Brooks, Ross**
74NHLActSta-32
740PCNHL-376

**Brooks, W.**
28V1282PauC-80

**Brophy, John**
84MapLeaP-4
87MapLeaPLA-28
88MapLeaPLA-28
89HamRoaA-2
90HamRoaA-60
91HamRoaA-19
92HamRoaA-20
93HamRoaA-18
94HamRoaA-1
95HamRoaA-2
96HamRoaA-HRA21

**Bros, Michal**
95CzeAPSE-120
95UppDec-541
95UppDecElelce-541
95UppDecElelceG-541
96CzeAPSE-278

**Brossart, Willie**
73MapLeaP-2
74NHLActSta-254
74NHLActStaU-41

**Brosseau, david**
98ChaChe-4

**Brost, Todd**
90AlbIntTC-12
91AlbIntTC-2
93AlbIntTC-2
930PCPreTC-8
93Pow-479
93Ult-459
94HunBli-5

**Brostrom, Anders**
71SweHocS-264
72SweHocS-242
83SweSemE-228

**Brostrom, Bjarne**
69SweHocS-223
71SweHocS-369

**Broten, Aaron**
81RocPos-2
820PC-136
830PC-227
830PCSti-226

84DevPos-10
850PC-249
850PCSti-62
86DevPol-6
870PC-46
870PCSti-62
87PanSti-78
87Top-46
88DevCar-3
880PC-138
880PCSti-76
88PanSti-271
88Top-138
89DevCar-4
890PC-180
890PC-308
890PCSti-88
89PanSti-254
89Top-180
90Bow-185
90BowTif-185
90NordPet-1
900PC-118
900PCPre-10
90PanSti-247
90ProSet-131
90ProSet-530
90Sco-162
90ScoCan-162
90ScoHotRS-72
90ScoRoo-21T
90Top-118
90TopTif-118
90UppDec-210
90UppDecP-210
91Bow-162
91PanSti-105
91ScoAme-307
91ScoCan-250
91ScoCan-337
94MinGolG-6
**Broten, Neal**
81NorStaPos-4
81SweSemHVS-99
82NorStaPos-4
82NorStaPos-6
820PC-164
820PCSti-190
83NorStaPos-5
83NorStaPos-5
830PC-168
830PCSti-20
83PufSti-13
84NorSta7E-1
84NorStaPos-5
840PC-96
840PCSti-46
84Top-72
85NorStaPos-6
850PC-124
850PCSti-40
85Top-124
86NorSta7E-1
860PC-99
860PCSti-166
86Top-99
87NorStaPos-10
870PC-11
870PCSti-52
87PanSti-297
87Top-11
88FriLayS-7
88NorStaADA-3
880PC-144
880PCSti-201
88PanSti-92
88Top-144
890PC-87
890PC-306
890PCSti-202
89PanSti-107
89SweSemWCS-165
89Top-87
90Bow-178
90BowTif-178
900PC-90
90PanSti-261
90ProSet-132
90Sco-144
90ScoCan-144
90Top-90
90TopTif-90
90UppDec-48
90UppDecF-48
91Bow-121
91Bow-420
910PC-420
91PanSti-107
91Par-80
91ParFre-80
91Pin-161
91PinFre-161
91ProSet-112
91ProSetFre-112
91ProSetPla-143
91ProSetPla-188
94SweSemE-280
94SweSemWCS-140
91Top-420
91UppDec-232
91UppDecF-232

92Bow-81
920PC-62
92PanSti-89
92PanStiFre-89
92Par-313
92ParEmel-313
92Pin-209
92PinFre-209
92Sco-32
92ScoCan-32
92StaClu-90
92Top-309
92TopGol-309G
92Ult-189
92UppDec-206
930PCPre-131
930PCPreG-131
93PanSti-272
93Par-54
93ParEmel-54
93Pin-334
93PinCan-334
93Pow-57
93Sco-166
93ScoCan-166
93StaClu-28
93StaCluFDI-28
93StaCluFDIO-28
93StaCluO-28
93TopPre-131
93TopPreG-131
93Ult-296
93UppDec-109
93UppDecSP-34
94CanGamNHLP-76
94Don-67
94Fla-39
94Lea-246
94MinGolG-6
940PCPre-74
940PCPreSE-74
94Par-53
94ParGol-53
94Pin-293
94PinArtP-293
94PinRinC-293
94Sco-113
94ScoGol-113
94ScoPla-113
94ScoPlaTS-113
94StaHoc-3
94StaScoS-113
94TopPre-74
94TopPreSE-74
94Ult-48
94UppDec-273
94UppDecElelce-273
94UppDecSPI-SP18
94UppDecSPIDC-SP18
95BeAPla-42
95BeAPIaG-S42
95BeAPSig-S42
95BeAPSigDC-S42
95CanGamNHLP-157
95ColCho-285
95ColChoPC-285
95ColChoPCP-285
95Don-259
95Emo-95
95Lea-286
95LeaRoaCup-7
95Met-82
95ParInt-120
95ParIntEl-120
95Pin-117
95PinArtP-117
95PinRinC-117
95PlaOneoOne-276
95Sco-265
95ScoBlaIce-265
95ScoBlaIceAP-265
95SigRooMI-3
95SigRooMI-4
95SigRooSMIS-3
95SigRooSMIS-4
95SkyImp-91
95Ult-87
95UltGolM-87
95UltGolM-187
95UppDec-114
95UppDecElelce-114
95UppDecElelceG-114
96ColCho-152
96StaPos-3
97PacDynBKS-28

**Broten, Paul**
89ProIHL-28
89RanMarMB-37
90Bow-224
90BowTif-224
90ScoRoo-41T
91Par-336
91ParFre-336
91StaClu-76
91UppDec-550
91UppDecF-550
92Bow-265
920PC-364
92Pin-212
92PinFre-212
92Sco-353
92ScoCan-353
92StaClu-109
92Top-355
92TopGol-355G

92Ult-134
92Ult-353
92UppDec-148
93Par-324
93ParEmel-324
93Sco-658
93ScoCan-297
93ScoCan-658
93ScoGol-658
93UppDec-468
94Lea-409
94MinGolG-6
940PCPre-261
940PCPreSE-261
94Par-60
94ParGol-60
94Pin-433
94PinArtP-433
94PinRinC-433
94StaHoc-4
94StaPinS-433
94StaPinS-NNO
94StaPos-1
94TopPre-261
94TopPreSE-261
94UppDec-15
94UppDecElelce-15
98GerDELE-110

**Broughton, George**
12C57-39

**Brousseau, Jason**
907thInnSMC-67
907thInnSQMJHL-57
917thInnSQMJHL-230
92ForWorF-3
93ForWorF-4
94JohChi-2

**Brousseau, Nicolas**
94CenHocL-39

**Brousseau, Paul**
907thInnSQMJHL-177
917thInnSQMJHL-206
94ClaProP-152
97PinIns-141

**Brower, Scott**
90ProAHLIHL-302
93FinnSIS-256
94CenHocL-40

**Brown, Adam**
34BeeGro1P-90
44BeeGro2P-83
51Par-30

**Brown, Alan**
94HunBli-6

**Brown, Andy**
72SarProSta-83
740PCWHA-58

**Brown, Arnie**
63RochAme-6
64BeeGro3P-121
64CocCap-75
64Top-34
65Coc-76
65Top-90
66Top-90
66TopUSAT-48
67Top-89
680PC-68
68ShiCoi-98
68Top-68
690PC-34
69Top-34
70ColSta-76
70DadCoo-10
70EssPowPla-184
700PC-66
70Top-66
710PC-14
71SarProSta-57
71Top-14
71TorSun-86
720PC-144
72SarProSta-72
72Top-111
730PC-225
74NHLActSta-14
94ParTalB-97
95Par66-86
95Par66Coi-86

**Brown, Bob**
917thInnSCHLAW-19
95TriAme-8

**Brown, Bobby**
95SlaMemC-36
96RoaExp-10
97GuiFla-12

**Brown, Brad**
917thInnSOHL-53
93Cla-100
93NorBayC-1
93NorBayC-25
94Cla-16
94ClaDraGol-16
94NorBayC-4
95Cla-90
95SigRooCP-3
95SigRooFF-FF2
95SigRooFFS-FF2
97PacInvNRB-100
97UppDec-296
98PacDynI-93
98PacDynIIB-93
98PacDynIR-93

98PacOmeH-57
98PacOmeODI-57
98PacOmeR-57
98PacOme-292
98PacUppDecE-292
98UppDecE1o1-292
98UppDecGR-292

**Brown, Cal**
90ProAHLIHL-171

**Brown, Cam**
88BraWheK-23
89BraWheK-8
90ProAHLIHL-336
91ProAHLCHL-598
94EriPan-9

**Brown, Connie**
34BeeGro1P-91

**Brown, Craig**
92WesMic-5
93WesMic-4

**Brown, Curtis**
95DonEliWJ-11
95PriAlbR-2
95SigRoo-63
95SigRooSig-63
95Ult-333
95UppDec-531
95UppDecElelce-307
95UppDecElelce-531
95UppDecElelceG-307
95UppDecElelceG-531
96FlePic-150
96LeaPre-142
96LeaPrePP-142
96MetUni-172
96Pin-227
96PinArtP-227
96PinFoi-227
96PinPreS-227
96PinRinC-227
96SP-14
96Sum-185
96SumArtP-185
96SumIce-185
96SumMet-185
96SumPreS-185
96Ult-14
96UltGolM-14
96UltRoo-3
96UppDec-226
96Zen-145
96ZenArtP-145
97Be A PPAD-53
97Be A PPAPD-53
97BeAPIa-53
97BeAPIaAut-53
97UppDec-230
980-PChr-185
980-PChrR-185
98Pac-104
98PacIceB-104
98PacOmeH-21
98PacOmeODI-21
98PacOmeR-21
98PacRed-104
98Top-185
98TopO-P-185
99Pac-35
99PacAur-15
99PacAurPD-15
99PacCop-35
99PacGol-35
99PacIceB-35
99PacPreD-35

**Brown, Dan**
897thInnSOHL-99
94CenHocL-41

**Brown, Dave**
81SasBla-7
83SprInd-8
85FlyPos-2
86FlyPos-2
880ilTeal-3
880ilTenAnn-145
88PanSti-319
890ilTeal-3
900ilGA-3
90ProSet-440
91FlyJCP-3
910ilPanTS-3
91ProSet-452
91ScoCan-634
91ScoRoo-84T
92FlyJCP-6
92FlyUppDS-6
92FlyUppDS-30
94Lea-428

**Brown, Doug**
88DevCar-4
880PC-115
880PCSti-23
880PCSti-80
88PanSti-291
88Top-115
89DevCar-5
890PC-242
90Dev-3
900PC-117
90PanSti-67
90ProSet-163
90Top-117
90TopTif-117
90UppDec-159
90UppDecF-159

- 91Bow-285
- 91OPC-42
- 91Pin-363
- 91PinFre-363
- 91ProSet-138
- 91ProSetFre-138
- 91ScoAme-163
- 91StaClu-47
- 91Top-42
- 91UppDec-214
- 91UppDecF-214
- 92Bow-126
- 92OPC-333
- 92Sco-118
- 92ScoCan-118
- 92StaClu-331
- 92Top-139
- 92TopGol-139G
- 93Don-258
- 93Lea-378
- 93Par-424
- 93ParEmel-424
- 93PenFoo-7
- 93Pow-411
- 93Sco-582
- 93ScoCan-582
- 93ScoGol-582
- 93Ult-393
- 93UppDec-459
- 94Don-213
- 94FinnJaaK-117
- 94Lea-116
- 94OPCPre-263
- 94OPCPreSE-263
- 94ParSE-SE135
- 94ParSEG-SE135
- 94Pin-197
- 94PinArtP-197
- 94PinRinC-197
- 94Sco-15
- 94ScoGol-15
- 94ScoPla-15
- 94ScoPlaTS-15
- 94TopPre-263
- 94TopPreSE-263
- 94UppDec-422
- 94UppDecEleIce-422
- 95ColCho-47
- 95ColChoPC-47
- 95ColChoPCP-47
- 95Sco-193
- 95ScoBlaIce-193
- 95ScoBlaIceAP-193
- 95SweGloWC-114
- 95Top-81
- 95TopOPCi-81
- 95TopPowL-8PL
- 95UppDec-79
- 95UppDecEleIce-79
- 95UppDecEleIceG-79
- 96BeAPAut-43
- 96BeAPAutSil-43
- 96BeAPla-43
- 97PacInvNRB-67
- 97ScoRedW-13
- 97ScoRedWPla-13
- 97ScoRedWPre-13
- 98Fin-10
- 98FinNo P-10
- 98FinNo PR-10
- 98FinRef-10
- 98Pac-187
- 98PacIceB-187
- 98PacRed-187
- 98UppDec-267
- 98UppDecE-267
- 98UppDecE1o1-267
- 98UppDecGR-267
- 98UppDecM-76
- 98UppDecMGS-76
- 98UppDecMSS-76
- 98UppDecMSS-76
- 99Pac-134
- 99PacCop-134
- 99PacGol-134
- 99PacIceB-134
- 99PacPreD-134

**Brown, Eric**
- 93WatBlaH-4

**Brown, George A.**
- 34BeeGro1P-140

**Brown, George V**
- 83HalFP-L2
- 85HalFC-152

**Brown, Greg**
- 90OPCPre-11
- 90ProSet-590
- 90SabBluS-4
- 90SabCam-4
- 90ScoRoo-96T
- 91ProAHLCHL-18
- 91RochAmeDD-1
- 91RochAmeKod-3
- 91RochAmePos-3
- 91ScoCan-518
- 92RochAmeDD-2
- 92RochAmeKod-4
- 95SweLeaE-287
- 95SweUppDE-176
- 98GerDELE-94

**Brown, Ivan**
- 95GuiFla-18

**Brown, Jason**

- 91AirCanSJHL-B46
- 92MPSPhoSJHL-18

**Brown, Jeff**
- 84SudWol-7
- 85NordMcD-2
- 85NordTeal-3
- 85SudWol-20
- 86NordGenF-3
- 86NordMcD-3
- 86NordTeal-1
- 87NordGenF-2
- 88NordGenF-3
- 88NordTeal-5
- 880PC-201
- 88OPCSti-192
- 88PanSti-349
- 89Kra-28
- 89Nord-3
- 89NordGenF-2
- 89NordPol-1
- 890PC-28
- 890PCSti-193
- 89PanSti-325
- 89Top-28
- 90BluKod-3
- 90Bow-25
- 90BowTif-25
- 900PC-220
- 900PC-295
- 90PanSti-274
- 90ProSet-260
- 90Sco-41
- 90ScoCan-41
- 90Top-220
- 90Top-295
- 90TopTif-295
- 90UppDec-191
- 90UppDecF-191
- 91BluPos-3
- 91Bow-385
- 910PC-222
- 91PanSti-23
- 91Par-156
- 91ParFre-156
- 91Pin-72
- 91PinFre-72
- 91ProSet-212
- 91ProSetFre-212
- 91ProSetPla-114
- 91ScoAme-276
- 91ScoCan-496
- 91StaClu-148
- 91Top-222
- 91UppDec-211
- 91UppDecF-211
- 92Bow-247
- 92PanSti-25
- 92PanStiFre-25
- 92Pin-13
- 92PinFre-13
- 92ProSet-158
- 92Sco-220
- 92ScoCan-220
- 92StaClu-188
- 92Top-174
- 92TopGol-174G
- 92Ult-183
- 93Don-293
- 93Don-499
- 93Lea-29
- 930PCPre-363
- 930PCPre-381
- 930PCPreG-363
- 930PCPreG-381
- 93PanSti-165
- 93Par-173
- 93ParEmel-173
- 93Pin-39
- 93PinCan-39
- 93Pow-207
- 93Sco-194
- 93ScoCan-194
- 93StaClu-188
- 93StaCluFDI-188
- 93StaCluFDIO-188
- 93StaCluFin-2
- 93StaCluO-188
- 93TopPre-363
- 93TopPre-381
- 93TopPreG-363
- 93TopPreG-381
- 93Ult-223
- 93UppDec-130
- 93UppDecSP-135
- 94CanGamNHLP-313
- 94CanuProI-4
- 94Don-109
- 94EASpo-121
- 94Fla-188
- 94Fle-222
- 94Lea-247
- 94LeaLim-18
- 940PCPre-272
- 940PCPre-487
- 940PCPreSE-272
- 940PCPreSE-487
- 94Par-244
- 94ParGol-244
- 94ParVin-V45
- 94Pin-34
- 94PinArtP-34
- 94PinRinC-34
- 94Sel-110
- 94SelGol-110

- 94SP-123
- 94SPDieCut-123
- 94TopPre-272
- 94TopPre-487
- 94TopPreSE-272
- 94TopPreSE-487
- 94Ult-221
- 94UppDec-34
- 94UppDecEleIce-34
- 94UppDecSPI-SP81
- 94UppDecSPIDC-SP81
- 95CanGamNHLP-276
- 95CanuBuiDA-8
- 95ColCho-301
- 95ColChoPC-301
- 95ColChoPCP-301
- 95Don-183
- 95DonEli-78
- 95DonEliDCS-78
- 95DonEliDCU-78
- 95Emo-177
- 95ImpSti-126
- 95Lea-245
- 95Met-148
- 95ParInt-365
- 95ParIntEI-365
- 95Pin-29
- 95PinArtP-29
- 95PinRinC-29
- 95PlaOneoOne-206
- 95Sco-23
- 95ScoBlaIce-23
- 95ScoBlaIceAP-23
- 95SkyImp-166
- 95StaCluMO-23
- 95Top-268
- 95TopOPCi-268
- 95Ult-165
- 95UltGolM-165
- 95UppDec-352
- 95UppDecEleIce-352
- 95UppDecEleIceG-352
- 95UppDecSpe-SE84
- 95UppDecSpeEdiG-SE84
- 96ColCho-120
- 96FlePic-64
- 96MetUni-65
- 96Pin-12
- 96PinArtP-12
- 96PinFoi-12
- 96PinPreS-12
- 96PinRinC-12
- 96PlaOneoOne-396
- 96Sco-87
- 96ScoArtPro-87
- 96ScoDeaCAP-87
- 96ScoGolB-87
- 96ScoSpeAP-87
- 96SkyImp-51
- 96TeaOut-83
- 96Ult-72
- 96UltGolM-72
- 96UppDec-73
- 97Be A PPAD-89
- 97Be A PPAPD-89
- 97BeAPla-89
- 97BeAPlaAut-89
- 97BeAPlaAut-89
- 97CarHur-1
- 97PacDynBKS-16
- 98BowCHL-4
- 98BowCHLGA-4
- 98BowCHLOI-4
- 98BowChrC-4
- 98BowChrCGA-4
- 98BowChrCGAR-4
- 98BowChrCOI-4
- 98BowChrCOIR-4
- 98BowChrCR-4
- 98Pac-438
- 98PacIceB-438
- 98PacPar-243
- 98PacParC-243
- 98PacParEG-243
- 98PacParH-243
- 98PacParIB-243
- 98PacParS-243
- 98PacRed-438

**Brown, Jeffrey**
- 94SarSti-21
- 95BowDraPro-P5
- 95Cla-96
- 95Sla-347
- 95Sla-439

**Brown, Jeremy**
- 92WesMic-6
- 93WesMic-5

**Brown, Jerry**
- 34BeeGro1P-92

**Brown, Jim**
- 907thInnSOHL-298
- 917thInnSOHL-288
- 93WowSouPla-2
- 94HamRoaA-18

**Brown, Joel**
- 82KinCan-4
- 83KinCan-18
- 84KitRan-14

**Brown, Keith**
- 80BlaBroBac-1
- 80BlaWhiBor-3
- 80OPC-98
- 80Top-98
- 81BlaBorPos-2
- 81BlaBroBac-1
- 810PC-55

- 810PCSti-115
- 81Top-W67
- 82OPC-62
- 83BlaBorPos-2
- 83OPC-98
- 84OPC-33
- 84OPCSti-28
- 84Top-28
- 85OPC-59
- 85Top-59
- 86BlaCok-3
- 86OPC-206
- 87OPC-47
- 87PanSti-233
- 87Top-47
- 88BlaCok-2
- 89BlaCok-23
- 89BlaCok-23
- 90Bow-10
- 90BowTif-10
- 90OPC-276
- 90PanSti-192
- 90ProSet-49
- 90Sco-161
- 90ScoCan-161
- 90Top-276
- 90TopTif-276
- 91BlaCok-2
- 91Pin-21
- 91Par-261
- 91ParFre-261
- 91Pin-154
- 91Pin-370
- 91PinFre-154
- 91PinFre-370
- 91ProSet-371
- 91ProSetFre-371
- 91ScoAme-76
- 91ScoCan-76
- 92Bow-4
- 92OPC-48
- 92PanSti-13
- 92PanStiFre-13
- 92Par-274
- 92ParEmel-274
- 92Pin-92
- 92PinFre-92
- 92Sco-68
- 92ScoCan-68
- 92StaClu-274
- 92Top-52
- 92TopGol-52G
- 93Pin-422
- 93PinCan-422
- 93Sco-384
- 93Sco-569
- 93ScoCan-384
- 93ScoCan-569
- 93ScoGol-569
- 93StaClu-58
- 93StaClu-281
- 93StaCluFDI-58
- 93StaCluFDI-281
- 93StaCluFDIO-58
- 93StaCluO-58
- 93StaCluO-281
- 93Ult-322
- 94Fle-78
- 94Pin-368
- 94PinArtP-368
- 94PinRinC-368
- 94Ult-295

**Brown, Kevin**
- 93Cla-17
- 93Cla-33
- 93DetJrRW-17
- 94Cla-36
- 94ClaDraGol-36
- 94ClaTri-T31
- 94Fin-15
- 94FinRef-15
- 94FinSupTW-15
- 94Lea-457
- 94LeaLim-7
- 94ParSE-SE77
- 94ParSEG-SE77
- 94UppDec-249
- 94UppDecEleIce-249
- 95ColEdgI-182
- 95Don-168
- 95Ima-28
- 95ImaGol-28
- 95Lea-38
- 95PhoRoa-5
- 95Pin-215
- 95PinArtP-215
- 95PinRinC-215
- 95Sco-301
- 95ScoBlaIce-301
- 95ScoBlaIceAP-301
- 96SprFai-44

**Brown, Kevin A.**
- 907thInnSOHL-255
- 917thInnSOHL-108
- 917thInnSOHL-218
- 94DayBom-12
- 95DayBom-7
- 98UppDecM-84
- 98UppDecMGS-84
- 98UppDecMSS-84
- 98UppDecMSS-84

**Brown, Larry**
- 70EssPowPla-130
- 71SarProSta-159

- 71TorSun-190
- 72SarProSta-95
- 740PCNHL-271
- 750PCNHL-377
- 760PCNHL-355
- 770PCNHL-289
- 780PC-361
- 790PC-323

**Brown, Lisa**
- 94ClaWomOH-W24

**Brown, Mike**
- 95RedDeerR-5
- 97BowCHL-126
- 97BowCHLAu-6
- 97BowCHLBB-13
- 97BowCHLBowBesAR-13
- 97BowCHLBowBesR-13
- 97BowCHLOPC-126

**Brown, Newell**
- 52JunBluT-15

**Brown, Ryan**
- 917thInnSWHL-127

**Brown, Rich**
- 94SarSti-27
- 95Sla-354
- 96St.JohML-4
- 97St.JohML-4

**Brown, Rob**
- 84KamBla-4
- 85KamBla-4
- 86KamBla-3
- 87PenKod-2
- 880PC-109
- 880PCSti-63
- 880PCSti-131
- 880PCSti-237
- 88PanSti-336
- 88Top-109
- 890PC-193
- 890PCSti-117
- 890PCSti-163
- 890PCSti-236
- 890PCSti-256
- 89PanSti-186
- 89PanSti-310
- 89PenCokE-2
- 89PenFoo-1
- 89Top-193
- 89TopStiIns-8
- 90Bow-202
- 90BowHatTri-3
- 90BowTif-202
- 90OPC-19
- 90PanSti-128
- 90ProSet-229
- 90Sco-105
- 90ScoCan-105
- 90ScoHotRS-51
- 90ScoYouS-5
- 90Top-19
- 90TopTif-19
- 90UppDec-142
- 90UppDecF-142
- 90WhaJr7E-3
- 91Bow-16
- 910PC-83
- 91PanSti-315
- 91Par-60
- 91Par-258
- 91ParFre-60
- 91ParFre-258
- 91Pin-141
- 91PinFre-141
- 91ProSet-80
- 91ProSetFre-80
- 91ProSetFre-606
- 91ProSetPla-42
- 91ScoAme-246
- 91ScoCan-466
- 91StaClu-200
- 91Top-83
- 91UppDec-198
- 91UppDecF-198
- 91WhaJr7E-4
- 92Bow-168
- 92OPC-170
- 92PanSti-10
- 92PanStiFre-10
- 92Pin-331
- 92PinFre-331
- 92Sco-244
- 92ScoCan-244
- 92ScoShaCan-1
- 92StaClu-295
- 92Top-72
- 92TopGol-72G
- 92Ult-33
- 92UppDec-387
- 94Lea-540
- 94Ult-304
- 94UppDec-403
- 94UppDecEleIce-403
- 95ColEdgI-104
- 95ColEdgIQ-IR4
- 96ColEdgFI-13
- 97Be A PPAD-48
- 97Be A PPAPD-48
- 97BeAPla-48
- 97BeAPlaAut-48
- 97PacOme-183
- 97PacOmeC-183
- 97PacOmeDG-183
- 97PacOmeEG-183
- 97PacOmeG-183

- 97PacOmeIB-183
- 97ScoPen-19
- 97ScoPenPla-19
- 97ScoPenPre-19
- 98Be A PPA-265
- 98Be A PPAA-265
- 98Be A PPAAF-265
- 98Be A PPSE-265
- 98Be APG-265
- 98Pac-349
- 98PacIceB-349
- 98PacRed-349
- 99Pac-335
- 99PacCop-335
- 99PacGol-335
- 99PacIceB-335
- 99PacPreD-335

**Brown, Robert**
- 52JunBluT-15

**Brown, Sean (DEF)**
- 95Cla-20
- 95Cla-83
- 95Sla-352
- 96OilPos-8
- 97Don-208
- 97DonPreProG-208
- 97DonPreProS-208
- 98PacOmeH-91
- 98PacOmeODI-91
- 98PacOmeR-91
- 98UppDecGR-276

**Brown, Sean (FWD)**
- 907thInnSOHL-203
- 91OshGen-12
- 92OshGenS-3
- 93OshGen-8
- 94KnoChe-8
- 96RoaExp-18
- 98UppDec-276
- 98UppDecE-276
- 98UppDecE1o1-276

**Brown, Steve**
- 95VanVooRHI-20

**Brown, Tom**
- 94SarSti-6
- 95Sla-335
- 96SudWol-4
- 96SudWolP-6
- 98ChaChe-5

**Brown, Walter A**
- 83HalFP-2
- 85HalFC-78

**Browne, Bill**
- 96SauSteMG-2
- 96SauSteMGA-2

**Browne, Cecil**
- 23CreSel-7
- 23V1281PauC-5
- 24CreSel-6
- 28V1282PauC-63

**Brownlee, Brent**
- 907thInnSOHL-128
- 917thInnSOHL-364

**Brownlee, Pat**
- 98ChaChe-6

**Brownschidle, Jack**
- 78BluPos-6
- 78OPC-379
- 79OPC-278
- 80OPC-101
- 80Top-101
- 810PC-302
- 82OPC-300
- 83OPC-311
- 84WhaJunW-1
- 85WhaJunW-1

**Browter, Scott**
- 89ProIHL-36

**Brubaker, Jeff**
- 81CanaPos-4
- 84MapLeaP-5
- 85MapLeaP-5
- 88OilTenAnn-19
- 88ProAHL-18

**Bruce, David**
- 82KitRan-11
- 83KitRan-11
- 84FreExp-7
- 85FreExp-2
- 86FreExp-3
- 87CanuSheOil-5
- 88CanuMoh-7
- 88PanSti-137
- 89ProIHL-173
- 90BluKod-4
- 90ProAHLIHL-86
- 91Par-384
- 91ParFre-384
- 91ProSet-485
- 91ProSetFre-485
- 91ProSetPla-227
- 91ScoCan-644
- 92Bow-358
- 92OPC-246
- 92PanSti-126
- 92PanStiFre-126
- 92Pin-159
- 92PinFre-159
- 92Sco-301
- 92ScoCan-301
- 93StaClu-284

- 92Top-448
- 92TopGol-448G
- 92Ult-191
- 92UppDec-102
- 98GerDELE-69

**Brucks, Derrick**
- 91AirCanSJHL-E41

**Bruggemann, Lars**
- 94GerDELE-284
- 95GerDELE-297
- 96GerDELE-324
- 98GerDELE-29

**Bruininks, Brett**
- 98FloEve-1

**Bruininks, Brian**
- 92DalFre-5
- 93DalFre-4

**Bruk, David**
- 94CzeAPSE-86
- 95CzeAPSE-44
- 95FinnSemWC-157

**Brule, Eric**
- 907thInnSQMJHL-26
- 917thInnSMC-28
- 91ProAHLCHL-302
- 92ForWorF-4

**Brumby, David**
- 95LetHur-4

**Brummer, Johan**
- 89SweSemE-44
- 90SweSemE-194
- 91SweSemE-273
- 92SweSemE-296
- 93SweSemE-261
- 94SweLeaE-95
- 95SweLeaE-229
- 95SweUppDE-93

**Brumwell, Murray**
- 83OPC-228
- 83OPCSti-179
- 88ProAHL-338
- 89ProAHL-9
- 90ProAHLIHL-435

**Bruna, Miroslav**
- 95CzeAPSE-197
- 96CzeAPSE-332

**Brunchk, Bedrich**
- 72SweSemWC-35
- 74SweSemHVS-74

**Bruneau, Paul**
- 897thInnNHL-141

**Brunel, Craig**
- 96PriAlbR-3
- 96PriAlbROC-3

**Brunet, Benoit**
- 88ProAHL-278
- 89ProAHL-186
- 90CanaPos-3
- 91UppDec-469
- 91UppDecF-469
- 92Bow-414
- 92CanaPos-3
- 92DurPan-19
- 92OPC-352
- 92StaClu-134
- 92Top-137
- 92TopGol-137G
- 92Ult-101
- 92UppDec-80
- 93CanaMol-2
- 93CanaPos-3
- 93Don-166
- 93DurSco-8
- 93Lea-360
- 93PCCanHF-31
- 930PCPre-84
- 930PCPreG-84
- 93PanSti-20
- 93Par-375
- 93ParEmel-375
- 93Pow-366
- 93StaClu-422
- 93StaCluFDI-422
- 93StaCluO-422
- 93TopPre-84
- 93TopPreG-84
- 93Ult-349
- 93UppDec-415
- 94CanaPos-4
- 940PCPre-94
- 940PCPreSE-94
- 94Pin-452
- 94PinArtP-452
- 94PinRinC-452
- 94StaClu-227
- 94StaCluFDI-227
- 94StaCluMOMS-227
- 94StaCluSTWC-227
- 94TopPre-94
- 94TopPreSE-94
- 95BeAPla-86
- 95BeAPSig-86
- 95BeAPSigDC-S86
- 95CanaPos-3
- 95CanaShe-2
- 95CanGamNHLP-146
- 95ColCho-35
- 95ColChoPC-35
- 95ColChoPCP-35
- 95Don-367
- 95Met-75
- 95ParInt-116
- 95ParIntEI-116
- 95PlaOneoOne-162

☐ 95Top-87
☐ 95TopOPCI-87
☐ 95Ult-255
☐ 95UppDec-156
☐ 95UppDecElelce-156
☐ 95UppDecElelceG-156
☐ 96CanaPos-4
☐ 96CanaShe-2
☐ 97CanaPos-3
☐ 97ScoCan-18
☐ 97ScoCanPla-18
☐ 98Be A PPA-70
☐ 98Be A PPAA-70
☐ 98Be A PPAAF-70
☐ 98Be A PPTBASG-70
☐ 98Be APG-70
☐ 98Pac-248
☐ 98PacIceB-248
☐ 98PacOmeH-118
☐ 98PacOmeODI-118
☐ 98PacOmeR-118
☐ 98PacRed-248
☐ 98ScoCanPre-18
☐ 99Pac-201
☐ 99PacCop-201
☐ 99PacGol-201
☐ 99PacIceB-201
☐ 99PacPreD-201
**Brunet, Gerry**
☐ 51LavDaiLSJ-58
**Bruneteau, Mud**
☐ 34BeeGro1P-93
☐ 36V356WorG-47
☐ 39OPCV3011-43
☐ 40OPCV3012-138
**Brunetta, Mario**
☐ 87NordGenF-3
☐ 88NordGenF-4
☐ 88NordTeal-6
☐ 89HalCit-3
☐ 89ProAHL-159
☐ 90PanSti-152
☐ 96GerDELE-24
☐ 98GerDELE-163
**Brunette, Andrew**
☐ 907thInnSOHL-277
☐ 917thInnSOHL-284
☐ 93OweSouPla-3
☐ 94PorPir-3
☐ 95PorPir-6
☐ 96ColEdgFL-47
☐ 96Fle-124
☐ 96FleCalCan-1
☐ 96PorPir-19
☐ 96SkyImp-147
☐ 96Ult-173
☐ 96UltGolM-173
☐ 96UppDec-184
☐ 97PacInvNRB-207
☐ 97PacOme-237
☐ 97PacOmeC-237
☐ 97PacOmeDG-237
☐ 97PacOmeEG-237
☐ 97PacOmeG-237
☐ 97PacOmeIB-237
☐ 97PinIns-111
☐ 97UppDec-382
☐ 98Pac-439
☐ 98PacAur-99
☐ 98PacCroR-72
☐ 98PacCroRLS-72
☐ 98PacDynI-100
☐ 98PacDynIIB-100
☐ 98PacDynIR-100
☐ 98PacIceB-439
☐ 98PacOmeH-127
☐ 98PacOmeODI-127
☐ 98PacOmeR-127
☐ 98PacPar-121
☐ 98PacParC-121
☐ 98PacParEG-121
☐ 98PacParH-121
☐ 98PacParIB-121
☐ 98PacParS-121
☐ 98PacRed-439
☐ 98PacRev-77
☐ 98PacRevIS-77
☐ 98PacRevR-77
☐ 98SP Aut-46
☐ 98UppDec-301
☐ 98UppDecE-301
☐ 98UppDecE1o1-301
☐ 98UppDecGR-301
☐ 98UppDecM-113
☐ 98UppDecMGS-113
☐ 98UppDecMSS-113
☐ 98UppDecMSS-113
☐ 99Pac-220
☐ 99PacAur-6
☐ 99PacAurPD-6
☐ 99PacCop-220
☐ 99PacGol-220
☐ 99PacIceB-220
☐ 99PacPreD-220
☐ 99SP AutPS-46
**Brunner, Gerhard**
☐ 98GerDELE-314
**Brunner, Markus**
☐ 907thInnSOHL-328
☐ 917thInnSOHL-151
☐ 91OshGen-15
☐ 91OshGenS-19
**Bruns, Roger**
☐ 94GerDELE-437
**Brunsing, Frank**
☐ 94GerDELE-224
**Brus, Kjell**
☐ 69SweHocS-114
☐ 70SweHocS-74
☐ 71SweHocS-164
☐ 72SweHocS-163
☐ 72SweSemWC-63
☐ 73SweHocS-53
☐ 73SweWorCS-53
☐ 74SweHocS-205
**Bruselinck, Derek**
☐ 92MPSPhoSJHL-151
**Brush, Matt**
☐ 98FloEve-2
**Brux, Arno**
☐ 94GerDELE-333
☐ 95GerDELE-237
**Bryan, Shawn**
☐ 90ProAHLIHL-496
**Bryan, Tim**
☐ 95Sla-430
**Bryden, Rob**
☐ 88FliSpi-2
☐ 89ProAHL-287
**Brydge, Bill**
☐ 23V1281PauC-19
☐ 33V129-22
☐ 33V252CanG-5
☐ 33V357IceK-2
☐ 34DiaMatS-6
☐ 35DiaMatT2-5
☐ 35DiaMatT3-4
☐ 35DiaMatTI-5
**Brydges, Paul**
☐ 88ProAHL-246
☐ 89ProAHL-27
☐ 93GueSto-27
☐ 94GueSto-28
**Brydges, Scott**
☐ 82OshGen-7
☐ 83OshGen-11
**Brydson, Glenn**
☐ 33OPCV304B-64
☐ 33V252CanG-6
☐ 33V357IceK-39
☐ 34BeeGro1P-42
☐ 35DiaMatT4-2
☐ 35DiaMatT5-1
☐ 35DiaMatTI-6
☐ 37DiaMatT6-1
**Brylin, Sergei**
☐ 92Cla-47
☐ 92RusStaRA-23
☐ 92RusStaRA-5
☐ 93Pin-509
☐ 93PinCan-509
☐ 93UppDec-276
☐ 94UppDec-329
☐ 94UppDecElelce-329
☐ 95ColCho-296
☐ 95ColChoPC-296
☐ 95ColChoPCP-296
☐ 95Don-52
☐ 95Lea-40
☐ 95ParInt-119
☐ 95ParIntEl-119
☐ 95Pin-120
☐ 95PinArtP-120
☐ 95PinGloG-18
☐ 95PinRinC-120
☐ 95PlaOneoOne-277
☐ 95Sco-274
☐ 95ScoBlaIce-274
☐ 95ScoBlaIceAP-274
☐ 95Top-35
☐ 95TopNewG-2NG
☐ 95TopOPCI-35
☐ 95Ult-88
☐ 95UltGolM-88
☐ 95UppDec-31
☐ 95UppDecElelce-31
☐ 95UppDecElelceG-31
☐ 96ClaGol-47
☐ 96Dev-18
☐ 97ScoDev-19
☐ 97ScoDevPla-19
☐ 97ScoDevPre-19
☐ 98Be A PPA-231
☐ 98Be A PPAA-231
☐ 98Be A PPAAF-231
☐ 98Be A PPSE-231
☐ 98Be APG-231
☐ 98UppDec-311
☐ 98UppDecE-311
☐ 98UppDecE1o1-311
☐ 98UppDecGR-311
**Bryner, Anders**
☐ 67SweHoc-216
☐ 69SweHocS-258
**Bubla, Jiri**
☐ 72SweSemWC-38
☐ 74SweHocS-11
☐ 74SweSemHVS-53
☐ 79PanSti-76
☐ 81CanuSilD-20
☐ 81CanuTeal-4
☐ 82Canu-3
☐ 83Canu-2
☐ 83OPC-347
☐ 83OPCSti-143
☐ 83Vac-102
☐ 84Canu-3
☐ 84OPC-315
☐ 85Canu-2
**Bubola, Adrian**
☐ 91BriColJHL-9
**Buchal, Jaroslav**
☐ 95CzeAPSE-164
☐ 96CzeAPSE-187
**Buchanan, Bucky**
☐ 51LavDaiQSHL-56
☐ 51LavDaiS-29
**Buchanan, Greg**
☐ 91BriColJHL-6
☐ 92BriColJHL-211
**Buchanan, Jeff**
☐ 89SasBla-17
☐ 907thInnSWHL-89
☐ 90SasBla-4
☐ 917thInnSWHL-102
☐ 91SasBla-4
☐ 95Indlce-3
**Buchanan, Kirk**
☐ 92BriColJHL-188
**Buchanan, Ron**
☐ 72CleCruWHA-1
☐ 72CruCleWHAL-1
☐ 73QuaOatWHA-36
☐ 74OPCWHA-23
☐ 75OPCWHA-39
**Buchanan, Trevor**
☐ 88KamBla-5
☐ 89VicCou-3
☐ 94CenHocL-73
**Buchberger, Kelly**
☐ 88OilTeal-4
☐ 88OilTenAnn-133
☐ 89OilTeal-4
☐ 90OilIGA-4
☐ 90ProSet-441
☐ 91OilIGA-2
☐ 91OilPanTS-4
☐ 91OilTeal-3
☐ 91Par-275
☐ 91ParFre-275
☐ 91ProSet-385
☐ 91ProSetFre-385
☐ 91ScoCan-429
☐ 92Bow-393
☐ 92OilIGA-3
☐ 92OilTeal-1
☐ 92OPC-125
☐ 92Pin-95
☐ 92PinFre-95
☐ 92ProSet-48
☐ 92Sco-126
☐ 92ScoCan-126
☐ 92ScoSha-11
☐ 92ScoShaCan-11
☐ 92StaClu-235
☐ 92Top-455
☐ 92TopGol-455G
☐ 92Ult-291
☐ 92UppDec-123
☐ 93PanSti-241
☐ 93Pin-58
☐ 93PinCan-58
☐ 93Pow-340
☐ 93Sco-317
☐ 93ScoCan-317
☐ 93Ult-314
☐ 93UppDec-197
☐ 94CanGamNHLP-98
☐ 94Don-18
☐ 94Lea-333
☐ 94OPCPre-404
☐ 94OPCPreSE-404
☐ 94Pin-332
☐ 94PinArtP-332
☐ 94PinRinC-332
☐ 94StaClu-121
☐ 94StaCluFDI-121
☐ 94StaCluMOMS-121
☐ 94StaCluSTWC-121
☐ 94TopPre-404
☐ 94TopPreSE-404
☐ 94Ult-290
☐ 94UppDec-134
☐ 94UppDecElelce-134
☐ 95CanGamNHLP-111
☐ 95ColCho-310
☐ 95ColChoPC-310
☐ 95ColChoPCP-310
☐ 95ParInt-77
☐ 95ParIntEl-77
☐ 95Top-298
☐ 95TopOPCI-298
☐ 95UppDec-121
☐ 95UppDecElelce-121
☐ 95UppDecElelceG-121
☐ 96ColCho-94
☐ 96KraUppD-36
☐ 96OilPos-16
☐ 97Be A PPAD-150
☐ 97Be A PPAPD-150
☐ 97BeAPla-150
☐ 97BeAPlaAut-150
☐ 97Pac-268
☐ 97PacCop-268
☐ 97PacDyn-47
☐ 97PacDynC-47
☐ 97PacDynDG-47
☐ 97PacDynEG-47
☐ 97PacDynIB-47
☐ 97PacDynR-47
☐ 97PacDynSil-47
☐ 97PacDynTan-49
☐ 97PacEmeGre-268
☐ 97PacIceB-268
☐ 97PacOme-89
☐ 97PacOmeC-89
☐ 97PacOmeDG-89
☐ 97PacOmeEG-89
☐ 97PacOmeG-89
☐ 97PacOmeIB-89
☐ 97PacRed-268
☐ 97PacSil-268
☐ 97SPAut-64
☐ 97UppDec-278
☐ 98Be A PPA-201
☐ 98Be A PPAA-201
☐ 98Be A PPAAF-201
☐ 98Be A PPSE-201
☐ 98Be APG-201
☐ 98O-PChr-22
☐ 98O-PChrR-22
☐ 98Pac-205
☐ 98PacAur-70
☐ 98PacIceB-205
☐ 98PacPar-84
☐ 98PacParC-84
☐ 98PacParEG-84
☐ 98PacParH-84
☐ 98PacParIB-84
☐ 98PacParS-84
☐ 98PacRed-205
☐ 98Top-22
☐ 98TopO-P-22
☐ 98UppDec-93
☐ 98UppDecE-93
☐ 98UppDecE1o1-93
☐ 98UppDecGR-93
☐ 99PacAur-7
☐ 99PacAurPD-7
**Bucher, Laurent**
☐ 91UppDec-668
☐ 91UppDecCWJC-29
☐ 91UppDecF-668
☐ 93SwiHNL-421
**Buchko, Berkeley**
☐ 96MedHatT-1
**Buchwieser, H.**
☐ 95GerDELE-352
**Buck, David**
☐ 93MinDul-3
**Buckberger, Ashley**
☐ 917thInnSWHL-193
☐ 95SlaMemC-18
**Buckland, Frank**
☐ 83HalFP-O6
☐ 85HalFC-216
**Buckland, Wyatt**
☐ 907thInnSOHL-278
☐ 917thInnSOHL-287
☐ 94TolSto-2
**Buckle, Chad**
☐ 92BriColJHL-196
**Buckley, David**
☐ 89HamRoaA-3
☐ 90HamRoaA-43
**Buckley, Jerry**
☐ 95DayBom-26
**Buckley, Tom**
☐ 94DetJrRW-10
☐ 95Sla-77
☐ 95SlaMemC-84
☐ 96SprFal-14
**Buckman, Chris**
☐ 92BriColJHL-139
**Bucyk, Johnny (John)**
☐ 44BeeGro2P-8
☐ 44BeeGro2P-156
☐ 57BruTealss-4
☐ 57Top-10
☐ 58Top-40
☐ 59Top-23
☐ 60ShiCoi-104
☐ 60Top-11
☐ 60TopSta-6
☐ 61ShiCoi-7
☐ 61Top-8
☐ 62Top-11
☐ 62TopHocBuc-4
☐ 63Top-11
☐ 63TorSta-8
☐ 64BeeGro3P-3
☐ 64CocCap-6
☐ 64Top-100
☐ 65Coc-6
☐ 65Top-101
☐ 66Top-39
☐ 66TopUSAT-39
☐ 67Top-42
☐ 68OPC-5
☐ 68OPC-210
☐ 68ShiCoi-6
☐ 68Top-5
☐ 69OPC-26
☐ 69Top-26
☐ 70BruPos-7
☐ 70BruTealss-2
☐ 70ColSta-46
☐ 70DadCoo-11
☐ 70EssPowPla-60
☐ 70OPC-2
☐ 70PosCerS-1
☐ 70SarProSta-8
☐ 70Top-2
☐ 71BruTealss-6
☐ 71OPC-35
☐ 71OPC-249
☐ 71OPC-255
☐ 71SarProSta-9
☐ 71Top-1
☐ 71Top-2
☐ 71Top-3
☐ 71Top-35
☐ 71TorSun-5
☐ 72OPC-1
☐ 72SarProSta-16
☐ 72Top-60
☐ 73MacMil-2
☐ 73OPC-147
☐ 73Top-26
☐ 74NHLActSta-31
☐ 74OPCNHL-28
☐ 74OPCNHL-239
☐ 74OPCNHL-245
☐ 74Top-28
☐ 74Top-239
☐ 74Top-245
☐ 75OPCNHL-9
☐ 75OPCNHL-314
☐ 75Top-9
☐ 75Top-314
☐ 76OPCNHL-95
☐ 76OPCNHL-381
☐ 76Top-95
☐ 76TopGlol-14
☐ 77OPCNHL-155
☐ 77Top-155
☐ 81TCMA-5
☐ 83HalFP-J4
☐ 85HalFC-181
☐ 91BruSpoAL-5
☐ 93ZelMasH-2
☐ 93ZelMasoHS-2
☐ 94ParMisL-56
☐ 94ParTalB-1
☐ 94ParTalBM-SL1
☐ 95Par66-5
☐ 95Par66Coi-5
☐ 97PinBee-58
☐ 97PinBeeGOA-58
☐ 97PinBeeGP-58
☐ 99RetHoc-105
☐ 99UppDecCL-46
☐ 99UppDecCLCLC-46
☐ 99UppDecES-6
☐ 99UppDecRG-105
☐ 99UppDecRII-JOB
☐ 99UppDecRIL1-JOB
☐ 99UppDecRP-105
**Bucyk, Randy**
☐ 85CanaPos-3
☐ 86SheCan-8
☐ 88SalLakCGE-16
☐ 89ProIHL-205
☐ 90ProAHLIHL-608
**Buczkowski, Paul**
☐ 917thInnSWHL-105
☐ 91SasBla-24
☐ 93SasBla-5
☐ 95SasBla-6
**Buda, Dave**
☐ 89ProAHL-54
**Budai, Jeff**
☐ 917thInnSWHL-269
**Budeau, Dennis**
☐ 91AirCanSJHL-D18
**Budy, Tim**
☐ 89ProAHL-226
**Buetow, Jason**
☐ 907thInnSOHL-279
☐ 917thInnSOHL-286
**Buettgen, Jim**
☐ 85MonGolF-13
**Buffey, Vern**
☐ 61SudWol-3
☐ 62SudWol-5
**Buhler, Scott**
☐ 95MedHatT-4
☐ 96MedHatT-2
**Buie, Chris**
☐ 92BriColJHL-107
**Bujar, Krzysztof**
☐ 89SweSemWCS-142
**Bukac, Ludek**
☐ 94GerDELE-369
☐ 96CzeAPSE-334
**Bukta, Mike**
☐ 89NasKni-3
**Bulis, Jan**
☐ 95BowDraPro-P6
☐ 95Sla-24
☐ 97BowCHL-1
☐ 97BowCHLOPC-1
☐ 97DonPri-174
☐ 97DonPriSoA-174
☐ 97Kat-168
☐ 97KatGol-168
☐ 97KatSil-168
☐ 97Pin-24
☐ 97PinArtP-24
☐ 97PinPrePBB-24
☐ 97PinPrePBC-24
☐ 97PinPrePBM-24
☐ 97PinPrePBY-24
☐ 97PinPrePFC-24
☐ 97PinPrePFM-24
☐ 97PinPrePFY-24
☐ 97PinPrePla-24
☐ 97PinRinC-24
☐ 97SPAut-198
☐ 97UppDec-381
☐ 97UppDecBD-89
☐ 97UppDecBDDD-89
☐ 97UppDecBDQD-89
☐ 97UppDecBDTD-89
☐ 97UppDecIce-59
☐ 97UppDecIceP-59
☐ 97UppDecIPS-59
☐ 98Pac-440
☐ 98PacIceB-440
☐ 98PacRed-440
☐ 98SPxFin-89
☐ 98SPxFin-131
☐ 98SPxFinR-89
☐ 98SPxFinR-131
☐ 98SPxFinS-89
☐ 98SPxFinS-131
☐ 98UC-216
☐ 98UD ChoPCR-216
☐ 98UD ChoR-216
☐ 98UD3-29
☐ 98UD3-89
☐ 98UD3-149
☐ 98UD3DieC-29
☐ 98UD3DieC-89
☐ 98UD3DieC-149
☐ 98UppDec-202
☐ 98UppDecE-202
☐ 98UppDecE1o1-202
☐ 98UppDecGR-202
☐ 99Pac-438
☐ 99PacCop-438
☐ 99PacGol-438
☐ 99PacIceB-438
☐ 99PacPreD-438
☐ 99UppDecM-218
☐ 99UppDecMGS-218
☐ 99UppDecMSS-218
☐ 99UppDecMSS-218
**Buljin, Vladislav**
☐ 91UppDecCWJC-2
**Bullard, Mike**
☐ 82OPC-262
☐ 82OPC-264
☐ 82OPCSti-149
☐ 82PosCer-15
☐ 83OPC-277
☐ 83OPCSti-235
☐ 83PenCok-3
☐ 83PenHeiP-4
☐ 83PenTealP-4
☐ 83PufSti-9
☐ 847EDis-39
☐ 84OPC-172
☐ 84OPC-365
☐ 84OPCSti-118
☐ 84PenHeiP-3
☐ 84Top-123
☐ 85OPC-67
☐ 85OPCSti-104
☐ 85Top-67
☐ 86OPC-83
☐ 86OPCSti-228
☐ 86Top-83
☐ 87BluTealss-2
☐ 87FlamRedRP-3
☐ 87OPC-210
☐ 87OPCSti-37
☐ 88BluTealss-2
☐ 88OPC-152
☐ 88OPCSti-93
☐ 88OPCSti-119
☐ 88PanSti-8
☐ 88Top-152
☐ 89FlyPos-3
☐ 89OPC-21
☐ 89OPCSti-104
☐ 89Top-21
☐ 90Bow-114
☐ 90BowTif-114
☐ 90OPC-274
☐ 90PanSti-119
☐ 90ProSet-211
☐ 90Top-274
☐ 90TopTif-274
☐ 90UppDec-230
☐ 90UppDecF-230
☐ 91MapLeaP-4
☐ 91Par-397
☐ 91ParFre-397
☐ 91Pin-69
☐ 91PinFre-69
☐ 91ProSet-496
☐ 91ProSetFre-496
☐ 91ProSetPla-233
☐ 91ScoCan-590
☐ 91ScoRoo-40T
☐ 92Sco-218
☐ 92ScoCan-218
☐ 92StaClu-494
☐ 92Top-146
☐ 92TopGol-146G
☐ 94GerDELE-258
☐ 95GerDELE-256
☐ 96GerDELE-144
☐ 98GerDELE-156
**Buller, Hy**
☐ 44BeeGro2P-300
☐ 51Par-91
☐ 52Par-98
☐ 53Par-58
**Bulley, Ted**
☐ 78OPC-217
☐ 78Top-217
☐ 79OPC-128
☐ 79Top-128
☐ 80OPC-229
☐ 80Top-229
☐ 81BlaBorPos-3
☐ 81OPC-56
☐ 81Top-W68
☐ 82Cap-2
☐ 82OPC-360
☐ 82PosCer-4
☐ 83PenCok-4
☐ 83PenTealP-5
**Bullock, Greg**
☐ 95Cla-71
☐ 95ClaAut-2
☐ 96St.JohML-6
☐ 98GerDELE-290
**Bumstead, Geoff**
☐ 92CorBigRed-3
☐ 93CorBigRed-3
☐ 95AlaGolKin-3
**Bumstead, Larry**
☐ 82BraWheK-20
**Burakovsky, Mikael**
☐ 95SweLeaE-263
☐ 95SweLeaER-7
**Burakovsky, Robert**
☐ 85SwePanS-141
☐ 86SwePanS-157
☐ 87SwePanS-157
☐ 89SweSemE-16
☐ 90SweSemE-85
☐ 91SweSemE-189
☐ 91SweSemWCS-44
☐ 92SweSemE-221
☐ 93Lea-429
☐ 93Par-144
☐ 93ParEmel-144
☐ 93SenKraS-4
☐ 93Ult-379
☐ 93UppDec-498
☐ 93UppDecSP-106
☐ 94ClaProP-166
☐ 95SweLeaE-262
☐ 95SweLeaEFF-9
☐ 95SweUppDE-149
**Burch, Billy**
☐ 23V1451-35
☐ 24C144ChaCig-9
☐ 24V130MapC-21
☐ 24V1452-13
☐ 83HalFP-E3
☐ 85HalFC-64
**Burchell, Skippy (Fred)**
☐ 52St.LawS-6
☐ 62QueAce-4
☐ 63QueAce-3
☐ 63QueAceQ-2
**Burchill, Rick**
☐ 89JohChi-19
**Burda, Vaclav**
☐ 95CzeAPSE-272
☐ 96CzeAPSE-127
**Bure, Pavel**
☐ 90UppDec-526
☐ 90UppDecF-526
☐ 91CanuAutC-2
☐ 91CanuMol-2
☐ 91CanuMol-3
☐ 91CanuTeal8-2
☐ 91Gil-10
☐ 91OPCPre-67
☐ 91Par-404
☐ 91Par-446
☐ 91Par-462
☐ 91ParFre-404
☐ 91ParFre-446
☐ 91ParFre-462
☐ 91Pin-315
☐ 91PinFre-315
☐ 91ProSet-564
☐ 91ProSetFre-564
☐ 91ProSetPla-272
☐ 91RusStaRA-1
☐ 91RusTriBur-6
☐ 91RusTriBur-7
☐ 91RusTriBur-8
☐ 91RusTriBur-9
☐ 91RusTriBur-10
☐ 91ScoRoo-49T
☐ 91StaPicH-25
☐ 91SweSemWCS-89
☐ 91UppDec-54
☐ 91UppDec-555
☐ 91UppDec-647
☐ 91UppDecF-54
☐ 91UppDecF-555
☐ 91UppDecF-647
☐ 92Bow-154
☐ 92CanuRoaTA-4
☐ 92Cla-AU2
☐ 92OPC-25
☐ 92OPC-324
☐ 92OPC25Al-25
☐ 92OPCPreSP-10
☐ 92OPCTroW-1
☐ 92PanSti-271
☐ 92PanSti-290
☐ 92PanSti-C
☐ 92PanStiFre-271
☐ 92PanStiFre-290
☐ 92PanStiFre-C
☐ 92Par-188
☐ 92Par-234
☐ 92Par-460
☐ 92Par-506
☐ 92ParEmel-188
☐ 92ParEmel-234
☐ 92ParEmel-460
☐ 92ParEmel-506
☐ 92Pin-110
☐ 92PinCanPP-1

❑ 92PinFre-110
❑ 92PinTea2-8
❑ 92PinTea2F-8
❑ 92PinTeaP-4
❑ 92PinTeaPF-4
❑ 92ProSet-192
❑ 92ProSetAW-CC3
❑ 92ProSetGTL-13
❑ 92ProSetRGL-2
❑ 92Sco-14
❑ 92Sco-504
❑ 92Sco-523
❑ 92ScoCan-14
❑ 92ScoCan-504
❑ 92ScoCan-523
❑ 92ScoCanPS-2
❑ 92ScoYouS-30
❑ 92SeaPat-31
❑ 92StaClu-246
❑ 92StaClu-489
❑ 92Top-8
❑ 92Top-353
❑ 92TopGol-8G
❑ 92TopGol-353G
❑ 92TriFroRWP-5
❑ 92TriFroRWP-6
❑ 92Ult-219
❑ 92UltAwaW-9
❑ 92UltImp-2
❑ 92UltRoo-3
❑ 92UppDec-156
❑ 92UppDec-362
❑ 92UppDec-431
❑ 92UppDec-SP2
❑ 92UppDecERT-ERT1
❑ 92UppDecES-E2
❑ 92UppDecWJG-WG5
❑ 93Cla-117
❑ 93Cla-AU2
❑ 93ClaCraNum-N6
❑ 93ClaPromo-3
❑ 93Don-351
❑ 93DonIceKin-8
❑ 93DonSpeP-X
❑ 93Kra-3
❑ 93Kra-51
❑ 93Lea-10
❑ 93LeaGolAS-8
❑ 93McDUppD-2
❑ 93OPCPre-260
❑ 93OPCPre-440
❑ 93OPCPreBG-7
❑ 93OPCPreG-260
❑ 93OPCPreG-440
❑ 93PanSti-O
❑ 93Par-211
❑ 93ParEasWesS-W2
❑ 93ParEmel-211
❑ 93ParUSACG-G7
❑ 93Pin-320
❑ 93Pin2HS-320
❑ 93PinAllS-31
❑ 93PinAllSC-31
❑ 93PinCan-320
❑ 93PinNifFif-6
❑ 93PinTea2-3
❑ 93PinTea2C-3
❑ 93PinTeaP-10
❑ 93PinTeaPC-10
❑ 93Pow-248
❑ 93PowGloG-1
❑ 93PowPoiL-1
❑ 93Sco-333
❑ 93ScoCan-333
❑ 93ScoDreTea-19
❑ 93ScoFra-22
❑ 93ScoIntS-1
❑ 93ScoIntSC-1
❑ 93SeaPat-2
❑ 93StaClu-480
❑ 93StaCluAS-6
❑ 93StaCluFDI-480
❑ 93StaCluO-480
❑ 93TopPre-260
❑ 93TopPre-440
❑ 93TopPreG-260
❑ 93TopPreG-440
❑ 93Ult-37
❑ 93UltAllS-17
❑ 93UltRedLS-2
❑ 93UltSpeM-1
❑ 93UppDec-35
❑ 93UppDec-307
❑ 93UppDecFH-30
❑ 93UppDecLAS-21
❑ 93UppDecNB-HB5
❑ 93UppDecNR-15
❑ 93UppDecSilSka-H2
❑ 93UppDecSilSkaG-H2
❑ 93UppDecSP-162
❑ 94-ActPacM-MM3
❑ 94BAPUpCP-UC3
❑ 94BeAPla-R35
❑ 94BeAPla-R177
❑ 94CanGamNHLP-266
❑ 94CanGamNHLP-341
❑ 94CanGamNHLP-376
❑ 94CanuProl-5
❑ 94ClaProPIH-LP22
❑ 94Don-19
❑ 94DonDom-8
❑ 94DonEliIns-3
❑ 94EASpo-143
❑ 94Fin-24
❑ 94FinBowB-B11
❑ 94FinBowBR-B11
❑ 94FinDivFCC-20
❑ 94FinRef-24
❑ 94FinSupTW-24
❑ 94Fla-189
❑ 94FlaHotN-1
❑ 94FlaScoP-1
❑ 94Fle-223
❑ 94FleHea-1
❑ 94HocWit-7
❑ 94KenStaLA-3
❑ 94KenStaLC-1
❑ 94Kra-68
❑ 94Lea-10
❑ 94LeaFirOIce-3
❑ 94LeaGolS-4
❑ 94LeaLim-100
❑ 94LeaLimG-10
❑ 94LeaLimI-24
❑ 94McDUppD-McD23
❑ 94OPCPre-39
❑ 94OPCPre-151
❑ 94OPCPre-325
❑ 94OPCPre-415
❑ 94OPCPreSE-39
❑ 94OPCPreSE-151
❑ 94OPCPreSE-325
❑ 94OPCPreSE-415
❑ 94Par-297
❑ 94ParCratGB-24
❑ 94ParCratGG-24
❑ 94ParCratGR-24
❑ 94ParGol-297
❑ 94ParSE-SE187
❑ 94ParSEES-ES15
❑ 94ParSEG-SE187
❑ 94ParVin-V18
❑ 94Pin-140
❑ 94Pin-MVPC
❑ 94PinArtP-140
❑ 94PinBoo-BR13
❑ 94PinGam-GR4
❑ 94PinNorLig-NL17
❑ 94PinRinC-140
❑ 94PinTeaP-TP12
❑ 94PinTeaPDP-TP12
❑ 94PosCerBB-5
❑ 94Sco-78
❑ 94Sco-190
❑ 94Sco90PC-5
❑ 94ScoDreTea-DT24
❑ 94ScoFra-TF24
❑ 94ScoGol-190
❑ 94ScoPla-190
❑ 94ScoPlaTS-190
❑ 94Sel-92
❑ 94SelFirLin-6
❑ 94SelGol-92
❑ 94SP-121
❑ 94SPDieCut-121
❑ 94SPPre-16
❑ 94SPPreDC-16
❑ 94StaClu-10
❑ 94StaCluDD-3
❑ 94StaCluDDMO-3
❑ 94StaCluFDI-10
❑ 94StaCluFI-5
❑ 94StaCluFIMO-5
❑ 94StaCluMO-4
❑ 94StaCluMOMS-10
❑ 94StaCluST-24
❑ 94StaCluSTWC-10
❑ 94TopFinB-4
❑ 94TopFinI-1
❑ 94TopPre-39
❑ 94TopPre-151
❑ 94TopPre-325
❑ 94TopPre-415
❑ 94TopPreGTG-5
❑ 94TopPreSE-39
❑ 94TopPreSE-151
❑ 94TopPreSE-325
❑ 94TopPreSE-415
❑ 94Ult-222
❑ 94UltAllS-7
❑ 94UltRedLS-2
❑ 94UltScoK-1
❑ 94UltSpeM-1
❑ 94UppDec-227
❑ 94UppDec-469
❑ 94UppDecEleIce-90
❑ 94UppDecEleIce-227
❑ 94UppDecEleIce-469
❑ 94UppDecNBAP-20
❑ 94UppDecPH-H2
❑ 94UppDecPH-H19
❑ 94UppDecPHEG-H2
❑ 94UppDecPHEG-H19
❑ 94UppDecPHES-H2
❑ 94UppDecPHES-H19
❑ 94UppDecPHG-H2
❑ 94UppDecPHG-H19
❑ 94UppDecPR-R1
❑ 94UppDecPR-R25
❑ 94UppDecPR-R31
❑ 94UppDecPR-R53
❑ 94UppDecPRE-R1
❑ 94UppDecPRE-R25
❑ 94UppDecPRE-R31
❑ 94UppDecPRE-R53
❑ 94UppDecPreRG-R1
❑ 94UppDecPreRG-R25
❑ 94UppDecPreRG-R31
❑ 94UppDecPreRG-R53
❑ 94UppDecSPI-SP171
❑ 94UppDecSPIDC-SP171
❑ 95BAPLetL-LL7
❑ 95Bow-65
❑ 95BowAllFoi-65
❑ 95BowBes-BB13
❑ 95BowBesRef-BB13
❑ 95CanGamNHLP-21
❑ 95CanGamNHLP-274
❑ 95CanuBuiDA-10
❑ 95ColCho-45
❑ 95ColChoCTG-C1
❑ 95ColChoCTG-C1B
❑ 95ColChoCTG-C1C
❑ 95ColChoCTGGB-C1
❑ 95ColChoCTGGR-C1
❑ 95ColChoCTGSB-C1
❑ 95ColChoCTGSR-C1
❑ 95ColChoPC-45
❑ 95ColChoPCP-45
❑ 95Don-170
❑ 95DonDom-6
❑ 95DonEli-77
❑ 95DonEliDCS-77
❑ 95DonEliDCU-77
❑ 95Emo-178
❑ 95EmoXci-16
❑ 95Fin-75
❑ 95Fin-187
❑ 95FinRef-75
❑ 95FinRef-187
❑ 95GerDELE-442
❑ 95Ima-10
❑ 95Ima-100
❑ 95ImaCleE-CE10
❑ 95ImaGol-10
❑ 95ImaGol-100
❑ 95ImaPlaPl-PL1
❑ 95ImpSti-123
❑ 95ImpStiDCS-14
❑ 95KenStaLA-3
❑ 95Kra-77
❑ 95Lea-135
❑ 95LeaFirOIce-1
❑ 95LeaFreFra-8
❑ 95LeaLim-17
❑ 95McDPin-MCD-8
❑ 95Met-149
❑ 95MetHM-1
❑ 95MetIS-1
❑ 95NHLAcePC-9D
❑ 95NHLCooT-10
❑ 95NHLCooT-RP10
❑ 95ParInt-248
❑ 95ParInt-482
❑ 95ParIntCCGS1-5
❑ 95ParIntCCSS1-5
❑ 95ParIntEl-248
❑ 95ParIntEl-482
❑ 95ParIntNHLAS-3
❑ 95Pin-1
❑ 95PinArtP-1
❑ 95PinCleS-12
❑ 95PinFan-12
❑ 95PinGloG-1
❑ 95PinRinC-1
❑ 95PinRoa2-8
❑ 95PlaOneoOne-100
❑ 95PlaOneoOne-207
❑ 95PlaOneoOne-316
❑ 95ProMag-26
❑ 95Sco-135
❑ 95ScoBlaIce-135
❑ 95ScoBlaIceAP-135
❑ 95ScoBorBat-11
❑ 95ScoDreTea-10
❑ 95ScoLam-2
❑ 95SelCer-16
❑ 95SelCerGT-5
❑ 95SelCerMG-16
❑ 95SelCerP-5
❑ 95SkyImp-167
❑ 95SkyImpCI-9
❑ 95SkyImpIQ-3
❑ 95SP-149
❑ 95SPHol-FX20
❑ 95SPHolSpFX-FX20
❑ 95SPStaEto-E29
❑ 95SPStaEtoG-E29
❑ 95StaClu-186
❑ 95StaCluEN-EN1
❑ 95StaCluMO-41
❑ 95StaCluMOMS-186
❑ 95StaCluNem-N4
❑ 95Sum-7
❑ 95SumArtP-7
❑ 95SumGM-7
❑ 95SumIce-7
❑ 95SumMadH-7
❑ 95SweGloWC-174
❑ 95Top-20
❑ 95Top-300
❑ 95TopCanG-5CG
❑ 95TopHidGem-5HG
❑ 95TopMarMPB-20
❑ 95TopMysF-M15
❑ 95TopMysFR-M15
❑ 95TopOPCI-20
❑ 95TopOPCI-300
❑ 95TopPro-PF11
❑ 95TopSupSki-30
❑ 95TopSupSkiPla-30
❑ 95Ult-166
❑ 95Ult-379
❑ 95UltGolM-166
❑ 95UppDec-214
❑ 95UppDec-406
❑ 95UppDecEleIce-214
❑ 95UppDecEleIce-406
❑ 95UppDecEleIceG-214
❑ 95UppDecEleIceG-406
❑ 95UppDecFreFra-F10
❑ 95UppDecFreFraJ-F10
❑ 95UppDecNHLAS-AS4
❑ 95UppDecPRE-R9
❑ 95UppDecPRE-R26
❑ 95UppDecPreR-R9
❑ 95UppDecPreR-R26
❑ 95UppDecSpeE-SE172
❑ 95UppDecSpeEdiG-SE172
❑ 95Zen-9
❑ 95ZenZT-12
❑ 96BeAPBisITB-18
❑ 96BeAPLH-4B
❑ 96BeAPLHAut-4B
❑ 96BeAPLHAutSil-4B
❑ 96CanuPos-96
❑ 96ColCho-266
❑ 96ColCho-333
❑ 96ColChoCTG-C17A
❑ 96ColChoCTG-C17B
❑ 96ColChoCTG-C17C
❑ 96ColChoCTGE-CR17
❑ 96ColChoCTGEG-CR17
❑ 96ColChoCTGG-C17A
❑ 96ColChoCTGG-C17B
❑ 96ColChoCTGG-C17C
❑ 96ColChoMVP-UD22
❑ 96ColChoMVPG-UD22
❑ 96ColChoSti-S16
❑ 96Don-65
❑ 96DonCanI-59
❑ 96DonCanIGPP-59
❑ 96DonCanIRPP-59
❑ 96DonDom-7
❑ 96DonEli-103
❑ 96DonEliDCS-103
❑ 96DonEliIns-1
❑ 96DonEliInsG-1
❑ 96DonEliS-1
❑ 96DonPrePro-65
❑ 96Fla-93
❑ 96FlaBluI-93
❑ 96FlaCenIS-1
❑ 96Fle-111
❑ 96FleArtRos-1
❑ 96FlePea-1
❑ 96FlePicDL-4
❑ 96FlePicF5-5
❑ 96HocGreC-3
❑ 96HocGreCG-3
❑ 96Lea-15
❑ 96LeaLeaAL-9
❑ 96LeaLeaALP-P9
❑ 96LeaLim-32
❑ 96LeaLimG-32
❑ 96LeaLimStu-10
❑ 96LeaPre-94
❑ 96LeaPreP-15
❑ 96LeaPrePP-94
❑ 96LeaPreSP-3
❑ 96LeaPreVP-9
❑ 96LeaPreVPG-9
❑ 96LeaSwe-13
❑ 96LeaSwe(-13
❑ 96MetUni-155
❑ 96MetUniIC-2
❑ 96MetUniICSP-2
❑ 96MetUniLW-2
❑ 96MetUniLWSP-2
❑ 96NHLACEPC-6
❑ 96NHLProSTA-26
❑ 96Pin-175
❑ 96Pin-248
❑ 96PinArtP-175
❑ 96PinArtP-248
❑ 96PinByTN-15
❑ 96PinByTNP-15
❑ 96PinFan-FC14
❑ 96PinFoi-175
❑ 96PinFoi-248
❑ 96PinMcD-27
❑ 96PinMin-7
❑ 96PinMinB-7
❑ 96PinMinCoiB-7
❑ 96PinMinCoiGP-7
❑ 96PinMinCoiN-7
❑ 96PinMinCoiS-7
❑ 96PinMinCoiSG-7
❑ 96PinMinG-7
❑ 96PinMinS-7
❑ 96PinPreS-175
❑ 96PinPreS-248
❑ 96PinRinC-175
❑ 96PinRinC-248
❑ 96PlaOneoOne-438
❑ 96Sco-35
❑ 96ScoArtPro-35
❑ 96ScoDeaCAP-35
❑ 96ScoDreTea-10
❑ 96ScoGolB-35
❑ 96ScoSpeAP-35
❑ 96ScoSudDea-6
❑ 96SelCer-34
❑ 96SelCerAP-34
❑ 96SelCerBlu-34
❑ 96SelCerCor-7
❑ 96SelCerMB-34
❑ 96SelCerMG-34
❑ 96SelCerMR-34
❑ 96SelCerRed-34
❑ 96SkyImp-131
❑ 96SkyImpCI-1
❑ 96SkyImpVer-1
❑ 96SP-157
❑ 96SPCleWin-CW16
❑ 96SPSPxFor-2
❑ 96SPx-46
❑ 96SPxGol-46
❑ 96Sum-42
❑ 96SumArtP-42
❑ 96SumIce-42
❑ 96SumMet-42
❑ 96SumPreS-42
❑ 96SweSemW-142
❑ 96TeaOut-33
❑ 96TopNHLP-15
❑ 96TopPicFT-FT13
❑ 96TopPicOI-15
❑ 96Ult-167
❑ 96UltGolM-167
❑ 96UltMr.Mom-2
❑ 96UppDec-347
❑ 96UppDecBD-176
❑ 96UppDecBDG-176
❑ 96UppDecBDRFTC-RC14
❑ 96UppDecGJ-GJ10
❑ 96UppDecHH-HH14
❑ 96UppDecHHG-HH14
❑ 96UppDecHHS-HH14
❑ 96UppDecIce-105
❑ 96UppDecIcePar-105
❑ 96UppDecLSH-LS18
❑ 96UppDecLSHF-LS18
❑ 96UppDecLSHS-LS18
❑ 96UppDecSS-SS1A
❑ 96Zen-3
❑ 96ZenArtP-3
❑ 96ZenZT-8
❑ 97BeAPlaPOT-12
❑ 97ColCho-255
❑ 97ColChoCTG-C24A
❑ 97ColChoCTG-C24B
❑ 97ColChoCTG-C24C
❑ 97ColChoCTGE-CR24
❑ 97ColChoSta-SQ59
❑ 97ColChoSti-S25
❑ 97Don-187
❑ 97DonCanI-18
❑ 97DonCanIDS-18
❑ 97DonCanIPS-18
❑ 97DonEli-4
❑ 97DonEli-118
❑ 97DonEliAsp-4
❑ 97DonEliAsp-118
❑ 97DonEliC-20
❑ 97DonEliMC-20
❑ 97DonEliPN-12A
❑ 97DonEliPN-12B
❑ 97DonEliPN-12C
❑ 97DonEliPNDC-12A
❑ 97DonEliPNDC-12B
❑ 97DonEliPNDC-12C
❑ 97DonEliS-4
❑ 97DonEliS-118
❑ 97DonLim-7
❑ 97DonLim-104
❑ 97DonLim-153
❑ 97DonLimExp-7
❑ 97DonLimExp-104
❑ 97DonLimExp-153
❑ 97DonLimFOTG-66
❑ 97DonLin2L-11
❑ 97DonLin2LDC-11
❑ 97DonPre-25
❑ 97DonPre-194
❑ 97DonPreCttC-25
❑ 97DonPreCttC-194
❑ 97DonPreDWT-5
❑ 97DonPreLotT-4A
❑ 97DonPreProG-187
❑ 97DonPreProS-187
❑ 97DonPreT-17
❑ 97DonPreTB-17
❑ 97DonPreTBC-17
❑ 97DonPreTPC-17
❑ 97DonPreTPG-17
❑ 97DonPri-15
❑ 97DonPri-211
❑ 97DonPriDD-3
❑ 97DonPriODI-13
❑ 97DonPriP-5
❑ 97DonPriS-5
❑ 97DonPriSB-5
❑ 97DonPriSG-5
❑ 97DonPriSoA-15
❑ 97DonPriSoA-211
❑ 97DonPriSS-5
❑ 97DonRedAle-6
❑ 97EssOlyHH-38
❑ 97EssOlyHHF-38
❑ 97HigMinHMC-2
❑ 97Kat-145
❑ 97KatGol-145
❑ 97KatSil-145
❑ 97Lea-60
❑ 97LeaFirOnIce-8
❑ 97LeaFraMat-60
❑ 97LeaFraMDC-60
❑ 97LeaInt-60
❑ 97LeaIntUI-60
❑ 97McD-3
❑ 97Pac-96
❑ 97PacCarSup-20
❑ 97PacCarSupM-20
❑ 97PacCop-96
❑ 97PacCroR-133
❑ 97PacCroRBoSDC-19
❑ 97PacCroRCCJ-10
❑ 97PacCroRCCJG-10
❑ 97PacCroRCCJS-10
❑ 97PacCroREG-133
❑ 97PacCroRHTDC-18
❑ 97PacCroRIB-133
❑ 97PacCroRLCDC-19
❑ 97PacCroRS-133
❑ 97PacDyn-125
❑ 97PacDynBKS-95
❑ 97PacDynC-125
❑ 97PacDynDD-15A
❑ 97PacDynDG-125
❑ 97PacDynEG-125
❑ 97PacDynIB-125
❑ 97PacDynKotN-10
❑ 97PacDynR-125
❑ 97PacDynSil-125
❑ 97PacDynTan-14
❑ 97PacEmeGre-96
❑ 97PacGolCroDC-20
❑ 97PacIceB-96
❑ 97PacInv-140
❑ 97PacInvAZ-23
❑ 97PacInvC-140
❑ 97PacInvEG-140
❑ 97PacInvIB-140
❑ 97PacInvNRB-201
❑ 97PacInvOTG-20
❑ 97PacInvR-140
❑ 97PacInvS-140
❑ 97PacOme-228
❑ 97PacOmeC-228
❑ 97PacOmeDG-228
❑ 97PacOmeEG-228
❑ 97PacOmeG-228
❑ 97PacOmeGFDCC-18
❑ 97PacOmeIB-228
❑ 97PacOmeSil-11
❑ 97PacOmeSLC-19
❑ 97PacOmeTL-19
❑ 97PacPar-186
❑ 97PacParBNDC-19
❑ 97PacParC-186
❑ 97PacParDG-186
❑ 97PacParEG-186
❑ 97PacParIB-186
❑ 97PacParP-19
❑ 97PacParRed-186
❑ 97PacParSil-186
❑ 97PacRed-96
❑ 97PacRev-139
❑ 97PacRev1AGD-18
❑ 97PacRevC-139
❑ 97PacRevE-139
❑ 97PacRevIB-139
❑ 97PacRevNID-10
❑ 97PacRevR-139
❑ 97PacRevS-139
❑ 97PacRevTCL-25
❑ 97PacSil-96
❑ 97PacSlaSDC-11A
❑ 97PacTeaCCC-25
❑ 97Pin-41
❑ 97PinArtP-41
❑ 97PinBee-15
❑ 97PinBeeGP-15
❑ 97PinCer-45
❑ 97PinCerMB-45
❑ 97PinCerMG-45
❑ 97PinCerMR-45
❑ 97PinCerR-45
❑ 97PinEpiGO-21
❑ 97PinEpiGP-21
❑ 97PinEpiME-21
❑ 97PinEpiMO-21
❑ 97PinEpiMP-21
❑ 97PinEpiPE-21
❑ 97PinEpiPO-21
❑ 97PinEpiPP-21
❑ 97PinEpiSE-21
❑ 97PinEpiSO-21
❑ 97PinEpiSP-21
❑ 97PinIns-11
❑ 97PinInsC-13
❑ 97PinInsCC-11
❑ 97PinInsCG-13
❑ 97PinInsEC-11
❑ 97PinInsT-12
❑ 97PinMin-17
❑ 97PinMinB-17
❑ 97PinMinCBP-17
❑ 97PinMinCGPP-17
❑ 97PinMinCNSP-17
❑ 97PinMinCoiB-17
❑ 97PinMinCoiGP-17
❑ 97PinMinCoiN-17
❑ 97PinMinCoiSG-17
❑ 97PinMinCoiSS-17
❑ 97PinMinGolTea-17
❑ 97PinMinMC-6
❑ 97PinMinMin-6
❑ 97PinMinSilTea-17
❑ 97PinPowPac-14
❑ 97PinPrePBB-41
❑ 97PinPrePBC-41
❑ 97PinPrePBM-41
❑ 97PinPrePBY-41
❑ 97PinPrePFC-41
❑ 97PinPrePFM-41
❑ 97PinPrePFY-41
❑ 97PinPrePla-41
❑ 97PinRinC-41
❑ 97PinTotCMPG-45
❑ 97PinTotCPB-45
❑ 97PinTotCPG-45
❑ 97PinTotCPR-45
❑ 97PosPin-17
❑ 97Sco-96
❑ 97Sco-261
❑ 97ScoArtPro-96
❑ 97ScoCanPla-1
❑ 97ScoCanPre-1
❑ 97ScoCanu-1
❑ 97ScoGolBla-96
❑ 97SP AutI-I36
❑ 97SPAut-156
❑ 97SPAutID-I36
❑ 97SPAutIE-I36
❑ 97SPx-47
❑ 97SPxBro-47
❑ 97SPxDim-SPX6
❑ 97SPxGol-47
❑ 97SPxGraF-47
❑ 97SPxSil-47
❑ 97SPxSte-47
❑ 97Stu-14
❑ 97StuHarH-18
❑ 97StuPor-14
❑ 97StuPrePG-14
❑ 97StuPrePS-14
❑ 97StuSil-9
❑ 97StuSil8-9
❑ 97TopHocMC-3
❑ 97TopHocMC-4
❑ 97UppDec-168
❑ 97UppDecBD-115
❑ 97UppDecBDDD-115
❑ 97UppDecBDPC-PC9
❑ 97UppDecBDPCDD-PC9
❑ 97UppDecBDPCM-PC9
❑ 97UppDecBDPCQD-PC9
❑ 97UppDecBDPCTD-PC9
❑ 97UppDecBDQD-115
❑ 97UppDecBDTD-115
❑ 97UppDecCtAG-8
❑ 97UppDecCtAG-AR8
❑ 97UppDecDV-10
❑ 97UppDecDVSM-10
❑ 97UppDecGDM-168
❑ 97UppDecIce-86
❑ 97UppDecIceP-86
❑ 97UppDecIPS-86
❑ 97UppDecSG-SG58
❑ 97UppDecSSM-SS24
❑ 97UppDecSSW-SS24
❑ 97UppDecTS-10
❑ 97UppDecTSL2-10
❑ 97UppDecTSS-5C
❑ 97Zen-34
❑ 97Zen5x7-59
❑ 97ZenGolImp-59
❑ 97ZenSilImp-59
❑ 97ZenZGol-34
❑ 97ZenZSil-34
❑ 98Be A PPA-211
❑ 98Be A PPAA-211
❑ 98Be A PPAAF-211
❑ 98Be A PPAJ-AS19
❑ 98Be A PPGUJA-G10
❑ 98Be A PPGUJC-G10
❑ 98Be A PPPH-H12
❑ 98Be A PPPUJC-P4
❑ 98Be A PPSE-211
❑ 98Be APG-211
❑ 98BowBes-58
❑ 98BowBesAR-58
❑ 98BowBesMIF-F14
❑ 98BowBesMIFAR-F14
❑ 98BowBesMIFR-F14
❑ 98BowBesR-58
❑ 98Fin-105
❑ 98FinDouMF-M43
❑ 98FinDouMF-M46
❑ 98FinDouMF-M48
❑ 98FinDouMF-M49
❑ 98FinDouSMFR-M43
❑ 98FinDouSMFR-M46
❑ 98FinDouSMFR-M48
❑ 98FinDouSMFR-M49
❑ 98FinNo P-105
❑ 98FinNo PR-105
❑ 98FinRedL-R4
❑ 98FinRedLR-R4
❑ 98FinRef-105
❑ 98McD-14
❑ 98O-PChr-180
❑ 98O-PChrR-180
❑ 98O-PChrSB-SB15
❑ 98O-PChrSBR-SB15
❑ 98Pac-10
❑ 98PacAur-188
❑ 98PacAurALC-18
❑ 98PacAurC-17
❑ 98PacAurCF-47
❑ 98PacAurCFC-47
❑ 98PacAurCFIB-47
❑ 98PacAurCFR-47
❑ 98PacAurCFS-47
❑ 98PacAurMAC-18
❑ 98PacCraCA-10
❑ 98PacCroR-134
❑ 98PacCroRLS-134
❑ 98PacDynI-187
❑ 98PacDynI-17
❑ 98PacDynIIB-187
❑ 98PacDynIR-187
❑ 98PacEO P-12

98PacGolCD-33
98PacIceB-10
98PacOmeCS-5
98PacOmeCSG-5
98PacOmeCSG-5
98PacOmeCSR-5
98PacOmeEP1o1-12
98PacOmePtF-4
98PacOmeH-99
98PacOmeO-17
98PacOmeODI-99
98PacOmeP-11
98PacOmePI-20
98PacOmePIB-20
98PacOmeR-99
98PacPar-234
98PacParC-234
98PacParEG-234
98PacParH-234
98PacParIB-234
98PacParS-234
98PacParSDDC-18
98PacRed-10
98PacRev-59
98PacRevIS-59
98PacRevR-59
98PacTeaC-26
98PacTim-19
98PacTitl-17
98PinEpiGE-21
98RevThrPA-30
98RevThrPA-30
98SP Aut-86
98SP AutSM-S17
98SP AutSotTG-PB
98SPxFin-84
98SPxFin1
98SPxFin-170
98SPxFinR-84
98SPxFinR-91
98SPxFinR-170
98SPxFinS-84
98SPxFinS-91
98SPxFinS-170
98SPXTopF-58
98SPXTopPF-58
98SPXTopPHH-H29
98SPXTopPLI-L10
98SPXTopPR-58
98SSASotT-PB
98Top-180
98TopGolLC1-74
98TopGolLC1B-74
98TopGolLC1BOoO-74
98TopGolLC1OoO-74
98TopGolLC1ROoO-74
98TopGolLC2-74
98TopGolLC2B-74
98TopGolLC2BOoO-74
98TopGolLC2OoO-74
98TopGolLC2R-74
98TopGolLC2ROoO-74
98TopGolLC3-74
98TopGolLC3B-74
98TopGolLC3BOoO-74
98TopGolLC3OoO-74
98TopGolLC3R-74
98TopGolLC3ROoO-74
98TopLocL-L14
98TopMysFB-M3
98TopMysFBR-M3
98TopMysFG-M3
98TopMysFGR-M3
98TopMysFS-M3
98TopMysFSR-M3
98TopO-P-180
98TopSeaB-SB15
98UC-208
98UCMBH-BH30
98UCSB-SQ2
98UCSG-SQ2
98UCSG-SQ2
98UCSR-SQ2
98UD ChoPCR-208
98UD ChoR-208
98UppDec-18
98UppDec-193
98UppDecE-18
98UppDecE-193
98UppDecE1o1-18
98UppDecE1o1-193
98UppDecFF-FF13
98UppDecFF-FF13
98UppDecFFQ1-FF13
98UppDecFFQ2-FF13
98UppDecFIT-FT24
98UppDecFITQ1-FT24
98UppDecFITQ2-FT24
98UppDecFITQ3-FT24
98UppDecGN-GN28
98UppDecGN-GN29
98UppDecGN-GN30
98UppDecGNQ1-GN28
98UppDecGNQ1-GN29
98UppDecGNQ1-GN30
98UppDecGNQ2-GN28
98UppDecGNQ2-GN29
98UppDecGNQ2-GN30
98UppDecGNQ3-GN28
98UppDecGNQ3-GN29
98UppDecGNQ3-GN30
98UppDecGR-18
98UppDecGR-193
98UppDecLSH-LS26

98UppDecLSHQ1-LS26
98UppDecLSHQ2-LS26
98UppDecLSHQ3-LS26
98UppDecM-85
98UppDecM1-M10
98UppDecM2-M10
98UppDecMGS-85
98UppDecMOH-OT11
98UppDecMS-S8
98UppDecMSS-85
98UppDecMSS-85
98UppDecWFG-WF28
98UppDecWFP-WF28
99AurSty-11
99Pac-169
99PacAur-61
99PacAurCC-7
99PacAurCF-14
99PacAurCFC-14
99PacAurCFPB-14
99PacAurPD-61
99PacCop-169
99PacGol-169
99PacGolCD-19
99PacHomA-11
99PacIceB-169
99PacPasAP-14
99PacPreD-169
99PacTeal-12
99RetHoc-36
99SP AutPS-86
99UppDecCL-59
99UppDecCLL-59
99UppDecEotG-E6
99UppDecM-85
99UppDecM2CN-9
99UppDecM9S-S10
99UppDecMGS-GU4
99UppDecMGS-85
99UppDecMGSA-GU4
99UppDecMHoG-H3
99UppDecMPS-PB
99UppDecMSS-85
99UppDecMSS-85
99UppDecMT-MVP10
99UppDecRG-G6B
99UppDecRG-36
99UppDecRGI-G6B
99UppDecRII-PAB
99UppDecRIL1-PAB
99UppDecRP-36

**Bure, Valeri**
917thInnSWHL-1
91UppDec-647
91UppDecF-647
92Cla-14
92Cla-AU2
92ClaLPs-LP9
93Cla-18
93Par-509
93Par-528
93ParEmel-509
93ParEmel-528
93Pin-501
93PinCan-501
93UppDec-571
94BeAPla-R159
94Cla-30
94ClaDraGol-30
94ClaROYS-R4
94ClaTri-T34
94Fin-48
94FinRef-48
94FinSupTW-48
94Fla-86
94FreCan-6
94Lea-471
940PCPre-337
940PCPreSE-337
94ParSE-SE87
94ParSEG-SE87
94Pin-492
94PinArtP-492
94PinRinC-492
94Sco-215
94ScoGol-215
94ScoPla-215
94Sel-187
94SelGol-187
94SPPre-11
94SPPreDC-11
94TopPre-337
94TopPreSE-337
94Ult-311
94UppDec-255
94UppDecEIeIce-255
94UppDecPC-C8
94UppDecPCEG-C8
94UppDecPCES-C8
94UppDecSPI-SP131
94UppDecSPIDC-SP131
95BeAPla-34
95BeAPSig-S34
95BeAPSigDC-S34
95Bow-160
95BowAllFoi-160
95BowBes-BB28
95BowBesRef-BB28
95CanaPos-4
95CanaShe-1
95CanGamNHLP-147
95ColCho-119
95ColChoPC-119
95ColChoPCP-119
95ColEdgI-40

95ColEdgIC-C11
95ColEdgIQ-IR10
95Don-102
95Fin-34
95FinnSemWC-134
95FinRef-34
95Ima-77
95ImaGol-77
95Lea-39
95McDPin-MCD-34
95ParInt-114
95ParInt-511
95ParIntEI-114
95ParIntEI-511
95Pin-174
95PinArtP-174
95PinGloG-22
95PinRinC-174
95ProMag-21
95Sco-138
95ScoBlaIce-138
95ScoBlaIceAP-138
95SelCer-131
95SelCerMG-131
95SP-74
95StaClu-220
95StaCluMOMS-220
95Sum-197
95SumArtP-197
95SumIce-197
95Top-358
95TopOPCI-358
95Ult-256
95UppDec-304
95UppDecEIeIce-304
95UppDecEIeIceG-304
95UppDecSpeE-SE46
95UppDecSpeEdiG-SE46
95Zen-125
96CanaPos-5
96CanaShe-3
96ClaGol-14
96ColCho-141
96DonCanI-69
96DonCanIGPP-69
96DonCanIRPP-69
96DonEli-119
96DonEliDCS-119
96DonRatR-3
96Fle-52
96Fle-136
96FlePic-124
96FleRooSen-3
96Lea-207
96LeaLim-62
96LeaLimG-62
96LeaPre-88
96LeaPreP-207
96LeaPrePP-88
96LeaPreSG-43
96LeaPreSte-43
96NHLProSTA-21
96Pin-209
96PinFoi-209
96PinPreS-209
96PinRinC-209
96Sco-245
96ScoArtPro-245
96ScoDeaCAP-245
96ScoGolB-245
96ScoSpeAP-245
96SelCer-18
96SelCerAP-18
96SelCerBlu-18
96SelCerMB-18
96SelCerMG-18
96SelCerMR-18
96SelCerRed-18
96SkyImp-60
96SkyImp-167
96SkyImpNHLF-4
96SP-80
96SPHolCol-HC16
96Sum-160
96SumArtP-160
96SumIce-160
96SumMet-160
96SumPreS-160
96TopPicRS-RS8
96UppDec-283
96UppDecGN-X29
96Zen-9
96ZenArtP-9
96ZenAss-15
97CanaPos-4
97ColCho-132
97Don-8
97DonEli-57
97DonEliAsp-57
97DonEliS-57
97DonLim-7
97DonLimExp-7
97DonPre-75
97DonPreCttC-75
97DonPreProG-8
97DonPreProS-8
97DonPri-95
97DonPriSoA-95
97Kat-73
97KatGol-73
97KatSil-73
97Pac-116
97PacCop-116

97PacEmeGre-116
97PacIceB-116
97PacRed-116
97PacSil-116
97Sco-231
97ScoCan-10
97ScoCanPla-10
97SPAut-78
97UppDecBD-6
97UppDecBDDD-6
97UppDecBDQD-6
97UppDecBDTD-6
98Be A PPA-170
98Be A PPAA-170
98Be A PPAAF-170
98Be A PPSE-170
98Be APG-170
98PacOmeH-30
98PacOmeODI-30
98PacOmeR-30
98ScoCanPre-10
98SPxFin-14
98SPxFinR-14
98SPxFinS-14
98UC-31
98UD ChoPCR-31
98UD ChoR-31
98UDCP-31
98UppDec-52
98UppDecC-52
98UppDecE1o1-52
98UppDecGR-52
98UppDecM-30
98UppDecMGS-30
98UppDecMSS-30
98UppDecMSS-30
99Pac-52
99PacAur-20
99PacCop-52
99PacGol-52
99PacIceB-52
99PacPreD-52
99RetHoc-11
99UppDecM-29
99UppDecMGS-29
99UppDecMSS-29
99UppDecMSS-29
99UppDecRG-11
99UppDecRP-11

**Bureau, Marc**
88SalLakCGE-24
89ProIHL-208
90ProAHLIHL-603
90Sco-423
90ScoCan-423
91Bow-126
910PC-93
91Par-302
91ParFre-302
91Pin-335
91PinFre-335
91ProSet-544
91ProSetFre-544
91ScoCan-476
91StaClu-322
91Top-93
91UppDec-274
91UppDecF-274
92Bow-382
92LigShe-7
920PC-78
92Par-400
92ParEmel-400
92StaClu-30
92Top-179
92TopGol-179G
93LigSealR-4
930PCPre-344
930PCPreG-344
93Par-461
93ParEmel-461
93Pin-321
93PinCan-321
93StaClu-134
93StaCluFDI-134
93StaCluFDIO-134
93StaCluO-134
93TopPreG-344
94LigPhoA-5
95CanaPos-5
96BeAPAut-82
96BeAPAutSil-82
96BeAPla-82
96CanaPos-6
96CanaShe-4
97CanaPos-5
97ScoCan-19
97ScoCanPla-19
980-PChr-140
980-PChrR-140
98ScoCanPre-19
98Top-140
98TopO-P-140

**Bureaux, Peter**
96KitRan-4

**Burfoot, Scott**
94EriPan-17
95FliGen-4
96RicRen-1

**Burger, Jiri**
95CzeAPSE-88
96CzeAPSE-88

**Burgess, Don**

740PCWHA-32
770PCWHA-66

**Burgess, Tim**
82OshGen-16

**Burgess, Trevor**
907thInnSOHL-329
917thInnSOHL-162
91OshGen-3
91OshGenS-10
92OshGenS-19
93GreMon-2
95ForWorFT-6
96GerDELE-132

**Burgess, Van**
907thInnSWHL-45
917thInnSWHL-170
93PriAlbR-3

**Burgoyne, Jaret**
89VicCou-4

**Burgoyne, Ryan**
93LonKni-6
95Sla-162

**Burke, Adam**
96WhaBobS-2

**Burke, Claude**
36V356WorG-112

**Burke, Dave**
92GreMon-15

**Burke, Don**
94CenHocL-5

**Burke, Eddie**
34DiaMatS-7
35DiaMatTI-7

**Burke, Greg**
92BirBul-17
93BirBul-17
93DayBom-28
96GerDELE-111

**Burke, Jim**
90ProAHLIHL-174
91ProAHLCHL-111

**Burke, Justin**
907thInnSWHL-63

**Burke, Marty**
27LaPat-11
33V252CanG-7
33V288HamG-3
33V357IceK-14
34BeeGro1P-43
34DiaMatS-8
35DiaMatT2-6
35DiaMatT3-5
35DiaMatT4-3
35DiaMatT5-2
35DiaMatTI-8
36V356WorG-72
37DiaMatT6-2

**Burke, Sean**
88DevCar-5
88FriLayS-38
880PC-94
880PCSti-82
880PCSti-158
88PanSti-267
88Top-94
89DevCar-6
89Kra-53
89KraAllSS-6
890PC-92
890PCSti-34
890PCSti-86
890PCSti-203
89PanSti-185
89PanSti-256
89Top-92
90Dev-4
90Kra-4
900PC-140
90PanSti-77
90ProSet-164
90Sco-34
90ScoCan-34
90ScoHotRS-17
90ScoYouS-11
90Top-140
90TopTif-140
90UppDec-66
90UppDecF-66
91AlbIntTC-3
91Bow-275
910PC-67
91PanSti-212
91ProSet-132
91ProSetFre-132
91ScoAme-245
91ScoCan-465
91StaClu-76
91Top-67
91UppDec-183
91UppDecF-183
92Cla-117
92Kra-28
920PCPre-92
92Par-57
92ParEmel-57
92ParPre-PV2
92Pin-295
92PinFre-295
92ScoCanO-13
92Ult-68
92UppDec-518
92WhaDai-2
93Don-141
93Lea-132
930PCPre-241

930PCPreG-241
93PanSti-131
93Pin-31
93PinCan-31
93Pow-103
93Sco-126
93ScoCan-126
93ScoFra-8
93StaClu-207
93StaCluFDI-207
93StaCluFDIO-207
93StaCluO-207
93TopPre-241
93TopPreG-241
93Ult-15
93WhaCok-1
94BeAPASig-53
94CanGamNHLP-281
94Don-158
94EASpo-60
94Fla-70
94Fle-84
94Kra-36
94Lea-85
940PCPre-542
940PCPreSE-542
94ParSE-SE71
94ParSEG-SE71
94Pin-114
94PinArtP-114
94PinGoaG-GT12
94PinRinC-114
94Sco-84
94ScoGol-84
94ScoPla-84
94ScoPlaTS-84
94Sel-127
94SelGol-127
94SP-51
94SPDieCut-51
94StaClu-171
94StaCluFDI-171
94StaCluMOMS-171
94StaCluST-10
94StaCluSTWC-171
94TopPre-542
94TopPreSE-542
94Ult-87
94UppDec-158
94UppDecEIeIce-158
95Bow-26
95BowAllFoi-26
95CanGamNHLP-131
95ColCho-199
95ColChoPC-199
95ColChoPCP-199
95Don-28
95DonBetTP-8
95DonEli-107
95DonEliDCS-107
95DonEliDCU-107
95Emo-73
95Fin-132
95FinRef-132
95ImpSti-54
95Kra-15
95Lea-63
95LeaLim-14
95Met-63
95ParInt-96
95ParIntEI-96
95Pin-124
95PinArtP-124
95PinMas-9
95PinRinC-124
95PlaOneoOne-45
95ProMag-126
95Sco-32
95Sco-320
95ScoBlaIce-32
95ScoBlaIce-320
95ScoBlaIceAP-32
95ScoBlaIceAP-320
95SelCer-100
95SelCerMG-100
95SkyImp-71
95SkyImpD-4
95SP-65
95StaClu-29
95StaCluMOMS-29
95Sum-125
95SumArtP-125
95SumIce-125
95SumInTheCre-13
95Top-135
95TopOPCI-135
95TopSupSki-76
95TopSupSkiPla-76
95Ult-65
95Ult-367
95UltGolM-65
95UltPrePadMen-3
95UltPrePadMenGM-3
95UppDec-130
95UppDecEIeIce-130
95UppDecEIeIceG-130
95UppDecSpeE-SE39
95UppDecSpeEdiG-SE39
95Zen-100
96BeAPAut-18
96BeAPAutSil-18
96BeAPla-18
96ClaGol-117
96ColCho-119
96ColCho-319

96Don-121
96DonCanI-66
96DonCanIGPP-66
96DonCanIRPP-66
96DonEli-51
96DonEliDCS-51
96DonPrePro-121
96Fle-45
96FleVez-2
96Lea-85
96LeaPre-85
96LeaPreP-85
96LeaPrePP-85
96MetUni-66
96NHLProSTA-126
96Pin-37
96PinArtP-37
96PinFoi-37
96PinPreS-37
96PinRinC-37
96Sco-46
96ScoArtPro-46
96ScoDeaCAP-46
96ScoGolB-46
96ScoSpeAP-46
96SelCer-44
96SelCerAP-44
96SelCerBlu-44
96SelCerMB-44
96SelCerMG-44
96SelCerMR-44
96SelCerRed-44
96SkyImp-52
96SkyImpZH-2
96SP-70
96Sum-109
96SumArtP-109
96SumIce-109
96SumMet-109
96SumPreS-109
96SweSemW-77
96Ult-73
96UltGolM-73
96UppDec-72
96UppDecIce-26
96UppDecIcePar-26
96WhaBobS-1
97CarHur-2
97ColCho-111
97Don-128
97DonCanI-99
97DonCanIDS-99
97DonCanIPS-99
97DonEli-39
97DonEliAsp-39
97DonEliS-39
97DonLim-119
97DonLim-194
97DonLimExp-119
97DonLimExp-194
97DonPre-104
97DonPreCttC-104
97DonPreProG-128
97DonPreProS-128
97DonPri-44
97DonPriSoA-44
97Kat-25
97KatGol-25
97KatSil-25
97Lea-63
97LeaFraMat-63
97LeaFraMDC-63
97LeaInt-63
97LeaIntUI-63
97Pac-81
97PacCop-81
97PacDyn-20
97PacDynC-20
97PacDynDG-20
97PacDynEG-20
97PacDynIB-20
97PacDynR-20
97PacDynSil-20
97PacDynTan-37
97PacEmeGre-81
97PacIceB-81
97PacInv-22
97PacInvC-22
97PacInvEG-22
97PacInvIB-22
97PacInvS-22
97PacOme-229
97PacOmeDG-229
97PacOmeEG-229
97PacOmeG-229
97PacOmeIB-229
97PacRed-81
97PacRev-140
97PacRevC-140
97PacRevE-140
97PacRevIB-140
97PacRevS-140
97PacSil-81
97Pin-42
97PinArtP-42
97PinCer-25
97PinCerMB-25
97PinCerMG-25
97PinCerMR-25
97PinCerR-25
97PinIns-30
97PinInsCC-30

- 97PinInsEC-30
- 97PinPrePBB-42
- 97PinPrePBC-42
- 97PinPrePBM-42
- 97PinPrePBY-42
- 97PinPrePFC-42
- 97PinPrePFM-42
- 97PinPrePFY-42
- 97PinPrePla-42
- 97PinRinC-42
- 97PinTotCMPG-25
- 97PinTotCPB-25
- 97PinTotCPG-25
- 97PinTotCPR-25
- 97Sco-1
- 97ScoArtPro-1
- 97ScoGolBla-1
- 97Stu-62
- 97StuPrePG-62
- 97StuPrePS-62
- 97UppDec-31
- 98Be A PPA-209
- 98Be A PPAA-209
- 98Be A PPAAF-209
- 98Be A PPSE-209
- 98Be APG-209
- 98O-PChr-19
- 98O-PChrR-19
- 98Pac-321
- 98PacCroR-56
- 98PacCroRLS-56
- 98PacDynIB-78
- 98PacDynIIB-78
- 98PacDynIR-78
- 98PacIceB-321
- 98PacOmeH-100
- 98PacOmeODI-100
- 98PacOmeR-100
- 98PacRed-321
- 98PacRev-60
- 98PacRevIS-60
- 98PacRevR-60
- 98Top-19
- 98TopO-P-19
- 98UC-147
- 98UC-252
- 98UD ChoPCR-147
- 98UD ChoPCR-252
- 98UD ChoR-147
- 98UD ChoR-252
- 99Pac-170
- 99PacAur-62
- 99PacAurPD-62
- 99PacCop-170
- 99PacGol-170
- 99PacIceB-170
- 99PacPreD-170

**Burke, Tim**
- 77NovScoV-4
- 90Dev-5

**Burkett, Michael**
- 93MicSta-2

**Burkhard, Alfred**
- 94GerDELE-25

**Burkholder, Barry**
- 83KinCan-17
- 84KinCan-12
- 85KinCan-12

**Burkholder, Dave**
- 95Sla-204

**Burkitt, Noel**
- 95Sla-400
- 95SudWol-13
- 95SudWolP-4

**Burkitt, Toby**
- 907thInnSOHL-354
- 917thInnSOHL-356

**Burlin, Borje**
- 67SweHoc-182
- 69SweHocS-238
- 71SweHocS-229
- 72SweHocSf-217
- 73SweHocS-73
- 73SweWorCS-73
- 74SweHocS-207

**Burlin, Dick**
- 89SweSemE-201

**Burman, Michael**
- 907thInnSOHL-304
- 917thInnSOHL-62
- 93NorBayC-11
- 94KnoChe-24
- 95RicRen-18

**Burn, Arren**
- 93HumHawP-9

**Burnett, Garrett**
- 94KitRanU-35

**Burnett, George**
- 897thInnSOHL-124
- 89NiaFalT-5
- 917thInnSCHLAW-7
- 917thInnSOHL-203
- 95BinRan-2
- 96BinRan-3
- 97GueSto-27

**Burnett, Mathew**
- 920tt672A-4

**Burnham, Brad**
- 91FerStaB-6

**Burnie, Stu**
- 88ProAHL-306

**Burns, Bob**
- 94GerDELE-416
- 96GerDELE-291

**Burns, Charlie**

---

- 44BeeGro2P-9
- 58Top-43
- 59Top-40
- 60Top-24
- 60TopSta-7
- 61ShiCoi-4
- 61Top-11
- 62Top-15
- 63Top-9
- 680PC-108
- 68Top-108
- 690PC-129
- 69Top-129
- 70ColSta-19
- 70DadCoo-12
- 70EssPowPla-169
- 700PC-44
- 700PCDec-13
- 70SarProSta-87
- 70Top-44
- 710PC-238
- 71SarProSta-87
- 71Top-21
- 71TorSun-127
- 720PC-178
- 72SarProSta-106

**Burns, Darren**
- 87BroBra-10
- 88BroBra-11

**Burns, Lance**
- 907thInnSWHL-130
- 917thInnSWHL-346

**Burns, Norm**
- 34BeeGro1P-263

**Burns, Pat**
- 88CanaPos-2
- 89CanaKra-1
- 89CanaPos-2
- 90CanaPos-4
- 90ProSet-669
- 91CanaPos-3
- 93Kra-31
- 94MapLeaK-6
- 94MapLeaPP-30

**Burns, R.R.**
- 95GerDELE-383

**Burns, Robin**
- 74NHLActSta-289
- 750PCNHL-104
- 75Top-104

**Burns, Sean**
- 89WinSpi-1
- 907thInnSOHL-177

**Burr, Shawn**
- 83KitRan-18
- 84KitRan-22
- 85KitRan-21
- 870PC-164
- 870PCMin-5
- 870PCSti-125
- 87PanSti-247
- 87RedWinLC-4
- 87Top-164
- 880PC-78
- 88PanSti-41
- 88RedWinLC-2
- 88Top-78
- 890PC-101
- 890PCSti-252
- 89PanSti-63
- 89RedWinLC-2
- 89Top-101
- 90Bow-232
- 90BowTif-232
- 900PC-74
- 90PanSti-213
- 90ProSet-66
- 90Sco-49
- 90ScoCan-49
- 90ScoHotRS-21
- 90Top-74
- 90TopTif-74
- 90UppDec-111
- 90UppDecF-111
- 91Bow-43
- 910PC-184
- 91PanSti-135
- 91Par-45
- 91ParFre-45
- 91Pin-86
- 91PinFre-86
- 91ProSet-58
- 91ProSetFre-58
- 91RedWinLC-1
- 91ScoAme-54
- 91ScoCan-54
- 91StaClu-101
- 91Top-184
- 91UppDec-315
- 91UppDecF-315
- 92Bow-122
- 920PC-24
- 92Pin-171
- 92PinFre-171
- 92ProSet-45
- 92Sco-207
- 92ScoCan-207
- 92StaClu-126
- 92Top-178
- 92TopGol-178G
- 92Ult-44
- 93Lea-296
- 930PCPre-83
- 930PCPreG-83
- 93Par-328

---

- 93ParEmel-328
- 93Pin-93
- 93PinCan-93
- 93Sco-175
- 93ScoCan-175
- 93StaClu-313
- 93StaCluFDI-313
- 93StaCluO-313
- 93TopPre-83
- 93TopPreG-83
- 93UppDec-91
- 94BeAPSig-93
- 94Lea-368
- 94LigPos-3
- 94Par-62
- 94ParGol-62
- 94Pin-318
- 94PinArtP-318
- 94PinRinC-318
- 94SarSti-29
- 94UppDec-484
- 94UppDecEleIce-484
- 95LigTeal-5
- 95ParInt-461
- 95ParIntEl-461
- 95Sco-13
- 95ScoBlaIce-13
- 95ScoBlaIceAP-13
- 95UppDec-355
- 95UppDecBlaIceG-355
- 95UppDecEleIceG-355
- 96BeAPAut-191
- 96BeAPAutSil-191
- 96BeAPla-191
- 96ColOcho-254
- 97Pac-152
- 97PacCop-152
- 97PacEmeGre-152
- 97PacIceB-152
- 97PacPar-163
- 97PacParC-163
- 97PacParDG-163
- 97PacParEG-163
- 97PacParIB-163
- 97PacParRed-163
- 97PacParSil-163
- 97PacRed-152
- 97PacSil-152
- 98Be A PPA-121
- 98Be A PPAA-121
- 98Be A PPAAF-121
- 98Be A PPTBASG-121
- 98Be APG-121

**Burridge, Randy**
- 860PC-70
- 86Top-70
- 88BruSpoA-2
- 880PC-33
- 880PCSti-29
- 88PanSti-208
- 88Top-33
- 89BruSpoA-3
- 890PC-121
- 890PCSti-28
- 89PanSti-197
- 89Top-121
- 90BruSpoA-4
- 900PC-190
- 90ProSet-2
- 90Sco-72
- 90ScoCan-72
- 90Top-190
- 90TopTif-190
- 90UppDec-196
- 90UppDecF-196
- 91Bow-349
- 91CapJun5-4
- 91CapKod-4
- 910PC-358
- 910PCPre-43
- 91PanSti-174
- 91Par-190
- 91ParFre-190
- 91Pin-55
- 91PinFre-55
- 91ProSet-510
- 91ProSetFre-4
- 91ProSetFre-510
- 91ProSetPla-241
- 91ScoAme-102
- 91ScoCan-102
- 91ScoCan-564
- 91ScoRoo-14T
- 91StaClu-119
- 91Top-358
- 91UppDec-567
- 91UppDecF-567
- 92Bow-29
- 92Bow-225
- 92CapKod-4
- 920PC-370
- 92PanSti-163
- 92PanStiFre-163
- 92Pin-115
- 92PinFre-115
- 92Sco-297
- 92ScoCan-297
- 92Top-83
- 92TopGol-83G
- 92UppDec-153
- 93Don-503
- 93Par-492

---

- 93ParEmel-492
- 93Pin-418
- 93PinCan-418
- 93Pow-464
- 93Sco-370
- 93ScoCan-370
- 93StaClu-416
- 93StaCluFDI-416
- 93StaCluO-416
- 93Ult-444
- 93UppDec-504
- 94CanGamNHLP-243
- 94Don-66
- 94Fla-197
- 94Lea-291
- 94Pin-110
- 94PinArtP-110
- 94PinRinC-110
- 94Sco-90
- 94ScoGol-90
- 94ScoPla-90
- 94ScoPlaTS-90
- 94StaClu-163
- 94StaCluFDI-163
- 94StaCluMOMS-163
- 94StaCluSTWC-163
- 95BeAPla-114
- 95BeAPSig-S114
- 95BeAPSigDC-S114
- 95Fin-21
- 95FinRef-21
- 95Met-13
- 95ParInt-293
- 95ParIntEl-293
- 95Sco-164
- 95ScoBlaIce-164
- 95ScoBlaIceAP-164
- 95Ult-210
- 95UppDec-320
- 95UppDecEleIce-320
- 95UppDecEleIceG-320
- 95UppDecSpeE-SE99
- 95UppDecSpeEdiG-SE99
- 96ColOcho-28
- 96Don-127
- 96DonPrePro-127
- 96Lea-121
- 96LeaPreP-121
- 96Pin-198
- 96PinArtP-198
- 96PinFoi-198
- 96PinPreS-198
- 96PinRinC-198
- 96Sco-52
- 96ScoArtPro-52
- 96ScoDeaCAP-52
- 96ScoGolB-52
- 96ScoSpeAP-52
- 96Sum-26
- 96SumArtP-26
- 96SumIce-26
- 96SumMet-26
- 96SumPreS-26
- 97Be A PPAD-79
- 97Be A PPAPD-79
- 97BeAPla-79
- 97BeAPlaAut-79
- 97PacInvNRB-18
- 97ScoSab-6
- 97ScoSabPla-6
- 97ScoSabPre-6

**Burrowes, Guy**
- 71RocAme-2

**Burrows, Dave**
- 71PenPos-3
- 720PC-133
- 72SarProSta-182
- 72Top-82
- 730PC-140
- 73Top-27
- 74NHLActSta-220
- 740PCNHL-147
- 74OPCNHL-241
- 74PenPos-3
- 74Top-137
- 74Top-241
- 750PCNHL-186
- 75Top-186
- 760PCNHL-83
- 76Top-83
- 77Coc-2
- 770PCNHL-66
- 77PenPucB-4
- 77Top-66
- 78MapLeaP-5
- 780PC-254
- 78Top-254
- 79MapLeaP-6
- 800PC-147
- 80Top-147

**Burstrom, Anders**
- 94SweLeaE-173
- 95SweLeaE-250

**Burt, Adam**
- 90Bow-292
- 90BowTif-252
- 900PC-431
- 90ProSet-447
- 90Sco-370
- 90ScoCan-370
- 90UppDec-324
- 90UppDecF-324
- 91PanSti-318
- 91Par-291
- 91ParFre-291

---

- 91Pin-77
- 91PinFre-77
- 91ScoCan-449
- 91WhaJr7E-5
- 92PanSti-264
- 92PanStiFre-264
- 92Sco-261
- 92ScoCan-261
- 92StaClu-139
- 92Top-283
- 92TopGol-283G
- 92Ult-69
- 92WhaDai-3
- 93Don-139
- 93Lea-280
- 93Pin-313
- 93PinCan-313
- 93Sco-307
- 93ScoCan-307
- 93WhaCok-2
- 94Pin-356
- 94PinArtP-356
- 94PinRinC-356
- 95Pin-200
- 95PinArtP-200
- 95PinRinC-200
- 95PlaOneoOne-155
- 95Top-184
- 95TopOPCI-184
- 95UppDec-303
- 95UppDecEleIce-303
- 95UppDecEleIceG-303
- 96BeAPAut-117
- 96BeAPAutSil-117
- 96BeAPla-117
- 97CarHur-3
- 97PacInvNRB-34
- 99Pac-300
- 99PacCop-300
- 99PacGol-300
- 99PacIceB-300
- 99PacPreD-300

**Burt, Wade**
- 96KamBla-6

**Burton, Archie**
- 52JunBluT-16

**Burton, Cumming**
- 52JunBluT-8

**Burton, James**
- 95FinnSemWC-184
- 95PhoRoa-6
- 95SweGloWC-188
- 96SweSemW-213

**Burton, Joe**
- 920klCitB-3
- 94CenHocL-56

**Busch, R.**
- 95GerDELE-288

**Bush, Eddie**
- 34BeeGro1P-94
- 61HamRed-2

**Busillo, Giuseppe**
- 98GerDELE-105

**Busillo, Joe**
- 897thInnSOHL-3
- 89OshGen-3
- 89OshGenP-3
- 907thInnSMC-86
- 907thInnSOHL-154
- 917thInnSMC-3
- 96GerDELE-354

**Busniuk, Ron**
- 74FigSaiWHA-5

**Buswell, Walter**
- 34BeeGro1P-141
- 35DiaMatT3-6
- 36V356WorG-32
- 370PCV304E-174
- 38QuaOatP-5
- 390PCV3011-32

**Butcher, Garth**
- 81RegPat-2
- 82Canu-4
- 83Canu-3
- 83Vac-103
- 84Canu-4
- 84KelWin-49
- 85Canu-3
- 86Canu-2
- 87CanuSheOil-6
- 870PCSti-200

---

- 87PanSti-343
- 88CanuMoh-8
- 880PC-202
- 880PCSti-54
- 88PanSti-134
- 89CanuMoh-1
- 890PCSti-72
- 89PanSti-158
- 90CanuMoh-4
- 900PC-150
- 90ProSet-295
- 90Sco-18
- 90ScoCan-18
- 90Top-150
- 90TopTif-150
- 90UppDec-98
- 90UppDecF-98
- 91BluPos-4
- 91Bow-383
- 91CanuPanTS-5
- 910PC-204
- 91PanSti-28
- 91Par-374
- 91ParFre-374
- 91Pin-85
- 91Pin-409
- 91PinFre-85
- 91PinFre-409
- 91ProSet-210
- 91ProSet-583
- 91ProSetFre-210
- 91ProSetFre-583
- 91ProSetPla-223
- 91ScoAme-24
- 91ScoCan-24
- 91StaClu-223
- 91Top-204
- 91UppDec-397
- 91UppDecF-397
- 92Bow-124
- 920PC-280
- 92PanSti-24
- 92PanStiFre-24
- 92Par-390
- 92ParEmel-390
- 92Pin-72
- 92PinFre-72
- 92ProSet-160
- 92Sco-65
- 92ScoCan-65
- 92StaClu-287
- 92Top-281
- 92TopGol-281G
- 92Ult-184
- 93Don-289
- 93Don-417
- 93Lea-239
- 930PCPre-316
- 930PCPreG-316
- 93PanSti-164
- 93Par-449
- 93ParEmel-449
- 93Pin-66
- 93PinAllS-24
- 93PinAllSC-24
- 93PinCan-66
- 93Pow-208
- 93Sco-173
- 93ScoCan-173
- 93StaClu-21
- 93StaCluFDI-21
- 93StaCluFDIO-21
- 93StaCluO-21
- 93TopPre-316
- 93TopPreG-316
- 93Ult-27
- 94EASpo-122
- 94Lea-466
- 94MapLeaK-7
- 94MapLeaP-2
- 94MapLeaPP-5
- 940PCPre-441
- 940PCPreSE-441
- 94Par-188
- 94ParGol-188
- 94Pin-394
- 94PinArtP-394
- 94PinRinC-394
- 94Sco-13
- 94ScoGol-13
- 94ScoPla-13
- 94ScoPlaTS-13
- 94TopPre-441
- 94TopPreSE-441
- 95Pin-53
- 95PinArtP-53
- 95PinRinC-53

**Butenschon, Sven**
- 95SlaMemC-33
- 96CleLum-5
- 98UppDec-10
- 98UppDecE-10
- 98UppDecE1o1-10
- 98UppDecGR-10

**Butko, Sergej**
- 95CzeAPSE-158
- 95CzeAPSE-174

**Butler, Jerome (Jerry)**
- 74NHLActSta-181
- 74OPCNHL-393
- 750PCNHL-167
- 75Top-167
- 760PCNHL-336
- 770PCNHL-349
- 78MapLeaP-6

---

- 780PC-304
- 79MapLeaP-7
- 790PC-393
- 80CanuSilD-6
- 80CanuTeal-6
- 800PC-351
- 80PepCap-105
- 81CanuSilD-5
- 81CanuTeal-5
- 810PC-332
- 82Jet-3
- 93MinDul-4

**Butler, Rob**
- 95Sla-395
- 95SudWol-16
- 95SudWolP-5
- 96SouCarS-22

**Butler, Rod**
- 93WatBlaH-5

**Butler, Stan**
- 95Sla-255

**Butorac, Ali**
- 81OshGen-4
- 83BelBul-19

**Butorac, Tony**
- 80SauSteMG-15

**Butsayev, Slava (Vyatcheslav)**
- 910PCIns-12R
- 91SweSemWCS-90
- 92FlyUppDS-41
- 92FlyUppDS-43
- 920PCPre-31
- 92Par-363
- 92ParEmel-363
- 92RusStaRA-14
- 92RusStaRA-6
- 92Ult-153
- 92UppDec-503
- 93Cla-87
- 93ClaProPBC-BC14
- 93ClaProPro-131
- 93Lea-307
- 930PCPre-79
- 930PCPreG-79
- 93Par-151
- 93ParEmel-151
- 93Sco-656
- 93ScoCan-656
- 93ScoGol-656
- 93StaClu-94
- 93StaCluFDI-94
- 93StaCluFDIO-94
- 93StaCluO-94
- 93TopPre-79
- 93TopPreG-79
- 93Ult-385
- 93UppDec-406
- 94FinnJaaK-148
- 94Par-213
- 94ParGol-213
- 94Pin-498
- 94PinArtP-498
- 94PinRinC-498
- 94UppDec-417
- 94UppDecEleIce-417

**Butt, Jamie**
- 92TacRoc-3
- 93TacRoc-2

**Butt, Kevin**
- 897thInnSOHL-18
- 89OshGen-18
- 89OshGenP-15
- 907thInnSMC-76
- 917thInnSOHL-101

**Butterfield, Jack**
- 83HalFP-M2
- 85HalFC-167

**Butters, Wm.**
- 90ProAHLIHL-551
- 91GreMon-3

**Butz, Rob**
- 94TriAme-4
- 95St.JohML-3
- 96St.JohML-7

**Buzak, Mike**
- 90ForSasTra-1
- 93MicSta-3
- 95ColEdgI-91

**Buzan, Garrett**
- 96DenUniPio-5

**Buzek, Petr**
- 94CzeAPSE-167
- 94SP-155
- 94SPDieCut-155
- 95Cla-52
- 95ClaAut-3
- 98UppDec-82
- 98UppDecE-82
- 98UppDecE1o1-82
- 98UppDecGR-82

**Byakin, Ilya**
- 89RusNatT-1
- 910PCIns-13R
- 91SweSemWCS-83
- 93Don-427
- 93Par-341
- 93ParEmel-341
- 93Pow-341
- 93Sco-619
- 93ScoCan-619
- 93ScoGol-619
- 93SweSemWCS-131
- 940PCPre-223
- 940PCPreSE-223

❑ 94TopPre-223
❑ 94TopPreSE-223
❑ 94Ult-70
❑ 95FinnSemWC-124
❑ 95SweLeaE-261
❑ 95SweUppDE-136
❑ 96SweSemW-138
**Byalsin, Igor**
❑ 90OPCRedA-1R
**Byce, John**
❑ 90Bow-38
❑ 90BowTif-38
❑ 90BruSpoA-5
❑ 90ScoRoo-62T
❑ 90UppDec-25
❑ 90UppDecF-25
❑ 91ProAHLCHL-59
❑ 93SweSemE-113
**Bye, Carlos**
❑ 917thInnSWHL-217
**Bye, Karyn**
❑ 94ClaWomOH-W27
**Byers, Jerry**
❑ 74NHLActSta-2
❑ 74OPCNHL-273
**Byers, Lyndon**
❑ 81RegPat-3
❑ 82RegPat-20
❑ 83RegPat-20
❑ 86MonGolF-19
❑ 88BruSpoA-3
❑ 89BruSpoA-4
❑ 90BruSpoA-6
❑ 90OPC-464
❑ 90ProSet-3
❑ 93LasVegThu-5
**Byers, Mike**
❑ 68ShiCoi-175
❑ 70ColSta-55
❑ 70EssPowPla-161
❑ 70OPC-160
❑ 71OPC-34
❑ 71Top-34
❑ 71TorSun-107
❑ 72ShaLosAW-1
❑ 72WhaNewEWHA-1
**Bykov, Slava (Viacheslav)**
❑ 83RusNatT-4
❑ 87RusNatT-4
❑ 89RusNatT-2
❑ 89SweSemWCS-92
❑ 90OPCRedA-10R
❑ 91SweSemWCS-100
❑ 93SweSemWCS-147
❑ 93SwiHNL-46
❑ 94FinnJaaK-145
❑ 95FinnSemWC-138
❑ 95SweGloWC-180
❑ 95SwiHNL-71
❑ 96SweSemW-151
**Bylsma, Dan**
❑ 92GreMon-6
❑ 93GreMon-3
❑ 95PhoRoa-7
❑ 96UppDec-276
❑ 97Be A PPAD-29
❑ 97Be A PPAPD-29
❑ 97BeAPla-29
❑ 97BeAPlaAut-29
**Bylsma, Sheldon**
❑ 91AirCanSJHL-D29
❑ 92MPSPhoSJHL-167
**Bylund, Agne**
❑ 69SweHocS-204
**Bylund, Lars**
❑ 65SweCorI-89
❑ 67SweHoc-43
❑ 69SweHocS-57
❑ 70SweHocS-20
❑ 71SweHocS-97
**Byram, Shawn**
❑ 88ProAHL-323
❑ 89ProAHL-235
❑ 91ProAHLCHL-482
❑ 92IndIce-5
**Byrne, Paddy**
❑ 36ProvRed-2
**Byrnes, Jason**
❑ 94KitRan-7
❑ 95Sla-146
❑ 96KitRan-3
**Byron, Wally**
❑ 24CreFal-2
❑ 24HolCre-8
**Bystrom, Lars**
❑ 83SweSemE-168
❑ 85SwePanS-217
❑ 86SwePanS-209
❑ 87SwePanS-205
❑ 89SweSemE-182
❑ 90SweSemE-17
❑ 91SweSemE-216
❑ 92SweSemE-245
❑ 93SweSemE-213
❑ 94SweLeaE-92
❑ 94SweLeaESS-9
❑ 95SweLeaE-109
❑ 95SweUppDE-169
**Bystrom, Sven**
❑ 65SweCorI-72
**Bzdel, Gerald**
❑ 88ProAHL-97
❑ 89HalCit-4
❑ 89ProAHL-174
❑ 90HalCit-3
❑ 90ProAHLIHL-444
❑ 91ProAHLCHL-529
**Bzdel, Mike**
❑ 92BriColJHL-150
**Cabana, Chad**
❑ 917thInnSWHL-298
❑ 94TriAme-5
**Cabana, Clint**
❑ 95MedHatT-5
**Cadden, Cory**
❑ 93KnoChe-2
❑ 94KnoChe-23
❑ 96SouCarS-30
**Cadieux, Steve**
❑ 90CinCyc-26
❑ 91CinCyc-3
**Cadotte, Mark**
❑ 95Sla-78
❑ 96DetWha-2
**Caffery, Jack**
❑ 44BeeGro2P-10
❑ 52JunBluT-154
❑ 55Par-19
❑ 55ParQuaO-19
❑ 57Top-8
❑ 94ParMisL-12
**Caffery, Terry**
❑ 69OPC-135
❑ 69SweHocS-351
❑ 72WhaNewEWHA-2
**Cagas, Pavel**
❑ 94CzeAPSE-1
❑ 95CzeAPSE-101
❑ 96GerDELE-226
**Cahan, Larry**
❑ 44BeeGro2P-301A
❑ 44BeeGro2P-301B
❑ 44BeeGro2P-387
❑ 55Par-16
❑ 55ParQuaO-16
❑ 57Top-59
❑ 58Top-23
❑ 61ShiCoi-95
❑ 61Top-52
❑ 62Top-48
❑ 63Top-51
❑ 64BeeGro3P-122
❑ 68OPC-35
❑ 68Top-35
❑ 70DadCoo-13
❑ 70EssPowPla-147
❑ 70OPC-164
❑ 70SarProSta-79
❑ 71TorSun-108
❑ 72OPC-307
❑ 94ParMisL-87
**Cahill, Chris**
❑ 95AlaGolKin-4
**Cahill, Darcy**
❑ 87KinCan-16
❑ 907thInnSOHL-204
❑ 94HumHawP-15
**Cahoon, Jim**
❑ 77NovScoV-5
**Cain, Aaron**
❑ 91AirCanSJHL-A39
❑ 92MPSPhoSJHL-23
**Cain, Dutch**
❑ 24C144ChaCig-10
❑ 24V130MapC-16
❑ 24V1452-35
**Cain, Herb**
❑ 34BeeGro1P-191
❑ 34SweCap-16
❑ 35OPCV304C-77
❑ 36OPCV304D-110
❑ 36V356WorG-46
❑ 37OPCV304E-172
❑ 38QuaOatP-6
❑ 39OPCV3011-42
**Cain, Kelly**
❑ 85LonKni-22
❑ 86KitRan-20
**Cain, Paul**
❑ 90RicRen-7
**Cairns, Eric**
❑ 917thInnSOHL-31
❑ 93DetJrRW-7
❑ 94BinRan-1
❑ 95BinRan-4
❑ 97Be A PPAD-28
❑ 97Be A PPAPD-28
❑ 97BeAPla-28
❑ 97BeAPlaAut-28
❑ 97Pac-301
❑ 97PacCop-301
❑ 97PacEmeGre-301
❑ 97PacIceB-301
❑ 97PacRed-301
❑ 97PacSil-301
**Cairns, Trevor**
❑ 93TacRoc-3
**Caissie, Jeremy**
❑ 917thInnSQMJHL-279
**Cajanek, Petr**
❑ 94CzeAPSE-202
❑ 94ParSE-SE214
❑ 94ParSEG-SE214
❑ 94UppDec-507
❑ 94UppDecEleIce-507
❑ 95CzeAPSE-46
**Calce, Luigi**
❑ 917thInnSOHL-282
❑ 93OweSouPla-4
**Calder, Frank**
❑ 83HalFP-B3
❑ 85HalFC-18
❑ 92HalFL-36
**Calder, Glenn**
❑ 91BriColJHL-79
❑ 92BriColJHL-98
**Calder, Kyle**
❑ 96RegPat-8
**Calder, Pierre**
❑ 907thInnSQMJHL-61
**Calder, Shane**
❑ 907thInnSWHL-73
❑ 90SasBla-13
❑ 917thInnSWHL-109
❑ 91SasBla-11
❑ 93SasBla-6
**Caldr, Vladimir**
❑ 94CzeAPSE-286
❑ 95CzeAPSE-51
❑ 96CzeAPSE-237
**Calen, Kenneth**
❑ 69SweHocS-225
❑ 71SweHocS-370
**Callahan, Gary**
❑ 84BelBul-24
❑ 86KitRan-24
❑ 88ProAHL-64
**Callahan, Greg**
❑ 96WheNai-20
**Callahan, Jack**
❑ 94KnoChe-14
❑ 95SigRooA-11
❑ 95SigRooAPC-11
**Callander, Drew**
❑ 79CanuRoyB-4
**Callander, Jock**
❑ 81RegPat-4
❑ 87PenKod-4
❑ 88ProIHL-44
❑ 90ProAHLIHL-371
❑ 91ProAHLCHL-291
❑ 92ProSet-175
❑ 93CleLum-13
❑ 93CleLumPos-4
❑ 93UppDec-10
❑ 95CleLum-8
❑ 95ColEdgI-115
❑ 96CleLum-7
**Callighen, Brett**
❑ 79OilPos-1
❑ 79OPC-315
❑ 80OPC-114
❑ 80PepCap-23
❑ 80Top-114
❑ 81OilRedR-18
❑ 81OPC-110
❑ 81OPCSti-212
❑ 81PosSta-20
❑ 82OPC-103
❑ 82PosCer-6
❑ 88OilTenAnn-50
**Callinan, Jeff**
❑ 91MinGolG-4
❑ 92MinGolG-5
❑ 93MinGolG-6
❑ 94MinGolG-7
❑ 95BirBul-18
**Caloun, Jan**
❑ 91UppDecCWJC-91
❑ 92Cla-38
❑ 95ColEdgI-144
❑ 95FinnSemWC-159
❑ 95Ima-23
❑ 95ImaGol-23
❑ 95ImaPlaPr-PR10
❑ 96ClaGol-38
❑ 96ColEdgFL-16
❑ 96KenTho-3
❑ 96Lea-217
❑ 96LeaPreP-217
❑ 96MetUni-173
❑ 96Pin-229
❑ 96PinArtP-229
❑ 96PinFoi-229
❑ 96PinPreS-229
❑ 96PinRinC-229
❑ 96Sum-187
❑ 96SumArtP-187
❑ 96SumIce-187
❑ 96SumMet-187
❑ 96SumPreS-187
❑ 96UppDec-195
**Calverly, Chris**
❑ 84VicCou-4
**Calvert, Jeff**
❑ 907thInnSWHL-159
❑ 917thInnSWHL-153
❑ 92TacRoc-4
❑ 93TacRoc-4
**Camazzola, Jim**
❑ 93SweSemWCS-212
❑ 98GerDELE-272
**Cambell, Terry**
❑ 94GerDELE-407
**Cambio, Chris**
❑ 89NasKni-4
**Cameron, Al**
❑ 77OPCNHL-48
❑ 77Top-48
❑ 78OPC-396
❑ 79JetPos-2
❑ 80JetPos-2
❑ 80PepCap-122
**Cameron, Angus**
❑ 34BeeGro1P-264
**Cameron, Craig**
❑ 72OPC-13
❑ 72Top-22
❑ 73OPC-42
❑ 73Top-147
❑ 74NHLActSta-166
❑ 74NHLActStaU-17
❑ 74OPCNHL-263
❑ 74Top-263
❑ 75OPCNHL-239
❑ 75Top-239
❑ 76OPCNHL-327
**Cameron, Dave**
❑ 81RocPos-3
❑ 82PosCer-11
❑ 96LetHur-2
❑ 98BowCHL-141
❑ 98BowCHLAuB-A29
❑ 98BowCHLAuG-A29
❑ 98BowCHLAuS-A29
❑ 98BowCHLGA-141
❑ 98BowCHLOI-141
❑ 98BowChrC-141
❑ 98BowChrCGA-141
❑ 98BowChrCGAR-141
❑ 98BowChrCOI-141
❑ 98BowChrCOIR-141
❑ 98BowChrCR-141
**Cameron, Harry**
❑ 83HalFP-G4
❑ 85HalFC-95
**Cameron, Julian**
❑ 907thInnSMC-52
**Cameron, Malcolm**
❑ 93HunBli-6
❑ 96ForWorF-1
**Cameron, Randy**
❑ 83BraWheK-22
❑ 84KelWin-7
**Cammock, Dave**
❑ 917thInnSWHL-36
**Campbell, Angus**
❑ 10C56-9
❑ 83HalFP-I4
❑ 85HalFC-125
**Campbell, Bill**
❑ 86SheCan-9
**Campbell, Brian**
❑ 95Sla-275
❑ 98BowCHL-23
❑ 98BowCHLGA-23
❑ 98BowCHLOI-23
❑ 98BowChrC-23
❑ 98BowChrCGA-23
❑ 98BowChrCGAR-23
❑ 98BowChrCOI-23
❑ 98BowChrCOIR-23
❑ 98BowChrCR-23
**Campbell, Bryan**
❑ 69OPC-106
❑ 70BlaBor-2
❑ 70EssPowPla-120
❑ 71OPC-214
❑ 71TorSun-64
❑ 73OPCWHAP-19
❑ 73QuaOatWHA-13
❑ 74OPCWHA-6
❑ 75OPCWHA-31
❑ 75StiKah-2
❑ 76OPCWHA-16
❑ 77OPCWHA-22
**Campbell, Cameron**
❑ 92BriColJHL-28
**Campbell, Cassie**
❑ 94ClaWomOH-W5
❑ 97ColCho-281
❑ 97EssOlyHH-59
❑ 97EssOlyHHF-59
**Campbell, Clarence**
❑ 83HalFP-A3
❑ 85HalFC-4
**Campbell, Colin**
❑ 74PenPos-4
❑ 75OPCNHL-346
❑ 76OPCNHL-372
❑ 76RocCokCan-3
❑ 76RocPucBuc-4
❑ 77PenPucB-6
❑ 78OPC-269
❑ 79OilPos-2
❑ 79OPC-339
❑ 80CanuSilD-7
❑ 80CanuTeal-7
❑ 80OPC-380
❑ 80PepCap-106
❑ 81CanuSilD-14
❑ 81CanuTeal-6
❑ 81OPC-333
❑ 82OPC-82
❑ 83OPC-119
❑ 84OPC-51
❑ 84Top-39
❑ 88OilTenAnn-123
**Campbell, Earl**
❑ 24C144ChaCig-11
**Campbell, Ed**
❑ 96BinRan-5
**Campbell, Jason**
❑ 93OweSouPla-5
❑ 95Sla-292
**Campbell, Jim**
❑ 917thInnSQMJHL-209
❑ 91AreDraPic-21
❑ 91Cla-25
❑ 91StaPicH-62
❑ 91UltDra-19
❑ 91UppDecCWJC-71
❑ 92UppDec-605
❑ 93Pow-499
❑ 93StaCluTUSA-2
❑ 93TopPreTUSA-17
❑ 93Ult-479
❑ 94ClaProPIA-IA12
❑ 94ClaProPIH-LP1
❑ 94FreCan-7
❑ 95FreCan-5
❑ 96BeAPLH-7A
❑ 96BeAPLHAut-7A
❑ 96BeAPLHAutSil-7A
❑ 96ColCho-360
❑ 96DonCanI-132
❑ 96DonCanIGPP-132
❑ 96DonCanIRPP-132
❑ 96DonEli-142
❑ 96DonEliAsp-7
❑ 96DonEliDCS-142
❑ 96Fla-123
❑ 96FlaBlul-123
❑ 96HocGreC-22
❑ 96HocGreCG-22
❑ 96LeaPre-147
❑ 96LeaPrePP-147
❑ 96PinMin-30
❑ 96PinMinB-30
❑ 96PinMinCoiB-30
❑ 96PinMinCoiGP-30
❑ 96PinMinCoiN-30
❑ 96PinMinCoiS-30
❑ 96PinMinCoiSG-30
❑ 96PinMinG-30
❑ 96PinMinS-30
❑ 96SelCer-106
❑ 96SelCerAP-106
❑ 96SelCerBlu-106
❑ 96SelCerMB-106
❑ 96SelCerMG-106
❑ 96SelCerMR-106
❑ 96SelCerRed-106
❑ 96SP-187
❑ 96Ult-144
❑ 96UltGolM-144
❑ 96UltRoo-4
❑ 96UppDec-328
❑ 96UppDecBD-142
❑ 96UppDecBDG-142
❑ 96UppDecIce-64
❑ 96UppDecIcePar-64
❑ 96Zen-129
❑ 96ZenArtP-129
❑ 97ColCho-228
❑ 97Don-111
❑ 97DonCanI-9
❑ 97DonCanIDS-9
❑ 97DonCanIPS-9
❑ 97DonEli-78
❑ 97DonEliAsp-78
❑ 97DonEliS-78
❑ 97DonLim-51
❑ 97DonLim-67
❑ 97DonLim-99
❑ 97DonLimExp-51
❑ 97DonLimExp-67
❑ 97DonLimExp-99
❑ 97DonPre-98
❑ 97DonPreCttC-98
❑ 97DonPreProG-111
❑ 97DonPreProS-111
❑ 97DonPri-94
❑ 97DonPriSoA-94
❑ 97Kat-127
❑ 97KatGol-127
❑ 97KatSil-127
❑ 97Lea-54
❑ 97LeaFraMat-54
❑ 97LeaFraMDC-54
❑ 97LeaInt-54
❑ 97LeaIntUI-54
❑ 97Pac-332
❑ 97PacCop-332
❑ 97PacCroR-113
❑ 97PacCroREG-113
❑ 97PacCroRIB-113
❑ 97PacCroRS-113
❑ 97PacDyn-105
❑ 97PacDyn-143
❑ 97PacDynC-105
❑ 97PacDynC-143
❑ 97PacDynDD-14A
❑ 97PacDynDG-105
❑ 97PacDynDG-143
❑ 97PacDynEG-105
❑ 97PacDynEG-143
❑ 97PacDynIB-105
❑ 97PacDynIB-143
❑ 97PacDynR-105
❑ 97PacDynR-143
❑ 97PacDynSil-105
❑ 97PacDynSil-143
❑ 97PacDynTan-18
❑ 97PacDynTan-58
❑ 97PacEmeGre-332
❑ 97PacIceB-332
❑ 97PacInv-117
❑ 97PacInvC-117
❑ 97PacInvEG-117
❑ 97PacInvFP-30
❑ 97PacInvIB-117
❑ 97PacInvR-117
❑ 97PacInvS-117
❑ 97PacOme-189
❑ 97PacOmeC-189
❑ 97PacOmeDG-189
❑ 97PacOmeEG-189
❑ 97PacOmeG-189
❑ 97PacOmeIB-189
❑ 97PacPar-155
❑ 97PacParC-155
❑ 97PacParDG-155
❑ 97PacParEG-155
❑ 97PacParIB-155
❑ 97PacParRed-155
❑ 97PacParSil-155
❑ 97PacRed-332
❑ 97PacRev-117
❑ 97PacRevC-117
❑ 97PacRevE-117
❑ 97PacRevIB-117
❑ 97PacRevR-117
❑ 97PacRevS-117
❑ 97PacSil-332
❑ 97Pin-130
❑ 97PinCer-52
❑ 97PinCerMB-52
❑ 97PinCerMG-52
❑ 97PinCerMR-52
❑ 97PinCerR-52
❑ 97PinIns-66
❑ 97PinInsCC-66
❑ 97PinInsEC-66
❑ 97PinPrePBB-130
❑ 97PinPrePBC-130
❑ 97PinPrePBM-130
❑ 97PinPrePBY-130
❑ 97PinPrePFC-130
❑ 97PinPrePFM-130
❑ 97PinPrePFY-130
❑ 97PinPrePla-130
❑ 97PinTotCMPG-52
❑ 97PinTotCPB-52
❑ 97PinTotCPG-52
❑ 97PinTotCPR-52
❑ 97Sco-215
❑ 97ScoBlu-4
❑ 97ScoBluPla-4
❑ 97ScoBluPre-4
❑ 97SPAut-137
❑ 97Stu-34
❑ 97StuPrePG-34
❑ 97StuPrePS-34
❑ 97UppDec-143
❑ 97UppDecGDM-143
❑ 97UppDecIce-13
❑ 97UppDecIceP-13
❑ 97UppDecIPS-13
❑ 97UppDecSG-SG46
❑ 97UppDecTSS-15A
❑ 98Be A PPA-125
❑ 98Be A PPAA-125
❑ 98Be A PPAAF-125
❑ 98Be A PPTBASG-125
❑ 98Be APG-125
❑ 98Fin-118
❑ 98FinNo P-118
❑ 98FinNo PR-118
❑ 98FinRef-118
❑ 98Pac-362
❑ 98PacAur-158
❑ 98PacCroR-113
❑ 98PacCroRLS-113
❑ 98PacDynI-155
❑ 98PacDynIIB-155
❑ 98PacDynIR-155
❑ 98PacIceB-362
❑ 98PacPar-198
❑ 98PacParC-198
❑ 98PacParEG-198
❑ 98PacParH-198
❑ 98PacParIB-198
❑ 98PacParS-198
❑ 98PacRed-362
❑ 98UC-189
❑ 98UD ChoPCR-189
❑ 98UD ChoR-189
❑ 98UppDec-178
❑ 98UppDecE-178
❑ 98UppDecE1o1-178
❑ 98UppDecGR-178
❑ 98UppDecM-183
❑ 98UppDecMGS-183
❑ 98UppDecMSS-183
❑ 98UppDecMSS-183
**Campbell, Ken**
❑ 66TulOil-1
**Campbell, Peter**
❑ 96SudWol-5
❑ 96SudWolP-7
❑ 97SudWolP-4
**Campbell, Ryan**
❑ 94GuiFla-13
❑ 95GuiFla-5
❑ 96GuiFla-5
❑ 97GuiFla-6
**Campbell, Scott**
❑ 78JetPos-2
❑ 79JetPos-3
❑ 80JetPos-3
❑ 80PepCap-123
❑ 897thInnSOHL-103
❑ 907thInnSOHL-355
❑ 917thInnSOHL-201
❑ 93MusFur-13
❑ 94GerDELE-7
❑ 94MusFur-6
❑ 95GerDELE-4
❑ 96GerDELE-4
**Campbell, Spiff**
❑ 24V1452-8
**Campbell, Terry**
❑ 96GerDELE-16
**Campbell, Wade**
❑ 82Jet-4
❑ 83Jet-4
❑ 83OPC-382
❑ 83Vac-124
❑ 84OPC-336
❑ 86MonGolF-16
❑ 89ProAHL-130
❑ 90ProAHLIHL-221
**Campeau, Christian**
❑ 907thInnSQMJHL-72
❑ 917thInnSQMJHL-35
**Campeau, Jason**
❑ 917thInnSOHL-152
❑ 91OshGen-17
❑ 91OshGenS-25
❑ 92OshGenS-25
❑ 93NorBayC-7
❑ 94NorBayC-8
**Campeau, Tod**
❑ 44BeeGro2P-226
❑ 45QuaOatP-66
❑ 51LavDaiQSHL-43
❑ 52St.LawS-77
**Campese, Bruno**
❑ 95SweGloWC-227
❑ 96GerDELE-2
❑ 96SweSemW-175
**Canale, Joe**
❑ 907thInnSQMJHL-43
❑ 917thInnSCHLAW-27
❑ 917thInnSMC-46
❑ 917thInnSQMJHL-97
❑ 96SarSti-5
**Canderyd, Stefan**
❑ 71SweHocS-331
❑ 72SweHocS-147
❑ 74SweHocS-209
**Cannon, Jason**
❑ 95Sla-15
**Cantu, Kris**
❑ 94NorBayC-13
❑ 95Sla-219
❑ 96SeaThu-31
**Capek, Ivo**
❑ 94CzeAPSE-71
❑ 95CzeAPSE-269
❑ 96CzeAPSE-311
**Capel, John**
❑ 82NorBayC-2
❑ 83NorBayC-5
**Capello, Jeff**
❑ 88ProAHL-262
**Capla, Boris**
❑ 94GerDELE-391
**Caplette, Guy**
❑ 88RivDu R-8
**Caplice, Shawn**
❑ 907thInnSOHL-28
❑ 917thInnSOHL-223
❑ 92Ott672A-5
**Capprini, Joe**
❑ 91RicRen-13
**Caprice, Frank**
❑ 81FreExp-13
❑ 82FreExp-13
❑ 83FreExp-2
❑ 84Canu-5
❑ 85Canu-4
❑ 86Canu-3
❑ 86FreExp-4
❑ 87CanuSheOil-7
❑ 87PanSti-339
❑ 89ProAHL-72
**Capson, Greg**
❑ 92GreMon-17
❑ 93GreMon-4
**Capuano, Dave**
❑ 89ProIHL-145
❑ 90CanuMoh-5
❑ 90OPC-170
❑ 90ProSet-543
❑ 90ScoRoo-105T
❑ 90Top-170
❑ 90TopTif-170
❑ 91Bow-323
❑ 91CanuPanTS-6
❑ 91OPC-318
❑ 91PanSti-41
❑ 91ProSet-237
❑ 91ProSetFre-237
❑ 91ScoAme-86
❑ 91ScoCan-86
❑ 91StaClu-53
❑ 91Top-318
❑ 91UppDec-202
❑ 91UppDecF-202
**Capuano, Jack**
❑ 88ProAHL-232
❑ 91ProAHLCHL-55
❑ 95TalTigS-23
**Caputo, Dino**
❑ 89VicCou-5
❑ 907thInnSWHL-245
**Caravaggio, Luciano**
❑ 93MicTecH-21
**Carbonneau, Guy**
❑ 82CanaPos-3
❑ 82CanaSte-2
❑ 83CanaPos-3
❑ 83OPC-185

❑ 83OPCSti-180
❑ 83Vac-41
❑ 84CanaPos-1
❑ 84CanaPos-2
❑ 84OPC-257
❑ 84OPCSti-160
❑ 857ECreCar-10
❑ 85CanaPla-1
❑ 85CanaPla-7
❑ 85CanaPos-4
❑ 85CanaPro-1
❑ 85OPC-233
❑ 85OPCSti-135
❑ 86CanaPos-1
❑ 86KraDra-5
❑ 86OPC-176
❑ 86OPCSti-7
❑ 86Top-176
❑ 87CanaPos-2
❑ 87CanaVacS-14
❑ 87CanaVacS-15
❑ 87CanaVacS-16
❑ 87CanaVacS-21
❑ 87CanaVacS-23
❑ 87CanaVacS-62
❑ 87CanaVacS-63
❑ 87OPC-232
❑ 87OPCSti-7
❑ 87PanSti-64
❑ 87ProAll-2
❑ 88CanaPos-3
❑ 88OPC-203
❑ 88OPCMin-4
❑ 88OPCSti-41
❑ 88OPCSti-209
❑ 88PanSti-256
❑ 88PanSti-407
❑ 89CanaKra-2
❑ 89CanaPos-3
❑ 89CanaProF-21
❑ 89Kra-19
❑ 89OPC-53
❑ 89OPCSti-48
❑ 89OPCSti-213
❑ 89PanSti-241
❑ 89PanSti-381
❑ 89Top-53
❑ 90Bow-44
❑ 90BowTif-44
❑ 90CanaPos-5
❑ 90OPC-93
❑ 90PanSti-58
❑ 90ProSet-146
❑ 90Sco-91
❑ 90ScoCan-91
❑ 90ScoHotRS-43
❑ 90Top-93
❑ 90TopTif-93
❑ 90UppDec-188
❑ 90UppDecF-188
❑ 91Bow-338
❑ 91CanaPanTS-2
❑ 91CanaPos-4
❑ 91Kra-79
❑ 91OPC-54
❑ 91OPCPre-152
❑ 91PanSti-197
❑ 91Par-92
❑ 91Par-466
❑ 91ParFre-92
❑ 91ParFre-466
❑ 91Pin-130
❑ 91Pin-374
❑ 91PinFre-130
❑ 91PinFre-374
❑ 91ProSet-130
❑ 91ProSet-345
❑ 91ProSet-576
❑ 91ProSetFre-130
❑ 91ProSetFre-345
❑ 91ProSetFre-576
❑ 91ProSetPC-15
❑ 91ProSetPla-63
❑ 91ScoAme-19
❑ 91ScoCan-19
❑ 91StaClu-41
❑ 91Top-54
❑ 91UppDec-265
❑ 91UppDecF-265
❑ 92Bow-38
❑ 92CanaPos-4
❑ 92DurPan-1
❑ 92OPC-206
❑ 92PanSti-149
❑ 92PanStiFre-149
❑ 92Par-485
❑ 92Par-508
❑ 92ParEmel-485
❑ 92ParEmel-508
❑ 92Pin-43
❑ 92PinFre-43
❑ 92ProSet-88
❑ 92ProSetAW-CC5
❑ 92Sco-269
❑ 92Sco-524
❑ 92ScoCan-269
❑ 92ScoCan-524
❑ 92StaClu-260
❑ 92StaClu-289
❑ 92Top-125
❑ 92TopGol-125G
❑ 92Ult-102
❑ 92UltAwaW-3
❑ 92UppDec-260
❑ 92UppDec-439
❑ 93CanaMol-3
❑ 93CanaPos-4
❑ 93Don-450
❑ 93DurSco-9
❑ 93Kra-47
❑ 93OPCCanHF-9
❑ 93OPCPre-250
❑ 93OPCPreG-250
❑ 93PanSti-19
❑ 93Par-372
❑ 93ParEmel-372
❑ 93Pin-280
❑ 93Pin2HS-280
❑ 93PinCan-280
❑ 93PinCap-12
❑ 93PinCapC-12
❑ 93Pow-126
❑ 93Sco-51
❑ 93ScoCan-51
❑ 93StaClu-1
❑ 93StaCluFDI-1
❑ 93StaCluFDIO-1
❑ 93StaCluO-1
❑ 93TopPre-250
❑ 93TopPreG-250
❑ 93Ult-350
❑ 93UppDecNR-9
❑ 94BeAPla-R67
❑ 94BeAPSig-106
❑ 94Lea-23
❑ 94OPCPre-282
❑ 94OPCPreSE-282
❑ 94ParSE-SE155
❑ 94ParSEG-SE155
❑ 94Pin-372
❑ 94PinArtP-372
❑ 94PinRinC-372
❑ 94Sco-46
❑ 94ScoGol-46
❑ 94ScoPla-46
❑ 94ScoPlaTS-46
❑ 94StaClu-174
❑ 94StaCluFDI-174
❑ 94StaCluMOMS-174
❑ 94StaCluSTWC-174
❑ 94TopPre-282
❑ 94TopPreSE-282
❑ 94UppDec-122
❑ 94UppDecElelce-122
❑ 95ColCho-302
❑ 95ColChoPC-302
❑ 95ColChoPCP-302
❑ 95ParInt-332
❑ 95ParIntEl-332
❑ 95Pin-144
❑ 95PinArtP-144
❑ 95PinRinC-144
❑ 95Sco-280
❑ 95ScoBlaIce-280
❑ 95ScoBlaIceAP-280
❑ 95StaCluM-M12
❑ 95Ult-228
❑ 95UppDec-273
❑ 95UppDecElelce-273
❑ 95UppDecElelceG-273
❑ 96ColCho-73
❑ 96StaPos-4
❑ 97Be A PPAD-194
❑ 97Be A PPAPD-194
❑ 97BeAPla-194
❑ 97BeAPlaAut-194
❑ 97Pac-292
❑ 97PacCop-292
❑ 97PacEmeGre-292
❑ 97PacIceB-292
❑ 97PacRed-292
❑ 97PacSil-292
❑ 98Be A PPA-39
❑ 98Be A PPAA-39
❑ 98Be A PPAAF-39
❑ 98Be A PPTBASG-39
❑ 98Be APG-39
❑ 98O-PChr-106
❑ 98O-PChrR-106
❑ 98Pac-173
❑ 98PacIceB-173
❑ 98PacRed-173
❑ 98Top-106
❑ 98TopO-P-106

**Cardarelli, Joe**
❑ 95SpoChi-21

**Cardiff, Jim**
❑ 73QuaOatWHA-31

**Cardiff, Mark**
❑ 907thInnSOHL-256

**Cardinal, Carson**
❑ 91AirCanSJHL-E5
❑ 92MPSPhoSJHL-13

**Cardinal, Curtis**
❑ 93RedDeeR-3

**Cardinal, Eric**
❑ 907thInnSQMJHL-110
❑ 917thInnSQMJHL-232

**Cardinal, Reg**
❑ 93MaiBlaB-59

**Cardwell, Justin**
❑ 93WesMic-6

**Careau, Sylvain**
❑ 917thInnSQMJHL-93

**Carey, Jason**
❑ 917thInnSWHL-285

**Carey, Jim**
❑ 94Fle-233
❑ 94PorPir-4
❑ 94SP-128
❑ 94SPDieCut-128
❑ 95BeAPla-189
❑ 95BeAPSig-S189
❑ 95BeAPSigDC-S189
❑ 95Bow-74
❑ 95BowAllFoi-74
❑ 95CanGamNHLP-28
❑ 95CanGamNHLP-287
❑ 95Cap-4
❑ 95ColCho-30
❑ 95ColCho-369
❑ 95ColCho-375
❑ 95ColChoPC-30
❑ 95ColChoPC-369
❑ 95ColChoPC-375
❑ 95ColChoPCP-30
❑ 95ColChoPCP-369
❑ 95ColChoPCP-375
❑ 95ColEdgI-52
❑ 95ColEdgIC-C5
❑ 95ColEdgIQ-IR8
❑ 95ColEdgITW-G7
❑ 95Don-189
❑ 95DonBetTP-6
❑ 95DonDom-4
❑ 95DonEli-69
❑ 95DonEliDCS-69
❑ 95DonEliDCU-69
❑ 95DonEliPW-10
❑ 95DonRooTea-1
❑ 95Emo-186
❑ 95EmoXci-19
❑ 95Fin-66
❑ 95FinRef-66
❑ 95Ima-4
❑ 95Ima-99
❑ 95ImaCleE-CE4
❑ 95ImaGol-4
❑ 95ImaGol-99
❑ 95ImaPlaPr-PR2
❑ 95ImpSti-131
❑ 95Kra-20
❑ 95Lea-78
❑ 95LeaFreFra-1
❑ 95LeaGolS-1
❑ 95LeaLim-55
❑ 95LeaLimSS-1
❑ 95LeaStuR-1
❑ 95McDPin-MCD-40
❑ 95Met-157
❑ 95NHLAcePC-6S
❑ 95ParInt-492
❑ 95ParIntCCGS1-16
❑ 95ParIntCCSS1-16
❑ 95ParIntEl-492
❑ 95ParIntGP-5
❑ 95ParIntPTP-PP36
❑ 95Pin-138
❑ 95PinArtP-138
❑ 95PinFan-20
❑ 95PinMas-3
❑ 95PinRinC-138
❑ 95PinRoa2-9
❑ 95PlaOneoOne-104
❑ 95PlaOneoOne-213
❑ 95ProMag-32
❑ 95Sco-78
❑ 95Sco-317
❑ 95ScoBlaIce-78
❑ 95ScoBlaIce-317
❑ 95ScoBlaIceAP-78
❑ 95ScoBlaIceAP-317
❑ 95ScoDreTea-12
❑ 95SelCer-12
❑ 95SelCerFut-2
❑ 95SelCerMG-12
❑ 95SelCerP-12
❑ 95SigRoo-44
❑ 95SigRooSig-44
❑ 95SkyImp-175
❑ 95SkyImp-228
❑ 95SkyImpD-2
❑ 95SP-156
❑ 95StaClu-115
❑ 95StaCluGTSC-GT6
❑ 95StaCluMO-48
❑ 95StaCluMOMS-115
❑ 95Sum-51
❑ 95SumArtP-51
❑ 95SumIce-51
❑ 95SumInTheCre-6
❑ 95Top-210
❑ 95Top-383
❑ 95TopMarMPB-383
❑ 95TopNewG-1NG
❑ 95TopOPCI-210
❑ 95TopOPCI-383
❑ 95TopSupSki-73
❑ 95TopSupSkiPla-73
❑ 95TopYouS-YS8
❑ 95Ult-173
❑ 95Ult-320
❑ 95Ult-368
❑ 95UltAllRoo-1
❑ 95UltAllRooGM-1
❑ 95UltGolM-173
❑ 95UltPrePadMen-4
❑ 95UltPrePadMenGM-4
❑ 95UppDec-344
❑ 95UppDecElelce-344
❑ 95UppDecElelceG-344
❑ 95UppDecFreFra-F20
❑ 95UppDecFreFraJ-F20
❑ 95UppDecPHE-H16
❑ 95UppDecSpeE-SE87
❑ 95UppDecSpeEdiG-SE87
❑ 95UppPreHV-H16
❑ 95Zen-5
❑ 95ZenZT-18
❑ 96BeAPStaTP-8
❑ 96ColCho-278
❑ 96ColCho-334
❑ 96ColChoSti-S17
❑ 96Don-33
❑ 96DonBetPip-3
❑ 96DonCanI-79
❑ 96DonCanIGPP-79
❑ 96DonCanIRPP-79
❑ 96DonDom-1
❑ 96DonEli-19
❑ 96DonEliDCS-19
❑ 96DonEliPW-3
❑ 96DonEliPW-P3
❑ 96DonPrePro-33
❑ 96Fla-98
❑ 96FlaBluI-98
❑ 96FlaHotG-3
❑ 96Fle-116
❑ 96Fle-144
❑ 96Fle-145
❑ 96Fle-146
❑ 96FlePicF5-6
❑ 96FlePicJE-12
❑ 96FleVez-3
❑ 96KraUppD-50
❑ 96Lea-68
❑ 96LeaLim-16
❑ 96LeaLimG-16
❑ 96LeaLimStu-5
❑ 96LeaPre-23
❑ 96LeaPreMM-1
❑ 96LeaPreP-68
❑ 96LeaPrePP-23
❑ 96LeaPreSG-21
❑ 96LeaPreSte-21
❑ 96LeaShuDow-10
❑ 96LeaSwe-9
❑ 96LeaSwe(-9
❑ 96MetUni-162
❑ 96MetUniAP-3
❑ 96MetUniAPSP-3
❑ 96MetUniIC-3
❑ 96MetUniICSP-3
❑ 96NHLACEPC-7
❑ 96NHLProSTA-32
❑ 96Pin-105
❑ 96PinArtP-105
❑ 96PinFoi-105
❑ 96PinMas-2
❑ 96PinMasDC-2
❑ 96PinMcD-32
❑ 96PinMin-28
❑ 96PinMinB-28
❑ 96PinMinCoiB-28
❑ 96PinMinCoiGP-28
❑ 96PinMinCoiN-28
❑ 96PinMinCoiS-28
❑ 96PinMinCoiSG-28
❑ 96PinMinG-28
❑ 96PinMinS-28
❑ 96PinPreS-105
❑ 96PinRinC-105
❑ 96PinTro-5
❑ 96PlaOneoOne-426
❑ 96Sco-74
❑ 96ScoArtPro-74
❑ 96ScoDeaCAP-74
❑ 96ScoGolB-74
❑ 96ScoNetW-3
❑ 96ScoSpeAP-74
❑ 96ScoSudDea-2
❑ 96SelCer-29
❑ 96SelCerAP-29
❑ 96SelCerBlu-29
❑ 96SelCerFre-3
❑ 96SelCerMB-29
❑ 96SelCerMG-29
❑ 96SelCerMR-29
❑ 96SelCerRed-29
❑ 96SkyImp-137
❑ 96SkyImpZH-3
❑ 96SP-164
❑ 96SPGamFil-GF13
❑ 96SPx-48
❑ 96SPxGol-48
❑ 96Sum-94
❑ 96SumArtP-94
❑ 96SumIce-94
❑ 96SumInTheCre-6
❑ 96SumInTheCrePS-6
❑ 96SumMet-94
❑ 96SumPreS-94
❑ 96SumUnt-94
❑ 96SweSemW-157
❑ 96SweSemWSG-SG5
❑ 96TeaOut-68
❑ 96TopNHLP-13
❑ 96TopPicID-ID9
❑ 96TopPicOI-13
❑ 96Ult-174
❑ 96UltCleThelce-1
❑ 96UltGolM-174
❑ 96UppDec-174
❑ 96UppDecBD-147
❑ 96UppDecBDG-147
❑ 96UppDecIce-72
❑ 96UppDecIcePar-72
❑ 96UppDecSS-SS14A
❑ 96Zen-7
❑ 96ZenArtP-7
❑ 96ZenZT-15
❑ 97ColCho-17
❑ 97ColChoSta-SQ57
❑ 97Don-22
❑ 97DonCanI-59
❑ 97DonCanIDS-59
❑ 97DonCanIPS-59
❑ 97DonLim-14
❑ 97DonLim-131
❑ 97DonLimExp-14
❑ 97DonLimExp-131
❑ 97DonLimFOTG-54
❑ 97DonPre-43
❑ 97DonPreCG-13
❑ 97DonPreCGP-13
❑ 97DonPreCttC-43
❑ 97DonPreProG-22
❑ 97DonPreProS-22
❑ 97Kat-9
❑ 97KatGol-9
❑ 97KatSil-9
❑ 97Lea-71
❑ 97Lea-P10
❑ 97LeaFraMat-71
❑ 97LeaFraMDC-71
❑ 97LeaInt-71
❑ 97LeaIntUI-71
❑ 97LeaPipDre-10
❑ 97Pac-23
❑ 97PacCop-23
❑ 97PacDyn-8
❑ 97PacDynBKS-6
❑ 97PacDynC-8
❑ 97PacDynDD-2B
❑ 97PacDynDG-8
❑ 97PacDynEG-8
❑ 97PacDynIB-8
❑ 97PacDynR-8
❑ 97PacDynSil-8
❑ 97PacDynSto-2
❑ 97PacDynTan-17
❑ 97PacEmeGre-23
❑ 97PacIceB-23
❑ 97PacInv-8
❑ 97PacInvC-8
❑ 97PacInvEG-8
❑ 97PacInvIB-8
❑ 97PacInvNRB-11
❑ 97PacInvR-8
❑ 97PacInvS-8
❑ 97PacPar-10
❑ 97PacParC-10
❑ 97PacParDG-10
❑ 97PacParEG-10
❑ 97PacParIB-10
❑ 97PacParRed-10
❑ 97PacParSil-10
❑ 97PacRed-23
❑ 97PacSil-23
❑ 97Pin-83
❑ 97PinArtP-83
❑ 97PinCer-15
❑ 97PinCerMB-15
❑ 97PinCerMG-15
❑ 97PinCerMR-15
❑ 97PinCerR-15
❑ 97PinIns-62
❑ 97PinInsCC-62
❑ 97PinInsEC-62
❑ 97PinInsSto-7
❑ 97PinInsSUG-3A/B
❑ 97PinInsSUG-3C/D
❑ 97PinPrePBB-83
❑ 97PinPrePBC-83
❑ 97PinPrePBM-83
❑ 97PinPrePBY-83
❑ 97PinPrePFC-83
❑ 97PinPrePFM-83
❑ 97PinPrePFY-83
❑ 97PinPrePla-83
❑ 97PinRinC-83
❑ 97PinTotCMPG-15
❑ 97PinTotCPB-15
❑ 97PinTotCPG-15
❑ 97PinTotCPR-15
❑ 97Sco-14
❑ 97ScoArtPro-14
❑ 97ScoBru-2
❑ 97ScoBruPla-2
❑ 97ScoBruPre-2
❑ 97ScoGolBla-14
❑ 97ScoNetW-2
❑ 97Stu-45
❑ 97StuPrePG-45
❑ 97StuPrePS-45

**Carignan, Patrick**
❑ 917thInnSQMJHL-160

**Caris, Ingemar**
❑ 65SweCorl-167
❑ 67SweHoc-284
❑ 69SweHocS-331
❑ 70SweHocS-243
❑ 71SweHocS-302

**Carkner, Terry**
❑ 87NordGenF-4
❑ 89FlyPos-4
❑ 89OPC-3
❑ 89PanSti-297
❑ 89Top-3
❑ 90FlyPos-4
❑ 90OPC-381
❑ 90PanSti-114
❑ 90ProSet-212
❑ 90Sco-47
❑ 90ScoCan-47
❑ 90Top-381
❑ 90TopTif-381
❑ 90UppDec-398
❑ 90UppDecF-398
❑ 91Bow-232
❑ 91FlyJCP-4
❑ 91OPC-291
❑ 91PanSti-235
❑ 91Par-342
❑ 91ParFre-342
❑ 91Pin-51
❑ 91PinFre-51
❑ 91ProSet-173
❑ 91ProSetFre-173
❑ 91ProSetPla-212
❑ 91ScoAme-64
❑ 91ScoCan-64
❑ 91StaClu-219
❑ 91Top-291
❑ 91UppDec-204
❑ 91UppDecF-204
❑ 92Bow-129
❑ 92FlyJCP-7
❑ 92FlyUppDS-15
❑ 92FlyUppDS-25
❑ 92FlyUppDS-38
❑ 92OPC-180
❑ 92PanSti-190
❑ 92PanStiFre-190
❑ 92Par-362
❑ 92ParEmel-362
❑ 92Pin-63
❑ 92PinFre-63
❑ 92ProSet-269
❑ 92Sco-66
❑ 92ScoCan-66
❑ 92StaClu-463
❑ 92Top-465
❑ 92TopGol-465G
❑ 92Ult-370
❑ 93Don-422
❑ 93OPCPre-152
❑ 93OPCPreG-152
❑ 93PanSti-54
❑ 93Par-332
❑ 93ParEmel-332
❑ 93Pin-286
❑ 93PinCan-286
❑ 93Pow-328
❑ 93Sco-233
❑ 93Sco-508
❑ 93ScoCan-233
❑ 93ScoCan-508
❑ 93ScoGol-508
❑ 93StaClu-252
❑ 93StaCluFDI-252
❑ 93StaCluO-252
❑ 93TopPre-152
❑ 93TopPreG-152
❑ 93Ult-304
❑ 94BeAPla-R167
❑ 94BeAPSig-144
❑ 94OPCPre-359
❑ 94OPCPreSE-359
❑ 94Par-69
❑ 94ParGol-69
❑ 94Pin-221
❑ 94PinArtP-221
❑ 94PinRinC-221
❑ 94TopPre-359
❑ 94TopPreSE-359
❑ 94UppDec-467
❑ 94UppDecElelce-467
❑ 95ColCho-113
❑ 95ColChoPC-113
❑ 95ColChoPCP-113
❑ 95ParInt-354
❑ 95ParIntEl-354
❑ 95UppDec-286
❑ 95UppDecElelce-286
❑ 95UppDecElelceG-286
❑ 96ColCho-109
❑ 97Be A PPAD-195
❑ 97Be A PPAPD-195
❑ 97BeAPla-195
❑ 97BeAPlaAut-195
❑ 97PacInvNRB-84
❑ 97UppDec-283
❑ 98Be A PPA-207
❑ 98Be A PPAA-207
❑ 98Be A PPAAF-207
❑ 98Be A PPSE-207
❑ 98Be APG-207

**Carlberg, Anders**
❑ 65SweCorl-138B

**Carleton, Wayne**
❑ 67Top-77
❑ 68PosCerM-4
❑ 68ShiCoi-160
❑ 69MapLeaWBG-3
❑ 69OPC-184
❑ 70BruPos-8
❑ 70BruTealss-11
❑ 70EssPowPla-62
❑ 70OPC-9
❑ 70SarProSta-6
❑ 70Top-9
❑ 70TopStiS-3
❑ 71LetActR-18
❑ 71OPC-178
❑ 71SarProSta-131
❑ 71TorSun-43
❑ 72NatOttWHA-4
❑ 72OPC-337
❑ 72SluCupWHA-4
❑ 73OPCWHAP-8
❑ 74OPCWHA-45
❑ 75OPCWHA-43
❑ 91UltOriS-47
❑ 91UltOriSF-47

**Carlson, Don**
❑ 90ArilIce-4
❑ 91ArilIce-2

**Carlson, Jack**
❑ 80NorStaPos-4
❑ 81NorStaPos-5

**Carlson, Kent**
❑ 83CanaPos-4
❑ 83Vac-42
❑ 84CanaPos-3

**Carlson, Steve**
❑ 89JohChi-36
❑ 91JohChi-1

**Carlsson, Ake**
❑ 69SweHocS-39
❑ 71SweHocS-138
❑ 72SweHocS-125

**Carlsson, Anders**
❑ 83SweSemE-62
❑ 84SweSemE-239
❑ 85SwePanS-240
❑ 88DevCar-6
❑ 88ProAHL-339
❑ 89SweSemE-38
❑ 90SweSemE-185
❑ 91SweSemE-354
❑ 91SweSemWCS-48
❑ 92SweSemE-61
❑ 93SweSemE-48
❑ 94SweLeaE-210
❑ 95SweLeaE-236
❑ 95SweLeaEC-5
❑ 95SweUppDE-102

**Carlsson, Arne**
❑ 65SweCorl-168
❑ 67SweHoc-4
❑ 67SweHoc-285
❑ 69SweHocS-184
❑ 69SweHocS-332
❑ 69SweWorC-101
❑ 70SweHocS-133
❑ 70SweHocS-277
❑ 71SweHocS-7
❑ 71SweHocS-225
❑ 72SweHocS-213
❑ 72SweSemWC-50
❑ 73SweHocS-61
❑ 73SweWorCS-61
❑ 74SweHocS-162
❑ 74SweSemHVS-3

**Carlsson, Bjorn**
❑ 83SweSemE-94
❑ 84SweSemE-94
❑ 85SwePanS-83
❑ 86SwePanS-73
❑ 87SwePanS-14
❑ 89SweSemE-228
❑ 90SweSemE-65
❑ 91SweSemE-240

**Carlsson, Calle**
❑ 92UppDec-228

**Carlsson, Clarence**
❑ 65SweCorl-202
❑ 67SweHoc-151

**Carlsson, Hans**
❑ 65SweCorl-38B
❑ 65SweCorl-73
❑ 67SweHoc-183
❑ 69SweHocS-239
❑ 70SweHocS-137
❑ 71SweHocS-230
❑ 72SweHocS-218
❑ 73SweHocS-69
❑ 73SweWorCS-69
❑ 74SweHocS-210

**Carlsson, Jan**
❑ 83SweSemE-224

**Carlsson, Kurt**
❑ 73SweHocS-23
❑ 73SweWorCS-23
❑ 83SweSemE-242

**Carlsson, Leif**
❑ 83SweSemE-108
❑ 84SweSemE-108
❑ 85SwePanS-96
❑ 85SwePanS-233
❑ 86SwePanS-90
❑ 87SwePanS-94
❑ 89SweSemE-268
❑ 90SweSemE-29
❑ 91SweSemE-84
❑ 92SweSemE-106
❑ 93SweSemE-78
❑ 95SweLeaE-219
❑ 95SweUppDE-63
❑ 96GerDELE-29
❑ 98GerDELE-175

**Carlsson, Leif R.**
❑ 83SweSemE-209
❑ 84SweSemE-234

**Carlsson, Lennart**
❑ 69SweHocS-226
❑ 71SweHocS-371

**Carlsson, Nicklas**
❑ 86SwePanS-122

**Carlsson, Nils**
❑ 67SweHoc-134
❑ 69SweHocS-146
❑ 71SweHocS-350

**Carlsson, Per-Olof**

83SweSemE-141
84SweSemE-161
85SwePanS-146
86SwePanS-153
87SwePanS-163
89SweSemE-133
90SweSemE-212
91SweSemE-141
92SweSemE-168

**Carlsson, Roland**
94FinnSIS-79
95FinnSIS-5

**Carlsson, Rolf**
72SweHocS-139

**Carlsson, Stefan**
65SweCorl-81B

**Carlsson, Stig**
64SweCorl-64
65SweCorl-64
67SweHoc-184
69SweHocS-240

**Carlsson, Thomas**
64SweCorl-96
65SweCorl-96A
67SweHoc-62
69SweHocS-95
70SweHocS-51
70SweHocS-138
71SweHocS-118
71SweHocS-231
72SweHocS-98
72SweHocS-99
73SweHocS-211
73SweWorCS-211
74SweHocS-163
89SweSemE-224
91SweSemE-233
93SweSemE-249
94SweLeaE-129

**Carlstrom, P.A.**
65SweCorl-46

**Carlyle, Randy**
76MapLeaP-4
77MapLeaP-2
78OPC-312
79OPC-124
79Top-124
80OPC-367
81OPC-256
81OPCSti-183
81OPCSti-255
81PosSta-8
81Top-E112
82OPC-265
82OPC-266
82OPCSti-144
82PosCer-15
83OPC-278
83OPCSti-227
83PenCok-6
83PenHeiP-5
83PenTealP-7
83PufSti-12
84JetPol-5
84OPC-337
84OPCSti-291
84PenHeiP-5
85JetPol-4
85JetSilD-2
85OPC-57
85OPCSti-251
85Top-57
86JetBor-4
86KraDra-6
86OPC-144
86OPCSti-107
86Top-144
87Jet-4
87OPC-9
87OPCSti-248
87PanSti-360
87Top-9
88JetPol-3
88OPC-204
88OPCSti-148
88PanSti-149
89JetSaf-6
89Kra-47
89OPC-291
89OPCSti-143
89PanSti-168
90JetIGA-5
90OPC-51
90PanSti-314
90ProSet-325
90Sco-136
90ScoCan-136
90Top-51
90TopTif-51
90UppDec-331
90UppDecF-331
91Bow-199
91JetIGA-4
91JetPanTS-4
91OPC-72
91PanSti-76
91Par-418
91ParFre-418
91Pin-288
91PinFre-288
91ProSet-273
91ProSetFre-273
91ScoAme-125
91ScoCan-125
91StaClu-94
91Top-72
92Bow-287
92OPC-12
92Pin-87
92PinFre-87
92ProSet-265
92Sco-167
92ScoCan-167
92StaClu-332
92Top-147
92TopGol-147G
93OPCPre-86
93OPCPreG-86
93PinAllS-27
93PinAllSC-27
93TopPre-86
93TopPreG-86
95JetTealss-4

**Carlyle, Steve**
69SweHocS-352

**Carmichael, Bruce**
61UniOilW-5

**Carnazzola, Jimmy**
95SweGloWC-234

**Carnback, Patrik**
89SweSemE-276
90SweSemE-37
91SweSemE-287
91SweSemWCS-46
92FreCan-4
93ClaProPro-105
93Don-6
93OPCPre-379
93OPCPreG-379
93Par-8
93ParEmel-8
93Pow-281
93Sco-615
93ScoCan-615
93ScoGol-615
93StaClu-434
93StaCluFDI-434
93StaCluO-434
93SweSemWCS-43
93TopPre-379
93TopPreG-379
93Ult-251
93UppDec-463
94Don-29
94DucCarJr-1
94Fle-1
94Lea-102
94OPCFinIns-1
94Par-7
94ParGol-7
94ParVin-V28
94Pin-189
94PinArtP-189
94PinRinC-189
94StaClu-53
94StaCluFDI-53
94StaCluMOMS-53
94StaCluSTWC-53
94SweLeaE-270
94UppDec-475
94UppDecEleIce-475
95ColCho-42
95ColChoPC-42
95ColChoPCP-42
95FinnSemWC-74
95ParInt-1
95ParIntEl-1
95PlaOneoOne-111
95ProMag-41
95SweGloWC-41
95SweUppDE-241
95Top-335
95TopOPCI-335
95UppDec-180
95UppDecEleIce-180
95UppDecEleIceG-180
96GerDELE-359
96NHLProSTA-41
96SweSemW-63

**Carnegie, Herbie**
51LaVDaiQSHL-16
52St.LawS-53

**Carnelley, Todd**
84KamBla-5
85KamBla-5

**Carney, Keith**
91RochAmeKod-6
91RochAmePos-4
92Cla-102
92OPCPre-81
92Par-15
92ParEmel-15
92Pin-229
92ProSet-223
92Sco-461
92ScoCan-461
92Ult-13
92UppDec-402
93BlaCok-22
93Don-412
93UppDec-516
94FliGen-5
94Lea-359
94Par-50
94ParGol-50
94UppDec-449
94UppDecEleIce-449
95BeAPla-9
95BeAPSig-S9
95BeAPSigDC-S9
95UppDec-435
95UppDecEleIce-435
95UppDecEleIceG-435
96ClaGol-102
97PacInvNRB-41
97PacOme-47
97PacOmeC-47
97PacOmeDG-47
97PacOmeEG-47
97PacOmeIB-47
98UC-155
98UD ChoPCR-155
98UD ChoR-155
98UppDec-343
98UppDecE-343
98UppDecEc1o1-343
98UppDecGR-343
99Pac-316
99PacCop-316
99PacGol-316
99PacIceB-316
99PacPreD-316

**Caron, Alain**
72NordPos-5
72OPC-324
73NordTeal-6
73QuaOatWHA-38

**Caron, Christian**
917thInnSQMJHL-92

**Caron, Daniel**
77GraVic-3

**Caron, Jacques**
71BluPos-4
72BluWhiBor-1
72OPC-140
72OPCPlaC-18
72SarProSta-193
72Top-86
73CanuRoyB-3
89ProAHL-301
96Dev-NNO

**Caron, Martin**
907thInnSQMJHL-203

**Caron, Pat**
907thInnSMC-64

**Caron, Sebastien**
92QueIntP-15

**Carpano, Andrea**
93SauSteMG-1

**Carpenter, Bob (Bobby)**
81Cap-2
82Cap-3
82OPC-361
82OPCSti-154
82PosCer-20
83OPC-366
83OPCSti-206
83PufSti-20
84CapPizH-1
84OPC-194
84OPCSti-132
85CapPizH-1
85OPC-26
85OPCBoxB-C
85OPCSti-112
85Top-26
85TopBoxB-C
86CapPol-3
86OPC-150
86OPCSti-200
86Top-150
87OPC-30
87OPC-30
88KinSmo-3
88OPC-72
88OPCSti-153
88PanSti-74
88Top-72
89BruSpoA-5
89OPC-167
89PanSti-196
89SweSemWCS-168
89Top-167
90Bow-30
90BowTif-30
90BruSpoA-7
90OPC-139
90PanSti-7
90ProSet-4
90Sco-16
90ScoCan-16
90Top-139
90TopTif-139
90UppDec-158
90UppDecF-158
91BruSpoA-5
91OPC-404
91OPCPre-148
91PanSti-181
91Par-226
91ParFre-226
91Pin-99
91Pin-396
91PinFre-99
91PinFre-396
91ProSet-349
91ProSetFre-349
91ScoAme-162
91ScoCan-162
91StaClu-161
91Top-404
92Bow-10
92CapKod-5
92OPC-131
92OPCPre-78
92PanSti-140
92PanStiFre-140
92Pin-315
92PinFre-315
92Sco-142
92ScoCan-142
92StaClu-122
92Top-378
92TopGol-378G
92UppDec-478
93Lea-421
93OPCPre-413
93OPCPreG-413
93Sco-267
93Sco-578
93ScoCan-267
93ScoCan-578
93ScoGol-578
93StaClu-175
93StaCluFDI-175
93StaCluFDIO-175
93StaCluO-175
93TopPre-413
93TopPreG-413
94HocWit-68
94Lea-436
94ParSE-SE96
94ParSEG-SE96
94Pin-201
94PinArtP-201
94PinRinC-201
94StaClu-158
94StaCluFDI-158
94StaCluMOMS-158
94StaCluSTWC-158
95BeAPla-11
95BeAPSig-S11
95BeAPSigDC-S11
95Ult-188
95UltGolM-188
95UppDec-183
95UppDecEleIce-183
95UppDecEleIceG-183
96BeAPAut-125
96BeAPAutSil-125
96BeAPla-125
96Dev-19
97PacInvNRB-109
97ScoDev-18
97ScoDevPla-18
97ScoDevPre-18
98Be A PPA-228
98Be A PPAA-228
98Be A PPAAF-228
98Be A PPSE-228
98Be APG-228

**Carpenter, Doug**
84DevPos-NNO
88ProAHL-119
91ProAHLCHL-382

**Carpenter, Steven**
92NorMicW-2
93NorMicW-3
94NorBayC-9
95RicRen-12
95Sla-214

**Carper, Brandon**
95TolSto-3

**Carr, Allan**
95Sla-334

**Carr, Gene**
71TorSun-236
74NHLActSta-111
74OPCNHL-320
75OPCNHL-343
76OPCNHL-290
77OPCNHL-298
78OPC-14
78Top-14

**Carr, Lorne**
34BeeGro1P-218
34BeeGro1P-304
35DiaMatT2-7
35DiaMatT3-7
35DiaMatTI-9
36V356WorG-26
39OPCV3011-62
45QuaOatP-13

**Carr, Mike**
92Ott672A-6

**Carrie, Dave**
87SudWol-15
89SauSteMG-19

**Carrier, Mario**
93DruVol-26

**Carriere, Larry**
72OPC-282
73OPC-260
74NHLActSta-46
74OPCNHL-43
74Top-43
75OPCNHL-154
75Top-154
76OPCNHL-297
77CanuRoyB-2
77OPCNHL-304
78OPC-272
92SpoFla-2

**Carriere, Tom**
92WesMic-7
93WesMic-7

**Carrol, Lorne**
24CreFal-9

**Carroll, Billy**
83IslTealss-3
83OPC-5
84IslIsIN-4
84OilRedR-20
84OilTeal-2
85OPC-203
85OPCSti-224
88OilTenAnn-16

**Carroll, George**
24C144ChaCig-12
24V130MapC-20
24V1452-42

**Carroll, Greg**
79OPC-184
79Top-184

**Carroll, Ken**
94SarSti-2
95Sla-181

**Carruthers, Dwight**
69SeaTotW-18

**Carse, Bill**
34BeeGro1P-44
39OPCV3011-80

**Carse, Bob**
34BeeGro1P-45
45QuaOatP-67

**Carson, Davie**
93SeaThu-3

**Carson, Gerald**
33V252CanG-8
33V357IceK-24
34BeeGro1P-192
34DiaMatS-9
34SweCap-1
35DiaMatTI-10

**Carson, Jimmy**
86Kin20tATI-2
87KinTeal4-2
87OPC-92
87OPCMin-6
87OPCSti-126
87OPCSti-210
87PanSti-279
87Top-92
88OilTeal-5
88OilTenAnn-53
88OPC-9
88OPCMin-5
88OPCSti-158
88PanSti-75
88Top-9
89OPC-127
89OPCSti-222
89PanSti-72
89RedWinLC-3
89SweSemWCS-163
89Top-127
90Bow-229
90BowTif-229
90Kra-5
90OPC-231
90OPCPre-12
90PanSti-214
90ProSet-67
90Sco-64
90ScoCan-64
90ScoHotRS-28
90Top-231
90TopTif-231
90UppDec-132
90UppDecF-132
91Bow-52
91OPC-104
91OPCPre-167
91PanSti-139
91Par-43
91ParFre-43
91Pin-173
91PinFre-173
91ProSet-55
91ProSetFre-55
91ProSetPla-33
91RedWinLC-2
91ScoAme-224
91ScoCan-224
91StaClu-121
91SweSemWCS-150
91Top-104
91UppDec-161
91UppDecF-161
92Bow-108
92OPC-152
92PanSti-114
92PanStiFre-114
92Par-308
92ParEmel-308
92Pin-329
92PinFre-329
92Sco-9
92ScoCan-9
92ScoSha-9
92ScoShaCan-9
92StaClu-277
92Top-398
92TopGol-398G
92Ult-45
92UppDec-253
93Don-159
93Don-500
93Lea-149
93OPCPre-376
93OPCPreG-376
93PanSti-204
93Par-368
93ParEmel-368
93Pin-285
93PinCan-285
93Pow-114
93Sco-109
93Sco-572
93ScoCan-572
93ScoGol-572
93StaClu-118
93StaCluFDI-118
93StaCluFDIO-118
93StaCluO-118
93SweSemWCS-187
93TopPre-376
93TopPreG-376
93Ult-42
94Fle-85
94HocWit-62
94OPCPre-326
94OPCPreSE-326
94Par-239
94ParGol-239
94ParSE-SE69
94ParSEG-SE69
94Pin-436
94PinArtP-436
94PinRinC-436
94TopPre-326
94TopPreSE-326
94Ult-299
94UppDec-198
94UppDecEleIce-198
95ColCho-180
95ColChoPC-180
95ColChoPCP-180
95Don-359
95Lea-308
95UppDecEleIce-328
95UppDecEleIceG-328

**Carson, Lindsay**
83FlyJCP-4
83OPC-261
83OPCSti-181
85FlyPos-3
86FlyPos-3
88ProAHL-58

**Carter, Anson**
93DonTeaC-7
93MicSta-4
93Pin-469
93PinCan-469
93UppDec-531
96LeaPre-146
96LeaPrePP-146
96PorPir-33
96SelCer-94
96SelCerAP-94
96SelCerBlu-94
96SelCerMB-94
96SelCerMG-94
96SelCerMR-94
96SelCerRed-94
96UppDec-358
96Zen-122
96ZenArtP-122
97Be A PPAD-67
97Be A PPAPD-67
97BeAPla-67
97BeAPlaAut-67
97ColCho-13
97Don-118
97DonCanl-73
97DonCanIDS-73
97DonCanIPS-73
97DonLim-107
97DonLimExp-107
97DonPre-29
97DonPreCttC-29
97DonPreProG-118
97DonPreProS-118
97DonPri-89
97DonPriSoA-89
97Lea-85
97LeaFraMat-85
97LeaFraMDC-85
97LeaInt-85
97LeaIntUI-85
97Pac-131
97PacCop-131
97PacCroR-8
97PacCroREG-8
97PacCroRIB-8
97PacCroRS-8
97PacEmeGre-131
97PacIceB-131
97PacOme-13
97PacOmeC-13
97PacOmeDG-13
97PacOmeEG-13
97PacOmeG-13
97PacOmeIB-13
97PacPar-11
97PacParC-11
97PacParDG-11
97PacParEG-11
97PacParIB-11
97PacParRed-11
97PacParSil-11
97PacRed-131
97PacSil-131
97PinIns-171
97ScoBru-8
97ScoBruPla-8
97ScoBruPre-8
97Stu-33
97StuPrePG-33
97StuPrePS-33
97UppDec-11
98Fin-21
98FinNo P-21
98FinNo PR-21
98FinRef-21
98Pac-73
98PacAur-9
98PacDynI-10
98PacDynIIB-10
98PacDynIR-10
98PacIceB-73
98PacOmeH-13
98PacOmeODI-13
98PacOmeR-13
98PacPar-11
98PacParC-11
98PacParEG-11
98PacParH-11
98PacParIB-11
98PacParS-11
98PacRed-73
98PacRev-8
98PacRevIS-8
98PacRevR-8
98UppDecM-18
98UppDecMGS-18
98UppDecMSS-18
98UppDecMSS-18
99Pac-21
99PacAur-11
99PacAurPD-11
99PacCop-21
99PacGol-21
99PacIceB-21
99PacPreD-21
99UppDecM-14
99UppDecMGS-14
99UppDecMSS-14
99UppDecMSS-14

**Carter, Billy**
60ShiCoi-115
63QueAce-4
63QueAceQ-3

**Carter, Dan**
95TolSto-6

**Carter, John**
86MonGolF-28
88BruPos-3
88ProAHL-163
89BruSpoA-6
90Bow-39
90BowTif-39
90BruSpoA-8
90PanSti-8
90ProSet-5
90Sco-283
90ScoCan-283
90UppDec-211
90UppDecF-211
91OPC-300
91ScoCan-557
91ScoRoo-7T
91Top-300
92Ult-399

**Carter, Lyle**
71TorSun-44

**Carter, Ron**
88OilTenAnn-98

**Carter, Shawn**
91BriColJHL-97
96St.JohML-8
97St.JohML-6

**Carter, Tim**
96ForWorF-2

**Carter, Warren**
95AlaGolKin-5

**Caruso, Brian**
93MinDul-5
95ForWorFT-16
96ForWorF-10

**Caruso, Jamie**
897thInnSOHL-156
907thInnSOHL-305
917thInnSOHL-88

**Carvel, Tim**
93RenEng-5

**Carver, Orrin**
52JunBluT-97

**Carveth, Joe**
34BeeGro1P-95
40OPCV3012-123
44BeeGro2P-227
45QuaOatP-68
51CleBar-9
76OldTim-4

**Carvil, Stewart**
93HumHawP-7

**Casale, Agostino**
96GerDELE-122

**Casavant, Mario**
77GraVic-4

**Casey, Gerald**
52JunBluT-95

**Casey, Jon**
85NorStaPos-7
88NorStaADA-4
89OPC-48
89OPCSti-197
89PanSti-114

❑ 89Top-48
❑ 90Bow-183
❑ 90BowTif-183
❑ 90OPC-269
❑ 90OPC-305
❑ 90OPCBoxB-B
❑ 90PanSti-254
❑ 90ProSet-133
❑ 90Sco-182
❑ 90ScoCan-182
❑ 90ScoHotRS-80
❑ 90Top-269
❑ 90Top-305
❑ 90TopBoxB-B
❑ 90TopTif-269
❑ 90UppDec-385
❑ 90UppDecF-385
❑ 91Bow-119
❑ 91Kra-75
❑ 91OPC-237
❑ 91OPCPre-112
❑ 91PanSti-118
❑ 91Par-77
❑ 91ParFre-77
❑ 91Pin-144
❑ 91PinFre-144
❑ 91ProSet-111
❑ 91ProSetFre-111
❑ 91ProSetPla-56
❑ 91ScoAme-191
❑ 91ScoCan-191
❑ 91StaClu-138
❑ 91Top-237
❑ 91UppDec-205
❑ 91UppDecF-205
❑ 92Bow-269
❑ 92Kra-27
❑ 92OPC-16
❑ 92OPCPreSP-7
❑ 92PanSti-87
❑ 92PanStiFre-87
❑ 92Par-73
❑ 92Pin-42
❑ 92PinFre-42
❑ 92ProSet-82
❑ 92Sco-249
❑ 92ScoCan-249
❑ 92SeaPat-64
❑ 92StaClu-198
❑ 92Top-379
❑ 92TopGol-379G
❑ 92Ult-90
❑ 92UppDec-190
❑ 93Don-16
❑ 93Lea-322
❑ 93McDUppD-3
❑ 93OPCPre-437
❑ 93OPCPreG-437
❑ 93PanSti-276
❑ 93Par-12
❑ 93ParEmel-12
❑ 93Pin-357
❑ 93PinAllS-41
❑ 93PinAllS-49
❑ 93PinAllSC-41
❑ 93PinAllSC-49
❑ 93PinCan-357
❑ 93Pow-17
❑ 93Sco-193
❑ 93Sco-526
❑ 93ScoCan-193
❑ 93ScoCan-526
❑ 93ScoGol-526
❑ 93StaClu-303
❑ 93StaClu-456
❑ 93StaCluFDI-303
❑ 93StaCluFDI-456
❑ 93StaCluO-303
❑ 93StaCluO-456
❑ 93TopPre-437
❑ 93TopPreG-437
❑ 93Ult-91
❑ 93Ult-266
❑ 93UppDec-507
❑ 93UppDecLAS-40
❑ 93UppDecSP-8
❑ 94EASpo-36
❑ 94OPCPre-229
❑ 94OPCPreSE-229
❑ 94ParSE-SE158
❑ 94ParSEG-SE158
❑ 94Pin-393
❑ 94PinArtP-393
❑ 94PinRinC-393
❑ 94Sco-111
❑ 94ScoGol-111
❑ 94ScoPla-111
❑ 94ScoPlaTS-111
❑ 94StaClu-184
❑ 94StaCluFDI-184
❑ 94StaCluMOMS-184
❑ 94StaCluSTWC-184
❑ 94TopPre-229
❑ 94TopPreSE-229
❑ 94UppDec-206
❑ 94UppDecEleIce-206
❑ 95ColEdgI-176
❑ 95ParInt-177
❑ 95ParIntEl-177
❑ 95PeoRiv-1
❑ 95PlaOneoOne-194
❑ 95Sco-290
❑ 95ScoBlaIce-290
❑ 95ScoBlaIceAP-290

❑ 95UppDec-70
❑ 95UppDecEleIce-70
❑ 95UppDecEleIceG-70
❑ 96BeAPAut-63
❑ 96BeAPAutSil-63
❑ 96BeAPla-63
❑ 96Don-37
❑ 96DonPrePro-37
❑ 96Lea-89
❑ 96LeaPreP-89
❑ 96Sco-214
❑ 96ScoArtPro-214
❑ 96ScoDeaCAP-214
❑ 96ScoGolB-214
❑ 96ScoSpeAP-214
❑ 97PacInvNRB-167
**Cashman, Wayne**
❑ 70BruPos-4
❑ 70BruTeaIss-12
❑ 70EssPowPla-63
❑ 70OPC-7
❑ 70OPC-233
❑ 70Top-7
❑ 71BruTeaIss-9
❑ 71OPC-129
❑ 71Top-129
❑ 71TorSun-6
❑ 72OPC-68
❑ 72OPCTeaC-4
❑ 72SarProSta-18
❑ 72Top-29
❑ 73MacMil-3
❑ 73OPC-85
❑ 73Top-166
❑ 74LipSou-9
❑ 74NHLActSta-30
❑ 74OPCNHL-206
❑ 74Top-206
❑ 75OPCNHL-63
❑ 75Top-63
❑ 76OPCNHL-165
❑ 76Top-165
❑ 77OPCNHL-234
❑ 77Top-234
❑ 77TopGloS-1
❑ 77TopOPCGlo-1
❑ 78OPC-124
❑ 78Top-124
❑ 79OPC-79
❑ 79Top-79
❑ 80OPC-318
❑ 81OPC-11
❑ 82OPC-8
❑ 82PosCer-1
❑ 91BruSpoAL-6
❑ 91FutTreC72-25
❑ 92LigShe8
❑ 93LigSealR-5
❑ 94LigPhoA-6
❑ 94ParTalB-18
**Casselman, Mike**
❑ 96CinCyc-17
❑ 98GerDELE-74
**Cassels, Andrew**
❑ 89ProAHL-191
❑ 90CanaPos-6
❑ 90ProSet-615
❑ 90Sco-422
❑ 90ScoCan-422
❑ 90UppDec-265
❑ 90UppDecF-265
❑ 91Bow-340
❑ 91CanaPanTS-3
❑ 91OPC-176
❑ 91OPCPre-72
❑ 91Par-285
❑ 91ParFre-285
❑ 91ProSet-395
❑ 91ProSetFre-395
❑ 91ScoCan-238
❑ 91ScoCan-607
❑ 91ScoRoo-57T
❑ 91StaClu-329
❑ 91Top-176
❑ 91UppDec-379
❑ 91UppDec-551
❑ 91UppDecF-379
❑ 91UppDecF-551
❑ 91WhaJr7E-6
❑ 92Bow-387
❑ 92OPC-222
❑ 92Par-298
❑ 92ParEmel-298
❑ 92Sco-323
❑ 92ScoCan-323
❑ 92StaClu-39
❑ 92Top-23
❑ 92TopGol-23G
❑ 92Ult-70
❑ 92UppDec-288
❑ 92WhaDai-4
❑ 93Don-142
❑ 93Lea-50
❑ 93OPCPre-65
❑ 93OPCPreG-65
❑ 93PanSti-123
❑ 93Par-359
❑ 93ParEmel-359
❑ 93Pin-103
❑ 93PinCan-103
❑ 93Pow-104
❑ 93Sco-64
❑ 93ScoCan-164
❑ 93StaClu-74
❑ 93StaCluFDI-74

❑ 93StaCluFDIO-74
❑ 93StaCluO-74
❑ 93TopPre-65
❑ 93TopPreG-65
❑ 93Ult-33
❑ 93UppDec-346
❑ 94WhaCok-3
❑ 94CanGamNHLP-113
❑ 94Don-178
❑ 94EASpo-57
❑ 94Fla-71
❑ 94Fle-86
❑ 94Lea-276
❑ 94OPCPre-227
❑ 94OPCPreSE-227
❑ 94Par-97
❑ 94ParGol-97
❑ 94ParVin-V58
❑ 94Pin-319
❑ 94PinArtP-319
❑ 94PinRinC-319
❑ 94Sco-34
❑ 94ScoGol-34
❑ 94ScoPla-34
❑ 94ScoPlaTS-34
❑ 94Sel-141
❑ 94SelGol-141
❑ 94SP-50
❑ 94SPDieCut-50
❑ 94TopPre-227
❑ 94TopPreSE-227
❑ 94Ult-300
❑ 94UppDec-317
❑ 94UppDecEleIce-317
❑ 94UppDecSPI-SP32
❑ 94UppDecSPIDC-SP32
❑ 95BeAPla-30
❑ 95BeAPSig-S30
❑ 95BeAPSigDC-S30
❑ 95Bow-4
❑ 95BowAllFoi-4
❑ 95CanGamNHLP-124
❑ 95ColCho-52
❑ 95ColChoPC-52
❑ 95ColChoPCP-52
❑ 95Don-148
❑ 95Emo-74
❑ 95Fin-74
❑ 95FinRef-74
❑ 95Kra-62
❑ 95Lea-147
❑ 95Met-64
❑ 95ParInt-364
❑ 95ParIntEI-364
❑ 95PlaOneoOne-46
❑ 95ProMag-127
❑ 95Sco-136
❑ 95ScoBlaIce-136
❑ 95ScoBlaIceAP-136
❑ 95SkyImp-72
❑ 95SP-61
❑ 95StaClu-61
❑ 95StaCluMOMS-61
❑ 95Sum-158
❑ 95SumArtP-158
❑ 95SumIce-158
❑ 95Top-30
❑ 95TopOPCI-30
❑ 95TopSupSki-4
❑ 95TopSupSkiPla-4
❑ 95Ult-66
❑ 95UltGolM-66
❑ 95UppDec-492
❑ 95UppDecEleIce-311
❑ 95UppDecEleIceG-311
❑ 95UppDecSpeE-SE36
❑ 95UppDecSpeEdiG-SE36
❑ 96ColCho-115
❑ 96Don-162
❑ 96DonPrePro-162
❑ 96Fla-41
❑ 96FlaBluI-41
❑ 96Fle-46
❑ 96FlePic-104
❑ 96Lea-78
❑ 96LeaPreP-78
❑ 96NHLProSTA-127
❑ 96Pin-82
❑ 96PinArtP-82
❑ 96PinFoi-82
❑ 96PinPreS-82
❑ 96PinPreSB-82
❑ 96PinRinC-82
❑ 96Sco-146
❑ 96ScoArtPro-146
❑ 96ScoDeaCAP-146
❑ 96ScoGolB-146
❑ 96ScoSpeAP-146
❑ 96SkyImp-53
❑ 96SP-72
❑ 96Sum-44
❑ 96SumArtP-44
❑ 96SumIce-44
❑ 96SumMet-44
❑ 96SumPreS-44
❑ 96UppDec-74
❑ 96UppDecBD-123
❑ 96UppDecBDG-123
❑ 96WhaBobS-3
❑ 97Be A PPAD-8
❑ 97Be A PPAPD-8
❑ 97BeAPla-8
❑ 97BeAPlaAut-8
❑ 97ColCho-113
❑ 97Don-146
❑ 97DonCanI-66

❑ 97BlaCok-3
❑ 88ProIHL-96
❑ 89ProIHL-51
❑ 94IndIce-2
❑ 95IndIce-4
**Cassivi, Frederic**
❑ 95ThuBayS-4
❑ 96SyrCru-30
❑ 98CinCyc-2
**Cast, Paul**
❑ 94HumHawP-21
**Castella, Reuben**
❑ 917thInnSOHL-174
**Castellan, Jason**
❑ 907thInnSOHL-280
**Caswell, Roy**
❑ 82BraWheK-14
**Catellier, Chris**
❑ 89VicCou-6
❑ 907thInnSWHL-238
❑ 917thInnSWHL-53
**Catenacci, Maurizio**
❑ 96GerDELE-100
**Catenaro, Angelo**
❑ 84BelBul-17
**Caton, Murray**
❑ 91BriColJHL-8
**Cattarinich, Joseph**
❑ 1OC56-16
❑ 83HalFP-M3
❑ 85HalFC-168
**Caufield, Jay**
❑ 89PenFoo-12
❑ 90ProSet-504
❑ 91PenCokE-16
❑ 92PenCokC-3
**Causey, Carey**
❑ 91BriColJHL-113
**Cava, Peter**
❑ 95SauSteMG-1
❑ 95Sla-365
❑ 96SauSteMG-3
❑ 96SauSteMGA-3
❑ 98BowCHL-18
❑ 98BowCHLGA-18
❑ 98BowCHLOI-18
❑ 98BowChrC-18
❑ 98BowChrCGA-18
❑ 98BowChrCGAR-18
❑ 98BowChrCOI-18
❑ 98BowChrCOIR-18
**Cavallin, Mark**
❑ 94CenHocL-94
**Cavallini, Gino**
❑ 84MonGolP-26
❑ 85FlamRedRP-6
❑ 87BluKod-5
❑ 87BluTeaIss-3
❑ 87OPC-146
❑ 87PanSti-315
❑ 87Top-146
❑ 88BluKod-17
❑ 88BluTeaIss-3
❑ 88OPC-149
❑ 88PanSti-103
❑ 88Top-149
❑ 89BluKod-17
❑ 89OPC-176
❑ 89PanSti-123
❑ 89Top-176
❑ 90BluKod-5
❑ 90OPC-36
❑ 90PanSti-265
❑ 90ProSet-261
❑ 90Sco-63
❑ 90ScoCan-63
❑ 90ScoHotRS-27
❑ 90Top-36
❑ 90TopTif-36
❑ 90UppDec-38
❑ 91BluPos-5
❑ 91Bow-368
❑ 91OPC-281
❑ 91PanSti-24
❑ 91Pin-216
❑ 91PinFre-216
❑ 91ProSet-218
❑ 91ProSetFre-218
❑ 91ScoAme-258
❑ 91ScoAme-308
❑ 91ScoCan-338
❑ 91ScoCan-478
❑ 91StaClu-34
❑ 91Top-281
❑ 91UppDec-187
❑ 91UppDec-646
❑ 91UppDecF-187
❑ 91UppDecF-646
❑ 92NorPet-3
❑ 92Sco-42
❑ 92ScoCan-42
❑ 92StaClu-480
❑ 92Top-234
❑ 92TopGol-234G
❑ 93OPCPre-232
❑ 93OPCPreG-232
❑ 93Sco-414
❑ 93ScoCan-414
❑ 93StaClu-152
❑ 93StaCluFDI-152
❑ 93StaCluFDIO-152
❑ 93StaCluO-152
❑ 93TopPre-232

❑ 93TopPreG-232
❑ 94MilAdm-4
❑ 95ColEdgI-159
❑ 95MilAdmBO-3
❑ 96GerDELE-152
**Cavallini, Paul**
❑ 87BluKod-4
❑ 87BluTealsS-4
❑ 88BluKod-14
❑ 88BluTeaIss-4
❑ 89BluKod-14
❑ 89OPC-269
❑ 89PanSti-127
❑ 90BluKod-6
❑ 90Bow-22
❑ 90BowTif-22
❑ 90OPC-57
❑ 90PanSti-276
❑ 90ProSet-262
❑ 90ProSet-353
❑ 90Sco-185
❑ 90Sco-349
❑ 90ScoCan-185
❑ 90ScoCan-349
❑ 90Top-57
❑ 90TopTif-57
❑ 90UppDec-281
❑ 90UppDecF-281
❑ 91BluPos-6
❑ 91Bow-378
❑ 91OPC-328
❑ 91PanSti-35
❑ 91Par-154
❑ 91ParFre-154
❑ 91Pin-182
❑ 91Pin-411
❑ 91PinFre-182
❑ 91PinFre-411
❑ 91ProSet-214
❑ 91ProSetPla-224
❑ 91ProSetSLM-2
❑ 91ScoAme-107
❑ 91ScoAme-308
❑ 91ScoCan-107
❑ 91ScoCan-338
❑ 91StaClu-48
❑ 91SweSemWCS-59
❑ 91Top-328
❑ 91UppDec-184
❑ 91UppDec-646
❑ 91UppDecF-184
❑ 92Bow-193
❑ 92CapKod-6
❑ 92OPC-379
❑ 92PanSti-23
❑ 92PanStiFre-23
❑ 92Pin-319
❑ 92PinFre-319
❑ 92ProSet-159
❑ 92Sco-22
❑ 92ScoCan-22
❑ 92StaClu-447
❑ 92Top-233
❑ 92TopGol-233G
❑ 92Ult-185
❑ 92Ult-432
❑ 92UppDec-212
❑ 93Don-88
❑ 93Lea-397
❑ 93Par-50
❑ 93ParEmel-50
❑ 93Pin-370
❑ 93PinCan-370
❑ 93Pow-321
❑ 93Sco-172
❑ 93Sco-538
❑ 93ScoCan-172
❑ 93ScoCan-538
❑ 93ScoGol-538
❑ 93UppDec-441
❑ 93UppDecSP-35
❑ 94CanGamNHLP-82
❑ 94Don-135
❑ 94Lea-79
❑ 94OPCPre-246
❑ 94OPCPreSE-246
❑ 94ParSE-SE42
❑ 94ParSEG-SE42
❑ 94ParVin-V12
❑ 94Pin-81
❑ 94PinArtP-81
❑ 94PinRinC-81
❑ 94Sco-94
❑ 94ScoGol-94
❑ 94ScoPla-94
❑ 94ScoPlaTS-94
❑ 94StaHoc-5
❑ 94StaPos-2
❑ 94StaScoS-94
❑ 94TopPre-246
❑ 94TopPreSE-246
❑ 94Ult-49
❑ 94UppDec-311
❑ 94UppDecEleIce-311
❑ 94UppDecSPI-SP108
❑ 94UppDecSPIDC-SP108
**Cavanagh, Chad**
❑ 95Sla-164
❑ 96DetWha-3
**Cavanagh, Pat**
❑ 89HamRoaA-4
❑ 90HamRoaA-53
❑ 92-TulOil-2

**Cavanaugh, Mike**
❑ 87KinCan-15
❑ 907thInnSOHL-29
**Cech, Roman**
❑ 94CzeAPSE-165
❑ 95CzeAPSE-181
❑ 96CzeAPSE-171
**Cech, Vratislav**
❑ 96KitRan-5
❑ 97BowCHL-155
❑ 97BowCHLAu-35
❑ 97BowCHLOPC-155
**Cech, Zdenek**
❑ 94CzeAPSE-294
❑ 95CzeAPSE-28
**Cechmanek, Roman**
❑ 94CzeAPSE-228
❑ 95CzeAPSE-3
❑ 96CzeAPSE-214
❑ 96CzeAPSE-337
**Cedergren, Henrik**
❑ 83SweSemE-71
❑ 84SweSemE-23
**Cederholm, Hans**
❑ 83SweSemE-5
❑ 84SweSemE-6
❑ 85SwePanS-5
❑ 87SwePanS-8
**Cefalo, Marco**
❑ 96PriAlbROC-4
**Ceglarski, Len**
❑ 90ProSet-385A
❑ 90ProSet-385B
**Cej, Jeff**
❑ 917thInnSWHL-305
**Celio, Manuele**
❑ 91SweSemWCS-192
❑ 93SweSemWCS-124
❑ 93SwiHNL-18
❑ 95SwiHNL-16
**Celio, Nicola**
❑ 91UppDec-665
❑ 91UppDecCWJC-26
❑ 91UppDecF-665
❑ 93SwiHNL-146
❑ 95SwiHNL-198
**Cella, Tony**
❑ 80SauSteMG-4
❑ 81SauSteMG-4
❑ 82SauSteMG-5
**Cely, Zdenek**
❑ 94CzeAPSE-180
❑ 95CzeAPSE-213
**Centrone, Marc**
❑ 81RegPat-5
❑ 82RegPat-18
❑ 83RegPat-18
**Ceresino, Ray**
❑ 44BeeGro2P-388
❑ 51CleBar-15
**Cermak, David**
❑ 94CzeAPSE-61
❑ 95CzeAPSE-89
❑ 96CzeAPSE-86
**Cernich, Kord**
❑ 90ProAHLIHL-6
❑ 91ProAHLCHL-211
❑ 91ProAHLCHL-330
❑ 97AncAce-4
**Cernich, Frantisek**
❑ 79PanSti-91
❑ 82SweSemHVS-91
**Cerniglia, Mike**
❑ 95NorlowH-2
**Cernosek, Marek**
❑ 96CzeAPSE-273
**Cerny, Frantisek**
❑ 82SweSemHVS-88
**Cerny, Josef**
❑ 69SweHocS-22
❑ 69SweWorC-147
❑ 70SweHocS-353
❑ 71SweHocS-49
❑ 72SweSemWC-34
❑ 74SweSemHVS-70
**Cerny, Michal**
❑ 92UppDec-603
❑ 94CzeAPSE-126
**Cerny, Milan**
❑ 94CzeAPSE-150
**Cerny, Otakar**
❑ 94CzeAPSE-54
**Cerny, Robert**
❑ 96SloPeeWT-5
**Cerven, Martin**
❑ 95SpoChi-10
❑ 96SeaThu-14
❑ 97BowCHL-90
❑ 97BowCHLOPC-90
**Chabot, Frederic**
❑ 89ProIHL-135
❑ 90ProAHLIHL-66
❑ 92FreCan-6
❑ 96ColEdgFL-17
❑ 97Be A PPAD-169
❑ 97Be A PPAPD-169
❑ 97BeAPla-169
❑ 97BeAPlaAut-169
**Chabot, John**
❑ 83CanaPos-5
❑ 84OPC-258
❑ 85OPC-244
❑ 85OPCSti-101
❑ 86OPCSti-230
❑ 86PenKod-5

❑ 87OPC-32
❑ 87OPCSti-169
❑ 87PanSti-151
❑ 87RedWinLC-5
❑ 87Top-32
❑ 88OPC-39
❑ 88PanSti-42
❑ 88RedWinLC-3
❑ 88Top-39
❑ 89OPC-225
❑ 89RedWinLC-4
❑ 90Bow-236
❑ 90BowTif-236
❑ 90OPC-163
❑ 90PanSti-216
❑ 90ProAHLIHL-488
❑ 90ProSet-68
❑ 90Sco-277
❑ 90ScoCan-277
❑ 90Top-163
❑ 90TopTif-163
❑ 90UppDec-113
❑ 90UppDecF-113
❑ 91UppDec-393
❑ 91UppDecF-393
❑ 94GerDELE-67
❑ 95GerDELE-67
❑ 96GerDELE-263
❑ 98GerDELE-134
**Chabot, Lorne**
❑ 23V1281PauC-15
❑ 32O'KeeMapL-1
❑ 33OPCV304A-18
❑ 33V129-45
❑ 33V252CanG-9
❑ 33V288HamG-30
❑ 33V357IceK-71
❑ 34BeeGro1P-46
❑ 34DiaMatS-10
❑ 34SweCap-33
❑ 35DiaMatT2-8
❑ 35DiaMatT3-8
❑ 35DiaMatTI-11
❑ 55Par-21
❑ 55ParQuaO-21
**Chabot, Nicolas**
❑ 96RimOce-7
❑ 96RimOceQPP-7
**Chad, John**
❑ 34BeeGro1P-47
**Chadney, Randy**
❑ 917thInnSWHL-55
**Chadwick, Bill**
❑ 83HalFP-E4
❑ 85HalFC-65
**Chadwick, Ed**
❑ 44BeeGro2P-389
❑ 52JunBluT-157
❑ 57Par-M24
❑ 57Par-M25
❑ 57Par-T2
❑ 58Par-12
❑ 59Par-5
❑ 61ShiCoi-20
❑ 84NovScoO-25
❑ 94ParMisL-128
**Chagnon, Paul**
❑ 94FreCan-8
❑ 95FreCan-6
**Chainey, Alain**
❑ 87NordGenF-31
❑ 89Nord-4
❑ 917thInnSQMJHL-182
**Chalanek, Miroslav**
❑ 94CzeAPSE-15
**Chalifoux, Denis**
❑ 907thInnSMC-70
❑ 907thInnSQMJHL-51
❑ 91ProAHLCHL-106
**Challice, Ben**
❑ 94GuiFla-1
**Chalmers, William**
❑ 52JunBluT-52
**Chaloner, Kane**
❑ 917thInnSWHL-58
**Chalupa, Milan**
❑ 79PanSti-79
❑ 82SweSemHVS-80
**Chamberlain, Curtis**
❑ 83SasBla-17
❑ 84SasBlaS-2
**Chamberlain, Murph**
❑ 34BeeGro1P-143
❑ 34BeeGro1P-305
❑ 37OPCV304E-147
❑ 38QuaOatP-7
❑ 39OPCV3011-12
❑ 44BeeGro2P-228
❑ 45QuaOatP-69A
❑ 45QuaOatP-69B
❑ 45QuaOatP-69C
❑ 61SudWol-4
❑ 62SudWol-6
**Chambers, Dave**
❑ 90NordPet-2
❑ 90ProSet-675
**Chambers, Shawn**
❑ 88NorStaADA-5
❑ 89OPC-142
❑ 89PanSti-111
❑ 89Top-142
❑ 90Bow-180
❑ 90BowTif-180
❑ 90OPC-192
❑ 90PanSti-252
❑ 90ProSet-134
❑ 90Sco-57
❑ 90ScoCan-57
❑ 90Top-192
❑ 90TopTif-192
❑ 90UppDec-106
❑ 90UppDecF-106
❑ 91CapJun5-5
❑ 91CapKod-5
❑ 91ScoCan-572
❑ 92LigShe-9
❑ 92Par-406
❑ 92ParEmel-406
❑ 92Sco-508
❑ 92ScoCan-508
❑ 92UppDec-104
❑ 93Don-325
❑ 93Lea-40
❑ 93LigKasK-2
❑ 93LigSealR-6
❑ 93OPCPre-101
❑ 93OPCPreG-101
❑ 93PanSti-219
❑ 93Pin-87
❑ 93PinCan-87
❑ 93Pow-229
❑ 93Sco-391
❑ 93ScoCan-391
❑ 93StaClu-412
❑ 93StaCluFDI-412
❑ 93StaCluO-412
❑ 93TopPre-101
❑ 93TopPreG-101
❑ 93Ult-75
❑ 93UppDec-68
❑ 94CanGamNHLP-227
❑ 94Don-72
❑ 94Fla-171
❑ 94Fle-204
❑ 94Lea-332
❑ 94OPCPre-174
❑ 94OPCPreSE-174
❑ 94Par-223
❑ 94ParGol-223
❑ 94Pin-97
❑ 94PinArtP-97
❑ 94PinRinC-97
❑ 94Sco-153
❑ 94ScoGol-153
❑ 94ScoPla-153
❑ 94ScoPlaTS-153
❑ 94TopPre-174
❑ 94TopPreSE-174
❑ 94Ult-203
❑ 95Don-126
❑ 95Emo-96
❑ 95FinnSemWC-109
❑ 95Lea-234
❑ 95ParInt-392
❑ 95ParIntEl-392
❑ 95Sco-86
❑ 95ScoBlaIce-86
❑ 95ScoBlaIceAP-86
❑ 95SkyImp-92
❑ 95Ult-259
❑ 95UppDec-148
❑ 95UppDecEleIce-148
❑ 95UppDecEleIceG-148
❑ 96BeAPAut-75
❑ 96BeAPAutSil-75
❑ 96BeAPla-75
❑ 96Dev-29
❑ 96UppDec-287
❑ 98Pac-174
❑ 98PacIceB-174
❑ 98PacRed-174
**Champagne, Andrew**
❑ 66TulOil-2
**Channell, Craig**
❑ 89ProIHL-134
**Chapdelaine, Rene**
❑ 89ProAHL-21
❑ 90ProAHLIHL-429
❑ 92PhoRoa-4
❑ 93PeoRiv-3
❑ 95PeoRiv-2
**Chapman, Art**
❑ 33V357IceK-32
❑ 34BeeGro1P-219
❑ 34DiaMatS-11
❑ 35DiaMatT2-9
❑ 35DiaMatT3-9
❑ 35DiaMatTI-12
❑ 35OPCV304C-94
❑ 36V356WorG-42
❑ 39OPCV3011-18
**Chapman, Blair**
❑ 77OPCNHL-174
❑ 77PenPucB-9
❑ 77Top-174
❑ 78OPC-33
❑ 78Top-33
❑ 79OPC-21
❑ 79Top-21
❑ 80OPC-48
❑ 80Top-48
❑ 81OPC-291
❑ 81Top-W115
**Chapman, Brian**
❑ 88ProAHL-67
❑ 89ProAHL-299
❑ 90ProAHLIHL-190
❑ 91ProAHLCHL-109
❑ 93PhoRoa-2
❑ 95PhoRoa-8
**Chapman, Craig**
❑ 907thInnSWHL-2
❑ 917thInnSWHL-122
**Chapman, Drew**
❑ 94GuiFla-7
❑ 95GuiFla-11
**Chapman, Phil**
❑ 52JunBluT-89
**Chappot, Roger**
❑ 72SweSemWC-149
**Chaput, Dan**
❑ 91FerStaB-7
❑ 93HamRoaA-4
**Chaput, Martin**
❑ 907thInnSQMJHL-46
❑ 917thInnSQMJHL-233
**Chara, Zdeno**
❑ 97SPAut-186
❑ 98BowBes-134
❑ 98BowBesAR-134
❑ 98BowBesR-134
❑ 98Pac-276
❑ 98PacIceB-276
❑ 98PacRed-276
❑ 98SPxFinS-52
❑ 98SPxFinR-52
❑ 98SPxFinS-52
❑ 98UC-124
❑ 98UD ChoPCR-124
❑ 98UD ChoR-124
❑ 98UD3-20
❑ 98UD3-80
❑ 98UD3-140
❑ 98UD3DieC-20
❑ 98UD3DieC-80
❑ 98UD3DieC-140
❑ 98UppDec-126
❑ 98UppDecE-126
❑ 98UppDecE1o1-126
❑ 98UppDecGR-126
❑ 99Pac-252
❑ 99PacCop-252
❑ 99PacGol-252
❑ 99PacIceB-252
❑ 99PacPreD-252
❑ 99UppDecM-130
❑ 99UppDecMGS-130
❑ 99UppDecMSS-130
❑ 99UppDecMSS-130
**Charbonneau, Alain**
❑ 98Vald'OF-5
**Charbonneau, Jocelyn**
❑ 917thInnSQMJHL-66
**Charbonneau, Jose**
❑ 86SheCan-10
❑ 87CanaPos-3
❑ 88CanaPos-4
❑ 88ProAHL-295
❑ 89ProIHL-181
❑ 90AlbIntTC-13
❑ 93Par-484
❑ 93ParEmel-484
❑ 93Pow-457
❑ 93Sco-638
❑ 93ScoCan-638
❑ 93ScoGol-638
❑ 93Ult-438
❑ 93UppDec-503
❑ 95GerDELE-257
❑ 96GerDELE-145
❑ 98GerDELE-141
**Charbonneau, Louis-Philippe**
❑ 95RoaExp-8
❑ 95SlaMemC-72
**Charbonneau, Patrice**
❑ 917thInnSQMJHL-251
❑ 93DruVol-17
**Charbonneau, Ron**
❑ 94GuiFla-10
**Charbonneau, Stephane**
❑ 907thInnSQMJHL-40
❑ 917thInnSMC-43
❑ 91ProAHLCHL-536
❑ 93PhoRoa-3
❑ 94EriPan-19
❑ 95PorPir-7
**Charland, Carl**
❑ 95SlaMemC-63
**Charlebois, Bob**
❑ 72NatOttWHA-5
❑ 72OPC-309
❑ 73QuaOatWHA-23
**Charles, Richard**
❑ 97FifFly-8
**Charlesworth, Todd**
❑ 82OshGen-22
❑ 83OshGen-3
❑ 88ProIHL-45
❑ 89ProAHL-139
❑ 90ProAHLIHL-2
❑ 93MusFur-17
❑ 94MusFur-9
**Charrois, Martin**
❑ 907thInnSQMJHL-9
❑ 917thInnSMC-52
**Charrois, Yvan**
❑ 907thInnSQMJHL-105
**Charron, Craig**
❑ 91CinCyc-4
❑ 94DayBom-5
❑ 95RochAmeSS-1
**Charron, Eric**
❑ 90ProAHLIHL-56
❑ 91ProAHLCHL-89
❑ 92FreCan-5
❑ 94Fle-205
❑ 94LigPhoA-7
❑ 94OPCPre-343
❑ 94OPCPreSE-343
❑ 94TopPre-343
❑ 94TopPreSE-343
❑ 94Ult-371
❑ 94UppDec-489
❑ 94UppDecEleIce-489
**Charron, Guy**
❑ 69CanaPosC-5
❑ 71SarProSta-60
❑ 71TorSun-87
❑ 72OPC-223
❑ 72SarProSta-80
❑ 73OPC-220
❑ 73RedWinMP-4
❑ 73RedWinTI-5
❑ 74NHLActSta-94
❑ 74NHLActStaU-14
❑ 74OPCNHL-57
❑ 74Top-57
❑ 75OPCNHL-32
❑ 75OPCNHL-319
❑ 75Top-32
❑ 75Top-319
❑ 76OPCNHL-186
❑ 76OPCNHL-384
❑ 76Top-186
❑ 77OPCNHL-145
❑ 77Top-145
❑ 78OPC-22
❑ 78Top-22
❑ 79OPC-152
❑ 79PanSti-62
❑ 79Top-152
❑ 80OPC-352
❑ 90FlamIGA-2
❑ 91FlamIGA-28
❑ 92FlamIGA-27
**Charron, Jonathan**
❑ 98Vald'OF-26
**Charron, Yves**
❑ 917thInnSQMJHL-31
**Chartier, Christian**
❑ 96SasBla-6
❑ 97UppDec-402
**Chartier, Dave**
❑ 80JetPos-4
❑ 81SasBla-6
❑ 83SasBla-10
**Chartier, Scott**
❑ 91BriColJHL-35
❑ 91BriColJHL-158
❑ 92WesMic-8
❑ 93Cla-61
❑ 94ClaAut-NNO
**Chartrain, Andre**
❑ 81FreExp-16
❑ 82FreExp-16
❑ 83FreExp-17
**Chartrand, Brad**
❑ 92CorBigRed-4
❑ 93CorBigRed-4
**Chartrand, Derek**
❑ 96SudWol-27
**Chartrand, Jacques**
❑ 52St.LawS-27
**Chartrand, Rick**
❑ 89RayJrC-4
**Chartrand, Simon**
❑ 89RayJrC-5
**Chartraw, Rick**
❑ 74CanaPos-3
❑ 75OPCNHL-388
❑ 76CanaPos-3
❑ 76OPCNHL-244
❑ 76Top-244
❑ 77CanaPos-3
❑ 77OPCNHL-363
❑ 78CanaPos-2
❑ 78OPC-238
❑ 78Top-238
❑ 79CanaPos-1
❑ 79OPC-243
❑ 79Top-243
❑ 80CanaPos-3
❑ 80OPC-364
❑ 82PosCer-8
❑ 83OilMcD-6
❑ 88OilTenAnn-96
**Chase, Don**
❑ 96WheNai-9
**Chase, Kelly**
❑ 88ProIHL-81
❑ 89BluKod-39
❑ 90Bow-14
❑ 90BowTif-14
❑ 90OPC-432
❑ 90ProAHLIHL-87
❑ 91BluPos-7
❑ 91OPC-23
❑ 91Top-23
❑ 93Don-483
❑ 94Don-157
❑ 94Lea-396
❑ 96BeAPAut-60
❑ 96BeAPAutSil-60
❑ 96BeAPla-60
❑ 96ColCho-122
❑ 96WhaBobS-4
❑ 97PacPar-156
❑ 97PacParC-156
❑ 97PacParDG-156
❑ 97PacParEG-156
❑ 97PacParIB-156
❑ 97PacParRed-156
❑ 97PacParSil-156
❑ 98Be A PPA-276
❑ 98Be A PPAA-276
❑ 98Be A PPAAF-276
❑ 98Be A PPSE-276
❑ 98Be APG-276
❑ 98Pac-363
❑ 98PacIceB-363
❑ 98PacPar-199
❑ 98PacParC-199
❑ 98PacParEG-199
❑ 98PacParH-199
❑ 98PacParIB-199
❑ 98PacParS-199
❑ 98PacRed-363
**Chase, Tim**
❑ 93KnoChe-3
❑ 96LouRiv-18
**Chasle, Yvon**
❑ 52JunBluT-134
**Chasse, Denis**
❑ 907thInnSQMJHL-13
❑ 917thInnSMC-54
❑ 91ProAHLCHL-535
❑ 93ClaProPro-79
❑ 94FinBowB-R15
❑ 94FinBowBR-R15
❑ 94Fle-184
❑ 94UppDec-414
❑ 94UppDecEleIce-414
❑ 95Don-164
❑ 95Lea-132
❑ 95SkyImpNHLF-5
❑ 95Ult-137
❑ 95UltGolM-137
❑ 95UppDec-416
❑ 95UppDecEleIce-416
❑ 95UppDecEleIceG-416
**Chateau, Brooke**
❑ 98ChaChe-7
**Chattington, Terrance**
❑ 52JunBluT-57
**Chaulk, Colin**
❑ 95Sla-123
**Chebaturkin, Vladimir**
❑ 93Cla-37
❑ 98Pac-277
❑ 98PacIceB-277
❑ 98PacRed-277
**Checco, Nick**
❑ 93MinGolG-7
❑ 94MinGolG-8
❑ 95MinGolG-9
❑ 96MinGolGCAS-6
❑ 98FloEve-3
**Checknita, Paul**
❑ 87KamBla-2
❑ 88LetHur-4
**Cheechoo, Jonathan**
❑ 98BowCHL-142
❑ 98BowCHL-164
❑ 98BowCHLAuB-A25
❑ 98BowCHLAuG-A25
❑ 98BowCHLAuS-A25
❑ 98BowCHLGA-142
❑ 98BowCHLGA-164
❑ 98BowCHLOI-142
❑ 98BowCHLOI-164
❑ 98BowCHLSC-SC18
❑ 98BowChrC-142
❑ 98BowChrC-164
❑ 98BowChrCGA-142
❑ 98BowChrCGA-164
❑ 98BowChrCGAR-142
❑ 98BowChrCGAR-164
❑ 98BowChrCOI-142
❑ 98BowChrCOI-164
❑ 98BowChrCOIR-142
❑ 98BowChrCOIR-164
❑ 98BowChrCR-142
❑ 98BowChrCR-164
❑ 98O-PChr-230
❑ 98O-PChrR-230
❑ 98Top-230
❑ 98TopO-P-230
**Cheevers, Gerry**
❑ 61SudWol-5
❑ 62SudWol-7
❑ 63RochAme-7
❑ 65Coc-1
❑ 65Top-31
❑ 67Top-99
❑ 68OPC-140
❑ 68ShiCoi-4
❑ 68Top-1
❑ 69OPC-22
❑ 69OPCFou-12
❑ 69Top-22
❑ 70BruPos-3
❑ 70BruTeaIss-13
❑ 70ColSta-71
❑ 70DadCoo-14
❑ 70EssPowPla-72
❑ 70OPC-1
❑ 70SarProSta-15
❑ 70Top-1
❑ 71BruTeaIss-20
❑ 71LetActR-8
❑ 71OPC-54
❑ 71SarProSta-16
❑ 71Top-4
❑ 71Top-54
❑ 71TorSun-7
❑ 72OPC-340
❑ 72SluCupWHA-5
❑ 72SweSemWC-188
❑ 73OPCWHAP-6
❑ 73QuaOatWHA-8
❑ 74OPCWHA-30
❑ 74TeaCanLWHA-3
❑ 75HerSta-1
❑ 75OPCWHA-20
❑ 75OPCWHA-67
❑ 76OPCNHL-120
❑ 76Top-120
❑ 77OPCNHL-260
❑ 77Top-260
❑ 77TopGloS-2
❑ 77TopOPCGlo-2
❑ 78OPC-140
❑ 78Top-140
❑ 79OPC-85
❑ 79Top-85
❑ 80OPC-168
❑ 80Top-168
❑ 85HalFC-250
❑ 91BruSpoAL-7
❑ 91StaPicH-61
❑ 92FutTre76CC-109
❑ 92OPC-343
❑ 92OPC25AI-5
❑ 94HocWit-81
❑ 94ParTalBFS-FS2
❑ 94ZelMasH-2
❑ 94ZelMasoHS-2
❑ 95Par66-16
❑ 95Par66-PR16
❑ 95Par66Coi-16
❑ 95Par66P-1
❑ 99RetHoc-92
❑ 99UppDecRG-92
❑ 99UppDecRII-GC
❑ 99UppDecRIL1-GC
❑ 99UppDecRP-92
**Chelios, Chris**
❑ 83CanaPos-6
❑ 84CanaPos-4
❑ 84OPC-259
❑ 85CanaPla-4
❑ 85CanaPla-7
❑ 85CanaPos-5
❑ 85CanaPro-2
❑ 85OPC-51
❑ 85OPCBoxB-D
❑ 85OPCSti-125
❑ 85Top-51
❑ 85TopBoxB-D
❑ 86CanaPos-2
❑ 86KraDra-7
❑ 86OPC-171
❑ 86OPCSti-6
❑ 86Top-171
❑ 87CanaPos-4
❑ 87CanaVacS-78
❑ 87CanaVacS-79
❑ 87CanaVacS-82
❑ 87CanaVacS-83
❑ 87OPC-106
❑ 87OPCSti-9
❑ 87PanSti-58
❑ 87ProAll-3
❑ 87Top-106
❑ 88CanaPos-5
❑ 88OPC-49
❑ 88OPCSti-51
❑ 88PanSti-253
❑ 88Top-49
❑ 89CanaKra-3
❑ 89CanaPos-4
❑ 89CanaProF-24
❑ 89Kra-20
❑ 89OPC-174
❑ 89OPC-307
❑ 89OPCSti-47
❑ 89OPCSti-56
❑ 89OPCSti-156
❑ 89OPCSti-198
❑ 89OPCSti-212
❑ 89PanSti-237
❑ 89PanSti-379
❑ 89SweSemWCS-157
❑ 89Top-174
❑ 89TopStiIns-1
❑ 90BlaCok-5
❑ 90Bow-42
❑ 90Bow-46
❑ 90BowTif-42
❑ 90BowTif-46
❑ 90Kra-6
❑ 90Kra-81
❑ 90OPC-29
❑ 90OPCPre-13
❑ 90PanSti-49
❑ 90ProSet-147A
❑ 90ProSet-147B
❑ 90ProSet-368
❑ 90ProSet-427
❑ 90Sco-15
❑ 90ScoCan-15
❑ 90ScoHotRS-9
❑ 90ScoRoo-4T
❑ 90Top-29
❑ 90TopTif-29
❑ 90UppDec-174
❑ 90UppDec-422
❑ 90UppDec-491
❑ 90UppDecF-174
❑ 90UppDecF-422
❑ 90UppDecF-491
❑ 91BlaCok-4
❑ 91Bow-398
❑ 91Gil-16
❑ 91Kra-18
❑ 91McDUppD-22
❑ 91McDUppD-H2
❑ 91OPC-233
❑ 91OPC-268
❑ 91OPCPre-17
❑ 91OPCPre-150
❑ 91PanSti-10
❑ 91PanSti-329
❑ 91Par-32
❑ 91Par-461
❑ 91ParFre-32
❑ 91Pin-58
❑ 91PinB-B9
❑ 91PinBFre-B9
❑ 91PinFre-58
❑ 91ProSet-48
❑ 91ProSet-278
❑ 91ProSetFre-48
❑ 91ProSetFre-278
❑ 91ProSetNHLAS-AC15
❑ 91ProSetPla-25
❑ 91ScoAme-235
❑ 91ScoCan-455
❑ 91StaClu-6
❑ 91SweSemWCS-130
❑ 91Top-233
❑ 91Top-268
❑ 91UppDec-37
❑ 91UppDec-354
❑ 91UppDecF-37
❑ 91UppDecF-354
❑ 92Bow-43
❑ 92Bow-201
❑ 92HumDum1-3
❑ 92Kra-38
❑ 92McDUppD-3
❑ 92OPC-13
❑ 92PanSti-11
❑ 92PanSti-286
❑ 92PanStiFre-11
❑ 92PanStiFre-286
❑ 92Par-29
❑ 92Par-457
❑ 92ParCheP-CP16
❑ 92ParEmel-29
❑ 92ParEmel-457
❑ 92Pin-109
❑ 92PinFre-109
❑ 92PinTeaPF-2
❑ 92ProSet-34
❑ 92Sco-2
❑ 92Sco-497
❑ 92ScoCan-2
❑ 92ScoCan-497
❑ 92ScoCanPS-1
❑ 92ScoUSAG-2
❑ 92SeaPat-4
❑ 92StaClu-87
❑ 92Top-98
❑ 92TopGol-98G
❑ 92Ult-34
❑ 92UltAllS-7
❑ 92UppDec-159
❑ 92UppDec-629
❑ 92UppDecWJG-WG3
❑ 93AmeLicSPC-3
❑ 93BlaCok-2
❑ 93Cla-118
❑ 93Cla-AU3
❑ 93Don-65
❑ 93DonIceKin-5
❑ 93Kra-70
❑ 93Lea-51
❑ 93LeaGolAS-2
❑ 93McDUppD-H5
❑ 93OPCPre-94
❑ 93OPCPre-237
❑ 93OPCPreG-94
❑ 93OPCPreG-237
❑ 93PanSti-153
❑ 93Par-45
❑ 93ParEmel-45
❑ 93Pin-181
❑ 93Pin-223
❑ 93Pin-233
❑ 93PinAllS-26
❑ 93PinAllSC-26
❑ 93PinCan-181
❑ 93PinCan-223
❑ 93PinCan-233
❑ 93Pow-47
❑ 93Sco-101
❑ 93ScoCan-101
❑ 93ScoDreTea-3
❑ 93StaClu-147
❑ 93StaClu-420
❑ 93StaClu-459
❑ 93StaCluFDI-147
❑ 93StaCluFDI-420
❑ 93StaCluFDI-459
❑ 93StaCluFDIO-147
❑ 93StaCluO-147
❑ 93StaCluO-420
❑ 93StaCluO-459
❑ 93SweSemWCS-172
❑ 93TopPre-94
❑ 93TopPre-237
❑ 93TopPreG-94
❑ 93TopPreG-237

93Ult-40
93UltAllS-14
93UltAwaW-2
93UppDec-129
93UppDecAW-AW5
93UppDecGGO-GG2
93UppDecLAS-22
93UppDecSP-28
94BeAPla-R97
94BeAPla-R109
94CanGamNHLP-73
94Don-118
94DonDom-6
94EASpo-25
94EASpo-186
94Fin-34
94FinnJaaK-111
94FinnJaaK-338
94FinRef-34
94Fla-32
94Fle-39
94HocWit-12
94Kra-2
94Lea-7
94LeaLim-83
94McDUppD-McD16
94OPCPre-475
94OPCPre-486
94OPCPreSE-475
94OPCPreSE-486
94Par-45
94ParGol-45
94Pin-94
94PinArtP-94
94PinBoo-BR4
94PinRinC-94
94PinTeaP-TP3
94PinTeaPDP-TP3
94PosCerBB-6
94Sco-189
94ScoChelt-Cl17
94ScoDreTea-DT8
94ScoGol-189
94ScoPla-189
94ScoPlaTS-189
94Sel-31
94SelFirLin-9
94SelGol-31
94SP-23
94SPDieCut-23
94StaClu-70
94StaCluDD-5
94StaCluDDMO-5
94StaCluFDI-70
94StaCluMO-2
94StaCluMOMS-70
94StaCluSTWC-70
94TopPre-475
94TopPre-486
94TopPreSE-475
94TopPreSE-486
94Ult-40
94UltAllS-8
94UppDec-26
94UppDecEleIce-26
94UppDecNBAP-2
94UppDecPC-C29
94UppDecPCEG-C29
94UppDecPH-H7
94UppDecPHEG-H7
94UppDecPHES-H7
94UppDecPHG-H7
94UppDecSPI-SP16
94UppDecSPIDC-SP16
95BeAPla-211
95BeAPSig-S211
95BeAPSigDC-S211
95Bow-12
95BowAllFoi-12
95CanGamNHLP-12
95CanGamNHLP-70
95ColCho-37
95ColCho-380
95ColChoPC-37
95ColChoPC-380
95ColChoPCP-37
95ColChoPCP-380
95Don-91
95DonDom-7
95DonEli-61
95DonEliDCS-61
95DonEliDCU-61
95DonProPoi-4
95Emo-28
95EmoXci-20
95Fin-19
95Fin-121
95FinnSemWC-104
95FinRef-19
95FinRef-121
95ImpSti-22
95ImpStiDCS-10
95KenStaLA-4
95KenStaLC-4
95Kra-44
95Lea-142
95LeaGolS-2
95LeaLim-40
95LeaRoaCup-6
95McDPin-MCD-23
95Met-24
95MetIS-2
95NHLAcePC-9S
95NHLCooT-11

95NHLCooT-RP11
95ParInt-38
95ParIntCCGS2-13
95ParIntCCSS2-13
95ParIntEl-38
95ParIntNHLAS-4
95ParIntPTP-PP20
95Pin-50
95PinArtP-50
95PinFirS-9
95PinFulC-6
95PinRinC-50
95PlaOneoOne-22
95PosUppD-15
95ProMag-7
95Sco-3
95ScoBlaIce-3
95ScoBlaIceAP-3
95ScoPro-3
95SelCer-2
95SelCerDS-4
95SelCerDSG-4
95SelCerMG-2
95SkyImp-28
95SP-23
95SPHol-FX3
95SPHolSpFX-FX3
95StaClu-10
95StaCluFea-F2
95StaCluMO-8
95StaCluMOMS-10
95Sum-39
95SumArtP-39
95SumGM-3
95SumIce-39
95SweGloWC-107
95SwiHNL-544
95Top-8
95Top-230
95TopHomGUSA-HGA6
95TopMarMPB-8
95TopMysF-M18
95TopMysFR-M18
95TopOPCi-8
95TopOPCi-230
95TopRinL-9RL
95TopSupSki-50
95TopSupSkiPla-50
95Ult-8
95Ult-380
95UppDec-170
95UppDec-238
95UppDecAGPRW-9
95UppDecEleIce-170
95UppDecEleIce-238
95UppDecEleIceG-170
95UppDecEleIceG-238
95UppDecNHLAS-AS2
95UppDecPHE-H34
95UppDecPreH-H34
95UppDecSpeE-SE17
95UppDecSpeEdiG-SE17
95Zen-37
96ColCho-47
96ColCho-301
96ColCho-313
96ColChoMVP-UD31
96ColChoMVPG-UD31
96Don-71
96DonCanI-56
96DonCanIGP-56
96DonCanIRPP-56
96DonDom-3
96DonEli-20
96DonEliDCS-20
96DonEliP-11
96DonHitLis-6
96DonPrePro-71
96DurAllT-DC8
96Fla-15
96FlaBluI-15
96Fle-16
96Fle-140
96FleNor-2
96FlePicDL-2
96FlePicF5-7
96HocGreC-4
96HocGreCG-4
96KraUppD-27
96KraUppD-38
96KraUppD-42
96Lea-46
96LeaLim-1
96LeaLimG-1
96LeaPre-19
96LeaPreP-46
96LeaPrePP-19
96LeaPreSG-7
96LeaPreSte-7
96MetUni-26
96MetUniCS-1
96MetUniCSSP-1
96NHLACEPC-8
96NHLProSTA-7
96Pin-34
96PinArtP-34
96PinFan-FC11
96PinFoi-34
96PinMcD-8
96PinMin-22
96PinMinB-22
96PinMinCoiB-22
96PinMinCoiGP-22
96PinMinCoiN-22

96PinMinCoiS-22
96PinMinCoiSG-22
96PinMinG-22
96PinMinS-22
96PinPreS-34
96PinRinC-34
96PinTro-8
96PlaOneoOne-370
96PosUppD-2
96Sco-36
96ScoArtPro-36
96ScoChelt-15
96ScoDeaCAP-36
96ScoGolB-36
96ScoSpeAP-36
96ScoSup-8
96SelCer-27
96SelCerAP-27
96SelCerBlu-27
96SelCerMB-27
96SelCerMG-27
96SelCerMR-27
96SelCerRed-27
96SkyImp-18
96SkyImpB-2
96SkyImpNHLF-5
96SP-27
96SPCleWin-CW18
96SPHolCol-HC6
96SPx-6
96SPxGol-6
96TopNHLP-19
96TopPicFT-FT6
96TopPicID-ID3
96TopPicOI-19
96Ult-30
96UltGolM-30
96UltPow-2
96UltPowBL-2
96UppDec-31
96UppDecBDG-145
96UppDecBDG-145
96UppDecGN-X11
96UppDecIce-10
96UppDecIcePar-10
96UppDecPP-P15
96UppDecSS-SS27A
96Zen-68
96ZenArtP-68
96ZenChaS-12
96ZenChaSD-12
97Be A PPAD-11
97Be A PPAPD-11
97BeAPla-11
97BeAPlaAut-11
97ColCho-46
97ColChoSta-SQ11
97ColChoSti-S7
97Don-37
97DonCanI-120
97DonCanIDS-120
97DonCanIPS-120
97DonCanISCS-4
97DonEli-31
97DonEliAsp-31
97DonEliS-31
97DonLim-16
97DonLim-87
97DonLim-166
97DonLim-175
97DonLimExp-16
97DonLimExp-87
97DonLimExp-166
97DonLimExp-175
97DonLimFOTG-58
97DonLin2L-13
97DonLin2LDC-13
97DonPre-127
97DonPre-171
97DonPreCttC-127
97DonPreCttC-171
97DonPreProG-37
97DonPreProS-37
97DonPri-99
97DonPriOD-24
97DonPriP-23
97DonPriS-23
97DonPriSB-23
97DonPriSG-23
97DonPriSoA-99
97DonPriSS-23
97EssOlyHH-30
97EssOlyHHF-30
97Kat-32
97KatGol-32
97KatSil-32
97Lea-64
97LeaFraMat-64
97LeaFraMDC-64
97LeaInt-64
97LeaIntUI-64
97Pac-7
97PacCop-7
97PacCroR-28
97PacCroRBoaSDC-4
97PacCroREG-28
97PacCroRIB-28

97PacCroRS-28
97PacDyn-25
97PacDynBKS-20
97PacDynC-25
97PacDynDG-25
97PacDynEG-25
97PacDynIB-25
97PacDynR-25
97PacDynSil-25
97PacDynTan-35
97PacEmeGre-7
97PacGolCroDC-6
97PacIceB-7
97PacInv-28
97PacInvC-28
97PacInvEG-28
97PacInvFP-6
97PacInvIB-28
97PacInvNRB-42
97PacInvR-28
97PacInvS-28
97PacOme-48
97PacOme-245
97PacOmeC-48
97PacOmeC-245
97PacOmeDG-48
97PacOmeDG-245
97PacOmeEG-48
97PacOmeEG-245
97PacOmeG-48
97PacOmeG-245
97PacOmeIB-48
97PacOmeIB-245
97PacOmeSLC-4
97PacPar-41
97PacParC-41
97PacParDG-41
97PacParEG-41
97PacParIB-41
97PacParSil-41
97PacRed-7
97PacRev-28
97PacRev1AGD-5
97PacRevC-28
97PacRevE-28
97PacRevIB-28
97PacRevR-28
97PacRevS-28
97PacRevTCL-6
97PacSil-7
97PacTeaCCC-6
97Pin-65
97PinArtP-65
97PinBee-25
97PinBeeGP-25
97PinCer-74
97PinCerGT-5
97PinCerMB-74
97PinCerMG-74
97PinCerMR-74
97PinCerR-74
97PinCerT-5
97PinIns-18
97PinInsCC-18
97PinInsEC-18
97PinPrePBB-65
97PinPrePBC-65
97PinPrePBM-65
97PinPrePBY-65
97PinPrePFC-65
97PinPrePFM-65
97PinPrePFY-65
97PinPrePla-65
97PinRinC-65
97PinTeaP-3
97PinTeaPM-3
97PinTeaPP-3
97PinTeaPPM-3
97PinTotCMPG-74
97PinTotCPB-74
97PinTotCPG-74
97PinTotCPR-74
97PosPin-12
97Sco-90
97ScoArtPro-90
97ScoChel-9
97ScoGolBla-90
97SP AutI-I3
97SPAut-30
97SPAutID-I3
97SPAutIE-I3
97SPAutSotT-CC
97SPx-9
97SPxBro-9
97SPxDim-SPX10
97SPxGol-9
97SPxGraF-9
97SPxSil-9
97SPxSte-9
97Stu-30
97StuPor-28
97StuPrePG-30
97StuPrePS-30
97UppDec-36
97UppDec-394
97UppDecBD-19
97UppDecBDD-29
97UppDecBDDD-29
97UppDecBDTD-29
97UppDecIce-67
97UppDecIceP-67
97UppDecIPS-67
97UppDecSG-SG7
97UppDecTSS-4C

97Zen-14
97Zen5x7-39
97ZenGolImp-39
97ZenSilImp-39
97ZenZGol-14
97ZenZSil-14
98Be A PPA-180
98Be A PPAA-180
98Be A PPAAF-180
98Be A PPAGUSC-S19
98Be A PPAJ-AS21
98Be A PPPH-H14
98Be A PPSE-180
98Be APG-180
98BowBes-29
98BowBesAR-29
98BowBesR-29
98Fin-127
98FinNo P-127
98FinNo PR-127
98FinRef-127
98O-PChr-166
98O-PChrBM-B2
98O-PChrBMR-B2
98O-PChrR-166
98Pac-7
98PacAur-39
98PacAurCF-10
98PacAurCFC-10
98PacAurCFIB-10
98PacAurCFR-10
98PacAurCFS-10
98PacCroR-28
98PacCroRLS-28
98PacCroRPotG-5
98PacDyni-39
98PacDynIIB-39
98PacDynIR-39
98PacDynITC-6
98PacGolCD-7
98PacIceB-7
98PacOmeH-49
98PacOmeO-6
98PacOmeODI-49
98PacOmePI-2
98PacOmePIB-2
98PacOmeR-49
98PacPar-44
98PacParEG-44
98PacParH-44
98PacParIB-44
98PacParS-44
98PacParTCD-6
98PacRed-7
98PacRev-29
98PacRevIS-29
98PacRevR-29
98PacRevS-8
98PacTeaC-6
98RevThrPA-3
98RevThrPA-3
98SP Aut-19
98SP AutA-8
98SP AutA-9
98SPxFin-120
98SPxFinR-120
98SPxFinS-120
98SPXTopP-12
98SPXTopPF-12
98SPXTopPR-12
98Top-166
98TopBoaM-B2
98TopGolLC1-3
98TopGolLC1B-3
98TopGolLC1BOoO-3
98TopGolLC1OoO-3
98TopGolLC1R-3
98TopGolLC1RoO-3
98TopGolLC2-3
98TopGolLC2B-3
98TopGolLC2BOoO-3
98TopGolLC2OoO-3
98TopGolLC2R-3
98TopGolLC2RoO-3
98TopGolLC3-3
98TopGolLC3B-3
98TopGolLC3BOoO-3
98TopGolLC3OoO-3
98TopGolLC3R-3
98TopGolLC3RoO-3
98TopMysFB-M17
98TopMysFBR-M17
98TopMysFG-M17
98TopMysFGR-M17
98TopMysFS-M17
98TopMysFSR-M17
98TopO-P-166
98UC-46
98UC-223
98UCMBH-BH23
98UD ChoPCR-46
98UD ChoPCR-223
98UD ChoR-46
98UD ChoR-223
98UppDec-65
98UppDecBD-19
98UppDecDD-19
98UppDecE-65
98UppDecE101-65
98UppDecFIT-FT21
98UppDecFITQ1-FT21
98UppDecFITQ2-FT21
98UppDecFITQ3-FT21
98UppDecGR-65

98UppDecM-44
98UppDecMGS-44
98UppDecMSS-44
98UppDecMSS-44
98UppDecQD-19
98UppDecTD-19
99Pac-135
99PacAur-49
99PacAurPD-49
99PacCop-135
99PacGol-135
99PacGolCD-16
99PacIceB-135
99PacPreD-135
99RetHoc-31
99SP AutPS-19
99UppDecCL-42
99UppDecCLCLC-42
99UppDecES-24
99UppDecM-73
99UppDecMGS-73
99UppDecMSS-73
99UppDecMSS-73
99UppDecRG-31
99UppDecRP-31

**Chelios, Steve**
91NasKni-13

**Chelodi, Armando**
94FinnJaaK-309

**Cherbayev, Alexander**
91UppDec-657
91UppDecCWJC-18
91UppDecF-657
92Cla-49
92RusStaRA-7
93Cla-38
93SweSemWCS-137
93UppDec-279
94ClaProP-194
94Fin-14
94FinRef-14
94FinSupTW-14
94Lea-465
94UppDec-263
94UppDecEleIce-263
94UppDecPC-C12
94UppDecPCEG-C12
94UppDecPCES-C12
96ClaGol-49

**Cheredaryk, Steve**
95SigRoo-43
95SigRooSig-43
96SprFal-5

**Cherneski, Stefan**
97BeeAutA-63
97BowCHL-117
97BowCHLB-10
97BowCHLBowBesAR-10
97BowCHLBowBesR-10
97BowCHLOPC-117
97PinBee-63
97PinBeeGP-63
98BowCHL-76
98BowCHLGA-76
98BowCHLOI-76
98BowChrC-76
98BowChrCGA-76
98BowChrCGAR-76
98BowChrCOI-76
98BowChrCOIR-76
98BowChrCR-76

**Chernik, Alexander**
89RusNatT-3
89SweSemWCS-100

**Cherniwchan, Al**
85BraWheK-12

**Chernomaz, Rich**
81VicCou-4
82VicCou-3
84DevPos-3
88SalLakCGE-6
89ProIHL-198
90ProAHLIHL-607
91ProAHLCHL-586
93St.JohML-4
94St.JohML-4
95GerDELE-403
96GerDELE-311
98GerDELE-205

**Cherrey, Scott**
93NorBayC-15
94NorBayC-18
95SauSteMG-2
95SigRoo-5
95SigRooSig-5
95Sla-371

**Cherry, Dick**
69OPC-173

**Cherry, Don**
52JunBluT-100
63RochAme-8
74OPCNHL-161
74Top-161
92ParChEP-NNO
92ParCheP-NNO
92ParCheP-NNO
92ParChePH-D20
96DurAllT-DC21
96DurAllT-DC22

**Cherviakov, Alexei**
93SweSemWCS-130

**Chervyakov, Denis**
93ClaProPro-69
96KenTho-4

**Chettleburgh, Mike**

83BraAle-29

**Chevalier, Robert**
52JunBluT-68

**Cheveldae, Tim**
88ProAHL-19
89ProAHL-326
90OPC-430
90PanSti-212
90ProSet-602
90Sco-87
90ScoCan-87
90UppDec-393
90UppDecR-393
91Bow-47
91OPC-35
91OPCPre-175
91PanSti-136
91Par-39
91Par-441
91ParFre-39
91ParFre-441
91Pin-21
91PinFre-21
91ProSet-57
91ProSetFre-57
91ProSetPC-7
91ProSetPla-31
91ProSetPla-280
91ScoAme-272
91ScoCan-492
91ScoYouS-25
91StaClu-224
91Top-35
91UppDec-129
91UppDecF-129
92Bow-202
92Bow-420
92Kra-28
92OPC-128
92PanSti-111
92PanStiFre-111
92ParEmel-37
92Pin-37
92Pin-269
92PinFre-37
92PinFre-269
92PinTea2-20
92PinTea2F-20
92ProSet-43
92ProSet-251
92Sco-275
92Sco-417
92ScoCan-275
92ScoCan-417
92ScoYouS-21
92SeaPat-7
92StaClu-199
92Top-225
92Top-310
92TopGol-225G
92TopGol-310G
92Ult-46
92UppDec-5
92UppDec-197
93Don-96
93Don-507
93Lea-195
93OPCPre-66
93OPCPreG-66
93PanSti-254
93Par-59
93ParEmel-59
93Pin-282
93PinCan-282
93Pow-67
93Sco-68
93ScoCan-68
93StaClu-166
93StaCluFDI-166
93StaCluFDIO-166
93StaCluO-166
93TopPre-66
93TopPreG-66
93Ult-14
93UppDec-9
94CanGamNHLP-297
94Don-325
94EASpo-42
94Fla-205
94Kra-37
94Lea-81
94OPCPre-502
94OPCPreSE-502
94ParSE-SE203
94ParSEG-SE203
94Pin-130
94PinArtP-130
94PinRinC-130
94Sel-102
94SelGol-102
94StaClu-217
94StaCluFDI-217
94StaCluMOMS-217
94StaCluSTWC-217
94TopPre-502
94TopPreSE-502
94Ult-240
94UppDecEleIce-75
94UppDecSPI-SP178
94UppDecSPIDC-SP178
95BeAPla-76
95BeAPSig-S76
95BeAPSigDC-S76

❑ 95CanGamNHLP-296
❑ 95ColCho-319
❑ 95ColChoPC-319
❑ 95ColChoPCP-319
❑ 95ImaPlaPl-PL8
❑ 95JetReaC-1
❑ 95JetTealss-3
❑ 95Kra-39
❑ 95ParInt-234
❑ 95ParIntEl-234
❑ 95Pin-136
❑ 95PinArtP-136
❑ 95PinRinC-136
❑ 95PlaOneoOne-325
❑ 95ProMag-61
❑ 95Sco-212
❑ 95ScoBlaIce-212
❑ 95ScoBlaIceAP-212
❑ 95Top-291
❑ 95TopOPCI-291
❑ 95UppDec-452
❑ 95UppDecEleIce-452
❑ 95UppDecEleIceG-452
❑ 95UppDecSpeE-SE179
❑ 95UppDecSpeEdiG-SE179
❑ 96NHLProSTA-61
❑ 96PlaOneoOne-406
**Cheveldayoff, Kevin**
❑ 88BraWheK-1
❑ 90ProAHLIHL-507
❑ 91ProAHLCHL-459
**Chevrefils, Real**
❑ 44BeeGro2P-11
❑ 52Par-80
❑ 53Par-89
❑ 54Par-63
❑ 54Top-6
❑ 55BruPho-4
❑ 57BruTealss-5
❑ 57Top-1
❑ 94ParMisL-8
**Chevrier, Alain**
❑ 85DevPos-4
❑ 86DevPol-7
❑ 86OPC-225
❑ 87OPC-58
❑ 87OPCSti-63
❑ 87PanSti-73
❑ 87Top-58
❑ 88JetPol-4
❑ 89BlaCok-19
❑ 89OPC-132
❑ 89PanSti-54
❑ 89Top-132
❑ 90OPC-436
❑ 90ProSet-230
**Chevrier, Wally**
❑ 61SudWol-6
❑ 62SudWol-8
**Cheyne, Travis**
❑ 91AirCanSJHL-E8
❑ 92MPSPhoSJHL-25
**Chiasson, Dan**
❑ 84SudWol-6
**Chiasson, Pascal**
❑ 917thInnSQMJHL-253
**Chiasson, Steve**
❑ 87RedWinLC-6
❑ 88RedWinLC-4
❑ 89OPC-164
❑ 89PanSti-62
❑ 89RedWinLC-5
❑ 89Top-164
❑ 90Bow-234
❑ 90BowTif-234
❑ 90OPC-94
❑ 90PanSti-207
❑ 90ProSet-69
❑ 90Sco-214
❑ 90ScoCan-214
❑ 90Top-94
❑ 90TopTif-94
❑ 90UppDec-96
❑ 90UppDecF-96
❑ 91OPC-508
❑ 91PanSti-143
❑ 91Par-268
❑ 91ParFre-268
❑ 91Pin-298
❑ 91PinFre-298
❑ 91RedWinLC-3
❑ 91ScoAme-293
❑ 91ScoCan-513
❑ 91Top-508
❑ 91UppDec-283
❑ 91UppDecF-283
❑ 92Bow-91
❑ 92OPC-160
❑ 92PanSti-120
❑ 92PanStiFre-120
❑ 92Par-282
❑ 92ParEmel-282
❑ 92Pin-339
❑ 92PinFre-339
❑ 92Sco-185
❑ 92ScoCan-185
❑ 92StaClu-105
❑ 92Top-37
❑ 92TopGol-37G
❑ 92Ult-282
❑ 92UppDec-546
❑ 93Don-97
❑ 93Lea-111
❑ 93OPCPre-196
❑ 93OPCPreG-196
❑ 93PanSti-251
❑ 93Par-55
❑ 93ParEmel-55
❑ 93Pin-194
❑ 93PinAllS-23
❑ 93PinAllSC-23
❑ 93PinCan-194
❑ 93Pow-68
❑ 93Sco-221
❑ 93ScoCan-221
❑ 93StaClu-247
❑ 93StaCluFDI-247
❑ 93StaCluFDIO-247
❑ 93StaCluO-247
❑ 93TopPre-196
❑ 93TopPreG-196
❑ 93Ult-305
❑ 93UppDec-345
❑ 94BeAPla-R83
❑ 94BeAPSig-130
❑ 94EASpo-38
❑ 94Fle-28
❑ 94Lea-487
❑ 94OPCPre-327
❑ 94OPCPreSE-327
❑ 94Par-68
❑ 94ParGol-68
❑ 94Pin-376
❑ 94PinArtP-376
❑ 94PinRinC-376
❑ 94Sco-45
❑ 94ScoGol-45
❑ 94ScoPla-45
❑ 94ScoPlaTS-45
❑ 94TopPre-327
❑ 94TopPreSE-327
❑ 94Ult-268
❑ 94UppDec-197
❑ 94UppDecEleIce-197
❑ 94UppDecSPI-SP101
❑ 94UppDecSPIDC-SP101
❑ 95ColCho-43
❑ 95ColChoPC-43
❑ 95ColChoPCP-43
❑ 95Don-69
❑ 95Emo-20
❑ 95Lea-193
❑ 95ParInt-298
❑ 95ParIntEl-298
❑ 95Pin-189
❑ 95PinArtP-189
❑ 95PinRinC-189
❑ 95PlaOneoOne-15
❑ 95Sco-146
❑ 95ScoBlaIce-146
❑ 95ScoBlaIceAP-146
❑ 95SkyImp-20
❑ 95Top-129
❑ 95TopOPCI-129
❑ 95Ult-23
❑ 95UltGolM-23
❑ 95UppDec-10
❑ 95UppDecEleIce-10
❑ 95UppDecEleIceG-10
❑ 96Don-120
❑ 96DonPrePro-120
❑ 96Sco-235
❑ 96ScoArtPro-235
❑ 96ScoDeaCAP-235
❑ 96ScoGolB-235
❑ 96ScoSpeAP-235
❑ 96SP-22
❑ 96TopNHLP-125
❑ 96TopPicOI-125
❑ 96UppDec-26
❑ 97Be A PPAD-202
❑ 97Be A PPAPD-202
❑ 97BeAPla-202
❑ 97BeAPlaAut-202
❑ 97CarHur-4
❑ 98Pac-129
❑ 98PacIceB-129
❑ 98PacRed-129
**Chibirev, Igor**
❑ 90OPCRedA-8R
❑ 91OPCIns-14R
❑ 93ClaProPro-98
❑ 93Don-436
❑ 93Pow-350
❑ 94ClaProP-61
❑ 94Par-98
❑ 94ParGol-98
**Chighisola, Mike**
❑ 90CinCyc-24
❑ 91HamRoaA-2
**Chimera, Jason**
❑ 96MedHatT-3
**Chin, Colin**
❑ 89ProIHL-123
❑ 90ProAHLIHL-540
❑ 91ProAHLCHL-250
❑ 94ClaProP-81
**Chin, Nick**
❑ 94FinnJaaK-318
**Ching, Shu**
❑ 79PanSti-360
**Chinn, Nicky**
❑ 97SheSte-6
❑ 97SheSte-7
**Chipman, Jason**
❑ 907thInnSOHL-53
❑ 92BriColJHL-208
**Chipperfield, Ron**
❑ 74OPCWHA-42
❑ 75OPCWHA-4
❑ 76OPCWHA-32
❑ 77OPCWHA-10
❑ 79OilPos-3
❑ 80NordPos-4
❑ 80OPC-280
❑ 88OilTenAnn-74
**Chisholm, Lex**
❑ 34BeeGro1P-306
❑ 40OPCV3012-148
**Chitaroni, Mario**
❑ 84SudWol-5
❑ 85SudWol-13
❑ 86SudWol-8
❑ 87FliSpi-1
❑ 88ProAHL-198
❑ 93SweSemWCS-224
❑ 94FinnJaaK-307
❑ 96GerDELE-44
❑ 96SweSemW-181
❑ 98GerDELE-178
**Chitaroni, Terry**
❑ 88SudWol-15
❑ 89SudWol-24
❑ 907thInnSOHL-380
❑ 90SudWol-15
❑ 917thInnSMC-121
❑ 917thInnSOHL-250
❑ 91StaPicH-15
❑ 91SudWol-15
❑ 91UltDra-49
❑ 93ClaProPro-92
❑ 93St.JohML-5
❑ 94BraSmo-11
**Chlad, Martin**
❑ 94CzeAPSE-47
❑ 95CzeAPSE-77
❑ 96CzeAPSE-75
**Chlubna, Tomas**
❑ 94CzeAPSE-132
❑ 96CzeAPSE-204
**Chokan, Dale**
❑ 907thInnSOHL-205
❑ 917thInnSOHL-116
**Cholette, Jules**
❑ 36V356WorG-127
**Cholewa, Marek**
❑ 89SweSemWCS-132
**Choquette, Darin**
❑ 84VicCou-5
**Chorney, Grant**
❑ 86RegPat-2
❑ 89SasBla-18
**Chorney, Marc**
❑ 82PosCer-15
❑ 83PenHeiP-6
❑ 83PenTealP-8
**Chorske, Tom**
❑ 89CanaPos-5
❑ 90CanaPos-7
❑ 90OPC-490
❑ 90ProSet-616
❑ 91Bow-345
❑ 91CanaPanTS-4
❑ 91OPC-287
❑ 91OPCPre-91
❑ 91Par-95
❑ 91ParFre-95
❑ 91Pin-295
❑ 91PinFre-295
❑ 91ScoCan-613
❑ 91ScoRoo-63T
❑ 91StaClu-276
❑ 91Top-287
❑ 91UppDec-427
❑ 91UppDecF-427
❑ 92Pin-293
❑ 92PinFre-293
❑ 92Sco-184
❑ 92ScoCan-184
❑ 92StaClu-351
❑ 92Top-313
❑ 92TopGol-313G
❑ 92Ult-112
❑ 93OPCPre-524
❑ 93OPCPreG-524
❑ 93Par-384
❑ 93ParEmel-384
❑ 93Pow-375
❑ 93TopPre-524
❑ 93TopPreG-524
❑ 93UppDec-416
❑ 94CanGamNHLP-349
❑ 94Lea-262
❑ 94OPCPre-131
❑ 94OPCPreSE-131
❑ 94Pin-182
❑ 94PinArtP-182
❑ 94PinRinC-182
❑ 94TopPre-131
❑ 94TopPreSE-131
❑ 94UppDec-191
❑ 94UppDecEleIce-191
❑ 95BeAPla-43
❑ 95BeAPSig-S43
❑ 95BeAPSigDC-S43
❑ 95ColCho-237
❑ 95ColChoPC-237
❑ 95ColChoPCP-237
❑ 95Sco-284
❑ 95ScoBlaIce-284
❑ 95ScoBlaIceAP-284
❑ 95Sen-5
❑ 96Pin-26
❑ 96PinArtP-26
❑ 96PinFoi-26
❑ 96PinPreS-26
❑ 96PinRinC-26
❑ 96SenPizH-3
❑ 97Be A PPAD-207
❑ 97Be A PPAPD-207
❑ 97BeAPla-207
❑ 97BeAPlaAut-207
❑ 97PacInvNRB-132
❑ 98Pac-278
❑ 98PacIceB-278
❑ 98PacRed-278
**Chotowetz, Kelly**
❑ 89RegPat-1
❑ 907thInnSWHL-172
**Chouinard, David (Dave)**
❑ 907thInnSQMJHL-240
❑ 917thInnSQMJHL-134
**Chouinard, Eric**
❑ 97UppDec-408
❑ 98BowBes-139
❑ 98BowBesAR-139
❑ 98BowBesR-139
❑ 98BowCHL-104
❑ 98BowCHL-143
❑ 98BowCHLAuB-A15
❑ 98BowCHLAuG-A15
❑ 98BowCHLAuS-A15
❑ 98BowCHLGA-104
❑ 98BowCHLGA-143
❑ 98BowCHLOI-104
❑ 98BowCHLOI-143
❑ 98BowChrC-104
❑ 98BowChrC-143
❑ 98BowChrCGA-104
❑ 98BowChrCGA-143
❑ 98BowChrCGAR-104
❑ 98BowChrCGAR-143
❑ 98BowChrCOI-104
❑ 98BowChrCOI-143
❑ 98BowChrCOIR-104
❑ 98BowChrCOIR-143
❑ 98BowChrCR-104
❑ 98BowChrCR-143
❑ 98FinFutF-F13
❑ 98FinFutFR-F13
❑ 98QueRem-5
❑ 99QuePeeWHWCCS-26
**Chouinard, Guy**
❑ 76OPCNHL-316
❑ 77OPCNHL-237
❑ 77Top-237
❑ 78OPC-340
❑ 79FlamPos-3
❑ 79FlaTeal-4
❑ 79OPC-60
❑ 79Top-60
❑ 80FlamPos-2
❑ 80OPC-45
❑ 80PepCap-2
❑ 80Top-45
❑ 81FlamPos-3
❑ 81OPC-33
❑ 81OPCSti-219
❑ 81Top-6
❑ 82OPC-41
❑ 82OPCSti-215
❑ 82PosCer-3
❑ 83OPC-78
❑ 92QueIntPWG-NNO
❑ 99QuePeeWHWCCS-2
**Chouinard, Jacques**
❑ 80QueRem-2
**Chouinard, Marc**
❑ 95Cla-29
❑ 95ClaCHLAS-AS18
**Chouinard, Mathieu**
❑ 97UppDec-399
❑ 98BowCHL-82
❑ 98BowCHL-159
❑ 98BowCHLAuB-A9
❑ 98BowCHLAuG-A9
❑ 98BowCHLAuS-A9
❑ 98BowCHLGA-82
❑ 98BowCHLGA-159
❑ 98BowCHLOI-82
❑ 98BowCHLOI-159
❑ 98BowChrC-82
❑ 98BowChrC-159
❑ 98BowChrCGA-82
❑ 98BowChrCGA-159
❑ 98BowChrCGAR-82
❑ 98BowChrCGAR-159
❑ 98BowChrCOI-82
❑ 98BowChrCOI-159
❑ 98BowChrCOIR-82
❑ 98BowChrCOIR-159
❑ 98BowChrCR-82
❑ 98BowChrCR-159
❑ 98FinFutF-F12
❑ 98FinFutFR-F12
❑ 99QuePeeWHWCCS-25
**Choules, Gregg**
❑ 84ChiSag-6
**Chowaniec, Stefan**
❑ 79PanSti-127
**Chretien, Claude**
❑ 51LavDaiLSJ-19
**Christensen, Matt**
❑ 85MinDul-15
**Christensen, Ted**
❑ 95ColCho-349
❑ 95ColChoPC-349
❑ 95ColChoPCP-349
**Christensen, Troy**
❑ 96DayBom-19
**Christian, Brandon**
❑ 94JohChi-3
❑ 95ThuBayS-5
**Christian, Dave**
❑ 80JetPos-5
❑ 80OPC-176
❑ 80PepCap-124
❑ 80Top-176
❑ 80USAOlyTMP-14
❑ 81JetPos-3
❑ 81OPC-359
❑ 81OPC-360
❑ 81OPC-378
❑ 81OPCSti-136
❑ 81SweSemHVS-96
❑ 81Top-7
❑ 81Top-66
❑ 82Jet-5
❑ 82OPC-377
❑ 82OPCSti-206
❑ 82PosCer-21
❑ 83OPC-367
❑ 84CapPizH-2
❑ 84OPC-195
❑ 84OPCSti-133
❑ 84Top-142
❑ 85CapPizH-2
❑ 85OPC-99
❑ 85OPCSti-110
❑ 85Top-99
❑ 86CapKod-4
❑ 86CapPol-4
❑ 86OPC-21
❑ 86OPCBoxB-C
❑ 86OPCSti-248
❑ 86Top-21
❑ 86TopBoxB-C
❑ 87CapKod-27
❑ 87CapTealss-3
❑ 87OPC-88
❑ 87OPCSti-235
❑ 87PanSti-184
❑ 87Top-88
❑ 88CapBor-1
❑ 88CapSmo-1
❑ 88OPC-14
❑ 88OPCSti-70
❑ 88PanSti-369
❑ 88Top-14
❑ 89BruSpoAU-2
❑ 89CapTealss-2
❑ 89OPC-159
❑ 89OPCSti-78
❑ 89PanSti-345
❑ 89SweSemWCS-166
❑ 89Top-159
❑ 90Bow-40
❑ 90BowTif-40
❑ 90BruSpoA-9
❑ 90OPC-263
❑ 90PanSti-18
❑ 90ProSet-6
❑ 90Sco-295
❑ 90ScoCan-295
❑ 90Top-263
❑ 90TopTif-263
❑ 90UppDec-61
❑ 90UppDecF-61
❑ 91BluPos-8
❑ 91Bow-358
❑ 91OPC-276
❑ 91OPCPre-53
❑ 91PanSti-173
❑ 91Par-159
❑ 91ParFre-159
❑ 91Pin-244
❑ 91PinFre-244
❑ 91ProSet-11
❑ 91ProSet-297
❑ 91ProSet-471
❑ 91ProSetFre-11
❑ 91ProSetFre-297
❑ 91ProSetFre-471
❑ 91ProSetPla-110
❑ 91ScoAme-292
❑ 91ScoCan-589
❑ 91ScoRoo-39T
❑ 91StaClu-95
❑ 91SweSemWCS-142
❑ 91Top-276
❑ 91UppDec-541
❑ 91UppDecF-541
❑ 92Bow-6
❑ 92OPC-289
❑ 92OPCPre-1
❑ 92Pin-193
❑ 92PinFre-193
❑ 92Sco-198
❑ 92ScoCan-198
❑ 92StaClu-216
❑ 92Top-21
❑ 92TopGol-21G
❑ 92Ult-273
❑ 92UppDec-194
❑ 93BlaCok-9
❑ 93OPCPre-118
❑ 93OPCPreG-118
❑ 93Sco-440
❑ 93ScoCan-440
❑ 93TopPre-118
❑ 93TopPreG-118
❑ 94FinnJaaK-127
❑ 95ColEdgI-164
❑ 95Ima-26
❑ 95ImaGol-26
❑ 95SigRooMI-5
❑ 95SigRooMI-6
❑ 95SigRooSMIS-5
❑ 95SigRooSMIS-6
**Christian, Gord**
❑ 93JohChi-7
❑ 94JohChi-7
**Christian, Jeff**
❑ 90ProAHLIHL-572
❑ 91ProAHLCHL-415
❑ 95CleLum-9
❑ 96CleLum-8
**Christian, Lou**
❑ 84NovScoO-26
**Christian, Marc**
❑ 93MinDul-7
**Christian, Matt**
❑ 93MinDul-6
**Christian, Mike**
❑ 96GueSto-13
**Christian, Tim**
❑ 91FerStaB-8
❑ 95RoaExp-11
❑ 96RoaExp-24
**Christiansen, Hal**
❑ 89RegPat-2
❑ 907thInnSWHL-164
❑ 917thInnSWHL-225
**Christiansen, Keith**
❑ 72FigSaiPos-4
❑ 72SweSemWC-124
**Christiansson, Jan**
❑ 67SweHoc-234
**Christiansson, Jens**
❑ 84SweSemE-156
❑ 86SwePanS-143
**Christie, Jason**
❑ 88SasBla-21
❑ 89SasBla-22
❑ 94PorPir-5
❑ 95PorPir-8
❑ 96PorPir-21
**Christie, Mike**
❑ 74NHLActSta-61
❑ 74OPCNHL-278
❑ 75OPCNHL-366
❑ 76OPCNHL-333
❑ 76OPCNHL-383
❑ 77OPCNHL-357
❑ 78OPC-291
❑ 79OPC-345
❑ 79Roc-4
❑ 80OPC-358
**Christie, Ryan**
❑ 95Sla-293
**Christion, Scott**
❑ 91AirCanSJHL-B18
❑ 91AirCanSJHL-D17
❑ 91AirCanSJHLAS-16
❑ 91AirCanSJHLAS-49
**Christoff, Steve**
❑ 80NorStaPos-5
❑ 80OPC-103
❑ 80Top-103
❑ 80USAOlyTMP-13
❑ 81NorStaPos-6
❑ 81OPC-160
❑ 81SweSemHVS-101
❑ 81Top-W104
❑ 82OPC-42
❑ 82OPCSti-194
❑ 82PosCer-9
❑ 83OPC-169
❑ 84OPC-81
❑ 95SigRooMI-7
❑ 95SigRooMI-8
❑ 95SigRooSMIS-7
❑ 95SigRooSMIS-8
**Christoffer, Justin**
❑ 91AirCanSJHL-C37
**Christopher, Des**
❑ 907thInnSWHL-207
**Christy, Frankie**
❑ 51BufBis-3
**Chrun, Mike**
❑ 89SpoChi-1
❑ 907thInnSWHL-188
❑ 917thInnSWHL-203
**Chrystal, Bob**
❑ 51CleBar-17
❑ 54Par-69
❑ 54Top-2
**Chubarov, Artem**
❑ 97UppDecBD-69
❑ 97UppDecBDDD-69
❑ 97UppDecBDQD-69
❑ 97UppDecBDTD-69
❑ 98UC-284
❑ 98UD ChoPCR-284
❑ 98UD ChoR-284
**Chun, Ta**
❑ 79PanSti-357
**Chunchukov, Alexsandr**
❑ 94RalIce-3
**Church, Brad**
❑ 93PriAlbR-4
❑ 94PriAlbR-3
❑ 95Cla-17
❑ 95ClaIceBre-BK15
❑ 95Ima-82
❑ 95ImaGol-82
❑ 95ImaPlaPDC-PD5
❑ 95PriAlbR-3
❑ 96ClaIceBreDC-BK15
❑ 96PorPir-12
**Church, Jack**
❑ 34BeeGro1P-307
❑ 39OPCV3011-52
**Churla, Shane**
❑ 83MedHatT-2
❑ 87FlamRedRP-4
❑ 90ProSet-135
❑ 91ScoCan-542
❑ 92Par-316
❑ 92ParEmel-316
❑ 92Ult-315
❑ 93OPCPre-368
❑ 93OPCPreG-368
❑ 93Par-316
❑ 93ParEmel-316
❑ 93Sco-425
❑ 93ScoCan-425
❑ 93TopPre-368
❑ 93TopPreG-368
❑ 94BeAPSig-169
❑ 94Lea-364
❑ 94ParSE-SE41
❑ 94ParSEG-SE41
❑ 94Pin-516
❑ 94PinArtP-516
❑ 94PinRinC-516
❑ 94StaClu-21
❑ 94StaCluFDI-21
❑ 94StaCluMOMS-21
❑ 94StaCluSTWC-21
❑ 94StaHoc-6
❑ 94StaPos-3
❑ 94StaScoS-NNO
❑ 94Ult-278
❑ 94UppDec-186
❑ 94UppDecEleIce-186
❑ 95ParInt-61
❑ 95ParIntEl-61
❑ 95PlaOneoOne-246
❑ 95ProMag-21
❑ 95UppDec-458
❑ 95UppDecEleIce-458
❑ 95UppDecEleIceG-458
❑ 96NHLProSTA-121
❑ 96Pin-191
❑ 96PinArtP-191
❑ 96PinFoi-191
❑ 96PinPreS-191
❑ 96PinRinC-191
❑ 96PlaOneoOne-365
❑ 97Be A PPAD-182
❑ 97Be A PPAPD-182
❑ 97BeAPla-182
❑ 97BeAPlaAut-182
❑ 97PacInvNRB-123
❑ 97UppDec-317
**Chychrun, Jeff**
❑ 83KinCan-8
❑ 84KinCan-18
❑ 85KinCan-18
❑ 89FlyPos-5
❑ 90FlyPos-5
❑ 90OPC-465
❑ 90ProSet-213
❑ 90Sco-138
❑ 90ScoCan-138
❑ 90UppDec-446
❑ 90UppDecF-446
❑ 91ScoCan-626
❑ 92Bow-257
❑ 92DurPan-33
❑ 92Sco-364
❑ 92ScoCan-364
❑ 92StaClu-298
❑ 92Top-196
❑ 92TopGol-196G
**Chynoweth, Dean**
❑ 85MedHatT-9
❑ 89Isl-2
❑ 90ProAHLIHL-511
❑ 91ProAHLCHL-463
❑ 94OPCPre-45
❑ 94OPCPreSE-45
❑ 94TopPre-45
❑ 94TopPreSE-45
❑ 97Be A PPAD-246
❑ 97Be A PPAPD-246
❑ 97BeAPla-246
❑ 97BeAPlaAut-246
❑ 97Pac-340
❑ 97PacCop-340
❑ 97PacEmeGre-340
❑ 97PacIceB-340
❑ 97PacRed-340
❑ 97PacSil-340
❑ 97UppDec-222
**Chynoweth, Ed**
❑ 917thInnSMC-71
❑ 917thInnSWHL-120
**Chyzowski, Barry**
❑ 89ProIHL-42
**Chyzowski, Dave**
❑ 87KamBla-3
❑ 88KamBla-6
❑ 89Isl-3
❑ 907thInnSMC-3
❑ 90OPC-146
❑ 90ProAHLIHL-509
❑ 90ProSet-483
❑ 90Sco-372
❑ 90ScoCan-372
❑ 90ScoYouS-12
❑ 90Top-146
❑ 90TopTif-146
❑ 90UppDec-228

90UppDecF-228
91Bow-229
91OPC-435
91PanSti-253
91ProAHLCHL-471
91ScoCan-443
91StaClu-250
91Top-435
91UppDec-281
91UppDecF-281
95AdiRedW-3
98KanCitB-20

**Chyzowski, Ron**
88ProAHL-292

**Ciarcia, Jerry**
82SweSemHVS-142

**Ciavaglia, Peter**
91ProAHLCHL-12
91RochAmeDD-2
91RochAmeKod-7
91RochAmePos-5
92Cla-103
92RochAmeDD-3
92RochAmeKod-5
93Sco-474
93ScoCan-474
93SweSemE-135
95ColEdgI-121
96ClaGol-103
96DetVip-2

**Ciccarelli, Dino**
81NorStaPos-7
81OPC-161
81Top-W105
82McDSti-7
82NorStaPos-5
82NorStaPos-6
82OPC-162
82OPC-165
82OPCSti-189
82PosCer-9
83NorStaPos-6
83OPC-164
83OPC-170
83OPCSti-118
83OPCSti-119
83PufSti-15
847EDis-27
84KelAccD-1
84NorSta7E-12
84NorStaPos-6
84OPC-97
84OPCSti-47
84Top-73
857ECreCar-9
85NorSta7E-1
85NorStaPos-8
85OPC-13
85OPCSti-39
85Top-13
86NorSta7E-6
86OPC-138
86OPCSti-169
86Top-138
87NorStaPos-11
87OPC-81
87OPCMin-7
87OPCSti-57
87OPCSti-118
87PanSti-293
87Top-81
88NorStaADA-6
88OPC-175
88OPCSti-202
88PanSti-93
88Top-175
89CapKod-22
89CapTealss-3
89OPC-41
89OPCSti-75
89PanSti-342
89Top-41
90Bow-69
90BowHatTri-15
90BowTif-69
90CapKod-4
90CapPos-4
90CapSmo-4
90Kra-7
90OPC-100
90OPCPre-14
90PanSti-161
90ProSet-308
90Sco-230
90ScoCan-230
90ScoHotRS-94
90Top-100
90TopTeaSL-6
90TopTif-100
90UppDec-76
90UppDecF-76
91Bow-302
91CapJun5-6
91CapKod-6
91Kra-14
91OPC-429
91PanSti-207
91Par-193
91ParFre-193
91Pin-128
91PinFre-128
91ProSet-258
91ProSetFre-258
91ProSetPla-131
91ScoAme-128

91ScoCan-128
91StaClu-118
91Top-429
91UppDec-276
91UppDecF-276
92Bow-176
92OPC-249
92OPCPre-44
92PanSti-160
92PanStiFre-160
92Par-45
92ParEmel-45
92Pin-311
92PinFre-311
92Sco-395
92ScoCan-395
92StaClu-399
92Top-318
92TopGol-318G
92Ult-47
92Ult-283
92UppDec-461
93Don-98
93Lea-18
93OPCPre-49
93OPCPreG-49
93PanSti-245
93Par-60
93ParChePH-D5
93ParEmel-60
93Pin-127
93Pin-239
93PinCan-127
93PinCan-239
93Pow-60
93Sco-214
93ScoCan-214
93StaClu-294
93StaCluO-294
93TopPre-49
93TopPreG-49
93Ult-32
93UppDec-136
93UppDecSP-41
94BeAPla-R39
94BeAPla-R129
94CanGamNHLP-86
94Don-86
94EASpo-41
94Fla-46
94Fle-57
94Lea-44
94OPCPre-541
94OPCPreSE-541
94Par-65
94ParGol-65
94ParSEV-2
94Pin-241
94PinArtP-241
94PinRinC-241
94SarSti-29
94Sco-19
94Sco-243
94Sco-246
94ScoGol-19
94ScoGol-243
94ScoGol-246
94ScoPla-19
94ScoPla-243
94ScoPla-246
94ScoTaTS-19
94ScoTaTS-243
94ScoTaTS-246
94Sel-118
94SelGol-118
94SelPro-118
94StaClu-191
94StaCluFDI-191
94StaCluMOMS-191
94StaCluSTWC-191
94TopPre-541
94TopPreSE-541
94Ult-58
94UppDec-5
94UppDecEleIce-5
94UppDecSPI-SP112
94UppDecSPIDC-SP112
95BeAPla-49
95BeAPSig-S49
95BeAPSigDC-S49
95CanGamNHLP-99
95ColCho-89
95ColChoPC-89
95ColChoPCP-89
95Don-30
95Emo-51
95Lea-190
95ParInt-339
95ParIntEl-339
95Pin-74
95PinArtP-74
95PinRinC-74
95PlaOneoOne-251
95Sco-247
95ScoBlaIce-247
95ScoBlaIceAP-247
95SelCer-102
95SelCerMG-102
95SkyImp-50
95StaClu-150
95StaCluMOMS-150
95StaCluPS-PS7
95Sum-65
95SumArtP-65

95SumIce-65
95Top-77
95TopOPCI-77
95Ult-232
95UppDec-431
95UppDecEleIce-431
95UppDecEleIceG-431
95UppDecSpeE-SE28
95UppDecSpeEdiG-SE28
95Zen-51
95ZenGifG-16
96ColCho-88
96Don-150
96DonPrePro-150
96Fla-86
96FlaBluI-86
96Lea-16
96LeaPreP-16
96MetUni-143
96Pin-31
96PinArtP-31
96PinFoi-31
96PinPreS-31
96PinRinC-31
96Sco-101
96ScoArtPro-101
96ScoDeaCAP-101
96ScoGolB-101
96ScoSpeAP-101
96SP-147
96TopPic5C-FC4
96Ult-156
96UltGolM-156
96UppDec-196
96UppDec-336
96UppDecBD-148
96UppDecBDG-148
96UppDecIce-66
96UppDecIcePar-66
96UppDecPP-P22
96Zen-87
96ZenArtP-87
97ColCho-237
97ColChoCTG-C22A
97ColChoCTG-C22B
97ColChoCTG-C22C
97ColChoCTGE-CR22
97ColChoSta-SQ22
97ColChoSti-S22
97Don-177
97DonCanI-77
97DonCanIDS-77
97DonCanIPS-77
97DonEli-43
97DonEliAsp-43
97DonEliS-43
97DonLim-25
97DonLimExp-25
97DonPre-51
97DonPreCttC-51
97DonPreProG-177
97DonPreProS-177
97DonPri-66
97DonPriSoA-66
97Kat-134
97KatGol-134
97KatSil-134
97Lea-83
97LeaFraMat-83
97LeaFraMDC-83
97LeaInt-83
97LeaIntUI-83
97Pac-15
97PacCop-15
97PacCroR-124
97PacCroREG-124
97PacCroRIB-124
97PacCroRS-124
97PacDyn-115
97PacDynBKS-88
97PacDynC-115
97PacDynDG-115
97PacDynEG-115
97PacDynIB-115
97PacDynR-115
97PacDynSil-115
97PacDynTan-57
97PacEmeGre-15
97PacIceB-15
97PacInv-129
97PacInvAZ-22
97PacInvC-129
97PacInvIB-129
97PacInvNRB-183
97PacInvR-129
97PacInvS-129
97PacOme-97
97PacOmeC-97
97PacOmeDG-97
97PacOmeEG-97
97PacOmeIB-97
97PacPar-171
97PacParC-171
97PacParDG-171
97PacParEG-171
97PacParIB-171
97PacParRed-171
97PacParSil-171
97PacRed-15
97PacRevC-58
97PacRevIB-58

97PacRevR-58
97PacRevS-58
97PacSil-15
97PacTeaCCC-23
97Pin-68
97PinArtP-68
97PinBee-29
97PinBeeGP-29
97PinCer-105
97PinCerMB-105
97PinCerMG-105
97PinCerMR-105
97PinCerR-105
97PinPrePBB-68
97PinPrePBC-68
97PinPrePBM-68
97PinPrePBY-68
97PinPrePFC-68
97PinPrePFM-68
97PinPrePFY-68
97PinPrePla-68
97PinTotCMPG-105
97PinTotCPB-105
97PinTotCPG-105
97PinTotCPR-105
97Sco-119
97ScoArtPro-119
97ScoChel-15
97ScoGolBla-119
97SP AutI-I27
97SPAut-148
97SPAutID-I27
97SPAutIE-I27
97Stu-65
97StuPrePG-65
97StuPrePS-65
97UppDec-154
97UppDec-199
97UppDecBD-21
97UppDecBDDD-21
97UppDecBDQD-21
97UppDecBDTD-21
97UppDecCtAg-17
97UppDecCtAgA-AR17
97UppDecGDM-154
97UppDecIce-22
97UppDecIceP-22
97UppDecIPS-22
97Zen-47
97ZenZGol-47
97ZenZSil-47
98Be A PPAM-M3
98Be A PPAM-M9
98BowBes-68
98BowBesAR-68
98BowBesR-68
98Fin-5
98FinNo P-5
98FinNo PR-5
98FinRef-5
98O-PChr-119
98O-PChrR-119
98Pac-22
98PacAur-78
98PacAurCF-22
98PacAurCFC-22
98PacAurCFIB-22
98PacAurCFR-22
98PacAurCFS-22
98PacCroR-57
98PacCroRLS-57
98PacDynI-79
98PacDynIIB-79
98PacDynIR-79
98PacDynITC-11
98PacIceB-22
98PacOmeH-101
98PacOmeODI-101
98PacOmeR-101
98PacPar-94
98PacParC-94
98PacParEG-94
98PacParH-94
98PacParIB-94
98PacParS-94
98PacParTCD-11
98PacRed-22
98PacRev-61
98PacRevIS-61
98PacRevR-61
98Top-119
98TopO-P-119
98UC-93
98UD ChoPCR-93
98UD ChoR-93
98UDCP-93
99Pac-171
99PacCop-171
99PacGol-171
99PacIceB-171
99PacPreD-171

**Ciccarello, Joe**
93MinDul-8

**Ciccone, Enrico**
90ProAHLIHL-120
91UppDec-51
91UppDecF-51
92OPCPre-122
92UppDec-90
93Lea-375
93LigSealR-7
93Par-219
93ParEmel-219

93UppDec-528
94BeAPla-R16
94BeAPSig-132
94LigPhoA-8
94UppDec-460
94UppDecEleIce-460
95CanGamNHLP-254
95ColCho-152
95ColChoPC-152
95ColChoPCP-152
95LigTeal-6
95Sco-382
95UppDecEleIce-382
95UppDecEleIceG-382
96BeAPAut-129
96BeAPAutSil-129
96BeAPla-129
96UppDec-238
97CarHur-5
97PacInvNRB-43
98Pac-397
98PacIceB-397
98PacRed-397

**Cichocki, Chris**
86OPC-41
86OPCSti-124
86Top-41
88ProAHL-327
90ProAHLIHL-14
91ProAHLCHL-206
92BinRan-9
96CinCyc-33
98CinCyc-27

**Cierny, Jozef**
92Cla-35
92RochAmeDD-4
92RochAmeKod-6
93Cla-127
94CapBreO-5
94ClaProP-86
94Sco-217
94ScoGol-217
94ScoPla-217
96ClaGol-35
98GerDELE-255

**Ciesla, Hank**
44BeeGro2P-84
52JunBluT-32
58Top-49
63Par-51
94ParMisL-29

**Ciger, Zdeno**
90Dev-6
90OPCPre-15
90ProSet-619
90ScoRoo-82T
90UppDec-429
90UppDecF-429
91Bow-280
91ScoCan-405
91StaClu-379
91Top-352
91UppDec-385
91UppDecF-385
92OilTeal-2
92OPC-88
92PanSti-175
92PanStiFre-175
92Par-286
92ParEmel-286
92Pin-302
92PinFre-302
92Sco-534
92ScoCan-534
92StaClu-228
92Top-496
92TopGol-496G
92Ult-113
92UppDec-457
93Don-113
93Lea-197
93OPCPre-456
93OPCPreG-456
93PanSti-239
93Par-336
93ParEmel-336
93Pow-78
93Sco-388
93ScoCan-388
93StaClu-73
93StaCluFDI-73
93StaCluFDIO-73
93StaCluO-73
93TopPre-456
93TopPreG-456
93Ult-315
93UppDec-330
94Don-274
94FinnJaaK-198
94Lea-65
94Par-76
94ParGol-76
94Pin-70
94PinArtP-70
94PinRinC-70
94Sco-122
94ScoGol-122
94ScoPlaTS-122
94StaClu-229
94StaCluFDI-229
94StaCluMOMS-229
94StaCluSTWC-229
94Ult-71

94UppDec-28
94UppDecEleIce-28
95BeAPla-137
95BeAPSig-S137
95BeAPSigDC-S137
95Don-360
95DonEli-24
95DonEliDCS-24
95DonEliDCU-24
95Fin-107
95FinRef-107
95Met-53
95ParInt-79
95ParIntEl-79
95SloAPSNT-23
95SP-53
95StaClu-127
95StaCluMOMS-127
95Ult-237
96ColCho-95
96Don-203
96DonPrePro-203
96FlePic-96
96Lea-76
96LeaPreP-76
96Pin-148
96PinArtP-148
96PinFoi-148
96PinPreS-148
96PinRinC-148
96Sco-20
96ScoArtPro-20
96ScoDeaCAP-20
96ScoGolB-20
96ScoSpeAP-20
96Sum-19
96SumArtP-19
96SumIce-19
96SumMet-19
96SumPreS-19
96SweSemW-229

**Cihal, Miroslav**
95CzeAPSE-230

**Cihlar, Jiri**
94CzeAPSE-177
95CzeAPSE-189

**Cijan, Thomas**
95AusNatTea-2

**Cikl, Igor**
95CzeAPSE-113

**Cimellaro, Tony**
907thInnSOHL-54
917thInnSOHL-109
96GerDELE-109

**Cimetta, Rob**
89BruSpoA-7
90OPC-288
90Top-288
90TopTif-288
91Bow-160
91MapLeaP-5
910PC-256
910PCPre-160
91StaClu-9
91Top-256
92St.JohML-3
92StaClu-83
92Top-181
92TopGol-181G
94GerDELE-280
95GerDELE-276
96GerDELE-181
98GerDELE-113

**Cinibulk, Martin**
96CzeAPSE-122

**Cipolla, Jason**
95SouCarS-6
96St.JohML-9

**Cipriano, Mark**
89VicCou-7
907thInnSWHL-242

**Ciprick, Trent**
84BraWheK-15

**Circelli, Anthony**
93SweSemWCS-215
95FinnSemV-173
95SweGloWC-229

**Cirella, Joe**
80OshGen-12
81RocPos-4
82OPC-137
82OshGen-5
82PosCer-1
83CanNatJ-2
84DevPos-2
84OPC-110
84OPCSti-74
84Top-85
85OPC-98
85Top-98
86DevPol-8
86OPC-163
86OPCSti-198
86Top-163
87OPC-170
87OPCSti-61
87Top-170
88DevCar-7
88OPC-188
88OPCSti-79
88PanSti-268
88Top-188
89Nord-5

89NordGenF-3
89NordPol-2
89OPC-130
89Top-130
90NordPet-3
90NordTeal-1
90OPC-107
90PanSti-141
90ProSet-243
90Sco-305C
90ScoCan-305C
90Top-107
90TopTif-107
90UppDec-293
90UppDecF-293
90NordPanTS-1
910PC-502
91Par-340
91ParFre-340
91ScoCan-441
91Top-502
92Sco-369
92ScoCan-369
92StaClu-479
92Top-163
92TopGol-163G
93Lea-269
930PCPre-41
930PCPre-414
930PCPreG-41
930PCPreG-414
93PanTeal-1
93Par-347
93ParEmel-347
93Pin-346
93PinCan-346
93PinExp-3
93Pow-91
93Sco-515
93ScoCan-515
93ScoGol-515
93StaClu-2
93StaCluFDI-2
93StaCluFDIO-2
93StaCluO-2
93TopPre-41
93TopPreG-41
93TopPreG-414
93UppDec-65
94EASpo-49
94Pin-308
94PinArtP-308
94PinRinC-308
95MilAdmBO-4
96GerDELE-346

**Cirelli, Anthony**
96GerDELE-223

**Cirillo, Ryan**
95Sla-191

**Cirjak, John**
95SpoChi-16
97BowCHL-95
97BowCHLOPC-95

**Cirone, Frank**
94Rallce-4

**Cirone, Jason**
907thInnSOHL-30
907thInnSOHL-178
91MonHaw-2
91ProAHLCHL-183
91UppDec-605
91UppDecF-605
95BufStaRHI-34
98KanCitB-24

**Cisar, Marian**
97BeeAutA-67
97PinBee-67
97PinBeeGP-67
98BowCHL-58
98BowCHLGA-58
98BowCHLOI-58
98BowChrC-58
98BowChrCGA-58
98BowChrCOI-58
98BowChrCOIR-58
98BowChrCR-58
98UppDec-303
98UppDecE-303
98UppDecE101-303
98UppDecGR-303

**Clackson, Kim**
78JetPos-3
80NordPos-5
80PepCap-62
810PC-271

**Claesson, Anders**
67SweHoc-217
69SweHocS-259
70SweHocS-148
71SweHocS-241

**Claesson, Jan**
83SweSemE-91
84SweSemE-91
85SwePanS-234

**Claesson, Stefan**
89SweSemE-9
90SweSemE-82
91SweSemE-234

**Clague, Jason**
93RedDeeR-4

**Clancy, Chris**
907thInnSOHL-31
917thInnSOHL-16

❑ 91CorRoy-20
**Clancy, Greg**
❑ 897thInnSOHL-59
❑ 907thInnSOHL-81
**Clancy, King**
❑ 23V1451-3
❑ 24C144ChaCig-13
❑ 24V1452-3
❑ 32O'KeeMapL-7
❑ 33OPCV304A-31
❑ 33V129-8
❑ 33V252CanG-10
❑ 33V288HamG-17
❑ 33V3572IceKP-1
❑ 33V357IceK-13
❑ 34BeeGro1P-308
❑ 34SweCap-44
❑ 36ChaPos-5
❑ 36OPCV304D-125
❑ 36V356WorG-29
❑ 55Par-33
❑ 55ParQuaO-33
❑ 59Par-50
❑ 60Top-47
❑ 60TopSta-8
❑ 61YorYelB-39
❑ 63Par-20
❑ 69MapLeaWBG-4
❑ 80MapLeaP-6
❑ 83HalFP-C3
❑ 85HalFC-33
❑ 92HalFL-8
❑ 94ParMisLP-P4
❑ 94ParTalB-132
**Clancy, Terry**
❑ 69MapLeaWBG-5
❑ 72MapLeaP-2
**Clantara, Roland**
❑ 51LavDaiLSJ-52
**Clapper, Dit**
❑ 33OPCV304A-8
❑ 33V129-36
❑ 33V252CanG-11
❑ 33V357IceK-1
❑ 34BeeGro1P-8
❑ 34DiaMatS-12
❑ 36V356WorG-36
❑ 39OPCV3011-95
❑ 60Top-26
❑ 60TopSta-9
❑ 83HalFP-F3
❑ 85HalFC-79
❑ 91BruSpoAL-8
❑ 94ParTalBG-8
❑ 99UppDecCL-44
❑ 99UppDecCLCLC-44
**Claringbull, Mike**
❑ 85MedHatT-1
**Clark, Andrew**
❑ 93SauSteMG-18
❑ 94GueSto-10
❑ 95GueSto5A-2
❑ 95Sla-90
❑ 96GerDELE-307
**Clark, Brett**
❑ 97CanaPos-6
❑ 98Be A PPA-220
❑ 98Be A PPAA-220
❑ 98Be A PPAAF-220
❑ 98Be A PPSE-220
❑ 98Be APG-220
❑ 98UppDecM-105
❑ 98UppDecMGS-105
❑ 98UppDecMSS-105
❑ 98UppDecMSS-105
**Clark, Dean**
❑ 84KamBla-6
❑ 88OilTenAnn-100
**Clark, Don**
❑ 95SasBla-7
**Clark, Donn**
❑ 81SasBla-4
❑ 917thInnSWHL-149
**Clark, George**
❑ 23CreSel-5
❑ 95GerDELE-359
**Clark, Gord**
❑ 86LonKni-30
**Clark, Herb**
❑ 10C56-11
**Clark, Jason**
❑ 96WheNai-21
❑ 98GerDELE-3
**Clark, Kerry**
❑ 88ProAHL-319
❑ 89ProAHL-248
❑ 90ProAHLIHL-620
❑ 91ProAHLCHL-584
❑ 93PorPir-18
❑ 94ClaEnf-E7
❑ 94PorPir-6
❑ 95ColEdgI-171
**Clark, Norbert**
❑ 51LavDaiLSJ-20
**Clark, Ron**
❑ 89RayJrC-6
**Clark, Wendel**
❑ 83SasBla-8
❑ 84SasBlaS-3
❑ 85MapLeaP-6
❑ 86KraDra-8
❑ 86MapLeaP-4
❑ 86OPC-149
❑ 86OPCSti-125
❑ 86OPCSti-141
❑ 86Top-149
❑ 87MapLeaP-2
❑ 87MapLeaPLA-6
❑ 87MapLeaPO-2
❑ 87OPC-12
❑ 87OPCSti-152
❑ 87PanSti-330
❑ 87ProAll-10
❑ 87Top-12
❑ 88FriLayS-29
❑ 88MapLeaPLA-2
❑ 88OPCSti-172
❑ 88PanSti-121
❑ 89Kra-34
❑ 89PanSti-144
❑ 90Bow-159
❑ 90BowTif-159
❑ 90OPC-79
❑ 90PanSti-286
❑ 90ProSet-276
❑ 90Sco-171
❑ 90ScoCan-171
❑ 90Top-79
❑ 90TopTif-79
❑ 90UppDec-3
❑ 90UppDecF-3
❑ 91Bow-156
❑ 91Gil-11
❑ 91Kra-42
❑ 91MapLeaP-6
❑ 91MapLeaPTS-3
❑ 91OPC-464
❑ 91OPCPre-116
❑ 91OPCPre-177
❑ 91PanSti-102
❑ 91Par-170
❑ 91ParFre-170
❑ 91Pin-250
❑ 91PinFre-250
❑ 91ProSet-225
❑ 91ProSet-585
❑ 91ProSetFre-225
❑ 91ProSetFre-585
❑ 91ProSetPla-120
❑ 91ScoAme-116
❑ 91ScoCan-116
❑ 91ScoKel-3
❑ 91StaClu-124
❑ 91Top-464
❑ 91UppDec-386
❑ 91UppDecF-386
❑ 92Bow-325
❑ 92HumDum1-4
❑ 92MapLeaK-8
❑ 92OPC-96
❑ 92PanSti-79
❑ 92PanStiFre-79
❑ 92Par-179
❑ 92ParCheP-CP11
❑ 92ParEmel-179
❑ 92Pin-276
❑ 92PinFre-276
❑ 92ProSet-189
❑ 92Sco-110
❑ 92ScoCan-110
❑ 92SeaPat-70
❑ 92StaClu-204
❑ 92Top-325
❑ 92TopGol-325G
❑ 92Ult-208
❑ 92UppDec-89
❑ 93Don-337
❑ 93Kra-34
❑ 93Lea-166
❑ 93OPCPre-359
❑ 93OPCPreF-9
❑ 93OPCPreG-359
❑ 93PanSti-227
❑ 93Par-475
❑ 93ParEmel-475
❑ 93ParFirO-F9
❑ 93Pin-157
❑ 93PinCan-157
❑ 93PinCap-23
❑ 93PinCapC-23
❑ 93Pow-241
❑ 93Sco-137
❑ 93ScoBla-1
❑ 93ScoCan-137
❑ 93StaClu-192
❑ 93StaCluFDI-192
❑ 93StaCluFDIO-192
❑ 93StaCluO-192
❑ 93TopPre-359
❑ 93TopPreF-9
❑ 93TopPreG-359
❑ 93Ult-146
❑ 93UppDec-340
❑ 93UppDecNR-6
❑ 94BeAPla-R72
❑ 94BeAPla-R142
❑ 94CanGamNHLP-194
❑ 94Fin-103
❑ 94FinRef-103
❑ 94FinSupTW-103
❑ 94Fla-142
❑ 94Fle-173
❑ 94FleSlaA-1
❑ 94Kra-3
❑ 94Lea-542
❑ 94LeaLim-31
❑ 94McDUppD-McD24
❑ 94NordBurK-3
❑ 94OPCPre-55
❑ 94OPCPre-297
❑ 94OPCPre-345
❑ 94OPCPreSE-55
❑ 94OPCPreSE-297
❑ 94ParSE-SE146
❑ 94ParSEG-SE146
❑ 94Pin-385
❑ 94PinArtP-385
❑ 94PinGam-GR13
❑ 94PinNorLig-NL5
❑ 94PinRinC-385
❑ 94Sco-3
❑ 94ScoChelt-CI13
❑ 94ScoGol-3
❑ 94ScoHobS-3
❑ 94ScoPla-3
❑ 94ScoPlaTS-3
❑ 94Sel-20
❑ 94SelGol-20
❑ 94SP-97
❑ 94SPDieCut-97
❑ 94TopFinI-10
❑ 94TopPre-55
❑ 94TopPre-297
❑ 94TopPre-345
❑ 94TopPreSE-55
❑ 94TopPreSE-297
❑ 94Ult-172
❑ 94Ult-354
❑ 94UppDec-115
❑ 94UppDecElelce-115
❑ 94UppDecSPI-SP154
❑ 94UppDecSPIDC-SP154
❑ 95BeAPla-55
❑ 95BeAPSig-S55
❑ 95BeAPSigDC-S55
❑ 95Bow-45
❑ 95BowAllFoi-45
❑ 95CanGamNHLP-174
❑ 95ColCho-103
❑ 95ColChoPC-103
❑ 95ColChoPCP-103
❑ 95Don-193
❑ 95Don-389
❑ 95DonEli-27
❑ 95DonEliDCS-27
❑ 95DonEliDCU-27
❑ 95Fin-87
❑ 95FinRef-87
❑ 95ImpSti-76
❑ 95Kra-9
❑ 95Lea-207
❑ 95LeaLim-70
❑ 95Met-89
❑ 95ParInt-399
❑ 95ParIntEl-399
❑ 95PinFan-21
❑ 95PinFirS-8
❑ 95PlaOneoOne-279
❑ 95ProMag-57
❑ 95Sco-57
❑ 95ScoBlaIce-57
❑ 95ScoBlaIceAP-57
❑ 95SelCer-82
❑ 95SelCerMG-82
❑ 95SkyImp-99
❑ 95StaClu-155
❑ 95StaCluFea-F8
❑ 95StaCluMO-18
❑ 95StaCluMOMS-155
❑ 95StaCluPS-PS8
❑ 95Sum-131
❑ 95SumArtP-131
❑ 95SumIce-131
❑ 95SumMadH-8
❑ 95Top-269
❑ 95TopHomGC-HGC2
❑ 95TopOPCI-269
❑ 95TopSupSki-45
❑ 95TopSupSkiPla-45
❑ 95Ult-129
❑ 95Ult-265
❑ 95UltGolM-129
❑ 95UppDec-325
❑ 95UppDecElelce-325
❑ 95UppDecElelceG-325
❑ 95UppDecSpeE-SE139
❑ 95UppDecSpeEdiG-SE139
❑ 95Zen-94
❑ 95ZenGifG-3
❑ 96ColCho-258
❑ 96Don-98
❑ 96DonCanI-29
❑ 96DonCanIGPP-29
❑ 96DonCanIRPP-29
❑ 96DonDom-6
❑ 96DonEli-98
❑ 96DonEliDCS-98
❑ 96DonHitLis-2
❑ 96DonPrePro-98
❑ 96Fla-89
❑ 96FlaBlul-89
❑ 96FlePic-130
❑ 96Lea-166
❑ 96LeaLim-12
❑ 96LeaLimG-12
❑ 96LeaLimStu-20
❑ 96LeaPre-87
❑ 96LeaPreP-166
❑ 96LeaPrePP-87
❑ 96LeaPreSG-48
❑ 96LeaPreSte-48
❑ 96MapLeaP-1
❑ 96MapLeaP-3
❑ 96MetUni-148
❑ 96NHLProSTA-57
❑ 96Pin-196
❑ 96PinArtP-196
❑ 96PinFoi-196
❑ 96PinPreS-196
❑ 96PinRinC-196
❑ 96PlaOneoOne-411
❑ 96Sco-42
❑ 96ScoArtPro-42
❑ 96ScoChelt-7
❑ 96ScoDeaCAP-42
❑ 96ScoGolB-42
❑ 96ScoSpeAP-42
❑ 96SelCer-65
❑ 96SelCer-P65
❑ 96SelCerAP-65
❑ 96SelCerAP-65B
❑ 96SelCerBlu-65
❑ 96SelCerMB-65
❑ 96SelCerMG-65
❑ 96SelCerMR-65
❑ 96SelCerRed-65
❑ 96SkyImp-125
❑ 96SP-150
❑ 96Sum-140
❑ 96SumArtP-140
❑ 96SumIce-140
❑ 96SumMet-140
❑ 96SumPreS-140
❑ 96Ult-162
❑ 96UltGolM-162
❑ 96UppDec-342
❑ 96UppDecBD-107
❑ 96UppDecBDG-107
❑ 96UppDecGN-X15
❑ 96Zen-24
❑ 96ZenArtP-24
❑ 97ColCho-246
❑ 97Don-57
❑ 97DonCanI-80
❑ 97DonCanIDS-80
❑ 97DonCanIPS-80
❑ 97DonLim-40
❑ 97DonLimExp-40
❑ 97DonPreProG-57
❑ 97DonPreProS-57
❑ 97DonPri-150
❑ 97DonPriSoA-150
❑ 97Kat-139
❑ 97KatGol-139
❑ 97KatSil-139
❑ 97Pac-17
❑ 97PacCop-17
❑ 97PacCroR-129
❑ 97PacCroREG-129
❑ 97PacCroRIB-129
❑ 97PacCroRS-129
❑ 97PacDyn-121
❑ 97PacDynC-121
❑ 97PacDynDG-121
❑ 97PacDynEG-121
❑ 97PacDynIB-121
❑ 97PacDynR-121
❑ 97PacDynSil-121
❑ 97PacDynTan-27
❑ 97PacEmeGre-17
❑ 97PacIceB-17
❑ 97PacInv-136
❑ 97PacInvC-136
❑ 97PacInvEG-136
❑ 97PacInvIB-136
❑ 97PacInvR-136
❑ 97PacInvS-136
❑ 97PacOme-218
❑ 97PacOmeC-218
❑ 97PacOmeDG-218
❑ 97PacOmeEG-218
❑ 97PacOmeG-218
❑ 97PacOmeIB-218
❑ 97PacPar-179
❑ 97PacParC-179
❑ 97PacParDG-179
❑ 97PacParEG-179
❑ 97PacParIB-179
❑ 97PacParRed-179
❑ 97PacParSil-179
❑ 97PacRed-17
❑ 97PacRev-133
❑ 97PacRevC-133
❑ 97PacRevE-133
❑ 97PacRevIB-133
❑ 97PacRevR-133
❑ 97PacRevS-133
❑ 97PacSil-17
❑ 97PacSlaSDC-10A
❑ 97Pin-185
❑ 97PinCer-71
❑ 97PinCerMB-71
❑ 97PinCerMG-71
❑ 97PinCerMR-71
❑ 97PinCerR-71
❑ 97PinIns-89
❑ 97PinInsCC-89
❑ 97PinInsEC-89
❑ 97PinPrePBB-185
❑ 97PinPrePBC-185
❑ 97PinPrePBM-185
❑ 97PinPrePBY-185
❑ 97PinPrePFC-185
❑ 97PinPrePFM-185
❑ 97PinPrePFY-185
❑ 97PinPrePla-185
❑ 97PinTotCMPG-71
❑ 97PinTotCPB-71
❑ 97PinTotCPG-71
❑ 97PinTotCPR-71
❑ 97Sco-128
❑ 97ScoArtPro-128
❑ 97ScoGolBla-128
❑ 97ScoMapL-5
❑ 97ScoMapLPla-5
❑ 97ScoMapLPre-5
❑ 97SPAut-152
❑ 97UppDec-164
❑ 98Be A PPA-280
❑ 98Be A PPAA-280
❑ 98Be A PPAAF-280
❑ 98Be A PPSE-280
❑ 98Be APG-280
❑ 98BowBes-19
❑ 98BowBesAR-19
❑ 98BowBesR-19
❑ 98O-PChr-142
❑ 98O-PChrR-142
❑ 98Pac-411
❑ 98PacCroR-123
❑ 98PacCroRLS-123
❑ 98PacDynI-171
❑ 98PacDynIIB-171
❑ 98PacDynIR-171
❑ 98PacIceB-411
❑ 98PacOmeH-217
❑ 98PacOmeODI-217
❑ 98PacOmeR-217
❑ 98PacRed-411
❑ 98PacRev-131
❑ 98PacRevIS-131
❑ 98PacRevR-131
❑ 98SP Aut-79
❑ 98Top-142
❑ 98TopO-P-142
❑ 98UC-202
❑ 98UD ChoPCR-202
❑ 98UD ChoR-202
❑ 98UppDec-188
❑ 98UppDecBD-79
❑ 98UppDecDD-79
❑ 98UppDecE-188
❑ 98UppDecE-369
❑ 98UppDecE1o1-188
❑ 98UppDecE1o1-369
❑ 98UppDecGR-188
❑ 98UppDecGR-369
❑ 98UppDecM-190
❑ 98UppDecMGS-190
❑ 98UppDecMSS-190
❑ 98UppDecMSS-190
❑ 98UppDecQD-79
❑ 98UppDecTD-79
❑ 99Pac-136
❑ 99PacCop-136
❑ 99PacGol-136
❑ 99PacIceB-136
❑ 99PacPreD-136
❑ 99SP AutPS-79
❑ 99UppDecM-76
❑ 99UppDecMGS-76
❑ 99UppDecMPS-WC
❑ 99UppDecMSS-76
❑ 99UppDecMSS-76
**Clarke, Bobby**
❑ 70DadCoo-15
❑ 70EssPowPla-211
❑ 70OPC-195
❑ 70SarProSta-148
❑ 71OPC-114
❑ 71OPCTBoo-10
❑ 71SarProSta-152
❑ 71Top-114
❑ 71TorSun-191
❑ 72FlyMigM-2
❑ 72OPC-14
❑ 72OPCTeaC-5
❑ 72SarProSta-162
❑ 72Top-90
❑ 73FlyLin-4
❑ 73MacMil-4
❑ 73OPC-50
❑ 73OPC-134
❑ 73OPC-135
❑ 73Top-2
❑ 73Top-3
❑ 73Top-50
❑ 74LipSou-21
❑ 74NHLActSta-216
❑ 74OPCNHL-3
❑ 74OPCNHL-135
❑ 74OPCNHL-154
❑ 74OPCNHL-260
❑ 74Top-3
❑ 74Top-135
❑ 74Top-154
❑ 74Top-260
❑ 75FlyCanDC-4
❑ 75HerSta-21
❑ 75OPCNHL-209
❑ 75OPCNHL-250
❑ 75OPCNHL-286
❑ 75OPCNHL-325
❑ 75Top-209
❑ 75Top-250
❑ 75Top-286
❑ 75Top-325
❑ 76OPCNHL-2
❑ 76OPCNHL-3
❑ 76OPCNHL-70
❑ 76OPCNHL-215
❑ 76OPCNHL-391
❑ 76Top-2
❑ 76Top-3
❑ 76Top-70
❑ 76Top-215
❑ 76TopGlol-1
❑ 77Coc-3
❑ 77OPCNHL-115
❑ 77Top-115
❑ 77TopGloS-3
❑ 77TopOPCGlo-3
❑ 78OPC-215
❑ 78Top-215
❑ 79OPC-125
❑ 79Top-125
❑ 80OPC-55
❑ 80OPCSup-16
❑ 80Top-55
❑ 81OPC-240
❑ 81OPCSti-178
❑ 81PosSta-7
❑ 81Top-E103
❑ 82OPC-248
❑ 82OPCSti-115
❑ 82PosCer-14
❑ 83FlyJCP-5
❑ 83OPC-262
❑ 83OPCSti-12
❑ 83OPCSti-198
❑ 83OPCSti-302
❑ 83PufSti-7
❑ 84KelWin-41
❑ 85FlyPos-4
❑ 85HalFC-258
❑ 88EssAllSta-5
❑ 89FlyPos-6
❑ 90ProSet-651
❑ 90ProSet-657
❑ 90UppDec-509
❑ 90UppDecF-509
❑ 91FutTreC72-57
❑ 91Kra-54
❑ 91Kra-67
❑ 92FlyUppDS-44
❑ 92FutTre76CC-177
❑ 92HalFL-16
❑ 92OPC-43
❑ 92OPC25AI-3
❑ 92Par-468
❑ 92ParEmel-468
❑ 94HocWit-80
❑ 99RetHoc-99
❑ 99UppDecCL-24
❑ 99UppDecCLCLC-24
❑ 99UppDecES-14
❑ 99UppDecJotC-JC1
❑ 99UppDecRG-G2B
❑ 99UppDecRG-99
❑ 99UppDecRGI-G2B
❑ 99UppDecRII-BC
❑ 99UppDecRIL1-BC
❑ 99UppDecRP-99
❑ 99UppDecRTotC-TC10
**Clarke, Chris**
❑ 91ProAHLCHL-560
❑ 95GerDELE-363
**Clarke, Doug**
❑ 88SalLakCGE-14
**Clarke, Jason**
❑ 917thInnSOHL-202
❑ 94RoaExp-11
❑ 95RoaExp-16
**Clarke, Jim**
❑ 75RoaPhoWHA-26
❑ 81RegPat-10
**Clarke, Joe**
❑ 93SauSteMGM-8
**Clarke, Mike**
❑ 75HamFin-2
**Clarke, Taylor**
❑ 96RicRen-2
**Clarke, Todd**
❑ 83Ott67-4
❑ 84KinCan-20
❑ 85KinCan-20
**Clarke, Wayne**
❑ 93RenEng-6
**Clarke, Will**
❑ 96DayBom-10
**Clatney, Paul**
❑ 95MadMon-16
**Clause, Greg**
❑ 75HamFin-3
**Clauss, Karl**
❑ 91KnoChe-4
**Clayton, Mike**
❑ 84MonGolF-12
**Clayton, Travis**
❑ 99WicThu-2
**Clearwater, Ray**
❑ 72CleCruWHA-2
**Cleary, Dan (Daniel)**
❑ 95Cla-83
❑ 95ClaCHLAS-AS11
❑ 95SigRooA-15
❑ 95SigRooAP-P3
❑ 95SigRooAPC-15
❑ 95Sla-39
❑ 95UppDec-507
❑ 95UppDecElelce-507
❑ 95UppDecElelceG-507
❑ 97Be A PPAD-224
❑ 97Be A PPAPD-224
❑ 97BeAPla-224
❑ 97BeAPlaAut-224
❑ 97BowCHL-2
❑ 97BowCHL-121
❑ 97BowCHLAu-121
❑ 97BowCHLBB-7
❑ 97BowCHLBowBesAR-7
❑ 97BowCHLBowBesR-7
❑ 97BowCHLOPC-2
❑ 97BowCHLOPC-121
❑ 97ColCho-307
❑ 97DonEli-37
❑ 97DonEli-123
❑ 97DonEliAsp-37
❑ 97DonEliAsp-123
❑ 97DonEliBttF-4
❑ 97DonEliBttFA-4
❑ 97DonEliC-10
❑ 97DonEliMC-10
❑ 97DonEliS-37
❑ 97DonEliS-123
❑ 97DonLimFOTG-68
❑ 97DonPre-152
❑ 97DonPre-199
❑ 97DonPreCttC-152
❑ 97DonPreCttC-199
❑ 97DonPreLotT-6C
❑ 97DonPri-166
❑ 97DonPri-217
❑ 97DonPriSoA-166
❑ 97DonPriSoA-217
❑ 97Kat-33
❑ 97KatGol-33
❑ 97KatSil-33
❑ 97Lea-159
❑ 97Lea-200
❑ 97LeaFraMat-159
❑ 97LeaFraMat-200
❑ 97LeaFraMDC-159
❑ 97LeaFraMDC-200
❑ 97LeaInt-150
❑ 97LeaIntUI-150
❑ 97McD-36
❑ 97PacDyn-NNO
❑ 97PacDynC-NNO
❑ 97PacDynDG-NNO
❑ 97PacDynEG-NNO
❑ 97PacDynIB-NNO
❑ 97PacDynR-NNO
❑ 97PacDynSil-NNO
❑ 97PacPar-42
❑ 97PacParC-42
❑ 97PacParDG-42
❑ 97PacParEG-42
❑ 97PacParIB-42
❑ 97PacParRed-42
❑ 97PacParSil-42
❑ 97Pin-10
❑ 97PinArtP-10
❑ 97PinCerRR-E
❑ 97PinCerRRG-E
❑ 97PinCerRRMG-E
❑ 97PinPrePBB-10
❑ 97PinPrePBC-10
❑ 97PinPrePBM-10
❑ 97PinPrePBY-10
❑ 97PinPrePFC-10
❑ 97PinPrePFM-10
❑ 97PinPrePFY-10
❑ 97PinPrePla-10
❑ 97PinRinC-10
❑ 97Sco-61
❑ 97ScoArtPro-61
❑ 97ScoGolBla-61
❑ 97SPAut-177
❑ 97UppDec-247
❑ 97UppDecIce-38
❑ 97UppDecIceP-38
❑ 97UppDecIPS-38
❑ 98BowBes-103
❑ 98BowBesAR-103
❑ 98BowBesR-103
❑ 98FinFutF-F17
❑ 98FinFutFR-F17
❑ 98SPxFin-20
❑ 98SPxFin-128
❑ 98SPxFinR-20
❑ 98SPxFinR-128
❑ 98SPxFinS-20
❑ 98SPxFinS-128
❑ 98TopGolLC1-38
❑ 98TopGolLC1B-38
❑ 98TopGolLC1BOoO-38
❑ 98TopGolLC1OoO-38
❑ 98TopGolLC1R-38
❑ 98TopGolLC1ROoO-38
❑ 98TopGolLC2-38
❑ 98TopGolLC2B-38
❑ 98TopGolLC2BOoO-38
❑ 98TopGolLC2OoO-38
❑ 98TopGolLC2R-38
❑ 98TopGolLC2ROoO-38
❑ 98TopGolLC3-38
❑ 98TopGolLC3B-38
❑ 98TopGolLC3BOoO-38
❑ 98TopGolLC3OoO-38
❑ 98TopGolLC3R-38
❑ 98TopGolLC3ROoO-38
❑ 98UC-44
❑ 98UD ChoPCR-44
❑ 98UD ChoR-44
❑ 98UppDec-4
❑ 98UppDecE-4
❑ 98UppDecE1o1-4
❑ 98UppDecGR-4
❑ 98UppDecM-47
❑ 98UppDecMGS-47
❑ 98UppDecMSS-47
❑ 98UppDecMSS-47
❑ 99RetHoc-34

❏ 99UppDecM-77
❏ 99UppDecMGS-77
❏ 99UppDecMSS-77
❏ 99UppDecMSS-77
❏ 99UppDecRG-34
❏ 99UppDecRP-34
**Cleary, Joe**
❏ 92IndIce-6
**Cleghorn, Odie**
❏ 10C55SweCP-25
❏ 11C55-25
❏ 12C57-50
❏ 23V1451-18
❏ 24C144ChaCig-14
❏ 24V1452-45
**Cleghorn, Sprague**
❏ 10C55SweCP-24
❏ 11C55-24
❏ 12C57-15
❏ 23V1451-11
❏ 24C144ChaCig-15
❏ 24V130MapC-15
❏ 24V1452-49
❏ 60TopSta-10
❏ 83HalFP-E5
❏ 85HalFC-66
**Clemens, Kevin**
❏ 87RegPat-1
**Clement, Bill**
❏ 72SarProSta-168
❏ 73FlyLin-5
❏ 74NHLActSta-204
❏ 740PCNHL-357
❏ 750PCNHL-189
❏ 75Top-189
❏ 760PCNHL-82
❏ 76Top-82
❏ 770PCNHL-292
❏ 780PC-364
❏ 79FlamPos-4
❏ 79FlaTeal-5
❏ 790PC-295
❏ 80FlamPos-3
❏ 800PC-376
❏ 80PepCap-3
❏ 81FlamPos-4
❏ 810PC-39
❏ 820PC-44
❏ 92Par-478
❏ 92ParEmel-478
**Clement, Patrick**
❏ 917thInnSMC-31
❏ 917thInnSQMJHL-85
**Clement, Sean**
❏ 88ProAHL-185
**Clements, Scott**
❏ 88ProIHL-7
**Clifford, Brian**
❏ 93MicSta-5
❏ 96TolSto-11
**Clifford, Chris**
❏ 83KinCan-14
❏ 84KinCan-7
❏ 85KinCan-7
❏ 86KinCan-9
❏ 88ProIHL-97
❏ 89ProIHL-144
❏ 90ProAHLIHL-372
**Climie, Ron**
❏ 72NatOttWHA-6
❏ 720PC-318
❏ 730PCWHAP-12
❏ 740PCWHA-15
❏ 750PCWHA-52
**Cline, Bruce**
❏ 50QueCit-4
❏ 51LavDaiS-70
❏ 52St.LawS-23
❏ 94ParMisL-106
**Cline, Walter**
❏ 55MonRoy-1
**Clouston, Shaun**
❏ 86PorWinH-4
❏ 87PorWinH-6
❏ 88PorWinH-6
❏ 89ProIHL-166
❏ 90ProAHLIHL-333
❏ 92-TulOil-3
❏ 94CenHocL-95
**Cloutier, Colin**
❏ 92BraWheK-2
❏ 95SigRoo-4
❏ 95SigRooSig-4
❏ 95SlaMemC-45
**Cloutier, Dan**
❏ 93SauSteMG-3
❏ 93SauSteMGM-27
❏ 94Cla-22
❏ 94ClaDraGol-22
❏ 94Fin-145
❏ 94FinRef-145
❏ 94FinSupTW-145
❏ 94ParSE-SE210
❏ 94ParSEG-SE210
❏ 94Pin-522
❏ 94PinArtP-522
❏ 94PinRinC-522
❏ 94SP-146
❏ 94SPDieCut-146
❏ 94UppDec-498
❏ 94UppDecEIeIce-498
❏ 95Cla-95
❏ 95DonCanWJT-2
❏ 95GueSto5A-22
❏ 95Ima-49

❏ 95ImaGol-49
❏ 95SauSteMG-3
❏ 95Sla-95
❏ 95Sla-357
❏ 95TopCanWJ-18CJ
❏ 96BinRan-6
❏ 97PacRev-85
❏ 97PacRevC-85
❏ 97PacRevE-85
❏ 97PacRevIB-85
❏ 97PacRevR-85
❏ 97PacRevS-85
❏ 97UppDecBD-78
❏ 97UppDecBDDD-78
❏ 97UppDecBDQD-78
❏ 97UppDecBDTD-78
❏ 98BowBes-116
❏ 98BowBesAR-116
❏ 98BowBesMIF-F9
❏ 98BowBesMIFAR-F9
❏ 98BowBesMIFR-F9
❏ 98BowBesR-116
❏ 98Pac-291
❏ 98PacIceB-291
❏ 98PacOmeH-154
❏ 98PacOmeODI-154
❏ 98PacOmeR-154
❏ 98Par-150
❏ 98PacParC-150
❏ 98PacParEG-150
❏ 98PacParH-150
❏ 98PacParIB-150
❏ 98PacParS-150
❏ 98PacRed-291
❏ 98SPxFin-125
❏ 98SPxFinR-125
❏ 98SPxFinS-125
❏ 98UC-131
❏ 98UD ChoPCR-131
❏ 98UD ChoR-131
❏ 98UD3-25
❏ 98UD3-85
❏ 98UD3-145
❏ 98UD3DieC-25
❏ 98UD3DieC-85
❏ 98UD3DieC-145
❏ 98UDCP-131
❏ 98UppDec-134
❏ 98UppDecE-134
❏ 98UppDecE101-134
❏ 98UppDecGR-134
❏ 99Pac-267
❏ 99PacCop-267
❏ 99PacGol-267
❏ 99PacIceB-267
❏ 99PacPreD-267
**Cloutier, Denis**
❏ 907thInnSWHL-111
**Cloutier, Eric**
❏ 95LouIceGP-3
**Cloutier, Francois**
❏ 95SlaMemC-65
**Cloutier, Jacques**
❏ 82SabMilP-9
❏ 86SabBluS-5
❏ 86SabBluSSma-5
❏ 87PanSti-21
❏ 87SabBluS-5
❏ 87SabWonBH-6
❏ 88ProAHL-248
❏ 88SabBluS-5
❏ 88SabWonBH-5
❏ 89BlaCok-11
❏ 90BlaCok-11
❏ 90Bow-11
❏ 90BowTif-11
❏ 900PC-378
❏ 90PanSti-197
❏ 90ProSet-428
❏ 90Top-378
❏ 90TopTif-378
❏ 90UppDec-114
❏ 90UppDecF-114
❏ 91Bow-146
❏ 91NordPet-3
❏ 910PC-286
❏ 91Par-368
❏ 91ParFre-368
❏ 91ProSetPla-219
❏ 91ScoCan-236
❏ 91StaClu-166
❏ 91Top-286
❏ 92Bow-332
❏ 92DurPan-46
❏ 92NorPet-4
❏ 920PC-113
❏ 92Sco-378
❏ 92ScoCan-378
❏ 92StaClu-118
❏ 92Top-66
❏ 92TopGol-66G
❏ 92UppDec-324
❏ 93DurSco-18
**Cloutier, Nichol**
❏ 907thInnSQMJHL-243
**Cloutier, Patrick**
❏ 907thInnSQMJHL-216
**Cloutier, Real**
❏ 740PCWHA-63
❏ 750PCWHA-16
❏ 76NordMarA-7
❏ 76NordPos-10
❏ 760PCWHA-1
❏ 760PCWHA-3
❏ 760PCWHA-76

❏ 770PCWHA-8
❏ 790PC-239
❏ 79Top-239
❏ 80NordPos-6
❏ 800PC-178
❏ 800PC-238
❏ 80PepCap-63
❏ 80Top-178
❏ 80Top-238
❏ 81NordPos-4
❏ 810PCSti-74
❏ 81PosSta-17
❏ 82NordPos-4
❏ 820PC-279
❏ 820PC-280
❏ 820PCSti-23
❏ 82PosCer-18
❏ 83NordPos-4
❏ 830PC-62
❏ 830PCSti-246
❏ 83PufSti-10
❏ 84Top-15
**Cloutier, Rejean**
❏ 84NovScoO-5
❏ 86SheCan-11
**Cloutier, Sylvain**
❏ 917thInnSOHL-350
❏ 92Cla-22
❏ 93GueSto-9
❏ 95AdiRedW-4
❏ 96ClaGol-22
**Clowes, Luke**
❏ 92WinSpi-3
❏ 93WinSpi-22
❏ 94WinSpi-24
**Clukey, Barry**
❏ 93MaiBlaB-43
**Clune, Art**
❏ 52JunBluT-152
**Clune, Walter**
❏ 51LavDaiQSHL-96
❏ 51LavDaiS-96
❏ 52St.LawS-12
**Clymer, Ben**
❏ 95DonEliiWJ-27
❏ 96MinGolGCAS-7
**Coakley, Chris**
❏ 93WatBlaH-6
**Coalter, Brandon**
❏ 95Sla-237
**Coalter, Gary**
❏ 74NHLActSta-290
❏ 740PCNHL-17
❏ 74Top-17
❏ 750PCNHL-334
**Coates, Brandon**
❏ 917thInnSWHL-35
**Cocciolo, Vince**
❏ 89PorWinH-2
**Cochrane, Glen**
❏ 82PosCer-14
❏ 83FlyJCP-6
❏ 85Canu-5
❏ 86Canu-4
❏ 86KraDra-9
❏ 880ilTenAnn-101
**Coci, Eric**
❏ 907thInnSQMJHL-128
**Cockburn, Bill**
❏ 24CreFal-1
**Cockell, Matt**
❏ 96SasBla-7
**Code, Chris**
❏ 907thInnSOHL-206
**Code, Tony**
❏ 93WesMic-8
**Coffey, Paul**
❏ 80PepCap-2
❏ 810ilRedR-7
❏ 810PC-111
❏ 820ilRedR-7
❏ 820PC-101
❏ 820PC-102
❏ 820PCSti-104
❏ 820PCSti-105
❏ 820PCSti-160
❏ 82PosCer-4
❏ 83Ess-5
❏ 830ilMcD-25
❏ 830PC-25
❏ 830PCSti-94
❏ 830PCSti-95
❏ 83PufSti-3
❏ 83Vac-22
❏ 847EDis-14
❏ 84KelAccD-5A
❏ 84KelAccD-5B
❏ 840ilRedR-7
❏ 840ilTeal-3
❏ 840PC-217
❏ 840PC-239
❏ 840PCSti-134
❏ 840PCSti-251
❏ 840PCSti-252
❏ 84Top-50
❏ 84Top-163
❏ 857ECreCar-6
❏ 850ilRedR-7
❏ 850PC-85
❏ 850PCSti-56
❏ 850PCSti-124
❏ 850PCSti-191
❏ 850PCSti-217

❏ 85Top-85
❏ 85TopStiIns-4
❏ 86KraDra-10
❏ 860ilRedR-7
❏ 860ilTeal-7
❏ 860PC-137
❏ 860PCSti-68
❏ 860PCSti-112
❏ 860PCSti-188
❏ 86Top-137
❏ 86TopStiIns-5
❏ 870PC-99
❏ 870PCMin-8
❏ 870PCSti-89
❏ 87PanSti-256
❏ 87PenKod-5
❏ 87ProAll-14
❏ 87Top-99
❏ 88EssAllSta-6
❏ 88FriLayS-24
❏ 880ilTenAnn-54
❏ 880ilTenAnn-64
❏ 880PC-179
❏ 880PCMin-6
❏ 880PCSti-233
❏ 88PanSti-333
❏ 88Top-179
❏ 89Kra-54
❏ 89KraAllSS-3
❏ 890PC-95
❏ 890PCSti-237
❏ 89PanSti-183
❏ 89PanSti-311
❏ 89PenFoo-4
❏ 89SweSemWCS-59
❏ 89Top-95
❏ 90Bow-211
❏ 90BowTif-211
❏ 90Kra-8
❏ 90Kra-82
❏ 900PC-116
❏ 900PC-202
❏ 900PCBoxB-C
❏ 900PCPre-16
❏ 90PanSti-135
❏ 90PanSti-324
❏ 90PenFoo-2
❏ 90ProSet-231
❏ 90ProSet-361
❏ 90Sco-6
❏ 90Sco-319
❏ 90Sco-332
❏ 90ScoCan-6
❏ 90ScoCan-319
❏ 90ScoCan-332
❏ 90ScoHotRS-65
❏ 90Top-116
❏ 90Top-202
❏ 90TopBoxB-C
❏ 90TopTif-116
❏ 90TopTif-202
❏ 90UppDec-124
❏ 90UppDec-498
❏ 90UppDecF-124
❏ 90UppDecF-498
❏ 91Bow-81
❏ 91Gil-37
❏ 91Kra-74
❏ 91McDUppD-11
❏ 910PC-183
❏ 910PC-384
❏ 910PC-504
❏ 910PCPre-79
❏ 91PanSti-276
❏ 91PanSti-336
❏ 91Par-140
❏ 91Par-212
❏ 91Par-225
❏ 91Par-297
❏ 91ParFre-140
❏ 91ParFre-212
❏ 91ParFre-225
❏ 91ParFre-297
❏ 91PenFooCS-11
❏ 91Pin-186
❏ 91Pin-377
❏ 91PinFre-186
❏ 91PinFre-377
❏ 91ProSet-190
❏ 91ProSet-312
❏ 91ProSetFre-190
❏ 91ProSetFre-312
❏ 91ProSetPC-21
❏ 91ProSetPla-94
❏ 91ProSetPlaPC-PC12
❏ 91ScoAme-115
❏ 91ScoAme-372
❏ 91ScoCan-115
❏ 91ScoFan-9
❏ 91ScoNat-9
❏ 91ScoNatCWC-9
❏ 91StaClu-212
❏ 91SweSemWCS-58
❏ 91Top-183
❏ 91Top-504
❏ 91UppDec-11
❏ 91UppDec-501
❏ 91UppDecF-11
❏ 91UppDecF-177
❏ 91UppDecF-501
❏ 91UppDecF-615

❏ 92Bow-181
❏ 92Bow-226
❏ 92Kra-39
❏ 92McDUppD-17
❏ 920PC-5
❏ 920PC-187
❏ 920PC-318
❏ 920PC25AI-14
❏ 920PCPreSP-4
❏ 92PanSti-72
❏ 92PanSti-278
❏ 92PanStiFre-72
❏ 92PanStiFre-278
❏ 92Par-63
❏ 92Par-276
❏ 92Par-458
❏ 92ParEmel-63
❏ 92ParEmel-276
❏ 92ParEmel-458
❏ 92Pin-50
❏ 92PinFre-50
❏ 92PinTeaP-3
❏ 92PinTeaPF-3
❏ 92ProSet-71
❏ 92Sco-265
❏ 92Sco-441
❏ 92ScoCan-265
❏ 92ScoCan-441
❏ 92StaClu-169
❏ 92Top-5
❏ 92Top-182
❏ 92TopGol-5G
❏ 92TopGol-182G
❏ 92Ult-80
❏ 92UltAllS-1
❏ 92UppDec-116
❏ 93Don-99
❏ 93Kra-4
❏ 93Lea-67
❏ 93LeaGolAS-7
❏ 93McDUppD-4
❏ 930PCPre-145
❏ 930PCPreG-145
❏ 93PanSti-183
❏ 93PanSti-252
❏ 93Par-56
❏ 93ParChePH-D8
❏ 93ParEmel-56
❏ 93Pin-80
❏ 93PinAllS-43
❏ 93PinAllSC-43
❏ 93PinCan-80
❏ 93PinTeaP-8
❏ 93PinTeaPC-8
❏ 93Pow-70
❏ 93Sco-106
❏ 93ScoCan-106
❏ 93ScoDreTea-8
❏ 93SeaPat-3
❏ 93StaClu-450
❏ 93StaCluAS-2
❏ 93StaCluFDI-450
❏ 93StaCluFin-4
❏ 93StaCluO-450
❏ 93SweSemWCS-197
❏ 93TopPre-145
❏ 93TopPreBG-6
❏ 93TopPreG-145
❏ 93Ult-71
❏ 93UppDec-315
❏ 93UppDecGGO-GG6
❏ 93UppDecLAS-23
❏ 93UppDecSP-42
❏ 94BeAPA99A-G2
❏ 94BeAPla-R91
❏ 94CanGamNHLP-93
❏ 94Don-54
❏ 94DonDom-6
❏ 94EASpo-37
❏ 94Fin-68
❏ 94Fin-99
❏ 94FinnJaaK-86
❏ 94FinnJaaK-337
❏ 94FinRef-68
❏ 94FinRef-99
❏ 94FinRinL-6
❏ 94FinSupTW-68
❏ 94FinSupTW-99
❏ 94Fla-47
❏ 94Fle-58
❏ 94HocWit-46
❏ 94Lea-168
❏ 94LeaFirOIce-8
❏ 94LeaLim-75
❏ 94McDUppD-McD19
❏ 940PCPre-15
❏ 940PCPre-489
❏ 940PCPreSE-15
❏ 940PCPreSE-489
❏ 94Par-63
❏ 94ParGol-63
❏ 94ParSEV-15
❏ 94Pin-429
❏ 94PinArtP-429
❏ 94PinRinC-429
❏ 94ScoDreTea-DT6
❏ 94Sel-72
❏ 94SelGol-72
❏ 94SP-36
❏ 94SPDieCut-36
❏ 94StaCluMO-3
❏ 94TopPre-15
❏ 94TopPre-489
❏ 94TopPreSE-15
❏ 94TopPreSE-489

❏ 94Ult-59
❏ 94UltAllS-9
❏ 94UppDec-24
❏ 94UppDecEIeIce-24
❏ 94UppDecPC-23
❏ 94UppDecPC-31
❏ 94UppDecPCEG-31
❏ 94UppDecSPI-SP22
❏ 94UppDecSPIDC-SP22
❏ 95Bow-1
❏ 95BowAllFoi-41
❏ 95CanGamNHLP-13
❏ 95CanGamNHLP-102
❏ 95ColCho-18
❏ 95ColCho-379
❏ 95ColCho-390
❏ 95ColChoCTG-C29
❏ 95ColChoCTG-C29B
❏ 95ColChoCTG-C29C
❏ 95ColChoCTGGB-C29
❏ 95ColChoCTGGR-C29
❏ 95ColChoCTGSB-C29
❏ 95ColChoCTGSR-C29
❏ 95ColChoPC-18
❏ 95ColChoPC-379
❏ 95ColChoPC-390
❏ 95ColChoPCP-18
❏ 95ColChoPCP-379
❏ 95ColChoPCP-390
❏ 95Don-119
❏ 95DonDom-7
❏ 95DonEli-85
❏ 95DonEliCE-13
❏ 95DonEliDCS-85
❏ 95DonEliDCU-85
❏ 95DonEliIns-5
❏ 95DonIgn-2
❏ 95Emo-52
❏ 95Fin-137
❏ 95FinnSemWC-82
❏ 95FinRef-137
❏ 95ImpSti-39
❏ 95ImpStiDCS-5
❏ 95Kra-43
❏ 95Kra-64
❏ 95Lea-144
❏ 95LeaFirOIce-4
❏ 95LeaGolS-2
❏ 95LeaLim-24
❏ 95LeaRoaCup-5
❏ 95McDPin-MCD-4
❏ 95Met-44
❏ 95NHLAcePC-1C
❏ 95ParInt-66
❏ 95ParIntCCGS1-8
❏ 95ParIntCCSS1-8
❏ 95ParIntEI-66
❏ 95ParIntNHLAS-5
❏ 95ParIntPTP-PP19
❏ 95ParIntTW-4
❏ 95Pin-14
❏ 95PinArtP-14
❏ 95PinRinC-14
❏ 95PlaOneoOne-33
❏ 95PlaOneoOne-143
❏ 95PosUppD-16
❏ 95ProMag-101
❏ 95Sco-24
❏ 95ScoBlaIce-24
❏ 95ScoBlaIceAP-24
❏ 95ScoGolBla-5
❏ 95SelCer-21
❏ 95SelCerMG-21
❏ 95SkyImp-51
❏ 95SP-45
❏ 95SPHol-FX6
❏ 95SPHolSpFX-FX6
❏ 95SPStaEto-E13
❏ 95SPStaEtoG-E13
❏ 95StaClu-34
❏ 95StaCluM-M11
❏ 95StaCluMO-30
❏ 95StaCluMOMS-34
❏ 95StaCluPS-PS4
❏ 95Sum-16
❏ 95Sum-198
❏ 95SumArtP-16
❏ 95SumArtP-198
❏ 95SumGM-9
❏ 95SumIce-16
❏ 95SumIce-198
❏ 95SweGloWC-76
❏ 95Top-4
❏ 95Top-265
❏ 95TopHomGC-HGC11
❏ 95TopMarMPB-4
❏ 95TopOPCI-4
❏ 95TopOPCI-265
❏ 95TopPro-PF12
❏ 95TopSupSki-29
❏ 95TopSupSkiPla-29
❏ 95Ult-44
❏ 95UltGolM-44
❏ 95UltPow-3
❏ 95UppDec-226
❏ 95UppDec-248
❏ 95UppDec-396
❏ 95UppDecEIeIce-226
❏ 95UppDecEIeIce-248
❏ 95UppDecEIeIce-396
❏ 95UppDecEIeIceG-226
❏ 95UppDecEIeIceG-248
❏ 95UppDecEIeIceG-396
❏ 95UppDecFreFra-F17
❏ 95UppDecFreFraJ-F17

❏ 95UppDecNHLAS-AS1
❏ 95UppDecPHE-H3
❏ 95UppDecPHE-H31
❏ 95UppDecPRE-R12
❏ 95UppDecPreR-H31
❏ 95UppDecPreR-R12
❏ 95UppDecSpeE-SE118
❏ 95UppDecSpeEdiG-SE118
❏ 95UppPreHV-H3
❏ 95Zen-2
❏ 96ColCho-85
❏ 96ColCho-316
❏ 96ColChoMVP-UD28
❏ 96ColChoMVPG-UD28
❏ 96Don-238
❏ 96DonCanI-9
❏ 96DonCanI-149
❏ 96DonCanIGPP-9
❏ 96DonCanIGPP-149
❏ 96DonCanIRPP-149
❏ 96DonDom-3
❏ 96DonEli-72
❏ 96DonEliDCS-72
❏ 96DonEliP-5
❏ 96DonPrePro-140
❏ 96DonPrePro-238
❏ 96DurAIIT-DC1
❏ 96DurL'EB-JB1
❏ 96Fla-66
❏ 96FlaBluI-66
❏ 96FlaHotN-2
❏ 96Fle-29
❏ 96Fle-140
❏ 96FleNor-3
❏ 96FlePic-20
❏ 96FlePicF5-8
❏ 96FlePicJE-18
❏ 96FlyPos-3
❏ 96Lea-164
❏ 96LeaLeaAL-4
❏ 96LeaLeaALP-P4
❏ 96LeaLim-18
❏ 96LeaLimG-18
❏ 96LeaLimStu-4
❏ 96LeaPre-101
❏ 96LeaPreP-164
❏ 96LeaPrePP-101
❏ 96MetUni-67
❏ 96MetUniIC-4
❏ 96MetUniICSP-4
❏ 96NHLProSTA-101
❏ 96Pin-14
❏ 96PinArtP-14
❏ 96PinFan-72
❏ 96PinFoi-14
❏ 96PinMcD-3
❏ 96PinMin-20
❏ 96PinMinB-20
❏ 96PinMinCoiB-20
❏ 96PinMinCoiGP-20
❏ 96PinMinCoiN-20
❏ 96PinMinCoiSG-20
❏ 96PinMinG-20
❏ 96PinMinS-20
❏ 96PinPreS-14
❏ 96PinRinC-14
❏ 96PinTeaP-7
❏ 96PosUppD-4
❏ 96Sco-142
❏ 96ScoArtPro-142
❏ 96ScoDeaCAP-142
❏ 96ScoGolB-142
❏ 96ScoSpeAP-142
❏ 96ScoSup-6
❏ 96SelCer-89
❏ 96SelCerBlu-89
❏ 96SelCerMB-89
❏ 96SelCerMG-89
❏ 96SelCerMR-89
❏ 96SelCerRed-89
❏ 96SkyImp-33
❏ 96SkyImpNHLF-6
❏ 96SPCleWin-CW13
❏ 96SPGamFil-GF19
❏ 96SPx-15
❏ 96SPxGol-15
❏ 96SPxHolIH-HH4
❏ 96StaCluMO-5
❏ 96Sum-3
❏ 96SumArtP-3
❏ 96SumIce-3
❏ 96SumMet-3
❏ 96SumPreS-3
❏ 96SweSemW-79
❏ 96TeaOut-49
❏ 96TopPicF-FT-FT7
❏ 96Ult-122
❏ 96UltGolM-74
❏ 96UltPow-3
❏ 96UltPowBL-3
❏ 96UppDec-268
❏ 96UppDecBD-151
❏ 96UppDecBDG-151
❏ 96UppDecGN-X9
❏ 96UppDecLSH-LS10
❏ 96UppDecLSHF-LS10
❏ 96UppDecLSHS-LS10
❏ 96UppDecSS-SS20A
❏ 96Zen-48
❏ 96ZenArtP-48
❏ 96ZenChaS-4

❑ 96ZenChaSD-4
❑ 97Be A PPAD-12
❑ 97Be A PPAPD-12
❑ 97BeAPla-12
❑ 97BeAPlaAut-12
❑ 97BeAPlaTAN-11
❑ 97ColCho-189
❑ 97Don-63
❑ 97DonCanI-64
❑ 97DonCanIDS-64
❑ 97DonCanINP-23
❑ 97DonCanIPS-64
❑ 97DonCanISCS-30
❑ 97DonEli-63
❑ 97DonEliAsp-63
❑ 97DonEliS-63
❑ 97DonLim-6
❑ 97DonLim-100
❑ 97DonLim-108
❑ 97DonLimExp-6
❑ 97DonLimExp-100
❑ 97DonLimExp-108
❑ 97DonLimFOTG-12
❑ 97DonLin2L-15
❑ 97DonLin2LDC-15
❑ 97DonPre-12
❑ 97DonPreCttC-12
❑ 97DonPreProG-63
❑ 97DonPreProS-63
❑ 97DonPri-110
❑ 97DonPriSoA-110
❑ 97Kat-103
❑ 97KatGol-103
❑ 97KatSil-103
❑ 97Lea-21
❑ 97LeaFraMat-21
❑ 97LeaFraMDC-21
❑ 97LeaInt-21
❑ 97LeaIntUI-21
❑ 97Pac-77
❑ 97PacCop-77
❑ 97PacEmeGre-77
❑ 97PacIceB-77
❑ 97PacInv-99
❑ 97PacInvC-99
❑ 97PacInvEG-99
❑ 97PacInvIB-99
❑ 97PacInvNRB-140
❑ 97PacInvR-99
❑ 97PacInvS-99
❑ 97PacOme-161
❑ 97PacOmeC-161
❑ 97PacOmeDG-161
❑ 97PacOmeEG-161
❑ 97PacOmeG-161
❑ 97PacOmeIB-161
❑ 97PacRed-77
❑ 97PacRev-98
❑ 97PacRevC-98
❑ 97PacRevE-98
❑ 97PacRevIB-98
❑ 97PacRevR-98
❑ 97PacRevS-98
❑ 97PacSil-77
❑ 97Pin-153
❑ 97PinCer-102
❑ 97PinCerMB-102
❑ 97PinCerMG-102
❑ 97PinCerMR-102
❑ 97PinCerR-102
❑ 97PinIns-160
❑ 97PinPrePBB-153
❑ 97PinPrePBC-153
❑ 97PinPrePBM-153
❑ 97PinPrePBY-153
❑ 97PinPrePFC-153
❑ 97PinPrePFM-153
❑ 97PinPrePFY-153
❑ 97PinPrePla-153
❑ 97PinTotCMPG-102
❑ 97PinTotCPB-102
❑ 97PinTotCPG-102
❑ 97PinTotCPR-102
❑ 97Sco-166
❑ 97ScoFly-11
❑ 97ScoFlyPla-11
❑ 97ScoFlyPre-11
❑ 97SPAut-113
❑ 97Stu-85
❑ 97StuPrePG-85
❑ 97StuPrePS-85
❑ 97UppDec-329
❑ 97UppDecGDM-329
❑ 98Be A PPA-177
❑ 98Be A PPAA-177
❑ 98Be A PPAAF-177
❑ 98Be A PPAJ-AS11
❑ 98Be A PPAM-M14
❑ 98Be A PPPH-H9
❑ 98Be A PPSE-177
❑ 98Be APG-177
❑ 98McDGreT-T10
❑ 98O-PChr-10
❑ 98O-PChrR-10
❑ 98Pac-322
❑ 98PacIceB-322
❑ 98PacOmeH-39
❑ 98PacOmeODI-39
❑ 98PacOmeR-39
❑ 98PacPar-45
❑ 98PacParC-45
❑ 98PacParEG-45
❑ 98PacParH-45
❑ 98PacParIB-45
❑ 98PacParS-45
❑ 98PacRed-322
❑ 98Top-10
❑ 98TopO-P-10
❑ 98UC-151
❑ 98UD ChoPCR-151
❑ 98UD ChoR-151
❑ 98UDCP-151
❑ 98UppDec-66
❑ 98UppDecE-66
❑ 98UppDecE1o1-66
❑ 98UppDecGR-66
❑ 99Pac-68
❑ 99PacCop-68
❑ 99PacGol-68
❑ 99PacIceB-68
❑ 99PacPreD-68
❑ 99UppDecCL-29
❑ 99UppDecCLCLC-29
**Coffin, Brodie**
❑ 93LonKni-7
**Coghill, Trent**
❑ 89SasBla-16
❑ 907thInnSWHL-81
❑ 90SasBla-15
**Cohagen, Perry**
❑ 92HarCri-5
**Cohen, Paul**
❑ 90ProAHLIHL-505
❑ 91NasKni-17
❑ 98GerDELE-56
**Colagiacomo, Adam**
❑ 95Cla-88
❑ 95Sla-170
❑ 95Sla-NNO
❑ 96UppDec-369
❑ 96UppDecBD-24
❑ 96UppDecBDG-24
❑ 97BowCHL-145
❑ 97BowCHLAu-25
❑ 97BowCHLBB-12
❑ 97BowCHLBowBesAR-12
❑ 97BowCHLBowBesR-12
❑ 97BowCHLOPC-145
**Colborne, Brett**
❑ 91AirCanSJHL-E35
❑ 92MPSPhoSJHL-105
**Colbourne, Darren**
❑ 92DayBom-4
❑ 93RicRen-19
❑ 94ClaProP-243
**Coldwell, Daryl**
❑ 81VicCou-5
**Cole, Alaine**
❑ 907thInnSQMJHL-190
**Cole, Danton**
❑ 89ProAHL-30
❑ 90JetIGA-6
❑ 90OPCPre-17
❑ 90UppDec-517
❑ 90UppDecF-517
❑ 91Bow-202
❑ 91JetIGA-5
❑ 91JetPanTS-5
❑ 91OPC-27
❑ 91PanSti-72
❑ 91ProSet-263
❑ 91ProSetFre-263
❑ 91ScoCan-240
❑ 91StaClu-342
❑ 91Top-27
❑ 91UppDec-210
❑ 91UppDecF-210
❑ 92LigShe-10
❑ 92PanSti-56
❑ 92PanStiFre-56
❑ 92Par-408
❑ 92ParEmel-408
❑ 93Don-491
❑ 93LigSealR-8
❑ 93Par-464
❑ 93ParEmel-464
❑ 93Pow-441
❑ 93Sco-655
❑ 93ScoCan-655
❑ 93ScoGol-655
❑ 93StaClu-239
❑ 93StaCluFDI-239
❑ 93StaCluFDIO-239
❑ 93StaCluO-239
❑ 94CanGamNHLP-222
❑ 94Don-172
❑ 94Lea-259
❑ 94OPCPre-11
❑ 94OPCPreSE-11
❑ 94ParSE-SE169
❑ 94ParSEG-SE169
❑ 94Pin-45
❑ 94PinArtP-45
❑ 94PinRinC-45
❑ 94Sco-131
❑ 94ScoGol-131
❑ 94ScoPla-131
❑ 94ScoPlaTS-131
❑ 94TopPre-11
❑ 94TopPreSE-11
❑ 94Ult-204
❑ 94UppDec-126
❑ 94UppDecEleIce-126
❑ 96GerDELE-88
❑ 96GraRapG-3
**Cole, Jeff**
❑ 91AirCanSJHL-C36
❑ 91AirCanSJHLAS-5
**Cole, Lee**
❑ 95SauSteMG-4
❑ 95Sla-373
**Cole, Mike**
❑ 92BriColJHL-217
**Cole, Patrick**
❑ 907thInnSQMJHL-252
**Cole, Tom**
❑ 92NasKni-4
**Coleman, Jon**
❑ 93DonTeaUSA-4
❑ 93Pin-481
❑ 93PinCan-481
❑ 93UppDec-563
**Coleman, Mike**
❑ 91ProAHLCHL-510
**Coles, Bruce**
❑ 91JohChi-6
❑ 94JohChi-5
**Coles, Jason**
❑ 907thInnSOHL-257
❑ 917thInnSOHL-209
**Collard, Geoff**
❑ 94DubFigS-7
**Colley, Kevin**
❑ 98BowCHL-37
❑ 98BowCHLGA-37
❑ 98BowCHLOI-37
❑ 98BowChrC-37
❑ 98BowChrCGA-37
❑ 98BowChrCGAR-37
❑ 98BowChrCOI-37
❑ 98BowChrCOIR-37
❑ 98BowChrCR-37
**Colley, Tom**
❑ 89NewHavN-3
**Collin, Christer**
❑ 71SweHocS-384
❑ 72SweHocS-258
**Collin, Curtis**
❑ 82KinCan-3
❑ 83NorBayC-6
**Collin, Eryc**
❑ 96RimOce-8
❑ 96RimOceQPP-8
**Collin, Mikael**
❑ 71SweHocS-221
❑ 72SweHocS-211
❑ 73SweHocS-60
❑ 73SweWorCS-60
❑ 74SweHocS-139
**Collins, Bill**
❑ 68ShiCoi-68
❑ 69CanaPosC-6
❑ 69OPC-126
❑ 70EssPowPla-7
❑ 70SarProSta-104
❑ 71OPC-139
❑ 71SarProSta-49
❑ 71TorSun-88
❑ 72OPC-265
❑ 72SarProSta-71
❑ 73OPC-163
❑ 73RedWinMP-5
❑ 73RedWinTI-6
❑ 73Top-158
❑ 74NHLActSta-250
❑ 74OPCNHL-364
❑ 81RedWinOld-10
**Collins, Gary**
❑ 52JunBluT-121
❑ 57Par-T23
**Collins, Ken**
❑ 52JunBluT-115
❑ 95GerDELE-7
**Collins, Kevin**
❑ 90ProSet-683
**Collins, Maurice**
❑ 52JunBluT-65
**Collyard, Bob**
❑ 74NHLActSta-319
❑ 79PanSti-216
❑ 81MilAdm-14
**Colman, Mike**
❑ 90KanCitBla-14
❑ 90ProAHLIHL-599
**Colombi, Carlo**
❑ 917thInnSQMJHL-4
**Columbus, Jeff**
❑ 87SauSteMG-24
**Colville, Mac**
❑ 34BeeGro1P-265
❑ 36V356WorG-89
❑ 39OPCV3011-90
**Colville, Neil**
❑ 34BeeGro1P-266
❑ 36OPCV304D-105
❑ 36V356WorG-91
❑ 39OPCV3011-39
❑ 83HalFP-A4
❑ 85HalFC-5
**Colvin, John**
❑ 89SpoChi-2
**Colwill, Les**
❑ 58Top-19
**Comeau, Marcel**
❑ 78LouGea-2
❑ 88SasBla-3
❑ 90ProAHLIHL-440
❑ 917thInnSWHL-148
❑ 92TacRoc-6
❑ 93TacRoc-5
**Comeau, Rey**
❑ 72Flam-3
❑ 72OPC-239
❑ 73OPC-29
❑ 73Top-29
❑ 74NHLActSta-3
❑ 74OPCNHL-296
❑ 75OPCNHL-248
❑ 75Top-248
❑ 76OPCNHL-343
❑ 77OPCNHL-346
❑ 78OPC-293
❑ 79OPC-385
**Comfort, Fred**
❑ 23V1281PauC-8
❑ 24CreSel-9
**Comley, Rick**
❑ 92NorMicW-28
❑ 93NorMicW-32
**Comploi, Giorgio**
❑ 93SweSemWCS-216
❑ 94FinnJaaK-296
**Conacher, Brian**
❑ 64BeeGro3P-159
❑ 65MapLeaWB-5
❑ 67Top-17
❑ 67YorActOct-1
❑ 67YorActOct-6
❑ 68ShiCoi-167
❑ 69MapLeaWBG-6
❑ 71OPC-138
❑ 71TorSun-89
❑ 72NatOttWHA-7
**Conacher, Chuck (Charlie)**
❑ 320'KeeMapL-9
❑ 33OPCV304A-34
❑ 33V129-5
❑ 33V252CanG-12
❑ 33V288HamG-49
❑ 34BeeGro1P-309
❑ 34SweCap-45
❑ 36ChaPos-9
❑ 36OPCV304D-123
❑ 36V356WorG-1
❑ 37OPCV304E-138
❑ 39OPCV3011-59
❑ 55Par-26
❑ 55ParQuaO-26
❑ 83HalFP-A5
❑ 85HalFC-6
❑ 91ProSet-338
❑ 91ProSetFre-338
❑ 92HalFL-14
❑ 99UppDecCL-38
❑ 99UppDecCLCLC-38
**Conacher, Jim**
❑ 44BeeGro2P-85
❑ 51Par-105
❑ 52Par-103
**Conacher, John**
❑ 44BeeGro2P-157
**Conacher, Lionel**
❑ 33V252CanG-13
❑ 34DiaMatS-13
❑ 34SweCap-17
❑ 36OPCV304D-102
❑ 36TriPos-1
❑ 36V356WorG-10
❑ 94ParTalBG-12
**Conacher, Pat**
❑ 83MonAlp-14
❑ 83OilMcD-11
❑ 84NovScoO-7
❑ 88DevCar-8
❑ 88OilTenAnn-139
❑ 89DevCar-7
❑ 89ProAHL-219
❑ 90Dev-7
❑ 90ProSet-477
❑ 91ProSet-427
❑ 91ProSetFre-427
❑ 91ScoCan-654
❑ 91StaClu-387
❑ 92OPCPre-49
❑ 92Sco-544
❑ 92ScoCan-544
❑ 93Don-153
❑ 93Lea-380
❑ 93OPCPre-252
❑ 93OPCPreG-252
❑ 93Par-363
❑ 93ParEmel-363
❑ 93Pow-358
❑ 93StaClu-179
❑ 93StaCluFDI-179
❑ 93StaCluFDIO-179
❑ 93StaCluO-179
❑ 93TopPre-252
❑ 93TopPreG-252
❑ 93Ult-342
❑ 94BeAP99A-G4
❑ 94CanGamNHLP-122
❑ 94Par-107
❑ 94ParGol-107
❑ 94Pin-403
❑ 94PinArtP-403
❑ 94PinRinC-403
❑ 94StaClu-237
❑ 94StaCluFDI-237
❑ 94StaCluMOMS-237
❑ 94StaCluSTWC-237
❑ 95BeAPla-92
❑ 95BeAPSig-S92
❑ 95BeAPSigDC-S92
❑ 95CanGamNHLP-136
❑ 95PlaOneoOne-268
**Conacher, Pete**
❑ 44BeeGro2P-86
❑ 44BeeGro2P-390
❑ 52Par-33
❑ 53Par-70
❑ 54Par-86
❑ 54Top-33
❑ 57Par-T14
**Conacher, Roy**
❑ 34BeeGro1P-9
❑ 39OPCV3011-91
❑ 44BeeGro2P-87
❑ 48ExhCan-50
❑ 51Par-50
❑ 91BruSpoAL-12
**Concannon, Rob**
❑ 95SouCarS-8
❑ 96SouCarS-21
**Conlan, Wayne**
❑ 93MaiBlaB-44
**Conn, Joe**
❑ 44BeeGro2P-88
**Conn, Red (Hugh)**
❑ 34DiaMatS-14
❑ 35DiaMatTI-13
**Conn, Rob**
❑ 91ProAHLCHL-494
❑ 92Indlce-7
❑ 94Indlce-3
**Connell, Alex**
❑ 24C144ChaCig-16
❑ 24V1452-10
❑ 33V252CanG-14
❑ 34BeeGro1P-194
❑ 34SweCap-18
❑ 60TopSta-11
❑ 83HalFP-M4
❑ 85HalFC-169
**Connelly, Jack**
❑ 23CreSel-8
**Connelly, Jim**
❑ 52JunBluT-51
**Connelly, Wayne**
❑ 44BeeGro2P-12A
❑ 44BeeGro2P-12B
❑ 61Par-44
❑ 62Top-18
❑ 64BeeGro3P-4
❑ 66Top-40
❑ 68OPC-50
❑ 68ShiCoi-62
❑ 68Top-50
❑ 69OPC-60
❑ 69Top-60
❑ 70DadCoo-16
❑ 70EssPowPla-141
❑ 70OPC-159
❑ 70RedWinM-2
❑ 70SarProSta-54
❑ 71OPC-237
❑ 71SarProSta-186
❑ 71Top-127
❑ 71TorSun-237
❑ 72FigSaiPos-5
❑ 72OPC-296
❑ 72SluCupWHA-6
❑ 73QuaOatWHA-35
❑ 74FigSaiWHA-6
❑ 74OPCWHA-54
❑ 76OPCWHA-122
❑ 95Par66-20
❑ 95Par66Coi-20
**Connolly, Bert**
❑ 35DiaMatT2-10
❑ 35DiaMatT3-10
❑ 35DiaMatTI-14
**Connolly, Tim**
❑ 98SPXTopP-86
❑ 98SPXTopPF-86
❑ 98SPXTopPR-86
❑ 98UppDecBD-117
❑ 98UppDecDD-117
❑ 98UppDecQD-117
❑ 98UppDecTD-117
**Connor, Cam**
❑ 74PhoRoaWP-2
❑ 75OPCWHA-48
❑ 75RoaPhoWHA-17
❑ 76OPCWHA-89
❑ 78CanaPos-3
❑ 79OilPos-4
❑ 79OPC-138
❑ 79Top-138
❑ 80OPC-387
❑ 88OilTenAnn-134
**Connors, Bobby**
❑ 23V1281PauC-12
**Conroy, Allan (Al)**
❑ 82MedHatT-1
❑ 83MedHatT-23
❑ 85MedHatT-6
❑ 89ProAHL-314
❑ 90ProAHLIHL-473
❑ 91ProAHLCHL-267
❑ 92TopGol-525G
❑ 93OPCPre-352
❑ 93OPCPreG-352
❑ 93TopPre-352
❑ 93TopPreG-352
**Conroy, Craig**
❑ 92ClaKni-3
❑ 94Cla-51
❑ 94ClaAllAme-AA1
❑ 94ClaDraGol-51
❑ 94FreCan-9
❑ 95ColEdgI-41
❑ 95Don-169
❑ 95FreCan-7
❑ 95Ima-64
❑ 95ImaAut-64A
❑ 95ImaGol-64
❑ 95Lea-85
❑ 95Pin-218
❑ 95PinArtP-218
❑ 95PinRinC-218
❑ 95Sco-297
❑ 95ScoBlaIce-297
❑ 95ScoBlaIceAP-297
❑ 95Top-187
❑ 95TopOPCI-187
❑ 97Be A PPAD-59
❑ 97Be A PPAPD-59
❑ 97BeAPla-59
❑ 97BeAPlaAut-59
❑ 97PacInvNRB-168
❑ 98Be A PPA-277
❑ 98Be A PPAA-277
❑ 98Be A PPAAF-277
❑ 98Be A PPSE-277
❑ 98Be APG-277
❑ 98O-PChr-47
❑ 98O-PChrR-47
❑ 98Pac-364
❑ 98PacIceB-364
❑ 98PacPar-200
❑ 98PacParC-200
❑ 98PacParEG-200
❑ 98PacParH-200
❑ 98PacParIB-200
❑ 98PacParS-200
❑ 98PacRed-364
❑ 98Top-47
❑ 98TopO-P-47
❑ 99Pac-353
❑ 99PacCop-353
❑ 99PacGol-353
❑ 99PacIceB-353
❑ 99PacPreD-353
**Constant, Chris**
❑ 89BraWheK-6
❑ 907thInnSWHL-229
❑ 90BraWheK-23
❑ 917thInnSWHL-209
**Constantin, Charles**
❑ 76NordMarA-8
❑ 76NordPos-11
**Constantine, Kevin**
❑ 90ProAHLIHL-121
**Conti, Leonardo**
❑ 96GerDELE-3
❑ 98GerDELE-278
**Contini, Joe**
❑ 75HamFin-4
**Converse, Trevor**
❑ 91AirCanSJHL-D15
❑ 91RicRen-14
**Convery, Brandon**
❑ 907thInnSOHL-381
❑ 90SudWol-12
❑ 917thInnSOHL-258
❑ 91SudWol-16
❑ 93DonTeaC-8
❑ 93NiaFalT-11
❑ 93NiaFalT-28
❑ 93Pin-470
❑ 93PinCan-470
❑ 93UppDec-548
❑ 94Cla-82
❑ 94ClaDraGol-82
❑ 94ClaProP-59
❑ 94ClaTri-T67
❑ 94Lea-483
❑ 94OPCPre-386
❑ 94OPCPreSE-386
❑ 94St.JohML-5
❑ 94TopPre-386
❑ 94TopPreSE-386
❑ 94UppDec-259
❑ 94UppDecEleIce-259
❑ 95ColEdgI-18
❑ 95St.JohML-4
❑ 96DonCanI-144
❑ 96DonCanIGPP-144
❑ 96DonCanIRPP-144
❑ 96FlePic-146
❑ 96LeaGolR-7
❑ 96LeaPre-132
❑ 96LeaPrePP-132
❑ 96Pin-241
❑ 96PinArtP-241
❑ 96PinFoi-241
❑ 96PinPreS-241
❑ 96PinRinC-241
❑ 96St.JohML-10
❑ 96Sum-174
❑ 96SumArtP-174
❑ 96SumIce-174
❑ 96SumMet-174
❑ 96SumPreS-174
❑ 96UppDec-186
❑ 96Zen-132
❑ 96ZenArtP-132
❑ 97Don-85
❑ 97DonLim-167
❑ 97DonLimExp-167
❑ 97DonPreProG-85
❑ 97DonPreProS-85
❑ 97PacInvNRB-192
❑ 97PinIns-152
❑ 97Sco-164
❑ 97ScoMapL-14
❑ 97ScoMapLPla-14
❑ 97ScoMapLPre-14
**Conway, Kevin**
❑ 81SauSteMG-7
❑ 82SauSteMG-6
❑ 83KinCan-16
❑ 94FinnJaaK-324
**Cook, Bill**
❑ 23V1281PauC-35
❑ 24V130MapC-6
❑ 24V1452-24
❑ 33OPCV304A-38
❑ 33V129-31
❑ 33V357IceK-30
❑ 34BeeGro1P-267
❑ 34DiaMatS-15
❑ 34SweCap-40
❑ 35DiaMatT2-11
❑ 35DiaMatT2-12
❑ 35DiaMatT3-11
❑ 36ChaPos-6
❑ 60Top-10
❑ 60TopSta-12
❑ 83HalFP-I5
❑ 85HalFC-126
❑ 94ParMisLP-P8
❑ 99UppDecCL-45
❑ 99UppDecCLCLC-45
**Cook, Brad**
❑ 93DetJrRW-13
**Cook, Brian**
❑ 94CenHocL-42
**Cook, Bun**
❑ 33OPCV304B-72
❑ 33V129-46
❑ 33V252CanG-15
❑ 33V357IceK-66
❑ 34BeeGro1P-10
❑ 34DiaMatS-16
❑ 34SweCap-41
❑ 35DiaMatT2-13
❑ 35DiaMatT3-12
❑ 35DiaMatTI-15
❑ 36ChaPos-10
❑ 36V356WorG-68
❑ 51CleBar-1
❑ 94ParTalBG-10
**Cook, Cam**
❑ 92MPSPhoSJHL-150
**Cook, Dean**
❑ 86KamBla-4
❑ 87KamBla-4
❑ 88KamBla-7
❑ 89ProIHL-187
**Cook, Joe**
❑ 917thInnSOHL-163
❑ 91OshGen-23
❑ 91OshGenS-3
❑ 92OshGenS-7
❑ 94ClaProP-231
**Cook, Michel**
❑ 91AirCanSJHL-B42
❑ 91AirCanSJHLAS-32
❑ 91AirCanSJHLAS-45
❑ 92MPSPhoSJHL-156
**Cook, Tom**
❑ 34BeeGro1P-195
❑ 34DiaMatS-17
❑ 35DiaMatT2-14
❑ 35DiaMatT3-13
❑ 35DiaMatT4-4
❑ 35DiaMatT5-3
❑ 35DiaMatTI-16
❑ 36V356WorG-43
❑ 37DiaMatT6-3
❑ 37OPCV304E-180
**Cooke, Jamie**
❑ 91ProAHLCHL-282
**Cooke, Matt**
❑ 95Sla-415
❑ 97BowCHL-22
❑ 97BowCHLOPC-22
❑ 98BowCHL-11
❑ 98BowCHLGA-11
❑ 98BowCHLOI-11
❑ 98BowChrC-11
❑ 98BowChrCGA-11
❑ 98BowChrCGAR-11
❑ 98BowChrCOI-11
❑ 98BowChrCOIR-11
❑ 98BowChrCR-11
❑ 98PacDynI-188
❑ 98PacDynIIB-188
❑ 98PacDynIR-188
❑ 98PacOmeH-242
❑ 98PacOmeODI-242
❑ 98PacOmeR-242
❑ 98UC-268
❑ 98UD ChoPCR-268
❑ 98UD ChoR-268
❑ 98UppDec-381
❑ 98UppDecE-381
❑ 98UppDecE1o1-381
❑ 98UppDecGR-381
**Cool, Eric**
❑ 917thInnSQMJHL-192
**Cooley, Gaye**
❑ 71RocAme-3
**Coombs, Joe**
❑ 95Sla-49
**Cooney, Matt**
❑ 93CorBigRed-5
**Cooper, Carson**
❑ 24C144ChaCig-17
❑ 24V130MapC-9
❑ 24V1452-21
**Cooper, David**
❑ 907thInnSWHL-38

917thInnSWHL-319
93RochAmeKod-8
94ClaProP-210
94ClaTri-T7
95RochAmeSS-2
96St.JohML-11
97St.JohML-7
97UppDec-193
**Cooper, Ian**
94FinnJaaK-330
**Cooper, Jeff**
88ProIHL-46
**Cooper, Joe**
34BeeGro1P-268
**Cooper, John**
93WinSpi-23
94WinSpi-25
**Cooper, Kory**
95Sla-31
97BowCHL-20
97BowCHLOPC-20
**Cooper, Stephen**
94FinnJaaK-314
**Coopman, Todd**
897thInnSOHL-128
89NiaFalT-6
890shGenP-21
907thInnSOHL-258
**Copeland, Todd**
90ProAHLIHL-573
91ProAHLCHL-418
**Copija, Miroslaw**
89SweSemWCS-141
**Copley, John**
89KitRan-11
907thInnSMC-42
907thInnSOHL-179
917thInnSOHL-178
**Copley, Randy**
98BowCHL-114
98BowCHL-125
98BowCHLAuB-A34
98BowCHLAuG-A34
98BowCHLAuS-A34
98BowCHLGA-114
98BowCHLGA-125
98BowCHLOI-114
98BowCHLOI-125
98BowChrC-114
98BowChrC-125
98BowChrCGA-114
98BowChrCGA-125
98BowChrCGAR-114
98BowChrCGAR-125
98BowChrCOI-114
98BowChrCOI-125
98BowChrCOIR-114
98BowChrCOIR-125
98BowChrCR-114
98BowChrCR-125
**Copp, Bob**
34BeeGro1P-310
**Coppo, Paul**
69SweWorC-179
69SweWorC-184
**Coram, Greg**
82Ott67-2
83Ott67-5
84Ott67-5
**Corbeau, Bert**
23V1451-25
24C144ChaCig-18
24V1452-58
**Corbeil, Justin**
86SudWol-4
87SudWol-5
**Corbet, Rene**
917thInnSMC-63
917thInnSMC-105
917thInnSQMJHL-287
91AreDraPic-18
91Cla-21
91StaPicH-31
91UltDra-20
93Par-433
93ParEmel-433
93Pin-448
93PinCan-448
93UppDec-339
94Cla-98
94ClaDraGol-98
94ClaProP-130
94ClaTri-T55
94Fin-97
94FinRef-97
94FinSupTW-97
94Fla-143
94Par-193
94ParGol-193
94Pin-460
94PinArtP-460
94PinRinC-460
94PinRooTP-6
94Sco-236
94ScoGol-236
94ScoPla-236
94ScoPlaTS-236
94Sel-197
94SelGol-197
94UppDec-179
94UppDecEleIce-179
95BeAPla-78
95BeAPSig-S78
95BeAPSigDC-S78
95ColEdgI-27

95Don-371
95Emo-35
95Ima-78
95ImaGol-78
95UppDec-100
95UppDecEleIce-100
95UppDecEleIceG-100
97Be A PPAD-205
97Be A PPAPD-205
97BeAPla-205
97PacInvNRB-50
97ScoAva-14
97ScoAvaPla-14
97ScoAvaPre-14
98Pac-158
98PacIceB-158
98PacRed-158
99Pac-54
99PacCop-54
99PacGol-54
99PacIceB-54
99PacPreD-54
99UppDecM-36
99UppDecMGS-36
99UppDecMGS-36
99UppDecMSS-36
**Corbett, Mike**
63RochAme-9
96DenUniPio-3
**Corbett, Peter**
91ProAHLCHL-437
**Corbett, Scott**
95Sla-350
96SarSti-6
**Corbin, Victor**
51LavDaiLSJ-36
**Corbin, Yvan**
907thInnSQMJHL-179
917thInnSOHL-81
**Cordery, Bill**
94WheThu-22
**Corey, Ronald**
88CanaPos-6
89CanaPos-6
90CanaPos-8
91CanaPos-5
96CanaPos-7
**Corkum, Bob**
89ProAHL-278
90ProAHLIHL-280
90SabCam-5
90UppDec-35
90UppDecF-35
91Par-238
91ParFre-238
91ProAHLCHL-8
91RochAmeDD-3
91RochAmeKod-8
91RochAmePos-6
92SabBluS-4
92SabJubF-13
92StaClu-179
92Top-74
92TopGol-74G
93Don-10
93DucMilCap-5
93Par-6
93ParEmel-6
93Pow-282
93Sco-637
93ScoCan-637
93ScoGol-637
93StaClu-284
93StaCluFDI-284
93StaCluO-284
94CanGamNHLP-28
94Don-96
94DucCarJr-2
94Fin-72
94FinRef-72
94FinSupTW-72
94Fla-1
94Fle-2
94Lea-299
94OPCPre-31
94OPCPreSE-31
94ParSE-SE2
94ParSEG-SE2
94Pin-144
94PinArtP-144
94PinRinC-144
94Sco-158
94ScoGol-158
94ScoPla-158
94ScoPlaTS-158
94SP-4
94SPDieCut-4
94StaCluST-1
94TopPre-31
94TopPreSE-31
94Ult-1
94UppDec-413
94UppDecEleIce-413
95BeAPla-112
95BeAPSig-S112
95BeAPSigDC-S112
95ColCho-14
95ColChoPC-14
95ColChoPCP-14
95Don-112
95KenStaLA-5
95Lea-300
95Pin-121
95PinArtP-121

95PinRinC-121
95PlaOneoOne-221
95Sco-42
95ScoBlaIce-42
95ScoBlaIceAP-42
95Top-59
95TopOPCI-59
95UppDec-149
95UppDecEleIce-149
95UppDecEleIceG-149
96PlaOneoOne-415
97Be A PPAD-117
97Be A PPAPD-117
97BeAPla-117
97BeAPlaAut-117
97Pac-226
97PacCop-226
97PacEmeGre-226
97PacIceB-226
97PacRed-226
97PacSil-226
98Pac-334
98PacIceB-334
98PacRed-334
99Pac-317
99PacCop-317
99PacGol-317
99PacIceB-317
99PacPreD-317
**Cormier, Dan**
84MonGolF-18
**Cormier, Derek**
98GerDELE-293
**Cormier, Michel**
74RoaPhoRoaWP-3
750PCWHA-74
75RoaPhoWHA-16
76RoaPhoWHA-74
**Cornacchia, David**
97SudWolP-17
**Cornacchia, Rick**
83KinCan-26
84KinCan-2
890shGenP-13
907thInnSMC-75
907thInnSOHL-349
917thInnSOHL-171
930shGen-26
**Cornelius, Jeff**
907thInnSOHL-55
85KinCan-10
**Cornforth, Mark**
96ProBru-2
**Cornier, Sylvain**
907thInnSQMJHL-197
**Cornish, Clair**
897thInnSOHL-17
890shGen-5
890shGenP-17
907thInnSMC-98
907thInnSOHL-330
**Corpse, Keli**
907thInnSOHL-55
917thInnSOHL-224
93KinFro-22
95FreCan-8
96GraRapG-4
96WheNai-8
**Corrigan, Jason**
897thInnSOHL-153
**Corrigan, Mike**
70CanuRoyB-2
70EssPowPla-47
700PC-227
71CanuRoyB-2
710PC-157
71SarProSta-224
720PC-74
72SarProSta-94
72Top-89
730PC-48
73Top-48
74NHLActSta-109
740PCNHL-37
74Top-37
750PCNHL-361
760PCNHL-268
760PCNHL-386
770PCNHL-236
77PenPucB-27
77Top-236
**Corriveau, Andre**
51LavDaiQSHL-74
52St.LawS-24
55MonRoy-2
**Corriveau, Luc**
90MonAAA-8
**Corriveau, Rick**
897thInnSOHL-47
907thInnSOHL-129
90Sco-396
90ScoCan-396
917thInnSOHL-200
92TolSto-24
93TolSto-25
94TolSto-3
95BufStaRHI-72
**Corriveau, Yvon**
86CapPol-5
88CapBor-2
88CapSmo-2
89CapTeaIss-4
900PC-364
90ProSet-100
90Sco-302A
90ScoCan-302A

90Top-364
90TopTif-364
90WhaJr7E-4
91UppDec-407
91UppDecF-407
920PCPre-74
92PanSti-259
92PanStiFre-259
92Par-295
92ParEmel-295
92Sco-541
92ScoCan-541
92StaClu-476
92Top-474
92TopGol-474G
92UppDec-460
930PCPre-208
930PCPreG-208
93StaClu-9
93StaCluFDI-9
93StaCluFDIO-9
93StaCluO-9
93TopPre-208
93TopPreG-208
96DetVip-3
96GerDELE-170
**Corsi, Jim**
82SweSemHVS-122
88OilTenAnn-115
**Corso, Daniel**
95BowDraPro-P7
95UppDec-510
95UppDecEleIce-510
95UppDecEleIceG-510
97BowCHL-71
97BowCHLOPC-71
98BowCHL-89
98BowCHLGA-89
98BowCHLOI-89
98BowChrC-89
98BowChrCGA-89
98BowChrCGAR-89
98BowChrCOI-89
98BowChrCOIR-89
98BowChrCR-89
98UC-269
98UD ChoPCR-269
98UD ChoR-269
99QuePeeWEHWCCS-14
**Corson, Shayne**
83BraAle-2
86CanaPos-3
87CanaPos-3
87CanaVacS-49
87CanaVacS-50
88CanaPos-7
89CanaKra-4
89CanaPos-7
89CanaProF-27
89Kra-21
890PC-248
890PCSti-49
89PanSti-242
90Bow-41
90BowTif-41
90CanaPos-9
900PC-58
90PanSti-54
90ProSet-148
90ProSet-369A
90ProSet-369B
90Sco-213
90ScoCan-213
90ScoHotRS-91
90Top-58
90TopTif-58
90UppDec-280
90UppDecF-280
91Bow-328
91CanaPanTS-5
91CanaPos-6
91Kra-29
910PC-157
910PC-298
910PCPre-161
91PanSti-196
91Par-86
91ParFre-86
91Pin-102
91PinFre-102
91ProSet-413
91ProSetFre-413
91ScoAme-65
91ScoCan-65
91StaClu-9
91Top-157
91UppDec-282
91UppDec-505
91UppDecF-282
91UppDecF-505
92Bow-82
92HumDum2-2
920ilIGA-4
920PC-231
92PanSti-150
92PanStiFre-150
92Par-53
92ParEmel-53
92Pin-323
92PinFre-323
92ProSet-89
92Sco-158
92ScoCan-158

92StaClu-221
92Top-201
92TopGol-201G
92Ult-57
92Ult-292
92UppDec-330
92UppDec-541
93Don-114
93Lea-46
930PCPre-38
930PCPreG-38
93PanSti-236
93Par-338
93ParEmel-338
93Pin-249
93PinCan-249
93Pow-79
93Sco-108
93ScoCan-108
93ScoDynDC-7
93StaClu-40
93StaCluFDI-40
93StaCluFDIO-40
93StaCluO-40
93TopPre-38
93TopPreG-38
93Ult-51
93UppDec-132
93UppDecNR-13
93UppDecSP-49
94BeAPSig-172
94CanGamNHLP-99
94Don-221
94EASpo-46
94Fin-74
94FinRef-74
94FinnJaaK-93
94FinSupTW-74
94Fla-57
94Fle-69
94Lea-164
940PCPre-210
940PCPreSE-210
94Par-75
94ParGol-75
94ParVin-V3
94Pin-44
94PinArtP-44
94PinRinC-44
94Sco-174
94ScoGol-174
94ScoPla-174
94ScoPlaTS-174
94Sel-47
94SelGol-47
94SP-42
94SPDieCut-42
94StaCluMO-12
94TopPre-210
94TopPreSE-210
94Ult-291
94UppDec-351
94UppDecEleIce-351
94UppDecSPI-SP116
94UppDecSPIDC-SP116
95Bow-11
95BowAllFoi-11
95CanGamNHLP-241
95ColCho-146
95ColChoPC-146
95ColChoPCP-146
95Don-376
95Emo-145
95Fin-18
95FinnSemWC-91
95FinRef-18
95Lea-123
95Met-122
95ParInt-174
95ParIntEl-174
95PlaOneoOne-86
95Sco-245
95ScoBlaIce-245
95ScoBlaIceAP-245
95SelCer-101
95SelCerMG-101
95SkyImp-138
95SP-122
95SPAut-84
95TopOPCI-55
95Top-55
95Top-229
95TopOPCI-229
95Ult-53
95Ult-296
95UltGolM-53
95UppDec-101
95UppDecEleIce-101
95UppDecEleIceG-101
95UppDecSpeE-SE159
95UppDecSpeEdiG-SE159
95Zen-98

96DonCanI-43
96DonCanIGPP-43
96DonCanIRPP-43
96DonEli-58
96DonEliDCS-58
96DonPrePro-55
96Fle-95
96Lea-163
96LeaLim-66
96LeaLimG-66
96LeaPre-26
96LeaPreP-163
96LeaPrePP-26
96MetUni-130
96Pin-104
96PinArtP-104
96PinFoi-104
96PinPreS-104
96PinRinC-104
96Sco-78
96ScoArtPro-78
96ScoDeaCAP-78
96ScoGolB-78
96ScoSpeAP-78
96SelCer-73
96SelCerAP-73
96SelCerBlu-73
96SelCerMB-73
96SelCerMG-73
96SelCerMR-73
96SelCerRed-73
96SkyImp-110
96SP-84
96Sum-137
96SumArtP-137
96SumIce-137
96SumMet-137
96SumPreS-137
96TeaOut-11
96TopNHLP-139
96TopPicOI-139
96Ult-85
96UltGolM-86
96UppDec-139
96UppDecBD-119
96UppDecBDG-119
96Zen-107
96ZenArtP-107
97CanaPos-7
97ColCho-137
97Don-42
97DonLim-172
97DonLimExp-172
97DonPreProG-42
97DonPreProS-42
97Pac-246
97PacCop-246
97PacCroR-67
97PacCroREG-67
97PacCroRIB-67
97PacCroRS-67
97PacEmeGre-246
97PacIceB-246
97PacOme-116
97PacOmeC-116
97PacOmeDG-116
97PacOmeEG-116
97PacOmeG-116
97PacOmeIB-116
97PacOmeTL-11
97PacPar-93
97PacParC-93
97PacParDG-93
97PacParEG-93
97PacParIB-93
97PacParRed-93
97PacParSil-93
97PacRed-246
97PacRev-69
97PacRevC-69
97PacRevE-69
97PacRevEB-69
97PacRevIB-69
97PacRevR-69
97PacRevS-69
97PacSil-246
97ScoCan-12
97ScoCanPla-12
97SPAut-84
97UppDec-298
97UppDecBD-107
97UppDecBDDD-107
97UppDecBDQD-107
97UppDecBDTD-107
97Zen-67
97Zen5x7-34
97ZenGolImp-34
97ZenSilImp-34
97ZenZGol-67
97ZenZSil-67
98BowBes-98
98BowBesAR-98
98BowBesR-98
98Pac-249
98PacAur-92
98PacAurMAC-11
98PacCroR-67
98PacCroRLS-67
98PacDynI-94
98PacDynIIB-94
98PacDynIR-94
98PacIceB-249
98PacOmeH-119
98PacOmeODI-119
98PacOmeR-119
98PacPar-111

98PacParC-111
98PacParEG-111
98PacParH-111
98PacParIB-111
98PacParS-111
98PacRed-249
98PacRev-71
98PacRevIS-71
98PacRevR-71
98ScoCanPre-12
98UC-103
98UD ChoPCR-103
98UD ChoR-103
98UDCP-103
98UppDec-291
98UppDecE-291
98UppDecE101-291
98UppDecG-291
98UppDecM-109
98UppDecMGS-109
98UppDecMSS-109
98UppDecMSS-109
99Pac-202
99PacAur-73
99PacAurPD-73
99PacCop-202
99PacGol-202
99PacIceB-202
99PacPreD-202
**Cort, Joel**
94GueSto-6
95GueSto5A-12
95Sla-86
96GueSto-6
96GueStoPC-5
**Cortes, Mike**
85MinDul-14
**Corvo, Joe**
96UppDecIce-145
**Cossette, Bryan**
91AirCanSJHL-D44
92MPSPhoSJHL-9
**Cossette, Jean Marie**
52JunBluT-39
62QueAce-5
**Costea, Mark**
96AlaGolKin-1
**Costello, Les**
44BeeGro2P-391
45QuaOatP-14
**Costello, Murray**
44BeeGro2P-9
52JunBluT-156
94ParMisL-60
**Costello, Rich**
840PC-298
**Cota, Darren**
85MedHatT-20
**Cote, Alain**
790PC-324
80NordPos-7
81NordPos-5
810PC-272
82NordPos-5
820PC-281
830PC-291
83NordPos-5
83Vac-63
84NordPos-5
840PC-278
85NordGenF-4
85NordMcD-3
85NordPla-6
85NordPro-5
85NordTeal-4
850PC-205
850PCSti-149
86KraDra-11
86NordGenF-4
86NordMcD-4
86NordTeal-2
86NordYumY-1
860PC-233
860PCSti-20
87NordGenF-5
87NordYumY-1
870PC-254
87PanSti-169
88NordGenF-6
88NordTeal-7
880PC-205
880PCSti-186
88PanSti-352
89ProAHL-102
907thInnSQMJHL-89
90ProAHLIHL-54
917thInnSQMJHL-25
917thInnSQMJHL-54
91CanaPos-7
910PCPre-188
91ProSet-417
91ProSetFre-417
92FreCan-7
93DurSco-19
94ThuBayS-7
**Cote, Andre**
81FreExp-24
82FreExp-24
83FreExp-24
**Cote, Bart**
89BraWheK-9
907thInnSWHL-219
90BraWheK-4
917thInnSMC-94
**Cote, Benoit**

❏ 97BowCHL-128
❏ 97BowCHLAu-8
❏ 97BowCHLOPC-128

**Cote, Brandin**
❏ 98SP Aut-124
❏ 98UppDec-401
❏ 98UppDecE-401
❏ 98UppDecE1o1-401
❏ 98UppDecGR-401
❏ 99SP AutPS-124

**Cote, Martin**
❏ 84RicRiv-3

**Cote, Michael (Mike)**
❏ 907thInnSOHL-331
❏ 917thInnSOHL-344
❏ 91OshGenS-18

**Cote, Patrick**
❏ 95Cla-33
❏ 97Be A PPAD-235
❏ 97Be A PPAPD-235
❏ 97BeAPla-235
❏ 97BeAPlaAut-235
❏ 98PacOmeH-134
❏ 98PacOmeODI-134
❏ 98PacOmeR-134
❏ 98UppDec-304
❏ 98UppDecE-304
❏ 98UppDecE1o1-304
❏ 98UppDecGR-304
❏ 99Pac-221
❏ 99PacCop-221
❏ 99PacGol-221
❏ 99PacIceB-221
❏ 99PacPreD-221

**Cote, Ray**
❏ 83MonAlp-23
❏ 84NovScoO-6
❏ 88OilTenAnn-140

**Cote, Roger**
❏ 80QueRem-3

**Cote, Steven**
❏ 92QueIntP-26

**Cote, Sylvain**
❏ 81FreExp-3
❏ 82FreExp-3
❏ 84WhaJunW-2
❏ 85WhaJunW-2
❏ 86WhaJunT-4
❏ 87WhaJunBK-3
❏ 88PanSti-237
❏ 88WhaJunGR-3
❏ 89OPC-162
❏ 89PanSti-229
❏ 89Top-162
❏ 89WhaJunM-3
❏ 90ProSet-448
❏ 90Sco-83
❏ 90ScoCan-83
❏ 90WhaJr7E-5
❏ 91Bow-17
❏ 91CapJun5-7
❏ 91CapKod-7
❏ 91OPC-249
❏ 91Pin-221
❏ 91PinFre-221
❏ 91ProSet-82
❏ 91ProSet-512
❏ 91ProSetFre-82
❏ 91ProSetFre-512
❏ 91ScoAme-129
❏ 91ScoCan-129
❏ 91ScoCan-596
❏ 91ScoRoo-46T
❏ 91StaClu-183
❏ 91Top-249
❏ 92Bow-115
❏ 92CapKod-7
❏ 92DurPan-34
❏ 92OPC-277
❏ 92Par-431
❏ 92ParEmel-431
❏ 92Pin-182
❏ 92PinFre-182
❏ 92Sco-78
❏ 92ScoCan-78
❏ 92StaClu-145
❏ 92Top-428
❏ 92TopGol-428G
❏ 92Ult-433
❏ 93Don-367
❏ 93DurSco-35
❏ 93Lea-52
❏ 93OPCPre-138
❏ 93OPCPreG-138
❏ 93Par-489
❏ 93ParEmel-489
❏ 93Pin-258
❏ 93PinCan-258
❏ 93Pow-259
❏ 93Sco-92
❏ 93Sco-450
❏ 93ScoCan-92
❏ 93ScoCan-450
❏ 93StaClu-66
❏ 93StaCluFDI-66
❏ 93StaCluFDIO-66
❏ 93StaCluO-66
❏ 93TopPre-138
❏ 93TopPreG-138
❏ 93Ult-445
❏ 94BeAPSig-166
❏ 94CanGamNHLP-249
❏ 94Don-153
❏ 94Fla-198
❏ 94Fle-234

❏ 94Lea-140
❏ 94OPCPre-208
❏ 94OPCPreSE-208
❏ 94ParSE-SE193
❏ 94ParSEG-SE193
❏ 94Pin-33
❏ 94PinArtP-33
❏ 94PinRinC-33
❏ 94Sel-128
❏ 94SelGol-128
❏ 94SelPro-128
❏ 94TopPre-208
❏ 94TopPreSE-208
❏ 94Ult-232
❏ 94UppDec-354
❏ 94UppDecEleIce-354
❏ 95Cap-5
❏ 95ColCho-284
❏ 95ColChoPC-284
❏ 95ColChoPCP-284
❏ 95Fin-37
❏ 95FinRef-37
❏ 95Lea-218
❏ 95Met-158
❏ 95ParInt-222
❏ 95ParIntEI-222
❏ 95Pin-65
❏ 95PinArtP-65
❏ 95PinRinC-65
❏ 95PlaOneoOne-321
❏ 95Sco-183
❏ 95ScoBlaIce-183
❏ 95ScoBlaIceAP-183
❏ 95StaClu-23
❏ 95StaCluMOMS-23
❏ 95Ult-321
❏ 95UppDec-133
❏ 95UppDecEleIce-133
❏ 95UppDecEleIceG-133
❏ 95UppDecSpE-SE176
❏ 95UppDecSpEdiG-SE176
❏ 96ColCho-207
❏ 96SkyImp-138
❏ 96TopNHLP-153
❏ 96TopPicOI-153
❏ 97Pac-207
❏ 97PacCop-207
❏ 97PacEmeGre-207
❏ 97PacIceB-207
❏ 97PacRed-207
❏ 97PacSil-207
❏ 98Pac-412
❏ 98PacIceB-412
❏ 98PacRed-412
❏ 99Pac-404
❏ 99PacCop-404
❏ 99PacGol-404
❏ 99PacIceB-404
❏ 99PacPreD-404

**Cotton, Baldy (Harold)**
❏ 320'KeeMapL-8
❏ 33OPCV304A-35
❏ 33V129-12
❏ 33V288HamG-39
❏ 33V357IceK-33
❏ 34BeeGro1P-311
❏ 36V356WorG-35
❏ 55Par-32
❏ 55ParQuaO-32

**Coughlin, Ben**
❏ 92HarCri-6

**Coulis, Tim**
❏ 84SprInd-10
❏ 85NorStaPos-9

**Coulombe, Serge**
❏ 90RayJrC-4

**Coulter, Arthur (Art)**
❏ 34BeeGro1P-269
❏ 35DiaMatT2-15
❏ 35DiaMatT3-14
❏ 35DiaMatTI-17
❏ 35OPCV304C-93
❏ 39OPCV3011-34
❏ 83HalFP-J5
❏ 85HalFC-185

**Coupal, Gary**
❏ 92SudWol-21
❏ 93SudWol-17
❏ 93SudWolP-16
❏ 93SudWolP-4

**Courcy, Bob**
❏ 62QueAce-6
❏ 69SeaTotW-3

**Cournoyer, Bertrand**
❏ 88RivDu R-9

**Cournoyer, Yvan**
❏ 64BeeGro3P-101
❏ 64CanaPos-4
❏ 64CocCap-63
❏ 65Coc-63
❏ 65Top-76
❏ 66Top-72
❏ 66TopUSAT-13
❏ 67CanalGA-12
❏ 67Top-70
❏ 67YorActOct-28
❏ 67YorActOct-29
❏ 67YorActOct-30
❏ 68CanalGA-12
❏ 68CanaPosBW-3
❏ 68OPC-62
❏ 68PosCerM-5
❏ 68ShiCoi-87
❏ 68Top-62
❏ 69CanaPosC-7

❏ 69OPC-6
❏ 69OPC-221
❏ 69OPCFou-3
❏ 69OPCSta-4
❏ 69Top-6
❏ 70CanaPin-2
❏ 70ColSta-60
❏ 70DadCoo-17
❏ 70EssPowPla-9
❏ 70OPC-50
❏ 70OPCDec-23
❏ 70SarProSta-109
❏ 70Top-50
❏ 71Baz-15
❏ 71CanaPos-3
❏ 71ColHea-1
❏ 71FriLay-1
❏ 71LetActR-15
❏ 71MatMinRec-1
❏ 71OPC-15
❏ 71OPC-260
❏ 71OPCPos-4
❏ 71SarProSta-102
❏ 71Top-15
❏ 71TorSun-148
❏ 72CanaPos-4
❏ 72CanGreWLP-2
❏ 72OPC-29
❏ 72OPC-44
❏ 72OPC-250
❏ 72OPCTeaC-6
❏ 72SarProSta-117
❏ 72SweSemWC-204
❏ 72Top-10
❏ 72Top-131
❏ 73CanaPos-4
❏ 73MacMil-5
❏ 73OPC-157
❏ 73Top-115
❏ 74CanaPos-4
❏ 74LipSou-13
❏ 74NHLActSta-148
❏ 74OPCNHL-124
❏ 74OPCNHL-140
❏ 74Top-124
❏ 74Top-140
❏ 75CanaPos-4
❏ 75HerSta-8
❏ 75OPCNHL-70
❏ 75Top-70
❏ 76CanaPos-4
❏ 76OPCNHL-30
❏ 76Top-30
❏ 77CanaPos-4
❏ 77OPCNHL-230
❏ 77Spo-1
❏ 77Top-230
❏ 78CanaPos-4
❏ 78OPC-60
❏ 78Top-60
❏ 83HalFP-K1
❏ 85HalFC-136
❏ 88EssAllSta-7
❏ 91FutTreC72-82
❏ 92SpoFla-12
❏ 93OPCCanHF-23
❏ 93OPCCanP-1
❏ 93ZelMasH-3
❏ 93ZelMasoHS-3
❏ 94ParTalB-75
❏ 94ParTalB-80
❏ 94ParTalBA-A2
❏ 95Par66-60
❏ 95Par66Coi-60
❏ 96CanaPos-9

**Cournoyer, Yves**
❏ 88RivDu R-10

**Courteau, Maurice**
❏ 51LavDaiLSJ-59

**Courteau, Yves**
❏ 84MonGolF-17
❏ 85MonGolF-24

**Courtemanche, Dave**
❏ 81KinCan-3

**Courtemanche, Marc**
❏ 77GraVic-5

**Courtemanche, Yves**
❏ 77GraVic-6

**Courtenay, Ed**
❏ 89ProIHL-80
❏ 90ProAHLIHL-116
❏ 91ProAHLCHL-507
❏ 91UppDec-517
❏ 91UppDecF-517
❏ 92OPCPre-8
❏ 92UppDec-507
❏ 93Lea-145
❏ 93PanSti-261
❏ 93Pow-217
❏ 93StaClu-72
❏ 93StaCluFDI-72
❏ 93StaCluFDIO-72
❏ 93StaCluO-72
❏ 93Ult-8
❏ 96SouCarS-27
❏ 96SheSte-20

**Courtnall, Geoff**
❏ 81VicCou-6
❏ 82VicCou-4
❏ 84VicCou-6
❏ 85MonGolF-11
❏ 88CapBor-3
❏ 88CapGSmo-3
❏ 88OilTenAnn-88

❏ 88OPCSti-222
❏ 89CapKod-14
❏ 89CapTeaIss-5
❏ 89OPC-111
❏ 89OPCSti-80
❏ 89OPCSti-107
❏ 89OPCSti-164
❏ 89OPCSti-246
❏ 89PanSti-340
❏ 89Top-111
❏ 89TopStiIns-9
❏ 90BluKod-7
❏ 90Bow-73
❏ 90BowTif-73
❏ 90Kra-9
❏ 90OPC-273
❏ 90OPCPre-18
❏ 90PanSti-159
❏ 90ProSet-309
❏ 90ProSet-521
❏ 90Sco-124
❏ 90ScoRoo-5T
❏ 90Top-273
❏ 90TopTif-273
❏ 90UppDec-238
❏ 90UppDec-438
❏ 90UppDecF-238
❏ 90UppDecF-438
❏ 91Bow-318
❏ 91CanuAutC-4
❏ 91CanuTeal8-4
❏ 91Kra-15
❏ 91OPC-305
❏ 91OPCPre-101
❏ 91PanSti-38
❏ 91Par-186
❏ 91ParFre-186
❏ 91Pin-263
❏ 91PinFre-263
❏ 91ProSet-245
❏ 91ProSetFre-245
❏ 91ProSetPla-123
❏ 91ScoAme-150
❏ 91ScoAme-380
❏ 91ScoCan-150
❏ 91ScoCan-220
❏ 91StaClu-149
❏ 91UppDec-467
❏ 91UppDecF-467
❏ 92Bow-345
❏ 92CanuRoaTA-5
❏ 92OPC-176
❏ 92PanSti-29
❏ 92PanStiFre-29
❏ 92Par-189
❏ 92ParEmel-189
❏ 92Pin-187
❏ 92PinFre-187
❏ 92ProSet-198
❏ 92Sco-234
❏ 92ScoCan-234
❏ 92StaClu-265
❏ 92Top-472
❏ 92TopGol-472G
❏ 92Ult-220
❏ 92UppDec-39
❏ 92UppDec-240
❏ 92Don-352
❏ 93Lea-72
❏ 93OPCPre-337
❏ 93OPCPreG-337
❏ 93PanSti-170
❏ 93Par-216
❏ 93ParEmel-216
❏ 93Pin-132
❏ 93PinCan-132
❏ 93Pow-249
❏ 93Sco-78
❏ 93ScoCan-78
❏ 93StaClu-413
❏ 93StaCluFDI-413
❏ 93StaCluO-413
❏ 93TopPre-337
❏ 93TopPreG-337
❏ 93Ult-76
❏ 93UppDec-114
❏ 93UppDecSP-163
❏ 94BeAPla-R6
❏ 94BeAPSig-135
❏ 94CanGamNHLP-329
❏ 94CanuProl-6
❏ 94Don-50
❏ 94EASpo-142
❏ 94Fin-83
❏ 94FinRef-83
❏ 94FinSupTW-83
❏ 94Fle-224
❏ 94Lea-63
❏ 94LeaLim-69
❏ 94OPCPre-186
❏ 94OPCPre-525
❏ 94OPCPreSE-186
❏ 94OPCPreSE-525
❏ 94Par-240
❏ 94ParGol-240
❏ 94Pin-276
❏ 94PinArtP-276
❏ 94PinRinC-276
❏ 94PosCerBB-7
❏ 94Sco-161
❏ 94ScoGol-161
❏ 94ScoPla-161
❏ 94ScoPlaTS-161

❏ 94Sel-137
❏ 94SelGol-137
❏ 94SP-125
❏ 94SPDieCut-125
❏ 94TopPre-186
❏ 94TopPre-525
❏ 94TopPreSE-186
❏ 94TopPreSE-525
❏ 94Ult-382
❏ 94UppDec-286
❏ 94UppDecEleIce-286
❏ 94UppDecSPI-SP82
❏ 94UppDecSPIDC-SP82
❏ 95CanGamNHLP-240
❏ 95CanuBuiDA-14
❏ 95ColCho-31
❏ 95ColChoPC-31
❏ 95ColChoPCP-31
❏ 95Don-238
❏ 95Emo-146
❏ 95Fin-49
❏ 95FinRef-49
❏ 95Lea-233
❏ 95LeaLim-3
❏ 95ParInt-448
❏ 95ParIntEI-448
❏ 95PlaOneoOne-87
❏ 95PlaOneoOne-305
❏ 95ProMag-11
❏ 95ProMag-128
❏ 95Sco-255
❏ 95ScoBlaIce-255
❏ 95ScoBlaIceAP-255
❏ 95SkyImp-139
❏ 95SP-128
❏ 95Sum-119
❏ 95SumArtP-119
❏ 95SumIce-119
❏ 95Top-276
❏ 95TopOPCI-276
❏ 95Ult-167
❏ 95Ult-297
❏ 95UltGolM-167
❏ 95UppDec-120
❏ 95UppDecEleIce-120
❏ 95UppDecEleIceG-120
❏ 95Zen-58
❏ 96ColCho-229
❏ 96Don-54
❏ 96DonEli-43
❏ 96DonEliDCS-43
❏ 96DonPrePro-54
❏ 96Lea-158
❏ 96LeaPreP-158
❏ 96NHLProSTA-11
❏ 96Pin-146
❏ 96PinArtP-146
❏ 96PinFoi-146
❏ 96PinPreS-146
❏ 96PinRinC-146
❏ 96Sco-32
❏ 96ScoArtPro-32
❏ 96ScoDeaCAP-32
❏ 96ScoGolB-32
❏ 96ScoSpeAP-32
❏ 96SkyImp-111
❏ 96TopNHLP-149
❏ 96TopPicOI-149
❏ 96UppDec-327
❏ 97ColCho-227
❏ 97Don-47
❏ 97DonLim-24
❏ 97DonLimExp-24
❏ 97DonPreProG-47
❏ 97DonPreProS-47
❏ 97Pac-62
❏ 97PacCop-62
❏ 97PacEmeGre-62
❏ 97PacIceB-62
❏ 97PacInv-118
❏ 97PacInvC-118
❏ 97PacInvEG-118
❏ 97PacInvIB-118
❏ 97PacInvR-118
❏ 97PacInvS-118
❏ 97PacOme-190
❏ 97PacOmeC-190
❏ 97PacOmeDG-190
❏ 97PacOmeEG-190
❏ 97PacOmeG-190
❏ 97PacOmeIB-190
❏ 97PacPar-157
❏ 97PacParC-157
❏ 97PacParDG-157
❏ 97PacParEG-157
❏ 97PacParIB-157
❏ 97PacParRed-157
❏ 97PacParSil-157
❏ 97PacRed-62
❏ 97PacRevC-118
❏ 97PacRevE-118
❏ 97PacRevEIB-118
❏ 97PacRevIB-118
❏ 97PacRevR-118
❏ 97PacRevS-118
❏ 97PacSil-62
❏ 97PacSlaSDC-9A
❏ 97Sco-184
❏ 97ScoBlu-15
❏ 97ScoBluPla-15
❏ 97ScoBluPre-15
❏ 98Be A PPA-124
❏ 98Be A PPAA-124
❏ 98Be A PPAAF-124
❏ 98Be A PPTBASG-124

❏ 98Be APG-124
❏ 98O-PChr-139
❏ 98O-PChrR-139
❏ 98Pac-365
❏ 98PacAur-159
❏ 98PacDynI-156
❏ 98PacDynIIB-156
❏ 98PacDynIR-156
❏ 98PacIceB-365
❏ 98PacPar-201
❏ 98PacParC-201
❏ 98PacParEG-201
❏ 98PacParH-201
❏ 98PacParS-201
❏ 98PacRed-365
❏ 98Top-139
❏ 98TopO-P-139
❏ 98UC-190
❏ 98UD ChoPCR-190
❏ 98UD ChoR-190
❏ 98UDCP-190
❏ 98UppDec-357
❏ 98UppDecE-357
❏ 98UppDecE1o1-357
❏ 98UppDecGR-357
❏ 99Pac-354
❏ 99PacCop-354
❏ 99PacGol-354
❏ 99PacIceB-354
❏ 99PacPreD-354

**Courtnall, Russ**
❏ 82VicCou-5
❏ 83VicCou-5
❏ 84KelWin-37
❏ 84VicCou-7
❏ 85MapLeaP-6
❏ 85MapLeaP-7
❏ 85MapLeaP-8
❏ 85OPCSti-20
❏ 86KraDra-12
❏ 86MapLeaP-5
❏ 86OPC-174
❏ 86OPCSti-149
❏ 86Top-174
❏ 87MapLeaP-3
❏ 87MapLeaPLA-30
❏ 87MapLeaPO-3
❏ 87OPC-62
❏ 87OPCBoxB-P
❏ 87OPCSti-164
❏ 87PanSti-327
❏ 87Top-62
❏ 87TopBoxB-P
❏ 88CanaPos-8
❏ 88MapLeaPLA-30
❏ 88OPC-183
❏ 88OPCSti-175
❏ 88PanSti-122
❏ 88Top-183
❏ 89CanaKra-5
❏ 89CanaPos-8
❏ 89CanaProF-6
❏ 89Kra-22
❏ 89OPC-239
❏ 89OPCSti-53
❏ 90Bow-47
❏ 90BowTif-47
❏ 90CanaPos-10
❏ 90OPC-124
❏ 90PanSti-56
❏ 90ProSet-149
❏ 90Sco-148
❏ 90ScoCan-148
❏ 90Top-124
❏ 90TopTif-124
❏ 90UppDec-259
❏ 90UppDecF-259
❏ 91Bow-346
❏ 91Bow-414
❏ 91CanaPanTS-6
❏ 91CanaPos-8
❏ 91Kra-49
❏ 91OPC-119
❏ 91OPCPre-58
❏ 91OPCPre-194
❏ 91PanSti-186
❏ 91Par-308
❏ 91ParFre-308
❏ 91Pin-254
❏ 91PinFre-254
❏ 91ProSet-126
❏ 91ProSetFre-126
❏ 91ProSetPla-62
❏ 91ScoAme-42
❏ 91ScoAme-380
❏ 91ScoCan-42
❏ 91ScoCan-270
❏ 91StaClu-43
❏ 91Top-119
❏ 91TopTeaSL-18
❏ 91UppDec-87
❏ 91UppDec-168
❏ 91UppDecF-87
❏ 91UppDecF-168
❏ 92Bow-45
❏ 92HumDum2-3
❏ 92OPC-284
❏ 92OPCPre-204
❏ 92PanSti-154
❏ 92PanStiFre-154
❏ 92Par-78
❏ 92ParEmel-78
❏ 92Pin-337
❏ 92PinFre-337

❏ 92Sco-4
❏ 92ScoCan-4
❏ 92SeaPat-33
❏ 92StaClu-152
❏ 92Top-276
❏ 92TopGol-276G
❏ 92Ult-91
❏ 92Ult-316
❏ 92UppDec-94
❏ 92UppDec-441
❏ 93Don-80
❏ 93Kra-5
❏ 93Lea-65
❏ 93OPCPre-153
❏ 93OPCPreG-153
❏ 93PanSti-268
❏ 93Par-53
❏ 93ParEmel-53
❏ 93Pin-268
❏ 93PinCan-268
❏ 93Pow-58
❏ 93Sco-130
❏ 93ScoCan-130
❏ 93StaClu-55
❏ 93StaCluFDI-55
❏ 93StaCluFDIO-55
❏ 93StaCluO-55
❏ 93TopPre-153
❏ 93TopPreG-153
❏ 93Ult-50
❏ 93UltSpeM-2
❏ 93UppDec-32
❏ 93UppDecSP-36
❏ 94BeAPla99A-G5
❏ 94BeAPla-R27
❏ 94CanGamNHLP-77
❏ 94Don-167
❏ 94EASpo-35
❏ 94Fin-54
❏ 94FinnJaaK-98
❏ 94FinRef-54
❏ 94FinSupTW-54
❏ 94Fla-40
❏ 94Fle-48
❏ 94Lea-126
❏ 94LeaLim-35
❏ 94OPCPre-395
❏ 94OPCPreSE-395
❏ 94Par-52
❏ 94ParGol-52
❏ 94ParSEV-30
❏ 94Pin-133
❏ 94PinArtP-133
❏ 94PinRinC-133
❏ 94PosCerBB-8
❏ 94Sco-43
❏ 94ScoGol-43
❏ 94ScoPla-43
❏ 94ScoPlaTS-43
❏ 94Sel-70
❏ 94SelGol-70
❏ 94StaClu-170
❏ 94StaCluFDI-170
❏ 94StaCluMO-19
❏ 94StaCluMOMS-170
❏ 94StaCluSTWC-170
❏ 94StaHoc-7
❏ 94StaPinS-133
❏ 94StaPinS-NNO
❏ 94StaScoS-43
❏ 94TopPre-395
❏ 94TopPreSE-395
❏ 94Ult-279
❏ 94UltSpeM-2
❏ 94UppDec-31
❏ 94UppDecEleIce-31
❏ 94UppDecSPI-SP19
❏ 94UppDecSPIDC-SP19
❏ 95BeAPla-65
❏ 95BeAPSig-S65
❏ 95BeAPSigDC-S65
❏ 95CanGamNHLP-275
❏ 95ColCho-267
❏ 95ColChoPC-267
❏ 95ColChoPCP-267
❏ 95Don-199
❏ 95Emo-179
❏ 95FinnSemWC-95
❏ 95Lea-51
❏ 95Met-150
❏ 95ParInt-210
❏ 95ParIntEI-210
❏ 95Sco-242
❏ 95ScoBlaIce-242
❏ 95ScoBlaIceAP-242
❏ 95SkyImp-166
❏ 95StaClu-9
❏ 95StaCluMOMS-9
❏ 95Sum-128
❏ 95SumArtP-128
❏ 95SumIce-128
❏ 95Top-194
❏ 95TopOPCI-194
❏ 95TopSupSki-11
❏ 95TopSupSkiPla-11
❏ 95Ult-168
❏ 95UltGolM-168
❏ 95UppDec-317
❏ 95UppDecEleIce-317
❏ 95UppDecEleIceG-317
❏ 95Zen-115
❏ 96CanuPos-9
❏ 96ColCho-276
❏ 96Don-194
❏ 96DonPrePro-194

96Lea-29
96LeaPreP-29
96MetUni-156
96Pin-75
96PinArtP-75
96PinFoi-75
96PinPreS-75
96PinRinC-75
96Sco-109
96ScoArtPro-109
96ScoDeaCAP-109
96ScoGolB-109
96ScoSpeAP-109
96SkyImp-132
96SP-161
96Sum-22
96SumArtP-22
96SumIce-22
96SumMet-22
96SumPreS-22
96TopNHLP-107
96TopPicOI-107
96UppDec-350
97ColCho-166
97Pac-275
97PacCop-275
97PacEmeGre-275
97PacIceB-275
97PacRed-275
97PacRev-64
97PacRevC-64
97PacRevE-64
97PacRevIB-64
97PacRevR-64
97PacRevS-64
97PacSil-275
98O-PChr-188
98O-PChrR-188
98Pac-233
98PacIceB-233
98PacPar-103
98PacParC-103
98PacParEG-103
98PacParH-103
98PacParIB-103
98PacParS-103
98PacRed-233
98Top-188
98TopO-P-188
99Pac-188
99PacCop-188
99PacGol-188
99PacIceB-188
99PacPreD-188
**Courtney, Ken**
52JunBluT-93
**Courville, Larry**
917thInnSOHL-15
91CorRoy-19
94Fin-156
94FinRef-156
94FinSupTW-156
94Pin-540
94PinArtP-540
94PinRinC-540
94SP-150
94SPDieCut-150
95Cla-50
95ColEdgI-88
95DonCanWJT-11
95TopCanWJ-3CJ
96Pin-235
96PinArtP-235
96PinFoi-235
96PinPreS-235
96PinRinC-235
96SyrCru-35
97Sco-57
97ScoArtPro-57
97ScoCanPla-13
97ScoCanPre-13
97ScoCanu-13
97ScoGolB-57
**Cousineau, Bryan**
91MapLeaP-7
**Cousineau, Marcel**
907thInnSQMJHL-133
91Cla-50
91StaPicH-47
91UltDra-45
93St.JohML-6
94ClaProP-111
94St.JohML-6
95St.JohML-5
96BeAPAut-213
96BeAPAutSil-213
96BeAPla-213
96UppDecBD-63
96UppDecBDG-63
97Don-198
97DonCanI-147
97DonCanIDS-147
97DonCanILG-10
97DonCanILGP-10
97DonCanIPS-147
97DonLim-86
97DonLim-116
97DonLim-160
97DonLimExp-86
97DonLimExp-116
97DonLimExp-160
97DonLimFOTG-39
97DonMed-7
97DonPre-158
97DonPreCttC-158

97DonPreProG-198
97DonPreProS-198
97DonRatR-7
97Lea-114
97LeaFraMat-114
97LeaFraMDC-114
97LeaInt-114
97LeaIntUI-114
97PacOme-219
97PacOmeC-219
97PacOmeDG-219
97PacOmeEG-219
97PacOmeG-219
97PacOmeIB-219
97PinIns-69
97PinInsCE-69
97PinInsEC-69
97PinInsSto-22
97PinInsSUG-4A/B
97PinInsSUG-4C/D
97Sco-23
97ScoArtPro-23
97ScoGolBla-23
97ScoMapL-3
97ScoMapLPla-3
97ScoMapLPre-3
97St.JohML-8
**Coutineir, Francis**
907thInnSQMJHL-95
**Coutu, Billy**
23V1451-17
24C144ChaCig-19
24V1452-44
**Couture, Doc (Gerry)**
44BeeGro2P-90
44BeeGro2P-158
44BeeGro2P-229
45QuaOatP-70
51BufBis-4
51Par-7
52Par-41
53Par-84
**Couture, Guillame**
97RimOce-4
**Couture, Lolo (Rosario)**
34DiaMatS-18
35DiaMatT2-16
35DiaMatT3-15
35DiaMatTI-18
**Couturier, Sylvain**
84RicRiv-4
88ProAHL-211
89ProAHL-7
90ProAHLIHL-360
91UppDec-491
91UppDecF-491
92PhoRoa-5
94MilAdm-5
95MilAdmBO-5
96MilAdmBO-5
98GerDELE-127
**Couvrette, Michel**
94CenHocL-96
**Coveny, Chris**
917thInnSOHL-302
92Ott672A-7
**Coveny, Michael**
95SlaMemC-51
**Cowan, Dave**
85MinDul-7
**Cowan, Jeff**
93GueSto-20
94GueSto-23
95Cla-82
95Sla-23
96RoaExp-17
**Cowan, Sean**
92Rallce-2
92Rallce-33
**Cowick, Bruce**
74CapWhiB-8
740PCNHL-386
**Cowie, Rob**
91MonHaw-3
91ProAHLCHL-174
95ColEdgI-183
95Ima-57
95ImaGol-56
95PhoRoa-9
98GerDELE-155
**Cowley, Bill**
34BeeGro1P-11
35DiaMatTI-19
390PCV3011-98
83HalFP-M5
85HalFC-170
91BruSpoAL-9
91BruSpoAL-12
**Cowley, Wayne**
88SalLakCGE-5
89ProIHL-206
96GerDELE-204
**Cowmedow, Lee**
97FitFly-7
**Cox, Allan**
907thInnSOHL-306
917thInnSOHL-56
**Cox, Danny**
23V1281PauC-18
330PCV304A-1
33V129-48
33V252CanG-16
33V357IceK-69
**Cox, Peter**
907thInnSWHL-158

917thInnSWHL-45
**Cox, Tim**
907thInnSWHL-91
90SasBla-20
**Coxe, Craig**
83BelBul-22
84FreExp-27
85Canu-6
86Canu-5
87BluTeaIss-6
87CanuSheOil-8
88BluKol-15
88BluTeaIss-5
89CanuMoh-6
90CanuMoh-6
900PC-339
90ProSet-544
90TopTif-339
91CanuPanTS-7
910PC-447
91ProAHLCHL-520
91ProSet-329
91ProSetFre-329
91Top-447
91UppDec-60
91UppDecF-60
**Coyne, Colleen**
94ClaWomOH-W26
**Craas, Morgan**
84SweSemE-134
**Crabo, Sven**
70SweHocS-186
71SweHocS-272
**Craievich, David (Dave)**
897thInnSOHL-13
89OshGen-13
89OshGenP-2
907thInnSMC-84
907thInnNHL-332
91CinCyc-5
91ProAHLCHL-422
92BirBul-8
93BirBul-8
94BirBul-5
**Craig, Bob**
71RocAme-4
**Craig, Glen**
89WinSpi-2
907thInnSOHL-102
917thInnSOHL-30
**Craig, Jim**
79FlamPos-5
79FlaTeaI-6
800PC-22
80Top-22
80USAOlyTMP-1
95SigRooMI-9
95SigRooMI-10
95SigRooSMIS-9
95SigRooSMIS-10
**Craig, Mike**
897thInnSOHL-9
89OshGen-9
89OshGenP-23
907thInnSMC-90
900PCPreV-19
90ProSet-613
90ScoRoo-59T
90UppDec-472
90UppDecF-472
91Bow-130
910PC-187
91Par-301
91Pin-219
91PinFre-219
91ProSet-405
91ProSetFre-405
91ProSetPla-189
91ScoAme-181
91ScoCan-181
91StaClu-344
91Top-187
91UppDec-125
91UppDecF-125
92Bow-334
920PC-103
92PanSti-95
92PanStiFre-95
92Par-314
92ParEmel-314
92Pin-99
92PinFre-99
92Sco-271
92ScoCan-271
92StaClu-268
92Top-238
92TopGol-238G
92Ult-317
92UppDec-65
93Don-81
93Lea-88
930PCPre-309
930PCPreG-309
93PanSti-271
93Par-323
93ParEmel-323
93Pin-314
93PinCan-314
93Pow-322
93Sco-156
93ScoCan-156

93StaClu-355
93StaCluFDI-355
93StaCluO-355
93TopPre-309
93TopPreG-309
93Ult-297
93UppDec-191
94CanGamNHLP-231
94Lea-510
94MapLeaK-8
94MapLeaPP-21
940PCPre-538
940PCPreSE-538
94Par-54
94Pin-399
94PinArtP-399
94PinRinC-399
94StaHoc-3
94TopPre-538
94TopPreSE-538
94UppDec-213
94UppDecEleIce-213
95BeAPla-17
95BeAPSig-S17
95BeAPSigDC-S17
97Pac-309
97PacCop-309
97PacEmeGre-309
97PacIceB-309
97PacRed-309
97PacSil-309
97ScoMapL-11
97ScoMapLPla-11
97ScoMapLPre-11
**Craigdallie, Marty**
91AirCanSJHL-E31
92BriColJHL-66
**Craighead, John**
91BriColJHL-165
91BriColJHL-NNO
93RicRen-5
96St.JohML-12
**Craigwell, Dale**
897thInnSOHL-4
89OshGen-4
890shGenP-11
907thInnSMC-85
907thInnSOHL-85
90UppDec-464
90UppDecF-464
917thInnSCHLAW-2
91Par-389
91ParFre-389
91ProAHLCHL-516
92Bow-198
920PC-271
92PanSti-133
92PanStiFre-133
92Par-168
92ParEmel-168
92Sco-466
92ScoCan-466
92StaClu-464
92Top-60
92TopGol-60G
92Ult-192
92UppDec-40
930PCPre-348
930PCPreG-348
93TopPre-348
93TopPreG-348
93UppDec-56
94UppDec-380
94UppDecEleIce-380
95ColEdgI-189
98GerDELE-285
**Crandall, Chip**
830shGen-29
**Crane, Brian**
93MicSta-6
**Crane, Corey**
92SudWol-13
**Crane, Derrick**
907thInnSOHL-130
917thInnSOHL-375
**Crane, Todd**
95Sla-163
**Cranston, Sid**
82BraWheK-7
**Cranston, Tim**
93SheSte-3
94FinnJaaK-320
94SheSte-11
97SheSte-16
97SheSte-2
**Crashley, Bart**
67Top-105
720PC-295
72ShaLosAW-2
**Craven, Murray**
82MedHatT-2
83MedHatT-1
830PC-120
84KelWin-44
85FlyPos-5
850PC-53
850PCSti-95
85Top-53
86FlyPos-4
860PC-167
860PCSti-244
86Top-167
870PC-22
870PCSti-69

87PanSti-133
87Top-22
880PCBoxB-J
880PCBoxB-J
880PCSti-98
88PanSti-320
88Top-79
88TopBoxB-J
89FlyPos-7
890PC-44
89Top-44
900PC-318
90PanSti-116
90ProSet-214
90Sco-56
90ScoCan-56
90Top-318
90TopTif-318
90UppDec-6
90UppDecF-6
910PC-254
91PanSti-234
91Par-288
91ParFre-288
91Pin-177
91PinFre-177
91ProSet-175
91ProSet-393
91ProSetFre-175
91ProSetFre-393
91ScoAme-262
91ScoCan-482
91StaClu-176
91Top-254
91UppDec-306
91UppDecF-306
91WhaJr7E-7
92Bow-280
920PC-127
920PCPreSP-3
92PanSti-262
92PanStiFre-262
92Par-55
92Par-495
92ParEmel-55
92ParEmel-495
92Pin-281
92PinFre-281
92ProSet-60
92Sco-18
92ScoCan-18
92StaClu-442
92Top-248
92TopGol-248G
92Ult-71
92UppDec-49
92WhaDai-5
93Don-353
93Lea-5
930PCPre-400
930PCPreG-400
93PanSti-169
93Par-208
93ParEmel-208
93Pin-88
93PinCan-88
93Pow-448
93Sco-49
93ScoCan-49
93StaClu-264
93StaCluFDI-264
93StaCluO-264
93TopPre-400
93TopPreG-400
93Ult-439
93UppDec-410
94Don-131
94Lea-121
940PCPre-47
940PCPreSE-47
94Par-242
94ParGol-242
94Pin-291
94PinArtP-291
94PinRinC-291
94Sco-109
94ScoGol-109
94ScoPla-109
94ScoPlaTS-109
94StaClu-255
94StaCluFDI-255
94StaCluMOMS-255
94StaCluSTWC-255
94TopPre-47
94TopPreSE-47
94Ult-223
94UppDec-45
94UppDecEleIce-45
95BeAPla-46
95BeAPSig-S46
95BeAPSigDC-S46
95ColCho-120
95ColChoPC-120
95ColChoPCP-120
95Don-46
95Lea-6
95ParInt-313
95ParIntEI-313
95Pin-179
95PinArtP-179

95PinRinC-179
95Sco-214
95ScoBlaIce-214
95ScoBlaIceAP-214
95Top-52
95TopOPCI-52
95UppDec-151
95UppDecEleIce-151
95UppDecEleIceG-151
96Pin-162
96PinArtP-162
96PinFoi-162
96PinPreS-162
96PinRinC-162
96TeaOut-13
97Pac-238
97PacCop-238
97PacEmeGre-238
97PacIceB-238
97PacRed-238
97PacSil-238
98Be A PPA-118
98Be A PPAA-118
98Be A PPAAF-118
98Be A PPTBASG-118
98Be APG-118
98Pac-378
98PacIceB-378
98PacRed-378
**Crawford, Austin**
93WatBlaH-7
**Crawford, Bob**
83WhaJunHC-1
840PC-68
840PCSti-197
84Top-53
84WhaJunW-3
850PC-162
850PCSti-167
85Top-162
85WhaJunW-3
86CapKod-5
**Crawford, Derek**
92DalFre-6
92DayBom-5
93DalFre-5
94CenHocL-6
**Crawford, Floyd**
51LavDiaQSHL-25
**Crawford, Glenn**
94WinSpi-8
95Cla-98
95Sla-411
95Sla-438
95UppDec-520
95UppDecEleIce-520
95UppDecEleIceG-520
**Crawford, Jack**
400PCV3012-134
**Crawford, Jeff**
81RegPat-9
82RegPat-22
83RegPat-22
94HunBli-28
**Crawford, John**
34BeeGro1P-12
44BeeGro2P-14
**Crawford, Lou**
85NovScoO-10
88ProAHL-10
89ProAHL-56
90ProAHLIHL-138
91ProAHLCHL-62
**Crawford, Marc**
81CanuSilD-3
81FreExp-17
82FreExp-17
820PC-342
82PosCer-19
83Canu-4
84FreExp-23
85FreExp-4
85FreExp-5
907thInnSOHL-50
91ProAHLCHL-357
92St.JohML-4
93St.JohML-7
96KraUppD-41
97AvaPin-1
**Crawford, Red (Kenneth)**
52JunBluT-181
**Crawford, Rusty**
23V1281PauC-70
83HalFP-E6
85HalFC-67
**Crawford, Wayne**
96GuiFla-3
**Creagh, Brendan**
93GreMon-5
94GreMon-19
95BirBul-12
**Creamer, Bob**
92NasKni-7
**Creamer, Pierre**
907thInnSMC-50
**Creightney, Nigel**
92BriColJHL-239
**Creighton, Adam**
81Ott67-2
82Ott67-3
83Ott67-6
84SabBluS-3
85SabBluS-4

86SabBluS-6
86SabBluSSma-6
87PanSti-31
87SabBluS-6
88PanSti-225
88SabWonBH-6
890PC-218
89PanSti-51
90BlaCok-14
90Bow-9
90BowTif-9
900PC-83
90PanSti-193
90ProSet-50
90Sco-82
90ScoCan-82
90Top-83
90TopTif-83
90UppDec-4
90UppDecF-4
91Bow-394
91Kra-47
910PC-314
910PCPre-171
91PanSti-13
91Par-113
91ParFre-113
91Pin-82
91PinFre-82
91ProSet-42
91ProSet-437
91ProSetFre-42
91ProSetFre-437
91ProSetPC-17
91ScoAme-265
91ScoCan-485
91ScoRoo-21T
91StaClu-89
91Top-314
91UppDec-254
91UppDecF-254
92Bow-88
92LigShe-11
920PC-85
920PCPre-61
92PanSti-204
92PanStiFre-204
92Par-172
92ParEmel-172
92Pin-199
92PinFre-199
92ProSet-103
92Sco-144
92ScoCan-144
92StaClu-45
92Top-451
92TopGol-451G
92Ult-409
92UppDec-311
93Don-326
93Lea-85
93LigKasK-4
93LigSealR-9
93PanSti-215
93Pin-272
93PinCan-272
93Sco-86
93ScoCan-86
93StaClu-5
93StaCluFDI-5
93StaCluFDIO-5
93StaCluO-5
94Fle-185
94Par-222
94ParGol-222
94StaClu-23
94StaCluFDI-23
94StaCluMOMS-23
94StaCluSTWC-23
94UppDec-348
94UppDecEeIce-348
95BeAPla-142
95BeAPSig-S142
95BeAPSigDC-S142
95CanGamNHLP-234
95ColCho-229
95ColChoPC-229
95ColChoPCP-229
95Don-336
95ParInt-444
95ParIntEI-444
95Sco-283
95ScoBlaIce-283
95ScoBlaIceAP-283
95UppDec-375
95UppDecEleIce-375
95UppDecEleIceG-375
96Pin-80
96PinArtP-80
96PinFoi-80
96PinPreS-80
96PinRinC-80
**Creighton, Dave**
44BeeGro2P-15A
44BeeGro2P-15B
44BeeGro2P-392
52Par-76
53Par-85
54Par-58
57Top-66
60Par-10
94ParMisL-99
**Cressman, Glen**

- 52JunBluT-127

**Cressman, Matt**
- 93WesMic-9

**Crettenain, Yves**
- 93SweSemWCS-260

**Crha, Jiri**
- 74SweHocS-10
- 79MapLeaP-8
- 79PanSti-75
- 80PepCap-83
- 81OPC-315
- 81OPCSti-106

**Crichton, Cory**
- 88KamBla-8

**Crimin, Derek**
- 91AirCanSJHL-B45
- 91AirCanSJHLAS-27
- 91AirCanSJHLAS-41
- 92MPSPhoSJHL-65

**Crisp, Terry**
- 68ShiCoi-156
- 70EssPowPla-245
- 70SarProSta-182
- 71BluPos-5
- 71OPC-127
- 71SarProSta-179
- 71TorSun-238
- 72OPC-88
- 72SarProSta-128
- 72Top-103
- 73FlyLin-6
- 74NHLActSta-203
- 74OPCNHL-352
- 75FlyCanDC-5
- 75OPCNHL-337
- 80SauSteMG-24
- 81SauSteMG-8
- 82SauSteMG-8
- 84SauSteMG-5
- 85MonGolF-1
- 85MonGolF-3
- 86MonGolF-1
- 87FlamRedRP-5
- 91AlbIntTC-4
- 92LigShe-12
- 93LigSealR-10
- 94LigPhoA-9
- 94LigPos-4

**Crisp, Tony**
- 87KitRan-13

**Cristofoli, Ed**
- 89ProAHL-194
- 90ProAHLIHL-72

**Croce, Pat**
- 85FlyPos-6
- 86FlyPos-5

**Crocker, Corey**
- 95Sla-312

**Crockett, Ken**
- 91BriColJHL-31

**Crocock, Rob**
- 83BelBul-21

**Croghan, Morris**
- 36V356WorG-103

**Crombeen, Mike**
- 78BluPos-7
- 82PosCer-17
- 83OPC-312
- 83OPCSti-126
- 83WhaJunHC-2
- 84WhaJunW-4

**Crombie, Chris**
- 897thInnSOHL-30
- 907thInnSOHL-131
- 917thInnSOHL-374

**Cronin, Shawn**
- 88ProAHL-45
- 89JetSaf-7
- 90Bow-128
- 90BowTif-128
- 90JetIGA-7
- 90ProSet-559
- 91JetIGA-6
- 91JetPanTS-6
- 91Par-423
- 91ParFre-423
- 91ProSet-268
- 91ProSetFre-268
- 91ScoCan-423
- 91UppDec-478
- 91UppDecF-478
- 92FlyJCP-8
- 92FlyUppDS-16
- 92OPCPre-42
- 92Sco-366
- 92ScoCan-366
- 92StaClu-471
- 92Top-489
- 92TopGol-489G

**Crook, Ken**
- 88BroBra-19

**Croon, Ulf**
- 69SweHocS-129
- 70SweHocS-89

**Cross, Cory**
- 94LigPhoA-10
- 94LigPos-5
- 94UppDec-340
- 94UppDecElelce-340
- 95Ima-88
- 95ImaGol-88
- 95Lea-275
- 95LigTeal-7
- 95Top-44
- 95TopOPCI-44
- 96BeAPAut-143
- 96BeAPAutSil-143
- 96BeAPla-143
- 97PacInvNRB-184
- 97UppDec-365
- 98Be A PPA-128
- 98Be A PPAA-128
- 98Be A PPAAF-128
- 98Be A PPTBASG-128
- 98Be APG-128
- 99Pac-386
- 99PacCop-386
- 99PacGol-386
- 99PacIceB-386
- 99PacPreD-386

**Cross, Nick**
- 96GuiFla-11

**Crossman, Doug**
- 81BlaBorPos-4
- 82OPC-63
- 82PosCer-4
- 83FlyJCP-7
- 83OPC-263
- 84OPC-157
- 85FlyPos-7
- 86FlyPos-6
- 86OPCSti-237
- 87OPC-182
- 87PanSti-125
- 87Top-182
- 88KinSmo-4
- 88OPCSti-100
- 88Top-197
- 89Isl-4
- 90Bow-115
- 90BowTif-115
- 90Kra-10
- 90OPC-72
- 90PanSti-91
- 90ProSet-179
- 90Sco-59
- 90ScoCan-59
- 90ScoRoo-52T
- 90Top-72
- 90TopTif-72
- 90UppDec-7
- 90UppDec-419
- 90UppDecF-7
- 90UppDecF-419
- 90WhaJr7E-6
- 91OPC-341
- 91ScoAme-38
- 91ScoCan-38
- 91Top-341
- 92OPCPre-59
- 92Par-388
- 92ParEmel-388
- 92ProSet-180
- 92Ult-410
- 93OPCPre-159
- 93OPCPreG-159
- 93PeoRiv-4
- 93Sco-25
- 93ScoCan-25
- 93TopPre-159
- 93TopPreG-159

**Croteau, Gary**
- 70EssPowPla-104
- 70OPC-189
- 70SarProSta-141
- 71LetActR-12
- 71OPC-17
- 71SarProSta-133
- 71Top-17
- 71TorSun-45
- 72OPC-3
- 72SarProSta-48
- 72SweSemWC-180
- 72Top-83
- 73OPC-228
- 74NHLActSta-295
- 74OPCNHL-36
- 74Top-36
- 76OPCNHL-283
- 76RocCokCan-4
- 76RocPucBuc-5
- 77OPCNHL-52
- 77RocCokCan-3
- 77Top-52
- 78OPC-362
- 79OPC-158
- 79Roc-5
- 79Top-158

**Croteau, Paul**
- 95RoaExp-6

**Crowder, Bruce**
- 82OPC-9
- 82PosCer-1
- 83BruTealss-2
- 83OPC-46

**Crowder, Keith**
- 82OPC-10
- 82OPCSti-80
- 83BruTealss-3
- 83OPC-47
- 83OPCSti-56
- 84OPC-2
- 84Top-2
- 85OPC-159
- 85OPCSti-163
- 85Top-159
- 86OPC-130
- 86OPCSti-37

**Crowder, Keith** (continued)
- 86Top-130
- 87OPC-194
- 87OPCSti-136
- 87PanSti-14
- 87Top-194
- 88BruSpoA-4
- 88OPC-206
- 88PanSti-209
- 89KinSmo-10
- 89OPC-199
- 90OPC-476

**Crowder, Troy**
- 90Dev-8
- 90ProSet-620
- 90ScoRoo-43T
- 90UppDec-441
- 90UppDecF-441
- 91OPC-374
- 91OPCPre-169
- 91ScoCan-602
- 91ScoRoo-52T
- 91Top-374
- 91UppDec-342
- 91UppDecF-342
- 95UppDecElelce-437
- 95UppDecElelceG-437
- 96CanuPos-18

**Crowdis, Lou**
- 51BufBis-5

**Crowe, Phil**
- 92ProRoa-6
- 93Don-446
- 96DetVip-4
- 97PacDynBKS-65

**Crowe, Rick**
- 91BriColJHL-3

**Crowley, Joe**
- 917thInnSQMJHL-203
- 92IndIce-8

**Crowley, Mike**
- 94MinGolG-9
- 96MinGolGCAS-8
- 98Pac-47
- 98PacIceB-47
- 98PacRed-47
- 98UppDec-8
- 98UppDecE-8
- 98UppDecE1o1-8
- 98UppDecGR-8
- 98UppDecM-5
- 98UppDecMGS-5
- 98UppDecMSS-5
- 98UppDecMSS-5

**Crowley, Nick**
- 95MinGolG-10

**Crowley, Ted**
- 92St.JohML-5
- 93ClaProPro-112
- 93Pow-500
- 93StaCluTUSA-3
- 93TopPreTUSA-12
- 93Ult-480
- 94Par-93
- 94ParGol-93
- 94Sco-233
- 94ScoGol-233
- 94ScoPla-233
- 94ScoPlaTS-233
- 94UppDec-442
- 94UppDecElelce-442
- 96CinCyc-4

**Crowley, Wayne**
- 90ProAHLIHL-609

**Crowther, Cory**
- 92BriColJHL-103

**Crozier, Joe**
- 51LavDaiQSHL-3
- 52St.LawS-43
- 56QueAce-4
- 63RochAme-10
- 80MapLeaP-8
- 82KitRan-4

**Crozier, Roger**
- 64BeeGro3P-66
- 64CocCap-37
- 64Top-47
- 65Coc-37
- 65Top-42
- 66Top-43
- 66TopUSAT-43
- 67Top-48
- 68OPC-23
- 68OPCPucSti-10
- 68ShiCoi-35
- 68Top-23
- 69OPC-55
- 69OPCFou-15
- 69Top-55
- 70ColSta-83
- 70DadCoo-18
- 70EssPowPla-73
- 70OPC-145
- 70Top-145
- 71Baz-32
- 71LetActR-3
- 71OPC-36
- 71OPCTBoo-5
- 71SabPos-4
- 71SarProSta-27
- 71Top-36
- 71TorSun-24
- 72OPC-50
- 72SabPepPB-1
- 72SarProSta-32
- 72SweSemWC-165
- 72Top-31
- 73OPC-153
- 73SabBel-1
- 73SabPos-1
- 73Top-108
- 74NHLActSta-45
- 75OPCNHL-350
- 93SabNoc-1
- 94ParTalB-53
- 94ParTalB-157
- 94ParTalB-158
- 94ParTalBM-AS1
- 94ParTalBM-TW5
- 95Par66-56
- 95Par66Coi-56

**Cruickshank, Curtis**
- 97BowCHL-139
- 97BowCHLAu-19
- 97BowCHLBB-19
- 97BowCHLBowBesAR-19
- 97BowCHLBowBesR-19
- 97BowCHLOPC-139

**Cruickshank, Gord**
- 89ProAHL-62

**Crumley, Chad**
- 92MPSPhoSJHL-66

**Crummer, Bob**
- 97GueSto-17

**Crump, Lionel**
- 95NorlowH-3

**Crutchfield, Nels**
- 34SweCap-2

**Crystal, Bob**
- 44BeeGro2P-302

**Cucksey, Don**
- 91RayJrC-2

**Cucuz, Sasha**
- 94SarSti-26

**Cude, Wilf (Wilfred)**
- 34BeeGro1P-144
- 34SweCap-3
- 35DiaMatT2-17
- 35DiaMatT3-16
- 35DiaMatTI-20
- 35OPCV304C-73
- 36OPCV304D-120
- 36V356WorG-9
- 37OPCV304E-149
- 38QuaOatP-8

**Culhane, Jim**
- 88ProAHL-70
- 89ProAHL-298
- 90ProAHLIHL-504
- 91ProAHLCHL-454

**Culic, Chet**
- 93MinDul-6

**Cull, Dean**
- 907thInnSOHL-389
- 91RayJrC-9

**Cull, Trent**
- 907thInnSOHL-281
- 917thInnSOHL-177
- 93KinFro-19
- 94St.JohML-7
- 95St.JohML-6
- 96St.JohML-13

**Cullen, Barry**
- 44BeeGro2P-393
- 57Par-T21
- 58Par-31
- 59Top-25
- 60Par-32
- 60ShiCoi-47
- 94ParMisL-120

**Cullen, Brian**
- 44BeeGro2P-304
- 44BeeGro2P-394
- 52JunBluT-25
- 55Par-13
- 55ParQuaO-13
- 57Par-M22
- 57Par-T9
- 58Par-36
- 58Par-50
- 59Top-55
- 60ShiCoi-99
- 94ParMisL-118

**Cullen, John**
- 87FllSpi-2
- 89OPC-145
- 89OPCSti-64
- 89OPCSti-231
- 89PanSti-316
- 89PenFoo-9
- 89Top-145
- 90Bow-210
- 90BowTif-210
- 90OPC-208
- 90OPCPre-20
- 90PanSti-125
- 90PenFoo-10
- 90ProSet-232
- 90Sco-281
- 90Top-208
- 90TopTif-208
- 90UppDec-12
- 90UppDecF-12
- 91Bow-1
- 91Kra-24
- 91OPC-226
- 91OPCPre-127
- 91PanSti-314
- 91Par-59
- 91ParFre-59
- 91Pin-125
- 91Pin-391
- 91PinFre-125
- 91PinFre-391
- 91ProSet-85
- 91ProSet-302
- 91ProSetCC-CC9
- 91ProSetCCF-CC9
- 91ProSetFre-85
- 91ProSetFre-302
- 91ProSetPla-175
- 91ScoAme-7
- 91ScoAme-421
- 91ScoCan-7
- 91ScoCan-311
- 91ScoYouS-5
- 91SweSemWCS-72
- 91Top-226
- 91UppDec-84
- 91UppDec-235
- 91UppDecF-84
- 91UppDecF-235
- 91WhaJr7E-8
- 92Bow-194
- 92Bow-227
- 92MapLeaK-9
- 92McDUppD-18
- 92OPC-104
- 92PanSti-257
- 92PanStiFre-257
- 92Par-180
- 92ParEmel-180
- 92Pin-285
- 92PinFre-285
- 92ProSet-57
- 92Sco-150
- 92Sco-425
- 92ScoCan-150
- 92ScoCan-425
- 92SeaPat-45
- 92Top-132
- 92TopGol-132G
- 92Ult-72
- 92Ult-419
- 92UppDec-304
- 92UppDec-465
- 93Don-334
- 93Lea-245
- 93OPCPre-479
- 93OPCPreG-479
- 93PanSti-226
- 93Par-473
- 93ParEmel-473
- 93Pin-388
- 93PinCan-388
- 93Sco-189
- 93ScoBla-16
- 93ScoCan-189
- 93StaCluFDI-209
- 93StaCluFDIO-209
- 93StaCluO-209
- 93TopPre-479
- 93TopPreG-479
- 93Ult-20
- 93UppDec-395
- 94BeAPSig-105
- 94Lea-412
- 94LigPos-6
- 94OPCPre-423
- 94OPCPreSE-423
- 94ParSE-SE140
- 94ParSEG-SE140
- 94PenFoo-7
- 94Pin-397
- 94PinArtP-397
- 94PinRinC-397
- 94SP-91
- 94SPDieCut-91
- 94TopPre-423
- 94TopPreSE-423
- 94Ult-348
- 94UppDec-281
- 94UppDecElelce-281
- 95ColGamNHLP-248
- 95ColCho-181
- 95ColChoPC-181
- 95ColChoPCP-181
- 95Don-156
- 95Lea-181
- 95LigTeal-8
- 95ParInt-463
- 95ParIntEl-463
- 95Sco-105
- 95ScoBlaIce-105
- 95ScoBlaIceAP-105
- 95Top-74
- 95TopOPCI-74
- 95UppDec-358
- 95UppDecElelce-358
- 95UppDecElelceG-358
- 96Fla-87
- 96FlaBlul-87
- 97Pac-282
- 97PacCop-282
- 97PacDyn-116
- 97PacDynC-116
- 97PacDynEG-116
- 97PacDynIB-116
- 97PacDynR-116
- 97PacDynSil-116
- 97PacDynTan-53
- 97PacEmeGre-282
- 97PacIceB-282
- 97PacInv-130
- 97PacInvC-130
- 97PacInvEG-130
- 97PacInvIB-130
- 97PacInvS-130
- 97PacRed-282
- 97PacSil-282
- 97Sco-155
- 97ScoArtPro-155
- 97ScoGolBla-155
- 98PacDynI-172
- 98PacDynIIB-172
- 98PacDynIR-172
- 98UppDec-365
- 98UppDecE-365
- 98UppDecE1o1-365
- 98UppDecGR-365

**Cullen, Justin**
- 907thInnSOHL-229
- 90KitRan-25
- 917thInnSOHL-95

**Cullen, Matt**
- 95DonEliWJ-33
- 97PacOme-1
- 97PacOmeC-1
- 97PacOmeDG-1
- 97PacOmeEG-1
- 97PacOmeG-1
- 97PacOmeIB-1
- 97ScoMigDPla-5
- 97ScoMigDPre-5
- 97ScoMigDuc-5
- 98Fin-53
- 98FinNo P-53
- 98FinNo PR-53
- 98FinRef-53
- 98Pac-45
- 98PacIceB-45
- 98PacRed-45
- 98UC-7
- 98UD ChoPCR-7
- 98UD ChoR-7
- 98UD3-16
- 98UD3-76
- 98UD3-136
- 98UD3DieC-16
- 98UD3DieC-76
- 98UD3DieC-136
- 98UppDec-32
- 98UppDecE-32
- 98UppDecE1o1-32
- 98UppDecGR-32

**Cullen, Peter**
- 95NorlowH-4

**Cullen, Ray**
- 68OPC-54
- 68ShiCoi-71
- 68Top-54
- 69OPC-130
- 69OPCFou-15
- 69OPCSta-5
- 69Top-130
- 70CanuRoyB-3
- 70ColSta-15
- 70DadCoo-19
- 70EssPowPla-45
- 70OPC-228
- 70OPCDec-31
- 70SarProSta-9

**Cullic, Chet**
- 96LouRiv-17

**Cullimore, Jassen**
- 897thInnSOHL-116
- 907thInnSOHL-356
- 917thInnSOHL-146
- 91AreDraPic-22
- 91Cla-26
- 91PetPet-21
- 91StaPicH-71
- 91UltDra-23
- 91UppDec-72
- 91UppDec-690
- 91UppDecCWJC-64
- 91UppDecF-72
- 91UppDecF-690
- 92HamCan-4
- 94BeAPSig-80
- 94Lea-488
- 94OPCPre-477
- 94OPCPreSE-477
- 94ParSE-SE191
- 94ParSEG-SE191
- 94TopPre-477
- 94TopPreSE-477
- 94UppDec-247
- 94UppDecElelce-247
- 95ColEdgI-89
- 95Don-175
- 95Ima-53
- 95ImaGol-53
- 95Lea-25
- 95Top-101
- 95TopOPCI-101
- 96CanaPos-10
- 96CanaShe-6
- 97CanaPos-8
- 97PacInvNRB-101

**Cumming, Scott**
- 85LonKni-29

**Cummings, Burton**
- 91JetIGA-7
- 91ProSetPla-290

**Cummings, Don**
- 28V1282PauC-52

**Cummins, Jim**
- 92Cla-94
- 93LigSealR-11
- 93StaClu-448
- 93StaCluFDI-448
- 93StaCluO-448
- 94Lea-434
- 96ClaGol-94
- 97Be A PPAD-80
- 97Be A PPAPD-80
- 97BeAPla-80
- 97BeAPlaAut-80
- 97PacInvNRB-44
- 98Pac-335
- 98PacIceB-335
- 98PacRed-335
- 99Pac-318
- 99PacCop-318
- 99PacIceB-318
- 99PacPreD-318

**Cunderlik, Roman**
- 95SloAPSNT-7

**Cunneyworth, Randy**
- 86PenKod-6
- 87OPC-150
- 87PanSti-148
- 87PenKod-6
- 87PenMask-2
- 87Top-150
- 88OPC-19
- 88OPCSti-231
- 88PanSti-337
- 88Top-19
- 89JetSaf-8
- 89Kra-48
- 89OPC-63
- 89Top-63A
- 89Top-63B
- 89WhaJunM-4
- 90OPC-67
- 90ProSet-101
- 90Sco-276
- 90ScoCan-276
- 90Top-67
- 90TopTif-67
- 90UppDec-268
- 90UppDecF-268
- 90WhaJr7E-7
- 91PanSti-320
- 91Par-284
- 91ParFre-284
- 91ProSet-392
- 91ProSetFre-392
- 91ScoCan-424
- 91WhaJr7E-9
- 92PanSti-260
- 92PanStiFre-260
- 92Ult-73
- 92WhaDai-6
- 93Don-413
- 93OPCPre-423
- 93OPCPreG-423
- 93StaClu-341
- 93StaCluFDI-341
- 93StaCluO-341
- 93TopPre-423
- 93TopPreG-423
- 93WhaCok-4
- 94Pin-406
- 94PinArtP-406
- 94PinRinC-406
- 94SenBelM-9
- 94StaClu-38
- 94StaCluFDI-38
- 94StaCluMOMS-38
- 94StaCluSTWC-38
- 94Ult-336
- 95BeAPla-81
- 95BeAPSig-S81
- 95BeAPSigDC-S81
- 95ParInt-421
- 95ParIntEl-421
- 95ProMag-112
- 95Sen-6
- 96ColCho-178
- 96KraUppD-34
- 96NHLProSTA-112
- 96SenPizH-4
- 96UppDec-111
- 97Be A PPAD-175
- 97Be A PPAPD-175
- 97BeAPla-175
- 97BeAPlaAut-175

- 97Pac-198
- 97PacCop-198
- 97PacEmeGre-198
- 97PacRed-198
- 97PacIceB-198
- 97PacSil-198
- 97Sco-161

**Cunniff, John**
- 72WhaNewEWHA-3
- 89DevCar-8
- 90Dev-9
- 90ProSet-670

**Cunningham, Bob**
- 61ShiCoi-96
- 97AncAce-5

**Cunningham, Les**
- 34BeeGro1P-49
- 39OPCV3O11-78

**Cunningham, Rick**
- 72NatOttWHA-8

**Curcio, Patrick**
- 98GerDELE-199

**Curley, Brendan**
- 93HamRoaA-7
- 94HamRoaA-16

**Curley, Cindy**
- 94ClaWomOH-W31

**Curran, Brian**
- 870PC-90
- 87PanSti-95
- 87Top-90
- 88MapLeaPLA-26
- 90ProSet-277
- 90SabBluS-5
- 91MapLeaPTS-4
- 91ProAHLCHL-2
- 91RochAmeDD-4
- 91RochAmeKod-9
- 94PorPir-7
- 95PorPir-10

**Curran, Jack**
- 63RochAme-11

**Curran, Mike**
- 69SweWorC-15
- 69SweWorC-92
- 72FigSaiPos-6
- 72SweSemWC-118
- 74FigSaiWHA-7
- 92FutTrePS-1

**Currie, Alex**
- 10C55SweCP-13
- 11C55-13
- 12C57-32

**Currie, Dan**
- 87SauSteMG-2
- 88ProAHL-75
- 89ProAHL-136
- 90ProAHLIHL-222
- 91ProAHLCHL-228
- 91UppDec-347
- 91UppDecF-347
- 92OilGA-13
- 93ClaProPro-150
- 93PhoRoa-4
- 95ColEdgI-105
- 98GerDELE-198

**Currie, Glen**
- 81Cap-3
- 82Cap-4
- 82PosCer-20
- 84CapPizH-3

**Currie, Jason**
- 92ClaKni-4
- 94RicRen-19

**Currie, Sheldon**
- 81MilAdm-11

**Currie, Tony**
- 78BluPos-8
- 800PC-384
- 81FreExp-7
- 810PC-292
- 81Top-W116
- 82FreExp-7
- 820PC-341
- 83FreExp-11
- 84NovScoO-22
- 84WhaJunW-5
- 85FreExp-9

**Curry, Busher (Floyd James)**
- 44BeeGro2P-230
- 45QuaOatP-60C
- 45QuaOatP-71A
- 45QuaOatP-71B
- 48ExhCan-27
- 51Par-2
- 52Par-7
- 53Par-35
- 54Par-15
- 54Par-89
- 55Par-40
- 55Par-76
- 55ParQuaO-40
- 55ParQuaO-76
- 57Par-M20
- 63QueAce-5
- 63QueAceQ-4
- 94ParMisL-78

**Curry, Dave**
- 83BraWheK-23
- 85BraWheK-6

**Curth, Christian**
- 94GerDELE-15
- 95GerDELE-130
- 96GerDELE-320

**Curtin, Luke**
- 94Sel-153
- 94SelGol-153
- 95BowDraPro-P8

**Curtis, Joel**
- 830shGen-8

**Curtis, Paul**
- 70EssPowPla-150
- 710PC-4
- 71SarProSta-77
- 71TorSun-109
- 720PC-266
- 72SarProSta-85

**Cushenan, Ian**
- 44BeeGro2P-231
- 44BeeGro2P-305
- 58Par-24
- 63Par-49

**Cusson, Charles**
- 87BroBra-22
- 88BroBra-8

**Cusson, Mathieu**
- 95SasBla-8
- 96SasBla-8

**Cuthbert, Cam**
- 93RenEng-7

**Cutts, Don**
- 880ilTenAnn-152

**Cyr, Denis**
- 80FlamPos-4
- 81FlamPos-5
- 820PC-43
- 82PosCer-3
- 83BlaBorPos-3

**Cyr, Paul**
- 81VicCou-7
- 82VicCou-6
- 83CanNatJ-3
- 84KelWin-31
- 84SabBluS-4
- 850PCSti-183
- 85SabBluS-5
- 85SabBluSS-5
- 860PC-200
- 86SabBluS-7
- 86SabBluSSma-7
- 87PanSti-33
- 90ProSet-449
- 90ScoRoo-72T
- 90WhaJr7E-8
- 91Bow-20
- 910PC-73
- 91PanSti-321
- 91ProAHLCHL-100
- 91ProSet-88
- 91ProSetFre-88
- 91ScoCan-413
- 91StaClu-279
- 91Top-73
- 91WhaJr7E-10

**Cyr, Raymond**
- 52JunBluT-81

**Cyrenne, Cory**
- 98BowCHL-74
- 98BowCHLGA-74
- 98BowCHLOI-74
- 98BowChrC-74
- 98BowChrCGA-74
- 98BowChrCGAR-74
- 98BowChrCOI-74
- 98BowChrCOIR-74
- 98BowChrCR-74

**Czapka, Ludvik**
- 89SweSemWCS-137

**Czerkawski, Mariusz**
- 91SweSemE-73
- 93SweSemE-69
- 94Don-138
- 94FinBowB-R20
- 94FinBowBR-R20
- 94Fla-9
- 94Fle-10
- 94Lea-82
- 94LeaLim-29
- 940PCPre-293
- 940PCPreSE-293
- 94Par-20
- 94ParGol-20
- 94ParSEES-ES5
- 94ParVin-V55
- 94Pin-246
- 94Pin1HS-246
- 94PinArtP-246
- 94PinArtP-467
- 94PinInC-246
- 94PinInC-467
- 94PinRooTP-12
- 94Sco-227
- 94ScoGol-227
- 94ScoPla-227
- 94ScoPlaTS-227
- 94Sel-190
- 94SelGol-190
- 94SelYouExp-YE11
- 94SP-10
- 94SPDieCut-10
- 94TopPre-293
- 94TopPreSE-293
- 94Ult-11
- 94UppDec-239
- 94UppDec-534
- 94UppDec-543
- 94UppDecEIeIce-239
- 94UppDecEIeIce-534
- 94UppDecEIeIce-543
- 94UppDecPC-C5
- 94UppDecPCEG-C5
- 94UppDecPCES-C5
- 94UppDecSPI-SP5
- 94UppDecSPIDC-SP5
- 95ColCho-50
- 95ColChoPC-50
- 95ColChoPCP-50
- 95Don-21
- 95FinnSISL-63
- 95Lea-55
- 95LeaStuR-17
- 95McDPin-MCD-37
- 95ParInt-18
- 95ParInt-345
- 95ParIntEI-18
- 95ParIntEI-345
- 95Pin-185
- 95PinArtP-185
- 95PinFan-4
- 95PinGloG-24
- 95PinRinC-185
- 95PlaOneoOne-117
- 95Sco-143
- 95ScoBlaIce-143
- 95ScoBlaIceAP-143
- 95SkyImpNHLF-1
- 95Top-153
- 95TopNewG-19NG
- 95TopOPCI-153
- 95TopPowL-7PL
- 95Ult-9
- 95UltAllRoo-2
- 95UltAllRooGM-2
- 95UltGolM-9
- 95UppDec-189
- 95UppDecEIeIce-189
- 95UppDecEIeIceG-189
- 95UppDecSpE-SE6
- 95UppDecSpEdiG-SE6
- 96BeAPAut-166
- 96BeAPAutSil-166
- 96BeAPla-166
- 96ColCho-93
- 96DonCanI-96
- 96DonCanIGPP-96
- 96DonCanIRPP-96
- 96OilPos-21
- 96Pin-167
- 96PinArtP-167
- 96PinFoi-167
- 96PinPreS-167
- 96PinRinC-167
- 96PlaOneoOne-368
- 96SP-59
- 96UppDecBD-122
- 96UppDecBDG-122
- 97ColCho-93
- 97Pac-216
- 97PacCop-216
- 97PacEmeGre-216
- 97PacIceB-216
- 97PacRed-216
- 97PacSil-216
- 97Pin-122
- 97PinIns-158
- 97PinPrePBB-122
- 97PinPrePBC-122
- 97PinPrePBM-122
- 97PinPrePBY-122
- 97PinPrePFC-122
- 97PinPrePFM-122
- 97PinPrePFY-122
- 97PinPrePla-122
- 97Sco-208
- 98Pac-279
- 98PacIceB-279
- 98PacPar-141
- 98PacParC-141
- 98PacParEG-141
- 98PacParH-141
- 98PacParIB-141
- 98PacParS-141
- 98PacRed-279
- 99Pac-253
- 99PacAur-89
- 99PacAurPD-89
- 99PacCop-253
- 99PacIceB-253
- 99PacPreD-253

**D'Alessio, Corrie**
- 91ProAHLCHL-616

**D'Alvise, Dan**
- 81SweSemHVS-87

**D'Amico, John**
- 93ActPacHOFI-5

**D'Amour, Claud**
- 86SudWol-28

**D'Amour, Marc**
- 80SauSteMG-25
- 81SauSteMG-9
- 85FlamRedRP-7
- 86MonGolF-14
- 88ProAHL-133
- 89ProAHL-352
- 91ProAHLCHL-264

**d'Amour, Sylvain**
- 77GraVic-7

**D'Arcy, Ryan**
- 92WesMic-9
- 93WesMic-11

**d'Orsonnens, Martin**
- 92ClaKni-13
- 92ClaKni-24
- 93Rallce-4
- 94JohChi-7

**Da Corte, Luigi**
- 94FinnJaaK-293

**Dabanovich, Jamie**
- 91KnoChe-11

**Dachyshyn, Dean**
- 83MonAlp-22
- 84NovScoO-13
- 85NovScoO-4

**Dackell, Andreas**
- 91SweSemE-51
- 92SweSemE-64
- 93SweSemE-37
- 94SweLeaE-49
- 94SweLeaEGC-2
- 95FinnSemWC-70
- 95SweGloWC-44
- 95SweLeaE-18
- 95SweLeaEC-10
- 95SweUppDE-36
- 95SweUppDETNA-NA3
- 96BeAPAut-109
- 96BeAPAutSil-109
- 96BeAPla-109
- 96DonCanI-134
- 96DonCanIGPP-134
- 96DonCanIRPP-134
- 96Lea-211
- 96LeaPreP-211
- 96Sco-260
- 96ScoArtPro-260
- 96ScoDeaCAP-260
- 96ScoGolB-260
- 96ScoSpeAP-260
- 96SkyImp-56
- 96TopPicRS-RS14
- 96UppDecBD-65
- 96UppDecBDG-65
- 96UppDecIce-31
- 96UppDecIcePar-31
- 97BeAPlaSTP-15
- 97ColCho-128
- 97Don-20
- 97DonEli-60
- 97DonEliAsp-60
- 97DonEliS-60
- 97DonLim-63
- 97DonLimExp-63
- 97DonPre-71
- 97DonPreCttC-71
- 97DonPreProG-20
- 97DonPreProS-20
- 97DonPri-104
- 97DonPriPG-14
- 97DonPriPGP-14
- 97DonPriSoA-104
- 97Pac-141
- 97PacCop-141
- 97PacCroR-9
- 97PacCroRFODC-2
- 97PacCroRIB-9
- 97PacCroRS-9
- 97PacEmeGre-141
- 97PacIceB-141
- 97PacOme-14
- 97PacOmeC-14
- 97PacOmeDG-14
- 97PacOmeEG-14
- 97PacOmeG-14
- 97PacOmeIB-14
- 97PacRed-141
- 97PacRev-8
- 97PacRevC-8
- 97PacRevE-8
- 97PacRevIB-8
- 97PacRevR-8
- 97PacRevRtSD-2
- 97PacRevS-8
- 97PacSil-141
- 97Sco-47
- 97ScoArtPro-47
- 97ScoBru-13
- 97ScoBruPla-13
- 97UppDec-331
- 97UppDecE-331
- 97UppDecE1o1-331
- 97UppDecGR-331
- 98Pac-286
- 99PacAur-89
- 99PacAurPD-89
- 99PacCop-286
- 99PacGol-286
- 99PacPreD-286

**Dacosta, Jeff**
- 93KinFro-6
- 95Sla-111

**Dadswell, Doug**
- 86MonGolF-3
- 87FlamRedRP-6
- 90AlbIntTC-2
- 91CinCyc-6

**Dafoe, Byron**
- 87PorWinH-7
- 88PorWinH-7
- 89PorWinH-3
- 91ProAHLCHL-548
- 93ClaProPro-73
- 93PorPir-22
- 94Don-175
- 94Lea-283
- 940PCPre-42
- 940PCPreODI-14
- 940PCPreOMC-14
- 940PCPreOMR-14
- 94TopPreSE-42
- 94UppDec-447
- 94UppDecEIeIce-447
- 95Bow-97
- 95BowAllFoi-97
- 95BowBes-BB23
- 95BowBesRef-BB23
- 95Don-362
- 95DonEliR-5
- 95Met-173
- 95ParInt-375
- 95ParIntEI-375
- 95SelCer-120
- 95SelCerMG-120
- 95SP-70
- 95Sum-192
- 95SumArtP-192
- 95SumIce-192
- 95Top-293
- 95TopOPCI-293
- 95Ult-334
- 95UppDec-460
- 95UppDecEIeIce-460
- 95UppDecEIeIceG-460
- 95Zen-133
- 96BeAPAut-30
- 96BeAPAutSil-30
- 96BeAPla-30
- 96Don-221
- 96DonPrePro-221
- 96MetUni-116
- 96UppDec-303
- 96Zen-121
- 96ZenArtP-121
- 97ColCho-175
- 97Don-113
- 97DonLim-137
- 97DonLimExp-137
- 97DonPre-113
- 97DonPreProG-113
- 97DonPreProS-113
- 97Pac-278
- 97PacCop-278
- 97PacEmeGre-278
- 97PacIceB-278
- 97PacOme-154
- 97PacOmeDG-154
- 97PacOmeEG-154
- 97PacOmeG-154
- 97PacOmeIB-154
- 97PacRed-278
- 97PacSil-278
- 97Sco-203
- 97SPAut-109
- 97UppDec-323
- 98Pac-308
- 98PacAur-129
- 98PacIceB-308
- 98PacPar-162
- 98PacParC-162
- 98PacParEG-162
- 98PacParGSLC-2
- 98PacParH-162
- 98PacParIB-162
- 98PacParS-162
- 98PacRed-308
- 98PacRev-9
- 98PacRevIS-9
- 98PacRevR-9
- 98SP AutSotTG-BD
- 98SPxFin-7
- 98SPxFinR-7
- 98SPxFinS-7
- 98SSASotT-BD
- 98Top-3
- 98TopO-P-3
- 98UC-10
- 98UD ChoPCR-10
- 98UD ChoR-10
- 98UppDec-221
- 98UppDecE-221
- 98UppDecE1o1-221
- 98UppDecGR-221
- 98UppDecM-14
- 98UppDecMGS-14
- 98UppDecMSS-14
- 98UppDecMSS-14
- 99Pac-22
- 99PacAur-12
- 99PacAurGU-2
- 99PacAurPD-12
- 99PacCop-22
- 99PacGol-22
- 99PacGolCD-4
- 99PacIceB-22
- 99PacIn-tCN-2
- 99PacPreD-22
- 99UppDecMLL-LL4

**Dagenais, Emile**
- 51LavDalS-106
- 52St.LawS-67

**Dagenais, Mike**
- 897thInnSOHL-102
- 90ProAHLIHL-407
- 91ProAHLCHL-528
- 93CleLum-6
- 93CleLumPos-5

**Dagenais, Pierre**
- 97BeeAutA-74
- 97PinBee-74
- 97PinBeeGP-74
- 98BowCHL-100
- 98BowCHLGA-100
- 98BowCHLOI-100
- 98BowChrC-100
- 98BowChrCGA-100
- 98BowChrCGAR-100
- 98BowChrCOI-100
- 98BowChrCOIR-100
- 98BowChrCR-100

**Dahl, Kevin**
- 91AlbIntTC-5
- 92FlamIGA-23
- 920PCPre-22
- 92Par-261
- 92ParEmel-261
- 92Ult-266
- 92UppDec-493
- 930PCPre-362
- 930PCPreSE-362
- 93Par-298
- 93ParEmel-298
- 93Sco-423
- 93ScoCan-423
- 93StaClu-423
- 93StaCluFDI-432
- 93StaCluO-432
- 93TopPre-362
- 93TopPreG-362
- 93Ult-23
- 96LasVegThu-3

**Dahlberg, Lennart**
- 83SweSemE-34
- 84SweSemE-33

**Dahlen, Ulf**
- 85SwePanS-38
- 86SwePanS-27
- 880PC-47
- 880PCMin-7
- 880PCSti-126
- 880PCSti-258
- 88PanSti-305
- 88Top-47
- 890PC-2
- 89PanSti-288
- 89RanMarMB-16
- 89Top-2
- 90Bow-176
- 90BowTif-176
- 900PC-12
- 90ProSet-136
- 90Sco-2
- 90Top-12
- 90TopTif-12
- 90UppDec-283
- 90UppDecF-283
- 91Bow-127
- 91Bow-422
- 910PC-177
- 91PanSti-109
- 91Par-76
- 91ParFre-76
- 91Pin-152
- 91PinFre-152
- 91ProSet-106
- 91ProSetFre-106
- 91ProSetPla-186
- 91ScoAme-164
- 91ScoCan-164
- 91StaClu-55
- 91Top-177
- 91UppDec-348
- 91UppDecF-348
- 92Bow-143
- 920PC-129
- 92PanSti-92
- 92PanStiFre-92
- 92Par-310
- 92ParEmel-310
- 92Pin-68
- 92ProSet-80
- 92Sco-330
- 92ScoCan-330
- 92StaClu-207
- 92Top-28
- 92TopGol-28G
- 92Ult-92
- 92UppDec-250
- 93Don-78
- 93Don-488
- 93Lea-198
- 930PCPre-75
- 930PCPreG-75
- 93PanSti-270
- 93Par-322
- 93ParEmel-322
- 93Pin-248
- 93PinCan-248
- 93Pow-59
- 93Sco-107
- 93ScoCan-107
- 93ScoIntS-13
- 93ScoIntSC-13
- 93StaClu-238
- 93StaClu-428
- 93StaCluFDI-238
- 93StaCluFDI-428
- 93StaCluFDIO-238
- 93StaCluO-238
- 93StaCluO-428
- 93SweSemE-312
- 93SweSemWCS-34
- 93TopPre-75
- 93TopPreG-75
- 93Ult-81
- 93UppDec-360
- 94CanGamNHLP-63
- 94Don-57
- 94Fla-161
- 94Fle-194
- 94Lea-25
- 94LeaLim-76
- 940PCPre-299
- 940PCPreSE-299
- 94Par-215
- 94ParGol-215
- 94ParSEES-ES6
- 94Pin-48
- 94PinArtP-48
- 94PinRinC-48
- 94PinWorEdi-WE4
- 94Sel-123
- 94SelGol-123
- 94StaHoc-9
- 94TopPre-299
- 94TopPreSE-299
- 94Ult-192
- 94UppDec-16
- 94UppDecEIeIce-16
- 94UppDecSPI-SP70
- 94UppDecSPIDC-SP70
- 95CanGamNHLP-228
- 95ColCho-297
- 95ColChoPC-297
- 95ColChoPCP-297
- 95Don-92
- 95Emo-154
- 95ImpSti-109
- 95Kra-65
- 95Lea-157
- 95Met-128
- 95ParInt-245
- 95ParInt-452
- 95ParIntEI-245
- 95ParIntEI-452
- 95Pin-13
- 95PinArtP-13
- 95PinRinC-13
- 95PlaOneoOne-190
- 95ProMag-116
- 95Sco-137
- 95ScoBlaIce-137
- 95ScoBlaIceAP-137
- 95SelCer-25
- 95SelCerMG-25
- 95SkyImp-146
- 95StaCluMO-42
- 95Sum-15
- 95SumArtP-15
- 95SumIce-15
- 95SweGloWC-48
- 95Top-227
- 95TopOPCI-227
- 95Ult-144
- 95UltGolM-144
- 95UppDec-381

❑ 95UppDecEleIce-381
❑ 95UppDecEleIceG-381
❑ 95UppDecSpeE-SE72
❑ 95UppDecSpeEdiG-SE72
❑ 95Zen-7
❑ 96BeAPAut-35
❑ 96BeAPAutSil-35
❑ 96BeAPla-35
❑ 96ColCho-243
❑ 96Don-115
❑ 96DonPrePro-115
❑ 96Lea-55
❑ 96LeaPreP-55
❑ 96NHLProSTA-116
❑ 96Sco-234
❑ 96ScoArtPro-234
❑ 96ScoDeaCAP-234
❑ 96ScoGolB-234
❑ 96ScoSpeAP-234
❑ 96SweSemW-60
❑ 97ColCho-48
❑ 97Pac-74
❑ 97PacCop-74
❑ 97PacEmeGre-74
❑ 97PacIceB-74
❑ 97PacRed-74
❑ 97PacSil-74
❑ 97Sco-252

**Dahlgren, Lars**
❑ 67SweHoc-252
❑ 69SweHocS-297
❑ 70SweHocS-204
❑ 71SweHocS-292
❑ 72SweHocS-78

**Dahlin, Hakan**
❑ 72SweHocS-198

**Dahlin, Kjell**
❑ 83SweSemE-113
❑ 84SweSemE-113
❑ 85CanaPos-6
❑ 85CanaPos-7
❑ 85CanaPro-3
❑ 85SwePanS-111
❑ 85SwePanS-112
❑ 86CanaPos-4
❑ 86KraDra-13
❑ 86OPC-15
❑ 86OPC-262
❑ 86OPCSti-18
❑ 86OPCSti-126
❑ 86Top-15
❑ 87CanaPos-6
❑ 87CanaVacS-39
❑ 87CanaVacS-40
❑ 87OPCSti-14
❑ 89SweSemE-88
❑ 90SweSemE-262
❑ 91SweSemE-95
❑ 92SweSemE-123
❑ 93SweSemE-95

**Dahllof, Hakan**
❑ 70SweHocS-90
❑ 71SweHocS-182
❑ 72SweHocS-171
❑ 74SweHocS-211

**Dahllof, Hans**
❑ 64SweCorI-87
❑ 65SweCorI-87
❑ 67SweHoc-44
❑ 69SweHocS-59
❑ 70SweHocS-19

**Dahlquist, Chris**
❑ 87PenKod-7
❑ 90OPC-528
❑ 90ProSet-464
❑ 91Bow-128
❑ 91OPC-142
❑ 91ProSet-408
❑ 91ProSetFre-408
❑ 91ScoAme-365
❑ 91ScoCan-404
❑ 91StaClu-314
❑ 91Top-142
❑ 91UppDec-307
❑ 91UppDecF-307
❑ 92Bow-359
❑ 92FlamIGA-24
❑ 92OPC-22
❑ 92OPCPre-38
❑ 92Pin-167
❑ 92PinFre-167
❑ 92Sco-294
❑ 92ScoCan-294
❑ 92StaClu-57
❑ 92Top-231
❑ 92TopGol-231G
❑ 92Ult-267
❑ 93Pin-414
❑ 93PinCan-414
❑ 93Sco-314
❑ 93ScoCan-314
❑ 93StaClu-266
❑ 93StaCluFDI-266
❑ 93StaCluO-266
❑ 94Lea-386
❑ 94Pin-402
❑ 94PinArtP-402
❑ 94PinRinC-402
❑ 94SenBelM-10
❑ 95CanGamNHLP-197
❑ 96LasVegThu-4

**Dahlstrom, Cully**
❑ 34BeeGro1P-50
❑ 35DiaMatT5-4
❑ 37DiaMatT6-4
❑ 39OPCV3011-44
❑ 39OPCV3011-46
❑ 40OPCV3012-137

**Dahlstrom, Lars**
❑ 91SweSemE-293
❑ 92SweSemE-321
❑ 93SweSemE-286
❑ 94SweLeaE-94

**Dahlstrom, Ole Eskild**
❑ 93SweSemWCS-240
❑ 94FinnJaaK-259

**Daigle, Alain**
❑ 75OPCNHL-394
❑ 76OPCNHL-156
❑ 76Top-156
❑ 77OPCNHL-208
❑ 77Top-208
❑ 78OPC-117
❑ 78Top-117
❑ 79OPC-227
❑ 79Top-227

**Daigle, Alexandre**
❑ 917thInnSQMJHL-270
❑ 92UppDec-587
❑ 93Cla-1
❑ 93Cla-34
❑ 93Cla-50
❑ 93Cla-51
❑ 93Cla-52
❑ 93Cla-53
❑ 93Cla-54
❑ 93Cla-114
❑ 93ClaCraNum-N1
❑ 93ClaPre-HK1
❑ 93ClaPromo-1
❑ 93ClaTopTen-DP1
❑ 93Don-237
❑ 93Don-393
❑ 93DonEli-2
❑ 93DonRatR-1
❑ 93DonSpeP-P
❑ 93DurSco-1
❑ 93Kra-6
❑ 93Lea-311
❑ 93LeaFrePhe-1
❑ 93LeaStuS-9
❑ 93OPCPre-405
❑ 93OPCPreF-1
❑ 93OPCPreG-405
❑ 93Par-244
❑ 93ParCalC-C1
❑ 93ParCalCG-C1
❑ 93ParChePH-D11
❑ 93ParEasWesS-E3
❑ 93ParEmel-244
❑ 93ParFirO-F1
❑ 93ParUSACG-G6
❑ 93Pin-236
❑ 93Pin-AU1
❑ 93Pin2HS-SR1
❑ 93PinCan-236
❑ 93PinCan-AU1
❑ 93PinDaiED-1
❑ 93PinPow-1
❑ 93PinSupR-1
❑ 93PinSupRC-1
❑ 93Pow-396
❑ 93PowRooS-3
❑ 93Sco-496
❑ 93Sco-587
❑ 93Sco-NNO
❑ 93ScoCan-496
❑ 93ScoCan-587
❑ 93ScoCan-NNO
❑ 93ScoDynDC-3
❑ 93ScoGol-587
❑ 93ScoProP-587
❑ 93SenKraS-5
❑ 93StaClu-300
❑ 93StaCluFDI-300
❑ 93StaCluO-300
❑ 93TopPre-405
❑ 93TopPreF-1
❑ 93TopPreG-405
❑ 93Ult-380
❑ 93UltWavF-3
❑ 93UppDec-170
❑ 93UppDec-250
❑ 93UppDecPOE-E15
❑ 93UppDecSilSka-R3
❑ 93UppDecSilSkaG-R3
❑ 93UppDecSP-107
❑ 94BeAPla-R30
❑ 94CanGamNHLP-353
❑ 94ClaProP-13
❑ 94Don-211
❑ 94Fin-88
❑ 94Fin-155
❑ 94FinRef-88
❑ 94FinRef-155
❑ 94FinSupTW-88
❑ 94FinSupTW-155
❑ 94Fla-120
❑ 94FlaScoP-2
❑ 94Fle-143
❑ 94HocWit-91
❑ 94Lea-119
❑ 94LeaGolR-5
❑ 94LeaLim-87
❑ 94McDUppD-McD36
❑ 94OPCFinIns-7
❑ 94OPCPre-140
❑ 94OPCPre-195
❑ 94OPCPreSE-140
❑ 94OPCPreSE-195
❑ 94Par-285
❑ 94ParGol-285
❑ 94ParSE-SE119
❑ 94ParSEG-SE119
❑ 94ParVin-V42
❑ 94Pin-2
❑ 94Pin-461
❑ 94Pin-531
❑ 94Pin1HS-2
❑ 94PinArtP-2
❑ 94PinArtP-461
❑ 94PinArtP-531
❑ 94PinGam-GR6
❑ 94PinNorLig-NL6
❑ 94PinRinC-2
❑ 94PinRinC-461
❑ 94PinRinC-531
❑ 94Sco-248
❑ 94ScoDreTea-DT21
❑ 94ScoFra-TF16
❑ 94ScoGol-248
❑ 94ScoHobS-TF16
❑ 94ScoPla-248
❑ 94ScoPlaTS-248
❑ 94Sel-3
❑ 94SelGol-3
❑ 94SenBelM-11
❑ 94SP-81
❑ 94SP-136
❑ 94SPDieCut-81
❑ 94SPDieCut-136
❑ 94StaClu-110
❑ 94StaCluFDI-110
❑ 94StaCluMO-50
❑ 94StaCluMOMS-110
❑ 94StaCluSTWC-110
❑ 94TopPre-140
❑ 94TopPre-195
❑ 94TopPreSE-140
❑ 94TopPreSE-195
❑ 94Ult-146
❑ 94UltAllRoo-3
❑ 94UppDec-87
❑ 94UppDecEleIce-87
❑ 94UppDecIG-IG10
❑ 94UppDecNBAP-3
❑ 94UppDecSPI-SP54
❑ 94UppDecSPIDC-SP54
❑ 95BeAPla-188
❑ 95BeAPSig-S188
❑ 95BeAPSigDC-S188
❑ 95CanGamNHLP-190
❑ 95ColCho-208
❑ 95ColChoPC-208
❑ 95ColChoPCP-208
❑ 95Don-160
❑ 95DonCanWJT-16
❑ 95Emo-123
❑ 95ImpSti-86
❑ 95Kra-10
❑ 95Kra-63
❑ 95Lea-179
❑ 95LeaLim-38
❑ 95McDPin-MCD-38
❑ 95Met-104
❑ 95NHLAcePC-4D
❑ 95ParInt-150
❑ 95ParIntEl-150
❑ 95Pin-7
❑ 95PinArtP-7
❑ 95PinFan-3
❑ 95PinRinC-7
❑ 95PlaOneoOne-73
❑ 95PlaOneoOne-178
❑ 95ProMag-113
❑ 95Sco-18
❑ 95ScoBlaIce-18
❑ 95ScoBlaIceAP-18
❑ 95SelCer-22
❑ 95SelCerMG-22
❑ 95Sen-7
❑ 95SkyImp-118
❑ 95SP-103
❑ 95StaClu-97
❑ 95StaCluMOMS-97
❑ 95Sum-21
❑ 95SumArtP-21
❑ 95SumIce-21
❑ 95Top-342
❑ 95TopCanWJ-5CJ
❑ 95TopHomGC-HGC14
❑ 95TopOPCI-342
❑ 95TopSupSki-24
❑ 95TopSupSkiPla-24
❑ 95Ult-111
❑ 95UltGolM-111
❑ 95UltHigSpe-6
❑ 95UltRisS-2
❑ 95UltRisSGM-2
❑ 95UppDec-271
❑ 95UppDecEleIce-271
❑ 95UppDecEleIceG-271
❑ 95UppDecSpeE-SE60
❑ 95UppDecSpeEdiG-SE60
❑ 95UppDecWJA-4
❑ 95Zen-22
❑ 96ColCho-180
❑ 96ColCho-325
❑ 96Don-204
❑ 96DonCanI-104
❑ 96DonCanIGPP-104
❑ 96DonCanIRPP-104
❑ 96DonEli-84
❑ 96DonEliDCS-84
❑ 96DonPrePro-204
❑ 96Lea-80
❑ 96LeaPreP-80
❑ 96MetUni-105
❑ 96NHLProSTA-113
❑ 96Pin-133
❑ 96PinArtP-133
❑ 96PinFoi-133
❑ 96PinPreS-133
❑ 96PinRinC-133
❑ 96Sco-66
❑ 96ScoArtPro-66
❑ 96ScoDeaCAP-66
❑ 96ScoGolB-66
❑ 96ScoSpeAP-66
❑ 96SenPizH-6
❑ 96SkyImp-88
❑ 96SP-106
❑ 96Sum-106
❑ 96SumArtP-106
❑ 96SumIce-106
❑ 96SumMet-106
❑ 96SumPreS-106
❑ 96Ult-116
❑ 96UltGolM-117
❑ 96UppDec-302
❑ 96UppDecBD-91
❑ 96UppDecBDG-91
❑ 97ColCho-174
❑ 97ColChoSta-SQ25
❑ 97Don-78
❑ 97DonCanI-122
❑ 97DonCanIDS-122
❑ 97DonCanINP-15
❑ 97DonCanIPS-122
❑ 97DonEli-24
❑ 97DonEliAsp-24
❑ 97DonEliS-24
❑ 97DonLim-161
❑ 97DonLimExp-161
❑ 97DonPre-48
❑ 97DonPreCttC-48
❑ 97DonPreProG-78
❑ 97DonPreProS-78
❑ 97DonPri-22
❑ 97DonPriSoA-22
❑ 97Kat-98
❑ 97KatGol-98
❑ 97KatSil-98
❑ 97Lea-26
❑ 97LeaFraMat-26
❑ 97LeaFraMDC-26
❑ 97LeaInt-26
❑ 97LeaIntUI-26
❑ 97Pac-250
❑ 97PacCop-250
❑ 97PacCroR-90
❑ 97PacCroREG-90
❑ 97PacCroRIB-90
❑ 97PacCroRS-90
❑ 97PacDyn-84
❑ 97PacDynC-84
❑ 97PacDynDG-84
❑ 97PacDynEG-84
❑ 97PacDynIB-84
❑ 97PacDynR-84
❑ 97PacDynSil-84
❑ 97PacDynTan-54
❑ 97PacEmeGre-250
❑ 97PacIceB-250
❑ 97PacInv-93
❑ 97PacInvC-93
❑ 97PacInvEG-93
❑ 97PacInvFP-23
❑ 97PacInvIB-93
❑ 97PacInvR-93
❑ 97PacInvS-93
❑ 97PacPar-124
❑ 97PacParC-124
❑ 97PacParDG-124
❑ 97PacParEG-124
❑ 97PacParIB-124
❑ 97PacParRed-124
❑ 97PacParSil-124
❑ 97PacRed-250
❑ 97PacRev-99
❑ 97PacRevC-99
❑ 97PacRevE-99
❑ 97PacRevIB-99
❑ 97PacRevR-99
❑ 97PacRevS-99
❑ 97PacSil-250
❑ 97PacTeaCCC-17
❑ 97Pin-159
❑ 97PinCer-98
❑ 97PinCerMB-98
❑ 97PinCerMG-98
❑ 97PinCerMR-98
❑ 97PinCerR-98
❑ 97PinHocMC-3
❑ 97PinHocMC-4
❑ 97PinIns-109
❑ 97PinPrePBB-159
❑ 97PinPrePBC-159
❑ 97PinPrePBM-159
❑ 97PinPrePBY-159
❑ 97PinPrePFC-159
❑ 97PinPrePFM-159
❑ 97PinPrePFY-159
❑ 97PinPrePla-159
❑ 97PinTotCMPG-98
❑ 97PinTotCPB-98
❑ 97PinTotCPG-98
❑ 97PinTotCPR-98
❑ 97Sco-101
❑ 97ScoArtPro-101
❑ 97ScoGolBla-101
❑ 97SPAut-107
❑ 97Stu-92
❑ 97StuPrePG-92
❑ 97StuPrePS-92
❑ 97UppDec-117
❑ 98Fin-24
❑ 98FinNo P-24
❑ 98FinNo PR-24
❑ 98FinRef-24
❑ 98Pac-323
❑ 98PacAur-136
❑ 98PacDynI-134
❑ 98PacDynIIB-134
❑ 98PacDynIR-134
❑ 98PacIceB-323
❑ 98PacPar-170
❑ 98PacParC-170
❑ 98PacParEG-170
❑ 98PacParH-170
❑ 98PacParIB-170
❑ 98PacParS-170
❑ 98PacRed-323
❑ 98SPxFin-61
❑ 98SPxFinR-61
❑ 98SPxFinS-61
❑ 98UC-148
❑ 98UD ChoPCR-148
❑ 98UD ChoR-148
❑ 98UppDec-144
❑ 98UppDecE-144
❑ 98UppDecE1o1-144
❑ 98UppDecGR-144
❑ 98UppDecM-189
❑ 98UppDecMGS-189
❑ 98UppDecMSS-189
❑ 98UppDecMSS-189
❑ 99Pac-387
❑ 99PacCop-387
❑ 99PacGol-387
❑ 99PacIceB-387
❑ 99PacPreD-387

**Daigle, Chris**
❑ 97BowCHL-79
❑ 97BowCHLOPC-79
❑ 98Vald'OF-1

**Daigneault, J.J.**
❑ 84Canu-6
❑ 85Canu-7
❑ 86FlyPos-7
❑ 88ProAHL-136
❑ 88ProAHL-271
❑ 89CanaKra-6
❑ 89CanaPos-9
❑ 90CanaPos-11
❑ 90ProSet-466
❑ 91CanaPanTS-7
❑ 91CanaPos-9
❑ 91OPC-456
❑ 91PanSti-192
❑ 91Par-312
❑ 91ParFre-312
❑ 91ProSet-124
❑ 91ProSetFre-124
❑ 91ScoCan-520
❑ 91Top-456
❑ 91UppDec-170
❑ 91UppDecF-170
❑ 92Bow-371
❑ 92CanaPos-5
❑ 92DurPan-35
❑ 92OPC-304
❑ 92Par-324
❑ 92ParEmel-324
❑ 92Sco-311
❑ 92ScoCan-311
❑ 92StaClu-308
❑ 92Top-334
❑ 92TopGol-334G
❑ 92Ult-326
❑ 92UppDec-331
❑ 93CanaMol-5
❑ 93CanaPos-5
❑ 93DurSco-10
❑ 93Lea-437
❑ 93OPCCanHF-25
❑ 93OPCPre-372
❑ 93OPCPreG-372
❑ 93Par-377
❑ 93ParEmel-377
❑ 93Pin-311
❑ 93PinCan-311
❑ 93Pow-367
❑ 93Sco-299
❑ 93ScoCan-299
❑ 93StaClu-475
❑ 93StaCluFDI-475
❑ 93StaCluO-475
❑ 93TopPre-372
❑ 93TopPreG-372
❑ 93Ult-351
❑ 94CanaPos-5
❑ 94Lea-407
❑ 94Pin-224
❑ 94PinArtP-224
❑ 94PinRinC-224
❑ 94StaClu-52
❑ 94StaCluFDI-52
❑ 94StaCluMOMS-52
❑ 94StaCluSTWC-52
❑ 94UppDec-341
❑ 94UppDecEleIce-341
❑ 95CanGamNHLP-153
❑ 95ParInt-442
❑ 95ParIntEl-442
❑ 95PlaOneoOne-163
❑ 96BeAPAut-34
❑ 96BeAPAutSil-34
❑ 96BeAPla-34
❑ 96PlaOneoOne-377
❑ 97PacDynBKS-1
❑ 97Sco-254
❑ 97ScoMigDPla-8
❑ 97ScoMigDPre-8
❑ 97ScoMigDuc-8
❑ 97UppDec-212
❑ 98Be A PPA-76
❑ 98Be A PPAA-76
❑ 98Be A PPAAF-76
❑ 98Be A PPTBASG-76
❑ 98Be APG-76
❑ 98UppDec-305
❑ 98UppDecE-305
❑ 98UppDecE1o1-305
❑ 98UppDecGR-305

**Daigneault, Paul**
❑ 907thInnSQMJHL-171

**Dailey, Bob**
❑ 73CanuRoyB-4
❑ 74CanuRoyB-4
❑ 74NHLActSta-280
❑ 74OPCNHL-240
❑ 74Top-240
❑ 75CanuRoyB-5
❑ 75OPCNHL-231
❑ 75Top-231
❑ 76CanuRoyB-2
❑ 76OPCNHL-350
❑ 77OPCNHL-98
❑ 77Top-98
❑ 78OPC-131
❑ 78Top-131
❑ 79OPC-226
❑ 79Top-226
❑ 80OPC-131
❑ 80Top-131
❑ 81OPC-241
❑ 81Top-E104

**Dainville, Bob**
❑ 52St.LawS-89

**Dairon, Michael**
❑ 92BriColJHL-123

**Dale, Andrew**
❑ 93SudWol-12
❑ 93SudWolP-12
❑ 94SudWol-11
❑ 94SudWolP-5
❑ 95Sla-142
❑ 95Sla-394
❑ 95SudWol-21
❑ 95SudWolP-6

**Dale, Jack**
❑ 69SeaTotW-13

**Daley, Joe**
❑ 68OPC-188
❑ 69OPC-152
❑ 70SarProSta-17
❑ 71OPC-137
❑ 71SarProSta-62
❑ 71TorSun-90
❑ 74OPCWHA-38
❑ 75OPCWHA-101
❑ 76OPCWHA-6
❑ 76OPCWHA-20
❑ 76OPCWHA-61
❑ 77OPCWHA-9
❑ 78JetPos-4

**Dalgard, Christer**
❑ 83SweSemE-102
❑ 84SweSemE-100
❑ 85SwePanS-92
❑ 86SwePanS-85
❑ 87SwePanS-90

**Dalgarno, Brad**
❑ 89OPC-246
❑ 90ProSet-482
❑ 91StaClu-371
❑ 92Par-336
❑ 92ParEmel-336
❑ 93Don-197
❑ 93Lea-320
❑ 93OPCPre-223
❑ 93OPCPreG-223
❑ 93Par-393
❑ 93ParEmel-393
❑ 93Pin-333
❑ 93PinCan-333
❑ 93Sco-374
❑ 93ScoCan-374
❑ 93StaClu-167
❑ 93StaCluFDI-167
❑ 93StaCluFDIO-167
❑ 93StaCluO-167
❑ 93TopPre-223
❑ 93TopPreG-223
❑ 93Ult-364
❑ 93UppDec-219
❑ 94CanGamNHLP-153
❑ 94Pin-238
❑ 94PinArtP-238
❑ 94PinRinC-238
❑ 94StaClu-259
❑ 94StaCluFDI-259
❑ 94StaCluMOMS-259
❑ 94StaCluSTWC-259
❑ 95BeAPla-10
❑ 95BeAPSig-S10
❑ 95BeAPSigDC-S10

**Dallaire, Henri (G.)**
❑ 10C55SweCP-39
❑ 11C55-39
❑ 12C57-7

**Dallaire, Stacy**
❑ 917thInnSQMJHL-147

**Dallas, Darcy**
❑ 93NorMicW-4

**Dallman, Marty**
❑ 88ProAHL-223
❑ 94FinnJaaK-250
❑ 95SweGloWC-187

**Dallman, Rod**
❑ 84PriAlbRS-4
❑ 88ProAHL-316
❑ 89ProAHL-245
❑ 91ProAHLCHL-278

**Dalmad, Duncan**
❑ 95Sla-159

**Dalman, Daddy**
❑ 23V1281PauC-13

**Dalpiaz, Claus**
❑ 93SweSemWCS-270
❑ 94FinnJaaK-231
❑ 95AusNatTea-3
❑ 95GerDELE-361
❑ 95SweGloWC-181
❑ 96GerDELE-184
❑ 96SweSemW-210
❑ 98GerDELE-308

**Dalton, Ray**
❑ 98QueRem-6

**Daly, Craig**
❑ 90CinCyc-41

**Dam, Trevor**
❑ 86LonKni-21
❑ 897thInnSOHL-25
❑ 90ProAHLIHL-403
❑ 91ProAHLCHL-483
❑ 92IndIce-9

**Dame, Bunny**
❑ 34BeeGro1P-145

**Dame, George**
❑ 28V1282PauC-83

**Dameworth, Chad**
❑ 92NorMicW-3
❑ 93NorMicW-5
❑ 96WheNai-22

**Damphouse, Jean-Francois**
❑ 97BowCHL-160
❑ 97BowCHLOPC-160

**Damphousse, Vincent**
❑ 86MapLeaP-6
❑ 87MapLeaP-4
❑ 87MapLeaPLA-17
❑ 87MapLeaPO-4
❑ 87OPC-243
❑ 87OPCSti-128
❑ 87PanSti-333
❑ 88MapLeaPLA-17
❑ 88OPC-207
❑ 88OPCSti-171
❑ 88PanSti-123
❑ 89Kra-35
❑ 89OPC-272
❑ 89OPCSti-179
❑ 89PanSti-134
❑ 90Bow-163
❑ 90BowHatTri-6
❑ 90BowTif-163
❑ 90OPC-121
❑ 90OPC-241
❑ 90OPCPre-21
❑ 90PanSti-291
❑ 90ProSet-278
❑ 90Sco-95
❑ 90ScoCan-95
❑ 90ScoHotRS-47
❑ 90Top-121
❑ 90Top-241
❑ 90TopTif-121
❑ 90UppDec-224
❑ 90UppDec-484
❑ 90UppDecF-224
❑ 90UppDecF-484
❑ 91Bow-170
❑ 91Kra-84
❑ 91MapLeaPTS-5
❑ 91McDUppD-16
❑ 91OilIGA-3
❑ 91OilTeal-4
❑ 91OPC-299
❑ 91OPCPre-104
❑ 91PanSti-92
❑ 91Par-48
❑ 91ParFre-48
❑ 91Pin-91
❑ 91PinFre-91
❑ 91ProSet-224
❑ 91ProSet-292
❑ 91ProSet-381
❑ 91ProSetFre-224
❑ 91ProSetFre-293
❑ 91ProSetFre-381
❑ 91ProSetPla-35
❑ 91ScoAme-300
❑ 91ScoAme-338
❑ 91ScoCan-368
❑ 91ScoCan-609
❑ 91ScoRoo-59T
❑ 91StaClu-146
❑ 91Top-299
❑ 91TopTeaSL-9
❑ 91UppDec-136
❑ 91UppDec-535
❑ 91UppDecF-136
❑ 91UppDecF-535

❑ 92Bow-203A
❑ 92Bow-203B
❑ 92Bow-329
❑ 92CanaPos-6
❑ 92DurPan-20
❑ 92McDUppD-4
❑ 92OPC-192
❑ 92OPCPre-3
❑ 92PanSti-104
❑ 92PanStiFre-104
❑ 92Par-86
❑ 92Par-496
❑ 92ParEmel-86
❑ 92ParEmel-496
❑ 92Pin-261
❑ 92Pin-349
❑ 92PinFre-261
❑ 92PinFre-349
❑ 92ProSetGTL-5
❑ 92Sco-170
❑ 92ScoCan-170
❑ 92StaClu-191
❑ 92Top-55
❑ 92TopGol-55G
❑ 92Ult-103
❑ 92UppDec-6
❑ 92UppDec-307
❑ 92UppDec-476
❑ 93CanaMol-4
❑ 93CanaPos-6
❑ 93Don-172
❑ 93DurSco-11
❑ 93KraRec-1
❑ 93Lea-4
❑ 93OPCCanHF-38
❑ 93OPCPre-233
❑ 93OPCPreBG-2
❑ 93OPCPreG-233
❑ 93PanSti-13
❑ 93Par-104
❑ 93ParEmel-104
❑ 93Pin-85
❑ 93Pin-232
❑ 93PinCan-85
❑ 93PinCan-232
❑ 93PinTeaP-10
❑ 93PinTeaPC-10
❑ 93Pow-127
❑ 93Sco-244
❑ 93ScoCan-244
❑ 93StaClu-240
❑ 93StaCluFDI-240
❑ 93StaCluFDIO-240
❑ 93StaCluO-240
❑ 93TopPre-233
❑ 93TopPreG-233
❑ 93Ult-79
❑ 93UppDec-295
❑ 93UppDec-380
❑ 93UppDecHT-HT8
❑ 93UppDecNR-25
❑ 93UppDecSP-77
❑ 94BeAPla-R102
❑ 94BeAPla-R112
❑ 94BeAPSig-120
❑ 94CanaPos-6
❑ 94CanGamNHLP-133
❑ 94Don-226
❑ 94EASpo-70
❑ 94Fin-98
❑ 94FinRef-98
❑ 94FinSupTW-98
❑ 94Fla-87
❑ 94Fle-103
❑ 94HocWit-72
❑ 94Kra-16
❑ 94Lea-69
❑ 94LeaLim-90
❑ 94McDUppD-McD29
❑ 94OPCPre-65
❑ 94OPCPreSE-65
❑ 94Par-115
❑ 94ParGol-115
❑ 94ParVin-V23
❑ 94Pin-4
❑ 94Pin1HS-4
❑ 94PinArtP-4
❑ 94PinNorLig-NL3
❑ 94PinRinC-4
❑ 94Sco-165
❑ 94Sco90PC-20
❑ 94ScoGol-165
❑ 94ScoPla-165
❑ 94ScoPlaTS-165
❑ 94Sel-59
❑ 94SelGol-59
❑ 94SP-58
❑ 94SPDieCut-58
❑ 94TopFinI-22
❑ 94TopPre-65
❑ 94TopPreSE-65
❑ 94Ult-107
❑ 94UppDec-280
❑ 94UppDecElelce-280
❑ 94UppDecSPI-SP39
❑ 94UppDecSPIDC-SP39
❑ 95CanaPos-6
❑ 95CanaShe-11
❑ 95CanGamNHLP-148
❑ 95ColCho-320
❑ 95ColChoPC-320
❑ 95ColChoPCP-320
❑ 95Don-202
❑ 95DonEli-96
❑ 95DonEliDCS-96
❑ 95DonEliDCU-96
❑ 95Emo-87
❑ 95Fin-52
❑ 95FinRef-52
❑ 95GerDELE-443
❑ 95ImpSti-67
❑ 95Lea-302
❑ 95LeaLim-4
❑ 95Met-76
❑ 95ParInt-110
❑ 95ParIntEl-110
❑ 95Pin-84
❑ 95PinArtP-84
❑ 95PinRinC-84
❑ 95PlaOneoOne-53
❑ 95PosUppD-4
❑ 95ProMag-22
❑ 95Sco-36
❑ 95ScoBlaIce-36
❑ 95ScoBlaIceAP-36
❑ 95SelCer-75
❑ 95SelCerMG-75
❑ 95SkyImp-84
❑ 95SP-75
❑ 95StaClu-159
❑ 95StaCluMOMS-159
❑ 95Sum-64
❑ 95SumArtP-64
❑ 95SumIce-64
❑ 95Top-270
❑ 95TopOPCI-270
❑ 95TopPowL-9PL
❑ 95Ult-80
❑ 95UltGolM-80
❑ 95UppDec-66
❑ 95UppDecElelce-66
❑ 95UppDecElelceG-66
❑ 95UppDecSpeE-SE133
❑ 95UppDecSpeEdiG-SE133
❑ 95Zen-77
❑ 96CanaPos-11
❑ 96CanaShe-7
❑ 96ColCho-138
❑ 96Don-35
❑ 96DonCanI-53
❑ 96DonCanIGPP-53
❑ 96DonCanIRPP-53
❑ 96DonPrePro-35
❑ 96DurL'EB-JB15
❑ 96Fla-47
❑ 96FlaBluI-47
❑ 96Fle-53
❑ 96FlePic-36
❑ 96HocGreC-5
❑ 96HocGreCG-5
❑ 96KraUppD-37
❑ 96Lea-79
❑ 96LeaLim-84
❑ 96LeaLimG-84
❑ 96LeaPre-25
❑ 96LeaPreP-79
❑ 96LeaPrePP-25
❑ 96MetUni-79
❑ 96NHLACEPC-9
❑ 96NHLProSTA-22
❑ 96Pin-72
❑ 96PinArtP-72
❑ 96PinFoi-72
❑ 96PinPreS-72
❑ 96PinRinC-72
❑ 96PosUppD-4
❑ 96Sco-50
❑ 96ScoArtPro-50
❑ 96ScoDeaCAP-50
❑ 96ScoGolB-50
❑ 96ScoSpeAP-50
❑ 96SelCer-37
❑ 96SelCerAP-37
❑ 96SelCerBlu-37
❑ 96SelCerMB-37
❑ 96SelCerMG-37
❑ 96SelCerMR-37
❑ 96SelCerRed-37
❑ 96SkyImp-61
❑ 96Sum-136
❑ 96SumArtP-136
❑ 96SumIce-136
❑ 96SumMet-136
❑ 96SumPreS-136
❑ 96Ult-86
❑ 96UltGolM-87
❑ 96UppDec-86
❑ 96UppDecBD-25
❑ 96UppDecBDG-25
❑ 96UppDecIce-32
❑ 96UppDecIcePar-32
❑ 96Zen-100
❑ 96ZenArtP-100
❑ 97Be A PPAD-157
❑ 97Be A PPAPD-157
❑ 97BeAPla-157
❑ 97BeAPlaAut-157
❑ 97CanaPos-9
❑ 97ColCho-130
❑ 97ColChoSta-SQ32
❑ 97Don-173
❑ 97DonCanI-115
❑ 97DonCanIDS-115
❑ 97DonCanINP-29
❑ 97DonCanIPS-115
❑ 97DonEli-81
❑ 97DonEliAsp-81
❑ 97DonEliS-81
❑ 97DonLim-137
❑ 97DonLimExp-137
❑ 97DonPre-140
❑ 97DonPreCttC-140
❑ 97DonPreProG-173
❑ 97DonPreProS-173
❑ 97DonPri-164
❑ 97DonPriSoA-164
❑ 97Kat-74
❑ 97KatGol-74
❑ 97KatSil-74
❑ 97Lea-109
❑ 97LeaFraMat-109
❑ 97LeaFraMDC-109
❑ 97LeaInt-109
❑ 97LeaIntUI-109
❑ 97McD-21
❑ 97Pac-25
❑ 97PacCop-25
❑ 97PacCroR-68
❑ 97PacCroREG-68
❑ 97PacCroRIB-68
❑ 97PacCroRS-68
❑ 97PacDyn-62
❑ 97PacDynBKS-48
❑ 97PacDynC-62
❑ 97PacDynDG-62
❑ 97PacDynEG-62
❑ 97PacDynIB-62
❑ 97PacDynR-62
❑ 97PacDynSil-62
❑ 97PacDynTan-46
❑ 97PacEmeGre-25
❑ 97PacIceB-25
❑ 97PacInv-70
❑ 97PacInvC-70
❑ 97PacInvEG-70
❑ 97PacInvIB-70
❑ 97PacInvNRB-102
❑ 97PacInvR-70
❑ 97PacInvS-70
❑ 97PacOme-117
❑ 97PacOmeC-117
❑ 97PacOmeDG-117
❑ 97PacOmeEG-117
❑ 97PacOmeG-117
❑ 97PacOmeIB-117
❑ 97PacPar-94
❑ 97PacParC-94
❑ 97PacParDG-94
❑ 97PacParEG-94
❑ 97PacParIB-94
❑ 97PacParRed-94
❑ 97PacParSil-94
❑ 97PacRed-25
❑ 97PacRev-70
❑ 97PacRevC-70
❑ 97PacRevE-70
❑ 97PacRevIB-70
❑ 97PacRevR-70
❑ 97PacRevS-70
❑ 97PacSil-25
❑ 97PacSlaSDC-4B
❑ 97Pin-85
❑ 97PinArtP-85
❑ 97PinCer-72
❑ 97PinCerMB-72
❑ 97PinCerMG-72
❑ 97PinCerMR-72
❑ 97PinCerR-72
❑ 97PinIns-36
❑ 97PinInsCC-36
❑ 97PinInsEC-36
❑ 97PinPrePBB-85
❑ 97PinPrePBC-85
❑ 97PinPrePBM-85
❑ 97PinPrePBY-85
❑ 97PinPrePFC-85
❑ 97PinPrePFM-85
❑ 97PinPrePFY-85
❑ 97PinPrePla-85
❑ 97PinRinC-85
❑ 97PinTotCMPG-72
❑ 97PinTotCPB-72
❑ 97PinTotCPG-72
❑ 97PinTotCPR-72
❑ 97PosPin-9
❑ 97Sco-112
❑ 97ScoArtPro-112
❑ 97ScoCan-4
❑ 97ScoCanPla-4
❑ 97ScoChel-11
❑ 97ScoGolBla-112
❑ 97SPAut-82
❑ 97Stu-76
❑ 97StuPrePG-76
❑ 97StuPrePS-76
❑ 97UppDec-86
❑ 97Zen-39
❑ 97Zen5x7-57
❑ 97ZenGolImp-57
❑ 97ZenSilImp-57
❑ 97ZenZGol-39
❑ 97ZenZSil-39
❑ 98Be A PPA-217
❑ 98Be A PPAA-217
❑ 98Be A PPAAF-217
❑ 98Be A PPSE-217
❑ 98Be APG-217
❑ 98BowBes-14
❑ 98BowBesAR-14
❑ 98BowBesR-14
❑ 98Fin-9
❑ 98FinNo P-9
❑ 98FinNo PR-9
❑ 98FinRef-9
❑ 98O-PChr-118
❑ 98O-PChrR-118
❑ 98Pac-250
❑ 98PacAur-93
❑ 98PacCroR-68
❑ 98PacCroRLS-68
❑ 98PacDynI-95
❑ 98PacDynIIB-95
❑ 98PacDynIR-95
❑ 98PacIceB-250
❑ 98PacOmeH-120
❑ 98PacOmeODI-120
❑ 98PacOmeR-120
❑ 98PacPar-112
❑ 98PacParC-112
❑ 98PacParEG-112
❑ 98PacParH-112
❑ 98PacParIB-112
❑ 98PacParS-112
❑ 98PacRed-250
❑ 98PacRev-72
❑ 98PacRevIS-72
❑ 98PacRevR-72
❑ 98ScoCanPre-4
❑ 98SP Aut-43
❑ 98SPXTopP-32
❑ 98SPXTopPF-32
❑ 98SPXTopPR-32
❑ 98Top-118
❑ 98TopGolLC1-67
❑ 98TopGolLC1B-67
❑ 98TopGolLC1BOoO-67
❑ 98TopGolLC1OoO-67
❑ 98TopGolLC1R-67
❑ 98TopGolLC1ROoO-67
❑ 98TopGolLC2-67
❑ 98TopGolLC2B-67
❑ 98TopGolLC2BOoO-67
❑ 98TopGolLC2OoO-67
❑ 98TopGolLC2R-67
❑ 98TopGolLC2ROoO-67
❑ 98TopGolLC3-67
❑ 98TopGolLC3B-67
❑ 98TopGolLC3BOoO-67
❑ 98TopGolLC3OoO-67
❑ 98TopGolLC3R-67
❑ 98TopGolLC3ROoO-67
❑ 98TopO-P-118
❑ 98UC-110
❑ 98UD ChoPCR-110
❑ 98UD ChoR-110
❑ 98UppDec-110
❑ 98UppDecBD-43
❑ 98UppDecDD-43
❑ 98UppDecE-110
❑ 98UppDecE1o1-110
❑ 98UppDecGR-110
❑ 98UppDecM-101
❑ 98UppDecMGS-101
❑ 98UppDecMSS-101
❑ 98UppDecMSS-101
❑ 98UppDecQD-43
❑ 98UppDecTD-43
❑ 99Pac-369
❑ 99PacAur-119
❑ 99PacAurPD-119
❑ 99PacCop-369
❑ 99PacGol-369
❑ 99PacIceB-369
❑ 99PacPreD-369
❑ 99RetHoc-69
❑ 99SP AutPS-43
❑ 99UppDecM-173
❑ 99UppDecMGS-173
❑ 99UppDecMSS-173
❑ 99UppDecMSS-173
❑ 99UppDecRG-69
❑ 99UppDecRP-69

**Dampier, Alex**
❑ 93SheSte-16
❑ 94SheSte-1
❑ 97SheSte-21
❑ 97SheSte-24

**Dan, Steeler**
❑ 94SheSte-20
❑ 97SheSte-24
❑ 97SheSte-23

**Danby, John**
❑ 72WhaNewEWHA-4

**Dancause, Carl**
❑ 92QueIntP-11

**Dandenault, Eric**
❑ 907thInnSQMJHL-10
❑ 917thInnSMC-53
❑ 91ProAHLCHL-277
❑ 96CinCyc-37
❑ 98CinCyc-4

**Dandenault, Mathieu**
❑ 95Bow-114
❑ 95BowAllFoi-114
❑ 95Don-234
❑ 95LeaLim-37
❑ 95ParInt-335
❑ 95ParIntEl-335
❑ 95SP-43
❑ 95StaClu-213
❑ 95StaCluMOMS-213
❑ 95UppDec-497
❑ 95UppDecElelce-497
❑ 95UppDecElelceG-497
❑ 96BeAPAut-95
❑ 96BeAPAutSil-95
❑ 96BeAPla-95
❑ 98UppDec-84
❑ 98UppDecE-84
❑ 98UppDecE1o1-84
❑ 98UppDecGR-84

**Dandurand, Leo**
❑ 27LaPat-16
❑ 83HalFP-G5
❑ 85HalFC-96

**Daneyko, Ken**
❑ 86DevPol-9
❑ 87PanSti-76
❑ 88DevCar-9
❑ 89DevCar-9
❑ 89OPC-243
❑ 89PanSti-258
❑ 90Dev-10
❑ 90ProSet-165
❑ 90Sco-178
❑ 90ScoCan-178
❑ 90UppDec-427
❑ 90UppDecF-427
❑ 91Bow-284
❑ 91OPC-118
❑ 91PanSti-218
❑ 91Par-317
❑ 91ParFre-317
❑ 91Pin-142
❑ 91PinFre-142
❑ 91ProSet-139
❑ 91ProSetFre-139
❑ 91ScoAme-46
❑ 91ScoCan-46
❑ 91StaClu-103
❑ 91Top-118
❑ 91UppDec-435
❑ 91UppDecF-435
❑ 92Par-332
❑ 92ParEmel-332
❑ 92Pin-354
❑ 92PinFre-354
❑ 92Sco-53
❑ 92ScoCan-53
❑ 92Top-357
❑ 92TopGol-357G
❑ 92Ult-335
❑ 92UppDec-259
❑ 93OPCPre-236
❑ 93OPCPreG-236
❑ 93Par-387
❑ 93ParEmel-387
❑ 93Pin-134
❑ 93PinCan-134
❑ 93Sco-286
❑ 93ScoCan-286
❑ 93StaClu-206
❑ 93StaCluFDI-206
❑ 93StaCluFDIO-206
❑ 93StaCluO-206
❑ 93TopPre-236
❑ 93TopPreG-236
❑ 93Ult-358
❑ 94Lea-336
❑ 94OPCPre-79
❑ 94OPCPreSE-79
❑ 94Par-131
❑ 94ParGol-131
❑ 94Pin-330
❑ 94PinArtP-330
❑ 94PinRinC-330
❑ 94Sco-142
❑ 94ScoGol-142
❑ 94ScoPla-142
❑ 94ScoPlaTS-142
❑ 94TopPre-79
❑ 94TopPreSE-79
❑ 94Ult-318
❑ 95BeAPla-48
❑ 95BeAPSig-S48
❑ 95BeAPSigDC-S48
❑ 95Pin-177
❑ 95PinArtP-177
❑ 95PinRinC-177
❑ 95Top-188
❑ 95TopOPCI-188
❑ 95Ult-189
❑ 95UltGolM-189
❑ 96Dev-3
❑ 97Pac-325
❑ 97PacCop-325
❑ 97PacEmeGre-325
❑ 97PacIceB-325
❑ 97PacRed-325
❑ 97PacSil-325
❑ 97ScoDev-20
❑ 97ScoDevPla-20
❑ 97ScoDevPre-20
❑ 97UppDec-305
❑ 98O-PChr-101
❑ 98O-PChrR-101
❑ 98Top-101
❑ 98TopO-P-101
❑ 99Pac-236
❑ 99PacCop-236
❑ 99PacGol-236
❑ 99PacIceB-236
❑ 99PacPreD-236

**Daniel, Jarrod**
❑ 917thInnSWHL-184

**Daniels, Bob**
❑ 91FerStaB-9

**Daniels, Jeff**
❑ 88ProIHL-47
❑ 89ProIHL-146
❑ 91PenCokE-43
❑ 91ProAHLCHL-298
❑ 91ScoAme-400
❑ 91ScoCan-290
❑ 91UppDec-564
❑ 91UppDecF-564
❑ 92OPCPre-58
❑ 92Par-492
❑ 92ParEmel-492
❑ 92PenCokC-4
❑ 92Ult-377
❑ 92UppDec-508
❑ 93Lea-251
❑ 93OPCPre-343
❑ 93OPCPreG-343
❑ 93Par-429
❑ 93ParEmel-429
❑ 93PenFoo-11
❑ 93StaClu-483
❑ 93StaCluFDI-483
❑ 93StaCluO-483
❑ 93TopPre-343
❑ 93TopPreG-343
❑ 93UppDec-87
❑ 96SprFal-27

**Daniels, Kimbi**
❑ 907thInnSWHL-46
❑ 907thInnSWHL-72
❑ 91FlyJCP-5
❑ 91Par-346
❑ 91ParFre-346
❑ 91Pin-336
❑ 91PinFre-336
❑ 91ScoAme-399
❑ 91ScoCan-289
❑ 91UppDec-492
❑ 91UppDec-687
❑ 91UppDecCWJC-61
❑ 91UppDecF-492
❑ 91UppDecF-687
❑ 92StaClu-453
❑ 92UppDec-75

**Daniels, Mark**
❑ 91AirCanSJHL-D21

**Daniels, Scott**
❑ 86KamBla-5
❑ 88RegPat-3
❑ 89RegPat-3
❑ 90ProAHLIHL-192
❑ 91ProAHLCHL-112
❑ 95UppDec-328
❑ 96BeAPAut-170
❑ 96BeAPAutSil-170
❑ 96BeAPla-170
❑ 96FlyPos-4
❑ 96WhaBobS-5
❑ 97Be A PPAD-116
❑ 97Be A PPAPD-116
❑ 97BeAPla-116
❑ 97BeAPlaAut-116
❑ 98Be A PPA-229
❑ 98Be A PPAA-229
❑ 98Be A PPAAF-229
❑ 98Be A PPSE-229
❑ 98Be APG-229

**Daniels, Wayne**
❑ 91OshGen-22

**Danielsson, Ake**
❑ 69SweHocS-115
❑ 70SweHocS-72
❑ 71SweHocS-161
❑ 72SweHocS-156
❑ 73SweHocS-209
❑ 73SweWorCS-209
❑ 74SweHocS-165

**Danielsson, Bert**
❑ 69SweHocS-276

**Danielsson, Bjorn**
❑ 95ColCho-342
❑ 95ColChoPC-342
❑ 95ColChoPCP-342

**Danielsson, Gert**
❑ 69SweHocS-277

**Danielsson, Jan**
❑ 71SweHocS-209
❑ 72SweHocS-205

**Danielsson, Lars**
❑ 70SweHocS-3
❑ 71SweHocS-77
❑ 72SweHocS-52
❑ 73SweHocS-192
❑ 73SweWorCS-192
❑ 74SweHocS-164

**Danielsson, Martin**
❑ 92SweSemE-134

**Dano, Jozef**
❑ 95SloAPSNT-25
❑ 96SweSemW-236

**Danskin, Ruichard**
❑ 96FifFly-14

**Danyluk, Cam**
❑ 89PorWinH-4
❑ 907thInnSWHL-210
❑ 907thInnSWHL-320
❑ 917thInnSMC-84
❑ 917thInnSWHL-335

**Daoust, Andre**
❑ 69ColChe-4

**Daoust, Dan**
❑ 82CanaPos-4
❑ 82MapLeaP-7
❑ 83MapLeaP-3
❑ 83OPC-328
❑ 83OPCSti-28
❑ 83OPCSti-29
❑ 83Vac-83
❑ 84KelAccD-5B
❑ 84MapLeaP-7
❑ 84OPC-299
❑ 84OPCSti-9
❑ 84OPCSti-10
❑ 84Top-137
❑ 85MapLeaP-9
❑ 85OPC-164
❑ 85OPCSti-11
❑ 85Top-164
❑ 86KraDra-14
❑ 86OPC-241
❑ 86OPCSti-146
❑ 87MapLeaP-5
❑ 87MapLeaPLA-20
❑ 87MapLeaPO-5
❑ 88MapLeaPLA-20
❑ 88OPCSti-169
❑ 88PanSti-124
❑ 89OPC-277
❑ 89OPCSti-177
❑ 93SwiHNL-449
❑ 95SwiHNL-328

**Daoust, Eddy**
❑ 51LavDaiLSJ-1

**Dapuzzo, Pat**
❑ 90ProSet-684

**Darby, Craig**
❑ 93Cla-62
❑ 93FreCan-5
❑ 94Cla-86
❑ 94ClaAut-86
❑ 94ClaDraGol-86
❑ 94ClaProP-110
❑ 94FreCan-10
❑ 94UppDec-452
❑ 94UppDecElelce-452
❑ 95ColEdgI-92
❑ 95Ima-33
❑ 95ImaGol-33
❑ 95Pin-213
❑ 95PinArtP-213
❑ 95PinRinC-213
❑ 95Sco-305
❑ 95ScoBlaIce-305
❑ 95ScoBlaIceAP-305

**Darby, Kevin**
❑ 93FreCan-6

**Dark, Michael**
❑ 87BluKod-6
❑ 88SalLakCGE-2

**Darling, Dion**
❑ 94FreCan-11
❑ 95FreCan-9

**Darragh, Harold**
❑ 32O'KeeMapL-16

**Darragh, Jack**
❑ 10C55SweCP-17
❑ 11C55-17
❑ 12C57-29
❑ 23V1451-4
❑ 83HalFP-N3
❑ 85HalFC-199

**Dartsch, David**
❑ 96RicRen-3

**Darveau, Guy**
❑ 89ProAHL-193

**Dashney, Chris**
❑ 99WicThu-3

**Daskalakis, Cleon**
❑ 85MonGolF-14
❑ 86MonGolF-18

**Daugherty, Brent**
❑ 84SudWol-4
❑ 85SudWol-11
❑ 86SudWol-6

**Davey, Neil**
❑ 84PriAlbRS-5

**Daviault, Alex**
❑ 90KnoChe-118

**Davidson, Bob**
❑ 34BeeGro1P-312
❑ 36OPCV304D-100
❑ 36V356WorG-48
❑ 37OPCV304E-136
❑ 38QuaOatP-9
❑ 39OPCV3011-5
❑ 45QuaOatP-15
❑ 91UltOriS-33
❑ 91UltOriSF-33

**Davidson, Gord**
❑ 34BeeGro1P-270

**Davidson, John**
❑ 73BluWhiBor-3
❑ 74NHLActSta-239
❑ 74OPCNHL-11
❑ 74Top-11
❑ 75OPCNHL-183
❑ 75Top-183
❑ 76OPCNHL-204
❑ 76Top-204
❑ 77Coc-5
❑ 77OPCNHL-28
❑ 77Top-28
❑ 78OPC-211
❑ 78Top-211
❑ 79OPC-110
❑ 79Top-110
❑ 80OPC-190
❑ 80Top-190
❑ 81OPC-222
❑ 81Top-E95

**Davidson, Lee**
❑ 90MonHaw-2
❑ 90ProAHLIHL-256
❑ 91BriColJHL-159
❑ 91MonHaw-4
❑ 91ProAHLCHL-166
❑ 98GerDELE-189

**Davidson, Rick**
❑ 84VicCou-8
**Davidson, Ron**
❑ 81SweSemHVS-81
**Davidson, Scotty**
❑ 83HalFP-K2
❑ 85HalFC-137
**Davidson, Shawna**
❑ 94ClaWomOH-W25
**Davidson, Ty**
❑ 92BriColJHL-126
**Davidsson, Johan**
❑ 92SweSemE-353
❑ 93Par-538
❑ 93ParEmel-538
❑ 93SweSemE-118
❑ 94ParSE-SE236
❑ 94ParSEG-SE236
❑ 94SweLeaE-242
❑ 94SweLeaENHLD-2
❑ 95SigRoo-57
❑ 95SigRooSig-57
❑ 95SweGloWC-62
❑ 95SweLeaE-53
❑ 95SweUppDE-86
❑ 95SweUppDETNA-NA10
❑ 98BowBes-125
❑ 98BowBesAR-125
❑ 98BowBesR-125
❑ 98PacOmeH-9
❑ 98PacOmeODI-9
❑ 98PacOmeR-9
❑ 98SP Aut-91
❑ 98UppDec-211
❑ 98UppDecBD-3
❑ 98UppDecDD-3
❑ 98UppDecE-211
❑ 98UppDecE1o1-211
❑ 98UppDecGR-211
❑ 98UppDecM-4
❑ 98UppDecMGS-4
❑ 98UppDecMSS-4
❑ 98UppDecMSS-4
❑ 98UppDecQD-3
❑ 98UppDecTD-3
❑ 99Pac-2
❑ 99PacCop-2
❑ 99PacGol-2
❑ 99PacIceB-2
❑ 99PacPreD-2
❑ 99SP AutPS-91
❑ 99UppDecM-10
❑ 99UppDecMGS-10
❑ 99UppDecMSS-10
❑ 99UppDecMSS-10
**Davidsson, Mats**
❑ 65SweCorl-207
❑ 67SweHoc-266
❑ 69SweHocS-227
❑ 71SweHocS-372
**Davie, Bob**
❑ 34DiaMatS-19
**Davies, Curly**
❑ 52JunBluT-128
**Davies, Dan**
❑ 92BriColJHL-29
**Davies, Dave**
❑ 74SioCitM-2
**Davies, Greg**
❑ 83VicCou-6
❑ 87KamBla-5
❑ 88ProIHL-48
**Davies, Mark**
❑ 92BriColJHL-194
**Davis, Bob**
❑ 23V1281PauC-54
**Davis, Jean-Paul**
❑ 897thInnSOHL-6
❑ 89OshGen-6
❑ 907thInnSMC-80
❑ 907thInnSOHL-334
❑ 917thInnSOHL-164
❑ 91OshGen-27
❑ 91OshGenS-24
**Davis, Justin**
❑ 95Sla-115
❑ 96SauSteMG-4
❑ 96SauSteMGA-4
**Davis, Kelly**
❑ 81IndChe-3
❑ 82IndChe-1
**Davis, Lorne**
❑ 44BeeGro2P-232
**Davis, Malcolm**
❑ 84SabBluS-5
❑ 85OPCSti-186
❑ 85SabBluS-6
❑ 85SabBluSS-6
**Davis, Rick**
❑ 92CorBigRed-5
**Davis, Ryan**
❑ 95Sla-290
**Davis, Scott**
❑ 907thInnSWHL-16
**Davis, Troy**
❑ 92NorDakFS-6
**DaVita, David**
❑ 91ProAHLCHL-17
**Davydkin, Nikolai**
❑ 89SweSemE-31
❑ 91SweSemE-32
**Davydov, Evgeny**
❑ 90OPCRedA-18R
❑ 91Par-422
❑ 91ParFre-422
❑ 91RusStaRA-2
❑ 91SweSemWCS-92
❑ 92OPCPre-66
❑ 92Par-211
❑ 92Par-226
❑ 92ParEmel-211
❑ 92ParEmel-226
❑ 92Pin-226
❑ 92PinFre-226
❑ 92ProSet-244
❑ 92Sco-456
❑ 92ScoCan-456
❑ 92Top-115
❑ 92TopGol-115G
❑ 92Ult-441
❑ 92UppDec-420
❑ 92UppDecCC-CC19
❑ 92UppDecER-ER17
❑ 92UppDecES-E8
❑ 93Don-127
❑ 93Lea-24
❑ 93OPCPre-200
❑ 93OPCPre-444
❑ 93OPCPreG-200
❑ 93OPCPreG-444
❑ 93PanSti-194
❑ 93Par-78
❑ 93ParEmel-78
❑ 93Pin-109
❑ 93PinCan-109
❑ 93Pow-269
❑ 93Pow-397
❑ 93Sco-114
❑ 93Sco-499
❑ 93ScoCan-114
❑ 93ScoCan-499
❑ 93ScoGol-499
❑ 93StaClu-34
❑ 93StaClu-487
❑ 93StaCluFDI-34
❑ 93StaCluFDI-487
❑ 93StaCluFDIO-34
❑ 93StaCluO-34
❑ 93StaCluO-487
❑ 93TopPre-200
❑ 93TopPre-444
❑ 93TopPreG-200
❑ 93TopPreG-444
❑ 93Ult-58
❑ 93Ult-323
❑ 93UppDec-443
❑ 93UppDecSP-55
❑ 94OPCPre-518
❑ 94OPCPreSE-518
❑ 94Par-161
❑ 94ParGol-161
❑ 94Pin-202
❑ 94PinArtP-202
❑ 94PinRinC-202
❑ 94StaClu-66
❑ 94StaCluFDI-66
❑ 94StaCluMOMS-66
❑ 94StaCluSTWC-66
❑ 94TopPre-518
❑ 94TopPreSE-518
❑ 94Ult-147
❑ 94UppDec-49
❑ 94UppDecEleIce-49
**Davydov, Vitalij**
❑ 69SweHocS-2
❑ 69SweWorC-21
❑ 69SweWorC-74
❑ 69SweWorC-121
❑ 69SweWorC-122
❑ 69SweWorC-131
❑ 70SweHocS-315
❑ 71SweHocS-29
❑ 72SweSemWC-2
❑ 73SweHocS-122
❑ 73SweWorCS-122
❑ 74SweSemHVS-43
**Dawe, Jason**
❑ 897thInnSOHL-106
❑ 907thInnSOHL-357
❑ 917thInnSMC-113
❑ 917thInnSOHL-145
❑ 91AreDraPic-26
❑ 91Cla-31
❑ 91PetPet-1
❑ 91StaPicH-59
❑ 91UltDra-27
❑ 91UltDra-86
❑ 91UppDec-75
❑ 91UppDecF-75
❑ 93Cla-19
❑ 93Don-404
❑ 93PetPet-27
❑ 93UppDec-254
❑ 94ClaProP-88
❑ 94Don-245
❑ 94Lea-48
❑ 94OPCPre-149
❑ 94OPCPreSE-149
❑ 94ParSE-SE20
❑ 94ParSEG-SE20
❑ 94Pin-366
❑ 94PinArtP-366
❑ 94PinRinC-366
❑ 94TopPre-149
❑ 94TopPreSE-149
❑ 94Ult-21
❑ 94UppDec-167
❑ 94UppDecEleIce-167
❑ 95BeAPla-50
❑ 95BeAPSig-S50
❑ 95BeAPSigDC-S50
❑ 95ColEdgIC-C20
❑ 95Don-315
❑ 95Fin-158
❑ 95FinRef-158
❑ 95LeaLim-111
❑ 95Met-14
❑ 95ParInt-24
❑ 95ParIntEl-24
❑ 95Pin-123
❑ 95PinArtP-123
❑ 95PinRinC-123
❑ 95PlaOneoOne-230
❑ 95StaClu-147
❑ 95StaCluMOMS-147
❑ 95Top-128
❑ 95TopOPCI-128
❑ 95TopPowL-6PL
❑ 95Ult-16
❑ 95Ult-211
❑ 95UltGolM-16
❑ 95UppDec-61
❑ 95UppDecEleIce-61
❑ 95UppDecEleIceG-61
❑ 95UppDecSpeE-SE100
❑ 95UppDecSpeEdiG-SE100
❑ 96ColCho-31
❑ 96Don-165
❑ 96DonPrePro-165
❑ 96Fle-9
❑ 96FlePic-122
❑ 96Lea-93
❑ 96LeaPreP-93
❑ 96MetUni-13
❑ 96Pin-10
❑ 96PinArtP-10
❑ 96PinFoi-10
❑ 96PinPreS-10
❑ 96PinRinC-10
❑ 96PlaOneoOne-421
❑ 96Sco-59
❑ 96ScoArtPro-59
❑ 96ScoDeaCAP-59
❑ 96ScoGolB-59
❑ 96ScoSpeAP-59
❑ 96Ult-15
❑ 96UltGolM-15
❑ 96UppDec-19
❑ 96UppDecBD-139
❑ 96UppDecBDG-139
❑ 97ColCho-32
❑ 97Kat-14
❑ 97KatGol-14
❑ 97KatSil-14
❑ 97Pac-314
❑ 97PacCop-314
❑ 97PacCroR-12
❑ 97PacCroREG-12
❑ 97PacCroRIB-12
❑ 97PacCroRS-12
❑ 97PacEmeGre-314
❑ 97PacIceB-314
❑ 97PacInv-11
❑ 97PacInvC-11
❑ 97PacInvEG-11
❑ 97PacInvIB-11
❑ 97PacInvR-11
❑ 97PacInvS-11
❑ 97PacOme-20
❑ 97PacOmeC-20
❑ 97PacOmeDG-20
❑ 97PacOmeEG-20
❑ 97PacOmeG-20
❑ 97PacOmeIB-20
❑ 97PacPar-18
❑ 97PacParC-18
❑ 97PacParDG-18
❑ 97PacParEG-18
❑ 97PacParIB-18
❑ 97PacParRed-18
❑ 97PacParSil-18
❑ 97PacRed-314
❑ 97PacRev-13
❑ 97PacRevC-13
❑ 97PacRevE-13
❑ 97PacRevIB-13
❑ 97PacRevR-13
❑ 97PacRevS-13
❑ 97PacSil-314
❑ 97Sco-204
❑ 97ScoSab-7
❑ 97ScoSabPla-7
❑ 97ScoSabPre-7
❑ 97SPAut-13
❑ 97UppDec-19
❑ 97UppDecBD-30
❑ 97UppDecBDDD-30
❑ 97UppDecBDQD-30
❑ 97UppDecBDTD-30
❑ 98O-PChr-202
❑ 98O-PChrR-202
❑ 98Pac-280
❑ 98PacAur-115
❑ 98PacIceB-280
❑ 98PacPar-142
❑ 98PacParC-142
❑ 98PacParEG-142
❑ 98PacParH-142
❑ 98PacParIB-142
❑ 98PacParS-142
❑ 98PacRed-280
❑ 98Top-202
❑ 98TopO-P-202
❑ 98UppDec-129
❑ 98UppDecE-129
❑ 98UppDecE1o1-129
❑ 98UppDecGR-129
**Dawe, Wade**
❑ 95Sla-317
**Dawes, Robert**
❑ 44BeeGro2P-395
**Dawkins, Mark**
❑ 917thInnSWHL-310
**Dawson, Mike**
❑ 907thInnSOHL-56
❑ 917thInnSOHL-233
**Dawson, Wade**
❑ 91ProAHLCHL-162
**Day, Eric**
❑ 96MinGolGCAS-9
**Day, Hap (Clarence)**
❑ 24C144ChaCig-20
❑ 32O'KeeMapL-4
❑ 33OPCV304A-32
❑ 33V129-2
❑ 33V252CanG-17
❑ 33V288HamG-33
❑ 33V3572IceKP-2
❑ 33V357IceK-10
❑ 34BeeGro1P-313
❑ 36V356WorG-52
❑ 55Par-34
❑ 55ParQuaO-34
❑ 83HalFP-F4
❑ 85HalFC-80
❑ 94ParMisL-134
**Day, Joe**
❑ 90ProAHLIHL-181
❑ 91ProAHLCHL-103
❑ 91UppDec-516
❑ 91UppDecF-516
❑ 91WhaJr7E-11
❑ 94Par-138
❑ 94ParGol-138
**Dayley, Cory**
❑ 92BriColJHL-112
**Dayley, Wade**
❑ 91BriColJHL-47
❑ 92BriColJHL-116
**Dayman, Ryan**
❑ 92BriColJHL-31
**Daze, Eric**
❑ 94Fin-157
❑ 94FinRef-157
❑ 94FinSupTW-157
❑ 94LeaLimWJC-2
❑ 94Pin-529
❑ 94PinArtP-529
❑ 94PinRinC-529
❑ 94UppDec-497
❑ 94UppDecEleIce-497
❑ 95BAPLetL-LL4
❑ 95BeAPla-170
❑ 95BeAPSig-S170
❑ 95BeAPSigDC-S170
❑ 95Bow-125
❑ 95BowAllFoi-125
❑ 95BowBes-BB18
❑ 95BowBesRef-BB18
❑ 95ColCho-411
❑ 95Don-345
❑ 95DonCanWJT-15
❑ 95DonEli-63
❑ 95DonEliDCS-63
❑ 95DonEliDCU-63
❑ 95DonEliR-1
❑ 95DonRatRoo-6
❑ 95EmoGen-2
❑ 95Fin-3
❑ 95FinRef-3
❑ 95Ima-14
❑ 95ImaGol-14
❑ 95Lea-226
❑ 95LeaLim-65
❑ 95LeaLimRP-6
❑ 95LeaStuR-11
❑ 95Met-174
❑ 95ParInt-45
❑ 95ParIntCCGS2-16
❑ 95ParIntCCSS2-16
❑ 95ParIntEl-45
❑ 95ParIntPTP-PP40
❑ 95Pin-203
❑ 95PinArtP-203
❑ 95PinRinC-203
❑ 95PlaOneoOne-234
❑ 95Sco-312
❑ 95ScoBlaIce-312
❑ 95ScoBlaIceAP-312
❑ 95SelCer-132
❑ 95SelCerMG-132
❑ 95SkyImp-193
❑ 95SkyImpNHLF-17
❑ 95SP-22
❑ 95StaClu-195
❑ 95StaCluMOMS-195
❑ 95Sum-190
❑ 95SumArtP-190
❑ 95SumIce-190
❑ 95Top-26
❑ 95TopCanWJ-19CJ
❑ 95TopOPCI-26
❑ 95Ult-32
❑ 95Ult-335
❑ 95UltExtAtt-2
❑ 95UltGolM-32
❑ 95UppDec-268
❑ 95UppDecEleIce-268
❑ 95UppDecEleIceG-268
❑ 95UppDecPHE-H29
❑ 95UppDecPreH-H29
❑ 95Zen-122
❑ 95ZenRooRC-13
❑ 96ColCho-45
❑ 96ColCho-313
❑ 96ColChoCTG-C20A
❑ 96ColChoCTG-C20B
❑ 96ColChoCTG-C20C
❑ 96ColChoCTGG-C20A
❑ 96ColChoCTGG-C20B
❑ 96ColChoCTGG-C20C
❑ 96ColChoMVP-UD37
❑ 96ColChoMVPG-UD37
❑ 96DonCanI-20
❑ 96DonCanIGPP-20
❑ 96DonCanIOC-14
❑ 96DonCanIRPP-20
❑ 96DonDom-10
❑ 96DonEli-71
❑ 96DonEliAsp-1
❑ 96DonEliDCS-71
❑ 96DonHitLis-12
❑ 96DonRatR-1
❑ 96DurL'EB-JB4
❑ 96Fla-16
❑ 96FlaBluI-16
❑ 96FlaHotN-3
❑ 96Fle-17
❑ 96Fle-136
❑ 96FlePicF5-9
❑ 96FlePicFF-4
❑ 96FlePicJE-19
❑ 96FleRooSen-4
❑ 96Lea-202
❑ 96LeaLim-37
❑ 96LeaLimBTB-10
❑ 96LeaLimBTBLE-10
❑ 96LeaLimBTBP-P10
❑ 96LeaLimG-37
❑ 96LeaPre-61
❑ 96LeaPre-149
❑ 96LeaPreP-202
❑ 96LeaPrePP-61
❑ 96LeaPrePP-149
❑ 96LeaPreSG-25
❑ 96LeaPreSte-25
❑ 96LeaSwe-7
❑ 96LeaSwe(-7
❑ 96LeaTheBO.-2
❑ 96MetUni-27
❑ 96NHLACEPC-10
❑ 96Pin-212
❑ 96PinArtP-212
❑ 96PinByTN-11
❑ 96PinByTNP-11
❑ 96PinFoi-212
❑ 96PinMcD-3
❑ 96PinPreS-212
❑ 96PinRinC-212
❑ 96PinTeaP-10
❑ 96Sco-236
❑ 96ScoArtPro-236
❑ 96ScoChelt-16
❑ 96ScoDeaCAP-236
❑ 96ScoGolB-236
❑ 96ScoSam-236
❑ 96ScoSpeAP-236
❑ 96SelCer-79
❑ 96SelCerAP-79
❑ 96SelCerBlu-79
❑ 96SelCerMB-79
❑ 96SelCerMR-79
❑ 96SelCerRed-79
❑ 96SkyImp-19
❑ 96SkyImp-168
❑ 96SkyImpNHLF-7
❑ 96SP-26
❑ 96SPCleWin-CW20
❑ 96SPHolCol-HC2
❑ 96SPx-50
❑ 96SPx-GF1
❑ 96SPxGol-50
❑ 96StaCluMO-50
❑ 96Sum-151
❑ 96SumArtP-151
❑ 96SumHigV-7
❑ 96SumHigVM-7
❑ 96SumIce-151
❑ 96SumMet-151
❑ 96SumPreS-151
❑ 96TeaOut-9
❑ 96TopNHLP-77
❑ 96TopPicOI-77
❑ 96TopPicRS-RS4
❑ 96Ult-31
❑ 96UltGolM-31
❑ 96UppDec-29
❑ 96UppDec-359
❑ 96UppDecGN-X19
❑ 96UppDecIce-79
❑ 96UppDecIcePar-79
❑ 96UppDecLSH-LS15
❑ 96UppDecLSHF-LS15
❑ 96UppDecLSHS-LS15
❑ 96UppDecSS-SS18B
❑ 96Zen-99
❑ 96ZenArtP-99
❑ 96ZenZT-14
❑ 97BeAPlaTAN-2
❑ 97ColCho-53
❑ 97ColChoSta-SQ15
❑ 97Don-192
❑ 97DonCanI-21
❑ 97DonCanIDS-21
❑ 97DonCanIPS-21
❑ 97DonLim-65
❑ 97DonLimExp-65
❑ 97DonPre-116
❑ 97DonPreCttC-116
❑ 97DonPreProG-192
❑ 97DonPreProS-192
❑ 97DonPri-26
❑ 97DonPriSoA-26
❑ 97Lea-97
❑ 97LeaFraMat-97
❑ 97LeaFraMDC-97
❑ 97LeaInt-97
❑ 97LeaIntUI-97
❑ 97Pac-108
❑ 97PacCop-108
❑ 97PacCroR-29
❑ 97PacCroREG-29
❑ 97PacCroRIB-29
❑ 97PacCroRS-29
❑ 97PacDyn-26
❑ 97PacDynC-26
❑ 97PacDynDG-26
❑ 97PacDynEG-26
❑ 97PacDynIB-26
❑ 97PacDynR-26
❑ 97PacDynSil-26
❑ 97PacDynTan-31
❑ 97PacEmeGre-108
❑ 97PacIceB-108
❑ 97PacInv-29
❑ 97PacInvC-29
❑ 97PacInvEG-29
❑ 97PacInvIB-29
❑ 97PacInvR-29
❑ 97PacInvS-29
❑ 97PacOme-49
❑ 97PacOmeC-49
❑ 97PacOmeDG-49
❑ 97PacOmeEG-49
❑ 97PacOmeG-49
❑ 97PacOmeIB-49
❑ 97PacPar-43
❑ 97PacParC-43
❑ 97PacParDG-43
❑ 97PacParEG-43
❑ 97PacParIB-43
❑ 97PacParRed-43
❑ 97PacParSil-43
❑ 97PacRed-108
❑ 97PacRev-29
❑ 97PacRevC-29
❑ 97PacRevE-29
❑ 97PacRevIB-29
❑ 97PacRevR-29
❑ 97PacRevS-29
❑ 97PacSil-108
❑ 97Pin-121
❑ 97PinCer-122
❑ 97PinCerMB-122
❑ 97PinCerMG-122
❑ 97PinCerMR-122
❑ 97PinCerR-122
❑ 97PinIns-88
❑ 97PinInsCC-88
❑ 97PinInsEC-88
❑ 97PinPrePBB-121
❑ 97PinPrePBC-121
❑ 97PinPrePBM-121
❑ 97PinPrePBY-121
❑ 97PinPrePFC-121
❑ 97PinPrePFM-121
❑ 97PinPrePFY-121
❑ 97PinPrePla-121
❑ 97PinTotCMPG-122
❑ 97PinTotCPB-122
❑ 97PinTotCPG-122
❑ 97PinTotCPR-122
❑ 97Sco-193
❑ 97SPAut-31
❑ 97UppDec-41
❑ 97UppDecBD-63
❑ 97UppDecBDDD-63
❑ 97UppDecBDQD-63
❑ 97UppDecBDTD-63
❑ 97Zen-55
❑ 97Zen5x7-54
❑ 97ZenGolImp-54
❑ 97ZenSilImp-54
❑ 97ZenZGol-55
❑ 97ZenZSil-55
❑ 98Be A PPA-179
❑ 98Be A PPAA-179
❑ 98Be A PPAAF-179
❑ 98Be A PPSE-179
❑ 98Be APG-179
❑ 98Fin-66
❑ 98FinNo P-66
❑ 98FinNo PR-66
❑ 98FinRef-66
❑ 98O-PChr-195
❑ 98O-PChrR-195
❑ 98Pac-143
❑ 98PacAur-40
❑ 98PacCroR-29
❑ 98PacCroRLS-29
❑ 98PacDynI-40
❑ 98PacDynIIB-40
❑ 98PacDynIR-40
❑ 98PacIceB-143
❑ 98PacOmeH-50
❑ 98PacOmeODI-50
❑ 98PacOmeR-50
❑ 98PacPar-46
❑ 98PacParC-46
❑ 98PacParEG-46
❑ 98PacParH-46
❑ 98PacParIB-46
❑ 98PacParS-46
❑ 98PacRed-143
❑ 98PacRev-30
❑ 98PacRevIS-30
❑ 98PacRevR-30
❑ 98Top-195
❑ 98TopGolLC1-98
❑ 98TopGolLC1B-98
❑ 98TopGolLC1BOoO-98
❑ 98TopGolLC1OoO-98
❑ 98TopGolLC1R-98
❑ 98TopGolLC1ROoO-98
❑ 98TopGolLC2-98
❑ 98TopGolLC2B-98
❑ 98TopGolLC2BOoO-98
❑ 98TopGolLC2OoO-98
❑ 98TopGolLC2R-98
❑ 98TopGolLC2ROoO-98
❑ 98TopGolLC3-98
❑ 98TopGolLC3B-98
❑ 98TopGolLC3BOoO-98
❑ 98TopGolLC3OoO-98
❑ 98TopGolLC3R-98
❑ 98TopGolLC3ROoO-98
❑ 98UC-45
❑ 98UD ChoPCR-45
❑ 98UD ChoR-45
❑ 98UDCP-45
❑ 98UppDec-68
❑ 98UppDecE-68
❑ 98UppDecE1o1-68
❑ 98UppDecGR-68
❑ 98UppDecM-48
❑ 98UppDecMGS-48
❑ 98UppDecMSS-48
❑ 98UppDecMSS-48
❑ 99Pac-85
❑ 99PacCop-85
❑ 99PacGol-85
❑ 99PacIceB-85
❑ 99PacPreD-85
**De Jonge, Gavin**
❑ 93HumHawP-2
❑ 94HumHawP-NNO
**De Piero, Bob**
❑ 82SweSemHVS-140
**De Raaf, Helmut**
❑ 91SweSemWCS-152
❑ 93SweSemWCS-149
❑ 94GerDELE-78
❑ 95GerDELE-76
**de Ruiter, Chris**
❑ 92ClaKni-18
**De Santis, Mark**
❑ 94ClaProP-77
**De Toni, Lino**
❑ 93SweSemWCS-223
❑ 94FinnJaaK-306
**Dea, Billy**
❑ 44BeeGro2P-159
❑ 44BeeGro2P-306
❑ 57Top-39
❑ 68OPC-190
❑ 70EssPowPla-142
❑ 70OPC-30
❑ 70SarProSta-53
❑ 70Top-30
❑ 76OldTim-5
❑ 81RedWinOld-11
❑ 94ParMisL-47
**Deacon, Don**
❑ 39OPCV3011-70
**Deadmarsh, Adam**
❑ 917thInnSWHL-32
❑ 92UppDec-609
❑ 93Cla-20
❑ 93DonTeaUSA-5
❑ 93Pin-491
❑ 93PinCan-491
❑ 93UppDec-562
❑ 94BeAPla-R165
❑ 94ClaTri-T55
❑ 94Fin-31
❑ 94Fin-118
❑ 94FinBowB-R13
❑ 94FinBowBR-R13
❑ 94FinRef-31
❑ 94FinRef-118
❑ 94FinSupTW-31
❑ 94FinSupTW-118
❑ 94Fla-144
❑ 94Fle-174
❑ 94Lea-442
❑ 94LeaLimWJUSA-4
❑ 94NordBurK-4
❑ 94OPCPre-449
❑ 94OPCPreSE-449
❑ 94ParSE-SE144
❑ 94ParSE-SE246
❑ 94ParSEG-SE144
❑ 94ParSEG-SE246
❑ 94Pin-253
❑ 94PinArtP-253
❑ 94PinRinC-253
❑ 94Sel-179
❑ 94SelGol-179
❑ 94SPPre-15
❑ 94SPPreDC-15
❑ 94TopPre-449
❑ 94TopPreSE-449
❑ 94Ult-355
❑ 94UppDec-261

❑ 94UppDec-562
❑ 94UppDecEleIce-261
❑ 94UppDecEleIce-562
❑ 94UppDecSPI-SP155
❑ 94UppDecSPIDC-SP155
❑ 95BeAPla-186
❑ 95BeAPSig-S186
❑ 95BeAPSigDC-S186
❑ 95CanGamNHLP-81
❑ 95ColCho-294
❑ 95ColCho-360
❑ 95ColChoPC-294
❑ 95ColChoPC-360
❑ 95ColChoPCP-294
❑ 95ColChoPCP-360
❑ 95Don-145
❑ 95Ima-60
❑ 95ImaAut-60A
❑ 95ImaGol-60
❑ 95Lea-72
❑ 95Met-30
❑ 95ParInt-54
❑ 95ParIntEl-54
❑ 95Pin-72
❑ 95PinArtP-72
❑ 95PinRinC-72
❑ 95PlaOneoOne-136
❑ 95Sco-168
❑ 95ScoBlaIce-168
❑ 95ScoBlaIceAP-168
❑ 95ScoChelt-6
❑ 95SkyImpNHLF-4
❑ 95SP-33
❑ 95Top-288
❑ 95TopNewG-6NG
❑ 95TopOPCI-288
❑ 95Ult-130
❑ 95UltGolM-130
❑ 95UppDec-65
❑ 95UppDecEleIce-65
❑ 95UppDecEleIceG-65
❑ 95UppDecSpeE-SE22
❑ 95UppDecSpeEdiG-SE22
❑ 96ColCho-58
❑ 96Don-145
❑ 96DonPrePro-145
❑ 96MetUni-30
❑ 96Pin-43
❑ 96PinArtP-43
❑ 96PinFoi-43
❑ 96PinPreS-43
❑ 96PinRinC-43
❑ 96Sco-93
❑ 96ScoArtPro-93
❑ 96ScoDeaCAP-93
❑ 96ScoGolB-93
❑ 96ScoSpeAP-93
❑ 96SP-36
❑ 96SPCleWin-CW17
❑ 96TopNHLP-103
❑ 96TopPicOI-103
❑ 96Ult-34
❑ 96UltGolM-34
❑ 96UppDec-41
❑ 96UppDecBD-81
❑ 96UppDecBDG-81
❑ 96UppDecGN-X25
❑ 96UppDecPP-P23
❑ 97Be A PPAD-52
❑ 97Be A PPAPD-52
❑ 97BeAPla-52
❑ 97BeAPlaAut-52
❑ 97ColCho-57
❑ 97ColChoSta-SQ45
❑ 97Don-161
❑ 97DonCanI-126
❑ 97DonCanIDS-126
❑ 97DonCanIPS-126
❑ 97DonEli-75
❑ 97DonEliAsp-75
❑ 97DonEliS-75
❑ 97DonLim-95
❑ 97DonLim-132
❑ 97DonLim-161
❑ 97DonLimExp-95
❑ 97DonLimExp-132
❑ 97DonLimExp-161
❑ 97DonPre-53
❑ 97DonPreCttC-53
❑ 97DonPreProG-161
❑ 97DonPreProS-161
❑ 97DonPri-163
❑ 97DonPriSoA-163
❑ 97DonRedAle-1
❑ 97Kat-37
❑ 97KatGol-37
❑ 97KatSil-37
❑ 97Lea-57
❑ 97LeaFraMat-57
❑ 97LeaFraMDC-57
❑ 97LeaInt-57
❑ 97LeaIntUI-57
❑ 97Pac-47
❑ 97PacCop-47
❑ 97PacCroR-32
❑ 97PacCroREG-32
❑ 97PacCroRIB-32
❑ 97PacCroRS-32
❑ 97PacEmeGre-47
❑ 97PacIceB-47
❑ 97PacInv-33
❑ 97PacInvC-33
❑ 97PacInvEG-33
❑ 97PacInvIB-33
❑ 97PacInvR-33
❑ 97PacInvS-33
❑ 97PacOme-55
❑ 97PacOmeC-55
❑ 97PacOmeDG-55
❑ 97PacOmeEG-55
❑ 97PacOmeG-55
❑ 97PacOmeIB-55
❑ 97PacPar-48
❑ 97PacParC-48
❑ 97PacParDG-48
❑ 97PacParEG-48
❑ 97PacParIB-48
❑ 97PacParRed-48
❑ 97PacParSil-48
❑ 97PacRed-47
❑ 97PacSil-47
❑ 97Pin-114
❑ 97PinCer-112
❑ 97PinCerMB-112
❑ 97PinCerMG-112
❑ 97PinCerMR-112
❑ 97PinCerR-112
❑ 97PinIns-170
❑ 97PinPrePBB-114
❑ 97PinPrePBC-114
❑ 97PinPrePBM-114
❑ 97PinPrePBY-114
❑ 97PinPrePFC-114
❑ 97PinPrePFM-114
❑ 97PinPrePFY-114
❑ 97PinPrePla-114
❑ 97PinTotCMPG-112
❑ 97PinTotCPB-112
❑ 97PinTotCPG-112
❑ 97PinTotCPR-112
❑ 97Sco-146
❑ 97ScoArtPro-146
❑ 97ScoAva-8
❑ 97ScoAvaPla-8
❑ 97ScoAvaPre-8
❑ 97ScoGolBla-146
❑ 97SPAut-40
❑ 97Stu-70
❑ 97StuPrePG-70
❑ 97StuPrePS-70
❑ 97UppDec-46
❑ 97UppDecBD-75
❑ 97UppDecBDDD-75
❑ 97UppDecBDQD-75
❑ 97UppDecBDTD-75
❑ 97UppDecIce-18
❑ 97UppDecIceP-18
❑ 97UppDecIPS-18
❑ 97UppDecTSS-13A
❑ 98Be A PPA-36
❑ 98Be A PPAA-36
❑ 98Be A PPAAF-36
❑ 98Be A PPTBASG-36
❑ 98Be APG-36
❑ 98Fin-79
❑ 98FinNo P-79
❑ 98FinNo PR-79
❑ 98FinRef-79
❑ 98Pac-18
❑ 98PacAur-45
❑ 98PacDynI-45
❑ 98PacDynIIB-45
❑ 98PacDynIR-45
❑ 98PacIceB-18
❑ 98PacOmeH-58
❑ 98PacOmeODI-58
❑ 98PacOmeR-58
❑ 98PacPar-53
❑ 98PacParC-53
❑ 98PacParEG-53
❑ 98PacParH-53
❑ 98PacParIB-53
❑ 98PacParS-53
❑ 98PacRed-18
❑ 98PacRev-33
❑ 98PacRevIS-33
❑ 98PacRevR-33
❑ 98SP Aut-23
❑ 98SP AutSotTG-AD
❑ 98SSASotT-AD
❑ 98UC-57
❑ 98UD ChoPCR-57
❑ 98UD ChoR-57
❑ 98UppDec-72
❑ 98UppDecE-72
❑ 98UppDecE1o1-72
❑ 98UppDecGR-72
❑ 98UppDecM-58
❑ 98UppDecMGS-58
❑ 98UppDecMSS-58
❑ 98UppDecMSS-58
❑ 99Pac-101
❑ 99PacAur-35
❑ 99PacAurPD-35
❑ 99PacCop-101
❑ 99PacGol-101
❑ 99PacIceB-101
❑ 99PacPreD-101
❑ 99RetHoc-23
❑ 99SP AutPS-23
❑ 99UppDecM-57
❑ 99UppDecMGS-57
❑ 99UppDecMSS-57
❑ 99UppDecMSS-57
❑ 99UppDecRG-23
❑ 99UppDecRP-23

**Deadmarsh, Butch**
❑ 74OPCNHL-73
❑ 75OPCWHA-59
❑ 76OPCWHA-53

**Deadmarsh, Jake**
❑ 95SigRooA-12
❑ 95SigRooAPC-12
❑ 96KamBla-7

**Dean, Barry**
❑ 75RoaPhoWHA-21
❑ 76RocCokCan-5
❑ 77OPCNHL-183
❑ 77Top-183
❑ 78OPC-142
❑ 78Top-142
❑ 79OPC-318

**Dean, Bob**
❑ 61HamRed-3

**Dean, Kevin**
❑ 91ProAHLCHL-417
❑ 95Top-208
❑ 95TopOPCI-208
❑ 96Dev-28
❑ 97Be A PPAD-57
❑ 97Be A PPAPD-57
❑ 97BeAPla-57
❑ 97BeAPlaAut-57
❑ 98Be A PPA-82
❑ 98Be A PPAA-82
❑ 98Be A PPAAF-82
❑ 98Be A PPTBASG-82
❑ 98Be APG-82

**DeAngelis, Mike**
❑ 85MinDul-3
❑ 93SweSemWCS-214
❑ 95FinnSemWC-172

**Deasley, Bryan**
❑ 90ProAHLIHL-619
❑ 91ProAHLCHL-580

**Deazley, Mark**
❑ 897thInnSOHL-10
❑ 89OshGen-10
❑ 89OshGenP-19
❑ 907thInnSMC-97
❑ 907thInnSOHL-335
❑ 917thInnSOHL-153
❑ 91OshGen-26
❑ 91OshGenS-17
❑ 92TolSto-12
❑ 93TolSto-14
❑ 95TalTigS-6

**Debenedet, Nelson**
❑ 74NHLActSta-232
❑ 74OPCNHL-293
❑ 74PenPos-5
❑ 81RedWinOld-12

**DeBlois, Lucien**
❑ 78OPC-136
❑ 78Top-136
❑ 79Roc-6
❑ 80OPC-146
❑ 80Top-146
❑ 81JetPos-4
❑ 81OPC-74
❑ 81OPCSti-232
❑ 81Top-W79
❑ 82Jet-6
❑ 82OPC-379
❑ 82OPCSti-212
❑ 82PosCer-21
❑ 83Jet-5
❑ 83OPC-378
❑ 83OPC-383
❑ 83OPCSti-285
❑ 83Vac-125
❑ 84CanaPos-5
❑ 84OPC-260
❑ 84OPCSti-290
❑ 85CanaPos-8
❑ 85CanaPro-4
❑ 89Nord-6
❑ 89NordGenF-4
❑ 89NordPol-3
❑ 90NordPet-4
❑ 90NordTeal-2
❑ 90OPC-441
❑ 90PanSti-140
❑ 90ProSet-244
❑ 90ProSet-531
❑ 90UppDec-363
❑ 90UppDecF-363
❑ 91MapLeaP-8
❑ 91OPC-102
❑ 91PanSti-100
❑ 91ProSet-491
❑ 91ProSetFre-491
❑ 91ScoCan-395
❑ 91Top-102
❑ 92DurPan-2
❑ 92Sco-371
❑ 92ScoCan-371

**DeBoer, Peter (Pete)**
❑ 89ProIHL-169
❑ 90ProAHLIHL-330
❑ 93DetJrRW-24
❑ 95Sla-80
❑ 95SlaMemC-100
❑ 96DetWha-21

**Debol, Dave**
❑ 79OPC-363
❑ 79PanSti-215
❑ 80OPC-381

**Debrie, Darren**
❑ 95Sla-270

**DeBrusk, Louie**
❑ 897thInnSOHL-28
❑ 907thInnSOHL-132
❑ 91OilIGA-4
❑ 91OilTeal-5
❑ 91Par-281
❑ 91ParFre-281
❑ 91Pin-347
❑ 91PinFre-347
❑ 91ProSet-535
❑ 91ProSetFre-535
❑ 91UppDec-249
❑ 91UppDec-526
❑ 91UppDecF-249
❑ 91UppDecF-526
❑ 92Bow-318
❑ 92OilIGA-5
❑ 92OilTeal-4
❑ 92StaClu-290
❑ 92Top-392
❑ 92TopGol-392G
❑ 92UppDec-467
❑ 93Don-108
❑ 93Lea-225
❑ 93OPCPre-319
❑ 93OPCPreG-319
❑ 93Par-337
❑ 93ParEmel-337
❑ 93TopPre-319
❑ 93TopPreG-319
❑ 93UppDec-79
❑ 94BeAPla-R89
❑ 94BeAPSig-29
❑ 94Lea-532
❑ 94UppDec-485
❑ 94UppDecEleIce-485
❑ 95ColCho-87
❑ 95ColChoPC-87
❑ 95ColChoPCP-87
❑ 95ParInt-81
❑ 95ParIntEl-81
❑ 96ColCho-100
❑ 96OilPos-29
❑ 97PacDynBKS-37
❑ 97PacOme-211
❑ 97PacOmeC-211
❑ 97PacOmeDG-211
❑ 97PacOmeEG-211
❑ 97PacOmeG-211
❑ 97PacOmeIB-211
❑ 98Pac-398
❑ 98PacIceB-398
❑ 98PacRed-398

**DeBus, Steve**
❑ 94MinGolG-10
❑ 95MinGolG-11
❑ 96MinGolGCAS-10

**Debusschere, Dave**
❑ 91AirCanSJHL-D46
❑ 92MPSPhoSJHL-8

**Decaen, Steve**
❑ 917thInnSQMJHL-153

**DeCarle, Mike**
❑ 89ProIHL-104
❑ 91NasKni-19
❑ 92NasKni-15

**Decary, Ed**
❑ 10C56-13

**DeCecco, Bret**
❑ 96SeaThu-16
❑ 97UppDec-409
❑ 98BowBes-149
❑ 98BowBesAR-149
❑ 98BowBesR-149
❑ 98BowCHL-59
❑ 98BowCHLGA-59
❑ 98BowCHLOI-59
❑ 98BowChrC-59
❑ 98BowChrCGA-59
❑ 98BowChrCGAR-59
❑ 98BowChrCOI-59
❑ 98BowChrCOIR-59
❑ 98BowChrCR-59

**Decelles, Luc**
❑ 93DruVol-20

**Dechaine, Chris**
❑ 92MPSPhoSJHL-107

**DeCiantis, Rob**
❑ 94KitRan-21
❑ 95Cla-87
❑ 95Sla-141
❑ 96KitRan-6

**Deck, Kim**
❑ 87KamBla-6
❑ 88KamBla-9
❑ 89PorWinH-5
❑ 907thInnSWHL-156
❑ 907thInnSWHL-323

**Decker, Todd**
❑ 87KamBla-7

**DeCoff, Mike**
❑ 89OshGenP-4
❑ 907thInnSOHL-155
❑ 917thInnSMC-15

**Decorby, Ian**
❑ 94EriPan-20

**DeCosty, Derek**
❑ 92WheThu-4
❑ 93WheThu-4
❑ 94WheThu-6
❑ 96GuiFla-17

**Deeks, Alain**
❑ 92HamCan-5
❑ 94KnoChe-16

**Defazio, Dan**
❑ 82OshGen-14

**DeFazio, Jerrett**
❑ 897thInnSOHL-57
❑ 907thInnSOHL-82

**Defelice, Norman**
❑ 44BeeGro2P-66A
❑ 52JunBluT-18

**Defrenza, Fran**
❑ 907thInnSWHL-98
❑ 917thInnSWHL-54

**Defty, Ian**
❑ 97KinHaw-19

**Degaetano, Phil**
❑ 88ProAHL-164
❑ 94FinnJaaK-294

**Degagne, Rob**
❑ 82NorBayC-3
❑ 83NorBayC-7

**Degagne, Shawn**
❑ 96KitRan-7

**Degerstedt, Patrik**
❑ 93SweSemE-91
❑ 98GerDELE-289

**DeGiacomo, Dwight**
❑ 90MicTecHus-3

**Degner, Terry**
❑ 907thInnSWHL-99
❑ 917thInnSWHL-290

**DeGrace, Yanick**
❑ 907thInnSQMJHL-170
❑ 917thInnSQMJHL-208

**DeGray, Dale**
❑ 80OshGen-11
❑ 81OshGen-14
❑ 82OshGen-4
❑ 84MonGolF-11
❑ 85MonGolF-20
❑ 87MapLeaPLA-25
❑ 88KinSmo-5
❑ 89OPC-18
❑ 89Top-18
❑ 90ProAHLIHL-279
❑ 92SanDieG-5
❑ 95ColEdgI-111
❑ 96CinCyc-51

**Deguise, Michel**
❑ 88RivDu R-11

**Dehaime, Trevor**
❑ 907thInnSQMJHL-210

**Dehart, John**
❑ 91BriColJHL-99
❑ 91BriColJHL-159
❑ 91BriColJHL-164
❑ 92CorBigRed-6
❑ 93CorBigRed-6

**Deis, Tyler**
❑ 92MPSPhoSJHL-52

**Deiter, Thomas**
❑ 94GerDELE-432

**DeJordy, Denis**
❑ 61Top-37
❑ 62Top-25
❑ 63Top-24
❑ 64BeeGro3P-32
❑ 64CocCap-36
❑ 64Top-22
❑ 65Top-113
❑ 66Top-115
❑ 66TopUSAT-50
❑ 67Top-65
❑ 67Top-115
❑ 68OPC-12
❑ 68ShiCoi-20
❑ 68Top-12
❑ 69OPC-66
❑ 69OPCFou-7
❑ 69Top-66
❑ 70ColSta-84
❑ 70DadCoo-20
❑ 70EssPowPla-162
❑ 70OPC-31
❑ 70SarProSta-73
❑ 70Top-31
❑ 71Baz-8
❑ 71CanaPos-4
❑ 71OPC-63
❑ 71Top-63
❑ 71TorSun-110
❑ 72OPC-184
❑ 72SarProSta-130
❑ 72Top-144
❑ 73RedWinTI-7
❑ 94ParTalB-28
❑ 95Par66-39
❑ 95Par66Coi-39

**Del Monte, Dion**
❑ 96GerDELE-331
❑ 97SheSte-10

**Delaronde, Shane**
❑ 95Sla-10

**Delarosbil, Raymond**
❑ 907thInnSQMJHL-178
❑ 917thInnSQMJHL-155
❑ 93DruVol-18

**Delcourt, Grant**
❑ 84KelWin-18

**Delesoy, Jason**
❑ 92BriColJHL-16

**Deleurme, Jason**
❑ 93TacRoc-6
❑ 98BowCHL-49
❑ 98BowCHLGA-49
❑ 98BowCHLOI-49
❑ 98BowChrC-49
❑ 98BowChrCGA-49
❑ 98BowChrCGAR-49
❑ 98BowChrCOI-49
❑ 98BowChrCOIR-49
❑ 98BowChrCR-49

**Delfino, David**
❑ 93SweSemWCS-209
❑ 94FinnJaaK-291

**DelGuidice, Matt**
❑ 90ProAHLIHL-125
❑ 91OPCPre-96
❑ 91Par-1
❑ 91ParFre-1
❑ 91ProSet-521
❑ 91ProSetFre-521
❑ 91UppDec-463
❑ 91UppDecF-463
❑ 93RalIce-3
❑ 95RoaExp-3

**Delianedis, Dan**
❑ 88ProAHL-330

**DeLisle, Joe**
❑ 85MinDul-29

**Delisle, Jonathan**
❑ 95SlaMemC-70
❑ 97BowCHL-55
❑ 97BowCHLOPC-55

**Delisle, Xavier**
❑ 94ParSE-SE255
❑ 94ParSEG-SE255
❑ 94SP-178
❑ 94SPDieCut-178

**Deliva, Joey**
❑ 917thInnSQMJHL-204

**Dell'Jannone, Patrick**
❑ 82SweSemHVS-133

**Dellaire, Stacy**
❑ 907thInnSQMJHL-172

**Delmonte, Dan**
❑ 93PetPet-24
❑ 94SarSti-17

**Delmore, Andy**
❑ 93NorBayC-5
❑ 95SigRooA-13
❑ 95SigRooAPC-13
❑ 95Sla-336
❑ 96SarSti-7
❑ 97BowCHL-34
❑ 97BowCHLOPC-34

**Delorimiere, Bob**
❑ 94BraSmo-2
❑ 96ForWorF-6

**Delorme, Gilbert**
❑ 81CanaPos-5
❑ 82CanaPos-5
❑ 82CanaSte-3
❑ 83CanaPos-7
❑ 83OPC-186
❑ 83OPCSti-70
❑ 83Vac-43
❑ 85NordGenF-5
❑ 85NordMcD-4
❑ 85NordPro-6
❑ 85NordTeal-5
❑ 86NordGenF-5
❑ 86NordMcD-5
❑ 86NordYumY-2
❑ 86OPC-234
❑ 86OPCSti-28
❑ 87RedWinLC-7
❑ 88RedWinLC-5
❑ 89PenFoo-6B
❑ 90OPC-517
❑ 91ProAHLCHL-300
❑ 92CleLum-6
❑ 93CleLum-3
❑ 93CleLumPos-6

**Delorme, Marc**
❑ 94BraSmo-19

**Delorme, Rene**
❑ 77GraVic-8

**Delorme, Ron**
❑ 77RocCokCan-4
❑ 78OPC-323
❑ 79OPC-284
❑ 79Roc-7
❑ 80OPC-321
❑ 81OPC-82
❑ 81OPCSti-231
❑ 82Canu-5
❑ 82OPC-347
❑ 82PosCer-19
❑ 83Canu-5
❑ 83OPC-348
❑ 83Vac-104
❑ 84Canu-7
❑ 84KelWin-39
❑ 84OPC-205

**Delparte, Guy**
❑ 76RocCokCan-6
❑ 76RocPucBuc-6

**Delvecchio, Alex**
❑ 44BeeGro2P-160
❑ 51Par-63
❑ 52Par-53
❑ 53Par-47
❑ 54Par-36
❑ 54Par-90
❑ 54Top-39
❑ 57Top-34
❑ 58Top-52
❑ 59Top-8
❑ 60Par-36
❑ 60ShiCoi-44
❑ 61Par-25
❑ 61ShiCoi-70
❑ 62Par-32
❑ 62YorIroOTra-21
❑ 63ChePho-9
❑ 63Par-50
❑ 63TorSta-9
❑ 63YorWhiB-50
❑ 64BeeGro3P-67A
❑ 64BeeGro3P-67B
❑ 64CocCap-45B
❑ 64Top-95
❑ 64TorSta-8
❑ 65Coc-44
❑ 65Top-47
❑ 66Top-102
❑ 66TopUSAT-63
❑ 67Top-51
❑ 68OPC-28
❑ 68ShiCoi-37
❑ 68Top-28
❑ 69OPC-157
❑ 69OPC-206
❑ 69OPCFou-18
❑ 69Top-64
❑ 70ColSta-4
❑ 70DadCoo-21
❑ 70EssPowPla-135
❑ 70OPC-157
❑ 70RedWinM-3
❑ 70SarProSta-59
❑ 71Baz-7
❑ 71OPC-37
❑ 71OPCTBoo-12
❑ 71SarProSta-55
❑ 71Top-37
❑ 71TorSun-91
❑ 72OPC-26
❑ 72SarProSta-76
❑ 72SweSemWC-193
❑ 72Top-141
❑ 73OPC-1
❑ 73RedWinTI-8
❑ 73Top-141
❑ 74OPCNHL-222
❑ 74Top-222
❑ 76OldTim-6
❑ 81RedWinOld-13
❑ 83HalFP-E7
❑ 85HalFC-230
❑ 90ProSet-652
❑ 90ProSet-658
❑ 91ParPHC-PHC2
❑ 91ParPHCF-PHC2
❑ 91StaPicH-10
❑ 91UltOriS-68
❑ 91UltOriSF-68
❑ 92ParParR-PR19
❑ 94ParMisL-59
❑ 94ParTalB-56
❑ 95Par66-53
❑ 95Par66-127
❑ 95Par66Coi-53
❑ 99RetHoc-89
❑ 99UppDecRG-89
❑ 99UppDecRII-AD
❑ 99UppDecRIL1-AD
❑ 99UppDecRP-89

**DeMaio, Frank**
❑ 90ArIIce-6

**DeMarco, Ab**
❑ 69SweHocS-353
❑ 69SweWorC-32
❑ 71OPC-90
❑ 71TorSun-169
❑ 73BluWhiBor-4
❑ 73OPC-118
❑ 73Top-118
❑ 74CanuRoyB-5
❑ 74NHLActSta-218
❑ 74NHLActStaU-38
❑ 74OPCNHL-89
❑ 74Top-89
❑ 75CanuRoyB-6
❑ 75OPCNHL-78
❑ 75Top-78
❑ 76OPCNHL-374
❑ 77OPCNHL-283

**DeMarco, Ab Sr.**
❑ 39OPCV3011-82
❑ 51BufBis-8

**Demarski, Matt**
❑ 96LetHur-3
❑ 98FloEve-4

**DeMartinis, Lucio**
❑ 98Vald'OF-11

**DeMeres, Tony**
❑ 34BeeGro1P-146
❑ 40OPCV3012-144

**Demers, Jacques**
❑ 81FreExp-12
❑ 82FreExp-12
❑ 87RedWinLC-8
❑ 88RedWinLC-6
❑ 89RedWinLC-19
❑ 92CanaPos-8
❑ 93CanaPos-7
❑ 93Kra-32
❑ 93OPCCanHF-10
❑ 94CanaPos-7

**Demers, Normand**
❑ 907thInnSMC-73
❑ 907thInnSQMJHL-83

**Demin, Vassili**
❑ 94EriPan-6

**Demitra, Pavol**
❑ 92UppDec-602
❑ 93Don-240
❑ 93Lea-366
❑ 93Par-140
❑ 93ParEmel-140
❑ 93Pin-446

❑ 93PinCan-446
❑ 93Sco-624
❑ 93ScoCan-624
❑ 93ScoGol-624
❑ 93SenKraS-6
❑ 93UppDec-372
❑ 93UppDecSP-108
❑ 94Don-133
❑ 94Fin-111
❑ 94FinRef-111
❑ 94FinSupTW-111
❑ 94Fle-144
❑ 94Lea-115
❑ 94OPCPre-336
❑ 94OPCPreSE-336
❑ 94ParSE-SE121
❑ 94ParSEG-SE121
❑ 94Sel-185
❑ 94SelGol-185
❑ 94TopPre-336
❑ 94TopPreSE-336
❑ 94Ult-337
❑ 94UppDec-216
❑ 94UppDecElelce-216
❑ 94UppDecSPI-SP145
❑ 94UppDecSPIDC-SP145
❑ 95CanGamNHLP-195
❑ 95ColEdgI-48
❑ 95ParInt-149
❑ 95ParIntEl-149
❑ 96GraRapG-5
❑ 96LasVegThu-5
❑ 97Be A PPAD-146
❑ 97Be A PPAPD-146
❑ 97BeAPla-146
❑ 97BeAPlaAut-146
❑ 97ColCho-232
❑ 97PacCroR-114
❑ 97PacCroREG-114
❑ 97PacCroRIB-114
❑ 97PacCroRS-114
❑ 97PacOme-191
❑ 97PacOmeC-191
❑ 97PacOmeDG-191
❑ 97PacOmeEG-191
❑ 97PacOmeG-191
❑ 97PacOmeIB-191
❑ 97ScoBlu-18
❑ 97ScoBluPla-18
❑ 97ScoBluPre-18
❑ 97SPAut-142
❑ 97UppDec-146
❑ 98Be A PPA-126
❑ 98Be A PPAA-126
❑ 98Be A PPAAF-126
❑ 98Be A PPTBASG-126
❑ 98Be APG-126
❑ 98Fin-62
❑ 98FinNo P-62
❑ 98FinNo PR-62
❑ 98FinRef-62
❑ 98Pac-38
❑ 98PacIceB-38
❑ 98PacOmeH-201
❑ 98PacOmeODI-201
❑ 98PacOmeR-201
❑ 98PacPar-202
❑ 98PacParC-202
❑ 98PacParEG-202
❑ 98PacParH-202
❑ 98PacParIB-202
❑ 98PacParS-202
❑ 98PacRed-38
❑ 98PacRev-121
❑ 98PacRevIS-121
❑ 98PacRevR-121
❑ 98SP Aut-74
❑ 98SPxFin-76
❑ 98SPxFinR-76
❑ 98SPxFinS-76
❑ 98TopGolLC1-29
❑ 98TopGolLC1B-29
❑ 98TopGolLC1BOoO-29
❑ 98TopGolLC1OoO-29
❑ 98TopGolLC1R-29
❑ 98TopGolLC1ROoO-29
❑ 98TopGolLC2-29
❑ 98TopGolLC2B-29
❑ 98TopGolLC2BOoO-29
❑ 98TopGolLC2OoO-29
❑ 98TopGolLC2R-29
❑ 98TopGolLC2ROoO-29
❑ 98TopGolLC3-29
❑ 98TopGolLC3B-29
❑ 98TopGolLC3BOoO-29
❑ 98TopGolLC3OoO-29
❑ 98TopGolLC3R-29
❑ 98TopGolLC3ROoO-29
❑ 98UC-186
❑ 98UD ChoPCR-186
❑ 98UD ChoR-186
❑ 98UppDec-173
❑ 98UppDecE-173
❑ 98UppDecE1o1-173
❑ 98UppDecGR-173
❑ 98UppDecM-185
❑ 98UppDecMGS-185
❑ 98UppDecMSS-185
❑ 98UppDecMSS-185
❑ 99Pac-355
❑ 99PacAur-124
❑ 99PacAurPD-124
❑ 99PacCop-355
❑ 99PacGol-355
❑ 99PacIceB-355
❑ 99PacPreD-355
❑ 99RetHoc-70
❑ 99SP AutPS-74
❑ 99UppDecM-182
❑ 99UppDecMGS-182
❑ 99UppDecMPS-PD
❑ 99UppDecMSS-182
❑ 99UppDecMSS-182
❑ 99UppDecRG-70
❑ 99UppDecRP-70

**Demmans, Trevor**
❑ 92MPSPhoSJHL-118

**Demmel, Franz**
❑ 94GerDELE-220
❑ 95GerDELE-216
❑ 96GerDELE-360

**Dempsey, Ed**
❑ 96KamBla-8

**Dempsey, Nathan**
❑ 917thInnSWHL-221
❑ 94St.JohML-8
❑ 95St.JohML-7
❑ 96St.JohML-14
❑ 97St.JohML-9

**Denham, Jeff**
❑ 91BriColJHL-37

**Denis, Louis**
❑ 36V356WorG-125
❑ 51LavDaiQSHL-97
❑ 51LavDaiS-97
❑ 52St.LawS-13

**Denis, Marc**
❑ 95DonEliWJ-1
❑ 95UppDec-529
❑ 95UppDecElelce-529
❑ 95UppDecElelceG-529
❑ 96ColCho-363
❑ 96UppDecBD-130
❑ 96UppDecBDG-130
❑ 96UppDecIce-117
❑ 97BowCHL-61
❑ 97BowCHLOPC-61
❑ 97ColCho-302
❑ 97Don-202
❑ 97DonCanI-145
❑ 97DonCanIDS-145
❑ 97DonCanILG-12
❑ 97DonCanILGP-12
❑ 97DonCanIPS-145
❑ 97DonEliBttF-2
❑ 97DonEliBttFA-2
❑ 97DonLim-47
❑ 97DonLim-127
❑ 97DonLimExp-47
❑ 97DonLimExp-127
❑ 97DonLimFOTG-47
❑ 97DonMed-4
❑ 97DonPre-145
❑ 97DonPre-187
❑ 97DonPreCG-10
❑ 97DonPreCGP-10
❑ 97DonPreCttC-145
❑ 97DonPreCttC-187
❑ 97DonPreProG-202
❑ 97DonPreProS-202
❑ 97DonPriPG-18
❑ 97DonPriPGP-18
❑ 97DonRatR-4
❑ 97Lea-105
❑ 97Lea-148
❑ 97LeaFraMat-105
❑ 97LeaFraMat-148
❑ 97LeaFraMDC-105
❑ 97LeaFraMDC-148
❑ 97LeaInt-105
❑ 97LeaIntUI-105
❑ 97PinIns-64
❑ 97PinInsCC-64
❑ 97PinInsEC-64
❑ 97ScoAva-3
❑ 97ScoAvaPla-3
❑ 97ScoAvaPre-3
❑ 97Stu-25
❑ 97StuPor-26
❑ 97StuPrePG-25
❑ 97StuPrePS-25
❑ 97UppDecIce-31
❑ 97UppDecIceP-31
❑ 97UppDecIPS-31
❑ 97UppDecTSS-12B
❑ 98PacOmeH-59
❑ 98PacOmeODI-59
❑ 98PacOmeR-59
❑ 98UppDec-25
❑ 98UppDec-75
❑ 98UppDecE-25
❑ 98UppDecE-75
❑ 98UppDecE1o1-25
❑ 98UppDecE1o1-75
❑ 98UppDecGN-GN9
❑ 98UppDecGNQ1-GN9
❑ 98UppDecGNQ2-GN9
❑ 98UppDecGNQ3-GN9
❑ 98UppDecGR-25
❑ 98UppDecGR-75

**Denisov, Dmitri**
❑ 95SwiHNL-199
❑ 96SweSemW-155

**Denisov, Mikhail**
❑ 74SweHocS-74

**Denneny, Corbett**
❑ 23V1451-40

**Denneny, Cy**
❑ 23V1451-10
❑ 24C144ChaCig-21
❑ 24V1452-7
❑ 60Top-8
❑ 60TopSta-13
❑ 83HalFP-K3
❑ 85HalFC-138

**Dennis, Danny (Daniel)**
❑ 91AirCanSJHL-E20
❑ 92MPSPhoSJHL-20

**Dennis, Duane**
❑ 94CapBreO-6

**Dennison, Heath**
❑ 92BriColJHL-158

**Dennison, Joe**
❑ 12C57-42

**Denomme, C.J.**
❑ 917thInnSOHL-74

**Denomme, Jason**
❑ 98OshGenP-8
❑ 907thInnSOHL-156
❑ 917thInnSMC-9
❑ 917thInnSOHL-328

**Dent, Ted**
❑ 93JohChi-5
❑ 94JohChi-6

**Denzin, Drew**
❑ 93MicWol-4

**Deobald, Lonny**
❑ 92MPSPhoSJHL-56

**DePalma, Larry**
❑ 87NorStaPos-12
❑ 88NorStaADA-7
❑ 89ProIHL-79
❑ 90ProAHLIHL-111
❑ 91ProAHLCHL-524
❑ 96MilAdmBO-4

**DePourcq, John**
❑ 94CenHocL-110
❑ 95LouIceG-2
❑ 95LouIceGP-4

**DeProfio, Chris**
❑ 96LouRiv-13
❑ 97LouRivF-16

**Deraspe, Patrick**
❑ 917thInnSQMJHL-185

**Derkatch, Dale**
❑ 81RegPat-8
❑ 82RegPat-13
❑ 83CanNatJ-4
❑ 83RegPat-13
❑ 94GerDELE-305
❑ 95GerDELE-191

**Derksen, Devin**
❑ 907thInnSWHL-100
❑ 93RicRen-8

**Derksen, Duane**
❑ 92Cla-91
❑ 95MadMon-1
❑ 96ClaGol-91

**Derlago, Bill**
❑ 78CanuRoyB-3
❑ 79CanuRoyB-5
❑ 80MapLeaP-9
❑ 80OPC-11
❑ 80PepCap-84
❑ 80Top-11
❑ 81MapLeaP-6
❑ 81OPC-305
❑ 81OPCSti-99
❑ 81OPCSti-108
❑ 81Top-8
❑ 82MapLeaP-8
❑ 82MapLeaP-9
❑ 82OPC-319
❑ 82OPC-320
❑ 82OPCSti-67
❑ 82OPCSti-68
❑ 82PosCer-18
❑ 83Ess-6
❑ 83MapLeaP-4
❑ 83OPC-327
❑ 83OPCSti-35
❑ 83PufSti-1
❑ 83Vac-84
❑ 847EDis-45
❑ 84KelWin-27
❑ 84MapLeaP-8
❑ 84OPC-300
❑ 84OPCSti-14
❑ 85OPC-71
❑ 85OPCSti-7
❑ 85Top-71
❑ 86JetBor-5
❑ 86KraDra-15
❑ 86NordTeal-3
❑ 86OPC-254
❑ 86OPCSti-105
❑ 87OPCSti-224

**Derndtsson, Peter**
❑ 92SweSemE-314

**Dernestal, Stefan**
❑ 91SweSemE-227

**DeRouville, Philippe**
❑ 917thInnSQMJHL-131
❑ 93UppDec-260
❑ 95CleLum-10
❑ 95ColEdgI-116
❑ 95Don-206
❑ 95Lea-111
❑ 95Pin-214
❑ 95PinArtP-214
❑ 95PinRinC-214
❑ 95Sco-291
❑ 95ScoBlaIce-291
❑ 95ScoBlaIceAP-291
❑ 97Don-197
❑ 97DonCanILG-11
❑ 97DonCanILGP-11
❑ 97DonPreProG-197
❑ 97DonPreProS-197

**Derraugh, Doug**
❑ 95GerDELE-375
❑ 96GerDELE-196

**DeSantis, Mark**
❑ 907thInnSOHL-32
❑ 917thInnSOHL-3
❑ 91CorRoy-2
❑ 94ClaEnf-E10
❑ 94GreMon-18

**Desaulniers, Gerard**
❑ 51LavDaiQSHL-93
❑ 51LavDaiS-93
❑ 52St.LawS-4

**Desbiens, Robert**
❑ 51LavDaiLSJ-4

**Deschamps, Marc**
❑ 92WheThu-5

**Deschamps, Robert**
❑ 897thInnSOHL-158
❑ 907thInnSOHL-282

**Deschaume, Laurent**
❑ 93SweSemWCS-261

**Descoteaux, Matthieu**
❑ 95BowDraPro-P9

**Desgagne, Marc**
❑ 917thInnSQMJHL-7

**Desilets, Joffre**
❑ 34BeeGro1P-147
❑ 36OPCV304D-114
❑ 37OPCV304E-156

**Desilets, Mike**
❑ 52JunBluT-158

**Desjardine, Ken**
❑ 72NordPos-6
❑ 73NordTeal-7

**Desjardines, Mario**
❑ 86KamBla-6

**Desjardins, Eric**
❑ 88CanaPos-9
❑ 89CanaKra-7
❑ 89CanaPos-10
❑ 90CanaPos-12
❑ 90OPC-425
❑ 90ProSet-467
❑ 90ScoRoo-58T
❑ 90UppDec-428
❑ 90UppDecF-428
❑ 91Bow-329
❑ 91CanaPanTS-8
❑ 91CanaPos-10
❑ 91Gil-27
❑ 91OPC-14
❑ 91OPCPre-157
❑ 91PanSti-189
❑ 91Par-85
❑ 91ParFre-85
❑ 91Pin-73
❑ 91PinFre-73
❑ 91ProSet-118
❑ 91ProSetFre-118
❑ 91ProSetPla-193
❑ 91ScoAme-119
❑ 91ScoCan-119
❑ 91ScoYouS-23
❑ 91StaClu-214
❑ 91Top-14
❑ 91UppDec-360
❑ 91UppDec-504
❑ 91UppDecF-360
❑ 91UppDecF-504
❑ 92Bow-228
❑ 92Bow-311
❑ 92CanaPos-7
❑ 92DurPan-36
❑ 92OPC-360
❑ 92PanSti-156
❑ 92PanStiFre-156
❑ 92Par-80
❑ 92ParEmel-80
❑ 92Pin-16
❑ 92PinFre-16
❑ 92PinTea2-9
❑ 92PinTea2F-9
❑ 92ProSet-86
❑ 92Sco-23
❑ 92ScoCan-23
❑ 92ScoYouS-28
❑ 92StaClu-326
❑ 92Top-192
❑ 92TopGol-192G
❑ 92Ult-104
❑ 92UppDec-268
❑ 93CanaPos-8
❑ 93Don-173
❑ 93DurSco-12
❑ 93Lea-203
❑ 93OPCCanHF-20
❑ 93OPCPre-32
❑ 93OPCPreG-32
❑ 93PanSti-21
❑ 93Par-102
❑ 93ParEmel-102
❑ 93Pin-59
❑ 93PinCan-59
❑ 93Pow-128
❑ 93Sco-128
❑ 93ScoCan-128
❑ 93StaClu-170
❑ 93StaCluFDI-170
❑ 93StaCluFDIO-170
❑ 93StaCluO-170
❑ 93SweSemWCS-195
❑ 93TopPre-32
❑ 93TopPreG-32
❑ 93Ult-94
❑ 93UppDec-184
❑ 94BeAPla-R105
❑ 94CanaPos-8
❑ 94CanGamNHLP-139
❑ 94Don-177
❑ 94EASpo-67
❑ 94FinnJaaK-87
❑ 94Fla-88
❑ 94Fle-151
❑ 94Lea-433
❑ 94Par-118
❑ 94ParGol-118
❑ 94Pin-106
❑ 94PinArtP-106
❑ 94PinRinC-106
❑ 94Sco-110
❑ 94ScoGol-110
❑ 94ScoPla-110
❑ 94ScoPlaTS-110
❑ 94Sel-113
❑ 94SelGol-113
❑ 94StaClu-263
❑ 94StaCluFDI-263
❑ 94StaCluMOMS-263
❑ 94StaCluSTWC-263
❑ 94Ult-108
❑ 94UppDec-279
❑ 94UppDecElelce-279
❑ 95CanGamNHLP-209
❑ 95ColCho-105
❑ 95ColChoPC-105
❑ 95ColChoPCP-105
❑ 95Don-151
❑ 95Emo-130
❑ 95Fin-174
❑ 95FinRef-174
❑ 95ImpSti-93
❑ 95Lea-70
❑ 95Met-109
❑ 95ParInt-428
❑ 95ParIntEl-428
❑ 95Pin-110
❑ 95PinArtP-110
❑ 95PinRinC-110
❑ 95PlaOneoOne-75
❑ 95PosUppD-5
❑ 95Sco-207
❑ 95ScoBlaIce-207
❑ 95ScoBlaIceAP-207
❑ 95SkyImp-124
❑ 95SP-112
❑ 95StaClu-125
❑ 95StaCluMOMS-125
❑ 95Top-290
❑ 95TopOPCI-290
❑ 95Ult-116
❑ 95UltGolM-116
❑ 95UppDec-186
❑ 95UppDecElelce-186
❑ 95UppDecElelceG-186
❑ 95UppDecNHLAS-AS9
❑ 95UppDecSpeE-SE150
❑ 95UppDecSpeEdiG-SE150
❑ 96BeAPAut-40
❑ 96BeAPAutSil-40
❑ 96BeAPla-40
❑ 96ColCho-195
❑ 96Don-25
❑ 96DonPrePro-25
❑ 96Fle-79
❑ 96FleNor-4
❑ 96FlyPos-5
❑ 96Lea-27
❑ 96LeaPre-32
❑ 96LeaPreP-27
❑ 96LeaPrePP-32
❑ 96MetUni-110
❑ 96Pin-169
❑ 96PinArtP-169
❑ 96PinFoi-169
❑ 96PinPreS-169
❑ 96PinRinC-169
❑ 96Sco-159
❑ 96ScoArtPro-159
❑ 96ScoDeaCAP-159
❑ 96ScoGolB-159
❑ 96ScoSpeAP-159
❑ 96SkyImp-93
❑ 96SkyImpNHLF-8
❑ 96SP-113
❑ 96StaCluMO-41
❑ 96SweSemW-83
❑ 96TeaOut-86
❑ 96TopNHLP-93
❑ 96TopPicOI-93
❑ 96Ult-123
❑ 96UltGolM-123
❑ 96UppDec-123
❑ 96UppDecBD-37
❑ 96UppDecBDG-37
❑ 96UppDecIce-47
❑ 96UppDecIcePar-47
❑ 97ColChoWD-W15
❑ 97Don-141
❑ 97DonLim-80
❑ 97DonLimExp-80
❑ 97DonPreProG-141
❑ 97DonPreProS-141
❑ 97EssOlyHH-13
❑ 97EssOlyHHF-13
❑ 97Pac-121
❑ 97PacCop-121
❑ 97PacEmeGre-121
❑ 97PacIceB-121
❑ 97PacOme-162
❑ 97PacOmeC-162
❑ 97PacOmeDG-162
❑ 97PacOmeEG-162
❑ 97PacOmeG-162
❑ 97PacOmeIB-162
❑ 97PacRed-121
❑ 97PacSil-121
❑ 97Sco-196
❑ 97ScoFly-7
❑ 97ScoFlyPla-7
❑ 97ScoFlyPre-7
❑ 97UppDec-332
❑ 98Be A PPA-253
❑ 98Be A PPAA-253
❑ 98Be A PPAAF-253
❑ 98Be A PPSE-253
❑ 98Be APG-253
❑ 98Fin-102
❑ 98FinNo P-102
❑ 98FinNo PR-102
❑ 98FinRef-102
❑ 98O-PChr-35
❑ 98O-PChrR-35
❑ 98Pac-324
❑ 98PacAur-137
❑ 98PacIceB-324
❑ 98PacOmeH-173
❑ 98PacOmeODI-173
❑ 98PacOmeR-173
❑ 98PacPar-171
❑ 98PacParC-171
❑ 98PacParEG-171
❑ 98PacParH-171
❑ 98PacParIB-171
❑ 98PacParS-171
❑ 98PacRed-324
❑ 98Top-35
❑ 98TopO-P-35
❑ 98UppDec-150
❑ 98UppDecE-150
❑ 98UppDecE1o1-150
❑ 98UppDecGR-150
❑ 98UppDecM-154
❑ 98UppDecMGS-154
❑ 98UppDecMSS-154
❑ 98UppDecMSS-154
❑ 99Pac-301
❑ 99PacAur-104
❑ 99PacAurPD-104
❑ 99PacCop-301
❑ 99PacGol-301
❑ 99PacIceB-301
❑ 99PacPreD-301
❑ 99UppDecM-152
❑ 99UppDecMGS-152
❑ 99UppDecMSS-152
❑ 99UppDecMSS-152

**Desjardins, Gerry**
❑ 69OPC-99
❑ 69OPCFou-14
❑ 69OPCSta-6
❑ 69Top-99
❑ 70ColSta-67
❑ 70EssPowPla-109
❑ 70OPC-152
❑ 70SarProSta-45
❑ 72OPC-119
❑ 72SarProSta-129
❑ 72Top-38
❑ 73OPC-178
❑ 73Top-114
❑ 75OPCNHL-125
❑ 75Top-125
❑ 76OPCNHL-230
❑ 76Top-230
❑ 77OPCNHL-150
❑ 77Top-150

**Desjardins, Martin**
❑ 88ProAHL-293
❑ 89CanaPos-11
❑ 90ProAHLIHL-410
❑ 91ProAHLCHL-484
❑ 93SwiHNL-424
❑ 95SwiHNL-248

**Desjardins, Norman**
❑ 89ProAHL-189
❑ 90ProAHLIHL-69
❑ 91ProAHLCHL-75

**Desjardins, Stephane**
❑ 907thInnSQMJHL-5
❑ 917thInnSMC-61
❑ 917thInnSQMJHL-286
❑ 94RoaExp-12

**Desjardins, Valerie**
❑ 92QueIntP-19

**Deslauriers, Jacques**
❑ 51LavDaiQSHL-82
❑ 52St.LawS-25
❑ 55MonRoy-3

**Desloges, Steve**
❑ 74SioCitM-3

**Desmarais, Matt**
❑ 92MPSPhoSJHL-46

**Desnoyers, David**
❑ 90MonAAA-9
❑ 917thInnSQMJHL-3

**Desouza, Ray**
❑ 92NasKni-8
❑ 94CenHocL-7

**Despatis, Chris**
❑ 95Sla-276

**Desrochers, Eric**
❑ 907thInnSQMJHL-191

**DesRochers, Patrick**
❑ 95Sla-332
❑ 96SarSti-8
❑ 96UppDec-371
❑ 97BowCHL-40
❑ 97BowCHLOPC-40
❑ 98BowCHL-139
❑ 98BowCHLAuB-A20
❑ 98BowCHLAuG-A20
❑ 98BowCHLAuS-A20
❑ 98BowCHLGA-139
❑ 98BowCHLOI-139
❑ 98BowCHLSC-SC5
❑ 98BowChrC-139
❑ 98BowChrCGA-139
❑ 98BowChrCGAR-139
❑ 98BowChrCOI-139
❑ 98BowChrCOIR-139
❑ 98BowChrCR-139
❑ 98FinFutF-F11
❑ 98FinFutFR-F11

**Desrosiers, Dennis**
❑ 78LouGea-3
❑ 90CinCyc-38
❑ 91CinCyc-7

**Desrosiers, Gilles**
❑ 51LavDaiLSJ-3

**Desrosiers, Joe**
❑ 86SudWol-30
❑ 897thInnSOHL-95

**Desrosiers, Julien**
❑ 97RimOce-24

**Desrosiers, Louis**
❑ 52JunBluT-47

**Desyatkov, Pavel**
❑ 93Pin-505
❑ 93PinCan-505

**Deuling, Jarrett**
❑ 907thInnSWHL-308
❑ 93KamBla-3
❑ 96KenTho-5

**Deutscher, Torsten**
❑ 94GerDELE-36
❑ 95GerDELE-29

**Devaney, John**
❑ 81SweSemHVS-85

**Devereaux, Boyd**
❑ 95BowDraPro-P10
❑ 95Cla-87
❑ 95Sla-149
❑ 95Sla-432
❑ 96CEFLAuHP-2
❑ 96KitRan-8
❑ 96KitRan-9
❑ 96OilPos-19
❑ 96UppDecBD-86
❑ 96UppDecBDG-86
❑ 96UppDecIce-122
❑ 97Be A PPAD-237
❑ 97Be A PPAPD-237
❑ 97BeAPla-237
❑ 97BeAPlaAut-237
❑ 97BowCHL-23
❑ 97BowCHLOPC-23
❑ 97ColCho-311
❑ 97DonEli-90
❑ 97DonEliAsp-90
❑ 97DonEliS-90
❑ 97DonPri-184
❑ 97DonPriSoA-184
❑ 97Kat-56
❑ 97KatGol-56
❑ 97KatSil-56
❑ 97Lea-149
❑ 97LeaFraMat-149
❑ 97LeaFraMDC-149
❑ 97PacPar-73
❑ 97PacParC-73
❑ 97PacParDG-73
❑ 97PacParEG-73
❑ 97PacParIB-73
❑ 97PacParRed-73
❑ 97PacParSil-73
❑ 97Pin-13
❑ 97PinArtP-13
❑ 97PinCerRR-J
❑ 97PinCerRRG-J
❑ 97PinCerRRMG-J
❑ 97PinPrePBB-13
❑ 97PinPrePBC-13
❑ 97PinPrePBM-13
❑ 97PinPrePBY-13
❑ 97PinPrePFC-13
❑ 97PinPrePFM-13
❑ 97PinPrePFY-13
❑ 97PinPrePla-13
❑ 97PinRinC-13
❑ 97Sco-73
❑ 97ScoArtPro-73
❑ 97ScoGolBla-73
❑ 97SPAut-181
❑ 97UppDecBD-146
❑ 97UppDecBDDD-146
❑ 97UppDecBDQD-146
❑ 97UppDecBDTD-146
❑ 97Zen-93
❑ 97ZenZGol-93
❑ 97ZenZSil-93
❑ 98O-PChr-21
❑ 98O-PChrR-21
❑ 98Top-21
❑ 98TopO-P-21

**Devereaux, John**

- 88FliSpi-3
- 91GreMon-4

**Devine, Kevin**
- 76SanDieMW-1
- 81IndChe-4
- 82IndChe-2

**Devjatov, Vladimir**
- 73SweHocS-129
- 73SweWorCS-129

**Devlin, Vince**
- 92BriColJHL-216
- 92BriColJHL-227

**DeVries, Greg**
- 93NiaFalT-5
- 94CapBreO-7
- 96OilPos-5
- 96UppDec-191
- 97Be A PPAD-78
- 97Be A PPAPD-78
- 97BeAPla-78
- 97BeAPlaAut-78
- 97PacInvNRB-76
- 98UppDecM-56
- 98UppDecMGS-56
- 98UppDecMSS-56
- 98UppDecMSS-56

**DeVuono, Lenny (Len)**
- 907thInnSOHL-93
- 907thInnSOHL-230
- 90KitRan-7

**DeWaele, Kirk**
- 93LetHur-2

**Dewar, Jeff**
- 93SeaThu-4

**Dewitz, Dieter**
- 70SweHocS-368

**DeWolf, Josh**
- 95Cla-59

**DeWolf, Karl**
- 94FreNatT-8

**Dewsbury, Al**
- 44BeeGro2P-91
- 51Par-38
- 52Par-17
- 53Par-78
- 54Par-78
- 94ParMisL-22

**Dexheimer, Alexander**
- 98GerDELE-218

**Dextater, Bill**
- 83KinCan-28

**Dexter, Jason**
- 95BirBul-19

**Dey, Edgar**
- 10C56-6

**Deyell, Mark**
- 93SasBla-3
- 93SasBla-7
- 95SasBla-9
- 96St.JohML-15
- 97St.JohML-10

**Dezaine, Joel**
- 95Sla-158

**Dezainde, Norman (Norm)**
- 907thInnSOHL-231
- 90KitRan-15
- 917thInnSOHL-82
- 93KitRan-8
- 94TolSto-4
- 95SigRoo-24
- 95SigRooSig-24
- 95TolSto-14
- 96TolSto-22

**Di Fiore, Ralph**
- 94FinnJaaK-295

**Diachuk, Ed**
- 61UniOilW-2

**Dibley, Gord**
- 67ColChe-5

**Dicasmirro, Nate**
- 95NorlowH-5

**Dick, Harry**
- 51BufBis-6

**Dickens, Ernie**
- 34BeeGro1P-314
- 44BeeGro2P-92

**Dickenson, Herb**
- 52Par-57

**Dickie, Gary**
- 86RegPat-3
- 87RegPat-2
- 88RegPat-4

**Dickie, Gord**
- 917thInnSOHL-289
- 93KitRan-6

**Dickie, J.J.**
- 96SauSteMG-5
- 96SauSteMGA-5

**Dickie, Kevin**
- 91AirCanSJHLAS-3
- 91AirCanSJHLAS-47

**Dickinson, Brian**
- 89RayJrC-7

**Dickson, Darryl**
- 91AirCanSJHL-D47
- 92MPSPhoSJHL-24

**Diduck, Gerald**
- 85IsIIsIN-18
- 89Isl-5
- 89OPC-182
- 89OPCSti-117
- 89PanSti-274
- 89Top-182
- 90CanaPos-13
- 90CanuMoh-7

- 900PC-421
- 900PCPre-22
- 90PanSti-85
- 90ProSet-180
- 90ProSet-468
- 90Sco-139
- 90ScoCan-139
- 90ScoRoo-23T
- 90UppDec-390
- 90UppDecF-390
- 91CanaPanTS-9
- 91CanuAutC-5
- 91CanuTeal8-5
- 91OPC-280
- 91Par-407
- 91ParFre-407
- 91Pin-211
- 91PinFre-211
- 91ProSet-502
- 91ProSetFre-502
- 91ScoCan-243
- 91Top-280
- 92Bow-65
- 92CanuRoaTA-6
- 92OPC-309
- 92Par-419
- 92ParEmel-419
- 92Pin-81
- 92PinFre-81
- 92Sco-34
- 92ScoCan-34
- 92StaClu-97
- 92Top-44
- 92TopGol-44G
- 92Ult-424
- 93Don-360
- 93Lea-387
- 93Pin-291
- 93PinCan-291
- 93Pow-250
- 93Sco-356
- 93ScoCan-356
- 93Ult-440
- 94CanuProI-7
- 94Lea-402
- 94Pin-359
- 94PinArtP-359
- 94PinRinC-359
- 94StaClu-91
- 94StaCluFDI-91
- 94StaCluMOMS-91
- 94StaCluSTWC-91
- 95Lea-313
- 95ParIntEI-368
- 95Top-247
- 95TopOPCI-247
- 95Ult-245
- 96BeAPAut-167
- 96BeAPAutSil-167
- 96BeAPla-167
- 96WhaBobS-6
- 97Be A PPAD-55
- 97Be A PPAPD-55
- 97BeAPla-55
- 97BeAPlaAut-55

**Diduck, Judy**
- 94ClaWomOH-W12
- 97ColCho-283

**Dieard, Jean-Francis**
- 907thInnSQMJHL-121

**Diener, Derek**
- 93LetHur-3
- 95LetHur-5

**Dietrich, Don**
- 83SprInd-21

**Dietrich, Lou**
- 52JunBluT-13

**Dietrich, Shawn**
- 89SpoChi-3
- 907thInnSWHL-198
- 917thInnSWHL-200

**Dietsch, Andre**
- 94GerDELE-34
- 95GerDELE-26

**DiFazio, Alberto**
- 82SweSemHVS-136

**DiFronzo, Michele**
- 94ClaWomOH-W32

**Dilio, Frank**
- 83HalFP-F5
- 85HalFC-81

**Dillabough, Bob**
- 63Par-47
- 64BeeGro3P-5
- 65Coc-15
- 65Top-39
- 66Top-98
- 68OPC-191
- 69OPC-150
- 70DadCoo-22
- 70SarProSta-217
- 72CleCruWHA-3
- 72CruCleWHAL-2

**Dillon, Cecil**
- 330PCV304B-71
- 33V129-32
- 33V252CanG-18
- 33V357IceK-15
- 34BeeGro1P-271
- 34DiaMatS-20
- 35DiaMatT2-18
- 35DiaMatT2-19
- 35DiaMatT3-17

**Dillon, Wayne**

- 740PCWHA-3
- 750PCNHL-363
- 760PCNHL-9
- 76Top-9
- 770PCNHL-166
- 77Top-166
- 780PC-73
- 78Top-73
- 79JetPos-4
- 790PC-359

**Dimaio, Rob**
- 84KamBla-7
- 85MedHatT-5
- 88ProAHL-310
- 89ProAHL-234
- 90OPCPre-27
- 90ProAHLIHL-512
- 90ProSet-625
- 90UppDec-225
- 90UppDecF-225
- 91Par-325
- 91ParFre-325
- 91ProSet-430
- 91ProSetFre-430
- 91UppDec-481
- 91UppDecF-481
- 92Bow-403
- 92LigShe-13
- 92OPCPre-62
- 92Par-402
- 92ParEmel-402
- 92StaClu-33
- 92Top-488
- 92TopGol-488G
- 92UppDec-529
- 93LigKasK-5
- 93OPCPre-242
- 93OPCPreG-242
- 93PanSti-218
- 93Par-124
- 93Par-196
- 93ParEmel-196
- 93StaClu-182
- 93StaCluFDI-182
- 93StaCluFDIO-182
- 93StaCluO-182
- 93TopPre-242
- 93TopPreG-242
- 93UppDec-176
- 94Lea-549
- 940PCPre-114
- 940PCPreSE-114
- 94Pin-360
- 94PinArtP-360
- 94PinRinC-360
- 94TopPre-114
- 94TopPreSE-114
- 95BeAPla-105
- 95BeAPSig-S105
- 95BeAPSigDC-S105
- 95ParInt-431
- 95ParIntEI-431
- 95Top-92
- 95TopOPCI-92
- 95UppDec-336
- 95UppDecElelce-336
- 95UppDecElelceG-336
- 97Be A PPAD-6
- 97Be A PPAPD-6
- 97BeAPla-6
- 97BeAPlaAut-6
- 97Pac-287
- 97PacCop-287
- 97PacEmeGre-287
- 97PacIceB-287
- 97PacRed-287
- 97PacSil-287
- 97ScoBru-9
- 97ScoBruPla-9
- 97ScoBruPre-9
- 98Be A PPA-7
- 98Be A PPAA-7
- 98Be A PPAAF-7
- 98Be A PPTBASG-7
- 98Be APG-7
- 98Fin-61
- 98FinNo P-61
- 98FinNo PR-61
- 98FinRef-61
- 98Pac-75
- 98PacIceB-75
- 98PacRed-75

**Dimbat, Andreas**
- 95GerDELE-68
- 96GerDELE-264

**Dimitri, Dave**
- 93HunBli-7

**Dimme, Birley**
- 52JunBluT-55

**Dimuzio, Frank**
- 88ProAHL-31
- 93SweSemWCS-217
- 94FinnJaaK-300
- 98GerDELE-201

**Dineen, Bill**
- 44BeeGro2P-162
- 52JunBluT-147
- 53Par-127
- 54Par-48
- 54Top-57
- 57Top-49
- 60CleBar-3
- 62QueAce-7A
- 62QueAce-7B
- 63QueAce-4
- 63QueAceQ-5

- 88ProAHL-2
- 92FlyUppDS-20
- 92FlyUppDS-34
- 92Sco-517
- 92ScoCan-517
- 93ParParR-PR62
- 94ParMisL-50

**Dineen, Gord**
- 80SauSteMG-3
- 81SauSteMG-10
- 82IndChe-3
- 85IsIIsIN-19
- 89OPC-256
- 900PC-470
- 90ProSet-233
- 90UppDec-369
- 90UppDecF-369
- 91ProAHLCHL-306
- 92DurPan-37
- 92SanDieG-6
- 92SenKraS-7
- 94StaClu-219
- 94StaCluFDI-219
- 94StaCluFDIO-43
- 94StaCluO-43
- 94StaCluMOMS-219
- 94StaCluSTWC-219
- 95ColEdgI-192

**Dineen, Kevin**
- 85OPC-34
- 85OPCSti-168
- 85Top-34
- 85WhaJunW-4
- 86OPC-88
- 86OPCSti-56
- 86Top-88
- 86WhaJunT-5
- 870PC-124
- 870PCSti-202
- 87PanSti-44
- 87Top-124
- 87WhaJunBK-4
- 88FriLayS-28
- 88OPC-36
- 880PCSti-269
- 88PanSti-240
- 88Top-36
- 88WhaJunGR-4
- 890PC-304
- 890PCBoxB-M
- 890PCSti-270
- 89PanSti-219
- 89Top-20
- 89TopBoxB-M
- 89WhaJunM-5
- 90Bow-261
- 90BowHatTri-7
- 90BowTif-261
- 90Kra-11
- 900PC-213
- 90PanSti-43
- 90ProSet-102
- 90Sco-212
- 90ScoCan-212
- 90ScoHotRS-90
- 90Top-213
- 90TopTif-213
- 90UppDec-266
- 90UppDecF-266
- 90WhaJr7E-9
- 91Bow-6
- 91FlyJCP-6
- 91Kra-86
- 910PC-285
- 91PanSti-323
- 91Par-348
- 91ParFre-348
- 91Pin-246
- 91PinFre-246
- 91ProSet-89
- 91ProSetFre-89
- 91ProSet-451
- 91ProSetFre-451
- 91ProSetNHLSA-AC17
- 91ProSetPla-46
- 91ScoAme-118
- 91ScoCan-118
- 91ScoKel-11
- 91StaClu-162
- 91SweSemWCS-71
- 91Top-285
- 91UppDec-105
- 91UppDec-530
- 91UppDecF-105
- 91UppDecF-530
- 92Bow-121
- 92DurPan-12
- 92FlyJCP-9
- 92FlyUppDS-1
- 92FlyUppDS-20
- 92FlyUppDS-25
- 920PC-200
- 92PanSti-186
- 92PanStiFre-186
- 92Par-127
- 92ParEmel-127
- 92Pin-14
- 92PinFre-14
- 92ProSet-134
- 92Sco-284
- 92ScoCan-284
- 92StaClu-365
- 92Top-131

- 92TopGol-131G
- 92Ult-154
- 92UppDec-256
- 93Don-249
- 93DurSco-37
- 93Kra-33
- 93Lea-156
- 93LeaHatTA-6
- 93OPCPre-167
- 93OPCPreG-167
- 93YouSti-49
- 93Par-421
- 93ParEmel-421
- 93Pin-276
- 93PinCan-276
- 93PinCap-17
- 93PinCapC-17
- 93Pow-179
- 93Sco-122
- 93ScoCan-122
- 93StaClu-43
- 93StaCluFDI-43
- 93StaCluFDIO-43
- 93StaCluO-43
- 93TopPre-167
- 93TopPreG-167
- 93Ult-107
- 93UppDec-212
- 94CanGamNHLP-357
- 94Don-36
- 94Lea-167
- 940PCPre-207
- 940PCPreSE-207
- 94Par-172
- 94ParGol-172
- 94Pin-426
- 94PinArtP-426
- 94PinRinC-426
- 94Sco-197
- 94ScoGol-197
- 94ScoPla-197
- 94ScoPlaTS-197
- 94Sel-142
- 94SelGol-142
- 94SelPro-142
- 94TopPre-207
- 94TopPreSE-207
- 94Ult-156
- 94UppDec-431
- 94UppDecElelce-431
- 94CanGamNHLP-207
- 95ColEdgI-130
- 95ColEdgIC-C3
- 95Don-212
- 95Ima-21
- 95ImaGol-21
- 95ImaPlaPI-PL3
- 95Lea-205
- 95ParInt-366
- 95ParIntEI-366
- 95Pin-150
- 95PinArtP-150
- 95PinRinC-150
- 95Sco-277
- 95ScoBlaIce-277
- 95ScoBlaIceAP-277
- 95Top-143
- 95TopOPCI-143
- 96KraUppD-33
- 96SP-71
- 96UppDec-270
- 96UppDecBD-72
- 96UppDecBDG-72
- 97ColCho-109
- 97Kat-26
- 97KatGol-26
- 97KatSil-26
- 97Pac-218
- 97PacCop-218
- 97PacCroR-22
- 97PacCroREG-22
- 97PacCroRIB-22
- 97PacCroRS-22
- 97PacEmeGre-218
- 97PacIceB-218
- 97PacOme-43
- 97PacOmeC-43
- 97PacOmeDG-43
- 97PacOmeEG-43
- 97PacOmeG-43
- 97PacOmeIB-43
- 97PacPar-33
- 97PacParC-33
- 97PacParDG-33
- 97PacParEG-33
- 97PacParIB-33
- 97PacParRed-33
- 97PacParSil-33
- 97PacRed-218
- 97PacSil-218
- 97UppDec-241
- 980-PChr-173
- 980-PChrR-173
- 98Pac-130
- 98PacAur-30
- 98PacDynI-30
- 98PacDynIIB-30
- 98PacDynIR-30
- 98PacIceB-130
- 98PacPar-34
- 98PacParC-34
- 98PacParEG-34
- 98PacParH-34
- 98PacParIB-34

- 98PacParS-34
- 98PacRed-130
- 98Top-173
- 98Top0-P-173
- 99Pac-69
- 99PacCop-69
- 99PacGol-69
- 99PacIceB-69
- 99PacPreD-69

**Dineen, Peter**
- 83MonAlp-8
- 88ProAHL-21
- 89ProAHL-327
- 90ProAHLIHL-306

**Dineen, Shawn**
- 83MonAlp-25
- 89ProIHL-120

**Dingman, Chris**
- 92BraWheK-3
- 94Cla-17
- 94ClaDraGol-17
- 94ClaTri-T10
- 95SigRoo-20
- 95SigRooSig-20
- 95SlaMemC-43
- 97Be A PPAD-216
- 97Be A PPAPD-216
- 97BeAPla-216
- 97BeAPlaAut-216
- 97Lea-158
- 97LeaFraMat-158
- 97LeaFraMDC-158
- 97PacCroR-17
- 97PacCroREG-17
- 97PacCroRIB-17
- 97PacCroRS-17
- 97PacPar-27
- 97PacParC-27
- 97PacParDG-27
- 97PacParEG-27
- 97PacParIB-27
- 97PacParRed-27
- 97PacParSil-27
- 97Pin-7
- 97PinArtP-7
- 97PinPrePBB-7
- 97PinPrePBC-7
- 97PinPrePBM-7
- 97PinPrePBY-7
- 97PinPrePFC-7
- 97PinPrePFM-7
- 97PinPrePFY-7
- 97PinRinC-7
- 97Sco-55
- 97ScoArtPro-55
- 97ScoGolBla-55
- 97UppDec-234

**Dingwall, Richard**
- 96FitFly-8

**Dinsmore, Charlie (Charles A)**
- 24C144ChaCig-22
- 24V130MapC-17
- 24V1452-40

**Dion, Michel**
- 760PCWHA-6
- 760PCWHA-114
- 770PCWHA-62
- 790PC-316
- 80NordPos-8
- 800PC-223
- 80Top-223
- 820PC-267
- 820PCSti-146
- 820PCSti-168
- 82PosCer-15
- 830PC-279
- 830PCSti-234
- 83PenCok-7
- 83PenHeiP-7
- 83PenTealP-9
- 840PC-173
- 84PenHeiP-6

**Dion, Steven**
- 907thInnSQMJHL-141
- 917thInnSQMJHL-221

**Dion, Tom**
- 92WheThu-6

**Dionne, Gilbert**
- 88KitRan-18
- 89KitRan-19
- 907thInnSMC-39
- 90ProAHLIHL-62
- 91Par-313
- 91Par-447
- 91ParFre-313
- 91ParFre-447
- 91ProAHLCHL-73
- 91UppDec-448
- 91UppDecF-448
- 92Bow-439
- 92CanaPos-9
- 92DurPan-21
- 92HumDum1-5
- 920PC-307
- 92PanSti-272
- 92PanStiFre-272
- 92PanSti-M
- 92PanStiFre-M
- 92Par-81
- 92Par-237
- 92ParEmel-81
- 92ParEmel-237
- 92ParPre-PV3

- 92Pin-5
- 92PinFre-5
- 92PinTea2-29
- 92PinTea2F-29
- 92ProSet-92
- 92ProSetRGL-6
- 92Sco-331
- 92ScoCan-331
- 92ScoSha-7
- 92ScoYouS-9
- 92SeaPat-24
- 92StaClu-403
- 92Top-13
- 92Top-19
- 92TopGol-13G
- 92TopGol-19G
- 92Ult-105
- 92UltRoo-4
- 92UppDec-356
- 92UppDec-427
- 92UppDec-625
- 92UppDecDecAR-AR2
- 93CanaPos-9
- 93ClaProPro-87
- 93Don-174
- 93DurSco-13
- 93Lea-117
- 930PCPre-480
- 930PCPreG-480
- 93PanSti-18
- 93Par-101
- 93ParEmel-101
- 93Pin-199
- 93PinCan-199
- 93Pow-368
- 93Sco-178
- 93ScoCan-178
- 93StaClu-115
- 93StaCluFDI-115
- 93StaCluFDIO-115
- 93StaCluO-115
- 93TopPre-480
- 93TopPreG-480
- 93Ult-141
- 93UppDec-117
- 94BeAPla-R22
- 94CanaPos-9
- 94CanGamNHLP-134
- 94Fle-152
- 940PCPre-366
- 940PCPreSE-366
- 94ParSE-SE91
- 94ParSEG-SE91
- 94ParVin-V14
- 94Pin-422
- 94PinArtP-422
- 94PinRinC-422
- 94TopPre-366
- 94TopPreSE-366
- 94Ult-109
- 94UppDec-57
- 94UppDec-384
- 94UppDecElelce-57
- 94UppDecElelce-384
- 98CinCyc-5

**Dionne, Marcel**
- 71ColHea-2
- 710PC-133
- 71TorSun-92
- 720PC-8
- 72Top-18
- 730PC-17
- 73RedWinTI-9
- 73Top-17
- 74NHLActSta-105
- 740PCNHL-84
- 74Top-72
- 74Top-84
- 750PCNHL-140
- 750PCNHL-210
- 750PCNHL-318
- 75Top-140
- 75Top-210
- 75Top-318
- 760PCNHL-91
- 760PCNHL-386
- 76Top-91
- 76TopGloI-4
- 77Coc-6
- 770PCNHL-1
- 770PCNHL-3
- 770PCNHL-240
- 77Top-1
- 77Top-2
- 77Top-3
- 77Top-240
- 77TopGloS-4
- 77TopOPCGlo-4
- 780PC-120
- 78Top-120
- 790PC-1
- 790PC-2
- 790PC-5
- 790PC-160
- 79PanSti-61
- 79Top-1
- 79Top-2
- 79Top-5
- 79Top-160
- 80KinCarN-1

❑ 80OPC-20
❑ 80OPC-81
❑ 80OPC-162
❑ 80OPC-163
❑ 80OPC-165
❑ 80OPCSup-8
❑ 80Top-20
❑ 80Top-81
❑ 80Top-162
❑ 80Top-163
❑ 80Top-165
❑ 81OPC-141
❑ 81OPC-150
❑ 81OPC-156
❑ 81OPC-391
❑ 81OPCSti-147
❑ 81OPCSti-235
❑ 81OPCSti-267
❑ 81PosSta-12
❑ 81Top-9
❑ 81Top-54
❑ 81Top-W125
❑ 82NeiGre-12
❑ 82OPC-149
❑ 82OPC-152
❑ 82OPC-153
❑ 82OPCSti-230
❑ 82PosCer-8
❑ 83OPC-150
❑ 83OPC-151
❑ 83OPC-152
❑ 83OPC-211
❑ 83OPCSti-1
❑ 83OPCSti-294
❑ 83OPCSti-295
❑ 83OPCSti-323
❑ 83OPCSti-324
❑ 83PufSti-11
❑ 847EDis-24
❑ 84KelAccD-2
❑ 84KinSmo-2
❑ 84OPC-82
❑ 84OPCSti-264
❑ 84OPCSti-265
❑ 84Top-64
❑ 857ECreCar-8
❑ 85OPC-90
❑ 85OPCBoxB-E
❑ 85OPCSti-235
❑ 85Top-90
❑ 85TopBoxB-E
❑ 86OPC-30
❑ 86OPCSti-88
❑ 86Top-30
❑ 87OPC-129
❑ 87OPCSti-34
❑ 87PanSti-113
❑ 87Top-129
❑ 88EssAllSta-8
❑ 88FriLayS-34
❑ 88OPC-13
❑ 88OPCMin-8
❑ 88OPCSti-244
❑ 88PanSti-190
❑ 88Top-13
❑ 90ProSet-653
❑ 91FutTreC72-91
❑ 91Kra-85
❑ 91Pin-385
❑ 91PinFre-385
❑ 91UppDec-636
❑ 91UppDecF-636
❑ 92FutTre76CC-139
❑ 92FutTre76CC-179
❑ 92OPC-294
❑ 92OPC25AI-4
❑ 93ZelMasH-4
❑ 93ZelMasoHS-4
❑ 98KinLA TC-2
❑ 99RetHoc-103
❑ 99UppDecCL-39
❑ 99UppDecCLCLC-39
❑ 99UppDecES-8
❑ 99UppDecRG-103
❑ 99UppDecRII-MD
❑ 99UppDecRIL1-MD
❑ 99UppDecRM-RM2
❑ 99UppDecRP-103

**Dionne, Vincent**
❑ 92QueIntP-1

**Dipietro, Paul**
❑ 86SudWol-21
❑ 87SudWol-22
❑ 88SudWol-22
❑ 89SudWol-15
❑ 90ProAHLIHL-68
❑ 91Pin-350
❑ 91PinFre-350
❑ 91ProAHLCHL-70
❑ 91ProSet-546
❑ 91ProSetFre-546
❑ 92FreCan-8
❑ 92Par-489
❑ 92ParEmel-489
❑ 92StaClu-98
❑ 92Top-361
❑ 92TopGol-361G
❑ 93CanaPos-10
❑ 93ClaProPro-104
❑ 93Lea-248
❑ 93OPCPre-288
❑ 93OPCPreG-288
❑ 93Par-108
❑ 93ParEmel-108
❑ 93Pin-114
❑ 93PinCan-114
❑ 93Pow-369
❑ 93Sco-494
❑ 93ScoCan-494
❑ 93StaClu-194
❑ 93StaCluFDI-194
❑ 93StaCluFDIO-194
❑ 93StaCluO-194
❑ 93SudWol-24
❑ 93TopPre-288
❑ 93TopPreG-288
❑ 93Ult-159
❑ 93UppDec-108
❑ 94CanaPos-10
❑ 94MapLeaK-9
❑ 94MapLeaPP-25
❑ 94OPCPre-252
❑ 94OPCPreSE-252
❑ 94Pin-443
❑ 94PinArtP-443
❑ 94PinRinC-443
❑ 94TopPre-252
❑ 94TopPreSE-252

**Dirk, Robert**
❑ 87BluTeaIss-6
❑ 88BluTeaIss-6
❑ 89ProIHL-8
❑ 90BluKod-8
❑ 90ProSet-522
❑ 91CanuAutC-6
❑ 91CanuTeal8-6
❑ 91OPC-493
❑ 91Par-403
❑ 91ParFre-403
❑ 91ScoCan-508
❑ 91Top-493
❑ 92CanuRoaTA-7
❑ 92Par-425
❑ 92ParEmel-425
❑ 92Sco-279
❑ 92ScoCan-279
❑ 92Top-437
❑ 92TopGol-437G
❑ 92Ult-425
❑ 93OPCPre-284
❑ 93OPCPreG-284
❑ 93Pin-327
❑ 93PinCan-327
❑ 93Sco-288
❑ 93ScoCan-288
❑ 93TopPre-284
❑ 93TopPreG-284
❑ 94CanuProI-8
❑ 94DucCarJr-3
❑ 94Pin-405
❑ 94PinArtP-405
❑ 94PinRinC-405
❑ 95BeAPla-159
❑ 95BeAPSig-S159
❑ 95BeAPSigDC-S159
❑ 95UppDec-432
❑ 95UppDecEleIce-432
❑ 95UppDecEleIceG-432

**DiRoberto, Torrey**
❑ 95SeaThu-7
❑ 96SeaThu-18

**Disher, Jason**
❑ 93KinFro-9
❑ 95ThuBayS-6

**Disiewich, Jason**
❑ 91BriColJHL-55
❑ 92BriColJHL-94
❑ 92BriColJHL-111
❑ 93DayBom-8

**Disschops, Jake**
❑ 86SudWol-31

**Diviney, Norm**
❑ 50QueCit-5

**Divis, Reinhard**
❑ 95AusNatTea-4

**Divisek, Michal**
❑ 95SeaThu-8
❑ 96CzeAPSE-223

**DiVita, David**
❑ 91RochAmeDD-5
❑ 91RochAmeKod-10
❑ 91RochAmePos-7
❑ 92RochAmeDD-5
❑ 92RochAmeKod-7

**Divjak, Dan**
❑ 90ArilIce-5
❑ 91ArilIce-6
❑ 91ArilIce-18
❑ 92ArilIce-8

**Djelloul, Serge**
❑ 94FreNatT-9

**Djoos, Par**
❑ 86SwePanS-40
❑ 87SwePanS-50
❑ 89SweSemE-29
❑ 90OPCPre-24
❑ 90ProSet-603
❑ 90ScoRoo-107T
❑ 92BinRan-20
❑ 92Sco-372
❑ 92ScoCan-372
❑ 92StaClu-492
❑ 92Top-93
❑ 92TopGol-93G
❑ 93SweSemWCS-30
❑ 93SwiHNL-89
❑ 94SweLeaE-164
❑ 95SweLeaE-140
❑ 95SweUppDE-203

**Dlouhy, Jan**
❑ 94CzeAPSE-53
❑ 95CzeAPSE-79
❑ 96CzeAPSE-79

**Dmitriev, Igor**
❑ 74SweHocS-61
❑ 89RusNatT-4

**Doak, Gary**
❑ 67Top-97
❑ 68OPC-138
❑ 68ShiCoi-14
❑ 69OPC-202
❑ 70BruTeaIss-3
❑ 70CanuRoyB-4
❑ 70DadCoo-23
❑ 70EssPowPla-38
❑ 70OPC-114
❑ 70SarProSta-218
❑ 70Top-114
❑ 71CanuRoyB-21
❑ 71OPC-87
❑ 71SarProSta-214
❑ 71Top-87
❑ 72OPC-73
❑ 72Top-81
❑ 73RedWinTI-10
❑ 74OPCNHL-361
❑ 75OPCNHL-358
❑ 76OPCNHL-7
❑ 76Top-7
❑ 77OPCNHL-181
❑ 77Top-181
❑ 78OPC-305
❑ 80OPC-374

**Doan, Shane**
❑ 93KamBla-4
❑ 95BeAPla-172
❑ 95BeAPSig-S172
❑ 95BeAPSigDC-S172
❑ 95Bow-149
❑ 95BowAllFoi-149
❑ 95BowBes-BB24
❑ 95BowBesRef-BB24
❑ 95Cla-7
❑ 95ClaCHLAS-AS5
❑ 95ClaIceBre-BK7
❑ 95ColCho-403
❑ 95Don-210
❑ 95DonEli-109
❑ 95DonEliDCS-109
❑ 95DonEliDCU-109
❑ 95DonEliR-13
❑ 95DonRatRoo-8
❑ 95Fin-22
❑ 95FinRef-22
❑ 95Ima-85
❑ 95ImaGol-85
❑ 95JetTeaIss-5
❑ 95LeaLim-7
❑ 95Met-175
❑ 95ParInt-267
❑ 95ParIntEl-267
❑ 95SelCer-114
❑ 95SelCerMG-114
❑ 95SigRooA-14
❑ 95SigRooAPC-14
❑ 95SkyImp-226
❑ 95SlaMemC-15
❑ 95StaClu-207
❑ 95StaCluMOMS-207
❑ 95Sum-188
❑ 95SumArtP-188
❑ 95SumIce-188
❑ 95Top-314
❑ 95TopOPCI-314
❑ 95TopSupSkiSR-SR8
❑ 95Ult-336
❑ 95UltHigSpe-7
❑ 95UppDec-269
❑ 95UppDecEleIce-269
❑ 95UppDecEleIceG-269
❑ 95UppDecPHE-H27
❑ 95UppDecPreH-H27
❑ 95Zen-132
❑ 95ZenRooRC-15
❑ 96ClaIceBreDC-BK7
❑ 96ColCho-205
❑ 96Sco-262
❑ 96ScoArtPro-262
❑ 96ScoDeaCAP-262
❑ 96ScoGolB-262
❑ 96ScoSpeAP-262
❑ 96UppDec-314
❑ 97Pac-330
❑ 97PacCop-330
❑ 97PacEmeGre-330
❑ 97PacIceB-330
❑ 97PacInvNRB-149
❑ 97PacRed-330
❑ 97PacSil-330
❑ 97UppDec-131
❑ 99Pac-319
❑ 99PacCop-319
❑ 99PacGol-319
❑ 99PacIceB-319
❑ 99PacPreD-319

**Dobbin, Brian**
❑ 82KinCan-11
❑ 85LonKni-10
❑ 89ProAHL-341
❑ 90ProAHLIHL-33
❑ 91ProAHLCHL-375
❑ 94MilAdm-6

**Dobbyn, Josh**
❑ 96RegPat-9

**Dobek, Bob**
❑ 76SanDieMW-2

**Dobni, Evans**
❑ 81RegPat-7

**Dobrescu, Jay**
❑ 91AirCanSJHL-E2
❑ 92MPSPhoSJHL-7

**Dobrochotov, Viktor**
❑ 74SweHocS-88

**Dobrota, Andrej**
❑ 917thInnSQMJHL-132

**Dobry, Ivan**
❑ 95SloPeeWT-4

**Dobrzynski, Ralf**
❑ 94GerDELE-209

**Dobson, Jim**
❑ 83FreExp-6
❑ 84FreExp-11

**Dodunski, Colin**
❑ 91FerStaB-10

**Doers, Mike**
❑ 94DayBom-10

**Doherty, Kevin**
❑ 88BroBra-6

**Doherty, Paul**
❑ 907thInnSOHL-103
❑ 93OshGen-20

**Dohler, Udo**
❑ 94GerDELE-111
❑ 95GerDELE-27
❑ 96GerDELE-25

**Doig, Jason**
❑ 94ClaCHLP-CP4
❑ 94ParSE-SE254
❑ 94ParSEG-SE254
❑ 94Sel-161
❑ 94SelGol-161
❑ 94SP-177
❑ 94SPDieCut-177
❑ 95Bow-120
❑ 95BowAllFoi-120
❑ 95Cla-31
❑ 95ClaCHLAS-AS15
❑ 95ColCho-407
❑ 95Don-253
❑ 95Ima-12
❑ 95ImaCleE-CE18
❑ 95ImaGol-12
❑ 95ImaPlaPDC-PD9
❑ 95JetTeaIss-6
❑ 95ParInt-529
❑ 95ParIntEl-529
❑ 95StaClu-222
❑ 95StaCluMOMS-222
❑ 95Top-355
❑ 95TopOPCI-355
❑ 95Ult-337
❑ 95UppDec-499
❑ 95UppDecEleIce-499
❑ 95UppDecEleIceG-499
❑ 96Fle-125
❑ 96FleCalCan-2
❑ 96SkyImp-148
❑ 96UppDecIce-119
❑ 97BowCHL-48
❑ 97BowCHLOPC-48
❑ 98Pac-336
❑ 98PacIceB-336
❑ 98PacRed-336

**Doiron, Shane**
❑ 907thInnSQMJHL-130
❑ 917thInnSQMJHL-201

**Dolak, Thomas**
❑ 98GerDELE-61
❑ 98GerDELE-331

**Dolan, Mick**
❑ 91FerStaB-11

**Dolana, Libor**
❑ 91SweSemWCS-120
❑ 93SwiHNL-351
❑ 94CzeAPSE-14
❑ 95CzeAPSE-186
❑ 96CzeAPSE-321

**Dolezal, Jiri**
❑ 89SweSemWCS-193
❑ 94GerDELE-334
❑ 95FinnSemWC-153
❑ 95GerDELE-304

**Doll, Andre**
❑ 92CorBigRed-7
❑ 93CorBigRed-7

**Dollard, David**
❑ 92BriColJHL-52

**Dollas, Bobby**
❑ 86SheCan-12
❑ 87MonHaw-4
❑ 88ProAHL-100
❑ 93DucMilCap-2
❑ 93OPCPre-491
❑ 93OPCPreG-491
❑ 93Pow-283
❑ 93StaClu-463
❑ 93StaCluFDI-463
❑ 93StaCluO-463
❑ 93TopPre-491
❑ 93TopPreG-491
❑ 94CanGamNHLP-366
❑ 94DucCarJr-4
❑ 94Fla-2
❑ 94Lea-383
❑ 94OPCPre-264
❑ 94OPCPreSE-264
❑ 94Pin-41
❑ 94PinArtP-41
❑ 94PinRinC-41
❑ 94TopPre-264
❑ 94TopPreSE-264
❑ 94UppDec-13
❑ 94UppDecEleIce-13
❑ 95ColCho-289
❑ 95ColChoPC-289
❑ 95ColChoPCP-289
❑ 95Duc-1
❑ 95Emo-1
❑ 95PlaOneoOne-112
❑ 95SkyImp-1
❑ 95UppDec-395
❑ 95UppDecEleIce-395
❑ 95UppDecEleIceG-395
❑ 96BeAPAut-96
❑ 96BeAPAutSil-96
❑ 96BeAPla-96
❑ 96Duc-2
❑ 96Pin-157
❑ 96PinArtP-157
❑ 96PinFoi-157
❑ 96PinPreS-157
❑ 96PinRinC-157
❑ 97Pac-41
❑ 97PacCop-41
❑ 97PacEmeGre-41
❑ 97PacIceB-41
❑ 97PacRed-41
❑ 97PacSil-41
❑ 98Be A PPA-266
❑ 98Be A PPAA-266
❑ 98Be A PPAAF-266
❑ 98Be A PPSE-266
❑ 98Be APG-266

**Dombkiewicz, Mike**
❑ 96GueSto-9
❑ 97GueSto-9

**Dome, Robert**
❑ 97DonPre-163
❑ 97DonPreCttC-163
❑ 97DonPri-169
❑ 97DonPriSoA-169
❑ 97Pin-21
❑ 97PinArtP-21
❑ 97PinPrePBB-21
❑ 97PinPrePBC-21
❑ 97PinPrePBM-21
❑ 97PinPrePBY-21
❑ 97PinPrePFC-21
❑ 97PinPrePFM-21
❑ 97PinPrePFY-21
❑ 97PinPrePla-21
❑ 97PinRinC-21
❑ 97ScoPen-16
❑ 97ScoPenPla-16
❑ 97ScoPenPre-16
❑ 97SPAut-128
❑ 97UppDec-346
❑ 97UppDecBD-88
❑ 97UppDecBDDD-88
❑ 97UppDecBDQD-88
❑ 97UppDecBDTD-88
❑ 98Pac-350
❑ 98PacIceB-350
❑ 98PacRed-350
❑ 98SPxFin-67
❑ 98SPxFin-147
❑ 98SPxFinR-67
❑ 98SPxFinR-147
❑ 98SPxFinS-67
❑ 98SPxFinS-147
❑ 98UC-171
❑ 98UD ChoPCR-171
❑ 98UD ChoR-171
❑ 98UD3-9
❑ 98UD3-69
❑ 98UD3-129
❑ 98UD3DieC-9
❑ 98UD3DieC-69
❑ 98UD3DieC-129
❑ 98UDCP-171
❑ 98UppDec-164
❑ 98UppDecE-164
❑ 98UppDecE1o1-164
❑ 98UppDecGN-GN22
❑ 98UppDecGNQ1-GN22
❑ 98UppDecGNQ2-GN22
❑ 98UppDecGNQ3-GN22
❑ 98UppDecGR-164
❑ 98UppDecM-166
❑ 98UppDecMGS-166
❑ 98UppDecMSS-166
❑ 98UppDecMSS-166
❑ 99QuePeeWHWCCS-8

**Domenichelli, Hnat**
❑ 93KamBla-5
❑ 95DonEliWJ-12
❑ 95SlaMemC-13
❑ 95UppDec-539
❑ 95UppDecEleIce-539
❑ 95UppDecEleIceG-539
❑ 96DonCanI-122
❑ 96DonCanIGPP-122
❑ 96DonCanIRPP-122
❑ 96LeaLimR-4
❑ 96LeaLimRG-4
❑ 96LeaPre-121
❑ 96LeaPrePP-121
❑ 96MetUni-175
❑ 96SprFal-11
❑ 96Ult-74
❑ 96UltGolM-75
❑ 96UppDec-272
❑ 97ColCho-33
❑ 97Don-196
❑ 97DonCanI-131
❑ 97DonCanIDS-131
❑ 97DonCanIPS-131
❑ 97DonLim-45
❑ 97DonLimExp-45
❑ 97DonPreProG-196
❑ 97DonPreProS-196
❑ 97Lea-79
❑ 97LeaFraMat-79
❑ 97LeaFraMDC-79
❑ 97LeaInt-79
❑ 97LeaIntUI-79
❑ 97Pac-237
❑ 97PacCop-237
❑ 97PacEmeGre-237
❑ 97PacIceB-237
❑ 97PacRed-237
❑ 97PacSil-237
❑ 97PinIns-93
❑ 97Sco-68
❑ 97ScoArtPro-68
❑ 97ScoGolBla-68
❑ 97UppDec-22
❑ 98Pac-116
❑ 98PacIceB-116
❑ 98PacRed-116
❑ 98UppDec-53
❑ 98UppDecE-53
❑ 98UppDecE1o1-53
❑ 98UppDecGR-53

**Domi, Tie**
❑ 89ProAHL-127
❑ 90OPCPre-25
❑ 90ProAHLIHL-22
❑ 91Par-333
❑ 91ParFre-333
❑ 91ProSet-440
❑ 91ProSetFre-440
❑ 92Par-434
❑ 92ParEmel-434
❑ 92Sco-408
❑ 92ScoCan-408
❑ 92Top-395
❑ 92TopGol-395G
❑ 92UppDec-99
❑ 93Don-381
❑ 93JetRuf-8
❑ 93Lea-216
❑ 93OPCPre-513
❑ 93OPCPreG-513
❑ 93Par-230
❑ 93ParEmel-230
❑ 93Pin-295
❑ 93PinCan-295
❑ 93Sco-312
❑ 93ScoCan-312
❑ 93TopPre-513
❑ 93TopPreG-513
❑ 94BeAPla-R65
❑ 94BeAPla-R168
❑ 94BeAPSig-143
❑ 94CanGamNHLP-250
❑ 94CanGamNHLP-344
❑ 94Don-60
❑ 94Lea-318
❑ 94MapLeaK-10
❑ 94MapLeaPP-24
❑ 94OPCPre-444
❑ 94OPCPreSE-444
❑ 94ParSE-SE202
❑ 94ParSEG-SE202
❑ 94Pin-344
❑ 94PinArtP-344
❑ 94PinRinC-344
❑ 94Sco-123
❑ 94ScoGol-123
❑ 94ScoPla-123
❑ 94ScoPlaTS-123
❑ 94TopPre-444
❑ 94TopPreSE-444
❑ 94Ult-392
❑ 94UppDec-409
❑ 94UppDecEleIce-409
❑ 95CanGamNHLP-263
❑ 95ColCho-242
❑ 95ColChoPC-242
❑ 95ColChoPCP-242
❑ 95Don-225
❑ 95ParInt-205
❑ 95ParIntEl-205
❑ 95Pin-159
❑ 95PinArtP-159
❑ 95PinFulC-9
❑ 95PinRinC-159
❑ 95PlaOneoOne-94
❑ 95Sco-275
❑ 95ScoBlaIce-275
❑ 95ScoBlaIceAP-275
❑ 95Ult-159
❑ 95UltGolM-159
❑ 96BeAPAut-47
❑ 96BeAPAutSil-47
❑ 96BeAPla-47
❑ 96ColCho-261
❑ 96DurAllT-DC13
❑ 96MapLeaP-4
❑ 96UppDec-201
❑ 96UppDecIce-68
❑ 96UppDecIcePar-68
❑ 97ColCho-253
❑ 97Kat-140
❑ 97KatGol-140
❑ 97KatSil-140
❑ 97Pac-65
❑ 97PacCop-65
❑ 97PacEmeGre-65
❑ 97PacIceB-65
❑ 97PacOme-220
❑ 97PacOmeC-220
❑ 97PacOmeDG-220
❑ 97PacOmeEG-220
❑ 97PacOmeG-220
❑ 97PacOmeIB-220
❑ 97PacRed-65
❑ 97PacRev-134
❑ 97PacRevC-134
❑ 97PacRevE-134
❑ 97PacRevIB-134
❑ 97PacRevR-134
❑ 97PacRevS-134
❑ 97PacSil-65
❑ 97Sco-219
❑ 97ScoMapL-8
❑ 97ScoMapLPla-8
❑ 97ScoMapLPre-8
❑ 97UppDec-196
❑ 97UppDec-368
❑ 98Pac-28
❑ 98PacAur-180
❑ 98PacAurFL-10
❑ 98PacAurFLIB-10
❑ 98PacAurFLR-10
❑ 98PacCroR-129
❑ 98PacCroRLS-129
❑ 98PacDynI-178
❑ 98PacDynIIB-178
❑ 98PacDynIR-178
❑ 98PacIceB-28
❑ 98PacOmeH-226
❑ 98PacOmeODI-226
❑ 98PacOmeR-226
❑ 98PacPar-225
❑ 98PacParC-225
❑ 98PacParEG-225
❑ 98PacParH-225
❑ 98PacParIB-225
❑ 98PacParS-225
❑ 98PacRed-28
❑ 98PacRev-136
❑ 98PacRevIS-136
❑ 98PacRevR-136
❑ 98RevThrPA-9
❑ 98RevThrPA-9
❑ 98UC-204
❑ 98UD ChoPCR-204
❑ 98UD ChoR-204
❑ 98UppDec-189
❑ 98UppDecE-189
❑ 98UppDecE1o1-189
❑ 98UppDecGR-189
❑ 99Pac-405
❑ 99PacCop-405
❑ 99PacGol-405
❑ 99PacIceB-405
❑ 99PacPreD-405
❑ 99UppDecMPS-TD

**Domke, H.**
❑ 95GerDELE-348

**Domonsky, Brad**
❑ 95Sla-402
❑ 95SudWol-2
❑ 95SudWolP-7
❑ 96SudWol-6
❑ 96SudWolP-8

**Donaghue, Mike**
❑ 99WicThu-4

**Donahue, Mark**
❑ 907thInnSOHL-104
❑ 93KitRan-16

**Donald, Darren**
❑ 91AirCanSJHL-E46

**Donald, Derek**
❑ 92DayBom-7
❑ 93DayBom-15
❑ 96AncAce-2
❑ 97AncAce-6

**Donaldson, Craig**
❑ 897thInnSOHL-7
❑ 89OshGen-7
❑ 89OshGenP-7
❑ 907thInnSMC-79

**Donaldson, Dale**
❑ 93RedDeeR-5

**Donatelli, Clark**
❑ 90Bow-181
❑ 90BowTif-181
❑ 90OPC-458
❑ 90ProAHLIHL-316

**Donato, Ted**
❑ 91Par-230
❑ 91ParFre-230
❑ 92BruPos-2
❑ 92OPCPre-30
❑ 92Par-8
❑ 92ParEmel-8
❑ 92ProSet-221
❑ 92Sco-479
❑ 92ScoCan-479
❑ 92StaClu-271
❑ 92Ult-251
❑ 92UppDec-202
❑ 92UppDec-393
❑ 92UppDecGHS-G20
❑ 93Don-25
❑ 93Lea-54
❑ 93OPCPre-146
❑ 93OPCPreG-146
❑ 93PanSti-8
❑ 93Par-283
❑ 93ParEmel-283
❑ 93Pin-102

❑ 93PinCan-102
❑ 93Pow-18
❑ 93Sco-262
❑ 93ScoCan-262
❑ 93StaClu-83
❑ 93StaCluFDI-83
❑ 93StaCluFDIO-83
❑ 93StaCluO-83
❑ 93TopPre-146
❑ 93TopPreG-146
❑ 93Ult-267
❑ 93UppDec-143
❑ 94BeAPSig-141
❑ 94CanGamNHLP-43
❑ 94Don-155
❑ 94FinnSIS-357
❑ 94FinnSISGS-1
❑ 94Lea-49
❑ 94OPCPre-88
❑ 94OPCPreSE-88
❑ 94ParSE-SE14
❑ 94ParSEG-SE14
❑ 94Pin-146
❑ 94PinArtP-146
❑ 94PinRinC-146
❑ 94Sco-27
❑ 94ScoGol-27
❑ 94ScoPla-27
❑ 94ScoPlaTS-27
❑ 94TopPre-88
❑ 94TopPreSE-88
❑ 94Ult-12
❑ 94UppDec-61
❑ 94UppDecEleIce-61
❑ 95ColCho-76
❑ 95ColChoPC-76
❑ 95ColChoPCP-76
❑ 95Don-263
❑ 95FinnSISL-97
❑ 95Lea-326
❑ 95ParInt-17
❑ 95ParIntEl-17
❑ 95Sco-28
❑ 95ScoBlaIce-28
❑ 95ScoBlaIceAP-28
❑ 95Top-324
❑ 95TopOPCI-324
❑ 95Ult-204
❑ 95UppDec-80
❑ 95UppDecEleIce-80
❑ 95UppDecEleIceG-80
❑ 95UppDecSpeE-SE97
❑ 95UppDecSpeEdiG-SE97
❑ 96BeAPAut-37
❑ 96BeAPAutSil-37
❑ 96BeAPla-37
❑ 96ColCho-19
❑ 96Don-211
❑ 96DonPrePro-211
❑ 96Sco-30
❑ 96ScoArtPro-30
❑ 96ScoDeaCAP-30
❑ 96ScoGolB-30
❑ 96ScoSpeAP-30
❑ 96SP-13
❑ 96UppDec-221
❑ 97ColCho-14
❑ 97Don-108
❑ 97DonLim-118
❑ 97DonLimExp-118
❑ 97DonPreProG-108
❑ 97DonPreProS-108
❑ 97Kat-10
❑ 97KatGol-10
❑ 97KatSil-10
❑ 97Pac-209
❑ 97PacCop-209
❑ 97PacCroR-10
❑ 97PacCroREG-10
❑ 97PacCroRIB-10
❑ 97PacCroRS-10
❑ 97PacEmeGre-209
❑ 97PacIceB-209
❑ 97PacInv-9
❑ 97PacInvC-9
❑ 97PacInvEG-9
❑ 97PacInvIB-9
❑ 97PacInvR-9
❑ 97PacInvS-9
❑ 97PacOme-15
❑ 97PacOmeC-15
❑ 97PacOmeDG-15
❑ 97PacOmeEG-15
❑ 97PacOmeG-15
❑ 97PacOmeIB-15
❑ 97PacPar-12
❑ 97PacParC-12
❑ 97PacParDG-12
❑ 97PacParEG-12
❑ 97PacParIB-12
❑ 97PacParRed-12
❑ 97PacParSil-12
❑ 97PacRed-209
❑ 97PacRev-9
❑ 97PacRevC-9
❑ 97PacRevE-9
❑ 97PacRevIB-9
❑ 97PacRevR-9
❑ 97PacRevS-9
❑ 97PacSil-209
❑ 97PinCer-87
❑ 97PinCerMB-87
❑ 97PinCerMG-87
❑ 97PinCerMR-87
❑ 97PinCerR-87
❑ 97PinIns-101
❑ 97PinTotCMPG-87
❑ 97PinTotCPB-87
❑ 97PinTotCPG-87
❑ 97PinTotCPR-87
❑ 97Sco-171
❑ 97ScoBru-6
❑ 97ScoBruPla-6
❑ 97ScoBruPre-6
❑ 97SPAut-7
❑ 97UppDec-221
❑ 98Pac-76
❑ 98PacAur-11
❑ 98PacIceB-76
❑ 98PacOmeH-145
❑ 98PacOmeODI-145
❑ 98PacOmeR-145
❑ 98PacPar-13
❑ 98PacParC-13
❑ 98PacParEG-13
❑ 98PacParH-13
❑ 98PacParIB-13
❑ 98PacParS-13
❑ 98PacRed-76
❑ 98UC-11
❑ 98UD ChoPCR-11
❑ 98UD ChoR-11
❑ 98UDCP-11
❑ 98UppDec-217
❑ 98UppDecE-217
❑ 98UppDecE1o1-217
❑ 98UppDecGR-217

**Donnelly, Dave**
❑ 86BlaCok-4
❑ 88OilTenAnn-150
❑ 90ProAHLIHL-131

**Donnelly, Gord**
❑ 84FreExp-6
❑ 84NordPos-6
❑ 85FreExp-20
❑ 85NordMcD-5
❑ 85NordTeal-6
❑ 86NordGenF-6
❑ 86NordTeal-4
❑ 87NordGenF-6
❑ 88NordGenF-7
❑ 88NordTeal-8
❑ 89JetSaf-9
❑ 90JetIGA-8
❑ 90ProSet-560
❑ 91JetPanTS-7
❑ 91ProSet-357
❑ 91ProSetFre-357
❑ 91SabBluS-4
❑ 91SabPepC-4
❑ 91UppDec-305
❑ 91UppDecF-305
❑ 92DurPan-13
❑ 92SabBluS-5
❑ 92SabJubF-3
❑ 92Ult-259
❑ 93StaClu-396
❑ 93StaCluFDI-396
❑ 93StaCluO-396
❑ 94StaPos-4

**Donnelly, John**
❑ 72NatOttWHA-9

**Donnelly, Mike**
❑ 87SabBluS-7
❑ 88ProAHL-263
❑ 88SabBluS-6
❑ 89ProAHL-274
❑ 90ProAHLIHL-428
❑ 91Par-294
❑ 91ParFre-294
❑ 91Pin-299
❑ 91PinFre-299
❑ 91ProSet-399
❑ 91ProSetFre-399
❑ 91ProSetPla-183
❑ 91ScoCan-499
❑ 91UppDec-420
❑ 91UppDecF-420
❑ 92Bow-342
❑ 92OPC-151
❑ 92Pin-98
❑ 92PinFre-98
❑ 92Sco-67
❑ 92ScoCan-67
❑ 92StaClu-411
❑ 92Top-121
❑ 92TopGol-121G
❑ 92Ult-81
❑ 93Don-155
❑ 93Lea-282
❑ 93OPCPre-33
❑ 93OPCPreG-33
❑ 93Par-369
❑ 93ParEmel-369
❑ 93Pin-172
❑ 93PinCan-172
❑ 93Pow-359
❑ 93Sco-176
❑ 93ScoCan-176
❑ 93StaClu-374
❑ 93StaCluFDI-374
❑ 93StaCluO-374
❑ 93TopPre-33
❑ 93TopPreG-33
❑ 94CanGamNHLP-123
❑ 94Don-287
❑ 94Fla-78
❑ 94Lea-106
❑ 94OPCPre-308
❑ 94OPCPreSE-308
❑ 94Pin-223
❑ 94PinArtP-223
❑ 94PinRinC-223
❑ 94StaClu-14
❑ 94StaCluFDI-14
❑ 94StaCluMOMS-14
❑ 94StaCluSTWC-14
❑ 94StaPos-5
❑ 94TopPre-308
❑ 94TopPreSE-308
❑ 94Ult-97
❑ 94UppDec-199
❑ 94UppDecEleIce-199
❑ 95BeAPla-80
❑ 95BeAPSig-S80
❑ 95BeAPSigDC-S80
❑ 95CanGamNHLP-87
❑ 95ColCho-263
❑ 95ColChoPC-263
❑ 95ColChoPCP-263
❑ 95Don-232
❑ 95Lea-217
❑ 95ParInt-57
❑ 95ParIntEl-57
❑ 95Pin-156
❑ 95PinArtP-156
❑ 95PinRinC-156
❑ 95Sco-147
❑ 95ScoBlaIce-147
❑ 95ScoBlaIceAP-147
❑ 95UppDec-87
❑ 95UppDecEleIce-87
❑ 95UppDecEleIceG-87
❑ 96DetVip-5

**Donnelly, Pete**
❑ 73QuaOatWHA-29

**Donnelly, Trueman**
❑ 36V356WorG-134

**Donovan, Rob**
❑ 94BirBul-6
❑ 95BirBul-7

**Donovan, Ryan**
❑ 91BriColJHL-109
❑ 92BriColJHL-171

**Donovan, Shean**
❑ 92Ott672A-9
❑ 94Fin-158
❑ 94FinRef-158
❑ 94FinSupTW-158
❑ 94Pin-539
❑ 94PinArtP-539
❑ 94PinRinC-539
❑ 94SP-149
❑ 94SPDieCut-149
❑ 94UppDec-366
❑ 94UppDecEleIce-366
❑ 95BeAPla-3
❑ 95BeAPSig-S3
❑ 95BeAPSigDC-S3
❑ 95Bow-140
❑ 95BowAllFoi-140
❑ 95Cla-92
❑ 95Don-77
❑ 95DonCanWJT-19
❑ 95Fin-163
❑ 95FinRef-163
❑ 95Ima-46
❑ 95ImaAut-46A
❑ 95ImaGol-46
❑ 95Lea-47
❑ 95ParInt-458
❑ 95ParIntEl-458
❑ 95Pin-211
❑ 95PinArtP-211
❑ 95PinRinC-211
❑ 95Sco-307
❑ 95ScoBlaIce-307
❑ 95ScoBlaIceAP-307
❑ 95StaClu-114
❑ 95StaCluMOMS-114
❑ 95Sum-177
❑ 95SumArtP-177
❑ 95SumIce-177
❑ 95Top-42
❑ 95TopCanWJ-13CJ
❑ 95TopOPCI-42
❑ 95UppDec-131
❑ 95UppDecEleIce-131
❑ 95UppDecEleIceG-131
❑ 96ColCho-234
❑ 96UppDec-149
❑ 97Be A PPAD-142
❑ 97Be A PPAPD-142
❑ 97BeAPla-142
❑ 97BeAPlaAut-142
❑ 97PacInvNRB-176
❑ 97UppDec-152
❑ 98Pac-159
❑ 98PacIceB-159
❑ 98PacRed-159
❑ 98UppDec-251
❑ 98UppDecE-251
❑ 98UppDecE1o1-251
❑ 98UppDecGR-251

**Dontigny, Steve**
❑ 917thInnSQMJHL-60

**Doolan, John**
❑ 98KanCitB-27

**Dopita, Jiri**
❑ 94GerDELE-43
❑ 95CzeAPSE-20
❑ 96CzeAPSE-230
❑ 96SweSemW-122

**Dopita, Lubos**
❑ 94CzeAPSE-267

**Dopson, Rob**
❑ 90ProAHLIHL-370
❑ 91ProAHLCHL-301
❑ 92CleLum-15
❑ 93CleLum-22
❑ 93CleLumPos-7
❑ 95ColEdgI-131

**Doraty, Ken**
❑ 320'KeeMapL-NNO
❑ 33OPCV304A-4
❑ 33V129-14
❑ 33V357IceK-49

**Dorchak, Dean**
❑ 89PorWinH-6
❑ 907thInnSWHL-321

**Dore, Andre**
❑ 82PosCer-13
❑ 83NordPos-6
❑ 83OPC-313
❑ 84OPC-279

**Dore, Daniel**
❑ 88NordGenF-8
❑ 88NordTeal-9
❑ 89Nord-7
❑ 89NordGenF-5
❑ 89NordPol-4
❑ 90HalCit-4
❑ 90NordTeal-3
❑ 90UppDec-255
❑ 90UppDecF-255
❑ 91NordPanTS-2
❑ 91ProAHLCHL-539

**Dore, Mike**
❑ 90RayJrC-5
❑ 91RayJrC-4

**Dorey, Jim**
❑ 68MapLeaWB-2
❑ 69OPC-45
❑ 70ColSta-79
❑ 70EssPowPla-23
❑ 70MapLeaP-1
❑ 70OPC-106
❑ 70SarProSta-197
❑ 70Top-106
❑ 71MapLeaP-2
❑ 71OPC-57
❑ 71SarProSta-201
❑ 71Top-57
❑ 71TorSun-255
❑ 72OPC-339
❑ 72SweSemWC-168
❑ 72WhaNewEWHA-5
❑ 73QuaOatWHA-47
❑ 75OPCWHA-94
❑ 76NordPos-12
❑ 76OPCWHA-24

**Dorian, Dan**
❑ 93HumHawP-21

**Dorion, Dan**
❑ 88ProAHL-340

**Dorn, Konrad**
❑ 95AusNatTea-5

**Dornhoefer, Gary**
❑ 64BeeGro3P-6
❑ 64CocCap-5
❑ 64Top-72
❑ 65Top-38
❑ 68OPC-94
❑ 68ShiCoi-126
❑ 68Top-94
❑ 69OPC-94
❑ 69Top-94
❑ 70ColSta-40
❑ 70DadCoo-24
❑ 70EssPowPla-208
❑ 70FlyPos-2
❑ 70OPC-85
❑ 70OPCDec-33
❑ 70SarProSta-149
❑ 70Top-85
❑ 71LetActR-3
❑ 71OPC-202
❑ 71SarProSta-151
❑ 71Top-89
❑ 71TorSun-192
❑ 72FlyMigM-3
❑ 72OPC-146
❑ 72SarProSta-161
❑ 72SweSemWC-179
❑ 72Top-41
❑ 73OPC-182
❑ 73Top-167
❑ 74NHLActSta-213
❑ 74OPCNHL-44
❑ 74Top-44
❑ 75FlyCanDC-6
❑ 75OPCNHL-129
❑ 75Top-129
❑ 76OPCNHL-256
❑ 76Top-256
❑ 77OPCNHL-202
❑ 77Top-202
❑ 94ParTalB-20

**Dorochin, I.**
❑ 95GerDELE-46

**Dorofeyev, Igor**
❑ 91OPCIns-32R
❑ 92UppDec-352

**Dorohoy, Eddie**
❑ 44BeeGro2P-233
❑ 45QuaOatP-72

**Dortigny, Steve**
❑ 907thInnSQMJHL-193

**Dorval, Sebastien**
❑ 92QueIntP-42

**Dosdall, Cory**
❑ 907thInnSWHL-169
❑ 917thInnSWHL-308

**Dostal, David**
❑ 96CzeAPSE-118

**Doucet, Benoit**
❑ 85MonGolF-26
❑ 94FinnJaaK-281
❑ 94GerDELE-86
❑ 95GerDELE-91
❑ 95GerDELE-431
❑ 96GerDELE-279
❑ 96SweSemW-196

**Doucet, Dany**
❑ 92QueIntP-10

**Doucet, Dave**
❑ 91AirCanSJHL-C6
❑ 92MPSPhoSJHL-81

**Doucet, Wayne**
❑ 86SudWol-20
❑ 90ProAHLIHL-497
❑ 90Sco-397
❑ 90ScoCan-397
❑ 91ProAHLCHL-461

**Doucette, Dave**
❑ 89SauSteMG-27
❑ 92DalFre-7
❑ 93DalFre-6
❑ 94CenHocL-111

**Douglas, Jordy**
❑ 79OPC-335
❑ 80OPC-97
❑ 80Top-97
❑ 81OPCSti-65
❑ 82NorStaPos-7
❑ 82PosCer-7
❑ 83NorStaPos-7
❑ 84OPC-338

**Douglas, Kent**
❑ 44BeeGro2P-396
❑ 62YorIroOTra-13
❑ 63ChePho-10
❑ 63MapLeaWB-5
❑ 63Par-7
❑ 63Par-67
❑ 63TorSta-10
❑ 63YorWhiB-13
❑ 64BeeGro3P-160
❑ 64CocCap-102
❑ 65Coc-101
❑ 65Top-14
❑ 66Top-82
❑ 68OPC-26
❑ 68ShiCoi-39
❑ 68Top-26
❑ 94ParTalB-109
❑ 95Par66-105
❑ 95Par66Coi-105

**Douglas, Layne**
❑ 91AirCanSJHL-A22
❑ 91AirCanSJHLAS-19
❑ 91AirCanSJHLAS-41

**Douglas, Les (Leslie)**
❑ 51LavDaiQSHL-100
❑ 51LavDaiS-100
❑ 52St.LawS-5

**Douglas, Lester (Les)**
❑ 34BeeGro1P-99
❑ 40OPCV3012-129

**Douglas, Ryan**
❑ 92BriColJHL-157
❑ 93PetPet-21
❑ 93SauSteMG-2
❑ 94FliGen-6

**Doull, Doug**
❑ 917thInnSOHL-114

**Dourion, George**
❑ 897thInnSOHL-71
❑ 907thInnSOHL-207
❑ 917thInnSOHL-266
❑ 91SudWol-12

**Douris, Peter**
❑ 86SheCan-13
❑ 87MonHaw-5
❑ 88ProIHL-83
❑ 89BruSpoAU-3
❑ 90BruSpoA-10
❑ 90OPCPre-26
❑ 90ProSet-407
❑ 91BruSpoA-6
❑ 91OPCPre-141
❑ 91ProAHLCHL-64
❑ 91ProSet-347
❑ 91ProSetFre-347
❑ 91ScoCan-633
❑ 91UppDec-403
❑ 91UppDec-601
❑ 91UppDecF-403
❑ 91UppDecF-601
❑ 92PanSti-141
❑ 92PanStiFre-141
❑ 92Sco-384
❑ 92ScoCan-384
❑ 92StaClu-402
❑ 92Top-190
❑ 92TopGol-190G
❑ 93OPCPre-265
❑ 93OPCPreG-265
❑ 93Pow-284
❑ 93TopPre-265
❑ 93TopPreG-265
❑ 94CanGamNHLP-30
❑ 94DucCarJr-5
❑ 94Lea-397
❑ 94OPCPre-184
❑ 94OPCPreSE-184
❑ 94TopPre-184
❑ 94TopPreSE-184
❑ 95BeAPla-25
❑ 95BeAPSig-S25
❑ 95BeAPSigDC-S25
❑ 95ParInt-278
❑ 95ParIntEl-278
❑ 95PlaOneoOne-222
❑ 96MilAdmBO-5
❑ 98GerDELE-70

**Douris, Yvon**
❑ 77KalWin-8

**Dowd, Bill**
❑ 81Ott67-3
❑ 82Ott67-4

**Dowd, Jim**
❑ 91ProAHLCHL-423
❑ 93ClaProPro-22
❑ 93Pow-376
❑ 94BeAPSig-91
❑ 94ClaProP-44
❑ 94Don-47
❑ 94Lea-307
❑ 94OPCPre-321
❑ 94OPCPreSE-321
❑ 94Par-279
❑ 94ParGol-279
❑ 94ParSE-SE98
❑ 94ParSEG-SE98
❑ 94Pin-439
❑ 94PinArtP-439
❑ 94PinRinC-439
❑ 94StaClu-194
❑ 94StaCluFDI-194
❑ 94StaCluMOMS-194
❑ 94StaCluSTWC-194
❑ 94TopPre-321
❑ 94TopPreSE-321
❑ 94Ult-116
❑ 94UppDec-410
❑ 94UppDecEleIce-410
❑ 95ParInt-485
❑ 95ParIntEl-485
❑ 95StaClu-91
❑ 95StaCluMOMS-91
❑ 95Top-316
❑ 95TopOPCI-316
❑ 95Ult-260
❑ 97Be A PPAD-111
❑ 97Be A PPAPD-111
❑ 97BeAPla-111
❑ 97BeAPlaAut-111

**Downey, Aaron**
❑ 95HamRoaA-20
❑ 96HamRoaA-HRA20

**Downey, Brian**
❑ 93ThuBayS-11
❑ 95MadMon-2

**Downey, Jason**
❑ 907thInnSQMJHL-176
❑ 917thInnSQMJHL-154
❑ 93DayBom-4
❑ 94DayBom-4
❑ 95DayBom-8
❑ 96DayBom-18

**Doyle, Jason**
❑ 95BowDraPro-P11
❑ 95Cla-88
❑ 95SauSteMG-5
❑ 95Sla-375

**Doyle, Joe**
❑ 94SarSti-5

**Doyle, Paul**
❑ 95Sla-144
❑ 95Sla-434

**Doyle, Perry**
❑ 94SheSte-14
❑ 97SheSte-19

**Doyle, Robin**
❑ 88ProAHL-22
❑ 93SweSemWCS-272
❑ 94FinnJaaK-233
❑ 95AusNatTea-6
❑ 96SweSemW-29
❑ 98GerDELE-139

**Doyle, Shane**
❑ 84BelBul-13
❑ 88ProIHL-10

**Doyle, Stephen**
❑ 95SolBar-13

**Doyle, Trevor**
❑ 93KinFro-5

**Doyon, Mario**
❑ 88ProIHL-98
❑ 89ProIHL-66
❑ 90HalCit-5
❑ 90ProAHLIHL-443
❑ 91ProAHLCHL-364
❑ 91UppDec-411
❑ 91UppDecF-411
❑ 93FreCan-7

**Drabek, Adam**
❑ 96CzeAPSE-285

**Drader, Daryl**
❑ 77RocAme-6

**Drag, Milan**
❑ 89VicCou-8

**Dragan, Jaromir**
❑ 95SloAPSNT-5
❑ 96SweSemW-220

**Dragicevic, Milan**
❑ 86RegPat-4
❑ 87RegPat-3
❑ 89SpoChi-4

**Dragon, Joe**
❑ 86SudWol-11
❑ 94ClaProP-237

**Drainville, Francois**
❑ 97RimOce-20

**Drainville, Robert**
❑ 51LavDaiS-39

**Draisaitl, Peter**
❑ 89SweSemWCS-124
❑ 91SweSemWCS-166
❑ 94GerDELE-208
❑ 95GerDELE-209
❑ 95GerDELE-437
❑ 96GerDELE-353
❑ 98GerDELE-323

**Drake, Clare**
❑ 89JetSaf-29
❑ 90JetIGA-9

**Drake, Dallas**
❑ 92Cla-86
❑ 93ClaProPBC-BC19
❑ 93ClaProPLP-LP5
❑ 93ClaProPro-15
❑ 93Don-100
❑ 93Don-508
❑ 93Lea-148
❑ 93OPCPre-365
❑ 93OPCPreG-365
❑ 93Par-61
❑ 93ParEmel-61
❑ 93Pin-28
❑ 93PinCan-28
❑ 93Pow-71
❑ 93Sco-246
❑ 93ScoCan-246
❑ 93StaClu-484
❑ 93StaCluFDI-484
❑ 93StaCluO-484
❑ 93TopPre-365
❑ 93TopPreG-365
❑ 93Ult-104
❑ 93UppDec-50
❑ 93UppDecNB-HB4
❑ 93UppDecSP-43
❑ 94CanGamNHLP-251
❑ 94ClaAut-NNO
❑ 94Fla-206
❑ 94Lea-380
❑ 94OPCPre-64
❑ 94OPCPreSE-64
❑ 94Par-261
❑ 94ParGol-261
❑ 94ParVin-V90
❑ 94Pin-225
❑ 94PinArtP-225
❑ 94PinRinC-225
❑ 94TopPre-64
❑ 94TopPreSE-64
❑ 94Ult-241
❑ 94UppDec-360
❑ 94UppDecEleIce-360
❑ 95BeAPla-83
❑ 95BeAPSig-S83
❑ 95BeAPSigDC-S83
❑ 95CanGamNHLP-288
❑ 95ColCho-269
❑ 95ColChoPC-269
❑ 95ColChoPCP-269
❑ 95JetReaC-2
❑ 95JetTeaIss-7
❑ 95Lea-268
❑ 95ParInt-503
❑ 95ParIntEl-503
❑ 95Pin-25
❑ 95PinArtP-25
❑ 95PinRinC-25
❑ 95PlaOneoOne-326
❑ 95ProMag-62
❑ 95Top-328
❑ 95TopOPCI-328
❑ 95Ult-326
❑ 95UppDec-17
❑ 95UppDecEleIce-17
❑ 95UppDecEleIceG-17
❑ 95UppDecSpeE-SE178
❑ 95UppDecSpeEdiG-SE178
❑ 96ClaGol-86
❑ 96NHLProSTA-62
❑ 96PlaOneoOne-405
❑ 97ColCho-197
❑ 97PacInvNRB-150
❑ 97PacOme-172
❑ 97PacOmeC-172
❑ 97PacOmeDG-172
❑ 97PacOmeEG-172
❑ 97PacOmeG-172
❑ 97PacOmeIB-172
❑ 97UppDec-338
❑ 98Be A PPA-257
❑ 98Be A PPAA-257
❑ 98Be A PPAAF-257
❑ 98Be A PPSE-257
❑ 98Be APG-257
❑ 98O-PChr-107
❑ 98O-PChrR-107
❑ 98Pac-337
❑ 98PacIceB-337
❑ 98PacOmeH-183
❑ 98PacOmeODI-183
❑ 98PacOmeR-183
❑ 98PacPar-180
❑ 98PacParC-180
❑ 98PacParEG-180
❑ 98PacParH-180

❑ 98PacParIB-180
❑ 98PacParS-180
❑ 98PacRed-337
❑ 98Top-107
❑ 98TopO-P-107
❑ 98UppDec-342
❑ 98UppDecE-342
❑ 98UppDecE1o1-342
❑ 98UppDecGR-342
❑ 99Pac-320
❑ 99PacCop-320
❑ 99PacGol-320
❑ 99PacIceB-320
❑ 99PacPreD-320

**Drapeau, Etienne**
❑ 95BowDraPro-P12
❑ 95ClaCHLAS-AS16
❑ 95UppDec-514
❑ 95UppDecEleIce-514
❑ 95UppDecEleIceG-514

**Drapeau, Gaston**
❑ 80QueRem-4
❑ 907thInnSQMJHL-180
❑ 917thInnSQMJHL-124

**Draper, Dave**
❑ 83BraAle-13

**Draper, Kris**
❑ 907thInnSOHL-83
❑ 90JetIGA-10
❑ 90Sco-404
❑ 90ScoCan-404
❑ 90UppDec-466
❑ 90UppDecF-466
❑ 90UppDecF-473
❑ 91JetPanTS-8
❑ 91MonHaw-5
❑ 91ProAHLCHL-177
❑ 92OPC-374
❑ 92OPCPre-27
❑ 92Top-249
❑ 92TopGol-249G
❑ 93Don-423
❑ 94BeAPSig-25
❑ 94Don-182
❑ 94Lea-28
❑ 94StaClu-72
❑ 94StaCluFDI-72
❑ 94StaCluMOMS-72
❑ 94StaCluSTWC-72
❑ 94UppDec-492
❑ 94UppDecEleIce-492
❑ 95CanGamNHLP-94
❑ 95UppDec-459
❑ 95UppDecEleIce-459
❑ 95UppDecEleIceG-459
❑ 96Don-169
❑ 96DonCanI-92
❑ 96DonCanIGPP-92
❑ 96DonCanIRPP-92
❑ 96DonPrePro-169
❑ 96Lea-119
❑ 96LeaPreP-119
❑ 96RedWinDNFP-1
❑ 96Sco-192
❑ 96ScoArtPro-192
❑ 96ScoDeaCAP-192
❑ 96ScoGolB-192
❑ 96ScoSpeAP-192
❑ 96UppDecBD-33
❑ 96UppDecBDG-33
❑ 97Be A PPAD-20
❑ 97Be A PPAPD-20
❑ 97BeAPla-20
❑ 97BeAPlaAut-20
❑ 97PacInvNRB-68
❑ 97ScoRedW-12
❑ 97ScoRedWPla-12
❑ 97ScoRedWPre-12
❑ 97UppDec-62
❑ 98Be A PPA-200
❑ 98Be A PPAA-200
❑ 98Be A PPAAF-200
❑ 98Be A PPSE-200
❑ 98Be APG-200
❑ 98O-PChr-168
❑ 98O-PChrR-168
❑ 98Pac-188
❑ 98PacIceB-188
❑ 98PacRed-188
❑ 98Top-168
❑ 98TopO-P-168
❑ 98UppDec-268
❑ 98UppDecE-268
❑ 98UppDecE1o1-268
❑ 98UppDecGR-268
❑ 99Pac-137
❑ 99PacCop-137
❑ 99PacGol-137
❑ 99PacIceB-137
❑ 99PacPreD-137

**Draper, Tom**
❑ 88ProAHL-180
❑ 89JetSaf-10
❑ 90ProAHLIHL-554
❑ 91Par-240
❑ 91Par-448
❑ 91ParFre-240
❑ 91ParFre-448
❑ 91Pin-341
❑ 91PinFre-341
❑ 91ProAHLCHL-20
❑ 91RochAmeDD-6
❑ 91RochAmePos-8
❑ 91SabBluS-5
❑ 91SabPepC-5
❑ 91UppDec-552
❑ 91UppDecF-552
❑ 92Bow-56
❑ 92OPC-376
❑ 92PanSti-243
❑ 92PanStiFre-243
❑ 92ProSet-14
❑ 92Sco-530
❑ 92ScoCan-530
❑ 92StaClu-395
❑ 92Top-278
❑ 92TopGol-278G
❑ 92Ult-14
❑ 92UppDec-201
❑ 92UppDec-361
❑ 95ColEdgI-160
❑ 95MilAdmBO-6

**Draxler, M.**
❑ 95GerDELE-377

**Drayna, D.J.**
❑ 95NorIowH-6

**Dreger, Barry**
❑ 88BraWheK-10

**Dreger, Ron**
❑ 81SasBla-12
❑ 83SasBla-19
❑ 84SasBlaS-4

**Dreveny, Greg**
❑ 897thInnSOHL-92
❑ 907thInnSOHL-2
❑ 917thInnSOHL-112
❑ 92SudWol-25

**Drevitch, Scott**
❑ 88ProAHL-160
❑ 89ProAHL-76
❑ 91RicRen-4
❑ 92RicRen-3

**Drevitch, Todd**
❑ 91RicRen-6
❑ 92ForWorF-5

**Drillon, Gordie (Gordon)**
❑ 34BeeGro1P-148
❑ 34BeeGro1P-315
❑ 37OPCV304E-142
❑ 38QuaOatP-10
❑ 39OPCV3011-4
❑ 40OPCV3012-110
❑ 55Par-25
❑ 55ParQuaO-25
❑ 83HalFP-H3
❑ 85HalFC-109

**Drinkwater, C.G.**
❑ 83HalFP-J6
❑ 85HalFC-186

**Driscoll, Chris**
❑ 907thInnSOHL-283

**Driscoll, Peter**
❑ 76OPCWHA-45
❑ 79OilPos-5
❑ 88OilTenAnn-7

**Driscoll, Steve**
❑ 84FreExp-15

**Driver, Bruce**
❑ 84DevPos-23
❑ 85OPC-127
❑ 85Top-127
❑ 86DevPol-10
❑ 86OPC-19
❑ 86Top-19
❑ 87OPC-79
❑ 87OPCSti-60
❑ 87PanSti-74
❑ 87Top-79
❑ 88DevCar-10
❑ 88OPC-157
❑ 88OPCSti-77
❑ 88PanSti-269
❑ 88Top-157
❑ 89DevCar-10
❑ 90Bow-87
❑ 90BowTif-87
❑ 90Dev-11
❑ 90OPC-172
❑ 90PanSti-69
❑ 90ProSet-166
❑ 90Sco-109
❑ 90ScoCan-109
❑ 90Top-172
❑ 90TopTif-172
❑ 90UppDec-373
❑ 90UppDecF-373
❑ 91Bow-281
❑ 91OPC-294
❑ 91PanSti-225
❑ 91Par-322
❑ 91ParFre-322
❑ 91Pin-63
❑ 91PinFre-63
❑ 91ProSet-140
❑ 91ProSet-577
❑ 91ProSetFre-140
❑ 91ProSetFre-577
❑ 91ProSetPla-69
❑ 91ScoAme-89
❑ 91ScoCan-89
❑ 91StaClu-122
❑ 91Top-294
❑ 91UppDec-292
❑ 91UppDecF-292
❑ 92PanSti-178
❑ 92PanStiFre-178
❑ 92Par-333
❑ 92ParEmel-333
❑ 92Pin-278
❑ 92PinFre-278
❑ 92ProSet-99
❑ 92Sco-251
❑ 92ScoCan-251
❑ 92StaClu-376
❑ 92Top-384
❑ 92TopGol-384G
❑ 92Ult-336
❑ 92UppDec-200
❑ 93Don-185
❑ 93Lea-56
❑ 93OPCPre-377
❑ 93OPCPreG-377
❑ 93PanSti-44
❑ 93Pin-277
❑ 93PinCan-277
❑ 93Pow-135
❑ 93Sco-263
❑ 93ScoCan-263
❑ 93StaClu-126
❑ 93StaCluFDI-126
❑ 93StaCluFDIO-126
❑ 93StaCluO-126
❑ 93TopPre-377
❑ 93TopPreG-377
❑ 93Ult-214
❑ 94CanGamNHLP-150
❑ 94Lea-377
❑ 94OPCPre-292
❑ 94OPCPreSE-292
❑ 94Pin-126
❑ 94PinArtP-126
❑ 94PinRinC-126
❑ 94Sco-115
❑ 94ScoGol-115
❑ 94ScoPla-115
❑ 94ScoPlaTS-115
❑ 94StaClu-35
❑ 94StaCluFDI-35
❑ 94StaCluMOMS-35
❑ 94StaCluSTWC-35
❑ 94TopPre-292
❑ 94TopPreSE-292
❑ 95BeAPla-147
❑ 95BeAPSig-S147
❑ 95BeAPSigDC-S147
❑ 95ParInt-413
❑ 95ParIntEl-413
❑ 95Sco-257
❑ 95ScoBlaIce-257
❑ 95ScoBlaIceAP-257
❑ 95Ult-190
❑ 95UltGolM-190
❑ 96FlePic-156
❑ 97Be A PPAD-87
❑ 97Be A PPAPD-87
❑ 97BeAPla-87
❑ 97BeAPlaAut-87
❑ 97PacInvNRB-124
❑ 97ScoRan-11
❑ 97ScoRanPla-11
❑ 97ScoRanPre-11
❑ 97UppDec-110
❑ 98O-PChr-41
❑ 98O-PChrR-41
❑ 98Pac-292
❑ 98PacIceB-292
❑ 98PacRed-292
❑ 98Top-41
❑ 98TopO-P-41

**Drolet, Nancy**
❑ 94ClaWomOH-W18
❑ 97ColCho-277
❑ 97EssOlyHH-56
❑ 97EssOlyHHF-56

**Drolet, Rene**
❑ 77RocAme-7
❑ 77RocAme-8

**Droppa, Ivan**
❑ 91UppDecCWJC-98
❑ 92IndIce-10
❑ 93Cla-128
❑ 93ClaProPro-149
❑ 93Don-414
❑ 93Par-42
❑ 93ParEmel-42
❑ 93Ult-288
❑ 94IndIce-4
❑ 94Lea-112
❑ 94Par-49
❑ 94ParGol-49
❑ 94StaClu-252
❑ 94StaCluFDI-252
❑ 94StaCluMOMS-252
❑ 94StaCluSTWC-252
❑ 94UppDec-435
❑ 94UppDecEleIce-435
❑ 95IndIce-5
❑ 98GerDELE-267

**Drouillard, Phil**
❑ 82NorBayC-4

**Drouin, Claude**
❑ 80QueRem-5

**Drouin, Eric**
❑ 96RimOce-9
❑ 96RimOceQPP-9
❑ 97BowCHL-67
❑ 97BowCHLOPC-67
❑ 97RimOce-22
❑ 98BowCHL-111
❑ 98BowCHLGA-111
❑ 98BowCHLOI-111
❑ 98BowChrC-111
❑ 98BowChrCGA-111
❑ 98BowChrCGAR-111
❑ 98BowChrCOI-111
❑ 98BowChrCOIR-111
❑ 98BowChrCR-111

**Drouin, Jude**
❑ 70ColSta-18
❑ 70OPC-171
❑ 70SarProSta-88
❑ 71LetActR-21
❑ 71OPC-68
❑ 71OPCTBoo-21
❑ 71SarProSta-81
❑ 71Top-68
❑ 71TorSun-128
❑ 72OPC-47
❑ 72SarProSta-100
❑ 72Top-153
❑ 73NorStaAP-2
❑ 73NorStaP-3
❑ 73OPC-125
❑ 73Top-125
❑ 74NHLActSta-139
❑ 74NHLActStaU-24
❑ 74OPCNHL-255
❑ 74Top-255
❑ 75OPCNHL-224
❑ 75Top-224
❑ 76OPCNHL-106
❑ 76Top-106
❑ 77OPCNHL-182
❑ 77Top-182
❑ 78OPC-93
❑ 78Top-93
❑ 79JetPos-5
❑ 79OPC-329
❑ 80JetPos-6
❑ 80OPC-285
❑ 80PepCap-125

**Drouin, P.C.**
❑ 92CorBigRed-8
❑ 96ProBru-17

**Drouin, Paul**
❑ 36V356WorG-50
❑ 37OPCV304E-158
❑ 38QuaOatP-11
❑ 39OPCV3011-24

**Drouin, Polly**
❑ 34BeeGro1P-149

**Drozdetski, Nikolai**
❑ 81SweSemHVS-49
❑ 82SweSemHVS-63

**Drozdiak, Dean**
❑ 83VicCou-7

**Druce, John**
❑ 89CapKod-19
❑ 89ProAHL-100
❑ 90BowHatTri-16
❑ 90CapKod-5
❑ 90CapPos-5
❑ 90CapSmo-5
❑ 90OPC-298
❑ 90ProSet-310
❑ 90Sco-246
❑ 90ScoCan-246
❑ 90ScoYouS-25
❑ 90Top-298
❑ 90TopTif-298
❑ 90UppDec-371
❑ 90UppDecF-371
❑ 91Bow-293
❑ 91Bow-413
❑ 91CapJun5-8
❑ 91CapKod-8
❑ 91OPC-206
❑ 91PanSti-200
❑ 91Par-415
❑ 91ParFre-415
❑ 91Pin-395
❑ 91PinFre-395
❑ 91ProSet-251
❑ 91ProSetFre-251
❑ 91ProSetPla-129
❑ 91ScoAme-180
❑ 91ScoCan-180
❑ 91StaClu-331
❑ 91Top-206
❑ 91UppDec-151
❑ 91UppDecF-151
❑ 92Bow-180
❑ 92OPC-105
❑ 92OPCPre-80
❑ 92Par-437
❑ 92ParEmel-437
❑ 92Pin-185
❑ 92PinFre-185
❑ 92Sco-121
❑ 92ScoCan-121
❑ 92StaClu-405
❑ 92Top-188
❑ 92TopGol-188G
❑ 92Ult-442
❑ 92UppDec-205
❑ 93Pow-360
❑ 94CanGamNHLP-124
❑ 94Don-223
❑ 94Lea-131
❑ 94OPCPreSE-549
❑ 94Pin-304
❑ 94PinArtP-304
❑ 94PinRinC-304
❑ 94StaClu-71
❑ 94StaCluFDI-71
❑ 94StaCluMOMS-71
❑ 94StaCluSTWC-71
❑ 94TopPreSE-549
❑ 94Ult-98
❑ 95CanGamNHLP-135
❑ 95ColCho-135
❑ 95ColChoPC-135
❑ 95ColChoPCP-135
❑ 95Lea-107
❑ 95Pin-113
❑ 95PinArtP-113
❑ 95PinRinC-113
❑ 95Top-111
❑ 95TopOPCI-111
❑ 96FlyPos-6
❑ 97PacDynBKS-69
❑ 97ScoFly-19
❑ 97ScoFlyPla-19
❑ 97ScoFlyPre-19

**Druken, Harold**
❑ 96DetWha-4
❑ 96UppDec-380
❑ 97BowCHL-146
❑ 97BowCHLAu-26
❑ 97BowCHLOPC-146
❑ 98SPXTopP-64
❑ 98SPXTopPF-64
❑ 98SPXTopPR-64
❑ 98UppDecBD-91
❑ 98UppDecDD-91
❑ 98UppDecQD-91
❑ 98UppDecTD-91

**Drulia, Stan**
❑ 84BelBul-9
❑ 88NiaFalT-16
❑ 89ProAHL-138
❑ 90KnoChe-107
❑ 91ProAHLCHL-379
❑ 92OPCPre-105
❑ 92Par-177
❑ 92ParEmel-177
❑ 92UppDec-487
❑ 93Par-191
❑ 93ParEmel-191
❑ 95ColEdgI-100
❑ 95ColEdgIQ-IR6
❑ 96DetVip-6

**Drummond, Kurt**
❑ 95SwiCurB-3

**Drury, Bryan**
❑ 907thInnSOHL-284

**Drury, Chris**
❑ 93Cla-101
❑ 95DonEliWJ-34
❑ 95UppDec-569
❑ 95UppDecEleIce-569
❑ 95UppDecEleIceG-569
❑ 98BowBes-102
❑ 98BowBesA-A8A
❑ 98BowBesA-A8B
❑ 98BowBesAAR-A8A
❑ 98BowBesAAR-A8B
❑ 98BowBesAR-102
❑ 98BowBesAR-A8A
❑ 98BowBesAR-A8B
❑ 98BowBesP-BP7
❑ 98BowBesPAR-BP7
❑ 98BowBesPR-BP7
❑ 98BowBesR-102
❑ 98PacCroR-32
❑ 98PacCroRLS-32
❑ 98PacCroRRC-1
❑ 98PacDynI-46
❑ 98PacDynIIB-46
❑ 98PacDynIR-46
❑ 98PacDynIR-1
❑ 98PacOmeH-67
❑ 98PacOmeODI-67
❑ 98PacOmeR-67
❑ 98PacRev-34
❑ 98PacRevIS-34
❑ 98PacRevR-34
❑ 98SP Aut-96
❑ 98SP AutSS-SS20
❑ 98SPXTopP-17
❑ 98SPXTopPF-17
❑ 98SPXTopPR-17
❑ 98UppDec-415
❑ 98UppDecBD-24
❑ 98UppDecDD-24
❑ 98UppDecE-415
❑ 98UppDecE1o1-415
❑ 98UppDecGN-GN21
❑ 98UppDecGNQ1-GN21
❑ 98UppDecGNQ2-GN21
❑ 98UppDecGNQ3-GN21
❑ 98UppDecGR-415
❑ 98UppDecM-54
❑ 98UppDecM1-M11
❑ 98UppDecM2-M11
❑ 98UppDecMGS-54
❑ 98UppDecMP-CD
❑ 98UppDecMSS-54
❑ 98UppDecMSS-54
❑ 98UppDecP-P26
❑ 98UppDecPQ1-P26
❑ 98UppDecPQ2-P26
❑ 98UppDecPQ3-P26
❑ 98UppDecQD-24
❑ 98UppDecTD-24
❑ 98UppDecWFG-WF16
❑ 98UppDecWFP-WF16
❑ 99Pac-102
❑ 99PacAur-36
❑ 99PacAurPD-36
❑ 99PacCop-102
❑ 99PacGol-102
❑ 99PacGolCD-7
❑ 99PacIceB-102
❑ 99PacPreD-102
❑ 99SP AutPS-96
❑ 99UppDecCL-74
❑ 99UppDecCLCLC-74
❑ 99UppDecM-54
❑ 99UppDecM2CN-10
❑ 99UppDecMPS-54
❑ 99UppDecMPS-CD
❑ 99UppDecMSS-54
❑ 99UppDecMSS-54

**Drury, Ted**
❑ 92HarCri-7
❑ 92UppDec-396
❑ 93Cla-63
❑ 93Don-58
❑ 93Don-437
❑ 93DonRatR-14
❑ 93Lea-424
❑ 93Par-35
❑ 93ParEmel-35
❑ 93Pin-447
❑ 93PinCan-447
❑ 93Pow-303
❑ 93Sco-608
❑ 93ScoCan-608
❑ 93ScoGol-608
❑ 93StaClu-443
❑ 93StaCluFDI-443
❑ 93StaCluO-443
❑ 93Ult-280
❑ 93UltWavF-4
❑ 93UppDec-466
❑ 93UppDecSP-20
❑ 94BeAPSig-34
❑ 94ClaAut-NNO
❑ 94ClaProP-14
❑ 94ClaProPIH-LP2
❑ 94Don-186
❑ 94Lea-22
❑ 94OPCPre-157
❑ 94OPCPreSE-157
❑ 94Par-96
❑ 94ParGol-96
❑ 94Pin-187
❑ 94PinArtP-187
❑ 94PinRinC-187
❑ 94TopPre-157
❑ 94TopPreSE-157
❑ 94Ult-88
❑ 94UppDec-205
❑ 94UppDecEleIce-205
❑ 95ParInt-422
❑ 95ParIntEl-422
❑ 95Sen-8
❑ 95UppDec-298
❑ 95UppDecEleIce-298
❑ 95UppDecEleIceG-298
❑ 96ColCho-183
❑ 96Duc-5
❑ 96UppDec-115
❑ 97Be A PPAD-84
❑ 97Be A PPAPD-84
❑ 97BeAPla-84
❑ 97BeAPlaAut-84
❑ 97ColCho-6
❑ 97Pac-312
❑ 97PacCop-312
❑ 97PacEmeGre-312
❑ 97PacIceB-312
❑ 97PacRed-312
❑ 97PacSil-312
❑ 97ScoMigDPla-11
❑ 97ScoMigDPre-11
❑ 97ScoMigDuc-11
❑ 98Be A PPA-5
❑ 98Be A PPAA-5
❑ 98Be A PPAAF-5
❑ 98Be A PPTBASG-5
❑ 98Be APG-5
❑ 98O-PChr-212
❑ 98O-PChrR-212
❑ 98Top-212
❑ 98TopO-P-212

**Dryden, Dave**
❑ 64BeeGro3P-33
❑ 65Coc-36
❑ 67Top-57
❑ 68OPC-150
❑ 68ShiCoi-30
❑ 70ColSta-80
❑ 71OPC-159
❑ 71SabPos-5
❑ 71SarProSta-32
❑ 71TorSun-25
❑ 72OPC-241
❑ 72SarProSta-34
❑ 73OPC-63
❑ 73SabPos-2
❑ 73Top-187
❑ 74OPCWHA-20
❑ 75OPCWHA-104
❑ 76OPCWHA-85
❑ 77OPCWHA-28
❑ 79OilPos-6
❑ 79OPC-71
❑ 79Top-71
❑ 88OilTenAnn-90

**Dryden, Ken**
❑ 69SweWorC-26
❑ 69SweWorC-93
❑ 70CanaPin-3
❑ 71CanaPos-5
❑ 71ColHea-3
❑ 71FriLay-2
❑ 71LetActR-2
❑ 71LetActR-22
❑ 71OPC-45
❑ 71OPCPos-22
❑ 71OPCTBoo-17
❑ 71Top-45
❑ 71TorSun-149
❑ 72CanaPos-5
❑ 72CanGreWLP-3
❑ 72OPC-145
❑ 72OPC-247
❑ 72OPCPlaC-12
❑ 72OPCTeaC-7
❑ 72SarProSta-124
❑ 72SweHocS-111
❑ 72Top-127
❑ 72Top-160
❑ 73OPC-136
❑ 73Top-4
❑ 73Top-10
❑ 74CanaPos-5
❑ 74LipSou-19
❑ 74NHLActSta-158
❑ 74OPCNHL-155
❑ 74Top-155
❑ 75CanaPos-5
❑ 75OPCNHL-35
❑ 75OPCNHL-213
❑ 75Top-35
❑ 75Top-213
❑ 76CanaPos-5
❑ 76OPCNHL-6
❑ 76OPCNHL-200
❑ 76Top-6
❑ 76Top-200
❑ 76TopGloI-5
❑ 77CanaPos-5
❑ 77OPCNHL-6
❑ 77OPCNHL-8
❑ 77OPCNHL-100
❑ 77Spo-2
❑ 77Top-6
❑ 77Top-8
❑ 77Top-100
❑ 77TopGloS-5
❑ 77TopOPCGlo-5
❑ 78CanaPos-5
❑ 78OPC-50
❑ 78OPC-68
❑ 78OPC-70
❑ 78OPC-330
❑ 78Top-50
❑ 78Top-68
❑ 78Top-70
❑ 79OPC-6
❑ 79OPC-8
❑ 79OPC-150
❑ 79Top-6
❑ 79Top-8A
❑ 79Top-8B
❑ 79Top-150
❑ 83HalFP-N4
❑ 85HalFC-196
❑ 88EssAllSta-9
❑ 91FutTreC72-85
❑ 91SweSemWCS-236
❑ 93OPCCanHF-51
❑ 96SweSemWHL-HL1
❑ 99RetHoc-101
❑ 99UppDecCL-23
❑ 99UppDecCLCLC-23
❑ 99UppDecEotG-E5
❑ 99UppDecES-15
❑ 99UppDecRII-KD
❑ 99UppDecRIL1-KD
❑ 99UppDecRM-RM5
❑ 99UppDecRP-101

**Duba, Lukas**
❑ 96CzeAPSE-236

**Dube, Christian**
❑ 94ParSE-SE258
❑ 94ParSEG-SE258
❑ 94Sel-166
❑ 94SelGol-166
❑ 94SP-179
❑ 94SPDieCut-179
❑ 95Cla-34
❑ 95DonEliWJ-13
❑ 95SP-171
❑ 96ColCho-357
❑ 96DonCanI-146
❑ 96DonCanIGPP-146
❑ 96DonCanIRPP-146
❑ 96DonEli-137
❑ 96DonEliAsp-25
❑ 96DonEliDCS-137
❑ 96LeaPre-135
❑ 96LeaPrePP-135
❑ 96MetUni-176
❑ 96SelCer-95
❑ 96SelCerAP-95
❑ 96SelCerBlu-95
❑ 96SelCerMB-95
❑ 96SelCerMG-95
❑ 96SelCerMR-95
❑ 96SelCerRed-95
❑ 96SP-183
❑ 96Ult-104
❑ 96UltGolM-105
❑ 96UltRoo-5
❑ 96UppDec-296
❑ 96UppDecBD-79
❑ 96UppDecBDG-79
❑ 96UppDecIce-136
❑ 96Zen-135
❑ 96ZenArtP-135

□ 97DonLim-46
□ 97DonLimExp-46
□ 97PacPar-113
□ 97PacParC-113
□ 97PacParDG-113
□ 97PacParEG-113
□ 97PacParIB-113
□ 97PacParSil-113
□ 97ScoRan-14
□ 97ScoRanPla-14
□ 97ScoRanPre-14
□ 97UppDec-105
□ 97UppDecGDM-105
**Dube, Dany**
□ 92AlbIntTC-7
□ 93AlbIntTC-3
□ 97ColCho-288
**Dube, Gilles**
□ 44BeeGro2P-234
□ 51LavDaiS-50
□ 52St.LawS-75
**Dube, Norm**
□ 77OPCWHA-54
**Dube, Roger**
□ 93SweSemWCS-262
□ 94FreNatT-10
**Dube, Yanick**
□ 917thInnSQMJHL-227
□ 93DonTeaC-9
□ 93Par-512
□ 93ParEmel-512
□ 93Pin-471
□ 93PinCan-471
□ 93UppDec-533
□ 94ClaCHLAS-C2
□ 95SigRoo-3
□ 95SigRooCP-4
□ 95SigRooSig-3
**Dubeau, Martin**
□ 92QueIntP-24
**Dubek, Vladimir**
□ 95SloPeeWT-6
**Duberman, Justin**
□ 92CleLum-18
□ 93ClaProPro-116
□ 93CleLum-11
□ 93CleLumPos-8
□ 93Don-471
□ 95SouCarS-22
**Dubinsky, Mike**
□ 92BraWheK-4
□ 95SigRoo-42
□ 95SigRooSig-42
□ 95SlaMemC-37
**Dubinsky, Steve**
□ 92ClaKni-5
□ 92ClaKni-24
□ 93Cla-64
□ 93Don-70
□ 93Par-40
□ 93ParEmel-40
□ 93UppDec-477
□ 94ClaProP-7
□ 94Don-26
□ 94IndIce-5
□ 94Lea-426
□ 94OPCPre-233
□ 94OPCPreSE-233
□ 94TopPre-233
□ 94TopPreSE-233
□ 95IndIce-6
□ 97Be A PPAD-166
□ 97Be A PPAPD-166
□ 97BeAPla-166
□ 97BeAPlaAut-166
□ 97PacDynBKS-21
**Dubkov, Ilja**
□ 93RoaExp-7
□ 94RoaExp-15
□ 95RoaExp-10
□ 96RoaExp-21
**Dubois, Eric**
□ 907thInnSMC-68
□ 907thInnSQMJHL-55
□ 91GreMon-5
□ 98Vald'OF-25
**Dubois, Guy**
□ 72SweSemWC-152
**Dubois, Robert**
□ 93OshGen-16
□ 95Sla-30
**Duce, Bryan**
□ 95Sla-145
□ 96KitRan-10
**Ducharme, Bruno**
□ 907thInnSQMJHL-202
□ 917thInnSQMJHL-250
**Ducharme, Sylvain**
□ 917thInnSQMJHL-278
□ 93DruVol-7
**Duchesne, Alexandre**
□ 90MonAAA-10
□ 917thInnSQMJHL-290
□ 93DruVol-24
**Duchesne, Eric**
□ 907thInnSQMJHL-37
□ 917thInnSQMJHL-84
**Duchesne, Gaetan**
□ 80QueRem-6
□ 81Cap-4
□ 82PosCer-20
□ 84CapPizH-4
□ 85CapPizH-3
□ 86CapKod-6

□ 86CapPol-6
□ 87NordGenF-7
□ 87PanSti-183
□ 88NordGenF-7
□ 88NordGenF-9
□ 88OPC-208
□ 88OPCSti-187
□ 88PanSti-353
□ 89OPCSti-194
□ 90OPC-319
□ 90PanSti-256
□ 90ProSet-137
□ 90Sco-375
□ 90ScoCan-375
□ 90Top-319
□ 90TopTif-319
□ 90UppDec-108
□ 90UppDecF-108
□ 91Bow-120
□ 91OPC-433
□ 91PanSti-117
□ 91Par-305
□ 91ParFre-305
□ 91ProSet-110
□ 91ProSetFre-110
□ 91ScoCan-440
□ 91StaClu-153
□ 91Top-433
□ 91UppDec-207
□ 91UppDecF-207
□ 92Bow-266
□ 92DurPan-22
□ 92OPC-143
□ 92Pin-198
□ 92PinFre-198
□ 92Sco-338
□ 92ScoCan-338
□ 92StaClu-307
□ 92Top-406
□ 92TopGol-406G
□ 92Ult-318
□ 92UppDec-469
□ 93Don-301
□ 93DurSco-40
□ 93Lea-339
□ 93PanSti-273
□ 93Par-456
□ 93ParEmel-456
□ 93Pin-377
□ 93PinCan-377
□ 93Pow-433
□ 93Sco-226
□ 93Sco-545
□ 93ScoCan-226
□ 93ScoCan-545
□ 93ScoGol-545
□ 94CanGamNHLP-211
□ 94Lea-547
□ 94OPCPre-232
□ 94OPCPreSE-232
□ 94Pin-219
□ 94PinArtP-219
□ 94PinRinC-219
□ 94Sco-196
□ 94ScoGol-196
□ 94ScoPla-196
□ 94ScoPlaTS-196
□ 94TopPre-232
□ 94TopPreSE-232
□ 95CanGamNHLP-119
**Duchesne, Paul**
□ 51LavDaiLSJ-45
**Duchesne, Steve**
□ 86Kin20tATI-3
□ 87KinTeal4-3
□ 88KinSmo-6
□ 88OPC-182
□ 88OPCSti-152
□ 88PanSti-70
□ 88Top-182
□ 89KinSmo-14
□ 89Kra-58
□ 89OPC-123
□ 89OPCSti-65
□ 89OPCSti-150
□ 89OPCSti-165
□ 89PanSti-93
□ 89PanSti-176
□ 89Top-123
□ 89TopStiIns-10
□ 90Bow-146
□ 90BowTif-146
□ 90KinSmo-15
□ 90Kra-65
□ 90OPC-86
□ 90PanSti-241
□ 90ProSet-115
□ 90ProSet-350
□ 90Sco-26
□ 90ScoCan-26
□ 90ScoHotRS-15
□ 90Top-86
□ 90TopTif-86
□ 90UppDec-136
□ 90UppDecF-136
□ 91Bow-191
□ 91FlyJCP-7
□ 91OPC-31
□ 91OPCPre-13
□ 91PanSti-80
□ 91Par-125
□ 91ParFre-125
□ 91Pin-42
□ 91PinFre-42
□ 91ProSet-96

□ 91ProSet-448
□ 91ProSetFre-96
□ 91ProSetFre-448
□ 91ProSetPla-86
□ 91ScoAme-205
□ 91ScoCan-205
□ 91ScoCan-569
□ 91ScoRoo-19T
□ 91StaClu-98
□ 91SweSemWCS-61
□ 91Top-31
□ 91UppDec-570
□ 91UppDecF-570
□ 92Bow-31
□ 92DurPan-38
□ 92NorPet-5
□ 92OPC-296
□ 92OPCPre-130
□ 92PanSti-192
□ 92PanStiFre-192
□ 92Par-143
□ 92ParEmel-143
□ 92Pin-320
□ 92PinFre-320
□ 92ProSet-137
□ 92Sco-151
□ 92ScoCan-151
□ 92StaClu-313
□ 92Top-271
□ 92TopGol-271G
□ 92Ult-384
□ 92UppDec-513
□ 93Don-276
□ 93Don-484
□ 93Lea-176
□ 93McDUppD-14
□ 93OPCPre-151
□ 93OPCPreG-151
□ 93PanSti-76
□ 93Par-168
□ 93ParEmel-168
□ 93Pin-78
□ 93PinAllS-16
□ 93PinAllSC-16
□ 93PinCan-78
□ 93Pow-197
□ 93Sco-190
□ 93ScoCan-190
□ 93StaCluAS-8
□ 93SweSemWCS-194
□ 93TopPre-151
□ 93TopPreBG-2
□ 93TopPreG-151
□ 93Ult-7
□ 93UppDec-217
□ 93UppDecLAS-2
□ 94BeAPla-R64
□ 94BeAPSig-137
□ 94CanGamNHLP-210
□ 94Don-304
□ 94EASpo-109
□ 94Fla-152
□ 94Fle-186
□ 94HocWit-8
□ 94Lea-3
□ 94LeaLim-93
□ 94OPCPre-401
□ 94OPCPreSE-401
□ 94Par-205
□ 94ParGol-205
□ 94ParVin-V26
□ 94Pin-108
□ 94PinArtP-108
□ 94PinRinC-108
□ 94PosCerBB-9
□ 94Sco-52
□ 94ScoGol-52
□ 94ScoPla-52
□ 94ScoPlaTS-52
□ 94Sel-145
□ 94SelGol-145
□ 94StaClu-81
□ 94StaCluFDI-81
□ 94StaCluMOMS-81
□ 94StaCluSTWC-81
□ 94TopPre-401
□ 94TopPreSE-401
□ 94Ult-182
□ 94UppDec-108
□ 94UppDecEleIce-108
□ 94UppDecSPI-SP158
□ 94UppDecSPIDC-SP158
□ 95CanGamNHLP-196
□ 95ColCho-279
□ 95ColChoPC-279
□ 95ColChoPCP-279
□ 95Don-278
□ 95Emo-124
□ 95Fin-17
□ 95FinRef-17
□ 95ImpSti-87
□ 95ImpStiDCS-15
□ 95Lea-143
□ 95Met-105
□ 95ParInt-153
□ 95ParIntEI-153
□ 95PlaOneoOne-88
□ 95PosUppD-3
□ 95Sco-99
□ 95ScoBlaIce-99
□ 95ScoBlaIceAP-99
□ 95Sen-9
□ 95SkyImp-119
□ 95StaClu-126
□ 95StaCluMOMS-126

□ 95Sum-145
□ 95SumArtP-145
□ 95SumIce-145
□ 95Top-102
□ 95Top-337
□ 95TopOPCI-102
□ 95TopOPCI-337
□ 95Ult-138
□ 95Ult-279
□ 95UltGoIM-138
□ 95UppDec-49
□ 95UppDecEleIce-49
□ 95UppDecEleIceG-49
□ 95UppDecSpeE-SE147
□ 95UppDecSpeEdiG-SE147
□ 95Zen-111
□ 96BeAPAut-141
□ 96BeAPAutSil-141
□ 96BeAPla-141
□ 96ColCho-182
□ 96Don-182
□ 96DonPrePro-182
□ 96Fle-75
□ 96MetUni-106
□ 96PlaOneoOne-347
□ 96PosUppD-5
□ 96Sco-62
□ 96ScoArtPro-62
□ 96ScoDeaCAP-62
□ 96ScoGolB-62
□ 96ScoSpeAP-62
□ 96SenPizH-7
□ 96SkyImp-89
□ 96SweSemW-49
□ 96TeaOut-57
□ 96TopNHLP-73
□ 96TopPicOI-73
□ 96Ult-117
□ 96UltGoIM-118
□ 96UppDec-304
□ 97ColCho-179
□ 97Pac-302
□ 97PacCop-302
□ 97PacCroR-115
□ 97PacCroREG-115
□ 97PacCroRIB-115
□ 97PacCroRS-115
□ 97PacEmeGre-302
□ 97PacIceB-302
□ 97PacInv-94
□ 97PacInvC-94
□ 97PacInvEG-94
□ 97PacInvIB-94
□ 97PacInvR-94
□ 97PacInvS-94
□ 97PacOme-192
□ 97PacOmeC-192
□ 97PacOmeDG-192
□ 97PacOmeEG-192
□ 97PacOmeIB-192
□ 97PacRed-302
□ 97PacRev-119
□ 97PacRevC-119
□ 97PacRevE-119
□ 97PacRevIB-119
□ 97PacRevR-119
□ 97PacRevS-119
□ 97PacSil-302
□ 97Pin-142
□ 97PinIns-136
□ 97PinPrePBB-142
□ 97PinPrePBC-142
□ 97PinPrePBM-142
□ 97PinPrePBY-142
□ 97PinPrePFC-142
□ 97PinPrePFM-142
□ 97PinPrePFY-142
□ 97PinPrePla-142
□ 97Sco-230
□ 97ScoBlu-16
□ 97ScoBluPla-16
□ 97ScoBluPre-16
□ 97SPAut-144
□ 97UppDec-114
□ 98Be A PPA-215
□ 98Be A PPAA-215
□ 98Be A PPAAF-215
□ 98Be A PPSE-215
□ 98BeAPG-215
□ 98O-PChr-44
□ 98O-PChrR-44
□ 98Pac-366
□ 98PacIceB-366
□ 98PacRed-366
□ 98Top-44
□ 98TopO-P-44
□ 98UC-182
□ 98UD ChoPCR-182
□ 98UD ChoR-182
□ 98UppDec-286
□ 98UppDecE101-286
□ 98UppDecE-286
□ 98UppDecM-93
□ 98UppDecMGS-93
□ 98UppDecMSS-93
**Ducolon, Toby**
□ 88ProIHL-92
□ 89ProIHL-12
**Duda, Jason**
□ 93SasBla-8
□ 99WicThu-5
**Dudik, Dimitri**

□ 98GerDELE-265
**Dudley, George S**
□ 83HalFP-E8
□ 85HalFC-68
**Dudley, Rhett**
□ 99WicThu-6
**Dudley, Rick**
□ 74NHLActSta-39
□ 740PCNHL-268
□ 750PCWHA-58
□ 75StiKah-3
□ 760PCWHA-17
□ 76StiKah-1
□ 79OPC-37
□ 79Top-37
□ 80OPC-355
□ 81OPC-362
□ 88ProAHL-201
□ 89NewHavN-14
□ 89SabCam-5
□ 90ProSet-662
□ 90SabCam-9
□ 92SanDieG-7
□ 93PhoRoa-5
□ 93SabNoc-2
**Due-Boje, Christian**
□ 84SweSemE-129
□ 86SwePanS-64
□ 87SwePanS-75
□ 89SweSemE-15
□ 90SweSemE-278
□ 91SweSemE-61
□ 92SweSemE-77
□ 93SweSemE-52
□ 94FinnJaaK-55
□ 94SweLeaE-109
□ 94SweLeaEGC-4
□ 95SweLeaE-28
□ 95SweUppDE-39
□ 98GerDELE-300
**Dueling, Jarrett**
□ 917thInnSWHL-93
**Duerden, Dave**
□ 95Cla-94
□ 95Sla-321
□ 97BowCHL-3
□ 97BowCHLOPC-3
**Dufalt, Pascal**
□ 907thInnSQMJHL-76
**Duff, Dick**
□ 44BeeGro2P-397
□ 55Par-18
□ 55ParQua0-18
□ 57Par-T3
□ 58Par-29
□ 59Par-38
□ 60Par-12
□ 60ShiCoi-2
□ 60YorPreP-8
□ 61Par-12
□ 61ShiCoi-53
□ 61YorYelB-2
□ 62Par-2
□ 62ShiMetC-12
□ 62YorIroOTra-7
□ 63ChePho-11
□ 63MapLeaWB-6
□ 63Par-4
□ 63Par-64
□ 63TorSta-11
□ 63YorWhiB-9
□ 64BeeGro3P-102
□ 64BeeGro3P-123
□ 64CanaPos-5
□ 64CocCap-79
□ 65Coc-60
□ 65Top-7
□ 66CanalGA-3
□ 66Top-71
□ 67CanalGA-8
□ 67PosFliB-6
□ 67Top-2
□ 67YorActOct-26
□ 68CanalGA-8
□ 68CanaPosBW-4
□ 68OPC-161
□ 68ShiCoi-85
□ 69OPC-11
□ 70DadCoo-25
□ 70SarProSta-65
□ 71OPC-164
□ 71SabPos-6
□ 71SarProSta-24
□ 71TorSun-26
□ 80MapLeaP-10
□ 92ParParR-PR24
□ 94ParMisL-126
□ 94ParMisL-167
□ 94ParTalB-106
□ 95Par66-78
□ 95Par66Coi-78
**Duff, John**
□ 91FerStaB-17
**Duff, Les**
□ 52JunBluT-155
□ 63RochAme-12
**Duffus, Parris**
□ 91AirCanSJHL-D49
□ 92PeoRivC-2
□ 93PeoRiv-5
□ 94ClaProP-68
□ 96LasVegThu-6
□ 97PinIns-75
□ 97PinInsCC-75

□ 97PinInsEC-75
□ 98GerDELE-119
**Duffy, Ben**
□ 85MinDul-31
**Duffy, Francois**
□ 92QueIntP-25
**Dufour, Guy**
□ 720PC-328
□ 730PCWHAP-3
**Dufour, Luc**
□ 83BruTealss-4
□ 83OPC-48
□ 83OPCSti-172
□ 83OPCSti-182
□ 84NordPos-7
□ 84OPC-3
**Dufour, Luc F.**
□ 84ChiSag-8
**Dufour, Marc**
□ 61SudWol-7
□ 62SudWol-9
**Dufour, Marcel**
□ 51LavDaiLSJ-8
**Dufour, Michel**
□ 83FreExp-3
**Dufresne, Dan**
□ 91AirCanSJHL-A36
□ 92CorBigRed-9
□ 93CorBigRed-8
**Dufresne, Donald**
□ 88ProAHL-298
□ 89CanaPos-12
□ 90CanaPos-14
□ 90ProSet-469
□ 90ScoRoo-35T
□ 90UppDec-332
□ 90UppDecF-332
□ 91CanaPanTS-10
□ 91CanaPos-11
□ 91ProSet-418
□ 91ProSetFre-418
□ 91ScoCan-392
□ 92CanaPos-10
□ 92DurPan-39
□ 93Lea-355
□ 93Par-467
□ 93ParEmel-467
□ 93Ult-422
□ 94BeAPSig-45
□ 96OilPos-34
**Duggan, Brad**
□ 81SasBla-5
**Dugre, Yvan**
□ 51LavDaiQSHL-49
**Duguay, Ron**
□ 780PC-177
□ 78Top-177
□ 790PC-208
□ 79Top-208
□ 80OPC-37
□ 80Top-37
□ 81OPC-223
□ 81OPCSti-171
□ 81Top-E96
□ 820PC-217
□ 820PC-221
□ 820PCSti-134
□ 82PosCer-13
□ 83OPC-121
□ 83PufSti-13
□ 84OPC-52
□ 84OPCSti-42
□ 84Top-40
□ 857ECreCar-5
□ 85OPC-116
□ 85OPCSti-32
□ 85Top-116
□ 86PenKod-7
□ 87OPC-110
□ 87PanSti-119
□ 87RedWinLC-9
□ 87Top-110
□ 88KinSmo-7
□ 89PanSti-96
□ 91ProAHLCHL-317
**Duguid, Lorne**
□ 33OPCV304B-58
□ 33V252CanG-19
□ 33V357IceK-52
**Duhaime, Trevor**
□ 917thInnSQMJHL-165
□ 92ForWorF-6
□ 92HamRoaA-6
**Duhart, Jim**
□ 93FliGen-9
□ 94FliGen-7
□ 95FliGen-25
**Dumaine, Trent**
□ 91AirCanSJHL-E24
**Dumart, Porky (Woody)**
□ 34BeeGro1P-13
□ 36ProvRed-3
□ 39OPCV3011-94
□ 44BeeGro2P-16
□ 51Par-28
□ 52Par-72
□ 53Par-96
□ 91BruSpoAL-36
□ 94Koll-1
□ 94ParMisLP-P9
**Dumas, Denis Jr.**
□ 77GraVic-9
**Dumas, Mark**
□ 88ProAHL-69
**Dumas, Rob**

□ 91NasKni-11
□ 92NasKni-11
□ 95VanVooRHI-11
**Dumba, Jared**
□ 96SasBla-9
**Dumonski, Steve**
□ 95Sla-67
□ 96DetWha-5
**Dumont, Jean-Pierre**
□ 95BowDraPro-P13
□ 97BeeAutA-68
□ 97BowCHL-60
□ 97BowCHLOPC-60
□ 97PinBee-68
□ 97PinBeeGP-68
□ 98SP Aut-94
□ 98SPXTopP-11
□ 98SPXTopPH-11
□ 98SPXTopPR-11
□ 98UC-271
□ 98UD ChoPCR-271
□ 98UD ChoR-271
□ 99Pac-86
□ 99PacAur-31
□ 99PacAurPD-31
□ 99PacCop-86
□ 99PacGol-86
□ 99PacIceB-86
□ 99PacPreD-86
□ 99SP AutPS-94
□ 99UppDecM-44
□ 99UppDecMGS-44
□ 99UppDecMSS-44
□ 99UppDecMSS-44
**Dumont, Louis**
□ 907thInnSWHL-222
□ 917thInnSWHL-222
**Dumoulin, Mario**
□ 917thInnSQMJHL-260
**Dunbar, Dale**
□ 85FreExp-24
**Duncalfe, Darren**
□ 91AirCanSJHL-E26
**Duncan, Brett**
□ 93SeaThu-5
□ 94Rallce-5
□ 95St.JohF-5
**Duncan, Glen**
□ 81IndChe-5
□ 82IndChe-4
**Duncan, Iain**
□ 87Jet-5
□ 87MonHaw-6
□ 88JetPol-5
□ 88OPC-209
□ 88OPCSti-108
□ 88OPCSti-132
□ 88OPCSti-140
□ 88OPCSti-238
□ 88PanSti-154
□ 89JetSaf-11
□ 89OPC-293
□ 89OPCSti-136
□ 89PanSti-170
□ 90JetIGA-11
□ 90MonHaw-3
□ 90ProAHLIHL-249
□ 92TolSto-19
□ 94TolSto-5
**Duncan, Trevor**
□ 89RayJrC-8
**Duncanson, Craig**
□ 85SudWol-19
□ 89KinSmo-19
□ 90MonHaw-4
□ 90ProAHLIHL-248
□ 91BalSki-13
□ 91ProAHLCHL-566
□ 92BinRan-4
□ 94BinRan-2
**Dundas, R.J. (Rocky)**
□ 82RegPar-7
□ 83RegPar-7
□ 84KelWin-17
□ 88ProAHL-285
**Dunderdale, Tom**
□ 10C55SweCP-6
□ 10C56-14
□ 11C55-6
□ 12C57-5
□ 83HalFP-I6
□ 85HalFC-127
**Dunham, Mike**
□ 91UppDec-693
□ 91UppDecCWJC-80
□ 91UppDecF-693
□ 92MaiBlaB-2
□ 92MaiBlaB-18
□ 93Cla-56
□ 93Pow-501
□ 93StaCluTUSA-4
□ 93TopPreTUSA-1
□ 93Ult-481
□ 94ClaAut-NNO
□ 94ClaProPIA-IA13
□ 94ClaProPIH-LP3
□ 94FinnJaaK-108
□ 95ColEdgI-6
□ 95ColEdgIP-PR3
□ 95ColEdgITW-G10
□ 95Ima-61
□ 95ImaGol-61
□ 96BeAPAut-212
□ 96BeAPAutSil-212
□ 96BeAPla-212

96ColEdgFL-3
97ColEdgPC-1
96Dev-1
96UppDecBD-3
96UppDecBDG-3
97Be A PPAD-110
97Be A PPAPD-110
97BeAPla-110
97BeAPlaAut-110
97Don-93
97DonCanI-87
97DonCanIDS-87
97DonCanIPS-87
97DonEli-59
97DonEliAsp-59
97DonEliS-59
97DonLim-78
97DonLim-194
97DonLimExp-78
97DonLimExp-194
97DonLimFOTG-41
97DonPre-40
97DonPreCG-17
97DonPreCGP-17
97DonPreCttC-40
97DonPreProG-93
97DonPreProS-93
97DonPri-86
97DonPriSoA-86
97Lea-104
97LeaFraMat-104
97LeaFraMDC-104
97LeaInt-104
97LeaIntUI-104
97LeaPipDre-16
97PacDynBKS-106
97Pin-79
97PinArtP-79
97PinPrePBB-79
97PinPrePBC-79
97PinPrePBM-79
97PinPrePBY-79
97PinPrePFC-79
97PinPrePFM-79
97PinPrePFY-79
97PinPrePla-79
97PinRinC-79
97Sco-45
97Sco-269
97ScoArtPro-45
97ScoDev-13
97ScoDevPla-13
97ScoDevPre-13
97ScoGolBla-45
97Stu-56
97StuPrePG-56
97StuPrePS-56
98Be A PPA-72
98Be A PPAA-72
98Be A PPAAF-72
98Be A PPTBASG-72
98Be APG-72
98BowBes-75
98BowBesAR-75
98BowBesR-75
98Pac-262
98PacAur-100
98PacCroR-73
98PacCroRLS-73
98PacDynI-101
98PacDynIIB-101
98PacDynIR-101
98PacDynITC-14
98PacIceB-262
98PacOmeH-128
98PacOmeODI-128
98PacOmeR-128
98PacPar-122
98PacParC-122
98PacParEG-122
98PacParGSLC-9
98PacParH-122
98PacParIB-122
98PacParS-122
98PacRed-262
98PacRev-78
98PacRevIS-78
98PacRevR-78
98SP Aut-44
98SPXTopP-34
98SPXTopPF-34
98SPXTopPR-34
98TopGolLC1-83
98TopGolLC1B-83
98TopGolLC1BooO-83
98TopGolLC1OoO-83
98TopGolLC1R-83
98TopGolLC1RooO-83
98TopGolLC2-83
98TopGolLC2B-83
98TopGolLC2BooO-83
98TopGolLC2OoO-83
98TopGolLC2R-83
98TopGolLC2RooO-83
98TopGolLC3-83
98TopGolLC3B-83
98TopGolLC3BooO-83
98TopGolLC3OoO-83
98TopGolLC3R-83
98TopGolLC3RooO-83
98UppDec-210
98UppDecBD-47
98UppDecDD-47
98UppDecE-210

98UppDecE1o1-210
98UppDecGR-210
98UppDecM-110
98UppDecMGS-110
98UppDecMP-MD
98UppDecMSS-110
98UppDecMSS-110
98UppDecQD-47
98UppDecTD-47
99Pac-222
99PacAur-78
99PacAurPD-78
99PacCop-222
99PacGol-222
99PacHomaA-14
99PacIceB-222
99PacPreD-222
99PacTeaL-15
99SP AutPS-44
99UppDecRG-44
99UppDecRP-44

**Dunk, Brett**
87BroBra-21

**Dunlop, Blake**
74NHLActSta-140
740PCNHL-308
750PCNHL-16
75Top-16
760PCNHL-263
76Top-263
790PC-174
79Top-174
800PC-370
810PC-293
810PCSti-131
81Top-W117
820PC-301
820PCSti-199
82PosCer-17
830PC-314
830PCSti-131
83PufSti-13
92BluUDBB-5

**Dunn, Dave**
73CanuRoyB-5
74MapLeaP-2
74NHLActSta-271
74NHLActStaU-35
740PCNHL-152
74Top-152
75MapLeaP-5
750PCNHL-187
75Top-187

**Dunn, Jamie**
91AirCanSJHL-E48
92MPSPhoSJHL-161

**Dunn, Jay**
91AirCanSJHL-A28
91AirCanSJHLAS-2

**Dunn, Jimmy**
83HalFP-07
85HalFC-217

**Dunn, Pat**
69SeaTotW-19
93SweSemWCS-263
94FreNatT-11

**Dunn, Richie**
800PC-109
80Top-109
810PC-29
820PC-45
82PosCer-2
830PC-137
83WhaJunHC-3
840PC-69
88ProAHL-259
89ProAHL-259

**Dunnigan, Dave**
91BriColJHL-65

**Dunphy, Serge**
92OshGenS-21
95Sla-404

**Dunstan, Geordie**
92BriColJHL-102

**Dunville, Doug**
66TulOil-3

**Dupere, David**
92QuelntP-14

**Dupere, Denis**
71MapLeaP-3
710PC-200
71TorSun-256
72MapLeaP-3
720PC-167
72SarProSta-210
73MapLeaP-3
730PC-210
74CapWhiB-9
740PCNHL-105
740PCNHL-219
74Top-105
74Top-219
750PCNHL-159
750PCNHL-382
75Top-159
760PCNHL-334
76RocCokCan-7
770PCNHL-388
77RocCanCan-5
780PC-283

**Duperron, Christian**
84ChiSag-7

**Dupont, Andre**

71BluPos-6
720PC-16
72SarProSta-194
72Top-19
730PC-113
73Top-183
74NHLActSta-211
740PCNHL-67
74Top-67
75FlyCanDC-7
750PCNHL-56
750PCNHL-211
75Top-56
75Top-211
760PCNHL-131
76Top-131
770PCNHL-164
77Top-164
780PC-98
78Top-98
790PC-178
79Top-178
80NordPos-9
80PepCap-64
81NordPos-6
810PC-273
82NordPos-6
820PC-282
82PosCer-16
83NordPos-7

**Dupont, George**
94CenHocL-57

**Dupont, Jerome**
81BlaBorPos-5
83BlaBorPos-4
86MapLeaP-7

**Dupont, Micki**
96KamBla-10

**Dupont, Norm (Normand)**
77NovScoV-6
79CanaPos-2
80JetPos-7
80PepCap-126
81JetPos-5
810PC-363
810PCSti-139
82Jet-7
820PC-378
82PosCer-21
83WhaJunHC-4

**Dupont, Yannick**
96RimOce-10
96RimOceQPP-10

**Dupre, Yanick**
907thInnSQMJHL-200
917thInnSMC-59
917thInnSMC-126
917thInnSQMJHL-284
91Cla-41
910PCPre-16
91StaPicH-44
91UltDra-36
91UltDra-88
92StaClu-137
92Top-515
92TopGol-515G
92UppDec-421

**Dupuis, Bob**
880IlTenAnn-118

**Dupuis, Guy**
90ProAHLIHL-478
91ProAHLCHL-137

**Dupuis, Lori**
97ColCho-291

**Dupuis, Marc**
95Sla-38

**Durand, Brian**
85MinDul-25

**Durand, Eric**
93SweSemWCS-253

**Durbano, Steve**
72BluWhiBor-2
73BluWhiBor-5
730PC-124
73Top-168
74NHLActSta-225
740PCNHL-106
74PenPos-6
74Top-106
760PCNHL-4
760PCNHL-19
760PCNHL-384
76RocPucBuc-7
76Top-4
76Top-19

**Durdle, Darren**
96GerDELE-27
98GerDELE-172

**Duris, M.**
95GerDELE-108

**Duris, Peter**
96SloPeeWT-6

**Duris, Vitezslav**
80MapLeaP-11
80PepCap-85
810PC-316
82MapLeaP-10

**Durnan, Bill**
44BeeGro2P-235
45QuaOatP-73A
45QuaOatP-73B
45QuaOatP-73C
45QuaOatP-73D
55Par-63
55ParQuaO-63

83HalFP-K4
85HalFC-139
91Kra-37
93HigLinGG-12
930PCCanHF-47
94ParTalBG-6
99UppDecCL-34
99UppDecCLLC-34

**Durocher, Andre**
907thInnSQMJHL-257

**Durocher, Steve**
92QuelntP-55

**Durroulin, Mario**
907thInnSQMJHL-120

**Dusablon, Benoit**
98Vald'OF-2

**Duschene, Donat**
51LavDaiQSHL-20

**Dussault, Normand**
44BeeGro2P-236
45QuaOatP-74A
45QuaOatP-74B
51LavDaiQSHL-22
52St.LawS-96

**Dustin, Bobby**
92MinGolG-6
93MinGolG-8
94MinGolG-11
95MinGolG-12

**Duthie, Ryan**
917thInnSWHL-17
94St.JohF-3
95AdiRedW-3

**Dutiaume, Mark**
95Cla-37
95SlaMemC-41

**Dutiaume, Todd**
917thInnSWHL-198
92BraWheK-5

**Dutil, Christian**
91AirCanSJHL-A33
92MPSPhoSJHL-158

**Dutkowski, Duke**
23V1281PauC-26
33V252CanG-20
33V357IceK-56
34DiaMatS-21

**Dutton, Red (Mervyn)**
23V1281PauC-62
33V129-23
33V252CanG-21
33V357IceK-25
34BeeGro1P-222
34DiaMatS-22
35DiaMatT2-20
35DiaMatT3-18
35DiaMatTI-21
36V356WorG-14
60Top-16
83HalFP-A6
85HalFC-7

**Duus, Jesper**
87SwePanS-95
89SweSemE-79
90SweSemE-254
91SweSemE-85
92SweSemE-105
93SweSemE-77
94SweLeaE-122
95SweLeaE-217
95SweUppDE-57
96GerDELE-185
96GerDELE-301

**Duval, Jon**
907thInnSWHL-39
917thInnSWHL-315
94BirBul-7

**Duval, Luc**
84ChiSag-9

**Duval, Murray**
907thInnSMC-21
907thInnSWHL-302
91ProAHLCHL-312

**Duzkin, Viktor**
73SweWorCS-100

**Dvorak, Filip**
96CzeAPSE-283
96CzeAPSE-281
96KitRan-11

**Dvorak, Miroslav**
74SweHocS-119
79PanSti-78
81SweSemHVS-57
82SweSemHVS-83
83FlyJCP-8

**Dvorak, Radek**
95BeAPla-163
95BeAPSig-S163
95BeAPSigDC-S163
95Bow-130
95BowAllFoi-130
95BowBes-BB22
95BowBesRef-BB22
95Cla-10
95ClaAut-4
95ColCho-398
95Don-277
95DonEli-19
95DonEliDCS-19
95DonEliP-C4
95DonRatRoo-10
95Fin-125

95FinRef-125
95LeaLim-10
95LeaLimRP-7
95Met-176
95ParInt-260
95ParInt-508
95ParIntEl-260
95ParIntEl-508
95ParIntPTP-PP45
95SelCer-133
95SelCerMG-133
95SigRooSig-39
95SkyImp-200
95SP-59
95StaClu-200
95StaCluMOMS-200
95Sum-169
95SumArtP-169
95SumIce-169
95Top-319
95TopOPCI-319
95TopSupSkiSR-SR10
95Ult-338
95UltExtAtt-3
95UppDec-260
95UppDecEleIce-260
95UppDecEleIceG-260
95UppDecPHE-H26
95UppDecPreH-H26
95Zen-147
95ZenRooRC-2
96ClalceBreDC-BK9
96Don-213
96DonEli-105
96DonEliDCS-105
96DonPrePro-213
96Lea-160
96LeaPreP-160
96MetUni-57
96Sco-247
96ScoArtPro-247
96ScoDeaCAP-247
96ScoGolB-247
96ScoSpeAP-247
96SkyImp-44
96Sum-169
96SumArtP-169
96SumIce-169
96SumMet-169
96SumPreS-169
96Ult-64
96UltGolM-64
97ColCho-103
97Pac-50
97PacCop-50
97PacEmeGre-50
97PacIceB-50
97PacRed-50
97PacSil-50
97Sco-221
97UppDec-71
98Pac-220
98PacIceB-220
98PacRed-220
98UppDec-280
98UppDecE-280
98UppDecE1o1-280
98UppDecGR-280
99Pac-172
99PacCop-172
99PacGol-172
99PacIceB-172
99PacPreD-172

**Dvorak, Todd**
95MadMon-12

**Dwyer, Don**
92DalFre-8
93DalFre-7

**Dwyer, Gordie**
95SlaMemC-61
97BowCHL-53
97BowCHLOPC-53

**Dwyer, John**
94DubFigS-8

**Dyck, Ed**
72CanuRoyB-5

**Dyck, Joel**
907thInnSWHL-57
917thInnSWHL-138

**Dyck, Larry**
88ProIHL-41
89ProIHL-93
90ProAHLIHL-104
91ProAHLCHL-143

**Dyck, Mike**
86RegPat-5
87RegPat-5
88RegPat-5
96MedHatT-4

**Dyck, Paul**
907thInnSWHL-160
91ProAHLCHL-304
92CleLum-25
93CleLum-4
93CleLumPos-9

**Dye, Babe**
23V1451-23
24C144ChaCig-23
24V1452-54
83HalFP-C4
85HalFC-34

**Dyer, Dean**
89VicCou-9

**Dyer, Kelly**
95Fin-125

94ClaWomOH-W22

**Dyhr, Nick**
92MPSPhoSJHL-70

**Dykeman, Rob**
907thInnSOHL-33
917thInnSMC-36
917thInnSOHL-20
91CorRoy-26

**Dykhuis, Karl**
907thInnSQMJHL-229
90AlbIntTC-4
90Sco-437
90ScoCan-437
90UppDec-471
90UppDecF-471
91AlbIntTC-9
910PC-172
91Par-262
91ParFre-262
91Top-172
91UppDec-688
91UppDecCWJC-62
91UppDecF-688
92Sco-462
92ScoCan-462
92Ult-274
92UppDec-404
93Pow-48
93UppDec-106
94IndIce-6
94ParSE-SE34
94ParSEG-SE34
95BeAPla-75
95BeAPSig-S75
95BeAPSigDC-S75
95Lea-264
95Top-118
95TopOPCI-118
95Ult-283
96FlyPos-7
96UppDec-311
97PacInvNRB-141
97PacOme-209
97PacOmeC-209
97PacOmeDG-209
97PacOmeEG-209
97PacOmeG-209
97PacOmeIB-209
97PacPar-172
97PacParC-172
97PacParDG-172
97PacParEG-172
97PacParIB-172
97PacParRed-172
97PacParSil-172
98Be A PPA-255
98Be A PPAA-255
98Be A PPAAF-255
98Be A PPSE-255
98Be APG-255
98Fin-122
98FinNo P-122
98FinNo PR-122
98FinRef-122
98Pac-399
98PacAur-173
98PacIceB-399
98PacPar-217
98PacParC-217
98PacParEG-217
98PacParH-217
98PacParIB-217
98PacParS-217
98PacRed-399

**Dykstra, Steven (Steve)**
85SabBluS-7
85SabBluSS-7
86SabBluS-8
86SabBluSSma-8
870PCSti-146
87SabWonBH-8
880IlTenAnn-38
90ProAHLIHL-317
95ForWorFT-5

**Dylevsky, Andrej**
92NasKni-18

**Dylla, E.**
95GerDELE-22

**Dziedzic, Joe**
91MinGolG-5
92MinGolG-7
93MinGolG-9
94Cla-37
94ClaDraGol-37
95Don-235
95PenFoo-13
95SigRoo-67
95SigRooSig-67
95Top-336
95TopOPCI-336
95Ult-339
95UppDec-429
95UppDecEleIce-429
95UppDecEleIceG-429
96BeAPAut-149
96BeAPAutSil-149
96BeAPla-149
96ColCho-216
96UppDec-136
97ColCho-213
97Pac-305
97PacEmeGre-305
97PacIceB-305

97PacRed-305
97PacSil-305

**Dzikowski, John**
83BraWheK-4
84BraWheK-7
85BraWheK-7

**Dzurilla, Vladimir**
69SweHocS-23
69SweWorC-1
69SweWorC-156
70SweHocS-100
70SweHocS-101
70SweHocS-102
70SweHocS-103
70SweHocS-104
70SweHocS-105
70SweHocS-106
70SweHocS-107
70SweHocS-108
70SweHocS-109
70SweHocS-110
70SweHocS-111
70SweHocS-345
92FutTre76CC-152

**Eagan, Joe**
92DalFre-9

**Eagles, Mike**
82KitRan-19
83CanNatJ-5
83FreExp-20
84FreExp-20
85NordGenF-6
85NordMcD-6
85NordPro-7
85NordTeal-7
86NordGenF-7
86NordMcD-6
86NordTeal-5
87NordGenF-4
870PC-253
87PanSti-170
88BlaCok-4
880PCSti-191
88PanSti-354
89ProIHL-68
90ProAHLIHL-395
91JetIGA-8
91Par-420
91ParFre-420
91ProSet-518
91ProSetFre-518
91ScoCan-414
91UppDec-523
91UppDecF-523
92Sco-345
92ScoCan-345
93JetRuf-9
930PCPre-116
930PCPreG-116
93Par-229
93ParEmel-229
93Sco-429
93ScoCan-429
93StaClu-14
93StaCluFDI-14
93StaCluFDIO-14
93StaCluO-14
93TopPre-116
93TopPreG-116
94BeAPSig-157
95Cap-6
97Be A PPAD-149
97Be A PPAPD-149
97BeAPla-149
97BeAPlaAut-149
97PacDynBKS-101

**Eakin, Bruce**
81SasBla-9
84MonGolF-22
85NovScoO-27
94GerDELE-91
95GerDELE-93
96GerDELE-234

**Eakins, Dallas**
88ProAHL-34
89ProAHL-41
90MonHaw-5
90ProAHLIHL-253
91MonHaw-6
91ProAHLCHL-58
97Be A PPAD-86
97Be A PPAPD-86
97BeAPla-86
97BeAPlaAut-86

**Earhart, Barry**
86LonKni-9

**Earl, Tom**
72WhaNewEWHA-6

**East, John**
897thInnSOHL-62
90HamRoaA-45
91HamRoaA-3

**Eastland, Mike**
94MapLeaPP-4

**Eastwood, Mike**
91ProAHLCHL-358
92MapLeaK-10
92Par-494
92ParEmel-494
92St.JohML-6
93ScoBla-19
93UppDec-57
94CanGamNHLP-232
94Lea-378
94MapLeaG-5

Elik, Todd • 497

❑ 94ParSE-SE183
❑ 94ParSEG-SE183
❑ 94StaClu-167
❑ 94StaCluFDI-167
❑ 94StaCluMOMS-167
❑ 94StaCluSTWC-167
❑ 95BeAPla-102
❑ 95BeAPSig-S102
❑ 95BeAPSigDC-S102
❑ 95CanGamNHLP-290
❑ 95Don-207
❑ 95JetReaC-3
❑ 95JetTeaIss-8
❑ 95Lea-299
❑ 95PlaOneoOne-216
❑ 95UppDec-292
❑ 95UppDecEleIce-292
❑ 95UppDecEleIceG-292
❑ 96PlaOneoOne-399
❑ 97PacInvNRB-125
**Eaton, J.D.**
❑ 907thInnSOHL-382
❑ 90SudWol-20
❑ 917thInnSOHL-42
**Eatough, Jeff**
❑ 82NorBayC-5
**Eaves, Mike**
❑ 79PanSti-222
❑ 80NorStaPos-6
❑ 80OPC-206
❑ 80Top-206
❑ 81NorStaPos-8
❑ 81OPC-171
❑ 82NorStaPos-8
❑ 83OPC-79
❑ 83Vac-4
❑ 84OPC-221
❑ 84OPCSti-244
❑ 85OPC-213
❑ 89FlyPos-8
❑ 90ProAHLIHL-26
❑ 91ProAHLCHL-286
**Eaves, Murray**
❑ 83OPC-384
❑ 88ProAHL-12
❑ 89ProAHL-324
**Eberle, Derek**
❑ 907thInnSWHL-184
❑ 917thInnSWHL-229
**Eberle, Jorg**
❑ 91SweSemWCS-188
❑ 92UppDec-384
❑ 93SweSemWCS-122
❑ 93SwiHNL-96
❑ 95FinnSemWC-192
❑ 95SweGloWC-210
❑ 95SwiHNL-147
❑ 95SwiHNL-508
**Ebermann, Bohuslav**
❑ 79PanSti-89
❑ 96CzeAPSE-286
**Ecclestone, Tim**
❑ 68OPC-178
❑ 69OPC-179
❑ 70ColSta-58
❑ 70DadCoo-26
❑ 70EssPowPla-246
❑ 70OPC-102
❑ 70SarProSta-188
❑ 70Top-102
❑ 70TopStiS-4
❑ 71Baz-27
❑ 71LetActR-9
❑ 71OPC-52
❑ 71SarProSta-56
❑ 71Top-52
❑ 71TorSun-93
❑ 72OPC-55
❑ 72SarProSta-78
❑ 72Top-33
❑ 73OPC-144
❑ 73RedWinTI-11
❑ 73Top-124
❑ 74NHLActSta-255
❑ 74OPCNHL-323
❑ 76OPCNHL-351
❑ 77OPCNHL-364
**Eckmaier, Beppi**
❑ 98GerDELE-313
**Eckmaier, J.**
❑ 95GerDELE-382
**Edberg, Rolf**
❑ 70SweHocS-8
❑ 71SweHocS-83
❑ 72SweHocS-62
❑ 73SweHocS-200
❑ 73SweWorCS-200
❑ 74SweHocS-212
❑ 79PanSti-194
❑ 80OPC-65
❑ 80Top-65
❑ 82SweSemHVS-21
❑ 84SweSemE-140
**Eddolls, Frank**
❑ 44BeeGro2P-307
❑ 45QuaOatP-75
❑ 51Par-89
**Edenvik, Curt**
❑ 65SweCorI-172
❑ 67SweHoc-26
❑ 69SweHocS-40
❑ 71SweHocS-332
❑ 72SweHocS-142
**Edenvik, Per**
❑ 71SweHocS-333
❑ 72SweHocS-143
**Eder, Stephan**
❑ 94GerDELE-332
**Edestrand, Darryl**
❑ 71OPC-187
❑ 71PenPos-4
❑ 71TorSun-213
❑ 72OPC-195
❑ 72SarProSta-181
❑ 73OPC-216
❑ 74NHLActSta-34
❑ 74OPCNHL-313
❑ 75OPCNHL-11
❑ 75Top-11
❑ 76OPCNHL-179
❑ 76Top-179
❑ 77OPCNHL-321
❑ 77RocAme-9
❑ 78OPC-377
❑ 79OPC-280
**Edgar, Trevor**
❑ 95Sla-241
**Edgerton, Devin**
❑ 92WheThu-7
❑ 95PhoRoa-10
**Edholm, Mats**
❑ 87SwePanS-261
**Edin, Lage**
❑ 67SweHoc-117
❑ 69SweHocS-130
❑ 70SweHocS-85
❑ 71SweHocS-178
❑ 72SweHocS-168
❑ 73SweHocS-227
❑ 73SweWorCS-227
**Edlund, Hans**
❑ 83SweSemE-42
❑ 84SweSemE-42
❑ 85SwePanS-37
❑ 86SwePanS-22
❑ 87SwePanS-37
**Edlund, Jan**
❑ 69SweHocS-205
**Edlund, Par**
❑ 85SwePanS-44
❑ 86SwePanS-17
❑ 87SwePanS-40
❑ 90SweSemE-46
❑ 91SweSemE-297
❑ 92SweSemE-322
❑ 93SweSemE-287
❑ 94SweLeaE-106
❑ 95SweLeaE-142
❑ 95SweUppDE-216
**Edmond, Dominic**
❑ 84RicRiv-5
**Edmundson, Gary**
❑ 44BeeGro2P-398
❑ 59Par-48
❑ 60Par-5
❑ 60ShiCoi-14
❑ 61UniOilW-9
**Edmundson, Mark**
❑ 92Ott672A-10
**Edqvist, Sten**
❑ 65SweCorI-90B
**Edstrom, Anders**
❑ 67SweHoc-199
**Edstrom, Lars**
❑ 89SweSemE-166
❑ 90SweSemE-244
❑ 91SweSemE-165
❑ 92SweSemE-192
❑ 93SweSemE-163
❑ 94SweLeaE-176
❑ 95SweLeaE-202
❑ 95SweUppDE-214
**Edstrom, Peter**
❑ 83SweSemE-48
❑ 84SweSemE-48
❑ 85SwePanS-42
❑ 86SwePanS-25
❑ 87SwePanS-39
**Edstrom, Tomas**
❑ 86SwePanS-189
**Edur, Tom**
❑ 76RocCokCan-8
❑ 76RocPucBuc-8
❑ 77OPCNHL-169
❑ 77RocCokCan-6
❑ 77Top-169
❑ 78OPC-119
❑ 78Top-119
**Edwards, Dave**
❑ 89OshGenP-14
**Edwards, Don**
❑ 77OPCNHL-201
❑ 77Top-201
❑ 78OPC-70
❑ 78OPC-150
❑ 78OPC-336
❑ 78Top-70
❑ 78Top-150
❑ 79OPC-105
❑ 79SabBel-1
❑ 79SabMilP-1
❑ 79Top-105
❑ 80OPC-92
❑ 80OPC-166
❑ 80OPC-215
❑ 80Top-92
❑ 80Top-166
❑ 80Top-215
❑ 81OPC-21
❑ 81OPC-389
❑ 81OPCSti-55
❑ 81SabMilP-3
❑ 81Top-E75
❑ 82FlamDol-2
❑ 82OPC-46
❑ 82OPCSti-124
❑ 82PosCer-2
❑ 83OPC-80
❑ 83PufSti-2
❑ 83Vac-5
❑ 84OPC-222
❑ 85MapLeaP-10
❑ 85OPC-183
❑ 86OPCSti-139
**Edwards, Gary**
❑ 71LetActR-23
❑ 71OPC-155
❑ 71TorSun-111
❑ 72OPC-113
❑ 72OPCPlaC-9
❑ 72Top-151
❑ 73OPC-199
❑ 74NHLActSta-113
❑ 75OPCNHL-105
❑ 75Top-105
❑ 76OPCNHL-365
❑ 77OPCNHL-345
❑ 78NorStaCD-5
❑ 78OPC-6
❑ 78Top-6
❑ 79NorStaPos-3
❑ 80NorStaPos-7
❑ 80OPC-335
❑ 88OilTenAnn-78
**Edwards, Jeff**
❑ 93OmaLan-5
**Edwards, Marv**
❑ 52JunBluT-17
❑ 69MapLeaWBG-7
❑ 69OPC-185
❑ 72SarProSta-49
**Edwards, Paul**
❑ 80OshGen-10
❑ 81OshGen-8
**Edwards, Ray**
❑ 92DayBom-8
❑ 93DayBom-13
❑ 94HunBli-7
**Edwards, Roy**
❑ 67Top-106
❑ 68OPC-144
❑ 68ShiCoi-40
❑ 69OPC-56
❑ 69Top-56
❑ 70DadCoo-27
❑ 70EssPowPla-144
❑ 70OPC-21
❑ 70RedWinM-4
❑ 70SarProSta-62
❑ 70Top-21
❑ 71Baz-21
❑ 71OPC-99
❑ 71PenPos-5
❑ 71SarProSta-167
❑ 71Top-99
❑ 71TorSun-214
❑ 72SarProSta-174
❑ 72SweSemWC-192
❑ 73OPC-82
❑ 73Top-82
**Edwards, Troy**
❑ 91AirCanSJHL-A44
❑ 92MPSPhoSJHL-1
**Egan, Pat**
❑ 34BeeGro1P-223
❑ 44BeeGro2P-17
❑ 44BeeGro2P-308
**Egeland, Allan**
❑ 907thInnSWHL-126
❑ 917thInnSWHL-169
❑ 92TacRoc-8
❑ 93TacRoc-7
**Egeland, Tracy**
❑ 90ProAHLIHL-404
❑ 91ProAHLCHL-481
❑ 92IndIce-11
**Egen, Ulrich**
❑ 82SweSemHVS-109
**Egers, Jack**
❑ 70EssPowPla-195
❑ 71BluPos-7
❑ 71TorSun-170
❑ 72BluWhiBor-3
❑ 72OPC-107
❑ 72SarProSta-196
❑ 72Top-147
❑ 73OPC-79
❑ 73Top-79
❑ 74CapWhiB-10
❑ 74NHLActSta-315
❑ 74OPCNHL-93
❑ 74Top-93
❑ 75OPCNHL-134
❑ 75Top-134
**Egger, Karlheinz**
❑ 72SweSemWC-101
**Ego, Klaus**
❑ 72SweSemWC-103
**Ehlers, Heinz**
❑ 85SwePanS-150
❑ 86SwePanS-155
❑ 87SwePanS-159
❑ 89SweSemE-15
❑ 90SweSemE-88
❑ 92SweSemE-262
❑ 98GerDELE-125
**Ehman, Gerry**
❑ 44BeeGro2P-399
❑ 59Par-19
❑ 60Par-8
❑ 60ShiCoi-19
❑ 63RochAme-13
❑ 68OPC-84
❑ 68ShiCoi-109
❑ 68Top-84
❑ 69OPC-83
❑ 69Top-83
❑ 70DadCoo-28
❑ 70EssPowPla-98
❑ 70OPC-187
❑ 70SarProSta-144
**Ehrenverth, Edgar**
❑ 61SudWol-10
❑ 62SudWol-10
**Ehrmantraut, Lyle**
❑ 91AirCanSJHL-E18
❑ 92MPSPhoSJHL-57
**Eichenmann, Zdenek**
❑ 94CzeAPSE-14
❑ 95CzeAPSE-114
❑ 96CzeAPSE-84
**Eichstadt, Scott**
❑ 91ProAHLCHL-99
**Eigner, Trent**
❑ 94HunBli-8
**Eigner, Ty**
❑ 93ForWorF-5
**Eimannsberger, Johann**
❑ 72SweSemWC-100
**Einarsson, Roland**
❑ 67SweHoc-63
❑ 69SweHocS-96
❑ 70SweHocS-48
❑ 71SweHocS-115
❑ 72SweHocS-96
❑ 73SweHocS-208
❑ 73SweWorCS-208
**Einhorn, Andrew**
❑ 97GuiFla-11
**Eirickson, Shane**
❑ 85BraWheK-23
**Eisebitt, Torsten**
❑ 94GerDELE-398
❑ 95GerDELE-418
**Eiselt, Vaclav**
❑ 94CzeAPSE-273
❑ 95CzeAPSE-144
❑ 96CzeAPSE-91
**Eisenhut, Neil**
❑ 91ProAHLCHL-599
❑ 92HamCan-6
❑ 93Pow-459
❑ 94ClaProP-199
❑ 94St.JohF-4
❑ 95ColEdgI-172
❑ 98GerDELE-24
**Ek, Marko**
❑ 93FinnJyvHS-149
❑ 93FinnSIS-151
❑ 94FinnSIS-131
❑ 96FinnSISR-117
**Ekelund, Peter**
❑ 89SweSemE-119
❑ 90SweSemE-120
❑ 91SweSemE-125
❑ 92SweSemE-138
❑ 93SwiHNL-400
❑ 94SweLeaE-293
❑ 95SweLeaE-58
❑ 95SweUppDE-87
**Ekenberg, Arne**
❑ 67SweHoc-152
**Eklof, Ake**
❑ 64SweCorI-161
❑ 65SweCorI-161
❑ 67SweHoc-118
❑ 69SweHocS-131
❑ 70SweHocS-86
❑ 71SweHocS-125
❑ 72SweHocS-104
❑ 73SweHocS-220
❑ 73SweWorCS-220
❑ 74SweHocS-213
**Eklof, Rolf**
❑ 65SweCorI-104A
**Eklund, Kjell**
❑ 67SweHoc-135
❑ 69SweHocS-147
**Eklund, Pelle (Per-Erik)**
❑ 83SweSemE-16
❑ 84SweSemE-14
❑ 85FlyPos-8
❑ 85SwePanS-119
❑ 85SwePanS-120
❑ 86FlyPos-8
❑ 86OPCSti-127
❑ 87OPC-89
❑ 87OPCMin-9
❑ 87PanSti-132
❑ 87Top-89
❑ 88OPC-211
❑ 89FlyPos-9
❑ 89OPCSti-105
❑ 89PanSti-296
❑ 89SweSemWCS-19
❑ 90Bow-107
❑ 90BowTif-107
❑ 90FlyPos-7
❑ 90OPC-254
❑ 90PanSti-113
❑ 90ProSet-215
❑ 90Sco-308A
❑ 90ScoCan-308A
❑ 90Top-254
❑ 90TopTif-254
❑ 90UppDec-138
❑ 90UppDecF-138
❑ 91Bow-241
❑ 91FlyJCP-9
❑ 91OPC-111
❑ 91PanSti-228
❑ 91Par-128
❑ 91ParFre-128
❑ 91Pin-134
❑ 91PinFre-134
❑ 91ProSet-179
❑ 91ProSetFre-179
❑ 91ProSetPla-89
❑ 91ScoAme-91
❑ 91ScoCan-91
❑ 91StaClu-182
❑ 91SweSemE-358
❑ 91SweSemWCS-210
❑ 91Top-111
❑ 91UppDec-103
❑ 91UppDecF-103
❑ 92Bow-179
❑ 92FlyJCP-10
❑ 92FlyUppDS-29
❑ 92OPC-242
❑ 92PanSti-189
❑ 92PanStiFre-189
❑ 92Pin-149
❑ 92PinFre-149
❑ 92Sco-173
❑ 92ScoCan-173
❑ 92StaClu-154
❑ 92Top-117
❑ 92TopGol-117G
❑ 92Ult-155
❑ 93Don-250
❑ 93Lea-177
❑ 93OPCPre-449
❑ 93OPCPreG-449
❑ 93PanSti-51
❑ 93Par-147
❑ 93ParEmel-147
❑ 93Pin-256
❑ 93PinCan-256
❑ 93Pow-180
❑ 93Sco-181
❑ 93ScoCan-181
❑ 93StaClu-289
❑ 93StaCluFDI-289
❑ 93StaCluO-289
❑ 93SweSemWCS-39
❑ 93TopPre-449
❑ 93TopPreG-449
❑ 93Ult-386
❑ 93UppDec-120
❑ 94Par-56
❑ 94ParGol-56
❑ 94SweLeaE-243
❑ 95SweGloWC-53
❑ 95SweLeaE-71
❑ 95SweLeaE-NNO
❑ 95SweLeaEC-13
❑ 95SweLeaEM-11
❑ 95SweUppDE-101
❑ 95SweUppDE-228
❑ 95SweUppDE-254
❑ 96SweSemCDT-10
❑ 96SweSemW-66
❑ 96SweSemWAS-AS5
**Eklund, Per**
❑ 94SweLeaE-194
❑ 94SweLeaERR-5
❑ 95SweLeaE-34
❑ 95SweUppDE-50
❑ 95SweUppDE-222
❑ 95SweUppDETNA-NA5
❑ 96SweSemW-69
**Eklund, Thom**
❑ 83SweSemE-37
❑ 84SweSemE-231
❑ 85SwePanS-229
❑ 86SwePanS-259
❑ 87SwePanS-245
❑ 89SweSemE-226
❑ 89SweSemWCS-13
❑ 90SweSemE-61
❑ 91SweSemE-238
**Ekman, Kenneth**
❑ 67SweHoc-153
❑ 70SweHocS-180
❑ 71SweHocS-265
❑ 72SweHocS-243
❑ 72SweSemWC-64
❑ 74SweHocS-166
**Ekroth, Peter**
❑ 83SweSemE-202
❑ 84SweSemE-226
❑ 85SwePanS-226
❑ 86SwePanS-252
❑ 89SweSemE-270
❑ 90SweSemE-55
❑ 91SweSemE-231
**Ekrt, Martin**
❑ 96GerDELE-329
**Eksell, Ake**
❑ 84SweSemE-97
**Elander, Peter**
❑ 83SweSemE-236
**Elcombe, Kelly**
❑ 81FreExp-11
❑ 82FreExp-11
**Eldebrink, Anders**
❑ 81CanuSilD-17
❑ 81CanuTeal-7
❑ 81FreExp-9
❑ 82FreExp-9
❑ 83SweSemE-198
❑ 84SweSemE-222
❑ 85SwePanS-121
❑ 85SwePanS-122
❑ 85SwePanS-223
❑ 86SwePanS-248
❑ 87SwePanS-235
❑ 89SweSemE-219
❑ 89SweSemWCS-9
❑ 93SweSemWCS-20
❑ 93SwiHNL-11
❑ 95SweUppDE1DS-DS6
❑ 95SwiHNL-515
❑ 95SwiHNL-537
**Elder, Brian**
❑ 95SlaMemC-27
❑ 97BowCHL-102
❑ 97BowCHLOPC-102
**Elders, Jason**
❑ 92BriColJHL-241
**Eley, Mike**
❑ 95MedHatT-6
❑ 96MedHatT-5
**Elias, Patrik**
❑ 94CzeAPSE-64
❑ 96Dev-22
❑ 97Be A PPAD-228
❑ 97Be A PPAPD-228
❑ 97BeAPla-228
❑ 97BeAPlaAut-228
❑ 97BeAPlaPOT-16
❑ 97BeeAutA-53
❑ 97DonEli-65
❑ 97DonEliAsp-65
❑ 97DonEliS-65
❑ 97DonPri-170
❑ 97DonPriDD-24
❑ 97DonPriSoA-170
❑ 97Kat-80
❑ 97KatGol-80
❑ 97KatSil-80
❑ 97PacCroR-74
❑ 97PacCroREG-74
❑ 97PacCroRIB-74
❑ 97PacCroRS-74
❑ 97PacInvNRB-111
❑ 97PacOme-128
❑ 97PacOmeC-128
❑ 97PacOmeDG-128
❑ 97PacOmeEG-128
❑ 97PacOmeG-128
❑ 97PacOmeIB-128
❑ 97PacRev-76
❑ 97PacRevC-76
❑ 97PacRevE-76
❑ 97PacRevIB-76
❑ 97PacRevR-76
❑ 97PacRevS-76
❑ 97PinBee-53
❑ 97PinBeeGP-53
❑ 97PinBeeGT-20
❑ 97PinBeeT-20
❑ 97SP AutI-I6
❑ 97SPAut-185
❑ 97SPAutID-I6
❑ 97SPAutIE-I6
❑ 97UppDec-189
❑ 97UppDecBD-44
❑ 97UppDecBDDD-44
❑ 97UppDecBDPC-PC8
❑ 97UppDecBDPCDD-PC8
❑ 97UppDecBDPCM-PC8
❑ 97UppDecBDPCQD-PC8
❑ 97UppDecBDPCTD-PC8
❑ 97UppDecBDQD-44
❑ 97UppDecBDTD-44
❑ 97UppDecIce-60
❑ 97UppDecIceP-60
❑ 97UppDecILL-L7A
❑ 97UppDecILL2-L7A
❑ 97UppDecIPS-60
❑ 97Zen-81
❑ 97Zen5x7-69
❑ 97ZenGolImp-69
❑ 97ZenRooR-14
❑ 97ZenSilImp-69
❑ 97ZenZGol-81
❑ 97ZenZSil-81
❑ 97ZenZT-16
❑ 97ZenZTG-16
❑ 98Be A PPA-81
❑ 98Be A PPAA-81
❑ 98Be A PPAAF-81
❑ 98Be A PPTBASG-81
❑ 98Be APG-81
❑ 98BowBes-26
❑ 98BowBesAR-26
❑ 98BowBesP-BP3
❑ 98BowBesPAR-BP3
❑ 98BowBesPR-BP3
❑ 98BowBesR-26
❑ 98Fin-59
❑ 98FinCen-C1
❑ 98FinCenR-C1
❑ 98FinNo P-59
❑ 98FinNo PR-59
❑ 98FinRef-59
❑ 98O-PChr-62
❑ 98O-PChrR-62
❑ 98O-PChrSB-SB9
❑ 98O-PChrSBR-SB9
❑ 98Pac-26
❑ 98PacAur-109
❑ 98PacAurCF-27
❑ 98PacAurCFC-27
❑ 98PacAurCFIB-27
❑ 98PacAurCFR-27
❑ 98PacAurCFS-27
❑ 98PacCroR-79
❑ 98PacCroRLS-79
❑ 98PacDynI-109
❑ 98PacDynIIB-109
❑ 98PacDynIR-109
❑ 98PacGolCD-19
❑ 98PacIceB-26
❑ 98PacOmeH-137
❑ 98PacOmeODI-137
❑ 98PacOmeR-137
❑ 98PacPar-133
❑ 98PacParC-133
❑ 98PacParEG-133
❑ 98PacParH-133
❑ 98PacParIB-133
❑ 98PacParS-133
❑ 98PacRed-26
❑ 98PacRev-84
❑ 98PacRevIS-84
❑ 98PacRevR-84
❑ 98SP Aut-50
❑ 98SPxFin-49
❑ 98SPxFin-123
❑ 98SPxFinR-49
❑ 98SPxFinR-123
❑ 98SPxFinS-49
❑ 98SPxFinS-123
❑ 98Top-62
❑ 98TopAut-A7
❑ 98TopGolLC1-37
❑ 98TopGolLC1B-37
❑ 98TopGolLC1BOoO-37
❑ 98TopGolLC1OoO-37
❑ 98TopGolLC1R-37
❑ 98TopGolLC1ROoO-37
❑ 98TopGolLC2-37
❑ 98TopGolLC2B-37
❑ 98TopGolLC2BOoO-37
❑ 98TopGolLC2OoO-37
❑ 98TopGolLC2R-37
❑ 98TopGolLC2ROoO-37
❑ 98TopGolLC3-37
❑ 98TopGolLC3B-37
❑ 98TopGolLC3BOoO-37
❑ 98TopGolLC3OoO-37
❑ 98TopGolLC3R-37
❑ 98TopGolLC3ROoO-37
❑ 98TopO-P-62
❑ 98TopSeaB-SB9
❑ 98UC-114
❑ 98UCSB-SQ12
❑ 98UCSG-SQ12
❑ 98UCSG-SQ12
❑ 98UCSR-SQ12
❑ 98UD ChoPCR-114
❑ 98UD ChoR-114
❑ 98UD3-10
❑ 98UD3-70
❑ 98UD3-130
❑ 98UD3DieC-10
❑ 98UD3DieC-70
❑ 98UD3DieC-130
❑ 98UppDec-119
❑ 98UppDecE-119
❑ 98UppDecE1o1-119
❑ 98UppDecFF-FF15
❑ 98UppDecFFQ1-FF15
❑ 98UppDecFFQ2-FF15
❑ 98UppDecGR-119
❑ 98UppDecM-116
❑ 98UppDecMGS-119
❑ 98UppDecMSS-119
❑ 98UppDecMSS-119
❑ 99Pac-237
❑ 99PacAur-85
❑ 99PacAurPD-85
❑ 99PacCop-237
❑ 99PacGol-237
❑ 99PacIceB-237
❑ 99PacPreD-237
❑ 99SP AutPS-50
❑ 99UppDecCL-80
❑ 99UppDecCLCLC-80
❑ 99UppDecM-116
❑ 99UppDecMGS-116
❑ 99UppDecMSS-116
❑ 99UppDecMSS-116
**Eliasson, Magnus**
❑ 95SweUppDE-91
**Eliasson, Roger**
❑ 83SweSemE-154
❑ 85SwePanS-204
**Elich, Matt**
❑ 95Sla-418
❑ 97BowCHL-124
❑ 97BowCHLAu-4
❑ 97BowCHLOPC-124
**Eligh, Jarrett**
❑ 88BroBra-16
**Elik, Todd**
❑ 83KinCan-15
❑ 84KinCan-8
❑ 89ProAHL-10
❑ 90Bow-151
❑ 90BowTif-151

□ 90KinSmo-5
□ 90OPC-352
□ 90ProSet-116
□ 90Sco-297
□ 90ScoCan-297
□ 90Top-352
□ 90TopTif-352
□ 90UppDec-233
□ 90UppDecF-233
□ 91Bow-185
□ 91OPC-251
□ 91OPCPre-74
□ 91PanSti-85
□ 91Par-300
□ 91ParFre-300
□ 91Pin-264
□ 91PinFre-264
□ 91ProSet-94
□ 91ProSet-410
□ 91ProSetFre-94
□ 91ProSetFre-410
□ 91ProSetPla-57
□ 91ScoAme-83
□ 91ScoCan-83
□ 91ScoCan-563
□ 91ScoRoo-13T
□ 91StaClu-310
□ 91Top-251
□ 91UppDec-544
□ 91UppDecF-544
□ 92Bow-317
□ 92OilTeal-5
□ 92OPC-20
□ 92Par-77
□ 92Par-292
□ 92ParEmel-77
□ 92ParEmel-292
□ 92Pin-207
□ 92PinFre-207
□ 92Sco-307
□ 92ScoCan-307
□ 92StaClu-226
□ 92Top-97
□ 92TopGol-97G
□ 92Ult-93
□ 92UppDec-210
□ 93Don-489
□ 93PanSti-238
□ 93Par-71
□ 93ParEmel-71
□ 93Pin-202
□ 93PinCan-202
□ 93Pow-80
□ 93Pow-434
□ 93Sco-185
□ 93Sco-581
□ 93ScoCan-185
□ 93ScoCan-581
□ 93ScoGol-581
□ 93StaClu-363
□ 93StaCluFDI-363
□ 93StaCluO-363
□ 94CanGamNHLP-212
□ 94Don-163
□ 94Fla-162
□ 94Lea-226
□ 94OPCPre-76
□ 94OPCPreSE-76
□ 94Par-210
□ 94ParGol-210
□ 94Pin-275
□ 94PinArtP-275
□ 94PinRinC-275
□ 94Sco-125
□ 94ScoGol-125
□ 94ScoPla-125
□ 94ScoPlaTS-125
□ 94TopPre-76
□ 94TopPreSE-76
□ 94Ult-193
□ 94UppDec-363
□ 94UppDecEleIce-363
□ 95BeAPla-89
□ 95BeAPSig-S89
□ 95BeAPSigDC-S89
□ 95Don-388
□ 95Lea-165
□ 95PlaOneoOne-118
□ 95Sco-58
□ 95ScoBlaIce-58
□ 95ScoBlaIceAP-58
□ 95UppDec-479
□ 95UppDecEleIce-479
□ 95UppDecEleIceG-479

**Eliot, Darren**
□ 84KinSmo-18
□ 86Kin20tATI-4
□ 87KinTeal4-4
□ 87PanSti-272

**Ellacott, Ken**
□ 82Canu-6

**Ellett, Bob**
□ 71RocAme-5
□ 84Ott67-6

**Ellett, David (Dave)**
□ 84JetPol-6
□ 85JetPol-5
□ 85JetSiID-3
□ 85OPC-185
□ 86JetBor-6
□ 87Jet-6
□ 87OPC-35
□ 87OPCSti-251
□ 87PanSti-358
□ 87Top-35
□ 88JetPol-6
□ 88OPC-167
□ 88OPCSti-150
□ 88PanSti-150
□ 88Top-167
□ 89JetSaf-12
□ 89Kra-49
□ 89OPC-69
□ 89OPCSti-139
□ 89PanSti-167
□ 89Top-69
□ 90Bow-132
□ 90BowTif-132
□ 90OPC-104
□ 90PanSti-310
□ 90ProSet-326
□ 90ProSet-532
□ 90Sco-65
□ 90ScoCan-65
□ 90ScoHotRS-29
□ 90ScoRoo-67T
□ 90Top-104
□ 90TopTif-104
□ 90UppDec-71
□ 90UppDec-413
□ 90UppDecF-71
□ 90UppDecF-413
□ 91Bow-163
□ 91Gil-17
□ 91JetPanTS-9
□ 91MapLeaP-9
□ 91OPC-381
□ 91OPCPre-180
□ 91PanSti-94
□ 91Par-172
□ 91ParFre-172
□ 91Pin-111
□ 91PinFre-111
□ 91ProSet-230
□ 91ProSetFre-230
□ 91ProSetPla-116
□ 91ScoAme-275
□ 91ScoCan-495
□ 91ScoKel-23
□ 91StaClu-274
□ 91SweSemWCS-62
□ 91Top-381
□ 91UppDec-96
□ 91UppDec-196
□ 91UppDecF-96
□ 91UppDecF-196
□ 92Bow-204
□ 92Bow-291
□ 92HumDum2-4
□ 92MapLeaK-11
□ 92McDUppD-5
□ 92OPC-9
□ 92PanSti-83
□ 92PanStiFre-83
□ 92Par-181
□ 92ParEmel-181
□ 92Pin-273
□ 92PinFre-273
□ 92ProSet-186
□ 92Sco-152
□ 92ScoCan-152
□ 92StaClu-283
□ 92Top-30
□ 92TopGol-30G
□ 92Ult-209
□ 92UppDec-214
□ 93Don-344
□ 93Lea-86
□ 93OPCPre-297
□ 93OPCPreG-297
□ 93PanSti-231
□ 93Par-205
□ 93ParEmel-205
□ 93Pin-262
□ 93PinCan-262
□ 93Pow-243
□ 93Sco-119
□ 93ScoBla-20
□ 93ScoCan-119
□ 93StaClu-469
□ 93StaCluFDI-469
□ 93StaCluO-469
□ 93TopPre-297
□ 93TopPreG-297
□ 93Ult-38
□ 93UppDec-215
□ 93UppDecSP-157
□ 94BeAPla-R50
□ 94BeAPSig-65
□ 94CanGamNHLP-238
□ 94Don-230
□ 94EASpo-134
□ 94Fla-178
□ 94Fle-213
□ 94Lea-35
□ 94MapLeaG-6
□ 94MapLeaPP-3
□ 94Par-227
□ 94ParGol-227
□ 94ParVin-V8
□ 94Pin-209
□ 94PinArtP-209
□ 94PinRinC-209
□ 94Sco-83
□ 94ScoGol-83
□ 94ScoPla-83
□ 94ScoPlaTS-83
□ 94StaClu-42
□ 94StaCluFDI-42
□ 94StaCluMOMS-42
□ 94StaCluSTWC-42
□ 94Ult-213
□ 94UppDec-67
□ 94UppDecEleIce-67
□ 94UppDecNBAP-4
□ 95CanGamNHLP-264
□ 95ColCho-162
□ 95ColChoPC-162
□ 95ColChoPCP-162
□ 95Don-340
□ 95ParInt-475
□ 95ParIntEl-475
□ 95Sco-129
□ 95ScoBlaIce-129
□ 95ScoBlaIceAP-129
□ 95Top-207
□ 95TopOPCI-207
□ 95UppDec-144
□ 95UppDecEleIce-144
□ 95UppDecEleIceG-144
□ 96BeAPAut-177
□ 96BeAPAutSil-177
□ 96BeAPla-177
□ 96UppDec-344
□ 97PacInvNRB-112
□ 97PacPar-13
□ 97PacParC-13
□ 97PacParDG-13
□ 97PacParEG-13
□ 97PacParIB-13
□ 97PacParRed-13
□ 97PacParSil-13
□ 97ScoBru-16
□ 97ScoBruPla-16
□ 97ScoBruPre-16
□ 98O-PChr-6
□ 98O-PChrR-6
□ 98Pac-78
□ 98PacAur-12
□ 98PacIceB-78
□ 98PacPar-14
□ 98PacParC-14
□ 98PacParEG-14
□ 98PacParH-14
□ 98PacParIB-14
□ 98PacParS-14
□ 98PacRed-78
□ 98Top-6
□ 98TopO-P-6

**Ellingsen, Age**
□ 87SwePanS-33

**Elliott, Chaucer**
□ 83HalFP-M6
□ 85HalFC-171

**Elliott, Paul**
□ 96LetHur-4

**Elliott, Warren**
□ 70FlyPos-3

**Ellis, Aaron**
□ 93DetJrRW-3
□ 93DonTeaUSA-6
□ 93Pin-479
□ 93PinCan-479
□ 93UppDec-554

**Ellis, Ron**
□ 63MapLeaWB-7
□ 64BeeGro3P-161
□ 64CocCap-97
□ 65Coc-95
□ 65MapLeaWB-6
□ 65MapLeaWB-7
□ 65Top-82
□ 66Top-81
□ 67PosFliB-8
□ 67Top-14
□ 67YorActOct-16
□ 67YorActOct-17
□ 67YorActOct-22
□ 68OPC-126
□ 68PosCerM-6
□ 68ShiCoi-165
□ 68Top-126
□ 69MapLeaWBG-8
□ 69MapLeaWBG-9
□ 69MapLeaWBG-10
□ 69OPC-46
□ 69Top-46
□ 70ColSta-54
□ 70DadCoo-29
□ 70EssPowPla-22
□ 70MapLeaP-2
□ 70OPC-221
□ 70OPCDec-46
□ 70PosCerS-2
□ 70SarProSta-200
□ 70TopStiS-5
□ 71Baz-34
□ 71FriLay-7
□ 71LetActR-22
□ 71MapLeaP-4
□ 71OPC-113
□ 71SarProSta-203
□ 71Top-113
□ 71TorSun-257
□ 72KellroT-1
□ 72MapLeaP-4
□ 72MapLeaP-5
□ 72OPC-36
□ 72OPCTeaC-8
□ 72SarProSta-201
□ 72SweSemWC-166
□ 72Top-152
□ 73MacMil-6
□ 73MapLeaP-4
□ 73OPC-55
□ 73Top-55
□ 74LipSou-6
□ 74MapLeaP-3
□ 74NHLActSta-270
□ 74OPCNHL-12
□ 74Top-12
□ 75OPCNHL-59
□ 75Top-59
□ 77MapLeaP-3
□ 77OPCNHL-311
□ 78MapLeaP-7
□ 78OPC-92
□ 78Top-92
□ 79MapLeaP-9
□ 79OPC-373
□ 80OPC-329
□ 80PepCap-86
□ 91FutTreC72-76
□ 91UltOriS-34
□ 91UltOriSF-34
□ 94ParTalB-125
□ 94ParTalB-162
□ 94ParTalB-168
□ 95Par66-106
□ 95Par66Coi-106

**Ellstrom, Sven-Allan**
□ 71SweHocS-361

**Elmer, W.D.**
□ 23V1281PauC-34

**Elo, Hans-Goran**
□ 84SweSemE-123
□ 86SwePanS-58
□ 87SwePanS-69

**Elomo, Miikka**
□ 94Fin-143
□ 94FinRef-143
□ 94FinSupTW-143
□ 95Cla-22
□ 95ClaIceBre-BK10
□ 95ColCho-333
□ 95ColChoPC-333
□ 95ColChoPCP-333
□ 95FinnSIS-336
□ 95FinnSISDD-3
□ 95UppDec-546
□ 95UppDecEleIce-546
□ 95UppDecEleIceG-546
□ 96ClaIceBreDC-BK10
□ 96FinnSISR-148
□ 96FinnSISRRE-5
□ 96PorPir-20

**Elomo, Teemu**
□ 97UppDecBD-15
□ 97UppDecBDDD-15
□ 97UppDecBDQD-15
□ 97UppDecBDTD-15
□ 98UC-276
□ 98UD ChoPCR-276
□ 98UD ChoR-276

**Eloranta, Kari**
□ 81SweSemHVS-21
□ 83OPC-81
□ 83OPCSti-270
□ 83Vac-6
□ 84OPC-223
□ 85SwePanS-184
□ 86SwePanS-113
□ 89SweSemWCS-31
□ 92SweSemE-254
□ 93SweSemE-227
□ 94FinnSIS-362
□ 94SweLeaE-10

**Eloranta, Mikko**
□ 95FinnSIS-243
□ 96FinnSISRRE-2

**Elsener, Dan**
□ 93FliGen-6

**Elsner, Alexandr**
□ 95CzeAPSE-206

**Elters, Helmut**
□ 94GerDELE-360

**Eltner, M.**
□ 95GerDELE-177

**Elvenes, Roger**
□ 92SweSemE-268
□ 93SweSemE-230
□ 94SweLeaE-33
□ 94SweLeaESS-10
□ 95SweLeaE-121
□ 95SweUppDE-179

**Elvenes, Stefan**
□ 92SweSemE-267
□ 93SweSemE-237
□ 94FinnJaaK-76
□ 94SweLeaE-81
□ 94SweLeaETG-4
□ 95SweLeaE-264
□ 95SweLeaEFF-9
□ 95SweUppDE-150

**Elvenes, Tord**
□ 93SweSemE-239

**Elynuik, Pat**
□ 84PriAlbRS-6
□ 87Jet-7
□ 88JetPol-7
□ 89JetSaf-13
□ 89OPC-94
□ 89OPCSti-35
□ 89OPCSti-66
□ 89OPCSti-142
□ 89OPCSti-206
□ 89PanSti-165
□ 89Top-94
□ 90Bow-137
□ 90BowTif-137
□ 90JetIGA-12
□ 90Kra-12
□ 90OPC-71
□ 90OPCPre-28
□ 90PanSti-312
□ 90ProSet-327
□ 90Sco-205
□ 90ScoCan-205
□ 90ScoHotRS-86
□ 90ScoYouS-28
□ 90Top-71
□ 90TopTif-71
□ 90UppDec-74
□ 90UppDecF-74
□ 91Bow-198
□ 91JetIGA-9
□ 91JetPanTS-10
□ 91OPC-326
□ 91PanSti-66
□ 91Par-202
□ 91ParFre-202
□ 91Pin-117
□ 91Pin-416
□ 91PinFre-117
□ 91PinFre-416
□ 91ProSet-262
□ 91ProSetFre-262
□ 91ProSetPla-136
□ 91ScoAme-295
□ 91ScoAme-341
□ 91ScoCan-371
□ 91ScoCan-515
□ 91ScoYouS-34
□ 91StaClu-132
□ 91Top-326
□ 91UppDec-109
□ 91UppDecF-109
□ 92Bow-270
□ 92CapKod-8
□ 92OPC-201
□ 92OPCPre-119
□ 92PanSti-54
□ 92PanStiFre-54
□ 92Par-205
□ 92ParEmel-205
□ 92Pin-53
□ 92PinFre-53
□ 92ProSet-214
□ 92Sco-233
□ 92ScoCan-233
□ 92ScoSha-23
□ 92StaClu-410
□ 92Top-56
□ 92TopGol-56G
□ 92Ult-434
□ 92UppDec-312
□ 92UppDec-537
□ 93Don-368
□ 93Lea-6
□ 93LigSealR-12
□ 93OPCPre-51
□ 93OPCPreG-51
□ 93PanSti-29
□ 93Par-224
□ 93ParEmel-224
□ 93Pin-382
□ 93PinCan-382
□ 93Pow-260
□ 93Pow-442
□ 93Sco-223
□ 93Sco-580
□ 93ScoCan-223
□ 93ScoCan-580
□ 93ScoGol-580
□ 93StaClu-49
□ 93StaClu-447
□ 93StaCluFDI-49
□ 93StaCluFDI-447
□ 93StaCluFDIO-49
□ 93StaCluO-49
□ 93StaCluO-447
□ 93TopPre-51
□ 93TopPreG-51
□ 93Ult-67
□ 93UppDec-75
□ 94BeAPSig-164
□ 94Fle-145
□ 94Lea-535
□ 94OPCPre-107
□ 94OPCPreSE-107
□ 94Pin-381
□ 94PinArtP-381
□ 94PinRinC-381
□ 94SenBelM-12
□ 94TopPre-107
□ 94TopPreSE-107
□ 94Ult-338
□ 94UppDec-421
□ 94UppDecEleIce-421
□ 95ColCho-39
□ 95ColChoPC-39
□ 95ColChoPCP-39

**Emberg, Eddie**
□ 51LavDaiQSHL-108

**Emerson, Nelson**
□ 90ProAHLIHL-88
□ 90Sco-383
□ 90ScoCan-383
□ 91BluPos-9
□ 91OPCPre-138
□ 91Par-151
□ 91ParFre-151
□ 91Pin-314
□ 91PinFre-314
□ 91ProSet-557
□ 91ProSetFre-557
□ 91ProSetPla-269
□ 91ScoCan-550
□ 91ScoRoo-89T
□ 91UppDec-445
□ 91UppDecF-445
□ 92Bow-40
□ 92OPC-181
□ 92PanSti-B
□ 92PanStiFre-B
□ 92Par-152
□ 92Par-232
□ 92ParEmel-152
□ 92ParEmel-232
□ 92Pin-36
□ 92PinAmePP-1
□ 92PinFre-36
□ 92ProSet-161
□ 92ProSetGTL-9
□ 92ProSetRGL-5
□ 92Sco-376
□ 92Sco-505
□ 92ScoCan-376
□ 92ScoCan-505
□ 92ScoYouS-13
□ 92SeaPat-16
□ 92StaClu-306
□ 92Top-11
□ 92Top-480
□ 92TopGol-11G
□ 92TopGol-480G
□ 92Ult-393
□ 92UltRoo-5
□ 92UppDec-18
□ 92UppDec-166
□ 93Don-383
□ 93JetRuf-10
□ 93Lea-75
□ 93OPCPre-35
□ 93OPCPreG-35
□ 93PanSti-159
□ 93Par-497
□ 93ParEmel-497
□ 93Pin-245
□ 93PinCan-245
□ 93Pow-209
□ 93Pow-472
□ 93Sco-28
□ 93Sco-506
□ 93ScoCan-28
□ 93ScoCan-506
□ 93ScoGol-506
□ 93StaClu-223
□ 93StaCluFDI-223
□ 93StaCluFDIO-223
□ 93StaCluO-223
□ 93TopPre-35
□ 93TopPreG-35
□ 93Ult-45
□ 93Ult-453
□ 93UppDec-342
□ 93UppDecSP-175
□ 94CanGamNHLP-252
□ 94Don-297
□ 94Fle-240
□ 94Lea-80
□ 94OPCPre-352
□ 94OPCPreSE-352
□ 94Par-267
□ 94ParGol-267
□ 94ParSEV-33
□ 94Pin-325
□ 94PinArtP-325
□ 94PinRinC-325
□ 94Sco-41
□ 94ScoGol-41
□ 94ScoPla-41
□ 94ScoPlaTS-41
□ 94Sel-125
□ 94SelGol-125
□ 94SP-135
□ 94SPDieCut-135
□ 94StaClu-240
□ 94StaCluFDI-240
□ 94StaCluMOMS-240
□ 94StaCluSTWC-240
□ 94TopPre-352
□ 94TopPreSE-352
□ 94Ult-242
□ 94UppDec-47
□ 94UppDecEleIce-47
□ 94UppDecSPI-SP179
□ 94UppDecSPIDC-SP179
□ 95BeAPla-38
□ 95BeAPSig-S38
□ 95BeAPSigDC-S38
□ 95ColCho-196
□ 95ColChoPC-196
□ 95ColChoPCP-196
□ 95Don-7
□ 95Don-365
□ 95Emo-192
□ 95Fin-102
□ 95FinRef-102
□ 95Lea-163
□ 95Met-65
□ 95ParInt-367
□ 95ParIntEl-367
□ 95PlaOneoOne-217
□ 95Sco-259
□ 95ScoBlaIce-259
□ 95ScoBlaIceAP-259
□ 95SkyImp-73
□ 95SP-63
□ 95StaClu-38
□ 95StaCluMOMS-38
□ 95Sum-132
□ 95SumArtP-132
□ 95SumIce-132
□ 95Top-311
□ 95TopOPCI-311
□ 95Ult-179
□ 95Ult-246
□ 95UltGolM-179
□ 95UppDec-178
□ 95UppDec-311
□ 95UppDecEleIce-178
□ 95UppDecEleIce-471
□ 95UppDecEleIceG-178
□ 95UppDecEleIceG-471
□ 95UppDecSpeE-SE126
□ 95UppDecSpeEdiG-SE126
□ 95Zen-43
□ 96ColCho-116
□ 96Don-73
□ 96DonPrePro-73
□ 96MetUni-68
□ 96Pin-60
□ 96PinArtP-60
□ 96PinFoi-60
□ 96PinPreS-60
□ 96PinRinC-60
□ 96PlaOneoOne-400
□ 96Sco-37
□ 96ScoArtPro-37
□ 96ScoDeaCAP-37
□ 96ScoGolB-37
□ 96ScoSpeAP-37
□ 96TopNHLP-135
□ 96TopPicOI-135
□ 96UppDec-269
□ 96WhaBobS-7
□ 97CarHur-7
□ 97ColCho-115
□ 97DonPri-135
□ 97DonPriSoA-135
□ 97Pac-349
□ 97PacCop-349
□ 97PacCroR-23
□ 97PacCroREG-23
□ 97PacCroRIB-23
□ 97PacCroRS-23
□ 97PacEmeGre-349
□ 97PacIceB-349
□ 97PacInvNRB-35
□ 97PacOme-39
□ 97PacOmeC-39
□ 97PacOmeDG-39
□ 97PacOmeEG-39
□ 97PacOmeG-39
□ 97PacOmeIB-39
□ 97PacPar-34
□ 97PacParC-34
□ 97PacParDG-34
□ 97PacParEG-34
□ 97PacParIB-34
□ 97PacParRed-34
□ 97PacParSil-34
□ 97PacRed-349
□ 97PacSil-349
□ 97UppDec-243
□ 97UppDecIce-1
□ 97UppDecIceP-1
□ 97UppDecIPS-1
□ 98O-PChr-218
□ 98O-PChrR-218
□ 98Pac-131
□ 98PacAur-31
□ 98PacIceB-131
□ 98PacOmeH-51
□ 98PacOmeODI-51
□ 98PacOmeR-51
□ 98PacPar-35
□ 98PacParC-35
□ 98PacParEG-35
□ 98PacParH-35
□ 98PacParIB-35
□ 98PacParS-35
□ 98PacRed-131
□ 98Top-218
□ 98TopO-P-218
□ 98UC-43
□ 98UD ChoPCR-43
□ 98UD ChoR-43
□ 98UDCP-43
□ 98UppDec-60
□ 98UppDecE-60
□ 98UppDecE1o1-60
□ 98UppDecGR-60

**Emma, David**
□ 91ScoAme-330
□ 92UppDec-462
□ 93OPCPre-448
□ 93OPCPreG-448
□ 93Pow-377
□ 93Sco-468
□ 93ScoCan-468
□ 93TopPre-448
□ 93TopPreG-448
□ 94ClaProP-98
□ 94Fla-93
□ 94Ult-319
□ 95UppDec-155
□ 95UppDecEleIce-155
□ 95UppDecEleIceG-155
□ 96ProBru-10

**Emmett, Rick**
□ 93PetPet-14
□ 94KitRan-13
□ 94WinSpi-21

**Emmons, Gary**
89ProIHL-83
91ProAHLCHL-506
98KanCitB-26
**Emmons, John**
92UppDec-608
93DonTeaUSA-7
93Pin-492
93PinCan-492
93UppDec-557
96DayBom-13
**Emms, Hap (Leighton)**
330PCV304A-40
33V252CanG-22
33V357IceK-55
34BeeGro1P-224
35DiaMatT2-21
35DiaMatT3-19
36V356WorG-59
**Emond, Patrick**
84ChiSag-10
**Empey, Larry**
91AirCanSJHL-E12
92MPSPhoSJHL-39
94EriPan-5
**Enander, Mikael**
89SweSemE-36
91SweSemE-36
92SweSemE-57
93SweSemE-33
94SweLeaE-182
**Endean, Craig**
86RegPat-6
87RegPat-5
89ProIHL-131
**Engblom, Borje**
71SweHocS-389
**Engblom, Brian**
77CanaPos-6
78CanaPos-6
79CanaPos-3
790PC-361
80CanaPos-4
800PC-304
80PepCap-42
81CanaPos-6
810PC-175
810PCSti-33
81Top-10
82Cap-5
82McDSti-29
820PC-362
82PosCer-10
830PC-368
830PCSti-203
83PufSti-20
84KinSmo-3
840PC-83
840PCSti-271
84Top-65
850PC-5
850PCSti-233
85Top-5
86FlamRedR-5
860PC-40
860PCSti-46
86Top-40
**Engblom, David**
95SweUppDE-11
**Engel, Alexander**
94GerDELE-154
95GerDELE-151
96GerDELE-228
**Engelbrecht, Bernhard**
79PanSti-97
82SweSemHVS-102
94GerDELE-337
**Engevik, Glen**
89NasKni-6
**Engfer, Jon**
95TalTigS-2
**English, John**
83SauSteMG-4
88ProAHL-193
**Englund, Bo**
64SweCorI-17
64SweCorI-52
65SweCorI-17
65SweCorI-52
67SweHoc-267
69SweHocS-116
**Englund, Christer**
71SweHocS-390
73SweHocS-206
73SweWorCS-206
**Englund, Patric**
89SweSemE-21
90SweSemE-92
91SweSemE-22
92SweSemE-47
94SweLeaE-96
95SweLeaE-164
95SweUppDE-17
**Engman, Petri**
94FinnSIS-333
95FinnSIS-17
**Engqvist, Knut**
92BriColJHL-25
**Engstrom, Mikael**
91SweSemE-174
92SweSemE-196
93SweSemE-166
94SweLeaE-114
**Enio, Jim**
44BeeGro2P-163

**Ennis, Jim**
880ilTenAnn-92
88ProAHL-88
89ProAHL-300
**Ens, Kelly**
88LetHur-5
89LetHur-4
90ProAHLIHL-193
91ProAHLCHL-113
**Ensom, Jim**
93NorBayC-8
94KitRanU-33
95Sla-285
**Epantchinsev, Vadim**
94ParSE-SE231
94ParSEG-SE231
94SP-170
94SPDieCut-164
94UppDec-514
94UppDecEleIce-514
95SigRoo-50
95SigRooSig-50
**Epoch, Paul**
86KitRan-14
**Eppers, Henrik**
93PetPet-13
**Epstein, Nikolai**
74SweHocS-50
**Equale, Ryan**
96RoaExp-12
**Erasmas, Ryan**
91BriColJHL-98
**Erb, Jamie**
93RalIce-5
**Erdall, Rick**
89SweSemE-113
90SweSemE-144
91SweSemE-196
**Erdman, Josh**
907thInnSWHL-330
**Erdmann, Alexander**
96GerDELE-164
**Eremenko, Rick**
91BriColJHL-17
**Erickson, Autry**
60ShiCoi-112
61ShiCoi-18
**Erickson, Bryan**
850PC-80
85Top-80
86Kin20tATI-5
860PC-101
860PCSti-93
86Top-101
87KinTeal4-5
870PC-100
87PanSti-282
87Top-130
91JetIGA-10
91ProSet-516
91ProSetFre-516
91ScoCan-657
93JetRuf-11
930PCPre-294
930PCPreG-294
93TopPre-294
93TopPreG-294
**Erickson, Chad**
91ProAHLCHL-421
93RalIce-4
95BirBul-21
**Erickson, Grant**
72CleCruWHA-4
**Erickson, Kyle**
93MinDul-9
**Erickson, Patrik**
87SwePanS-60
89SweSemE-42
90SweSemE-186
91SweSemE-15
91SweSemE-355
91SweSemWCS-47
92SweSemE-43
93SweSemE-72
94SweLeaE-98
95SweGloWC-54
95SweLeaE-36
95SweLeaEFF-13
95SweUppDE-54
**Erickson, Roland**
79PanSti-193
**Ericsson, Arne**
65SweCorI-91
**Ericsson, Bo**
82SweSemHVS-11
83SweSemE-6
84SweSemE-224
86SwePanS-251
87SwePanS-238
**Ericsson, Jan**
83SweSemE-24
87SweHoc-235
93SweSemE-233
**Ericsson, Rolf**
83SweSemE-18
**Erikksson, Anders**
98UppDec-88
98UppDecE1o1-88
**Eriksen, Tommie**
90ProAHLIHL-185
**Eriksson, Anders**
91SweSemE-327
92SweSemE-230
93Cla-129

93Par-540
93ParEmel-540
93SweSemE-200
94ParSE-SE233
94ParSEG-SE233
94SP-170
94SPDieCut-170
94SweLeaE-32
94UppDec-518
94UppDecEleIce-518
95AdiRedW-6
95ColEdgI-2
95ColCho-356
96ColEdgFL-4
96DonCanI-145
96DonCanIGPP-145
96DonCanIPP-145
96DonEli-129
96DonEliDCS-129
96FlePic-180
96Lea-214
96LeaPre-125
96LeaPreP-214
96LeaPrePP-125
96MetUni-177
96Pin-219
96PinArtP-219
96PinFoi-219
96PinPreS-219
96PinRinC-219
96SelCer-92
96SelCerAP-92
96SelCerBlu-92
96SelCerMB-92
96SelCerMG-92
96SelCerMR-92
96SelCerRed-92
96SP-176
96SPSPxFor-4
96Sum-190
96SumArtP-190
96SumIce-190
96SumMet-190
96SumPreS-190
96SweSemW-55
96Ult-49
96UltGoIM-49
96UltRoo-6
96UppDec-183
96UppDecGN-X22
96UppDecIce-83
96UppDecIcePar-83
96Zen-137
96ZenArtP-137
97Be A PPAD-180
97Be A PPAPD-180
97BeAPla-180
97BeAPlaAut-180
97Don-174
97DonLim-54
97DonLimExp-54
97DonPreProG-174
97DonPreProS-174
97PacPar-64
97PacParC-64
97PacParDG-64
97PacParEG-64
97PacParIB-64
97PacParRed-64
97PacParSil-64
97SPAut-56
98O-PChr-25
98O-PChrR-25
98Pac-189
98PacIceB-189
98PacPar-73
98PacParC-73
98PacParEG-73
98PacParH-73
98PacParIB-73
98PacParS-73
98PacRed-189
98SPxFin-129
98SPxFinR-129
98SPxFinS-129
98Top-25
98TopO-P-25
98UD3-28
98UD3-88
98UD3-148
98UD3DieC-28
98UD3DieC-88
98UD3DieC-148
98UppDecGR-88
99Pac-87
99PacCop-87
99PacGol-87
99PacIceB-87
99PacPreD-87
**Eriksson, Bengt**
67SweHoc-235
69SweHocS-278
71SweHocS-273
**Eriksson, Bjorn**
95SweLeaE-212
**Eriksson, Bo**
71SweHocS-391
72SweSemE-259
84SweSemE-178
85SwePanS-159
85SwePanS-227
86SwePanS-170
87SwePanS-193
**Eriksson, Clas**

90SweSemE-270
91SweSemE-100
92SweSemE-118
93SweSemE-90
94SweLeaE-87
95SweLeaE-45
95SweUppDE-71
**Eriksson, Eddy**
89SweSemE-110
90SweSemE-115
91SweSemE-121
92SweSemE-139
**Eriksson, Hakan**
83SweSemE-88
**Eriksson, Hans**
64SweCorI-35
64SweCorI-81
65SweCorI-35
65SweCorI-81A
67SweHoc-27
69SweHocS-41
73SweHocS-46
73SweWorCS-46
83SweSemE-133
**Eriksson, Jan**
81SweSemHVS-5
82SweSemHVS-7
83SweSemE-4
84SweSemE-3
85SwePanS-6
87SwePanS-247
89SweSemE-242
90SweSemE-160
**Eriksson, Jonas**
92SweSemE-102
93SweSemE-75
94SweLeaE-113
94SweLeaECS-4
95SweUppDE1DS-DS11
96GerDELE-227
**Eriksson, Jorgen**
89SweSemE-178
90SweSemE-10
91SweSemE-206
92SweSemE-229
93SweSemE-7
**Eriksson, Karl-Olof**
69SweHocS-298
70SweHocS-198
71SweHocS-284
**Eriksson, Karl-Ove**
67SweHoc-253
**Eriksson, Kent**
83SweSemE-233
**Eriksson, Kjell**
67SweHoc-86
**Eriksson, Lars Bertil**
67SweHoc-200
**Eriksson, Lars Erik**
73SweHocS-171
73SweWorCS-171□
   83SweSemE-51
84SweSemE-50
85SwePanS-31
87SwePanS-47
89SweSemE-27
90SweSemE-176
91SweSemE-29
**Eriksson, Leif**
65SweCorI-188
67SweHoc-168
86SwePanS-144
**Eriksson, Lennart**
71SweHocS-323
72SweHocS-138
**Eriksson, Markus**
92SweSemE-354
93SweSemE-142
94SweLeaE-289
95SweLeaE-66
**Eriksson, Mats**
74SweHocS-392
72SweHocS-263
**Eriksson, Niklas**
89SweSemE-135
90SweSemE-210
91SweSemE-147
92SweSemE-165
93SweSemE-114
94FinnJaaK-72
94SweLeaE-41
94SweLeaEGC-16
95SweLeaE-70
95SweLeaEG-7
95SweUppDE-103
**Eriksson, Owe**
84SweSemE-62
85SwePanS-62
**Eriksson, Patrik**
86SwePanS-49
**Eriksson, Peter**
84SweSemE-71
86SwePanS-53
86SwePanS-125
86SwePanS-131
87SwePanS-62
87SwePanS-117
87SwePanS-122
89OilTeal-5
89SweSemE-45
90SweSemE-110
90SweSemE-193
90UppDec-145

90UppDecF-145
91SweSemE-47
91SweSemE-115
92SweSemE-145
93SweSemE-114
95SweUppDE1DS-DS16
**Eriksson, Robin**
83SweSemE-114
84SweSemE-127
**Eriksson, Roland**
72SweHocS-43
72SweHocS-264
73SweHocS-25
73SweWorCS-25
74SweHocS-214
770PCNHL-123
77Top-123
78CanuRoyB-4
780PC-241
78Top-241
790PC-350
83SweSemE-135
85SwePanS-192
**Eriksson, Tomaz**
86SwePanS-61
86SwePanS-77
89SweSemE-236
90SweSemE-67
91SweSemE-237
**Eriksson, Tommy**
67SweHoc-268
69SweHocS-312
70SweHocS-215
71SweHocS-362
72SweHocS-187
72SweHocS-273
82SweSemHVS-15
83FlyJCP-9
840PC-158
85FlyPos-9
85SwePanS-215
87SwePanS-74
89SweSemE-52
89SweSemWCS-12
90SweSemE-275
91SweSemE-57
91SweSemE-321
91SweSemWCS-30
92SweSemE-83
93SweSemE-56
94SweLeaE-262
**Eriksson, Ulf**
65SweCorI-142
**Erixon, Jan**
82SweSemHVS-24
87PanSti-120
88PanSti-306
890PC-96
89RanMarMB-20
90PanSti-104
90ProSet-195
90Sco-272
90ScoCan-272
90ScoCan-343
90Top-187
90TopTif-187
90UppDec-366
90UppDecF-366
91Bow-77
910PC-152
91PanSti-283
91Pin-187
91PinFre-187
91ScoAme-264
91ScoCan-484
91StaClu-151
91Top-152
91UppDec-178
91UppDecF-178
92Bow-253
920PC-207
92PanSti-241
92PanStiFre-241
92Pin-191
92PinFre-191
92Sco-362
92ScoCan-362
92StaClu-161
92Top-153
92TopGol-153G
93Sco-287
93ScoCan-287
93SweSemWCS-35
**Ernlund, Hans-Olov**
70SweHocS-115
71SweHocS-204
72SweHocS-183
**Ernst, Bingo**
51LavDaiQSHL-83
52St.LawS-26
**Errey, Bob**
83PenCok-8
83PenTealP-10
84PenHeiP-7
86PenKod-8
87PanSti-152
87PenKod-8
87PenMask-3
890PC-50
890PCSti-233

89PanSti-315
89PenFoo-8
89Top-50
90Bow-212
90BowTif-212
900PC-230
90PanSti-133
90ProSet-234
90Sco-255
90ScoCan-255
90Top-230
90TopTif-230
91Bow-85
910PC-94
91PanSti-279
91Par-138
91ParFre-138
91Pin-257
91PinFre-257
91ProSet-187
91ProSetFre-187
91ProSetPla-215
91ScoAme-169
91ScoCan-169
91StaClu-191
91Top-94
92Bow-304
92DurPan-23
920PC-323
92Par-374
92ParEmel-374
92PenCokC-5
92PenFoo-2
92Pin-310
92PinFre-310
92Sco-287
92ScoCan-287
92StaClu-170
92Top-95
92TopGol-95G
93Lea-377
93Par-453
93ParEmel-453
93Pin-410
93PinCan-410
93PinCap-21
93PinCapC-21
93Pow-435
93Sco-208
93ScoCan-208
93ScoCan-566
93ScoGol-566
93StaClu-404
93StaCluFDI-404
93StaCluO-404
94CanGamNHLP-361
94Lea-398
940PCPre-331
940PCPreSE-331
94ParSE-SE161
94ParSEG-SE161
94Pin-192
94PinArtP-192
94PinRinC-192
94Sco-87
94ScoGol-87
94ScoPla-87
94ScoPlaTS-87
94StaClu-37
94StaCluFDI-37
94StaCluMOMS-37
94StaCluSTWC-37
94TopPre-331
94TopPreSE-331
94UppDec-401
94UppDecEleIce-401
95Lea-315
95Sco-174
95ScoBlaIce-174
95ScoBlaIceAP-174
96BeAPAut-197
96BeAPAutSil-197
96BeAPla-197
97PacInvNRB-177
**Erskine, John**
98BowCHL-134
98BowCHLAuB-A24
98BowCHLAuG-A24
98BowCHLAuS-A24
98BowCHLGA-134
98BowCHLOI-134
98BowChrC-134
98BowChrCGA-134
98BowChrCGAR-134
98BowChrCOI-134
98BowChrCOIR-134
98BowChrCR-134
**Erskine, Wayne**
84KinCan-19
85KinCan-19
86KinCan-17
**Ertel, Tyler**
87KitRan-14
897thInnSOHL-151
907thInnSOHL-180
**Eruzione, Mike**
80USAOlyTMP-2
81SweSemHVS-104
91NasKni-24
95SigRooMI-11
95SigRooMI-12
95SigRooMI-47
95SigRooSMIS-11
95SigRooSMIS-12

**Esau, Leonard (Len)**
90ProAHLIHL-150
91ProAHLCHL-352
94Par-37
94ParGol-37
94St.JohF-5
96DetVip-7
**Esbjorn, Lars-Erik**
73SweHocS-147
73SweWorCS-147
74SweHocS-167
**Esbjors, Joacim**
89SweSemE-267
90SweSemE-32
91SweSemE-281
92SweSemE-303
93SweSemE-269
94FinnJaaK-61
94SweLeaE-195
95SweLeaE-144
95SweUppDE-205
**Esbjors, Jonas**
91SweSemE-299
92SweSemE-318
93SweSemE-283
94SweLeaE-206
95SweLeaE-146
**Esche, Robert**
95Sla-57
96DetWha-6
97BowCHL-41
97BowCHLOPC-41
98BowCHL-1
98BowCHLGA-1
98BowCHLOI-1
98BowChrC-1
98BowChrCGA-1
98BowChrCGAR-1
98BowChrCOI-1
98BowChrCOIR-1
98BowChrCR-1
99Pac-332
99PacCop-332
99PacGol-332
99PacIceB-332
99PacPreD-332
99RetHoc-65
99UppDecM-160
99UppDecMGS-160
99UppDecMSS-160
99UppDecMSS-160
99UppDecRG-65
99UppDecRP-65
**Eskrzycki, Andrzej**
79PanSti-123
**Esmantovich, Igor**
900PC-479
**Espe, David (Dave)**
89HalCit-5
89ProAHL-161
90HalCit-6
90ProAHLIHL-442
91ProAHLCHL-531
**Esposito, Phil**
63ChePho-12
64BeeGro3P-34A
64BeeGro3P-34B
64CocCap-24
65Coc-25
65Top-116
66Top-63
67Top-32
680PC-7
680PC-208
680PCPucSti-5
68ShiCoi-8
68Top-7
690PC-30
690PC-205A
690PC-205B
690PC-214
690PCFou-18
690PCSta-7
69Top-30
70BruPos-13
70BruTealss-4
70DadCoo-30
70EssPowPla-58
700PC-11
700PC-233
700PC-237
700PCDec-6
70SarProSta-14
70Top-11
70TopStiS-6
71Baz-1
71BruTealss-4
71MatMinRec-3
710PC-20
710PC-247
710PC-253
710PCPos-21
71SarProSta-7
71SweHocS-199
71Top-1
71Top-2
71Top-3
71Top-20
71TorSun-8
72KellroT-2
720PC-76
720PC-111
720PC-230
720PC-272

❏ 72OPC-280
❏ 72OPC-283
❏ 72OPCPlaC-2
❏ 72OPCTeaC-9
❏ 72SweHocS-115
❏ 72SweSemWC-184
❏ 72Top-61
❏ 72Top-62
❏ 72Top-63
❏ 72Top-124
❏ 72Top-150
❏ 73OPC-120
❏ 73OPC-133
❏ 73OPC-134
❏ 73OPC-135
❏ 73OPC-138
❏ 73Top-1
❏ 73Top-2
❏ 73Top-3
❏ 73Top-6
❏ 73Top-120
❏ 74NHLActSta-26
❏ 74OPCNHL-1
❏ 74OPCNHL-3
❏ 74OPCNHL-28
❏ 74OPCNHL-129
❏ 74OPCNHL-200
❏ 74OPCNHL-244
❏ 74OPCNHL-246
❏ 74Top-1
❏ 74Top-3
❏ 74Top-28
❏ 74Top-129
❏ 74Top-200
❏ 74Top-244
❏ 74Top-246
❏ 75OPCNHL-200A
❏ 75OPCNHL-200B
❏ 75OPCNHL-208
❏ 75OPCNHL-210
❏ 75OPCNHL-212
❏ 75OPCNHL-292
❏ 75OPCNHL-314
❏ 75Top-200
❏ 75Top-208
❏ 75Top-210
❏ 75Top-212
❏ 75Top-292
❏ 75Top-314
❏ 76OPCNHL-5
❏ 76OPCNHL-245
❏ 76OPCNHL-390
❏ 76Top-5
❏ 76Top-245
❏ 76TopGloI-7
❏ 77OPCNHL-5
❏ 77OPCNHL-55
❏ 77Spo-3
❏ 77Top-5
❏ 77Top-55
❏ 78OPC-2
❏ 78OPC-67
❏ 78OPC-100
❏ 78Top-2
❏ 78Top-67
❏ 78Top-100
❏ 79OPC-220
❏ 79Top-220
❏ 80OPC-100
❏ 80OPC-149
❏ 80OPCSup-14
❏ 80Top-100
❏ 80Top-149
❏ 82NeiGre-36
❏ 85HalFC-244
❏ 87SauSteMG-15
❏ 88EssAllSta-10
❏ 90ProSet-403
❏ 90UppDec-510
❏ 90UppDecF-510
❏ 91BruSpoAL-10
❏ 91FutTreC72-40
❏ 91FutTreC72-70
❏ 91FutTreC72-84
❏ 91FutTreC72P-2
❏ 91ProSet-594
❏ 91ProSetFre-594
❏ 91SweSemWCS-240
❏ 92FutTre76CC-102
❏ 92FutTre76CC-139
❏ 92FutTre76CC-153
❏ 92HalFL-7
❏ 92LigShe-14
❏ 92OPC-283
❏ 92OPC25AI-10
❏ 93LigSealR-13
❏ 94LigPhoA-11
❏ 94LigPos-7
❏ 94ParTalB-29
❏ 94ParTalBA-A4
❏ 95FanPhiE-1
❏ 95FanPhiE-2
❏ 95FanPhiE-3
❏ 95FanPhiE-4
❏ 95FanPhiE-5
❏ 95Par66-33
❏ 95Par66Coi-33
❏ 98O-PChrBRtP-10
❏ 98O-PChrBRtPR-10
❏ 98TopBlaFTPA-10
❏ 98TopBlaFTPA-10
❏ 99RetHoc-94
❏ 99UppDecCA-C8
❏ 99UppDecCL-19

❏ 99UppDecCLCLC-19
❏ 99UppDecES-18
❏ 99UppDecRG-G9A
❏ 99UppDecRG-94
❏ 99UppDecRGI-G9A
❏ 99UppDecRII-PE
❏ 99UppDecRIL1-PE
❏ 99UppDecRM-RM4
❏ 99UppDecRP-94

**Esposito, Tony**
❏ 69OPC-138
❏ 70DadCoo-31
❏ 70EssPowPla-126
❏ 70OPC-153
❏ 70OPC-234
❏ 70OPC-247
❏ 70OPC-250
❏ 70OPCDec-32
❏ 70SarProSta-33
❏ 70TopStiS-7
❏ 71Baz-29
❏ 71LetActR-13
❏ 71MatMinRec-2
❏ 71OPC-110
❏ 71OPCPos-8
❏ 71OPCTBoo-13
❏ 71SarProSta-44
❏ 71SweHocS-195
❏ 71Top-4
❏ 71Top-5
❏ 71Top-6
❏ 71Top-110
❏ 71TorSun-65
❏ 72OPC-137
❏ 72OPC-196
❏ 72OPC-226
❏ 72OPC-286
❏ 72OPCTeaC-10
❏ 72SarProSta-66
❏ 72SweSemWC-231
❏ 72Top-20
❏ 72Top-64
❏ 72Top-121
❏ 73BluWhiBor-23
❏ 73OPC-90
❏ 73OPC-136
❏ 73Top-4
❏ 74LipSou-45
❏ 74NHLActSta-78
❏ 74OPCNHL-170
❏ 74Top-170
❏ 75OPCNHL-240
❏ 75Top-240
❏ 76OPCNHL-100
❏ 76Top-100
❏ 76TopGloI-3
❏ 77OPCNHL-170
❏ 77Spo-3
❏ 77Top-170
❏ 78OPC-250
❏ 78Top-250
❏ 78Top-70
❏ 79OPC-8
❏ 79OPC-80
❏ 79Top-8A
❏ 79Top-8B
❏ 79Top-80
❏ 80BlaWhiBor-4
❏ 80OPC-86
❏ 80OPC-150
❏ 80OPC-168
❏ 80OPCSup-4
❏ 80Top-86
❏ 80Top-150
❏ 80Top-168
❏ 81BlaBorPos-6
❏ 81OPC-54
❏ 81OPC-67
❏ 81OPCSti-113
❏ 81Top-11
❏ 81Top-W126
❏ 82OPC-64
❏ 82PosCer-4
❏ 83BlaBorPos-5
❏ 83OPC-99
❏ 83PufSti-13
❏ 88EssAllSta-11
❏ 90ProSet-699
❏ 91FutTreC72-96
❏ 91Pin-388
❏ 91PinFre-388
❏ 92LigShe-15
❏ 92OPC-194
❏ 92OPC25AI-2
❏ 93HigLinGG-8
❏ 93LigSealR-14
❏ 94LigPhoA-12
❏ 94LigPos-8
❏ 96SweSemWHL-HL7
❏ 98BlaLeg-1
❏ 99RetHoc-107
❏ 99UppDecES-17
❏ 99UppDecRG-107
❏ 99UppDecRII-TE
❏ 99UppDecRIL1-TE
❏ 99UppDecRP-107

**Esselmont, Ryan**
❏ 92BriColJHL-49
**Esselmont, Shea**
❏ 907thInnSMC-4
❏ 917thInnSWHL-62
**Esselmont, Todd**

❏ 907thInnSMC-5
❏ 907thInnSWHL-65
**Essensa, Bob**
❏ 87MonHaw-7
❏ 89JetSaf-14
❏ 89OPCSti-63
❏ 89OPCSti-205
❏ 89PanSti-173
❏ 89ProAHL-34
❏ 90Bow-131
❏ 90BowTif-131
❏ 90JetIGA-13
❏ 90OPC-119
❏ 90OPCPre-29
❏ 90PanSti-311
❏ 90ProSet-328
❏ 90Sco-112
❏ 90Sco-324
❏ 90ScoCan-112
❏ 90ScoCan-324
❏ 90Top-119
❏ 90TopTif-119
❏ 90UppDec-122
❏ 90UppDec-337
❏ 90UppDecF-122
❏ 90UppDecF-337
❏ 91Bow-193
❏ 91Gil-8
❏ 91JetIGA-11
❏ 91OPC-307
❏ 91PanSti-75
❏ 91Par-199
❏ 91ParFre-199
❏ 91Pin-66
❏ 91PinFre-66
❏ 91ProSet-266
❏ 91ProSet-602
❏ 91ProSetFre-266
❏ 91ProSetFre-602
❏ 91ProSetPla-135
❏ 91ProSetPla-285
❏ 91ProSetPre-266
❏ 91ScoAme-251
❏ 91ScoCan-471
❏ 91ScoYouS-17
❏ 91StaClu-152
❏ 91Top-307
❏ 91UppDec-101
❏ 91UppDecF-101
❏ 92Bow-306
❏ 92Kra-26
❏ 92OPC-226
❏ 92PanSti-51
❏ 92PanStiFre-51
❏ 92Par-207
❏ 92ParEmel-207
❏ 92Pin-190
❏ 92PinFre-190
❏ 92ProSet-211
❏ 92ProSet-267
❏ 92Sco-123
❏ 92ScoCan-123
❏ 92StaClu-210
❏ 92Top-183
❏ 92TopGol-183G
❏ 92Ult-240
❏ 92UppDec-217
❏ 93Don-382
❏ 93JetRuf-12
❏ 93KraRec-2
❏ 93Lea-38
❏ 93OPCPre-161
❏ 93OPCPreG-161
❏ 93PanSti-199
❏ 93Par-234
❏ 93ParEmel-234
❏ 93Pin-133
❏ 93PinCan-133
❏ 93Pow-270
❏ 93Sco-26
❏ 93ScoCan-26
❏ 93StaClu-254
❏ 93StaCluFDI-254
❏ 93StaCluO-254
❏ 93TopPre-161
❏ 93TopPreG-161
❏ 93Ult-89
❏ 93UppDec-144
❏ 94EASpo-150
❏ 94Lea-93
❏ 94Par-64
❏ 94ParGol-64
❏ 94Pin-428
❏ 94PinArtP-428
❏ 94PinRinC-428
❏ 94Sco-191
❏ 94ScoGol-191
❏ 94ScoPla-191
❏ 94ScoPlaTS-191
❏ 95ColEdgI-126
❏ 96OilPos-30
❏ 97Be A PPAD-185
❏ 97Be A PPAPD-185
❏ 97BeAPla-185
❏ 97BeAPlaAut-185
❏ 97PacInvNRB-77
❏ 98Pac-206
❏ 98PacCroR-50
❏ 98PacCroRLS-50
❏ 98PacDynI-70
❏ 98PacDynIB-70
❏ 98PacDynIR-70
❏ 98PacIceB-206
❏ 98PacRed-206
**Essex, Brad**

❏ 96PeoRiv-4
❏ 96PeoRivPA-4
**Estevez, Emilio**
❏ 92DisMigDM-2
**Etcher, Fred**
❏ 52JunBluT-96
**Etches, Derek**
❏ 89SudWol-11
❏ 907thInnSOHL-383
❏ 90SudWol-11
❏ 917thInnSOHL-43
**Ethier, Martin**
❏ 97BowCHL-47
❏ 97BowCHLOPC-47
**Ethier, Neil**
❏ 89SudWol-16
**Ethier, Trevor**
❏ 93SasBla-9
**Ettles, Blair**
❏ 92CorBigRed-10
❏ 93CorBigRed-9
**Eustache, Eddie**
❏ 52JunMinBluT-167
**Evaldson, Ove**
❏ 67SweHoc-169
**Evans, Chris**
❏ 72BluWhiBor-4
❏ 72OPC-236
❏ 72SarProSta-192
❏ 73BluWhiBor-6
❏ 73OPC-208
❏ 74NHLActSta-306
❏ 74NHLActStaU-31
❏ 74OPCNHL-59
❏ 74Top-59
❏ 76OPCWHA-22
**Evans, Cory**
❏ 917thInnSOHL-372
❏ 93WinSpi-16
❏ 94WinSpi-18
**Evans, Daryl**
❏ 83OPC-153
❏ 83OPCSti-144
❏ 84KinSmo-4
❏ 88ProAHL-231
❏ 89NewHavN-4
**Evans, Doug**
❏ 87BluKod-7
❏ 87BluTealss-7
❏ 88BluKod-32
❏ 88BluTealss-7
❏ 90JetIGA-14
❏ 90OPC-413
❏ 90ProSet-561
❏ 91Bow-203
❏ 91JetIGA-12
❏ 91JetPanTS-11
❏ 91MicWol-1
❏ 91OPC-438
❏ 91ScoCan-399
❏ 91StaClu-321
❏ 91Top-438
❏ 92DayBom-9
❏ 92FlyJCP-11
❏ 92FlyUppDS-24
❏ 92OPCPre-45
❏ 93OPCPre-203
❏ 93OPCPreG-203
❏ 93PeoRiv-7
❏ 93TopPre-203
❏ 93TopPreG-203
❏ 94GreMon-17
❏ 95ColEdgI-177
❏ 95PeoRiv-3
❏ 96PeoRiv-5
❏ 96PeoRivPA-5
**Evans, Frank**
❏ 89SpoChi-5
❏ 907thInnSWHL-196
❏ 917thInnSCHLAW-18
❏ 917thInnSMC-75
❏ 917thInnSWHL-8
❏ 94LasVegThu-5
**Evans, Jack**
❏ 44BeeGro2P-93
❏ 44BeeGro2P-309A
❏ 44BeeGro2P-309B
❏ 51Par-90
❏ 53Par-54
❏ 54Par-72
❏ 54Top-14
❏ 57Top-55
❏ 58Top-31
❏ 59Top-30
❏ 59Top-48
❏ 60ShiCoi-76
❏ 60Top-30
❏ 60TopSta-14
❏ 61ShiCoi-39
❏ 62Top-26
❏ 94ParMisL-101
**Evans, Jimmy**
❏ 28V1282PauC-60
**Evans, Kevin**
❏ 89ProIHL-76
❏ 90ProAHLIHL-100
❏ 91ProAHLCHL-511
❏ 91ScoCan-650
❏ 93PeoRiv-8
**Evans, Mike**
❏ 91AirCanSJHL-C3
❏ 92MPSPhoSJHL-100
**Evans, Shawn**
❏ 94MilAdm-300
❏ 89ProAHL-244

❏ 91ProAHLCHL-96
❏ 94MilAdm-7
**Evans, Stan**
❏ 23V1281PauC-60
**Evans, Stewart**
❏ 34BeeGro1P-196
❏ 34SweCap-19
❏ 36V356WorG-67
❏ 37OPCV304E-164
❏ 38QuaOatP-12
**Evans, Terry**
❏ 77KalWin-7
**Evans-Harvey, Ronnie**
❏ 94GuiFla-14
❏ 95GuiFla-7
**Evason, Dean**
❏ 84SudWol-2
❏ 85SudWol-6
❏ 87OPC-166
❏ 87PanSti-47
❏ 87Top-166
❏ 87WhaJunBK-5
❏ 88WhaJunGR-5
❏ 89WhaJunM-6
❏ 90Bow-262
❏ 90BowTif-262
❏ 90OPC-376
❏ 90PanSti-44
❏ 90ProSet-103
❏ 90Sco-259A
❏ 90Sco-259B
❏ 90ScoCan-259A
❏ 90ScoCan-259B
❏ 90Top-376
❏ 90UppDec-192
❏ 90UppDecF-192
❏ 90WhaJr7E-10
❏ 91Bow-10
❏ 91OPC-325
❏ 91OPCPre-36
❏ 91PanSti-312
❏ 91Par-388
❏ 91ParFre-388
❏ 91Pin-153
❏ 91PinFre-153
❏ 91ProSet-84
❏ 91ProSetFre-84
❏ 91ProSetPla-230
❏ 91ScoAme-17
❏ 91ScoCan-17
❏ 91ScoCan-641
❏ 91ScoRoo-91T
❏ 91ShaSanJSA-4
❏ 91StaClu-145
❏ 91Top-325
❏ 91UppDec-127
❏ 91UppDec-560
❏ 91UppDecF-127
❏ 91UppDecF-560
❏ 92Bow-133
❏ 92OPC-381
❏ 92PanSti-131
❏ 92PanStiFre-131
❏ 92Par-392
❏ 92ParEmel-392
❏ 92Pin-169
❏ 92PinFre-169
❏ 92Sco-103
❏ 92ScoCan-103
❏ 92StaClu-11
❏ 92Top-304
❏ 92TopGol-304G
❏ 92Ult-193
❏ 92UppDec-281
❏ 93Don-86
❏ 93PanSti-259
❏ 93Par-319
❏ 93ParEmel-319
❏ 93Pin-384
❏ 93PinCan-384
❏ 93Pow-323
❏ 93Sco-353
❏ 93Sco-550
❏ 93ScoCan-353
❏ 93ScoCan-550
❏ 93ScoGol-550
❏ 93Ult-298
❏ 94BeAPSig-138
❏ 94CanGamNHLP-78
❏ 94Lea-45
❏ 94OPCPre-361
❏ 94OPCPreSE-361
❏ 94ParSE-SE46
❏ 94ParSEG-SE46
❏ 94Pin-346
❏ 94PinArtP-346
❏ 94PinRinC-346
❏ 94StaClu-82
❏ 94StaCluFDI-82
❏ 94StaCluMOMS-82
❏ 94StaCluSTWC-82
❏ 94StaHoc-10
❏ 94StaPos-6
❏ 94TopPre-361
❏ 94TopPreSE-361
❏ 94Ult-50
❏ 94UppDec-48
❏ 94UppDecEeIce-48
❏ 95ColCho-300
❏ 95ColChoPC-300
❏ 95ParInt-36
❏ 95ParIntEl-36
❏ 95UppDec-22
❏ 95UppDecEeIce-22

❏ 95UppDecEeIceG-22
❏ 98GerDELE-68
**Evensson, Conny**
❏ 67SweHoc-87
❏ 71SweHocS-150
❏ 72SweHocS-133
❏ 73SweHocS-178
❏ 73SweWorCS-178
❏ 74SweHocS-215
❏ 84SweSemE-121
❏ 85SwePanS-90
❏ 86SwePanS-83
❏ 91SweSemE-359
❏ 93SwiHNL-6
**Evoy, Sean**
❏ 84SudWol-2
❏ 85SudWol-6
**Evtuschevsi, Greg**
❏ 84KamBla-8
**Evtushevski, Greg**
❏ 94GerDELE-229
❏ 95GerDELE-165
❏ 96GerDELE-240
❏ 98GerDELE-44
**Ewacha, Rod**
❏ 90MicTecHus-4
❏ 91MicTecHus-3
**Ewen, Dean**
❏ 89ProAHL-242
❏ 91ProAHLCHL-452
❏ 98LasVegT-4
**Ewen, Todd**
❏ 87BluKod-8
❏ 87BluTealss-8
❏ 88BluKod-21
❏ 88BluTealss-8
❏ 89CanaKra-8
❏ 90CanaPos-15
❏ 90ProSet-470A
❏ 90ProSet-470B
❏ 91CanaPanTS-11
❏ 91CanaPos-12
❏ 91ProSet-419
❏ 91ProSetFre-419
❏ 91StaClu-340
❏ 92CanaPos-11
❏ 92Pin-250
❏ 92PinFre-250
❏ 92UppDec-549
❏ 93Don-9
❏ 93Lea-427
❏ 93OPCPre-369
❏ 93OPCPreG-369
❏ 93Par-5
❏ 93ParEmel-5
❏ 93PinCan-409
❏ 93Pow-285
❏ 93Sco-565
❏ 93ScoCan-565
❏ 93ScoGol-565
❏ 93StaClu-309
❏ 93StaCluFDI-309
❏ 93StaCluO-309
❏ 93TopPre-369
❏ 93TopPreG-369
❏ 93Ult-252
❏ 93UppDec-449
❏ 94DucCarJr-6
❏ 94OPCPre-119
❏ 94OPCPreSE-119
❏ 94Pin-503
❏ 94PinArtP-503
❏ 94PinRinC-503
❏ 94TopPre-119
❏ 94TopPreSE-119
❏ 94Ult-2
❏ 94UppDec-427
❏ 94UppDecEeIce-427
❏ 95BeAPla-155
❏ 95BeAPSig-S155
❏ 95BeAPSigDC-S155
❏ 95UppDec-340
❏ 95UppDecEeIce-340
❏ 95UppDecEeIceG-340
❏ 96ColCho-11
❏ 97PacInvNRB-178
**Ewing, Steve**
❏ 86KitRan-29
**Exantus, Paul-Emile**
❏ 907thInnSQMJHL-265
❏ 917thInnSQMJHL-296
**Exelby, Randy**
❏ 88ProAHL-272
❏ 89ProIHL-115
❏ 90KanCitBla-7
❏ 90ProAHLIHL-589
**Eysselt, Jan**
❏ 95GerDELE-287
❏ 96GerDELE-315
**Ezinicki, Bill**
❏ 44BeeGro2P-400
❏ 45QuaOatP-16A
❏ 45QuaOatP-16B
❏ 45QuaOatP-16C
❏ 45QuaOatP-16D
**Faassen, Danny (Dan)**
❏ 907thInnSWHL-205
❏ 917thInnSWHL-19
**Fabian, Petr**
❏ 94CzeAPSE-103
❏ 96CzeAPSE-108
**Fabian, Sean**
❏ 91MinGolG-6
**Fabrizio, Dino**

❏ 92QueIntP-41
**Fadejev, Michail**
❏ 95CzeAPSE-166
❏ 96CzeAPSE-333
**Fader, Duncan**
❏ 93KinFro-15
❏ 95Sla-135
**Fafard, Dominic**
❏ 94WheThu-14
**Fafard, Perry**
❏ 84BraWheK-12
**Fagan, Andrew**
❏ 95Sla-165
**Fagerlund, Bjorn**
❏ 67SweHoc-88
❏ 71SweHocS-137
❏ 73SweHocS-172
❏ 73SweWorCS-172
❏ 74SweHocS-140
**Fagerlund, Rickard**
❏ 64SweCorl-62
❏ 65SweCorl-62
**Fagerstrom, Ake**
❏ 70SweHocS-4
❏ 71SweHocS-78
❏ 72SweHocS-53
❏ 73SweHocS-194
❏ 73SweWorCS-194
**Fagerstrom, Kristian**
❏ 94FinnSIS-336
❏ 95FinnSIS-7
**Fagerstrom, Veli-Pekka**
❏ 95FinnSIS-6
**Fagioli, Luciano**
❏ 87SudWol-12
**Fahey, Rebecca**
❏ 97ColCho-292
**Fahl, Dustin**
❏ 92NorMicW-4
**Fahrutdinov, Mishat**
❏ 89SweSemE-262
❏ 90SweSemE-162
❏ 91SweSemE-264
❏ 92SweSemE-287
❏ 93SweSemE-254
❏ 94SweLeaE-47
❏ 95SweLeaE-129
❏ 95SweUppDE-195
**Fair, Keith**
❏ 93SweSemWCS-119
❏ 93SwiHNL-147
❏ 95SwiHNL-148
**Fair, Quinn**
❏ 91AirCanSJHL-C9
**Fairbairn, Bill**
❏ 70EssPowPla-187
❏ 70SarProSta-123
❏ 71OPC-215
❏ 71SarProSta-123
❏ 71TorSun-171
❏ 72OPC-87
❏ 72SarProSta-150
❏ 73OPC-41
❏ 73Top-41
❏ 74NHLActSta-184
❏ 74OPCNHL-231
❏ 74Top-231
❏ 75OPCNHL-109
❏ 75Top-109
❏ 76OPCNHL-57
❏ 76Top-57
❏ 77OPCNHL-303
❏ 77Top-255
❏ 78OPC-267
**Fairchild, Kelly**
❏ 94Cla-71
❏ 94ClaDraGol-71
❏ 94St.JohML-9
❏ 95SigRoo-23
❏ 95SigRooSig-23
❏ 95St.JohML-4
❏ 96ColEdgFL-5
**Falesy, Kevin**
❏ 87KinCan-17
❏ 89KitRan-27
**Falk, Niklas**
❏ 95SweLeaE-186
❏ 95SweLeaE-3
❏ 95SweUppDE-48
**Falk, Stefan**
❏ 86SwePanS-134
❏ 87SwePanS-125
❏ 89SweSemE-117
❏ 91SweSemE-126
❏ 92SweSemE-147
❏ 93SweSemE-116
❏ 95SweLeaE-54
❏ 95SweUppDE-84
**Falkenberg, Bob**
❏ 68OPC-141
❏ 72OPC-310
**Falkman, Craig**
❏ 72FigSaiPos-7
❏ 72SweSemWC-127
**Falloon, Pat**
❏ 89SpoChi-6
❏ 907thInnSWHL-189
❏ 90UppDec-469
❏ 90UppDecF-469
❏ 917thInnSCHLAW-12
❏ 917thInnSOHL-12
❏ 917thInnSMC-100
❏ 91AreDraPic-1
❏ 91AreDraPic-32

- 91AreDraPic-HOLO
- 91Cla-2
- 91ClaPromo-2
- 91Gil-3
- 91Kra-8
- 91OPCPre-56
- 91Par-160
- 91ParFre-160
- 91Pin-329
- 91PinFre-329
- 91ProSet-558
- 91ProSetCC-CC3
- 91ProSetCCF-CC3
- 91ProSetFre-558
- 91ProSetPla-271
- 91ScoCan-640
- 91ScoRoo-90T
- 91ShaSanJSA-5
- 91StaPicH-2
- 91StaPicH-36
- 91UltDra-2
- 91UltDra-56
- 91UltDra-58
- 91UltDra-78
- 91UltDra-80
- 91UltDraP-1
- 91UppDec-593
- 91UppDecF-593
- 92Bow-361
- 92HumDum1-6
- 92OPC-227
- 92OPCPreSP-12
- 92PanSti-K
- 92PanStiFre-273
- 92PanStiFre-K
- 92Par-161
- 92Par-233
- 92ParEmel-161
- 92ParEmel-233
- 92Pin-9
- 92Pin-238
- 92PinFre-9
- 92PinFre-238
- 92PinTea2-26
- 92PinTea2F-26
- 92ProSet-166
- 92ProSetGTL-10
- 92ProSetRGL-4
- 92Sco-125
- 92Sco-436
- 92ScoCan-125
- 92ScoCan-436
- 92ScoYouS-14
- 92SeaPat-62
- 92StaClu-56
- 92StaClu-259
- 92Top-7
- 92Top-418
- 92TopGol-7G
- 92TopGol-418G
- 92Ult-194
- 92UltRoo-6
- 92UppDec-19
- 92UppDec-286
- 92UppDec-355
- 92UppDec-386
- 92UppDecWJG-WG13
- 93Don-308
- 93DonSpeP-T
- 93Kra-7
- 93Lea-49
- 93LeaStuS-2
- 93OPCPre-259
- 93OPCPreG-259
- 93PanSti-W
- 93Par-183
- 93ParEmel-183
- 93Pin-20
- 93PinCan-20
- 93PinTea2-26
- 93PinTea2C-26
- 93Pow-218
- 93Sco-133
- 93ScoCan-133
- 93ScoFra-19
- 93StaClu-224
- 93StaCluFDI-224
- 93StaCluFDIO-224
- 93StaCluO-224
- 93TopPre-259
- 93TopPreG-259
- 93Ult-56
- 93UppDec-39
- 93UppDecFH-29
- 93UppDecLAS-52
- 93UppDecSP-141
- 94CanGamNHLP-214
- 94Don-83
- 94EASpo-119
- 94Fin-32
- 94FinRef-32
- 94FinSupTW-32
- 94Fla-163
- 94Fle-195
- 94HocWit-98
- 94Lea-95
- 94LeaLim-14
- 94OPCPre-521
- 94OPCPreSE-521
- 94ParSE-SE165
- 94ParSEG-SE165
- 94ParVin-V70
- 94Pin-173
- 94PinArtP-173
- 94PinRinC-173
- 94Sco-152
- 94ScoGol-152
- 94ScoPla-152
- 94ScoPlaTS-152
- 94Sel-116
- 94SelGol-116
- 94StaClu-62
- 94StaCluFDI-62
- 94StaCluMOMS-62
- 94StaCluSTWC-62
- 94TopPre-521
- 94TopPreSE-521
- 94Ult-364
- 94UppDec-307
- 94UppDecEleIce-307
- 95BeAPla-95
- 95BeAPSig-S95
- 95BeAPSigDC-S95
- 95CanGamNHLP-227
- 95ColCho-188
- 95ColChoPC-188
- 95ColChoPCP-188
- 95Don-213
- 95ImpSti-107
- 95Lea-241
- 95ParIntEl-424
- 95ParIntEl-424
- 95PlaOneoOne-82
- 95ProMag-117
- 95Sco-184
- 95ScoBlaIce-184
- 95ScoBlaIceAP-184
- 95Top-147
- 95TopOPCI-147
- 95Ult-284
- 95UppDec-483
- 95UppDecEleIce-318
- 95UppDecEleIceG-318
- 96ColCho-194
- 96Don-208
- 96DonPrePro-208
- 96FlePic-102
- 96FlyPos-8
- 96Lea-102
- 96LeaPreP-102
- 96NHLProSTA-117
- 96Pin-115
- 96PinArtP-115
- 96PinFoi-115
- 96PinPreS-115
- 96PinRinC-115
- 96PlaOneoOne-361
- 96Sco-21
- 96ScoArtPro-21
- 96ScoDeaCAP-21
- 96ScoGolB-21
- 96ScoSpeAP-21
- 96UppDec-122
- 97Pac-199
- 97PacCop-199
- 97PacEmeGre-199
- 97PacIceB-199
- 97PacRed-199
- 97PacSil-199
- 97ScoFly-16
- 97ScoFlyPla-16
- 97ScoFlyPre-16
- 98Be A PPA-205
- 98Be A PPAA-205
- 98Be A PPAAF-205
- 98Be A PPSE-205
- 98Be APG-205
- 98O-PChr-182
- 98O-PChrR-182
- 98Top-182
- 98TopO-P-182
- 99Pac-153
- 99PacCop-153
- 99PacGol-153
- 99PacIceB-153
- 99PacPreD-153

**Falta, Pavel**
- 94CzeAPSE-163

**Fancy, Jeff**
- 907thInnSWHL-106
- 917thInnSWHL-66

**Fandul, Vjatcheslav**
- 93FinnJyvHS-353
- 93FinnSIS-220
- 94FinnSIS-327
- 94FinnSISFi-3
- 95FinnSIS-127
- 95FinnSIS-370

**Farda, Richard**
- 69SweHocS-24
- 69SweWorC-81
- 69SweWorC-146
- 70SweHocS-354
- 71SweHocS-50
- 72SweSemWC-31
- 74SweHocS-18
- 74SweSemHVS-63
- 95CzeAPSE-123

**Farell, Brian**
- 92HarCri-8

**Farelli, Cary**
- 82SweSemHVS-137

**Farkas, Jeff**
- 95DonEliWJ-35
- 97UppDecBD-125
- 97UppDecBDD-125
- 97UppDecBDQD-125
- 97UppDecBDTD-125
- 98UC-306

- 98UD ChoPCR-306
- 98UD ChoR-306

**Farmer, Sean**
- 95SlaMemC-59

**Farrell, Arthur F**
- 83HalFP-L3
- 85HalFC-153

**Farrell, Brian**
- 94Cla-33
- 94ClaDraGol-33

**Farrell, Scott**
- 89SpoChi-7

**Farris, Kevin**
- 85NovScoO-23

**Farrish, Dave**
- 77OPCNHL-179
- 77Top-179
- 78OPC-41
- 78Top-41
- 79OPC-299
- 80MapLeaP-12
- 80OPC-311
- 80PepCap-87
- 81OPC-317
- 83MapLeaP-5
- 83OPC-329
- 83Vac-85
- 84OPC-301
- 88ProAHL-36
- 89ProAHL-49
- 90ManHaw-6
- 90ProAHLIHL-263
- 91ManHaw-7
- 91ProAHLCHL-187

**Fata, Rico**
- 95SauSteMG-6
- 95Sla-369
- 97BowCHL-24
- 97BowCHLOPC-24
- 97UppDec-410
- 98Be A PPA-171
- 98Be A PPAA-171
- 98Be A PPAAF-171
- 98Be A PPSE-171
- 98Be APG-171
- 98BowBes-114
- 98BowBesAR-114
- 98BowBesR-114
- 98BowCHL-131
- 98BowCHLAuB-A40
- 98BowCHLAuG-A40
- 98BowCHLAuS-A40
- 98BowCHLGA-131
- 98BowCHLOI-131
- 98BowCHLSC-SC16
- 98BowChrC-131
- 98BowChrCGA-131
- 98BowChrCGAR-131
- 98BowChrCOI-131
- 98BowChrCOIR-131
- 98BowChrCR-131
- 98FinFutF-F6
- 98FinFutFR-F6
- 98O-PChr-225
- 98O-PChrR-225
- 98PacCroR-17
- 98PacCroRLS-17
- 98PacDynI-24
- 98PacDynIIB-24
- 98PacDynIR-24
- 98PacOmeH-38
- 98PacOmeODI-38
- 98PacOmeR-38
- 98SP Aut-92
- 98Top-225
- 98TopGolLC1-46
- 98TopGolLC1B-46
- 98TopGolLC1BOoO-46
- 98TopGolLC1OoO-46
- 98TopGolLC1R-46
- 98TopGolLC1ROoO-46
- 98TopGolLC2-46
- 98TopGolLC2B-46
- 98TopGolLC2BOoO-46
- 98TopGolLC2OoO-46
- 98TopGolLC2R-46
- 98TopGolLC2ROoO-46
- 98TopGolLC3-46
- 98TopGolLC3B-46
- 98TopGolLC3BOoO-46
- 98TopGolLC3OoO-46
- 98TopGolLC3R-46
- 98TopGolLC3ROoO-46
- 98TopO-P-225
- 98UppDec-413
- 98UppDecBD-11
- 98UppDecDD-11
- 98UppDecE-413
- 98UppDecE101-413
- 98UppDecGN-GN20
- 98UppDecGNQ1-GN20
- 98UppDecGNQ2-GN20
- 98UppDecGNQ3-GN20
- 98UppDecGR-413
- 98UppDecM-27
- 98UppDecMGS-27
- 98UppDecMP-RF
- 98UppDecMSS-27
- 98UppDecP-P30
- 98UppDecPQ1-P30
- 98UppDecPQ2-P30
- 98UppDecPQ3-P30
- 98UppDecQD-11
- 98UppDecTD-11

- 99Pac-66
- 99PacCop-66
- 99PacGol-66
- 99PacIceB-66
- 99PacPreD-66
- 99QuePeeWHWCCS-24
- 99SP AutPS-92
- 99UppDecM-34
- 99UppDecMGS-34
- 99UppDecMSS-34
- 99UppDecMSS-34

**Fatrola, Richard**
- 897thInnSOHL-73
- 907thInnSOHL-4
- 95MusFur-12

**Faubert, Mario**
- 78OPC-296
- 81OPC-261
- 81OPCSti-189

**Faulkner, Alex**
- 44BeeGro2P-164
- 63Par-42
- 63YorWhiB-49
- 64BeeGro3P-68

**Faulkner, Andy**
- 91BriColJHL-52
- 91BriColJHL-153

**Fausel, Shane**
- 91AriIce-13

**Fauss, Ted**
- 83NovScoV-21
- 750PCWHA-122

**Faust, Andre**
- 92Par-365
- 92ParEmel-365
- 93ClaProPro-47
- 93Par-419
- 93ParEmel-419
- 93Pin-209
- 93PinCan-209
- 93StaClu-462
- 93StaCluFDI-462
- 93StaCluO-462
- 93UppDec-63
- 94Don-184
- 96GerDELE-20
- 96GerDELE-P5

**Faust, Elliott**
- 95Sla-206

**Fauteux, Jonathan**
- 98Vald'OF-6

**Favaro, Randy**
- 95SpoChi-11

**Favell, Doug**
- 68ShiCoi-127
- 69OPC-88
- 69Top-88
- 70ColSta-91
- 70DadCoo-32
- 70EssPowPla-199
- 70FlyPos-4
- 70OPC-199
- 70OPCDec-35
- 70SarProSta-152
- 71LetActR-11
- 71LetActR-21
- 710PC-72
- 71SarProSta-156
- 71Top-72
- 71TorSun-193
- 72FlyMigM-4
- 720PC-89
- 72OPCPlaC-16
- 72SarProSta-157
- 72Top-74
- 73MapLeaP-5
- 73MapLeaP-6
- 730PC-158
- 73Top-119
- 74NHLActSta-262
- 740PCNHL-4
- 740PCNHL-46
- 74Top-4
- 74Top-46
- 75MapLeaP-6
- 750PCNHL-381
- 760PCNHL-292
- 76RocCokCan-9
- 76RocPucBuc-9
- 77Coc-7
- 77OPCNHL-370
- 77RocCokCan-7
- 780PC-54
- 78Top-54
- 790PC-274

**Favot, Tim**
- 897thInnSOHL-166
- 907thInnSOHL-307
- 917thInnSOHL-262
- 91SudWol-17

**Fawcett, Len**
- 86KitRan-9

**Feamster, Dave**
- 83BlaBorPos-6
- 83OPC-100

**Fearns, Kent**
- 95Cla-72
- 95ClaAut-5

**Feasby, Scott**
- 897thInnSOHL-88
- 93MusFur-12
- 94MusFur-5
- 95MusFur-9

**Featherstone, Glen**
- 88ProIHL-71
- 90BluKod-9

- 900PC-387
- 90ProSet-523
- 90ScoRoo-25T
- 90Top-387
- 90TopTif-387
- 91Bow-371
- 91BruSpoA-7
- 910PC-436
- 91OPCPre-66
- 91ScoCan-587
- 91ScoRoo-37T
- 91StaClu-319
- 91Top-436
- 930PCPre-14
- 930PCPreG-14
- 93Pow-288
- 93StaClu-372
- 93StaCluFDI-372
- 93StaCluO-372
- 93TopPre-14
- 93TopPreG-14
- 94BeAPSig-81
- 95ParInt-363
- 95ParIntEl-363
- 96WhaBobS-8

**Featherstone, Tony**
- 70EssPowPla-103
- 71Top-106
- 73NorStaP-4
- 750PCWHA-122

**Federenko, Brad**
- 91AirCanSJHL-B32
- 91AirCanSJHLAS-12
- 93MinDul-10

**Federko, Bernie**
- 770PCNHL-312
- 78BluPos-10
- 780PC-143
- 78Top-143
- 790PC-215
- 79Top-215
- 80OPC-71
- 800PC-136
- 800PCSup-18
- 80Top-71
- 80Top-136
- 810PC-288
- 810PC-300
- 810PC-304
- 810PCSti-128
- 81Top-12
- 81Top-62
- 81Top-W127
- 820PC-302
- 820PC-303
- 820PCSti-197
- 82PosCer-17
- 830PC-315
- 830PCSti-125
- 83PufSti-18
- 840PC-184
- 840PC-367
- 840PCSti-54
- 840PCSti-55
- 84Top-131
- 850PC-104
- 850PCSti-53
- 85Top-104
- 860PCSti-174
- 86Top-105
- 87BluKod-9
- 87BluTealss-9
- 870PC-83
- 870PCSti-24
- 87PanSti-312
- 87Top-83
- 88BluKod-24
- 88BluTealss-9
- 88FriLayS-4
- 880PCBoxB-E
- 880PCSti-21
- 88PanSti-104
- 88Top-81
- 88TopBoxB-E
- 890PC-107
- 890PCSti-247
- 89RedWinLC-6
- 89Top-107
- 90Bow-238
- 90BowTif-238
- 900PC-191
- 90PanSti-209
- 90ProSet-70
- 90Sco-252
- 90ScoCan-252
- 90Top-191
- 90TopTif-191
- 90UppDec-58
- 90UppDecF-58
- 91ProSet-597
- 91ProSetFre-597
- 92BluUDBB-14
- 94HocWit-47

**Fedorchuk, Dean**
- 94Cla-52
- 94ClaDraGol-52
- 94DayBom-14

**Fedorko, Mike**
- 75HamFin-5
- 917thInnSWHL-262
- 91PriAlbR-1

**Fedorov, Anton**
- 91MicWol-3
- 93MicWol-5
- 94RalIce-6

**Fedorov, Juri**
- 74SweHocS-87
- 79PanSti-146
- 80USSOlyTMP-1

**Fedorov, Sergei**
- 89RusNatT-5
- 900PCPre-30
- 900PCRedA-19R
- 90ProSet-604
- 90ScoRoo-20T
- 90ScoYouS-9
- 90UppDec-521
- 90UppDec-525
- 90UppDecF-521
- 90UppDecF-525
- 91Bow-90
- 91Gil-12
- 91Kra-51
- 910PC-8
- 910PC-401
- 91OPCPre-68
- 91OPCPre-173
- 91PanSti-145
- 91PanSti-340
- 91Par-38
- 91ParFre-38
- 91ParPHC-PHC5
- 91ParPHCF-PHC5
- 91Pin-157
- 91PinFre-157
- 91ProSet-53
- 91ProSetFre-53
- 91ProSetNHLAS-AC10
- 91ProSetPla-30
- 91ProSetPla-277
- 91ProSetPlaPC-PC7
- 91RedWinLC-4
- 91RusStaNHL-1
- 91RusStaRA-3
- 91RusTriBur-NNO
- 91RusTriFed-1
- 91RusTriFed-2
- 91RusTriFed-3
- 91RusTriFed-4
- 91RusTriFed-5
- 91RusTrilrb-NNO
- 91RusTriKam-NNO
- 91RusTriSem-NNO
- 91ScoAme-250
- 91ScoAme-352
- 91ScoAme-408
- 91ScoCan-298
- 91ScoCan-382
- 91ScoCan-470
- 91ScoHotC-4
- 91ScoYouS-1
- 91StaClu-316
- 91StaPicH-30
- 91SweSemWCS-219
- 91Top-8
- 91Top-401
- 91UppDec-6
- 91UppDec-40
- 91UppDec-82
- 91UppDec-144
- 91UppDec-631
- 91UppDecES-9
- 91UppDecESF-9
- 91UppDecF-6
- 91UppDecF-40
- 91UppDecF-82
- 91UppDecF-144
- 91UppDecF-631
- 92Bow-205
- 92Bow-416
- 92HumDum2-5
- 92McDUppD-6
- 92OPC-195
- 920PCPreSP-20
- 92PanSti-113
- 92PanSti-291
- 92PanStiFre-113
- 92PanStiFre-291
- 92Par-39
- 92Par-219
- 92ParEmel-39
- 92ParEmel-219
- 92Pin-20
- 92PinFre-20
- 92PinTea2-30
- 92PinTea2F-30
- 92ProSet-40
- 92Sco-252
- 92ScoCan-252
- 92ScoYouS-5
- 92SeaPat-5
- 92StaClu-244
- 92StaClu-300
- 92Top-252
- 92TopGol-252G
- 92Ult-48
- 92UltImp-3
- 92UppDec-157
- 92UppDec-632
- 92UppDecES-E1
- 92UppDecWJG-WG16
- 93Don-101
- 93DonEli-U2
- 93Lea-129
- 930PCPre-318
- 930PCPre-441

- 930PCPreG-318
- 930PCPreG-441
- 93PanSti-246
- 93Par-58
- 93ParEasWesS-W10
- 93ParEmel-58
- 93Pin-54
- 93PinCan-54
- 93PinTea2-24
- 93PinTea2C-24
- 93Pow-72
- 93PowGam-1
- 93PowGloG-2
- 93PowSlaA-3
- 93Sco-250
- 93ScoCan-250
- 93ScoDynDUS-9
- 93ScoIntS-3
- 93ScoIntSC-3
- 93StaClu-45
- 93StaCluFDI-45
- 93StaCluFDIO-45
- 93StaCluO-45
- 93TopPre-318
- 93TopPre-441
- 93TopPreG-318
- 93TopPreG-441
- 93Ult-121
- 93UltSpeM-3
- 93UppDec-171
- 93UppDecNR-12
- 93UppDecSP-44
- 94ActPacBHP-1
- 94BAPUpCP-UC7
- 94BeAP99A-G6
- 94BeAPla-R145
- 94CanGamNHLP-87
- 94CanGamNHLP-267
- 94CanGamNHLP-331
- 94CanGamNHLP-360
- 94Don-173
- 94DonDom-5
- 94DonEliIns-4
- 94DonIceMas-2
- 94EASpo-40
- 94Fin-65
- 94FinBowB-B7
- 94FinBowBR-B7
- 94FinDivFCC-13
- 94FinnJaaK-146
- 94FinnJaaK-348
- 94FinRef-65
- 94FinSupTW-65
- 94Fla-48
- 94Fla-213
- 94Fla-214
- 94Fla-215
- 94Fla-216
- 94Fla-217
- 94Fla-218
- 94Fla-219
- 94Fla-220
- 94Fla-221
- 94FlaCenS-2
- 94FlaScoP-3
- 94Fle-59
- 94FleHea-2
- 94HocWit-69
- 94KenStaLA-4
- 94KenStaLC-2
- 94Kra-59
- 94Kra-69
- 94Lea-155
- 94LeaFirOIce-1
- 94LeaGolS-1
- 94LeaLim-81
- 94LeaLimG-9
- 94LeaLimI-7
- 94McDUppD-McD12
- 94OPCPre-40
- 94OPCPre-276
- 94OPCPre-520
- 94OPCPreSE-40
- 94OPCPreSE-276
- 94OPCPreSE-520
- 94Par-305
- 94ParCratGB-7
- 94ParCratGG-7
- 94ParCratGR-7
- 94ParGol-305
- 94ParSE-SE50
- 94ParSEES-ES16
- 94ParSEG-SE50
- 94ParVin-V59
- 94Pin-150
- 94PinArtP-150
- 94PinGam-GR3
- 94PinRinC-150
- 94PinTea-TP8
- 94PinTeaPDP-TP8
- 94PinWorEdi-WE5
- 94PosCerBB-10
- 94Sco90PC-2
- 94ScoDreTea-DT12
- 94ScoFra-TF7
- 94Sel-10
- 94SelGol-10
- 94SP-33
- 94SPDieCut-33
- 94SPPre-24
- 94SPPreDC-24
- 94StaClu-250
- 94StaClu-268
- 94StaCluFDI-250

**Fedosov, Vladimir**

**Fedotov, Alexander**

**Fedotov, Anatoli**

**Fedotov, Sergei**

**Fedulov, Igor**

**Fedyk, Brent**

96ScoDeaCAP-191
96ScoGolB-191
96ScoSpeAP-191
96PupDec-46
99Pac-268
99PacCop-268
99PacGol-268
99PacIceB-268
99PacPreD-268
**Feher, Artie**
84BraWheK-8
85BraWheK-8
**Feiffer, Jason**
91AirCanSJHL-A21
91AirCanSJHLAS-31
**Felicetti, Dino**
96GerDELE-124
**Felix, Chris**
81SauSteMG-11
82SauSteMG-8
83SauSteMG-5
84SauSteMG-6
87SauSteMG-11
88ProAHL-29
89ProAHL-83
90ProAHLIHL-213
95SwiHNL-490
**Feller, J.**
95GerDELE-347
**Felli, Christian**
92CorBigRed-11
93CorBigRed-10
**Felski, Sven**
94GerDELE-39
95GerDELE-37
96GerDELE-36
98GerDELE-158
98GerDELE-316
**Felsner, Brian**
97PacOme-50
97PacOmeC-50
97PacOmeDG-50
97PacOmeEG-50
97PacOmeG-50
97PacOmeIB-50
**Felsner, Denny**
91MicWol-2
92Cla-63
92Cla-64
92Par-493
92ParEmel-493
92PeoRivC-5
92Pin-413
92PinFre-413
92Sco-481
92ScoCan-481
92Top-514
92TopGol-514G
92UppDec-413
93Par-267
93ParEmel-267
93PeoRiv-10
94ClaProP-189
94OPCPre-436
94OPCPreSE-436
94ParSE-SE151
94ParSEG-SE151
94TopPre-436
94TopPreSE-436
94UppDec-114
94UppDecEIeIce-114
96ClaGol-63
96ClaGol-64
96MilAdmBO-6
**Feltendahl, Lars-Olof**
69SweHocS-313
**Fendt, Torsten**
95GerDELE-9
96GerDELE-7
**Fennig, Wade**
89RegPat-4
90ForSasTra-2
**Fenton, Eric**
92MaiBlaB-11
93PorPir-13
94ClaAut-NNO
95PeoRiv-4
96MilAdmBO-7
**Fenton, Paul**
85WhaJunW-5
88OPC-213
89JetSaf-15
90Bow-139
90BowTif-139
90OPC-313
90PanSti-313
90ProSet-329
90ProSet-533A
90ProSet-533B
90Sco-156
90ScoCan-156
90ScoRoo-57T
90Top-313
90TopTif-313
90UppDec-92
90UppDecF-92
91Bow-256
91JetPanTS-12
91JetPanTS-G
91OPC-331
91OPCPre-187
91ScoAme-14
91ScoCan-14
91ScoCan-593
91ShaSanJSA-6

91StaClu-327
91Top-331
92OPC-380
92Sco-257
92ScoCan-257
92Top-173
92TopGol-173G
**Fenyves, Dave**
85SabBluS-8
85SabBluSS-8
86SabBluS-9
86SabBluSSma-9
88ProAHL-131
89ProAHL-335
90ProAHLIHL-32
91ProAHLCHL-283
**Fera, Rick**
83SauSteMG-6
84KinCan-13
94FinnJaaK-325
**Ferding, Curt**
69SweHocS-228
**Ference, Andrew**
96UppDec-374
97BowCHL-100
97BowCHLOPC-100
98BowCHL-48
98BowCHLGA-48
98BowCHLOI-48
**Ference, Brad**
97BowCHL-133
97BowCHLAu-13
97BowCHLBB-9
97BowCHLBowBesAR-9
97BowCHLBowBesR-9
97BowCHLOPC-133
98BowCHL-43
98BowCHLGA-43
98BowCHLOI-43
98BowCHLSC-SC6
98BowChrC-43
98BowChrCGA-43
98BowChrCGAR-43
98BowChrCOI-43
98BowChrCOIR-43
98BowChrCR-43
98UC-261
98UD ChoPCR-261
98UD ChoR-261
**Fergin, Tony**
93CorBigRed-11
**Fergus, Tom**
82OPC-11
82OPCSti-88
82PosCer-1
83BruTealss-5
83OPC-49
83OPCSti-55
84OPC-84
84OPCSti-189
84Top-3
85MapLeaP-11
85OPC-113
85OPCSti-164
85Top-113
86KraDra-16
86MapLeaP-8
86OPC-84
86OPCSti-143
86Top-84
87MapLeaP-6
87MapLeaPLA-7
87MapLeaPO-6
87OPC-120
87OPCSti-159
87PanSti-332
87Top-120
88MapLeaPLA-3
88OPC-214
88OPCSti-170
89OPC-103
89OPCSti-173
89PanSti-135
89Top-103
90Bow-157
90BowTif-157
90OPC-63
90PanSti-282
90ProSet-279A
90ProSet-279B
90Sco-285
90ScoCan-285
90Top-63
90TopTif-63
90UppDec-83
90UppDecF-83
91MapLeaP-10
91Par-400
91ParFre-400
91ProSet-234
91ProSetFre-234
91ProSetPla-238
91ScoCan-234
91UppDec-384
91UppDecF-384
92Bow-273
92OPC-356
92Sco-190
92ScoCan-190
92StaClu-278
92Top-311
92TopGol-311G
92Ult-426

93SwiHNL-122
95SwiHNL-540
**Ferguson, Bob**
95Indice-23
98FloEve-7
**Ferguson, Craig**
92FreCan-9
93FreCan-8
94ClaProP-45
94FreCan-12
94Lea-525
**Ferguson, Dallas**
97AncAce-7
**Ferguson, Dan**
89SauSteMG-24
907thInnSOHL-358
**Ferguson, George**
72MapLeaP-6
74MapLeaP-4
74MapLeaP-4
74NHLActStaU-36
74OPCNHL-302
75MapLeaP-7
75OPCNHL-77
75Top-77
76MapLeaP-5
76OPCNHL-286
77MapLeaP-4
77OPCNHL-266
78OPC-395
79OPC-139
79Top-139
80OPC-44
80Top-44
81OPC-262
81OPCSti-184
82NorStaPos-9
82OPC-268
82OPCSti-150
82PosCer-15
83NorStaPos-8
83OPC-171
**Ferguson, Ian**
83OshGen-4
**Ferguson, Jeff**
88LetHur-6
89SpoChi-8
**Ferguson, John**
44BeeGro2P-237
60CleBar-4
63ChePho-13
63Par-33
63Par-92
64BeeGro3P-103
64CanaPos-6
64CocCap-71
64Top-4
65CanaSteG-3
65Coc-70
65Top-10
66CanaIGA-9
66Top-70
66TopUSAT-65
67CanaIGA-22
67Top-69
67YorActOct-16
67YorActOct-21
68CanaIGA-22
68CanaPosBW-5
68OPC-20
68PosCerM-7
68ShiCoi-84
69CanaPosC-8
69OPC-7
69Top-7
70CanaPin-4
70DadCoo-33
70EssPowPla-15
70OPC-264
79JetPos-6
83Jet-6
84JetPol-7
85JetPol-6
86JetBor-7
89ProAHL-198
90ProAHLIHL-60
91ProAHLCHL-74
91UltiOriS-9
91UltiOriSF-9
94ParTalB-66
95Par66-59
95Par66Coi-59
**Ferguson, Kyle**
93MicTecH-19
96SouCarS-16
**Ferguson, Lorne**
44BeeGro2P-19
51Par-35
54Top-31
57Top-40
58Top-55
94ParMisL-54
**Ferguson, Norm**
69OPC-146
70ColSta-56
70DadCoo-34
70SarProSta-142
71OPC-179
71SarProSta-136
71TorSun-46
72SweSemWC-173
75OPCWHA-92
76SanDieMW-3
77OPCWHA-52

90ProAHLIHL-241
91ProAHLCHL-236
**Ferguson, Scott**
917thInnSWHL-77
93KamBla-6
99Pac-3
99PacCop-3
99PacGol-3
99PacIceB-3
99PacPreD-3
**Ferguson, Tim**
94GerDELE-23
95GerDELE-20
96GerDELE-17
98FloEve-6
**Ferland, Jeannot**
907thInnSQMJHL-259
917thInnSQMJHL-187
**Fermoyle, Andy**
96NorlowH-7
**Fernandez, Emmanuel (Manny)**
917thInnSQMJHL-242
93DonTeaC-10
93Pin-457
93PinCan-457
93UppDec-536
95ColEdgI-139
95ColEdgIQ-IR1
95ColEdgITW-G2
95Don-10
95Ima-24
95ImaGol-24
95ImaPlaPr-PR9
95Lea-169
95ParInt-63
95ParIntEI-63
95Pin-216
95PinArtP-216
95PinRinC-216
95Sco-299
95ScoBlaIce-299
95ScoBlaIceAP-299
95SkyImpNHLF-14
96DonCanILG-8
97PacOme-68
97PacOmeC-68
97PacOmeDG-68
97PacOmeEG-68
97PacOmeG-68
97PacOmeIB-68
99Pac-175
98PacIceB-175
98PacRed-175
99UppDecM-67
99UppDecMGS-67
99UppDecMSS-67
99UppDecMSS-67
**Ferner, Mark**
84KamBla-9
88ProAHL-253
89ProAHL-89
90ProAHLIHL-208
91BalSki-10
91ProAHLCHL-568
930PCPre-478
930PCPreG-478
93Par-275
93ParEmel-275
93StaClu-342
93StaCluFDI-342
93StaCluO-342
93TopPre-478
93TopPreG-478
**Fernqvist, Lars**
83SweSemE-197
**Fernstrom, Allan**
67SweHoc-136
**Fernstrom, Hans-Erik**
65SweCorI-106
67SweHoc-170
**Ferone, Paul**
95SeaThu-9
96SeaThu-7
**Ferranti, Steve**
93MicSta-7
97LouRivF-9
**Ferraro, Chris**
91UppDec-648
91UppDecCWJC-74
91UppDecF-648
92MaiBlaB-25
92Pac-502
93StaCluTUSA-5
93TopPreTUSA-5
93Ult-482
94Cla-39
94ClaAut-39
94ClaDraGol-39
94ClaProPIH-LP4
94FinnJaaK-129
95BinRan-5
95ColEdgI-18
96BinRan-7
96ColEdgFL-6
96Lea-229
96LeaPreP-229
96Pin-233
97PacDynBKS-60
**Ferraro, Peter**
91UppDec-648

91UppDec-696
91UppDecCWJC-83
91UppDecF-648
91UppDecF-696
92MaiBlaB-26
93Pow-503
93StaCluTUSA-6
93TopPreTUSA-15
93Ult-483
94Cla-38
94ClaAut-38
94ClaDraGol-38
94ClaProPIA-IA10
94ClaProPIH-LP5
94FinnJaaK-132
94BinRan-6
95Bow-134
95BowAllFoi-134
95ColEdgI-17
95ParInt-532
95ParIntEI-532
95SkyImp-211
96BinRan-8
96ColEdgFL-7
96Fle-126
96FleCalCan-3
96FlePic-140
96FleProShe-3
96LeaGolR-4
96MetUni-178
96Pin-218
96PinArtP-218
96PinFoi-218
96PinPreS-218
96PinRinC-218
96SkyImp-149
96Sum-181
96SumIce-181
96SumMet-181
96SumPreS-181
98Be A PPA-161
98Be A PPAA-161
98Be A PPAAF-161
98Be A PPSE-161
**Ferraro, Ray**
83BraWheK-20
85WhaJunW-6
86OPC-160
86OPCSti-57
86Top-160
87OPC-109
87Top-109
87WhaJunBK-6
88OPC-114
88OPCSti-268
88PanSti-241
88Top-114
88WhaJunGR-6
89OPC-70
89OPCSti-263
89PanSti-222
89Top-70
89WhaJunM-7
90Bow-258
90BowTif-258
90OPC-336
90PanSti-45
90ProSet-144
90Sco-134
90ScoCan-134
90ScoRoo-15T
90Top-336
90TopTif-336
90UppDec-289
90UppDecF-289
91Bow-212
91OPC-304
91PanSti-250
91Par-110
91ParFre-110
91Pin-123
91PinFre-123
91ProSet-156
91ProSetFre-156
91ProSetPla-76
91ScoAme-48
91ScoCan-48
91StaClu-3
91Top-304
91UppDec-311
91UppDecF-311
92Bow-128
92Bow-229
92HumDum1-7
92OPC-42
92OPCPreSP-1
92PanSti-198
92PanStiFre-198
92Par-98
92Par-499
92ParEmel-98
92ParEmel-499
92Pin-154
92PinFre-154
92ProSet-105
92Sco-298
92ScoCan-298
92ScoSha-3
92ScoShaCan-3
92StaClu-123
92Top-324

92TopGol-324G
92Ult-123
92UppDec-12
92UppDec-193
93Don-198
93Lea-121
930PCPre-349
930PCPreG-349
93Par-123
93ParEmel-123
93Pin-48
93PinCan-48
93Pow-382
93Sco-60
93ScoCan-60
93StaClu-50
93StaCluFDI-50
93StaCluFDIO-50
93StaCluMasP-6
93StaCluMasPW-6
93StaCluO-50
93TopPre-349
93TopPreG-349
93Ult-16
93UppDec-153
93UppDecSP-90
94BeAPSig-92
94CanGamNHLP-154
94Don-162
94Fle-120
94HocWit-84
94Lea-334
940PCPre-335
940PCPreSE-335
94Par-134
94ParGol-134
94ParVin-V86
94Pin-314
94PinArtP-314
94PinRinC-314
94Sel-41
94SelGol-41
94SP-69
94SPDieCut-69
94StaClu-20
94StaCluFDI-20
94StaCluMOMS-20
94StaCluSTWC-20
94TopPre-335
94TopPreSE-335
94Ult-324
94UppDec-14
94UppDecEIeIce-14
95CanGamNHLP-178
95ColCho-33
95ColChoPC-33
95ColChoPCP-33
95Don-144
95Don-297
95Emo-111
95Fin-36
95FinRef-36
95Kra-74
95Lea-284
95Met-94
95ParInt-409
95ParIntEI-409
95PlaOneoOne-173
95Sco-66
95ScoBlaIce-66
95ScoBlaIceAP-66
95SkyImp-107
95StaClu-120
95StaCluMOMS-120
95Sum-108
95SumArtP-108
95SumIce-108
95Top-245
95TopOPCI-245
95TopSupSki-23
95TopSupSkiPla-23
95Ult-93
95Ult-273
95UltGoIM-93
95UppDec-90
95UppDecEIeIce-90
95UppDecEIeIceG-90
95UppDecSpeSE-143
95UppDecSpeEdiG-SE143
96BeAPAut-139
96BeAPAutSil-139
96BeAPla-139
96ColCho-131
96ColCho-320
96Don-183
96DonPrePro-183
96Fle-49
96LeaPre-16
96LeaPrePP-16
96NHLACEPC-12
96Pin-29
96PinArtP-29
96PinFoi-29
96PinPreS-29
96PinRinC-29
96PlaOneoOne-380
96Sco-107
96ScoArtPro-107
96ScoDeaCAP-107
96ScoGolB-107
96ScoSpeAP-107
96SkyImp-57
96TopNHLP-119
96TopPicOI-119
96UppDec-273

96UppDecBD-74
96UppDecBG-74
97DonCanI-98
97DonCanIDS-98
97DonCanIPS-98
97Pac-53
97PacCop-53
97PacDyn-59
97PacDynBKS-45
97PacDynC-59
97PacDynDG-59
97PacDynEG-59
97PacDynIB-59
97PacDynR-59
97PacDynSil-59
97PacDynTan-49
97PacEmeGre-53
97PacIceB-53
97PacInv-66
97PacInvC-66
97PacInvEG-66
97PacInvIB-66
97PacInvR-66
97PacInvS-66
97PacRed-53
97PacSil-53
97Pin-146
97PinCer-82
97PinCerMB-82
97PinCerMG-82
97PinCerMR-82
97PinCerR-82
97PinIns-180
97PinPrePBB-146
97PinPrePBC-146
97PinPrePBM-146
97PinPrePBY-146
97PinPrePFC-146
97PinPrePFM-146
97PinPrePFY-146
97PinPrePla-146
97PinTotCMPG-82
97PinTotCPB-82
97PinTotCPG-82
97PinTotCPR-82
97Sco-189
99Pac-189
99PacCop-189
99PacGol-189
99PacIceB-189
99PacPreD-189
**Ferras, Joe**
88ProAHL-24
**Ferreira, Brian**
91JohChi-12
92NasKni-12
**Ferschweiler, Pat**
92WesMic-10
93RoaExp-8
94RoaExp-18
98KanCitB-10
**Ferster, Ryan**
96GuiFla-10
**Feser, Collin**
84PriAlbRS-7
**Feser, Till**
94GerDELE-283
95GerDELE-278
96GerDELE-175
**Fess, Chris**
94KnoChe-18
**Fetisov, Slava (Vyacheslav)**
79PanSti-141
81SweSemHVS-39
82SweSemHVS-53
83RusNatT-5
87RusNatT-5
89DevCar-11
89RusNatT-6
89SweSemWCS-87
90Bow-80
90BowTif-80
90Dev-12
90OPC-27
90PanSti-75
90PanSti-339
90ProSet-167A
90ProSet-167B
90Sco-62
90ScoCan-62
90Top-27
90TopTif-27
90UppDec-176
90UppDecF-176
91Bow-273
91OPC-175
91Par-96
91ParFre-96
91Pin-101
91PinFre-101
91ProSet-142
91ProSetFre-142
91ProSetPla-199
91RusStaNHL-2
91RusStaRA-4
91ScoAme-184
91ScoCan-184
91StaClu-24
91SweSemWCS-213
91Top-175
91UppDec-410
91UppDecF-410
92Bow-145
92OPC-162

❑ 92Par-334
❑ 92ParEmel-334
❑ 92Pin-299
❑ 92PinFre-299
❑ 92ProSet-96
❑ 92Sco-97
❑ 92ScoCan-97
❑ 92StaClu-392
❑ 92Top-458
❑ 92TopGol-458G
❑ 92Ult-337
❑ 92UppDec-278
❑ 93Pin-397
❑ 93PinCan-397
❑ 93Pow-136
❑ 93Sco-229
❑ 93ScoCan-229
❑ 93StaClu-265
❑ 93StaCluFDI-265
❑ 93StaCluO-265
❑ 94EASpo-74
❑ 94EASpo-208
❑ 94UppDec-434
❑ 94UppDecElelce-434
❑ 95CanGamNHLP-100
❑ 95Don-272
❑ 95Lea-280
❑ 95ParInt-68
❑ 95ParInt-249
❑ 95ParIntEl-68
❑ 95ParIntEl-249
❑ 95SweGloWC-236
❑ 96Don-28
❑ 96DonEli-99
❑ 96DonEliDCS-99
❑ 96DonPrePro-28
❑ 96Fla-27
❑ 96FlaBlul-27
❑ 96Fle-143
❑ 96Lea-42
❑ 96LeaLim-26
❑ 96LeaLimG-26
❑ 96LeaPre-34
❑ 96LeaPreP-42
❑ 96LeaPrePP-34
❑ 96Sco-73
❑ 96ScoArtPro-73
❑ 96ScoDeaCAP-73
❑ 96ScoGolB-73
❑ 96ScoSpeAP-73
❑ 96Sum-128
❑ 96SumArtP-128
❑ 96SumIce-128
❑ 96SumMet-128
❑ 96SumPreS-128
❑ 96UppDecBD-2
❑ 96UppDecBDG-2
❑ 97Pac-111
❑ 97PacCop-111
❑ 97PacEmeGre-111
❑ 97PacIceB-111
❑ 97PacOme-78
❑ 97PacOmeC-78
❑ 97PacOmeDG-78
❑ 97PacOmeEG-78
❑ 97PacOmeG-78
❑ 97PacOmeIB-78
❑ 97PacRed-111
❑ 97PacRev-46
❑ 97PacRevC-46
❑ 97PacRevE-46
❑ 97PacRevIB-46
❑ 97PacRevR-46
❑ 97PacRevS-46
❑ 97PacSil-111
❑ 97PosPin-24
❑ 97ScoRedW-11
❑ 97ScoRedWPla-11
❑ 97ScoRedWPre-11
❑ 98Pac-190
❑ 98PacIceB-190
❑ 98PacRed-190

**Fetta, Joey**
❑ 98QueRem-7

**Fetterman, Matt**
❑ 95NorIowH-8

**Fewster, Neil**
❑ 917thInnSOHL-208
❑ 93NiaFalT-15
❑ 94GueSto-11

**Fiander, Craig**
❑ 93FreCan-9

**Fiatt, Brian**
❑ 92-TulOil-4

**Ficenek, Jakub**
❑ 95CzeAPSE-129

**Fichaud, Eric**
❑ 94Cla-14
❑ 94ClaCHLAS-C3
❑ 94ClaCHLP-CP2
❑ 94ClaDraGol-14
❑ 94ClaTri-T67
❑ 94Fin-77
❑ 94FinRef-77
❑ 94FinSupTW-77
❑ 94Fla-179
❑ 94Lea-443
❑ 94LeaLim-45
❑ 94LeaPhe-7
❑ 94OPCPre-533
❑ 94OPCPreSE-533
❑ 94ParSE-SE174
❑ 94ParSEG-SE174
❑ 94Pin-493
❑ 94PinArtP-493
❑ 94PinRinC-493
❑ 94Sel-188
❑ 94SelGol-188
❑ 94TopPre-533
❑ 94TopPreSE-533
❑ 94Ult-376
❑ 94UppDec-338
❑ 94UppDecElelce-338
❑ 95Bow-155
❑ 95BowAllFoi-155
❑ 95CanGamNHLP-177
❑ 95ColEdgI-93
❑ 95ColEdgITW-G11
❑ 95DonEliR-6
❑ 95Ima-13
❑ 95ImaGol-13
❑ 95ParInt-537
❑ 95ParIntEl-537
❑ 95SP-90
❑ 96BeAPAut-214
❑ 96BeAPAutSil-214
❑ 96BeAPla-214
❑ 96ColCho-155
❑ 96ColCho-323
❑ 96ColEdgFL-8
❑ 96ColEdgPC-2
❑ 96DonCanI-120
❑ 96DonCanIGPP-120
❑ 96DonCanILG-6
❑ 96DonCanIRPP-120
❑ 96DonEli-132
❑ 96DonEliAsp-14
❑ 96DonEliDCS-132
❑ 96DonRatR-8
❑ 96Fla-115
❑ 96FlaBlul-115
❑ 96Fle-127
❑ 96FleCalCan-4
❑ 96IslPos-4
❑ 96LeaGolR-9
❑ 96LeaLim-69
❑ 96LeaLimG-69
❑ 96LeaPre-119
❑ 96LeaPrePP-119
❑ 96LeaPreSG-53
❑ 96LeaPreSte-53
❑ 96MetUni-179
❑ 96Pin-228
❑ 96PinArtP-228
❑ 96PinFoi-228
❑ 96PinPreS-228
❑ 96PinRinC-228
❑ 96Sco-256
❑ 96ScoArtPro-256
❑ 96ScoDeaCAP-256
❑ 96ScoGolB-256
❑ 96ScoSpeAP-256
❑ 96SelCer-103
❑ 96SelCerAP-103
❑ 96SelCerBlu-103
❑ 96SelCerMB-103
❑ 96SelCerMG-103
❑ 96SelCerMR-103
❑ 96SelCerRed-103
❑ 96SkyImp-150
❑ 96SP-92
❑ 96Sum-178
❑ 96SumArtP-178
❑ 96SumIce-178
❑ 96SumMet-178
❑ 96SumPreS-178
❑ 96TopPicRS-RS15
❑ 96Ult-100
❑ 96UltGolM-101
❑ 96UltRoo-7
❑ 96UppDec-96
❑ 96UppDecBD-105
❑ 96UppDecBDG-105
❑ 96UppDecGN-X27
❑ 96UppDecSS-SS12B
❑ 96Zen-116
❑ 96ZenArtP-116
❑ 97ColCho-153
❑ 97Don-183
❑ 97DonCanILG-8
❑ 97DonCanILGP-8
❑ 97DonEli-87
❑ 97DonEliAsp-87
❑ 97DonEliS-87
❑ 97DonLim-59
❑ 97DonLim-124
❑ 97DonLim-174
❑ 97DonLimExp-59
❑ 97DonLimExp-124
❑ 97DonLimExp-174
❑ 97DonLimFOTG-56
❑ 97DonPre-49
❑ 97DonPreCG-8
❑ 97DonPreCGP-8
❑ 97DonPreCttC-49
❑ 97DonPreProG-183
❑ 97DonPreProS-183
❑ 97DonPri-40
❑ 97DonPriPG-12
❑ 97DonPriPGP-12
❑ 97DonPriSoA-40
❑ 97Kat-86
❑ 97KatGol-86
❑ 97KatSil-86
❑ 97Lea-20
❑ 97LeaFraMat-20
❑ 97LeaFraMDC-20
❑ 97LeaInt-20
❑ 97LeaIntUI-20
❑ 97LeaPipDre-15
❑ 97Pac-274
❑ 97PacCop-274
❑ 97PacEmeGre-274
❑ 97PacIceB-274
❑ 97PacRed-274
❑ 97PacSil-274
❑ 97Pin-66
❑ 97PinArtP-66
❑ 97PinIns-31
❑ 97PinInsCC-31
❑ 97PinInsEC-31
❑ 97PinInsSUG-5A/B
❑ 97PinInsSUG-5C/D
❑ 97PinPrePBB-66
❑ 97PinPrePBC-66
❑ 97PinPrePBM-66
❑ 97PinPrePBY-66
❑ 97PinPrePFC-66
❑ 97PinPrePFM-66
❑ 97PinPrePFY-66
❑ 97PinPrePla-66
❑ 97PinRinC-66
❑ 97Sco-26
❑ 97ScoArtPro-26
❑ 97ScoGolBla-26
❑ 97Stu-91
❑ 97StuPrePG-91
❑ 97StuPrePS-91
❑ 97UppDec-102
❑ 98Be A PPA-227
❑ 98Be A PPAA-227
❑ 98Be A PPAAF-227
❑ 98Be A PPSE-227
❑ 98Be APG-227

**Fichuk, Pete**
❑ 72SweSemWC-131

**Fidler, Mike**
❑ 77OPCNHL-290
❑ 78OPC-84
❑ 78Top-84
❑ 79NorStaPos-4
❑ 79OPC-219
❑ 79PanSti-217
❑ 79Top-219
❑ 81OPC-136

**Fiebelkorn, Jed**
❑ 91MinGolG-7
❑ 92MinGolG-8
❑ 93MinGolG-10
❑ 94MinGolG-12

**Field, Wilfy**
❑ 34BeeGro1P-225
❑ 39OPCV3011-64

**Fielder, Guyle**
❑ 57Top-36

**Fife, Jeff**
❑ 897thInnSOHL-93
❑ 897thInnSOHL-197

**Figliomeni, Mike**
❑ 93MicTecH-6

**Figliuzzi, Stefano**
❑ 93SweSemWCS-227
❑ 94FinnJaaK-302
❑ 95SweGloWC-233
❑ 96GerDELE-120
❑ 96SweSemW-178

**Fihnn, Kjell**
❑ 65SweCorI-48B
❑ 67SweHoc-102
❑ 72SweHocS-265

**Filatov, Anatoli**
❑ 93NiaFalT-22

**Filimonov, Dmitri**
❑ 91StaPicH-19
❑ 91UppDec-3
❑ 91UppDecF-3
❑ 92RusStaRA-6
❑ 93Don-239
❑ 93Lea-400
❑ 93OPCPre-496
❑ 93OPCPreG-496
❑ 93Par-139
❑ 93ParEmel-139
❑ 93Pin-450
❑ 93PinCan-450
❑ 93Pow-398
❑ 93Sco-598
❑ 93ScoCan-598
❑ 93ScoGol-598
❑ 93SenKraS-8
❑ 93StaClu-468
❑ 93StaCluFDI-468
❑ 93StaCluO-468
❑ 93SweSemWCS-132
❑ 93TopPre-496
❑ 93TopPreG-496
❑ 93Ult-381
❑ 93UppDec-405
❑ 93UppDecSP-109
❑ 94Don-97
❑ 94Par-162
❑ 94ParGol-162
❑ 94UppDec-178
❑ 94UppDecElelce-178
❑ 95IndIce-7

**Filion, Maurice**
❑ 72NordPos-7
❑ 73NordTeal-8

**Filip, Jan**
❑ 94CzeAPSE-27

**Filip, Martin**
❑ 96CzeAPSE-111

**Filip, Milan**
❑ 94CzeAPSE-39

**Filipek, Daryl**
❑ 91FerStaB-13

**Filipenko, Mark**
❑ 92BriColJHL-132

**Filipenko, Wayne**
❑ 91AirCanSJHL-A20

**Filipowicz, Jayme**
❑ 94DubFigS-9

**Filippin, J. Christophe**
❑ 94FreNatT-12

**Filippov, Alexander**
❑ 73SweHocS-124
❑ 73SweWorCS-124

**Fillion, Bob**
❑ 44BeeGro2P-238
❑ 45QuaOatP-76A
❑ 45QuaOatP-76B
❑ 45QuaOatP-76C
❑ 45QuaOatP-76D
❑ 48ExhCan-6

**Fillion, Claude**
❑ 95HamRoaA-11

**Fillon, Pierre**
❑ 907thInnSQMJHL-169

**Findlay, Tim**
❑ 94WinSpi-26
❑ 95SigRoo-61
❑ 95SigRooSig-61
❑ 95Sla-429

**Fink, Patrik**
❑ 94CzeAPSE-178
❑ 95CzeAPSE-194
❑ 96CzeAPSE-328

**Finkbeiner, Lloyd**
❑ 51BufBis-7
❑ 51LavDaiQSHL-90

**Finlay, Andy**
❑ 96FifFly-7
❑ 97FifFly-9

**Finley, Brian**
❑ 98BowCHL-21
❑ 98BowCHL-161
❑ 98BowCHLGA-21
❑ 98BowCHLGA-161
❑ 98BowCHLOI-21
❑ 98BowCHLOI-161
❑ 98BowCHLSC-SC17
❑ 98BowChrC-21
❑ 98BowChrC-161
❑ 98BowChrCGA-21
❑ 98BowChrCGA-161
❑ 98BowChrCGAR-21
❑ 98BowChrCGAR-161
❑ 98BowChrCOI-21
❑ 98BowChrCOI-161
❑ 98BowChrCOIR-21
❑ 98BowChrCOIR-161
❑ 98BowChrCR-21
❑ 98BowChrCR-161
❑ 98O-PChr-240
❑ 98O-PChrR-240
❑ 98SP Aut-114
❑ 98SP AutSotTG-BF
❑ 98SPXTopP-61
❑ 98SPXTopPF-61
❑ 98SPXTopPR-61
❑ 98SSASotT-BF
❑ 98Top-240
❑ 98TopO-P-240
❑ 98UppDec-391
❑ 98UppDecBD-96
❑ 98UppDecDD-96
❑ 98UppDecE-391
❑ 98UppDecE1o1-391
❑ 98UppDecGR-391
❑ 98UppDecQD-96
❑ 98UppDecTD-96
❑ 99SP AutPS-114

**Finley, Jeff**
❑ 86PorWinH-5
❑ 88ProAHL-308
❑ 89ProAHL-252
❑ 90ProAHLIHL-503
❑ 91ProAHLCHL-470
❑ 92StaClu-426
❑ 93Pow-405
❑ 96BeAPAut-156
❑ 96BeAPAutSil-156
❑ 96BeAPla-156
❑ 97PacInvNRB-151

**Finn, Ron**
❑ 90ProSet-685

**Finn, Sean**
❑ 89JohChi-35

**Finn, Shannon**
❑ 95PeoRiv-5
❑ 96MilAdmBO-8

**Finn, Steven**
❑ 85NordGenF-7
❑ 85NordPro-8
❑ 86FreExp-6
❑ 86NordMcD-7
❑ 86NordTeal-6
❑ 87NordGenF-9
❑ 88NordGenF-10
❑ 88NordTeal-11
❑ 88PanSti-350
❑ 89Nord-8
❑ 89NordGenF-6
❑ 89NordPol-5
❑ 89OPCSti-191
❑ 90NordPet-5
❑ 90NordTeal-4
❑ 90ProSet-514
❑ 91Bow-140
❑ 91NordPanTS-3
❑ 91NordPet-4
❑ 91OPC-139
❑ 91PanSti-261
❑ 91Pin-138
❑ 91PinFre-138
❑ 91ProSet-204
❑ 91ProSetFre-204
❑ 91ScoAme-278
❑ 91ScoCan-498
❑ 91StaClu-56
❑ 91Top-139
❑ 91UppDec-340
❑ 91UppDecF-340
❑ 92Bow-185
❑ 92DurPan-40
❑ 92NorPet-6
❑ 92OPC-7
❑ 92PanSti-216
❑ 92PanStiFre-216
❑ 92Par-379
❑ 92ParEmel-379
❑ 92Sco-44
❑ 92ScoCan-44
❑ 92StaClu-384
❑ 92Top-449
❑ 92TopGol-449G
❑ 93DurSco-20
❑ 93Lea-422
❑ 93OPCPre-326
❑ 93OPCPreG-326
❑ 93PanSti-75
❑ 93Pin-307
❑ 93PinCan-307
❑ 93Sco-322
❑ 93ScoCan-322
❑ 93StaClu-464
❑ 93StaCluFDI-464
❑ 93StaCluMasP-21
❑ 93StaCluMasPW-21
❑ 93StaCluO-464
❑ 93TopPre-326
❑ 93TopPreG-326
❑ 94NordBurK-5
❑ 94OPCPre-398
❑ 94OPCPreSE-398
❑ 94Pin-312
❑ 94PinArtP-312
❑ 94PinRinC-312
❑ 94StaClu-192
❑ 94StaCluFDI-192
❑ 94StaCluMOMS-192
❑ 94StaCluSTWC-192
❑ 94TopPre-398
❑ 94TopPreSE-398
❑ 96BeAPAut-188
❑ 96BeAPAutSil-188
❑ 96BeAPla-188
❑ 96ColCho-132
❑ 97PacInvNRB-93

**Finney, Mark**
❑ 96GuiFla-9

**Finnie, John**
❑ 907thInnSMC-28

**Finnigan, Frank**
❑ 24C144ChaCig-24
❑ 24V1452-9
❑ 32O'KeeMapL-12
❑ 33OPCV304A-25
❑ 33V129-26
❑ 33V252CanG-23
❑ 34BeeGro1P-316
❑ 35DiaMatTI-22

**Finnstrom, Johan**
❑ 94SweLeaE-202
❑ 94SweLeaENHLD-4
❑ 95SigRoo-6
❑ 95SigRooSig-6
❑ 95SweLeaE-115
❑ 95SweUppDE-173

**Finsted, Morten**
❑ 93SweSemWCS-248
❑ 94FinnJaaK-260
❑ 95FinnSemWC-180

**Fiore, Tony**
❑ 92-TulOil-5

**Fiorentino, Peter**
❑ 87SauSteMG-23
❑ 89ProIHL-46
❑ 90ProAHLIHL-5
❑ 91ProAHLCHL-190
❑ 92BinRan-18
❑ 94BinRan-3
❑ 95LasVegThu-2
❑ 96BinRan-9

**Fioretti, Mark**
❑ 84KelWin-8

**Firsov, Anatoli**
❑ 69SweHocS-3
❑ 69SweWorC-21
❑ 69SweWorC-63
❑ 69SweWorC-68
❑ 69SweWorC-121
❑ 69SweWorC-132
❑ 69SweWorC-139
❑ 70SweHocS-323
❑ 71SweHocS-35
❑ 72SweSemWC-11
❑ 73SweHocS-99
❑ 73SweWorCS-99
❑ 74SweSemHVS-42
❑ 91SweSemWCS-243
❑ 96SweSemWHL-HL5

**Firth, Jason**
❑ 88KitRan-13
❑ 897thInnSOHL-184
❑ 89KitRan-14
❑ 907thInnSMC-33
❑ 907thInnSOHL-232
❑ 90KitRan-12
❑ 917thInnSOHL-59
❑ 94ThuBayS-12
❑ 95ThuBayS-7

**Fischer, Jiri**
❑ 98BowCHLAuB-A19
❑ 98BowCHLAuG-A19
❑ 98BowCHLAuS-A19
❑ 98BowChrC-155
❑ 98BowChrCGA-155
❑ 98BowChrCGAR-155
❑ 98BowChrCOI-155
❑ 98BowChrCOIR-155
❑ 98BowChrCR-155
❑ 98O-PChr-242
❑ 98O-PChrR-242
❑ 98Top-242
❑ 98TopO-P-242

**Fischer, Kai**
❑ 95GerDELE-77
❑ 96GerDELE-271

**Fischer, Lubomir**
❑ 94CzeAPSE-277
❑ 95CzeAPSE-99

**Fischer, Ron**
❑ 89SweSemWCS-112
❑ 94GerDELE-379
❑ 95GerDELE-366

**Fiset, Mike**
❑ 85KinCan-24
❑ 86KinCan-24
❑ 87KinCan-24

**Fiset, Stephane**
❑ 89Nord-9
❑ 89NordGenF-7
❑ 89NordPol-6
❑ 90HalCit-7
❑ 90NordTeal-5
❑ 90OPC-312
❑ 90ProAHLIHL-466
❑ 90Sco-415
❑ 90ScoCan-415
❑ 90ScoYouS-22
❑ 90Top-312
❑ 90TopTif-312
❑ 91NordPet-5
❑ 91PanSti-258
❑ 91Par-363
❑ 91ParFre-363
❑ 91ProAHLCHL-530
❑ 91UppDec-452
❑ 91UppDecF-452
❑ 92Bow-398
❑ 92DurPan-47
❑ 92NorPet-7
❑ 92OPC-75
❑ 92PanSti-207
❑ 92PanStiFre-207
❑ 92Par-378
❑ 92ParEmel-378
❑ 92ProSet-152
❑ 92Sco-354
❑ 92ScoCan-354
❑ 92StaClu-196
❑ 92Top-285
❑ 92TopGol-285G
❑ 93Don-274
❑ 93DurSco-21
❑ 93Kra-52
❑ 93Lea-301
❑ 93OPCPre-165
❑ 93OPCPreG-165
❑ 93Par-164
❑ 93ParEmel-164
❑ 93Pin-115
❑ 93PinCan-115
❑ 93PinMas-6
❑ 93Pow-199
❑ 93Sco-379
❑ 93ScoCan-379
❑ 93StaClu-315
❑ 93StaCluFDI-315
❑ 93StaCluO-315
❑ 93TopPre-165
❑ 93TopPreG-165
❑ 93Ult-55
❑ 93UppDec-203
❑ 94CanGamNHLP-292
❑ 94Don-225
❑ 94Fla-145
❑ 94Fle-175
❑ 94Kra-38
❑ 94Lea-329
❑ 94NordBurK-6
❑ 94OPCPre-333
❑ 94OPCPreSE-333
❑ 94Pin-102
❑ 94PinArtP-102
❑ 94PinRinC-102
❑ 94Sco-126
❑ 94ScoGol-126
❑ 94ScoPla-126
❑ 94ScoPlaTS-126
❑ 94SP-99
❑ 94SPDieCut-99
❑ 94StaClu-246
❑ 94StaCluFDI-246
❑ 94StaCluMOMS-246
❑ 94StaCluSTWC-246
❑ 94TopPre-333
❑ 94TopPreSE-333
❑ 94Ult-173
❑ 94Ult-249
❑ 94UppDec-450
❑ 94UppDecElelce-450
❑ 95BeAPla-121
❑ 95BeAPSig-S121
❑ 95BeAPSigDC-S121
❑ 95CanGamNHLP-82
❑ 95ColCho-150
❑ 95ColChoPC-150
❑ 95ColChoPCP-150
❑ 95Don-390
❑ 95Kra-26
❑ 95Met-31
❑ 95ParInt-317
❑ 95ParIntEl-317
❑ 95ProMag-1
❑ 95Sco-205
❑ 95ScoBlaIce-205
❑ 95ScoBlaIceAP-205
❑ 95SP-34
❑ 95StaClu-53
❑ 95StaCluMOMS-53
❑ 95Sum-160
❑ 95SumArtP-160
❑ 95SumIce-160
❑ 95SumInTheCre-8
❑ 95Top-284
❑ 95TopOPCI-284
❑ 95Ult-131
❑ 95Ult-220
❑ 95Ult-369
❑ 95UltGolM-131
❑ 95UppDec-397
❑ 95UppDecElelce-397
❑ 95UppDecElelceG-397
❑ 95UppDecSpeE-SE23
❑ 95UppDecSpeEdiG-SE23
❑ 95Zen-119
❑ 96ColCho-59
❑ 96Don-186
❑ 96DonCanI-17
❑ 96DonCanIGPP-17
❑ 96DonCanILG-5
❑ 96DonCanIRPP-17
❑ 96DonEli-13
❑ 96DonEliDCS-13
❑ 96DonEliPW-10
❑ 96DonEliPW-P10
❑ 96DonPrePro-186
❑ 96Lea-188
❑ 96LeaLim-72
❑ 96LeaLimG-72
❑ 96LeaPre-57
❑ 96LeaPreP-188
❑ 96LeaPrePP-57
❑ 96LeaPreSG-15
❑ 96LeaPreSte-15
❑ 96MetUni-74
❑ 96NHLProSTA-1
❑ 96PinMas-8
❑ 96PinMasDC-8
❑ 96Sco-17
❑ 96ScoArtPro-17
❑ 96ScoDeaCAP-17
❑ 96ScoGolB-17
❑ 96ScoNetW-10
❑ 96ScoSpeAP-17
❑ 96SelCer-8
❑ 96SelCerAP-8
❑ 96SelCerBlu-8
❑ 96SelCerMB-8
❑ 96SelCerMG-8
❑ 96SelCerMR-8
❑ 96SelCerRed-8
❑ 96SP-77
❑ 96Sum-98
❑ 96SumArtP-98
❑ 96SumIce-98
❑ 96SumMet-98
❑ 96SumPreS-98
❑ 96Ult-78
❑ 96UltGolM-79
❑ 96UppDec-274
❑ 96UppDecBD-85
❑ 96UppDecBDG-85
❑ 96Zen-20
❑ 96ZenArtP-20
❑ 97Don-179
❑ 97DonCanI-30
❑ 97DonCanIDS-30
❑ 97DonCanILG-5
❑ 97DonCanILGP-5
❑ 97DonCanIPS-30
❑ 97DonEli-54
❑ 97DonEliAsp-54
❑ 97DonEliS-54
❑ 97DonLim-150
❑ 97DonLim-180
❑ 97DonLimExp-150
❑ 97DonLimExp-180
❑ 97DonPre-136
❑ 97DonPreCttC-136
❑ 97DonPreProG-179
❑ 97DonPreProS-179
❑ 97DonPri-96
❑ 97DonPriSoA-96
❑ 97Kat-69
❑ 97KatGol-69
❑ 97KatSil-69
❑ 97Lea-93
❑ 97LeaFraMat-93
❑ 97LeaFraMDC-93
❑ 97LeaInt-93
❑ 97LeaIntUI-93
❑ 97Pac-245

□ 97PacCop-245
□ 97PacEmeGre-245
□ 97PacIceB-245
□ 97PacInv-67
□ 97PacInvEG-67
□ 97PacInvIB-67
□ 97PacInvNB-67
□ 97PacInvR-67
□ 97PacInvS-67
□ 97PacOme-107
□ 97PacOmeC-107
□ 97PacOmeDG-107
□ 97PacOmeEG-107
□ 97PacOmeG-107
□ 97PacOmeIB-107
□ 97PacPar-88
□ 97PacParC-88
□ 97PacParEG-88
□ 97PacParH-88
□ 97PacParIB-88
□ 97PacParRed-88
□ 97PacParSil-88
□ 97PacRed-245
□ 97PacSil-245
□ 97Pin-52
□ 97PinArtP-52
□ 97PinCer-14
□ 97PinCerMB-14
□ 97PinCerMG-14
□ 97PinCerMR-14
□ 97PinCerR-14
□ 97PinIns-23
□ 97PinInsCC-23
□ 97PinInsEC-23
□ 97PinPrePBB-52
□ 97PinPrePBC-52
□ 97PinPrePBM-52
□ 97PinPrePBY-52
□ 97PinPrePFC-52
□ 97PinPrePFM-52
□ 97PinPrePFY-52
□ 97PinPrePSa-52
□ 97PinRinC-52
□ 97PinTotCMPG-14
□ 97PinTotCPB-14
□ 97PinTotCPG-14
□ 97PinTotCPR-14
□ 97Sco-35
□ 97ScoArtPro-35
□ 97ScoGolBla-35
□ 97SPAut-76
□ 97Stu-52
□ 97StuPrePG-52
□ 97StuPrePS-52
□ 98Be A PPA-214
□ 98Be A PPAA-214
□ 98Be A PPAAF-214
□ 98Be A PPSE-214
□ 98Be APG-214
□ 98Pac-234
□ 98PacAur-86
□ 98PacDynI-87
□ 98PacDynIIB-87
□ 98PacDynIR-87
□ 98PacIceB-234
□ 98PacOmeH-110
□ 98PacOmeODI-110
□ 98PacOmeR-110
□ 98PacPar-104
□ 98PacParC-104
□ 98PacParEG-104
□ 98PacParH-104
□ 98PacParIB-104
□ 98PacParS-104
□ 98PacRed-234
□ 98PacRev-66
□ 98PacRevIS-66
□ 98PacRevR-66
□ 98UC-97
□ 98UD ChoPCR-97
□ 98UD ChoR-97
□ 98UppDec-288
□ 98UppDecE-288
□ 98UppDecE1o1-288
□ 98UppDecGR-288
□ 99Pac-190
□ 99PacCop-190
□ 99PacGol-190
□ 99PacIceB-190
□ 99PacPreD-190
**Fishback, Bruce**
□ 85MinDul-16
**Fisher, Craig**
□ 90OPC-126
□ 90ProAHLIHL-30
□ 90Sco-412
□ 90ScoCan-412
□ 90Top-126
□ 90TopTif-126
□ 90UppDec-155
□ 90UppDecF-155
□ 91ProAHLCHL-233
□ 94IndIce-7
□ 95ColEdgI-173
□ 95Ima-22
□ 95ImaGol-22
□ 96ColEdgFL-18
**Fisher, Dunc**
□ 44BeeGro2P-310
□ 51Par-24
**Fisher, Jiri**
□ 98BowCHL-155
□ 98BowCHLGA-155
□ 98BowCHLOI-155
**Fisher, Mike**

□ 97SudWolP-10
**Fisher, Shane**
□ 96AlaGolKin-2
**Fitchner, Bob**
□ 76NordMarA-9
□ 76NordPos-13
**Fitzgerald, Brian**
□ 89ProAHL-223
**Fitzgerald, Randy**
□ 96DetWha-8
**Fitzgerald, Rob**
□ 95Sla-48
**Fitzgerald, Rusty**
□ 93MinDul-11
□ 95Lea-316
□ 95Top-209
□ 95TopOPCI-209
□ 95UppDec-142
□ 95UppDecEleIce-142
□ 95UppDecEleIceG-142
□ 96CleLum-9
**Fitzgerald, Tom**
□ 88ProAHL-321
□ 89Isl-6
□ 89ProAHL-239
□ 90Bow-116
□ 90BowTif-116
□ 91OPC-279
□ 91ProSet-431
□ 91ProSetFre-431
□ 91Top-279
□ 91UppDec-389
□ 91UppDecF-389
□ 92Bow-369
□ 92OPC-394
□ 92StaClu-102
□ 92Top-31
□ 92TopGol-31G
□ 92Ult-342
□ 92UppDec-52
□ 93Don-121
□ 93Lea-221
□ 93OPCPre-338
□ 93OPCPreG-338
□ 93PanTeal-2
□ 93Par-348
□ 93ParEmel-348
□ 93Pin-390
□ 93PinCan-390
□ 93Sco-493
□ 93Sco-554
□ 93ScoCan-493
□ 93ScoCan-554
□ 93ScoGol-554
□ 93StaClu-392
□ 93StaCluFDI-392
□ 93StaCluO-392
□ 93TopPre-338
□ 93TopPreG-338
□ 93Ult-324
□ 94Lea-516
□ 94OPCPre-53
□ 94OPCPreSE-53
□ 94ParSE-SE64
□ 94ParSEG-SE64
□ 94Pin-207
□ 94PinArtP-207
□ 94PinRinC-207
□ 94Sco-163
□ 94ScoGol-163
□ 94ScoPla-163
□ 94ScoPlaTS-163
□ 94TopPre-53
□ 94TopPreSE-53
□ 94UppDec-320
□ 94UppDecEleIce-320
□ 95ParInt-352
□ 95ParIntEI-352
□ 95Top-294
□ 95TopOPCI-294
□ 95UppDec-436
□ 95UppDecEleIce-436
□ 95UppDecEleIceG-436
□ 96BeAPAut-4
□ 96BeAPAutSil-4
□ 96BeAPla-4
□ 96Pin-57
□ 96PinArtP-57
□ 96PinFoi-57
□ 96PinPreS-57
□ 96PinRinC-57
□ 96UppDec-69
□ 97Pac-113
□ 97PacCop-113
□ 97PacEmeGre-113
□ 97PacIceB-113
□ 97PacRed-113
□ 97PacSil-113
□ 97UppDec-286
□ 98Be A PPA-73
□ 98Be A PPAA-73
□ 98Be A PPAAF-73
□ 98Be A PPTBASG-73
□ 98Be APG-73
□ 98PacAur-101
□ 98PacCroR-74
□ 98PacCroRLS-74
□ 98PacDynI-102
□ 98PacDynIIB-102
□ 98PacDynIR-102
□ 98PacPar-123
□ 98PacParC-123
□ 98PacParEG-123
□ 98PacParH-123
□ 98PacParIB-123

□ 98PacParS-123
□ 98PacParTCD-14
□ 99Pac-223
□ 99PacCop-223
□ 99PacGol-223
□ 99PacIceB-223
□ 99PacPreD-223
**Fitzpatrick, Blaine**
□ 95SauSteMG-7
□ 95Sla-377
**Fitzpatrick, Mark**
□ 85MedHatT-23
□ 88KinSmo-8
□ 88ProAHL-209
□ 89Isl-7
□ 89PanSti-265
□ 90Bow-119
□ 90BowTif-119
□ 90OPC-395
□ 90PanSti-86
□ 90ProSet-181
□ 90Sco-102A
□ 90Sco-102B
□ 90ScoCan-102A
□ 90ScoCan-102B
□ 90ScoHotRS-50
□ 90ScoYouS-32
□ 90Top-395
□ 90TopTif-395
□ 90UppDec-37
□ 90UppDecF-37
□ 91Bow-213
□ 91OPC-47
□ 91ProAHLCHL-472
□ 91ScoAme-266
□ 91ScoCan-486
□ 91StaClu-345
□ 91Top-47
□ 91UppDec-602
□ 91UppDecF-602
□ 92Bow-394
□ 92Kra-32
□ 92OPC-204
□ 92PanSti-195
□ 92PanStiFre-195
□ 92Par-99
□ 92ParEmel-99
□ 92Pin-24
□ 92PinFre-24
□ 92ProSet-107
□ 92Sco-210
□ 92Sco-526
□ 92ScoCan-210
□ 92ScoCan-526
□ 92StaClu-12
□ 92Top-216
□ 92TopGol-216G
□ 92Ult-124
□ 92UltAwaW-7
□ 92UppDec-332
□ 93Don-133
□ 93Lea-335
□ 93PanSti-66
□ 93Par-344
□ 93ParEmel-344
□ 93Pin-369
□ 93PinCan-369
□ 93Pow-92
□ 93Sco-171
□ 93Sco-537
□ 93ScoCan-171
□ 93ScoCan-537
□ 93ScoGol-537
□ 93StaClu-307
□ 93StaCluFDI-307
□ 93StaCluO-307
□ 94Don-235
□ 94EASpo-202
□ 94Lea-308
□ 94OPCPre-82
□ 94Par-87
□ 94ParGol-87
□ 94Pin-236
□ 94PinArtP-236
□ 94PinRinC-236
□ 94Ult-296
□ 94UppDec-457
□ 94UppDecEleIce-457
□ 94UppDecSPI-SP120
□ 94UppDecSPIDC-SP120
□ 95Don-301
□ 95Lea-120
□ 95ParInt-88
□ 95ParIntEI-88
□ 95Pin-175
□ 95PinArtP-175
□ 95PinMas-7
□ 95PinRinC-175
□ 95Sco-173
□ 95ScoBlaIce-173
□ 95ScoBlaIceAP-173
□ 95Top-183
□ 95TopOPCI-183
□ 95UppDec-423
□ 95UppDecEleIce-423
□ 95UppDecEleIceG-423
□ 96BeAPAut-10
□ 96BeAPAutSil-10
□ 96BeAPla-10
□ 97Sco-234
□ 98Be A PPA-182
□ 98Be A PPAA-182
□ 98Be A PPAAF-182
□ 98Be A PPSE-182
□ 98Be APG-182

□ 98O-PChr-194
□ 98O-PChrR-194
□ 98Top-194
□ 98TopO-P-194
□ 99Pac-88
□ 99PacCop-88
□ 99PacGol-88
□ 99PacIceB-88
□ 99PacPreD-88
**Fitzpatrick, Rory**
□ 92SudWol-5
□ 93SudWol-5
□ 93SudWolP-5
□ 94Fin-115
□ 94FinRef-115
□ 94FinSupTW-115
□ 94LeaLimWJUSA-5
□ 94SlaPro-7
□ 94SP-192
□ 94SPDieCut-192
□ 94SudWol-3
□ 94SudWolP-18
□ 95FreCan-10
□ 95ParInt-535
□ 95ParIntEI-535
□ 96CanaShe-8
**Fitzpatrick, Ross**
□ 83SprInd-15
□ 89ProAHL-340
□ 90ProAHLIHL-23
□ 91ProAHLCHL-207
**Fitzsimmons, Jason**
□ 90thInnSWHL-162
□ 91thInnSWHL-280
□ 90SouCarS-31
**Fizzell, Bert**
□ 67ColChe-6
□ 69ColChe-5
**Fizzell, Kris**
□ 94PriAlbR-4
□ 95PriAlbR-4
**Fjallby, Claes-Ove**
□ 71SweHocS-352
**Flaherty, Joe**
□ 88ProAHL-169
**Flaherty, Ray**
□ 80OshGen-2
**Flaherty, Wade**
□ 90KanCitBla-3
□ 90ProAHLIHL-601
□ 91ProAHLCHL-517
□ 95ColCho-97
□ 95ColChoPC-97
□ 95Don-280
□ 95ParInt-189
□ 95ParIntEI-189
□ 95Pin-173
□ 95PinArtP-173
□ 95PinRinC-173
□ 95Top-249
□ 95TopOPCI-249
□ 95UppDec-57
□ 95UppDecEleIce-57
□ 97PacInvNRB-179
□ 98Pac-281
□ 98PacIceB-281
□ 98PacRed-281
□ 99Pac-254
□ 99PacCop-254
□ 99PacGol-254
□ 99PacIceB-254
□ 99PacPreD-254
**Flaman, Dallas**
□ 95PriAlbR-5
□ 96PriAlbR-4
□ 96PriAlbROC-5
**Flaman, Fernie (Fern)**
□ 44BeeGro2P-20
□ 44BeeGro2P-401
□ 45QuaOatP-17
□ 51Par-80
□ 52Par-47
□ 53Par-14
□ 54Par-20
□ 54Top-25
□ 55BruPho-5
□ 57Par-4
□ 58Top-56
□ 59Top-29
□ 60ShiCoi-102
□ 60Top-57
□ 61Top-21
□ 90Sco-357
□ 90ScoCan-357
□ 91BruSpoAL-11
□ 91BruSpoAL-35
□ 91UltOriS-48
□ 91UltOriS-76
□ 91UltOriSF-48
□ 91UltOriSF-76
□ 93ParParR-PR45
□ 94ParMisL-2
**Flanagan, Dave**
□ 91ProAHLCHL-128
**Flanagan, Joe**
□ 92BirBul-4
□ 93BirBul-4
**Flanagan, Mike**
□ 89HamRoaA-5
**Flasar, Ales**
□ 94CzeAPSE-3
**Flatley, Patrick (Pat)**

□ 83CanNatJ-6
□ 84OPC-124
□ 85IsIIsIN-4
□ 85OPC-83
□ 85OPCSti-73
□ 85Top-83
□ 86OPC-162
□ 86OPCSti-207
□ 86Top-162
□ 87OPC-136
□ 87OPCSti-245
□ 87PanSti-101
□ 87Top-136
□ 88OPC-191
□ 88PanSti-286
□ 88Top-191
□ 89Isl-8
□ 89OPC-250
□ 89PanSti-272
□ 90Bow-124
□ 90BowTif-124
□ 90OPC-350
□ 90PanSti-82
□ 90ProSet-182
□ 90Sco-174
□ 90ScoCan-174
□ 90Top-350
□ 90TopTif-350
□ 90UppDec-118
□ 90UppDecF-118
□ 91Bow-218
□ 91PanSti-245
□ 91Par-111
□ 91ParFre-111
□ 91Pin-67
□ 91Pin-405
□ 91PinFre-67
□ 91PinFre-405
□ 91ProSet-152
□ 91ProSet-578
□ 91ProSetFre-152
□ 91ProSetFre-578
□ 91ProSetPla-77
□ 91ScoAme-29
□ 91ScoCan-29
□ 91StaClu-20
□ 91Top-343
□ 91UppDec-226
□ 91UppDecF-226
□ 92Bow-134
□ 92PanSti-201
□ 92PanStiFre-201
□ 92Par-342
□ 92ParEmel-342
□ 92Pin-44
□ 92PinFre-44
□ 92ProSet-102
□ 92Sco-99
□ 92ScoCan-99
□ 92StaClu-477
□ 92Top-135
□ 92TopGol-135G
□ 92Ult-125
□ 93Don-199
□ 93Kra-29
□ 93Lea-43
□ 93OPCPre-28
□ 93OPCPreG-28
□ 93PanSti-60
□ 93Par-391
□ 93ParEmel-391
□ 93Pin-203
□ 93PinCan-203
□ 93PinCap-14
□ 93PinCapC-14
□ 93Pow-146
□ 93Sco-220
□ 93ScoCan-220
□ 93StaClu-24
□ 93StaCluFDI-24
□ 93StaCluFDIO-24
□ 93StaCluO-24
□ 93TopPre-28
□ 93TopPreG-28
□ 93Ult-34
□ 93UppDec-210
□ 94CanGamNHLP-155
□ 94Fla-102
□ 94Fle-121
□ 94Lea-381
□ 94OPCPre-178
□ 94OPCPreSE-178
□ 94ParSE-SE103
□ 94ParSEG-SE103
□ 94Pin-176
□ 94PinArtP-176
□ 94PinRinC-176
□ 94Sco-116
□ 94ScoGol-116
□ 94ScoPla-116
□ 94ScoPlaTS-116
□ 94TopPre-178
□ 94TopPreSE-178
□ 94Ult-125
□ 94UppDec-371
□ 94UppDecEleIce-371
□ 95BeAPla-13
□ 95BeAPSig-S13
□ 95BeAPSigDC-S13
□ 95CanGamNHLP-173
□ 95ColCho-202
□ 95ColChoPC-202
□ 95ColChoPCP-202
□ 95Don-227

□ 95Emo-104
□ 95Lea-151
□ 95ParInt-403
□ 95ParIntEI-403
□ 95Pin-30
□ 95PinArtP-30
□ 95PinRinC-30
□ 95PlaOneoOne-62
□ 95ProMag-58
□ 95Sco-196
□ 95ScoBlaIce-196
□ 95ScoBlaIceAP-196
□ 95SkyImp-100
□ 95Top-139
□ 95TopOPCI-139
□ 95UppDec-106
□ 95UppDecEleIce-106
□ 95UppDecEleIceG-106
□ 96NHLProSTA-58
□ 97PacInvNRB-126
□ 97ScoRan-12
□ 97ScoRanPla-12
□ 97ScoRanPre-12
**Fleetwood, Brent**
□ 87PorWinH-8
□ 88PorWinH-8
□ 89PorWinH-7
□ 94CenHocL-43
**Fleming, Adam**
□ 95Sla-128
**Fleming, Bob**
□ 87FliSpi-3
**Fleming, Gavin**
□ 96FitFly-1
**Fleming, Gerry**
□ 92FreCan-10
□ 93ClaPro-37
□ 93FreCan-10
□ 94CanaPos-11
**Fleming, Reg**
□ 44BeeGro2P-94
□ 60ShiCoi-78
□ 61ShiCoi-24
□ 61Top-26
□ 62Top-42
□ 62TopHocBuc-5
□ 63Top-31
□ 64BeeGro3P-7
□ 64BeeGro3P-124
□ 64CocCap-14
□ 64Top-35
□ 65Coc-12
□ 65Top-104
□ 66Top-93
□ 66TopUSAT-54
□ 67Top-30
□ 68OPC-167
□ 68ShiCoi-96
□ 69OPC-95
□ 69OPCFou-2
□ 69Top-95
□ 70DadCoo-35
□ 70EssPowPla-79
□ 70OPC-128
□ 70OPCDec-12
□ 70Top-128
□ 72OPC-316
□ 73QuaOatWHA-45
□ 94ParTalB-8
□ 95Par66-83
□ 95Par66Coi-83
**Fleming, Ryan**
□ 93MicSta-8
**Fleming, Wayne**
□ 90AlbIntTC-22
□ 91AlbIntTC-7
□ 92SweSemE-329
□ 93SweSemE-294
□ 94SweLeaE-300
**Flemming, Markus**
□ 94GerDELE-288
□ 94GerDELE-265
**Flemming, Michael**
□ 94GerDELE-412
**Flesch, John**
□ 74NHLActStaU-18
□ 75OPCNHL-353
□ 81MilAdm-5
**Fletcher, Cliff**
□ 91MapLeaP-11
**Fletcher, Craig**
□ 917thInnSWHL-57
□ 92BriColJHL-125
**Fletcher, John**
□ 90CinCyc-37
□ 91JohChi-3
**Fletcher, Scott**
□ 95SpoChi-2
**Fletcher, Steven**
□ 86SheCan-14
□ 88ProAHL-171
□ 89ProAHL-347
□ 90ProAHLIHL-457
□ 91ProAHLCHL-256
**Flett, Bill**
□ 68OPC-159
□ 68ShiCoi-57
□ 69OPC-102
□ 69Top-102
□ 70DadCoo-36
□ 70EssPowPla-157
□ 70OPC-161
□ 70SarProSta-75
□ 70TopStiS-8

□ 71OPC-47
□ 71SarProSta-67
□ 71Top-47
□ 71TorSun-112
□ 72OPC-187
□ 72SarProSta-164
□ 72SweSemWC-226
□ 72Top-139
□ 73FlyLin-7
□ 73OPC-20
□ 73Top-20
□ 74MapLeaP-6
□ 74MapLeaP-7
□ 74NHLActSta-268
□ 74OPCNHL-64
□ 74Top-64
□ 75OPCNHL-349
□ 76OPCNHL-332
□ 79OilPos-7
□ 79OPC-266
□ 88OilTenAnn-71
**Flett, Josh**
□ 92BriColJHL-6
**Flett, Will**
□ 66TulOil-4
**Fleury, Carl**
□ 917thInnSQMJHL-104
□ 94RoaExp-7
**Fleury, Chris**
□ 95UppDec-518
□ 95UppDecEleIce-518
□ 95UppDecEleIceG-518
**Fleury, Sylvain**
□ 92OklCitB-4
□ 98UppDecWFP-WF19
**Fleury, Theo (Theoren)**
□ 88SalLakCGE-8
□ 89Kra-2
□ 89OPC-232
□ 90Bow-102
□ 90BowTif-102
□ 90FlamIGA-3
□ 90OPC-386
□ 90PanSti-176
□ 90ProSet-33
□ 90Sco-226
□ 90ScoCan-226
□ 90ScoYouS-6
□ 90Top-386
□ 90TopTif-386
□ 90UppDec-47
□ 90UppDec-478
□ 90UppDecF-47
□ 90UppDecF-478
□ 91Bow-249
□ 91Bow-270
□ 91FlamIGA-19
□ 91FlamPanTS-1
□ 91Gil-4
□ 91Kra-13
□ 91McDUppD-18
□ 91OPC-282
□ 91OPC-322
□ 91OPCPre-92
□ 91PanSti-51
□ 91Par-22
□ 91ParFre-22
□ 91Pin-190
□ 91Pin-358
□ 91PinFre-190
□ 91PinFre-358
□ 91ProSet-28
□ 91ProSet-274
□ 91ProSetFre-28
□ 91ProSetFre-274
□ 91ProSetNHLSA-AC20
□ 91ProSetPC-4
□ 91ProSetPla-16
□ 91ScoAme-226
□ 91ScoAme-407
□ 91ScoCan-297
□ 91ScoHotC-7
□ 91ScoYouS-4
□ 91StaClu-355
□ 91Top-282
□ 91Top-322
□ 91TopTeaSL-14
□ 91UppDec-80
□ 91UppDec-245
□ 91UppDec-506
□ 91UppDec-630
□ 91UppDecF-245
□ 91UppDecF-506
□ 91UppDecF-630
□ 92Bow-206
□ 92Bow-355
□ 92FlamIGA-20
□ 92HumDum1-8
□ 92JofKoh-1
□ 92McDUppD-7
□ 92OPC-99
□ 92PanSti-46
□ 92PanStiFre-46
□ 92Par-19
□ 92ParEmel-19
□ 92Pin-125
□ 92ProSet-23
□ 92Sco-280
□ 92ScoCan-280
□ 92StaClu-2
□ 92TopGol-220G

❑ 92Ult-21
❑ 92UppDec-285
❑ 93AmeLicSPC-1
❑ 93Don-46
❑ 93DonSpeP-D
❑ 93Kra-8
❑ 93Lea-154
❑ 93OPCPre-100
❑ 93OPCPreBG-13
❑ 93OPCPreG-100
❑ 93PanSti-179
❑ 93Par-28
❑ 93ParEmeI-28
❑ 93Pin-79
❑ 93PinCan-79
❑ 93Pow-36
❑ 93Sco-191
❑ 93Sco-441
❑ 93ScoCan-191
❑ 93ScoCan-441
❑ 93StaClu-390
❑ 93StaCluFDI-390
❑ 93StaCluMasP-17
❑ 93StaCluMasPW-17
❑ 93StaCluO-390
❑ 93TopPre-100
❑ 93TopPreG-100
❑ 93TopPrePS-100
❑ 93Ult-41
❑ 93UppDec-3
❑ 93UppDec-229
❑ 93UppDec-288
❑ 93UppDecGGO-GG7
❑ 93UppDecNR-28
❑ 93UppDecSP-21
❑ 94BeAPla-R23
❑ 94BeAPSig-123
❑ 94CanGamNHLP-54
❑ 94Don-99
❑ 94EASpo-23
❑ 94Fin-28
❑ 94FinBowB-B4
❑ 94FinBowB-X21
❑ 94FinBowBR-B4
❑ 94FinBowBR-X21
❑ 94FinnJaaK-96
❑ 94FinnJaaK-357
❑ 94FinRef-28
❑ 94FinSupTW-28
❑ 94Fla-24
❑ 94Fle-29
❑ 94FleHocT-1
❑ 94FleHocT-2
❑ 94FleHocT-3
❑ 94FleHocT-4
❑ 94FleHocT-5
❑ 94FleHocT-6
❑ 94FleHocT-7
❑ 94FleHocT-8
❑ 94FleHocT-9
❑ 94FleHocT-10
❑ 94FleHocT-11
❑ 94FleHocT-12
❑ 94FleHocT-13
❑ 94FleHocT-14
❑ 94HocWit-94
❑ 94Kra-4
❑ 94Lea-55
❑ 94LeaLim-99
❑ 94OPCPre-295
❑ 94OPCPreSE-295
❑ 94ParSE-SE28
❑ 94ParSEG-SE28
❑ 94ParVin-V20
❑ 94Pin-38
❑ 94PinArtP-38
❑ 94PinNorLig-NL15
❑ 94PinRinC-38
❑ 94PosCerBB-11
❑ 94Sco-69
❑ 94ScoChelt-CI15
❑ 94ScoFra-TF4
❑ 94ScoGol-69
❑ 94ScoPla-69
❑ 94ScoPlaTS-69
❑ 94Sel-109
❑ 94SelGol-109
❑ 94SP-17
❑ 94SPDieCut-17
❑ 94StaClu-25
❑ 94StaCluFDI-25
❑ 94StaCluMOMS-25
❑ 94StaCluST-4
❑ 94StaCluSTWC-25
❑ 94TopFinI-19
❑ 94TopPre-295
❑ 94TopPreGTG-7
❑ 94TopPreSE-295
❑ 94Ult-29
❑ 94UppDec-315
❑ 94UppDec-566
❑ 94UppDecEleIce-315
❑ 94UppDecEleIce-566
❑ 94UppDecNBAP-21
❑ 94UppDecPR-R41
❑ 94UppDecPR-R58
❑ 94UppDecPRE-R41
❑ 94UppDecPRE-R58
❑ 94UppDecPreRG-R41
❑ 94UppDecPreRG-R58
❑ 94UppDecSPI-SP11
❑ 94UppDecSPIDC-SP11
❑ 95Bow-52
❑ 95BowAllFoi-52
❑ 95CanGamNHLP-17
❑ 95ColCho-201
❑ 95ColCho-384
❑ 95ColChoCTG-C11
❑ 95ColChoCTG-C11B
❑ 95ColChoCTG-C11C
❑ 95ColChoCTGGB-C11
❑ 95ColChoCTGGR-C11
❑ 95ColChoCTGSB-C11
❑ 95ColChoCTGSR-C11
❑ 95ColChoPC-201
❑ 95ColChoPC-384
❑ 95ColChoPCP-201
❑ 95ColChoPCP-384
❑ 95ColEdgILL-L9
❑ 95Don-289
❑ 95DonEli-106
❑ 95DonEliDCS-106
❑ 95DonEliDCU-106
❑ 95DonMar-6
❑ 95DonProPoi-12
❑ 95Emo-21
❑ 95EmoXci-1
❑ 95Fin-30
❑ 95Fin-181
❑ 95FinnSemWC-96
❑ 95FinnSISL-81
❑ 95FinnSISLSS-9
❑ 95FinRef-30
❑ 95FinRef-181
❑ 95FleMetPP-3
❑ 95ImpSti-15
❑ 95KenStaLA-7
❑ 95KenStaLC-5
❑ 95Kra-49
❑ 95Kra-58
❑ 95Lea-115
❑ 95LeaFirOIce-5
❑ 95LeaGolS-5
❑ 95LeaLim-6
❑ 95Met-18
❑ 95MetHM-3
❑ 95MetIW-3
❑ 95NHLAcePC-13S
❑ 95NoFeaAdCa-2
❑ 95ParInt-29
❑ 95ParIntEl-29
❑ 95Pin-6
❑ 95PinArtP-6
❑ 95PinFan-9
❑ 95PinFirS-15
❑ 95PinRinC-6
❑ 95PlaOneoOne-16
❑ 95ProMag-46
❑ 95Sco-121
❑ 95ScoBlaIce-121
❑ 95ScoBlaIceAP-121
❑ 95ScoGolBla-13
❑ 95ScoLam-13
❑ 95SelCer-5
❑ 95SelCerDS-13
❑ 95SelCerDSG-13
❑ 95SelCerMG-5
❑ 95SkyImp-21
❑ 95SkyImpIQ-13
❑ 95SkyImpPP-1
❑ 95SP-16
❑ 95SPStaEto-E6
❑ 95SPStaEtoG-E6
❑ 95StaClu-165
❑ 95StaCluEN-EN5
❑ 95StaCluMO-33
❑ 95StaCluMOMS-165
❑ 95StaCluMPT-2
❑ 95Sum-8
❑ 95SumArtP-8
❑ 95SumIce-8
❑ 95SweGloWC-83
❑ 95Top-25
❑ 95Top-382
❑ 95TopCanG-6CG
❑ 95TopHidGem-1HG
❑ 95TopHomGC-HGC5
❑ 95TopMarMPB-382
❑ 95TopOPCI-25
❑ 95TopOPCI-382
❑ 95TopSupSki-35
❑ 95TopSupSkiPla-35
❑ 95Ult-24
❑ 95Ult-382
❑ 95UltCreCra-3
❑ 95UltGolM-24
❑ 95UltRedLS-2
❑ 95UltRedLSGM-2
❑ 95UppDec-179
❑ 95UppDec-235
❑ 95UppDecAGPRW-13
❑ 95UppDecEleIce-179
❑ 95UppDecEleIce-235
❑ 95UppDecEleIceG-179
❑ 95UppDecEleIceG-235
❑ 95UppDecFreFra-F12
❑ 95UppDecFreFraJ-F12
❑ 95UppDecNHLAS-AS11
❑ 95UppDecPRE-R8
❑ 95UppDecPreR-R8
❑ 95UppDecSpeE-SE101
❑ 95UppDecSpeEdiG-SE101
❑ 95Zen-11
❑ 96BeAPAut-159
❑ 96BeAPAutSil-159
❑ 96BeAPBisITB-4
❑ 96BeAPla-159
❑ 96ColCho-35
❑ 96ColCho-300
❑ 96ColCho-312
❑ 96ColChoBlo-35
❑ 96ColChoBloBi-2
❑ 96ColChoMVP-UD11
❑ 96ColChoMVPG-UD11
❑ 96ColChoSti-S20
❑ 96Don-159
❑ 96DonCanI-78
❑ 96DonCanIGPP-78
❑ 96DonCanIOC-5
❑ 96DonCanIRPP-78
❑ 96DonEli-54
❑ 96DonEliDCS-54
❑ 96DonHitLis-20
❑ 96DonPrePro-159
❑ 96Fla-11
❑ 96FlaBluI-11
❑ 96Fle-12
❑ 96FleArtRos-3
❑ 96FlePic-24
❑ 96FlePicF5-11
❑ 96FlePicJE-2
❑ 96HocGreC-7
❑ 96HocGreCG-7
❑ 96KraUppD-8
❑ 96KraUppD-36
❑ 96KraUppD-65
❑ 96Lea-61
❑ 96LeaLim-67
❑ 96LeaLimG-67
❑ 96LeaPre-67
❑ 96LeaPreP-61
❑ 96LeaPrePP-67
❑ 96LeaPreSG-47
❑ 96LeaPreSte-47
❑ 96MetUni-18
❑ 96NHLACEPC-13
❑ 96NHLProSTA-46
❑ 96Pin-6
❑ 96PinArtP-6
❑ 96PinFoi-6
❑ 96PinMcD-15
❑ 96PinPreS-6
❑ 96PinRinC-6
❑ 96PosUppD-6
❑ 96Sco-12
❑ 96ScoArtPro-12
❑ 96ScoChelt-13
❑ 96ScoDeaCAP-12
❑ 96ScoGolB-12
❑ 96ScoSpeAP-12
❑ 96SelCer-75
❑ 96SelCerAP-75
❑ 96SelCerBlu-75
❑ 96SelCerMB-75
❑ 96SelCerMG-75
❑ 96SelCerMR-75
❑ 96SelCerRed-75
❑ 96SkyImp-13
❑ 96SP-20
❑ 96SPCleWin-CW14
❑ 96SPGamFil-GF15
❑ 96SPx-5
❑ 96SPxGol-5
❑ 96StaCluMO-7
❑ 96Sum-91
❑ 96SumArtP-91
❑ 96SumIce-91
❑ 96SumMet-91
❑ 96SumPreS-91
❑ 96SweSemW-87
❑ 96TeaOut-4
❑ 96TopPicTS-TS14
❑ 96Ult-21
❑ 96UltGolM-21
❑ 96UppDec-22
❑ 96UppDec-208
❑ 96UppDecBD-70
❑ 96UppDecBDG-70
❑ 96UppDecGJ-GJ12
❑ 96UppDecGN-X30
❑ 96UppDecIce-9
❑ 96UppDecIcePar-9
❑ 96UppDecLSH-LS9
❑ 96UppDecLSHF-LS9
❑ 96UppDecLSHS-LS9
❑ 96UppDecPP-P14
❑ 96UppDecSS-SS4A
❑ 96Zen-55
❑ 96ZenArtP-55
❑ 96ZenAss-11
❑ 97ColCho-40
❑ 97ColChoCTG-C14A
❑ 97ColChoCTG-C14B
❑ 97ColChoCTG-C14C
❑ 97ColChoCTGE-CR14
❑ 97ColChoSta-SQ64
❑ 97ColChoWD-W11
❑ 97Don-160
❑ 97DonCanI-23
❑ 97DonCanIDS-23
❑ 97DonCanINP-19
❑ 97DonCanIPS-23
❑ 97DonEli-74
❑ 97DonEliAsp-74
❑ 97DonEliS-74
❑ 97DonLim-24
❑ 97DonLim-157
❑ 97DonLim-177
❑ 97DonLimExp-24
❑ 97DonLimExp-157
❑ 97DonLimExp-177
❑ 97DonPre-138
❑ 97DonPreCttC-138
❑ 97DonPreProG-160
❑ 97DonPreProS-160
❑ 97DonPri-141
❑ 97DonPriSoA-141
❑ 97EssOlyHH-12
❑ 97EssOlyHHF-12
❑ 97Kat-20
❑ 97KatGol-20
❑ 97KatSil-20
❑ 97Lea-136
❑ 97LeaFraMat-136
❑ 97LeaFraMDC-136
❑ 97LeaInt-136
❑ 97LeaIntUI-136
❑ 97McD-2
❑ 97McDGamFil-9
❑ 97Pac-45
❑ 97PacCop-45
❑ 97PacCroR-18
❑ 97PacCroREG-18
❑ 97PacCroRIB-18
❑ 97PacCroRS-18
❑ 97PacDyn-15
❑ 97PacDyn-137
❑ 97PacDynC-15
❑ 97PacDynC-137
❑ 97PacDynDD-4A
❑ 97PacDynDG-15
❑ 97PacDynDG-137
❑ 97PacDynEG-15
❑ 97PacDynEG-137
❑ 97PacDynIB-15
❑ 97PacDynIB-137
❑ 97PacDynR-15
❑ 97PacDynR-137
❑ 97PacDynSil-15
❑ 97PacDynSil-137
❑ 97PacDynTan-23
❑ 97PacDynTan-35
❑ 97PacEmeGre-45
❑ 97PacIceB-45
❑ 97PacInv-16
❑ 97PacInvC-16
❑ 97PacInvEG-16
❑ 97PacInvIB-16
❑ 97PacInvR-16
❑ 97PacInvS-16
❑ 97PacOme-29
❑ 97PacOmeC-29
❑ 97PacOmeDG-29
❑ 97PacOmeEG-29
❑ 97PacOmeG-29
❑ 97PacOmeIB-29
❑ 97PacOmeSLC-3
❑ 97PacOmeTL-3
❑ 97PacPar-28
❑ 97PacParC-28
❑ 97PacParDG-28
❑ 97PacParEG-28
❑ 97PacParIB-28
❑ 97PacParRed-28
❑ 97PacParSil-28
❑ 97PacRed-45
❑ 97PacRev-17
❑ 97PacRev1AGD-4
❑ 97PacRevC-17
❑ 97PacRevE-17
❑ 97PacRevIB-17
❑ 97PacRevR-17
❑ 97PacRevS-17
❑ 97PacRevTCL-4
❑ 97PacSil-45
❑ 97Pin-103
❑ 97PinBee-18
❑ 97PinBeeGP-18
❑ 97PinCer-42
❑ 97PinCerMB-42
❑ 97PinCerMG-42
❑ 97PinCerMR-42
❑ 97PinCerR-42
❑ 97PinIns-40
❑ 97PinInsCC-40
❑ 97PinInsEC-40
❑ 97PinPrePBB-103
❑ 97PinPrePBC-103
❑ 97PinPrePBM-103
❑ 97PinPrePBY-103
❑ 97PinPrePFC-103
❑ 97PinPrePFM-103
❑ 97PinPrePFY-103
❑ 97PinPrePla-103
❑ 97PinTotCMPG-42
❑ 97PinTotCPB-42
❑ 97PinTotCPG-42
❑ 97PinTotCPR-42
❑ 97Sco-97
❑ 97ScoArtPro-97
❑ 97ScoGolBla-97
❑ 97SP AutI-I20
❑ 97SPAut-18
❑ 97SPAutID-I20
❑ 97SPAutIE-I20
❑ 97SPx-6
❑ 97SPxBro-6
❑ 97SPxDim-SPX14
❑ 97SPxGol-6
❑ 97SPxGraF-6
❑ 97SPxSil-6
❑ 97SPxSte-6
❑ 97Stu-81
❑ 97StuPrePG-81
❑ 97StuPrePS-81
❑ 97UppDec-232
❑ 97UppDecBD-143
❑ 97UppDecBDDD-143
❑ 97UppDecBDQD-143
❑ 97UppDecBDTD-143
❑ 97UppDecDV-9
❑ 97UppDecDVSM-9
❑ 97UppDecGDM-232
❑ 97UppDecIce-64
❑ 97UppDecIceP-64
❑ 97UppDecIPS-64
❑ 97Zen-12
❑ 97Zen5x7-46
❑ 97ZenGolImp-46
❑ 97ZenSilImp-46
❑ 97ZenZGol-12
❑ 97ZenZSil-12
❑ 98Be A PPA-168
❑ 98Be A PPAA-168
❑ 98Be A PPAAF-168
❑ 98Be A PPSE-168
❑ 98Be APG-168
❑ 98BowBes-31
❑ 98BowBesAR-31
❑ 98BowBesR-31
❑ 98Fin-2
❑ 98FinNo P-2
❑ 98FinNo PR-2
❑ 98FinRef-2
❑ 98JelSpo-2
❑ 98McD-2
❑ 98O-PChr-27
❑ 98O-PChrR-27
❑ 98Pac-117
❑ 98PacAur-24
❑ 98PacAurCF-8
❑ 98PacAurCFC-8
❑ 98PacAurCFIB-8
❑ 98PacAurCFR-8
❑ 98PacAurCFS-8
❑ 98PacCroR-18
❑ 98PacCroRLS-18
❑ 98PacCroRPotG-4
❑ 98PacDynI-25
❑ 98PacDynIIB-25
❑ 98PacDynIR-25
❑ 98PacDynITC-4
❑ 98PacGolCD-6
❑ 98PacIceB-117
❑ 98PacOmeH-31
❑ 98PacOmeO-5
❑ 98PacOmeODI-31
❑ 98PacOmeR-31
❑ 98PacPar-27
❑ 98PacParC-27
❑ 98PacParEG-27
❑ 98PacParH-27
❑ 98PacParIB-27
❑ 98PacParS-27
❑ 98PacParTCD-4
❑ 98PacRed-117
❑ 98PacRev-18
❑ 98PacRevADC-6
❑ 98PacRevCTL-3
❑ 98PacRevIS-18
❑ 98PacRevR-18
❑ 98PacRevS-6
❑ 98PacTeaC-4
❑ 98RevThrPA-2
❑ 98RevThrPA-2
❑ 98SP Aut-12
❑ 98SPxFin-12
❑ 98SPxFin-107
❑ 98SPxFin-167
❑ 98SPxFinR-12
❑ 98SPxFinR-107
❑ 98SPxFinR-167
❑ 98SPxFinS-12
❑ 98SPxFinS-107
❑ 98SPxFinS-167
❑ 98SPXTopP-7
❑ 98SPXTopPF-7
❑ 98SPXTopPHH-H6
❑ 98SPXTopPLI-L11
❑ 98SPXTopPPS-PS19
❑ 98SPXTopPR-7
❑ 98Top-27
❑ 98TopBlaLGR'-GR7
❑ 98TopGolLC1-8
❑ 98TopGolLC1B-8
❑ 98TopGolLC1BOoO-8
❑ 98TopGolLC1OoO-8
❑ 98TopGolLC1R-8
❑ 98TopGolLC1ROoO-8
❑ 98TopGolLC2-8
❑ 98TopGolLC2B-8
❑ 98TopGolLC2BOoO-8
❑ 98TopGolLC2OoO-8
❑ 98TopGolLC2R-8
❑ 98TopGolLC2ROoO-8
❑ 98TopGolLC3-8
❑ 98TopGolLC3B-8
❑ 98TopGolLC3BOoO-8
❑ 98TopGolLC3OoO-8
❑ 98TopGolLC3R-8
❑ 98TopGolLC3ROoO-8
❑ 98TopGolLGR'-GR7
❑ 98TopGolLGR'BOoO-GR7
❑ 98TopGolLGR'OoO-GR7
❑ 98TopGolLGR'ROoO-GR7
❑ 98TopO-P-27
❑ 98TopRedLGR'-GR7
❑ 98UC-34
❑ 98UCMBH-BH25
❑ 98UCSB-SQ13
❑ 98UCSG-SQ13
❑ 98UCSG-SQ13
❑ 98UCSR-SQ13
❑ 98UD ChoPCR-34
❑ 98UD ChoR-34
❑ 98UD3-40
❑ 98UD3-100
❑ 98UD3-160
❑ 98UD3DieC-40
❑ 98UD3DieC-100
❑ 98UD3DieC-160
❑ 98UppDec-232
❑ 98UppDecBD-13
❑ 98UppDecDD-13
❑ 98UppDecE-232
❑ 98UppDecE1o1-232
❑ 98UppDecFF-FF28
❑ 98UppDecFF-FF28
❑ 98UppDecFFQ1-FF28
❑ 98UppDecFFQ2-FF28
❑ 98UppDecFIT-FT5
❑ 98UppDecFITQ1-FT5
❑ 98UppDecFITQ2-FT5
❑ 98UppDecFITQ3-FT5
❑ 98UppDecGR-232
❑ 98UppDecLSH-LS6
❑ 98UppDecLSHQ1-LS6
❑ 98UppDecLSHQ2-LS6
❑ 98UppDecLSHQ3-LS6
❑ 98UppDecM-57
❑ 98UppDecMGS-57
❑ 98UppDecMSS-57
❑ 98UppDecMSS-57
❑ 98UppDecP-P27
❑ 98UppDecPQ1-P27
❑ 98UppDecPQ2-P27
❑ 98UppDecPQ3-P27
❑ 98UppDecQD-13
❑ 98UppDecTD-13
❑ 98UppDecWFG-WF19
❑ 99AurSty-4
❑ 99Pac-103
❑ 99PacAur-37
❑ 99PacAurCF-6
❑ 99PacAurCFC-6
❑ 99PacAurCFPB-6
❑ 99PacAurPD-37
❑ 99PacCop-103
❑ 99PacGol-103
❑ 99PacGolCD-8
❑ 99PacIceB-103
❑ 99PacPasAP-5
❑ 99PacPreD-103
❑ 99RetHoc-22
❑ 99SP AutPS-12
❑ 99UppDecM-53
❑ 99UppDecMGS-53
❑ 99UppDecMPS-TF
❑ 99UppDecMSS-53
❑ 99UppDecMSS-53
❑ 99UppDecRG-G7B
❑ 99UppDecRG-22
❑ 99UppDecRGI-G7B
❑ 99UppDecRP-22

**Flichel, Marty**
❑ 92TacRoc-9
❑ 93TacRoc-8
❑ 96DayBom-17

**Flichel, Todd**
❑ 87MonHaw-8
❑ 88ProAHL-170
❑ 89ProAHL-37
❑ 90MonHaw-8
❑ 90ProAHLIHL-247
❑ 91ProAHLCHL-246
❑ 93RochAmeKod-9

**Fliegauf, Charly**
❑ 94GerDELE-26

**Flinn, Tyson**
❑ 95Sla-385
❑ 95SudWol-4
❑ 95SudWolP-8
❑ 96SudWolP-9

**Flint, Calvin**
❑ 89BraWheK-13
❑ 907thInnSWHL-232
❑ 90BraWheK-21

**Flintoft, Rob**
❑ 87PorWinH-9
❑ 88PorWinH-9

**Flinton, Eric**
❑ 95Cla-73
❑ 95ClaAut-6
❑ 96BinRan-10

**Flockhart, Rob**
❑ 77CanuRoyB-3
❑ 84SprInd-13

**Flockhart, Ron**
❑ 82OPC-249
❑ 82OPCSti-113
❑ 83OPC-264
❑ 83OPCSti-192
❑ 83PenCok-9
❑ 84CanaPos-6
❑ 84KelWin-46
❑ 84OPC-174
❑ 84OPCSti-115
❑ 84OPCSti-116
❑ 84PenHeiP-8
❑ 84Top-124
❑ 85OPC-171
❑ 85OPCSti-128
❑ 86OPC-144
❑ 86OPCSti-176
❑ 86Top-146
❑ 87BluKod-10
❑ 87OPC-103
❑ 87OPCSti-25
❑ 87PanSti-317
❑ 87Top-103
❑ 92DalFre-10
❑ 93DalFre-18
❑ 94CenHocL-8

**Flomenhoft, Steven**
❑ 92HarCri-9
❑ 93KnoChe-4
❑ 94KnoChe-12

**Florence, Andrew**
❑ 98BowChrC-48
❑ 98BowChrCGA-48
❑ 98BowChrCGAR-48
❑ 98BowChrCOI-48
❑ 98BowChrCOIR-48
❑ 98BowChrCR-48

**Florio, Perry**
❑ 91JohChi-20
❑ 93JohChi-18
❑ 94JohChi-8

**Floyd, Larry**
❑ 88ProAHL-90
❑ 89ProIHL-113
❑ 91ProAHLCHL-314
❑ 92SanDieG-8

**Floyd, Lloyd**
❑ 90ProAHLIHL-319

**Flugge, Christian**
❑ 94GerDELE-327

**Flyers, Fife**
❑ 97FifFly-1

**Flynn, Billy**
❑ 94GerDELE-53

**Flynn, Brendan**
❑ 91RicRen-3
❑ 92RicRen-4
❑ 93RicRen-14
❑ 95GerDELE-25
❑ 95RicRen-9

**Flynn, Danny (Dan)**
❑ 897thInnSOHL-96
❑ 93SauSteMG-30

**Flynn, Michael**
❑ 97LouRivF-6

**Flynn, Norman**
❑ 907thInnSQMJHL-238

**Focht, Dan**
❑ 95BowDraPro-P20
❑ 95TriAme-10

**Fogal, Ron**
❑ 71RocAme-6

**Fogarty, Bryan**
❑ 85KinCan-13
❑ 86KinCan-12
❑ 87KinCan-21
❑ 88NiaFalT-14
❑ 89HalCit-6
❑ 89Nord-10
❑ 89ProAHL-168
❑ 90Bow-173
❑ 90BowTif-173
❑ 90NordPet-6
❑ 90NordTeal-6
❑ 90PanSti-144
❑ 90ProSet-515
❑ 90Sco-54
❑ 90ScoCan-54
❑ 90UppDec-548
❑ 90UppDecF-548
❑ 91Bow-149
❑ 91NordPanTS-4
❑ 91NordPet-6
❑ 91OPC-500
❑ 91PanSti-259
❑ 91Par-146
❑ 91ParFre-146
❑ 91Pin-59
❑ 91PinFre-59
❑ 91ProSet-200
❑ 91ProSetFre-200
❑ 91ProSetPla-103
❑ 91ScoAme-237
❑ 91ScoCan-457
❑ 91Top-500
❑ 91UppDec-337
❑ 91UppDecF-337
❑ 92PenCokC-6
❑ 94CanaPos-12
❑ 95ColEdgI-165

**Foglietta, Bob**
❑ 86PorWinH-6
❑ 94FinnJaaK-301

**Foglietta, Joe**
❑ 93SweSemWCS-220

**Fogolin, Lee**
❑ 44BeeGro2P-95
❑ 44BeeGro2P-165
❑ 51Par-46
❑ 52Par-55
❑ 53Par-72
❑ 54Par-84
❑ 74NHLActSta-42
❑ 75OPCNHL-306
❑ 75Top-306
❑ 76OPCNHL-253
❑ 76Top-253
❑ 77OPCNHL-94
❑ 77Top-94
❑ 78OPC-27
❑ 78Top-27
❑ 79OilPos-8
❑ 79OPC-183
❑ 79Top-183
❑ 80OPC-63
❑ 80PepCap-25
❑ 80Top-63
❑ 81OilRedR-2

❑ 81OilWesEM-1
❑ 81OPC-112
❑ 81OPCSti-215
❑ 82OilRedR-2
❑ 82OPC-104
❑ 82OPCSti-106
❑ 82PosCer-6
❑ 83OilDol-H18
❑ 83OilMcD-12
❑ 83OPC-26
❑ 83OPCSti-17
❑ 83OPCSti-100
❑ 83Vac-23
❑ 84OilRedR-2
❑ 84OilTeal-4
❑ 84OPC-240
❑ 84OPCSti-254
❑ 85OilRedR-2
❑ 85OPC-235
❑ 85OPCSti-218
❑ 86OilRedR-2
❑ 86OilTeal-2
❑ 86OPC-210
❑ 86OPCSti-71
❑ 88OilTenAnn-42
**Fois, Jordan**
❑ 87SudWol-6
❑ 88SudWol-6
❑ 90RicRen-12
**Fokin, Sergei**
❑ 92SweSemE-279
❑ 93SweSemE-244
❑ 94SweLeaE-185
❑ 95SweLeaE-40
❑ 95SweUppDE-58
**Folden, Brian**
❑ 93WatBlaH-10
**Foley, Colin**
❑ 907thInnSWHL-319
❑ 917thInnSWHL-37
❑ 96AlaGolKin-3
**Foley, Gerry**
❑ 57Top-57
❑ 94ParMisL-94
**Foley, Paul**
❑ 75HamFin-6
**Foley, Rick**
❑ 72OPC-80
❑ 72SarProSta-165
❑ 72Top-98
**Foligno, Mike**
❑ 79RedWinP-3
❑ 80OPC-16
❑ 80OPC-187
❑ 80Top-16
❑ 80Top-187
❑ 81OPC-87
❑ 81OPCSti-122
❑ 81Top-W87
❑ 82OPC-26
❑ 82OPCSti-120
❑ 82PosCer-2
❑ 82SabMilP-12
❑ 83OPC-63
❑ 83OPCSti-237
❑ 83PufSti-7
❑ 84OPC-20
❑ 84OPCSti-212
❑ 84SabBluS-6
❑ 84Top-16
❑ 85OPC-17
❑ 85OPCSti-174
❑ 85SabBluS-9
❑ 85SabBluSS-9
❑ 85Top-17
❑ 86OPC-127
❑ 86OPCBoxB-D
❑ 86OPCSti-42
❑ 86SabBluS-10
❑ 86SabBluSSma-10
❑ 86Top-127
❑ 86TopBoxB-D
❑ 87OPC-40
❑ 87OPCSti-150
❑ 87PanSti-29
❑ 87SabBluS-8
❑ 87SabWonBH-9
❑ 87Top-40
❑ 88FriLayS-18
❑ 88OPC-184
❑ 88OPCSti-257
❑ 88PanSti-226
❑ 88SabBluS-7
❑ 88SabWonBH-7
❑ 88Top-184
❑ 89OPC-78
❑ 89OPCSti-260
❑ 89PanSti-210
❑ 89SabBluS-4
❑ 89SabCam-6
❑ 89Top-78
❑ 90Bow-247
❑ 90BowTif-247
❑ 90OPC-123
❑ 90PanSti-25
❑ 90ProSet-20
❑ 90SabCam-7
❑ 90Sco-133
❑ 90ScoCan-133
❑ 90Top-123
❑ 90TopTif-123
❑ 90UppDec-378
❑ 90UppDecF-378
❑ 91Bow-169
❑ 91MapLeaP-12
❑ 91OPC-18
❑ 91Pin-292
❑ 91PinFre-292
❑ 91ScoCan-248
❑ 91StaClu-29
❑ 91Top-18
❑ 91UppDec-212
❑ 91UppDecF-212
❑ 92PanSti-84
❑ 92PanStiFre-84
❑ 92Par-415
❑ 92ParEmel-415
❑ 92Ult-420
❑ 93Don-433
❑ 93OPCPre-262
❑ 93OPCPreG-262
❑ 93PanSti-228
❑ 93PanTeal-3
❑ 93Pow-346
❑ 93SabNoc-3
❑ 93Sco-387
❑ 93Sco-647
❑ 93ScoBla-21
❑ 93ScoCan-387
❑ 93ScoCan-647
❑ 93ScoGol-647
❑ 93TopPre-262
❑ 93TopPreG-262
❑ 93UppDec-155
❑ 94StaCluST-9
❑ 95St.JohML-24
**Folk, Trevor**
❑ 99WicThu-7
**Folkesson, Osten**
❑ 67SweHoc-254
❑ 69SweHocS-299
**Folkett, Curtis**
❑ 88BraWheK-16
❑ 91AirCanSJHL-C15
**Folta, Petr**
❑ 94CzeAPSE-134
**Fomradas, Blaine**
❑ 91AirCanSJHL-D34
**Foneir, Sebastein**
❑ 907thInnSQMJHL-81
**Fonso, Antonio**
❑ 94GerDELE-408
**Fontaine, Dave**
❑ 93AmoLesFAM-6
**Fontaine, Len**
❑ 72OPC-244
**Fontas, Jon**
❑ 78LouGea-4
**Fonteyne, Val**
❑ 44BeeGro2P-166
❑ 60Par-21
❑ 60ShiCoi-48
❑ 61Par-21
❑ 61ShiCoi-67
❑ 62Par-27
❑ 63Top-61
❑ 64BeeGro3P-69
❑ 64CocCap-83
❑ 65Coc-45
❑ 66Top-108
❑ 68OPC-109
❑ 68ShiCoi-137
❑ 68Top-109
❑ 69OPC-119
❑ 69Top-119
❑ 70OPC-208
❑ 70SarProSta-176
❑ 71OPC-189
❑ 71PenPos-6
❑ 71SarProSta-163
❑ 72OPC-319
❑ 94ParTalB-95
❑ 95Par66-57
❑ 95Par66Coi-57
**Fontinato, Lou**
❑ 44BeeGro2P-239
❑ 44BeeGro2P-311
❑ 57Top-64
❑ 58Top-41
❑ 59Top-5
❑ 60ShiCoi-97
❑ 60Top-61
❑ 61ShiCoi-111
❑ 61YorYelB-40
❑ 62Par-52
❑ 62ShiMetC-23
❑ 81TCMA-4
❑ 91UltOriS-19
❑ 91UltOriSF-19
❑ 93OPCCanHF-52
❑ 93ParParR-PR61
❑ 94ParMisL-93
**Foote, Adam**
❑ 89SauSteMG-15
❑ 907thInnSOHL-157
❑ 917thInnSMC-5
❑ 91NordPet-7
❑ 91Par-371
❑ 91ParFre-371
❑ 91Pin-337
❑ 91PinFre-337
❑ 91ProSetPla-268
❑ 91UppDec-529
❑ 91UppDecF-529
❑ 92NorPet-8
❑ 92Sco-131
❑ 92ScoCan-131
❑ 92StaClu-468
❑ 92TopGol-528G
❑ 93Don-272
❑ 93Lea-229
❑ 93Pin-26
❑ 93PinCan-26
❑ 93Pow-418
❑ 93Sco-149
❑ 93ScoCan-149
❑ 93StaClu-496
❑ 93StaCluFDI-496
❑ 93StaCluO-496
❑ 94BeAPla-R42
❑ 94BeAPSig-2
❑ 94Lea-529
❑ 94NordBurK-7
❑ 94Pin-432
❑ 94PinArtP-432
❑ 94PinRinC-432
❑ 94Sco-151
❑ 94ScoGol-151
❑ 94ScoPla-151
❑ 94ScoPlaTS-151
❑ 95Pin-195
❑ 95PinArtP-195
❑ 95PinRinC-195
❑ 95UppDec-204
❑ 95UppDecEleIce-204
❑ 95UppDecEleIceG-204
❑ 96BeAPAut-196
❑ 96BeAPAutSil-196
❑ 96BeAPla-196
❑ 96MetUni-31
❑ 96SP-38
❑ 96UppDecBD-52
❑ 96UppDecBDG-52
❑ 97ColCho-64
❑ 97ColChoWD-W16
❑ 97EssOlyHH-21
❑ 97EssOlyHHF-21
❑ 97Pac-135
❑ 97PacCop-135
❑ 97PacEmeGre-135
❑ 97PacIceB-135
❑ 97PacRed-135
❑ 97PacSil-135
❑ 97Sco-257
❑ 97ScoAva-12
❑ 97ScoAvaPla-12
❑ 97ScoAvaPre-12
❑ 97UppDec-255
❑ 98Be A PPA-33
❑ 98Be A PPAA-33
❑ 98Be A PPAAF-33
❑ 98Be A PPTBASG-33
❑ 98Be APG-33
❑ 98O-PChr-189
❑ 98O-PChrR-189
❑ 98Pac-52
❑ 98PacIceB-52
❑ 98PacPar-54
❑ 98PacParC-54
❑ 98PacParEG-54
❑ 98PacParH-54
❑ 98PacParIB-54
❑ 98PacParS-54
❑ 98PacRed-52
❑ 98Top-189
❑ 98TopO-P-189
❑ 98UC-228
❑ 98UD ChoPCR-228
❑ 98UD ChoR-228
❑ 99Pac-104
❑ 99PacCop-104
❑ 99PacGol-104
❑ 99PacIceB-104
❑ 99PacPreD-104
**Forbes, Colin**
❑ 97PacOme-163
❑ 97PacOmeC-163
❑ 97PacOmeDG-163
❑ 97PacOmeEG-163
❑ 97PacOmeG-163
❑ 97PacOmeIB-163
❑ 97UppDec-191
❑ 98O-PChr-49
❑ 98O-PChrR-49
❑ 98Pac-325
❑ 98PacIceB-325
❑ 98PacPar-172
❑ 98PacParC-172
❑ 98PacParEG-172
❑ 98PacParH-172
❑ 98PacParIB-172
❑ 98PacParS-172
❑ 98PacRed-325
❑ 98Top-49
❑ 98TopO-P-49
❑ 98UppDec-335
❑ 98UppDecE-335
❑ 98UppDecE1o1-335
❑ 98UppDecGR-335
❑ 98UppDecM-151
❑ 98UppDecMGS-151
❑ 98UppDecMSS-151
❑ 98UppDecMSS-151
❑ 99Pac-388
❑ 99PacCop-388
❑ 99PacGol-388
❑ 99PacIceB-388
❑ 99PacPreD-388
**Forbes, Dave**
❑ 74NHLActSta-29
❑ 74OPCNHL-266
❑ 75OPCNHL-173
❑ 75Top-173
❑ 76OPCNHL-246
❑ 76Top-246
❑ 77OPCNHL-143
❑ 77Top-143
❑ 78OPC-167
❑ 78Top-167
**Forbes, Ian**
❑ 97GueSto-10
**Forbes, Mike**
❑ 81OilRedR-26
❑ 88OilTenAnn-72
**Forbes, Vernon**
❑ 23V1451-29
❑ 24C144ChaCig-25
❑ 24V130MapC-25
❑ 24V1452-11
**Forch, Libor**
❑ 94CzeAPSE-241
❑ 95CzeAPSE-14
**Ford, Brian**
❑ 83FreExp-4
❑ 83Vac-64
❑ 89ProAHL-268
**Ford, Colin**
❑ 87SauSteMG-18
**Ford, George**
❑ 52St.LawS-59
**Ford, John**
❑ 52JunBluT-114
**Ford, Mike**
❑ 76OPCWHA-75
**Ford, Pat**
❑ 92NorMicW-29
❑ 93NorMicW-30
**Forestell, Brian**
❑ 89WinSpi-3
❑ 907thInnSOHL-181
**Forsander, Johan**
❑ 97UppDecBD-99
❑ 97UppDecBDDD-99
❑ 97UppDecBDQD-99
❑ 97UppDecBDTD-99
❑ 98UC-293
❑ 98UD ChoPCR-293
❑ 98UD ChoR-293
**Forsberg, Bjorn**
❑ 71SweHocS-342
**Forsberg, Jonas**
❑ 92SweSemE-349
❑ 94ParSE-SE245
❑ 94ParSEG-SE245
❑ 94SweLeaE-170
❑ 95SweGloWC-55
❑ 95SweLeaE-27
❑ 95SweLeaES-9
❑ 98UD ChoS-1
**Forsberg, Kent**
❑ 92SweSemE-332
❑ 93SweSemE-297
**Forsberg, Pasi**
❑ 93FinnJyvHS-298
❑ 93FinnSIS-74
**Forsberg, Per**
❑ 83SweSemE-150
❑ 86SwePanS-201
❑ 87SwePanS-197
**Forsberg, Peter**
❑ 91AreDraPic-4
❑ 91Cla-5
❑ 91StaPicH-35
❑ 91SweSemE-213
❑ 91UltDra-5
❑ 91UltDra-61
❑ 91UltDra-74
❑ 91UppDec-64
❑ 91UppDecF-64
❑ 92SweSemE-242
❑ 92SweSemE-347
❑ 92UppDec-235
❑ 92UppDec-369
❑ 92UppDec-375
❑ 92UppDec-595
❑ 93SweSemE-209
❑ 93SweSemE-301
❑ 93SweSemE-302
❑ 93SweSemE-305
❑ 93SweSemE-311
❑ 93SweSemWCS-13
❑ 94BeAPla-R152
❑ 94Fin-1
❑ 94FinBowB-R12
❑ 94FinBowB-X22
❑ 94FinBowBR-R12
❑ 94FinBowBR-X22
❑ 94FinnJaaK-75
❑ 94FinnJaaK-355
❑ 94FinRef-1
❑ 94FinSupTW-1
❑ 94Fla-146
❑ 94Fle-176
❑ 94FleRooS-2
❑ 94Lea-475
❑ 94LeaLim-116
❑ 94LeaLimI-28
❑ 94LeaPhe-3
❑ 94McDUppD-McD31
❑ 94NordBurK-8
❑ 94OPCPre-385
❑ 94OPCPre-425
❑ 94OPCPreSE-385
❑ 94OPCPreSE-425
❑ 94ParSE-SE149
❑ 94ParSEES-ES1
❑ 94ParSEG-SE149
❑ 94Pin-266
❑ 94Pin-479
❑ 94PinArtP-266
❑ 94PinArtP-479
❑ 94PinRinC-266
❑ 94PinRinC-479
❑ 94PinRooTP-9
❑ 94ScoTopRR-2
❑ 94Sel-175
❑ 94SelGol-175
❑ 94SelYouExp-YE7
❑ 94SP-96
❑ 94SPDieCut-96
❑ 94SPPre-2
❑ 94SPPreDC-2
❑ 94SweLeaE-189
❑ 94SweLeaEGC-19
❑ 94SweLeaEGS-3
❑ 94TopFinB-17
❑ 94TopPre-385
❑ 94TopPre-425
❑ 94TopPreSE-385
❑ 94TopPreSE-425
❑ 94Ult-356
❑ 94UltPro-1
❑ 94UppDec-245
❑ 94UppDec-528
❑ 94UppDec-555
❑ 94UppDecEleIce-245
❑ 94UppDecEleIce-528
❑ 94UppDecEleIce-555
❑ 94UppDecPC-C1
❑ 94UppDecPCEG-C1
❑ 94UppDecPCES-C1
❑ 94UppDecPH-H10
❑ 94UppDecPHEG-H10
❑ 94UppDecPHES-H10
❑ 94UppDecPHG-H10
❑ 94UppDecSPI-SP156
❑ 94UppDecSPIDC-SP156
❑ 95Bow-85
❑ 95BowAllFoi-85
❑ 95BowBes-BB1
❑ 95BowBesRef-BB1
❑ 95CanGamNHLP-29
❑ 95CanGamNHLP-77
❑ 95ColCho-26
❑ 95ColCho-371
❑ 95ColCho-391
❑ 95ColChoCTG-C20
❑ 95ColChoCTG-C20B
❑ 95ColChoCTG-C20C
❑ 95ColChoCTGGB-C20
❑ 95ColChoCTGGR-C20
❑ 95ColChoCTGSB-C20
❑ 95ColChoCTGSR-C20
❑ 95ColChoPC-26
❑ 95ColChoPC-371
❑ 95ColChoPC-391
❑ 95ColChoPCP-26
❑ 95ColChoPCP-371
❑ 95ColChoPCP-391
❑ 95Don-65
❑ 95DonDom-1
❑ 95DonEli-39
❑ 95DonEliCE-4
❑ 95DonEliDCS-39
❑ 95DonEliDCU-39
❑ 95DonRooTea-2
❑ 95Emo-36
❑ 95EmoXci-14
❑ 95Fin-26
❑ 95Fin-100
❑ 95FinnSemWC-64
❑ 95FinRef-26
❑ 95FinRef-100
❑ 95ImpSti-28
❑ 95Kra-11
❑ 95Lea-20
❑ 95LeaFirOIce-6
❑ 95LeaLim-2
❑ 95LeaLimSG-4
❑ 95LeaStuR-2
❑ 95McDPin-MCD-7
❑ 95Met-32
❑ 95MetIS-4
❑ 95MetWin-1
❑ 95NHLAcePC-9H
❑ 95NHLCooT-10
❑ 95NHLCooT-RP12
❑ 95ParInt-237
❑ 95ParInt-316
❑ 95ParIntAS-4
❑ 95ParIntCCGS1-13
❑ 95ParIntCCGS2-6
❑ 95ParIntCCSS1-13
❑ 95ParIntCCSS2-6
❑ 95ParIntEI-237
❑ 95ParIntEI-316
❑ 95ParIntPTP-PP4
❑ 95ParIntPTP-PP13
❑ 95ParIntTW-3
❑ 95PinCleS-8
❑ 95PinFan-25
❑ 95PinFirS-11
❑ 95PinRoa2-15
❑ 95PlaOneoOne-25
❑ 95PlaOneoOne-137
❑ 95PlaOneoOne-239
❑ 95ProMag-2
❑ 95Sco-31
❑ 95ScoBlaIce-31
❑ 95ScoBlaIceAP-31
❑ 95ScoChelt-7
❑ 95ScoDreTea-5
❑ 95ScoGolBla-10
❑ 95SelCer-68
❑ 95SelCerFut-1
❑ 95SelCerMG-68
❑ 95SelCerP-68
❑ 95SkyImp-35
❑ 95SkyImp-229
❑ 95SkyImpIQ-8
❑ 95SP-29
❑ 95SPHol-FX4
❑ 95SPHolSpFX-FX4
❑ 95SPStaEto-E10
❑ 95SPStaEtoG-E10
❑ 95StaClu-105
❑ 95StaCluGTSC-GT4
❑ 95StaCluMO-47
❑ 95StaCluMOMS-105
❑ 95StaCluNem-N9
❑ 95Sum-117
❑ 95SumArtP-117
❑ 95SumIce-117
❑ 95SweGloWC-21
❑ 95SweGloWC-253
❑ 95SweGloWC-254
❑ 95SweGloWC-255
❑ 95SweGloWC-270
❑ 95SweGloWC-NNO
❑ 95SweUppDE-234
❑ 95Top-359
❑ 95Top-380
❑ 95TopMarMPB-380
❑ 95TopNewG-10NG
❑ 95TopOPCI-359
❑ 95TopOPCI-380
❑ 95TopSupSki-18
❑ 95TopSupSkiPla-18
❑ 95TopYouS-YS4
❑ 95Ult-132
❑ 95Ult-383
❑ 95UltAllRoo-3
❑ 95UltAllRooGM-3
❑ 95UltExtAtt-5
❑ 95UltGolM-132
❑ 95UltHigSpe-8
❑ 95UppDec-90
❑ 95UppDecAGPRW-11
❑ 95UppDecEleIce-430
❑ 95UppDecEleIceG-430
❑ 95UppDecFreFra-F1
❑ 95UppDecFreFraJ-F1
❑ 95UppDecNHLAS-AS17
❑ 95UppDecPHE-H8
❑ 95UppDecPRE-R25
❑ 95UppDecPRE-R37
❑ 95UppDecPRF-R54
❑ 95UppDecPreR-R25
❑ 95UppDecPreR-R37
❑ 95UppDecPreR-R54
❑ 95UppDecSpeE-SE21
❑ 95UppDecSpeEdiG-SE21
❑ 95UppPreHV-H8
❑ 95UppPreRP-R37
❑ 95UppPreRP-R54
❑ 95Zen-70
❑ 95ZenZT-8
❑ 96BeAPBisITB-5
❑ 96BeAPLH-2B
❑ 96BeAPLHAut-2B
❑ 96BeAPLHAutSil-2B
❑ 96ColCho-63
❑ 96ColCho-298
❑ 96ColCho-314
❑ 96ColChoMVP-UD3
❑ 96ColChoMVPG-UD3
❑ 96ColChoSti-S3
❑ 96Don-139
❑ 96DonCanI-6
❑ 96DonCanIGPP-6
❑ 96DonCanIRPP-6
❑ 96DonEli-12
❑ 96DonEliDCS-12
❑ 96DonEliS-7
❑ 96DonGoTS-10
❑ 96DonHitLis-14
❑ 96DonPrePro-139
❑ 96DurL'EB-JB8
❑ 96Fla-18
❑ 96FlaBluI-18
❑ 96FlaCenIS-3
❑ 96FlaNowAT-3
❑ 96Fle-20
❑ 96Fle-139
❑ 96FleArtRos-4
❑ 96FlePea-3
❑ 96FlePicDL-3
❑ 96FlePicF5-12
❑ 96KraUppD-48
❑ 96Lea-159
❑ 96LeaLeaAL-6
❑ 96LeaLeaALP-P6
❑ 96LeaLim-29
❑ 96LeaLimBTB-8
❑ 96LeaLimBTBLE-8
❑ 96LeaLimBTBP-P8
❑ 96LeaLimG-29
❑ 96LeaPre-110
❑ 96LeaPreP-159
❑ 96LeaPrePP-110
❑ 96LeaPreSG-60
❑ 96LeaPreSP-6
❑ 96LeaPreSte-60
❑ 96LeaTheBO.-8
❑ 96MetUni-32
❑ 96MetUniCS-2
❑ 96MetUniCSSP-2
❑ 96MetUniLW-4
❑ 96MetUniLWSP-4
❑ 96NHLACEPC-14
❑ 96NHLProSTA-2
❑ 96Pin-78
❑ 96Pin-249
❑ 96PinArtP-78
❑ 96PinArtP-249
❑ 96PinFan-FC15
❑ 96PinFoi-78
❑ 96PinFoi-249
❑ 96PinMcD-28
❑ 96PinMin-6
❑ 96PinMinB-6
❑ 96PinMinCoiB-6
❑ 96PinMinCoiGP-6
❑ 96PinMinCoiN-6
❑ 96PinMinCoiS-6
❑ 96PinMinCoiSG-6
❑ 96PinMinG-6
❑ 96PinMinS-6
❑ 96PinPreS-78
❑ 96PinPreS-249
❑ 96PinRinC-78
❑ 96PinRinC-249
❑ 96PinTeaP-2
❑ 96PlaOneoOne-357
❑ 96Sco-99
❑ 96ScoArtPro-99
❑ 96ScoChelt-2
❑ 96ScoDeaCAP-99
❑ 96ScoDreTea-4
❑ 96ScoGolB-99
❑ 96ScoSpeAP-99
❑ 96SelCerCor-15
❑ 96SkyImp-22
❑ 96SkyImpB-3
❑ 96SkyImpVer-3
❑ 96SP-33
❑ 96SPGamFil-GF2
❑ 96SPSPxFor-1
❑ 96SPx-8
❑ 96SPxGol-8
❑ 96StaCluMO-20
❑ 96Sum-142
❑ 96SumArtP-142
❑ 96SumHigV-6
❑ 96SumHigVM-6
❑ 96SumIce-142
❑ 96SumMet-142
❑ 96SumPreS-142
❑ 96SumUnt-5
❑ 96SweSemCDT-8
❑ 96SweSemW-57
❑ 96SweSemW-74
❑ 96SweSemWNS-NS1
❑ 96TeaOut-29
❑ 96TopNHLP-5
❑ 96TopPicFT-FT16
❑ 96TopPicOI-5
❑ 96TopPicTS-TS7
❑ 96Ult-35
❑ 96UltCleTheIce-2
❑ 96UltGolM-35
❑ 96UppDec-239
❑ 96UppDecBD-171
❑ 96UppDecBDG-171
❑ 96UppDecBDRFTC-RC7
❑ 96UppDecGN-X2
❑ 96UppDecHH-HH7
❑ 96UppDecHHG-HH7
❑ 96UppDecHHS-HH7
❑ 96UppDecIce-81
❑ 96UppDecIcePar-81
❑ 96UppDecLSH-LS8
❑ 96UppDecLSHF-LS8
❑ 96UppDecLSHS-LS8
❑ 96UppDecSS-SS8A
❑ 96Zen-76
❑ 96ZenArtP-76
❑ 96ZenChaS-9
❑ 96ZenChaSD-9
❑ 97BeAPlaPOT-11
❑ 97ColCho-54
❑ 97ColChoCTG-C21A
❑ 97ColChoCTG-C21B
❑ 97ColChoCTG-C21C
❑ 97ColChoCTGE-CR21
❑ 97ColChoSta-SQ71
❑ 97ColChoSti-S21
❑ 97Don-1
❑ 97DonCanI-6
❑ 97DonCanIDS-6
❑ 97DonCanIPS-6
❑ 97DonCanISCS-18
❑ 97DonEli-1
❑ 97DonEliAsp-1
❑ 97DonEliBttF-5
❑ 97DonEliBttFA-5
❑ 97DonEliC-23
❑ 97DonEliIns-7
❑ 97DonEliMC-23
❑ 97DonEliPN-1A
❑ 97DonEliPN-1B
❑ 97DonEliPN-1C
❑ 97DonEliPNDC-1A
❑ 97DonEliPNDC-1B
❑ 97DonEliPNDC-1C
❑ 97DonEliS-1
❑ 97DonLim-2
❑ 97DonLim-48
❑ 97DonLim-109
❑ 97DonLimExp-2
❑ 97DonLimExp-48
❑ 97DonLimExp-109
❑ 97DonLimFOTG-72
❑ 97DonLin2L-4
❑ 97DonLin2LDC-4

97DonPre-2
97DonPre-173
97DonPreCttC-2
97DonPreCttC-173
97DonPreDWT-4
97DonPrePM-12
97DonPreProS-1
97DonPreT-9
97DonPreTB-9
97DonPreTBC-9
97DonPreTPC-9
97DonPreTPG-9
97DonPri-8
97DonPri-185
97DonPriDD-10
97DonPriODl-8
97DonPriS-10
97DonPriSB-10
97DonPriSG-10
97DonPriSoA-8
97DonPriSoA-185
97DonPriSS-10
97EssOlyHH-43
97EssOlyHHF-43
97Kat-38
97KatGol-38
97KatSil-38
97Lea-3
97Lea-170
97LeaBanSea-13
97LeaFirOnlce-12
97LeaFraMat-3
97LeaFraMat-170
97LeaFraMDC-3
97LeaFraMDC-170
97LeaInt-3
97LeaIntUl-3
97McD-15
97Pac-21
97PacCarSup-4
97PacCarSupM-4
97PacCop-21
97PacCraChoAwa-4
97PacCroR-33
97PacCroRBoSDC-5
97PacCroRCCJ-4
97PacCroRCCJG-4
97PacCroRCCJS-4
97PacCroREG-33
97PacCroRHTDC-4
97PacCroRIB-33
97PacCroRLCDC-5
97PacCroRS-33
97PacDyn-29
97PacDyn-138
97PacDynBKS-24
97PacDynC-29
97PacDynC-138
97PacDynDD-5A
97PacDynDG-29
97PacDynDG-138
97PacDynEG-29
97PacDynEG-138
97PacDynIB-29
97PacDynIB-138
97PacDynKotN-2
97PacDynR-29
97PacDynR-138
28PacDynSil-29
97PacDynSil-138
97PacDynTan-5
97PacDynTan-25
97PacEmeGre-21
97PacGolCroDC-7
97PacIceB-21
97PacInv-34
97PacInvAZ-5
97PacInvC-34
97PacInvEG-34
77PacInvFP-7
97PacInvIB-34
97PacInvNRB-51
97PacInvNRB-216
97PacInvOTG-5
97PacInvR-34
97PacInvS-34
97PacOme-56
97PacOmeC-56
97PacOmeDG-56
97PacOmeEG-56
97PacOmeG-56
97PacOmeGFDCC-3
97PacOmeIB-56
97PacOmeSil-3
97PacOmeSLC-5
97PacPar-49
97PacParBNDC-5
97PacParC-49
97PacParDG-49
97PacParEG-49
97PacParIB-49
97PacParP-5
97PacParRed-49
97PacParSil-49
97PacRed-21
97PacRev-32
97PacRev1AGD-6
97PacRevC-32
97PacRevE-32
97PacRevIB-32
97PacRevNID-3
97PacRevR-32

97PacRevS-32
97PacSil-21
97PacSlaSDC-2A
97Pin-73
97Pin-191
97PinArtP-73
97PinBee-9
97PinBeeGP-9
97PinBeeGT-9
97PinBeeT-9
97PinCer-32
97PinCerGT-10
97PinCerMB-32
97PinCerMG-32
97PinCerMR-32
97PinCerR-32
97PinCerT-10
97PinEpiGO-14
97PinEpiGP-14
97PinEpiME-14
97PinEpiMO-14
97PinEpiMP-14
97PinEpiPE-14
97PinEpiPO-14
97PinEpiPP-14
97PinEpiSE-14
97PinEpiSO-14
97PinEpiSP-14
97PinIns-8
97PinIns-P8
97PinInsC-16
97PinInsCG-16
97PinInsCG-16
97PinInsEC-8
97PinInsT-5
97PinMin-3
97PinMinB-3
97PinMinCBP-3
97PinMinCGPP-3
97PinMinCNSP-3
97PinMinCoiB-3
97PinMinCoiGP-3
97PinMinCoiN-3
97PinMinCoiSG-3
97PinMinCoiSS-3
97PinMinGolTea-3
97PinMinMC-2
97PinMinMin-2
97PinMinSilTea-3
97PinPowPac-19
97PinPrePBB-73
97PinPrePBB-191
97PinPrePBC-73
97PinPrePBC-191
97PinPrePBM-73
97PinPrePBM-191
97PinPrePBY-73
97PinPrePBY-191
97PinPrePFC-73
97PinPrePFC-191
97PinPrePFM-73
97PinPrePFM-191
97PinPrePFY-73
97PinPrePFY-191
97PinPrePla-73
97PinPrePla-191
97PinRinC-73
97PinTeaP-7
97PinTeaPM-7
97PinTeaPP-7
97PinTeaPPM-7
97PinTotCMPG-32
97PinTotCPB-32
97PinTotCPG-32
97PinTotCPR-32
97PosPin-20
97Sco-83
97Sco-PR83
97ScoArtPro-83
97ScoAva-4
97ScoAvaPla-4
97ScoAvaPre-4
97ScoGolBla-83
97SP Autl-I12
97SPAut-36
97SPAutlD-I12
97SPAutlE-I12
97SPx-11
97SPxBro-11
97SPxDim-SPX16
97SPxGol-11
97SPxGraF-11
97SPxSil-11
97SPxSte-11
97Stu-15
97StuHarH-16
97StuPor-15
97StuPrePG-15
97StuPrePS-15
97StuSil-13
97StuSil8-13
97UppDec-252
97UppDecBD-106
97UppDecBDG-106
97UppDecBDPC-106
97UppDecBDPCDD-PC11
97UppDecBDPCM-PC11
97UppDecBDPCQD-PC11
97UppDecBDPCTD-PC11
97UppDecBDQD-106
97UppDecBDTD-106
97UppDecDV-14
97UppDecDVSM-14
97UppDecGDM-252
97UppDecIC-IC12

97UppDecIC2-IC12
97UppDecIce-61
97UppDecIceP-61
97UppDecILL-L4B
97UppDecILL2-L4B
97UppDecIPS-61
97UppDecSG-SG21
97UppDecSSM-SS21
97UppDecSSW-SS21
97UppDecTS-21
97UppDecTSL2-21
97UppDecTSS-1C
97Zen-2
97Zen5x7-19
97ZenChaTC-12
97ZenGolImp-19
97ZenSilImp-19
97ZenZGol-2
97ZenZSil-2
97ZenT-5
97ZenZT5x7-5
97ZenZTG-5
98Be A PPA-35
98Be A PPAA-35
98Be A PPAAF-35
98Be A PPAGUSC-S2
98Be A PPAJ-AS2
98Be A PPPGUJC-G7
98Be A PPPH-H2
98Be A PPPPUJC-P22
98Be APG-35
98BowBes-12
98BowBesAR-12
98BowBesMIF-F6
98BowBesMIFAR-F6
98BowBesMIFR-F6
98BowBesR-12
98BowBesSBB-SB8
98BowBesSBBAR-SB8
98BowBesSBBR-SB8
98CroRoyCCAJG-4
98CroRoyCCAJG-4
98CroRoyCCAJB-4
98CroRoyCCAJP-4
98CroRoyCCAJR-4
98Fin-6
98FinCen-C7
98FinCenR-C7
98FinDouMF-M21
98FinDouMF-M25
98FinDouMF-M26
98FinDouMF-M27
98FinDouSMFR-M21
98FinDouSMFR-M25
98FinDouSMFR-M26
98FinDouSMFR-M27
98FinNo P-6
98FinNo PR-6
98FinRef-6
98McD-7
98O-PChr-1
98O-PChrR-1
98O-PChrSB-SB21
98O-PChrSBR-SB21
98Pac-21
98PacAur-46
98PacAurALC-5
98PacAurC-4
98PacAurCF-11
98PacAurCFC-11
98PacAurCFIB-11
98PacAurCFR-11
98PacAurFL-2
98PacAurFLIB-2
98PacAurFLR-2
98PacAurMAC-5
98PacAurNC-3
98PacCroR-33
98PacCroRCCA-4
98PacCroRCCAJ-4
98PacCroRLL-4
98PacCroRMP-4
98PacCroRPP-4
98PacDynI-47
98PacDynI-5
98PacDynIAR-4
98PacDynIARB-4
98PacDynIARIB-4
98PacDynIARR-4
98PacDynIARS-4
98PacDynIFT-5
98PacDynIIB-47
98PacDynIIP-3
98PacDynIR-47
98PacEO P-4
98PacGolCD-8
98PacIceB-21
98PacOmeEP1o1-4
98PacOmeFtF-8
98PacOmeH-60
98PacOmeODI-60
98PacOmeP-4
98PacOmePI-25
98PacOmePIB-25
98PacOmeR-60
98PacPar-55
98PacParC-55
98PacParEG-55
98PacParH-55
98PacParHoFB-3
98PacParHoFBPP-3

98PacParIB-55
98PacParIG-2
98PacParIGG-2
98PacParIGS-2
98PacParS-55
98PacParSDDC-4
98PacRed-21
98PacRev-35
98PacRevADC-7
98PacRevCTL-4
98PacRevIS-35
98PacRevNI-3
98PacRevR-35
98PacRevS-10
98PacTim-3
98PacTitl-5
98PinEpiGE-14
98RevThrPA-23
98RevThrPA-23
98SP Aut-20
98SP AutSM-S19
98SP AutSS-SS6
98SPxFin-95
98SPxFin-166
98SPxFin-178
98SPxFinR-95
98SPxFinR-166
98SPxFinR-178
98SPxFinS-95
98SPxFinS-166
98SPxFinS-178
98SPXTopP-13
98SPXTopPF-13
98SPXTopPHH-H10
98SPXTopPLI-L28
98SPXTopPPS-PS23
98SPXTopPR-13
98Top-1
98TopGolLC1-21
98TopGolLC1B-21
98TopGolLC1BOoO-21
98TopGolLC1OoO-21
98TopGolLC1ROoO-21
98TopGolLC1R-21
98TopGolLC1ROoO-21
98TopGolLC2-21
98TopGolLC2B-21
98TopGolLC2BOoO-21
98TopGolLC2OoO-21
98TopGolLC2R-21
98TopGolLC2ROoO-21
98TopGolLC3-21
98TopGolLC3B-21
98TopGolLC3BOoO-21
98TopGolLC3OoO-21
98TopGolLC3R-21
98TopGolLC3ROoO-21
98TopIceA2-I8
98TopLocL-L1
98TopMysFB-M8
98TopMysFBR-M8
98TopMysFG-M8
98TopMysFGR-M8
98TopMysFS-M8
98TopMysFSR-M8
98TopO-P-1
98TopSeaB-SB21
98UC-56
98UC-229
98UC-241
98UCMBH-BH14
98UCSB-SQ20
98UCSG-SQ20
98UCSG-SQ20
98UCSR-SQ20
98UD ChoPCR-56
98UD ChoPCR-229
98UD ChoPCR-241
98UD ChoR-56
98UD ChoR-229
98UD ChoR-241
98UD3-33
98UD3-93
98UD3-153
98UD3DieC-33
98UD3DieC-93
98UD3DieC-153
98UppDec-29
98UppDec-69
98UppDecBD-21
98UppDecE-29
98UppDecE-69
98UppDecE1o1-29
98UppDecE1o1-69
98UppDecFF-FF17
98UppDecFF-FF17
98UppDecFFQ1-FF17
98UppDecFFQ2-FF17
98UppDecFIT-FT2
98UppDecFITQ1-FT2
98UppDecFITQ2-FT2
98UppDecFITQ3-FT2
98UppDecGN-GN25
98UppDecGN-GN26
98UppDecGN-GN27
98UppDecGNQ1-GN25
98UppDecGNQ1-GN26
98UppDecGNQ1-GN27
98UppDecGNQ2-GN25
98UppDecGNQ2-GN26
98UppDecGNQ2-GN27
98UppDecGNQ3-GN25
98UppDecGNQ3-GN26
98UppDecGNQ3-GN27
98UppDecGR-29

98UppDecGR-69
98UppDecLSH-LS12
98UppDecLSHQ1-LS12
98UppDecLSHQ2-LS12
98UppDecLSHQ3-LS12
98UppDecM-51
98UppDecM1-M28
98UppDecM2-M28
98UppDecMGS-51
98UppDecMOH-OT8
98UppDecMPG-PG9
98UppDecMS-S5
98UppDecMSF-F14
98UppDecMSS-51
98UppDecP-P11
98UppDecPQ1-P11
98UppDecPQ2-P11
98UppDecPQ3-P11
98UppDecQD-21
98UppDecTD-21
98UppDecWFG-WF7
98UppDecWFP-WF7
99AurSty-5
99Pac-105
99PacAur-38
99PacAurCC-4
99PacAurCF-7
99PacAurCFC-7
99PacAurCFPB-7
99PacAurCP-4
99PacAurPD-38
99PacGolCop-105
99PacCra-3
99PacGol-105
99PacGolCD-9
99PacIceB-105
99PacPasAP-6
99PacPreD-105
99RetHoc-19
99SP AutPS-20
99UppDecCL-54
99UppDecCLCLC-54
99UppDecM-52
99UppDecM9S-S6
99UppDecMGS-52
99UppDecMHoG-H6
99UppDecMSS-52
99UppDecMSS-52
99UppDecRG-19
99UppDecRP-19

**Forseth, Jody**
91AirCanSJHL-E43
**Forsey, Jack**
34BeeGro1P-317
**Forslund, Tomas**
89SweSemE-134
90SweSemE-209
91FlamIGA-2
91oLoCroC-9
91Par-20
91ParFre-20
91Pin-333
91PinFre-333
91ProSet-527
91ProSetFre-527
91ScoCan-629
91ScoRoo-79T
91UppDec-27
91UppDecF-27
91UppDecF-586
92Bow-384
92OPC-70
92PanSti-D
92PanStiFre-D
92StaClu-280
92Top-186
98UD3-33
92UppDec-3
92UppDec-429
92UppDecERT-ERT6
93ClaProPBC-BC15
93ClaProPro-139
93SweSemE-143
93SweSemWCS-41
94FinnJaaK-77
94SweLeaE-65
95FinnSemWC-69
95SweGloWC-46
95SweLeaE-242
95SweLeaEFF-7
95SweUppDE-112
96GerDELE-357
96SweSemW-67
98GerDELE-88
**Forsman, Jonny**
83SweSemE-185
84SweSemE-208
86SwePanS-232
87SwePanS-222
89SweSemW-67
**Forss, Matti**
93FinnSIS-200
93FinnSIS-387
95FinnSISL-36
**Forster, Nathan**
96SeaThu-4
**Forsythe, Trevor**
91KnoChe-8
**Fortier, Dave**
740PCNHL-382
750PCNHL-336

76CanuRoyB-3
760PCNHL-328
**Fortier, Francois**
98BowCHL-90
98BowCHLGA-90
98BowCHLOI-90
98BowChrC-90
98BowChrCGA-90
98BowChrCGAR-90
98BowChrCOI-90
98BowChrCOIR-90
98BowChrCR-90
**Fortier, Marc**
84ChiSag-11
88NordGenF-11
88NordTeal-7
88ProAHL-114
89Nord-11
89NordGenF-8
89NordPol-7
89OPC-262
89OPCSti-189
89PanSti-335
90Bow-167
90BowTif-167
90NordPet-7
90NordTeal-7
90OPC-176
90PanSti-153
90ProSet-245A
90ProSet-245B
90Sco-78
90ScoCan-78
90Top-176
90TopTif-176
91NordPanTS-5
91NordPet-8
92ProSet-128
92StaClu-173
92Top-226
92TopGol-226G
93PhoRoa-6
95SwiHNL-42
98GerDELE-164
**Fortier, Sebastien**
917thInnSQMJHL-39
93WheThu-10
**Fortin, Dany**
917thInnSQMJHL-18
**Fortin, Emile**
36V356WorG-122
**Fortin, Jean-Francois**
96UppDec-375
96UppDecBD-4
96UppDecBDG-4
97BowCHL-46
97BowCHL-157
97BowCHLBB-17
97BowCHLBowBesAR-17
97BowCHLBowBesR-17
97BowCHLOPC-46
97BowCHLOPC-157
**Forton, Yvan**
51LavDaiLSJ-55
**Foster, Corey**
89ProAHL-146
90ProAHLIHL-231
91FlyJCP-9
91Par-344
91ParFre-344
91Pin-332
91PinFre-332
91ProSet-551
91ProSetFre-551
91ProSetPla-265
91UppDec-591
91UppDecF-591
92UppDec-53
95CleLum-11
96CleLum-10
**Foster, Darryl**
93NiaFalT-3
94DetJrRW-2
95Cla-89
95SlaMemC-76
**Foster, David**
91AirCanSJHL-D9
92MPSPhoSJHL-33
**Foster, Dwight**
780PC-171
81OPC-3
81OPCSti-52
81RocPos-5
81Top-E67
82OPC-138
82PosCer-11
83OPC-122
83OPCSti-133
84OPC-53
84Top-41
85OPC-14
85Top-14
87PanSti-17
87RedWinLC-10
**Foster, Jerry**
89ProAHL-74
**Foster, Kurtis**
98SP Aut-116
98SP AutSotTG-KF
98SSASotT-KF
98UppDec-393
98UppDecE-393
98UppDecE1o1-393
98UppDecGR-393
99SP AutPS-116

**Foster, Norm**
88ProAHL-154
89ProAHL-60
90ProAHLIHL-135
91ProAHLCHL-225
91UppDec-465
91UppDecF-465
**Fotheringham, Shawn**
92ClaKni-6
**Fotiu, Nick**
750PCWHA-108
770PCNHL-11
77Top-11
780PC-367
790PC-286
800PC-184
80Top-184
820PC-222
82PosCer-13
830PC-243
850PC-22
85Top-22
86FlamRedR-6
880IlTenAnn-143
89ProAHL-107
92NasKni-2
**Fountain, Mike**
907thInnSOHL-336
917thInnSOHL-170
910shGen-1
910shGenS-22
91UppDecCWJC-52
92AlbIntTC-8
92HamCan-7
93ClaProPro-106
94ClaProP-175
94ClaTri-T70
96CanuPos-30
96SP-162
96SyrCru-1
97Don-218
97DonCanI-136
97DonCanIDS-136
97DonCanIIS-136
97DonPreProG-218
97DonPreProS-218
97PinIns-76
97PinInsCG-76
97PinInsEC-76
**Fournel, Dan**
94HunBli-9
95SouCarS-9
96SouCarS-11
**Fournier, Jack**
12C57-36
**Fournier, Marc**
83SauSteMG-7
**Fournier, Rob**
88NiaFalT-10
897thInnSOHL-171
**Fournier, Wade**
95LouIceG-3
95LouIceGP-5
**Fowler, Bob**
89ProHL-129
**Fowler, Dan**
91ProAHLCHL-32
**Fowler, Heck (Norman)**
24C144ChaCig-26
24V130MapC-3
24V1452-30
24V1282PauC-87
**Fowler, Jimmy (James)**
28V1282PauC-74
34BeeGro1P-318
360PCV304D-103
370PCV304E-135
38QuaOatP-13
390PCV3011-55
**Fowler, Rob**
87MonHaw-9
**Fox, Greg**
77NovScoV-7
790PC-116
79Top-116
80BlaBroBac-2
80BlaWhiBor-5
800PC-268
81BlaBorPos-7
81BlaBroBac-2
81OPC-69
820PC-65
82PosCer-4
830PC-101
840PC-175
84PenHeiP-9
**Fox, Jim**
810PC-153
820PC-154
820PCSti-235
82PosCer-8
830PC-154
830PCSti-293
83PufSti-7
84KinSmo-5
840PC-84
840PCSti-268
84Top-66
850PC-61
850PCSti-236
85Top-61
86Kin20tATI-6
860PC-215
860PCSti-89
87KinTeal4-6

87OPC-75
87OPCSti-216
87PanSti-281
87Top-75
88KinSmo-9
88OPC-139
88OPCSti-154
88PanSti-76
88Top-139

**Foy, Chris**
93RicRen-18
94RicRen-5
95SouCarS-14

**Foyston, Frank**
83HalFP-B4
85HalFC-20

**Fragapane, Eric**
92QueIntP-33

**Francella, Giullio**
82SweSemHVS-130

**Franceschetti, Lou**
86CapKod-7
86CapPol-7
87CapKod-25
87CapTeaIss-4
87PanSti-188
88CapBor-4
88CapSmo-4
88ProAHL-39
90Bow-164
90BowTif-164
90OPC-303
90PanSti-289
90ProSet-280
90SabBluS-6
90Sco-266
90ScoCan-266
90Top-303
90TopTif-303
90UppDec-396
90UppDecF-396
91MapLeaPTS-6
91OPC-354
91ProAHLCHL-360
91RochAmeKod-11
91RochAmePos-9
91ScoCan-388
91Top-354
91UppDec-399
91UppDecF-399

**Franche, Delphis**
51LavDaiQSHL-27
52St.LawS-91

**Francis, Bob**
90ProAHLIHL-611
94St.JohF-6
96ProBru-NNO

**Francis, Emile**
66Top-21
74OPCNHL-9
74Top-9
83HalFP-I7
85HalFC-231
92HalFL-10

**Francis, Ron**
80SauSteMG-14
81SauSteMG-12
82OPC-123
82OPCSti-129
82PosCer-7
82WhaJunHC-3
83OPC-138
83OPCSti-255
83PufSti-18
83WhaJunHC-5
847EDis-22
84KelAccD-4
84OPC-70
84OPCSti-196
84Top-54
84WhaJunW-6
857ECreCar-7
85OPC-140
85OPCBoxB-F
85OPCSti-172
85Top-140
85TopBoxB-F
85WhaJunW-7
86OPC-43
86OPCSti-51
86Top-43
86WhaJunT-8
87OPC-187
87OPCBoxB-J
87OPCMin-10
87OPCSti-206
87PanSti-43
87SauSteMG-8
87Top-187
87TopBoxB-J
87WhaJunBK-7
88FriLayS-20
88OPC-52
88OPCBoxB-A
88OPCSti-264
88PanSti-242
88Top-52
88TopBoxB-A
88WhaJunGR-7
89OPC-175
89OPCSti-269
89PanSti-221
89SauSteMG-13
89Top-175
89WhaJunM-8
90Bow-254
90BowTif-254
90Kra-13
90Kra-83
90OPC-311
90OPCPre-32
90PanSti-39
90ProSet-105
90ProSet-367
90Sco-70
90ScoCan-70
90ScoHotRS-37
90Top-311
90TopTeaSL-21
90TopTif-311
90UppDec-67
90UppDec-314
90UppDecF-67
90UppDecF-314
90WhaJr7E-11
91Bow-90
91OPC-130
91OPCPre-120
91PanSti-281
91Par-353
91ParFre-353
91PenCokE-10
91PenFoo-3
91PenFooCS-5
91Pin-167
91PinFre-167
91ProSet-188
91ProSetFre-188
91ProSetPla-214
91ScoAme-267
91ScoCan-487
91StaClu-73
91Top-130
91UppDec-299
91UppDecF-299
92Bow-123
92OPC-188
92PanSti-224
92PanStiFre-224
92Par-141
92ParEmel-141
92PenCokC-7
92PenFoo-7
92Pin-303
92PinFre-303
92ProSet-144
92Sco-267
92Sco-518
92ScoCan-267
92StaClu-352
92Top-322
92TopGol-322G
92Ult-163
92UppDec-291
93Don-261
93Lea-161
93OPCPre-424
93OPCPreG-424
93PanSti-81
93Par-160
93ParEmel-160
93PenFoo-14
93PenSti-2
93Pin-74
93PinCan-74
93Pow-188
93Sco-151
93ScoCan-151
93StaClu-385
93StaCluFDI-385
93StaCluO-385
93TopPre-424
93TopPreG-424
93Ult-44
93UppDec-351
94CanGamNHLP-183
94Don-122
94FinRinL-16
94Fla-134
94Fle-162
94HocWit-53
94Lea-235
94LeaLim-30
94OPCPre-139
94OPCPreSE-139
94Par-176
94ParGol-176
94PenFoo-9
94Pin-72
94PinArtP-72
94PinRinC-72
94Sco-244
94Sco90PC-18
94ScoGol-244
94ScoPla-244
94ScoPlaTS-244
94Sel-84
94SelGol-84
94SP-92
94SPDieCut-92
94StaClu-96
94StaCluFDI-96
94StaCluMOMS-96
94StaCluST-18
94StaCluSTWC-96
94TopPre-139
94TopPreSE-139
94Ult-163
94UppDec-12
94UppDecEleIce-12
94UppDecSPI-SP150
94UppDecSPIDC-SP150
95BeAPla-8
95BeAPSig-S8
95BeAPSigDC-S8
95Bow-31
95BowAllFoi-31
95CanGamNHLP-215
95ColCho-200
95ColCho-393
95ColChoPC-200
95ColChoPC-393
95ColChoPCP-200
95ColChoPCP-393
95Don-94
95DonEli-40
95DonEliDCS-40
95DonEliDCU-40
95DonIgn-10
95Emo-136
95EmoXce-7
95EmoXci-11
95Fin-127
95FinRef-127
95ImpSti-98
95Lea-45
95LeaLim-23
95Met-116
95MetIW-4
95NHLAcePC-7C
95ParInt-164
95ParIntEl-164
95ParIntPTP-PP47
95ParIntTW-6
95PenFoo-1
95Pin-39
95PinArtP-39
95PinRinC-39
95PlaOneoOne-77
95ProMag-91
95Sco-187
95ScoBlaIce-187
95ScoBlaIceAP-187
95SelCer-52
95SelCerDS-2
95SelCerDSG-2
95SelCerMG-52
95SkyImp-130
95SP-115
95StaClu-22
95StaCluMO-22
95StaCluMOMS-22
95StaCluPS-PS3
95Sum-42
95SumArtP-42
95SumIce-42
95Top-244
95TopOPCI-244
95TopPowL-5PL
95Ult-122
95Ult-384
95UltExtAtt-6
95UltGolM-122
95UltPrePiv-2
95UltPrePivGM-2
95UppDec-46
95UppDec-255
95UppDecAGPRW-23
95UppDecEleIce-46
95UppDecEleIce-255
95UppDecEleIceG-46
95UppDecEleIceG-255
95UppDecNHLAS-AS18
95UppDecPRE-R11
95UppDecPreR-R11
95UppDecSpeE-SE66
95UppDecSpeEdiG-SE66
95UppPreRP-R59
95Zen-35
96ColCho-212
96ColCho-328
96ColChoMVP-UD2
96ColChoMVPG-UD2
96Don-149
96DonCanI-93
96DonCanIGPP-93
96DonCanIRPP-93
96DonDom-4
96DonEli-40
96DonEliDCS-40
96DonPrePro-149
96Fla-75
96FlaBluI-75
96Fle-85
96Fle-137
96Fle-139
96FleArtRos-5
96FlePic-16
96FlePicF5-13
96FlePicFF-7
96FlePicJE-16
96KraUppD-44
96Lea-11
96LeaLim-52
96LeaLimG-52
96LeaPre-62
96LeaPreP-11
96LeaPrePP-62
96LeaPreSG-6
96LeaPreSte-6
96MetUni-125
96MetUniCS-3
96MetUniCSSP-3
96MetUniLW-5
96MetUniLWSP-5
96NHLACEPC-15
96NHLProSTA-91
96PenTri-1
96Pin-143
96PinArtP-143
96PinFoi-143
96PinPreS-143
96PinRinC-143
96PlaOneoOne-360
96Sco-56
96ScoArtPro-56
96ScoDeaCAP-56
96ScoGolB-56
96ScoSpeAP-56
96SelCer-12
96SelCerAP-12
96SelCerBlu-12
96SelCerMB-12
96SelCerMG-12
96SelCerMR-12
96SelCerRed-12
96SkyImp-100
96SkyImpB-4
96SP-127
96StaCluMO-45
96Sum-10
96SumArtP-10
96SumIce-10
96SumMet-10
96SumPreS-10
96SumUnt-4
96Ult-139
96UltGolM-139
96UltMr.Mom-3
96UppDec-133
96UppDecBD-101
96UppDecBDG-101
96UppDecIce-55
96UppDecIcePar-55
96Zen-10
96ZenArtP-10
96ZenChaS-7
96ZenChaSD-7
97ColCho-204
97ColChoSta-SQ54
97Don-137
97DonCanI-44
97DonCanIDS-44
97DonCanINP-20
97DonCanIPS-44
97DonEli-113
97DonEliAsp-113
97DonEliS-113
97DonLim-199
97DonLimExp-199
97DonPre-142
97DonPreCttC-142
97DonPreProG-137
97DonPreProS-137
97DonPri-77
97DonPriSoA-77
97Kat-116
97KatGol-116
97KatSil-116
97Lea-44
97LeaFraMat-44
97LeaFraMDC-44
97LeaInt-44
97LeaIntUI-44
97Pac-123
97PacCop-123
97PacCroR-109
97PacCroREG-109
97PacCroRIB-109
97PacCroRS-109
97PacDyn-100
97PacDynC-100
97PacDynDG-100
97PacDynEG-100
97PacDynIB-100
97PacDynR-100
97PacDynSil-100
97PacDynTan-63
97PacEmeGre-123
97PacIceB-123
97PacInv-111
97PacInvAZ-19
97PacInvC-111
97PacInvEG-111
97PacInvIB-111
97PacInvR-111
97PacInvS-111
97PacOme-184
97PacOmeC-184
97PacOmeDG-184
97PacOmeEG-184
97PacOmeG-184
97PacOmeIB-184
97PacPar-148
97PacParC-148
97PacParDG-148
97PacParEG-148
97PacParIB-148
97PacParRed-148
97PacParSil-148
97PacRed-123
97PacRev-112
97PacRevC-112
97PacRevE-112
97PacRevIB-112
97PacRevR-112
97PacRevS-112
97PacSil-123
97PacSlaSDC-8B
97Pin-78
97PinArtP-78
97PinBee-49
97PinBeeGP-49
97PinCer-121
97PinCerMB-121
97PinCerMG-121
97PinCerMR-121
97PinCerR-121
97PinIns-52
97PinInsCC-52
97PinInsEC-52
97PinPrePBB-78
97PinPrePBC-78
97PinPrePBM-78
97PinPrePBY-78
97PinPrePFC-78
97PinPrePFM-78
97PinPrePFY-78
97PinPrePla-78
97PinRinC-78
97PinTotCMPG-121
97PinTotCPB-121
97PinTotCPG-121
97PinTotCPR-121
97Sco-132
97ScoArtPro-132
97ScoGolBla-132
97ScoPen-5
97ScoPenPla-5
97ScoPenPre-5
97SPAut-126
97SPx-41
97SPxBro-41
97SPxGol-41
97SPxGraF-41
97SPxSil-41
97SPxSte-41
97Stu-74
97StuPrePG-74
97StuPrePS-74
97UppDec-135
97UppDecBD-11
97UppDecBDDD-11
97UppDecBDQD-11
97UppDecBDTD-11
97UppDecGDM-135
97UppDecIce-65
97UppDecIceP-65
97UppDecIPS-65
97UppDecSSM-SS25
97UppDecSSW-SS25
97Zen-50
97Zen5x7-53
97ZenGolImp-53
97ZenSilImp-53
97ZenZGol-50
97ZenZSil-50
98Be A PPA-174
98Be A PPAA-174
98Be A PPAAF-174
98Be A PPAM-M12
98Be A PPSE-174
98Be APG-174
98BowBes-50
98BowBesAR-50
98BowBesR-50
98Fin-50
98FinNo P-50
98FinNo PR-50
98FinRef-50
98O-PChr-4
98O-PChrR-4
98O-PChrSB-SB22
98O-PChrSBR-SB22
98Pac-351
98PacCroR-22
98PacCroRLS-22
98PacDynI-31
98PacDynIIB-31
98PacDynIR-31
98PacIceB-351
98PacOmeH-40
98PacOmeODI-40
98PacOmeR-40
98PacRed-351
98PacRev-23
98PacRevIS-23
98PacRevR-23
98SP Aut-14
98SP AutSM-S21
98Top-4
98TopGolLC1-22
98TopGolLC1B-22
98TopGolLC1BOoO-22
98TopGolLC1OoO-22
98TopGolLC1R-22
98TopGolLC1ROoO-22
98TopGolLC2-22
98TopGolLC2B-22
98TopGolLC2BOoO-22
98TopGolLC2OoO-22
98TopGolLC2R-22
98TopGolLC2ROoO-22
98TopGolLC3-22
98TopGolLC3B-22
98TopGolLC3BOoO-22
98TopGolLC3OoO-22
98TopGolLC3R-22
98TopGolLC3ROoO-22
98TopO-P-4
98TopSeaB-SB22
98UC-169
98UD ChoPCR-169
98UD ChoR-169
98UppDec-241
98UppDecBD-14
98UppDecDD-14
98UppDecE-241
98UppDecE1o1-241
98UppDecGR-241
98UppDecLSH-LS8
98UppDecLSHQ1-LS8
98UppDecLSHQ2-LS8
98UppDecLSHQ3-LS8
98UppDecM-35
98UppDecMGS-35
98UppDecMSS-35
98UppDecMSS-35
98UppDecQD-14
98UppDecTD-14
99Pac-70
99PacAur-25
99PacAurPD-25
99PacCop-70
99PacGol-70
99PacIceB-70
99PacPreD-70
99SP AutPS-14
99UppDecM-40
99UppDecMGS-40
99UppDecMSS-40
99UppDecMSS-40

**Francis, Ronny (Swede)**
65SweCorI-117B

**Francis, Todd**
83BraAle-27
94BraSmo-3

**Francois, Jean**
88RivDu R-23
97BowCHLAu-37
97BowCHLAu-160
99QuePeeWHWCCS-18

**Francz, R.**
95GerDELE-19

**Franek, Petr**
94CzeAPSE-204
95CzeAPSE-151
98LasVegT-5

**Frank, Jeff**
82RegPat-17
83RegPat-17

**Frank, Mark**
82MedHatT-3

**Franke, Peter**
94GerDELE-410
95GerDELE-408
96GerDELE-70

**Franklin, T.**
85HalFC-62

**Franks, Jim**
34BeeGro1P-272

**Franks, Mark**
907thInnSWHL-74
90SasBla-18
917thInnSWHL-116
91SasBla-17
92BraWheK-6
93HunBli-8
94HunBli-10

**Frankum, Paul**
95SolBar-6

**Frantti, Gordon**
91ProAHLCHL-515
94HunBli-11

**Franz, Georg**
89SweSemWCS-117
91SweSemWCS-175
93SweSemWCS-165
94FinnJaaK-283
94GerDELE-254
95GerDELE-252
96GerDELE-141

**Franzen, Rikard**
87SwePanS-9
89SweSemE-8
90SweSemE-81
91SweSemE-7
92SweSemE-33
94SweLeaE-108
94SweLeaESS-1
95SweLeaE-165
95SweLeaEM-13
95SweUppDE-4
95SweUppDE-219
95SweUppDE-249
96SweSemCDT-4
96SweSemW-51
98UD ChoS-2

**Franzi, Marcel**
95SwiHNL-451

**Frappier, Shawn**
92SudWol-7
93SudWol-7
93SudWolP-7
94SudWol-6
94SudWolP-19
95Sla-12

**Fraser, Barry**
88OilTenAnn-158

**Fraser, Chas.**
23V1451-39

**Fraser, Chris**
89WinSpi-4

**Fraser, Craig**
897thInnSOHL-74
907thInnSOHL-5
917thInnSOHL-34

**Fraser, Curt**
78CanuRoyB-5
79CanuRoyB-6
79OPC-117
79Top-117
80CanuSilD-8
80CanuTeal-8
80OPC-287
80PepCap-107
81CanuSilD-2
81CanuTeal-8
81OPC-334
82Canu-7
82OPC-343
82OPCSti-244
82PosCer-19
82VicCou-7
83BlaBorPos-7
83OPC-102
84OPC-34
84Top-29
85OPC-3
85OPCSti-24
85Top-3
86BlaCok-5
86OPC-31
86Top-31
87BlaCok-5
87PanSti-231
88NorStaADA-8
90ProAHLIHL-327
91ProAHLCHL-619

**Fraser, Iain**
897thInnSOHL-19
897thInnSOHL-186
897thInnSOHL-198
89OshGen-19
89OshGenP-25
907thInnSMC-89
91ProAHLIHL-468
93ClaProPro-49
93Don-478
93OPCPre-525
93OPCPreG-525
93Par-434
93ParCalC-C19
93ParCalCG-C19
93ParEmel-434
93Pow-419
93PowRooS-4
93Sco-625
93ScoCan-625
93ScoGol-625
93StaClu-485
93StaCluFDI-485
93StaCluO-485
93TopPre-525
93TopPreG-525
93Ult-73
93Ult-400
93UltPro-1
93UppDec-337
94ClaProP-15
94Don-270
94Lea-105
94OPCFinIns-6
94OPCPre-7
94OPCPreSE-7
94Par-187
94Par-280
94ParGol-187
94ParGol-280
94Pin-513
94PinArtP-513
94PinRinC-513
94StaClu-32
94StaCluFDI-32
94StaCluMOMS-32
94StaCluSTWC-32
94TopPre-7
94TopPreSE-7
94Ult-174
94UppDec-162
94UppDecEleIce-162
96KenTho-6

**Fraser, Kerry**
90ProSet-686

**Fraser, Legs**
51LavDaiQSHL-104

**Fraser, Scott**
94FreCan-13
95FreCan-11
98Pac-207
98PacIceB-207
98PacRed-207

**Fraser, Scott Jr.**
80QueRem-7

**Fraser, Scotty (Scott)**
23V1281PauC-53

**Fraser, Trever**
917thInnSWHL-171
92TacRoc-10
93TacRoc-9

**Fraszko, Adam**
89SweSemWCS-146

**Frawley, Dan**
83SprInd-9
86PenKod-9
87PanSti-153
87PenKod-9
87PenMask-4
88PanSti-338
89ProIHL-160
90ProAHLIHL-274
91ProAHLCHL-3
91RochAmeDD-8
91RochAmeKod-12
91RochAmePos-10

❑ 92RochAmeDD-6
❑ 92RochAmeKod-8
❑ 95RochAmeSS-3
**Frayn, Robert**
❑ 897thInnSOHL-175
❑ 907thInnSOHL-6
❑ 917thInnSOHL-184
**Frazer, Fritz**
❑ 51LavDaiQSHL-106
**Freadrich, Kyle**
❑ 96RegPat-17
**Frechette, Yanick**
❑ 907thInnSQMJHL-60
❑ 917thInnSQMJHL-237
**Frederick, Joe**
❑ 92NorMicW-5
❑ 93Cla-65
❑ 94ClaProP-131
**Frederick, Troy**
❑ 88BraWheK-8
❑ 89BraWheK-2
❑ 90ProAHLIHL-596
❑ 91ProAHLCHL-512
❑ 94CenHocL-22
❑ 95ForWorFT-9
**Fredericks, Ray**
❑ 51LavDaiS-104
❑ 52St.LawS-70
**Frederickson, Frank**
❑ 24HolCre-5
❑ 60Top-34
❑ 60TopSta-15
❑ 83HalFP-D3
❑ 85HalFC-49
**Fredriksson, Dennis**
❑ 91SweSemE-300
**Freer, Mark**
❑ 88ProAHL-126
❑ 89ProAHL-337
❑ 90ProAHLIHL-47
❑ 91Par-343
❑ 91ParFre-343
❑ 91ProAHLCHL-279
❑ 92Par-354
❑ 92ParEmel-354
❑ 92ProSet-127
❑ 92UppDec-445
❑ 93OPCPre-142
❑ 93OPCPreG-142
❑ 93PanSti-118
❑ 93StaClu-29
❑ 93StaCluFDI-29
❑ 93StaCluFDIO-29
❑ 93StaCluO-29
❑ 93TopPre-142
❑ 93TopPreG-142
❑ 95ColEdgI-132
**Freitag, Wayne**
❑ 63QueAce-7
❑ 63QueAceQ-6
**French, Chris**
❑ 96AlaGolKin-4
**French, John**
❑ 72WhaNewEWHA-7
❑ 73QuaOatWHA-33
❑ 74OPCWHA-33
❑ 76OPCWHA-105
**Frenette, Derek**
❑ 91ProAHLCHL-27
❑ 92PeoRivC-6
❑ 93PeoRiv-11
**Frescoln, Chris**
❑ 93MicWol-6
**Frestadius, Robert**
❑ 83SweSemE-157
❑ 86SwePanS-194
❑ 87SwePanS-196
❑ 89SweSemE-173
**Frew, Irv**
❑ 35DiaMatT2-22
❑ 35DiaMatT3-20
❑ 35DiaMatTI-23
**Frid, Rob**
❑ 93LonKni-8
❑ 97LouRivF-20
**Friday, Bill**
❑ 61SudWol-9
❑ 62SudWol-11
❑ 91UltOriS-85
❑ 91UltOriSF-85
**Friday, Bob**
❑ 51LavDaiQSHL-87
**Fridfinson, Wally**
❑ 24CreFal-3
❑ 24HolCre-1
**Fridgen, Dan**
❑ 82WhaJunHC-5
❑ 93RenEng-9
**Friesen, Curtis**
❑ 907thInnSWHL-47
**Friesen, Jeff**
❑ 93Cla-102
❑ 93ClaCla94-CL3
❑ 93ClaPromo-2
❑ 93DonTeaC-11
❑ 93Par-505
❑ 93ParEmel-505
❑ 93Pin-472
❑ 93PinCan-472
❑ 93UppDec-532
❑ 93UppDecPOE-E8
❑ 94BeAPla-R164
❑ 94Cla-10
❑ 94ClaAut-10
❑ 94ClaCHLAS-C4
❑ 94ClaDraGol-10
❑ 94ClaProP-202
❑ 94ClaProP-209
❑ 94ClaProP-AU3
❑ 94ClaROYS-R5
❑ 94ClaTri-T61
❑ 94Fin-11
❑ 94Fin-159
❑ 94FinBowB-R14
❑ 94FinBowBR-R14
❑ 94FinRef-11
❑ 94FinRef-159
❑ 94FinSupTW-11
❑ 94FinSupTW-159
❑ 94Fla-164
❑ 94Fle-196
❑ 94FleRooS-3
❑ 94Lea-482
❑ 94LeaLimWJC-3
❑ 94LeaPhe-9
❑ 94OPCPre-547
❑ 94OPCPreSE-547
❑ 94ParSE-SE166
❑ 94ParSEG-SE166
❑ 94Pin-252
❑ 94Pin-532
❑ 94PinArtP-252
❑ 94PinArtP-532
❑ 94PinRinC-252
❑ 94PinRinC-532
❑ 94PinRooTP-7
❑ 94Sco-203
❑ 94ScoGol-203
❑ 94ScoPla-203
❑ 94ScoTopRR-8
❑ 94Sel-176
❑ 94SelGol-176
❑ 94SelYouExp-YE9
❑ 94SP-145
❑ 94SPDieCut-145
❑ 94TopPre-547
❑ 94TopPreSE-547
❑ 94Ult-365
❑ 94UppDec-237
❑ 94UppDec-526
❑ 94UppDecEleIce-237
❑ 94UppDecEleIce-526
❑ 94UppDecSPI-SP161
❑ 94UppDecSPIDC-SP161
❑ 95Bow-84
❑ 95BowAllFoi-84
❑ 95CanGamNHLP-30
❑ 95CanGamNHLP-223
❑ 95ColCho-309
❑ 95ColCho-372
❑ 95ColChoPC-309
❑ 95ColChoPC-372
❑ 95ColChoPCP-309
❑ 95ColChoPCP-372
❑ 95Don-162
❑ 95DonCanWJT-21
❑ 95DonProPoi-11
❑ 95DonRooTea-7
❑ 95Emo-155
❑ 95Fin-27
❑ 95FinRef-27
❑ 95Ima-2
❑ 95ImaAut-2A
❑ 95ImaCleE-CE2
❑ 95ImaGol-2
❑ 95Lea-21
❑ 95LeaLim-62
❑ 95LeaStuR-7
❑ 95McDPin-MCD-31
❑ 95Met-129
❑ 95ParInt-182
❑ 95ParIntEl-182
❑ 95Pin-55
❑ 95PinArtP-55
❑ 95PinRinC-55
❑ 95PlaOneoOne-83
❑ 95ProMag-118
❑ 95Sco-91
❑ 95ScoBlaIce-91
❑ 95ScoBlaIceAP-91
❑ 95ScoChelt-10
❑ 95ScoGolBla-11
❑ 95SelCer-56
❑ 95SelCerMG-56
❑ 95SkyImp-147
❑ 95SkyImp-235
❑ 95SP-133
❑ 95StaClu-106
❑ 95StaCluMOMS-106
❑ 95Sum-68
❑ 95SumArtP-68
❑ 95SumIce-68
❑ 95Top-360
❑ 95TopCanWJ-15CJ
❑ 95TopNewG-18NG
❑ 95TopOPCI-360
❑ 95TopSupSki-69
❑ 95TopSupSkiPla-69
❑ 95TopYouS-YS6
❑ 95Ult-145
❑ 95UltAllRoo-4
❑ 95UltAllRooGM-4
❑ 95UltGolM-145
❑ 95UppDec-134
❑ 95UppDecEleIce-134
❑ 95UppDecEleIceG-134
❑ 95UppDecSpeE-SE74
❑ 95UppDecSpeEdiG-SE74
❑ 95UppDecWJA-13
❑ 95Zen-65
❑ 96BeAPAut-190
❑ 96BeAPAutSil-190
❑ 96BeAPla-190
❑ 96ColCho-238
❑ 96Don-79
❑ 96DonEli-53
❑ 96DonEliDCS-53
❑ 96DonPrePro-79
❑ 96Lea-87
❑ 96LeaLim-83
❑ 96LeaLimG-83
❑ 96LeaPre-97
❑ 96LeaPreP-87
❑ 96LeaPrePP-97
❑ 96NHLProSTA-118
❑ 96Pin-18
❑ 96PinArtP-18
❑ 96PinFoi-18
❑ 96PinPreS-18
❑ 96PinRinC-18
❑ 96PlaOneoOne-362
❑ 96Sco-4
❑ 96ScoArtPro-4
❑ 96ScoDeaCAP-4
❑ 96ScoGolB-4
❑ 96ScoSpeAP-4
❑ 96SelCer-61
❑ 96SelCerAP-61
❑ 96SelCerBlu-61
❑ 96SelCerMB-61
❑ 96SelCerMG-61
❑ 96SelCerMR-61
❑ 96SelCerRed-61
❑ 96SkyImp-116
❑ 96SP-143
❑ 96Sum-144
❑ 96SumArtP-144
❑ 96SumIce-144
❑ 96SumMet-144
❑ 96SumPreS-144
❑ 96UppDec-332
❑ 96UppDecIce-58
❑ 96UppDecIcePar-58
❑ 96Zen-89
❑ 96ZenArtP-89
❑ 97ColCho-215
❑ 97ColChoSta-SQ10
❑ 97Don-55
❑ 97DonCanI-81
❑ 97DonCanIDS-81
❑ 97DonCanIPS-81
❑ 97DonEli-93
❑ 97DonEliAsp-93
❑ 97DonEliS-93
❑ 97DonLim-72
❑ 97DonLim-196
❑ 97DonLimExp-72
❑ 97DonLimExp-196
❑ 97DonPre-14
❑ 97DonPreCttC-14
❑ 97DonPreProG-55
❑ 97DonPreProS-55
❑ 97DonPri-70
❑ 97DonPriSoA-70
❑ 97Lea-102
❑ 97LeaFraMat-102
❑ 97LeaFraMDC-102
❑ 97LeaInt-102
❑ 97LeaIntUI-102
❑ 97Pac-63
❑ 97PacCop-63
❑ 97PacCroR-119
❑ 97PacCroREG-119
❑ 97PacCroRIB-119
❑ 97PacCroRS-119
❑ 97PacDyn-110
❑ 97PacDynC-110
❑ 97PacDynDG-110
❑ 97PacDynEG-110
❑ 97PacDynIB-110
❑ 97PacDynR-110
❑ 97PacDynSil-110
❑ 97PacDynTan-60
❑ 97PacEmeGre-63
❑ 97PacIceB-63
❑ 97PacInv-124
❑ 97PacInvC-124
❑ 97PacInvEG-124
❑ 97PacInvIB-124
❑ 97PacInvR-124
❑ 97PacInvS-124
❑ 97PacOme-200
❑ 97PacOmeC-200
❑ 97PacOmeDG-200
❑ 97PacOmeEG-200
❑ 97PacOmeG-200
❑ 97PacOmeIB-200
❑ 97PacPar-164
❑ 97PacParC-164
❑ 97PacParDG-164
❑ 97PacParEG-164
❑ 97PacParIB-164
❑ 97PacParRed-164
❑ 97PacParSil-164
❑ 97PacRed-63
❑ 97PacRev-123
❑ 97PacRevC-123
❑ 97PacRevE-123
❑ 97PacRevIB-123
❑ 97PacRevR-123
❑ 97PacRevS-123
❑ 97PacSil-63
❑ 97Pin-119
❑ 97PinCer-81
❑ 97PinCerMB-81
❑ 97PinCerMG-81
❑ 97PinCerMR-81
❑ 97PinCerR-81
❑ 97PinIns-121
❑ 97PinPrePBB-119
❑ 97PinPrePBC-119
❑ 97PinPrePBM-119
❑ 97PinPrePBY-119
❑ 97PinPrePFC-119
❑ 97PinPrePFM-119
❑ 97PinPrePFY-119
❑ 97PinPrePla-119
❑ 97PinTotCMPG-81
❑ 97PinTotCPB-81
❑ 97PinTotCPG-81
❑ 97PinTotCPR-81
❑ 97Sco-170
❑ 97SPAut-134
❑ 97Stu-98
❑ 97StuPrePG-98
❑ 97StuPrePS-98
❑ 97UppDec-358
❑ 97Zen-33
❑ 97ZenZGol-33
❑ 97ZenZSil-33
❑ 98Be A PPA-267
❑ 98Be A PPAA-267
❑ 98Be A PPAAF-267
❑ 98Be A PPSE-267
❑ 98Be APG-267
❑ 98BowBes-41
❑ 98BowBesAR-41
❑ 98BowBesR-41
❑ 98Fin-32
❑ 98FinNo P-32
❑ 98FinNo PR-32
❑ 98FinRef-32
❑ 98O-PChr-128
❑ 98O-PChrR-128
❑ 98Pac-379
❑ 98PacAur-166
❑ 98PacCroR-118
❑ 98PacCroRLS-118
❑ 98PacDynI-164
❑ 98PacDynIIB-164
❑ 98PacDynIR-164
❑ 98PacIceB-379
❑ 98PacOmeH-209
❑ 98PacOmeODI-209
❑ 98PacOmeR-209
❑ 98PacPar-209
❑ 98PacParC-209
❑ 98PacParEG-209
❑ 98PacParH-209
❑ 98PacParIB-209
❑ 98PacParS-209
❑ 98PacRed-379
❑ 98PacRev-126
❑ 98PacRevIS-126
❑ 98PacRevR-126
❑ 98SP Aut-76
❑ 98Top-128
❑ 98TopGolLC1-60
❑ 98TopGolLC1B-60
❑ 98TopGolLC1BOoO-60
❑ 98TopGolLC1OoO-60
❑ 98TopGolLC1R-60
❑ 98TopGolLC1ROoO-60
❑ 98TopGolLC2-60
❑ 98TopGolLC2B-60
❑ 98TopGolLC2BOoO-60
❑ 98TopGolLC2OoO-60
❑ 98TopGolLC2R-60
❑ 98TopGolLC2ROoO-60
❑ 98TopGolLC3-60
❑ 98TopGolLC3B-60
❑ 98TopGolLC3BOoO-60
❑ 98TopGolLC3OoO-60
❑ 98TopGolLC3R-60
❑ 98TopGolLC3ROoO-60
❑ 98TopO-P-128
❑ 98UC-174
❑ 98UD ChoPCR-174
❑ 98UD ChoR-174
❑ 98UppDec-351
❑ 98UppDecE-351
❑ 98UppDecE1o1-351
❑ 98UppDecGR-351
❑ 98UppDecM-174
❑ 98UppDecMGS-174
❑ 98UppDecMSS-174
❑ 98UppDecMSS-174
❑ 99Pac-370
❑ 99PacAur-120
❑ 99PacAurPD-120
❑ 99PacCop-370
❑ 99PacGol-370
❑ 99PacIceB-370
❑ 99PacPreD-370
❑ 99RetHoc-68
❑ 99SP AutPS-76
❑ 99UppDecM-175
❑ 99UppDecMGS-175
❑ 99UppDecMPS-JF
❑ 99UppDecMSS-175
❑ 99UppDecMSS-175
❑ 99UppDecRG-68
❑ 99UppDecRP-68
**Friesen, Karl**
❑ 89SweSemWCS-103
❑ 91SweSemWCS-154
❑ 94GerDELE-314
❑ 95GerDELE-360
**Friesen, Rob**
❑ 94GuiFla-6
**Friesen, Terry**
❑ 95SwiCurB-4
❑ 98BowCHL-62
❑ 98BowCHLGA-62
❑ 98BowCHLOI-62
❑ 98BowChrC-62
❑ 98BowChrCGA-62
❑ 98BowChrCGAR-62
❑ 98BowChrCOI-62
❑ 98BowChrCOIR-62
❑ 98BowChrCR-62
**Friest, Ron**
❑ 82NorStaPos-10
**Frig, Len**
❑ 74NHLActSta-69
❑ 74OPCNHL-242
❑ 74Top-242
❑ 75OPCNHL-174
❑ 75Top-174
❑ 76OPCNHL-197
❑ 77OPCNHL-384
**Friman, Jerry**
❑ 92SweSemE-96
❑ 93SweSemE-68
**Friman, Kari-Pekka**
❑ 93FinnJyvHS-225
❑ 93FinnSIS-190
❑ 94FinnSIS-104
❑ 95FinnSIS-175
❑ 95FinnSIS-340
**Fritz, George**
❑ 94GerDELE-430
❑ 95GerDELE-397
**Fritz, Tommy**
❑ 89SweSemE-105
❑ 90SweSemE-108
❑ 91SweSemE-112
❑ 92SweSemE-129
**Frkan, Jan**
❑ 96SloPeeWT-7
**Froese, Bob**
❑ 78LouGea-5
❑ 83FlyJCP-10
❑ 83OPC-265
❑ 83OPCSti-183
❑ 84OPC-159
❑ 84OPCSti-113
❑ 84Top-117
❑ 85FlyPos-10
❑ 86OPC-55
❑ 86OPC-263
❑ 86OPC-264
❑ 86OPCSti-182
❑ 86OPCSti-186
❑ 86OPCSti-193
❑ 86OPCSti-236
❑ 86Top-55
❑ 86TopStiIns-7
❑ 87OPC-195
❑ 87Top-195
❑ 88PanSti-299
❑ 89PanSti-284
❑ 89RanMarMB-33
**Froese, Colin**
❑ 91AirCanSJHL-E13
❑ 92MPSPhoSJHL-37
**Froh, David**
❑ 93OshGen-5
❑ 95Sla-192
**Frolikov, Alexei**
❑ 90OPC-502
**Frolov, Anatoli**
❑ 74SweHocS-48
**Frolov, Dmitri**
❑ 90OPC-523
❑ 92UppDec-348
❑ 94FinnJaaK-151
❑ 95FinnSemWC-130
❑ 96GerDELE-210
**Frosch, Frantisek**
❑ 94GerDELE-428
❑ 95GerDELE-391
❑ 96GerDELE-76
❑ 98GerDELE-35
**Frutel, Christian**
❑ 94GerDELE-315
**Fry, Curtis**
❑ 92BriColJHL-51
**Fry, Rick**
❑ 89PorWinH-8
**Fryar, Mike**
❑ 95NorlowH-9
**Frycer, Miroslav**
❑ 81NordPos-7
❑ 81SweSemHVS-65
❑ 82MapLeaP-11
❑ 82MapLeaP-12
❑ 82OPC-321
❑ 82OPCSti-65
❑ 82PosCer-18
❑ 83MapLeaP-6
❑ 83OPC-330
❑ 83OPCSti-38
❑ 83Vac-86
❑ 84MapLeaP-9
❑ 85MapLeaP-12
❑ 85OPC-198
❑ 85OPCSti-21
❑ 86MapLeaP-9
❑ 86OPC-68
❑ 86OPCSti-142
❑ 86Top-68
❑ 87MapLeaP-7
❑ 87MapLeaPLA-15
❑ 87MapLeaPO-7
❑ 87OPCSti-158
❑ 88OilTeal-6
❑ 88OilTenAnn-153
**Frydl, Karel**
❑ 96CzeAPSE-104
**Frykbo, Anders**
❑ 86SwePanS-266
❑ 89SweSemE-233
❑ 90SweSemE-72
❑ 91SweSemE-245
**Frylen, Edvin**
❑ 92SweSemE-280
❑ 92SweSemE-351
❑ 93Par-536
❑ 93ParEmel-536
❑ 93SweSemE-245
❑ 93UppDec-572
❑ 94SweLeaE-105
❑ 94SweLeaENHLD-5
❑ 95SigRoo-17
❑ 95SigRooSig-17
❑ 95SweLeaE-299
❑ 95SweUppDE-188
**Ftorek, Robbie**
❑ 74PhoRoaWP-4
❑ 75OPCWHA-19
❑ 75RoaPhoWHA-8
❑ 76OPCWHA-13
❑ 76RoaPhoWHA-3
❑ 77OPCWHA-35
❑ 79OPC-267
❑ 80NordPos-10
❑ 80OPC-35
❑ 80PepCap-65
❑ 80Top-35
❑ 81OPC-274
❑ 81OPCSti-72
❑ 81PosSta-24
❑ 82OPC-223
❑ 82PosCer-13
❑ 83OPC-244
❑ 88KinSmo-10
❑ 89HalCit-7
❑ 89ProAHL-157
❑ 90NordPet-8
❑ 92FutTre76CC-189
❑ 96Dev-NNO
**Fuchs, Andrej**
❑ 94GerDELE-351
❑ 95GerDELE-323
❑ 96GerDELE-101
**Fuchs, Boris**
❑ 94GerDELE-356
❑ 95GerDELE-326
❑ 96GerDELE-103
**Fuchs, Lothar**
❑ 70SweHocS-375
**Fuhr, Grant**
❑ 81OilRedR-1
❑ 81OilWesEM-2
❑ 82OilRedR-31
❑ 82OPC-105
❑ 82OPCSti-95
❑ 82OPCSti-161
❑ 82PosCer-6
❑ 82VicCou-8
❑ 83OilMcD-19
❑ 83OPC-27
❑ 83Vac-24
❑ 84OilRedR-31
❑ 84OilTeal-5
❑ 84OPC-241
❑ 84OPCSti-259
❑ 85OilRedR-31
❑ 85OPC-207
❑ 85OPCSti-221
❑ 86KraDra-17
❑ 86OilRedR-31
❑ 86OilTeal-31
❑ 86OPC-56
❑ 86OPCSti-67
❑ 86OPCSti-121
❑ 86Top-56
❑ 87OilTeal-31
❑ 87OPC-178
❑ 87OPCSti-85
❑ 87PanSti-254
❑ 87Top-178
❑ 88EssAllSta-12
❑ 88OilTeal-7
❑ 88OilTenAnn-65
❑ 88OilTenAnn-130
❑ 88OPC-59
❑ 88OPCMin-9
❑ 88OPCSti-122
❑ 88OPCSti-212
❑ 88OPCSti-223
❑ 88PanSti-52
❑ 88PanSti-188
❑ 88PanSti-403
❑ 88Top-59
❑ 88TopStiIns-6
❑ 89Kra-11
❑ 89OilTeal-6
❑ 89OPC-192
❑ 89OPCSti-228
❑ 89SweSemWCS-53
❑ 89Top-192
❑ 90Bow-189
❑ 90BowTif-189
❑ 90OPC-321
❑ 90PanSti-230
❑ 90ProSet-82
❑ 90Sco-275
❑ 90ScoCan-275
❑ 90Top-321
❑ 90TopTif-321
❑ 90UppDec-264
❑ 90UppDecF-264
❑ 91Bow-111
❑ 91Bow-407
❑ 91Gil-19
❑ 91Kra-9
❑ 91MapLeaP-13
❑ 91OPC-84
❑ 91OPCPre-100
❑ 91OPCPre-191
❑ 91Par-175
❑ 91ParFre-175
❑ 91Pin-168
❑ 91PinFre-168
❑ 91ProSet-78
❑ 91ProSet-494
❑ 91ProSetFre-78
❑ 91ProSetFre-494
❑ 91ProSetPC-27
❑ 91ProSetPla-117
❑ 91ScoAme-114
❑ 91ScoCan-114
❑ 91ScoCan-608
❑ 91ScoRoo-58T
❑ 91StaClu-258
❑ 91Top-84
❑ 91UppDec-264
❑ 91UppDec-553
❑ 91UppDecF-264
❑ 91UppDecF-553
❑ 92Bow-114
❑ 92HumDum1-9
❑ 92Kra-35
❑ 92OPC-31
❑ 92OPC-119
❑ 92OPC25Al-15
❑ 92PanSti-75
❑ 92PanStiFre-75
❑ 92Par-182
❑ 92Par-250
❑ 92Par-497
❑ 92ParEmel-182
❑ 92ParEmel-250
❑ 92ParEmel-497
❑ 92ParPre-PV5
❑ 92Pin-267
❑ 92Pin-301
❑ 92PinFre-267
❑ 92PinFre-301
❑ 92ProSet-183
❑ 92Sco-20
❑ 92Sco-437
❑ 92ScoCan-20
❑ 92ScoCan-437
❑ 92SeaPat-54
❑ 92StaClu-412
❑ 92Top-350
❑ 92TopGol-350G
❑ 92Ult-210
❑ 92UppDec-271
❑ 93Don-34
❑ 93HigLinGG-3
❑ 93KenStaLA-3
❑ 93Lea-66
❑ 93LeaPaiWar-5
❑ 93OPCPre-218
❑ 93OPCPreG-218
❑ 93PanSti-108
❑ 93Par-22
❑ 93ParChePH-D7
❑ 93ParEmel-22
❑ 93Pin-65
❑ 93PinCan-65
❑ 93PinMas-1
❑ 93Pow-27
❑ 93PowNet-3
❑ 93SabNoc-4
❑ 93Sco-75
❑ 93ScoCan-75
❑ 93StaClu-260
❑ 93StaCluFDI-260
❑ 93StaCluMasP-15
❑ 93StaCluMasPW-15
❑ 93StaCluO-260
❑ 93TopPre-218
❑ 93TopPreG-218
❑ 93Ult-13
❑ 93UppDec-163
❑ 93UppDecGGO-GG10
❑ 93UppDecSP-15
❑ 94BeAP99A-G7
❑ 94CanGamNHLP-273
❑ 94CanGamNHLP-333
❑ 94Don-212
❑ 94EASpo-18
❑ 94FinRinL-4
❑ 94HocWit-40
❑ 94KenStaLC-3
❑ 94Lea-78
❑ 94OPCPre-80
❑ 94Pin-421
❑ 94PinArtP-421
❑ 94PinRinC-421
❑ 94Sel-93
❑ 94SelGol-93
❑ 94TopPre-80
❑ 94Ult-262
❑ 95BeAPla-196
❑ 95BeAPSig-S196
❑ 95BeAPSigDC-S196
❑ 95Bow-25
❑ 95BowAllFoi-25
❑ 95CanGamNHLP-8

❑ 95CanGamNHLP-245
❑ 95Don-310
❑ 95DonEli-42
❑ 95DonEliDCS-42
❑ 95DonEliDCU-42
❑ 95DonEliPW-9
❑ 95DonEliPW-P9
❑ 95Fin-113
❑ 95FinRef-113
❑ 95Kra-28
❑ 95Met-123
❑ 95NoFeaAdCa-1
❑ 95ParInt-443
❑ 95ParIntEl-443
❑ 95ParIntPTP-PP9
❑ 95ParIntPTP-PP34
❑ 95Sco-228
❑ 95ScoBlaIce-228
❑ 95ScoBlaIceAP-228
❑ 95SP-126
❑ 95StaClu-24
❑ 95StaCluMOMS-24
❑ 95Top-242
❑ 95TopOPCI-242
❑ 95TopSupSki-88
❑ 95TopSupSkiPla-88
❑ 95Ult-298
❑ 95UppDec-484
❑ 95UppDecEleIce-484
❑ 95UppDecEleIceG-484
❑ 95UppDecSpeE-SE158
❑ 95UppDecSpeEdiG-SE158
❑ 95Zen-107
❑ 96BeAPStaTP-9
❑ 96ColCho-224
❑ 96Don-117
❑ 96DonCanI-109
❑ 96DonCanI-148
❑ 96DonCanIGPP-109
❑ 96DonCanIGPP-148
❑ 96DonCanIRPP-109
❑ 96DonCanIRPP-148
❑ 96DonEli-29
❑ 96DonEliDCS-29
❑ 96DonEliP-12
❑ 96DonPrePro-117
❑ 96Fla-80
❑ 96FlaBluI-80
❑ 96Fle-96
❑ 96Lea-64
❑ 96LeaLim-48
❑ 96LeaLimG-48
❑ 96LeaPreP-64
❑ 96MetUni-131
❑ 96NHLACEPC-16
❑ 96Pin-181
❑ 96PinArtP-181
❑ 96PinFoi-181
❑ 96PinPreS-181
❑ 96PinRinC-181
❑ 96Sco-91
❑ 96ScoArtPro-91
❑ 96ScoDeaCAP-91
❑ 96ScoGolB-91
❑ 96ScoSpeAP-91
❑ 96SelCer-35
❑ 96SelCerAP-35
❑ 96SelCerBlu-35
❑ 96SelCerMB-35
❑ 96SelCerMG-35
❑ 96SelCerMR-35
❑ 96SelCerRed-35
❑ 96SkyImp-112
❑ 96SP-133
❑ 96SPxHolH-HH10
❑ 96Sum-14
❑ 96SumArtP-14
❑ 96SumIce-14
❑ 96SumMet-14
❑ 96SumPreS-14
❑ 96TeaOut-66
❑ 96TopPicID-ID15
❑ 96Ult-145
❑ 96UltGolM-145
❑ 96UppDec-140
❑ 96UppDecBD-128
❑ 96UppDecBDG-128
❑ 96UppDecGN-X33
❑ 96UppDecIce-62
❑ 96UppDecIcePar-62
❑ 96Zen-82
❑ 96ZenArtP-82
❑ 96ZenChaS-3
❑ 96ZenChaS-P3
❑ 96ZenChaSD-3
❑ 97ColCho-225
❑ 97Don-153
❑ 97DonCanI-95
❑ 97DonCanIDS-95
❑ 97DonCanIPS-95
❑ 97DonEli-110
❑ 97DonEliAsp-110
❑ 97DonEliS-110
❑ 97DonLim-32
❑ 97DonLimExp-32
❑ 97DonLimFOTG-45
❑ 97DonPre-60
❑ 97DonPreCttC-60
❑ 97DonPreProG-153
❑ 97DonPreProS-153
❑ 97DonPri-82
❑ 97DonPriPG-19
❑ 97DonPriPGP-19
❑ 97DonPriSoA-82
❑ 97Kat-128
❑ 97KatGol-128
❑ 97KatSil-128
❑ 97Lea-123
❑ 97LeaFraMat-123
❑ 97LeaFraMDC-123
❑ 97LeaInt-123
❑ 97LeaIntUI-123
❑ 97Pac-228
❑ 97PacCop-228
❑ 97PacCroR-116
❑ 97PacCroREG-116
❑ 97PacCroRFODC-17
❑ 97PacCroRIB-116
❑ 97PacCroRS-116
❑ 97PacDyn-106
❑ 97PacDynC-106
❑ 97PacDynDG-106
❑ 97PacDynEG-106
❑ 97PacDynIB-106
❑ 97PacDynR-106
❑ 97PacDynSil-106
❑ 97PacDynSto-19
❑ 97PacDynTan-18
❑ 97PacEmeGre-228
❑ 97PacIceB-228
❑ 97PacInTheCLC-18
❑ 97PacInv-119
❑ 97PacInvC-119
❑ 97PacInvEG-119
❑ 97PacInvIB-119
❑ 97PacInvR-119
❑ 97PacInvS-119
❑ 97PacOme-193
❑ 97PacOmeC-193
❑ 97PacOmeDG-193
❑ 97PacOmeEG-193
❑ 97PacOmeG-193
❑ 97PacOmeIB-193
❑ 97PacPar-158
❑ 97PacParC-158
❑ 97PacParDG-158
❑ 97PacParEG-158
❑ 97PacParGSL-18
❑ 97PacParIB-158
❑ 97PacParRed-158
❑ 97PacParSil-158
❑ 97PacRed-228
❑ 97PacRev-120
❑ 97PacRevC-120
❑ 97PacRevE-120
❑ 97PacRevIB-120
❑ 97PacRevR-120
❑ 97PacRevRtSD-17
❑ 97PacRevS-120
❑ 97PacSil-228
❑ 97Pin-81
❑ 97PinArtP-81
❑ 97PinBee-44
❑ 97PinBeeGP-44
❑ 97PinCer-10
❑ 97PinCerMB-10
❑ 97PinCerMG-10
❑ 97PinCerMR-10
❑ 97PinCerR-10
❑ 97PinIns-51
❑ 97PinInsCC-51
❑ 97PinInsEC-51
❑ 97PinInsSto-20
❑ 97PinInsSUG-6A/B
❑ 97PinInsSUG-6C/D
❑ 97PinMas-10
❑ 97PinMasDC-10
❑ 97PinMasJ-10
❑ 97PinPrePBB-81
❑ 97PinPrePBC-81
❑ 97PinPrePBM-81
❑ 97PinPrePBY-81
❑ 97PinPrePFC-81
❑ 97PinPrePFM-81
❑ 97PinPrePFY-81
❑ 97PinPrePla-81
❑ 97PinRinC-81
❑ 97PinTin-2
❑ 97PinTotCMPG-10
❑ 97PinTotCPB-10
❑ 97PinTotCPG-10
❑ 97PinTotCPR-10
❑ 97Sco-5
❑ 97ScoArtPro-5
❑ 97ScoBlu-11
❑ 97ScoBluPla-11
❑ 97ScoBluPre-11
❑ 97ScoGolBla-5
❑ 97ScoNetW-10
❑ 97SPAut-143
❑ 97SPAutSotT-GF
❑ 97Stu-102
❑ 97StuPrePG-102
❑ 97StuPrePS-102
❑ 97UppDec-145
❑ 97UppDecBD-148
❑ 97UppDecBDDD-148
❑ 97UppDecBDQD-148
❑ 97UppDecBDTD-148
❑ 97Zen-60
❑ 97Zen5x7-14
❑ 97ZenGolImp-14
❑ 97ZenSilImp-14
❑ 97ZenZGol-60
❑ 97ZenZSil-60
❑ 98Be A PPA-122
❑ 98Be A PPAA-122
❑ 98Be A PPAAF-122
❑ 98Be A PPTBASG-122
❑ 98Be APG-122
❑ 98BowBes-22
❑ 98BowBesAR-22
❑ 98BowBesR-22
❑ 98Fin-27
❑ 98FinNo P-27
❑ 98FinNo PR-27
❑ 98FinRef-27
❑ 98McDGreT-T7
❑ 98O-PChr-114
❑ 98O-PChrBFtP-5
❑ 98O-PChrBFtPR-5
❑ 98O-PChrR-114
❑ 98Pac-31
❑ 98PacAur-160
❑ 98PacAurCF-41
❑ 98PacAurCFC-41
❑ 98PacAurCFIB-41
❑ 98PacAurCFR-41
❑ 98PacAurCFS-41
❑ 98PacCroR-114
❑ 98PacCroRLS-114
❑ 98PacDynI-157
❑ 98PacDynIIB-157
❑ 98PacDynIIW-8
❑ 98PacDynIR-157
❑ 98PacDynITC-22
❑ 98PacIceB-31
❑ 98PacOmeH-202
❑ 98PacOmeODI-202
❑ 98PacOmeR-202
❑ 98PacPar-203
❑ 98PacParC-203
❑ 98PacParEG-203
❑ 98PacParGSLC-17
❑ 98PacParH-203
❑ 98PacParIB-203
❑ 98PacParS-203
❑ 98PacParTCD-22
❑ 98PacRed-31
❑ 98PacRev-122
❑ 98PacRevIS-122
❑ 98PacRevR-122
❑ 98SPxFin-77
❑ 98SPxFinR-77
❑ 98SPxFinS-77
❑ 98Top-114
❑ 98TopBlaFTP-5
❑ 98TopGolLC1-95
❑ 98TopGolLC1B-95
❑ 98TopGolLC1BOoO-95
❑ 98TopGolLC1OoO-95
❑ 98TopGolLC1R-95
❑ 98TopGolLC1ROoO-95
❑ 98TopGolLC2-95
❑ 98TopGolLC2B-95
❑ 98TopGolLC2BOoO-95
❑ 98TopGolLC2OoO-95
❑ 98TopGolLC2R-95
❑ 98TopGolLC2ROoO-95
❑ 98TopGolLC3-95
❑ 98TopGolLC3B-95
❑ 98TopGolLC3BOoO-95
❑ 98TopGolLC3OoO-95
❑ 98TopGolLC3R-95
❑ 98TopGolLC3ROoO-95
❑ 98TopO-P-114
❑ 98UppDec-362
❑ 98UppDecE-362
❑ 98UppDecE1o1-362
❑ 98UppDecGR-362
❑ 99Pac-356
❑ 99PacAur-125
❑ 99PacAurGU-17
❑ 99PacAurPD-125
❑ 99PacCop-356
❑ 99PacGol-356
❑ 99PacIceB-356
❑ 99PacIn tCN-17
❑ 99PacPreD-356
❑ 99PacTeaL-23
❑ 99UppDecM-185
❑ 99UppDecMGS-185
❑ 99UppDecMSS-185
❑ 99UppDecMSS-185

**Fujita, Ryan**
❑ 907thInnSWHL-105
❑ 917thInnSWHL-110
❑ 91SasBla-19

**Fujtsawa, Yoshifumi**
❑ 96AlaGolKin-5

**Fukami, Scott**
❑ 88LetHur-7
❑ 907thInnSWHL-259
❑ 917thInnSWHL-69

**Fukushima, Shane**
❑ 95NorIowH-10

**Fullan, Larry**
❑ 74NHLActSta-324

**Fullum, Rival**
❑ 87KitRan-12
❑ 88KitRan-12
❑ 89KitRan-13
❑ 907thInnSMC-46
❑ 907thInnSOHL-24
❑ 907thInnSOHL-182
❑ 917thInnSOHL-21
❑ 91CorRoy-16
❑ 93WheThu-UD4
❑ 94ThuBayS-8
❑ 95ThuBayS-8

**Funk, Florian**
❑ 94GerDELE-136
❑ 95GerDELE-138
❑ 96GerDELE-35
❑ 98GerDELE-169

**Funk, Lorenz**
❑ 72SweSemWC-102
❑ 79PanSti-105
❑ 94GerDELE-81
❑ 95GerDELE-87
❑ 96GerDELE-34
❑ 98GerDELE-168

**Furey, Kirk**
❑ 93OweSouPla-8

**Furlan, Frank**
❑ 89HamRoaA-6

**Furrer, Gaston**
❑ 72SweSemWC-140

**Fusco, Mark**
❑ 84WhaJunW-7
❑ 85OPC-74
❑ 85Top-74

**Fuster, Marco**
❑ 91RicRen-17

**Fyfuglien, Jamie**
❑ 91AirCanSJHL-C21

**Gabler, Michael**
❑ 94GerDELE-293

**Gabriel, Jeff**
❑ 93RenEng-10
❑ 94GreMon-16

**Gador, Rob**
❑ 90CinCyc-28

**Gadowsky, Guy**
❑ 91RicRen-18
❑ 92RicRen-5

**Gadsby, Bill**
❑ 44BeeGro2P-96
❑ 44BeeGro2P-167
❑ 44BeeGro2P-312
❑ 51Par-37
❑ 52Par-56
❑ 53Par-76
❑ 54Par-87
❑ 54Top-20
❑ 57Top-65
❑ 58Top-34
❑ 59Top-62
❑ 60ShiCoi-90
❑ 60Top-22
❑ 61Par-27
❑ 61ShiCoi-79
❑ 62Par-25
❑ 62YorIroOTra-31
❑ 63ChePho-14
❑ 63Par-59
❑ 63TorSta-12
❑ 63YorWhiB-39
❑ 64BeeGro3P-70
❑ 64CocCap-40
❑ 64Top-96
❑ 65Coc-40
❑ 65Top-44
❑ 76OldTim-7
❑ 81RedWinOld-4
❑ 83HalFP-H4
❑ 85HalFC-110
❑ 91Kra-74
❑ 91UltOriS-69
❑ 91UltOriSF-69
❑ 92ParParR-PR9
❑ 94ParMisL-89
❑ 94ParMisL-137
❑ 94ParTalB-54

**Gaetz, Link**
❑ 88NorStaADA-9
❑ 89ProIHL-88
❑ 90OPCPre-33
❑ 90ProAHLIHL-110
❑ 90Sco-411
❑ 90ScoCan-411
❑ 91OPCIns-1S
❑ 91Pin-339
❑ 91Pin-412
❑ 91PinFre-339
❑ 91PinFre-412
❑ 91ProSet-561
❑ 91ProSetFre-561
❑ 91ShaSanJSA-7
❑ 94CenHocL-74

**Gaffar, Shayne**
❑ 907thInnSOHL-34
❑ 917thInnSOHL-12
❑ 91CorRoy-15

**Gage, Joaquin**
❑ 917thInnSWHL-46
❑ 93PriAlbR-5
❑ 94CapBreO-8
❑ 95Bow-154
❑ 95BowAllFoi-154
❑ 95Don-237
❑ 95Lea-255
❑ 95ParInt-343
❑ 95ParIntEl-343

**Gage, Jody**
❑ 88ProAHL-266
❑ 89ProAHL-276
❑ 90ProAHLIHL-285
❑ 91ProAHLCHL-21
❑ 91RochAmeDD-7
❑ 91RochAmeKod-13
❑ 92RochAmeDD-7
❑ 92RochAmeKod-9
❑ 93RochAmeKod-10
❑ 94ClaProP-82
❑ 95ColEdgI-63
❑ 95RochAmeSS-4

**Gaggi, Jason**
❑ 95Sla-32
❑ 96SudWol-7
❑ 96SudWolP-10

**Gagne, Art**
❑ 23V1281PauC-31
❑ 27LaPat-2

**Gagne, Dominic**
❑ 90MonAAA-11

**Gagne, Don**
❑ 89HamRoaA-7
❑ 90CinCyc-22

**Gagne, Jacque**
❑ 56QueAce-5

**Gagne, Luc**
❑ 94SudWol-13
❑ 94SudWolP-6
❑ 95Sla-398
❑ 95SudWol-5
❑ 95SudWolP-9
❑ 96SudWol-8
❑ 96SudWolP-11

**Gagne, Martin**
❑ 907thInnSQMJHL-39
❑ 917thInnSMC-42

**Gagne, Mausime**
❑ 907thInnSQMJHL-124

**Gagne, Paul**
❑ 81OPC-75
❑ 81OPCSti-233
❑ 81RocPos-6
❑ 81Top-W80
❑ 82OPC-139
❑ 84DevPos-17
❑ 85DevPos-5
❑ 85OPC-163
❑ 85OPCSti-60
❑ 85Top-163
❑ 88ProAHL-237
❑ 89ProAHL-122
❑ 93SwiHNL-252
❑ 95SwiHNL-452

**Gagne, Remi**
❑ 83NovScoV-14

**Gagne, Simon**
❑ 97UppDec-411
❑ 98BowBes-140
❑ 98BowBesAR-140
❑ 98BowBesR-140
❑ 98BowCHL-107
❑ 98BowCHL-126
❑ 98BowCHLAuB-A36
❑ 98BowCHLAuG-A36
❑ 98BowCHLAuS-A36
❑ 98BowCHLGA-107
❑ 98BowCHLGA-126
❑ 98BowCHLOI-107
❑ 98BowCHLOI-126
❑ 98BowChrC-107
❑ 98BowChrC-126
❑ 98BowChrCGA-107
❑ 98BowChrCGA-126
❑ 98BowChrCGAR-107
❑ 98BowChrCGAR-126
❑ 98BowChrCOI-107
❑ 98BowChrCOI-126
❑ 98BowChrCOIR-107
❑ 98BowChrCOIR-126
❑ 98BowChrCR-107
❑ 98BowChrCR-126
❑ 98QueRem-8
❑ 99QuePeeWHWCCS-28

**Gagne, Wayne**
❑ 88ProIHL-77

**Gagner, Dave**
❑ 87NorStaPos-13
❑ 88NorStaADA-10
❑ 88OPC-215
❑ 89OPC-109
❑ 89OPCBoxB-N
❑ 89OPCSti-203
❑ 89PanSti-103
❑ 89Top-109
❑ 89TopBoxB-N
❑ 90Bow-186
❑ 90BowTif-186
❑ 90OPC-168
❑ 90PanSti-248
❑ 90ProSet-138
❑ 90Sco-108
❑ 90ScoCan-108
❑ 90ScoHotRS-52
❑ 90Top-168
❑ 90TopTif-168
❑ 90UppDec-248
❑ 90UppDecF-248
❑ 91Bow-131
❑ 91Bow-419
❑ 91OPC-74
❑ 91OPCPre-128
❑ 91PanSti-112
❑ 91Par-78
❑ 91ParFre-78
❑ 91Pin-71
❑ 91PinFre-71
❑ 91ProSet-108
❑ 91ProSet-288
❑ 91ProSetFre-108
❑ 91ProSetFre-288
❑ 91ProSetPla-60
❑ 91ScoAme-72
❑ 91ScoCan-72
❑ 91StaClu-117
❑ 91Top-74
❑ 91TopTeaSL-7
❑ 91UppDec-86
❑ 91UppDec-180
❑ 91UppDecF-86
❑ 91UppDecF-180
❑ 92Bow-171
❑ 92HumDum2-6
❑ 92OPC-80
❑ 92PanSti-90
❑ 92PanStiFre-90
❑ 92Par-311
❑ 92ParEmel-311
❑ 92Pin-85
❑ 92PinFre-85
❑ 92ProSet-77
❑ 92Sco-227
❑ 92ScoCan-227
❑ 92StaClu-121
❑ 92Top-254
❑ 92TopGol-254G
❑ 92Ult-94
❑ 92UppDec-174
❑ 93Don-83
❑ 93Lea-128
❑ 93OPCPre-183
❑ 93OPCPreG-183
❑ 93PanSti-269
❑ 93Par-317
❑ 93ParEmel-317
❑ 93Pin-77
❑ 93PinCan-77
❑ 93Pow-60
❑ 93Sco-98
❑ 93ScoCan-98
❑ 93StaClu-436
❑ 93StaCluFDI-436
❑ 93StaCluO-436
❑ 93TopPre-183
❑ 93TopPreG-183
❑ 93Ult-92
❑ 93UppDec-145
❑ 94BeAPla-R5
❑ 94BeAPSig-77
❑ 94CanGamNHLP-79
❑ 94Don-164
❑ 94EASpo-34
❑ 94Fle-49
❑ 94Lea-319
❑ 94OPCPre-298
❑ 94OPCPreSE-298
❑ 94Par-58
❑ 94ParGol-58
❑ 94Pin-334
❑ 94PinArtP-334
❑ 94PinRinC-334
❑ 94Sel-6
❑ 94SelGol-6
❑ 94SP-30
❑ 94SPDieCut-30
❑ 94StaClu-45
❑ 94StaCluFDI-45
❑ 94StaCluMOMS-45
❑ 94StaCluSTWC-45
❑ 94StaHoc-11
❑ 94StaPinS-334
❑ 94StaPinS-NNO
❑ 94StaPos-7
❑ 94TopPre-298
❑ 94TopPreSE-298
❑ 94Ult-51
❑ 94UppDec-382
❑ 94UppDecEleIce-382
❑ 95Bow-33
❑ 95BowAllFoi-33
❑ 95CanGamNHLP-86
❑ 95ColCho-7
❑ 95ColChoPC-7
❑ 95ColChoPCP-7
❑ 95Don-58
❑ 95Emo-45
❑ 95Fin-31
❑ 95FinRef-31
❑ 95Kra-57
❑ 95Lea-22
❑ 95Met-38
❑ 95ParInt-471
❑ 95ParIntEl-471
❑ 95Pin-125
❑ 95PinArtP-125
❑ 95PinRinC-125
❑ 95PlaOneoOne-30
❑ 95Sco-93
❑ 95ScoBlaIce-93
❑ 95ScoBlaIceAP-93
❑ 95SkyImp-44
❑ 95StaClu-31
❑ 95StaCluMOMS-31
❑ 95Sum-53
❑ 95SumArtP-53
❑ 95SumIce-53
❑ 95Top-254
❑ 95TopOPCI-254
❑ 95Ult-229
❑ 95UppDec-370
❑ 95UppDecEleIce-370
❑ 95UppDecEleIceG-370
❑ 95UppDecSpeE-SE24
❑ 95UppDecSpeEdiG-SE24
❑ 95Zen-56
❑ 95ZenGifG-11
❑ 96ColCho-260
❑ 96Don-170
❑ 96DonPrePro-170
❑ 96Fla-12
❑ 96FlaBluI-12
❑ 96KraUppD-64
❑ 96MetUni-19
❑ 96Pin-39
❑ 96PinArtP-39
❑ 96PinFoi-39
❑ 96PinPreS-39
❑ 96PinRinC-39
❑ 96PlaOneoOne-337
❑ 96Sco-14
❑ 96ScoArtPro-14
❑ 96ScoDeaCAP-14
❑ 96ScoGolB-14
❑ 96ScoSpeAP-14
❑ 96Sum-80
❑ 96SumArtP-80
❑ 96SumIce-80
❑ 96SumMet-80
❑ 96SumPreS-80
❑ 96Ult-22
❑ 96UltGolM-22
❑ 97Be A PPAD-174
❑ 97Be A PPAPD-174
❑ 97BeAPla-174
❑ 97BeAPlaAut-174
❑ 97ColCho-38
❑ 97Don-80
❑ 97DonPreProG-80
❑ 97DonPreProS-80
❑ 97DonPri-103
❑ 97DonPriSoA-103
❑ 97Pac-159
❑ 97PacCop-159
❑ 97PacCroR-56
❑ 97PacCroREG-56
❑ 97PacCroRIB-56
❑ 97PacCroRS-56
❑ 97PacEmeGre-159
❑ 97PacIceB-159
❑ 97PacInv-17
❑ 97PacInvC-17
❑ 97PacInvEG-17
❑ 97PacInvIB-17
❑ 97PacInvR-17
❑ 97PacInvS-17
❑ 97PacOme-98
❑ 97PacOmeC-98
❑ 97PacOmeDG-98
❑ 97PacOmeEG-98
❑ 97PacOmeG-98
❑ 97PacOmeIB-98
❑ 97PacPar-79
❑ 97PacParC-79
❑ 97PacParDG-79
❑ 97PacParEG-79
❑ 97PacParIB-79
❑ 97PacParRed-79
❑ 97PacParSil-79
❑ 97PacRed-159
❑ 97PacRev-59
❑ 97PacRevC-59
❑ 97PacRevE-59
❑ 97PacRevIB-59
❑ 97PacRevR-59
❑ 97PacRevS-59
❑ 97PacSil-159
❑ 97Pin-156
❑ 97PinCer-47
❑ 97PinCerMB-47
❑ 97PinCerMG-47
❑ 97PinCerMR-47
❑ 97PinCerR-47
❑ 97PinIns-181
❑ 97PinPrePBB-156
❑ 97PinPrePBC-156
❑ 97PinPrePBM-156
❑ 97PinPrePBY-156
❑ 97PinPrePFC-156
❑ 97PinPrePFM-156
❑ 97PinPrePFY-156
❑ 97PinPrePla-156
❑ 97PinTotCMPG-47
❑ 97PinTotCPB-47
❑ 97PinTotCPG-47
❑ 97PinTotCPR-47
❑ 97Sco-79
❑ 97ScoArtPro-79
❑ 97ScoGolBla-79
❑ 97UppDecBD-58
❑ 97UppDecBDDD-58
❑ 97UppDecBDQD-58
❑ 97UppDecBDTD-58
❑ 97Zen-75
❑ 97Zen5x7-35
❑ 97ZenGolImp-35
❑ 97ZenSilImp-35
❑ 97ZenZGol-75
❑ 97ZenZSil-75
❑ 98Be A PPA-57
❑ 98Be A PPAA-57
❑ 98Be A PPAAF-57
❑ 98Be A PPTBASG-57
❑ 98Be APG-57
❑ 98Fin-114
❑ 98FinNo P-114
❑ 98FinNo PR-114
❑ 98FinRef-114
❑ 98Pac-221
❑ 98PacAur-79
❑ 98PacDynI-80
❑ 98PacDynIIB-80
❑ 98PacDynIR-80
❑ 98PacIceB-221
❑ 98PacPar-95
❑ 98PacParC-95
❑ 98PacParEG-95
❑ 98PacParH-95
❑ 98PacParIB-95
❑ 98PacParS-95
❑ 98PacRed-221

❑ 98UC-92
❑ 98UD ChoPCR-92
❑ 98UD ChoR-92
❑ 99Pac-422
❑ 99PacCop-422
❑ 99PacGol-422
❑ 99PacIceB-422
❑ 99PacPreD-422
**Gagner, Ken**
❑ 83BraAle-25
**Gagnier, Francis**
❑ 92QueIntP-34
**Gagnon, Chad**
❑ 97RimOce-45
**Gagnon, Dave**
❑ 90ProAHLIHL-491
❑ 91ScoAme-387
❑ 91ScoCan-277
❑ 94RoaExp-2
❑ 96RoaExp-1
**Gagnon, Francois**
❑ 907thInnSQMJHL-263
❑ 917thInnSQMJHL-15
❑ 94CenHocL-44
**Gagnon, Germaine**
❑ 72OPC-200
❑ 72SarProSta-133
❑ 73OPC-161
❑ 73Top-178
❑ 74NHLActSta-85
❑ 74OPCNHL-344
❑ 75OPCNHL-101
❑ 75Top-101
**Gagnon, Gerry**
❑ 51LavDaiLSJ-11
**Gagnon, Jacques**
❑ 51LavDaiQSHL-21
**Gagnon, Jean-Francois**
❑ 917thInnSQMJHL-169
**Gagnon, Joel**
❑ 92OshGenS-22
❑ 93OshGen-2
❑ 94NorBayC-1
**Gagnon, Johnny**
❑ 33OPCV304A-19
❑ 33V129-43
❑ 33V357IceK-21
❑ 34BeeGro1P-151
❑ 34DiaMatS-23
❑ 35DiaMatT2-23
❑ 35DiaMatT3-21
❑ 36V356WorG-83
❑ 37OPCV304E-154
❑ 38QuaOatP-14
❑ 39OPCV3011-25
❑ 55Par-65
❑ 55ParQuaO-65
**Gagnon, Marc**
❑ 91BriColJHL-140
❑ 91BriColJHL-146
❑ 91BriColJHL-156
**Gagnon, Ovila**
❑ 52JunBluT-162
**Gagnon, Pascal**
❑ 917thInnSQMJHL-46
**Gagnon, Paul**
❑ 51LavDaiLSJ-6
**Gagnon, Paul-Sebastien**
❑ 93AmoLesFAM-7
**Gagnon, Pierre**
❑ 86SudWol-16
❑ 87SudWol-16
❑ 88KitRan-21
❑ 907thInnSQMJHL-3
❑ 917thInnSMC-50
❑ 917thInnSQMJHL-292
**Gagnon, Sean**
❑ 917thInnSOHL-264
❑ 91SudWol-5
❑ 93SauSteMG-7
❑ 93SauSteMGM-7
❑ 94DayBom-11
❑ 95DayBom-17
❑ 95DayBom-P1
**Gagnon, Simon**
❑ 92QueIntP-3
**Gagnon, Yannick**
❑ 93DruVol-3
**Gahn, Kristian**
❑ 90SweSemE-95
❑ 91SweSemE-24
❑ 92SweSemE-48
❑ 92UppDec-232
❑ 94SweLeaE-118
❑ 95SweLeaE-279
❑ 95SweUppDE-159
**Gailer, Peter**
❑ 82SweSemHVS-104
**Gailloux, Kris**
❑ 92BriColJHL-224
**Gainer, Clayton**
❑ 93WheThu-16
**Gainey, Bob**
❑ 73CanaPos-5
❑ 74CanaPos-6
❑ 74OPCNHL-388
❑ 75CanaPos-6
❑ 75OPCNHL-278
❑ 75Top-278
❑ 76CanaPos-6
❑ 76OPCNHL-44
❑ 76OPCNHL-217
❑ 76Top-44
❑ 76Top-217
❑ 77CanaPos-7
❑ 77OPCNHL-129
❑ 77Top-129
❑ 78CanaPos-7
❑ 78OPC-76
❑ 78Top-76
❑ 79CanaPos-4
❑ 79OPC-170
❑ 79Top-170
❑ 80CanaPos-5
❑ 80OPC-58
❑ 80OPCSup-9
❑ 80PepCap-43
❑ 80Top-58
❑ 81CanaPos-7
❑ 81OPC-176
❑ 81OPC-194
❑ 81OPCSti-30
❑ 81OPCSti-43
❑ 81OPCSti-269
❑ 81Top-13
❑ 82CanaPos-6
❑ 82CanaSte-4
❑ 82McDSti-12
❑ 82OPC-181
❑ 82OPCSti-36
❑ 82PosCer-10
❑ 83CanaPos-8
❑ 83Ess-7
❑ 83OPC-187
❑ 83OPCSti-66
❑ 83Vac-44
❑ 847EDis-29
❑ 84CanaPos-7
❑ 84KelAccD-3A
❑ 84OPC-261
❑ 84OPCSti-153
❑ 85CanaPla-1
❑ 85CanaPla-7
❑ 85CanaPos-9
❑ 85CanaPos-10
❑ 85CanaPro-5
❑ 85OPC-169
❑ 85OPCSti-138
❑ 86CanaPos-5
❑ 86KraDra-18
❑ 86OPC-96
❑ 86OPCSti-12
❑ 86Top-96
❑ 87CanaPos-7
❑ 87CanaVacS-12
❑ 87CanaVacS-13
❑ 87CanaVacS-18
❑ 87CanaVacS-53
❑ 87CanaVacS-88
❑ 87OPC-228
❑ 87OPCSti-12
❑ 87PanSti-69
❑ 88CanaPos-10
❑ 88OPC-216
❑ 88OPCSti-42
❑ 89CanaProF-23
❑ 89OPCSti-58
❑ 90ProSet-668
❑ 91Kra-39
❑ 92FutTre76CC-140
❑ 93OPCCanHF-16
❑ 93OPCCanHF-59
❑ 93UppDecLAS-41
❑ 94StaHoc-12
❑ 96StaPos-5
**Gainey, Steve**
❑ 96KamBla-11
**Gainor, Dutch (Norman)**
❑ 34SweCap-20
❑ 36V356WorG-98
**Galanov, Maxim**
❑ 98PacOmeH-200
❑ 98PacOmeODI-200
❑ 98PacOmeR-200
**Galarneau, Danny**
❑ 91AirCanSJHL-B39
❑ 92MPSPhoSJHL-160
**Galarneau, Michel**
❑ 82WhaJunHC-4
❑ 94FreNatT-13
**Galati, Mike**
❑ 95GueSto5A-29
**Galbraith, Walter**
❑ 33OPCV304A-7
❑ 38BruGarMS-2
**Galchenyuk, Alex (Alexander)**
❑ 91OPCIns-33R
❑ 92UppDec-353
❑ 93ClaProPro-96
**Galiamoutsas, Hakan**
❑ 98GerDELE-128
**Galkin, Andrej**
❑ 94CzeAPSE-239
❑ 95CzeAPSE-15
❑ 96CzeAPSE-232
**Gallace, Richard**
❑ 917thInnSOHL-119
**Gallace, Steve**
❑ 95Sla-295
**Gallagher, John**
❑ 34BeeGro1P-226
❑ 36OPCV304D-108
❑ 36V356WorG-41
**Gallagher, Matt**
❑ 89NasKni-7
**Gallagher, Ray**
❑ 87BroBra-12
❑ 88BroBra-1
❑ 93HunBli-9
❑ 94FliGen-8
**Gallant, Chester**
❑ 94SudWolP-7
❑ 95Sla-201
**Gallant, Gerard**
❑ 87OPC-67
❑ 87OPCSti-106
❑ 87PanSti-245
❑ 87RedWinLC-11
❑ 87Top-67
❑ 88OPC-12
❑ 88OPCSti-254
❑ 88PanSti-43
❑ 88RedWinLC-7
❑ 88Top-12
❑ 89OPC-172
❑ 89OPC-302
❑ 89OPCSti-32
❑ 89OPCSti-157
❑ 89OPCSti-253
❑ 89PanSti-58
❑ 89RedWinLC-7
❑ 89Top-172
❑ 89TopStiIns-2
❑ 90Bow-237
❑ 90BowTif-237
❑ 90Kra-14
❑ 90OPC-322
❑ 90PanSti-205
❑ 90ProSet-71
❑ 90Sco-180
❑ 90ScoCan-180
❑ 90ScoHotRS-78
❑ 90Top-322
❑ 90TopTif-322
❑ 90UppDec-134
❑ 90UppDecF-134
❑ 91Bow-56
❑ 91Kra-83
❑ 91OPC-443
❑ 91PanSti-142
❑ 91Par-269
❑ 91ParFre-269
❑ 91Pin-205
❑ 91PinFre-205
❑ 91ProSet-63
❑ 91ProSetFre-63
❑ 91RedWinLC-5
❑ 91ScoAme-34
❑ 91ScoCan-34
❑ 91StaClu-165
❑ 91Top-443
❑ 92Bow-169
❑ 92OPC-163
❑ 92PanSti-116
❑ 92PanStiFre-116
❑ 92Pin-135
❑ 92PinFre-135
❑ 92Sco-119
❑ 92ScoCan-119
❑ 92StaClu-218
❑ 92Top-92
❑ 92TopGol-92G
❑ 92Ult-284
❑ 92UppDec-246
❑ 93Don-320
❑ 93Lea-310
❑ 93LigSealR-15
❑ 93OPCPre-511
❑ 93OPCPreG-511
❑ 93Pin-404
❑ 93PinCan-404
❑ 93Pow-230
❑ 93Sco-402
❑ 93Sco-560
❑ 93ScoCan-402
❑ 93ScoCan-560
❑ 93StaClu-16
❑ 93StaClu-346
❑ 93StaCluFDI-16
❑ 93StaCluFDI-346
❑ 93StaCluFDIO-16
❑ 93StaCluO-16
❑ 93StaCluO-346
❑ 93TopPre-511
❑ 93TopPreG-511
**Gallant, Gordie**
❑ 74FigSaiWHA-8
❑ 75OPCWHA-96
❑ 76OPCWHA-4
**Gallant, Shaun**
❑ 95Sla-282
**Gallant, Trevor**
❑ 917thInnSOHL-80
❑ 93KitRan-10
❑ 94KitRan-11
❑ 94NorBayC-10
❑ 95Sla-217
**Gallentine, Brian**
❑ 92WesMic-11
❑ 93WesMic-12
❑ 95RoaExp-12
**Galley, Garry**
❑ 84KinSmo-6
❑ 86Kin20tATI-7
❑ 87CapKod-2
❑ 87CapTeaIss-5
❑ 87KinTeal4-7
❑ 88BruPos-4
❑ 89BruSpoA-8
❑ 89BruSpoA-11
❑ 90OPC-331
❑ 90ProSet-7A
❑ 90ProSet-7B
❑ 90Sco-253
❑ 90ScoCan-253
❑ 90Top-331
❑ 90TopTif-331
❑ 90UppDec-379
❑ 90UppDecF-379
❑ 91Bow-360
❑ 91OPC-86
❑ 91PanSti-175
❑ 91Par-7
❑ 91Par-350
❑ 91ParFre-7
❑ 91ParFre-350
❑ 91Pin-171
❑ 91PinFre-171
❑ 91ProSet-7
❑ 91ProSet-298
❑ 91ProSetFre-7
❑ 91ProSetFre-298
❑ 91ProSetPla-211
❑ 91ScoAme-71
❑ 91ScoCan-71
❑ 91StaClu-175
❑ 91Top-86
❑ 91UppDec-439
❑ 91UppDec-607
❑ 91UppDecF-439
❑ 91UppDecF-607
❑ 92Bow-11
❑ 92DurPan-41
❑ 92FlyJCP-13
❑ 92FlyUppDS-18
❑ 92FlyUppDS-37A
❑ 92OPC-317
❑ 92Par-364
❑ 92ParEmel-364
❑ 92Pin-103
❑ 92PinFre-103
❑ 92Sco-19
❑ 92ScoCan-19
❑ 92StaClu-424
❑ 92Top-360
❑ 92TopGol-360G
❑ 92Ult-156
❑ 92UppDec-319
❑ 93Don-251
❑ 93DurSco-38
❑ 93Lea-120
❑ 93OPCPre-255
❑ 93OPCPreG-255
❑ 93PanSti-53
❑ 93Par-423
❑ 93ParEmel-423
❑ 93Pin-72
❑ 93PinCan-72
❑ 93Pow-182
❑ 93Sco-143
❑ 93ScoCan-143
❑ 93StaClu-381
❑ 93StaCluFDI-381
❑ 93StaCluO-381
❑ 93TopPre-255
❑ 93TopPreG-255
❑ 93Ult-124
❑ 93UppDec-90
❑ 94BeAPSig-62
❑ 94CanGamNHLP-182
❑ 94Don-166
❑ 94EASpo-97
❑ 94Fle-153
❑ 94Lea-264
❑ 94LeaLim-5
❑ 94OPCPre-535
❑ 94OPCPreSE-535
❑ 94ParSE-SE128
❑ 94ParSEG-SE128
❑ 94ParVin-V87
❑ 94Pin-27
❑ 94PinArtP-27
❑ 94PinRinC-27
❑ 94Sco-26
❑ 94ScoGol-26
❑ 94ScoPla-26
❑ 94ScoPlaTS-26
❑ 94Sel-117
❑ 94SelGol-117
❑ 94StaCluMO-29
❑ 94TopPre-535
❑ 94TopPreSE-535
❑ 94Ult-157
❑ 94UppDec-19
❑ 94UppDecEleIce-19
❑ 95CanGamNHLP-46
❑ 95ColCho-73
❑ 95ColChoPC-73
❑ 95ColChoPCP-73
❑ 95Don-116
❑ 95Emo-15
❑ 95Lea-30
❑ 95ParInt-21
❑ 95ParIntEl-21
❑ 95Pin-4
❑ 95PinArtP-4
❑ 95PinRinC-4
❑ 95PlaOneoOne-124
❑ 95Sco-112
❑ 95ScoBlaIce-112
❑ 95ScoBlaIceAP-112
❑ 95SkyImp-15
❑ 95StaClu-3
❑ 95StaCluMOMS-3
❑ 95Top-155
❑ 95TopOPCI-155
❑ 95TopSupSki-37
❑ 95TopSupSkiPla-37
❑ 95Ult-17
❑ 95UltGolM-17
❑ 95UppDec-198
❑ 95UppDecEleIce-198
❑ 95UppDecEleIceG-198
❑ 95UppDecSpeE-SE8
❑ 95UppDecSpeEdiG-SE8
❑ 96Don-106
❑ 96DonPrePro-106
❑ 96Lea-8
❑ 96LeaPreP-8
❑ 96Pin-69
❑ 96PinPreS-69
❑ 96Sco-131
❑ 96ScoArtPro-131
❑ 96ScoDeaCAP-131
❑ 96ScoGolB-131
❑ 96ScoSpeAP-131
❑ 96TopNHLP-95
❑ 96TopPicOI-95
❑ 97ColCho-30
❑ 97Pac-288
❑ 97PacCop-288
❑ 97PacEmeGre-288
❑ 97PacIceB-288
❑ 97PacOme-108
❑ 97PacOmeC-108
❑ 97PacOmeDG-108
❑ 97PacOmeEG-108
❑ 97PacOmeG-108
❑ 97PacOmeIB-108
❑ 97PacPar-89
❑ 97PacParC-89
❑ 97PacParDG-89
❑ 97PacParEG-89
❑ 97PacParIB-89
❑ 97PacParRed-89
❑ 97PacParSil-89
❑ 97PacRed-288
❑ 97PacSil-288
❑ 97SPAut-73
❑ 98Fin-31
❑ 98FinNo P-31
❑ 98FinNo PR-31
❑ 98FinRef-31
❑ 98Pac-235
❑ 98PacIceB-235
❑ 98PacRed-235
**Gallinger, Don**
❑ 34BeeGro1P-14
**Galloway, Kyle**
❑ 93RoaExp-9
**Gallstedt, Niklas**
❑ 84SweSemE-228
❑ 85SwePanS-224
❑ 89SweSemE-32
❑ 90SweSemE-179
❑ 91SweSemE-33
❑ 92SweSemE-59
❑ 93SweSemE-40
**Galuppo, Sandy**
❑ 92DayBom-10
❑ 94BirBul-8
**Galvas, David**
❑ 96CzeAPSE-105
**Gamache, Jean-Guy**
❑ 52JunBluT-35
**Gamache, Simon**
❑ 98Vald'OF-17
**Gamble, Bruce**
❑ 44BeeGro2P-21
❑ 60ShiCoi-119
❑ 62Top-3
❑ 64BeeGro3P-162
❑ 65MapLeaWB-10
❑ 67Top-18
❑ 68OPC-197
❑ 68PosCerM-8
❑ 68ShiCoi-173
❑ 69MapLeaWBG-11
❑ 69MapLeaWBG-12
❑ 69OPC-44
❑ 69OPCFou-4
❑ 69Top-44
❑ 70ColSta-82
❑ 70DadCoo-37
❑ 70EssPowPla-36
❑ 70MapLeaP-3
❑ 70OPC-105
❑ 70OPCDec-44
❑ 70SarProSta-193
❑ 70Top-105
❑ 71OPC-201
❑ 71OPCPos-16
❑ 71SarProSta-160
❑ 71Top-104
❑ 71TorSun-194
❑ 95Par66-118
❑ 95Par66Coi-118
**Gamble, Dick**
❑ 44BeeGro2P-240
❑ 45QuaOatP-77
❑ 48ExhCan-7
❑ 51Par-16
❑ 52Par-5
❑ 53Par-18
❑ 54Top-1
❑ 63RochAme-14
**Gamble, Troy**
❑ 85MedHatT-15
❑ 89ProIHL-178
❑ 90CanuMoh-8
❑ 90CanuMol-2
❑ 90OPCPre-34
❑ 90ProSet-641
❑ 90ScoRoo-32T
❑ 90UppDec-434
❑ 90UppDecF-434
❑ 91Bow-315
❑ 91CanuAutC-7
❑ 91CanuPanTS-8
❑ 91CanuTeal8-7
❑ 91OPC-446
❑ 91PanSti-37
❑ 91Par-402
❑ 91ParFre-402
❑ 91ProSet-238
❑ 91ProSetFre-238
❑ 91ProSetPla-121
❑ 91ScoAme-282
❑ 91ScoCan-502
❑ 91ScoYouS-29
❑ 91StaClu-218
❑ 91Top-446
❑ 91UppDec-120
❑ 91UppDecF-120
❑ 92Bow-410
❑ 92HamCan-8
❑ 92Top-412
❑ 92TopGol-412G
❑ 95ColEdgI-133
❑ 95ColEdgITW-G4
**Gambucci, Gary**
❑ 69SweWorC-19
❑ 72SweSemWC-123
❑ 74FigSaiWHA-9
**Ganchar, Perry**
❑ 81SasBla-22
❑ 86SheCan-15
❑ 89ProIHL-148
❑ 90ProAHLIHL-379
❑ 91ProAHLCHL-292
❑ 92CleLum-10
❑ 93CleLum-16
❑ 93CleLumPos-10
❑ 95CleLum-12
**Gani, Darren**
❑ 83BelBul-25
❑ 84BelBul-22
**Gans, David (Dave)**
❑ 81OshGen-11
❑ 82OshGen-19
❑ 83OshGen-27
**Ganster, Friedrich**
❑ 93SweSemWCS-277
**Gant, Kevin**
❑ 85KitRan-8
**Ganz, Bryan**
❑ 92NorMicW-6
❑ 93NorMicW-6
**Garanin, Evgeny**
❑ 92RusStaRA-8
**Garatti, Jason**
❑ 93MinDul-12
**Garbutt, Murray**
❑ 907thInnSWHL-25
❑ 917thInnSMC-90
❑ 91ProAHLCHL-514
❑ 93HunBli-10
**Gardiner, Bert**
❑ 34BeeGro1P-152
**Gardiner, Bruce**
❑ 96SenPizH-8
❑ 97Be A PPAD-51
❑ 97Be A PPAPD-51
❑ 97BeAPla-51
❑ 97BeAPlaAut-51
❑ 97Pac-172
❑ 97PacCop-172
❑ 97PacEmeGre-172
❑ 97PacIceB-172
❑ 97PacRed-172
❑ 97PacSil-172
❑ 97UppDec-115
❑ 98Be A PPA-97
❑ 98Be A PPAA-97
❑ 98Be A PPAAF-97
❑ 98Be A PPTBASG-97
❑ 98Be APG-97
❑ 98Pac-309
❑ 98PacIceB-309
❑ 98PacRed-309
❑ 99Pac-287
❑ 99PacCop-287
❑ 99PacGol-287
❑ 99PacIceB-287
❑ 99PacPreD-287
**Gardiner, Chuck (Charlie)**
❑ 23CreSel-9
❑ 28V1282PauC-89
❑ 33V252CanG-24
❑ 34DiaMatS-24
❑ 60Top-32
❑ 60TopSta-16
❑ 83HalFP-I8
❑ 85HalFC-128
**Gardiner, Herb**
❑ 23V1281PauC-63
❑ 27LaPat-9
❑ 60Top-44
❑ 60TopSta-17
❑ 83HalFP-L4
❑ 85HalFC-154
**Gardiner, Jeff**
❑ 897thInnSOHL-159
❑ 907thInnSOHL-105
❑ 917thInnSOHL-44
**Gardiner, Scott**
❑ 83BelBul-5
**Gardner, Bill**
❑ 81BlaBorPos-8
❑ 82PosCer-4
❑ 83BlaBorPos-8
❑ 83OPC-103
❑ 83PenHeiP-8
❑ 84OPC-35
❑ 86WhaJunT-9
❑ 88ProIHL-99
**Gardner, Cal**
❑ 44BeeGro2P-22
❑ 44BeeGro2P-402
❑ 45QuaOatP-18A
❑ 45QuaOatP-18B
❑ 45QuaOatP-60A
❑ 45QuaOatP-60B
❑ 45QuaOatP-60D
❑ 48ExhCan-30
❑ 51Par-85
❑ 52Par-30
❑ 53Par-99
❑ 54Par-53
❑ 54Top-47
❑ 55BruPho-6
❑ 60CleBar-5
❑ 93ParParR-PR57
❑ 94ParMisL-10
**Gardner, Dave**
❑ 73CanaPos-6
❑ 74NHLActSta-244
❑ 74NHLActStaU-6
❑ 74OPCNHL-47
❑ 74Top-47
❑ 75OPCNHL-119
❑ 75Top-119
❑ 76OPCNHL-274
❑ 77OPCNHL-258
❑ 77Top-258
❑ 78OPC-278
❑ 91AirCanSJHL-A23
**Gardner, George**
❑ 70CanuRoyB-5
❑ 70OPC-224
❑ 70SarProSta-222
❑ 71CanuRoyB-18
❑ 71LetActR-16
❑ 71OPC-235
❑ 71SarProSta-213
❑ 71TorSun-277
❑ 72CanuNal-2
❑ 72ShaLosAW-3
**Gardner, Jimmy (James)**
❑ 10C55SweCP-36
❑ 11C55-36
❑ 12C57-24
❑ 83HalFP-M7
❑ 85HalFC-172
**Gardner, Joel**
❑ 90ProAHLIHL-381
❑ 91KnoChe-13
❑ 92RalIce-3
❑ 92RalIce-27
**Gardner, Paul**
❑ 76RocCokCan-10
❑ 77OPCNHL-24
❑ 77RocCokCan-8
❑ 77Top-24
❑ 78OPC-88
❑ 78Top-88
❑ 79MapLeaP-10
❑ 79OPC-5
❑ 79Top-5
❑ 81OPC-257
❑ 81OPCSti-187
❑ 81Top-E113
❑ 82OPC-236
❑ 82OPC-269
❑ 82OPCSti-145
❑ 82PosCer-15
❑ 83OPC-219
❑ 83OPC-275
❑ 83OPC-280
❑ 83OPCSti-230
❑ 83PenTeaP-11
❑ 83PufSti-10
❑ 89ProAHL-113
❑ 93PorPir-4
❑ 96PorPir-NNO
**Gardner, Ryan**
❑ 95Sla-166
**Gare, Danny**
❑ 75OPCNHL-64
❑ 75Top-64
❑ 76OPCNHL-222
❑ 76OPCNHL-380
❑ 76Top-222
❑ 78OPC-209
❑ 78Top-209
❑ 79OPC-61
❑ 79SabBel-2
❑ 79Top-61
❑ 80OPC-38
❑ 80OPC-88
❑ 80OPC-161
❑ 80OPC-167
❑ 80OPC-260
❑ 80Top-38
❑ 80Top-88
❑ 80Top-161
❑ 80Top-167
❑ 80Top-260
❑ 81OPC-20
❑ 81OPC-27
❑ 81OPC-28
❑ 81OPCSti-53
❑ 81Top-14
❑ 81Top-47

❑ 81Top-E127
❑ 82OPC-83
❑ 82OPCSti-184
❑ 82PosCer-5
❑ 83OPC-123
❑ 83OPCSti-135
❑ 83PufSti-17
❑ 84KelWin-23
❑ 84OPC-54
❑ 84Top-42
❑ 85OPC-37
❑ 85OPCSti-35
❑ 85Top-37
❑ 86OilRedR-18
❑ 86OPC-69
❑ 86OPCSti-159
❑ 86Top-69
❑ 88OilTenAnn-20
❑ 93LigSealR-16
❑ 93SabNoc-5
❑ 94LigPhoA-13
**Gare, Morey**
❑ 92NorMicW-30
❑ 93NorMicW-31
**Gareau, Guy**
❑ 51LavDaiLSJ-2
**Gariepy, Ray**
❑ 44BeeGro2P-23
**Garland, Scott**
❑ 76MapLeaP-6
❑ 76OPCNHL-243
❑ 77OPCNHL-302
❑ 78OPC-274
**Garnea, Jean-Francois**
❑ 92QueIntP-53
**Garnelle, Dick**
❑ 56QueAce-6
**Garner, Tyrone**
❑ 95Sla-232
❑ 99Pac-66
❑ 99PacCop-66
❑ 99PacGol-66
❑ 99PacIceB-66
❑ 99PacPreD-66
**Garon, Mathieu**
❑ 95BowDraPro-P14
❑ 95UppDec-525
❑ 95UppDecEleIce-525
❑ 95UppDecEleIceG-525
❑ 97BeeAutA-71
❑ 97PinBee-71
❑ 97PinBeeGP-71
❑ 97Zen-98
❑ 97Zen5x7-78
❑ 97ZenGolImp-78
❑ 97ZenSilImp-78
❑ 97ZenZGol-98
❑ 97ZenZSil-98
❑ 98BowBes-145
❑ 98BowBesAR-145
❑ 98BowBesR-145
❑ 98BowCHL-81
❑ 98BowCHLGA-81
❑ 98BowCHLOI-81
❑ 98BowCHLSC-SC21
❑ 98BowChrC-81
❑ 98BowChrCGA-81
❑ 98BowChrCGAR-81
❑ 98BowChrCOI-81
❑ 98BowChrCOIR-81
❑ 98BowChrCR-81
❑ 98UC-260
❑ 98UD ChoPCR-260
❑ 98UD ChoR-260
**Garpenlov, Johan**
❑ 86SwePanS-81
❑ 87SwePanS-79
❑ 89SweSemE-67
❑ 90OPCPre-35
❑ 90ProSet-605
❑ 90ScoRoo-17T
❑ 90UppDec-521
❑ 90UppDec-523
❑ 90UppDecF-521
❑ 90UppDecF-523
❑ 91Bow-45
❑ 91OPC-278
❑ 91PanSti-144
❑ 91Par-385
❑ 91ParFre-385
❑ 91ProSet-56
❑ 91ProSetFre-56
❑ 91ProSetPla-29
❑ 91RedWinLC-6
❑ 91ScoAme-204
❑ 91ScoCan-204
❑ 91StaClu-268
❑ 91SweSemE-353
❑ 91SweSemWCS-212
❑ 91Top-278
❑ 91UppDec-28
❑ 91UppDec-167
❑ 91UppDecES-15
❑ 91UppDecESF-15
❑ 91UppDecF-28
❑ 91UppDecF-167
❑ 92Bow-400
❑ 92Par-397
❑ 92ParEmel-397
❑ 92Pin-122
❑ 92PinFre-122
❑ 92Sco-406
❑ 92ScoCan-406
❑ 92StaClu-212
❑ 92Top-359
❑ 92TopGol-359G
❑ 92Ult-400
❑ 92UppDec-59
❑ 93Don-309
❑ 93Lea-133
❑ 93OPCPre-53
❑ 93OPCPreG-53
❑ 93PanSti-257
❑ 93Pin-63
❑ 93PinCan-63
❑ 93Pow-219
❑ 93Sco-183
❑ 93ScoCan-183
❑ 93StaClu-44
❑ 93StaCluFDI-44
❑ 93StaCluFDIO-44
❑ 93StaCluO-44
❑ 93SweSemWCS-38
❑ 93TopPre-53
❑ 93TopPreG-53
❑ 93Ult-83
❑ 93UppDecSP-142
❑ 94BeAPla-R38
❑ 94BeAPSig-61
❑ 94CanGamNHLP-215
❑ 94Don-301
❑ 94EASpo-118
❑ 94Fla-165
❑ 94Lea-234
❑ 94OPCPre-201
❑ 94OPCPreSE-201
❑ 94Par-209
❑ 94ParGol-209
❑ 94Pin-296
❑ 94PinArtP-296
❑ 94PinRinC-296
❑ 94Sco-176
❑ 94ScoGol-176
❑ 94ScoPla-176
❑ 94ScoPlaTS-176
❑ 94SP-45
❑ 94SPDieCut-45
❑ 94TopPre-201
❑ 94TopPreSE-201
❑ 94Ult-194
❑ 94UppDec-64
❑ 94UppDecEleIce-64
❑ 95CanGamNHLP-120
❑ 95ColCho-240
❑ 95ColChoPC-240
❑ 95ColChoPCP-240
❑ 95Don-322
❑ 95Lea-282
❑ 95ParInt-90
❑ 95ParIntEl-90
❑ 95StaClu-62
❑ 95StaCluMOMS-62
❑ 95SweGloWC-36
❑ 95SweUppDE-242
❑ 95Top-56
❑ 95TopOPCI-56
❑ 95UppDec-129
❑ 95UppDecEleIce-129
❑ 95UppDecEleIceG-129
❑ 96BeAPAut-67
❑ 96BeAPAutSil-67
❑ 96BeAPla-67
❑ 96ColCho-106
❑ 97Pac-348
❑ 97PacCop-348
❑ 97PacEmeGre-348
❑ 97PacIceB-348
❑ 97PacRed-348
❑ 97PacSil-348
**Garrett, John**
❑ 74FigSaiWHA-10
❑ 75OPCWHA-12
❑ 76OPCWHA-55
❑ 77OPCWHA-23
❑ 79OPC-293
❑ 80OPC-77
❑ 80Top-77
❑ 81OPC-137
❑ 81OPCSti-68
❑ 82NordPos-7
❑ 82OPC-283
❑ 83Canu-6
❑ 83NordPos-8
❑ 83OPC-349
❑ 83OPCSti-275
❑ 83Vac-105
❑ 84Canu-8
❑ 84OPC-317
❑ 85OPC-220
**Garrett, Red**
❑ 34BeeGro1P-273
**Garthe, M.**
❑ 95GerDELE-45
**Gartner, Mike**
❑ 80OPC-49
❑ 80OPC-195
❑ 80Top-49
❑ 80Top-195
❑ 81Cap-5
❑ 81OPC-347
❑ 81OPCSti-190
❑ 81Top-E117
❑ 82Cap-6
❑ 82NeiGre-14
❑ 82OPC-363
❑ 82OPCSti-153
❑ 82PosCer-20
❑ 83OPC-364
❑ 83OPC-369
❑ 83OPCSti-207
❑ 83PufSti-21
❑ 847EDis-53
❑ 84CapPizH-5
❑ 84KelAccD-4
❑ 84OPC-197
❑ 84OPC-370
❑ 84OPCSti-131
❑ 84Top-143
❑ 857ECreCar-20
❑ 85CapPizH-4
❑ 85OPC-46
❑ 85OPCSti-111
❑ 85Top-46
❑ 86CapKod-8
❑ 86CapPol-8
❑ 86OPC-59
❑ 86OPCSti-251
❑ 86Top-59
❑ 87CapKod-11
❑ 87CapTeaIss-6
❑ 87OPC-168
❑ 87OPCSti-239
❑ 87PanSti-180
❑ 87Top-168
❑ 88CapBor-5
❑ 88CapSmo-5
❑ 88FriLayS-13
❑ 88OPC-50
❑ 88OPCBoxB-N
❑ 88OPCSti-67
❑ 88PanSti-370
❑ 88Top-50
❑ 88TopBoxB-N
❑ 89OPC-30
❑ 89OPCSti-196
❑ 89PanSti-104
❑ 89SweSemWCS-75
❑ 89Top-30
❑ 90Bow-220
❑ 90BowHatTri-8
❑ 90BowHatTri-17
❑ 90BowTif-220
❑ 90Kra-69
❑ 90OPC-373
❑ 90OPCPre-36
❑ 90PanSti-103
❑ 90ProSet-196
❑ 90ProSet-351
❑ 90Sco-130
❑ 90Sco-333
❑ 90ScoCan-130
❑ 90ScoCan-333
❑ 90ScoHotRS-60
❑ 90Top-373
❑ 90TopTif-373
❑ 90UppDec-277
❑ 90UppDecF-277
❑ 91Bow-74
❑ 91Kra-27
❑ 91OPC-46
❑ 91OPCPre-147
❑ 91OPCPre-164
❑ 91PanSti-292
❑ 91Par-122
❑ 91Par-430
❑ 91ParFre-122
❑ 91ParFre-430
❑ 91Pin-202
❑ 91PinFre-202
❑ 91ProSet-167
❑ 91ProSet-604
❑ 91ProSetFre-167
❑ 91ProSetFre-604
❑ 91ProSetPla-84
❑ 91ProSetPlaPC-PC11
❑ 91ScoAme-135
❑ 91ScoCan-135
❑ 91StaClu-51
❑ 91Top-46
❑ 91UppDec-247
❑ 91UppDecF-247
❑ 92Bow-146
❑ 92OPC-245
❑ 92OPC-300
❑ 92PanSti-237
❑ 92PanStiFre-237
❑ 92Par-108
❑ 92ParEmel-108
❑ 92Pin-94
❑ 92PinFre-94
❑ 92ProSet-113
❑ 92ProSet-256
❑ 92Sco-50
❑ 92Sco-443
❑ 92Sco-445
❑ 92ScoCan-50
❑ 92ScoCan-443
❑ 92ScoCan-445
❑ 92StaClu-311
❑ 92Top-264
❑ 92Top-404
❑ 92TopGol-264G
❑ 92TopGol-404G
❑ 92Ult-135
❑ 92UppDec-34
❑ 92UppDec-126
❑ 93Don-218
❑ 93Don-494
❑ 93Lea-213
❑ 93McDUppD-15
❑ 93OPCPre-375
❑ 93OPCPre-384
❑ 93OPCPreG-375
❑ 93OPCPreG-384
❑ 93PanSti-91
❑ 93Par-400
❑ 93ParEmel-400
❑ 93Pin-27
❑ 93Pin-241
❑ 93PinAllS-8
❑ 93PinAllS-46
❑ 93PinAllSC-8
❑ 93PinAllSC-46
❑ 93PinCan-27
❑ 93PinCan-241
❑ 93Pow-157
❑ 93Sco-2
❑ 93Sco-447
❑ 93ScoCan-2
❑ 93ScoCan-447
❑ 93ScoSam-2
❑ 93StaClu-110
❑ 93StaCluAS-22
❑ 93StaCluFDI-110
❑ 93StaCluFDIO-110
❑ 93StaCluFin-6
❑ 93StaCluO-110
❑ 93TopPre-375
❑ 93TopPre-384
❑ 93TopPreG-375
❑ 93TopPreG-384
❑ 93Ult-25
❑ 93UltRedLS-3
❑ 93UltSpeM-4
❑ 93UppDec-205
❑ 93UppDecLAS-38
❑ 93UppDecNR-26
❑ 93UppDecSP-98
❑ 94BeAPla-R127
❑ 94CanGamNHLP-233
❑ 94Don-111
❑ 94EASpo-89
❑ 94Fin-96
❑ 94FinRef-96
❑ 94FinSupTW-96
❑ 94Fla-180
❑ 94Fle-214
❑ 94Lea-135
❑ 94LeaFirOIce-11
❑ 94MapLeaG-7
❑ 94MapLeaK-11
❑ 94MapLeaPP-21A
❑ 94OPCPre-253
❑ 94OPCPreSE-253
❑ 94Par-228
❑ 94ParGol-228
❑ 94ParSEV-29
❑ 94Pin-31
❑ 94PinArtP-31
❑ 94PinRinC-31
❑ 94Sco-112
❑ 94Sco-242
❑ 94ScoGol-112
❑ 94ScoGol-242
❑ 94ScoPla-112
❑ 94ScoPla-242
❑ 94ScoPlaTS-112
❑ 94ScoPlaTS-242
❑ 94Sel-95
❑ 94SelGol-95
❑ 94TopPre-253
❑ 94TopPreSE-253
❑ 94Ult-214
❑ 94UltRedLS-3
❑ 94UppDec-32
❑ 94UppDec-230
❑ 94UppDecEleIce-32
❑ 94UppDecEleIce-230
❑ 94UppDecNBAP-22
❑ 94UppDecSPI-SP78
❑ 94UppDecSPIDC-SP78
❑ 95CanGamNHLP-261
❑ 95ColCho-149
❑ 95ColChoPC-149
❑ 95ColChoPCP-149
❑ 95Don-293
❑ 95Emo-169
❑ 95Fin-8
❑ 95FinRef-8
❑ 95Lea-37
❑ 95LeaLim-109
❑ 95Met-142
❑ 95ParInt-206
❑ 95ParIntEl-206
❑ 95Pin-75
❑ 95PinArtP-75
❑ 95PinRinC-75
❑ 95PlaOneoOne-95
❑ 95Sco-204
❑ 95ScoBlaIce-204
❑ 95ScoBlaIceAP-204
❑ 95SelCer-54
❑ 95SelCerMG-54
❑ 95SkyImp-159
❑ 95StaClu-162
❑ 95StaCluMOMS-162
❑ 95Sum-143
❑ 95SumArtP-143
❑ 95SumIce-143
❑ 95SweGloWC-85
❑ 95Top-98
❑ 95TopOPCI-98
❑ 95TopSupSki-28
❑ 95TopSupSkiPla-28
❑ 95Ult-311
❑ 95UppDec-110
❑ 95UppDecEleIce-110
❑ 95UppDecEleIceG-110
❑ 95Zen-62
❑ 96BeAPAut-25
❑ 96BeAPAutSil-25
❑ 96BeAPla-25
❑ 96Don-206
❑ 96DonCanI-18
❑ 96DonCanIGPP-18
❑ 96DonCanIRPP-18
❑ 96DonEli-123
❑ 96DonEliDCS-123
❑ 96DonPrePro-206
❑ 96DurL'EB-JB9
❑ 96FlaNowAT-1
❑ 96FlePic-170
❑ 96Lea-91
❑ 96LeaPreP-91
❑ 96MetUni-116
❑ 96NHLACEPC-17
❑ 96Pin-35
❑ 96PinArtP-35
❑ 96PinFoi-35
❑ 96PinPreS-35
❑ 96PinRinC-35
❑ 96PlaOneoOne-349
❑ 96Sco-154
❑ 96ScoArtPro-154
❑ 96ScoDeaCAP-154
❑ 96ScoGolB-154
❑ 96ScoSpeAP-154
❑ 96SkyImpB-5
❑ 96SP-123
❑ 96StaCluMO-22
❑ 96Sum-28
❑ 96SumArtP-28
❑ 96SumIce-28
❑ 96SumMet-28
❑ 96SumPreS-28
❑ 96TeaOut-36
❑ 96TopPic5C-FC2
❑ 96Ult-130
❑ 96UltGolM-130
❑ 96UppDec-316
❑ 96UppDecBD-42
❑ 96UppDecBDG-42
❑ 96UppDecIce-52
❑ 96UppDecIcePar-52
❑ 97ColCho-196
❑ 97Don-110
❑ 97DonCanI-54
❑ 97DonCanI-149
❑ 97DonCanIDS-54
❑ 97DonCanIDS-149
❑ 97DonCanIPS-54
❑ 97DonCanIPS-149
❑ 97DonEli-147
❑ 97DonEliAsp-147
❑ 97DonEliS-147
❑ 97DonLim-40
❑ 97DonLimExp-40
❑ 97DonPre-47
❑ 97DonPreCttC-47
❑ 97DonPreProG-110
❑ 97DonPreProS-110
❑ 97DonPri-93
❑ 97DonPriSoA-93
❑ 97Kat-109
❑ 97KatGol-109
❑ 97KatSil-109
❑ 97Pac-22
❑ 97PacCop-22
❑ 97PacCroR-102
❑ 97PacCroREG-102
❑ 97PacCroRIB-102
❑ 97PacCroRS-102
❑ 97PacDyn-95
❑ 97PacDynBKS-74
❑ 97PacDynC-95
❑ 97PacDynDG-95
❑ 97PacDynEG-95
❑ 97PacDynIB-95
❑ 97PacDynR-95
❑ 97PacDynSil-95
❑ 97PacDynTan-65
❑ 97PacEmeGre-22
❑ 97PacIceB-22
❑ 97PacInv-106
❑ 97PacInvC-106
❑ 97PacInvEG-106
❑ 97PacInvIB-106
❑ 97PacInvNRB-152
❑ 97PacInvR-106
❑ 97PacInvS-106
❑ 97PacOme-173
❑ 97PacOmeC-173
❑ 97PacOmeDG-173
❑ 97PacOmeEG-173
❑ 97PacOmeG-173
❑ 97PacOmeIB-173
❑ 97PacPar-139
❑ 97PacParC-139
❑ 97PacParDG-139
❑ 97PacParEG-139
❑ 97PacParIB-139
❑ 97PacParRed-139
❑ 97PacParSil-139
❑ 97PacRed-22
❑ 97PacRev-105
❑ 97PacRevC-105
❑ 97PacRevE-105
❑ 97PacRevIB-105
❑ 97PacRevR-105
❑ 97PacRevS-105
❑ 97PacSil-22
❑ 97PacSlaSDC-7C
❑ 97Pin-137
❑ 97PinCer-85
❑ 97PinCerMB-85
❑ 97PinCerMG-85
❑ 97PinCerMR-85
❑ 97PinCerR-85
❑ 97PinIns-97
❑ 97PinPrePBB-137
❑ 97PinPrePBC-137
❑ 97PinPrePBM-137
❑ 97PinPrePBY-137
❑ 97PinPrePFC-137
❑ 97PinPrePFM-137
❑ 97PinPrePFY-137
❑ 97PinPrePla-137
❑ 97PinTotCMPG-85
❑ 97PinTotCPB-85
❑ 97PinTotCPG-85
❑ 97PinTotCPR-85
❑ 97Sco-139
❑ 97ScoArtPro-139
❑ 97ScoGolBla-139
❑ 97SPAut-124
❑ 97Stu-89
❑ 97StuPrePG-89
❑ 97StuPrePS-89
❑ 97UppDec-128
❑ 98Pac-338
❑ 98PacIceB-338
❑ 98PacRed-338
❑ 99RetHoc-110
❑ 99UppDecRG-110
❑ 99UppDecRII-MG
❑ 99UppDecRIL1-MG
❑ 99UppDecRP-110
**Gartshore, David**
❑ 91LakSupSL-9
**Garver, Jon**
❑ 93WatBlaH-9
**Garvey, Brendan**
❑ 92OklCitB-5
**Garvey, Liam**
❑ 91MicTecHus-30
❑ 93MicTecH-18
❑ 96PeoRiv-6
❑ 96PeoRivPA-6
❑ 98GerDELE-256
**Garvin, Scott**
❑ 92BriColJHL-231
**Garwasiuk, Ron**
❑ 77RocAme-10
**Garzone, Matt**
❑ 96RicRen-6
**Gasparini, Tony**
❑ 93OmaLan-6
**Gassoff, Bob**
❑ 74NHLActSta-243
❑ 75OPCNHL-58
❑ 75Top-58
❑ 76OPCNHL-301
❑ 76OPCNHL-393
❑ 77OPCNHL-4
❑ 77Top-4
❑ 92BluUDBB-13
**Gassoff, Brad**
❑ 76CanuRoyB-4
❑ 77CanCanDC-2
❑ 77CanuRoyB-4
❑ 78OPC-388
❑ 79OPC-353
**Gatenby, Dan**
❑ 87SudWol-3
**Gathercole, Philip**
❑ 917thInnSQMJHL-235
**Gatherum, Dave**
❑ 51LavDaiS-66
❑ 52St.LawS-107
**Gatto, Greg**
❑ 907thInnSWHL-315
❑ 917thInnSWHL-10
**Gatzos, Steve**
❑ 80SauSteMG-10
❑ 83PenCok-10
❑ 83PenTealP-12
❑ 84PenHeiP-10
**Gaucher, Ryan**
❑ 96SasBla-10
**Gaucher, Yves**
❑ 84RicRiv-6
**Gaudet, Denis**
❑ 93NorBayC-17
**Gaudet, Kevin**
❑ 96GerDELE-203
❑ 98GerDELE-202
**Gaudet, Marc-Andre**
❑ 97BowCHL-66
❑ 97BowCHLOPC-66
❑ 98BowCHL-91
❑ 98BowCHLGA-91
❑ 98BowCHLOI-91
❑ 98BowChrC-91
❑ 98BowChrCGA-91
❑ 98BowChrCGAR-91
❑ 98BowChrCOI-91
❑ 98BowChrCOIR-91
❑ 98BowChrCR-91
**Gaudette, Andre**
❑ 72NordPos-8
❑ 73NordTeal-9
❑ 74OPCWHA-46
**Gaudreau, Robert (Rob)**
❑ 92Cla-82
❑ 93ClaProPLP-LP3
❑ 93ClaProPProt-PR3
❑ 93ClaProPro-16
❑ 93ClaProPro-140
❑ 93Don-310
❑ 93Lea-9
❑ 93OPCPre-199
❑ 93OPCPreG-199
❑ 93PanSti-258
❑ 93Par-189
❑ 93ParEmel-189
❑ 93Pin-41
❑ 93PinCan-41
❑ 93Pow-220
❑ 93PowSecYS-1
❑ 93Sco-247
❑ 93ScoCan-247
❑ 93StaClu-174
❑ 93StaCluFDI-174
❑ 93StaCluFDIO-174
❑ 93StaCluO-174
❑ 93TopPre-199
❑ 93TopPreG-199
❑ 93Ult-98
❑ 93UltPro-2
❑ 93UppDec-149
❑ 93UppDecHT-HT9
❑ 93UppDecNB-HB2
❑ 93UppDecSP-143
❑ 94BeAPSig-85
❑ 94Fle-146
❑ 94Lea-39
❑ 94OPCPre-4
❑ 94OPCPreSE-4
❑ 94Par-207
❑ 94ParGol-207
❑ 94Pin-349
❑ 94PinArtP-349
❑ 94PinRinC-349
❑ 94SenBelM-13
❑ 94TopPre-4
❑ 94TopPreSE-4
❑ 94UppDec-182
❑ 94UppDec-277
❑ 94UppDecEleIce-182
❑ 94UppDecEleIce-277
❑ 95ColCho-158
❑ 95ColChoPC-158
❑ 95ColChoPCP-158
❑ 95Sco-141
❑ 95ScoBlaIce-141
❑ 95ScoBlaIceAP-141
❑ 95Sen-10
❑ 95Top-117
❑ 95TopOPCI-117
❑ 95UppDec-164
❑ 95UppDecEleIce-164
❑ 95UppDecEleIceG-164
❑ 96ClaGol-82
**Gaudreault, Armand**
❑ 51LavDaiQSHL-14
**Gaudreault, Leonard (Leon)**
❑ 27LaPat-13
❑ 51LavDaiLSJ-32
**Gaul, Horace**
❑ 10C56-31
**Gaul, Michael**
❑ 917thInnSQMJHL-236
❑ 94KnoChe-19
**Gaulin, Jean-Marc**
❑ 81FreExp-22
❑ 82FreExp-22
❑ 83FreExp-21
❑ 84NordPos-8
❑ 85FreExp-26
❑ 85NordGenF-8
❑ 86FreExp-8
**Gaume, Dallas**
❑ 88ProAHL-61
**Gaumond, Alexandre**
❑ 917thInnSQMJHL-295
**Gaus, Thomas**
❑ 94GerDELE-417
❑ 95GerDELE-388
❑ 96GerDELE-296
**Gauthier, Alain**
❑ 907thInnSQMJHL-251
❑ 917thInnSQMJHL-249
**Gauthier, Daniel**
❑ 90KnoChe-106
❑ 91ProAHLCHL-296
❑ 92CleLum-22
❑ 93ClaProPro-23
❑ 94IndIce-8
❑ 95IndIce-8
**Gauthier, Denis**
❑ 93DruVol-14
❑ 95Cla-19
❑ 95ClaCHLAS-AS14
❑ 95DonEliWJ-5
❑ 95UppDec-533
❑ 95UppDecEleIce-533
❑ 95UppDecEleIceG-533
❑ 98Pac-118
❑ 98PacIceB-118
❑ 98PacRed-118
❑ 98UppDec-50
❑ 98UppDecE-50
❑ 98UppDecE1o1-50
❑ 98UppDecGR-50
**Gauthier, Derek**
❑ 907thInnSOHL-233
❑ 90KitRan-17
❑ 917thInnSOHL-84
❑ 94BraSmo-8
❑ 97AncAce-8
**Gauthier, Don**
❑ 89RayJrC-9
**Gauthier, Fern**
❑ 44BeeGro2P-168

**Gauthier, Gerard**
- 90ProSet-687

**Gauthier, Jean**
- 61ShiCoi-120
- 61YorYelB-42
- 63ChePho-15
- 63Par-28
- 63Par-87
- 63QueAce-8
- 63QueAceQ-7
- 63YorWhiB-29

**Gauthier, Luc**
- 86SheCan-16
- 88ProAHL-299
- 89ProAHL-197
- 90ProAHLIHL-55
- 91ProAHLCHL-76
- 92FreCan-11
- 93FreCan-11
- 94FreCan-14
- 95FreCan-29

**Gauthier, Sean**
- 907thInnSOHL-57
- 91MonHaw-9
- 91ProAHLCHL-180
- 95SouCarS-23

**Gauthier, Steven**
- 84ChiSag-12

**Gauvreau, Brent**
- 98BowCHL-144
- 98BowCHLAuB-A37
- 98BowCHLAuS-A37
- 98BowCHLGA-144
- 98BowChrC-144
- 98BowChrCGA-144
- 98BowChrCGAR-144
- 98BowChrCOI-144
- 98BowChrCOIR-144
- 98BowChrCR-144

**Gavey, Aaron**
- 917thInnSOHL-316
- 93Cla-21
- 93DonTeaC-12
- 93Pin-473
- 93PinCan-473
- 93SauSteMG-20
- 93SauSteMGM-22
- 93UppDec-545
- 94BeAPla-R156
- 94Cla-115
- 94ClaCHLAS-C5
- 94ClaDraGol-115
- 94ClaROYS-R6
- 94ClaTri-T64
- 94Fla-172
- 94Lea-452
- 94LeaLim-118
- 94OPCPre-536
- 94OPCPreSE-536
- 94Pin-251
- 94PinArtP-251
- 94PinRinC-251
- 94Sco-207
- 94ScoGol-207
- 94ScoPla-207
- 94Sel-180
- 94SelGol-180
- 94TopPre-536
- 94TopPreSE-536
- 95BeAPla-165
- 95BeAPSig-S165
- 95BeAPSigDC-S165
- 95Bow-121
- 95BowAllFoi-121
- 95ColEdgI-101
- 95Don-369
- 95Fin-28
- 95FinRef-28
- 95LigTeal-9
- 95ParInt-527
- 95ParIntEI-527
- 95SkyImp-221
- 95SP-138
- 95StaClu-138
- 95StaCluMOMS-138
- 95UppDec-417
- 95UppDecEIeIce-417
- 95UppDecEIeIceG-417
- 96ColCho-249
- 96DonEli-64
- 96DonEliDCS-64
- 96Lea-167
- 96LeaPreP-167
- 96Sco-259
- 96ScoArtPro-259
- 96ScoDeaCAP-259
- 96ScoGolB-259
- 96ScoSpeAP-259
- 96Sum-158
- 96SumArtP-158
- 96SumIce-158
- 96SumMet-158
- 96SumPreS-158
- 97PacInvNRB-27
- 97UppDec-28

**Gavin, Stewart**
- 80MapLeaP-19
- 80PepCap-88
- 81MapLeaP-7
- 82MapLeaP-13
- 82PosCer-18
- 83MapLeaP-7
- 83OPC-331

**Gebauer, A.**
- 83Vac-87
- 84MapLeaP-10
- 840PC-302
- 85OPCSti-17
- 86WhaJunT-10
- 87OPC-61
- 87PanSti-49
- 87Top-61
- 87WhaJunBK-8
- 88NorStaADA-11
- 880PC-217
- 890PC-214
- 89PanSti-113
- 900PC-402
- 90PanSti-260
- 90ProSet-139
- 90Sco-244
- 90ScoCan-244
- 90UppDec-150
- 90UppDecF-150
- 91ProSet-404
- 91ProSetFre-404
- 91ScoCan-433
- 92Sco-117
- 92ScoCan-117

**Gawley, Sean**
- 917thInnSOHL-298

**Gebauer, A.**
- 95GerDELE-350

**Gebel, Martin**
- 94GerDELE-237
- 95GerDELE-240
- 96GerDELE-73

**Gecse, Derek**
- 91BriColJHL-101

**Gecse, Dorel**
- 918riColJHL-72

**Geddes, Paul**
- 94GerDELE-323
- 95GerDELE-299
- 96GerDELE-325

**Gee, George**
- 44BeeGro2P-97
- 44BeeGro2P-169
- 51Par-43
- 52Par-36
- 53Par-83
- 54Par-80

**Geekie, Craig**
- 917thInnSWHL-213
- 92BraWheK-7

**Geesink, Tony**
- 84OIt67-7

**Geffert, Pavel**
- 94CzeAPSE-87
- 96CzeAPSE-131

**Gegenfurther, Christian**
- 94GerDELE-383
- 95GerDELE-367
- 96GerDELE-189
- 98GerDELE-310

**Gehrig, Mario**
- 94GerDELE-276
- 95GerDELE-273
- 96GerDELE-168
- 98GerDELE-122
- 98GerDELE-336

**Gelati, Mike**
- 95Sla-300

**Geldart, Greg**
- 95TalTigS-14

**Gelinas, Martin**
- 88OilTenAnn-73
- 89OilTeal-7
- 90Bow-190
- 90BowTif-190
- 90OilIGA-5
- 900PC-64
- 90ProSet-83
- 90Sco-301C
- 90ScoCan-301C
- 90ScoYouS-21
- 90Top-64
- 90UppDec-23
- 90UppDecF-23
- 91Bow-102
- 91OilIGA-5
- 91OilPanTS-5
- 91OilTeal-6
- 910PC-244
- 91PanSti-128
- 91Par-283
- 91ParFre-283
- 91Pin-93
- 91PinFre-93
- 91ProSet-66
- 91ProSetFre-66
- 91ScoAme-159
- 91ScoCan-159
- 91ScoYouS-14
- 91StaClu-11
- 91Top-244
- 91UppDec-266
- 91UppDecF-266
- 92OilIGA-6
- 920PC-19
- 92PanSti-106
- 92PanStiFre-106
- 92Pin-166
- 92PinFre-166
- 92Sco-281
- 92ScoCan-281
- 92StaClu-314
- 92Top-292

**Gelinas, Martin** (cont.)
- 92TopGol-292G
- 92UppDec-282
- 93Don-271
- 93Don-501
- 93DurSco-22
- 93Lea-396
- 93Par-166
- 93ParEmeI-166
- 93Pin-366
- 93PinCan-366
- 93Sco-408
- 93ScoCan-408
- 93ScoCan-534
- 93ScoGol-534
- 93Ult-401
- 93UppDec-322
- 93UppDecSP-127
- 94CanGamNHLP-335
- 94CanuProI-9
- 94Lea-138
- 94OPCPre-101
- 94OPCPreSE-101
- 94ParSE-SE184
- 94ParSEG-SE184
- 94ParVin-V36
- 94Pin-324
- 94PinArtP-324
- 94PinRinC-324
- 94TopPre-101
- 94TopPreSE-101
- 94Ult-383
- 94UppDec-54
- 94UppDecEIeIce-54
- 94UppDecSPI-SP172
- 94UppDecSPIDC-SP172
- 95BeAPla-149
- 95BeAPSig-S149
- 95BeAPSigDC-S149
- 95CanGamNHLP-273
- 95CanuBuiDA-9
- 95ColCho-176
- 95ColChoPC-176
- 95ColChoPCP-176
- 95Don-223
- 95ParInt-480
- 95ParIntEI-480
- 95Pin-161
- 95PinArtP-161
- 95PinRinC-161
- 95Top-176
- 95TopOPCI-176
- 95UppDec-359
- 95UppDecEIeIce-359
- 95UppDecEIeIceG-359
- 96CanuPos-23
- 96Don-133
- 96DonPrePro-133
- 96Lea-127
- 96LeaPreP-127
- 96Pin-83
- 96PinArtP-83
- 96PinFoi-83
- 96PinPreS-83
- 96PinRinC-83
- 96Sco-98
- 96ScoArtPro-98
- 96ScoDeaCAP-98
- 96ScoGolB-98
- 96ScoSpeAP-98
- 96Sum-79
- 96SumArtP-79
- 96SumIce-79
- 96SumMet-79
- 96SumPreS-79
- 96UppDec-171
- 97CarHur-8
- 97ColCho-257
- 97ColChoSta-SQ8
- 97Don-41
- 97DonCanI-61
- 97DonCanIDS-61
- 97DonCanIPS-61
- 97DonLim-185
- 97DonLimExp-185
- 97DonPre-83
- 97DonPreCttC-83
- 97DonPreProG-41
- 97DonPreProS-41
- 97Lea-37
- 97LeaFraMat-37
- 97LeaFraMDC-37
- 97LeaInt-37
- 97LeaIntUI-37
- 97Pac-67
- 97PacCop-67
- 97PacCroR-134
- 97PacCroREG-134
- 97PacCroRIB-134
- 97PacCroRS-134
- 97PacDyn-126
- 97PacDynC-126
- 97PacDynDG-126
- 97PacDynEG-126
- 97PacDynIB-126
- 97PacDynR-126
- 97PacDynSil-126
- 97PacDynTan-60
- 97PacEmeGre-67
- 97PacIceB-67
- 97PacInv-141
- 97PacInvC-141
- 97PacInvEG-141
- 97PacInvIB-141
- 97PacInvR-141

**Gelinas, Martin** (cont.)
- 97PacInvS-141
- 97PacOme-40
- 97PacOmeC-40
- 97PacOmeDG-40
- 97PacOmeEG-40
- 97PacOmeG-40
- 97PacOmeIB-40
- 97PacPar-187
- 97PacParC-187
- 97PacParDG-187
- 97PacParEG-187
- 97PacParIB-187
- 97PacParRed-187
- 97PacParSil-187
- 97PacRed-67
- 97PacRev-22
- 97PacRevC-22
- 97PacRevEmt-22
- 97PacRevIB-22
- 97PacRevR-22
- 97PacRevS-22
- 97PacSil-67
- 97Pin-168
- 97PinCer-113
- 97PinCerMB-113
- 97PinCerMG-113
- 97PinCerMR-113
- 97PinCerR-113
- 97PinIns-103
- 97PinPrePBB-168
- 97PinPrePBC-168
- 97PinPrePBM-168
- 97PinPrePBY-168
- 97PinPrePFC-168
- 97PinPrePFM-168
- 97PinPrePFY-168
- 97PinPrePla-168
- 97PinTotCMPG-113
- 97PinTotCPB-113
- 97PinTotCPG-113
- 97PinTotCPR-113
- 97Sco-133
- 97ScoArtPro-133
- 97ScoCanPla-5
- 97ScoCanPre-5
- 97ScoCanu-5
- 97ScoGolBla-133
- 97UppDec-167
- 97UppDec-200
- 98Fin-8
- 98FinNo P-8
- 98FinNo PR-8
- 98FinRef-8
- 98Pac-132
- 98PacAur-32
- 98PacDynI-32
- 98PacDynIIB-32
- 98PacDynIR-32
- 98PacIceB-132
- 98PacOmeH-41
- 98PacOmeR-41
- 98PacPar-36
- 98PacParC-36
- 98PacParEG-36
- 98PacParH-36
- 98PacParIB-36
- 98PacParS-36
- 98PacRed-132
- 98UppDec-238
- 98UppDecE-238
- 98UppDecE1o1-238
- 98UppDecGR-238
- 98UppDecM-39
- 98UppDecMGS-39
- 98UppDecMSS-39
- 98UppDecMSS-39
- 99Pac-71
- 99PacCop-71
- 99PacGol-71
- 99PacIceB-71
- 99PacPreD-71

**Gelinas, Ryan**
- 95Sla-406

**Gelineau, Jack**
- 44BeeGro2P-24
- 48ExhCan-47
- 51LavDaiQSHL-4
- 51LavDaiS-4
- 51St.LawS-37

**Gendron, Bryan**
- 897thInnSOHL-120
- 907thInnSOHL-359
- 917thInnSOHL-141
- 91PetPet-11

**Gendron, Edgard**
- 51LavDaiLSJ-50

**Gendron, Jean-Guy**
- 44BeeGro2P-25
- 44BeeGro2P-313
- 52JunBluT-40
- 57Top-52
- 58Top-51
- 59Top-24
- 60ShiCoi-109
- 60Top-31
- 60YorPreP-9
- 61ShiCoi-93
- 61Top-57
- 62Top-16
- 63Top-16
- 63TorSta-23
- 64BeeGro3P-8
- 64QueAce-4

**Gendron, Jean-Guy** (cont.)
- 65QueAce-4
- 680PC-185
- 690PC-169
- 690PCFou-11
- 69Top-96
- 70DadCoo-38
- 70EssPowPla-207
- 700PC-86
- 70SarProSta-157
- 70Top-86
- 710PC-204
- 71SarProSta-153
- 71TorSun-195
- 72FlyMigM-5
- 72NordPos-9
- 720PC-302
- 72SluCupWHA-7
- 72SweSemWC-170
- 73NordTeal-10

**Gendron, Martin**
- 907thInnSQMJHL-234
- 917thInnSQMJHL-27
- 92Cla-23
- 93Cla-131
- 93DonTeaC-13
- 93Pin-474
- 93PinCan-474
- 93Pow-480
- 93Ult-460
- 93UppDec-259
- 93UppDec-540
- 94ClaProPIH-LP12
- 94PorPir-8
- 95Cap-7
- 95Don-47
- 95ParInt-489
- 95ParIntEI-489
- 95Pin-201
- 95PinArtP-201
- 95PinRinC-201
- 95PorPir-11
- 95Sco-315
- 95ScoBIaIce-315
- 95ScoBIaIceAP-315
- 95SkyImp-224
- 95Ult-174
- 95UltGoIM-174
- 96ClaGol-23
- 96LasVegThu-7

**Gendron, Pierre**
- 917thInnSQMJHL-133

**Genest, Marc**
- 96SouCarS-10

**Genest, Patrick**
- 907thInnSQMJHL-366
- 917thInnSQMJHL-188

**Genik, Jason**
- 92BriColJHL-182

**Genovy, Al**
- 77KalWin-13

**Gentile, Flavio**
- 91Arilce-17

**Genze, Alexander**
- 94GerDELE-297
- 95GerDELE-197
- 96GerDELE-428

**Geoffrion, BoomBoom (Bernie)**
- 44BeeGro2P-241
- 45QuaOatP-78
- 48ExhCan-8
- 48ExhCan-61
- 51Par-14
- 52Par-3
- 53Par-29
- 54Par-100
- 55Par-43
- 55Par-70
- 55ParQuaO-43
- 55ParQuaO-70
- 57Par-M2
- 57Par-M24
- 58Par-28
- 59Par-33
- 60Par-46
- 60Par-59
- 60ShiCoi-28
- 60YorPreP-10
- 61Par-35
- 61ShiCoi-104
- 61YorYelB-28
- 62Par-48
- 62Par-53
- 62ShiMetC-34
- 62YorIroOTra-12
- 63ChePho-16
- 63Par-29
- 63Par-88
- 63TorSta-14
- 63YorWhiB-20
- 64BeeGro3P-125
- 64BeeGro3P-189
- 64QueAce-5
- 65QueAce-5
- 66Top-85
- 66TopUSAT-36
- 67Top-29
- 72Flam-4
- 74OPCNHL-147
- 74Top-147
- 79CanaPos-5
- 83HalFP-M8
- 85HalFC-166

**Geoffrion, Dan (Danny)**
- 79CanaPos-6
- 80JetPos-8
- 80PepCap-127
- 81OPC-364
- 81OPCSti-141

**George, Chris**
- 94SarSti-10
- 95Sla-7

**George, Darcy**
- 92BriColJHL-174

**George, Justin**
- 93NorMicW-7
- 95SolBar-11

**George, Zac**
- 92BriColJHL-26

**Gerard, Dean**
- 91AirCanSJHL-A32
- 91AirCanSJHL-B32
- 91AirCanSJHLAS-8
- 92MPSPhoSJHL-45

**Gerard, Eddie**
- 12C57-34
- 23V1451-1
- 60TopSta-18
- 83HalFP-N5
- 85HalFC-200

**Gerbe, Joseph**
- 96GueSto-12
- 97GueSto-11

**Gerebi, Nick**
- 91MinGolG-8

**Geremia, Ryan**
- 95SwiCurB-5

**Gerhardsson, Peter**
- 94SweLeaE-249
- 95SweLeaE-158

**Geris, Dave**
- 93WinSpi-20
- 94WinSpi-22
- 95Sla-425

**Gerlitz, H.**
- 28V1282PauC-58

**Gerlitz, J.**
- 28V1282PauC-57

**Gerlitz, J.**
- 28V1282PauC-54

**Germain, Claude**
- 51LavDaiLSJ-57

**Germain, Daniel**
- 917thInnSQMJHL-252

**Germain, Eric**
- 88ProAHL-205
- 89ProAHL-12
- 90ProAHLIHL-19
- 93AmoLesFAM-8
- 93RicRen-17

**Gernander, Ken**
- 91MonHaw-10
- 91ProAHLCHL-178
- 94BinRan-4
- 95BinRan-8
- 96BinRan-12

**Gerow, Rod**
- 85LonKni-24

**Gerrits, Brian**
- 86PorWinH-7
- 88SasBla-16

**Gerse, Dave**
- 88RegPat-6

**Gerum, Christian**
- 94GerDELE-322
- 95GerDELE-291
- 96GerDELE-318

**Gervais, Eddy**
- 917thInnSQMJHL-79

**Gervais, Gaston**
- 51LavDaiQSHL-84

**Gervais, George**
- 91AirCanSJHL-B34

**Gervais, Guy**
- 50QueCit-6
- 51LavDaiLSJ-40

**Gervais, Shawn**
- 92BriColJHL-168
- 93SeaThu-6
- 95SeaThu-10

**Gervais, Victor**
- 90ProAHLIHL-201
- 91HamRoaA-4
- 91ProAHLCHL-558
- 92HamRoaA-9

**Gervais, Victor** (cont.)
- 93CleLum-15
- 93HamRoaA-9
- 95CleLum-13
- 96HamRoaA-HRA9
- 98GerDELE-140

**Gesce, Derek**
- 92BriColJHL-9

**Getliffe, Ray**
- 34BeeGro1P-15
- 34BeeGro1P-153
- 390PCV3011-29
- 400PCV3012-147

**Giacomin, Ed**
- 64BeeGro3P-126
- 65Coc-73
- 65Top-21
- 66Top-23
- 67Top-85
- 67Top-123
- 680PC-67
- 680PC-205
- 68ShiCoi-95
- 68Top-67
- 690PC-33
- 690PC-217
- 690PCFou-5
- 690PCSta-8
- 69Top-33
- 70ColSta-70
- 70DadCoo-39
- 70EssPowPla-181
- 700PC-68
- 700PC-244
- 700PCDec-42
- 70PosCerS-3
- 70SarProSta-115
- 70Top-68
- 70TopStiS-9
- 71LetActR-10
- 71MatMinRec-4
- 710PC-220
- 710PC-248
- 710PC-250
- 710PCTBoo-7
- 71SarProSta-128
- 71Top-2
- 71Top-5
- 71Top-6
- 71Top-90
- 71TorSun-172
- 720PC-173
- 72SarProSta-147
- 72SweSemWC-213
- 72Top-165
- 730PC-160
- 73Top-140
- 74LipSou-26
- 74NHLActSta-189
- 74OPCNHL-160
- 74Top-160
- 75OPCNHL-55
- 75Top-55
- 760PCNHL-160
- 76Top-160
- 770PCNHL-70
- 77Top-70
- 81RedWinOld-2
- 85HalFC-259
- 91UltOriS-20
- 91UltOriSBB-1
- 91UltOriSF-20
- 92HalFL-31
- 95Par66-93
- 95Par66Coi-93
- 95ZelMasoH-2

**Giammarco, Franco**
- 86KinCan-7
- 87KinCan-7

**Gianini, Tiziano**
- 91UppDec-670
- 91UppDecWJC-31
- 91UppDecF-670
- 93SwiHNL-142
- 95SwiHNL-189

**Giannetti, Mark**
- 93SudWol-13
- 93SudWolP-13

**Giarard, Dary**
- 907thInnSQMJHL-21

**Giard, Stephane**
- 917thInnSQMJHL-52

**Gibb, Myles**
- 91AirCanSJHL-B27

**Gibbons, Brian**
- 72NatOttWHA-10

**Gibbons, Jeff**
- 92TolSto-6

**Gibbs, Barry**
- 70EssPowPla-164
- 70NorStaP-1
- 70SarProSta-91
- 71SarProSta-95
- 71TorSun-129
- 720PC-101
- 72SarProSta-108
- 72Top-169
- 73NorStaAP-3
- 73NorStaP-5
- 730PC-174
- 73Top-30
- 74NHLActSta-137
- 74NHLActStaU-1
- 74OPCNHL-203
- 74Top-203
- 75OPCNHL-214

□ 75Top-214
**Gibbs, Richard**
□ 92MPSPhoSJHL-135
**Gibson, Don**
□ 90CanuMoh-9
□ 90ProAHLIHL-340
□ 91ProAHLCHL-610
□ 91UppDec-495
□ 91UppDecF-495
**Gibson, Doug**
□ 750PCNHL-375
**Gibson, Jack**
□ 72NatOttWHA-11
□ 83HalFP-N6
□ 83Jet-7
□ 85HalFC-201
**Gibson, Jason**
□ 97AncAce-9
**Gibson, Mike**
□ 86RegPat-7
**Gibson, Steve**
□ 907thInnSOHL-183
□ 917thInnSOHL-176
□ 92WinSpi-25
□ 93WheThu-UD5
□ 94WheThu-7
**Gibson, Wade**
□ 897thInnSOHL-66
□ 907thInnSOHL-84
□ 917thInnSOHL-73
□ 93SauSteMG-21
□ 93SauSteMGM-23
**Gidlund, Lars**
□ 65SweCorl-154
**Gies, Jeff**
□ 93SauSteMG-14
□ 95SauSteMG-8
□ 95Sla-368
**Giesebrecht, Bert**
□ 51LavDaiS-60
**Giesebrecht, Gus**
□ 34BeeGro1P-100
□ 390PCV3011-69
**Giesebrecht, Jack**
□ 51LavDaiS-112
□ 52St.LawS-62
**Giffin, Bob**
□ 83Ott67-7
□ 84Ott67-8
**Giffin, Lee**
□ 83OshGen-22
□ 88ProIHL-49
□ 89ProIHL-37
□ 90KanCitBla-18
□ 90ProAHLIHL-584
□ 91ProAHLCHL-464
**Giffin, Rob**
□ 93PetPet-4
□ 95Sla-311
**Gignac, Chris**
□ 917thInnSOHL-307
**Gignac, Jean-Guy**
□ 52JunBluT-74
**Giguere, Jean Sebastien**
□ 94ParSE-SE270
□ 94ParSEG-SE270
□ 95Cla-13
□ 95ClaCHLAS-AS13
□ 95ClaIceBre-BK12
□ 96ClaIceBreDC-BK12
□ 96UppDecIce-25
□ 96UppDecIcePar-25
□ 97BowCHL-62
□ 97BowCHLOPC-62
□ 97Don-200
□ 97DonCanI-146
□ 97DonCanIDS-146
□ 97DonCanILG-4
□ 97DonCanILGP-4
□ 97DonCanIPS-146
□ 97DonLim-29
□ 97DonLim-102
□ 97DonLimExp-29
□ 97DonLimExp-102
□ 97DonLimFOTG-9
□ 97DonMed-10
□ 97DonPre-160
□ 97DonPreCttC-160
□ 97DonPreProG-200
□ 97DonPreProS-200
□ 97DonRatR-10
□ 97PinIns-63
□ 97PinInsCC-63
□ 97PinInsEC-63
□ 97PinInsSto-13
□ 97Stu-73
□ 97StuPrePG-73
□ 97StuPrePS-73
□ 98PacOmeH-32
□ 98PacOmeODI-32
□ 98PacOmeR-32
□ 98PacRev-19
□ 98PacRevIS-19
□ 98PacRevR-19
□ 98UppDec-13
□ 98UppDecE-13
□ 98UppDecE1o1-13
□ 98UppDecGN-GN7
□ 98UppDecGNQ1-GN7

□ 98UppDecGNQ2-GN7
□ 98UppDecGNQ3-GN7
□ 98UppDecGR-13
□ 98UppDecM-32
□ 98UppDecMGS-32
□ 98UppDecMSS-32
□ 98UppDecMSS-32
□ 99Pac-55
□ 99PacAur-21
□ 99PacAurPD-21
□ 99PacCop-55
□ 99PacGol-55
□ 99PacIceB-55
□ 99PacPreD-55
□ 99UppDecM-35
□ 99UppDecMGS-35
□ 99UppDecMSS-35
□ 99UppDecMSS-35
**Giguere, Stephane**
□ 88FliSpi-4
**Gilbert, Ed**
□ 74NHLActSta-302
□ 750PCNHL-370
□ 760PCNHL-329
**Gilbert, Gilles**
□ 71TorSun-130
□ 730PC-74
□ 73Top-74
□ 74NHLActSta-24
□ 740PCNHL-10
□ 740PCNHL-132
□ 74Top-10
□ 74Top-132
□ 750PCNHL-45
□ 75Top-45
□ 760PCNHL-255
□ 76Top-255
□ 770PCNHL-125
□ 77Top-125
□ 780PC-68
□ 780PC-95
□ 78Top-68
□ 78Top-95
□ 790PC-209
□ 79Top-209
□ 800PC-175
□ 80Top-175
□ 810PC-88
□ 810PCSti-123
□ 81Top-W88
□ 820PC-84
□ 92SpoFla-6
**Gilbert, Greg**
□ 82IndChe-5
□ 84IslIsIN-5
□ 840PC-125
□ 840PCSti-90
□ 84Top-93
□ 85IslIsIN-5
□ 850PC-126
□ 850PCSti-75
□ 85Top-126
□ 880PC-83
□ 88PanSti-287
□ 88Top-83
□ 89BlaCok-8
□ 90BlaCok-8
□ 900PC-255
□ 90PanSti-196
□ 90ProSet-429
□ 90Sco-264
□ 90ScoCan-264
□ 90Top-255
□ 90TopTif-255
□ 91BlaCok-6
□ 910PC-149
□ 91ProSet-372
□ 91ProSetFre-372
□ 91ScoCan-539
□ 91StaClu-242
□ 91Top-149
□ 92Sco-134
□ 92ScoCan-134
□ 92StaClu-323
□ 92Top-218
□ 92TopGol-218G
□ 92Ult-275
□ 93Lea-348
□ 930PCPre-216
□ 930PCPreG-216
□ 93Par-404A
□ 93ParEmeI-404A
□ 93Pin-405
□ 93PinCan-405
□ 93Sco-305
□ 93ScoCan-305
□ 93ScoGol-561
□ 93StaClu-37
□ 93StaCluFDI-37
□ 93StaCluFDIO-37
□ 93StaCluO-37
□ 93TopPre-216
□ 93TopPreG-216
□ 93UppDec-404
□ 94Lea-341
□ 940PCPre-169
□ 940PCPreSE-169
□ 94ParSE-SE111
□ 94ParSEG-SE111
□ 94Pin-415
□ 94PinArtP-415
□ 94PinRinC-415

□ 94TopPre-169
□ 94TopPreSE-169
□ 95Top-96
□ 95TopOPCI-96
**Gilbert, Greg (Minors)**
□ 74SioCitM-4
**Gilbert, Rod**
□ 44BeeGro2P-314
□ 61Top-62
□ 62Top-59
□ 63Top-57
□ 64BeeGro3P-127
□ 64CocCap-77
□ 64Top-24
□ 64TorSta-9
□ 65Coc-79
□ 65Top-91
□ 66Top-26
□ 66TopUSAT-26
□ 67Top-90
□ 680PC-72
□ 680PC-209
□ 680PCPucSti-9
□ 68Top-72
□ 690PC-37
□ 690PCFou-12
□ 690PCSta-9
□ 69Top-37
□ 70ColSta-53
□ 70DadCoo-40
□ 70EssPowPla-185
□ 700PC-63
□ 700PCDec-39
□ 70SarProSta-122
□ 70Top-63
□ 70TopStiS-10
□ 71Baz-30
□ 71LetActR-14
□ 710PC-123
□ 710PCPos-7
□ 710PCTBoo-18
□ 71SarProSta-113
□ 71Top-123
□ 71TorSun-173
□ 72KellroT-3
□ 720PC-153
□ 720PC-229
□ 720PCTeaC-11
□ 72SarProSta-141
□ 72SweHocS-116
□ 72Top-80
□ 72Top-125
□ 73MacMil-7
□ 730PC-156
□ 73Top-88
□ 74LipSou-40
□ 74NHLActSta-188
□ 740PCNHL-141
□ 740PCNHL-201
□ 74Top-141
□ 74Top-201
□ 750PCNHL-225
□ 750PCNHL-324
□ 75Top-225
□ 75Top-324
□ 760PCNHL-90
□ 760PCNHL-390
□ 76Top-90
□ 76TopGloI-18
□ 77Coc-8
□ 770PCNHL-25
□ 77Top-25
□ 83HalFP-H5
□ 85HalFC-111
□ 90UppDec-512
□ 90UppDecF-512
□ 91FutTreC72-74
□ 91Kra-82
□ 91ProSet-593
□ 91ProSetFre-593
□ 91ProSetNHLSA-AC23
□ 91StaPicH-7
□ 92ZelMasH-2
□ 92ZelMasoHS-2
□ 94ParTalB-104
□ 94ParTalBA-B1
□ 94ParTalBM-SL5
□ 95Par66-79
□ 95Par66Coi-79
□ 95ScoRedW-14
□ 95ScoRedWPla-14
□ 97ScoRedWPre-14
**Gilbertson, Stan**
□ 71LetActR-19
□ 710PC-183
□ 71TorSun-47
□ 720PC-70
□ 72SarProSta-52
□ 72Top-101
□ 730PC-212
□ 74NHLActSta-60
□ 740PCNHL-223
□ 74Top-223
□ 750PCNHL-382
□ 760PCNHL-187
□ 76Top-187
□ 77Top-203
**Gilchrist, Brent**
□ 84KelWin-16
□ 88CanaPos-11
□ 89CanaKra-9
□ 89CanaPos-13
□ 90CanaPos-16
□ 900PC-422
□ 90ProSet-471
□ 90ScoRoo-88T
□ 91Bow-336

□ 91CanaPanTS-12
□ 91CanaPos-13
□ 910PC-90
□ 91Par-315
□ 91ParFre-315
□ 91Pin-236
□ 91PinFre-236
□ 91ProSet-414
□ 91ProSetFre-414
□ 91ProSetPla-192
□ 91ScoCan-259
□ 91Top-90
□ 92Bow-322
□ 920ilIGA-7
□ 920PC-221
□ 920PCPre-129
□ 92PanSti-153
□ 92PanStiFre-153
□ 92Pin-357
□ 92PinFre-357
□ 92ProSet-90
□ 92Sco-46
□ 92ScoCan-46
□ 92StaClu-449
□ 92Top-386
□ 92TopGol-386G
□ 92UppDec-459
□ 93Par-52
□ 93ParEmeI-52
□ 93Pin-415
□ 93PinCan-415
□ 93Pow-324
□ 93Sco-206
□ 93ScoCan-206
□ 93UppDec-329
□ 94Fle-50
□ 94Lea-340
□ 94Par-55
□ 94ParGol-55
□ 94ParVin-V21
□ 94Pin-185
□ 94PinArtP-185
□ 94PinRinC-185
□ 94StaClu-143
□ 94StaCluFDI-143
□ 94StaCluMOMS-143
□ 94StaCluSTWC-143
□ 94StaHoc-13
□ 94StaPinS-185
□ 94StaPinS-NNO
□ 94StaPos-8
□ 94UppDec-347
□ 94UppDecEleIce-347
□ 95BeAPla-71
□ 95BeAPSig-S71
□ 95BeAPSigDC-S71
□ 95ParInt-326
□ 95ParIntEl-326
□ 95Sco-261
□ 95ScoBlaIce-261
□ 95ScoBlaIceAP-261
□ 95StaScoS-261
□ 95UppDec-326
□ 95UppDecEleIce-326
□ 95UppDecEleIceG-326
□ 95JetTealss-9
□ 96Sco-49
□ 96ScoArtPro-49
□ 96ScoDeaCAP-49
□ 96ScoGolB-49
□ 96ScoSpeAP-49
□ 96StaPos-5
□ 97Be A PPAD-85
□ 97Be A PPAPD-85
□ 97BeAPla-85
□ 97BeAPlaAut-85
□ 97Pac-136
□ 97PacCop-136
□ 97PacEmeGre-136
□ 97PacIceB-136
□ 97PacOme-79
□ 97PacOmeC-79
□ 97PacOmeDG-79
□ 97PacOmeEG-79
□ 97PacOmeG-79
□ 97PacOmeIB-79
□ 97PacRed-136
□ 97PacSil-79
□ 97ScoRedW-14
□ 97ScoRedWPla-14
□ 97ScoRedWPre-14
□ 980-PChr-95
□ 980-PChrR-95
□ 98Pac-191
□ 98PacIceB-191
□ 98PacRed-191
□ 98Top-95
□ 98TopO-P-95
**Giles, Andy**
□ 93HumHawP-16
**Giles, Curt**
□ 80NorStaPos-8
□ 81NorStaPos-9
□ 82NorStaPos-11
□ 820PC-166
□ 82PosCer-9
□ 83NorStaPos-9
□ 84NorStaPos-7
□ 84NorStaPos-8
□ 85NorSta7E-3
□ 85NorStaPos-10
□ 850PC-96
□ 85Top-96
□ 860PC-119
□ 860PCSti-172

□ 86Top-119
□ 87NorStaPos-14
□ 87PanSti-110
□ 88NorStaADA-12
□ 890PC-213
□ 89PanSti-112
□ 900PC-228
□ 90PanSti-250
□ 90ProSet-140
□ 90Sco-94
□ 90ScoCan-94
□ 90Top-228
□ 90TopTif-228
□ 90UppDec-9
□ 90UppDecF-9
□ 91AlbIntTC-8
□ 910PC-17
□ 91ProSet-114
□ 91ProSetFre-114
□ 91ScoAme-137
□ 91ScoCan-137
□ 91Top-17
□ 92StaClu-64
□ 92Top-202
□ 92TopGol-202G
**Gilhen, Randy**
□ 86SheCan-17
□ 87MonHaw-10
□ 88JetPol-8
□ 900PC-250
□ 90ProSet-506
□ 90Top-250
□ 90TopTif-250
□ 91Bow-84
□ 910PC-418
□ 910PCPre-123
□ 91Par-335
□ 91ParFre-335
□ 91Pin-238
□ 91PinFre-238
□ 91ProSetFre-403
□ 91ScoAme-157
□ 91ScoCan-157
□ 91ScoCan-566
□ 91ScoRoo-16T
□ 91StaClu-275
□ 91Top-418
□ 91UppDec-603
□ 91UppDecF-603
□ 92Bow-327
□ 920PC-26
□ 92Pin-126
□ 92PinFre-126
□ 92Sco-268
□ 92ScoCan-268
□ 92StaClu-318
□ 92Top-27
□ 92TopGol-27G
□ 92UppDec-82
□ 93Pow-93
□ 93Sco-643
□ 93ScoCan-643
□ 93ScoGol-643
□ 93UppDec-481
□ 93JetTealss-9
**Gill, Hal**
□ 97PacOme-16
□ 97PacOmeC-16
□ 97PacOmeDG-16
□ 97PacOmeG-16
□ 97PacOmeIB-16
□ 98UppDecM-17
□ 98UppDecMGS-17
□ 98UppDecMSS-17
□ 98UppDecMSS-17
□ 99Pac-23
□ 99PacCop-23
□ 99PacGol-23
□ 99PacIceB-23
□ 99PacPreD-23
**Gill, Todd**
□ 86MapLeaP-10
□ 87MapLeaP-8
□ 87MapLeaPLA-13
□ 87MapLeaPo-8
□ 870PCSti-163
□ 88MapLeaPLA-12
□ 89PanSti-143
□ 90ProSet-534
□ 91Bow-171
□ 91MapLeaP-14
□ 91MapLeaPTS-7
□ 910PC-361
□ 91Par-393
□ 91ParFre-393
□ 91Pin-278
□ 91PinFre-278
□ 91ProSet-226
□ 91ProSetFre-226
□ 91ScoCan-521
□ 91StaClu-336
□ 91Top-361
□ 92Bow-375
□ 92PanSti-82
□ 92PanStiFre-82
□ 92Pin-290
□ 92PinFre-290
□ 92Sco-196
□ 92ScoCan-196
□ 92StaClu-261
□ 92Top-374

□ 92TopGol-374G
□ 93Don-335
□ 93Lea-22
□ 930PCPre-4
□ 930PCPreG-4
□ 93Pin-68
□ 93PinCan-68
□ 93Pow-449
□ 93Sco-292
□ 93ScoBla-22
□ 93ScoCan-292
□ 93StaClu-62
□ 93StaCluFDI-62
□ 93StaCluFDIO-62
□ 93StaCluO-62
□ 93TopPre-4
□ 93TopPreG-4
□ 93Ult-77
□ 94BeAP99A-G8
□ 94BeAPla-R24
□ 94BeAPSig-104
□ 94CanGamNHLP-239
□ 94EASpo-133
□ 94Lea-497
□ 94MapLeaG-8
□ 94MapLeaK-12
□ 94MapLeaP-1
□ 94MapLeaPP-8
□ 940PCPre-189
□ 940PCPreSE-189
□ 94Par-233
□ 94ParGol-233
□ 94Pin-181
□ 94PinArtP-181
□ 94PinRinC-181
□ 94Sco-55
□ 94ScoGol-55
□ 94ScoPla-55
□ 94ScoPlaTS-55
□ 94TopPre-189
□ 94TopPreSE-189
□ 94Ult-215
□ 94UppDec-440
□ 94UppDecEleIce-440
□ 95CanGamNHLP-265
□ 95ColCho-101
□ 95ColChoPC-101
□ 95ColChoPCP-101
□ 95Don-14
□ 95Emo-170
□ 95ImaPlaPI-PL10
□ 95Lea-278
□ 95ParInt-202
□ 95ParIntEl-202
□ 95Pin-171
□ 95PinArtP-171
□ 95PinRinC-171
□ 95Sco-162
□ 95ScoBlaIce-162
□ 95ScoBlaIceAP-162
□ 95SkyImp-160
□ 95Top-124
□ 95TopOPCI-124
□ 95UppDec-117
□ 95UppDecEleIce-117
□ 95UppDecEleIceG-117
□ 96BeAPAut1-1
□ 96BeAPAutSil-1
□ 96BeAPla-1
□ 96Don-15
□ 96DonEli-79
□ 96DonEliDCS-79
□ 96DonPrePro-15
□ 96Pin-176
□ 96PinArtP-176
□ 96PinFoi-176
□ 96PinPreS-176
□ 96PinRinC-176
□ 96Sco-208
□ 96ScoArtPro-208
□ 96ScoDeaCAP-208
□ 96ScoGolB-208
□ 96ScoSpeAP-208
□ 96Sum-4
□ 96SumArtP-4
□ 96SumIce-4
□ 96SumMet-4
□ 96SumPreS-4
□ 96Zen-14
□ 96ZenArtP-14
□ 97Pac-98
□ 97PacCop-98
□ 97PacEmeGre-98
□ 97PacIceB-98
□ 97PacRed-98
□ 97PacSil-98
□ 97UppDec-151
□ 98Be A PPA-127
□ 98Be A PPAAF-127
□ 98Be A PPTBASG-127
□ 98Be APG-127
□ 98Pac-367
□ 98PacIceB-367
□ 98PacRed-367
**Gillam, Sean**
□ 95SpoChi-19
**Gilliard, Tony**
□ 82NorBayC-6
**Gillies, Clark**
□ 74NHLActSta-163
□ 750PCNHL-199
□ 750PCNHL-323
□ 75Top-199
□ 75Top-323

□ 760PCNHL-126
□ 760PCNHL-216
□ 760PCNHL-389
□ 76Top-126
□ 76Top-216
□ 770PCNHL-250
□ 77Top-250
□ 77TopGloS-6
□ 77TopOPCGlo-6
□ 780PC-220
□ 780PC-327
□ 78Top-220
□ 79IslTrans-3
□ 790PC-130
□ 79Top-130
□ 800PC-75
□ 80Top-75
□ 810PC-202
□ 810PCSti-164
□ 81Top-E88
□ 82McdSti-13
□ 820PC-201
□ 820PCSti-54
□ 820PCSti-55
□ 82PosCer-12
□ 83IslTealss-4
□ 830PC-6
□ 830PCSti-84
□ 83PufSti-20
□ 84IslIsIN-6
□ 840PC-126
□ 84Top-94
□ 85IslIsIN-6
□ 850PC-81
□ 850PCSti-68
□ 85Top-81
□ 860PC-141
□ 860PCSti-205
□ 86SabBluS-11
□ 86SabBluSSma-11
□ 86Top-141
□ 870PC-96
□ 87PanSti-34
□ 87SabBluS-9
□ 87SabWonBH-10
□ 87Top-96
□ 88EssAllSta-13
□ 880PC-80
□ 88Top-80
□ 91UppDec-640
□ 91UppDecF-640
□ 93IslCheBA-3
**Gilligan, William**
□ 79PanSti-223
**Gillingham, Todd**
□ 907thInnSQMJHL-174
□ 91ProAHLCHL-351
□ 93St.JohMl-8
□ 95ColEagl-151
□ 97St.JohML-11
**Gillis, Errol**
□ 23V1281PauC-4
□ 24CreSel-7
**Gillis, Jere**
□ 77CanCanDC-3
□ 77CanuRoyB-5
□ 78CanuRoyB-6
□ 780PC-109
□ 78Top-109
□ 79CanuRoyB-7
□ 790PC-322
□ 800PC-283
□ 810PC-232
□ 82PosCer-16
□ 83Canu-7
□ 83Vac-106
□ 84FreExp-11
□ 840PC-318
□ 85FreExp-11
**Gillis, Mike**
□ 79Roc-8
□ 810PC-12
□ 82PosCer-1
**Gillis, Paul**
□ 82NorBayC-7
□ 83NordPos-9
□ 84NordPos-9
□ 85NordGenF-9
□ 85NordMcD-7
□ 85NordPro-9
□ 85NordTeal-8
□ 850PCSti-150
□ 86NordGenF-8
□ 86NordMcD-8
□ 86NordTeal-7
□ 86NordYumY-3
□ 860PC-168
□ 860PCSti-24
□ 86Top-168
□ 87NordGenF-10
□ 87NordYumY-2
□ 870PC-247
□ 870PCSti-221
□ 87PanSti-167
□ 88NordGenF-12
□ 88NordTeal-13
□ 89Kra-29
□ 89Nord-12
□ 89NordGenF-9
□ 89NordProB-9
□ 890PC-265
□ 890PCSti-183
□ 89PanSti-330
□ 90Bow-165

90BowTif-165
90NordPet-9
90NordTeal-8
90OPC-22
90OPC-122
90PanSti-143
90ProSet-246
90Sco-141
90ScoCan-141
90Top-22
90Top-122
90TopTif-22
90UppDec-49
90UppDecF-49
91NordPanTS-6
91OPC-469
91ProAHLCHL-489
91ScoAme-364
91ScoCan-403
91Top-469
91WhaJr7E-12
92WhaDai-7

**Gillis, Ryan**
93NorBayC-10
94NorBayC-12
95Sla-218
96DayBom-16

**Gillow, Russ**
72ShaLosAW-4

**Gilmore, Dave**
917thInnSOHL-363
93LonKni-9
95Cla-88

**Gilmore, Tom**
72ShaLosAW-5

**Gilmour, Billy (HL)**
10C55SweCP-22
11C55-22
83HalFP-D4
85HalFC-50

**Gilmour, Darryl**
86PorWinH-8
88ProAHL-122
90ProAHLIHL-427
91ProAHLCHL-403
92PhoRoa-7
94MusFur-12

**Gilmour, Doug**
84OPC-185
84OPCSti-60
85OPC-76
85OPCSti-48
85Top-76
86OPC-93
86OPCSti-177
86Top-93
87BluKod-11
87OPC-175
87OPCBoxB-E
87OPCMin-11
87OPCSti-27
87PanSti-311
87Top-175
87TopBoxB-E
88FriLayS-8
88OPC-56
88OPCSti-20
88PanSti-105
88Top-56
89Kra-1
89OPC-74
89OPCSti-103
89PanSti-28
89Top-74
90Bow-96
90BowTif-96
90FlamIGA-4
90OPC-136
90PanSti-172
90ProSet-34
90Sco-155
90ScoCan-155
90ScoHotRS-69
90Top-136
90TopTif-136
90UppDec-271
90UppDecF-271
91Bow-255
91FlamIGA-3
91FlamPanTS-2
91Kra-78
91OPC-208
91PanSti-59
91Par-26
91Par-396
91ParFre-26
91ParFre-396
91Pin-92
91PinFre-92
91ProSet-34
91ProSetFre-34
91ProSetPla-234
91ScoAme-218
91ScoCan-218
91StaClu-96
91Top-208
91UppDec-188
91UppDec-558
91UppDecF-558
92BluUDBB-2
92Bow-83
92HumDum2-7
92MapLeaK-12
92OPC-177

92OPCPreSP-8
92PanSti-77
92PanStiFre-77
92Par-183
92Par-502
92ParCheP-CP1
92ParCheP-CP1993
92ParEmel-183
92ParEmel-502
92Pin-279
92PinCanPP-3
92PinFre-279
92ProSet-184
92ProSetGTL-11
92Sco-40
92Sco-43
92ScoCan-40
92ScoCan-43
92SeaPat-55
92StaClu-359
92Top-122
92TopGol-122G
92Ult-211
92UppDec-21
92UppDec-215
92UppDec-639
93Cla-119
93Cla-AU4
93Don-341
93DonEli-7
93Kra-9
93Kra-53
93KraRec-3
93Lea-93
93LeaGolAS-6
93LeaStuS-1
93McDUppD-5
93OPCPre-390
93OPCPreBG-11
93OPCPreG-390
93PanSti-T
93Par-469
93ParChePH-D9
93ParEasWesS-W4
93ParEmel-469
93ParUSACG-G10
93Pin-100
93Pin-226
93PinAllS-44
93PinAllSC-44
93PinCan-100
93PinCan-226
93Pow-244
93PowGam-2
93PowPoiL-2
93Sco-66
93ScoBla-2
93ScoCan-66
93ScoDynDC-1
93ScoFra-21
93SeaPat-4
93StaClu-140
93StaClu-149
93StaCluAS-17
93StaCluFDI-140
93StaCluFDI-149
93StaCluFDIO-140
93StaCluFDIO-149
93StaCluMasP-2
93StaCluMasPW-2
93StaCluO-140
93StaCluO-149
93TopPre-390
93TopPreG-390
93Ult-110
93UltAllS-16
93UltAwaW-3
93UltPreP-1
93UppDec-306
93UppDec-382
93UppDecAW-AW6
93UppDecLAS-24
93UppDecNL-NL5
93UppDecNR-5
93UppDecNR-21
93UppDecNR-21
93UppDecSilSka-R7
93UppDecSilSkaG-R7
93UppDecSP-158
94ActPacBHP-2
94BAPUpCP-UC10
94BeAPla-R1
94BeAPla-R111
94BeAPla-R180
94BeAPSig-1
94CanGamNHLHP-45
94CanGamNHLHP-234
94Cla-AU1
94ClaAut-NNO
94Don-8
94DonIceMas-3
94EASpo-135
94Fin-100
94FinBowB-B19
94FinBowB-X22
94FinBowBR-B19
94FinBowBR-X22
94FinRef-100
94FinSupTW-100
94Fla-181
94FlaCenS-3
94Fle-215
94FleHea-3
94HocWit-61
94KenStaLA-5

94KenStaLC-4
94Kra-17
94Lea-99
94LeaFirOIce-5
94LeaGolS-2
94LeaLim-8
94LeaLimG-9
94LeaLimI-23
94MapLeaG-9
94MapLeaK-13
94MapLeaP-1
94MapLeaP-2
94MapLeaPP-2
94McDUppD-McD28
94OPCPre-225
94OPCPre-279
94OPCPreSE-225
94OPCPreSE-279
94Par-313
94ParCratGB-23
94ParCratGG-23
94ParCratGR-23
94ParGol-313
94ParSE-SE176
94ParSEG-SE176
94ParVin-V80
94Pin-135
94PinArtP-135
94PinGam-GR11
94PinNorLig-NL8
94PinRinC-135
94PinTeaP-TP10
94PinTeaPDP-TP10
94PinWorEdi-WE2
94PosCerBB-12
94Sco-185
94Sco90PC-4
94ScoDreTea-DT13
94ScoFra-TF23
94ScoGol-185
94ScoPla-185
94ScoPlaTS-185
94Sel-69
94SelGol-69
94SP-115
94SPDieCut-115
94SPPre-21
94SPPreDC-21
94StaCluMO-21
94StaCluST-23
94TopHidGem-3HG
94TopPre-225
94TopPre-279
94Pow-244
94PowPreSE-225
94PowPreSE-279
94Ult-216
94UltPreP-3
94UltScoK-3
94UppDec-138
94UppDecEleIce-138
94UppDecNBAP-41
94UppDecNBAP-42
94UppDecNBAP-43
94UppDecNBAP-44
94UppDecNBAP-45
94UppDecPC-C18
94UppDecPCEG-C18
94UppDecPH-H3
94UppDecPH-H21
94UppDecPHEG-H3
94UppDecPHEG-H21
94UppDecPHES-H3
94UppDecPHES-H21
94UppDecPHG-H3
94UppDecPHG-H21
94UppDecPR-R11
94UppDecPR-R27
94UppDecPR-R49
94UppDecPR-R56
94UppDecPRE-R11
94UppDecPRE-R27
94UppDecPRE-R49
94UppDecPRE-R56
94UppDecPreRG-R11
94UppDecPreRG-R27
94UppDecPreRG-R49
94UppDecPreRG-R56
94UppDecSPI-SP167
94UppDecSPIDC-SP167
95Bow-18
95BowAllFoi-18
95CanGamNHLP-22
95CanGamNHLP-257
95ColCho-5
95ColChoCTG-C21
95ColChoCTG-C21B
95ColChoCTG-C21C
95ColChoCTGGB-C21
95ColChoCTGGR-C21
95ColChoCTGSR-C21
95ColChoPC-5
95ColChoPC-359
95ColChoPCP-5
95ColChoPCP-359
95DonDom-5
95DonEli-92
95DonEliDCS-92
95DonEliDCU-92
95DonIgn-3
95Emo-171
95Fin-55
95Fin-170

95FinRef-55
95FinRef-170
95ImpSti-117
95Kra-14
95Lea-211
95LeaLim-72
95McDPin-MCD-9
95Met-143
95NHLAcePC-3H
95NHLACEPC-18
95NHLCooT-17
95NHLCooT-RP17
95ParInt-199
95ParIntCCGS1-12
95ParIntCCSS1-12
95ParIntEI-199
95Pin-61
95PinArtP-61
95PinCleS-6
95PinFirS-3
95PinRinC-61
95PlaOneoOne-96
95PlaOneoOne-202
95PlaOneoOne-315
95PosUppD-18
95ProMag-77
95Sco-73
95Sco-202
95ScoBlaIce-73
95ScoBlaIceAP-73
95ScoBorBat-5
95ScoDreTea-6
95SelCer-48
95SelCer-53
95SelCerDS-1
95SelCerDSG-1
95SelCerMG-48
95SkyImp-161
95SkyImpCI-8
95SP-144
95StaClu-184
95StaCluEN-EN8
95StaCluMO-44
95StaCluMOMS-184
95StaCluMPT-3
95StaCluNem-N7
95Sum-62
95SumArtP-62
95SumIce-62
95SweGloWC-93
95WiHNL-545
95Top-234
95TopHomGC-HGC4
95TopOPCI-234
95TopPro-PF17
95TopRinL-8RL
95TopSupSki-14
95TopSupSkiPla-14
95Ult-160
95UltGolM-160
95UppDec-240
95UppDec-291
95UppDecAGPRW-10
95UppDecEleIce-240
95UppDecEleIce-291
95UppDecEleIceG-240
95UppDecEleIceG-291
95UppDecSpeE-SE80
95UppDecSpeEdiG-SE80
95Zen-54
96BeAPAut-22
96BeAPAutSil-22
96BeAPla-22
96ColCho-256
96ColCho-332
96ColChoCTG-C2A
96ColChoCTG-C2B
96ColChoCTG-C2C
96ColChoCTGE-CR2
96ColChoCTGEG-CR2
96ColChoCTGG-C2A
96ColChoCTGG-C2B
96ColChoCTGG-C2C
96ColChoMVP-UD45
96ColChoMVPG-UD45
96Don-46
96Don-239
96DonCanI-112
96DonCanIGPP-112
96DonCanIOC-9
96DonCanIRPP-112
96DonDom-6
96DonEli-44
96DonEliCS-44
96DonEliP-6
96DonHitLis-15
96DonPrePro-46
96DonPrePro-239
96DurIAIIT-DC7
96DurL'EB-JB7
96Fla-90
96FlaBlul-90
96Fle-107
96FlePCC-8
96FlePic-68
96HocGreC-8
96HocGreCG-8
96KraVapGol-37
96Lea-74
96LeaFirOI-10
96LeaLeaAL-14
96LeaLeaALP-14
96LeaLim-70
96LeaLimBTB-4
96LeaLimBTBLE-4
96LeaLimBTBP-P4

96LeaLimG-70
96LeaPre-104
96LeaPreP-74
96LeaPrePP-104
96LeaPreSG-10
96LeaPreSte-10
96MapLeaP-1
96MetUni-149
96NHLLACEPC-18
96NHLProSTA-77
96Pin-127
96PinArtP-127
96PinByTN-7
96PinByTNP-7
96PinFoi-127
96PinMcD-14
96PinPreS-127
96PinRinC-127
96PlaOneoOne-356
96PosUppD-7
96Sco-95
96ScoArtPro-95
96ScoChelt-9
96ScoDeaCAP-95
96ScoGolB-95
96ScoSpeAP-95
96SelCer-15
96SelCerAP-15
96SelCerBlu-15
96SelCerMB-15
96SelCerMG-15
96SelCerMR-15
96SelCerRed-15
96SkyImp-126
96SkyImpB-15
96SP-152
96SPGamFil-GF16
96SPHolCol-HC3
96SPx-45
96SPxGol-45
96SPxHolH-HH9
96Sum-118
96SumArtP-118
96SumIce-118
96SumMet-118
96SumPreS-118
96Ult-163
96UltGolM-163
96UppDec-162
96UppDecBD-28
96UppDecBDG-28
96UppDecGJ-GJ3
96UppDecGN-X10
96UppDecIce-69
96UppDecIcePar-69
96UppDecLSH-LS11
96UppDecLSHF-LS11
96UppDecLSHS-LS11
96UppDecPP-P29
96UppDecSS-SS4B
96Zen-47
96ZenArtP-47
96ZenChaS-13
96ZenChaSD-13
97BeAPlaTAN-7
97ColCho-139
97ColChoCTG-C13A
97ColChoCTG-C13B
97ColChoCTG-C13C
97ColChoCTGE-CR13
97ColChoSta-SQ70
97ColChoSti-S24
97Don-10
97DonCanI-49
97DonCanIDS-49
97DonCanINP-9
97DonCanIPS-49
97DonCanISCS-13
97DonEli-73
97DonEliAsp-73
97DonEliS-73
97DonLim-66
97DonLim-82
97DonLim-155
97DonLimExp-66
97DonLimExp-82
97DonLimExp-155
97DonLimFOTG-19
97DonLin2L-7
97DonLin2LDC-7
97DonPre-69
97DonPreCttC-69
97DonPreProG-10
97DonPreProS-10
97DonPri-52
97DonPriSoA-52
97Kat-81
97KatGol-81
97KatSil-81
97Lea-80
97LeaFraMat-80
97LeaFraMDC-80
97LeaInt-80
97LeaIntUI-80
97Pac-93
97PacCarSup-11
97PacCarSupM-11
97PacCop-93
97PacCroR-75
97PacCroREG-75
97PacCroRIB-75
97PacCroRS-75
97PacDyn-69
97PacDynC-69
97PacDynDG-69

97PacDynEG-69
97PacDynIB-69
97PacDynR-69
97PacDynSil-69
97PacEmeGre-93
97PacIceB-93
97PacInv-77
97PacInvC-77
97PacInvEG-77
97PacInvIB-77
97PacInvNRB-113
97PacInvR-77
97PacInvS-77
97PacOme-129
97PacOmeC-129
97PacOmeDG-129
97PacOmeEG-129
97PacOmeG-129
97PacOmeIB-129
97PacOmeSLC-11
97PacPar-102
97PacParBNDC-13
97PacParC-102
97PacParDG-102
97PacParEG-102
97PacParIB-102
97PacParRed-102
97PacParSil-102
97PacRed-93
97PacRev-77
97PacRevC-77
97PacRevE-77
97PacRevIB-77
97PacRevR-77
97PacRevS-77
97PacSil-93
97Pin-39
97PinArtP-39
97PinBee-47
97PinBeeGP-47
97PinCer-51
97PinCerMB-51
97PinCerMG-51
97PinCerMR-51
97PinCerR-51
97PinEpiG-24
97PinEpiGP-24
97PinEpiME-24
97PinEpiMO-24
97PinEpiMP-24
97PinEpiPE-24
97PinEpiPO-24
97PinEpiPP-24
97PinEpiSE-24
97PinEpiSO-24
97PinEpiSP-24
97PinIns-39
97PinInsCC-73
97PinInsEC-73
97PinPrePBB-39
97PinPrePBC-39
97PinPrePBM-39
97PinPrePBY-39
97PinPrePFC-39
97PinPrePFM-39
97PinPrePFY-39
97PinPrePla-39
97PinRinC-39
97PinTeaP-9
97PinTeaPM-9
97PinTeaPP-9
97PinTeaPPM-9
97PinTotCMPG-51
97PinTotCPB-51
97PinTotCPG-51
97PinTotCPR-51
97Sco-93
97ScoArtPro-93
97ScoChel-6
97ScoDev-1
97ScoDevPla-1
97ScoDevPre-1
97ScoGolBla-93
97SPAut-88
97SPx-25
97SPxBro-25
97SPxDinDim-SPX5
97SPxGol-25
97SPxGraF-25
97SPxSil-25
97SPxSte-25
97Stu-93
97StuPrePG-93
97StuPrePS-93
97TopHocMC-7
97TopHocMC-8
97UppDec-91
97UppDec-198
97UppDecBDDD-70
97UppDecBDQD-70
97UppDecBDTD-70
97UppDecGDM-91
97UppDecIce-82
97UppDecIce-P82
97UppDecIPS-82
97UppDecSG-SG33
97UppDecSSM-SS16
97UppDecSSW-SS16
97UppDecTSS-18B
97Zen-46
97Zen5x7-12
97ZenGolImp-12
97ZenSilImp-12

97ZenZGol-46
97ZenZSii-46
98Be A PPA-178
98Be a PPA-178
98Be A PPAAF-178
98Be a PPPH-H18
98Be a PPSE-178
98Be APG-178
98BowBes-13
98BowBesAR-13
98BowBesR-13
98Fin-54
98FinNo P-54
98FinNo PR-54
98FinRef-54
98Pac-93
98PacCroR-30
98PacCroRLS-30
98PacCroRPotG-6
98PacDynI-41
98PacDynIFT-4
98PacDynIIB-41
98PacDynIR-41
98PacGolCD-20
98PacIceB-93
98PacOmeH-52
98PacOmeO-7
98PacOmeODI-52
98PacOmeR-52
98PacPar-47
98PacParC-47
98PacParEG-47
98PacParH-47
98PacParIB-47
98PacParS-47
98PacRed-93
98PacRev-31
98PacRevIS-31
98PacRevR-31
98PacRevS-9
98PacTim-10
98PinEpiGE-24
98SP Aut-18
98SP AutA-5
98SP AutSM-S4
98SP AutSS-SS30
98SPxFin-47
98SPxFinAR-47
98SPxFinR-47
98SPxFinS-47
98SPXTopP-10
98SPXTopPF-10
98SPXTopPHH-H7
98SPXTopPLI-L25
98SPXTopPR-10
98TopGolLC1-64
98TopGolLC1B-64
98TopGolLC1BOoO-64
98TopGolLC1OoO-64
98TopGolLC1R-64
98TopGolLC1ROoO-64
98TopGolLC2-64
98TopGolLC2B-64
98TopGolLC2BOoO-64
98TopGolLC2OoO-64
98TopGolLC2R-64
98TopGolLC2ROoO-64
98TopGolLC3-64
98TopGolLC3B-64
98TopGolLC3BOoO-64
98TopGolLC3OoO-64
98TopGolLC3R-64
98TopGolLC3ROoO-64
98UC-117
98UD ChoPCR-117
98UD ChoR-117
98UD3-50
98UD3-110
98UD3-170
98UD3DieC-50
98UD3DieC-110
98UD3DieC-170
98UppDec-63
98UppDecBD-18
98UppDecBD-18
98UppDecDD-18
98UppDecE-63
98UppDecE1o1-63
98UppDecFIT-FT16
98UppDecFITQ1-FT16
98UppDecFITQ2-FT16
98UppDecFITQ3-FT16
98UppDecGJ-GJ18
98UppDecLSH-LS7
98UppDecLSHQ1-LS7
98UppDecLSHQ2-LS7
98UppDecLSHQ3-LS7
98UppDecM-43
98UppDecM1-M25
98UppDecM2-M25
98UppDecMGS-43
98UppDecMSS-43
98UppDecP-P15
98UppDecPQ1-P15
98UppDecPQ2-P15
98UppDecPQ3-P15
98UppDecQD-18
98UppDecTD-18
98Pac-89
98PacAur-32
99PacAurPD-32
99PacCop-89
99PacGol-89
99PacHomaA-6

❑ 99PacIceB-89
❑ 99PacPreD-89
❑ 99PacTeaL-7
❑ 99RetHoc-18
❑ 99SP AutPS-18
❑ 99UppDecM-48
❑ 99UppDecMGS-48
❑ 99UppDecMSS-48
❑ 99UppDecMSS-48
❑ 99UppDecRG-18
❑ 99UppDecRP-18
**Gimaev, Irek**
❑ 80USSOlyTMP-2
❑ 83RusNatT-6
**Gingras, Gaston**
❑ 80CanaPos-6
❑ 80OPC-322
❑ 80PepCap-44
❑ 81CanaPos-8
❑ 81OPC-182
❑ 82CanaPos-7
❑ 82MapLeaP-14
❑ 82MapLeaP-15
❑ 82OPC-182
❑ 83MapLeaP-8
❑ 83OPC-332
❑ 83OPCSti-40
❑ 83Vac-88
❑ 84OPC-303
❑ 85CanaPos-11
❑ 86KraDra-19
❑ 87BluKod-12
❑ 87BluTealss-10
❑ 87OPC-229
❑ 87OPCSti-8
❑ 88BluKod-23
❑ 88BluTealss-10
❑ 88OPC-35
❑ 88Top-35
❑ 89OPC-270
❑ 89OPCSti-21
❑ 95FreCan-12
**Gingras, Michel**
❑ 907thInnSMC-62
**Ginnell, Erin**
❑ 86RegPat-8
**Gionta, Brian**
❑ 98UC-298
❑ 98UD ChoPCR-298
❑ 98UD ChoR-298
**Girard, Bob**
❑ 76OPCNHL-362
❑ 77OPCNHL-255
❑ 78OPC-339
**Girard, Dany**
❑ 917thInnSQMJHL-78
**Girard, Frederic**
❑ 96RimOce-11
❑ 96RimOceQPP-11
**Girard, Jonathan**
❑ 97UppDec-403
❑ 98BowCHL-97
❑ 98BowCHL-135
❑ 98BowCHLAuB-A30
❑ 98BowCHLAuG-A30
❑ 98BowCHLAuS-A30
❑ 98BowCHLGA-97
❑ 98BowCHLGA-135
❑ 98BowCHLOI-97
❑ 98BowCHLOI-135
❑ 98BowCHLSC-SC13
❑ 98BowChrC-97
❑ 98BowChrC-135
❑ 98BowChrCGA-97
❑ 98BowChrCGA-135
❑ 98BowChrCGAR-97
❑ 98BowChrCGAR-135
❑ 98BowChrCOI-97
❑ 98BowChrCOI-135
❑ 98BowChrCOIR-97
❑ 98BowChrCOIR-135
❑ 98BowChrCR-97
❑ 98BowChrCR-135
❑ 98UppDec-222
❑ 98UppDecE-222
❑ 98UppDecE1o1-222
❑ 98UppDecGR-222
❑ 99Pac-32
❑ 99PacCop-32
❑ 99PacGol-32
❑ 99PacIceB-32
❑ 99PacPreD-32
❑ 99QuePeeWHWCCS-30
❑ 99UppDecM-19
❑ 99UppDecMGS-19
❑ 99UppDecMSS-19
❑ 99UppDecMSS-19
**Girard, Ken**
❑ 57Par-T18
❑ 94ParMisL-132
**Girard, Luc**
❑ 98Vald'OF-16
**Girard, Rick**
❑ 917thInnSWHL-176
❑ 93DonTeaC-14
❑ 93Pin-475
❑ 93PinCan-475
❑ 93UppDec-539
❑ 94ClaTri-T70
❑ 96SyrCru-37
❑ 98GerDELE-274
**Girard, Roland**
❑ 51LavDaiLSJ-43
**Girgan, Kyle**
❑ 92MPSPhoSJHL-128
**Girhiny, Richard**
❑ 907thInnSOHL-259
❑ 95MusFur-5
**Girouard, Guy**
❑ 92OklCitB-6
**Giroux, Larry**
❑ 73BluWhiBor-7
❑ 74NHLActSta-242
❑ 75OPCNHL-273
❑ 75Top-273
❑ 78BluPos-12
**Giroux, Rejean**
❑ 72NordPos-10
❑ 73NordTeal-11
**Given, Jason**
❑ 91BriColJHL-103
❑ 92BriColJHL-122
**Glad, Jarkko**
❑ 93FinnSIS-118
❑ 94FinnSIS-231
❑ 95FinnSIS-275
**Gladney, Bob**
❑ 78LouGea-7
**Gladney, Jason**
❑ 917thInnSOHL-92
❑ 93KitRan-1
❑ 93KitRan-19
❑ 95TolSto-15
❑ 96TolSto-23
**Gladu, Patrick**
❑ 95TolSto-7
**Gladu, Paul**
❑ 51CleBar-19
**Glass, Pud (Frank)**
❑ 10C55SweCP-34
❑ 10C56-5
❑ 11C55-34
❑ 12C57-21
**Glaude, Gerard**
❑ 51LavDaiQSHL-32
**Glazov, Sergei**
❑ 73SweHocS-106
❑ 73SweWorCS-106
**Gleason, Todd**
❑ 907thInnSOHL-208
❑ 917thInnSOHL-339
**Gleason, Trent**
❑ 89WinSpi-5
❑ 907thInnSOHL-106
**Gleason, Troy**
❑ 907thInnSOHL-107
**Glennie, Brian**
❑ 69MapLeaWBG-13
❑ 69MapLeaWBG-14
❑ 69MapLeaWBM-1
❑ 70EssPowPla-34
❑ 70OPC-216
❑ 70SarProSta-196
❑ 71MapLeaP-5
❑ 71OPC-197
❑ 71TorSun-258
❑ 72MapLeaP-7
❑ 72MapLeaP-8
❑ 72OPC-216
❑ 72SarProSta-205
❑ 72Top-37
❑ 73MacMil-8
❑ 73MapLeaP-7
❑ 73OPC-170
❑ 73Top-163
❑ 74MapLeaP-8
❑ 74NHLActSta-267
❑ 74OPCNHL-310
❑ 75MapLeaP-8
❑ 75OPCNHL-365
❑ 76MapLeaP-7
❑ 76OPCNHL-99
❑ 76Top-99
❑ 77Coc-9
❑ 77MapLeaP-5
❑ 77OPCNHL-275
❑ 78OPC-345
❑ 79OPC-341
❑ 91FutTreC72-88
**Glennon, Matt**
❑ 91JohChi-17
❑ 91ProAHLCHL-58
**Glickman, Jason**
❑ 89RegPat-5
**Glines, Matt**
❑ 92AriIce-14
**Glover, Chris**
❑ 83BraAle-21
**Glover, Fred**
❑ 44BeeGro2P-170
❑ 51Par-60
❑ 52Par-40
❑ 60CleBar-6
**Glover, Howie**
❑ 44BeeGro2P-171
❑ 44BeeGro2P-315
❑ 60ShiCoi-57
❑ 61Par-19
❑ 61ShiCoi-65
❑ 62Par-28
**Glover, Mike**
❑ 87SauSteMG-3
❑ 88ProAHL-82
**Glowa, Kelly**
❑ 82BraWheK-11
❑ 93SwiHNL-329
❑ 95SwiHNL-358
**Glynn, Brian**
❑ 87FlamRedRP-7
❑ 89ProIHL-191
❑ 91Bow-132
❑ 91OPC-506
❑ 91PanSti-114
❑ 91ProSet-406
❑ 91ProSetFre-406
❑ 91ScoCan-446
❑ 91StaClu-388
❑ 91Top-506
❑ 91UppDec-158
❑ 91UppDecF-158
❑ 92Bow-379
❑ 92OilIGA-8
❑ 92OilTeal-6
❑ 92Par-287
❑ 92ParEmel-287
❑ 92Pin-136
❑ 92PinFre-136
❑ 92Sco-361
❑ 92ScoCan-361
❑ 92StaClu-472
❑ 92Top-198
❑ 92TopGol-198G
❑ 92Ult-58
❑ 92UppDec-64
❑ 93Don-236
❑ 93Par-141
❑ 93ParEmel-141
❑ 93Pow-399
❑ 93SenKraS-9
❑ 93UppDec-458
❑ 94CanuProI-10
❑ 96WhaBobS-9
**Gobel, Eric**
❑ 84RicRiv-7
**Gobel, T.**
❑ 95GerDELE-337
**Gober, Mike**
❑ 88ProAHL-5
❑ 89ProAHL-313
❑ 90ProAHLIHL-312
❑ 91KnoChe-6
**Goc, Sascha**
❑ 96GerDELE-294
❑ 99QuePeeWHWCCS-15
**Godard, Chris**
❑ 92BriColJHL-207
**Godbout, Brent**
❑ 93MinGolG-13
❑ 94MinGolG-13
❑ 96MinGolGCAS-11
**Godbout, Daniel**
❑ 917thInnSOHL-102
❑ 94KitRan-4
**Godbout, Jason**
❑ 94MinGolG-14
❑ 95MinGolG-13
❑ 96MinGolGCAS-12
**Godden, Ernie**
❑ 92WinSpi-15
**Godfrey, Warren**
❑ 44BeeGro2P-26A
❑ 44BeeGro2P-26B
❑ 44BeeGro2P-26C
❑ 44BeeGro2P-172
❑ 52Par-85
❑ 53Par-95
❑ 54Par-56
❑ 54Top-50
❑ 57Top-41
❑ 58Top-58
❑ 59Top-27
❑ 60Par-30
❑ 60ShiCoi-49
❑ 61Par-30
❑ 61ShiCoi-62
❑ 62Par-36
❑ 62Top-4
❑ 62TopHocBuc-6
❑ 64BeeGro3P-9
❑ 64BeeGro3P-71
❑ 65Coc-38
❑ 93ParParR-PR54
❑ 94ParMisL-51
❑ 94ParTalB-63
**Godynyuk, Alexander**
❑ 91MapLeaP-15
❑ 91OPC-471
❑ 91Pin-318
❑ 91PinFre-318
❑ 91ProSet-563
❑ 91ProSetFre-563
❑ 91ProSetPla-251
❑ 91ScoAme-391
❑ 91ScoCan-281
❑ 91Top-471
❑ 91UppDec-466
❑ 91UppDec-609
❑ 91UppDecES-16
❑ 91UppDecESF-16
❑ 91UppDecF-466
❑ 91UppDecF-609
❑ 92FlamIGA-18
❑ 92OPC-10
❑ 92StaClu-88
❑ 92Top-256
❑ 92TopGol-256G
❑ 93Don-135
❑ 93Don-438
❑ 93OPCPre-289
❑ 93OPCPreG-289
❑ 93Par-74
❑ 93ParEmel-74
❑ 93StaClu-268
❑ 93StaCluFDI-268
❑ 93StaCluO-268
❑ 93TopPre-289
❑ 93TopPreG-289
❑ 93Ult-325
❑ 93UppDec-469
❑ 93WhaCok-5
❑ 94BeAPSig-67
❑ 94Don-202
❑ 94Fla-72
❑ 94Lea-29
❑ 94Par-100
❑ 94ParGol-100
❑ 94Pin-286
❑ 94PinArtP-286
❑ 94PinRinC-286
❑ 94Ult-89
❑ 94UppDec-188
❑ 94UppDecEleIce-188
❑ 96BeAPAut-83
❑ 96BeAPAutSil-83
❑ 96BeAPla-83
**Goebel, Bryce**
❑ 917thInnSWHL-104
❑ 91SasBla-6
**Goegan, Grant**
❑ 82SweSemHVS-141
**Goegan, Peter (Pete)**
❑ 44BeeGro2P-173
❑ 58Top-47
❑ 59Top-4
❑ 60Par-34
❑ 60ShiCoi-50
❑ 61Par-23
❑ 61ShiCoi-75
❑ 63Par-43
❑ 63YorWhiB-53
❑ 64BeeGro3P-72
❑ 94ParTalB-61
❑ 95Par66-54
❑ 95Par66Coi-54
**Goerlitz, M.**
❑ 95GerDELE-303
**Goertz, Dave**
❑ 81RegPat-6
❑ 82RegPat-4
❑ 83RegPat-4
❑ 84PriAlbRS-8
❑ 88ProIHL-50
❑ 89ProIHL-147
❑ 90ProAHLIHL-377
**Goetzinger, Jeremy**
❑ 96PriAlbR-5
❑ 96PriAlbROC-6
**Gofton, John**
❑ 61HamRed-4
**Gohde, Bob**
❑ 97LouRivF-10
**Goheen, Moose**
❑ 60Top-63
❑ 60TopSta-19
❑ 83HalFP-H6
❑ 85HalFC-112
**Golanov, Maxim**
❑ 93UppDec-273
❑ 95BinRan-7
❑ 96BinRan-11
**Golden, Mike**
❑ 89ProIHL-34
❑ 90ProAHLIHL-11
**Goldham, Bob**
❑ 34BeeGro1P-319
❑ 44BeeGro2P-98
❑ 44BeeGro2P-174
❑ 45QuaOatP-19A
❑ 45QuaOatP-19B
❑ 45QuaOatP-19C
❑ 51Par-67
❑ 52Par-64
❑ 53Par-49
❑ 54Par-39
❑ 54Top-46
**Goldie, Dan**
❑ 94ClaProP-233
**Goldmann, Rick (Erich)**
❑ 94GerDELE-289
❑ 95GerDELE-272
❑ 96GerDELE-171
**Goldsworthy, Bill**
❑ 68OPC-148
❑ 68ShiCoi-86
❑ 69OPC-195
❑ 70ColSta-52
❑ 70DadCoo-41
❑ 70EssPowPla-168
❑ 70NorStaP-2
❑ 70OPC-46
❑ 70SarProSta-95
❑ 70Top-46
❑ 71OPC-55
❑ 71SarProSta-86
❑ 71Top-55
❑ 71TorSun-131
❑ 72OPC-159
❑ 72OPCPlaC-10
❑ 72OPCTeaC-12
❑ 72SarProSta-104
❑ 72SweSemWC-220
❑ 72Top-115
❑ 73NorStaAP-4
❑ 73NorStaP-6
❑ 73OPC-62
❑ 73Top-62
❑ 74NHLActSta-127
❑ 74OPCNHL-1
❑ 74OPCNHL-112
❑ 74OPCNHL-134
❑ 74OPCNHL-220
❑ 74Top-1
❑ 74Top-112
❑ 74Top-134
❑ 74Top-220
❑ 75OPCNHL-180
❑ 75OPCNHL-321
❑ 75Top-180
❑ 75Top-321
❑ 76OPCNHL-169
❑ 76Top-169
❑ 77OPCNHL-99
❑ 77Top-99
❑ 91FutTreC72-79
**Goldsworthy, Leroy**
❑ 34BeeGro1P-53
❑ 35DiaMatT2-24
❑ 35DiaMatT3-22
❑ 35DiaMatTI-24
❑ 35OPCV304C-96
❑ 36V356WorG-73
❑ 51BufBis-9
**Goldsworthy, Sean**
❑ 94CenHocL-75
**Goldup, Glenn**
❑ 74CanaPos-7
❑ 74OPCNHL-275
❑ 75OPCNHL-391
❑ 78OPC-337
❑ 79OPC-376
❑ 80KinCarN-2
❑ 80OPC-382
**Goldup, Hank**
❑ 34BeeGro1P-274
❑ 34BeeGro1P-320
❑ 39OPCV3011-54
**Golembiewski, Leo**
❑ 90ArIce-1
❑ 90ArIce-2
❑ 91ArIce-1
❑ 91ArIce-18
❑ 92ArIce-1
**Golembrosky, Frank**
❑ 72NordPos-11
❑ 73NordTeal-12
**Golikov, Alexander**
❑ 74SweHocS-46
❑ 79PanSti-154
❑ 80USSOlyTMP-3
**Golikov, Vladimir**
❑ 74SweHocS-49
❑ 79PanSti-148
❑ 81SweSemHVS-52
❑ 82SweSemHVS-66
**Golonka, Jozef**
❑ 69SweHocS-25
❑ 69SweWorC-2
❑ 69SweWorC-7
❑ 69SweWorC-80
❑ 91SweSemWCS-248
❑ 94GerDELE-321
**Golosjumov, Sergei**
❑ 89SweSemWCS-80
**Goltz, Fred**
❑ 907thInnSOHL-58
❑ 94CenHocL-76
❑ 95LouIceG-4
**Goltz, Jeremy**
❑ 90ArIce-7
❑ 91ArIce-7
❑ 91ArIce-18
❑ 92ArIce-9
**Golubovsky, Yan**
❑ 94Cla-19
❑ 94ClaDraGol-19
❑ 94ClaTri-T19
❑ 95AdiRedW-7
❑ 95Ima-30
❑ 95ImaAut-30A
❑ 95ImaGol-30
❑ 98BowBes-104
❑ 98BowBesAR-104
❑ 98BowBesMIF-F8
❑ 98BowBesMIFAR-F8
❑ 98BowBesMIFR-F8
❑ 98BowBesR-104
❑ 98UppDec-11
❑ 98UppDecE-11
❑ 98UppDecE1o1-11
❑ 98UppDecGR-11
**Goman, Vesa**
❑ 95FinnSIS-361
❑ 96FinnSISR-156
**Gomes, Tom**
❑ 94CenHocL-58
**Gomez, Scott**
❑ 98BowCHL-145
❑ 98BowCHLAuB-A27
❑ 98BowCHLAuG-A27
❑ 98BowCHLAuS-A27
❑ 98BowCHLGA-145
❑ 98BowCHLOI-145
❑ 98BowCHLSC-SC19
❑ 98BowChrC-145
❑ 98BowChrCGA-145
❑ 98BowChrCGAR-145
❑ 98BowChrCOI-145
❑ 98BowChrCOIR-145
❑ 98BowChrCR-145
❑ 98O-PChr-232
❑ 98O-PChrR-232
❑ 98Top-232
❑ 98TopO-P-232
**Gonchar, Sergei**
❑ 92Cla-41
❑ 92Cla-43
❑ 92RusStaRA-9
❑ 93UppDec-272
❑ 94Cla-27
❑ 94ClaDraGol-27
❑ 94ClaProPIA-IA19
❑ 94ParSE-SE195
❑ 94ParSEG-SE195
❑ 94PorPir-9
❑ 94UppDec-264
❑ 94UppDecEleIce-264
❑ 95CanGamNHLP-286
❑ 95Cap-8
❑ 95ColEdgI-53
❑ 95Don-173
❑ 95Emo-187
❑ 95Ima-55
❑ 95ImaGol-55
❑ 95Lea-26
❑ 95Met-159
❑ 95ParInt-225
❑ 95ParIntEl-225
❑ 95Pin-71
❑ 95PinArtP-71
❑ 95PinRinC-71
❑ 95SkyImp-176
❑ 95Top-47
❑ 95TopOPCI-47
❑ 95Ult-322
❑ 95UppDec-305
❑ 95UppDecEleIce-305
❑ 95UppDecEleIceG-305
❑ 96BeAPAut-150
❑ 96BeAPAutSil-150
❑ 96BeAPla-150
❑ 96ClaGol-41
❑ 96ClaGol-43
❑ 96ColCho-286
❑ 96Fle-117
❑ 96FlePicF5-14
❑ 96FleRooSen-5
❑ 96MetUni-163
❑ 96Pin-40
❑ 96PinArtP-40
❑ 96PinFoi-40
❑ 96PinPreS-40
❑ 96PinRinC-40
❑ 96SkyImp-139
❑ 96SkyImpNHLF-9
❑ 96SP-165
❑ 96TeaOut-58
❑ 96TopNHLP-91
❑ 96TopPicOI-91
❑ 96Ult-175
❑ 96UltGolM-175
❑ 96UppDec-175
❑ 96UppDecIce-75
❑ 96UppDecIcePar-75
❑ 97ColCho-273
❑ 97Pac-103
❑ 97PacCop-103
❑ 97PacEmeGre-103
❑ 97PacIceB-103
❑ 97PacRed-103
❑ 97PacSil-103
❑ 97SPAut-166
❑ 97UppDec-180
❑ 98Be A PPA-299
❑ 98Be A PPAA-299
❑ 98Be A PPAAF-299
❑ 98Be A PPSE-299
❑ 98Be APG-299
❑ 98Pac-441
❑ 98PacAur-195
❑ 98PacIceB-441
❑ 98PacPar-244
❑ 98PacParC-244
❑ 98PacParEG-244
❑ 98PacParH-244
❑ 98PacParIB-244
❑ 98PacParS-244
❑ 98PacRed-441
❑ 98SP AutSotTG-SG
❑ 98SPxFin-90
❑ 98SPxFinR-90
❑ 98SPxFinS-90
❑ 98SSASotT-SG
❑ 98UppDec-201
❑ 98UppDecE-201
❑ 98UppDecE1o1-201
❑ 98UppDecGR-201
❑ 98UppDecM-211
❑ 98UppDecMGS-211
❑ 98UppDecMSS-211
❑ 98UppDecMSS-211
❑ 99Pac-439
❑ 99PacAur-147
❑ 99PacAurPD-147
❑ 99PacCop-439
❑ 99PacGol-439
❑ 99PacIceB-439
❑ 99PacPreD-439
❑ 99UppDecM-216
❑ 99UppDecMGS-216
❑ 99UppDecMPS-SG
❑ 99UppDecMSS-216
❑ 99UppDecMSS-216
**Goneau, Daniel**
❑ 93UppDecPOE-E5
❑ 96BeAPAut-107
❑ 96BeAPAutSil-107
❑ 96BeAPla-107
❑ 96ColCho-353
❑ 96DonCanI-126
❑ 96DonCanIGPP-126
❑ 96DonCanIRPP-126
❑ 96DonEli-143
❑ 96DonEliAsp-18
❑ 96DonEliDCS-143
❑ 96Fla-116
❑ 96FlaBluI-116
❑ 96LeaPre-145
❑ 96LeaPrePP-145
❑ 96MetUni-180
❑ 96SelCer-107
❑ 96SelCerAP-107
❑ 96SelCerBlu-107
❑ 96SelCerMB-107
❑ 96SelCerMG-107
❑ 96SelCerMR-107
❑ 96SelCerRed-107
❑ 96SP-184
❑ 96Ult-105
❑ 96UltGolM-106
❑ 96UltRoo-8
❑ 96UppDec-295
❑ 96UppDecIce-42
❑ 96UppDecIcePar-42
❑ 96Zen-148
❑ 96ZenArtP-148
❑ 97Don-190
❑ 97DonLim-148
❑ 97DonLimExp-148
❑ 97DonPreProG-190
❑ 97DonPreProS-190
❑ 97Pac-327
❑ 97PacCop-327
❑ 97PacEmeGre-327
❑ 97PacIceB-327
❑ 97PacRed-327
❑ 97PacSil-327
❑ 97ScoRan-18
❑ 97ScoRanPla-18
❑ 97ScoRanPre-18
❑ 98SPxFin-55
❑ 98SPxFin-141
❑ 98SPxFinR-55
❑ 98SPxFinR-141
❑ 98SPxFinS-55
❑ 98SPxFinS-141
❑ 98UC-137
❑ 98UD ChoPCR-137
❑ 98UD ChoR-137
**Good, Mikael**
❑ 83SweSemE-152
**Goodall, Glen**
❑ 90ProAHLIHL-482
❑ 91ProAHLCHL-191
**Goodall, Ron**
❑ 85KitRan-29
❑ 86KitRan-27
❑ 87KitRan-27
**Goodenough, Larry**
❑ 75FlyCanDC-8
❑ 75OPCNHL-373
❑ 76OPCNHL-96
❑ 76Top-96
❑ 77CanCanDC-4
❑ 77CanuRoyB-6
❑ 77OPCNHL-359
❑ 79OPC-383
**Goodfellow, Ebbie**
❑ 33OPCV304B-52
❑ 33V129-20
❑ 33V252CanG-25
❑ 33V288HamG-42
❑ 34BeeGro1P-101
❑ 34SweCap-37
❑ 36OPCV304D-117
❑ 36V356WorG-11
❑ 39OPCV3011-66
❑ 83HalFP-C5
❑ 85HalFC-35
**Goodkey, Mark**
❑ 90ForSasTra-3
**Goodman, Paul**
❑ 34BeeGro1P-54
❑ 40OPCV3012-150
**Goodwin, John**
❑ 80SauSteMG-16
❑ 83NovScoV-7
**Goold, Billy**
❑ 51LavDaiQSHL-89
**Gooldy, Eric**
❑ 96DetWha-9
**Gooley, Pat**
❑ 87BroBra-23
❑ 88BroBra-17
**Goralczyk, Felix**
❑ 69SweWorC-193
❑ 69SweWorC-200
**Goran, Lars**
❑ 65SweCorI-181
❑ 70SweHocS-190
❑ 72SweHocS-124
❑ 72SweHocS-249
❑ 73SweHocS-165
❑ 73SweHocS-174
❑ 73SweWorCS-165
❑ 73SweWorCS-174
❑ 74SweHocS-178
❑ 74SweHocS-255
❑ 95SweUppDE-217
**Goransson, Per**
❑ 83SweSemE-92
❑ 84SweSemE-92
❑ 86SwePanS-74
**Gorbachev, Sergei**
❑ 95SigRooFF-FF4
❑ 95SigRooFFS-FF4

**Gorbacov, Eduard**
- 96CzeAPSE-114

**Gordiouk, Viktor**
- 910PCIns-15R
- 91SweSemWCS-97
- 920PCPre-60
- 92Par-17
- 92SabJubF-6
- 92UppDec-579
- 92UppDecER-ER18
- 93ClaProPro-88
- 93Pow-28
- 93RochAmeKod-11
- 93Ult-120
- 93UltAllRoo-2
- 94Lea-468
- 940PCPre-456
- 940PCPreSE-456
- 94ParSE-SE23
- 94ParSEG-SE23
- 94TopPre-456
- 94TopPreSE-456
- 94Ult-263
- 95ColEdgI-149
- 96GerDELE-277

**Gordon, Bruce**
- 81SasBla-21

**Gordon, Chris**
- 91MicWol-4
- 93MicWol-7
- 94HunBli-12
- 95FliGen-19

**Gordon, Ian**
- 95SigRooA-16
- 95SigRooAPC-16
- 95St.JohF-6

**Gordon, Jack**
- 51CleBar-12
- 60CleBar-7
- 740PCNHL-238
- 74Top-238

**Gordon, Larry**
- 92CleLum-2

**Gordon, Rhett**
- 96SprFal-17

**Gordon, Robb**
- 92BriColJHL-147
- 95DonEliWJ-14
- 95UppDec-538
- 95UppDecEIeIce-538
- 95UppDecEIeIceG-538
- 96SyrCru-9

**Gordon, Scott**
- 86FreExp-9
- 88ProAHL-118
- 89HalCit-8
- 89ProAHL-153
- 90Bow-171
- 90BowTif-171
- 90HalCit-8
- 90NordPet-10
- 90ProAHLIHL-467
- 90ProSet-634
- 91NordPanTS-7
- 93KnoChe-5

**Gordon, Todd**
- 91GreMon-6
- 92GreMon-13

**Gorence, Tom**
- 790PC-51
- 79Top-51
- 800PC-368
- 810PC-250
- 820PC-250
- 88OilTenAnn-87

**Gorev, Roman**
- 94ClaProP-141

**Gorgenlander, Rudi**
- 94GerDELE-120
- 95GerDELE-109
- 96GerDELE-54

**Gorgi, Mark**
- 91AirCanSJHL-C31

**Goring, Butch**
- 710PC-152
- 71SarProSta-73
- 71TorSun-113
- 720PC-56
- 72SarProSta-92
- 72Top-72
- 730PC-155
- 73Top-138
- 74NHLActSta-119
- 740PCNHL-74
- 740PCNHL-98
- 74Top-74
- 74Top-98
- 750PCNHL-221
- 75Top-221
- 760PCNHL-239
- 76Top-239
- 77Coc-10
- 770PCNHL-67
- 77Top-67
- 780PC-151
- 78Top-151
- 790PC-98
- 79Top-98
- 800PC-254
- 80Top-254
- 810PC-203
- 810PCSti-20
- 81Top-E89
- 820PC-200

**82PosCer-12**
- 830PC-7
- 830PCSti-13
- 830PCSti-177
- 84IsIIsIN-7
- 84IsIIsIN-38
- 840PC-127
- 840PCSti-84
- 84Top-95
- 93LasVegThu-8

**Gorleau, Jason**
- 97BowCHL-63
- 97BowCHLOPC-63

**Gorman, Dave**
- 74PhoRoaWP-5
- 75RoaPhoWHA-10

**Gorman, Jeff**
- 907thInnSWHL-274
- 90PriAlbR-3
- 917thInnSWHL-260
- 91PriAlbR-2
- 93PriAlbR-6

**Gorman, Mike**
- 98BowCHL-12
- 98BowCHLGA-12
- 98BowCHLOI-12
- 98BowChrC-12
- 98BowChrCGA-12
- 98BowChrCGAR-12
- 98BowChrCOI-12
- 98BowChrCOIR-12
- 98BowChrCR-12

**Gorman, Sean**
- 92OklCitB-7
- 94CenHocL-59

**Gorman, Tommy**
- 36V356WorG-17
- 83HalFP-H7
- 85HalFC-113

**Gorokhov, Ilja**
- 95SP-181

**Gorski, Leroy**
- 81SasBla-3

**Gorski, Sheldon**
- 94CenHocL-77
- 96LouRiv-9
- 97LouRivF-7
- 97LouRivF-28

**Gorsky, Matt**
- 97LouRivF-26

**Gosdeck, Carsten**
- 98GerDELE-18

**Gosselin, David**
- 98BowCHL-109
- 98BowCHLGA-109
- 98BowCHLOI-109
- 98BowChrC-109
- 98BowChrCGA-109
- 98BowChrCGAR-109
- 98BowChrCOI-109
- 98BowChrCOIR-109
- 98BowChrCR-109

**Gosselin, Denis**
- 90RayJrC-6
- 91RayJrC-5

**Gosselin, Guy**
- 85MinDul-10
- 88ProAHL-181
- 89ProAHL-36

**Gosselin, Mario**
- 83CanNatJ-7
- 83NordPos-10
- 84NordPos-10
- 85NordGenF-10
- 85NordMcD-8
- 85NordPla-2
- 85NordPla-6
- 85NordPro-10
- 85NordTeal-9
- 850PC-18
- 850PCSti-146
- 85Top-18
- 86KraDra-20
- 86NordGenF-9
- 86NordMcD-9
- 86NordTeal-8
- 860PC-235
- 860PCSti-21
- 87NordGenF-11
- 87NordYumY-3A
- 87NordYumY-3B
- 870PC-250
- 870PCSti-231
- 87PanSti-157
- 88NordGenF-13
- 88NordTeal-14
- 880PC-173
- 880PCSti-193
- 88PanSti-347
- 88Top-173
- 89KinSmo-18
- 890PC-258
- 900PC-442
- 90ProAHLIHL-349
- 90UppDec-91
- 90UppDecF-91
- 91ProAHLIHL-115

**Gosselin, Steve**
- 907thInnSQMJHL-23
- 917thInnSQMJHL-86

**Gossmann, Carsten**
- 94GerDELE-97
- 95GerDELE-78

**Gotaas, Steve**
- 84PriAlbRS-9

**88ProIHL-51**
- 90ProAHLIHL-112
- 91ProAHLCHL-157
- 93LasVegThu-9

**Gottselig, Johnny**
- 33V252CanG-26
- 34BeeGro1P-55
- 34DiaMatS-25
- 35DiaMatT2-25
- 35DiaMatT3-23
- 35DiaMatT4-5
- 35DiaMatT5-5
- 35DiaMatTI-25
- 350PCV304C-80
- 36V356WorG-55
- 37DiaMatT6-5
- 390PCV3011-50

**Gotziaman, Chris**
- 92NorDakFS-7
- 95FliGen-16

**Goudie, Brian**
- 917thInnSMC-7
- 917thInnSOHL-336
- 93HamRoaA-5
- 94HamRoaA-9
- 95RicRen-8
- 96RicRen-7

**Goudreau, Marcel**
- 69ColChe-6

**Gould, Bob**
- 82Cap-7
- 82PosCer-20
- 84CapPizH-6
- 84CapPizH-5
- 840PC-196
- 85CapPizH-5
- 86CapKod-9
- 86CapPol-9
- 87CapKod-23
- 87CapTealss-7
- 870PC-55
- 870PCSti-237
- 87Top-55
- 88CapBor-6
- 88CapSmo-6
- 89BruSpoA-9
- 890PC-289
- 900PC-398
- 90ProAHLIHL-144

**Gould, John**
- 74CanuRoyB-6
- 74NHLActSta-278
- 740PCNHL-381
- 75CanuRoyB-7
- 750PCNHL-266
- 75Top-266
- 76CanuRoyB-5
- 760PCNHL-85
- 76Top-85
- 770PCNHL-382
- 780PC-309
- 790PC-282

**Gould, Justin**
- 96ProBru-9

**Goulet, Bob**
- 89JohChi-20

**Goulet, Michel**
- 80NordPos-11
- 800PC-67
- 80PepCap-66
- 80Top-67
- 81NordPos-8
- 810PC-275
- 810PCSti-75
- 82McDSti-14
- 82McDSti-19
- 82NordPos-8
- 820PC-284
- 820PCSti-25
- 83Ess-8
- 83NordPos-11
- 830PC-287
- 830PC-288
- 830PC-292
- 830PCSti-166
- 830PCSti-249
- 830PCSti-250
- 83PufSti-15
- 83Vac-65
- 847FEdis-15
- 84KelAccD-1
- 84NordPos-11
- 840PC-207
- 840PC-280
- 840PC-366
- 840PC-384
- 840PC-391
- 840PCSti-64
- 840PCSti-140
- 840PCSti-168
- 840PCSti-169
- 84Top-129
- 84Top-153
- 857ECreCar-15
- 857ECreCar-16
- 85NordGenF-11
- 85NordMcD-9
- 85NordPro-11
- 85NordTeal-10
- 850PC-150
- 850PCSti-141
- 85Top-150
- 86KraDra-21
- 86NordGenF-10
- 86NordMcD-10

**86NordTeal-9**
- 86NordYumY-4
- 860PC-92
- 860PCBoxB-E
- 860PCSti-22
- 860PCSti-113
- 86Top-92
- 86TopBoxB-E
- 86TopStiIns-2
- 87NordGenF-12
- 87NordYumY-4
- 870PC-77
- 870PCBoxB-M
- 870PCMin-2
- 870PCSti-113
- 870PCSti-225
- 87PanSti-163
- 87ProAll-11
- 87Top-77
- 87TopBoxB-M
- 87TopStiIns-6
- 88EssAllSta-14
- 88FriLayS-22
- 88NordGenF-14
- 88NordTeal-15
- 880PC-54
- 880PCMin-10
- 880PCSti-188
- 88PanSti-355
- 88Top-54
- 88TopStiIns-7
- 89Kra-30
- 89Nord-13
- 89NordGenF-10
- 89NordPol-9
- 890PC-57
- 890PCSti-186
- 89PanSti-326
- 89SweSemWCS-70
- 89Top-57
- 90BlaCok-13
- 90NordTeal-9
- 900PC-329
- 90ProSet-430
- 90Sco-221
- 90ScoCan-221
- 90Top-329
- 90TopTif-329
- 90UppDec-133
- 90UppDecF-133
- 91BlaCok-7
- 91Bow-392
- 91Kra-87
- 910PC-336
- 91PanSti-11
- 91Par-36
- 91Par-215
- 91Par-428
- 91Par-457
- 91ParFre-36
- 91ParFre-215
- 91ParFre-428
- 91Pin-109
- 91PinFre-109
- 91ProSet-50
- 91ProSetFre-50
- 91ProSetPla-46
- 91ProSetPlaPC-PC15
- 91ScoAme-201
- 91ScoAme-375
- 91ScoCan-201
- 91ScoCan-265
- 91StaClu-66
- 91Top-336
- 91UppDec-374
- 91UppDecF-374
- 92Bow-310
- 92DurPan-24
- 920PC-358
- 92PanSti-6
- 92PanStiFre-6
- 92Par-272
- 92ParEmel-272
- 92Pin-22
- 92PinAmePP-1
- 92PinFre-22
- 92ProSet-32
- 92Sco-202
- 92Sco-444
- 92ScoCan-202
- 92ScoCan-444
- 92StaClu-69
- 92Top-255
- 92Top-347
- 92TopGol-255G
- 92TopGol-347G
- 92Ult-35
- 92UppDec-113
- 93Don-701
- 93DurSco-42
- 93Lea-373
- 930PCPre-386
- 930PCPreG-386
- 93PanSti-148
- 93Par-313
- 93ParEmel-313
- 93Pin-399
- 93PinCan-399
- 93Pow-49
- 93Sco-153
- 93ScoCan-153
- 93StaClu-12
- 93StaCluFDI-12
- 93StaCluFDIO-12

**93StaCluO-12**
- 93TopPre-386
- 93TopPreG-386
- 93Ult-289
- 94EASpo-28
- 94HocWit-33
- 98HaloFM-1

**Goupille, Red (Cliff)**
- 34BeeGro1P-154
- 370PCV304E-178
- 390PCV3011-22
- 400PCV3012-120

**Gourlie, Bryan**
- 87PorWinH-10
- 88PorWinH-10
- 89PorWinH-9
- 907thInnSWHL-304

**Govedaris, Chris**
- 90Bow-259
- 90BowTif-259
- 90ProAHLIHL-187
- 90WhaJr7E-12
- 91ProAHLCHL-102
- 91ScoAme-325
- 91ScoCan-355
- 93ClaProPro-29
- 93St.JohML-9
- 94MilAdm-9
- 94Par-236
- 94ParGol-236
- 95ColEdgI-166
- 96GerDELE-45
- 98GerDELE-167

**Goverde, David**
- 88SudWol-2
- 89SudWol-19
- 90ProAHLIHL-352
- 91ProAHLCHL-399
- 92PhoRoa-8
- 93ClaProPro-54
- 93PhoRoa-7
- 95TolSto-20
- 96TolSto-35

**Gowan, Mark**
- 92SudWol-26

**Gowens, Mark**
- 93FliGen-17
- 94FliGen-9

**Goyer, Benoit**
- 90MonAAA-12

**Goyer, Gerry**
- 67Top-54

**Goyette, Danielle**
- 94ClaWomOH-W7
- 97ColCho-285

**Goyette, Phil**
- 44BeeGro2P-242
- 44BeeGro2P-317
- 52JunBluT-141
- 57Par-M11
- 58Par-47
- 59Par-2
- 60Par-50
- 60Par-58
- 60ShiCoi-27
- 60YorPreP-11
- 61Par-46
- 61ShiCoi-116
- 61YorYelB-30
- 62Par-37
- 62ShiMetC-28
- 63Top-58
- 64BeeGro3P-128
- 64CocCap-87
- 64Top-87
- 65Coc-87
- 65Top-92
- 66Top-28
- 66TopUSAT-28
- 67Top-25
- 680PC-73
- 68ShiCoi-97
- 68Top-73
- 690PC-21
- 690PCFou-6
- 69Top-21
- 70ColSta-10
- 70DadCoo-42
- 70EssPowPla-80
- 700PC-127
- 700PC-251
- 70Top-127
- 710PC-88
- 71SabPos-7
- 71SarProSta-30
- 71Top-88
- 71TorSun-27
- 72SweSemWC-196
- 91UltOriS-11
- 91UltOriSF-11
- 93ParParR-PR59
- 94ParMisL-74
- 94ParTalB-105
- 94ParTalB-173
- 95Par66-99
- 95Par66Coi-99

**Gozzi, Anders**
- 87SwePanS-15
- 89SweSemE-15
- 90SweSemE-190
- 91SweSemE-42
- 92SweSemE-67
- 93SweSemE-39
- 94SweLeaE-223
- 95SweLeaE-11

**95SweUppDE-10**
- 93TopPre-386
- 93TopPreG-386
- 93Ult-289

**Grabinsky, Jeff**
- 92BriColJHL-38

**Graboski, Tony**
- 34BeeGro1P-155

**Grachev, Vladimir**
- 92RusStaRA-24

**Gracie, Bob (Robert)**
- 320'KeeMapL-14
- 330PCV304B-66
- 33V129-40
- 33V252CanG-27
- 33V357IceK-53
- 34BeeGro1P-156
- 34BeeGro1P-197
- 34DiaMatS-26
- 35DiaMatTI-26
- 36V356WorG-38
- 370PCV304E-171
- 38QuaOatP-15

**Gradin, Henrik**
- 92SweSemE-247
- 93SweSemE-216

**Gradin, Peter**
- 83SweSemE-14
- 84SweSemE-13
- 85SwePanS-16
- 87SwePanS-13
- 89SweSemE-12
- 90SweSemE-46
- 91SweSemE-13

**Gradin, Thomas**
- 78CanuRoyB-7
- 79CanuRoyB-8
- 790PC-53
- 79PanSti-201
- 79Top-53
- 80CanuSilD-9
- 80CanuTeal-9
- 800PC-241
- 80PepCap-108
- 80Top-241
- 81CanuSilD-19
- 81CanuTeal-9
- 810PC-327
- 810PC-346
- 810PCSti-243
- 81Top-15
- 81Top-64
- 82Canu-8
- 820PC-337
- 820PC-344
- 820PC-345
- 820PCSti-240
- 82PosCer-19
- 82SweSemHVS-148
- 83Canu-8
- 830PC-350
- 830PCSti-273
- 83PufSti-3
- 83Vac-107
- 84Canu-9
- 84KelAccD-6
- 840PC-319
- 840PCSti-282
- 85Canu-8
- 850PC-16
- 850PCSti-240
- 85Top-16
- 87SwePanS-18
- 89SweSemE-13

**Graesen, Mats**
- 89SweSemE-284

**Graf, Kris**
- 95SpoChi-8

**Graham, Dave**
- 95GuiFla-17

**Graham, Dirk**
- 84SprInd-21
- 85NorSta7E-12
- 85NorStaPos-11
- 860PC-143
- 860PCSti-171
- 86Top-143
- 87NorStaPos-15
- 87PanSti-295
- 87Top-184
- 88BlaCok-5
- 880PC-135
- 880PCSti-7
- 88PanSti-25
- 88Top-135
- 89BlaCok-16
- 890PC-52
- 89PanSti-44
- 89Top-52
- 90BlaCok-1
- 90Bow-8
- 90BowTif-8
- 900PC-179
- 90PanSti-191
- 90ProSet-51
- 90Sco-17
- 90ScoCan-17
- 90Top-179
- 90TopTif-179
- 90UppDec-131
- 90UppDecF-131
- 91BlaCok-8
- 91Bow-397
- 910PC-217
- 910PC-430

**910PC-521**
- 910PCPre-131
- 91PanSti-16
- 91Par-33
- 91ParFre-33
- 91Pin-261
- 91PinFre-261
- 91ProSet-51
- 91ProSet-323
- 91ProSet-570
- 91ProSetFre-51
- 91ProSetFre-323
- 91ProSetFre-570
- 91ProSetNHLAS-AC12
- 91ProSetPla-23
- 91ScoAme-15
- 91ScoAme-432
- 91ScoCan-15
- 91ScoCan-322
- 91StaClu-181
- 91Top-217
- 91Top-521
- 91UppDec-271
- 91UppDec-502
- 91UppDecAWH-AW8
- 91UppDecF-271
- 91UppDecF-502
- 92Bow-68
- 920PC-210
- 92PanSti-7
- 92PanStiFre-7
- 92Par-271
- 92ParEmel-271
- 92Pin-173
- 92PinFre-173
- 92ProSet-38
- 92Sco-27
- 92ScoCan-27
- 92StaClu-342
- 92Top-376
- 92TopGol-376G
- 92Ult-36
- 92UppDec-272
- 93BlaCok-25
- 93Don-63
- 93Lea-270
- 930PCPre-88
- 930PCPreG-88
- 93PanSti-147
- 93Pin-24
- 93PinCan-24
- 93PinCap-5
- 93PinCapC-5
- 93Pow-50
- 93Sco-12
- 93ScoCan-12
- 93StaClu-90
- 93StaCluFDI-90
- 93StaCluFDIO-90
- 93StaCluO-90
- 93TopPre-88
- 93TopPreG-88
- 93Ult-61
- 93UppDec-328
- 94BeAPSig-78
- 94CanGamNHLP-66
- 94FinnJaaK-97
- 94Fla-33
- 94Fle-40
- 94Lea-335
- 940PCPre-67
- 940PCPreSE-67
- 94Pin-317
- 94PinArtP-317
- 94PinRinC-317
- 94Sco-56
- 94ScoGol-56
- 94ScoPla-56
- 94ScoPlaTS-56
- 94TopPre-67
- 94TopPreSE-67
- 94Ult-41

**Graham, Jimmy**
- 28V1282PauC-42
- 69ColChe-7

**Graham, John**
- 91BriColJHL-42
- 91BriColJHL-157

**Graham, Pat**
- 82PosCer-15
- 83MapLeaP-9
- 83PenHeiP-9

**Graham, Rob**
- 87SudWol-13

**Graham, Rod**
- 71RocAme-7
- 77RocAme-11
- 77RocAme-12
- 82KinCan-24

**Graham, Ross**
- 52JunBluT-7

**Grahame, Ron**
- 750PCWHA-9
- 750PCWHA-61
- 760PCWHA-107
- 780PC-219
- 78Top-219
- 80NordPos-12

**Grahling, Eric**
- 92HarCri-10

**Grahn, Christer**
- 70SweHocS-195
- 71SweHocS-281
- 72SweHocS-42
- 74SweHocS-141

**Grahn, Karl-Olov**
❑ 72SweHocS-67
**Granath, Einar**
❑ 67SweHoc-185
**Granato, Cammi**
❑ 93Cla-66
❑ 94ClaProP-248
❑ 94ClaWomOH-W37
❑ 95AHC-10
**Granato, Tony**
❑ 89OPC-161
❑ 89OPC-310
❑ 89OPCSti-10
❑ 89OPCSti-36
❑ 89OPCSti-150
❑ 89OPCSti-241
❑ 89PanSti-285
❑ 89Top-161
❑ 90Bow-140
❑ 90BowHatTri-18
❑ 90BowTif-140
❑ 90KinSmo-11
❑ 90OPC-62
❑ 90PanSti-239
❑ 90ProSet-117
❑ 90Sco-48
❑ 90ScoCan-48
❑ 90ScoYouS-33
❑ 90Top-62
❑ 90TopTif-62
❑ 90UppDec-272
❑ 90UppDecF-272
❑ 91Bow-192
❑ 91Kra-35
❑ 91OPC-88
❑ 91PanSti-83
❑ 91Par-66
❑ 91ParFre-66
❑ 91Pin-76
❑ 91PinFre-76
❑ 91ProSet-98
❑ 91ProSetFre-98
❑ 91ProSetPla-49
❑ 91ScoAme-57
❑ 91ScoCan-57
❑ 91StaClu-97
❑ 91SweSemWCS-147
❑ 91Top-88
❑ 91UppDec-172
❑ 91UppDec-508
❑ 91UppDecF-172
❑ 91UppDecF-508
❑ 92Bow-50
❑ 92OPC-65
❑ 92PanSti-68
❑ 92PanStiFre-68
❑ 92Par-301
❑ 92ParEmel-301
❑ 92Pin-69
❑ 92Pin-262
❑ 92PinFre-69
❑ 92PinFre-262
❑ 92ProSet-74
❑ 92Sco-243
❑ 92ScoCan-243
❑ 92ScoUSAG-4
❑ 92SeaPat-11
❑ 92StaClu-281
❑ 92Top-242
❑ 92TopGol-242G
❑ 92Ult-82
❑ 92UppDec-185
❑ 93Don-160
❑ 93Lea-201
❑ 93OPCPre-144
❑ 93OPCPre-504
❑ 93OPCPreG-144
❑ 93OPCPreG-504
❑ 93PanSti-203
❑ 93Par-93
❑ 93ParEmel-93
❑ 93Pin-137
❑ 93PinCan-137
❑ 93Pow-115
❑ 93Sco-52
❑ 93Sco-444
❑ 93ScoCan-52
❑ 93ScoCan-444
❑ 93StaClu-285
❑ 93StaCluFDI-285
❑ 93StaCluO-285
❑ 93SweSemWCS-181
❑ 93TopPre-144
❑ 93TopPre-504
❑ 93TopPreG-144
❑ 93TopPreG-504
❑ 93Ult-63
❑ 93UppDec-146
❑ 93UppDecSP-69
❑ 94BeAP99A-G9
❑ 94BeAPla-R98
❑ 94BeAPSig-114
❑ 94CanGamNHLP-125
❑ 94Don-145
❑ 94FinnJaaK-126
❑ 94HocWit-32
❑ 94Lea-229
❑ 94OPCPre-183
❑ 94OPCPreSE-183
❑ 94ParSE-SE83
❑ 94ParSEG-SE83
❑ 94ParVin-V76
❑ 94Pin-118
❑ 94PinArtP-118
❑ 94PinRinC-118
❑ 94Sco-71
❑ 94ScoGol-71
❑ 94ScoPla-71
❑ 94ScoPlaTS-71
❑ 94SP-56
❑ 94SPDieCut-56
❑ 94StaCluST-11
❑ 94TopPre-183
❑ 94TopPreSE-183
❑ 94Ult-305
❑ 94UppDec-29
❑ 94UppDecElelce-29
❑ 94UppDecSPI-SP126
❑ 94UppDecSPIDC-SP126
❑ 95CanGamNHLP-139
❑ 95ColCho-194
❑ 95ColChoPC-194
❑ 95ColChoPCP-194
❑ 95Don-111
❑ 95FinnSemWC-117
❑ 95ImaPlaPl-PL2
❑ 95Lea-174
❑ 95Met-70
❑ 95ParInt-376
❑ 95ParIntEl-376
❑ 95PlaOneoOne-49
❑ 95Sco-233
❑ 95ScoBlalce-233
❑ 95ScoBlalceAP-233
❑ 95StaClu-116
❑ 95StaCluMOMS-116
❑ 95Sum-100
❑ 95SumArtP-100
❑ 95SumIce-100
❑ 95SweGloWC-120
❑ 95Top-58
❑ 95TopOPCI-58
❑ 95Ult-249
❑ 95UppDec-201
❑ 95UppDecElelce-201
❑ 95UppDecElelceG-201
❑ 96BeAPAut-142
❑ 96BeAPAutSil-142
❑ 96BeAPla-142
❑ 96Fla-84
❑ 96FlaBlul-84
❑ 96PlaOneoOne-340
❑ 96SP-140
❑ 96UppDecBD-121
❑ 96UppDecBDG-121
❑ 97ColCho-218
❑ 97Don-121
❑ 97DonLim-144
❑ 97DonLimExp-144
❑ 97DonPreProG-121
❑ 97DonPreProS-121
❑ 97Pac-203
❑ 97PacCop-203
❑ 97PacDyn-111
❑ 97PacDynBKS-109
❑ 97PacDynC-111
❑ 97PacDynDG-111
❑ 97PacDynEG-111
❑ 97PacDynIB-111
❑ 97PacDynR-111
❑ 97PacDynSil-111
❑ 97PacDynTan-67
❑ 97PacEmeGre-203
❑ 97PacIceB-203
❑ 97PacInv-125
❑ 97PacInvC-125
❑ 97PacInvEG-125
❑ 97PacInvIB-125
❑ 97PacInvR-125
❑ 97PacInvS-125
❑ 97PacOme-201
❑ 97PacOmeC-201
❑ 97PacOmeDG-201
❑ 97PacOmeEG-201
❑ 97PacOmeG-201
❑ 97PacOmeIB-201
❑ 97PacPar-165
❑ 97PacParC-165
❑ 97PacParDG-165
❑ 97PacParEG-165
❑ 97PacParIB-165
❑ 97PacParRed-165
❑ 97PacParSil-165
❑ 97PacRed-203
❑ 97PacSil-203
❑ 97Pin-187
❑ 97PinIns-142
❑ 97PinPrePBB-187
❑ 97PinPrePBC-187
❑ 97PinPrePBM-187
❑ 97PinPrePBY-187
❑ 97PinPrePFC-187
❑ 97PinPrePFM-187
❑ 97PinPrePFY-187
❑ 97PinPrePla-187
❑ 97Sco-77
❑ 97ScoArtPro-77
❑ 97ScoGolBla-77
❑ 97SPAut-135
❑ 97UppDec-360
❑ 97UppDecGDM-360
❑ 98Be A PPA-272
❑ 98Be A PPAA-272
❑ 98Be A PPAAF-272
❑ 98Be A PPSE-272
❑ 98Be APG-272
❑ 98O-PChr-147
❑ 98O-PChrR-147
❑ 98Pac-380
❑ 98PacAur-167
❑ 98PacDynI-165
❑ 98PacDynIIB-165
❑ 98PacDynIR-165
❑ 98PacIceB-380
❑ 98PacPar-210
❑ 98PacParC-210
❑ 98PacParEG-210
❑ 98PacParH-210
❑ 98PacParIB-210
❑ 98PacParS-210
❑ 98PacRed-380
❑ 98Top-147
❑ 98TopO-P-147
❑ 98UppDec-352
❑ 98UppDecE-352
❑ 98UppDecE1o1-352
❑ 98UppDecGR-352
❑ 99Pac-371
❑ 99PacCop-371
❑ 99PacGol-371
❑ 99PacIceB-371
❑ 99PacPreD-371
**Granberg, Gunnar**
❑ 69SweHocS-241
❑ 70SweHocS-139
**Grand'maison, Dominic**
❑ 907thInnSQMJHL-247
❑ 917thInnSQMJHL-257
❑ 94CenHocL-45
❑ 95FliGen-12
**Grandberg, Geoff**
❑ 907thInnSWHL-208
❑ 917thInnSMC-83
❑ 917thInnSWHL-21
**Grandmaitre, Syl**
❑ 81KinCan-9
❑ 82KinCan-9
**Granholm, Svante**
❑ 67SweHoc-218
❑ 69SweHocS-333
❑ 70SweHocS-251
❑ 71SweHocS-309
❑ 72SweHocS-293
❑ 73SweHocS-145
❑ 73SweWorCS-145
❑ 74SweHocS-216
**Grankvist, Erik**
❑ 91SweSemE-153
❑ 92SweSemE-176
❑ 93SweSemE-147
❑ 94SweLeaE-27
❑ 95SweLeaE-247
**Granlund, Lars**
❑ 69SweHocS-97
❑ 71SweHocS-353
**Granlund, Mikael**
❑ 93FinnSIS-84
**Granqvist, Daniel**
❑ 93SweSemE-172
**Granstedt, Mikael**
❑ 83SweSemE-182
❑ 84SweSemE-205
❑ 86SwePanS-234
❑ 87SwePanS-220
❑ 89SweSemE-202
**Granstrom, Alf**
❑ 69SweHocS-78
**Granstrom, Lars-Olof**
❑ 69SweHocS-229
**Grant, Benny**
❑ 32O'KeeMapL-17
**Grant, Danny**
❑ 64CanaPos-7
❑ 67CanalGA-23
❑ 68OPC-52
❑ 68Top-52
❑ 69OPC-125
❑ 69OPC-208
❑ 69OPCFou-17
❑ 69OPCSta-10
❑ 69Top-125
❑ 70ColSta-36
❑ 70DadCoo-43
❑ 70EssPowPla-176
❑ 70NorStaP-3
❑ 70OPC-47
❑ 70SarProSta-92
❑ 70Top-47
❑ 70TopStiS-11
❑ 71LetActR-11
❑ 71OPC-79
❑ 71OPCTBoo-11
❑ 71SarProSta-85
❑ 71Top-79
❑ 71TorSun-132
❑ 72OPC-57
❑ 72SarProSta-103
❑ 72Top-39
❑ 73NorStaP-7
❑ 73OPC-214
❑ 73Top-161
❑ 74NHLActSta-98
❑ 74OPCNHL-112
❑ 74OPCNHL-174
❑ 74Top-112
❑ 74Top-174
❑ 75OPCNHL-49
❑ 75OPCNHL-212
❑ 75OPCNHL-318
❑ 75Top-49
❑ 75Top-212
❑ 75Top-318
❑ 76OPCNHL-16
❑ 76Top-16
❑ 77OPCNHL-147
❑ 77Top-147
❑ 78OPC-306
**Grant, Derek**
❑ 93NiaFalT-14
**Grant, Doug**
❑ 73RedWinMP-6
❑ 74NHLActSta-101
❑ 74OPCNHL-347
❑ 77OPCNHL-294
❑ 78OPC-373
**Grant, Joe**
❑ 81SweSemHVS-79
**Grant, Kevin**
❑ 86KitRan-8
❑ 87KitRan-8
❑ 88SudWol-5
❑ 89ProIHL-197
❑ 90ProAHLIHL-606
❑ 91ProAHLCHL-575
❑ 93PhoRoa-8
❑ 98GerDELE-257
**Grant, Lee**
❑ 92BriColJHL-48
**Grant, Michael**
❑ 83HalFP-O8
❑ 85HalFC-218
**Grant, Peter**
❑ 90MicTecHus-5
**Grassel, Corey**
❑ 95MadMon-6
**Grassie, Chris**
❑ 91NasKni-4
❑ 92NasKni-6
**Gratton, Benoit**
❑ 96PorPir-25
❑ 99Pac-440
❑ 99PacAur-148
❑ 99PacAurPD-148
❑ 99PacCop-440
❑ 99PacGol-440
❑ 99PacIceB-440
❑ 99PacPreD-440
**Gratton, Brad**
❑ 87KinCan-19
**Gratton, Chris**
❑ 917thInnSOHL-225
❑ 92UppDec-590
❑ 92UppDec-SP3
❑ 93Cla-3
❑ 93ClaTopTen-DP3
❑ 93Don-330
❑ 93Don-393
❑ 93DonRatR-2
❑ 93DonSpeP-V
❑ 93Lea-331
❑ 93LeaFrePhe-3
❑ 93LigKasK-3
❑ 93LigSealR-17
❑ 93OPCPre-410
❑ 93OPCPreG-410
❑ 93Par-250
❑ 93ParCalC-C3
❑ 93ParCalCG-C3
❑ 93ParChePH-D12
❑ 93ParEasWesS-E6
❑ 93ParEmel-250
❑ 93Pin-443
❑ 93PinCan-443
❑ 93PinSupR-3
❑ 93PinSupRC-3
❑ 93Pow-443
❑ 93PowRooS-5
❑ 93Sco-596
❑ 93ScoCan-596
❑ 93ScoGol-596
❑ 93StaClu-320
❑ 93StaCluFDI-320
❑ 93StaCluO-320
❑ 93TopPre-410
❑ 93TopPreG-410
❑ 93Ult-423
❑ 93UltWavF-5
❑ 93UppDec-78
❑ 93UppDecSilSka-R4
❑ 93UppDecSilSkaG-R4
❑ 93UppDecSP-149
❑ 94BeAPla-R110
❑ 94BeAPSig-116
❑ 94CanGamNHLP-223
❑ 94ClaAut-NNO
❑ 94ClaProP-16
❑ 94Don-189
❑ 94Fin-58
❑ 94FinRef-58
❑ 94FinSupTW-58
❑ 94Fla-173
❑ 94Fle-206
❑ 94Lea-86
❑ 94LeaGolR-4
❑ 94LeaLim-56
❑ 94LeaLimI-22
❑ 94LigHeaP-2
❑ 94LigPhoA-14
❑ 94LigPos-9
❑ 94OPCFinIns-20
❑ 94OPCPre-439
❑ 94OPCPreSE-439
❑ 94Par-220
❑ 94Par-282
❑ 94ParCratGB-22
❑ 94ParCratGG-22
❑ 94ParCratGR-22
❑ 94ParGol-220
❑ 94ParGol-282
❑ 94ParSEV-16
❑ 94Pin-19
❑ 94Pin-468
❑ 94PinArtP-19
❑ 94PinArtP-468
❑ 94PinRinC-19
❑ 94PinRinC-468
❑ 94Sel-77
❑ 94SelGol-77
❑ 94SP-111
❑ 94SPDieCut-111
❑ 94StaClu-112
❑ 94StaClu-195
❑ 94StaCluFDI-112
❑ 94StaCluFDI-195
❑ 94StaCluMOMS-112
❑ 94StaCluMOMS-195
❑ 94StaCluSTWC-112
❑ 94StaCluSTWC-195
❑ 94TopPre-439
❑ 94TopPreSE-439
❑ 94Ult-205
❑ 94UltAllRoo-4
❑ 94UltPow-3
❑ 94UppDec-345
❑ 94UppDecElelce-345
❑ 94UppDecNBAP-6
❑ 94UppDecSPI-SP75
❑ 94UppDecSPIDC-SP75
❑ 95CanGamNHLP-247
❑ 95ColCho-140
❑ 95ColCho-357
❑ 95ColChoPC-140
❑ 95ColChoPC-357
❑ 95ColChoPCP-140
❑ 95ColChoPCP-357
❑ 95Don-122
❑ 95Emo-163
❑ 95ImpSti-114
❑ 95Lea-133
❑ 95LeaLim-8
❑ 95LigTeal-10
❑ 95Met-136
❑ 95ParInt-462
❑ 95ParIntEl-462
❑ 95Pin-33
❑ 95PinArtP-33
❑ 95PinRinC-33
❑ 95PlaOneoOne-92
❑ 95ProMag-72
❑ 95Sco-39
❑ 95ScoBlalce-39
❑ 95ScoBlalceAP-39
❑ 95ScoChelt-4
❑ 95SkyImp-154
❑ 95StaClu-134
❑ 95StaCluMOMS-134
❑ 95Sum-45
❑ 95SumArtP-45
❑ 95SumIce-45
❑ 95Top-70
❑ 95TopOPCI-70
❑ 95Ult-151
❑ 95UltGolM-151
❑ 95UppDec-407
❑ 95UppDecElelce-407
❑ 95UppDecElelceG-407
❑ 95UppDecSpeE-SE75
❑ 95UppDecSpeEdiG-SE75
❑ 95Zen-15
❑ 96ColCho-245
❑ 96ColCho-331
❑ 96Don-173
❑ 96DonCanI-62
❑ 96DonCanIGPP-62
❑ 96DonCanIOC-8
❑ 96DonCanIRPP-62
❑ 96DonPrePro-173
❑ 96Lea-120
❑ 96LeaPreP-120
❑ 96MetUni-144
❑ 96NHLProSTA-72
❑ 96Pin-141
❑ 96PinArtP-141
❑ 96PinFoi-141
❑ 96PinPreS-141
❑ 96PinRinC-141
❑ 96Sco-148
❑ 96ScoArtPro-148
❑ 96ScoDeaCAP-148
❑ 96ScoGolB-148
❑ 96ScoSpeAP-148
❑ 96SkyImp-121
❑ 96SP-145
❑ 96SPHolCol-HC12
❑ 96TeaOut-23
❑ 96UppDec-337
❑ 96UppDecBD-77
❑ 96UppDecBDG-77
❑ 96UppDecGN-X32
❑ 96UppDecIce-65
❑ 96UppDecIcePar-65
❑ 96UppDecPP-P10
❑ 97Be A PPAD-137
❑ 97Be A PPAPD-137
❑ 97BeAPla-137
❑ 97BeAPlaAut-137
❑ 97ColCho-236
❑ 97ColChoSta-SQ61
❑ 97Don-56
❑ 97DonCanI-39
❑ 97DonCanIDS-39
❑ 97DonCanIPS-39
❑ 97DonEli-91
❑ 97DonEliAsp-91
❑ 97DonEliS-91
❑ 97DonLim-148
❑ 97DonLimExp-148
❑ 97DonPre-130
❑ 97DonPreCttC-130
❑ 97DonPreProG-56
❑ 97DonPreProS-56
❑ 97DonPri-118
❑ 97DonPriSoA-118
❑ 97Kat-104
❑ 97KatGol-104
❑ 97KatSil-104
❑ 97Lea-27
❑ 97LeaFraMat-27
❑ 97LeaFraMDC-27
❑ 97LeaInt-27
❑ 97LeaIntUI-27
❑ 97Pac-308
❑ 97PacCop-308
❑ 97PacCroR-96
❑ 97PacCroREG-96
❑ 97PacCroRIB-96
❑ 97PacCroRS-96
❑ 97PacDyn-117
❑ 97PacDynC-117
❑ 97PacDynDG-117
❑ 97PacDynEG-117
❑ 97PacDynIB-117
❑ 97PacDynR-117
❑ 97PacDynSil-117
❑ 97PacDynTan-62
❑ 97PacEmeGre-308
❑ 97PacIceB-308
❑ 97PacInv-131
❑ 97PacInvC-131
❑ 97PacInvEG-131
❑ 97PacInvIB-131
❑ 97PacInvR-131
❑ 97PacInvS-131
❑ 97PacOme-164
❑ 97PacOmeC-164
❑ 97PacOmeDG-164
❑ 97PacOmeEG-164
❑ 97PacOmeG-164
❑ 97PacOmeIB-164
❑ 97PacPar-131
❑ 97PacParC-131
❑ 97PacParDG-131
❑ 97PacParEG-131
❑ 97PacParIB-131
❑ 97PacParRed-131
❑ 97PacParSil-131
❑ 97PacRed-308
❑ 97PacRev-100
❑ 97PacRevC-100
❑ 97PacRevE-100
❑ 97PacRevIB-100
❑ 97PacRevR-100
❑ 97PacRevS-100
❑ 97PacSil-308
❑ 97Pin-183
❑ 97PinCer-84
❑ 97PinCerMB-84
❑ 97PinCerMG-84
❑ 97PinCerMR-84
❑ 97PinCerR-84
❑ 97PinIns-110
❑ 97PinPrePBB-183
❑ 97PinPrePBC-183
❑ 97PinPrePBM-183
❑ 97PinPrePBY-183
❑ 97PinPrePFC-183
❑ 97PinPrePFM-183
❑ 97PinPrePFY-183
❑ 97PinPrePla-183
❑ 97PinTotCMPG-84
❑ 97PinTotCPB-84
❑ 97PinTotCPG-84
❑ 97PinTotCPR-84
❑ 97Sco-168
❑ 97ScoFly-6
❑ 97ScoFlyPla-6
❑ 97ScoFlyPre-6
❑ 97SPAut-112
❑ 97SPx-45
❑ 97SPxBro-45
❑ 97SPxGol-45
❑ 97SPxGraF-45
❑ 97SPxSil-45
❑ 97SPxSte-45
❑ 97Stu-90
❑ 97StuPrePG-90
❑ 97StuPrePS-90
❑ 97UppDec-155
❑ 97UppDec-327
❑ 97Zen-56
❑ 97ZenZGol-56
❑ 97ZenZSil-56
❑ 98Be A PPA-101
❑ 98Be A PPAA-101
❑ 98Be A PPAAF-101
❑ 98Be A PPTBASG-101
❑ 98Be APG-101
❑ 98Fin-139
❑ 98FinNo P-139
❑ 98FinNo PR-139
❑ 98FinRef-139
❑ 98Pac-55
❑ 98PacAur-138
❑ 98PacDynI-135
❑ 98PacDynIIB-135
❑ 98PacDynIR-135
❑ 98PacIceB-55
❑ 98PacOmeH-218
❑ 98PacOmeODI-218
❑ 98PacOmeR-218
❑ 98PacPar-173
❑ 98PacParC-173
❑ 98PacParEG-173
❑ 98PacParH-173
❑ 98PacParIB-173
❑ 98PacParS-173
❑ 98PacRed-55
❑ 98UC-150
❑ 98UD ChoPCR-150
❑ 98UD ChoR-150
❑ 98UppDec-149
❑ 98UppDecE-149
❑ 98UppDecE1o1-149
❑ 98UppDecGR-149
❑ 98UppDecM-192
❑ 98UppDecMGS-192
❑ 98UppDecMSS-192
❑ 98UppDecMSS-192
❑ 99Pac-389
❑ 99PacAur-129
❑ 99PacAurPD-129
❑ 99PacCop-389
❑ 99PacGol-389
❑ 99PacIceB-389
❑ 99PacPreD-389
❑ 99UppDecM-193
❑ 99UppDecMGS-193
❑ 99UppDecMSS-193
❑ 99UppDecMSS-193
**Gratton, Danny (Dan)**
❑ 82OshGen-12
❑ 83OshGen-9
❑ 88ProAHL-210
**Gratton, Gilles**
❑ 72NatOttWHA-12
❑ 74OPCWHA-65
❑ 76OPCNHL-28
❑ 76Top-28
❑ 77OPCNHL-207
❑ 77Top-207
**Gratton, Mike**
❑ 90RayJrC-7
**Gratton, Norm**
❑ 74NHLActSta-47
❑ 74NHLActStaU-19
❑ 74OPCNHL-288
❑ 75OPCNHL-34
❑ 75Top-34
**Graul, Thomas**
❑ 94GerDELE-38
❑ 95GerDELE-31
**Gravel, Florian**
❑ 51LavDaiLSJ-53
**Gravel, Francois**
❑ 88ProAHL-275
❑ 89ProAHL-184
❑ 98GerDELE-192
**Gravel, Greg**
❑ 80OshGen-18
❑ 81OshGen-16
**Gravelle, Dan**
❑ 93GreMon-6
❑ 94ClaProP-234
**Gravelle, Leo**
❑ 44BeeGro2P-243
❑ 45QuaOatP-79A
❑ 45QuaOatP-79B
❑ 45QuaOatP-79C
❑ 51LavDaiQSHL-109
❑ 52St.LawS-61
**Graves, Adam**
❑ 87RedWinLC-12
❑ 88RedWinLC-8
❑ 89OilTeal-8
❑ 90OilIGA-6
❑ 90OPC-251
❑ 90OPC-480
❑ 90ProSet-84
❑ 90Sco-163
❑ 90ScoCan-163
❑ 90Top-251
❑ 90UppDec-344
❑ 90UppDecF-344
❑ 91Bow-97
❑ 91OilPanTS-6
❑ 91OPC-167
❑ 91OPCPre-28
❑ 91PanSti-122
❑ 91Par-339
❑ 91ParFre-339
❑ 91Pin-16
❑ 91PinFre-16
❑ 91ProSet-67
❑ 91ProSet-443
❑ 91ProSetFre-67
❑ 91ProSetFre-443
❑ 91ProSetPla-207
❑ 91ScoAme-358
❑ 91ScoCan-235
❑ 91ScoCan-594
❑ 91ScoRoo-44T
❑ 91StaClu-332
❑ 91Top-167
❑ 91UppDec-268
❑ 91UppDec-574
❑ 91UppDecF-268
❑ 91UppDecF-574
❑ 92Bow-373
❑ 92OPC-158
❑ 92PanSti-238
❑ 92PanStiFre-238
❑ 92Par-346
❑ 92ParEmel-346
❑ 92Pin-108
❑ 92PinFre-108

92ProSet-115
92Sco-71
92ScoCan-71
92ScoCan-75
92StaClu-150
92Top-329
92TopGol-329G
92Ult-136
92UppDec-388
92UppDec-453
92WinSpi-5
93ClaTeaCan-TC7
93Don-219
93Kra-10
93Lea-130
93OPCPre-106
93OPCPreG-106
93PanSti-92
93Par-134
93ParEmel-134
93Pin-99
93PinCan-99
93Pow-158
93Sco-35
93ScoCan-35
93ScoDynDUS-5
93StaClu-270
93StaCluFDI-270
93StaCluMasP-18
93StaCluMasPW-18
93StaCluO-270
93TopPre-106
93TopPreG-106
93Ult-43
93UppDec-128
93UppDecHT-HT1
93UppDecSP-99
94BeAPla-R117
94CanGamNHLP-259
94CanGamNHLP-352
94Don-43
94Fin-23
94FinDivFCC-9
94FinRef-23
94FinRinL-20
94FinSupTW-23
94Fla-111
94Fle-132
94FleFraFut-3
94HocWit-86
94Kra-62
94Lea-255
94LeaLim-73
94McDUppD-McD2
94OPCPre-128
94OPCPre-350
94OPCPreSE-128
94OPCPreSE-350
94Par-147
94Par-307
94ParCratGB-15
94ParCratGG-15
94ParCratGR-15
94ParGol-147
94ParGol-307
94ParSEV-41
94Pin-62
94PinArtP-62
94PinGam-GR15
94PinRinC-62
94PinTeaP-TP6
94PinTeaPDP-TP6
94Sco-164
94ScoChelt-CI9
94ScoDreTea-DT9
94ScoGol-164
94ScoPla-164
94ScoPlaTS-164
94Sel-48
94SelGol-48
94SP-77
94SPDieCut-77
94StaClu-9
94StaClu-265
94StaCluFDI-9
94StaCluFDI-265
94StaCluMO-35
94StaCluMOMS-9
94StaCluMOMS-265
94StaCluSTWC-9
94StaCluSTWC-265
94TopFinl-7
94TopPre-128
94TopPre-350
94TopPreSE-128
94TopPreSE-350
94Ult-137
94UltAwaW-4
94UltPow-4
94UltRedLS-4
94UppDec-10
94UppDecEleIce-10
94UppDecG-IG7
94UppDecPR-R5
94UppDecPR-R38
94UppDecPRE-R5
94UppDecPRE-R38
94UppDecPreRG-R38
94UppDecSPI-SP140
94UppDecSPIDC-SP140
94BeAPla-212
95BeAPSig-S212
95BeAPSigDC-S212

95Bow-54
95BowAllFoi-54
95CanGamNHLP-179
95ColCho-277
95ColCho-358
95ColChoPC-277
95ColChoPC-358
95ColChoPCP-277
95ColChoPCP-358
95ColEdgILL-L1
95Don-82
95DonEli-10
95DonEliDCS-10
95DonEliDCU-10
95Emo-112
95KenStaLA-8
95KenStaLC-6
95Lea-152
95LeaLim-11
95ParIntF-137
95ParIntE-137
95Pin-45
95PinArtP-45
95PinRinC-45
95PlaOneoOne-66
95ProMag-96
95Sco-2
95ScoBlaIce-2
95ScoBlaIceAP-2
95SelCer-47
95SelCerMG-47
95SkyImp-108
95SP-98
95StaClu-57
95StaCluMOMS-57
95Sum-66
95SumArtP-66
95SumIce-66
95SweGloWC-96
95Top-295
95TopHomGC-HGC26
95TopOPCI-295
95TopPowL-3PL
95Ult-274
95UppDec-224
95UppDec-239
95UppDec-329
95UppDecEleIce-224
95UppDecEleIce-239
95UppDecEleIce-329
95UppDecEleIceG-224
95UppDecEleIceG-239
95UppDecEleIceG-329
95UppDecSpeE-SE57
95UppDecSpeEdiG-SE57
95Zen-33
95ZenGifG-17
96ColCho-174
96ColCho-324
96Don-66
96DonEli-107
96DonEliDCS-107
96DonPrePro-66
96Fle-67
96FlePic-90
96KraUppD-34
96Lea-20
96LeaPreP-20
96NHLProSTA-96
96Pin-9
96PinArtP-9
96PinFoi-9
96PinPreS-9
96PinRinC-9
96Sco-81
96ScoArtPro-81
96ScoDeaCAP-81
96ScoGolB-81
96ScoSpeAP-81
96SelCer-51
96SelCerAP-51
96SelCerBlu-51
96SelCerMB-51
96SelCerMG-51
96SelCerMR-51
96SelCerRed-51
96SkyImp-78
96SP-103
96Sum-120
96SumArtP-120
96SumIce-120
96SumMet-120
96SumPreS-120
96TeaOut-6
96UppDec-297
96UppDecBD-9
96UppDecBDG-9
96UppDecIce-44
96UppDecIcePar-44
96UppDecPP-P5
97Be A PPAD-58
97Be A PPAPD-58
97BeAPla-58
97BeAPlaAut-58
97ColCho-163
97Don-70
97DonCanI-97
97DonCanIDS-97
97DonCanIPS-97
97DonEli-47
97DonEliS-47
97DonEliAsp-47
97DonLim-18
97DonLimExp-18
97DonPre-133

97DonPreCttC-133
97DonPreProG-70
97DonPreProS-70
97DonPri-83
97DonPriSoA-83
97Kat-91
97KatGol-91
97KatSil-91
97Lea-89
97LeaFraMat-89
97LeaFraMDC-89
97LeaInt-89
97LeaIntUI-89
97Pac-26
97PacCop-26
97PacCroR-83
97PacCroREG-83
97PacCroRIB-83
97PacCroRS-83
97PacDyn-77
97PacDynC-77
97PacDynDG-77
97PacDynEG-77
97PacDynIB-77
97PacDynR-77
97PacDynSil-77
97PacDynTan-69
97PacEmeGre-26
97PacInv-85
97PacInvC-85
97PacInvEG-85
97PacInvIB-85
97PacInvNRB-127
97PacInvR-85
97PacInvS-85
97PacOme-144
97PacOmeC-144
97PacOmeDG-144
97PacOmeEG-144
97PacOmeG-144
97PacOmeIB-144
97PacPar-114
97PacParC-114
97PacParDG-114
97PacParEG-114
97PacParIB-114
97PacParRed-114
97PacParSil-114
97PacRed-26
97PacRev-86
97PacRevC-86
97PacRevE-86
97PacRevIB-86
97PacRevR-86
97PacRevS-86
97PacSil-26
97Pin-174
97PinCer-96
97PinCerMB-96
97PinCerMG-96
97PinCerMR-96
97PinCerR-96
97PinIns-104
97PinPrePBB-174
97PinPrePBC-174
97PinPrePBM-174
97PinPrePBY-174
97PinPrePFC-174
97PinPrePFM-174
97PinPrePFY-174
97PinPrePla-174
97PinTotCMPG-96
97PinTotCPB-96
97PinTotCPG-96
97PinTotCPR-96
97Sco-142
97ScoArtPro-142
97ScoGolBla-142
97ScoRan-4
97ScoRanPla-4
97ScoRanPre-4
97SPAut-103
97UppDec-108
97UppDecBD-2
97UppDecBDDD-2
97UppDecBDQD-2
97UppDecBDTD-2
98Be A PPA-91
98Be A PPAA-91
98Be A PPAAF-91
98Be A PPTBASG-91
98Be APG-91
98BowBes-81
98BowBesAR-81
98BowBesR-81
98O-PChr-89
98O-PChrR-89
98Pac-293
98PacAur-121
98PacCroR-87
98PacCroRLS-87
98PacDynI-120
98PacDynIIB-120
98PacDynIR-120
98PacIceB-293
98PacOmeH-155
98PacOmeODI-155
98PacOmeR-155
98PacPar-151
98PacParC-151
98PacParEG-151
98PacParH-151
98PacParIB-151

98PacParS-151
98PacRed-293
98Top-89
98TopGolLC1-41
98TopGolLC1B-41
98TopGolLC1Ooo-41
98TopGolLC1OoO-41
98TopGolLC1R-41
98TopGolLC1ROoO-41
98TopGolLC2-41
98TopGolLC2B-41
98TopGolLC2BOoO-41
98TopGolLC2Ooo-41
98TopGolLC2OoO-41
98TopGolLC3-41
98TopGolLC3B-41
98TopGolLC3BOoO-41
98TopGolLC3Ooo-41
98TopGolLC3OoO-41
98TopO-P-89
98UC-134
98UD ChoPCR-134
98UD ChoR-134
99Pac-269
99PacAur-93
99PacAurPD-93
99PacCop-269
99PacGol-269
99PacIceB-269
99PacPreD-269
99UppDecM-135
99UppDecMGS-135
99UppDecMSS-135
99UppDecMSS-135

**Graves, Hilliard**
73OPC-110
73Top-110
74OPCNHL-306
75OPCNHL-62
75Top-62
76OPCNHL-273
77CanCanDC-5
77CanuRoyB-7
77OPCNHL-286
78CanuRoyB-8
78OPC-357
79JetPos-7
79OPC-294

**Graves, Steve**
81SauSteMG-13
82SauSteMG-9
83SauSteMG-8
84NovScoO-9
85NovScoO-17
86OilRedR-15
88OilTenAnn-32
90ProAHLIHL-362

**Gray, Alex**
23V1281PauC-20

**Gray, Brandon**
93OshGen-6

**Gray, John**
75RoaPhoWHA-15
76OPCWHA-25
78JetPos-5

**Gray, Mike**
917thInnSWHL-5
93SasBla-10

**Gray, Roy**
93LonKni-10
93LonKni-24
95Sla-261

**Gray, Terry**
61Top-16
62QueAce-8
62Top-20
63QueAce-9
63QueAceQ-8
64QueAce-6
65QueAce-6
68OPC-44
68Top-44

**Grayling, Ted**
91AirCanSJHL-D11
92MPSPhoSJHL-75

**Greco, Gus**
82SauSteMG-10
83SauSteMG-9

**Greco, Piero**
97SheSte-21

**Gredder, Mike**
82IndChe-6

**Green, Cory**
92BriColJHL-106

**Green, Darryl**
95Sla-366

**Green, David (Dave)**
91BriColJHL-100
92BriColJHL-73
92ClaKni-7
93WinSpi-9
94WinSpi-11

**Green, Dustin**
91BriColJHL-26
92BriColJHL-55

**Green, Josh**
95BowDraPro-P15
95Cla-60
95ClaAut-7
95MedHatT-7
96ColEdgSS&D-4
96MedHatT-6
98BowBes-119

98BowBesAR-119
98BowBesR-119
98PacDynI-88
98PacDynIIB-88
98PacDynIR-88
98PacOmeH-116
98PacOmeODI-116
98PacOmeR-116
98SP Aut-99
98UppDec-418
98UppDecE-418
98UppDecE101-418
98UppDecGN-GN13
98UppDecGNQ1-GN13
98UppDecGNQ2-GN13
98UppDecGNQ3-GN13
98UppDecGR-418
98UppDecM-98
98UppDecMGS-98
98UppDecMSS-98
98UppDecMSS-98
99SP AutPS-99
99UppDecM-94
99UppDecMGS-94
99UppDecMGS-94
99UppDecMSS-94
99UppDecMSS-94

**Green, Mark**
89SpoChi-9
91JohChi-16

**Green, Red**
23V1451-31
24C144ChaCig-27
24V130MapC-10
24V1452-15

**Green, Rick**
77OPCNHL-245
77Top-245
78OPC-363
79OPC-309
80OPC-33
80Top-33
81Cap-6
81OPC-348
81OPCSti-193
81Top-E118
82CanaPos-8
82CanaSte-5
82OPC-183
82OPCSti-156
82PosCer-20
83CanaPos-9
83OPC-188
84CanaPos-8
84OPC-262
85CanaPos-12
85CanaPos-13
85CanaPro-6
86CanaPos-6
86KraDra-22
87CanaPos-8
87CanaVacS-65
87CanaVacS-68
87CanaVacS-70
870PC-234
870PCSti-11
87PanSti-60
88CanaPos-12
900PCPre-37
90ProSet-436
90ScoRoo-84T
91PanSti-147
91RedWinLC-7

**Green, Scott**
84SauSteMG-7
88ProAHL-204
92NorMicW-7
93NorMicW-8

**Green, Shawn**
82VicCou-9

**Green, Shayne**
89VicCou-10
907thInnSWHL-256
917thInnSWHL-89
92DayBom-11
95VanVooRHI-10

**Green, Shorty**
23V1451-30
24C144ChaCig-28
24V130MapC-22
24V1452-14
83HalFP-K5
85HalFC-140

**Green, Ted**
61ShiCoi-16
61Top-2
62Top-7
62TopHocBuc-7
63Top-7
64BeeGro3P-10
64CocCap-3
64Top-32
64TorSta-10
65Coc-3
65Top-98
66Top-37
66TopUSAT-37
67Top-94
68OPC-4
68ShiCoi-12
68Top-4
690PC-23
690PC-218
690PCFou-6
69Top-23
70BruPos-19

70DadCoo-44
70EssPowPla-57
700PC-134
70SarProSta-4
71BruTeaIss-3
710PC-173
71SarProSta-6
71TorSun-9
72SluCupWHA-8
72WhaNewEWHA-8
750PCWHA-57
760PCWHA-112
78JetPos-9
81OilRedR-xx
820ilRedR-NNO
830ilMcD-20
840ilRedR-NNO
860ilRedR-NNO
880ilTenAnn-57
900ilIGA-7
910ilIGA-27
920ilIGA-27
94ParTalB-3
95Par66-6
95Par66Coi-6

**Green, Travis**
89SpoChi-9
90ProAHLIHL-510
91ProAHLCHL-467
92Par-343
92ParEmel-343
92Ult-343
93ClaProPro-126
93Don-200
93Lea-127
93OPCPre-489
93OPCPreG-489
93Par-126
93ParEmel-126
93Pow-383
93Sco-661
93ScoCan-661
93ScoGol-661
93StaClu-394
93StaCluFDI-394
93StaCluO-394
93TopPre-489
93TopPreG-489
93Ult-365
93UppDec-59
94CanGamNHLP-156
94Don-75
94Lea-288
94Par-137
94ParGol-137
94Pin-216
94PinArtP-216
94PinRinC-216
94StaClu-236
94StaCluFDI-236
94StaCluMOMS-236
94StaCluSTWC-236
94Ult-126
94UppDec-220
94UppDecEleIce-220
95BeAPla-15
95BeAPSig-S15
95BeAPSigDC-S15
95CanGamNHLP-170
95Don-208
95Fin-79
95FinRef-79
95LeaLim-100
95Met-90
95ParInt-400
95ParIntEI-400
95PlaOneoOne-280
95SP-87
95Sum-60
95SumArtP-60
95SumIce-60
95Top-89
95TopOPCI-89
95Ult-266
95UltHigSpe-12
95UppDec-473
95UppDecEleIce-473
95UppDecEleIceG-473
95UppDecSpeE-SE138
95UppDecSpeEdiG-SE138
96ColCho-157
96Don-175
96DonPrePro-175
96Fle-64
96FlePic-70
96IsIPos-5
96Lea-131
96LeaPre-5
96LeaPreP-5
96MetUni-92
96NHLACEPC-19
96Pin-70
96PinArtP-70
96PinFoi-70
96PinPreS-70
96PinRinC-70
96PlaOneoOne-418
96Sco-15
96ScoArtP-15
96ScoDeaCAP-15
96ScoGolB-15
96ScoSpeAP-15
96SkyImp-75
96SP-94

96Sum-61
96SumArtP-61
96SumIce-61
96SumMet-61
96SumPreS-61
96Ult-101
96UltGolM-102
96UppDec-290
96Zen-26
96ZenArtP-26
97Be A PPAD-63
97Be A PPAPD-63
97BeAPla-63
97BeAPlaAut-63
97ColCho-160
97ColChoSta-SQ39
97Don-62
97DonCanI-65
97DonCanIDS-65
97DonCanIPS-65
97DonLim-59
97DonLim-110
97DonLimExp-59
97DonLimExp-110
97DonPreProG-62
97DonPreProS-62
97DonPri-62
97DonPriSoA-102
97Kat-87
97KatGol-87
97KatSil-87
97Pac-170
97PacCop-170
97PacDyn-73
97PacDynC-73
97PacDynDG-73
97PacDynEG-73
97PacDynIB-73
97PacDynR-73
97PacDynSil-73
97PacDynTan-72
97PacEmeGre-170
97PacIceB-170
97PacInv-81
97PacInvC-81
97PacInvEG-81
97PacInvIB-81
97PacInvR-81
97PacInvS-81
97PacOme-137
97PacOmeC-137
97PacOmeDG-137
97PacOmeEG-137
97PacOmeG-137
97PacOmeIB-137
97PacPar-108
97PacParC-108
97PacParDG-108
97PacParEG-108
97PacParIB-108
97PacParRed-108
97PacParSil-108
97PacRed-170
97PacRev-81
97PacRevC-81
97PacRevE-81
97PacRevIB-81
97PacRevR-81
97PacRevS-81
97PacSil-170
97Pin-167
97PinCer-123
97PinCerMB-123
97PinCerMG-123
97PinCerMR-123
97PinCerR-123
97PinIns-130
97PinPrePBB-167
97PinPrePBC-167
97PinPrePBM-167
97PinPrePBY-167
97PinPrePFC-167
97PinPrePFM-167
97PinPrePFY-167
97PinPrePla-167
97PinTotCMPG-123
97PinTotCPB-123
97PinTotCPG-123
97PinTotCPR-123
97Sco-173
97SPAut-94
97UppDec-307
98Be A PPA-155
98Be A PPAA-155
98Be A PPAAF-155
98Be A PPSE-155
98BeAPG-155
98O-PChr-162
98O-PChrR-162
98Pac-50
98PacAur-1
98PacCroR-1
98PacCroRLS-1
98PacDynI-1
98PacDynIIB-1
98PacDynIR-1
98PacIceB-50
98PacOmeH-1
98PacOmeODI-1
98PacOmeR-1
98PacPar-1
98PacParC-1
98PacParEG-1
98PacParH-1
98PacParIB-1

- 98PacParS-1
- 98PacRed-50
- 98SpxFin-4
- 98SpxFinR-4
- 98SpxFinS-4
- 98Top-162
- 98TopO-P-162
- 98UC-5
- 98UD ChoPCR-5
- 98UD ChoR-5
- 98UDCP-5
- 98UppDec-215
- 98UppDecE-215
- 98UppDecE101-215
- 98UppDecGR-215
- 99Pac-4
- 99PacCop-4
- 99PacGol-4
- 99PacIceB-4
- 99PacPreD-4

**Greenan, Roy**
- 52JunBluT-122

**Greenberg, Steve**
- 89HamRoaA-8
- 90HamRoaA-46

**Greene, Matt**
- 93WesMic-13

**Greenlaw, Jeff**
- 86CapKod-10
- 88ProAHL-30
- 89ProAHL-79
- 90ProAHLIHL-210
- 91CapJun5-9
- 91ProAHLCHL-547
- 96CinCyc-29

**Greenlay, Mike**
- 88SasBla-5
- 89ProAHL-133
- 90KnoChe-119
- 90ProAHLIHL-225
- 91KnoChe3-1

**Greenough, Glenn**
- 84SudWol-10
- 85SudWol-12

**Greenough, Nick**
- 98Vald'OF-10

**Greenway, Dave**
- 93RedDeeR-6

**Greenwood, Jeff**
- 91AirCanSJHL-B32
- 91AirCanSJHL-D20
- 92MPSPhoSJHL-119

**Greer, Brian**
- 95MusFur-17

**Gregg, Randy**
- 81SweSemHVS-77
- 82OilRedR-21
- 83OilMcD-14
- 830PC-28
- 83OPCSti-145
- 83Vac-25
- 84OilRedR-21
- 84OilTeal-6
- 84OPC-242
- 84OPCSti-257
- 85OilRedR-21
- 85OPC-199
- 85OPCSti-225
- 86OilRedR-21
- 86OilTeal-21
- 87OPCSti-94
- 88OilTeal-8
- 88OilTenAnn-13
- 89OilTeal-9
- 89OPC-229
- 90OPC-275
- 90PanSti-231
- 90Sco-306C
- 90SccoCan-306C
- 90Top-275
- 90TopTif-275
- 91CanuAutC-8
- 91CanuTeal8-8
- 91Pin-415
- 91PinFre-415
- 91ScoCan-598
- 91ScoRoo-48T

**Gregg, Vic**
- 52St.LawS-64

**Gregga, Shamus**
- 93HamRoaA-17

**Gregoire, Bill**
- 84VicCou-9

**Gregoire, Jean-Francois**
- 907thInnSQMJHL-82
- 917thInnSQMJHL-65

**Gregor, Colin**
- 88LetHur-8
- 907thInnSWHL-254
- 93RicRen-6
- 94HamRoaA-4
- 95BirBul-9

**Gregory, Dave**
- 95GuiFla-1

**Gregory, Jim**
- 73MapLeaP-8

**Gregson, Terry**
- 90ProSet-688

**Greig, Mark**
- 88LetHur-9
- 89LetHur-9
- 90ProAHLIHL-180
- 90Sco-431
- 90ScoCan-431
- 91Pin-352

- 91PinFre-352
- 91ProSet-537
- 91ProSetFre-537
- 91ScoAme-383
- 91UppDec-456
- 91UppDecF-456
- 91WhaJr7E-13
- 920PC-186
- 920PCPre-99
- 92StaClu-421
- 92Top-175
- 92TopGol-175G
- 93Don-137
- 93Don-495
- 93Lea-412
- 930PCPre-301
- 930PCPreG-301
- 93StaClu-386
- 93StaCluFDI-386
- 93StaCluO-386
- 93TopPre-301
- 93TopPreG-301
- 93Ult-334
- 93WhaCok-6
- 94Lea-522
- 94St.JohF-7

**Grein, Andre**
- 94GerDELE-228
- 95GerDELE-237
- 96GerDELE-78

**Grenemo, Arne**
- 67SweHoc-236

**Grenier, David**
- 95FreCan-13

**Grenier, Lucien**
- 71SarProSta-76
- 71TorSun-114
- 72SarProSta-1

**Grenier, Martin**
- 98QueRem-9

**Grenier, Richard**
- 76NordMarA-10
- 76NordPos-14
- 760PCWHA-59

**Grenier, Tony**
- 84PriAlbRS-10

**Grenville, Chris**
- 917thInnSOHL-315
- 95BirBul-8

**Greschner, Ron**
- 750PCNHL-146
- 75Top-146
- 760PCNHL-154
- 76Top-154
- 770PCNHL-256
- 77Top-256
- 780PC-154
- 78Top-154
- 790PC-78
- 79Top-78
- 800PC-248
- 80Top-248
- 810PC-224
- 810PCSti-167
- 81Top-E97
- 820PC-224
- 82PosCer-13
- 84OPC-141
- 85OPC-182
- 860PC-18
- 86Top-18
- 870PC-159
- 87Top-159
- 89RanMarMB-4
- 900PC-447
- 90ProSet-197

**Gretzky, Brent**
- 897thInnSOHL-75
- 907thInnSOHL-9
- 917thInnSOHL-99
- 92UppDec-37
- 93Don-318
- 93Par-248
- 93ParCalC-C14
- 93ParCalCG-C14
- 93ParEmel-248
- 93Pin-429
- 93PinCan-429
- 93Sco-606
- 93ScoCan-606
- 93ScoGol-606
- 93Ult-424
- 93UppDec-354
- 93UppDecSP-150
- 94BeAPla-R161
- 94BeAPSig-154
- 94Cla-99
- 94ClaDraGol-99
- 94ClaTri-T64
- 940PCPre-209
- 940PCPreSE-209
- 94Par-218
- 94Par-295
- 94ParGol-218
- 94ParGol-295
- 94ParVin-V62
- 94TopPre-209
- 94TopPreSE-209
- 94UppDec-69
- 94UppDecEleIce-69
- 95ColCho-281
- 95ColChoPC-281

- 95ColChoPCP-281
- 95ColEdgI-82
- 95Ima-17
- 95ImaGol-17
- 95St.JohML-9
- 96LasVegThu-8

**Gretzky, Keith**
- 87FliSpi-4
- 89ProIHL-101
- 91ProAHLCHL-322
- 92Cla-118
- 92SanDieG-9
- 92UppDec-37
- 93ClaPro-99
- 96ClaGol-118

**Gretzky, Walter**
- 98McDGreT-T1

**Gretzky, Wayne**
- 790ilPos-9
- 790PC-18
- 79Top-18
- 800PC-3
- 800PC-87
- 800PC-163
- 800PC-182
- 800PC-250
- 800PCSup-7
- 80Top-3
- 80Top-87
- 80Top-162
- 80Top-163
- 80Top-182
- 80Top-250
- 810PC-3
- 810ilRedR-99
- 810ilRedR-99
- 810ilRedR-99
- 810ilRedR-99
- 810ilWesEM-3
- 81Top-16
- 81Top-52
- 82McDSti-20
- 82McDSti-22
- 82NeiGre-1
- 82NeiGre-2
- 82NeiGre-3
- 82NeiGre-4
- 82NeiGre-5
- 82NeiGre-6
- 82NeiGre-7
- 82NeiGre-8
- 82NeiGre-9
- 82NeiGre-10
- 82NeiGre-11
- 82NeiGre-12
- 82NeiGre-13
- 82NeiGre-14
- 82NeiGre-15
- 82NeiGre-16
- 82NeiGre-17
- 82NeiGre-18
- 82NeiGre-19
- 82NeiGre-20
- 82NeiGre-21
- 82NeiGre-22
- 82NeiGre-23
- 82NeiGre-24
- 82NeiGre-25
- 82NeiGre-26
- 82NeiGre-27
- 82NeiGre-28
- 82NeiGre-29
- 82NeiGre-30
- 82NeiGre-31
- 82NeiGre-32
- 82NeiGre-33
- 82NeiGre-34
- 82NeiGre-35
- 82NeiGre-36
- 82NeiGre-37
- 82NeiGre-38
- 82NeiGre-39
- 82NeiGre-40
- 82NeiGre-41
- 82NeiGre-42
- 82NeiGre-43
- 82NeiGre-44
- 82NeiGre-45
- 82NeiGre-46
- 82NeiGre-47
- 82NeiGre-48
- 82NeiGre-49
- 82NeiGre-50
- 820ilRedR-99
- 820ilRedR-99
- 820ilRedR-99
- 820ilRedR-99
- 820PC-1
- 820PC-99
- 820PC-106
- 820PC-107
- 820PC-235
- 820PC-237
- 820PC-240
- 820PC-242
- 820PC-243
- 820PCSti-97

- 820PCSti-98
- 820PCSti-256
- 820PCSti-257
- 820PCSti-258
- 820PCSti-259
- 82PosCer-6
- 83BelBul-27
- 830ilDol-H14
- 830ilMcD-21
- 830PC-22
- 830PC-23
- 830PC-29
- 830PC-204
- 830PC-212
- 830PC-215
- 830PC-216
- 830PC-217
- 830PCSti-9
- 830PCSti-89
- 830PCSti-90
- 830PCSti-161
- 830PCSti-301
- 830PCSti-307
- 830PCSti-325
- 830PCSti-326
- 83PufSti-1
- 83Vac-26
- 847EDis-16
- 847EDis-NNO
- 840ilRedR-99
- 840ilRedR-99
- 840ilRedR-99
- 840ilRedR-99
- 840PC-208
- 840PC-243
- 840PC-373
- 840PC-374
- 840PC-380
- 840PC-381
- 840PC-382
- 840PC-383
- 840PC-388
- 840PCSti-63
- 840PCSti-138
- 840PCSti-226
- 840PCSti-229
- 840PCSti-255
- 840PCSti-256
- 84Top-51
- 84Top-154
- 85IsIIsINT-21
- 85IsIIsINT-29
- 850ilRedR-99
- 850ilRedR-99
- 850ilRedR-99
- 850PC-120
- 850PC-257
- 850PC-258
- 850PC-259
- 850PCBoxB-G
- 850PCSti-5
- 850PCSti-54
- 850PCSti-120
- 850PCSti-198
- 850PCSti-202
- 850PCSti-222
- 85Top-120
- 85TopBoxB-G
- 85TopStiIns-2
- 86KraDra-8
- 860ilRedR-99
- 860ilRedR-99
- 860ilTeal-99
- 860PC-3
- 860PC-259
- 860PC-260
- 860PCBoxB-F
- 860PCSti-72
- 860PCSti-115
- 860PCSti-183
- 860PCSti-191
- 860PCSti-195
- 86Top-3
- 86TopBoxB-F
- 86TopStiIns-3
- 870ilTeal-99
- 870PC-53
- 870PCBoxB-A
- 870PCMin-13
- 870PCSti-86
- 870PCSti-115
- 870PCSti-174
- 870PCSti-180
- 870PCSti-181
- 87PanSti-192
- 87PanSti-197
- 87PanSti-198
- 87PanSti-199
- 87PanSti-200
- 87PanSti-261
- 87PanSti-371
- 87PanSti-373
- 87PanSti-389
- 87SauSteMG-29
- 87Top-53
- 87TopBoxB-A
- 87TopStiIns-5
- 88EssAllSta-15
- 88KinSmo-11
- 880ilTenAnn-46
- 880ilTenAnn-55

- 880ilTenAnn-137
- 880PC-120
- 880PCBoxB-B
- 880PCMin-11
- 880PCSti-1
- 880PCSti-121
- 880PCSti-224
- 88PanSti-58
- 88PanSti-178
- 88PanSti-181
- 88PanSti-193
- 88Top-120
- 88TopBoxB-B
- 88TopStiIns-8
- 89ActPacPro-1
- 89KinSmo-1
- 89KinSmoG8-NNO
- 89Kra-59
- 89KraAllSS-2
- 890PC-156
- 890PC-320
- 890PC-325
- 890PCBoxB-E
- 890PCSti-47
- 890PCSti-154
- 890PCSti-166
- 890PCSti-209
- 89PanSti-87
- 89PanSti-179
- 89PanSti-374
- 89SweSemWCS-65
- 89Top-156
- 89TopBoxB-E
- 89TopStiIns-11
- 90BowTif-143
- 90KinSmo-1
- 90Kra-15
- 90Kra-66
- 900PC-1
- 900PC-2
- 900PC-3
- 900PC-120
- 900PC-199
- 900PC-522
- 900PCBoxB-D
- 900PCPre-38
- 90PanSti-242
- 90PanSti-332
- 90ProSet-118
- 90ProSet-340
- 90ProSet-388
- 90ProSet-394
- 90ProSet-703
- 90ProSetPM-P2
- 90Sco-321
- 90Sco-336
- 90Sco-338
- 90Sco-347
- 90Sco-352
- 90Sco-353
- 90Sco-361
- 90ScoCan-1
- 90ScoCan-321
- 90ScoCan-336
- 90ScoCan-338
- 90ScoCan-347
- 90ScoCan-352
- 90ScoCan-353
- 90ScoCan-361
- 90ScoHotRS-1
- 90ScoPro-1A
- 90ScoPro-1B
- 90ScoRoo-110T
- 90Top-1
- 90Top-2
- 90Top-3
- 90Top-120
- 90Top-199
- 90TopBoxB-D
- 90TopTeaSL-12
- 90UppDec-54
- 90UppDec-205
- 90UppDec-307
- 90UppDec-476
- 90UppDec-545
- 90UppDecF-54
- 90UppDecF-205
- 90UppDecF-307
- 90UppDecF-476
- 90UppDecF-545
- 90UppDecHol-1
- 90UppDecHol-2
- 90UppDecHol-3
- 90UppDecP-241A
- 91Bow-173
- 91Bow-176
- 91Kra-65
- 91McDUppD-17
- 91McDUppD-H1
- 910PC-201
- 910PC-224
- 910PC-257
- 910PC-258
- 910PC-321
- 910PC-520
- 910PC-522
- 910PC-524
- 910PCPre-3

- 91PanSti-78
- 91PanSti-327
- 91Par-73
- 91Par-207
- 91Par-222
- 91Par-429
- 91Par-433
- 91Par-465
- 91ParFre-73
- 91ParFre-207
- 91ParFre-222
- 91ParFre-429
- 91ParFre-433
- 91ParFre-465
- 91Pin-100
- 91Pin-381
- 91PinB-B11
- 91PinBFre-B11
- 91PinFre-100
- 91PinFre-381
- 91ProSet-101
- 91ProSet-285
- 91ProSet-324
- 91ProSet-574
- 91ProSetCC-CC5
- 91ProSetCCF-CC5
- 91ProSetFre-101
- 91ProSetFre-285
- 91ProSetFre-324
- 91ProSetFre-574
- 91ProSetNHLAS-AC4
- 91ProSetPC-11
- 91ProSetPla-52
- 91ProSetPla-142
- 91ProSetPlaPC-PC4
- 91ProSetPlaPC-PC14
- 91ScoAme-100
- 91ScoAme-346
- 91ScoAme-405
- 91ScoAme-406
- 91ScoAme-413
- 91ScoAme-422
- 91ScoAme-427
- 91ScoAme-434
- 91ScoCan-100
- 91ScoCan-295
- 91ScoCan-296
- 91ScoCan-303
- 91ScoCan-312
- 91ScoCan-317
- 91ScoCan-376
- 91ScoCan-1
- 91ScoHotC-2
- 91ScoNat-1
- 91ScoNatCWC-1
- 91StaClu-1
- 91SweSemWCS-64
- 91Top-201
- 91Top-224
- 91Top-257
- 91Top-258
- 91Top-321
- 91Top-520
- 91Top-522
- 91Top-524
- 91TopBowPS-2
- 91TopTeaSL-10
- 91UppDec-13
- 91UppDec-38
- 91UppDec-45
- 91UppDec-437
- 91UppDec-501
- 91UppDec-621
- 91UppDec-SP1
- 91UppDecAWH-AW1
- 91UppDecAWH-AW6
- 91UppDecBB-1
- 91UppDecCWJC-NNO1
- 91UppDecCWJC-NNO2
- 91UppDecF-13
- 91UppDecF-38
- 91UppDecF-437
- 91UppDecF-501
- 91UppDecF-621
- 92Bow-1
- 92Bow-207
- 92Hig5Pre-P1
- 92HumDum1-10
- 92Kra-40
- 920PC-15
- 920PC-220
- 920PC25AI-12
- 92PanSti-64
- 92PanSti-287
- 92PanStiFre-64
- 92PanStiFre-287
- 92Par-65
- 92Par-509
- 92ParEmel-65
- 92ParEmel-509
- 92Pin-200
- 92Pin-249
- 92PinFre-200
- 92PinFre-249
- 92PinTeaP-5
- 92PinTeaPF-5
- 92ProSet-66
- 92ProSet-246
- 92ProSetGTL-6
- 92Sco-1
- 92Sco-412
- 92Sco-426
- 92Sco-525
- 92ScoCan-1

- 92ScoCan-412
- 92ScoCan-426
- 92ScoCan-525
- 92SeaPat-9
- 92StaClu-18
- 92StaClu-256
- 92Top-1
- 92Top-123
- 92TopGol-1G
- 92TopGol-123G
- 92Ult-83
- 92UltAllS-10
- 92UltAwaW-6
- 92UppDec-25
- 92UppDec-33
- 92UppDec-37
- 92UppDec-423
- 92UppDec-435
- 92UppDec-621
- 92UppDecAWT-W1
- 92UppDecGHS-G5
- 92UppDecShe-5
- 92UppDecWGH-10
- 92UppDecWGH-11
- 92UppDecWGH-12
- 92UppDecWGH-13
- 92UppDecWGH-14
- 92UppDecWGH-15
- 92UppDecWGH-16
- 92UppDecWGH-17
- 92UppDecWGH-18
- 92UppDecWGJG-WG10
- 93Don-152
- 93Don-395
- 93DonEli-10
- 93DonIceKin-4
- 93DonSpeP-K
- 93Kra-34
- 93Kra-54
- 93Lea-304
- 93LeaGolAS-6
- 93LeaStuS-4
- 930PCPre-330
- 930PCPre-380
- 930PCPreBG-1
- 930PCPreG-330
- 930PCPreG-380
- 93PanSti-R
- 93Par-99
- 93ParChePH-D1
- 93ParEasWesS-W1
- 93ParEmel-99
- 93ParUSACG-G1
- 93Pin-237
- 93Pin-400
- 93Pin-512
- 93PinAllS-45
- 93PinAllSC-45
- 93PinCan-237
- 93PinCan-400
- 93PinCan-512
- 93PinCap-11
- 93PinCapC-11
- 93PinTeaP-5
- 93PinTeaPC-5
- 93Pow-116
- 93PowGam-3
- 93PowPoiL-3
- 93Sco-300
- 93Sco-662
- 93ScoCan-300
- 93ScoCan-662
- 93ScoDreTea-11
- 93ScoDynDUS-7
- 93ScoFra-9
- 93ScoGol-662
- 93SeaPat-5
- 93StaClu-200
- 93StaCluAS-23
- 93StaCluFDI-200
- 93StaCluFDIO-200
- 93StaCluFin-1
- 93StaCluMasP-8
- 93StaCluMasPW-8
- 93StaCluO-200
- 93SweSemWCS-199
- 93TopPre-330
- 93TopPre-380
- 93TopPreBG-7
- 93TopPreBG-A
- 93TopPreG-330
- 93TopPreG-380
- 93Ult-114
- 93Ult-C3C
- 93UltAllS-15
- 93UltPreP-2
- 93UltScoK-2
- 93UppDec-99
- 93UppDec-*99B
- 93UppDec-**99B
- 93UppDecGBB-1
- 93UppDecGS-1
- 93UppDecLAS-25
- 93UppDecNB-HB9
- 93UppDecNL-NL1
- 93UppDecSilSka-R1
- 93UppDecSilSka-NNO
- 93UppDecSilSka-NNO
- 93UppDecSilSkaG-R1
- 93UppDecSP-70
- 93BAPUppCP-UC1
- 94BeAPA99A-G1
- 94BeAPla-R99
- 94BeAPla-R147
- 94BeAPla-R176

❑ 94BeAPSig-108
❑ 94CanGamNHLP-126
❑ 94CanGamNHLP-268
❑ 94CokMilGP-1
❑ 94CokMilGP-2
❑ 94CokMilGP-3
❑ 94CokMilGP-4
❑ 94CokMilGP-5
❑ 94CokMilGP-6
❑ 94CokMilGP-7
❑ 94CokMilGP-8
❑ 94CokMilGP-9
❑ 94CokMilGP-10
❑ 94CokMilGP-11
❑ 94CokMilGP-12
❑ 94CokMilGP-13
❑ 94CokMilGP-14
❑ 94CokMilGP-15
❑ 94CokMilGP-16
❑ 94CokMilGP-17
❑ 94CokMilGP-18
❑ 94Don-127
❑ 94DonDom-5
❑ 94DonEliIns-5
❑ 94DonIceMas-4
❑ 94EASpo-63
❑ 94EASpo-192
❑ 94Fin-41
❑ 94FinDivFCC-18
❑ 94FinnJaaK-99
❑ 94FinnJaaK-344
❑ 94FinRef-41
❑ 94FinRinL-5
❑ 94FinSupTW-41
❑ 94Fla-79
❑ 94FlaCenS-4
❑ 94FlaHotN-2
❑ 94Fle-94
❑ 94FleHea-4
❑ 94HocWit-99
❑ 94KinUppDST-NNO
❑ 94Kra-5
❑ 94Kra-63
❑ 94Lea-345
❑ 94LeaFirOIce-4
❑ 94LeaGolS-1
❑ 94LeaLim-10
❑ 94LeaLimG-7
❑ 94LeaLimI-11
❑ 94OPCPre-130
❑ 94OPCPre-150
❑ 94OPCPre-154
❑ 94OPCPre-280
❑ 94OPCPre-375
❑ 94OPCPreSE-130
❑ 94OPCPreSE-150
❑ 94OPCPreSE-154
❑ 94OPCPreSE-280
❑ 94OPCPreSE-375
❑ 94Par-103
❑ 94Par-306
❑ 94ParCratGB-11
❑ 94ParCratGB-28
❑ 94ParCratGG-11
❑ 94ParCratGG-28
❑ 94ParCratGR-11
❑ 94ParCratGR-28
❑ 94ParGol-103
❑ 94ParGol-306
❑ 94ParSE-NNO
❑ 94ParSEV-20
❑ 94Pin-200
❑ 94PinArtP-200
❑ 94PinRinC-200
❑ 94PinTeaP-TP9
❑ 94PinTeaPDP-TP9
❑ 94PosCerBB-13
❑ 94Sco-241
❑ 94Sco90PC-1
❑ 94ScoDreTea-DT14
❑ 94ScoFra-TF11
❑ 94ScoGol-241
❑ 94ScoPla-241
❑ 94ScoPlaTS-241
❑ 94Sel-83
❑ 94SelFirLin-11
❑ 94SelGol-83
❑ 94SP-54A
❑ 94SP-54B
❑ 94SP-SP1
❑ 94SPDieCut-54
❑ 94SPPre-17
❑ 94SPPreDC-17
❑ 94StaClu-99
❑ 94StaClu-270
❑ 94StaCluFDI-99
❑ 94StaCluFDI-270
❑ 94StaCluFI-4
❑ 94StaCluFIMO-4
❑ 94StaCluMO-5
❑ 94StaCluMOMS-99
❑ 94StaCluMOMS-270
❑ 94StaCluSTWC-99
❑ 94StaCluSTWC-270
❑ 94TopPre-130
❑ 94TopPre-150
❑ 94TopPre-154
❑ 94TopPre-280
❑ 94TopPre-375
❑ 94TopPreGTG-1
❑ 94TopPreSE-130
❑ 94TopPreSE-150
❑ 94TopPreSE-154
❑ 94TopPreSE-280
❑ 94TopPreSE-375
❑ 94Ult-306
❑ 94UltAllS-10
❑ 94UltAwaW-5
❑ 94UltPreP-4
❑ 94UltScoK-4
❑ 94UppDec-1
❑ 94UppDec-226
❑ 94UppDec-228
❑ 94UppDec-541
❑ 94UppDecEleIce-1
❑ 94UppDecEleIce-226
❑ 94UppDecEleIce-228
❑ 94UppDecEleIce-541
❑ 94UppDecG24KG-1
❑ 94UppDecIG-IG15
❑ 94UppDecNBAP-7
❑ 94UppDecPC-C16
❑ 94UppDecPCEG-C16
❑ 94UppDecPH-H1
❑ 94UppDecPH-H16
❑ 94UppDecPHEG-H1
❑ 94UppDecPHEG-H16
❑ 94UppDecPHES-H1
❑ 94UppDecPHES-H16
❑ 94UppDecPHG-H1
❑ 94UppDecPHG-H16
❑ 94UppDecPR-R19
❑ 94UppDecPR-R21
❑ 94UppDecPR-R42
❑ 94UppDecPR-R59
❑ 94UppDecPRE-R19
❑ 94UppDecPRE-R21
❑ 94UppDecPRE-R42
❑ 94UppDecPRE-R59
❑ 94UppDecPreRG-R19
❑ 94UppDecPreRG-R21
❑ 94UppDecPreRG-R42
❑ 94UppDecPreRG-R59
❑ 94UppDecSPI-SP36
❑ 94UppDecSPIDC-SP36
❑ 95BAPLetL-LL2
❑ 95BeAPGreGM-GM1
❑ 95BeAPGreGM-GM2
❑ 95BeAPGreGM-GM3
❑ 95BeAPGreGM-GM4
❑ 95BeAPGreGM-GM5
❑ 95BeAPGreGM-GM6
❑ 95BeAPGreGM-GM7
❑ 95BeAPGreGM-GM8
❑ 95BeAPGreGM-GM9
❑ 95BeAPGreGM-GM10
❑ 95BeAPla-97
❑ 95BeAPSig-S97
❑ 95BeAPSig-*S97
❑ 95BeAPSigDC-S97
❑ 95Bow-1
❑ 95BowAllFoi-1
❑ 95BowBes-BB5
❑ 95BowBesRef-BB5
❑ 95CanGamNHLP-1
❑ 95CanGamNHLP-132
❑ 95ColCho-1
❑ 95ColCho-361
❑ 95ColCho-395
❑ 95ColCho-396
❑ 95ColChoCTG-C3
❑ 95ColChoCTG-C3B
❑ 95ColChoCTG-C3C
❑ 95ColChoCTGGB-C3
❑ 95ColChoCTGGR-C3
❑ 95ColChoCTGSB-C3
❑ 95ColChoCTGSR-C3
❑ 95ColChoPC-1
❑ 95ColChoPC-361
❑ 95ColChoPC-395
❑ 95ColChoPC-396
❑ 95ColChoPCP-1
❑ 95ColChoPCP-361
❑ 95ColChoPCP-395
❑ 95ColChoPCP-396
❑ 95Don-13
❑ 95DonDom-5
❑ 95DonEli-58
❑ 95DonEliCE-3
❑ 95DonEliDCS-58
❑ 95DonEliDCS-58U
❑ 95DonEliDCU-58
❑ 95DonEliDCU-58U
❑ 95DonEliIns-7
❑ 95Emo-81
❑ 95EmoXce-4
❑ 95EmoXci-5
❑ 95Fin-5
❑ 95Fin-180
❑ 95FinnSemWC-99
❑ 95FinRef-5
❑ 95FinRef-180
❑ 95ImpSti-57
❑ 95ImpStiDCS-21
❑ 95Kra-53
❑ 95Lea-89
❑ 95LeaFirOIce-10
❑ 95LeaLim-87
❑ 95LeaLimSG-3
❑ 95Met-71
❑ 95MetHM-4
❑ 95MetIS-5
❑ 95NHLAcePC-1D
❑ 95NHLCooT-2
❑ 95NHLCooT-RP2
❑ 95ParInt-100
❑ 95ParInt-449
❑ 95ParIntCCGS1-6
❑ 95ParIntCCGS2-10
❑ 95ParIntCCSS1-6
❑ 95ParIntCCSS2-10
❑ 95ParIntEI-100
❑ 95ParIntEI-449
❑ 95ParIntNHLAS-1
❑ 95Pin-101
❑ 95PinArtP-101
❑ 95PinCleS-9
❑ 95PinFan-13
❑ 95PinFirS-2
❑ 95PinRinC-101
❑ 95PlaOneoOne-50
❑ 95PlaOneoOne-159
❑ 95PlaOneoOne-269
❑ 95PosUppD-17
❑ 95PosUppD-AU17
❑ 95ProMag-67
❑ 95Sco-250
❑ 95ScoBlaIce-250
❑ 95ScoBlaIceAP-250
❑ 95ScoBorBat-2
❑ 95ScoDreTea-1
❑ 95ScoLam-1
❑ 95SelCer-23
❑ 95SelCerGT-2
❑ 95SelCerMG-23
❑ 95SkyImp-79
❑ 95SkyImpCI-4
❑ 95SkyImpIQ-6
❑ 95SP-66A
❑ 95SP-127
❑ 95SP-GC1
❑ 95SPHol-FX10
❑ 95SPHolSpFX-FX10
❑ 95SPStaEto-E17
❑ 95SPStaEtoG-E17
❑ 95StaClu-173
❑ 95StaCluM-M1
❑ 95StaCluMO-32
❑ 95StaCluMOMS-173
❑ 95StaCluNem-N2
❑ 95Sum-24
❑ 95SumArtP-24
❑ 95SumGM-18
❑ 95SumIce-24
❑ 95SweGloWC-99
❑ 95SweGloWC-265
❑ 95SweGloWC-266
❑ 95SweGloWC-267
❑ 95Top-85
❑ 95Top-375
❑ 95TopHomGC-HGC20
❑ 95TopMarMPB-375
❑ 95TopMysF-M1
❑ 95TopMysFR-M1
❑ 95TopOPCI-85
❑ 95TopOPCI-375
❑ 95TopPro-PF1
❑ 95TopRinL-10RL
❑ 95TopSupSki-15
❑ 95TopSupSkiPla-15
❑ 95Ult-74
❑ 95Ult-385
❑ 95UltExtAtt-7
❑ 95UltGolM-74
❑ 95UltPrePiv-3
❑ 95UltPrePivGM-3
❑ 95UltUltHP-2
❑ 95UltUltV-2
❑ 95UppDec-99
❑ 95UppDec-222
❑ 95UppDec-252
❑ 95UppDecAGPRW-1
❑ 95UppDecEleIce-99
❑ 95UppDecEleIce-222
❑ 95UppDecEleIce-252
❑ 95UppDecEleIceG-99
❑ 95UppDecEleIceG-222
❑ 95UppDecEleIceG-252
❑ 95UppDecFreFra-F2
❑ 95UppDecFreFraJ-F2
❑ 95UppDecGreCol-G1
❑ 95UppDecGreCol-G2
❑ 95UppDecGreCol-G3
❑ 95UppDecGreCol-G4
❑ 95UppDecGreCol-G5
❑ 95UppDecGreCol-G6
❑ 95UppDecGreCol-G7
❑ 95UppDecGreCol-G8
❑ 95UppDecGreCol-G9
❑ 95UppDecGreCol-G10
❑ 95UppDecGreCol-G11
❑ 95UppDecGreCol-G12
❑ 95UppDecGreCol-G13
❑ 95UppDecGreCol-G14
❑ 95UppDecGreCol-G15
❑ 95UppDecGreCol-G16
❑ 95UppDecGreCol-G17
❑ 95UppDecGreCol-G18
❑ 95UppDecGreCol-G19
❑ 95UppDecGreCol-G20
❑ 95UppDecGreColJ-G1
❑ 95UppDecGreColJ-G2
❑ 95UppDecGreColJ-G3
❑ 95UppDecGreColJ-G4
❑ 95UppDecGreColJ-G5
❑ 95UppDecGreColJ-G6
❑ 95UppDecGreColJ-G7
❑ 95UppDecGreColJ-G8
❑ 95UppDecGreColJ-G9
❑ 95UppDecGreColJ-G10
❑ 95UppDecGreColJ-G11
❑ 95UppDecGreColJ-G12
❑ 95UppDecGreColJ-G13
❑ 95UppDecGreColJ-G14
❑ 95UppDecGreColJ-G15
❑ 95UppDecGreColJ-G16
❑ 95UppDecGreColJ-G17
❑ 95UppDecGreColJ-G18
❑ 95UppDecGreColJ-G19
❑ 95UppDecGreColJ-G20
❑ 95UppDecNHLAS-AS5
❑ 95UppDecPHE-H7
❑ 95UppDecPRE-R13
❑ 95UppDecPRE-R23
❑ 95UppDecPRE-R31
❑ 95UppDecPRE-R41
❑ 95UppDecPRE-R51
❑ 95UppDecPreR-R13
❑ 95UppDecPreR-R23
❑ 95UppDecPreR-R31
❑ 95UppDecPreR-R41
❑ 95UppDecPreR-R51
❑ 95UppDecSpeE-SE128
❑ 95UppDecSpeEdiG-SE128
❑ 95UppPreHV-H7
❑ 95UppPreRP-R31
❑ 95UppPreRP-R41
❑ 95UppPreRP-R51
❑ 95Zen-13
❑ 95ZenZT-4
❑ 96BeAPBisITB-1
❑ 96ColCho-222
❑ 96ColCho-290
❑ 96ColCho-329
❑ 96ColCho-336
❑ 96ColCho-P222
❑ 96ColCho-NNO1
❑ 96ColCho-NNO2
❑ 96ColChoBlo-170
❑ 96ColChoBloBi-1
❑ 96ColChoCTG-C1A
❑ 96ColChoCTG-C1B
❑ 96ColChoCTG-C1C
❑ 96ColChoCTGE-CR1
❑ 96ColChoCTGEG-CR1
❑ 96ColChoCTGG-C1A
❑ 96ColChoCTGG-C1B
❑ 96ColChoCTGG-C1C
❑ 96ColChoMVP-UD1
❑ 96ColChoMVPG-UD1
❑ 96ColChoSti-S1
❑ 96Don-93
❑ 96DonCanI-93
❑ 96DonCanIGPP-5
❑ 96DonCanIOC-7
❑ 96DonCanIRPP-5
❑ 96DonDom-5
❑ 96DonEli-10
❑ 96DonEliDCS-10
❑ 96DonEliIns-2
❑ 96DonEliInsG-2
❑ 96DonEliP-1
❑ 96DonPrePro-93
❑ 96Fla-59
❑ 96FlaBluI-59
❑ 96FlaHotN-4
❑ 96FlaNowAT-1
❑ 96Fle-68
❑ 96FleArtRos-6
❑ 96FlePCC-4
❑ 96FlePea-4
❑ 96FlePic-8
❑ 96FlePicDL-1
❑ 96FlePicF5-15
❑ 96HocGreC-9
❑ 96HocGreCG-9
❑ 96Lea-140
❑ 96LeaFirOI-5
❑ 96LeaLeaAL-8
❑ 96LeaLeaALP-P8
❑ 96LeaLim-7
❑ 96LeaLimG-7
❑ 96LeaLimStu-3
❑ 96LeaPre-112
❑ 96LeaPreP-140
❑ 96LeaPrePP-112
❑ 96LeaPreSP-5
❑ 96LeaPreVP-1
❑ 96LeaPreVPG-1
❑ 96MetUni-96
❑ 96MetUniLW-6
❑ 96MetUniLWSP-6
❑ 96NHLACEPC-20
❑ 96NHLProSTA-67
❑ 96Pin-1
❑ 96PinArtP-1
❑ 96PinByTN-9
❑ 96PinByTNP-9
❑ 96PinFan-FC5
❑ 96PinFoi-1
❑ 96PinPreS-1
❑ 96PinRinC-1
❑ 96PinTeaP-1
❑ 96PlaOneoOne-430
❑ 96PosUppD-8
❑ 96Sco-41
❑ 96ScoArtPro-41
❑ 96ScoDeaCAP-41
❑ 96ScoDreTea-8
❑ 96ScoGolB-41
❑ 96ScoSpeAP-41
❑ 96ScoSudDea-12
❑ 96SelCer-4
❑ 96SelCerAP-4
❑ 96SelCerBlu-4
❑ 96SelCerCor-4
❑ 96SelCerMB-4
❑ 96SelCerMG-4
❑ 96SelCerMR-4
❑ 96SelCerRed-4
❑ 96SkyImp-79
❑ 96SkyImpCI-3
❑ 96SkyImpVer-4
❑ 96SP-99
❑ 96SP-P99
❑ 96SPCleWin-CW1
❑ 96SPGamFil-GF1
❑ 96SPHolCol-HC1
❑ 96SPInsInf-IN1
❑ 96SPInsInfG-IN1
❑ 96SPSPxFor-1
❑ 96SPSPxFor-5
❑ 96SPSPxForAut-1
❑ 96SPx-39
❑ 96SPx-P39
❑ 96SPx-GF1
❑ 96SPx-GS1
❑ 96SPx-GT1
❑ 96SPxGol-39
❑ 96SPxHolH-HH7
❑ 96StaCluMO-1
❑ 96Sum-67
❑ 96SumArtP-67
❑ 96SumHigV-5
❑ 96SumHigVM-5
❑ 96SumIce-67
❑ 96SumMet-67
❑ 96SumPreS-67
❑ 96SumUnt-12
❑ 96SweSemW-99
❑ 96TeaOut-19
❑ 96TopPic5C-FC1
❑ 96TopPicFT-FT10
❑ 96TopPicTS-TS2
❑ 96Ult-106
❑ 96UltGolM-107
❑ 96UltPow-5
❑ 96UltPowRL-2
❑ 96UppDec-108
❑ 96UppDec-361
❑ 96UppDecB-5
❑ 96UppDecBD-180
❑ 96UppDecBDP-P180
❑ 96UppDecBDG-180
❑ 96UppDecBDRFTC-RC1
❑ 96UppDecGN-X1
❑ 96UppDecHH-HH1
❑ 96UppDecHHG-HH1
❑ 96UppDecHHS-HH1
❑ 96UppDecIce-112
❑ 96UppDecIceDF-S1
❑ 96UppDecIcePar-112
❑ 96UppDecIceSCF-S1
❑ 96UppDecLSH-LS1
❑ 96UppDecLSHF-LS1
❑ 96UppDecLSHS-LS1
❑ 96UppDecSS-SS5A
❑ 96Zen-13
❑ 96ZenArtP-13
❑ 96ZenChaS-2
❑ 96ZenChaSD-2
❑ 97BeAPlaPOT-1
❑ 97BeAPlaTAN-8
❑ 97ColCho-167
❑ 97ColCho-312
❑ 97ColChoCTG-C1A
❑ 97ColChoCTG-C1B
❑ 97ColChoCTG-C1C
❑ 97ColChoCTGE-CR1
❑ 97ColChoMM-MM1
❑ 97ColChoMM-MM2
❑ 97ColChoMM-MM3
❑ 97ColChoMM-MM4
❑ 97ColChoMM-MM5
❑ 97ColChoSta-SQ90
❑ 97ColChoSti-S1
❑ 97ColChoWD-W1
❑ 97Don-143
❑ 97DonCanI-5
❑ 97DonCanIDS-5
❑ 97DonCanINP-1
❑ 97DonCanIPS-5
❑ 97DonCanISCS-28
❑ 97DonEli-9
❑ 97DonEli-143
❑ 97DonEliAsp-9
❑ 97DonEliAsp-143
❑ 97DonEliC-19
❑ 97DonEliIns-1
❑ 97DonEliMC-19
❑ 97DonEliS-9
❑ 97DonEliS-143
❑ 97DonLim-4
❑ 97DonLim-97
❑ 97DonLim-200
❑ 97DonLimExp-4
❑ 97DonLimExp-97
❑ 97DonLimExp-200
❑ 97DonLimFOTG-1
❑ 97DonLimFOTG-34
❑ 97DonLin2L-1
❑ 97DonLin2LDC-1
❑ 97DonPre-4
❑ 97DonPre-172
❑ 97DonPreCttC-4
❑ 97DonPreCttC-172
❑ 97DonPreDWT-1
❑ 97DonPreDWT-12
❑ 97DonPreLotT-6A
❑ 97DonPrePM-3
❑ 97DonPreProG-143
❑ 97DonPreProS-143
❑ 97DonPreT-23
❑ 97DonPreTB-3
❑ 97DonPreTB-23
❑ 97DonPreTBC-3
❑ 97DonPreTBC-23
❑ 97DonPreTPC-3
❑ 97DonPreTPC-23
❑ 97DonPreTPG-3
❑ 97DonPreTPG-23
❑ 97DonPri-10
❑ 97DonPri-199
❑ 97DonPriDD-8
❑ 97DonPriODI-10
❑ 97DonPriP-7
❑ 97DonPriS-7
❑ 97DonPriSB-7
❑ 97DonPriSG-7
❑ 97DonPriSoA-10
❑ 97DonPriSoA-199
❑ 97DonPriSS-7
❑ 97Kat-92
❑ 97Kat-157
❑ 97KatGol-92
❑ 97KatGol-157
❑ 97KatSil-92
❑ 97KatSil-157
❑ 97Lea-8
❑ 97Lea-175
❑ 97LeaBanSea-3
❑ 97LeaFirOnIce-1
❑ 97LeaFraMat-8
❑ 97LeaFraMat-175
❑ 97LeaFraMDC-8
❑ 97LeaFraMDC-175
❑ 97LeaInt-8
❑ 97LeaIntUI-8
❑ 97McD-1
❑ 97McDGamFil-1
❑ 97Pac-99
❑ 97PacCarSup-12
❑ 97PacCarSupM-12
❑ 97PacCop-99
❑ 97PacCraChoAwa-7
❑ 97PacCroR-84
❑ 97PacCroRBoSDC-14
❑ 97PacCroRCCJ-7
❑ 97PacCroRCCJS-7
❑ 97PacCroREG-84
❑ 97PacCroRHTDC-11
❑ 97PacCroRIB-84
❑ 97PacCroRLCDC-11
❑ 97PacCroRS-84
❑ 97PacDyn-78
❑ 97PacDyn-140
❑ 97PacDynBKS-59
❑ 97PacDynC-78
❑ 97PacDynC-140
❑ 97PacDynDD-10A
❑ 97PacDynDG-78
❑ 97PacDynDG-140
❑ 97PacDynEG-78
❑ 97PacDynEG-140
❑ 97PacDynIB-78
❑ 97PacDynIB-140
❑ 97PacDynKotN-6
❑ 97PacDynR-78
❑ 97PacDynR-140
❑ 97PacDynSil-78
❑ 97PacDynSil-140
❑ 97PacDynTan-1
❑ 97PacDynTan-19
❑ 97PacEmeGre-99
❑ 97PacGolCroDC-15
❑ 97PacIceB-99
❑ 97PacInv-86
❑ 97PacInvAZ-14
❑ 97PacInvC-86
❑ 97PacInvEG-86
❑ 97PacInvFP-21
❑ 97PacInvIB-86
❑ 97PacInvNRB-128
❑ 97PacInvNRB-218
❑ 97PacInvOTG-12
❑ 97PacInvR-86
❑ 97PacInvS-86
❑ 97PacOme-145
❑ 97PacOme-250
❑ 97PacOmeC-145
❑ 97PacOmeC-250
❑ 97PacOmeDG-145
❑ 97PacOmeDG-250
❑ 97PacOmeEG-145
❑ 97PacOmeEG-250
❑ 97PacOmeG-145
❑ 97PacOmeG-250
❑ 97PacOmeGFDCC-11
❑ 97PacOmeIB-145
❑ 97PacOmeIB-250
❑ 97PacOmeSil-8
❑ 97PacOmeSLC-13
❑ 97PacOmeTL-14
❑ 97PacPar-115
❑ 97PacParBNDC-14
❑ 97PacParC-115
❑ 97PacParCG-10
❑ 97PacParDG-115
❑ 97PacParEG-115
❑ 97PacParIB-115
❑ 97PacParP-13
❑ 97PacParRed-115
❑ 97PacParSil-115
❑ 97PacRed-99
❑ 97PacRev-87
❑ 97PacRev1AGD-14
❑ 97PacRevC-87
❑ 97PacRevE-87
❑ 97PacRevIB-87
❑ 97PacRevNID-7
❑ 97PacRevR-87
❑ 97PacRevS-87
❑ 97PacRevTCL-16
❑ 97PacSil-99
❑ 97PacSlaSDC-5A
❑ 97PacTeaCCC-16
❑ 97Pin-67
❑ 97Pin-192
❑ 97PinArtP-67
❑ 97PinBee-33
❑ 97PinBeeGP-33
❑ 97PinBeeGT-7
❑ 97PinBeeT-7
❑ 97PinCer-100
❑ 97PinCerGT-7
❑ 97PinCerMB-100
❑ 97PinCerMG-100
❑ 97PinCerMR-100
❑ 97PinCerR-100
❑ 97PinCerT-7
❑ 97PinEpiGO-1
❑ 97PinEpiGP-1
❑ 97PinEpiME-1
❑ 97PinEpiMO-1
❑ 97PinEpiMP-1
❑ 97PinEpiPE-1
❑ 97PinEpiPO-1
❑ 97PinEpiPP-1
❑ 97PinEpiSE-1
❑ 97PinEpiSO-1
❑ 97PinEpiSP-1
❑ 97PinIns-3
❑ 97PinInsC-18
❑ 97PinInsCC-3
❑ 97PinInsCG-18
❑ 97PinInsEC-3
❑ 97PinInsT-1
❑ 97PinMin-18
❑ 97PinMinB-18
❑ 97PinMinCBP-18
❑ 97PinMinCGPP-18
❑ 97PinMinCNSP-18
❑ 97PinMinCoiB-18
❑ 97PinMinCoiGP-18
❑ 97PinMinCoiN-18
❑ 97PinMinCoiSG-18
❑ 97PinMinCoiSS-18
❑ 97PinMinGolTea-18
❑ 97PinMinSilTea-18
❑ 97PinPowPac-17
❑ 97PinPrePBB-67
❑ 97PinPrePBB-192
❑ 97PinPrePBC-67
❑ 97PinPrePBC-192
❑ 97PinPrePBM-67
❑ 97PinPrePBM-192
❑ 97PinPrePBY-67
❑ 97PinPrePBY-192
❑ 97PinPrePFC-67
❑ 97PinPrePFC-192
❑ 97PinPrePFM-67
❑ 97PinPrePFM-192
❑ 97PinPrePFY-67
❑ 97PinPrePFY-192
❑ 97PinPrePla-67
❑ 97PinPrePla-192
❑ 97PinRinC-67
❑ 97PinTeaP-4
❑ 97PinTeaPM-4
❑ 97PinTeaPP-4
❑ 97PinTeaPPM-4
❑ 97PinTotCMPG-100
❑ 97PinTotCPB-100
❑ 97PinTotCPG-100
❑ 97PinTotCPR-100
❑ 97Sco-99
❑ 97ScoArtPro-99
❑ 97ScoGolBla-99
❑ 97ScoRan-1
❑ 97ScoRanPla-1
❑ 97ScoRanPre-1
❑ 97SP AutI-I26
❑ 97SPAut-99
❑ 97SPAutAut-1
❑ 97SPAutAut-2
❑ 97SPAutAut-3
❑ 97SPAutAut-4
❑ 97SPAutAut-5
❑ 97SPAutAut-6
❑ 97SPAutAut-7
❑ 97SPAutAut-8
❑ 97SPAutAut-9
❑ 97SPAutAut-10
❑ 97SPAutAut-11
❑ 97SPAutID-I26
❑ 97SPAutIE-I26
❑ 97SPAutMoaL-M6
❑ 97SPAutSotT-WG
❑ 97SPAutTra-T1
❑ 97SPx-30
❑ 97SPx-30S
❑ 97SPxBro-30
❑ 97SPxDim-SPX1
❑ 97SPxDuo-1
❑ 97SPxDuoAut-1
❑ 97SPxGol-30
❑ 97SPxGraF-30
❑ 97SPxSil-30
❑ 97SPxSte-30
❑ 97Stu-1
❑ 97Stu-109
❑ 97StuHarH-1
❑ 97StuPor-1

❑ 97StuPrePG-1
❑ 97StuPrePG-109
❑ 97StuPrePS-1
❑ 97StuPrePS-109
❑ 97StuSil-1
❑ 97StuSil8-1
❑ 97TopHocMC-9
❑ 97TopHocMC-10
❑ 97UppDec-109
❑ 97UppDec-209
❑ 97UppDec-419
❑ 97UppDecBD-144
❑ 97UppDecBDDD-144
❑ 97UppDecBDPC-PC1
❑ 97UppDecBDPCDD-PC1
❑ 97UppDecBDPCM-PC1
❑ 97UppDecBDPCQD-PC1
❑ 97UppDecBDPCTD-PC1
❑ 97UppDecBDQD-144
❑ 97UppDecBDTD-144
❑ 97UppDecCtAG-20
❑ 97UppDecCtAG-AR20
❑ 97UppDecDV-1
❑ 97UppDecDV-RT1
❑ 97UppDecDVDM-DM1
❑ 97UppDecDVSM-1
❑ 97UppDecGDM-109
❑ 97UppDecGJ-GJ8
❑ 97UppDecGJ-GJ8S
❑ 97UppDecIC-IC1
❑ 97UppDecIC2-IC1
❑ 97UppDecIce-90
❑ 97UppDecIceP-90
❑ 97UppDecILL-L1B
❑ 97UppDecILL2-L1B
❑ 97UppDecIPS-90
❑ 97UppDecSG-SG1
❑ 97UppDecSSM-SS1
❑ 97UppDecSSW-SS1
❑ 97UppDecTS-1
❑ 97UppDecTSL2-1
❑ 97UppDecTSS-1B
❑ 97Zen-4
❑ 97Zen5x7-1
❑ 97ZenChaTC-2
❑ 97ZenGolImp-1
❑ 97ZenSilImp-1
❑ 97ZenZGol-4
❑ 97ZenZSil-4
❑ 97ZenZT-2
❑ 97ZenZT5x7-2
❑ 97ZenZTG-2
❑ 98Be A PPA-90
❑ 98Be A PPAA-90
❑ 98Be A PPAAF-90
❑ 98Be A PPAGUSC-S23
❑ 98Be A PPAJ-AS25
❑ 98Be A PPAM-M1
❑ 98Be A PPAM-M7
❑ 98Be A PPGUJA-G1
❑ 98Be A PPPGUJC-G1
❑ 98Be A PPPH-H3
❑ 98Be A PPPPUJC-P24
❑ 98Be A PPTBASG-90
❑ 98Be APG-90
❑ 98BowBes-3
❑ 98BowBesAR-3
❑ 98BowBesMIF-F15
❑ 98BowBesMIFAR-F15
❑ 98BowBesMIFR-F15
❑ 98BowBesR-3
❑ 98CroRoyCCAJG-8
❑ 98CroRoyCCAJG-8
❑ 98CroRoyCCAJLB-8
❑ 98CroRoyCCAJP-8
❑ 98CroRoyCCAJR-8
❑ 98Fin-64
❑ 98FinDouMF-M1
❑ 98FinDouMF-M5
❑ 98FinDouMF-M8
❑ 98FinDouMF-M9
❑ 98FinDouSMFR-M1
❑ 98FinDouSMFR-M5
❑ 98FinDouSMFR-M8
❑ 98FinDouSMFR-M9
❑ 98FinNo P-64
❑ 98FinNo PR-64
❑ 98FinOve-4
❑ 98FinOveR-4
❑ 98FinRedL-R9
❑ 98FinRedLR-R9
❑ 98FinRef-64
❑ 98JelSpo-3
❑ 98McD-1
❑ 98McDGreM-M1
❑ 98McDGreM-M2
❑ 98McDGreM-M3
❑ 98McDGreM-M4
❑ 98McDGreM-M5
❑ 98McDGreM-M6
❑ 98McDGreM-M7
❑ 98McDGreM-M8
❑ 98McDGreM-M9
❑ 98McDGreM-M10
❑ 98O-PChr-219
❑ 98O-PChrBFtP-1
❑ 98O-PChrBFtPR-1
❑ 98O-PChrR-219
❑ 98O-PChrSB-SB20
❑ 98O-PChrSBR-SB20
❑ 98Pac-99
❑ 98PacAur-122
❑ 98PacAurALC-13
❑ 98PacAurC-12
❑ 98PacAurCF-30
❑ 98PacAurCFC-30
❑ 98PacAurCFIB-30
❑ 98PacAurCFR-30
❑ 98PacAurCFS-30
❑ 98PacAurFL-9
❑ 98PacAurFLIB-9
❑ 98PacAurFLR-9
❑ 98PacAurMAC-13
❑ 98PacAurNC-8
❑ 98PacAurT-122
❑ 98PacCraCA-7
❑ 98PacCroR-88
❑ 98PacCroRCCA-8
❑ 98PacCroRCCAJ-8
❑ 98PacCroRLL-8
❑ 98PacCroRLS-88
❑ 98PacCroRMP-14
❑ 98PacCroRPP-16
❑ 98PacDynI-121
❑ 98PacDynI-13
❑ 98PacDynIAR-8
❑ 98PacDynIARB-8
❑ 98PacDynIARIB-8
❑ 98PacDynIARR-8
❑ 98PacDynIARS-8
❑ 98PacDynIFT-13
❑ 98PacDynIIB-121
❑ 98PacDynIM-121
❑ 98PacDynIPP-8
❑ 98PacDynIR-121
❑ 98PacDynITC-17
❑ 98PacEO P-14
❑ 98PacGolCD-23
❑ 98PacIceB-99
❑ 98PacOmeCS-7
❑ 98PacOmeCSG-7
❑ 98PacOmeCSG-7
❑ 98PacOmeCSR-7
❑ 98PacOmeEP1o1-14
❑ 98PacOmeFtF-2
❑ 98PacOmeH-156
❑ 98PacOmeO-23
❑ 98PacOmeODI-156
❑ 98PacOmeP-13
❑ 98PacOmePI-26
❑ 98PacOmePIB-26
❑ 98PacOmeR-156
❑ 98PacOmeSE-156
❑ 98PacPar-152
❑ 98PacParC-152
❑ 98PacParEG-152
❑ 98PacParH-152
❑ 98PacParHoFB-7
❑ 98PacParHoFBPP-7
❑ 98PacParIB-152
❑ 98PacParIG-7
❑ 98PacParIGG-7
❑ 98PacParIGS-7
❑ 98PacParS-152
❑ 98PacParSDDC-12
❑ 98PacParTCD-17
❑ 98PacRed-99
❑ 98PacRev-92
❑ 98PacRevADC-8
❑ 98PacRevCTL-11
❑ 98PacRevIS-92
❑ 98PacRevNI-8
❑ 98PacRevR-92
❑ 98PacRevS-23
❑ 98PacTeaC-17
❑ 98PacTim-11
❑ 98PacTitI-13
❑ 98PinEpiGE-1
❑ 98RanPowP-NYR1
❑ 98RevThrPA-27
❑ 98RevThrPA-27
❑ 98SP Aut-56
❑ 98SP AutA-1
❑ 98SP AutA-10
❑ 98SP AutA-11
❑ 98SP AutSM-S28
❑ 98SP AutSM-S29
❑ 98SP AutSM-S30
❑ 98SP AutSotTG-WG
❑ 98SP AutSS-SS1
❑ 98SPxFin-53
❑ 98SPxFin-99
❑ 98SPxFin-151
❑ 98SPxFin-180
❑ 98SPxFin-S99
❑ 98SPxFinR-53
❑ 98SPxFinR-99
❑ 98SPxFinR-151
❑ 98SPxFinR-180
❑ 98SPxFinS-53
❑ 98SPxFinS-99
❑ 98SPxFinS-151
❑ 98SPxFinS-180
❑ 98SPXTopP-38
❑ 98SPXTopPF-38
❑ 98SPXTopPHH-H18
❑ 98SPXTopPLI-L27
❑ 98SPXTopPPS-PS1
❑ 98SPXTopPPS-PS16
❑ 98SPXTopPR-38
❑ 98SPXTopPYotGO-WG1
❑ 98SPXTopPYotGO-WG2
❑ 98SPXTopPYotGO-WG3
❑ 98SPXTopPYotGO-WG4
❑ 98SPXTopPYotGO-WG5
❑ 98SPXTopPYotGO-WG6
❑ 98SPXTopPYotGO-WG7
❑ 98SPXTopPYotGO-WG8
❑ 98SPXTopPYotGO-WG9
❑ 98SPXTopPYotGO-WG10
❑ 98SPXTopPYotGO-WG11
❑ 98SPXTopPYotGO-WG12
❑ 98SPXTopPYotGO-WG13
❑ 98SPXTopPYotGO-WG14
❑ 98SPXTopPYotGO-WG15
❑ 98SPXTopPYotGO-WG16
❑ 98SPXTopPYotGO-WG17
❑ 98SPXTopPYotGO-WG18
❑ 98SPXTopPYotGO-WG19
❑ 98SPXTopPYotGO-WG20
❑ 98SPXTopPYotGO-WG21
❑ 98SPXTopPYotGO-WG22
❑ 98SPXTopPYotGO-WG23
❑ 98SPXTopPYotGO-WG24
❑ 98SPXTopPYotGO-WG25
❑ 98SPXTopPYotGO-WG26
❑ 98SPXTopPYotGO-WG27
❑ 98SPXTopPYotGO-WG28
❑ 98SPXTopPYotGO-WG29
❑ 98SPXTopPYotGO-WG30
❑ 98SSASotT-WG
❑ 98Top-219
❑ 98TopBlaFTP-1
❑ 98TopGolLC1-4
❑ 98TopGolLC1B-4
❑ 98TopGolLC1BOoO-4
❑ 98TopGolLC1OoO-4
❑ 98TopGolLC1R-4
❑ 98TopGolLC1ROoO-4
❑ 98TopGolLC2-4
❑ 98TopGolLC2B-4
❑ 98TopGolLC2BOoO-4
❑ 98TopGolLC2OoO-4
❑ 98TopGolLC2R-4
❑ 98TopGolLC2ROoO-4
❑ 98TopGolLC3-4
❑ 98TopGolLC3B-4
❑ 98TopGolLC3BOoO-4
❑ 98TopGolLC3OoO-4
❑ 98TopGolLC3R-4
❑ 98TopGolLC3ROoO-4
❑ 98TopLocL-L7
❑ 98TopMysFB-M4
❑ 98TopMysFBR-M4
❑ 98TopMysFG-M4
❑ 98TopMysFGR-M4
❑ 98TopMysFS-M4
❑ 98TopMysFSR-M4
❑ 98TopO-P-219
❑ 98TopSeaB-SB20
❑ 98UC-128
❑ 98UC-225
❑ 98UC-236
❑ 98UC-308
❑ 98UCMBH-BH1
❑ 98UCSB-SQ1
❑ 98UCSG-SQ1
❑ 98UCSG-SQ1
❑ 98UCSR-SQ1
❑ 98UD ChoPCR-128
❑ 98UD ChoPCR-225
❑ 98UD ChoPCR-236
❑ 98UD ChoPCR-308
❑ 98UD ChoR-128
❑ 98UD ChoR-225
❑ 98UD ChoR-236
❑ 98UD ChoR-308
❑ 98UD3-31
❑ 98UD3-91
❑ 98UD3-151
❑ 98UD3DieC-31
❑ 98UD3DieC-91
❑ 98UD3DieC-151
❑ 98UppDec-135
❑ 98UppDec-207
❑ 98UppDec-388
❑ 98UppDec-390
❑ 98UppDecBD-55
❑ 98UppDecBDYotGO-1
❑ 98UppDecBDYotGO-2
❑ 98UppDecBDYotGO-3
❑ 98UppDecBDYotGO-4
❑ 98UppDecBDYotGO-5
❑ 98UppDecBDYotGO-6
❑ 98UppDecBDYotGO-7
❑ 98UppDecBDYotGO-8
❑ 98UppDecBDYotGO-9
❑ 98UppDecBDYotGO-10
❑ 98UppDecBDYotGO-11
❑ 98UppDecBDYotGO-12
❑ 98UppDecBDYotGO-13
❑ 98UppDecBDYotGO-14
❑ 98UppDecBDYotGO-15
❑ 98UppDecBDYotGO-16
❑ 98UppDecBDYotGO-17
❑ 98UppDecBDYotGO-18
❑ 98UppDecBDYotGO-19
❑ 98UppDecBDYotGO-20
❑ 98UppDecBDYotGO-21
❑ 98UppDecBDYotGO-22
❑ 98UppDecBDYotGO-23
❑ 98UppDecBDYotGO-24
❑ 98UppDecBDYotGO-25
❑ 98UppDecBDYotGO-26
❑ 98UppDecBDYotGO-27
❑ 98UppDecBDYotGO-28
❑ 98UppDecBDYotGO-29
❑ 98UppDecBDYotGO-30
❑ 98UppDecBDYotGO-31
❑ 98UppDecBDYotGO-32
❑ 98UppDecBDYotGO-33
❑ 98UppDecBDYotGO-34
❑ 98UppDecBDYotGO-35
❑ 98UppDecBDYotGO-36
❑ 98UppDecBDYotGO-37
❑ 98UppDecBDYotGO-38
❑ 98UppDecBDYotGO-39
❑ 98UppDecBDYotGO-40
❑ 98UppDecBDYotGO-41
❑ 98UppDecBDYotGO-42
❑ 98UppDecBDYotGO-43
❑ 98UppDecBDYotGO-44
❑ 98UppDecBDYotGO-45
❑ 98UppDecBDYotGO-46
❑ 98UppDecBDYotGO-47
❑ 98UppDecBDYotGO-48
❑ 98UppDecBDYotGO-49
❑ 98UppDecBDYotGO-50
❑ 98UppDecBDYotGO-51
❑ 98UppDecBDYotGO-52
❑ 98UppDecBDYotGO-53
❑ 98UppDecBDYotGO-54
❑ 98UppDecBDYotGO-55
❑ 98UppDecBDYotGO-56
❑ 98UppDecBDYotGO-57
❑ 98UppDecBDYotGO-58
❑ 98UppDecBDYotGO-59
❑ 98UppDecBDYotGO-60
❑ 98UppDecBDYotGO-61
❑ 98UppDecBDYotGO-62
❑ 98UppDecBDYotGO-63
❑ 98UppDecBDYotGO-64
❑ 98UppDecBDYotGO-65
❑ 98UppDecBDYotGO-66
❑ 98UppDecBDYotGO-67
❑ 98UppDecBDYotGO-68
❑ 98UppDecBDYotGO-69
❑ 98UppDecBDYotGO-70
❑ 98UppDecBDYotGO-71
❑ 98UppDecBDYotGO-72
❑ 98UppDecBDYotGO-73
❑ 98UppDecBDYotGO-74
❑ 98UppDecBDYotGO-75
❑ 98UppDecBDYotGO-76
❑ 98UppDecBDYotGO-77
❑ 98UppDecBDYotGO-78
❑ 98UppDecBDYotGO-79
❑ 98UppDecBDYotGO-80
❑ 98UppDecBDYotGO-81
❑ 98UppDecBDYotGO-82
❑ 98UppDecBDYotGO-83
❑ 98UppDecBDYotGO-84
❑ 98UppDecBDYotGO-85
❑ 98UppDecBDYotGO-86
❑ 98UppDecBDYotGO-87
❑ 98UppDecBDYotGO-88
❑ 98UppDecBDYotGO-89
❑ 98UppDecBDYotGO-90
❑ 98UppDecBDYotGO-91
❑ 98UppDecBDYotGO-92
❑ 98UppDecBDYotGO-93
❑ 98UppDecBDYotGO-94
❑ 98UppDecBDYotGO-95
❑ 98UppDecBDYotGO-96
❑ 98UppDecBDYotGO-97
❑ 98UppDecBDYotGO-98
❑ 98UppDecBDYotGO-99
❑ 98UppDecDD-55
❑ 98UppDecE-135
❑ 98UppDecE-207
❑ 98UppDecE-388
❑ 98UppDecE-390
❑ 98UppDecE1o1-135
❑ 98UppDecE1o1-207
❑ 98UppDecE1o1-388
❑ 98UppDecE1o1-390
❑ 98UppDecFF-FF1
❑ 98UppDecFF-FF1
❑ 98UppDecFFQ1-FF1
❑ 98UppDecFFQ2-FF1
❑ 98UppDecFIT-FT30
❑ 98UppDecFITQ1-FT30
❑ 98UppDecFITQ2-FT30
❑ 98UppDecFITQ3-FT30
❑ 98UppDecGJ-GJ1
❑ 98UppDecGJ-GJA2
❑ 98UppDecGJ-GJA4
❑ 98UppDecGN-GN1
❑ 98UppDecGN-GN2
❑ 98UppDecGN-GN3
❑ 98UppDecGNQ1-GN1
❑ 98UppDecGNQ1-GN2
❑ 98UppDecGNQ1-GN3
❑ 98UppDecGNQ2-GN1
❑ 98UppDecGNQ2-GN2
❑ 98UppDecGNQ2-GN3
❑ 98UppDecGNQ3-GN1
❑ 98UppDecGNQ3-GN2
❑ 98UppDecGNQ3-GN3
❑ 98UppDecGR-135
❑ 98UppDecGR-207
❑ 98UppDecGR-388
❑ 98UppDecGR-390
❑ 98UppDecGR-NNO
❑ 98UppDecLSH-LS1
❑ 98UppDecLSHQ1-LS1
❑ 98UppDecLSHQ2-LS1
❑ 98UppDecLSHQ3-LS1
❑ 98UppDecM-132
❑ 98UppDecM-218
❑ 98UppDecM-219
❑ 98UppDecM-220
❑ 98UppDecM1-M27
❑ 98UppDecM2-M27
❑ 98UppDecMD-D1
❑ 98UppDecMD-D2
❑ 98UppDecMD-D3
❑ 98UppDecMD-D4
❑ 98UppDecMD-D5
❑ 98UppDecMD-D6
❑ 98UppDecMD-D7
❑ 98UppDecMD-D8
❑ 98UppDecMD-D9
❑ 98UppDecMD-D10
❑ 98UppDecMD-D11
❑ 98UppDecMD-D12
❑ 98UppDecMD-D13
❑ 98UppDecMD-D14
❑ 98UppDecMD-D15
❑ 98UppDECMGS-WG
❑ 98UppDecMGS-132
❑ 98UppDecMGS-218
❑ 98UppDecMGS-219
❑ 98UppDecMGS-220
❑ 98UppDecMOH-OT5
❑ 98UppDecMP-WG
❑ 98UppDecMS-S2
❑ 98UppDecMSF-F12
❑ 98UppDecMSS-132
❑ 98UppDecMSS-218
❑ 98UppDecMSS-219
❑ 98UppDecMSS-220
❑ 98UppDecMSS-132
❑ 98UppDecMSS-218
❑ 98UppDecMSS-219
❑ 98UppDecMSS-220
❑ 98UppDecP-P9
❑ 98UppDecPQ1-P9
❑ 98UppDecPQ2-P9
❑ 98UppDecPQ3-P9
❑ 98UppDecQD-55
❑ 98UppDecTD-55
❑ 98UppDecWFG-WF18
❑ 98UppDecWFP-WF18
❑ 98UppDecYotGO-GO1
❑ 98UppDecYotGO-GO2
❑ 98UppDecYotGO-GO3
❑ 98UppDecYotGO-GO4
❑ 98UppDecYotGO-GO5
❑ 98UppDecYotGO-GO6
❑ 98UppDecYotGO-GO7
❑ 98UppDecYotGO-GO8
❑ 98UppDecYotGO-GO9
❑ 98UppDecYotGO-GO10
❑ 98UppDecYotGO-GO11
❑ 98UppDecYotGO-GO12
❑ 98UppDecYotGO-GO13
❑ 98UppDecYotGO-GO14
❑ 98UppDecYotGO-GO15
❑ 98UppDecYotGO-GO16
❑ 98UppDecYotGO-GO17
❑ 98UppDecYotGO-GO18
❑ 98UppDecYotGO-GO19
❑ 98UppDecYotGO-GO20
❑ 98UppDecYotGO-GO21
❑ 98UppDecYotGO-GO22
❑ 98UppDecYotGO-GO23
❑ 98UppDecYotGO-GO24
❑ 98UppDecYotGO-GO25
❑ 98UppDecYotGO-GO26
❑ 98UppDecYotGO-GO27
❑ 98UppDecYotGO-GO28
❑ 98UppDecYotGO-GO29
❑ 98UppDecYotGO-GO30
❑ 98UppDecYotGOQ1-GO1
❑ 98UppDecYotGOQ1-GO2
❑ 98UppDecYotGOQ1-GO3
❑ 98UppDecYotGOQ1-GO4
❑ 98UppDecYotGOQ1-GO5
❑ 98UppDecYotGOQ1-GO6
❑ 98UppDecYotGOQ1-GO7
❑ 98UppDecYotGOQ1-GO8
❑ 98UppDecYotGOQ1-GO9
❑ 98UppDecYotGOQ1-GO10
❑ 98UppDecYotGOQ1-GO11
❑ 98UppDecYotGOQ1-GO12
❑ 98UppDecYotGOQ1-GO13
❑ 98UppDecYotGOQ1-GO14
❑ 98UppDecYotGOQ1-GO15
❑ 98UppDecYotGOQ1-GO16
❑ 98UppDecYotGOQ1-GO17
❑ 98UppDecYotGOQ1-GO18
❑ 98UppDecYotGOQ1-GO19
❑ 98UppDecYotGOQ1-GO20
❑ 98UppDecYotGOQ1-GO21
❑ 98UppDecYotGOQ1-GO22
❑ 98UppDecYotGOQ1-GO23
❑ 98UppDecYotGOQ1-GO24
❑ 98UppDecYotGOQ1-GO25
❑ 98UppDecYotGOQ1-GO26
❑ 98UppDecYotGOQ1-GO27
❑ 98UppDecYotGOQ1-GO28
❑ 98UppDecYotGOQ1-GO29
❑ 98UppDecYotGOQ1-GO30
❑ 98UppDecYotGOQ2-GO1
❑ 98UppDecYotGOQ2-GO2
❑ 98UppDecYotGOQ2-GO3
❑ 98UppDecYotGOQ2-GO4
❑ 98UppDecYotGOQ2-GO5
❑ 98UppDecYotGOQ2-GO6
❑ 98UppDecYotGOQ2-GO7
❑ 98UppDecYotGOQ2-GO8
❑ 98UppDecYotGOQ2-GO9
❑ 98UppDecYotGOQ2-GO10
❑ 98UppDecYotGOQ2-GO11
❑ 98UppDecYotGOQ2-GO12
❑ 98UppDecYotGOQ2-GO13
❑ 98UppDecYotGOQ2-GO14
❑ 98UppDecYotGOQ2-GO15
❑ 98UppDecYotGOQ2-GO16
❑ 98UppDecYotGOQ2-GO17
❑ 98UppDecYotGOQ2-GO18
❑ 98UppDecYotGOQ2-GO19
❑ 98UppDecYotGOQ2-GO20
❑ 98UppDecYotGOQ2-GO21
❑ 98UppDecYotGOQ2-GO22
❑ 98UppDecYotGOQ2-GO23
❑ 98UppDecYotGOQ2-GO24
❑ 98UppDecYotGOQ2-GO25
❑ 98UppDecYotGOQ2-GO26
❑ 98UppDecYotGOQ2-GO27
❑ 98UppDecYotGOQ2-GO28
❑ 98UppDecYotGOQ2-GO29
❑ 98UppDecYotGOQ2-GO30
❑ 98UppDecYotGOQ3-GO1
❑ 98UppDecYotGOQ3-GO2
❑ 98UppDecYotGOQ3-GO3
❑ 98UppDecYotGOQ3-GO4
❑ 98UppDecYotGOQ3-GO5
❑ 98UppDecYotGOQ3-GO6
❑ 98UppDecYotGOQ3-GO7
❑ 98UppDecYotGOQ3-GO8
❑ 98UppDecYotGOQ3-GO9
❑ 98UppDecYotGOQ3-GO10
❑ 98UppDecYotGOQ3-GO11
❑ 98UppDecYotGOQ3-GO12
❑ 98UppDecYotGOQ3-GO13
❑ 98UppDecYotGOQ3-GO14
❑ 98UppDecYotGOQ3-GO15
❑ 98UppDecYotGOQ3-GO16
❑ 98UppDecYotGOQ3-GO17
❑ 98UppDecYotGOQ3-GO18
❑ 98UppDecYotGOQ3-GO19
❑ 98UppDecYotGOQ3-GO20
❑ 98UppDecYotGOQ3-GO21
❑ 98UppDecYotGOQ3-GO22
❑ 98UppDecYotGOQ3-GO23
❑ 98UppDecYotGOQ3-GO24
❑ 98UppDecYotGOQ3-GO25
❑ 98UppDecYotGOQ3-GO26
❑ 98UppDecYotGOQ3-GO27
❑ 98UppDecYotGOQ3-GO28
❑ 98UppDecYotGOQ3-GO29
❑ 98UppDecYotGOQ3-GO30
❑ 99PinTeaP-H1
❑ 99RetHoc-49
❑ 99SP AutPS-56
❑ 99UppDecCA-C1
❑ 99UppDecCA-C2
❑ 99UppDecCA-C3
❑ 99UppDecCL-1
❑ 99UppDecCL-51
❑ 99UppDecCL-81
❑ 99UppDecCL-82
❑ 99UppDecCL-83
❑ 99UppDecCL-84
❑ 99UppDecCL-85
❑ 99UppDecCL-86
❑ 99UppDecCL-87
❑ 99UppDecCL-88
❑ 99UppDecCL-89
❑ 99UppDecCL-90
❑ 99UppDecCLACT-AC1
❑ 99UppDecCLCLC-1
❑ 99UppDecCLCLC-51
❑ 99UppDecCLCLC-81
❑ 99UppDecCLCLC-82
❑ 99UppDecCLCLC-83
❑ 99UppDecCLCLC-84
❑ 99UppDecCLCLC-85
❑ 99UppDecCLCLC-86
❑ 99UppDecCLCLC-87
❑ 99UppDecCLCLC-88
❑ 99UppDecCLCLC-89
❑ 99UppDecCLCLC-90
❑ 99UppDecEotG-E1
❑ 99UppDecES-19
❑ 99UppDecGM-GM1
❑ 99UppDecGM-GM2
❑ 99UppDecGM-GM3
❑ 99UppDecGM-GM4
❑ 99UppDecGM-GM5
❑ 99UppDecGM-GM6
❑ 99UppDecGM-GM7
❑ 99UppDecGM-GM8
❑ 99UppDecGM-GM9
❑ 99UppDecGM-GM10
❑ 99UppDecM-1
❑ 99UppDecM-131
❑ 99UppDecM-219
❑ 99UppDecM-220
❑ 99UppDecM9S-S1
❑ 99UppDecMGS-GU6
❑ 99UppDecMGS-1
❑ 99UppDecMGS-131
❑ 99UppDecMGS-219
❑ 99UppDecMGS-220
❑ 99UppDecMGUSA-GU6
❑ 99UppDecMHoG-H1
❑ 99UppDecMLO-LO1
❑ 99UppDecMLO-LO2
❑ 99UppDecMLO-LO3
❑ 99UppDecMLO-LO4
❑ 99UppDecMLO-LO5
❑ 99UppDecMLO-LO6
❑ 99UppDecMLO-LO7
❑ 99UppDecMLO-LO8
❑ 99UppDecMLO-LO9
❑ 99UppDecMLO-LO10
❑ 99UppDecMPS-WG
❑ 99UppDecMSS-1
❑ 99UppDecMSS-131
❑ 99UppDecMSS-219
❑ 99UppDecMSS-220
❑ 99UppDecMSS-1
❑ 99UppDecMSS-131
❑ 99UppDecMSS-219
❑ 99UppDecMSS-220
❑ 99UppDecMT-MVP1
❑ 99UppDecRDR-DR9
❑ 99UppDecRDRI-DR9
❑ 99UppDecREG-EG1
❑ 99UppDecREG-EG2
❑ 99UppDecREG-EG3
❑ 99UppDecREG-EG4
❑ 99UppDecREG-EG5
❑ 99UppDecREG-EG6
❑ 99UppDecREG-EG7
❑ 99UppDecREG-EG8
❑ 99UppDecREG-EG9
❑ 99UppDecREG-EG10
❑ 99UppDecREGI-EG1
❑ 99UppDecREGI-EG2
❑ 99UppDecREGI-EG3
❑ 99UppDecREGI-EG4
❑ 99UppDecREGI-EG5
❑ 99UppDecREGI-EG6
❑ 99UppDecREGI-EG7
❑ 99UppDecREGI-EG8
❑ 99UppDecREGI-EG9
❑ 99UppDecREGI-EG10
❑ 99UppDecRG-49
❑ 99UppDecRII-WG
❑ 99UppDecRIL1-WG
❑ 99UppDecRM-RM1
❑ 99UppDecRP-49
❑ 99UppDecRTotC-TC9

**Greyeyes, Mark**

❑ 87PorWinH-11
❑ 88PorWinH-11

**Grieco, Scott**

❑ 93LetHur-4
❑ 95LetHur-6

**Grier, Mike**

❑ 96BeAPAut-220
❑ 96BeAPAutSil-220
❑ 96BeAPla-220
❑ 96DonCanI-141
❑ 96DonCanIGPP-141
❑ 96DonCanIRPP-141
❑ 96Fla-110
❑ 96FlaBluI-110
❑ 96MetUni-181
❑ 96OilPos-25
❑ 96SelCer-101
❑ 96SelCerAP-101
❑ 96SelCerBlu-101
❑ 96SelCerMB-101
❑ 96SelCerMG-101
❑ 96SelCerMR-101
❑ 96SelCerRed-101
❑ 96SP-177
❑ 96Ult-58
❑ 96UltGolM-58
❑ 96UltRoo-9
❑ 96UppDec-259
❑ 96UppDecBD-15
❑ 96UppDecBDG-15
❑ 96UppDecIce-86
❑ 96UppDecIcePar-86
❑ 96UppDecPP-P13
❑ 97ColCho-88
❑ 97ColChoSta-SQ24
❑ 97Don-94
❑ 97DonCanI-121
❑ 97DonCanIDS-121
❑ 97DonCanIPS-121
❑ 97DonEli-62
❑ 97DonEliAsp-62
❑ 97DonEliS-62
❑ 97DonLim-27
❑ 97DonLim-50
❑ 97DonLim-199
❑ 97DonLimExp-27
❑ 97DonLimExp-50
❑ 97DonLimExp-199
❑ 97DonLimFOTG-22
❑ 97DonPre-44
❑ 97DonPreCttC-44
❑ 97DonPreProG-94
❑ 97DonPreProS-94
❑ 97DonPri-59
❑ 97DonPriSoA-59
❑ 97Lea-81
❑ 97LeaBanSea-23
❑ 97LeaFraMat-81
❑ 97LeaFraMDC-81
❑ 97LeaInt-81
❑ 97LeaIntUI-81
❑ 97Pac-164
❑ 97PacCop-164
❑ 97PacDyn-48
❑ 97PacDynC-48
❑ 97PacDynDG-48
❑ 97PacDynEG-48
❑ 97PacDynIB-48
❑ 97PacDynR-48
❑ 97PacDynSil-48
❑ 97PacDynTan-10
❑ 97PacEmeGre-164
❑ 97PacIceB-164
❑ 97PacInv-55
❑ 97PacInvC-55
❑ 97PacInvEG-55
❑ 97PacInvIB-55
❑ 97PacInvOTG-10
❑ 97PacInvR-55
❑ 97PacInvS-55
❑ 97PacOme-90
❑ 97PacOmeC-90
❑ 97PacOmeDG-90
❑ 97PacOmeEG-90
❑ 97PacOmeG-90
❑ 97PacOmeIB-90
❑ 97PacPar-74

❑ 97PacParC-74
❑ 97PacParDG-74
❑ 97PacParEG-74
❑ 97PacParIB-74
❑ 97PacParRed-74
❑ 97PacParSil-74
❑ 97PacRed-164
❑ 97PacSil-164
❑ 97Pin-177
❑ 97PinCer-73
❑ 97PinCerMB-73
❑ 97PinCerMG-73
❑ 97PinCerMR-73
❑ 97PinCerR-73
❑ 97PinIns-85
❑ 97PinInsCC-85
❑ 97PinInsEC-85
❑ 97PinInsT-29
❑ 97PinPrePBB-177
❑ 97PinPrePBC-177
❑ 97PinPrePBM-177
❑ 97PinPrePBY-177
❑ 97PinPrePFC-177
❑ 97PinPrePFM-177
❑ 97PinPrePFY-177
❑ 97PinPrePla-177
❑ 97PinTotCMPG-73
❑ 97PinTotCPB-73
❑ 97PinTotCPG-73
❑ 97PinTotCPR-73
❑ 97Sco-153
❑ 97ScoArtPro-153
❑ 97ScoChel-10
❑ 97ScoGolBla-153
❑ 97SPAut-63
❑ 97SPAutSotT-MG
❑ 97Stu-51
❑ 97StuHarH-22
❑ 97StuPrePG-51
❑ 97StuPrePS-51
❑ 97UppDec-67
❑ 97UppDec-207
❑ 97UppDecSG-SG25
❑ 97UppDecTSS-16A
❑ 98Be A PPA-54
❑ 98Be A PPAA-54
❑ 98Be A PPAAF-54
❑ 98Be A PPTBASG-54
❑ 98Be APG-54
❑ 98O-PChr-31
❑ 98O-PChrR-31
❑ 98Pac-208
❑ 98PacAur-71
❑ 98PacDynI-71
❑ 98PacDynIIB-71
❑ 98PacDynIR-71
❑ 98PacIceB-208
❑ 98PacPar-85
❑ 98PacParC-85
❑ 98PacParEG-85
❑ 98PacParH-85
❑ 98PacParIB-85
❑ 98PacParS-85
❑ 98PacRed-208
❑ 98Top-31
❑ 98TopO-P-31
❑ 98UppDec-94
❑ 98UppDecE-94
❑ 98UppDecE1o1-94
❑ 98UppDecGR-94
❑ 98UppDecM-81
❑ 98UppDecMGS-81
❑ 98UppDecMSS-81
❑ 98UppDecMSS-81
❑ 99Pac-154
❑ 99PacAur-57
❑ 99PacAurPD-57
❑ 99PacCop-154
❑ 99PacGol-154
❑ 99PacIceB-154
❑ 99PacPreD-154
❑ 99UppDecM-81
❑ 99UppDecMGS-81
❑ 99UppDecMSS-81
❑ 99UppDecMSS-81

**Grieve, Brent**
❑ 897thInnSOHL-22
❑ 89OshGen-22
❑ 89OshGenP-26
❑ 907thInnSMC-92
❑ 90ProAHLIHL-506
❑ 91ProAHLCHL-453
❑ 92Cla-100
❑ 94BeAPSig-42
❑ 94ClaProP-128
❑ 94Lea-485
❑ 94OPCPre-99
❑ 94OPCPre-431
❑ 94OPCPreSE-99
❑ 94OPCPreSE-431
❑ 94Par-79
❑ 94ParGol-79
❑ 94StaClu-257
❑ 94StaCluFDI-257
❑ 94StaCluMOMS-257
❑ 94StaCluSTWC-257
❑ 94TopPre-99
❑ 94TopPre-431
❑ 94TopPreSE-99
❑ 94TopPreSE-431
❑ 94Ult-274
❑ 94UppDec-396
❑ 94UppDecEleIce-396
❑ 95UppDec-307
❑ 96ClaGol-100

**Grieve, Brian**
❑ 897thInnSOHL-12
❑ 89OshGen-12
❑ 89OshGenP-9
❑ 907thInnSMC-81
❑ 907thInnSOHL-337
❑ 917thInnSOHL-165
❑ 91OshGen-2
❑ 91OshGen-28
❑ 91OshGenS-16

**Griffis, Si**
❑ 83HalFP-L5
❑ 85HalFC-155

**Griffiths, Frank**
❑ 93ActPacHOFI-8

**Griffiths, Tuffy**
❑ 36V356WorG-132

**Grigg, Kody**
❑ 94NorBayC-21

**Grigg, Reggie**
❑ 62QueAce-9

**Grigg, Vic**
❑ 51LavDaiQSHL-102

**Grillo, Dean**
❑ 92NorDakFS-8
❑ 94Cla-42
❑ 94ClaDraGol-42
❑ 96KenTho-7

**Grills, Chad**
❑ 917thInnSOHL-135
❑ 91PetPet-4
❑ 93PetPet-11
❑ 93SauSteMG-22
❑ 95FliGen-6

**Grimes, Jake**
❑ 897thInnSOHL-76
❑ 907thInnSOHL-8
❑ 917thInnSOHL-111
❑ 94ClaProP-43
❑ 94ThuBayS-6

**Grimes, Kevin**
❑ 97BowCHL-136
❑ 97BowCHLAu-16
❑ 97BowCHLOPC-136

**Grimson, Stu**
❑ 82RegPat-8
❑ 83RegPat-8
❑ 88SalLakCGE-12
❑ 89ProIHL-199
❑ 90BlaCok-19
❑ 91BlaCok-9
❑ 91UppDec-416
❑ 91UppDecF-416
❑ 93Don-15
❑ 93DucMilCap-3
❑ 93Kra-11
❑ 93Lea-330
❑ 93OPCPre-357
❑ 93OPCPreG-357
❑ 93Par-277
❑ 93ParEmel-277
❑ 93Pin-401
❑ 93PinCan-401
❑ 93Pow-1
❑ 93Sco-558
❑ 93ScoCan-558
❑ 93ScoGol-558
❑ 93TopPre-357
❑ 93TopPreG-357
❑ 93Ult-253
❑ 94CanGamNHLP-33
❑ 94Par-3
❑ 94ParGol-3
❑ 94Pin-512
❑ 94PinArtP-512
❑ 94PinRinC-512
❑ 95BeAPla-224
❑ 95BeAPSig-S224
❑ 95BeAPSigDC-S224
❑ 97CarHur-9
❑ 97Kat-27
❑ 97KatGol-27
❑ 97KatSil-27
❑ 97Pac-296
❑ 97PacCop-296
❑ 97PacEmeGre-296
❑ 97PacIceB-296
❑ 97PacRed-296
❑ 97PacSil-296
❑ 97UppDec-33
❑ 98Be A PPA-152
❑ 98Be A PPAA-152
❑ 98Be A PPAAF-152
❑ 98Be A PPSE-152
❑ 98Be APG-152
❑ 98O-PChr-96
❑ 98O-PChrR-96
❑ 98Pac-133
❑ 98PacIceB-133
❑ 98PacOmeH-2
❑ 98PacOmeODI-2
❑ 98PacOmeR-2
❑ 98PacRed-133
❑ 98Top-96
❑ 98TopO-P-96
❑ 99Pac-5
❑ 99PacCop-5
❑ 99PacGol-5
❑ 99PacIceB-5
❑ 99PacPreD-5

**Gringras, Gaston**
❑ 87CanaPos-9

**Grisdale, John**
❑ 72MapLeaP-9
❑ 74CanuRoyB-7
❑ 75CanuRoyB-8
❑ 75OPCNHL-339
❑ 76CanuRoyB-6
❑ 77CanuRoyB-8
❑ 77OPCNHL-277
❑ 78CanuRoyB-9
❑ 78OPC-318

**Grise, Patrick**
❑ 88RivDu R-12
❑ 907thInnSQMJHL-62
❑ 917thInnSQMJHL-30

**Grnak, Marianne**
❑ 94ClaWomOH-W16

**Groeneveld, Phil**
❑ 95ForWorFT-3

**Groger, Thomas**
❑ 94GerDELE-12
❑ 95GerDELE-322

**Groke, Jamie**
❑ 85LonKni-20

**Groleau, Francois**
❑ 907thInnSQMJHL-225
❑ 917thInnSQMJHL-55
❑ 91ArenDraPic-29
❑ 91Cla-35
❑ 91StaPicH-23
❑ 91UltDra-30
❑ 94ClaProP-47
❑ 94St.JohF-8
❑ 98GerDELE-281

**Groleau, Jason**
❑ 95SlaMemC-54

**Groleau, Marius**
❑ 51LavDaiS-36

**Groleau, Samuel**
❑ 917thInnSQMJHL-159

**Gromling, Dimtri**
❑ 98GerDELE-286

**Gronau, Mark**
❑ 94GerDELE-72
❑ 95GerDELE-51

**Gronberg, Jan**
❑ 86SwePanS-54

**Gronborg, Rikard**
❑ 92SweSemE-257

**Grondin, Jimmy**
❑ 96RimOce-12
❑ 96RimOceQPP-12
❑ 97RimOce-11

**Grondin, Philippe**
❑ 96RimOceU-3
❑ 97RimOce-27

**Grondin, Pierre**
❑ 77GraVic-10

**Gronman, Tuomas**
❑ 917thInnSWHL-154
❑ 91UppDec-677
❑ 91UppDecCWJC-40
❑ 91UppDecF-677
❑ 93FinnJyvHS-231
❑ 93FinnSIS-188
❑ 93Par-523
❑ 93ParEmel-523
❑ 93UppDec-270
❑ 94FinnSIS-314
❑ 94FinnSISH-4
❑ 95FinnSemWC-3
❑ 95FinnSemWC-225
❑ 95FinnSIS-126
❑ 95FinnSISDT-1
❑ 95FinnSISL-4
❑ 96DonCanI-139
❑ 96DonCanIGPP-139
❑ 96DonCanIRPP-139
❑ 96FinnSISRS-4
❑ 96SelCer-105
❑ 96SelCerAP-105
❑ 96SelCerBlu-105
❑ 96SelCerMB-105
❑ 96SelCerMG-105
❑ 96SelCerMR-105
❑ 96SelCerRed-105
❑ 96UppDec-237
❑ 98KanCitB-6
❑ 98UppDec-163
❑ 98UppDecE-163
❑ 98UppDecE1o1-163
❑ 98UppDecGR-163

**Gronstrand, Jari**
❑ 88NordGenF-15
❑ 88NordTeal-16
❑ 89Nord-14
❑ 89NordGenF-11
❑ 91SweSemE-158
❑ 93FinnSIS-65
❑ 94GerDELE-400

**Gronvall, Janne**
❑ 91UppDec-672
❑ 91UppDecCWJC-35
❑ 91UppDecF-672
❑ 92Cla-32
❑ 93FinnJyvHS-291
❑ 93FinnSIS-64
❑ 94FinnSIS-159
❑ 94FinnSIS-175
❑ 94St.JohML-10
❑ 95ColEdgI-80
❑ 95FinnSISL-75
❑ 95St.JohML-10
❑ 96ClaGol-32

**Grosek, Michal**
❑ 93TacRoc-10
❑ 94ClaProP-9
❑ 94Fin-64
❑ 94FinRef-64
❑ 94FinSupTW-64
❑ 94Fle-241
❑ 94OPCPre-531
❑ 94OPCPreSE-531
❑ 94Par-266
❑ 94ParGol-266
❑ 94Pin-482
❑ 94PinArtP-482
❑ 94PinRinC-482
❑ 94TopPre-531
❑ 94TopPreSE-531
❑ 94Ult-393
❑ 94UppDec-433
❑ 94UppDecEleIce-433
❑ 95ColEdgI-68
❑ 95Don-125
❑ 95Lea-53
❑ 95ParInt-231
❑ 95ParIntEl-231
❑ 95UppDec-111
❑ 95UppDecEleIce-111
❑ 95UppDecEleIceG-111
❑ 97Be A PPAD-187
❑ 97Be A PPAPD-187
❑ 97BeAPla-187
❑ 97BeAPlaAut-187
❑ 97PacCroR-13
❑ 97PacCroREG-13
❑ 97PacCroRIB-13
❑ 97PacCroRS-13
❑ 97PacInvNRB-19
❑ 97PacOme-21
❑ 97PacOmeC-21
❑ 97PacOmeDG-21
❑ 97PacOmeEG-21
❑ 97PacOmeG-21
❑ 97PacOmeIB-21
❑ 97Sco-255
❑ 97ScoSab-8
❑ 97ScoSabPla-8
❑ 97ScoSabPre-8
❑ 98O-PChr-152
❑ 98O-PChrR-152
❑ 98Pac-105
❑ 98PacAur-16
❑ 98PacCroR-12
❑ 98PacCroRLS-12
❑ 98PacDynI-17
❑ 98PacDynIIB-17
❑ 98PacDynIR-17
❑ 98PacIceB-105
❑ 98PacOmeH-22
❑ 98PacOmeODI-22
❑ 98PacOmeR-22
❑ 98PacPar-18
❑ 98PacParC-18
❑ 98PacParEG-18
❑ 98PacParH-18
❑ 98PacParIB-18
❑ 98PacParS-18
❑ 98PacRed-105
❑ 98PacRev-13
❑ 98PacRevIS-13
❑ 98PacRevR-13
❑ 98SP Aut-10
❑ 98Top-152
❑ 98TopO-P-152
❑ 98UppDecM-25
❑ 98UppDecMGS-25
❑ 98UppDecMSS-25
❑ 98UppDecMSS-25
❑ 99Pac-36
❑ 99PacCop-36
❑ 99PacGol-36
❑ 99PacIceB-36
❑ 99PacPreD-36
❑ 99SP AutPS-10
❑ 99UppDecM-28
❑ 99UppDecMGS-28
❑ 99UppDecMSS-28
❑ 99UppDecMSS-28

**Gross, Lloyd**
❑ 34DiaMatS-27

**Gross, Pavel**
❑ 94GerDELE-277
❑ 95GerDELE-274
❑ 96GerDELE-169
❑ 98GerDELE-230

**Grosse, Erwin**
❑ 51LavDaiQSHL-64
❑ 52St.LawS-104

**Grossi, Dino**
❑ 94ClaProP-137

**Grossmann, Vitalij**
❑ 94GerDELE-161

**Grossmann, W.**
❑ 95GerDELE-161

**Grosso, Don**
❑ 34BeeGro1P-102
❑ 40OPCV3012-128

**Groten, Richard**
❑ 90ForSasTra-4

**Grotnes, Pal**
❑ 93SweSemE-313

**Groulx, Danny**
❑ 98Vald'OF-4

**Groulx, Wayne**
❑ 81SauSteMG-14
❑ 82SauSteMG-11
❑ 83SauSteMG-11
❑ 84SauSteMG-8
❑ 93SweSemWCS-278
❑ 94FinnJaaK-239

**Gruba, Tony**
❑ 94DayBom-15

**Grubb, Colin**
❑ 96FifFly-5

**Gruber, Bucky**
❑ 95NorIowH-11

**Gruden, John**
❑ 91FerStaB-14
❑ 94Cla-53
❑ 94ClaAllAme-AA2
❑ 94ClaDraGol-53
❑ 94Don-179
❑ 94Fle-11
❑ 94Lea-192
❑ 94OPCPre-447
❑ 94OPCPreSE-447
❑ 94TopPre-447
❑ 94TopPreSE-447
❑ 94Ult-254
❑ 95Top-104
❑ 95TopOPCI-104
❑ 96ProBru-4

**Gruen, Danny**
❑ 75OPCWHA-128

**Gruhl, Scott**
❑ 88ProIHL-52
❑ 89ProIHL-150
❑ 90ProAHLIHL-382
❑ 91ProAHLCHL-254
❑ 93ClaProPro-122
❑ 94RicRen-6
❑ 95RicRen-14
❑ 96RicRen-8

**Grundmann, Olaf**
❑ 94GerDELE-219
❑ 95GerDELE-196
❑ 96GerDELE-339

**Grundstrom, Goran**
❑ 83SweSemE-54

**Gruth, Henryk**
❑ 79PanSti-121
❑ 89SweSemWCS-133

**Gruttaduria, Mike**
❑ 95ForWorFT-14

**Gryp, Bob**
❑ 74NHLActSta-323
❑ 75OPCNHL-348

**Gschwill, Timo**
❑ 94GerDELE-191
❑ 95GerDELE-176

**Guadette, Andre**
❑ 73QuaOatWHA-22

**Guay, Bernard**
❑ 50QueCit-7

**Guay, Francois**
❑ 88ProAHL-267
❑ 89ProAHL-273
❑ 90ProAHLIHL-291
❑ 96GerDELE-172
❑ 98GerDELE-42

**Guay, Marc-Andre**
❑ 92QueIntP-36

**Guay, Paul**
❑ 84OPC-160
❑ 86Kin20tATI-8
❑ 87KinTeal4-8
❑ 88ProAHL-161
❑ 89ProAHL-212
❑ 90ProAHLIHL-513
❑ 91ProAHLCHL-611

**Gudas, Leo**
❑ 89SweSemWCS-186
❑ 93SwiHNL-194
❑ 94FinnJaaK-166
❑ 95SweGloWC-148
❑ 96SweSemW-112
❑ 98GerDELE-279

**Gudmundsson, Peter**
❑ 72SweHocS-157
❑ 73SweHocS-47
❑ 73SweWorCS-47
❑ 74SweHocS-217

**Guellet, Stephane**
❑ 907thInnSQMJHL-125

**Guenette, Luc**
❑ 85FreExp-17

**Guenette, Steve**
❑ 87PenKod-10
❑ 90ProAHLIHL-627
❑ 91ProAHLCHL-150

**Guenette, Sylvain**
❑ 92QueIntP-5

**Guennelon, Gerald**
❑ 94FinnJaaK-219
❑ 94FreNatT-14
❑ 95SweGloWC-206

**Guerard, Daniel**
❑ 93Cla-132

**Guerard, Stephane**
❑ 87NordGenF-13
❑ 88NordGenF-16
❑ 88NordTeal-17
❑ 89Nord-15
❑ 89NordGenF-12
❑ 89NordPol-10
❑ 90HalCit-9
❑ 90NordTeal-10
❑ 91NordPanTS-8

**Guerin, Bill**
❑ 91Par-453
❑ 91ParFre-453
❑ 92Cla-105
❑ 92OPC-308
❑ 92OPCPre-120
❑ 92Par-97
❑ 92ParEmel-97
❑ 92ProSet-230
❑ 92Sco-470
❑ 92ScoCan-470
❑ 92StaClu-17
❑ 92Top-516
❑ 92TopGol-516G
❑ 92Ult-338
❑ 92UppDec-411
❑ 93Don-186
❑ 93Lea-7
❑ 93OPCPre-421
❑ 93OPCPreG-421
❑ 93Par-382
❑ 93ParEmel-382
❑ 93Pin-305
❑ 93PinCan-305
❑ 93Sco-395
❑ 93ScoCan-395
❑ 93StaClu-467
❑ 93StaCluFDI-467
❑ 93StaCluO-467
❑ 93TopPre-421
❑ 93TopPreG-421
❑ 93Ult-359
❑ 94BeAPSig-50
❑ 94CanGamNHLP-350
❑ 94Don-62
❑ 94Fla-94
❑ 94Fle-112
❑ 94Lea-146
❑ 94OPCPre-231
❑ 94OPCPreSE-231
❑ 94Par-127
❑ 94ParGol-127
❑ 94Pin-23
❑ 94PinArtP-23
❑ 94PinRinC-23
❑ 94TopPre-231
❑ 94TopPreSE-231
❑ 94Ult-117
❑ 94UppDec-359
❑ 94UppDecEleIce-359
❑ 95CanGamNHLP-166
❑ 95ColCho-60
❑ 95ColChoPC-60
❑ 95ColChoPCP-60
❑ 95Don-35
❑ 95Fin-82
❑ 95FinRef-82
❑ 95Lea-201
❑ 95ParInt-124
❑ 95ParIntEl-124
❑ 95Pin-32
❑ 95PinArtP-32
❑ 95PinRinC-32
❑ 95PlaOneoOne-58
❑ 95Sco-106
❑ 95ScoBlaIce-106
❑ 95ScoBlaIceAP-106
❑ 95SP-82
❑ 95StaClu-130
❑ 95StaCluMOMS-130
❑ 95Sum-111
❑ 95SumArtP-111
❑ 95SumIce-111
❑ 95Top-88
❑ 95TopOPCI-88
❑ 95TopSupSki-44
❑ 95TopSupSkiPla-44
❑ 95Ult-191
❑ 95Ult-261
❑ 95UltGolM-191
❑ 95UppDec-373
❑ 95UppDecEleIce-373
❑ 95UppDecEleIceG-373
❑ 95UppDecSpeE-SE48
❑ 95UppDecSpeEdiG-SE48
❑ 96BeAPAut-29
❑ 96BeAPAutSil-29
❑ 96BeAPla-29
❑ 96ClaGol-105
❑ 96ColCho-146
❑ 96Dev-12
❑ 96Don-180
❑ 96DonEli-69
❑ 96DonEliDCS-69
❑ 96DonPrePro-180
❑ 96Fla-53
❑ 96FlaBluI-53
❑ 96LeaPre-108
❑ 96LeaPrePP-108
❑ 96Pin-170
❑ 96PinArtP-170
❑ 96PinFoi-170
❑ 96PinPreS-170
❑ 96PinRinC-170
❑ 96Sco-197
❑ 96ScoArtPro-197
❑ 96ScoDeaCAP-197
❑ 96ScoGolB-197
❑ 96ScoSpeAP-197
❑ 96SelCer-26
❑ 96SelCerAP-26
❑ 96SelCerBlu-26
❑ 96SelCerMB-26
❑ 96SelCerMG-26
❑ 96SelCerMR-26
❑ 96SelCerRed-26
❑ 96SkyImp-69
❑ 96SP-91
❑ 96TopNHLP-141
❑ 96TopPicOI-141
❑ 96UppDec-90
❑ 96UppDecBD-112
❑ 96UppDecBDG-112
❑ 96UppDecIce-35
❑ 96UppDecIcePar-35
❑ 96UppDecPP-P11
❑ 96Zen-106
❑ 96ZenArtP-106
❑ 97ColCho-147
❑ 97ColChoSta-SQ21
❑ 97Kat-82
❑ 97KatGol-82
❑ 97KatSil-82
❑ 97Pac-117
❑ 97PacCop-117
❑ 97PacEmeGre-117
❑ 97PacIceB-117
❑ 97PacOme-91
❑ 97PacOmeC-91
❑ 97PacOmeDG-91
❑ 97PacOmeEG-91
❑ 97PacOmeG-91
❑ 97PacOmeIB-91
❑ 97PacRed-117
❑ 97PacRev-54
❑ 97PacRevC-54
❑ 97PacRevE-54
❑ 97PacRevIB-54
❑ 97PacRevR-54
❑ 97PacRevS-54
❑ 97PacSil-117
❑ 97Pin-136
❑ 97PinIns-131
❑ 97PinPrePBB-136
❑ 97PinPrePBC-136
❑ 97PinPrePBM-136
❑ 97PinPrePBY-136
❑ 97PinPrePFC-136
❑ 97PinPrePFM-136
❑ 97PinPrePFY-136
❑ 97PinPrePla-136
❑ 97Sco-199
❑ 97ScoDev-5
❑ 97ScoDevPla-5
❑ 97ScoDevPre-5
❑ 97SPAut-86
❑ 97UppDecBD-38
❑ 97UppDecBDDD-38
❑ 97UppDecBDQD-38
❑ 97UppDecBDTD-38
❑ 97UppDecTSS-13C
❑ 98Be A PPA-53
❑ 98Be A PPAA-53
❑ 98Be A PPAAF-53
❑ 98Be A PPTBASG-53
❑ 98Be APG-53
❑ 98Fin-12
❑ 98FinNo P-12
❑ 98FinNo PR-12
❑ 98FinPro-PP5
❑ 98FinRef-12
❑ 98Pac-209
❑ 98PacAur-72
❑ 98PacCroR-51
❑ 98PacCroRLS-51
❑ 98PacDynI-72
❑ 98PacDynIIB-72
❑ 98PacDynIR-72
❑ 98PacIceB-209
❑ 98PacOmeH-92
❑ 98PacOmeODI-92
❑ 98PacOmeR-92
❑ 98PacPar-86
❑ 98PacParC-86
❑ 98PacParEG-86
❑ 98PacParH-86
❑ 98PacParIB-86
❑ 98PacParS-86
❑ 98PacRed-209
❑ 98PacRev-54
❑ 98PacRevIS-54
❑ 98PacRevR-54
❑ 98SP Aut-34
❑ 98SPxFin-36
❑ 98SPxFinR-36
❑ 98SPxFinS-36
❑ 98SPXTopP-26
❑ 98SPXTopPF-26
❑ 98SPXTopPR-26
❑ 98TopGolLC1-75
❑ 98TopGolLC1B-75
❑ 98TopGolLC1BOoO-75
❑ 98TopGolLC1OoO-75
❑ 98TopGolLC1R-75
❑ 98TopGolLC1ROoO-75
❑ 98TopGolLC2-75
❑ 98TopGolLC2B-75
❑ 98TopGolLC2BOoO-75
❑ 98TopGolLC2OoO-75
❑ 98TopGolLC2R-75
❑ 98TopGolLC2ROoO-75
❑ 98TopGolLC3-75
❑ 98TopGolLC3B-75
❑ 98TopGolLC3BOoO-75
❑ 98TopGolLC3OoO-75
❑ 98TopGolLC3R-75
❑ 98TopGolLC3ROoO-75
❑ 98UC-84
❑ 98UD ChoPCR-84
❑ 98UD ChoR-84
❑ 98UppDec-92
❑ 98UppDecBD-35
❑ 98UppDecDD-35
❑ 98UppDecE-92
❑ 98UppDecE1o1-92
❑ 98UppDecGR-92
❑ 98UppDecM-80
❑ 98UppDecMGS-80
❑ 98UppDecMPG-PG14

98UppDecMSS-80
98UppDecMSS-80
98UppDecQD-35
98UppDecTD-35
99Pac-155
99PacAur-56
99PacAurPD-56
99PacCop-155
99PacGol-155
99PacHomaA-10
99PacIceB-155
99PacPreD-155
99PacTeaL-11
99RetHoc-33
99SP AutPS-34
99UppDecM-78
99UppDecMGS-78
99UppDecMSS-78
99UppDecMSS-78
99UppDecRG-33
99UppDecRP-33
**Guetens, Vern**
94EriPan-16
**Guevremont, Jocelyn**
71CanuRoyB-4
71OPC-232
71TorSun-278
72CanuRoyB-6
72OPC-37
72SarProSta-222
72Top-75
73CanuRoyB-6
73OPC-143
73Top-142
74LipSou-48
74NHLActSta-276
74NHLActStaU-3
74OPCNHL-122
74Top-122
75OPCNHL-216
75Top-216
76OPCNHL-108
76Top-108
77OPCNHL-242
77Top-242
78OPC-94
78Top-94
79OPC-381
91FutTreC72-33
**Guidolin, Aldo**
44BeeGro2P-318
52St.LawS-17B
53Par-66
60CleBar-8
**Guidolin, Bep**
34BeeGro1P-17
44BeeGro2P-99
51LavDaiS-114
51Par-42
52St.LawS-65
74OPCNHL-34
74Top-34
**Guillaume, Olivier**
91thInnSQMJHL-248
**Guillet, Robert**
88RivDu R-13
907thInnSQMJHL-241
917thInnSQMJHL-129
92FreCan-12
93FreCan-12
95MilAdmBO-7
98GerDELE-111
**Guilmette, Yves**
77KalWin-12
**Guindon, Bob**
72NordPos-12
73NordTeal-13
740PCWHA-26
78JetPos-7
**Guinn, Rob**
94SarSti-20
95Cla-96
95Sla-47
**Guirestante, John**
93LonKni-11
93LonKni-25
93NorBayC-19
94NorBayC-22
**Guitard, Dean**
87SudWol-19
**Guite, Pierre**
72NordPos-13
73NordTeal-14
750PCWHA-17
75StiKah-4
760PCWHA-123
**Gula, Ladislav**
94CzeAPSE-94
**Gulash, Garry**
92BriColJHL-10
96RicRen-9
**Gulda, Peter**
94GerDELE-262
95FinnSemWC-166
95GerDELE-247
96GerDELE-139
98GerDELE-81
98GerDELE-328
**Gullberg, Weine**
71SweHocS-334
72SweHocS-144
**Gullion, Brett**
90ForSasTra-5
**Gulutzan, Glen**
907thInnSWHL-222
90BraWheK-24
917thInnSWHL-112
91SasBla-13
**Gunis, Michal**
96SloPeeWT-9
**Gunler, Joakim**
92SweSemE-183
93SweSemE-157
**Gunn, Jim**
83VicCou-8
**Gunn, Roydon**
84PriAlbRS-11
**Gunnar, Lars**
72SweHocS-206
79PanSti-198
**Gunnarsson, Soren**
71SweHocS-266
72SweHocS-244
74SweHocS-168
**Gunther, Petri**
96DenUniPio-4
**Guntner, Michael**
93SweSemWCS-276
94FinnJaaK-234
95AusNatTea-7
**Gunville, Ron**
89LetHur-6
91AirCanSJLH-D15
**Guolla, Steve**
93MicSta-9
96KenTho-8
97ColCho-220
97Pac-281
97PacCop-281
97PacDyn-112
97PacDynC-112
97PacDynDG-112
97PacDynEG-112
97PacDynIB-112
97PacDynR-112
97PacDynSil-112
97PacDynTan-66
97PacEmeGre-281
97PacIceB-281
97PacInv-126
97PacInvC-126
97PacInvEG-126
97PacInvIB-126
97PacInvR-126
97PacInvS-126
97PacRed-281
97PacSil-281
97UppDec-148
**Gurejev, Vladimir**
73SweHocS-118
73SweWorCS-118
**Guren, Milos (Miloslav)**
94CzeAPSE-186
94SP-154
94SPDieCut-154
95CzeAPSE-35
95SigRoo-56
95SigRooSig-56
98UppDec-296
98UppDecE-296
98UppDecE101-296
98UppDecGR-296
99Pac-216
99PacCop-216
99PacGol-216
99PacIceB-216
99PacPreD-216
**Gusarov, Alexei**
87RusNatT-6
89RusNatT-7
89SweSemWCS-82
91Bow-145
91NordPet-9
91OPC-355
91PanSti-260
91Par-364
91ParFre-364
91Pin-230
91PinFre-230
91ProSet-207
91ProSetFre-207
91ProSetPla-221
91RusStaNHL-7
91RusStaRA-5
91ScoAme-326
91ScoCan-356
91StaClu-330
91Top-355
91UppDec-365
91UppDecF-365
92NorPet-9
920PC-389
92PanSti-215
92PanStiFre-215
92Pin-161
92PinFre-161
92ProSet-147
92Sco-264
92ScoCan-264
92StaClu-451
92Ult-173
92UppDec-127
930PCPre-293
930PCPreG-293
93Par-441
93ParEmel-441
93Pin-261
93PinCan-261
93Pow-420
93Sco-260
93ScoCan-260
93StaClu-424
93StaCluFDI-424
93StaCluO-424
93TopPre-293
93TopPreG-293
93UppDec-362
94Don-216
94FinnJaaK-159
94Lea-408
94NordBurK-9
94ParSE-SE148
94ParSEG-SE148
94Pin-164
94PinArtP-164
94PinRinC-164
94StaClu-67
94StaCluFDI-67
94StaCluMOMS-67
94StaCluSTWC-67
95SweGloWC-168
97Be A PPAD-196
97Be A PPAPD-196
97BeAPla-196
97BeAPlaAut-196
97PacInvNRB-52
98Be A PPA-183
98Be A PPAA-183
98Be A PPAAF-183
98Be A PPSE-183
98Be APG-183
**Gusev, Alexander**
73SweHocS-82
73SweWorCS-82
74SweHocS-4
74SweSemHVS-30
91FutTreC72-19
**Gusev, Sergei**
74SweHocS-43
98Be A PPA-192
98Be A PPAA-192
98Be A PPAAF-192
98Be A PPSE-192
98Be APG-192
98PacDynI-54
98PacDynIIB-54
98PacDynIR-54
98PacOmeI-78
98PacOmeODI-78
98PacOmeR-78
**Gusmanov, Ravil**
91UppDecCWJC-3
94Cla-73
94ClaDraGol-73
94ClaTri-T76
94Fin-107
94FinRef-107
94FinSupTW-107
940PCPre-323
940PCPreSE-323
94ParSE-SE205
94ParSEG-SE205
94TopPre-323
94TopPreSE-323
94UppDec-254
94UppDecEIeIce-254
**Gustafsson, Cory**
92HarCri-11
**Gustafson, Jon**
91RicRen-16
92RicRen-6
93RicRen-20
94CenHocL-9
**Gustafsson, Bengt**
800PC-222
80Top-222
81OPC-353
82Cap-8
820PC-364
820PCSti-157
82PosCer-20
830PC-370
84CapPizH-7
840PC-198
840PCSti-130
84Top-144
85CapPizH-6
87CapKod-16
87CapTealss-7
88CapBor-7
88CapSmo-7
880PC-151
88PanSti-371
88Top-151
89SweSemE-89
90SweSemE-259
910PCIns-2S
91SweSemE-91
91SweSemE-348
91SweSemWCS-45
92SweSemE-116
93SweSemWCS-15
**Gustafsson, Claes**
87SwePanS-263
**Gustafsson, Lennart**
67SweHoc-45
**Gustafsson, Magnus**
90SweSemE-220
**Gustafsson, Per**
89SweSemE-104
90SweSemE-106
91SweSemE-111
92SweSemE-131
93SweSemE-104
94SweLeaE-276
95SweLeaE-231
95SweLeaEFF-6
95SweLeaEM-15
95SweLeaUppDE-76
95SweUppDE-226
95SweUppDE-253
95SweUppDETNA-NA11
96MetUni-58
96SP-179
96UppDec-267
96UppDecBD-40
96UppDecBDG-40
97Be A PPAD-69
97Be A PPAPD-69
97BeAPla-69
97BeAPlaAut-69
97Pac-165
97PacCop-165
97PacEmeGre-165
97PacIceB-165
97PacRed-165
97PacSil-165
97St.JohML-12
**Gustafsson, Peter**
89SweSemE-46
90SweSemE-192
91SweSemE-45
92SweSemE-70
**Gustafsson, Tomas**
84SweSemE-158
**Gustavson, Ben**
95Sla-268
**Gustavson, Stefan**
90SweSemE-291
94SweLeaE-296
95SweLeaE-10
95SweUppDE-9
**Gustavsson, Bengt**
67SweHoc-137
69SweHocS-148
71SweHocS-262
**Gustavsson, Bengt-Ake**
67SweHoc-5
67SweHoc-138
69SweHocS-149
70SweHocS-112
71SweHocS-201
72SweHocS-181
82SweSemHVS-146
89SweSemWCS-20
**Gustavsson, Charles**
67SweHoc-201
**Gustavsson, Gote**
70SweHocS-219
72SweHocS-279
**Gustavsson, Jakob**
83SweSemE-27
84SweSemE-27
85SwePanS-25
86SwePanS-4
**Gustavsson, Kjell-Ove**
65SweCorI-98
67SweHoc-266
71SweHocS-310
**Gustavsson, Lars Ake**
70SweHocS-113
71SweHocS-202
73SweHocS-213
73SweWorCS-213
**Gustavsson, Lars-Anders**
69SweHocS-279
70SweHocS-187
72SweHocS-101
**Gustavsson, Lennart**
69SweHocS-117
71SweHocS-324
72SweHocS-355
**Gustavsson, Patrik**
90SweSemE-119
91SweSemE-195
**Gustavsson, Per**
95ColCho-343
95ColChoPC-343
95ColChoPCP-343
**Gustavsson, Peter**
83SweSemE-243
89SweSemE-282
**Gustavsson, Thomas**
83SweSemE-211
93SweSemE-109
95SweLeaE-225
95SweUppDE-82
**Guttler, Georg**
94GerDELE-165
95GerDELE-155
**Guy, Kevan**
82MedHatT-4
83MedHatT-14
85MonGolF-16
86MonGolF-10
88CanuMoh-9
89ProIHL-177
90CanuMoh-10
90ProSet-545
91CanuPanTS-9
91ProAHLCHL-576
**Guy, Mark**
897thInnSOHL-27
907thInnSOHL-133
**Guzda, Brad**
98LasVegT-6
**Guze, Ray**
92BriColJHL-120
93LasVegThu-10
94LasVegThu-6
95GerDELE-15
**Gylywoychuk, Dwayne**
89BraWheK-19
907thInnSWHL-218
90BraWheK-13
917thInnSWHL-210
92BraWheK-8
94GreMon-15
95DayBom-30
**Gyori, Arpad**
94CzeAPSE-115
96CzeAPSE-254
**Gyori, Dylan**
95TriAme-11
96UppDec-381
98BowCHL-51
98BowCHLGA-51
98BowCHLOI-51
98BowChrC-51
98BowChrCGA-51
98BowChrCGAR-51
98BowChrCOI-51
98BowChrCOIR-51
**Haakana, Kari**
93FinnSIS-264
94FinnSIS-121
95FinnSIS-285
96FinnSISR-84
98GerDELE-309
**Haake, Bernd**
94GerDELE-199
95GerDELE-194
96GerDELE-337
**Haakstad, Jason**
92BriColJHL-47
**Haanpaa, Ari**
91SweSemWCS-13
93FinnJyvHS-287
93FinnSIS-76
94FinnSIS-22
93FinnSIS-320
95FinnSISL-79
**Haapakoski, Mikko**
93FinnSIS-378
93SweSemWCS-49
93SwiHNL-65
94FinnJaaK-6
95FinnSemWC-48
95SwiHNL-88
**Haapalainen, Hannu**
74SweSemHVS-94
**Haapaniemi, Miro**
93FinnSIS-103
94FinnSIS-96
95FinnSIS-210
**Haapsaari, Tommi**
93FinnJyvHS-296
93FinnSIS-67
94FinnSIS-60
95FinnSIS-112
**Haarmann, Mark**
830shGen-7
**Haarstad, Tor**
65SweCorI-155
**Haas, Dave (David)**
85LonKni-14
88ProAHL-79
89ProAHL-141
90ProAHLIHL-220
91ProAHLCHL-224
98GerDELE-186
**Haas, Julius**
69SweWorC-151
70SweHocS-355
**Haas, Rostislav**
96CzeAPSE-98
**Habscheid, Marc**
81SasBla-14
820ilRedR-23
83MonAlp-26
84NovScoO-14
84OilRedR-23
88NorStaADA-13
88OilTenAnn-59
89OPC-151
890PCSti-198
89RedWinLC-8
89Top-151
90Bow-228
90BowTif-228
900PC-342
90PanSti-204
90ProSet-437
90ScoRoo-24T
90Top-342
90TopTif-342
90UppDec-374
90UppDecF-374
910PC-250
91PanSti-138
91ProSet-365
91ProSetFre-365
91RedWinLC-8
91ScoCan-583
91ScoRoo-33T
91Top-250
92Sco-546
92ScoCan-546
**Hachborn, Len**
83SprInd-4
90ProAHLIHL-4
91ProAHLIHL-318
**Hackett, Jeff**
88ProAHL-304
89PanSti-276
89ProAHL-236
900PCPre-99
90ProSet-624
90Sco-388
90ScoCan-388
91Bow-219
910PC-382
910PCPre-108
91PanSti-240
91Pin-119
91PinFre-119
91ProSet-331
91ProSetFre-331
91ProSetPla-226
91ScoAme-367
91ScoCan-326
91ScoCan-642
91ScoRoo-92T
91ShaSanJSA-8
91Top-382
91UppDec-58
91UppDecF-58
92Bow-348
92Kra-29
920PC-218
92PanSti-123
92PanStiFre-123
92Par-162
92ParEmel-162
92Pin-105
92PinFre-105
92ProSet-171
92Sco-82
92ScoCan-82
92StaClu-108
92Top-185
92TopGol-185G
92Ult-195
92UppDec-308
93BlaCok-19
93Don-61
93Lea-319
93Par-312
93ParEmel-312
93Pin-373
93PinCan-373
93Pow-312
93Sco-38
93ScoCan-38
93ScoCan-541
93ScoGol-541
93StaClu-326
93StaCluFDI-326
93StaCluO-326
94Don-35
94Lea-218
95ParInt-44
95ParIntEI-44
95UppDec-387
95UppDecEIeIce-387
95UppDecEIeIceG-387
96BeAPAut-42
96BeAPAutSil-42
96BeAPla-42
96ColCho-54
96Don-88
96DonPrePro-88
96Fle-147
96Lea-54
96LeaPreP-54
96Pin-110
96PinArtP-110
96PinFoi-110
96PinPreS-110
96PinRinC-110
96Sco-85
96ScoArtPro-85
96ScoDeacAP-85
96ScoGolB-85
96ScoSpeAP-85
96UppDec-30
97ColCho-47
97Don-116
97DonCanI-101
97DonCanIDS-101
97DonCanIPS-101
97DonLim-160
97DonLimExp-160
97DonPre-139
97DonPreCttC-139
97DonPreProG-116
97DonPrePros-116
97DonPri-68
97DonPriSoA-68
97Kat-34
97KatGol-34
97KatSil-34
97Lea-32
97LeaFraMat-32
97LeaFraMDC-32
97LeaInt-32
97LeaIntUI-32
97Pac-160
97PacCop-160
97PacCroR-30
97PacCroREG-30
97PacCroRIB-30
97PacCroRS-30
97PacDyn-27
97PacDynC-27
97PacDynDG-27
97PacDynEG-27
97PacDynIB-27
97PacDynR-27
97PacDynSil-27
97PacDynSto-5
97PacDynTan-39
97PacEmeGre-160
97PacIceB-160
97PacInTheCLC-4
97PacInv-30
97PacInvC-30
97PacInvEG-30
97PacInvIB-30
97PacInvR-30
97PacOme-51
97PacOmeC-51
97PacOmeDG-51
97PacOmeEG-51
97PacOmeG-51
97PacOmeIB-51
97Par-44
97ParC-44
97ParDG-44
97ParEG-44
97ParGSL-4
97ParIB-44
97ParRed-44
97ParSil-44
97PacRev-30
97PacRevC-30
97PacRevE-30
97PacRevIB-30
97PacRevR-30
97PacRevRStD-4
97PacRevS-30
97PacSil-160
97Pin-72
97PinArtP-72
97PinCer-30
97PinCerMB-30
97PinCerMG-30
97PinCerMR-30
97PinCerR-30
97PinIns-41
97PinInsCC-41
97PinInsEC-41
97PinInsSto-8
97PinInsSUG-7A/B
97PinInsSUG-7C/D
97PinMas-7
97PinMasDC-7
97PinMasJ-7
97PinMasPro-7
97PinPrePBB-72
97PinPrePBC-72
97PinPrePBM-72
97PinPrePBY-72
97PinPrePFC-72
97PinPrePFM-72
97PinPrePFY-72
97PinPrePla-72
97PinRinC-72
97PinTin-3
97PinTotCMPG-30
97PinTotCPB-30
97PinTotCPG-30
97PinTotCPR-30
97Sco-15
97ScoArtPro-15
97ScoGolBla-15
97UppDec-38
98Be A PPA-27
98Be A PPAA-27
98Be A PPAAF-27
98Be A PPTBASG-27
98Be APG-27
98BowBes-63
98BowBesAR-63
98BowBesR-63
98Fin-86
98FinNo P-86
98FinNo PR-86
98FinRef-86
98O-PChr-93
98O-PChrR-93
98O-PChrSB-SB5
98O-PChrSBR-SB5
98Pac-144
98PacAur-41
98PacCroR-69
98PacCroRLS-69
98PacDynI-42
98PacDynIIB-42
98PacDynIR-42
98PacIceB-144
98PacOmeH-121
98PacOmeODI-121
98PacOmeR-121
98PacPar-48
98PacParC-48
98PacParGSLC-5
98PacParIB-48
98PacParS-48
98PacRed-144
98PacRev-73
98PacRevIS-73
98PacRevR-73

98SPxFin-21
98SPxFinR-21
98SPxFinS-21
98Top-93
98TopO-P-93
98TopSeaB-SB5
98UC-49
98UD ChoPCR-49
98UD ChoR-49
99Pac-203
99PacAur-74
99PacAurGU-10
99PacAurPD-74
99PacCop-203
99PacGol-203
99PacIceB-203
99PacIn tCN-9
99PacPreD-203
99UppDecM-104
99UppDecMGS-104
99UppDecMPS-JH
99UppDecMSS-104
99UppDecMSS-104

**Hacquoil, Frank**
23V1281PauC-59

**Hadamczik, Alois**
94CzeAPSE-287
95CzeAPSE-219

**Haddad, John**
95AlaGolKin-6

**Hadden, Greg**
92NorMicW-8
93NorMicW-9
95RicRen-1

**Hadfield, Vic**
44BeeGro2P-319
61ShiCoi-97
62Top-60
63Top-54
64BeeGro3P-129
64CocCap-81
64Top-62
65Coc-82
65Top-27
66Top-86
66TopUSAT-19
67Top-88
68OPC-171
68ShiCoi-105
68Top-74
69OPC-38
69Top-38
70ColSta-45
70DadCoo-45
70EssPowPla-188
70OPC-62
70SarProSta-126
70Top-62
71LetActR-4
71OPC-9
71SarProSta-121
71Top-9
71TorSun-174
720PC-31
720PC-250
720PC-272
720PCTeaC-13
72SarProSta-151
72SweHocS-117
72Top-61
72Top-110
72Top-132
73OPC-108
73Top-181
74NHLActSta-233
74OPCNHL-65
74PenPos-7
74Top-65
75OPCNHL-165
75Top-165
760PCNHL-226
76Top-226
91FutTreC72-36
91UltOriS-21
91UltOriSF-21
94ParTalB-90
95Par66-98
95Par66Coi-98

**Hadraschek, C.**
95GerDELE-36

**Haegglund, Roger**
84FreExp-4

**Haelzle, Jason**
92WinSpi-4

**Hagg, Lars**
65SweCorl-65

**Haggerty, Ryan**
95ColEdgl-3
96WheNai-33

**Haggerty, Sean**
93Cla-103
93DetJrRW-21
93DetJrRW-23
94Fin-119
94FinRef-119
94FinSupTW-119
94LeaLimWJUSA-6
94SP-191
94SPDieCut-191
95Cla-84
95SigRoo-51
95SigRooSig-51
95Sla-69
95Sla-NNO
95SlaMemC-97

96KenTho-9
96Pin-215
96PinArtP-215
96PinFoi-215
96PinRinC-215
96Sum-177
96SumArtP-177
96SumIce-177
96SumMet-177
96SumPreS-177

**Hagglund, Roger**
83SweSemE-231
86SwePanS-11
87SwePanS-30

**Haggroth, Lennart**
64SweCorl-12
64SweCorl-136
65SweCorl-12
65SweCorl-136
69SweHocS-79
96SweSemWHL-HL10

**Haggstrom, Olle**
84SweSemE-203

**Haglsperger, J.**
95GerDELE-355

**Hagman, Matti**
79PanSti-172
80PepCap-26
81OilRedR-10
81OPC-113
82OPC-108
82OPCSti-103
82PosCer-6
82SweSemHVS-156
88OilTenAnn-58
92FutTre76CC-148
92FutTre76CC-187
96FinnSISR-199

**Hagrenius, Jonathan**
92SweSemE-309

**Hagstrom, Anders**
67SweHoc-6
67SweHoc-255
69SweHocS-300
70SweHocS-199
71SweHocS-285
72SweHocS-68

**Hagstrom, Lars**
65SweCorl-160

**Hagstrom, Peter**
92SweSemE-122
95SweUppDE1DS-DS13

**Hague, Alan**
93SheSte-2
94SheSte-13
95SolBar-10

**Haider, Reinhard**
94GerDELE-29

**Haidy, Sam**
82SauSteMG-12
83SauSteMG-11

**Haig, John**
97FifFly-15

**Haig, Scot**
93OmaLan-8

**Haight, Steve**
92OshGenS-12

**Hainsworth, George**
23V1281PauC-39
27LaPat-8
330PCV304A-15
33V129-13
33V252CanG-28
34BeeGro1P-321
55Par-59
55ParQuaO-59
83HalFP-J7
85HalFC-187
94ParMisLP-P2

**Hajdu, Richard**
83VicCou-9
84VicCou-10

**Hajdusek, Stanislav**
82SweSemHVS-81

**Hajt, Bill**
750PCNHL-233
75Top-233
760PCNHL-128
76Top-128
770PCNHL-27
77Top-27
780PC-108
78Top-108
790PC-221
79Top-221
800PC-337
81SabMIIP-9
82PosCer-2
830PC-64
84KelWin-50
840PC-21
840PCSti-214
84SabBluS-7
84Top-7
850PC-119
850PCSti-176
85SabBluS-10
85SabBluS-10
85Top-119
860PC-52
86SabBluS-12
86SabBluSSma-12
86Top-52
87PanSti-26

**Hajt, Chris**
94GueSto-7
95BowDraPro-P16
95Cla-61
95Cla-85
95GueSto5A-13
95Sla-87
95Sla-436
96ColEdgSS&D-5
96GueSto-7
96GueSto-35
96GueStoPC-11
97BowCHL-35
97BowCHLOPC-35
97GueSto-7
98BowCHL-2
98BowCHLGA-2
98BowCHLOI-2
98BowChrC-2
98BowChrCGA-2
98BowChrCGAR-2
98BowChrCOI-2
98BowChrCOIR-2
98BowChrCR-2
98UC-299
98UD ChoPCR-299
98UD ChoR-299

**Hakanen, Timo**
95ColCho-327
95ColChoPC-327
95ColChoPCP-327
95FinnSIS-366
95FinnSISDD-9
96FinnSISR-159

**Hakansson, Anders**
81NorStaPos-10
83PenHeiP-10
84KinSmo-7
840PC-85

**Hakansson, Jonas**
91SweSemE-199
92SweSemE-216

**Hakansson, Mikael**
91SweSemE-329
92SweSemE-94
93Par-539
93ParEmel-539
93SweSemE-66
94SweLeaE-208
95SweLeaE-106
95SweUppDE-164

**Hakstol, Dave**
92IndIce-12

**Hakulinen, Markku**
82SweSemHVS-47

**Hala, Jiri**
94CzeAPSE-96

**Hale, Larry**
70EssPowPla-215
70SarProSta-155
71SarProSta-154
71TorSun-196
720PC-53
72Top-44

**Hale, Rob**
88LetHur-10
89LetHur-7

**Haley, John**
90RicRen-16

**Haley, Mike**
95SpoChi-17

**Halfnight, Ashlin**
93DonTeaUSA-8
93Pin-482
93PinCan-482

**Halifax, Sean**
93RedDeeR-8

**Halkidis, Bob**
85LonKni-7
85SabBluS-11
85SabBluSS-11
86SabBluS-13
86SabBluSSma-13
87SabBluS-10
88SabBluS-8
88SabWonBH-8
89ProAHL-270
91MapLeaP-16
92ProSet-190
94LigPhoA-15
98GerDELE-91

**Halko, Steve**
93MicWol-8
96SprFal-20
97CarHur-10

**Hall, Billy**
917thInnSOHL-297
92Ott672A-11

**Hall, Chris**
92OshGenS-8
93OshGen-23
95SlaMemC-53

**Hall, Dean**
89JohChi-28

**Hall, Del**
75RoaPhoWHA-9
760PCWHA-78
76RoaPhoWHA-4

**Hall, Glenn**
44BeeGro2P-100
44BeeGro2P-175
57Top-20
58Top-13
59Top-28
59Top-32

60ShiCoi-61
60Top-25
60TopSta-20
61ShiCoi-29
61Top-22
61Top-32
61Top-44
62EIProDis-2
62ShiMetC-49
62Top-24
62TopHocBuc-8
63ChePho-17
63Top-23
63TorSta-15
64BeeGro3P-35
64CocCap-19
64Top-12
64Top-110
64TorSta-17
65Coc-19
65Top-55
66Top-54
66Top-126
67Top-65
67Top-129
68OPC-215
68OPCPucSti-13
68ShiCoi-151
68Top-111
69OPC-12
69OPC-207
69OPC-211
69OPCSta-11
69Top-12
70EssPowPla-235
70OPC-210
70OPCDec-27
72SweSemWC-187
83HalFP-H8
85HalFC-114
91AriIce-19
91StaPicH-52
92BluUDBB-1
94ParMisL-46
94ParMisL-141
94ParMisL-146
94ParMisL-158
94ParMisL-159
94ParTalB-32
94ParTalB-133
94ParTalB-165
94ParTalB-166
95Par66-31
95Par66-121
95Par66Coi-31
98BlaLeg-2
99RetHoc-93
99UppDecCL-17
99UppDecCLCLC-17
99UppDecRG-93
99UppDecRG-G3A
99UppDecRGI-G3A
99UppDecRP-93

**Hall, Jason**
90RayJrC-8
91RayJrC-6

**Hall, Joe**
10C55SweCP-2
11C55-2
12C57-16

**Hall, John**
90RicRen-16

**Hall, Murray**
44BeeGro2P-101
62Top-43
64BeeGro3P-36
64BeeGro3P-73
66Top-105
70CanuRoyB-6
70EssPowPla-51
700PC-118
70SarProSta-224
70Top-118
71CanuRoyB-3
710PC-109
71SarProSta-211
71Top-109
71TorSun-279
720PC-294
72SarProSta-212
73QuaOatWHA-14

**Hall, Randy**
897thInnSOHL-132
89NiaFalT-7
907thInnSOHL-74
917thInnSOHL-210
93NiaFalT-26

**Hall, Scott**
92BriColJHL-219

**Hall, Taylor**
81RegPat-15
82RegPat-19
83RegPat-19
84Canu-10
85Canu-9
86Canu-9
86FreExp-10
90ProAHLIHL-303
92-TulOil-8
94CenHocL-97

**Hall, Todd**
91UppDecCWJC-77

**Hallback, Mathias**
92SweSemE-98

93SweSemE-71
94SweLeaE-241

**Hallegard, Jeff**
83SweSemE-98
86SwePanS-76

**Haller, Kevin**
88RegPat-7
90ProAHLIHL-265
91Bow-28
91OPC-473
91Pin-307
91PinFre-307
91ProSet-525
91ProSetFre-525
91ProSetPla-250
91RochAmeKod-14
92Bow-301
92CanaPos-12
92OPC-290
92Pin-211
92PinFre-211
92Sco-159
92ScoCan-159
92StaClu-38
92Top-445
92TopGol-445G
92Ult-327
92UppDec-479
93CanaMol-6
93CanaPos-11
93Don-168
93Lea-223
930PCCanHF-8
930PCPre-339
930PCPreG-339
93Par-376
93ParEmel-376
93Pin-193
93PinCan-193
93Pow-370
93Sco-268
93ScoCan-268
93StaClu-53
93StaCluFDI-53
93StaCluFDIO-53
93StaCluU0-53
93TopPre-339
93TopPreG-339
93Ult-352
93UppDec-333
94BeAPla-R56
94BeAPSig-56
94Lea-371
94OPCPre-351
94OPCPreSE-351
94Par-120
94ParGol-120
94ParSE-SE126
94ParSEG-SE126
94Pin-373
94PinArtP-373
94PinRinC-373
94TopPre-351
94TopPreSE-351
94UppDec-144
94UppDecEIeIce-144
94UppDecNBAP-23
95ColCho-295
95ColChoPC-295
95ColChoPCP-295
95ParInt-430
95ParIntEI-430
95PlaOneoOne-292
95Top-178
95TopOPCI-178
95UppDec-357
95UppDecEIeIce-357
95UppDecEIeIceG-357
97Be A PPAD-98
97Be A PPAPD-98
97BeAPla-98
97BeAPlaAut-98
97CarHur-11
97PacInvNRB-36
97UppDec-242
99Pac-6
99PacCop-6
99PacGol-6
99PacIceB-6
99PacPreD-6

**Hallgren, Rolf**
67SweHoc-28

**Hallin, Mats**
81IndChe-6
82IndChe-7
83IslTeaIss-5
830PC-8
830PCSti-184
84IsIsIlN-8
85IsIsIlN-7
85NorStaPos-12
87SwePanS-241
90SweSemE-137
91SweSemE-187

**Halme, Jari**
94FinnSIS-37

**Halonen, Marko**

93FinnSIS-205
93FinnSIS-262

**Halonen, Mikko**
93FinnJyvHS-208
93FinnSIS-225
94FinnSIS-172
94FinnSIS-334

**Halpenny, Scott**
87BroBra-11

**Haltia, Patrik**
90SweSemE-250
91SweSemE-81
92SweSemE-103
94SweLeaE-215
94SweLeaENHLD-7
94SweLeaERR-8
95SweLeaE-39
95SweLeaES-5

**Halttunen, Niko**
94Fin-132
94FinRef-132
94FinSupTW-132
94ParSE-SE220
94ParSEG-SE220
95FinnSIS-51

**Halverson, Don**
95PriAlbR-6
96PriAlbR-6
96PriAlbROC-7

**Halverson, Trevor**
897thInnSOHL-157
907thInnSOHL-308
91AreDraPic-16
91BalSki-3
91Cla-18
91ProAHLCHL-555
91StaPicH-14
91UltDra-17
91UltDra-73
94HamRoaA-7
95HamRoaA-16
96PorPir-28

**Halward, Doug**
760PCNHL-306
77RocAme-13
780PC-392
80KinCarN-3
800PC-207
80Top-207
81CanuSIID-6
81CanuTeal-10
810PC-335
82Canu-9
82PosCer-19
83Canu-9
830PC-351
830PCSti-278
84Canu-11
840PC-320
840PCSti-278
85Canu-10
850PC-189
850PCSti-243
86KraDra-24
860PC-248
860PCSti-97
87RedWinLC-13
880ilTeal-9
880ilTenAnn-157
880PC-113
88Top-113

**Ham, Zach**
94DubFigS-10

**Hamalainen, Erik**
93FinnJyvHS-106
93FinnSIS-12
93FinnSIS-362
93FinnSIS-374
94FinnSIS-98
95FinnBecAC-4
95FinnKarWCL-1
95FinnSIS-178
95FinnSISGC-5
95SweLeaE-163
95SweUppDE-2
96SweSemW-4

**Hamalainen, Jarkko**
93FinnJyvHS-265
93FinnSIS-287

**Hamalainen, Tero**
95FinnSIS-209
96FinnSISR-14
96FinnSISRRE-4

**Hamalainen, Tommi**
93FinnSIS-90

**Haman, Radek**
95CzeAPSE-215

**Hamel, Denis**
97BowCHL-70
97BowCHLOPC-70

**Hamel, Gilles**
840PC-22
84SabBluS-8
850PCSti-185
85SabBluS-13
85SabBluS-12
86Jet-8
87Jet-8

870PC-218
870PCSti-253
87PanSti-366
88KinSmo-12
88ProAHL-174

**Hamel, Jean**
72BluWhiBor-5
73BluWhiBor-8
74NHLActSta-91
740PCNHL-383
750PCNHL-257
75Top-257
760PCNHL-340
770PCNHL-348
780PC-281
790PC-262
79RedWinP-4
79Top-262
810PC-97
82NordPos-9
83CanaPos-10
83NordPos-12
83Vac-45
84CanaPos-9
840PC-263
840PCSti-158
88ProAHL-289
89ProAHL-201
917thInnSQMJHL-294
93DruVol-25

**Hamel, Pierre**
79JetPos-8
80JetPos-9
800PC-205
80PepCap-128
80Top-205
810PC-365
810PCSti-143

**Hamelin, Craig**
93RenEng-11

**Hamelin, Hugo**
917thInnSQMJHL-101

**Hamelin, Richard**
907thInnSQMJHL-187
917thInnSQMJHL-56

**Hamill, Red**
34BeeGro1P-18
44BeeGro2P-102

**Hamilton, Al**
680PC-70
690PC-192
70DadCoo-46
70EssPowPla-77
70SarProSta-22
710PC-49
71SarProSta-23
71Top-49
71TorSun-28
72SluCupWHA-9
73QuaOatWHA-16
740PCWHA-29
74TeaCanLWHA-4
750PCWHA-49
760PCWHA-97
770PCWHA-40
790ilPos-10
790PC-355
880ilTenAnn-63

**Hamilton, Bob**
61HamRed-6
61HamRed-5
61HamRed-8

**Hamilton, Colin**
96FifFly-6
97FifFly-18

**Hamilton, Dave**
917thInnSWHL-51

**Hamilton, Gord**
820tt67-5
830tt67-8
830tt67-9
94SarSti-28

**Hamilton, Hugh**
94ParSE-SE253
94ParSEG-SE253
95SigRoo-16
95SigRooSig-16
95SpoChi-3
96UppDecIce-124
97BowCHL-83
97BowCHLOPC-83
98FloEve-8

**Hamilton, Jack**
51LavDaiS-65
52St.LawS-101

**Hamilton, Jim**
77PenPucB-23
83PenCok-11
83PenTeaIP-13

**Hamilton, Lee**
95LetHur-7

**Hamilton, Reg**
34BeeGro1P-322
370PCV304-137
38QuaOatP-16
390PCV3011-1
400PCV3012-119

**Hamilton, Steve**
92NorMicW-9
93NorMicW-10

**Hamm, Trent**
91AirCanSJHL-C14
94AirCanSJHLAS-8

**Hammarstrom, Inge**
67SweHoc-7
67SweHoc-219

❑ 69SweHocS-58
❑ 70SweHocS-26
❑ 71SweHocS-13
❑ 71SweHocS-103
❑ 72SweHocS-11
❑ 72SweHocS-89
❑ 72SweSemWC-61
❑ 73MapLeaP-9
❑ 73SweHocS-12
❑ 73SweHocS-164
❑ 73SweWorCS-12
❑ 73SweWorCS-164
❑ 74MapLeaP-9
❑ 74NHLActSta-258
❑ 74OPCNHL-88
❑ 74SweHocS-313
❑ 74Top-88
❑ 75MapLeaP-9
❑ 75MapLeaP-10
❑ 75OPCNHL-168
❑ 75Top-168
❑ 76MapLeaP-8
❑ 76OPCNHL-358
❑ 77MapLeaP-6
❑ 77OPCNHL-320
❑ 78BluPos-13
❑ 78OPC-53
❑ 78Top-53
**Hammarstrom, Peter**
❑ 89SweSemE-18
❑ 90SweSemE-90
❑ 91SweSemE-14
❑ 92SweSemE-38
❑ 93SweSemE-111
❑ 94SweLeaE-88
❑ 95SweLeaE-52
❑ 95SweUppDE-85
**Hammer, Rolf**
❑ 94GerDELE-189
❑ 95GerDELE-189
❑ 96GerDELE-128
**Hammond, Ken**
❑ 88OilTenAnn-52
❑ 89ProAHL-128
❑ 90ProAHLIHL-141
❑ 91ProSet-484
❑ 91ProSetFre-484
❑ 91ScoCan-647
❑ 91ScoRoo-97T
❑ 91ShaSanJSA-9
❑ 92Par-358
❑ 92ParEmel-358
❑ 92ParPre-PV4
❑ 92Sen-4
**Hammond, Russ**
❑ 92CorBigRed-12
**Hammond, Scott**
❑ 82Ott67-16
❑ 83Ott67-10
**Hampe, Kevin**
❑ 92HarCri-12
**Hampeis, Lada**
❑ 93TacRoc-11
**Hampson, Ted**
❑ 44BeeGro2P-320
❑ 44BeeGro2P-403
❑ 59Par-34
❑ 60ShiCoi-98
❑ 61ShiCoi-92
❑ 61Top-59
❑ 62Top-55
❑ 63YorWhiB-52
❑ 64BeeGro3P-74
❑ 67Top-108
❑ 68OPC-85
❑ 68ShiCoi-111
❑ 68Top-85
❑ 69OPC-86
❑ 69OPCFou-7
❑ 69OPCSta-12
❑ 69Top-86
❑ 70ColSta-9
❑ 70DadCoo-47
❑ 70EssPowPla-100
❑ 70OPC-190
❑ 70SarProSta-137
❑ 71OPC-101
❑ 71SarProSta-94
❑ 71Top-101
❑ 71TorSun-133
❑ 72FigSaiPos-8
❑ 72SweSemWC-176
❑ 73QuaOatWHA-4
❑ 95Par66-47
❑ 95Par66Coi-47
**Hampton, Rick**
❑ 74NHLActSta-68
❑ 74OPCNHL-329
❑ 75OPCNHL-65
❑ 75Top-65
❑ 76OPCNHL-113
❑ 76OPCNHL-383
❑ 76Top-113
❑ 77OPCNHL-63
❑ 77Top-63
❑ 78OPC-174
❑ 78Top-174
❑ 79OPC-330
❑ 79PanSti-54
**Hamr, Radek**
❑ 93ClaProPro-142
❑ 93Lea-265
❑ 93Par-143
❑ 93ParEmel-143
❑ 93Sco-476
❑ 93ScoCan-476
❑ 93UppDec-34
❑ 94ClaProP-87
❑ 95CzeAPSE-276
❑ 96CzeAPSE-128
**Hamrlik, Martin**
❑ 91Cla-27
❑ 91StaPicH-18
❑ 93ClaProPro-62
❑ 95PeoRiv-6
**Hamrlik, Roman**
❑ 91UppDecCWJC-88
❑ 92Cla-1
❑ 92Cla-60
❑ 92ClaLPs-LP1
❑ 92ClaPromo-1
❑ 92LigShe-16
❑ 92OPCPre-46
❑ 92OPCPreTR-2
❑ 92Par-173
❑ 92Par-443
❑ 92ParEmel-173
❑ 92ParEmel-443
❑ 92Pin-408
❑ 92PinFre-408
❑ 92Ult-201
❑ 92UltImp-4
❑ 92UppDec-555
❑ 92UppDec-631
❑ 92UppDecCC-CC8
❑ 92UppDecER-ER11
❑ 93Cla-120
❑ 93ClaProPBC-BC3
❑ 93ClaProPro-50
❑ 93Don-327
❑ 93Lea-151
❑ 93LigSealR-18
❑ 93OPCPre-281
❑ 93OPCPre-323
❑ 93OPCPreF-2
❑ 93OPCPreG-281
❑ 93OPCPreG-323
❑ 93Par-190
❑ 93ParEmel-190
❑ 93ParFirO-F2
❑ 93Pin-34
❑ 93PinCan-34
❑ 93PinTea2-18
❑ 93PinTea2C-18
❑ 93Pow-231
❑ 93Sco-131
❑ 93ScoCan-131
❑ 93StaClu-75
❑ 93StaCluFDI-75
❑ 93StaCluFDIO-75
❑ 93StaCluO-75
❑ 93SweSemWCS-101
❑ 93TopPre-281
❑ 93TopPre-323
❑ 93TopPreF-2
❑ 93TopPreG-281
❑ 93TopPreG-323
❑ 93Ult-108
❑ 93UppDec-158
❑ 93UppDecSP-151
❑ 94BeAPla-R9
❑ 94Don-128
❑ 94EASpo-128
❑ 94Fle-207
❑ 94Lea-132
❑ 94LigPhoA-16
❑ 94LigPos-10
❑ 94OPCPre-54
❑ 94OPCPreSE-54
❑ 94ParSE-SE171
❑ 94ParSEG-SE171
❑ 94ParVin-V53
❑ 94Pin-123
❑ 94PinArtP-123
❑ 94PinRinC-123
❑ 94Sco-48
❑ 94ScoGol-48
❑ 94ScoPla-48
❑ 94ScoPlaTS-48
❑ 94SP-112
❑ 94SPDieCut-112
❑ 94TopPre-54
❑ 94TopPreSE-54
❑ 94Ult-206
❑ 94UppDec-174
❑ 94UppDecElelce-174
❑ 94UppDecSPI-SP164
❑ 94UppDecSPIDC-SP164
❑ 95BeAPla-133
❑ 95BeAPSig-S133
❑ 95BeAPSigDC-S133
❑ 95Bow-82
❑ 95BowAllFoi-82
❑ 95CanGamNHLP-255
❑ 95ColCho-92
❑ 95ColChoPC-92
❑ 95ColChoPCP-92
❑ 95Don-256
❑ 95DonEli-36
❑ 95DonEliDCS-36
❑ 95DonEliDCU-36
❑ 95Emo-164
❑ 95Fin-93
❑ 95FinRef-93
❑ 95ImpSti-112
❑ 95ImpStiDCS-20
❑ 95Lea-295
❑ 95LeaLim-33
❑ 95LigTeal-11
❑ 95Met-137
❑ 95MetIS-6
❑ 95ParInt-198
❑ 95ParIntEl-198
❑ 95ParIntPTP-PP25
❑ 95Pin-59
❑ 95PinArtP-59
❑ 95PinFan-11
❑ 95PinRinC-59
❑ 95PlaOneoOne-310
❑ 95ProMag-73
❑ 95Sco-185
❑ 95ScoBlaIce-185
❑ 95ScoBlaIceAP-185
❑ 95SelCer-20
❑ 95SelCerMG-20
❑ 95SkyImp-155
❑ 95SP-135
❑ 95SPStaEto-E25
❑ 95SPStaEtoG-E25
❑ 95StaClu-89
❑ 95StaCluMO-11
❑ 95StaCluMOMS-89
❑ 95Sum-56
❑ 95SumArtP-56
❑ 95SumIce-56
❑ 95SweGloWC-149
❑ 95Top-193
❑ 95TopOPCI-193
❑ 95TopYouS-YS13
❑ 95Ult-152
❑ 95UltGolM-152
❑ 95UltHigSpe-9
❑ 95UltRisS-3
❑ 95UltRisSGM-3
❑ 95UppDec-152
❑ 95UppDecElelce-152
❑ 95UppDecElelceG-152
❑ 95UppDecNHLAS-AS8
❑ 95UppDecPHE-H39
❑ 95UppDecPreH-H39
❑ 95UppDecSpeE-SE76
❑ 95UppDecSpeEdiG-SE76
❑ 95Zen-112
❑ 96ClaGol-1
❑ 96ClaGol-60
❑ 96ColCho-244
❑ 96ColCho-331
❑ 96ColChoBlo-244
❑ 96ColChoMVP-UD25
❑ 96ColChoMVPG-UD25
❑ 96ColChoSti-S18
❑ 96Don-84
❑ 96DonCanI-44
❑ 96DonCanIGPP-44
❑ 96DonCanIRPP-44
❑ 96DonEli-23
❑ 96DonEliDCS-23
❑ 96DonHitLis-16
❑ 96DonPrePro-84
❑ 96Fla-88
❑ 96FlaBlul-88
❑ 96Fle-104
❑ 96FlePicDL-6
❑ 96FlePicF5-16
❑ 96Lea-118
❑ 96LeaLim-4
❑ 96LeaLimG-4
❑ 96LeaPre-90
❑ 96LeaPreP-118
❑ 96LeaPrePP-90
❑ 96LeaPreSG-44
❑ 96LeaPreSte-44
❑ 96MetUni-145
❑ 96NHLACEPC-21
❑ 96NHLProSTA-73
❑ 96Pin-178
❑ 96PinArtP-178
❑ 96PinFoi-178
❑ 96PinPreS-178
❑ 96PinRinC-178
❑ 96PlaOneoOne-416
❑ 96Sco-127
❑ 96ScoArtPro-127
❑ 96ScoDeaCAP-127
❑ 96ScoGolB-127
❑ 96ScoSpeAP-127
❑ 96SelCer-48
❑ 96SelCerAP-48
❑ 96SelCerBlu-48
❑ 96SelCerMB-48
❑ 96SelCerMG-48
❑ 96SelCerMR-48
❑ 96SelCerRed-48
❑ 96SkyImp-122
❑ 96SP-144
❑ 96SPHolCol-HC22
❑ 96SPx-42
❑ 96SPxGol-42
❑ 96StaCluMO-37
❑ 96Sum-132
❑ 96SumArtP-132
❑ 96SumIce-132
❑ 96SumMet-132
❑ 96SumPreS-132
❑ 96TeaOut-75
❑ 96TopNHLP-35
❑ 96TopPicFT-FT9
❑ 96TopPicOI-35
❑ 96Ult-157
❑ 96UltGolM-157
❑ 96UltPow-6
❑ 96UltPowBL-4
❑ 96UppDec-153
❑ 96UppDec-367
❑ 96UppDecBD-143
❑ 96UppDecBDG-143
❑ 96UppDecGN-X8
❑ 96UppDecIce-102
❑ 96UppDecIcePar-102
❑ 96UppDecSS-SS13A
❑ 96Zen-92
❑ 96ZenArtP-92
❑ 97Be A PPAD-147
❑ 97Be A PPAPD-147
❑ 97BeAPla-147
❑ 97BeAPlaAut-147
❑ 97ColCho-240
❑ 97ColChoSta-SQ44
❑ 97Don-112
❑ 97DonCanI-123
❑ 97DonCanIDS-123
❑ 97DonCanIPS-123
❑ 97DonEli-94
❑ 97DonEliAsp-94
❑ 97DonEliS-94
❑ 97DonLim-146
❑ 97DonLimExp-146
❑ 97DonPre-141
❑ 97DonPreCttC-141
❑ 97DonPreProG-112
❑ 97DonPreProS-112
❑ 97DonPri-120
❑ 97DonPriSoA-120
❑ 97EssOlyHH-53
❑ 97EssOlyHHF-53
❑ 97Kat-135
❑ 97KatGol-135
❑ 97KatSil-135
❑ 97Lea-76
❑ 97LeaFraMat-76
❑ 97LeaFraMDC-76
❑ 97LeaInt-76
❑ 97LeaIntUI-76
❑ 97Pac-100
❑ 97PacCop-100
❑ 97PacCroR-125
❑ 97PacCroREG-125
❑ 97PacCroRIB-125
❑ 97PacCroRS-125
❑ 97PacDyn-118
❑ 97PacDynC-118
❑ 97PacDynDG-118
❑ 97PacDynEG-118
❑ 97PacDynIB-118
❑ 97PacDynR-118
❑ 97PacDynSil-118
❑ 97PacDynTan-61
❑ 97PacEmeGre-100
❑ 97PacIceB-100
❑ 97PacInv-132
❑ 97PacInvC-132
❑ 97PacInvEG-132
❑ 97PacInvIB-132
❑ 97PacInvR-132
❑ 97PacInvS-132
❑ 97PacOme-92
❑ 97PacOmeC-92
❑ 97PacOmeDG-92
❑ 97PacOmeEG-92
❑ 97PacOmeG-92
❑ 97PacOmeIB-92
❑ 97PacPar-173
❑ 97PacParC-173
❑ 97PacParDG-173
❑ 97PacParEG-173
❑ 97PacParIB-173
❑ 97PacParRed-173
❑ 97PacParSil-173
❑ 97PacRed-100
❑ 97PacRev-53
❑ 97PacRevC-53
❑ 97PacRevE-53
❑ 97PacRevIB-53
❑ 97PacRevR-53
❑ 97PacRevS-53
❑ 97PacSil-100
❑ 97Pin-175
❑ 97PinIns-162
❑ 97PinPrePBB-175
❑ 97PinPrePBC-175
❑ 97PinPrePBM-175
❑ 97PinPrePBY-175
❑ 97PinPrePFC-175
❑ 97PinPrePFM-175
❑ 97PinPrePFY-175
❑ 97PinPrePla-175
❑ 97Sco-214
❑ 97SPAut-149
❑ 97Stu-75
❑ 97StuPrePG-75
❑ 97StuPrePS-75
❑ 97UppDec-157
❑ 97UppDec-363
❑ 97UppDecBD-142
❑ 97UppDecBDDD-142
❑ 97UppDecBDQD-142
❑ 97UppDecBDTD-142
❑ 97UppDecSG-SG47
❑ 98Be A PPA-52
❑ 98Be A PPAA-52
❑ 98Be A PPAAF-52
❑ 98Be A PPTBASG-52
❑ 98Be APG-52
❑ 98Pac-219
❑ 98PacAur-73
❑ 98PacDynI-73
❑ 98PacDynIIB-73
❑ 98PacDynIR-73
❑ 98PacIceB-219
❑ 98PacOmeH-93
❑ 98PacOmeODI-93
❑ 98PacOmeR-93
❑ 98PacPar-87
❑ 98PacParC-87
❑ 98PacParEG-87
❑ 98PacParH-87
❑ 98PacParIB-87
❑ 98PacParS-87
❑ 98PacRed-219
❑ 98UC-80
❑ 98UD ChoPCR-80
❑ 98UD ChoR-80
❑ 98UppDec-96
❑ 98UppDecE-96
❑ 98UppDecE1o1-96
❑ 98UppDecGR-96
❑ 98UppDecM-83
❑ 98UppDecMGS-83
❑ 98UppDecMSS-83
❑ 98UppDecMSS-83
❑ 99Pac-156
❑ 99PacCop-156
❑ 99PacGol-156
❑ 99PacIceB-156
❑ 99PacPreD-156
**Hamway, Mark**
❑ 84SprInd-18
**Hanas, Trevor**
❑ 917thInnSWHL-218
❑ 93SasBla-11
❑ 95LetHur-8
❑ 96PeoRiv-7
❑ 96PeoRivPA-7
**Hanchuk, Jason**
❑ 93MicTecH-5
❑ 96LouRiv-5
**Hancock, Quinn**
❑ 98BowCHL-57
❑ 98BowCHLGA-57
❑ 98BowCHLOI-57
❑ 98BowChrC-57
❑ 98BowChrCGA-57
❑ 98BowChrCGAR-57
❑ 98BowChrCOI-57
❑ 98BowChrCOIR-57
❑ 98BowChrCR-57
**Hand, Tony**
❑ 94FinnJaaK-323
❑ 97SheSte-7
❑ 97SheSte-9
**Handley, Pete**
❑ 82NorBayC-8
**Handrick, Jorg**
❑ 96GerDELE-147
**Handy, Ron**
❑ 80SauSteMG-17
❑ 82KinCan-5
❑ 84SprInd-14
❑ 88ProIHL-16
❑ 89ProIHL-140
❑ 90KanCitBla-5
❑ 90ProAHLIHL-582
❑ 91ProAHLCHL-513
❑ 92PeoRivC-7
❑ 94CenHocL-112
❑ 94SheSte-6
❑ 95LouIceG-5
❑ 95LouIceGP-6
**Handzus, Michal**
❑ 98BowBes-132
❑ 98BowBesAR-132
❑ 98BowBesR-132
❑ 98PacDynI-158
❑ 98PacDynIIB-158
❑ 98PacDynIR-158
❑ 98SP Aut-108
❑ 98UppDec-363
❑ 98UppDecE-363
❑ 98UppDecE1o1-363
❑ 98UppDecGR-363
❑ 98UppDecM-182
❑ 98UppDecMGS-182
❑ 98UppDecMSS-182
❑ 98UppDecMSS-182
❑ 99Pac-357
❑ 99PacCop-357
❑ 99PacGol-357
❑ 99PacIceB-357
❑ 99PacPreD-357
❑ 99SP AutPS-108
❑ 99UppDecM-189
❑ 99UppDecMGS-189
❑ 99UppDecMSS-189
❑ 99UppDecMSS-189
**Haney, Merv**
❑ 917thInnSWHL-251
❑ 91PriAlbR-3
❑ 93PriAlbR-7
**Hanft, Jorg**
❑ 89SweSemWCS-111
❑ 95GerDELE-271
❑ 95GerDELE-436
**Hangsleben, Al**
❑ 79OPC-307
❑ 81OPC-354
❑ 81OPCSti-197
**Hanig, Gustav**
❑ 72SweSemWC-108
**Hanisz, Andrezej**
❑ 89SweSemWCS-129
❑ 94GerDELE-361
**Hankela, Timo**
❑ 93FinnJyvHS-284
❑ 93FinnSIS-59
**Hankinson, Ben**
❑ 91ProAHLCHL-413
❑ 93Pin-210
❑ 93PinCan-210
❑ 94LigPhoA-17
❑ 95AdiRedW-8
❑ 96GraRapG-7
**Hankinson, Casey**
❑ 94MinGolG-15
❑ 95DonEliWJ-36
❑ 95MinGolG-14
❑ 96MinGolGCAS-13
**Hankinson, Peter**
❑ 90MonHaw-9
❑ 90ProAHLIHL-254
❑ 90ProAHLIHL-547
❑ 91ProAHLCHL-239
❑ 92SanDieG-10
**Hankkio, Greg**
❑ 85KitRan-14
❑ 86LonKni-25
**Hanley, Tim**
❑ 89ProAHL-238
❑ 91LakSupSL-10
❑ 95RoaExp-17
**Hanley, William**
❑ 85HalFC-251
**Hanlon, Glen**
❑ 78CanuRoyB-10
❑ 79CanuRoyB-9
❑ 79OPC-337
❑ 80CanuSilD-10
❑ 80CanuTeal-10
❑ 80OPC-141
❑ 80OPCSup-22
❑ 80Top-141
❑ 81CanuSilD-7
❑ 81CanuTeal-11
❑ 81OPC-336
❑ 81OPCSti-245
❑ 84OPC-142
❑ 84OPCSti-98
❑ 84Top-106
❑ 85OPC-149
❑ 85OPCSti-87
❑ 85Top-149
❑ 87OPC-89
❑ 87OPCMin-14
❑ 87OPCSti-109
❑ 87PanSti-238
❑ 87RedWinLC-14
❑ 87Top-89
❑ 88OPC-150
❑ 88PanSti-36
❑ 88RedWinLC-10
❑ 88Top-150
❑ 89OPC-144
❑ 89PanSti-65
❑ 89RedWinLC-9
❑ 89Top-144
❑ 90OPC-266
❑ 90PanSti-203
❑ 90ProAHLIHL-305
❑ 90ProSet-72
❑ 90Sco-228
❑ 90ScoCan-228
❑ 90Top-266
❑ 90TopTif-266
❑ 90UppDec-395
❑ 90UppDecF-395
**Hanlon, James**
❑ 90KnoChe-112
❑ 94GerDELE-244
❑ 95GerDELE-229
❑ 96GerDELE-80
**Hanna, John**
❑ 44BeeGro2P-244
❑ 58Top-7
❑ 59Top-31
❑ 59Top-53
❑ 60ShiCoi-85
❑ 62QueAce-10
❑ 63QueAce-10
❑ 63QueAceQ-9
❑ 64BeeGro3P-104
❑ 64QueAce-7
❑ 65QueAce-7
❑ 69SeaTotW-11
❑ 83Ott67-11
❑ 84Ott67-9
❑ 88ProAHL-74
**Hannah, Andrew**
❑ 97GuiFla-3
**Hannah, Shaun**
❑ 92CorBigRed-13
❑ 93CorBigRed-12
**Hannan, Dave**
❑ 83OPC-281
❑ 83PenCok-12
❑ 83PenHeiP-11
❑ 83PenTealP-14
❑ 86PenKod-10
❑ 87OilTeal-12
❑ 87PanSti-154
❑ 88OilTenAnn-83
❑ 89OPC-257
❑ 90OPC-449
❑ 90ProSet-535
❑ 91Bow-155
❑ 91MapLeaP-17
❑ 91MapLeaPTS-8
❑ 91OPC-360
❑ 91Pin-413
❑ 91PinFre-413
❑ 91ScoCan-241
❑ 91StaClu-220
❑ 91Top-360
❑ 91UppDec-312
❑ 91UppDecF-312
❑ 92SabBluS-6
❑ 92Sco-538
❑ 92ScoCan-538
❑ 92Sen-5
❑ 93StaClu-47
❑ 93StaCluFDI-47
❑ 93StaCluFDIO-47
❑ 93StaCluO-47
❑ 94OPCPre-118
❑ 94OPCPreSE-118
❑ 94Pin-446
❑ 94PinArtP-446
❑ 94PinRinC-446
❑ 94TopPre-118
❑ 94TopPreSE-118
❑ 96SenPizH-9
**Hannan, Scott**
❑ 98PacDynI-166
❑ 98PacDynIIB-166
❑ 98PacDynIR-166
❑ 98UppDec-353
❑ 98UppDecE-353
❑ 98UppDecE1o1-353
❑ 98UppDecGR-353
❑ 99Pac-385
❑ 99PacCop-385
❑ 99PacGol-385
❑ 99PacIceB-385
❑ 99PacPreD-385
❑ 99UppDecM-180
❑ 99UppDecMGS-180
❑ 99UppDecMSS-180
❑ 99UppDecMSS-180
**Hannigan, Gord**
❑ 44BeeGro2P-404
❑ 45QuaOatP-20
❑ 52Par-54
❑ 53Par-3
❑ 54Par-27
**Hannigan, Pat**
❑ 61ShiCoi-83
❑ 61Top-58
❑ 62Top-64
❑ 68ShiCoi-134
**Hannon, Brian**
❑ 89ProIHL-136
❑ 94GerDELE-170
❑ 95GerDELE-120
**Hansch, Randy**
❑ 83VicCou-10
❑ 84VicCou-11
❑ 85KamBla-6
❑ 90ProAHLIHL-490
**Hansen, Ivan**
❑ 83SweSemE-138
❑ 85SwePanS-194
❑ 86SwePanS-123
❑ 87SwePanS-160
**Hansen, Kevin**
❑ 95Sla-388
❑ 95SudWol-8
❑ 95SudWolP-10
❑ 96SudWol-9
❑ 96SudWolP-12
**Hansen, Mark**
❑ 91AirCanSJHL-E33
**Hansen, Matt**
❑ 91LakSupSL-11
**Hansen, Rick**
❑ 91ProSetPla-296
**Hansen, Ronny**
❑ 89SweSemE-261
❑ 90SweSemE-169
**Hansen, Tavis**
❑ 93TacRoc-12
❑ 95ColEdgI-69
❑ 95Lea-214
❑ 96SprFal-19
**Hanson, Dave**
❑ 82IndChe-8
**Hanson, Devon**
❑ 93SasBla-12
**Hanson, Greg**
❑ 93MinDul-13
**Hanson, Keith**
❑ 84MonGolF-16
**Hanson, Michael**
❑ 95Sla-342
❑ 96SarSti-9
**Hanson, Tom**
❑ 85MinDul-13
**Hansson, Bo**
❑ 64SweCorI-37
❑ 65SweCorI-37
❑ 67SweHoc-29
❑ 69SweHocS-42
❑ 70SweHocS-9
❑ 71SweHocS-84
**Hansson, Gote**
❑ 64SweCorI-103
❑ 65SweCorI-103
❑ 67SweHoc-139
❑ 69SweHocS-150
❑ 70SweHocS-117
❑ 71SweHocS-211
❑ 72SweHocS-188
**Hansson, Hans**
❑ 69SweHocS-151
❑ 70SweHocS-121
❑ 71SweHocS-212
❑ 72SweHocS-189
❑ 74SweHocS-218

95SelCerMG-62
95SkyImp-45
95SkyImp-233
95SP-39
95StaClu-103
95StaCluMOMS-103
95StaScoS-38
95Sum-148
95SumArtP-148
95SumIce-148
95SumMadH-15
95Top-356
95TopCanWJ-10CJ
95TopHomGC-HGC17
95TopNewG-17NG
95TopOPCI-356
95TopSupSki-68
95TopSupSkiPla-68
95Ult-37
95UltCreCra-4
95UltGolM-37
95UltHigSpe-10
95UppDec-199
95UppDecEIeIce-199
95UppDecEIeIceG-199
95UppDecSpeE-SE114
95UppDecSpeEdiG-SE114
95UppDecWJA-14
95Zen-75
95ZenGifG-10
96ColCho-67
96ColCho-315
96Don-94
96DonPrePro-94
96Lea-145
96LeaPre-114
96LeaPreP-145
96LeaPrePP-114
96NHLProSTA-122
96Pin-52
96PinArtP-52
96PinFoi-52
96PinPreS-52
96PinRinC-52
96Sco-86
96ScoArtPro-86
96ScoDeaCAP-86
96ScoGolB-86
96ScoSpeAP-86
96SP-42
96StaPos-7
96StaScoS-86
96Sum-46
96SumArtP-46
96SumIce-46
96SumMet-46
96SumPreS-46
96UppDec-45
96UppDecPP-P30
97BeA PPAD-96
97BeA PPAPD-96
97BeAPIa-96
97BeAPIaAut-96
97ColCho-75
97Don-68
97DonPre-144
97DonPreCttC-144
97DonPreProG-68
97DonPreProS-68
97DonPri-157
97DonPriSoA-157
97PacInvNRB-60
97UppDec-55
98PacOmeH-157
98PacOmeODI-157
98PacOmeR-157
98PacRev-93
98PacRevIS-93
98PacRevR-93
98RanPowP-NYR2
98UppDec-323
98UppDecE-323
98UppDecE1o1-323
98UppDecGR-323
98UppDecM-138
98UppDecMGS-138
98UppDecMSS-138
98UppDecMSS-138
99Pac-270
99PacCop-270
99PacGol-270
99PacIceB-270
99PacPreD-270

**Hascak, Oto**
90SweSemE-62
91SweSemE-235
91SweSemWCS-116
93SweSemE-288
94GerDELE-179
95GerDELE-181
95SloAPSNT-16
96CzeAPSE-226
96SweSemW-235

**Hasek, Dominik**
89SweSemWCS-178
90ProAHLIHL-409
91Par-263
91Par-449
91ParFre-263
91ParFre-449
91ProAHLCHL-500
91ProSet-529
91ProSetFre-529
91ProSetPla-252
91ScoAme-316

91ScoCan-346
91SweSemWCS-103
91UppDec-335
91UppDecES-14
91UppDecESF-14
91UppDecF-335
92Bow-428
92Kra-30
92OPC-301
92OPCPre-50
92PanSti-292
92PanStiFre-292
92SabBluS-7
92SabJubF-4
92Sco-373
92ScoCan-373
92StaClu-107
92Top-136
92TopGol-136G
92UppDec-92
92UppDec-366
92UppDec-506
92UppDecART-AR6
92UppDecART-AR7
92UppDecERT-ERT3
92UppDecES-E3
93Lea-256
93OPCPre-320
93OPCPre-463
93OPCPreG-320
93OPCPreG-463
93Pin-403
93PinCan-403
93Pow-297
93SabLimETI-2
93SabNoc-6
93Sco-281
93ScoCan-281
93StaClu-178
93StaCluFDI-178
93StaCluFDIO-178
93StaCluO-178
93TopPre-320
93TopPre-463
93TopPreG-320
93TopPreG-463
93Ult-274
93UppDec-387
94CanGamNHLP-274
94CanGamNHLP-332
94CanGamNHLP-333
94Don-94
94DonDom-3
94DonMasM-3
94EASpo-211
94Fin-43
94FinnJaaK-163
94FinnJaaK-333
94FinRef-43
94FinSupTW-43
94Fla-17
94FlaHotN-3
94Fle-20
94FleNet-3
94Kra-39
94Kra-60
94Kra-70
94Lea-120
94LeaCreP-6
94LeaGolS-8
94LeaLim-102
94LeaLimI-3
940PCPre-35
940PCPre-80
940PCPre-152
940PCPre-156
940PCPre-312
940PCPre-440
940PCPreSE-35
940PCPreSE-80
940PCPreSE-152
940PCPreSE-156
940PCPreSE-312
940PCPreSE-440
94Par-24
94ParGol-24
94ParSEES-ES19
94ParVin-V1
94Pin-175
94Pin-MVPU
94PinArtP-175
94PinGoaG-GT1
94PinRinC-175
94PinWorEdi-WE6
94Sco-78
94ScoGol-78
94ScoPla-78
94ScoPlaTS-78
94Sel-52
94SelGol-52
94SP-14
94SPDieCut-14
94SPPre-19
94SPPreDC-19
94StaClu-125
94StaClu-179
94StaClu-269
94StaCluFDI-125
94StaCluFDI-179
94StaCluFDI-269
94StaCluMOMS-125
94StaCluMOMS-179
94StaCluMOMS-269
94StaCluSTWC-125

94StaCluSTWC-179
94StaCluSTWC-269
94TopPre-35
94TopPre-80
94TopPre-152
94TopPre-156
94TopPre-312
94TopPre-440
94TopPreSE-35
94TopPreSE-80
94TopPreSE-152
94TopPreSE-156
94TopPreSE-312
94TopPreSE-440
94Ult-22
94UltAwaW-6
94UltGloGre-2
94UltPrePM-1
94UppDec-233
94UppDec-285
94UppDec-545
94UppDecEIeIce-233
94UppDecEIeIce-285
94UppDecEIeIce-545
94UppDecPH-H31
94UppDecPHEG-H31
94UppDecPHES-H31
94UppDecPHG-H31
94UppDecSPI-SP8
94UppDecSPIDC-SP8
95BeAPla-192
95BeAPSig-S192
95BeAPSigDC-S192
95Bow-56
95BowAllFoi-56
95CanGamNHLP-14
95CanGamNHLP-48
95ColCho-258
95ColCho-367
95ColCho-381
95ColCho-394
95ColChoPC-258
95ColChoPC-367
95ColChoPC-381
95ColChoPC-394
95ColChoPCP-258
95ColChoPCP-367
95ColChoPCP-381
95ColChoPCP-394
95Don-33
95DonBetTP-2
95DonDom-4
95DonEli-30
95DonEliDCS-30
95DonEliDCU-30
95Emo-16
95Fin-72
95Fin-90
95FinnSemWC-141
95FinnSemWC-214
95FinRef-72
95FinRef-90
95ImpSti-12
95KenStaLA-9
95KenStaLC-7
95Kra-16
95Kra-45
95Lea-56
95LeaGolS-1
95LeaLim-76
95LeaLimSS-5
95McDCDPin-MCD-28
95Met-15
95MetIS-7
95NHLAcePC-13D
95ParInt-236
95ParInt-291
95ParIntAS-1
95ParIntCCGS2-5
95ParIntCCSS2-5
95ParIntEI-236
95ParIntEI-291
95ParIntGP-4
95ParIntPTP-PP28
95ParIntTW-5
95Pin-139
95PinArtP-139
95PinCleS-15
95PinFan-17
95PinFirS-14
95PinGloG-19
95PinRinC-139
95PlaOneoOne-12
95PlaOneoOne-125
95ProMag-107
95Sco-200
95Sco-325
95ScoBalce-200
95ScoBalce-325
95ScoBalceAP-200
95ScoBalceAP-325
95SelCer-89
95SelCerMG-89
95SkyImp-16
95SkyImpD-1
95SP-13
95StaClu-60
95StaCluM-M10
95StaCluMO-12
95StaCluMOMS-60
95StaCluNem-N6
95Sum-159
95SumArtP-159
95SumIce-159
95SumInTheCre-2

95SweGloWC-145
95Top-2
95Top-302
95TopHidGem-4HG
95TopMarMPB-2
95TopMysF-M19
95TopMysFR-M19
95TopOPCI-2
95TopOPCI-302
95TopPro-PF14
95TopSupSki-75
95TopSupSkiPla-75
95Ult-18
95Ult-370
95UltGolM-18
95UltPrePadMen-5
95UltPrePadMenGM-5
95UltUltHP-3
95UltUltV-3
95UppDec-104
95UppDecEIeIce-104
95UppDecEIeIceG-104
95UppDecFreFra-F11
95UppDecFreFraJ-F11
95UppDecNHLAS-AS20
95UppDecPHE-H13
95UppDecSpeE-SE98
95UppDecSpeEdiG-SE98
95UppPreHV-H13
95Zen-109
96BeAPStaTP-11
96ColCho-30
96ColCho-311
96Don-192
96DonCanI-60
96DonCanIGPP-60
96DonCanIRPP-60
96DonEli-37
96DonEliDCS-37
96DonPrePro-192
96Fla-8
96FlaBluI-8
96FlaHotG-4
96Fle-10
96Fle-147
96FlePicDL-6
96FleVez-4
96KraUppD-18
96Lea-19
96LeaLim-21
96LeaLimG-21
96LeaPreMM-7
96LeaPreP-19
96LeaPrePP-91
96LeaPreSG-52
96LeaPreSte-52
96MetUni-14
96MetUniAP-4
96MetUniAPSP-4
96MetUniCS-4
96MetUniCSSP-4
96NHLProSTA-107
96Pin-106
96PinArtP-106
96PinFoi-106
96PinMin-2
96PinMinB-2
96PinMinCoiB-2
96PinMinCoiGP-2
96PinMinCoiN-2
96PinMinCoiSG-2
96PinMinG-2
96PinMinS-2
96PinPreS-106
96PinRinC-106
96Sco-18
96ScoArtPro-18
96ScoDeaCAP-18
96ScoGolB-18
96ScoNetW-4
96ScoSpeAP-18
96ScoSudDea-3
96SelCer-74
96SelCerAP-74
96SelCerBlu-74
96SelCerFre-5
96SelCerMB-74
96SelCerMG-74
96SelCerMR-74
96SelCerRed-74
96SkyImp-74
96SkyImpZH-4
96SP-17
96SPHolCol-HC30
96SPSPxFor-3
96StaCluMO-42
96Sum-2
96SumArtP-2
96SumIce-2
96SumInTheCre-14
96SumInTheCrePS-14
96SumMet-2
96SumPreS-2
96SweSemW-103
96SweSemWSG-SG1
96TeaOut-69
96TopPicID-ID10
96Ult-16
96UltCleTheIce-3
96UltGolM-16
96UppDec-222
96UppDecBDG-156
96UppDecBDG-156

96UppDecGN-X28
96UppDecIce-5
96UppDecIcePar-5
96UppDecSS-SS26A
96Zen-15
96ZenArtP-15
96ZenBePlaSTP-2
97ColCho-22
97ColChoSta-SQ81
97ColChoSti-S30
97Don-9
97DonBetTP-4
97DonCanI-10
97DonCanIDS-10
97DonCanIPS-10
97DonCanISCS-22
97DonEli-30
97DonEliAsp-30
97DonEliC-6
97DonEliIns-11
97DonEliMC-6
97DonEliS-30
97DonLim-76
97DonLim-86
97DonLim-147
97DonLimExp-76
97DonLimExp-86
97DonLimExp-147
97DonLimFOTG-65
97DonPre-1
97DonPre-169
97DonPreCG-6
97DonPreCGP-6
97DonPreCttC-1
97DonPreCttC-169
97DonPreProG-9
97DonPreProS-9
97DonPri-80
97DonPriODI-22
97DonPriP-31
97DonPriPGP-13
97DonPriS-31
97DonPriSB-31
97DonPriSG-31
97DonPriSoA-80
97DonPriSS-31
97EssOlyHH-54
97EssOlyHHF-54
97Kat-15
97KatGol-15
97KatSil-15
97Lea-2
97Lea-169
97LeaFraMat-2
97LeaFraMat-169
97LeaFraMDC-2
97LeaFraMDC-169
97LeaInt-2
97LeaIntUI-2
97LeaPipDre-1
97McD-26
97Pac-39
97PacCop-39
97PacCraChoAwa-2
97PacCroR-14
97PacCroREG-14
97PacCroRFODC-3
97PacCroRIB-14
97PacCroRS-14
97PacDyn-10
97PacDyn-136
97PacDynBKS-10
97PacDynBKS-104
97PacDynC-10
97PacDynC-136
97PacDynDD-3A
97PacDynDG-10
97PacDynDG-136
97PacDynEG-10
97PacDynEG-136
97PacDynIB-10
97PacDynIB-136
97PacDynR-10
97PacDynR-136
97PacDynSil-10
97PacDynSil-136
97PacDynSto-3
97PacDynTan-4
97PacDynTan-21
97PacEmeGre-39
97PacGolCroDC-3
97PacInTheCLC-2
97PacInv-12
97PacInvCI-12
97PacInvEG-12
97PacInvFP-4
97PacInvIB-12
97PacInvNRB-20
97PacInvR-12
97PacInvS-12
97PacOme-22
97PacOmeC-22
97PacOmeDG-22
97PacOmeEG-22
97PacOmeIB-22
97PacOmeNSZ-1
97PacPar-19
97PacParBNDC-4
97PacParC-19
97PacParDG-19
97PacParGSL-2

97PacParIB-19
97PacParP-4
97PacParRed-19
97PacParSil-19
97PacRed-39
97PacRev-14
97PacRev1AGD-3
97PacRevC-14
97PacRevE-14
97PacRevIB-14
97PacRevR-14
97PacRevRtSD-3
97PacRevS-14
97PacSil-39
97PacTeaCCC-3
97Pin-28
97PinArtP-28
97PinBee-24
97PinBeeGP-24
97PinCer-1
97PinCerGT-4
97PinCerMB-1
97PinCerMG-1
97PinCerMR-1
97PinCerR-1
97PinCerT-4
97PinEpiGO-22
97PinEpiGP-22
97PinEpiME-22
97PinEpiMO-22
97PinEpiMP-22
97PinEpiPE-22
97PinEpiPO-22
97PinEpiPP-22
97PinEpiSE-22
97PinEpiSO-22
97PinEpiSP-22
97PinIns-2
97PinInsCC-2
97PinInsEC-2
97PinInsSto-3
97PinInsT-15
97PinMin-8
97PinMinB-8
97PinMinCBP-8
97PinMinCGPP-8
97PinMinCNSP-8
97PinMinCoiB-8
97PinMinCoiGP-8
97PinMinCoiN-8
97PinMinCoiSG-8
97PinMinCoiSS-8
97PinMinGolTea-8
97PinMinMC-5
97PinMinMin-5
97PinMinSilTea-8
97PinPowPac-4
97PinPrePBB-28
97PinPrePBC-28
97PinPrePBM-28
97PinPrePBY-28
97PinPrePFC-28
97PinPrePFM-28
97PinPrePFY-28
97PinPrePla-28
97PinRinC-28
97PinTeaP-2
97PinTeaPM-2
97PinTeaPPM-2
97PinTotCMPG-1
97PinTotCPB-1
97PinTotCPG-1
97PinTotCPR-1
97PosPin-16
97Sco-39
97Sco-266
97ScoArtPro-39
97ScoGolBla-39
97ScoNetW-17
97ScoSab-1
97ScoSabPla-1
97ScoSabPre-1
97SP Autl-I34
97SPAut-14
97SPAutID-I34
97SPAutIE-I34
97SPx-4
97SPxBro-4
97SPxDuo-9
97SPxGol-4
97SPxGraF-4
97SPxSil-4
97SPxSte-4
97Stu-2
97StuPor-2
97StuPrePG-2
97StuPrePS-2
97StuSil-7
97StuSil8-7
97UppDec-225
97UppDecBD-20
97UppDecBDDD-20
97UppDecBDQD-20
97UppDecBDTD-20
97UppDecDV-24
97UppDecDVSM-24
97UppDecGDM-225
97UppDecGJ-GJ3
97UppDecIC-IC5
97UppDecIC2-IC5
97UppDecIce-87
97UppDecIPS-87
97UppDecPS-87
97UppDecSG-SG39

97UppDecTS-18
97UppDecTSL2-18
97UppDecTSS-2A
97Zen-20
97Zen5x7-62
97ZenGolImp-62
97ZenSilImp-62
97ZenZGol-20
97ZenZSil-20
98Be A PPA-162
98Be A PPAA-162
98Be A PPAAF-162
98Be A PPAGUSC-S18
98Be A PPAJ-AS20
98Be A PPSE-162
98Be AGP-162
98BowBes-11
98BowBesA-A1A
98BowBesA-A1B
98BowBesAAR-A1A
98BowBesAAR-A1B
98BowBesAR-11
98BowBesAR-A1A
98BowBesAR-A1B
98BowBesMIF-F9
98BowBesMIFAR-F9
98BowBesMIFR-F9
98BowBesR-11
98BowBesSBB-SB1
98BowBesSBBAR-SB1
98BowBesSBBR-SB1
98CroRoyCCAJG-3
98CroRoyCCAJG-3
98CroRoyCCAJLB-3
98CroRoyCCAJP-3
98CroRoyCCAJR-3
98Fin-4
98FinDouMF-M2
98FinDouMF-M5
98FinDouMF-M6
98FinDouMF-M7
98FinDouSMFR-M2
98FinDouSMFR-M5
98FinDouSMFR-M6
98FinDouSMFR-M7
98FinNo P-4
98FinNo PR-4
98FinOve-2
98FinOveR-2
98FinRef-4
98LunGoaG-3
98LunGoaGS-3
98McD-16
980-PChr-163
980-PChrR-163
980-PChrSB-SB1
980-PChrSBR-SB1
98Pac-39
98PacAur-17
98PacAurALC-4
98PacAurC-3
98PacAurCF-6
98PacAurCFC-6
98PacAurCFIB-6
98PacAurCFR-6
98PacAurCFS-6
98PacAurFL-1
98PacAurFLIB-1
98PacAurFLR-1
98PacAurNC-2
98PacCraCA-2
98PacCroR-13
98PacCroRCCA-3
98PacCroRCCAJ-3
98PacCroRLL-3
98PacCroRLS-13
98PacCroRMP-3
98PacCroRPP-2
98PacDynI-4
98PacDynIARB-3
98PacDynIARB-3
98PacDynIARR-3
98PacDynIARS-3
98PacDynIIB-18
98PacDynIIW-1
98PacDynIPP-2
98PacDynIR-18
98PacDynITC-3
98PacEO P-3
98PacGolCD-4
98PacIceB-39
98PacOmeCS-2
98PacOmeCSG-2
98PacOmeCSG-2
98PacOmeCSR-2
98PacOmeEP1o1-3
98PacOmePtF-3
98PacOmeH-23
98PacOme0-4
98PacOmeODI-23
98PacOmeP-3
98PacOmePI-21
98PacOmePIB-21
98PacOmeR-23
98PacPar-19
98PacParC-19
98PacParGSLC-3
98PacParH-19
98PacParHoFB-2
98PacParHoFBPP-2
98PacParIB-19
98PacParS-19

❑ 98PacParTCD-3
❑ 98PacRed-39
❑ 98PacRev-14
❑ 98PacRevADC-9
❑ 98PacRevIS-14
❑ 98PacRevNI-2
❑ 98PacRevR-14
❑ 98PacRevS-4
❑ 98PacTeaC-3
❑ 98PacTim-2
❑ 98PacTitl-4
❑ 98PacTroW-2
❑ 98PinEpiGE-22
❑ 98RevThrPA-11
❑ 98RevThrPA-11
❑ 98SP Aut-8
❑ 98SP AutSM-S3
❑ 98SP AutSS-SS7
❑ 98SPxFin-8
❑ 98SPxFin-103
❑ 98SPxFin-159
❑ 98SPxFin-173
❑ 98SPxFinR-8
❑ 98SPxFinR-103
❑ 98SPxFinR-159
❑ 98SPxFinR-173
❑ 98SPxFinS-8
❑ 98SPxFinS-103
❑ 98SPxFinS-159
❑ 98SPxFinS-173
❑ 98SPXTopP-6
❑ 98SPXTopPF-6
❑ 98SPXTopPHH-H5
❑ 98SPXTopPLI-L6
❑ 98SPXTopPPS-PS4
❑ 98SPXTopPR-6
❑ 98Top-163
❑ 98TopAut-A8
❑ 98TopGolLC1-34
❑ 98TopGolLC1B-34
❑ 98TopGolLC1BOoO-34
❑ 98TopGolLC1OoO-34
❑ 98TopGolLC1R-34
❑ 98TopGolLC1ROoO-34
❑ 98TopGolLC2-34
❑ 98TopGolLC2B-34
❑ 98TopGolLC2BOoO-34
❑ 98TopGolLC2OoO-34
❑ 98TopGolLC2R-34
❑ 98TopGolLC2ROoO-34
❑ 98TopGolLC3-34
❑ 98TopGolLC3B-34
❑ 98TopGolLC3BOoO-34
❑ 98TopGolLC3OoO-34
❑ 98TopGolLC3R-34
❑ 98TopGolLC3ROoO-34
❑ 98TopLocL-L5
❑ 98TopMysFB-M7
❑ 98TopMysFBR-M7
❑ 98TopMysFG-M7
❑ 98TopMysFGR-M7
❑ 98TopMysFS-M7
❑ 98TopMysFSR-M7
❑ 98TopO-P-163
❑ 98TopSeaB-SB1
❑ 98UC-23
❑ 98UC-221
❑ 98UC-244
❑ 98UCMBH-BH18
❑ 98UCSB-SQ4
❑ 98UCSG-SQ4
❑ 98UCSG-SQ4
❑ 98UCSR-SQ4
❑ 98UD ChoPCR-23
❑ 98UD ChoPCR-221
❑ 98UD ChoPCR-244
❑ 98UD ChoR-23
❑ 98UD ChoR-221
❑ 98UD ChoR-244
❑ 98UD3-57
❑ 98UD3-117
❑ 98UD3-177
❑ 98UD3DieC-57
❑ 98UD3DieC-117
❑ 98UD3DieC-177
❑ 98UDCP-23
❑ 98UppDec-20
❑ 98UppDec-44
❑ 98UppDecBD-10
❑ 98UppDecDD-10
❑ 98UppDecE-20
❑ 98UppDecE-44
❑ 98UppDecE1o1-20
❑ 98UppDecE1o1-44
❑ 98UppDecFIT-FT10
❑ 98UppDecFITQ1-FT10
❑ 98UppDecFITQ2-FT10
❑ 98UppDecFITQ3-FT10
❑ 98UppDecGJ-GJ17
❑ 98UppDecGR-20
❑ 98UppDecGR-44
❑ 98UppDecLSH-LS27
❑ 98UppDecLSHQ1-LS27
❑ 98UppDecLSHQ2-LS27
❑ 98UppDecLSHQ3-LS27
❑ 98UppDecM-21
❑ 98UppDecM1-M6
❑ 98UppDecM2-M6
❑ 98UppDecMGS-21
❑ 98UppDecMOH-OT7
❑ 98UppDecMSF-F4
❑ 98UppDecMSS-21
❑ 98UppDecMSS-21
❑ 98UppDecP-P17
❑ 98UppDecPQ1-P17
❑ 98UppDecPQ2-P17
❑ 98UppDecPQ3-P17
❑ 98UppDecQD-10
❑ 98UppDecTD-10
❑ 98UppDecWFG-WF4
❑ 98UppDecWFP-WF4
❑ 99AurSty-3
❑ 99Pac-37
❑ 99PacAur-16
❑ 99PacAurCC-3
❑ 99PacAurCF-4
❑ 99PacAurCFC-4
❑ 99PacAurCFPB-4
❑ 99PacAurCP-3
❑ 99PacAurCPP-3
❑ 99PacAurGU-3
❑ 99PacAurPD-16
❑ 99PacCop-37
❑ 99PacCra-2
❑ 99PacGol-37
❑ 99PacGolCD-5
❑ 99PacHomaA-3
❑ 99PacIceB-37
❑ 99PacIn tCN-3
❑ 99PacPasAP-4
❑ 99PacPreD-37
❑ 99PacTeaL-4
❑ 99RetHoc-7
❑ 99SP AutPS-8
❑ 99UppDecCL-52
❑ 99UppDecCLCLC-52
❑ 99UppDecM-21
❑ 99UppDecMGS-21
❑ 99UppDecMLL-LL1
❑ 99UppDecMSS-21
❑ 99UppDecMSS-21
❑ 99UppDecMT-MVP3
❑ 99UppDecRDR-DR8
❑ 99UppDecRDRI-DR8
❑ 99UppDecRG-G10B
❑ 99UppDecRG-7
❑ 99UppDecRGI-G10B
❑ 99UppDecRP-7
❑ 99UppDecRTotC-TC8

**Haskett, Chris**
❑ 95Sla-189

**Hass, W.**
❑ 52JunBluT-27

**Hassan, Sana**
❑ 95GerDELE-405
❑ 96GerDELE-301

**Hassard, Bob**
❑ 44BeeGro2P-406
❑ 45QuaOatP-21
❑ 52Par-105
❑ 53Par-4

**Hasselblad, Peter**
❑ 89SweSemE-78
❑ 90SweSemE-253
❑ 92SweSemE-206
❑ 93SweSemE-176
❑ 94SweLeaE-31
❑ 95SweLeaE-267
❑ 95SweUppDE-135

**Hassinen, Jani**
❑ 93FinnJyvHS-57
❑ 93FinnSIS-246
❑ 94Fin-136
❑ 94FinnSIS-42
❑ 94FinRef-136
❑ 94FinSupTW-136
❑ 95FinnSIS-23

**Hassleblad, Peter**
❑ 95SweLeaEFF-14

**Hassman, Jeff**
❑ 91AirCanSJHL-A14

**Hastman, Darren**
❑ 907thInnSWHL-112
❑ 917thInnSWHL-294

**Hatch, Chris**
❑ 91AirCanSJHL-B48
❑ 92MPSPhoSJHL-15

**Hatcher, Derian**
❑ 897thInnSOHL-154
❑ 907thInnSOHL-309
❑ 90Sco-430
❑ 90ScoCan-430
❑ 90UppDec-359
❑ 90UppDecF-359
❑ 91OPCPre-143
❑ 91Par-75
❑ 91ParFre-75
❑ 91Pin-328
❑ 91PinFre-328
❑ 91ProSet-543
❑ 91ProSetFre-543
❑ 91ProSetPla-258
❑ 91ScoCan-656
❑ 91ScoRoo-106T
❑ 91UppDec-546
❑ 91UppDecF-546
❑ 92Bow-365
❑ 92OPC-123
❑ 92PanSti-H
❑ 92PanStiFre-H
❑ 92Par-72
❑ 92ParEmel-72
❑ 92Pin-34
❑ 92PinFre-34
❑ 92ProSet-75
❑ 92Sco-51
❑ 92ScoCan-51
❑ 92StaClu-414
❑ 92Top-405
❑ 92TopGol-405G
❑ 92Ult-319
❑ 92UppDec-287
❑ 93Don-77
❑ 93Lea-212
❑ 93OPCPre-520
❑ 93OPCPreG-520
❑ 93PanSti-274
❑ 93Par-46
❑ 93ParEmel-46
❑ 93Pin-57
❑ 93PinCan-57
❑ 93Pow-61
❑ 93Sco-168
❑ 93ScoCan-168
❑ 93StaClu-494
❑ 93StaCluFDI-494
❑ 93StaCluO-494
❑ 93TopPre-520
❑ 93TopPreG-520
❑ 93Ult-39
❑ 93UppDec-204
❑ 93UppDecSP-37
❑ 94BeAPla-R15
❑ 94BeAPla-R136
❑ 94BeAPSig-125
❑ 94CanGamNHLP-83
❑ 94Don-317
❑ 94EASpo-194
❑ 94Fle-52
❑ 94Lea-286
❑ 94LeaLim-25
❑ 94OPCPre-332
❑ 94OPCPreSE-332
❑ 94ParSE-SE45
❑ 94ParSEG-SE45
❑ 94ParVin-V30
❑ 94Pin-55
❑ 94PinArtP-55
❑ 94PinRinC-55
❑ 94Sco-148
❑ 94ScoGol-148
❑ 94ScoPla-148
❑ 94ScoPlaTS-148
❑ 94Sel-50
❑ 94SelGol-50
❑ 94StaClu-107
❑ 94StaCluFDI-107
❑ 94StaCluMOMS-107
❑ 94StaCluSTWC-107
❑ 94StaHoc-14
❑ 94StaPinS-35
❑ 94StaPinS-NNO
❑ 94StaPos-10
❑ 94StaScoS-148
❑ 94TopPre-332
❑ 94TopPreSE-332
❑ 94Ult-52
❑ 94UppDec-127
❑ 94UppDecEleIce-127
❑ 94UppDecNBAP-24
❑ 94UppDecSPI-SP20
❑ 94UppDecSPIDC-SP20
❑ 95ColCho-224
❑ 95ColChoPC-224
❑ 95ColChoPCP-224
❑ 95Don-326
❑ 95Emo-47
❑ 95Lea-279
❑ 95Met-40
❑ 95ParInt-58
❑ 95ParIntEl-58
❑ 95Pin-70
❑ 95PinArtP-70
❑ 95PinRinC-70
❑ 95PlaOneoOne-140
❑ 95ProMag-123
❑ 95Sco-225
❑ 95ScoBlaIce-225
❑ 95ScoBlaIceAP-225
❑ 95ScoChelt-8
❑ 95SkyImp-46
❑ 95SP-40
❑ 95StaClu-78
❑ 95StaCluMOMS-78
❑ 95StaScoS-225
❑ 95Sum-72
❑ 95SumArtP-72
❑ 95SumIce-72
❑ 95SweGloWC-109
❑ 95Top-197
❑ 95TopOPCI-197
❑ 95Ult-38
❑ 95UltGolM-38
❑ 95UppDec-3
❑ 95UppDecEleIce-3
❑ 95UppDecEleIceG-3
❑ 95UppDecSpeE-SE112
❑ 95UppDecSpeEdiG-SE112
❑ 96ColCho-70
❑ 96DonCanI-4
❑ 96DonCanIGPP-4
❑ 96DonCanIRPP-4
❑ 96DonEli-28
❑ 96DonEliDCS-28
❑ 96Fla-22
❑ 96FlaBluI-22
❑ 96Fle-26
❑ 96LeaPre-80
❑ 96LeaPrePP-80
❑ 96MetUni-39
❑ 96NHLProSTA-123
❑ 96SkyImp-29
❑ 96SP-45
❑ 96StaPos-8
❑ 96StaScoS-NNO
❑ 96Sum-29
❑ 96SumArtP-29
❑ 96SumIce-29
❑ 96SumMet-29
❑ 96SumPreS-29
❑ 96TeaOut-80
❑ 96Ult-42
❑ 96UltGolM-42
❑ 96UppDec-44
❑ 96UppDecPP-P27
❑ 96Zen-19
❑ 96ZenArtP-19
❑ 97ColCho-70
❑ 97Don-168
❑ 97DonCanI-124
❑ 97DonCanIDS-124
❑ 97DonCanIPS-124
❑ 97DonEli-32
❑ 97DonEliAsp-32
❑ 97DonEliS-32
❑ 97DonLim-21
❑ 97DonLimExp-21
❑ 97DonPre-21
❑ 97DonPreCttC-21
❑ 97DonPreProG-168
❑ 97DonPreProS-168
❑ 97DonPri-30
❑ 97DonPriSoA-30
❑ 97EssOlyHH-32
❑ 97EssOlyHHF-32
❑ 97Kat-44
❑ 97KatGol-44
❑ 97KatSil-44
❑ 97Lea-144
❑ 97LeaFraMat-144
❑ 97LeaFraMDC-144
❑ 97LeaInt-144
❑ 97LeaIntUI-144
❑ 97Pac-214
❑ 97PacCop-214
❑ 97PacCroR-40
❑ 97PacCroREG-40
❑ 97PacCroRIB-40
❑ 97PacCroRS-40
❑ 97PacDyn-35
❑ 97PacDynC-35
❑ 97PacDynDG-35
❑ 97PacDynEG-35
❑ 97PacDynIB-35
❑ 97PacDynR-35
❑ 97PacDynSil-35
❑ 97PacDynTan-38
❑ 97PacEmeGre-214
❑ 97PacIceB-214
❑ 97PacOme-69
❑ 97PacOmeC-69
❑ 97PacOmeDG-69
❑ 97PacOmeEG-69
❑ 97PacOmeG-69
❑ 97PacOmeIB-69
❑ 97PacPar-57
❑ 97PacParC-57
❑ 97PacParDG-57
❑ 97PacParEG-57
❑ 97PacParIB-57
❑ 97PacParRed-57
❑ 97PacParSil-57
❑ 97PacRed-214
❑ 97PacSil-214
❑ 97Pin-182
❑ 97PinCer-54
❑ 97PinCerMB-54
❑ 97PinCerMG-54
❑ 97PinCerMR-54
❑ 97PinCerR-54
❑ 97PinIns-138
❑ 97PinPrePBB-182
❑ 97PinPrePBC-182
❑ 97PinPrePBM-182
❑ 97PinPrePBY-182
❑ 97PinPrePFC-182
❑ 97PinPrePFM-182
❑ 97PinPrePFY-182
❑ 97PinPrePla-182
❑ 97PinTotCMPG-54
❑ 97PinTotCPB-54
❑ 97PinTotCPG-54
❑ 97PinTotCPR-54
❑ 97Sco-198
❑ 97SPAut-45
❑ 97Stu-96
❑ 97StuPrePG-96
❑ 97StuPrePS-96
❑ 97UppDec-51
❑ 97UppDec-397
❑ 97UppDecBD-94
❑ 97UppDecBDDD-94
❑ 97UppDecBDQD-94
❑ 97UppDecBDTD-94
❑ 97UppDecIce-2
❑ 97UppDecIceP-2
❑ 97UppDecIPS-2
❑ 97UppDecTSS-20A
❑ 98Be A PPA-194
❑ 98Be A PPAA-194
❑ 98Be A PPAAF-194
❑ 98Be A PPSE-194
❑ 98Be APG-194
❑ 98Fin-39
❑ 98FinNo P-39
❑ 98FinNo PR-39
❑ 98FinRef-39
❑ 98O-PChr-148
❑ 98O-PChrBM-B13
❑ 98O-PChrBMR-B13
❑ 98O-PChrR-148
❑ 98Pac-176
❑ 98PacAur-54
❑ 98PacDynI-55
❑ 98PacDynIIB-55
❑ 98PacDynIR-55
❑ 98PacIceB-176
❑ 98PacOmeH-69
❑ 98PacOmeODI-69
❑ 98PacOmeR-69
❑ 98PacPar-63
❑ 98PacParC-63
❑ 98PacParEG-63
❑ 98PacParH-63
❑ 98PacParIB-63
❑ 98PacParS-63
❑ 98PacRed-176
❑ 98Top-148
❑ 98TopBoaM-B13
❑ 98TopO-P-148
❑ 98UC-65
❑ 98UD ChoPCR-65
❑ 98UD ChoR-65
❑ 98UDCP-65
❑ 98UppDec-259
❑ 98UppDecE-259
❑ 98UppDecE1o1-259
❑ 98UppDecGJ-GJ9
❑ 98UppDecGR-259
❑ 98UppDecM-66
❑ 98UppDecMGS-66
❑ 98UppDecMSS-66
❑ 98UppDecMSS-66
❑ 99Pac-118
❑ 99PacCop-118
❑ 99PacGol-118
❑ 99PacIceB-118
❑ 99PacPreD-118
❑ 99UppDecM-65
❑ 99UppDecMGS-65
❑ 99UppDecMSS-65
❑ 99UppDecMSS-65

**Hatcher, Kevin**
❑ 83NorBayC-8
❑ 86CapKod-11
❑ 86CapPol-10
❑ 87CapKod-4
❑ 87CapTeaIss-9
❑ 87OPC-68
❑ 87PanSti-179
❑ 87Top-68
❑ 88CapBor-8
❑ 88CapSmo-8
❑ 88OPC-86
❑ 88PanSti-365
❑ 88Top-86
❑ 89CapKod-4
❑ 89CapTeaIss-6
❑ 89OPC-146
❑ 89PanSti-347
❑ 89Top-146
❑ 90Bow-70
❑ 90BowTif-70
❑ 90CapKod-6
❑ 90CapPos-6
❑ 90CapSmo-6
❑ 90OPC-147
❑ 90PanSti-167
❑ 90ProSet-311
❑ 90ProSet-376
❑ 90Sco-90
❑ 90ScoCan-90
❑ 90ScoHotRS-42
❑ 90Top-147
❑ 90TopTif-147
❑ 90UppDec-109
❑ 90UppDec-486
❑ 90UppDecF-109
❑ 90UppDecF-486
❑ 91Bow-296
❑ 91Bow-409
❑ 91CapJun5-10
❑ 91CapKod-9
❑ 91Gil-36
❑ 91Kra-20
❑ 91OPC-310
❑ 91OPCPre-88
❑ 91PanSti-198
❑ 91Par-191
❑ 91ParFre-191
❑ 91Pin-131
❑ 91PinFre-131
❑ 91ProSet-249
❑ 91ProSet-316
❑ 91ProSetFre-249
❑ 91ProSetFre-316
❑ 91ProSetPC-29
❑ 91ProSetPla-127
❑ 91ProSetPla-281
❑ 91ScoAme-20
❑ 91ScoAme-340
❑ 91ScoCan-20
❑ 91ScoCan-370
❑ 91ScoKel-7
❑ 91StaClu-140
❑ 91SweSemWCS-136
❑ 91Top-310
❑ 91TopTeaSL-16
❑ 91UppDec-98
❑ 91UppDec-361
❑ 91UppDec-511
❑ 91UppDecF-98
❑ 91UppDecF-361
❑ 91UppDecF-511
❑ 92Bow-230
❑ 92Bow-271
❑ 92CapKod-9
❑ 92HumDum1-11
❑ 92McDUppD-19
❑ 92OPC-145
❑ 92PanSti-167
❑ 92PanStiFre-167
❑ 92Par-198
❑ 92ParEmel-198
❑ 92Pin-11
❑ 92PinFre-11
❑ 92ProSet-204
❑ 92Sco-273
❑ 92Sco-439
❑ 92ScoCan-273
❑ 92ScoCan-439
❑ 92ScoUSAG-13
❑ 92SeaPat-48
❑ 92StaClu-301
❑ 92Top-149
❑ 92TopGol-149G
❑ 92Ult-231
❑ 92UppDec-198
❑ 93Don-369
❑ 93Kra-33
❑ 93Lea-34
❑ 93OPCPre-435
❑ 93OPCPreG-435
❑ 93PanSti-C
❑ 93Par-221
❑ 93ParEmel-221
❑ 93Pin-90
❑ 93PinCan-90
❑ 93PinCap-25
❑ 93PinCapC-25
❑ 93Pow-261
❑ 93Sco-136
❑ 93Sco-450
❑ 93ScoCan-136
❑ 93ScoCan-450
❑ 93ScoFra-23
❑ 93StaClu-153
❑ 93StaCluFDI-153
❑ 93StaCluFDIO-153
❑ 93StaCluO-153
❑ 93SweSemWCS-175
❑ 93TopPre-435
❑ 93TopPreG-435
❑ 93Ult-118
❑ 93UppDec-140
❑ 93UppDecSP-169
❑ 94BeAPla-R131
❑ 94BeAPSig-48
❑ 94CanGamNHLP-363
❑ 94Don-199
❑ 94EASpo-151
❑ 94Fin-17
❑ 94FinnJaaK-114
❑ 94FinnJaaK-342
❑ 94FinRef-17
❑ 94FinSupTW-17
❑ 94Fle-53
❑ 94HocWit-17
❑ 94Lea-369
❑ 94Par-259
❑ 94ParGol-259
❑ 94ParVin-V54
❑ 94Pin-345
❑ 94PinArtP-345
❑ 94PinRinC-345
❑ 94Sel-148
❑ 94SelGol-148
❑ 94SP-31
❑ 94SPDieCut-31
❑ 94StaClu-220
❑ 94StaCluFDI-220
❑ 94StaCluMOMS-220
❑ 94StaCluSTWC-220
❑ 94StaPos-11
❑ 94Ult-233
❑ 94UppDec-332
❑ 94UppDecEleIce-332
❑ 94UppDecSPI-SP86
❑ 94UppDecSPI-SP110
❑ 94UppDecSPIDC-SP86
❑ 94UppDecSPIDC-SP110
❑ 95Bow-48
❑ 95BowAllFoi-48
❑ 95CanGamNHLP-89
❑ 95ColCho-186
❑ 95ColChoPC-186
❑ 95ColChoPCP-186
❑ 95Don-95
❑ 95DonEli-17
❑ 95DonEliDCS-17
❑ 95DonEliDCU-17
❑ 95Emo-48
❑ 95Fin-148
❑ 95FinnSemWC-106
❑ 95FinRef-148
❑ 95ImpSti-34
❑ 95Lea-117
❑ 95Met-41
❑ 95ParInt-56
❑ 95ParIntEl-56
❑ 95Pin-10
❑ 95PinArtP-10
❑ 95PinRinC-10
❑ 95PlaOneoOne-248
❑ 95Sco-12
❑ 95ScoBlaIce-12
❑ 95ScoBlaIceAP-12
❑ 95SelCer-41
❑ 95SelCerMG-41
❑ 95SkyImp-47
❑ 95SP-37
❑ 95StaClu-42
❑ 95StaCluMO-28
❑ 95StaCluMOMS-42
❑ 95StaScoS-12
❑ 95Sum-41
❑ 95SumArtP-41
❑ 95SumIce-41
❑ 95SweGloWC-105
❑ 95Top-273
❑ 95TopOPCI-273
❑ 95TopSupSki-53
❑ 95TopSupSkiPla-53
❑ 95Ult-230
❑ 95UppDec-256
❑ 95UppDec-309
❑ 95UppDecEleIce-256
❑ 95UppDecEleIce-309
❑ 95UppDecEleIceG-256
❑ 95UppDecEleIceG-309
❑ 95UppDecSpeE-SE25
❑ 95UppDecSpeEdiG-SE25
❑ 95Zen-44
❑ 96BeAPAut-14
❑ 96BeAPAutSil-14
❑ 96BeAPla-14
❑ 96ColCho-71
❑ 96Don-29
❑ 96DonEli-24
❑ 96DonEliDCS-24
❑ 96DonPrePro-29
❑ 96Fla-76
❑ 96FlaBluI-76
❑ 96FlePicF5-17
❑ 96Lea-48
❑ 96LeaPreP-48
❑ 96MetUni-126
❑ 96Pin-3
❑ 96PinArtP-3
❑ 96PinFoi-3
❑ 96PinPreS-3
❑ 96PinRinC-3
❑ 96PlaOneoOne-408
❑ 96Sco-117
❑ 96ScoArtPro-117
❑ 96ScoDeaCAP-117
❑ 96ScoGolB-117
❑ 96ScoSpeAP-117
❑ 96SP-130
❑ 96StaCluMO-11
❑ 96SweSemW-163
❑ 96TopNHLP-33
❑ 96TopPicOI-33
❑ 96Ult-140
❑ 96UltGolM-140
❑ 96UppDec-319
❑ 96UppDecBD-54
❑ 96UppDecBDG-54
❑ 96UppDecPP-P21
❑ 97ColCho-207
❑ 97Don-26
❑ 97DonLim-21
❑ 97DonLimExp-21
❑ 97DonPre-70
❑ 97DonPreCttC-70
❑ 97DonPreProG-26
❑ 97DonPreProS-26
❑ 97DonPri-100
❑ 97DonPriSoA-100
❑ 97EssOlyHH-31
❑ 97EssOlyHHF-31
❑ 97Kat-117
❑ 97KatGol-117
❑ 97KatSil-117
❑ 97Lea-129
❑ 97LeaFraMat-129
❑ 97LeaFraMDC-129
❑ 97LeaInt-129
❑ 97LeaIntUI-129
❑ 97Pac-227
❑ 97PacCop-227
❑ 97PacDyn-101
❑ 97PacDynC-101
❑ 97PacDynDG-101
❑ 97PacDynEG-101
❑ 97PacDynIB-101
❑ 97PacDynR-101
❑ 97PacDynSil-101
❑ 97PacDynTan-62
❑ 97PacEmeGre-227
❑ 97PacIceB-227
❑ 97PacInv-112
❑ 97PacInvC-112
❑ 97PacInvEG-112
❑ 97PacInvIB-112
❑ 97PacInvR-112
❑ 97PacInvS-112
❑ 97PacOme-185
❑ 97PacOmeC-185
❑ 97PacOmeDG-185
❑ 97PacOmeEG-185
❑ 97PacOmeG-185
❑ 97PacOmeIB-185
❑ 97PacPar-149
❑ 97PacParC-149
❑ 97PacParDG-149
❑ 97PacParEG-149
❑ 97PacParIB-149
❑ 97PacParRed-149
❑ 97PacParSil-149
❑ 97PacRed-227
❑ 97PacSil-227
❑ 97Pin-171
❑ 97PinCer-86
❑ 97PinCerMB-86

❑ 97PinCerMG-86
❑ 97PinCerMR-86
❑ 97PinCerR-86
❑ 97PinIns-98
❑ 97PinPrePBB-171
❑ 97PinPrePBC-171
❑ 97PinPrePBM-171
❑ 97PinPrePBY-171
❑ 97PinPrePFC-171
❑ 97PinPrePFM-171
❑ 97PinPrePFY-171
❑ 97PinPrePla-171
❑ 97PinTotCMPG-86
❑ 97PinTotCPB-86
❑ 97PinTotCPG-86
❑ 97PinTotCPR-86
❑ 97Sco-222
❑ 97ScoPen-8
❑ 97ScoPenPla-8
❑ 97ScoPenPre-8
❑ 97SPAut-127
❑ 97UppDec-343
❑ 98Be A PPA-112
❑ 98Be A PPAA-112
❑ 98Be A PPAAF-112
❑ 98Be A PPTBASG-112
❑ 98Be APG-112
❑ 98BowBes-24
❑ 98BowBesAR-24
❑ 98BowBesR-24
❑ 98O-PChr-73
❑ 98O-PChrBM-B14
❑ 98O-PChrBMR-B14
❑ 98O-PChrR-73
❑ 98Pac-352
❑ 98PacAur-153
❑ 98PacDynI-149
❑ 98PacDynIIB-149
❑ 98PacDynIR-149
❑ 98PacIceB-352
❑ 98PacPar-191
❑ 98PacParC-191
❑ 98PacParEG-191
❑ 98PacParH-191
❑ 98PacParIB-191
❑ 98PacParS-191
❑ 98PacRed-352
❑ 98Top-73
❑ 98TopBoaM-B14
❑ 98TopO-P-73
❑ 98UC-172
❑ 98UD ChoPCR-172
❑ 98UD ChoR-172
❑ 98UppDec-159
❑ 98UppDec-348
❑ 98UppDecE-159
❑ 98UppDecE-348
❑ 98UppDecE1o1-159
❑ 98UppDecE1o1-348
❑ 98UppDecGR-159
❑ 98UppDecGR-348
❑ 99Pac-336
❑ 99PacCop-336
❑ 99PacGol-336
❑ 99PacIceB-336
❑ 99PacPreD-336
**Hatcher, Mark**
❑ 82NorBayC-9
❑ 83NorBayC-9
❑ 88ProAHL-35
**Hatinen, Markus**
❑ 94FinnSIS-253
**Hatzkin, Ben**
❑ 74TeaCanLWHA-7
**Hauer, Brett**
❑ 93Cla-67
❑ 93LasVegThu-11
❑ 93MinDulCom-3
❑ 93Pow-504
❑ 93StaCluTUSA-7
❑ 93TopPreTUSA-20
❑ 93Ult-484
❑ 94ClaAut-NNO
❑ 94SweLeaE-268
**Haugh, Tom**
❑ 67SweHoc-154
**Hausler, Oliver**
❑ 94GerDELE-382
**Hauswirth, Mike**
❑ 90MicTecHus-7
❑ 91MicTecHus-5
**Hautamaa, Juha**
❑ 93FinnSIS-130
❑ 94FinnSIS-120
❑ 95FinnSIS-41
❑ 95FinnSISL-105
❑ 95FinnSISSpo-8
**Havanov, Alexander**
❑ 92BirBul-9
❑ 93BirBul-9
**Havel, Jan**
❑ 69SweHocS-26
❑ 69SweWorC-10
❑ 71SweHocS-51
❑ 72SweSemWC-29
❑ 74SweSemHVS-71
**Havelid, Niclas**
❑ 91SweSemE-11
❑ 92SweSemE-35
❑ 94SweLeaE-36
❑ 95SweLeaE-5
❑ 95SweUppDE-5
**Havenhand, Andy**
❑ 93SheSte-1
❑ 94SheSte-23

❑ 95SolBar-5
**Haviland, Kyle**
❑ 94CenHocL-46
❑ 95MusFur-3
**Hawerchuk, Dale**
❑ 81JetPos-6
❑ 82Jet-8
❑ 82Jet-9
❑ 82OPC-3
❑ 82OPC-374
❑ 82OPC-380
❑ 82OPC-381
❑ 82OPCSti-204
❑ 82OPCSti-249
❑ 82PosCer-1
❑ 83Ess-9
❑ 83Jet-8
❑ 83OPC-377
❑ 83OPC-385
❑ 83OPCSti-282
❑ 83PufSti-5
❑ 83Vac-126
❑ 84JetPol-8
❑ 84KelAccD-5A
❑ 84KelAccD-5B
❑ 84OPC-339
❑ 84OPC-393
❑ 84OPCSti-284
❑ 84OPCSti-285
❑ 84Top-152
❑ 857ECreCar-21
❑ 85JetPol-7
❑ 85JetSIID-4
❑ 85OPC-109
❑ 85OPCSti-248
❑ 85Top-109
❑ 85TopStiIns-8
❑ 86JetBor-9
❑ 86KraDra-25
❑ 86OPC-74
❑ 86OPCSti-104
❑ 86Top-74
❑ 87Jet-9
❑ 87OPC-149
❑ 87OPCBoxB-I
❑ 87OPCSti-255
❑ 87PanSti-363
❑ 87ProAll-7
❑ 87Top-149
❑ 87TopBoxB-I
❑ 88EssAllSta-16
❑ 88FriLayS-9
❑ 88JetPol-9
❑ 88OPC-65
❑ 88OPCBoxB-K
❑ 88OPCMin-12
❑ 88OPCSti-143
❑ 88PanSti-155
❑ 88Top-65
❑ 88TopBoxB-K
❑ 89JetSaf-16
❑ 89Kra-50
❑ 89OPC-122
❑ 89OPCSti-134
❑ 89PanSti-162
❑ 89SweSemWCS-67
❑ 89Top-122
❑ 90Bow-129
❑ 90BowTif-129
❑ 90Kra-10
❑ 90OPC-141
❑ 90OPCPre-40
❑ 90PanSti-317
❑ 90ProSet-330A
❑ 90ProSet-330B
❑ 90ProSet-415
❑ 90SabBluS-8
❑ 90SabCam-9
❑ 90Sco-50
❑ 90ScoCan-50
❑ 90ScoHotRS-22
❑ 90ScoRoo-2T
❑ 90Top-141
❑ 90TopTeaSL-11
❑ 90TopTif-141
❑ 90UppDec-53
❑ 90UppDec-443
❑ 90UppDecF-53
❑ 90UppDecF-443
❑ 91Bow-31
❑ 91Kra-36
❑ 91OPC-32
❑ 91OPC-65
❑ 91OPCPre-1
❑ 91PanSti-296
❑ 91Par-18
❑ 91Par-216
❑ 91ParFre-18
❑ 91ParFre-216
❑ 91Pin-80
❑ 91PinFre-80
❑ 91ProSet-24
❑ 91ProSetFre-24
❑ 91ProSetPla-11
❑ 91SabBluS-7
❑ 91SabPepC-7
❑ 91ScoAme-259
❑ 91ScoAme-376
❑ 91ScoCan-266
❑ 91ScoCan-429
❑ 91StaClu-312
❑ 91Top-65
❑ 91TopTeaSL-2
❑ 91UppDec-12

❑ 91UppDec-79
❑ 91UppDec-126
❑ 91UppDecF-12
❑ 91UppDecF-79
❑ 91UppDecF-126
❑ 92Bow-308
❑ 92OPC-212
❑ 92PanSti-247
❑ 92PanStiFre-247
❑ 92Par-11
❑ 92ParEmel-11
❑ 92Pin-316
❑ 92PinFre-316
❑ 92ProSet-12
❑ 92SabBluS-8
❑ 92SabJubF-5
❑ 92Sco-272
❑ 92ScoCan-272
❑ 92SeaPat-68
❑ 92StaClu-419
❑ 92Top-296
❑ 92TopGol-296G
❑ 92Ult-15
❑ 92UppDec-302
❑ 93Don-35
❑ 93Lea-71
❑ 93OPCPre-7
❑ 93OPCPreF-11
❑ 93OPCPreG-7
❑ 93PanSti-102
❑ 93Par-23
❑ 93ParEmel-23
❑ 93Pin-260
❑ 93PinCan-260
❑ 93Pow-29
❑ 93SabLimETI-3
❑ 93SabNoc-7
❑ 93Sco-159
❑ 93ScoCan-159
❑ 93StaCluFDI-220
❑ 93StaCluFDIO-220
❑ 93StaCluO-220
❑ 93TopPre-7
❑ 93TopPreF-11
❑ 93TopPreG-7
❑ 93Ult-149
❑ 93UppDec-411
❑ 93UppDecSP-16
❑ 94BeAPla-R7
❑ 94BeAPSig-5
❑ 94CanGamNHLP-46
❑ 94Don-44
❑ 94EASpo-16
❑ 94FinnJaaK-89
❑ 94Fla-18
❑ 94Fle-21
❑ 94HocWit-22
❑ 94Lea-313
❑ 94LeaLim-94
❑ 94OPCPre-320
❑ 94OPCPreSE-320
❑ 94Par-29
❑ 94ParGol-29
❑ 94Pin-43
❑ 94PinArtP-43
❑ 94PinRinC-43
❑ 94Sco-192
❑ 94ScoGol-192
❑ 94ScoPla-192
❑ 94ScoPlaTS-192
❑ 94Sel-42
❑ 94SelGol-42
❑ 94SP-15
❑ 94SPDieCut-15
❑ 94StaClu-248
❑ 94StaCluFDI-248
❑ 94StaCluMOMS-248
❑ 94StaCluSTWC-248
❑ 94TopPre-320
❑ 94TopPreSE-320
❑ 94Ult-23
❑ 94UppDec-102
❑ 94UppDecEleIce-102
❑ 94UppDecSPI-SP9
❑ 94UppDecSPIDC-SP9
❑ 95CanGamNHLP-238
❑ 95ColCho-245
❑ 95ColChoPC-245
❑ 95ColChoPCP-245
❑ 95Don-384
❑ 95DonEli-100
❑ 95DonEliDCS-100
❑ 95DonEliDCU-100
❑ 95Emo-147
❑ 95Fin-153
❑ 95FinRef-153
❑ 95ImpSti-103
❑ 95Lea-184
❑ 95Met-124
❑ 95ParInt-180
❑ 95ParIntEI-180
❑ 95PlaOneoOne-306
❑ 95Sco-222
❑ 95ScoBlaIce-222
❑ 95ScoBlaIceAP-222
❑ 95SelCer-97
❑ 95SelCerMG-97
❑ 95SkyImp-140
❑ 95SP-123
❑ 95StaClu-46
❑ 95StaCluMOMS-46
❑ 95Sum-95
❑ 95SumArtP-95
❑ 95SumIce-95

❑ 95Top-271
❑ 95TopOPCI-271
❑ 95Ult-299
❑ 95UppDec-38
❑ 95UppDecEleIce-38
❑ 95UppDecEleIceG-38
❑ 96BeAPAut-203
❑ 96BeAPAutSil-203
❑ 96BeAPla-203
❑ 96ColCho-196
❑ 96Don-90
❑ 96DonPrePro-90
❑ 96Fla-67
❑ 96FlaBluI-67
❑ 96FlePic-120
❑ 96FlyPos-9
❑ 96Lea-124
❑ 96LeaPreP-124
❑ 96MetUni-111
❑ 96Pin-44
❑ 96PinArtP-44
❑ 96PinFoi-44
❑ 96PinPreS-44
❑ 96PinRinC-44
❑ 96PlaOneoOne-409
❑ 96Sco-51
❑ 96ScoArtPro-51
❑ 96ScoDeaCAP-51
❑ 96ScoGolB-51
❑ 96ScoSpeAP-51
❑ 96SkyImp-94
❑ 96TopPic5C-FC8
❑ 96UppDec-120
❑ 96UppDecIce-50
❑ 96UppDecIcePar-50
❑ 97ColCho-190
❑ 97Don-36
❑ 97Pac-225
❑ 97PacCop-225
❑ 97PacEmeGre-225
❑ 97PacIceB-225
❑ 97PacRed-225
❑ 97PacSil-225
**Hawes, Chris**
❑ 917thInnSWHL-71
**Hawes, Mike**
❑ 89SpoChi-10
**Hawgood, Greg**
❑ 84KamBla-10
❑ 85KamBla-7
❑ 86KamBla-8
❑ 88ProAHL-168
❑ 89BruSpoA-10
❑ 89OPC-81
❑ 89OPCSti-67
❑ 89OPCSti-207
❑ 89PanSti-189
❑ 89Top-81
❑ 90OPC-236
❑ 90PanSti-10
❑ 90ProSet-442
❑ 90ScoRoo-79T
❑ 90Top-236
❑ 90TopTif-236
❑ 90UppDec-391
❑ 90UppDecF-391
❑ 91ProAHLCHL-226
❑ 92FlyUppDS-40
❑ 92oilIGA-9
❑ 92Par-361
❑ 92ParEmel-361
❑ 92StaClu-495
❑ 92Top-358
❑ 92TopGol-358G
❑ 93Don-245
❑ 93Lea-266
❑ 93OPCPre-422
❑ 93OPCPreG-422
❑ 93Pow-347
❑ 93Sco-396
❑ 93Sco-642
❑ 93ScoCan-396
❑ 93ScoCan-642
❑ 93ScoGol-642
❑ 93TopPre-422
❑ 93TopPreG-422
❑ 93Ult-388
❑ 94Lea-534
❑ 94Par-181
❑ 94ParGol-181
❑ 94PenFoo-2
❑ 95ColEdgI-152
❑ 95LasVegThu-3
❑ 96ColEdgFL-25
**Hawkins, Richard**
❑ 85KitRan-27
**Hawkins, Shawn**
❑ 89RayJrC-10
**Hawkins, Todd**
❑ 84BelBul-26
❑ 87FliSpi-5
❑ 89ProIHL-183
❑ 90ProAHLIHL-324
❑ 91ProAHLCHL-342
❑ 92St.JohML-7
❑ 93CleLum-9
❑ 93CleLumPos-11
❑ 96CinCyc-12
❑ 96CinCyc-6
**Hawley, Joe**
❑ 897thInnSOHL-105
❑ 907thInnSOHL-361
❑ 91ProAHLCHL-44
❑ 92PeoRivC-8
❑ 93MusFur-14

**Hawley, Kent**
❑ 88ProAHL-138
❑ 89ProAHL-348
❑ 90ProAHLIHL-40
❑ 95MadMon-9
**Haworth, Alan**
❑ 81SabMilP-5
❑ 82Cap-9
❑ 84CapPizH-8
❑ 84OPC-199
❑ 85CapPizH-7
❑ 85OPC-117
❑ 85OPCSti-108
❑ 85Top-117
❑ 86CapKod-12
❑ 86CapPol-11
❑ 86OPC-107
❑ 86OPCSti-255
❑ 86Top-107
❑ 87NordGenF-14
❑ 87NordYumY-5
❑ 87PanSti-187
❑ 88OPC-131
❑ 88OPCSti-195
❑ 88PanSti-55
❑ 88Top-131
**Haworth, Gordie (Gordon)**
❑ 50QueCit-8
❑ 51LavDaiS-68
❑ 52St.LawS-22
❑ 61UniOilW-6
**Hawryliw, Neil**
❑ 81IndChe-7
**Hawryluk, Neil**
❑ 89LetHur-8
**Hay, Charles**
❑ 83HalFP-C6
❑ 85HalFC-36
**Hay, Don**
❑ 95SlaMemC-25
**Hay, Dwayne**
❑ 94GueSto-9
❑ 95Cla-38
❑ 95GueStoSA-3
❑ 95Sla-89
❑ 96GueSto-22
❑ 96GueSto-35
❑ 96GueStoPC-9
❑ 96UppDecIce-123
❑ 97BowCHL-25
❑ 97BowCHLOPC-25
**Hay, George**
❑ 23V1281PauC-28
❑ 60Top-15
❑ 60TopSta-23
❑ 83HalFP-G7
❑ 85HalFC-98
**Hay, Red (Bill)**
❑ 44BeeGro2P-103
❑ 60ShiCoi-77
❑ 60Top-6
❑ 60TopSta-22
❑ 61ShiCoi-34
❑ 61Top-35
❑ 62Top-35
❑ 62TopHocBuc-9
❑ 63ChePho-20
❑ 63Top-34
❑ 63TorSta-17
❑ 64BeeGro3P-37
❑ 64CocCap-26
❑ 64Top-7
❑ 64TorSta-13
❑ 65Coc-28
❑ 65Top-62
❑ 94ParTalB-42
❑ 95Par66-30
❑ 95Par66Coi-30
**Hay, Scott**
❑ 94SarSti-3
**Hayden, Brian**
❑ 95Sla-153
**Hayden, Jamie**
❑ 907thInnSWHL-171
❑ 93ThuBayS-2
**Hayden, Steve**
❑ 92CorBigRed-14
**Hayes, Bobby**
❑ 93WatBlaH-11
**Hayes, Robert (James)**
❑ 51LavDaiLSJ-5
❑ 51LavDaiQSHL-8
**Hayko, Rick**
❑ 85MinDul-9
**Haynes, Paul**
❑ 33V357IceK-6
❑ 34BeeGro1P-157
❑ 34SweCap-21
❑ 35DiaMatT2-26
❑ 35DiaMatT3-24
❑ 350PCV304C-95
❑ 36V356WorG-33
❑ 370PCV304E-155
❑ 38QuaOatP-17
❑ 390PCV3011-31
❑ 400PCV3012-112
**Hayton, Bryan**
❑ 96KitRan-13
**Hayward, Brian**
❑ 83Jet-9
❑ 83Vac-127
❑ 84JetPol-8
❑ 85JetPol-9
❑ 85OPC-226
❑ 86CanaPos-7
❑ 86KraDra-26

❑ 86OPC-255
❑ 87CanaPos-10
❑ 87CanaVacS-61
❑ 87CanaVacS-67
❑ 87CanaVacS-77
❑ 87CanaVacS-84
❑ 87OPC-230
❑ 87OPCMin-15
❑ 87OPCSti-175
❑ 87OPCSti-184
❑ 87PanSti-55
❑ 87PanSti-376A
❑ 88CanaPos-13
❑ 88OPC-195
❑ 88OPCMin-13
❑ 88OPCSti-52
❑ 88PanSti-214
❑ 88PanSti-251
❑ 88PanSti-402
❑ 88Top-195
❑ 89CanaKra-10
❑ 89CanaPos-14
❑ 89OPC-237
❑ 89OPCSti-50
❑ 89PanSti-246
❑ 90OPC-23
❑ 90PanSti-61
❑ 90ProSet-150
❑ 90Sco-304C
❑ 90ScoCan-304C
❑ 90ScoRoo-78T
❑ 90Top-23
❑ 90TopTif-23
❑ 90UppDec-171
❑ 90UppDec-449
❑ 90UppDecF-171
❑ 90UppDecF-449
❑ 91Bow-122
❑ 91OPC-178
❑ 91PanSti-106
❑ 91Pin-83
❑ 91PinFre-83
❑ 91ProSet-327
❑ 91ProSetFre-327
❑ 91ScoAme-211
❑ 91ScoCan-211
❑ 91ScoCan-554
❑ 91ScoRoo-4T
❑ 91ShaSanJSA-10
❑ 91StaClu-19
❑ 91Top-178
❑ 91UppDec-59
❑ 91UppDecF-59
❑ 92Bow-60
❑ 92Pin-266
❑ 92PinFre-266
❑ 92StaClu-364
❑ 92Top-436
❑ 92TopGol-436G
❑ 93PanSti-265
**Hayward, Rick**
❑ 86SheCan-19
❑ 89ProIHL-207
❑ 90ProAHLIHL-345
❑ 91ProAHLCHL-469
❑ 95CleLum-14
❑ 96CleLum-11
❑ 98GerDELE-144
**Hazelhurst, Mark**
❑ 96GuiFla-18
**Head, Barry**
❑ 74SioCitM-5
**Head, Don**
❑ 44BeeGro2P-28
❑ 61ShiCoi-11
❑ 61Top-17
❑ 69SeaTotW-1
**Headley, Curly**
❑ 23V1281PauC-37
❑ 24C144ChaCig-29
❑ 24V130MapC-4
**Headley, Gopher**
❑ 24V1452-23
**Healey, Grant**
❑ 90RayJrC-9
❑ 91RayJrC-7
**Healey, Paul**
❑ 93PriAlbR-9
❑ 94PriAlbR-5
❑ 95ColEdgI-44
❑ 97Don-205
❑ 97DonPreProG-205
❑ 97DonPreProS-205
**Healy, Glenn**
❑ 88KinSmo-13
❑ 88OPCSti-123
❑ 88OPCSti-255
❑ 88PanSti-68
❑ 89Isl-9
❑ 89PanSti-97
❑ 90OPC-400
❑ 90PanSti-88
❑ 90ProSet-183
❑ 90Sco-294
❑ 90ScoCan-294
❑ 90UppDec-18
❑ 90UppDecF-18
❑ 91Bow-224
❑ 91OPC-368
❑ 91PanSti-249
❑ 91Par-107
❑ 91ParFre-107
❑ 91Pin-185
❑ 91PinFre-185
❑ 91ProSet-153

❑ 91ProSetFre-153
❑ 91ProSetPC-18
❑ 91ProSetPla-73
❑ 91ScoAme-68
❑ 91ScoCan-68
❑ 91StaClu-369
❑ 91Top-368
❑ 91UppDec-224
❑ 91UppDecF-224
❑ 92Bow-434
❑ 92OPC-262
❑ 92Par-341
❑ 92Par-505
❑ 92ParEmel-341
❑ 92ParEmel-505
❑ 92Pin-121
❑ 92PinFre-121
❑ 92Sco-188
❑ 92ScoCan-188
❑ 92StaClu-356
❑ 92Top-305
❑ 92TopGol-305G
❑ 92Ult-126
❑ 93Don-211
❑ 93OPCPre-486
❑ 93OPCPreG-486
❑ 93PanSti-65
❑ 93Par-405
❑ 93ParEmel-405
❑ 93Pin-365
❑ 93PinCan-365
❑ 93Pow-390
❑ 93Sco-177
❑ 93Sco-533
❑ 93ScoCan-177
❑ 93ScoCan-533
❑ 93ScoGol-533
❑ 93StaClu-453
❑ 93StaCluFDI-453
❑ 93StaCluO-453
❑ 93TopPre-486
❑ 93TopPreG-486
❑ 93Ult-106
❑ 93Ult-371
❑ 93UppDec-321
❑ 94BeAPla-R13
❑ 94BeAPSig-28
❑ 94CanGamNHLP-287
❑ 94Don-283
❑ 94EASpo-84
❑ 94Lea-310
❑ 94OPCPre-388
❑ 94OPCPreSE-388
❑ 94ParSE-SE117
❑ 94ParSEG-SE117
❑ 94Pin-430
❑ 94PinArtP-430
❑ 94PinRinC-430
❑ 94TopPre-388
❑ 94TopPreSE-388
❑ 94UppDec-455
❑ 94UppDecEleIce-455
❑ 95ColCho-272
❑ 95ColChoPC-272
❑ 95ColChoPCP-272
❑ 95Don-54
❑ 95ParInt-406
❑ 95ParIntEI-406
❑ 95Pin-91
❑ 95PinArtP-91
❑ 95PinRinC-91
❑ 95Sco-273
❑ 95ScoBlaIce-273
❑ 95ScoBlaIceAP-273
❑ 95Top-292
❑ 95TopOPCI-292
❑ 95Ult-101
❑ 95UltGolM-101
❑ 95UppDec-30
❑ 95UppDecEleIce-30
❑ 95UppDecEleIceG-30
❑ 96BeAPAut-140
❑ 96BeAPAutSil-140
❑ 96BeAPla-140
❑ 96Don-212
❑ 96DonPrePro-212
❑ 96Sco-34
❑ 96ScoArtPro-34
❑ 96ScoDeaCAP-34
❑ 96ScoGolB-34
❑ 96ScoSpeAP-34
❑ 96UppDec-202
❑ 97PacDynBKS-61
❑ 97PacPar-180
❑ 97PacParC-180
❑ 97PacParDG-180
❑ 97PacParEG-180
❑ 97PacParIB-180
❑ 97PacParRed-180
❑ 97PacParSil-180
❑ 97Sco-22
❑ 97ScoArtPro-22
❑ 97ScoGolBla-22
❑ 97ScoMapL-2
❑ 97ScoMapLPla-2
❑ 97ScoMapLPre-2
**Heaney, Geraldine**
❑ 94ClaWomOH-W19
❑ 97ColCho-282
❑ 97EssOlyHH-57
❑ 97EssOlyHHF-57
**Heaney, Mike**
❑ 95LouIceG-6
❑ 95LouIceGP-7

**Heaphy, Shawn**
❑ 91ProAHLCHL-588
❑ 93ClaProPro-141
❑ 93LasVegThu-12
**Hearn, Donny (Don)**
❑ 91BriColJHL-36
❑ 92BriColJHL-58
**Hearn, Jamie**
❑ 92OklCitB-8
❑ 94CenHocL-47
❑ 95FliGen-22
❑ 95MusFur-16
**Heaslip, Mark**
❑ 76OPCNHL-376
❑ 79OPC-320
**Heasty, John**
❑ 93FliGen-10
**Heath, Randy**
❑ 86SwePanS-235
**Heathwood, Steve**
❑ 74SioCitM-6
**Heatley, Murray**
❑ 74FigSaiWHA-12
❑ 75OPCWHA-53
**Heaton, Scott**
❑ 94SheSte-18
❑ 97SheSte-15
**Hebenton, Andy**
❑ 44BeeGro2P-29
❑ 44BeeGro2P-322
❑ 57Top-58
❑ 58Top-46
❑ 59Top-16
❑ 60ShiCoi-91
❑ 60Top-42
❑ 60TopSta-24
❑ 61ShiCoi-90
❑ 61Top-55
❑ 62Top-54
❑ 62TopHocBuc-10
❑ 63Top-15
❑ 64BeeGro3P-11
❑ 94ParMisL-97
**Hebenton, Clay**
❑ 76RoaPhoWHA-5
**Hebert, Andre**
❑ 77GraVic-11
**Hebert, Guy**
❑ 89ProIHL-5
❑ 90ProAHLIHL-89
❑ 91ProAHLCHL-29
❑ 92Bow-32
❑ 92OPC-116
❑ 92OPCPre-40
❑ 92Par-386
❑ 92ParEmel-386
❑ 92Sco-460
❑ 92ScoCan-460
❑ 92StaClu-401
❑ 92Top-112
❑ 92TopGol-112G
❑ 92Ult-394
❑ 92UppDec-501
❑ 93Don-13
❑ 93Lea-356
❑ 93OPCPre-519
❑ 93OPCPreG-519
❑ 93Par-279
❑ 93ParEmel-279
❑ 93Pin-167
❑ 93PinCan-167
❑ 93PinExp-1
❑ 93Pow-2
❑ 93Sco-426
❑ 93Sco-489
❑ 93Sco-502
❑ 93ScoCan-426
❑ 93ScoCan-489
❑ 93ScoCan-502
❑ 93ScoGol-502
❑ 93StaClu-295
❑ 93StaCluFDI-295
❑ 93StaCluO-295
❑ 93TopPre-519
❑ 93TopPreG-519
❑ 93Ult-254
❑ 93UppDec-1
❑ 94BeAPla-R47
❑ 94BeAPSig-99
❑ 94CanGamNHLP-269
❑ 94Don-81
❑ 94DucCarJr-9
❑ 94EASpo-6
❑ 94Fin-20
❑ 94FinRef-20
❑ 94FinSupTW-20
❑ 94Fla-3
❑ 94Kra-40
❑ 94KraGoaM-2
❑ 94Lea-142
❑ 94LeaLimI-1
❑ 94OPCPre-338
❑ 94OPCPreSE-338
❑ 94ParSE-SE1
❑ 94ParSEG-SE1
❑ 94Pin-15
❑ 94PinArtP-15
❑ 94PinMas-MA4
❑ 94PinRinC-15
❑ 94Sco-42
❑ 94ScoFra-TF1
❑ 94ScoGol-42
❑ 94ScoPla-42
❑ 94ScoPlaTS-42
❑ 94Sel-79
❑ 94SelGol-79
❑ 94SP-5
❑ 94SPDieCut-5
❑ 94StaClu-6
❑ 94StaCluFDI-6
❑ 94StaCluMOMS-6
❑ 94StaCluSTWC-6
❑ 94TopPre-338
❑ 94TopPreSE-338
❑ 94Ult-3
❑ 94UppDec-3
❑ 94UppDecEleIce-3
❑ 95ColCho-287
❑ 95ColChoPC-287
❑ 95ColChoPCP-287
❑ 95Don-71
❑ 95DonEliPW-5
❑ 95Emo-2
❑ 95Fin-122
❑ 95FinnSemWC-210
❑ 95FinRef-122
❑ 95Kra-37
❑ 95Lea-271
❑ 95Met-1
❑ 95ParInt-4
❑ 95ParIntEl-4
❑ 95Pin-143
❑ 95PinArtP-143
❑ 95PinRinC-143
❑ 95PlaOneoOne-1
❑ 95PlaOneoOne-113
❑ 95ProMag-42
❑ 95Sco-94
❑ 95ScoBlaIce-94
❑ 95ScoBlaIceAP-94
❑ 95SkyImp-2
❑ 95SP-3
❑ 95StaClu-82
❑ 95StaCluMOMS-82
❑ 95Sum-58
❑ 95SumArtP-58
❑ 95SumIce-58
❑ 95Top-112
❑ 95TopOPCI-112
❑ 95Ult-1
❑ 95UltGolM-1
❑ 95UppDec-467
❑ 95UppDecEleIce-467
❑ 95UppDecEleIceG-467
❑ 95UppDecSpeE-SE3
❑ 95UppDecSpeEdiG-SE3
❑ 95Zen-99
❑ 96BeAPAut-61
❑ 96BeAPAutSil-61
❑ 96BeAPla-61
❑ 96ColCho-5
❑ 96ColCho-309
❑ 96Don-164
❑ 96DonPrePro-164
❑ 96Duc-21
❑ 96Fla-1
❑ 96FlaBluI-1
❑ 96Fle-1
❑ 96Fle-147
❑ 96KraUppD-16
❑ 96Lea-88
❑ 96LeaPreP-88
❑ 96MetUni-1
❑ 96NHLProSTA-42
❑ 96Pin-88
❑ 96PinArtP-88
❑ 96PinFoi-88
❑ 96PinPreS-88
❑ 96PinRinC-88
❑ 96Sco-13
❑ 96ScoArtPro-13
❑ 96ScoDeaCAP-13
❑ 96ScoGolB-13
❑ 96ScoSpeAP-13
❑ 96SkyImp-1
❑ 96SP-5
❑ 96Sum-75
❑ 96SumArtP-75
❑ 96SumIce-75
❑ 96SumMet-75
❑ 96SumPreS-75
❑ 96TeaOut-72
❑ 96Ult-1
❑ 96UltGolM-1
❑ 96UppDec-2
❑ 96UppDecBD-53
❑ 96UppDecBDG-53
❑ 97BeAPlaSTP-1
❑ 97ColCho-1
❑ 97ColChoSta-SQ42
❑ 97Don-167
❑ 97DonCanI-37
❑ 97DonCanIDS-37
❑ 97DonCanIPS-37
❑ 97DonEli-45
❑ 97DonEliAsp-45
❑ 97DonEliS-45
❑ 97DonLim-102
❑ 97DonLimExp-102
❑ 97DonPre-129
❑ 97DonPreCttC-129
❑ 97DonPreProG-167
❑ 97DonPreProS-167
❑ 97DonPri-124
❑ 97DonPriPG-20
❑ 97DonPriPGP-20
❑ 97DonPriSoA-124
❑ 97Kat-1
❑ 97KatGol-1
❑ 97KatSil-1
❑ 97Lea-72
❑ 97LeaFraMat-72
❑ 97LeaFraMDC-72
❑ 97LeaInt-72
❑ 97LeaIntUI-72
❑ 97LeaPipDre-7
❑ 97Pac-260
❑ 97PacCop-260
❑ 97PacCroR-1
❑ 97PacCroREG-1
❑ 97PacCroRFODC-1
❑ 97PacCroRIB-1
❑ 97PacCroRS-1
❑ 97PacDyn-2
❑ 97PacDynC-2
❑ 97PacDynDG-2
❑ 97PacDynEG-2
❑ 97PacDynIB-2
❑ 97PacDynR-2
❑ 97PacDynSil-2
❑ 97PacDynSto-1
❑ 97PacDynTan-24
❑ 97PacEmeGre-260
❑ 97PacIceB-260
❑ 97PacInTheCLC-1
❑ 97PacInv-2
❑ 97PacInvC-2
❑ 97PacInvEG-2
❑ 97PacInvIB-2
❑ 97PacInvR-2
❑ 97PacInvS-2
❑ 97PacOme-2
❑ 97PacOmeC-2
❑ 97PacOmeDG-2
❑ 97PacOmeEG-2
❑ 97PacOmeG-2
❑ 97PacOmeIB-2
❑ 97PacPar-1
❑ 97PacParC-1
❑ 97PacParDG-1
❑ 97PacParEG-1
❑ 97PacParGSL-1
❑ 97PacParIB-1
❑ 97PacParRed-1
❑ 97PacParSil-1
❑ 97PacRed-260
❑ 97PacRev-1
❑ 97PacRevC-1
❑ 97PacRevE-1
❑ 97PacRevIB-1
❑ 97PacRevR-1
❑ 97PacRevRtSD-1
❑ 97PacRevS-1
❑ 97PacSil-260
❑ 97Pin-90
❑ 97PinArtP-90
❑ 97PinCer-19
❑ 97PinCerMB-19
❑ 97PinCerMG-19
❑ 97PinCerMR-19
❑ 97PinCerR-19
❑ 97PinIns-70
❑ 97PinIns-P70
❑ 97PinInsC-11
❑ 97PinInsCC-70
❑ 97PinInsCG-11
❑ 97PinInsEC-70
❑ 97PinInsSto-6
❑ 97PinInsSUG-8A/B
❑ 97PinInsSUG-8C/D
❑ 97PinMas-6
❑ 97PinMasDC-6
❑ 97PinMasJ-6
❑ 97PinMasPro-6
❑ 97PinPrePBB-90
❑ 97PinPrePBC-90
❑ 97PinPrePBM-90
❑ 97PinPrePBY-90
❑ 97PinPrePFC-90
❑ 97PinPrePFM-90
❑ 97PinPrePFY-90
❑ 97PinPrePla-90
❑ 97PinRepMas-2
❑ 97PinRinC-90
❑ 97PinTin-4
❑ 97PinTotCMPG-19
❑ 97PinTotCPB-19
❑ 97PinTotCPG-19
❑ 97PinTotCPR-19
❑ 97Sco-6
❑ 97ScoArtPro-6
❑ 97ScoGolBla-6
❑ 97ScoMigDPla-14
❑ 97ScoMigDPre-14
❑ 97ScoMigDuc-14
❑ 97ScoNetW-1
❑ 97SPAutSotT-GH
❑ 97Stu-37
❑ 97StuPrePG-37
❑ 97StuPrePS-37
❑ 97UppDec-6
❑ 97UppDecBD-34
❑ 97UppDecBDDD-34
❑ 97UppDecBDQD-34
❑ 97UppDecBDTD-34
❑ 97Zen-66
❑ 97Zen5x7-11
❑ 97ZenGolImp-11
❑ 97ZenSilImp-11
❑ 97ZenZGol-66
❑ 97ZenZSil-66
❑ 98Be A PPA-4
❑ 98Be A PPAA-4
❑ 98Be A PPAAF-4
❑ 98Be A PPTBASG-4
❑ 98Be APG-4
❑ 98Fin-58
❑ 98FinNo P-58
❑ 98FinNo PR-58
❑ 98FinRef-58
❑ 98O-PChr-48
❑ 98O-PChrR-48
❑ 98Pac-54
❑ 98PacAur-2
❑ 98PacCroR-2
❑ 98PacCroRLS-2
❑ 98PacDynI-2
❑ 98PacDynIIB-2
❑ 98PacDynIR-2
❑ 98PacIceB-54
❑ 98PacOmeH-3
❑ 98PacOmeODI-3
❑ 98PacOmeR-3
❑ 98PacPar-2
❑ 98PacParC-2
❑ 98PacParEG-2
❑ 98PacParGSLC-1
❑ 98PacParH-2
❑ 98PacParIB-2
❑ 98PacParS-2
❑ 98PacRed-54
❑ 98PacRev-1
❑ 98PacRevIS-1
❑ 98PacRevR-1
❑ 98SP Aut-3
❑ 98SPxFin-2
❑ 98SPxFinR-2
❑ 98SPxFinS-2
❑ 98Top-48
❑ 98TopGolLC1-57
❑ 98TopGolLC1B-57
❑ 98TopGolLC1BOoO-57
❑ 98TopGolLC1OoO-57
❑ 98TopGolLC1R-57
❑ 98TopGolLC1ROoO-57
❑ 98TopGolLC2-57
❑ 98TopGolLC2B-57
❑ 98TopGolLC2BOoO-57
❑ 98TopGolLC2OoO-57
❑ 98TopGolLC2R-57
❑ 98TopGolLC2ROoO-57
❑ 98TopGolLC3-57
❑ 98TopGolLC3B-57
❑ 98TopGolLC3BOoO-57
❑ 98TopGolLC3OoO-57
❑ 98TopGolLC3R-57
❑ 98TopGolLC3ROoO-57
❑ 98TopO-P-48
❑ 98UC-1
❑ 98UD ChoPCR-1
❑ 98UD ChoR-1
❑ 98UDCP-1
❑ 98UppDec-212
❑ 98UppDecE-212
❑ 98UppDecE1o1-212
❑ 98UppDecGR-212
❑ 98UppDecM-6
❑ 98UppDecMGS-6
❑ 98UppDecMSS-6
❑ 98UppDecMSS-6
❑ 99Pac-7
❑ 99PacAur-1
❑ 99PacAurGU-1
❑ 99PacAurPD-1
❑ 99PacCop-7
❑ 99PacGol-7
❑ 99PacIceB-7
❑ 99PacIn tCN-1
❑ 99PacPreD-7
❑ 99SP AutPS-3
❑ 99UppDecM-6
❑ 99UppDecMGS-6
❑ 99UppDecMSS-6
❑ 99UppDecMSS-6
**Hebert, Ian**
❑ 94BirBul-10
❑ 95BirBul-16
**Hebert, Patrick**
❑ 907thInnSQMJHL-195
**Hebert, Roland**
❑ 51LavDaiQSHL-19
**Hebky, David**
❑ 917thInnSWHL-56
❑ 92BriColJHL-215
**Hecht, Jochen**
❑ 94GerDELE-282
❑ 95GerDELE-277
❑ 95SigRooA-17
❑ 95SigRooAPC-17
❑ 96GerDELE-173
❑ 99Pac-367
❑ 99PacCop-367
❑ 99PacGol-367
❑ 99PacIceB-367
❑ 99PacPreD-367
❑ 99UppDecM-188
❑ 99UppDecMGS-188
❑ 99UppDecMSS-188
❑ 99UppDecMSS-188
**Hedberg, Anders**
❑ 69SweHocS-132
❑ 69SweWorC-112
❑ 70SweHocS-91
❑ 70SweHocS-282
❑ 71SweHocS-14
❑ 71SweHocS-150
❑ 72SweHocS-12
❑ 72SweHocS-172
❑ 72SweSemWC-69
❑ 73SweHocS-17
❑ 73SweHocS-215
❑ 73SweWorCS-17
❑ 73SweWorCS-215
❑ 74OPCWHA-17
❑ 74SweHocS-23
❑ 74SweHocS-219
❑ 74SweSemHVS-12
❑ 75OPCWHA-40
❑ 75OPCWHA-72
❑ 76OPCWHA-66
❑ 76OPCWHA-125
❑ 77OPCWHA-3
❑ 78OPC-25
❑ 78Top-25
❑ 79OPC-240
❑ 79Top-240
❑ 80OPC-73
❑ 80OPCSup-15
❑ 80Top-73
❑ 81OPC-225
❑ 81OPC-237
❑ 81OPCSti-166
❑ 81Top-58
❑ 81Top-E98
❑ 82OPC-225
❑ 83OPC-245
❑ 83OPCSti-215
❑ 83PufSti-19
❑ 84OPC-143
❑ 84OPCSti-102
❑ 84Top-107
❑ 85OPCSti-200
❑ 91SweSemWCS-235
❑ 92FutTre76CC-141
❑ 95SweGloWC-70
**Hedberg, Goran**
❑ 69SweHocS-206
**Hedberg, Jan**
❑ 65SweCorI-137
**Hedberg, Johan**
❑ 92SweSemE-152
❑ 93SweSemE-122
❑ 94SweLeaE-40
❑ 94SweLeaECS-7
❑ 95SweGloWC-6
❑ 95SweLeaE-61
❑ 95SweLeaES-7
❑ 95SweUppDE-94
**Hedberg, Ove**
❑ 65SweCorI-44B
❑ 67SweHoc-30
❑ 69SweHocS-43
**Hede, Niklas**
❑ 94FinnSIS-328
❑ 95FinnSIS-223
❑ 96GerDELE-43
❑ 98GerDELE-161
**Hedell, Jan**
❑ 85SwePanS-182
❑ 86SwePanS-114
❑ 87SwePanS-113
**Hedenstrom, Lars**
❑ 64SweCorI-83
❑ 65SweCorI-83
❑ 67SweHoc-46
❑ 69SweHocS-60
❑ 70SweHocS-21
**Hedenstrom, Per**
❑ 83SweSemE-64
❑ 84SweSemE-64
❑ 85SwePanS-56
**Hedican, Bret**
❑ 92Cla-87
❑ 92Par-385
❑ 92ParEmel-385
❑ 92Pin-228
❑ 92PinFre-228
❑ 92ProSet-240
❑ 92Sco-471
❑ 92ScoCan-471
❑ 92StaClu-203
❑ 92Top-517
❑ 92TopGol-517G
❑ 92UppDec-414
❑ 93Don-291
❑ 93Lea-286
❑ 93OPCPre-224
❑ 93OPCPreG-224
❑ 93Par-177
❑ 93ParEmel-177
❑ 93Pin-315
❑ 93PinCan-315
❑ 93Pow-210
❑ 93StaClu-81
❑ 93StaCluFDI-81
❑ 93StaCluFDIO-81
❑ 93StaCluO-81
❑ 93TopPre-224
❑ 93TopPreG-224
❑ 93Ult-66
❑ 93UppDec-185
❑ 94Lea-425
❑ 94OPCPre-162
❑ 94OPCPreSE-162
❑ 94Par-243
❑ 94ParGol-243
❑ 94Pin-369
❑ 94PinArtP-369
❑ 94PinRinC-369
❑ 94StaClu-27
❑ 94StaCluFDI-27
❑ 94StaCluMOMS-27
❑ 94StaCluSTWC-27
❑ 94TopPre-162
❑ 94TopPreSE-162
❑ 94Ult-224
❑ 94UppDec-398
❑ 94UppDecEleIce-398
❑ 95BeAPla-19
❑ 95BeAPSig-S19
❑ 95BeAPSigDC-S19
❑ 95CanuBuiDA-3
❑ 95ColCho-255
❑ 95ColChoPC-255
❑ 95ColChoPCP-255
❑ 95ParInt-216
❑ 95ParIntEl-216
❑ 95PlaOneoOne-317
❑ 95Top-72
❑ 95TopOPCI-72
❑ 95Ult-316
❑ 95UppDec-95
❑ 95UppDecEleIce-95
❑ 95UppDecEleIceG-95
❑ 96CanuPos-3
❑ 96ClaGol-87
❑ 96UppDec-173
❑ 97Pac-284
❑ 97PacCop-284
❑ 97PacEmeGre-284
❑ 97PacIceB-284
❑ 97PacRed-284
❑ 97PacSil-284
❑ 97SPAut-158
❑ 98O-PChr-81
❑ 98O-PChrR-81
❑ 98Pac-426
❑ 98PacIceB-426
❑ 98PacOmeH-102
❑ 98PacOmeODI-102
❑ 98PacOmeR-102
❑ 98PacRed-426
❑ 98Top-81
❑ 98TopO-P-81
❑ 98UppDec-196
❑ 98UppDecE-196
❑ 98UppDecE1o1-196
❑ 98UppDecGR-196
**Hedican, Tom**
❑ 93LonKni-27
**Hedin, Pierre**
❑ 97UppDecBD-36
❑ 97UppDecBDDD-36
❑ 97UppDecBDQD-36
❑ 97UppDecBDTD-36
❑ 98UC-291
❑ 98UD ChoPCR-291
❑ 98UD ChoR-291
**Hedin, Thomas**
❑ 83SweSemE-46
❑ 84SweSemE-46
❑ 86SwePanS-233
❑ 87SwePanS-225
**Hedington, Steve**
❑ 83OshGen-10
❑ 86SudWol-14
**Hedlund, Anders**
❑ 65SweCorI-166
❑ 71SweHocS-343
**Hedlund, Henrik**
❑ 64SweCorI-144
❑ 65SweCorI-144
❑ 67SweHoc-287
❑ 69SweHocS-334
❑ 70SweHocS-252
❑ 71SweHocS-311
❑ 72SweHocS-294
❑ 73SweHocS-141
❑ 73SweWorCS-141
❑ 74SweHocS-220
**Hedlund, Karl-Soren**
❑ 65SweCorI-138A
❑ 65SweCorI-201
❑ 67SweHoc-269
❑ 69SweHocS-314
❑ 70SweHocS-216
**Hedlund, Leif**
❑ 83SweSemE-190
❑ 84SweSemE-213
**Hedlund, Mattias**
❑ 93SweSemE-74
**Hedlund, Tommy**
❑ 89SweSemE-10
❑ 95SweLeaE-160
❑ 95SweUppDE-7
**Hedman, Glenn**
❑ 89SweSemE-200
❑ 93SweSemE-11
**Hedman, Kjell**
❑ 67SweHoc-31
❑ 69SweHocS-44
❑ 70SweHocS-2
**Hedqvist, Nils-Arne**
❑ 71SweHocS-335
❑ 72SweHocS-149
❑ 74SweHocS-221
**Hedson, David**
❑ 72SarProSta-134
**Hedstrom, Kjell-Ake**
❑ 67SweHoc-186
**Heed, Jonas**
❑ 84SweSemE-229
❑ 85SwePanS-225
❑ 86SwePanS-255
❑ 87SwePanS-237
❑ 89SweSemE-221
❑ 90SweSemE-30
❑ 91SweSemE-280
❑ 92SweSemE-305
**Heed, Klas**
❑ 85SwePanS-185
❑ 86SwePanS-116
❑ 89SweSemE-102
❑ 90SweSemE-105
❑ 91SweSemE-109
❑ 92SweSemE-128
**Heeney, Bob**
❑ 85BraWheK-4
**Heer, De**
❑ 79PanSti-282
**Heerema, Jeff**
❑ 98BowBes-147
❑ 98BowBesAR-147
❑ 98BowBesR-147
❑ 98BowCHL-146
❑ 98BowCHLAuB-A31
❑ 98BowCHLAuG-A31
❑ 98BowCHLAuS-A31
❑ 98BowCHLGA-146
❑ 98BowCHLOI-146
❑ 98BowChrC-146
❑ 98BowChrCGA-146
❑ 98BowChrCGAR-146
❑ 98BowChrCOI-146
❑ 98BowChrCOIR-146
❑ 98BowChrCR-146
❑ 98FinFutF-F9
❑ 98FinFutFR-F9
❑ 98O-PChr-233
❑ 98O-PChrR-233
❑ 98Top-233
❑ 98TopO-P-233
**Heffernan, Gerry**
❑ 34BeeGro1P-158
**Heffernan, Jimmy**
❑ 36V356WorG-130
**Hefford, Jayna**
❑ 97ColCho-289
**Hegberg, Jason**
❑ 96LetHur-5
**Hegberg, Rob**
❑ 94PriAlbR-6
**Hegen, Dieter**
❑ 89SweSemWCS-114
❑ 91SweSemWCS-173
❑ 92UppDec-370
❑ 93SweSemWCS-158
❑ 94FinnJaaK-287
❑ 94GerDELE-311
❑ 95GerDELE-94
❑ 95GerDELE-433
❑ 95SweGloWC-225
❑ 96GerDELE-281
❑ 96SweSemW-198
❑ 98GerDELE-292
❑ 98GerDELE-338
**Hegen, Gerhard**
❑ 94GerDELE-169
❑ 95GerDELE-148
**Hehr, Jason**
❑ 92NorMicW-11
❑ 93NorMicW-13
**Heidt, Michael**
❑ 89SweSemWCS-113
❑ 91SweSemWCS-159
❑ 93SweSemWCS-151
❑ 94GerDELE-275
❑ 95GerDELE-246
❑ 96GerDELE-138
**Heidt, Robert**
❑ 94GerDELE-24
❑ 95GerDELE-21
**Heikkila, Kari**
❑ 82SweSemHVS-28
❑ 84SweSemE-175
❑ 85SwePanS-161
**Heikkinen, Kari**
❑ 93FinnJyvHS-292
❑ 93FinnSIS-70
❑ 94FinnSIS-11
**Heikkinen, Markku**
❑ 93FinnJyvHS-136
❑ 93FinnSIS-139
❑ 94FinnSIS-3
**Heil, Jeff**
❑ 98ChaChe-8
**Heiland, Jason**
❑ 94CenHocL-10
**Heinanen, Jokke**
❑ 93FinnJyvHS-352
❑ 93FinnSIS-224
❑ 94FinnSIS-116
❑ 94FinnSISJ-2
❑ 95FinnSIS-356
❑ 95FinnSISL-24
❑ 95FinnSISP-1
❑ 96FinnSISR-154
**Heindl, Bill**
❑ 69SweHocS-355
**Heine, Pete**
❑ 92WheThu-8
**Heinisto, Pasi**
❑ 93FinnSIS-269
❑ 94FinnSIS-288
**Heinola, Arto**
❑ 87SwePanS-267
**Heinold, Peter**
❑ 94GerDELE-434
**Heinrich, Lionel**
❑ 55BruPho-7
**Heinrichs, Marco**
❑ 94GerDELE-213
**Heins, Shawn**
❑ 917thInnSOHL-131
❑ 91PetPet-25

□ 92WinSpi-27
□ 99Pac-385
□ 99PacCop-385
□ 99PacGol-385
□ 99PacIceB-385
□ 99PacPreD-385
**Heinze, Stephen (Steve)**
□ 91Par-232
□ 91ParFre-232
□ 92OPC-92
□ 92OPCPre-24
□ 92Par-247
□ 92ParEmel-247
□ 92ProSet-220
□ 92Sco-476
□ 92ScoCan-476
□ 92StaClu-166
□ 92Top-519
□ 92TopGol-519G
□ 92Ult-3
□ 92UppDec-400
□ 92UppDecACH-3
□ 93Lea-116
□ 93OPCPre-378
□ 93OPCPreG-378
□ 93Pin-53
□ 93PinCan-53
□ 93Pow-289
□ 93Sco-251
□ 93ScoCan-251
□ 93StaClu-15
□ 93StaCluFDI-15
□ 93StaCluFDIO-15
□ 93StaClu0-15
□ 93TopPre-378
□ 93TopPreG-378
□ 94BeAPSig-161
□ 94CanGamNHLP-348
□ 94Lea-404
□ 94OPCPre-387
□ 94OPCPreSE-387
□ 94Pin-341
□ 94PinArtP-341
□ 94PinRinC-341
□ 94StaClu-137
□ 94StaCluFDI-137
□ 94StaCluMOMS-137
□ 94StaCluSTWC-137
□ 94TopPre-387
□ 94TopPreSE-387
□ 94UppDec-327
□ 94UppDecEIeIce-327
□ 95Sum-87
□ 95SumArtP-87
□ 95SumIce-87
□ 95Top-278
□ 95TopOPCI-278
□ 95UppDec-293
□ 95UppDecEIeIce-293
□ 95UppDecEIeIceG-293
□ 96BeAPAut-154
□ 96BeAPAutSil-154
□ 96BeAPla-154
□ 97ColCho-20
□ 97Pac-261
□ 97PacCop-261
□ 97PacEmeGre-261
□ 97PacIceB-261
□ 97PacRed-261
□ 97PacSil-261
□ 97ScoBru-10
□ 97ScoBruPla-10
□ 97ScoBruPre-10
□ 98Be A PPA-157
□ 98Be A PPAA-157
□ 98Be A PPAAF-157
□ 98Be A PPSE-157
□ 98Be APG-157
□ 98Pac-79
□ 98PacIceB-79
□ 98PacOmeH-15
□ 98PacOmeODI-15
□ 98PacOmeR-15
□ 98PacRed-79
□ 98UppDec-42
□ 98UppDecE-42
□ 98UppDecE1o1-42
□ 98UppDecGR-42
□ 99Pac-24
□ 99PacCop-24
□ 99PacGol-24
□ 99PacIceB-24
□ 99PacPreD-24
**Heinzle, Karl**
□ 94FinnJaaK-248
□ 95AusNatTea-8
**Heisig, Branjo**
□ 94GerDELE-394
□ 95GerDELE-164
□ 96GerDELE-238
**Heiskala, Earl**
□ 61HamRed-8
□ 69OPC-170
□ 70EssPowPla-212
□ 70FlyPos-5
□ 70OPC-193
□ 72ShaLosAW-6
**Heiskanen, Arto**
□ 93FinnJyvHS-347
□ 93FinnSIS-230
□ 94FinnSIS-30
□ 95FinnSIS-176
□ 95FinnSISL-27
**Heiss, Joseph**
□ 91SweSemWCS-153

□ 94FinnJaaK-272
□ 94GerDELE-200
□ 95FinnSemWC-165
□ 95GerDELE-195
□ 95GerDELE-429
□ 95SweGloWC-218
□ 96GerDELE-338
□ 98GerDELE-93
□ 98GerDELE-325
**Heistad, Jeramie**
□ 917thInnSWHL-324
**Heisten, Barrett**
□ 98SPXTopP-85
□ 98SPXTopPF-85
□ 98SPXTopPR-85
□ 98UppDecBD-116
□ 98UppDecDD-116
□ 98UppDecQD-116
□ 98UppDecTD-116
**Hejduk, Milan**
□ 94CzeAPSE-34
□ 95SigRoo-52A
□ 95SigRoo-52B
□ 95SigRooSig-52
□ 96CzeAPSE-157
□ 98Be A PPA-187
□ 98Be A PPAA-187
□ 98Be A PPAAF-187
□ 98Be A PPSE-187
□ 98Be APG-187
□ 98BowBes-110
□ 98BowBesAR-110
□ 98BowBesR-110
□ 98PacCroR-34
□ 98PacCroRLS-34
□ 98PacCroRRC-2
□ 98PacDynI-48
□ 98PacDynIIB-48
□ 98PacDynIR-48
□ 98PacDynIR-2
□ 98PacOmeH-67
□ 98PacOmeODI-67
□ 98PacOmeR-67
□ 98PacRev-36
□ 98PacRevIS-36
□ 98PacRevR-36
□ 98SP Aut-95
□ 98SPXTopP-16
□ 98SPXTopPF-16
□ 98SPXTopPR-16
□ 98TopGolLC1-90
□ 98TopGolLC1B-90
□ 98TopGolLC1BOoO-90
□ 98TopGolLC1OoO-90
□ 98TopGolLC1R-90
□ 98TopGolLC1ROoO-90
□ 98TopGolLC2-90
□ 98TopGolLC2B-90
□ 98TopGolLC2BOoO-90
□ 98TopGolLC2OoO-90
□ 98TopGolLC2R-90
□ 98TopGolLC2ROoO-90
□ 98TopGolLC3-90
□ 98TopGolLC3B-90
□ 98TopGolLC3BOoO-90
□ 98TopGolLC3OoO-90
□ 98TopGolLC3R-90
□ 98TopGolLC3ROoO-90
□ 98UppDec-247
□ 98UppDecE-247
□ 98UppDecE1o1-247
□ 98UppDecGR-247
□ 98UppDecM-55
□ 98UppDecMGS-55
□ 98UppDecMSS-55
□ 98UppDecMSS-55
□ 99Pac-106
□ 99PacAur-39
□ 99PacAurPD-39
□ 99PacGolCD-10
□ 99SP AutPS-95
□ 99UppDecCL-75
□ 99UppDecCLCLC-75
□ 99UppDecM-58
□ 99UppDecMGS-58
□ 99UppDecMSS-58
□ 99UppDecMSS-58
**Hejna, Tony**
□ 90ProAHLIHL-90
**Helander, Hannu**
□ 82SweSemHVS-34
**Helander, Peter**
□ 81SweSemHVS-8
□ 82SweSemHVS-9
**Helber, Mike**
□ 91MicWol-6
**Held, Daniel**
□ 89SweSemWCS-125
□ 94GerDELE-46
□ 95GerDELE-16
**Helenefors, Allan**
□ 69SweHocS-242
□ 70SweHocS-134
**Helenius, Sami**
□ 93FinnJyvHS-266
□ 94St.JohF-9
□ 95St.JohF-7
□ 98LasVegT-7
**Helin, Jimi**
□ 93FinnJyvHS-206
□ 93FinnSIS-263
**Helinski, Jon**
□ 84KitRan-18
**Helisten, Mikko**
□ 94Fin-131

□ 94FinRef-131
□ 94FinnSupTW-131
□ 94ParSE-SE219
□ 94ParSEG-SE219
□ 95FinnSIS-319
**Heljemo, Claes**
□ 89SweSemE-98
**Hellenberg, Par**
□ 89SweSemE-241
□ 90SweSemE-151
□ 91SweSemE-253
**Heller, Ott**
□ 330PCV304A-16
□ 33V129-34
□ 33V252CanG-29
□ 34BeeGro1P-275
□ 34DiaMatS-28
□ 35DiaMatT2-27
□ 35DiaMatT3-25
□ 35DiaMatTI-27
□ 36V356WorG-87
□ 390PCV3011-33
□ 400PCV3012-142
**Hellgren, Ari**
□ 81SweSemHVS-19
**Hellgren, Jens**
□ 83SweSemE-240
□ 84SweSemE-184
□ 85SweSemE-173
□ 86SweSemE-185
□ 87SweSemE-164
□ 89SweSemE-164
□ 90SweSemE-243
□ 91SweSemE-173
**Hellgren, Roger**
□ 84SweSemE-8
□ 85SweSemS-10
**Helling, Kjell**
□ 71SweHocS-95
**Hellkvist, Stefan**
□ 89SweSemE-253
□ 90SweSemE-166
□ 91SweSemE-271
□ 92SweSemE-291
□ 93SweSemE-257
□ 94SweLeaE-71
□ 95SweLeaE-239
□ 95SweUppDE-107
**Hellman, Bjorn**
□ 83SweSemE-7
□ 84SweSemE-5
□ 85SweSemS-8
□ 87SweSemS-12
**Hellmann, Kenneth**
□ 69SweHocS-167
**Hellsing, Torbjorn**
□ 70SweHocS-131
**Hellstrom, Lars**
□ 83SweSemE-169
**Helman, Harry**
□ 23V1451-5
**Helmer, Bryan**
□ 98BowBes-131
□ 98BowBesAR-131
□ 98BowBesR-131
□ 98LasVegT-8
**Helmer, Tim**
□ 82NorBayC-10
□ 83NorBayC-10
□ 83Ott67-12
□ 84Ott67-10
**Helminen, Raimo**
□ 89SweSemWCS-39
□ 90SweSemE-135
□ 91SweSemE-186
□ 91SweSemWCS-24
□ 92SweSemE-210
□ 93SweSemE-180
□ 93SweSemWCS-63
□ 94FinnJaaK-30
□ 94FinnSIS-363
□ 94SweLeaE-67
□ 94SweLeaEP-4
□ 95FinnKarWCL-2
□ 95FinnSemWC-14
□ 95FinnSISGC-12
□ 95SweLeaE-96
□ 95SweLeaEC-6
□ 95SweLeaEM-10
□ 95SweUppDE-141
□ 95SweUppDE-232
□ 96SweSemW-14
**Helmuth, Andy**
□ 84Ott67-11
**Hemenway, Ken**
□ 93OmaLan-9
**Hemming, Jonas**
□ 96FinnSISR-120
**Hemstrom, Jens**
□ 90SweSemE-147
□ 93SweSemE-187
□ 94SweLeaE-219
□ 95SweUppDE-181
**Henchberger, Lloyd**
□ 51LavDaiQSHL-66
**Henckle, James**
□ 87KinCan-13
**Hendelis, Andris**
□ 74SweHocS-72
**Henderson, Archie**
□ 82WhaJunHC-6
□ 84NovScoO-12
□ 89NasKni-8

**Henderson, Burt**
□ 92BriColJHL-70
□ 93TacRoc-13
□ 98CinCyc-8
**Henderson, Garfield**
□ 917thInnSWHL-0
□ 92MPSPhoSJHL-55
**Henderson, Jay**
□ 95RedDeeR-6
□ 98BowCHL-77
□ 98BowCHLJA-77
□ 98BowCHLOI-77
□ 98BowChrC-77
□ 98BowChrCGA-77
□ 98BowChrCGAR-77
□ 98BowChrCOI-77
□ 98BowChrCOIR-77
□ 98BowChrCR-77
**Henderson, John**
□ 51Par-23
**Henderson, Murray**
□ 44BeeGro2P-30
**Henderson, Paul**
□ 61HamRed-9
□ 63ChePho-21
□ 64BeeGro3P-76
□ 64CocCap-52
□ 64TorSta-14
□ 65Coc-50
□ 65Top-51
□ 66Top-46
□ 66TopUSAT-46
□ 67Top-103
□ 68MapLeaWB-3
□ 680PC-127
□ 68PosCerM-11
□ 68ShiCoi-161
□ 68Top-127
□ 690PC-47
□ 69Top-47
□ 70DadCoo-50
□ 70EssPowPla-30
□ 70MapLeaP-5
□ 70OPC-27
□ 70PosCerS-4
□ 70SarProSta-105
□ 71ColHea-4
□ 71FriLay-8
□ 71LetActR-22
□ 71MapLeaP-7
□ 71OPC-67
□ 71SarProSta-200
□ 71Top-67
□ 71TorSun-260
□ 72MapLeaP-10
□ 72MapLeaP-11
□ 720PC-126
□ 720PCPlaC-19
□ 720PCTeaC-14
□ 72SarProSta-203
□ 72Top-73
□ 73MacMil-9
□ 73MapLeaP-10
□ 73OPC-7
□ 73Top-7
□ 740PCNHL-219
□ 740PCWHA-57
□ 74TeaCanLWHA-8
□ 74Top-219
□ 750PCWHA-42
□ 760PCWHA-84
□ 770PCWHA-31
□ 91FutTreC72-63
□ 91FutTreC72-71
□ 91FutTreC72-81
□ 91FutTreC72-98
□ 91FutTreC72-P1
□ 91FutTreC72P7-3
□ 92FutTre76CC-105
□ 94ParTalB-50
□ 95Par66-40
□ 95Par66Coi-40
□ 97PinCerSS-1
□ 97PinCerSS-2
□ 97PinCerSS-3
□ 97PinCerSS-4
□ 97PinCerSS-5
**Henderson, Ryan**
□ 96SasBla-11
**Henderson, Todd**
□ 95AlaGolKin-2
□ 95AlaGolKin-6
**Hendrick, Jorg**
□ 94GerDELE-266
□ 95GerDELE-259
□ 98GerDELE-72
**Hendrickson, Dan**
□ 93MinGolG-12
□ 94MinGolG-12
□ 95MinGolG-15
□ 96MinGolGCAS-14
**Hendrickson, Darby**
□ 91MinGolG-9
□ 92MinGolG-9
□ 93Pow-505
□ 93StaCluTUSA-8
□ 93TopPreTUSA-4
□ 93Ult-485
□ 94Cla-104
□ 94ClaDraGol-104
□ 94ClaProPIH-LP6
□ 94MapLeaPP-29
□ 94St.JohML-12
□ 95Bow-129

□ 72SweHocS-266
**Henry, Alex**
□ 98BowCHL-156
□ 98BowCHLAuB-A17
□ 98BowCHLAuG-A17
□ 98BowCHLAuS-A17
□ 98BowCHLGA-156
□ 98BowCHLOI-156
□ 98BowChrC-156
□ 98BowChrCGA-156
□ 98BowChrCGAR-156
□ 98BowChrCOI-156
□ 98BowChrCOIR-156
□ 98BowChrCR-156
**Henry, Camille**
□ 44BeeGro2P-323
□ 50QueCit-9
□ 52JunBluT-73A
□ 52JunBluT-73B
□ 54Par-73
□ 54Top-32
□ 57Top-63
□ 58Top-54
□ 59Top-28
□ 59Top-46
□ 60ShiCoi-83
□ 60Top-53
□ 60TopSta-25
□ 61ShiCoi-87
□ 61Top-56
□ 62Top-62
□ 63Top-56
□ 63TorSta-18
□ 64BeeGro3P-38
□ 64BeeGro3P-131
□ 64CocCap-88
□ 64Top-14
□ 65Top-58
□ 67Top-26
□ 680PC-116
□ 68Top-116
□ 690PC-17
□ 69Top-17
□ 91UltOriS-22
□ 91UltOriSF-22
□ 93ParParR-PR50
□ 94ParMisL-100
□ 94ParTalB-107
**Henry, Dale**
□ 83SasBla-11
□ 84SprInd-17
□ 88ProAHL-322
□ 89ProAHL-231
□ 90ProAHLIHL-529
□ 94CenHocL-79
□ 94ClaEnf-E3
**Henry, Daryl**
□ 83MedHatT-19
**Henry, Frederic**
□ 97BowCHL-43
□ 97BowCHLOPC-43
**Henry, Jim**
□ 34BeeGro1P-276A
□ 34BeeGro1P-276B
□ 44BeeGro2P-31
□ 44BeeGro2P-104
□ 51Par-9
□ 52Par-74
□ 53Par-86
□ 54Par-49
□ 54Top-37
□ 92ParParR-PR7
**Henry, Nick**
□ 95SolBar-2
**Henry, Shane**
□ 94RicRen-2
**Henrikson, Gunnar**
□ 91BriColJHL-141
**Henriksson, Hannu**
□ 93FinnJyvHS-76
□ 93FinnSIS-114
□ 94FinnSIS-128
□ 95FinnSIS-30
□ 95FinnSIS-177
□ 95FinnSISL-102
□ 96FinnSISRS-1
**Henriksson, Kristian**
□ 84SweSemE-82
**Henriksson, Lars-Olof**
□ 67SweHoc-202
**Henriksson, Leif**
□ 67SweHoc-8
□ 67SweHoc-288
□ 69SweHocS-185
□ 69SweHocS-335
□ 69SweWorC-104
□ 70SweHocS-253
□ 71SweHocS-312
□ 72SweHocS-295
□ 73SweHocS-140
□ 74SweHocS-222
**Henriksson, Lennart**
□ 91SweSemE-214
**Henriksson, Olle**
□ 71SweHocS-394

**Herbst, A.**
□ 95GerDELE-179
**Herbst, Abe**
□ 96SarSti-10
□ 97UppDec-404
**Herbst, Marco**
□ 94GerDELE-141
□ 95GerDELE-125
□ 96GerDELE-205
**Herczeg, Don**
□ 83MedHatT-3
**Hergesheimer, Phil**
□ 34BeeGro1P-56
□ 400PCV3012-143
**Hergesheimer, Wally (Walter)**
□ 44BeeGro2P-324
□ 51Par-100
□ 52Par-20
□ 53Par-67
□ 54Par-71
□ 54Top-22
□ 57Top-33
□ 94ParMisL-26
**Hergott, Orrin**
□ 91AirCanSJHL-B51
**Herlick, Darcy**
□ 91AirCanSJHL-D1
□ 92MPSPhoSJHL-147
**Herlofsky, Derek**
□ 95DayBom-3
□ 96DayBom-20
**Hermansson, Dan**
□ 83SweSemE-207
□ 84SweSemE-232
**Hermansson, Hakan**
□ 83SweSemE-100
□ 93SweSemE-20
**Hermansson, Jorgen**
□ 93SweSemE-8
**Hermansson, Lennart**
□ 90SweSemE-142
□ 92SweSemE-238
□ 93SweSemE-207
□ 94SweLeaE-80
**Hermsdorf, Steve**
□ 92HarCri-13
**Hern, Riley**
□ 10C55SweCP-32
□ 10C56-22
□ 11C55-32
□ 83HalFP-K6
□ 85HalFC-232
**Herniman, Scott**
□ 88SudWol-25
**Herniman, Steve**
□ 87SauSteMG-19
□ 88KitRan-27
□ 91ProAHLCHL-146
□ 93MusFur-20
□ 94MusFur-16
□ 95MusFur-18
**Heron, Chris**
□ 96UppDec-382
**Heron, Red (Bob)**
□ 34BeeGro1P-323
□ 390PCV3011-53
□ 400PCV3012-140
**Heroux, Yves**
□ 84ChiSag-13
□ 86FreExp-11
□ 88FliSpi-6
□ 90ProAHLIHL-96
□ 90ProAHL-518
□ 91ProAHLCHL-34
□ 96GerDELE-18
**Herperger, Chris**
□ 907thInnSWHL-67
□ 917thInnSWHL-189
□ 93SeaThu-7
□ 95ColEdgI-45
**Herr, Craig**
□ 95RoaExp-21
**Herr, Matt**
□ 95DonEliWJ-37
□ 98PacCroR-141
□ 98PacCroRLS-141
□ 98PacDynI-194
□ 98PacDynIIB-194
□ 98PacDynIR-194
□ 98PacOmeH-246
□ 98PacOmeODI-246
□ 98PacOmeR-246
□ 98SP Aut-113
□ 98UppDec-386
□ 98UppDecE-386
□ 98UppDecE1o1-386
□ 98UppDecGR-386
□ 98UppDecM-214
□ 98UppDecMGS-214
□ 98UppDecMSS-214
□ 98UppDecMSS-214
□ 99SP AutPS-113
**Herrera, Mike**
□ 94DubFigS-11
**Herriman, Don**
□ 73QuaOatWHA-46
**Herrington, Rob**
□ 92BriColJHL-183
**Herron, Denis**
□ 74NHLActSta-234
□ 74NHLActStaU-16
□ 740PCNHL-45
□ 74Top-45
□ 750PCNHL-68

❏ 75Top-68
❏ 76OPCNHL-55
❏ 76Top-55
❏ 77OPCNHL-119
❏ 77PenPucB-1
❏ 77Top-119
❏ 78OPC-172
❏ 78Top-172
❏ 79CanaPos-7
❏ 79OPC-94
❏ 79PanSti-52
❏ 79Top-94
❏ 80CanaPos-7
❏ 80OPC-130
❏ 80PepCap-45
❏ 80Top-130
❏ 80Top-166
❏ 81CanaPos-9
❏ 81OPCSti-258
❏ 82OPC-239
❏ 82OPC-241
❏ 82OPC-270
❏ 82OPCSti-41
❏ 82OPCSti-252
❏ 83PenCok-13
❏ 83PenHeiP-12
❏ 83PenTealP-15
❏ 84KelAccD-5B
❏ 84OPC-176
❏ 84OPCSti-122
❏ 84PenHeiP-11
❏ 85OPC-186

**Hersh, Harold**
❏ 91 7thInnSQMJHL-219A
❏ 91 7thInnSQMJHL-219B
❏ 95FreCan-14
❏ 95SlaMemC-57

**Herter, Jason**
❏ 90UppDec-325
❏ 90UppDecF-325
❏ 91ProAHLCHL-600
❏ 92HamCan-9
❏ 93ClaProPro-58
❏ 98GerDELE-71

**Hervey, Matt**
❏ 83VicCou-11
❏ 87MonHaw-11
❏ 88ProAHL-186
❏ 89ProAHL-40
❏ 90MonHaw-10
❏ 90ProAHLIHL-251
❏ 91ProAHLCHL-63

**Herzig, Falk**
❏ 94GerDELE-402
❏ 95GerDELE-421

**Hes, Jiri**
❏ 94CzeAPSE-257
❏ 95CzeAPSE-130

**Heschuk, Brad**
❏ 88KamBla-11

**Heshka, Scott**
❏ 92MPSPhoSJHL-159

**Hess, Bob**
❏ 75OPCNHL-264
❏ 75Top-264
❏ 76OPCNHL-277
❏ 77OPCNHL-394
❏ 78OPC-358

**Hess, Manuel**
❏ 94GerDELE-190
❏ 95GerDELE-190
❏ 96GerDELE-129

**Hessel, Mats**
❏ 83SweSemE-13
❏ 84SweSemE-12
❏ 85SwePanS-15
❏ 87SwePanS-21

**Hettle, Fred**
❏ 90 7thInnSWHL-300
❏ 91 7thInnSWHL-271

**Heward, Jamie**
❏ 87RegPat-7
❏ 88RegPat-8
❏ 89RegPat-6
❏ 90 7thInnSWHL-167
❏ 91ProAHLCHL-308
❏ 92CleLum-7
❏ 93ClaProPro-107
❏ 93CleLum-20
❏ 93CleLumPos-12
❏ 95St.JohML-12
❏ 95St.JohML-16
❏ 98BowBes-74
❏ 98BowBesAR-74
❏ 98BowBesR-74
❏ 99Pac-224
❏ 99PacCop-224
❏ 99PacGol-224
❏ 99PacIceB-224
❏ 99PacPreD-224

**Hewer, Oak**
❏ 96SauSteMG-6
❏ 96SauSteMGA-6

**Hewitson, Bobby**
❏ 83HalFP-F6
❏ 85HalFC-82

**Hewitt, Foster**
❏ 34BeeGro1P-356
❏ 38QuaOatP-18
❏ 83HalFP-A7
❏ 85HalFC-8
❏ 92HalFL-13

**Hewitt, William A**
❏ 83HalFP-G8

**Hextall, Bryan**
❏ 34BeeGro1P-277
❏ 390PCV3011-86
❏ 69OPC-154
❏ 70DadCoo-51
❏ 70EssPowPla-223
❏ 70OPC-94
❏ 70Top-94
❏ 71LetActR-13
❏ 71OPC-16
❏ 71PenPos-8
❏ 71SarProSta-173
❏ 71Top-16
❏ 71TorSun-216
❏ 72OPC-174
❏ 72SarProSta-173
❏ 72Top-157
❏ 73OPC-43
❏ 73Top-43
❏ 75OPCNHL-26A
❏ 75OPCNHL-26B
❏ 75Top-26
❏ 76OPCNHL-13
❏ 76Top-13
❏ 83HalFP-K7
❏ 85HalFC-141
❏ 92HalFL-28

**Hextall, Dennis**
❏ 69OPC-107
❏ 69Top-107
❏ 70EssPowPla-107
❏ 70OPC-186
❏ 70SarProSta-133
❏ 71OPC-244
❏ 71Top-128
❏ 72OPC-225
❏ 72SweSemWC-172
❏ 73NorStaAP-5
❏ 73NorStaP-9
❏ 73OPC-115
❏ 73Top-136
❏ 74NHLActSta-129
❏ 74OPCNHL-2
❏ 74OPCNHL-112
❏ 74OPCNHL-115
❏ 74Top-2
❏ 74Top-112
❏ 74Top-115
❏ 75OPCNHL-310
❏ 75OPCNHL-321
❏ 75Top-310
❏ 75Top-321
❏ 76OPCNHL-32
❏ 76Top-32
❏ 77OPCNHL-197
❏ 77Top-197
❏ 78OPC-48
❏ 78Top-48
❏ 79OPC-392
❏ 81RedWinOld-14

**Hextall, Donevan**
❏ 90 7thInnSWHL-277
❏ 90PriAlbR-4
❏ 91 7thInnSCHLAW-15
❏ 91 7thInnSWHL-266
❏ 91AreDraPic-24
❏ 91Cla-29
❏ 91PriAlbR-4
❏ 91StaPicH-11
❏ 91UltDra-25
❏ 93Rallce-7

**Hextall, Ron**
❏ 82BraWheK-23
❏ 83BraWheK-24
❏ 86FlyPos-9
❏ 87OPC-169
❏ 87OPCMin-16
❏ 87OPCSti-1
❏ 87OPCSti-101
❏ 87OPCSti-114
❏ 87OPCSti-129
❏ 87OPCSti-182
❏ 87PanSti-123
❏ 87PanSti-191
❏ 87PanSti-378
❏ 87Top-169
❏ 87TopStiIns-2
❏ 88EssAllSta-17
❏ 88FriLayS-37
❏ 88OPC-34
❏ 88OPCMin-14
❏ 88OPCSti-103
❏ 88PanSti-315
❏ 88Top-34
❏ 89FlyPos-10
❏ 89OPC-155
❏ 89OPC-311
❏ 89OPCSti-111
❏ 89PanSti-302
❏ 89SweSemWCS-55
❏ 89Top-155
❏ 90Bow-105
❏ 90BowTif-105
❏ 90FlyPos-8
❏ 90Kra-17
❏ 90OPC-243
❏ 90OPCPre-41
❏ 90PanSti-118
❏ 90ProSet-216
❏ 90Sco-25
❏ 90ScoCan-25
❏ 90ScoHotRS-14
❏ 90Top-243
❏ 90TopTif-243

❏ 90UppDec-227
❏ 90UppDecF-227
❏ 91Bow-234
❏ 91FlyJCP-10
❏ 91OPC-470
❏ 91OPCPre-38
❏ 91PanSti-227
❏ 91Par-126
❏ 91ParFre-126
❏ 91Pin-118
❏ 91PinFre-118
❏ 91ProSet-176
❏ 91ProSetFre-176
❏ 91ProSetPla-87
❏ 91ScoAme-239
❏ 91ScoCan-459
❏ 91StaClu-173
❏ 91Top-470
❏ 91UppDec-327
❏ 91UppDecF-327
❏ 92Bow-195
❏ 92Kra-31
❏ 92NorPet-10
❏ 92OPC-84
❏ 92OPCPre-57
❏ 92Par-144
❏ 92ParChe P-CP20
❏ 92ParEmel-144
❏ 92Pin-340
❏ 92PinFre-340
❏ 92ProSet-129
❏ 92Sco-104
❏ 92StaClu-288
❏ 92Top-40
❏ 92TopGol-40G
❏ 92Ult-174
❏ 92Ult-385
❏ 92UppDec-532
❏ 93Don-196
❏ 93HigLinGG-4
❏ 93Lea-341
❏ 93OPCPre-468
❏ 93OPCPreG-468
❏ 93PanSti-77
❏ 93Par-118
❏ 93ParEmel-118
❏ 93Pin-376
❏ 93PinCan-376
❏ 93PinMas-8
❏ 93Pow-147
❏ 93Sco-152
❏ 93ScoCan-152
❏ 93ScoCan-544
❏ 93ScoGol-544
❏ 93StaClu-433
❏ 93StaCluFDI-433
❏ 93StaCluO-433
❏ 93TopPre-468
❏ 93TopPreG-468
❏ 93Ult-366
❏ 93UppDec-434
❏ 94CanGamNHLP-372
❏ 94Don-147
❏ 94EASpo-114
❏ 94Fla-127
❏ 94Fle-154
❏ 94Kra-41
❏ 94Lea-50
❏ 94Lea-495
❏ 94Par-136
❏ 94ParGol-136
❏ 94ParSE-SE130
❏ 94ParSEG-SE130
❏ 94Pin-274
❏ 94PinArtP-274
❏ 94PinMas-MA6
❏ 94PinRinC-274
❏ 94Sco-140
❏ 94ScoGol-140
❏ 94ScoPla-140
❏ 94ScoPlaTS-140
❏ 94Sel-67
❏ 94SelGol-67
❏ 94SP-87
❏ 94SPDieCut-87
❏ 94StaClu-51
❏ 94StaClu-182
❏ 94StaCluFDI-51
❏ 94StaCluFDI-182
❏ 94StaCluMOMS-51
❏ 94StaCluMOMS-182
❏ 94StaCluSTWC-51
❏ 94StaCluSTWC-182
❏ 94Ult-127
❏ 94Ult-343
❏ 94UppDec-170
❏ 94UppDecEleIce-170
❏ 94UppDecSPI-SP147
❏ 94UppDecSPIDC-SP147
❏ 95BeAPla-198
❏ 95BeAPSig-S198
❏ 95BeAPSigDC-S198
❏ 95Bow-38
❏ 95BowAllFoi-38
❏ 95CanGamNHLP-210
❏ 95ColCho-203
❏ 95ColChoPC-203
❏ 95ColChoPCP-203
❏ 95Don-147
❏ 95DonEli-108
❏ 95DonEliDCS-108
❏ 95DonEliDCU-108
❏ 95DonEliPW-8

❏ 95Emo-131
❏ 95Fin-86
❏ 95FinRef-86
❏ 95ImaPlaPI-PL4
❏ 95Kra-27
❏ 95Lea-192
❏ 95LeaIntLSS-7
❏ 95Met-110
❏ 95ParInt-159
❏ 95ParIntEI-159
❏ 95ParIntPTP-PP33
❏ 95Pin-95
❏ 95PinArtP-95
❏ 95PinMas-8
❏ 95PinRinC-95
❏ 95PlaOneoOne-181
❏ 95ProMag-52
❏ 95Sco-195
❏ 95ScoBlaIce-195
❏ 95ScoBlaIceAP-195
❏ 95SelCer-78
❏ 95SelCerMG-78
❏ 95SkyImp-125
❏ 95SP-109
❏ 95StaClu-33
❏ 95StaCluMOMS-33
❏ 95Sum-133
❏ 95SumArtP-133
❏ 95SumIce-133
❏ 95SumInTheCre-10
❏ 95Top-167
❏ 95TopHidGem-12HG
❏ 95TopOPCI-167
❏ 95TopSupSki-77
❏ 95TopSupSkiPla-77
❏ 95Ult-117
❏ 95Ult-371
❏ 95UltGolM-117
❏ 95UppDec-428
❏ 95UppDecEleIce-428
❏ 95UppDecEleIceG-428
❏ 95UppDecSpeE-SE65
❏ 95UppDecSpeEdiG-SE65
❏ 95Zen-97
❏ 96BeAPStaTP-3
❏ 96ColCho-191
❏ 96ColCho-326
❏ 96Don-61
❏ 96DonCanI-51
❏ 96DonCanIGPP-51
❏ 96DonCanIRPP-51
❏ 96DonEli-2
❏ 96DonEliDCS-2
❏ 96DonPrePro-61
❏ 96Fla-68
❏ 96FlaBluI-68
❏ 96Fle-80
❏ 96Fle-144
❏ 96Fle-145
❏ 96FlePic-80
❏ 96FlePicF5-18
❏ 96FlePicFF-3
❏ 96FleVez-5
❏ 96FlyPos-10
❏ 96Lea-194
❏ 96LeaLim-35
❏ 96LeaLimG-35
❏ 96LeaPre-77
❏ 96LeaPreP-194
❏ 96LeaPrePP-77
❏ 96LeaPreSG-9
❏ 96LeaPreSte-9
❏ 96LeaShuDow-14
❏ 96MetUni-112
❏ 96MetUniAP-5
❏ 96MetUniAPSP-5
❏ 96NHLProSTA-52
❏ 96Pin-101
❏ 96PinArtP-101
❏ 96PinFoi-101
❏ 96PinMas-6
❏ 96PinMasDC-6
❏ 96PinPreS-101
❏ 96PinRinC-101
❏ 96Sco-80
❏ 96ScoArtPro-80
❏ 96ScoDeaCAP-80
❏ 96ScoGolB-80
❏ 96ScoNetW-11
❏ 96ScoSpeAP-80
❏ 96ScoSudDea-14
❏ 96ScoSup-9
❏ 96SelCerAP-63
❏ 96SelCerBlu-63
❏ 96SelCerFre-13
❏ 96SelCerMB-63
❏ 96SelCerMG-63
❏ 96SelCerMR-63
❏ 96SelCerRed-63
❏ 96SkyImp-95
❏ 96SkyImpZH-5
❏ 96SP-116
❏ 96Sum-100
❏ 96SumArtP-100
❏ 96SumIce-100
❏ 96SumInTheCre-16
❏ 96SumInTheCrePS-16
❏ 96SumMet-100
❏ 96SumPreS-100
❏ 96SumUnt-18
❏ 96TeaOut-64
❏ 96TopPicID-ID11
❏ 96Ult-124

❏ 96UltGolM-124
❏ 96UppDec-119
❏ 96UppDec-197
❏ 96UppDecSS-SS22B
❏ 96Zen-46
❏ 96ZenArtP-46
❏ 97ColCho-188
❏ 97Don-114
❏ 97DonCanI-48
❏ 97DonCanIDS-48
❏ 97DonCanINP-26
❏ 97DonCanIPS-48
❏ 97DonEli-35
❏ 97DonEliAsp-35
❏ 97DonEliS-35
❏ 97DonLim-89
❏ 97DonLimExp-89
❏ 97DonLimFOTG-52
❏ 97DonPre-96
❏ 97DonPreCG-14
❏ 97DonPreCGP-14
❏ 97DonPreCttC-96
❏ 97DonPreProG-114
❏ 97DonPreProS-114
❏ 97DonPri-48
❏ 97DonPriPG-9
❏ 97DonPriPGP-9
❏ 97DonPriSoA-48
❏ 97Kat-105
❏ 97KatGol-105
❏ 97KatSil-105
❏ 97Lea-52
❏ 97LeaFraMat-52
❏ 97LeaFraMDC-52
❏ 97LeaInt-52
❏ 97LeaIntUI-52
❏ 97Pac-27
❏ 97PacCop-27
❏ 97PacCroR-97
❏ 97PacCroREG-97
❏ 97PacCroRFODC-13
❏ 97PacCroRIB-97
❏ 97PacCroRS-97
❏ 97PacDynC-89
❏ 97PacDynD-89
❏ 97PacDynDG-89
❏ 97PacDynEG-89
❏ 97PacDynIB-89
❏ 97PacDynR-89
❏ 97PacDynSil-89
❏ 97PacDynSto-15
❏ 97PacDynTan-55
❏ 97PacEmeGre-27
❏ 97PacIceB-27
❏ 97PacInTheCLC-14
❏ 97PacInv-100
❏ 97PacInvC-100
❏ 97PacInvEG-100
❏ 97PacInvIB-100
❏ 97PacInvR-100
❏ 97PacInvS-100
❏ 97PacOme-165
❏ 97PacOmeC-165
❏ 97PacOmeDG-165
❏ 97PacOmeEG-165
❏ 97PacOmeG-165
❏ 97PacOmeIB-165
❏ 97PacOmeNSZ-9
❏ 97PacPar-132
❏ 97PacParC-132
❏ 97PacParDG-132
❏ 97PacParEG-132
❏ 97PacParGSL-14
❏ 97PacParIB-132
❏ 97PacParRed-132
❏ 97PacParSil-132
❏ 97PacRed-27
❏ 97PacRev-101
❏ 97PacRevC-101
❏ 97PacRevE-101
❏ 97PacRevIB-101
❏ 97PacRevR-101
❏ 97PacRevRtSD-14
❏ 97PacRevS-101
❏ 97PacSil-27
❏ 97Pin-100
❏ 97PinArtP-100
❏ 97PinIns-22
❏ 97PinInsCC-22
❏ 97PinInsEC-22
❏ 97PinInsSto-18
❏ 97PinPrePBB-100
❏ 97PinPrePBC-100
❏ 97PinPrePBM-100
❏ 97PinPrePBY-100
❏ 97PinPrePFC-100
❏ 97PinPrePFM-100
❏ 97PinPrePFY-100
❏ 97PinPrePla-100
❏ 97PinRinC-100
❏ 97Sco-27
❏ 97ScoArtPro-27
❏ 97ScoFly-1
❏ 97ScoFlyPla-1
❏ 97ScoFlyPre-1
❏ 97ScoGolBla-27
❏ 97SPAut-116
❏ 97Stu-43
❏ 97StuPrePG-43
❏ 97StuPrePS-43
❏ 98Be A PPA-99
❏ 98Be A PPAA-99
❏ 98Be A PPAAF-99
❏ 98Be A PPTBASG-99
❏ 98Be APG-99

❏ 98Pac-326
❏ 98PacAur-139
❏ 98PacCroR-98
❏ 98PacCroRLS-98
❏ 98PacDynl-136
❏ 98PacDynIB-136
❏ 98PacDynIR-136
❏ 98PacIceB-326
❏ 98PacOmeH-174
❏ 98PacOmeODI-174
❏ 98PacOmeR-174
❏ 98PacPar-174
❏ 98PacParC-174
❏ 98PacParEG-174
❏ 98PacParH-174
❏ 98PacParIB-174
❏ 98PacParS-174
❏ 98PacRed-326
❏ 98PacRev-104
❏ 98PacRevIS-104
❏ 98PacRevR-104
❏ 99Pac-302
❏ 99PacCop-302
❏ 99PacGol-302
❏ 99PacIceB-302
❏ 99PacPreD-302

**Heyliger, Vic**
❏ 35DiaMatT5-6
❏ 37DiaMatT6-6

**Hibbert, Jimmy**
❏ 93NiaFaIT-2
❏ 97SheSte-1

**Hicke, Bill**
❏ 44BeeGro2P-248
❏ 59Par-31
❏ 60Par-40
❏ 60Par-56
❏ 60ShiCoi-38
❏ 60YorPreP-14
❏ 61Par-38
❏ 61ShiCoi-108
❏ 61YorYelB-16
❏ 62Par-40
❏ 62ShiMetC-38
❏ 63ChePho-22
❏ 63Par-25
❏ 63Par-84
❏ 63YorWhiB-30
❏ 64BeeGro3P-107
❏ 64BeeGro3P-132
❏ 64CocCap-60
❏ 64Top-98
❏ 65Coc-83
❏ 65Top-30
❏ 68OPC-86
❏ 68ShiCoi-118
❏ 68Top-86
❏ 69OPC-145
❏ 69OPCFou-6
❏ 69Top-84
❏ 70DadCoo-52
❏ 70EssPowPla-99
❏ 70OPC-76
❏ 70OPCDec-38
❏ 70SarProSta-143
❏ 70Top-76
❏ 70TopStiS-12
❏ 71OPC-142
❏ 71SarProSta-175
❏ 71TorSun-217
❏ 72OPC-327
❏ 94ParTalB-86
❏ 95Par66-91
❏ 95Par66Coi-91

**Hicke, Ernie**
❏ 70EssPowPla-105
❏ 71OPC-61
❏ 71SarProSta-139
❏ 71Top-61
❏ 71TorSun-48
❏ 72OPC-72
❏ 72SarProSta-3
❏ 72Top-154
❏ 73OPC-18
❏ 73Top-18
❏ 74NHLActSta-165
❏ 74NHLActStaU-20
❏ 74OPCNHL-387
❏ 75OPCNHL-71
❏ 75Top-71
❏ 76OPCNHL-87
❏ 76Top-87
❏ 77OPCNHL-132
❏ 77Top-132

**Hickey, Greg**
❏ 75HamFin-7

**Hickey, Les**
❏ 51BufBis-10

**Hickey, Pat**
❏ 74OPCWHA-24
❏ 75OPCNHL-345
❏ 76OPCNHL-107
❏ 76Top-107
❏ 77OPCNHL-221
❏ 77Top-221
❏ 78OPC-112
❏ 78Top-112
❏ 79OPC-86
❏ 79PanSti-68
❏ 79Top-86
❏ 80MapLeaP-15
❏ 80OPC-28
❏ 80PepCap-89
❏ 80Top-28

❏ 81OPC-318
❏ 81OPCSti-104
❏ 82OPC-304
❏ 88ProAHL-212
❏ 92HamCan-10

**Hicks, Alex**
❏ 92TolSto-21
❏ 93TolSto-23
❏ 94LasVegThu-7
❏ 95BufStaRHI-94
❏ 95ParInt-271
❏ 95ParIntEI-271
❏ 96ColCho-9
❏ 96UppDec-6
❏ 97Be A PPAD-177
❏ 97Be A PPAPD-177
❏ 97BeAPla-177
❏ 97BeAPlaAut-177
❏ 97PacInvNRB-159
❏ 97ScoPen-15
❏ 97ScoPenPla-15
❏ 97ScoPenPre-15
❏ 98Pac-353
❏ 98PacIceB-353
❏ 98PacRed-353

**Hicks, Doug**
❏ 77OPCNHL-361
❏ 78OPC-228
❏ 78Top-228
❏ 79OIIPos-11
❏ 79OPC-379
❏ 80OPC-221
❏ 80Top-221
❏ 81OIIRedR-5
❏ 81OPC-114
❏ 82OPC-365
❏ 82PosCer-20
❏ 88OIITenAnn-95

**Hicks, Glen**
❏ 78JetPos-8
❏ 79RedWinP-5
❏ 81OPC-98

**Hicks, Greg**
❏ 52JunBluT-124
❏ 60CleBar-9

**Hicks, Wayne**
❏ 63QueAce-12
❏ 63QueAceQ-11
❏ 64QueAce-9
❏ 65QueAce-8
❏ 70OPC-95
❏ 70Top-95

**Hidlebaugh, Mike**
❏ 91AirCanSJHL-C50

**Hiemer, Manuel**
❏ 96GerDELE-186

**Hiemer, Uli**
❏ 84DevPos-28
❏ 86DevPol-11
❏ 86OPC-226
❏ 89SweSemWCS-108
❏ 91SweSemWCS-155
❏ 93SweSemWCS-153
❏ 94FinnJaaK-277
❏ 94GerDELE-94
❏ 95GerDELE-84

**Hietala, Tommi**
❏ 93ThuBayS-16

**Higgins, Jack**
❏ 52JunBluT-105

**Higgins, Matt**
❏ 95BowDraPro-P17
❏ 98BowBes-135
❏ 98BowBesAR-135
❏ 98BowBesR-135
❏ 98PacOmeI-122
❏ 98PacOmeODI-122
❏ 98PacOmeR-122
❏ 98SPxFin-45
❏ 98SPxFinR-45
❏ 98SPxFinS-45
❏ 98UC-107
❏ 98UD ChoPCR-107
❏ 98UD ChoR-107
❏ 99Pac-204
❏ 99PacCop-204
❏ 99PacGol-204
❏ 99PacIceB-204
❏ 99PacPreD-204

**Higgins, Paul**
❏ 82MapLeaP-17

**Higgins, Tim**
❏ 80BlaWhiBor-6
❏ 81BlaBorPos-9
❏ 81OPC-57
❏ 81Top-W69
❏ 82OPC-66
❏ 82OPCSti-177
❏ 82PosCer-4
❏ 83OPC-104
❏ 84DevPos-20
❏ 84OPC-111
❏ 86OPC-227
❏ 87PanSti-269
❏ 87RedWinLC-15

**Hilbert, Andy**
❏ 98SPXTopP-87
❏ 98SPXTopPF-87
❏ 98SPXTopPR-87
❏ 98UppDecBD-118
❏ 98UppDecDD-118
❏ 98UppDecQD-118
❏ 98UppDecTD-118

**Hildebrand, Ike**
❏ 44BeeGro2P-325

❑ 51CleBar-4
❑ 54Par-83
**Hildebrandt, Roy**
❑ 89RayJrC-11
**Hilger, Raimond**
❑ 92UppDec-373
❑ 93SweSemWCS-163
❑ 94FinnJaaK-288
❑ 94GerDELE-380
❑ 95FinnSemWC-169
❑ 95GerDELE-378
❑ 96GerDELE-199
❑ 98GerDELE-299
**Hill, Al**
❑ 79OPC-166
❑ 79Top-166
❑ 80OPC-348
❑ 88ProAHL-140
❑ 89ProAHL-359
❑ 90ProAHLIHL-20
❑ 91ProAHLCHL-213
❑ 96CinCyc-NNO
**Hill, Jeff**
❑ 90MicTecHus-10
❑ 91MicTecHus-6
❑ 93MicTecH-13
**Hill, Keith**
❑ 90ForSasTra-6
**Hill, Kiley**
❑ 917thInnSOHL-314
❑ 93SauSteMGM-24
❑ 94SudWolP-8
**Hill, Mel**
❑ 34BeeGro1P-19
❑ 34BeeGro1P-324
❑ 39OPCV3011-96
❑ 45QuaOatP-22
❑ 91BruSpoAL-12
**Hill, Sean**
❑ 91ProAHLCHL-84
❑ 92CanaPos-13
❑ 92Cla-101
❑ 92Par-487
❑ 92ParEmel-487
❑ 92Ult-328
❑ 92UppDec-392
❑ 92UppDec-523
❑ 93Don-7
❑ 93Lea-353
❑ 93OPCCanHF-19
❑ 93OPCPre-312
❑ 93OPCPreG-312
❑ 93Par-2
❑ 93ParEmel-2
❑ 93Pin-147
❑ 93PinCan-147
❑ 93Pow-3
❑ 93Sco-490
❑ 93Sco-500
❑ 93ScoCan-490
❑ 93ScoCan-500
❑ 93ScoGol-500
❑ 93StaClu-387
❑ 93StaCluFDI-387
❑ 93StaCluO-387
❑ 93TopPre-312
❑ 93TopPreG-312
❑ 93Ult-182
❑ 93Ult-255
❑ 93UppDec-16
❑ 93UppDecSP-1
❑ 94Fla-121
❑ 94Fle-147
❑ 94Lea-476
❑ 94OPCPre-545
❑ 94Par-6
❑ 94ParGol-6
❑ 94ParSE-SE124
❑ 94ParSEG-SE124
❑ 94Pin-395
❑ 94PinArtP-395
❑ 94PinRinC-395
❑ 94SenBelM-14
❑ 94StaClu-28
❑ 94StaCluFDI-28
❑ 94StaCluMOMS-28
❑ 94StaCluSTWC-28
❑ 94TopPre-545
❑ 94Ult-339
❑ 94UppDec-161
❑ 94UppDecElelce-161
❑ 95BeAPla-74
❑ 95BeAPSig-S74
❑ 95BeAPSigDC-S74
❑ 95CanGamNHLP-198
❑ 95ColCho-65
❑ 95ColChoPC-65
❑ 95ColChoPCP-65
❑ 95ParInt-416
❑ 95ParIntEl-416
❑ 95Pin-93
❑ 95PinArtP-93
❑ 95PinRinC-93
❑ 95PlaOneoOne-287
❑ 95Sen-11
❑ 95Top-329
❑ 95TopOPCI-329
❑ 95UppDec-323
❑ 95UppDecElelce-323
❑ 95UppDecElelceG-323
❑ 96ClaGol-101
❑ 96SenPizH-10
❑ 96UppDec-117
❑ 97CarHur-12
❑ 97PacInvNRB-133
❑ 98Be A PPA-173
❑ 98Be A PPAA-173
❑ 98Be A PPAAF-173
❑ 98Be A PPSE-173
❑ 98Be APG-173
**Hill, Tim**
❑ 93PetPet-6
**Hillblom, Niklas**
❑ 90SweSemE-219
**Hillebrandt, Jon**
❑ 93Cla-68
❑ 93StaCluTUSA-9
❑ 93TopPreTUSA-10
❑ 94ClaAut-NNO
❑ 94ClaProP-162
❑ 95BinRan-14
❑ 96PeoRiv-8
❑ 96PeoRivPA-8
**Hiller, Bernd**
❑ 70SweHocS-376
**Hiller, Dutch**
❑ 34BeeGro1P-278
❑ 39OPCV3011-89
❑ 45QuaOatP-82
❑ 94Koll-2
**Hiller, Guido**
❑ 94GerDELE-45
**Hiller, Jim**
❑ 92OPCPre-34
❑ 92Par-70
❑ 92Par-281
❑ 92ParEmel-70
❑ 92ParEmel-281
❑ 92Pin-399
❑ 92PinFre-399
❑ 92Ult-307
❑ 92UppDec-560
❑ 94BinRan-5
❑ 94ClaProP-117
❑ 96GerDELE-195
❑ 98GerDELE-294
**Hillgren, Kenneth**
❑ 67SweHoc-171
**Hillier, Craig**
❑ 95BowDraPro-P18
❑ 95Sla-257
❑ 97BeeAutA-64
❑ 97PinBee-64
❑ 97PinBeeGP-64
**Hillier, Randy**
❑ 83BruTealss-6
❑ 85OPC-212
❑ 86PenKod-11
❑ 87PanSti-145
❑ 87PenKod-11
❑ 88OPC-158
❑ 88Top-158
❑ 89OPC-126
❑ 89PenFoo-11
❑ 89Top-126
❑ 90OPC-408
❑ 90PanSti-137
❑ 90PenFoo-3
❑ 90ProSet-507
❑ 90Sco-76
❑ 90ScoCan-76
❑ 91OPCPre-122
❑ 91Pin-281
❑ 91PinFre-281
❑ 91ProSet-360
❑ 91ProSetFre-360
❑ 91ProSetPla-158
❑ 91SabBluS-8
❑ 91SabPepC-8
❑ 91ScoCan-580
❑ 91ScoRoo-30T
**Hillkvist, S.**
❑ 95SweLeaEFF-7
**Hillman, Bud (Floyd)**
❑ 52JunBluT-83
❑ 56QueAce-7
**Hillman, Jim**
❑ 93MinGolG-13
**Hillman, John**
❑ 93MinGolG-14
**Hillman, Larry**
❑ 44BeeGro2P-32
❑ 44BeeGro2P-176
❑ 44BeeGro2P-407
❑ 52JunBluT-3
❑ 57BruTealss-8
❑ 57Top-17
❑ 58Top-25
❑ 60YorPreP-15
❑ 61Par-14
❑ 61ShiCoi-59
❑ 61YorYelB-31
❑ 62Par-17
❑ 62ShiMetC-17
❑ 63MapLeaWB-10
❑ 63RochAme-15
❑ 63YorWhiB-11
❑ 64BeeGro3P-164
❑ 65MapLeaWB-8
❑ 67Top-80
❑ 67YorActOct-29
❑ 68OPC-48
❑ 68ShiCoi-74
❑ 68Top-48
❑ 69MapLeaWBG-16
❑ 69OPC-90
❑ 69OPCFou-4
❑ 69Top-90
❑ 70DadCoo-53
❑ 70EssPowPla-201
❑ 70FlyPos-6
❑ 70OPC-81
❑ 70SarProSta-158
❑ 70Top-81
❑ 71OPC-168
❑ 71SarProSta-75
❑ 71TorSun-115
❑ 72OPC-176
❑ 72SarProSta-39
❑ 72SweSemWC-178
❑ 78JetPos-9
❑ 91UltOriS-36
❑ 91UltOriSF-36
❑ 94ParMisL-55
❑ 94ParTalB-118
❑ 95Par66-104
❑ 95Par66Coi-104
**Hillman, Wayne**
❑ 44BeeGro2P-105
❑ 61ShiCoi-21
❑ 61Top-38
❑ 62Top-31
❑ 63ChePho-23
❑ 63Top-27
❑ 64BeeGro3P-39
❑ 64BeeGro3P-133
❑ 64CocCap-34
❑ 64Top-41
❑ 64TorSta-15
❑ 65Coc-74
❑ 66Top-87
❑ 66TopUSAT-34
❑ 67PosFliB-12
❑ 67Top-22
❑ 68OPC-47
❑ 68Top-47
❑ 69OPC-91
❑ 69Top-91
❑ 70DadCoo-54
❑ 70EssPowPla-203
❑ 70OPC-198
❑ 70SarProSta-160
❑ 71Baz-26
❑ 71OPC-62
❑ 71SarProSta-146
❑ 71Top-62
❑ 71TorSun-197
❑ 72OPC-255
❑ 72SarProSta-156
❑ 94ParTalB-41
❑ 95Par66-84
❑ 95Par66Coi-84
**Hillock, Mike**
❑ 91AirCanSJHL-C12
❑ 92MPSPhoSJHL-67
❑ 93NorMicW-14
**Hiltner, Mike**
❑ 90KanCitBla-13
❑ 90ProAHLIHL-594
❑ 91NasKni-15
**Hilton, Kevin**
❑ 93DonTeaUSA-9
❑ 93MicWol-9
❑ 93Pin-493
❑ 93PinCan-493
❑ 93UppDec-567
**Hilton, Mark**
❑ 91NasKni-8
❑ 94CenHocL-113
❑ 95ForWorFT-15
**Himes, Normie**
❑ 33OPCV304A-29
❑ 33V129-21
❑ 33V252CanG-30
❑ 33V357IceK-44
❑ 34DiaMatS-29
❑ 35DiaMatTI-28
❑ 36V356WorG-92
**Hindmarch, Dave**
❑ 81SweSemHVS-89
❑ 83OPC-82
❑ 83Vac-7
❑ 84OPC-224
**Hindrikes, Yngve**
❑ 71SweHocS-395
❑ 72SweHocS-267
**Hinka, Jaroslav**
❑ 96CzeAPSE-139
**Hinks, Rod**
❑ 907thInnSOHL-384
❑ 90SudWol-10
❑ 917thInnSOHL-252
❑ 91SudWol-18
❑ 92SudWol-18
❑ 93OweSouPla-6
❑ 93OweSouPla-11
❑ 94JohChi-9
**Hinse, Andre**
❑ 75OPCWHA-35
❑ 76RoaPhoWHA-6
**Hinterstocker, H.**
❑ 79PanSti-109
**Hinterstocker, M.**
❑ 79PanSti-106
**Hinz, Chad**
❑ 96UppDec-383
❑ 98BowCHL-80
❑ 98BowCHLGA-80
❑ 98BowCHLOI-80
❑ 98BowChrC-80
❑ 98BowChrCGA-80
❑ 98BowChrCGAR-80
❑ 98BowChrCOI-80
❑ 98BowChrCOIR-80
❑ 98BowChrCR-80
**Hirche, Claus**
❑ 69SweWorC-170
❑ 69SweWorC-174
❑ 70SweHocS-365
**Hirsch, Corey**
❑ 88KamBla-12
❑ 907thInnSMC-25
❑ 907thInnSWHL-306
❑ 917thInnSWHL-76
❑ 92BinRan-22
❑ 92Par-344
❑ 92ParEmel-344
❑ 92UppDec-463
❑ 93AlbIntTC-5
❑ 93Cla-133
❑ 93ClaProPBC-BC5
❑ 93ClaProPro-65
❑ 93ClaProPro-74
❑ 93Don-216
❑ 93Lea-313
❑ 93OPCPreTC-18
❑ 93Pin-220
❑ 93PinCan-220
❑ 93Pow-482
❑ 93Sco-453
❑ 93ScoCan-453
❑ 93Ult-64
❑ 93Ult-462
❑ 93UltAllRoo-3
❑ 94BinRan-6
❑ 94Cla-85
❑ 94ClaDraGol-85
❑ 94ClaProPIA-IA2
❑ 94ClaProPIH-LP14
❑ 94ClaTri-T43
❑ 94FinnJaaK-80
❑ 94Par-149
❑ 94ParGol-149
❑ 94PinRooTP-1
❑ 94ScoTeaC-CT4
❑ 94Ult-330
❑ 94UppDec-218
❑ 94UppDecElelce-218
❑ 95Bow-145
❑ 95BowAllFoi-145
❑ 95ColEdgI-19
❑ 95Ima-62
❑ 95ImaGol-62
❑ 95ParInt-483
❑ 95ParIntEl-483
❑ 95SelCer-143
❑ 95SelCerMG-143
❑ 95SP-151
❑ 95Sum-184
❑ 95SumArtP-184
❑ 95SumIce-184
❑ 95UppDec-405
❑ 95UppDecElelce-405
❑ 95UppDecElelceG-405
❑ 95Zen-134
❑ 96BeAPAut-51
❑ 96BeAPAutSil-51
❑ 96BeAPla-51
❑ 96CanuPos-31
❑ 96ColCho-272
❑ 96Don-179
❑ 96DonCanI-73
❑ 96DonCanIGPP-73
❑ 96DonCanIRPP-73
❑ 96DonEli-34
❑ 96DonEliDCS-34
❑ 96DonPrePro-179
❑ 96Fla-94
❑ 96FlaBluI-94
❑ 96Lea-152
❑ 96LeaLim-89
❑ 96LeaLimG-89
❑ 96LeaPre-33
❑ 96LeaPreP-152
❑ 96LeaPrePP-33
❑ 96LeaPreSG-3
❑ 96LeaPreSte-3
❑ 96LeaShuDow-12
❑ 96Pin-211
❑ 96PinArtP-211
❑ 96PinFoi-211
❑ 96PinPreS-211
❑ 96PinRinC-211
❑ 96Sco-149
❑ 96ScoArtPro-149
❑ 96ScoDeaCAP-149
❑ 96ScoGolB-149
❑ 96ScoNetW-16
❑ 96ScoSpeAP-149
❑ 96ScoSudDea-13
❑ 96SelCer-71
❑ 96SelCerAP-71
❑ 96SelCerBlu-71
❑ 96SelCerMB-71
❑ 96SelCerMG-71
❑ 96SelCerMR-71
❑ 96SelCerRed-71
❑ 96SP-159
❑ 96Sum-125
❑ 96SumArtP-125
❑ 96SumIce-125
❑ 96SumInTheCre-15
❑ 96SumInTheCrePS-15
❑ 96SumMet-125
❑ 96SumPreS-125
❑ 96TopPicRS-RS16
❑ 96UppDec-168
❑ 96UppDecBD-131
❑ 96UppDecBDG-131
❑ 96UppDecIce-71
❑ 96UppDecIcePar-71
❑ 96Zen-75
❑ 96ZenArtP-75
❑ 97ColCho-258
❑ 97Don-162
❑ 97DonCanI-109
❑ 97DonCanIDS-109
❑ 97DonCanIPS-109
❑ 97DonLim-10
❑ 97DonLimExp-10
❑ 97DonPreProG-162
❑ 97DonPreProS-162
❑ 97Lea-146
❑ 97LeaFraMat-146
❑ 97LeaFraMDC-146
❑ 97LeaInt-146
❑ 97LeaIntUI-146
❑ 97Pac-180
❑ 97PacCop-180
❑ 97PacEmeGre-180
❑ 97PacIceB-180
❑ 97PacRed-180
❑ 97PacSil-180
❑ 97PinIns-29
❑ 97PinInsCC-29
❑ 97PinInsEC-29
❑ 97PinInsSUG-9A/B
❑ 97PinInsSUG-9C/D
❑ 97Sco-12
❑ 97ScoArtPro-12
❑ 97ScoCanPla-11
❑ 97ScoCanPre-11
❑ 97ScoCanu-11
❑ 97ScoGolBla-12
❑ 97UppDec-171
❑ 98PacOmeH-235
❑ 98PacOmeODI-235
❑ 98PacOmeR-235
**Hirsch, Greg**
❑ 92MaiBlaB-35
**Hirsch, Tom**
❑ 84NorStaPos-10
❑ 84OPC-99
❑ 85NorStaPos-14
❑ 87NorStaPos-17
**Hirschfeld, Bert**
❑ 45QuaOatP-83
**Hirsimaki, Jari**
❑ 94FinnSIS-240
❑ 95FinnSIS-143
❑ 95FinnSISL-99
❑ 95FinnSISSpo-7
**Hirsimaki, Jukka**
❑ 83SweSemE-203
**Hirvonen, Raimo**
❑ 82SweSemHVS-31
**Hirvonen, Timo**
❑ 93FinnJyvHS-207
❑ 93FinnSIS-268
❑ 94FinnSIS-106
❑ 95FinnSIS-294
❑ 96FinnSISR-94
**Hirvonen, Tomi**
❑ 95ColCho-338
❑ 95ColChoPC-338
❑ 95ColChoPCP-338
❑ 95FinnSIS-242
❑ 95FinnSISDD-11
❑ 96FinnSISR-36
**Hislop, Jamie**
❑ 79OPC-380
❑ 80NordPos-13
❑ 80OPC-327
❑ 80PepCap-67
❑ 81FlamPos-6
❑ 81OPC-40
❑ 82OPC-47
❑ 82PosCer-3
❑ 83OPC-83
❑ 83Vac-8
❑ 89ProIHL-200
❑ 90ProAHLIHL-612
❑ 92FlamIGA-29
**Hitchcock, Ken**
❑ 84KamBla-11
❑ 85KamBla-8
❑ 92FlyUppDS-34
❑ 96StaPos-9
**Hitchen, Allan**
❑ 95Sla-306
**Hitchins, Kelly**
❑ 85BraWheK-1
❑ 88BraWheK-20
**Hitchman, Fred**
❑ 24C144ChaCig-31
❑ 33OPCV304A-5
**Hitchman, Lionel**
❑ 23V1451-8
❑ 24V1452-4
❑ 33V357IceK-34
❑ 34DiaMatS-30
❑ 38BruGarMS-3
❑ 91BruSpoAL-13
**Hjalm, Michael**
❑ 83SweSemE-162
❑ 84SweSemE-37
❑ 85SwePanS-39
❑ 86SwePanS-21
❑ 87SwePanS-198
❑ 89SweSemE-180
❑ 90SweSemE-13
❑ 92SweSemE-263
❑ 93SweSemE-231
❑ 94SweLeaE-263
❑ 95SweLeaE-123
❑ 95SweLeaEFF-11
❑ 95SweUppDE-180
**Hjalmar, Hans**
❑ 86SwePanS-243
❑ 87SwePanS-219
❑ 89SweSemE-204
❑ 90SweSemE-242
**Hjalmarsson, Mats**
❑ 91SweSemE-301
❑ 92SweSemE-316
**Hjarpe, Hakan**
❑ 85SwePanS-211
**Hjelm, Hans**
❑ 70SweHocS-220
**Hjerpe, Hakan**
❑ 82SweSemHVS-36
**Hjertaas, Troy**
❑ 907thInnSWHL-282
❑ 90PriAlbR-5
❑ 917thInnSWHL-252
❑ 91PriAlbR-5
**Hlady, Scott**
❑ 92BraWheK-9
**Hlavac, Jan**
❑ 94CzeAPSE-84
❑ 94ParSE-SE213
❑ 94ParSEG-SE213
❑ 94SP-158
❑ 94SPDieCut-158
❑ 94UppDec-508
❑ 94UppDecElelce-508
❑ 95Cla-25
❑ 96CzeAPSE-138
**Hlinka, Ivan**
❑ 70SweHocS-356
❑ 71SweHocS-52
❑ 72SweSemWC-40
❑ 74SweHocS-14
❑ 74SweSemHVS-66
❑ 79PanSti-83
❑ 81CanuSilD-4
❑ 81SweSemHVS-72
❑ 82Canu-10
❑ 82OPC-346
❑ 82PosCer-19
❑ 91SweSemWCS-250
❑ 92FutTre76CC-128
**Hlinka, Jiri**
❑ 94CzeAPSE-262
❑ 95CzeAPSE-142
**Hlinka, Michal**
❑ 94CzeAPSE-117
❑ 95CzeAPSE-221
**Hlinka, Miroslav**
❑ 94CzeAPSE-90
❑ 96CzeAPSE-136
**Hlusek, Stefan**
❑ 96SloPeeWT-10
**Hlushko, Todd**
❑ 897thInnSOHL-41
❑ 90ProAHLIHL-202
❑ 91BalSki-9
❑ 91ProAHLCHL-567
❑ 92AlbIntTC-9
❑ 93AlbIntTC-6
❑ 93Don-469
❑ 93OPCPreTC-12
❑ 93Pow-483
❑ 93Ult-463
❑ 94ParSE-SE25
❑ 94ParSEG-SE25
❑ 94ScoTeaC-CT9
❑ 94St.JohF-10
❑ 95St.JohF-8
❑ 96Sum-194
❑ 96SumArtP-194
❑ 96SumIce-194
❑ 96SumMet-194
❑ 96SumPreS-194
❑ 97PacInvNRB-28
**Hlynsky, Bill**
❑ 81SasBla-18
**Hnidy, Shane**
❑ 917thInnSWHL-177
❑ 93PriAlbR-10
❑ 94PriAlbR-7
❑ 95PriAlbR-7
**Hnilicka, Milan**
❑ 91UppDecCWJC-87
❑ 93RicRen-12
❑ 96CzeAPSE-74
**Hoad, Jeff**
❑ 89BraWheK-10
❑ 907thInnSWHL-221
❑ 90BraWheK-1
❑ 917thInnSWHL-215
❑ 92BraWheK-10
**Hoard, Brian**
❑ 87SauSteMG-34
❑ 88ProAHL-239
❑ 89ProAHL-111
**Hober, Dan**
❑ 86SwePanS-245
**Hobin, Mike**
❑ 76RoaPhoWHA-7
❑ 77NovScoV-8
**Hobson, Chris**
❑ 93HumHawP-3
❑ 94HumHawP-16
❑ 97KinHaw-10
**Hobson, Doug**
❑ 84PriAlbRS-12
❑ 88ProIHL-53
**Hobson, Jonathon**
❑ 96KamBla-12
**Hock, Robert**
❑ 94FinnJaaK-282
❑ 94GerDELE-375
❑ 95GerDELE-356
**Hocking, Justin**
❑ 90ForSasTra-7
❑ 917thInnSWHL-12
❑ 92Cla-16
❑ 94Lea-479
❑ 94UppDec-210
❑ 94UppDecElelce-210
❑ 96ClaGol-16
**Hodek, Petr**
❑ 94CzeAPSE-99
**Hodge, Charlie**
❑ 44BeeGro2P-251A
❑ 44BeeGro2P-251B
❑ 52JunBluT-129
❑ 55Par-69
❑ 55ParQuaO-69
❑ 57Par-M17
❑ 58Par-17
❑ 59Par-16
❑ 60ShiCoi-39
❑ 60YorPreP-16
❑ 62QueAce-12
❑ 63ChePho-24
❑ 63QueAce-13
❑ 63QueAce-14
❑ 63QueAceQ-12
❑ 63QueAceQ-13
❑ 64BeeGro3P-108
❑ 64CocCap-55
❑ 64Top-17
❑ 64TorSta-16
❑ 65CanaSteG-4
❑ 65Coc-55
❑ 65Top-67
❑ 66Top-65
❑ 68OPC-78
❑ 68OPCPucSti-12
❑ 68ShiCoi-116
❑ 68Top-78
❑ 69OPC-77
❑ 69OPCFou-8
❑ 69Top-77
❑ 70CanuRoyB-7
❑ 70ColSta-68
❑ 70DadCoo-55
❑ 70EssPowPla-37
❑ 70OPC-229
❑ 70SarProSta-211
❑ 94ParMisLFS-FS6
❑ 94ParTalB-82
❑ 94ParTalB-139
❑ 94ParTalB-148
❑ 95Par66-70
❑ 95Par66Coi-70
**Hodge, Dan**
❑ 96PeoRiv-9
❑ 96PeoRivPA-9
**Hodge, Ken**
❑ 64BeeGro3P-40
❑ 65Coc-29
❑ 65Top-65
❑ 66Top-114
❑ 67Top-98
❑ 68OPC-8
❑ 68ShiCoi-10
❑ 68Top-8
❑ 69OPC-27
❑ 69OPCFou-2
❑ 69OPCSta-13
❑ 69Top-27
❑ 70BruPos-10
❑ 70BruTealss-14
❑ 70ColSta-62
❑ 70DadCoo-56
❑ 70EssPowPla-59
❑ 70OPC-8
❑ 70OPC-233
❑ 70PosCerS-5
❑ 70SarProSta-10
❑ 70Top-8
❑ 71BruTealss-5
❑ 71OPC-115
❑ 71OPC-254
❑ 71SarProSta-8
❑ 71Top-115
❑ 71TorSun-10
❑ 72OPC-49
❑ 72OPC-169
❑ 72SarProSta-22
❑ 72Top-166
❑ 73OPC-26
❑ 73Top-133
❑ 74LipSou-28
❑ 74NHLActSta-28
❑ 74OPCNHL-128
❑ 74OPCNHL-230
❑ 74Top-128
❑ 74Top-230
❑ 75OPCNHL-215
❑ 75Top-215
❑ 76OPCNHL-25
❑ 76Top-25
❑ 77OPCNHL-192
❑ 77Top-192
❑ 91UltOriS-49
❑ 91UltOriSF-49
❑ 92Ult-411
❑ 94ParTalBFS-FS3
❑ 95Par66-23
❑ 95Par66Coi-23
**Hodge, Ken CO**

❑ 917thInnSWHL-44
**Hodge, Ken Jr.**
❑ 88ProIHL-28
❑ 89ProIHL-89
❑ 90BruSpoA-12
❑ 90ProAHLIHL-134
❑ 90ProSet-587
❑ 90ScoRoo-85T
❑ 90UppDec-529
❑ 90UppDecF-529
❑ 91Bow-347
❑ 91Bow-362
❑ 91BruSpoA-8
❑ 91Kra-17
❑ 91OPC-5
❑ 91OPC-440
❑ 91OPCPre-41
❑ 91OPCPre-154
❑ 91PanSti-178
❑ 91PanSti-341
❑ 91Par-2
❑ 91ParFre-2
❑ 91ParPHC-PHC3
❑ 91ParPHCF-PHC3
❑ 91Pin-203
❑ 91PinFre-203
❑ 91ProSet-3
❑ 91ProSetFre-3
❑ 91ProSetNHLAS-AC11
❑ 91ProSetPla-6
❑ 91ProSetPlaPC-PC9
❑ 91ScoAme-113
❑ 91ScoAme-353
❑ 91ScoCan-113
❑ 91ScoCan-383
❑ 91ScoYouS-9
❑ 91StaClu-357
❑ 91Top-5
❑ 91Top-440
❑ 91UppDec-41
❑ 91UppDec-251
❑ 91UppDecF-41
❑ 91UppDecF-251
❑ 92Pin-390
❑ 92PinFre-390
❑ 92ProSet-182
❑ 92Sco-274
❑ 92ScoCan-274
❑ 92Top-306
❑ 92TopGol-306G
❑ 92UppDec-254
❑ 96GerDELE-110
**Hodge, Rob**
❑ 93WesMic-14
**Hodgen, Jeff**
❑ 897thInnSOHL-46
**Hodges, Bob**
❑ 90ProSet-689
**Hodges, Matthew**
❑ 97SudWolP-21
**Hodgson, Dan**
❑ 84KelWin-56
❑ 84PriAlbRS-13
❑ 85MapLeaP-13
❑ 93SwiHNL-429
❑ 95SwiHNL-124
❑ 95SwiHNL-521
**Hodgson, Ted**
❑ 51LavDaiQSHL-62
❑ 52St.LawS-106
❑ 72CleCruWHA-5
❑ 72CruCleWHAL-3
**Hodson, Jason**
❑ 92BriColJHL-104
**Hodson, Kevin**
❑ 907thInnSOHL-158
❑ 917thInnSMC-2
❑ 917thInnSOHL-320
❑ 92IndIce-13
❑ 93SauSteMGM-28
❑ 94ClaProP-218
❑ 94ClaTri-T19
❑ 95AdiRedW-9
❑ 95ColEdgI-3
❑ 95ColEdgITW-G12
❑ 95ParInt-525
❑ 95ParIntEl-525
❑ 96BeAPAut-218
❑ 96BeAPAutSil-218
❑ 96BeAPla-218
❑ 96BeAPla-P218
❑ 96Don-230
❑ 96DonCanI-136
❑ 96DonCanIGPP-136
❑ 96DonCanIRPP-136
❑ 96DonPrePro-230
❑ 96Fla-108
❑ 96FlaBluI-108
❑ 96LeaGolR-2
❑ 96LeaPre-137
❑ 96LeaPrePP-137
❑ 96Pin-238
❑ 96PinArtP-238
❑ 96PinFoi-238
❑ 96PinPreS-238
❑ 96PinRinC-238
❑ 96Sum-183
❑ 96SumArtP-183
❑ 96SumIce-183
❑ 96SumMet-183
❑ 96SumPreS-183
❑ 96UppDec-253
❑ 96Zen-136
❑ 96ZenArtP-136
❑ 97Don-199
❑ 97DonLim-17
❑ 97DonLim-89
❑ 97DonLimExp-17
❑ 97DonLimExp-89
❑ 97DonPreProG-199
❑ 97DonPreProS-199
❑ 97DonPri-65
❑ 97DonPriSoA-65
❑ 97PacOme-80
❑ 97PacOmeC-80
❑ 97PacOmeDG-80
❑ 97PacOmeEG-80
❑ 97PacOmeG-80
❑ 97PacOmeIB-80
❑ 97Pin-47
❑ 97PinArtP-47
❑ 97PinInsSto-10
❑ 97PinPrePBB-47
❑ 97PinPrePBC-47
❑ 97PinPrePBM-47
❑ 97PinPrePBY-47
❑ 97PinPrePFC-47
❑ 97PinPrePFM-47
❑ 97PinPrePFY-47
❑ 97PinPrePla-47
❑ 97PinRinC-47
❑ 97Sco-24
❑ 97ScoArtPro-24
❑ 97ScoGolBla-24
❑ 97ScoRedW-18
❑ 97ScoRedWPla-18
❑ 97ScoRedWPre-18
❑ 97SPAut-179
❑ 97UppDec-272
❑ 97UppDecIce-33
❑ 97UppDecIceP-33
❑ 97UppDecIPS-33
❑ 98Pac-192
❑ 98PacIceB-192
❑ 98PacPar-75
❑ 98PacParC-75
❑ 98PacParEG-75
❑ 98PacParH-75
❑ 98PacParIB-75
❑ 98PacParS-75
❑ 98PacRed-192
❑ 99Pac-390
❑ 99PacAur-130
❑ 99PacAurPD-130
❑ 99PacCop-390
❑ 99PacGol-390
❑ 99PacIceB-390
❑ 99PacPreD-390
❑ 99UppDecM-195
❑ 99UppDecMGS-195
❑ 99UppDecMSS-195
❑ 99UppDecMSS-195
**Hoekstra, Cecil**
❑ 55MonRoy-4
❑ 60ShiCoi-79
**Hoekstra, Ed**
❑ 62QueAce-13
❑ 63QueAce-15
❑ 63QueAceQ-14
❑ 64QueAce-10
❑ 65QueAce-9
❑ 68OPC-98
❑ 68ShiCoi-124
❑ 68Top-98
**Hofbauer, Patrik**
❑ 93SweSemE-2
❑ 95SweLeaE-184
**Hoff, Geir**
❑ 93SweSemWCS-237
❑ 94FinnJaaK-263
❑ 95SweGloWC-193
**Hoffart, Randy**
❑ 84SasBlaS-5
❑ 85BraWheK-24
**Hoffman, Aaron**
❑ 91BriColJHL-66
❑ 92BriColJHL-80
**Hoffman, Kevin**
❑ 95VanVooRHI-17
**Hoffman, Matt**
❑ 897thInnSOHL-15
❑ 89OshGen-15
❑ 89OshGenP-6
❑ 907thInnSMC-94
❑ 907thInnSOHL-338
❑ 917thInnSOHL-154
❑ 91OshGen-7
❑ 91OshGenS-9
❑ 93JohChi-6
❑ 94JohChi-10
**Hoffman, Mike**
❑ 87FliSpi-6
❑ 88FliSpi-7
❑ 88FliSpi-19
**Hoffmann, Jim**
❑ 94GerDELE-187
❑ 95GerDELE-187
❑ 96GerDELE-126
**Hoffmann, L.**
❑ 95GerDELE-73
**Hoffmann, Oliver**
❑ 91SweSemWCS-199
❑ 93SwiHNL-22
❑ 95SwiHNL-20
**Hoffmeyer, Bob**
❑ 84DevPos-21
❑ 88DevCar-11
❑ 89ProAHL-208
❑ 91ProAHLCHL-161
**Hofford, Jim**
❑ 86SabBluS-14
❑ 86SabBluSSma-14
❑ 88ProAHL-256
❑ 89ProAHL-281
**Hoffort, Bruce**
❑ 89ProAHL-350
❑ 90OPCPre-42
❑ 90ProAHLIHL-36
❑ 90Sco-413
❑ 90ScoCan-413
❑ 90UppDec-135
❑ 90UppDecF-135
❑ 91ProAHLCHL-326
**Hofherr, Anton**
❑ 72SweSemWC-104
**Hofherr, Franz**
❑ 72SweSemWC-112
**Hofmann, Peter**
❑ 93SwiHNL-479
❑ 94GerDELE-406
**Hofner, Ernst**
❑ 82SweSemHVS-114
❑ 94GerDELE-368
❑ 95GerDELE-358
❑ 98GerDELE-341
**Hofverberg, Sture**
❑ 65SweCorI-140
**Hogaboam, Bill**
❑ 73RedWinMP-8
❑ 74NHLActSta-99
❑ 74OPCNHL-84
❑ 74OPCNHL-116
❑ 74Top-84
❑ 74Top-116
❑ 75OPCNHL-67
❑ 75Top-67
❑ 76OPCNHL-73
❑ 76OPCNHL-387
❑ 76Top-73
❑ 77OPCNHL-148
❑ 77Top-148
❑ 79OPC-362
**Hogan, Matt**
❑ 94SarSti-25
**Hogan, Peter**
❑ 95Sla-242
❑ 98BowCHL-26
❑ 98BowCHLGA-26
❑ 98BowCHLOI-26
❑ 98BowChrC-26
❑ 98BowChrCGA-26
❑ 98BowChrCGAR-26
❑ 98BowChrCOI-26
❑ 98BowChrCOIR-26
❑ 98BowChrCR-26
**Hogan, Tim**
❑ 91MicWol-7
❑ 93MicWol-10
**Hoganson, Dale**
❑ 70EssPowPla-146
❑ 70SarProSta-68
❑ 71CanaPos-7
❑ 71OPC-149
❑ 71TorSun-116
❑ 75OPCWHA-2
❑ 80NordPos-14
❑ 80OPC-155
❑ 80PepCap-68
❑ 80Top-155
❑ 81OPC-276
**Hogardh, Peter**
❑ 95SweLeaE-200
❑ 95SweUppDE-215
**Hogasta, Goran**
❑ 79PanSti-184
**Hogden, Jeff**
❑ 91CinCyc-9
**Hogg, Jeff**
❑ 82OshGen-2
❑ 83KinCan-25
**Hogg, Murray**
❑ 93GueSto-21
❑ 95Sla-53
❑ 96ForWorF-5
**Hogg, Steve**
❑ 87BroBra-18
❑ 93PetPet-17
❑ 95Sla-319
**Hoggarth, Ron**
❑ 90ProSet-690
**Hoglund, Jonas**
❑ 90SweSemE-269
❑ 91SweSemE-99
❑ 92SweSemE-115
❑ 92UppDec-222
❑ 93SweSemE-96
❑ 94SweLeaE-242
❑ 95SweLeaE-213
❑ 95SweUppDE-68
❑ 95SweUppDETNA-NA8
❑ 96BeAPLH-8A
❑ 96BeAPLHAut-8A
❑ 96BeAPLHAutSil-8A
❑ 96ColCho-355
❑ 96DonCanI-140
❑ 96DonCanIGPP-140
❑ 96DonCanIRPP-140
❑ 96DonEli-146
❑ 96DonEliAsp-12
❑ 96DonEliDCS-146
❑ 96LeaLimR-10
❑ 96LeaLimRG-10
❑ 96LeaPre-124
❑ 96LeaPrePP-124
❑ 96SelCer-102
❑ 96SelCerAP-102
❑ 96SelCerBlu-102
❑ 96SelCerMB-102
❑ 96SelCerMG-102
❑ 96SelCerMR-102
❑ 96SelCerRed-102
❑ 96SP-172
❑ 96Ult-23
❑ 96UltGolM-23
❑ 96UppDec-232
❑ 96UppDecBD-44
❑ 96UppDecBDG-44
❑ 96UppDecGN-X38
❑ 96Zen-117
❑ 96ZenArtP-117
❑ 97ColCho-43
❑ 97Don-169
❑ 97DonCanI-36
❑ 97DonCanIDS-36
❑ 97DonCanIPS-36
❑ 97DonLim-88
❑ 97DonLimExp-88
❑ 97DonPreProG-169
❑ 97DonPreProS-169
❑ 97Pac-185
❑ 97PacCop-185
❑ 97PacDyn-16
❑ 97PacDynC-16
❑ 97PacDynDG-16
❑ 97PacDynEG-16
❑ 97PacDynIB-16
❑ 97PacDynR-16
❑ 97PacDynSil-16
❑ 97PacDynTan-36
❑ 97PacEmeGre-185
❑ 97PacIceB-185
❑ 97PacInv-18
❑ 97PacInvC-18
❑ 97PacInvEG-18
❑ 97PacInvIB-18
❑ 97PacInvR-18
❑ 97PacInvS-18
❑ 97PacPar-29
❑ 97PacParC-29
❑ 97PacParDG-29
❑ 97PacParEG-29
❑ 97PacParIB-29
❑ 97PacParRed-29
❑ 97PacParSil-29
❑ 97PacRed-185
❑ 97PacSil-185
❑ 97PinIns-129
❑ 97Sco-181
❑ 97UppDec-27
❑ 98UppDec-116
❑ 98UppDecE-116
❑ 98UppDecE1o1-116
❑ 98UppDecGR-116
**Hoglund, Patrik**
❑ 91SweSemE-160
❑ 92SweSemE-178
❑ 93SweSemE-149
❑ 94SweLeaE-266
❑ 95SweUppDE-115
**Hogosta, Goran**
❑ 71SweHocS-381
❑ 72SweHocS-256
❑ 74SweHocS-143
❑ 81SweSemHVS-1
**Hogstrom, Jerk**
❑ 91SweSemE-285
**Hogue, Benoit**
❑ 88SabBluS-10
❑ 88SabWonBH-10
❑ 89OPC-201
❑ 89OPCSti-37
❑ 89OPCSti-77
❑ 89OPCSti-225
❑ 89SabBluS-6
❑ 89SabCam-8
❑ 90OPC-215
❑ 90ProSet-416
❑ 90SabBluS-9
❑ 90SabCam-10
❑ 90Top-215
❑ 90TopTif-215
❑ 90UppDec-402
❑ 90UppDecF-402
❑ 91Bow-38
❑ 91NordPanTS-E
❑ 91NordPanTS-F
❑ 91OPC-292
❑ 91OPCPre-179
❑ 91PanSti-300
❑ 91Par-332
❑ 91ParFre-332
❑ 91Pin-146
❑ 91PinFre-146
❑ 91ProSet-17
❑ 91ProSet-435
❑ 91ProSetFre-17
❑ 91ProSetFre-435
❑ 91ProSetPla-200
❑ 91ScoAme-134
❑ 91ScoCan-134
❑ 91ScoRoo-108T
❑ 91ScoYouS-31
❑ 91StaClu-157
❑ 91Top-292
❑ 91UppDec-159
❑ 91UppDecF-159
❑ 92Bow-28
❑ 92DurPan-3
❑ 92OPC-132
❑ 92PanSti-197
❑ 92PanStiFre-197
❑ 92Par-104
❑ 92ParEmel-104
❑ 92Pin-62
❑ 92PinFre-62
❑ 92ProSet-108
❑ 92Sco-276
❑ 92ScoCan-276
❑ 92ScoSha-21
❑ 92ScoShaCan-21
❑ 92StaClu-425
❑ 92Top-103
❑ 92TopGol-103G
❑ 92Ult-127
❑ 92UppDec-325
❑ 93Don-201
❑ 93DurSco-29
❑ 93Lea-155
❑ 93OPCPre-140
❑ 93OPCPreG-140
❑ 93PanSti-59
❑ 93Par-396
❑ 93ParEmel-396
❑ 93Pin-18
❑ 93PinCan-18
❑ 93Pow-148
❑ 93Sco-16
❑ 93ScoCan-16
❑ 93StaClu-76
❑ 93StaCluFDI-76
❑ 93StaCluFDIO-76
❑ 93StaCluO-76
❑ 93TopPre-140
❑ 93TopPreG-140
❑ 93Ult-123
❑ 93UppDec-456
❑ 94CanGamNHLP-374
❑ 94Don-188
❑ 94EASpo-83
❑ 94Lea-124
❑ 94LeaLim-20
❑ 94MapLeaK-15
❑ 94MapLeaPP-28
❑ 94OPCPre-26
❑ 94OPCPreSE-26
❑ 94ParSE-SE106
❑ 94ParSEG-SE106
❑ 94Pin-129
❑ 94PinArtP-129
❑ 94PinRinC-129
❑ 94Sel-130
❑ 94SelGol-130
❑ 94TopPre-26
❑ 94TopPreSE-26
❑ 94Ult-128
❑ 94UppDec-436
❑ 94UppDecEleIce-436
❑ 95BeAPla-126
❑ 95BeAPSig-S126
❑ 95BeAPSigDC-S126
❑ 95CanGamNHLP-258
❑ 95ColCho-72
❑ 95ColChoPC-72
❑ 95ColChoPCP-72
❑ 95Don-70
❑ 95ImaPlaPl-PL7
❑ 95Lea-134
❑ 95ParInt-330
❑ 95ParIntEl-330
❑ 95Pin-186
❑ 95PinArtP-186
❑ 95PinRinC-186
❑ 95Sco-262
❑ 95ScoBlaIce-262
❑ 95ScoBlaIceAP-262
❑ 95Top-71
❑ 95TopOPCI-71
❑ 95Ult-312
❑ 95UppDec-351
❑ 95UppDecEleIce-351
❑ 95UppDecEleIceG-351
❑ 95UppDecSpeE-SE171
❑ 95UppDecSpeEdiG-SE171
❑ 96ColCho-72
❑ 96Don-135
❑ 96DonPrePro-135
❑ 96FlePic-136
❑ 96Lea-137
❑ 96LeaPreP-137
❑ 96Pin-73
❑ 96PinArtP-73
❑ 96PinFoi-73
❑ 96PinPreS-73
❑ 96PinRinC-73
❑ 96Sco-141
❑ 96ScoArtPro-141
❑ 96ScoDeaCAP-141
❑ 96ScoGolB-141
❑ 96ScoSpeAP-141
❑ 96StaPos-10
❑ 96Sum-56
❑ 96SumArtP-56
❑ 96SumIce-56
❑ 96SumMet-56
❑ 96SumPreS-56
❑ 96UppDec-247
❑ 97Be A PPAD-152
❑ 97Be A PPAPD-152
❑ 97BeAPla-152
❑ 97BeAPlaAut-152
❑ 97Pac-240
❑ 97PacCop-240
❑ 97PacEmeGre-240
❑ 97PacIceB-240
❑ 97PacRed-240
❑ 97PacSil-240
❑ 97Sco-217
❑ 98Pac-177
❑ 98PacIceB-177
❑ 98PacRed-177
❑ 99Pac-119
❑ 99PacCop-119
❑ 99PacGol-119
❑ 99PacIceB-119
❑ 99PacPreD-119
**Hogue, Russell**
❑ 93PriAlbR-11
❑ 94PriAlbR-8
❑ 95PriAlbR-8
❑ 96PriAlbR-7
❑ 96PriAlbROC-8
**Hohenadl, Frank**
❑ 94GerDELE-212
❑ 98GerDELE-304
**Hohenberger, Herbert**
❑ 90ProAHLIHL-63
❑ 94GerDELE-216
❑ 95AusNatTea-9
❑ 95GerDELE-204
❑ 95SweGloWC-186
❑ 96GerDELE-345
❑ 96SweSemW-214
**Hohenberger, Martin**
❑ 95SigRooA-18
❑ 95SigRooAPC-18
❑ 96LetHur-6
**Hohendahl, F.**
❑ 95GerDELE-340
**Hoiness, Brent**
❑ 91AirCanSJHL-A43
❑ 92MPSPhoSJHL-91
**Hokanson, Jeff**
❑ 91BriColJHL-139
**Hokegard, Joakim**
❑ 83SweSemE-221
**Holan, Milos**
❑ 93Cla-134
❑ 93Don-244
❑ 93Par-268
❑ 93ParEmel-268
❑ 93Pin-427
❑ 93PinCan-427
❑ 93SweSemWCS-91
❑ 93Ult-389
❑ 93UltWavF-6
❑ 93UppDec-523
❑ 93UppDecSP-115
❑ 94ClaProP-70
❑ 94Don-10
❑ 94Lea-289
❑ 95ColCho-265
❑ 95ColChoPC-265
❑ 95ColChoPCP-265
❑ 95Don-339
❑ 95Lea-324
❑ 95ParInt-2
❑ 95ParIntEl-2
❑ 95Top-173
❑ 95TopOPCI-173
❑ 95Ult-2
❑ 95UltGolM-2
❑ 95UppDec-77
❑ 95UppDecEleIce-77
❑ 95UppDecEleIceG-77
❑ 96Don-20
❑ 96DonPrePro-20
❑ 96Sco-211
❑ 96ScoArtPro-211
❑ 96ScoDeaCAP-211
❑ 96ScoGolB-211
❑ 96ScoSpeAP-211
**Holden, Barney**
❑ 10C55SweCP-3
❑ 10C56-4
❑ 11C55-3
**Holden, Cory**
❑ 95GerDELE-315
❑ 96GerDELE-97
**Holden, Josh**
❑ 95BowDraPro-P19
❑ 95Cla-62
❑ 95ClaAut-8
❑ 95UppDec-513
❑ 95UppDecEleIce-513
❑ 95UppDecEleIceG-513
❑ 96ColEdgSS&D-6
❑ 96RegPat-1
❑ 97BeeAutA-66
❑ 97BowCHL-114
❑ 97BowCHLOPC-114
❑ 97PinBee-66
❑ 97PinBeeGP-66
❑ 97UppDecBD-45
❑ 97UppDecBDDD-45
❑ 97UppDecBDQD-45
❑ 97UppDecBDTD-45
❑ 97Zen-100
❑ 97Zen5x7-80
❑ 97ZenGolImp-80
❑ 97ZenSilImp-80
❑ 97ZenZGol-100
❑ 97ZenZSil-100
❑ 98BowCHL-73
❑ 98BowCHLGA-73
❑ 98BowCHLOI-73
❑ 98BowChrC-73
❑ 98BowChrCGA-73
❑ 98BowChrCGAR-73
❑ 98BowChrCOI-73
❑ 98BowChrCOIR-73
❑ 98BowChrCR-73
❑ 98SP Aut-112
❑ 98UC-253
❑ 98UD ChoPCR-253
❑ 98UD ChoR-253
❑ 98UppDecM-207
❑ 98UppDecMGS-207
❑ 98UppDecMSS-207
❑ 98UppDecMSS-207
❑ 99Pac-423
❑ 99PacCop-423
❑ 99PacGol-423
❑ 99PacIceB-423
❑ 99PacPreD-423
❑ 99SP AutPS-112
❑ 99UppDecM-211
❑ 99UppDecMGS-211
❑ 99UppDecMSS-211
❑ 99UppDecMSS-211
**Holden, Mark**
❑ 83NovScoV-1
❑ 84NovScoO-1
**Holden, Paul**
❑ 897thInnSOHL-24
❑ 90ProAHLIHL-431
❑ 91ProAHLCHL-396
❑ 93St.JohML-10
**Holdien, Dean**
❑ 88SasBla-10
❑ 89SasBla-10
**Holdridge, Kevin**
❑ 96DetWha-10
**Holdsworth, Brent**
❑ 93LonKni-12
**Holecek, Jiri**
❑ 71SweHocS-43
❑ 72SweHocS-21
❑ 72SweHocS-45
❑ 72SweSemWC-22
❑ 73SweHocS-27
❑ 73SweWorCS-27
❑ 74SweHocS-109
❑ 74SweSemHVS-51
❑ 79PanSti-74
❑ 91SweSemWCS-246
**Holecko, Peter**
❑ 96SloPeeWT-11
**Holeczy, Roger**
❑ 94DubFigS-12
**Holeczy, Steve**
❑ 94DubFigS-13
**Holick, Mark**
❑ 84SasBlaS-6
❑ 93DalFre-8
**Holik, Bobby**
❑ 90OPCPre-43
❑ 90ProSet-609
❑ 90ScoRoo-10T
❑ 90ScoYouS-34
❑ 90UppDec-534
❑ 90UppDecF-534
❑ 90WhaJr7E-13
❑ 91Bow-18
❑ 91OPC-7
❑ 91OPC-56
❑ 91PanSti-316
❑ 91PanSti-342
❑ 91Par-290
❑ 91ParFre-290
❑ 91Pin-65
❑ 91PinFre-65
❑ 91ProSet-79
❑ 91ProSetFre-79
❑ 91ProSetPla-43
❑ 91ScoAme-153
❑ 91ScoCan-153
❑ 91ScoYouS-36
❑ 91StaClu-299
❑ 91SweSemWCS-224
❑ 91Top-7
❑ 91Top-56
❑ 91UppDec-233
❑ 91UppDecES-3
❑ 91UppDecESF-3
❑ 91UppDecF-233
❑ 91WhaJr7E-14
❑ 92Bow-407
❑ 92OPC-254
❑ 92OPCPre-77
❑ 92PanSti-261
❑ 92PanSti-293
❑ 92PanStiFre-261
❑ 92PanStiFre-293
❑ 92Par-96
❑ 92ParEmel-96
❑ 92Pin-277
❑ 92PinFre-277
❑ 92ProSet-61
❑ 92Sco-128
❑ 92ScoCan-128
❑ 92StaClu-106
❑ 92Top-330
❑ 92TopGol-330G
❑ 92Ult-339
❑ 92UppDec-252
❑ 92UppDec-500
❑ 93Don-183
❑ 93Lea-227
❑ 93OPCPre-52
❑ 93OPCPre-322
❑ 93OPCPreG-52
❑ 93OPCPreG-322
❑ 93Par-385
❑ 93ParEmel-385
❑ 93Pin-71

❑ 93PinCan-71
❑ 93Pow-378
❑ 93Sco-198
❑ 93ScoCan-198
❑ 93StaClu-159
❑ 93StaCluFDI-159
❑ 93StaCluFDIO-159
❑ 93StaCluO-159
❑ 93TopPre-52
❑ 93TopPre-322
❑ 93TopPreG-52
❑ 93TopPreG-322
❑ 93Ult-360
❑ 93UppDec-218
❑ 94CanGamNHLP-144
❑ 94Don-90
❑ 94Lea-252
❑ 94OPCPre-315
❑ 94OPCPreSE-315
❑ 94Par-128
❑ 94ParGol-128
❑ 94Pin-347
❑ 94PinArtP-347
❑ 94PinRinC-347
❑ 94StaClu-129
❑ 94StaCluFDI-129
❑ 94StaCluMOMS-129
❑ 94StaCluSTWC-129
❑ 94TopPre-315
❑ 94TopPreSE-315
❑ 94UppDec-314
❑ 94UppDecEleIce-314
❑ 95BeAPla-202
❑ 95BeAPSig-S202
❑ 95BeAPSigDC-S202
❑ 95CanGamNHLP-159
❑ 95ColCho-185
❑ 95ColChoPC-185
❑ 95ColChoPCP-185
❑ 95Don-220
❑ 95ParInt-125
❑ 95ParIntEl-125
❑ 95Top-303
❑ 95TopOPCI-303
❑ 95TopPowL-10PL
❑ 95Ult-262
❑ 95UppDec-365
❑ 95UppDecEleIce-365
❑ 95UppDecEleIceG-365
❑ 96Dev-16
❑ 96SP-87
❑ 97Be A PPAD-201
❑ 97Be A PPAPD-201
❑ 97BeAPla-201
❑ 97BeAPlaAut-201
❑ 97ColCho-143
❑ 97Don-140
❑ 97DonPreProG-140
❑ 97DonPreProS-140
❑ 97DonPri-158
❑ 97DonPriSoA-158
❑ 97Pac-55
❑ 97PacCop-55
❑ 97PacCroR-76
❑ 97PacCroREG-76
❑ 97PacCroRIB-76
❑ 97PacCroRS-76
❑ 97PacDyn-70
❑ 97PacDynC-70
❑ 97PacDynDG-70
❑ 97PacDynEG-70
❑ 97PacDynIB-70
❑ 97PacDynR-70
❑ 97PacDynSil-70
❑ 97PacDynTan-45
❑ 97PacEmeGre-55
❑ 97PacIceB-55
❑ 97PacInv-78
❑ 97PacInvC-78
❑ 97PacInvEG-78
❑ 97PacInvIB-78
❑ 97PacInvR-78
❑ 97PacInvS-78
❑ 97PacOme-130
❑ 97PacOmeC-130
❑ 97PacOmeDG-130
❑ 97PacOmeEG-130
❑ 97PacOmeG-130
❑ 97PacOmeIB-130
❑ 97PacPar-103
❑ 97PacParC-103
❑ 97PacParDG-103
❑ 97PacParEG-103
❑ 97PacParIB-103
❑ 97PacParRed-103
❑ 97PacParSil-103
❑ 97PacRed-55
❑ 97PacRev-78
❑ 97PacRevC-78
❑ 97PacRevE-78
❑ 97PacRevIB-78
❑ 97PacRevR-78
❑ 97PacRevS-78
❑ 97PacSil-55
❑ 97Sco-183
❑ 97ScoDev-2
❑ 97ScoDevPla-2
❑ 97ScoDevPre-2
❑ 97SPAut-89
❑ 97UppDec-304
❑ 97Zen-68
❑ 97ZenZGol-68
❑ 97ZenZSil-68
❑ 98BowBes-53
❑ 98BowBesAR-53
❑ 98BowBesR-53
❑ 98Fin-95
❑ 98FinNo P-95
❑ 98FinNo PR-95
❑ 98FinRef-95
❑ 98O-PChr-131
❑ 98O-PChrR-131
❑ 98Pac-263
❑ 98PacAur-110
❑ 98PacCroR-80
❑ 98PacCroRLS-80
❑ 98PacDynI-110
❑ 98PacDynIIB-110
❑ 98PacDynIR-110
❑ 98PacIceB-263
❑ 98PacOmeH-138
❑ 98PacOmeODI-138
❑ 98PacOmeR-138
❑ 98PacPar-134
❑ 98PacParC-134
❑ 98PacParEG-134
❑ 98PacParH-134
❑ 98PacParIB-134
❑ 98PacParS-134
❑ 98PacRed-263
❑ 98PacRev-85
❑ 98PacRevADC-10
❑ 98PacRevIS-85
❑ 98PacRevR-85
❑ 98Top-131
❑ 98TopO-P-131
❑ 98UC-115
❑ 98UD ChoPCR-115
❑ 98UD ChoR-115
❑ 98UDCP-115
❑ 98UppDec-313
❑ 98UppDecE-313
❑ 98UppDecE1o1-313
❑ 98UppDecGR-313
❑ 98UppDecM-121
❑ 98UppDecMGS-121
❑ 98UppDecMSS-121
❑ 98UppDecMSS-121
❑ 99DevPowP-NJD4
❑ 99Pac-238
❑ 99PacAur-86
❑ 99PacAurPD-86
❑ 99PacCop-238
❑ 99PacGol-238
❑ 99PacIceB-238
❑ 99PacPreD-238

**Holik, Jaroslav**
❑ 69SweHocS-27
❑ 69SweWorC-6
❑ 69SweWorC-78
❑ 69SweWorC-149
❑ 70SweHocS-357
❑ 72SweHocS-24
❑ 74SweHocS-115
❑ 74SweSemHVS-60
❑ 94CzeAPSE-291

**Holik, Jiri**
❑ 69SweHocS-28
❑ 69SweWorC-3
❑ 69SweWorC-150
❑ 70SweHocS-358
❑ 71SweHocS-53
❑ 72SweHocS-25
❑ 72SweSemWC-39
❑ 74SweHocS-116
❑ 74SweSemHVS-61
❑ 95CzeAPSE-196
❑ 96CzeAPSE-331

**Holk, Brian**
❑ 907thInnSOHL-260

**Holland, Bob**
❑ 77NovScoV-9
❑ 81IndChe-8
❑ 82IndChe-9

**Holland, Dennis**
❑ 86PorWinH-9
❑ 87PorWinH-12
❑ 88PorWinH-12
❑ 89ProAHL-322
❑ 90ProAHLIHL-471
❑ 91ProAHLCHL-593

**Holland, Derek**
❑ 96MedHatT-7

**Holland, Jason**
❑ 93KamBla-8
❑ 95DonEliWJ-6
❑ 95SigRoo-11
❑ 95SigRooSig-11
❑ 95SlaMemC-3
❑ 95UppDec-537
❑ 95UppDecEleIce-537
❑ 95UppDecEleIceG-537
❑ 96KenTho-10
❑ 97Don-214
❑ 97DonCanI-144
❑ 97DonCanIDS-144
❑ 97DonCanIPS-144
❑ 97DonPreProG-214
❑ 97DonPreProS-214
❑ 98UppDec-224
❑ 98UppDecE-224
❑ 98UppDecE1o1-224
❑ 98UppDecGR-224

**Holland, Jerry**
❑ 75OPCNHL-392
❑ 76OPCNHL-315

**Hollenstein, Felix**
❑ 91SweSemWCS-194
❑ 93SweSemWCS-127
❑ 93SwiHNL-23
❑ 95FinnSemWC-191
❑ 95SwiHNL-21

**Hollett, Flash (Frank)**
❑ 34BeeGro1P-325
❑ 35OPCV304C-83
❑ 36V356WorG-62
❑ 39OPCV3011-41

**Hollett, Steve**
❑ 84SauSteMG-9
❑ 89ProAHL-97

**Holley, Pat**
❑ 87SudWol-20

**Hollinger, Terry**
❑ 88RegPat-9
❑ 89RegPat-7
❑ 907thInnSWHL-165
❑ 917thInnSWHL-354
❑ 92PeoRivC-9
❑ 93PeoRiv-12
❑ 94ClaProP-171
❑ 94Par-204
❑ 94ParGol-204
❑ 95RochAmeSS-5

**Hollinger, Todd**
❑ 91AirCanSJHL-A27

**Hollingshead, Kelly**
❑ 91AirCanSJHL-B20

**Hollingworth, Bucky**
❑ 54Top-12
❑ 94ParMisL-62

**Hollinworth, Gordie**
❑ 52JunBluT-131

**Hollis, Scott**
❑ 897thInnSOHL-11
❑ 89OshGen-11
❑ 89OshGenP-3
❑ 907thInnSMC-96
❑ 907thInnSOHL-339
❑ 917thInnSOHL-155
❑ 91OshGen-11
❑ 91OshGenS-1
❑ 92OshGenS-20
❑ 93LasVegThu-13
❑ 95AdiRedW-10
❑ 98LasVegT-9

**Holloway, Bruce**
❑ 81RegPat-13
❑ 83FreExp-13
❑ 84FreExp-3

**Holman, Jim**
❑ 92WesMic-12
❑ 93WesMic-15

**Holmberg, Erik**
❑ 83SweSemE-167
❑ 84SweSemE-68
❑ 85SwePanS-64
❑ 86SwePanS-269
❑ 89SweSemE-237
❑ 90SweSemE-14
❑ 91SweSemE-212
❑ 92SweSemE-246
❑ 93SweSemE-215

**Holmberg, Jorgen**
❑ 83SweSemE-89
❑ 84SweSemE-89
❑ 85SwePanS-81
❑ 89SweSemE-260
❑ 90SweSemE-165
❑ 91SweSemE-270

**Holmberg, Mikael**
❑ 85SwePanS-108
❑ 86SwePanS-106
❑ 87SwePanS-104
❑ 89SweSemE-92
❑ 90SweSemE-266
❑ 94SweLeaE-198
❑ 95SweLeaE-68
❑ 95SweUppDE-109

**Holmberg, Niklas**
❑ 83SweSemE-125
❑ 84SweSemE-148

**Holmes, Chuck**
❑ 69SeaTotW-2

**Holmes, Daril**
❑ 84KinCan-25
❑ 85KinCan-25
❑ 86KinCan-13

**Holmes, Darren**
❑ 91BriColJHL-46

**Holmes, Hap**
❑ 83HalFP-L6
❑ 85HalFC-156

**Holmes, James**
❑ 52JunBluT-54

**Holmes, Mark**
❑ 88SalLakCGE-22

**Holmes, Tom**
❑ 92HarCri-14
❑ 96RicRen-11

**Holmes, Warren**
❑ 78LouGea-8
❑ 95Sla-243

**Holmgren, Leif**
❑ 72SweHocS-64
❑ 73SweHocS-196
❑ 73SweWorCS-196
❑ 74SweHocS-223
❑ 79PanSti-192
❑ 81SweSemHVS-14
❑ 82SweSemHVS-23
❑ 83SweSemE-20
❑ 91SweSemE-302
❑ 92SweSemE-324

**Holmgren, Niclas**
❑ 86SwePanS-10

**Holmgren, Paul**
❑ 77OPCNHL-307
❑ 78OPC-234
❑ 78Top-234
❑ 79OPC-156
❑ 79Top-156
❑ 80OPC-164
❑ 80OPC-172
❑ 80Top-164
❑ 80Top-172
❑ 81OPC-242
❑ 81OPCSti-179
❑ 81Top-E105
❑ 82OPC-251
❑ 82OPCSti-116
❑ 82PosCer-14
❑ 83OPC-266
❑ 84NorSta7E-7
❑ 84NorStaPos-11
❑ 84OPC-100
❑ 84Top-74
❑ 85FlyPos-12
❑ 85IsIIsINT-11
❑ 86FlyPos-10
❑ 89FlyPos-11
❑ 90ProSet-673
❑ 92WhaDai-8

**Holmgren, Rune**
❑ 69SweHocS-231

**Holmqvist, Leif**
❑ 64SweCorI-6
❑ 64SweCorI-107
❑ 65SweCorI-6
❑ 65SweCorI-31B
❑ 65SweCorI-107A
❑ 67SweHoc-9
❑ 67SweHoc-32
❑ 69SweHocS-45
❑ 69SweHocS-186
❑ 69SweWorC-38
❑ 69SweWorC-44
❑ 69SweWorC-53
❑ 69SweWorC-103
❑ 70SweHocS-1
❑ 70SweHocS-62
❑ 70SweHocS-63
❑ 70SweHocS-64
❑ 70SweHocS-65
❑ 70SweHocS-120
❑ 70SweHocS-273
❑ 71SweHocS-2
❑ 71SweHocS-75
❑ 72SweHocS-2
❑ 72SweHocS-51
❑ 72SweSemWC-42
❑ 73SweHocS-190
❑ 73SweWorCS-190
❑ 74SweHocS-316
❑ 81SweSemHVS-109
❑ 91SweSemWCS-231
❑ 95SweGloWC-64

**Holmqvist, Mikael**
❑ 98UC-289
❑ 98UD ChoPCR-289
❑ 98UD ChoR-289

**Holmstedt, Kenneth**
❑ 71SweHocS-321
❑ 72SweHocS-136
❑ 74SweHocS-142

**Holmstrom, Borje**
❑ 67SweHoc-220

**Holmstrom, Christer**
❑ 72SweHocS-274

**Holmstrom, Tomas**
❑ 94SweLeaE-218
❑ 94SweLeaENHLD-9
❑ 94SweLeaERR-3
❑ 95SigRooA-19
❑ 95SigRooAPC-19
❑ 95SweGloWC-50
❑ 95SweLeaE-54
❑ 95SweLeaEFF-8
❑ 95SweUppDE-123
❑ 95SweUppDETNA-NA15
❑ 96DonCanI-129
❑ 96DonCanIGPP-129
❑ 96DonCanIRPP-129
❑ 96Fla-107
❑ 96FlaBluI-107
❑ 96LeaLimR-9
❑ 96LeaLimRG-9
❑ 96SelCer-97
❑ 96SelCerAP-97
❑ 96SelCerBlu-97
❑ 96SelCerMB-97
❑ 96SelCerMG-97
❑ 96SelCerMR-97
❑ 96SelCerRed-97
❑ 96SweSemW-70
❑ 96UppDec-255
❑ 96Zen-118
❑ 96ZenArtP-118
❑ 97Be A PPAD-188
❑ 97Be A PPAPD-188
❑ 97BeAPla-188
❑ 97BeAPlaAut-188
❑ 97Pac-319
❑ 97PacCop-319
❑ 97PacEmeGre-319
❑ 97PacIceB-319
❑ 97PacRed-319
❑ 97PacSil-319
❑ 97ScoRedW-16
❑ 97ScoRedWPla-16
❑ 97ScoRedWPre-16
❑ 98Be A PPA-196
❑ 98Be A PPAA-196
❑ 98Be A PPAAF-196
❑ 98Be A PPSE-196
❑ 98Be APG-196
❑ 98Pac-193
❑ 98PacIceB-193
❑ 98PacRed-193
❑ 98SP AutSotTG-TH
❑ 98SSASotT-TH
❑ 98UppDec-89
❑ 98UppDecE-89
❑ 98UppDecE1o1-89
❑ 98UppDecGR-89
❑ 98UppDecM-74
❑ 98UppDecMGS-74
❑ 98UppDecMSS-74
❑ 98UppDecMSS-74
❑ 99Pac-139
❑ 99PacCop-139
❑ 99PacGol-139
❑ 99PacIceB-139
❑ 99PacPreD-139
❑ 99UppDecM-75
❑ 99UppDecMGS-75
❑ 99UppDecMSS-75
❑ 99UppDecMSS-75

**Holocek, Jiri**
❑ 96SweSemWHL-HL16

**Holowatiuk, Bill**
❑ 92CorBigRed-15
❑ 93CorBigRed-13

**Holscher, Henrik**
❑ 94GerDELE-313
❑ 95GerDELE-305
❑ 96GerDELE-333

**Holt, Barton**
❑ 92MPSPhoSJHL-133

**Holt, Randy**
❑ 77OPCNHL-34
❑ 77Top-34
❑ 78CanuRoyB-11
❑ 78OPC-341
❑ 79OPC-4
❑ 79Top-4
❑ 80FlamPos-5
❑ 80PepCap-4
❑ 81Cap-7
❑ 81OPC-41
❑ 82Cap-10
❑ 82PosCer-20
❑ 83FlyJCP-11
❑ 83OPC-220

**Holt, Todd**
❑ 907thInnSWHL-48
❑ 917thInnSWHL-192

**Holtby, Greg**
❑ 83SasBla-5
❑ 84SasBlaS-7

**Holum, Dave**
❑ 95RoaExp-4

**Holunga, Shane**
❑ 91AirCanSJHL-C45
❑ 91AirCanSJHLAS-20

**Holway, Albert**
❑ 24C144ChaCig-32
❑ 24V1452-56

**Holy, Karel**
❑ 81SweSemHVS-66

**Holy, Robert**
❑ 94CzeAPSE-23

**Holzer, David**
❑ 89LetHur-9

**Holzer, M.**
❑ 95GerDELE-346

**Holzinger, Brian**
❑ 91UppDecCWJC-72
❑ 95BeAPla-161
❑ 95BeAPSig-S161
❑ 95BeAPSigDC-S161
❑ 95Bow-165
❑ 95BowAllFoi-165
❑ 95CanGamNHLP-39
❑ 95Cla-74
❑ 95ClaAut-9
❑ 95ClaIceBre-BK18
❑ 95Don-298
❑ 95Emo-17
❑ 95EmoGen-1
❑ 95Fin-67
❑ 95FinRef-67
❑ 95Lea-250
❑ 95LeaStuR-14
❑ 95Met-177
❑ 95ParInt-27
❑ 95ParIntEl-27
❑ 95Pin-205
❑ 95PinArtP-205
❑ 95PinRinC-205
❑ 95PlaOneoOne-126
❑ 95Sco-310
❑ 95ScoBlaIce-310
❑ 95ScoBlaIceAP-310
❑ 95SelCer-110
❑ 95SelCerFut-6
❑ 95SelCerMG-110
❑ 95SkyImp-190
❑ 95SkyImpNHLF-15
❑ 95SP-14
❑ 95StaClu-194
❑ 95StaCluMOMS-194
❑ 95Sum-168
❑ 95SumArtP-168
❑ 95SumIce-168
❑ 95Top-24
❑ 95TopOPCI-24
❑ 95Ult-19
❑ 95Ult-341
❑ 95UltGolM-19
❑ 95UppDec-88
❑ 95UppDecEleIce-88
❑ 95UppDecEleIceG-88
❑ 95Zen-126
❑ 95ZenRooRC-5
❑ 96ClaIceBreDC-BK18
❑ 96ColCho-24
❑ 96ColCho-342
❑ 96Don-226
❑ 96DonPrePro-226
❑ 96Lea-212
❑ 96LeaPreP-212
❑ 96Sco-266
❑ 96ScoArtPro-266
❑ 96ScoDeaCAP-266
❑ 96ScoGolB-266
❑ 96ScoSpeAP-266
❑ 96SP-18
❑ 96SPHolCol-HC19
❑ 96UppDec-16
❑ 96UppDecBD-118
❑ 96UppDecBDG-118
❑ 97Be A PPAD-34
❑ 97Be A PPAPD-34
❑ 97BeAPla-34
❑ 97BeAPlaAut-34
❑ 97ColCho-25
❑ 97ColChoSta-SQ14
❑ 97Don-74
❑ 97DonLim-58
❑ 97DonLim-184
❑ 97DonLimExp-58
❑ 97DonLimExp-184
❑ 97DonPre-93
❑ 97DonPreCttC-93
❑ 97DonPreProG-74
❑ 97DonPreProS-74
❑ 97DonPri-69
❑ 97DonPriSoA-69
❑ 97Lea-120
❑ 97LeaFraMat-120
❑ 97LeaFraMDC-120
❑ 97LeaInt-120
❑ 97LeaIntUI-120
❑ 97Pac-158
❑ 97PacCop-158
❑ 97PacDyn-11
❑ 97PacDynC-11
❑ 97PacDynDG-11
❑ 97PacDynEG-11
❑ 97PacDynIB-11
❑ 97PacDynR-11
❑ 97PacDynSil-11
❑ 97PacDynTan-32
❑ 97PacEmeGre-158
❑ 97PacIceB-158
❑ 97PacOme-23
❑ 97PacOmeC-23
❑ 97PacOmeDG-23
❑ 97PacOmeEG-23
❑ 97PacOmeG-23
❑ 97PacOmeIB-23
❑ 97PacPar-20
❑ 97PacParC-20
❑ 97PacParDG-20
❑ 97PacParEG-20
❑ 97PacParIB-20
❑ 97PacParRed-20
❑ 97PacParSil-20
❑ 97PacRed-158
❑ 97PacSil-158
❑ 97PinCer-118
❑ 97PinCerMB-118
❑ 97PinCerMG-118
❑ 97PinCerMR-118
❑ 97PinCerR-118
❑ 97PinIns-163
❑ 97PinTotCMPG-118
❑ 97PinTotCPB-118
❑ 97PinTotCPG-118
❑ 97PinTotCPR-118
❑ 97Sco-172
❑ 97ScoSab-9
❑ 97ScoSabPla-9
❑ 97ScoSabPre-9
❑ 97SPAut-16
❑ 97SPAutSotT-BH
❑ 97UppDec-15
❑ 97UppDecIce-19
❑ 97UppDecIceP-19
❑ 97UppDecIPS-19
❑ 97UppDecSG-SG49
❑ 98Be A PPA-15
❑ 98Be A PPAA-15
❑ 98Be A PPAAF-15
❑ 98Be A PPTBASG-15
❑ 98Be APG-15
❑ 98Pac-106
❑ 98PacAur-18
❑ 98PacDynI-19
❑ 98PacDynIIB-19
❑ 98PacDynIR-19
❑ 98PacIceB-106
❑ 98PacOmeH-24
❑ 98PacOmeODI-24
❑ 98PacOmeR-24
❑ 98PacPar-20
❑ 98PacParC-20
❑ 98PacParEG-20
❑ 98PacParH-20
❑ 98PacParIB-20
❑ 98PacParS-20
❑ 98PacRed-106
❑ 98UC-21
❑ 98UD ChoPCR-21
❑ 98UD ChoR-21
❑ 98UDCP-21
❑ 98UppDec-47
❑ 98UppDecBD-9
❑ 98UppDecDD-9
❑ 98UppDecE-47
❑ 98UppDecE1o1-47
❑ 98UppDecGR-47
❑ 98UppDecM-20
❑ 98UppDecMGS-20
❑ 98UppDecMSS-20
❑ 98UppDecMSS-20
❑ 98UppDecQD-9
❑ 98UppDecTD-9
❑ 99Pac-38
❑ 99PacCop-38
❑ 99PacGol-38
❑ 99PacIceB-38
❑ 99PacPreD-38

**Holzmann, Georg**
❑ 82SweSemHVS-120
❑ 89SweSemWCS-118
❑ 93SweSemWCS-160
❑ 94GerDELE-64
❑ 95GerDELE-63
❑ 96GerDELE-249

**Honkavaara, Aarne**
❑ 96FinnSISR-187

**Honkonen, Mikko**
❑ 95FinnSIS-76
❑ 96FinnSISR-76

**Honneger, Doug**
❑ 93SwiHNL-40
❑ 95FinnSemWC-190

**Hood, Bruce**
❑ 91UltOriS-86
❑ 91UltOriSF-86

**Hood, Murray**
❑ 89HamRoaA-9
❑ 90HamRoaA-49
❑ 91HamRoaA-5

**Hooey, Todd**
❑ 82OshGen-10
❑ 84MonGolF-19

**Hooge, Clint**
❑ 91AirCanSJHL-D30
❑ 92MPSPhoSJHL-84

**Hooper, Dale**
❑ 96DayBom-9

**Hooper, Tom**
❑ 83HalFP-M9
❑ 85HalFC-173

**Hoople, Ryan**
❑ 95LetHur-9
❑ 96LetHur-7
❑ 97BowCHL-101
❑ 97BowCHLOPC-101

**Hooson, Bill**
❑ 917thInnSWHL-270

**Hoover, David**
❑ 84KinCan-14

**Hoover, Ron**
❑ 89ProAHL-65
❑ 90ProAHLIHL-126
❑ 91UppDec-287
❑ 91UppDecF-287
❑ 92PeoRivC-10
❑ 93PeoRiv-13
❑ 95PeoRiv-7

**Hoover, Tim**
❑ 82SauSteMG-13
❑ 83SauSteMG-12
❑ 84SauSteMG-10

**Hope, Jared**
❑ 95SpoChi-14

**Hopiavuori, Ralph**
❑ 72CleCruWHA-6

**Hopkins, Dean**
❑ 82PosCer-8
❑ 84NovScoO-20
❑ 85NovScoO-1
❑ 88OilTenAnn-135
❑ 88ProAHL-104
❑ 89HalCit-9
❑ 89ProAHL-164
❑ 90HalCit-10
❑ 90ProAHLIHL-446
❑ 91ProAHLCHL-545

**Hopkins, Larry**
❑ 78LouGea-9
❑ 81JetPos-7

**Hopkins, Tom**
❑ 897thInnSOHL-115

**Hoppe, Matthias**
❑ 89SweSemWCS-105
❑ 94GerDELE-435
❑ 95GerDELE-386
❑ 96GerDELE-293
❑ 98GerDELE-224

**Hopper, Rick**
❑ 907thInnSWHL-260
❑ 917thInnSWHL-50

**Hopramon, Ralph**
❑ 72CruCleWHA-5

**Horacek, Tony**
❑ 84KelWin-20
❑ 88ProAHL-139
❑ 90Bow-104
❑ 90BowTif-104
❑ 90FlyPos-9
❑ 90ProSet-499

91FlyJCP-11
91ProSet-455
91ProSetFre-455
92IndIce-14
94IndIce-9
96CinCyc-24
**Horachek, Peter**
88FliSpi-8
93FliGen-18
94FliGen-10
**Horak, Jakub**
93SwiHNL-113
95SwiHNL-192
**Horak, Michal**
96CzeAPSE-260
**Horak, Roman**
94CzeAPSE-113
95FinnSemWC-161
96CzeAPSE-130
96SweSemW-124
**Horan, Brian**
91ProAHLCHL-438
92NasKni-17
**Horava, Miloslav**
82SweSemHVS-79
89RanMarMB-6
900PC-337
90ProSet-198A
90ProSet-198B
90Top-337
90TopTif-337
90UppDec-13
90UppDecF-13
91SweSemE-203
92SweSemE-226
93SweSemE-198
94CzeAPSE-253
95CzeAPSE-127
**Horbul, Doug**
74NHLActSta-300
740PCNHL-317
**Hordal, Craig**
94PriAlbR-9
**Hordy, Mike**
81IndChe-9
**Horeck, Pete**
44BeeGro2P-33
44BeeGro2P-177
**Horesovsky, Josef**
69SweHocS-29
69SweWorC-79
69SweWorC-153
70SweHocS-348
71SweHocS-44
72SweHocS-22
72SweHocS-47
72SweSemWC-23
73SweHocS-228
73SweWorCS-28
74SweHocS-111
74SweSemHVS-54
**Horn, Alexander**
94GerDELE-424
**Horn, Bill**
92GreMon-3
93RochAmeKod-12
94GreMon-14
**Hornak, Ernest**
92ForWorF-8
**Horne, Buddy**
52JunBluT-119
**Horne, Kyle**
96FifFly-16
**Horner, Red**
320'KeeMapL-2
330PCV304A-10
33V129-1
33V252CanG-31
33V288HamG-21
33V357IceK-16
34BeeGro1P-326
34SweCap-46
360PCV304D-122
36V356WorG-8
370PCV304E-134
38QuaOatP-19
390PCV3011-10
83HalFP-H9
85HalFC-115
**Hornung, Blaire**
91AirCanSJHL-A7
**Hornung, Brad**
86RegPat-9
**Hornung, Larry**
71BluPos-8
720PC-317
73QuaOatPWHA-26
**Horny, Karel**
96CzeAPSE-112
**Hornya, Robert**
90ProAHLIHL-165
**Horton, Bill**
72CleCruWHA-7
72CruIceWHAL-4
**Horton, Tim**
44BeeGro2P-408
45QuaOatP-23
52Par-58
53Par-13
54Par-31
54Par-90
55Par-3
55ParQua0-3
57Par-T22
58Par-42

59Par-23
60Par-1
60ShiCoi-5
60YorPreP-17
61Par-1
61ShiCoi-44
61YorYelB-7
62Par-7
62ShiMetC-4
62YorIro0Tra-3
63ChePho-25
63Par-16
63Par-76
63TorSta-19
63YorWhiB-1
64BeeGro3P-165A
64BeeGro3P-165B
64CocCap-94
64Top-102
64Top-105
64TorSta-17
65Coc-94
65Top-79
66Top-80
67PosFliB-3
67Top-16
67Top-127
67YorActOct-3
67YorActOct-21
67YorActOct-25
67YorActOct-31
68MapLeaWB-4
680PC-123
680PC-201
680PCPucSti-18
68ShiCoi-172
68Top-123
69MapLeaWBG-17
690PC-182
690PC-213
690PCFou-1
69Top-45
70EssPowPla-183
700PC-59
70SarProSta-125
70Top-59
710PC-186
710PCPos-18
71SarProSta-169
71TorSun-218
720PC-197
72SarProSta-37
730PC-189
73SabPos-3
83HalFP-J8
85HalFC-188
91Kra-86
91UltOriS-37
91UltOriS-84
91UltOriS-97
91UltOriSF-37
91UltOriSF-84
91UltOriSF-97
92HalFL-24
92ParParR-PR16
92ParParR-PR34
93ParParRCI-3
93SabNoc-8
94ParMisL-127
94ParTalB-131
94ParTalB-135
95Par66-103
95Par66Coi-103
99UppDecCL-40
99UppDecCLCLC-40
**Horvath, Bronco**
44BeeGro2P-34
44BeeGro2P-107
44BeeGro2P-326
44BeeGro2P-409
57BruTealss-9
57Top-7
58Top-35
59Top-56
60ShiCoi-105
60Top-54
60TopSta-26
61ShiCoi-31
61Top-40
62Top-63
63RochAme-16
64BeeGro3P-166
94ParMisL-105
**Horvath, Jason**
917thInnSWHL-187
**Horvath, Tony**
75HamFin-8
**Horyna, Robert**
90NewSai-7
96CzeAPSE-266
**Hosek, Miroslav**
94CzeAPSE-259
**Hospodar, Ed**
800PC-366
810PC-233
82WhaJunHC-7
83WhaJunHC-6
85FlyPos-11
86FlyPos-11
87SabBluS-12
87SabWonBH-11
**Hossa, Marian**
97DonEli-28
97DonEliAsp-28

97DonEliS-28
97DonPre-162
97DonPreCttC-162
97PacDyn-NNO
97PacDynC-NNO
97PacDynEG-NNO
97PacDynIB-NNO
97PacDynIN-NNO
97PacDynSil-NNO
97PacPar-125
97PacParC-125
97PacParDG-125
97PacParEG-125
97PacParIB-125
97PacParRed-125
97PacParSil-125
97Pin-17
97PinArtP-17
97PinPrePBB-17
97PinPrePBC-17
97PinPrePBM-17
97PinPrePBY-17
97PinPrePFC-17
97PinPrePFM-17
97PinPrePFY-17
97PinPrePla-17
97PinRinC-17
97UppDec-326
98Be A PPA-249
98Be A PPAA-249
98Be A PPAAF-249
98Be A PPSE-249
98Be APG-249
98BowBes-107
98BowBesAR-107
98BowBesMIF-F13
98BowBesMIFAR-F13
98BowBesMIFR-F13
98BowBesR-107
98BowCHL-53
98BowCHLGA-53
98BowCHLOI-53
98BowCHLSC-SC7
98BowChrC-53
98BowChrCGA-53
98BowChrCGAR-53
98BowChrCOI-53
98BowChrCOIR-53
98BowChrCR-53
98FinFutF-F16
98FinFutFR-F16
98McD-23
980-PChr-104
980-PChrR-104
98PacOmeH-164
98PacOmeODI-164
98PacOmeR-164
98PacRev-99
98PacRevIS-99
98PacRevR-99
98SP AutSotTG-MH
98SPxFin-58
98SPxFin-140
98SPxFinR-58
98SPxFinR-140
98SPxFinS-58
98SPxFinS-140
98SSASotT-MH
98Top-104
98TopO-P-104
98UC-142
98UD ChoPCR-142
98UD ChoR-142
98UppDec-6
98UppDecE-6
98UppDecE1o1-6
98UppDecGN-GN2
98UppDecGNQ1-GN2
98UppDecGNQ2-GN2
98UppDecGNQ3-GN2
98UppDecGR-6
99Pac-288
99PacAur-99
99PacAurPD-99
99PacCop-288
99PacGol-288
99PacIceB-288
99PacPreD-288
99QuePeeWHWCCS-16
99RetHoc-56
99UppDecCL-73
99UppDecCLCLC-73
99UppDecM-144
99UppDecM2CN-8
99UppDecMGS-GU5
99UppDecMGS-144
99UppDecMGSA-GU5
99UppDecMSS-144
99UppDecMSS-144
99UppDecRG-56
99UppDecRGP-56
**Host, Charlie**
96DenUniPio-7
**Hostak, Martin**
90FlyPos-10
900PCPre-44
90ProSet-629
90ScoRoo-36T
90UppDec-542
90UppDecF-542
91Bow-233
91ProAHLCHL-285
91StaClu-337
91UppDec-473

91UppDecF-473
92SweSemE-236
93SweSemE-206
94FinnJaaK-189
94SweLeaE-238
95SweLeaE-104
95SweLeaEFF-10
95SweUppDE-162
96CzeAPSE-137
96SweSemW-121
**Hotham, Greg**
79MapLeaP-12
83PenHeiP-13
83PenTealP-16
84PenHeiP-12
88ProAHL-228
89ProAHL-118
**Houck, Paul**
88ProIHL-20
**Houda, Doug**
85MedHatT-2
88RedWinLC-9
89RedWinLC-10
900PC-410
90ProAHLIHL-479
90Sco-11
90ScoCan-11
910PC-512
91ProSet-81
91ProSetFre-81
91ScoCan-442
91Top-512
91WhaJr7E-15
92WhaDai-9
94Lea-523
96IslPos-6
97Be A PPAD-193
97Be A PPAPD-193
97BeAPla-193
97BeAPlaAut-193
97PacDynBKS-55
**Houde, Eric**
98Pac-251
98PacIceB-251
98PacRed-251
**Hougen, Jim**
82MedHatT-5
**Hough, Mike**
82KitRan-20
83FreExp-7
84FreExp-12
85FreExp-8
86FreExp-12
86NordGenF-11
86NordMcD-11
86NordTeal-10
87NordGenF-15
870PCSti-220
88ProAHL-98
89Nord-16
89NordGenF-13
89NordPol-11
890PC-266
90Bow-174
90BowTif-174
90NordPet-11
90NordTeal-11
900PC-427
90ProSet-247
90ProSet-516
91Bow-144
91NordPanTS-9
91NordPet-10
910PC-113
91PanSti-254
91Par-150
91ParFre-150
91Pin-194
91PinFre-194
91ProSet-463
91ProSet-582
91ProSetFre-463
91ProSetFre-582
91ProSetPla-217
91ScoAme-112
91ScoCan-112
91StaClu-80
91Top-113
91UppDec-562
91UppDecF-562
92Bow-178
92DurPan-25
92NorPet-11
920PC-392
92PanSti-211
92PanStiFre-211
92Par-380
92ParEmel-380
92Pin-113
92PinFre-113
92ProSet-154
92ProSet-266
92Sco-64
92ScoCan-64
92StaClu-434
92Top-297
92TopGol-297G
92Ult-175
93Don-122
93DurSco-45
93Lea-247
930PCPre-482
930PCPreG-482
93Pin-402
93PinCan-402

93Pow-94
93Sco-393
93Sco-559
93ScoCan-393
93ScoCan-559
93ScoGol-559
93StaClu-466
93StaCluFDI-466
93StaCluO-466
93TopPre-482
93TopPreG-482
94Lea-504
940PCPre-116
940PCPreSE-116
94Pin-333
94PinArtP-333
94PinRinC-333
94TopPre-116
94TopPreSE-116
94Ult-297
95BeAPla-122
95BeAPSig-S122
95BeAPSigDC-S122
96Pin-76
96PinArtP-76
96PinFoi-76
96PinPreS-76
96PinRinC-76
97PacDynBKS-40
98Fin-83
98FinNo P-83
98FinNo PR-83
98FinRef-83
**Houghton, Art**
92MPSPhoSJHL-68
**Houghton, Darren**
91AirCanSJHL-D13
92MPSPhoSJHL-79
**Houk, Rod**
87RegPat-8
88RegPat-10
92DayBom-12
**Houlder, Bill**
87CapKod-34
88ProAHL-37
89CapTealss-7
900PC-399
90ProAHLIHL-273
90ProSet-417
91ProAHLCHL-1
91RochAmePos-11
92SanDieG-11
93Don-8
93Lea-315
930PCPre-403
930PCPreG-403
93Par-272
93ParEmel-272
93Pow-4
93Sco-639
93ScoCan-639
93ScoGol-639
93StaClu-419
93StaCluFDI-419
93StaCluO-419
93TopPre-403
93TopPreG-403
93Ult-256
93UppDec-429
94BeAPSig-43
94LigPos-11
940PCPre-92
940PCPreSE-92
94Pin-206
94PinArtP-206
94PinRinC-206
94TopPre-92
94TopPreSE-92
94Ult-4
94Ult-362
94UppDec-183
94UppDecEleIce-183
95ColCho-243
95ColChoPC-243
95ColChoPCP-243
95LigTeal-12
95ParInt-464
95ParIntEl-464
95UppDec-475
95UppDecEleIce-475
95UppDecEleIceG-475
96UppDec-154
980-PChr-46
980-PChrR-46
98Pac-381
98PacIceB-381
98PacRed-381
98Top-46
98TopO-P-46
99Pac-372
99PacCop-372
99PacGol-372
99PacIceB-372
99PacPreD-372
**Houle, Butch (Gerard)**
52JunBluT-66
**Houle, Eric**
93AmoLesFAM-9
**Houle, Kevin**
86SheCan-20
**Houle, Rejean**
69CanaPosC-11
700PC-174
71CanaPos-8
710PC-147

71TorSun-151
72CanaPos-6
720PC-210
72SarProSta-125
740PCWHA-41
74TeaCanLWHA-9
750PCWHA-84
76CanaPos-7
760PCNHL-360
77CanaPos-8
770PCNHL-241
77Top-241
78CanaPos-8
780PC-227
78Top-227
79CanaPos-8
790PC-34
79Top-34
80CanaPos-8
800PC-261
80PepCap-46
80Top-261
81CanaPos-10
810PC-183
810PCSti-37
82CanaPos-9
820PC-184
92SpoFla-10
96CanaPos-12
**Houle, Yvan**
52JunBluT-46
**House, Bobby**
89SpoChi-11
907thInnSWHL-190
917thInnSWHL-208
91StaPicH-69
91UltDra-47
92BraWheK-11
94ClaProP-219
94IndIce-10
**Housley, Phil**
82SabMilP-11
830PC-65
830PCSti-238
83PufSti-12
840PC-23
840PCSti-203
840PCSti-204
84SabBluS-9
850PC-63
850PCSti-173
85SabBluS-13
85SabBluS-13
85Top-63
860PC-154
860PCSti-41
86SabBluS-15
86SabBluSSma-15
86Top-154
870PC-33
870PCMin-17
870PCSti-151
87PanSti-24
87SabBluS-13
87SabWonBH-12
87Top-33
880PC-119
880PCSti-255
88PanSti-220
88SabBluS-11
88SabWonBH-11
88Top-119
890PC-59
890PCSti-161
89PanSti-205
89SabBluS-7
89SabCam-9
89SweSemWCS-156
89Top-59
90Bow-239
90BowTif-239
90JetIGA-15
90Kra-18
90Kra-85
900PC-89
900PC-262
900PCPre-45
90PanSti-21
90ProSet-21A
90ProSet-21B
90ProSet-364
90ProSet-562
90Sco-145
90ScoCan-145
90ScoHotRS-63
90ScoRoo-3T
90Top-89
90Top-262
90TopTif-89
90UppDec-22
90UppDec-435
90UppDecF-22
90UppDecF-435
91Bow-197
91JetIGA-14
91JetPanTS-13
91JetPanTS-H
91Kra-33
910PC-395
910PCPre-50
91PanSti-65
91Par-205
91ParFre-205

91Pin-4
91PinFre-4
91ProSet-267
91ProSet-295
91ProSetFre-267
91ProSetFre-295
91ProSetPC-30
91ProSetPla-137
91ScoAme-271
91ScoCan-491
91StaClu-65
91SweSemWCS-133
91Top-395
91TopTeaSL-11
91UppDec-106
91UppDec-624
91UppDecF-106
91UppDecF-624
92Bow-20
92Bow-208
92HumDum2-8
92McDUppD-8
920PC-298
920PCPreSP-16
92PanSti-61
92PanStiFre-61
92Par-208
92ParEmel-208
92Pin-70
92PinFre-70
92ProSet-212
92ProSetGTL-14
92Sco-299
92Sco-440
92ScoCan-299
92ScoCan-440
92SeaPat-59
92StaClu-14
92Top-268
92Top-456
92TopGol-268G
92TopGol-456G
92Ult-241
92UppDec-24
92UppDec-276
92UppDec-628
93Don-294
93Lea-61
93McDUppD-6
930PCPre-36
930PCPre-503
930PCPreBG-4
930PCPreG-36
930PCPreG-503
93PanSti-133
93PanSti-196
93Par-174
93ParEmel-174
93Pin-351
93PinAllS-25
93PinAllSC-25
93PinCan-351
93Pow-271
93Pow-427
93Sco-232
93Sco-482
93Sco-520
93ScoCan-232
93ScoCan-482
93ScoCan-520
93ScoGol-520
93StaClu-104
93StaCluFDI-104
93StaCluFDIO-104
93StaCluO-104
93SweSemWCS-174
93TopPre-36
93TopPre-503
93TopPreBG-19
93TopPreG-36
93TopPreG-503
93Ult-100
93Ult-409
93UltAllS-18
93UppDec-525
93UppDecLaS-26
93UppDecSP-136
94BeAPla-R78
94EASpo-145
94Fin-91
94FinRef-91
94FinSupTW-91
94Fle-30
94HocWit-101
94Lea-450
94LeaLim-77
940PCPre-353
940PCPre-491
940PCPreSE-353
940PCPreSE-491
94Par-197
94ParGol-197
94ParSE-SE30
94ParSEG-SE30
94Pin-410
94PinArtP-410
94PinRinC-410
94Sel-146
94SelGol-146
94SP-19
94SPDieCut-19
94TopPre-353
94TopPre-491
94TopPreSE-353
94TopPreSE-491

- 94Ult-269
- 94UppDec-169
- 94UppDecElelce-169
- 94UppDecSPI-SP102
- 94UppDecSPIDC-SP102
- 95BeAPla-72
- 95BeAPSig-S72
- 95BeAPSigDC-S72
- 95ColCho-212
- 95ColChoPC-212
- 95ColChoPCP-212
- 95Don-74
- 95Emo-22
- 95Fin-7
- 95FinRef-7
- 95ImpSti-16
- 95Kra-13
- 95Lea-141
- 95Met-19
- 95ParInt-30
- 95ParIntEI-30
- 95PlaOneoOne-17
- 95PlaOneoOne-129
- 95Sco-45
- 95ScoBlaIce-45
- 95ScoBlaIceAP-45
- 95SelCer-86
- 95SelCerMG-86
- 95SkyImp-22
- 95SP-9
- 95StaClu-145
- 95StaCluMO-145
- 95StaCluMOMS-145
- 95Sum-40
- 95SumArtP-40
- 95SumIce-40
- 95SweGloWC-106
- 95SwiHNL-543
- 95Top-166
- 95TopOPCI-166
- 95TopSupSki-66
- 95TopSupSkiPla-66
- 95Ult-25
- 95UltGolM-25
- 95UppDec-294
- 95UppDecElelce-294
- 95UppDecEleIceG-294
- 95UppDecSpeE-SE13
- 95UppDecSpeEdiG-SE13
- 95Zen-104
- 96ColCho-150
- 96Don-201
- 96DonPrePro-201
- 96Fle-59
- 96FleNor-5
- 96FlePic-22
- 96Lea-65
- 96LeaPreP-65
- 96MetUni-164
- 96Pin-19
- 96PinArtP-19
- 96PinFoi-19
- 96PinPreS-19
- 96PinRinC-19
- 96PlaOneoOne-429
- 96Sco-153
- 96ScoArtPro-153
- 96ScoDeaCAP-153
- 96ScoGolB-153
- 96ScoSpeAP-153
- 96SkyImp-140
- 96SkyImpB-7
- 96SkyImpNHLF-10
- 96SP-167
- 96Sum-121
- 96SumArtP-121
- 96SumIce-121
- 96SumMet-121
- 96SumPreS-121
- 96SweSemW-161
- 96Ult-176
- 96UltGolM-176
- 96UppDec-261
- 96UppDecBD-96
- 96UppDecBDG-96
- 97ColCho-275
- 97Don-150
- 97DonPreProG-150
- 97DonPreProS-150
- 97Pac-259
- 97PacCop-259
- 97PacEmeGre-259
- 97PacIceB-259
- 97PacOme-238
- 97PacOmeC-238
- 97PacOmeDG-238
- 97PacOmeEG-238
- 97PacOmeG-238
- 97PacOmeIB-238
- 97PacRed-259
- 97PacRev-146
- 97PacRevC-146
- 97PacRevE-146
- 97PacRevIB-146
- 97PacRevR-146
- 97PacRevS-146
- 97PacSil-259
- 97SPAut-168
- 98Be A PPA-167
- 98Be A PPAA-167
- 98Be A PPAAF-167
- 98Be A PPAM-M16
- 98Be A PPSE-167
- 98Be A PPG-167
- 98Pac-96
- 98PacDynI-26
- 98PacDynIIB-26
- 98PacDynIR-26
- 98PacIceB-96
- 98PacRed-96
- 98UC-220
- 98UD ChoPCR-220
- 98UD ChoR-220
- 98UppDec-233
- 98UppDecE-233
- 98UppDecE1o1-233
- 98UppDecGR-233
- 98UppDecM-29
- 98UppDecMGS-29
- 98UppDecMSS-29
- 98UppDecMSS-29
- 99Pac-56
- 99PacAur-22
- 99PacAurPD-22
- 99PacCop-56
- 99PacGol-56
- 99PacIceB-56
- 99PacPreD-56
- 99UppDecM-30
- 99UppDecMGS-30
- 99UppDecMSS-30

**Houston, Ken**
- 770PCNHL-274
- 780PC-348
- 79FlamPos-6
- 79FlaTeal-7
- 790PC-310
- 80FlamPos-6
- 800PC-303
- 80PepCap-5
- 81FlamPos-7
- 82Cap-11
- 820PC-366
- 820PCSti-221
- 82PosCer-3
- 830PC-371
- 830PCSti-200

**Howald, Patrick**
- 93SweSemWCS-117
- 93SwiHNL-100
- 95SweGloWC-214
- 95SwiHNL-98

**Howarth, Todd**
- 93ThuBayS-9
- 94ThuBayS-1
- 95ThuBayS-9
- 99WicThu-8

**Howatt, Garry**
- 74NHLActSta-164
- 740PCNHL-375
- 750PCNHL-54
- 75Top-54
- 760PCNHL-206
- 760PCNHL-389
- 76Top-206
- 770PCNHL-194
- 77Top-194
- 780PC-29
- 78Top-29
- 790PC-205
- 79Top-205
- 800PC-386
- 820PC-140
- 820PCSti-133
- 82PosCer-7
- 830PC-229

**Howe, Corey**
- 92NorDakFS-9

**Howe, Gordie**
- 44BeeGro2P-178A
- 44BeeGro2P-178B
- 48ExhCan-44
- 48ExhCan-53
- 51Par-66
- 52Par-88
- 52RoyDesH-8
- 53Par-50
- 54Par-41
- 54Par-92
- 54Top-8
- 57Top-42
- 58Top-8
- 59Top-48
- 59Top-63
- 60Par-20
- 60ShiCoi-42
- 60WonBreL-1
- 60WonBrePP-1
- 61Par-20
- 61ShiCoi-66
- 62EIProDis-3
- 62Par-30
- 62Par-31
- 62ShiMetC-54
- 62YorIroOTra-19
- 63ChePho-26
- 63Par-55
- 63Top-31
- 63Top-58
- 63TorSta-20
- 64BeeGro3P-77A
- 64BeeGro3P-77B
- 64CocCap-44
- 64CocCap-45A
- 64Top-89
- 64TorSta-18
- 65Coc-43

- 65Top-108
- 65Top-122
- 66Top-109
- 66Top-121
- 66TopUSAT-23
- 67GenMil-2
- 67Top-43
- 67Top-131
- 680PC-29
- 680PC-203
- 680PCPucSti-22
- 68ShiCoi-44
- 68Top-29
- 690PC-61
- 690PC-193A
- 690PC-193B
- 690PC-215
- 690PCFou-14
- 690PCSta-14
- 69Top-61
- 70ColSta-47
- 70DadCoo-57
- 70EssPowPla-134
- 700PC-29
- 700PC-238
- 700PCDec-18
- 70RedWinM-5
- 70SarProSta-6
- 70Top-29
- 70TopStiS-13
- 71MatMinRec-5
- 710PC-262
- 710PCTBoo-23
- 71SweHocS-198
- 71Top-70
- 71TorSun-96
- 72SweSemWC-190
- 730PCWHAP-13
- 730PCWHAP-14
- 740PCWHA-1
- 750PCWHA-66
- 750PCWHA-100
- 760PCWHA-50
- 760PCWHA-72
- 770PCWHA-1
- 790PC-175
- 79Top-175
- 81RedWinOld-22
- 82NeiGre-10
- 83HalFP-B6
- 85HalFC-16
- 88EssAllSta-18
- 90ProSet-654
- 90ProSet-660
- 90WhaJr7E-14
- 91ParPHC-PHC1
- 91ParPHCF-PHC1
- 91ProSet-344
- 91ProSetFre-344
- 91SweSemWCS-238
- 92HalFL-9
- 92UppDecGHH-19
- 92UppDecGHH-20
- 92UppDecGHH-21
- 92UppDecGHH-22
- 92UppDecGHH-23
- 92UppDecGHH-24
- 92UppDecGHH-25
- 92UppDecGHH-26
- 92UppDecGHH-27
- 92UppDecShe-3
- 92UppDecShe-4
- 93ParChePH-D17
- 93ParParR-PR33
- 93ParParR-PR42
- 93ParParR-PR51
- 93ParParR-PR60
- 93ParParRCI-1
- 93ParParRCI-7
- 93UppDecLAS-42
- 93UppDecLAS-AU
- 94HocWit-9
- 94ParMisL-43
- 94ParMisL-145
- 94ParMisL-160
- 94ParMisL-162
- 94ParMisL-171
- 94ParMisLA-1
- 94ParTalB-46
- 94ParTalB-144
- 94ParTalB-154
- 94ParTalB-171
- 94ParTalB-177
- 94ParTalBA-A5
- 95Par66-42
- 95Par66-126
- 95Par66-142
- 95Par66-PR42
- 95Par66-MHA1
- 95Par66-MHA2
- 95Par66-MHA3
- 95Par66-MHA4
- 95Par66-MHA5
- 95Par66-MRH1
- 95Par66-MRH2
- 95Par66-MRH3
- 95Par66-MRH4
- 95Par66-MRH5
- 95Par66Coi-42
- 95Par66Coi-GH1
- 95Par66Coi-GH2
- 95Par66Coi-GH3
- 95Par66Coi-GH4
- 95Par66Coi-GH5
- 95Par66P-5

- 95ZelMasoH-3
- 97DonEliBttf-8
- 97DonEliBttFA-8
- 97HigMinHLMC-1
- 97HigMinHLMC-2
- 97SPAutMoaL-M1
- 97SPAutTra-T1
- 98Be A PPALGH-GH1
- 98Be A PPALGH-GH2
- 98McDGreT-T2
- 980-PChrBFtP-7
- 980-PChrBFtPR-7
- 98TopBlaFTP-7
- 98TopBlaFTPA-7
- 99RetHoc-82
- 99UppDecCA-C7
- 99UppDecCL-3
- 99UppDecCLACT-AC2
- 99UppDecCLCLC-3
- 99UppDecEotG-E4
- 99UppDecES-2
- 99UppDecRDR-DR11
- 99UppDecRDRI-DR11
- 99UppDecRG-G2A
- 99UppDecRG-82
- 99UppDecRGI-G2A
- 99UppDecRII-GH
- 99UppDecRIL1-GH
- 99UppDecRP-82
- 99UppDecRTotC-TC12

**Howe, Mark**
- 730PCWHAP-14
- 740PCWHA-1
- 74TeaCanLWHA-10
- 750PCWHA-7
- 760PCWHA-95
- 770PCWHA-25
- 790PC-216
- 79Top-216
- 800PC-91
- 800PC-160
- 80Top-91
- 80Top-160
- 810PC-128
- 810PCSti-62
- 810PCSti-145
- 81PosSta-11
- 81Top-E82
- 82McDSti-31
- 820PC-252
- 820PCSti-131
- 82PosCer-7
- 830PC-267
- 830PCSti-171
- 830PCSti-195
- 830PCSti-196
- 83PufSti-8
- 840PC-161
- 840PCSti-109
- 84Top-118
- 857ECreCar-14
- 85FlyPos-14
- 850PC-35
- 850PCSti-93
- 85Top-35
- 86FlyPos-12
- 860PC-123
- 860PCSti-116
- 860PCSti-184
- 860PCSti-246
- 86Top-123
- 86TopStilns-6
- 87OPC-54
- 870PCMin-18
- 870PCSti-100
- 870PCSti-112
- 870PCSti-176
- 87PanSti-124
- 87Top-54
- 87TopStilns-9
- 88EssAllSta-19
- 880PC-6
- 880PCSti-104
- 880PCSti-124
- 88PanSti-316
- 88Top-6
- 89FlyPos-12
- 890PC-191
- 890PCSti-109
- 89PanSti-300
- 89SweSemWCS-160
- 89Top-191
- 90FlyPos-11
- 90Kra-19
- 900PC-185
- 90PanSti-122
- 90ProSet-217
- 90Sco-220
- 90ScoCan-220
- 90ScoHotRS-92
- 90Top-185
- 90TopTif-185
- 90UppDec-261
- 90UppDecF-261
- 91FlyJCP-12
- 910PC-466
- 91Par-130
- 91ParFre-130
- 91Pin-297
- 91Pin-418
- 91PinFre-297
- 91PinFre-418
- 91ProSet-182
- 91ProSetFre-182

- 91ScoAme-252
- 91ScoCan-472
- 91SweSemWCS-134
- 91Top-466
- 92PanSti-191
- 92PanStiFre-191
- 92Par-279
- 92ParEmel-279
- 92Pin-244
- 92Pin-322
- 92PinFre-244
- 92PinFre-322
- 92Sco-217
- 92ScoCan-217
- 92Ult-285
- 92UppDec-530
- 93Lea-259
- 930PCPre-157
- 930PCPreG-157
- 93Pin-235
- 93Pin-254
- 93PinCan-235
- 93PinCan-254
- 93Pow-329
- 93Sco-91
- 93ScoCan-91
- 93StaClu-112
- 93StaCluFDI-112
- 93StaCluFDIO-112
- 93StaCluO-112
- 93TopPre-157
- 93TopPreG-157
- 94Pin-295
- 94PinArtP-295
- 94PinRinC-295
- 94UppDecNBAP-25

**Howe, Marty**
- 730PCWHAP-14
- 740PCWHA-1
- 74TeaCanLWHA-11
- 750PCWHA-15
- 760PCWHA-15
- 770PCWHA-65
- 790PC-46
- 79Top-46
- 800PC-139
- 830PCSti-54
- 83WhaJunHC-7
- 840PC-71
- 84Top-55

**Howe, Syd**
- 330PCV304A-24
- 33V357IceK-72
- 34BeeGro1P-104
- 35DiaMatTI-29
- 36V356WorG-75
- 390PCV3011-72
- 83HalFP-M10
- 85HalFC-174

**Howell, Harry**
- 44BeeGro2P-327
- 53Par-57
- 54Par-70
- 54Top-3
- 57Top-51
- 58Top-60
- 59Top-20
- 59Top-54
- 60ShiCoi-86
- 60Top-49
- 61ShiCoi-89
- 61Top-51
- 62Top-46
- 62TopHocBuc-11
- 63Top-48
- 64BeeGro3P-134
- 64CocCap-74
- 64Top-83
- 64TorSta-19
- 65Coc-75
- 65Top-22
- 66Top-91
- 66TopUSAT-18
- 67GenMil-3
- 67Top-84
- 67Top-119
- 67Top-121
- 680PC-69
- 68ShiCoi-103
- 68Top-69
- 690PC-79
- 69Top-79
- 70DadCoo-58
- 70EssPowPla-93
- 700PC-72
- 700PCDec-37
- 70SarProSta-134
- 70Top-72
- 710PC-153
- 71SarProSta-71
- 71TorSun-117
- 720PC-193
- 72SarProSta-90
- 81TCMA-6
- 83HalFP-F7
- 85HalFC-83
- 90UppDec-511
- 90UppDecF-511
- 91Kra-73
- 91UltOriS-23
- 91UltOriSF-23
- 92ParParR-PR15
- 93ParParRCI-6
- 94ParMisL-96

- 94ParTalB-92
- 95Par66-80
- 95Par66Coi-80

**Howse, Don**
- 77NovScoV-10

**Howse, Jason**
- 91BriColJHL-124

**Howson, Scott**
- 82IndChe-10
- 84SprInd-9

**Hoyda, Dave**
- 79JetPos-9
- 790PC-338
- 800PC-332
- 810PC-366

**Hoyle, Jimmy**
- 28V1282PauC-88

**Hrazdira, Richard**
- 96CzeAPSE-168

**Hrbaty, Jan**
- 69SweHocS-30
- 69SweWorC-11
- 70SweHocS-359
- 74SweHocS-120
- 94CzeAPSE-292
- 95CzeAPSE-175
- 96CzeAPSE-310

**Hrbek, Petr**
- 92Cla-39
- 93ClaProPro-67
- 94GerDELE-381
- 95FinnSemWC-163
- 95SweGloWC-160
- 96ClaGol-39
- 96CzeAPSE-180

**Hrdina, Jan**
- 95SeaThu-11
- 96CleLum-12
- 98PacCroR-109
- 98PacCroRLS-109
- 98PacDynI-150
- 98PacDynIIB-150
- 98PacDynIR-150
- 98PacDynIR-6
- 98PacOmeH-200
- 98PacOmeODI-200
- 98PacOmeR-200
- 98SP Aut-106
- 98UppDec-345
- 98UppDecE-345
- 98UppDecE1o1-345
- 98UppDecGR-345
- 99Pac-337
- 99PacCop-337
- 99PacGol-337
- 99PacIceB-337
- 99PacPreD-337
- 99SP AutPS-106
- 99UppDecM-169
- 99UppDecMGS-169
- 99UppDecMPS-JHR
- 99UppDecMSS-169
- 99UppDecMSS-169

**Hrdina, Jaroslav**
- 82SweSemHVS-97

**Hrdina, Jiri**
- 890PCSti-60
- 890PCSti-97
- 90FlamIGA-5
- 900PC-234
- 90PanSti-182
- 90ProSet-421
- 90Top-234
- 90TopTif-234
- 90UppDec-292
- 90UppDecF-292
- 91Bow-82
- 91FlamPanTS-3
- 910PC-213
- 91ProSet-461
- 91ProSetFre-461
- 91ScoCan-418
- 91StaClu-36
- 91Top-213
- 92StaClu-158
- 92Top-272
- 92TopGol-272G

**Hrechkosy, Dave**
- 74NHLActSta-59
- 750PCNHL-156
- 750PCNHL-316

**Hrechosky, Dave**
- 71RocMane-8

**Hreuss, Michael**
- 94GerDELE-304
- 95GerDELE-283
- 96GerDELE-89

**Hrivnak, Jim**
- 89ProAHL-93
- 90CapPos-7
- 90CapSmo-7
- 900PC-9
- 90ProAHLIHL-216
- 90ProSet-646
- 90Sco-386
- 90ScoCan-386
- 90Top-9
- 90TopTif-9
- 91Bow-305
- 91CapKod-10
- 910PC-487
- 91ProAHLCHL-549

- 91ProSet-509
- 91ProSetFre-509
- 91StaClu-264
- 91Top-487
- 91UppDec-343
- 91UppDec-343
- 92Bow-372
- 92CapKod-10
- 92Par-430
- 92ParEmel-430
- 92StaClu-325
- 92Top-18
- 92TopGol-18G
- 92Ult-435
- 92UppDec-151
- 93Lea-312
- 93Pin-407
- 93PinCan-407
- 93Pow-428
- 93Sco-201
- 93Sco-563
- 93ScoCan-201
- 93ScoCan-563
- 93ScoGol-563
- 93StaClu-421
- 93StaCluFDI-421
- 93StaCluO-421
- 93Ult-410
- 94MilAdm-10

**Hrkac, Tony**
- 87BluKod-13
- 87BluTealss-11
- 88BluKod-18
- 88BluTealss-11
- 880PC-129
- 880PCMin-15
- 880PCSti-19
- 880PCSti-36
- 880PCSti-129
- 88PanSti-106
- 88Top-129
- 89Nord-17
- 890PC-64
- 890PCSti-25
- 89PanSti-119
- 89Top-64
- 90Bow-172
- 90BowTif-172
- 90NordPet-12
- 90NordTeal-12
- 90PanSti-146
- 90ProSet-248
- 90Sco-256
- 90ScoCan-256
- 90UppDec-184
- 90UppDecF-184
- 91Bow-141
- 91NordPanTS-10
- 910PC-241
- 910PCPre-40
- 91ProSet-205
- 91ProSetFre-205
- 91ProSetPla-105
- 91ScoAme-122
- 91ScoCan-122
- 91ScoCan-555
- 91ScoRoo-5T
- 91ShaSanJSA-11
- 91StaClu-136
- 91Top-241
- 91UppDec-56
- 91UppDecF-56
- 92IndIce-15
- 92Sco-407
- 92ScoCan-407
- 92Top-524
- 92TopGol-524G
- 93Don-292
- 93Lea-329
- 93Par-448
- 93ParEmel-448
- 93Ult-411
- 94MilAdm-11
- 95ColEdgI-161
- 95ColEdgIP-PR6
- 95MilAdmBO-8
- 96MilAdmBO-9
- 98Pac-210
- 98PacIceB-210
- 98PacRed-210

**Hrstka, Ivo**
- 94CzeAPSE-20

**Hrubes, Milos**
- 96CzeAPSE-100

**Hrudey, Kelly**
- 81IndChe-10
- 82IndChe-11
- 83IsITeaIss-6
- 85IsIIsIN-26
- 850PC-122
- 850PCSti-79
- 85Top-122
- 860PC-27
- 860PCSti-212
- 86Top-27
- 870PC-119
- 870PCSti-242
- 87PanSti-90
- 87Top-119
- 880PC-155
- 880PCSti-109
- 88PanSti-283
- 88Top-155
- 89KinSmo-16
- 890PC-166

□ 89OPC-305
□ 89OPCSti-149
□ 89PanSti-89
□ 89Top-166
□ 90Bow-144
□ 90BowTif-144
□ 90KinSmo-17
□ 90OPC-103
□ 90PanSti-246
□ 90ProSet-119
□ 90Sco-115
□ 90ScoCan-115
□ 90ScoHotRS-55
□ 90Top-103
□ 90TopTif-103
□ 90UppDec-231
□ 90UppDecF-231
□ 91Bow-183
□ 91KinUppDST-NNO
□ 91OPC-195
□ 91PanSti-81
□ 91Par-71
□ 91ParFre-71
□ 91Pin-39
□ 91PinFre-39
□ 91ProSet-102
□ 91ProSetFre-102
□ 91ProSetPla-54
□ 91ProSetPlaPC-PC6
□ 91ScoAme-231
□ 91ScoCan-451
□ 91StaClu-120
□ 91Top-195
□ 91UppDec-262
□ 91UppDecF-262
□ 92Bow-42
□ 92Kra-32
□ 92OPC-44
□ 92PanSti-63
□ 92PanStiFre-63
□ 92Par-66
□ 92ParEmel-66
□ 92Pin-19
□ 92PinFre-19
□ 92ProSet-70
□ 92Sco-155
□ 92ScoCan-155
□ 92SeaPat-12
□ 92StaClu-391
□ 92Top-29
□ 92TopGol-29G
□ 92Ult-84
□ 92UppDec-270
□ 93Don-161
□ 93Kra-55
□ 93Lea-39
□ 93OPCPre-471
□ 93OPCPreG-471
□ 93PanSti-210
□ 93Par-97
□ 93ParEmel-97
□ 93Pin-252
□ 93PinCan-252
□ 93Pow-117
□ 93Sco-140
□ 93ScoCan-140
□ 93StaClu-54
□ 93StaCluFDI-54
□ 93StaCluFDIO-54
□ 93StaCluO-54
□ 93TopPre-471
□ 93TopPreG-471
□ 93Ult-131
□ 93UppDec-216
□ 93UppDecSP-71
□ 94BeAP99A-G13
□ 94BeAPSig-140
□ 94CanGamNHLP-282
□ 94Don-207
□ 94EASpo-66
□ 94Fla-80
□ 94Fle-95
□ 94HocWit-93
□ 94Kra-42
□ 94Lea-189
□ 94OPCPre-462
□ 94OPCPreSE-462
□ 94ParSel-SE81
□ 94ParSEG-SE81
□ 94Pin-292
□ 94PinArtP-292
□ 94PinMas-MA3
□ 94PinRinC-292
□ 94Sco-145
□ 94ScoGol-145
□ 94ScoPla-145
□ 94ScoPlaTS-145
□ 94Sel-34
□ 94SelGol-34
□ 94StaClu-208
□ 94StaCluFDI-208
□ 94StaCluMOMS-208
□ 94StaCluSTWC-208
□ 94TopPre-462
□ 94TopPreSE-462
□ 94Ult-99
□ 94UppDec-432
□ 94UppDecEleIce-432
□ 95CanGamNHLP-143
□ 95ColCho-147
□ 95ColChoPC-147
□ 95ColChoPCP-147
□ 95Don-215
□ 95ImpSti-61
□ 95Kra-36

□ 95ParInt-103
□ 95ParIntEl-103
□ 95Pin-122
□ 95PinArtP-122
□ 95PinRinC-122
□ 95PlaOneoOne-270
□ 95PosUppD-19
□ 95Sco-198
□ 95ScoBlaIce-198
□ 95ScoBlaIceAP-198
□ 95SelCer-65
□ 95SelCerMG-65
□ 95StaClu-8
□ 95StaCluMOMS-8
□ 95Sum-55
□ 95SumArtP-55
□ 95SumIce-55
□ 95TopSupSki-87
□ 95TopSupSkiPla-87
□ 95Ult-75
□ 95UltGolM-75
□ 95UppDec-145
□ 95UppDecEleIce-145
□ 95UppDecEleIceG-145
□ 95Zen-55
□ 96BeAPAut-45
□ 96BeAPAutSil-45
□ 96BeAPla-45
□ 96Don-209
□ 96DonCanI-36
□ 96DonCanIGPP-36
□ 96DonCanIRPP-36
□ 96DonEli-60
□ 96DonEliDCS-60
□ 96DonPrePro-209
□ 96Lea-109
□ 96LeaPre-39
□ 96LeaPreP-109
□ 96LeaPrePP-39
□ 96MetUni-136
□ 96Pin-120
□ 96PinArtP-120
□ 96PinFan-NNO1
□ 96PinFan-NNO2
□ 96PinFan-NNO3
□ 96PinFoi-120
□ 96PinMas-10
□ 96PinMasDC-10
□ 96PinPreS-120
□ 96PinRinC-120
□ 96PlaOneoOne-367
□ 96Sco-68
□ 96ScoArtPro-68
□ 96ScoDeaCAP-68
□ 96ScoGolB-68
□ 96ScoSpeAP-68
□ 96SelCer-87
□ 96SelCerAP-87
□ 96SelCerBlu-87
□ 96SelCerMB-87
□ 96SelCerMG-87
□ 96SelCerMR-87
□ 96SelCerRed-87
□ 96SP-141
□ 96Sum-126
□ 96SumArtP-126
□ 96SumIce-126
□ 96SumMet-126
□ 96SumPreS-126
□ 96Ult-150
□ 96UltGolM-150
□ 96UppDec-330
□ 96UppDecBD-62
□ 96UppDecBDG-62
□ 96Zen-57
□ 96ZenArtP-57
□ 97Don-92
□ 97DonLimFOTG-27
□ 97DonPrePro-92
□ 97DonPreProS-92
□ 97DonPri-85
□ 97DonPriSoA-85
□ 97Pac-337
□ 97PacCop-337
□ 97PacEmeGre-337
□ 97PacIceB-337
□ 97PacRed-337
□ 97PacSil-337
□ 97PinInsSUG-10A/B
□ 97PinInsSUG-10C/D
□ 97Sco-50
□ 97ScoArtPro-50
□ 97ScoGolBla-50
□ 97ShaFleAS-2
□ 98Pac-382
□ 98PacIceB-382
□ 98PacRed-382
**Hruska, David**
□ 95RedDeeR-7
□ 96CzeAPSE-234
**Hrycuik, Jim**
□ 74CapWHA-17
□ 74NHLActSta-322
**Hrycuik, Tony**
□ 92BriColJHL-144
**Hrycun, Kelly**
□ 96AlaGolKin-7
**Hrynewich, Steve**
□ 83Ott67-13
□ 84Ott67-12
**Hrynewich, Tim**
□ 83PenTealP-17
**Hryniuk, Brett**
□ 92NorDakFS-10
**Hrytsak, Rob**

□ 91JohChi-15
**Hsin, Cheng**
□ 79PanSti-359
**Huard, Billy (Bill)**
□ 89NasKni-9
□ 90ProAHLIHL-566
□ 91ProAHLCHL-414
□ 93Par-414
□ 93ParEmel-414
□ 93OPCSti-221
□ 93SenKraS-10
□ 93UppDec-485
□ 94SenBelM-15
□ 96StaPos-11
□ 97Be A PPAD-31
□ 97Be A PPAPD-31
□ 97BeAPla-31
□ 97BeAPlaAut-31
**Huard, Stephane**
□ 917thInnSQMJHL-16
**Hub, Jaroslav**
□ 94CzeAPSE-191
□ 95CzeAPSE-45
□ 96CzeAPSE-324
**Hubalek, Roman**
□ 91KnoChe-14
**Hubbard, Bill**
□ 93OmaLan-10
**Huber, Phil**
□ 87KamBla-9
□ 88KamBla-13
□ 907thInnSMC-6
□ 90RicRen-4
□ 91ProAHLCHL-458
□ 92RicRen-7
□ 95SigRoo-38
□ 95SigRooSig-38
□ 98GerDELE-7
**Huber, Willie**
□ 79OPC-17
□ 79RedWinP-7
□ 79Top-17
□ 80OPC-173
□ 80Top-173
□ 81OPC-89
□ 81OPCSti-126
□ 81Top-W89
□ 82OPC-85
□ 82OPCSti-185
□ 82PosCer-5
□ 83OPC-246
□ 83OPCSti-139
□ 83PufSti-21
□ 87CanuSheOil-9
□ 87OPC-93
□ 87OPCSti-34
□ 87PanSti-109
□ 87Top-93
**Hubick, Greg**
□ 75MapLeaP-11
**Hubinette, Per-Arne**
□ 67SweHoc-10
□ 67SweHoc-140
□ 69SweHocS-152
□ 70SweHocS-5
□ 71SweHocS-79
□ 72SweHocS-54
**Hubinette, Torbjorn**
□ 67SweHoc-119
□ 69SweHocS-133
□ 70SweHocS-92
□ 71SweHocS-184
**Huck, Fran**
□ 69SweHocS-356
□ 69SweWorC-25
□ 69SweWorC-34
□ 69SweWorC-95
□ 69SweWorC-187
□ 70EssPowPla-6
□ 72BluWhiBor-6
□ 73Top-63
□ 74FigSaiWHA-13
□ 740PCWHA-28
□ 75OPCWHA-121
**Huckle, Jeff**
□ 91AirCanSJHL-C24
**Hucko, Patrik**
□ 94CzeAPSE-189
**Hucul, Fred**
□ 44BeeGro2P-108
□ 51Par-45
□ 52Par-26
□ 53Par-71
**Huczkowski, Hans**
□ 93SweSemE-259
□ 95SweUppDE1DS-DS4
**Hudacek, Vladimir**
□ 94CzeAPSE-252
**Huddy, Charlie**
□ 81OilWesEM-5
□ 82OilRedR-22
□ 83OilMcD-9
□ 83OPC-30
□ 83OPCSti-96
□ 83Vac-27
□ 84OilRedR-22
□ 84OilTeal-8
□ 84OPC-244
□ 84OPCSti-258
□ 85OilRedR-22
□ 85OPC-187
□ 85OPCSti-216
□ 86OilRedR-22
□ 86OilTeal-22
□ 86OPC-211

□ 86OPCSti-69
□ 87OilTeal-22
□ 87OPC-207
□ 87OPCSti-87
□ 87PanSti-260
□ 88OilTeal-10
□ 88OilTenAnn-45
□ 88OPC-218
□ 88OPCSti-221
□ 88PanSti-53
□ 89Kra-12
□ 89OilTeal-10
□ 89OPC-158
□ 89OPCSti-220
□ 89PanSti-82
□ 89Top-158
□ 90OilIGA-8
□ 90OPC-344
□ 90PanSti-221
□ 90ProSet-85
□ 90Sco-199
□ 90ScoCan-199
□ 90Top-344
□ 90TopTif-344
□ 90UppDec-341
□ 90UppDecF-341
□ 91Bow-103
□ 91OilPanTS-7
□ 91OPCPre-125
□ 91PanSti-129
□ 91Par-298
□ 91ParFre-298
□ 91Pin-225
□ 91PinFre-225
□ 91ProSet-400
□ 91ProSetFre-400
□ 91ScoCan-247
□ 91ScoCan-570
□ 91ScoRoo-20T
□ 91StaClu-203
□ 91UppDec-569
□ 91UppDecF-569
□ 92Pin-143
□ 92PinFre-143
□ 92Sco-92
□ 92ScoCan-92
□ 92StaClu-372
□ 92Top-279
□ 92TopGol-279G
□ 92Ult-308
□ 93OPCPre-219
□ 93OPCPreG-219
□ 93Pin-296
□ 93PinCan-296
□ 93Pow-361
□ 93Sco-90
□ 93ScoCan-90
□ 93StaClu-308
□ 93StaCluFDI-308
□ 93StaCluO-308
□ 93TopPre-219
□ 93TopPreG-219
□ 93Ult-344
□ 94BeAP99A-G11
□ 94Pin-178
□ 94PinArtP-178
□ 94PinRinC-178
**Hudon, Gil**
□ 83SprInd-1
**Hudson, Dave**
□ 72OPC-211
□ 73OPC-234
□ 74NHLActSta-297
□ 74OPCWHA-335
□ 75OPCNHL-122
□ 75Top-122
□ 76OPCNHL-299
□ 76RocCokCan-11
□ 76RocPucBuc-10
□ 77OPCNHL-343
□ 77RocCokCan-9
□ 78OPC-299
**Hudson, Gordie**
□ 50QueCit-10
□ 51LavDaiS-117
□ 52St.LawS-46
**Hudson, Mike**
□ 85SudWol-15
□ 86SudWol-15
□ 88BlaCok-6
□ 89BlaCok-17
□ 90BlaCok-17
□ 90OPC-424
□ 90ProSet-431
□ 91BlaCok-10
□ 91Bow-399
□ 91OPC-495
□ 91Par-260
□ 91ParFre-260
□ 91Pin-38
□ 91PinFre-38
□ 91ProSet-369
□ 91ProSetFre-369
□ 91ScoCan-389
□ 91StaClu-22
□ 91Top-495
□ 92Bow-73
□ 92OilTeal-7
□ 92OPC-331
□ 92Pin-134
□ 92PinFre-134
□ 92Sco-156
□ 92ScoCan-156
□ 92StaClu-182
□ 92Top-172

□ 92TopGol-172G
□ 92Ult-37
□ 93Sco-659
□ 93ScoCan-659
□ 93ScoGol-659
□ 94BeAPla-R31
□ 94PenFoo-8
□ 98GerDELE-241
**Hudson, Rob**
□ 84Ott67-13
**Hueguenin, Rene**
□ 72SweSemWC-154
**Huettl, Dave**
□ 92NorMicW-12
**Huffman, Kerry**
□ 88PanSti-317
□ 89FlyPos-13
□ 90FlyPos-12
□ 90OPC-516
□ 91FlyJCP-13
□ 91Par-349
□ 91ParFre-349
□ 92NorPet-12
□ 92OPCPre-48
□ 92Par-382
□ 92ParEmel-382
□ 92ProSet-136
□ 92Sco-239
□ 92ScoCan-239
□ 92StaClu-381
□ 92Top-387
□ 92TopGol-387G
□ 92Ult-386
□ 92UppDec-444
□ 93Lea-291
□ 93OPCPre-43
□ 93OPCPreG-43
□ 93Sco-182
□ 93ScoCan-182
□ 93StaClu-33
□ 93StaCluFDI-33
□ 93StaCluFDIO-33
□ 93StaCluO-33
□ 93TopPre-43
□ 93TopPreG-43
□ 93Ult-402
□ 94BeAPSig-83
□ 94SenBelM-16
□ 94StaClu-127
□ 94StaCluFDI-127
□ 94StaCluMOMS-127
□ 94StaCluSTWC-127
□ 95Sen-12
□ 95Top-131
□ 95TopOPCI-131
□ 96LasVegThu-9
**Hughes, Brent**
□ 69OPC-144
□ 70SarProSta-147
□ 71OPC-205
□ 71SarProSta-147
□ 71TorSun-198
□ 72OPC-234
□ 72SarProSta-155
□ 73OPC-184
□ 73RedWinMP-9
□ 74NHLActSta-301
□ 74Top-73
□ 76OPCWHA-34
□ 76SanDieMW-4
□ 87MonHaw-12
□ 88ProAHL-184
□ 89JetSaf-17
□ 89ProAHL-31
□ 90MonHaw-11
□ 90ProAHLIHL-244
□ 90UppDec-333
□ 90UppDecF-333
□ 91BalSki-2
□ 91ProAHLCHL-561
□ 94Lea-218
□ 94Pin-510
□ 94PinArtP-510
□ 94PinRinC-510
□ 94StaClu-234
□ 94StaCluFDI-234
□ 94StaCluMOMS-234
□ 94StaCluSTWC-234
□ 94Ult-255
□ 96IslPos-7
□ 97PacDynBKS-35
**Hughes, Chuck E.**
□ 92BirBul-7
□ 93BirBul-7
**Hughes, Don**
□ 67SweHoc-270
**Hughes, Frank**
□ 76OPCWHA-81
□ 76RoaPhoWHA-8
**Hughes, Howie**
□ 68OPC-158
□ 69OPC-142
□ 70SarProSta-89
**Hughes, Jack**
□ 23V1281PauC-3
□ 24CreSel-2
□ 28V1282PauC-66
**Hughes, Jason**
□ 917thInnSOHL-273
□ 93KitRan-5
□ 94KitRan-6
**Hughes, John**
□ 74PhoRoaWP-6
□ 75OPCWHA-45

□ 75StiKah-5
□ 76OPCWHA-106
□ 76StiKah-3
□ 79CanuRoyB-10
□ 80PepCap-27
□ 88OilTenAnn-116
**Hughes, Pat**
□ 77NovScoV-11
□ 78CanaPos-9
□ 79OPC-65
□ 79Top-65
□ 80OPC-347
□ 81OilRedR-16
□ 82OilRedR-16
□ 82OPC-109
□ 82PosCer-6
□ 83OilMcD-15
□ 83OPC-31
□ 83OPC-213
□ 83OPCSti-327
□ 83OPCSti-328
□ 83Vac-28
□ 847EDis-18
□ 84OilRedR-16
□ 84OilTeal-9
□ 84OPC-245
□ 85OPCSti-229
□ 85SabBluS-14
□ 85SabBluSS-14
□ 88OilTenAnn-24
□ 88SudWol-17
□ 87SudWol-17
**Hughes, Ryan**
□ 91UppDecCWJC-47
□ 92CorBigRed-16
□ 93Cla-69
□ 94ClaAut-NNO
□ 94ClaProP-74
**Huikari, Juha**
□ 82SweSemHVS-33
**Huizenga, Kenny**
□ 97AncAce-3
**Hulbig, Joe**
□ 97PacDynBKS-38
**Hulett, Dean**
□ 91LakSupSL-13
□ 93Cla-70
□ 93PhoRoa-10
□ 94ClaAut-NNO
□ 94ClaProP-142
□ 95LouIceG-7
□ 95LouIceGP-8
**Hull, Bobby**
□ 44BeeGro2P-109A
□ 44BeeGro2P-109B
□ 58Top-66
□ 59Top-47
□ 60ShiCoi-63
□ 60Top-58
□ 60TopSta-28
□ 60WonBreL-2
□ 60WonBrePP-2
□ 61ShiCoi-25
□ 61Top-29
□ 62ShiMetC-47
□ 62ShiMetC-57
□ 62Top-33
□ 62TopHocBuc-12
□ 63ChePho-27
□ 63Top-33
□ 63TorSta-21
□ 64BeeGro3P-41A
□ 64BeeGro3P-41B
□ 64BeeGro3P-41C
□ 64BeeGro3P-41D
□ 64BeeGro3P-41E
□ 64BeeGro3P-41F
□ 64CocCap-25
□ 64Top-20
□ 64Top-107
□ 64TorSta-20
□ 65Coc-26
□ 65Top-59
□ 66Top-64
□ 66Top-112
□ 66Top-125
□ 66TopUSAT-40
□ 67Top-113
□ 67Top-124
□ 68OPC-16
□ 68OPC-204
□ 68OPCPucSti-3
□ 68ShiCoi-17
□ 68Top-16
□ 69OPC-70
□ 69OPC-216
□ 69OPCFou-9
□ 69OPCPos-9
□ 69Top-70
□ 70BlaBor-3
□ 70DadCoo-59
□ 70EssPowPla-116
□ 70OPC-15
□ 70OPC-235
□ 70OPCDec-30
□ 70Top-15
□ 70TopStiS-14
□ 71Baz-4
□ 71OPC-50
□ 71OPC-261
□ 71OPCPos-9
□ 71OPCTBoo-1
□ 71SarProSta-34

□ 71SweHocS-200
□ 71Top-1
□ 71Top-50
□ 71TorSun-66
□ 72KellroT-4
□ 72OPC-228
□ 72OPC-272
□ 72OPC-336
□ 72SluCupWHA-11
□ 72SweHocS-118
□ 72SweSemWC-228
□ 72Top-61
□ 72Top-126
□ 73OPCWHAP-16
□ 73QuaOatWHA-50
□ 74OPCWHA-50
□ 75OPCWHA-1
□ 75OPCWHA-65
□ 76OPCWHA-3
□ 76OPCWHA-5
□ 76OPCWHA-65
□ 76OPCWHA-100
□ 77OPCWHA-50
□ 79JetPos-10
□ 79OPC-185
□ 79Top-185
□ 85HalFC-242
□ 88EssAllSta-20
□ 91SweSemWCS-239
□ 91UltOriS-57
□ 91UltOriS-77
□ 91UltOriS-88
□ 91UltOriS-89
□ 91UltOriS-90
□ 91UltOriS-91
□ 91UltOriS-96
□ 91UltOriS-NNO
□ 91UltOriSBB-2
□ 91UltOriSF-57
□ 91UltOriSF-77
□ 91UltOriSF-82
□ 91UltOriSF-88
□ 91UltOriSF-89
□ 91UltOriSF-90
□ 91UltOriSF-91
□ 91UltOriSF-92
□ 91UltOriSF-96
□ 91UltOriSF-NNO
□ 92FutTre76CC-107
□ 92FutTre76CC-110
□ 92FutTre76CC-139
□ 92FutTre76CC-142
□ 92FutTre76CC-178
□ 93ActPacPro-1
□ 93ActPacPro-2
□ 93AmeLicSPC-P
□ 93UppDecLAS-43
□ 93ZelMasH-5
□ 93ZelMasoHS-5
□ 94ParTalB-25
□ 94ParTalB-136
□ 94ParTalBM-AA3
□ 94ParTalBM-AS5
□ 94ParTalBM-TW2
□ 94ParTalBM-TW6
□ 95Par66-21
□ 95Par66-124
□ 95Par66-129
□ 95Par66-130
□ 95Par66-141
□ 95Par66Coi-21
□ 97DonEliBtfP-6
□ 97DonEliBttFA-6
□ 97SPAutMoaL-M5
□ 97SPAutTra-T5
□ 97TopHocMC-11
□ 97TopHocMC-12
□ 98BaLeg-3
□ 98O-PChrBftP-9
□ 98O-PChrBftPH-9
□ 98TopBlaFTP-9
□ 98TopBlaFTPA-9
□ 98UppDecGJ-GJ3
□ 98UppDecGJ-GJA1
□ 99RetHoc-86
□ 99UppDecLB
□ 99UppDecCLACT-AC3
□ 99UppDecCLCLC-8
□ 99UppDecES-9
□ 99UppDecRG-86
□ 99UppDecRII-BOH
□ 99UppDecRIL1-BOH
□ 99UppDecRP-86
**Hull, Brett**
□ 85MinDul-28
□ 86MonGolF-20
□ 87BluTeaIss-12
□ 87FlamRedRP-8
□ 88BluKod-16
□ 88BluTeaIss-12
□ 88OPC-66
□ 88OPCMin-16
□ 88OPCSti-16
□ 88OPCSti-81
□ 88OPCSti-127
□ 88OPCSti-210
□ 88PanSti-107
□ 88Top-66
□ 89BluKod-16
□ 89OPC-186
□ 89OPCBoxB-F
□ 89OPCSti-22
□ 89PanSti-117

- 89SweSemWCS-167
- 89Top-186
- 89TopBoxB-F
- 90BluKod-10
- 90Bow-24
- 90BowHatTri-1
- 90BowTif-24
- 90HulColUMD-1
- 90HulColUMD-2
- 90HulColUMD-3
- 90HulColUMD-4
- 90HulColUMD-5
- 90HulColUMD-6
- 90HulColUMD-7
- 90HulColUMD-8
- 90HulColUMD-9
- 90HulColUMD-10
- 90HulColUMD-11
- 90HulColUMD-12
- 90Kra-20
- 90Kra-67
- 900PC-4
- 900PC-77
- 900PC-195
- 900PC-513
- 900PCPre-47
- 90PanSti-262
- 90PanSti-333
- 90ProSet-1A
- 90ProSet-263
- 90ProSet-342
- 90ProSet-378
- 90ProSet-395
- 90ProSetPM-P3
- 90Sco-300
- 90Sco-317
- 90Sco-346
- 90Sco-351
- 90Sco-366
- 90ScoCan-300
- 90ScoCan-317
- 90ScoCan-346
- 90ScoCan-351
- 90ScoCan-366
- 90ScoHotRS-100
- 90Top-4
- 90Top-77
- 90Top-195
- 90TopTeaSL-2
- 90TopTif-4
- 90TopTif-77
- 90TopTif-195
- 90UppDec-154
- 90UppDec-203
- 90UppDec-312
- 90UppDec-474
- 90UppDec-546
- 90UppDecF-154
- 90UppDecF-203
- 90UppDecF-312
- 90UppDecF-474
- 90UppDecF-546
- 90UppDecHol-4
- 90UppDecHol-6
- 91BluPos-10
- 91Bow-367
- 91Bow-375
- 91Gil-14
- 91Kra-66
- 91McDUppD-13
- 91McDUppD-H4
- 910PC-190
- 910PC-259
- 910PC-303
- 910PC-403
- 910PC-516
- 910PCPre-49
- 91PanSti-25
- 91PanSti-325
- 91Par-157
- 91Par-219
- 91Par-432
- 91Par-474
- 91ParFre-157
- 91ParFre-219
- 91ParFre-432
- 91ParFre-474
- 91ParPHC-PHC6
- 91ParPHCF-PHC6
- 91Pin-200
- 91Pin-356
- 91Pin-376
- 91PinB-B12
- 91PinBFre-B12
- 91PinFre-200
- 91PinFre-356
- 91PinFre-376
- 91ProSet-215
- 91ProSet-290
- 91ProSet-320
- 91ProSet-326
- 91ProSetCC-CC6
- 91ProSetCCF-CC6
- 91ProSetFre-215
- 91ProSetFre-290
- 91ProSetFre-320
- 91ProSetFre-326
- 91ProSetNHLAS-AC6
- 91ProSetNHLSA-AC18
- 91ProSetPC-24
- 91ProSetPla-109
- 91ProSetPla-282
- 91ProSetPlaPC-PC5
- 91ProSetSLM-4
- 91ScoAme-1
- 91ScoAme-337
- 91ScoAme-347
- 91ScoAme-371
- 91ScoAme-404
- 91ScoAme-412
- 91ScoAme-428
- 91ScoCan-1
- 91ScoCan-261
- 91ScoCan-294
- 91ScoCan-302
- 91ScoCan-335
- 91ScoCan-367
- 91ScoCan-377
- 91ScoFan-2
- 91ScoHotC-3
- 91ScoKel-21
- 91ScoNat-2
- 91ScoNatCWC-2
- 91StaClu-67
- 91SweSemWCS-144
- 91Top-190
- 91Top-259
- 91Top-303
- 91Top-403
- 91Top-510
- 91TopBowPS-9
- 91TopTeaSL-20
- 91UppDec-7
- 91UppDec-33
- 91UppDec-45
- 91UppDec-464
- 91UppDec-622
- 91UppDec-SP1
- 91UppDecAWH-AW3
- 91UppDecBB-2
- 91UppDecBHH-1
- 91UppDecBHH-2
- 91UppDecBHH-3
- 91UppDecBHH-4
- 91UppDecBHH-5
- 91UppDecBHH-6
- 91UppDecBHH-7
- 91UppDecBHH-8
- 91UppDecBHH-9
- 91UppDecBHH-AU1
- 91UppDecBHH-NNO
- 91UppDecBHHF-1
- 91UppDecBHHF-2
- 91UppDecBHHF-3
- 91UppDecBHHF-4
- 91UppDecBHHF-5
- 91UppDecBHHF-6
- 91UppDecBHHF-7
- 91UppDecBHHF-8
- 91UppDecBHHF-9
- 91UppDecBHHF-AU1
- 91UppDecF-7
- 91UppDecF-33
- 91UppDecF-45
- 91UppDecF-464
- 91UppDecF-622
- 92BluUDBB-12
- 92BluUDBB-NNO
- 92Bow-186
- 92Bow-209
- 92High5Pre-P3
- 92HumDum2-9
- 92Kra-41
- 92McDUppD-H2
- 920PC-87
- 920PC-124
- 920PC25AI-21
- 920PCPreSP-21
- 92PanSti-16
- 92PanSti-289
- 92PanStiFre-16
- 92PanStiFre-289
- 92Par-153
- 92Par-459
- 92ParEmel-153
- 92ParEmel-459
- 92Pin-100
- 92Pin-257
- 92PinFre-100
- 92PinFre-257
- 92PinTeaP-6
- 92PinTeaPF-6
- 92ProSet-156
- 92ProSet-245
- 92ProSetGTL-8
- 92Sco-350
- 92Sco-411
- 92Sco-435
- 92Sco-442
- 92Sco-500
- 92ScoCan-350
- 92ScoCan-411
- 92ScoCan-435
- 92ScoCan-442
- 92ScoCan-500
- 92SeaPat-13
- 92StaClu-1
- 92StaClu-258
- 92Top-2
- 92Top-260
- 92Top-340
- 92TopGol-2G
- 92TopGol-260G
- 92TopGol-340G
- 92UltAllS-12
- 92UppDec-29
- 92UppDec-423
- 92UppDec-620
- 92UppDecAWT-W2
- 92UppDecGHS-G7
- 93Don-286
- 93DonEli-5
- 93DonSpeP-U
- 93KenStaLA-4
- 93KenStaLC-3
- 93Kra-35
- 93Lea-255
- 93LeaGolIAS-3
- 93LeaStuS-8
- 93McDUppD-7
- 930PCPre-425
- 930PCPreBG-22
- 930PCPreG-425
- 93PanSti-N
- 93Par-180
- 93ParEasWesS-W7
- 93ParEmel-180
- 93ParUSACG-G4
- 93Pin-200
- 93PinAllS-34
- 93PinAllSC-34
- 93PinCan-200
- 93PinCap-20
- 93PinCapC-20
- 93PinNifFif-10
- 93PinTeaP-6
- 93Pow-211
- 93PowPoiL-4
- 93PowSlaA-4
- 93Sco-335
- 93ScoCan-335
- 93ScoDreTea-18
- 93ScoDynDUS-4
- 93ScoFra-18
- 93SeaPat-6
- 93StaClu-65
- 93StaCluAS-4
- 93StaCluFDI-65
- 93StaCluFDIO-65
- 93StaCluFin-3
- 93StaCluMasP-9
- 93StaCluMasPW-9
- 93StaCluO-65
- 93SweSemWCS-185
- 93TopPre-425
- 93TopPreBG-21
- 93TopPreBG-B
- 93TopPreG-425
- 93Ult-117
- 93UltRedLS-4
- 93UltScoK-3
- 93UppDec-160
- 93UppDec-232
- 93UppDecGGO-GG3
- 93UppDecLAS-21
- 93UppDecNB-HB3
- 93UppDecNL-NL2
- 93UppDecSilSka-R5
- 93UppDecSilSkaG-R5
- 93UppDecSP-137
- 94-ActPacM-MM2
- 94BeAP99A-G10
- 94BeAPla-R48
- 94CanGamNHLP-203
- 94DonDom-8
- 94EASpo-125
- 94Fin-42
- 94FinBowB-B15
- 94FinBowBR-B15
- 94FinDivFCC-15
- 94FinnJaaK-123
- 94FinnJaaK-347
- 94FinRef-42
- 94FinSupTW-42
- 94Fla-153
- 94FlaHotN-4
- 94Fle-187
- 94FleSlaA-2
- 94HocWit-97
- 94KenStaLA-6
- 94Kra-6
- 94Lea-16
- 94LeaGolS-4
- 94LeaLim-2
- 94LeaLimG-2
- 94McDUppD-McD13
- 940PCPre-417
- 940PCPre-465
- 940PCPreSE-417
- 940PCPreSE-465
- 94Par-309
- 94ParCratGB-20
- 94ParCratGG-20
- 94ParCratGR-20
- 94ParGol-309
- 94ParSE-SE154
- 94ParSEG-SE154
- 94ParVin-V35
- 94Pin-450
- 94PinArtP-450
- 94PinBoo-BR9
- 94PinRinC-450
- 94PinTeaP-TP11
- 94PinTeaPDP-TP11
- 94Sco-100
- 94ScoDreTea-DT22
- 94ScoFra-TF20
- 94ScoGol-100
- 94ScoPla-100
- 94ScoPlaTS-100
- 94Sel-97
- 94SelFirLin-12
- 94SelGol-97
- 94SP-100
- 94SPDieCut-100
- 94SPPre-29
- 94SPPreDC-29
- 94StaClu-100
- 94StaCluDD-3
- 94StaCluDDMO-3
- 94StaCluFDI-100
- 94StaCluFI-2
- 94StaCluFIMO-2
- 94StaCluMO-6
- 94StaCluMOMS-100
- 94StaCluMOMS-183
- 94StaCluSTWC-100
- 94TopFinB-8
- 94TopFinI-2
- 94TopPre-417
- 94TopPre-465
- 94TopPreGTG-3
- 94TopPreSE-417
- 94TopPreSE-465
- 94Ult-183
- 94UltAllS-11
- 94UltRedLS-5
- 94UppDec-229
- 94UppDec-333
- 94UppDec-569
- 94UppDecEleIce-229
- 94UppDecEleIce-333
- 94UppDecEleIce-569
- 94UppDecNBAP-8
- 94UppDecPC-C17
- 94UppDecPCEG-C17
- 94UppDecPR-R2
- 94UppDecPR-R32
- 94UppDecPR-R57
- 94UppDecPRE-R2
- 94UppDecPRE-R32
- 94UppDecPRE-R57
- 94UppDecPreRG-R2
- 94UppDecPreRG-R32
- 94UppDecPreRG-R57
- 94UppDecSPI-SP66
- 94UppDecSPIDC-SP66
- 95BeAPla-1
- 95BeAPSig-S1
- 95BeAPSigDC-S1
- 95Bow-43
- 95BowAllFoi-43
- 95CanGamNHLP-7
- 95CanGamNHLP-23
- 95CanGamNHLP-236
- 95ColCho-214
- 95ColCho-364
- 95ColChoCTG-C5
- 95ColChoCTG-C5C
- 95ColChoCTGGR-C5
- 95ColChoCTGGB-C5
- 95ColChoCTGSR-C5
- 95ColChoPC-214
- 95ColChoPC-364
- 95ColChoPCP-214
- 95ColChoPCP-364
- 95Don-68
- 95DonDom-6
- 95DonEli-7
- 95DonElICE-12
- 95DonEliDCS-7
- 95DonEliDCU-7
- 95DonMar-7
- 95DonProPoi-6
- 95Emo-148
- 95EmoXci-8
- 95Fin-10
- 95Fin-184
- 95FinnSemWC-113
- 95FinRef-10
- 95FinRef-184
- 95ImpSti-101
- 95ImpStiDCS-11
- 95KelDon-5
- 95KelDon-6
- 95KenStaLA-10
- 95Kra-66
- 95Lea-209
- 95LeaFlrOIce-9
- 95LeaGolS-6
- 95LeaLim-28
- 95LeaLimSG-10
- 95McDPin-MCD-6
- 95Met-125
- 95MetHM-5
- 95MetIS-8
- 95NHLAcePC-11D
- 95NHLCooT-15
- 95NHLCooT-RP15
- 95ParInt-172
- 95ParIntCCGS1-10
- 95ParIntCCSS1-10
- 95ParIntEl-172
- 95ParIntNHLAS-2
- 95ParIntPTP-PP54
- 95Pin-15
- 95PinArtP-15
- 95PinCleS-2
- 95PinFan-24
- 95PinFirS-12
- 95PinRinC-15
- 95PlaOneoOne-89
- 95PlaOneoOne-195
- 95PlaOneoOne-307
- 95ProMag-12
- 95Sco-235
- 95ScoBlaIce-235
- 95ScoBlaIceAP-235
- 95ScoBorBat-6
- 95ScoDreTea-9
- 95ScoLam-11
- 95SelCer-4
- 95SelCerGT-6
- 95SelCerMG-4
- 95SkyImp-141
- 95SkyImpIQ-2
- 95SP-121
- 95SPStaEto-E24
- 95SPStaEtoG-E24
- 95StaClu-183
- 95StaCluMO-37
- 95StaCluMOMS-183
- 95StaCluPS-PS9
- 95Sum-13
- 95SumArtP-13
- 95SumGolB-13
- 95SumGM-17
- 95SumIce-13
- 95SumMadH-2
- 95SweGloWC-115
- 95Top-10
- 95Top-372
- 95TopHidGem-10HG
- 95TopMarMPB-10
- 95TopMysF-M7
- 95TopMysFR-M7
- 95TopOPCI-10
- 95TopOPCI-372
- 95TopPro-PF19
- 95TopRinL-4RL
- 95TopSupSki-48
- 95TopSupSkiPla-48
- 95Ult-139
- 95Ult-386
- 95UltExtAtt-8
- 95UltGolM-139
- 95UltRedLS-3
- 95UltRedLSGM-3
- 95UppDec-233
- 95UppDec-251
- 95UppDec-486
- 95UppDecAGPRW-3
- 95UppDecEleIce-233
- 95UppDecEleIce-251
- 95UppDecEleIce-486
- 95UppDecEleIceG-233
- 95UppDecEleIceG-251
- 95UppDecEleIceG-486
- 95UppDecFreFra-F15
- 95UppDecFreFraJ-F15
- 95UppDecNHLAS-AS3
- 95UppDecPRE-R5
- 95UppDecPreR-R5
- 95UppDecSpeE-SE157
- 95UppDecSpeEdiG-SE157
- 95Zen-1
- 95ZenZT-15
- 96BeAPBisITB-14
- 96ColCho-223
- 96ColCho-329
- 96ColChoMVP-UD29
- 96ColChoMVPG-UD29
- 96ColChoSti-S2
- 96Don-197
- 96DonCanI-65
- 96DonCanIGPP-65
- 96DonCanIRPP-65
- 96DonEli-4
- 96DonEliDCS-4
- 96DonEliInS-4
- 96DonEliP-9
- 96DonGoTS-6
- 96DonPrePro-197
- 96DurAlIT-DC5
- 96DurL'EB-JB5
- 96Fla-81
- 96FlaBluI-81
- 96FlaCenIS-4
- 96Fle-97
- 96FleArtRos-7
- 96FlePicDL-10
- 96FlePicF5-19
- 96FlePicF-6
- 96HocGreC-10
- 96HocGreCG-10
- 96KraUppD-11
- 96Lea-45
- 96LeaLeaAL-3
- 96LeaLeaALP-P3
- 96LeaLim-24
- 96LeaLimG-24
- 96LeaLimStu-15
- 96LeaPre-106
- 96LeaPreP-45
- 96LeaPrePP-106
- 96LeaPreSP-9
- 96LeaPreVP-5
- 96LeaPreVPG-5
- 96LeaSwe-12
- 96LeaSwe(-12
- 96MetUni-132
- 96MetUni-187
- 96MetUniLW-7
- 96MetUniLWSP-7
- 96NHLACEPC-22
- 96NHLProSTA-12
- 96Pin-128
- 96PinArtP-128
- 96PinByTN-6
- 96PinByTN-P16
- 96PinByTNP-6
- 96PinFan-FC16
- 96PinFoi-128
- 96PinMcD-24
- 96PinMin-14
- 96PinMinB-14
- 96PinMinCoiB-14
- 96PinMinCoiGP-14
- 96PinMinCoiN-14
- 96PinMinCoiNG-14
- 96PinMinCoiSG-14
- 96PinMinG-14
- 96PinMinS-14
- 96PinPreS-128
- 96PinRinC-128
- 96PinTeaP-6
- 96PlaOneoOne-427
- 96Sco-19
- 96ScoArtPro-19
- 96ScoDeaCAP-19
- 96ScoGolB-19
- 96ScoSam-19
- 96ScoSpeAP-19
- 96ScoSud-11
- 96ScoSudDea-4
- 96SelCer-19
- 96SelCerAP-19
- 96SelCerBlu-19
- 96SelCerCor-6
- 96SelCerMB-19
- 96SelCerMG-19
- 96SelCerMR-19
- 96SelCerRed-19
- 96SkyImp-113
- 96SkyImpB-8
- 96SP-136
- 96SPGamFil-GF4
- 96SPSPxFor-2
- 96SPx-40
- 96SPxGol-40
- 96SPxHoIH-HH8
- 96StaCluMO-3
- 96Sum-35
- 96SumArtP-35
- 96SumHigV-16
- 96SumHigVM-16
- 96SumIce-35
- 96SumMet-35
- 96SumPreS-35
- 96SweSemW-164
- 96TeaOut-31
- 96TopNHLP-29
- 96TopPicFT-FT12
- 96TopPicOI-29
- 96TopPicTS-TS10
- 96Ult-146
- 96UltGolM-146
- 96UltMr.Mom-4
- 96UppDec-324
- 96UppDecBD-170
- 96UppDecBDG-170
- 96UppDecGJ-GJ2
- 96UppDecGN-X6
- 96UppDecHH-HH13
- 96UppDecHHG-HH13
- 96UppDecHHS-HH13
- 96UppDecIce-115
- 96UppDecIcePar-115
- 96UppDecSS-SS15B
- 96Zen-67
- 96ZenArtP-67
- 96ZenZT-7
- 97Be A PPAD-15
- 97Be A PPAPD-15
- 97BeAPla-15
- 97BeAPlaAut-15
- 97BeAPlaPOT-6
- 97BeAPlaTAN-13
- 97ColCho-224
- 97ColChoCTG-C26A
- 97ColChoCTG-C26B
- 97ColChoCTG-C26C
- 97ColChoCTGE-CR26
- 97ColChoSta-SQ76
- 97ColChoSti-S26
- 97Don-71
- 97DonCanI-17
- 97DonCanIDS-17
- 97DonCanIPS-17
- 97DonCanISCS-6
- 97DonEli-12
- 97DonEliAsp-12
- 97DonEliBttF-6
- 97DonEliBttFa-6
- 97DonEliS-12
- 97DonLim-20
- 97DonLim-51
- 97DonLim-185
- 97DonLimExp-20
- 97DonLimExp-51
- 97DonLimExp-185
- 97DonLimFOTG-20
- 97DonLimFOTG-28
- 97DonLimFOTG-38
- 97DonLin2L-18
- 97DonLin2LDC-18
- 97DonPre-15
- 97DonPre-193
- 97DonPreCttC-15
- 97DonPreCttC-193
- 97DonPreDWT-2
- 97DonPreLotT-3C
- 97DonPreProG-71
- 97DonPreProS-71
- 97DonPreT-18
- 97DonPreTB-18
- 97DonPreTBC-18
- 97DonPreTPC-18
- 97DonPreTPG-18
- 97DonPri-9
- 97DonPriDD-23
- 97DonPriODI-9
- 97DonPriP-28
- 97DonPriS-28
- 97DonPriSB-28
- 97DonPriSG-28
- 97DonPriSoA-9
- 97DonPriSS-28
- 97DonRedAle-5
- 97EssOlyHH-27
- 97EssOlyHHF-27
- 97HigMinHMC-4
- 97Kat-129
- 97Kat-163
- 97KatGol-129
- 97KatGol-163
- 97KatSil-129
- 97KatSil-163
- 97Lea-11
- 97Lea-178
- 97LeaBanSea-11
- 97LeaFraMat-11
- 97LeaFraMat-178
- 97LeaFraMDC-11
- 97LeaFraMDC-178
- 97LeaInt-11
- 97LeaIntUI-11
- 97McD-16
- 97Pac-16
- 97PacCarSup-18
- 97PacCarSupM-18
- 97PacCop-16
- 97PacCroR-117
- 97PacCroRBoSDC-18
- 97PacCroREG-117
- 97PacCroRHTDC-16
- 97PacCroRIB-117
- 97PacCroRLCDC-18
- 97PacCroRS-117
- 97PacDyn-143
- 97PacDynBKS-81
- 97PacDynC-107
- 97PacDynC-143
- 97PacDynDD-14B
- 97PacDynDG-107
- 97PacDynEG-107
- 97PacDynEG-143
- 97PacDynIB-107
- 97PacDynIB-143
- 97PacDynR-107
- 97PacDynR-143
- 97PacDynSil-107
- 97PacDynSil-143
- 97PacDynTan-18
- 97PacEmeGre-16
- 97PacGolCroDC-19
- 97PacIceB-16
- 97PacInv-120
- 97PacInvAZ-21
- 97PacInvEG-120
- 97PacInvFP-31
- 97PacInvIB-120
- 97PacInvNRB-169
- 97PacInvOTG-18
- 97PacInvR-120
- 97PacInvRB-120
- 97PacOme-194
- 97PacOmeC-194
- 97PacOmeDG-194
- 97PacOmeEG-194
- 97PacOmeG-194
- 97PacOmeGFDCC-17
- 97PacOmeIB-194
- 97PacPar-159
- 97PacParBNDC-18
- 97PacParC-159
- 97PacParDG-159
- 97PacParEG-159
- 97PacParIB-159
- 97PacParP-18
- 97PacParRed-159
- 97PacParSil-159
- 97PacRed-16
- 97PacRev-121
- 97PacRevC-121
- 97PacRevE-121
- 97PacRevIB-121
- 97PacRevR-121
- 97PacRevS-121
- 97PacRevTC-21
- 97PacSil-16
- 97PacSlaSDC-9C
- 97PacTeaCCC-21
- 97Pin-35
- 97PinArtP-35
- 97PinBee-35
- 97PinBeeGP-6
- 97PinBeeGT-14
- 97PinBeeT-14
- 97PinCer-70
- 97PinCerGT-19
- 97PinCerMB-70
- 97PinCerMG-70
- 97PinCerMR-70
- 97PinCerR-70
- 97PinCerT-19
- 97PinEpiGO-18
- 97PinEpiGE-18
- 97PinEpiME-18
- 97PinEpiMO-18

- 97PinEpiMP-18
- 97PinEpiPE-18
- 97PinEpiPO-18
- 97PinEpiPP-18
- 97PinEpiSE-18
- 97PinEpiSO-18
- 97PinEpiSP-18
- 97PinIns-12
- 97PinInsC-23
- 97PinInsCC-12
- 97PinInsCG-23
- 97PinInsEC-12
- 97PinInsT-19
- 97PinMin-23
- 97PinMinB-23
- 97PinMinCBP-23
- 97PinMinCGPP-23
- 97PinMinCNSP-23
- 97PinMinCoiB-23
- 97PinMinCoiGP-23
- 97PinMinCoiN-23
- 97PinMinCoiSG-23
- 97PinMinCoiSS-23
- 97PinMinGolTea-23
- 97PinMinMC-3
- 97PinMinMin-3
- 97PinMinSilTea-23
- 97PinPowPac-8
- 97PinPrePBB-35
- 97PinPrePBC-35
- 97PinPrePBM-35
- 97PinPrePBY-35
- 97PinPrePFC-35
- 97PinPrePFM-35
- 97PinPrePFY-35
- 97PinPrePla-35
- 97PinRinC-35
- 97PinTotCMPG-70
- 97PinTotCPB-70
- 97PinTotCPG-70
- 97PinTotCPR-70
- 97PosPin-11
- 97Sco-81
- 97ScoArtPro-81
- 97ScoBlu-1
- 97ScoBluPla-1
- 97ScoBluPre-1
- 97ScoGolBla-81
- 97SP AutI-I2
- 97SPAut-138
- 97SPAutID-I2
- 97SPAutIE-I2
- 97SPAutSotT-BH
- 97SPAutTra-T5
- 97SPx-43
- 97SPxBro-43
- 97SPxDim-SPX20
- 97SPxGol-43
- 97SPxGraF-43
- 97SPxSil-43
- 97SPxSte-43
- 97Stu-11
- 97StuHarH-20
- 97StuPor-11
- 97StuPrePG-11
- 97StuPrePS-11
- 97StuSil-8
- 97StuSil8-8
- 97TopHocMC-13
- 97TopHocMC-14
- 97UppDec-141
- 97UppDecBD-19
- 97UppDecBDDD-19
- 97UppDecBDPC-PC18
- 97UppDecBDPCDD-PC18
- 97UppDecBDPCM-PC18
- 97UppDecBDPCQD-PC18
- 97UppDecBDPCTD-PC18
- 97UppDecBDQD-19
- 97UppDecBDTD-19
- 97UppDecCtAG-3
- 97UppDecCtAG-AR3
- 97UppDecDV-25
- 97UppDecDVSM-25
- 97UppDecGDM-141
- 97UppDecIC-IC16
- 97UppDecIC2-IC16
- 97UppDecIce-66
- 97UppDecIceP-66
- 97UppDecILL-L8C
- 97UppDecILL2-L8C
- 97UppDecIPS-66
- 97UppDecSG-SG16
- 97UppDecSSM-SS4
- 97UppDecSSW-SS4
- 97UppDecTS-16
- 97UppDecTSL2-16
- 97UppDecTSS-9C
- 97Zen-25
- 97Zen5x7-48
- 97ZenChaTC-7
- 97ZenGolImp-48
- 97ZenSilImp-48
- 97ZenZGol-25
- 97ZenZSil-25
- 98Be A PPA-189
- 98Be A PPAA-189
- 98Be A PPAAF-189
- 98Be A PPAGUSC-S11
- 98Be A PPAJ-AS12
- 98Be A PPAM-M6
- 98Be A PPPGUJC-G18
- 98Be A PPPPUJC-P1
- 98Be A PPSE-189
- 98Be APG-189
- 98BowBes-10
- 98BowBesAR-10
- 98BowBesR-10
- 98Fin-19
- 98FinNo P-19
- 98FinNo PR-19
- 98FinRef-19
- 98McDGreT-T5
- 98O-PChr-30
- 98O-PChrBFtP-6
- 98O-PChrBFtPR-6
- 98O-PChrR-30
- 98Pac-16
- 98PacAur-55
- 98PacCroR-38
- 98PacCroRLS-38
- 98PacCroRMP-7
- 98PacCroRPotG-10
- 98PacCroRPP-6
- 98PacDynI-56
- 98PacDynIFT-7
- 98PacDynIIB-56
- 98PacDynIR-56
- 98PacEO P-7
- 98PacGolCD-30
- 98PacIceB-16
- 98PacOmeEP1o1-7
- 98PacOmeH-70
- 98PacOmeO-12
- 98PacOmeODI-70
- 98PacOmePI-9
- 98PacOmePIB-9
- 98PacOmeR-70
- 98PacPar-64
- 98PacParC-64
- 98PacParEG-64
- 98PacParH-64
- 98PacParIB-64
- 98PacParS-64
- 98PacRed-16
- 98PacRev-41
- 98PacRevCTL-6
- 98PacRevIS-41
- 98PacRevR-41
- 98PacRevS-14
- 98PacTeaC-22
- 98PacTim-17
- 98PinEpiGE-18
- 98SP Aut-24
- 98SP AutA-12
- 98SP AutSM-S2
- 98SP AutSotTG-BH
- 98SP AutSS-SS4
- 98SPxFin-97
- 98SPxFinR-97
- 98SPxFinS-97
- 98SPXTopP-19
- 98SPXTopPF-19
- 98SPXTopPHH-H12
- 98SPXTopPLI-L16
- 98SPXTopPPS-PS25
- 98SPXTopPR-19
- 98SSASotT-BH
- 98Top-30
- 98TopBlaFTP-6
- 98TopGolLC1-92
- 98TopGolLC1B-92
- 98TopGolLC1BOoO-92
- 98TopGolLC1OoO-92
- 98TopGolLC1R-92
- 98TopGolLC1ROoO-92
- 98TopGolLC2-92
- 98TopGolLC2B-92
- 98TopGolLC2BOoO-92
- 98TopGolLC2OoO-92
- 98TopGolLC2R-92
- 98TopGolLC2ROoO-92
- 98TopGolLC3-92
- 98TopGolLC3B-92
- 98TopGolLC3BOoO-92
- 98TopGolLC3OoO-92
- 98TopGolLC3R-92
- 98TopGolLC3ROoO-92
- 98TopO-P-30
- 98UC-183
- 98UCMBH-BH4
- 98UCSB-SQ22
- 98UCSG-SQ22
- 98UCSR-SQ22
- 98UD ChoPCR-183
- 98UD ChoR-183
- 98UD3-35
- 98UD3-95
- 98UD3-155
- 98UD3DieC-35
- 98UD3DieC-95
- 98UD3DieC-155
- 98UDCP-183
- 98UppDec-76
- 98UppDecBD-25
- 98UppDecDD-25
- 98UppDecE-76
- 98UppDecE1o1-76
- 98UppDecFF-FF7
- 98UppDecFF-FF7
- 98UppDecFFQ1-FF7
- 98UppDecFFQ2-FF7
- 98UppDecGR-76
- 98UppDecM-59
- 98UppDecM1-M16
- 98UppDecM2-M16
- 98UppDECMGS-BH
- 98UppDecMGS-59
- 98UppDecMSF-F1
- 98UppDecMSS-59
- 98UppDecMSS-59
- 98UppDecP-P2
- 98UppDecPQ1-P2
- 98UppDecPQ2-P2
- 98UppDecPQ3-P2
- 98UppDecQD-25
- 98UppDecTD-25
- 98UppDecWFG-WF26
- 98UppDecWFP-WF26
- 99Pac-120
- 99PacAur-44
- 99PacAurPD-44
- 99PacCop-120
- 99PacGol-120
- 99PacGolCD-14
- 99PacIceB-120
- 99PacPasAP-10
- 99PacPreD-120
- 99RetHoc-25
- 99SP AutPS-24
- 99UppDecCL-63
- 99UppDecCLCLC-63
- 99UppDecEotG-E7
- 99UppDecM-60
- 99UppDecMGS-60
- 99UppDecMHoG-H2
- 99UppDecMPS-BH
- 99UppDecMSS-60
- 99UppDecMSS-60
- 99UppDecRG-25
- 99UppDecRII-BRH
- 99UppDecRIL1-BRH
- 99UppDecRP-25

**Hull, Dennis**
- 64BeeGro3P-42
- 65Coc-27
- 65Top-64
- 66Top-113
- 66TopUSAT-1
- 67Top-56
- 68Bla-1
- 68OPC-153
- 68ShiCoi-27
- 68ShiCoi-28
- 69OPC-71
- 69Top-71
- 70BlaBor-4
- 70ColSta-32
- 70DadCoo-60
- 70EssPowPla-117
- 70OPC-14
- 70PosCerS-6
- 70SarProSta-36
- 70Top-14
- 71LetActR-16
- 71OPC-85
- 71SarProSta-46
- 71Top-85
- 71TorSun-67
- 72OPC-52
- 72OPCTeaC-15
- 72SarProSta-67
- 72Top-164
- 73OPC-171
- 73Top-60
- 74LipSou-17
- 74NHLActSta-73
- 74OPCNHL-150
- 74Top-150
- 75OPCNHL-254
- 75Top-254
- 76OPCNHL-195
- 76Top-195
- 76TopGloI-16
- 77OPCNHL-225
- 77Top-225
- 91FutTreC72-89
- 94ParTalB-39
- 95Par66-37
- 95Par66Coi-37

**Hull, Jody**
- 89PanSti-230
- 89WhaJunM-9
- 90OPCPre-46
- 90ProSet-490
- 90UppDec-322
- 90UppDecF-322
- 91ProAHLCHL-201
- 91ScoCan-524
- 91StaClu-100
- 92Par-119
- 92ParEmeI-119
- 92Sen-6
- 92UppDec-539
- 93Lea-157
- 93OPCPre-212
- 93OPCPreG-212
- 93PanSti-115
- 93Par-76
- 93ParEmeI-76
- 93Sco-320
- 93ScoCan-320
- 93StaClu-344
- 93StaCluFDI-344
- 93StaCluO-344
- 93TopPre-212
- 93TopPreG-212
- 93UppDec-112
- 93UppDec-510
- 94OPCPre-427
- 94OPCPreSE-427
- 94Par-89
- 94ParGol-89
- 94StaClu-199
- 94StaCluFDI-199
- 94StaCluMOMS-199
- 94StaCluSTWC-199
- 94TopPre-427
- 94TopPreSE-427
- 94UppDec-176
- 94UppDecEleIce-176
- 95BeAPla-110
- 95BeAPSig-S110
- 95BeAPSigDC-S110
- 95Fin-109
- 95FinRef-109
- 95Met-59
- 95ParInt-353
- 95ParIntEl-353
- 95ProMag-86
- 95SP-57
- 95Top-134
- 95TopOPCI-134
- 95Ult-241
- 95UppDec-50
- 95UppDecEleIce-50
- 95UppDecEleIceG-50
- 95UppDecSpeE-SE123
- 95UppDecSpeEdiG-SE123
- 96ColCho-107
- 96NHLProSTA-86
- 97PacDynBKS-41
- 99Pac-303
- 99PacCop-303
- 99PacGol-303
- 99PacIceB-303
- 99PacPreD-303

**Hulse, Cale**
- 917thInnSWHL-43
- 92Cla-21
- 94ClaProP-222
- 94Lea-481
- 94OPCPre-407
- 94OPCPreSE-407
- 94TopPre-407
- 94TopPreSE-407
- 95UppDec-437
- 96ClaGol-21
- 96ColCho-36
- 96Pin-242
- 96PinArtP-242
- 96PinFoi-242
- 96PinPreS-242
- 96PinRinC-242
- 97Be A PPAD-60
- 97Be A PPAPD-60
- 97BeAPla-60
- 97BeAPlaAut-60
- 97PacDynBKS-12
- 98O-PChr-32
- 98O-PChrR-32
- 98Pac-119
- 98PacIceB-119
- 98PacRed-119
- 98Top-32
- 98TopO-P-32

**Hulst, Kent**
- 89ProAHL-109
- 90NewSai-8
- 90ProAHLIHL-149
- 91ProAHLCHL-380
- 93PorPir-12
- 94PorPir-10
- 95PorPir-12
- 96PorPir-10

**Hultberg, John**
- 94DubFigS-14
- 95Sla-107

**Hulton, Jim**
- 86KitRan-19
- 87KitRan-20

**Hume, Fred**
- 83HalFP-A8
- 85HalFC-233

**Humeniuk, Scott**
- 91ProAHLCHL-97

**Humenny, Layne**
- 92MPSPhoSJHL-58

**Huml, Dusan**
- 94CzeAPSE-152

**Humphrey, Todd**
- 93FliGen-20
- 94FliGen-11

**Humphries, John**
- 83KinCan-21

**Hungle, Casey**
- 91BriColJHL-61
- 92BriColJHL-96
- 95TalTigS-16

**Hunt, Brian**
- 89ProAHL-38

**Hunt, Curtis**
- 84PriAlbRS-14
- 87FliSpi-7
- 89ProIHL-186
- 90ProAHLIHL-516
- 91ProAHLCHL-336
- 92St.JohML-8
- 93St.JohML-11

**Hunt, Greg**
- 91BriColJHL-83
- 92BriColJHL-173

**Hunter, Andria**
- 94ClaWomOH-W17

**Hunter, Bill**
- 74TeaCanLWHA-12

**Hunter, Brian**
- 93MicTecH-10

**Hunter, Dale**
- 80NordPos-15
- 80PepCap-69
- 81NordPos-9
- 81OPC-277
- 82NordPos-10
- 82OPC-285
- 82OPCSti-26
- 82PosCer-16
- 83Ess-10
- 83NordPos-13
- 83OPC-293
- 83Vac-66
- 84KelAccD-6
- 84NordPos-12
- 84OPC-281
- 84OPCSti-179
- 85NordGenF-13
- 85NordMcD-10
- 85NordPla-3
- 85NordPla-6
- 85NordPro-12
- 85NordTeal-11
- 85OPC-179
- 85OPCSti-151
- 86KraDra-27
- 86NordGenF-12
- 86NordMcD-12
- 86NordTeal-11
- 86NordYumY-5
- 86OPC-192
- 86OPCSti-32
- 86Top-192
- 87CapKod-32
- 87CapTealss-10
- 87OPC-245
- 87PanSti-168
- 88CapBor-9
- 88CapSmo-9
- 88OPC-70
- 88OPCSti-73
- 88PanSti-372
- 88Top-70
- 89CapKod-32
- 89CapTealss-8
- 89OPC-76
- 89PanSti-346
- 89Top-76
- 90Bow-71
- 90BowTif-71
- 90CapKod-32
- 90CapPos-8
- 90CapSmo-8
- 90OPC-129
- 90PanSti-168
- 90ProSet-312
- 90Sco-44
- 90ScoCan-44
- 90Top-129
- 90TopTif-129
- 90UppDec-219
- 90UppDecF-219
- 91Bow-303
- 91CapJun5-11
- 91CapKod-11
- 91OPC-229
- 91PanSti-203
- 91Par-195
- 91ParFre-195
- 91Pin-40
- 91PinFre-40
- 91ProSet-506
- 91ProSetFre-506
- 91ProSetPla-245
- 91ScoAme-56
- 91ScoAme-306
- 91ScoCan-56
- 91ScoCan-336
- 91StaClu-164
- 91Top-229
- 91UppDec-209
- 91UppDecF-209
- 92Bow-303
- 92CapKod-11
- 92OPC-18
- 92OPCPreSP-2
- 92PanSti-165
- 92PanStiFre-165
- 92ParCheP-CP7
- 92ParChePS-1
- 92Pin-104
- 92Pin-237
- 92PinFre-104
- 92PinFre-237
- 92ProSet-202
- 92Sco-231
- 92ScoCan-231
- 92ScoSha-4
- 92ScoShaCan-4
- 92StaClu-40
- 92Top-464
- 92TopGol-464G
- 92Ult-232
- 92UppDec-131
- 93Don-370
- 93Lea-118
- 93PanSti-26
- 93ParChePH-D6
- 93Pin-13
- 93PinCan-13
- 93Pow-262
- 93Sco-40
- 93ScoCan-40
- 93Ult-135
- 94CanGamNHLP-244
- 94Don-149
- 94Fla-199
- 94Fle-235
- 94Lea-183
- 94OPCPre-506
- 94OPCPreSE-506
- 94Par-254
- 94ParGol-254
- 94Pin-85
- 94PinArtP-85
- 94PinRinC-85
- 94Sco-143
- 94ScoGol-143
- 94ScoPla-143
- 94ScoPlaTS-143
- 94Sel-33
- 94SelGol-33
- 94SP-127
- 94SPDieCut-127
- 94StaClu-134
- 94StaCluFDI-134
- 94StaCluMOMS-134
- 94StaCluSTWC-134
- 94TopPre-506
- 94TopPreSE-506
- 94Ult-234
- 94UppDec-68
- 94UppDecEleIce-68
- 95BeAPla-213
- 95BeAPSig-S213
- 95BeAPSigDC-S213
- 95Cap-9
- 95ColCho-155
- 95ColChoPC-155
- 95ColChoPCP-155
- 95Don-12
- 95Emo-188
- 95Lea-215
- 95ParInt-223
- 95ParIntEl-223
- 95Pin-21
- 95PinArtP-21
- 95PinRinC-21
- 95PlaOneoOne-322
- 95ProMag-33
- 95Sco-107
- 95ScoBlaIce-107
- 95ScoBlaIceAP-107
- 95SkyImp-177
- 95SP-159
- 95Sum-5
- 95SumArtP-5
- 95SumIce-5
- 95Top-177
- 95TopOPCI-177
- 95Ult-175
- 95UltGolM-175
- 95UppDec-442
- 95UppDecEleIce-442
- 95UppDecEleIceG-442
- 95ZenGifG-12
- 96ColCho-288
- 96Don-199
- 96DonPrePro-199
- 96DurAllT-DC20
- 96Fla-99
- 96FlaBluI-99
- 96Lea-56
- 96LeaPreP-56
- 96NHLProSTA-33
- 96Sco-110
- 96ScoArtPro-110
- 96ScoDeaCAP-110
- 96ScoGolB-110
- 96ScoSpeAP-110
- 96UppDec-178
- 96UppDecBD-82
- 96UppDecBDG-82
- 97ColCho-271
- 97Don-195
- 97DonPreProG-195
- 97DonPreProS-195
- 97Pac-129
- 97PacCop-129
- 97PacCroR-139
- 97PacCroREG-139
- 97PacCroRIB-139
- 97PacCroRS-139
- 97PacEmeGre-129
- 97PacIceB-129
- 97PacInv-146
- 97PacInvC-146
- 97PacInvEG-146
- 97PacInvIB-146
- 97PacInvR-146
- 97PacInvS-146
- 97PacOme-239
- 97PacOmeC-239
- 97PacOmeDG-239
- 97PacOmeEG-239
- 97PacOmeG-239
- 97PacOmeIB-239
- 97PacPar-194
- 97PacParC-194
- 97PacParDG-194
- 97PacParEG-194
- 97PacParIB-194
- 97PacParRed-194
- 97PacParSil-194
- 97PacRed-129
- 97PacRev-147
- 97PacRevC-147
- 97PacRevE-147
- 97PacRevIB-147
- 97PacRevR-147
- 97PacRevS-147
- 97PacSil-129
- 97Sco-201
- 97UppDec-175
- 98Be A PPAM-M17
- 98O-PChr-58
- 98O-PChrR-58
- 98Pac-442
- 98PacIceB-442
- 98PacRed-442
- 98Top-58
- 98TopO-P-58
- 98UppDec-383
- 98UppDecE-383
- 98UppDecE1o1-383
- 98UppDecGR-383
- 99Pac-107
- 99PacCop-107
- 99PacGol-107
- 99PacIceB-107
- 99PacPreD-107

**Hunter, Dave**
- 79OilPos-12
- 79OPC-387
- 80OPC-293
- 80PepCap-28
- 81OilRedR-12
- 81OPC-115
- 82OilRedR-12
- 82OPC-110
- 82OPCSti-102
- 82PosCer-6
- 83OilDol-H16
- 83OilMcD-8
- 83OPC-32
- 83OPCSti-154
- 83Vac-29
- 84OilRedR-12
- 84OilTeal-10
- 84OPC-246
- 85OilRedR-12
- 86OilRedR-12
- 86OilTeal-12
- 87PanSti-268
- 87PenKod-12
- 88JetPol-10
- 88OilTeal-11
- 88OilTenAnn-40
- 88OPC-62
- 88OPCSti-235
- 88PanSti-339
- 88Top-62

**Hunter, Jim**
- 83NorBayC-11

**Hunter, Mark**
- 81CanaPos-11
- 82CanaPos-10
- 82CanaSte-6
- 82OPC-185
- 82PosCer-10
- 83CanaPos-11
- 83Vac-46
- 84CanaPos-10
- 85OPCSti-137
- 86OPC-57
- 86OPCSti-181
- 86Top-57
- 87BluKod-14
- 87OPC-50
- 87OPCSti-21
- 87PanSti-313
- 87Top-50
- 88OPC-187
- 88OPCSti-14
- 88PanSti-108
- 88Top-187
- 90FlamIGA-6
- 90ProSet-422
- 90ScoRoo-77T
- 91Bow-9
- 91FlamPanTS-4
- 91OPC-109
- 91Pin-253
- 91PinFre-253
- 91ProSet-390
- 91ProSetFre-390
- 91ScoAme-156
- 91ScoAme-306
- 91ScoCan-156
- 91ScoCan-336
- 91StaClu-15
- 91Top-109
- 91UppDec-479
- 91UppDecF-479
- 91WhaJr7E-16
- 92Sco-194
- 92ScoCan-194
- 92StaClu-396
- 92Top-36
- 92TopGol-36G
- 95Sla-355
- 96St.JohML-17

**Hunter, Tim**
- 85FlamRedRP-8
- 86FlamRedR-7
- 87FlamRedRP-9
- 87PanSti-216
- 90FlamIGA-7
- 90OPC-434
- 90ProSet-423
- 91FlamIGA-5
- 91FlamPanTS-5
- 91Pin-375
- 91PinFre-375
- 91ProSet-366
- 91ProSetFre-366

- 98TopGolLC2B-35
- 98TopGolLC2BOoO-35
- 98TopGolLC2OoO-35
- 98TopGolLC2R-35
- 98TopGolLC2ROoO-35
- 98TopGolLC3-35
- 98TopGolLC3B-35
- 98TopGolLC3BOoO-35
- 98TopGolLC3OoO-35
- 98TopGolLC3R-35
- 98TopGolLC3ROoO-35
- 98TopIceA2-I3
- 98TopO-P-52
- 98UC-35
- 98UD ChoPCR-35
- 98UD ChoR-35
- 98UDCP-35
- 98UppDec-55
- 98UppDecBD-12
- 98UppDecDD-12
- 98UppDecE-55
- 98UppDecE1o1-55
- 98UppDecGR-55
- 98UppDecM-34
- 98UppDecMGS-34
- 98UppDecMP-JI
- 98UppDecMSS-34
- 98UppDecMSS-34
- 98UppDecQD-12
- 98UppDecTD-12
- 99Pac-57
- 99PacAur-23
- 99PacAurPD-23
- 99PacCop-57
- 99PacGol-57
- 99PacHomaA-4
- 99PacIceB-57
- 99PacPreD-57
- 99PacTeaL-5
- 99RetHoc-12
- 99SP AutPS-13
- 99UppDecM-32
- 99UppDecMGS-32
- 99UppDecMSS-32
- 99UppDecMSS-32
- 99UppDecRG-12
- 99UppDecRP-12

**Ignatjev, Victor**
- 93ClaProPro-128
- 94CenHocL-60

**Ihnacak, Miroslav**
- 87PanSti-336
- 88ProAHL-14
- 89HalCit-10
- 89ProAHL-155
- 90HalCit-11
- 90ProAHLIHL-463

**Ihnacak, Peter**
- 82SweSemHVS-96
- 83OPCSti-32
- 83PufSti-3
- 85OPCSti-19
- 86MapLeaP-12
- 87MapLeaP-10
- 87MapLeaPLA-24
- 87MapLeaPO-10
- 87PanSti-334
- 89ProAHL-120
- 94GerDELE-240
- 95GerDELE-234
- 96GerDELE-85
- 98GerDELE-268

**Ikonen, Juha**
- 93FinnJyvHS-203
- 94FinnSIS-16
- 95FinnSIS-93
- 96FinnSISR-89

**Ikonen, Markku**
- 93FinnSIS-156
- 94FinnSIS-110
- 95FinnSIS-62

**Ilitch, Mike**
- 91ProSetNHLSA-AC22

**Illikainen, Darin**
- 85MinDul-8

**Ilmivalta, Pekka**
- 93FinnSIS-281

**Ilvasky, Slavomir**
- 94FinnJaaK-206

**Ilyin, Roman**
- 91OPCIns-34R

**Imbeau, Jean**
- 917thInnSQMJHL-67

**Imber, Shaun**
- 907thInnSOHL-159
- 917thInnSMC-19
- 917thInnSOHL-323

**Imdahl, Thomas**
- 94GerDELE-359
- 95GerDELE-231

**Imes, Chris**
- 91UppDecCWJC-75
- 92MaiBlaB-5
- 92MaiBlaB-19
- 93Pow-506
- 93StaCluTUSA-10
- 93TopPreTUSA-11
- 93Ult-486
- 95ColEdgI-168

**Imhauser, Peter**
- 86SwePanS-149
- 87SwePanS-155
- 90SweSemE-133

**Imlach, Punch**
- 51LavDaiQSHL-37
- 52St.LawS-54
- 59Par-15
- 60ShiCoi-20
- 61ShiCoi-57
- 61YorYelB-38
- 62ShiMetC-15
- 63ChePho-28
- 63Par-19
- 63Par-79
- 64Top-45
- 65Top-11
- 66Top-11
- 66TopUSAT-11
- 69MapLeaWBG-40
- 71SabPos-8
- 79MapLeaP-14
- 85HalFC-243
- 92HalFL-25

**Immonen, Santeri**
- 95FinnSIS-44

**Immonen, Waltteri**
- 93FinnJyvHS-110
- 93FinnSIS-8
- 93SweSemWCS-52
- 94FinnJaaK-19
- 94FinnSIS-24
- 95FinnSemWC-7
- 95FinnSIS-46
- 95FinnSISDT-2
- 95FinnSISL-11
- 96FinnSISR-45
- 96FinnSISRATG-3

**Imoo, Dusty**
- 88LetHur-12
- 89LetHur-10
- 907thInnSWHL-183
- 91ProAHLCHL-258

**Ing, Peter**
- 90OPCPre-49
- 90ProSet-639
- 90Sco-414
- 90ScoCan-414
- 90ScoRoo-11T
- 90UppDec-432
- 90UppDecF-432
- 91Bow-157
- 91MapLeaPTS-10
- 91OilIGA-6
- 91OilTeal-7
- 91OPC-145
- 91OPCPre-33
- 91PanSti-99
- 91ProSet-222
- 91ProSet-388
- 91ProSetFre-222
- 91ProSetFre-388
- 91ProSetPla-41
- 91ScoAme-55
- 91ScoCan-55
- 91ScoCan-612
- 91ScoRoo-62T
- 91ScoYouS-12
- 91StaClu-352
- 91Top-145
- 91UppDec-118
- 91UppDecF-118
- 92StaClu-347
- 92Top-423
- 92TopGol-423G
- 93LasVegThu-14

**Ingarfield, Earl**
- 44BeeGro2P-328A
- 44BeeGro2P-328B
- 58Top-18
- 59Top-10
- 60ShiCoi-92
- 61ShiCoi-82
- 61Top-49
- 62Top-51
- 62TopHocBuc-13
- 63Top-55
- 64BeeGro3P-135
- 64CocCap-80
- 64Top-65
- 65Coc-81
- 66Top-30
- 68OPC-102
- 68ShiCoi-136
- 68Top-102
- 69OPC-87
- 69OPCFou-9
- 69Top-87
- 70DadCoo-61
- 70EssPowPla-97
- 70OPC-191
- 70SarProSta-132
- 70TopStiS-15
- 72SweSemWC-177
- 94ParTalB-91
- 95Par66-87
- 95Par66Coi-87

**Inglis, Bill**
- 70OPC-130
- 70SarProSta-27
- 70Top-130

**Ingman, Jan**
- 83SweSemE-115
- 84SweSemE-115
- 85SwePanS-103
- 86SwePanS-99
- 89SweSemE-87
- 90SweSemE-264

**Ingraham, Cal**
- 92MaiBlaB-16
- 92MaiBlaB-34
- 93MaiBlaB-53
- 95TalTigS-12

**Ingram, Geoff**
- 897thInnSOHL-117

**Ingram, Jim**
- 91BriColJHL-56

**Ingram, Ron (Ronald)**
- 44BeeGro2P-179
- 63Par-54
- 63YorWhiB-54
- 64BeeGro3P-78
- 69SeaTotW-10
- 94ParMisL-33

**Ingvarsson, Ulf**
- 70SweHocS-205
- 71SweHocS-286
- 72SweHocS-71

**Inhacak, Miroslav**
- 85MapLeaP-15

**Inhacak, Peter**
- 82MapLeaP-18
- 83MapLeaP-11
- 83OPC-334
- 83Vac-90
- 84MapLeaP-12
- 85MapLeaP-16

**Inkinen, Mikko**
- 95FinnSIS-270
- 96FinnSISR-67

**Inkpen, Dave**
- 76OPCWHA-83
- 76StiKah-2
- 79OPC-321

**Innanen, Derek**
- 92WesMic-13
- 93WesMic-16

**Innes, Judson**
- 89PorWinH-11

**Inness, Gary**
- 74PenPos-8
- 75OPCNHL-227
- 75Top-227
- 76OPCNHL-331
- 77OPCWHA-18
- 79OPC-358

**Insam, Adolf**
- 82SweSemHVS-132

**Intranuovo, Ralph**
- 907thInnSOHL-160
- 917thInnSMC-20
- 917thInnSOHL-332
- 92Cla-27
- 93SauSteMGM-19
- 93UppDec-253
- 94CapBreO-10
- 94ClaProP-186
- 95ColEdgI-33
- 95Lea-35
- 95Sco-294
- 95ScoBlaIce-294
- 95ScoBlaIceAP-294
- 96ClaGol-27
- 96Don-232
- 96DonPrePro-232
- 96LeaGolR-5
- 96Pin-237
- 96PinArtP-237
- 96PinFoi-237
- 96PinPreS-237
- 96PinRinC-237
- 96Sco-263
- 96ScoArtPro-263
- 96ScoDeaCAP-263
- 96ScoGolB-263
- 96ScoSpeAP-263
- 96Sum-175
- 96SumArtP-175
- 96SumIce-175
- 96SumMet-175
- 96SumPreS-175
- 96UppDec-182

**Intwert, Dean**
- 89PorWinH-12
- 907thInnSWHL-326
- 917thInnSWHL-333

**Ioannou, Yianni**
- 93NiaFalT-8
- 95Cla-82

**Iob, Tony**
- 907thInnSOHL-60
- 917thInnSMC-22
- 917thInnSOHL-325
- 92RochAmeKod-11

**Ion, Mickey**
- 83HalFP-A9
- 85HalFC-9

**Iovio, Emilio**
- 96GerDELE-224

**Irbe, Arturs**
- 89RusNatT-8
- 90OPC-501
- 90OPCRedA-7R
- 91Pin-323
- 91PinFre-323
- 91ProSetPla-270
- 91RusTrilrb-16
- 91RusTrilrb-17
- 91RusTrilrb-18
- 91RusTrilrb-19
- 91RusTrilrb-20
- 91StaPicH-37
- 91SweSemWCS-77
- 91UppDec-532
- 91UppDecF-532
- 92Par-396
- 92ParEmel-396
- 92RusStaRA-13
- 92Sco-457
- 92ScoCan-457
- 92StaClu-131
- 92Top-29
- 92TopGol-25G
- 92TriFroRWP-23
- 92TriFroRWP-24
- 92Ult-401
- 92UltImp-5
- 93ClaProPro-117
- 93Don-311
- 93Lea-199
- 93OPCPre-110
- 93OPCPre-442
- 93OPCPreG-110
- 93OPCPreG-442
- 93Par-451
- 93ParEmel-451
- 93Pin-86
- 93PinCan-86
- 93Pow-221
- 93PowRisS-1
- 93Sco-377
- 93ScoCan-377
- 93StaClu-4
- 93StaCluFDI-4
- 93StaCluFDIO-4
- 93StaCluO-4
- 93TopPre-110
- 93TopPre-442
- 93TopPreG-110
- 93TopPreG-442
- 93Ult-145
- 93UppDec-125
- 94CanGamNHLP-294
- 94Don-7
- 94DonDom-7
- 94DonMasM-4
- 94EASpo-120
- 94Fin-104
- 94FinDivFCC-16
- 94FinRef-104
- 94FinSupTW-104
- 94Fla-166
- 94Fle-197
- 94FleFraFut-4
- 94FleNet-4
- 94KenStaLA-7
- 94Kra-43
- 94Lea-175
- 94LeaLim-74
- 94LeaLimI-21
- 94OPCPre-260
- 94OPCPreSE-260
- 94ParSE-SE162
- 94ParSEES-ES17
- 94ParSEG-SE162
- 94ParVin-V79
- 94Pin-121
- 94PinArtP-121
- 94PinGoaG-GT9
- 94PinRinC-121
- 94Sco-10
- 94ScoFra-TF21
- 94ScoGol-10
- 94ScoPla-10
- 94ScoPlaTS-10
- 94Sel-37
- 94SelGol-37
- 94SP-105
- 94SPDieCut-105
- 94StaClu-190
- 94StaCluDD-1
- 94StaCluDDMO-1
- 94StaCluFDI-190
- 94StaCluMO-17
- 94StaCluMOMS-190
- 94StaCluSTWC-190
- 94TopPre-260
- 94TopPreSE-260
- 94Ult-195
- 94UltGloGre-3
- 94UltPrePM-2
- 94UppDec-116
- 94UppDecElelce-116
- 94UppDecSPI-SP71
- 94UppDecSPIDC-SP71
- 95BeAPla-23
- 95BeAPSig-S23
- 95BeAPSigDC-S23
- 95CanGamNHLP-233
- 95ColCho-64
- 95ColChoPC-64
- 95ColChoPCP-64
- 95Don-239
- 95Emo-156
- 95ImpSti-108
- 95KenStaLC-8
- 95Kra-38
- 95Lea-267
- 95Met-130
- 95ParInt-188
- 95ParInt-251
- 95ParIntAS-1
- 95ParIntEl-188
- 95ParIntEl-251
- 95ParIntGP-10
- 95PinFan-7
- 95PlaOneoOne-84
- 95PlaOneoOne-191
- 95PlaOneoOne-302
- 95ProMag-119
- 95Sco-189
- 95ScoBlaIce-189
- 95ScoBlaIceAP-189
- 95SelCer-91
- 95SelCerMG-91
- 95SkyImp-148
- 95StaClu-58
- 95StaCluMOMS-58
- 95Sum-84
- 95SumArtP-84
- 95SumIce-84
- 95Top-296
- 95TopOPCI-296
- 95Ult-146
- 95UltGolM-146
- 95UppDec-403
- 95UppDecElelce-403
- 95UppDecElelceG-403
- 95UppDecSpeE-SE162
- 95UppDecSpeEdiG-SE162
- 95Zen-81
- 96NHLProSTA-119
- 96PlaOneoOne-345
- 96StaPos-12
- 96Sum-110
- 96SumArtP-110
- 96SumIce-110
- 96SumMet-110
- 96SumPreS-110
- 96UppDec-248
- 96Zen-60
- 96ZenArtP-60
- 97Pac-188
- 97PacCop-188
- 97PacEmeGre-188
- 97PacIceB-188
- 97PacRed-188
- 97PacSil-188
- 97Pin-74
- 97PinArtP-74
- 97PinIns-61
- 97PinInsCC-61
- 97PinInsEC-61
- 97PinPrePBB-74
- 97PinPrePBC-74
- 97PinPrePBM-74
- 97PinPrePBY-74
- 97PinPrePFC-74
- 97PinPrePFM-74
- 97PinPrePFY-74
- 97PinPrePla-74
- 97PinRinC-74
- 97Sco-7
- 97ScoArtPro-7
- 97ScoCanPla-12
- 97ScoCanPre-12
- 97ScoCanu-12
- 97ScoGolBla-7
- 97UppDec-377
- 98Be A PPA-172
- 98Be A PPAA-172
- 98Be A PPAAF-172
- 98Be A PPSE-172
- 98Be APG-172
- 98Pac-427
- 98PacCroR-23
- 98PacCroRLS-23
- 98PacDynI-33
- 98PacDynIIB-33
- 98PacDynIR-33
- 98PacIceB-427
- 98PacOmeH-42
- 98PacOmeODI-42
- 98PacOmeR-42
- 98PacPar-235
- 98PacParC-235
- 98PacParEG-235
- 98PacParH-235
- 98PacParIB-235
- 98PacParS-235
- 98PacRed-427
- 98PacRev-24
- 98PacRevADC-11
- 98PacRevIS-24
- 98PacRevR-24
- 99Pac-72
- 99PacAur-26
- 99PacAurGU-4
- 99PacAurPD-26
- 99PacCop-72
- 99PacGol-72
- 99PacHomaA-5
- 99PacIceB-72
- 99PacIn tCN-4
- 99PacPreD-72
- 99PacTeaL-6
- 99UppDecM-37
- 99UppDecMGS-37
- 99UppDecMSS-37
- 99UppDecMSS-37

**Ircandia, Len**
- 77KalWin-4

**Iredale, John**
- 94FinnJaaK-328

**Ironstone, Joe**
- 24V1452-1

**Irsag, Jake**
- 95Sla-44

**Irvin, Dick**
- 32O'KeeMapL-20
- 60Top-60
- 60TopSta-29
- 83HalFP-G10
- 85HalFC-101
- 98PinCBCHNiC-6

**Irvine, Jack**
- 51LavDaiQSHL-78
- 52St.LawS-31

**Irvine, Ted**
- 68OPC-39
- 68ShiCoi-51
- 68Top-39
- 69OPC-103
- 69Top-103
- 70EssPowPla-197
- 70OPC-65
- 70SarProSta-114
- 70Top-65
- 71OPC-74
- 71SarProSta-126
- 71TorSun-175
- 72OPC-212
- 72SarProSta-152
- 73OPC-248
- 74NHLActSta-195
- 74OPCNHL-264
- 74Top-264
- 75OPCNHL-244
- 75Top-244
- 76OPCNHL-347

**Irving, Berg**
- 28V1282PauC-62

**Irving, Stu**
- 78LouGea-10

**Irwin, Doug**
- 94GerDELE-326
- 95GerDELE-312

**Irwin, Ivan**
- 54Top-44
- 94ParMisL-107

**Irwin, Jack**
- 23V1281PauC-22

**Irwin, Joel**
- 92BriColJHL-62

**Irwin, Richard**
- 96GueSto-17

**Isaksson, Esa**
- 69SweHocS-367
- 71SweHocS-65
- 72SweSemWC-78

**Isaksson, Ulf**
- 82SweSemHVS-14
- 83SweSemE-17
- 84SweSemE-15

**Isbister, Brad**
- 95Cla-21
- 96UppDecIce-125
- 97Be A PPAD-226
- 97Be A PPAPD-226
- 97BeAPla-226
- 97BeAPlaAut-226
- 97BowCHL-92
- 97BowCHLOPC-92
- 97ColCho-305
- 97DonEli-46
- 97DonEliAsp-46
- 97DonEliS-46
- 97DonPre-154
- 97DonPreCttC-154
- 97DonPri-176
- 97DonPriSoA-176
- 97Kat-110
- 97KatGol-110
- 97KatSil-110
- 97Lea-162
- 97LeaFraMat-162
- 97LeaFraMDC-162
- 97PacCroR-103
- 97PacCroREG-103
- 97PacCroRIB-103
- 97PacCroRS-103
- 97PacPar-140
- 97PacParC-140
- 97PacParDG-140
- 97PacParEG-140
- 97PacParIB-140
- 97PacParRed-140
- 97PacParSil-140
- 97Pin-20
- 97PinArtP-20
- 97PinCerRR-I
- 97PinCerRRG-I
- 97PinCerRRMG-I
- 97PinPrePBB-20
- 97PinPrePBC-20
- 97PinPrePBM-20
- 97PinPrePBY-20
- 97PinPrePFC-20
- 97PinPrePFM-20
- 97PinPrePFY-20
- 97PinPrePla-20
- 97PinRinC-20
- 97Sco-72
- 97ScoArtPro-72
- 97ScoGolBla-72
- 97SPAut-189
- 97UppDec-340
- 97UppDecBD-24
- 97UppDecBDDD-24
- 97UppDecBDQD-24
- 97UppDecBDTD-24
- 97ZenRooR-7
- 98Be A PPA-109
- 98Be A PPAA-109
- 98Be A PPAAF-109
- 98Be A PPTBASG-109
- 98Be APG-109
- 98O-PChr-169
- 98O-PChrR-169
- 98Pac-339
- 98PacAur-144
- 98PacDynI-142
- 98PacDynIIB-142
- 98PacDynIR-142
- 98PacIceB-339
- 98PacPar-181
- 98PacParC-181
- 98PacParEG-181
- 98PacParH-181
- 98PacParIB-181
- 98PacParS-181
- 98PacRed-339
- 98SPxFin-65
- 98SPxFin-146
- 98SPxFinR-65
- 98SPxFinR-146
- 98SPxFinS-65
- 98SPxFinS-146
- 98Top-169
- 98TopO-P-169
- 98UC-161
- 98UD ChoPCR-161
- 98UD ChoR-161
- 98UD3-26
- 98UD3-86
- 98UD3-146
- 98UD3DieC-26
- 98UD3DieC-86
- 98UD3DieC-146
- 98UDCP-161
- 98UppDec-152
- 98UppDecE-152
- 98UppDecE1o1-152
- 98UppDecGN-GN11
- 98UppDecGNQ1-GN11
- 98UppDecGNQ2-GN11
- 98UppDecGNQ3-GN11
- 98UppDecGR-152
- 98UppDecM-159
- 98UppDecMGS-159
- 98UppDecMSS-159
- 98UppDecMSS-159
- 99UppDecM-128
- 99UppDecMGS-128
- 99UppDecMSS-128
- 99UppDecMSS-128

**Isen, Corey**
- 95Sla-178

**Iserhoff, Neil**
- 917thInnSOHL-156
- 91OshGen-8
- 91OshGenS-26
- 92OshGenS-26

**Isotalo, Jarkko**
- 94FinnSIS-284

**Israel, Aaron**
- 92HarCri-15
- 94Cla-119
- 94ClaDraGol-119
- 94JohChi-11

**Israel, Jamie**
- 89KitRan-20
- 907thInnSMC-34
- 907thInnSOHL-234
- 90KitRan-18

**Israelson, Larry**
- 75OPCWHA-46

**Issel, Jason**
- 93PriAlbR-12
- 94PriAlbR-10
- 95PriAlbR-9
- 96PriAlbR-8
- 96PriAlbROC-9

**Issel, Kim**
- 84PriAlbRS-15
- 88OilTenAnn-155
- 88ProAHL-86
- 89ProAHL-145
- 90Sco-409
- 90ScoCan-409

**Issila, Hannu**
- 82SweSemHVS-27

**Itamies, Iiro**
- 95FinnSIS-82
- 96FinnSISR-82

**Iuliano, Jerry**
- 83SauSteMG-13

**Ivan, Mark**
- 96LetHur-8

**Ivan, Tommy**
- 60ShiCoi-80
- 70BlaBor-5
- 83HalFP-L8
- 85HalFC-158
- 92HalFL-35
- 94ParMisL-42

**Ivan, Victor**
- 51Par-20

**Ivankovic, Frank**
- 95Sla-156

**Ivannikov, Valeri**
- 95FinnSemWC-122

**Ivanov, Denis**
- 96GueSto-5

**Ivany, Ron**
- 98GerDELE-225

**Ivarsson, Anders**
- 86SwePanS-50

**Ivarsson, Lars**
- 84SweSemE-54
- 85SwePanS-20
- 86SwePanS-33
- 87SwePanS-49
- 89SweSemE-99
- 90SweSemE-104
- 91SweSemE-108

92SweSemE-136
93SweSemE-250
94SweLeaE-23
95SweLeaE-128
95SweUppDE-187
**Ivarsson, Pierre**
90SweSemE-159
91SweSemE-263
92SweSemE-277
**Jaako, Kari**
85SwePanS-164
86SwePanS-186
87SwePanS-184
89SweSemE-162
90SweSemE-43
91SweSemE-291
**Jaaskelainen, Joonas**
94FinnSIS-226
95FinnSIS-290
96FinnSISR-88
**Jablonic, Don**
93MinDul-14
**Jablonski, Jeff**
91NasKni-10
92TolSto-16
95RoaExp-13
96RoaExp-15
**Jablonski, Pat**
88ProIHL-93
89BluKod-1
89ProIHL-3
90ProAHLIHL-97
91BluPos-11
91OPC-246
91OPCPre-29
91Pin-331
91PinFre-331
91ScoAme-329
91ScoCan-359
91Top-246
91UppDec-107
91UppDecF-107
92Bow-66
92LigShe-17
92OPC-311
92OPCPre-95
92Par-404
92ParEmel-404
92ProSet-178
92StaClu-231
92Top-396
92TopGol-396G
92Ult-202
92UppDec-458
93OPCPre-186
93OPCPreG-186
93Par-192
93ParEmel-192
93PinMas-5
93Pow-444
93Sco-349
93ScoCan-349
93TopPre-186
93TopPreG-186
93Ult-125
94Lea-446
95ParInt-386
95ParIntEl-386
96BeAPAut-99
96BeAPAutSil-99
96BeAPla-99
96CanaPos-13
**Jackman, Barrett**
98SP Aut-117
98SP AutSotTG-BJ
98SSASotT-BJ
98UppDec-394
98UppDecE-394
98UppDecE1o1-394
98UppDecGR-394
99SP AutPS-117
**Jackman, Jason**
94GueSto-13
95GueSto5A-4
95Sla-101
96GueSto-20
96GueStoPC-6
97GueSto-25
**Jackman, Richard**
95SauSteMG-9
95Sla-374
96CEFLAuHP-3
96SauSteMG-7
96SauSteMG-8
96SauSteMGA-7
96SauSteMGA-8
96UppDecIce-133
97BowCHL-36
97BowCHLOPC-36
98BowCHL-5
98BowCHLGA-5
98BowCHLOI-5
98BowChrC-5
98BowChrCGA-5
98BowChrCGAR-5
98BowChrCOIR-5
98BowChrCR-5
**Jackson, Art**
34BeeGro1P-327
350PCV304C-88
39OPCV3011-93
**Jackson, Busher (Harvey)**
320'KeeMapL-11
33OPCV304A-33

33V129-6
33V252CanG-32
33V288HamG-29
34BeeGro1P-231
34BeeGro1P-328
34SweCap-47
36OPCV304D-124
36TriPos-2
36V356WorG-51
37OPCV304E-139
38QuaOatP-20
39OPCV3011-20
55Par-22
55ParQuaO-22
83HalFP-M11
83HalFC-175
**Jackson, Dane**
92HamCan-11
94ClaProP-127
94Sco-216
94ScoGol-216
94ScoPla-216
94ScoPlaTS-216
95RochAmeSS-6
**Jackson, Don**
79PanSti-212
82OilRedR-29
83OilMcD-7
83OPC-33
83Vac-30
84OilRedR-29
84OilTeal-11
84OPC-247
85OilRedR-29
88OilTenAnn-76
90KnoChe-103
91NordPet-11
92NorPet-14
**Jackson, Harold**
35DiaMatT4-6
36OPCV304D-112
76OldTim-8
**Jackson, Jeff**
83BraAle-14
84MapLeaP-13
86MapLeaP-13
87NordGenF-16
88NordGenF-17
88NordTeal-18
88OPC-219
88OPCSti-190
89Nord-18
89NordGenF-14
89NordPol-12
89OPCSti-184
90HalCit-12
90NordTeal-13
90OPC-249
90ProAHLIHL-459
90Top-249
90TopTif-249
90UppDec-249
90UppDecF-291
91LakSupSL-14
91ProAHLCHL-365
**Jackson, Jim**
82Ott167-9
83OPC-84
83OPCSti-146
83Ott67-14
84OPC-225
84Ott67-14
88ProAHL-250
89ProAHL-279
**Jackson, Joshua**
92DisMigDM-3
**Jackson, Mike**
90NewSai-9
90ProAHLIHL-169
94CenHocL-48
**Jackson, Paul**
69ColChe-8
94CenHocL-80
94SheSte-3
**Jackson, Red (Walter)**
33V252CanG-33
34DiaMatS-31
**Jackson, Stan**
23V1451-27
24C144ChaCig-33
24V1452-60
**Jacob, Guy**
81OshGen-21
88FliSpi-9
**Jacobs, Tim**
76OPCNHL-370
**Jacobsen, Anders**
87SwePanS-253
**Jacobson, Garnet**
95PriAlbR-10
96PriAlbR-9
96PriAlbROC-10
**Jacobson, Ole**
65SweCorl-171
**Jacobson, Tommy**
95FinnSemWC-179
95SweLeaE-193
**Jacobsson, Bertil**
69SweHocS-244
70SweHocS-141
71SweHocS-233
**Jacobsson, Curt**
69SweHocS-280

70SweHocS-188
**Jacobsson, Lars-Erik**
71SweHocS-267
**Jacobsson, Leif**
69SweHocS-281
70SweHocS-189
**Jacobsson, Mats**
84SweSemE-36
**Jacobsson, Orjan**
92SweSemE-251
**Jacobsson, Peter**
89SweSemE-249
90SweSemE-158
91SweSemE-262
92SweSemE-283
93SweSemE-248
94SweLeaE-117
**Jacobsson, Sven-Ake**
71SweHocS-213
72SweHocS-190
74SweHocS-224
**Jacoby, Jake**
93WatBlaH-12
**Jacques, Alexandre**
97BowCHL-80
97BowCHLOPC-80
**Jacques, Daniel**
97GueSto-3
**Jacques, Steve**
90ProAHLIHL-358
**Jadamzik, R.**
95GerDELE-339
**Jagenstedt, Thomas**
84SweSemE-143
85SwePanS-20
**Jager, Rolf**
69SweHocS-208
70SweHocS-200
71SweHocS-287
87SwePanS-25
**Jagr, Jaromir**
900PCPre-50
90PenFoo-11
90ProSet-632
90ProSet-632B
90Sco-428
90ScoCan-428
90ScoRoo-70T
90UppDec-356
90UppDecF-356
91Bow-95
91Gil-34
91Kra-3
910PC-9
910PC-40
91OPCPre-24
91PenCokE-68
91PenFoo-11
91PenFooCS-7
91Pin-53
91PinFre-53
91ProSet-183
91ProSet-319
91ProSetFre-183
91ProSetPla-92
91ScoAme-98
91ScoAme-351
91ScoCan-98
91ScoCan-381
91ScoHotC-8
91ScoYouS-38
91StaClu-343
91StaPicH-70
91SweSemWCS-225
91Top-9
91Top-40
91UppDec-20
91UppDec-42
91UppDec-256
91UppDec-617
91UppDecES-6
91UppDecESF-6
91UppDecF-42
91UppDecF-42
91UppDecF-256
91UppDecF-617
92Bow-231
92Bow-302
92HumDum2-10
92Kra-42
92McDUppD-20
92OPC-102
92PanSti-282
92PanSti-294
92PanSti-S
92Par-174
92Par-314
92ParEmel-135
92ParEmel-220
92ParEmel-465
92PenCokC-8
92PenFoo-9
92Pin-275
92PinFre-275
92PiriTea2-15
92PinTea2F-15

92PinTeaP-6
92PinTeaPF-6
92ProSet-141
92Sco-113
92Sco-494
92ScoCan-113
92ScoCan-494
92ScoYouS-4
92SeaPat-35
92StaClu-498
92Top-24
92TopGol-24G
92Ult-164
92UltAllS-6
92UltImp-6
92UppDec-16
92UppDec-28
92UppDec-622
92UppDecAWT-W3
92UppDecES-E14
92UppDecWJG-WG6
93Don-270
93DonIceKin-3
93KenStaLA-5
93KenStaLC-4
93Kra-13
93Lea-346
93McDUppD-17
93OPCPre-105
93OPCPre-325
93OPCPreBG-19
93OPCPreG-105
93OPCPreG-325
93PanSti-82
93ParEmel-154
93PenSti-3
93Pin-195
93PinAllS-20
93PinAllSC-20
93PinCan-195
93PinTea2-12
93PinTea2C-12
93PinTeaP-6
93PinTeaP-6
93Pow-189
93PowGloG-3
93PowPoIL-5
93Sco-50
93ScoCan-50
93ScoIntS-9
93ScoIntSC-9
93SeaPat-7
93StaClu-98
93StaCluAS-4
93StaCluFDI-98
93StaCluFDIO-98
93StaCluO-98
93TopPre-105
93TopPre-325
93TopPreG-105
93TopPreG-325
93Ult-65
93UltRedLS-5
93UppDec-139
93UppDecFH-33
93UppDecLAS-3
93UppDecSilSka-R8
93UppDecSilSkaG-R8
93UppDecSP-121
94ActPacBPP-BP3
94BeAPla-R63
94CanGamNHLP-184
94CzeAPSE-68
94Don-159
94DonDom-4
94EASpo-107
94Fin-33
94FinBowB-B20
94FinBowBR-B20
94FinnJaaK-183
94FinnJaaK-351
94FinRef-33
94FinRinL-15
94FinSupTW-33
94Fle-163
94FleSlaA-4
94HocWit-107
94KenStaLA-8
94Kra-8
94Lea-151
94LeaGolS-15
94LeaLim-86
94LeaLimG-6
94McDUppD-McD10
94OPCPre-460
94OPCPreSE-460
94Par-174
94ParGol-174
94ParGol-314
94ParSEES-ES20
94ParSEV-42
94PenFoo-23
94Pin-98
94PinArtP-98
94PinGam-GR5
94PinRinC-98
94PinTeaP-TP11
94PinTeaPDP-TP11
94Sco-135
94Sco90PC-9
94ScoGol-135
94ScoPla-135

94ScoPlaTS-135
94Sel-60
94SelGol-60
94SP-89
94SPDieCut-89
94SPPre-26
94SPPreDC-26
94StaClu-68
94StaCluFDI-68
94StaCluMO-44
94StaCluMOMS-68
94StaCluSTWC-68
94TopFinB-1
94TopPre-460
94TopPreSE-460
94Ult-164
94UltGloGre-4
94UppDec-93
94UppDec-544
94UppDecEleIce-93
94UppDecEleIce-544
94UppDecPC-C24
94UppDecPCEG-C24
94UppDecPH-H24
94UppDecPHEG-H24
94UppDecPHES-H24
94UppDecPHG-H24
94UppDecPR-R18
94UppDecPR-R29
94UppDecPR-R39
94UppDecPRE-R18
94UppDecPRE-R29
94UppDecPRE-R39
94UppDecPreRG-R18
94UppDecPreRG-R29
94UppDecPreRG-R39
94UppDecSPI-SP60
94UppDecSPIDC-SP60
95BAPLetL-LL12
95Bow-57
95BowAllFoi-57
95BowBes-BB7
95BowBesRef-BB7
95CanGamNHLP-11
95CanGamNHLP-216
95ColCho-127
95ColCho-378
95ColCho-389
95ColChoCTG-C7
95ColChoCTG-C7B
95ColChoCTG-C7C
95ColChoCTGGB-C7
95ColChoCTGGR-C7
95ColChoCTGSB-C7
95ColChoCTGSR-C7
95ColChoPC-127
95ColChoPC-378
95ColChoPC-389
95ColChoPCP-127
95ColChoPCP-378
95ColChoPCP-389
95Don-142
95DonEli-35
95DonEliCE-6
95DonEliDCS-35
95DonEliDCU-35
95DonEliIns-10
95DonMar-5
95Emo-137
95EmoXci-9
95Fin-70
95Fin-185
95FinnSemWC-158
95FinRef-70
95FinRef-185
95ImpSti-96
95ImpStiDCS-23
95Kra-42
95Kra-78
95Lea-71
95LeaFreFra-4
95LeaGolS-5
95LeaLim-73
95LeaLimSG-8
95LeaRoaCup-3
95McDPin-MCD-1
95Met-117
95MetHM-6
95MetIS-9
95NHLAcePC-12D
95NHLCooT-20
95NHLCooT-RP20
95ParInt-165
95ParInt-244
95ParIntAS-5
95ParIntCCGS2-1
95ParIntCCSS2-1
95ParIntEl-165
95ParIntEl-244
95ParIntNHLAS-2
95ParIntPTP-PP7
95ParIntPTP-PP14
95ParIntTW-2
95PenFoo-5
95Pin-11
95PinArtP-11
95PinCleS-11
95PinGolG-2
95PinRinC-11
95PinRoa2-13
95PlaOneoOne-78
95PlaOneoOne-185
95PlaOneoOne-297
95ProMag-92

95Sco-1
95ScoBlaIce-1
95ScoBlaIceAP-1
95ScoBorBat-14
95ScoDreTea-8
95ScoLam-12
95SelCer-38
95SelCerGT-4
95SelCerMG-38
95SigRooAJJ-JJ1
95SigRooAJJ-JJ2
95SigRooAJJ-JJ3
95SigRooAJJ-JJ4
95SigRooAJJ-JJ5
95SkyImp-131
95SkyImpCI-2
95SkyImpIQ-1
95SP-114
95SPHol-FX18
95SPHolSpFX-FX18
95SPStaEto-E23
95SPStaEtoG-E23
95StaClu-70
95StaCluGTSC-GT3
95StaCluMO-5
95StaCluMOMS-70
95Sum-17
95SumArtP-17
95SumGM-12
95SumIce-17
95SumMadH-10
95SweGloWC-157
95Top-200
95Top-374
95TopMarMPB-374
95TopMysF-M8
95TopMysFR-M8
95TopOPCI-200
95TopOPCI-374
95TopPowL-5PL
95TopPro-PF4
95TopSupSki-20
95TopSupSkiPla-20
95TopYouS-YS15
95Ult-123
95Ult-387
95UltExtAtt-9
95UltGolM-123
95UltRedLS-4
95UltRedLSGM-4
95UltUltHP-4
95UltUltV-4
95UppDec-465
95UppDecAGPRW-17
95UppDecEleIce-465
95UppDecEleIceG-465
95UppDecFreFra-F4
95UppDecFreFraJ-F4
95UppDecNHLAS-AS3
95UppDecPHE-H2
95UppDecPRE-R3
95UppDecPRE-R22
95UppDecPRE-R38
95UppDecPRE-R46
95UppDecPreR-R3
95UppDecPreR-R22
95UppDecPreR-R38
95UppDecPreR-R46
95UppDecSpeE-SE153
95UppDecSpeEdiG-SE153
95UppPreHV-H2
95UppPreRP-R38
95UppPreRP-R46
95Zen-3
95ZenZT-11
95BeAPBisITB-9
96ColCho-211
96ColCho-294
96ColCho-328
96ColChoCTG-C6A
96ColChoCTG-C6B
96ColChoCTG-C6C
96ColChoCTGE-CR6
96ColChoCTGG-C6A
96ColChoCTGG-C6B
96ColChoCTGG-C6C
96ColChoMVP-UD43
96ColChoMVPG-UD43
96ColChoSti-S8
96Don-43
96DonCanI-1
96DonCanIGPP-1
96DonCanIRPP-1
96DonDom-4
96DonEli-8
96DonEliDCS-8
96DonEliP-8
96DonGoTS-5
96DonPrePro-43
96Fla-77
96FlaBlu-FF77
96FlaCenIS-5
96Fle-86
96Fle-137
96Fle-138
96Fle-139
96Fle-141
96Fle-142
96FleArtRos-8
96FlePea-5
96FlePicDL-6
96FlePicFS-20
96FlePicFF-5
96HocGreC-11

96HocGreCG-11
96KraUppD-32
96KraUppD-57
96Lea-106
96LeaLeaAL-5
96LeaLeaALP-P5
96LeaLim-11
96LeaLimG-11
96LeaPre-22
96LeaPreP-106
96LeaPrePP-22
96LeaPreSG-37
96LeaPreSP-8
96LeaPreSte-37
96LeaTheBO.-1
96MetUniI-127
96MetUniIC-6
96MetUniICSP-6
96MetUniLW-8
96MetUniLWSP-8
96NHLACEPC-23
96NHLProSTA-92
96PenTri-7
96Pin-102
96PinArtP-102
96PinByTN-8
96PinByTNP-8
96PinFan-FC7
96PinFoi-102
96PinMcD-23
96PinMin-4
96PinMin-8
96PinMinCoiB-4
96PinMinCoiGP-4
96PinMinCoiN-4
96PinMinCoiS-4
96PinMinCoiSG-4
96PinMinG-4
96PinMinS-4
96PinPreS-102
96PinRinC-102
96PinTeaP-6
96PlaOneoOne-433
96Sco-29
96ScoArtPro-29
96ScoDeaCAP-29
96ScoDreTea-7
96ScoGolB-29
96ScoSpeAP-29
96ScoSudDea-9
96SelCer-43
96SelCerAP-43
96SelCerBiu-43
96SelCerCor-3
96SelCerMB-43
96SelCerMG-43
96SelCerMR-43
96SelCerRed-43
96SkyImp-101
96SkyImpVer-5
96SP-126
96SPSPxFor-2
96SPSPxFor-5
96SPSPxForAut-2
96SPx-38
96SPxGol-38
96StaCluMO-25
96Sum-85
96SumArtP-85
96SumHigV-15
96SumHigVM-15
96SumIce-85
96SumMet-85
96SumPreS-85
96SumUnt-2
96SweSemW-125
96TeaOut-32
96TopNHLP-1
96TopPicFT-FT14
96TopPicOl-1
96TopPicTS-TS6
96Ult-141
96UltCleTheIce-4
96UltGolM-141
96UltMr.Mom-5
96UppDec-320
96UppDecBD-75
96UppDecBDG-75
96UppDecBDRFTC-RC5
96UppDecGJ-GJ4
96UppDecGN-X17
96UppDecHH-HH18
96UppDecHHG-HH18
96UppDecHHS-HH18
96UppDecIce-101
96UppDecIceCar-101
96UppDecIceSCF-S7
96UppDecLSH-LS4
96UppDecLSHF-LS4
96UppDecLSHS-LS4
96UppDecLSS-SS13B
96Zen-74
96ZenArtP-74
96ZenChaS-6
96ZenChaSD-6
97BeAPlaPOT-7
97BeAPlaTAN-20
97ColCho-205
97ColChoCTG-C28A
97ColChoCTG-C28B
97ColChoCTG-C28C
97ColChoCTGE-CR28

❑ 97ColChoSta-SQ89
❑ 97ColChoSti-S15
❑ 97Don-188
❑ 97DonCanI-8
❑ 97DonCanIDS-8
❑ 97DonCanIPS-8
❑ 97DonCanISCS-9
❑ 97DonEli-11
❑ 97DonEli-125
❑ 97DonEliAsp-11
❑ 97DonEliAsp-125
❑ 97DonEliBttF-4
❑ 97DonEliBttFA-4
❑ 97DonEliC-25
❑ 97DonEliIns-2
❑ 97DonEliMC-25
❑ 97DonEliPN-6A
❑ 97DonEliPN-6B
❑ 97DonEliPN-6C
❑ 97DonEliPNDC-6A
❑ 97DonEliPNDC-6B
❑ 97DonEliPNDC-6C
❑ 97DonEliS-11
❑ 97DonEliS-125
❑ 97DonLim-8
❑ 97DonLim-55
❑ 97DonLimExp-8
❑ 97DonLimExp-55
❑ 97DonLimFOTG-14
❑ 97DonLin2L-16
❑ 97DonLin2LDC-16
❑ 97DonPre-125
❑ 97DonPre-192
❑ 97DonPreCttC-125
❑ 97DonPreCttC-192
❑ 97DonPreDWT-7
❑ 97DonPreDWT-11
❑ 97DonPreLotT-1C
❑ 97DonPrePM-10
❑ 97DonPreProG-188
❑ 97DonPreProS-188
❑ 97DonPreT-14
❑ 97DonPreT-20
❑ 97DonPreTB-14
❑ 97DonPreTB-20
❑ 97DonPreTBC-14
❑ 97DonPreTBC-20
❑ 97DonPreTPC-14
❑ 97DonPreTPC-20
❑ 97DonPreTPG-14
❑ 97DonPreTPG-20
❑ 97DonPri-18
❑ 97DonPriDD-4
❑ 97DonPriODI-16
❑ 97DonPriP-4
❑ 97DonPriS-4
❑ 97DonPriSB-4
❑ 97DonPriSG-4
❑ 97DonPriSoA-18
❑ 97DonPriSS-4
❑ 97EssOlyHH-52
❑ 97EssOlyHHF-52
❑ 97HigMinHMC-5
❑ 97Kat-118
❑ 97Kat-162
❑ 97KatGol-118
❑ 97KatGol-162
❑ 97KatSil-118
❑ 97KatSil-162
❑ 97Lea-10
❑ 97Lea-177
❑ 97LeaBanSea-4
❑ 97LeaFirOnIce-3
❑ 97LeaFraMat-10
❑ 97LeaFraMat-177
❑ 97LeaFraMDC-10
❑ 97LeaFraMDC-177
❑ 97LeaInt-10
❑ 97LeaIntUI-10
❑ 97McD-20
❑ 97Pac-68
❑ 97PacCop-68
❑ 97PacCraChoAwa-10
❑ 97PacCroR-110
❑ 97PacCroRBoSDC-17
❑ 97PacCroRCCJ-9
❑ 97PacCroRCCJG-9
❑ 97PacCroRCCJS-9
❑ 97PacCroREG-110
❑ 97PacCroRHTDC-15
❑ 97PacCroRIB-110
❑ 97PacCroRLCDC-17
❑ 97PacCroRS-110
❑ 97PacDyn-102
❑ 97PacDyn-142
❑ 97PacDynBKS-77
❑ 97PacDynC-102
❑ 97PacDynC-142
❑ 97PacDynDD-13A
❑ 97PacDynDG-102
❑ 97PacDynDG-142
❑ 97PacDynEG-102
❑ 97PacDynEG-142
❑ 97PacDynIB-102
❑ 97PacDynIB-142
❑ 97PacDynKotN-9
❑ 97PacDynR-102
❑ 97PacDynR-142
❑ 97PacDynSil-102
❑ 97PacDynSil-142
❑ 97PacDynTan-5
❑ 97PacDynTan-22
❑ 97PacEmeGre-68
❑ 97PacGolCroDC-18
❑ 97PacIceB-68
❑ 97PacInv-113
❑ 97PacInvAZ-20
❑ 97PacInvC-113
❑ 97PacInvEG-113
❑ 97PacInvFP-28
❑ 97PacInvIB-113
❑ 97PacInvNRB-160
❑ 97PacInvNRB-220
❑ 97PacInvOTG-17
❑ 97PacInvR-113
❑ 97PacInvS-113
❑ 97PacOme-186
❑ 97PacOmeC-186
❑ 97PacOmeDG-186
❑ 97PacOmeEG-186
❑ 97PacOmeG-186
❑ 97PacOmeGFDCC-16
❑ 97PacOmeIB-186
❑ 97PacOmeSil-10
❑ 97PacOmeSLC-17
❑ 97PacPar-150
❑ 97PacParBNDC-17
❑ 97PacParC-150
❑ 97PacParDG-150
❑ 97PacParEG-150
❑ 97PacParIB-150
❑ 97PacParP-17
❑ 97PacParRed-150
❑ 97PacParSil-150
❑ 97PacRed-68
❑ 97PacRev-113
❑ 97PacRev1AGD-17
❑ 97PacRevC-113
❑ 97PacRevE-113
❑ 97PacRevIB-113
❑ 97PacRevNID-9
❑ 97PacRevR-113
❑ 97PacRevS-113
❑ 97PacRevTCL-20
❑ 97PacSil-68
❑ 97PacSlaSDC-8C
❑ 97PacTeaCCC-20
❑ 97Pin-30
❑ 97Pin-193
❑ 97PinArtP-30
❑ 97PinBee-7
❑ 97PinBeeGP-7
❑ 97PinBeeGT-10
❑ 97PinBeeT-10
❑ 97PinCer-35
❑ 97PinCerGT-14
❑ 97PinCerMB-35
❑ 97PinCerMG-35
❑ 97PinCerMR-35
❑ 97PinCerR-35
❑ 97PinCerT-14
❑ 97PinEpiGO-20
❑ 97PinEpiGP-20
❑ 97PinEpiME-20
❑ 97PinEpiMO-20
❑ 97PinEpiMP-20
❑ 97PinEpiPE-20
❑ 97PinEpiPO-20
❑ 97PinEpiPP-20
❑ 97PinEpiSE-20
❑ 97PinEpiSO-20
❑ 97PinEpiSP-20
❑ 97PinHocMC-5
❑ 97PinHocMC-6
❑ 97PinIns-6
❑ 97PinInsC-2
❑ 97PinInsCC-6
❑ 97PinInsCG-2
❑ 97PinInsEC-6
❑ 97PinInsT-10
❑ 97PinMin-22
❑ 97PinMinB-22
❑ 97PinMinCBP-22
❑ 97PinMinCGPP-22
❑ 97PinMinCNSP-22
❑ 97PinMinCoiB-22
❑ 97PinMinCoiGP-22
❑ 97PinMinCoiN-22
❑ 97PinMinCoiSG-22
❑ 97PinMinCoiSS-22
❑ 97PinMinGolTea-22
❑ 97PinMinSilTea-22
❑ 97PinPowPac-11
❑ 97PinPrePBB-30
❑ 97PinPrePBB-193
❑ 97PinPrePBC-30
❑ 97PinPrePBC-193
❑ 97PinPrePBM-30
❑ 97PinPrePBM-193
❑ 97PinPrePBY-30
❑ 97PinPrePBY-193
❑ 97PinPrePFC-30
❑ 97PinPrePFC-193
❑ 97PinPrePFM-30
❑ 97PinPrePFM-193
❑ 97PinPrePFY-30
❑ 97PinPrePFY-193
❑ 97PinPrePla-30
❑ 97PinPrePla-193
❑ 97PinRinC-30
❑ 97PinTeaP-6
❑ 97PinTeaPM-6
❑ 97PinTeaPP-6
❑ 97PinTeaPPM-6
❑ 97PinTotCMPG-35
❑ 97PinTotCPB-35
❑ 97PinTotCPG-35
❑ 97PinTotCPR-35
❑ 97PosPin-21
❑ 97Sco-82
❑ 97Sco-PR82
❑ 97ScoArtPro-82
❑ 97ScoChel-13
❑ 97ScoGolBla-82
❑ 97ScoPen-4
❑ 97ScoPenPla-4
❑ 97ScoPenPre-4
❑ 97SP AutI-I8
❑ 97SPAut-125
❑ 97SPAutID-I8
❑ 97SPAutIE-I8
❑ 97SPx-42
❑ 97SPxBro-42
❑ 97SPxDuo-2
❑ 97SPxDuoAut-2
❑ 97SPxGol-42
❑ 97SPxGraF-42
❑ 97SPxSil-42
❑ 97SPxSte-42
❑ 97Stu-5
❑ 97StuHarH-19
❑ 97StuPor-5
❑ 97StuPrePG-5
❑ 97StuPrePS-5
❑ 97StuSil-22
❑ 97StuSil8-22
❑ 97UppDec-342
❑ 97UppDecBD-72
❑ 97UppDecBDDD-72
❑ 97UppDecBDPC-PC20
❑ 97UppDecBDPCDD-PC20
❑ 97UppDecBDPCM-PC20
❑ 97UppDecBDPCQD-PC20
❑ 97UppDecBDPCTD-PC20
❑ 97UppDecBDQD-72
❑ 97UppDecBDTD-72
❑ 97UppDecCtAG-16
❑ 97UppDecCtAG-AR16
❑ 97UppDecDV-3
❑ 97UppDecDVDM-DM4
❑ 97UppDecDVSM-3
❑ 97UppDecGDM-342
❑ 97UppDecIC-IC18
❑ 97UppDecIC2-IC18
❑ 97UppDecIce-68
❑ 97UppDecIceP-68
❑ 97UppDecILL-L2C
❑ 97UppDecILL2-L2C
❑ 97UppDecIPS-68
❑ 97UppDecSG-SG38
❑ 97UppDecSSM-SS2
❑ 97UppDecSSW-SS2
❑ 97UppDecTS-3
❑ 97UppDecTSL2-3
❑ 97UppDecTSS-5B
❑ 97Zen-31
❑ 97Zen5x7-8
❑ 97ZenChaTC-3
❑ 97ZenGolImp-8
❑ 97ZenSilImp-8
❑ 97ZenZGol-31
❑ 97ZenZSil-31
❑ 98Be A PPA-261
❑ 98Be A PPAA-261
❑ 98Be A PPAAF-261
❑ 98Be A PPAGUSC-S17
❑ 98Be A PPAJ-AS18
❑ 98Be A PPPGUJC-G23
❑ 98Be A PPPH-H5
❑ 98Be A PPPPUJC-P7
❑ 98Be A PPSE-261
❑ 98Be APG-261
❑ 98BowBes-4
❑ 98BowBesA-A2A
❑ 98BowBesA-A2B
❑ 98BowBesAAR-A2A
❑ 98BowBesAAR-A2B
❑ 98BowBesAR-4
❑ 98BowBesAR-A2A
❑ 98BowBesAR-A2B
❑ 98BowBesMIF-F3
❑ 98BowBesMIFAR-F3
❑ 98BowBesMIFR-F3
❑ 98BowBesR-4
❑ 98BowBesSBB-SB6
❑ 98BowBesSBBAR-SB6
❑ 98BowBesSBBR-SB6
❑ 98CroRoyCCAJG-10
❑ 98CroRoyCCAJG-10
❑ 98CroRoyCCAJLB-10
❑ 98CroRoyCCAJP-10
❑ 98CroRoyCCAJR-10
❑ 98Fin-74
❑ 98FinCen-C13
❑ 98FinCenR-C13
❑ 98FinDouMF-M1
❑ 98FinDouMF-M2
❑ 98FinDouMF-M3
❑ 98FinDouMF-M4
❑ 98FinDouSMFR-M1
❑ 98FinDouSMFR-M2
❑ 98FinDouSMFR-M3
❑ 98FinDouSMFR-M4
❑ 98FinNo P-74
❑ 98FinNo PR-74
❑ 98FinOve-6
❑ 98FinOveR-6
❑ 98FinRedL-R1
❑ 98FinRedLR-R1
❑ 98FinRef-74
❑ 98McD-11
❑ 98O-PChr-111
❑ 98O-PChrR-111
❑ 98O-PChrSB-SB19
❑ 98O-PChrSBR-SB19
❑ 98Pac-68
❑ 98PacAur-154
❑ 98PacAurALC-16
❑ 98PacAurC-15
❑ 98PacAurCF-40
❑ 98PacAurCFC-40
❑ 98PacAurCFIB-40
❑ 98PacAurCFR-40
❑ 98PacAurCFS-40
❑ 98PacAurFL-8
❑ 98PacAurFLIB-8
❑ 98PacAurFLR-8
❑ 98PacAurMAC-16
❑ 98PacAurNC-10
❑ 98PacCraCA-9
❑ 98PacCroR-110
❑ 98PacCroRCCA-10
❑ 98PacCroRCCAJ-10
❑ 98PacCroRLL-10
❑ 98PacCroRLS-110
❑ 98PacCroRMP-17
❑ 98PacCroRPotG-21
❑ 98PacDynI-151
❑ 98PacDynI-16
❑ 98PacDynIAR-10
❑ 98PacDynIARB-10
❑ 98PacDynIARIB-10
❑ 98PacDynIARR-10
❑ 98PacDynIARS-10
❑ 98PacDynIFT-16
❑ 98PacDynIIB-151
❑ 98PacDynIPP-10
❑ 98PacDynIR-151
❑ 98PacDynITC-21
❑ 98PacEO P-18
❑ 98PacGolCD-29
❑ 98PacIceB-68
❑ 98PacOmeCS-9
❑ 98PacOmeCSG-9
❑ 98PacOmeCSG-9
❑ 98PacOmeCSR-9
❑ 98PacOmeEP1o1-18
❑ 98PacOmeFtF-3
❑ 98PacOmeH-195
❑ 98PacOmeO-30
❑ 98PacOmeODI-195
❑ 98PacOmeP-18
❑ 98PacOmePI-27
❑ 98PacOmePIB-27
❑ 98PacOmeR-195
❑ 98PacPar-192
❑ 98PacParC-192
❑ 98PacParEG-192
❑ 98PacParH-192
❑ 98PacParHoFB-9
❑ 98PacParHoFBPP-9
❑ 98PacParIB-192
❑ 98PacParS-192
❑ 98PacParSDDC-16
❑ 98PacParTCD-21
❑ 98PacRed-68
❑ 98PacRev-118
❑ 98PacRevADC-12
❑ 98PacRevCTL-16
❑ 98PacRevIS-118
❑ 98PacRevNI-10
❑ 98PacRevR-118
❑ 98PacRevS-31
❑ 98PacTeaC-21
❑ 98PacTim-16
❑ 98PacTitI-16
❑ 98PacTroW-3
❑ 98PinEpiGE-20
❑ 98RevThrPA-29
❑ 98RevThrPA-29
❑ 98SP Aut-70
❑ 98SP AutSM-S7
❑ 98SP AutSS-SS5
❑ 98SPxFin-94
❑ 98SPxFin-165
❑ 98SPxFin-174
❑ 98SPxFinR-94
❑ 98SPxFinR-165
❑ 98SPxFinR-174
❑ 98SPxFinS-94
❑ 98SPxFinS-165
❑ 98SPxFinS-174
❑ 98SPXTopP-49
❑ 98SPXTopPF-49
❑ 98SPXTopPHH-H25
❑ 98SPXTopPLI-L18
❑ 98SPXTopPPS-PS11
❑ 98SPXTopPR-49
❑ 98SPXTopPWM-JJ
❑ 98Top-111
❑ 98TopAut-A5
❑ 98TopBlaLGR'-GR5
❑ 98TopGolLC1-5
❑ 98TopGolLC1B-5
❑ 98TopGolLC1BOoO-5
❑ 98TopGolLC1OoO-5
❑ 98TopGolLC1R-5
❑ 98TopGolLC1ROoO-5
❑ 98TopGolLC2-5
❑ 98TopGolLC2B-5
❑ 98TopGolLC2BOoO-5
❑ 98TopGolLC2OoO-5
❑ 98TopGolLC2R-5
❑ 98TopGolLC2ROoO-5
❑ 98TopGolLC3-5
❑ 98TopGolLC3B-5
❑ 98TopGolLC3BOoO-5
❑ 98TopGolLC3OoO-5
❑ 98TopGolLC3R-5
❑ 98TopGolLC3ROoO-5
❑ 98TopGolLGR'-GR5
❑ 98TopGolLGR'BOoO-GR5
❑ 98TopGolLGR'OoO-GR5
❑ 98TopGolLGR'ROoO-GR5
❑ 98TopLocL-L4
❑ 98TopMysFB-M6
❑ 98TopMysFBR-M6
❑ 98TopMysFG-M6
❑ 98TopMysFGR-M6
❑ 98TopMysFS-M6
❑ 98TopMysFSR-M6
❑ 98TopO-P-111
❑ 98TopRedLGR'-GR5
❑ 98TopSeaB-SB19
❑ 98UC-168
❑ 98UC-226
❑ 98UCMBH-BH5
❑ 98UCSB-SQ16
❑ 98UCSG-SQ16
❑ 98UCSG-SQ16
❑ 98UCSR-SQ16
❑ 98UD ChoPCR-168
❑ 98UD ChoPCR-226
❑ 98UD ChoR-168
❑ 98UD ChoR-226
❑ 98UD3-32
❑ 98UD3-92
❑ 98UD3-152
❑ 98UD3DieC-32
❑ 98UD3DieC-92
❑ 98UD3DieC-152
❑ 98UppDec-27
❑ 98UppDec-161
❑ 98UppDecBD-69
❑ 98UppDecDD-69
❑ 98UppDecE-27
❑ 98UppDecE-161
❑ 98UppDecE1o1-27
❑ 98UppDecE1o1-161
❑ 98UppDecFF-FF4
❑ 98UppDecFF-FF4
❑ 98UppDecFFQ1-FF4
❑ 98UppDecFFQ2-FF4
❑ 98UppDecFIT-FT29
❑ 98UppDecFITQ1-FT29
❑ 98UppDecFITQ2-FT29
❑ 98UppDecFITQ3-FT29
❑ 98UppDecGJ-GJ15
❑ 98UppDecGN-GN22
❑ 98UppDecGN-GN23
❑ 98UppDecGN-GN24
❑ 98UppDecGNQ1-GN22
❑ 98UppDecGNQ1-GN23
❑ 98UppDecGNQ1-GN24
❑ 98UppDecGNQ2-GN22
❑ 98UppDecGNQ2-GN23
❑ 98UppDecGNQ2-GN24
❑ 98UppDecGNQ3-GN22
❑ 98UppDecGNQ3-GN23
❑ 98UppDecGNQ3-GN24
❑ 98UppDecGR-27
❑ 98UppDecGR-161
❑ 98UppDecLSH-LS3
❑ 98UppDecLSHQ1-LS3
❑ 98UppDecLSHQ2-LS3
❑ 98UppDecLSHQ3-LS3
❑ 98UppDecM-163
❑ 98UppDecM1-M18
❑ 98UppDecM2-M18
❑ 98UppDecMGS-163
❑ 98UppDecMOH-OT3
❑ 98UppDecMPG-PG10
❑ 98UppDecMSF-F11
❑ 98UppDecMSS-163
❑ 98UppDecMSS-163
❑ 98UppDecP-P10
❑ 98UppDecPQ1-P10
❑ 98UppDecPQ2-P10
❑ 98UppDecPQ3-P10
❑ 98UppDecQD-69
❑ 98UppDecTD-69
❑ 98UppDecWFG-WF25
❑ 98UppDecWFP-WF25
❑ 99AurSty-17
❑ 99Pac-338
❑ 99PacAur-116
❑ 99PacAurCC-10
❑ 99PacAurCF-18
❑ 99PacAurCFC-18
❑ 99PacAurCFPB-18
❑ 99PacAurCP-10
❑ 99PacAurCPP-10
❑ 99PacAurPD-116
❑ 99PacCop-338
❑ 99PacCra-9
❑ 99PacGol-338
❑ 99PacGolCD-31
❑ 99PacIceB-338
❑ 99PacPasAP-19
❑ 99PacPreD-338
❑ 99PacTeaL-22
❑ 99RetHoc-66
❑ 99SP AutPS-70
❑ 99UppDecCL-37
❑ 99UppDecCL-53
❑ 99UppDecCLCLC-37
❑ 99UppDecCLCLC-53
❑ 99UppDecEotG-E3
❑ 99UppDecM-165
❑ 99UppDecM2CN-6
❑ 99UppDecM9S-S2
❑ 99UppDecMGS-GU12
❑ 99UppDecMGS-165
❑ 99UppDecMGUSA-GU12
❑ 99UppDecMHoG-H9
❑ 99UppDecMPS-JJ
❑ 99UppDecMSS-165
❑ 99UppDecMSS-165
❑ 99UppDecMT-MVP8
❑ 99UppDecRDR-DR3
❑ 99UppDecRDRI-DR3
❑ 99UppDecRG-66
❑ 99UppDecRP-66
❑ 99UppDecRTotC-TC3

**Jakes, Tomas**
❑ 95CzeAPSE-26
❑ 96CzeAPSE-221

**Jakobsen, Tommy**
❑ 93SweSemWCS-233
❑ 94FinnJaaK-256
❑ 95SweGloWC-194
❑ 95SweUppDE-38
❑ 96GerDELE-11
❑ 96SweSemW-203
❑ 98GerDELE-288

**Jakobsson, Kurt**
❑ 67SweHoc-238
❑ 71SweHocS-274
❑ 72SweHocS-247

**Jakobsson, Lars-Erik**
❑ 69SweHocS-282
❑ 70SweHocS-181

**Jakobsson, Leif**
❑ 67SweHoc-239
❑ 71SweHocS-275
❑ 72SweHocS-248

**Jakobsson, Sven-Ake**
❑ 67SweHoc-141
❑ 69SweHocS-153
❑ 70SweHocS-122

**Jakobsson, Urban**
❑ 87SwePanS-269

**Jaks, Pauli**
❑ 91UppDec-663
❑ 91UppDecCWJC-24
❑ 91UppDecF-663
❑ 93PhoRoa-11
❑ 94ClaProP-80
❑ 94UppDec-387
❑ 94UppDecEleIce-387
❑ 95SwiHNL-187

**Jaks, Peter**
❑ 91SweSemWCS-197
❑ 93SwiHNL-150
❑ 95SwiHNL-205

**Jalava, Harri**
❑ 95FinnSIS-395

**Jalava, Tuomas**
❑ 95FinnSIS-348

**Jalbert, Craig**
❑ 95Sla-198

**Jalbert, Dean**
❑ 86SudWol-10

**Jalo, Risto**
❑ 88OilTenAnn-39
❑ 93FinnJyvHS-88
❑ 93FinnSIS-121
❑ 94FinnSIS-213
❑ 95FinnSIS-24
❑ 95FinnSIS-179
❑ 95FinnSISL-90
❑ 95FinnSISSpo-6
❑ 96FinnSISR-19

**Jalonen, Jukka**
❑ 93FinnJyvHS-73

**Jalonen, Kari**
❑ 82SweSemHVS-37
❑ 87SwePanS-223
❑ 88OilTenAnn-148
❑ 89SweSemWCS-42
❑ 93FinnSIS-386

**James, Angela**
❑ 94ClaWomOH-W6
❑ 97ColCho-276

**James, Brad**
❑ 90ProAHLIHL-137

**James, David**
❑ 83KinCan-22

**James, Gerry**
❑ 44BeeGro2P-411
❑ 57Par-T8
❑ 60Par-7
❑ 60ShiCoi-17
❑ 94ParMisL-117

**James, Graham**
❑ 907thInnSWHL-66

**James, Mike**
❑ 81Ott67-5
❑ 82Ott67-10
❑ 83Ott67-15
❑ 92RicRen-8

**James, Ryan**
❑ 95NorIowH-16

**Jamieson, Dusty**
❑ 97GueSto-23

**Jamsen, Lasse**
❑ 95FinnSIS-268
❑ 96FinnSISR-64

**Janasak, Steve**
❑ 81SweSemHVS-91
❑ 95SigRooMI-15
❑ 95SigRooMI-16
❑ 95SigRooSMIS-15
❑ 95SigRooSMIS-16

**Jancarik, Petr**
❑ 94CzeAPSE-29

**Janecek, Martin**
❑ 94CzeAPSE-22

**Janecky, Otakar**
❑ 89SweSemWCS-191
❑ 93FinnJyvHS-108
❑ 93FinnSIS-26
❑ 93FinnSIS-364
❑ 94FinnJaaK-188
❑ 94FinnSIS-91
❑ 94FinnSIS-373
❑ 94FinnSISFI-4
❑ 95FinnSIS-53
❑ 95FinnSIS-171
❑ 95FinnSIS-371
❑ 95FinnSISL-14
❑ 95FinnSISSpo-1
❑ 96FinnSISR-185
❑ 96FinnSISRMA-7

**Janecyk, Bob**
❑ 83BlaBorPos-9
❑ 84KinSmo-9
❑ 85OPC-223
❑ 85OPCSti-239
❑ 86Kin20tATI-10
❑ 86OPC-131
❑ 86OPCSti-91
❑ 86Top-131
❑ 87KinTeal4-10

**Janelle, Roland**
❑ 917thInnSCHLAW-29

**Janicki, Trevor**
❑ 93NorMicW-15

**Janikowski, Janusz**
❑ 94GerDELE-413
❑ 95GerDELE-419

**Janiszewski, Henryk**
❑ 79PanSti-120

**Jankowski, Lou**
❑ 44BeeGro2P-110
❑ 54Par-79
❑ 54Top-28

**Janku, Pavel**
❑ 94CzeAPSE-193
❑ 95CzeAPSE-40
❑ 96SweSemW-118

**Janney, Craig**
❑ 88BruPos-5
❑ 88BruSpoA-5
❑ 88BruSpoA-23
❑ 88OPCSti-90
❑ 89BruSpoA-11
❑ 89OPC-190
❑ 89OPC-298
❑ 89OPCSti-29
❑ 89OPCSti-35
❑ 89OPCSti-38
❑ 89OPCSti-175
❑ 89PanSti-198
❑ 89SweSemWCS-173
❑ 89Top-190
❑ 90Bow-33
❑ 90BowTif-33
❑ 90BruSpoA-13
❑ 90OPC-212
❑ 90PanSti-14
❑ 90ProSet-8
❑ 90Sco-118
❑ 90ScoCan-118
❑ 90ScoHotRS-58
❑ 90ScoYouS-30
❑ 90Top-212
❑ 90TopTif-212
❑ 90UppDec-234
❑ 90UppDecF-234
❑ 91Bow-355
❑ 91Kra-31
❑ 91OPC-41
❑ 91OPCPre-93
❑ 91PanSti-170
❑ 91Par-4
❑ 91Par-378
❑ 91ParFre-4
❑ 91ParFre-378
❑ 91Pin-57
❑ 91PinFre-57
❑ 91ProSet-2
❑ 91ProSetFre-2
❑ 91ProSetPla-3
❑ 91ScoAme-253
❑ 91ScoCan-473
❑ 91StaClu-147
❑ 91SweSemWCS-143
❑ 91Top-41
❑ 91UppDec-128
❑ 91UppDec-512
❑ 91UppDecF-128
❑ 91UppDecF-512
❑ 92Bow-14
❑ 92OPC-325
❑ 92PanSti-22
❑ 92PanStiFre-22
❑ 92Par-154
❑ 92ParEmel-154
❑ 92Pin-196
❑ 92PinFre-196
❑ 92ProSet-157
❑ 92Sco-285
❑ 92ScoCan-285
❑ 92ScoUSAG-11
❑ 92StaClu-41
❑ 92Top-134
❑ 92TopGol-134G
❑ 92Ult-187
❑ 92UppDec-125
❑ 93Don-295
❑ 93Lea-181
❑ 93OPCPre-120
❑ 93OPCPreG-120
❑ 93PanSti-157

93Par-443
93ParEmel-443
93Pin-130
93PinCan-130
93Pow-212
93Sco-186
93ScoCan-186
93ScoDynDUS-4
93StaClu-335
93StaCluFDI-335
93StaCluMasP-22
93StaCluMasPW-22
93StaCluO-335
93SweSemWCS-186
93TopPre-120
93TopPreG-120
93Ult-134
93UppDec-225
93UppDec-303
93UppDec-323
93UppDecSP-138
94BeAPla-R52
94CanGamNHLP-204
94Don-28
94EASpo-123
94FinnJaaK-119
94Fla-154
94HocWit-4
94Kra-18
94Lea-52
94LeaLim-91
94OPCPre-60
94OPCPreSE-60
94Par-200
94ParGol-200
94Pin-84
94PinArtP-84
94PinRinC-84
94Sco-127
94ScoGol-127
94ScoPla-127
94ScoPlaTS-127
94Sel-139
94SelGol-139
94SP-109
94SPDieCut-109
94TopPre-60
94TopPreSE-60
94Ult-363
94UppDec-18
94UppDecEleIce-18
94UppDecPR-R16
94UppDecPRE-R16
94UppDecPRERG-R16
94UppDecSPI-SP67
94UppDecSPIDC-SP67
95BeAPla-47
95BeAPSig-S47
95BeAPSigDC-S47
95Bow-3
95BowAllFoi-3
95CanGamNHLP-226
95ColCho-264
95ColChoPC-264
95ColChoPCP-264
95Don-137
95DonEli-33
95DonEliDCS-33
95DonEliDCU-33
95Emo-157
95Fin-4
95FinnSemWC-107
95FinRef-4
95ImpSti-106
95Lea-98
95LeaLim-13
95Met-131
95NHLAcePC-2H
95ParInt-455
95ParIntEl-455
95Pin-37
95PinArtP-37
95PinRinC-37
95PlaOneoOne-192
95ProMag-120
95Sco-15
95ScoBlaIce-15
95ScoBlaIceAP-15
95SelCer-33
95SelCerMG-33
95SkyImp-149
95StaClu-179
95StaCluMOMS-179
95Sum-49
95SumArtP-49
95SumIce-49
95SweGloWC-118
95Top-95
95TopOPCI-95
95TopSupSki-13
95TopSupSkiP-13
95Ult-147
95UltGolM-147
95UppDec-315
95UppDecEleIce-315
95UppDecEleIceG-315
95UppDecSpeE-SE73
95UppDecSpeEdiG-SE73
96ColCho-207
96Don-154
96DonEli-104
96DonEliDCS-104
96DonPrePro-154
96FlePic-60
96Lea-36

91UppDecF-228
92OPCPre-117
92WhaDai-10
93OPCPre-133
93PanSti-127
93Par-355
93ParEmel-355
93Sco-339
93ScoCan-339
93StaClu-180
93StaCluFDI-180
93StaCluFDIO-180
93StaCluO-180
93TopPre-133
93TopPreG-133
93UppDec-198
93WhaCok-7
94Lea-361
94ParSE-SE70
94ParSEG-SE70
94StaClu-212
94StaCluFDI-212
94StaCluMOMS-212
94StaCluSTWC-212
94UppDec-35
94UppDecEleIce-35
95UppDec-312
95UppDecEleIce-312
95UppDecEleIceG-312
96BeAPAut-199
96BeAPAutSil-199
96BeAPla-199
96WhaBobS-10
96Ult-131
96UltGolM-131
96UppDec-127
96UppDecBD-45
96UppDecBDG-45
96Zen-49
96ZenArtP-49
97ColCho-201
97Don-46
97DonLim-67
97DonLimExp-67
97DonPreProG-46
97DonPreProS-46
97DonPri-154
97DonPriSoA-154
97Pac-148
97PacCop-148
97PacEmeGre-148
97PacIceB-148
97PacRed-148
97PacRev-106
97PacRevC-106
97PacRevE-106
97PacRevIB-106
97PacRevR-106
97PacRevS-106
97PacSil-148
97Sco-154
97ScoArtPro-154
97ScoGolBla-154
97SPAut-123
97UppDec-334
98BowBes-94
98BowBesAR-94
98BowBesR-94
98Pac-340
98PacIceB-340
98PacRed-340
98SP Aut-80
98UC-156
98UD ChoPCR-156
98UD ChoR-156
98UppDec-366
98UppDecBD-81
98UppDecDD-81
98UppDecE-366
98UppDecE1o1-366
98UppDecGR-366
98UppDecQD-81
98UppDecTD-81
99SP AutPS-80

93WatBlaH-13
**Jarn, Heikki**
72SweSemWC-77
**Jarnberg, Per**
84SweSemE-58
**Jaroslav, Walter**
94GerDELE-32
**Jaroslavtsev, Viktor**
73SweHocS-119
73SweWorCS-119
**Jarrett, Doug**
64BeeGro3P-43
65Coc-34
66Top-111
67Top-112
68Bla-2
68OPC-13
68ShiCoi-26
68Top-13
69OPC-67
69OPCFou-6
69Top-67
70BlaBor-6
70DadCoo-62
70EssPowPla-112
70OPC-150
70SarProSta-34
71OPC-208
71SarProSta-41
71TorSun-68
72OPC-97
72SarProSta-58
73OPC-187
73Top-76
74NHLActSta-79
74OPC-351
75OPCNHL-333
94ParTalB-38
95Par66-27
95Par66Coi-27
**Jarrett, Gary**
67Top-44
68OPC-87
68ShiCoi-120
68Top-87
69OPC-85
69Top-85
70ColSta-49
70DadCoo-63
70EssPowPla-101
70OPC-75
70SarProSta-140
70Top-75
71OPC-93
71SarProSta-138
71Top-93
71TorSun-49
72CleCruWHA-8
73QuaOatWHA-27
74OPCWHA-61
75OPCWHA-87
**Jarry, Pierre**
72MapLeaP-12
72OPC-237
72SarProSta-208
73OPC-186
73RedWinMP-10
74NHLActSta-102
74OPCNHL-171
74Top-171
75OPCNHL-359A
75OPCNHL-359B
76OPCNHL-49
76Top-49
77OPCNHL-106
77Top-106
**Jarvela, Pekka**
89SweSemE-203
**Jarvenpaa, Hannu**
86JetBor-10
87Jet-10
88JetPol-11
89OPC-292
89OPCSti-145
91SweSemE-150
91SweSemWCS-23
93FinnSIS-273
94FinnSIS-23
94FinnSISH-17
95FinnSIS-181
**Jarvenpaa, Juha**
93FinnJyvHS-77
93FinnSIS-122
94FinnSIS-87
94FinnSIS-251
95FinnSIS-25
95FinnSISL-107
96FinnSISR-39
**Jarventie, Martti**
94Fin-130
94FinnSIS-235
94FinRef-130
94FinSupTW-130
95FinnSIS-32
96FinnSISR-98
**Jarvholm, Erik**
67SweHoc-256
69SweHocS-301
70SweHocS-201
71SweHocS-288
72SweHocS-69
**Jarvi, Iiro**
88NordGenF-18
88NordTeal-19

89Nord-19
89NordGenF-15
89NordPol-13
890PC-264
890PCSti-7
890PCSti-192
89PanSti-329
90NordTeal-14
900PC-52
90ProAHLIHL-451
90Top-52
90TopTif-52
93FinnJyvHS-19
93FinnSIS-106
94FinnSIS-31
94FinnSIS-379
95FinnSIS-213
95FinnSISL-45
96FinnSISRS-8
96GerDELE-60
**Jarvinen, Jari**
93FinnJyvHS-171
93FinnSIS-164
**Jarvinen, Pauli**
89SweSemWCS-46
90SweSemE-237
91SweSemE-164
91SweSemWCS-14
93FinnJyvHS-289
93FinnSIS-73
94FinnJaaK-50
94PanSni-75
94FinnSISFi-7
95FinnSIS-318
95FinnSISL-78
**Jarvinen, Timo**
93FinnSIS-209
**Jarvis, Doug**
75CanaPos-7
76OPCNHL-217
760PCNHL-313
76Top-217
77CanaPos-9
770PCNHL-139
77Top-139
78CanaPos-10
780PC-13
78Top-13
79CanaPos-9
790PC-112
79Top-112
80CanaPos-9
800PC-76
80PepCap-47
80Top-76
81CanaPos-12
810PC-184
810PCSti-34
82Cap-12
820PC-367
820PCSti-40
830PC-372
830PCSti-208
84CapPizH-9
840PC-200
840PCSti-129
840PCSti-234
84Top-145
85CapPizH-8
85OPC-151
850PCSti-109
85Top-151
860PC-28
86Top-28
86WhaJunT-11
870PC-95
870PCMin-19
870PCSti-183
870PCSti-207
87PanSti-52
87Top-95
87WhaJunBK-9
94StaHoc-15
**Jarvis, Wes**
81Cap-9
88ProAHL-230
89ProAHL-106
96KitRan-14
97BowCHL-158
97BowCHLAu-38
97BowCHLOPC-158
**Jasecko, Stanislav**
95SloAPSNT-8
96GaraRapG-8
**Jaskin, Alexei**
94CzeAPSE-233
95CzeAPSE-5
96CzeAPSE-219
**Jattne, Bert**
71SweHocS-76
73SweHocS-191
73SweWorCS-191
74SweHocS-144
**Jaufmann, Andrej**
94GerDELE-114
**Javanainen, Arto**
81SweSemHVS-33
82SweSemHVS-38
93FinnJyvHS-356
93FinnSIS-218

93FinnSIS-388
95FinnSISL-25
**Javeblad, Tomas**
85SwePanS-178
86SwePanS-111
87SwePanS-170
89SweSemE-147
90SweSemE-225
**Javin, Miroslav**
94CzeAPSE-124
95CzeAPSE-32
96CzeAPSE-314
**Jax, Fredrik**
90SweSemE-221
91SweSemE-145
92UppDec-230
94ClaProP-133
94FliGen-12
**Jax, Hans**
69SweHocS-118
70SweHocS-75
71SweHocS-165
72SweHocS-159
73SweHocS-54
73SweWorCS-54
74SweHocS-225
86SwePanS-162
**Jay, Bob**
90ProAHLIHL-550
91ProAHLCHL-252
93Par-361
93ParEmel-361
93PhoRoa-12
93UppDec-470
96DetVip-9
**Jaycock, Randy**
93DalFre-9
**Jean, Maxime**
917thInnSQMJHL-53
**Jedamzik, Rafael**
94GerDELE-83
**Jeffrey, Larry**
44BeeGro2P-180
62YorIroOTra-33
63Par-48
63YorWhiB-41
64BeeGro3P-79A
64BeeGro3P-79B
64BeeGro3P-167
64CocCap-47
64Top-29
64TorSta-21
65MapLeaWB-9
65Top-83
67Top-21
680PC-74
68ShiCoi-106
700PC-28
70Top-28
94ParTalB-59
95Par66-115
95Par66Coi-115
**Jeffrey, Mike**
87MonHaw-14
88ProAHL-158
89JohChi-33
**Jelinek, Tomas**
91SweSemWCS-122
92UppDec-497
93SweSemWCS-103
93UppDec-165
94CzeAPSE-261
94FinnJaaK-179
95CzeAPSE-138
95SweGloWC-153
96CzeAPSE-297
**Jenacek, Lubos**
94CzeAPSE-244
95CzeAPSE-16
**Jenkins, Craig**
89NasKni-10
**Jenkins, Jon**
83OshGen-15
94KnoChe-10
**Jenkins, Roger**
34BeeGro1P-160
34DiaMatS-32
34SweCap-4
35DiaMatTl-30
350PCV304C-92
**Jenkins, Scott**
907thInnSOHL-211
**Jenkins, Todd**
89NasKni-11
**Jennings, Grant**
83SasBla-3
84SasBlaS-8
89WhaJunM-10
900PC-510
90ProSet-106
90ScoRoo-31T
90WhaJr7E-15
910PC-468
91PenCoKE-3
91ScoCan-531
91Top-468
92PenCoKC-9
92Sco-542
92ScoCan-542
93Par-427
93ParEmel-427
93PenFoo-2
94BeAPSig-51
94MapLeaK-16
94MapLeaPP-27

94PenFoo-1
**Jennings, Jason**
92WesMic-14
93JohChi-10
94ClaProP-238
94JohChi-12
95VanVooRHI-9
**Jennings, William**
34BeeGro1P-105
83HalFP-K8
85HalFC-142
90UppDecF-209
**Jensen, Al**
81Cap-9
82PosCer-20
83OPC-373
830PCSti-202
84CapPizH-10
840PC-201
840PCSti-128
840PCSti-232
84Top-146
85CapPizH-9
86CapPol-12
860PC-135
860PCSti-252
86Top-135
**Jensen, Chris**
88ProAHL-125
89ProAHL-339
90ProAHLIHL-38
91ProAHLCHL-275
93ForWorF-7
93PorPir-5
94PorPir-11
**Jensen, Cody**
96RegPat-22
**Jensen, Darren**
860PCSti-187
**Jensen, David A**
84SprInd-5
84WhaJunW-4
86CapKod-13
86CapPol-13
87CapTealss-11
**Jensen, David H**
92UppDec-379
**Jensen, Eric**
93MicTecH-2
**Jensen, James**
94CenHocL-11
**Jensen, Steve**
770PCNHL-238
77Top-238
780PC-45
78Top-45
790PC-292
79PanSti-220
80KinCarN-5
800PC-294
810PC-154
82PosCer-8
**Jenson, Christian**
95VanVooRHI-3
**Jenson, Wade**
81VicCou-8
**Jerabek, Vladimir**
95CzeAPSE-173
96CzeAPSE-177
**Jernberg, Tomas**
83SweSemE-206
84SweSemE-225
86SwePanS-264
**Jerofejev, Dmitrij**
96CzeAPSE-199
**Jerome, Darcy**
907thInnSWHL-163
**Jerrard, Paul**
89ProIHL-96
91ProAHLCHL-151
**Jerwa, Joe**
34BeeGro1P-232
35DiaMatT2-29
35DiaMatT3-26
**Jesiolowski, David**
917thInnSWHL-274
93LetHur-5
**Jessee, Scott**
78LouGea-11
**Jessey, Ivan**
88LetHur-13
**Jessiman, Brent**
82BraWheK-16
83BraWheK-14
**Jestadt, Jeff**
91FerStaB-16
93RoaExp-10
94RoaExp-8
95RoaExp-1
**Jickling, Mike**
89SpoChi-12
907thInnSWHL-191
917thInnSMC-89
917thInnSWHL-7
98FloEve-9
**Jindrich, Robert**
95CzeAPSE-251
96CzeAPSE-296
**Jinman, Lee**
93NorBayC-14
94NorBayC-17
95Cla-90
95Sla-58
95Sla-223
**Jiranek, Martin**

❑ 92Cla-69
❑ 93PorPir-14
❑ 94ClaProP-169
❑ 96ClaGol-69
❑ 96GerDELE-327
❑ 98GerDELE-253
**Jirik, Jaroslav**
❑ 69SweHocS-31
❑ 69SweWorC-141
**Joanette, Kitoute**
❑ 51LavDaiQSHL-75
**Joanette, Rosario**
❑ 52St.LawS-20
**Jobe, Trevor**
❑ 88ProAHL-241
❑ 89HamRoaA-10
❑ 90ProAHLIHL-161
❑ 91RicRen-10
❑ 92NasKni-16
**Jodoin, Clement**
❑ 90HalCit-13
❑ 90ProAHLIHL-447
❑ 91ProAHLCHL-544
**Jodoin, Mark**
❑ 93WesMic-17
**Jodzio, Rick**
❑ 75OPCWHA-99
❑ 76OPCWHA-113
❑ 77RocCokCan-10
**Joelsson, Rolf**
❑ 67SweHoc-155
**Joffe, Aaron**
❑ 90AriIce-8
❑ 91AriIce-8
❑ 92AriIce-7
**Johannesen, Glen**
❑ 88ProIHL-14
**Johanneson, Connie**
❑ 23CreSel-11
❑ 28V1282PauC-68
**Johannson, Jim**
❑ 88SalLakCGE-17
❑ 89ProIHL-70
❑ 90ProAHLIHL-396
**Johansen, Roy**
❑ 93SweSemWCS-243
❑ 94FinnJaaK-264
**Johansen, Tom**
❑ 94FinnJaaK-269
**Johansen, Trevor**
❑ 77MapLeaP-7
❑ 78MapLeaP-10
❑ 78OPC-320
❑ 79Roc-9
**Johansson, Ake**
❑ 67SweHoc-202
**Johansson, Andreas**
❑ 91SweSemE-101
❑ 92SweSemE-113
❑ 93SweSemE-85
❑ 94FinnJaaK-70
❑ 94SweLeaE-51
❑ 95ColEdgI-94
❑ 96BeAPAut-103
❑ 96BeAPAutSil-103
❑ 96BeAPla-103
❑ 96SweSemW-64
❑ 97DonLim-121
❑ 97DonLim-159
❑ 97DonLimExp-121
❑ 97DonLimExp-159
❑ 97DonPri-134
❑ 97DonPriSoA-134
❑ 98PacOmeH-165
❑ 98PacOmeODI-165
❑ 98PacOmeR-165
❑ 99Pac-289
❑ 99PacCop-289
❑ 99PacGol-289
❑ 99PacIceB-289
❑ 99PacPreD-289
**Johansson, Antik (Anders)**
❑ 64SweCorI-36
❑ 65SweCorI-36
❑ 67SweHoc-33
❑ 69SweHocS-46
❑ 69SweHocS-336
❑ 70SweHocS-246
❑ 71SweHocS-303
❑ 72SweHocS-289
**Johansson, Arne**
❑ 67SweHoc-157
❑ 69SweHocS-316
❑ 70SweHocS-222
**Johansson, Bjorn**
❑ 65SweCorI-203
❑ 67SweHoc-156
❑ 69SweHocS-168
❑ 72SweHocS-5
❑ 72SweHocS-214
❑ 73SweHocS-5
❑ 73SweHocS-64
❑ 73SweWorCS-5
❑ 73SweWorCS-64
❑ 74SweHocS-170
❑ 74SweSemHVS-5
❑ 77RocAme-14
**Johansson, Calle**
❑ 83SweSemE-227
❑ 85SwePanS-30
❑ 86SwePanS-7
❑ 87SabBluS-14
❑ 87SabWonBH-13
❑ 88OPCSti-134
❑ 88OPCSti-254
❑ 88PanSti-221
❑ 88SabBluS-12
❑ 88SabWonBH-12
❑ 89CapKod-6
❑ 89CapTealss-9
❑ 89OPC-16
❑ 89Top-16
❑ 90Bow-75
❑ 90BowTif-75
❑ 90CapKod-9
❑ 90CapPos-10
❑ 90CapSmo-9
❑ 90OPC-164
❑ 90ProSet-313
❑ 90Sco-309A
❑ 90ScoCan-309A
❑ 90Top-164
❑ 90TopTif-164
❑ 90UppDec-149
❑ 90UppDecF-149
❑ 91Bow-294
❑ 91CapJun5-13
❑ 91CapKod-13
❑ 91OPC-126
❑ 91PanSti-205
❑ 91Par-410
❑ 91ParFre-410
❑ 91Pin-232
❑ 91PinFre-232
❑ 91ProSet-248
❑ 91ProSetFre-248
❑ 91ProSetPla-243
❑ 91ScoAme-155
❑ 91ScoCan-155
❑ 91StaClu-188
❑ 91SweSemE-340
❑ 91SweSemWCS-207
❑ 91Top-126
❑ 91UppDec-316
❑ 91UppDecF-316
❑ 92Bow-275
❑ 92CapKod-13
❑ 92OPC-223
❑ 92Par-201
❑ 92Pin-30
❑ 92PinFre-30
❑ 92ProSet-203
❑ 92Sco-209
❑ 92ScoCan-209
❑ 92StaClu-341
❑ 92SweSemE-341
❑ 92Top-498
❑ 92TopGol-498G
❑ 92Ult-234
❑ 92UppDec-139
❑ 93Don-372
❑ 93Lea-153
❑ 93OPCPre-278
❑ 93OPCPreG-278
❑ 93PanSti-31
❑ 93Pin-107
❑ 93PinCan-107
❑ 93Pow-465
❑ 93Sco-76
❑ 93ScoCan-76
❑ 93StaClu-451
❑ 93StaCluFDI-451
❑ 93StaCluO-451
❑ 93SweSemWCS-25
❑ 93TopPre-278
❑ 93TopPreG-278
❑ 94Don-243
❑ 94Lea-242
❑ 94OPCPre-59
❑ 94OPCPreSE-59
❑ 94ParSE-SE197
❑ 94ParSEG-SE197
❑ 94Pin-305
❑ 94PinArtP-305
❑ 94PinRinC-305
❑ 94TopPre-59
❑ 94TopPreSE-59
❑ 94Ult-235
❑ 95BeAPla-54
❑ 95BeAPSig-S54
❑ 95BeAPSigDC-S54
❑ 95CanGamNHLP-285
❑ 95Cap-10
❑ 95ColCho-130
❑ 95ColChoPC-130
❑ 95ColChoPCP-130
❑ 95Don-309
❑ 95Emo-189
❑ 95ImpSti-132
❑ 95Lea-298
❑ 95ParInt-218
❑ 95ParIntEI-218
❑ 95SkyImp-178
❑ 95SweGloWC-8
❑ 95Top-274
❑ 95TopOPCI-274
❑ 95Ult-176
❑ 95UltGolM-176
❑ 96MetUni-165
❑ 96Pin-85
❑ 96PinArtP-85
❑ 96PinFoi-85
❑ 96PinPreS-85
❑ 96PinRinC-85
❑ 96SweSemW-42
❑ 96TopNHLP-161
❑ 96TopPicOI-161
❑ 97PacInvNRB-208
❑ 97PacOme-240
❑ 97PacOmeC-240
❑ 97PacOmeDG-240
❑ 97PacOmeEG-240
❑ 97PacOmeG-240
❑ 97PacOmeIB-240
❑ 97SPAut-167
❑ 97UppDec-383
❑ 98Be A PPA-297
❑ 98Be A PPAA-297
❑ 98Be A PPAAF-297
❑ 98Be A PPSE-297
❑ 98Be APG-297
❑ 98Pac-6
❑ 98PacAur-196
❑ 98PacDynI-195
❑ 98PacDynIIB-195
❑ 98PacDynIR-195
❑ 98PacIceB-6
❑ 98PacPar-245
❑ 98PacParC-245
❑ 98PacParEG-245
❑ 98PacParH-245
❑ 98PacParIB-245
❑ 98PacParS-245
❑ 98PacRed-6
❑ 98UC-219
❑ 98UD ChoPCR-219
❑ 98UD ChoR-219
❑ 98UppDec-382
❑ 98UppDecE-382
❑ 98UppDecE1o1-382
❑ 98UppDecGR-382
❑ 99Pac-441
❑ 99PacCop-441
❑ 99PacGol-441
❑ 99PacIceB-441
❑ 99PacPreD-441
**Johansson, Christer**
❑ 69SweHocS-207
❑ 72SweHocS-205
❑ 74SweHocS-226
**Johansson, Daniel**
❑ 92SweSemE-252
❑ 92UppDec-599
❑ 93SweSemE-220
❑ 94SweLeaE-104
❑ 95SweGloWC-56
❑ 95SweLeaE-230
❑ 95SweUppDE-80
**Johansson, Frederik**
❑ 90SweSemE-146
❑ 94ParSE-SE241
❑ 94ParSEG-SE241
❑ 95SweUppDE-130
**Johansson, Glenn**
❑ 83SweSemE-208
❑ 84SweSemE-233
❑ 85SwePanS-230
❑ 86SwePanS-260
❑ 87SwePanS-242
**Johansson, Goran**
❑ 67SweHoc-142
❑ 69SweHocS-154
**Johansson, Gunnar**
❑ 72SweHocS-44
❑ 73SweHocS-187
❑ 73SweWorCS-187
❑ 74SweHocS-227
**Johansson, Hans**
❑ 83SweSemE-59
❑ 84SweSemE-59
**Johansson, Ingemar**
❑ 64SweCorI-32
❑ 65SweCorI-32
**Johansson, Jakob**
❑ 98SPXTopP-84
❑ 98SPXTopPF-84
❑ 98SPXTopPR-84
❑ 98UppDecBD-114
❑ 98UppDecDD-114
❑ 98UppDecQD-114
❑ 98UppDecTD-114
**Johansson, Jan**
❑ 67SweHoc-201
❑ 69SweHocS-260
❑ 70SweHocS-150
❑ 71SweHocS-243
❑ 71SweHocS-397
❑ 89SweSemE-211
**Johansson, Jens**
❑ 83SweSemE-174
❑ 84SweSemE-199
❑ 86SwePanS-202
❑ 87SwePanS-194
**Johansson, Kari**
❑ 69SweHocS-368
**Johansson, Kenneth**
❑ 85SwePanS-177
❑ 86SwePanS-112
❑ 87SwePanS-110
❑ 89SweSemE-97
❑ 90SweSemE-101
❑ 92SweSemE-249
❑ 93SweSemE-218
❑ 94SweLeaE-161
❑ 95SweLeaE-224
**Johansson, Kent**
❑ 89SweSemE-66
**Johansson, Kjell**
❑ 67SweHoc-48
❑ 73SweHocS-159
❑ 73SweWorCS-159
❑ 85SwePanS-158
**Johansson, Kjell-Ake**
❑ 84SweSemE-174
❑ 86SwePanS-171
**Johansson, Lars-Erik**
❑ 71SweHocS-313
❑ 73SweHocS-151
❑ 73SweWorCS-151
❑ 74SweHocS-228
**Johansson, Lars-Goran**
❑ 67SweHoc-240
❑ 69SweHocS-283
❑ 71SweHocS-276
**Johansson, Leif**
❑ 89SweSemE-213
**Johansson, Lennart**
❑ 64SweCorI-20
❑ 64SweCorI-85
❑ 65SweCorI-20
❑ 65SweCorI-85
❑ 67SweHoc-47
❑ 69SweHocS-62
❑ 70SweHocS-27
❑ 71SweHocS-104
❑ 71SweHocS-344
**Johansson, Martin**
❑ 72SweHocS-199
❑ 74SweHocS-171
**Johansson, Mattias**
❑ 91SweSemE-102
❑ 91SweSemE-330
❑ 92SweSemE-117
❑ 93Par-537
❑ 93ParEmel-537
❑ 93SweSemE-88
❑ 94SweLeaE-234
❑ 95SweLeaE-44
❑ 95SweLeaEG-5
❑ 95SweUppDE-69
**Johansson, Mikael**
❑ 83SweSemE-218
❑ 85SwePanS-86
❑ 86SwePanS-78
❑ 87SwePanS-82
❑ 89SweSemE-61
❑ 89SweSemWCS-22
❑ 90SweSemE-293
❑ 91SweSemE-65
❑ 91SweSemE-350
❑ 91SweSemWCS-43
❑ 93SweSemWCS-31
❑ 93SwiHNL-24
❑ 94SweLeaE-255
❑ 95FinnSemWC-68
❑ 95SweGloWC-30
❑ 95SweLeaE-119
❑ 95SwiHNL-1
❑ 95SwiHNL-527
❑ 95SwiHNL-539
❑ 96SweSemW-65
**Johansson, Nicke (Nils)**
❑ 64SweCorI-10
❑ 64SweCorI-152
❑ 65SweCorI-10
❑ 65SweCorI-152
❑ 67SweHoc-12
❑ 67SweHoc-120
❑ 69SweHocS-134
❑ 69SweHocS-188
❑ 69SweWorC-56
❑ 69SweWorC-60
❑ 69SweWorC-102
❑ 70SweHocS-278
❑ 71SweHocS-139
❑ 72SweHocS-123
❑ 73SweHocS-173
❑ 73SweWorCS-173
❑ 81SweSemHVS-113
**Johansson, Olof**
❑ 83SweSemE-212
**Johansson, Per-Johan**
❑ 72SweHocS-206
❑ 93SweSemE-41
❑ 94SweLeaE-251
❑ 95SweLeaE-174
**Johansson, Peter**
❑ 89SweSemE-24
❑ 90SweSemE-94
**Johansson, Roger**
❑ 86SwePanS-95
❑ 87SwePanS-105
❑ 90FlamIGA-8
❑ 90OPC-96
❑ 90ProSet-424
❑ 90ScoRoo-91T
❑ 90Top-96
❑ 90TopTif-96
❑ 91Bow-257
❑ 91FlamPanTS-6
❑ 91FlamPanTS-G
❑ 91OPC-53
❑ 91StaClu-375
❑ 91SweSemE-139
❑ 91Top-53
❑ 92FlamIGA-19
❑ 92Par-263
❑ 92ParEmel-263
❑ 92Ult-268
❑ 93OPCPre-253
❑ 93OPCPreG-253
❑ 93StaClu-133
❑ 93StaCluFDI-133
❑ 93StaCluFDIO-133
❑ 93StaCluO-133
❑ 93SweSemE-131
❑ 93SweSemWCS-29
❑ 93TopPre-253
❑ 93TopPreG-253
❑ 94FinnJaaK-62
❑ 94SweLeaE-259
❑ 94SweLeaEGC-21
❑ 94SweLeaEGS-6
❑ 95FinnSemWC-58
❑ 95SweGloWC-22
❑ 95SweLeaE-218
❑ 95SweLeaEC-9
❑ 95SweLeaEFF-5
❑ 95SweUppDE-62
❑ 96SweSemCDT-6
❑ 96SweSemW-54
**Johansson, Soren**
❑ 73SweHocS-225
❑ 73SweWorCS-225
❑ 74SweHocS-230
❑ 83SweSemE-225
**Johansson, Sten**
❑ 71SweHocS-151
**Johansson, Stig-Goran**
❑ 64SweCorI-74
❑ 65SweCorI-74
❑ 67SweHoc-13
❑ 67SweHoc-188
❑ 69SweHocS-189
❑ 69SweHocS-245
❑ 69SweWorC-37
❑ 69SweWorC-116
❑ 70SweHocS-142
❑ 70SweHocS-283
❑ 71SweHocS-15
❑ 71SweHocS-234
❑ 72SweHocS-13
❑ 72SweHocS-220
❑ 72SweHocS-221
❑ 72SweSemWC-47
❑ 73SweHocS-65
❑ 73SweWorCS-65
❑ 74SweHocS-229
❑ 74SweSemHVS-21
**Johansson, Sven Tumba**
❑ 64SweCorI-1
❑ 64SweCorI-125
❑ 65SweCorI-1
❑ 65SweCorI-125
❑ 81SweSemHVS-124
❑ 91SweSemWCS-233
❑ 95SweGloWC-68
**Johansson, Sven-Olov**
❑ 65SweCorI-149
**Johansson, Thomas**
❑ 90SweSemE-282
❑ 91SweSemE-64
❑ 92SweSemE-81
❑ 93SweSemE-55
❑ 94SweLeaE-121
❑ 95SweLeaE-30
❑ 95SweUppDE-40
**Johansson, Torbjorn**
❑ 95SweLeaE-243
❑ 95SweLeaER-5
❑ 95SweUppDE-96
**Johansson, Tord**
❑ 71SweHocS-205
❑ 72SweHocS-184
**Johansson, Ulf**
❑ 69SweHocS-169
**Johansson, Uno**
❑ 85SwePanS-193
**John, Bernie**
❑ 917thInnSOHL-249
❑ 91SudWol-6
❑ 92SudWol-8
**John, Peter**
❑ 96GerDELE-37
❑ 98GerDELE-180
**Johns, Don**
❑ 60ShiCoi-93
❑ 63Top-64
❑ 64BeeGro3P-136
❑ 64CocCap-76
❑ 65QueAce-10
❑ 94ParTalB-98
**Johnson, Al**
❑ 44BeeGro2P-181
❑ 61Par-22
❑ 61ShiCoi-72
**Johnson, Anders**
❑ 83SweSemE-96
❑ 85SwePanS-85
❑ 86SwePanS-79
❑ 87SwePanS-81
❑ 89SweSemE-69
❑ 90SweSemE-289
❑ 92SweSemE-42
❑ 94SweLeaE-283
**Johnson, Andy**
❑ 95Sla-323
**Johnson, Antony**
❑ 93HumHawP-12
❑ 94FinnJaaK-322
❑ 94HumHawP-12
**Johnson, Bill**
❑ 52St.LawS-60
**Johnson, Bob**
❑ 72BluWhiBor-8
❑ 74NHLActSta-230
❑ 74PenPos-9
❑ 81RedWinOld-1
❑ 85FlamRedRP-9
❑ 86FlamRedR-8
❑ 90PenFoo-7
❑ 90ProSet-674
**Johnson, Brent**
❑ 98UppDec-358
❑ 98UppDecE-358
❑ 98UppDecE1o1-358
❑ 98UppDecGR-358
❑ 99Pac-367
❑ 99PacCop-367
❑ 99PacGol-367
❑ 99PacIceB-367
❑ 99PacPreD-367
**Johnson, Brian**
❑ 85MinDul-18
**Johnson, Chad**
❑ 92NorDakFS-12
❑ 93ForWorF-8
**Johnson, Ching (Ivan)**
❑ 33OPCV304A-39
❑ 33V129-33
❑ 34BeeGro1P-279
❑ 34SweCap-42
❑ 35DiaMatT2-30
❑ 35DiaMatT3-27
❑ 35DiaMatTI-31
❑ 36TriPos-3
❑ 36V356WorG-21
❑ 83HalFP-D5
❑ 85HalFC-51
❑ 94ParTalBG-11
**Johnson, Clint**
❑ 95MinGolG-16
**Johnson, Cory**
❑ 917thInnSOHL-227
❑ 92NorDakFS-13
❑ 95MusFur-6
❑ 96GraRapG-11
**Johnson, Craig**
❑ 91MinGolG-10
❑ 92MinGolG-10
❑ 92OklCitB-9
❑ 92WinSpi-19
❑ 93Pow-507
❑ 93StaCluTUSA-11
❑ 93TopPreTUSA-19
❑ 93Ult-487
❑ 94BirBul-11
❑ 94ClaProPIA-IA14
❑ 94ClaProPIH-LP7
❑ 94Fla-155
❑ 94OPCPre-369
❑ 94OPCPreSE-369
❑ 94TopPre-369
❑ 94TopPreSE-369
❑ 94UppDec-253
❑ 94UppDecEleIce-253
❑ 95Lea-273
❑ 95Pin-208
❑ 95PinArtP-208
❑ 95PinRinC-208
❑ 95Sco-292
❑ 95ScoBlaIce-292
❑ 95ScoBlaIceAP-292
❑ 95SP-66B
❑ 95UppDec-139
❑ 95UppDecEleIce-139
❑ 95UppDecEleIceG-139
❑ 96ColCho-129
❑ 96UppDec-80
❑ 97Be A PPAD-100
❑ 97Be A PPAPD-100
❑ 97BeAPla-100
❑ 97BeAPlaAut-100
❑ 97PacDynBKS-46
❑ 98Pac-236
❑ 98PacIceB-236
❑ 98PacRed-236
❑ 99Pac-191
❑ 99PacCop-191
❑ 99PacGol-191
❑ 99PacIceB-191
❑ 99PacPreD-191
**Johnson, Danny (Dan)**
❑ 70CanuRoyB-8
❑ 70EssPowPla-44
❑ 70SarProSta-214
❑ 71OPC-95
❑ 71SarProSta-210
❑ 71TorSun-280
**Johnson, Dion**
❑ 91AirCanSJHL-A11
❑ 92MPSPhoSJHL-121
**Johnson, Gary**
❑ 83MedHatT-4
**Johnson, Greg**
❑ 90UppDec-460
❑ 90UppDecF-460
❑ 92NorDakFS-11
❑ 93ClaTeaCan-TC1
❑ 93Don-94
❑ 93Lea-370
❑ 93OPCPre-457
❑ 93OPCPreG-457
❑ 93Par-270
❑ 93ParEmel-270
❑ 93Pin-453
❑ 93PinCan-453
❑ 93Pow-330
❑ 93Sco-601
❑ 93ScoCan-601
❑ 93ScoGol-601
❑ 93StaClu-367
❑ 93StaCluFDI-367
❑ 93StaCluO-367
❑ 93TopPre-457
❑ 93TopPreG-457
❑ 93Ult-306
❑ 93UltWavF-7
❑ 93UppDec-452
❑ 94ClaProP-17
❑ 94Don-150
❑ 94Lea-355
❑ 94OPCPre-257
❑ 94OPCPreSE-257
❑ 94ParSE-SE48
❑ 94ParSEG-SE48
❑ 94Pin-511
❑ 94PinArtP-511
❑ 94PinRinC-511
❑ 94ScoTeaC-CT5
❑ 94TopPre-257
❑ 94TopPreSE-257
❑ 94Ult-283
❑ 94UppDec-212
❑ 94UppDecEleIce-212
❑ 95BeAPla-73
❑ 95BeAPSig-S73
❑ 95BeAPSigDC-S73
❑ 95ParInt-338
❑ 95ParIntEI-338
❑ 95Ult-233
❑ 95UppDec-308
❑ 95UppDec-334
❑ 95UppDecEleIce-334
❑ 95UppDecEleIceG-334
❑ 96ColCho-78
❑ 96Don-111
❑ 96DonPrePro-111
❑ 96FlePic-100
❑ 96Lea-33
❑ 96LeaPreP-33
❑ 96Pin-140
❑ 96PinArtP-140
❑ 96PinFoi-140
❑ 96PinPreS-140
❑ 96PinRinC-140
❑ 96Sco-132
❑ 96ScoArtPro-132
❑ 96ScoDeaCAP-132
❑ 96ScoGolB-132
❑ 96ScoSpeAP-132
❑ 96Sum-49
❑ 96SumArtP-49
❑ 96SumIce-49
❑ 96SumMet-49
❑ 96SumPreS-49
❑ 96UppDec-254
❑ 97ColCho-206
❑ 97ScoPen-11
❑ 97ScoPenPla-11
❑ 97ScoPenPre-11
❑ 97UppDec-134
❑ 98Be A PPA-225
❑ 98Be A PPAA-225
❑ 98Be A PPAAF-225
❑ 98Be A PPSE-225
❑ 98Be APG-225
❑ 98Pac-145
❑ 98PacCroR-75
❑ 98PacCroRLS-75
❑ 98PacIceB-145
❑ 98PacOmeH-129
❑ 98PacOmeODI-129
❑ 98PacOmeR-129
❑ 98PacRed-145
❑ 98UppDec-306
❑ 98UppDecE-306
❑ 98UppDecE1o1-306
❑ 98UppDecGR-306
❑ 98UppDecM-111
❑ 98UppDecMGS-111
❑ 98UppDecMSS-111
❑ 98UppDecMSS-111
❑ 99Pac-225
❑ 99PacCop-225
❑ 99PacGol-225
❑ 99PacIceB-225
❑ 99PacPreD-225
**Johnson, Jason**
❑ 93KitRan-23
**Johnson, Jeff**
❑ 90ProSet-249
**Johnson, Jim**
❑ 61SudWol-10
❑ 62SudWol-12
❑ 68OPC-186
❑ 69OPC-97
❑ 69Top-97
❑ 70EssPowPla-213
❑ 70SarProSta-153
❑ 71OPC-48
❑ 71SarProSta-148
❑ 71Top-48
❑ 71TorSun-199
❑ 72FigSaiPos-9
❑ 74FigSaiWHA-14
❑ 86OPC-231
❑ 86OPCSti-128
❑ 86PenKod-12
❑ 87OPC-196
❑ 87OPCSti-172
❑ 87PanSti-143
❑ 87PenKod-13
❑ 87PenMask-5
❑ 87Top-196
❑ 88OPC-148
❑ 88PanSti-334
❑ 88Top-148
❑ 89OPC-77
❑ 89PanSti-320
❑ 89PenFoo-2
❑ 89Top-77
❑ 90OPC-98
❑ 90ProSet-235
❑ 90Sco-202

❑ 90ScoCan-202
❑ 90Top-98
❑ 90TopTif-98
❑ 91OPC-426
❑ 91Par-303
❑ 91ParFre-303
❑ 91Pin-235
❑ 91PinFre-235
❑ 91ProSet-116
❑ 91ProSetFre-116
❑ 91ScoAme-52
❑ 91ScoCan-52
❑ 91Top-426
❑ 92Bow-177
❑ 92PanSti-94
❑ 92PanStiFre-94
❑ 92Pin-137
❑ 92PinFre-137
❑ 92ProSet-83
❑ 92Sco-161
❑ 92ScoCan-161
❑ 92StaClu-75
❑ 92Top-54
❑ 92TopGol-54G
❑ 92Ult-95
❑ 93OPCPre-98
❑ 93OPCPreG-98
❑ 93Pin-192
❑ 93PinCan-192
❑ 93Sco-144
❑ 93ScoCan-144
❑ 93StaClu-298
❑ 93StaCluFDI-298
❑ 93StaCluO-298
❑ 93TopPre-98
❑ 93TopPreG-98
❑ 94FinnJaaK-110
❑ 94Pin-440
❑ 94PinArtP-440
❑ 94PinRinC-440
❑ 94StaHoc-16
❑ 95Cap-11
❑ 97Be A PPAD-104
❑ 97Be A PPAPD-104
❑ 97BeAPla-104
❑ 97BeAPlaAut-104
❑ 97Pac-174
❑ 97PacCop-174
❑ 97PacEmeGre-174
❑ 97PacIceB-174
❑ 97PacRed-174
❑ 97PacSil-174
**Johnson, Joe**
❑ 97GuiFla-4
**Johnson, John**
❑ 897thInnSOHL-144
❑ 89NiaFalT-8
❑ 907thInnSOHL-261
❑ 91PetPet-26
❑ 92TolSto-13
❑ 93WheThu-11
**Johnson, Jonas**
❑ 91SweSemE-49
❑ 92SweSemE-71
❑ 93SweSemE-46
❑ 95SweLeaE-177
❑ 95SweUppDE-26
❑ 95SweUppDE-250
**Johnson, Karl**
❑ 91AirCanSJHL-E9
❑ 92MPSPhoSJHL-17
**Johnson, Kenny**
❑ 93HumHawP-1
❑ 99PacAur-90
❑ 99PacAurPD-90
**Johnson, Lance**
❑ 907thInnSMC-7
❑ 907thInnSWHL-288
❑ 917thInnSWHL-83
**Johnson, Mark**
❑ 79PanSti-213
❑ 80OPC-69
❑ 80Top-69
❑ 80USAOlyTMP-4
❑ 81SweSemHVS-100
❑ 82WhaJunHC-8
❑ 83OPC-140
❑ 83OPCSti-254
❑ 83PufSti-17
❑ 83WhaJunHC-8
❑ 84OPC-72
❑ 84OPCSti-193
❑ 84Top-56
❑ 84WhaJunW-9
❑ 85DevPos-6
❑ 85OPC-44
❑ 85OPCSti-50
❑ 85Top-44
❑ 86DevPol-12
❑ 86OPC-112
❑ 86OPCSti-200
❑ 86Top-112
❑ 87OPC-101
❑ 87OPCSti-64
❑ 87PanSti-83
❑ 87Top-101
❑ 88DevCar-13
❑ 88OPC-45
❑ 88Top-45
❑ 89DevCar-12
❑ 89OPC-244
❑ 89PanSti-260
❑ 89SweSemWCS-174
❑ 90OPC-178
❑ 90PanSti-66
❑ 90ProSet-168
❑ 90Top-178
❑ 90TopTif-178
❑ 90UppDec-180
❑ 90UppDecF-180
❑ 95MadMon-21
❑ 95SigRooMI-17
❑ 95SigRooMI-18
❑ 95SigRooSMIS-17
❑ 95SigRooSMIS-18
**Johnson, Matt**
❑ 93PetPet-22
❑ 94Cla-65
❑ 94ClaDraGol-65
❑ 94ClaTri-T31
❑ 94OPCPre-339
❑ 94OPCPreSE-339
❑ 94Pin-496
❑ 94PinArtP-496
❑ 94PinRinC-496
❑ 94TopPre-339
❑ 94TopPreSE-339
❑ 94UppDec-203
❑ 94UppDecEleIce-203
❑ 95Don-217
❑ 95Lea-64
❑ 96BeAPAut-215
❑ 96BeAPAutSil-215
❑ 96BeAPla-215
❑ 96ColEdgFL-28
❑ 97Pac-350
❑ 97PacCop-350
❑ 97PacEmeGre-350
❑ 97PacIceB-350
❑ 97PacRed-350
❑ 97PacSil-350
❑ 98UppDecM-100
❑ 98UppDecMGS-100
❑ 98UppDecMSS-100
❑ 98UppDecMSS-100
**Johnson, Mike (Michael)**
❑ 917thInnSOHL-300
❑ 92Ott672A-12
❑ 97Be A PPAD-218
❑ 97Be A PPAPD-218
❑ 97BeAPla-218
❑ 97BeAPlaAut-218
❑ 97BeAPlaPOT-18
❑ 97BeeAutA-54
❑ 97Kat-166
❑ 97KatGol-166
❑ 97KatSil-166
❑ 97Pac-335
❑ 97PacCop-335
❑ 97PacEmeGre-335
❑ 97PacIceB-335
❑ 97PacOme-221
❑ 97PacOmeC-221
❑ 97PacOmeDG-221
❑ 97PacOmeEG-221
❑ 97PacOmeG-221
❑ 97PacOmeIB-221
❑ 97PacRed-335
❑ 97PacSil-335
❑ 97PinBee-54
❑ 97PinBeeGP-54
❑ 97SPAut-194
❑ 97UppDecBD-118
❑ 97UppDecBDDD-118
❑ 97UppDecBDPC-PC27
❑ 97UppDecBDPCDD-PC27
❑ 97UppDecBDPCM-PC27
❑ 97UppDecBDPCQD-PC27
❑ 97UppDecBDPCTD-PC27
❑ 97UppDecBDQD-118
❑ 97UppDecBDTD-118
❑ 97UppDecIce-48
❑ 97UppDecIceP-48
❑ 97UppDecIPS-48
❑ 97Zen-82
❑ 97ZenGolImp-71
❑ 97ZenRooR-12
❑ 97ZenSilImp-71
❑ 97ZenZGol-82
❑ 97ZenZSil-82
❑ 97ZenZT-12
❑ 97ZenZTG-12
❑ 98Be A PPA-137
❑ 98Be A PPAA-137
❑ 98Be A PPAAF-137
❑ 98Be A PPTBASG-137
❑ 98Be APG-137
❑ 98BowBes-71
❑ 98BowBesAR-71
❑ 98BowBesP-BP1
❑ 98BowBesPAR-BP1
❑ 98BowBesPR-BP1
❑ 98BowBesR-71
❑ 98Fin-37
❑ 98FinCen-C16
❑ 98FinCenR-C16
❑ 98FinNo P-37
❑ 98FinNo PR-37
❑ 98FinRef-37
❑ 98GerDELE-194
❑ 98O-PChr-42
❑ 98O-PChrR-42
❑ 98O-PChrSB-SB7
❑ 98O-PChrSBR-SB7
❑ 98Pac-413
❑ 98PacAur-181
❑ 98PacCroR-130
❑ 98PacCroRLS-130
❑ 98PacDynI-179
❑ 98PacDynIIB-179
❑ 98PacDynIR-179
❑ 98PacIceB-413
❑ 98PacOmeH-227
❑ 98PacOmeODI-227
❑ 98PacOmeR-227
❑ 98PacPar-226
❑ 98PacParC-226
❑ 98PacParEG-226
❑ 98PacParH-226
❑ 98PacParIB-226
❑ 98PacParS-226
❑ 98PacRed-413
❑ 98PacRev-137
❑ 98PacRevIS-137
❑ 98PacRevR-137
❑ 98SP Aut-81
❑ 98SPxFin-81
❑ 98SPxFin-122
❑ 98SPxFinR-81
❑ 98SPxFinR-122
❑ 98SPxFinS-81
❑ 98SPxFinS-122
❑ 98Top-42
❑ 98TopGolLC1-66
❑ 98TopGolLC1B-66
❑ 98TopGolLC1BOoO-66
❑ 98TopGolLC1OoO-66
❑ 98TopGolLC1R-66
❑ 98TopGolLC1ROoO-66
❑ 98TopGolLC2-66
❑ 98TopGolLC2B-66
❑ 98TopGolLC2BOoO-66
❑ 98TopGolLC2OoO-66
❑ 98TopGolLC2R-66
❑ 98TopGolLC2ROoO-66
❑ 98TopGolLC3-66
❑ 98TopGolLC3B-66
❑ 98TopGolLC3BOoO-66
❑ 98TopGolLC3OoO-66
❑ 98TopGolLC3R-66
❑ 98TopGolLC3ROoO-66
❑ 98TopIceA2-I14
❑ 98TopO-P-42
❑ 98TopSeaB-SB7
❑ 98UC-199
❑ 98UCSB-SQ27
❑ 98UCSG-SQ27
❑ 98UCSG-SQ27
❑ 98UCSR-SQ27
❑ 98UD ChoPCR-199
❑ 98UD ChoR-199
❑ 98UD3-23
❑ 98UD3-83
❑ 98UD3-143
❑ 98UD3DieC-23
❑ 98UD3DieC-83
❑ 98UD3DieC-143
❑ 98UppDec-187
❑ 98UppDecE-187
❑ 98UppDecE1o1-187
❑ 98UppDecFF-FF27
❑ 98UppDecFF-FF27
❑ 98UppDecFFQ1-FF27
❑ 98UppDecFFQ2-FF27
❑ 98UppDecFIT-FT18
❑ 98UppDecFITQ1-FT18
❑ 98UppDecFITQ2-FT18
❑ 98UppDecFITQ3-FT18
❑ 98UppDecGR-187
❑ 98UppDecM-199
❑ 98UppDecMGS-199
❑ 98UppDecMP-MJ
❑ 98UppDecMSS-199
❑ 98UppDecMSS-199
❑ 99Pac-406
❑ 99PacAur-135
❑ 99PacAurPD-135
❑ 99PacCop-406
❑ 99PacGol-406
❑ 99PacIceB-406
❑ 99PacPreD-406
❑ 99SP AutPS-81
❑ 99UppDecM-202
❑ 99UppDecMGS-202
❑ 99UppDecMSS-202
❑ 99UppDecMSS-202
**Johnson, Moose (Ernest)**
❑ 10C55SweCP-28
❑ 10C56-30
❑ 11C55-28
❑ 12C57-25
❑ 60Top-4
❑ 60TopSta-30
❑ 83HalFP-A10
❑ 85HalFC-10
**Johnson, Norm**
❑ 57BruTealss-10
❑ 58Top-17
**Johnson, Perry**
❑ 96RegPat-6
❑ 98BowCHL-44
❑ 98BowCHLGA-44
❑ 98BowCHLOI-44
❑ 98BowChrC-44
❑ 98BowChrCGA-44
❑ 98BowChrCGAR-44
❑ 98BowChrCOI-44
❑ 98BowChrCOIR-44
❑ 98BowChrCR-44
**Johnson, Peter**
❑ 93HumHawP-NNO
❑ 94HumHawP-NNO
**Johnson, Red**
❑ 51LavDaiS-110
**Johnson, Ryan**
❑ 98UD3-2
❑ 98UD3-62
❑ 98UD3-122
❑ 98UD3DieC-2
❑ 98UD3DieC-62
❑ 98UD3DieC-122
❑ 98UppDec-15
❑ 98UppDec-283
❑ 98UppDecE-15
❑ 98UppDecE-283
❑ 98UppDecE1o1-15
❑ 98UppDecE1o1-283
❑ 98UppDecGR-15
❑ 98UppDecGR-283
**Johnson, Scott**
❑ 91HamRoaA-6
**Johnson, Shane**
❑ 917thInnSOHL-342
❑ 91AirCanSJHL-E4
❑ 92BriColJHL-69
**Johnson, Shaun**
❑ 93HumHawP-8
❑ 94HumHawP-8
**Johnson, Stephon**
❑ 93HumHawP-10
❑ 94HumHawP-10
**Johnson, Terry**
❑ 81FreExp-14
❑ 82FreExp-14
❑ 84OPC-186
❑ 86MapLeaP-14
**Johnson, Todd**
❑ 907thInnSWHL-148
❑ 917thInnSWHL-79
**Johnson, Tom**
❑ 44BeeGro2P-35
❑ 44BeeGro2P-252
❑ 45QuaOatP-84
❑ 48ExhCan-10
❑ 51Par-7
❑ 52Par-9
❑ 54Par-10
❑ 55Par-49
❑ 55Par-71
❑ 55ParQuaO-49
❑ 57Par-M6
❑ 58Par-7
❑ 58Par-10
❑ 59Par-10
❑ 60Par-44
❑ 60ShiCoi-25
❑ 60YorPreP-18
❑ 61Par-42
❑ 61ShiCoi-106
❑ 61YorYelB-11
❑ 62Par-50
❑ 62ShiMetC-36
❑ 63Top-4
❑ 64BeeGro3P-13
❑ 64CocCap-7
❑ 64Top-101
❑ 64TorSta-22
❑ 70BruPos-21
❑ 83HalFP-D6
❑ 85HalFC-52
❑ 93ParParR-PR55
❑ 94GueSto-15
❑ 94ParMisL-79
❑ 94ParMisL-143
❑ 94ParTalB-12
**Johnson, Troy**
❑ 92NorMicW-13
**Johnsson, Anders**
❑ 84SweSemE-84
**Johnsson, Jonas**
❑ 94SweLeaE-13
❑ 96GerDELE-150
**Johnsson, Kim**
❑ 95SweLeaE-266
❑ 95SweUppDE-134
**Johnsson, Kjell**
❑ 69SweHocS-61
❑ 70SweHocS-22
❑ 71SweHocS-98
❑ 72SweHocS-83
**Johnsson, Pierre**
❑ 93SweSemE-222
❑ 94SweLeaE-128
❑ 95SweLeaE-117
❑ 95SweUppDE-172
**Johnston, B.J.**
❑ 92OshGenS-14
❑ 93OshGen-19
❑ 94SarSti-18
❑ 95Sla-264
**Johnston, Bernhard**
❑ 94GerDELE-247
❑ 95GerDELE-241
**Johnston, Brent**
❑ 95Sla-281
**Johnston, Chris**
❑ 917thInnSWHL-201
❑ 92BraWheK-12
❑ 95DayBom-29
**Johnston, Eddie (Ed)**
❑ 44BeeGro2P-36
❑ 63Top-2
❑ 64BeeGro3P-12
❑ 64CocCap-1
❑ 64Top-21
❑ 65Top-97
❑ 66Top-99
❑ 66TopUSAT-64
❑ 67Top-96
❑ 68OPC-133
❑ 69OPC-200
❑ 70BruPos-2
❑ 70BruTealss-5
❑ 70DadCoo-64
❑ 70EssPowPla-55
❑ 70OPC-133
❑ 70SarProSta-5
❑ 71BruTealss-1
❑ 71LetActR-17
❑ 71OPC-172
❑ 71SarProSta-15
❑ 71Top-4
❑ 71TorSun-11
❑ 72OPC-261
❑ 72SarProSta-20
❑ 72Top-13
❑ 73MacMil-10
❑ 73MapLeaP-11
❑ 73OPC-23
❑ 73Top-23
❑ 74NHLActSta-246
❑ 74OPCNHL-265
❑ 75OPCNHL-185
❑ 75Top-185
❑ 76OPCNHL-285
❑ 77OPCNHL-276
❑ 83PenTeaIP-18
❑ 91FutTreC72-93
❑ 93Kra-36
❑ 93PenFoo-19
❑ 94ParTalB-15
❑ 94ParTalB-167
❑ 94ParTalB-168
❑ 94PenFoo-11
❑ 95Par66-18
❑ 95Par66Coi-18
❑ 95PenFoo-22
**Johnston, Glen**
❑ 87SauSteMG-35
**Johnston, Greg**
❑ 85MonGolF-19
❑ 87OPC-102
❑ 87Top-102
❑ 88BruPos-6
❑ 90NewSai-10
❑ 90ProAHLIHL-160
❑ 91ProAHLCHL-353
❑ 92Top-413
❑ 92TopGol-413G
❑ 94GerDELE-155
❑ 95GerDELE-156
❑ 96GerDELE-229
❑ 98GerDELE-43
**Johnston, Jay**
❑ 907thInnSOHL-225
**Johnston, Joey**
❑ 71OPC-182
❑ 71SarProSta-143
❑ 71TorSun-50
❑ 72OPC-96
❑ 72SarProSta-45
❑ 72Top-48
❑ 73OPC-172
❑ 73Top-143
❑ 74NHLActSta-57
❑ 74OPCNHL-56
❑ 74OPCNHL-185
❑ 74Top-56
❑ 74Top-185
❑ 75OPCNHL-193
❑ 75Top-193
❑ 76OPCNHL-325
**Johnston, Karl**
❑ 91ProAHLCHL-95
**Johnston, Kurt**
❑ 95Sla-125
**Johnston, Larry**
❑ 71SarProSta-65A
❑ 72SarProSta-82
❑ 73OPC-251
❑ 73RedWinMP-11
❑ 73RedWinTI-12
❑ 75OPCNHL-394
❑ 81RedWinOld-5
**Johnston, Marshall**
❑ 71SarProSta-141
❑ 71TorSun-51
❑ 72OPC-171
❑ 72SarProSta-44
❑ 73OPC-21
❑ 73Top-21
❑ 74OPCNHL-189
❑ 74Top-189
❑ 81RocPos-7
**Johnston, Marty**
❑ 98BowCHL-86
❑ 98BowCHLGA-86
❑ 98BowCHLOI-86
❑ 98BowChrC-86
❑ 98BowChrCGA-86
❑ 98BowChrCGAR-86
❑ 98BowChrCOI-86
❑ 98BowChrCOIR-86
❑ 98BowChrCR-86
**Johnston, Neil**
❑ 94PriAlbR-11
**Johnston, Randy**
❑ 81IndChe-11
❑ 82IndChe-12
**Johnston, Ryan**
❑ 96SasBla-12
**Johnston, Tyler**
❑ 92BriColJHL-15
**Johnston, Wingy (George)**
❑ 34BeeGro1P-58
**Johnstone, Chris**
❑ 93NiaFalT-27
❑ 95Sla-205
**Johnstone, Ed**
❑ 79OPC-179
❑ 79Top-179
❑ 80OPC-277
❑ 81OPC-226
❑ 81OPCSti-169
❑ 81Top-E99
❑ 82OPC-226
❑ 82OPCSti-139
❑ 82PosCer-13
❑ 83OPC-124
❑ 84OPC-55
❑ 84Top-43
❑ 89NewHavN-5
❑ 93JohChi-20
❑ 94JohChi-22
**Johnstone, Jeff**
❑ 93NiaFalT-10
❑ 95Cla-89
❑ 95Sla-193
**Jokela, Mikko**
❑ 98SPXTopP-72
❑ 98SPXTopPF-72
❑ 98SPXTopPR-72
❑ 98UppDecBD-99
❑ 98UppDecDD-99
❑ 98UppDecQD-99
❑ 98UppDecTD-99
**Jokiharju, Juha**
❑ 93FinnJyvHS-107
❑ 93FinnSIS-13
❑ 94FinnSIS-169
❑ 94FinnSIS-320
❑ 94FinnSIS-383
❑ 95SweLeaE-154
**Jokilahti, Jarmo**
❑ 93FinnJyvHS-140
❑ 93FinnSIS-140
**Jokinen, Jyrki**
❑ 93FinnJyvHS-143
❑ 93FinnSIS-157
❑ 94FinnSIS-130
**Jokinen, Olli**
❑ 97DonEli-72
❑ 97DonEliAsp-72
❑ 97DonEliS-72
❑ 97DonPre-147
❑ 97DonPre-196
❑ 97DonPreCttC-147
❑ 97DonPreCttC-196
❑ 97Lea-155
❑ 97LeaFraMat-155
❑ 97LeaFraMDC-155
❑ 97PacDyn-NNO
❑ 97PacDynC-NNO
❑ 97PacDynDG-NNO
❑ 97PacDynEG-NNO
❑ 97PacDynIB-NNO
❑ 97PacDynR-NNO
❑ 97PacDynSil-NNO
❑ 97PacPar-90
❑ 97PacParC-90
❑ 97PacParDG-90
❑ 97PacParEG-90
❑ 97PacParIB-90
❑ 97PacParRed-90
❑ 97PacParSil-90
❑ 97Pin-4
❑ 97PinArtP-4
❑ 97PinCerRR-F
❑ 97PinCerRRG-F
❑ 97PinCerRRMG-F
❑ 97PinPrePBB-4
❑ 97PinPrePBC-4
❑ 97PinPrePBM-4
❑ 97PinPrePBY-4
❑ 97PinPrePFC-4
❑ 97PinPrePFM-4
❑ 97PinPrePFY-4
❑ 97PinPrePla-4
❑ 97PinRinC-4
❑ 97Sco-65
❑ 97ScoArtPro-65
❑ 97ScoGolBla-65
❑ 97UppDec-288
❑ 97UppDecIce-58
❑ 97UppDecIceP-58
❑ 97UppDecILL-L9A
❑ 97UppDecILL2-L9A
❑ 97UppDecIPS-58
❑ 98BowBes-101
❑ 98BowBesAR-101
❑ 98BowBesMIF-F6
❑ 98BowBesMIFAR-F6
❑ 98BowBesMIFR-F6
❑ 98BowBesR-101
❑ 98FinFutF-F18
❑ 98FinFutFR-F18
❑ 98PacOmeH-117
❑ 98PacOmeODI-117
❑ 98PacOmeR-117
❑ 98PacRev-67
❑ 98PacRevIS-67
❑ 98PacRevR-67
❑ 98SP Aut-100
❑ 98SPxFin-139
❑ 98SPxFinR-139
❑ 98SPxFinS-139
❑ 98TopGolLC1-43
❑ 98TopGolLC1B-43
❑ 98TopGolLC1BOoO-43
❑ 98TopGolLC1OoO-43
❑ 98TopGolLC1R-43
❑ 98TopGolLC1ROoO-43
❑ 98TopGolLC2-43
❑ 98TopGolLC2B-43
❑ 98TopGolLC2BOoO-43
❑ 98TopGolLC2OoO-43
❑ 98TopGolLC2R-43
❑ 98TopGolLC2ROoO-43
❑ 98TopGolLC3-43
❑ 98TopGolLC3B-43
❑ 98TopGolLC3BOoO-43
❑ 98TopGolLC3OoO-43
❑ 98TopGolLC3R-43
❑ 98TopGolLC3ROoO-43
❑ 98UC-275
❑ 98UD ChoPCR-275
❑ 98UD ChoR-275
❑ 98UD3-11
❑ 98UD3-71
❑ 98UD3-131
❑ 98UD3DieC-11
❑ 98UD3DieC-71
❑ 98UD3DieC-131
❑ 98UppDec-12
❑ 98UppDecBD-42
❑ 98UppDecDD-42
❑ 98UppDecE-12
❑ 98UppDecE1o1-12
❑ 98UppDecGN-GN25
❑ 98UppDecGNQ1-GN25
❑ 98UppDecGNQ2-GN25
❑ 98UppDecGNQ3-GN25
❑ 98UppDecGR-12
❑ 98UppDecM-95
❑ 98UppDecMGS-95
❑ 98UppDecMSS-95
❑ 98UppDecMSS-95
❑ 98UppDecQD-42
❑ 98UppDecTD-42
❑ 99Pac-192
❑ 99PacCop-192
❑ 99PacGol-192
❑ 99PacIceB-192
❑ 99PacPreD-192
❑ 99SP AutPS-100
❑ 99UppDecM-97
❑ 99UppDecMGS-97
❑ 99UppDecMSS-97
❑ 99UppDecMSS-97
❑ 99UppDecRG-G8C
❑ 99UppDecRGI-G8C
**Joliat, Aurel**
❑ 23V1451-14
❑ 24C144ChaCig-34
❑ 24V130MapC-14
❑ 24V1452-48
❑ 27LaPat-4
❑ 33OPCV304B-50
❑ 33V252CanG-34
❑ 33V288HamG-27
❑ 33V3572IceKP-3
❑ 33V357IceK-3
❑ 34BeeGro1P-161
❑ 34DiaMatS-33
❑ 34SweCap-5
❑ 35DiaMatT2-31
❑ 35DiaMatT3-28
❑ 35DiaMatTI-32
❑ 36ChaPos-8
❑ 36OPCV304D-129
❑ 36V356WorG-65
❑ 37OPCV304E-152
❑ 55Par-58
❑ 55ParQuaO-58
❑ 83HalFP-D7
❑ 85HalFC-53
❑ 93OPCCanHF-21
❑ 93OPCCanHF-59
**Joly, Greg**
❑ 74CapWhiB-12
❑ 74NHLActSta-321
❑ 74OPCNHL-294
❑ 75OPCNHL-170
❑ 75Top-170
❑ 76OPCNHL-52
❑ 76Top-52
❑ 77OPCNHL-273
❑ 78OPC-148
❑ 78Top-148
❑ 79OPC-311
❑ 79RedWinP-6
❑ 80OPC-270
❑ 82OPC-86
❑ 82PosCer-5
**Jomphe, Daniel**
❑ 84ChiSag-14
**Jomphe, Jean-Francois**
❑ 907thInnSQMJHL-108
❑ 94ClaProP-123
❑ 96ColCho-8
❑ 96Duc-19
❑ 96UppDec-3
❑ 97PacInvNRB-3
**Jonak, Jiri**
❑ 94CzeAPSE-144
❑ 96CzeAPSE-193
**Jonasson, Antero**
❑ 67SweHoc-222
**Jonathan, Stan**
❑ 77OPCNHL-270
❑ 78OPC-181
❑ 78Top-181
❑ 79OPC-263
❑ 79Top-263
❑ 80OPC-113

❑ 80Top-113
❑ 81OPC-13
❑ 82PosCer-1
❑ 83PenHeiP-14
**Jones, Bob**
❑ 87SauSteMG-5
❑ 89SauSteMG-18
❑ 90ProAHLIHL-301
❑ 91ProAHLCHL-251
❑ 93MusFur-3
**Jones, Brad**
❑ 87SauSteMG-7
❑ 89ProAHL-42
❑ 90KinSmo-21
❑ 91Bow-181
❑ 91FlyJCP-14
❑ 91OPC-478
❑ 91OPCPre-115
❑ 91Par-127
❑ 91ParFre-127
❑ 91ProSet-456
❑ 91ProSetFre-456
❑ 91ScoCan-603
❑ 91ScoRoo-53T
❑ 91StaClu-368
❑ 91Top-478
❑ 91UppDec-304
❑ 91UppDecF-304
❑ 92StaClu-141
❑ 92Top-299
❑ 92TopGol-299G
❑ 95BinRan-9
❑ 96GerDELE-67
**Jones, Casey**
❑ 897thInnSOHL-174
**Jones, Chris**
❑ 91BriColJHL-62
❑ 92BriColJHL-105
**Jones, Corey**
❑ 89VicCou-12
❑ 907thInnSWHL-103
❑ 917thInnSWHL-26
**Jones, Daryl**
❑ 92MPSPhoSJHL-153
**Jones, Doug**
❑ 85KitRan-24
❑ 86KitRan-23
❑ 87KitRan-22
❑ 94FliGen-13
**Jones, Harald**
❑ 72SweSemWC-159
**Jones, Jim (Jimmy)**
❑ 10C56-19
❑ 77MapLeaP-8
❑ 78MapLeaP-11
❑ 78OPC-288
❑ 79MapLeaP-15
❑ 79OPC-288
**Jones, Keith**
❑ 92CapKod-14
❑ 92Cla-96
❑ 92OPCPre-14
❑ 92Par-427
❑ 92ParEmel-427
❑ 92Ult-436
❑ 92UppDec-533
❑ 93ClaProPro-43
❑ 93OPCPre-96
❑ 93OPCPreG-96
❑ 93Par-495
❑ 93ParEmel-495
❑ 93Pow-466
❑ 93Sco-417
❑ 93ScoCan-417
❑ 93StaClu-234
❑ 93StaCluFDI-234
❑ 93StaCluFDIO-234
❑ 93StaCluO-234
❑ 93TopPre-96
❑ 93TopPreG-96
❑ 93Ult-446
❑ 93UppDec-377
❑ 94BeAPSig-131
❑ 94Lea-506
❑ 94Pin-378
❑ 94PinArtP-378
❑ 94PinRinC-378
❑ 94UppDec-411
❑ 94UppDecElelce-411
❑ 95CanGamNHLP-282
❑ 95Cap-12
❑ 95ColCho-166
❑ 95ColChoPC-166
❑ 95ColChoPCP-166
❑ 95Don-282
❑ 95Lea-105
❑ 95Met-160
❑ 95ParInt-217
❑ 95ParIntEl-217
❑ 95Pin-27
❑ 95PinArtP-27
❑ 95PinRinC-27
❑ 95PlaOneoOne-323
❑ 95Sco-95
❑ 95ScoBlaIce-95
❑ 95ScoBlaIceAP-95
❑ 95StaClu-88
❑ 95StaCluMOMS-88
❑ 95Top-73
❑ 95TopOPCI-73
❑ 95UppDec-451
❑ 95UppDecElelce-451
❑ 95UppDecElelceG-451
❑ 95UppDecSpeE-SE85
❑ 95UppDecSpeEdiG-SE85
❑ 96BeAPAut-194
❑ 96BeAPAutSil-194
❑ 96BeAPla-194
❑ 96ClaGol-96
❑ 96ColCho-285
❑ 96Pin-93
❑ 96PinArtP-93
❑ 96PinFoi-93
❑ 96PinPreS-93
❑ 96PinRinC-93
❑ 96PlaOneoOne-423
❑ 96Sco-225
❑ 96ScoArtPro-225
❑ 96ScoDeaCAP-225
❑ 96ScoGolB-225
❑ 96ScoSpeAP-225
❑ 96UppDecBD-39
❑ 96UppDecBDG-39
❑ 97ColCho-59
❑ 97DonLim-18
❑ 97DonLimExp-18
❑ 97Pac-291
❑ 97PacCop-291
❑ 97PacEmeGre-291
❑ 97PacIceB-291
❑ 97PacRed-291
❑ 97PacSil-291
❑ 97Sco-250
❑ 97ScoAva-9
❑ 97ScoAvaPla-9
❑ 97ScoAvaPre-9
❑ 98PacOmeH-175
❑ 98PacOmeODI-175
❑ 98PacOmeR-175
❑ 98UppDecM-150
❑ 98UppDecMGS-150
❑ 98UppDecMSS-150
❑ 98UppDecMSS-150
❑ 99Pac-304
❑ 99PacCop-304
❑ 99PacGol-304
❑ 99PacIceB-304
❑ 99PacPreD-304
❑ 99UppDecM-151
❑ 99UppDecMGS-151
❑ 99UppDecMSS-151
❑ 99UppDecMSS-151
**Jones, Nick**
❑ 95RoaExp-19
**Jones, Ron**
❑ 75OPCNHL-247
❑ 75Top-247
❑ 89WinSpi-7
**Jones, Steve**
❑ 95Sla-329
**Jones, Todd**
❑ 92NorDakFS-14
**Jones, Ty**
❑ 95SpoChi-7
❑ 97BowCHL-142
❑ 97BowCHLAu-22
❑ 97BowCHLOPC-142
❑ 97UppDecBD-52
❑ 97UppDecBDDD-52
❑ 97UppDecBDQD-52
❑ 97UppDecBDTD-52
❑ 98PacDynI-43
❑ 98PacDynIIB-43
❑ 98PacDynIR-43
❑ 98UC-303
❑ 98UD ChoPCR-303
❑ 98UD ChoR-303
❑ 98UppDec-242
❑ 98UppDecE-242
❑ 98UppDecE1o1-242
❑ 98UppDecGN-GN14
❑ 98UppDecGNQ1-GN14
❑ 98UppDecGNQ2-GN14
❑ 98UppDecGNQ3-GN14
❑ 98UppDecGR-242
❑ 99Pac-99
❑ 99PacCop-99
❑ 99PacGol-99
❑ 99PacIceB-99
❑ 99PacPreD-99
❑ 99UppDecM-45
❑ 99UppDecMGS-45
❑ 99UppDecMSS-45
❑ 99UppDecMSS-45
**Jonsson, Hans**
❑ 83SweSemE-237
❑ 91SweSemE-210
❑ 92SweSemE-231
❑ 93SweSemE-201
❑ 94SweLeaE-44
❑ 95SweLeaE-102
❑ 95SweUppDE-156
**Jonsson, Jonas**
❑ 90SweSemE-121
❑ 91SweSemE-124
**Jonsson, Jorgen**
❑ 92SweSemE-272
❑ 93SweSemE-236
❑ 94SweLeaE-69
❑ 94SweLeaEGC-10
❑ 94SweLeaETG-5
❑ 95FinnSemWC-66
❑ 95SigRoo-46
❑ 95SigRooSig-46
❑ 95SweGloWC-38
❑ 95SweLeaE-215
❑ 95SweUppDE-72
❑ 95SweUppDETNA-NA9
**Jonsson, Kenny**
❑ 92SweSemE-253
❑ 92UppDec-596
❑ 93Cla-135
❑ 93Par-535
❑ 93ParEmel-535
❑ 93SweSemE-223
❑ 93SweSemE-304
❑ 94BeAPla-R154
❑ 94Cla-25
❑ 94ClaDraGol-25
❑ 94ClaROYS-R8
❑ 94ClaTri-T67
❑ 94Fin-5
❑ 94Fin-56
❑ 94FinBowB-R18
❑ 94FinBowBR-R18
❑ 94FinRef-5
❑ 94FinRef-56
❑ 94FinSupTW-5
❑ 94FinSupTW-56
❑ 94Fla-182
❑ 94Fle-216
❑ 94Lea-472
❑ 94LeaLim-115
❑ 94MapLeaK-17
❑ 94MapLeaPP-7
❑ 94OPCPre-329
❑ 94OPCPreSE-329
❑ 94ParSE-SE173
❑ 94ParSEG-SE173
❑ 94Pin-264
❑ 94Pin-476
❑ 94PinArtP-264
❑ 94PinArtP-476
❑ 94PinRinC-264
❑ 94PinRinC-476
❑ 94PinRooTP-4
❑ 94ScoTopRR-6
❑ 94Sel-172
❑ 94SelGol-172
❑ 94SelYouExp-YE4
❑ 94SPPre-7
❑ 94SPPreDC-7
❑ 94St.JohML-14
❑ 94SweLeaEGC-11
❑ 94TopPre-329
❑ 94TopPreSE-329
❑ 94Ult-377
❑ 94UppDec-238
❑ 94UppDec-530
❑ 94UppDec-560
❑ 94UppDecElelce-238
❑ 94UppDecElelce-530
❑ 94UppDecElelce-560
❑ 94UppDecPC-C11
❑ 94UppDecPCEG-C11
❑ 94UppDecPCES-C11
❑ 94UppDecSPI-SP168
❑ 94UppDecSPIDC-SP168
❑ 95BeAPla-180
❑ 95BeAPSig-S180
❑ 95BeAPSigDC-S180
❑ 95Bow-86
❑ 95BowAllFoi-86
❑ 95CanGamNHLP-31
❑ 95CanGamNHLP-267
❑ 95ColCho-137
❑ 95ColCho-373
❑ 95ColChoPC-137
❑ 95ColChoPC-373
❑ 95ColChoPCP-137
❑ 95ColChoPCP-373
❑ 95ColEdgIC-C4
❑ 95Don-115
❑ 95DonEli-4
❑ 95DonEliDCS-4
❑ 95DonEliDCU-4
❑ 95Emo-172
❑ 95Fin-29
❑ 95FinnSemWC-59
❑ 95FinRef-29
❑ 95Ima-59
❑ 95ImaAut-59A
❑ 95ImaGol-59
❑ 95Lea-24
❑ 95LeaLim-88
❑ 95McDPin-MCD-36
❑ 95Met-144
❑ 95ParInt-203
❑ 95ParIntEl-203
❑ 95Pin-130
❑ 95PinArtP-130
❑ 95PinRinC-130
❑ 95PlaOneoOne-203
❑ 95ProMag-78
❑ 95Sco-30
❑ 95ScoBlaIce-30
❑ 95ScoBlaIceAP-30
❑ 95SkyImp-162
❑ 95SkyImpNHLF-13
❑ 95SP-147
❑ 95StaClu-107
❑ 95StaCluMOMS-107
❑ 95SweGloWC-15
❑ 95SweUppDE-240
❑ 95Top-211
❑ 95TopNewG-9NG
❑ 95TopOPCI-211
❑ 95Ult-161
❑ 95UltGolM-161
❑ 95UppDec-463
❑ 95UppDecElelce-463
❑ 95UppDecElelceG-463
❑ 95UppDecSpeE-SE81
❑ 95UppDecSpeEdiG-SE81
❑ 96ColCho-159
❑ 96Don-74
❑ 96DonEli-117
❑ 96DonEliDCS-117
❑ 96DonPrePro-74
❑ 96Fle-65
❑ 96FlePic-92
❑ 96IslPos-8
❑ 96Lea-60
❑ 96LeaPre-28
❑ 96LeaPreP-60
❑ 96LeaPrePP-28
❑ 96MetUni-93
❑ 96NHLProSTA-78
❑ 96Pin-91
❑ 96PinArtP-91
❑ 96PinFoi-91
❑ 96PinPreS-91
❑ 96PinRinC-91
❑ 96Sco-168
❑ 96ScoArtPro-168
❑ 96ScoDeaCAP-168
❑ 96ScoGolB-168
❑ 96ScoSpeAP-168
❑ 96SkyImp-76
❑ 96SP-93
❑ 96SweSemW-53
❑ 96Ult-102
❑ 96UltGolM-103
❑ 96UppDec-101
❑ 96UppDecBD-73
❑ 96UppDecBDG-73
❑ 97ColCho-159
❑ 97EssOlyHH-46
❑ 97EssOlyHHF-46
❑ 97Kat-88
❑ 97KatGol-88
❑ 97KatSil-88
❑ 97PacInvNRB-116
❑ 97SPAut-95
❑ 97UppDec-312
❑ 97UppDecBD-10
❑ 97UppDecBDDD-10
❑ 97UppDecBDQD-10
❑ 97UppDecBDTD-10
❑ 98Be A PPA-87
❑ 98Be A PPAA-87
❑ 98Be A PPAF-87
❑ 98Be A PPTBASG-87
❑ 98Be APG-87
❑ 98Pac-282
❑ 98PacIceB-282
❑ 98PacOmeH-146
❑ 98PacOmeODI-146
❑ 98PacOmeR-146
❑ 98PacPar-143
❑ 98PacParC-143
❑ 98PacParEG-143
❑ 98PacParH-143
❑ 98PacParIB-143
❑ 98PacParS-143
❑ 98PacRed-282
❑ 98PacRev-87
❑ 98PacRevIS-87
❑ 98PacRevR-87
❑ 98TopGolLC1-27
❑ 98TopGolLC1B-27
❑ 98TopGolLC1BOoO-27
❑ 98TopGolLC1OoO-27
❑ 98TopGolLC1R-27
❑ 98TopGolLC1ROoO-27
❑ 98TopGolLC2-27
❑ 98TopGolLC2B-27
❑ 98TopGolLC2BOoO-27
❑ 98TopGolLC2OoO-27
❑ 98TopGolLC2R-27
❑ 98TopGolLC2ROoO-27
❑ 98TopGolLC3-27
❑ 98TopGolLC3B-27
❑ 98TopGolLC3BOoO-27
❑ 98TopGolLC3OoO-27
❑ 98TopGolLC3R-27
❑ 98TopGolLC3ROoO-27
❑ 98UC-125
❑ 98UD ChoPCR-125
❑ 98UD ChoR-125
❑ 98UDCP-125
❑ 98UppDec-318
❑ 98UppDecE-318
❑ 98UppDecE1o1-318
❑ 98UppDecGR-318
❑ 98UppDecM-130
❑ 98UppDecMGS-130
❑ 98UppDecMSS-130
❑ 98UppDecMSS-130
❑ 99Pac-255
❑ 99PacCop-255
❑ 99PacGol-255
❑ 99PacIceB-255
❑ 99PacPreD-255
❑ 99UppDecM-129
❑ 99UppDecMGS-129
❑ 99UppDecMSS-129
❑ 99UppDecMSS-129
**Jonsson, Kjell**
❑ 64SweCorI-82
❑ 64SweCorI-102
❑ 65SweCorI-82
❑ 65SweCorI-102
❑ 67SweHoc-289
❑ 69SweHocS-337
**Jonsson, Lennart**
❑ 83SweSemE-156
❑ 85SwePanS-207
**Jonsson, Ove**
❑ 67SweHoc-223
❑ 69SweHocS-261
**Jonsson, Pierre**
❑ 96GerDELE-94
**Jonsson, Stefan**
❑ 83SweSemE-204
❑ 84SweSemE-227
❑ 85SwePanS-228
❑ 86SwePanS-256
❑ 87SwePanS-240
❑ 89SweSemE-225
❑ 90SweSemE-54
❑ 91SweSemE-229
❑ 92SweSemE-185
❑ 93SweSemE-155
❑ 94SweLeaE-162
❑ 95SweLeaE-79
❑ 95SweUppDE-121
**Jonsson, Tomas**
❑ 81SweSemHVS-2
❑ 82OPC-202
❑ 82PosCer-12
❑ 83IslTeaIss-7
❑ 83OPC-9
❑ 83OPCSti-87
❑ 83SweSemE-181
❑ 84IslIslN-16
❑ 84OPC-128
❑ 85IslIslN-20
❑ 85OPC-154
❑ 85OPCSti-78
❑ 85Top-154
❑ 86OPC-78
❑ 86OPCSti-214
❑ 86Top-78
❑ 87OPC-190
❑ 87PanSti-92
❑ 87Top-190
❑ 88OilTeal-12
❑ 88OilTenAnn-149
❑ 88OPC-108
❑ 88Top-108
❑ 89SweSemE-124
❑ 89SweSemWCS-5
❑ 90SweSemE-202
❑ 91SweSemE-131
❑ 91SweSemE-342
❑ 91SweSemWCS-32
❑ 92SweSemE-153
❑ 93SweSemE-124
❑ 93SweSemWCS-5
❑ 94FinnJaaK-54
❑ 94SweLeaE-100
❑ 94SweLeaEGC-23
❑ 95SweGloWC-14
❑ 95SweLeaE-62
❑ 95SweLeaE-303
❑ 95SweLeaEC-1
❑ 95SweLeaEFF-15
❑ 95SweLeaEM-5
❑ 95SweUppDE-95
❑ 95SweUppDE-227
❑ 95SweUppDE-255
❑ 96SweSemCDT-3
❑ 96SweSemW-47
**Jooris, Mark**
❑ 95GerDELE-357
❑ 96GerDELE-217
**Jordan, Ric**
❑ 72WhaNewEWHA-9
**Jorde, Manfred**
❑ 94GerDELE-185
**Jorgenson, Ken**
❑ 82MedHatT-6
**Jorgenson, Kevin**
❑ 87PorWinH-13
❑ 88PorWinH-13
❑ 89PorWinH-13
**Jorgenson, Len**
❑ 88KamBla-14
**Jorgenson, Lynn**
❑ 78LouGea-12
**Jortikka, Hannu**
❑ 93SwiHNL-58
❑ 94SweLeaE-302
**Josefsson, Ola**
❑ 89SweSemE-71
❑ 90SweSemE-287
❑ 91SweSemE-68
❑ 92SweSemE-95
❑ 93SweSemE-67
❑ 94SweLeaE-74
❑ 95SweLeaE-187
❑ 95SweUppDE-49
**Joseph, Anthony**
❑ 90MonHaw-12
**Joseph, Chris**
❑ 88OilTeal-13
❑ 88OilTenAnn-2
❑ 88OPCSti-218
❑ 89OPCSti-225
❑ 89ProAHL-131
❑ 90OilIGA-9
❑ 90ProSet-443
❑ 90UppDec-323
❑ 90UppDecF-323
❑ 91Bow-108
❑ 91OilPanTS-8
❑ 91OilTeal-8
❑ 91OPC-432
❑ 91ScoCan-415
❑ 91StaClu-362
❑ 91Top-432
❑ 91UppDec-436
❑ 91UppDecF-436
❑ 92OilIGA-11
❑ 92OilTeal-8
❑ 92OPC-203
❑ 93Don-492
❑ 93LigSealR-19
❑ 93OPCPre-87
❑ 93OPCPreG-87
❑ 93Pow-445
❑ 93Sco-576
❑ 93ScoCan-576
❑ 93ScoGol-576
❑ 93TopPre-87
❑ 93TopPreG-87
❑ 94CanGamNHLP-228
❑ 94Don-253
❑ 94Lea-158
❑ 94OPCPre-374
❑ 94OPCPreSE-374
❑ 94ParSE-SE168
❑ 94ParSEG-SE168
❑ 94PenFoo-17
❑ 94Pin-156
❑ 94PinArtP-156
❑ 94PinRinC-156
❑ 94Sco-98
❑ 94ScoGol-98
❑ 94ScoPla-98
❑ 94ScoPlaTS-98
❑ 94StaClu-224
❑ 94StaCluFDI-224
❑ 94StaCluMOMS-224
❑ 94StaCluSTWC-224
❑ 94TopPre-374
❑ 94TopPreSE-374
❑ 94Ult-207
❑ 94UppDec-185
❑ 94UppDecElelce-185
❑ 95BeAPla-98
❑ 95BeAPSig-S98
❑ 95BeAPSigDC-S98
❑ 95Don-64
❑ 95ParInt-433
❑ 95ParIntEl-433
❑ 95PenFoo-19
❑ 95Top-93
❑ 95TopOPCI-93
❑ 95UppDec-449
❑ 95UppDecElelce-449
❑ 95UppDecElelceG-449
❑ 96CanuPos-32
❑ 97PacInvNRB-202
❑ 98CinCyc-9
**Joseph, Curtis**
❑ 89BluKod-31
❑ 89ProIHL-7
❑ 90BluKod-11
❑ 90OPC-171
❑ 90OPCPre-51
❑ 90PanSti-272
❑ 90ProSet-638
❑ 90Sco-151
❑ 90ScoCan-151
❑ 90ScoYouS-15
❑ 90Top-171
❑ 90TopTif-171
❑ 90UppDec-175
❑ 90UppDecF-175
❑ 91AirCanSJHL-A49
❑ 91BluPos-12
❑ 91OPC-417
❑ 91OPCPre-165
❑ 91PanSti-22
❑ 91Par-152
❑ 91ParFre-152
❑ 91Pin-105
❑ 91PinFre-105
❑ 91ProSet-473
❑ 91ProSetFre-473
❑ 91ProSetPla-225
❑ 91ScoAme-296
❑ 91ScoCan-516
❑ 91ScoYouS-19
❑ 91Top-417
❑ 91UppDec-139
❑ 91UppDecF-139
❑ 92BluUDBB-9
❑ 92Bow-368
❑ 92Kra-31
❑ 92OPC-339
❑ 92PanSti-15
❑ 92PanStiFre-15
❑ 92Par-155
❑ 92Par-503
❑ 92ParEmel-155
❑ 92ParEmel-503
❑ 92Pin-54
❑ 92Pin-264
❑ 92PinFre-54
❑ 92PinFre-264
❑ 92ProSet-164
❑ 92Sco-262
❑ 92ScoCan-262
❑ 92ScoYouS-17
❑ 92SeaPat-14
❑ 92StaClu-327
❑ 92Top-237
❑ 92TopGol-237G
❑ 92Ult-188
❑ 92UppDec-186
❑ 93Don-296
❑ 93Lea-2
❑ 93LeaPaiWar-2
❑ 93OPCPre-222
❑ 93OPCPre-272
❑ 93OPCPreG-222
❑ 93OPCPreG-272
❑ 93PanSti-166
❑ 93Par-175
❑ 93ParEmel-175
❑ 93Pin-15
❑ 93PinCan-15
❑ 93Pow-213
❑ 93PowGam-4
❑ 93PowNet-4
❑ 93Sco-116
❑ 93ScoCan-116
❑ 93StaClu-162
❑ 93StaCluFDI-162
❑ 93StaCluFDIO-162
❑ 93StaCluO-162
❑ 93TopPre-222
❑ 93TopPre-272
❑ 93TopPreBG-18
❑ 93TopPreG-222
❑ 93TopPreG-272
❑ 93Ult-172
❑ 93UppDec-157
❑ 93UppDecSP-139
❑ 94BeAPla-R71
❑ 94BeAPla-R101
❑ 94BeAPla-R174
❑ 94BeAPSig-109
❑ 94CanGamNHLP-293
❑ 94Don-287
❑ 94DonMasM-5
❑ 94EASpo-126
❑ 94Fin-29
❑ 94FinRef-29
❑ 94FinSupTW-29
❑ 94Fla-156
❑ 94Fle-188
❑ 94FleNet-5
❑ 94HocWit-35
❑ 94Kra-44
❑ 94KraGoaM-3
❑ 94Lea-208
❑ 94LeaCreP-3
❑ 94LeaGolS-7
❑ 94LeaLim-95
❑ 94OPCPre-340
❑ 94OPCPreSE-340
❑ 94Par-199
❑ 94ParGol-199
❑ 94ParVin-V17
❑ 94Pin-6
❑ 94Pin1HS-6
❑ 94PinArtP-6
❑ 94PinGoaG-GT13
❑ 94PinMas-MA10
❑ 94PinRinC-6
❑ 94PinTeaP-TP2
❑ 94PinTeaPDP-TP2
❑ 94Sco-181
❑ 94ScoGol-181
❑ 94ScoPla-181
❑ 94ScoPlaTS-181
❑ 94Sel-121
❑ 94SelGol-121
❑ 94SP-102
❑ 94SPDieCut-102
❑ 94StaClu-142
❑ 94StaCluFDI-142
❑ 94StaCluMO-22
❑ 94StaCluMOMS-142
❑ 94StaCluST-20
❑ 94StaCluSTWC-142
❑ 94TopPre-340
❑ 94TopPreSE-340
❑ 94Ult-184
❑ 94UltPrePM-3
❑ 94UppDec-91
❑ 94UppDecElelce-91
❑ 94UppDecPH-H33
❑ 94UppDecPHEG-H33
❑ 94UppDecPHES-H33
❑ 94UppDecPHG-H33
❑ 94UppDecSPI-SP68
❑ 94UppDecSPIDC-SP68
❑ 95ColCho-291
❑ 95ColChoPC-291
❑ 95ColChoPCP-291
❑ 95ColEdgILL-L6
❑ 95Don-135
❑ 95DonEli-59
❑ 95DonEliDCS-59
❑ 95DonEliDCU-59
❑ 95Emo-62
❑ 95Lea-281
❑ 95ParInt-350
❑ 95ParIntEl-350
❑ 95Sco-251
❑ 95ScoBlaIce-251
❑ 95ScoBlaIceAP-251
❑ 95SelCer-84
❑ 95SelCerMG-84
❑ 95SkyImp-60
❑ 95SP-54
❑ 95StaCluMO-29
❑ 95Top-215
❑ 95TopOPCI-215
❑ 95Ult-140
❑ 95UltGolM-140
❑ 95UltPrePadMen-6
❑ 95UltPrePadMenGM-6
❑ 95UppDec-296
❑ 96BeAPAut-206
❑ 96BeAPAutSil-206
❑ 96BeAPla-206
❑ 96BeAPStaTP-14
❑ 96ColCho-90
❑ 96ColCho-317

❑ 96ColEdgFL-29
❑ 96Don-110
❑ 96DonBetPip-8
❑ 96DonCanI-116
❑ 96DonCanIGPP-116
❑ 96DonCanIRPP-116
❑ 96DonEli-92
❑ 96DonEliDCS-92
❑ 96DonPrePro-110
❑ 96DurAllT-DC4
❑ 96Fla-33
❑ 96FlaBluI-33
❑ 96FlaHotG-5
❑ 96Fle-37
❑ 96FroFlaMas-2
❑ 96Lea-28
❑ 96LeaLim-90
❑ 96LeaLimG-90
❑ 96LeaPreMM-10
❑ 96LeaPreP-28
❑ 96LeaPreVP-13
❑ 96LeaPreVPG-13
❑ 96LeaShuDow-5
❑ 96MetUni-53
❑ 96OilPos-31
❑ 96Pin-164
❑ 96PinArtP-164
❑ 96PinFoi-164
❑ 96PinMcD-40
❑ 96PinPreS-164
❑ 96PinRinC-164
❑ 96PosUppD-9
❑ 96Sco-90
❑ 96ScoArtPro-90
❑ 96ScoDeaCAP-90
❑ 96ScoGolB-90
❑ 96ScoNetW-7
❑ 96ScoSpeAP-90
❑ 96ScoSudDea-6
❑ 96SelCer-66
❑ 96SelCerAP-66
❑ 96SelCerBlu-66
❑ 96SelCerFre-7
❑ 96SelCerMB-66
❑ 96SelCerMG-66
❑ 96SelCerMR-66
❑ 96SelCerRed-66
❑ 96SkyImp-42
❑ 96SP-54
❑ 96Sum-150
❑ 96SumArtP-150
❑ 96SumIce-150
❑ 96SumInTheCre-5
❑ 96SumInTheCrePS-5
❑ 96SumMet-150
❑ 96SumPreS-150
❑ 96TopNHLP-83
❑ 96TopPicOI-83
❑ 96Ult-59
❑ 96UltGolM-59
❑ 96UppDec-256
❑ 96UppDecBD-158
❑ 96UppDecBDG-158
❑ 96UppDecBDRFTC-RC17
❑ 96UppDecGN-X27
❑ 96UppDecIce-21
❑ 96UppDecIcePar-21
❑ 96Zen-112
❑ 96ZenArtP-112
❑ 97BeAPlaSTP-7
❑ 97ColCho-89
❑ 97ColChoSta-SQ31
❑ 97ColChoSti-S6
❑ 97ColChoWD-W19
❑ 97Don-43
❑ 97DonBetTP-8
❑ 97DonCanI-20
❑ 97DonCanIDS-20
❑ 97DonCanINP-27
❑ 97DonCanIPS-20
❑ 97DonCanISCS-2
❑ 97DonEli-19
❑ 97DonEliAsp-19
❑ 97DonEliC-29
❑ 97DonEliMC-29
❑ 97DonEliS-19
❑ 97DonLim-81
❑ 97DonLim-103
❑ 97DonLim-174
❑ 97DonLimExp-81
❑ 97DonLimExp-103
❑ 97DonLimExp-174
❑ 97DonLimFOTG-23
❑ 97DonPre-84
❑ 97DonPreCG-3
❑ 97DonPreCGP-3
❑ 97DonPreCttC-84
❑ 97DonPreProG-43
❑ 97DonPreProS-43
❑ 97DonPri-123
❑ 97DonPriPG-4
❑ 97DonPriPGP-4
❑ 97DonPriSoA-123
❑ 97EssOlyHH-18
❑ 97EssOlyHHF-18
❑ 97Kat-57
❑ 97KatGol-57
❑ 97KatSil-57
❑ 97Lea-16
❑ 97LeaFraMat-16
❑ 97LeaFraMDC-16
❑ 97LeaInt-16
❑ 97LeaIntUI-16
❑ 97LeaPipDre-4
❑ 97McD-27
❑ 97Pac-242
❑ 97PacCop-242
❑ 97PacCroR-53
❑ 97PacCroREG-53
❑ 97PacCroRFODC-8
❑ 97PacCroRIB-53
❑ 97PacCroRS-53
❑ 97PacDyn-49
❑ 97PacDynC-49
❑ 97PacDynDG-49
❑ 97PacDynEG-49
❑ 97PacDynIB-49
❑ 97PacDynR-49
❑ 97PacDynSil-49
❑ 97PacDynSto-9
❑ 97PacDynTan-11
❑ 97PacEmeGre-242
❑ 97PacIceB-242
❑ 97PacInTheCLC-9
❑ 97PacInv-56
❑ 97PacInvC-56
❑ 97PacInvEG-56
❑ 97PacInvIB-56
❑ 97PacInvR-56
❑ 97PacInvS-56
❑ 97PacOme-93
❑ 97PacOmeC-93
❑ 97PacOmeDG-93
❑ 97PacOmeEG-93
❑ 97PacOmeG-93
❑ 97PacOmeIB-93
❑ 97PacPar-75
❑ 97PacParC-75
❑ 97PacParDG-75
❑ 97PacParEG-75
❑ 97PacParGSL-8
❑ 97PacParIB-75
❑ 97PacParRed-75
❑ 97PacParSil-75
❑ 97PacRed-242
❑ 97PacRev-55
❑ 97PacRevC-55
❑ 97PacRevE-55
❑ 97PacRevIB-55
❑ 97PacRevR-55
❑ 97PacRevRtSD-8
❑ 97PacRevS-55
❑ 97PacSil-242
❑ 97PacTeaCCC-10
❑ 97Pin-93
❑ 97PinArtP-93
❑ 97PinBee-12
❑ 97PinBeeGP-12
❑ 97PinCer-18
❑ 97PinCerMB-18
❑ 97PinCerMG-18
❑ 97PinCerMR-18
❑ 97PinCerR-18
❑ 97PinEpiGO-17
❑ 97PinEpiGP-17
❑ 97PinEpiME-17
❑ 97PinEpiMO-17
❑ 97PinEpiMP-17
❑ 97PinEpiPE-17
❑ 97PinEpiPO-17
❑ 97PinEpiPP-17
❑ 97PinEpiSE-17
❑ 97PinEpiSO-17
❑ 97PinEpiSP-17
❑ 97PinIns-25
❑ 97PinInsC-24
❑ 97PinInsCC-25
❑ 97PinInsCG-24
❑ 97PinInsEC-25
❑ 97PinInsSto-12
❑ 97PinInsSUG-10A/B
❑ 97PinInsSUG-10C/D
❑ 97PinInsT-21
❑ 97PinMas-4
❑ 97PinMasDC-4
❑ 97PinMasJ-4
❑ 97PinMasPro-4
❑ 97PinMin-24
❑ 97PinMinB-24
❑ 97PinMinCBP-24
❑ 97PinMinCGPP-24
❑ 97PinMinCNSP-24
❑ 97PinMinCoiB-24
❑ 97PinMinCoiGP-24
❑ 97PinMinCoiN-24
❑ 97PinMinCoiSG-24
❑ 97PinMinCoiSS-24
❑ 97PinMinGolTea-24
❑ 97PinMinSilTea-24
❑ 97PinPowPac-22
❑ 97PinPrePBB-93
❑ 97PinPrePBC-93
❑ 97PinPrePBM-93
❑ 97PinPrePBY-93
❑ 97PinPrePFC-93
❑ 97PinPrePFM-93
❑ 97PinPrePFY-93
❑ 97PinPrePla-93
❑ 97PinRepMas-3
❑ 97PinRinC-93
❑ 97PinTeaP-2
❑ 97PinTeaPM-2
❑ 97PinTeaPP-2
❑ 97PinTeaPPM-2
❑ 97PinTin-5
❑ 97PinTotCMPG-18
❑ 97PinTotCPB-18
❑ 97PinTotCPG-18
❑ 97PinTotCPR-18
❑ 97Sco-31
❑ 97ScoArtPro-31
❑ 97ScoGolBla-31
❑ 97ScoNetW-5
❑ 97SPAut-60
❑ 97SPx-19
❑ 97SPxBro-19
❑ 97SPxDim-SPX9
❑ 97SPxGol-19
❑ 97SPxGraF-19
❑ 97SPxSil-19
❑ 97SPxSte-19
❑ 97Stu-29
❑ 97StuPrePG-29
❑ 97StuPrePS-29
❑ 97UppDec-273
❑ 97UppDecBD-126
❑ 97UppDecBDDD-126
❑ 97UppDecBDQD-126
❑ 97UppDecBDTD-126
❑ 97UppDecGDM-273
❑ 97UppDecIce-81
❑ 97UppDecIceP-81
❑ 97UppDecIPS-81
❑ 97UppDecSG-SG31
❑ 97UppDecTS-25
❑ 97UppDecTSL2-25
❑ 97UppDecTSS-10B
❑ 97Zen-17
❑ 97Zen5x7-38
❑ 97ZenGolImp-38
❑ 97ZenSilImp-38
❑ 97ZenZGol-17
❑ 97ZenZSil-17
❑ 98Be A PPA-284
❑ 98Be A PPAA-284
❑ 98Be A PPAAF-284
❑ 98Be A PPPH-H15
❑ 98Be A PPSE-284
❑ 98Be APG-284
❑ 98BowBes-20
❑ 98BowBesAR-20
❑ 98BowBesR-20
❑ 98Fin-36
❑ 98FinNo P-36
❑ 98FinNo PR-36
❑ 98FinRef-36
❑ 98JelSpo-4
❑ 98McD-18
❑ 98O-PChr-186
❑ 98O-PChrR-186
❑ 98O-PChrSB-SB4
❑ 98O-PChrSBR-SB4
❑ 98Pac-211
❑ 98PacAur-182
❑ 98PacCroR-131
❑ 98PacCroRLS-131
❑ 98PacCroRPotG-22
❑ 98PacDynI-180
❑ 98PacDynIIB-180
❑ 98PacDynIIW-9
❑ 98PacDynIR-180
❑ 98PacIceB-211
❑ 98PacOmeCS-10
❑ 98PacOmeCSG-10
❑ 98PacOmeCSG-10
❑ 98PacOmeCSR-10
❑ 98PacOmeH-228
❑ 98PacOmeO-32
❑ 98PacOmeODI-228
❑ 98PacOmePI-14
❑ 98PacOmePIB-14
❑ 98PacOmeR-228
❑ 98PacPar-227
❑ 98PacParC-227
❑ 98PacParEG-227
❑ 98PacParGSLC-19
❑ 98PacParH-227
❑ 98PacParIB-227
❑ 98PacParIG-10
❑ 98PacParIGG-10
❑ 98PacParIGS-10
❑ 98PacParS-227
❑ 98PacRed-211
❑ 98PacRev-138
❑ 98PacRevIS-138
❑ 98PacRevR-138
❑ 98PacRevS-33
❑ 98PinEpiGE-17
❑ 98RevThrPA-19
❑ 98RevThrPA-19
❑ 98SP Aut-82
❑ 98SP AutSotTG-CJ
❑ 98SP AutSS-SS27
❑ 98SPXTopP-54
❑ 98SPXTopPF-54
❑ 98SPXTopPHH-H28
❑ 98SPXTopPLI-L12
❑ 98SPXTopPPS-PS14
❑ 98SPXTopPR-54
❑ 98SPXTopPWM-CJ
❑ 98SSASotT-CJ
❑ 98Top-186
❑ 98TopGolLC1-39
❑ 98TopGolLC1B-39
❑ 98TopGolLC1BOoO-39
❑ 98TopGolLC1OoO-39
❑ 98TopGolLC1R-39
❑ 98TopGolLC1ROoO-39
❑ 98TopGolLC2-39
❑ 98TopGolLC2B-39
❑ 98TopGolLC2BOoO-39
❑ 98TopGolLC2OoO-39
❑ 98TopGolLC2R-39
❑ 98TopGolLC2ROoO-39
❑ 98TopGolLC3-39
❑ 98TopGolLC3B-39
❑ 98TopGolLC3BOoO-39
❑ 98TopGolLC3OoO-39
❑ 98TopGolLC3R-39
❑ 98TopGolLC3ROoO-39
❑ 98TopO-P-186
❑ 98TopSeaB-SB4
❑ 98UC-81
❑ 98UC-251
❑ 98UD ChoPCR-81
❑ 98UD ChoPCR-251
❑ 98UD ChoR-81
❑ 98UD ChoR-251
❑ 98UD3-41
❑ 98UD3-101
❑ 98UD3-161
❑ 98UD3DieC-41
❑ 98UD3DieC-101
❑ 98UD3DieC-161
❑ 98UDCP-81
❑ 98UppDec-191
❑ 98UppDecBD-83
❑ 98UppDecDD-83
❑ 98UppDecE-191
❑ 98UppDecE1o1-191
❑ 98UppDecGJ-GJ4
❑ 98UppDecGR-191
❑ 98UppDecLSH-LS29
❑ 98UppDecLSHQ1-LS29
❑ 98UppDecLSHQ2-LS29
❑ 98UppDecLSHQ3-LS29
❑ 98UppDecM-194
❑ 98UppDecM1-M12
❑ 98UppDecM2-M12
❑ 98UppDecMGS-194
❑ 98UppDecMSS-194
❑ 98UppDecMSS-194
❑ 98UppDecP-P20
❑ 98UppDecPQ1-P20
❑ 98UppDecPQ2-P20
❑ 98UppDecPQ3-P20
❑ 98UppDecQD-83
❑ 98UppDecTD-83
❑ 98UppDecWFG-WF13
❑ 98UppDecWFP-WF13
❑ 99AurSty-18
❑ 99Pac-407
❑ 99PacAur-136
❑ 99PacAurCF-19
❑ 99PacAurCFC-19
❑ 99PacAurCFPB-19
❑ 99PacAurGU-19
❑ 99PacAurPD-136
❑ 99PacCop-407
❑ 99PacCra-10
❑ 99PacGol-407
❑ 99PacGolCD-34
❑ 99PacIceB-407
❑ 99PacIn tCN-19
❑ 99PacPasAP-20
❑ 99PacPreD-407
❑ 99PacTeaL-26
❑ 99RetHoc-75
❑ 99SP AutPS-82
❑ 99UppDecM-198
❑ 99UppDecMGS-GU14
❑ 99UppDecMGS-198
❑ 99UppDecMGUSA-GU14
❑ 99UppDecMLL-LL6
❑ 99UppDecMSS-198
❑ 99UppDecMSS-198
❑ 99UppDecRG-75
❑ 99UppDecRII-CJ
❑ 99UppDecRIL1-CJ
❑ 99UppDecRP-75

**Joseph, Fabian**

❑ 82VicCou-10
❑ 83VicCou-12
❑ 88ProAHL-92
❑ 89ProAHL-137
❑ 91AlbIntTC-10
❑ 92ScoCanO-8
❑ 93AlbIntTC-7
❑ 93OPCPreTC-7
❑ 93Pow-484
❑ 93Ult-464
❑ 94MilAdm-12
❑ 94ScoTeaC-CT10
❑ 95ColEdgI-162
❑ 95MilAdmBO-9
❑ 96MilAdmBO-10

**Joseph, Tony**

❑ 89ProAHL-48
❑ 90ProAHLIHL-243
❑ 91ProAHLCHL-155

**Josephson, Mike**

❑ 91BriColJHL-75
❑ 91BriColJHL-166
❑ 93KamBla-11
❑ 95LetHur-10
❑ 96LetHur-9

**Joss, Eddie**

❑ 51LavDaiS-120

**Joss, Terry**

❑ 95Sla-407

**Jotkus, Pete**

❑ 36V356WorG-104

**Joubert, Jacques**

❑ 95PeoRiv-8
❑ 96MilAdmBO-11

**Jovanovski, Ed**

❑ 93WinSpi-1
❑ 94Cla-1
❑ 94ClaCHLAS-C6
❑ 94ClaDraD-5
❑ 94ClaDraD-6
❑ 94ClaDraD-7
❑ 94ClaDraGol-1
❑ 94ClaPic-CP11
❑ 94ClaProP-203
❑ 94ClaROYS-R9
❑ 94ClaTri-T25
❑ 94Fin-149
❑ 94FinRef-149
❑ 94FinSupTW-149
❑ 94LeaLimWJC-5
❑ 94ParSE-SE207
❑ 94ParSEG-SE207
❑ 94Pin-524
❑ 94PinArtP-524
❑ 94PinRinC-524
❑ 94SP-140
❑ 94SPDieCut-140
❑ 94TopFinB-21
❑ 94UppDec-496
❑ 94UppDecEleIce-496
❑ 94WinSpi-14
❑ 95BeAPla-178
❑ 95BeAPSig-S178
❑ 95BeAPSigDC-S178
❑ 95Bow-100
❑ 95BowAllFoi-100
❑ 95BowBes-BB19
❑ 95BowBesRef-BB19
❑ 95Cla-98
❑ 95ClaAut-10
❑ 95ClaCHLAS-AS9
❑ 95ClaIceBre-BK19
❑ 95ColCho-399
❑ 95DonCanWJT-6
❑ 95DonEli-68
❑ 95DonEliDCS-68
❑ 95DonEliDCU-68
❑ 95DonEliR-11
❑ 95EmoGen-9
❑ 95Fin-176
❑ 95FinRef-176
❑ 95Ima-15
❑ 95ImaCleE-CE17
❑ 95ImaGol-15
❑ 95Met-178
❑ 95ParInt-536
❑ 95ParIntEl-536
❑ 95ParIntPTP-PP42
❑ 95SelCer-137
❑ 95SelCerFut-10
❑ 95SelCerMG-137
❑ 95SkyImp-201
❑ 95SP-58
❑ 95StaClu-196
❑ 95StaCluGTSC-GT9
❑ 95StaCluMOMS-196
❑ 95Sum-171
❑ 95SumArtP-171
❑ 95SumIce-171
❑ 95Top-354
❑ 95TopCanWJ-22CJ
❑ 95TopOPCI-354
❑ 95TopSupSkiSR-SR1
❑ 95Ult-342
❑ 95UltExtAtt-10
❑ 95UppDec-501
❑ 95UppDecEleIce-501
❑ 95UppDecEleIceG-501
❑ 95UppDecPHE-H24
❑ 95UppDecPreH-H24
❑ 95Zen-121
❑ 95ZenRooRC-7
❑ 96ClaIceBreDC-BK19
❑ 96ColCho-105
❑ 96ColCho-318
❑ 96ColCho-340
❑ 96ColChoMVP-UD34
❑ 96ColChoMVPG-UD34
❑ 96DonCanI-35
❑ 96DonCanIGPP-35
❑ 96DonCanIRPP-35
❑ 96DonDom-10
❑ 96DonEli-82
❑ 96DonEliAsp-6
❑ 96DonEliDCS-82
❑ 96DonHitLis-3
❑ 96DonRatR-7
❑ 96Fla-37
❑ 96FlaBluI-37
❑ 96FlaHotN-5
❑ 96Fle-39
❑ 96FlePic-98
❑ 96FlePicF5-21
❑ 96FlePicJE-13
❑ 96FleRooSen-6
❑ 96KraUppD-55
❑ 96Lea-208
❑ 96LeaFirOI-13
❑ 96LeaLeaAL-19
❑ 96LeaLeaALP-P19
❑ 96LeaLim-14
❑ 96LeaLimBTB-7
❑ 96LeaLimBTBLE-7
❑ 96LeaLimBTBP-P7
❑ 96LeaLimG-14
❑ 96LeaPre-68
❑ 96LeaPreP-208
❑ 96LeaPrePP-68
❑ 96LeaPreVP-8
❑ 96LeaPreVPG-8
❑ 96MetUni-59
❑ 96MetUniCS-5
❑ 96MetUniCSSP-5
❑ 96NHLACEPC-24
❑ 96Pin-204
❑ 96PinArtP-204
❑ 96PinByTN-4
❑ 96PinByTNP-4
❑ 96PinFoi-204
❑ 96PinMcD-6
❑ 96PinPreS-204
❑ 96PinRinC-204
❑ 96PinTeaP-7
❑ 96PosUppD-10
❑ 96Sco-239
❑ 96ScoArtPro-239
❑ 96ScoChelt-12
❑ 96ScoDeaCAP-239
❑ 96ScoGolB-239
❑ 96ScoSpeAP-239
❑ 96SelCer-30
❑ 96SelCerAP-30
❑ 96SelCerBlu-30
❑ 96SelCerMB-30
❑ 96SelCerMG-30
❑ 96SelCerMR-30
❑ 96SelCerRed-30
❑ 96SkyImp-45
❑ 96SkyImpCI-5
❑ 96SkyImpNHLF-11
❑ 96SP-60
❑ 96SPGamFil-GF14
❑ 96StaCluMO-47
❑ 96Sum-163
❑ 96SumArtP-163
❑ 96SumIce-163
❑ 96SumMet-163
❑ 96SumPreS-163
❑ 96TeaOut-85
❑ 96TopPicFT-FT8
❑ 96TopPicID-ID5
❑ 96TopPicRS-RS11
❑ 96Ult-65
❑ 96UltGolM-65
❑ 96UltPow-7
❑ 96UltPowBL-5
❑ 96UppDec-66
❑ 96UppDec-362
❑ 96UppDecBD-18
❑ 96UppDecBDG-18
❑ 96UppDecBDRFTC-RC15
❑ 96UppDecGN-X11
❑ 96UppDecIce-88
❑ 96UppDecIceDF-S3
❑ 96UppDecIcePar-88
❑ 96UppDecIceSCF-S3
❑ 96UppDecPP-P8
❑ 96UppDecSS-SS3B
❑ 96Zen-45
❑ 96ZenArtP-45
❑ 97Be A PPAD-21
❑ 97Be A PPAPD-21
❑ 97BeAPla-21
❑ 97BeAPlaAut-21
❑ 97ColCho-101
❑ 97Don-144
❑ 97DonCanI-14
❑ 97DonCanIDS-14
❑ 97DonCanIPS-14
❑ 97DonEli-33
❑ 97DonEliAsp-33
❑ 97DonEliS-33
❑ 97DonLim-5
❑ 97DonLim-37
❑ 97DonLimExp-5
❑ 97DonLimExp-37
❑ 97DonPre-19
❑ 97DonPreCttC-19
❑ 97DonPreProG-144
❑ 97DonPreProS-144
❑ 97DonPri-27
❑ 97DonPriSoA-27
❑ 97Kat-61
❑ 97KatGol-61
❑ 97KatSil-61
❑ 97Lea-17
❑ 97LeaFraMat-17
❑ 97LeaFraMDC-17
❑ 97LeaInt-17
❑ 97LeaIntUI-17
❑ 97PacCroR-57
❑ 97PacCroREG-57
❑ 97PacCroRIB-57
❑ 97PacCroRS-57
❑ 97PacDyn-53
❑ 97PacDynC-53
❑ 97PacDynDG-53
❑ 97PacDynEG-53
❑ 97PacDynIB-53
❑ 97PacDynR-53
❑ 97PacDynSil-53
❑ 97PacDynTan-49
❑ 97PacInv-60
❑ 97PacInvC-60
❑ 97PacInvEG-60
❑ 97PacInvIB-60
❑ 97PacInvNRB-85
❑ 97PacInvR-60
❑ 97PacInvS-60
❑ 97PacOme-99
❑ 97PacOmeC-99
❑ 97PacOmeDG-99
❑ 97PacOmeEG-99
❑ 97PacOmeG-99
❑ 97PacOmeIB-99
❑ 97PacPar-80
❑ 97PacParC-80
❑ 97PacParDG-80
❑ 97PacParEG-80
❑ 97PacParIB-80
❑ 97PacParRed-80
❑ 97PacParSil-80
❑ 97PacRev-60
❑ 97PacRevC-60
❑ 97PacRevE-60
❑ 97PacRevIB-60
❑ 97PacRevR-60
❑ 97PacRevS-60
❑ 97Pin-113
❑ 97PinCer-48
❑ 97PinCerMB-48
❑ 97PinCerMG-48
❑ 97PinCerMR-48
❑ 97PinCerR-48
❑ 97PinIns-86
❑ 97PinInsCC-86
❑ 97PinInsEC-86
❑ 97PinPrePBB-113
❑ 97PinPrePBC-113
❑ 97PinPrePBM-113
❑ 97PinPrePBY-113
❑ 97PinPrePFC-113
❑ 97PinPrePFM-113
❑ 97PinPrePFY-113
❑ 97PinPrePla-113
❑ 97PinTotCMPG-48
❑ 97PinTotCPB-48
❑ 97PinTotCPG-48
❑ 97PinTotCPR-48
❑ 97Sco-235
❑ 97SPAut-65
❑ 97SPx-21
❑ 97SPxBro-21
❑ 97SPxGol-21
❑ 97SPxGraF-21
❑ 97SPxSil-21
❑ 97SPxSte-21
❑ 97Stu-39
❑ 97StuPrePG-39
❑ 97StuPrePS-39
❑ 97UppDec-284
❑ 97UppDec-389
❑ 97UppDecBD-141
❑ 97UppDecBDDD-141
❑ 97UppDecBDQD-141
❑ 97UppDecBDTD-141
❑ 97UppDecIce-26
❑ 97UppDecIceP-26
❑ 97UppDecIPS-26
❑ 97UppDecSG-SG15
❑ 98O-PChr-177
❑ 98O-PChrR-177
❑ 98Pac-222
❑ 98PacAur-80
❑ 98PacCroR-58
❑ 98PacCroRLS-58
❑ 98PacDynI-81
❑ 98PacDynIIB-81
❑ 98PacDynIR-81
❑ 98PacIceB-222
❑ 98PacPar-96
❑ 98PacParC-96
❑ 98PacParEG-96
❑ 98PacParH-96
❑ 98PacParIB-96
❑ 98PacParS-96
❑ 98PacRed-222
❑ 98SP Aut-37
❑ 98SP AutSotTG-EJ
❑ 98SPxFin-39
❑ 98SPxFinR-39
❑ 98SPxFinS-39
❑ 98SSASotT-EJ
❑ 98Top-177
❑ 98TopO-P-177
❑ 98UC-91
❑ 98UD ChoPCR-91
❑ 98UD ChoR-91
❑ 98UDCP-91
❑ 98UppDec-101
❑ 98UppDecBD-37
❑ 98UppDecDD-37
❑ 98UppDecE-101
❑ 98UppDecE1o1-101
❑ 98UppDecGR-101
❑ 98UppDecM-206
❑ 98UppDecMGS-206
❑ 98UppDecMSS-206
❑ 98UppDecMSS-206
❑ 98UppDecQD-37
❑ 98UppDecTD-37
❑ 99Pac-424
❑ 99PacCop-424
❑ 99PacGol-424
❑ 99PacIceB-424
❑ 99PacPreD-424
❑ 99SP AutPS-37
❑ 99UppDecM-209
❑ 99UppDecMGS-209
❑ 99UppDecMSS-209
❑ 99UppDecMSS-209

**Joyal, Ed (Eddie)**

❑ 63YorWhiB-48
❑ 64BeeGro3P-80A
❑ 64BeeGro3P-80B
❑ 64BeeGro3P-168
❑ 64CocCap-54
❑ 65Top-85
❑ 68OPC-40
❑ 68ShiCoi-55
❑ 68Top-40
❑ 69OPC-108
❑ 69OPCFou-5
❑ 69OPCSta-16

□ 69Top-108
□ 70EssPowPla-156
□ 70OPC-39
□ 70OPCDec-3
□ 70SarProSta-67
□ 70Top-39
□ 70TopStiS-16
□ 71OPC-23
□ 71SarProSta-74
□ 71Top-23
□ 71TorSun-118
□ 72SweSemWC-205
□ 75OPCWHA-36
**Joyal, Eric**
□ 907thInnSQMJHL-192
□ 917thInnSQMJHL-64
**Joyce, Bob**
□ 88BruPos-7
□ 88BruSpoA-6
□ 88BruSpoA-23
□ 88OPC-2
□ 88Top-2
□ 89BruSpoA-12
□ 89CapKod-27
□ 89OPC-73
□ 89OPCSti-4
□ 89OPCSti-31
□ 89PanSti-199
□ 89Top-73
□ 90ProAHLIHL-206
□ 90Sco-291
□ 90ScoCan-291
□ 91MonHaw-12
□ 91ProAHLCHL-172
□ 93LasVegThu-16
□ 94LasVegThu-8
□ 98GerDELE-82
**Joyce, Duane**
□ 89ProIHL-126
□ 90ProAHLIHL-105
□ 91ProAHLCHL-523
□ 96CinCyc-3
**Joyce, Graham**
□ 52JunBluT-120
**Joyce, John**
□ 94BirBul-12
□ 95BirBul-17
**Jubenville, Jeff**
□ 907thInnSWHL-3
□ 917thInnSWHL-123
□ 93TacRoc-14
**Juckes, Gordon W**
□ 44BeeGro2P-329
□ 83HalFP-K9
□ 85HalFC-143
**Judson, Rick**
□ 92TolSto-20
□ 93TolSto-22
□ 94TolSto-10
□ 95TolSto-12
□ 96TolSto-20
**Judza, Bill**
□ 45QuaOatP-24A
□ 45QuaOatP-24B
□ 45QuaOatP-60C
**Juhlin, Patrik**
□ 89SweSemE-250
□ 90SweSemE-171
□ 91SweSemE-266
□ 92SweSemE-286
□ 93SweSemE-252
□ 93SweSemWCS-11
□ 94Cla-80
□ 94ClaDraGol-80
□ 94ClaROYS-R10
□ 94ClaTri-T49
□ 94Fin-6
□ 94FinnJaaK-68
□ 94FinRef-6
□ 94FinSupTW-6
□ 94Fla-128
□ 94Fle-155
□ 94OPCPre-378
□ 94OPCPreSE-378
□ 94ParSE-SE133
□ 94ParSEG-SE133
□ 94SweLeaE-222
□ 94SweLeaEGC-18
□ 94SweLeaEGS-8
□ 94TopPre-378
□ 94TopPreSE-378
□ 94Ult-344
□ 94UppDec-246
□ 94UppDec-553
□ 94UppDecElelce-246
□ 94UppDecElelce-553
□ 94UppDecSPI-SP148
□ 94UppDecSPIDC-SP148
□ 95BeAPla-119
□ 95BeAPSig-S119
□ 95BeAPSigDC-S119
□ 95ColCho-236
□ 95ColChoPC-236
□ 95ColChoPCP-236
□ 95Don-60
□ 95FinnSemWC-76
□ 95Lea-44
□ 95ParInt-160
□ 95ParIntEl-160
□ 95SigRooFF-FF3
□ 95SigRooFFS-FF3
□ 95SweGloWC-31
□ 95SweUppDE-244
□ 96SweSemW-62
**Jukes, Gordon W.**
□ 74TeaCanLWHA-13
**Julian, Jason**
□ 917thInnSOHL-335
□ 92OshGenS-10
**Julien, Claude**
□ 83FreExp-16
□ 84FreExp-8
□ 85FreExp-15
□ 88ProAHL-105
□ 89HalCit-11
□ 89ProAHL-165
□ 90KanCitBla-12
□ 90ProAHLIHL-587
□ 91MonHaw-13
□ 91ProAHLCHL-171
**Julien, Stephane**
□ 907thInnSQMJHL-93
□ 917thInnSQMJHL-112
**Juneau, Joe**
□ 91AlbIntTC-11
□ 91Par-234
□ 91ParFre-234
□ 92Bow-292
□ 92BruPos-3
□ 92OPC-89
□ 92OPCPre-101
□ 92PanSti-L
□ 92PanStiFre-L
□ 92Par-2
□ 92ParEmel-2
□ 92Pin-221
□ 92PinFre-221
□ 92PinTea2-19
□ 92PinTea2F-19
□ 92ProSet-219
□ 92Sco-453
□ 92ScoCan-453
□ 92ScoCanO-2
□ 92ScoYouS-22
□ 92SeaPat-18
□ 92StaClu-297
□ 92Top-365
□ 92TopGol-365G
□ 92Ult-4
□ 92Ult-448
□ 92UppDec-354
□ 92UppDec-399
□ 92UppDec-455
□ 92UppDecACH-1
□ 92UppDecCC-CC9
□ 92UppDecGHS-G11
□ 93Don-26
□ 93Don-394
□ 93Don-504
□ 93DurSco-27
□ 93Kra-14
□ 93Lea-218
□ 93LeaGolR-2
□ 93OPCPre-125
□ 93OPCPre-299
□ 93OPCPreG-125
□ 93OPCPreG-299
□ 93PanSti-143
□ 93PanSti-A
□ 93Par-241
□ 93Par-280
□ 93ParEmel-241
□ 93ParEmel-280
□ 93Pin-5
□ 93Pin1S-3
□ 93PinCan-5
□ 93PinTea2-4
□ 93PinTea2C-4
□ 93Pow-19
□ 93PowPoiL-6
□ 93PowSecYS-2
□ 93Sco-330
□ 93ScoCan-330
□ 93SeaPat-8
□ 93StaClu-202
□ 93StaCluFDI-202
□ 93StaCluFDIO-202
□ 93StaCluO-202
□ 93TopPre-125
□ 93TopPre-299
□ 93TopPreBG-12
□ 93TopPreG-125
□ 93TopPreG-299
□ 93Ult-49
□ 93UppDec-282
□ 93UppDec-343
□ 93UppDecFH-35
□ 93UppDecLAS-53
□ 93UppDecNB-HB10
□ 93UppDecSP-9
□ 94BeAPla-R85
□ 94BeAPla-R100
□ 94CanGamNHLP-245
□ 94ClaProP-AU4
□ 94Don-258
□ 94EASpo-10
□ 94Fin-93
□ 94FinRef-93
□ 94FinSupTW-93
□ 94Fla-200
□ 94Fle-236
□ 94FleFraFut-5
□ 94Kra-19
□ 94Lea-62
□ 94LeaFirOIce-7
□ 94LeaLim-38
□ 94LeaLimI-25
□ 94OPCPre-100
□ 94OPCPreSE-100
□ 94ParCratGB-25
□ 94ParCratGG-25
□ 94ParCratGR-25
□ 94ParSE-SE198
□ 94ParSEG-SE198
□ 94ParSEV-17
□ 94Pin-7
□ 94Pin1HS-7
□ 94PinArtP-7
□ 94PinRinC-7
□ 94Sco-124
□ 94ScoFra-TF25
□ 94ScoGol-124
□ 94ScoPla-124
□ 94ScoPlaTS-124
□ 94Sel-86
□ 94SelGol-86
□ 94SP-126
□ 94SPDieCut-126
□ 94TopPre-100
□ 94TopPreSE-100
□ 94Ult-388
□ 94UppDec-88
□ 94UppDecElelce-88
□ 94UppDecNBAP-27
□ 94UppDecPR-R15
□ 94UppDecPRE-R15
□ 94UppDecPreRG-R15
□ 94UppDecSPI-SP175
□ 94UppDecSPIDC-SP175
□ 95BeAPla-58
□ 95BeAPSig-S58
□ 95BeAPSigDC-S58
□ 95Bow-39
□ 95BowAllFoi-39
□ 95CanGamNHLP-283
□ 95Cap-13
□ 95ColCho-118
□ 95ColChoPC-118
□ 95ColChoPCP-118
□ 95Don-136
□ 95DonEli-104
□ 95DonEliDCS-104
□ 95DonEliDCU-104
□ 95Emo-190
□ 95Fin-124
□ 95FinRef-124
□ 95ImpSti-129
□ 95ImpStiDCS-8
□ 95Kra-5
□ 95Lea-188
□ 95LeaLim-98
□ 95Met-161
□ 95ParInt-221
□ 95ParIntEl-221
□ 95PlaOneoOne-105
□ 95PosUppD-7
□ 95ProMag-34
□ 95Sco-256
□ 95ScoBlaIce-256
□ 95ScoBlaIceAP-256
□ 95SelCer-80
□ 95SelCerMG-80
□ 95SkyImp-179
□ 95SP-158
□ 95StaClu-187
□ 95StaCluMOMS-187
□ 95Sum-139
□ 95SumArtP-139
□ 95SumIce-139
□ 95Top-216
□ 95TopHomGC-HGC25
□ 95TopOPCI-216
□ 95TopSupSki-25
□ 95TopSupSkiPla-25
□ 95Ult-323
□ 95UppDec-25
□ 95UppDecElelce-25
□ 95UppDecElelceG-25
□ 95UppDecPRE-R17
□ 95UppDecPreR-R17
□ 95UppDecSpeE-SE86
□ 95UppDecSpeEdiG-SE86
□ 95Zen-96
□ 96ColCho-277
□ 96ColCho-334
□ 96Don-151
□ 96DonCanI-38
□ 96DonCanIGPP-38
□ 96DonCanIRPP-38
□ 96DonEli-90
□ 96DonEliDCS-90
□ 96DonPrePro-151
□ 96Fle-118
□ 96FlePic-108
□ 96Lea-21
□ 96LeaPre-49
□ 96LeaPreP-21
□ 96LeaPrePP-49
□ 96MetUni-166
□ 96NHLACEPC-25
□ 96NHLProSTA-34
□ 96Pin-160
□ 96PinArtP-160
□ 96PinFoi-160
□ 96PinPreS-160
□ 96PinRinC-160
□ 96Sco-144
□ 96ScoArtPro-144
□ 96ScoDeaCAP-144
□ 96ScoGolB-144
□ 96ScoSpeAP-144
□ 96SkyImp-141
□ 96SP-166
□ 96SPHolCol-HC17
□ 96Sum-7
□ 96SumArtP-7
□ 96SumIce-7
□ 96SumMet-7
□ 96SumPreS-7
□ 96SweSemW-92
□ 96TeaOut-44
□ 96Ult-177
□ 96UltGolM-177
□ 96UppDec-176
□ 96UppDecBD-90
□ 96UppDecBDG-90
□ 96UppDecGN-X40
□ 96Zen-27
□ 96ZenArtP-27
□ 97Be A PPAD-184
□ 97Be A PPAPD-184
□ 97BeAPla-184
□ 97BeAPlaAut-184
□ 97ColCho-268
□ 97Don-95
□ 97DonEli-41
□ 97DonEliAsp-41
□ 97DonEliS-41
□ 97DonLim-61
□ 97DonLimExp-61
□ 97DonPre-13
□ 97DonPreCttC-13
□ 97DonPreProG-95
□ 97DonPreProS-95
□ 97DonPri-137
□ 97DonPriSoA-137
□ 97Kat-152
□ 97KatGol-152
□ 97KatSil-152
□ 97Lea-53
□ 97LeaFraMat-53
□ 97LeaFraMDC-53
□ 97LeaInt-53
□ 97LeaIntUI-53
□ 97Pac-155
□ 97PacCop-155
□ 97PacCroR-140
□ 97PacCroREG-140
□ 97PacCroRIB-140
□ 97PacCroRS-140
□ 97PacDyn-131
□ 97PacDynC-131
□ 97PacDynDG-131
□ 97PacDynEG-131
□ 97PacDynIB-131
□ 97PacDynR-131
□ 97PacDynSil-131
□ 97PacDynTan-57
□ 97PacEmeGre-155
□ 97PacIceB-155
□ 97PacInv-147
□ 97PacInvC-147
□ 97PacInvEG-147
□ 97PacInvIB-147
□ 97PacInvR-147
□ 97PacInvS-147
□ 97PacOme-241
□ 97PacOmeC-241
□ 97PacOmeDG-241
□ 97PacOmeEG-241
□ 97PacOmeG-241
□ 97PacOmeIB-241
□ 97PacPar-195
□ 97PacParC-195
□ 97PacParDG-195
□ 97PacParEG-195
□ 97PacParIB-195
□ 97PacParRed-195
□ 97PacParSil-195
□ 97PacRed-155
□ 97PacRev-148
□ 97PacRevC-148
□ 97PacRevE-148
□ 97PacRevIB-148
□ 97PacRevR-148
□ 97PacRevS-148
□ 97PacSil-155
□ 97PacSlaSDC-12A
□ 97Pin-107
□ 97PinCer-63
□ 97PinCerMB-63
□ 97PinCerMG-63
□ 97PinCerMR-63
□ 97PinCerR-63
□ 97PinIns-151
□ 97PinPrePBB-107
□ 97PinPrePBC-107
□ 97PinPrePBM-107
□ 97PinPrePBY-107
□ 97PinPrePFC-107
□ 97PinPrePFM-107
□ 97PinPrePFY-107
□ 97PinPrePla-107
□ 97PinTotCMPG-63
□ 97PinTotCPB-63
□ 97PinTotCPG-63
□ 97PinTotCPR-63
□ 97Sco-140
□ 97ScoArtPro-140
□ 97ScoGolBla-140
□ 97SPAut-163
□ 97SPx-49
□ 97SPxBro-49
□ 97SPxGol-49
□ 97SPxGraF-49
□ 97SPxSil-49
□ 97SPxSte-49
□ 97Stu-68
□ 97StuPrePG-68
□ 97StuPrePS-68
□ 97UppDec-176
□ 97UppDecTSS-18C
□ 98Be A PPA-147
□ 98Be A PPAA-147
□ 98Be A PPAAF-147
□ 98Be A PPTBASG-147
□ 98Be APG-147
□ 98BowBes-93
□ 98BowBesAR-93
□ 98BowBesR-93
□ 98Fin-78
□ 98FinNo P-78
□ 98FinNo PR-78
□ 98FinRef-78
□ 98O-PChr-151
□ 98O-PChrR-151
□ 98Pac-90
□ 98PacAur-197
□ 98PacCroR-142
□ 98PacCroRLS-142
□ 98PacDynI-196
□ 98PacDynIIB-196
□ 98PacDynIR-196
□ 98PacIceB-90
□ 98PacOmeH-247
□ 98PacOmeODI-247
□ 98PacOmeR-247
□ 98PacPar-246
□ 98PacParC-246
□ 98PacParEG-246
□ 98PacParH-246
□ 98PacParIB-246
□ 98PacParS-246
□ 98PacRed-90
□ 98PacRev-147
□ 98PacRevIS-147
□ 98PacRevR-147
□ 98SP Aut-89
□ 98SP AutSotTG-JJ
□ 98SSASotT-JJ
□ 98Top-151
□ 98TopGolLC1-40
□ 98TopGolLC1B-40
□ 98TopGolLC1BOoO-40
□ 98TopGolLC1OoO-40
□ 98TopGolLC1R-40
□ 98TopGolLC1ROoO-40
□ 98TopGolLC2-40
□ 98TopGolLC2B-40
□ 98TopGolLC2BOoO-40
□ 98TopGolLC2OoO-40
□ 98TopGolLC2R-40
□ 98TopGolLC2ROoO-40
□ 98TopGolLC3-40
□ 98TopGolLC3B-40
□ 98TopGolLC3BOoO-40
□ 98TopGolLC3OoO-40
□ 98TopGolLC3R-40
□ 98TopGolLC3ROoO-40
□ 98TopO-P-151
□ 98UC-214
□ 98UD ChoPCR-214
□ 98UD ChoR-214
□ 98UppDec-203
□ 98UppDecE-203
□ 98UppDecE1o1-203
□ 98UppDecGR-203
□ 98UppDecM-216
□ 98UppDecMGS-216
□ 98UppDecMSS-216
□ 98UppDecMSS-216
□ 99Pac-39
□ 99PacAur-17
□ 99PacAurPD-17
□ 99PacCop-39
□ 99PacGol-39
□ 99PacIceB-39
□ 99PacPreD-39
□ 99QuePeeWHWCCS-5
□ 99RetHoc-9
□ 99SP AutPS-89
□ 99UppDecM-22
□ 99UppDecMGS-22
□ 99UppDecMSS-22
□ 99UppDecMSS-22
□ 99UppDecRG-9
□ 99UppDecRP-9
**Jungwirth, Thomas**
□ 94GerDELE-130
□ 95GerDELE-128
**Junker, Steve**
□ 89SpoChi-13
□ 907thInnSWHL-193
□ 917thInnSMC-80
□ 917thInnSWHL-9
□ 91UppDecCWJC-57
□ 93Don-202
□ 93Lea-402
□ 93Par-394
□ 93ParEmel-394
□ 93Ult-367
□ 93UppDec-241
□ 94ClaProP-193
□ 98GerDELE-75
**Junkin, Dale**
□ 907thInnSOHL-62
□ 917thInnSOHL-199
□ 93DetJrRW-9
□ 93NiaFalT-12
**Jurak, Milan**
□ 96CzeAPSE-284
**Jurik, Juraj**
□ 94CzeAPSE-197
□ 95CzeAPSE-121
□ 96CzeAPSE-107
**Jursinov, Vladimir**
□ 69SweHocS-5
□ 83RusNatT-21
□ 87RusNatT-24
□ 90OPC-494
□ 93FinnJyvHS-313
□ 93FinnSIS-28
□ 93FinnSIS-373
□ 94FinnSIS-398
□ 95FinnSIS-385
□ 95FinnSIS-396
**Jutila, Timo**
□ 89SweSemE-152
□ 90SweSemE-226
□ 91SweSemE-154
□ 91SweSemWCS-5
□ 93FinnJyvHS-285
□ 93FinnSIS-63
□ 93FinnSIS-368
□ 93SweSemWCS-53
□ 94FinnJaaK-5
□ 94FinnSIS-59
□ 94FinnSIS-162
□ 94FinnSISFI-6
□ 95FinnJaaKLAC-8
□ 95FinnKarWCL-3
□ 95FinnSemWC-5
□ 95FinnSemWC-202
□ 95FinnSIS-180
□ 95FinnSIS-312
□ 95FinnSISDT-8
□ 95FinnSISGC-6
□ 95FinnSISL-73
□ 95SweGloWC-130
□ 96FinnSISR-177
□ 96SweSemW-5
□ 96SweSemWAS-AS2
**Jutras, Claude**
□ 907thInnSQMJHL-11
□ 917thInnSMC-65
□ 917thInnSQMJHL-213
□ 94CapBreO-11
**Juzda, Bill**
□ 34BeeGro1P-280
□ 44BeeGro2P-412
□ 48ExhCan-31
□ 51Par-77
**Jylha, Juhani**
□ 69SweHocS-369
□ 69SweWorC-84
**Kabat, Kurt**
□ 92HamRoaA-8
**Kabayama, Matt**
□ 82MedHatT-7
□ 83MedHatT-17
**Kaberle, Frantisek**
□ 93UppDec-261
□ 94CzeAPSE-51
□ 95SweLeaE-272
□ 95SweUppDE-155
□ 95SweUppDETNA-NA18
□ 96SweSemW-106
**Kaberle, Frantisek Sr**
□ 79PanSti-80
□ 81SweSemHVS-58
**Kaberle, Tomas**
□ 95CzeAPSE-80
□ 96CzeAPSE-81
□ 98Be A PPA-287
□ 98Be A PPAA-287
□ 98Be A PPAAF-287
□ 98Be A PPSE-287
□ 98Be APG-287
□ 98PacCroRRC-9
□ 98PacDynI-181
□ 98PacDynIIB-181
□ 98PacDynIR-181
□ 98PacDynIR-9
□ 98PacOmeH-233
□ 98PacOmeODI-233
□ 98PacOmeR-233
□ 98PacRev-139
□ 98PacRevIS-139
□ 98PacRevR-139
□ 98SP Aut-110
□ 98SPXTopP-56
□ 98SPXTopPF-56
□ 98SPXTopPR-56
□ 98UppDec-375
□ 98UppDecBD-82
□ 98UppDecDD-82
□ 98UppDecE-375
□ 98UppDecE1o1-375
□ 98UppDecGR-375
□ 98UppDecM-197
□ 98UppDecMGS-197
□ 98UppDecMSS-197
□ 98UppDecMSS-197
□ 98UppDecQD-82
□ 98UppDecTD-82
□ 99Pac-408
□ 99PacCop-408
□ 99PacGol-408
□ 99PacIceB-408
□ 99PacPreD-408
□ 99SP AutPS-110
□ 99UppDecM-203
□ 99UppDecMGS-203
□ 99UppDecMPS-TK
□ 99UppDecMSS-203
□ 99UppDecMSS-203
**Kabrt, Pavel**
□ 96CzeAPSE-161
**Kachowski, Mark**
□ 84KamBla-12
□ 85KamBla-9
□ 87PenKod-14
□ 89ProIHL-159
□ 90ProAHLIHL-378
**Kachur, Eddie**
□ 94ParMisL-37
**Kachur, John**
□ 99WicThu-9
**Kachur, Trent**
□ 86RegPat-12
□ 87RegPat-10
**Kacir, Marian**
□ 93OweSouPla-6
□ 93OweSouPla-12
**Kadera, Roman**
□ 93UppDec-267
□ 94CzeAPSE-135
□ 95CzeAPSE-234
**Kadlec, Arnold**
□ 81SweSemHVS-59
□ 82SweSemHVS-82
**Kadlec, Drahomir**
□ 89SweSemWCS-187
□ 93SweSemWCS-92
□ 94FinnJaaK-170
□ 94GerDELE-176
□ 95FinnSemWC-144
□ 95GerDELE-172
□ 96CzeAPSE-344
□ 96GerDELE-115
**Kaebel, Butch**
□ 90KnoChe-110
□ 92BirBul-5
□ 93BirBul-5
□ 93PeoRiv-14
□ 96PeoRiv-10
□ 96PeoRivPA-10
**Kaebel, Karson**
□ 92NorMicW-14
□ 93NorMicW-16
□ 94DayBom-7
□ 96PeoRiv-11
□ 96PeoRivPA-11
**Kaebel, Klage**
□ 93OmaLan-11
**Kaese, Trent**
□ 87FliSpi-9
**Kahelin, Timo**
□ 93FinnJyvHS-255
□ 93FinnSIS-284
**Kahiluoto, Tommi**
□ 96FinnSISR-31
**Kaipainen, Matti**
□ 93FinnSIS-124
□ 94FinnSIS-69
□ 95FinnSIS-236
□ 96FinnSISR-34
**Kaiser, Vern**
□ 44BeeGro2P-253
□ 45QuaOatP-85
□ 51BufBis-11
**Kajer, Milos**
□ 94CzeAPSE-69
□ 95CzeAPSE-90
**Kajki, Milan**
□ 79PanSti-77
**Kajzerek, Marian**
□ 69SweWorC-196
**Kakko, Erik**
□ 93FinnJyvHS-316
□ 93FinnSIS-33
□ 94FinnSIS-269
□ 95FinnSIS-21
□ 96FinnSISR-146
**Kalawsky, Craig**
□ 86RegPat-13
□ 87RegPat-11
**Kales, Craig**
□ 82NorBayC-11
□ 83KinCan-20
**Kaleta, Alex**
□ 34BeeGro1P-59
□ 44BeeGro2P-330
**Kall, Per-Erik**
□ 69SweHocS-209
**Kallay, Ian**
□ 90ForSasTra-8
**Kallio, Markku**
□ 94FinnSIS-311
**Kallio, Tomi**
□ 95ColCho-334
□ 95ColChoPC-334
□ 95ColChoPCP-334
□ 95FinnSIS-335
□ 95FinnSISDD-5
□ 96FinnSISR-146
**Kalliomaki, Tuomas**
□ 93FinnJyvHS-172
□ 93FinnSIS-171
□ 95FinnSIS-350
**Kallioniemi, Riku**
□ 95FinnSIS-303
□ 96FinnSISR-97
**Kallur, Anders**
□ 79IslTrans-6
□ 80OPC-156
□ 80Top-156
□ 81OPC-204
□ 81OPCSti-162
□ 81Top-E90
□ 82OPC-203
□ 82OPCSti-57
□ 82PosCer-12
□ 84IslIsIN-9
□ 85IslIsIN-8

**Kalmikov, Konstantin**
❑ 96SudWol-11
❑ 96SudWolP-13
❑ 97SudWolP-5
**Kalt, Dieter**
❑ 93SweSemWCS-279
❑ 94FinnJaaK-241
❑ 95AusNatTea-10
❑ 95FinnSemWC-186
❑ 96GerDELE-178
❑ 96SweSemW-217
**Kalteva, Petri**
❑ 93FinnJyvHS-295
❑ 93FinnSIS-61
❑ 94FinnSIS-296
❑ 95FinnSIS-316
**Kambeitz, Jim**
❑ 83MedHatT-20
**Kamel, Noel**
❑ 92MPSPhoSJHL-73
**Kamenev, Vasili**
❑ 95SigRooFF-FF5
❑ 95SigRooFFS-FF5
**Kamensky, Valeri**
❑ 87RusNatT-7
❑ 89RusNatT-9
❑ 89SweSemWCS-91
❑ 90OPCRedA-4R
❑ 91Gil-30
❑ 91NordPet-12
❑ 91OPC-513
❑ 91Par-362
❑ 91ParFre-362
❑ 91Pin-340
❑ 91PinFre-340
❑ 91RusStaRA-6
❑ 91RusTriKam-1
❑ 91RusTriKam-2
❑ 91RusTriKam-3
❑ 91RusTriKam-4
❑ 91RusTriKam-5
❑ 91ScoRoo-76T
❑ 91SweSemWCS-88
❑ 91Top-513
❑ 91UppDec-273
❑ 91UppDec-SP1
❑ 91UppDecF-273
❑ 92Bow-432
❑ 92HumDum1-12
❑ 92NorPet-15
❑ 92OPC-266
❑ 92PanSti-295
❑ 92PanSti-R
❑ 92PanStiFre-295
❑ 92PanStiFre-R
❑ 92Par-230
❑ 92Par-377
❑ 92ParEmel-230
❑ 92ParEmel-377
❑ 92Pin-64
❑ 92PinFre-64
❑ 92ProSet-148
❑ 92Sco-360
❑ 92ScoCan-360
❑ 92ScoYouS-24
❑ 92StaClu-344
❑ 92Top-53
❑ 92TopGol-53G
❑ 92TriFroRWP-11
❑ 92TriFroRWP-12
❑ 92UppDec-27
❑ 92UppDecES-E20
❑ 93Don-277
❑ 93Lea-207
❑ 93OPCPre-85
❑ 93OPCPreG-85
❑ 93PanSti-72
❑ 93Par-438
❑ 93ParEmel-438
❑ 93Pin-244
❑ 93PinCan-244
❑ 93Pow-199
❑ 93Sco-326
❑ 93ScoCan-326
❑ 93StaClu-237
❑ 93StaCluFDI-237
❑ 93StaCluFDIO-237
❑ 93StaCluO-237
❑ 93TopPre-85
❑ 93TopPreG-85
❑ 93Ult-84
❑ 93UppDec-118
❑ 94BeAPSig-158
❑ 94CanGamNHLP-195
❑ 94Don-116
❑ 94FinnJaaK-157
❑ 94Fla-147
❑ 94Fle-177
❑ 94Lea-117
❑ 94NordBurK-10
❑ 94OPCPre-32
❑ 94OPCPreSE-32
❑ 94Par-190
❑ 94ParGol-190
❑ 94Pin-343
❑ 94PinArtP-343
❑ 94PinRinC-343
❑ 94Sel-144
❑ 94SelGol-144
❑ 94TopPre-32
❑ 94TopPreSE-32
❑ 94Ult-357
❑ 94UppDec-355
❑ 94UppDecElelce-355
❑ 95CanGamNHLP-74
❑ 95ColCho-221
❑ 95ColChoPC-221
❑ 95ColChoPCP-221
❑ 95Don-236
❑ 95DonEli-22
❑ 95DonEliDCS-22
❑ 95DonEliDCU-22
❑ 95Emo-37
❑ 95Fin-170
❑ 95FinnSemWC-131
❑ 95FinRef-164
❑ 95ImpSti-31
❑ 95Met-33
❑ 95ParInt-48
❑ 95ParIntEl-48
❑ 95PlaOneoOne-243
❑ 95Sco-268
❑ 95ScoBlaIce-268
❑ 95ScoBlaIceAP-268
❑ 95SelCer-105
❑ 95SelCerMG-105
❑ 95SkyImp-36
❑ 95StaClu-161
❑ 95StaCluMOMS-161
❑ 95Sum-6
❑ 95SumArtP-6
❑ 95SumIce-6
❑ 95SweGloWC-179
❑ 95SwiHNL-542
❑ 95Ult-221
❑ 95UppDec-489
❑ 95UppDecElelce-489
❑ 95UppDecElelceG-489
❑ 96BeAPAut-33
❑ 96BeAPAutSil-33
❑ 96BeAPla-33
❑ 96ColCho-62
❑ 96ColChoBlo-62
❑ 96Don-14
❑ 96DonCanI-32
❑ 96DonCanIGPP-32
❑ 96DonCanIRPP-32
❑ 96DonEli-118
❑ 96DonEliDCS-118
❑ 96DonPrePro-14
❑ 96Fle-21
❑ 96FleArtRos-9
❑ 96FlePicDL-9
❑ 96FlePicF5-22
❑ 96Lea-170
❑ 96LeaLim-81
❑ 96LeaLimG-81
❑ 96LeaPre-53
❑ 96LeaPreP-170
❑ 96LeaPrePP-53
❑ 96LeaPreSG-59
❑ 96LeaPreSte-59
❑ 96MetUni-33
❑ 96Pin-47
❑ 96PinArtP-47
❑ 96PinFoi-47
❑ 96PinPreS-47
❑ 96PinRinC-47
❑ 96PlaOneoOne-420
❑ 96Sco-157
❑ 96ScoArtPro-157
❑ 96ScoDeaCAP-157
❑ 96ScoGolB-157
❑ 96ScoSpeAP-157
❑ 96SelCer-67
❑ 96SelCerAP-67
❑ 96SelCerBlu-67
❑ 96SelCerMB-67
❑ 96SelCerMG-67
❑ 96SelCerMR-67
❑ 96SelCerRed-67
❑ 96SkyImp-23
❑ 96SkyImpB-9
❑ 96Sum-59
❑ 96SumArtP-59
❑ 96SumIce-59
❑ 96SumMet-59
❑ 96SumPreS-59
❑ 96SweSemW-149
❑ 96TopNHLP-39
❑ 96TopPicOI-39
❑ 96Ult-36
❑ 96UltGolM-36
❑ 96UppDec-241
❑ 96UppDecGN-X20
❑ 96Zen-8
❑ 96ZenArtP-8
❑ 97ColCho-58
❑ 97Don-132
❑ 97DonCanI-82
❑ 97DonCanIDS-82
❑ 97DonCanIPS-82
❑ 97DonEli-44
❑ 97DonEliAsp-44
❑ 97DonEliS-44
❑ 97DonLim-47
❑ 97DonLim-111
❑ 97DonLimExp-47
❑ 97DonLimExp-111
❑ 97DonPreProG-132
❑ 97DonPreProS-132
❑ 97DonPri-87
❑ 97DonPriSoA-87
❑ 97Pac-213
❑ 97PacCop-213
❑ 97PacCroR-34
❑ 97PacCroREG-34
❑ 97PacCroRIB-34
❑ 97PacCroRS-34
❑ 97PacDyn-30
❑ 97PacDynC-30
❑ 97PacDynDG-30
❑ 97PacDynEG-30
❑ 97PacDynIB-30
❑ 97PacDynR-30
❑ 97PacDynSil-30
❑ 97PacDynTan-42
❑ 97PacEmeGre-213
❑ 97PacIceB-213
❑ 97PacInv-35
❑ 97PacInvC-35
❑ 97PacInvEG-35
❑ 97PacInvIB-35
❑ 97PacInvR-35
❑ 97PacInvS-35
❑ 97PacOme-57
❑ 97PacOmeC-57
❑ 97PacOmeDG-57
❑ 97PacOmeEG-57
❑ 97PacOmeG-57
❑ 97PacOmeIB-57
❑ 97PacPar-50
❑ 97PacParC-50
❑ 97PacParDG-50
❑ 97PacParEG-50
❑ 97PacParIB-50
❑ 97PacParRed-50
❑ 97PacParSil-50
❑ 97PacRed-213
❑ 97PacRev-33
❑ 97PacRevC-33
❑ 97PacRevE-33
❑ 97PacRevIB-33
❑ 97PacRevR-33
❑ 97PacRevS-33
❑ 97PacSil-213
❑ 97Pin-186
❑ 97PinCer-67
❑ 97PinCerMB-67
❑ 97PinCerMG-67
❑ 97PinCerMR-67
❑ 97PinCerR-67
❑ 97PinIns-114
❑ 97PinPrePBB-186
❑ 97PinPrePBC-186
❑ 97PinPrePBM-186
❑ 97PinPrePBY-186
❑ 97PinPrePFC-186
❑ 97PinPrePFM-186
❑ 97PinPrePFY-186
❑ 97PinPrePla-186
❑ 97PinTotCMPG-67
❑ 97PinTotCPB-67
❑ 97PinTotCPG-67
❑ 97PinTotCPR-67
❑ 97Sco-186
❑ 97ScoAva-7
❑ 97ScoAvaPla-7
❑ 97ScoAvaPre-7
❑ 97SPAut-39
❑ 97UppDec-254
❑ 98Be A PPA-186
❑ 98Be A PPAA-186
❑ 98Be A PPAAF-186
❑ 98Be A PPSE-186
❑ 98Be APG-186
❑ 98BowBes-89
❑ 98BowBesAR-89
❑ 98BowBesR-89
❑ 98Fin-43
❑ 98FinNo P-43
❑ 98FinNo PR-43
❑ 98FinRef-43
❑ 98O-PChr-39
❑ 98O-PChrR-39
❑ 98Pac-160
❑ 98PacAur-47
❑ 98PacDynI-49
❑ 98PacDynIIB-49
❑ 98PacDynIR-49
❑ 98PacIceB-160
❑ 98PacPar-56
❑ 98PacParC-56
❑ 98PacParEG-56
❑ 98PacParH-56
❑ 98PacParIB-56
❑ 98PacParS-56
❑ 98PacRed-160
❑ 98SPxFin-23
❑ 98SPxFinR-23
❑ 98SPxFinS-23
❑ 98Top-39
❑ 98TopO-P-39
❑ 98UC-58
❑ 98UD ChoPCR-58
❑ 98UD ChoR-58
❑ 98UppDec-249
❑ 98UppDecE-249
❑ 98UppDecE1o1-249
❑ 98UppDecGR-249
❑ 99Pac-108
❑ 99PacCop-108
❑ 99PacGol-108
❑ 99PacIceB-108
❑ 99PacPreD-108
**Kames, Jaroslav**
❑ 94CzeAPSE-181
❑ 95CzeAPSE-29
**Kaminski, B.**
❑ 95GerDELE-35
**Kaminski, Darcy**
❑ 89LetHur-11
❑ 90HamRoaA-47
❑ 91HamRoaA-20
❑ 92NasKni-22
❑ 94CenHocL-114
**Kaminski, Ian**
❑ 92RusStaRA-33
**Kaminski, Kevin**
❑ 88SasBla-23
❑ 89HalCit-12
❑ 89Nord-20
❑ 89NordGenF-16
❑ 89ProAHL-170
❑ 90NordTeal-15
❑ 90ProAHLIHL-448
❑ 90ProAHLIHL-544
❑ 93Don-505
❑ 93Par-493
❑ 93ParEmel-493
❑ 93PorPir-21
❑ 94ClaEnf-E8
❑ 94PorPir-12
❑ 95Cap-14
❑ 96BeAPAut-86
❑ 96BeAPAutSil-86
❑ 96BeAPla-86
❑ 98LasVegT-10
**Kaminsky, Max**
❑ 34BeeGro1P-198
❑ 35DiaMatTI-33
**Kaminsky, Yan**
❑ 92UppDec-333
❑ 92UppDec-344
❑ 93Cla-88
❑ 93Don-456
❑ 93JetRuf-13
❑ 94ClaProP-185
❑ 94Lea-173
❑ 94OPCPre-399
❑ 94OPCPreSE-399
❑ 94Pin-263
❑ 94PinArtP-263
❑ 94PinRinC-263
❑ 94Sco-221
❑ 94ScoGol-221
❑ 94ScoPla-221
❑ 94ScoPlaTS-221
❑ 94TopPre-399
❑ 94TopPreSE-399
**Kammerer, Axel**
❑ 89SweSemWCS-123
❑ 94GerDELE-193
❑ 95GerDELE-328
❑ 96GerDELE-106
**Kampersal, Jeffery**
❑ 92RicRen-9
**Kampf, Radek**
❑ 96CzeAPSE-299
**Kampman, Bingo**
❑ 34BeeGro1P-329
❑ 38QuaOatP-21
❑ 39OPCV3011-3
❑ 40OPCV3012-109
**Kamppuri, Hannu**
❑ 82SweSemHVS-26
❑ 84DevPos-33
**Kamula, Pete**
❑ 52JunBluT-19
**Kane, Boyd**
❑ 96RegPat-12
❑ 98ChaChe-9
**Kane, Dan**
❑ 84MonGolF-7
**Kane, Shaun**
❑ 93RalIce-8
**Kangas, Pasi**
❑ 95FinnSIS-266
**Kangas, Vesa**
❑ 89SweSemE-161
**Kangasalusta, Pekka**
❑ 95FinnSIS-231
❑ 96FinnSISR-30
**Kangasniemi, Miska**
❑ 94Fin-134
❑ 94FinRef-134
❑ 94FinSupTW-134
❑ 95FinnSIS-60
**Kankovsky, Petr**
❑ 94CzeAPSE-192
❑ 95CzeAPSE-188
❑ 96CzeAPSE-323
**Kankovsky, Roman**
❑ 94CzeAPSE-190
❑ 95CzeAPSE-178
❑ 96CzeAPSE-313
**Kannegiesser, Sheldon**
❑ 71OPC-190
❑ 71PenPos-9
❑ 71TorSun-219
❑ 74NHLActSta-114
❑ 74OPCNHL-338
❑ 75OPCNHL-69
❑ 75Top-69
❑ 76OPCNHL-335
❑ 78OPC-310
**Kannewurf, Frank**
❑ 94GerDELE-37
❑ 95GerDELE-30
**Kannisto, Mika**
❑ 94FinnSIS-294
❑ 95FinnSIS-221
❑ 96FinnSISR-24
**Kantor, Robert**
❑ 95CzeAPSE-207
**Kapanen, Hannu**
❑ 93FinnJyvHS-163
❑ 95FinnSIS-389
**Kapanen, Kimmo**
❑ 93FinnSIS-162
❑ 94FinnSIS-229
❑ 95FinnSIS-2
**Kapanen, Sami**
❑ 91UppDec-674
❑ 91UppDecCWJC-37
❑ 91UppDecF-674
❑ 93FinnJyvHS-174
❑ 93FinnSIS-179
❑ 94FinnJaaK-39
❑ 94FinnSIS-163
❑ 94FinnSIS-209
❑ 94FinnSISFI-8
❑ 94FinnSISMN-5
❑ 94FinnSISS-5
❑ 95FinnBecAC-5
❑ 95FinnKarWCL-4
❑ 95FinnSemWC-24
❑ 95FinnSemWC-231
❑ 95FinnSIS-12
❑ 95FinnSISDD-6
❑ 95FinnSISGC-13
❑ 95FinnSISL-72
❑ 95FinnSISLSS-1
❑ 95ParInt-516
❑ 95ParIntEl-516
❑ 96BeAPAut-145
❑ 96BeAPAutSil-145
❑ 96BeAPla-145
❑ 96SweSemW-19
❑ 97CarHur-13
❑ 97DonPri-73
❑ 97DonPriSoA-73
❑ 97Pac-192
❑ 97PacCop-192
❑ 97PacEmeGre-192
❑ 97PacIceB-192
❑ 97PacOme-41
❑ 97PacOmeC-41
❑ 97PacOmeDG-41
❑ 97PacOmeEG-41
❑ 97PacOmeG-41
❑ 97PacOmeIB-41
❑ 97PacRed-192
❑ 97PacRev-23
❑ 97PacRevC-23
❑ 97PacRevE-23
❑ 97PacRevIB-23
❑ 97PacRevR-23
❑ 97PacRevS-23
❑ 97PacSil-192
❑ 97SPAut-27
❑ 97UppDec-239
❑ 97UppDecBD-147
❑ 97UppDecBDDD-147
❑ 97UppDecBDQD-147
❑ 97UppDecBDTD-147
❑ 97Zen-69
❑ 97ZenZGol-69
❑ 97ZenZSil-69
❑ 98Be A PPA-24
❑ 98Be A PPAA-24
❑ 98Be A PPAAF-24
❑ 98Be A PPTBASG-24
❑ 98Be APG-24
❑ 98BowBes-97
❑ 98BowBesAR-97
❑ 98BowBesR-97
❑ 98Fin-130
❑ 98FinNo P-130
❑ 98FinNo PR-130
❑ 98FinRef-130
❑ 98O-PChr-178
❑ 98O-PChrR-178
❑ 98Pac-134
❑ 98PacAur-33
❑ 98PacCroR-24
❑ 98PacCroRLS-24
❑ 98PacDynI-34
❑ 98PacDynIIB-34
❑ 98PacDynIR-34
❑ 98PacIceB-134
❑ 98PacOmeH-43
❑ 98PacOmeODI-43
❑ 98PacOmeR-43
❑ 98PacPar-37
❑ 98PacParC-37
❑ 98PacParEG-37
❑ 98PacParH-37
❑ 98PacParIB-37
❑ 98PacParS-37
❑ 98PacRed-134
❑ 98SP Aut-16
❑ 98SPxFin-16
❑ 98SPxFinR-16
❑ 98SPxFinS-16
❑ 98Top-178
❑ 98TopGolLC1-36
❑ 98TopGolLC1B-36
❑ 98TopGolLC1BOoO-36
❑ 98TopGolLC1OoO-36
❑ 98TopGolLC1R-36
❑ 98TopGolLC1ROoO-36
❑ 98TopGolLC2-36
❑ 98TopGolLC2B-36
❑ 98TopGolLC2BOoO-36
❑ 98TopGolLC2OoO-36
❑ 98TopGolLC2R-36
❑ 98TopGolLC2ROoO-36
❑ 98TopGolLC3-36
❑ 98TopGolLC3B-36
❑ 98TopGolLC3BOoO-36
❑ 98TopGolLC3OoO-36
❑ 98TopGolLC3R-36
❑ 98TopGolLC3ROoO-36
❑ 98TopO-P-178
❑ 98UC-40
❑ 98UD ChoPCR-40
❑ 98UD ChoR-40
❑ 98UppDec-57
❑ 98UppDecBD-17
❑ 98UppDecDD-17
❑ 98UppDecE-57
❑ 98UppDecE1o1-57
❑ 98UppDecGR-57
❑ 98UppDecM-38
❑ 98UppDecMGS-38
❑ 98UppDecMSS-38
❑ 98UppDecMSS-38
❑ 98UppDecQD-17
❑ 98UppDecTD-17
❑ 99Pac-73
❑ 99PacAur-27
❑ 99PacAurPD-27
❑ 99PacCop-73
❑ 99PacGol-73
❑ 99PacIceB-73
❑ 99PacPreD-73
❑ 99RetHoc-15
❑ 99SP AutPS-16
❑ 99UppDecM-39
❑ 99UppDecMGS-39
❑ 99UppDecMPS-SK
❑ 99UppDecMSS-39
❑ 99UppDecMSS-39
❑ 99UppDecRG-15
❑ 99UppDecRP-15
**Kapkaikin, Konstantin**
❑ 91OPCIns-51R
**Kapus, Richard**
❑ 93UppDec-265
**Kapusta, Tomas**
❑ 89ProAHL-147
❑ 90ProAHLIHL-235
❑ 91ProAHLCHL-231
❑ 93FinnJyvHS-48
❑ 93FinnSIS-250
❑ 93FinnSIS-361
❑ 93SweSemWCS-99
❑ 94FinnSIS-225
❑ 94FinnSISFI-9
❑ 95FinnSIS-357
❑ 95FinnSIS-372
❑ 95FinnSISL-87
❑ 96CzeAPSE-227
**Kapustin, Sergei**
❑ 74SweHocS-63
❑ 79PanSti-153
❑ 80USSOlyTMP-4
❑ 82SweSemHVS-71
❑ 83RusNatT-7
❑ 92FutTre76CC-144
**Karabin, Ladislav**
❑ 93CleLum-18
❑ 93CleLumPos-13
❑ 93Don-472
❑ 93Par-426
❑ 93ParEmel-426
❑ 93UppDec-467
❑ 94ClaProP-108
❑ 95RochAmeSS-7
**Karakas, Kraig**
❑ 93MinDul-15
**Karakas, Mike**
❑ 34BeeGro1P-60
❑ 35DiaMatT3-29
❑ 35DiaMatT4-7
❑ 35DiaMatT5-7
❑ 36OPCV304D-107
❑ 36V356WorG-123
❑ 37DiaMatT6-7
❑ 39OPCV3011-47
**Karalahti, Jere**
❑ 93FinnSIS-86
❑ 93FinnSIS-395
❑ 94Fin-126
❑ 94FinnSIS-2
❑ 94FinnSISJ-4
❑ 94FinRef-126
❑ 94FinSupTW-126
❑ 94ParSE-SE216
❑ 94ParSEG-SE216
❑ 95FinnSemWC-237
❑ 95FinnSIS-206
❑ 96FinnSISR-4
**Karalis, Tom**
❑ 85FreExp-21
❑ 86FreExp-13
❑ 87FliSpi-10
❑ 89ProIHL-117
❑ 90ProAHLIHL-549
❑ 91ProAHLCHL-176
❑ 92-TulOil-7
**Karam, Jake**
❑ 92CorBigRed-17
❑ 93CorBigRed-14
**Karamnov, Vitali**
❑ 92Par-387
❑ 92ParEmel-387
❑ 92Pin-398
❑ 92PinFre-398
❑ 92UppDec-341
❑ 92UppDec-510
❑ 93Don-287
❑ 93Lea-408
❑ 93OPCPre-292
❑ 93OPCPreG-292
❑ 93Par-444
❑ 93ParEmel-444
❑ 93Pow-429
❑ 93StaClu-478
❑ 93StaCluFDI-478
❑ 93StaCluO-478
❑ 93TopPre-292
❑ 93TopPreG-292
❑ 93Ult-412
❑ 93UppDec-338
❑ 96GerDELE-259
❑ 98GerDELE-37
**Karapuu, Mika**
❑ 93FinnSIS-44
❑ 96FinnSISR-121
**Karasek, Ryan**
❑ 94DubFigS-15
**Karcher, Carl**
❑ 94DucCarJr-27
**Karestal, Lars**
❑ 67SweHoc-203
**Karg, Steffen**
❑ 98GerDELE-220
**Karger, Reinhard**
❑ 69SweWorC-173
❑ 70SweHocS-377
**Kariya, Paul**
❑ 91BriColJHL-84
❑ 91BriColJHL-86
❑ 91BriColJHL-91
❑ 91BriColJHL-93
❑ 91BriColJHL-168
❑ 91UppDecCWJC-50
❑ 92MaiBlaB-20
❑ 92UppDec-586
❑ 92UppDec-SP3
❑ 93AlbIntTC-8
❑ 93Cla-4
❑ 93Cla-113
❑ 93ClaCraNum-N2
❑ 93ClaPromo-NNO
❑ 93ClaTeaCan-TC2
❑ 93ClaTopTen-DP4
❑ 93MaiBlaB-37
❑ 93MaiBlaB-41
❑ 93MaiBlaB-60
❑ 93MaiBlaB-61
❑ 93OPCPreTC-17
❑ 93Pow-485
❑ 93Ult-465
❑ 93UppDecPOE-E10
❑ 94BAPUpCP-UC9
❑ 94BeAPla-R103
❑ 94BeAPla-R126
❑ 94BeAPla-R151
❑ 94BeAPSig-151
❑ 94ClaProP-18
❑ 94ClaProPIA-IA3
❑ 94ClaProPIH-LP15
❑ 94DucCarJr-10
❑ 94Fin-7
❑ 94FinBowB-R1
❑ 94FinBowB-X21
❑ 94FinBowBR-R1
❑ 94FinBowBR-X21
❑ 94FinnJaaK-104
❑ 94FinRef-7
❑ 94FinSupTW-7
❑ 94Fla-4
❑ 94Fle-3
❑ 94FleRooS-5
❑ 94Lea-455
❑ 94LeaLim-107
❑ 94LeaLimG-5
❑ 94LeaLimI-27
❑ 94LeaPhe-5
❑ 94McDUppD-McD32
❑ 94OPCPre-405
❑ 94OPCPreSE-405
❑ 94ParSE-SE8
❑ 94ParSEG-SE8
❑ 94ParSEV-1
❑ 94Pin-265
❑ 94Pin-480
❑ 94PinArtP-265
❑ 94PinArtP-480
❑ 94PinRinC-265
❑ 94PinRinC-480
❑ 94PinRooTP-9
❑ 94ScoTeaC-CT1
❑ 94ScoTopRR-1
❑ 94Sel-173
❑ 94SelGol-173
❑ 94SelYouExp-YE5
❑ 94SP-1
❑ 94SPDieCut-1
❑ 94SPPre-1
❑ 94SPPreDC-1
❑ 94TopFinB-9
❑ 94TopPre-405
❑ 94TopPreSE-405
❑ 94UltPro-3
❑ 94UppDec-235
❑ 94UppDec-527
❑ 94UppDecElelce-235
❑ 94UppDecElelce-527
❑ 94UppDecPC-C2
❑ 94UppDecPCEG-C2
❑ 94UppDecPCES-C2
❑ 94UppDecPH-H14
❑ 94UppDecPHEG-H14
❑ 94UppDecPHES-H14
❑ 94UppDecPHG-H14
❑ 94UppDecSPI-SP91
❑ 94UppDecSPIDC-SP91
❑ 95BAPLetL-LL10
❑ 95Bow-90
❑ 95BowAllFoi-90
❑ 95BowBes-BB15

❑ 95BowBesRef-BB15
❑ 95CanGamNHLP-32
❑ 95ColCho-159
❑ 95ColCho-363
❑ 95ColCho-370
❑ 95ColChoCTG-C10
❑ 95ColChoCTG-C10B
❑ 95ColChoCTG-C10C
❑ 95ColChoCTGGB-C10
❑ 95ColChoCTGGR-C10
❑ 95ColChoCTGSB-C10
❑ 95ColChoCTGSR-C10
❑ 95ColChoPC-159
❑ 95ColChoPC-363
❑ 95ColChoPC-370
❑ 95ColChoPCP-159
❑ 95ColChoPCP-363
❑ 95ColChoPCP-370
❑ 95Don-57
❑ 95DonDom-6
❑ 95DonEli-31
❑ 95DonEliCE-5
❑ 95DonEliDCS-31
❑ 95DonEliDCU-31
❑ 95DonEliIns-6
❑ 95DonProPoi-19
❑ 95DonRooTea-3
❑ 95Emo-3
❑ 95EmoXci-15
❑ 95Fin-165
❑ 95Fin-189
❑ 95FinnSemWC-86
❑ 95FinnSemWC-206
❑ 95FinRef-165
❑ 95FinRef-189
❑ 95ImpSti-2
❑ 95ImpStiDCS-12
❑ 95Kra-55
❑ 95Lea-304
❑ 95LeaFirOIce-11
❑ 95LeaLim-9
❑ 95LeaLimSG-5
❑ 95LeaStuR-3
❑ 95McDPin-MCD-11
❑ 95Met-2
❑ 95MetHM-7
❑ 95NHLAcePC-7H
❑ 95NHLCooT-8
❑ 95NHLCooT-RP8
❑ 95ParInt-3
❑ 95ParIntCCGS1-4
❑ 95ParIntCCGS2-4
❑ 95ParIntCCSS1-4
❑ 95ParIntCCSS2-4
❑ 95ParIntEl-3
❑ 95ParIntPTP-PP15
❑ 95ParIntPTP-PP46
❑ 95Pin-2
❑ 95PinArtP-2
❑ 95PinCleS-3
❑ 95PinFan-26
❑ 95PinRinC-2
❑ 95PinRoa2-2
❑ 95PlaOneoOne-2
❑ 95PlaOneoOne-114
❑ 95PlaOneoOne-223
❑ 95PosUppD-20
❑ 95ProMag-43
❑ 95Sco-125
❑ 95ScoBlaIce-125
❑ 95ScoBlaIceAP-125
❑ 95ScoDreTea-7
❑ 95ScoGolBla-9
❑ 95SelCer-13
❑ 95SelCerFut-3
❑ 95SelCerMG-13
❑ 95SelCerP-13
❑ 95SkyImp-3
❑ 95SkyImp-230
❑ 95SkyImpCI-7
❑ 95SP-1
❑ 95SPHol-FX2
❑ 95SPHolSpFX-FX2
❑ 95SPStaEto-E1
❑ 95SPStaEtoG-E1
❑ 95StaClu-174
❑ 95StaCluGTSC-GT1
❑ 95StaCluMO-46
❑ 95StaCluMOMS-174
❑ 95StaCluNem-N9
❑ 95Sum-2
❑ 95SumArtP-2
❑ 95SumGM-19
❑ 95SumIce-2
❑ 95SweGloWC-91
❑ 95Top-7
❑ 95Top-217
❑ 95TopHomGC-HGC7
❑ 95TopMarMPB-7
❑ 95TopMysF-M13
❑ 95TopMysFR-M13
❑ 95TopNewG-5NG
❑ 95TopOPCI-7
❑ 95TopOPCI-217
❑ 95TopSupSki-16
❑ 95TopSupSkiPla-16
❑ 95TopYouS-YS1
❑ 95Ult-3
❑ 95Ult-388
❑ 95UltAllRoo-5
❑ 95UltAllRooGM-5
❑ 95UltExtAtt-11
❑ 95UltGolM-3
❑ 95UltHigSpe-11
❑ 95UppDec-206
❑ 95UppDec-245
❑ 95UppDecAGPRW-6
❑ 95UppDecEleIce-206
❑ 95UppDecEleIce-245
❑ 95UppDecEleIceG-206
❑ 95UppDecEleIceG-245
❑ 95UppDecFreFra-F9
❑ 95UppDecFreFraJ-F9
❑ 95UppDecNHLAS-AS14
❑ 95UppDecPRE-R43
❑ 95UppDecPreR-R43
❑ 95UppDecSpeE-SE1
❑ 95UppDecSpeEdiG-SE1
❑ 95UppDecWJA-5
❑ 95UppPreRP-R43
❑ 95Zen-17
❑ 95ZenZT-14
❑ 96BeAPBisITB-20
❑ 96BeAPLH-6B
❑ 96BeAPLHAut-6B
❑ 96BeAPLHAutSil-6B
❑ 96ColCho-1
❑ 96ColCho-289
❑ 96ColCho-309
❑ 96ColChoCTG-C24A
❑ 96ColChoCTG-C24B
❑ 96ColChoCTG-C24C
❑ 96ColChoCTGE-CR24
❑ 96ColChoCTGEG-CR24
❑ 96ColChoCTGG-C24A
❑ 96ColChoCTGG-C24B
❑ 96ColChoCTGG-C24C
❑ 96ColChoMVP-UD10
❑ 96ColChoMVPG-UD10
❑ 96ColChoSti-S14
❑ 96Don-142
❑ 96DonCanI-3
❑ 96DonCanIGPP-3
❑ 96DonCanIOC-2
❑ 96DonCanIRPP-3
❑ 96DonDom-8
❑ 96DonEli-1
❑ 96DonEliDCS-1
❑ 96DonEliS-5
❑ 96DonGoTS-8
❑ 96DonPrePro-142
❑ 96Duc-22
❑ 96DurL'EB-JB20
❑ 96Fla-2
❑ 96FlaBluI-2
❑ 96FlaCenIS-6
❑ 96Fle-2
❑ 96Fle-141
❑ 96FleArtRos-10
❑ 96FlePea-6
❑ 96FlePic-6
❑ 96FlePicDL-5
❑ 96FlePicF5-23
❑ 96FlePicJE-6
❑ 96HocGreC-12
❑ 96HocGreCG-12
❑ 96KraUppD-29
❑ 96KraUppD-33
❑ 96KraUppD-43
❑ 96Lea-176
❑ 96LeaFirOI-4
❑ 96LeaLim-17
❑ 96LeaLimG-17
❑ 96LeaPre-7
❑ 96LeaPreP-176
❑ 96LeaPrePP-7
❑ 96LeaPreSG-34
❑ 96LeaPreSP-11
❑ 96LeaPreSte-34
❑ 96LeaSwe-5
❑ 96LeaSwe(-5
❑ 96MetUni-2
❑ 96MetUniIC-7
❑ 96MetUniICSP-7
❑ 96MetUniLW-9
❑ 96MetUniLWSP-9
❑ 96NHLACEPC-26
❑ 96NHLProSTA-43
❑ 96Pin-184
❑ 96PinArtP-184
❑ 96PinFoi-184
❑ 96PinMcD-29
❑ 96PinMin-5
❑ 96PinMinB-5
❑ 96PinMinCoiB-5
❑ 96PinMinCoiGP-5
❑ 96PinMinCoiN-5
❑ 96PinMinCoiS-5
❑ 96PinMinCoiSG-5
❑ 96PinMinG-5
❑ 96PinMinS-5
❑ 96PinPreS-184
❑ 96PinRinC-184
❑ 96PinTeaP-5
❑ 96PinTro-2
❑ 96PlaOneoOne-353
❑ 96PosUppD-11
❑ 96Sco-8
❑ 96ScoArtPro-8
❑ 96ScoDeaCAP-8
❑ 96ScoDreTea-2
❑ 96ScoGolB-8
❑ 96ScoSpeAP-8
❑ 96ScoSudDea-13
❑ 96SelCer-14
❑ 96SelCerAP-14
❑ 96SelCerBlu-14
❑ 96SelCerCor-11
❑ 96SelCerMB-14
❑ 96SelCerMG-14
❑ 96SelCerMR-14
❑ 96SelCerRed-14
❑ 96SkyImp-2
❑ 96SkyImpCI-6
❑ 96SkyImpVer-6
❑ 96SP-1
❑ 96SPCleWin-CW5
❑ 96SPGamFil-GF9
❑ 96SPx-1
❑ 96SPxGol-1
❑ 96StaCluMO-2
❑ 96Sum-116
❑ 96SumArtP-116
❑ 96SumHigV-3
❑ 96SumHigVM-3
❑ 96SumIce-116
❑ 96SumMet-116
❑ 96SumPreS-116
❑ 96SumUnt-7
❑ 96SweSemW-94
❑ 96TeaOut-1
❑ 96TopPicFT-FT11
❑ 96TopPicTS-TS4
❑ 96Ult-2
❑ 96UltGolM-2
❑ 96UltPow-8
❑ 96UltPowRL-3
❑ 96UppDec-1
❑ 96UppDecB-4
❑ 96UppDecBD-175
❑ 96UppDecBDG-175
❑ 96UppDecBDRFTC-RC8
❑ 96UppDecGN-X1
❑ 96UppDecHH-HH9
❑ 96UppDecHHG-HH9
❑ 96UppDecHHS-HH9
❑ 96UppDecIce-76
❑ 96UppDecIceDF-S6
❑ 96UppDecIcePar-76
❑ 96UppDecIceSCF-S6
❑ 96UppDecLSH-LS12
❑ 96UppDecLSHF-LS12
❑ 96UppDecLSHS-LS12
❑ 96UppDecSS-SS1B
❑ 96Zen-90
❑ 96ZenArtP-90
❑ 96ZenZT-2
❑ 97BeAPlaPOT-5
❑ 97ColCho-9
❑ 97ColCho-318
❑ 97ColChoCTG-C9A
❑ 97ColChoCTG-C9B
❑ 97ColChoCTG-C9C
❑ 97ColChoCTGE-CR9
❑ 97ColChoSta-SQ85
❑ 97ColChoSti-S9
❑ 97ColChoWD-W5
❑ 97Don-7
❑ 97DonCanI-2
❑ 97DonCanIDS-2
❑ 97DonCanINP-3
❑ 97DonCanIPS-2
❑ 97DonCanISCS-20
❑ 97DonEli-7
❑ 97DonEli-136
❑ 97DonEliAsp-7
❑ 97DonEliAsp-136
❑ 97DonEliC-22
❑ 97DonEliIns-7
❑ 97DonEliMC-22
❑ 97DonEliPN-5A
❑ 97DonEliPN-5B
❑ 97DonEliPN-5C
❑ 97DonEliPNDC-5A
❑ 97DonEliPNDC-5B
❑ 97DonEliPNDC-5C
❑ 97DonEliS-7
❑ 97DonEliS-136
❑ 97DonLim-35
❑ 97DonLim-56
❑ 97DonLim-114
❑ 97DonLimExp-35
❑ 97DonLimExp-56
❑ 97DonLimExp-114
❑ 97DonLimFOTG-10
❑ 97DonLimFOTG-40
❑ 97DonLin2L-20
❑ 97DonLin2LDC-20
❑ 97DonPre-10
❑ 97DonPre-183
❑ 97DonPreCttC-10
❑ 97DonPreCttC-183
❑ 97DonPreDWT-2
❑ 97DonPreDWT-11
❑ 97DonPreLotT-4C
❑ 97DonPrePM-8
❑ 97DonPreProG-7
❑ 97DonPreProS-7
❑ 97DonPreT-2
❑ 97DonPreT-22
❑ 97DonPreTB-2
❑ 97DonPreTB-22
❑ 97DonPreTBC-2
❑ 97DonPreTBC-22
❑ 97DonPreTPC-2
❑ 97DonPreTPC-22
❑ 97DonPreTPG-2
❑ 97DonPreTPG-22
❑ 97DonPri-13
❑ 97DonPri-204
❑ 97DonPriDD-14
❑ 97DonPriODI-12
❑ 97DonPriP-13
❑ 97DonPriS-13
❑ 97DonPriSB-13
❑ 97DonPriSG-13
❑ 97DonPriSoA-13
❑ 97DonPriSoA-204
❑ 97DonPriSS-13
❑ 97EssOlyHH-9
❑ 97EssOlyHHF-9
❑ 97Kat-2
❑ 97Kat-159
❑ 97KatGol-2
❑ 97KatGol-159
❑ 97KatSil-2
❑ 97KatSil-159
❑ 97Lea-6
❑ 97Lea-173
❑ 97LeaBanSea-1
❑ 97LeaFirOnIce-16
❑ 97LeaFraMat-6
❑ 97LeaFraMat-173
❑ 97LeaFraMDC-6
❑ 97LeaFraMDC-173
❑ 97LeaInt-6
❑ 97LeaIntUI-6
❑ 97McD-9
❑ 97McDGamFil-6
❑ 97Pac-9
❑ 97PacCarSup-1
❑ 97PacCarSupM-1
❑ 97PacCop-9
❑ 97PacCraChoAwa-1
❑ 97PacCroR-2
❑ 97PacCroRBoSDC-1
❑ 97PacCroRCCJ-1
❑ 97PacCroRCCJG-1
❑ 97PacCroRCCJS-1
❑ 97PacCroREG-2
❑ 97PacCroRHTDC-1
❑ 97PacCroRIB-2
❑ 97PacCroRLCDC-1
❑ 97PacCroRS-2
❑ 97PacDyn-3
❑ 97PacDyn-135
❑ 97PacDynBKS-2
❑ 97PacDynBKS-103
❑ 97PacDynC-3
❑ 97PacDynC-135
❑ 97PacDynDD-1A
❑ 97PacDynDG-3
❑ 97PacDynDG-135
❑ 97PacDynEG-3
❑ 97PacDynEG-135
❑ 97PacDynIB-3
❑ 97PacDynIB-135
❑ 97PacDynKotN-1
❑ 97PacDynR-3
❑ 97PacDynR-135
❑ 97PacDynSil-3
❑ 97PacDynSil-135
❑ 97PacDynTan-2
❑ 97PacDynTan-24
❑ 97PacEmeGre-9
❑ 97PacGolCroDC-1
❑ 97PacIceB-9
❑ 97PacInv-3
❑ 97PacInvAZ-1
❑ 97PacInvC-3
❑ 97PacInvEG-3
❑ 97PacInvFP-1
❑ 97PacInvIB-3
❑ 97PacInvNRB-4
❑ 97PacInvNRB-215
❑ 97PacInvOTG-1
❑ 97PacInvR-3
❑ 97PacInvS-3
❑ 97PacOme-3
❑ 97PacOmeC-3
❑ 97PacOmeDG-3
❑ 97PacOmeEG-3
❑ 97PacOmeG-3
❑ 97PacOmeGFDCC-1
❑ 97PacOmeIB-3
❑ 97PacOmeSil-1
❑ 97PacOmeSLC-1
❑ 97PacOmeTL-1
❑ 97PacPar-2
❑ 97PacParBNDC-1
❑ 97PacParC-2
❑ 97PacParCG-1
❑ 97PacParDG-2
❑ 97PacParEG-2
❑ 97PacParIB-2
❑ 97PacParP-1
❑ 97PacParRed-2
❑ 97PacParSil-2
❑ 97PacRed-9
❑ 97PacRev-2
❑ 97PacRevC-2
❑ 97PacRevE-2
❑ 97PacRevIB-2
❑ 97PacRevNID-1
❑ 97PacRevR-2
❑ 97PacRevS-2
❑ 97PacRevTCL-1
❑ 97PacSil-9
❑ 97PacSlaSDC-1A
❑ 97Pin-53
❑ 97Pin-NNO
❑ 97PinArtP-53
❑ 97PinBee-31
❑ 97PinBeeGP-31
❑ 97PinBeeGT-1
❑ 97PinBeeT-1
❑ 97PinCer-34
❑ 97PinCerGT-9
❑ 97PinCerMB-34
❑ 97PinCerMG-34
❑ 97PinCerMR-34
❑ 97PinCerR-34
❑ 97PinCerT-9
❑ 97PinEpiGO-19
❑ 97PinEpiGP-19
❑ 97PinEpiME-19
❑ 97PinEpiMO-19
❑ 97PinEpiMP-19
❑ 97PinEpiPE-19
❑ 97PinEpiPO-19
❑ 97PinEpiPP-19
❑ 97PinEpiSE-19
❑ 97PinEpiSO-19
❑ 97PinEpiSP-19
❑ 97PinHocMC-7
❑ 97PinHocMC-8
❑ 97PinIns-10
❑ 97PinInsC-15
❑ 97PinInsCC-10
❑ 97PinInsCG-15
❑ 97PinInsEC-10
❑ 97PinInsT-4
❑ 97PinMin-2
❑ 97PinMinB-2
❑ 97PinMinCBP-2
❑ 97PinMinCGPP-2
❑ 97PinMinCNSP-2
❑ 97PinMinCoiB-2
❑ 97PinMinCoiGP-2
❑ 97PinMinCoiN-2
❑ 97PinMinCoiSG-2
❑ 97PinMinCoiSS-2
❑ 97PinMinGolTea-2
❑ 97PinMinSilTea-2
❑ 97PinPowPac-2
❑ 97PinPowPac-P2
❑ 97PinPrePBB-53
❑ 97PinPrePBC-53
❑ 97PinPrePBM-53
❑ 97PinPrePBY-53
❑ 97PinPrePFC-53
❑ 97PinPrePFM-53
❑ 97PinPrePFY-53
❑ 97PinPrePla-53
❑ 97PinRinC-53
❑ 97PinTeaP-4
❑ 97PinTeaPM-4
❑ 97PinTeaPP-4
❑ 97PinTeaPPM-4
❑ 97PinTotCMPG-34
❑ 97PinTotCPB-34
❑ 97PinTotCPG-34
❑ 97PinTotCPR-34
❑ 97PosPin-7
❑ 97Sco-84
❑ 97Sco-260
❑ 97Sco-270
❑ 97Sco-PR84
❑ 97ScoArtPro-84
❑ 97ScoGolBla-84
❑ 97ScoMigDPla-1
❑ 97ScoMigDPre-1
❑ 97ScoMigDuc-1
❑ 97SP AutI-I11
❑ 97SPAut-6
❑ 97SPAutID-I11
❑ 97SPAutIE-I11
❑ 97SPx-1
❑ 97SPxBro-1
❑ 97SPxDim-SPX19
❑ 97SPxGol-1
❑ 97SPxGraF-1
❑ 97SPxSil-1
❑ 97SPxSte-1
❑ 97Stu-4
❑ 97StuHarH-3
❑ 97StuPor-4
❑ 97StuPrePG-4
❑ 97StuPrePS-4
❑ 97StuSil-5
❑ 97StuSil8-5
❑ 97UppDec-211
❑ 97UppDecBD-14
❑ 97UppDecBDDD-14
❑ 97UppDecBDPC-PC26
❑ 97UppDecBDPCDD-PC26
❑ 97UppDecBDPCM-PC26
❑ 97UppDecBDPCQD-PC26
❑ 97UppDecBDPCTD-PC26
❑ 97UppDecBDQD-14
❑ 97UppDecBDTD-14
❑ 97UppDecCtAG-2
❑ 97UppDecCtAG-AR2
❑ 97UppDecDV-6
❑ 97UppDecDVSM-6
❑ 97UppDecGDM-211
❑ 97UppDecIC-IC9
❑ 97UppDecIC2-IC9
❑ 97UppDecIce-85
❑ 97UppDecIceP-85
❑ 97UppDecILL-L1A
❑ 97UppDecILL2-L1A
❑ 97UppDecIPS-85
❑ 97UppDecSG-SG9
❑ 97UppDecSSM-SS9
❑ 97UppDecSSW-SS9
❑ 97UppDecTS-9
❑ 97UppDecTSL2-9
❑ 97UppDecTSS-3C
❑ 97Zen-15
❑ 97Zen5x7-45
❑ 97ZenGolImp-45
❑ 97ZenSilImp-45
❑ 97ZenZGol-15
❑ 97ZenZSil-15
❑ 97ZenZT-6
❑ 97ZenZT5x7-6
❑ 97ZenZTG-6
❑ 98Be A PPA-2
❑ 98Be A PPAA-2
❑ 98Be A PPAAF-2
❑ 98Be A PPAGUSC-S7
❑ 98Be A PPAJ-AS7
❑ 98Be A PPGUJA-G12
❑ 98Be A PPPGUJC-G12
❑ 98Be A PPPPUJC-P18
❑ 98Be A PPTBASG-2
❑ 98Be APG-2
❑ 98BowBes-2
❑ 98BowBesAR-2
❑ 98BowBesMIF-F2
❑ 98BowBesMIFAR-F2
❑ 98BowBesMIFR-F2
❑ 98BowBesR-2
❑ 98BowBesSBB-SB9
❑ 98BowBesSBBAR-SB9
❑ 98BowBesSBBR-SB9
❑ 98CroRoyCCAJG-1
❑ 98CroRoyCCAJG-1
❑ 98CroRoyCCAJLB-1
❑ 98CroRoyCCAJP-1
❑ 98CroRoyCCAJR-1
❑ 98Fin-100
❑ 98FinCen-C10
❑ 98FinCenR-C10
❑ 98FinDouMF-M11
❑ 98FinDouMF-M12
❑ 98FinDouMF-M13
❑ 98FinDouMF-M14
❑ 98FinDouSMFR-M11
❑ 98FinDouSMFR-M12
❑ 98FinDouSMFR-M13
❑ 98FinDouSMFR-M14
❑ 98FinNo P-100
❑ 98FinNo PR-100
❑ 98FinRedL-R3
❑ 98FinRedLR-R3
❑ 98FinRef-100
❑ 98JelSpo-5
❑ 98McD-8
❑ 98O-PChr-53
❑ 98O-PChrR-53
❑ 98Pac-9
❑ 98PacAur-3
❑ 98PacAurALC-1
❑ 98PacAurC-1
❑ 98PacAurCF-1
❑ 98PacAurCFC-1
❑ 98PacAurCFIB-1
❑ 98PacAurCFR-1
❑ 98PacAurCFS-1
❑ 98PacAurMAC-1
❑ 98PacCroR-3
❑ 98PacCroRCCA-1
❑ 98PacCroRCCAJ-1
❑ 98PacCroRLL-1
❑ 98PacCroRLS-3
❑ 98PacCroRMP-1
❑ 98PacCroRPP-1
❑ 98PacDynI-3
❑ 98PacDynI-1
❑ 98PacDynIAR-1
❑ 98PacDynIARB-1
❑ 98PacDynIARIB-1
❑ 98PacDynIARR-1
❑ 98PacDynIARS-1
❑ 98PacDynIFT-1
❑ 98PacDynIIB-3
❑ 98PacDynIPP-1
❑ 98PacDynIR-3
❑ 98PacDynITC-1
❑ 98PacEO P-1
❑ 98PacGolCD-1
❑ 98PacIceB-9
❑ 98PacOmeCS-1
❑ 98PacOmeCSG-1
❑ 98PacOmeCSG-1
❑ 98PacOmeCSR-1
❑ 98PacOmeEP1o1-1
❑ 98PacOmeFtF-2
❑ 98PacOmeH-4
❑ 98PacOmeO-1
❑ 98PacOmeODI-4
❑ 98PacOmeP-1
❑ 98PacOmePI-28
❑ 98PacOmePIB-28
❑ 98PacOmeR-4
❑ 98PacPar-3
❑ 98PacParC-3
❑ 98PacParEG-3
❑ 98PacParH-3
❑ 98PacParIB-3
❑ 98PacParIG-1
❑ 98PacParIGG-1
❑ 98PacParIGS-1
❑ 98PacParS-3
❑ 98PacParSDDC-1
❑ 98PacRed-9
❑ 98PacRev-2
❑ 98PacRevADC-13
❑ 98PacRevCTL-1
❑ 98PacRevIS-2
❑ 98PacRevNI-1
❑ 98PacRevR-2
❑ 98PacRevS-1
❑ 98PacTeaC-1
❑ 98PacTitI-1
❑ 98PinEpiGE-19
❑ 98RevThrPA-21
❑ 98RevThrPA-21
❑ 98SP Aut-1
❑ 98SP AutSM-S16
❑ 98SP AutSS-SS8
❑ 98SPxFin-116
❑ 98SPxFin-153
❑ 98SPxFin-179
❑ 98SPxFinR-116
❑ 98SPxFinR-153
❑ 98SPxFinR-179
❑ 98SPxFinS-116
❑ 98SPxFinS-153
❑ 98SPxFinS-179
❑ 98SPXTopP-1
❑ 98SPXTopPF-1
❑ 98SPXTopPHH-H1
❑ 98SPXTopPLI-L3
❑ 98SPXTopPPS-PS18
❑ 98SPXTopPR-1
❑ 98Top-53
❑ 98TopBlaLGR'-GR4
❑ 98TopGolLC1-51
❑ 98TopGolLC1B-51
❑ 98TopGolLC1BOoO-51
❑ 98TopGolLC1OoO-51
❑ 98TopGolLC1R-51
❑ 98TopGolLC1ROoO-51
❑ 98TopGolLC2-51
❑ 98TopGolLC2B-51
❑ 98TopGolLC2BOoO-51
❑ 98TopGolLC2OoO-51
❑ 98TopGolLC2R-51
❑ 98TopGolLC2ROoO-51
❑ 98TopGolLC3-51
❑ 98TopGolLC3B-51
❑ 98TopGolLC3BOoO-51
❑ 98TopGolLC3OoO-51
❑ 98TopGolLC3R-51
❑ 98TopGolLC3ROoO-51
❑ 98TopGolLGR'-GR4
❑ 98TopGolLGR'BOoO-GR4
❑ 98TopGolLGR'OoO-GR4
❑ 98TopGolLGR'ROoO-GR4
❑ 98TopIceA2-I1
❑ 98TopO-P-53
❑ 98TopRedLGR'-GR4
❑ 98UC-4
❑ 98UC-224
❑ 98UC-240
❑ 98UCMBH-BH11
❑ 98UCSB-SQ25
❑ 98UCSG-SQ25
❑ 98UCSG-SQ25
❑ 98UCSR-SQ25
❑ 98UD ChoPCR-4
❑ 98UD ChoPCR-224
❑ 98UD ChoPCR-240
❑ 98UD ChoR-4
❑ 98UD ChoR-224
❑ 98UD ChoR-240
❑ 98UD3-34
❑ 98UD3-94
❑ 98UD3-154
❑ 98UD3DieC-34
❑ 98UD3DieC-94
❑ 98UD3DieC-154
❑ 98UppDec-17
❑ 98UppDec-31
❑ 98UppDecBD-1
❑ 98UppDecDD-1
❑ 98UppDecE-17
❑ 98UppDecE-31
❑ 98UppDecE1o1-17
❑ 98UppDecE1o1-31
❑ 98UppDecFF-FF8
❑ 98UppDecFF-FF8
❑ 98UppDecFFQ1-FF8
❑ 98UppDecFFQ2-FF8
❑ 98UppDecFIT-FT6
❑ 98UppDecFITQ1-FT6
❑ 98UppDecFITQ2-FT6
❑ 98UppDecFITQ3-FT6
❑ 98UppDecGN-GN19
❑ 98UppDecGN-GN20
❑ 98UppDecGN-GN21
❑ 98UppDecGNQ1-GN19
❑ 98UppDecGNQ1-GN20
❑ 98UppDecGNQ1-GN21
❑ 98UppDecGNQ2-GN19
❑ 98UppDecGNQ2-GN20
❑ 98UppDecGNQ2-GN21
❑ 98UppDecGNQ3-GN19
❑ 98UppDecGNQ3-GN20
❑ 98UppDecGNQ3-GN21
❑ 98UppDecGR-17
❑ 98UppDecGR-31
❑ 98UppDecLSH-LS17
❑ 98UppDecLSHQ1-LS17
❑ 98UppDecLSHQ2-LS17
❑ 98UppDecLSHQ3-LS17
❑ 98UppDecM-1
❑ 98UppDecM1-M3
❑ 98UppDecM2-M3
❑ 98UppDecMGS-1
❑ 98UppDecMOH-OT9
❑ 98UppDecMS-S6
❑ 98UppDecMSF-F6
❑ 98UppDecMSS-1
❑ 98UppDecMSS-1
❑ 98UppDecP-P21
❑ 98UppDecPQ1-P21
❑ 98UppDecPQ2-P21
❑ 98UppDecPQ3-P21
❑ 98UppDecQD-1
❑ 98UppDecTD-1
❑ 98UppDecWFG-WF1

❑ 98UppDecWFP-WF1
❑ 99AurSty-1
❑ 99Pac-8
❑ 99PacAur-2
❑ 99PacAurCC-1
❑ 99PacAurCF-1
❑ 99PacAurCFC-1
❑ 99PacAurCFPB-1
❑ 99PacAurCP-1
❑ 99PacAurCPP-1
❑ 99PacAurPD-2
❑ 99PacCop-8
❑ 99PacCra-1
❑ 99PacGol-8
❑ 99PacGolCD-1
❑ 99PacHomaA-1
❑ 99PacIceB-8
❑ 99PacPasAP-1
❑ 99PacPreD-8
❑ 99PacTeaL-1
❑ 99RetHoc-1
❑ 99SP AutPS-1
❑ 99UppDecCL-55
❑ 99UppDecCLCLC-55
❑ 99UppDecEotG-E1
❑ 99UppDecES-25
❑ 99UppDecM-4
❑ 99UppDecM2CN-3
❑ 99UppDecMGS-GU1
❑ 99UppDecMGS-4
❑ 99UppDecMGUSA-GU1
❑ 99UppDecMHoG-H8
❑ 99UppDecMSS-4
❑ 99UppDecMSS-4
❑ 99UppDecMT-MVP2
❑ 99UppDecRDR-DR4
❑ 99UppDecRDRI-DR4
❑ 99UppDecRG-G7C
❑ 99UppDecRG-1
❑ 99UppDecRGI-G7C
❑ 99UppDecRM-RM6
❑ 99UppDecRP-1
❑ 99UppDecRTotC-TC4
**Karjalainen, Kyosti**
❑ 87SwePanS-57
❑ 89SweSemE-40
❑ 90ProAHLIHL-350
❑ 91Par-295
❑ 91ParFre-295
❑ 91ProAHLCHL-398
❑ 91UppDec-606
❑ 91UppDecF-606
❑ 92SweSemE-193
❑ 92UppDec-111
❑ 92UppDecES-E6
❑ 93SweSemE-159
❑ 94SweLeaE-261
❑ 95SweLeaE-105
❑ 95SweUppDE-163
❑ 98GerDELE-277
**Karjalainen, Sami**
❑ 95FinnSIS-238
**Karjalainen, Vesa**
❑ 94FinnSIS-291
❑ 95FinnSIS-145
❑ 95FinnSISL-96
**Karlander, Al**
❑ 70EssPowPla-139
❑ 70SarProSta-58
❑ 71TorSun-97
❑ 73RedWinTI-13
❑ 76OPCWHA-104
**Karlander, Kory**
❑ 91AirCanSJHL-D4
❑ 91AirCanSJHLAS-15
❑ 91AirCanSJHLAS-47
❑ 92NorMicW-15
❑ 93NorMicW-17
**Karlberg, Micael**
❑ 91SweSemE-274
❑ 92SweSemE-293
❑ 93SweSemE-21
❑ 95SweLeaE-237
❑ 95SweUppDE-104
**Karlin, Mattias**
❑ 98UC-290
❑ 98UD ChoPCR-290
❑ 98UD ChoR-290
**Karlsson, Anders**
❑ 84SweSemE-133
**Karlsson, Andreas**
❑ 93SweSemE-141
❑ 94SweLeaE-226
❑ 94SweLeaERR-9
❑ 95SweLeaE-67
❑ 95SweUppDE-110
**Karlsson, Arne**
❑ 73SweHocS-3
❑ 73SweWorCS-3
**Karlsson, Bengt Ake**
❑ 71SweHocS-336
❑ 72SweHocS-105
❑ 73SweHocS-223
❑ 73SweWorCS-223
❑ 74SweHocS-232
**Karlsson, Bengt-Goran**
❑ 67SweHoc-158
❑ 69SweHocS-317
❑ 70SweHocS-223
❑ 72SweHocS-250
❑ 72SweSemWC-65
❑ 74SweHocS-231
**Karlsson, Berny**
❑ 64SweCorI-95
❑ 65SweCorI-95
❑ 67SweHoc-290
❑ 69SweHocS-170
❑ 70SweHocS-191
❑ 72SweHocS-251
**Karlsson, Bert-Olav**
❑ 90SweSemE-68
**Karlsson, Bertil**
❑ 64SweCorI-5
❑ 64SweCorI-113
❑ 65SweCorI-5
❑ 65SweCorI-113
❑ 67SweHoc-173
❑ 69SweHocS-63
❑ 69SweHocS-80
❑ 71SweHocS-277
**Karlsson, Christer**
❑ 71SweHocS-226
**Karlsson, Ingvar**
❑ 87SwePanS-67
**Karlsson, Jacob**
❑ 89SweSemE-84
❑ 90SweSemE-257
❑ 91SweSemE-88
❑ 92SweSemE-108
❑ 92UppDec-229
❑ 93SweSemE-81
❑ 95SweLeaE-291
**Karlsson, Jan**
❑ 83SweSemE-155
❑ 85SwePanS-206
❑ 89SweSemE-248
❑ 89SweSemE-266
❑ 90SweSemE-155
❑ 91SweSemE-260
**Karlsson, Jan-Ake**
❑ 71SweHocS-325
❑ 71SweHocS-398
❑ 72SweHocS-141
❑ 72SweHocS-268
**Karlsson, Lars**
❑ 83SweSemE-128
❑ 84SweSemE-31
❑ 84SweSemE-118
❑ 85SwePanS-29
❑ 86SwePanS-6
❑ 87SwePanS-29
❑ 89SweSemE-94
❑ 90SweSemE-265
❑ 91SweSemE-30
❑ 91SweSemE-93
❑ 92SweSemE-52
❑ 92SweSemE-121
❑ 93SweSemE-27
❑ 93SweSemE-94
❑ 94SweLeaE-231
❑ 95SweLeaE-168
**Karlsson, Marcus**
❑ 91SweSemE-326
❑ 95GerDELE-75
❑ 95SweLeaE-277
❑ 95SweLeaER-8
❑ 95SweUppDE-158
**Karlsson, Martin**
❑ 72SweHocS-207
❑ 73SweHocS-26
❑ 73SweWorCS-26
❑ 74SweHocS-233
❑ 96GerDELE-269
**Karlsson, Nils-Erik**
❑ 69SweHocS-171
**Karlsson, Ove**
❑ 83SweSemE-235
**Karlsson, Per**
❑ 73SweHocS-41
❑ 73SweWorCS-41
**Karlsson, Peter**
❑ 92SweSemE-282
❑ 93SweSemE-247
**Karlsson, Reine**
❑ 83SweSemE-215
❑ 84SweSemE-240
❑ 85SwePanS-238
❑ 86SwePanS-265
❑ 87SwePanS-249
**Karlsson, Roger**
❑ 92SweSemE-58
**Karlsson, Rolf**
❑ 67SweHoc-204
❑ 71SweHocS-326
❑ 84SweSemE-189
**Karlsson, Ronnie**
❑ 92SweSemE-28
**Karlsson, Stefan**
❑ 67SweHoc-49
❑ 69SweHocS-64
❑ 69SweHocS-190
❑ 69SweWorC-45
❑ 69SweWorC-118
❑ 70SweHocS-28
❑ 70SweHocS-284
❑ 71SweHocS-16
❑ 71SweHocS-105
❑ 72SweHocS-14
❑ 72SweHocS-94
❑ 72SweSemWC-51
❑ 73SweHocS-19
❑ 73SweHocS-167
❑ 73SweWorCS-19
❑ 73SweWorCS-167
❑ 74SweHocS-234
❑ 74SweSemHVS-14
❑ 84SweSemE-242
**Karlsson, Torgny**
❑ 86SwePanS-135
**Karlsson, Torsten**
❑ 67SweHoc-174
**Karlstad, Jon Magne**
❑ 93SweSemWCS-235
**Karmanos, Jason**
❑ 92HarCri-16
❑ 93DonTeaUSA-10
❑ 93Pin-494
❑ 93PinCan-494
**Karouk, Kenneth**
❑ 94GerDELE-174
**Karp, Herman**
❑ 71RocAme-9
**Karpa, Dave**
❑ 91FerStaB-17
❑ 92Cla-68
❑ 92NorPet-16
❑ 92Par-151
❑ 92ParEmel-151
❑ 92UppDec-517
❑ 93OPCPre-408
❑ 93OPCPreG-408
❑ 93Par-165
❑ 93ParEmel-165
❑ 93Pow-421
❑ 93Sco-611
❑ 93ScoCan-611
❑ 93ScoGol-611
❑ 93StaClu-296
❑ 93StaCluFDI-296
❑ 93StaCluO-296
❑ 93TopPre-408
❑ 93TopPreG-408
❑ 93Ult-97
❑ 93UltPro-3
❑ 93UppDec-375
❑ 94OPCPre-202
❑ 94OPCPreSE-202
❑ 94ParSE-SE145
❑ 94ParSEG-SE145
❑ 94TopPre-202
❑ 94TopPreSE-202
❑ 94UppDec-41
❑ 94UppDecElelce-41
❑ 95ColCho-192
❑ 95ColChoPC-192
❑ 95ColChoPCP-192
❑ 95Duc-2
❑ 95ParInt-273
❑ 95ParIntEl-273
❑ 95UppDec-119
❑ 95UppDecElelce-119
❑ 95UppDecElelceG-119
❑ 96BeAPAut-41
❑ 96BeAPAutSil-41
❑ 96BeAPla-41
❑ 96ClaGol-68
❑ 96Duc-17
❑ 97PacDynBKS-3
❑ 97ScoMigDPla-19
❑ 97ScoMigDPre-19
❑ 97ScoMigDuc-19
❑ 97UppDec-217
❑ 98Pac-57
❑ 98PacIceB-57
❑ 98PacRed-57
**Karpen, Mark**
❑ 90KanCitBla-17
❑ 93MusFur-8
❑ 94CenHocL-115
❑ 99WicThu-10
**Karpenko, Igor**
❑ 96LasVegThu-10
**Karpov, Valeri**
❑ 93Cla-90
❑ 94Cla-43
❑ 94ClaDraGol-43
❑ 94ClaProPIA-IA20
❑ 94ClaROYS-R11
❑ 94ClaTri-T1
❑ 94DucCarJr-11
❑ 94Fle-4
❑ 94Lea-486
❑ 94LeaLim-51
❑ 94LeaPhe-10
❑ 94OPCPre-284
❑ 94OPCPreSE-284
❑ 94ParSE-SE6
❑ 94ParSEG-SE6
❑ 94ParSEV-6
❑ 94Pin-486
❑ 94PinArtP-486
❑ 94PinRinC-486
❑ 94PinRooTP-11
❑ 94Sel-183
❑ 94SelGol-183
❑ 94TopPre-284
❑ 94TopPreSE-284
❑ 94UppDec-256
❑ 94UppDec-570
❑ 94UppDecElelce-256
❑ 94UppDecElelce-570
❑ 94UppDecPC-C6
❑ 94UppDecPCEG-C6
❑ 94UppDecPCES-C6
❑ 94UppDecSPI-SP92
❑ 94UppDecSPIDC-SP92
❑ 95BeAPla-205
❑ 95BeAPSig-S205
❑ 95BeAPSigDC-S205
❑ 95ColCho-211
❑ 95ColChoPC-211
❑ 95ColChoPCP-211
❑ 95Don-191
❑ 95Lea-80
❑ 95ParInt-277
❑ 95ParIntEl-277
❑ 95Sco-170
❑ 95ScoBlalce-170
❑ 95ScoBlalceAP-170
❑ 95Top-137
❑ 95TopOPCI-137
❑ 95UppDec-378
❑ 95UppDecElelce-378
❑ 95UppDecElelceG-378
❑ 95UppDecSpeE-SE93
❑ 95UppDecSpeEdiG-SE93
**Karpovtsev, Alexander**
❑ 91OPCIns-35R
❑ 92RusStaRA-10
❑ 92UppDec-351
❑ 93Cla-89
❑ 93Don-212
❑ 93OPCPre-358
❑ 93OPCPreG-358
❑ 93Par-269
❑ 93ParEmel-269
❑ 93Pin-437
❑ 93PinCan-437
❑ 93Pow-391
❑ 93Sco-591
❑ 93ScoCan-591
❑ 93ScoGol-591
❑ 93StaClu-291
❑ 93StaCluFDI-291
❑ 93StaCluO-291
❑ 93SweSemWCS-133
❑ 93TopPre-358
❑ 93TopPreG-358
❑ 93Ult-372
❑ 93UppDec-484
❑ 93UppDecSP-100
❑ 94ClaAllRT-AR6
❑ 94ClaProP-19
❑ 94Don-327
❑ 94FinnJaaK-138
❑ 94Lea-118
❑ 94OPCFinIns-4
❑ 94OPCPre-255
❑ 94OPCPreSE-255
❑ 94ParSE-SE114
❑ 94ParSEG-SE114
❑ 94Pin-364
❑ 94PinArtP-364
❑ 94PinRinC-364
❑ 94TopPre-255
❑ 94TopPreSE-255
❑ 94UppDec-288
❑ 94UppDecElelce-288
❑ 95CanGamNHLP-188
❑ 95ParInt-142
❑ 95ParIntEl-142
❑ 95UppDec-288
❑ 95UppDecElelce-288
❑ 95UppDecElelceG-288
❑ 96BeAPAut-118
❑ 96BeAPAutSil-118
❑ 96BeAPla-118
❑ 97ColCho-169
❑ 97Pac-223
❑ 97PacCop-223
❑ 97PacEmeGre-223
❑ 97PacIceB-223
❑ 97PacRed-223
❑ 97PacSil-223
❑ 97ScoRan-8
❑ 97ScoRanPla-8
❑ 97ScoRanPre-8
❑ 99Pac-409
❑ 99PacCop-409
❑ 99PacGol-409
❑ 99PacIceB-409
❑ 99PacPreD-409
**Karpuk, K.**
❑ 95GerDELE-222
**Karrbrandt, Thomas**
❑ 83SweSemE-230
**Karrenbauer, Bernd**
❑ 69SweWorC-176
❑ 70SweHocS-369
**Kartio, Dave**
❑ 74SioCitM-7
**Kasatonov, Alexei**
❑ 82SweSemHVS-57
❑ 83RusNatT-8
❑ 87RusNatT-8
❑ 89RusNatT-10
❑ 89SweSemWCS-81
❑ 90Dev-13
❑ 90OPC-358
❑ 90PanSti-335
❑ 90ProSet-169
❑ 90Sco-209
❑ 90ScoCan-209
❑ 90Top-358
❑ 90TopTif-358
❑ 90UppDec-286
❑ 90UppDecF-286
❑ 91Bow-276
❑ 91OPC-439
❑ 91PanSti-216
❑ 91Par-319
❑ 91ParFre-319
❑ 91Pin-255
❑ 91PinFre-255
❑ 91ProSetPla-198
❑ 91RusStaNHL-4
❑ 91RusStaRA-7
❑ 91ScoAme-194
❑ 91ScoCan-194
❑ 91StaClu-282
❑ 91SweSemWCS-214
❑ 91Top-439
❑ 91UppDec-185
❑ 91UppDecF-185
❑ 92Bow-323
❑ 92OPC-353
❑ 92PanSti-180
❑ 92PanStiFre-180
❑ 92Pin-289
❑ 92PinFre-289
❑ 92ProSet-101
❑ 92Sco-394
❑ 92ScoCan-394
❑ 92StaClu-406
❑ 92Top-152
❑ 92TopGol-152G
❑ 92Ult-340
❑ 92UppDec-96
❑ 93Don-5
❑ 93Lea-381
❑ 93OPCPre-492
❑ 93OPCPreG-492
❑ 93Par-276
❑ 93ParEmel-276
❑ 93Pin-359
❑ 93PinCan-359
❑ 93Pow-5
❑ 93Sco-61
❑ 93Sco-528
❑ 93ScoCan-61
❑ 93ScoCan-528
❑ 93ScoGol-528
❑ 93StaClu-332
❑ 93StaCluFDI-332
❑ 93StaCluO-332
❑ 93TopPre-492
❑ 93TopPreG-492
❑ 93Ult-257
❑ 93UppDec-474
❑ 94CanGamNHLP-37
❑ 94EASpo-1
❑ 94FinnJaaK-143
❑ 94Lea-473
❑ 94OPCPre-159
❑ 94OPCPreSE-159
❑ 94Par-195
❑ 94ParGol-195
❑ 94ParSE-SE9
❑ 94ParSEG-SE9
❑ 94Pin-398
❑ 94PinArtP-398
❑ 94PinRinC-398
❑ 94Sco-183
❑ 94ScoGol-183
❑ 94ScoPla-183
❑ 94ScoPlaTS-183
❑ 94StaCluMO-9
❑ 94TopPre-159
❑ 94TopPreSE-159
❑ 94Ult-257
❑ 94UppDec-208
❑ 94UppDecElelce-208
❑ 95CanGamNHLP-37
❑ 95ColCho-115
❑ 95ColChoPC-115
❑ 95ColChoPCP-115
❑ 95ParInt-15
❑ 95ParIntEl-15
❑ 95PlaOneoOne-6
❑ 95SweGloWC-237
❑ 95UppDec-69
❑ 95UppDecElelceG-69
**Kasik, Petr**
❑ 95CzeAPSE-81
❑ 96CzeAPSE-76
**Kasjajev, Alexander**
❑ 74SweHocS-51
**Kaski, Olli**
❑ 93FinnJyvHS-345
❑ 93FinnSIS-212
❑ 94FinnSIS-365
❑ 94SweLeaE-171
❑ 94SweLeaEFA-8
❑ 95FinnSemWC-32
❑ 95FinnSIS-353
❑ 95FinnSISDT-3
❑ 95FinnSISL-20
❑ 96GerDELE-154
❑ 98GerDELE-85
**Kasowski, Peter**
❑ 92DayBom-13
❑ 97GuiFla-10
**Kasparaitis, Darius**
❑ 91UppDec-650
❑ 91UppDecCWJC-11
❑ 91UppDecF-650
❑ 92Cla-4
❑ 92ClaLPs-LP4
❑ 92OPCPre-103
❑ 92Par-102
❑ 92Par-215
❑ 92ParEmel-102
❑ 92ParEmel-215
❑ 92Pin-407
❑ 92PinFre-407
❑ 92RusStaRA-1
❑ 92RusStaRA-11
❑ 92Ult-344
❑ 92UppDec-335
❑ 92UppDec-554
❑ 92UppDec-563
❑ 92UppDec-623
❑ 92UppDecCC-CC13
❑ 92UppDecER-ER7
❑ 93Don-203
❑ 93Lea-101
❑ 93LeaGolR-13
❑ 93OPCPre-112
❑ 93OPCPre-443
❑ 93OPCPreG-112
❑ 93OPCPreG-443
❑ 93Par-122
❑ 93ParEmel-122
❑ 93Pin-84
❑ 93PinCan-84
❑ 93Pow-149
❑ 93PowSecYS-3
❑ 93Sco-124
❑ 93ScoCan-124
❑ 93ScoIntS-17
❑ 93ScoIntSC-17
❑ 93StaClu-101
❑ 93StaCluFDI-101
❑ 93StaCluFDIO-101
❑ 93StaCluO-101
❑ 93SweSemWCS-146
❑ 93TopPre-112
❑ 93TopPre-443
❑ 93TopPreG-112
❑ 93TopPreG-443
❑ 93Ult-160
❑ 93UppDec-173
❑ 93UppDecSP-91
❑ 94BeAPla-R148
❑ 94BeAPSig-142
❑ 94CanGamNHLP-161
❑ 94Don-252
❑ 94EASpo-80
❑ 94Fle-122
❑ 94Lea-27
❑ 94OPCPre-211
❑ 94OPCPreSE-211
❑ 94Par-133
❑ 94ParGol-133
❑ 94ParSEV-27
❑ 94Pin-26
❑ 94PinArtP-26
❑ 94PinRinC-26
❑ 94Sco-11
❑ 94ScoChelt-CI3
❑ 94ScoGol-11
❑ 94ScoHobS-C13
❑ 94ScoPla-11
❑ 94ScoPlaTS-11
❑ 94StaCluST-14
❑ 94TopPre-211
❑ 94TopPreSE-211
❑ 94Ult-129
❑ 94UppDec-298
❑ 94UppDecElelce-298
❑ 94UppDecSPI-SP46
❑ 94UppDecSPIDC-SP46
❑ 95ColCho-2
❑ 95ColChoPC-2
❑ 95ColChoPCP-2
❑ 95Lea-235
❑ 95ParInt-402
❑ 95ParIntEl-402
❑ 95Sco-40
❑ 95ScoBlalce-40
❑ 95ScoBlalceAP-40
❑ 95UppDec-447
❑ 95UppDecElelce-447
❑ 95UppDecElelceG-447
❑ 96ClaGol-4
❑ 96ColCho-162
❑ 96SP-129
❑ 96TeaOut-59
❑ 96UppDec-291
❑ 96UppDecBD-61
❑ 96UppDecBDG-61
❑ 97Be A PPAD-159
❑ 97Be A PPAPD-159
❑ 97BeAPla-159
❑ 97BeAPlaAut-159
❑ 97ColCho-211
❑ 97Pac-61
❑ 97PacCop-61
❑ 97PacEmeGre-61
❑ 97PacIceB-61
❑ 97PacPar-151
❑ 97PacParC-151
❑ 97PacParDG-151
❑ 97PacParEG-151
❑ 97PacParIB-151
❑ 97PacParRed-151
❑ 97PacParSil-151
❑ 97PacRed-61
❑ 97PacSil-61
❑ 97Sco-162
❑ 97ScoPen-10
❑ 97ScoPenPla-10
❑ 97ScoPenPre-10
❑ 97UppDec-136
❑ 97UppDec-391
❑ 98Be A PPA-113
❑ 98Be A PPAA-113
❑ 98Be A PPAAF-113
❑ 98Be A PPTBASG-113
❑ 98Be APG-113
❑ 98Fin-25
❑ 98FinNo P-25
❑ 98FinNo PR-25
❑ 98FinRef-25
❑ 98Pac-354
❑ 98PacAur-155
❑ 98PacIceB-354
❑ 98PacPar-193
❑ 98PacParC-193
❑ 98PacParEG-193
❑ 98PacParH-193
❑ 98PacParIB-193
❑ 98PacParS-193
❑ 98PacRed-354
❑ 98UppDec-160
❑ 98UppDecE-160
❑ 98UppDecE1o1-160
❑ 98UppDecGJ-GJ22
❑ 98UppDecGR-160
❑ 99Pac-339
❑ 99PacCop-339
❑ 99PacGol-339
❑ 99PacIceB-339
❑ 99PacPreD-339
**Kasper, Oliver**
❑ 94GerDELE-352
**Kasper, Peter**
❑ 95AusNatTea-11
**Kasper, Steve**
❑ 81OPC-4
❑ 81OPCSti-51
❑ 81Top-E68
❑ 82OPC-12
❑ 82OPCSti-81
❑ 82OPCSti-253
❑ 82PosCer-1
❑ 83BruTealss-7
❑ 83OPC-50
❑ 83OPCSti-53
❑ 85OPC-79
❑ 85Top-79
❑ 86OPC-97
❑ 86OPCSti-40
❑ 86Top-97
❑ 87OPC-162
❑ 87OPCSti-66B
❑ 87PanSti-15
❑ 87Top-162
❑ 88BruPos-8
❑ 88BruSpoA-7
❑ 88OPC-176
❑ 88OPCSti-27
❑ 88PanSti-210
❑ 88Top-176
❑ 89KinSmo-5
❑ 89OPC-194
❑ 89OPCSti-152
❑ 89PanSti-92
❑ 89Top-194
❑ 90Bow-147
❑ 90BowTif-147
❑ 90KinSmo-7
❑ 90OPC-153
❑ 90PanSti-238
❑ 90ProSet-120
❑ 90Sco-247
❑ 90ScoCan-247
❑ 90Top-153
❑ 90TopTif-153
❑ 90UppDec-140
❑ 90UppDecF-140
❑ 91Bow-187
❑ 91FlyJCP-15
❑ 91OPC-302
❑ 91OPCPre-85
❑ 91PanSti-88
❑ 91ProSet-449
❑ 91ProSetFre-449
❑ 91ScoAme-256
❑ 91ScoCan-574
❑ 91ScoRoo-24T
❑ 91StaClu-139
❑ 91Top-302
❑ 91UppDec-576
❑ 91UppDecF-576
❑ 92Bow-33
❑ 92DurPan-4
❑ 92FlyUppDS-12
❑ 92LigShe-18
❑ 92Par-403
❑ 92ParEmel-403
❑ 92Sco-306
❑ 92ScoCan-306
❑ 92StaClu-71
❑ 92Top-150
❑ 92TopGol-150G
❑ 93OPCPre-73
❑ 93OPCPreG-73
❑ 93StaClu-122
❑ 93StaCluFDI-122
❑ 93StaCluFDIO-122
❑ 93StaCluO-122
❑ 93TopPre-73
❑ 93TopPreG-73
**Kasperczyk, Jedrzej**
❑ 89SweSemWCS-139
❑ 94GerDELE-156
❑ 95GerDELE-157
❑ 96GerDELE-212
**Kastak, Kamil**
❑ 92SweSemE-143
❑ 93FinnSIS-193
❑ 93SweSemWCS-107
❑ 94FinnJaaK-175
❑ 95SweGloWC-162
❑ 96CzeAPSE-178
**Kastelic, Ed**
❑ 84MonGolF-24
❑ 87CapKod-29
❑ 87CapTealss-12
❑ 89WhaJunM-11
❑ 90OPC-404
❑ 90ProSet-450
❑ 90WhaJr7E-16
❑ 91WhaJr7E-17

❑ 92PhoRoa-9
**Kastelic, Joe**
❑ 52JunBluT-31
**Kastner, Milan**
❑ 94CzeAPSE-91
**Kaszycki, Mike**
❑ 78OPC-171
❑ 78Top-171
❑ 79IslTrans-7
❑ 79OPC-87
❑ 79Top-87
❑ 80OPC-371
**Katelnikoff, Tracey**
❑ 88SasBla-18
**Kathan, Klaus**
❑ 98GerDELE-298
❑ 98GerDELE-326
**Kathan, Peter**
❑ 94GerDELE-173
**Kaufmann, Beat**
❑ 72SweSemWC-156
**Kauhanen, Ilpo**
❑ 907thInnSOHL-35
❑ 917thInnSOHL-19
❑ 91CorRoy-13
❑ 94FinnSIS-278
❑ 95FinnSIS-108
❑ 95FinnSISGG-10
❑ 96FinnSISR-122
❑ 96FinnSISRMA-3
**Kauhanen, Timo**
❑ 95FinnSIS-298
**Kauppila, Jari**
❑ 93FinnJyvHS-268
❑ 94FinnSIS-230
❑ 95FinnSIS-26
❑ 96FinnSISR-21
**Kautonen, Veli-Pekka**
❑ 93FinnJyvHS-299
❑ 93FinnSIS-68
❑ 94FinnSIS-265
❑ 95FinnSIS-198
❑ 96GerDELE-266
❑ 98GerDELE-33
**Kay, A.**
❑ 28V1282PauC-55
**Kayser, Steve**
❑ 84Ott67-15
**Kazatkjin, Yevgeny**
❑ 73SweHocS-110
❑ 73SweWorCS-110
**Kazuik, Garnet**
❑ 84BraWheK-1
**Kea, Ed**
❑ 75OPCNHL-383
❑ 76OPCNHL-361
❑ 77OPCNHL-301
❑ 78OPC-277
❑ 79OPC-390
❑ 81OPC-294
❑ 81Top-W118
❑ 82PosCer-17
**Kealty, Jeff**
❑ 93Cla-104
❑ 95DonEliWJ-28
**Kean, Mitch**
❑ 94HunBli-15
**Keane, Mike**
❑ 88CanaPos-14
❑ 89CanaKra-11
❑ 89CanaPos-15
❑ 90CanaPos-17
❑ 90OPC-325
❑ 90ProSet-151
❑ 90ScoRoo-102T
❑ 90Top-325
❑ 90TopTif-325
❑ 90UppDec-382
❑ 90UppDecF-382
❑ 91Bow-334
❑ 91CanaPanTS-13
❑ 91CanaPos-14
❑ 91OPC-434
❑ 91PanSti-190
❑ 91Par-311
❑ 91ParFre-311
❑ 91Pin-265
❑ 91PinFre-265
❑ 91ProSet-121
❑ 91ProSetFre-121
❑ 91ProSetPla-191
❑ 91ScoAme-360
❑ 91ScoCan-251
❑ 91StaClu-236
❑ 91Top-434
❑ 92Bow-290
❑ 92CanaPos-14
❑ 92HumDum1-13
❑ 92OPC-274
❑ 92Par-318
❑ 92ParEmel-318
❑ 92Pin-164
❑ 92PinFre-164
❑ 92Sco-179
❑ 92ScoCan-179
❑ 92StaClu-349
❑ 92Top-478
❑ 92TopGol-478G
❑ 92Ult-106
❑ 92UppDec-164
❑ 93CanaMol-7
❑ 93CanaPos-12
❑ 93Don-451
❑ 93Lea-279
❑ 93OPCPre-139
❑ 93OPCPreG-139
❑ 93Pin-339
❑ 93PinCan-339
❑ 93Pow-129
❑ 93Sco-170
❑ 93ScoCan-170
❑ 93StaClu-92
❑ 93StaCluFDI-92
❑ 93StaCluFDIO-92
❑ 93StaCluO-92
❑ 93TopPre-139
❑ 93TopPreG-139
❑ 93Ult-196
❑ 94CanaPos-13
❑ 94CanGamNHLP-135
❑ 94Don-134
❑ 94HocWit-63
❑ 94OPCPre-497
❑ 94OPCPreSE-497
❑ 94Pin-151
❑ 94PinArtP-151
❑ 94PinRinC-151
❑ 94Sco-187
❑ 94ScoGol-187
❑ 94ScoPla-187
❑ 94ScoPlaTS-187
❑ 94StaClu-18
❑ 94StaCluFDI-18
❑ 94StaCluMOMS-18
❑ 94StaCluSTWC-18
❑ 94TopPre-497
❑ 94TopPreSE-497
❑ 94Ult-110
❑ 95BeAPla-103
❑ 95BeAPSig-S103
❑ 95BeAPSigDC-S103
❑ 95CanaPos-7
❑ 95CanGamNHLP-149
❑ 95ColCho-153
❑ 95ColChoPC-153
❑ 95ColChoPCP-153
❑ 95Pin-83
❑ 95PinArtP-83
❑ 95PinRinC-83
❑ 95Sco-266
❑ 95ScoBlaIce-266
❑ 95ScoBlaIceAP-266
❑ 95StaClu-43
❑ 95StaCluMOMS-43
❑ 95Top-281
❑ 95TopOPCI-281
❑ 95UppDec-388
❑ 95UppDecEleIce-446
❑ 95UppDecEleIceG-446
❑ 97Be A PPAD-101
❑ 97Be A PPAPD-101
❑ 97BeAPla-101
❑ 97BeAPlaAut-101
❑ 97ColCho-63
❑ 97Pac-239
❑ 97PacCop-239
❑ 97PacEmeGre-239
❑ 97PacIceB-239
❑ 97PacRed-239
❑ 97PacSil-239
❑ 97ScoRan-3
❑ 97ScoRanPla-3
❑ 97ScoRanPre-3
❑ 97UppDec-315
❑ 98Be A PPA-42
❑ 98Be A PPAA-42
❑ 98Be A PPAAF-42
❑ 98Be A PPTBASG-42
❑ 98Be APG-42
❑ 98Pac-178
❑ 98PacIceB-178
❑ 98PacRed-178
❑ 98SPxFin-27
❑ 98SPxFinR-27
❑ 98SPxFinS-27
❑ 98UppDec-77
❑ 98UppDecE-77
❑ 98UppDecE1o1-77
❑ 98UppDecGR-77
❑ 99Pac-121
❑ 99PacCop-121
❑ 99PacGol-121
❑ 99PacIceB-121
❑ 99PacPreD-121
**Keans, Doug**
❑ 78LouGea-13
❑ 84OPC-5
❑ 84Top-4
❑ 85OPC-133
❑ 85Top-133
❑ 86OPC-22
❑ 86Top-22
❑ 87OPC-147
❑ 87OPCSti-139
❑ 87PanSti-4
❑ 87Top-147
❑ 88ProAHL-38
**Kearns, Dennis**
❑ 71CanuRoyB-13
❑ 71OPC-231
❑ 71TorSun-281
❑ 72CanuRoyB-8
❑ 72SarProSta-224
❑ 73CanuRoyB-7
❑ 73OPC-162
❑ 73Top-173
❑ 74CanuRoyB-8
❑ 74NHLActSta-288
❑ 74OPCNHL-366
❑ 75CanuRoyB-9
❑ 75OPCNHL-188
❑ 75Top-188
❑ 76CanuRoyB-7
❑ 76OPCNHL-338
❑ 76OPCNHL-395
❑ 77CanCanDC-6
❑ 77CanuRoyB-9
❑ 77OPCNHL-175
❑ 77Top-175
❑ 78CanuRoyB-12
❑ 78OPC-191
❑ 78Top-191
❑ 79CanuRoyB-11
❑ 79OPC-76
❑ 79PanSti-58
❑ 79Top-76
❑ 80CanuSilD-11
❑ 80CanuTeal-11
❑ 80OPC-392
❑ 80PepCap-109
❑ 81OPC-337
❑ 81OPCSti-249
**Keating, Jackie (Jack)**
❑ 34BeeGro1P-106
❑ 36ProvRed-4
❑ 39OPCV3011-67
**Keating, Mike**
❑ 75HamFin-9
**Keats, Duke**
❑ 23V1281PauC-45
❑ 83HalFP-D8
❑ 85HalFC-54
❑ 92HalFL-20
**Keczmer, Dan**
❑ 90ProAHLIHL-114
❑ 91OPCIns-3S
❑ 91WhaJr7E-18
❑ 93Don-406
❑ 93OPCPre-461
❑ 93OPCPreG-461
❑ 93Par-82
❑ 93ParEmel-82
❑ 93Pin-218
❑ 93PinCan-218
❑ 93Pow-304
❑ 93StaCluFDI-311
❑ 93TopPre-461
❑ 93TopPreG-461
❑ 93UppDec-249
❑ 94StaClu-262
❑ 94StaCluFDI-262
❑ 94StaCluMOMS-262
❑ 94StaCluSTWC-262
❑ 95UppDec-410
❑ 95UppDecEleIce-410
❑ 95UppDecEleIceG-410
**Keeling, Butch**
❑ 33OPCV304A-36
❑ 33V129-30
❑ 33V357IceK-20
❑ 34BeeGro1P-281
❑ 34DiaMatS-34
❑ 35DiaMatT2-32
❑ 35DiaMatT3-30
❑ 35DiaMatTI-34
❑ 36V356WorG-15
**Keenan, Cory**
❑ 87KitRan-11
❑ 88KitRan-11
❑ 897thInnSOHL-179
❑ 89KitRan-12
❑ 907thInnSMC-40
❑ 95SigRooA-20
❑ 95SigRooAPC-20
**Keenan, Larry**
❑ 61Par-13
❑ 61ShiCoi-55
❑ 61YorYelB-32
❑ 68OPC-115
❑ 68ShiCoi-155
❑ 68Top-115
❑ 70EssPowPla-90
❑ 70OPC-104
❑ 70Top-104
❑ 71SarProSta-31
❑ 71TorSun-29
**Keenan, Mike**
❑ 85FlyPos-15
❑ 86FlyPos-13
❑ 88BlaCok-7
❑ 89BlaCok-25
❑ 90BlaCok-25
❑ 91BlaCok-11
**Kehle, Markus**
❑ 94GerDELE-79
❑ 95GerDELE-298
**Kehle, Toni**
❑ 72SweSemWC-93
**Kehler, Drew**
❑ 96KamBla-13
**Kehoe, Rick**
❑ 72MapLeaP-13
❑ 72OPC-277
❑ 72SarProSta-209
❑ 73MacMil-11
❑ 73MapLeaP-12
❑ 73MapLeaP-13
❑ 73MapLeaP-14
❑ 73OPC-60
❑ 73Top-179
❑ 74NHLActSta-231
❑ 74OPCNHL-81
❑ 74PenPos-10
❑ 74Top-81
❑ 75OPCNHL-39
❑ 75Top-39
❑ 76OPCNHL-124
❑ 76Top-124
❑ 77OPCNHL-33
❑ 77PenPucB-17
❑ 77Top-33
❑ 78OPC-213
❑ 78Top-213
❑ 79OPC-109
❑ 79Top-109
❑ 80OPC-18
❑ 80OPC-117
❑ 80Top-18
❑ 80Top-117
❑ 81OPC-254
❑ 81OPC-260
❑ 81OPC-267
❑ 81OPCSti-182
❑ 81OPCSti-261
❑ 81Top-17
❑ 81Top-60
❑ 81Top-E128
❑ 82OPC-271
❑ 82OPCSti-143
❑ 82PosCer-15
❑ 83OPC-274
❑ 83OPC-282
❑ 83OPCSti-11
❑ 83OPCSti-231
❑ 83OPCSti-232
❑ 83PenHeiP-15
❑ 83PenTealP-19
❑ 83PufSti-8
❑ 847EDis-40
❑ 84KelAccD-5A
❑ 84OPC-177
❑ 84OPCSti-117
❑ 84PenHeiP-13
❑ 84Top-125
❑ 93PenFoo-6
❑ 95PenFoo-11
**Kehrer, Glen**
❑ 90HamRoaA-48
**Keijser, Kjell**
❑ 67SweHoc-64
❑ 71SweHocS-354
**Keiller, Ian**
❑ 917thInnSOHL-104
**Keiller, Jimmy**
❑ 36V356WorG-120
**Keimann, Dan**
❑ 98FloEve-20
**Keimu, Pekka**
❑ 70SweHocS-301
**Keinonen, Matti**
❑ 69SweHocS-370
❑ 69SweWorC-165
❑ 70SweHocS-302
❑ 72SweHocS-35
❑ 72SweSemWC-91
❑ 73SweHocS-37
❑ 73SweWorCS-37
**Kekalainen, Janne**
❑ 93FinnSIS-174
❑ 94FinnSIS-21
❑ 95FinnSIS-278
❑ 95FinnSISL-71
❑ 96FinnSISR-79
**Kekalainen, Jarmo**
❑ 91UppDec-108
❑ 91UppDecES-1
❑ 91UppDecESF-1
❑ 91UppDecF-108
❑ 93Par-410
❑ 93ParEmel-410
❑ 93SenKraS-11
❑ 93SweSemWCS-65
❑ 94ClaProP-198
❑ 94FinnJaaK-26
❑ 94FinnSIS-366
❑ 94SweLeaE-229
❑ 94SweLeaEFA-7
**Kelfer, Mike**
❑ 89ProAHL-246
❑ 90KanCitBla-16
❑ 90ProAHLIHL-592
**Kelham, A.J.**
❑ 917thInnSWHL-237
**Kelland, Chris**
❑ 93SheSte-11
❑ 94FinnJaaK-316
❑ 94SheSte-22
❑ 97SheSte-10
❑ 97SheSte-12
**Keller, Aaron**
❑ 93KamBla-12
❑ 95SlaMemC-7
**Keller, Florian**
❑ 94GerDELE-386
❑ 95GerDELE-374
❑ 96GerDELE-174
**Keller, Hans**
❑ 72SweSemWC-143
**Keller, John**
❑ 84KitRan-24
**Keller, Ryan**
❑ 91BriColJHL-57
❑ 92BriColJHL-213
**Kellett, Kevin**
❑ 95PriAlbR-11
❑ 96PriAlbR-10
❑ 96PriAlbROC-11
**Kellgren, Christer**
❑ 83SweSemE-232
**Kelln, Travis**
❑ 907thInnSWHL-21
**Kellogg, Allen**
❑ 52JunBluT-24
**Kellogg, Bob**
❑ 94ClaProP-63
❑ 94IndIce-11
**Kelly, Battleship (J. Bob)**
❑ 73BluWhiBor-10
❑ 74OPCNHL-143
❑ 74Top-143
❑ 75OPCNHL-263
❑ 75Top-263
❑ 76OPCNHL-261
❑ 76Top-261
❑ 77OPCNHL-14
❑ 77Top-14
❑ 78OPC-189
❑ 78Top-189
❑ 79OPC-306
**Kelly, Bob (Hound Dog)**
❑ 70EssPowPla-206
❑ 71OPC-203
❑ 71RocAme-10
❑ 71SarProSta-157
❑ 71TorSun-200
❑ 72SarProSta-163
❑ 73FlyLin-8
❑ 73OPC-253
❑ 74NHLActSta-200
❑ 74NHLActSta-223
❑ 74OPCNHL-380
❑ 74PenPos-11
❑ 75FlyCanDC-9
❑ 75OPCNHL-184
❑ 75Top-184
❑ 76OPCNHL-219
❑ 76Top-219
❑ 77OPCNHL-178
❑ 77Top-178
❑ 78OPC-71
❑ 78Top-71
❑ 79OPC-14
❑ 79Top-14
❑ 81OPC-349
❑ 81OPCSti-195
❑ 81Top-E119
❑ 92Par-477
❑ 92ParEmel-477
**Kelly, Brock**
❑ 89NasKni-12
❑ 91NasKni-16
**Kelly, Chuck**
❑ 67ColChe-7
**Kelly, Jim**
❑ 91ProSetPla-293
**Kelly, John P.**
❑ 82PosCer-8
**Kelly, Kendel**
❑ 92BriColJHL-2
**Kelly, Pat**
❑ 77RocCokCan-11
**Kelly, Paul**
❑ 88ProAHL-217
❑ 89ProAHL-3
❑ 93MusFur-10
❑ 94MusFur-13
❑ 95MusFur-7
**Kelly, Pep**
❑ 34BeeGro1P-330
❑ 35OPCV304C-87
❑ 36ChaPos-7
❑ 36V356WorG-86
❑ 37OPCV304E-145
❑ 38QuaOatP-22
❑ 39OPCV3011-9
**Kelly, Peter**
❑ 34BeeGro1P-107
❑ 34BeeGro1P-233
**Kelly, Red**
❑ 44BeeGro2P-182
❑ 44BeeGro2P-413A
❑ 44BeeGro2P-413B
❑ 51Par-55
❑ 52Par-67
❑ 52RoyDesH-7
❑ 53Par-40
❑ 54Par-42
❑ 54Par-91
❑ 54Top-5
❑ 57Top-48
❑ 58Top-61
❑ 59Top-65
❑ 60Par-9
❑ 60ShiCoi-4
❑ 60YorPreP-19
❑ 61Par-9
❑ 61ShiCoi-49
❑ 61YorYelB-21
❑ 62Par-5
❑ 62ShiMetC-9
❑ 62YorIroOTra-20
❑ 63ChePho-29
❑ 63MapLeaWB-11
❑ 63Par-3
❑ 63Par-63
❑ 63TorSta-22
❑ 63YorWhiB-12
❑ 64BeeGro3P-169
❑ 64CocCap-93
❑ 64Top-44
❑ 65Coc-93
❑ 65MapLeaWB-11
❑ 65Top-15
❑ 66Top-79
❑ 66TopUSAT-42
❑ 71PenPos-10
❑ 73MapLeaP-15
❑ 74OPCNHL-76
❑ 74Top-76
❑ 83HalFP-D9
❑ 85HalFC-55
❑ 90UppDec-502
❑ 90UppDecF-502
❑ 91Kra-81
❑ 91UltOriS-38
❑ 91UltOriS-79
❑ 91UltOriSF-38
❑ 91UltOriSF-79
❑ 92ParParR-PR10
❑ 93ParParR-PR58
❑ 94ParMisL-52
❑ 94ParMisL-142
❑ 94ParTalB-127
❑ 94ParTalB-165
❑ 94ZelMasH-3
❑ 94ZelMasoHS-3
❑ 95Par66-109
❑ 95Par66Coi-109
❑ 99RetHoc-98
❑ 99UppDecCL-22
❑ 99UppDecCLCLC-22
❑ 99UppDecRG-98
❑ 99UppDecRII-RK
❑ 99UppDecRIL1-RK
❑ 99UppDecRP-98
**Kelly, Steve**
❑ 93PriAlbR-13
❑ 94PriAlbR-12
❑ 95Cla-6
❑ 95ClaCHLAS-AS6
❑ 95ClaIceBre-BK6
❑ 95Ima-39
❑ 95ImaGol-39
❑ 95ImaPlaPDC-PD3
❑ 95PriAlbR-12
❑ 96ClaIceBreDC-BK6
❑ 96MetUni-183
❑ 96OilPos-10
❑ 97Don-216
❑ 97DonCanI-130
❑ 97DonCanIDS-130
❑ 97DonCanIPS-130
❑ 97DonLim-107
❑ 97DonLimExp-107
❑ 97DonMed-8
❑ 97DonPreProG-216
❑ 97DonPreProS-216
❑ 97DonRatR-8
❑ 97PinIns-117
❑ 97UppDec-188
**Kelman, Scott**
❑ 98SP Aut-125
❑ 98SP AutSotTG-SK
❑ 98SSASotT-SK
❑ 98UppDec-402
❑ 98UppDecE-402
❑ 98UppDecE1o1-402
❑ 98UppDecGR-402
❑ 99SP AutPS-125
**Kelman, Todd**
❑ 92BriColJHL-198
**Kelsey, Scot**
❑ 94CenHocL-81
**Kemp, Dylan**
❑ 95PriAlbR-13
❑ 96PriAlbROC-12
**Kemp, John**
❑ 82KinCan-13
**Kemper, Andrew**
❑ 917thInnSWHL-128
❑ 93SasBla-13
**Kempf, Markus**
❑ 94GerDELE-116
❑ 95GerDELE-117
**Kemppainen, Pasi**
❑ 94FinnSIS-310
❑ 95FinnSIS-282
**Kemppi, Miikka**
❑ 94FinnSIS-271
❑ 95FinnSIS-118
**Kenady, Chris**
❑ 95Cla-75
❑ 95ClaAut-11
**Kendall, Carl**
❑ 12C57-35
**Kendall, Jason**
❑ 93CorBigRed-15
**Kendall, William**
❑ 34BeeGro1P-331
❑ 34DiaMatS-35
❑ 35DiaMatT2-33
❑ 35DiaMatTI-35
**Kennedy, Bob**
❑ 88FliSpi-10
❑ 89JohChi-24
**Kennedy, Dean**
❑ 82BraWheK-3
❑ 86Kin20tATI-11
❑ 87KinTeal4-11
❑ 87PanSti-276
❑ 89SabBluS-8
❑ 89SabCam-10
❑ 90Bow-248
❑ 90BowTif-248
❑ 90ProSet-22
❑ 90SabBluS-10
❑ 90SabCam-11
❑ 90Sco-299
❑ 90ScoCan-299
❑ 90UppDec-380
❑ 90UppDecF-380
❑ 91JetIGA-15
❑ 91OPC-388
❑ 91ScoCan-431
❑ 91Top-388
❑ 92Pin-239
❑ 92PinFre-239
❑ 92Sco-211
❑ 92ScoCan-211
❑ 93JetRuf-14
❑ 93Kra-37
❑ 93Pin-178
❑ 93PinCan-178
❑ 93Sco-366
❑ 93ScoCan-366
❑ 94Lea-500
**Kennedy, Forbes**
❑ 44BeeGro2P-111
❑ 44BeeGro2P-183
❑ 57Top-50
❑ 58Top-11
❑ 59Top-52
❑ 63Top-19
❑ 64BeeGro3P-14
❑ 64CocCap-10
❑ 64TorSta-23
❑ 65Coc-8
❑ 68OPC-97
❑ 68ShiCoi-132
❑ 68Top-97
❑ 94ParMisL-35
❑ 94ParTalB-16
**Kennedy, Joey**
❑ 92BriColJHL-89
**Kennedy, Mike**
❑ 917thInnSWHL-131
❑ 94ClaProP-79
❑ 94Fle-54
❑ 94StaPos-12
❑ 94UppDec-326
❑ 94UppDecEleIce-326
❑ 95ColCho-205
❑ 95ColChoPC-205
❑ 95ColChoPCP-205
❑ 95ColEdgI-140
❑ 95ColEdgIC-C14
❑ 95Don-192
❑ 95Ima-73
❑ 95ImaGol-73
❑ 95Lea-7
❑ 95Top-27
❑ 95TopNewG-7NG
❑ 95TopOPCI-27
❑ 95Ult-39
❑ 95UltGolM-39
❑ 96StaPos-13
❑ 97St.JohML-13
**Kennedy, Ron**
❑ 77KalWin-5
❑ 95GerDELE-123
❑ 96GerDELE-22
**Kennedy, Sheldon**
❑ 89ProAHL-320
❑ 90OPC-520
❑ 91OPC-317
❑ 91ProAHLCHL-134
❑ 91RedWinLC-9
❑ 91Top-317
❑ 91UppDec-408
❑ 91UppDecF-408
❑ 92Top-368
❑ 92TopGol-368G
❑ 93Lea-246
❑ 93OPCPre-221
❑ 93OPCPreG-221
❑ 93Sco-361
❑ 93ScoCan-361
❑ 93TopPre-221
❑ 93TopPreG-221
❑ 94OPCPre-408
❑ 94OPCPreSE-408
❑ 94TopPre-408
❑ 94TopPreSE-408
❑ 94UppDec-437
❑ 94UppDecEleIce-437
❑ 97ColCho-21
❑ 97DonPreProG-36
❑ 97DonPreProS-36
❑ 97PacInvNRB-13
**Kennedy, Teeder (Ted)**
❑ 44BeeGro2P-414
❑ 45QuaOatP-25A
❑ 45QuaOatP-25B
❑ 45QuaOatP-25C
❑ 45QuaOatP-25D
❑ 45QuaOatP-25E
❑ 45QuaOatP-25F
❑ 48ExhCan-32
❑ 51Par-86
❑ 52Par-44
❑ 53Par-7
❑ 54Par-29
❑ 54Par-96
❑ 54Par-99
❑ 55Par-29
❑ 55ParQuaO-29
❑ 64BeeGro3P-170
❑ 83HalFP-E9
❑ 85HalFC-69
❑ 94ParMisL-116
**Kennedy, Troy**
❑ 85KamBla-10
❑ 88BraWheK-9
❑ 95GuiFla-12
**Kenney, Nick**

98CinCyc-24

**Kennholt, Kenneth**
89SweSemE-56
90SweSemE-277
91SweSemE-58
91SweSemE-344
91SweSemWCS-37
92SweSemE-79
93SweSemE-101
93SweSemWCS-3
94SweLeaE-5
95SweLeaE-50
95SweLeaEC-14
95SweLeaEFF-6
95SweUppDE-79

**Kennish, Ian**
92HarCri-17

**Kenny, Brendan**
92BriColJHL-65
93WesMic-18

**Kenny, Rob**
92BinRan-8
94BinRan-7

**Kenny, Shane**
93OweSouPla-13
95Cla-42
95Cla-93
95SigRooA-21
95SigRooAPC-21
95Sla-283
96SarSti-11

**Kent, Brian**
92OshGenS-23

**Keogan, Murray**
74OPCWHA-44
74PhoRoaWP-7
75RoaPhoWHA-11

**Keon, Dave**
44BeeGro2P-415
60WonBreL-3
60WonBrePP-3
60YorPreP-20
61Par-5
61ShiCoi-58
61YorYelB-27
62ElProDis-4
62Par-15
62ShiMetC-16
62ShiMetC-52
62ShiMetC-55
62YorIroOTra-9
63ChePho-30
63MapLeaWB-12
63MapLeaWB-13
63Par-75
63TorSta-23
63YorWhiB-6
64BeeGro3P-171A
64BeeGro3P-171B
64CocCap-99
64Top-94
64TorSta-24
65Coc-99
65CocBoo-B
65MapLeaWB-12
65Top-17
66Top-78
66TopUSAT-30
67PosFliB-6
67Top-11
67YorActOct-4
67YorActOct-13
67YorActOct-19
680PC-198
68OPCPucSti-19
68PosCerM-13
68ShiCoi-169
68Top-128
69MapLeaWBG-18
69MapLeaWBG-19
69MapLeaWBM-7
690PC-51
690PCFou-11
690PCSta-17
69Top-51
70DadCoo-65
70EssPowPla-27
700PC-219
700PCDec-47
70SarProSta-208
70TopStiS-17
71Baz-11
71LetActR-1
71MapLeaP-8
710PC-80
710PC-259
710PCPos-3
710PCTBoo-16
71SarProSta-206
71Top-80
71TorSun-261
72MapLeaP-14
72MapLeaP-15
720PC-108
720PC-209
72SarProSta-206
72SweSemWC-164
72Top-88
73MapLeaP-16
730PC-150
73Top-85
74LipSou-50
74MapLeaP-10
74MapLeaP-11
74NHLActSta-256

740PCNHL-151
74Top-151
750PCWHA-97
760PCWHA-52
790PC-279
800PC-272
810PC-129
81Top-E83
82PosCer-7
85HalFC-255
91UltOriS-39
91UltOriSF-39
92ParParR-PR21
92ParProS-2
93ParParR-PR67
94ParMisLFS-FS2
94ParTalB-111
94ParTalBA-A6
94ZelMasH-4
94ZelMasoHS-4
95Par66-100
95Par66Coi-100

**Kerch, Alexander**
900PC-474
94ClaProP-176

**Kerch, Kerry**
82KitRan-6

**Keresztes, Otto**
94GerDELE-347

**Kerr, Alan**
84SprInd-8
85IslsIsIN-9
880PC-63
880PCSti-106
88PanSti-288
88Top-63
89Isl-10
89PanSti-275
90Bow-118
90BowTif-118
900PC-50
90PanSti-89
90ProSet-184
90Sco-307A
90ScoCan-307A
90Top-50
90TopTif-50
90UppDec-388
90UppDecF-388
91Par-273
91ParFre-273
91ProSet-376
91ProSetFre-376
91ScoCan-571

**Kerr, Albert**
10C55SweCP-10
11C55-10
12C57-33

**Kerr, Allen**
907thInnSMC-58

**Kerr, Chris**
91BriColJHL-81
91BriColJHL-128
95Sla-421

**Kerr, Dave**
330PCV304B-59
33V252CanG-35
33V357IceK-19
34BeeGro1P-282
34SweCap-43
35DiaMatT2-34
35DiaMatT3-31
36V356WorG-53
390PCV3011-37
400PCV3012-139

**Kerr, Kevin**
83NorBayC-12
88ProAHL-252
90CinCyc-32
90ProAHLIHL-282
91CinCyc-10
92BirBul-15
93BirBul-15
93FliGen-13
94FliGen-14
95FliGen-2

**Kerr, Randy**
91AirCanSJHL-C7

**Kerr, Reg**
790PC-67
79Top-67
800PC-377
81BlaBorPos-11
810PC-58
810PCSti-118
81Top-W70
820PC-67
820PCSti-176
82PosCer-4
83MonAlp-11
88OilTenAnn-75

**Kerr, Scott**
83KitRan-14

**Kerr, Tim**
810PC-251
820PC-253
82PosCer-14
83FlyJCP-13
84TEDis-37
840PC-162
840PC-364
840PCSti-105
840PCSti-106
84Top-119
857ECreCar-14

85FlyPos-16
850PC-91
850PC-260
850PCBoxB-H
850PCSti-96
85Top-91
85TopBoxB-H
86FlyPos-14
860PC-134
860PC-261
860PCBoxB-G
860PCSti-240
86Top-134
86TopBoxB-G
870PC-144
870PCBoxB-B
870PCMin-20
870PCSti-103
87PanSti-128
87Top-144
87TopBoxB-B
87TopStiIns-10
88EssAllSta-21
88PanSti-321
89FlyPos-14
890PC-72
890PCBoxB-G
890PCSti-110
890PCSti-216
89PanSti-294
89PanSti-377
89Top-72
89TopBoxB-G
90FlyPos-13
900PC-210
90PanSti-120
90ProSet-218
90Sco-177
90ScoCan-177
90ScoHotRS-77
90Top-210
90TopTif-210
90UppDec-247
90UppDec-304
90UppDecF-247
90UppDecF-304
910PC-164
910PCPre-83
91PanSti-226
91Pin-52
91PinFre-52
91ProSet-180
91ProSetFre-180
91ProSetFre-446
91ProSetPla-80
91ScoAme-108
91ScoCan-108
91ScoCan-565
91ScoRoo-15T
91StaClu-130
91Top-164
920PCPre-127
92Pin-368
92PinFre-368
92Sco-93
92ScoCan-93
92Top-351
92TopGol-351G
92Ult-74
92WhaDai-11

**Kerrigan, Steve**
92DayBom-14
92DayBom-26

**Kersey, Jade**
91BriColJHL-44
92BriColJHL-99

**Kerth, Werner**
93SweSemWCS-280
94FinnJaaK-243
95AusNatTea-12
96SweSemW-218

**Kesa, Dan**
907thInnSWHL-271
90PriAlbR-6
917thInnSWHL-247
91PriAlbR-6
92HamCan-12
93Pow-460
94ClaProP-116
96DetVip-10
99Pac-340
99PacCop-340
99PacGol-340
99PacIceB-340
99PacPreD-340

**Keskinen, Esa**
89SweSemWCS-48
91SweSemWCS-19
93FinnJyvHS-318
93FinnSIS-40
93FinnSIS-360
93FinnSIS-370
93FinnSIS-372
94FinnJaaK-41
94FinnSIS-156
94FinnSIS-164
94FinnSIS-367
94FinnSISFI-10
94FinnSISS-7
94SweLeaE-177
94SweLeaEFA-2
95FinnKarWCL-5
95FinnSemWC-9
95FinnSISGC-14

95FinnSISL-8
95SweGloWC-144
95SweLeaE-56
95SweLeaE-306
95SweLeaEC-7
95SweLeaEM-6
95SweUppDE-89
95SweUppDE-225
95SweSemW-9

**Keskinen, Jere**
93FinnSIS-18

**Kessell, Rick**
72SarProSta-177

**Kesselring, Casey**
92MPSPhoSJHL-111

**Ketola, Stefan**
91SweSemE-75
92SweSemE-320
93SweSemE-285
94SweLeaE-269
95SweLeaE-24
95SweUppDE-29

**Ketola, Veli-Pekka**
69SweHocS-371
69SweWorC-158
70SweHocS-303
71SweHocS-65
72SweHocS-36
72SweSemWC-79
74SweHocS-108
74SweSemHVS-83
750PCWHA-15
760PCWHA-88
81RocPos-8
82SweSemHVS-162
91SweSemWCS-230
93FinnJyvHS-343
94FinnSIS-400
95FinnSIS-387
96FinnSISR-196
96SweSemWHL-HL13

**Ketter, Kerry**
72Flam-6

**Ketterer, Markus**
91SweSemWCS-2
91UppDec-23
91UppDecF-23
93Cla-39
93RochAmeKod-13
93SweSemWCS-45
94ClaProP-167
94FinnJaaK-4
95FinnSemWC-47
95SweGloWC-127
95SweLeaE-211
95SweUppDE-56
95SweUppDE-224
96SweSemW-32
96SweSemWSG-SG8

**Keyes, Tim**
95Sla-256

**Khabibulin, Nikolai**
91UppDec-652
91UppDecCWJC-13
91UppDecF-652
93SweSemWCS-129
94Fin-27
94FinnJaaK-135
94FinRef-27
94FinSupTW-27
94Fle-242
94UppDec-420
94UppDecEeIce-420
95BeAPla-176
95BeAPlaSigDC-176
95BeAPlaSigDC-S176
95Bow-89
95BowAllFoi-89
95ColCho-75
95ColChoPC-75
95ColChoPCP-75
95ColEdgI-70
95ColEdgIC-C12
95Don-185
95Emo-193
95Fin-63
95FinRef-63
95Ima-42
95ImaGol-42
95JetReaC-4
95JetTealss-10
95Lea-27
95Met-162
95ParInt-230
95ParIntEI-230
95Pin-118
95PinArtP-118
95PinRinC-118
95Sco-142
95ScoBlaIce-142
95ScoBlaIceAP-142
95SkyImp-181
95StaClu-157
95StaCluMOMS-157
95Top-48
95TopOPCI-48
95Ult-180
95UltGolM-180
95UppDecEeIce-85
95UppDecEleceG-85
96BeAPStaTP-7
96ColCho-204

96Don-172
96DonBetPip-9
96DonCanI-95
96DonCanIGPP-95
96DonCanIRPP-95
96DonDom-2
96DonEli-49
96DonEliDCS-49
96DonEliPW-P9
96DonPrePro-172
96Fla-71
96FlaBlul-71
96Fle-90
96FlePic-86
96Lea-63
96LeaLim-60
96LeaLimG-60
96LeaPre-10
96LeaPreMM-9
96LeaPreP-63
96LeaPrePP-10
96LeaPreSG-30
96LeaPreSte-30
96LeaShuDow-9
96LeaTheBO.-6
96MetUni-118
96Pin-161
96PinArtP-161
96PinFoi-161
96PinMas-7
96PinMasDC-7
96PinPreS-161
96PinRinC-161
96Sco-105
96ScoArtPro-105
96ScoDeaCAP-105
96ScoGolB-105
96ScoNetW-18
96ScoSpeAP-105
96ScoSudDea-15
96SelCer-17
96SelCerAP-17
96SelCerBlu-17
96SelCerMB-17
96SelCerMG-17
96SelCerMR-17
96SelCerRed-17
96SkyImp-105
96SP-120
96Sum-41
96SumArtP-41
96SumIce-41
96SumInTheCre-12
96SumInTheCrePS-12
96SumMet-41
96SumPreS-41
96SweSemW-129
96TeaOut-65
96Ult-132
96UltGolM-132
96UppDec-126
96UppDecBD-36
96UppDecBDG-36
96Zen-40
96ZenArtP-40
97BeA PPAD-13
97BeA PPAPD-13
97BeAPla-13
97BeAPlaAut-13
97BeAPlaSTP-13
97ColCho-193
97ColChoSta-SQ35
97Don-120
97DonCanI-75
97DonCanIDS-75
97DonCanIPS-75
97DonLim-124
97DonLimExp-124
97DonLimFOTG-30
97DonPre-101
97DonPreCttC-101
97DonPreProG-120
97DonPreProG-120
97DonPri-36
97DonPriSoA-36
97EssOlyHH-40
97EssOlyHHF-40
97Kat-111
97KatGol-111
97KatSil-111
97Lea-62
97LeaFraMat-62
97LeaFraMDC-62
97LeaInt-62
97LeaIntUI-62
97LeaPipDre-13
97Pac-6
97PacCop-6
97PacCroR-104
97PacCroREG-104
97PacCroRFODC-15
97PacCroRIB-104
97PacCroRS-104
97PacDyn-96
97PacDynDG-96
97PacDynEG-96
97PacDynIB-96
97PacDynR-96
97PacDynSil-96
97PacDynSto-17
97PacDynTan-64
97PacEmeGre-6

97PacIceB-6
97PacInTheCLC-16
97PacInv-107
97PacInvC-107
97PacInvEG-107
97PacInvIB-107
97PacInvNRB-153
97PacInvR-107
97PacInvS-107
97PacOme-174
97PacOmeC-174
97PacOmeDG-174
97PacOmeEG-174
97PacOmeG-174
97PacOmeIB-174
97PacPar-141
97PacParC-141
97PacParDG-141
97PacParEG-141
97PacParGSL-16
97PacParIB-141
97PacParRed-141
97PacParSil-141
97PacRed-6
97PacRev-107
97PacRevC-107
97PacRevE-107
97PacRevIB-107
97PacRevR-107
97PacRevRtSD-15
97PacRevS-107
97PacSil-6
97Pin-94
97PinArtP-94
97PinCer-16
97PinCerMB-16
97PinCerMG-16
97PinCerMR-16
97PinCerR-16
97PinIns-44
97PinInsCC-44
97PinInsEC-44
97PinInsSto-16
97PinInsSUG-9A/B
97PinInsSUG-9C/D
97PinMas-9
97PinMasDC-9
97PinMasJ-9
97PinMasPro-9
97PinPrePBB-94
97PinPrePBC-94
97PinPrePBM-94
97PinPrePBY-94
97PinPrePFC-94
97PinPrePFM-94
97PinPrePFY-94
97PinRinC-94
97PinTin-6
97PinTotCMPG-16
97PinTotCPB-16
97PinTotCPG-16
97PinTotCPR-16
97Sco-10
97ScoArtPro-10
97ScoGolBla-10
97ScoNetW-9
97SPAut-120
97SPAutSotT-NK
97Stu-63
97StuPrePG-63
97StuPrePS-63
97UppDec-129
97UppDecBD-53
97UppDecBDD-53
97UppDecBDDD-53
97UppDecBDTD-53
97Zen-76
97ZenZGol-76
97ZenZSil-76
98Be A PPA-108
98Be A PPAA-108
98Be A PPAAF-108
98Be A PPTBASG-108
98Be APG-108
98BowBes-23
98BowBesAR-23
98BowBesR-23
98Fin-15
98FinNo P-15
98FinNo PR-15
98FinRef-15
980-PChr-115
980-PChrR-115
98Pac-341
98PacAur-145
98PacCroR-103
98PacCroRLS-103
98PacDynl-143
98PacDynIIB-143
98PacDynIR-143
98PacIceB-341
98PacOmeH-184
98PacOmeO-2
98PacOmeODI-184
98PacOmeR-184
98PacPar-182
98PacParC-182
98PacParEG-182
98PacParGSLC-15
98PacParIB-182
98PacParS-182
98PacRed-341
98PacRev-110

98PacRevADC-14
98PacRevIS-110
98PacRevR-110
98PacRevS-28
98RevThrPA-18
98RevThrPA-18
98SP Aut-67
98SPxFin-66
98SPxFinS-66
98SPxFinS-66
98Top-115
98TopGolLC1-70
98TopGolLC1B-70
98TopGolLC1BOoO-70
98TopGolLC1OoO-70
98TopGolLC1R-70
98TopGolLC1ROoO-70
98TopGolLC2-70
98TopGolLC2B-70
98TopGolLC2BOoO-70
98TopGolLC2OoO-70
98TopGolLC2R-70
98TopGolLC2ROoO-70
98TopGolLC3-70
98TopGolLC3B-70
98TopGolLC3BOoO-70
98TopGolLC3OoO-70
98TopGolLC3R-70
98TopGolLC3ROoO-70
98TopLaceA2-I15
98TopO-P-115
98UC-162
98UD ChoPCR-162
98UD ChoR-162
98UppDec-157
98UppDecE-157
98UppDecEo1o1-157
98UppDecGR-157
98UppDecM-158
98UppDecMGS-158
98UppDecMSS-158
98UppDecMSS-158
99Pac-321
99PacAur-109
99PacAurGU-16
99PacAurPD-109
99PacCop-321
99PacGol-321
99PacIceB-321
99PacIn tCN-15
99PacPreD-321
99SP AutPS-67
99UppDecM-161
99UppDecMGS-161
99UppDecMSS-LL10
99UppDecMSS-161
99UppDecMSS-161

**Khaidarov, Ravil**
910PCIns-36R
91RusStaRA-8
92UppDec-347
94FinnJaaK-162

**Khalizov, Svatoslav**
89RusNatT-11

**Kharin, Sergei**
90JetIGA-16
90MonHaw-13
90ProAHLIHL-261
91ProAHLCHL-540
91ScoAme-394
91ScoCan-284
91UppDec-381
91UppDecF-381
93DayBom-14
95DayBom-9
95DayBom-P2

**Kharlamov, Alexander**
91FutTreC72-100
92RusStaRA-12
92RusStaRA-12
93Cla-105
93ParEmel-529
93Pin-504
93PinCan-504
94Cla-13
94ClaDraGol-13
94Sco-213
94ScoGol-213
94ScoPla-213
95ColEdgI-56
95PorPir-13
96PorPir-22

**Kharlamov, Valeri**
69SweHocS-1
69SweWorC-21
69SweWorC-30
69SweWorC-125
70SweHocS-322
71SweHocS-34
72SweHocS-30
72SweHocS-50
72SweSemWC-17
73SweHocS-87
73SweWorCS-87
74SweHocS-5
74SweSemHVS-34
79PanSti-151
81SweSemHVS-50
91FutTreC72-58
91FutTreC72-100
91SweSemWCS-244
92FutTre76CC-108
95SweGloWC-241

**Khlopotnov, Denis**

❑ 96UppDecIce-141
**Khmylev, Yuri**
❑ 87RusNatT-9
❑ 89RusNatT-12
❑ 89SweSemWCS-94
❑ 91OPCIns-16R
❑ 92Par-255
❑ 92ParEmel-255
❑ 92RusStaRA-13
❑ 92SabBluS-9
❑ 92SabJubF-6
❑ 92Ult-260
❑ 92UppDec-504
❑ 93Don-36
❑ 93Lea-211
❑ 93OPCPre-389
❑ 93OPCPreG-389
❑ 93PanSti-106
❑ 93Pin-201
❑ 93PinCan-201
❑ 93Pow-30
❑ 93Sco-302
❑ 93ScoCan-302
❑ 93StaClu-241
❑ 93StaCluFDI-241
❑ 93StaCluFDIO-241
❑ 93StaCluO-241
❑ 93TopPre-389
❑ 93TopPreG-389
❑ 93Ult-173
❑ 94CanGamNHLP-53
❑ 94Don-324
❑ 94Fle-22
❑ 94Lea-297
❑ 94OPCPre-14
❑ 94OPCPreSE-14
❑ 94Par-22
❑ 94ParGol-22
❑ 94Pin-69
❑ 94PinArtP-69
❑ 94PinRinC-69
❑ 94TopPre-14
❑ 94TopPreSE-14
❑ 94Ult-264
❑ 94UppDec-368
❑ 94UppDecEleIce-368
❑ 94UppDecSPI-SP98
❑ 94UppDecSPIDC-SP98
❑ 95BeAPla-4
❑ 95BeAPSig-S4
❑ 95BeAPSigDC-S4
❑ 95CanGamNHLP-45
❑ 95ColCho-23
❑ 95ColChoPC-23
❑ 95ColChoPCP-23
❑ 95Don-18
❑ 95ParInt-23
❑ 95ParIntEl-23
❑ 95PlaOneoOne-231
❑ 95ProMag-108
❑ 95Sco-61
❑ 95ScoBlaIce-61
❑ 95ScoBlaIceAP-61
❑ 95Top-371
❑ 95TopOPCI-371
❑ 95UppDec-27
❑ 95UppDecEleIce-27
❑ 95UppDecEleIceG-27
❑ 96Don-185
❑ 96DonPrePro-185
❑ 96NHLProSTA-108
❑ 96PlaOneoOne-414
❑ 96Sco-199
❑ 96ScoArtPro-199
❑ 96ScoDeaCAP-199
❑ 96ScoGolB-199
❑ 96ScoSpeAP-199
**Kholomeyev, Alex**
❑ 92ForWorF-9
❑ 94CenHocL-24
**Khomutov, Andrei**
❑ 82SweSemHVS-68
❑ 83RusNatT-9
❑ 87RusNatT-10
❑ 89RusNatT-13
❑ 89SweSemWCS-93
❑ 90OPCRedA-3R
❑ 91SweSemWCS-99
❑ 93SweSemWCS-148
❑ 93SwiHNL-48
❑ 94FinnJaaK-154
❑ 95FinnSemWC-139
❑ 95SweGloWC-178
❑ 95SwiHNL-74
❑ 95SwiHNL-513
❑ 96SweSemW-152
**Khristich, Dimitri**
❑ 89CapTeaIss-10
❑ 90CapKod-10
❑ 90OPCRedA-16R
❑ 90UppDec-537
❑ 90UppDecF-537
❑ 91Bow-307
❑ 91CapJun5-14
❑ 91CapKod-14
❑ 91OPC-78
❑ 91OPCPre-176
❑ 91Par-189
❑ 91ParFre-189
❑ 91Pin-162
❑ 91PinFre-162
❑ 91ProSet-260
❑ 91ProSetFre-260
❑ 91ProSetPla-242
❑ 91ScoAme-175
❑ 91ScoCan-175
❑ 91ScoYouS-6
❑ 91StaClu-359
❑ 91Top-78
❑ 91UppDec-157
❑ 91UppDecF-157
❑ 92Bow-427
❑ 92CapKod-15
❑ 92OPC-286
❑ 92PanSti-N
❑ 92PanStiFre-N
❑ 92Par-428
❑ 92ParEmel-428
❑ 92Pin-146
❑ 92PinFre-146
❑ 92PinTea2-25
❑ 92PinTea2F-25
❑ 92ProSet-208
❑ 92RusStaRA-3
❑ 92Sco-33
❑ 92ScoCan-33
❑ 92ScoSha-27
❑ 92ScoShaCan-27
❑ 92ScoYouS-15
❑ 92StaClu-86
❑ 92Top-470
❑ 92TopGol-470G
❑ 92Ult-235
❑ 92UltImp-7
❑ 92UppDec-219
❑ 93Don-373
❑ 93Lea-168
❑ 93OPCPre-210
❑ 93OPCPreG-210
❑ 93PanSti-28
❑ 93Par-220
❑ 93ParEmel-220
❑ 93Pin-44
❑ 93PinCan-44
❑ 93PinTea2-23
❑ 93PinTea2C-23
❑ 93Pow-264
❑ 93Sco-80
❑ 93ScoCan-80
❑ 93ScoIntS-20
❑ 93ScoIntSC-20
❑ 93StaClu-277
❑ 93StaCluFDI-277
❑ 93StaCluO-277
❑ 93TopPre-210
❑ 93TopPreG-210
❑ 93Ult-59
❑ 93UppDec-135
❑ 93UppDecSP-171
❑ 94CanGamNHLP-246
❑ 94Don-264
❑ 94EASpo-154
❑ 94Fla-201
❑ 94Fle-237
❑ 94Lea-190
❑ 94OPCPre-534
❑ 94OPCPreSE-534
❑ 94Par-252
❑ 94ParGol-252
❑ 94Pin-59
❑ 94PinArtP-59
❑ 94PinRinC-59
❑ 94Sco-118
❑ 94ScoGol-118
❑ 94ScoPla-118
❑ 94ScoPlaTS-118
❑ 94Sel-104
❑ 94SelGol-104
❑ 94SP-130
❑ 94SPDieCut-130
❑ 94StaClu-12
❑ 94StaCluFDI-12
❑ 94StaCluMOMS-12
❑ 94StaCluSTWC-12
❑ 94TopPre-534
❑ 94TopPreSE-534
❑ 94Ult-236
❑ 94UppDec-76
❑ 94UppDecEleIce-76
❑ 94UppDecSPI-SP87
❑ 94UppDecSPIDC-SP87
❑ 95BeAPla-36
❑ 95BeAPSig-S36
❑ 95BeAPSigDC-S36
❑ 95Bow-61
❑ 95BowAllFoi-61
❑ 95CanGamNHLP-133
❑ 95ColCho-183
❑ 95ColChoPC-183
❑ 95ColChoPCP-183
❑ 95Don-265
❑ 95Emo-82
❑ 95Fin-166
❑ 95FinRef-166
❑ 95ImpSti-60
❑ 95Lea-139
❑ 95Met-72
❑ 95ParInt-108
❑ 95ParIntEl-108
❑ 95Sco-151
❑ 95ScoBlaIce-151
❑ 95ScoBlaIceAP-151
❑ 95SkyImp-80
❑ 95SP-67
❑ 95StaClu-68
❑ 95StaCluMOMS-68
❑ 95Sum-153
❑ 95SumArtP-153
❑ 95SumIce-153
❑ 95Top-248
❑ 95TopOPCI-248
❑ 95Ult-250
❑ 95UppDec-287
❑ 95UppDecEleIce-287
❑ 95UppDecEleIceG-287
❑ 96ColCho-123
❑ 96ColCho-320
❑ 96Don-56
❑ 96DonCanI-105
❑ 96DonCanIGPP-105
❑ 96DonCanIRPP-105
❑ 96DonEli-70
❑ 96DonEliDCS-70
❑ 96DonPrePro-56
❑ 96Fla-46
❑ 96FlaBluI-46
❑ 96Fle-50
❑ 96FlePic-134
❑ 96Lea-168
❑ 96LeaPreP-79
❑ 96LeaPreP-168
❑ 96LeaPrePP-79
❑ 96MetUni-75
❑ 96Pin-190
❑ 96PinArtP-190
❑ 96PinFoi-190
❑ 96PinPreS-190
❑ 96PinRinC-190
❑ 96Sco-122
❑ 96ScoArtPro-122
❑ 96ScoDeaCAP-122
❑ 96ScoGolB-122
❑ 96ScoSpeAP-122
❑ 96SelCer-46
❑ 96SelCerAP-46
❑ 96SelCerBlu-46
❑ 96SelCerMB-46
❑ 96SelCerMG-46
❑ 96SelCerMR-46
❑ 96SelCerRed-46
❑ 96SkyImp-58
❑ 96Sum-27
❑ 96SumArtP-27
❑ 96SumIce-27
❑ 96SumMet-27
❑ 96SumPreS-27
❑ 96Ult-79
❑ 96UltGolM-80
❑ 96UppDec-76
❑ 96UppDecBD-108
❑ 96UppDecBDG-108
❑ 96Zen-88
❑ 96ZenArtP-88
❑ 97Be A PPAD-61
❑ 97Be A PPAPD-61
❑ 97BeAPla-61
❑ 97BeAPlaAut-61
❑ 97ColCho-119
❑ 97ColChoCTG-C17A
❑ 97ColChoCTG-C17B
❑ 97ColChoCTG-C17C
❑ 97ColChoCTGE-CR17
❑ 97ColChoSta-SQ27
❑ 97Don-89
❑ 97DonCanI-58
❑ 97DonCanIDS-58
❑ 97DonCanIPS-58
❑ 97DonLim-73
❑ 97DonLimExp-73
❑ 97DonPre-92
❑ 97DonPreCttC-92
❑ 97DonPrePro-89
❑ 97DonPreProS-89
❑ 97DonPri-39
❑ 97DonPriSoA-39
❑ 97Kat-11
❑ 97KatGol-11
❑ 97KatSil-11
❑ 97Lea-29
❑ 97LeaFraMat-29
❑ 97LeaFraMDC-29
❑ 97LeaInt-29
❑ 97LeaIntUI-29
❑ 97Pac-219
❑ 97PacCop-219
❑ 97PacDyn-60
❑ 97PacDynC-60
❑ 97PacDynDG-60
❑ 97PacDynEG-60
❑ 97PacDynIB-60
❑ 97PacDynR-60
❑ 97PacDynSil-60
❑ 97PacDynTan-36
❑ 97PacEmeGre-219
❑ 97PacIceB-219
❑ 97PacInv-68
❑ 97PacInvC-68
❑ 97PacInvEG-68
❑ 97PacInvIB-68
❑ 97PacInvR-68
❑ 97PacInvS-68
❑ 97PacOme-17
❑ 97PacOmeC-17
❑ 97PacOmeDG-7
❑ 97PacOmeDG-17
❑ 97PacOmeEG-17
❑ 97PacOmeG-7
❑ 97PacOmeG-17
❑ 97PacOmeIB-17
❑ 97PacPar-14
❑ 97PacParC-14
❑ 97PacParDG-14
❑ 97PacParEG-14
❑ 97PacParIB-14
❑ 97PacParRed-14
❑ 97PacParSil-14
❑ 97PacRed-219
❑ 97PacRev-10
❑ 97PacRevC-10
❑ 97PacRevE-10
❑ 97PacRevIB-10
❑ 97PacRevR-10
❑ 97PacRevS-10
❑ 97PacSil-219
❑ 97Pin-179
❑ 97PinCer-126
❑ 97PinCerMB-126
❑ 97PinCerMG-126
❑ 97PinCerMR-126
❑ 97PinCerR-126
❑ 97PinIns-124
❑ 97PinPrePBB-179
❑ 97PinPrePBC-179
❑ 97PinPrePBM-179
❑ 97PinPrePBY-179
❑ 97PinPrePFC-179
❑ 97PinPrePFM-179
❑ 97PinPrePFY-179
❑ 97PinPrePla-179
❑ 97PinTotCMPG-126
❑ 97PinTotCPB-126
❑ 97PinTotCPG-126
❑ 97PinTotCPR-126
❑ 97Sco-111
❑ 97ScoArtPro-111
❑ 97ScoBru-5
❑ 97ScoBruPla-5
❑ 97ScoBruPre-5
❑ 97ScoGolBla-111
❑ 97SPAut-12
❑ 97Stu-80
❑ 97StuPrePG-80
❑ 97StuPrePS-80
❑ 97UppDec-91
❑ 98Be A PPA-11
❑ 98Be A PPAA-11
❑ 98Be A PPAAF-11
❑ 98Be A PPTBASG-11
❑ 98Be APG-11
❑ 98Fin-117
❑ 98FinNo P-117
❑ 98FinNo PR-117
❑ 98FinRef-117
❑ 98O-PChr-164
❑ 98O-PChrR-164
❑ 98Pac-83
❑ 98PacAur-13
❑ 98PacCroR-9
❑ 98PacCroRLS-9
❑ 98PacDynI-11
❑ 98PacDynIIB-11
❑ 98PacDynIR-11
❑ 98PacIceB-83
❑ 98PacOmeH-16
❑ 98PacOmeODI-16
❑ 98PacOmeR-16
❑ 98PacPar-15
❑ 98PacParC-15
❑ 98PacParEG-15
❑ 98PacParH-15
❑ 98PacParIB-15
❑ 98PacParS-15
❑ 98PacRed-83
❑ 98PacRev-10
❑ 98PacRevIS-10
❑ 98PacRevR-10
❑ 98Top-164
❑ 98TopGolLC1-23
❑ 98TopGolLC1B-23
❑ 98TopGolLC1BOoO-23
❑ 98TopGolLC1OoO-23
❑ 98TopGolLC1R-23
❑ 98TopGolLC1ROoO-23
❑ 98TopGolLC2-23
❑ 98TopGolLC2B-23
❑ 98TopGolLC2BOoO-23
❑ 98TopGolLC2OoO-23
❑ 98TopGolLC2R-23
❑ 98TopGolLC2ROoO-23
❑ 98TopGolLC3-23
❑ 98TopGolLC3B-23
❑ 98TopGolLC3BOoO-23
❑ 98TopGolLC3OoO-23
❑ 98TopGolLC3R-23
❑ 98TopGolLC3ROoO-23
❑ 98TopO-P-164
❑ 98UC-12
❑ 98UD ChoPCR-12
❑ 98UD ChoR-12
❑ 98UppDecM-16
❑ 98UppDecMGS-16
❑ 98UppDecMSS-16
❑ 98UppDecMSS-16
❑ 99Pac-25
❑ 99PacCop-25
❑ 99PacGol-25
❑ 99PacIceB-25
❑ 99PacPreD-25
❑ 99UppDecM-17
❑ 99UppDecMGS-17
❑ 99UppDecMSS-17
❑ 99UppDecMSS-17
**Kiang, Hsi**
❑ 79PanSti-358
**Kibermanis, Chris**
❑ 93RedDeeR-9
❑ 95RedDeeR-8
**Kidd, Ian**
❑ 89ProIHL-182
❑ 90ProAHLIHL-323
❑ 91ProAHLCHL-601
**Kidd, Trevor**
❑ 88BraWheK-21
❑ 89BraWheK-1
❑ 907thInnSWHL-226
❑ 90BraWheK-15
❑ 90Sco-438
❑ 90ScoCan-438
❑ 90UppDec-463
❑ 90UppDecF-463
❑ 917thInnSMC-74
❑ 91AlbIntTC-12
❑ 91OPC-312
❑ 91ScoAme-381
❑ 91ScoCan-271
❑ 91Top-312
❑ 91UppDec-449
❑ 91UppDec-684
❑ 91UppDecCWJC-58
❑ 91UppDecF-449
❑ 91UppDecF-684
❑ 92ScoCanO-12
❑ 92Top-280
❑ 92TopGol-280G
❑ 92UppDec-134
❑ 92UppDec-385
❑ 93Lea-385
❑ 93Pow-305
❑ 93Sco-660
❑ 93ScoCan-660
❑ 93ScoGol-560
❑ 93ScoGol-660
❑ 93Ult-281
❑ 93UppDec-399
❑ 94BeAPSig-167
❑ 94CanGamNHLP-275
❑ 94Don-4
❑ 94Fla-25
❑ 94Fle-31
❑ 94Kra-45
❑ 94Lea-322
❑ 94OPCFinIns-5
❑ 94OPCPre-413
❑ 94OPCPreSE-413
❑ 94Par-288
❑ 94ParGol-288
❑ 94ParSE-SE24
❑ 94ParSEG-SE24
❑ 94Pin-365
❑ 94PinArtP-365
❑ 94PinMas-MA7
❑ 94PinRinC-365
❑ 94Sco-259
❑ 94ScoGol-259
❑ 94ScoPla-259
❑ 94ScoPlaTS-259
❑ 94SP-21
❑ 94SPDieCut-21
❑ 94StaClu-106
❑ 94StaCluFDI-106
❑ 94StaCluMOMS-106
❑ 94StaCluSTWC-106
❑ 94TopPre-413
❑ 94TopPreSE-413
❑ 94Ult-30
❑ 94UppDec-395
❑ 94UppDecEleIce-395
❑ 94UppDecSPI-SP12
❑ 94UppDecSPIDC-SP12
❑ 95ColCho-69
❑ 95ColChoPC-69
❑ 95ColChoPCP-69
❑ 95ColEdgIC-C21
❑ 95Don-31
❑ 95DonBetTP-4
❑ 95DonDom-8
❑ 95DonProPoi-16
❑ 95Emo-23
❑ 95ImpSti-17
❑ 95Kra-24
❑ 95Lea-83
❑ 95LeaLim-31
❑ 95Met-20
❑ 95ParInt-35
❑ 95ParIntEl-35
❑ 95ParIntGP-8
❑ 95Pin-151
❑ 95PinArtP-151
❑ 95PinRinC-151
❑ 95PlaOneoOne-233
❑ 95ProMag-47
❑ 95Sco-19
❑ 95ScoBlaIce-19
❑ 95ScoBlaIceAP-19
❑ 95ScoPro-19
❑ 95SelCer-40
❑ 95SelCerMG-40
❑ 95SkyImp-23
❑ 95SkyImpD-10
❑ 95SP-21
❑ 95StaClu-72
❑ 95StaCluMOMS-72
❑ 95Sum-138
❑ 95SumArtP-138
❑ 95SumIce-138
❑ 95Top-154
❑ 95TopCanG-4CG
❑ 95TopHomGC-HGC13
❑ 95TopOPCI-154
❑ 95TopSupSki-82
❑ 95TopSupSkiPla-82
❑ 95Ult-26
❑ 95UltGolM-26
❑ 95UltRisS-4
❑ 95UltRisSGM-4
❑ 95UppDec-143
❑ 95UppDec-229
❑ 95UppDecEleIce-143
❑ 95UppDecEleIce-229
❑ 95UppDecEleIceG-143
❑ 95UppDecEleIceG-229
❑ 95UppDecSpeE-SE15
❑ 95UppDecSpeEdiG-SE15
❑ 95UppDecWJA-10
❑ 95Zen-67
❑ 96BeAPAut-127
❑ 96BeAPAutSil-127
❑ 96BeAPla-127
❑ 96ColCho-34
❑ 96ColCho-312
❑ 96Don-160
❑ 96DonCanI-37
❑ 96DonCanIGPP-37
❑ 96DonCanIRPP-37
❑ 96DonEli-45
❑ 96DonEliDCS-45
❑ 96DonPrePro-160
❑ 96Fla-13
❑ 96FlaBluI-13
❑ 96Fle-13
❑ 96Lea-67
❑ 96LeaLim-25
❑ 96LeaLimG-25
❑ 96LeaPre-116
❑ 96LeaPreP-67
❑ 96LeaPrePP-116
❑ 96MetUni-20
❑ 96NHLProSTA-47
❑ 96Pin-174
❑ 96PinArtP-174
❑ 96PinFoi-174
❑ 96PinMcD-34
❑ 96PinPreS-174
❑ 96PinRinC-174
❑ 96Sco-58
❑ 96ScoArtPro-58
❑ 96ScoDeaCAP-58
❑ 96ScoGolB-58
❑ 96ScoSpeAP-58
❑ 96SelCer-21
❑ 96SelCerAP-21
❑ 96SelCerBlu-21
❑ 96SelCerMB-21
❑ 96SelCerMG-21
❑ 96SelCerMR-21
❑ 96SelCerRed-21
❑ 96SkyImp-14
❑ 96SP-21
❑ 96Sum-36
❑ 96SumArtP-36
❑ 96SumIce-36
❑ 96SumMet-36
❑ 96SumPreS-36
❑ 96TeaOut-73
❑ 96Ult-25
❑ 96UltGolM-25
❑ 96UppDec-25
❑ 96Zen-11
❑ 96ZenArtP-11
❑ 97CarHur-14
❑ 97ColCho-37
❑ 97Don-59
❑ 97DonCanI-60
❑ 97DonCanIDS-60
❑ 97DonCanIPS-60
❑ 97DonEli-107
❑ 97DonEliAsp-107
❑ 97DonEliS-107
❑ 97DonLim-10
❑ 97DonLimExp-10
❑ 97DonPre-73
❑ 97DonPreCttC-73
❑ 97DonPreProG-59
❑ 97DonPreProS-59
❑ 97DonPri-98
❑ 97DonPriSoA-98
❑ 97Lea-126
❑ 97LeaFraMat-126
❑ 97LeaFraMDC-126
❑ 97LeaInt-126
❑ 97LeaIntUI-126
❑ 97Pac-133
❑ 97PacCop-133
❑ 97PacCroR-24
❑ 97PacCroREG-24
❑ 97PacCroRIB-24
❑ 97PacCroRS-24
❑ 97PacDyn-18
❑ 97PacDynC-18
❑ 97PacDynDG-18
❑ 97PacDynEG-18
❑ 97PacDynIB-18
❑ 97PacDynR-18
❑ 97PacDynSil-18
❑ 97PacDynSto-4
❑ 97PacDynTan-23
❑ 97PacEmeGre-133
❑ 97PacIceB-133
❑ 97PacInTheCLC-3
❑ 97PacInv-20
❑ 97PacInvC-20
❑ 97PacInvEG-20
❑ 97PacInvIB-20
❑ 97PacInvR-20
❑ 97PacInvS-20
❑ 97PacOme-42
❑ 97PacOmeC-42
❑ 97PacOmeDG-42
❑ 97PacOmeEG-42
❑ 97PacOmeG-42
❑ 97PacOmeIB-42
❑ 97PacPar-35
❑ 97PacParC-35
❑ 97PacParDG-35
❑ 97PacParEG-35
❑ 97PacParGSL-3
❑ 97PacParIB-35
❑ 97PacParRed-35
❑ 97PacParSil-35
❑ 97PacRed-133
❑ 97PacRev-24
❑ 97PacRevC-24
❑ 97PacRevE-24
❑ 97PacRevIB-24
❑ 97PacRevR-24
❑ 97PacRevS-24
❑ 97PacSil-133
❑ 97Pin-60
❑ 97PinArtP-60
❑ 97PinCer-21
❑ 97PinCerMB-21
❑ 97PinCerMG-21
❑ 97PinCerMR-21
❑ 97PinCerR-21
❑ 97PinIns-87
❑ 97PinInsCC-87
❑ 97PinInsEC-87
❑ 97PinInsSUG-8A/B
❑ 97PinInsSUG-8C/D
❑ 97PinPrePBB-60
❑ 97PinPrePBC-60
❑ 97PinPrePBM-60
❑ 97PinPrePBY-60
❑ 97PinPrePFC-60
❑ 97PinPrePFM-60
❑ 97PinPrePFY-60
❑ 97PinPrePla-60
❑ 97PinRinC-60
❑ 97PinTotCMPG-21
❑ 97PinTotCPB-21
❑ 97PinTotCPG-21
❑ 97PinTotCPR-21
❑ 97Sco-37
❑ 97ScoArtPro-37
❑ 97ScoGolBla-37
❑ 97ScoNetW-3
❑ 97Stu-61
❑ 97StuPrePG-61
❑ 97StuPrePS-61
❑ 97UppDec-23
❑ 98Be A PPA-22
❑ 98Be A PPAA-22
❑ 98Be A PPAAF-22
❑ 98Be A PPTBASG-22
❑ 98Be APG-22
❑ 98BowBes-30
❑ 98BowBesAR-30
❑ 98BowBesR-30
❑ 98Fin-85
❑ 98FinNo P-85
❑ 98FinNo PR-85
❑ 98FinPro-PP4
❑ 98FinRef-85
❑ 98O-PChr-66
❑ 98O-PChrR-66
❑ 98Pac-135
❑ 98PacAur-34
❑ 98PacCroR-25
❑ 98PacCroRLS-25
❑ 98PacDynI-35
❑ 98PacDynIIB-35
❑ 98PacDynIR-35
❑ 98PacIceB-135
❑ 98PacOmeH-44
❑ 98PacOmeODI-44
❑ 98PacOmeR-44
❑ 98PacPar-38
❑ 98PacParC-38
❑ 98PacParEG-38
❑ 98PacParGSLC-4
❑ 98PacParH-38
❑ 98PacParIB-38
❑ 98PacParS-38
❑ 98PacRed-135
❑ 98PacRev-25
❑ 98PacRevIS-25
❑ 98PacRevR-25
❑ 98SPxFin-15
❑ 98SPxFinR-15
❑ 98SPxFinS-15
❑ 98Top-66
❑ 98TopO-P-66
❑ 98UC-42
❑ 98UD ChoPCR-42
❑ 98UD ChoR-42
❑ 98UppDec-58
❑ 98UppDecE-58
❑ 98UppDecE1o1-58
❑ 98UppDecGR-58
❑ 98UppDecM-36
❑ 98UppDecMGS-36
❑ 98UppDecMSS-36
❑ 98UppDecMSS-36
❑ 99Pac-74
❑ 99PacCop-74
❑ 99PacGol-74
❑ 99PacIceB-74
❑ 99PacPreD-74
**Kienass, Torsten**
❑ 94FinnJaaK-274
❑ 94GerDELE-48
❑ 95GerDELE-79
❑ 95GerDELE-435
❑ 96GerDELE-322
**Kiene, Chris**

❑ 89ProAHL-221
❑ 90ProAHLIHL-575
❑ 91MonHaw-14
❑ 91ProAHLCHL-165
**Kiereck, Matt**
❑ 92SudWol-14
**Kiessling, Udo**
❑ 79PanSti-100
❑ 82SweSemHVS-105
❑ 89SweSemWCS-107
❑ 91SweSemWCS-157
❑ 94GerDELE-268
❑ 95GerDELE-248
**Kihlstrom, Christer**
❑ 71SweHocS-337
❑ 72SweHocS-148
**Kihlstrom, Mats**
❑ 83SweSemE-200
❑ 84SweSemE-52
❑ 85SwePanS-51
❑ 86SwePanS-249
❑ 87SwePanS-236
❑ 89SweSemE-220
❑ 89SweSemWCS-7
❑ 90SweSemE-53
❑ 91SweSemE-228
**Kiili, Lasse**
❑ 69SweHocS-372
**Kiimalainen, Markku**
❑ 81SweSemHVS-27
❑ 82SweSemHVS-40
**Kikesch, Jeff**
❑ 97LouRivF-14
**Kilduff, David**
❑ 91BriColJHL-87
❑ 91BriColJHL-159
❑ 92BriColJHL-135
**Kiley, Chris**
❑ 93RenEng-12
**Kilger, Chad**
❑ 93KinFro-17
❑ 94Cla95DP-DP3
❑ 95BeAPla-167
❑ 95BeAPSig-S167
❑ 95BeAPSigDC-S167
❑ 95Bow-137
❑ 95BowAllFoi-137
❑ 95BowBes-BB25
❑ 95BowBesRef-BB25
❑ 95Cla-4
❑ 95Cla-86
❑ 95ClaCHLAS-AS10
❑ 95ClaIceBre-BK4
❑ 95Don-379
❑ 95DonEli-55
❑ 95DonEliDCS-55
❑ 95DonEliDCU-55
❑ 95DonEliR-9
❑ 95DonRatRoo-7
❑ 95EmoGen-10
❑ 95Fin-81
❑ 95FinRef-81
❑ 95Ima-84
❑ 95ImaGol-84
❑ 95ImaPlaPDC-PD7
❑ 95ImpSti-3
❑ 95LeaLim-34
❑ 95LeaLimRP-3
❑ 95Met-179
❑ 95ParInt-255
❑ 95ParInt-500
❑ 95ParIntEl-255
❑ 95ParIntEl-500
❑ 95SelCer-116
❑ 95SelCerMG-116
❑ 95SkyImp-188
❑ 95SkyImpNHLF-18
❑ 95SP-163
❑ 95StaClu-202
❑ 95StaCluMOMS-202
❑ 95Sum-179
❑ 95SumArtP-179
❑ 95SumIce-179
❑ 95Top-301
❑ 95TopOPCI-301
❑ 95TopSupSkiSR-SR5
❑ 95Ult-343
❑ 95UppDec-262
❑ 95UppDecEleIce-262
❑ 95UppDecEleIceG-262
❑ 95Zen-139
❑ 95ZenRooRC-12
❑ 96ClaIceBreDC-BK4
❑ 96ColCho-200
❑ 96ColCho-337
❑ 96Don-236
❑ 96DonPrePro-236
❑ 96Lea-203
❑ 96LeaPreP-203
❑ 96Sco-255
❑ 96ScoArtPro-255
❑ 96ScoDeaCAP-255
❑ 96ScoGolB-255
❑ 96ScoSpeAP-255
❑ 96Sum-155
❑ 96SumArtP-155
❑ 96SumIce-155
❑ 96SumMet-155
❑ 96SumPreS-155
❑ 96TopNHLP-151
❑ 96TopPicOI-151
❑ 96UppDec-130
❑ 97Don-175
❑ 97DonLim-73
❑ 97DonLimExp-73
❑ 97DonPreProG-175
❑ 97DonPreProS-175
❑ 97Lea-137
❑ 97LeaFraMat-137
❑ 97LeaFraMDC-137
❑ 97LeaInt-137
❑ 97LeaIntUI-137
❑ 97UppDec-130
❑ 98Pac-146
❑ 98PacIceB-146
❑ 98PacRed-146
❑ 98UppDec-244
❑ 98UppDecE-244
❑ 98UppDecE1o1-244
❑ 98UppDecGR-244
❑ 99Pac-157
❑ 99PacCop-157
❑ 99PacGol-157
❑ 99PacIceB-157
❑ 99PacPreD-157
**Killen, Frank**
❑ 93HumHawP-20
**Kilpatrick, Gary**
❑ 69SeaTotW-7
**Kilpatrick, Gen.J.R.**
❑ 83HalFP-H10
❑ 85HalFC-116
**Kilpio, Raimo**
❑ 96FinnSISR-189
**Kilrea, Brian**
❑ 82Ott67-11
❑ 83Ott67-16
❑ 85IsIIsN-30
❑ 907thInnSOHL-100
❑ 917thInnSOHL-309
❑ 92Ott672A-13
**Kilrea, Hec**
❑ 33V129-17
❑ 33V357IceK-64
❑ 34BeeGro1P-108
❑ 34BeeGro1P-332
❑ 35OPCV304C-86
❑ 36V356WorG-24
❑ 39OPCV3011-71
**Kilrea, Ken**
❑ 34BeeGro1P-109
**Kilrea, Wally**
❑ 33OPCV304B-63
❑ 33V357IceK-53
❑ 34BeeGro1P-110
**Kimble, Darin**
❑ 88ProAHL-110
❑ 89Nord-21
❑ 89NordGenF-17
❑ 89NordPol-14
❑ 90NordPet-13
❑ 90NordTeal-16
❑ 90OPC-437
❑ 90ProSet-517
❑ 91BluPos-13
❑ 91Bow-381
❑ 91NordPanTS-11
❑ 91OPC-156
❑ 91Par-377
❑ 91ParFre-377
❑ 91ScoCan-526
❑ 91StaClu-278
❑ 91Top-156
❑ 92StaClu-486
❑ 92Top-511
❑ 92TopGol-511G
❑ 93BlaCok-24
**Kimura, Kevin**
❑ 92BriColJHL-32
**Kinaschuk, Brett**
❑ 91AirCanSJHL-D5
❑ 92MPSPhoSJHL-30
**Kinaschuk, Kent**
❑ 92MPSPhoSJHL-36
**Kincaid, Cameron**
❑ 95Sla-428
**Kinch, Rob**
❑ 92MPSPhoSJHL-44
**Kindrachuk, Orest**
❑ 73FlyLin-9
❑ 74NHLActSta-212
❑ 74OPCNHL-334
❑ 75FlyCanDC-10
❑ 75OPCNHL-389
❑ 76OPCNHL-233
❑ 76Top-233
❑ 77OPCNHL-26
❑ 77Top-26
❑ 78OPC-114
❑ 78Top-114
❑ 79OPC-218
❑ 79Top-218
❑ 80OPC-292
❑ 92Par-476
❑ 92ParEmel-476
**Kinell, Bengt**
❑ 85SwePanS-191
**King, Archie**
❑ 75HamFin-10
**King, Dave**
❑ 89SweSemWCS-52
❑ 90AlbIntTC-21
❑ 91AlbIntTC-13
❑ 92FlamIGA-26
❑ 93Kra-38
**King, Derek**
❑ 84SauSteMG-11
❑ 88PanSti-289
❑ 89OPC-6
❑ 89OPCSti-116
❑ 89PanSti-271
❑ 89ProAHL-250
❑ 89Top-6
❑ 90OPC-128
❑ 90ProSet-185
❑ 90ScoRoo-86T
❑ 90Top-128
❑ 90TopTif-128
❑ 90UppDec-407
❑ 90UppDecF-407
❑ 91Bow-220
❑ 91OPC-455
❑ 91PanSti-247
❑ 91Par-108
❑ 91ParFre-108
❑ 91Pin-107
❑ 91PinFre-107
❑ 91ProSet-146
❑ 91ProSetFre-146
❑ 91ProSetPla-201
❑ 91ProSetPla-286
❑ 91ScoAme-167
❑ 91ScoCan-167
❑ 91StaClu-82
❑ 91Top-455
❑ 91UppDec-382
❑ 91UppDecF-382
❑ 92Bow-188
❑ 92OPC-79
❑ 92PanSti-199
❑ 92PanStiFre-199
❑ 92Par-100
❑ 92ParEmel-100
❑ 92Pin-17
❑ 92PinFre-17
❑ 92ProSet-110
❑ 92Sco-255
❑ 92ScoCan-255
❑ 92ScoSha-15
❑ 92ScoShaCan-15
❑ 92StaClu-82
❑ 92Top-431
❑ 92TopGol-431G
❑ 92Ult-128
❑ 92UppDec-191
❑ 93Don-204
❑ 93Lea-119
❑ 93OPCPre-176
❑ 93OPCPreG-176
❑ 93PanSti-58
❑ 93Par-119
❑ 93ParEmel-119
❑ 93Pin-128
❑ 93PinCan-128
❑ 93Pow-150
❑ 93Sco-48
❑ 93ScoCan-48
❑ 93ScoDynDC-9
❑ 93StaClu-215
❑ 93StaCluFDI-215
❑ 93StaCluFDIO-215
❑ 93StaCluO-215
❑ 93TopPre-176
❑ 93TopPreG-176
❑ 93Ult-176
❑ 93UppDec-417
❑ 94BeAPSig-6
❑ 94CanGamNHLP-157
❑ 94Don-30
❑ 94Fla-103
❑ 94Fle-123
❑ 94HocWit-28
❑ 94Lea-188
❑ 94OPCPre-304
❑ 94OPCPreSE-304
❑ 94Par-132
❑ 94ParGol-132
❑ 94Pin-302
❑ 94PinArtP-302
❑ 94PinRinC-302
❑ 94Sel-9
❑ 94SelGol-9
❑ 94StaClu-108
❑ 94StaCluFDI-108
❑ 94StaCluMOMS-108
❑ 94StaCluSTWC-108
❑ 94TopPre-304
❑ 94TopPreSE-304
❑ 94Ult-325
❑ 94UppDec-59
❑ 94UppDecEleIce-59
❑ 95CanGamNHLP-172
❑ 95Don-300
❑ 95ImpSti-77
❑ 95Lea-261
❑ 95ParInt-132
❑ 95ParIntEl-132
❑ 95Sco-238
❑ 95ScoBlaIce-238
❑ 95ScoBlaIceAP-238
❑ 95StaClu-81
❑ 95StaCluMOMS-81
❑ 95Top-202
❑ 95TopOPCI-202
❑ 96FifFly-4
❑ 96IsIPos-9
❑ 96SP-95
❑ 96UppDecIce-40
❑ 96UppDecIcePar-40
❑ 97Be A PPAD-40
❑ 97Be A PPAPD-40
❑ 97BeAPla-40
❑ 97BeAPlaAut-40
❑ 97ColCho-112
❑ 97Don-69
❑ 97DonPreProG-69
❑ 97DonPreProS-69
❑ 97FifFly-4
❑ 97PacInv-24
❑ 97PacInvC-24
❑ 97PacInvEG-24
❑ 97PacInvIB-24
❑ 97PacInvNRB-37
❑ 97PacInvR-24
❑ 97PacInvS-24
❑ 97PacPar-181
❑ 97PacParC-181
❑ 97PacParDG-181
❑ 97PacParEG-181
❑ 97PacParIB-181
❑ 97PacParRed-181
❑ 97PacParSil-181
❑ 97ScoMapL-18
❑ 97ScoMapLPla-18
❑ 97ScoMapLPre-18
❑ 98Be A PPA-135
❑ 98Be A PPAA-135
❑ 98Be A PPAAF-135
❑ 98Be A PPTBASG-135
❑ 98Be APG-135
❑ 98O-PChr-84
❑ 98O-PChrR-84
❑ 98Pac-414
❑ 98PacIceB-414
❑ 98PacPar-228
❑ 98PacParC-228
❑ 98PacParEG-228
❑ 98PacParH-228
❑ 98PacParIB-228
❑ 98PacParS-228
❑ 98PacRed-414
❑ 98Top-84
❑ 98TopO-P-84
❑ 98UppDec-373
❑ 98UppDecE-373
❑ 98UppDecE1o1-373
❑ 98UppDecGR-373
❑ 99Pac-410
❑ 99PacCop-410
❑ 99PacGol-410
❑ 99PacIceB-410
❑ 99PacPreD-410
**King, Frank**
❑ 44BeeGro2P-254
❑ 51LavDaiQSHL-10
**King, Kevin**
❑ 89SauSteMG-12
❑ 907thInnSOHL-70
❑ 907thInnSOHL-161
❑ 917thInnSOHL-228
**King, Kris**
❑ 88RedWinLC-11
❑ 89RanMarMB-12
❑ 90OPC-526
❑ 90ProSet-491
❑ 90ScoRoo-90T
❑ 90UppDec-440
❑ 90UppDecF-440
❑ 91Bow-59
❑ 91OPC-498
❑ 91Par-337
❑ 91ParFre-337
❑ 91Pin-362
❑ 91PinFre-362
❑ 91ProSet-445
❑ 91ProSetFre-445
❑ 91ScoAme-363
❑ 91ScoCan-402
❑ 91StaClu-26
❑ 91Top-498
❑ 91UppDec-330
❑ 91UppDecF-330
❑ 92Bow-380
❑ 92OPC-86
❑ 92Par-442
❑ 92ParEmel-442
❑ 92Pin-168
❑ 92Pin-253
❑ 92PinFre-168
❑ 92PinFre-253
❑ 92Sco-181
❑ 92ScoCan-181
❑ 92StaClu-187
❑ 92Top-509
❑ 92TopGol-509G
❑ 92UppDec-78
❑ 93Don-379
❑ 93JetRuf-15
❑ 93Lea-253
❑ 93Par-478B
❑ 93ParEmel-478B
❑ 93Pin-316
❑ 93PinCan-316
❑ 93Sco-362
❑ 93ScoCan-362
❑ 93UppDec-14
❑ 94BeAPSig-15
❑ 94Lea-395
❑ 94Par-269
❑ 94ParGol-269
❑ 94StaClu-124
❑ 94StaCluFDI-124
❑ 94StaCluMOMS-124
❑ 94StaCluSTWC-124
❑ 94UppDec-308
❑ 94UppDecEleIce-308
❑ 95ColCho-215
❑ 95ColChoPC-215
❑ 95ColChoPCP-215
❑ 95JetReaC-5
❑ 95JetTeaIss-11
❑ 95ParInt-502
❑ 95ParIntEl-502
❑ 95UppDec-141
❑ 95UppDecEleIce-141
❑ 95UppDecEleIceG-141
❑ 96KraUppD-35
❑ 96PinTro-7
❑ 97Be A PPAD-108
❑ 97Be A PPAPD-108
❑ 97BeAPla-108
❑ 97BeAPlaAut-108
❑ 97Pac-90
❑ 97PacCop-90
❑ 97PacEmeGre-90
❑ 97PacIceB-90
❑ 97PacRed-90
❑ 97PacSil-90
❑ 98Be A PPA-288
❑ 98Be A PPAA-288
❑ 98Be A PPAAF-288
❑ 98Be A PPSE-288
❑ 98Be APG-288
❑ 98O-PChr-160
❑ 98O-PChrR-160
❑ 98Pac-415
❑ 98PacIceB-415
❑ 98PacRed-415
❑ 98Top-160
❑ 98TopO-P-160
**King, Larry**
❑ 91ProSetPla-292
**King, Mike**
❑ 83KinCan-9
**King, Scott**
❑ 90HamRoaA-41
❑ 90ProAHLIHL-492
❑ 92StaClu-269
**King, Scott 2**
❑ 92TolSto-8
❑ 93SauSteMG-5
**King, Steven (Steve)**
❑ 69SweHocS-357
❑ 72NatOttWHA-13
❑ 82OshGen-13
❑ 83KinCan-19
❑ 91ProAHLCHL-199
❑ 92BinRan-13
❑ 92Par-347
❑ 92ParEmel-347
❑ 92Ult-355
❑ 92UppDec-575
❑ 93Cla-136
❑ 93ClaProPProt-PR1
❑ 93ClaProPro-60
❑ 93ClaProPro-74
❑ 93Don-1
❑ 93Lea-410
❑ 93OPCPre-303
❑ 93OPCPreG-303
❑ 93Par-1
❑ 93ParEmel-1
❑ 93Pin-345
❑ 93PinCan-345
❑ 93Pow-6
❑ 93Sco-382
❑ 93Sco-514
❑ 93ScoCan-382
❑ 93ScoCan-514
❑ 93ScoGol-514
❑ 93StaClu-377
❑ 93StaCluFDI-377
❑ 93StaCluO-377
❑ 93TopPre-303
❑ 93TopPreG-303
❑ 93Ult-258
❑ 93UppDec-24
❑ 94DucCarJr-12
❑ 94OPCPre-220
❑ 94OPCPreSE-220
❑ 94TopPre-220
❑ 94TopPreSE-220
❑ 96FifFly-19
❑ 97FifFly-11
**King, Wayne**
❑ 74NHLActSta-56
**Kinghan, Rob**
❑ 907thInnSOHL-36
❑ 917thInnSOHL-29
**Kinghorn, Ron**
❑ 91ProAHLCHL-433
**Kingston, George**
❑ 95GerDELE-428
**Kinisky, Al**
❑ 907thInnSWHL-4
❑ 917thInnSWHL-339
❑ 92BriColJHL-178
**Kinnear, Geordie**
❑ 907thInnSOHL-363
❑ 917thInnSOHL-132
❑ 91PetPet-24
**Kinney, Bonnie**
❑ 95SlaMemC-17
**Kinney, Donnie**
❑ 96KamBla-14
❑ 97BowCHL-91
❑ 97BowCHLOPC-91
**Kinney, Ken**
❑ 95VanVooRHI-18
**Kinniburgh, Todd**
❑ 89PorWinH-14
**Kiopini, Serge**
❑ 90MonAAA-13
**Kiprusoff, Marko**
❑ 91UppDec-671
❑ 91UppDecCWJC-34
❑ 91UppDecF-671
❑ 93FinnJyvHS-321
❑ 93FinnSIS-35
❑ 94FinnJaaK-18
❑ 94FinnSIS-7
❑ 94FinnSIS-161
❑ 94FinnSISND-2
❑ 95Bow-109
❑ 95BowAllFoi-109
❑ 95Don-351
❑ 95FinnBecAC-6
❑ 95FinnKarWCL-6
❑ 95FinnSemWC-2
❑ 95FinnSIS-163
❑ 95FinnSIS-200
❑ 95FinnSISGC-7
❑ 95FinnSISL-5
❑ 95ParInt-268
❑ 95ParIntEl-268
❑ 95StaClu-141
❑ 95StaCluMOMS-141
❑ 95SweGloWC-131
❑ 96Lea-233
❑ 96LeaPreP-233
❑ 96Pin-234
❑ 96PinArtP-234
❑ 96PinFoi-234
❑ 96PinPreS-234
❑ 96PinRinC-234
❑ 96SweSemW-2
❑ 96SweSemWAS-AS3
❑ 96UppDec-188
**Kiprusoff, Miikka**
❑ 94Fin-125
❑ 94FinRef-125
❑ 94FinSupTW-125
❑ 95FinnSIS-122
❑ 95FinnSISDD-8
**Kirby, Travis**
❑ 92MPSPhoSJHL-141
**Kiriakou, Lou**
❑ 84MonGolF-9
**Kirk, Bobby**
❑ 34BeeGro1P-283
**Kirk, Gavin**
❑ 72NatOttWHA-14
❑ 73QuaOatWHA-5
❑ 75OPCWHA-103
❑ 76OPCWHA-99
**Kirkpatrick, Bob**
❑ 34BeeGro1P-284
**Kirkpatrick, Dave**
❑ 92BriColJHL-5
**Kirkwood, Brad**
❑ 96GuiFla-16
**Kirsch, Rob**
❑ 93NorBayC-24
**Kirton, Douglas**
❑ 98GerDELE-149
**Kirton, Mark**
❑ 79MapLeaP-16
❑ 80MapLeaP-16
❑ 81OPC-90
❑ 81Top-W90
❑ 82OPC-87
❑ 82PosCer-5
❑ 83Canu-10
❑ 83OPC-352
❑ 83Vac-109
❑ 85FreExp-19
❑ 86FreExp-14
❑ 88ProAHL-227
**Kirton, Scott**
❑ 92BriColJHL-237
❑ 92NorDakFS-15
**Kirwan, Jeff**
❑ 95SwiCurB-7
**Kisil, John**
❑ 93MicTecH-17
**Kisilivich, Brent**
❑ 82MedHatT-8
❑ 83MedHatT-5
**Kisio, Kelly**
❑ 84OPC-56
❑ 84OPCSti-40
❑ 85OPC-101
❑ 85Top-101
❑ 86OPC-116
❑ 86OPCSti-163
❑ 86Top-116
❑ 87OPC-76
❑ 87OPCSti-28
❑ 87PanSti-115
❑ 87Top-76
❑ 88OPC-143
❑ 88OPCSti-239
❑ 88PanSti-307
❑ 88Top-143
❑ 89OPC-171
❑ 89PanSti-287
❑ 89RanMarMB-11
❑ 89Top-171
❑ 90OPC-239
❑ 90PanSti-94
❑ 90ProSet-200
❑ 90Sco-37
❑ 90ScoCan-37
❑ 90Top-239
❑ 90TopTif-239
❑ 90UppDec-296
❑ 90UppDecF-296
❑ 91Bow-72
❑ 91OPC-335
❑ 91OPCPre-69
❑ 91PanSti-291
❑ 91Par-165
❑ 91ParFre-165
❑ 91Pin-231
❑ 91PinFre-231
❑ 91ProSet-168
❑ 91ProSet-479
❑ 91ProSetFre-168
❑ 91ProSetFre-479
❑ 91ProSetPC-26
❑ 91ProSetPla-104
❑ 91ScoAme-288
❑ 91ScoCan-553
❑ 91ScoRoo-3T
❑ 91ShaSanJSA-12
❑ 91StaClu-186
❑ 91Top-335
❑ 91UppDec-515
❑ 91UppDecF-515
❑ 92Bow-166
❑ 92OPC-232
❑ 92PanSti-124
❑ 92PanStiFre-124
❑ 92Par-166
❑ 92ParEmel-166
❑ 92Pin-362
❑ 92PinFre-362
❑ 92ProSet-167
❑ 92Sco-57
❑ 92ScoCan-57
❑ 92StaClu-454
❑ 92Top-331
❑ 92TopGol-331G
❑ 92Ult-196
❑ 93Don-55
❑ 93Lea-208
❑ 93OPCPre-455
❑ 93OPCPreG-455
❑ 93PanSti-256
❑ 93Par-33
❑ 93ParEmel-33
❑ 93Pin-395
❑ 93PinAllS-30
❑ 93PinAllSC-30
❑ 93PinCan-395
❑ 93Pow-37
❑ 93Sco-27
❑ 93Sco-556
❑ 93ScoCan-27
❑ 93ScoCan-556
❑ 93ScoGol-556
❑ 93StaClu-30
❑ 93StaCluFDI-30
❑ 93StaCluFDIO-30
❑ 93StaCluO-30
❑ 93TopPre-455
❑ 93TopPreG-455
❑ 93Ult-155
❑ 93Ult-282
❑ 93UppDec-304
❑ 93UppDecLAS-28
❑ 94CanGamNHLP-55
❑ 94EASpo-117
❑ 94Lea-493
❑ 94Pin-306
❑ 94PinArtP-306
❑ 94PinRinC-306
❑ 95ColCho-193
❑ 95ColChoPC-193
❑ 95ColChoPCP-193
**Kister, Ed**
❑ 85LonKni-11
❑ 86KitRan-11
**Kit, Home**
❑ 94GuiFla-20
❑ 95GuiFla-19
❑ 96GuiFla-27
❑ 97GuiFla-22
**Kitchen, Bill**
❑ 83NovScoV-2
**Kitchen, Mike**
❑ 76RocCokCan-12
❑ 77OPCNHL-267
❑ 77RocCokCan-12
❑ 78OPC-338
❑ 79Roc-10
❑ 81OPC-83
❑ 81RocPos-9
❑ 82PosCer-11
**Kitchener, Craig**
❑ 80OshGen-3
**Kitching, Gary**
❑ 91FerStaB-18
**Kitteringham, Craig**
❑ 88ProAHL-135
**Kiuru, Jussi**
❑ 93FinnSIS-201
❑ 94FinnSIS-283
❑ 95FinnSIS-105
**Kivela, Antero**
❑ 79PanSti-163
**Kivela, Kimo**
❑ 67SweHoc-241
**Kivela, Teppo**
❑ 91SweSemWCS-15
❑ 93FinnJyvHS-23
❑ 93FinnSIS-95
❑ 94FinnSIS-210
❑ 94FinnSIS-375
❑ 94FinnSISH-10
❑ 95FinnSIS-155
❑ 95FinnSISL-23
❑ 96FinnSISR-155
**Kivell, Rob**
❑ 83VicCou-13

❑ 84VicCou-12
❑ 85MonGolF-10
**Kivi, Karri**
❑ 93FinnJyvHS-346
❑ 93FinnSIS-215
❑ 94FinnSIS-134
❑ 95FinnSIS-352
❑ 95FinnSISDT-3
❑ 96FinnSISR-153
**Kiviaho, Tommy**
❑ 93FinnJyvHS-257
❑ 93FinnSIS-293
❑ 94FinnSIS-338
❑ 94FinnSISH-16
❑ 95FinnSIS-36
❑ 96FinnSISR-8
**Kivila, Pasi**
❑ 93FinnJyvHS-58
❑ 93FinnSIS-248
❑ 94FinnSIS-83
**Kivinen, Teemu**
❑ 93FinnSIS-60
**Kjellberg, Patric**
❑ 89SweSemE-25
❑ 90SweSemE-91
❑ 91SweSemE-20
❑ 92CanaPos-15
❑ 92FreCan-13
❑ 92OPCPre-29
❑ 92UppDec-498
❑ 93ClaProPro-21
❑ 93SweSemE-117
❑ 93SweSemWCS-42
❑ 94FinnJaaK-78
❑ 94SweLeaE-16
❑ 94SweLeaEGC-17
❑ 94SweLeaETG-9
❑ 95SweLeaE-190
❑ 95SweLeaEC-2
❑ 95SweUppDE-53
❑ 98PacDynI-103
❑ 98PacDynIIB-103
❑ 98PacDynIR-103
❑ 99Pac-226
❑ 99PacCop-226
❑ 99PacGol-226
❑ 99PacIceB-226
❑ 99PacPreD-226
**Kjenstadt, Olaf**
❑ 917thInnSWHL-313
❑ 93SeaThu-10
❑ 94BirBul-14
❑ 95BirBul-20
❑ 98CinCyc-10
**Klaers, John**
❑ 94CenHocL-82
**Klapac, Filip**
❑ 96CzeAPSE-95
**Klapac, Jan**
❑ 69SweHocS-32
**Klapac, Jiri**
❑ 74SweSemHVS-62
**Klapstein, Terry**
❑ 89VicCou-13
**Klasnick, Rob**
❑ 93OmaLan-12
**Klasons, George**
❑ 77KalWin-1
**Klassen, Jason**
❑ 917thInnSWHL-248
❑ 91PriAlbR-7
**Klassen, Ralph**
❑ 76OPCNHL-282
❑ 77OPCNHL-372
❑ 78OPC-346
**Klassen, Todd**
❑ 907thInnSWHL-111
❑ 917thInnSWHL-295
**Klatt, Bill**
❑ 72FigSaiPos-10
**Klatt, Trent**
❑ 91MinGolG-11
❑ 91Par-452
❑ 91ParFre-452
❑ 92Cla-89
❑ 92Par-317
❑ 92ParEmel-317
❑ 92ProSet-229
❑ 92Sco-482
❑ 92ScoCan-482
❑ 92UppDec-62
❑ 93Don-82
❑ 93Lea-14
❑ 93OPCPre-523
❑ 93OPCPreG-523
❑ 93Par-48
❑ 93ParEmel-48
❑ 93Pow-62
❑ 93TopPre-523
❑ 93TopPreG-523
❑ 93Ult-157
❑ 93UltPro-4
❑ 93UppDec-152
❑ 94CanGamNHLP-143
❑ 94Don-37
❑ 94Lea-316
❑ 94OPCPre-46
❑ 94OPCPreSE-46
❑ 94ParSE-SE43
❑ 94ParSEG-SE43
❑ 94Pin-442
❑ 94PinArtP-442
❑ 94PinRinC-442
❑ 94SP-29
❑ 94SPDieCut-29
❑ 94StaCluST-6
❑ 94StaHoc-17
❑ 94StaPos-13
❑ 94TopPre-46
❑ 94TopPreSE-46
❑ 94Ult-53
❑ 94UppDec-374
❑ 94UppDecEleIce-374
❑ 95CanGamNHLP-88
❑ 95ColCho-36
❑ 95ColChoPC-36
❑ 95ColChoPCP-36
❑ 95Don-330
❑ 95Lea-57
❑ 95Pin-193
❑ 95PinArtP-193
❑ 95PinRinC-193
❑ 95Top-106
❑ 95TopOPCI-106
❑ 95UppDec-162
❑ 95UppDecEleIce-162
❑ 95UppDecEleIceG-162
❑ 96BeAPAut-157
❑ 96BeAPAutSil-157
❑ 96BeAPla-157
❑ 96ClaGol-89
❑ 96FlyPos-11
❑ 97ColCho-191
❑ 97Pac-251
❑ 97PacCop-251
❑ 97PacEmeGre-251
❑ 97PacIceB-251
❑ 97PacOme-166
❑ 97PacOmeC-166
❑ 97PacOmeDG-166
❑ 97PacOmeEG-166
❑ 97PacOmeG-166
❑ 97PacOmeIB-166
❑ 97PacRed-251
❑ 97PacSil-251
❑ 97ScoFly-8
❑ 97ScoFlyPla-8
❑ 97ScoFlyPre-8
❑ 97UppDec-120
❑ 98Pac-327
❑ 98PacIceB-327
❑ 98PacPar-175
❑ 98PacParC-175
❑ 98PacParEG-175
❑ 98PacParH-175
❑ 98PacParIB-175
❑ 98PacParS-175
❑ 98PacRed-327
**Klauda, Radek**
❑ 96CzeAPSE-210
**Klee, Ken**
❑ 93ClaProPro-82
❑ 93PorPir-6
❑ 94PorPir-13
❑ 95BeAPla-162
❑ 95BeAPSig-S162
❑ 95BeAPSigDC-S162
❑ 95Bow-163
❑ 95BowAllFoi-163
❑ 95Cap-15
❑ 95UppDec-128
❑ 95UppDecEleIce-128
❑ 95UppDecEleIceG-128
❑ 97Be A PPAD-91
❑ 97Be A PPAPD-91
❑ 97BeAPla-91
❑ 97BeAPlaAut-91
❑ 97PacInvNRB-209
❑ 97UppDec-386
❑ 98Be A PPA-149
❑ 98Be A PPAA-149
❑ 98Be A PPAAF-149
❑ 98Be A PPTBASG-149
❑ 98Be APG-149
❑ 99Pac-442
❑ 99PacCop-442
❑ 99PacGol-442
❑ 99PacIceB-442
❑ 99PacPreD-442
**Klein, Jim**
❑ 34BeeGro1P-234
❑ 34DiaMatS-36
**Klein, Lloyd**
❑ 35DiaMatT2-35
❑ 35DiaMatT3-32
❑ 35DiaMatTI-36
**Kleinendorst, Scot**
❑ 85WhaJunW-8
❑ 86WhaJunT-12
❑ 87WhaJunBK-10
❑ 88WhaJunGR-8
❑ 89CapKod-29
❑ 89CapTealss-11
**Kleisinger, Curtis**
❑ 91AirCanSJHL-B16
**Klemm, Jon**
❑ 89SpoChi-14
❑ 907thInnSWHL-197
❑ 917thInnSMC-71
❑ 917thInnSMC-77
❑ 91ProAHLCHL-534
❑ 94NordBurK-11
❑ 95SkyImp-194
❑ 95UppDec-93
❑ 95UppDecEleIce-93
❑ 95UppDecEleIceG-93
❑ 95UppDecSpeE-SE20
❑ 95UppDecSpeEdiG-SE20
❑ 96BeAPAut-144
❑ 96BeAPAutSil-144
❑ 96BeAPla-144
❑ 97PacDynBKS-25
❑ 98O-PChr-113
❑ 98O-PChrR-113
❑ 98Top-113
❑ 98TopO-P-113
**Klenner, Sebastian**
❑ 94GerDELE-405
**Kletzel, Dean**
❑ 95SlaMemC-39
**Kletzel, Derek**
❑ 907thInnSWHL-161
❑ 917thInnSWHL-283
**Klevakin, Dmitri**
❑ 94ParSE-SE232
❑ 94ParSEG-SE232
❑ 94SP-166
❑ 94SPDieCut-166
❑ 94UppDec-515
❑ 94UppDecEleIce-515
**Kliemann, Matthias**
❑ 94GerDELE-392
❑ 95GerDELE-415
**Klima, Petr**
❑ 86OPC-98
❑ 86OPCSti-129
❑ 86OPCSti-162
❑ 86Top-98
❑ 87OPC-26
❑ 87OPCSti-104
❑ 87PanSti-246
❑ 87RedWinLC-16
❑ 87Top-26
❑ 88OPC-28
❑ 88OPCSti-251
❑ 88PanSti-44
❑ 88RedWinLC-12
❑ 88Top-28
❑ 89OilTeal-11
❑ 90Bow-197
❑ 90BowTif-197
❑ 90OilIGA-10
❑ 90OPC-85
❑ 90PanSti-228
❑ 90ProSet-86
❑ 90Sco-232
❑ 90ScoCan-232
❑ 90Top-85
❑ 90TopTif-85
❑ 90UppDec-282
❑ 90UppDecF-282
❑ 91Bow-96
❑ 91Bow-104
❑ 91OilIGA-7
❑ 91OilPanTS-9
❑ 91OilTeal-9
❑ 91OPC-193
❑ 91OPCPre-61
❑ 91PanSti-126
❑ 91Par-280
❑ 91Par-458
❑ 91ParFre-280
❑ 91Pin-159
❑ 91PinFre-159
❑ 91ProSet-72
❑ 91ProSetFre-72
❑ 91ProSetPla-37
❑ 91ScoAme-136
❑ 91ScoCan-136
❑ 91ScoKel-17
❑ 91StaClu-61
❑ 91SweSemWCS-220
❑ 91Top-193
❑ 91UppDec-111
❑ 91UppDecF-111
❑ 92Bow-135
❑ 92OilIGA-10
❑ 92PanSti-105
❑ 92PanStiFre-105
❑ 92Par-54
❑ 92ParEmel-54
❑ 92Pin-344
❑ 92PinFre-344
❑ 92Sco-383
❑ 92ScoCan-383
❑ 92ScoSha-24
❑ 92ScoShaCan-24
❑ 92StaClu-368
❑ 92Top-26
❑ 92TopGol-26G
❑ 92Ult-59
❑ 92UltImp-8
❑ 92UppDec-551
❑ 93Don-317
❑ 93Lea-321
❑ 93LigSealR-20
❑ 93PanSti-234
❑ 93Par-195
❑ 93ParEmel-195
❑ 93Pin-349
❑ 93PinCan-349
❑ 93Pow-232
❑ 93Sco-242
❑ 93Sco-518
❑ 93ScoCan-242
❑ 93ScoCan-518
❑ 93ScoGol-518
❑ 93SweSemWCS-104
❑ 93Ult-425
❑ 93UppDec-291
❑ 93UppDec-526
❑ 93UppDecSP-152
❑ 94BeAPSig-155
❑ 94CanGamNHLP-224
❑ 94Don-249
❑ 94EASpo-47
❑ 94Fla-174
❑ 94Fle-208
❑ 94Lea-171
❑ 94LigPhoA-18
❑ 94OPCPre-318
❑ 94OPCPreSE-318
❑ 94Par-219
❑ 94ParGol-219
❑ 94Pin-311
❑ 94PinArtP-311
❑ 94PinRinC-311
❑ 94SP-110
❑ 94SPDieCut-110
❑ 94StaClu-136
❑ 94StaCluFDI-136
❑ 94StaCluMOMS-136
❑ 94StaCluST-22
❑ 94StaCluSTWC-136
❑ 94TopPre-318
❑ 94TopPreSE-318
❑ 94Ult-208
❑ 94UppDec-86
❑ 94UppDecEleIce-86
❑ 95Bow-22
❑ 95BowAllFoi-22
❑ 95CanGamNHLP-251
❑ 95ColCho-134
❑ 95ColChoPC-134
❑ 95ColChoPCP-134
❑ 95Don-110
❑ 95Emo-165
❑ 95Fin-112
❑ 95FinRef-112
❑ 95Lea-321
❑ 95LigTeal-13
❑ 95Met-138
❑ 95ParInt-197
❑ 95ParIntEl-197
❑ 95PlaOneoOne-311
❑ 95Sco-65
❑ 95ScoBlaIce-65
❑ 95ScoBlaIceAP-65
❑ 95SkyImp-156
❑ 95SP-136
❑ 95StaClu-185
❑ 95StaCluMOMS-185
❑ 95Sum-141
❑ 95SumArtP-141
❑ 95SumIce-141
❑ 95Top-238
❑ 95TopOPCI-238
❑ 95Ult-153
❑ 95UltGolM-153
❑ 95UppDec-118
❑ 95UppDecEleIce-118
❑ 95UppDecEleIceG-118
❑ 95UppDecSpeE-SE167
❑ 95UppDecSpeEdiG-SE167
❑ 96CleLum-13
❑ 96ColCho-246
❑ 96Don-196
❑ 96DonPrePro-196
❑ 96Lea-39
❑ 96LeaPreP-39
❑ 96MetUni-76
❑ 96OilPos-85
❑ 96Pin-79
❑ 96PinArtP-79
❑ 96PinFoi-79
❑ 96PinPreS-79
❑ 96PinRinC-79
❑ 96PlaOneoOne-404
❑ 96Sco-202
❑ 96ScoArtPro-202
❑ 96ScoDeaCAP-202
❑ 96ScoGolB-202
❑ 96ScoSpeAP-202
❑ 96UppDec-156
❑ 97Pac-347
❑ 97PacCop-347
❑ 97PacEmeGre-347
❑ 97PacIceB-347
❑ 97PacRed-347
❑ 97PacSil-347
**Klimentiev, Sergei**
❑ 95ColEdgI-64
❑ 95RochAmeSS-8
**Klimov, Konstantin**
❑ 73SweHocS-116
❑ 73SweWorCS-116
❑ 74SweHocS-62
**Klimovich, Sergei**
❑ 92Cla-46
❑ 92RusStaRA-30
❑ 92RusStaRA-14
❑ 92UppDec-339
❑ 93UppDec-275
❑ 94IndIce-12
❑ 95ColEdgI-135
❑ 95IndIce-10
❑ 96ClaGol-46
**Klimt, Tomas**
❑ 93UppDec-263
❑ 95CzeAPSE-256
❑ 96CzeAPSE-304
**Klippenstein, Wade**
❑ 95AlaGolKin-8
**Kloboucek, Jan**
❑ 92BriColJHL-222
**Kloboucek, Jiri**
❑ 92CorBigRed-18
❑ 93CorBigRed-3
**Klochkov, Vladislav**
❑ 96SasBla-13
**Klockare, Stefan**
❑ 90SweSemE-183
❑ 91SweSemE-38
❑ 92SweSemE-56
❑ 92UppDec-224
❑ 93SweSemE-32
❑ 94SweLeaE-73
❑ 95SweLeaE-16
❑ 95SweUppDE-24
**Kloepzig, Steve**
❑ 86PorWinH-10
❑ 87KamBla-10
**Kloiber, Ralph**
❑ 74SioCitM-8
**Klostreich, Page**
❑ 92NorDakFS-16
**Kluczkowski, Steve**
❑ 897thInnSOHL-54
**Klukay, Joe**
❑ 44BeeGro2P-38
❑ 44BeeGro2P-416
❑ 45QuaOatP-26A
❑ 45QuaOatP-26B
❑ 48ExhCan-33
❑ 51Par-74
❑ 52Par-75
❑ 53Par-94
❑ 54Par-54
❑ 55Par-6
❑ 55ParQuaO-6
❑ 76OldTim-9
❑ 81RedWinOld-18
**Kluzak, Gord**
❑ 83BruTealss-8
❑ 83OPC-51
❑ 83OPCSti-185
❑ 84OPC-6
❑ 84OPCSti-186
❑ 84Top-5
❑ 85OPC-167
❑ 86OPC-54
❑ 86Top-54
❑ 88BruPos-9
❑ 88BruSpoA-8
❑ 88OPC-23
❑ 88OPCSti-25
❑ 88PanSti-205
❑ 88Top-23
❑ 89BruSpoAU-4
❑ 90OPC-495
❑ 90ProSet-383
❑ 90Sco-367
❑ 90ScoCan-367
**Klyn, Brad**
❑ 91BriColJHL-161
❑ 92BriColJHL-161
**Klynck, Beryl**
❑ 52JunBluT-123
**Klyne, Lawrence**
❑ 92BriColJHL-91
**Knauft, Lorne**
❑ 93FliGen-15
❑ 94BraSmo-5
**Knesaurek, Robert (Rob)**
❑ 88SudWol-23
❑ 89SudWol-25
**Knibbs, Kalvin**
❑ 907thInnSWHL-26
**Knickle, Rick**
❑ 86SheCan-21
❑ 89ProIHL-26
❑ 90ProAHLIHL-515
❑ 91ProAHLCHL-320
❑ 92SanDieG-13
❑ 93ClaProPBC-BC12
❑ 93ClaProPro-121
❑ 93PhoRoa-13
❑ 93Sco-466
❑ 93ScoCan-466
❑ 95ColEdgI-122
❑ 95ColEdgITW-G3
❑ 96MilAdmBO-12
**Knight, Brad**
❑ 91BriColJHL-29
**Knight, Curtis**
❑ 91AirCanSJHL-A17
❑ 92MPSPhoSJHL-40
**Knight, Darryl**
❑ 96SarSti-12
**Knight, Jason**
❑ 917thInnSWHL-337
❑ 91SasBla-9
**Knight, Jeff**
❑ 907thInnSWHL-44
❑ 91AirCanSJHL-C39
❑ 91AirCanSJHLAS-38
**Knight, Keith**
❑ 82KinCan-15
**Knight, Terry**
❑ 83MedHatT-7
**Knights, Michael**
❑ 97KinHaw-4
**Knipscheer, Fred**
❑ 93Par-18
❑ 93ParEmel-18
❑ 94ClaAut-NNO
❑ 94ClaProP-60
❑ 94ClaTri-T4
❑ 94Lea-331
❑ 94Pin-249
❑ 94PinArtP-249
❑ 94PinRinC-249
❑ 94Sco-220
❑ 94ScoGol-220
❑ 94ScoPla-220
❑ 94ScoPlaTS-220
❑ 94StaClu-17
❑ 94StaCluFDI-17
❑ 94StaCluMOMS-17
❑ 94StaCluSTWC-17
❑ 95PlaOneoOne-227
**Knispscheer, Fred**
❑ 98CinCyc-11
**Knobloch, Thomas**
❑ 94GerDELE-401
❑ 95GerDELE-420
**Knopp, Kevin**
❑ 95SouCarS-20
❑ 96SouCarS-28
**Knorr, Derek**
❑ 91AirCanSJHL-D15
❑ 95FliGen-18
**Knott, Nick**
❑ 34BeeGro1P-235
**Knox, Blake**
❑ 907thInnSWHL-49
❑ 917thInnSWHL-139
**Knox, Cameron**
❑ 92BriColJHL-145
**Knox, Jason**
❑ 89VicCou-14
❑ 907thInnSWHL-248
❑ 90SasBla-7
❑ 917thInnSWHL-155
❑ 95VanVooRHI-6
**Knox, Paul**
❑ 52JunBluT-143
**Knox, Seymour**
❑ 93ActPacHOFI-7
**Knuble, Mike**
❑ 91MicWol-8
❑ 93MicWol-11
❑ 95AdiRedW-11
❑ 97Be A PPAD-43
❑ 97Be A PPAPD-43
❑ 97BeAPla-43
❑ 97BeAPlaAut-43
❑ 97Don-225
❑ 97DonLim-2
❑ 97DonLim-17
❑ 97DonLimExp-2
❑ 97DonLimExp-17
❑ 97DonPreProG-225
❑ 97DonPreProS-225
❑ 97PinIns-172
❑ 97ScoRedW-20
❑ 97ScoRedWPla-20
❑ 97ScoRedWPre-20
❑ 97SPAut-180
❑ 97UppDec-187
❑ 97UppDecIce-39
❑ 97UppDecIceP-39
❑ 97UppDecIPS-39
❑ 98Pac-194
❑ 98PacIceB-194
❑ 98PacRed-194
❑ 98UppDec-325
❑ 98UppDecE-325
❑ 98UppDecE1o1-325
❑ 98UppDecGR-325
❑ 98UppDecM-136
❑ 98UppDecMGS-136
❑ 98UppDecMSS-136
❑ 98UppDecMSS-136
❑ 99Pac-271
❑ 99PacCop-271
❑ 99PacGol-271
❑ 99PacIceB-271
❑ 99PacPreD-271
**Knutsen, Espen**
❑ 93SweSemWCS-241
❑ 94FinnJaaK-261
❑ 94SweLeaE-264
❑ 94SweLeaEFA-1
❑ 95SweGloWC-198
❑ 95SweGloWC-252
❑ 95SweLeaE-35
❑ 95SweLeaEFF-13
❑ 95SweUppDE-51
❑ 95SweUppDETNA-NA6
❑ 96SweSemW-206
❑ 97DonEli-106
❑ 97DonEli-144
❑ 97DonEliAsp-106
❑ 97DonEliAsp-144
❑ 97DonEliS-106
❑ 97DonEliS-144
❑ 97DonPre-161
❑ 97DonPreCttC-161
❑ 97DonPri-172
❑ 97DonPriDD-26
❑ 97DonPriSoA-172
❑ 97Kat-3
❑ 97KatGol-3
❑ 97KatSil-3
❑ 97PacDyn-NNO
❑ 97PacDynC-NNO
❑ 97PacDynDG-NNO
❑ 97PacDynEG-NNO
❑ 97PacDynIB-NNO
❑ 97PacDynR-NNO
❑ 97PacDynSil-NNO
❑ 97PacPar-3
❑ 97PacParC-3
❑ 97PacParDG-3
❑ 97PacParEG-3
❑ 97PacParIB-3
❑ 97PacParRed-3
❑ 97PacParSil-3
❑ 97Pin-1
❑ 97PinArtP-1
❑ 97PinCerRR-K
❑ 97PinCerRRG-K
❑ 97PinCerRRMG-K
❑ 97PinPrePBB-1
❑ 97PinPrePBC-1
❑ 97PinPrePBM-1
❑ 97PinPrePBY-1
❑ 97PinPrePFC-1
❑ 97PinPrePFM-1
❑ 97PinPrePFY-1
❑ 97PinPrePla-1
❑ 97PinRinC-1
❑ 97Sco-66
❑ 97ScoArtPro-66
❑ 97ScoGolBla-66
❑ 97ScoMigDPla-20
❑ 97ScoMigDPre-20
❑ 97ScoMigDuc-20
❑ 97SPAut-169
❑ 97UppDec-216
❑ 97UppDecBD-81
❑ 97UppDecBDDD-81
❑ 97UppDecBDQD-81
❑ 97UppDecBDTD-81
❑ 97UppDecIce-44
❑ 97UppDecIceP-44
❑ 97UppDecIPS-44
**Knutsson, Knut**
❑ 65SweCorI-60
**Knuude, Mike**
❑ 83BelBul-6
❑ 84BelBul-6
**Koberle, Walter**
❑ 72SweSemWC-115
❑ 79PanSti-111
**Kobrc, Roman**
❑ 92BriColJHL-233
**Kobzev, Igor**
❑ 74SweHocS-69
**Koch, Paul**
❑ 95TolSto-4
❑ 96TolSto-5
**Kochan, Dieter**
❑ 92BriColJHL-64
❑ 93NorMicW-18
❑ 97LouRivF-21
**Kochta, Jiri**
❑ 69SweWorC-155
❑ 70SweHocS-360
❑ 71SweHocS-54
❑ 72SweSemWC-28
❑ 73SweHocS-32
❑ 73SweWorCS-32
❑ 74SweHocS-110
❑ 74SweSemHVS-58
❑ 94GerDELE-390
❑ 95GerDELE-406
❑ 98GerDELE-19
**Kock, Jan**
❑ 73SweHocS-240
❑ 73SweWorCS-240
❑ 74SweHocS-172
❑ 83SweSemE-55
❑ 84SweSemE-55
**Kockare, Heimo**
❑ 65SweCorI-182
**Kocur, Joey (Joe)**
❑ 83SasBla-22
❑ 87PanSti-251
❑ 87RedWinLC-17
❑ 88RedWinLC-13
❑ 89PanSti-67
❑ 89RedWinLC-11
❑ 90OPC-55
❑ 90PanSti-211
❑ 90ProSet-73
❑ 90Sco-201
❑ 90ScoCan-201
❑ 90Top-55
❑ 90TopTif-55
❑ 90UppDec-411
❑ 90UppDecF-411
❑ 91Bow-69
❑ 91OPC-427
❑ 91Pin-240
❑ 91PinFre-240
❑ 91ScoAme-92
❑ 91ScoCan-92
❑ 91StaClu-365
❑ 91Top-427
❑ 92Bow-80
❑ 92OPC-169
❑ 92Pin-152
❑ 92PinFre-152
❑ 92Sco-24
❑ 92ScoCan-24
❑ 92StaClu-417
❑ 92Top-128
❑ 92TopGol-128G
❑ 93OPCPre-512
❑ 93OPCPreG-512
❑ 93Par-401
❑ 93ParEmel-401
❑ 93Pin-184
❑ 93PinCan-184
❑ 93Sco-270
❑ 93ScoCan-270
❑ 93TopPre-512
❑ 93TopPreG-512
❑ 94Pin-243
❑ 94PinArtP-243
❑ 94PinRinC-243
❑ 94StaClu-73
❑ 94StaCluFDI-73

❑ 97PinPrePFC-89
❑ 97PinPrePFM-89
❑ 97PinPrePFY-89
❑ 97PinPrePla-89
❑ 97PinRinC-89
❑ 97Sco-25
❑ 97ScoArtPro-25
❑ 97ScoGolBla-25
❑ 97Zen-59
❑ 97Zen5x7-30
❑ 97ZenGolImp-30
❑ 97ZenSilImp-30
❑ 97ZenZGol-59
❑ 97ZenZSil-59
❑ 98BowBes-59
❑ 98BowBesAR-59
❑ 98BowBesR-59
❑ 98Fin-126
❑ 98FinNo P-126
❑ 98FinNo PR-126
❑ 98FinRef-126
❑ 98LunGoaG-4
❑ 98LunGoaGS-4
❑ 98O-PChr-193
❑ 98O-PChrR-193
❑ 98Pac-37
❑ 98PacAur-198
❑ 98PacAurC-20
❑ 98PacAurCF-50
❑ 98PacAurCFC-50
❑ 98PacAurCFIB-50
❑ 98PacAurCFR-50
❑ 98PacAurCFS-50
❑ 98PacCroR-143
❑ 98PacCroRLS-143
❑ 98PacCroRPP-25
❑ 98PacDynI-197
❑ 98PacDynI-20
❑ 98PacDynIIB-197
❑ 98PacDynIIW-10
❑ 98PacDynIR-197
❑ 98PacGolCD-36
❑ 98PacIceB-37
❑ 98PacOmeH-248
❑ 98PacOmeODI-248
❑ 98PacOmeR-248
❑ 98PacPar-247
❑ 98PacParC-247
❑ 98PacParEG-247
❑ 98PacParGSLC-20
❑ 98PacParH-247
❑ 98PacParIB-247
❑ 98PacParS-247
❑ 98PacRed-37
❑ 98PacRev-148
❑ 98PacRevIS-148
❑ 98PacRevR-148
❑ 98PacTeaC-27
❑ 98PacTitI-20
❑ 98RevThrPA-20
❑ 98RevThrPA-20
❑ 98SP Aut-87
❑ 98SPxFin-88
❑ 98SPxFinR-88
❑ 98SPxFinS-88
❑ 98Top-193
❑ 98TopGolLC1-63
❑ 98TopGolLC1B-63
❑ 98TopGolLC1BOoO-63
❑ 98TopGolLC1OoO-63
❑ 98TopGolLC1R-63
❑ 98TopGolLC1ROoO-63
❑ 98TopGolLC2-63
❑ 98TopGolLC2B-63
❑ 98TopGolLC2BOoO-63
❑ 98TopGolLC2OoO-63
❑ 98TopGolLC2R-63
❑ 98TopGolLC2ROoO-63
❑ 98TopGolLC3-63
❑ 98TopGolLC3B-63
❑ 98TopGolLC3BOoO-63
❑ 98TopGolLC3OoO-63
❑ 98TopGolLC3R-63
❑ 98TopGolLC3ROoO-63
❑ 98TopMysFB-M2
❑ 98TopMysFBR-M2
❑ 98TopMysFG-M2
❑ 98TopMysFGR-M2
❑ 98TopMysFS-M2
❑ 98TopMysFSR-M2
❑ 98TopO-P-193
❑ 98UC-215
❑ 98UD ChoPCR-215
❑ 98UD ChoR-215
❑ 98UppDec-205
❑ 98UppDecBD-89
❑ 98UppDecDD-89
❑ 98UppDecE-205
❑ 98UppDecE1o1-205
❑ 98UppDecGR-205
❑ 98UppDecM-210
❑ 98UppDecMGS-210
❑ 98UppDecMSS-210
❑ 98UppDecMSS-210
❑ 98UppDecQD-89
❑ 98UppDecTD-89
❑ 99Pac-443
❑ 99PacAur-149
❑ 99PacAurGU-20
❑ 99PacAurPD-149
❑ 99PacCop-443
❑ 99PacGol-443
❑ 99PacIceB-443
❑ 99PacIn tCN-20
❑ 99PacPreD-443
❑ 99SP AutPS-87
❑ 99UppDecM-217
❑ 99UppDecMGS-217
❑ 99UppDecMSS-217
❑ 99UppDecMSS-217

**Komadoski, Neil**
❑ 73OPC-16
❑ 73Top-16
❑ 74NHLActSta-112
❑ 74OPCNHL-358
❑ 75OPCNHL-238
❑ 75Top-238
❑ 76OPCNHL-284
❑ 77OPCNHL-344
❑ 78OPC-382

**Komarniski, Zenith**
❑ 95TriAme-14
❑ 95UppDec-516
❑ 95UppDecEleIce-516
❑ 95UppDecEleIceG-516
❑ 97BowCHL-85
❑ 97BowCHLOPC-85
❑ 98BowCHL-46
❑ 98BowCHLGA-46
❑ 98BowCHLOI-46
❑ 98BowChrC-46
❑ 98BowChrCGA-46
❑ 98BowChrCGAR-46
❑ 98BowChrCOI-46
❑ 98BowChrCOIR-46
❑ 98BowChrCR-46
❑ 98UC-263
❑ 98UD ChoPCR-263
❑ 98UD ChoR-263

**Komarov, Pavel**
❑ 95BinRan-10

**Komma, Michael**
❑ 94GerDELE-61
❑ 95GerDELE-61

**Komonosky, Ward**
❑ 84PriAlbRS-16

**Kompon, Jamie**
❑ 90CinCyc-35

**Kondrashkin, Sergei**
❑ 93Par-532
❑ 93ParEmel-532
❑ 93Pin-511
❑ 93PinCan-511

**Konecny, Kamil**
❑ 96CzeAPSE-97

**Konecny, Michal**
❑ 95CzeAPSE-210

**Koniger, Stefan**
❑ 94GerDELE-125

**Konik, Brad**
❑ 92HarCri-18
❑ 96ProBru-27

**Konik, George**
❑ 72FigSaiPos-11
❑ 72SweSemWC-132

**Konovalenko, Viktor**
❑ 69SweWorC-130
❑ 70SweHocS-231
❑ 70SweHocS-232
❑ 70SweHocS-233
❑ 70SweHocS-234
❑ 70SweHocS-235
❑ 70SweHocS-236
❑ 70SweHocS-237
❑ 70SweHocS-238
❑ 70SweHocS-239
❑ 70SweHocS-240
❑ 70SweHocS-241
❑ 70SweHocS-242
❑ 70SweHocS-313
❑ 71SweHocS-26
❑ 72SweSemWC-1
❑ 74SweSemHVS-50

**Konowalchuk, Steve**
❑ 907thInnSWHL-312
❑ 917thInnSWHL-30
❑ 91Cla-46
❑ 91StaPicH-9
❑ 91UltDra-41
❑ 91UppDecCWJC-73
❑ 92CapKod-16
❑ 92OPCPre-15
❑ 92Par-202
❑ 92ParEmel-202
❑ 92Ult-437
❑ 92UppDec-418
❑ 93ClaProPro-102
❑ 93Par-223
❑ 93ParEmel-223
❑ 93Sco-458
❑ 93ScoCan-458
❑ 93StaClu-481
❑ 93StaCluFDI-481
❑ 93StaCluO-481
❑ 93UppDec-28
❑ 94Lea-423
❑ 94OPCPre-273
❑ 94OPCPreSE-273
❑ 94ParSE-SE192
❑ 94ParSEG-SE192
❑ 94Pin-348
❑ 94PinArtP-348
❑ 94PinRinC-348
❑ 94TopPre-273
❑ 94TopPreSE-273
❑ 94Ult-389
❑ 94UppDec-214
❑ 94UppDecEleIce-214
❑ 95CanGamNHLP-279
❑ 95Cap-17
❑ 95ColCho-318
❑ 95ColChoPC-318
❑ 95ColChoPCP-318
❑ 95Don-296
❑ 95Lea-323
❑ 95ParInt-493
❑ 95ParIntEl-493
❑ 95SP-160
❑ 95Ult-324
❑ 96BeAPAut-173
❑ 96BeAPAutSil-173
❑ 96BeAPla-173
❑ 96ColCho-281
❑ 96Pin-131
❑ 96PinArtP-131
❑ 96PinFoi-131
❑ 96PinPreS-131
❑ 96PinRinC-131
❑ 96Sco-135
❑ 96ScoArtPro-135
❑ 96ScoDeaCAP-135
❑ 96ScoGolB-135
❑ 96ScoSpeAP-135
❑ 96UppDec-179
❑ 97ColCho-274
❑ 97Pac-69
❑ 97PacCop-69
❑ 97PacDyn-132
❑ 97PacDynC-132
❑ 97PacDynDG-132
❑ 97PacDynEG-132
❑ 97PacDynIB-132
❑ 97PacDynR-132
❑ 97PacDynSil-132
❑ 97PacDynTan-58
❑ 97PacEmeGre-69
❑ 97PacIceB-69
❑ 97PacInv-148
❑ 97PacInvC-148
❑ 97PacInvEG-148
❑ 97PacInvIB-148
❑ 97PacInvR-148
❑ 97PacInvS-148
❑ 97PacPar-197
❑ 97PacParC-197
❑ 97PacParDG-197
❑ 97PacParEG-197
❑ 97PacParIB-197
❑ 97PacParRed-197
❑ 97PacParSil-197
❑ 97PacRed-69
❑ 97PacSil-69
❑ 97Sco-220
❑ 97UppDec-174
❑ 98Be A PPA-148
❑ 98Be A PPAA-148
❑ 98Be A PPAAF-148
❑ 98Be A PPTBASG-148
❑ 98Be APG-148
❑ 98Pac-443
❑ 98PacIceB-443
❑ 98PacPar-248
❑ 98PacParC-248
❑ 98PacParEG-248
❑ 98PacParH-248
❑ 98PacParIB-248
❑ 98PacParS-248
❑ 98PacRed-443
❑ 99Pac-444
❑ 99PacCop-444
❑ 99PacGol-444
❑ 99PacIceB-444
❑ 99PacPreD-444

**Konroyd, Steve**
❑ 80OshGen-9
❑ 81FlamPos-8
❑ 82OPC-48
❑ 83OPC-85
❑ 83Vac-9
❑ 84OPC-226
❑ 85FlamRedRP-10
❑ 87OPC-153
❑ 87Top-153
❑ 88OPC-171
❑ 88OPCSti-110
❑ 88PanSti-284
❑ 88Top-171
❑ 89BlaCok-21
❑ 89OPC-220
❑ 90BlaCok-21
❑ 90ProSet-52
❑ 90Sco-29
❑ 90ScoCan-29
❑ 91BlaCok-12
❑ 91OPC-366
❑ 91Par-287
❑ 91ParFre-287
❑ 91Pin-180
❑ 91PinFre-180
❑ 91ProSetPla-177
❑ 91ScoAme-189
❑ 91ScoCan-189
❑ 91Top-366
❑ 91WhaJr7E-19
❑ 92Bow-18
❑ 92OPC-238
❑ 92Par-299
❑ 92ParEmel-299
❑ 92Pin-352
❑ 92PinFre-352
❑ 92ProSet-62
❑ 92Sco-172
❑ 92ScoCan-172
❑ 92StaClu-236
❑ 92Top-411
❑ 92TopGol-411G
❑ 92Ult-300
❑ 92WhaDai-12
❑ 93Sco-219
❑ 93ScoCan-219
❑ 94OPCPre-394
❑ 94OPCPreSE-394
❑ 94Pin-339
❑ 94PinArtP-339
❑ 94PinRinC-339
❑ 94TopPre-394
❑ 94TopPreSE-394

**Konstantinov, Vladimir**
❑ 87RusNatT-11
❑ 89RusNatT-14
❑ 89SweSemWCS-86
❑ 90OPCRedA-21R
❑ 91OPCPre-118A
❑ 91OPCPre-118B
❑ 91OPCPre-155
❑ 91Par-46
❑ 91ParFre-46
❑ 91Pin-311
❑ 91PinFre-311
❑ 91ProSet-533
❑ 91ProSetFre-533
❑ 91ProSetPla-254
❑ 91RusStaNHL-5
❑ 91RusStaRA-9
❑ 91ScoCan-659
❑ 91ScoRoo-109T
❑ 91SweSemWCS-81
❑ 91UppDec-594
❑ 91UppDecF-594
❑ 92Bow-326
❑ 92OPC-267
❑ 92Par-283
❑ 92ParEmel-283
❑ 92Pin-76
❑ 92PinFre-76
❑ 92ProSet-44
❑ 92Sco-31
❑ 92Sco-503
❑ 92ScoCan-31
❑ 92ScoCan-503
❑ 92ScoYouS-23
❑ 92StaClu-418
❑ 92Top-14
❑ 92Top-165
❑ 92TopGol-14G
❑ 92TopGol-165G
❑ 92Ult-49
❑ 92UppDec-267
❑ 92UppDec-357
❑ 92UppDecART-AR5
❑ 92UppDecART-AR7
❑ 92UppDecAWT-W5
❑ 92UppDecES-E10
❑ 93Lea-237
❑ 93OPCPre-108
❑ 93OPCPreG-108
❑ 93Par-325
❑ 93ParEmel-325
❑ 93Pin-264
❑ 93PinCan-264
❑ 93Pow-73
❑ 93Sco-20
❑ 93ScoCan-20
❑ 93StaClu-333
❑ 93StaCluFDI-333
❑ 93StaCluO-333
❑ 93TopPre-108
❑ 93TopPreG-108
❑ 93Ult-150
❑ 93UppDec-366
❑ 94CanGamNHLP-94
❑ 94Fla-49
❑ 94Fle-60
❑ 94Lea-391
❑ 94OPCPre-448
❑ 94OPCPreSE-448
❑ 94ParSE-SE53
❑ 94ParSEG-SE53
❑ 94Pin-116
❑ 94PinArtP-116
❑ 94PinRinC-116
❑ 94Sco-96
❑ 94ScoGol-96
❑ 94ScoPla-96
❑ 94ScoPlaTS-96
❑ 94StaClu-159
❑ 94StaCluFDI-159
❑ 94StaCluMOMS-159
❑ 94StaCluSTWC-159
❑ 94TopPre-448
❑ 94TopPreSE-448
❑ 94Ult-61
❑ 94UppDec-189
❑ 94UppDecEleIce-189
❑ 95BeAPla-216
❑ 95BeAPSig-S216
❑ 95BeAPSigDC-S216
❑ 95Emo-54
❑ 95Lea-283
❑ 95Met-46
❑ 95ParInt-69
❑ 95ParIntEl-69
❑ 95Pin-129
❑ 95PinArtP-129
❑ 95PinRinC-129
❑ 95PlaOneoOne-145
❑ 95Sco-176
❑ 95ScoBlaIce-176
❑ 95ScoBlaIceAP-176
❑ 95SkyImp-53
❑ 95Ult-46
❑ 95UltGolM-46
❑ 95UppDec-190
❑ 95UppDecEleIce-190
❑ 95UppDecEleIceG-190
❑ 96ColCho-82
❑ 96ColCho-302
❑ 96ColCho-316
❑ 96Don-83
❑ 96DonPrePro-83
❑ 96Fle-31
❑ 96Fle-143
❑ 96FleNor-6
❑ 96Lea-110
❑ 96LeaPreP-110
❑ 96MetUni-46
❑ 96MetUniCS-6
❑ 96MetUniCSSP-6
❑ 96Pin-65
❑ 96PinArtP-65
❑ 96PinFoi-65
❑ 96PinPreS-65
❑ 96PinRinC-65
❑ 96Sco-84
❑ 96ScoArtPro-84
❑ 96ScoDeaCAP-84
❑ 96ScoGolB-84
❑ 96ScoSpeAP-84
❑ 96SkyImp-35
❑ 96SkyImpNHLF-12
❑ 96SP-53
❑ 96Sum-63
❑ 96SumArtP-63
❑ 96SumIce-63
❑ 96SumMet-63
❑ 96SumPreS-63
❑ 96TopNHLP-169
❑ 96TopPicOI-169
❑ 96Ult-51
❑ 96UltGolM-51
❑ 96UltPow-9
❑ 96UltPowBL-6
❑ 96UppDec-52
❑ 96UppDecBD-16
❑ 96UppDecBDG-16
❑ 96UppDecPP-P12
❑ 97ColCho-82
❑ 97ColChoSta-SQ33
❑ 97Don-65
❑ 97DonPreProG-65
❑ 97DonPreProS-65
❑ 97Pac-189
❑ 97PacCarSup-7
❑ 97PacCarSupM-7
❑ 97PacCop-189
❑ 97PacDyn-42
❑ 97PacDynC-42
❑ 97PacDynDD-7B
❑ 97PacDynDG-42
❑ 97PacDynEG-42
❑ 97PacDynIB-42
❑ 97PacDynR-42
❑ 97PacDynSil-42
❑ 97PacDynTan-26
❑ 97PacEmeGre-189
❑ 97PacIceB-189
❑ 97PacInv-47
❑ 97PacInvC-47
❑ 97PacInvEG-47
❑ 97PacInvFP-13
❑ 97PacInvIB-47
❑ 97PacInvR-47
❑ 97PacInvS-47
❑ 97PacRed-189
❑ 97PacSil-189
❑ 97PinIns-126
❑ 97Sco-228
❑ 97ScoRedW-9
❑ 97ScoRedWPla-9
❑ 97ScoRedWPre-9
❑ 97UppDec-63
❑ 97UppDec-203
❑ 97UppDecGDM-63

**Kontilla, Mikko**
❑ 93FinnSIS-20

**Kontny, Josef**
❑ 94GerDELE-152
❑ 95GerDELE-147

**Kontos, Chris**
❑ 87PenKod-15
❑ 89ProAHL-14
❑ 90ProAHLIHL-359
❑ 91AlbIntTC-14
❑ 92LigShe-19
❑ 92OPCPre-123
❑ 92Par-176
❑ 92ParEmel-176
❑ 92Ult-412
❑ 92UppDec-502
❑ 93AlbIntTC-9
❑ 93Lea-160
❑ 93OPCPre-215
❑ 93OPCPreG-215
❑ 93OPCPreTC-14
❑ 93PanSti-213
❑ 93Par-197
❑ 93ParEmel-197
❑ 93Pin-8
❑ 93PinCan-8
❑ 93Pow-233
❑ 93Sco-113
❑ 93ScoCan-113
❑ 93TopPre-215
❑ 93TopPreG-215
❑ 93Ult-162
❑ 93UppDec-54
❑ 94EASpo-131
❑ 94ScoTeaC-CT6

**Kontsek, Roman**
❑ 94FinnJaaK-204

**Konttila, Mikko**
❑ 93FinnSIS-19
❑ 94FinnSIS-111
❑ 94FinnSIS-350
❑ 95FinnSIS-280

**Koopman, Kevin**
❑ 907thInnSWHL-257
❑ 917thInnSWHL-188

**Koopmans, Brad**
❑ 91BriColJHL-70

**Kopec, Dan**
❑ 907thInnSWHL-227
❑ 90BraWheK-12
❑ 917thInnSWHL-204

**Kopf, Ernst**
❑ 92UppDec-372
❑ 93SweSemWCS-161
❑ 94FinnJaaK-284
❑ 94GerDELE-98
❑ 95FinnSemWC-168
❑ 96GerDELE-283

**Kopot, Artem**
❑ 91UppDecCWJC-9

**Kopriva, Bretislav**
❑ 94CzeAPSE-300
❑ 95CzeAPSE-124

**Kopta, Petr**
❑ 94GerDELE-425
❑ 95GerDELE-112
❑ 96GerDELE-55

**Korab, Jerry**
❑ 71TorSun-69
❑ 72OPC-285
❑ 73CanuRoyB-8
❑ 73OPC-203
❑ 74NHLActSta-43
❑ 74OPCNHL-354
❑ 75OPCNHL-192
❑ 75Top-192
❑ 76OPCNHL-27
❑ 76SabGla-1
❑ 76Top-27
❑ 77OPCNHL-128
❑ 77Top-128
❑ 78OPC-231
❑ 78Top-231
❑ 79OPC-74
❑ 79SabBel-3
❑ 79SabMilP-3
❑ 79Top-74
❑ 80KinCarN-6
❑ 80OPC-300
❑ 81OPC-145
❑ 81OPCSti-240
❑ 81Top-W97
❑ 82PosCer-8
❑ 83OPCSti-297

**Korbela, Jaroslav**
❑ 82SweSemHVS-95

**Korber, Daniel**
❑ 94GerDELE-279
❑ 95GerDELE-275
❑ 96GerDELE-171
❑ 98GerDELE-17

**Korchinkski, Larry**
❑ 83SasBla-16

**Kordic, Dan**
❑ 907thInnSWHL-40
❑ 91FlyJCP-16
❑ 91Pin-338
❑ 91PinFre-338
❑ 91ProSet-553
❑ 91ProSetFre-553
❑ 96FlyPos-12
❑ 97Be A PPAD-158
❑ 97Be A PPAPD-158
❑ 97BeAPla-158
❑ 97BeAPlaAut-158
❑ 97PacInvNRB-142

**Kordic, John**
❑ 85CanaPos-14
❑ 86CanaPos-8
❑ 87CanaPos-11
❑ 87CanaVacS-57
❑ 87CanaVacS-58
❑ 90OPC-401
❑ 90ProSet-536
❑ 91NordPet-13
❑ 91ProSet-468
❑ 91ProSetFre-468

**Korhonen, Markus**
❑ 95FinnSIS-136

**Korinek, Petr**
❑ 93FinnJyvHS-233
❑ 93FinnSIS-205
❑ 94FinnSIS-244
❑ 94FinnSISFI-13
❑ 95FinnSIS-78
❑ 95FinnSIS-374
❑ 95FinnSISL-68
❑ 96CzeAPSE-301

**Korn, Jim**
❑ 79RedWinP-8
❑ 81OPC-91
❑ 81OPCSti-127
❑ 81Top-W91
❑ 82MapLeaP-19
❑ 82OPC-323
❑ 83MapLeaP-12
❑ 83OPC-335
❑ 83Vac-91
❑ 84MapLeaP-14
❑ 84OPC-304
❑ 84OPCSti-17
❑ 85MapLeaP-17
❑ 86SabBluS-16
❑ 86SabBluSSma-16
❑ 88DevCar-14
❑ 89DevCar-13
❑ 89PanSti-261
❑ 90OPC-450

**Korney, Mike**
❑ 75OPCNHL-342

**Korol, Dave**
❑ 88ProAHL-13
❑ 89ProIHL-121
❑ 90ProAHLIHL-309
❑ 91ProAHLCHL-328

**Korolev, Andrei**
❑ 95SweLeaE-295
❑ 95SweUppDE-197

**Korolev, Evgeny**
❑ 95Sla-325

**Korolev, Igor**
❑ 91OPCIns-37R
❑ 92OPCPre-53
❑ 92Par-158
❑ 92ParEmel-158
❑ 92Pin-417
❑ 92PinFre-417
❑ 92RusStaRA-10
❑ 92RusStaRA-15
❑ 92Ult-395
❑ 92UppDec-338
❑ 92UppDec-581
❑ 92UppDecCC-CC2
❑ 92UppDecER-ER3
❑ 93Don-297
❑ 93Lea-96
❑ 93OPCPre-409
❑ 93OPCPreG-409
❑ 93Par-446
❑ 93ParEmel-446
❑ 93Pow-214
❑ 93Sco-271
❑ 93ScoCan-271
❑ 93StaClu-119
❑ 93StaCluFDI-119
❑ 93StaCluFDIO-119
❑ 93StaCluO-119
❑ 93SweSemWCS-145
❑ 93TopPre-409
❑ 93TopPreG-409
❑ 93Ult-185
❑ 93UppDec-353
❑ 94Don-239
❑ 94FinnJaaK-161
❑ 94Lea-90
❑ 94ParSE-SE156
❑ 94ParSEG-SE156
❑ 94StaClu-46
❑ 94StaCluFDI-46
❑ 94StaCluMOMS-46
❑ 94StaCluSTWC-46
❑ 94UppDec-184
❑ 94UppDec-344
❑ 94UppDecEleIce-184
❑ 94UppDecEleIce-344
❑ 95BeAPla-135
❑ 95BeAPSig-S135
❑ 95BeAPSigDC-S135
❑ 95Bow-9
❑ 95BowAllFoi-9
❑ 95CanGamNHLP-291
❑ 95ColCho-257
❑ 95ColChoPC-257
❑ 95ColChoPCP-257
❑ 95Don-352
❑ 95Fin-84
❑ 95FinRef-84
❑ 95JetReaC-6
❑ 95JetTeaIss-12
❑ 95Lea-48
❑ 95LeaLim-32
❑ 95Met-163
❑ 95ParInt-227
❑ 95ParIntEl-227
❑ 95PlaOneoOne-327
❑ 95SP-168
❑ 95StaClu-131
❑ 95StaCluMOMS-131
❑ 95Sum-28
❑ 95SumArtP-28
❑ 95SumIce-28
❑ 95Top-146
❑ 95TopOPCI-146
❑ 95Ult-327
❑ 95UppDec-299
❑ 95UppDecEleIce-299
❑ 95UppDecEleIceG-299
❑ 95UppDecSpeE-SE90
❑ 95UppDecSpeEdiG-SE90
❑ 95Zen-63
❑ 96ColCho-202
❑ 96PlaOneoOne-407
❑ 96SweSemW-145
❑ 97PacOme-222
❑ 97PacOmeC-222
❑ 97PacOmeDG-222
❑ 97PacOmeEG-222
❑ 97PacOmeG-222
❑ 97PacOmeIB-222
❑ 97PacRev-135
❑ 97PacRevC-135
❑ 97PacRevE-135

❑ 95BowAllFoi-77
❑ 95CanGamNHLP-97
❑ 95ColCho-32
❑ 95ColChoPC-32
❑ 95ColChoPCP-32
❑ 95ColEdgIC-C17
❑ 95Don-134
❑ 95DonEli-87
❑ 95DonEliDCS-87
❑ 95DonEliDCU-87
❑ 95Emo-55
❑ 95Fin-83
❑ 95FinnSemWC-137
❑ 95FinRef-83
❑ 95Lea-210
❑ 95LeaRoaCup-8
❑ 95Met-47
❑ 95ParInt-65
❑ 95ParIntEl-65
❑ 95Pin-128
❑ 95PinArtP-128
❑ 95PinRinC-128
❑ 95PlaOneoOne-254
❑ 95Sco-165
❑ 95ScoBlaIce-165
❑ 95ScoBlaIceAP-165
❑ 95SkyImp-54
❑ 95SP-49
❑ 95StaClu-84
❑ 95StaCluMOMS-84
❑ 95Sum-83
❑ 95SumArtP-83
❑ 95SumIce-83
❑ 95Top-322
❑ 95TopOPCI-322
❑ 95TopPowL-8PL
❑ 95Ult-47
❑ 95UltGolM-47
❑ 95UppDec-154
❑ 95UppDecEleIce-154
❑ 95UppDecEleIceG-154
❑ 95UppDecSpeE-SE117
❑ 95UppDecSpeEdiG-SE117
❑ 96ColCho-81
❑ 96ColChoCTG-C18A
❑ 96ColChoCTG-C18B
❑ 96ColChoCTG-C18C
❑ 96ColChoCTGE-CR18
❑ 96ColChoCTGEG-CR18
❑ 96ColChoCTGG-C18A
❑ 96ColChoCTGG-C18B
❑ 96ColChoCTGG-C18C
❑ 96Don-19
❑ 96DonCanI-71
❑ 96DonCanIGPP-71
❑ 96DonCanIRPP-71
❑ 96DonEli-81
❑ 96DonEliDCS-81
❑ 96DonPrePro-19
❑ 96Fle-32
❑ 96Lea-196
❑ 96LeaLim-88
❑ 96LeaLimG-88
❑ 96LeaPreP-196
❑ 96LeaPreSG-38
❑ 96LeaPreSte-38
❑ 96MetUni-47
❑ 96Pin-129
❑ 96PinArtP-129
❑ 96PinFoi-129
❑ 96PinPreS-129
❑ 96PinRinC-129
❑ 96Sco-158
❑ 96ScoArtPro-158
❑ 96ScoDeaCAP-158
❑ 96ScoGolB-158
❑ 96ScoSpeAP-158
❑ 96SkyImp-36
❑ 96SP-49
❑ 96Sum-84
❑ 96SumArtP-84
❑ 96SumIce-84
❑ 96SumMet-84
❑ 96SumPreS-84
❑ 96SweSemW-146
❑ 96TeaOut-8
❑ 96TopNHLP-67
❑ 96TopPicOI-67
❑ 96Ult-52
❑ 96UltGolM-52
❑ 96UppDec-251
❑ 96UppDecBD-113
❑ 96UppDecBDG-113
❑ 96Zen-22
❑ 96ZenArtP-22
❑ 97Be A PPAD-97
❑ 97Be A PPAPD-97
❑ 97BeAPla-97
❑ 97BeAPlaAut-97
❑ 97ColCho-85
❑ 97ColChoSta-SQ13
❑ 97Don-119
❑ 97DonCanISCS-25
❑ 97DonEli-25
❑ 97DonEliAsp-25
❑ 97DonEliS-25
❑ 97DonPre-134
❑ 97DonPreCttC-134
❑ 97DonPreProG-119
❑ 97DonPreProS-119
❑ 97DonPri-130
❑ 97DonPriSoA-130
❑ 97Kat-50
❑ 97KatGol-50
❑ 97KatSil-50
❑ 97Lea-31
❑ 97LeaFraMat-31
❑ 97LeaFraMDC-31
❑ 97LeaInt-31
❑ 97LeaIntUI-31
❑ 97Pac-267
❑ 97PacCop-267
❑ 97PacCroR-46
❑ 97PacCroREG-46
❑ 97PacCroRIB-46
❑ 97PacCroRS-46
❑ 97PacEmeGre-267
❑ 97PacIceB-267
❑ 97PacInv-48
❑ 97PacInvC-48
❑ 97PacInvEG-48
❑ 97PacInvIB-48
❑ 97PacInvR-48
❑ 97PacInvS-48
❑ 97PacOme-81
❑ 97PacOmeC-81
❑ 97PacOmeDG-81
❑ 97PacOmeEG-81
❑ 97PacOmeG-81
❑ 97PacOmeIB-81
❑ 97PacPar-66
❑ 97PacParC-66
❑ 97PacParDG-66
❑ 97PacParEG-66
❑ 97PacParIB-66
❑ 97PacParRed-66
❑ 97PacParSil-66
❑ 97PacRed-267
❑ 97PacSil-267
❑ 97Pin-117
❑ 97PinIns-116
❑ 97PinPrePBB-117
❑ 97PinPrePBC-117
❑ 97PinPrePBM-117
❑ 97PinPrePBY-117
❑ 97PinPrePFC-117
❑ 97PinPrePFM-117
❑ 97PinPrePFY-117
❑ 97PinPrePla-117
❑ 97Sco-209
❑ 97ScoRedW-7
❑ 97ScoRedWPla-7
❑ 97ScoRedWPre-7
❑ 97SPAut-50
❑ 97UppDec-271
❑ 97UppDecBD-129
❑ 97UppDecBDDD-129
❑ 97UppDecBDQD-129
❑ 97UppDecBDTD-129
❑ 97UppDecGDM-271
❑ 98Be A PPTBASG-49
❑ 98PacPar-76
❑ 98PacParC-76
❑ 98PacParEG-76
❑ 98PacParH-76
❑ 98PacParIB-76
❑ 98PacParS-76
❑ 98UDCP-78
❑ 98UppDecGR-264
❑ 99Pac-140
❑ 99PacCop-140
❑ 99PacIceB-140
❑ 99PacPreD-140

**Kozlov, Viktor**
❑ 92Cla-61
❑ 92Cla-62
❑ 92UppDec-613
❑ 93Cla-6
❑ 93ClaProPBC-BC9
❑ 93ClaProPLP-LP4
❑ 93ClaProPro-93
❑ 93ClaTopTen-DP6
❑ 93SweSemWCS-140
❑ 94BeAPla-R158
❑ 94BeAPSig-153A
❑ 94BeAPSig-153B
❑ 94Cla-113
❑ 94ClaDraGol-113
❑ 94ClaProPIA-IA17
❑ 94ClaROYS-R12
❑ 94ClaTri-T61
❑ 94Fin-46
❑ 94FinRef-46
❑ 94FinSupTW-46
❑ 94Lea-451
❑ 94LeaLim-21
❑ 94LeaPhe-8
❑ 94McDUppD-McD33
❑ 94ParSE-SE159
❑ 94ParSEG-SE159
❑ 94ParSEV-43
❑ 94Pin-477
❑ 94Pin-481
❑ 94PinArtP-477
❑ 94PinArtP-481
❑ 94PinRinC-477
❑ 94PinRinC-481
❑ 94PinRooTP-5
❑ 94ScoTopRR-10
❑ 94Sel-174
❑ 94SelGol-174
❑ 94SelYouExp-YE6
❑ 94SPPre-3
❑ 94SPPreDC-3
❑ 94Ult-366
❑ 94UltPro-4
❑ 94UppDec-265
❑ 94UppDecEleIce-265
❑ 94UppDecPC-C3
❑ 94UppDecPCEG-C3
❑ 94UppDecPCES-C3
❑ 94UppDecSPI-SP162
❑ 94UppDecSPIDC-SP162
❑ 95Bow-159
❑ 95BowAllFoi-159
❑ 95CanGamNHLP-229
❑ 95ColCho-252
❑ 95ColChoPC-252
❑ 95ColChoPCP-252
❑ 95ColEdgI-145
❑ 95ColEdgIC-C10
❑ 95ColEdgIP-PR4
❑ 95Don-171
❑ 95Lea-73
❑ 95LeaLim-77
❑ 95ParInt-187
❑ 95ParInt-515
❑ 95ParIntEl-187
❑ 95ParIntEl-515
❑ 95Pin-99
❑ 95PinArtP-99
❑ 95PinGloG-16
❑ 95PinRinC-99
❑ 95Sco-114
❑ 95ScoBlaIce-114
❑ 95ScoBlaIceAP-114
❑ 95StaClu-137
❑ 95StaCluMOMS-137
❑ 95Sum-142
❑ 95SumArtP-142
❑ 95SumIce-142
❑ 95Top-357
❑ 95TopOPCI-357
❑ 95UppDec-92
❑ 95UppDecEleIce-92
❑ 95UppDecEleIceG-92
❑ 96ClaGol-61
❑ 96ClaGol-62
❑ 96ColCho-237
❑ 96SweSemW-147
❑ 96UppDec-152
❑ 97ColCho-217
❑ 97DonLim-91
❑ 97DonLimExp-91
❑ 97Pac-125
❑ 97PacCop-125
❑ 97PacCroR-58
❑ 97PacCroREG-58
❑ 97PacCroRIB-58
❑ 97PacCroRS-58
❑ 97PacDyn-113
❑ 97PacDynC-113
❑ 97PacDynDG-113
❑ 97PacDynEG-113
❑ 97PacDynIB-113
❑ 97PacDynR-113
❑ 97PacDynSil-113
❑ 97PacDynTan-64
❑ 97PacEmeGre-125
❑ 97PacIceB-125
❑ 97PacPar-166
❑ 97PacParC-166
❑ 97PacParDG-166
❑ 97PacParEG-166
❑ 97PacParIB-166
❑ 97PacParRed-166
❑ 97PacParSil-166
❑ 97PacRed-125
❑ 97PacSil-125
❑ 97Sco-223
❑ 97SPAut-70
❑ 97UppDec-359
❑ 98Be A PPA-49
❑ 98Be A PPA-60
❑ 98Be A PPAA-49
❑ 98Be A PPAA-60
❑ 98Be A PPAAF-49
❑ 98Be A PPAAF-60
❑ 98Be A PPTBASG-60
❑ 98Be APG-49
❑ 98Be APG-60
❑ 98Fin-94
❑ 98FinNo P-94
❑ 98FinNo PR-94
❑ 98FinRef-94
❑ 98O-PChr-83
❑ 98O-PChrR-83
❑ 98Pac-196
❑ 98Pac-223
❑ 98PacAur-63
❑ 98PacAur-81
❑ 98PacCroR-59
❑ 98PacCroRLS-59
❑ 98PacDynI-63
❑ 98PacDynI-82
❑ 98PacDynIIB-63
❑ 98PacDynIIB-82
❑ 98PacDynIR-63
❑ 98PacDynIR-82
❑ 98PacIceB-196
❑ 98PacIceB-223
❑ 98PacOmeH-103
❑ 98PacOmeODI-103
❑ 98PacOmeR-103
❑ 98PacPar-97
❑ 98PacParC-97
❑ 98PacParEG-97
❑ 98PacParH-97
❑ 98PacParIB-97
❑ 98PacParS-97
❑ 98PacRed-196
❑ 98PacRed-223
❑ 98PacRev-62
❑ 98PacRevIS-62
❑ 98PacRevR-62
❑ 98Top-83
❑ 98TopO-P-83
❑ 98UC-78
❑ 98UD ChoPCR-78
❑ 98UD ChoR-78
❑ 98UppDec-98
❑ 98UppDec-264
❑ 98UppDecE-98
❑ 98UppDecE-264
❑ 98UppDecE1o1-98
❑ 98UppDecE1o1-264
❑ 98UppDecGR-98
❑ 99Pac-173
❑ 99PacAur-63
❑ 99PacAurPD-63
❑ 99PacCop-173
❑ 99PacGol-173
❑ 99PacIceB-173
❑ 99PacPreD-173
❑ 99UppDecM-86
❑ 99UppDecMGS-86
❑ 99UppDecMSS-86
❑ 99UppDecMSS-86

**Kozurok, Chico**
❑ 61SudWol-11
❑ 62SudWol-13

**Kraemer, Chris**
❑ 907thInnSOHL-163
❑ 917thInnSOHL-78

**Kraemer, Greg**
❑ 93KinFro-18

**Kraft, Ryan**
❑ 94MinGolG-17
❑ 95MinGolG-18
❑ 96MinGolGCAS-16

**Kraft, Thomas**
❑ 92BriColJHL-34

**Kraftcheck, Steve**
❑ 44BeeGro2P-331
❑ 44BeeGro2P-417
❑ 51Par-92
❑ 52Par-23
❑ 58Par-37

**Kraiger, Yogi**
❑ 51LavDaiQSHL-9
❑ 51LavDaiS-9
❑ 52St.LawS-48

**Krainz, Martin**
❑ 93SweSemWCS-274
❑ 94FinnJaaK-235
❑ 95AusNatTea-13

**Krajicek, Jan**
❑ 94CzeAPSE-188
❑ 95CzeAPSE-37

**Krajov, Vitali**
❑ 74SweHocS-89

**Krake, Paul**
❑ 92OklCitB-10
❑ 94CenHocL-49

**Krake, Skip**
❑ 67Top-93
❑ 68OPC-3
❑ 68OPC-43
❑ 68ShiCoi-60
❑ 68Top-3
❑ 68Top-43
❑ 69OPC-141
❑ 70DadCoo-66
❑ 70EssPowPla-82
❑ 70OPC-126
❑ 70SarProSta-24
❑ 70Top-126
❑ 72CleCruWHA-9

**Krakiwsky, Sean**
❑ 85MinDul-32

**Kral, Richard**
❑ 94CzeAPSE-43
❑ 95CzeAPSE-236

**Kralik, Jiri**
❑ 81SweSemHVS-55
❑ 82SweSemHVS-76

**Krall, Justin**
❑ 96PeoRivP-12
❑ 96PeoRivPA-12

**Kramer, Ted**
❑ 91MicWol-9
❑ 92PhoRoa-11

**Kramny, Tomas**
❑ 94CzeAPSE-121
❑ 96CzeAPSE-197

**Kramskoy, Vladimir**
❑ 93SweSemE-271

**Kranwinkel, Markus**
❑ 94GerDELE-226
❑ 94GerDELE-236

**Krasny, Tomas**
❑ 95CzeAPSE-216
❑ 96CzeAPSE-182

**Kratena, Ondrej**
❑ 95CzeAPSE-119
❑ 95UppDec-540
❑ 95UppDecEleIce-540
❑ 95UppDecEleIceG-540
❑ 96CzeAPSE-233

**Kratky, Petr**
❑ 95CzeAPSE-157
❑ 96CzeAPSE-176

**Kratoska, Ales**
❑ 96CzeAPSE-208

**Kratz, Michael**
❑ 94GerDELE-353

**Kraus, Richard**
❑ 92BriColJHL-186

**Krause, Sean**
❑ 91BriColJHL-60

**Krauss, Daryl**
❑ 91AirCanSJHL-B43
❑ 92MPSPhoSJHL-144

**Krauss, Rob**
❑ 90CinCyc-33
❑ 92BirBul-16
❑ 93BirBul-16

**Kravchuk, Igor**
❑ 90OPCRedA-11R
❑ 91OPCIns-19R
❑ 91Par-257
❑ 91Par-461
❑ 91ParFre-257
❑ 91RusStaRA-10
❑ 91SweSemWCS-82
❑ 92Bow-408
❑ 92OilTeal-9
❑ 92OPC-161
❑ 92PanSti-297
❑ 92PanSti-A
❑ 92PanStiFre-297
❑ 92PanStiFre-A
❑ 92Par-35
❑ 92Par-291
❑ 92ParEmel-35
❑ 92ParEmel-291
❑ 92Pin-225
❑ 92PinFre-225
❑ 92ProSet-35
❑ 92Sco-454
❑ 92ScoCan-454
❑ 92SeaPat-69
❑ 92StaClu-7
❑ 92Top-200
❑ 92TopGol-200G
❑ 92TriFroRWP-17
❑ 92TriFroRWP-18
❑ 92Ult-38
❑ 92UppDec-239
❑ 92UppDec-367
❑ 92UppDecES-E7
❑ 93Don-116
❑ 93Lea-163
❑ 93OPCPre-495
❑ 93OPCPreG-495
❑ 93Par-65
❑ 93ParEmel-65
❑ 93Pin-36
❑ 93PinCan-36
❑ 93Pow-81
❑ 93Sco-309
❑ 93ScoCan-309
❑ 93StaClu-204
❑ 93StaCluFDI-204
❑ 93StaCluFDIO-204
❑ 93StaCluO-204
❑ 93TopPre-495
❑ 93TopPreG-495
❑ 93Ult-80
❑ 93UppDec-174
❑ 94CanGamNHLP-367
❑ 94Don-259
❑ 94EASpo-44
❑ 94Fla-58
❑ 94Fle-70
❑ 94Lea-244
❑ 94OPCPre-172
❑ 94OPCPreSE-172
❑ 94ParSE-SE58
❑ 94ParSEG-SE58
❑ 94Pin-96
❑ 94PinArtP-96
❑ 94PinRinC-96
❑ 94Sco-33
❑ 94ScoGol-33
❑ 94ScoPla-33
❑ 94ScoPlaTS-33
❑ 94TopPre-172
❑ 94TopPreSE-172
❑ 94Ult-72
❑ 94UppDec-463
❑ 94UppDecEleIce-463
❑ 95CanGamNHLP-109
❑ 95Emo-63
❑ 95ParInt-74
❑ 95ParIntEl-74
❑ 95PlaOneoOne-148
❑ 95SkyImp-61
❑ 95SweGloWC-167
❑ 95Ult-54
❑ 95UltGolM-54
❑ 95UppDec-146
❑ 95UppDecEleIce-146
❑ 95UppDecEleIceG-146
❑ 96BeAPAut-3
❑ 96BeAPAutSil-3
❑ 96BeAPla-3
❑ 96PlaOneoOne-372
❑ 96SweSemW-132
❑ 97PacInvNRB-170
❑ 97PacOme-155
❑ 97PacOmeC-155
❑ 97PacOmeDG-155
❑ 97PacOmeEG-155
❑ 97PacOmeG-155
❑ 97PacOmeIB-155
❑ 97PacPar-126
❑ 97PacParC-126
❑ 97PacParDG-126
❑ 97PacParEG-126
❑ 97PacParIB-126
❑ 97PacParRed-126
❑ 97PacParSil-126
❑ 98O-PChr-36
❑ 98O-PChrR-36
❑ 98Pac-310
❑ 98PacAur-130
❑ 98PacCroR-93
❑ 98PacCroRLS-93
❑ 98PacDynI-127
❑ 98PacDynIIB-127
❑ 98PacDynIR-127
❑ 98PacIceB-310
❑ 98PacPar-163
❑ 98PacParC-163
❑ 98PacParEG-163
❑ 98PacParH-163
❑ 98PacParIB-163
❑ 98PacParS-163
❑ 98PacRed-310
❑ 98Top-36
❑ 98TopO-P-36
❑ 98UppDec-330
❑ 98UppDecE-330
❑ 98UppDecE1o1-330
❑ 98UppDecGR-330
❑ 99Pac-290
❑ 99PacCop-290
❑ 99PacGol-290
❑ 99PacIceB-290
❑ 99PacPreD-290

**Kravets, Mikhail**
❑ 91ProAHLCHL-505
❑ 92Cla-106
❑ 92UppDec-542
❑ 96ClaGol-106

**Krawinkel, Markus**
❑ 95GerDELE-221
❑ 96GerDELE-71

**Krayer, Paul**
❑ 89NasKni-13

**Krayzel, Ludek**
❑ 96CzeAPSE-205

**Krechin, Vladimir**
❑ 93Cla-41

**Kreis, Harold**
❑ 82SweSemHVS-106
❑ 89SweSemWCS-109
❑ 91SweSemWCS-156
❑ 94GerDELE-274
❑ 95GerDELE-266
❑ 96GerDELE-160

**Krejci, Lukas**
❑ 96SloPeeWT-13

**Krentz, Dale**
❑ 88ProAHL-15
❑ 89ProAHL-319
❑ 94GerDELE-281
❑ 95GerDELE-372

**Krepelka, Paul**
❑ 91HamRoaA-8
❑ 92HamRoaA-2

**Kress, Jamie**
❑ 92OshGenS-2

**Kretchine, Vladimir**
❑ 93WinSpi-17
❑ 94WinSpi-19
❑ 95Sla-422

**Kretschmer, Horst**
❑ 79PanSti-102

**Kreuser, Jeff**
❑ 98KanCitB-28

**Kreutzer, Christopher**
❑ 94GerDELE-80
❑ 95GerDELE-80

**Kreutzer, Daniel**
❑ 98GerDELE-257

**Kreutzer, Kevin**
❑ 98ChaChe-10

**Kreuzmann, Jaroslav**
❑ 94CzeAPSE-160
❑ 95CzeAPSE-261

**Krinner, Anton**
❑ 91SweSemWCS-171
❑ 94GerDELE-16
❑ 95GerDELE-144
❑ 96GerDELE-244

**Krisak, Patrik**
❑ 93UppDec-266

**Krisko, Dan**
❑ 907thInnSOHL-262
❑ 917thInnSOHL-216

**Kriss, Aaron**
❑ 95TalTigS-4

**Kristiansen, Erik**
❑ 87SwePanS-41
❑ 93SweSemWCS-238
❑ 94FinnJaaK-262

**Kristiansen, Pal**
❑ 94FinnJaaK-257

**Kristin, Miroslav**
❑ 96SloPeeWT-14

**Krivchenkov, Alexei**
❑ 95HamRoaA-13
❑ 96HamRoaA-HRA15

**Krivokrasov, Sergei**
❑ 91UppDec-658
❑ 91UppDecCWJC-19
❑ 91UppDecF-658
❑ 92Cla-42
❑ 92IndIce-16
❑ 92OPCPre-9
❑ 92Par-36
❑ 92ParEmel-36
❑ 92Pin-410
❑ 92PinFre-410
❑ 92TriFroRWP-9
❑ 92TriFroRWP-10
❑ 92Ult-276
❑ 92UppDec-582
❑ 92UppDecER-ER5
❑ 93Cla-138
❑ 93ClaProPro-38
❑ 93Don-74
❑ 93Lea-434
❑ 93Pin-419
❑ 93PinCan-419
❑ 93Pow-51
❑ 93Sco-464
❑ 93ScoCan-464
❑ 93Ult-112
❑ 94ClaProP-220
❑ 94Don-91
❑ 94Fle-41
❑ 94IndIce-13
❑ 94Lea-238
❑ 94OPCPre-513
❑ 94OPCPreSE-513
❑ 94ParSE-SE37
❑ 94ParSEG-SE37
❑ 94ParSEV-19
❑ 94PinRooTP-12
❑ 94TopPre-513
❑ 94TopPreSE-513
❑ 94UppDec-80
❑ 94UppDecEleIce-80
❑ 95BeAPla-187
❑ 95BeAPSig-S187
❑ 95BeAPSigDC-S187
❑ 95CanGamNHLP-65
❑ 95ColCho-96
❑ 95ColChoPC-96
❑ 95ColChoPCP-96
❑ 95Don-203
❑ 95Emo-29
❑ 95Lea-32
❑ 95LeaStuR-18
❑ 95ParInt-314
❑ 95ParIntEl-314
❑ 95Pin-154
❑ 95PinArtP-154
❑ 95PinRinC-154
❑ 95Sco-62
❑ 95ScoBlaIce-62
❑ 95ScoBlaIceAP-62
❑ 95SkyImp-29
❑ 95SkyImpNHLF-6
❑ 95TopNewG-16NG
❑ 95Ult-33
❑ 95UltGolM-33
❑ 95UppDec-11
❑ 95UppDecEleIce-11
❑ 95UppDecEleIceG-11
❑ 96ClaGol-42
❑ 97Pac-134
❑ 97PacCop-134
❑ 97PacEmeGre-134
❑ 97PacIceB-134
❑ 97PacPar-45
❑ 97PacParC-45
❑ 97PacParDG-45
❑ 97PacParEG-45
❑ 97PacParIB-45
❑ 97PacParRed-45
❑ 97PacParSil-45
❑ 97PacRed-134
❑ 97PacSil-134
❑ 97SPAut-34
❑ 97UppDec-37
❑ 98Be A PPA-223
❑ 98Be A PPAA-223
❑ 98Be A PPAAF-223
❑ 98Be A PPSE-223
❑ 98Be APG-223
❑ 98O-PChr-211
❑ 98O-PChrR-211
❑ 98Pac-147
❑ 98PacAur-102
❑ 98PacCroR-76
❑ 98PacCroRLS-76
❑ 98PacDynI-104
❑ 98PacDynIIB-104
❑ 98PacDynIR-104
❑ 98PacIceB-147
❑ 98PacOmeH-130
❑ 98PacOmeODI-130
❑ 98PacOmeR-130
❑ 98PacPar-124
❑ 98PacParC-124
❑ 98PacParEG-124
❑ 98PacParH-124
❑ 98PacParIB-124
❑ 98PacParS-124
❑ 98PacRed-147
❑ 98PacRev-79
❑ 98PacRevADC-15
❑ 98PacRevIS-79
❑ 98PacRevR-79
❑ 98SP Aut-45
❑ 98Top-211
❑ 98TopO-P-211
❑ 98UppDec-302
❑ 98UppDecBD-48
❑ 98UppDecDD-48
❑ 98UppDecE-302
❑ 98UppDecE1o1-302
❑ 98UppDecGR-302
❑ 98UppDecM-114
❑ 98UppDecMGS-114
❑ 98UppDecMSS-114
❑ 98UppDecMSS-114
❑ 98UppDecQD-48
❑ 98UppDecTD-48
❑ 99Pac-227
❑ 99PacAur-79

❑ 99PacAurPD-79
❑ 99PacCop-227
❑ 99PacGol-227
❑ 99PacIceB-227
❑ 99PacPreD-227
❑ 99SP AutPS-45
❑ 99UppDecM-109
❑ 99UppDecMGS-109
❑ 99UppDecMSS-109
❑ 99UppDecMSS-109
**Krivolapov, Viktor**
❑ 73SweHocS-109
❑ 73SweWorCS-109
**Kriz, Ondrej**
❑ 93DayBom-6
**Kriz, Pavel**
❑ 95SasBla-10
❑ 95SigRooA-22
❑ 95SigRooAPC-22
❑ 96CzeAPSE-150
**Krocak, Jiri**
❑ 95CzeAPSE-277
❑ 96CzeAPSE-126
**Krol, Joe**
❑ 34BeeGro1P-236
**Krolak, Curt**
❑ 92ForWorF-10
**Kromm, Bobby**
❑ 81RedWinOld-7
**Kromm, Rich (Richard)**
❑ 84OPC-227
❑ 85FlamRedRP-11
❑ 85OPC-222
❑ 86OPC-229
❑ 87PanSti-103
❑ 88ProAHL-318
❑ 89SweSemE-136
❑ 90ProAHLIHL-498
❑ 91ProAHLCHL-465
**Kromp, Wolfgang**
❑ 94FinnJaaK-249
**Kron, Robert**
❑ 89SweSemWCS-199
❑ 90CanuMoh-11
❑ 90OPCPre-52
❑ 90ProSet-642
❑ 90ScoRoo-65T
❑ 90UppDec-528
❑ 90UppDecF-528
❑ 91Bow-320
❑ 91CanuAutC-9
❑ 91CanuPanTS-10
❑ 91CanuTeal8-9
❑ 91OPC-52
❑ 91PanSti-47
❑ 91ParPHC-PHC4
❑ 91ParPHCF-PHC4
❑ 91ProSet-239
❑ 91ProSetFre-239
❑ 91ProSetPla-122
❑ 91ScoCan-257
❑ 91StaClu-240
❑ 91Top-52
❑ 91UppDec-225
❑ 91UppDecES-8
❑ 91UppDecESF-8
❑ 91UppDecF-225
❑ 92Bow-413
❑ 92CanuRoaTA-9
❑ 92OPC-2
❑ 92PanSti-33
❑ 92PanStiFre-33
❑ 92StaClu-155
❑ 92Top-80
❑ 92TopGol-80G
❑ 92UppDec-69
❑ 93Don-143
❑ 93Lea-171
❑ 93Par-90
❑ 93ParEmel-90
❑ 93Pin-421
❑ 93PinCan-421
❑ 93Pow-351
❑ 93Sco-428
❑ 93ScoCan-428
❑ 93UppDec-359
❑ 93UppDecSP-61
❑ 93WhaCok-8
❑ 94BeAPSig-66
❑ 94CanGamNHLP-114
❑ 94Don-114
❑ 94FinnJaaK-181
❑ 94Lea-101
❑ 94OPCPre-296
❑ 94OPCPreSE-296
❑ 94ParSE-SE76
❑ 94ParSEG-SE76
❑ 94Pin-336
❑ 94PinArtP-336
❑ 94PinRinC-336
❑ 94StaClu-146
❑ 94StaCluFDI-146
❑ 94StaCluMOMS-146
❑ 94StaCluSTWC-146
❑ 94TopPre-296
❑ 94TopPreSE-296
❑ 94Ult-90
❑ 94UppDec-408
❑ 94UppDecElelce-408
❑ 95ColCho-298
❑ 95ColChoPC-298
❑ 95ColChoPCP-298
❑ 95Don-231
❑ 95Lea-257
❑ 95ParInt-92
❑ 95ParIntEl-92
❑ 95Pin-85
❑ 95PinArtP-85
❑ 95PinRinC-85
❑ 95Sco-154
❑ 95ScoBlaIce-154
❑ 95ScoBlaIceAP-154
❑ 95Top-161
❑ 95TopOPCI-161
❑ 95UppDec-400
❑ 95UppDecElelce-400
❑ 95UppDecElelceG-400
❑ 96Lea-57
❑ 96LeaPreP-57
❑ 96Pin-132
❑ 96PinArtP-132
❑ 96PinFoi-132
❑ 96PinPreS-132
❑ 96PinRinC-132
❑ 96Sco-195
❑ 96ScoArtPro-195
❑ 96ScoDeaCAP-195
❑ 96ScoGolB-195
❑ 96ScoSpeAP-195
❑ 96WhaBobS-11
❑ 97Be A PPAD-140
❑ 97Be A PPAPD-140
❑ 97BeAPla-140
❑ 97BeAPlaAut-140
❑ 97CarHur-15
❑ 97Pac-114
❑ 97PacCop-114
❑ 97PacEmeGre-114
❑ 97PacIceB-114
❑ 97PacRed-114
❑ 97PacSil-114
❑ 98Be A PPA-25
❑ 98Be A PPAA-25
❑ 98Be A PPAAF-25
❑ 98Be A PPTBASG-25
❑ 98Be APG-25
❑ 98Fin-97
❑ 98FinNo P-97
❑ 98FinNo PR-97
❑ 98FinRef-97
❑ 98Pac-136
❑ 98PacAur-35
❑ 98PacDynI-36
❑ 98PacDynIIB-36
❑ 98PacDynIR-36
❑ 98PacIceB-136
❑ 98PacPar-39
❑ 98PacParC-39
❑ 98PacParEG-39
❑ 98PacParH-39
❑ 98PacParIB-39
❑ 98PacParS-39
❑ 98PacRed-136
❑ 99Pac-76
❑ 99PacCop-76
❑ 99PacGol-76
❑ 99PacIceB-76
❑ 99PacPreD-76
**Kroon, Jan-Olov**
❑ 67SweHoc-103
❑ 69SweHocS-119
❑ 70SweHocS-10
❑ 71SweHocS-85
❑ 72SweHocS-61
❑ 73SweHocS-199
❑ 73SweWorCS-199
❑ 74SweHocS-235
**Kroon, Ulf**
❑ 67SweHoc-121
**Krooshoop, Mike**
❑ 93KamBla-13
**Kropf, Barret**
❑ 91AirCanSJHL-A31
**Kropf, M.**
❑ 95GerDELE-380
**Kroseberg, Gunnar**
❑ 95MadMon-14
**Kroupa, Vlastimil**
❑ 93Don-315
❑ 93Lea-439
❑ 93Par-266
❑ 93ParEmel-266
❑ 93Ult-414
❑ 93UppDec-437
❑ 93UppDecSP-144
❑ 94ClaProP-4
❑ 94Don-277
❑ 94Lea-265
❑ 94LeaLim-64
❑ 94OPCPre-113
❑ 94OPCPreSE-113
❑ 94ParSE-SE167
❑ 94ParSEG-SE167
❑ 94Pin-242
❑ 94PinArtP-242
❑ 94PinRinC-242
❑ 94TopPre-113
❑ 94TopPreSE-113
❑ 94Ult-196
❑ 94UppDec-453
❑ 94UppDecElelce-453
❑ 98KanCitB-15
**Kruchkowski, Corey**
❑ 92BriColJHL-191
**Krueger, Shawn**
❑ 917thInnSOHL-276
**Krug, Jason**
❑ 91AirCanSJHL-E32
❑ 92MPSPhoSJHL-101
**Kruger, Martin**
❑ 71SweHocS-345
**Kruger, Raphael**
❑ 94GerDELE-372
❑ 95GerDELE-365
**Kruger, Trevor**
❑ 89HamRoaA-11
**Kruhlak, Rob**
❑ 92NorMicW-16
**Krulis, Jan**
❑ 94CzeAPSE-74
❑ 95CzeAPSE-82
❑ 96CzeAPSE-77
**Krull, Harald**
❑ 82SweSemHVS-108
**Krumpschmid, Norm**
❑ 94MusFur-11
**Krupp, Uwe**
❑ 86SabBluS-17
❑ 86SabBluSSma-17
❑ 87SabBluS-15
❑ 87SabWonBH-14
❑ 88OPC-220
❑ 88SabBluS-13
❑ 88SabWonBH-13
❑ 89PanSti-216
❑ 89SabBluS-9
❑ 89SabCam-11
❑ 90OPC-390
❑ 90PanSti-22
❑ 90ProSet-23
❑ 90SabBluS-11
❑ 90SabCam-12
❑ 90Sco-169
❑ 90ScoCan-169
❑ 90Top-390
❑ 90TopTif-390
❑ 90UppDec-187
❑ 90UppDecF-187
❑ 91Bow-26
❑ 91OPC-155
❑ 91OPCPre-140
❑ 91PanSti-305
❑ 91Par-109
❑ 91ParFre-109
❑ 91Pin-19
❑ 91PinFre-19
❑ 91ProSet-20
❑ 91ProSet-301
❑ 91ProSet-436
❑ 91ProSetFre-20
❑ 91ProSetFre-301
❑ 91ProSetFre-436
❑ 91ProSetPla-202
❑ 91ScoAme-84
❑ 91ScoCan-84
❑ 91ScoRoo-104T
❑ 91StaClu-62
❑ 91SweSemWCS-162
❑ 91Top-155
❑ 91UppDec-102
❑ 91UppDec-540
❑ 91UppDecF-102
❑ 91UppDecF-540
❑ 92Bow-349
❑ 92OPC-173
❑ 92PanSti-202
❑ 92PanStiFre-202
❑ 92Par-101
❑ 92Par-453
❑ 92ParEmel-101
❑ 92ParEmel-453
❑ 92Pin-86
❑ 92Pin-240
❑ 92PinFre-86
❑ 92PinFre-240
❑ 92ProSet-109
❑ 92Sco-77
❑ 92ScoCan-77
❑ 92StaClu-177
❑ 92Top-158
❑ 92TopGol-158G
❑ 92Ult-129
❑ 92UppDec-187
❑ 93Don-205
❑ 93Lea-57
❑ 93OPCPre-3
❑ 93OPCPreG-3
❑ 93Par-388
❑ 93ParEmel-388
❑ 93Pin-259
❑ 93PinCan-259
❑ 93Pow-151
❑ 93Sco-87
❑ 93ScoCan-87
❑ 93ScoIntS-11
❑ 93ScoIntSC-11
❑ 93StaClu-138
❑ 93StaCluFDI-138
❑ 93StaCluFDIO-138
❑ 93StaCluO-138
❑ 93SweSemWCS-168
❑ 93TopPre-3
❑ 93TopPreG-3
❑ 94BeAPSig-163
❑ 94CanGamNHLP-201
❑ 94Fle-179
❑ 94Lea-422
❑ 94NordBurK-13
❑ 94Pin-382
❑ 94PinArtP-382
❑ 94PinRinC-382
❑ 94StaClu-172
❑ 94StaCluFDI-172
❑ 94StaCluMOMS-172
❑ 94StaCluSTWC-172
❑ 94Ult-358
❑ 94UppDec-310
❑ 94UppDecElelce-310
❑ 95CanGamNHLP-79
❑ 95ColCho-80
❑ 95ColChoPC-80
❑ 95ColChoPCP-80
❑ 95Don-49
❑ 95Emo-38
❑ 95GerDELE-444
❑ 95Lea-266
❑ 95ParInt-50
❑ 95ParIntEl-50
❑ 95Pin-46
❑ 95PinArtP-46
❑ 95PinGloG-8
❑ 95PinRinC-46
❑ 95Sco-108
❑ 95ScoBlaIce-108
❑ 95ScoBlaIceAP-108
❑ 95UppDecElelce-388
❑ 95UppDecElelceG-388
❑ 96BeAPAut-87
❑ 96BeAPAutSil-87
❑ 96BeAPla-87
❑ 96ColCho-56
❑ 96Don-114
❑ 96DonPrePro-114
❑ 96Lea-49
❑ 96LeaPreP-49
❑ 96MetUni-34
❑ 96Pin-24
❑ 96PinArtP-24
❑ 96PinFoi-24
❑ 96PinPreS-24
❑ 96PinRinC-24
❑ 96Sco-175
❑ 96ScoArtPro-175
❑ 96ScoDeaCAP-175
❑ 96ScoGolB-175
❑ 96ScoSpeAP-175
❑ 96SkyImp-24
❑ 96Sum-38
❑ 96SumArtP-38
❑ 96SumIce-38
❑ 96SumMet-38
❑ 96SumPreS-38
❑ 96TopNHLP-163
❑ 96TopPicOI-163
❑ 96UppDec-39
❑ 97Pac-265
❑ 97PacCop-265
❑ 97PacEmeGre-265
❑ 97PacIceB-265
❑ 97PacInvNRB-53
❑ 97PacOme-58
❑ 97PacOmeC-58
❑ 97PacOmeDG-58
❑ 97PacOmeEG-58
❑ 97PacOmeG-58
❑ 97PacOmeIB-58
❑ 97PacRed-265
❑ 97PacSil-265
❑ 97ScoAva-15
❑ 97ScoAvaPla-15
❑ 97ScoAvaPre-15
❑ 98O-PChr-11
❑ 98O-PChrR-11
❑ 98Pac-161
❑ 98PacDynI-64
❑ 98PacDynIIB-64
❑ 98PacDynIR-64
❑ 98PacIceB-161
❑ 98PacRed-161
❑ 98Top-11
❑ 98TopO-P-11
❑ 98UppDec-269
❑ 98UppDecE-269
❑ 98UppDecE1o1-269
❑ 98UppDecGR-269
**Kruppke, Gord**
❑ 89ProAHL-312
❑ 90ProAHLIHL-469
❑ 91ProAHLCHL-138
❑ 93Sco-467
❑ 93ScoCan-467
**Kruse, Eric**
❑ 93MicSta-11
**Kruse, Paul**
❑ 88KamBla-15
❑ 907thInnSMC-8
❑ 90ProAHLIHL-621
❑ 91ProAHLCHL-581
❑ 92Cla-115
❑ 94Lea-352
❑ 95Lea-251
❑ 95Pin-66
❑ 95PinArtP-66
❑ 95PinRinC-66
❑ 95PlaOneoOne-130
❑ 95Top-51
❑ 95TopOPCI-51
❑ 96ClaGol-115
❑ 96IsIPos-10
❑ 97Be A PPAD-42
❑ 97Be A PPAPD-42
❑ 97BeAPla-42
❑ 97BeAPlaAut-42
❑ 97PacInvNRB-117
**Krushel, Rod**
❑ 91AirCanSJHL-A12
❑ 91AirCanSJHLAS-33
**Krushelnyski, Mike**
❑ 83BruTeaIss-9
❑ 83OPC-52
❑ 83OPCSti-43
❑ 84OilRedR-26
❑ 84OilTeal-12
❑ 84OPC-248
❑ 84OPCSti-188
❑ 84Top-6
❑ 85OilRedR-26
❑ 85OPC-49
❑ 85OPCSti-223
❑ 85Top-49
❑ 86KraDra-28
❑ 86OilRedR-26
❑ 86OilTeal-26
❑ 86OPC-193
❑ 86OPCSti-74
❑ 86Top-193
❑ 87OilTeal-26
❑ 87OPC-202
❑ 87OPCSti-90
❑ 87PanSti-266
❑ 88KinSmo-14
❑ 88OilTenAnn-79
❑ 88OPC-221
❑ 88OPCSti-226
❑ 89KinSmo-12
❑ 89OPC-104
❑ 89OPCSti-153
❑ 89PanSti-94
❑ 89Top-104
❑ 90Bow-145
❑ 90BowTif-145
❑ 90OPC-167
❑ 90PanSti-245
❑ 90ProSet-121A
❑ 90ProSet-121B
❑ 90ProSet-537
❑ 90Sco-227
❑ 90ScoCan-227
❑ 90ScoRoo-47T
❑ 90Top-167
❑ 90TopTif-167
❑ 90UppDec-394
❑ 90UppDecF-394
❑ 91Bow-166
❑ 91MapLeaP-19
❑ 91OPC-324
❑ 91OPCPre-189
❑ 91PanSti-97
❑ 91Pin-269
❑ 91PinFre-269
❑ 91ProSet-233
❑ 91ProSetFre-233
❑ 91ProSetPla-119
❑ 91ScoAme-33
❑ 91ScoCan-33
❑ 91StaClu-54
❑ 91Top-324
❑ 91UppDec-320
❑ 91UppDecF-320
❑ 92Bow-2
❑ 92DurPan-5
❑ 92OPC-335
❑ 92PanSti-78
❑ 92PanStiFre-78
❑ 92Par-411
❑ 92ParEmel-411
❑ 92Sco-283
❑ 92ScoCan-283
❑ 92StaClu-487
❑ 92Top-450
❑ 92TopGol-450G
❑ 92Ult-421
❑ 92UppDec-87
❑ 93DurSco-31
❑ 93OPCPre-169
❑ 93OPCPreG-169
❑ 93PanSti-229
❑ 93Pin-328
❑ 93PinCan-328
❑ 93Sco-367
❑ 93ScoBla-23
❑ 93ScoCan-367
❑ 93StaClu-306
❑ 93StaCluFDI-306
❑ 93StaCluO-306
❑ 93TopPre-169
❑ 93TopPreG-169
❑ 94BeAPSig-177
❑ 94Lea-438
**Krutov, Vladimir**
❑ 81SweSemHVS-45
❑ 82SweSemHVS-62
❑ 83RusNatT-10
❑ 87RusNatT-12
❑ 89CanuMoh-7
❑ 89Kra-40
❑ 89RusNatT-15
❑ 89SweSemWCS-89
❑ 90OPC-380
❑ 90PanSti-304
❑ 90PanSti-337
❑ 90ProSet-296
❑ 90Sco-273
❑ 90ScoCan-273
❑ 90Top-380
❑ 90TopTif-380
❑ 90UppDec-77
❑ 90UppDecF-77
❑ 95SweGloWC-240
**Kruzich, Gary**
❑ 88FliSpi-11
**Krygier, Bryan**
❑ 92NasKni-20
**Krygier, Todd**
❑ 88ProAHL-63
❑ 89ProAHL-294
❑ 89WhaJunM-12
❑ 90Bow-251
❑ 90BowTif-251
❑ 90OPC-260
❑ 90PanSti-35
❑ 90ProSet-107
❑ 90Sco-237
❑ 90ScoCan-237
❑ 90Top-260
❑ 90TopTif-260
❑ 90UppDec-417
❑ 90UppDecF-417
❑ 90WhaJr7E-17
❑ 91Bow-2
❑ 91CapJun5-15
❑ 91CapKod-15
❑ 91OPC-449
❑ 91PanSti-317
❑ 91Par-408
❑ 91ParFre-408
❑ 91Pin-242
❑ 91Pin-394
❑ 91PinFre-242
❑ 91PinFre-394
❑ 91ProSet-83
❑ 91ProSetFre-83
❑ 91ScoAme-97
❑ 91ScoCan-97
❑ 91ScoCan-637
❑ 91ScoRoo-87T
❑ 91StaClu-45
❑ 91Top-449
❑ 91UppDec-215
❑ 91UppDec-582
❑ 91UppDecF-215
❑ 91UppDecF-582
❑ 92CapKod-17
❑ 92Pin-204
❑ 92PinFre-204
❑ 92ProSet-270
❑ 92Sco-98
❑ 92ScoCan-98
❑ 92StaClu-474
❑ 92Top-502
❑ 92TopGol-502G
❑ 92Ult-438
❑ 93OPCPre-188
❑ 93OPCPreG-188
❑ 93Pow-467
❑ 93Sco-357
❑ 93ScoCan-357
❑ 93StaClu-337
❑ 93StaCluFDI-337
❑ 93StaCluO-337
❑ 93TopPre-188
❑ 93TopPreG-188
❑ 93Ult-448
❑ 93UppDec-207
❑ 94DucCarJr-13
❑ 94Par-258
❑ 94ParGol-258
❑ 94Pin-455
❑ 94PinArtP-455
❑ 94PinRinC-455
❑ 94StaClu-256
❑ 94StaCluFDI-256
❑ 94StaCluMOMS-256
❑ 94StaCluSTWC-256
❑ 94UppDec-477
❑ 94UppDecElelce-477
❑ 95BeAPla-93
❑ 95BeAPSig-S93
❑ 95BeAPSigDC-S93
❑ 95ColCho-241
❑ 95ColChoPC-241
❑ 95ColChoPCP-241
❑ 95Don-335
❑ 95Fin-114
❑ 95FinRef-114
❑ 95Met-3
❑ 95ParInt-276
❑ 95ParIntEl-276
❑ 95Pin-183
❑ 95PinArtP-183
❑ 95PinRinC-183
❑ 95PlaOneoOne-224
❑ 95SkyImp-4
❑ 95StaClu-19
❑ 95StaCluMOMS-19
❑ 95Top-163
❑ 95TopOPCI-163
❑ 95Ult-201
❑ 95UppDec-9
❑ 95UppDecElelce-9
❑ 95UppDecElelceG-9
❑ 96Don-202
❑ 96DonPrePro-202
❑ 96Lea-70
❑ 96LeaPreP-70
❑ 96PlaOneoOne-363
❑ 96Sco-203
❑ 96ScoArtPro-203
❑ 96ScoDeaCAP-203
❑ 96ScoGolB-203
❑ 96ScoSpeAP-203
❑ 97Pac-318
❑ 97PacCop-318
❑ 97PacEmeGre-318
❑ 97PacIceB-318
❑ 97PacRed-318
❑ 97PacSil-318
**Krykov, Valeri**
❑ 93FinnJyvHS-18
❑ 93FinnSIS-99
❑ 94FinnSIS-260
❑ 94FinnSISH-11
❑ 95FinnSIS-115
❑ 96FinnSISR-134
**Krylov, Gennady**
❑ 73SweHocS-115
❑ 73SweWorCS-115
**Krys, Mark**
❑ 91JohChi-4
❑ 93RochAmeKod-14
❑ 96SyrCru-5
❑ 98GerDELE-77
**Kryskow, Dave**
❑ 74CapWhiB-13
❑ 74NHLActSta-320
❑ 74NHLActStaU-10
❑ 74OPCNHL-62
❑ 74Top-62
❑ 75OPCNHL-158
❑ 75Top-158
**Krywulak, Jason**
❑ 907thInnSWHL-27
❑ 917thInnSWHL-178
**Kryznowski, Ed**
❑ 44BeeGro2P-39
❑ 51Par-33
❑ 52Par-29
**Kubicek, Michal**
❑ 94CzeAPSE-101
❑ 95CzeAPSE-62
**Kubina, Pavel**
❑ 98BowBes-133
❑ 98BowBesAR-133
❑ 98BowBesR-133
❑ 98PacOmeH-224
❑ 98PacOmeODI-224
❑ 98PacOmeR-224
❑ 98UppDec-368
❑ 98UppDecE-368
❑ 98UppDecE1o1-368
❑ 98UppDecGR-368
❑ 99Pac-391
❑ 99PacCop-391
❑ 99PacGol-391
❑ 99PacIceB-391
❑ 99PacPreD-391
❑ 99UppDecM-194
❑ 99UppDecMGS-194
❑ 99UppDecMSS-194
❑ 99UppDecMSS-194
**Kubox, Petr**
❑ 96CzeAPSE-222
**Kucera, Frantisek (Frank)**
❑ 89SweSemWCS-184
❑ 90OPCPre-53
❑ 90ProAHLIHL-411
❑ 90ProSet-599
❑ 91BlaCok-13
❑ 91Bow-404
❑ 91ProAHLCHL-495
❑ 91ScoCan-390
❑ 91UppDec-468
❑ 91UppDecF-468
❑ 92Bow-7
❑ 92Par-269
❑ 92ParEmel-269
❑ 92Sco-346
❑ 92ScoCan-346
❑ 92StaClu-438
❑ 92Top-520
❑ 92TopGol-520G
❑ 92Ult-277
❑ 93BlaCok-4
❑ 93Don-439
❑ 93Sco-372
❑ 93ScoCan-372
❑ 93StaClu-442
❑ 93StaCluFDI-442
❑ 93StaCluO-442
❑ 94CzeAPSE-79
❑ 94FinnJaaK-169
❑ 94Lea-392
❑ 94Pin-210
❑ 94PinArtP-210
❑ 94PinRinC-210
❑ 94StaClu-49
❑ 94StaCluFDI-49
❑ 94StaCluMOMS-49
❑ 94StaCluSTWC-49
❑ 95BeAPla-33
❑ 95BeAPSig-S33
❑ 95BeAPSigDC-S33
❑ 95CanGamNHLP-129
❑ 95ColCho-304
❑ 95ColChoPC-304
❑ 95ColChoPCP-304
❑ 95Emo-75
❑ 95FinnSemWC-146
❑ 95Lea-50
❑ 95PlaOneoOne-264
❑ 95Top-84
❑ 95TopOPCI-84
❑ 95Ult-67
❑ 95UltGolM-67
❑ 95UppDecElelce-424
❑ 95UppDecElelceG-424
❑ 96WhaBobS-12
**Kucera, Jiri**
❑ 89SweSemWCS-195
❑ 93FinnSIS-72
❑ 93SweSemWCS-98
❑ 94CzeAPSE-140
❑ 94FinnJaaK-190
❑ 94FinnSIS-14
❑ 94SweLeaE-187

□ 94SweLeaEFA-5
□ 95CzeAPSE-78
□ 95FinnSemWC-150
□ 95FinnSISL-76
□ 95SweGloWC-161
□ 95SweLeaE-83
□ 95SweUppDE-126
□ 96SweSemW-117
**Kucharcik, Tomas**
□ 94CzeAPSE-153
□ 95CzeAPSE-253
**Kucharzj, Jevgenij**
□ 74SweHocS-65
**Kucheran, Bob**
□ 800ShGen-5
**Kuchma, Bill**
□ 84Ott67-16
**Kuchyna, Petr**
□ 94CzeAPSE-170
□ 95CzeAPSE-273
□ 96SweSemW-110
**Kucko, Andrej**
□ 96SloPeeWT-15
**Kuda, Petr**
□ 94CzeAPSE-50
□ 95CzeAPSE-83
**Kudashov, Alexei**
□ 93Cla-42
□ 93Don-345
□ 93Par-260
□ 93ParEmel-260
□ 93Pin-445
□ 93PinCan-445
□ 93Sco-623
□ 93ScoCan-623
□ 93ScoGol-623
□ 93St.JohML-12
□ 93UppDec-427
□ 93UppDecSP-159
□ 94ClaProP-106
□ 94Don-84
□ 94Lea-181
□ 94MapLeaG-10
□ 94OPCPre-78
□ 94OPCPreSE-78
□ 94ParSE-SE180
□ 94ParSEG-SE180
□ 94St.JohML-16
□ 94TopPre-78
□ 94TopPreSE-78
□ 95ColEdgI-23
□ 96GerDELE-284
**Kudelski, Bob**
□ 88ProAHL-206
□ 89KinSmo-20
□ 90KinSmo-20
□ 90OPC-46
□ 90PanSti-232
□ 90ProSet-122
□ 90Sco-305A
□ 90ScoCan-305A
□ 90TopTif-46
□ 90UppDec-433
□ 90UppDecF-433
□ 91Bow-189
□ 91OPC-61
□ 91OPCPre-129
□ 91PanSti-87
□ 91Par-299
□ 91ParFre-299
□ 91Pin-113
□ 91PinFre-113
□ 91ProSet-99
□ 91ProSetFre-99
□ 91ProSetPla-181
□ 91ScoAme-154
□ 91ScoCan-154
□ 91StaClu-40
□ 91Top-61
□ 91UppDec-301
□ 91UppDecF-301
□ 92Bow-12
□ 92OPC-326
□ 92PanSti-69
□ 92PanStiFre-69
□ 92Par-357
□ 92ParEmel-357
□ 92Pin-84
□ 92PinFre-84
□ 92Sco-221
□ 92ScoCan-221
□ 92StaClu-149
□ 92Top-145
□ 92TopGol-145G
□ 93Don-232
□ 93Don-434
□ 93Lea-48
□ 93OPCPre-40
□ 93OPCPreG-40
□ 93PanSti-114
□ 93Par-408
□ 93ParEmel-408
□ 93Pin-38
□ 93PinCan-38
□ 93Pow-170
□ 93Pow-348
□ 93Sco-257
□ 93Sco-549
□ 93ScoCan-257
□ 93ScoCan-549
□ 93ScoGol-549
□ 93SenKraS-12
□ 93StaClu-120

□ 93StaCluFDI-120
□ 93StaCluFDIO-120
□ 93StaCluO-120
□ 93TopPre-40
□ 93TopPreG-40
□ 93Ult-85
□ 93UppDec-17
□ 93UppDecSP-110
□ 94CanGamNHLP-105
□ 94Don-227
□ 94EASpo-95
□ 94Fla-64
□ 94Fle-79
□ 94Lea-314
□ 94OPCPre-245
□ 94OPCPreSE-245
□ 94Par-83
□ 94ParGol-83
□ 94ParSEV-35
□ 94Pin-284
□ 94PinArtP-284
□ 94PinRinC-284
□ 94Sco-28
□ 94ScoGol-28
□ 94ScoPla-28
□ 94ScoPlaTS-28
□ 94Sel-55
□ 94SelGol-55
□ 94SP-46
□ 94SPDieCut-46
□ 94StaCluMO-43
□ 94TopFinI-23
□ 94TopPre-245
□ 94TopPreSE-245
□ 94Ult-80
□ 94UppDec-376
□ 94UppDecEleIce-376
□ 94UppDecSPI-SP29
□ 94UppDecSPIDC-SP29
□ 95ColCho-226
□ 95ColChoPC-226
□ 95ColChoPCP-226
□ 95PlaOneoOne-260
□ 95ProMag-87
□ 95UppDec-138
□ 95UppDecEleIce-138
□ 95UppDecEleIceG-138
□ 96NHLProSTA-87
**Kudinov, Andrei**
□ 94BinRan-8
□ 95BinRan-11
**Kudrna, Ladislav**
□ 95CzeAPSE-146
**Kuenzi, Werner**
□ 72SweSemWC-146
**Kufflick, Jerome**
□ 95SasBla-11
**Kuhl, Marcus**
□ 79PanSti-113
□ 82SweSemHVS-110
□ 94GerDELE-272
□ 95GerDELE-263
**Kuhn, Bernd**
□ 72SweSemWC-110
**Kuhn, Florian**
□ 96GerDELE-116
**Kuhn, Tyler**
□ 91AirCanSJHL-D45
□ 91AirCanSJHLAS-17
□ 92MPSPhoSJHL-19
**Kuhnhackl, Erich**
□ 79PanSti-103
□ 82SweSemHVS-112
□ 98GerDELE-340
**Kuhnhauser, Bernd**
□ 94GerDELE-87
□ 95GerDELE-92
□ 96GerDELE-428
□ 96GerDELE-280
□ 98GerDELE-303
**Kuhnke, Harald**
□ 94GerDELE-135
□ 95GerDELE-137
**Kuivalainen, Pasi**
□ 93FinnJyvHS-164
□ 93FinnSIS-161
□ 94FinnJaaK-2
□ 94FinnSIS-1
□ 94FinnSISMN-1
□ 94FinnSISNP-9
□ 95FinnSemWC-1
□ 95FinnSIS-272
□ 95FinnSISGG-9
□ 95FinnSISL-64
□ 96FinnSISRATG-5
□ 96FinnSISRMA-5
**Kujala, Petri**
□ 93FinnSIS-144
□ 95FinnSIS-269
**Kukacka, Zbynek**
□ 917thInnSOHL-306
□ 94CzeAPSE-82
□ 98GerDELE-76
**Kuki, Arto**
□ 94FinnSISND-4
□ 95FinnSIS-395
□ 96FinnSISRRE-7
**Kukuk, Philip**
□ 94GerDELE-20
**Kukulowicz, Adolph**
□ 52JunBluT-78
**Kulabuchov, Vadim**
□ 94CzeAPSE-270
□ 95GerDELE-426

**Kulagin, Boris**
□ 74SweHocS-66
**Kulak, Stu**
□ 81VicCou-9
□ 82VicCou-11
□ 83FreExp-23
□ 86Canu-7
□ 86OilRedR-8
□ 86OilTeal-8
□ 87NordGenF-17
□ 88OilTenAnn-44
□ 89ProAHL-33
□ 90KanCitBla-9
□ 90ProAHLIHL-586
□ 94CenHocL-83
**Kulich, Vladimir**
□ 95SloPeeWT-12
**Kulikov, Alexander**
□ 74SweHocS-84
**Kullman, Ed**
□ 44BeeGro2P-332
□ 51Par-101
□ 52Par-18
□ 53Par-61
**Kulmala, Arto**
□ 94FinnSIS-78
□ 95FinnSIS-114
□ 96FinnSISR-128
**Kulonen, Timo**
□ 93FinnJyvHS-226
□ 93FinnSIS-189
□ 94FinnSIS-237
□ 95FinnSIS-139
**Kultanen, Jarno**
□ 94FinnSIS-228
□ 95FinnSIS-73
**Kummer, Wolfgang**
□ 93SweSemWCS-164
□ 94GerDELE-96
□ 95GerDELE-97
□ 96GerDELE-131
□ 98GerDELE-312
**Kumpel, Mark**
□ 84FreExp-19
□ 85NordGenF-14
□ 85NordMcD-11
□ 85NordPro-13
□ 86NordGenF-13
□ 86NordMcD-13
□ 89JetSaf-18
□ 90JetIGA-17
□ 90OPC-444
□ 91JetPanTS-14
□ 91ProAHLCHL-184
**Kumstat, Pavel**
□ 96CzeAPSE-200
**Kunast, Christian**
□ 94GerDELE-265
□ 95GerDELE-243
□ 96GerDELE-114
□ 98GerDELE-84
**Kunce, Daniel**
□ 94GerDELE-183
□ 95GerDELE-175
□ 96GerDELE-133
□ 98GerDELE-266
**Kunce, G.**
□ 95GerDELE-174
□ 95GerDELE-433
**Kungle, Jeff**
□ 91AirCanSJHL-B41
□ 91AirCanSJHLAS-1
□ 96PeoRiv-13
□ 96PeoRivPA-14
**Kuntar, Les**
□ 92FreCan-14
□ 93ClaProPro-72
□ 93FreCan-13
□ 94Par-114
□ 94ParGol-114
□ 95ColEdgITW-G9
**Kuntos, Jiri**
□ 94CzeAPSE-7
□ 95CzeAPSE-106
**Kuntz, Al**
□ 51LavDaiS-108
□ 52St.LawS-66
**Kuntz, Dean**
□ 88SasBla-4
**Kuntz, Mark**
□ 85MedHatT-3
□ 88LetHur-14
□ 91RicRen-12
□ 92RicRen-10
**Kuokkonen, Jouni**
□ 96SeaThu-13
**Kuoppala, Ismo**
□ 94FinnSIS-354
□ 95FinnSIS-87
□ 96FinnSISR-52
**Kupacs, Artur**
□ 94GreMon-13
**Kupaks, Arturs**
□ 96TolSto-18
**Kupari, Marko**
□ 93FinnSIS-155
**Kupka, Tomas**
□ 94CzeAPSE-266
□ 95CzeAPSE-143
**Kurashov, Konstantin**
□ 90OPC-469
□ 91OPCIns-52R

**Kurawski, Mark**
□ 89ProIHL-52
**Kurjenniemi, Janne**
□ 95FinnSIS-66
**Kurkinen, Risto**
□ 90SweSemE-111
□ 91SweSemE-116
□ 91SweSemWCS-16
□ 93FinnJyvHS-189
□ 93FinnSIS-158
□ 94FinnSISFI-15
□ 95FinnSISL-51
**Kurri, Jari**
□ 80PepCap-29
□ 81OilRedR-17
□ 81OPC-107
□ 81OPCSti-11
□ 81OPCSti-211
□ 81Top-18
□ 82OilRedR-17
□ 82OPC-111
□ 82OPCSti-108
□ 82OPCSti-109
□ 82PosCer-6
□ 83OilMcD-5
□ 83OPC-34
□ 83OPCSti-104
□ 83PufSti-5
□ 83Vac-31
□ 847EDis-19
□ 84KelAccD-1
□ 84OilRedR-17
□ 84OilTeal-13
□ 84OPC-215
□ 84OPCSti-249
□ 84OPCSti-249
□ 84OPCSti-250
□ 84Top-52
□ 84Top-161
□ 857ECreCar-6
□ 85OilRedR-17
□ 85OPC-155
□ 85OPC-261
□ 85OPCSti-121
□ 85OPCSti-201
□ 85OPCSti-231
□ 85Top-155
□ 85TopStiIns-3
□ 86KraDra-29
□ 86OilRedR-17
□ 86OilTeal-17
□ 86OPC-208
□ 86OPC-258
□ 86OPCSti-73
□ 86OPCSti-73
□ 86OPCSti-118
□ 86OPCSti-185
□ 86Top-108
□ 86TopBoxB-H
□ 86TopStiIns-10
□ 87OilTeal-17
□ 87OPC-148
□ 87OPCMin-21
□ 87OPCSti-82
□ 87OPCSti-117
□ 87PanSti-262
□ 87Top-148
□ 87TopStiIns-4
□ 88EssAllSta-22
□ 88OilTeal-14
□ 88OilTenAnn-41
□ 88OPC-147
□ 88OPCSti-227
□ 88PanSti-59
□ 88Top-147
□ 89Kra-13
□ 89KraAllSS-5
□ 89OilTeal-12
□ 89OPC-43
□ 89OPCBoxB-I
□ 89OPCSti-221
□ 89PanSti-73
□ 89PanSti-181
□ 89Top-43
□ 89TopBoxB-I
□ 90Bow-191
□ 90BowHatTri-19
□ 90BowTif-191
□ 90Kra-68
□ 90OPC-5
□ 90OPC-108
□ 90PanSti-222
□ 90ProSet-87A
□ 90ProSet-87B
□ 90ProSet-348A
□ 90ProSet-348B
□ 90Sco-158
□ 90Sco-348
□ 90ScoCan-158
□ 90ScoCan-348
□ 90Top-5
□ 90Top-108
□ 90TopTif-108
□ 90UppDec-146
□ 90UppDecF-146
□ 91Kra-67
□ 91OPC-295
□ 91OPCPre-111
□ 91Par-72
□ 91Par-210
□ 91Par-223
□ 91ParFre-72
□ 91ParFre-210

□ 91ParFre-223
□ 91Pin-48
□ 91PinFre-48
□ 91ProSet-93
□ 91ProSetFre-93
□ 91ProSetPla-48
□ 91ScoAme-600
□ 91ScoCan-600
□ 91ScoRoo-50T
□ 91SweSemWCS-18
□ 91Top-295
□ 91UppDec-24
□ 91UppDec-366
□ 91UppDecF-24
□ 91UppDecF-366
□ 92Bow-94
□ 92KenPol-2
□ 92OPC-205
□ 92PanSti-66
□ 92PanStiFre-66
□ 92Par-67
□ 92Par-445
□ 92ParEmel-67
□ 92ParEmel-445
□ 92Pin-60
□ 92PinFre-60
□ 92ProSet-68
□ 92Sco-398
□ 92ScoCan-398
□ 92StaClu-138
□ 92Top-51
□ 92TopGol-51G
□ 92Ult-85
□ 92UltImp-11
□ 92UppDec-218
□ 92UppDecWJG-WG4
□ 93Cla-121
□ 93Don-151
□ 93Lea-240
□ 93McDUppD-8
□ 93OPCPre-206
□ 93OPCPreG-206
□ 93PanSti-202
□ 93Par-365
□ 93ParEmel-365
□ 93Pin-75
□ 93PinAllS-35
□ 93PinAllSC-35
□ 93PinCan-75
□ 93Pow-118
□ 93PowGloG-4
□ 93Sco-100
□ 93ScoCan-100
□ 93Sco-446
□ 93ScoCan-446
□ 93ScoDynDUS-7
□ 93ScoIntS-7
□ 93ScoIntSC-7
□ 93StaClu-400
□ 93StaCluAS-12
□ 93StaCluFDI-400
□ 93StaCluMasP-14
□ 93StaCluMasPW-14
□ 93StaCluO-400
□ 93SweSemWCS-67
□ 93TopPre-206
□ 93TopPreG-206
□ 93Ult-165
□ 93UppDec-332
□ 93UppDecLAS-29
□ 94BeAP99A-G16
□ 94BeAPla-R25
□ 94CanGamNHLP-127
□ 94Don-93
□ 94Fin-81
□ 94FinnJaaK-24
□ 94FinnJaaK-346
□ 94FinnSIS-207
□ 94FinnSISGS-2
□ 94FinRef-81
□ 94FinRinL-3
□ 94FinSupTW-81
□ 94Fla-81
□ 94Fle-96
□ 94HocWit-89
□ 94Lea-104
□ 94LeaLim-105
□ 94OPCPre-25
□ 94OPCPreSE-25
□ 94Par-104
□ 94ParGol-104
□ 94ParSEES-ES9
□ 94ParSEV-24
□ 94Pin-35
□ 94PinArtP-35
□ 94PinRinC-35
□ 94PinWorEdi-WE7
□ 94PosCerBB-14
□ 94Sco-114
□ 94ScoGol-114
□ 94ScoPla-114
□ 94ScoPlaTS-114
□ 94Sel-71
□ 94SelGol-71
□ 94SP-57
□ 94SPDieCut-57
□ 94TopPre-25
□ 94TopPreSE-25
□ 94Ult-100
□ 94UltGloGre-5
□ 94UltGloGreS-5
□ 94UppDec-293
□ 94UppDec-559
□ 94UppDecEleIce-293
□ 94UppDecEleIce-559
□ 94UppDecSPI-SP37
□ 94UppDecSPIDC-SP37

□ 95BeAPla-201
□ 95BeAPSig-S201
□ 95BeAPSigDC-S201
□ 95CanGamNHLP-134
□ 95ColCho-16
□ 95ColChoPC-16
□ 95ColChoPCP-16
□ 95Don-133
□ 95Emo-83
□ 95FinnJaaKLAC-2
□ 95FinnSemWC-17
□ 95FinnSemWC-204
□ 95FinnSISL-16
□ 95FinnSISLSS-7
□ 95FinnSISSpe-4
□ 95Lea-122
□ 95ParInt-102
□ 95ParIntEl-102
□ 95ParIntEl-239
□ 95Pin-22
□ 95PinArtP-22
□ 95PinGloG-4
□ 95PinRinC-22
□ 95PlaOneoOne-271
□ 95ProMag-68
□ 95Sco-115
□ 95ScoBlaIce-115
□ 95ScoBlaIceAP-115
□ 95SelCer-35
□ 95SelCerMG-35
□ 95SkyImp-81
□ 95StaClu-151
□ 95StaCluMOMS-151
□ 95Sum-32
□ 95SumArtP-32
□ 95SumIce-32
□ 95SweGloWC-137
□ 95Top-239
□ 95TopOPCI-239
□ 95UppDec-372
□ 95UppDecEleIce-372
□ 95UppDecEleIceG-372
□ 95UppDecSpE-SE41
□ 95UppDecSpEdiG-SE41
□ 95Zen-50
□ 96ColCho-173
□ 96DonCanI-49
□ 96DonCanIGPP-49
□ 96DonCanIRPP-49
□ 96DonEli-85
□ 96DonEliDCS-85
□ 96Duc-23
□ 96MetUni-3
□ 96NHLProSTA-68
□ 96PlaOneoOne-412
□ 96SelCer-86
□ 96SelCerAP-86
□ 96SelCerBlu-86
□ 96SelCerMB-86
□ 96SelCerMG-86
□ 96SelCerMR-86
□ 96SelCerRed-86
□ 96SP-3
□ 96Sum-47
□ 96SumArtP-47
□ 96SumIce-47
□ 96SumMet-47
□ 96SumPreS-47
□ 96SweSemW-24
□ 96SweSemWNS-NS4
□ 96TopPic5C-FC3
□ 96Ult-3
□ 96UltGolM-3
□ 96UppDec-212
□ 96UppDecGN-X24
□ 97Be A PPAD-7
□ 97Be A PPAPD-7
□ 97BeAPla-7
□ 97BeAPlaAut-7
□ 97ColCho-10
□ 97PacCroR-35
□ 97PacCroREG-35
□ 97PacCroRIB-35
□ 97PacCroRS-35
□ 97PacOme-59
□ 97PacOmeCop-59
□ 97PacOmeDG-59
□ 97PacOmeEG-59
□ 97PacOmeG-59
□ 97PacOmeIB-59
□ 97PacPar-51
□ 97PacParC-51
□ 97PacParDG-51
□ 97PacParEG-51
□ 97PacParIB-51
□ 97PacParRed-51
□ 97PacParSil-51
□ 97PacRev-34
□ 97PacRevC-34
□ 97PacRevE-34
□ 97PacRevIB-34
□ 97PacRevR-34
□ 97PacRevS-34
□ 97PacSlaSDC-1B
□ 97PinIns-113
□ 97ScoAva-5
□ 97ScoAvaPla-5
□ 97ScoAvaPre-5
□ 97SPAut-42
□ 98McDGreT-T9
□ 98Pac-162
□ 98PacIceB-162
□ 98PacRed-162

□ 98UppDecFIT-FT8
□ 98UppDecFITQ1-FT8
□ 98UppDecFITQ2-FT8
□ 98UppDecFITQ3-FT8
□ 99RetHoc-108
□ 99UppDecCL-48
□ 99UppDecCLCLC-48
□ 99UppDecRG-G8A
□ 99UppDecRG-108
□ 99UppDecRGI-G8A
□ 99UppDecRII-JK
□ 99UppDecRIL1-JK
□ 99UppDecRP-108
**Kurt, Gary**
□ 710PC-181
□ 720PC-306
□ 750PCWHA-126
□ 75RoaPhoWHA-1
□ 760PCWHA-102
□ 76RoaPhoWHA-10
**Kurtenbach, Orland**
□ 44BeeGro2P-40
□ 61ShiCoi-14
□ 61Top-15
□ 61UniOilW-11
□ 63Top-20
□ 64BeeGro3P-15
□ 64BeeGro3P-137
□ 64BeeGro3P-172
□ 64CocCap-4
□ 64Top-18
□ 64TorSta-25
□ 65Coc-105
□ 65MapLeaWB-13
□ 65Top-20
□ 66Top-25
□ 66TopUSAT-25
□ 67Top-87
□ 680PC-170
□ 68ShiCoi-100
□ 690PC-188
□ 70CanuRoyB-9
□ 70ColSta-23
□ 70DadCoo-67
□ 70EssPowPla-53
□ 700PC-117
□ 700PCDec-45
□ 70PosCerS-7
□ 70SarProSta-212
□ 70Top-117
□ 71Baz-13
□ 71CanuRoyB-6
□ 71LetActR-7
□ 710PC-42
□ 710PCPos-12
□ 710PCTBoo-20
□ 71SarProSta-216
□ 71Top-42
□ 71TorSun-282
□ 72CanuRoyB-9
□ 720PC-141
□ 720PC-149
□ 720PCPlaC-22
□ 72SarProSta-215
□ 72SweSemWC-209
□ 72Top-46
□ 73CanuRoyB-9
□ 73MacMil-11
□ 730PC-4
□ 73Top-157
**Kurtenbach, Terry**
□ 94GuiFla-3
□ 95GuiFla-4
□ 95GuiFla-26
□ 96GuiFla-4
□ 97GuiFla-5
**Kurtz, Justin**
□ 94ParSE-SE262
□ 94ParSEG-SE262
□ 95SigRooA-23
□ 95SigRooAPC-23
□ 95SlaMemC-32
□ 97BowCHL-111
□ 97BowCHLOPC-111
**Kurvers, Tom**
□ 84CanaPos-11
□ 85CanaPla-2
□ 85CanaPla-7
□ 85CanaPos-15
□ 85CanaPos-7
□ 85OPC-219
□ 85OPCSti-129
□ 86OPCSti-10
□ 86SabBluS-18
□ 86SabBluSSma-18
□ 88DevCar-15
□ 88OPC-222
□ 89OPC-9
□ 89OPCSti-44
□ 89PanSti-252
□ 89Top-9
□ 90CanuMoh-12
□ 90OPC-11
□ 90PanSti-287
□ 90ProSet-282
□ 90Sco-142
□ 90ScoCan-142
□ 90Top-11
□ 90TopTif-11
□ 90UppDec-160

❑ 90UppDecF-160
❑ 91Bow-319
❑ 91MapLeaPTS-11
❑ 91OPCPre-98
❑ 91PanSti-43
❑ 91Par-112
❑ 91ParFre-112
❑ 91Pin-7
❑ 91PinFre-7
❑ 91ProSet-244
❑ 91ProSet-428
❑ 91ProSetFre-244
❑ 91ProSetFre-428
❑ 91ScoAme-174
❑ 91ScoCan-174
❑ 91ScoCan-568
❑ 91ScoRoo-18T
❑ 92Bow-259
❑ 92OPC-202
❑ 92Pin-324
❑ 92PinFre-324
❑ 92Sco-232
❑ 92ScoCan-232
❑ 92StaClu-409
❑ 92Top-118
❑ 92TopGol-118G
❑ 92UppDec-292
❑ 93OPCPre-279
❑ 93OPCPreG-279
❑ 93Par-392
❑ 93ParEmel-392
❑ 93Pow-384
❑ 93StaClu-279
❑ 93StaCluFDI-279
❑ 93StaCluO-279
❑ 93TopPre-279
❑ 93TopPreG-279
❑ 93Ult-368
❑ 93UppDec-381
❑ 94DucCarJr-14
❑ 94Fle-5
❑ 94Lea-449
❑ 94ParSE-SE4
❑ 94ParSEG-SE4
❑ 94Pin-380
❑ 94PinArtP-380
❑ 94PinRinC-380
❑ 94UppDec-123
❑ 94UppDecEleIce-123
❑ 95StaCluMO-24
**Kurzawski, Mark**
❑ 88ProIHL-100
**Kushner, Dale**
❑ 85MedHatT-12
❑ 89ProAHL-243
❑ 90FlyPos-14
❑ 90OPCPre-54
❑ 90ProAHLIHL-28
❑ 91Bow-247
❑ 91OPC-415
❑ 91ProAHLCHL-268
❑ 91ScoCan-512
❑ 91StaClu-349
❑ 91Top-415
❑ 91UppDec-429
❑ 91UppDecF-429
❑ 94St.JohF-11
**Kuskin, Viktor**
❑ 71SweHocS-30
❑ 72SweSemWC-4
**Kuster, Henry**
❑ 95BowDraPro-P21
❑ 95Cla-63
❑ 95ClaAut-12
❑ 95ClaCHLAS-AS3
❑ 95MedHatT-9
❑ 96MedHatT-9
**Kustra, Damon**
❑ 89SasBla-3
**Kuusisaari, Juha**
❑ 95FinnSIS-346
**Kuusisto, Jarmo**
❑ 89SweSemWCS-36
❑ 93FinnJyvHS-230
❑ 93FinnSIS-186
❑ 94FinnSIS-5
❑ 94FinnSISMN-3
❑ 95FinnSIS-169
❑ 95FinnSIS-182
❑ 95FinnSISL-30
❑ 95FinnSISSpe-5
**Kuusisto, Riku**
❑ 93FinnSIS-274
**Kuwabara, Ryan**
❑ 897thInnSOHL-55
❑ 907thInnSOHL-85
❑ 917thInnSOHL-303
❑ 92FreCan-15
❑ 93FreCan-14
**Kuzela, Milan**
❑ 74SweHocS-12
**Kuzkin, Victor**
❑ 69SweHocS-6
❑ 73SweHocS-100
❑ 74SweSemHVS-45
❑ 91FutTreC72-41
**Kuzmin, Valeri**
❑ 74SweHocS-53
**Kuzminsky, Alexander**
❑ 91UppDec-656
❑ 91UppDecCWJC-17
❑ 91UppDecF-656
**Kuznetsov, Juri**
❑ 90OPC-489
❑ 93SweSemE-5
❑ 94FinnSIS-316
❑ 95FinnSIS-3
**Kuznetsov, Maxim**
❑ 94Sel-157
❑ 94SelGol-157
❑ 95SigRooFF-FF7
❑ 95SigRooFFS-FF7
**Kuznetsov, Viktor**
❑ 74SweHocS-54
**Kuznik, Greg**
❑ 95SeaThu-13
❑ 96SeaThu-22
❑ 98BowCHL-47
❑ 98BowCHLGA-47
❑ 98BowCHLOI-47
❑ 98BowChrC-47
❑ 98BowChrCGA-47
❑ 98BowChrCGAR-47
❑ 98BowChrCOI-47
❑ 98BowChrCOIR-47
❑ 98BowChrCR-47
❑ 98FloEve-11
**Kvalevog, Toby**
❑ 93DonTeaUSA-11
❑ 93Pin-480
❑ 93PinCan-480
❑ 93UppDec-555
**Kvartalnov, Andrei**
❑ 91OPCIns-53R
❑ 95SwiHNL-279
❑ 95SwiHNL-526
**Kvartalnov, Dmitri**
❑ 89RusNatT-16
❑ 91ProAHLCHL-313
❑ 92BruPos-4
❑ 92Cla-93
❑ 92Cla-120
❑ 92ClaLPs-LP6
❑ 92OPCPre-6
❑ 92Par-7
❑ 92Par-222
❑ 92ParEmel-7
❑ 92ParEmel-222
❑ 92Pin-405
❑ 92PinFre-405
❑ 92RusStaRA-9
❑ 92RusStaRA-18
❑ 92Ult-252
❑ 92UltImp-12
❑ 92UppDec-455
❑ 92UppDec-561
❑ 93ClaProPBC-BC17
❑ 93ClaProPro-32
❑ 93ClaProPro-AU1
❑ 93Don-27
❑ 93Lea-143
❑ 93OPCPre-197
❑ 93OPCPreG-197
❑ 93PanSti-7
❑ 93Par-287
❑ 93ParEmel-287
❑ 93Pin-161
❑ 93PinCan-161
❑ 93Pow-20
❑ 93PowSecYS-4
❑ 93Sco-187
❑ 93ScoCan-187
❑ 93TopPre-197
❑ 93TopPreG-197
❑ 93Ult-82
❑ 93UppDec-19
❑ 93UppDecLAS-55
❑ 94EASpo-195
❑ 95SwiHNL-206
❑ 96ClaGol-93
❑ 96ClaGol-120
**Kvasha, Oleg**
❑ 98Be A PPA-210
❑ 98Be A PPAA-210
❑ 98Be A PPAAF-210
❑ 98Be A PPSE-210
❑ 98Be APG-210
❑ 98BowBes-126
❑ 98BowBesAR-126
❑ 98BowBesR-126
❑ 98PacCroR-60
❑ 98PacCroRLS-60
❑ 98PacDynI-83
❑ 98PacDynIIB-83
❑ 98PacDynIR-83
❑ 98PacOmeH-108
❑ 98PacOmeODI-108
❑ 98PacOmeR-108
❑ 98SP Aut-98
❑ 98TopGolLC1-25
❑ 98TopGolLC1B-25
❑ 98TopGolLC1BOoO-25
❑ 98TopGolLC1OoO-25
❑ 98TopGolLC1R-25
❑ 98TopGolLC1ROoO-25
❑ 98TopGolLC2-25
❑ 98TopGolLC2B-25
❑ 98TopGolLC2BOoO-25
❑ 98TopGolLC2OoO-25
❑ 98TopGolLC2R-25
❑ 98TopGolLC2ROoO-25
❑ 98TopGolLC3-25
❑ 98TopGolLC3B-25
❑ 98TopGolLC3BOoO-25
❑ 98TopGolLC3OoO-25
❑ 98TopGolLC3R-25
❑ 98TopGolLC3ROoO-25
❑ 98UppDec-416
❑ 98UppDecE-416
❑ 98UppDecE1o1-416
❑ 98UppDecGN-GN24
❑ 98UppDecGNQ1-GN24
❑ 98UppDecGNQ2-GN24
❑ 98UppDecGNQ3-GN24
❑ 98UppDecGR-416
❑ 98UppDecM-92
❑ 98UppDecMGS-92
❑ 98UppDecMSS-92
❑ 98UppDecMSS-92
❑ 99Pac-174
❑ 99PacCop-174
❑ 99PacGol-174
❑ 99PacIceB-174
❑ 99PacPreD-174
❑ 99QuePeeWHWCCS-12
❑ 99SP AutPS-98
❑ 99UppDecM-89
❑ 99UppDecMGS-89
❑ 99UppDecMSS-89
❑ 99UppDecMSS-89
**Kverka, Jaromir**
❑ 94CzeAPSE-89
❑ 95CzeAPSE-191
**Kwasigroch, Piotr**
❑ 89SweSemWCS-148
❑ 94GerDELE-164
❑ 95GerDELE-163
❑ 96GerDELE-237
**Kwasniewski, Ken**
❑ 93RenEng-13
**Kwiatkowski, Darren**
❑ 87RegPat-14
**Kwiatkowski, Jason**
❑ 907thInnSWHL-276
❑ 90PriAlbR-7
❑ 917thInnSWHL-245
❑ 91PriAlbR-8
❑ 92TacRoc-11
**Kwiatkowski, Joel**
❑ 97BowCHL-84
❑ 97BowCHLOPC-84
❑ 98BowCHL-45
❑ 98BowCHLGA-45
❑ 98BowCHLOI-45
❑ 98BowChrC-45
❑ 98BowChrCGA-45
❑ 98BowChrCGAR-45
❑ 98BowChrCOI-45
❑ 98BowChrCOIR-45
❑ 98BowChrCR-45
**Kwong, Larry**
❑ 51LavDaiQSHL-73
❑ 52St.LawS-19
**Kyhos, Vladimir**
❑ 95CzeAPSE-149
❑ 96CzeAPSE-166
**Kyle, Doug**
❑ 83SasBla-20
**Kyle, Gus**
❑ 44BeeGro2P-333
**Kyle, Walt**
❑ 51Par-21
❑ 93SeaThu-11
**Kyle, William**
❑ 51LavDaiQSHL-39
**Kyndl, Roman**
❑ 96SloPeeWT-16
**Kypreos, Nick**
❑ 83NorBayC-13
❑ 89CapTeaIss-12
❑ 90Bow-67
❑ 90BowTif-67
❑ 90CapKod-11
❑ 90CapPos-11
❑ 90CapSmo-10
❑ 90OPC-440
❑ 90ProSet-551
❑ 91Bow-301
❑ 91CapJun5-16
❑ 91CapKod-16
❑ 91OPC-511
❑ 91PanSti-204
❑ 91Par-411
❑ 91ParFre-411
❑ 91ProSet-513
❑ 91ProSetFre-513
❑ 91ScoCan-432
❑ 91StaClu-307
❑ 91Top-511
❑ 92Par-297
❑ 92ParEmel-297
❑ 92Top-193
❑ 92TopGol-193G
❑ 92Ult-301
❑ 92UppDec-447
❑ 92WhaDai-13
❑ 93Don-140
❑ 93Lea-414
❑ 93Pin-83
❑ 93PinCan-83
❑ 93Pow-105
❑ 93Sco-404
❑ 93ScoCan-404
❑ 93UppDec-11
❑ 94BeAPla-R21
❑ 94BeAPSig-54
❑ 94Lea-406
❑ 94Pin-408
❑ 94PinArtP-408
❑ 94PinRinC-408
❑ 94StaClu-154
❑ 94StaCluFDI-154
❑ 94StaCluMOMS-154
❑ 94StaCluSTWC-154
❑ 95UppDec-493
❑ 95UppDecEleIce-493
❑ 95UppDecEleIceG-493
❑ 97Be A PPAD-128
❑ 97Be A PPAPD-128
❑ 97BeAPla-128
❑ 97BeAPlaAut-128
**Kyro, Roger**
❑ 92UppDec-226
❑ 93SweSemE-12
❑ 95SweLeaE-173
❑ 95SweUppDE-27
**Kysela, Daniel**
❑ 94CzeAPSE-118
❑ 96CzeAPSE-195
**Kysela, Robert**
❑ 94CzeAPSE-220
❑ 95CzeAPSE-170
❑ 96CzeAPSE-179
**Kyte, Jim**
❑ 82Jet-10
❑ 83Jet-10
❑ 83Vac-128
❑ 84JetPol-10
❑ 85JetPol-9
❑ 86JetBor-11
❑ 87Jet-11
❑ 87OPC-226
❑ 87PanSti-362
❑ 88JetPol-12
❑ 88OPCSti-145
❑ 89OPC-295
❑ 89OPCSti-140
❑ 90ProAHLIHL-374
❑ 91FlamIGA-6
❑ 91Pin-398
❑ 91PinFre-398
❑ 91ProSet-612
❑ 91ProSetFre-612
❑ 91ScoCan-547
❑ 93LasVegThu-17
❑ 94ClaEnf-E9
❑ 94LasVegThu-9
**L'Henry, Fabrice**
❑ 94FreNatT-17
**L'Heureux, Conrad**
❑ 51LavDaiLSJ-28
**L'Heureux, Wilf**
❑ 23V1281PauC-17
**Laaksonen, Antti**
❑ 96DenUniPio-6
❑ 98PacDynI-12
❑ 98PacDynIIB-12
❑ 98PacDynIR-12
❑ 98UppDec-223
❑ 98UppDecE-223
❑ 98UppDecE1o1-223
❑ 98UppDecGR-223
❑ 98UppDecTD-102
**Laaksonen, Mika**
❑ 94FinnSIS-137
❑ 95FinnSIS-71
❑ 96FinnSISR-73
**Laaksonen, Mikko**
❑ 95FinnSIS-347
**Laaksonen, Tom**
❑ 95FinnSIS-208
**Laamanen, Jukka**
❑ 95FinnSIS-263
❑ 96FinnSISR-57
**Laan, John**
❑ 94BraSmo-15
**Laapas, Marru**
❑ 95FinnSIS-33
❑ 96FinnSISR-140
**Laattikainen, Arto**
❑ 98SPXTopP-70
❑ 98SPXTopPF-70
❑ 98SPXTopPR-70
❑ 98UppDecBD-102
❑ 98UppDecQD-102
**Labadie, Michel**
❑ 52JunBluT-70
❑ 62QueAce-14
**Labanski, Greg**
❑ 95Sla-227
**Labarbera, Jason**
❑ 98BowCHL-140
❑ 98BowCHLAuB-A2
❑ 98BowCHLAuG-A2
❑ 98BowCHLAuS-A2
❑ 98BowCHLGA-140
❑ 98BowCHLOI-140
❑ 98BowChrC-140
❑ 98BowChrCGA-140
❑ 98BowChrCGAR-140
❑ 98BowChrCOI-140
❑ 98BowChrCOIR-140
❑ 98BowChrCR-140
**Labatte, Neil**
❑ 78BluPos-14
**Labbe, Jean-Francois**
❑ 907thInnSQMJHL-88
❑ 917thInnSQMJHL-122
❑ 93ThuBayS-1
**Labelle, Marc**
❑ 91ProAHLCHL-87
**Labelle, Serge**
❑ 917thInnSQMJHL-20
**Labenski, Greg**
❑ 98BowCHL-6
❑ 98BowCHLGA-6
❑ 98BowCHLOI-6
❑ 98BowChrC-6
❑ 98BowChrCGA-6
❑ 98BowChrCGAR-6
❑ 98BowChrCOI-6
❑ 98BowChrCOIR-6
❑ 98BowChrCR-6
**Laberge, Gilles**
❑ 84ChiSag-15
**Labine, Leo**
❑ 44BeeGro2P-41
❑ 44BeeGro2P-184
❑ 52Par-81
❑ 53Par-93
❑ 54Par-61
❑ 54Top-19
❑ 55BruPho-8
❑ 57BruTealss-11
❑ 57Top-9
❑ 58Top-4
❑ 59Top-7
❑ 60ShiCoi-117
❑ 60Top-13
❑ 61Par-33
❑ 61ShiCoi-64
❑ 61UniOilW-3
❑ 62Par-26
❑ 91UltOriS-50
❑ 91UltOriSF-50
❑ 93ParParRCI-10
❑ 94ParMisL-4
**Laborte, Benoit**
❑ 95FinnSemWC-198
**Labossiere, Gaston**
❑ 51LavDaiLSJ-51
**Labossiere, Gord**
❑ 44BeeGro2P-334
❑ 61SudWol-12
❑ 62SudWol-14
❑ 64BeeGro3P-138
❑ 65QueAce-11
❑ 68OPC-38
❑ 68ShiCoi-54
❑ 68Top-38
❑ 69OPC-109
❑ 69Top-109
❑ 70EssPowPla-152
❑ 70OPC-38
❑ 70Top-38
❑ 72OPC-303
❑ 75OPCWHA-89
**Labraaten, Dan**
❑ 70SweHocS-76
❑ 71SweHocS-17
❑ 71SweHocS-166
❑ 72SweHocS-161
❑ 72SweSemWC-67
❑ 73SweHocS-55
❑ 73SweWorCS-55
❑ 74SweHocS-236
❑ 74SweSemHVS-23
❑ 77OPCWHA-57
❑ 79OPC-92
❑ 79RedWinP-9
❑ 79Top-92
❑ 80OPC-217
❑ 80Top-217
❑ 81FlamPos-9
❑ 81OPC-42
❑ 83SweSemE-142
❑ 84SweSemE-163
❑ 85SwePanS-125
❑ 85SwePanS-126
❑ 85SwePanS-147
❑ 86SwePanS-150
❑ 87SwePanS-162
**Labraaten, Jan**
❑ 93SweSemE-317
❑ 95ColCho-353
❑ 95ColChoPC-353
❑ 95ColChoPCP-353
❑ 95SigRooA-24
❑ 95SigRooAPC-24
**Labraaten, Leif**
❑ 71SweHocS-152
❑ 72SweHocS-129
**Labraaten, Ulf**
❑ 83SweSemE-239
**Labranche, Emmanuel**
❑ 93DruVol-9
**Labre, Yvon**
❑ 73OPC-247
❑ 74CapWhiB-14
❑ 74OPCNHL-345
❑ 75OPCNHL-61
❑ 75Top-61
❑ 76OPCNHL-161
❑ 76OPCNHL-396
❑ 76Top-161
❑ 77OPCNHL-31
❑ 77Top-31
❑ 78OPC-324
❑ 79OPC-343
**Labrecque, Patrick**
❑ 907thInnSQMJHL-215
❑ 94FreCan-15
❑ 94WheThu-16
❑ 95FreCan-15
❑ 96Lea-224
❑ 96LeaPreP-224
❑ 96Pin-246
❑ 96PinArtP-246
❑ 96PinFoi-246
❑ 96PinPreS-246
❑ 96PinRinC-246
**Labrie, Guy**
❑ 51LavDaiQSHL-47
❑ 52St.LawS-74
**Labrier, Bob**
❑ 84KamBla-13
❑ 85KamBla-11
**Labrosse, Claude**
❑ 62QueAce-15
**LaCasse, Rene**
❑ 63QueAce-17
❑ 64QueAce-11
**Lach, Elmer**
❑ 34BeeGro1P-162
❑ 40OPCV3012-125
❑ 44BeeGro2P-255
❑ 45QuaOatP-86A
❑ 45QuaOatP-86B
❑ 45QuaOatP-86C
❑ 45QuaOatP-86D
❑ 48ExhCan-11
❑ 48ExhCan-60
❑ 51Par-1
❑ 52Par-6
❑ 53Par-30
❑ 53Par-31
❑ 83HalFP-I9
❑ 85HalFC-129
❑ 91ProSet-337
❑ 91ProSetFre-337
❑ 93OPCCanHF-34
❑ 93ParParR-PR36
❑ 94ParTalBG-4
**Lachance, Bob**
❑ 93DonTeaUSA-12
❑ 93Pin-495
❑ 93PinCan-495
❑ 93UppDec-564
**Lachance, Jimmy**
❑ 88RivDu R-14
**Lachance, Marcel**
❑ 77GraVic-12
**Lachance, Scott**
❑ 91AreDraPic-3
❑ 91Cla-4
❑ 91Par-326
❑ 91ParFre-326
❑ 91StaPicH-24
❑ 91UltDra-4
❑ 91UltDra-56
❑ 91UltDra-60
❑ 91UltDra-81
❑ 91UppDec-692
❑ 91UppDecCWJC-79
❑ 91UppDecF-692
❑ 92Bow-438
❑ 92OPC-390
❑ 92OPCPre-79
❑ 92PanSti-Q
❑ 92PanStiFre-Q
❑ 92Par-105
❑ 92ParEmel-105
❑ 92Pin-223
❑ 92Pin-244
❑ 92PinFre-223
❑ 92PinFre-244
❑ 92PinTea2-6
❑ 92PinTea2F-6
❑ 92ProSet-234
❑ 92Sco-449
❑ 92ScoCan-449
❑ 92ScoYouS-12
❑ 92SeaPat-52
❑ 92StaClu-201
❑ 92Top-366
❑ 92TopGol-366G
❑ 92Ult-130
❑ 92UppDec-360
❑ 92UppDec-398
❑ 92UppDec-409
❑ 92UppDec-571
❑ 92UppDecACH-4
❑ 92UppDecCC-CC16
❑ 93Don-206
❑ 93Lea-139
❑ 93OPCPre-257
❑ 93OPCPreG-257
❑ 93PanSti-63
❑ 93Par-120
❑ 93ParEmel-120
❑ 93Pin-62
❑ 93PinCan-62
❑ 93PinTea2-21
❑ 93PinTea2C-21
❑ 93Pow-152
❑ 93Sco-103
❑ 93ScoCan-103
❑ 93StaClu-465
❑ 93StaCluFDI-465
❑ 93StaCluMasP-16
❑ 93StaCluMasPW-16
❑ 93StaCluO-465
❑ 93TopPre-257
❑ 93TopPreG-257
❑ 93TopPrePS-257
❑ 93Ult-369
❑ 93UppDec-320
❑ 93UppDecSP-92
❑ 94BeAPla-R44
❑ 94BeAPSig-82
❑ 94Don-41
❑ 94Fle-124
❑ 94Lea-372
❑ 94OPCPre-66
❑ 94OPCPreSE-66
❑ 94Par-140
❑ 94ParGol-140
❑ 94Pin-193
❑ 94PinArtP-193
❑ 94PinRinC-193
❑ 94Sco-195
❑ 94ScoGol-195
❑ 94ScoPla-195
❑ 94ScoPlaTS-195
❑ 94TopPre-66
❑ 94TopPreSE-66
❑ 94Ult-326
❑ 94UppDec-412
❑ 94UppDecEleIce-412
❑ 95Don-353
❑ 95Lea-202
❑ 95Pin-167
❑ 95PinArtP-167
❑ 95PinRinC-167
❑ 95PlaOneoOne-281
❑ 95Sco-177
❑ 95ScoBlaIce-177
❑ 95ScoBlaIceAP-177
❑ 95SkyImp-101
❑ 95Ult-94
❑ 95UltGolM-94
❑ 95UppDec-390
❑ 95UppDecEleIce-390
❑ 95UppDecEleIceG-390
❑ 96BeAPAut-27
❑ 96BeAPAutSil-27
❑ 96BeAPla-27
❑ 96Fla-55
❑ 96FlaBluI-55
❑ 96IslPos-12
❑ 97Don-142
❑ 97DonLim-166
❑ 97DonLimExp-166
❑ 97DonPre-143
❑ 97DonPreCttC-143
❑ 97DonPreProG-142
❑ 97DonPreProS-142
❑ 97Lea-95
❑ 97LeaFraMat-95
❑ 97LeaFraMDC-95
❑ 97LeaInt-95
❑ 97LeaIntUI-95
❑ 97Pac-85
❑ 97PacCop-85
❑ 97PacEmeGre-85
❑ 97PacIceB-85
❑ 97PacRed-85
❑ 97PacSil-85
❑ 97Sco-259
❑ 98Be A PPA-84
❑ 98Be A PPAA-84
❑ 98Be A PPAAF-84
❑ 98Be A PPTBASG-84
❑ 98Be APG-84
**Lachborn, Len**
❑ 85FlyPos-11
**Lacher, Blaine**
❑ 91LakSupSL-15
❑ 94Cla-35
❑ 94ClaDraGol-35
❑ 94ClaROYS-R13
❑ 94ClaTri-T4
❑ 94Fin-95
❑ 94FinBowB-R3
❑ 94FinBowBR-R3
❑ 94FinRef-95
❑ 94FinSupTW-95
❑ 94Fle-13
❑ 94FleRooS-6
❑ 94SP-7
❑ 94SPDieCut-7
❑ 94SPPre-8
❑ 94SPPreDC-8
❑ 94UppDec-495
❑ 94UppDec-539
❑ 94UppDecEleIce-495
❑ 94UppDecEleIce-539
❑ 94UppDecSPI-SP95
❑ 94UppDecSPIDC-SP95
❑ 95CanGamNHLP-38
❑ 95ColCho-22
❑ 95ColChoPC-22
❑ 95ColChoPCP-22
❑ 95Don-123
❑ 95DonBetTP-1
❑ 95DonRooTea-5
❑ 95Emo-8
❑ 95Ima-9
❑ 95ImaAut-9A
❑ 95ImaCleE-CE9
❑ 95ImaGol-9
❑ 95Kra-19
❑ 95Lea-3
❑ 95LeaLim-41
❑ 95LeaStuR-5
❑ 95Met-7
❑ 95ParInt-14
❑ 95ParIntEl-14
❑ 95Pin-147
❑ 95PinArtP-147
❑ 95PinMas-1
❑ 95PinRinC-147
❑ 95PlaOneoOne-7
❑ 95PlaOneoOne-119
❑ 95ProMag-17
❑ 95Sco-17
❑ 95ScoBlaIce-17
❑ 95ScoBlaIceAP-17
❑ 95SkyImp-9
❑ 95SkyImp-232
❑ 95SkyImp-NNO
❑ 95SkyImpD-5
❑ 95SkyImpPP-1
❑ 95StaClu-104
❑ 95StaCluMO-50

- 95StaCluMOMS-104
- 95Sum-121
- 95SumArtP-127
- 95SumIce-127
- 95Top-23
- 95TopNewG-15NG
- 95TopOPCI-23
- 95Ult-10
- 95UltAllRoo-6
- 95UltAllRooGM-6
- 95UltGoIM-10
- 95UltPrePadMen-7
- 95UltPrePadMenGM-7
- 95UppDec-385
- 95UppDecElelce-385
- 95UppDecElelceG-385
- 95UppDecPHE-H15
- 95UppDecSpeE-SE7
- 95UppDecSpeEdiG-SE7
- 95UppPreHV-H15
- 95Zen-78
- 96NHLProSTA-17

**Lackey, Carl**
- 69SweWorC-17

**Lackey, Jerry**
- 69SweWorC-182

**Lackey, Miroslav**
- 69SweHocS-33
- 69SweWorC-142
- 70SweHocS-346

**Laco, Marek**
- 95SloPeeWT-13

**Lacombe, Frank**
- 72NordPos-14
- 73NordTeal-15
- 76NordPos-15

**Lacombe, Norm (Normand)**
- 85SabBluS-15
- 85SabBluS-15
- 86SabBluS-19
- 86SabBluSSma-19
- 87OilTeal-19
- 88OilTeal-15
- 88OilTenAnn-81
- 89OilTeal-13
- 89PanSti-84
- 90FlyPos-15
- 90ProSet-500
- 90ScoRoo-99T
- 91Bow-248
- 91OPC-357
- 91ScoCan-394
- 91StaClu-363
- 91Top-357

**Lacombe, Patrick**
- 917thInnSQMJHL-87

**Lacoste, Yvon**
- 65QueAce-12

**Lacour, Robin**
- 93DetJrRW-5
- 94KitRanU-32
- 95Sla-36
- 96SudWol-12
- 96SudWolP-14

**Lacoursiere, Joseph**
- 51LavDaiLSJ-16

**Lacouture, Dan**
- 94Sel-154
- 94SelGol-154
- 95Cla-64

**LaCouture, Dave**
- 92MaiBlaB-9
- 92MaiBlaB-24

**Lacroix, Andre**
- 68OPC-184
- 68ShiCoi-128
- 69OPC-98
- 69OPCFou-10
- 69OPCSta-18
- 69Top-98
- 70ColSta-29
- 70DadCoo-68
- 70EssPowPla-204
- 70FlyPos-7
- 70OPC-84
- 70SarProSta-154
- 70Top-84
- 70TopStiS-18
- 71OPC-33
- 71SarProSta-39
- 71Top-33
- 71TorSun-201
- 72SluCupWHA-12
- 73OPCWHAP-10
- 73QuaOatWHA-6
- 74MarSanDW-1
- 74OPCWHA-60
- 75OPCWHA-10
- 75OPCWHA-64
- 76OPCWHA-70
- 76OPCWHA-80
- 77OPCWHA-30
- 79OPC-107
- 79Top-107

**Lacroix, Daniel**
- 89ProIHL-31
- 90ProAHLIHL-7
- 91ProAHLCHL-194
- 92BinRan-19
- 92Cla-58
- 93Lea-351
- 94ClaEnf-E2
- 94ClaProP-69
- 94UppDec-283
- 94UppDecElelce-283

- 95BinRan-12
- 96BeAPAut-135
- 96BeAPAutSil-135
- 96BeAPla-135
- 96ClaGol-58
- 96FlyPos-13
- 97PacDynBKS-70
- 97PacInvNRB-143
- 97ScoFly-20
- 97ScoFlyPla-20
- 97ScoFlyPre-20

**Lacroix, Eric**
- 92Cla-58
- 92Cla-77
- 92St.JohML-9
- 93St.JohML-13
- 94BeAPSig-13
- 94ClaProP-164
- 94Fle-97
- 94Par-234
- 94ParGol-234
- 94UppDec-352
- 94UppDecElelce-352
- 95CanGamNHLP-142
- 95ColCho-276
- 95ColChoPC-276
- 95ColChoPCP-276
- 95ParInt-107
- 95ParIntEl-107
- 95Pin-82
- 95PinArtP-82
- 95PinRinC-82
- 95Top-32
- 95TopOPCI-32
- 95Ult-252
- 95UppDec-122
- 95UppDecElelce-122
- 95UppDecElelceG-122
- 96ClaGol-58
- 96ClaGol-77
- 96UppDec-244
- 97Pac-161
- 97PacCop-161
- 97PacEmeGre-161
- 97PacIceB-161
- 97PacRed-161
- 97PacSil-161
- 97ScoAva-13
- 97ScoAvaPla-13
- 97ScoAvaPre-13
- 98Be A PPA-38
- 98Be A PPAA-38
- 98Be A PPAAF-38
- 98Be A PPTBASG-38
- 98Be APG-38
- 98Pac-163
- 98PacIceB-163
- 98PacRed-163
- 98UppDec-71
- 98UppDecE-71
- 98UppDecE101-71
- 98UppDecGR-71

**Lacroix, Martin**
- 92Cla-78
- 96ClaGol-78

**Lacroix, Pierre**
- 80NordPos-16
- 80PepCap-70
- 81NordPos-10
- 81OPC-278
- 82OPC-286
- 83OPCSti-261
- 83WhaJunHC-10

**Lacroix, Renald**
- 51LavDaiS-116
- 52St.LawS-29

**Ladouceur, Randy**
- 84OPC-60
- 85OPC-216
- 87WhaJunBK-11
- 88WhaJunBR-9
- 89WhaJunM-13
- 90OPC-162
- 90PanSti-41
- 90ProSet-108
- 90Top-162
- 90TopTif-162
- 90UppDec-151
- 90UppDecF-151
- 90WhaJr7E-18
- 91Bow-5
- 91Par-289
- 91ParFre-289
- 91Pin-224
- 91PinFre-224
- 91ProSet-396
- 91ProSet-573
- 91ProSetFre-396
- 91ProSetFre-573
- 91ScoAme-436
- 91ScoCan-407
- 91WhaJr7E-20
- 92Bow-107
- 92OPC-299
- 92Pin-291
- 92PinFre-291
- 92Sco-61
- 92ScoCan-61
- 92StaClu-156
- 92Top-344
- 92TopGol-344G
- 92WhaDai-14
- 93OPCPre-469
- 93OPCPreG-469
- 93Pin-389

- 93PinCan-389
- 93Sco-553
- 93ScoCan-553
- 93ScoGol-553
- 93StaClu-271
- 93StaCluFDI-271
- 93StaCluO-271
- 93TopPre-469
- 93TopPreG-469
- 94CanGamNHLP-365
- 94DucCarJr-15
- 94EASpo-2
- 94ParSE-SE3
- 94ParSEG-SE3
- 94StaClu-69
- 94StaCluFDI-69
- 94StaCluMOMS-69
- 94StaCluSTWC-69
- 95BeAPla-37
- 95BeAPSig-S37
- 95BeAPSigDC-S37
- 95ParInt-7
- 95ParIntEl-7

**LaFayette, Justin**
- 91ProAHLCHL-493

**LaFayette, Nathan**
- 907thInnSOHL-25
- 907thInnSOHL-63
- 917thInnSCHLAW-3
- 917thInnSMC-114
- 917thInnSOHL-14
- 91CorRoy-18
- 91StaPich-56
- 91UltDra-46
- 92UppDec-588
- 93Cla-22
- 93PeoRiv-15
- 94CanGamNHLP-340
- 94CanuProl-12
- 94ClaProP-195
- 94Don-156
- 94Fla-190
- 94Lea-216
- 94OPCFinIns-22
- 94OPCPre-18
- 94OPCPreSE-18
- 94Par-247
- 94ParGol-247
- 94ParSEV-44
- 94Pin-453
- 94PinArtP-453
- 94PinRinC-453
- 94TopPre-18
- 94TopPreSE-18
- 94Ult-225
- 94UppDec-448
- 94UppDecElelce-448
- 95Ima-40
- 95ImaGol-40

**Laferriere, Rick**
- 81RocPos-10

**Laflamme, Christian**
- 93UppDecPOE-E6
- 95Cla-40
- 95Ima-87
- 95ImaGol-87
- 97PacOme-52
- 97PacOmeC-52
- 97PacOmeDG-52
- 97PacOmeEG-52
- 97PacOmeG-52
- 97PacOmelB-52
- 97UppDec-185
- 98Be A PPA-32
- 98Be A PPAA-32
- 98Be A PPAAF-32
- 98Be A PPTBASG-32
- 98Be APG-32
- 98Pac-148
- 98PacIceB-148
- 98PacRed-148
- 98UppDec-64
- 98UppDecE-64
- 98UppDecE101-64
- 98UppDecGR-64

**Laflamme, Daniel**
- 907thInnSQMJHL-103
- 917thInnSQMJHL-183

**LaFleur, Brian**
- 93MinGolG-15
- 94MinGolG-18
- 95MinGolG-19
- 96MinGolGCAS-17

**Lafleur, Guy**
- 70CanaPin-6
- 71CanaPos-9
- 71ColHea-5
- 71OPC-148
- 71OPCPos-13
- 71TorSun-152
- 72CanaPos-7
- 72CanaGreWLP-5
- 72OPC-59
- 72Top-79
- 73CanaPos-7
- 73OPC-72
- 73Top-72
- 74CanaPos-8
- 74NHLActSta-152
- 74OPCNHL-232
- 74Top-232
- 75CanaPos-8
- 75HerSta-9
- 75OPCNHL-126
- 75OPCNHL-208

- 75OPCNHL-290
- 75OPCNHL-322
- 75Top-126
- 75Top-208
- 75Top-290
- 75Top-322
- 76CanaPos-9
- 76OPCNHL-1
- 76OPCNHL-2
- 76OPCNHL-3
- 76OPCNHL-5
- 76OPCNHL-163
- 76OPCNHL-388
- 76Top-1
- 76Top-2
- 76Top-3
- 76Top-5
- 76Top-163
- 76TopGloI-11
- 77CanaPos-10
- 77OPCNHL-1
- 77OPCNHL-2
- 77OPCNHL-7
- 77OPCNHL-200
- 77OPCNHL-214
- 77OPCNHL-216
- 77OPCNHL-218
- 77Top-1
- 77Top-2
- 77Top-3
- 77Top-7
- 77Top-200
- 77Top-214
- 77Top-216
- 77Top-218
- 77TopGloS-7
- 77TopOPCGlo-7
- 78CanaPos-11
- 78OPC-3
- 78OPC-63
- 78OPC-64
- 78OPC-65
- 78OPC-69
- 78OPC-90
- 78OPC-326
- 78Top-3
- 78Top-63
- 78Top-64
- 78Top-65
- 78Top-69
- 78Top-90
- 79CanaPos-10
- 79OPC-1
- 79OPC-2
- 79OPC-3
- 79OPC-7
- 79OPC-200
- 79Top-1
- 79Top-2
- 79Top-3
- 79Top-7
- 79Top-200
- 80CanaPos-14
- 80OPC-10
- 80OPC-82
- 80OPC-162
- 80OPC-163
- 80OPC-216
- 80OPCSup-10
- 80Top-10
- 80Top-82
- 80Top-162
- 80Top-163
- 80Top-216
- 81CanaSti-13
- 81OPC-177
- 81OPC-195
- 81OPCSti-29
- 81OPCSti-41
- 81Top-19
- 82CanaPos-11
- 82CanaSte-8
- 82McDSti-8
- 82NeiGre-31
- 82OPC-186
- 82OPC-187
- 82OPCSti-28
- 82OPCSti-29
- 82PosCer-10
- 83CanaPos-12
- 83OPC-183
- 83OPC-189
- 83OPCSti-2
- 83OPCSti-58
- 83OPCSti-59
- 83PufSti-4
- 83Vac-47
- 84CanaPos-12
- 84KelAccD-3B
- 84OPC-264
- 84OPC-360
- 84OPCSti-149
- 84OPCSti-150
- 84Top-81
- 88EssAllSta-23
- 89Kra-31
- 89Nord-22
- 89NordGenF-18
- 89NordPol-15
- 89OPC-189
- 89OPCSti-245
- 89Top-189
- 90Kra-22
- 90NordPet-14

- 90OPC-142
- 90OPCPre-55
- 90PanSti-145
- 90ProSet-250
- 90Sco-290
- 90ScoCan-290
- 90ScoHotRS-96
- 90Top-142
- 90TopTif-142
- 90UppDec-162
- 90UppDecF-162
- 91Kra-66
- 91NordPanTS-12
- 91NordPanTS-C
- 91NordPanTS-D
- 91NordPanTS-G
- 91OPC-1
- 91OPC-2
- 91OPC-3
- 91ProSet-317
- 91ProSetFre-317
- 91ScoAme-401
- 91ScoAme-402
- 91ScoAme-403
- 91ScoCan-291
- 91ScoCan-292
- 91ScoCan-293
- 91Top-1
- 91Top-2
- 91Top-3
- 91UppDec-219
- 91UppDec-638
- 91UppDecF-219
- 91UppDecF-638
- 93AmeLicSPC-2
- 930PCCanHF-17
- 930PCCanHF-57
- 93TitGuyLl-1
- 94TitGuyL-1
- 94TitGuyL-2
- 94TitGuyL-3
- 94TitGuyL-4
- 94TitGuyL-5
- 94TitGuyL-6
- 94TitGuyL-7
- 94TitGuyL-8
- 94TitGuyL-9
- 94TitGuyL-10
- 94TitGuyL-11
- 94TitGuyL-12
- 94TitGuyL-13
- 94TitGuyL-14
- 94TitGuyL-15
- 94TitGuyL-16
- 94TitGuyL-17
- 94TitGuyL-18
- 94TitGuyL-19
- 94TitGuyL-21
- 94TitGuyL-22
- 94TitGuyL-23
- 94TitGuyL-24
- 96SweSemWHL-HL2
- 99UppDecCL-11
- 99UppDecCLCLC-11

**Lafoley, Grayson**
- 920tt672A-14

**LaFontaine, Pat**
- 84OPC-129
- 84OPC-392
- 84Top-96
- 85IsIlsIN-11
- 85OPC-137
- 85OPCSti-74
- 85Top-137
- 86OPC-2
- 86OPCSti-206
- 86Top-2
- 87OPC-173
- 87OPCMin-22
- 87OPCSti-243
- 87PanSti-98
- 87Top-173
- 88FriLayS-14
- 88OPC-123
- 88OPCBoxB-C
- 88OPCSti-111
- 88PanSti-290
- 88Top-123
- 88TopBoxB-C
- 89Isl-11
- 89OPC-60
- 89OPCSti-119
- 89PanSti-264
- 89SweSemWCS-164
- 89Top-60
- 90Bow-123
- 90BowHatTri-9
- 90BowTif-123
- 90Kra-23
- 90Kra-86
- 90OPC-184
- 90OPC-315
- 90OPCPre-56
- 90PanSti-81
- 90ProSet-186
- 90ProSet-372
- 90Sco-250
- 90ScoCan-250
- 90ScoHotRS-95
- 90Top-184
- 90Top-315
- 90TopTif-184
- 90UppDec-246

- 90UppDec-306
- 90UppDec-479
- 90UppDecF-246
- 90UppDecF-306
- 90UppDecF-479
- 91Bow-222
- 91Gil-23
- 91Kra-25
- 91McDUppD-6
- 91OPC-80
- 91OPCPre-64
- 91PanSti-243
- 91Par-16
- 91ParFre-16
- 91Pin-25
- 91PinFre-25
- 91ProSet-149
- 91ProSet-308
- 91ProSet-358
- 91ProSetFre-149
- 91ProSetFre-308
- 91ProSetFre-358
- 91ProSetPla-157
- 91ProSetPOTM-P5
- 91SabBluS-9
- 91SabPepC-9
- 91ScoAme-260
- 91ScoAme-332
- 91ScoCan-362
- 91ScoCan-480
- 91ScoKel-15
- 91ScoRoo-100T
- 91StaClu-123
- 91SweSemWCS-138
- 91Top-80
- 91TopBowPS-7
- 91TopTeaSL-12
- 91UppDec-253
- 91UppDec-556
- 91UppDecF-253
- 91UppDecF-556
- 92Bow-142
- 92HumDum2-11
- 92OPC-285
- 92OPCPreSP-17
- 92PanSti-246
- 92PanStiFre-246
- 92Par-12
- 92ParEmel-12
- 92Pin-7
- 92Pin-254
- 92PinFre-7
- 92PinFre-254
- 92ProSet-13
- 92SabBluS-10
- 92SabJubF-7
- 92Sco-6
- 92Sco-420
- 92ScoCan-6
- 92ScoCan-420
- 92ScoCanPS-1
- 92ScoCanPS-2
- 92ScoSha-8
- 92ScoShaCan-8
- 92ScoUSAG-1
- 92SeaPat-42
- 92StaClu-95
- 92Top-345
- 92TopGol-345G
- 92Ult-16
- 92UppDec-165
- 92UppDec-456
- 92UppDecGHS-G3
- 93Don-37
- 93DonIceKin-2
- 93KenStaLA-6
- 93KenStaLC-5
- 93Kra-39
- 93Lea-12
- 93LeaGolAS-1
- 93LeaStuS-3
- 93McDUppD-18
- 93OPCPre-171
- 93OPCPre-490
- 93OPCPreBG-14
- 93OPCPreG-171
- 93OPCPreG-490
- 93PanSti-101
- 93PanSti-137
- 93Par-289
- 93ParEasWesS-E8
- 93ParEmel-289
- 93Pin-300
- 93Pin2HS-300
- 93PinAllS-11
- 93PinAllSC-11
- 93PinCan-300
- 93PinCapC-3
- 93PinNifFif-12
- 93Pow-31
- 93PowPoiL-7
- 93SabNoc-9
- 93ScoCan-345
- 93ScoDreTea-13
- 93ScoDynDUS-2
- 93ScoFra-2
- 93StaClu-20
- 93StaClu-460
- 93StaCluFDI-20
- 93StaCluFDI-460
- 93StaCluFDIO-20
- 93StaCluMasP-1

- 93StaCluMasPW-1
- 93StaCluO-20
- 93StaCluO-460
- 93SweSemWCS-183
- 93TopPre-171
- 93TopPre-490
- 93TopPreG-171
- 93TopPreG-490
- 93Ult-219
- 93UltAllS-3
- 93UltAllS-4
- 93UltPreP-3
- 93UltScoK-1
- 93UltSpeM-9
- 93UppDec-137
- 93UppDec-221
- 93UppDec-287
- 93UppDecHT-HT10
- 93UppDecLAS-4
- 93UppDecSP-17
- 94BeAPla-R79
- 94BeAPla-R132
- 94BeAPSig-63
- 94CanGamNHLP-50
- 94Don-300
- 94EASpo-15
- 94Fin-70
- 94FinnJaaK-120
- 94FinnJaaK-359
- 94FinRef-70
- 94FinSupTW-70
- 94Fla-19
- 94FlaCenS-5
- 94Fle-23
- 94HocWit-105
- 94KenStaLA-9
- 94Kra-10
- 94Lea-278
- 94LeaGolS-14
- 94LeaLim-63
- 94OPCPre-180
- 94OPCPreSE-180
- 94Par-310
- 94ParCratGB-3
- 94ParCratGG-3
- 94ParCratSR-3
- 94ParGol-310
- 94ParSE-SE18
- 94ParSEG-SE18
- 94ParVin-V73
- 94Pin-350
- 94PinArtP-350
- 94PinGam-GR2
- 94PinRinC-350
- 94Sco-2
- 94ScoFra-TF3
- 94ScoGol-2
- 94ScoHobS-2
- 94ScoPla-2
- 94ScoPlaTS-2
- 94Sel-57
- 94SelGol-57
- 94SP-12
- 94SPDieCut-12
- 94TopPre-180
- 94TopPreGTG-6
- 94TopPreSE-180
- 94Ult-24
- 94UltPreP-5
- 94UltSpeM-5
- 94UppDec-17
- 94UppDecElelce-17
- 94UppDecIG-IG14
- 94UppDecNBAP-28
- 94UppDecPR-R17
- 94UppDecPR-R22
- 94UppDecPR-R47
- 94UppDecPR-R55
- 94UppDecPRE-R17
- 94UppDecPRE-R22
- 94UppDecPRE-R47
- 94UppDecPRE-R55
- 94UppDecPreRG-R17
- 94UppDecPreRG-R22
- 94UppDecPreRG-R47
- 94UppDecPreRG-R55
- 94UppDecSPI-SP99
- 94UppDecSPIDC-SP99
- 95Bow-29
- 95BowAllFoi-29
- 95CanGamNHLP-42
- 95ColCho-157
- 95ColChoCTG-C27
- 95ColChoCTG-C27B
- 95ColChoCTG-C27C
- 95ColChoCTGGB-C27
- 95ColChoCTGSB-C27
- 95ColChoCTGSB-C27
- 95ColChoCTGSR-C27
- 95ColChoPC-157
- 95ColChoPCP-157
- 95Don-172
- 95DonEli-75
- 95DonEliDCS-75
- 95DonEliDCU-75
- 95DonProPoi-2
- 95Emo-18
- 95Fin-40
- 95FinnSemWC-114
- 95FinRef-40
- 95FinRef-130
- 95ImpSti-11
- 95ImpStiDCS-3
- 95Lea-140

❑ 95LeaLim-113
❑ 95Met-16
❑ 95MetIS-11
❑ 95NHLAcePC-5S
❑ 95ParInt-20
❑ 95ParIntEl-20
❑ 95ParIntPTP-PP49
❑ 95Pin-54
❑ 95PinArtP-54
❑ 95PinRinC-54
❑ 95PlaOneoOne-13
❑ 95PlaOneoOne-127
❑ 95ProMag-109
❑ 95Sco-201
❑ 95ScoBlaIce-201
❑ 95ScoBlaIceAP-201
❑ 95ScoBorBat-7
❑ 95ScoGolBla-8
❑ 95SelCer-18
❑ 95SelCerMG-18
❑ 95SkyImp-17
❑ 95SP-12
❑ 95SPStaEto-E5
❑ 95SPStaEtoG-E5
❑ 95StaClu-164
❑ 95StaCluMOMS-164
❑ 95Sum-34
❑ 95SumArtP-34
❑ 95SumIce-34
❑ 95SweGloWC-116
❑ 95Top-13
❑ 95Top-250
❑ 95TopHomGUSA-HGA4
❑ 95TopMarMPB-13
❑ 95TopOPCI-13
❑ 95TopOPCI-250
❑ 95TopPowL-6PL
❑ 95TopRinL-5RL
❑ 95TopSupSki-5
❑ 95TopSupSkiPla-5
❑ 95Ult-20
❑ 95Ult-389
❑ 95UltGolM-20
❑ 95UppDec-386
❑ 95UppDecEleIce-386
❑ 95UppDecEleIceG-386
❑ 95UppDecPRE-R19
❑ 95UppDecPRE-R29
❑ 95UppDecPreR-R19
❑ 95UppDecPreR-R29
❑ 95UppDecSpeE-SE10
❑ 95UppDecSpeEdiG-SE10
❑ 95Zen-85
❑ 96BeAPLH-8B
❑ 96BeAPLHAut-8B
❑ 96BeAPLHAutSil-8B
❑ 96ColCho-23
❑ 96ColCho-311
❑ 96ColChoBlo-23
❑ 96ColChoMVP-UD40
❑ 96ColChoMVPG-UD40
❑ 96ColChoSti-S21
❑ 96Don-113
❑ 96DonCanI-11
❑ 96DonCanIGPP-11
❑ 96DonCanIRPP-11
❑ 96DonEli-101
❑ 96DonEliDCS-101
❑ 96DonEliP-10
❑ 96DonPrePro-113
❑ 96Fla-9
❑ 96FlaBluI-9
❑ 96Fle-11
❑ 96FleArtRos-11
❑ 96FlePic-38
❑ 96FlePicDL-10
❑ 96KraUppD-34
❑ 96Lea-44
❑ 96LeaLim-59
❑ 96LeaLimG-59
❑ 96LeaPre-11
❑ 96LeaPreP-44
❑ 96LeaPrePP-11
❑ 96LeaPreSG-22
❑ 96LeaPreSte-22
❑ 96MetUni-15
❑ 96MetUniIC-8
❑ 96MetUniICSP-8
❑ 96NHLACEPC-27
❑ 96NHLProSTA-109
❑ 96Pin-27
❑ 96PinArtP-27
❑ 96PinFoi-27
❑ 96PinPreS-27
❑ 96PinRinC-27
❑ 96Sco-139
❑ 96ScoArtPro-139
❑ 96ScoDeaCAP-139
❑ 96ScoGolB-139
❑ 96ScoSpeAP-139
❑ 96SelCer-9
❑ 96SelCerAP-9
❑ 96SelCerBlu-9
❑ 96SelCerMB-9
❑ 96SelCerMG-9
❑ 96SelCerMR-9
❑ 96SelCerRed-9
❑ 96SkyImp-11
❑ 96SkyImpB-10
❑ 96SP-15
❑ 96SPGamFil-GF18
❑ 96SPHolCol-HC8
❑ 96SPx-18
❑ 96SPxGol-18
❑ 96Sum-127
❑ 96SumArtP-127
❑ 96SumIce-127
❑ 96SumMet-127
❑ 96SumPreS-127
❑ 96SweSemW-165
❑ 96Ult-17
❑ 96UltGolM-17
❑ 96UltMr.Mom-6
❑ 96UppDec-15
❑ 96UppDecSS-SS17B
❑ 96Zen-83
❑ 96ZenArtP-83
❑ 96ZenAss-9
❑ 97BeAPlaPOT-15
❑ 97ColCho-31
❑ 97Don-133
❑ 97DonCanI-69
❑ 97DonCanIDS-69
❑ 97DonCanIPS-69
❑ 97DonEli-111
❑ 97DonEli-146
❑ 97DonEliAsp-111
❑ 97DonEliAsp-146
❑ 97DonEliS-111
❑ 97DonEliS-146
❑ 97DonLim-111
❑ 97DonLimExp-111
❑ 97DonPre-58
❑ 97DonPreCttC-58
❑ 97DonPreProG-133
❑ 97DonPreProS-133
❑ 97DonPri-160
❑ 97DonPriSoA-160
❑ 97Kat-93
❑ 97KatGol-93
❑ 97KatSil-93
❑ 97Lea-34
❑ 97LeaFraMat-34
❑ 97LeaFraMDC-34
❑ 97LeaInt-34
❑ 97LeaIntUI-34
❑ 97PacCroR-85
❑ 97PacCroREG-85
❑ 97PacCroRIB-85
❑ 97PacCroRLCDC-12
❑ 97PacCroRS-85
❑ 97PacOme-146
❑ 97PacOmeC-146
❑ 97PacOmeDG-146
❑ 97PacOmeEG-146
❑ 97PacOmeG-146
❑ 97PacOmeIB-146
❑ 97PacOmeSLC-14
❑ 97PacPar-117
❑ 97PacParC-117
❑ 97PacParDG-117
❑ 97PacParEG-117
❑ 97PacParIB-117
❑ 97PacParRed-117
❑ 97PacParSil-117
❑ 97PacRev-88
❑ 97PacRevC-88
❑ 97PacRevE-88
❑ 97PacRevIB-88
❑ 97PacRevR-88
❑ 97PacRevS-88
❑ 97Pin-69
❑ 97PinArtP-69
❑ 97PinBee-43
❑ 97PinBeeGP-43
❑ 97PinBeeGT-18
❑ 97PinBeeT-18
❑ 97PinCer-80
❑ 97PinCerMB-80
❑ 97PinCerMG-80
❑ 97PinCerMR-80
❑ 97PinCerR-80
❑ 97PinHocMC-9
❑ 97PinHocMC-10
❑ 97PinIns-39
❑ 97PinInsCC-39
❑ 97PinInsEC-39
❑ 97PinPrePBB-69
❑ 97PinPrePBC-69
❑ 97PinPrePBM-69
❑ 97PinPrePBY-69
❑ 97PinPrePFC-69
❑ 97PinPrePFM-69
❑ 97PinPrePFY-69
❑ 97PinPrePla-69
❑ 97PinRinC-69
❑ 97PinTotCMPG-80
❑ 97PinTotCPB-80
❑ 97PinTotCPG-80
❑ 97PinTotCPR-80
❑ 97Sco-104
❑ 97ScoArtPro-104
❑ 97ScoGolBla-104
❑ 97ScoRan-10
❑ 97ScoRanPla-10
❑ 97ScoRanPre-10
❑ 97SP AutI-I1
❑ 97SPAut-98
❑ 97SPAutID-I1
❑ 97SPAutIE-I1
❑ 97SPx-5
❑ 97SPxBro-5
❑ 97SPxGol-5
❑ 97SPxGraF-5
❑ 97SPxSil-5
❑ 97SPxSte-5
❑ 97Stu-50
❑ 97StuPrePG-50
❑ 97StuPrePS-50
❑ 97UppDec-318
❑ 97UppDecBD-133
❑ 97UppDecBDDD-133
❑ 97UppDecBDPC-PC22
❑ 97UppDecBDPCDD-PC22
❑ 97UppDecBDPCM-PC22
❑ 97UppDecBDPCQD-PC22
❑ 97UppDecBDPCTD-PC22
❑ 97UppDecBDQD-133
❑ 97UppDecBDTD-133
❑ 97UppDecIce-72
❑ 97UppDecIceP-72
❑ 97UppDecIPS-72
❑ 97Zen-44
❑ 97Zen5x7-26
❑ 97ZenChaTC-14
❑ 97ZenGolImp-26
❑ 97ZenSilImp-26
❑ 97ZenZGol-44
❑ 97ZenZSil-44
❑ 98Pac-295
❑ 98PacIceB-295
❑ 98PacPar-154
❑ 98PacParC-154
❑ 98PacParEG-154
❑ 98PacParH-154
❑ 98PacParIB-154
❑ 98PacParS-154
❑ 98PacRed-295
❑ 98PacTim-12
❑ 98SPxFin-56
❑ 98SPxFinR-56
❑ 98SPxFinS-56
❑ 98UC-130
❑ 98UD ChoPCR-130
❑ 98UD ChoR-130
❑ 98UppDec-133
❑ 98UppDecE-133
❑ 98UppDecE1o1-133
❑ 98UppDecGR-133

**LaForest, Bob**
❑ 82NorBayC-12

**LaForest, Mark**
❑ 82NorBayC-13
❑ 89ProAHL-124
❑ 90ProAHLIHL-13
❑ 90UppDec-81
❑ 90UppDecF-81
❑ 91ProAHLCHL-208
❑ 94MilAdm-13
❑ 95ColEdgI-163
❑ 95MilAdmBO-10

**Laforge, Alain**
❑ 86KinCan-28
❑ 88NiaFalT-21
❑ 89SudWol-7
❑ 907thInnSOHL-386
❑ 90SudWol-19

**Laforge, Bill**
❑ 80OshGen-17
❑ 88NiaFalT-22

**Laforge, Claude**
❑ 58Top-33
❑ 59Top-64
❑ 62Par-24
❑ 68ShiCoi-133

**Laforge, Marc**
❑ 84KinCan-16
❑ 85KinCan-16
❑ 86KinCan-16
❑ 88ProAHL-49
❑ 90ProAHLIHL-233
❑ 91ProAHLCHL-216
❑ 94CapBreO-12
❑ 97AncAce-10

**Lafoy, Mike**
❑ 82KinCan-20

**Laframboise, Pete (Peter)**
❑ 72OPC-263
❑ 72SarProSta-53
❑ 73OPC-244
❑ 74CapWhiB-15
❑ 74NHLActSta-317
❑ 74OPCNHL-166
❑ 74Top-166
❑ 75OPCNHL-364

**Lafrance, Darryl**
❑ 917thInnSOHL-157
❑ 91OshGen-14
❑ 91OshGenS-13
❑ 92OshGenS-17
❑ 93OshGen-14
❑ 95Cla-91
❑ 95FliGen-15

**Lafrance, Eric**
❑ 907thInnSQMJHL-183
❑ 917thInnSQMJHL-170

**Lafrance, Leo**
❑ 27LaPat-3

**Lafreniere, Chris**
❑ 907thInnSWHL-195
❑ 917thInnSMC-75

**Lafreniere, Jason**
❑ 83BraAle-6
❑ 85NordMcD-12
❑ 85NordTeal-13
❑ 86NordGenF-14
❑ 86NordTeal-12
❑ 87NordGenF-18
❑ 87OPCSti-130
❑ 87OPCSti-219
❑ 87PanSti-171
❑ 88OPC-223
❑ 88OPCSti-185
❑ 89ProIHL-25
❑ 90AlbIntTC-14
❑ 93Par-466
❑ 93ParEmel-466
❑ 98GerDELE-182

**Lafreniere, Marc**
❑ 90RayJrC-10
❑ 91RayJrC-8

**Lafreniere, Roger**
❑ 61HamRed-10

**Lagace, Jean-Guy**
❑ 74NHLActStaU-15
❑ 74OPCNHL-299
❑ 74PenPos-12
❑ 75OPCNHL-141
❑ 75Top-141

**Laganas, Chris**
❑ 91GreMon-7
❑ 92OklCitB-11
❑ 94CenHocL-61

**Laginski, Al**
❑ 89RayJrC-12

**LaGrand, Scott**
❑ 92Cla-79
❑ 96ClaGol-79

**Lahaye, Lester**
❑ 52JunBluT-45

**Lahey, Matthew**
❑ 95Sla-326
❑ 96SauSteMG-9
❑ 96SauSteMGA-9
❑ 97GueSto-15

**Lahey, Pat**
❑ 82SauSteMG-14
❑ 83SauSteMG-14

**Lahn, Stefan**
❑ 95GerDELE-290
❑ 96GerDELE-317

**Lahnalampi, Derek**
❑ 94NorBayC-3

**Lahtinen, Jouni**
❑ 95FinnSIS-239
❑ 96FinnSISR-37

**Lahtinen, Timo**
❑ 83SweSemE-219
❑ 84SweSemE-243
❑ 91SweSemE-309
❑ 92SweSemE-331
❑ 93SweSemE-296
❑ 98GerDELE-108

**Laidlaw, Ken**
❑ 69ColChe-9

**Laidlaw, Tom**
❑ 81OPC-234
❑ 82OPC-227
❑ 82PosCer-13
❑ 83OPC-247
❑ 84OPC-144
❑ 86OPC-147
❑ 86OPCSti-223
❑ 86Top-147
❑ 88KinSmo-15
❑ 88OPC-37
❑ 88PanSti-71
❑ 88Top-37
❑ 89KinSmo-23
❑ 89OPC-34
❑ 89Top-34
❑ 90KinSmo-12
❑ 90OPC-524
❑ 90ProSet-123
❑ 90Sco-69
❑ 90ScoCan-69
❑ 90UppDec-119
❑ 90UppDecF-119

**Laine, Erkki**
❑ 82SweSemHVS-43
❑ 84SweSemE-110
❑ 85SwePanS-104
❑ 86SwePanS-98
❑ 87SwePanS-100
❑ 89SweSemWCS-45
❑ 93FinnSIS-81
❑ 93FinnSIS-297

**Laine, Sami**
❑ 95FinnSIS-212
❑ 96FinnSISR-7

**Laird, Rob**
❑ 89CapKod-xx
❑ 90ProAHLIHL-217
❑ 91ProAHLCHL-571
❑ 95PhoRoa-23

**Laitinen, Kari**
❑ 89SweSemWCS-43

**Laitre, Martin**
❑ 907thInnSQMJHL-254

**Lajeunesse, Bruno**
❑ 907thInnSQMJHL-132

**Lajeunesse, Martin**
❑ 907thInnSQMJHL-242
❑ 917thInnSQMJHL-126

**Lajeunesse, Serge**
❑ 70EssPowPla-131
❑ 71OPC-136

**Lajoie, Claude**
❑ 84ChiSag-16

**Lajoie, Serge**
❑ 86KamBla-9

**Lake, Allan**
❑ 86KitRan-16
❑ 87KitRan-28

**Lake, Fred**
❑ 10C55SweCP-9
❑ 10C56-27
❑ 11C55-9
❑ 12C57-31

**Lakovic, Sasha**
❑ 94CenHocL-99
❑ 95LasVegThu-4

**Lakso, Bob**
❑ 88ProIHL-1
❑ 89ProIHL-125
❑ 90ProAHLIHL-542
❑ 91ProAHLCHL-257

**Laksola, Pekka**
❑ 93FinnJyvHS-290
❑ 93FinnSIS-66
❑ 94FinnSIS-64
❑ 94FinnSIS-377
❑ 95FinnSemWC-33
❑ 95FinnSIS-111
❑ 95FinnSIS-183
❑ 95FinnSISDT-8
❑ 95FinnSISL-74
❑ 96GerDELE-254

**Lala, Jiri**
❑ 81SweSemHVS-70
❑ 82SweSemHVS-89
❑ 89SweSemWCS-198
❑ 91SweSemWCS-114
❑ 94GerDELE-113
❑ 95GerDELE-115

**Lalancette, Jacques**
❑ 51LavDaiLSJ-24

**Lalande, Hector (Hec)**
❑ 52JunBluT-170
❑ 57Top-31
❑ 94ParMisL-38

**Laliberte, Hugues**
❑ 907thInnSQMJHL-213
❑ 917thInnSQMJHL-26

**Laliberte, Spike**
❑ 51LavDaiQSHL-59

**Lalime, Patrick**
❑ 917thInnSQMJHL-71
❑ 94HamRoaA-3
❑ 95CleLum-15
❑ 96BeAPLH-10A
❑ 96BeAPLHAut-10A
❑ 96BeAPLHAutSil-10A
❑ 96BeAPStaTP-1
❑ 96DonEli-133
❑ 96DonEliDCS-133
❑ 96Fla-121
❑ 96FlaBluI-121
❑ 96FlaHotG-6
❑ 96SelCer-108
❑ 96SelCerAP-108
❑ 96SelCerBlu-108
❑ 96SelCerMB-108
❑ 96SelCerMG-108
❑ 96SelCerMR-108
❑ 96SelCerRed-108
❑ 96Ult-142
❑ 96UltGolM-142
❑ 96UppDecBD-168
❑ 96UppDecBDG-168
❑ 96UppDecIce-54
❑ 96UppDecIcePar-54
❑ 97ColCho-208
❑ 97ColChoSta-SQ40
❑ 97Don-76
❑ 97DonCanILG-9
❑ 97DonCanILGP-9
❑ 97DonLim-142
❑ 97DonLim-159
❑ 97DonLimExp-142
❑ 97DonLimExp-159
❑ 97DonPreProG-76
❑ 97DonPreProS-76
❑ 97Lea-111
❑ 97LeaFraMat-111
❑ 97LeaFraMDC-111
❑ 97LeaInt-111
❑ 97LeaIntUI-111
❑ 97Pac-40
❑ 97PacCop-40
❑ 97PacDyn-103
❑ 97PacDyn-142
❑ 97PacDynBKS-78
❑ 97PacDynC-103
❑ 97PacDynC-142
❑ 97PacDynDD-13B
❑ 97PacDynDG-103
❑ 97PacDynDG-142
❑ 97PacDynEG-103
❑ 97PacDynEG-142
❑ 97PacDynIB-103
❑ 97PacDynIB-142
❑ 97PacDynR-103
❑ 97PacDynR-142
❑ 97PacDynSil-103
❑ 97PacDynSil-142
❑ 97PacDynSto-18
❑ 97PacDynTan-9
❑ 97PacDynTan-22
❑ 97PacEmeGre-40
❑ 97PacIceB-40
❑ 97PacInTheCLC-17
❑ 97PacInv-114
❑ 97PacInvC-114
❑ 97PacInvEG-114
❑ 97PacInvFP-29
❑ 97PacInvIB-114
❑ 97PacInvNRB-161
❑ 97PacInvR-114
❑ 97PacInvS-114
❑ 97PacRed-40
❑ 97PacSil-40
❑ 97PinCer-23
❑ 97PinCerMB-23
❑ 97PinCerMG-23
❑ 97PinCerMR-23
❑ 97PinCerR-23
❑ 97PinIns-67
❑ 97PinInsCC-67
❑ 97PinInsEC-67
❑ 97PinInsSUG-6A/B
❑ 97PinInsSUG-6C/D
❑ 97PinTotCMPG-23
❑ 97PinTotCPB-23
❑ 97PinTotCPG-23
❑ 97PinTotCPR-23
❑ 97Sco-40
❑ 97ScoArtPro-40
❑ 97ScoGolBla-40
❑ 97ScoPen-3
❑ 97ScoPenPla-3
❑ 97ScoPenPre-3
❑ 97UppDec-133
❑ 97UppDecGDM-133
❑ 97UppDecSG-SG40
❑ 97UppDecTSS-12A
❑ 98KanCitB-22

**Lalonde, Bobby**
❑ 71CanuRoyB-1
❑ 71TorSun-283
❑ 72CanuRoyB-10
❑ 72OPC-217
❑ 73CanuRoyB-10
❑ 73OPC-179
❑ 73Top-189
❑ 74CanuRoyB-9
❑ 74OPCNHL-392
❑ 75CanuRoyB-10
❑ 75OPCNHL-246
❑ 75Top-246
❑ 76CanuRoyB-8
❑ 76OPCNHL-278
❑ 77OPCNHL-313
❑ 78OPC-285
❑ 79OPC-326
❑ 80OPC-265

**Lalonde, Gregg**
❑ 94SudWolP-20
❑ 95Sla-384
❑ 95SudWol-9
❑ 95SudWolP-11

**Lalonde, Herve**
❑ 52JunBluT-38

**Lalonde, Newsy**
❑ 10C55SweCP-42
❑ 10C56-36
❑ 11C55-42
❑ 12C57-44
❑ 23V1281PauC-38
❑ 24V130MapC-27
❑ 27LaPat-17
❑ 55Par-55
❑ 55ParQuaO-55
❑ 60Top-48
❑ 60TopSta-31
❑ 83HalFP-E10
❑ 85HalFC-70
❑ 99UppDecCL-32
❑ 99UppDecCLCLC-32

**Lalonde, Pierre-Francois**
❑ 917thInnSQMJHL-205

**Lalonde, Robert**
❑ 72SarProSta-221

**Lalonde, Ron**
❑ 74NHLActSta-221
❑ 74NHLActStaU-42
❑ 74PenPos-13
❑ 75OPCNHL-152
❑ 75Top-152
❑ 76OPCNHL-339
❑ 77OPCNHL-378
❑ 78OPC-371

**Lalonde, Todd**
❑ 85SudWol-7
❑ 86SudWol-2
❑ 87SudWol-4
❑ 88SudWol-24
❑ 95Sla-405

**Lalor, Mike**
❑ 83NovScoV-12
❑ 85CanaPos-16
❑ 85CanaPro-8
❑ 86CanaPos-9
❑ 86KraDra-30
❑ 87CanaPos-12
❑ 87CanaVacS-22
❑ 87CanaVacS-59
❑ 87CanaVacS-60
❑ 88BluKod-26
❑ 88CanaPos-15
❑ 89BluKod-26
❑ 90CapKod-12
❑ 90CapPos-12
❑ 90CapSmo-11
❑ 90OPC-341
❑ 90OPCPre-57
❑ 90PanSti-267
❑ 90ProSet-264
❑ 90ProSet-552
❑ 90Sco-67
❑ 90ScoCan-67
❑ 90ScoRoo-98T
❑ 90Top-341
❑ 90TopTif-341
❑ 90UppDec-40
❑ 90UppDecF-40
❑ 91CapJun5-17
❑ 91OPC-483
❑ 91Par-427
❑ 91ParFre-427
❑ 91ProSet-255
❑ 91ProSetFre-255
❑ 91ScoAme-249
❑ 91ScoCan-469
❑ 91Top-483
❑ 92Bow-319
❑ 92Pin-123
❑ 92PinFre-123
❑ 92ProSet-268
❑ 92Sco-363
❑ 92ScoCan-363
❑ 92StaClu-190
❑ 92Top-140
❑ 92TopGol-140G
❑ 93Don-306
❑ 93Kra-40
❑ 93Lea-399
❑ 94StaPos-14
❑ 96StaPos-14

**Laluk, Laird**
❑ 95SasBla-12
❑ 96SasBla-14

**Laluk, Scott**
❑ 92BraWheK-14
❑ 95SlaMemC-29

**Lamarche, Martin**
❑ 917thInnSQMJHL-90

**Lamb, Garth**
❑ 89NasKni-14

**Lamb, Jeff**
❑ 88ProAHL-150
❑ 89ProIHL-110

**Lamb, Joe**
❑ 33OPCV304A-2
❑ 33V357IceK-41
❑ 34BeeGro1P-237
❑ 34DiaMatS-37
❑ 34SweCap-6
❑ 35DiaMatTI-37
❑ 36V356WorG-37
❑ 38BruGarMS-4

**Lamb, Mark**
❑ 82MedHatT-9
❑ 83MedHatT-8
❑ 84MonGolF-6
❑ 85MonGolF-7
❑ 88OilTeal-16
❑ 88OilTenAnn-61
❑ 88ProAHL-89
❑ 89OilTeal-14
❑ 90OilIGA-11
❑ 90OPC-25
❑ 90ProSet-88
❑ 90Sco-308C
❑ 90ScoCan-308C
❑ 90Top-25
❑ 90TopTif-25
❑ 91OilIGA-8
❑ 91OilPanTS-10
❑ 91OilTeal-10
❑ 91ScoCan-652
❑ 92OPC-322
❑ 92Par-116
❑ 92ParEmel-116
❑ 92Pin-374
❑ 92PinFre-374
❑ 92Sco-514
❑ 92ScoCan-514
❑ 92Sen-7
❑ 92Top-230
❑ 92TopGol-230G
❑ 93Don-230
❑ 93Lea-308
❑ 93OPCPre-271
❑ 93OPCPreG-271
❑ 93PanSti-117
❑ 93Pin-323
❑ 93PinCan-323
❑ 93PinCapC-16
❑ 93Pow-171
❑ 93Sco-407
❑ 93ScoCan-407
❑ 93SenKraS-13
❑ 93StaClu-172
❑ 93StaCluFDI-172
❑ 93StaCluFDIO-172
❑ 93StaCluO-172
❑ 93TopPre-271
❑ 93TopPreG-271
❑ 94CanGamNHLP-178
❑ 94Lea-337
❑ 94Pin-163
❑ 94PinArtP-163
❑ 94PinRinC-163
❑ 94StaClu-206
❑ 94StaCluFDI-206
❑ 94StaCluMOMS-206
❑ 94StaCluSTWC-206

**Lambert, Dan**
❑ 907thInnSOHL-164
❑ 91Pin-346
❑ 91PinFre-346
❑ 91UppDec-592
❑ 91UppDecF-592
❑ 92Bow-356
❑ 92OPC-357
❑ 92Top-364
❑ 92TopGol-364G
❑ 92UppDec-251
❑ 93FinnJyvHS-26
❑ 93FinnSIS-87
❑ 96ColEdgFL-30

**Lambert, Denny**
❑ 89SauSteMG-8

❑ 917thInnSMC-17
❑ 91ProAHLCHL-324
❑ 92SanDieG-14
❑ 95Bow-98
❑ 95BowAllFoi-98
❑ 95Top-286
❑ 95TopOPCI-286
❑ 95Ult-4
❑ 95UltGolM-4
❑ 96BeAPAut-68
❑ 96BeAPAutSil-68
❑ 96BeAPla-68
❑ 96SenPizH-11
❑ 97PacInvNRB-134
❑ 98Pac-311
❑ 98PacAur-103
❑ 98PacIceB-311
❑ 98PacOmeH-131
❑ 98PacOmeODI-131
❑ 98PacOmeR-131
❑ 98PacPar-125
❑ 98PacParC-125
❑ 98PacParEG-125
❑ 98PacParH-125
❑ 98PacParIB-125
❑ 98PacParS-125
❑ 98PacRed-311
❑ 99Pac-228
❑ 99PacCop-228
❑ 99PacGol-228
❑ 99PacIceB-228
❑ 99PacPreD-228

**Lambert, Judd**
❑ 92BriColJHL-42

**Lambert, Lane**
❑ 81SasBla-19
❑ 84OPC-57
❑ 87NordGenF-19
❑ 87RedWinLC-18
❑ 88NordGenF-19
❑ 88NordTeal-20
❑ 88OPC-224
❑ 88OPCSti-183
❑ 88PanSti-356
❑ 93SwiHNL-503
❑ 95SwiHNL-362
❑ 96CleLum-14

**Lambert, Ross**
❑ 83MonAlp-13
❑ 84NovScoO-23

**Lambert, Sylvio**
❑ 51LavDaiLSJ-21

**Lambert, Yves**
❑ 917thInnSQMJHL-272

**Lambert, Yvon**
❑ 73CanaPos-8
❑ 74CanaPos-9
❑ 74NHLActSta-147
❑ 74OPCNHL-342
❑ 75CanaPos-9
❑ 75OPCNHL-17
❑ 75Top-17
❑ 76CanaPos-10
❑ 76OPCNHL-232
❑ 76Top-232
❑ 77CanaPos-11
❑ 77OPCNHL-151
❑ 77Top-151
❑ 78CanaPos-12
❑ 78OPC-147
❑ 78Top-147
❑ 79CanaPos-11
❑ 79OPC-24
❑ 79Top-24
❑ 80CanaPos-11
❑ 80OPC-246
❑ 80PepCap-48
❑ 80Top-246
❑ 81OPC-185
❑ 81OPCSti-35
❑ 81SabMilP-16
❑ 82OPC-27
❑ 82OPCSti-125
❑ 82PosCer-2

**Lamby, Dick**
❑ 79PanSti-208

**Lamey, Rob**
❑ 96GuiFla-2

**Laming, Andrew**
❑ 917thInnSWHL-65

**Lamirande, Charles**
❑ 51LavDaiLSJ-31

**Lamirande, Gaston**
❑ 51LavDaiLSJ-39

**Lamirande, J.P.**
❑ 51LavDaiQSHL-31
❑ 52St.LawS-95

**Lammens, Hank**
❑ 88ProAHL-320
❑ 89ProAHL-233
❑ 92AlbIntTC-10
❑ 93Par-409
❑ 93ParEmel-409

**Lamoreux, Leo**
❑ 34BeeGro1P-163

**Lamoriello, Lou**
❑ 88DevCar-16
❑ 89DevCar-14
❑ 90Dev-14
❑ 96Dev-NNO

**Lamothe, Carl**
❑ 907thInnSQMJHL-255
❑ 917thInnSQMJHL-148

**Lamothe, Marc**
❑ 917thInnSOHL-240
❑ 93KinFro-2
❑ 94FreCan-16
❑ 95FreCan-16

**Lamoureux, Guillaume**
❑ 98Vald'OF-3

**Lamoureux, Leo**
❑ 45QuaOatP-87A
❑ 45QuaOatP-87B

**Lamoureux, Mitch**
❑ 80OshGen-15
❑ 81OshGen-6
❑ 83PenTealP-20
❑ 92SanDieG-15
❑ 96ProBru-22

**Lamoureux, Patrick**
❑ 917thInnSQMJHL-51

**Lampert, Reinhard**
❑ 93SweSemWCS-287
❑ 94FinnJaaK-247

**Lampinen, Juha**
❑ 93FinnJyvHS-85
❑ 93FinnSIS-113
❑ 94FinnSIS-54
❑ 95FinnSIS-232
❑ 96GerDELE-95

**Lampman, Josh**
❑ 93WatBlaH-15

**Lampman, Mike**
❑ 72BluWhiBor-9
❑ 73BluWhiBor-11
❑ 76OPCNHL-375
❑ 77OPCNHL-396

**Lampron, Patrick**
❑ 917thInnSQMJHL-98

**Landegren, Dan**
❑ 71SweHocS-235
❑ 72SweHocS-222
❑ 73SweHocS-75
❑ 73SweWorCS-75
❑ 74SweHocS-237

**Landeskog, Tony**
❑ 84SweSemE-130

**Landgren, Reine**
❑ 89SweSemE-232
❑ 90SweSemE-64
❑ 91SweSemE-242

**Landini, Mark**
❑ 94WheThu-23

**Landoli, Nicky**
❑ 94GuiFla-17

**Landon, Bruce**
❑ 72WhaNewEWHA-10
❑ 76OPCWHA-48

**Landon, Larry**
❑ 83NovScoV-23

**Landry, Eric**
❑ 93GueSto-10
❑ 95Sla-318
❑ 96RoaExp-3

**Landry, Jerome**
❑ 92QueIntP-4

**Landry, John**
❑ 82KinCan-17
❑ 84SudWol-11

**Landry, Roger**
❑ 52JunBluT-160

**Landry, Sean**
❑ 92QueIntP-21

**Landstrom, Kjell**
❑ 71SweHocS-236
❑ 72SweHocS-223
❑ 73SweHocS-76
❑ 73SweWorCS-76
❑ 74SweHocS-238

**Lane, Chris**
❑ 95SpoChi-4

**Lane, Gordie**
❑ 77OPCNHL-287
❑ 78OPC-284
❑ 79OPC-325
❑ 80OPC-323
❑ 81OPC-212
❑ 83OPC-10
❑ 84IslIsN-17
❑ 85IslIsN-21
❑ 85OPCSti-77

**Lane, Mitch**
❑ 93MicTecH-22

**Lang, Bill**
❑ 907thInnSOHL-310
❑ 917thInnSOHL-60
❑ 93NorBayC-9

**Lang, Chad**
❑ 917thInnSOHL-129
❑ 91PetPet-22
❑ 93PetPet-15
❑ 95Cla-94

**Lang, Karel**
❑ 82SweSemHVS-77
❑ 94GerDELE-225
❑ 95GerDELE-219
❑ 96GerDELE-69
❑ 98GerDELE-25

**Lang, Kjell**
❑ 69SweHocS-86

**Lang, Robert**
❑ 92OPCPre-47
❑ 92Par-64
❑ 92Par-227
❑ 92ParEmel-64
❑ 92ParEmel-227
❑ 92PhoRoa-12
❑ 92Pin-411
❑ 92PinFre-411
❑ 92UppDec-552
❑ 92UppDecER-ER4
❑ 93ClaProPro-46
❑ 93Sco-456
❑ 93ScoCan-456
❑ 93Ult-188
❑ 94BeAPSig-174
❑ 94CzeAPSE-222
❑ 94FinnJaaK-186
❑ 94Lea-429
❑ 94OPCPre-218
❑ 94OPCPreSE-218
❑ 94Par-286
❑ 94ParGol-286
❑ 94ParSE-SE78
❑ 94ParSEG-SE78
❑ 94Pin-413
❑ 94PinArtP-413
❑ 94PinRinC-413
❑ 94TopPre-218
❑ 94TopPreSE-218
❑ 94Ult-101
❑ 94UppDec-175
❑ 94UppDecEleIce-175
❑ 95ColCho-175
❑ 95ColChoPC-175
❑ 95ColChoPCP-175
❑ 95ParInt-101
❑ 95ParIntEI-101
❑ 95SweGloWC-155
❑ 95Top-186
❑ 95TopOPCI-186
❑ 95UppDec-281
❑ 95UppDecEleIce-281
❑ 95UppDecEleIceG-281
❑ 97Be A PPAD-14
❑ 97Be A PPAPD-14
❑ 97BeAPla-14
❑ 97BeAPlaAut-14
❑ 98Be A PPA-263
❑ 98Be A PPAA-263
❑ 98Be A PPAAF-263
❑ 98Be A PPSE-263
❑ 98Be APG-263
❑ 98Pac-355
❑ 98PacIceB-355
❑ 98PacOmeH-197
❑ 98PacOmeODI-197
❑ 98PacOmeR-197
❑ 98PacRed-355
❑ 99Pac-342
❑ 99PacCop-342
❑ 99PacGol-342
❑ 99PacIceB-342
❑ 99PacPreD-342

**Langager, Shane**
❑ 88SasBla-9
❑ 89SasBla-9

**Langauer, Michael**
❑ 907thInnSQMJHL-139

**Langbacka, Jan**
❑ 93FinnJyvHS-198
❑ 93FinnSIS-266
❑ 94FinnSIS-26

**Langdon, Darren**
❑ 92DayBom-16
❑ 94BinRan-9
❑ 95Bow-92
❑ 95BowAllFoi-92
❑ 95Don-224
❑ 95Lea-262
❑ 95Met-181
❑ 95ParInt-528
❑ 95ParIntEI-528
❑ 95SkyImp-212
❑ 95Top-116
❑ 95TopOPCI-116
❑ 95Ult-102
❑ 95Ult-345
❑ 95UltGolM-102
❑ 96BeAPAut-9
❑ 96BeAPAutSil-9
❑ 96BeAPla-9
❑ 98O-PChr-172
❑ 98O-PChrR-172
❑ 98Pac-296
❑ 98PacIceB-296
❑ 98PacRed-296
❑ 98Top-172
❑ 98TopO-P-172

**Langdon, Steve**
❑ 77RocAme-15

**Lange, Lennart**
❑ 64SweCorI-56
❑ 65SweCorI-56
❑ 67SweHoc-104
❑ 71SweHocS-355

**Lange, Patrick**
❑ 94GerDELE-195
❑ 95GerDELE-309

**Langelle, Pete**
❑ 34BeeGro1P-333
❑ 39OPCV3011-7
❑ 40OPCV3012-117

**Langen, Mike**
❑ 907thInnSWHL-270
❑ 91AirCanSJHL-A13

**Langenbrunner, Jamie**
❑ 93DonTeaUSA-13
❑ 93PetPet-20
❑ 93Pin-496
❑ 93PinCan-496
❑ 93UppDec-566
❑ 94Cla-24
❑ 94ClaDraGol-24
❑ 94ClaTri-T16
❑ 94Fin-120
❑ 94FinRef-120
❑ 94FinSupTW-120
❑ 94LeaLimWJUSA-7
❑ 94ParSEG-SE248
❑ 94ScoGol-211
❑ 94ScoPla-211
❑ 95Cla-94
❑ 95ColEdgI-141
❑ 95Ima-48
❑ 95ImaAut-48A
❑ 95ImaGol-48
❑ 95Sum-170
❑ 95SumArtP-170
❑ 95SumIce-170
❑ 95Ult-346
❑ 95UppDec-503
❑ 95UppDecEleIce-503
❑ 95UppDecEleIceG-503
❑ 96BeAPLH-6A
❑ 96BeAPLHAut-6A
❑ 96BeAPLHAutSil-6A
❑ 96ColCho-74
❑ 96ColEdgPC-6
❑ 96Don-218
❑ 96DonCanI-137
❑ 96DonCanIGPP-137
❑ 96DonCanIRPP-137
❑ 96DonEli-144
❑ 96DonEliAsp-21
❑ 96DonEliDCS-144
❑ 96DonProPre-218
❑ 96Fla-105
❑ 96FlaBluI-105
❑ 96Fle-129
❑ 96FleCalCan-6
❑ 96Lea-225
❑ 96LeaLimR-8
❑ 96LeaLimRG-8
❑ 96LeaPre-144
❑ 96LeaPreP-225
❑ 96LeaPrePP-144
❑ 96MetUni-184
❑ 96Pin-247
❑ 96PinArtP-247
❑ 96PinFoi-247
❑ 96PinPreS-247
❑ 96PinRinC-247
❑ 96Sco-254
❑ 96ScoArtPro-254
❑ 96ScoDeaCAP-254
❑ 96ScoGolB-254
❑ 96ScoSpeAP-254
❑ 96SelCer-115
❑ 96SelCerAP-115
❑ 96SelCerBlu-115
❑ 96SelCerMB-115
❑ 96SelCerMG-115
❑ 96SelCerMR-115
❑ 96SelCerRed-115
❑ 96SkyImp-152
❑ 96SP-46
❑ 96StaPos-15
❑ 96Sum-192
❑ 96SumArtP-192
❑ 96SumIce-192
❑ 96SumMet-192
❑ 96SumPreS-192
❑ 96Ult-43
❑ 96UltGolM-43
❑ 96UltRoo-11
❑ 96UppDec-48
❑ 96UppDecBD-126
❑ 96UppDecBDG-126
❑ 96UppDecIce-15
❑ 96UppDecIcePar-15
❑ 96Zen-139
❑ 96ZenArtP-139
❑ 97ColCho-69
❑ 97Don-97
❑ 97DonCanI-103
❑ 97DonCanIDS-103
❑ 97DonCanIPS-103
❑ 97DonLim-167
❑ 97DonLimExp-167
❑ 97DonPre-20
❑ 97DonPreCttC-20
❑ 97DonPreProG-97
❑ 97DonPreProS-97
❑ 97DonPri-79
❑ 97DonPriSoA-79
❑ 97Lea-46
❑ 97LeaFraMat-46
❑ 97LeaFraMDC-46
❑ 97LeaInt-46
❑ 97LeaIntUI-46
❑ 97Pac-110
❑ 97PacCop-110
❑ 97PacDyn-36
❑ 97PacDynC-36
❑ 97PacDynDG-36
❑ 97PacDynEG-36
❑ 97PacDynIB-36
❑ 97PacDynR-36
❑ 97PacDynSil-36
❑ 97PacDynTan-32
❑ 97PacEmeGre-110
❑ 97PacIceB-110
❑ 97PacInv-40
❑ 97PacInvC-40
❑ 97PacInvEG-40
❑ 97PacInvIB-40
❑ 97PacInvR-40
❑ 97PacInvS-40
❑ 97PacOme-70
❑ 97PacOmeC-70
❑ 97PacOmeDG-70
❑ 97PacOmeEG-70
❑ 97PacOmeG-70
❑ 97PacOmeIB-70
❑ 97PacPar-58
❑ 97PacParC-58
❑ 97PacParDG-58
❑ 97PacParEG-58
❑ 97PacParIB-58
❑ 97PacParRed-58
❑ 97PacParSil-58
❑ 97PacRed-110
❑ 97PacRev-41
❑ 97PacRevC-41
❑ 97PacRevE-41
❑ 97PacRevIB-41
❑ 97PacRevR-41
❑ 97PacRevS-41
❑ 97PacSil-110
❑ 97PinIns-100
❑ 97Sco-211
❑ 97SPAut-47
❑ 97SPAutSotT-JL
❑ 97UppDec-260
❑ 97Zen-61
❑ 97Zen5x7-51
❑ 97ZenGolImp-51
❑ 97ZenSilImp-51
❑ 97ZenZGol-61
❑ 97ZenZSil-61
❑ 98O-PChr-7
❑ 98O-PChrR-7
❑ 98Pac-15
❑ 98PacAur-56
❑ 98PacCroR-39
❑ 98PacCroRLS-39
❑ 98PacDynI-57
❑ 98PacDynIB-57
❑ 98PacDynIR-57
❑ 98PacIceB-15
❑ 98PacOmeH-71
❑ 98PacOmeODI-71
❑ 98PacOmeR-71
❑ 98PacPar-65
❑ 98PacParC-65
❑ 98PacParEG-65
❑ 98PacParH-65
❑ 98PacParIB-65
❑ 98PacParS-65
❑ 98PacRed-15
❑ 98PacRev-42
❑ 98PacRevIS-42
❑ 98PacRevR-42
❑ 98Top-7
❑ 98TopO-P-7
❑ 98UC-61
❑ 98UD ChoPCR-61
❑ 98UD ChoR-61
❑ 98UDCP-61
❑ 98UppDec-81
❑ 98UppDecE-81
❑ 98UppDecE1o1-81
❑ 98UppDecGR-81
❑ 99Pac-122
❑ 99PacAur-45
❑ 99PacAurPD-45
❑ 99PacCop-122
❑ 99PacGol-122
❑ 99PacIceB-122
❑ 99PacPreD-122
❑ 99UppDecM-64
❑ 99UppDecMGS-64
❑ 99UppDecMSS-64
❑ 99UppDecMSS-64

**Langevin, Chris**
❑ 85SabBluS-10
❑ 85SabBluSS-16

**Langevin, Dave**
❑ 79IslTrans-8
❑ 80OPC-188
❑ 80Top-188
❑ 81OPC-213
❑ 82OPC-204
❑ 82PosCer-12
❑ 83IslTeaIss-8
❑ 83OPC-11
❑ 83OPCSti-83
❑ 84IslIsN-18
❑ 85IslIsN-22
❑ 85NorSta7E-11
❑ 85NorStaPos-15
❑ 86OPC-218

**Langill, Eric**
❑ 92QueIntP-20

**Langille, Derek**
❑ 90NewSai-13
❑ 90ProAHLIHL-153
❑ 91MonHaw-16
❑ 91ProAHLCHL-173

**Langkow, Daymond**
❑ 93UppDecPOE-E7
❑ 94Cla95DP-DP4
❑ 94LigPos-12
❑ 94TriAme-6
❑ 95Cla-5
❑ 95ClaCHLAS-AS4
❑ 95ClaIceBre-BK5
❑ 95ColCho-402
❑ 95Don-324
❑ 95DonEliWJ-16
❑ 95Ima-83
❑ 95ImaCleE-CE12
❑ 95ImaGol-83
❑ 95ImaPlaPDC-PD6
❑ 95LeaLim-45
❑ 95Met-182
❑ 95ParInt-270
❑ 95ParIntEI-270
❑ 95SelCer-124
❑ 95SelCerMG-124
❑ 95SigRoo-22
❑ 95SigRooAP-P2
❑ 95SigRooSig-22
❑ 95SkyImp-222
❑ 95SP-139
❑ 95TriAme-15
❑ 95TriAme-30
❑ 95UppDec-270
❑ 95UppDec-526
❑ 95UppDecEleIce-270
❑ 95UppDecEleIce-526
❑ 95UppDecEleIceG-270
❑ 95UppDecEleIceG-526
❑ 95Zen-143
❑ 96ClaIceBreDC-BK5
❑ 96ColCho-346
❑ 96DonCanI-135
❑ 96DonCanIGPP-135
❑ 96DonCanIRPP-135
❑ 96DonEli-134
❑ 96DonEliAsp-13
❑ 96DonEliDCS-134
❑ 96Fle-130
❑ 96FleCalCan-7
❑ 96Lea-232
❑ 96LeaPre-140
❑ 96LeaPreP-232
❑ 96LeaPrePP-140
❑ 96MetUni-185
❑ 96Pin-240
❑ 96PinArtP-240
❑ 96PinFoi-240
❑ 96PinPreS-240
❑ 96PinRinC-240
❑ 96SelCer-117
❑ 96SelCerAP-117
❑ 96SelCerBlu-117
❑ 96SelCerMB-117
❑ 96SelCerMG-117
❑ 96SelCerMR-117
❑ 96SelCerRed-117
❑ 96SkyImp-153
❑ 96SP-146
❑ 96Sum-186
❑ 96SumArtP-186
❑ 96SumIce-186
❑ 96SumMet-186
❑ 96SumPreS-186
❑ 96Ult-158
❑ 96UltGolM-158
❑ 96UppDec-340
❑ 96UppDecBD-46
❑ 96UppDecBDG-46
❑ 96UppDecGN-X30
❑ 96Zen-141
❑ 96ZenArtP-141
❑ 97Be A PPAD-176
❑ 97Be A PPAPD-176
❑ 97BeAPla-176
❑ 97BeAPlaAut-176
❑ 97ColCho-243
❑ 97Don-18
❑ 97DonCanI-70
❑ 97DonCanIDS-70
❑ 97DonCanINP-21
❑ 97DonCanIPS-70
❑ 97DonEli-36
❑ 97DonEliAsp-36
❑ 97DonEliS-36
❑ 97DonLim-31
❑ 97DonLim-133
❑ 97DonLim-192
❑ 97DonLimExp-31
❑ 97DonLimExp-133
❑ 97DonLimExp-192
❑ 97DonLimFOTG-48
❑ 97DonPre-23
❑ 97DonPreCttC-23
❑ 97DonPreProG-18
❑ 97DonPreProS-18
❑ 97DonPri-21
❑ 97DonPriSoA-21
❑ 97Kat-136
❑ 97KatGol-136
❑ 97KatSil-136
❑ 97Lea-103
❑ 97LeaFraMat-103
❑ 97LeaFraMDC-103
❑ 97LeaInt-103
❑ 97LeaIntUI-103
❑ 97PacDyn-119
❑ 97PacDynC-119
❑ 97PacDynDG-119
❑ 97PacDynEG-119
❑ 97PacDynIB-119
❑ 97PacDynR-119
❑ 97PacDynSil-119
❑ 97PacDynTan-65
❑ 97PacInv-133
❑ 97PacInvC-133
❑ 97PacInvEG-133
❑ 97PacInvIB-133
❑ 97PacInvR-133
❑ 97PacInvS-133
❑ 97PacOme-210
❑ 97PacOmeC-210
❑ 97PacOmeDG-210
❑ 97PacOmeEG-210
❑ 97PacOmeG-210
❑ 97PacOmeIB-210
❑ 97PacPar-174
❑ 97PacParC-174
❑ 97PacParDG-174
❑ 97PacParEG-174
❑ 97PacParIB-174
❑ 97PacParRed-174
❑ 97PacParSil-174
❑ 97Pin-112
❑ 97PinIns-99
❑ 97PinPrePBB-112
❑ 97PinPrePBC-112
❑ 97PinPrePBM-112
❑ 97PinPrePBY-112
❑ 97PinPrePFC-112
❑ 97PinPrePFM-112
❑ 97PinPrePFY-112
❑ 97PinPrePla-112
❑ 97Sco-167
❑ 97SPAut-145
❑ 97Stu-48
❑ 97StuHarH-6
❑ 97StuPrePG-48
❑ 97StuPrePS-48
❑ 97UppDec-158
❑ 97UppDecIce-15
❑ 97UppDecIceP-15
❑ 97UppDecIPS-15
❑ 97UppDecSG-SG32
❑ 97UppDecTSS-15C
❑ 98Be A PPA-129
❑ 98Be A PPAA-129
❑ 98Be A PPAAF-129
❑ 98Be A PPTBASG-129
❑ 98Be APG-129
❑ 98O-PChr-72
❑ 98O-PChrR-72
❑ 98Pac-400
❑ 98PacIceB-400
❑ 98PacRed-400
❑ 98Top-72
❑ 98TopO-P-72
❑ 98UC-192
❑ 98UD ChoPCR-192
❑ 98UD ChoR-192
❑ 99Pac-305
❑ 99PacCop-305
❑ 99PacGol-305
❑ 99PacIceB-305
❑ 99PacPreD-305

**Langkow, Scott**
❑ 95ColEdgI-71
❑ 96SprFal-35
❑ 99Pac-332
❑ 99PacCop-332
❑ 99PacGol-332
❑ 99PacIceB-332
❑ 99PacPreD-332

**Langlais, Alain**
❑ 89NewHavN-6

**Langlois, Charlie**
❑ 24V130MapC-26
❑ 24V1452-17
❑ 27LaPat-12

**Langlois, Jocelyn**
❑ 907thInnSQMJHL-79
❑ 917thInnSQMJHL-107

**Langlois, Junior (Albert)**
❑ 44BeeGro2P-256
❑ 44BeeGro2P-335
❑ 58Par-5
❑ 59Par-45
❑ 60Par-39
❑ 60ShiCoi-24
❑ 60TopSta-32
❑ 60YorPreP-21
❑ 61Par-37
❑ 61ShiCoi-94
❑ 61Top-46
❑ 62Top-47
❑ 62TopHocBuc-14
❑ 63Top-49
❑ 64BeeGro3P-81
❑ 64CocCap-38
❑ 64Top-13
❑ 65Coc-2
❑ 65Top-33
❑ 94ParTalB-52

**Langlois, Louis C**
❑ 24C144ChaCig-35

**Langlois, Patrick**
❑ 92FreCan-16
❑ 93FreCan-15
❑ 94FreCan-17
❑ 95FreCan-17

**Langlois, Peter**
❑ 84KitRan-9

**Langner, Paul**
❑ 72SweSemWC-111

**Langway, Rod**
❑ 78CanaPos-13
❑ 79CanaPos-12
❑ 80CanaPos-12
❑ 80OPC-344
❑ 80PepCap-49
❑ 81CanaPos-14
❑ 81OPC-186
❑ 81OPCSti-39
❑ 82Cap-13
❑ 82McDSti-32
❑ 82OPC-368
❑ 82OPCSti-34
❑ 82PosCer-10
❑ 83OPC-207
❑ 83OPC-365

□ 83OPC-374
□ 83OPCSti-201
□ 83OPCSti-313
□ 83PufSti-19
□ 847EDis-54
□ 84CapPizH-11
□ 84OPC-202
□ 84OPC-210
□ 84OPC-377
□ 84OPCSti-125
□ 84OPCSti-126
□ 84OPCSti-230
□ 84Top-147
□ 84Top-156
□ 857ECreCar-20
□ 85CapPizH-10
□ 85OPC-8
□ 85OPCSti-105
□ 85OPCSti-113
□ 85Top-8
□ 85TopStiIns-10
□ 86CapKod-14
□ 86CapPol-14
□ 86OPC-164
□ 86OPCSti-249
□ 86Top-164
□ 87CapKod-5
□ 87CapTeaIss-13
□ 87OPC-108
□ 87OPCSti-236
□ 87PanSti-178
□ 87Top-108
□ 88CapBor-10
□ 88CapSmo-10
□ 88EssAllSta-24
□ 88OPC-192
□ 88OPCSti-69
□ 88PanSti-366
□ 88Top-192
□ 89CapKod-5
□ 89CapTeaIss-13
□ 89OPC-55
□ 89OPCSti-77
□ 89PanSti-350
□ 89SweSemWCS-159
□ 89Top-55
□ 90CapKod-13
□ 90CapPos-13
□ 90CapSmo-12
□ 90Kra-24
□ 90OPC-353
□ 90ProSet-314
□ 90Sco-20
□ 90ScoCan-20
□ 90ScoHotRS-11
□ 90Top-353
□ 90TopTif-353
□ 90UppDec-57
□ 90UppDec-309
□ 90UppDecF-57
□ 90UppDecF-309
□ 91CapJun5-18
□ 91CapKod-17
□ 91OPC-105
□ 91PanSti-209
□ 91Par-197
□ 91ParFre-197
□ 91Pin-195
□ 91PinFre-195
□ 91ProSet-259
□ 91ProSet-587
□ 91ProSetFre-259
□ 91ProSetFre-587
□ 91ScoAme-228
□ 91ScoCan-228
□ 91StaClu-225
□ 91Top-105
□ 91UppDec-314
□ 91UppDecF-314
□ 92Bow-279
□ 92CapKod-18
□ 92OPC-347
□ 92PanSti-169
□ 92PanStiFre-169
□ 92Par-433
□ 92ParEmel-433
□ 92Pin-131
□ 92PinFre-131
□ 92Sco-143
□ 92ScoCan-143
□ 92StaClu-215
□ 92Top-46
□ 92TopGol-46G
□ 93Sco-145
□ 93ScoCan-145
□ 94HocWit-26
□ 94RicRen-12
□ 96SweSemWHL-HL8
**Laniel, Marc**
□ 88ProAHL-328
□ 89ProAHL-227
□ 90ProAHLIHL-567
□ 93FreCan-16
□ 96CinCyc-26
□ 98GerDELE-214
**Lanigan, Gerry**
□ 94DetJrRW-8
□ 95Sla-18
□ 95SlaMemC-22
**Lanigan, Shane**
□ 96RegPat-3
**Lank, Jeff**
□ 917thInnSWHL-256
□ 93PriAlbR-9
□ 93PriAlbR-14

□ 94PriAlbR-13
**Lankshear, Mike**
□ 95GueSto5A-16
□ 95Sla-102
□ 96GueSto-24
□ 96GueStoPC-8
**Lanteigne, Eric**
□ 89RayJrC-13
**Lanthier, Jean-Marc**
□ 80QueRem-8
□ 83FreExp-5
□ 85Canu-11
□ 85FreExp-13
□ 86FreExp-15
□ 88ProAHL-155
□ 89ProAHL-220
**Lantz, Kent**
□ 86SwePanS-212
□ 89SweSemE-188
□ 90SweSemE-16
□ 91SweSemE-217
**Lanz, Rick**
□ 80CanuSilD-12
□ 80CanuTeal-12
□ 80shGen-24
□ 80PepCap-110
□ 81CanuSilD-1
□ 81CanuTeal-12
□ 81OPC-338
□ 82Canu-11
□ 82OPC-348
□ 83Canu-11
□ 83OPC-353
□ 83OPCSti-280
□ 83Vac-110
□ 84Canu-12
□ 84OPC-321
□ 84OPCSti-276
□ 85Canu-12
□ 85OPC-197
□ 86Canu-13
□ 86OPC-179
□ 86Top-179
□ 87MapLeaP-12
□ 87MapLeaPLA-11
□ 87MapLeaPO-12
□ 87OPC-239
□ 87OPCSti-157
□ 88MapLeaPLA-9
□ 880PC-225
□ 880PCSti-176
**Lanzinger, Gunter**
□ 95AusNatTea-14
**Lapensee, Bruno**
□ 86KitRan-25
**Laperriere, Dan (Daniel)**
□ 92Cla-57
□ 92Cla-75
□ 92OPCPre-39
□ 92PeoRivC-11
□ 92UppDec-525
□ 93Don-485
□ 93OPCPre-526
□ 93OPCPreG-526
□ 93PeoRiv-16
□ 93TopPre-526
□ 93TopPreG-526
□ 94ClaProP-184
□ 94Don-187
□ 94Lea-156
□ 94Sco-219
□ 94ScoPla-219
□ 94ScoPlaTS-219
□ 94StaClu-243
□ 94StaCluFDI-243
□ 94StaCluMOMS-243
□ 94StaCluSTWC-243
□ 96ClaGol-57
□ 96ClaGol-75
□ 96PorPir-24
□ 98GerDELE-206
**Laperriere, Gilles**
□ 52JunBluT-67
**Laperriere, Ian**
□ 907thInnSQMJHL-14
□ 917thInnSMC-56
□ 917thInnSQMJHL-281
□ 92Cla-57
□ 93DruVol-10
□ 94Cla-69
□ 94ClaDraGol-69
□ 94ClaTri-T58
□ 94Fle-189
□ 94Lea-484
□ 94OPCPre-307
□ 94OPCPreSE-307
□ 94SPPre-14
□ 94SPPreDC-14
□ 94TopPre-307
□ 94TopPreSE-307
□ 94UppDec-306
□ 94UppDecEleIce-306
□ 95CanGamNHLP-33
□ 95CanGamNHLP-235
□ 95ColCho-19
□ 95ColChoPC-19
□ 95ColEdgIC-C2
□ 95Don-5
□ 95Emo-149
□ 95Ima-7
□ 95ImaCleE-CE7
□ 95ImaGol-7
□ 95ImaPlaPr-PR3

□ 95Lea-99
□ 95LeaLim-53
□ 95LeaStuR-10
□ 95ParInt-176
□ 95ParIntEI-176
□ 95ParIntEI-408
□ 95Pin-127
□ 95PinArtP-127
□ 95PinRinC-127
□ 95PlaOneoOne-308
□ 95Sco-72
□ 95ScoBIaIce-72
□ 95ScoBIaIceAP-72
□ 95SkyImp-142
□ 95SkyImpNHLF-7
□ 95Top-347
□ 95TopNewG-20NG
□ 95TopOPCI-347
□ 95Ult-141
□ 95UltAllRoo-7
□ 95UltAllRooGM-7
□ 95UltGolM-141
□ 95UppDec-32
□ 95UppDecEleIce-32
□ 95UppDecEleIceG-32
□ 95UppDecSpeE-SE69
□ 95UppDecSpeEdIG-SE69
□ 96ClaGol-57
□ 96PlaOneoOne-403
□ 96UppDecBD-10
□ 96UppDecBDG-10
□ 96UppDecIce-30
□ 96UppDecIcePar-30
□ 97Be A PPAD-189
□ 97Be A PPAPD-189
□ 97BeAPla-189
□ 97BeAPlaAut-189
□ 97ColCho-120
□ 97PacDynBKS-47
□ 97UppDec-83
□ 98Be A PPA-65
□ 98Be A PPAA-65
□ 98Be A PPAAF-65
□ 98Be A PPTBASG-65
□ 98Be APG-65
□ 98Pac-237
□ 98PacIceB-237
□ 98PacRed-237
□ 98UppDec-108
□ 98UppDecE-108
□ 98UppDecE1o1-108
□ 98UppDecGR-108
**Laperriere, Jacques**
□ 44BeeGro2P-257
□ 63ChePho-31
□ 63Par-370
□ 63Par-86
□ 63YorWhiB-34
□ 64BeeGro3P-109
□ 64CanaPos-10
□ 64CocCap-56
□ 64Top-53
□ 64TorSta-26
□ 65CanaSteG-5
□ 65Coc-56
□ 65CocBoo-C
□ 65Top-3
□ 66Top-67
□ 66Top-122
□ 67CanalGA-2
□ 67PosFliB-4
□ 67Top-7
□ 67YorActOct-5
□ 67YorActOct-11
□ 67YorActOct-18
□ 68CanalGA-2
□ 68CanaPosBW-8
□ 68OPC-58
□ 68PosCerM-14
□ 68ShiCoi-78
□ 68Top-58
□ 69CanaPosC-12
□ 69OPC-3
□ 69OPCFou-2
□ 69Top-3
□ 70CanaPin-7
□ 70DadCoo-69
□ 70EssPowPla-2
□ 70OPC-52
□ 70OPC-245
□ 70OPCDec-20
□ 70PosCerS-8
□ 70SarProSta-97
□ 70Top-52
□ 70TopStiS-19
□ 71CanaPos-10
□ 71LetActR-2
□ 71OPC-144
□ 71SarProSta-108
□ 71TorSun-153
□ 72CanaPos-8
□ 72OPC-205
□ 72OPCPlaC-11
□ 72SarProSta-121
□ 72SweHocC-112
□ 72SweSemWC-225
□ 73CanaPos-9
□ 73OPC-40
□ 73Top-137
□ 74CanaPos-10
□ 74NHLActSta-154
□ 740PCNHL-202
□ 74Top-202
□ 81CanaPos-15

□ 82CanaPos-12
□ 83CanaPos-14
□ 83CanaPos-15
□ 84CanaPos-13
□ 85HalFC-260
□ 86CanaPos-10
□ 87CanaPos-13
□ 87CanaVacS-8
□ 87CanaVacS-11
□ 88CanaPos-16
□ 88EssAllSta-25
□ 89CanaPos-16
□ 90CanaPos-18
□ 91CanaPos-15
□ 92SpoFla-1
□ 93OPCCanHF-15
□ 93OPCCanHF-36
□ 94ParTalB-72
□ 94ParTalB-140
□ 94ParTalB-149
□ 94ParTalBM-AS3
□ 95Par66-65
□ 95Par66-122
□ 95Par66-128
□ 95Par66-PR128
□ 95Par66Coi-65
□ 95Par66P-3
□ 95ZelMasoH-4
**Lapeyre, Jody**
□ 95TriAme-16
**Lapin, Mikhail**
□ 92WesMic-15
**Lapin, Misha**
□ 93WesMic-19
**Laplante, Darryl**
□ 95Cla-49
□ 98UppDec-9
□ 98UppDecE-9
□ 98UppDecE1o1-9
□ 98UppDecGR-9
**Laplante, Eric**
□ 98QueRem-10
**LaPlante, Sebastien**
□ 93GreMon-7
**Laplante, Steve**
□ 917thInnSQMJHL-58
**Lapointe, Claude**
□ 89HalCit-13
□ 89ProAHL-166
□ 90HalCit-14
□ 90ProAHLIHL-445
□ 91NordPet-14
□ 91OPC-431
□ 91Par-370
□ 91PinFre-370
□ 91Pin-313
□ 91PinFre-313
□ 91ProSet-556
□ 91ProSetFre-556
□ 91ProSetPla-267
□ 91Top-431
□ 91UppDec-488
□ 91UppDecF-488
□ 92Bow-421
□ 92DurPan-6
□ 92NorPet-18
□ 92OPC-320
□ 92PanSti-213
□ 92Pin-141
□ 92PinFre-141
□ 92ProSet-151
□ 92ProSetRGL-12
□ 92Sco-219
□ 92ScoCan-219
□ 92StaClu-93
□ 92Top-94
□ 92TopGol-94G
□ 92Ult-176
□ 92UppDec-147
□ 93Don-285
□ 93DurSco-24
□ 93Lea-64
□ 93OPCPre-251
□ 93OPCPreG-251
□ 93Par-437
□ 93ParEmel-437
□ 93Pin-294
□ 93PinCan-294
□ 93Pow-422
□ 93Sco-352
□ 93ScoCan-352
□ 93TopPre-251
□ 93TopPreG-251
□ 93Ult-403
□ 94Lea-304
□ 94NordBurK-14
□ 94Pin-231
□ 94PinArtP-231
□ 94PinRinC-231
□ 94Sco-194
□ 94ScoGol-194
□ 94ScoPla-194
□ 94ScoPlaTS-194
□ 96BeAPlaAut-200
□ 96BeAPlaAutSil-200
□ 96IslPos-11
□ 97PacInvNRB-118
□ 97UppDec-311
□ 980-PChr-167
□ 980-PChrR-167
□ 98Top-167

□ 98TopO-P-167
□ 99Pac-256
□ 99PacCop-256
□ 99PacGol-256
□ 99PacIceB-256
□ 99PacPreD-256
**Lapointe, Guy**
□ 69CanaPosC-13
□ 70CanaPin-8
□ 70EssPowPla-5
□ 70OPC-177
□ 70SarProSta-105
□ 71CanaPos-11
□ 71OPC-145
□ 71SarProSta-98
□ 71TorSun-154
□ 72CanaPos-9
□ 72OPC-86
□ 72OPCTeaC-16
□ 72SarProSta-113
□ 72Top-57
□ 73CanaPos-10
□ 73MacMil-13
□ 73OPC-114
□ 73Top-170
□ 74CanaPos-11
□ 74LipSou-16
□ 74NHLActSta-150
□ 740PCNHL-70
□ 74Top-70
□ 75CanaPos-10
□ 750PCNHL-48
□ 750PCNHL-293
□ 75Top-198
□ 75Top-293
□ 76CanaPos-11
□ 760PCNHL-223
□ 76Top-223
□ 76TopGlol-17
□ 77CanaPos-12
□ 77Coc-13
□ 770PCNHL-60
□ 77Top-60
□ 78CanaPos-14
□ 780PC-260
□ 78Top-260
□ 79CanaPos-13
□ 79OPC-135
□ 79Top-135
□ 80CanaPos-13
□ 80OPC-201
□ 80PepCap-50
□ 80Top-201
□ 81CanaPos-16
□ 82OPC-305
□ 82PosCer-17
□ 84NordPos-13
□ 87NordGenF-31
□ 88EssAllSta-26
□ 88NordGenF-5
□ 89Nord-23
□ 91FutTreC72-92
□ 92FutTre76CC-171
□ 93ActPacHOFI-2
**Lapointe, Herve**
□ 907thInnSQMJHL-107
□ 917thInnSQMJHL-179
**Lapointe, Martin**
□ 907thInnSMC-61
□ 907thInnSQMJHL-25
□ 90UppDec-467
□ 90UppDecF-467
□ 917thInnSMC-102
□ 91AreDraPic-8
□ 91Cla-9
□ 91Gil-20
□ 91Par-267
□ 91ParFre-267
□ 91Pin-355
□ 91PinFre-355
□ 91ProSet-532
□ 91ProSetFre-532
□ 91RedWinLC-10
□ 91ScoCan-655
□ 91ScoRoo-105T
□ 91StaPicH-5
□ 91UltDra-9
□ 91UltDra-65
□ 91UppDec-63
□ 91UppDec-66
□ 91UppDec-685
□ 91UppDecCWJC-59
□ 91UppDecF-63
□ 91UppDecF-66
□ 91UppDecF-685
□ 92Pin-365
□ 92PinFre-365
□ 92ProSet-226
□ 92Sco-409
□ 92ScoCan-409
□ 92UppDec-405
□ 92UppDec-584
□ 93DurSco-6
□ 93Lea-336
□ 93Par-63
□ 93ParEmel-63
□ 93TopPreG-263G
□ 93UppDec-267
□ 94BeAPSig-133
□ 94ClaProP-173
□ 94Lea-201
□ 94Par-70
□ 94ParGol-70
□ 94Pin-449

□ 94PinArtP-449
□ 94PinRinC-449
□ 94StaClu-151
□ 94StaCluFDI-151
□ 94StaCluMOMS-151
□ 94StaCluSTWC-151
□ 94Ult-285
□ 94UppDec-406
□ 94UppDecEleIce-406
□ 95ColEdgI-4
□ 95ColEdgIQ-IR9
□ 95ParInt-340
□ 95ParIntEI-340
□ 95UppDec-200
□ 95UppDecEleIce-200
□ 95UppDecEleIceG-200
□ 95UppDecWJA-11
□ 96BeAPAut-128
□ 96BeAPAutSil-128
□ 96BeAPla-128
□ 96UppDecBD-13
□ 96UppDecBDG-13
□ 97ColCho-86
□ 97Pac-241
□ 97PacCop-241
□ 97PacEmeGre-241
□ 97PacIceB-241
□ 97PacRed-241
□ 97PacSil-241
□ 97ScoRedW-10
□ 97ScoRedWPla-10
□ 97ScoRedWPre-10
□ 97UppDec-58
□ 98Be A PPA-198
□ 98Be A PPAA-198
□ 98Be A PPAAF-198
□ 98Be A PPSE-198
□ 98Be APG-198
□ 98Pac-197
□ 98PacIceB-197
□ 98PacOmeH-81
□ 98PacOmeODI-81
□ 98PacOmeR-81
□ 98PacRed-197
□ 98UppDec-86
□ 98UppDecE-86
□ 98UppDecE1o1-86
□ 98UppDecGR-86
□ 99Pac-141
□ 99PacCop-141
□ 99PacGol-141
□ 99PacIceB-141
□ 99PacPreD-141
**Lapointe, Normand**
□ 750PCWHA-85
**Lapointe, Rick**
□ 760PCNHL-48
□ 76Top-48
□ 770PCNHL-152
□ 77Top-152A
□ 77Top-152B
□ 780PC-322
□ 79OPC-121
□ 79Top-121
□ 81OPC-295
□ 81OPCSti-134
□ 81Top-W119
□ 82NordPos-11
□ 82PosCer-17
□ 83FreExp-8
□ 83NordPos-14
□ 830PC-294
□ 84KinSmo-19
**Lapointe, Rodney**
□ 87SudWol-7
**Lapointe, Ron**
□ 89ProIHL-189
**Lapointe, Steve**
□ 907thInnSQMJHL-208
**Lapointe, Sylvain**
□ 917thInnSQMJHL-216
□ 93WheThu-17
**Laporte, Roger**
□ 88RivDu R-15
**Laporte, Yves**
□ 51LavDaiLSJ-56
**Lappin, Chris**
□ 92GreMon-18
**Lappin, Mike**
□ 92Cla-76
□ 92RalIce-37
□ 96ClaGol-76
**Lappin, Peter**
□ 88SalLakCGE-4
□ 89ProIHL-84
□ 90ProAHLIHL-109
□ 90Sco-403
□ 90ScoCan-403
□ 90UppDec-235
□ 90UppDecF-235
□ 910PCIns-5S
□ 91ProAHLCHL-522
**Laprade, Edgar**
□ 44BeeGro2P-336
□ 51Par-96
□ 52Par-100
□ 52RoyDesH-3
□ 54Top-56
□ 93ActPacHOFI-7
**Laprise, Sebastien**
□ 98Vald'OF-15
**Lapsjenkov, Gennadi**
□ 74SweHocC-37

□ 99Pac-158
□ 99PacCop-158
□ 99PacGol-158
□ 99PacPreD-158
**Larche, Roger**
□ 907thInnSQMJHL-15
□ 917thInnSMC-67
□ 917thInnSQMJHL-293
□ 92GreMon-10
□ 93RoaExp-11
**Larin, Daniel**
□ 92OklCityB-12
□ 96GerDELE-242
**Larionov, Igor**
□ 83RusNatT-11
□ 87RusNatT-13
□ 88CanuMoh-8
□ 89Kra-41
□ 89RusNatT-17
□ 89SweSemWCS-90
□ 90Bow-63
□ 90BowTif-63
□ 90CanuMoh-13
□ 90Kra-25
□ 90OPC-359
□ 90PanSti-294
□ 90PanSti-336
□ 90ProSet-297
□ 90Sco-123
□ 90ScoCan-123
□ 90Top-359
□ 90TopTif-359
□ 90UppDec-128
□ 90UppDecF-128
□ 91Bow-326
□ 91CanuAutC-10
□ 91CanuMol-4
□ 91CanuPanTS-11
□ 91CanuTeal8-10
□ 91OPC-480
□ 91PanSti-42
□ 91Par-406
□ 91ParFre-406
□ 91Pin-293
□ 91PinFre-293
□ 91ProSet-246
□ 91ProSetFre-246
□ 91ProSetPla-126
□ 91RusStaNHL-6
□ 91RusStaRA-11
□ 91ScoAme-168
□ 91ScoCan-168
□ 91StaClu-150
□ 91SweSemWCS-217
□ 91Top-480
□ 91UppDec-298
□ 91UppDecES-18
□ 91UppDecESF-18
□ 91UppDecF-298
□ 92Bow-350
□ 92OPC-159
□ 92PanSti-32
□ 92PanStiFre-32
□ 92Sco-58
□ 92ScoCan-58
□ 92ScoSha-13
□ 92ScoShaCan-13
□ 92StaClu-299
□ 92Top-512
□ 92TopGol-512G
□ 92TriFroRWP-1
□ 92TriFroRWP-2
□ 93Don-305
□ 93Lea-391
□ 93Par-185
□ 93ParEmel-185
□ 93Pin-367
□ 93PinCan-367
□ 93Pow-436
□ 93Sco-535
□ 93ScoCan-535
□ 93ScoDynDUS-8
□ 93ScoGol-535
□ 93Ult-415
□ 94CanGamNHLP-216
□ 94Don-106
□ 94FinnJaak-156
□ 94Lea-311
□ 94LeaLim-47
□ 94OPCPre-170
□ 94OPCPreSE-170
□ 94ParSE-SE164
□ 94ParSEG-SE164
□ 94ParVin-V88
□ 94Pin-74
□ 94PinArtP-74
□ 94PinRinC-74
□ 94Sco-61
□ 94ScoGol-61
□ 94ScoPla-61
□ 94ScoPlaTS-61
□ 94Sel-40
□ 94SelGol-40
□ 94TopPre-170
□ 94TopPreSE-170
□ 94Ult-197
□ 94UppDec-85
□ 94UppDecEleIce-85
□ 95BeAPla-206
□ 95BeAPlaC-S206
□ 95BeAPSigDC-S206
□ 95CanGamNHLP-222
□ 95ColCho-239
□ 95ColChoPC-239

95ColChoPCP-239
95Fin-57
95FinRef-57
95Lea-318
95ParInt-184
95ParInt-336
95ParIntEI-184
95ParIntEI-336
95Pin-81
95PinArtP-81
95PinRinC-81
95PlaOneoOne-85
95Sco-254
95ScoBlaIce-254
95ScoBlaIceAP-254
95Sum-76
95SumArtP-76
95SumIce-76
95SweGloWC-239
95Ult-234
95UppDec-213
95UppDecEleIce-213
95UppDecEleIce-349
95UppDecEleIceG-213
95UppDecEleIceG-349
96ColCho-83
96Don-167
96DonCanI-117
96DonCanIGPP-117
96DonCanIRPP-117
96DonEli-50
96DonEliDCS-50
96DonPrePro-167
96FilePic-110
96Lea-104
96LeaPre-75
96LeaPreP-104
96LeaPrePGP-75
96Pin-74
96PinArtP-74
96PinFoi-74
96PinPreS-74
96PinRinC-74
96PlaOneoOne-346
96Sco-178
96ScoArtPro-178
96ScoDeaCAP-178
96ScoGolB-178
96ScoSpeAP-178
96SelCer-62
96SelCerAP-62
96SelCerBlu-62
96SelCerMB-62
96SelCerMG-62
96SelCerMR-62
96SelCerRed-62
96Sum-40
96SumArtP-40
96SumIce-40
96SumMet-40
96SumPreS-40
96UppDec-51
96Zen-96
96ZenArtP-96
97DonLim-178
97DonLimExp-178
97DonPri-90
97DonPriSoA-90
97Pac-49
97PacCop-49
97PacEmeGre-49
97PacIceB-49
97PacOme-82
97PacOmeC-82
97PacOmeDG-82
97PacOmeEG-82
97PacOmeG-82
97PacOmeIB-82
97PacOmeR-82
97PacRed-49
97PacSil-49
97Pin-129
97PinIns-146
97PinPrePBB-129
97PinPrePBC-129
97PinPrePBM-129
97PinPrePBY-129
97PinPrePFC-129
97PinPrePFM-129
97PinPrePFY-129
97PinPrePla-129
97ScoRedW-5
97ScoRedWPla-5
97ScoRedWPre-5
97SPAut-54
97UppDecILL-L6B
97UppDecILL2-L6B
98Be A PPA-199
98Be A PPAA-199
98Be A PPAAF-199
98Be A PPSE-199
98Be APG-199
98Pac-198
98PacAur-64
98PacIceB-198
98PacOmeH-82
98PacOmeODI-82
98PacOmeR-82
98PacPar-77
98PacParEG-77
98PacParC-77
98PacParH-77
98PacParIB-77
98PacParS-77
98PacRed-198

98UC-71
98UD ChoPCR-71
98UD ChoR-71
98UDCP-71
98UppDec-261
98UppDecE-261
98UppDecE1o1-261
98UppDecGR-261
99Pac-142
99PacCop-142
99PacGol-142
99PacIceB-142
99PacPreD-142
99RetHoc-30
99UppDecM-74
99UppDecMGS-74
99UppDecMPS-IL
99UppDecMSS-74
99UppDecMSS-74
99UppDecRG-30
99UppDecRP-30

**Larivee, Francis**
95BowDraPro-P22
97St.JohML-14

**Larivee, Paul**
51LavDiaQSHL-79
52St.LawS-33

**Lariviere, Christian**
907thInnSQMJHL-221
917thInnSCHLAW-28
91JohChi-13
91FreCan-17

**Lariviere, Garry**
75RoaPhoWHA-4
76RoaPhoWHA-11
770PCWHA-26
790PC-291
80NordPos-17
80PepCap-71
810ilRedR-6
810ilWesEM-6
810PC-116
820ilRedR-6
820PC-116
82PosCer-4
880ilTenAnn-84

**Larkin, Bryan**
84SasBlaS-10

**Larkin, Huey**
80SauSteMG-9
81SauSteMG-15
82SauSteMG-15

**Larkin, Jim**
92BirBul-2
93BirBul-2
94BirBul-16

**Larkin, Mike**
96HamRoaA-HRA2

**Larkin, Wayne**
60CleBar-10

**Larmer, Jeff**
830PC-230
830PCSti-186
840PC-36
85NovScoO-2
91ProAHLCHL-613

**Larmer, Steve**
83BlaBorPos-11
830PC-105
830PC-206
830PCSti-108
830PCSti-312
83PufSti-17
840PC-37
840PCSti-29
84Top-30
850PC-132
850PCSti-28
85Top-132
86BlaCok-6
860PC-139
860PCSti-157
86Top-139
87BlaCok-6
870PC-59
870PCSti-81
87PanSti-226
87Top-59
88BlaCok-8
880PC-154
880PCMin-17
880PCSti-12
88PanSti-26
88Top-154
89BlaCok-3
890PC-179
890PCBoxB-J
890PCSti-17
89PanSti-43
89Top-179
89TopBoxB-J
90BlaCok-3
90Bow-5
90BowTif-5
90Kra-26
900PC-56
900PCPre-58
900PCPreSE-58
90PanSti-194
90ProSet-53A
90ProSet-53B
90ProSet-345
90Sco-135
90ScoCan-135
90ScoHotRS-61
90Top-56

90TopTeaSL-1
90TopTif-56
90UppDec-242
90UppDec-499
90UppDecF-242
90UppDecF-499
91BlaCok-14
91Bow-395
91Bow-405
91Kra-69
91McDUppD-15
910PC-75
910PCPre-60
910PCPre-135
91PanSti-8
91Par-34
91Par-457
91ParFre-34
91Pin-29
91Pin-357
91PinFre-29
91PinFre-357
91ProSet-49
91ProSet-279
91ProSetFre-49
91ProSetFre-279
91ProSetPla-28
91ProSetPla-287
91ProSetNHLAS-AC13
91ScoAme-140
91ScoCan-140
91StaClu-209
91SweSemWCS-73
91Top-75
91TopTeaSL-21
91UppDec-15
91UppDec-257
91UppDecF-15
91UppDecF-257
92Bow-61
920PC-32
92PanSti-5
92PanStiFre-5
92Par-30
92ParEmel-30
92Pin-74
92PinFre-74
92ProSet-31
92Sco-266
92ScoCan-266
92SeaPat-2
92StaClu-54
92Top-497
92TopGol-497G
92Ult-39
92UppDec-4
92UppDec-135
92UppDecGHS-G6
93Don-461
930PCPre-240
930PCPreG-240
93PanSti-146
93Par-404B
93ParEmel-404B
93Pin-356
93PinCan-356
93Pow-52
93Pow-392
93Sco-3
93Sco-525
93ScoCan-3
93ScoCan-525
93ScoDreTea-22
93ScoGol-525
93ScoSam-3
93StaClu-236
93StaClu-398
93StaCluFDI-236
93StaCluFDI-398
93StaCluFDIO-236
93StaCluO-236
93StaCluO-398
93TopPre-240
93TopPreG-240
93Ult-129
93Ult-373
93UppDec-172
93UppDec-471
93UppDecHT-HT14
93UppDecNR-22
94BeAPP99A-G12
94BeAPla-R169
94BeAPSig-146
94CanGamNHLP-164
94Don-231
94EASpo-29
94Fin-63
94FinnJaaK-90
94FinRef-63
94FinnSupTW-63
94Fla-113
94Fle-134
94HocWit-43
94Lea-270
940PCPre-418
940PCPre-532
940PCPreSE-418
940PCPreSE-532
94Par-146
94ParGol-146
94Pin-88
94PinArtP-88
94PinRinC-88
94Sco-40
94ScoGol-40

94ScoPla-40
94ScoPlaTS-40
94Sel-112
94SelGol-112
94StaClu-242
94StaCluFDI-242
94StaCluMOMS-242
94StaCluST-15
94StaCluSTWC-242
94TopPre-418
94TopPre-532
94TopPreSE-418
94TopPreSE-532
94Ult-138
94UppDec-40
94UppDecEleIce-40
95ColCho-154
95ColChoPC-154
95ColChoPCP-154
95Don-2
95Emo-114
95FinnSemWC-100
95Lea-178
95Sco-211
95ScoBlaIce-211
95ScoBlaIceAP-211
95TopHidGem-7HG
95Ult-103
95UltGolM-103
95BlaLeg-4

**Larner, Don**
96LasVegThu-11
96TolSto-32

**Larney, Rob**
97GuiFla-2

**Laroche, Jean-Francois**
917thInnSQMJHL-62

**Larochelle, Allan**
83SasBla-23

**Larochelle, Claude**
50QueCit-11
78LouGea-14

**Larochelle, Dany**
917thInnSQMJHL-81

**Larochelle, Martin**
917thInnSQMJHL-137

**Larochelle, Wildor**
27LaPat-7
330PCV304A-21
33V288HamG-14
33V357IceK-28
34DiaMatS-38
34SweCap-7
35DiaMatT2-36
35DiaMatT3-33
35DiaMatT4-8
35DiaMatTI-38
36V356WorG-34

**Larocque, Andre**
80QueRem-10

**Larocque, Bunny (Michel)**
73CanaPos-11
74CanaPos-12
74NHLActSta-149
740PCNHL-297
75CanaPos-11
750PCNHL-362
76CanaPos-12
760PCNHL-6
760PCNHL-79
76Top-6
76Top-79
77CanaPos-13
770PCNHL-6
770PCNHL-177
77Top-6
77Top-177
78CanaPos-15
780PC-158
78Top-158
79CanaPos-14
790PC-296
80CanaPos-14
810PC-319
810PCSti-105
810PCSti-259
82MapLeaP-20
82MapLeaP-21
820PC-324
820PCSti-77
82PosCer-18

**Larocque, Denis**
88ProAHL-219
89ProIHL-33
90MonHaw-14
90ProAHLIHL-257
92DayBom-17

**Larocque, Mario**
95BowDraPro-P23
99Pac-400
99PacCop-400
99PacGol-400
99PacIceB-400
99PacPreD-400

**Larocque, Stephane**
917thInnSQMJHL-259
96ForWor-4

**Laroruk, Cam**
84KelWin-19

**Larose, Benoit**
907thInnSQMJHL-59
917thInnSCHLAW-23
917thInnSQMJHL-247

**Larose, Claude**

64BeeGro3P-110A
64BeeGro3P-110B
64CanaPos-11
64CocCap-62
65Coc-62
65Top-75
66CanaIGA-5
66Top-10
67CanaIGA-11
67Top-4
680PC-51
68ShiCoi-69
68Top-51
69CanaPosC-14
690PC-194
690PCFou-12
69Top-126
70EssPowPla-10
700PC-56
70Top-56
71CanaPos-12
710PC-146
71SarProSta-106
71TorSun-155
72CanaPos-10
720PC-231
72SarProSta-122
72SweSemWC-199
73CanaPos-12
74CanaPos-13
74NHLActSta-157
74NHLActStaU-32
740PCNHL-124
74Top-124
750PCNHL-112
75StiKah-6
75Top-112
760PCNHL-310
76StiKah-4
770PCNHL-167
770PCWHA-43
77Top-167
88ProAHL-60
88ProAHL-282
94ParTalB-71
95Par66-69
95Par66Coi-69

**Larose, Guy**
87MonHaw-15
88ProAHL-182
89ProAHL-29
90JetIGA-18
90MonHaw-15
90ProAHLIHL-259
91Par-399
91ParFre-399
91ProAHLCHL-195
92Bow-281
920PC-269
920PCPre-128
92StaClu-237
92Top-47
92TopGol-47G
92UppDec-527

**Larose, Paul**
72NordPos-15
73NordTeal-16

**Larose, Ray**
64QueAce-12
69SeaTotW-12

**Larouche, Mike**
83NorBayC-14

**Larouche, Pierre**
74PenPos-14
750PCNHL-305
75Top-305
760PCNHL-1
760PCNHL-5
760PCNHL-199
760PCNHL-392
76Top-1
76Top-5
76Top-199
77CanaPos-14
770PCNHL-102
77PenPucB-10
77Top-102
78CanaPos-16
780PC-35
78Top-35
79CanaPos-15
790PC-233
79Top-233
80CanaPos-15
800PC-151
800PC-216
80PepCap-51
80Top-151
80Top-216
810PC-187
810PCSti-38
820PC-125
820PCSti-127
82PosCer-7
82WhaJunHC-10
83PufSti-13
840PC-145
840PC-363
840PCSti-103
84Top-108
850PC-54
850PCSti-85
85Top-54

**Larsson, Bengt**
67SweHoc-34

**Larsson, Bjorn**
64SweCorI-3
64SweCorI-43
65SweCorI-3

87PanSti-116

**Larouche, Steve**
907thInnSQMJHL-30
917thInnSMC-29
91ProAHLCHL-83
92FreCan-17
93ClaProPro-78
94ClaProP-160
95BinRan-13
95Don-39
95Emo-125
95Ima-31
95ImaGol-31
95Lea-94
95Pin-209
95PinArtP-209
95PinRinC-209
95PlaOneoOne-179
95ProMag-114
95Sco-302
95ScoBlaIce-302
95ScoBlaIceAP-302
95Top-38
95TopOPCI-38
95Ult-112
95UltGolM-112
95UppDec-89
95UppDecEleIce-89
95UppDecEleIceG-89
96NHLProSTA-114

**Larrivee, Jacques**
93AmoLesFAM-10

**Larsen, Brad**
94ParSE-SE269
94ParSEG-SE269
94Sel-164
94SelGol-164
94SP-187
94SPDieCut-187
95Cla-45
95DonEliWJ-17
95SigRooA-25
95SigRooAPC-25
95SwiCurB-8
95UppDec-534
95UppDecEleIce-534
95UppDecEleIceG-534
96UppDecIce-134

**Larsen, Greg**
83NorBayC-15

**Larson, Brett**
93MinDul-16
95MadMon-15

**Larson, Dave**
92MinGolG-6
93MinGolG-16
94MinGolG-19
95MinGolG-20

**Larson, Dean**
96AncAce-4
97AncAce-11

**Larson, Jon**
92NorDakFS-17
93KnoChe-6
94RoaExp-6
95RoaExp-18

**Larson, Norman**
34BeeGro1P-238
400PCV3012-127

**Larson, Reed**
780PC-226
78Top-226
790PC-213
79RedWinP-11
79Top-213
800PC-43
80Top-43
810PC-92
810PCSti-124
81Top-W92
820PC-88
820PC-89
820PCSti-180
82PosCer-5
830PC-125
830PCSti-134
83PufSti-18
84KelAccD-2
840PC-58
840PCSti-36
84Top-44
850PC-55
850PCSti-33
85Top-55
860PC-114
860PCSti-39
86Top-110
870PC-131
870PCSti-142
87PanSti-7
88BruSpoA-9
880ilTenAnn-56
880PC-145
88Top-145

65SweCorI-43
65SweCorI-187
69SweHocS-47

**Larsson, Bo**
83SweSemE-76
84SweSemE-122

**Larsson, Carl-Erik**
84SweSemE-168
86SwePanS-158
87SwePanS-164
90SweSemE-143

**Larsson, Curt**
65SweCorI-175
67SweHoc-189
69SweHocS-246
70SweHocS-130
71SweHocS-223
72SweHocS-212
73SweHocS-59
73SweWorCS-59
74SweHocS-9
74SweHocS-145
74SweSemHVS-24

**Larsson, Ivar**
64SweCorI-151
65SweCorI-151
67SweHoc-122
69SweHocS-135
70SweHocS-84
71SweHocS-176
72SweHocS-166
74SweHocS-146

**Larsson, Jan**
84SweSemE-65
86SwePanS-52
87SwePanS-63
89SweSemE-41
90SweSemE-188
91SweSemE-41
92SweSemE-66
93SweSemWCS-16
93SwiHNL-103
95FinnSemWC-73
95SweLeaE-274
95SweLeaEC-8
95SweUppDE-165

**Larsson, Jorgen**
87SwePanS-254

**Larsson, Kjell**
65SweCorI-76
67SweHoc-159
85SwePanS-220
95SwiHNL-56

**Larsson, Lars-Erik**
67SweHoc-160
71SweHocS-322

**Larsson, Nisse**
67SweHoc-50

**Larsson, Ove**
71SweHocS-251
72SweHocS-233
73SweHocS-241
73SweWorCS-241
74SweHocS-239

**Larsson, Peter**
86SwePanS-268
87SwePanS-246
89SweSemE-235
90SweSemE-189
91SweSemE-43
92SweSemE-72
93SweSemE-47
94SweLeaE-193
94SweLeaEP-5
95SweLeaE-23
95SweUppDE-34

**Larsson, Robert**
86SwePanS-226
89SweSemE-195

**Larsson, Rolf**
65SweCorI-116B
67SweHoc-175
69SweHocS-172
71SweHocS-252

**Larsson, Stefan**
83SweSemE-229
86SwePanS-156
89SweSemE-273
90SweSemE-34
91SweSemE-282
92SweSemE-308
93SweSemE-275
93SweSemWCS-7
94SweLeaE-34
95SweGloWC-25
95SweLeaE-139
95SweLeaEFF-4
95SweUppDE-208

**Larsson, Stig**
67SweHoc-65
69SweHocS-98
70SweHocS-55
71SweHocS-126
72SweHocS-110
73SweHocS-212
73SweWorCS-212
74SweHocS-240

**Larsson, Tore**
69SweHocS-173

**Larsson, Ulf**
67SweHoc-257
69SweHocS-302
70SweHocS-206
73SweHocS-293

**Larsson, Urban**

❑ 83SweSemE-109
**Larsson, Vilgot**
❑ 65SweCorI-48A
**Lartama, Mika**
❑ 93FinnJyvHS-49
❑ 93FinnSIS-249
❑ 95FinnSISL-85
**Larter, Tyler**
❑ 84SauSteMG-12
❑ 87SauSteMG-4
❑ 88ProAHL-32
❑ 89ProAHL-94
❑ 90ProAHLIHL-207
❑ 91MonHaw-17
❑ 91ProAHLCHL-181
**Larway, Don**
❑ 77OPCWHA-48
**Lascala, Frank**
❑ 90RicRen-15
❑ 92DalFre-11
❑ 93DalFre-10
❑ 94CenHocL-12
❑ 96GerDELE-220
**Laskoski, Gary**
❑ 83OPC-156
❑ 83OPCSti-296
**Lassila, Hannu**
❑ 81SweSemHVS-20
**Laszkiewicz, Leszek**
❑ 98GerDELE-261
**Latal, Jaromir**
❑ 94CzeAPSE-5
**Latal, Jiri**
❑ 89ProAHL-344
❑ 90FlyPos-16
❑ 90OPCPre-59
❑ 90ProSet-501
❑ 90UppDec-410
❑ 90UppDecF-410
❑ 91FlyJCP-17
❑ 91OPC-444
❑ 91ProSet-454
❑ 91ProSetFre-454
❑ 91ScoCan-540
❑ 91Top-444
❑ 91UppDec-404
❑ 91UppDecF-404
❑ 95CzeAPSE-103
❑ 95CzeAPSE-104
❑ 96CzeAPSE-263
**Latendresse, Mike**
❑ 92MaiBlaB-21
❑ 93MaiBlaB-42
❑ 94TolSto-11
❑ 95BirBul-10
**Laterreur, Yan**
❑ 917thInnSQMJHL-261
**Latos, Jim**
❑ 84SasBlaS-11
❑ 86PorWinH-11
❑ 89ProIHL-30
❑ 90KanCitBla-20
❑ 90ProAHLIHL-585
❑ 94CenHocL-116
❑ 95LouIceG-8
❑ 95LouIceGP-9
**Latta, Dave (David)**
❑ 83KitRan-19
❑ 84KitRan-23
❑ 85KitRan-22
❑ 86KitRan-22
❑ 87NordGenF-20
❑ 88NordGenF-20
❑ 88NordTeal-21
❑ 89Nord-24
❑ 89NordGenF-19
❑ 89NordPol-16
❑ 90HalCit-15
❑ 90NordTeal-17
❑ 90ProAHLIHL-461
❑ 91ProAHLCHL-376
❑ 97AncAce-12
**Latta, Ken**
❑ 80SauSteMG-21
❑ 81SauSteMG-16
**Latti, Petri**
❑ 93FinnSIS-204
❑ 94FinnSIS-356
❑ 95FinnSIS-100
❑ 96FinnSISR-104
**Latto, Gordon**
❑ 96FifFly-13
❑ 97FifFly-13
**Latulippe, Martin**
❑ 93DruVol-5
**Latvala, Jan**
❑ 93FinnSIS-138
❑ 94FinnSIS-29
❑ 95FinnSIS-262
❑ 96FinnSISR-60
**Lauer, Brad**
❑ 88OPC-226
❑ 90OPC-217
❑ 90ProAHLIHL-501
❑ 90Top-217
❑ 90TopTif-217
❑ 91BlaCok-15
❑ 91ProAHLCHL-490
❑ 91ProSet-375
❑ 91ProSetFre-375
❑ 91StaClu-142
❑ 92IndIce-17
❑ 95CleLum-16
❑ 96CleLum-15
**Laufman, Ken**
❑ 52St.LawS-56
**Laughlin, Craig**
❑ 81CanaPos-17
❑ 82Cap-14
❑ 82PosCer-10
❑ 83OPC-375
❑ 84CapPizH-12
❑ 84OPC-203
❑ 85CapPizH-11
❑ 85OPC-190
❑ 86CapKod-15
❑ 86CapPol-15
❑ 86OPC-35
❑ 86OPCSti-253
❑ 86Top-35
❑ 87CapKod-18
❑ 87CapTeaIss-14
❑ 87OPC-161
❑ 87PanSti-182
❑ 87Top-161
❑ 88MapLeaPLA-18
❑ 89OPC-275
❑ 89OPCSti-171
**Laughlin, Dan**
❑ 95MadMon-10
**Laughton, Mike**
❑ 69OPC-148
❑ 70OPC-74
❑ 70SarProSta-136
❑ 70Top-74
❑ 74MarSanDW-2
**Laukkanen, Janne**
❑ 91UppDec-22
❑ 91UppDecF-22
❑ 93Cla-43
❑ 93FinnJyvHS-46
❑ 93FinnSIS-239
❑ 93FinnSIS-367
❑ 93SweSemWCS-54
❑ 94Cla-102
❑ 94ClaDraGol-102
❑ 94Fin-8
❑ 94FinnJaaK-17
❑ 94FinRef-8
❑ 94FinSupTW-8
❑ 94Fla-148
❑ 94Lea-447
❑ 94NordBurK-15
❑ 94OPCPre-411
❑ 94OPCPreSE-411
❑ 94ParSE-SE142
❑ 94ParSEG-SE142
❑ 94Pin-485
❑ 94PinArtP-485
❑ 94PinRinC-485
❑ 94PinRooTP-3
❑ 94Sel-181
❑ 94SelGol-181
❑ 94SelYouExp-YE3
❑ 94TopPre-411
❑ 94TopPreSE-411
❑ 94Ult-359
❑ 94UppDec-251
❑ 94UppDec-565
❑ 94UppDecEleIce-251
❑ 94UppDecEleIce-565
❑ 94UppDecSPI-SP157
❑ 94UppDecSPIDC-SP157
❑ 95ColEdgI-28
❑ 95FinnSemWC-12
❑ 95FinnSISL-83
❑ 95FinnSISLLG-2
❑ 95Ima-63
❑ 95ImaGol-63
❑ 95Lea-46
❑ 95ParInt-52
❑ 95ParIntEl-52
❑ 95SweGloWC-134
❑ 95UppDec-123
❑ 95UppDecEleIce-123
❑ 95UppDecEleIceG-123
❑ 96ColCho-187
❑ 96SenPizH-12
❑ 96SweSemW-29
❑ 96UppDec-116
❑ 97Be A PPAD-90
❑ 97Be A PPAPD-90
❑ 97BeAPla-90
❑ 97BeAPlaAut-90
❑ 97PacInvNRB-135
❑ 98O-PChr-153
❑ 98O-PChrR-153
❑ 98Pac-312
❑ 98PacIceB-312
❑ 98PacRed-312
❑ 98Top-153
❑ 98TopO-P-153
❑ 98UppDec-141
❑ 98UppDecE-141
❑ 98UppDecE1o1-141
❑ 98UppDecGR-141
**Laukkanen, Jari**
❑ 93FinnJyvHS-17
❑ 93FinnSIS-100
❑ 94FinnSIS-84
❑ 95FinnSIS-9
❑ 96FinnSISR-10
**Laurence, Red (Don)**
❑ 79OPC-369
❑ 81IndChe-12
❑ 82IndChe-13
**Laurie, Rob**
❑ 93JohChi-16
❑ 94JohChi-13
❑ 95TolSto-1
**Laurila, Harri**
❑ 93FinnJyvHS-135
❑ 93FinnSIS-146
❑ 93SweSemWCS-55
❑ 94FinnJaaK-13
❑ 94FinnSIS-170
❑ 94FinnSIS-326
❑ 95FinnSemWC-36
❑ 95FinnSIS-151
❑ 95FinnSIS-184
❑ 95FinnSISL-47
❑ 96FinnSISR-125
**Laurila, Marty**
❑ 93WatBlaH-16
**Laurin, Don**
❑ 88BraWheK-15
**Laurin, Steve**
❑ 90ProAHLIHL-555
**Laus, Paul**
❑ 88NiaFalT-17
❑ 897thInnSOHL-142
❑ 89NiaFalT-9
❑ 90KnoChe-102
❑ 90ProAHLIHL-534
❑ 91ProAHLCHL-293
❑ 92CleLum-3
❑ 93OPCPre-402
❑ 93OPCPreG-402
❑ 93PanTeal-4
❑ 93StaClu-292
❑ 93StaCluFDI-292
❑ 93StaCluO-292
❑ 93TopPre-402
❑ 93TopPreG-402
❑ 94Don-201
❑ 95CanGamNHLP-121
❑ 95PlaOneoOne-41
❑ 96BeAPAut-192
❑ 96BeAPAutSil-192
❑ 96BeAPla-192
❑ 97PacDynBKS-42
❑ 97PacRev-61
❑ 97PacRevC-61
❑ 97PacRevE-61
❑ 97PacRevIB-61
❑ 97PacRevR-61
❑ 97PacRevS-61
❑ 97UppDec-75
❑ 98Pac-224
❑ 98PacAur-82
❑ 98PacDynI-84
❑ 98PacDynIIB-84
❑ 98PacDynIR-84
❑ 98PacIceB-224
❑ 98PacOmeH-104
❑ 98PacOmeODI-104
❑ 98PacOmeR-104
❑ 98PacPar-98
❑ 98PacParC-98
❑ 98PacParEG-98
❑ 98PacParH-98
❑ 98PacParIB-98
❑ 98PacParS-98
❑ 98PacRed-224
❑ 99Pac-175
❑ 99PacCop-175
❑ 99PacGol-175
❑ 99PacIceB-175
❑ 99PacPreD-175
**Lauzon, Serge**
❑ 84ChiSag-17
**Lavalee, Charlie**
❑ 83MonAlp-27
**Lavallee, Kevin**
❑ 80FlamPos-8
❑ 80PepCap-6
❑ 81FlamPos-10
❑ 81OPC-43
❑ 82OPC-49
❑ 82OPCSti-220
❑ 82PosCer-3
❑ 83OPC-157
❑ 84OPC-183
❑ 86PenKod-13
❑ 94GerDELE-100
❑ 95GerDELE-142
**Lavallee, Martin**
❑ 907thInnSQMJHL-24
❑ 907thInnSQMJHL-184
❑ 917thInnSMC-27
❑ 917thInnSQMJHL-168
**Lavallere, Sebastein**
❑ 907thInnSQMJHL-185
**LaVarre, Mark**
❑ 83NorBayC-16
❑ 85NovScoO-8
❑ 87BlaCok-7
❑ 88ProAHL-68
**Lave, Rob**
❑ 93NorBayC-3
**Lavell, Mike**
❑ 95Sla-274
**Lavender, Brian**
❑ 71BluPos-9
❑ 72OPC-270
❑ 73RedWinTI-14
**Lavigne, Eric**
❑ 907thInnSQMJHL-150
❑ 917thInnSQMJHL-214
❑ 91AreDraPic-19
❑ 91Cla-22
❑ 91StaPicH-42
❑ 91UltDra-21
❑ 93PhoRoa-15
❑ 94ClaProP-191
**Lavinsh, Rodrigo**
❑ 94RalIce-8
❑ 95TalTigS-1
**Laviolette, Jack**
❑ 10C55SweCP-45
❑ 10C56-21
❑ 11C55-45
❑ 12C57-46
❑ 27LaPat-19
❑ 83HalFP-L9
❑ 85HalFC-159
**Laviolette, Kerry**
❑ 83SasBla-9
**Laviolette, Peter**
❑ 89ProIHL-43
❑ 90ProAHLIHL-16
❑ 91ProAHLCHL-197
❑ 93Pow-508
❑ 93StaCluTUSA-12
❑ 93TopPreTUSA-3
❑ 93Ult-488
❑ 96ProBru-6
**Laviolette, Ted**
❑ 90MonAAA-14
**Lavitt, Sam**
❑ 51BufBis-12
**Lavoie, Daryl**
❑ 92WinSpi-13
❑ 93WinSpi-5
**Lavoie, Dominic**
❑ 88ProIHL-74
❑ 89BluKod-38
❑ 89ProIHL-20
❑ 90Bow-26
❑ 90BowTif-26
❑ 90ProAHLIHL-95
❑ 90Sco-416
❑ 90ScoCan-416
❑ 92Ult-145
❑ 93Lea-415
❑ 93Par-366
❑ 93ParEmel-366
❑ 93PhoRoa-16
❑ 93UppDec-444
**Lavoie, Etienne**
❑ 907thInnSQMJHL-230
❑ 917thInnSQMJHL-127
**Lavoie, Roberto**
❑ 80QueRem-11
❑ 93SwiHNL-288
**Lavoie, Yannick**
❑ 93AmoLesFAM-11
**Law, Brian**
❑ 91BriColJHL-151
**Law, Kirby**
❑ 93SasBla-14
❑ 95LetHur-11
❑ 96LetHur-10
**Lawless, Paul**
❑ 83OPC-141
❑ 85WhaJunW-9
❑ 86WhaJunT-13
❑ 87PanSti-48
❑ 87WhaJunBK-12
❑ 95ColEdgI-112
❑ 96CinCyc-13
**Lawrence, Brett**
❑ 91KnoChe-18
**Lawrence, Derek**
❑ 92BriColJHL-220
**Lawrence, Mark**
❑ 88NiaFalT-5
❑ 897thInnSOHL-131
❑ 89NiaFalT-10
❑ 907thInnSOHL-108
❑ 917thInnSOHL-40
❑ 94ClaProP-172
❑ 94UppDec-260
❑ 94UppDecEleIce-260
❑ 95Lea-59
❑ 99Pac-257
❑ 99PacCop-257
❑ 99PacGol-257
❑ 99PacIceB-257
❑ 99PacPreD-257
**Lawson, Danny**
❑ 70EssPowPla-179
❑ 71SabPos-9
❑ 71TorSun-30
❑ 72SluCupWHA-13
❑ 73QuaOatWHA-48
❑ 74OPCWHA-25
❑ 75OPCWHA-86
❑ 76OPCWHA-8
**Lawson, Eddie**
❑ 63RochAme-17
**Lawson, Jeff**
❑ 91AirCanSJHL-E40
❑ 92MPSPhoSJHL-124
**Lawson, Tom**
❑ 84Ott67-18
**Lawton, Brian**
❑ 83NorStaPos-11
❑ 84NorStaPos-12
❑ 85NorStaPos-16
❑ 87NorStaPos-18
❑ 87OPC-145
❑ 87PanSti-300
❑ 87Top-145
❑ 88OPC-20
❑ 88OPCSti-198
❑ 88PanSti-94
❑ 88Top-20
❑ 89BruSpoAU-5
❑ 89Nord-25
❑ 89OPC-91
❑ 89SweSemWCS-172
❑ 89Top-91
❑ 90ProAHLIHL-355
❑ 91Par-167
❑ 91ParFre-167
❑ 91ProSet-482
❑ 91ProSetFre-482
❑ 91ScoCan-648
❑ 91ScoRoo-98T
❑ 91ShaSanJSA-13
❑ 91UppDec-572
❑ 91UppDecF-572
❑ 92Bow-254
❑ 92OPC-276
❑ 92PanSti-132
❑ 92PanStiFre-132
❑ 92Par-163
❑ 92ParEmel-163
❑ 92Pin-71
❑ 92PinFre-71
❑ 92ProSet-173
❑ 92Sco-343
❑ 92ScoCan-343
❑ 92StaClu-171
❑ 92Top-435
❑ 92TopGol-435G
❑ 92Ult-197
**Laxdal, Derek**
❑ 83BraWheK-19
❑ 84BraWheK-11
❑ 85BraWheK-11
❑ 88MapLeaPLA-21
❑ 89OPC-169
❑ 89OPCSti-181
❑ 89ProAHL-108
❑ 89Top-169
❑ 90ProAHLIHL-494
❑ 91ProAHLCHL-466
❑ 92AlbIntTC-11
❑ 94RoaExp-16
**Lay, Mike**
❑ 82MedHatT-10
❑ 83MedHatT-21
❑ 94GerDELE-269
❑ 95GerDELE-401
❑ 96GerDELE-309
**Laycock, R.**
❑ 95GerDELE-18
**Laycock, Travis**
❑ 907thInnSWHL-272
❑ 90PriAlbR-8
❑ 917thInnSWHL-255
❑ 91PriAlbR-10
**Laycoe, Hal**
❑ 44BeeGro2P-42
❑ 44BeeGro2P-258
❑ 45QuaOatP-88A
❑ 45QuaOatP-88B
❑ 48ExhCan-12
❑ 51Par-25
❑ 52Par-71
❑ 53Par-87
❑ 54Par-52
❑ 54Top-38
❑ 55BruPho-9
**Laylin, Cory**
❑ 91MinGolG-12
**Layton, Ian**
❑ 907thInnSWHL-154
**Layzell, Brad**
❑ 93RenEng-14
❑ 94FreCan-18
❑ 96MilAdmBO-13
**Lazaro, Jeff**
❑ 90ProAHLIHL-124
❑ 91Bow-352
❑ 91BruSpoA-9
❑ 91OPC-380
❑ 91ProAHLCHL-65
❑ 91ProSet-13
❑ 91ProSetFre-13
❑ 91ScoCan-445
❑ 91StaClu-397
❑ 91Top-380
❑ 91UppDec-364
❑ 91UppDecF-364
❑ 92PanSti-139
❑ 92PanStiFre-139
❑ 92Top-224
❑ 92TopGol-224G
❑ 93Pow-509
❑ 93TopPreTUSA-21
❑ 93Ult-489
❑ 94FinnJaaK-131
❑ 95FinnSemWC-119
❑ 95GerDELE-329
❑ 96GerDELE-107
**Leach, Brenn**
❑ 82VicCou-12
❑ 83VicCou-14
**Leach, Jamie**
❑ 88NiaFalT-12
❑ 89ProIHL-143
❑ 90OPC-377
❑ 90OPCPre-60
❑ 90Sco-420
❑ 90ScoCan-420
❑ 90Top-377
❑ 90TopTif-377
❑ 91OPC-492
❑ 91PenCokE-20
❑ 91StaClu-296
❑ 91Top-492
❑ 91UppDec-447
❑ 91UppDecF-447
❑ 92Bow-320
❑ 92StaClu-329
❑ 92Top-362
❑ 92TopGol-362G
❑ 92UppDec-168
❑ 93TopPreG-528G
❑ 95RochAmeSS-9
**Leach, Jay**
❑ 91ProAHLCHL-116
**Leach, Reggie**
❑ 70BruPos-9
❑ 71BruTeaIss-19
❑ 71OPC-175
❑ 71TorSun-12
❑ 72OPC-51
❑ 72SarProSta-54
❑ 72Top-17
❑ 73OPC-84
❑ 73Top-84
❑ 74NHLActSta-201
❑ 74OPCNHL-95
❑ 74Top-95
❑ 75FlyCanDC-11
❑ 75HerSta-22
❑ 75OPCNHL-166
❑ 75OPCNHL-325
❑ 75Top-166
❑ 75Top-325
❑ 76OPCNHL-1
❑ 76OPCNHL-65
❑ 76OPCNHL-110
❑ 76OPCNHL-215
❑ 76OPCNHL-391
❑ 76Top-1
❑ 76Top-65
❑ 76Top-110
❑ 76Top-215
❑ 76TopGloI-21
❑ 77OPCNHL-185
❑ 77Top-185
❑ 77TopGloS-8
❑ 77TopOPCGlo-8
❑ 78OPC-165
❑ 78Top-165
❑ 79OPC-95
❑ 79Top-95
❑ 80OPC-70
❑ 80OPC-249
❑ 80Top-70
❑ 80Top-249
❑ 81OPC-243
❑ 81OPCSti-181
❑ 81Top-E106
❑ 82OPC-90
❑ 82PosCer-14
❑ 83OPCSti-9
❑ 92FutTre76CC-172
❑ 92Par-471
❑ 92ParEmel-471
❑ 93ParChePH-D19
**Leach, Steve (Stephen)**
❑ 86CapPol-16
❑ 88CapBor-11
❑ 88CapSmo-11
❑ 89CapKod-21
❑ 89CapTeaIss-14
❑ 89OPC-67
❑ 89OPCSti-79
❑ 89PanSti-349
❑ 89Top-67
❑ 90CapKod-14
❑ 90CapPos-14
❑ 90CapSmo-13
❑ 90OPC-235
❑ 90PanSti-166
❑ 90ProSet-315
❑ 90Sco-279
❑ 90ScoCan-279
❑ 90Top-235
❑ 90TopTif-235
❑ 91Bow-306
❑ 91BruSpoA-10
❑ 91OPC-100
❑ 91OPCPre-12
❑ 91PanSti-211
❑ 91Par-6
❑ 91ParFre-6
❑ 91Pin-46
❑ 91PinFre-46
❑ 91ProSet-253
❑ 91ProSet-346
❑ 91ProSetFre-253
❑ 91ProSetFre-346
❑ 91ProSetPla-151
❑ 91ScoCan-576
❑ 91ScoRoo-26T
❑ 91StaClu-226
❑ 91Top-100
❑ 92Bow-298
❑ 92BruPos-5
❑ 92OPC-112
❑ 92Par-241
❑ 92ParEmel-241
❑ 92Pin-73
❑ 92PinFre-73
❑ 92ProSet-6
❑ 92Sco-54
❑ 92ScoCan-54
❑ 92StaClu-68
❑ 92Top-16
❑ 92TopGol-16G
❑ 92Ult-5
❑ 92UppDec-61
❑ 93Don-28
❑ 93Lea-3
❑ 93OPCPre-507
❑ 93OPCPreG-507
❑ 93PanSti-5
❑ 93Par-285
❑ 93ParEmel-285
❑ 93Pin-73
❑ 93PinCan-73
❑ 93Pow-21
❑ 93Sco-88
❑ 93ScoCan-88
❑ 93StaClu-187
❑ 93StaCluFDI-187
❑ 93StaCluFDIO-187
❑ 93StaCluO-187
❑ 93TopPre-507
❑ 93TopPreG-507
❑ 93Ult-268
❑ 94Lea-420
❑ 94OPCPre-268
❑ 94OPCPreSE-268
❑ 94Pin-298
❑ 94PinArtP-298
❑ 94PinRinC-298
❑ 94Sco-79
❑ 94ScoGol-79
❑ 94ScoPla-79
❑ 94ScoPlaTS-79
❑ 94TopPre-268
❑ 94TopPreSE-268
❑ 94UppDec-342
❑ 94UppDecEleIce-342
❑ 95BeAPla-109
❑ 95BeAPSig-S109
❑ 95BeAPSigDC-S109
❑ 95ParInt-284
❑ 95ParIntEl-284
❑ 95UppDec-453
❑ 95UppDecEleIce-453
❑ 95UppDecEleIceG-453
❑ 96UppDec-142
❑ 97CarHur-16
❑ 97PacInvNRB-171
❑ 97PacPar-36
❑ 97PacParC-36
❑ 97PacParDG-36
❑ 97PacParEG-36
❑ 97PacParIB-36
❑ 97PacParRed-36
❑ 97PacParSil-36
❑ 98O-PChr-28
❑ 98O-PChrR-28
❑ 98Top-28
❑ 98TopO-P-28
**Leader, Al**
❑ 83HalFP-M12
❑ 85HalFC-176
**Leahy, Greg**
❑ 87PorWinH-14
❑ 88PorWinH-14
❑ 89PorWinH-15
❑ 907thInnSWHL-75
❑ 90SasBla-11
**Leary, Denis**
❑ 94BeAPla-R141
**Leask, Rob**
❑ 907thInnSOHL-212
❑ 917thInnSOHL-166
❑ 91OshGen-9
❑ 93JohChi-19
❑ 94JohChi-14
❑ 96GerDELE-31
❑ 98GerDELE-177
**Leavins, Jim**
❑ 90SweSemE-252
**Lebeau, Patrick**
❑ 90ProAHLIHL-73
❑ 91ProAHLCHL-72
❑ 91ScoAme-390
❑ 91ScoCan-280
❑ 91StaClu-373
❑ 91UppDec-453
❑ 91UppDec-644
❑ 91UppDecF-453
❑ 91UppDecF-644
❑ 93ClaProPro-28
❑ 93UppDec-499
❑ 95SwiHNL-46
**Lebeau, Stephan**
❑ 88ProAHL-281
❑ 89CanaKra-12
❑ 89CanaPos-17
❑ 90Bow-53
❑ 90BowTif-53
❑ 90CanaPos-19
❑ 90OPC-388
❑ 90ProSet-152
❑ 90Sco-262
❑ 90ScoCan-262
❑ 90Top-388
❑ 90TopTif-388
❑ 90UppDec-51
❑ 90UppDecF-51
❑ 91Bow-333
❑ 91CanaPanTS-14
❑ 91CanaPos-16
❑ 91Kra-26
❑ 91OPC-135
❑ 91PanSti-191
❑ 91Par-87
❑ 91ParFre-87
❑ 91Pin-139
❑ 91PinFre-139
❑ 91ProSet-120
❑ 91ProSetFre-120

❑ 91ProSetPla-190
❑ 91ScoAme-274
❑ 91ScoCan-494
❑ 91ScoYouS-7
❑ 91StaClu-283
❑ 91Top-135
❑ 91UppDec-261
❑ 91UppDec-644
❑ 91UppDecF-261
❑ 91UppDecF-644
❑ 92Bow-346
❑ 92CanaPos-16
❑ 92DurPan-7
❑ 92OPC-293
❑ 92PanSti-151
❑ 92PanStiFre-151
❑ 92Par-82
❑ 92ParEmel-82
❑ 92Pin-341
❑ 92PinFre-341
❑ 92Sco-246
❑ 92ScoCan-246
❑ 92StaClu-431
❑ 92Top-69
❑ 92TopGol-69G
❑ 92Ult-329
❑ 92UppDec-213
❑ 93CanaPos-13
❑ 93Don-175
❑ 93DurSco-14
❑ 93Lea-190
❑ 93OPCCanHF-7
❑ 93OPCPre-462
❑ 93OPCPreG-462
❑ 93PanSti-16
❑ 93Par-374
❑ 93ParEmel-374
❑ 93Pin-136
❑ 93PinCan-136
❑ 93Pow-130
❑ 93Sco-72
❑ 93ScoCan-72
❑ 93StaClu-343
❑ 93StaCluFDI-343
❑ 93StaCluO-343
❑ 93TopPre-462
❑ 93TopPreG-462
❑ 93Ult-241
❑ 93UppDec-402
❑ 93UppDecSP-78
❑ 94CanGamNHLP-32
❑ 94Don-234
❑ 94DucCarJr-16
❑ 94EASpo-209
❑ 94Lea-162
❑ 94OPCPre-63
❑ 94OPCPreSE-63
❑ 94Par-2
❑ 94ParCratGB-1
❑ 94ParCratGG-1
❑ 94ParCratGR-1
❑ 94ParGol-2
❑ 94ParSEV-11
❑ 94Pin-67
❑ 94PinArtP-67
❑ 94PinRinC-67
❑ 94Sco-128
❑ 94ScoGol-128
❑ 94ScoPla-128
❑ 94ScoPlaTS-128
❑ 94Sel-65
❑ 94SelGol-65
❑ 94SP-3
❑ 94SPDieCut-3
❑ 94TopPre-63
❑ 94TopPreSE-63
❑ 94Ult-5
❑ 94UppDec-53
❑ 94UppDecEleIce-53
❑ 94UppDecSPI-SP2
❑ 94UppDecSPIDC-SP2
❑ 95SwiHNL-150
❑ 95Ult-5
❑ 95UltGolM-5

**Lebedev, Gennady**
❑ 90OPC-508

**Lebedev, Yuri**
❑ 73SweHocS-94
❑ 73SweWorCS-94
❑ 74SweHocS-60
❑ 74SweSemHVS-40
❑ 79PanSti-156
❑ 81SweSemHVS-47
❑ 82SweSemHVS-74
❑ 91FutTreC72-37

**Lebel, Bobby**
❑ 96RimOce-13

**Lebel, Layne**
❑ 90MicTecHus-10
❑ 91MicTecHus-7
❑ 93MicTecH-15
❑ 94CenHocL-50

**Lebel, Robert**
❑ 83HalFP-H11
❑ 85HalFC-117

**LeBlanc, Bill**
❑ 51LavDaiQSHL-7

**Leblanc, Carl**
❑ 907thInnSQMJHL-66
❑ 917thInnSQMJHL-29
❑ 93KnoChe-7
❑ 94KnoChe-15
❑ 95SouCarS-16

**LeBlanc, Dan**
❑ 897thInnSOHL-43

**Leblanc, Dennis**
❑ 907thInnSQMJHL-224

**Leblanc, Francois**
❑ 907thInnSQMJHL-45

**LeBlanc, J.P.**
❑ 72ShaLosAW-7
❑ 73QuaOatWHA-42
❑ 74OPCWHA-36
❑ 76OPCNHL-326
❑ 77OPCNHL-133
❑ 77Top-133

**Leblanc, Jacques**
❑ 907thInnSQMJHL-211

**LeBlanc, Jean**
❑ 86FreExp-16

**Leblanc, Jeff**
❑ 98QueRem-11

**LeBlanc, John**
❑ 88OilTeal-17
❑ 89ProAHL-149
❑ 91MonHaw-18
❑ 91ProAHLCHL-169
❑ 92Bow-419
❑ 92OPC-287
❑ 92StaClu-388
❑ 92Top-98
❑ 92TopGol-88G

**LeBlanc, Michel**
❑ 95FinnSemWC-197

**Leblanc, Mike**
❑ 89RayJrC-14

**Leblanc, Ray**
❑ 83KitRan-30
❑ 87FliSpi-11
❑ 89ProIHL-67
❑ 90ProAHLIHL-553
❑ 91Par-255
❑ 91ParFre-255
❑ 91ProAHLCHL-502
❑ 92IndIce-18
❑ 92Sco-486
❑ 92ScoCan-486
❑ 92UppDec-381
❑ 95ColEdgITW-G1

**Leboda, Ted**
❑ 67ColChe-8

**Lebold, Dan**
❑ 96KitRan-15

**LeBoutillier, Pete**
❑ 93RedDeeR-10
❑ 93RedDeeR-11
❑ 97ScoMigDPla-17
❑ 97ScoMigDPre-17
❑ 97ScoMigDuc-17

**Lebrasseur, Pascal**
❑ 907thInnSQMJHL-17
❑ 917thInnSQMJHL-76

**Lebreau, Jean**
❑ 907thInnSQMJHL-267

**Lebrecque, Patrick**
❑ 91ProAHLCHL-532
❑ 95UppDec-379
❑ 95UppDecEleIce-379
❑ 95UppDecEleIceG-379

**Lebrun, Al**
❑ 61Top-61
❑ 62Top-50

**Lebrun, J.C.**
❑ 51LavDaiS-94

**LeBrun, Sean**
❑ 89ProAHL-247
❑ 90ProAHLIHL-495
❑ 91ProAHLCHL-474
❑ 92RicRen-11

**Lebsack, Greg**
❑ 83SasBla-18

**Lecavalier, Vincent**
❑ 96RimOce-14
❑ 96RimOceQPP-13
❑ 97BowCHL-69
❑ 97BowCHLOPC-69
❑ 97RimOce-4
❑ 97UppDec-412
❑ 97UppDecBD-150
❑ 97UppDecBDDD-150
❑ 97UppDecBDQD-150
❑ 97UppDecBDTD-150
❑ 97Zen-95
❑ 97Zen5x7-75
❑ 97ZenGolImp-75
❑ 97ZenSilImp-75
❑ 97ZenZGol-95
❑ 97ZenZSil-95
❑ 98Be A PPA-279
❑ 98Be A PPAA-279
❑ 98Be A PPAAF-279
❑ 98Be A PPSE-279
❑ 98Be APG-279
❑ 98BowBes-109
❑ 98BowBesAR-109
❑ 98BowBesMIF-F5
❑ 98BowBesMIFAR-F5
❑ 98BowBesMIFR-F5
❑ 98BowBesP-BP10
❑ 98BowBesPAR-BP10
❑ 98BowBesPR-BP10
❑ 98BowBesR-109
❑ 98BowCHL-103
❑ 98BowCHL-128
❑ 98BowCHLAuB-A10
❑ 98BowCHLAuG-A10
❑ 98BowCHLAuS-A10
❑ 98BowCHLGA-103
❑ 98BowCHLGA-128
❑ 98BowCHLOI-103
❑ 98BowCHLOI-128
❑ 98BowCHLSC-SC12
❑ 98BowChrC-103
❑ 98BowChrC-128
❑ 98BowChrCGA-103
❑ 98BowChrCGA-128
❑ 98BowChrCGAR-103
❑ 98BowChrCGAR-128
❑ 98BowChrCOI-103
❑ 98BowChrCOI-128
❑ 98BowChrCOIR-103
❑ 98BowChrCOIR-128
❑ 98BowChrCR-103
❑ 98BowChrCR-128
❑ 98FinFutF-F3
❑ 98FinFutFR-F3
❑ 98O-PChr-224
❑ 98O-PChrR-224
❑ 98PacCroR-124
❑ 98PacCroRLS-124
❑ 98PacCroRPP-21
❑ 98PacCroRRC-8
❑ 98PacDynI-173
❑ 98PacDynIFT-17
❑ 98PacDynIIB-173
❑ 98PacDynIR-173
❑ 98PacDynIR-8
❑ 98PacDynITC-24
❑ 98PacOmeH-219
❑ 98PacOmeO-31
❑ 98PacOmeODI-219
❑ 98PacOmePI-3
❑ 98PacOmePIB-3
❑ 98PacOmeR-219
❑ 98PacRev-133
❑ 98PacRevCTL-17
❑ 98PacRevIS-133
❑ 98PacRevR-133
❑ 98PacRevS-32
❑ 98SP Aut-109
❑ 98SP AutSM-S27
❑ 98SP AutSotTG-VL
❑ 98SP AutSS-SS18
❑ 98SPXTopP-53
❑ 98SPXTopPF-53
❑ 98SPXTopPHH-H26
❑ 98SPXTopPLI-L1
❑ 98SPXTopPPS-PS12
❑ 98SPXTopPR-53
❑ 98SSASotT-VL
❑ 98Top-224
❑ 98TopGolLC1-61
❑ 98TopGolLC1B-61
❑ 98TopGolLC1BOoO-61
❑ 98TopGolLC1OoO-61
❑ 98TopGolLC1R-61
❑ 98TopGolLC1ROoO-61
❑ 98TopGolLC2-61
❑ 98TopGolLC2B-61
❑ 98TopGolLC2BOoO-61
❑ 98TopGolLC2OoO-61
❑ 98TopGolLC2R-61
❑ 98TopGolLC2ROoO-61
❑ 98TopGolLC3-61
❑ 98TopGolLC3B-61
❑ 98TopGolLC3BOoO-61
❑ 98TopGolLC3OoO-61
❑ 98TopGolLC3R-61
❑ 98TopGolLC3ROoO-61
❑ 98TopO-P-224
❑ 98UC-259
❑ 98UD ChoPCR-259
❑ 98UD ChoR-259
❑ 98UppDec-414
❑ 98UppDecBD-80
❑ 98UppDecDD-80
❑ 98UppDecE-414
❑ 98UppDecE1o1-414
❑ 98UppDecGJ-GJ2
❑ 98UppDecGJ-GJA3
❑ 98UppDecGN-GN3
❑ 98UppDecGNQ1-GN3
❑ 98UppDecGNQ2-GN3
❑ 98UppDecGNQ3-GN3
❑ 98UppDecGR-414
❑ 98UppDecM-187
❑ 98UppDecM1-M1
❑ 98UppDecM2-M1
❑ 98UppDECMGS-VL
❑ 98UppDECMGS-VLA
❑ 98UppDecMGS-187
❑ 98UppDecMP-VL
❑ 98UppDecMPG-PG5
❑ 98UppDecMS-S1
❑ 98UppDecMSF-F3
❑ 98UppDecMSS-187
❑ 98UppDecMSS-187
❑ 98UppDecP-P16
❑ 98UppDecPQ1-P16
❑ 98UppDecPQ2-P16
❑ 98UppDecPQ3-P16
❑ 98UppDecQD-80
❑ 98UppDecTD-80
❑ 98UppDecWFG-WF5
❑ 98UppDecWFP-WF5
❑ 99Pac-392
❑ 99PacAur-131
❑ 99PacAurPD-131
❑ 99PacCop-392
❑ 99PacGol-392
❑ 99PacGolCD-32
❑ 99PacIceB-392
❑ 99PacPreD-392
❑ 99PacTeaL-25
❑ 99QuePeeWHWCCS-22
❑ 99RetHoc-72
❑ 99SP AutPS-109
❑ 99UppDecCL-72
❑ 99UppDecCLCLC-72
❑ 99UppDecM-190
❑ 99UppDecM2CN-5
❑ 99UppDecMGS-190
❑ 99UppDecMSS-190
❑ 99UppDecMSS-190
❑ 99UppDecRG-G5C
❑ 99UppDecRG-72
❑ 99UppDecRGI-G5C
❑ 99UppDecRII-VL
❑ 99UppDecRIL1-VL
❑ 99UppDecRP-72
❑ 99UppDecRTotC-TC1

**Lechl, Jurgen**
❑ 94GerDELE-329
❑ 95GerDELE-302
❑ 96GerDELE-330

**Lechtaler, Christian**
❑ 91SweSemE-298

**Lecklin, Kimmo**
❑ 93FinnSIS-30
❑ 94FinnSIS-47

**Leclair, Alain**
❑ 90RayJrC-11

**Leclair, Jackie**
❑ 44BeeGro2P-259
❑ 51LavDaiQSHL-12
❑ 51LavDaiS-98
❑ 52St.LawS-57
❑ 55Par-36
❑ 55ParQuaO-36
❑ 94ParMisL-83

**LeClair, John**
❑ 91Bow-344
❑ 91CanaPos-17
❑ 91OPC-209
❑ 91OPCPre-105
❑ 91OPCPre-186
❑ 91Par-84
❑ 91ParFre-84
❑ 91Pin-322
❑ 91PinFre-322
❑ 91ProSet-545
❑ 91ProSetFre-545
❑ 91ProSetPla-259
❑ 91ScoAme-313
❑ 91ScoCan-343
❑ 91Top-209
❑ 91UppDec-345
❑ 91UppDecF-345
❑ 92Bow-8
❑ 92CanaPos-17
❑ 92OPC-386
❑ 92Par-326
❑ 92ParEmel-326
❑ 92StaClu-181
❑ 92Top-500
❑ 92TopGol-500G
❑ 92Ult-330
❑ 92UppDec-55
❑ 93CanaPos-14
❑ 93Don-176
❑ 93Lea-98
❑ 93OPCPre-181
❑ 93OPCPreG-181
❑ 93Par-107
❑ 93ParEmel-107
❑ 93Pin-112
❑ 93PinCan-112
❑ 93Sco-318
❑ 93ScoCan-318
❑ 93StaClu-95
❑ 93StaCluFDI-95
❑ 93StaCluFDIO-95
❑ 93StaCluO-95
❑ 93TopPre-181
❑ 93TopPreG-181
❑ 93Ult-215
❑ 93UppDec-167
❑ 93UppDecSP-79
❑ 94CanaPos-13
❑ 94CanGamNHLP-136
❑ 94ClaProP-54
❑ 94Don-98
❑ 94Fle-156
❑ 94Lea-5
❑ 94OPCPre-117
❑ 94OPCPreSE-117
❑ 94Par-111
❑ 94ParGol-111
❑ 94Pin-272
❑ 94PinArtP-272
❑ 94PinRinC-272
❑ 94SP-85
❑ 94SPDieCut-85
❑ 94TopPre-117
❑ 94TopPreSE-117
❑ 94Ult-111
❑ 94UppDec-330
❑ 94UppDecEleIce-330
❑ 95BeAPla-130
❑ 95BeAPSig-S130
❑ 95BeAPSigDC-S130
❑ 95Bow-63
❑ 95BowAllFoi-63
❑ 95CanGamNHLP-10
❑ 95CanGamNHLP-206
❑ 95ColCho-261
❑ 95ColCho-376
❑ 95ColChoCTG-C23
❑ 95ColChoCTG-C23B
❑ 95ColChoCTG-C23C
❑ 95ColChoCTGGB-C23
❑ 95ColChoCTGGR-C23
❑ 95ColChoCTGSB-C23
❑ 95ColChoCTGSR-C23
❑ 95ColChoPC-261
❑ 95ColChoPC-376
❑ 95ColChoPCP-261
❑ 95ColChoPCP-376
❑ 95Don-114
❑ 95DonDom-2
❑ 95DonEli-56
❑ 95DonEliDCS-56
❑ 95DonEliDCU-56
❑ 95Emo-132
❑ 95Fin-60
❑ 95Fin-179
❑ 95FinRef-60
❑ 95FinRef-179
❑ 95ImpSti-92
❑ 95Kra-46
❑ 95Lea-95
❑ 95LeaLim-85
❑ 95McDPin-MCD-20
❑ 95Met-111
❑ 95MetIW-5
❑ 95NHLAcePC-12S
❑ 95ParInt-157
❑ 95ParIntEl-157
❑ 95Pin-51
❑ 95PinArtP-51
❑ 95PinRinC-51
❑ 95PinRoa2-16
❑ 95PlaOneoOne-293
❑ 95ProMag-53
❑ 95Sco-9
❑ 95ScoBlaIce-9
❑ 95ScoBlaIceAP-9
❑ 95SelCer-44
❑ 95SelCerMG-44
❑ 95SkyImp-126
❑ 95SkyImp-244
❑ 95SP-108
❑ 95StaClu-77
❑ 95StaCluMOMS-77
❑ 95StaCluPS-PS6
❑ 95Sum-75
❑ 95SumArtP-75
❑ 95SumIce-75
❑ 95SumMadH-3
❑ 95Top-65
❑ 95TopHomGUSA-HGA9
❑ 95TopOPCI-65
❑ 95TopPowL-1PL
❑ 95TopSupSki-42
❑ 95TopSupSkiPla-42
❑ 95Ult-118
❑ 95UltCreCra-5
❑ 95UltGolM-118
❑ 95UltRedLS-5
❑ 95UltRedLSGM-5
❑ 95UppDec-7
❑ 95UppDec-247
❑ 95UppDecAGPRW-24
❑ 95UppDecEleIce-7
❑ 95UppDecEleIce-247
❑ 95UppDecEleIceG-7
❑ 95UppDecEleIceG-247
❑ 95UppDecNHLAS-AS14
❑ 95UppDecSpeE-SE63
❑ 95UppDecSpeEdiG-SE63
❑ 95Zen-59
❑ 95ZenGifG-7
❑ 96BeAPBisITB-17
❑ 96ColCho-190
❑ 96ColCho-326
❑ 96ColChoCTG-C12A
❑ 96ColChoCTG-C12B
❑ 96ColChoCTG-C12C
❑ 96ColChoCTGE-CR12
❑ 96ColChoCTGEG-CR12
❑ 96ColChoCTGG-C12A
❑ 96ColChoCTGG-C12B
❑ 96ColChoCTGG-C12C
❑ 96ColChoMVP-UD8
❑ 96ColChoMVPG-UD8
❑ 96Don-36
❑ 96DonCanI-100
❑ 96DonCanIGPP-100
❑ 96DonCanIRPP-100
❑ 96DonEli-57
❑ 96DonEliDCS-57
❑ 96DonHitLis-13
❑ 96DonPrePro-36
❑ 96Fla-69
❑ 96FlaBluI-69
❑ 96Fle-81
❑ 96Fle-142
❑ 96FleArtRos-12
❑ 96FlePic-30
❑ 96FlePicDL-7
❑ 96FlePicF5-24
❑ 96FlePicFF-1
❑ 96FleProShe-1
❑ 96FleProShe-2
❑ 96FlyPos-14
❑ 96KraUppD-57
❑ 96Lea-83
❑ 96LeaLim-15
❑ 96LeaLimG-15
❑ 96LeaPre-105
❑ 96LeaPreP-83
❑ 96LeaPrePP-105
❑ 96LeaPreSG-39
❑ 96LeaPreSte-39
❑ 96MetUni-113
❑ 96MetUniLW-10
❑ 96MetUniLWSP-10
❑ 96NHLProSTA-53
❑ 96Pin-49
❑ 96PinArtP-49
❑ 96PinFoi-49
❑ 96PinMcD-4
❑ 96PinPreS-49
❑ 96PinRinC-49
❑ 96Sco-161
❑ 96ScoArtPro-161
❑ 96ScoDeaCAP-161
❑ 96ScoGolB-161
❑ 96ScoSpeAP-161
❑ 96SelCer-33
❑ 96SelCerAP-33
❑ 96SelCerBlu-33
❑ 96SelCerMB-33
❑ 96SelCerMG-33
❑ 96SelCerMR-33
❑ 96SelCerRed-33
❑ 96SkyImp-96
❑ 96SkyImp-S1
❑ 96SkyImp-NNO
❑ 96SkyImpB-11
❑ 96SP-112
❑ 96SPGamFil-GF17
❑ 96SPx-34
❑ 96SPxGol-34
❑ 96StaCluMO-43
❑ 96Sum-6
❑ 96SumArtP-6
❑ 96SumIce-6
❑ 96SumMet-6
❑ 96SumPreS-6
❑ 96TeaOut-3
❑ 96TopPicTS-TS1
❑ 96Ult-125
❑ 96Ult-S125
❑ 96UltCleTheIce-5
❑ 96UltGolM-125
❑ 96UppDec-118
❑ 96UppDec-368
❑ 96UppDecBD-110
❑ 96UppDecBDG-110
❑ 96UppDecIce-98
❑ 96UppDecIceDF-S10
❑ 96UppDecIcePar-98
❑ 96UppDecIceSCF-S10
❑ 96UppDecPP-P3
❑ 96Zen-17
❑ 96ZenArtP-17
❑ 96ZenAss-10
❑ 97Be A PPAD-250
❑ 97Be A PPAPD-250
❑ 97BeAPla-250
❑ 97BeAPlaAut-250
❑ 97BeAPlaPOT-9
❑ 97ColCho-182
❑ 97ColChoSta-SQ52
❑ 97Don-29
❑ 97Don-229
❑ 97DonCanI-93
❑ 97DonCanIDS-93
❑ 97DonCanIPS-93
❑ 97DonCanISCS-29
❑ 97DonEli-71
❑ 97DonEliAsp-71
❑ 97DonEliS-71
❑ 97DonLim-15
❑ 97DonLim-90
❑ 97DonLim-94
❑ 97DonLim-168
❑ 97DonLimExp-15
❑ 97DonLimExp-90
❑ 97DonLimExp-94
❑ 97DonLimExp-168
❑ 97DonLimFOTG-63
❑ 97DonPre-76
❑ 97DonPreCttC-76
❑ 97DonPreLotT-3A
❑ 97DonPreProG-29
❑ 97DonPreProG-229
❑ 97DonPreProS-29
❑ 97DonPreProS-229
❑ 97DonPri-132
❑ 97DonPri-205
❑ 97DonPriDD-28
❑ 97DonPriODI-26
❑ 97DonPriP-21
❑ 97DonPriS-21
❑ 97DonPriSB-21
❑ 97DonPriSG-21
❑ 97DonPriSoA-132
❑ 97DonPriSoA-205
❑ 97DonPriSS-21
❑ 97DonRedAle-7
❑ 97EssOlyHH-25
❑ 97EssOlyHHF-25
❑ 97Kat-106
❑ 97KatGol-106
❑ 97KatSil-106
❑ 97Lea-100
❑ 97LeaBanSea-7
❑ 97LeaFraMat-100
❑ 97LeaFraMDC-100
❑ 97LeaInt-100
❑ 97LeaIntUI-100
❑ 97Pac-10
❑ 97PacCarSup-14
❑ 97PacCarSupM-14
❑ 97PacCop-10
❑ 97PacCroR-98
❑ 97PacCroREG-98
❑ 97PacCroRHTDC-12
❑ 97PacCroRIB-98
❑ 97PacCroRLCDC-13
❑ 97PacCroRS-98
❑ 97PacDyn-90
❑ 97PacDyn-141
❑ 97PacDynBKS-71
❑ 97PacDynC-90
❑ 97PacDynC-141
❑ 97PacDynDG-90
❑ 97PacDynDG-141
❑ 97PacDynEG-90
❑ 97PacDynEG-141
❑ 97PacDynIB-90
❑ 97PacDynIB-141
❑ 97PacDynR-90
❑ 97PacDynR-141
❑ 97PacDynSil-90
❑ 97PacDynSil-141
❑ 97PacDynTan-15
❑ 97PacDynTan-20
❑ 97PacEmeGre-10
❑ 97PacIceB-10
❑ 97PacInv-101
❑ 97PacInvAZ-17
❑ 97PacInvC-101
❑ 97PacInvEG-101
❑ 97PacInvFP-24
❑ 97PacInvIB-101
❑ 97PacInvNRB-144
❑ 97PacInvR-101
❑ 97PacInvS-101
❑ 97PacOme-167
❑ 97PacOmeC-167
❑ 97PacOmeDG-167
❑ 97PacOmeEG-167
❑ 97PacOmeG-167
❑ 97PacOmeGFDCC-12
❑ 97PacOmeIB-167
❑ 97PacOmeSLC-15
❑ 97PacPar-133
❑ 97PacParC-133
❑ 97PacParDG-133
❑ 97PacParEG-133
❑ 97PacParIB-133
❑ 97PacParP-14
❑ 97PacParRed-133
❑ 97PacParSil-133
❑ 97PacRed-10
❑ 97PacRev-102
❑ 97PacRev1AGD-15
❑ 97PacRevC-102
❑ 97PacRevE-102
❑ 97PacRevIB-102
❑ 97PacRevR-102
❑ 97PacRevS-102
❑ 97PacSil-10
❑ 97PacSlaSDC-6C
❑ 97Pin-57
❑ 97Pin-196
❑ 97PinArtP-57
❑ 97PinBee-5
❑ 97PinBeeGP-5
❑ 97PinBeeGT-12
❑ 97PinBeeT-12
❑ 97PinCer-119
❑ 97PinCerGT-20
❑ 97PinCerMB-119
❑ 97PinCerMG-119
❑ 97PinCerMR-119
❑ 97PinCerR-119
❑ 97PinCerT-20
❑ 97PinEpiGO-23
❑ 97PinEpiGP-23
❑ 97PinEpiME-23
❑ 97PinEpiMO-23
❑ 97PinEpiMP-23
❑ 97PinEpiPE-23
❑ 97PinEpiPO-23
❑ 97PinEpiPP-23
❑ 97PinEpiSE-23
❑ 97PinEpiSO-23
❑ 97PinEpiSP-23
❑ 97PinIns-58
❑ 97PinInsC-6
❑ 97PinInsCC-58
❑ 97PinInsCG-6
❑ 97PinInsEC-58
❑ 97PinInsT-25
❑ 97PinMin-20
❑ 97PinMinB-20
❑ 97PinMinCBP-20
❑ 97PinMinCGPP-20
❑ 97PinMinCNSP-20
❑ 97PinMinCoiB-20
❑ 97PinMinCoiGP-20
❑ 97PinMinCoiN-20
❑ 97PinMinCoiSG-20
❑ 97PinMinCoiSS-20
❑ 97PinMinGolTea-20
❑ 97PinMinSilTea-20
❑ 97PinPowPac-23
❑ 97PinPrePBB-57
❑ 97PinPrePBB-196
❑ 97PinPrePBC-57
❑ 97PinPrePBC-196
❑ 97PinPrePBM-57
❑ 97PinPrePBM-196
❑ 97PinPrePBY-57
❑ 97PinPrePBY-196
❑ 97PinPrePFC-57
❑ 97PinPrePFC-196
❑ 97PinPrePFM-57
❑ 97PinPrePFM-196
❑ 97PinPrePFY-57
❑ 97PinPrePFY-196

97PinPrePla-57
97PinPrePla-196
97PinRinC-57
97PinTeaP-8
97PinTeaPM-8
97PinTeaPP-8
97PinTeaPPM-8
97PinTotCMPG-119
97PinTotCPB-119
97PinTotCPG-119
97PinTotCPR-119
97Sco-108
97ScoArtPro-108
97ScoChel-5
97ScoFly-4
97ScoFlyPla-4
97ScoFlyPre-4
97ScoGolBla-108
97SP Autl-I17
97SPAut-114
97SPAutiD-I17
97SPAutiE-I17
97SPx-38
97SPxBro-38
97SPxGol-38
97SPxGraF-38
97SPxSil-38
97SPxSte-38
97Stu-22
97StuPor-25
97StuPrePG-22
97StuPrePS-22
97StuSil-15
97StuSil-18-15
97UppDec-123
97UppDecBcD-65
97UppDecBDDD-65
97UppDecBDPC-PC6
97UppDecBDPCDD-PC6
97UppDecBDPCM-PC6
97UppDecBDPCQD-PC6
97UppDecBDPCTD-PC6
97UppDecBDQD-65
97UppDecBDTD-65
97UppDecCtAG-15
97UppDecCtAG-AR15
97UppDecIce-75
97UppDecIceP-75
97UppDecILL-L8A
97UppDecILL2-L8A
97UppDecIPS-75
97UppDecSG-SG50
97UppDecTS-20
97UppDecTSL2-20
97UppDecTSS-9B
97Zen-8
97Zen5x7-47
97ZenChaTC-8
97ZenGolImp-47
97ZenSilImp-47
97ZenZGol-8
97ZenZSil-8
97ZenZT-7
97ZenZT5x7-7
97ZenZTG-7
98Be A PPA-250
98Be A PPAA-250
98Be A PPAAF-250
98Be A PPAGUSC-S20
98Be A PPAJ-AS22
98Be A PPGUJA-G5
98Be A PPPGUJC-G5
98Be A PPPPUJC-P13
98Be A PPSE-250
98Be APG-250
98BowBes-7
98BowBesAR-7
98BowBesMIF-F1
98BowBesMIFAR-F1
98BowBesMIFR-F1
98BowBesR-7
98Fin-51
98FinDouMF-M41
98FinDouMF-M45
98FinDouMF-M46
98FinDouMF-M47
98FinDouSMFR-M41
98FinDouSMFR-M45
98FinDouSMFR-M46
98FinDouSMFR-M47
98FinNo P-51
98FinNo PR-51
98FinRedL-R16
98FinRedLR-R16
98FinRef-51
980-PChr-60
980-PChrR-60
980-PChrSB-SB16
980-PChrSB-SB28
980-PChrSBR-SB16
980-PChrSBR-SB28
98Pac-51
98PacAur-140
98PacAurALC-14
98PacAurC-13
98PacAurCF-35
98PacAurCFC-35
98PacAurCFIB-35
98PacAurCFR-35
98PacAurCFS-35
98PacAurMAC-14
98PacCroR-99
98PacCroRLS-99
98PacCroRMP-15
98PacCroRPotG-17

98PacCroRPP-18
98PacDynl-137
98PacDynl-14
98PacDynlIFT-14
98PacDynlIB-137
98PacDynlIR-137
98PacEO P-15
98PacIceB-51
98PacOmeEP1o1-15
98PacOmeHF-9
98PacOmeH-176
98PacOmeO-25
98PacOmeODI-176
98PacOmeP-15
98PacOmePI-15
98PacOmePIB-15
98PacOmeR-176
98PacPar-176
98PacParC-176
98PacParEG-176
98PacParH-176
98PacParIB-176
98PacParS-176
98PacParSDDC-13
98PacRed-51
98PacRev-105
98PacRevADC-16
98PacRevCTL-13
98PacRevIS-105
98PacRevR-105
98PacRevS-25
98PacTim-13
98PacTitl-14
98PinEpiGE-23
98RevThrPA-28
98RevThrPA-28
98SP Aut-63
98SP AutSM-S9
98SP AutSS-SS11
98SPxFin-60
98SPxFin-102
98SPxFin-164
98SPxFinR-60
98SPxFinR-102
98SPxFinR-164
98SPxFinS-60
98SPxFinS-102
98SPxFinS-164
98SPXTopP-44
98SPXTopPF-44
98SPXTopPHH-H22
98SPXTopPLI-L24
98SPXTopPPS-PS9
98SPXTopPR-44
98SPXTopPWM-JL
98Top-60
98TopAut-A3
98TopGolC-15
98TopGolC1B-86
98TopGolC1BOoO-86
98TopGolC1OoO-86
98TopGolC1R-86
98TopGolC1ROoO-86
98TopGolC2-86
98TopGolC2BOoO-86
98TopGolC2OoO-86
98TopGolC2ROoO-86
98TopGolC3-86
98TopGolC3B-86
98TopGolC3OoO-86
98TopGolC3R-86
98TopGolC3ROoO-86
98TopGolGR'-GR2
98TopGolGR'BOoO-GR2
98TopGolGR'OoO-GR2
98TopGolGR'ROoO-GR2
98TopMysFB-M10
98TopMysFBR-M10
98TopMysFG-M10
98TopMysFGR-M10
98TopMysFS-M10
98TopMysFSR-M10
98TopO-P-60
98TopRedLGR'-GR2
98TopSeaB-SB16
98TopSeaB-SB28
98UC-153
98UC-235
98UCMBH-BH6
98UCSB-SQ15
98UCSG-SQ15
98UCSG-SQ15
98UCSR-SQ15
98UD ChoPCR-153
98UD ChoPCR-235
98UD ChoR-153
98UD ChoR-235
98UD3-56
98UD3-116
98UD3-176
98UD3DieC-56
98UD3DieC-116
98UD3DieC-176
98UDCP-153
98UDCP-322
98UppDec-143
98UppDecBD-63
98UppDecDD-63
98UppDecE-143
98UppDecE1o1-143
98UppDecFF-FF25

98UppDecFF-FF25
98UppDecFFQ1-FF25
98UppDecFFQ2-FF25
98UppDecFIT-FT27
98UppDecFITQ1-FT27
98UppDecFITQ2-FT27
98UppDecFITQ3-FT27
98UppDecGR-143
98UppDecLSH-LS25
98UppDecLSHQ1-LS25
98UppDecLSHQ2-LS25
98UppDecLSHQ3-LS25
98UppDecM-148
98UppDecM1-M24
98UppDecM2-M24
98UppDECMGS-JL
98UppDecMGS-148
98UppDecMOH-OT14
98UppDecMPG-PG6
98UppDecMSS-148
98UppDecMSS-148
98UppDecP-P25
98UppDecPQ1-P25
98UppDecPQ2-P25
98UppDecPQ3-P25
98UppDecQD-63
98UppDecTD-63
98UppDecWFG-WF22
98UppDecWFP-WF22
99AurSty-14
99Pac-306
99PacAur-105
99PacAurCC-8
99PacAurCF-16
99PacAurCFC-16
99PacAurCFPB-16
99PacAurCP-8
99PacAurCPP-8
99PacAurPD-105
99PacCop-306
99PacGol-306
99PacGolCD-25
99PacIceB-306
99PacPasAP-16
99PacPreD-306
99RetHoc-60
99SP AutPS-63
99UppDecCL-68
99UppDecCLCLC-68
99UppDecM-148
99UppDecMGS-148
99UppDecMSS-148
99UppDecMSS-148
99UppDecRG-60
99UppDecRP-60

**Leclair, Nelson**
67ColChe-9

**Leclerc, Jean**
52JunBluT-43

**Leclerc, Martin-Benoit**
92QueIntP-7

**LeClerc, Mike**
95Cla-47
95SlaMemC-38
97UppDec-181
98BowBes-117
98BowBesAR-117
98BowBesMIF-F2
98BowBesMIFAR-F2
98BowBesMIFR-F2
98BowBesR-117
98UppDec-213
98UppDecE-213
98UppDecE1o1-213
98UppDecGR-213

**Leclerc, Paul**
51LavDaiQSHL-80
52St.LawS-18

**Leclerc, Renald**
76OPCWHA-28

**Leclerc, Roland**
52JunBluT-79

**Lecompte, Eric**
917thInnSQMJHL-217
93Cla-23
94Cla-41
94ClaDraGol-41
94ClaTri-T13
95ColEdgl-136
95IndIce-11
96ColEdgFL-31

**Lecours, Danny**
81MilAdm-10

**Lecuyer, Doug**
80BlaWhiBor-7
81OPC-367

**Ledlin, Frederik**
94GerDELE-201

**Ledock, Rene**
94GerDELE-140

**Leduc, Battleship (Albert)**
27LaPat-10
33OPCV304A-46
33V129-27
55Par-61
55ParQua0-61

**Leduc, Bob**
72NatOttWHA-15
72OPC-322
73OPCWHAP-9

**Leduc, Mike**
91BriColJHL-69

**Leduc, Rich**
75OPCWHA-113
76OPCWHA-41

77OPCWHA-13
79OPC-283
80NordPos-18
80OPC-122
80PepCap-72
80Top-122

**Ledyard, Grant**
86Kin20tATl-12
87KinTeal4-12
87PanSti-273
88CapBor-12
88CapSmo-12
89SabBluS-10
89SabCam-12
90OPC-406
90ProSet-24
90SabBluS-12
90SabCam-13
91Bow-40
91OPC-386
91Par-241
91ParFre-241
91SabBluS-10
91SabPepC-10
91StaClu-169
91Top-386
92OPC-393
92PanSti-244
92PanStiFre-244
92Pin-205
92PinFre-205
92SabBluS-11
92Sco-358
92ScoCan-358
92StaClu-79
92Top-321
92TopGol-321G
93Don-89
93Lea-394
93Par-321
93ParEmel-321
93Pin-413
93PinCan-413
93Pow-325
93Sco-568
93ScoCan-568
93ScoGol-568
93Ult-299
94CanGamNHLP-84
94Don-312
94Fla-42
94Lea-263
94OPCPre-98
94OPCPreSE-98
94Pin-204
94PinArtP-204
94PinRinC-204
94StaHoc-18
94StaPos-15
94TopPre-98
94Ult-54
95BeAPla-104
95BeAPSig-S104
95BeAPSigDC-S104
95CanGamNHLP-90
95PlaOneoOne-141
95Top-157
95TopOPCI-157
95Ult-40
95UltGolM-40
96StaPos-16
97Pac-345
97PacCop-345
97PacEmeGre-345
97PacIceB-345
97PacRed-345
97PacSil-345
97ScoCanPla-15
97ScoCanPre-15
97ScoCanu-15
98Pac-84
98PacIceB-84
98PacRed-84

**Lee, Bill**
52JunBluT-144

**Lee, Peter**
78OPC-244
78Top-244
79OPC-45
79Top-45
80OPC-278
81OPC-258
81OPCSti-185
81Top-E114
82PosCer-15
83PenHeiP-16

**Lee, Phil**
95SolBar-8

**Lee, Steve**
77KalWin-11

**Leeb, Brad**
95RedDeeR-9

**Leeb, Greg**
55SpoChi-15
97BowCHL-94
97BowCHLOPC-94
98BowCHL-55
98BowCHLGA-55
98BowCHLOI-55

98BowChrC-55
98BowChrCGA-55
98BowChrCGAR-55
98BowChrCOIR-55
98BowChrCR-55

**Leefe, Erik**
95SasBla-13

**Leek, Mikael**
83SweSemE-145

**Leeman, Gary**
81RegPat-12
82RegPat-14
83CanNatJ-8
83MapLeaf-13
83RegPat-14
84MapLeaf-15
84OPC-305
85MapLeaP-19
86KraDra-31
86MapLeaP-16
87MapLeaf-13
87MapLeaPLA-10
87MapLeaPO-13
87OPC-240
87OPCSti-161
87PanSti-331
88MapLeaPLA-8
88OPC-11
88OPCSti-178
88PanSti-125
88Top-11
89Kra-36
89OPC-22
89OPCSti-168
89PanSti-133
89Top-22
90Bow-155
90BowHatTri-10
90BowTif-155
90Kra-27
90OPC-135
90PanSti-279
90ProSet-283
90Sco-40
90ScoCan-40
90ScoHotRS-20
90ScoPro-40
90Top-135
90TopTeaSL-13
90TopTif-135
90UppDec-243
90UppDecF-243
90UppDecF-310
91Bow-161
91Kra-10
91MapLeaP-21
91MapLeaPTS-12
91MapLeaPTS-H
91OPC-188
91OPCPre-106
91OPCPre-134
91Par-173
91ParFre-173
91ParFre-254
91Pin-31
91PinFre-31
91ProSet-231
91ProSetFre-231
91ProSetPla-162
91ScoAme-77
91ScoCan-77
91StaClu-158
91Top-188
91UppDec-35
91UppDec-153
91UppDec-610
91UppDecF-35
92Bow-192
92FlamIGA-3
92OPC-33
92PanSti-41
92PanStiFre-41
92Par-323
92ParEmel-323
92Pin-184
92PinFre-184
92Sco-171
92ScoCan-171
92StaClu-272
92Top-85
92TopGol-85G
92Ult-22
92UppDec-66
92Pin-15
92PinFre-15
93OPCPre-397
93OPCPreG-397
93Sco-147
93ScoCan-147
93StaClu-244
93StaCluFDI-244
93StaCluFDIO-244
93StaCluO-244
93TopPre-397
93TopPreG-397
93Ult-353
94BeAPSig-73
94GerDELE-188

**Leeming, Bob**
89WinSpi-8

**Leetch, Brian**
88OPCSti-189

88PanSti-301
89OPC-136
89OPC-321
89OPC-326
89OPCSti-39
89OPCSti-91
89OPCSti-215
89OPCSti-240
89PanSti-279
89PanSti-378
89RanMarMB-2
89SweSemWCS-161
89Top-136
90Bow-215A
90Bow-215B
90BowTif-215A
90BowTif-215B
90Kra-28
90OPCPre-61
90PanSti-95
90ProSet-201
90ProSet-373
90Sco-225
90ScoCan-225
90ScoHotRS-93
90ScoYouS-2
90Top-221
90TopTif-221
90UppDec-253
90UppDec-315
90UppDecF-253
90UppDecF-315
90UppDecF-485
91Bow-75
91McDUppD-D2
91OPC-108
91OPC-215
91OPC-269
91OPCPre-57
91OPCPre-183
91PanSti-284
91Par-119
91Par-438
91Par-464
91Par-471
91ParFre-119
91ParFre-438
91ParFre-464
91ParFre-471
91ParPHC-PHC8
91ParPHCF-PHC8
91Pin-136
91PinB-B3
91PinBFre-B3
91PinFre-136
91ProSet-159
91ProSetFre-159
91ProSetFre-309
91ProSetPla-9
91ProSetPla-284
91ScoAme-5
91ScoAme-333
91ScoAme-343
91ScoCan-5
91ScoCan-363
91ScoCan-373
91ScoKel-8
91StaClu-201
91SweSemWCS-131
91Top-108
91Top-269
91TopTeaSL-4
91UppDec-35
91UppDec-153
91UppDec-600
91UppDec-612
91UppDecF-35
91UppDecF-153
91UppDecF-610
91UppDecF-612
92Bow-149
92Bow-232
92HumDum1-14
92McDUppD-H4
92OPC-378
92OPCTroW-2
92PanSti-239
92PanStiFre-239
92Par-110
92ParEmel-110
92ParEmel-467
92Par-467
92Pin-15
92PinFre-15
92PinTeaP-3
92PinTeaPF-3
92ProSet-112
92ProSetAW-CC4
92Sco-375
92Sco-416
92Sco-491
92Sco-522
92ScoCan-375
92ScoCan-416
92ScoCan-491
92ScoCan-522
92ScoUSAG-8
92SeaPat-28
92StaClu-73
92StaClu-248
92Top-261

92Top-293
92TopGol-261G
92TopGol-293G
92Ult-138
92UltAwaW-2
92UppDec-34
92UppDec-284
92UppDec-434
92UppDec-640
92UppDecWJG-WG15
93Don-221
93Lea-70
930PCPre-505
930PCPre-505
930PCPreG-25
930PCPreG-505
93PanSti-96
93Par-131
93ParEmel-131
93Pin-275
93Pin2HS-275
93PinCan-275
93PinTeaP-2
93PinTeaPC-2
93Pow-160
93PowSlaA-6
93Sco-235
93ScoCan-235
93ScoDreTea-6
93ScoFra-13
93StaClu-88
93StaCluFDI-88
93StaCluFDIO-88
93StaCluO-88
93SweSemWCS-171
93TopPre-25
93TopPre-505
93TopPreG-25
93TopPreG-505
93Ult-132
93UppDec-348
93UppDecLAS-5
93UppDecSP-102
94BeAPla-R46
94BeAPla-R149
94BeAPSig-46
94CanGamNHLP-170
94CanGamNHLP-260
94CanGamNHLP-327
94CanGamNHLP-334
94Don-152
94DonDom-2
94EASpo-85
94Fin-49
94FinBowB-B12
94FinBowB-X24
94FinBowBR-B12
94FinBowBR-X24
94FinnJaaK-113
94FinnJaaK-339
94FinRef-49
94FinSupTW-49
94Fla-114
94FlaScoP-5
94Fle-135
94FleHea-5
94HocWit-71
94KenStaLA-10
94KenStaLC-5
94Kra-64
94Lea-403
94LeaGolS-6
94LeaLim-33
94McDUppD-McD6
940PCPre-37
940PCPre-450
940PCPre-485
940PCPre-500
940PCPreSE-37
940PCPreSE-450
940PCPreSE-485
940PCPreSE-500
94Par-151
94ParGol-151
94ParVin-V15
94Pin-155
94PinArtP-155
94PinRinC-155
94PinTeaP-TP4
94PinTeaPDP-TP4
94PinWorEdi-WE15
94Sco-184
94ScoDreTea-DT4
94ScoGol-184
94ScoPla-184
94ScoPlaTS-184
94Sel-24
94SelFirLin-3
94SelGol-24
94SP-74
94SPDieCut-74
94StaClu-55
94StaClu-150
94StaCluFDI-55
94StaCluFDI-150
94StaCluFDIO-150
94StaCluFI-7
94StaCluMO-24
94StaCluMOMS-55
94StaCluMOMS-150
94StaCluST-15
94StaCluSTWC-55
94StaCluSTWC-150
94TopFinB-14
94TopPre-37

❑ 94TopPre-120
❑ 94TopPre-450
❑ 94TopPre-485
❑ 94TopPre-500
❑ 94TopPreSE-37
❑ 94TopPreSE-450
❑ 94TopPreSE-485
❑ 94TopPreSE-500
❑ 94Ult-139
❑ 94UltAllS-2
❑ 94UltAwaW-7
❑ 94UltSpeM-6
❑ 94UppDec-231
❑ 94UppDec-444
❑ 94UppDecEleIce-231
❑ 94UppDecEleIce-444
❑ 94UppDecNBAP-9
❑ 94UppDecPC-C28
❑ 94UppDecPCEG-C28
❑ 94UppDecPH-H11
❑ 94UppDecPHEG-H11
❑ 94UppDecPHES-H11
❑ 94UppDecPHG-H11
❑ 94UppDecPR-R13
❑ 94UppDecPR-R45
❑ 94UppDecPR-R51
❑ 94UppDecPRE-R13
❑ 94UppDecPRE-R45
❑ 94UppDecPRE-R51
❑ 94UppDecPreRG-R13
❑ 94UppDecPreRG-R45
❑ 94UppDecPreRG-R51
❑ 94UppDecSPI-SP50
❑ 94UppDecSPIDC-SP50
❑ 95Bow-32
❑ 95BowAllFoi-32
❑ 95BowBes-BB14
❑ 95BowBesRef-BB14
❑ 95CanGamNHLP-186
❑ 95ColCho-247
❑ 95ColChoPC-247
❑ 95ColChoPCP-247
❑ 95Don-181
❑ 95DonDom-3
❑ 95DonEli-98
❑ 95DonEliDCS-98
❑ 95DonEliDCU-98
❑ 95DonProPoi-5
❑ 95Emo-115
❑ 95EmoXci-6
❑ 95Fin-41
❑ 95Fin-115
❑ 95FinnSemWC-105
❑ 95FinRef-41
❑ 95FinRef-115
❑ 95ImpSti-79
❑ 95ImpStiDCS-7
❑ 95Lea-93
❑ 95LeaGolS-3
❑ 95LeaLim-90
❑ 95Met-96
❑ 95MetHM-8
❑ 95MetIS-12
❑ 95NHLAcePC-6C
❑ 95ParInt-144
❑ 95ParIntCCGS2-14
❑ 95ParIntCCSS2-14
❑ 95ParIntEl-144
❑ 95ParIntPTP-PP21
❑ 95Pin-133
❑ 95PinArtP-133
❑ 95PinFirS-6
❑ 95PinRinC-133
❑ 95PlaOneoOne-68
❑ 95PlaOneoOne-174
❑ 95PlaOneoOne-283
❑ 95ProMag-97
❑ 95Sco-124
❑ 95ScoBlaIce-124
❑ 95ScoBlaIceAP-124
❑ 95SelCer-27
❑ 95SelCerMG-27
❑ 95SigRooCF-CF3
❑ 95SigRooCFS-CF3
❑ 95SkyImp-110
❑ 95SP-94
❑ 95SPStaEto-E20
❑ 95SPStaEtoG-E20
❑ 95StaClu-30
❑ 95StaCluM-M8
❑ 95StaCluMO-3
❑ 95StaCluMOMS-30
❑ 95StaCluNem-N5
❑ 95Sum-23
❑ 95SumArtP-23
❑ 95SumGM-4
❑ 95SumIce-23
❑ 95SweGloWC-103
❑ 95Top-75
❑ 95TopHomGUSA-HGA1
❑ 95TopMysF-M16
❑ 95TopMysFR-M16
❑ 95TopOPCI-75
❑ 95TopPro-PF2
❑ 95TopSupSki-19
❑ 95TopSupSkiPla-19
❑ 95Ult-104
❑ 95Ult-390
❑ 95UltGolM-104
❑ 95UltUltHP-5
❑ 95UltUltV-5
❑ 95UppDec-236
❑ 95UppDec-487
❑ 95UppDecAGPRW-25
❑ 95UppDecEleIce-236
❑ 95UppDecEleIce-487
❑ 95UppDecEleIceG-236
❑ 95UppDecEleIceG-487
❑ 95UppDecFreFra-F18
❑ 95UppDecFreFraJ-F18
❑ 95UppDecNHLAS-AS7
❑ 95UppDecPHE-H33
❑ 95UppDecPRE-R18
❑ 95UppDecPreH-H33
❑ 95UppDecPreR-R18
❑ 95UppDecSpeE-SE55
❑ 95UppDecSpeEdiG-SE55
❑ 95Zen-32
❑ 96BeAPAut-55
❑ 96BeAPAutSil-55
❑ 96BeAPla-55
❑ 96BeAPla-P55
❑ 96ColCho-169
❑ 96ColCho-303
❑ 96ColCho-324
❑ 96ColChoCTG-C27A
❑ 96ColChoCTG-C27B
❑ 96ColChoCTG-C27C
❑ 96ColChoCTGE-CR27
❑ 96ColChoCTGEG-CR27
❑ 96ColChoCTGG-C27A
❑ 96ColChoCTGG-C27B
❑ 96ColChoCTGG-C27C
❑ 96ColChoMVP-UD30
❑ 96ColChoMVPG-UD30
❑ 96Don-13
❑ 96DonCanI-108
❑ 96DonCanIGPP-108
❑ 96DonCanIRPP-108
❑ 96DonEli-125
❑ 96DonEliDCS-125
❑ 96DonPrePro-13
❑ 96Fla-60
❑ 96FlaBluI-60
❑ 96Fle-70
❑ 96Fle-140
❑ 96FleNor-7
❑ 96FlePic-12
❑ 96FlePicF5-25
❑ 96FlePicJE-17
❑ 96KraUppD-1
❑ 96Lea-165
❑ 96LeaLim-82
❑ 96LeaLimG-82
❑ 96LeaPre-42
❑ 96LeaPreP-165
❑ 96LeaPrePP-42
❑ 96LeaPreSG-23
❑ 96LeaPreSte-23
❑ 96MetUni-98
❑ 96MetUniIC-9
❑ 96MetUniICSP-9
❑ 96NHLACEPC-28
❑ 96NHLProSTA-97
❑ 96Pin-193
❑ 96PinArtP-193
❑ 96PinFoi-193
❑ 96PinMcD-20
❑ 96PinPreS-193
❑ 96PinRinC-193
❑ 96Sco-179
❑ 96ScoArtPro-179
❑ 96ScoDeaCAP-179
❑ 96ScoGolB-179
❑ 96ScoSpeAP-179
❑ 96SelCer-76
❑ 96SelCerAP-76
❑ 96SelCerBlu-76
❑ 96SelCerMB-76
❑ 96SelCerMG-76
❑ 96SelCerMR-76
❑ 96SelCerRed-76
❑ 96SkyImp-81
❑ 96SkyImpNHLF-14
❑ 96SP-101
❑ 96SPx-26
❑ 96SPxGol-26
❑ 96StaCluMO-33
❑ 96Sum-96
❑ 96SumArtP-96
❑ 96SumIce-96
❑ 96SumMet-96
❑ 96SumPreS-96
❑ 96SweSemW-160
❑ 96TeaOut-78
❑ 96TopPicFT-FT5
❑ 96TopPicID-ID1
❑ 96Ult-108
❑ 96UltGolM-109
❑ 96UltPow-10
❑ 96UltPowBL-7
❑ 96UppDec-300
❑ 96UppDecBD-12
❑ 96UppDecBDG-12
❑ 96UppDecGN-X23
❑ 96UppDecIce-43
❑ 96UppDecIcePar-43
❑ 96UppDecSS-SS7B
❑ 96Zen-85
❑ 96ZenArtP-85
❑ 97ColCho-162
❑ 97ColChoSta-SQ20
❑ 97Don-156
❑ 97Don-230
❑ 97DonCanI-88
❑ 97DonCanIDS-88
❑ 97DonCanIPS-88
❑ 97DonEli-40
❑ 97DonEli-116
❑ 97DonEliAsp-40
❑ 97DonEliAsp-116
❑ 97DonEliC-30
❑ 97DonEliMC-30
❑ 97DonEliS-40
❑ 97DonEliS-116
❑ 97DonLim-70
❑ 97DonLim-179
❑ 97DonLim-182
❑ 97DonLimExp-70
❑ 97DonLimExp-179
❑ 97DonLimExp-182
❑ 97DonLimFOTG-64
❑ 97DonLin2L-3
❑ 97DonLin2LDC-3
❑ 97DonPre-22
❑ 97DonPre-188
❑ 97DonPreCttC-22
❑ 97DonPreCttC-188
❑ 97DonPreProG-156
❑ 97DonPreProG-230
❑ 97DonPreProS-156
❑ 97DonPreProS-230
❑ 97DonPri-74
❑ 97DonPriP-22
❑ 97DonPriS-22
❑ 97DonPriSB-22
❑ 97DonPriSG-22
❑ 97DonPriSoA-74
❑ 97DonPriSS-22
❑ 97EssOlyHH-29
❑ 97EssOlyHHF-29
❑ 97Kat-94
❑ 97KatGol-94
❑ 97KatSil-94
❑ 97Lea-117
❑ 97LeaBanSea-17
❑ 97LeaFraMat-117
❑ 97LeaFraMDC-117
❑ 97LeaInt-117
❑ 97LeaIntUI-117
❑ 97Pac-2
❑ 97PacCop-2
❑ 97PacCroR-86
❑ 97PacCroRBoSDC-15
❑ 97PacCroREG-86
❑ 97PacCroRIB-86
❑ 97PacCroRS-86
❑ 97PacDyn-80
❑ 97PacDynBKS-62
❑ 97PacDynBKS-108
❑ 97PacDynC-80
❑ 97PacDynDG-80
❑ 97PacDynEG-80
❑ 97PacDynIB-80
❑ 97PacDynR-80
❑ 97PacDynSil-80
❑ 97PacDynTan-19
❑ 97PacEmeGre-2
❑ 97PacIceB-2
❑ 97PacInv-88
❑ 97PacInvAZ-15
❑ 97PacInvC-88
❑ 97PacInvEG-88
❑ 97PacInvIB-88
❑ 97PacInvNRB-129
❑ 97PacInvR-88
❑ 97PacInvS-88
❑ 97PacOme-147
❑ 97PacOmeC-147
❑ 97PacOmeDG-147
❑ 97PacOmeEG-147
❑ 97PacOmeG-147
❑ 97PacOmeIB-147
❑ 97PacPar-118
❑ 97PacParC-118
❑ 97PacParDG-118
❑ 97PacParEG-118
❑ 97PacParIB-118
❑ 97PacParRed-118
❑ 97PacParSil-118
❑ 97PacRed-2
❑ 97PacRev-89
❑ 97PacRevC-89
❑ 97PacRevE-89
❑ 97PacRevIB-89
❑ 97PacRevR-89
❑ 97PacRevS-89
❑ 97PacSil-2
❑ 97PacSlaSDC-5C
❑ 97Pin-92
❑ 97Pin-195
❑ 97PinArtP-92
❑ 97PinBee-28
❑ 97PinBeeGP-28
❑ 97PinCer-36
❑ 97PinCerGT-6
❑ 97PinCerMB-36
❑ 97PinCerMG-36
❑ 97PinCerMR-36
❑ 97PinCerR-36
❑ 97PinCerT-6
❑ 97PinIns-20
❑ 97PinInsCC-20
❑ 97PinInsEC-20
❑ 97PinMin-19
❑ 97PinMinB-19
❑ 97PinMinCBP-19
❑ 97PinMinCGPP-19
❑ 97PinMinCNSP-19
❑ 97PinMinCoiB-19
❑ 97PinMinCoiGP-19
❑ 97PinMinCoiN-19
❑ 97PinMinCoiSG-19
❑ 97PinMinCoiSS-19
❑ 97PinMinGolTea-19
❑ 97PinMinSilTea-19
❑ 97PinPrePBB-92
❑ 97PinPrePBB-195
❑ 97PinPrePBC-92
❑ 97PinPrePBC-195
❑ 97PinPrePBM-92
❑ 97PinPrePBM-195
❑ 97PinPrePBY-92
❑ 97PinPrePBY-195
❑ 97PinPrePFC-92
❑ 97PinPrePFC-195
❑ 97PinPrePFM-92
❑ 97PinPrePFM-195
❑ 97PinPrePFY-92
❑ 97PinPrePFY-195
❑ 97PinPrePla-92
❑ 97PinPrePla-195
❑ 97PinRinC-92
❑ 97PinTeaP-3
❑ 97PinTeaPM-3
❑ 97PinTeaPP-3
❑ 97PinTeaPPM-3
❑ 97PinTotCMPG-36
❑ 97PinTotCPB-36
❑ 97PinTotCPG-36
❑ 97PinTotCPR-36
❑ 97PosPin-4
❑ 97Sco-126
❑ 97ScoArtPro-126
❑ 97ScoGolBla-126
❑ 97ScoRan-2
❑ 97ScoRanPla-2
❑ 97ScoRanPre-2
❑ 97SP AutI-I39
❑ 97SPAut-100
❑ 97SPAutID-I39
❑ 97SPAutIE-I39
❑ 97SPx-33
❑ 97SPxBro-33
❑ 97SPxGol-33
❑ 97SPxGraF-33
❑ 97SPxSil-33
❑ 97SPxSte-33
❑ 97Stu-86
❑ 97StuPor-35
❑ 97StuPrePG-86
❑ 97StuPrePS-86
❑ 97StuSil-23
❑ 97StuSil8-23
❑ 97UppDec-316
❑ 97UppDecBD-33
❑ 97UppDecBDDD-33
❑ 97UppDecBDPC-PC10
❑ 97UppDecBDPCDD-PC10
❑ 97UppDecBDPCM-PC10
❑ 97UppDecBDPCQD-PC10
❑ 97UppDecBDPCTD-PC10
❑ 97UppDecBDQD-33
❑ 97UppDecBDTD-33
❑ 97UppDecCtAG-19
❑ 97UppDecCtAG-AR19
❑ 97UppDecDV-12
❑ 97UppDecDVSM-12
❑ 97UppDecGDM-316
❑ 97UppDecGJ-GJ14
❑ 97UppDecIce-76
❑ 97UppDecIceP-76
❑ 97UppDecILL-L10A
❑ 97UppDecILL2-L10A
❑ 97UppDecIPS-76
❑ 97UppDecSG-SG22
❑ 97UppDecSSM-SS5
❑ 97UppDecSSW-SS5
❑ 97UppDecTS-28
❑ 97UppDecTSL2-28
❑ 97UppDecTSS-4B
❑ 97Zen-13
❑ 97Zen5x7-65
❑ 97ZenGolImp-65
❑ 97ZenSilImp-65
❑ 97ZenZGol-13
❑ 97ZenZSil-13
❑ 98Be A PPA-238
❑ 98Be A PPAA-238
❑ 98Be A PPAAF-238
❑ 98Be A PPPH-H16
❑ 98Be A PPSE-238
❑ 98Be APG-238
❑ 98BowBes-25
❑ 98BowBesAR-25
❑ 98BowBesMIF-F7
❑ 98BowBesMIFR-F7
❑ 98BowBesR-25
❑ 98Fin-137
❑ 98FinNo P-137
❑ 98FinNo PR-137
❑ 98FinPro-PP6
❑ 98FinRef-137
❑ 98McDGreT-T4
❑ 98O-PChr-75
❑ 98O-PChrBM-B3
❑ 98O-PChrBMR-B3
❑ 98O-PChrR-75
❑ 98Pac-297
❑ 98PacAur-124
❑ 98PacCroR-89
❑ 98PacCroRLS-89
❑ 98PacDynI-123
❑ 98PacDynIIB-123
❑ 98PacDynIR-123
❑ 98PacIceB-297
❑ 98PacOmeH-158
❑ 98PacOmeODI-158
❑ 98PacOmeR-158
❑ 98PacPar-155
❑ 98PacParC-155
❑ 98PacParEG-155
❑ 98PacParH-155
❑ 98PacParIB-155
❑ 98PacParS-155
❑ 98PacRed-297
❑ 98PacRev-94
❑ 98PacRevIS-94
❑ 98PacRevR-94
❑ 98RanPowP-NYR3
❑ 98SP Aut-57
❑ 98SP AutSS-SS17
❑ 98SPxFin-111
❑ 98SPxFinR-111
❑ 98SPxFinS-111
❑ 98SPXTopP-39
❑ 98SPXTopPF-39
❑ 98SPXTopPPS-PS6
❑ 98SPXTopPR-39
❑ 98Top-75
❑ 98TopAut-A9
❑ 98TopBoaM-B3
❑ 98TopGolLC1-85
❑ 98TopGolLC1B-85
❑ 98TopGolLC1BOoO-85
❑ 98TopGolLC1OoO-85
❑ 98TopGolLC1R-85
❑ 98TopGolLC1ROoO-85
❑ 98TopGolLC2-85
❑ 98TopGolLC2B-85
❑ 98TopGolLC2BOoO-85
❑ 98TopGolLC2OoO-85
❑ 98TopGolLC2R-85
❑ 98TopGolLC2ROoO-85
❑ 98TopGolLC3-85
❑ 98TopGolLC3B-85
❑ 98TopGolLC3BOoO-85
❑ 98TopGolLC3OoO-85
❑ 98TopGolLC3R-85
❑ 98TopGolLC3ROoO-85
❑ 98TopO-P-75
❑ 98UC-129
❑ 98UC-238
❑ 98UCMBH-BH29
❑ 98UCSB-SQ7
❑ 98UCSG-SQ7
❑ 98UCSG-SQ7
❑ 98UCSR-SQ7
❑ 98UD ChoPCR-129
❑ 98UD ChoPCR-238
❑ 98UD ChoR-129
❑ 98UD ChoR-238
❑ 98UppDec-322
❑ 98UppDecBD-56
❑ 98UppDecDD-56
❑ 98UppDecE-322
❑ 98UppDecE1o1-322
❑ 98UppDecGR-322
❑ 98UppDecLSH-LS13
❑ 98UppDecLSHQ1-LS13
❑ 98UppDecLSHQ2-LS13
❑ 98UppDecLSHQ3-LS13
❑ 98UppDecM-133
❑ 98UppDecMGS-133
❑ 98UppDecMSS-133
❑ 98UppDecMSS-133
❑ 98UppDecQD-56
❑ 98UppDecTD-56
❑ 99Pac-272
❑ 99PacAur-94
❑ 99PacAurPD-94
❑ 99PacCop-272
❑ 99PacGol-272
❑ 99PacIceB-272
❑ 99PacPreD-272
❑ 99RetHoc-51
❑ 99SP AutPS-57
❑ 99UppDecM-132
❑ 99UppDecMGS-132
❑ 99UppDecMSS-132
❑ 99UppDecMSS-132
❑ 99UppDecRG-G1B
❑ 99UppDecRG-51
❑ 99UppDecRGI-G1B
❑ 99UppDecRP-51

**Lefebvre, Fredrick**
❑ 88RivDu R-16
❑ 907thInnSQMJHL-194

**Lefebvre, Guy**
❑ 907thInnSQMJHL-96

**Lefebvre, Jean-Sebastien**
❑ 917thInnSQMJHL-144

**Lefebvre, Martin**
❑ 907thInnSQMJHL-186

**Lefebvre, Nicolas**
❑ 907thInnSQMJHL-84
❑ 907thInnSQMJHL-248
❑ 917thInnSQMJHL-266

**LeFebvre, Patrice**
❑ 90ProAHLIHL-337
❑ 93LasVegThu-18
❑ 94LasVegThu-11
❑ 95ColEdgI-153
❑ 95LasVegThu-5
❑ 96LasVegThu-12
❑ 98LasVegT-11

**Lefebvre, Stephane**
❑ 83NovScoV-4
❑ 93GueSto-19

**Lefebvre, Sylvain**
❑ 88ProAHL-297
❑ 89CanaKra-13
❑ 89CanaPos-18
❑ 90Bow-48
❑ 90BowTif-48
❑ 90CanaPos-20
❑ 90OPC-159
❑ 90PanSti-59
❑ 90ProSet-472
❑ 90Sco-307C
❑ 90ScoCan-307C
❑ 90Top-159
❑ 90TopTif-159
❑ 90UppDec-421
❑ 90UppDecF-421
❑ 91Bow-332
❑ 91CanaPanTS-15
❑ 91CanaPos-18
❑ 91OPC-489
❑ 91Par-307
❑ 91ParFre-307
❑ 91ScoCan-245
❑ 91StaClu-208
❑ 91Top-489
❑ 91UppDec-171
❑ 91UppDecF-171
❑ 92Bow-307
❑ 92MapLeaK-13
❑ 92OPC-303
❑ 92OPCPre-108
❑ 92Par-416
❑ 92ParEmel-416
❑ 92Sco-405
❑ 92ScoCan-405
❑ 92StaClu-367
❑ 92Top-341
❑ 92TopGol-341G
❑ 93Don-331
❑ 93Lea-267
❑ 93OPCPre-331
❑ 93OPCPreG-331
❑ 93Pin-317
❑ 93PinCan-317
❑ 93Pow-450
❑ 93Sco-359
❑ 93ScoBla-12
❑ 93ScoCan-359
❑ 93StaClu-48
❑ 93StaCluFDI-48
❑ 93StaCluFDIO-48
❑ 93StaCluO-48
❑ 93TopPre-331
❑ 93TopPreG-331
❑ 93Ult-430
❑ 94BeAPla-R66
❑ 94BeAPSig-41
❑ 94Fla-149
❑ 94Fle-180
❑ 94Lea-507
❑ 94NordBurK-16
❑ 94OPCPre-364
❑ 94OPCPreSE-364
❑ 94Pin-379
❑ 94PinArtP-379
❑ 94PinRinC-379
❑ 94TopPre-364
❑ 94TopPreSE-364
❑ 94Ult-176
❑ 94Ult-360
❑ 94UppDec-335
❑ 94UppDecEleIce-335
❑ 95Don-288
❑ 95Lea-292
❑ 95ParInt-321
❑ 95ParIntEl-321
❑ 95Pin-131
❑ 95PinArtP-131
❑ 95PinRinC-131
❑ 95PlaOneoOne-26
❑ 95Sco-192
❑ 95ScoBlaIce-192
❑ 95ScoBlaIceAP-192
❑ 95Top-279
❑ 95TopOPCI-279
❑ 95Ult-221
❑ 95UppDec-342
❑ 95UppDecEleIce-342
❑ 95UppDecEleIceG-342
❑ 96BeAPAut-54
❑ 96BeAPAutSil-54
❑ 96BeAPla-54
❑ 96Don-81
❑ 96DonPrePro-81
❑ 96Lea-98
❑ 96LeaPreP-98
❑ 96Sco-226
❑ 96ScoArtPro-226
❑ 96ScoDeaCAP-226
❑ 96ScoGolB-226
❑ 96ScoSpeAP-226
❑ 96Sum-149
❑ 96SumArtP-149
❑ 96SumIce-149
❑ 96SumMet-149
❑ 96SumPreS-149
❑ 97PacInvNRB-54
❑ 97ScoAva-16
❑ 97ScoAvaPla-16
❑ 97ScoAvaPre-16
❑ 98Be A PPA-184
❑ 98Be A PPAA-184
❑ 98Be A PPAAF-184
❑ 98Be A PPSE-184
❑ 98Be APG-184
❑ 99Pac-109
❑ 99PacCop-109
❑ 99PacGol-109
❑ 99PacIceB-109
❑ 99PacPreD-109

**Lefley, Bryan**
❑ 72OPC-252
❑ 72SarProSta-139
❑ 74NHLActSta-299
❑ 76OPCNHL-159
❑ 76RocCokCan-13
❑ 76RocPucBuc-11
❑ 77OPCNHL-297
❑ 77RocCokCan-13
❑ 78OPC-370
❑ 95SwiHNL-84

**Lefley, Chuck**
❑ 69SweHocS-358
❑ 72CanaPos-11
❑ 73CanaPos-13
❑ 73OPC-44
❑ 73Top-154
❑ 74CanaPos-14
❑ 74NHLActSta-155
❑ 74NHLActStaU-33
❑ 74OPCNHL-178
❑ 74Top-178
❑ 75OPCNHL-282
❑ 75Top-282
❑ 76OPCNHL-63
❑ 76OPCNHL-393
❑ 76Top-63
❑ 77OPCNHL-340
❑ 80OPC-395

**Lefreniere, Jason**
❑ 87NordYumY-6

**Legace, Manny**
❑ 907thInnSOHL-263
❑ 917thInnSOHL-217
❑ 92UppDec-585
❑ 93AlbIntTC-10
❑ 93Cla-24
❑ 93NiaFalT-25
❑ 93OPCPreTC-2
❑ 94ClaProPIA-IA5
❑ 94ClaProPIH-LP16
❑ 94ScoTeaC-CT20
❑ 95UppDecWJA-2
❑ 96ColEdgFL-9
❑ 96ColEdgPC-3
❑ 96SprFal-30
❑ 98PacCroR-63
❑ 98PacCroRLS-63
❑ 98PacCroRRC-4
❑ 99UppDecM-99
❑ 99UppDecMGS-99
❑ 99UppDecMSS-99
❑ 99UppDecMSS-99

**Legault, Alexandre**
❑ 907thInnSQMJHL-7
❑ 917thInnSMC-51
❑ 917thInnSQMJHL-193

**Legault, Derek**
❑ 92QueIntP-18

**Legault, Jay**
❑ 95Sla-239
❑ 97BowCHL-148
❑ 97BowCHLAu-28
❑ 97BowCHLOPC-148
❑ 98BowCHL-20
❑ 98BowCHLGA-20
❑ 98BowCHLOI-20
❑ 98BowChrC-20
❑ 98BowChrCGA-20
❑ 98BowChrCGAR-20
❑ 98BowChrCOI-20
❑ 98BowChrCOIR-20
❑ 98BowChrCR-20

**Legault, Marc**
❑ 917thInnSQMJHL-211

**Legault, Paul**
❑ 50QueCit-13

**Leger, Bob**
❑ 51LavDaiS-95
❑ 52St.LawS-102

**Leger, Germain**
❑ 51LavDaiQSHL-26

**Leger, Roger**
❑ 44BeeGro2P-260
❑ 45QuaOatP-89A
❑ 45QuaOatP-89B
❑ 45QuaOatP-89C
❑ 52St.LawS-9

**Legg, Mike**
❑ 93MicWol-12

**Legge, Barry**
❑ 80JetPos-10
❑ 80PepCap-129

**Legge, Randy**
❑ 76SanDieMW-5

**Leggett, Alan**
❑ 91ProAHLCHL-315
❑ 92RalIce-5
❑ 92RalIce-30
❑ 93RalIce-9

**Leggett, Casey**
❑ 97RimOce-55

**Legwand, David A**
❑ 97UppDecBD-35
❑ 97UppDecBDDD-35
❑ 97UppDecBDQD-35
❑ 97UppDecBDTD-35
❑ 98BowBes-136
❑ 98BowBesAR-136
❑ 98BowBesR-136
❑ 98BowCHL-14
❑ 98BowCHL-147
❑ 98BowCHLAuB-A11
❑ 98BowCHLAuG-A11
❑ 98BowCHLAuS-A11

□ 98BowCHLGA-14
□ 98BowCHLGA-147
□ 98BowCHLOI-14
□ 98BowCHLOI-147
□ 98BowChrC-14
□ 98BowChrC-147
□ 98BowChrCGA-14
□ 98BowChrCGA-147
□ 98BowChrCGAR-14
□ 98BowChrCGAR-147
□ 98BowChrCOI-14
□ 98BowChrCOI-147
□ 98BowChrCOIR-147
□ 98BowChrCR-14
□ 98BowChrCR-147
□ 98FinFutF-F1
□ 98FinFutFR-F1
□ 98O-PChr-234
□ 98O-PChrR-234
□ 98SPXTopP-88
□ 98SPXTopPF-88
□ 98SPXTopPR-88
□ 98Top-234
□ 98TopO-P-234
□ 98UC-302
□ 98UD ChoPCR-302
□ 98UD ChoR-302
□ 98UppDecBD-115
□ 98UppDecDD-115
□ 98UppDecQD-115
□ 98UppDecTD-115
□ 99Pac-229
□ 99PacAur-80
□ 99PacAurPD-80
□ 99PacCop-229
□ 99PacGol-229
□ 99PacGolCD-20
□ 99PacIceB-229
□ 99PacPreD-229
□ 99QuePeeWHWCCS-23
□ 99UppDecCL-77
□ 99UppDecCLCLC-77
□ 99UppDecM-110
□ 99UppDecM2CN-1
□ 99UppDecMGS-110
□ 99UppDecMSS-110
□ 99UppDecMSS-110

**Lehkonen, Timo**
□ 93FinnSIS-375
□ 94FinnSIS-219

**Lehman, Hugh**
□ 60Top-38
□ 60TopSta-33
□ 83HalFP-N7
□ 85HalFC-202

**Lehmann, Tommy**
□ 83SweSemE-22
□ 84SweSemE-20
□ 85SwePanS-19
□ 90SweSemE-89
□ 91SweSemE-18
□ 92SweSemE-239
□ 94SweLeaE-72
□ 95SweLeaE-159
□ 95SweUppDE-15

**Lehner, Josef**
□ 94GerDELE-58
□ 95GerDELE-53
□ 96GerDELE-252
□ 98GerDELE-322

**Lehoux, Guy**
□ 917thInnSMC-55
□ 91ProAHLCHL-350
□ 92St.JohML-10
□ 93St.JohML-14
□ 94St.JohML-17
□ 95St.JohML-14
□ 96St.JohML-19
□ 98GerDELE-215

**Lehoux, Jason**
□ 96RimOceU-4

**Lehtera, Tero**
□ 91UppDecCWJC-32
□ 93FinnJyvHS-197
□ 93FinnSIS-272
□ 94FinnSIS-9
□ 94FinnSISFI-16
□ 94FinnSISND-6
□ 94SweLeaE-200
□ 94SweLeaEFA-10
□ 95FinnKarWCL-8
□ 95FinnSemWC-27
□ 95FinnSIS-257
□ 95FinnSISGC-16
□ 95FinnSISL-62
□ 96FinnSISR-49
□ 96SweSemW-17

**Lehtinen, Jere**
□ 92Cla-31
□ 92UppDec-615
□ 93FinnJyvHS-322
□ 93FinnSIS-47
□ 94Cla-72
□ 94ClaDraGol-72
□ 94ClaProPIA-IA16
□ 94ClaTri-T16
□ 94FinnJaaK-29
□ 94FinnSIS-20
□ 94FinnSIS-155
□ 94FinnSIS-157
□ 95BeAPla-175
□ 95BeAPSig-S175
□ 95BeAPSigDC-S175
□ 95Bow-150

□ 95BowAllFoi-150
□ 95Don-332
□ 95Fin-53
□ 95FinnBecAC-2
□ 95FinnKarWCL-9
□ 95FinnSemWC-20
□ 95FinnSemWC-232
□ 95FinnSIS-164
□ 95FinnSISGC-17
□ 95FinnSISL-9
□ 95FinnSISSpe-7
□ 95FinRef-53
□ 95LeaLim-39
□ 95Met-183
□ 95MetIS-13
□ 95ParInt-265
□ 95ParIntEl-265
□ 95ParIntEl-518
□ 95SkyImp-195
□ 95SP-41
□ 95StaClu-199
□ 95StaCluMOMS-199
□ 95Sum-173
□ 95SumArtP-173
□ 95SumIce-173
□ 95Ult-347
□ 95UppDec-398
□ 95UppDecElelce-398
□ 95UppDecElelceG-398
□ 95Zen-145
□ 96ClaGol-31
□ 96ColCho-75
□ 96DonCanI-111
□ 96DonCanIGPP-111
□ 96DonCanIRPP-111
□ 96DonEli-77
□ 96DonEliAsp-10
□ 96DonEliDCS-77
□ 96DonRatR-4
□ 96PlePic-144
□ 96Lea-201
□ 96LeaLim-77
□ 96LeaLimG-77
□ 96LeaPre-47
□ 96LeaPreP-201
□ 96LeaPrePP-47
□ 96LeaPreSG-63
□ 96LeaPreSte-63
□ 96Sco-246
□ 96ScoArtPro-246
□ 96ScoDeaCAP-246
□ 96ScoGolB-246
□ 96ScoSpeAP-246
□ 96StaPos-17
□ 96StaScoS-246
□ 96Sum-153
□ 96SumArtP-153
□ 96SumIce-153
□ 96SumMet-153
□ 96SumPreS-153
□ 96SweSemW-20
□ 96SweSemW-37
□ 96SweSemWAS-AS4
□ 96TopPicRS-RS2
□ 96UppDec-49
□ 96UppDecBD-87
□ 96UppDecBDG-87
□ 96Zen-51
□ 96ZenArtP-51
□ 97Be A PPAD-123
□ 97Be A PPAPD-123
□ 97BeAPla-123
□ 97BeAPlaAut-123
□ 97ColCho-74
□ 97Don-30
□ 97DonEli-68
□ 97DonEliAsp-68
□ 97DonEliS-68
□ 97DonLim-135
□ 97DonLimExp-135
□ 97DonPre-65
□ 97DonPreCttC-65
□ 97DonPreProG-30
□ 97DonPreProS-30
□ 97DonPri-63
□ 97DonPriSoA-63
□ 97Kat-45
□ 97KatGol-45
□ 97KatSil-45
□ 97Lea-98
□ 97LeaFraMat-98
□ 97LeaFraMDC-98
□ 97LeaInt-98
□ 97LeaIntUI-98
□ 97PacInvNRB-61
□ 97PacOme-71
□ 97PacOmeC-71
□ 97PacOmeDG-71
□ 97PacOmeEG-71
□ 97PacOmeIB-71
□ 97PacPar-59
□ 97PacParC-59
□ 97PacParDG-59
□ 97PacParEG-59
□ 97PacParIB-59
□ 97PacParRed-59
□ 97PacParSil-59
□ 97PacRev-42
□ 97PacRevC-42
□ 97PacRevEB-42
□ 97PacRevIB-42
□ 97PacRevR-42
□ 97PacRevS-42

□ 97Pin-118
□ 97PinIns-187
□ 97PinPreBB-118
□ 97PinPrePBC-118
□ 97PinPrePBM-118
□ 97PinPrePBY-118
□ 97PinPrePFC-118
□ 97PinPrePFM-118
□ 97PinPrePFY-118
□ 97PinPrePla-118
□ 97Sco-188
□ 97SPAut-48
□ 97UppDec-52
□ 97UppDecBD-40
□ 97UppDecBDDD-40
□ 97UppDecBDQD-40
□ 97UppDecBDTD-40
□ 97UppDecSG-SG26
□ 97UppDecTSS-8C
□ 98Be A PPA-44
□ 98Be A PPAA-44
□ 98Be A PPAAF-44
□ 98Be A PPTBASG-44
□ 98Be APG-44
□ 98BowBes-76
□ 98BowBesAR-76
□ 98BowBesR-76
□ 98Pac-179
□ 98PacAur-57
□ 98PacCroR-40
□ 98PacCroRLS-40
□ 98PacDynI-58
□ 98PacDynIIB-58
□ 98PacDynIR-58
□ 98PacIceB-75
□ 98PacOmeH-72
□ 98PacOmeODI-72
□ 98PacOmeR-72
□ 98PacPar-66
□ 98PacParC-66
□ 98PacParEG-66
□ 98PacParH-66
□ 98PacParIB-66
□ 98PacParS-66
□ 98PacRed-179
□ 98PacRev-43
□ 98PacRevIS-43
□ 98PacRevR-43
□ 98SP Aut-27
□ 98SPxFin-28
□ 98SPxFinR-28
□ 98SPxFinS-28
□ 98UC-68
□ 98UD ChoPCR-68
□ 98UD ChoR-68
□ 98UppDec-258
□ 98UppDecE-258
□ 98UppDecE101-258
□ 98UppDecGR-258
□ 98UppDecM-67
□ 98UppDecMGS-67
□ 98UppDecMSS-67
□ 98UppDecMSS-67
□ 99Pac-123
□ 99PacAur-46
□ 99PacAurPD-46
□ 99PacCop-123
□ 99PacGol-123
□ 99PacIceB-123
□ 99PacPreD-123
□ 99SP AutPS-27
□ 99UppDecM-63
□ 99UppDecMGS-63
□ 99UppDecMSS-63
□ 99UppDecMSS-63

**Lehtinen, Mika**
□ 94FinnSIS-321
□ 95FinnSIS-325
□ 96FinnSISR-136

**Lehto, Joni**
□ 897thInnSOHL-53
□ 907thInnSOHL-86
□ 91ProAHLCHL-455
□ 91RicRen-5
□ 94FinnSIS-343
□ 95FinnSIS-162
□ 95FinnSIS-299
□ 95FinnSISDT-4
□ 95FinnSISL-31
□ 95FinnSISP-3
□ 96FinnSISR-176
□ 96FinnSISRS-9
□ 96GerDELE-66
□ 96SweSemW-33

**Lehto, Markus**
□ 80OshGen-14

□ 94FinnSIS-342
□ 94FinnSISH-19
□ 95FinnSIS-109
□ 96FinnSISR-126

**Lehtonen, Vesa**
□ 94FinnSIS-306

**Leibel, Brian**
□ 87RegPat-15
□ 88RegPat-12

**Leidborg, Gunnar**
□ 82SweSemHVS-3
□ 83SweSemE-1
□ 84SweSemE-1
□ 85SwePanS-4
□ 94GerDELE-5
□ 95GerDELE-384
□ 98GerDELE-291

**Leier, Dan**
□ 83SasBla-6

**Leimu, Pekka**
□ 69SweHocS-374
□ 69SweWorC-161

**Leinonen, Marko**
□ 93FinnSIS-137
□ 95FinnSIS-261
□ 96FinnSISR-55

**Leinonen, Mikko**
□ 79PanSti-178
□ 81SweSemHVS-28
□ 82OPC-4
□ 82SweSemHVS-160
□ 83OPC-248

**Leinonen, Sami**
□ 94FinnSIS-202
□ 95FinnSIS-141

**Leiter, Bob**
□ 63Top-14
□ 64BeeGro3P-16
□ 64CocCap-18
□ 64Top-63
□ 71PenPos-11
□ 71TorSun-220
□ 72Flam-5
□ 72OPC-218
□ 72SarProSta-9
□ 73OPC-117
□ 73Top-117
□ 74NHLActSta-15
□ 74OPCNHL-51
□ 74Top-51
□ 75OPCNHL-191
□ 75Top-191
□ 94ParTalB-11

**Leiter, Ken**
□ 84SprInd-6
□ 87OPCSti-131
□ 87PanSti-93

**Leitza, Brian**
□ 98KanCitB-2

**Lejczyk, Leszek**
□ 89SweSemWCS-127

**Lekkerimaki, Sami**
□ 93FinnJyvHS-267
□ 93FinnSIS-292

**Leksell, Sture**
□ 67SweHoc-105

**Leksola, Pekka**
□ 94FinnJaaK-16

**Lekun, Mike**
□ 80OshGen-19
□ 81OshGen-15

**Lelacheur, Robert**
□ 88SasBla-11
□ 89SasBla-11
□ 907thInnSWHL-82
□ 90SasBla-9

**Lemaire, Ed**
□ 85SudWol-17

**Lemaire, Jacques**
□ 64CanaPos-12
□ 67CanaIGA-25
□ 67Top-3
□ 68CanaIGA-25
□ 68CanaPosBW-9
□ 68OPC-63
□ 68PosCerM-45
□ 68ShiCoi-88
□ 68Top-63
□ 69CanaPosC-15
□ 69OPC-8
□ 69Top-8
□ 70CanaPin-9
□ 70ColSta-30
□ 70DadCoo-70
□ 70OPC-57
□ 70OPCDec-19
□ 70PosCerS-9
□ 70SarProSta-103
□ 70Top-57
□ 70TopStiS-20
□ 71CanaPos-13
□ 71LetActR-15
□ 71OPC-71
□ 71SarProSta-105
□ 71Top-71
□ 71TorSun-156
□ 72CanaPos-12
□ 72OPC-77
□ 72SarProSta-115
□ 72SweSemWC-208
□ 72Top-25
□ 73CanaPos-14
□ 73MacMil-14
□ 73OPC-56

□ 73Top-56
□ 74CanaPos-15
□ 74LipSou-38
□ 74NHLActSta-145
□ 74OPCNHL-24
□ 74Top-24
□ 75CanaPos-12
□ 75HerSta-10
□ 75OPCNHL-258
□ 75Top-258
□ 76CanaPos-13
□ 76OPCNHL-129
□ 76Top-129
□ 77CanaPos-15
□ 77OPCNHL-254
□ 77Top-254
□ 78CanaPos-17
□ 78OPC-180
□ 78Top-180
□ 83CanaPos-13
□ 84CanaPos-14
□ 85HalFC-245
□ 930PCCanHF-62
□ 94Kra-61
□ 94ParTalBFS-FS1
□ 96Dev-NNO

**Lemanowicz, David**
□ 91BriColJHL-18
□ 95SpoChi-1

**Lemanski, Casey**
□ 92BriColJHL-163

**LeMarque, Eric**
□ 91GreMon-8
□ 94FreNatT-15

**Lemay, Dave**
□ 907thInnSOHL-37
□ 917thInnSOHL-5
□ 91CorRoy-5
□ 930weSouPla-15
□ 95BufStaRHI-37

**Lemay, Marc**
□ 80QueRem-12

**Lemay, Moe**
□ 81Ott67-6
□ 82Canu-12
□ 83FreExp-12
□ 84Canu-13
□ 84OPC-322
□ 85Canu-13
□ 85OPC-173
□ 85OPCSti-246
□ 86Canu-8
□ 86OPC-249
□ 88OilTenAnn-43
□ 96GerDELE-215

**Lemay, Yanick**
□ 907thInnSQMJHL-223
□ 917thInnSQMJHL-17

**Lembke, Jeff**
□ 92NorDakFS-18

**Lemelin, Jacques**
□ 72NordPos-16

**Lemelin, Reggie (Rejean)**
□ 80FlamPos-7
□ 81FlamPos-11
□ 81OPC-44
□ 82OPC-50
□ 83OPC-86
□ 83OPCSti-266
□ 83Vac-10
□ 84OPC-228
□ 84OPCSti-240
□ 84Top-25
□ 85OPC-95
□ 85OPCSti-210
□ 85Top-95
□ 86FlamRedR-9
□ 86KraDra-32
□ 86OPC-102
□ 86OPCSti-83
□ 86Top-102
□ 87PanSti-204
□ 88BruPos-10
□ 88BruSpoA-10
□ 88OPC-186
□ 88OPCMin-18
□ 88OPCSti-24
□ 88PanSti-203
□ 88Top-186
□ 89BruSpoA-13
□ 89BruSpoAU-12
□ 89OPC-40
□ 89PanSti-195
□ 89Top-40
□ 90Bow-32
□ 90BowTif-32
□ 90BruSpoA-14
□ 90BruSpoA-26
□ 90OPC-343
□ 90OPC-486
□ 90PanSti-13
□ 90ProSet-9
□ 90ProSet-382
□ 90Sco-159
□ 90Sco-365
□ 90ScoCan-159
□ 90ScoCan-365
□ 90Top-343
□ 90TopTif-343
□ 90UppDec-209
□ 90UppDec-215
□ 90UppDecF-215
□ 91Bow-354

□ 91OPC-497
□ 91PanSti-172
□ 91ScoAme-127
□ 91ScoCan-127
□ 91StaClu-23
□ 91Top-497
□ 92DurPan-48

**Lemelin, Roger**
□ 76RocPucBuc-12

**Lemieux, Alain**
□ 85FreExp-7
□ 86NordMcD-14

**Lemieux, Andre**
□ 77GraVic-13

**Lemieux, Bob**
□ 77KalWin-3

**Lemieux, Carl**
□ 84RicRiv-8

**Lemieux, Claude**
□ 85CanaPos-1
□ 86CanaPos-11
□ 86KraDra-33
□ 87CanaPos-14
□ 87CanaVacS-31
□ 87OPC-227
□ 87OPCSti-19
□ 87PanSti-63
□ 88CanaPos-17
□ 88OPC-227
□ 88OPCSti-43
□ 88PanSti-257
□ 89CanaKra-14
□ 89CanaPos-19
□ 89OPC-234
□ 89OPCSti-52
□ 89PanSti-240
□ 90Dev-19
□ 90OPC-451
□ 90OPCPre-62
□ 90ProSet-153
□ 90ProSet-478
□ 90Sco-111
□ 90ScoCan-111
□ 90ScoRoo-9T
□ 90UppDec-447
□ 90UppDecF-447
□ 91Bow-271
□ 91Bow-277
□ 91OPC-394
□ 91PanSti-224
□ 91Par-101
□ 91ParFre-101
□ 91Pin-70
□ 91PinFre-70
□ 91ProSet-135
□ 91ProSetFre-135
□ 91ProSetPla-196
□ 91ScoAme-22
□ 91ScoCan-22
□ 91StaClu-18
□ 91Top-394
□ 91UppDec-294
□ 91UppDecF-294
□ 92Bow-49
□ 92DurPan-14
□ 92OPC-67
□ 92PanSti-172
□ 92PanStiFre-172
□ 92Par-89
□ 92ParEmel-89
□ 92Pin-259
□ 92PinFre-259
□ 92PinFre-284
□ 92ProSet-98
□ 92Sco-8
□ 92ScoCan-8
□ 92StaClu-50
□ 92Top-43
□ 92TopGol-43G
□ 92UppDec-163
□ 93Don-187
□ 93DurSco-47
□ 93Lea-125
□ 93OPCPre-134
□ 93OPCPreG-134
□ 93PanSti-35
□ 93Par-110
□ 93ParEmel-110
□ 93Pin-251
□ 93PinCan-251
□ 93Pow-137
□ 93Sco-160
□ 93ScoCan-160
□ 93StaClu-39
□ 93StaCluFDI-39
□ 93StaCluFDIO-39
□ 93StaCluO-39
□ 93TopPre-134
□ 93TopPreG-134
□ 93Ult-5
□ 93UppDec-296
□ 93UppDec-391
□ 93UppDecSP-83
□ 94BeAPSig-27
□ 94CanGamNHLP-145
□ 94Don-82
□ 94EASpo-77
□ 94Fle-113
□ 94Lea-185
□ 94OPCPre-204
□ 94OPCPreSE-204
□ 94Par-129
□ 94ParGol-129

□ 94ParVin-V59
□ 94Pin-287
□ 94PinArtP-287
□ 94PinInC-287
□ 94ScoChelt-CI16
□ 94Sel-73
□ 94SelGol-73
□ 94TopPre-204
□ 94TopPreSE-204
□ 94Ult-118
□ 94UppDec-303
□ 94UppDecElelce-303
□ 95Bow-13
□ 95BowAllFoi-13
□ 95ColCho-262
□ 95ColCho-392
□ 95ColChoCTG-C28
□ 95ColChoCTGG-C28
□ 95ColChoCTGGB-C28
□ 95ColChoCTGGR-C28
□ 95ColChoCTGSB-C28
□ 95ColChoCTGSR-C28
□ 95ColChoPC-262
□ 95ColChoPC-392
□ 95ColChoPCP-262
□ 95ColChoPCP-392
□ 95Don-343
□ 95DonEli-44
□ 95DonEliS-44
□ 95DonEliDCU-44
□ 95Emo-97
□ 95Fin-47
□ 95FinRef-47
□ 95ImaPlaPl-PL5
□ 95Kra-79
□ 95Lea-311
□ 95LeaLim-27
□ 95LeaRoaCup-10
□ 95Met-34
□ 95MetIW-6
□ 95NHLAcePC-4H
□ 95ParInt-319
□ 95ParIntEl-319
□ 95Pin-119
□ 95PinArtP-119
□ 95PinFirS-10
□ 95PinRinC-119
□ 95PlaOneoOne-244
□ 95ProMag-3
□ 95Sco-269
□ 95ScoBlaIce-269
□ 95ScoBlaIceAP-269
□ 95SelCer-99
□ 95SelCerDS-19
□ 95SelCerDSG-19
□ 95SelCerMG-99
□ 95SkyImp-37
□ 95SP-35
□ 95StaClu-189
□ 95StaCluMOMS-189
□ 95StaCluNem-N3
□ 95Sum-129
□ 95SumArtP-129
□ 95SumIce-129
□ 95Top-114
□ 95TopOPCI-114
□ 95Ult-192
□ 95Ult-223
□ 95UltCreCra-6
□ 95UltGoIM-192
□ 95UppDec-44
□ 95UppDec-258
□ 95UppDec-456
□ 95UppDecElelce-44
□ 95UppDecElelce-258
□ 95UppDecElelce-456
□ 95UppDecElelceG-44
□ 95UppDecElelceG-258
□ 95UppDecElelceG-456
□ 95UppDecSpeE-SE50
□ 95UppDecSpeE-SE50
□ 95UppDecSpeEdiG-SE50
□ 95UppDecSpeEdiG-SE108
□ 95Zen-116
□ 95ZenGifG-4
□ 96ColCho-57
□ 96ColChoMVP-UD6
□ 96ColChoMVPG-UD6
□ 96Don-23
□ 96DonCanI-115
□ 96DonCanIGPP-115
□ 96DonCanIRPP-115
□ 96DonEli-110
□ 96DonEliDCS-110
□ 96DonHitLis-18
□ 96DonPrePro-23
□ 96Fle-22
□ 96Fle-142
□ 96Lea-24
□ 96LeaLim-46
□ 96LeaLimBTB-6
□ 96LeaLimBTBLE-6
□ 96LeaLimBTBP-P6
□ 96LeaLimG-46
□ 96LeaPre-24
□ 96LeaPreP-24
□ 96LeaPrePP-24
□ 96LeaPreSG-31
□ 96LeaPreSte-31
□ 96MetUni-35
□ 96NHLProSTA-3
□ 96Pin-113
□ 96PinArtP-113
□ 96PinFoi-113

96PinPreS-113
96PinRinC-113
96Sco-116
96ScoArtPro-116
96ScoDeaCAP-116
96ScoGolB-116
96ScoSpeAP-116
96SelCer-53
96SelCerAP-53
96SelCerBlu-53
96SelCerMB-53
96SelCerMG-53
96SelCerMR-53
96SelCerRed-53
96SkyImp-25
96SkyImpB-12
96SP-39
96Sum-113
96SumArtP-113
96SumIce-113
96SumMet-113
96SumPreS-113
96SweSemW-91
96TeaOut-37
96TopNHLP-89
96TopPicOI-89
96Ult-37
96UltGolM-37
96UppDec-207
96UppDec-243
96UppDecPP-P17
96Zen-102
96ZenArtP-102
96ZenChaS-10
96ZenChaSD-10
97ColCho-62
97Don-88
97DonCanINP-25
97DonLim-15
97DonLimExp-15
97DonPre-126
97DonPreCttC-126
97DonPreProG-88
97DonPreProS-88
97DonPri-127
97DonPriSoA-127
97Kat-39
97KatGol-39
97KatSil-39
97Pac-3
97PacCop-3
97PacCroR-36
97PacCroREG-36
97PacCroRIB-36
97PacCroRS-36
97PacDyn-31
97PacDynC-31
97PacDynD-5B
97PacDynDG-31
97PacDynEG-31
97PacDynIB-31
97PacDynR-31
97PacDynSil-31
97PacDynTan-25
97PacEmeGre-3
97PacIceB-3
97PacInv-36
97PacInvAZ-6
97PacInvC-36
97PacInvEG-36
97PacInvFP-8
97PacInvIB-36
97PacInvR-36
97PacInvS-36
97PacOme-60
97PacOmeC-60
97PacOmeDG-60
97PacOmeEG-60
97PacOmeG-60
97PacOmeIB-60
97PacPar-52
97PacParC-52
97PacParDG-52
97PacParEG-52
97PacParIB-52
97PacParRed-52
97PacParSil-52
97PacRed-3
97PacRev-35
97PacRevC-35
97PacRevE-35
97PacRevIB-35
97PacRevR-35
97PacRevS-35
97PacSil-3
97PacSlaSDC-2C
97Pin-163
97PinCer-129
97PinCerMB-129
97PinCerMG-129
97PinCerMR-129
97PinCerR-129
97PinIns-156
97PinPrePBB-163
97PinPrePBC-163
97PinPrePBM-163
97PinPrePBY-163
97PinPrePFC-163
97PinPrePFM-163
97PinPrePFY-163
97PinPrePla-163
97PinTotCMPG-129
97PinTotCPB-129
97PinTotCPG-129
97PinTotCPR-129

97Sco-158
97ScoArtPro-158
97ScoAva-11
97ScoAvaPla-11
97ScoAvaPre-11
97ScoGolBla-158
97SPAut-38
97Stu-78
97StuPrePG-78
97StuPrePS-78
97UppDec-47
97UppDec-202
97UppDecGDM-47
97Zen-57
97Zen5x7-36
97ZenGolImp-36
97ZenSillmp-36
97ZenZGol-57
97ZenZSil-57
98O-PChr-65
98O-PChrR-65
98Pac-164
98PacAur-48
98PacDynI-50
98PacDynIIB-50
98PacDynIR-50
98PacIceB-164
98PacOmeH-61
98PacOmeODI-61
98PacOmeR-61
98PacPar-57
98PacParC-57
98PacParEG-57
98PacParH-57
98PacParIB-57
98PacParS-57
98PacRed-164
98PacRevIS-37
98PacRevR-37
98Top-65
98TopO-P-65
98UC-55
98UD ChoPCR-55
98UD ChoR-55
98UDCP-55
98UppDec-73
98UppDecE-73
98UppDecE1o1-73
98UppDecGR-73
99Pac-110
99PacAur-40
99PacAurPD-40
99PacCop-110
99PacGol-110
99PacIceB-110
99PacPreD-110

**Lemieux, Jean**
74NHLActSta-13
750PCNHL-367
760PCNHL-272

**Lemieux, Jocelyn**
87BluKod-15
87PanSti-319
88ProAHL-291
89CanaPos-20
90BlaCok-12
900PC-237
90PanSti-190
90ProSet-432
90ScoRoo-66T
90Top-237
90TopTif-237
90UppDec-544
90UppDecF-544
91BlaCok-16
910PC-453
91Par-256
91ParFre-256
91ScoCan-447
91StaClu-356
91Top-453
91UppDec-438
91UppDecF-438
92Bow-72
92DurPan-15
920PC-153
92PanSti-8
92PanStiFre-8
92Par-275
92ParEmel-275
92Sco-309
92ScoCan-309
92StaClu-446
92Top-300
92TopGol-300G
93BlaCok-21
93Don-440
93DurSco-43
930PCPre-295
930PCPreG-295
93PanSti-152
93Par-43
93ParEmel-43
93Pin-302
93PinCan-302
93Sco-420
93ScoCan-420
93StaCluFDI-255
93StaCluO-255
93TopPre-295
93TopPreG-295
94BeAPSig-129

94CanGamNHLP-115
94Lea-502
94OPCPre-122
94OPCPreSE-122
94Pin-89
94PinArtP-89
94PinRinC-89
94TopPre-122
94TopPreSE-122
94UppDec-372
94UppDecElelce-372
95ColCho-138
95ColChoPC-138
95ColChoPCP-138
95ParInt-393
95ParIntEl-393
95Pin-62
95PinArtP-62
95PinRinC-62
95UppDecElelce-491
95UppDecElelceG-491
96ColCho-42
96PacAur-48
96WhaBobS-13

**Lemieux, Mario**
83CanNatJ-9
857ECreCar-15
850PC-9
850PC-262
850PCBoxB-I
850PCSti-97
850PCSti-199
85Top-9
85TopBoxB-I
860PC-122
860PCBoxB-I
860PCSti-120
860PCSti-335
86PenKod-14
86Top-122
86TopBoxB-I
86TopStiIns-9
870PC-15
870PCMin-23
870PCSti-120
870PCSti-170
87PanSti-146
87PenKod-16
87PenMask-6
87ProAll-5
87Top-15
87TopStiIns-15
88EssAllSta-27
88FriLayS-1
880PC-1
880PCMin-19
880PCSti-116
880PCSti-204
880PCSti-210
880PCSti-211
880PCSti-232
88PanSti-340
88PanSti-400
88PanSti-401
88Top-1
88TopStiIns-2
89ActPacPro-2
89ActPacPro-3
89Kra-55
89KraAllSS-5
890PC-1
890PC-312
890PC-319
890PC-327
890PCBoxB-A
890PCSti-55
890PCSti-158
890PCSti-199
890PCSti-208
890PCSti-238
89PanSti-184
89PanSti-309
89PanSti-375
89PenCokE-3
89PenFoo-10
89SweSemWCS-64
89Top-1
89TopBoxB-A
89TopStiIns-3
90Bow-204
90BowHatTri-2
90BowTif-204
90Kra-29
90Kra-87
900PC-175
900PCBoxB-G
900PCPre-63
90PanSti-136
90PanSti-326
90PenFoo-13
90ProSet-236
90ProSet-362
90Sco-2
90Sco-337
90ScoCan-2
90ScoCan-337
90ScoHotRS-34
90Top-175
90TopBoxB-G
90TopTeaSL-17
90TopTif-175
90UppDec-59
90UppDec-144
90UppDec-305
90UppDecF-59
90UppDecF-144

90UppDecF-305
91Bow-87
91Bow-425
91Gil-33
91Kra-1
910PC-153
910PC-523
910PCPre-114
91PanSti-268
91Par-137
91Par-459
91Par-467
91ParFre-137
91ParFre-459
91ParFre-467
91ParPHCF-PHC7
91ParPHCF-PHC7
91PenCokE-66
91PenFoo-4
91PenFooCS-8
91Pin-1
91Pin-380
91PinB-B5
91PinBFre-B5
91PinFre-1
91PinFre-380
91ProSet-194
91ProSet-318
91ProSet-581
91ProSetFre-194
91ProSetFre-318
91ProSetFre-581
91ProSetPla-91
91ProSetPla-144
91ProSetPOTM-P3
91ScoAme-200
91ScoAme-425
91ScoAme-426
91ScoCan-200
91ScoCan-315
91ScoCan-365
91ScoHotC-5
91StaClu-174
91Top-153
91Top-523
91TopBowPS-1
91UppDec-47
91UppDec-156
91UppDec-611
91UppDecAWH-AW9
91UppDecF-45
91UppDecF-47
91UppDecF-156
91UppDecF-611
92AllWorMLP-1A
92AllWorMLP-1B
92AllWorMLP-1C
92AllWorMLP-1D
92AllWorMLP-1E
92AllWorMLP-1F
92Bow-189
92Bow-233
92Bow-440
92Cla-66
92Cla-SP
92Cla-AU1
92ClaCanML-1
92ClaCanML-2
92ClaCanML-3
92ClaGolP-NNO
92ClaPromo-2
92DurPan-8
92Hig5Pre-P2
92HumDum2-12
92JofKoh-3
92KelPos-1
92Kra-43
92McDUppD-21
920PC-138
920PC-240
920PC-292
920PC25AI-18
920PCPreSP-22
92PanSti-220
92PanSti-280
92PanStiFre-220
92PanStiFre-280
92Par-136
92Par-462
92Par-498
92ParEmel-136
92ParEmel-462
92ParEmel-498
92PenCokC-10
92PenFoo-1
92Pin-300
92PinFre-300
92ProSet-1
92ProSet-139
92Sco-390
92Sco-413
92Sco-433
92Sco-448
92Sco-519
92ScoCan-390
92ScoCan-413
92ScoCan-433
92ScoCan-448
92ScoCan-519
92SeaPat-34
92StaClu-94
92StaClu-251
92Top-212

92Top-265
92Top-504
92TopGol-212G
92TopGol-265G
92TopGol-504G
92Ult-165
92UltAllS-4
92UltAwaW-5
92UppDec-26
92UppDec-433
92UppDec-436
92UppDec-454
92UppDecGHS-G9
92UppDecWJG-WG11
93Don-262
93DonEli-1
93DonIceKin-7
93DonSpeP-R
93DonSpeP-NNO
93KenStaLA-7
93KenStaLC-6
93Kra-43
93Kra-56
93Kra-71
93Lea-1
93Lea-210
93Lea-NNO
93LeaGolAS-1
93LeaHatTA-1
93LeaHatTA-4
93LeaMarLem-1
93LeaMarLem-2
93LeaMarLem-3
93LeaMarLem-4
93LeaMarLem-5
93LeaMarLem-6
93LeaMarLem-7
93LeaMarLem-8
93LeaMarLem-9
93LeaMarLem-10
93McDUppD-H1
930PCPre-37
930PCPre-91
930PCPre-220
930PCPreBG-18
930PCPreF-10
930PCPreG-37
930PCPreG-185
930PCPreG-220
93PanSti-136
93PanSti-H
93Par-425
93ParChePH-D2
93ParEasWesS-E2
93ParEmel-425
93ParFirO-F10
93ParUSACG-G2
93PenFoo-1
93PenSti-4
93Pin-221
93Pin-230
93Pin-310
93PinCan-221
93PinCan-230
93PinCan-310
93PinCap-18
93PinCapC-18
93PinTeaP-5
93PinTeaPC-5
93Pow-190
93PowGam-5
93PowPoiL-8
93Sco-350
93Sco-479
93Sco-480
93ScoCan-350
93ScoCan-479
93ScoCan-480
93ScoDreTea-10
93ScoDynDC-8
93ScoFra-F16
93SeaPat-9
93StaClu-143
93StaClu-146
93StaClu-148
93StaClu-310
93StaCluAS-23
93StaCluFDI-143
93StaCluFDI-146
93StaCluFDI-310
93StaCluFDIO-143
93StaCluFDIO-146
93StaCluFDIO-148
93StaCluFin-10
93StaCluO-143
93StaCluO-146
93StaCluO-148
93StaCluO-310
93SweSemWCS-198
93TopPre-37
93TopPre-91
93TopPre-185
93TopPre-220
93TopPreBG-9
93TopPreBG-6
93TopPreF-10
93TopPreG-37
93TopPreG-185
93TopPreG-220
93Ult-116

93UltAwaW-4
93UltPreP-4
93UltRedLS-6
93UltScoK-4
93UppDec-301
93UppDec-407
93UppDecAW-AW1
93UppDecLAS-6
93UppDecNB-HB7
93UppDecPOE-E13
93UppDecSilSka-H1
93UppDecSilSkaG-H1
93UppDecSP-122
94BeAPla-R69
94CanGamNHLP-185
94Don-5
94DonDom-1
94DonEliIns-6
94DonIceMas-5
94EASpo-105
94EASpo-189
94Fla-135
94FlaCenS-6
94FlaHotN-5
94HocWit-66
94KenStaLA-11
94KenStaLC-6
94Lea-1
94LeaFirOIce-9
94LeaGolS-11
94LeaLim-1
94LeaLimG-1
94LeaLimI-18
940PCPre-250
940PCPreSE-250
94Par-296
94ParCratGB-18
94ParCratGG-18
94ParCratGR-18
94ParGol-296
94ParVin-V6
94Pin-170
94PinArtP-170
94PinRinC-170
94PinTeaP-TP10
94PinTeaPDP-TP10
94PinWorEdi-WE8
94ScoDreTea-DT15
94ScoFra-TF18
94StaClu-60
94StaCluFDI-60
94StaCluFI-1
94StaCluFIMO-1
94StaCluMOMS-60
94StaCluSTWC-60
94TopFinB-16
94TopPre-250
94TopPreSE-250
94Ult-165
94UltScoK-5
94UppDec-22
94UppDecElelce-22
94UppDecSPI-SP61
94UppDecSPIDC-SP61
95BAPLetL-LL11
95Bow-40
95BowAllFoi-40
95BowBes-BB10
95BowBesRef-BB10
95CanGamNHLP-2
95CanGamNHLP-211
95ColCho-256
95ColChoCTG-C25
95ColChoCTGGB-C25
95ColChoCTGGR-C25
95ColChoCTGSB-C25
95ColChoCTGSR-C25
95ColChoPC-256
95ColChoPCP-256
95Don-270
95DonDom-1
95DonEli-51
95DonEliCE-2
95DonEliDCS-51
95DonEliDCS-66
95DonEliDCS-66U
95DonEliDCU-51
95DonEliDCU-66
95DonEliDCU-66U
95DonEliIns-9
95DonEliLLS-1
95DonEliLLS-2
95DonEliLLS-3
95DonEliLLS-4
95DonEliLLS-5
95DonEliLLS-6
95DonEliLLS-7
95DonProPoi-14
95Emo-138
95EmoXce-8
95EmoXci-10
95Fin-150
95FinnSemWC-93
95FinRef-190
95ImpSti-97
95ImpStiDCS-24
95KelDon-1
95KelDon-2
95KelDon-3

95KelDon-4
95Kra-8
95Lea-1
95Lea-NNO
95LeaFreFra-7
95LeaLemB-1
95LeaLemB-2
95LeaLemB-3
95LeaLemB-4
95LeaLemB-5
95LeaLemB-6
95LeaLemB-7
95LeaLemB-8
95LeaLemB-9
95LeaLemB-10
95LeaLim-1
95LeaLimSG-1
95McDPin-MCD-15
95Met-118
95MetHM-9
95MetIS-14
95NHLAcePC-12H
95NHLCooT-4
95NHLCooT-RP4
95ParInt-170
95ParIntCCGS1-3
95ParIntCCSS1-3
95ParIntEl-170
95ParIntNHLAS-1
95ParIntPTP-PP2
95ParIntPTP-PP11
95PenFoo-23
95Pin-192
95PinArtP-192
95PinCleS-13
95PinFan-8
95PinFirS-13
95PinRinC-192
95PlaOneoOne-79
95PlaOneoOne-186
95PlaOneoOne-298
95ProMag-93
95SelCer-1
95SelCerGT-3
95SelCerMG-1
95SkyImp-132
95SkyImpCl-3
95SkyImpQ-7
95SP-113
95SPHol-FX17
95SPHolSpFX-FX17
95SPStaEto-E22
95SPStaEtoG-E22
95StaClu-180
95StaCluM-M2
95StaCluMOMS-180
95StaCluNem-N2
95Sum-118
95SumArtP-118
95SumGM-10
95SumIce-118
95SweGloWC-87
95Top-100
95TopHomGC-HGC30
95TopMysF-M2
95TopMysFR-M2
95TopOPCI-100
95TopPro-PF15
95TopRinL-2RL
95TopSupSki-1
95TopSupSkiPla-1
95Ult-288
95Ult-391
95UltExtAtt-13
95UltUltHP-6
95UltUltV-6
95UppDec-84
95UppDec-231
95UppDecAGPRW-16
95UppDecElelce-84
95UppDecElelce-231
95UppDecElelceG-84
95UppDecElelceG-231
95UppDecFreFra-F16
95UppDecFreFraJ-F16
95UppDecNHLAS-AS5
95UppDecPHE-H4
95UppDecPRE-R32
95UppDecPRE-R42
95UppDecPRE-R53
95UppDecPreR-R32
95UppDecPreR-R42
95UppDecPreR-R53
95UppDecSpeE-SE152
95UppDecSpeEdiG-SE152
95UppPreHV-H4
95UppPreRP-R32
95UppPreRP-R42
95UppPreRP-R53
95Zen-108
95ZenZT-3
96BeAPBisiTB-2
96ClaGol-66
96ColCho-210
96ColCho-293
96ColCho-335
96ColChoCTG-C5A
96ColChoCTG-C5B
96ColChoCTGE-CR5
96ColChoCTGEG-CR5
96ColChoCTGG-C5B
96ColChoCTGG-C5C
96ColChoSti-S7

❑ 96Don-131
❑ 96DonCanI-31
❑ 96DonCanIGPP-31
❑ 96DonCanIMLS-1
❑ 96DonCanIMLS-2
❑ 96DonCanIMLS-3
❑ 96DonCanIMLS-4
❑ 96DonCanIMLS-5
❑ 96DonCanIMLS-6
❑ 96DonCanIMLS-7
❑ 96DonCanIMLS-8
❑ 96DonCanIMLS-9
❑ 96DonCanIMLS-10
❑ 96DonCanIMLS-11
❑ 96DonCanIMLS-12
❑ 96DonCanIMLS-13
❑ 96DonCanIMLS-14
❑ 96DonCanIMLS-15
❑ 96DonCanIMLS-16
❑ 96DonCanIMLS-17
❑ 96DonCanIMLS-18
❑ 96DonCanIMLS-19
❑ 96DonCanIMLS-20
❑ 96DonCanIMLS-21
❑ 96DonCanIMLS-22
❑ 96DonCanIMLS-23
❑ 96DonCanIMLS-24
❑ 96DonCanIMLS-25
❑ 96DonCanIOC-13
❑ 96DonCanIRPP-31
❑ 96DonDom-4
❑ 96DonEli-109
❑ 96DonEliDCS-109
❑ 96DonEliHTH-1
❑ 96DonEliHTH-2
❑ 96DonEliHTH-3
❑ 96DonEliHTH-4
❑ 96DonEliHTH-5
❑ 96DonEliHTH-6
❑ 96DonEliHTH-NNO
❑ 96DonEliHTH-NNO
❑ 96DonEliP-4
❑ 96DonGoTS-1
❑ 96DonPrePro-131
❑ 96Fla-78
❑ 96FlaBluI-78
❑ 96FlaHotN-7
❑ 96FlaNowAT-2
❑ 96Fle-87
❑ 96Fle-137
❑ 96Fle-138
❑ 96Fle-139
❑ 96Fle-141
❑ 96FleArtRos-13
❑ 96FlePCC-3
❑ 96FlePea-7
❑ 96FlePicDL-1
❑ 96FlePicF5-26
❑ 96HocGreC-13
❑ 96HocGreCG-13
❑ 96KraUppD-22
❑ 96KraUppD-28
❑ 96KraUppD-37
❑ 96KraUppD-54
❑ 96KraUppD-56
❑ 96KraUppD-67
❑ 96Lea-84
❑ 96LeaFirOI-1
❑ 96LeaLim-85
❑ 96LeaLimG-85
❑ 96LeaLimStu-7
❑ 96LeaPre-113
❑ 96LeaPreP-84
❑ 96LeaPrePP-113
❑ 96LeaPreSP-2
❑ 96LeaPreVP-6
❑ 96LeaPreVPG-6
❑ 96LeaSwe-1
❑ 96LeaSwe(-1
❑ 96MapLeaP-2
❑ 96MetUni-128
❑ 96MetUniIC-10
❑ 96MetUniICSP-10
❑ 96MetUniLW-11
❑ 96MetUniLWSP-11
❑ 96NHLACEPC-29
❑ 96NHLProSTA-93
❑ 96PenTri-8
❑ 96Pin-86
❑ 96PinArtP-86
❑ 96PinFan-FC4
❑ 96PinFoi-86
❑ 96PinMcD-21
❑ 96PinMin-1
❑ 96PinMinB-1
❑ 96PinMinCoiB-1
❑ 96PinMinCoiGP-1
❑ 96PinMinCoiN-1
❑ 96PinMinCoiS-1
❑ 96PinMinCoiSG-1
❑ 96PinMinG-1
❑ 96PinMinS-1
❑ 96PinPreS-86
❑ 96PinRinC-86
❑ 96PinTeaP-2
❑ 96PinTro-1
❑ 96PlaOneoOne-436
❑ 96Sco-6
❑ 96ScoArtPro-6
❑ 96ScoDeaCAP-6
❑ 96ScoDreTea-6
❑ 96ScoGolB-6
❑ 96ScoSpeAP-6
❑ 96ScoSudDea-7
❑ 96SelCer-10
❑ 96SelCerAP-10
❑ 96SelCerBlu-10
❑ 96SelCerCor-2
❑ 96SelCerMB-10
❑ 96SelCerMG-10
❑ 96SelCerMR-10
❑ 96SelCerRed-10
❑ 96SkyImp-102
❑ 96SkyImpCI-7
❑ 96SkyImpVer-7
❑ 96SP-125
❑ 96SPCleWin-CW3
❑ 96SPSPxFor-1
❑ 96SPx-37
❑ 96SPxGol-37
❑ 96SPxHolH-HH6
❑ 96StaCluMO-24
❑ 96Sum-32
❑ 96SumArtP-32
❑ 96SumHigV-8
❑ 96SumHigVM-8
❑ 96SumIce-32
❑ 96SumMet-32
❑ 96SumPreS-32
❑ 96SumUnt-1
❑ 96SweSemW-85
❑ 96TeaOut-17
❑ 96TopNHLP-3
❑ 96TopPic5C-FC5
❑ 96TopPicFT-FT15
❑ 96TopPicOI-3
❑ 96Ult-143
❑ 96UltGolM-143
❑ 96UltPow-11
❑ 96UltPowRL-4
❑ 96UppDec-321
❑ 96UppDecBD-166
❑ 96UppDecBDG-166
❑ 96UppDecBDRFTC-RC3
❑ 96UppDecGJ-GJ6
❑ 96UppDecHH-HH16
❑ 96UppDecHHG-HH16
❑ 96UppDecHHS-HH16
❑ 96UppDecIce-114
❑ 96UppDecIceDF-S7
❑ 96UppDecIcePar-114
❑ 96UppDecIceSCF-S7
❑ 96UppDecLSH-LS3
❑ 96UppDecLSHF-LS3
❑ 96UppDecLSHS-LS3
❑ 96UppDecSS-SS5B
❑ 96Zen-114
❑ 96ZenArtP-114
❑ 96ZenChaS-5
❑ 96ZenChaSD-5
❑ 97BeAPLemDC-1
❑ 97BeAPLemDC-2
❑ 97FooSanMC-1
❑ 97FooSanMC-2
❑ 97HigMinHMC-6
❑ 97HigMinHMC-7
❑ 97HigMinHMC-8
❑ 97PinMarMom-1
❑ 97PinMarMom-2
❑ 97PinMarMom-3
❑ 97PinMarMom-4
❑ 97PinMarMom-5
❑ 97PinMarMom-6
❑ 97PinMarMom-7
❑ 97PinMarMom-8
❑ 97PinMarMom-9
❑ 97PinMarMom-10
❑ 97PinMarMom-11
❑ 97PinMarMom-12
❑ 97PinMarMom-13
❑ 97PinMarMom-14
❑ 97PinMarMom-15
❑ 97PinMarMom-16
❑ 97PinMarMom-17
❑ 97PinMarMom-18
❑ 97PinMarMom-XXX
❑ 97TopHocMC-15
❑ 97TopHocMC-16
❑ 98Be A PPPL-L1
❑ 98Be A PPPL-L2
❑ 98Be A PPPL-L3
❑ 98Be A PPPL-L4
❑ 98McDGreT-T12
❑ 99RetHoc-83
❑ 99UppDecCL-4
❑ 99UppDecCLACT-AC7
❑ 99UppDecCLCLC-4
❑ 99UppDecEotG-E3
❑ 99UppDecES-3
❑ 99UppDecJotC-JC5
❑ 99UppDecRDR-DR12
❑ 99UppDecRDRI-DR12
❑ 99UppDecRG-G5B
❑ 99UppDecRG-83
❑ 99UppDecRGI-G5B
❑ 99UppDecRII-ML
❑ 99UppDecRIL1-ML
❑ 99UppDecRM-RM3
❑ 99UppDecRP-83
❑ 99UppDecRTotC-TC13

**Lemieux, Real**
❑ 68OPC-36
❑ 68ShiCoi-50
❑ 68Top-36
❑ 69OPC-190
❑ 70SarProSta-70
❑ 71OPC-154
❑ 71SarProSta-72
❑ 71TorSun-119
❑ 72SarProSta-91
❑ 73OPC-122
❑ 73Top-122
❑ 75OPCNHL-274
❑ 75Top-274

**Lemieux, Richard**
❑ 72CanuRoyB-11
❑ 72OPC-202
❑ 72SarProSta-218
❑ 73CanuRoyB-11
❑ 73OPC-53
❑ 73Top-53
❑ 74NHLActSta-298
❑ 74OPCNHL-114
❑ 74Top-114
❑ 76OPCWHA-74

**Lemoine, J. Philippe**
❑ 93SweSemWCS-254
❑ 94FinnJaaK-213
❑ 94FreNatT-16

**Lemonde, Bernie**
❑ 50QueCit-12
❑ 51LavDaiS-90

**Lempiainen, Mikko**
❑ 93FinnJyvHS-204
❑ 93FinnSIS-271

**Lempio, Joachin**
❑ 94GerDELE-128

**Lenardon, Tim**
❑ 88ProAHL-347
❑ 91ProAHLCHL-149

**Lenarduzzi, Mike**
❑ 89OshGenP-12
❑ 907thInnSOHL-165
❑ 917thInnSMC-1
❑ 917thInnSOHL-310
❑ 93Par-87
❑ 93ParEmel-87
❑ 93Pin-207
❑ 93PinCan-207
❑ 93Ult-72
❑ 93UltPro-5

**Lendick, Mathieu**
❑ 98Vald'OF-S2

**Lendzyk, Taras**
❑ 91AirCanSJHL-B13
❑ 91AirCanSJHLAS-37
❑ 93MinDul-17
❑ 96SouCarS-35

**Lener, Slavomir**
❑ 92FlamIGA-28
❑ 96CzeAPSE-119
❑ 96CzeAPSE-335

**Lentz, Charlie**
❑ 93OmaLan-15

**Leonard, Gerry**
❑ 69SeaTotW-5

**Leong, Bo**
❑ 69SweHocS-303

**Leonhardt, Bjorn**
❑ 96GerDELE-183
❑ 98GerDELE-193

**Leonov, Dmitri**
❑ 95SpoChi-5

**Leonov, Yuri**
❑ 91OPCIns-39R
❑ 93SwiHNL-152

**Leoppky, Mark**
❑ 92MPSPhoSJHL-26

**Lepage, Bertrand**
❑ 52JunBluT-69

**Lepage, Martin**
❑ 907thInnSQMJHL-138
❑ 917thInnSQMJHL-207
❑ 96WheNai-25

**Lepage, Pierre**
❑ 77GraVic-14

**Lepine, Jos.**
❑ 51LavDaiQSHL-46

**Lepine, Pit**
❑ 27LaPat-5
❑ 33OPCV304A-20
❑ 33V129-42
❑ 33V252CanG-36
❑ 33V288HamG-23
❑ 33V357IceK-46
❑ 34BeeGro1P-164
❑ 34DiaMatS-39
❑ 34SweCap-8
❑ 35DiaMatT2-37
❑ 35DiaMatT3-34
❑ 35DiaMatTI-39
❑ 36V356WorG-78
❑ 37OPCV304E-159

**Lepisto, Jussi**
❑ 84SweSemE-151
❑ 85SwePanS-135

**Lepler, P.J.**
❑ 96RicRen-13
❑ 97LouRivF-3

**Leppa, Henry**
❑ 74SweHocS-100
❑ 74SweSemHVS-84

**Leppanen, Antti**
❑ 74SweHocS-104
❑ 74SweSemHVS-97

**Leppanen, Reijo**
❑ 81SweSemHVS-29
❑ 82SweSemHVS-45

**Leroux, Francois**
❑ 88OilTenAnn-147
❑ 90ProAHLIHL-239
❑ 90Sco-393
❑ 90ScoCan-393
❑ 91ProAHLCHL-215
❑ 92OilTeal-10
❑ 92WesMic-16
❑ 93Par-412
❑ 93ParEmel-412
❑ 94PenFoo-13
❑ 95PenFoo-6
❑ 95PlaOneoOne-81
❑ 96BeAPAut-112
❑ 96BeAPAutSil-112
❑ 96BeAPla-112
❑ 97PacInvNRB-162

**Leroux, Jean-Yves**
❑ 97Be A PPAD-45
❑ 97Be A PPAPD-45
❑ 97BeAPla-45
❑ 97BeAPlaAut-45
❑ 97Don-211
❑ 97DonPre-157
❑ 97DonPreCttC-157
❑ 97DonPreProG-211
❑ 97DonPreProS-211
❑ 97Lea-161
❑ 97LeaFraMat-161
❑ 97LeaFraMDC-161
❑ 97PinIns-186
❑ 97UppDec-249
❑ 98Pac-149
❑ 98PacAur-42
❑ 98PacIceB-149
❑ 98PacPar-49
❑ 98PacParC-49
❑ 98PacParEG-49
❑ 98PacParH-49
❑ 98PacParIB-49
❑ 98PacParS-49
❑ 98PacRed-149
❑ 98UC-52
❑ 98UD ChoPCR-52
❑ 98UD ChoR-52
❑ 99Pac-90
❑ 99PacCop-90
❑ 99PacGol-90
❑ 99PacIceB-90
❑ 99PacPreD-90

**LeRoux, Rod**
❑ 96SeaThu-3

**Leschasin, Ryan**
❑ 92ForWorF-11
❑ 93ForWorF-5
❑ 94CenHocL-13

**Leschyshyn, Curtis**
❑ 88NordGenF-21
❑ 88NordTeal-22
❑ 89Nord-26
❑ 89NordGenF-20
❑ 89NordPol-17
❑ 89PanSti-334
❑ 90NordPet-15
❑ 90NordTeal-18
❑ 90OPC-216
❑ 90PanSti-150
❑ 90ProSet-251
❑ 90Sco-92
❑ 90ScoCan-92
❑ 90ScoHotRS-44
❑ 90Top-216
❑ 90TopTif-216
❑ 90UppDec-295
❑ 90UppDecF-295
❑ 91Bow-142
❑ 91NordPanTS-13
❑ 91NordPet-15
❑ 91OPC-39
❑ 91PanSti-256
❑ 91Par-367
❑ 91ParFre-367
❑ 91Pin-258
❑ 91PinFre-258
❑ 91ProSet-198
❑ 91ProSetFre-198
❑ 91ScoAme-58
❑ 91ScoCan-58
❑ 91StaClu-156
❑ 91Top-39
❑ 91UppDec-413
❑ 91UppDecF-413
❑ 92Bow-335
❑ 92NorPet-19
❑ 92OPC-306
❑ 92PanSti-217
❑ 92PanStiFre-217
❑ 92Pin-46
❑ 92PinFre-46
❑ 92Sco-87
❑ 92ScoCan-87
❑ 92StaClu-413
❑ 92Top-124
❑ 92TopGol-124G
❑ 93Don-273
❑ 93Lea-305
❑ 93OPCPre-487
❑ 93OPCPreG-487
❑ 93Par-436
❑ 93ParEmel-436
❑ 93Pin-49
❑ 93PinCan-49
❑ 93Pow-423
❑ 93Sco-42
❑ 93ScoCan-42
❑ 93StaClu-336
❑ 93StaCluFDI-336
❑ 93StaCluO-336
❑ 93TopPre-487
❑ 93TopPreG-487
❑ 93Ult-404
❑ 93UppDec-133
❑ 94CanGamNHLP-202
❑ 94EASpo-110
❑ 94Lea-548
❑ 94NordBurK-17
❑ 94OPCPre-62
❑ 94OPCPreSE-62
❑ 94Pin-24
❑ 94PinArtP-24
❑ 94PinRinC-24
❑ 94Sco-64
❑ 94ScoGol-64
❑ 94ScoPla-64
❑ 94ScoPlaTS-64
❑ 94TopPre-62
❑ 94TopPreSE-62
❑ 95BeAPla-129
❑ 95BeAPSig-S129
❑ 95BeAPSigDC-S129
❑ 95CanGamNHLP-80
❑ 95ColCho-305
❑ 95ColChoPC-305
❑ 95ColChoPCP-305
❑ 95Emo-39
❑ 95PlaOneoOne-240
❑ 95Sco-153
❑ 95ScoBlaIce-153
❑ 95ScoBlaIceAP-153
❑ 95SkyImp-38
❑ 95Ult-133
❑ 95UltGolM-133
❑ 96Don-48
❑ 96DonPrePro-48
❑ 96Lea-126
❑ 96LeaPreP-126
❑ 96Sco-216
❑ 96ScoArtPro-216
❑ 96ScoDeaCAP-216
❑ 96ScoGolB-216
❑ 96ScoSpeAP-216
❑ 96UppDecBD-7
❑ 96UppDecBDG-7
❑ 97CarHur-17
❑ 97PacInvNRB-38
❑ 97UppDec-35

**Lesieur, Art**
❑ 35DiaMatT2-38
❑ 35DiaMatT3-35
❑ 36ProvRed-5

**Leska, Petr**
❑ 94FliGen-15
❑ 95CzeAPSE-50

**Leslie, Alex**
❑ 52JunBluT-21

**Leslie, Glen**
❑ 85LonKni-18

**Leslie, Lance**
❑ 94ThuBayS-14
❑ 96KenTho-11
❑ 96LouRiv-22
❑ 97LouRivF-22
❑ 99WicThu-11

**Leslie, Laura**
❑ 94ClaWomOH-W11

**Leslie, Lee J**
❑ 907thInnSWHL-275
❑ 90PriAlbR-9
❑ 917thInnSWHL-243
❑ 91PriAlbR-11
❑ 92Cla-26
❑ 92PeoRivC-12
❑ 95PeoRiv-9
❑ 96ClaGol-26

**Lessard, David**
❑ 917thInnSQMJHL-288

**Lessard, Jim**
❑ 91BriColJHL-43
❑ 91BriColJHL-169
❑ 94DayBom-6

**Lessard, Mario**
❑ 79OPC-389
❑ 80KinCarN-7
❑ 81OPC-146
❑ 81OPCSti-238
❑ 81Top-W98
❑ 82OPC-156
❑ 82OPCSti-236
❑ 82PosCer-8

**Lessard, Owen**
❑ 90ProAHLIHL-405
❑ 91ProAHLCHL-478
❑ 92IndIce-19

**Lessard, Richard (Rick)**
❑ 84Ott67-19
❑ 88SalLakCGE-18
❑ 89ProIHL-196
❑ 90ProAHLIHL-605
❑ 91ProAHLCHL-519
❑ 91ProSet-560
❑ 91ProSetFre-560
❑ 91UppDec-520
❑ 91UppDecF-520

**Lessard, Stephane**
❑ 80QueRem-13

**Lessor, Douglas**
❑ 52JunBluT-48

**Lestander, Roland**
❑ 69SweHocS-174
❑ 72SweHocS-196

**Lester, Don**
❑ 94RicRen-8
❑ 95AlaGolKin-10

**Lesueur, Percy**
❑ 10C55SweCP-16
❑ 10C56-2
❑ 11C55-16
❑ 12C57-27
❑ 83HalFP-C7
❑ 85HalFC-37

**Lesuk, Bill**
❑ 71TorSun-202
❑ 72FlyMigM-6
❑ 72OPC-245
❑ 73OPC-205
❑ 74CapWhiB-16
❑ 76OPCWHA-121
❑ 78JetPos-10
❑ 79JetPos-11
❑ 79OPC-312

**Leswick, Jack**
❑ 34DiaMatS-40

**Leswick, Tony**
❑ 44BeeGro2P-185
❑ 44BeeGro2P-337
❑ 51Par-59
❑ 52Par-65
❑ 52RoyDesH-1
❑ 53Par-43
❑ 54Par-45
❑ 54Top-45

**Letang, Alan**
❑ 917thInnSOHL-26
❑ 91CorRoy-25
❑ 94SarSti-24
❑ 95FreCan-18

**Letendre, Luce**
❑ 97ColCho-290

**Letourneau, Mathieu**
❑ 93AmoLesFAM-12

**Letourneau, Ray**
❑ 91ProAHLCHL-263

**Letowski, Trevor**
❑ 94SarSti-13
❑ 95Sla-341
❑ 96SarSti-13
❑ 96SarSti-14
❑ 96UppDecIce-121
❑ 97BowCHL-26
❑ 97BowCHLOPC-26
❑ 99UppDecM-164
❑ 99UppDecMGS-164
❑ 99UppDecMSS-164
❑ 99UppDecMSS-164

**Leuenberger, Marc**
❑ 91SweSemWCS-187
❑ 93SwiHNL-49
❑ 95SwiHNL-95

**Leuenberger, Sven**
❑ 91SweSemWCS-180
❑ 93SweSemWCS-115
❑ 93SwiHNL-92
❑ 95SwiHNL-90

**Leurs, Frank**
❑ 70FlyPos-3

**Levac, Frederic**
❑ 96RimOce-15
❑ 96RimOceQPP-14

**Levasseur, Chris**
❑ 87MonHaw-16

**Levasseur, Rob**
❑ 89NasKni-15

**Levasseur, Vincent**
❑ 93AmoLesFAM-13

**Leveille, Normand**
❑ 82OPC-13

**Leven, Jonas**
❑ 89SweSemE-123
❑ 90SweSemE-201
❑ 91SweSemE-130
❑ 92SweSemE-151

**Leveque, Guy**
❑ 907thInnSOHL-38
❑ 917thInnSMC-116
❑ 917thInnSOHL-11
❑ 91AreDraPic-30
❑ 91Cla-36
❑ 91CorRoy-7
❑ 91StaPicH-67
❑ 91UltDra-31
❑ 92PhoRoa-13
❑ 92UppDec-576
❑ 93ClaProPro-124
❑ 93PhoRoa-14
❑ 93UppDec-236
❑ 93UppDec-246
❑ 94ClaProP-163
❑ 94St.JohML-18

**Lever, Don**
❑ 72CanuRoyB-12
❑ 72OPC-259
❑ 73CanuRoyB-12
❑ 73OPC-111
❑ 73Top-111
❑ 74CanuRoyB-10
❑ 74NHLActSta-287
❑ 74OPCNHL-94
❑ 74Top-94
❑ 75CanuRoyB-11
❑ 75OPCNHL-206
❑ 75OPCNHL-329
❑ 75Top-206
❑ 75Top-329
❑ 76CanuRoyB-9
❑ 76OPCNHL-53
❑ 76Top-53
❑ 77CanCanDC-7
❑ 77CanuRoyB-10
❑ 77OPCNHL-111
❑ 77Top-111
❑ 78CanuRoyB-13
❑ 78OPC-86
❑ 78Top-86
❑ 79CanuRoyB-12
❑ 79FlamPos-7
❑ 79OPC-203
❑ 79PanSti-65
❑ 79Top-203
❑ 80FlamPos-9
❑ 80OPC-124
❑ 80PepCap-7
❑ 80Top-124
❑ 81OPC-45
❑ 81RocPos-11
❑ 82OPC-141
❑ 82OPCSti-224
❑ 82PosCer-11
❑ 83OPC-224
❑ 83OPC-231
❑ 83OPCSti-218
❑ 83PufSti-7
❑ 84DevPos-9
❑ 84OPC-112
❑ 84OPCSti-70
❑ 84Top-86
❑ 85OPC-238
❑ 87SabWonBH-15
❑ 88SabWonBH-14
❑ 90ProAHLIHL-293
❑ 91ProAHLCHL-23
❑ 91RochAmeKod-1
❑ 91RochAmePos-12

**Levesque, Ben**
❑ 82KinCan-25
❑ 83KinCan-3

**Levesque, Francois**
❑ 96RimOce-16
❑ 96RimOceQPP-15

**Levesque, Guildor**
❑ 51LavDaiLSJ-38
❑ 51LavDaiQSHL-29

**Levesque, Jonathan**
❑ 93AmoLesFAM-14
❑ 96RimOceU-5

**Levesque, Michel**
❑ 84RicRiv-9

**Levesque, Paul**
❑ 80QueRem-14

**Levie, Craig**
❑ 81JetPos-8
❑ 82Jet-11
❑ 82OPC-382
❑ 83NorStaPos-12
❑ 85NorStaPos-17

**Levins, Scott**
❑ 90MonHaw-16
❑ 90ProAHLIHL-258
❑ 91MonHaw-19
❑ 91ProAHLCHL-182
❑ 93Don-130
❑ 93Don-466
❑ 93Par-80
❑ 93ParEmel-80
❑ 93Sco-617
❑ 93ScoCan-617
❑ 93ScoGol-617
❑ 93Ult-326
❑ 93UppDec-433
❑ 93UppDecSP-56
❑ 94Don-119
❑ 94Par-155
❑ 94Par-292
❑ 94ParGol-155
❑ 94ParGol-292
❑ 94SenBelM-17
❑ 94Ult-148
❑ 94UppDec-295
❑ 94UppDecEleIce-295
❑ 95PlaOneoOne-180
❑ 95Sen-13
❑ 96SprFal-22

**Levinsky, Alex**
❑ 32O'KeeMapL-3
❑ 33OPCV304A-11
❑ 33V129-9
❑ 33V288HamG-36
❑ 33V357IceK-47
❑ 34BeeGro1P-63
❑ 35DiaMatT2-39
❑ 35DiaMatT2-40
❑ 35DiaMatT3-36
❑ 35DiaMatT4-9
❑ 35DiaMatT5-8
❑ 36V356WorG-61
❑ 37DiaMatT6-8
❑ 94ParTalBG-2

**Levo, Tapio**
❑ 79PanSti-168
❑ 81RocPos-12
❑ 81SweSemHVS-24
❑ 82SweSemHVS-154
❑ 83PufSti-10

**Levonen, Jari**
❑ 93FinnJyvHS-359
❑ 93FinnSIS-221
❑ 94FinnSIS-15
❑ 94FinnSISH-9
❑ 95FinnSIS-155
❑ 95FinnSISL-26
❑ 96FinnSISR-160

**Levonen, Jarno**
❑ 93FinnSIS-222
❑ 94FinnSIS-258
❑ 95FinnSIS-277
❑ 96FinnSISR-80

**Levy, Jeff**
❑ 93ClaProPro-52

❑ 93DayBom-2
❑ 94HunBli-16
**Lewicki, Danny**
❑ 44BeeGro2P-338
❑ 44BeeGro2P-418
❑ 45QuaOatP-27
❑ 51Par-71
❑ 54Top-23
❑ 57Top-61
❑ 58Top-6
❑ 62QueAce-16
❑ 94ParMisL-98
**Lewis, Adam**
❑ 96KitRan-16
**Lewis, Bob**
❑ 91BriColJHL-94
**Lewis, Dave**
❑ 74NHLActSta-177
❑ 74OPCNHL-324
❑ 75OPCNHL-108
❑ 75Top-108
❑ 76OPCNHL-221
❑ 76Top-221
❑ 77OPCNHL-116
❑ 77Top-116
❑ 78OPC-162
❑ 78Top-162
❑ 79IslTrans-9
❑ 79OPC-44
❑ 79Top-44
❑ 80KinCarN-8
❑ 80OPC-196
❑ 80Top-196
❑ 82OPC-157
❑ 82PosCer-8
❑ 83OPC-158
❑ 84DevPos-25
❑ 84OPC-113
❑ 84Top-87
❑ 85OPC-66
❑ 85OPCSti-59
❑ 85Top-66
❑ 86OPC-85
❑ 86OPCSti-197
❑ 86Top-85
❑ 87OPC-37
❑ 87PanSti-242
❑ 87Top-37
**Lewis, Herbie**
❑ 34BeeGro1P-111
❑ 34SweCap-38
❑ 36TriPos-4
❑ 36V356WorG-64
**Lewis, Randy**
❑ 90MicTecHus-11
❑ 91MicTecHus-8
❑ 91MicTecHus-9
**Lewis, Robert**
❑ 92DalFre-12
❑ 93DalFre-11
**Lewis, Roger**
❑ 93NorMicW-19
**Ley, Rick**
❑ 68MapLeaWB-5
❑ 69MapLeaWBG-20
❑ 69OPC-183
❑ 70DadCoo-71
❑ 70EssPowPla-20
❑ 70MapLeaP-6
❑ 70OPC-106
❑ 70SarProSta-198
❑ 70Top-108
❑ 71MapLeaP-9
❑ 71OPC-194
❑ 71SarProSta-195
❑ 71TorSun-262
❑ 72WhaNewEWHA-11
❑ 73QuaOatWHA-25
❑ 74TeaCanLWHA-14
❑ 75OPCWHA-14
❑ 76OPCWHA-101
❑ 79OPC-314
❑ 80OPC-198
❑ 80Top-198
❑ 81OPCSti-64
❑ 90ProSet-666
**Leyte, Copper**
❑ 50QueCit-14
❑ 51LavDaiQSHL-6
❑ 52St.LawS-52
**Lhenry, Fabrice**
❑ 98GerDELE-138
**Liapkin, Yuri**
❑ 72SweSemWC-14
❑ 73SweHocS-84
❑ 73SweWorCS-84
❑ 74SweSemHVS-32
❑ 91FutTreC72-83
**Liba, Igor**
❑ 82SweSemHVS-98
**Liberts, Juris**
❑ 74SweHocS-68
**Libett, Nick**
❑ 68ShiCoi-49
❑ 69OPC-162
❑ 70EssPowPla-138
❑ 70OPC-158
❑ 70SarProSta-60
❑ 71OPC-140
❑ 71SarProSta-53
❑ 71TorSun-98
❑ 72OPC-45
❑ 72SarProSta-75
❑ 72Top-67
❑ 73OPC-49
❑ 73RedWinMP-12
❑ 73RedWinTI-15
❑ 73Top-49
❑ 74NHLActSta-92
❑ 74OPCNHL-193
❑ 74Top-193
❑ 75OPCNHL-13
❑ 75Top-13
❑ 76OPCNHL-171
❑ 76Top-171
❑ 77OPCNHL-103
❑ 77Top-103
❑ 78OPC-251
❑ 78Top-251
❑ 79OPC-198
❑ 79Top-198
❑ 81RedWinOld-15
**Lichnovsky, Marcel**
❑ 94GerDELE-399
❑ 95GerDELE-414
**Liddington, Bob**
❑ 70MapLeaP-7
❑ 75OPCWHA-105
❑ 76RoaPhoWHA-12
**Lidgren, Joakim**
❑ 93SweSemE-10
❑ 95SweLeaE-241
❑ 95SweUppDE-100
**Lidster, Doug**
❑ 84Canu-14
❑ 85Canu-14
❑ 85OPC-241
❑ 86Canu-14
❑ 86KraDra-34
❑ 86OPC-32
❑ 86OPCSti-102
❑ 86Top-32
❑ 87CanuSheOil-10
❑ 87OPC-256
❑ 87OPCSti-191
❑ 87PanSti-341
❑ 88CanuMoh-10
❑ 88OPC-228
❑ 88OPCSti-63
❑ 88PanSti-135
❑ 89CanuMoh-9
❑ 89OPC-284
❑ 89OPCSti-69
❑ 90Bow-56
❑ 90BowTif-56
❑ 90CanuMoh-14
❑ 90CanuMol-3
❑ 90OPC-207
❑ 90PanSti-295
❑ 90ProSet-298
❑ 90Sco-73
❑ 90ScoCan-73
❑ 90Top-207
❑ 90TopTif-207
❑ 90UppDec-60
❑ 90UppDecF-60
❑ 91Bow-317
❑ 91CanuAutC-11
❑ 91CanuPanTS-12
❑ 91CanuTeal8-11
❑ 91OPC-179
❑ 91PanSti-40
❑ 91Par-184
❑ 91ParFre-184
❑ 91Pin-189
❑ 91PinFre-189
❑ 91ProSet-247
❑ 91ProSetFre-247
❑ 91ScoAme-215
❑ 91ScoCan-215
❑ 91StaClu-72
❑ 91Top-179
❑ 91UppDec-290
❑ 91UppDecF-290
❑ 92Bow-267
❑ 92CanuRoaTA-10
❑ 92OPC-51
❑ 92PanSti-37
❑ 92PanStiFre-37
❑ 92Pin-147
❑ 92PinFre-147
❑ 92ProSet-199
❑ 92Sco-124
❑ 92ScoCan-124
❑ 92StaClu-404
❑ 92Top-403
❑ 92TopGol-403G
❑ 92Ult-221
❑ 93Lea-365
❑ 93OPCPre-315
❑ 93OPCPreG-315
❑ 93PanSti-176
❑ 93Par-403
❑ 93ParEmel-403
❑ 93Pin-355
❑ 93PinCan-355
❑ 93Sco-65
❑ 93Sco-524
❑ 93ScoCan-65
❑ 93ScoCan-524
❑ 93ScoGol-524
❑ 93StaClu-406
❑ 93StaCluFDI-406
❑ 93StaCluO-406
❑ 93TopPre-315
❑ 93TopPreG-315
❑ 93Ult-374
❑ 94BeAPSig-23
❑ 94EASpo-140
❑ 94Lea-353
❑ 94Pin-409
❑ 94PinArtP-409
❑ 94PinRinC-409
❑ 94StaClu-122
❑ 94StaCluFDI-122
❑ 94StaCluMOMS-122
❑ 94StaCluSTWC-122
❑ 94UppDec-400
❑ 94UppDecElelce-400
❑ 95ParInt-412
❑ 95ParIntEl-412
❑ 95UppDec-401
❑ 95UppDecElelce-401
❑ 95UppDecElelceG-401
❑ 97Be A PPAD-208
❑ 97Be A PPAPD-208
❑ 97BeAPla-208
❑ 97BeAPlaAut-208
❑ 97PacInvNRB-130
**Lidstrom, Nicklas**
❑ 89SweSemE-247
❑ 90SweSemE-152
❑ 91OPCPre-117
❑ 91OPCPre-163
❑ 91Par-37
❑ 91Par-445
❑ 91ParFre-37
❑ 91ParFre-445
❑ 91Pin-320
❑ 91PinFre-320
❑ 91ProSet-531
❑ 91ProSet-610
❑ 91ProSetFre-531
❑ 91ProSetFre-610
❑ 91ProSetPla-253
❑ 91RedWinLC-11
❑ 91ScoCan-621
❑ 91ScoRoo-71T
❑ 91SweSemE-255
❑ 91SweSemE-322
❑ 91SweSemE-341
❑ 91SweSemWCS-31
❑ 91UppDec-26
❑ 91UppDec-584
❑ 91UppDec-587
❑ 91UppDecF-26
❑ 91UppDecF-584
❑ 91UppDecF-587
❑ 92Bow-305
❑ 92OPC-369
❑ 92PanSti-274
❑ 92PanSti-298
❑ 92PanSti-J
❑ 92PanStiFre-274
❑ 92PanStiFre-298
❑ 92PanStiFre-J
❑ 92Par-42
❑ 92Par-239
❑ 92Par-451
❑ 92ParEmel-42
❑ 92ParEmel-239
❑ 92ParEmel-451
❑ 92Pin-8
❑ 92PinFre-8
❑ 92PinTea2-3
❑ 92PinTea2F-3
❑ 92ProSet-42
❑ 92ProSetGTL-4
❑ 92Sco-391
❑ 92Sco-502
❑ 92ScoCan-391
❑ 92ScoCan-502
❑ 92ScoYouS-11
❑ 92StaClu-43
❑ 92StaClu-253
❑ 92Top-9
❑ 92Top-440
❑ 92TopGol-9G
❑ 92TopGol-440G
❑ 92Ult-51
❑ 92UltImp-13
❑ 92UltRoo-7
❑ 92UppDec-178
❑ 92UppDec-363
❑ 92UppDecART-AR4
❑ 92UppDecART-AR7
❑ 92UppDecAWT-W4
❑ 92UppDecERT-ERT2
❑ 92UppDecES-E9
❑ 93Don-102
❑ 93Lea-89
❑ 93OPCPre-9
❑ 93OPCPreG-9
❑ 93PanSti-253
❑ 93Par-62
❑ 93ParEmel-62
❑ 93Pin-98
❑ 93PinCan-98
❑ 93PinTea2-6
❑ 93PinTea2C-6
❑ 93Pow-74
❑ 93Sco-158
❑ 93ScoCan-158
❑ 93StaClu-196
❑ 93StaClu-429
❑ 93StaCluFDI-196
❑ 93StaCluFDI-429
❑ 93StaCluFDIO-196
❑ 93StaCluO-196
❑ 93StaCluO-429
❑ 93SweSemWCS-23
❑ 93TopPre-9
❑ 93TopPreG-9
❑ 93Ult-220
❑ 93UppDec-150
❑ 94BeAPSig-162
❑ 94CanGamNHLP-95
❑ 94Don-194
❑ 94Fle-62
❑ 94Lea-141
❑ 94OPCPre-52
❑ 94OPCPreSE-52
❑ 94Par-61
❑ 94ParGol-61
❑ 94ParSEES-ES4
❑ 94Pin-66
❑ 94PinArtP-66
❑ 94PinRinC-66
❑ 94PinWorEdi-WE16
❑ 94Sco-119
❑ 94ScoGol-119
❑ 94ScoPla-119
❑ 94ScoPlaTS-119
❑ 94Sel-134
❑ 94SelGol-134
❑ 94StaClu-228
❑ 94StaCluFDI-228
❑ 94StaCluMOMS-228
❑ 94StaCluSTWC-228
❑ 94SweLeaE-285
❑ 94SweLeaEGS-4
❑ 94TopPre-52
❑ 94TopPreSE-52
❑ 94Ult-62
❑ 94UppDec-112
❑ 94UppDecElelce-112
❑ 94UppDecSPI-SP114
❑ 94UppDecSPIDC-SP114
❑ 95CanGamNHLP-101
❑ 95ColCho-228
❑ 95ColChoPC-228
❑ 95ColChoPCP-228
❑ 95Don-83
❑ 95DonEli-2
❑ 95DonEliDCS-2
❑ 95DonEliDCU-2
❑ 95Emo-56
❑ 95Fin-69
❑ 95FinnSemWC-57
❑ 95FinRef-69
❑ 95ImpSti-41
❑ 95Lea-228
❑ 95Met-48
❑ 95ParInt-64
❑ 95ParInt-252
❑ 95ParIntAS-2
❑ 95ParIntEl-64
❑ 95ParIntEl-252
❑ 95ParIntPTP-PP24
❑ 95Pin-180
❑ 95PinArtP-180
❑ 95PinGloG-23
❑ 95PinRinC-180
❑ 95PlaOneoOne-146
❑ 95ProMag-103
❑ 95Sco-51
❑ 95ScoBlaIce-51
❑ 95ScoBlaIceAP-51
❑ 95SkyImp-55
❑ 95SP-42
❑ 95StaClu-129
❑ 95StaCluMOMS-129
❑ 95SweGloWC-9
❑ 95SweUppDE-239
❑ 95Top-107
❑ 95TopOPCI-107
❑ 95UppDec-34
❑ 95UppDecElelce-34
❑ 95UppDecElelceG-34
❑ 95UppDecNHLAS-AS7
❑ 95UppDecPHE-H36
❑ 95UppDecPreH-H36
❑ 95UppDecSpeE-SE29
❑ 95UppDecSpeEdiG-SE29
❑ 96ColCho-86
❑ 96ColChoMVP-UD33
❑ 96ColChoMVPG-UD33
❑ 96Don-119
❑ 96DonPrePro-119
❑ 96Fla-28
❑ 96FlaBlu-28
❑ 96FlePic-34
❑ 96Lea-75
❑ 96LeaPreP-75
❑ 96MetUni-48
❑ 96NHLProSTA-103
❑ 96Pin-28
❑ 96PinArtP-28
❑ 96PinFan-FC12
❑ 96PinFoi-28
❑ 96PinPreS-28
❑ 96PinRinC-28
❑ 96Sco-176
❑ 96ScoArtPro-176
❑ 96ScoDeaCAP-176
❑ 96ScoGolB-176
❑ 96ScoSpeAP-176
❑ 96SkyImp-37
❑ 96SkyImpB-13
❑ 96SP-52
❑ 96StaCluMO-19
❑ 96Sum-112
❑ 96SumArtP-112
❑ 96SumIce-112
❑ 96SumMet-112
❑ 96SumPreS-112
❑ 96SweSemW-45
❑ 96SweSemWNS-NS5
❑ 96TeaOut-51
❑ 96Ult-53
❑ 96UltGolM-53
❑ 96UltPow-12
❑ 96UltPowBL-8
❑ 96UppDec-56
❑ 96UppDecBD-50
❑ 96UppDecBDG-50
❑ 96UppDecGN-X22
❑ 97ColCho-81
❑ 97ColChoSta-SQ5
❑ 97DonLim-146
❑ 97DonLimExp-146
❑ 97DonPri-43
❑ 97DonPriSoA-43
❑ 97EssOlyHH-45
❑ 97EssOlyHHF-45
❑ 97Pac-78
❑ 97PacCop-78
❑ 97PacCroR-47
❑ 97PacCroREG-47
❑ 97PacCroRIB-47
❑ 97PacCroRS-47
❑ 97PacEmeGre-78
❑ 97PacIceB-78
❑ 97PacInv-49
❑ 97PacInvC-49
❑ 97PacInvEG-49
❑ 97PacInvIB-49
❑ 97PacInvR-49
❑ 97PacInvS-49
❑ 97PacOme-83
❑ 97PacOmeC-83
❑ 97PacOmeDG-83
❑ 97PacOmeEG-83
❑ 97PacOmeG-83
❑ 97PacOmeGFDCC-6
❑ 97PacOmeIB-83
❑ 97PacPar-67
❑ 97PacParC-67
❑ 97PacParDG-67
❑ 97PacParEG-67
❑ 97PacParIB-67
❑ 97PacParRed-67
❑ 97PacParSil-67
❑ 97PacRed-78
❑ 97PacRev-47
❑ 97PacRevC-47
❑ 97PacRevE-47
❑ 97PacRevIB-47
❑ 97PacRevR-47
❑ 97PacRevS-47
❑ 97PacSil-78
❑ 97PinCer-75
❑ 97PinCerMB-75
❑ 97PinCerMG-75
❑ 97PinCerMR-75
❑ 97PinCerR-75
❑ 97PinIns-91
❑ 97PinTotCMPG-75
❑ 97PinTotCPB-75
❑ 97PinTotCPG-75
❑ 97PinTotCPR-75
❑ 97PosPin-14
❑ 97Sco-182
❑ 97ScoRedW-4
❑ 97ScoRedWPla-4
❑ 97ScoRedWPre-4
❑ 97SPAut-53
❑ 97SPAutSotT-NL
❑ 97UppDec-267
❑ 97UppDecBD-119
❑ 97UppDecBDDD-119
❑ 97UppDecBDPC-PC19
❑ 97UppDecBDPCDD-PC19
❑ 97UppDecBDPCM-PC19
❑ 97UppDecBDPCQD-PC19
❑ 97UppDecBDPCTD-PC19
❑ 97UppDecBDQD-119
❑ 97UppDecBDTD-119
❑ 97UppDecGDM-267
❑ 97UppDecIce-5
❑ 97UppDecIceP-5
❑ 97UppDecILL-L10C
❑ 97UppDecILL2-L10C
❑ 97UppDecIPS-5
❑ 97UppDecSG-SG45
❑ 97UppDecTSS-14C
❑ 97Zen-58
❑ 97Zen5x7-55
❑ 97ZenGollmp-55
❑ 97ZenSilImp-55
❑ 97ZenZGol-58
❑ 97ZenZSil-58
❑ 98Be A PPA-197
❑ 98Be A PPAA-197
❑ 98Be A PPAAF-197
❑ 98Be A PPSE-197
❑ 98Be APG-197
❑ 98BowBes-47
❑ 98BowBesAR-47
❑ 98BowBesMIF-F8
❑ 98BowBesMIFAR-F8
❑ 98BowBesMIFR-F8
❑ 98BowBesR-47
❑ 98BowBesSBB-SB4
❑ 98BowBesSBBAR-SB4
❑ 98BowBesSBBR-SB4
❑ 98Fin-119
❑ 98FinNo P-119
❑ 98FinNo PR-119
❑ 98FinRef-119
❑ 98O-PChr-203
❑ 98O-PChrBM-B6
❑ 98O-PChrBMR-B6
❑ 98O-PChrR-203
❑ 98Pac-5
❑ 98PacAur-65
❑ 98PacAurCF-17
❑ 98PacAurCFC-17
❑ 98PacAurCFIB-17
❑ 98PacAurCFR-17
❑ 98PacAurCFS-17
❑ 98PacCroR-45
❑ 98PacCroRLS-45
❑ 98PacDynI-65
❑ 98PacDynIIB-65
❑ 98PacDynIR-65
❑ 98PacIceB-5
❑ 98PacOmeH-83
❑ 98PacOmeODI-83
❑ 98PacOmeR-83
❑ 98PacPar-78
❑ 98PacParC-78
❑ 98PacParEG-78
❑ 98PacParH-78
❑ 98PacParIB-78
❑ 98PacParS-78
❑ 98PacRed-5
❑ 98PacRev-48
❑ 98PacRevADC-17
❑ 98PacRevIS-48
❑ 98PacRevR-48
❑ 98PacTroW-6
❑ 98SP Aut-32
❑ 98SP AutSotTG-NL
❑ 98SPxFin-33
❑ 98SPxFin-112
❑ 98SPxFinR-33
❑ 98SPxFinR-112
❑ 98SPxFinS-33
❑ 98SPxFinS-112
❑ 98SPXTopP-25
❑ 98SPXTopPF-25
❑ 98SPXTopPR-25
❑ 98SSASotT-NL
❑ 98Top-203
❑ 98TopBoaM-B6
❑ 98TopGolLC1-58
❑ 98TopGolLC1B-58
❑ 98TopGolLC1BOoO-58
❑ 98TopGolLC1OoO-58
❑ 98TopGolLC1R-58
❑ 98TopGolLC1ROoO-58
❑ 98TopGolLC2-58
❑ 98TopGolLC2B-58
❑ 98TopGolLC2BOoO-58
❑ 98TopGolLC2OoO-58
❑ 98TopGolLC2R-58
❑ 98TopGolLC2ROoO-58
❑ 98TopGolLC3-58
❑ 98TopGolLC3B-58
❑ 98TopGolLC3BOoO-58
❑ 98TopGolLC3OoO-58
❑ 98TopGolLC3R-58
❑ 98TopGolLC3ROoO-58
❑ 98TopMysFB-M15
❑ 98TopMysFBR-M15
❑ 98TopMysFG-M15
❑ 98TopMysFGR-M15
❑ 98TopMysFS-M15
❑ 98TopMysFSR-M15
❑ 98TopO-P-203
❑ 98UC-77
❑ 98UC-233
❑ 98UD ChoPCR-77
❑ 98UD ChoPCR-233
❑ 98UD ChoR-77
❑ 98UD ChoR-233
❑ 98UppDec-83
❑ 98UppDecBD-31
❑ 98UppDecDD-31
❑ 98UppDecE-83
❑ 98UppDecE1o1-83
❑ 98UppDecFF-FF29
❑ 98UppDecFF-FF29
❑ 98UppDecFFQ1-FF29
❑ 98UppDecFFQ2-FF29
❑ 98UppDecGR-83
❑ 98UppDecM-70
❑ 98UppDecMGS-70
❑ 98UppDecMSS-70
❑ 98UppDecMSS-70
❑ 98UppDecQD-31
❑ 98UppDecTD-31
❑ 99Pac-143
❑ 99PacAur-51
❑ 99PacAurPD-51
❑ 99PacCop-143
❑ 99PacGol-143
❑ 99PacIceB-143
❑ 99PacPreD-143
❑ 99SP AutPS-32
❑ 99UppDecM-72
❑ 99UppDecMGS-72
❑ 99UppDecMSS-72
❑ 99UppDecMSS-72
❑ 99UppDecRII-NL
❑ 99UppDecRIL1-NL
**Liebsch, Ulrich**
❑ 91SweSemWCS-168
❑ 95GerDELE-69
**Lievers, Brett**
❑ 96ColEdgFL-32
**Lightbody, Quade**
❑ 93PetPet-25
❑ 94DetJrRW-3
❑ 95Sla-9
❑ 95SlaMemC-77
**Liikkanen, Jari**
❑ 94FinnSIS-218
**Liimatainen, Petri**
❑ 89SweSemE-6
❑ 90SweSemE-80
❑ 91SweSemE-5
❑ 92SweSemE-32
❑ 93SweSemE-175
❑ 94SweLeaE-19
❑ 96GerDELE-77
❑ 98GerDELE-20
**Liksiutkin, Viktor**
❑ 74SweHocS-45
**Lilja, Andreas**
❑ 95SweLeaE-259
**Lilja, Karl-Erik**
❑ 65SweCorl-70A
❑ 83SweSemE-81
❑ 84SweSemE-81
❑ 85SwePanS-72
❑ 86SwePanS-65
❑ 87SwePanS-71
❑ 89SweSemE-58
**Lilja, Tomas**
❑ 89SweSemE-155
❑ 90SweSemE-230
❑ 91SweSemE-155
❑ 92SweSemE-184
❑ 93SweSemE-154
❑ 94SweLeaE-227
**Lilley, John**
❑ 91UppDecCWJC-70
❑ 93Pow-510
❑ 93StaCluTUSA-13
❑ 93StaCluTUSA-14
❑ 93TopPreTUSA-8
❑ 93Ult-490
❑ 94ClaAut-NNO
❑ 94Don-260
❑ 94DucCarJr-17
❑ 94FinnJaaK-130
❑ 94Fle-6
❑ 94Lea-178
❑ 94OPCPre-499
❑ 94OPCPreSE-499
❑ 94Par-8
❑ 94ParGol-8
❑ 94Sco-228
❑ 94ScoGol-228
❑ 94ScoPla-228
❑ 94ScoPlaTS-228
❑ 94Sel-191
❑ 94SelGol-191
❑ 94StaClu-139
❑ 94StaCluFDI-139
❑ 94StaCluMOMS-139
❑ 94StaCluSTWC-139
❑ 94TopPre-499
❑ 94TopPreSE-499
❑ 94Ult-251
❑ 94UppDec-165
❑ 94UppDecElelce-165
❑ 95FinnSemWC-111
❑ 98GerDELE-59
**Lilley, Les**
❑ 52JunBluT-140
**Lillie, Jeff**
❑ 93KitRan-25
**Lillie, Shawn**
❑ 90RicRen-8
❑ 91KnoChe-12
**Lilljebjorn, Ake**
❑ 83SweSemE-52
❑ 84SweSemE-51
❑ 85SwePanS-48
❑ 86SwePanS-30
❑ 87SwePanS-5
❑ 89SweSemE-2
❑ 90SweSemE-27
❑ 91SweSemE-277
❑ 92SweSemE-150
❑ 93SweSemE-123
❑ 94SweLeaE-102
❑ 94SweLeaECS-6
❑ 96GerDELE-270
**Lilyholm, Len**
❑ 72FigSaiPos-12
❑ 72SweSemWC-125
**Limatainen, P.**
❑ 95GerDELE-226
**Lind, Juha**
❑ 93FinnSIS-24
❑ 94FinnSIS-49
❑ 94FinnSIS-153
❑ 94FinnSISH-1
❑ 95FinnSemWC-235
❑ 95FinnSIS-50
❑ 95FinnSISLLG-8
❑ 96FinnSISR-186
❑ 97DonPre-164
❑ 97DonPreCttC-164
❑ 97Lea-160
❑ 97LeaFraMat-160
❑ 97LeaFraMDC-160
❑ 97PacOme-72
❑ 97PacOmeC-72
❑ 97PacOmeDG-72
❑ 97PacOmeEG-72
❑ 97PacOmeG-72
❑ 97PacOmeIB-72
❑ 97Pin-2
❑ 97PinArtP-2
❑ 97PinPrePBB-2
❑ 97PinPrePBC-2
❑ 97PinPrePBM-2
❑ 97PinPrePBY-2
❑ 97PinPrePFC-2
❑ 97PinPrePFM-2

□ 98Pac-212
□ 98PacIceB-212
□ 98PacRed-212
□ 99Pac-259
□ 99PacCop-259
□ 99PacGol-259
□ 99PacIceB-259
□ 99PacPreD-259
**Lindgren, Niclas**
□ 84SweSemE-236
□ 85SwePanS-235
□ 86SwePanS-262
□ 87SwePanS-248
**Lindgren, Peter**
□ 84SweSemE-128
□ 85SwePanS-75
**Lindgren, Terry**
□ 93RedDeeR-12
□ 95RedDeeR-10
□ 96LouRiv-8
□ 97LouRivF-5
**Lindgren, Tommie**
□ 67SweHoc-67
□ 72SweHocS-227
□ 73SweHocS-230
□ 73SweWorCS-230
**Lindgren, Tore**
□ 89SweSemE-244
□ 90SweSemE-157
□ 91SweSemE-261
**Lindh, Fredrik**
□ 92SweSemE-355
□ 94SweLeaE-201
**Lindh, Mats**
□ 72SweHocS-16
□ 72SweHocS-296
□ 73SweHocS-153
□ 73SweWorCS-153
□ 74SweHocS-242
□ 74SweSemHVS-25
**Lindh, Patrik**
□ 89SweSemE-238
**Lindh, Rune**
□ 67SweHoc-36
**Lindholm, Jan**
□ 83SweSemE-31
□ 84SweSemE-30
□ 85SwePanS-28
**Lindholm, Mikael**
□ 86SwePanS-51
□ 89KinSmo-3
□ 90ProAHLIHL-351
□ 91SweSemE-40
□ 92SweSemE-73
□ 95SweLeaE-248
□ 95SweUppDE-124
**Lindkvist, Gunnar**
□ 71SweHocS-86
**Lindkvist, Lennart**
□ 67SweHoc-207
**Lindman, Mikael**
□ 86SwePanS-225
□ 89SweSemE-33
□ 90SweSemE-180
□ 91SweSemE-34
□ 92SweSemE-54
□ 93SweSemE-29
□ 94SweLeaE-37
□ 95SweLeaE-178
□ 95SweUppDE-21
**Lindmark, Orjan**
□ 84SweSemE-157
□ 85SwePanS-139
□ 86SwePanS-147
□ 87SwePanS-153
□ 89SweSemE-130
□ 90SweSemE-208
□ 91SweSemE-136
□ 92SweSemE-159
□ 93SweSemE-129
□ 94SweLeaE-124
□ 95SweLeaE-64
□ 95SweUppDE-98
□ 98GerDELE-52
**Lindmark, Peter**
□ 82SweSemHVS-1
□ 84SweSemE-99
□ 85SwePanS-91
□ 85SwePanS-115
□ 85SwePanS-116
□ 86SwePanS-84
□ 87SwePanS-89
□ 89SweSemWCS-3
□ 90SweSemE-125
□ 91SweSemE-176
□ 91SweSemE-337
□ 91SweSemWCS-27
□ 92SweSemE-199
□ 93SweSemE-170
□ 94SweLeaE-75
□ 94SweLeaECS-1
□ 95SweLeaE-257
□ 95SweLeaEC-4
**Lindquist, Fredrik**
□ 91Cla-44
□ 91SweSemE-72
□ 91UltDra-39
□ 92SweSemE-97
□ 93SweSemE-70
□ 94SweLeaE-86
□ 95SweLeaE-189
□ 95SweLeaEG-3
□ 95SweUppDETNA-NA7
□ 98BowBes-122
□ 98BowBesAR-122
□ 98BowBesMIF-F4
□ 98BowBesMIFAR-F4
□ 98BowBesMIFR-F4
□ 98BowBesR-122
□ 98UppDec-270
□ 98UppDecE-270
□ 98UppDecE1o1-270
□ 98UppDecGR-270
**Lindqvist, Kenneth**
□ 87SwePanS-258
**Lindqvist, Roger**
□ 69SweHocS-120
□ 70SweHocS-77
□ 71SweHocS-167
□ 73SweHocS-50
**Lindroos, Jari**
□ 93FinnJyvHS-137
□ 93FinnSIS-154
□ 94FinnSIS-25
□ 94FinnSIS-374
□ 95FinnSIS-186
□ 95FinnSIS-252
□ 95FinnSISL-50
□ 96FinnSISR-51
□ 96FinnSISRMA-9
**Lindros, Brett**
□ 93AlbIntTC-11
□ 93KinFro-23
□ 93OPCPreTC-1
□ 93Pin-NNO
□ 93Pin-NNO
□ 93Pow-486
□ 93Ult-466
□ 94BeAPla-R153
□ 94ClaProP-204
□ 94ClaProPIH-LP17
□ 94Fin-9
□ 94FinBowB-R10
□ 94FinBowBR-R10
□ 94FinnJaaK-106
□ 94FinRef-9
□ 94FinSupTW-9
□ 94Fla-104
□ 94Fle-125
□ 94FleRooS-7
□ 94Lea-445
□ 94LeaLim-50
□ 94LeaPhe-2
□ 94McDUppD-McD34
□ 94OPCPre-384
□ 94OPCPre-514
□ 94OPCPreSE-384
□ 94OPCPreSE-514
□ 94ParSE-SE109
□ 94ParSEG-SE109
□ 94ParSEV-36
□ 94Pin-257
□ 94Pin-478
□ 94PinArtP-257
□ 94PinArtP-478
□ 94PinRinC-257
□ 94PinRinC-478
□ 94PinRooTP-11
□ 94ScoTeaC-CT24
□ 94ScoTopRR-3
□ 94Sel-178
□ 94SelGol-178
□ 94SelYouExp-YE12
□ 94SP-70
□ 94SPDieCut-70
□ 94SPPre-10
□ 94SPPreDC-10
□ 94TopPre-384
□ 94TopPre-514
□ 94TopPreSE-384
□ 94TopPreSE-514
□ 94Ult-327
□ 94UltPro-5
□ 94UppDec-240
□ 94UppDec-537
□ 94UppDec-551
□ 94UppDecEleIce-240
□ 94UppDecEleIce-537
□ 94UppDecEleIce-551
□ 94UppDecPC-C7
□ 94UppDecPCEG-C7
□ 94UppDecPCES-C7
□ 94UppDecSPI-SP136
□ 94UppDecSPIDC-SP136
□ 95CanGamNHLP-171
□ 95ColCho-129
□ 95ColChoPC-129
□ 95ColChoPCP-129
□ 95Don-174
□ 95Emo-105
□ 95FinnSemWC-101
□ 95Lea-15
□ 95LeaLim-86
□ 95McDPin-MCD-33
□ 95ParInt-133
□ 95ParIntEl-133
□ 95PinFulC-7
□ 95PlaOneoOne-63
□ 95PlaOneoOne-171
□ 95ProMag-56
□ 95Sco-14
□ 95ScoBlaIce-14
□ 95ScoBlaIceAP-14
□ 95ScoChelt-3
□ 95SelCer-61
□ 95SelCerMG-61
□ 95SkyImp-102
□ 95SkyImpNHLF-12
□ 95StaClu-108
□ 95StaCluMOMS-108
□ 95Sum-104
□ 95SumArtP-104
□ 95SumIce-104
□ 95Top-41
□ 95TopOPCI-41
□ 95Ult-95
□ 95Ult-267
□ 95UltGolM-95
□ 95UppDec-82
□ 95UppDec-257
□ 95UppDecEleIce-82
□ 95UppDecEleIce-257
□ 95UppDecEleIceG-82
□ 95UppDecEleIceG-257
□ 95UppDecSpeE-SE54
□ 95UppDecSpeEdiG-SE54
□ 95Zen-84
□ 96NHLProSTA-56
**Lindros, Eric**
□ 897thInnSOHL-1
□ 897thInnSOHL-188
□ 897thInnSOHL-195
□ 897thInnSOHL-196
□ 89OshGen-1
□ 89OshGenP-31
□ 907thInnSMC-88
□ 907thInnSMC-99
□ 907thInnSOHL-1
□ 90Sco-330C
□ 90Sco-440A
□ 90Sco-440C
□ 90Sco-B1
□ 90Sco-B2
□ 90Sco-B3
□ 90Sco-B4
□ 90Sco-B5
□ 90ScoCan-330C
□ 90ScoCan-440A
□ 90ScoCan-440C
□ 90ScoCan-B1
□ 90ScoCan-B2
□ 90ScoCan-B3
□ 90ScoCan-B4
□ 90ScoCan-B5
□ 90ScoRoo-88T
□ 90ScoYouS-40
□ 90UppDec-451
□ 90UppDec-473
□ 90UppDecF-473
□ 917thInnSCHLAW-1
□ 917thInnSCHLAW-8
□ 917thInnSCHLAW-10
□ 917thInnSMC-96
□ 917thInnSMC-119
□ 91Cla-1
□ 91ClaPromo-1
□ 91OshGen-21
□ 91OshGenS-15
□ 91Pin-365
□ 91PinFre-365
□ 91ScoAme-354
□ 91ScoAme-355
□ 91ScoAme-356
□ 91ScoCan-329
□ 91ScoCan-330
□ 91ScoCan-384
□ 91ScoCan-385
□ 91ScoEriL-1
□ 91ScoEriL-2
□ 91ScoEriL-3
□ 91ScoHotC-1
□ 91ScoRoo-88T
□ 91ScoYouS-30
□ 91UppDec-7
□ 91UppDec-9
□ 91UppDecF-7
□ 91UppDecF-9
□ 92Bow-442
□ 92FlyJCP-15
□ 92FlyUppDS-11
□ 92FlyUppDS-31
□ 92FlyUppDS-42
□ 92JofKoh-4
□ 92OPCPre-102
□ 92OPCPreTR-1
□ 92PanSti-P
□ 92PanStiFre-P
□ 92Par-128
□ 92ParChePH-CP6
□ 92ParEmel-128
□ 92Pin-88
□ 92Pin-236
□ 92PinAmePP-1
□ 92PinEriL-1
□ 92PinEriL-2
□ 92PinEriL-3
□ 92PinEriL-4
□ 92PinEriL-5
□ 92PinEriL-6
□ 92PinEriL-7
□ 92PinEriL-8
□ 92PinEriL-9
□ 92PinEriL-10
□ 92PinEriL-11
□ 92PinEriL-12
□ 92PinEriL-13
□ 92PinEriL-14
□ 92PinEriL-15
□ 92PinEriL-16
□ 92PinEriL-17
□ 92PinEriL-18
□ 92PinEriL-19
□ 92PinEriL-20
□ 92PinEriL-21
□ 92PinEriL-22
□ 92PinEriL-23
□ 92PinEriL-24
□ 92PinEriL-25
□ 92PinEriL-26
□ 92PinEriL-27
□ 92PinEriL-28
□ 92PinEriL-29
□ 92PinEriL-30
□ 92PinFre-88
□ 92PinFre-236
□ 92PinTea2-1
□ 92PinTea2F-1
□ 92PinTeaP-5
□ 92PinTeaPF-5
□ 92ProSet-236
□ 92Sco-432
□ 92Sco-550
□ 92Sco-NNO
□ 92ScoCan-432
□ 92ScoCan-550
□ 92ScoCanO-1
□ 92ScoYouS-1
□ 92SeaPat-38
□ 92StaClu-501
□ 92Top-529
□ 92TopGol-529G
□ 92Ult-157
□ 92UppDec-88
□ 92UppDec-470
□ 92UppDecCC-CC6
□ 92UppDecGHS-G14
□ 92UppDecWJG-WG12
□ 93Don-242
□ 93DonEli-4
□ 93DonIceKin-9
□ 93DonSpeP-Q
□ 93KenStaLA-8
□ 93KenStaLC-7
□ 93Kra-15
□ 93Kra-57
□ 93Lea-233
□ 93LeaGolR-3
□ 93LeaHatTA-7
□ 93LeaStuS-10
□ 93OPCPre-121
□ 93OPCPre-310
□ 93OPCPreBG-12
□ 93OPCPreF-3
□ 93OPCPreG-121
□ 93OPCPreG-310
□ 93PanSti-144
□ 93PanSti-E
□ 93Par-236
□ 93Par-416
□ 93ParChePH-D15
□ 93ParEasWesS-E1
□ 93ParEmel-236
□ 93ParEmel-416
□ 93ParFirO-F3
□ 93ParUSACG-G3
□ 93Pin-1
□ 93Pin-AU2
□ 93Pin-NNO
□ 93Pin-NNO
□ 93Pin-NNO
□ 93Pin1S-4
□ 93PinCan-1
□ 93PinCan-AU2
□ 93PinPow-1
□ 93PinTea2-1
□ 93PinTea2C-1
□ 93PinTeaP-11
□ 93PinTeaPC-11
□ 93Pow-183
□ 93PowGam-4
□ 93PowSecYS-5
□ 93Sco-1
□ 93Sco-NNO
□ 93ScoCan-1
□ 93ScoCan-NNO
□ 93ScoDreTea-12
□ 93ScoDynDUS-1
□ 93ScoFra-15
□ 93ScoSam-1
□ 93SeaPat-10
□ 93StaClu-10
□ 93StaCluFDI-10
□ 93StaCluFDIO-10
□ 93StaCluMasP-5
□ 93StaCluMasPW-5
□ 93StaCluO-10
□ 93SweSemWCS-201
□ 93TopPre-121
□ 93TopPre-310
□ 93TopPreBG-13
□ 93TopPreBG-B
□ 93TopPreF-3
□ 93TopPreG-121
□ 93TopPreG-310
□ 93Ult-161
□ 93Ult-249
□ 93UltPreP-5
□ 93UppDec-30
□ 93UppDec-280
□ 93UppDecFH-31
□ 93UppDecLAS-56
□ 93UppDecNB-HB8
□ 93UppDecNR-23
□ 93UppDecPOE-E12
□ 93UppDecSilSka-H3
□ 93UppDecSilSkaG-H3
□ 93UppDecSP-116
□ 94BAPUpCP-UC2
□ 94BeAPla-R106
□ 94BeAPla-R178
□ 94CanGamNHLP-358
□ 94Don-137
□ 94DonDom-1
□ 94DonEliIns-7
□ 94DonIceMas-6
□ 94EASpo-99
□ 94Fin-38
□ 94FinBowB-B16
□ 94FinBowBR-B16
□ 94FinDivFCC-8
□ 94FinnJaaK-88
□ 94FinnJaaK-360
□ 94FinRef-38
□ 94FinSupTW-38
□ 94Fla-129
□ 94FlaCenS-7
□ 94FlaScoP-6
□ 94Fle-157
□ 94FleHea-6
□ 94HocWit-88
□ 94KenStaLA-12
□ 94KenStaLC-7
□ 94Kra-21
□ 94Lea-415
□ 94LeaFirOIce-6
□ 94LeaGolS-11
□ 94LeaLim-58
□ 94LeaLimG-4
□ 94LeaLimI-17
□ 94McDUppD-McD9
□ 94OPCPre-241
□ 94OPCPre-400
□ 94OPCPreSE-241
□ 94OPCPreSE-400
□ 94Par-301
□ 94ParCratGB-17
□ 94ParCratGG-17
□ 94ParCratGR-17
□ 94ParGol-301
□ 94ParSE-SE131
□ 94ParSEG-SE131
□ 94ParVin-V69
□ 94Pin-1
□ 94Pin1HS-1
□ 94PinArtP-1
□ 94PinBoo-BR16
□ 94PinGam-GR16
□ 94PinRinC-1
□ 94PinTeaP-TP8
□ 94PinTeaPDP-TP8
□ 94PinWorEdi-WE14
□ 94PosCerBB-15
□ 94Sco-1
□ 94Sco90PC-12
□ 94ScoChelt-CI1
□ 94ScoDreTea-DT19
□ 94ScoFra-TF17
□ 94ScoGol-1
□ 94ScoHobS-1
□ 94ScoPla-1
□ 94ScoPlaTS-1
□ 94Sel-100
□ 94SelFirLin-5
□ 94SelGol-100
□ 94SP-84
□ 94SPDieCut-84
□ 94SPPre-30
□ 94SPPreDC-30
□ 94StaClu-88
□ 94StaClu-203
□ 94StaCluDD-2
□ 94StaCluDDMO-2
□ 94StaCluFDI-88
□ 94StaCluFDI-203
□ 94StaCluMO-28
□ 94StaCluMOMS-88
□ 94StaCluMOMS-203
□ 94StaCluST-17
□ 94StaCluSTWC-88
□ 94StaCluSTWC-203
□ 94TopFinB-2
□ 94TopFinI-12
□ 94TopPre-241
□ 94TopPre-400
□ 94TopPreGTG-10
□ 94TopPreSE-241
□ 94TopPreSE-400
□ 94Ult-345
□ 94UltAllS-3
□ 94UltPow-5
□ 94UltPreP-6
□ 94UltScoK-6
□ 94UppDec-98
□ 94UppDecEleIce-98
□ 94UppDecNBAP-29
□ 94UppDecPC-C23
□ 94UppDecPCEG-C23
□ 94UppDecPH-H8
□ 94UppDecPH-H23
□ 94UppDecPHEG-H8
□ 94UppDecPHEG-H23
□ 94UppDecPHES-H8
□ 94UppDecPHES-H23
□ 94UppDecPHG-H8
□ 94UppDecPHG-H23
□ 94UppDecPR-R9
□ 94UppDecPR-R28
□ 94UppDecPRE-R9
□ 94UppDecPRE-R28
□ 94UppDecPreRG-R9
□ 94UppDecPreRG-R28
□ 94UppDecSPI-SP149
□ 94UppDecSPIDC-SP149
□ 95BAPLetL-LL14
□ 95Bow-71
□ 95BowAllFoi-71
□ 95BowBes-BB3
□ 95BowBesRef-BB3
□ 95CanGamNHLP-9
□ 95CanGamNHLP-201
□ 95ColCho-57
□ 95ColCho-377
□ 95ColCho-388
□ 95ColChoCTG-C4
□ 95ColChoCTG-C4B
□ 95ColChoCTG-C4C
□ 95ColChoCTGGB-C4
□ 95ColChoCTGGR-C4
□ 95ColChoCTGSB-C4
□ 95ColChoCTGSR-C4
□ 95ColChoPC-57
□ 95ColChoPC-377
□ 95ColChoPC-388
□ 95ColChoPCP-57
□ 95ColChoPCP-377
□ 95ColChoPCP-388
□ 95Don-1
□ 95DonDom-1
□ 95DonEli-88
□ 95DonEli-110
□ 95DonEliCE-1
□ 95DonEliDCS-88
□ 95DonEliDCS-88U
□ 95DonEliDCS-110
□ 95DonEliDCU-88
□ 95DonEliDCU-88U
□ 95DonEliDCU-110
□ 95DonEliIns-8
□ 95DonEliLLS-1E
□ 95DonEliLLS-2E
□ 95DonEliLLS-3E
□ 95DonEliLLS-4E
□ 95DonEliLLS-5E
□ 95DonEliLLS-6E
□ 95DonEliLLS-7E
□ 95DonMar-3
□ 95DonProPoi-13
□ 95Emo-133
□ 95EmoNteP-4
□ 95EmoXce-6
□ 95Fin-1
□ 95Fin-88
□ 95FinnSemWC-94
□ 95FinRef-1
□ 95FinRef-88
□ 95ImpSti-90
□ 95ImpStiDCS-17
□ 95Kra-41
□ 95Kra-72
□ 95Lea-82
□ 95LeaFirOIce-2
□ 95LeaGolS-4
□ 95LeaLim-99
□ 95LeaLimSG-2
□ 95LeaRoaCup-4
□ 95McDPin-MCD-2
□ 95Met-112
□ 95MetIW-7
□ 95MetWin-4
□ 95NHLAcePC-1H
□ 95NHLCooT-9
□ 95NHLCooT-RP9
□ 95ParInt-154
□ 95ParIntCCGS1-1
□ 95ParIntCCGS2-11
□ 95ParIntCCSS1-1
□ 95ParIntCCSS2-11
□ 95ParIntEl-154
□ 95ParIntPTP-PP1
□ 95ParIntPTP-PP10
□ 95ParIntTW-1
□ 95Pin-9
□ 95PinArtP-9
□ 95PinCleS-4
□ 95PinFan-27
□ 95PinRinC-9
□ 95PinRoa2-1
□ 95PlaOneoOne-76
□ 95PlaOneoOne-182
□ 95PlaOneoOne-294
□ 95PosUppD-6
□ 95ProMag-54
□ 95Sco-150
□ 95ScoBlaIce-150
□ 95ScoBlaIceAP-150
□ 95ScoChelt-1
□ 95ScoDreTea-3
□ 95ScoLam-15
□ 95SelCer-15
□ 95SelCerGT-1
□ 95SelCerMG-15
□ 95SkyImp-127
□ 95SkyImpCI-1
□ 95SkyImpIQ-4
□ 95SP-106
□ 95SPHol-FX16
□ 95SPHolSpFX-FX16
□ 95SPStaEto-E21
□ 95SPStaEtoG-E21
□ 95StaClu-181
□ 95StaCluMO-15
□ 95StaCluMOMS-181
□ 95StaCluNem-N1
□ 95StaCluPS-PS2
□ 95Sum-19
□ 95SumArtP-19
□ 95SumGM-5
□ 95SumIce-19
□ 95SumMadH-1
□ 95SweGloWC-88
□ 95SweGloWC-262
□ 95SweGloWC-263
□ 95SweGloWC-264
□ 95Top-1
□ 95Top-327
□ 95TopHomGC-HGC6
□ 95TopMarMPB-1
□ 95TopMysF-M4
□ 95TopMysFR-M4
□ 95TopOPCI-1
□ 95TopOPCI-327
□ 95TopPowL-1PL
□ 95TopPro-PF7
□ 95TopSupSki-40
□ 95TopSupSkiPla-40
□ 95Ult-119
□ 95Ult-392
□ 95UltCreCra-8
□ 95UltGolM-119
□ 95UltPrePiv-4
□ 95UltPrePivGM-4
□ 95UltRedLS-6
□ 95UltRedLSGM-6
□ 95UltUltHP-7
□ 95UltUltV-7
□ 95UppDec-374
□ 95UppDecAGPRW-18
□ 95UppDecEleIce-374
□ 95UppDecEleIceG-374
□ 95UppDecFreFra-F3
□ 95UppDecFreFraJ-F3
□ 95UppDecNHLAS-AS17
□ 95UppDecPHE-H1
□ 95UppDecPRE-R2
□ 95UppDecPRE-R21
□ 95UppDecPRE-R33
□ 95UppDecPRE-R52
□ 95UppDecPreR-R2
□ 95UppDecPreR-R21
□ 95UppDecPreR-R33
□ 95UppDecPreR-R52
□ 95UppDecSpeE-SE148
□ 95UppDecSpeEdiG-SE148
□ 95UppPreHV-H1
□ 95UppPreRP-R33
□ 95UppPreRP-R52
□ 95Zen-6
□ 95ZenZT-7
□ 96BeAPBisITB-3
□ 96BeAPLH-7B
□ 96BeAPLHAut-7B
□ 96BeAPLHAutSil-7B
□ 96ColCho-188
□ 96ColCho-291
□ 96ColCho-335
□ 96ColChoCTG-C28A
□ 96ColChoCTG-C28B
□ 96ColChoCTG-C28C
□ 96ColChoCTGE-CR28
□ 96ColChoCTGEG-CR28
□ 96ColChoCTGG-C28A
□ 96ColChoCTGG-C28B
□ 96ColChoCTGG-C28C
□ 96ColChoSti-S9
□ 96Don-137
□ 96DonCanI-7
□ 96DonCanIGPP-7
□ 96DonCanIOC-11
□ 96DonCanIRPP-7
□ 96DonDom-5
□ 96DonEli-7
□ 96DonEli-149
□ 96DonEliDCS-7
□ 96DonEliDCS-149
□ 96DonEliHTH-*1
□ 96DonEliHTH-*2
□ 96DonEliHTH-*3
□ 96DonEliHTH-*4
□ 96DonEliHTH-*5
□ 96DonEliHTH-*6
□ 96DonEliHTH-NNO
□ 96DonEliHTH-NNO
□ 96DonEliIns-9
□ 96DonEliInsG-9
□ 96DonEliS-8
□ 96DonGoTS-9
□ 96DonHitLis-1
□ 96DonHitLis-P1
□ 96DonPrePro-137
□ 96DurAllT-DC6
□ 96Fla-70
□ 96FlaBluI-70
□ 96FlaHotN-8
□ 96FlaNowAT-3
□ 96Fle-82
□ 96FleArtRos-14
□ 96FlePCC-1
□ 96FlePea-8
□ 96FlePic-4
□ 96FlePicDL-1
□ 96FlePicF5-28
□ 96FlyPos-15
□ 96HocGreC-14
□ 96HocGreCG-14
□ 96KraUppD-7
□ 96KraUppD-37
□ 96KraUppD-58
□ 96KraUppD-68
□ 96Lea-148
□ 96Lea-240
□ 96LeaFirOI-8
□ 96LeaLeaAL-10
□ 96LeaLeaALP-P10
□ 96LeaLim-47
□ 96LeaLim-NNO

**Lindsay, Evan**
96PriAlbR-11
96PriAlbROC-13
98BowCHL-61
98BowCHLGA-61
98BowCHLOI-61
98BowChrC-61
98BowChrCGA-61
98BowChrCGAR-61
98BowChrCOI-61
98BowChrCOIR-61
98BowChrCR-61
**Lindsay, Jeff**
90KnoChe-105
**Lindsay, Ryan**
93OshGen-25
95Sla-253
**Lindsay, Scott**
90ForSasTra-9
917thInnSWHL-322
**Lindsay, Ted**
44BeeGro2P-112
44BeeGro2P-186
48ExhCan-45
51Par-56
52Par-87
52RoyDesH-5
53Par-52
54Par-46
54Top-51
57Top-21
58Top-63
59Top-6
64BeeGro3P-82
64CocCap-48
64Top-82
76OldTim-10
83HalFP-L10
85HalFC-151
91Kra-70
91UltOriS-70
91UltOriS-94
91UltOriSF-70
91UltOriSF-94
92HalFL-19
92ParParR-PR31
92ZelMasH-3
92ZelMasoHS-3
93ParParR-PR49
94ParMisL-44
94ParMisL-140
94ParTalR-64
97PinBee-60
97PinBeeGOA-60
97PinBeeGP-60
99RetHoc-97
99UppDecCL-21
99UppDecCLACT-AC9
99UppDecCLCLC-21
99UppDecEotG-E8
99UppDecES-5
99UppDecRG-97
99UppDecRII-TL
99UppDecRIL1-TL
99UppDecRP-97
**Lindskog, Lars**
84SweSemE-132
**Lindstahl, Sam**
84SweSemE-220
85SwePanS-221
86SwePanS-246
87SwePanS-213
89SweSemE-192
90SweSemE-76
91SweSemE-3
92SweSemE-27
94SweLeaE-11
95SweUppDE1DS-DS9
**Lindstedt, Johan**
90SweSemE-294
91SweSemE-74
**Lindster, Thomas**
85SwePanS-195
86SwePanS-132
87SwePanS-121
**Lindstrom, Billy**
70SweHocS-255
**Lindstrom, Curt**
95FinnKarWCL-10
**Lindstrom, Eje**
65SweCorl-174
**Lindstrom, Evert**
71SweHocS-315
72SweHocS-297
73SweHocS-150
73SweWorCS-150
**Lindstrom, Orjan**
71SweHocS-253
72SweHocS-235
73SweHocS-236
73SweWorCS-236
74SweHocS-244
**Lindstrom, Roger**
83SweSemE-12
84SweSemE-11
85SwePanS-12
**Lindstrom, Seppo**
69SweHocS-375
69SweWorC-20
70SweHocS-296
71SweHocS-62
72SweHocS-108
72SweSemWC-73
74SweHocS-107
74SweSemHVS-77

**Lindstrom, Soren**
65SweCorl-158
**Lindstrom, Sven Bertil**
65SweHocS-64
69SweHocS-81
71SweHocS-127
73SweHocS-217
73SweWorCS-217
**Lindstrom, Willy**
71SweHocS-316
72SweHocS-298
73SweHocS-22
73SweHocS-149
73SweWorCS-22
73SweWorCS-149
74SweHocS-243
74SweSemHVS-17
77OPCWHA-39
78JetPos-11
79JetPos-12
79OPC-368
80JetPos-11
80OPC-142
80Top-142
81JetPos-9
81OPC-368
82Jet-12
82OPC-384
82OPCSti-209
82PosCer-21
830ilMcD-17
83OPC-35
83OPCSti-91
83Vac-32
840ilRedR-19
840ilTeal-14
84OPC-250
84OPCSti-260
85OPC-217
85OPCSti-226
86OPC-232
86OPCSti-227
86PenKod-15
87SwePanS-58
880ilTenAnn-23
89SweSemE-39
**Linesman, Ted**
83KinCan-8
84KinCan-27
85KinCan-27
86KinCan-29
**Linford, Dave**
88KamBla-16
**Ling, David**
93KinFro-16
95Cla-86
95ColEdgI-77
95St.JohF-12
96ColEdgFL-10
97ScoCan-16
97ScoCanPla-16
98KanCitB-12
98ScoCanPre-16
**Ling, Jamie**
91AirCanSJHL-A29
91AirCanSJHLAS-25
91AirCanSJHLAS-49
**Lingemann, Boris**
95GerDELE-90
96GerDELE-288
**Lingren, Steve**
917thInnSWHL-61
94DayBom-16
95DayBom-6
95DayBom-24
96DayBom-3
**Link, Brad**
99WicThu-12
**Linna, Kaj**
95Cla-76
**Linnell, Derek**
92Rallce-7
92Rallce-24
93Rallce-10
94Rallce-9
95AlaGolKin-11
**Linnonmaa, Harri**
70SweHocS-305
71SweHocS-67
72SweSemWC-80
74SweHocS-36
74SweSemHVS-85
**Linqvist, Roger**
73SweWorCS-50
**Linse, Martin**
83SweSemE-93
**Linseman, Ken**
79OPC-241
79Top-241
80OPC-24
80Top-24
81OPC-244
81OPCSti-176
81Top-E107
82OilRedR-13
82OPC-115
82OPCSti-112
82PosCer-24
830ilDol-H17
830ilMcD-1
83OPC-36
83OPCSti-102
83PufSti-6
83Vac-33

84OPC-7
87PanSti-16
88BruPos-11
88BruSpoA-11
880ilTenAnn-47
88OPC-118
88PanSti-211
88Top-118
89BruSpoA-14
89OPC-62
89OPCSti-26
89PanSti-190
89Top-62
900ilIGA-12
90OPC-345
90PanSti-111
90ProSet-219
90ProSet-444
90Sco-380
90ScoCan-380
90ScoRoo-95T
90Top-345
90TopTif-345
91Bow-105
910ilPanTS-11
91OPC-146
91ScoAme-359
91ScoCan-214
91ScoCan-622
91StaClu-299
91Top-146
**Linseman, Mike**
81KinCan-12
**Linseman, Steve**
83BraAle-15
84BelBul-18
**Linteau, Richard**
80QueRem-15
**Lipensky, Ales**
96CzeAPSE-282
**Lipina, Petr**
96CzeAPSE-71
**Lipsett, Chris**
91BriColJHL-161
92ClaKni-9
96RoaExp-23
**Liptrott, Peter**
86KinCan-8
87KinCan-8
94BraSmo-4
96LouRiv-4
**LiPuma, Chris**
88KitRan-25
89KitRan-25
907thInnSMC-44
907thInnSOHL-295
90KitRan-24
917thInnSOHL-94
93ClaProPro-118
93Don-493
93LigSealR-21
93Pin-208
93PinCan-208
93Pow-446
93Ult-178
93UltAllRoo-5
94ClaProP-20
94Ult-372
96KenTho-12
**Lirette, Noel**
69ColChe-10
**Liscombe, Carl**
34BeeGro1P-112
390PCV3011-74
**Liska, Jaroslav**
95CzeAPSE-52
96CzeAPSE-238
**Lisko, Craig**
99FerStaB-20
**Listwan, Darryn**
91AirCanSJHL-B32
91AirCanSJHL-E14
**Lisy, Peter**
85KitRan-20
86LonKni-18
**Litke, Dane**
98FloEve-12
**Litma, Lasse**
79PanSti-169
81SweSemHVS-22
82SweSemHVS-35
91Bow-290
91CapJun5-19
91CapKod-18
910PC-154
91Par-196
91ParFre-196
91Pin-169
91PinFre-169
91ProSetPlaPC-PC16
91ScoAme-99
91ScoCan-99
91StaClu-10
91Top-154
91UppDec-259
91UppDecF-259
92BluUDBB-4
92Sco-368
92ScoCan-368
92Top-307
92TopGol-307G
**Livernoche, Patrick**
93DruVol-19
**Ljungberg, Christer**
91SweSemE-248
**Ljungberg, Thomas**

59Top-61
60ShiCoi-62
60Top-21
61Par-28
61ShiCoi-71
62Par-12
62ShiMetC-18
63ChePho-32
63Par-6
63Par-66
64BeeGro3P-173
91UltOriS-58
91UltOriSF-58
93ParParR-PR66
94ParMisL-24
**Liukka, Simo**
96FinnSISR-114
**Lius, Joni**
93FinnJyvHS-142
93FinnSIS-152
94FinnSIS-17
95FinnSIS-64
95FinnSISL-49
**Liut, Mike**
80OPC-31
80Top-31
81OPC-289
81OPC-301
810PCSti-129
81OPCSti-153
81PosSta-13
81Top-20
81Top-W128
82OPC-306
82OPCSti-196
82PosCer-17
830PC-309
830PC-316
830PCSti-129
83PufSti-14
840PC-187
840PCSti-57
84Top-132
857ECreCar-7
85OPC-88
85OPCSti-169
85Top-88
85WhaJunW-10
86OPC-133
860PCSti-52
86Top-133
86WhaJunT-14
87OPC-152
87OPCMin-24
87OPCSti-121
870PCSti-209
87PanSti-38
87Top-152
87TopStiIns-8
87WhaJunBK-13
88OPC-127
88OPCMin-20
880PCSti-263
88PanSti-235
88Top-127
88WhaJunGR-10
89CapKod-1
89OPC-97
89OPC-317
89OPCSti-267
89Top-97
89WhaJunM-14
90Bow-66
90BowTif-66
90CapKod-15
90CapPos-15
90CapSmo-14
90Kra-31
900PC-44
90PanSti-165
90ProSet-316
90Sco-68
90ScoCan-68
90ScoCan-354
90ScoHotRS-32
90Top-44
90TopTif-44
90UppDec-127
90UppDecF-127

85SwePanS-190
86SwePanS-124
87SwePanS-243
89SweSemE-230
90SweSemE-112
91SweSemE-119
92SweSemE-148
93SweSemE-119
94SweLeaE-64
**Ljusterang, Per**
89SweSemE-154
90SweSemE-227
91SweSemE-157
92SweSemE-259
93SweSemE-224
**Loach, Lonnie**
88FliSpi-12
88ProIHL-101
89ProIHL-60
90ProAHLIHL-538
91ProAHLCHL-120
92Cla-95
92Par-305
92ParEmel-305
92Ult-146
92Ult-309
92UppDec-466
93Pow-7
95ColEdgI-123
96ClaGol-95
**Loach, Mike**
93WinSpi-11
95Sla-288
**Locas, Jacques**
45QuaOatP-90
48ExhCan-13
51LavDaiQSHL-95
51LavDaiS-57
52St.LawS-81
750PCWHA-129
75StiKah-7
76StiKah-5
**Lochead, Billy**
74NHLActSta-97
740PCNHL-318
750PCNHL-103
75Top-103
760PCNHL-122
76Top-122
770PCNHL-212
77Top-212
780PC-122
78Top-122
79OPC-301
94GerDELE-343
95GerDELE-308
96GerDELE-91
**Locke, Steve**
88NiaFalT-23
**Locker, Derek**
93MinDul-18
**Lockett, Ken**
74CanuRoyB-11
74NHLActSta-282
75CanuRoyB-12
76SanDieMW-6
**Lockhart, Tommy**
83HalFP-C8
85HalFC-38
**Locking, Norm**
35DiaMatT2-41
35DiaMatT3-37
35DiaMatTI-40
**Lockridge, Tim**
81IndChe-13
82IndChe-14
**Lockwood, Joe**
88ProIHL-32
**Lococo, Mike**
81SauSteMG-17
82SauSteMG-16
83SauSteMG-15
**Loder, Jeff**
86RoaExp-7
**Lodin, Hans**
86SwePanS-203
87SwePanS-193
89SweSemE-175
90SweSemE-8
91SweSemE-204
92SweSemE-227
93SweSemE-127
94SweLeaE-112
95SweLeaE-63
95SweUppDE-97
**Loen, Matt**
95MadMon-17
**Loeppky, Mark**
91AirCanSJHL-E7
**Loewen, Darcy**
89ProAHL-269
90ProAHLIHL-284
90SabCam-14
91ProAHLCHL-4
91RochAmeDD-10
91RochAmeKod-16
91UppDec-421
91UppDecF-421

93ParEmel-407
93SenKraS-14
93StaCluFDI-318
93StaCluO-318
93TopPre-184
93TopPreG-184
94LasVegThu-12
95LasVegThu-6
96LasVegThu-13
**Loewen, Jamie**
95AlaGolKin-12
**Lofgren, Bengt**
69SweHocS-304
**Lofqvist, William**
67SweHoc-176
69SweHocS-69
70SweHocS-18
71SweHocS-3
71SweHocS-96
72SweHocS-81
73SweHocS-2
73SweHocS-155
73SweWorCS-2
73SweWorCS-155
74SweHocS-147
74SweSemHVS-2
**Lofroth, Shawn**
96AlaGolKin-8
**Lofstedt, Borje**
69SweHocS-87
**Lofstrom, Jonas**
95SweLeaE-169
95SweUppDE-28
**Lofstrom, Per**
95SweLeaE-176
95SweUppDE-25
**Lofthouse, Mark**
80OPC-331
88ProAHL-132
89NewHavN-7
**Logan, Bob**
87SabWonBH-16
88ProAHL-215
**Logan, Dan**
86RegPat-14
**Logan, Dave**
780PC-343
80CanuSIID-14
80CanuTeal-14
80PepCap-112
**Logan, Jim**
52JunBluT-151
**Logan, Tim**
87RegPat-16
**Loges, Al**
93MicWol-13
**Lohko, Timo**
96FinnSISR-113
**Lohman, Lars**
65SweCorl-190
**Loi, Brad**
84RicRiv-10
**Loicq, Paul**
83HalFP-F8
85HalFC-234
**Loikala, Jani-Matti**
95FinnSIS-249
**Loiselle, Claude**
87PanSti-85
88DevCar-17
88PanSti-273
89Nord-27
89NordGenF-21
89NordPol-18
90Bow-175
90BowTif-175
90NordPet-16
90NordTeal-19
90PanSti-151
90ProSet-252
90Sco-207
90ScoCan-207
90UppDec-338
90UppDecF-338
91MapLeaP-22
91NordPanTS-14
91Pin-296
91PinFre-296
91ProSet-493
91ProSetFre-493
91ScoCan-532
92Pin-219
92PinFre-219
92Sco-328
92ScoCan-328
92Top-338
92TopGol-338G
930PCPre-328
930PCPreG-328
93TopPre-328
93TopPreG-328
**Loiselle, Pierre**
98QueRem-12
**Loisette, Jean-Marie**
56QueAce-9
**Lojkin, Alexei**
95FreCan-19
**Loksa, Michal**
95SloPeeWT-14
**Loktev, Konstantin**
73SweHocS-98
73SweWorCS-98
**Lomakin, Andrei**
89SweSemWCS-98

90OPC-472
91FlyJCP-18
910PCIns-40R
91OPCPre-178
91Par-131
91ParFre-131
91Pin-305
91PinFre-305
91ProSetPla-208
91RusStaRA-12
91ScoCan-660
91ScoRoo-110T
91StaPicH-17
91UppDec-518
91UppDecF-518
92Bow-286
92FlyJCP-16
92FlyUppDS-18
92FlyUppDS-43
92OPC-37
92PanSti-193
92PanStiFre-193
92Pin-162
92PinFre-162
92Sco-129
92ScoCan-129
92StaClu-115
92Top-380
92TopGol-380G
92TriFroRWP-3
92TriFroRWP-4
92Ult-372
92UppDec-428
92UppDecES-E17
93Don-128
93Lea-401
930PCPre-82
930PCPreG-82
93PanSti-52
93PanTeal-6
93Par-349
93ParEmel-349
93Pin-360
93PinCan-360
93Pow-96
93Sco-529
93ScoCan-529
93ScoGol-529
93StaClu-57
93StaClu-402
93StaCluFDI-57
93StaCluFDI-402
93StaCluFDIO-57
93StaCluO-57
93StaCluO-402
93SweSemWCS-143
93TopPre-82
93TopPreG-82
93Ult-327
93UppDec-102
94CanGamNHLP-106
94Don-85
94EASpo-52
94FinnJaaK-160
94Lea-302
940PCPreS-177
940PCPreSE-177
94Par-84
94ParGol-84
94Pin-337
94PinArtP-337
94PinRinC-337
94TopPre-177
94TopPreSE-177
94Ult-81
94UppDec-471
94UppDecEleIce-471
95SwiHNL-68
95SweUppDE-39
**Lombardo, Joe**
95Sla-389
95SudWol-3
95SudWolP-12
96SudWolP-15
**Lomow, Boyd**
83BraWheK-13
84BraWheK-21
**Lomow, Byron**
83BraWheK-6
84BraWheK-3
85BraWheK-3
89ProIHL-141
90ProAHLIHL-526
**Loney, Brian**
94ClaProP-217
95ParInt-481
95ParIntEl-481
96SyrCru-17
**Loney, Troy**
83PenCok-14
83PenTealP-21
87PenKod-17
88PanSti-341
89PanSti-319
89PenFoo-13B
900PC-347
90PanSti-138
90ProSet-237
90Sco-371
90ScoCan-371
90Top-347
90TopTif-347
90UppDec-367
90UppDecF-367
91Par-352

Luckner, Harald • 585


❑ 91ParFre-352
❑ 91PenCokE-24
❑ 91PenFoo-7
❑ 91ScoCan-522
❑ 91UppDec-489
❑ 91UppDecF-489
❑ 92PenCokC-11
❑ 92PenFoo-8
❑ 92Sco-348
❑ 92ScoCan-348
❑ 92StaClu-357
❑ 92Top-397
❑ 92TopGol-397G
❑ 92Ult-378
❑ 92UppDec-208
❑ 93Kra-41
❑ 93OPCPre-340
❑ 93OPCPreG-340
❑ 93Par-9
❑ 93ParEmel-9
❑ 93PenSti-5
❑ 93Pin-379
❑ 93PinCan-379
❑ 93PinCap-1
❑ 93PinCapC-1
❑ 93Pow-8
❑ 93Sco-547
❑ 93ScoCan-547
❑ 93ScoGol-547
❑ 93StaClu-395
❑ 93StaCluFDI-395
❑ 93StaCluO-395
❑ 93TopPre-340
❑ 93TopPreG-340
❑ 93Ult-259
❑ 93UppDec-438
❑ 93UppDecSP-2
❑ 94BeAPSig-84
❑ 94EASpo-4
❑ 94Lea-435
❑ 94OPCPre-363
❑ 94OPCPreSE-363
❑ 94Par-5
❑ 94ParGol-5
❑ 94Pin-396
❑ 94PinArtP-396
❑ 94PinRinC-396
❑ 94Sco-67
❑ 94ScoGol-67
❑ 94ScoPla-67
❑ 94ScoPlaTS-67
❑ 94TopPre-363
❑ 94TopPreSE-363
❑ 94UppDec-385
❑ 94UppDecEleIce-385

**Long, Andrew**
❑ 94GueSto-26
❑ 95GueSto5A-7
❑ 95Sla-103
❑ 96GueSto-25
❑ 97GueSto-18
❑ 98BowCHL-17
❑ 98BowCHLGA-17
❑ 98BowCHLOI-17
❑ 98BowChrC-17
❑ 98BowChrCGA-17
❑ 98BowChrCGAR-17
❑ 98BowChrCOI-17
❑ 98BowChrCOIR-17
❑ 98BowChrCR-17

**Long, Barry**
❑ 72OPC-288
❑ 75OPCWHA-69
❑ 75OPCWHA-90
❑ 76OPCWHA-7
❑ 78JetPos-12
❑ 79RedWinP-10
❑ 80JetPos-12
❑ 80OPC-258
❑ 80PepCap-131
❑ 80Top-258
❑ 81OPC-369
❑ 81OPCSti-142
❑ 83Jet-11
❑ 84JetPol-23
❑ 85JetPol-23

**Long, Bill**
❑ 86LonKni-13

**Long, Eric**
❑ 94RalIce-10

**Long, Stan**
❑ 51BufBis-13

**Long, Ted**
❑ 75HamFin-11

**Longauer, Michal**
❑ 917thInnSQMJHL-202

**Longbroek, David**
❑ 92BriColJHL-45

**Longman, Gary**
❑ 69ColChe-11

**Longo, Chris**
❑ 897thInnSOHL-114
❑ 897thInnSOHL-178
❑ 907thInnSOHL-364
❑ 917thInnSOHL-128
❑ 91PetPet-7
❑ 93PorPir-17
❑ 94ClaProP-89
❑ 94PorPir-14
❑ 96SprFal-16

**Longo, Mike**
❑ 90RayJrC-12
❑ 91RayJrC-9

**Longstaff, David**
❑ 97SheSte-8

**Longstaff, Scott**
❑ 91BriColJHL-2

**Longtry, Doc**
❑ 23V1281PauC-57

**Lonn, Anders**
❑ 95SweUppDE1DS-DS12

**Lonn, Mats**
❑ 64SweCorI-8
❑ 65SweCorI-8
❑ 67SweHoc-144
❑ 69SweHocS-156
❑ 70SweHocS-124
❑ 71SweHocS-214
❑ 72SweHocS-191

**Lonnberg, Harri**
❑ 93FinnSIS-225
❑ 94FinnSIS-221
❑ 95FinnSIS-308
❑ 95FinnSISP-4

**Lonsberry, Ross**
❑ 67Top-35
❑ 69OPC-104
❑ 69Top-104
❑ 70EssPowPla-151
❑ 70OPC-37
❑ 70SarProSta-66
❑ 70Top-37
❑ 71OPC-121
❑ 71SarProSta-69
❑ 71Top-121
❑ 71TorSun-120
❑ 72OPC-166
❑ 72SarProSta-166
❑ 72SweSemWC-206
❑ 72Top-112
❑ 73FlyLin-10
❑ 73OPC-36
❑ 73Top-36
❑ 74NHLActSta-199
❑ 74OPCNHL-144
❑ 74Top-144
❑ 75FlyCanDC-12
❑ 75OPCNHL-110
❑ 75Top-110
❑ 76OPCNHL-201
❑ 76Top-201
❑ 77OPCNHL-257
❑ 77Top-257
❑ 78OPC-186
❑ 78Top-186
❑ 79OPC-58
❑ 79Top-58
❑ 80OPC-388
❑ 81OPC-263

**Lonsinger, Bryan**
❑ 92HarCri-19

**Loob, Hakan**
❑ 82SweSemHVS-22
❑ 83Vac-11
❑ 84OPC-229
❑ 84OPCSti-242
❑ 85FlamRedRP-13
❑ 85OPC-184
❑ 86FlamRedR-10
❑ 86KraDra-35
❑ 87FlamRedRP-10
❑ 87FlamRedRP-11
❑ 87OPC-208
❑ 87OPCSti-44
❑ 87PanSti-214
❑ 88OPC-110
❑ 88OPCBoxB-O
❑ 88OPCMin-21
❑ 88OPCSti-94
❑ 88OPCSti-118
❑ 88PanSti-9
❑ 88Top-110
❑ 88TopBoxB-O
❑ 88TopStiIns-3
❑ 89SweSemE-91
❑ 90SweSemE-260
❑ 91SweSemE-92
❑ 91SweSemE-315
❑ 91SweSemE-318
❑ 91SweSemE-325
❑ 91SweSemE-347
❑ 91SweSemWCS-38
❑ 92SweSemE-111
❑ 92SweSemE-337
❑ 92SweSemE-340
❑ 92SweSemE-346
❑ 93SweSemE-84
❑ 93SweSemE-303
❑ 93SweSemWCS-9
❑ 94FinnJaaK-64
❑ 94SweLeaE-39
❑ 94SweLeaEGC-8
❑ 94SweLeaEP-6
❑ 94SweLeaETG-2
❑ 95FinnSemWC-75
❑ 95SweGloWC-52
❑ 95SweGloWC-246
❑ 95SweLeaE-1
❑ 95SweLeaE-305
❑ 95SweLeaEC-3
❑ 95SweLeaEFF-5
❑ 95SweLeaEM-9
❑ 95SweUppDE-64
❑ 95SweUppDE-223
❑ 95SweUppDE-252

**Loob, Jan**
❑ 86SwePanS-267

**Loob, Peter**
❑ 83SweSemE-205
❑ 84FreExp-14
❑ 86SwePanS-261

**Loof, Mattias**
❑ 92SweSemE-171
❑ 93SweSemE-140
❑ 94SweLeaE-247
❑ 95SweLeaE-293
❑ 95SweUppDE-198

**Looney, Shelley**
❑ 94ClaWomOH-W34

**Loong, Arne**
❑ 65SweCorI-63A
❑ 65SweCorI-126B

**Loov, Mats**
❑ 83SweSemE-146
❑ 84SweSemE-166
❑ 85SwePanS-151
❑ 86SwePanS-129
❑ 87SwePanS-120
❑ 89SweSemE-108
❑ 90SweSemE-114
❑ 92SweSemE-266
❑ 93SweSemE-240
❑ 94SweLeaE-93
❑ 94SweLeaETG-10
❑ 95SweLeaE-122
❑ 95SweLeaEFF-11
❑ 95SweUppDE-185

**Lopatka, Geoff**
❑ 92CorBigRed-19
❑ 93CorBigRed-17

**Loponen, Jouni**
❑ 94FinnSIS-286
❑ 95FinnSIS-59
❑ 95FinnSISL-48
❑ 96FinnSISR-58

**Lopresti, Peter (Pete)**
❑ 76OPCNHL-184
❑ 76Top-184
❑ 77OPCNHL-13
❑ 77Top-13
❑ 78OPC-230
❑ 78Top-230
❑ 79OPC-364
❑ 79PanSti-206
❑ 88OilTenAnn-122

**LoPresti, Sam**
❑ 34BeeGro1P-64

**Lord, Adam**
❑ 92BriColJHL-160

**Lord, Lars-Erik**
❑ 90SweSemE-200

**Lord, Philippe**
❑ 96RimOce-17
❑ 96RimOceQPP-16

**Lorentz, Dave**
❑ 897thInnSOHL-109

**Lorentz, Jim**
❑ 70EssPowPla-249
❑ 70OPC-209
❑ 70SarProSta-192
❑ 71OPC-227
❑ 71SabPos-10
❑ 71SarProSta-192
❑ 71Top-13
❑ 71TorSun-239
❑ 72OPC-116
❑ 72SarProSta-36
❑ 72Top-68
❑ 73OPC-75
❑ 73SabBel-2
❑ 73SabPos-4
❑ 73Top-171
❑ 74NHLActSta-48
❑ 74OPCNHL-61
❑ 74Top-61
❑ 75OPCNHL-28
❑ 75Top-28
❑ 76OPCNHL-162
❑ 76Top-162
❑ 77OPCNHL-58
❑ 77Top-58
❑ 78OPC-161
❑ 78Top-161

**Lorentz, Tom**
❑ 85MinDul-20

**Lorenz, Danny**
❑ 91ProAHLCHL-457
❑ 92Ult-345
❑ 93ClaProPro-132
❑ 93Lea-343
❑ 95ColEdgI-113
❑ 96MilAdmBO-14
❑ 98GerDELE-244

**Lorenzo, Johnny**
❑ 907thInnSQMJHL-196
❑ 917thInnSQMJHL-70

**Loretto, Chuck**
❑ 94CenHocL-100

**Lorimer, Bob**
❑ 79IslTrans-10
❑ 79OPC-181
❑ 79Top-181
❑ 80OPC-138
❑ 80Top-138
❑ 81OPC-214
❑ 81RocPos-13
❑ 82OPC-142
❑ 82OPCSti-228
❑ 82PosCer-11
❑ 83OPC-232
❑ 84DevPos-4
❑ 84OPC-114

**Loring, Al**
❑ 88ProAHL-208

**Loring, Brad**
❑ 907thInnSWHL-119
❑ 91BriColJHL-145
❑ 92BriColJHL-36

**Lorrain, Rod**
❑ 34BeeGro1P-165
❑ 37OPCV304E-176
❑ 38QuaOatP-23
❑ 39OPCV3011-23

**Losch, Mike**
❑ 94GerDELE-49
❑ 95GerDELE-43

**Loth, Andreas**
❑ 94GerDELE-257
❑ 95GerDELE-255

**Lotvonen, Kimmo**
❑ 95FinnSIS-301
❑ 96FinnSISR-96

**Loubier, Yves**
❑ 917thInnSQMJHL-274

**Loucks, Bob**
❑ 89LetHur-12
❑ 907thInnSWHL-137
❑ 907thInnSWHL-149
❑ 917thInnSWHL-359
❑ 95TriAme-17

**Loucks, Scott**
❑ 907thInnSWHL-296
❑ 917thInnSWHL-87
❑ 93KamBla-14

**Louder, Greg**
❑ 94WheThu-10

**Loughlin, Clem**
❑ 35DiaMatT4-10

**Loustel, Ron**
❑ 81SasBla-23
❑ 82BraWheK-22

**Louttit, Eddie**
❑ 52JunBluT-11

**Louttit, Paul**
❑ 81Ott67-7
❑ 82Ott67-12

**Lovdal, Orjan**
❑ 95SweGloWC-191

**Love, Brad**
❑ 917thInnSOHL-198

**Love, Dominik**
❑ 94HumHawP-23
❑ 97KinHaw-7

**Love, Tyler**
❑ 96SasBla-15

**Loveday, Lowell**
❑ 83MonAlp-6
❑ 84NovScoO-4

**Lovell, Greg**
❑ 93KinFro-1

**Lovell, John**
❑ 917thInnSOHL-25
❑ 91CorRoy-6
❑ 93GueSto-28
❑ 95Sla-305

**Lovell, Tim**
❑ 93MaiBlaB-52

**Loven, Fredrik**
❑ 95ColCho-351
❑ 95ColChoPC-351
❑ 95ColChoPCP-351
❑ 95SP-188

**Lovgren, Bengt**
❑ 67SweHoc-258
❑ 70SweHocS-209
❑ 71SweHocS-296
❑ 72SweHocS-72
❑ 74SweHocS-250

**Lovsin, Dave**
❑ 91AirCanSJHL-D17
❑ 91AirCanSJHL-D32

**Lovsin, Ken**
❑ 90ProAHLIHL-195
❑ 91BalSki-5
❑ 91ProAHLCHL-557
❑ 93AlbIntTC-12
❑ 93OPCPreTC-4
❑ 93Pow-487
❑ 93Ult-467
❑ 94ScoTeaC-CT16

**Low, Ron**
❑ 72MapLeaP-16
❑ 72OPC-258
❑ 74CapWhiB-17
❑ 74NHLActSta-308
❑ 74OPCNHL-39
❑ 74Top-39
❑ 75OPCNHL-25
❑ 75Top-25
❑ 76OPCNHL-69
❑ 76Top-69
❑ 77OPCNHL-305
❑ 78OPC-237
❑ 78Top-237
❑ 79OPC-348
❑ 80OPC-333
❑ 80PepCap-30
❑ 81OilRedR-30
❑ 82OilRedR-30
❑ 82OPC-112
❑ 82OPCSti-107
❑ 83OPC-233
❑ 84DevPos-30
❑ 84OPC-115
❑ 85NovScoO-25
❑ 88OilTenAnn-36
❑ 90OilIGA-13
❑ 91OilIGA-28
❑ 92OilIGA-28

**Lowe, Darren**
❑ 87FliSpi-12
❑ 88ProAHL-152
❑ 89ProIHL-45
❑ 90ProAHLIHL-310

**Lowe, Jason**
❑ 91BriColJHL-28

**Lowe, Kevin**
❑ 79OilPos-13
❑ 80PepCap-31
❑ 81OilRedR-4
❑ 81OPC-117
❑ 82OilRedR-4
❑ 82OPC-113
❑ 82OPCSti-96
❑ 82PosCer-6
❑ 83OilMcD-13
❑ 83OPC-37
❑ 83OPCSti-101
❑ 83Vac-34
❑ 847EDis-20
❑ 84KelAccD-3A
❑ 84KelAccD-3B
❑ 84OilRedR-4
❑ 84OilTeal-15
❑ 84OPC-251
❑ 84OPCSti-253
❑ 85OilRedR-4
❑ 85OPC-239
❑ 85OPCSti-219
❑ 86KraDra-36
❑ 86OilRedR-4
❑ 86OilTeal-4
❑ 86OPC-197
❑ 86OPCSti-70
❑ 86Top-197
❑ 87OilTeal-4
❑ 87OPC-200
❑ 87OPCMin-25
❑ 87OPCSti-84
❑ 87PanSti-257
❑ 88OilTeal-18
❑ 88OilTenAnn-5
❑ 88OPC-229
❑ 88OPCSti-219
❑ 88PanSti-54
❑ 89Kra-14
❑ 89KraAllSS-6
❑ 89OilTeal-15
❑ 89OPC-227
❑ 89OPCSti-224
❑ 89PanSti-79
❑ 89PanSti-180
❑ 89SweSemWCS-62
❑ 90Bow-198
❑ 90BowTif-198
❑ 90OilIGA-14
❑ 90OPC-307
❑ 90PanSti-224
❑ 90PanSti-330
❑ 90ProSet-89
❑ 90ProSet-339
❑ 90ProSet-380
❑ 90Sco-170
❑ 90ScoCan-170
❑ 90ScoHotRS-75
❑ 90Top-307
❑ 90TopTif-307
❑ 90UppDec-262
❑ 90UppDecF-262
❑ 91Bow-115
❑ 91OilIGA-9
❑ 91OilPanTS-12
❑ 91OilTeal-11
❑ 91OPC-220
❑ 91PanSti-131
❑ 91Par-51
❑ 91ParFre-51
❑ 91Pin-188
❑ 91Pin-371
❑ 91PinFre-188
❑ 91PinFre-371
❑ 91ProSet-76
❑ 91ProSet-572
❑ 91ProSetFre-76
❑ 91ProSetFre-572
❑ 91ProSetPla-38
❑ 91ScoAme-109
❑ 91ScoCan-109
❑ 91StaClu-179
❑ 91Top-220
❑ 91UppDec-186
❑ 91UppDecF-186
❑ 92Bow-99
❑ 92DurPan-42
❑ 92OPC-302
❑ 92PanSti-107
❑ 92PanStiFre-107
❑ 92Par-348
❑ 92ParEmel-348
❑ 92Pin-338
❑ 92PinFre-338
❑ 92Sco-39
❑ 92ScoCan-39
❑ 92StaClu-385
❑ 92Top-290
❑ 92TopGol-290G
❑ 92Ult-60
❑ 92Ult-356
❑ 93OPCPre-464
❑ 93OPCPreG-464
❑ 93PanSti-97
❑ 93Pin-11
❑ 93PinAllS-3
❑ 93PinAllSC-3
❑ 93PinCan-11
❑ 93Pow-393
❑ 93Sco-112
❑ 93ScoCan-112
❑ 93StaClu-165
❑ 93StaCluAS-19
❑ 93StaCluFDI-165
❑ 93StaCluFDIO-165
❑ 93StaCluO-165
❑ 93TopPre-464
❑ 93TopPreG-464
❑ 93Ult-375
❑ 94CanGamNHLP-171
❑ 94FinRinL-2
❑ 94ParSE-SE112
❑ 94ParSEG-SE112
❑ 94Pin-338
❑ 94PinArtP-338
❑ 94PinRinC-338
❑ 94StaClu-173
❑ 94StaCluFDI-173
❑ 94StaCluMOMS-173
❑ 94StaCluSTWC-173
❑ 94UppDec-393
❑ 94UppDecEleIce-393
❑ 95BeAPla-40
❑ 95BeAPSig-S40
❑ 95BeAPSigDC-S40
❑ 95Pin-89
❑ 95PinArtP-89
❑ 95PinRinC-89
❑ 95Sco-248
❑ 95ScoBlaIce-248
❑ 95ScoBlaIceAP-248
❑ 95UppDec-414
❑ 95UppDecEleIce-414
❑ 95UppDecEleIceG-414
❑ 96OilPos-4
❑ 97PacInvNRB-78
❑ 97UppDec-279

**Lowe, Ross**
❑ 44BeeGro2P-262
❑ 45QuaOatP-91

**Lowe, Steve**
❑ 95Cla-95
❑ 95SauSteMG-10
❑ 95Sla-174
❑ 98KanCitB-16

**Lowes, Bob**
❑ 95SlaMemC-50

**Lowgren, Torgny**
❑ 92SweSemE-271
❑ 95SweLeaE-238
❑ 95SweUppDE-106

**Lowrey, Frock (Fred)**
❑ 24C144ChaCig-36
❑ 24V130MapC-28
❑ 24V1452-36

**Lowry, David (Dave)**
❑ 85Canu-15
❑ 86Canu-9
❑ 87CanuSheOil-11
❑ 87PanSti-353
❑ 88ProIHL-67
❑ 89BluKod-10
❑ 90BluKod-12
❑ 90Bow-15
❑ 90BowTif-15
❑ 90OPC-370
❑ 90ProSet-265
❑ 90ScoRoo-38T
❑ 90Top-370
❑ 90TopTif-370
❑ 90UppDec-349
❑ 90UppDecF-349
❑ 91BluPos-14
❑ 91Bow-373
❑ 91OPC-180
❑ 91PanSti-32
❑ 91Par-376
❑ 91ParFre-376
❑ 91Pin-276
❑ 91PinFre-276
❑ 91ScoAme-149
❑ 91ScoCan-149
❑ 91StaClu-303
❑ 91Top-180
❑ 92Bow-370
❑ 92OPC-219
❑ 92PanSti-21
❑ 92PanStiFre-21
❑ 92Sco-109
❑ 92ScoCan-109
❑ 92StaClu-10
❑ 92Top-42
❑ 92TopGol-42G
❑ 93Don-125
❑ 93Lea-238
❑ 93OPCPre-244
❑ 93OPCPreG-244
❑ 93Par-79
❑ 93ParEmel-79
❑ 93Pin-408
❑ 93PinCan-408
❑ 93PinExp-4
❑ 93Pow-97
❑ 93Sco-564
❑ 93ScoCan-564
❑ 93ScoGol-564
❑ 93StaClu-121
❑ 93StaClu-379
❑ 93StaCluFDI-121
❑ 93StaCluFDI-379
❑ 93StaCluFDIO-121
❑ 93StaCluO-121
❑ 93StaCluO-379
❑ 93TopPre-244
❑ 93TopPreG-244
❑ 93TopPrePS-244
❑ 93UppDec-67
❑ 94BeAPSig-102
❑ 94CanGamNHLP-107
❑ 94Don-20
❑ 94Lea-414
❑ 94OPCPre-89
❑ 94OPCPreSE-89
❑ 94Pin-184
❑ 94PinArtP-184
❑ 94PinRinC-184
❑ 94Sco-81
❑ 94ScoGol-81
❑ 94ScoPla-81
❑ 94ScoPlaTS-81
❑ 94TopPre-89
❑ 94TopPreSE-89
❑ 94Ult-82
❑ 94UppDec-291
❑ 94UppDecEleIce-291
❑ 95CanGamNHLP-118
❑ 95ColCho-299
❑ 95ColChoPC-299
❑ 95ColChoPCP-299
❑ 95Don-222
❑ 95Lea-256
❑ 95Pin-199
❑ 95PinArtP-199
❑ 95PinRinC-199
❑ 95PlaOneoOne-261
❑ 95Sco-218
❑ 95ScoBlaIce-218
❑ 95ScoBlaIceAP-218
❑ 95UppDec-175
❑ 95UppDecEleIce-175
❑ 95UppDecEleIceG-175
❑ 96Don-174
❑ 96DonPrePro-174
❑ 96Lea-125
❑ 96LeaPreP-125
❑ 96Pin-81
❑ 96PinArtP-81
❑ 96PinFoi-81
❑ 96PinPreS-81
❑ 96PinRinC-81
❑ 96Sco-194
❑ 96ScoArtPro-194
❑ 96ScoDeaCAP-194
❑ 96ScoGolB-194
❑ 96ScoSpeAP-194
❑ 96UppDec-264
❑ 97Be A PPAD-183
❑ 97Be A PPAPD-183
❑ 97BeAPla-183
❑ 97BeAPlaAut-183
❑ 97PacInvNRB-87

**Loxam, Ryan**
❑ 91BriColJHL-51
❑ 92BriColJHL-210

**Loyer, Pat**
❑ 83BraWheK-7
❑ 84BraWheK-7

**Lozinski, Larry**
❑ 81OPC-99

**Lubina, Ladislav**
❑ 91SweSemWCS-121
❑ 94CzeAPSE-45
❑ 96CzeAPSE-153

**Lubiniecki, Daryl**
❑ 81SasBla-13

**Lucak, Josef**
❑ 95CzeAPSE-222

**Luce, Don**
❑ 70EssPowPla-136
❑ 71OPC-166
❑ 71SarProSta-26
❑ 71TorSun-31
❑ 72OPC-95
❑ 72SabPepPB-2
❑ 72SarProSta-33
❑ 72Top-106
❑ 73OPC-38
❑ 73SabPos-5
❑ 73Top-38
❑ 74NHLActSta-52
❑ 74OPCNHL-79
❑ 74Top-79
❑ 75OPCNHL-113
❑ 75Top-113
❑ 76OPCNHL-94
❑ 76Top-94
❑ 77OPCNHL-231
❑ 77Top-231
❑ 78OPC-58
❑ 78Top-58
❑ 79OPC-194
❑ 79Top-194
❑ 80OPC-302
❑ 81MapLeaP-9
❑ 81OPC-147
❑ 81Top-W99
❑ 93SabNoc-10

**Luce, Scott**
❑ 87SudWol-24

**Luchinkin, Sergei**
❑ 95SigRooCP-1
❑ 95SigRooFF-FF8
❑ 95SigRooFFS-FF8

**Luchkow, Faron**
❑ 90ForSasTra-10

**Luckner, Harald**
❑ 82SweSemHVS-25
❑ 83SweSemE-111

□ 98UppDecQD-92
□ 98UppDecTD-92
□ 98Vald'OF-9
**Luovi, Mikko**
□ 91UppDecCWJC-33
□ 93FinnJyvHS-82
□ 93FinnSIS-120
□ 93UppDec-271
□ 94FinnSIS-267
□ 94FinnSISH-14
□ 95FinnSIS-309
□ 96FinnSISR-99
**Lupaschuk, Ross**
□ 98SP Aut-118
□ 98SP AutSotTG-RL
□ 98SSASotT-RL
□ 98UppDec-395
□ 98UppDecE-395
□ 98UppDecE1o1-395
□ 98UppDecGR-395
□ 99SP AutPS-118
**Lupien, Camille**
□ 51LavDaiLSJ-26
**Lupien, Gilles**
□ 77CanaPos-16
□ 78CanaPos-18
□ 79CanaPos-16
□ 80OPC-298
**Lupien, Steve**
□ 907thInnSQMJHL-2
□ 917thInnSMC-49
**Lupul, Gary**
□ 80CanuSilD-15
□ 80CanuTeal-15
□ 81CanuSilD-18
□ 81CanuTeal-13
□ 81FreExp-5
□ 82FreExp-5
□ 82OPC-354
□ 82PosCer-19
□ 82VicCou-13
□ 83Canu-12
□ 83OPC-355
□ 83Vac-111
□ 847EDis-49
□ 84Canu-15
□ 84KelWin-32
□ 84OPC-323
□ 85Canu-16
□ 85FreExp-6
**Lupzig, Andreas**
□ 94GerDELE-210
□ 95GerDELE-210
□ 95GerDELE-429
□ 96GerDELE-355
□ 98GerDELE-104
□ 98GerDELE-320
**Lusth, Mats**
□ 83SweSemE-106
□ 84SweSemE-106
□ 85SwePanS-95
□ 86SwePanS-87
□ 87SwePanS-93
□ 90SweSemE-129
□ 91SweSemE-181
□ 92SweSemE-205
□ 93SwiHNL-469
□ 94SweLeaE-236
□ 95SweLeaE-300
□ 95SweUppDE-192
**Lutchenko, Vladimir**
□ 69SweHocS-7
□ 69SweWorC-21
□ 69SweWorC-69
□ 69SweWorC-129
□ 69SweWorC-132
□ 70SweHocS-316
□ 71SweHocS-31
□ 72SweSemWC-3
□ 73SweHocS-80
□ 73SweWorCS-80
□ 74SweSemHVS-28
□ 79PanSti-142
□ 81SweSemHVS-40
□ 91FutTreC72-42
**Lutes, Craig**
□ 907thInnSOHL-342
□ 917thInnSOHL-353
□ 91OshGenS-12
□ 92WinSpi-6
□ 93WinSpi-6
□ 94BirBul-17
□ 95BirBul-15
**Luther, Gary**
□ 87SauSteMG-30
**Luthi, Freddy**
□ 91SweSemWCS-189
□ 93SweSemWCS-121
□ 93SwiHNL-201
□ 95SweGloWC-211
□ 95SwiHNL-76
**Luthi, Peter**
□ 72SweSemWC-144
**Lutter, Peter**
□ 94GerDELE-362
□ 95GerDELE-317
□ 96GerDELE-98
□ 98GerDELE-15
**Lutz, Rainer**
□ 94GerDELE-309
**Luza, Patrik**
□ 91UppDecCWJC-90
**Lyasenko, Roman**
□ 96UppDecIce-144
**Lyck, Jan Erik**
□ 64SweCorI-80
□ 65SweCorI-80
□ 67SweHoc-54
□ 69SweHocS-68
□ 70SweHocS-32
□ 71SweHocS-109
□ 72SweHocS-93
□ 73SweHocS-166
□ 73SweWorCS-166
**Lycka, Jaroslav**
□ 81SweSemHVS-62
**Lydman, Toni**
□ 95UppDec-551
□ 95UppDecEleIce-551
□ 95UppDecEleIceG-551
**Lyle, George**
□ 80OPC-379
□ 81OPC-100
□ 82PosCer-7
□ 82WhaJunHC-11
**Lyle, Justin**
□ 93OmaLan-16
**Lylyk, David**
□ 94GueSto-21
**Lynch, John (Jack)**
□ 72OPC-160
□ 73OPC-232
□ 74NHLActSta-107
□ 74NHLActStaU-43
□ 74OPCNHL-331
□ 75OPCNHL-116
□ 75Top-116
□ 76OPCNHL-288
□ 77OPCNHL-369
**Lynn, Vic**
□ 44BeeGro2P-421
□ 45QuaOatP-29A
□ 45QuaOatP-29B
□ 45QuaOatP-29C
**Lyons, Corey**
□ 88LetHur-15
□ 89LetHur-13
□ 90ProAHLIHL-615
□ 91ProAHLCHL-583
**Lyons, Craig**
□ 907thInnSWHL-301
□ 917thInnSWHL-85
**Lyons, Marc**
□ 84KinCan-11
□ 85KinCan-11
□ 86KinCan-22
□ 93TolSto-21
**Lyons, Mike**
□ 96MinGolGCAS-18
**Lysak, Brett**
□ 96RegPat-20
**Lysen, Goran**
□ 65SweCorI-51
□ 67SweHoc-106
**Lysenko, Alexander**
□ 90OPC-500
**Lysenko, Ilya**
□ 93SudWol-18
□ 93SudWolP-17
**Lysiak, Tom**
□ 74NHLActSta-18
□ 74OPCNHL-14
□ 74OPCNHL-68
□ 74Top-14
□ 74Top-68
□ 75OPCNHL-230
□ 75OPCNHL-313
□ 75Top-230
□ 75Top-313
□ 76OPCNHL-174
□ 76OPCNHL-379
□ 76Top-174
□ 77OPCNHL-127
□ 77Top-127
□ 78OPC-97
□ 78Top-97
□ 79OPC-41
□ 79PanSti-59
□ 79Top-41
□ 80OPC-247
□ 80Top-247
□ 81BlaBorPos-13
□ 81OPC-59
□ 81OPC-73
□ 81OPCSti-114
□ 81Top-49
□ 81Top-W71
□ 82OPC-68
□ 82OPCSti-14
□ 82OPCSti-174
□ 82PosCer-4
□ 83BlaBorPos-13
□ 83OPC-107
□ 83OPCSti-110
□ 83PufSti-15
□ 84OPC-39
□ 84OPCSti-31
□ 84Top-31
□ 85OPC-23
□ 85Top-23
**Lyulin, Andrei**
□ 95SweUppDE-189
**Maatinen, Pasi**
□ 95FinnSIS-240
**Maatta, Borje**
□ 67SweHoc-242
□ 69SweHocS-285
□ 70SweHocS-183
□ 71SweHocS-269
□ 72SweHocS-245
**Maatta, Eilert**
□ 64SweCorI-28
□ 65SweCorI-28
□ 65SweCorI-63B
□ 67SweHoc-190
□ 69SweHocS-247
□ 70SweHocS-135
□ 71SweHocS-227
□ 81SweSemHVS-119
**Maatta, Soren**
□ 64SweCorI-71
□ 65SweCorI-71
□ 67SweHoc-191
□ 69SweHocS-248
□ 70SweHocS-143
□ 71SweHocS-237
**Maattanen, Pasi**
□ 93FinnJyvHS-84
□ 93FinnSIS-129
□ 94FinnSIS-28
**MacAdam, Al**
□ 74NHLActSta-65
□ 74OPCNHL-301
□ 75OPCNHL-253
□ 75Top-253
□ 76OPCNHL-237
□ 76OPCNHL-383
□ 76Top-237
□ 77OPCNHL-149
□ 77Top-149A
□ 77Top-149B
□ 78NorStaCD-4
□ 78OPC-381
□ 79NorStaPos-6
□ 79OPC-104
□ 79Top-104
□ 80NorStaPos-10
□ 80OPC-34
□ 80OPC-139
□ 80Top-34
□ 80Top-139
□ 81NorStaPos-12
□ 81OPC-163
□ 81OPCSti-90
□ 81Top-W107
□ 82NorStaPos-13
□ 82OPC-171
□ 82PosCer-9
□ 83NorStaPos-14
□ 83OPC-173
□ 84Canu-16
□ 84OPC-324
□ 84Top-75
□ 85FreExp-27
□ 85OPC-209
□ 85OPCSti-242
□ 97St.JohML-15
**MacAdam, Don**
□ 90ProAHLIHL-240
□ 94MilAdm-14
**MacArthur, Ken**
□ 90AlbIntTC-6
**MacAulay, Anthony**
□ 94HamRoaA-12
**MacAusland, Lennie (Len)**
□ 907thInnSWHL-58
□ 917thInnSWHL-185
**Macchio, Ralph**
□ 91ProSetPla-295
**MacDermid, Paul**
□ 85WhaJunW-11
□ 86WhaJunT-15
□ 87WhaJunBK-14
□ 88PanSti-243
□ 88WhaJunGR-11
□ 89OPC-183
□ 89OPCSti-266
□ 89PanSti-227
□ 89Top-183
□ 89WhaJunM-15
□ 90JetIGA-19
□ 90OPC-338
□ 90ProSet-331
□ 90Sco-296
□ 90ScoCan-296
□ 90Top-338
□ 90TopTif-338
□ 90UppDec-218
□ 90UppDecF-218
□ 91Bow-195
□ 91CapKod-19
□ 91JetIGA-16
□ 91JetPanTS-15
□ 91OPC-463
□ 91PanSti-69
□ 91Pin-279
□ 91PinFre-279
□ 91ProSet-269
□ 91ProSetFre-269
□ 91ScoAme-219
□ 91ScoCan-219
□ 91StaClu-254
□ 91Top-463
□ 92Bow-282
□ 92CapKod-19
□ 92Sco-59
□ 92ScoCan-59
□ 92StaClu-178
□ 92Top-391
□ 92TopGol-391G
□ 92Ult-439
□ 94NordBurK-18
**MacDonagh, Bill**
□ 51LavDaiQSHL-52
**MacDonald, Aaron**
□ 95Cla-32
□ 95SwiCurB-9
**MacDonald, B.J. (Blair)**
□ 76OPCWHA-93
□ 77OPCWHA-16
□ 79OilPos-15
□ 80OPC-32
□ 80PepCap-33
□ 80Top-32
□ 81CanuSilD-21
□ 81CanuTeal-14
□ 81FreExp-2
□ 81OPC-340
□ 82FreExp-2
□ 82OPC-350
□ 88OilTenAnn-99
□ 89ProIHL-164
□ 90ProAHLIHL-390
**MacDonald, Brett**
□ 83NorBayC-17
□ 85KitRan-12
□ 86FreExp-17
□ 87FliSpi-13
□ 88FliSpi-13
□ 91ProAHLCHL-430
□ 95FliGen-20
**MacDonald, Brian**
□ 83BraAle-12
**MacDonald, Bruce**
□ 92TolSto-18
□ 93TolSto-20
**MacDonald, Chris**
□ 95Sla-129
**MacDonald, Clint**
□ 91BriColJHL-120
□ 92BriColJHL-133
**MacDonald, Craig**
□ 99Pac-83
□ 99PacCop-83
□ 99PacGol-83
□ 99PacIceB-83
□ 99PacPreD-83
**MacDonald, Dave**
□ 94SudWol-2
□ 94SudWolP-25
□ 95Sla-381
□ 95SudWol-20
□ 95SudWolP-13
**MacDonald, David**
□ 96GueSto-3
**MacDonald, Doug**
□ 92Cla-92
□ 92RochAmeDD-10
□ 92RochAmeKod-13
□ 93RochAmeKod-15
□ 93UppDec-97
□ 96CinCyc-44
□ 96ClaGol-92
□ 98CinCyc-12
**MacDonald, Garett**
□ 92NorMicW-17
□ 94RicRen-10
□ 95RicRen-16
**MacDonald, Garrett**
□ 93NorMicW-20
**MacDonald, Jack**
□ 10C55SweCP-8
□ 11C55-8
□ 12C57-17
**MacDonald, Jason**
□ 907thInnSOHL-311
□ 917thInnSOHL-277
□ 93OweSouPla-6
□ 93OweSouPla-16
□ 94Cla-118
□ 94ClaDraGol-118
□ 95AdiRedW-12
**MacDonald, Kevin**
□ 88ProIHL-54
□ 89ProAHL-24
□ 89RayJrC-15
□ 90ProAHLIHL-366
□ 91ProAHLCHL-388
□ 95ColEdgI-106
**MacDonald, Kilby**
□ 34BeeGro1P-285
□ 39OPCV3011-87
**MacDonald, Lanny**
□ 99RetHoc-95
□ 99UppDecRDR-DR13
□ 99UppDecRDRI-DR13
□ 99UppDecRG-95
□ 99UppDecRII-LM
□ 99UppDecRIL1-LM
□ 99UppDecRP-95
**MacDonald, Leonard**
□ 89SudWol-14
□ 907thInnSOHL-184
□ 917thInnSOHL-185
**MacDonald, Lowell**
□ 61HamRed-11
□ 66TulOil-6
□ 68OPC-42
□ 68ShiCoi-56
□ 68Top-42
□ 70OPC-206
□ 72OPC-214
□ 73OPC-128
□ 73Top-128
□ 74NHLActSta-229
□ 74OPCNHL-30
□ 74OPCNHL-133
□ 74OPCNHL-183
□ 74PenPos-15
□ 74Top-30
□ 74Top-133
□ 74Top-183
□ 75OPCNHL-204
□ 75Top-204
□ 76OPCNHL-33
□ 76OPCNHL-218
□ 76Top-33
□ 76Top-218
□ 77OPCNHL-390
□ 77PenPucB-18
□ 94ParTalB-60
**MacDonald, Parker**
□ 44BeeGro2P-190
□ 44BeeGro2P-430
□ 55Par-9
□ 55Par-77
□ 55ParQuaO-9
□ 55ParQuaO-77
□ 60ShiCoi-59
□ 61ShiCoi-69
□ 62YorIroOTra-27
□ 63ChePho-33
□ 63Par-44
□ 63TorSta-24
□ 63YorWhiB-40
□ 64BeeGro3P-17
□ 64BeeGro3P-83
□ 64CocCap-53
□ 64Top-11
□ 64TorSta-27
□ 65Coc-14
□ 65Top-105
□ 68OPC-55
□ 68ShiCoi-70
□ 68Top-55
□ 73NorStaP-10
□ 89NewHavN-15
□ 94ParMisL-104
□ 94ParTalB-44
□ 95Par66-55
□ 95Par66Coi-55
**Macdonald, Paul**
□ 917thInnSQMJHL-200
**MacDonald, Ryan**
□ 94DetJrRW-4
□ 95Sla-212
□ 95SlaMemC-78
**MacDonald, Todd**
□ 92TacRoc-12
□ 93TacRoc-15
□ 95ColEdgI-24
□ 96CinCyc-1
**MacDonald, Tom**
□ 907thInnSOHL-166
□ 917thInnSMC-14
□ 917thInnSOHL-322
□ 93SauSteMG-15
□ 93SauSteMGM-17
□ 96LouRiv-20
**MacDonald, Wayne**
□ 90ForSasTra-11
**MacDonald, Willie**
□ 87KamBla-11
**MacEachern, Greg**
□ 907thInnSMC-57
□ 907thInnSQMJHL-77
□ 92-TulOil-8
**MacEachern, Liam**
□ 94SudWol-18
□ 94SudWolP-9
□ 95Sla-397
□ 95SudWol-10
□ 95SudWolP-14
**MacEachern, Shane**
□ 88ProIHL-70
□ 94BraSmo-16
**Macek, Petr**
□ 94CzeAPSE-254
□ 95CzeAPSE-132
**Macera, Mark**
□ 99WicThu-13
**MacFarland, Bill**
□ 69SeaTotW-20
**MacFarlane, Eon**
□ 92BriColJHL-200
**MacGillivray, Bill**
□ 92NorMicW-18
□ 93NorMicW-21
**MacGillvray, John**
□ 52JunBluT-165
**MacGregor, Blair**
□ 83MedHatT-6
**MacGregor, Brad**
□ 88ProAHL-96
**MacGregor, Bruce**
□ 44BeeGro2P-191
□ 61ShiCoi-73
□ 62Par-23
□ 62YorIroOTra-36
□ 63ChePho-34
□ 63Par-41
□ 63YorWhiB-51
□ 64BeeGro3P-84A
□ 64BeeGro3P-84B
□ 64CocCap-49
□ 64Top-76
□ 65Coc-48
□ 65Top-110
□ 66Top-104
□ 66TopUSAT-56
□ 67Top-102
□ 68OPC-30
□ 68ShiCoi-41
□ 68Top-30
□ 69OPC-63
□ 69Top-63
□ 70DadCoo-72
□ 70EssPowPla-137
□ 70OPC-27
□ 70RedWinM-6
□ 70SarProSta-51
□ 70Top-27
□ 71OPC-216
□ 71SarProSta-124
□ 71TorSun-176
□ 72OPC-103
□ 72SarProSta-153
□ 73OPC-201
□ 74OPCWHA-2
□ 75OPCWHA-22
□ 88OilTenAnn-154
□ 94ParTalB-47
□ 95Par66-49
□ 95Par66Coi-49
**MacGuigan, Garth**
□ 81IndChe-14
□ 82IndChe-15
**Mach, Miroslav**
□ 94CzeAPSE-63
□ 95CzeAPSE-91
□ 96CzeAPSE-300
**Machac, Oldrich**
□ 69SweHocS-34
□ 69SweWorC-154
□ 70SweHocS-349
□ 71SweHocS-45
□ 72SweSemWC-24
□ 73SweHocS-29
□ 73SweWorCS-29
□ 74SweHocS-13
□ 74SweSemHVS-55
**Machacek, Martin**
□ 93MicTecH-24
**Machalek, Robert**
□ 95CzeAPSE-108
**Macho, Michal**
□ 96SloPeeWT-17
**Machulda, Vladimir**
□ 94CzeAPSE-225
□ 95CzeAPSE-172
**MacInnes, John**
□ 91MicTecHus-10
**MacInnis, Al**
□ 82KitRan-17
□ 85FlamRedRP-16
□ 85OPC-237
□ 85OPCSti-211
□ 86FlamRedR-11
□ 86OPC-173
□ 86OPCSti-86
□ 86Top-173
□ 87FlamRedRP-12
□ 87OPC-72
□ 87OPCMin-26
□ 87OPCSti-40
□ 87OPCSti-123
□ 87PanSti-205
□ 87Top-72
□ 87TopStiIns-9
□ 88FriLayS-31
□ 88OPC-231
□ 88OPCMin-22
□ 88OPCSti-92
□ 88PanSti-5
□ 89Kra-3
□ 89OPC-49
□ 89OPCSti-5
□ 89OPCSti-21
□ 89OPCSti-95
□ 89OPCSti-159
□ 89OPCSti-161
□ 89PanSti-20
□ 89PanSti-32
□ 89SweSemWCS-56
□ 89Top-49
□ 89TopStiIns-4
□ 90Bow-93
□ 90BowTif-93
□ 90FlamIGA-9
□ 90FlamIGA-13
□ 90Kra-33
□ 90OPC-127
□ 90OPC-197
□ 90OPCBoxB-H
□ 90OPCPre-65
□ 90PanSti-185
□ 90PanSti-328
□ 90ProSet-35
□ 90ProSet-337
□ 90Sco-5
□ 90Sco-314
□ 90Sco-335
□ 90ScoCan-5
□ 90ScoCan-314
□ 90ScoCan-335
□ 90ScoHotRS-36
□ 90Top-127
□ 90Top-197
□ 90TopBoxB-H
□ 90TopTif-127
□ 90TopTif-197
□ 90UppDec-143
□ 90UppDec-319
□ 90UppDec-497
□ 90UppDecF-143
□ 90UppDecF-319
□ 90UppDecF-497
□ 91Bow-262
□ 91FlamIGA-7
□ 91FlamPanTS-7
□ 91Gil-7
□ 91Kra-32
□ 91McDUppD-23
□ 91OPC-262
□ 91OPC-491
□ 91OPCPre-81
□ 91PanSti-50
□ 91PanSti-330
□ 91Par-28
□ 91ParFre-28
□ 91Pin-220
□ 91Pin-399
□ 91PinB-B8
□ 91PinBFre-B8
□ 91PinFre-220
□ 91PinFre-399
□ 91ProSet-33
□ 91ProSet-275
□ 91ProSetFre-33
□ 91ProSetFre-275
□ 91ProSetNHLAS-AC8
□ 91ProSetPC-5
□ 91ProSetPla-19
□ 91ProSetPla-276
□ 91ScoAme-2
□ 91ScoAme-409
□ 91ScoAme-417
□ 91ScoCan-2
□ 91ScoCan-299
□ 91ScoCan-333
□ 91ScoFan-4
□ 91ScoKel-16
□ 91ScoNat-4
□ 91ScoNatCWC-4
□ 91StaClu-79
□ 91SweSemWCS-57
□ 91Top-262
□ 91Top-491
□ 91UppDec-8
□ 91UppDec-243
□ 91UppDec-632
□ 91UppDecF-8
□ 91UppDecF-243
□ 91UppDecF-632
□ 92Bow-51
□ 92Bow-211
□ 92FlamIGA-22
□ 92HumDum2-14
□ 92McDUppD-10
□ 92OPC-330
□ 92PanSti-49
□ 92PanSti-285
□ 92PanStiFre-49
□ 92PanStiFre-285
□ 92Par-20
□ 92ParEmel-20
□ 92Pin-83
□ 92PinFre-83
□ 92ProSet-22
□ 92Sco-302
□ 92Sco-421
□ 92Sco-496
□ 92ScoCan-302
□ 92ScoCan-421
□ 92ScoCan-496
□ 92SeaPat-60
□ 92StaClu-128
□ 92Top-452
□ 92TopGol-452G
□ 92Ult-23
□ 92UltAllS-8
□ 92UppDec-257
□ 93Don-47
□ 93KraRec-5
□ 93Lea-180
□ 93OPCPre-276
□ 93OPCPreG-276
□ 93PanSti-P
□ 93Par-36
□ 93ParChePH-D3
□ 93ParEmel-36
□ 93Pin-155
□ 93PinCan-155
□ 93Pow-38
□ 93PowSlaA-7
□ 93Sco-121
□ 93ScoCan-121
□ 93ScoDreTea-4
□ 93ScoFra-3
□ 93StaClu-105
□ 93StaCluFDI-105
□ 93StaCluFDIO-105
□ 93StaCluO-105
□ 93SweSemWCS-193
□ 93TopPre-276
□ 93TopPreG-276
□ 93Ult-113
□ 93UppDec-412
□ 93UppDecNR-19
□ 93UppDecSP-22
□ 94BeAP99A-G14
□ 94CanGamNHLP-264
□ 94DonDom-6
□ 94EASpo-20
□ 94FinDivFCC-12
□ 94FinnJaaK-84
□ 94FinnJaaK-340
□ 94Fla-157
□ 94Fle-190
□ 94FleSlaA-5
□ 94HocWit-90
□ 94Lea-461
□ 94LeaLim-79
□ 94McDUppD-McD15
□ 94OPCPre-110

94OPCPre-127
94OPCPre-347
94OPCPre-488
94OPCPreSE-110
94OPCPreSE-127
94OPCPreSE-347
94OPCPreSE-488
94Par-35
94ParGol-35
94ParSE-SE152
94ParSEG-SE152
94Pin-387
94PinArtP-387
94PinBoo-BR3
94PinRinC-387
94Sco-120
94ScoDreTea-DT7
94ScoGol-120
94ScoPla-120
94ScoPlaTS-120
94Sel-28
94SelGol-28
94SP-104
94SPDieCut-104
94StaClu-56
94StaCluFDI-56
94StaCluMO-7
94StaCluMOMS-56
94StaCluSTWC-56
94TopPre-110
94TopPre-127
94TopPre-347
94TopPre-488
94TopPreSE-110
94TopPreSE-127
94TopPreSE-347
94TopPreSE-488
94Ult-185
94UppDec-150
94UppDec-232
94UppDecEleIce-150
94UppDecEleIce-232
94UppDecPC-C33
94UppDecPCEG-C33
94UppDecPR-R46
94UppDecPRE-R46
94UppDecPreRG-R46
94UppDecSPI-SP159
94UppDecSPIDC-SP159
95BeAPla-134
95BeAPSig-S134
95BeAPSigDC-S134
95Bow-16
95BowAllFoi-16
95CanGamNHLP-242
95ColCho-313
95ColChoPC-313
95ColChoPCP-313
95Don-205
95DonDom-7
95DonEli-15
95DonEliDCS-15
95DonEliDCU-15
95Emo-150
95Fin-48
95FinnSemWC-85
95FinRef-48
95ImpSti-102
95Lea-312
95LeaLim-95
95Met-126
95NHLAcePC-2D
95ParInt-178
95ParIntEl-178
95Pin-79
95PinArtP-79
95PinRinC-79
95PlaOneoOne-90
95ProMag-13
95Sco-46
95ScoBlaIce-46
95ScoBlaIceAP-46
95SelCer-72
95SelCerMG-72
95SkyImp-143
95SP-125
95StaClu-13
95StaCluMO-34
95StaCluMOMS-13
95Sum-90
95SumArtP-90
95SumGM-14
95SumIce-90
95SweGloWC-79
95Top-145
95TopHomGC-HGC22
95TopOPCI-145
95TopSupSki-49
95TopSupSkiPla-49
95Ult-300
95UppDec-290
95UppDecEleIce-290
95UppDecEleIceG-290
95UppDecSpeE-SE71
95UppDecSpeEdiG-SE71
95Zen-40
96ColCho-228
96ColCho-329
96Don-12
96DonCanI-15
96DonCanIGPP-15
96DonCanIRPP-15
96DonEli-67
96DonEliDCS-67
96DonPrePro-12
96Fla-82
96FlaBluI-82
96Fle-98
96KraUppD-35
96Lea-174
96LeaPreP-174
96MetUni-133
96NHLProSTA-13
96Pin-153
96PinArtP-153
96PinFoi-153
96PinPreS-153
96PinRinC-153
96PosUppD-13
96Sco-114
96ScoArtPro-114
96ScoDeaCAP-114
96ScoGolB-114
96ScoSpeAP-114
96SkyImp-114
96StaCluMO-9
96SweSemW-81
96TeaOut-77
96TopNHLP-49
96TopPicOI-49
96Ult-147
96UltGolM-147
96UppDec-141
96Zen-18
96ZenArtP-18
97Be A PPAD-125
97Be A PPAPD-125
97BeAPla-125
97BeAPlaAut-125
97ColCho-234
97Don-122
97DonCanI-55
97DonCanIDS-55
97DonCanIPS-55
97DonPre-132
97DonPreCttC-132
97DonPreProG-122
97DonPreProS-122
97DonPri-144
97DonPriSoA-144
97Kat-130
97KatGol-130
97KatSil-130
97Pac-202
97PacCop-202
97PacEmeGre-202
97PacIceB-202
97PacOme-195
97PacOmeC-195
97PacOmeDG-195
97PacOmeEG-195
97PacOmeG-195
97PacOmeIB-195
97PacRed-202
97PacSil-202
97Pin-116
97PinCer-120
97PinCerMB-120
97PinCerMG-120
97PinCerMR-120
97PinCerR-120
97PinIns-116
97PinPrePBB-116
97PinPrePBC-116
97PinPrePBM-116
97PinPrePBY-116
97PinPrePFC-116
97PinPrePFM-116
97PinPrePFY-116
97PinPrePla-116
97PinTotCMPG-120
97PinTotCPB-120
97PinTotCPG-120
97PinTotCPR-120
97Sco-248
97ScoBlu-6
97ScoBluPla-6
97ScoBluPre-6
97SPAut-140
97UppDec-352
98Be A PPA-274
98Be A PPAA-274
98Be A PPAAF-274
98Be A PPAM-M22
98Be A PPSE-274
98Be APG-274
98BowBes-57
98BowBesAR-57
98BowBesR-57
98Fin-88
98FinNo P-88
98FinNo PR-88
98FinRef-88
98O-PChr-100
98O-PChrR-100
98Pac-368
98PacAur-161
98PacCroR-115
98PacCroRLS-115
98PacDynI-159
98PacDynIIB-159
98PacDynIR-159
98PacIceB-368
98PacOmeH-203
98PacOmeODI-203
98PacOmeR-203
98PacPar-204
98PacParC-204
98PacParEG-204
98PacParH-204
98PacParIB-204
98PacParS-204
98PacRed-368
98PacRev-123
98PacRevADC-19
98PacRevIS-123
98PacRevR-123
98SP Aut-72
98SPXTopP-51
98SPXTopPF-51
98SPXTopPR-51
98Top-100
98TopGolLC1-15
98TopGolLC1B-15
98TopGolLC1BOoO-15
98TopGolLC1OoO-15
98TopGolLC1R-15
98TopGolLC1ROoO-15
98TopGolLC2-15
98TopGolLC2B-15
98TopGolLC2BOoO-15
98TopGolLC2OoO-15
98TopGolLC2R-15
98TopGolLC2ROoO-15
98TopGolLC3-15
98TopGolLC3B-15
98TopGolLC3BOoO-15
98TopGolLC3OoO-15
98TopGolLC3R-15
98TopGolLC3ROoO-15
98TopO-P-100
98UC-188
98UD ChoPCR-188
98UD ChoR-188
98UppDec-176
98UppDecBD-77
98UppDecDD-77
98UppDecE-176
98UppDecE1o1-176
98UppDecGJ-GJ8
98UppDecGR-176
98UppDecM-179
98UppDecMGS-179
98UppDecMSS-179
98UppDecMSS-179
98UppDecQD-77
98UppDecTD-77
99Pac-358
99PacAur-126
99PacAurPD-126
99PacCop-358
99PacGol-358
99PacIceB-358
99PacPreD-358
99RetHoc-71
99SP AutPS-72
99UppDecM-183
99UppDecMGS-183
99UppDecMSS-183
99UppDecMSS-183
99UppDecRG-71
99UppDecRIL1-AM
99UppDecRP-71

**MacInnis, Ian**
81KinCan-7

**MacInnis, Rob**
83KitRan-4
88ProAHL-73
90ProAHLIHL-532
93RicRen-7

**MacIntosh, Andy**
92BriColJHL-153

**MacIntyre, Andy**
907thInnSWHL-6
917thInnSWHL-98
91SasBla-18
93SasBla-15
94IndIce-14
95IndIce-12

**MacIntyre, Dave**
91JohChi-8
95PeoRiv-10
98GerDELE-114

**MacIntyre, Duncan (Dunc)**
83BelBul-12
84BelBul-5
85FreExp-10
86FreExp-18

**MacIntyre, Jason**
93HamRoaA-16
94HamRoaA-17
95HamRoaA-8

**MacIsaac, Al**
91HamRoaA-9
96HamRoaA-HRA22

**MacIsaac, Bob**
917thInnSOHL-263
91SudWol-7
92SudWol-3
93SudWol-23
93SudWolP-25

**MacIsaac, Dave**
92MaiBlaB-23
93MaiBlaB-45
95MilAdmBO-11

**MacIsaac, Todd**
917thInnSWHL-348
93LetHur-6

**Maciver, Norm**
85MinDul-5
88PanSti-302
89ProAHL-140
90ProAHLIHL-224
91Bow-99
91OilIGA-10
91OilTeal-12
91Par-282
91ParFre-282
91ScoCan-434
92Bow-425
92OPC-344
92OPCPre-107
92Par-117
92ParEmel-117
92Pin-157
92PinFre-157
92ProSet-50
92Sco-349
92ScoCan-349
92Sen-9
92StaClu-46
92Top-96
92TopGol-96G
92Ult-61
92Ult-363
92UppDec-511
93Don-233
93Lea-189
93OPCPre-64
93OPCPreG-64
93PanSti-112
93Par-137
93ParEmel-137
93Pin-120
93PinCan-120
93Pow-172
93Sco-123
93ScoCan-123
93SenKraS-15
93StaClu-267
93StaCluFDI-267
93StaCluO-267
93TopPre-64
93TopPreG-64
93Ult-143
93UppDec-299
93UppDec-335
93UppDecSP-111
94BeAPSig-127
94CanGamNHLP-175
94Don-273
94EASpo-91
94Fla-122
94Lea-68
94OPCPre-49
94OPCPreSE-49
94Par-154
94ParGol-154
94Pin-80
94PinArtP-80
94PinRinC-80
94Sco-24
94ScoGol-24
94ScoPla-24
94ScoPlaTS-24
94SenBelM-18
94TopPre-49
94TopPreSE-49
94Ult-149
94UppDec-466
94UppDecEleIce-466
95ColCho-270
95ColChoPC-270
95ColChoPCP-270
95ParInt-171
95ParInt-499
95ParIntEl-171
95ParIntEl-499
95PenFoo-8
95Pin-170
95PinArtP-170
95PinRinC-170
95Sco-276
95ScoBlaIce-276
95ScoBlaIceAP-276
95Ult-289
96BeAPAut-133
96BeAPAutSil-133
96BeAPla-133
96ColCho-208
96Don-69
96DonPrePro-69
96FlePic-112
96Lea-35
96LeaPreP-35
96Sco-167
96ScoArtPro-167
96ScoDeaCAP-167
96ScoGolB-167
96ScoSpeAP-167
97Pac-60
97PacCop-60
97PacEmeGre-60
97PacIceB-60
97PacRed-60
97PacSil-60

**Mackay, Brian**
52JunBluT-133

**Mackay, Calum**
44BeeGro2P-271
45QuaOatP-92
51BufBis-14
51Par-9
54Par-11
55Par-41
55ParQuaO-41

**Mackay, Dave**
34BeeGro1P-65

**MacKay, Kevin**
89WinSpi-9
907thInnSOHL-186
917thInnSOHL-190

**MacKay, Mark**
95GerDELE-404
96GerDELE-312
98GerDELE-203
98GerDELE-337

**MacKay, Mickey**
83HalFP-N8
85HalFC-203

**MacKay, Murdo**
45QuaOatP-93

**Mackegard, Jens**
87SwePanS-259
87SwePanS-260

**Mackeigan, Jack**
82VicCou-14
83VicCou-15

**Mackell, Fleming**
44BeeGro2P-45
44BeeGro2P-422
45QuaOatP-30A
45QuaOatP-30B
48ExhCan-34
51Par-83
52Par-82
53Par-91A
53Par-91B
54Par-50
54Top-36
55BruTeaIss-12
57Top-16
58Top-29
59Top-19
59Top-60
61UniOilW-7
91BruSpoAL-14
94ParMisL-3

**MacKellar, Peter**
93SauSteMG-9
93SauSteMGM-5
95Sla-289

**MacKenzie, Bill**
33V357IceK-61
34BeeGro1P-199
36OPCV304D-111
36V356WorG-44
37OPCV304E-151
39OPCV3011-81

**MacKenzie, Brian**
917thInnSOHL-267

**MacKenzie, Derek**
97SudWolP-12
98SP Aut-127
98SP AutSotTG-DMA
98SSASotT-DMA
98UppDec-404
98UppDecE-404
98UppDecE1o1-404
98UppDecGR-404
99SP AutPS-127

**MacKenzie, Jean-Marc**
83SauSteMG-16
84SauSteMG-13
86LonKni-10

**MacKenzie, Ken**
907thInnSOHL-399
917thInnSOHL-265

**MacKenzie, Robert**
917thInnSOHL-285

**MacKenzie, Roddie**
95SlaMemC-66

**Mackey, David (Dave)**
82VicCou-15
83VicCou-16
85MedHatT-22
88ProIHL-103
90ProAHLIHL-328
91ProAHLCHL-31
92PeoRivC-13
93PeoRiv-17
94Lea-280
94MilAdm-15
94OPCPre-48
94OPCPreSE-48
94Par-202
94ParGol-202
94TopPre-48
94TopPreSE-48
95MilAdmBO-13
96MilAdmBO-16

**Mackey, Kevin**
95NorIowH-18

**Mackie, Dub**
23V1281PauC-14

**MacKinnon, Paul**
78JetPos-14

**MacLean, Cail**
93KinFro-12
95Sla-117

**MacLean, Dave**
81OshGen-17
83BelBul-4
84BelBul-11

**Maclean, Donald**
95Cla-30
95SigRooA-26
95SigRooAPC-26
97Be A PPAD-241
97Be A PPAPD-241
97BeAPla-241
97BeAPlaAut-241
97Kat-70
97KatGol-70
97KatSil-70
97PacCroR-63
97PacCroREG-63
97PacCroRIB-63
97PacCroRS-63
97Pin-14
97PinArtP-14
97PinPrePBB-14
97PinPrePBC-14
97PinPrePBM-14
97PinPrePBY-14
97PinPrePFC-14
97PinPrePFM-14
97PinPrePFY-14
97PinPrePla-14
97PinRinC-14
97SPAut-184
97UppDec-292
97UppDecBD-57
97UppDecBDDD-57
97UppDecBDQD-57
97UppDecBDTD-57
97UppDecIce-53
97UppDecIceP-53
97UppDecIPS-53
98Pac-238
98PacIceB-238
98PacRed-238
98UC-102
98UD ChoPCR-102
98UD ChoR-102
98UppDec-106
98UppDecE-106
98UppDecE1o1-106
98UppDecGR-106

**MacLean, John**
81OshGen-19
82OshGen-15
84DevPos-15
86DevPol-14
86OPC-37
86Top-37
87OPC-191
87PanSti-80
87Top-191
88DevCar-18
88OPC-10
88OPCSti-78
88PanSti-274
88Top-10
89DevCar-15
89OPC-102
89OPCSti-87
89PanSti-249
89Top-102
90Bow-83
90BowTif-83
90Dev-17
90OPC-224
90PanSti-74
90ProSet-170
90Sco-190
90ScoCan-190
90ScoHotRS-83
90Top-224
90TopTif-224
90UppDec-161
90UppDecF-161
91Bow-272
91Bow-289
91OPC-239
91OPCPre-4
91PanSti-213
91Pin-115
91PinFre-115
91ProSet-136
91ProSet-307
91ProSetFre-136
91ProSetFre-307
91ProSetPla-70
91ScoAme-210
91ScoCan-210
91ScoKel-13
91StaClu-144
91Top-239
91TopTeaSL-15
91UppDec-88
91UppDec-169
91UppDecF-88
91UppDecF-169
92Bow-130
92Par-90
92ParEmel-90
92Pin-351
92PinFre-351
92Sco-30
92ScoCan-30
92StaClu-28
92Top-273
92TopGol-273G
92Ult-115
92UppDec-521
93Don-184
93Lea-264
93OPCPre-193
93OPCPreG-193
93PanSti-40
93Par-115
93ParEmel-115
93Pin-183
93PinCan-183
93Pow-138
93Sco-81
93ScoCan-81
93StaClu-287
93StaCluFDI-287
93StaCluO-287
93TopPre-193
93TopPreG-193
93Ult-53
93UppDec-134
94BeAPSig-134
94CanGamNHLP-146
94Don-151
94Fin-90
94FinRef-90
94FinSupTW-90
94Fla-95
94Fle-114
94Lea-204
94LeaLim-92
94OPCPre-175
94OPCPreSE-175
94Par-125
94ParGol-125
94Pin-101
94PinArtP-101
94PinRinC-101
94Sco-172
94ScoGol-172
94ScoPla-172
94ScoPlaTS-172
94Sel-136
94SelGol-136
94SP-65
94SPDieCut-65
94TopPre-175
94TopPreSE-175
94Ult-119
94UppDec-8
94UppDecEleIce-8
94UppDecSPI-SP133
94UppDecSPIDC-SP133
95Bow-27
95BowAllFoi-27
95CanGamNHLP-160
95ColCho-34
95ColChoPC-34
95ColChoPCP-34
95Don-88
95DonEli-23
95DonEliDCS-23
95DonEliDCU-23
95Emo-98
95Fin-38
95FinRef-38
95Lea-176
95Met-83
95ParInt-123
95ParIntEl-123
95Pin-26
95PinArtP-26
95PinRinC-26
95PlaOneoOne-278
95ProMag-37
95Sco-77
95ScoBlaIce-77
95ScoBlaIceAP-77
95SelCer-92
95SelCerMG-92
95SkyImp-93
95SP-78
95StaClu-26
95StaCluMOMS-26
95Sum-106
95SumArtP-106
95SumIce-106
95Top-140
95TopOPCI-140
95TopSupSki-62
95TopSupSkiPla-62
95Ult-89
95Ult-193
95UltGolM-89
95UltGolM-193
95UppDec-74
95UppDecEleIce-74
95UppDecEleIceG-74
95UppDecSpeE-SE134
95UppDecSpeEdiG-SE134
95Zen-69
96Dev-15
96Don-146
96DonPrePro-146
96Lea-195
96LeaPreP-195
96NHLProSTA-37
96Pin-149
96PinArtP-149
96PinFoi-149
96PinPreS-149
96PinRinC-149
96Sco-143
96ScoArtPro-143
96ScoDeaCAP-143
96ScoGolB-143
96ScoSpeAP-143
96Sum-143
96SumArtP-143
96SumIce-143
96SumMet-143
96SumPreS-143
96UppDec-95
97ColCho-146
97Don-155
97DonLim-60
97DonLimExp-60
97DonPreProG-155
97DonPreProS-155
97Pac-169

97PacCop-169
97PacDyn-71
97PacDynC-71
97PacDynDG-71
97PacDynEG-71
97PacDynIB-71
97PacDynR-71
97PacDynSil-71
97PacDynTan-48
97PacEmeGre-169
97PacOme-202
97PacOmeDG-202
97PacOmeEG-202
97PacOmeG-202
97PacOmeIB-202
97PacOmeC-202
97PacPar-104
97PacParC-104
97PacParDG-104
97PacParEG-104
97PacParIB-104
97PacParRed-104
97PacParSil-104
97PacRed-169
97PacRev-124
97PacRevC-124
97PacRevE-124
97PacRevIB-124
97PacRevR-124
97PacRevS-124
97PacSil-169
97Pin-184
97PinCer-91
97PinCerMB-91
97PinCerMG-91
97PinCerMR-91
97PinCerR-91
97PinIns-145
97PinPrePBB-184
97PinPrePBC-184
97PinPrePBM-184
97PinPrePBY-184
97PinPrePFC-184
97PinPrePFM-184
97PinPrePFY-184
97PinPrePla-184
97PinTotCMPG-91
97PinTotCPB-91
97PinTotCPG-91
97PinTotCPR-91
97Sco-141
97ScoArtPro-141
97ScoDev-4
97ScoDevPla-4
97ScoDevPre-4
97ScoGolBla-141
97UppDec-94
97UppDecBD-68
97UppDecBDDD-68
97UppDecBDQD-68
97UppDecBDTD-68
98Pac-384
98PacIceB-384
98PacRed-384
98UC-176
98UD ChoPCR-176
98UD ChoR-176
98UppDec-320
98UppDecE-320
98UppDecE1o1-320
98UppDecGR-320
99Pac-273
99PacAur-95
99PacAurPD-95
99PacCop-273
99PacGol-273
99PacIceB-273
99PacPreD-273

**MacLean, Paul**
81JetPos-12
81SweSemHVS-86
82Jet-15
82OPC-386
82OPCSti-208
82PosCer-21
83Jet-14
83OPC-388
83OPCSti-283
83PufSti-6
83Vac-131
847EDis-59
84JetPol-13
84KelAccD-2
84OPC-342
84OPC-371
84OPCSti-289
857ECreCar-21
85JetPol-10
85JetSilD-5
85OPC-145
85OPCSti-250
85Top-145
86JetBor-12
86KraDra-38
86OPC-114
86OPCSti-108
86Top-114
87Jet-12
87OPC-91
87OPCSti-252
87PanSti-364
87Top-91
88OPC-38
88OPCMin-23
88OPCSti-144
88PanSti-156
88RedWinLC-14
88Top-38
89BluKod-15
89OPC-129
89OPCSti-18
89Top-129
90BluKod-13
90Bow-18
90BowTif-18
90OPC-110
90PanSti-271
90ProSet-266
90Sco-203
90ScoCan-203
90Top-110
90TopTif-110
90UppDec-330
90UppDecF-330
93PeoRiv-18
98KanCitB-25

**MacLean, Paul (juniors)**
87BroBra-6
88BroBra-9

**MacLean, Terry**
88ProIHL-86
89ProIHL-10
92-TulOil-9

**MacLeish, Rick**
710PC-207
71TorSun-203
720PC-105
72SarProSta-167
73FlyLin-11
730PC-133
730PC-138
730PC-146
73Top-1
73Top-6
73Top-135
74LipSou-20
74NHLActSta-210
740PCNHL-6
740PCNHL-163
74Top-6
74Top-163
75FlyCanDC-13
75HerSta-23
750PCNHL-20
75Top-20
760PCNHL-121
76Top-121
770PCNHL-7
770PCNHL-15
77Top-7
77Top-15
77TopGloS-9
77TopOPCGlo-9
780PC-125
78Top-125
790PC-75
79Top-75
800PC-115
80Top-115
810PC-133
81Top-E108
820PC-273
82OPCSti-147
92Par-472
92ParEmel-472

**MacLellan, Brian**
84KinSmo-11
84OPC-85
85OPC-204
86NorSta7E-2
86OPC-33
86Top-33
87NorStaPos-19
870PC-31
87PanSti-294
87Top-31
88NorStaADA-16
880PC-193
880PCSti-197
88PanSti-95
88Top-193
89OPC-208
90FlamIGA-10
900PC-286
90ProSet-36
90ScoRoo-56T
90Top-286
90TopTif-286
90UppDec-372
90UppDecF-372
91Bow-269
91FlamPanTS-8
910PC-50
91ScoCan-582
91ScoRoo-32T
91StaClu-206
91Top-50

**MacLellan, Scott**
81KinCan-2
82KinCan-21
91RayJrC-10

**MacLeod, Jeff**
89GerDELE-53

**MacLeod, Pat**
87KamBla-12
88KamBla-17
89ProIHL-90
90ProAHLIHL-108
910PCPre-87
91Par-161
91ParFre-161
91ProAHLCHL-525
91ProSet-559
91ProSetFre-559
91ScoCan-645
91ScoRoo-95T
91ShaSanJSA-14
91UppDec-578
91UppDecF-578
92Bow-433
920PC-273
92StaClu-336
92Top-317
92TopGol-317G
92UppDec-146
94MilAdm-16
98CinCyc-13

**MacMillan, Billy (Bill)**
69MapLeaWBM-3
70EssPowPla-33
70SarProSta-205
71MapLeaP-10
71SarProSta-198
71TorSun-263
72Flam-7
720PC-98
72SarProSta-5
72Top-77
74NHLActSta-170
740PCNHL-339
760PCNHL-312
81RocPos-14

**MacMillan, Bob**
72FigSaiPos-13
760PCNHL-38
76Top-38
770PCNHL-141
77Top-141
780PC-82
78Top-82
79FlamPos-8
79FlaTeal-9
790PC-210
79PanSti-66
79Top-210
80FlamPos-10
800PC-267
80PepCap-8
810PC-46
81RocPos-15
820PC-143
820PCSti-225
82PosCer-11
830PC-234
83OPCSti-220
83PufSti-11
840PC-40
84OPCSti-72
850PC-193

**MacMillan, Darren**
91AirCanSJHL-E38

**Macmillan, Garry**
69ColChe-12

**MacMillan, Jason**
95Sla-315

**MacMillan, Johnny (John)**
44BeeGro2P-423
61ShiCoi-56
62ShiMetC-14
63ChePho-38
63Par-15

**MacMillan, Tavis**
95SigRooA-27
95SigRooAPC-27

**MacMillan, Todd**
91AirCanSJHL-E15

**MacMillan, Travis**
95AlaGolKin-13

**MacNab, Brent**
56QueAce-10

**MacNair, Scott**
94RalIce-11

**MacNamara, Jerry**
52JunBluT-153

**MacNeil, Al**
44BeeGro2P-118A
44BeeGro2P-118B
44BeeGro2P-263
44BeeGro2P-424
57Par-T19
61ShiCoi-119
61YorYelB-36
62ShiMetC-40
62Top-32
63Top-28
64BeeGro3P-45
64BeeGro3P-139
64CocCap-33
64Top-26
64TorSta-28
65Coc-33
65Top-57
66Top-89
69CanaPosC-16
77NovScoV-14
94ParMisL-121
95Par66-94
95Par66Coi-94

**MacNeil, Bernie**
75StiKah-8

**MacNeil, Ian**
95Sla-247

**MacNevin, Troy**
84KinCan-29
85KinCan-29
86KinCan-15

**Macoun, Jamie**
83Vac-12
840PC-230
85FlamRedRP-17
850PC-201
850PCSti-212
86FlamRedR-12
860PC-203
86OPCSti-85
870PC-214
87OPCSti-48
87PanSti-208
890PC-207
89PanSti-38
90FlamIGA-11
900PC-265
90PanSti-178
90ProSet-37
90Sco-216
90ScoCan-216
90Top-265
90TopTif-265
90UppDec-101
90UppDecF-101
91FlamIGA-8
91FlamPanTS-9
910PC-168
91PanSti-61
91Pin-114
91PinFre-114
91ProSet-38
91ProSetFre-38
91ProSetPla-235
91ScoAme-346
91ScoCan-504
91StaClu-160
91Top-168
91UppDec-412
91UppDecF-412
92Bow-9
92MapLeaK-14
920PC-371
92Pin-294
92PinFre-294
92ProSet-188
92Sco-88
92ScoCan-88
92StaClu-309
92Top-348
92TopGol-348G
92Ult-212
930PCPre-517
93OPCPreG-517
93PanSti-230
93Pin-131
93PinCan-131
93Pow-451
93Sco-224
93ScoBla-11
93ScoCan-224
93TopPre-517
93TopPreG-517
93Ult-431
94CanGamNHLP-240
94Lea-418
94MapLeaG-11
94MapLeaK-18
94MapLeaP-1
94MapLeaPP-10
940PCPre-102
94OPCPreSE-102
94ParSE-SE179
94ParSEG-SE179
94Pin-297
94PinArtP-297
94PinRinC-297
94Sco-106
94ScoGol-106
94ScoPla-106
94ScoPlaTS-106
94TopPre-102
94TopPreSE-102
94Ult-217
95BeAPla-218
95BeAPSig-S218
95BeAPSigDC-S218
95UppDec-331
95UppDecEleIce-331
95UppDecEleIceG-331
96UppDec-166
97Pac-231
97PacCop-231
97PacEmeGre-231
97PacIceB-231
97PacRed-231
97PacSil-231

**Macphee, Wayne**
83NorBayC-18
94BraSmo-18

**MacPherson, Alex**
71BluPos-16

**MacPherson, B.J.**
907thInnSOHL-343
917thInnSOHL-158
910shGen-16
910shGenS-5
920shGenS-13
93NorBayC-13
94TolSto-13
95TolSto-9

**MacPherson, Blair**
85KitRan-26

**MacPherson, Bud**
44BeeGro2P-264
51Par-6
52Par-11
53Par-22
55Par-47
85ParQuaO-47

**MacPherson, Donald**
907thInnSOHL-87

**MacPherson, Duncan**
83SasBla-4
84SasBlaS-12
88ProAHL-307

**MacPherson, James**
45QuaOatP-94

**Macpherson, Scott**
98CinCyc-26

**MacQuisten, Doug**
36V356WorG-105

**MacRae, Jim**
81FreExp-25
82FreExp-25

**MacSwain, Steve**
96AncAce-5
97AncAce-13

**MacTavish, Craig**
85OilRedR-14
86OilRedR-14
86OilTeal-14
860PC-178
860PCSti-76
86Top-178
870ilTeal-14
870PC-203
87OPCSti-91
87PanSti-267
88OilTeal-19
880ilTenAnn-21
880PC-232
880PCSti-217
88PanSti-60
890ilTeal-16
890PC-230
89OPCSti-226
89PanSti-78
90Bow-193
90BowTif-193
900ilIGA-15
900PC-189
90PanSti-220
90ProSet-90
90Sco-258
90ScoCan-258
90Top-189
90TopTif-189
90UppDec-169
90UppDecF-169
91Bow-100
910ilIGA-11
910ilPanTS-13
910ilTeal-13
910PC-63
91PanSti-132
91Par-276
91ParFre-276
91Pin-215
91PinFre-215
91ProSet-77
91ProSetFre-77
91ScoAme-202
91ScoCan-202
91StaClu-133
91Top-63
91UppDec-284
91UppDecF-284
92Bow-118
920ilIGA-12
920ilTeal-11
920PC-118
92PanSti-101
92PanStiFre-101
92Par-48
92ParEmel-48
92Pin-78
92PinFre-78
92Sco-303
92ScoCan-303
92StaClu-125
92Top-336
92TopGol-336G
92Ult-294
92UppDec-425
93Don-462
93Kra-48
930PCPre-23
93OPCPreG-23
93PanSti-240
93Par-342
93ParEmel-342
93Pin-96
93PinCan-96
93PinCap-8
93PinCapC-8
93Pow-82
93Sco-8
93ScoCan-8
93StaClu-410
93StaCluFDI-410
93StaCluO-410
93TopPre-23
93TopPreG-23
93Ult-316
93UppDec-111
94BeAPSig-72
94FinRinL-8
94Lea-514
940PCPre-103
94OPCPreSE-103
94Par-145
94ParGol-145
94ParSE-SE132
94ParSEG-SE132
94Pin-392
94PinArtP-392
94PinRinC-392
94Sco-85
94ScoGol-85
94ScoPla-85
94ScoPlaTS-85
94TopPre-103
94TopPreSE-103
94UppDec-225
94UppDecEleIce-225
95Pin-148
95PinArtP-148
95PinRinC-148
95Sco-249
95ScoBlaIce-249
95ScoBlaIceAP-249
96ColCho-227
96Don-103
96DonPreePro-103
96Lea-192
96LeaPreP-192
96Sco-230
96ScoArtPro-230
96ScoDeaCAP-230
96ScoGolB-230
96ScoSpeAP-230
96StaCluMO-23

**MacVicar, Andy**
89SudWol-18

**MacWilliams, Mike**
88FliSpi-14
91ProAHLCHL-348

**Macy, Erik**
95NorlowH-19

**Madden, Chris**
96GueSto-21
97GueSto-4

**Madden, John**
93MicWol-15
99Pac-239
99PacCop-239
99PacIceB-239
99PacPreD-239
99RetHoc-47
99UppDecM-122
99UppDecMGS-122
99UppDecMSS-122
99UppDecMSS-122
99UppDecRG-47
99UppDecRP-47

**Madeley, Darrin**
91LakSupSL-16
92Cla-65
93ClaProPro-17
93ClaProPro-40
93Don-229
93Lea-299
930PCPre-283
93OPCPreG-283
93Par-142
93ParEmel-142
93Pin-211
93PinCan-211
93Pow-400
93Sco-462
93ScoCan-462
93SenKraS-16
93StaClu-431
93StaCluO-431
93TopPre-283
93TopPreG-283
93Ult-382
93UppDec-61
94Lea-300
940PCPre-109
94OPCPreSE-109
94ParSE-SE120
94ParSEG-SE120
94Pin-459
94PinArtP-459
94PinRinC-459
94Sco-51
94ScoGol-51
94ScoPla-51
94ScoPlaTS-51
94SenBelM-19
94TopPre-109
94TopPreSE-109
94Ult-340
95UppDec-158
95UppDecEleIce-158
95UppDecEleIceG-158
96ClaGol-65

**Mader, Bob**
52JunBluT-87

**Madia, Rob**
94CenHocL-14

**Madill, Jeff**
88ProAHL-335
89ProAHL-204
90ProAHLIHL-571
910PCIns-6S
91ProAHLCHL-521
95ColEdgI-191

**Madore, Stephane**
917thInnSQMJHL-151
96LouRiv-16
97LouRivF-15

**Magarrell, Adam**
95SigRoo-53
95SigRooSig-53
95SpoChi-22

**Maggs, Darryl**
71TorSun-71

**Magliarditi, Marc**
95DonEliWJ-24
98FloEve-13

**Magnertoft, Marcus**
93SweSemE-181
94SweLeaE-237
95SweLeaE-89
95SweUppDE-143

**Magnusson, Keith**
70BlaBor-7
70DadCoo-73
70EssPowPla-111
700PC-151
70SarProSta-35
710PC-69
71SarProSta-48
71Top-69
71TorSun-72
720PC-71
720PC-268
72SarProSta-5
72SweSemWC-230
72Top-65
72Top-87
730PC-151
73Top-44
74NHLActSta-88
740PCNHL-75
74Top-75
750PCNHL-176
75Top-176
760PCNHL-125
76Top-125
770PCNHL-89
77Top-89
780PC-34
78Top-34
80BlaBroBac-5
81BlaBorPos-14
81BlaBroBac-5

**Magnussen, Trond**
92SweSemE-312
93SweSemWCS-244
94FinnJaaK-265
95SweGloWC-196
96SweSemW-207

**Magnusson, Ingemar**
67SweHoc-89

**Magnusson, Mikael**
92SweSemE-85
93SweSemE-58
94SweLeaE-3
95SweLeaE-29
95SweUppDE-43

**Magnusson, Steve**
91MinGolG-13
91SweSemE-106
92MinGolG-11
93MinGolG-17
94CenHocL-51

**Maguire, Bill**
82NorBayC-14

**Maguire, Derek**
92HarCri-20
94Cla-56
94ClaDraGol-56
94FreCan-19

**Maguire, Kevin**
87SabBluS-17
87SabWonBH-18
88SabBluS-15
88SabWonBH-16
89SabBluS-11
89SabCam-13
90ProSet-538
91Bow-172
91MapLeaPTS-13
91ProAHLCHL-347

**Mahaffy, Johnny**
36V356WorG-133
51LavDaiQSHL-55

**Maher, Jeremy**
92QueIntP-22

**Maher, Jim**
92PhoRoa-14
93PhoRoa-17
94TolSto-14

**Mahon, Dan**
82KinCan-14

**Mahon, Mark**
96GerDELE-219
83NorStaPos-15

**Mahoney, Bill**
83NorStaPos-15

**Mahoney, Scott**
89SudWol-5

**Mahovlich, Frank**
44BeeGro2P-425
57Par-T17
58Par-33
59Par-24
60Par-2
60ShiCoi-12
60YorPreP-22
61Par-2
61ShiCoi-43
61YorYelB-3

62ElProDis-5
62Par-4
62Par-18
62ShiMetC-3
62ShiMetC-53
62YorIroOTra-11
63ChePho-35
63MapLeaWB-14
63MapLeaWB-15
63Par-17
63Par-77
63TorSta-25
63YorWhiB-5
64BeeGro3P-174A
64BeeGro3P-174B
64CocCap-108
64Top-85
64TorSta-29
65Coc-107
65Top-81
66Top-77
66Top-131
66TopUSAT-51
67PosFliB-5
67Top-79
67YorActOct-18
67YorActOct-20
67YorActOct-28
67YorActOct-35
68OPC-17
68OPCPucSti-2
68ShiCoi-45
68Top-31
69CanaPosC-17
69MapLeaWBG-21
69OPC-62
69OPC-222
69OPCFou-4
69OPCSta-19
69Top-62
70CanaPin-10
70DadCoo-74
70EssPowPla-143
70OPC-22
70OPC-242
70OPCDec-17
70PosCerS-10
70RedWinM-7
70SarProSta-63
70Top-22
70TopStiS-21
71Baz-2
71CanaPos-14
71ColHea-6
71FriLay-3
71LetActR-8
71OPC-105
71SarProSta-104
71Top-105
71TorSun-157
72CanaPos-13
72KellroT-5
72OPC-102
72OPC-128
72OPCTeaC-17
72SarProSta-120
72SweHocS-119
72SweSemWC-195
72Top-140
73CanaPos-15
73MacMil-15
73OPC-145
73Top-40
74OPCNHL-124
74OPCWHA-40
74TeaCanLWHA-15
74Top-124
75OPCWHA-110
76OPCWHA-111
77OPCWHA-61
81TCMA-10
83HalFP-I10
85HalFC-121
88EssAllSta-28
91FutTreC72-26
91FutTreC72-30
91Kra-87
91StaPicH-27
91UltOriSF-40
91UltOriSF-40
92ParParR-PR29
92ZelMasH-4
92ZelMasoHS-4
93OPCCanHF-24
93OPCCanHF-39
93ParParR-PR44
93UppDecLAS-44
94HocWit-56
94ParMisLA-6
94ParMisLFS-FS5
94ParTalB-130
94ParTalB-143
94ParTalBM-SL6
95Par66-102
95Par66-145
95Par66Coi-102
99UppDecCL-27
99UppDecCLCLC-27
99UppDecES-10

**Mahovlich, Peter (Pete)**
64BeeGro3P-85
66Top-103
66TopUSAT-21
68OPC-143

68ShiCoi-36
69CanaPosC-18
70CanaPin-11
70EssPowPla-14
70OPC-58
70PosCerS-11
70SarProSta-102
70Top-58
71CanaPos-15
71OPC-84
71SarProSta-99
71Top-84
71TorSun-158
72CanaPos-14
72CanGreWLP-4
72OPC-124
72OPCTeaC-18
72SarProSta-114
72Top-42
73CanaPos-16
73MacMil-16
73OPC-164
73Top-186
74CanaPos-16
74LipSou-39
74NHLActSta-146
74OPCNHL-97
74Top-97
75CanaPos-13
75HerSta-11
75OPCNHL-50
75OPCNHL-209
75OPCNHL-322
75Top-50
75Top-209
75Top-322
76CanaPos-14
76OPCNHL-2
76OPCNHL-15
76OPCNHL-388
76Top-2
76Top-15
77OPCNHL-205
77Top-205
78OPC-51
78Top-51
79OPC-187
79Top-187
80OPC-72
80OPCSup-6
80Top-72
91FutTreC72-27
91FutTreC72-30
92ForWorF-12
92FutTre76CC-180
95Par66-46
95Par66Coi-46

**Maia, Pierrick**
94FinnJaaK-223
94FreNatT-18
95SweGloWC-202

**Maidl, Anton**
94GerDELE-138
95GerDELE-131

**Maier, Arno**
93SweSemWCS-281
94FinnJaaK-245

**Maier, Kim**
91AirCanSJHL-A42
91AirCanSJHLAS-24
91AirCanSJHLAS-47
91AirCanSJHLAS-48
92WheThu-9
93KnoChe-8

**Mailhot, Jacques**
88ProAHL-103
89ProIHL-119
91ProAHLCHL-431

**Maillet, Chris**
93RedDeeR-13

**Maillet, Claude**
92GreMon-14

**Mailloux, Chris**
93DetJrRW-4

**Mailloux, Robert**
95Sla-114
98BowCHL-33
98BowCHLGA-33
98BowCHLOI-33
98BowChrC-33
98BowChrCGA-33
98BowChrCGAR-33
98BowChrCOI-33
98BowChrCOIR-33
98BowChrCR-33

**Mainer, Petr**
94CzeAPSE-100
95CzeAPSE-225

**Mair, Adam**
95Sla-298
97BowCHL-144
97BowCHLAu-24
97BowCHLOPC-144

**Mair, Jim (James)**
72OPC-232
72SarProSta-140

**Mair, Michael**
82SweSemHVS-135

**Maisonneuve, Roger**
52JunBluT-88

**Maitland, Shane**
907thInnSWHL-194
917thInnSMC-93
917thInnSWHL-15

**Majaury, Craig**
86LonKni-20

**Majic, Ron**
91NasKni-6
93HunBli-15
94HamRoaA-20

**Majic, Xavier**
93RenEng-16

**Major, Bruce**
90ProAHLIHL-545

**Major, Mark**
90ProAHLIHL-380
91ProAHLCHL-294
92CleLum-24
95AdiRedW-13
95BufStaRHI-32

**Majorov, Boris**
93FinnJyvHS-283
93FinnSIS-57
94FinnSIS-397

**Makarov, Nikolai**
82SweSemHVS-75

**Makarov, Sergei**
79PanSti-157
81SweSemHVS-51
82SweSemHVS-60
83RusNatT-12
87RusNatT-14
89Kra-4
89RusNatT-18
89SweSemWCS-96
90Bow-92
90BowTif-92
90FlamIGA-12
90FlamIGA-13
90OPC-60
90OPC-503
90OPCBoxB-P
90PanSti-184
90PanSti-334
90ProSet-38
90ProSet-379
90ProSet-396
90Sco-71
90Sco-329
90Sco-350
90Sco-362
90ScoCan-71
90ScoCan-329
90ScoCan-350
90ScoCan-362
90ScoHotRS-99
90Top-60
90TopBoxB-P
90TopTif-60
90UppDec-123
90UppDec-202
90UppDec-336
90UppDecF-123
90UppDecF-202
90UppDecF-336
91Bow-250
91Bow-264
91FlamIGA-9
91FlamPanTS-10
91OPC-482
91OPCPre-45
91PanSti-9
91Par-247
91ParFre-247
91Pin-271
91PinFre-271
91ProSet-39
91ProSetFre-39
91ProSetPla-15
91RusStaNHL-7
91RusStaRA-13
91ScoAme-51
91ScoCan-51
91StaClu-31
91SweSemWCS-216
91Top-482
91UppDec-321
91UppDecF-321
92Bow-53
92FlamIGA-15
92OPC-90
92PanSti-47
92PanStiFre-47
92Par-25
92ParEmel-25
92Pin-335
92PinFre-335
92ProSet-24
92Sco-382
92ScoCan-382
92ScoSha-2
92ScoShaCan-2
92StaClu-217
92Top-467
92TopGol-467G
92Ult-24
92UppDec-314
92UppDecES-E16
93Don-304
93Lea-384

93PanSti-183
93Par-188
93ParEmel-188
93Pin-362
93PinCan-362
93Pow-222
93Sco-33
93Sco-531
93ScoCan-33
93ScoCan-531
93ScoDynDUS-8
93ScoGol-531
93Ult-416
93UppDec-446
93UppDecSP-145
94CanGamNHLP-217
94Don-103
94FinnJaaK-155
94Fla-167
94Fle-198
94Lea-282
94OPCPre-396
94OPCPreSE-396
94Par-211
94ParGol-211
94Pin-152
94PinArtP-152
94PinRinC-152
94Sei-8
94SelGol-8
94SP-107
94SPDieCut-107
94StaClu-123
94StaCluFDI-123
94StaCluMOMS-123
94StaCluST-21
94StaCluSTWC-123
94TopPre-396
94TopPreSE-396
94Ult-198
94UppDec-124
94UppDecEIeIce-124
94UppDecSPI-SP72
94UppDecSPIDC-SP72
95ColCho-207
95ColChoPC-207
95ColChoPCP-207
95Emo-158
95Lea-293
95Sco-159
95ScoBlaIce-159
95ScoBlaIceAP-159
95SweGloWC-238
95Top-171
95TopOPCI-171
95Ult-148
95UltGolM-148
95UppDec-24
95UppDecEIeIce-24
95UppDecEIeIceG-24
**Makarov, Sergei B**
900PC-485
**Makatsch, Rainer**
72SweSemWC-116
**Makela, Erkki**
93FinnJyvHS-259
**Makela, Jarno**
93FinnSIS-228
94FinnSIS-247
95FinnSIS-158
**Makela, Mikko**
87PanSti-100
88OPC-44
88OPCSti-44
88PanSti-291
88Top-44
89Isl-12
89KinSmo-22
89OPC-247
89OPCSti-112
89PanSti-270
89SweSemWCS-41
90OPC-229
90OPCPre-66
90PanSti-237
90ProSet-418
90SabBluS-13
90SabCam-15
90ScoRoo-26T
90Top-229
90TopTif-229
91Bow-36
91OPC-503
91PanSti-302
91ScoCan-549
91StaClu-261
91Top-503
93SweSemE-192
93SweSemWCS-68
94FinnJaaK-31
94FinnSIS-345
94FinnSISGS-5
94Lea-515
94Ult-258
95FinnSemWC-42
95FinnSISL-106
95SweGloWC-142
96GerDELE-286
**Makela, Seppo**
93FinnSIS-380
**Makela, Timo**
91GreMon-9
**Maki, Brent**
83OshGen-23

**Maki, Chico**
44BeeGro2P-119A
44BeeGro2P-119B
61ShiCoi-28
62Top-37
63ChePho-36
63Top-41
64BeeGro3P-46A
64BeeGro3P-46B
64CocCap-30
64Top-73
64TorSta-30
65Coc-31
65Top-117
66Top-110
66TopUSAT-53
67Top-111
68Bla-3
68OPC-17
68ShiCoi-23
68Top-17
69OPC-137
70DadCoo-75
70EssPowPla-122
70OPC-149
70SarProSta-46
71CanuRoyB-20
71OPC-210
71SarProSta-36
71TorSun-73
72OPC-198
72SarProSta-60
73OPC-227
74NHLActSta-90
74OPCNHL-395
94ParTalB-24
95Par66-32
95Par66Coi-32
**Maki, Timo**
93FinnJyvHS-194
93FinnSIS-257
94FinnSIS-312
**Maki, Wayne**
67Top-55
68ShiCoi-19
70CanuRoyB-19
70EssPowPla-46
70OPC-116
70Top-116
71CanuRoyB-20
71OPC-58
71SarProSta-217
71Top-58
71TorSun-284
72CanuNal-3
72CanuRoyB-13
72OPC-84
72SarProSta-216
72SweSemWC-221
72Top-32
**Maki-Kokkila, Kimmo**
93FinnJyvHS-209
93FinnSIS-270
94FinnSIS-323
95FinnSIS-207
**Makiaho, Toni**
94Fin-139
94FinnSIS-272
94FinRef-139
94FinSupTW-139
95FinnSIS-27
96FinnSISR-23
**Makila, Rainer**
50QueCit-15
51LavDaiLSJ-41
**Makinen, Kari**
93FinnJyvHS-253
**Makinen, Marko**
95FinnSIS-333
95FinnSISDD-4
97LouRivF-11
**Makinen, Timo**
96FinnSISR-116
**Makitalo, Jarmo**
82SweSemHVS-41
83SweSemE-217
84SweSemE-230
85SwePanS-152
86SwePanS-152
87SweSemS-161
89SweSemE-137
92SweSemE-173
93SweSemE-144
94FinnSIS-368
94SweLeaE-77
**Makitalo, Jukka**
94FinnSIS-340
**Makkonen, Kari**
79OilRev-16
88OilTenAnn-144
**Malac, Pavel**
94CzeAPSE-182
95CzeAPSE-30
**Malakhov, Vladimir**
900PCRedA-2R
91SweSemWCS-80
91UppDec-1
91UppDecF-1
920PCPre-89
92Par-339
92ParEmel-339
92Pin-409
92PinFre-409
92RusStaRA-28

92RusStaRA-19
92TriFroRWP-19
92TriFroRWP-20
92Ult-346
92UltImp-14
92UppDec-554
92UppDec-577
92UppDecCC-CC12
92UppDecER-ER15
92UppDecGHS-G12
93ClaProPBC-BC4
93ClaProPro-55
93Don-207
93Lea-32
93LeaGolR-9
930PCPre-129
930PCPre-445
930PCPre-515
930PCPreG-129
930PCPreG-445
930PCPreG-515
93Par-125
93Par-239
93ParEmel-125
93ParEmel-239
93Pin-104
93PinCan-104
93Pow-153
93PowSecYS-6
93Sco-157
93ScoCan-157
93StaClu-248
93StaCluFDI-248
93StaCluFDIO-248
93StaCluO-248
93SweSemWCS-142
93TopPre-129
93TopPre-445
93TopPre-515
93TopPreG-129
93TopPreG-445
93TopPreG-515
93Ult-235
93UppDec-29
93UppDec-283
93UppDecLAS-57
93UppDecSP-93
94BeAPla-R125
94BeAPASig-121
94CanGamNHLP-162
94Don-307
94EASpo-79
94FinnJaaK-137
94FinnJaaK-341
94Fla-105
94Fle-126
94Lea-194
94OPCPre-546
94OPCPreSE-546
94ParSE-SE108
94ParSEG-SE108
94ParVin-V77
94Pin-104
94PinArtP-104
94PinBoo-BR2
94PinRinC-104
94Sco-62
94ScoGol-62
94ScoPla-62
94ScoPlaTS-62
94SP-60
94SPDieCut-60
94StaClu-144
94StaCluFDI-144
94StaCluMOMS-144
94StaCluSTWC-144
94TopPre-546
94TopPreSE-546
94Ult-130
94UppDec-139
94UppDecEIeIce-139
94UppDecSPI-SP47
94UppDecSPIDC-SP47
95CanaPos-9
95CanaShe-7
95CanGamNHLP-151
95ColCho-143
95ColChoPC-143
95ColChoPCP-143
95Don-4
95Emo-88
95Lea-149
95ParInt-115
95ParIntEl-115
95PlaOneoOne-273
95Sco-117
95ScoBlaIce-117
95ScoBlaIceAP-117
95SkyImp-85
95Sum-157
95SumArtP-157
95SumIce-157
95SweGloWC-166
95Top-113
95TopOPCI-113
95Ult-81
95UltGolM-81
95UppDec-466
95UppDecEIeIce-466
95UppDecEIeIceG-466
95UppDecSpeE-SE45
95UppDecSpeEdiG-SE45
96CanaPos-16
96CanaShe-10
96ColCho-139

96FlePic-118
96SweSemW-135
96TeaOut-55
96UppDec-84
97BeA PPAD-133
97BeA PPAPD-133
97BeAPla-133
97CanaPos-11
97Kat-76
97KatGol-76
97KatSil-76
97PacInvNRB-103
97PacOme-119
97PacOmeC-119
97PacOmeDG-119
97PacOmeEG-119
97PacOmeG-119
97PacOmeIB-119
97Sco-247
97ScoCan-11
97ScoCanPla-11
97SPAut-83
98BeA PPA-222
98BeA PPAA-222
98BeA PPAAF-222
98BeA PPSE-222
98BeA APP-222
98Fin-57
98FinNo P-57
98FinNo PR-57
98FinRef-57
98Pac-253
98PacIceB-253
98PacPar-114
98PacParC-114
98PacParEG-114
98PacParH-114
98PacParIB-114
98PacParS-114
98PacRed-253
98ScoCanPre-11
98UC-104
98UD ChoPCR-104
98UD ChoR-104
98UppDec-112
98UppDecE-112
98UppDecE1o1-112
98UppDecGR-112
99Pac-206
99PacCop-206
99PacGol-206
99PacIceB-206
99PacPreD-206
99UppDecM-102
99UppDecMGS-102
99UppDecMSS-102
99UppDecMSS-102
**Malanson, Robert**
907thInnSQMJHL-153
**Malanson, Stan**
907thInnSQMJHL-231
**Malarchuk, Clint**
81FreExp-6
82FreExp-4
82NordPos-12
83NordPos-15
84FreExp-10
85NordGenF-15
85NordMcD-13
85NordPla-6
85NordPro-14
85NordTeal-14
86KraDra-39
86NordGenF-15
86NordMcD-15
86NordTeal-14
86NordYumY-6
86OPC-47
86OPCSti-33
86Top-47
87CapKod-30
87CapTealss-15
87OPC-246
87PanSti-158
88CapBor-13
88CapSmo-13
88OPC-25
88OPCSti-72
88PanSti-363
88Top-25
89OPC-170
89SabBluS-12
89SabCam-14
89Top-170
90OPC-371
90PanSti-26
90ProSet-25
90SabBluS-14
90SabCam-16
90Sco-289
90ScoCan-289
90Top-371
90TopTif-371
90UppDec-399
90UppDecF-399
91Bow-23
91OPC-97
91PanSti-301
91Par-244
91ParFre-244
91Pin-103
91Pin-397
91PinFre-103
91PinFre-397

91ProSetPla-159
91SabBluS-11
91SabPepC-11
91ScoAme-438
91ScoCan-419
91StaClu-251
91Top-97
91UppDec-368
91UppDecF-368
92Bow-30
92SanDieG-16
92Sco-138
92ScoCan-138
92StaClu-186
92Top-363
92TopGol-363G
93LasVegThu-19
94ClaProP-85
94LasVegThu-14
95LasVegThu-24
96LasVegThu-14
**Malcolm, Bob**
71RocAme-12
**Malenfant, Dave**
96RimOce-18
96RimOceQPP-17
97RimOce-14
**Malenfant, Ken**
91AirCanSJHL-D27
**Malenfant, Ray**
36V356WorG-108
**Maley, Brennan**
90ProAHLIHL-562
**Maley, David**
85CanaPos-19
87CanaPos-16
88DevCar-19
89DevCar-16
90Dev-16
90OPC-438
90ProSet-171A
90ProSet-171B
90Sco-310A
90ScoCan-310A
91OPC-476
91Par-99
91ParFre-99
91Pin-272
91PinFre-272
91ProSet-421
91ProSetFre-421
91ScoCan-426
91Top-476
92Sco-370
92ScoCan-370
93StaClu-259
93StaCluFDI-259
93StaCluO-259
**Malgin, Albert**
91OPCIns-54R
93SwiHNL-308
95SwiHNL-280
**Malgunas, Kevin**
907thInnSWHL-5
917thInnSWHL-156
92RicRen-12
93HamRoaA-13
**Malgunas, Stewart**
90ProAHLIHL-487
91ProAHLCHL-123
93Don-470
93OPCPre-516
93OPCPreG-516
93Par-420
93ParEmel-420
93Sco-612
93ScoCan-612
93ScoGol-612
93StaClu-409
93StaCluFDI-409
93StaCluO-409
93TopPre-516
93TopPreG-516
93Ult-390
93UppDec-425
94Lea-170
95JetTeaIss-13
96PorPir-4
**Malhotra, Manny**
96GueSto-8
96GueSto-32
96GueStoPC-10
97GueSto-8
97UppDec-413
97UppDecBD-79
97UppDecBDDD-79
97UppDecBDQD-79
97UppDecBDTD-79
97Zen-96
97Zen5x7-76
97ZenGolImp-76
97ZenSilImp-76
97ZenZGol-96
97ZenZSil-96
98Be A PPA-241
98Be A PPAA-241
98Be A PPAAF-241
98Be A PPSE-241
98Be APG-241
98BowBes-106
98BowBesA-A10A
98BowBesA-A10B
98BowBesAAR-A10A
98BowBesAAR-A10B
98BowBesAR-106
98BowBesAR-A10A
98BowBesAR-A10B
98BowBesP-BP6
98BowBesPAR-BP6
98BowBesPR-BP6
98BowBesR-106
98BowCHL-10
98BowCHL-148
98BowCHLAuB-A5
98BowCHLAuG-A5
98BowCHLAuS-A5
98BowCHLGA-10
98BowCHLGA-148
98BowCHLOI-10
98BowCHLOI-148
98BowCHLSC-SC2
98BowChrC-10
98BowChrC-148
98BowChrCGA-10
98BowChrCGA-148
98BowChrCGAR-10
98BowChrCGAR-148
98BowChrCOI-10
98BowChrCOI-148
98BowChrCOIR-10
98BowChrCOIR-148
98BowChrCR-10
98BowChrCR-148
98FinFutF-F2
98FinFutFR-F2
98O-PChr-235
98O-PChrR-235
98PacCroR-90
98PacCroRLS-90
98PacCroRRC-6
98PacDynI-124
98PacDynIIB-124
98PacDynIR-124
98PacOmeH-159
98PacOmeODI-159
98PacOmeR-159
98PacRev-95
98PacRevIS-95
98PacRevR-95
98SP Aut-101
98SP AutSotTG-MM
98SPXTopP-40
98SPXTopPF-40
98SPXTopPR-40
98SSASotT-MM
98Top-235
98TopGolLC1-93
98TopGolLC1B-93
98TopGolLC1BOoO-93
98TopGolLC1OoO-93
98TopGolLC1R-93
98TopGolLC1ROoO-93
98TopGolLC2-93
98TopGolLC2B-93
98TopGolLC2BOoO-93
98TopGolLC2OoO-93
98TopGolLC2R-93
98TopGolLC2ROoO-93
98TopGolLC3-93
98TopGolLC3B-93
98TopGolLC3BOoO-93
98TopGolLC3OoO-93
98TopGolLC3R-93
98TopGolLC3ROoO-93
98TopO-P-235
98UC-255
98UD ChoPCR-255
98UD ChoR-255
98UppDec-420
98UppDecBD-57
98UppDecDD-57
98UppDecE-420
98UppDecE1o1-420
98UppDecGJ-GJ11
98UppDecGN-GN6
98UppDecGNQ1-GN6
98UppDecGNQ2-GN6
98UppDecGNQ3-GN6
98UppDecGR-420
98UppDecM-134
98UppDecM1-M8
98UppDecM2-M8
98UppDecMGS-134
98UppDecMP-MM
98UppDecMSS-134
98UppDecMSS-134
98UppDecP-P12
98UppDecPQ1-P12
98UppDecPQ2-P12
98UppDecPQ3-P12
98UppDecQD-57
98UppDecTD-57
98UppDecWFG-WF14
98UppDecWFP-WF14
99Pac-274
99PacCop-274
99PacGol-274
99PacIceB-274
99PacPreD-274
99SP AutPS-101
99UppDecM-136
99UppDecMGS-136
99UppDecMSS-136
99UppDecMSS-136
**Malik, Marek**
94ParSE-SE212
94ParSEG-SE212
94UppDec-482
94UppDec-506
94UppDec-558
94UppDecEleIce-482
94UppDecEleIce-506
94UppDecEleIce-558
95Don-150
95ParInt-99
95ParIntEI-99
95Sco-298
95ScoBlaIce-298
95ScoBlaIceAP-298
95Top-57
95TopOPCI-57
95UppDec-58
95UppDecEleIce-58
95UppDecEleIceG-58
96BeAPAut-110
96BeAPAutSil-110
96BeAPla-110
96ColCho-118
96Lea-227
96LeaPreP-227
96Pin-225
96PinArtP-225
96PinFoi-225
96PinPreS-225
96PinRinC-225
96WhaBobS-14
97Pac-322
97PacCop-322
97PacEmeGre-322
97PacIceB-322
97PacRed-322
97PacSil-322
**Malinowski, Merlin**
81OPC-76
81OPCSti-228
81RocPos-16
81Top-W81
82OPC-128
82OPCSti-229
82PosCer-11
83OPC-142
**Malinsky, Jiri**
94CzeAPSE-26
96CzeAPSE-147
**Malkoc, Dean**
907thInnSMC-16
907thInnSWHL-69
91ProAHLCHL-409
94IndIce-15
95StaClu-221
95StaCluMOMS-221
95UppDec-330
95UppDecEleIce-330
95UppDecEleIceG-330
97Be A PPAD-23
97Be A PPAPD-23
97BeAPla-23
97BeAPlaAut-23
**Malkov, Petr**
93SwiHNL-153
95SwiHNL-184
**Mall, Station**
82SauSteMG-24
**Mallen, Ken**
10C55SweCP-7
11C55-7
**Mallett, Kurt**
94RicRen-9
95RicRen-10
**Mallette, Troy**
87SauSteMG-20
89RanMarMB-26
90Bow-219
90BowTif-219
90OPC-277
90PanSti-100
90ProSet-492
90RayJrC-13
90Sco-288
90ScoCan-288
90Top-277
90TopTif-277
90UppDec-11
90UppDecF-11
91Bow-65
91OilIGA-12
91OilTeaI-14
91OPC-474
91OPCPre-39
91PanSti-295
91ProSet-157
91ProSetFre-157
91ScoAme-178
91ScoCan-178
91ScoCan-601
91StaClu-134
91Top-474
91UppDec-326
91UppDecF-326
92StaClu-432
92Top-335
92TopGol-335G
93Don-227
93Lea-228
93Par-413
93ParEmel-413
93Pow-401
93SenKraS-17
93StaClu-444
93StaCluFDI-444
93StaCluO-444
93UppDec-418
94CanGamNHLP-354
94Don-329
94Lea-358
94OPCPre-303
94OPCPreSE-303
94Par-160
94ParGol-160
94SenBelM-20
94StaClu-94
94StaCluFDI-94
94StaCluMOMS-94
94StaCluSTWC-94
94TopPre-303
94TopPreSE-303
94Ult-150
94UppDec-196
94UppDecEleIce-196
95Sen-14
95UppDec-461
95UppDecEleIce-461
95UppDecEleIceG-461
96BeAPAut-72
96BeAPAutSil-72
96BeAPla-72
97PacInvNRB-14
**Mallgrave, Matt**
92HarCri-21
93St.JohML-15
94ClaProP-109
94HamRoaA-19
**Mallon, Jason**
95RicRen-13
**Malloy, Mike**
88RobBra-13
**Malmberg, Ove**
64SweCorI-2
64SweCorI-130
65SweCorI-2
65SweCorI-130
**Malmstrom, Par**
71SweHocS-99
**Malo, Andre**
97SheSte-11
97SheSte-15
97SheSte-17
**Malo, Gaeten**
94GerDELE-60
95GerDELE-60
96GerDELE-257
**Malone, Cliff**
51LavDaiQSHL-91
52St.LawS-15
**Malone, Greg**
77PenPucB-12
78OPC-233
78Top-233
79OPC-9
79Top-9
80OPC-186
80Top-186
81OPC-264
82OPC-272
82PosCer-15
83OPC-284
83OPCSti-229
83PenHeiP-17
83PufSti-7
83WhaJunHC-11
83WhaJunHC-12
84OPC-74
84OPCSti-194
84Top-57
84WhaJunW-11
85OPC-118
85OPCSti-166
85Top-118
85WhaJunW-12
86FreExp-19
**Malone, Joe**
10C55SweCP-4
11C55-4
12C57-48
23V1451-13
60Top-3
60TopSta-34
83HalFP-N9
85HalFC-204
91ProSet-332
91ProSetFre-332
93OPCCanHF-55
99UppDecCL-41
99UppDecCLCLC-41
**Malone, Scott**
94BinRan-10
94Cla-66
94ClaDraGol-66
94ClaTri-T43
95BinRan-15
**Maloney, Dan**
71TorSun-74
72OPC-264
72SarProSta-70
73OPC-32
73Top-32
74NHLActSta-121
74OPCNHL-172
74Top-172
75OPCNHL-177
75Top-177
76OPCNHL-101
76Top-101
77OPCNHL-172
77Top-172
78MapLeaP-12
78OPC-21
78Top-21
79MapLeaP-17
79OPC-271
80OPC-118
80PepCap-90
80Top-118
81MapLeaP-10
81OPC-320
81OPCSti-102
82MapLeaP-22
82OPC-326
82OPCSti-72
83MapLeaP-14
84MapLeaP-16
86JetBor-3
88JetPol-13
**Maloney, Darren**
91AirCanSJHL-B22
91AirCanSJHLAS-43
92MPSPhoSJHL-71
93WesMic-20
96PeoRiv-15
96PeoRivPA-16
**Maloney, Dave**
76OPCNHL-181
76Top-181
77Coc-14
77OPCNHL-41
77Top-41
77TopGloS-10
77TopOPCGlo-10
78OPC-221
78Top-221
79OPC-159
79Top-159
80OPC-7
80Top-7
81OPC-227
81OPCSti-173
81Top-E100
82OPC-228
82OPCSti-140
82PosCer-13
83OPC-249
83OPCSti-211
84OPC-146
85OPC-89
85OPCSti-177
85Top-89
**Maloney, Don**
79OPC-42
79OPC-162
79Top-42
79Top-162
80OPC-231
80Top-231
81OPC-228
81OPCSti-170
81Top-E101
82OPC-229
82OPCSti-137
82PosCer-13
83OPC-250
83OPCSti-212
83PufSti-21
847EDis-36
84OPC-147
84OPCSti-95
84OPCSti-96
84Top-109
85OPC-94
85Top-94
86OPC-81
86Top-81
87OPC-49
87OPCSti-29
87PanSti-117
87Top-49
88PanSti-308
89Isl-13
89PanSti-231
90Bow-117
90BowTif-117
90OPC-31
90PanSti-84
90ProSet-187
90Sco-303A
90ScoCan-303A
90Top-31
90TopTif-31
90UppDec-20
90UppDecF-20
**Maloney, Phil**
44BeeGro2P-46
44BeeGro2P-426
45QuaOatP-31
74OPCNHL-104
74Top-104
**Maltais, Dominic**
907thInnSQMJHL-85
917thInnSQMJHL-108
93ForWorF-10
94CenHocL-25
95HamRoaA-7
96HamRoaA-HRA17
**Maltais, Frederic**
88RivDu R-17
**Maltais, Steve**
89CapKod-26
89ProAHL-85
90ProAHLIHL-205
90Sco-417
90ScoCan-417
91ProAHLCHL-156
92LigShe-20
95ColEdgI-107
**Maltby, Kirk**
907thInnSOHL-287
917thInnSOHL-278
92Cla-20
93Don-428
93OPCPre-290
93OPCPreG-290
93OweSouPla-18
93Sco-627
93ScoCan-627
93ScoGol-627
93StaClu-299
93StaCluFDI-299
93StaCluO-299
93TopPre-290
93TopPreG-290
93UppDec-520
94BeAPSig-38
94ClaProP-21
94Don-53
94Lea-230
94OPCPre-72
94OPCPreSE-72
94Pin-441
94PinArtP-441
94PinRinC-441
94TopPre-72
94TopPreSE-72
94UppDec-472
94UppDecEleIce-472
95ColCho-191
95ColChoPC-191
95ColChoPCP-191
95Pin-126
95PinArtP-126
95PinRinC-126
95PlaOneoOne-149
95Top-133
95TopOPCI-133
95UppDec-41
95UppDecEleIce-41
95UppDecEleIceG-41
96ClaGol-20
96PlaOneoOne-373
96RedWinDNFP-1
97ColCho-84
97PacDynBKS-33
97PacInvNRB-71
97ScoRedW-15
97ScoRedWPla-15
97ScoRedWPre-15
97UppDec-61
98Pac-199
98PacIceB-199
98PacRed-199
**Maltsev, Alexander**
69SweHocS-8
69SweWorC-67
69SweWorC-121
69SweWorC-124
69SweWorC-131
69SweWorC-133
70SweHocS-325
71SweHocS-36
72SweHocS-31
72SweHocS-50
72SweSemWC-10
73SweHocS-89
73SweWorCS-89
74SweHocS-8
74SweSemHVS-36
79PanSti-155
81SweSemHVS-46
82SweSemHVS-67
83RusNatT-13
91FutTreC72-20
91SweSemWCS-245
92FutTre76CC-161
92FutTre76CC-190
92FutTre76CC-200
92FutTrePS-1
96SweSemWHL-HL6
**Maluta, Ray**
77RocAme-16
**Maly, Miroslav**
84SprInd-20
94GerDELE-331
95GerDELE-297
96GerDELE-321
**Malykhin, Igor**
90OPCRedA-15R
91OPCIns-20R
93ClaProPro-86
**Malysiak, Andrzej**
79PanSti-128
**Manberg, Kenneth**
69SweHocS-177
**Manderville, Kent**
90UppDec-465
90UppDecF-465
91AlbIntTC-16
91Par-392
91ParFre-392
92MapLeaK-15
92OPC-14
92OPCPre-23
92Par-184
92ParEmel-184
92Sco-458
92ScoCan-458
92ScoCanO-10
92St.JohML-11
92StaClu-339
92Top-148
92TopGol-148G
92UppDec-32
93Par-204
93ParEmel-204
93ScoBla-10
93StaClu-417
93StaCluFDI-417
93StaCluO-417
93UppDec-420
94BeAPSig-156
94CanGamNHLP-235
94Lea-526
94MapLeaG-12
94MapLeaPP-17
94OPCPre-474
94OPCPreSE-474
94Par-235
94ParGol-235
94Pin-454
94PinArtP-454
94PinRinC-454
94StaClu-253
94StaCluFDI-253
94StaCluMOMS-253
94StaCluSTWC-253
94TopPre-474
94TopPreSE-474
94UppDec-131
94UppDecEleIce-131
95ColEdgI-83
95St.JohML-15
96SprFal-10
97Be A PPAD-165
97Be A PPAPD-165
97BeAPla-165
97BeAPlaAut-165
97CarHur-18
97ColCho-118
97Pac-289
97PacCop-289
97PacEmeGre-289
97PacIceB-289
97PacRed-289
97PacSil-289
99Pac-77
99PacCop-77
99PacGol-77
99PacIceB-77
99PacPreD-77
99RetHoc-13
99UppDecRG-13
99UppDecRP-13
**Mandich, Dan**
82NorStaPos-14
83NorStaPos-16
84NorStaPos-13
85NorStaPos-18
**Mando, DJ (Dean)**
95Sla-420
**Maneluk, George**
88ProAHL-317
89ProAHL-241
90ProAHLIHL-500
91ProAHLCHL-370
94CenHocL-117
95LouIceG-9
95LouIceGP-10
**Maneluk, Mike**
917thInnSWHL-199
92BraWheK-15
95ColEdgI-13
98BowBes-112
98BowBesAR-112
98BowBesR-112
98PacDynI-139
98PacDynIIB-139
98PacDynIR-139
98PacDynIR-5
98PacOmeH-53
98PacOmeODI-53
98PacOmeR-53
98SP Aut-93
98UppDec-332
98UppDecE-332
98UppDecE1o1-332
98UppDecGR-332
98UppDecM-49
98UppDecMGS-49
98UppDecMSS-49
98UppDecMSS-49
99SP AutPS-93
**Manery, Kris**
78NorStaCD-8
78OPC-107
78Top-107
79NorStaPos-7
79OPC-151
79Top-151
80JetPos-14
80PepCap-132
81OPC-371
**Manery, Randy**
72Flam-8
72OPC-260
72SarProSta-10
73OPC-131
73Top-131
74NHLActSta-9
74OPCNHL-86
74Top-86
75OPCNHL-44
75Top-44
76OPCNHL-24
76Top-24
77OPCNHL-389
78OPC-266
79OPC-317
80OPC-342

**Manganaro, Sal**
❑ 96DayBom-21
**Mangold, Pat**
❑ 84KamBla-14
**Maniago, Cesare**
❑ 44BeeGro2P-265
❑ 44BeeGro2P-427
❑ 61YorYelB-41
❑ 63Par-40
❑ 63Par-99
❑ 64BeeGro3P-140
❑ 68OPC-45
❑ 68ShiCoi-66
❑ 68Top-45
❑ 69OPC-121
❑ 69OPCFou-11
❑ 69Top-121
❑ 70ColSta-63
❑ 70EssPowPla-180
❑ 70NorStaP-5
❑ 70OPC-173
❑ 70SarProSta-81
❑ 71LetActR-24
❑ 71OPC-117
❑ 71SarProSta-92
❑ 71Top-5
❑ 71Top-117
❑ 71TorSun-136
❑ 72OPC-138
❑ 72SarProSta-110
❑ 72Top-104
❑ 73NorStaAP-6
❑ 73NorStaP-11
❑ 73OPC-127
❑ 73Top-146
❑ 74LipSou-27
❑ 74NHLActSta-138
❑ 74OPCNHL-26
❑ 74Top-26
❑ 75OPCNHL-261
❑ 75Top-261
❑ 76CanuRoyB-10
❑ 76OPCNHL-240
❑ 76Top-240
❑ 77CanCanDC-8
❑ 77CanuRoyB-11
❑ 77OPCNHL-23
❑ 77Top-23
❑ 95Par66-97
❑ 95Par66Coi-97
**Manlow, Eric**
❑ 917thInnSOHL-87
❑ 93KitRan-1
❑ 93KitRan-24
❑ 94DetJrRW-11
❑ 94KitRan-26
❑ 95ColEdgI-137
❑ 95IndIce-13
❑ 95SlaMemC-85
**Mann, Cameron**
❑ 93PetPet-16
❑ 95Sla-313
❑ 95Sla-NNO
❑ 96UppDecIce-130
❑ 97BowCHL-4
❑ 97BowCHLOPC-4
❑ 97ColCho-306
❑ 97UppDecBD-138
❑ 97UppDecBDDD-138
❑ 97UppDecBDQD-138
❑ 97UppDecBDTD-138
❑ 98BowBes-127
❑ 98BowBesAR-127
❑ 98BowBesR-127
❑ 98McD-26
❑ 98Pac-85
❑ 98PacIceB-85
❑ 98PacRed-85
❑ 98SPxFin-126
❑ 98SPxFinR-126
❑ 98SPxFinS-126
❑ 98UC-17
❑ 98UD ChoPCR-17
❑ 98UD ChoR-17
❑ 98UD3-19
❑ 98UD3-79
❑ 98UD3-139
❑ 98UD3DieC-19
❑ 98UD3DieC-79
❑ 98UD3DieC-139
❑ 98UppDec-2
❑ 98UppDecE-2
❑ 98UppDecE1o1-2
❑ 98UppDecGR-2
❑ 98UppDecM-11
❑ 98UppDecMGS-11
❑ 98UppDecMSS-11
❑ 98UppDecMSS-11
❑ 99Pac-26
❑ 99PacCop-26
❑ 99PacGol-26
❑ 99PacIceB-26
❑ 99PacPreD-26
**Mann, Jimmy**
❑ 79JetPos-14
❑ 80JetPos-15
❑ 80OPC-164
❑ 80OPC-353
❑ 80PepCap-133
❑ 80Top-164
❑ 81JetPos-13
❑ 81OPC-372
❑ 82Jet-16
❑ 83Jet-15
❑ 83NordPos-16
❑ 84NordPos-14
❑ 85NordGenF-16
❑ 85NordPro-15
❑ 86NordMcD-16
❑ 88ProIHL-21
**Mann, Norm**
❑ 34BeeGro1P-335A
❑ 34BeeGro1P-335B
**Mann, Pavel**
❑ 94GerDELE-344
❑ 95GerDELE-318
**Mann, Stephan**
❑ 94GerDELE-203
❑ 95GerDELE-206
❑ 96GerDELE-349
**Mannberg, Niklas**
❑ 83SweSemE-187
❑ 84SweSemE-210
❑ 86SwePanS-237
❑ 87SwePanS-228
❑ 89SweSemE-209
**Manness, Alan**
❑ 96KamBla-15
**Manninen, Kevin**
❑ 90MicTecHus-16
**Manninen, Mika**
❑ 93FinnSIS-110
❑ 94FinnSIS-108
❑ 94FinnSISJ-7
❑ 94FinnSISNP-1
❑ 95FinnSIS-29
**Manning, Blair**
❑ 95SeaThu-14
**Manno, Bob**
❑ 77CanuRoyB-12
❑ 78CanuRoyB-15
❑ 78OPC-349
❑ 79CanuRoyB-14
❑ 79OPC-270
❑ 80CanuSilD-16
❑ 81MapLeaP-11
❑ 81OPC-396
❑ 82OPC-325
❑ 82OPCSti-71
❑ 82PosCer-18
❑ 83OPC-132
❑ 84OPC-59
❑ 85OPC-134
❑ 85Top-134
❑ 98GerDELE-154
**Mansi, Moe**
❑ 88FliSpi-15
❑ 93SweSemWCS-226
❑ 94FinnJaaK-304
❑ 96GerDELE-121
❑ 96SweSemW-179
**Mansoff, Jason**
❑ 92BriColJHL-78
❑ 93MaiBlaB-40
**Manson, Dave**
❑ 84PriAlbRS-17
❑ 86BlaCok-8
❑ 87BlaCok-9
❑ 88BlaCok-9
❑ 89BlaCok-24
❑ 89OPC-150
❑ 89OPCSti-13
❑ 89PanSti-47
❑ 89Top-150
❑ 90BlaCok-24
❑ 90OPC-363
❑ 90OPC-397
❑ 90PanSti-199
❑ 90ProSet-54A
❑ 90ProSet-54B
❑ 90Sco-193
❑ 90ScoCan-193
❑ 90Top-363
❑ 90UppDec-85
❑ 90UppDecF-85
❑ 91Bow-389
❑ 91OilIGA-13
❑ 91OilTeal-15
❑ 91OPC-409
❑ 91OPCPre-137
❑ 91PanSti-15
❑ 91Par-49
❑ 91ParFre-49
❑ 91Pin-62
❑ 91PinFre-62
❑ 91ProSet-41
❑ 91ProSet-389
❑ 91ProSetFre-41
❑ 91ProSetFre-389
❑ 91ProSetPla-172
❑ 91ScoAme-152
❑ 91ScoCan-152
❑ 91ScoCan-624
❑ 91ScoRoo-74T
❑ 91StaClu-308
❑ 91Top-409
❑ 91UppDec-280
❑ 91UppDec-548
❑ 91UppDecF-280
❑ 91UppDecF-548
❑ 92Bow-339
❑ 92OilIGA-14
❑ 92OilTeal-12
❑ 92OPC-56
❑ 92PanSti-108
❑ 92PanStiFre-108
❑ 92Par-47
❑ 92ParCheP-CP15
❑ 92ParEmel-47
❑ 92Pin-334
❑ 92PinFre-334
❑ 92ProSet-55
❑ 92Sco-214
❑ 92ScoCan-214
❑ 92SeaPat-56
❑ 92StaClu-436
❑ 92Top-389
❑ 92TopGol-389G
❑ 92Ult-62
❑ 92UppDec-84
❑ 93Don-109
❑ 93Don-509
❑ 93Lea-159
❑ 93McDUppD-9
❑ 93OPCPre-71
❑ 93OPCPreG-71
❑ 93PanSti-242
❑ 93Par-335
❑ 93ParEmel-335
❑ 93Pin-363
❑ 93PinAllS-38
❑ 93PinAllSC-38
❑ 93PinCan-363
❑ 93Pow-83
❑ 93Sco-127
❑ 93ScoCan-127
❑ 93StaClu-183
❑ 93StaCluFDI-183
❑ 93StaCluFDIO-183
❑ 93StaCluO-183
❑ 93TopPre-71
❑ 93TopPreG-71
❑ 93Ult-93
❑ 93UppDec-358
❑ 93UppDecLAS-30
❑ 93UppDecSP-50
❑ 94BeAPla-R41
❑ 94BeAPSig-95
❑ 94CanGamNHLP-257
❑ 94Don-242
❑ 94EASpo-43
❑ 94Fla-207
❑ 94Fle-243
❑ 94Lea-239
❑ 94OPCPre-121
❑ 94OPCPreSE-121
❑ 94Par-262
❑ 94ParGol-262
❑ 94ParVin-V9
❑ 94Pin-51
❑ 94PinArtP-51
❑ 94PinRinC-51
❑ 94Sel-13
❑ 94SelGol-13
❑ 94SP-134
❑ 94SPDieCut-134
❑ 94StaClu-61
❑ 94StaCluFDI-61
❑ 94StaCluMOMS-61
❑ 94StaCluSTWC-61
❑ 94TopPre-121
❑ 94TopPreSE-121
❑ 94Ult-243
❑ 94UppDec-63
❑ 94UppDecEleIce-63
❑ 94UppDecNBAP-30
❑ 94UppDecSPI-SP180
❑ 94UppDecSPIDC-SP180
❑ 95CanGamNHLP-295
❑ 95ColCho-230
❑ 95ColChoPC-230
❑ 95ColChoPCP-230
❑ 95Don-317
❑ 95Emo-194
❑ 95JetReaC-7
❑ 95JetTeaIss-14
❑ 95Lea-158
❑ 95ParInt-233
❑ 95ParIntEI-233
❑ 95Pin-103
❑ 95PinArtP-103
❑ 95PinRinC-103
❑ 95PlaOneoOne-218
❑ 95Sco-59
❑ 95ScoBlaIce-59
❑ 95ScoBlaIceAP-59
❑ 95SkyImp-182
❑ 95Top-120
❑ 95TopOPCI-120
❑ 95Ult-181
❑ 95UltGolM-181
❑ 95UppDec-51
❑ 95UppDecEleIce-51
❑ 95UppDecEleIceG-51
❑ 96BeAPAut-57
❑ 96BeAPAutSil-57
❑ 96BeAPla-57
❑ 96CanaPos-17
❑ 96CanaShe-11
❑ 96MetUni-119
❑ 96PlaOneoOne-401
❑ 96Ult-133
❑ 96UltGolM-133
❑ 96UppDec-317
❑ 97CanaPos-12
❑ 97ColCho-136
❑ 97PacDynBKS-49
❑ 97ScoCan-17
❑ 97ScoCanPla-17
❑ 98Be A PPA-67
❑ 98Be A PPAA-67
❑ 98Be A PPAAF-67
❑ 98Be A PPTBASG-67
❑ 98Be APG-67
❑ 98O-PChr-165
❑ 98O-PChrR-165
❑ 98Pac-254
❑ 98PacIceB-254
❑ 98PacParC-115
❑ 98PacParC-115
❑ 98PacParEG-115
❑ 98PacParH-115
❑ 98PacParIB-115
❑ 98PacParS-115
❑ 98PacRed-254
❑ 98ScoCanPre-17
❑ 98Top-165
❑ 98TopO-P-165
❑ 98UC-108
❑ 98UD ChoPCR-108
❑ 98UD ChoR-108
❑ 98UppDec-113
❑ 98UppDecE-113
❑ 98UppDecE1o1-113
❑ 98UppDecGR-113
❑ 99Pac-91
❑ 99PacCop-91
❑ 99PacGol-91
❑ 99PacIceB-91
❑ 99PacPreD-91
**Mansson, Johan**
❑ 91SweSemE-178
❑ 92SweSemE-201
**Mantha, Billy**
❑ 24V1452-50
**Mantha, Carl**
❑ 907thInnSMC-51
❑ 907thInnSQMJHL-48
**Mantha, Georges**
❑ 33OPCV304A-22
❑ 33V252CanG-37
❑ 33V357IceK-26
❑ 34BeeGro1P-166
❑ 34DiaMatS-41
❑ 34SweCap-9
❑ 35DiaMatT2-42
❑ 35DiaMatT3-38
❑ 35DiaMatTI-41
❑ 36V356WorG-45
❑ 37OPCV304E-153
❑ 38QuaOatP-24
❑ 39OPCV3011-26
**Mantha, Maurice**
❑ 52JunBluT-169
❑ 60CleBar-11
**Mantha, Moe**
❑ 80JetPos-16
❑ 80PepCap-134
❑ 81OPC-373
❑ 83Jet-16
❑ 83Vac-132
❑ 85OPC-125
❑ 85OPCSti-98
❑ 85Top-125
❑ 86OPC-45
❑ 86OPCSti-231
❑ 86PenKod-16
❑ 86Top-45
❑ 87OPC-51
❑ 87OPCSti-171
❑ 87PanSti-142
❑ 87Top-51
❑ 88NorStaADA-17
❑ 88OilTenAnn-34
❑ 88OPC-30
❑ 88OPCSti-200
❑ 88Top-30
❑ 89JetSaf-19
❑ 90JetIGA-20
❑ 90OPC-354
❑ 90ProSet-332
❑ 90Sco-310C
❑ 90ScoCan-310C
❑ 90Top-354
❑ 90TopTif-354
❑ 91Bow-205
❑ 91JetIGA-17
❑ 91JetPanTS-16
❑ 91OPC-477
❑ 91ScoCan-506
❑ 91StaClu-287
❑ 91Top-477
**Mantha, Sylvio**
❑ 23V1451-12
❑ 24C144ChaCig-37
❑ 27LaPat-1
❑ 33V288HamG-18
❑ 33V357IceK-42
❑ 34BeeGro1P-167
❑ 34DiaMatS-42
❑ 34SweCap-10
❑ 35DiaMatT2-43
❑ 35DiaMatT3-39
❑ 35DiaMatTI-42
❑ 35OPCV304C-82
❑ 36TriPos-5
❑ 55Par-60
❑ 55ParQuaO-60
❑ 83HalFP-F9
❑ 85HalFC-84
**Mantione, Joe**
❑ 83KitRan-1
**Mara, Paul**
❑ 96SudWol-13
❑ 96SudWolP-16
❑ 96UppDecIce-149
❑ 97BowCHL-16
❑ 97BowCHL-137
❑ 97BowCHLBB-3
❑ 97BowCHLBowBesAR-3
❑ 97BowCHLBowBesR-3
❑ 97BowCHLOPC-16
❑ 97BowCHLOPC-137
❑ 97SudWolP-16
❑ 98UC-297
❑ 98UD ChoPCR-297
❑ 98UD ChoR-297
❑ 99Pac-400
❑ 99PacAur-132
❑ 99PacAurPD-132
❑ 99PacCop-400
❑ 99PacGol-400
❑ 99PacIceB-400
❑ 99PacPreD-400
❑ 99QuePeeWHWCCS-17
❑ 99UppDecCL-76
❑ 99UppDecCLCLC-76
❑ 99UppDecM-191
❑ 99UppDecM2CN-7
❑ 99UppDecMGS-191
❑ 99UppDecMSS-191
❑ 99UppDecMSS-191
**Maracle, Norm**
❑ 917thInnSWHL-117
❑ 91SasBla-3
❑ 93SasBla-16
❑ 95AdiRedW-14
❑ 98Pac-200
❑ 98PacIceB-200
❑ 98PacOmeH-89
❑ 98PacOmeODI-89
❑ 98PacOmeR-89
❑ 98PacRed-200
❑ 98PacRev-49
❑ 98PacRevIS-49
❑ 98PacRevR-49
❑ 98SPxFin-144
❑ 98SPxFinR-144
❑ 98SPxFinS-144
❑ 98UppDec-3
❑ 98UppDecE-3
❑ 98UppDecE1o1-3
❑ 98UppDecGR-3
❑ 98UppDecM-75
❑ 98UppDecMGS-75
❑ 98UppDecMSS-75
❑ 98UppDecMSS-75
**Marak, Zbynek**
❑ 94CzeAPSE-238
❑ 95CzeAPSE-19
**Maranduik, Bill**
❑ 93KinFro-13
**Marble, Evan**
❑ 907thInnSWHL-59
❑ 917thInnSWHL-321
❑ 98GerDELE-79
**Marc, Rob**
❑ 96KitRan-17
**Marcel, Paul**
❑ 34SweCap-13
**Marcetta, Milan**
❑ 68ShiCoi-67
**March, Mush (Harold)**
❑ 34BeeGro1P-67
❑ 34DiaMatS-43
❑ 34SweCap-34
❑ 35DiaMatT2-44
❑ 35DiaMatT3-40
❑ 35DiaMatT4-11
❑ 35DiaMatT5-43
❑ 35DiaMatTI-43
❑ 36ChaPos-2
❑ 36V356WorG-74
❑ 37DiaMatT6-9
❑ 39OPCV3011-45
**Marchant, Eddy**
❑ 91AirCanSJHL-C47
❑ 93RedDeeR-14
**Marchant, Gordon**
❑ 71BluPos-10
**Marchant, Todd**
❑ 92ClaKni-10
❑ 92UppDec-606
❑ 93Pow-511
❑ 93StaCluTUSA-15
❑ 93TopPreTUSA-14
❑ 93Ult-497
❑ 94CapBreO-13
❑ 94Cla-88
❑ 94ClaDraGol-88
❑ 94ClaProPIA-IA8
❑ 94ClaProPIH-LP8
❑ 94FinBowB-R19
❑ 94FinBowBR-R19
❑ 94Fle-71
❑ 94Lea-505
❑ 94ParSE-SE61
❑ 94ParSEG-SE61
❑ 94Sco-226
❑ 94ScoGol-226
❑ 94ScoPla-226
❑ 94ScoPlaTS-226
❑ 94SPPre-4
❑ 94SPPreDC-4
❑ 94UppDec-159
❑ 94UppDec-323
❑ 94UppDecEleIce-159
❑ 94UppDecEleIce-323
❑ 95BeAPla-190
❑ 95BeAPSig-S190
❑ 95BeAPSigDC-S190
❑ 95CanGamNHLP-107
❑ 95ColCho-210
❑ 95ColChoPC-210
❑ 95ColChoPCP-210
❑ 95ColEdgI-34
❑ 95ColEdgIC-C6
❑ 95ColEdgIP-PR1
❑ 95Don-200
❑ 95DonRooTea-8
❑ 95Emo-64
❑ 95Ima-8
❑ 95ImaCleE-CE8
❑ 95ImaGol-8
❑ 95ImaPlaPr-PR5
❑ 95Lea-61
❑ 95LeaStuR-8
❑ 95Met-54
❑ 95ParInt-347
❑ 95ParIntEI-347
❑ 95Pin-76
❑ 95PinArtP-76
❑ 95PinRinC-76
❑ 95ProMag-83
❑ 95Sco-34
❑ 95ScoBlaIce-34
❑ 95ScoBlaIceAP-34
❑ 95SkyImp-62
❑ 95SkyImp-234
❑ 95SkyImpNHLF-10
❑ 95StaClu-102
❑ 95StaCluMO-49
❑ 95StaCluMOMS-102
❑ 95Top-29
❑ 95TopNewG-3NG
❑ 95TopOPCI-29
❑ 95Ult-55
❑ 95UltAllRoo-8
❑ 95UltAllRooGM-8
❑ 95UltGolM-55
❑ 95UppDec-71
❑ 95UppDecEleIce-71
❑ 95UppDecEleIceG-71
❑ 95UppDecSpeE-SE121
❑ 95UppDecSpeEdiG-SE121
❑ 96ColCho-97
❑ 96Don-53
❑ 96DonPrePro-53
❑ 96Lea-153
❑ 96LeaPreP-153
❑ 96NHLProSTA-83
❑ 96OilPos-26
❑ 96Pin-117
❑ 96PinArtP-117
❑ 96PinFoi-117
❑ 96PinPreS-117
❑ 96PinRinC-117
❑ 96Sco-217
❑ 96ScoArtPro-217
❑ 96ScoDeaCAP-217
❑ 96ScoGolB-217
❑ 96ScoSpeAP-217
❑ 96UppDec-59
❑ 97Be A PPAD-72
❑ 97Be A PPAPD-72
❑ 97BeAPla-72
❑ 97BeAPlaAut-72
❑ 97Don-184
❑ 97DonLim-144
❑ 97DonLimExp-144
❑ 97DonPreProG-184
❑ 97DonPreProS-184
❑ 97Pac-320
❑ 97PacCop-320
❑ 97PacEmeGre-320
❑ 97PacIceB-320
❑ 97PacRed-320
❑ 97PacSil-320
❑ 97Pin-127
❑ 97PinPrePBB-127
❑ 97PinPrePBC-127
❑ 97PinPrePBM-127
❑ 97PinPrePBY-127
❑ 97PinPrePFC-127
❑ 97PinPrePFM-127
❑ 97PinPrePFY-127
❑ 97PinPrePla-127
❑ 97Sco-243
❑ 97UppDec-64
❑ 97UppDecGDM-64
❑ 98Be A PPA-55
❑ 98Be A PPAA-55
❑ 98Be A PPAAF-55
❑ 98Be A PPTBASG-55
❑ 98Be APG-55
❑ 98O-PChr-64
❑ 98O-PChrR-64
❑ 98Pac-213
❑ 98PacIceB-213
❑ 98PacPar-88
❑ 98PacParC-88
❑ 98PacParEG-88
❑ 98PacParH-88
❑ 98PacParIB-88
❑ 98PacParS-88
❑ 98PacRed-213
❑ 98Top-64
❑ 98TopO-P-64
❑ 98UppDec-275
❑ 98UppDecE-275
❑ 98UppDecE1o1-275
❑ 98UppDecGR-275
❑ 99Pac-159
❑ 99PacCop-159
❑ 99PacGol-159
❑ 99PacIceB-159
❑ 99PacPreD-159
**Marchessault, Alain**
❑ 87BroBra-8
**Marchessault, Richard**
❑ 87BroBra-16
**Marchetti, Giovanni**
❑ 94FinnJaaK-298
**Marchi, De**
❑ 79PanSti-392
**Marchinko, Brian**
❑ 72OPC-179
❑ 72SarProSta-136
**Marchment, Bryan**
❑ 89ProAHL-44
❑ 90JetIGA-21
❑ 90MonHaw-17
❑ 90ProAHLIHL-250
❑ 91BlaCok-17
❑ 91Bow-208
❑ 91OPC-116
❑ 91OPCPre-99
❑ 91ScoAme-314
❑ 91ScoCan-344
❑ 91ScoCan-606
❑ 91ScoRoo-56T
❑ 91StaClu-384
❑ 91Top-116
❑ 92Bow-418
❑ 92Par-267
❑ 92ParEmel-267
❑ 92Sco-288
❑ 92ScoCan-288
❑ 92StaClu-148
❑ 92Top-501
❑ 92TopGol-501G
❑ 92Ult-278
❑ 93Don-73
❑ 93Lea-224
❑ 93Pin-283
❑ 93PinCan-283
❑ 93Pow-352
❑ 93Sco-386
❑ 93Sco-577
❑ 93ScoCan-386
❑ 93ScoCan-577
❑ 93ScoGol-577
❑ 93StaClu-161
❑ 93StaCluFDI-161
❑ 93StaCluFDIO-161
❑ 93StaCluO-161
❑ 93Ult-335
❑ 93WhaCok-9
❑ 94Lea-127
❑ 94Pin-407
❑ 94PinArtP-407
❑ 94PinRinC-407
❑ 94Sco-107
❑ 94ScoGol-107
❑ 94ScoPla-107
❑ 94ScoPlaTS-107
❑ 94StaClu-84
❑ 94StaCluFDI-84
❑ 94StaCluMOMS-84
❑ 94StaCluSTWC-84
❑ 95BeAPla-39
❑ 95BeAPSig-S39
❑ 95BeAPSigDC-S39
❑ 95ColCho-67
❑ 95ColChoPC-67
❑ 95ColChoPCP-67
❑ 95Sco-270
❑ 95ScoBlaIce-270
❑ 95ScoBlaIceAP-270
❑ 95Ult-238
❑ 95UppDec-371
❑ 95UppDecEleIce-371
❑ 95UppDecEleIceG-371
❑ 96ColCho-99
❑ 96OilPos-24
❑ 97PacInvNRB-79
❑ 97UppDec-69
❑ 97UppDec-392
❑ 97UppDecBD-66
❑ 97UppDecBDDD-66
❑ 97UppDecBDQD-66
❑ 97UppDecBDTD-66
❑ 98Pac-385
❑ 98PacIceB-385
❑ 98PacOmeH-210
❑ 98PacOmeODI-210
❑ 98PacOmeR-210
❑ 98PacRed-385
❑ 98UppDec-356
❑ 98UppDecE-356
❑ 98UppDecE1o1-356
❑ 98UppDecGR-356
❑ 99Pac-374
❑ 99PacCop-374
❑ 99PacGol-374
❑ 99PacIceB-374
❑ 99PacPreD-374
**Marcinczak, Marek**
❑ 79PanSti-125
**Marcinko, Miroslav**
❑ 94FinnJaaK-196
❑ 96SweSemW-226
**Marcinyshyn, David (Dave)**
❑ 85KamBla-12
❑ 86KamBla-10
❑ 88ProAHL-342
❑ 89ProAHL-215
❑ 90OPCPre-67
❑ 90ProSet-623
❑ 91ProAHLCHL-543
❑ 92BinRan-16
❑ 94MilAdm-17
❑ 96CinCyc-27
❑ 98GerDELE-213
**Marcogliese, Jan**

❑ 92QueIntP-35
**Marcolini, Steve**
❑ 84KitRan-8
❑ 85KitRan-7
❑ 86LonKni-19
**Marcon, Lou**
❑ 59Top-49
**Marcotte, Donald (Don)**
❑ 70BruPos-6
❑ 70BruTeaIss-6
❑ 70EssPowPla-70
❑ 70OPC-138
❑ 71BruTeaIss-16
❑ 71OPC-176
❑ 71TorSun-13
❑ 72OPC-219
❑ 72SarProSta-27
❑ 73Top-89
❑ 74NHLActSta-21
❑ 74OPCNHL-221
❑ 74Top-221
❑ 75OPCNHL-269
❑ 75Top-269
❑ 76OPCNHL-234
❑ 76Top-234
❑ 77OPCNHL-165
❑ 77Top-165
❑ 78OPC-236
❑ 78Top-236
❑ 79OPC-99
❑ 79Top-99
❑ 80OPC-336
❑ 81OPC-14
❑ 82OPC-14
❑ 82OPCSti-91
❑ 91BruSpoAL-15
**Marcotte, Gaston**
❑ 52JunBluT-14
**Marcotte, Jacques**
❑ 52JunBluT-82
**Marcotte, Real**
❑ 51LavDaiLSJ-13
**Marcoux, Christian**
❑ 93DruVol-16
**Marcoux, Eric**
❑ 907thInnSQMJHL-201
❑ 917thInnSQMJHL-289
**Marcoux, Henri**
❑ 94GerDELE-256
❑ 95GerDELE-254
❑ 96GerDELE-143
**Marcus, Borje**
❑ 69SweHocS-157
❑ 70SweHocS-125
❑ 71SweHocS-215
**Marczell, Arthur**
❑ 95AusNatTea-16
**Marecek, Pavel**
❑ 94CzeAPSE-123
**Marek, Peter**
❑ 94WheThu-9
**Marengere, Steve**
❑ 83NovScoV-6
**Marentette, Mark**
❑ 90CinCyc-34
**Marett, Geb**
❑ 92HarCri-22
**Margettie, Don**
❑ 93LonKni-13
**Marha, Josef**
❑ 93Par-516
❑ 93ParEmel-516
❑ 94CzeAPSE-171
❑ 94SP-157
❑ 94SPDieCut-157
❑ 95ClaAut-13
❑ 97ScoAva-10
❑ 97ScoAvaPla-10
❑ 97ScoAvaPre-10
❑ 97UppDec-256
❑ 98Pac-59
❑ 98PacIceB-59
❑ 98PacPar-4
❑ 98PacParC-4
❑ 98PacParEG-4
❑ 98PacParH-4
❑ 98PacParIB-4
❑ 98PacParS-4
❑ 98PacRed-59
❑ 98SPxFin-3
❑ 98SPxFin-124
❑ 98SPxFinR-3
❑ 98SPxFinR-124
❑ 98SPxFinS-3
❑ 98SPxFinS-124
❑ 98UC-3
❑ 98UD ChoPCR-3
❑ 98UD ChoR-3
❑ 98UD3-3
❑ 98UD3-63
❑ 98UD3-123
❑ 98UD3DieC-3
❑ 98UD3DieC-63
❑ 98UD3DieC-123
❑ 98UppDec-33
❑ 98UppDec-216
❑ 98UppDecE-33
❑ 98UppDecE-216
❑ 98UppDecE1o1-33
❑ 98UppDecE1o1-216
❑ 98UppDecGR-33
❑ 98UppDecGR-216
❑ 99Pac-92
❑ 99PacCop-92
❑ 99PacGol-92
❑ 99PacIceB-92
❑ 99PacPreD-92
**Maric, Rob**
❑ 94KitRan-25
❑ 95Sla-136
**Marietti, Brett**
❑ 917thInnSOHL-371
❑ 95SouCarS-17
❑ 96SouCarS-24
**Marijarvi, Juha-Matti**
❑ 93FinnJyvHS-81
❑ 93FinnSIS-117
**Marik, Michal**
❑ 95CzeAPSE-245
❑ 96CzeAPSE-289
**Marin, Alexei**
❑ 91SweSemWCS-78
**Marini, Hector**
❑ 83OPC-235
❑ 83OPCSti-221
❑ 83PufSti-8
**Marinier, Roch**
❑ 84ChiSag-18
**Marinucci, Chris**
❑ 93MinDul-19
❑ 93MinDulCom-1
❑ 94Cla-100
❑ 94ClaAllAme-AA3
❑ 94ClaDraGol-100
❑ 94ClaTri-T40
❑ 95ColEdgI-193
❑ 95Don-6
❑ 95Ima-95
❑ 95ImaAut-95A
❑ 95ImaCleE-CE19
❑ 95ImaGol-95
❑ 95ImaPlaPr-PR7
❑ 95Lea-92
❑ 95ParInt-401
❑ 95ParIntEl-401
❑ 95Pin-206
❑ 95PinArtP-206
❑ 95PinRinC-206
❑ 95Sco-309
❑ 95ScoBlaIce-309
❑ 95ScoBlaIceAP-309
❑ 95Top-62
❑ 95TopOPCI-62
**Mario, Frank**
❑ 51LavDaiS-14
❑ 52St.LawS-51
**Mariucci, John**
❑ 34BeeGro1P-68
❑ 85HalFC-254
❑ 95AHC-3
**Marjamaki, Pekka**
❑ 69SweHocS-376
❑ 69SweWorC-163
❑ 70SweHocS-297
❑ 71SweHocS-64
❑ 72SweHocS-34
❑ 72SweSemWC-75
❑ 74SweHocS-105
❑ 74SweSemHVS-78
❑ 79PanSti-167
❑ 96FinnSISR-195
**Mark, Gordon**
❑ 84KamBla-15
❑ 94Par-80
❑ 94ParGol-80
**Mark, Len**
❑ 84KamBla-16
❑ 85KamBla-13
❑ 86KamBla-11
**Markarian, Ralph**
❑ 52JunBluT-178
**Marker, Gus**
❑ 34BeeGro1P-200
❑ 34BeeGro1P-239
❑ 34BeeGro1P-336
❑ 34SweCap-22
❑ 35OPCV304C-78
❑ 37OPCV304E-173
❑ 39OPCV3011-16
❑ 40OPCV3012-113
**Market, Hasty**
❑ 88KamBla-25
**Markkanen, Jussi**
❑ 94Fin-124
❑ 94FinRef-124
❑ 94FinSupTW-124
❑ 94ParSE-SE215
❑ 94ParSEG-SE215
❑ 95FinnSIS-311
**Markkanen, Mikko**
❑ 95ColCho-326
❑ 95ColChoPC-326
❑ 95ColChoPCP-326
❑ 95FinnSIS-334
❑ 95FinnSISDD-12
**Marklund, Jorgen**
❑ 83SweSemE-193
❑ 84SweSemE-216
❑ 86SwePanS-240
❑ 87SwePanS-227
**Marklund, Lars**
❑ 83SweSemE-175
❑ 84SweSemE-200
❑ 86SwePanS-222
❑ 87SwePanS-214
❑ 89SweSemE-199
**Markov, Andrei**
❑ 96UppDecIce-142
**Markov, Daniil**
❑ 97St.JohML-16
❑ 98Be A PPA-283
❑ 98Be A PPAA-283
❑ 98Be A PPAAF-283
❑ 98Be A PPSE-283
❑ 98Be APG-283
❑ 98BowBes-123
❑ 98BowBesAR-123
❑ 98BowBesMIF-F7
❑ 98BowBesMIFAR-F7
❑ 98BowBesMIFR-F7
❑ 98BowBesR-123
❑ 98Pac-417
❑ 98PacIceB-417
❑ 98PacOmeH-233
❑ 98PacOmeODI-233
❑ 98PacOmeR-233
❑ 98PacRed-417
❑ 98UppDec-372
❑ 98UppDecE-372
❑ 98UppDecE1o1-372
❑ 98UppDecGR-372
❑ 99UppDecM-197
❑ 99UppDecMGS-197
❑ 99UppDecMSS-197
❑ 99UppDecMSS-197
**Markov, Valentin**
❑ 73SweHocS-112
❑ 73SweWorCS-112
**Markov, Vladimir**
❑ 74SweHocS-79
**Markov, Zdenek**
❑ 97St.JohML-17
**Markovich, Mike**
❑ 93TolSto-11
**Marks, Jack**
❑ 12C57-38
**Marks, John**
❑ 74NHLActSta-80
❑ 74OPCNHL-282
❑ 75OPCNHL-121
❑ 75Top-121
❑ 76OPCNHL-114
❑ 76Top-114
❑ 77OPCNHL-47
❑ 77Top-47
❑ 78OPC-157
❑ 78Top-157
❑ 79OPC-16
❑ 79Top-16
❑ 80BlaWhiBor-8
❑ 80OPC-194
❑ 80Top-194
❑ 81BlaBorPos-15
❑ 81IndChe-15
❑ 81OPC-70
❑ 91ProAHLCHL-503
**Markus, Todd**
❑ 91AirCanSJHL-B31
**Markwart, Kelly**
❑ 88RegPat-14
❑ 89RegPat-9
❑ 907thInnSWHL-175
❑ 90SasBla-17
**Markwart, Nevin**
❑ 82RegPat-15
❑ 83RegPat-15
❑ 84OPC-8
❑ 84Top-7
❑ 89BruSpoA-16
❑ 90BruSpoA-15
❑ 90ProSet-408
❑ 91OPC-238
❑ 91Top-238
**Marleau, Patrick**
❑ 95SeaThu-15
❑ 96SeaThu-12
❑ 96UppDec-384
❑ 96UppDecBD-103
❑ 96UppDecBDG-103
❑ 97Be A PPAD-221
❑ 97Be A PPAPD-221
❑ 97BeAPla-221
❑ 97BeAPlaAut-221
❑ 97BowCHL-88
❑ 97BowCHL-141
❑ 97BowCHLBB-2
❑ 97BowCHLBowBesAR-2
❑ 97BowCHLBowBesR-2
❑ 97BowCHLOPC-88
❑ 97BowCHLOPC-141
❑ 97ColCho-304
❑ 97DonEli-99
❑ 97DonEli-128
❑ 97DonEli-145
❑ 97DonEliAsp-99
❑ 97DonEliAsp-128
❑ 97DonEliAsp-145
❑ 97DonEliBttF-3
❑ 97DonEliBttFA-3
❑ 97DonEliC-11
❑ 97DonEliMC-11
❑ 97DonEliS-99
❑ 97DonEliS-128
❑ 97DonEliS-145
❑ 97DonLim-200
❑ 97DonLimExp-200
❑ 97DonPre-150
❑ 97DonPre-198
❑ 97DonPreCttC-150
❑ 97DonPreCttC-198
❑ 97DonPreLotT-5C
❑ 97DonPri-175
❑ 97DonPri-195
❑ 97DonPri-216
❑ 97DonPriDD-18
❑ 97DonPriODI-29
❑ 97DonPriP-18
❑ 97DonPriS-18
❑ 97DonPriSB-18
❑ 97DonPriSG-18
❑ 97DonPriSoA-175
❑ 97DonPriSoA-195
❑ 97DonPriSoA-216
❑ 97DonPriSS-18
❑ 97Kat-121
❑ 97KatGol-121
❑ 97KatSil-121
❑ 97Lea-154
❑ 97LeaFraMat-154
❑ 97LeaFraMDC-154
❑ 97McD-34
❑ 97PacCroR-120
❑ 97PacCroREG-120
❑ 97PacCroRIB-120
❑ 97PacCroRS-120
❑ 97PacDyn-NNO
❑ 97PacDynC-NNO
❑ 97PacDynDG-NNO
❑ 97PacDynEG-NNO
❑ 97PacDynIB-NNO
❑ 97PacDynR-NNO
❑ 97PacDynSil-NNO
❑ 97PacOme-203
❑ 97PacOmeC-203
❑ 97PacOmeDG-203
❑ 97PacOmeEG-203
❑ 97PacOmeG-203
❑ 97PacOmeIB-203
❑ 97PacPar-167
❑ 97PacParC-167
❑ 97PacParDG-167
❑ 97PacParEG-167
❑ 97PacParIB-167
❑ 97PacParRed-167
❑ 97PacParSil-167
❑ 97PacRev-125
❑ 97PacRevC-125
❑ 97PacRevE-125
❑ 97PacRevIB-125
❑ 97PacRevR-125
❑ 97PacRevS-125
❑ 97Pin-12
❑ 97PinArtP-12
❑ 97PinCerRR-C
❑ 97PinCerRRG-C
❑ 97PinCerRRMG-C
❑ 97PinPrePBB-12
❑ 97PinPrePBC-12
❑ 97PinPrePBM-12
❑ 97PinPrePBY-12
❑ 97PinPrePFC-12
❑ 97PinPrePFM-12
❑ 97PinPrePFY-12
❑ 97PinPrePla-12
❑ 97PinRinC-12
❑ 97SPAut-191
❑ 97UppDec-354
❑ 97UppDecBD-140
❑ 97UppDecBDDD-140
❑ 97UppDecBDQD-140
❑ 97UppDecBDTD-140
❑ 97UppDecGDM-354
❑ 97UppDecIce-41
❑ 97UppDecIceP-41
❑ 97UppDecIPS-41
❑ 97UppDecSG-SG3
❑ 97Zen-84
❑ 97ZenRooR-10
❑ 97ZenZGol-84
❑ 97ZenZSil-84
❑ 98Be A PPA-120
❑ 98Be A PPAA-120
❑ 98Be A PPAAF-120
❑ 98Be A PPTBASG-120
❑ 98Be APG-120
❑ 98BowBes-60
❑ 98BowBesAR-60
❑ 98BowBesP-BP4
❑ 98BowBesPAR-BP4
❑ 98BowBesPR-BP4
❑ 98BowBesR-60
❑ 98Fin-18
❑ 98FinCen-C12
❑ 98FinCenR-C12
❑ 98FinNo P-18
❑ 98FinNo PR-18
❑ 98FinRef-18
❑ 98O-PChr-170
❑ 98O-PChrR-170
❑ 98O-PChrSB-SB10
❑ 98O-PChrSBR-SB10
❑ 98Pac-386
❑ 98PacAur-168
❑ 98PacAurCF-43
❑ 98PacAurCFC-43
❑ 98PacAurCFIB-43
❑ 98PacAurCFR-43
❑ 98PacAurCFS-43
❑ 98PacCroR-119
❑ 98PacCroRLS-119
❑ 98PacDynI-167
❑ 98PacDynIIB-167
❑ 98PacDynIR-167
❑ 98PacIceB-386
❑ 98PacOmeH-211
❑ 98PacOmeODI-211
❑ 98PacOmeR-211
❑ 98PacPar-211
❑ 98PacParC-211
❑ 98PacParEG-211
❑ 98PacParH-211
❑ 98PacParIB-211
❑ 98PacParS-211
❑ 98PacParTCD-23
❑ 98PacRed-386
❑ 98PacRev-127
❑ 98PacRevIS-127
❑ 98PacRevR-127
❑ 98PacTeaC-23
❑ 98SP Aut-75
❑ 98SPxFin-73
❑ 98SPxFin-130
❑ 98SPxFinR-73
❑ 98SPxFinR-130
❑ 98SPxFinS-73
❑ 98SPxFinS-130
❑ 98SPXTopP-50
❑ 98SPXTopPF-50
❑ 98SPXTopPR-50
❑ 98Top-170
❑ 98TopGolLC1-94
❑ 98TopGolLC1B-94
❑ 98TopGolLC1BOoO-94
❑ 98TopGolLC1OoO-94
❑ 98TopGolLC1R-94
❑ 98TopGolLC1ROoO-94
❑ 98TopGolLC2-94
❑ 98TopGolLC2B-94
❑ 98TopGolLC2BOoO-94
❑ 98TopGolLC2OoO-94
❑ 98TopGolLC2R-94
❑ 98TopGolLC2ROoO-94
❑ 98TopGolLC3-94
❑ 98TopGolLC3B-94
❑ 98TopGolLC3BOoO-94
❑ 98TopGolLC3OoO-94
❑ 98TopGolLC3R-94
❑ 98TopGolLC3ROoO-94
❑ 98TopO-P-170
❑ 98TopSeaB-SB10
❑ 98UC-173
❑ 98UD ChoPCR-173
❑ 98UD ChoR-173
❑ 98UD3-4
❑ 98UD3-64
❑ 98UD3-124
❑ 98UD3DieC-4
❑ 98UD3DieC-64
❑ 98UD3DieC-124
❑ 98UDCP-173
❑ 98UppDec-26
❑ 98UppDec-171
❑ 98UppDecDD-72
❑ 98UppDecDD-72
❑ 98UppDecE-26
❑ 98UppDecE-171
❑ 98UppDecE1o1-26
❑ 98UppDecE1o1-171
❑ 98UppDecGN-GN10
❑ 98UppDecGNQ1-GN10
❑ 98UppDecGNQ2-GN10
❑ 98UppDecGNQ3-GN10
❑ 98UppDecGR-26
❑ 98UppDecGR-171
❑ 98UppDecM-170
❑ 98UppDecMGS-170
❑ 98UppDecMPG-PG13
❑ 98UppDecMSS-170
❑ 98UppDecMSS-170
❑ 98UppDecQD-72
❑ 98UppDecTD-72
❑ 99Pac-375
❑ 99PacAur-121
❑ 99PacAurPD-121
❑ 99PacCop-375
❑ 99PacGol-375
❑ 99PacIceB-375
❑ 99PacPreD-375
❑ 99SP AutPS-75
❑ 99UppDecM-176
❑ 99UppDecMGS-176
❑ 99UppDecMSS-176
❑ 99UppDecMSS-176
**Marois, Dan (Daniel)**
❑ 88MapLeaPLA-15
❑ 89Kra-37
❑ 89OPC-273
❑ 89OPCSti-102
❑ 89OPCSti-172
❑ 89OPCSti-239
❑ 89PanSti-137
❑ 90Bow-160
❑ 90BowTif-160
❑ 90OPC-267
❑ 90PanSti-284
❑ 90ProSet-284
❑ 90Sco-122
❑ 90ScoCan-122
❑ 90ScoYouS-3
❑ 90Top-267
❑ 90TopTif-267
❑ 90UppDec-179
❑ 90UppDecF-179
❑ 91Bow-165
❑ 91MapLeaP-23
❑ 91MapLeaPTS-14
❑ 91OPC-212
❑ 91PanSti-95
❑ 91Par-329
❑ 91ParFre-329
❑ 91Pin-27
❑ 91PinFre-27
❑ 91ProSet-223
❑ 91ProSetFre-223
❑ 91ProSetPla-118
❑ 91ScoAme-254
❑ 91ScoCan-474
❑ 91StaClu-197
❑ 91Top-212
❑ 91UppDec-331
❑ 91UppDecF-331
❑ 92Bow-245
❑ 92DurPan-16
❑ 92OPC-58
❑ 92Pin-139
❑ 92PinFre-139
❑ 92Sco-63
❑ 92ScoCan-63
❑ 92StaClu-63
❑ 92Top-49
❑ 92TopGol-49G
❑ 92UppDec-71
❑ 93Don-17
❑ 93Par-282
❑ 93ParEmel-282
❑ 94Par-18
❑ 94ParGol-18
**Marois, Jean**
❑ 51LavDaiQSHL-2
❑ 52St.LawS-36
**Marois, Jerome**
❑ 98QueRem-13
**Marois, Mario**
❑ 80PepCap-113
❑ 81NordPos-11
❑ 81OPC-279
❑ 82NordPos-13
❑ 82OPC-287
❑ 82PosCer-16
❑ 83NordPos-17
❑ 83OPC-295
❑ 83Vac-67
❑ 84NordPos-15
❑ 84OPC-282
❑ 84OPCSti-166
❑ 84OPCSti-167
❑ 85JetPol-11
❑ 85NordGenF-17
❑ 85NordPro-16
❑ 85OPC-194
❑ 85OPCSti-144
❑ 86JetBor-13
❑ 86KraDra-40
❑ 87Jet-13
❑ 87OPC-220
❑ 87OPCSti-250
❑ 87PanSti-359
❑ 88JetPol-14
❑ 88OPC-233
❑ 88OPCSti-142
❑ 88PanSti-151
❑ 89Nord-28
❑ 89NordGenF-22
❑ 89NordPol-19
❑ 89OPC-260
❑ 89OPCSti-185
❑ 89PanSti-336
❑ 90BluKod-14
❑ 90NordTeal-20
❑ 90OPC-158
❑ 90ProSet-253
❑ 90ProSet-524
❑ 90Sco-229
❑ 90ScoCan-229
❑ 90ScoRoo-94T
❑ 90Top-158
❑ 90TopTif-158
❑ 90UppDec-8
❑ 90UppDecF-8
❑ 91Bow-380
❑ 91OPC-82
❑ 91ProSet-477
❑ 91ProSetFre-477
❑ 91ScoCan-546
❑ 91StaClu-12
❑ 91Top-82
❑ 92HamCan-14
❑ 92HamCan-29
**Maroste, Mark**
❑ 94GerDELE-137
❑ 95GerDELE-40
**Marotte, Gilles**
❑ 66Top-36
❑ 67Top-59
❑ 68Bla-4
❑ 68OPC-14
❑ 68ShiCoi-30
❑ 68Top-14
❑ 69OPC-68
❑ 69Top-68
❑ 70ColSta-65
❑ 70DadCoo-76
❑ 70EssPowPla-148
❑ 70OPC-34
❑ 70SarProSta-78
❑ 70Top-34
❑ 71LetActR-1
❑ 71OPC-151
❑ 71SarProSta-70
❑ 72OPC-27
❑ 72SarProSta-89
❑ 72SweSemWC-202
❑ 72Top-167
❑ 73OPC-5
❑ 73Top-188
❑ 74NHLActSta-197
❑ 74OPCNHL-373
❑ 75OPCNHL-164
❑ 75Top-164
❑ 76OPCNHL-192
❑ 76Top-192
❑ 91UltOriS-59
❑ 91UltOriSF-59
❑ 95Par66-17
❑ 95Par66Coi-17
**Marouelli, Dan**
❑ 90ProSet-692
**Marple, Stan**
❑ 97GuiFla-21
**Marquet, Sebastien**
❑ 93SweSemWCS-256
**Marquette, Dale**
❑ 88ProIHL-104
❑ 89ProIHL-64
**Marrietti, Brett**
❑ 907thInnSOHL-134
**Marrin, Peter**
❑ 76OPCWHA-96
❑ 77OPCWHA-51
**Marriott, Jamie**
❑ 91BriColJHL-38
**Mars, Gunnar**
❑ 69SweHocS-121
**Marsh, Blair**
❑ 92BriColJHL-235
❑ 93MaiBlaB-56
**Marsh, Brad**
❑ 79FlamPos-9
❑ 79FlaTeal-8
❑ 80FlamPos-12
❑ 80OPC-338
❑ 80PepCap-9
❑ 81OPC-47
❑ 81OPCSti-225
❑ 82OPC-254
❑ 82PosCer-14
❑ 83FlyJCP-15
❑ 83OPC-269
❑ 84OPC-163
❑ 85FlyPos-18
❑ 85OPC-72
❑ 85Top-72
❑ 86FlyPos-15
❑ 86OPC-175
❑ 86OPCSti-235
❑ 86Top-175
❑ 87OPC-128
❑ 87PanSti-127
❑ 87Top-128
❑ 88MapLeaPLA-25
❑ 88OPC-64
❑ 88OPCSti-101
❑ 88Top-64
❑ 89OPC-276
❑ 89OPCSti-175
❑ 89PanSti-141
❑ 90Bow-158
❑ 90BowTif-158
❑ 90OPC-155
❑ 90PanSti-277
❑ 90ProSet-285
❑ 90Sco-219
❑ 90ScoCan-219
❑ 90Top-155
❑ 90TopTif-155
❑ 90UppDec-199
❑ 90UppDecF-199
❑ 91MapLeaPTS-15
❑ 91OPC-19
❑ 91Pin-361
❑ 91Pin-401
❑ 91PinFre-361
❑ 91PinFre-401
❑ 91ProSet-378
❑ 91ProSetFre-378
❑ 91ScoCan-416
❑ 91Top-19
❑ 92Par-123
❑ 92ParEmel-123
❑ 92Pin-378
❑ 92PinFre-378
❑ 92ProSet-126
❑ 92ProSet-264
❑ 92Sco-293
❑ 92ScoCan-293
❑ 92Sen-10
❑ 92StaClu-482
❑ 92Top-215
❑ 92TopGol-215G
❑ 92Ult-364
❑ 93PinAllS-10
❑ 93PinAllSC-10
❑ 93Sco-392
❑ 93ScoCan-392
❑ 93SenKraS-18
❑ 93StaCluAS-15
❑ 94SenBelM-21
❑ 95Sen-15
**Marsh, Peter**
❑ 79JetPos-15
❑ 79OPC-147
❑ 79Top-147
❑ 80BlaBroBac-6
❑ 80OPC-314
❑ 81BlaBorPos-16
❑ 81BlaBroBac-6
❑ 81OPC-71
❑ 83BlaBorPos-14
**Marsh, Ryan**
❑ 94TriAme-7
**Marshall, Bert**
❑ 64BeeGro3P-86
❑ 65Coc-39
❑ 66Top-50
❑ 67Top-46

❑ 68OPC-79
❑ 68ShiCoi-117
❑ 68Top-79
❑ 69OPC-80
❑ 69OPCFou-17
❑ 69Top-80
❑ 70DadCoo-77
❑ 70OPC-188
❑ 70SarProSta-131
❑ 71Baz-25
❑ 71OPC-73
❑ 71SarProSta-134
❑ 71Top-73
❑ 71TorSun-52
❑ 72OPC-130
❑ 72SarProSta-47
❑ 72Top-162
❑ 73OPC-51
❑ 73Top-51
❑ 74NHLActSta-174
❑ 74OPCNHL-177
❑ 74Top-177
❑ 75OPCNHL-72
❑ 75Top-72
❑ 76OPCNHL-62
❑ 76Top-62
❑ 77OPCNHL-206
❑ 77Top-206
❑ 78OPC-49
❑ 78Top-49
❑ 81RocPos-17
**Marshall, Bobby**
❑ 94St.JohF-12
❑ 98GerDELE-14
**Marshall, Charles**
❑ 52JunBluT-20
**Marshall, Chris**
❑ 90CinCyc-29
❑ 91CinCyc-13
❑ 92BirBul-12
❑ 92RalIce-25
❑ 93BirBul-12
**Marshall, Don**
❑ 44BeeGro2P-266
❑ 44BeeGro2P-340
❑ 55Par-35
❑ 55ParQuaO-35
❑ 57Par-M8
❑ 58Par-44
❑ 59Par-37
❑ 60Par-42
❑ 60Par-57
❑ 60Par-59
❑ 60ShiCoi-23
❑ 60YorPreP-23
❑ 61Par-40
❑ 61ShiCoi-103
❑ 61YorYelB-6
❑ 62Par-43
❑ 62ShiMetC-33
❑ 62YorIroOTra-28
❑ 63Top-59
❑ 64BeeGro3P-141
❑ 64CocCap-89
❑ 64Top-97
❑ 65Coc-89
❑ 65Top-29
❑ 66Top-24
❑ 66TopUSAT-24
❑ 67Top-23
❑ 67Top-130
❑ 68OPC-75
❑ 68ShiCoi-99
❑ 68Top-75
❑ 69OPC-39
❑ 69Top-39
❑ 70ColSta-27
❑ 70DadCoo-78
❑ 70EssPowPla-88
❑ 70OPC-129
❑ 70Top-129
❑ 71MapLeaP-11
❑ 71OPC-199
❑ 71SarProSta-208
❑ 71TorSun-264
❑ 72SweSemWC-197
❑ 91UltOriS-13
❑ 91UltOriSF-13
❑ 94ParMisL-76
❑ 94ParTalB-88
❑ 95Par66-82
❑ 95Par66Coi-82
**Marshall, Grant**
❑ 907thInnSOHL-88
❑ 917thInnSOHL-299
❑ 92Cla-13
❑ 92Ott672A-15
❑ 93Cla-140
❑ 93St.JohML-16
❑ 94ClaProP-188
❑ 95Bow-162
❑ 95BowAllFoi-162
❑ 95Lea-327
❑ 95ParInt-533
❑ 95ParIntEl-533
❑ 95UppDec-362
❑ 95UppDecEleIce-362
❑ 95UppDecEleIceG-362
❑ 96BeAPAut-146
❑ 96BeAPAutSil-146
❑ 96BeAPla-146
❑ 96ClaGol-13
❑ 96ColCho-77
❑ 96Don-222
❑ 96DonPrePro-222
❑ 96Lea-169
❑ 96LeaPreP-169
❑ 96Sco-261
❑ 96ScoArtPro-261
❑ 96ScoDeaCAP-261
❑ 96ScoGolB-261
❑ 96ScoSpeAP-261
❑ 96StaPos-19
❑ 96UppDec-47
❑ 98UppDecM-64
❑ 98UppDecMGS-64
❑ 98UppDecMSS-64
❑ 98UppDecMSS-64
❑ 99Pac-125
❑ 99PacCop-125
❑ 99PacGol-125
❑ 99PacIceB-125
❑ 99PacPreD-125
**Marshall, Jack**
❑ 10C55SweCP-29
❑ 10C56-33
❑ 10C56-35
❑ 11C55-29
❑ 83HalFP-C9
❑ 85HalFC-39
**Marshall, Jason**
❑ 907thInnSWHL-117
❑ 90UppDec-453
❑ 90UppDecF-453
❑ 91ProAHLCHL-25
❑ 91ScoAme-388
❑ 91ScoCan-278
❑ 92PeoRivC-14
❑ 92UppDec-66
❑ 93AlbIntTC-13
❑ 93Pow-488
❑ 93Ult-468
❑ 94FinnJaaK-105
❑ 95Lea-190
❑ 96Duc-15
❑ 97Be A PPAD-54
❑ 97Be A PPAPD-54
❑ 97BeAPla-54
❑ 97BeAPlaAut-54
❑ 97PacInvNRB-5
❑ 98Be A PPA-1
❑ 98Be A PPAA-1
❑ 98Be A PPAAF-1
❑ 98Be A PPTBASG-1
❑ 98Be APG-1
❑ 98Pac-60
❑ 98PacIceB-60
❑ 98PacRed-60
**Marshall, Paul**
❑ 81MapLeaP-12
❑ 90ProAHLIHL-297
❑ 92BirBul-10
❑ 93BirBul-10
**Marshall, Rick**
❑ 907thInnSOHL-10
❑ 917thInnSOHL-105
❑ 92WinSpi-18
**Marshall, Willie**
❑ 55Par-17
❑ 55ParQuaO-17
❑ 58Par-19
**Marson, Mike**
❑ 74CapWhiB-19
❑ 74NHLActSta-313
❑ 75OPCNHL-43
❑ 75Top-43
**Martak, Igor**
❑ 95SloPeeWT-15
**Martan, John**
❑ 52JunBluT-109
**Martel, Jake**
❑ 95Sla-215
**Martel, Jocelyn**
❑ 907thInnSQMJHL-258
**Martell, Steve**
❑ 897thInnSOHL-34
❑ 907thInnSOHL-135
❑ 91ProAHLCHL-559
❑ 92HamRoaA-18
**Martensson, Leif**
❑ 71SweHocS-297
**Martensson, Ulf**
❑ 67SweHoc-107
❑ 69SweHocS-122
❑ 70SweHocS-78
❑ 71SweHocS-168
❑ 72SweHocS-162
❑ 73SweHocS-52
❑ 73SweWorCS-52
❑ 74SweHocS-251
**Marthinsen, Jim**
❑ 93SweSemWCS-229
❑ 94FinnJaaK-251
❑ 95FinnSemWC-177
❑ 95SweGloWC-190
❑ 96SweSemW-202
**Martikainen, Kari**
❑ 93FinnJyvHS-105
❑ 93FinnSIS-11
❑ 94FinnSIS-95
❑ 95FinnSIS-48
**Martin, Blake**
❑ 907thInnSOHL-64
**Martin, Brian**
❑ 83BelBul-7
❑ 89HamRoaA-13
❑ 90HamRoaA-58
❑ 91HamRoaA-10
❑ 92HamRoaA-13
**Martin, Chris**
❑ 82KitRan-29
**Martin, Clare George**
❑ 44BeeGro2P-192
❑ 51Par-39
**Martin, Craig**
❑ 907thInnSQMJHL-228
❑ 91ProAHLCHL-241
❑ 94ClaEnf-E6
❑ 94ClaProP-78
❑ 95BufStaRHI-61
❑ 95Lea-189
❑ 95ParInt-229
❑ 95ParIntEl-229
❑ 95Top-94
❑ 95TopOPCI-94
❑ 98GerDELE-118
**Martin, Don**
❑ 86LonKni-16
❑ 88ProAHL-94
❑ 89ProIHL-102
**Martin, Frank**
❑ 44BeeGro2P-47
❑ 53Par-97
❑ 54Top-30
❑ 62QueAce-17
❑ 63QueAce-16
❑ 63QueAceQ-15
❑ 94ParMisL-34
**Martin, Grant**
❑ 81FreExp-15
❑ 82FreExp-15
❑ 83FreExp-18
❑ 84FreExp-22
❑ 94GerDELE-436
❑ 95GerDELE-399
❑ 96GerDELE-308
**Martin, Jacques**
❑ 88BlaCok-10
❑ 89BlaCok-27
❑ 90NordPet-17
❑ 91NordPet-16
❑ 92NorPet-21
❑ 96SenPizH-13
**Martin, Jason**
❑ 91AirCanSJHL-D7
**Martin, Jeff**
❑ 95Sla-423
**Martin, Matt**
❑ 92MaiBlaB-4
❑ 93Cla-57
❑ 93Don-497
❑ 93Par-471
❑ 93ParEmeI-471
❑ 93Sco-635
❑ 93ScoCan-635
❑ 93ScoGol-635
❑ 93StaCluTUSA-16
❑ 93TopPreTUSA-23
❑ 93Ult-432
❑ 93UppDec-447
❑ 94ClaProP-150
❑ 94ClaProPIA-IA9
❑ 94ClaProPIH-LP9
❑ 94Don-34
❑ 94Lea-159
❑ 94MapLeaPP-23
❑ 94OPCPreSE-550
❑ 94St.JohML-19
❑ 94TopPreSE-550
❑ 97PacInvNRB-194
**Martin, Mike**
❑ 92WinSpi-2
❑ 93WinSpi-4
❑ 94WinSpi-5
❑ 95Cla-9
❑ 95Cla-98
❑ 95SigRooA-28
❑ 95SigRooAPC-28
❑ 95Sla-408
❑ 95Sla-NNO
❑ 96BinRan-13
**Martin, Neal**
❑ 93SauSteMGM-10
❑ 94SudWol-5
❑ 94SudWolP-21
❑ 95Sla-387
❑ 95SudWol-14
❑ 95SudWolP-15
❑ 96HamRoaA-HRA6
**Martin, Pete Jr.**
❑ 81VicCou-10
**Martin, Pete V.**
❑ 36V356WorG-31
**Martin, Peter (Swiss)**
❑ 93SwiHNL-289
❑ 95SwiHNL-318
**Martin, Pit**
❑ 61HamRed-12
❑ 63ChePho-37
❑ 64BeeGro3P-87
❑ 64CocCap-43
❑ 64Top-1
❑ 65Top-52
❑ 66Top-41
❑ 67Top-116
❑ 68OPC-18
❑ 68ShiCoi-22
❑ 68Top-18
❑ 69OPC-75
❑ 69Top-75
❑ 70BlaBor-8
❑ 70ColSta-31
❑ 70DadCoo-79
❑ 70EssPowPla-114
❑ 70OPC-18
❑ 70OPC-253
❑ 70SarProSta-39
❑ 70Top-18
❑ 71OPC-39
❑ 71SarProSta-42
❑ 71Top-39
❑ 71TorSun-75
❑ 72OPC-24
❑ 72SarProSta-68
❑ 72SweSemWC-224
❑ 72Top-99
❑ 73OPC-73
❑ 73Top-164
❑ 74LipSou-37
❑ 74NHLActSta-87
❑ 74OPCNHL-58
❑ 74Top-58
❑ 75OPCNHL-48
❑ 75Top-48
❑ 76OPCNHL-76
❑ 76OPCNHL-382
❑ 76Top-76
❑ 77Coc-15
❑ 77OPCNHL-135
❑ 77Top-135
❑ 78CanuRoyB-16
❑ 78OPC-286
❑ 90UppDec-513
❑ 90UppDecF-513
❑ 94ParTalB-51
❑ 95Par66-1
❑ 95Par66Coi-1
**Martin, Richard (Rick)**
❑ 71ColHea-7
❑ 71OPC-161
❑ 71OPCPos-6
❑ 71SabPos-11
❑ 71TorSun-32
❑ 72OPC-157
❑ 72OPC-182
❑ 72OPCPlaC-4
❑ 72SabPepPB-3
❑ 72SabPepPB-4
❑ 72SarProSta-35
❑ 72Top-145
❑ 73MacMil-17
❑ 73OPC-173
❑ 73SabBel-3
❑ 73SabPos-6
❑ 73Top-155
❑ 74LipSou-33
❑ 74NHLActSta-53
❑ 74OPCNHL-42
❑ 74OPCNHL-127
❑ 74OPCNHL-190
❑ 74Top-42
❑ 74Top-127
❑ 74Top-190
❑ 75OPCNHL-175
❑ 75OPCNHL-208
❑ 75OPCNHL-212
❑ 75OPCNHL-289
❑ 75OPCNHL-315
❑ 75Top-175
❑ 75Top-208
❑ 75Top-212
❑ 75Top-289
❑ 75Top-315
❑ 76OPCNHL-5
❑ 76OPCNHL-210
❑ 76OPCNHL-214
❑ 76OPCNHL-380
❑ 76SabGla-2
❑ 76Top-5
❑ 76Top-210
❑ 76Top-214
❑ 76TopGloI-19
❑ 77OPCNHL-180
❑ 77Top-180
❑ 77TopGloS-11
❑ 77TopOPCGlo-11
❑ 78OPC-80
❑ 78Top-80
❑ 79OPC-149
❑ 79SabBel-4
❑ 79Top-149
❑ 80OPC-51
❑ 80SabMilP-8
❑ 80Top-51
❑ 91FutTreC72-49
❑ 92FutTre76CC-125
❑ 93SabNoc-11
**Martin, Ronnie**
❑ 33V357IceK-7
❑ 34BeeGro1P-240
❑ 34DiaMatS-44
**Martin, Ronny (DEL)**
❑ 94GerDELE-196
❑ 95GerDELE-413
**Martin, Terry**
❑ 77OPCNHL-318
❑ 78OPC-118
❑ 78Top-118
❑ 79MapLeaP-18
❑ 80MapLeaP-17
❑ 80PepCap-91
❑ 81MapLeaP-13
❑ 81OPC-321
❑ 82MapLeaP-23
❑ 82OPC-329
❑ 82OPCSti-66
❑ 82PosCer-18
❑ 83MapLeaP-15
❑ 83OPC-336
❑ 83Vac-92
❑ 84NovScoO-24
❑ 84OPC-306
❑ 88OilTenAnn-146
❑ 89ProAHL-261
❑ 90ProAHLIHL-292
❑ 91ProAHLCHL-22
❑ 91RochAmeKod-2
❑ 91RochAmePos-14
❑ 92RochAmeKod-2
❑ 93RochAmeKod-2
❑ 94MapLeaK-19
**Martin, Tom**
❑ 83VicCou-17
❑ 90ProAHLIHL-419
**Martin, Tom (WHA)**
❑ 72NatOttWHA-16
**Martineau, Andre**
❑ 98QueRem-14
**Martineau, Don**
❑ 74NHLActSta-144
**Martineau, Patrice**
❑ 907thInnSQMJHL-28
❑ 917thInnSMC-38
❑ 917thInnSQMJHL-88
**Martinec, Patrik**
❑ 94CzeAPSE-85
❑ 96CzeAPSE-134
**Martinec, Tomas**
❑ 94CzeAPSE-18
❑ 94GerDELE-181
❑ 95CzeAPSE-117
❑ 95GerDELE-184
❑ 96CzeAPSE-156
❑ 96CzeAPSE-158
**Martinec, Vladimir**
❑ 71SweHocS-55
❑ 72SweSemWC-30
❑ 73SweHocS-30
❑ 73SweWorCS-30
❑ 74SweHocS-17
❑ 74SweSemHVS-56
❑ 79PanSti-86
❑ 92FutTre76CC-156
**Martinec, Vladislav**
❑ 69SweWorC-151
❑ 70SweHocS-361
**Martinek, Radek**
❑ 96CzeAPSE-248
**Martinelle, Per**
❑ 83SweSemE-21
❑ 84SweSemE-19
❑ 85SwePanS-18
❑ 87SwePanS-16
**Martini, Darcy**
❑ 90MicTecHus-14
❑ 91MicTecHus-11
❑ 91MicTecHus-12
❑ 91MicTecHus-34
❑ 94CapBreO-14
❑ 98GerDELE-187
**Martini, Mario**
❑ 83BelBul-15
❑ 84SudWol-3
**Martino, Tony**
❑ 92-TulOil-4
❑ 94CenHocL-101
**Martins, Steve**
❑ 92HarCri-23
❑ 96SprFal-12
❑ 96WhaBobS-15
**Martinson, Joel**
❑ 91AirCanSJHL-C29
**Martinson, Steven (Steve)**
❑ 88CanaPos-19
❑ 88ProAHL-294
❑ 89CanaPos-23
❑ 90ProAHLIHL-308
❑ 91ProAHLCHL-319
❑ 92SanDieG-17
**Martinsson, Per**
❑ 85SwePanS-129
❑ 86SwePanS-128
**Martone, Mike**
❑ 95Sla-308
**Marts, Par**
❑ 72SweHocS-282
❑ 74SweHocS-252
**Marttila, Jukka**
❑ 91SweSemWCS-8
**Marttila, Niko**
❑ 93FinnJyvHS-50
❑ 93FinnSIS-241
❑ 94FinnSIS-12
❑ 95FinnSIS-18
**Martynyuk, Alexander**
❑ 72SweSemWC-15
❑ 73SweHocS-92
❑ 73SweWorCS-92
❑ 74SweSemHVS-39
❑ 91FutTreC72-50
**Maruca, David**
❑ 96RegPat-5
**Maruk, Dennis**
❑ 76OPCNHL-86
❑ 76Top-86
❑ 77OPCNHL-21
❑ 77Top-21
❑ 78OPC-141
❑ 78Top-141
❑ 79OPC-223
❑ 79PanSti-60
❑ 79Top-223
❑ 80OPC-284
❑ 81Cap-10
❑ 81OPC-350
❑ 81OPC-357
❑ 81OPCSti-191
❑ 81Top-65
❑ 81Top-E120
❑ 82Cap-15
❑ 82OPC-359
❑ 82OPC-369
❑ 82OPC-370
❑ 82OPCSti-151
❑ 83NorStaPos-17
❑ 83OPC-174
❑ 83OPCSti-204
❑ 83OPCSti-205
❑ 83PufSti-18
❑ 84NorSta7E-9
❑ 84NorStaPos-14
❑ 84OPC-101
❑ 84OPCSti-48
❑ 84Top-76
❑ 85NorStaPos-19
❑ 85OPC-111
❑ 85Top-111
❑ 86NorSta7E-8
❑ 86OPC-60
❑ 86OPCSti-170
❑ 86Top-60
❑ 87NorStaPos-20
❑ 87OPC-117
❑ 87OPCSti-50
❑ 87PanSti-298
❑ 87Top-117
**Marusak, Jiri**
❑ 95CzeAPSE-38
**Maruschak, Duane**
❑ 89LetHur-14
❑ 907thInnSWHL-133
**Marvel, Chris**
❑ 93OmaLan-17
**Marvin, Willy**
❑ 96MinGolGCAS-19
**Marx, Gord**
❑ 95LasVegThu-7
**Masa, Martin**
❑ 92BriColJHL-60
❑ 94CenHocL-26
**Masak, Martin**
❑ 95CzeAPSE-63
❑ 96CzeAPSE-247
**Masjin, Alexei**
❑ 74SweHocS-90
**Maskarinec, Martin**
❑ 91SweSemWCS-110
❑ 94CzeAPSE-183
❑ 95CzeAPSE-128
**Maslennikov, Igor**
❑ 90OPCRedA-14R
❑ 91OPCIns-21R
❑ 91SweSemWCS-91
**Maslov, Nikolai**
❑ 91OPCIns-55R
**Masnick, Paul**
❑ 44BeeGro2P-267
❑ 45QuaOatP-95
❑ 51Par-8
❑ 52St.LawS-11
❑ 54Par-13
**Mason, Bob**
❑ 86CapKod-16
❑ 87BlaCok-10
❑ 87OPCSti-238
❑ 87PanSti-175
❑ 88NordGenF-22
❑ 88NordTeal-23
❑ 88PanSti-20
❑ 89CapTealss-15
❑ 89OPCSti-188
❑ 89PanSti-344
❑ 89ProAHL-88
❑ 91ProAHLCHL-617
❑ 92HamCan-15
❑ 94MilAdm-18
**Mason, Charley**
❑ 35DiaMatT2-45
❑ 35DiaMatT3-41
❑ 35DiaMatT3-42
❑ 35DiaMatTI-44
**Mason, Doug**
❑ 917thInnSOHL-256
❑ 98GerDELE-41
**Mason, Ron**
❑ 93MicSta-12
❑ 95AHC-6
**Mason, Wes**
❑ 94SarSti-19
❑ 95BowDraPro-P24
❑ 95Sla-349
❑ 95Sla-435
❑ 96SarSti-15
**Massa, Rob**
❑ 94SarSti-15
**Masse, Gerrard**
❑ 92WinSpi-12
**Masse, Mike**
❑ 92MPSPhoSJHL-87
**Masse, Patrice**
❑ 80QueRem-16
**Massey, Jeff**
❑ 94CenHocL-27
❑ 95ForWorFT-11
**Masson, Dale**
❑ 907thInnSMC-24
❑ 907thInnSWHL-294
❑ 917thInnSWHL-86
**Massy, Didier**
❑ 91SweSemWCS-183
**Mastad, Milt**
❑ 91BriColJHL-111
❑ 93SeaThu-12
❑ 96ProBru-28
**Masters, Chris**
❑ 94DubFigS-17
**Masters, Kevin**
❑ 907thInnSWHL-147
❑ 917thInnSWHL-267
**Masterson, Matt**
❑ 95Sla-413
**Matatall, Bruce**
❑ 91AirCanSJHL-B47
❑ 92MPSPhoSJHL-64
**Matatall, Craig**
❑ 91AirCanSJHL-C1
❑ 91AirCanSJHLAS-29
❑ 91AirCanSJHLAS-49
**Matechuk, Rod**
❑ 84SasBlaS-13
**Mateka, Eddie**
❑ 52JunBluT-30
**Materi, Lee**
❑ 92MPSPhoSJHL-69
**Mathers, Frank**
❑ 44BeeGro2P-428
❑ 45QuaOatP-32
❑ 88ProAHL-146
**Mathers, Mike**
❑ 907thInnSWHL-299
❑ 917thInnSWHL-81
**Mathias, Trevor**
❑ 91AirCanSJHL-C42
**Mathiasen, Dwight**
❑ 87PenKod-18
**Mathies, Jeremy**
❑ 91AirCanSJHL-D33
**Mathieson, Jim**
❑ 86RegPat-15
❑ 87RegPat-17
❑ 88RegPat-15
❑ 89RegPat-10
❑ 90ProAHLIHL-197
❑ 91BalSki-8
❑ 91ProAHLCHL-554
❑ 93PorPir-9
❑ 94PorPir-15
❑ 95PorPir-14
**Mathieu, Alexandre**
❑ 97BowCHL-123
❑ 97BowCHLAu-3
❑ 97BowCHLOPC-123
❑ 98BowCHL-115
❑ 98BowCHLGA-115
❑ 98BowCHLOI-115
❑ 98BowChrC-115
❑ 98BowChrCGA-115
❑ 98BowChrCGAR-115
❑ 98BowChrCOI-115
❑ 98BowChrCOIR-115
❑ 98BowChrCR-115
**Mathieu, Gilbert**
❑ 72SweSemWC-160
**Mathieu, Marquis**
❑ 907thInnSQMJHL-114
❑ 917thInnSQMJHL-162
❑ 93WheThu-13
❑ 94TolSto-16
**Mathieu, Nando**
❑ 72SweSemWC-138
**Matier, Mark**
❑ 907thInnSOHL-167
❑ 917thInnSMC-18
❑ 917thInnSOHL-326
❑ 93SauSteMGM-3
**Matikainen, Pentti**
❑ 89SweSemWCS-27
❑ 93FinnJyvHS-43
❑ 93FinnSIS-233
❑ 93SweSemWCS-88
❑ 96GerDELE-46
**Matikainen, Petri**
❑ 94FinnSIS-233
❑ 95FinnSIS-70
❑ 96GerDELE-255
**Matsos, David**
❑ 89SauSteMG-23
❑ 907thInnSOHL-168
❑ 917thInnSMC-10
❑ 917thInnSOHL-329
❑ 93SauSteMGM-12
**Matte, Christian**
❑ 97Don-207
❑ 97DonCanI-137
❑ 97DonCanIDS-137
❑ 97DonCanIPS-137
❑ 97DonMed-6
❑ 97DonPreProG-207
❑ 97DonPreProS-207
❑ 97DonRatR-6
❑ 97UppDec-257
**Matte, David**
❑ 92QueIntP-57
**Matte, Joe**
❑ 34BeeGro1P-69
**Matteau, Stephane**
❑ 89ProIHL-192
❑ 90FlamIGA-14
❑ 90OPCPre-68
❑ 90ProSet-593
❑ 90Sco-381
❑ 90ScoCan-381
❑ 90UppDec-535
❑ 90UppDecF-535
❑ 91Bow-258

**McAneeley, Ted • 595**


❑ 91FlamIGA-10
❑ 91FlamPanTS-11
❑ 91OPC-383
❑ 91PanSti-62
❑ 91Par-259
❑ 91ParFre-259
❑ 91ProSet-27
❑ 91ProSetFre-27
❑ 91ScoCan-242
❑ 91StaClu-391
❑ 91Top-383
❑ 91UppDec-121
❑ 91UppDecF-121
❑ 92Bow-340
❑ 92OPC-69
❑ 92Par-268
❑ 92ParEmel-268
❑ 92Pin-180
❑ 92PinFre-180
❑ 92Sco-543
❑ 92ScoCan-543
❑ 92StaClu-363
❑ 92Top-463
❑ 92TopGol-463G
❑ 92Ult-279
❑ 92UppDec-540
❑ 93BlaCok-13
❑ 93Don-463
❑ 93DurSco-44
❑ 93Lea-114
❑ 93OPCPre-415
❑ 93OPCPreG-415
❑ 93PanSti-150
❑ 93Par-41
❑ 93ParEmel-41
❑ 93Pin-344
❑ 93PinCan-344
❑ 93Pow-313
❑ 93Sco-398
❑ 93ScoCan-398
❑ 93StaClu-127
❑ 93StaCluFDI-127
❑ 93StaCluFDIO-127
❑ 93StaCluO-127
❑ 93TopPre-415
❑ 93TopPreG-415
❑ 93Ult-290
❑ 93UppDec-214
❑ 94CanGamNHLP-165
❑ 94Don-15
❑ 94Lea-32
❑ 94OPCPre-317
❑ 94OPCPreSE-317
❑ 94Par-150
❑ 94ParGol-150
❑ 94Pin-329
❑ 94PinArtP-329
❑ 94PinRinC-329
❑ 94StaClu-216
❑ 94StaCluFDI-216
❑ 94StaCluMOMS-216
❑ 94StaCluSTWC-216
❑ 94TopPre-317
❑ 94TopPreSE-317
❑ 94Ult-332
❑ 94UppDec-136
❑ 94UppDecEleIce-136
❑ 95BeAPla-5
❑ 95BeAPSig-S5
❑ 95BeAPSigDC-S5
❑ 95ParInt-446
❑ 95ParIntEl-446
❑ 95Sco-227
❑ 95ScoBlaIce-227
❑ 95ScoBlaIceAP-227
❑ 95UppDec-60
❑ 95UppDecEleIce-60
❑ 95UppDecEleIceG-60
❑ 96BeAPAut-169
❑ 96BeAPAutSil-169
❑ 96BeAPla-169
❑ 96ColCho-230
❑ 96UppDec-326
❑ 97Pac-280
❑ 97PacCop-280
❑ 97PacEmeGre-280
❑ 97PacIceB-280
❑ 97PacPar-168
❑ 97PacParC-168
❑ 97PacParDG-168
❑ 97PacParEG-168
❑ 97PacParIB-168
❑ 97PacParRed-168
❑ 97PacParSil-168
❑ 97PacRed-280
❑ 97PacSil-280
❑ 98Pac-387
❑ 98PacIceB-387
❑ 98PacPar-212
❑ 98PacParC-212
❑ 98PacParEG-212
❑ 98PacParH-212
❑ 98PacParIB-212
❑ 98PacParS-212
❑ 98PacRed-387
❑ 98UppDec-355
❑ 98UppDecE-355
❑ 98UppDecE1o1-355
❑ 98UppDecGR-355
❑ 99Pac-376
❑ 99PacCop-376
❑ 99PacGol-376
❑ 99PacIceB-376
❑ 99PacPreD-376

**Mattersdorfer, Darcy**
❑ 917thInnSWHL-70

**Matteucci, Mike**
❑ 91AirCanSJHL-D43
❑ 91AirCanSJHLAS-21
❑ 91AirCanSJHLAS-47
❑ 91AirCanSJHLAS-48
❑ 91LakSupSL-17

**Matthews, Jamie**
❑ 89SudWol-8
❑ 907thInnSOHL-387
❑ 90SudWol-9
❑ 917thInnSMC-124
❑ 917thInnSOHL-261
❑ 91Cla-37
❑ 91StaPicH-6
❑ 91SudWol-19
❑ 91UltDra-32
❑ 91UppDec-76
❑ 91UppDecF-76
❑ 92SudWol-10
❑ 93SudWol-16
❑ 93SudWolP-9

**Matthews, Jeff**
❑ 93RenEng-17

**Matthews, Ronnie**
❑ 51LavDaiS-40
❑ 52St.LawS-86

**Matthies, Jeremy**
❑ 92MPSPhoSJHL-155

**Mattila, Hannu**
❑ 93FinnJyvHS-78
❑ 93FinnSIS-127
❑ 94FinnSIS-76
❑ 95FinnSIS-38
❑ 96FinnSISR-35

**Mattis, Mike**
❑ 93MicSta-13

**Mattiussi, Dick**
❑ 69OPC-147
❑ 70EssPowPla-96
❑ 70OPC-192
❑ 70SarProSta-139

**Mattsson, Jesper**
❑ 91SweSemE-198
❑ 91SweSemE-332
❑ 92SweSemE-217
❑ 93Cla-141
❑ 93SweSemE-188
❑ 94ParSE-SE244
❑ 94ParSEG-SE244
❑ 94SP-171
❑ 94SPDieCut-171
❑ 94SweLeaE-280
❑ 94UppDec-519
❑ 94UppDecEleIce-519
❑ 95ColEdgI-76
❑ 95St.JohF-13
❑ 95SweGloWC-61
❑ 95SweLeaE-92

**Mattsson, Markus**
❑ 78JetPos-15
❑ 80JetPos-17
❑ 80OPC-394
❑ 80PepCap-135
❑ 81OPC-374
❑ 82SweSemHVS-159

**Mattsson, Torbjorn**
❑ 83SweSemE-57
❑ 84SweSemE-57
❑ 85SwePanS-54
❑ 86SwePanS-34
❑ 87SwePanS-256
❑ 90SweSemE-83

**Matulik, Ivan**
❑ 89ProAHL-150
❑ 90ProAHLIHL-527
❑ 91ProAHLCHL-537
❑ 93SheSte-8
❑ 95VanVooRHI-12

**Matusovich, Scott**
❑ 92BirBul-6
❑ 92NasKni-5
❑ 93BirBul-6
❑ 94WheThu-18

**Matuszek, Mike**
❑ 897thInnSOHL-170

**Matvichuk, Alexandre**
❑ 93SeaThu-24
❑ 94NorBayC-11
❑ 95Sla-216
❑ 96TolSto-17

**Matvichuk, Richard**
❑ 89SasBla-15
❑ 907thInnSWHL-83
❑ 90SasBla-14
❑ 917thInnSMC-108
❑ 917thInnSWHL-113
❑ 91AreDraPic-6
❑ 91Cla-7
❑ 91SasBla-14
❑ 91StaPicH-57
❑ 91UltDra-7
❑ 91UltDra-63
❑ 91UppDecCWJC-48
❑ 92OPCPre-83
❑ 92Par-74
❑ 92ParEmel-74
❑ 92Pin-391
❑ 92PinFre-391
❑ 92Ult-321
❑ 92UppDec-505
❑ 93Don-418
❑ 93Pin-182
❑ 93PinCan-182
❑ 93Sco-285
❑ 93ScoCan-285
❑ 93Ult-180
❑ 93UppDec-55
❑ 94ClaProP-151
❑ 94Don-303
❑ 94Lea-269
❑ 94OPCPre-187
❑ 94OPCPreSE-187
❑ 94Par-57
❑ 94ParGol-57
❑ 94StaPos-17
❑ 94TopPre-187
❑ 94TopPreSE-187
❑ 94UppDec-157
❑ 94UppDecEleIce-157
❑ 95ParInt-328
❑ 95ParIntEl-328
❑ 95PlaOneoOne-249
❑ 95UppDec-37
❑ 95UppDecEleIce-37
❑ 95UppDecEleIceG-37
❑ 96BeAPAut-195
❑ 96BeAPAutSil-195
❑ 96BeAPla-195
❑ 96Don-97
❑ 96DonPrePro-97
❑ 96Sco-229
❑ 96ScoArtPro-229
❑ 96ScoDeaCAP-229
❑ 96ScoGolB-229
❑ 96ScoSpeAP-229
❑ 96StaPos-20
❑ 97Don-193
❑ 97DonPreProG-193
❑ 97DonPreProS-193
❑ 97PacDynBKS-29
❑ 98O-PChr-210
❑ 98O-PChrR-210
❑ 98Top-210
❑ 98TopO-P-210
❑ 98UppDec-255
❑ 98UppDecE-255
❑ 98UppDecE1o1-255
❑ 98UppDecGR-255

**Matwijiw, Stan**
❑ 917thInnSWHL-261
❑ 91PriAlbR-12
❑ 93LetHur-7
❑ 94FliGen-16

**Maudie, Bob**
❑ 93KamBla-16
❑ 95SlaMemC-22
❑ 96BinRan-14

**Maurer, A.**
❑ 95GerDELE-349

**Maurice, Mike**
❑ 85KinCan-22
❑ 86KinCan-19
❑ 92HamCan-16
❑ 94ClaProP-64

**Maurice, Paul**
❑ 93DetJrRW-23
❑ 94DetJrRW-25
❑ 95SlaMemC-99
❑ 96WhaBobS-16
❑ 97CarHur-27

**Mavety, Larry**
❑ 83BelBul-29
❑ 84BelBul-3
❑ 907thInnSOHL-23
❑ 917thInnSOHL-110

**Maxner, Wayne**
❑ 85SudWol-5
❑ 86LonKni-4
❑ 897thInnSOHL-48
❑ 917thInnSOHL-192

**Maxwell, Brad**
❑ 78NorStaCD-6
❑ 78OPC-83
❑ 78Top-83
❑ 79NorStaPos-8
❑ 79OPC-231
❑ 79PanSti-56
❑ 79Top-231
❑ 80NorStaPos-11
❑ 80OPC-152
❑ 80Top-152
❑ 81NorStaPos-13
❑ 81OPC-102
❑ 82NorStaPos-15
❑ 82OPC-168
❑ 82PosCer-9
❑ 83NorStaPos-18
❑ 83OPC-175
❑ 84NordPos-16
❑ 84NorStaPos-15
❑ 84OPC-102
❑ 84OPCSti-50
❑ 84Top-77
❑ 85MapLeaP-20
❑ 85MapLeaP-21
❑ 85OPC-224
❑ 85OPCSti-154
❑ 86Canu-10
❑ 86OPC-242
❑ 86OPCSti-145

**Maxwell, Bryan**
❑ 76OPCWHA-54
❑ 78OPC-216
❑ 78Top-216
❑ 81JetPos-14
❑ 82Jet-17
❑ 82OPC-387
❑ 82PosCer-21
❑ 83PenCok-15
❑ 84PenHeiP-14
❑ 85MedHatT-16
❑ 88KinSmo-16
❑ 907thInnSWHL-209
❑ 917thInnSMC-95
❑ 917thInnSWHL-3
❑ 95LetHur-12
❑ 96LetHur-19

**Maxwell, Dennis**
❑ 917thInnSOHL-205
❑ 92SudWol-22
❑ 94SarSti-22
❑ 95Cla-96

**Maxwell, F.G.**
❑ 85HalFC-177

**Maxwell, Kevin**
❑ 81NorStaPos-14
❑ 81RocPos-18
❑ 81SweSemHVS-83
❑ 82PosCer-11

**Maxwell, Pete**
❑ 74SioCitM-9

**Maxwell, Robert**
❑ 52JunBluT-29

**Maxwell, Steamer**
❑ 83HalFP-M13

**Maxwell, Wayne**
❑ 96FifFly-10
❑ 97FifFly-3

**May, Alan**
❑ 88OilTenAnn-159
❑ 88ProAHL-78
❑ 89CapKod-16
❑ 89CapTealss-16
❑ 90Bow-78
❑ 90BowTif-78
❑ 90CapKod-16
❑ 90CapPos-16
❑ 90CapSmo-15
❑ 90PanSti-160
❑ 90ProSet-317
❑ 90UppDec-240
❑ 90UppDecF-240
❑ 91Bow-295
❑ 91CapJun5-20
❑ 91CapKod-20
❑ 91OPC-57
❑ 91Par-417
❑ 91ParFre-417
❑ 91ProSet-508
❑ 91ProSet-614
❑ 91ProSetFre-508
❑ 91ProSetFre-614
❑ 91ScoCan-545
❑ 91StaClu-288
❑ 91Top-57
❑ 92CapKod-20
❑ 92Sco-357
❑ 92ScoCan-357
❑ 93Don-419
❑ 93OPCPre-518
❑ 93OPCPreG-518
❑ 93Sco-430
❑ 93ScoCan-430
❑ 93TopPre-518
❑ 93TopPreG-518

**May, Bob**
❑ 93HunBli-16

**May, Brad**
❑ 88NiaFalT-2
❑ 897thInnSOHL-125
❑ 89NiaFalT-11
❑ 907thInnSOHL-264
❑ 90Sco-427
❑ 90ScoCan-427
❑ 90UppDec-455
❑ 90UppDecF-455
❑ 91Par-10
❑ 91ParFre-10
❑ 91Pin-302
❑ 91PinFre-302
❑ 91ProSet-523
❑ 91ProSetFre-523
❑ 91SabBluS-12
❑ 91SabPepC-12
❑ 91ScoCan-628
❑ 91ScoRoo-78T
❑ 91UppDec-596
❑ 91UppDecF-596
❑ 92Bow-374
❑ 92OPC-256
❑ 92PanSti-252
❑ 92PanStiFre-252
❑ 92Par-240
❑ 92Par-257
❑ 92ParEmel-240
❑ 92ParEmel-257
❑ 92Pin-197
❑ 92PinFre-197
❑ 92SabBluS-12
❑ 92SabJubF-8
❑ 92Sco-96
❑ 92ScoCan-96
❑ 92StaClu-51
❑ 92Top-34
❑ 92TopGol-34G
❑ 92Ult-17
❑ 92UppDec-74
❑ 93Don-38
❑ 93Lea-47
❑ 93OPCPre-192
❑ 93OPCPreG-192
❑ 93Par-27
❑ 93ParEmel-27
❑ 93Pin-141
❑ 93PinCan-141
❑ 93Pow-298
❑ 93SabNoc-12
❑ 93Sco-269
❑ 93ScoCan-269
❑ 93StaClu-203
❑ 93StaCluFDI-203
❑ 93StaCluFDIO-203
❑ 93StaCluO-203
❑ 93TopPre-192
❑ 93TopPreG-192
❑ 93UppDec-201
❑ 94BeAPla-R26
❑ 94BeAPSig-22
❑ 94CanGamNHLP-362
❑ 94Don-76
❑ 94Fle-24
❑ 94Lea-215
❑ 94OPCPre-409
❑ 94OPCPreSE-409
❑ 94Par-26
❑ 94ParGol-26
❑ 94Pin-194
❑ 94PinArtP-194
❑ 94PinRinC-194
❑ 94Sco-104
❑ 94ScoGol-104
❑ 94ScoPla-104
❑ 94ScoPlaTS-104
❑ 94StaClu-2
❑ 94StaCluFDI-2
❑ 94StaCluMOMS-2
❑ 94StaCluSTWC-2
❑ 94TopPre-409
❑ 94TopPreSE-409
❑ 94Ult-25
❑ 94UppDec-391
❑ 94UppDecEleIce-391
❑ 95Don-93
❑ 95Lea-224
❑ 95ParInt-289
❑ 95ParIntEl-289
❑ 95Sco-288
❑ 95ScoBlaIce-288
❑ 95ScoBlaIceAP-288
❑ 95StaClu-79
❑ 95StaCluMOMS-79
❑ 95Sum-70
❑ 95SumArtP-70
❑ 95SumIce-70
❑ 95UppDec-468
❑ 95UppDecEleIce-468
❑ 95UppDecEleIceG-468
❑ 96BeAPAut-52
❑ 96BeAPAutSil-52
❑ 96BeAPla-52
❑ 96BeAPla-P52
❑ 96ColCho-29
❑ 96Don-189
❑ 96DonPrePro-189
❑ 96Lea-4
❑ 96LeaPreP-4
❑ 96Sco-48
❑ 96ScoArtPro-48
❑ 96ScoDeaCAP-48
❑ 96ScoGolB-48
❑ 96ScoSpeAP-48
❑ 97PacDynBKS-11
❑ 97ScoSab-10
❑ 97ScoSabPla-10
❑ 97ScoSabPre-10
❑ 98Be A PPA-293
❑ 98Be A PPAA-293
❑ 98Be A PPAAF-293
❑ 98Be A PPSE-293
❑ 98Be APG-293
❑ 98Pac-429
❑ 98PacIceB-429
❑ 98PacRed-429
❑ 98UppDec-380
❑ 98UppDecE-380
❑ 98UppDecE1o1-380
❑ 98UppDecGR-380

**May, Darrell**
❑ 88ProIHL-94

**May, Mike**
❑ 91FerStaB-21

**Mayasich, John**
❑ 69SweWorC-177

**Maye, Chris**
❑ 93RenEng-18

**Mayer, Derek**
❑ 89ProAHL-329
❑ 91ProAHLCHL-135
❑ 92AlbIntTC-12
❑ 93AlbIntTC-14
❑ 93Don-467
❑ 93OPCPreTC-6
❑ 93Pow-489
❑ 93Ult-469
❑ 94Par-156
❑ 94ParGol-156
❑ 94ParVin-V60
❑ 94Sco-223
❑ 94ScoGol-223
❑ 94ScoPla-223
❑ 94ScoPlaTS-223
❑ 94ScoTeaC-CT17
❑ 94StaClu-251
❑ 94StaCluFDI-251
❑ 94StaCluMOMS-251
❑ 94StaCluSTWC-251
❑ 94UppDec-107
❑ 94UppDecEleIce-107
❑ 95FinnSIS-315
❑ 95FinnSIS-375
❑ 96FinnSISRS-5
❑ 96GerDELE-30
❑ 98GerDELE-160

**Mayer, Gil**
❑ 60CleBar-12

**Mayer, Hans-Jorg**
❑ 91UppDec-682
❑ 91UppDecCWJC-45
❑ 91UppDecF-682
❑ 94GerDELE-184
❑ 95GerDELE-185
❑ 96GerDELE-123

**Mayer, Pat**
❑ 88ProIHL-55

**Mayer, Stefan**
❑ 94GerDELE-28
❑ 95GerDELE-8
❑ 96GerDELE-9
❑ 98GerDELE-16

**Mayer, Thierry**
❑ 917thInnSQMJHL-218
❑ 95GerDELE-102

**Mayers, Jamal**
❑ 92WesMic-17
❑ 93WesMic-21
❑ 97Don-223
❑ 97DonPreProG-223
❑ 97DonPreProS-223
❑ 99Pac-359
❑ 99PacCop-359
❑ 99PacGol-359
❑ 99PacIceB-359
❑ 99PacPreD-359

**Mayes, David**
❑ 96SouCarS-12

**Maynard, Geordie**
❑ 907thInnSOHL-288
❑ 917thInnSOHL-281

**Maynard, Niall**
❑ 95Sla-265

**Maynort, Bruno**
❑ 95FinnSemWC-196

**Mayo, Kevin**
❑ 85BraWheK-9

**Mayo, Matthew**
❑ 93NiaFalT-18

**Mayr, Jorg**
❑ 94GerDELE-201
❑ 95GerDELE-199
❑ 96GerDELE-341
❑ 98GerDELE-100
❑ 98GerDELE-318

**Maznick, Paul**
❑ 48ExhCan-15

**Mazur, Eddie**
❑ 44BeeGro2P-268
❑ 51BufBis-15
❑ 53Par-20
❑ 54Par-4
❑ 60CleBar-13

**Mazur, Jay**
❑ 89ProIHL-176
❑ 90CanuMoh-17
❑ 91Bow-322
❑ 91OPC-28
❑ 91ProAHLCHL-612
❑ 91StaClu-272
❑ 91Top-28
❑ 91UppDec-378
❑ 91UppDecF-378
❑ 92HamCan-17
❑ 95RochAmeSS-10

**Mazutinec, Shane**
❑ 88LetHur-16

**Mazzoli, Pat**
❑ 91FerStaB-22

**McAdam, Don**
❑ 91ProAHLCHL-235

**McAdam, Gary**
❑ 77OPCNHL-253
❑ 77Top-253
❑ 78OPC-42
❑ 78Top-42
❑ 79OPC-72
❑ 79Top-72
❑ 80OPC-288
❑ 81FlamPos-13
❑ 81OPC-93
❑ 81Top-W93
❑ 82PosCer-3
❑ 84OPC-117

**McAleavy, Tony**
❑ 97KinHaw-16

**McAlendin, Marlin**
❑ 52JunBluT-6

**McAllister, Chris**
❑ 95Cla-35
❑ 96SyrCru-28

**McAlpine, Chris**
❑ 91MinGolG-14
❑ 92MinGolG-12
❑ 93MinGolG-18
❑ 94Cla-54
❑ 94ClaAllAme-AA4
❑ 94ClaDraGol-54
❑ 95ColEdgI-7
❑ 95Don-113
❑ 95Ima-80
❑ 95ImaAut-80A
❑ 95ImaGol-80
❑ 95Lea-14
❑ 95Pin-210
❑ 95PinArtP-210
❑ 95PinRinC-210
❑ 95Sco-293
❑ 95ScoBlaIce-293
❑ 95ScoBlaIceAP-293
❑ 95Top-61
❑ 95TopOPCI-61
❑ 97Be A PPAD-82
❑ 97Be A PPAPD-82
❑ 97BeAPla-82
❑ 97BeAPlaAut-82
❑ 97ScoBlu-14
❑ 97ScoBluPla-14
❑ 97ScoBluPre-14
❑ 97UppDec-348

**McAlpine, Mike**
❑ 92MinGolG-22
❑ 93MinGolG-19

**McAmmond, Dave**
❑ 91AirCanSJHL-B26

**McAmmond, Dean**
❑ 907thInnSWHL-267
❑ 90PriAlbR-11
❑ 917thInnSMC-109
❑ 917thInnSWHL-254
❑ 91AreDraPic-17
❑ 91Cla-19
❑ 91PriAlbR-13
❑ 91StaPicH-66
❑ 91UltDra-18
❑ 91UltDra-74
❑ 92ProSet-224
❑ 92Sco-469
❑ 92ScoCan-469
❑ 92Ult-40
❑ 92UppDec-403
❑ 93Don-110
❑ 93Lea-436
❑ 93OPCPre-366
❑ 93OPCPreG-366
❑ 93Par-64
❑ 93ParCalC-C9
❑ 93ParCalCG-C9
❑ 93ParEmel-64
❑ 93TopPre-366
❑ 93TopPreG-366
❑ 93Ult-317
❑ 93UppDec-480
❑ 93UppDecSP-51
❑ 94Don-123
❑ 94Fla-59
❑ 94Lea-298
❑ 94ParSE-SE62
❑ 94ParSEG-SE62
❑ 94Pin-358
❑ 94PinArtP-358
❑ 94PinRinC-358
❑ 94StaClu-147
❑ 94StaCluFDI-147
❑ 94StaCluMOMS-147
❑ 94StaCluSTWC-147
❑ 94Ult-292
❑ 94UppDec-386
❑ 94UppDecEleIce-386
❑ 95PlaOneoOne-257
❑ 95UppDec-363
❑ 95UppDecEleIce-363
❑ 95UppDecEleIceG-363
❑ 96BeAPAut-126
❑ 96BeAPAutSil-126
❑ 96BeAPla-126
❑ 96OilPos-37
❑ 96PlaOneoOne-419
❑ 96UppDec-257
❑ 97ColCho-97
❑ 97PacInvNRB-80
❑ 97SPAut-62
❑ 97UppDec-275
❑ 98BowBes-90
❑ 98BowBesAR-90
❑ 98BowBesR-90
❑ 98Pac-214
❑ 98PacIceB-214
❑ 98PacPar-89
❑ 98PacParC-89
❑ 98PacParEG-89
❑ 98PacParH-89
❑ 98PacParIB-89
❑ 98PacParS-89
❑ 98PacRed-214
❑ 98UC-79
❑ 98UD ChoPCR-79
❑ 98UD ChoR-79
❑ 98UppDec-271
❑ 98UppDecE-271
❑ 98UppDecE1o1-271
❑ 98UppDecGR-271
❑ 99Pac-93
❑ 99PacCop-93
❑ 99PacGol-93
❑ 99PacIceB-93
❑ 99PacPreD-93

**McAndrew, Hazen**
❑ 34BeeGro1P-241

**McAneeley, Ted**
❑ 72OPC-242
❑ 73OPC-37
❑ 73Top-37
❑ 74NHLActSta-66
❑ 74OPCNHL-148
❑ 74Top-148

**McArter, Joel**
❑ 92CorBigRed-20
❑ 93CorBigRed-18

**McArthur, Darryl**
❑ 95GueSto5A-17
❑ 95Sla-84

96GueSto-16
97GueSto-20
**McArthur, Dean**
82MedHatT-11
**McArthur, Dustin**
94SarSti-14
96PeoRiv-18
96PeoRivPA-17
**McArthur, Mark**
93GueSto-3
94GueSto-2
95ColEdgI-194
95SigRoo-69A
95SigRoo-69B
95SigRooSig-69
96ColEdgFL-33
**McAusland, Darren**
907thInnSWHL-7
917thInnSWHL-135
93PorPir-16
94PorPir-16
94WheThu-12
95PorPir-15
96PorPir-16
**McBain, Andrew**
82NorBayC-15
83Jet-17
83Vac-133
84JetPol-14
84OPC-343
85JetPol-12
86JetBor-14
87Jet-14
87PanSti-370
88FriLaysI-12
88JetPol-15
88OPC-105
88OPCSti-147
88PanSti-157
88Top-105
89OPC-38
89OPC-318
89OPCSti-135
89PenFoo-13A
89Top-38
90CanuMoh-18
90OPC-248
90PanSti-297
90ProSet-301A
90ProSet-301B
90Sco-257
90ScoCan-257
90Top-248
90TopTif-248
91CanuPanTS-15
91ProAHLCHL-605
91ProSet-500
91ProSetFre-500
92ProSet-120
92Sen-11
92Ult-147
930PCPre-238
930PCPreG-238
93TopPre-238
93TopPreG-238
94LasVegThu-15
940PCPre-77
940PCPreSE-77
94TopPre-77
94TopPreSE-77
95ColEdgI-127
**McBain, Jason**
907thInnSWHL-132
917thInnSWHL-48
92Cla-25
93DonTeaUSA-14
93Pin-483
93PinCan-483
93UppDec-552
95ColEdgI-72
96ClaGoI-25
96SprFal-25
96UppDec-189
98LasVegI-12
**McBain, Mike**
93RedDeeR-15
94ParSE-SE252
94ParSEG-SE252
94Sel-167
94SelGoI-167
94SP-176
94SPDieCut-176
95Cla-27
95DonEliWJ-29
95RedDeeR-11
95UppDec-570
95UppDecEleIce-570
95UppDecEleIceG-570
97BowCHL-103
97BowCHLOPC-103
98Pac-401
98PacIceB-401
98PacRed-401
**McBean, Wayne**
85MedHatT-18
88KinSmo-17
89ProAHL-237
90ProAHLIHL-502
90ProSet-485
91Bow-217
91OPC-62
91Par-330
91ParFre-330
91ProSet-144
91ProSetFre-144

91ScoCan-530
91StaClu-353
91Top-62
92OPC-50
92StaClu-397
92Top-443
92TopGoI-443G
93Lea-413
93StaClu-493
93StaCluFDI-493
93StaCluO-493
**McBride, Daryn**
90ProAHLIHL-363
91CinCyc-14
**McBurney, Jim**
52JunBluT-182
**McBurnie, Bob**
91BriColJHL-107
**McCabe, Bryan**
917thInnSWHL-331
93DonTeaC-16
93Pin-462
93PinCan-462
93UppDec-549
94Fin-150
94FinRef-150
94FinSupTW-150
94ParSE-SE209
94ParSEG-SE209
94Pin-523
94PinArtP-523
94PinRinC-523
94SP-153
94SPDieCut-153
94UppDec-502
94UppDecEleIce-502
95Bow-96
95BowAllFoi-96
95CanGamNHLP-175
95ColCho-404
95Don-333
95DonCanWJT-8
95Fin-54
95FinRef-54
95Ima-91
95ImaGoI-91
95ParInt-256
95ParIntEI-256
95SelCer-126
95SelCerMG-126
95SkyImp-209
95SlaMemC-34
95SP-91
95StaClu-93
95StaCluMOMS-93
95Sum-172
95SumArtP-172
95SumIce-172
95Top-312
95TopCanWJ-7CJ
95TopOPCI-312
95Ult-348
95UppDec-496
95UppDecEleIce-496
95UppDecEleIceG-496
95Zen-138
96BeAPAut-162
96BeAPAutSil-162
96BeAPla-162
96ColCho-161
96Don-217
96DonPrePro-217
96IsIPos-13
96Lea-161
96LeaPreP-161
96MetUni-94
96Sco-253
96ScoArtPro-253
96ScoDeaCAP-253
96ScoGoIB-253
96ScoSpeAP-253
96Sum-157
96SumArtP-157
96SumIce-157
96SumMet-157
96SumPreS-157
96TopNHLP-175
96TopPicOI-175
96UppDec-99
97ColCho-157
97Kat-89
97KatGoI-89
97KatSil-89
97Pac-118
97PacCop-118
97PacEmeGre-118
97PacIceB-118
97PacOme-138
97PacOmeC-138
97PacOmeDG-138
97PacOmeEG-138
97PacOmeG-138
97PacOmeIB-138
97PacRed-118
97PacSil-118
97UppDec-100
98Pac-430
98PacIceB-430
98PacRed-430
99Pac-425
99PacCop-425
99PacGoI-425
99PacIceB-425
99PacPreD-425
**McCabe, Scott**

91LakSupSL-18
**McCabe, Tony**
907thInnSOHL-236
90KitRan-11
917thInnSOHL-77
**McCaffrey, Albert**
24C144ChaCig-38
24VI452-57
**McCaffrey, Kevin**
92WesMic-18
**McCague, Mark**
907thInnSOHL-65
**McCague, Peter**
95Sla-224
**McCaig, Doug**
34BeeGro1P-114
44BeeGro2P-120
**McCaig, Rob**
94CenHocL-15
95LouIceG-10
95LouIceGP-11
**McCallion, Paul**
907thInnSOHL-237
90KitRan-21
917thInnSOHL-86
96GuiFla-21
**McCallum, Andy**
52St.LawS-93
**McCallum, Dunc**
61SudWol-13
62SudWol-15
68ShiCoi-143
70EssPowPla-222
710PC-132
71Top-132
**McCallum, Scott**
95TriAme-18
**McCambridge, Keith**
917thInnSWHL-186
95SlaMemC-5
95St.JohF-14
**McCammon, Bob**
85OilRedR-NNO
**McCann, Gordon**
91AirCanSJHL-C8
92MPSPhoSJHL-83
**McCann, Sean**
92HarCri-24
94Cla-55
94ClaAllAme-AA5
94ClaDraGoI-55
96GraRapG-10
**McCartan, Jack**
44BeeGro2P-341
60ShiCoi-81
60Top-39
72FigSaiPos-14
**McCarthy, Doug**
95VanVooRHI-5
**McCarthy, Jeremiah**
95DonEliWJ-30
**McCarthy, Joe**
93Rallce-11
**McCarthy, Kevin**
79CanuRoyB-15
790PC-287
80CanuSiID-17
80CanuTeal-16
800PC-21
80PepCap-114
80Top-21
81CanuSiID-22
81CanuTeal-15
810PC-341
810PCSti-248
82Canu-14
820PC-351
820PCSti-246
82PosCer-19
83Canu-13
830PC-356
830PCSti-279
83PufSti-6
840PC-178
840PCSti-119
84Top-126
88ProAHL-143
89ProAHL-360
**McCarthy, Sandy**
907thInnSMC-53
907thInnSQMJHL-54
917thInnSQMJHL-228
91Cla-42
91UppDec-1
91UppDecF-77
93Cla-142
93Don-59
93Lea-358
93Par-30
93ParEmel-30
93Pow-306
93Sco-633
93ScoCan-633
93ScoGoI-633
93StaCluFDI-441
93UppDec-493
94ClaProP-22
94Don-39
94Lea-411
95BeAPla-217
95BeAPSig-S217
95BeAPSigDC-S217
95UppDec-361
95UppDecEleIce-361

95UppDecEleIceG-361
96ColCho-43
96Don-42
96DonPrePro-42
96Sco-215
96ScoArtPro-215
96ScoDeaCAP-215
96ScoGoIB-215
96ScoSpeAP-215
96UppDec-23
97Kat-22
97KatGoI-22
97KatSil-22
97SPAut-21
97UppDec-25
98Be A PPA-282
98Be A PPAA-282
98Be A PPAAF-282
98Be A PPSE-282
98Be APG-282
98Fin-124
98FinNo P-124
98FinNo PR-124
98FinRef-124
980-PChr-82
980-PChrR-82
98Pac-402
98PacIceB-402
98PacOmeH-220
98PacOmeODI-220
98PacOmeR-220
98PacPar-218
98PacParC-218
98PacParEG-218
98PacParH-218
98PacParIB-218
98PacParS-218
98PacRed-402
98Top-82
98TopO-P-82
98UppDec-184
98UppDecE-184
98UppDecE1o1-184
98UppDecGR-184
99Pac-308
99PacCop-308
99PacGoI-308
99PacIceB-308
99PacPreD-308
**McCarthy, Steven**
98SP Aut-119
98SP AutSotTG-SM
98SSASotT-SM
98UppDec-396
98UppDecE-396
98UppDecE1o1-396
98UppDecGR-396
99SP AutPS-119
**McCarthy, Tom**
79NorStaPos-9
80NorStaPos-12
800PC-9
80OshGen-23
80Top-93
81NorStaPos-15
810PC-164
810PCSti-95
81Top-W108
82NorStaPos-16
820PC-169
82PosCer-9
82PosSti-19
830PC-176
83OPCSti-115
84NorSta7E-10
84NorStaPos-16
840PC-103
840PCSti-52
84Top-78
85NorStaPos-20
870PC-38
870PCSti-141
87PanSti-13
87Top-38
88BruSpoA-12
**McCarthy, Tom (50s)**
57Top-37
**McCarty, Darren**
897thInnSOHL-77
907thInnSOHL-12
917thInnSOHL-113
93ClaProPro-147
93Don-103
93Lea-435
930PCPre-412
930PCPreG-412
93Par-265
93ParEmel-265
93Pow-333
93Sco-631
93ScoCan-631
93ScoGoI-631
93StaClu-441
93StaCluO-441
93Ult-307
93UppDec-508
94CanGamNHLP-89
94Don-237
94Lea-197
94OPCFinIns-19
940PCPre-203

940PCPreSE-203
94Pin-180
94PinArtP-180
94PinRinC-180
94Sco-258
94ScoGoI-258
94ScoPla-258
94ScoPlaTS-258
94TopPre-203
94TopPreSE-203
94Ult-63
94UppDec-365
94UppDecElelce-365
95CanGamNHLP-103
95ColEdgIC-C19
95Don-313
95Lea-320
95ParInt-341
95ParIntEI-341
95Pin-176
95PinArtP-176
95PinRinC-176
95Top-28
95TopOPCI-28
95Ult-235
95UltCreCra-9
95UppDec-301
95UppDecEleIce-301
95UppDecEleIceG-301
96BeAPAut-175
96BeAPAutSil-175
96BeAPla-175
96ColCho-89
96RedWinDNFP-1
96UppDec-55
97ColCho-83
97Don-107
97DonEli-84
97DonEliAsp-84
97DonEliS-84
97DonLim-72
97DonLimExp-72
97DonPre-114
97DonPrePro-107
97DonPreProG-107
97DonPreHoS-107
97DonPri-146
97DonPriSoA-146
97Kat-51
97KatGoI-51
97KatSil-51
97Lea-88
97LeaFraMat-88
97LeaFraMDC-88
97LeaInt-88
97LeaIntUI-88
97Pac-163
97PacCop-163
97PacCroR-48
97PacCroREG-48
97PacCroRIB-48
97PacCroRS-48
97PacEmeGre-163
97PacIceB-163
97PacOme-84
97PacOmeC-84
97PacOmeDG-84
97PacOmeEG-84
97PacOmeG-84
97PacOmeIB-84
97PacPar-68
97PacParC-68
97PacParDG-68
97PacParEG-68
97PacParIB-68
97PacParRed-68
97PacParSil-68
97PacRed-163
97PacRev-48
97PacRevC-48
97PacRevE-48
97PacRevIB-48
97PacRevR-48
97PacRevS-48
97PacSil-163
97Pin-176
97PinPrePBB-176
97PinPrePBC-176
97PinPrePBM-176
97PinPrePBY-176
97PinPrePFC-176
97PinPrePFM-176
97PinPrePFY-176
97PinPrePla-176
97Sco-190
97ScoRedW-6
97ScoRedWPla-6
97ScoRedWPre-6
97SPAut-57
97SPAutSotT-DM
97UppDec-59
97UppDec-390
97UppDecGDM-59
98Be A PPA-50
98Be A PPAA-50
98Be A PPAAF-50
98Be A PPTBASG-50
98Be APG-50
98BowBes-79
98BowBesAR-79
98BowBesR-79
980-PChr-105
980-PChrR-105
98Pac-201
98PacAur-66

98PacCroR-46
98PacCroRLS-46
98PacDynI-66
98PacDynIIB-66
98PacDynIR-66
98PacIceB-201
98PacOmeH-84
98PacOmeODI-84
98PacOmeR-84
98PacPar-79
98PacParC-79
98PacParEG-79
98PacParH-79
98PacParIB-79
98PacParS-79
98PacRed-201
98PacRev-50
98PacRevIS-50
98PacRevR-50
98RevThrPA-4
98RevThrPA-4
98Top-105
98TopO-P-105
98UC-72
98UD ChoPCR-72
98UD ChoR-72
98UppDec-266
98UppDecE-266
98UppDecE1o1-266
98UppDecGR-266
98UppDecM-73
98UppDecMGS-73
98UppDecMSS-73
98UppDecMSS-73
99Pac-144
99PacAur-52
99PacAurPD-52
99PacCop-144
99PacGoI-144
99PacIceB-144
99PacPreD-144
**McCaskill, Ted**
72ShaLosAW-9
**McCaughey, Brad**
88ProIHL-80
92PhoRoa-15
96AlaGoIKin-9
**McCauley, Alyn**
94Cla95DP-DP5
94ParSE-SE264
94ParSEG-SE264
94Sel-162
94SelGoI-162
94SP-183
94SPDieCut-183
95Cla-53
95ClaG-92
95DonEliWJ-18
95SigRoo-47
95SigRooSig-47
95Sla-278
95SP-173
96UppDecBD-78
96UppDecBDG-78
96UppDecIce-129
97Be A PPAD-222
97Be A PPAPD-222
97BeAPla-222
97BeAPlaAut-222
97BeeAutA-55
97BowCHL-5
97BowCHLOPC-5
97ColCho-299
97DonEli-38
97DonEliAsp-38
97DonEliAsp-117
97DonEliS-38
97DonEliS-117
97DonPre-153
97DonPreCttC-153
97DonPri-81
97DonPri-206
97DonPri-220
97DonPriDD-20
97DonPriSoA-181
97DonPriSoA-206
97DonPriSoA-220
97Kat-141
97KatGoI-141
97KatSil-141
97Lea-152
97LeaFraMat-152
97LeaFraMDC-152
97PacCroR-130
97PacCroREG-130
97PacCroRIB-130
97PacCroRS-130
97PacDyn-NNO
97PacDynC-NNO
97PacDynDG-NNO
97PacDynEG-NNO
97PacDynIB-NNO
97PacDynIR-NNO
97PacDynR-NNO
97PacDynSil-NNO
97PacPar-182
97PacParC-182
97PacParDG-182
97PacParEG-182
97PacParIB-182
97PacParRed-182
97PacParSil-182
97Pin-18
97PinArtP-18

97PinBee-55
97PinBeeGP-55
97PinCerRR-G
97PinCerRRMG-G
97PinMin-28
97PinMinB-28
97PinMinCBP-28
97PinMinCGPP-28
97PinMinCNSP-28
97PinMinCoiB-28
97PinMinCoiGP-28
97PinMinCoiN-28
97PinMinCoiSG-28
97PinMinCoiSS-28
97PinMinSilTea-28
97PinPrePBB-18
97PinPrePBC-18
97PinPrePBM-18
97PinPrePBY-18
97PinPrePFC-18
97PinPrePFM-18
97PinPrePFY-18
97PinPrePla-18
97PinRinC-18
97Sco-52
97ScoArtPro-52
97ScoGoIBla-52
97ScoMapL-17
97ScoMapLPla-17
97ScoMapLPre-17
97SPAut-195
97UppDec-371
97UppDecBDB-128
97UppDecBDDD-128
97UppDecBDQD-128
97UppDecBDTD-128
97Zen-88
97Zen5x7-71
97ZenRooR-11
97ZenSilImp-70
97ZenZGoI-88
97ZenZSiI-88
98Be A PPA-138
98Be A PPAA-138
98Be A PPAAF-138
98Be A PPTBASG-138
98Be APG-138
980-PChr-79
980-PChrR-79
98Pac-418
98PacDynI-183
98PacDynIIB-183
98PacDynIR-183
98PacIceB-418
98PacOmeH-230
98PacOmeODI-230
98PacOmeR-230
98PacRed-418
98SPxFin-83
98SPxFin-132
98SPxFinR-83
98SPxFinR-132
98SPxFinS-83
98SPxFinS-132
98Top-79
98TopGoILC1-79
98TopGoILC1B-79
98TopGoILC1BOo0-79
98TopGoILC1R-79
98TopGoILC1ROo0-79
98TopGoILC2-79
98TopGoILC2B-79
98TopGoILC2Oo0-79
98TopGoILC2R-79
98TopGoILC2R0o0-79
98TopGoILC3-79
98TopGoILC3B-79
98TopGoILC3BOo0-79
98TopGoILC3R-79
98TopGoILC3ROo0-79
98TopO-P-79
98UC-200
98UD ChoPCR-200
98UD ChoR-200
98UD3-8
98UD3-68
98UD3-128
98UD3DieC-8
98UD3DieC-68
98UD3DieC-128
98UppDec-185
98UppDecE1o1-185
98UppDecGR-185
98UppDecM-198
98UppDecM-AM
98UppDecMGS-198
98UppDecMSS-198
98UppDecMSS-198
99Pac-413
99PacCop-413
99PacGoI-413
99PacIceB-413
**McCauley, Bill**
93DetJrRW-10
94DetJrRW-10
95SlaMemC-86
96ProBru-19
**McCauley, Wes**

□ 75Top-14
□ 77OPCNHL-352
**McElwee, Matt**
□ 95DayBom-10
**McEwen, Bobby**
□ 97KinHaw-2
**McEwen, Brad**
□ 91AirCanSJHLAS-23
□ 92MPSPhoSJHL-95
**McEwen, Dennis**
□ 86LonKni-23
□ 89HamRoaA-14
□ 90HamRoaA-50
□ 91HamRoaA-11
□ 93HamRoaA-8
□ 94HamRoaA-14
**McEwen, Doug**
□ 94FinnJaaK-326
**McEwen, Hugh**
□ 90MicTecHus-16
□ 91MicTecHus-14
**McEwen, Michael (Mike)**
□ 77OPCNHL-232
□ 77Top-232
□ 78OPC-187
□ 78Top-187
□ 79OPC-66
□ 79Roc-12
□ 79Top-66
□ 80OPC-185
□ 80Top-185
□ 81OPC-215
□ 82OPC-207
□ 82PosCer-12
□ 86WhaJunT-16
□ 91ProAHLCHL-374
□ 94CenHocL-62
**McFadden, Jim**
□ 44BeeGro2P-122
□ 44BeeGro2P-193
□ 51Par-44
□ 52Par-38
□ 53Par-77
**McFadyen, Don**
□ 35DiaMatT2-46
□ 35DiaMatT3-43
□ 35DiaMatTI-45
**McFarlane, Mark**
□ 907thInnSWHL-51
**McFatridge, Sean**
□ 917thInnSWHL-108
□ 91SasBla-20
□ 92BraWheK-16
**McFee, Dale**
□ 84PriAlbRS-18
**McGarry, Pat**
□ 93ForWorF-12
□ 94CenHocL-29
**McGarvey, Willie**
□ 897thInnSOHL-111
**McGee, Frank**
□ 83HalFP-D10
□ 85HalFC-56
**McGeough, Jim**
□ 89ProIHL-116
□ 90ProAHLIHL-315
□ 92RicRen-13
□ 94CenHocL-16
□ 99WicThu-15
**McGhan, Mike**
□ 93PriAlbR-15
□ 94PriAlbR-14
□ 95PriAlbR-14
**McGill, Bob**
□ 81MapLeaP-14
□ 82MapLeaP-24
□ 82OPC-327
□ 82PosCer-18
□ 84MapLeaP-17
□ 85MapLeaP-22
□ 85OPCSti-15
□ 87BlaCok-11
□ 88BlaCok-11
□ 89BlaCok-10
□ 90BlaCok-10
□ 90ProSet-55A
□ 90ProSet-55B
□ 90ScoRoo-49T
□ 91OPC-216
□ 91OPCPre-8
□ 91Pin-98
□ 91PinFre-98
□ 91ProSet-47
□ 91ProSet-480
□ 91ProSetFre-47
□ 91ProSetFre-480
□ 91ScoAme-368
□ 91ScoCan-327
□ 91ScoCan-560
□ 91ScoRoo-10T
□ 91ShaSanJSA-15
□ 91Top-216
□ 91UppDec-62
□ 91UppDecF-62
□ 92Bow-429
□ 92Sco-386
□ 92ScoCan-386
□ 92StaClu-483
□ 92Top-209
□ 92TopGol-209G
**McGill, Jack**
□ 34SweCap-11
□ 35DiaMatT2-47
□ 35DiaMatT3-44
□ 35DiaMatTI-46
□ 35OPCV304C-74
□ 36V356WorG-77
**McGill, Ryan**
□ 89ProIHL-56
□ 90ProAHLIHL-394
□ 91ProAHLCHL-498
□ 92FlyJCP-17
□ 92FlyUppDS-23
□ 92FlyUppDS-31
□ 92Par-366
□ 92ParEmel-366
□ 92Ult-373
□ 92UppDec-494
□ 93Par-415
□ 93ParEmel-415
□ 93Sco-649
□ 93ScoCan-649
□ 93ScoGol-649
□ 93Ult-177
□ 94UppDec-160
□ 94UppDecEleIce-160
**McGillis, Dan**
□ 96OilPos-23
□ 97Be A PPAD-131
□ 97Be A PPAPD-131
□ 97BeAPla-131
□ 97BeAPlaAut-131
□ 97Pac-294
□ 97PacCop-294
□ 97PacEmeGre-294
□ 97PacIceB-294
□ 97PacRed-294
□ 97PacSil-294
□ 98Pac-328
□ 98PacIceB-328
□ 98PacRed-328
□ 98UppDecM-153
□ 98UppDecMGS-153
□ 98UppDecMSS-153
□ 98UppDecMSS-153
□ 99Pac-309
□ 99PacCop-309
□ 99PacGol-309
□ 99PacIceB-309
□ 99PacPreD-309
**McGillvary, Glen**
□ 92MPSPhoSJHL-85
**McGimsie, Billy**
□ 83HalFP-E11
□ 85HalFC-71
**McGinn, Mark**
□ 92OklCitB-13
□ 94CenHocL-52
**McGlynn, Dick**
□ 72SweSemWC-133
**McGlynn, Peter (Pete)**
□ 897thInnSOHL-70
□ 907thInnSOHL-89
□ 917thInnSOHL-241
**McGowan, Cal**
□ 88KamBla-19
□ 907thInnSMC-9
□ 907thInnSWHL-293
□ 91ProAHLCHL-152
□ 95BinRan-16
**McGowan, Everett**
□ 28V1282PauC-81
**McGrath, Bobby**
□ 89HamRoaA-15
**McGrath, Peter**
□ 83NorBayC-19
**Mcgrattan, Brian**
□ 97GueSto-19
**McGregor, Brian**
□ 77RocAme-17
**McGregor, Percy**
□ 23V1281PauC-50
**McGrinder, Steve**
□ 90CinCyc-19
**McGuffin, Matt**
□ 907thInnSOHL-39
□ 917thInnSOHL-6
**McGuigan, Bill**
□ 94KitRan-18
□ 94SlaPro-3
□ 96AlaGolKin-10
**McGuire, E.J.**
□ 85FlyPos-20
□ 86FlyPos-17
□ 88BlaCok-12
□ 89BlaCok-26
□ 90BlaCok-27
□ 91ProAHLCHL-67
□ 95Sla-105
□ 96GueSto-28
**McGuire, Mickey**
□ 91BriColJHL-54
□ 92BriColJHL-136
**McGuire, Pierre**
□ 93WhaCok-11
**McHugh, Justin**
□ 91MinGolG-15
□ 92MinGolG-13
□ 93MinGolG-20
□ 94MinGolG-20
**McHugh, Mike**
□ 88ProIHL-35
□ 89ProIHL-86
□ 90ProAHLIHL-113
□ 91OPCIns-7S
□ 91ScoCan-651
**Mclantyre, Ian**
□ 917thInnSQMJHL-180
**McIlhargey, Jack**
□ 75FlyCanDC-14
□ 77CanCanDC-9
□ 77CanuRoyB-13
□ 78CanuRoyB-17
□ 78OPC-294
□ 79CanuRoyB-16
□ 79OPC-367
□ 91ProAHLCHL-618
□ 92HamCan-18
□ 96SyrCru-NNO
**McInenly, Bert**
□ 33OPCV304A-41
□ 36ProvRed-6
**McInerney, Eoin**
□ 95Sla-157
□ 96SarSti-18
**McInnes, Darin**
□ 86RegPat-16
**McInness, Paul**
□ 94SarSti-12
□ 95Sla-34
**McInnis, Marty**
□ 91Par-327
□ 91ParFre-327
□ 92Bow-352
□ 92OPC-135
□ 92OPCPre-12
□ 92Par-106
□ 92ParEmel-106
□ 92ProSet-233
□ 92Sco-465
□ 92ScoCan-465
□ 92StaClu-213
□ 92Top-302
□ 92TopGol-302G
□ 92Ult-347
□ 92UppDec-394
□ 92UppDec-410
□ 93ClaProPro-133
□ 93Don-457
□ 93OPCPre-57
□ 93OPCPreG-57
□ 93PanSti-62
□ 93Par-390
□ 93ParEmel-390
□ 93Pow-385
□ 93Sco-405
□ 93ScoCan-405
□ 93StaClu-257
□ 93StaCluFDI-257
□ 93StaCluO-257
□ 93TopPre-57
□ 93TopPreG-57
□ 93Ult-370
□ 93UppDec-392
□ 94BeAPla-R4
□ 94BeAPSig-14
□ 94CanGamNHLP-158
□ 94Don-311
□ 94Fla-106
□ 94Lea-157
□ 94OPCPre-244
□ 94OPCPreSE-244
□ 94ParSE-SE104
□ 94ParSEG-SE104
□ 94Pin-153
□ 94PinArtP-153
□ 94PinRinC-153
□ 94Sco-88
□ 94ScoGol-88
□ 94ScoPla-88
□ 94ScoPlaTS-88
□ 94TopPre-244
□ 94TopPreSE-244
□ 94Ult-131
□ 94UppDec-106
□ 94UppDecEleIce-106
□ 95ColCho-59
□ 95ColChoPC-59
□ 95ColChoPCP-59
□ 95ParInt-134
□ 95ParIntEl-134
□ 95Sco-217
□ 95ScoBlaIce-217
□ 95ScoBlaIceAP-217
□ 95Top-323
□ 95TopOPCI-323
□ 95UppDec-52
□ 95UppDecEleIce-52
□ 95UppDecEleIceG-52
□ 96ColCho-160
□ 96IslPos-14
□ 96Pin-62
□ 96PinArtP-62
□ 96PinFoi-62
□ 96PinPreS-62
□ 96PinRinC-62
□ 96UppDec-102
□ 97ColCho-42
□ 97PacRev-19
□ 97PacRevC-19
□ 97PacRevE-19
□ 97PacRevIB-19
□ 97PacRevR-19
□ 97PacRevS-19
□ 97Sco-210
□ 97UppDec-26
□ 98Be A PPA-19
□ 98Be A PPAA-19
□ 98Be A PPAAF-19
□ 98Be A PPTBASG-19
□ 98Be APG-19
□ 98O-PChr-103
□ 98O-PChrR-103
□ 98Pac-121
□ 98PacAur-26
□ 98PacIceB-121
□ 98PacOmeH-5
□ 98PacOmeODI-5
□ 98PacOmeR-5
□ 98PacPar-29
□ 98PacParC-29
□ 98PacParEG-29
□ 98PacParH-29
□ 98PacParIB-29
□ 98PacParS-29
□ 98PacRed-121
□ 98PacRev-3
□ 98PacRevIS-3
□ 98PacRevR-3
□ 98Top-103
□ 98TopO-P-103
□ 98UppDecM-7
□ 98UppDecMGS-7
□ 98UppDecMSS-7
□ 98UppDecMSS-7
□ 99Pac-9
□ 99PacAur-3
□ 99PacAurPD-3
□ 99PacCop-9
□ 99PacGol-9
□ 99PacIceB-9
□ 99PacPreD-9
**McIntosh, Bob**
□ 91AirCanSJHL-D17
□ 91AirCanSJHL-D31
**McIntosh, Don**
□ 52JunBluT-90
**McIntosh, Murray**
□ 94GerDELE-162
□ 95GerDELE-154
**McIntosh, Paul**
□ 78LouGea-15
**McIntyre, Ian**
□ 90MonAAA-15
□ 96SyrCru-11
□ 96WheNai-11
**McIntyre, Jack**
□ 44BeeGro2P-48
□ 52Par-77
□ 54Par-83
□ 54Top-43
□ 57Top-28
□ 60Par-24
□ 60ShiCoi-46
□ 94ParMisL-27
**McIntyre, John**
□ 89ProAHL-121
□ 90KinSmo-22
□ 90OPC-382
□ 90ProSet-457
□ 90ScoRoo-46T
□ 90Top-382
□ 90TopTif-382
□ 91Bow-180
□ 91MapLeaPTS-16
□ 91OPC-37
□ 91Par-296
□ 91ParFre-296
□ 91ProSet-401
□ 91ProSetFre-401
□ 91ScoAme-182
□ 91ScoCan-182
□ 91StaClu-324
□ 91Top-37
□ 91UppDec-218
□ 91UppDecF-218
□ 92Bow-336
□ 92Pin-214
□ 92PinFre-214
□ 92Sco-347
□ 92ScoCan-347
□ 92StaClu-117
□ 92Top-369
□ 92TopGol-369G
□ 92UppDec-118
□ 93Par-482
□ 93ParEmel-482
□ 93UppDec-527
□ 94Lea-365
□ 94StaClu-244
□ 94StaCluFDI-244
□ 94StaCluMOMS-244
□ 94StaCluSTWC-244
□ 94UppDec-478
□ 94UppDecEleIce-478
□ 95CanuBuiDA-15
**McIntyre, Larry**
□ 69MapLeaWBM-4
□ 72MapLeaP-18
**McIntyre, Lloyd**
□ 28V1282PauC-48
□ 36V356WorG-121
**McIntyre, Robb**
□ 91FerStaB-23
□ 94KnoChe-21
□ 94St.JohML-20
**McIvor, Trevor**
□ 897thInnSOHL-16
□ 89OshGen-16
□ 89OshGenP-22
□ 907thInnSMC-95
□ 907thInnSOHL-109
**McKave, Todd**
□ 92BriColJHL-229
**McKay, Bill**
□ 92MPSPhoSJHL-14
**McKay, Bruce**
□ 81MilAdm-7
**McKay, Doug**
□ 88DevCar-20
□ 89ProAHL-287
**McKay, Ken**
□ 95RedDeeR-13
**McKay, Martin**
□ 93SheSte-15
□ 94FinnJaaK-311
□ 94SheSte-24
□ 96FifFly-15
□ 97SheSte-1
**McKay, Michael**
□ 95SlaMemC-75
**McKay, Murdo**
□ 51LavDaiQSHL-5
□ 52St.LawS-45
**McKay, Randy**
□ 71SabPos-12
□ 88ProAHL-20
□ 89ProAHL-318
□ 90Bow-227
□ 90BowTif-227
□ 91ProSet-422
□ 91ProSetFre-422
□ 91ScoCan-604
□ 91ScoRoo-54T
□ 91UppDec-313
□ 91UppDecF-313
□ 92Bow-296
□ 92Par-331
□ 92ParEmel-331
□ 92Sco-339
□ 92ScoCan-339
□ 92StaClu-450
□ 92Top-106
□ 92TopGol-106G
□ 93Don-454
□ 93Pin-322
□ 93PinCan-322
□ 93Sco-319
□ 93ScoCan-319
□ 94Lea-400
□ 94OPCPre-271
□ 94OPCPreSE-271
□ 94Pin-222
□ 94PinArtP-222
□ 94PinRinC-222
□ 94TopPre-271
□ 94TopPreSE-271
□ 95BeAPla-52
□ 95BeAPSig-S52
□ 95BeAPSigDC-S52
□ 95CanGamNHLP-162
□ 95Emo-99
□ 95Lea-314
□ 95Pin-92
□ 95PinArtP-92
□ 95PinRinC-92
□ 95SkyImp-94
□ 95StaClu-153
□ 95StaCluMOMS-153
□ 95Top-201
□ 95TopOPCI-201
□ 95TopPowL-10PL
□ 95UppDec-444
□ 95UppDecEleIce-444
□ 95UppDecEleIceG-444
□ 96ColCho-154
□ 96Dev-21
□ 97Be A PPAD-160
□ 97Be A PPAPD-160
□ 97BeAPla-160
□ 97BeAPlaAut-160
□ 97PacInvNRB-114
□ 97PacOme-131
□ 97PacOmeC-131
□ 97PacOmeDG-131
□ 97PacOmeEG-131
□ 97PacOmeG-131
□ 97PacOmeIB-131
□ 97ScoDev-12
□ 97ScoDevPla-12
□ 97ScoDevPre-12
□ 98Be A PPA-80
□ 98Be A PPAA-80
□ 98Be A PPAAF-80
□ 98Be A PPTBASG-80
□ 98Be APG-80
□ 98O-PChr-90
□ 98O-PChrR-90
□ 98O-PChrSB-SB29
□ 98O-PChrSBR-SB29
□ 98Pac-264
□ 98PacAur-111
□ 98PacIceB-264
□ 98PacPar-135
□ 98PacParC-135
□ 98PacParEG-135
□ 98PacParH-135
□ 98PacParIB-135
□ 98PacParS-135
□ 98PacRed-264
□ 98Top-90
□ 98TopGolLC1-28
□ 98TopGolLC1B-28
□ 98TopGolLC1BOoO-28
□ 98TopGolLC1OoO-28
□ 98TopGolLC1R-28
□ 98TopGolLC1ROoO-28
□ 98TopGolLC2-28
□ 98TopGolLC2B-28
□ 98TopGolLC2BOoO-28
□ 98TopGolLC2OoO-28
□ 98TopGolLC2R-28
□ 98TopGolLC2ROoO-28
□ 98TopGolLC3-28
□ 98TopGolLC3B-28
□ 98TopGolLC3BOoO-28
□ 98TopGolLC3OoO-28
□ 98TopGolLC3R-28
□ 98TopGolLC3ROoO-28
□ 98TopO-P-90
□ 98TopSeaB-SB29
□ 99Pac-240
□ 99PacCop-240
□ 99PacGol-240
□ 99PacIceB-240
□ 99PacPreD-240
**McKay, Ray**
□ 71TorSun-33
**McKay, Ross**
□ 90ProAHLIHL-177
**McKay, Scott**
□ 897thInnSOHL-35
□ 907thInnSOHL-136
□ 917thInnSOHL-376
□ 94ClaProP-216
□ 94GreMon-12
**McKechney, Garnet**
□ 82KitRan-13
□ 83KitRan-10
□ 84KitRan-3
**McKechnie, Craig**
□ 91AirCanSJHL-A8
□ 92MPSPhoSJHL-149
**McKechnie, Darrin**
□ 86RegPat-17
□ 87RegPat-18
**McKechnie, Walt**
□ 70ColSta-1
□ 70EssPowPla-177
□ 70OPC-172
□ 70SarProSta-89
□ 71Baz-28
□ 71LetActR-5
□ 71OPC-124
□ 71OPCPos-17
□ 71SarProSta-129
□ 71TorSun-53
□ 72OPC-192
□ 72SarProSta-43
□ 73OPC-152
□ 73Top-127
□ 74NHLActSta-27
□ 74NHLActStaU-11
□ 74OPCNHL-56
□ 74Top-56
□ 75OPCNHL-194
□ 75Top-194
□ 76OPCNHL-196
□ 76OPCNHL-385
□ 76Top-196
□ 77OPCNHL-32
□ 77Top-32
□ 78MapLeaP-14
□ 78OPC-344
□ 79MapLeaP-20
□ 79OPC-68
□ 79Top-68
□ 80OPC-378
□ 82OPC-91
□ 82OPCSti-186
□ 82PosCer-5
□ 83PufSti-14
**McKee, Brian**
□ 90ProAHLIHL-552
□ 91ProAHLCHL-40
□ 92PeoRivC-15
**McKee, Corey**
□ 91AirCanSJHL-A25
**McKee, Jay**
□ 93SudWol-3
□ 93SudWolP-3
□ 94SudWolP-22
□ 95Sla-183
□ 95Sla-NNO
□ 96Fle-131
□ 96MetUni-186
□ 96Pin-222
□ 96PinArtP-222
□ 96PinFoi-222
□ 96PinPreS-222
□ 96PinRinC-222
□ 96SkyImp-154
□ 96Ult-18
□ 96UltGolM-18
□ 96UltRoo-12
□ 97Be A PPAD-122
□ 97Be A PPAPD-122
□ 97BeAPla-122
□ 97BeAPlaAut-122
□ 97UppDec-231
□ 99Pac-40
□ 99PacCop-40
□ 99PacGol-40
□ 99PacIceB-40
□ 99PacPreD-40
**McKee, Mike**
□ 93Don-479
□ 93Pow-424
□ 93Sco-630
□ 93ScoCan-630
□ 93ScoGol-630
□ 94ClaProP-91
**McKegney, Tony**
□ 79SabBel-5
□ 80OPC-144
□ 80Top-144
□ 81OPC-22
□ 81OPCSti-57
□ 81SabMilP-11
□ 81Top-E76
□ 82OPC-29
□ 82OPCSti-122
□ 82PosCer-2
□ 82SabMilP-13
□ 83OPC-60
□ 83OPC-296
□ 83OPCSti-239
□ 83PufSti-17
□ 83Vac-68
□ 84NorStaPos-17
□ 84OPC-283
□ 84OPCSti-171
□ 85NorSta7E-5
□ 85NorStaPos-21
□ 85OPC-156
□ 85OPCSti-45
□ 85Top-156
□ 87BluKod-16
□ 87BluTeaIss-13
□ 87OPC-172
□ 87PanSti-118
□ 87Top-172
□ 88BluKod-10
□ 88BluTeaIss-13
□ 88OPC-4
□ 88OPCSti-17
□ 88PanSti-109
□ 88Top-4
□ 89Nord-29
□ 89OPC-4
□ 89Top-4
□ 90Bow-168
□ 90BowTif-168
□ 90NordPet-18
□ 90NordTeal-21
□ 90OPC-333
□ 90PanSti-149
□ 90ProSet-254
□ 90Sco-311C
□ 90ScoCan-311C
□ 90Top-333
□ 90TopTif-333
□ 90UppDec-340
□ 90UppDecF-340
□ 91Bow-387
□ 91NordPanTS-15
□ 91OPC-484
□ 91ScoAme-104
□ 91ScoCan-104
□ 91StaClu-281
□ 91Top-484
**McKenna, Paul**
□ 92BriColJHL-7
**McKenna, Sean**
□ 84SabBluS-10
□ 85SabBluS-17
□ 85SabBluSS-17
□ 86Kin20tATI-14
□ 87KinTeal4-14
□ 87PanSti-284
□ 88MapLeaPLA-27
□ 88ProAHL-226
□ 89ProAHL-115
**McKenna, Steve**
□ 92MPSPhoSJHL-108
□ 97Be A PPAD-244
□ 97Be A PPAPD-244
□ 97BeAPla-244
□ 97BeAPlaAut-244
□ 97PacOme-109
□ 97PacOmeC-109
□ 97PacOmeDG-109
□ 97PacOmeEG-109
□ 97PacOmeG-109
□ 97PacOmeIB-109
□ 98Pac-239
□ 98PacIceB-239
□ 98PacRed-239
**McKenney, Don**
□ 44BeeGro2P-49
□ 44BeeGro2P-343
□ 44BeeGro2P-431
□ 52JunBluT-111
□ 54Top-35
□ 55BruPho-11
□ 57BruTeaIss-13
□ 57Top-13
□ 58Top-62
□ 59Top-9
□ 60ShiCoi-108
□ 60Top-40
□ 60TopSta-35
□ 61ShiCoi-6
□ 61Top-12
□ 62Top-10
□ 62TopHocBuc-16
□ 63MapLeaWB-16
□ 63Top-53
□ 64BeeGro3P-175A
□ 64BeeGro3P-175B
□ 64CocCap-101
□ 64Top-81
□ 64TorSta-31
□ 65Top-112
□ 91BruSpoAL-16
□ 94ParMisL-6
□ 94ParTalB-112
**McKenney, Sam**
□ 96DayBom-14
**McKenny, Jim**
□ 66TulOil-7
□ 68ShiCoi-174
□ 69MapLeaWBG-22
□ 70DadCoo-82
□ 70EssPowPla-29

❑ 70MapLeaP-8
❑ 70SarProSta-201
❑ 71MapLeaP-12
❑ 71OPC-43
❑ 71SarProSta-194
❑ 71Top-43
❑ 71TorSun-265
❑ 72MapLeaP-19
❑ 72MapLeaP-20
❑ 72OPC-83
❑ 72SarProSta-198
❑ 72SweSemWC-189
❑ 72Top-54
❑ 73MacMil-18
❑ 73MapLeaP-18
❑ 73OPC-39
❑ 73Top-39
❑ 74LipSou-23
❑ 74MapLeaP-13
❑ 74NHLActSta-260
❑ 74OPCNHL-198
❑ 74Top-198
❑ 75MapLeaP-13
❑ 75OPCNHL-311
❑ 75Top-311
❑ 76MapLeaP-10
❑ 76OPCNHL-302
❑ 77MapLeaP-10
❑ 77OPCNHL-374

**McKenzie, Bill**
❑ 76OPCNHL-267
❑ 78OPC-275
❑ 79Roc-13

**McKenzie, Gordon**
❑ 24CreFal-12

**McKenzie, Jim**
❑ 89ProAHL-302
❑ 90ProAHLIHL-175
❑ 90WhaJr7E-19
❑ 91Bow-7
❑ 91OPC-24
❑ 91ProSet-391
❑ 91ProSetFre-391
❑ 91StaClu-354
❑ 91Top-24
❑ 91UppDec-494
❑ 91UppDecF-494
❑ 91WhaJr7E-21
❑ 92WhaDai-15
❑ 93Par-357
❑ 93ParEmel-357
❑ 93UppDec-23
❑ 94Par-178
❑ 94ParGol-178
❑ 94PenFoo-20
❑ 95JetTealss-15
❑ 96BeAPAut-69
❑ 96BeAPAutSil-69
❑ 96BeAPla-69
❑ 97UppDec-337
❑ 99Pac-10
❑ 99PacCop-10
❑ 99PacGol-10
❑ 99PacIceB-10
❑ 99PacPreD-10
❑ 99RetHoc-3
❑ 99UppDecRG-3
❑ 99UppDecRP-3

**McKenzie, John**
❑ 60Par-37
❑ 60ShiCoi-43
❑ 61Par-34
❑ 63Top-42
❑ 64BeeGro3P-47
❑ 64CocCap-32
❑ 64Top-30
❑ 64TorSta-32
❑ 65Coc-84
❑ 65Top-94
❑ 66Top-97
❑ 66TopUSAT-66
❑ 67Top-39
❑ 68OPC-9
❑ 68ShiCoi-11
❑ 68Top-9
❑ 69OPC-28
❑ 69Top-28
❑ 70BruPos-12
❑ 70BruTealss-15
❑ 70ColSta-59
❑ 70DadCoo-83
❑ 70EssPowPla-68
❑ 70OPC-6
❑ 70OPC-241
❑ 70SarProSta-9
❑ 70Top-6
❑ 71BruTealss-14
❑ 71OPC-82
❑ 71SarProSta-3
❑ 71Top-82
❑ 71TorSun-14
❑ 72OPC-338
❑ 72SluCupWHA-14
❑ 72SweSemWC-185
❑ 74TeaCanLWHA-16
❑ 75OPCWHA-77
❑ 76OPCWHA-103
❑ 77OPCWHA-41
❑ 91UltOriS-52
❑ 91UltOriSF-52
❑ 94ParTalB-36
❑ 95Par66-10
❑ 95Par66Coi-10

**McKichan, Steve**
❑ 90ProAHLIHL-341

**McKie, Ryan**
❑ 95Sla-177
❑ 97SudWolP-18

**McKillop, Bob**
❑ 907thInnSOHL-66

**McKillop, Larry**
❑ 71RocAme-11

**McKim, Andrew**
❑ 90ProAHLIHL-626
❑ 91ProAHLCHL-343
❑ 93ClaProPro-14
❑ 94Par-16
❑ 94ParGol-16
❑ 95SwiHNL-503
❑ 96GerDELE-38
❑ 96SweSemWAS-AS6
❑ 98GerDELE-159

**McKinlay, Mike**
❑ 91BriColJHL-125
❑ 92BriColJHL-164

**McKinley, Barry**
❑ 93ThuBayS-12
❑ 94ThuBayS-5
❑ 95ThuBayS-11

**McKinley, Rob**
❑ 84KamBla-17
❑ 85KamBla-14
❑ 86KamBla-12
❑ 86RegPat-18
❑ 87RegPat-19

**McKinney, Bryan**
❑ 94GueSto-4
❑ 95GueSto5A-18
❑ 95Sla-88

**McKinnon, Alex**
❑ 24V1452-16

**McKinnon, Brian**
❑ 82Ott67-13
❑ 83Ott67-18

**McKinnon, Kenny**
❑ 36V356WorG-118

**McKinnon, Kevin**
❑ 92NorDakFS-20
❑ 94EriPan-10

**McKinnon, Robert**
❑ 24C144ChaCig-39

**McKnight, Wes**
❑ 34BeeGro1P-357

**McLaren, Don**
❑ 81Ott67-8
❑ 82Ott67-14
❑ 83Ott67-19
❑ 93SwiHNL-402
❑ 95SwiHNL-48

**McLaren, Kyle**
❑ 93TacRoc-16
❑ 95BeAPla-173
❑ 95BeAPSig-S173
❑ 95BeAPSigDC-S173
❑ 95Bow-151
❑ 95BowAllFoi-151
❑ 95CanGamNHLP-35
❑ 95Don-334
❑ 95DonEliR-15
❑ 95Fin-111
❑ 95FinRef-111
❑ 95Met-184
❑ 95ParInt-262
❑ 95ParIntEl-262
❑ 95SelCer-139
❑ 95SelCerMG-139
❑ 95SkyImp-189
❑ 95SP-8
❑ 95StaClu-63
❑ 95StaCluMOMS-63
❑ 95Sum-194
❑ 95SumArtP-194
❑ 95SumIce-194
❑ 95Top-309
❑ 95TopOPCI-309
❑ 95TopSupSkiSR-SR9
❑ 95Ult-349
❑ 95UppDec-421
❑ 95UppDecElelce-421
❑ 95UppDecElelceG-421
❑ 95Zen-127
❑ 95ZenRooRC-17
❑ 96ColCho-15
❑ 96ColCho-341
❑ 96Don-219
❑ 96DonPrePro-219
❑ 96Fle-5
❑ 96Lea-142
❑ 96LeaPreP-142
❑ 96MetUni-8
❑ 96Sco-258
❑ 96ScoArtPro-258
❑ 96ScoDeaCAP-258
❑ 96ScoGolB-258
❑ 96ScoSpeAP-258
❑ 96SkyImp-6
❑ 96SP-8
❑ 96Sum-159
❑ 96SumArtP-159
❑ 96SumIce-159
❑ 96SumMet-159
❑ 96SumPreS-159
❑ 96TopPicRS-RS13
❑ 96Ult-9
❑ 96UltGolM-9
❑ 96UppDec-9
❑ 96UppDecGN-X37
❑ 96UppDecSS-SS25B
❑ 97ColCho-15
❑ 97DonLim-106
❑ 97DonLimExp-106
❑ 97DonPre-107
❑ 97DonPreCttC-107
❑ 97Pac-42
❑ 97PacCop-42
❑ 97PacEmeGre-42
❑ 97PacIceB-42
❑ 97PacRed-42
❑ 97PacSil-42
❑ 97ScoBru-19
❑ 97ScoBruPla-19
❑ 97ScoBruPre-19
❑ 97SPAut-11
❑ 97UppDec-13
❑ 97UppDecBD-54
❑ 97UppDecBDDD-54
❑ 97UppDecBDQD-54
❑ 97UppDecBDTD-54
❑ 98Pac-86
❑ 98PacIceB-86
❑ 98PacRed-86
❑ 98UC-16
❑ 98UD ChoPCR-16
❑ 98UD ChoR-16
❑ 98UppDec-219
❑ 98UppDecE-219
❑ 98UppDecE1o1-219
❑ 98UppDecGR-219
❑ 98UppDecM-15
❑ 98UppDecMGS-15
❑ 98UppDecMSS-15
❑ 98UppDecMSS-15
❑ 99Pac-27
❑ 99PacCop-27
❑ 99PacGol-27
❑ 99PacIceB-27
❑ 99PacPreD-27
❑ 99UppDecM-16
❑ 99UppDecMGS-16
❑ 99UppDecMSS-16
❑ 99UppDecMSS-16

**McLaren, Steve**
❑ 93NorBayC-4
❑ 94NorBayC-5
❑ 95Indlce-14

**McLarren, Rick**
❑ 92BriColJHL-141

**McLarty, Jim**
❑ 91AirCanSJHL-C20
❑ 91AirCanSJHLAS-9

**McLaughlin, Maj. F**
❑ 83HalFP-J9
❑ 85HalFC-189

**McLaughlin, Mike**
❑ 92RochAmeDD-11
❑ 92RochAmeKod-14
❑ 94BinRan-12

**McLaughlin, Peter**
❑ 92HarCri-25

**McLay, Dave**
❑ 86PorWinH-12

**McLean, Brett**
❑ 95UppDec-506
❑ 95UppDecElelce-506
❑ 95UppDecElelceG-506
❑ 98UC-270
❑ 98UD ChoPCR-270
❑ 98UD ChoR-270

**McLean, Darren**
❑ 91AirCanSJHL-C25
❑ 92MPSPhoSJHL-12

**McLean, Greg**
❑ 93KitRan-4
❑ 94KitRan-5
❑ 96WheNai-4

**McLean, Hugh**
❑ 62SudWol-17

**McLean, Jack**
❑ 34BeeGro1P-338

**McLean, Jeff**
❑ 92Cla-85
❑ 94ClaProP-139
❑ 96ClaGol-85

**McLean, Jim**
❑ 91AirCanSJHL-B6

**McLean, Keith**
❑ 92HarCri-26

**McLean, Kirk**
❑ 83OshGen-2
❑ 87CanuSheOil-12
❑ 88CanuMoh-12
❑ 88OPCSti-1
❑ 88OPCSti-55
❑ 88OPCSti-138
❑ 88OPCSti-140
❑ 88PanSti-132
❑ 89CanuMoh-11
❑ 89Kra-43
❑ 89OPC-61
❑ 89OPCSti-64
❑ 89PanSti-155
❑ 89Top-61
❑ 90Bow-57
❑ 90BowTif-57
❑ 90CanuMoh-19
❑ 90CanuMol-5
❑ 90CanuMol-6
❑ 90Kra-70
❑ 90OPC-257
❑ 90OPCPre-70
❑ 90PanSti-296
❑ 90ProSet-302
❑ 90ProSet-355
❑ 90Sco-93
❑ 90ScoCan-93
❑ 90ScoHotRS-46
❑ 90Top-257
❑ 90TopTif-257
❑ 90UppDec-278
❑ 90UppDecF-278
❑ 91Bow-310
❑ 91CanuAutC-14
❑ 91CanuMol-6
❑ 91CanuPanTS-G
❑ 91CanuTeal8-14
❑ 91OPC-221
❑ 91OPCPre-158
❑ 91PanSti-45
❑ 91Par-181
❑ 91Par-440
❑ 91ParFre-181
❑ 91ParFre-440
❑ 91Pin-158
❑ 91PinFre-158
❑ 91ProSet-501
❑ 91ProSet-603
❑ 91ProSet-AU501
❑ 91ProSetFre-501
❑ 91ProSetFre-603
❑ 91ProSetFre-AU501
❑ 91ProSetPC-28
❑ 91ProSetPCP-1
❑ 91ProSetPla-239
❑ 91ProSetPOTM-P1
❑ 91ScoAme-261
❑ 91ScoCan-481
❑ 91StaClu-105
❑ 91Top-221
❑ 91UppDec-191
❑ 91UppDecF-191
❑ 92Bow-212
❑ 92Bow-285
❑ 92CanuRoaTA-13
❑ 92HumDum1-15
❑ 92Kra-29
❑ 92OPC-342
❑ 92OPC-349
❑ 92PanSti-27
❑ 92PanStiFre-27
❑ 92Par-192
❑ 92ParEmel-192
❑ 92Pin-246
❑ 92Pin-330
❑ 92PinFre-246
❑ 92PinFre-330
❑ 92ProSet-193
❑ 92ProSet-250
❑ 92ProSet-AU239
❑ 92Sco-385
❑ 92ScoCan-385
❑ 92SeaPat-71
❑ 92StaClu-193
❑ 92Top-130
❑ 92Top-270
❑ 92TopGol-130G
❑ 92TopGol-270G
❑ 92Ult-224
❑ 92UppDec-22
❑ 92UppDec-299
❑ 93Don-355
❑ 93Kra-58
❑ 93Lea-55
❑ 93LeaPaiWar-3
❑ 93OPCPre-113
❑ 93OPCPreG-113
❑ 93PanSti-177
❑ 93Par-213
❑ 93ParEmel-213
❑ 93Pin-158
❑ 93PinCan-158
❑ 93PinTeaP-7
❑ 93PinTeaPC-7
❑ 93Pow-253
❑ 93Sco-47
❑ 93ScoCan-47
❑ 93StaClu-163
❑ 93StaCluFDI-163
❑ 93StaCluFDIO-163
❑ 93StaCluO-163
❑ 93SweSemWCS-190
❑ 93TopPre-113
❑ 93TopPreG-113
❑ 93Ult-29
❑ 93UppDec-156
❑ 93UppDecNR-7
❑ 93UppDecSP-165
❑ 94BeAPla-R73
❑ 94BeAPla-R107
❑ 94CanGamNHLP-270
❑ 94CanuProl-15
❑ 94Don-22
❑ 94DonMasM-6
❑ 94EASpo-144
❑ 94Fin-61
❑ 94FinRef-61
❑ 94FinSupTW-61
❑ 94Fla-193
❑ 94Fle-227
❑ 94FleNet-6
❑ 94Kra-46
❑ 94Lea-109
❑ 94LeaCreP-7
❑ 94LeaLim-23
❑ 94OPCPre-85
❑ 94OPCPre-397
❑ 94OPCPreSE-85
❑ 94OPCPreSE-397
❑ 94Par-238
❑ 94ParGol-238
❑ 94ParSEV-10
❑ 94Pin-60
❑ 94PinArtP-60
❑ 94PinGoaG-GT11
❑ 94PinRinC-60
❑ 94Sco-60
❑ 94ScoGol-60
❑ 94ScoPla-60
❑ 94ScoPlaTS-60
❑ 94Sel-64
❑ 94SelGol-64
❑ 94SP-124
❑ 94SPDieCut-124
❑ 94StaClu-188
❑ 94StaClu-223
❑ 94StaCluFDI-188
❑ 94StaCluFDI-223
❑ 94StaCluMOMS-188
❑ 94StaCluMOMS-223
❑ 94StaCluSTWC-188
❑ 94StaCluSTWC-223
❑ 94TopPre-85
❑ 94TopPre-397
❑ 94TopPreSE-85
❑ 94TopPreSE-397
❑ 94Ult-228
❑ 94UppDec-133
❑ 94UppDecElelce-133
❑ 94UppDecPH-H34
❑ 94UppDecPHEG-H34
❑ 94UppDecPHES-H34
❑ 94UppDecPHG-H34
❑ 94UppDecSPI-SP84
❑ 94UppDecSPIDC-SP84
❑ 95BeAPla-200
❑ 95BeAPSig-S200
❑ 95BeAPSigDC-S200
❑ 95CanGamNHLP-278
❑ 95CanuBuiDA-1
❑ 95ColCho-71
❑ 95ColChoPC-71
❑ 95ColChoPCP-71
❑ 95Don-16
❑ 95Emo-181
❑ 95Fin-161
❑ 95FinRef-161
❑ 95ImpSti-127
❑ 95Kra-18
❑ 95Lea-102
❑ 95LeaLim-67
❑ 95McDPin-MCD-30
❑ 95Met-152
❑ 95ParInt-213
❑ 95ParIntEl-213
❑ 95ParIntGP-11
❑ 95Pin-132
❑ 95PinArtP-132
❑ 95PinRinC-132
❑ 95PlaOneoOne-101
❑ 95ProMag-28
❑ 95Sco-49
❑ 95ScoBlaIce-49
❑ 95ScoBlaIceAP-49
❑ 95SelCer-63
❑ 95SelCerMG-63
❑ 95SkyImp-170
❑ 95SkyImpD-12
❑ 95SP-152
❑ 95StaClu-41
❑ 95StaCluMOMS-41
❑ 95StaCluMPT-5
❑ 95Sum-69
❑ 95SumArtP-69
❑ 95SumIce-69
❑ 95SumInTheCre-14
❑ 95Top-277
❑ 95TopHidGem-13HG
❑ 95TopOPCI-277
❑ 95TopSupSki-89
❑ 95TopSupSkiPla-89
❑ 95Ult-170
❑ 95Ult-373
❑ 95UltGolM-170
❑ 95UppDec-136
❑ 95UppDecElelce-136
❑ 95UppDecElelceG-136
❑ 95UppDecSpeE-SE83
❑ 95UppDecSpeEdiG-SE83
❑ 95Zen-57
❑ 96CanuPos-1
❑ 96ColCho-271
❑ 96Don-3
❑ 96DonCanI-33
❑ 96DonCanIGPP-33
❑ 96DonCanIRPP-33
❑ 96DonEli-121
❑ 96DonEliDCS-121
❑ 96DonPrePro-3
❑ 96Fle-113
❑ 96Lea-43
❑ 96LeaPreP-43
❑ 96MetUni-158
❑ 96NHLProSTA-28
❑ 96Pin-90
❑ 96PinArtP-90
❑ 96PinFoi-90
❑ 96PinPreS-90
❑ 96PinRinC-90
❑ 96Sco-155
❑ 96ScoArtPro-155
❑ 96ScoDeaCAP-155
❑ 96ScoGolB-155
❑ 96ScoSpeAP-155
❑ 96SelCer-22
❑ 96SelCerAP-22
❑ 96SelCerBlu-22
❑ 96SelCerMB-22
❑ 96SelCerMG-22
❑ 96SelCerMR-22
❑ 96SelCerRed-22
❑ 96SkyImp-134
❑ 96Sum-68
❑ 96SumArtP-68
❑ 96SumIce-68
❑ 96SumMet-68
❑ 96SumPreS-68
❑ 96TeaOut-67
❑ 96Ult-169
❑ 96UltGolM-169
❑ 96UppDec-348
❑ 97Be A PPAD-118
❑ 97Be A PPAPD-118
❑ 97BeAPla-118
❑ 97BeAPlaAut-118
❑ 97Don-189
❑ 97DonCanI-79
❑ 97DonCanIDS-79
❑ 97DonCanIPS-79
❑ 97DonLim-3
❑ 97DonLimExp-3
❑ 97DonPreProG-189
❑ 97DonPreProS-189
❑ 97DonPri-162
❑ 97DonPriSoA-162
❑ 97Kat-147
❑ 97KatGol-147
❑ 97KatSil-147
❑ 97Lea-74
❑ 97LeaFraMat-74
❑ 97LeaFraMDC-74
❑ 97LeaInt-74
❑ 97LeaIntUI-74
❑ 97Pac-258
❑ 97PacCop-258
❑ 97PacDyn-128
❑ 97PacDynC-128
❑ 97PacDynDG-128
❑ 97PacDynEG-128
❑ 97PacDynIB-128
❑ 97PacDynR-128
❑ 97PacDynSil-128
❑ 97PacDynTan-56
❑ 97PacEmeGre-258
❑ 97PacIceB-258
❑ 97PacInv-143
❑ 97PacInvC-143
❑ 97PacInvEG-143
❑ 97PacInvIB-143
❑ 97PacInvR-143
❑ 97PacInvS-143
❑ 97PacPar-189
❑ 97PacParC-189
❑ 97PacParDG-189
❑ 97PacParEG-189
❑ 97PacParIB-189
❑ 97PacParRed-189
❑ 97PacParSil-189
❑ 97PacRed-258
❑ 97PacSil-258
❑ 97Pin-88
❑ 97PinArtP-88
❑ 97PinCer-27
❑ 97PinCerMB-27
❑ 97PinCerMG-27
❑ 97PinCerMR-27
❑ 97PinCerR-27
❑ 97PinIns-60
❑ 97PinInsCC-60
❑ 97PinInsEC-60
❑ 97PinPrePBB-88
❑ 97PinPrePBC-88
❑ 97PinPrePBM-88
❑ 97PinPrePBY-88
❑ 97PinPrePFC-88
❑ 97PinPrePFM-88
❑ 97PinPrePFY-88
❑ 97PinPrePla-88
❑ 97PinRinC-88
❑ 97PinTotCMPG-27
❑ 97PinTotCPB-27
❑ 97PinTotCPG-27
❑ 97PinTotCPR-27
❑ 97Sco-43
❑ 97ScoArtPro-43
❑ 97ScoCanPla-10
❑ 97ScoCanPre-10
❑ 97ScoCanu-10
❑ 97ScoGolBla-43
❑ 97SPAut-159
❑ 97Stu-88
❑ 97StuPrePG-88
❑ 97StuPrePS-88
❑ 97UppDec-375
❑ 97UppDecBD-31
❑ 97UppDecBDDD-31
❑ 97UppDecBDQD-31
❑ 97UppDecBDTD-31
❑ 98Pac-225
❑ 98PacIceB-225
❑ 98PacRed-225
❑ 99Pac-177
❑ 99PacCop-177
❑ 99PacGol-177
❑ 99PacIceB-177
❑ 99PacPreD-177

**McLean, Sean**
❑ 92QueIntP-47

**McLeary, Mark**
❑ 82VicCou-16

**McLellan, Cam**
❑ 89RegPat-11

**McLellan, Dusty**
❑ 91BriColJHL-25
❑ 91BriColJHL-155
❑ 92BriColJHL-204
❑ 93JohChi-11

**Mclellan, Jim**
❑ 61HamRed-13

**McLellan, Todd**
❑ 83SasBla-14
❑ 84SasBlaS-14
❑ 88ProAHL-303

**McLelland, Kevin**
❑ 89RedWinLC-12

**McLemman, Jamal**
❑ 99PacCop-360

**McLennan, Jamie**
❑ 89LetHur-15
❑ 907thInnSWHL-129
❑ 917thInnSCHLAW-16
❑ 917thInnSMC-79
❑ 91Cla-40
❑ 91RicRen-20
❑ 91StaPicH-32
❑ 91UltDra-35
❑ 93Don-458
❑ 93Pow-386
❑ 94CanGamNHLP-286
❑ 94ClaProP-112
❑ 94Don-88
❑ 94Fla-107
❑ 94Fle-127
❑ 94Kra-47
❑ 94Lea-74
❑ 94OPCFinIns-21
❑ 94OPCPre-143
❑ 94OPCPreSE-143
❑ 94Pin-250
❑ 94PinArtP-250
❑ 94PinRinC-250
❑ 94Sco-224
❑ 94ScoGol-224
❑ 94ScoPla-224
❑ 94ScoPlaTS-224
❑ 94Sel-189
❑ 94SelGol-189
❑ 94TopPre-143
❑ 94TopPreSE-143
❑ 94Ult-328
❑ 94UppDec-252
❑ 94UppDecElelce-252
❑ 94UppDecSPI-SP137
❑ 94UppDecSPIDC-SP137
❑ 95ParInt-404
❑ 95ParIntEl-404
❑ 97Be A PPAD-107
❑ 97Be A PPAPD-107
❑ 97BeAPla-107
❑ 97BeAPlaAut-107
❑ 97ScoBlu-20
❑ 97ScoBluPla-20
❑ 97ScoBluPre-20
❑ 98Be A PPA-273
❑ 98Be A PPAA-273
❑ 98Be A PPAAF-273
❑ 98Be A PPSE-273
❑ 98Be APG-273
❑ 98Pac-369
❑ 98PacAur-162
❑ 98PacDynI-160
❑ 98PacDynIIB-160
❑ 98PacDynIR-160
❑ 98PacIceB-369
❑ 98PacOmeH-204
❑ 98PacOmeODI-204
❑ 98PacOmeR-204
❑ 98PacPar-205
❑ 98PacParC-205
❑ 98PacParEG-205
❑ 98PacParH-205
❑ 98PacParIB-205
❑ 98PacParS-205
❑ 98PacRed-369
❑ 98UC-187
❑ 98UD ChoPCR-187
❑ 98UD ChoR-187
❑ 98UppDec-361
❑ 98UppDecE-361
❑ 98UppDecE1o1-361
❑ 98UppDecGR-361
❑ 99Pac-360
❑ 99PacIceB-360
❑ 99PacPreD-360

**McLennen, Blondie**
❑ 28V1282PauC-45

**McLeod, Al**
❑ 75OPCWHA-88
❑ 75RoaPhoWHA-3
❑ 76OPCWHA-47

**McLeod, Don**
❑ 74OPCWHA-48
❑ 74TeaCanLWHA-17
❑ 75OPCWHA-32
❑ 76OPCWHA-129
❑ 77OPCWHA-14

**McLeod, Jack**
❑ 44BeeGro2P-344
❑ 51Par-98
❑ 52Par-102

**McLeod, Jimmy**
❑ 72SluCupWHA-15
❑ 73QuaOatWHA-17

**McLeod, Pete**
❑ 85LonKni-15

**McLlwain, Dave**
❑ 84KitRan-21

87PenKod-19
880PC-132
88ProlHL-56
88Top-132
89JetSaf-20
90Bow-136
90BowTif-136
90JetIGA-22
900PC-299
90PanSti-319
90ProSet-333
90Sco-231A
90Sco-231B
90ScoCan-231B
90Top-299
90TopTif-299
90UppDec-216
90UppDecF-216
91Bow-196
91JetPanTS-17
910PC-95
91PanSti-73
91ProSet-434
91ProSetFre-434
91ScoCan-233
91ScoRoo-102T
91StaClu-202
91Top-95
91UppDec-222
91UppDec-527
91UppDecF-222
91UppDecF-527
92MapLeaK-16
92Sco-122
92ScoCan-122
92StaClu-491
92Top-393
92TopGol-393G
92UppDec-93
93Pow-402
93Sco-418
93Sco-583
93ScoBla-9
93ScoCan-418
93ScoCan-583
93ScoGol-583
93SenKraS-19
93UppDec-524
94BeAPSig-9
94CanGamNHLP-355
94Don-315
94Fla-123
94Lea-260
940PCPre-446
940PCPreSE-446
94Par-157
94ParGol-157
94Pin-54
94PinArtP-54
94PinRinC-54
94SenBelM-22
94StaClu-31
94StaCluFDI-31
94StaCluMOMS-31
94StaCluSTWC-31
94TopPre-446
94TopPreSE-446
94UppDec-423
94UppDecElelce-423
95CleLum-17
96CleLum-16

**McMahon, Mark**
95Sla-137
96KitRan-18
98BowCHL-3
98BowCHLGA-3
98BowCHLOI-3
98BowChrC-3
98BowChrCGA-3
98BowChrCGAR-3
98BowChrCOI-3
98BowChrCOIR-3
98BowChrCR-3

**McMahon, Mike**
45QuaOatP-97
61SudWol-15
62SudWol-18
65Coc-78
65Top-24
680PC-46
68ShiCoi-72
68Top-46
70DadCoo-84
700PC-143
70SarProSta-28
72FigSaiPos-15
720PC-305
74FigSaiWHA-16

**McManus, Sammy**
36V356WorG-79

**McManus, Tyler**
92CorBigRed-21
93CorBigRed-19

**McMaster, Geoff**
91AirCanSJHL-D15

**McMasters, Jim**
72CruCleWHAL-6

**McMeekin, Ken**
52JunBluT-179

**McMichel, Scott**
83BelBul-18

**McMillan, Casey**
86KamBla-13
88LetHur-17

**McMillan, Paul**
91BriColJHL-108
**McMillan, Tyler**
91AirCanSJHL-A4
92MPSPhoSJHL-146
**McMillen, Dave**
907thInnSWHL-253
917thInnSWHL-157
92TacRoc-13
**McMorran, Larry**
93LetHur-8
93SeaThu-13
**McMorris, Doyle**
95LetHur-13
**McMulkin, John**
917thInnSWHL-175
**McMullen, Bryan**
95GueSto5A-23
**McMullen, John**
96Dev-NNO
**McMunn, Harold**
23CenCsel-13
24HolCre-2
28V1282PauC-70
**McMurchy, Tom**
82BraWheK-12
83Sprlnd-10
85NovScoO-18
880ilTenAnn-31
**McMurtry, Chris**
917thInnSOHL-340
93SudWol-4
93SudWolP-4
94CenHocL-63
**McNab, Max**
44BeeGro2P-194
**McNab, Peter**
750PCNHL-252
75Top-252
760PCNHL-118
76Top-118
770PCNHL-7
770PCNHL-18
77Top-7
77Top-18
780PC-212
78Top-212
790PC-39
79Top-39
800PC-94
800PC-167
800PC-220
80Top-94
80Top-167
80Top-220
810PC-5
810PCSti-47
81Top-E69
820PC-16
820PCSti-83
820PCSti-84
82PosCer-1
83BruTealss-10
830PC-53
830PCSti-51
84Canu-17
840PC-326
850PCSti-244
86DevPoi-15
**McNabney, Sid**
51BufBis-16
**McNamara, George**
83HalFP-O10
85HalFC-220
**McNamara, Gerry**
80MapLeaP-18
**McNamara, Harold**
10C56-32
**McNamara, Len**
907thInnSOHL-299
**McNamee, Peter**
75RoaPhoWHA-7
**McNeil, Al**
79FlaTeal-10
**McNeil, Douglas**
51LavDuQSHL-99
**McNeil, Gerry**
44BeeGro2P-272
45QuaOatP-60A
45QuaOatP-60D
45QuaOatP-98
48ExhCan-16
51Par-15
51Par-52
52Par-12
53Par-25
54Par-1
55MonRoy-5
55Par-52
93ParParR-PR35
**McNeil, Shawn**
95SlaMemC-24
96KamBla-16
97BowCHL-99
97BowCHLOPC-99
98BowCHL-71
98BowCHLGA-71
98BowCHLOI-71
98BowChrC-71
98BowChrCGA-71
98BowChrCGAR-71
98BowChrCOI-71
98BowChrCOIR-71
98BowChrCR-71

**McNeil, Steve**
94GerDELE-264
**McNeill, Bill**
57Top-44
59Top-41
63Par-56
94ParMisL-48
**McNeill, Jay**
96RicRen-14
**McNeill, Mike**
89ProlHL-72
90BlaCok-15
90ProSet-600
91Bow-143
91NordPet-17
910PC-408
91ProSet-467
91ProSetFre-467
91StaClu-241
91Top-408
91UppDec-524
91UppDecF-524
92Bow-424
92StaClu-294
92Top-166
92TopGol-166G
94MilAdm-19
95MilAdmBO-12
96MilAdmBO-17
98GerDELE-19
**McNelis, Bill**
93WatBlaH-18
**McNicoll, Kaven**
92QueIntP-13
**McNutt, Steve**
907thInnSWHL-110
**McPhee, George**
850PC-252
**McPhee, Michael (Mike)**
83NovScoV-19
84CanaPos-16
85CanaPos-20
85CanaPro-10
850PC-225
86CanaPos-13
86KraDra-42
860PC-221
860PCSti-15
87CanaPos-17
87CanaVacS-17
87CanaVacS-29
87CanaVacS-37
87CanaVacS-38
87PanSti-66
88CanaPos-20
880PC-237
880PCSti-47
88PanSti-258
89CanaKra-16
89CanaPos-24
89CanaProF-35
89KraAllSS-1
890PC-84
890PCSti-59
89PanSti-243
89Top-84
90Bow-43
90BowTif-43
90CanaPos-21
900PC-137
90PanSti-63
90ProSet-155
90Top-137
90TopTif-137
90UppDec-384
90UppDecF-384
91Bow-339
91CanaPanTS-16
91CanaPos-19
910PC-252
91PanSti-188
91Par-310
91ParFre-310
91Pin-147
91PinFre-147
91ProSet-129
91ProSetFre-129
91ScoCan-147
91ScoCan-147
91StaClu-210
91Top-252
91UppDec-487
91UppDecF-487
92Bow-89
920PC-199
92Pin-342
92PinFre-342
92Sco-91
92ScoCan-91
92StaClu-452
92Top-45
92TopGol-45G
92Ult-322
92UppDec-538
930PCPre-214
930PCPreG-214
93Par-51
93ParEmel-51
93Pin-163
93PinCan-163
93Pow-326
93Sco-85
93StaClu-6
93StaCluFDI-6

93StaCluFDIO-6
93StaCluO-6
93TopPreG-214
93TopPreG-214
93Ult-300
93UppDec-43
94CanGamNHLP-80
94Lea-203
940PCPre-163
940PCPreSE-163
94Pin-105
94PinArtP-105
94PinRinC-105
94Sco-17
94ScoGol-17
94ScoPla-17
94ScoPlaTS-17
94StaHoc-20
94StaScoS-17
94TopPre-163
94TopPreSE-163
95SumGM-21
**McPherson, Bud**
48ExhCan-14
**McPherson, Darwin**
84BraWheK-19
88SasBla-25
89ProlHL-2
90ProAHLIHL-94
92DayBom-18
93DayBom-16
**McPolin, Justin**
95Sla-172
**McQuat, Jason**
92OshGenS-9
93OshGen-24
95LouIceG-11
95LouIceGP-12
**McQuat, Rob**
92OshGenS-6
93OshGen-18
**McQueen, Dave**
95Sla-330
**McRae, Basil**
81FreExp-10
82FreExp-10
83MapLeaP-16
86NordTeal-14
87NorStaPos-21
870PCSti-227
88NorStaADA-18
890PC-216
89PanSti-109
90Bow-187
90BowTif-187
900PC-151
90PanSti-249
90ProSet-141
90Sco-261
90ScoCan-261
90Top-151
90TopTif-151
90UppDec-30
90UppDecF-30
91PanSti-119
91ProSet-409
91ProSetFre-409
91ScoCan-391
91UppDec-388
91UppDecF-388
92Par-391
92ParEmel-391
92ProSet-176
92Sco-356
92Sco-509
92ScoCan-356
92ScoCan-509
93Pow-430
93Sco-436
93ScoCan-436
93StaClu-273
93StaCluO-273
95BeAPla-6
95BeAPSigDC-S6
**McRae, Chris**
89ProAHL-308
90ProAHLIHL-472
91ProAHLCHL-240
**McRae, Gord**
74MapLeaP-14
75MapLeaP-14
750PCNHL-203
75Top-203
76MapLeaP-14
760PCNHL-337
77MapLeaP-11
**McRae, Ken**
85SudWol-14
86SudWol-12
88ProAHL-49
89Nord-30
89NordGenF-23
89NordPol-20
90NordTeal-22
900PC-411
90ProSet-255
91Nord-16
91NordPet-18
91ProAHLCHL-542
92St.JohML-13
93St.JohML-17
95PhoRoa-11
**McReavy, Pat**

34BeeGro1P-24
34BeeGro1P-116
**McReynolds, Brian**
89JetSaf-21
89ProAHL-47
90ProAHLIHL-24
91ProAHLCHL-209
91UppDec-434
91UppDecF-434
92BinRan-15
93PhoRoa-18
95SweLeaE-260
95SweUppDE-147
98GerDELE-103
**McSheffrey, Bryan**
72CanuRoyB-14
73CanuRoyB-14
730PC-219
74NHLActSta-285
74NHLActStaU-4
**McSorley, Chris**
87FliSpi-14
88ProlHL-8
90RicRen-18
92TolSto-2
93TolSto-2
94LasVegThu-16
94LasVegThu-23
96LasVegThu-15
**McSorley, Marty**
83PenCok-16
83PenTealP-23
84PenHelP-15
850ilRedR-33
860ilRedR-33
860ilTeal-33
870ilTeal-33
870PC-205
88KinSmo-18
880ilTenAnn-37
89KinSmo-17
89PanSti-99
90KinSmo-18
900PC-17
900PC-392
90PanSti-234
90ProSet-124
90Sco-271
90ScoCan-271
90Top-17
90Top-392
90TopTif-392
90UppDec-212
90UppDecF-212
91Bow-184
910PC-225
910PC-322
91PanSti-84
91Par-69
91ParFre-69
91Pin-35
91PinFre-35
91ProSet-100
91ProSetFre-100
91ProSetNHLSA-AC21
91ProSetPla-184
91ScoAme-217
91ScoAme-407
91ScoCan-217
91ScoCan-297
91StaClu-267
91Top-225
91UppDec-199
91UppDecF-199
92Bow-35
920PC-261
92PanSti-73
92PanStiFre-73
92Par-304
92ParCheP-CP17
92ParEmel-304
92Pin-156
92PinFre-156
92ProSet-69
92Sco-26
92ScoCan-26
92StaClu-481
92Top-171
92TopGol-171G
92Ult-310
92UppDec-322
93Don-256
93Don-447
93Lea-352
930PCPre-395
930PCPreG-395
930PanSti-208
93Par-161
93ParEmel-161
93PenFoo-5
93Pin-374
93PinCan-374
93Pow-191
93Sco-212
93Sco-542
93ScoCan-212
93ScoCan-542
93ScoGol-542
93StaClu-155
93StaCluFDI-155
93StaCluFDIO-155
93StaCluFin-8
93StaCluO-155
93TopPre-395
93TopPreG-395

93Ult-227
93Ult-394
93UppDec-487
93UppDecGG-GG9
94BeAPla-R10
94BeAPla-R150
94CanGamNHLP-130
94Don-168
94EASpo-62
94FinRinL-11
94Fla-82
94Fle-98
94Lea-174
940PCPre-146
940PCPreSE-146
94Par-106
94ParGol-106
94Pin-61
94PinArtP-61
94PinRinC-61
94PosCerBB-16
94Sco-20
94ScoGol-20
94ScoPla-20
94ScoPlaTS-20
94Sel-124
94SelGol-124
94TopPre-146
94TopPreSE-146
94Ult-102
94UppDec-33
94UppDecElelce-33
94UppDecSPI-SP127
94UppDecSPIDC-SP127
95BeAPla-225
95BeAPSig-S225
95BeAPSigDC-S225
95CanGamNHLP-140
95ColCho-44
95ColChoPC-44
95ColChoPCP-44
95ColEdgILL-L2
95Don-354
95Lea-309
95ParInt-105
95ParIntEl-105
95Pin-36
95PinArtP-36
95PinRinC-36
95PlaOneoOne-51
95Sco-92
95ScoBlalce-92
95ScoBlalceAP-92
95Top-162
95TopUPCI-162
95Ult-76
95UltGolM-76
95UppDec-193
95UppDecElelce-193
95UppDecSpeE-SE129
95UppDecSpeEdiG-SE129
96ColCho-172
96DurAlIT-DC9
96FlePic-166
96KraUppD-62
96Pin-67
96PinArtP-67
96PinFoi-67
96PinPreS-67
96PinRinC-67
96UppDec-106
96UppDecIce-60
96UppDecIcePar-60
97ColCho-221
97Kat-122
97KatGol-122
97KatSil-122
97Pac-333
97PacCop-333
97PacEmeGre-333
97PacIceB-333
97PacOme-204
97PacOmeC-204
97PacOmeDG-204
97PacOmeEG-204
97PacOmeG-204
97PacOmeIB-204
97PacRed-333
97PacSil-333
98McDGreT-T3
980-PChr-155
980-PChrR-155
98PacAur-169
98PacIceB-388
98PacPar-213
98PacParC-213
98PacParEG-213
98PacParH-213
98PacParIB-213
98PacParS-213
98PacRed-388
98SP AutSotTG-MMC
98SSASotT-MMC
98Top-155
98TopO-P-155
**McSween, Don**
88ProAHL-255
89ProAHL-280
90ProAHLIHL-290
91RochAmeDD-11
91RochAmeKod-18

91RochAmePos-15
92SanDieG-19
94CanGamNHLP-179
94DucCarJr-19
94UppDec-301
94UppDecEleIce-301
96GraRapG-13
**McSweyn, Ralph**
690PC-96
70SarProSta-145
72ShaLosAW-8
**McTamney, Joey**
897thInnSOHL-63
93DalFre-12
**McTavish, Dale**
897thInnSOHL-110
907thInnSOHL-365
917thInnSOHL-127
91PetPet-16
**McTavish, Gord**
77NovScoV-15
79JetPos-16
**McVeigh, Rabbit (Charley)**
23V1281PauC-27
330PCV304A-44
33V357IceK-38
34BeeGro1P-242
34DiaMatS-45
35DiaMatTl-47
36V356WorG-93
**McVey, Ward**
24CreFal-7
**McVie, Tom**
69SeaToW-14
79JetPos-17
88ProAHL-341
89ProAHL-214
90ProAHLIHL-564
96WheNai-NNO
**Mead, Scott**
92MPSPhoSJHL-123
**Meadmore, Neil**
88ProAHL-173
89ProAHL-39
**Meagher, Maurice**
917thInnSWHL-345
**Meagher, Rick**
77NovScoV-16
820PC-144
84DevPos-16
87BluKod-17
87BluTealss-14
87PanSti-316
88BluKod-22
88BluTealss-14
880PC-235
88PanSti-110
89BluKod-22
890PC-116
89PanSti-125
89Top-116
90BluKod-16
900PC-125
900PC-488
90PanSti-273
90ProSet-267
90ProSet-389
90Sco-267
90Sco-359
90ScoCan-267
90ScoCan-359
90Top-125
90TopTif-125
90UppDec-208
90UppDec-285
90UppDecF-285
910PC-58
91ProSetSLM-3
91StaClu-85
91Top-58
92BluUDBB-23
92PeoRivC-16
**Means, Eric**
91MinGolG-16
92MinGolG-14
93MinGolG-21
**Mearns, Rick**
917thInnSWHL-33
**Mears, Glen**
94FliGen-17
95TolSto-5
**Measures, Allan**
93FinnJyvHS-86
93FinnSIS-119
94FinnSIS-61
95FinnSIS-33
95FinnSIS-39
95FinnSISL-103
**Meciar, Stanislav**
93FinnJyvHS-350
93FinnSIS-216
94SweLeaE-174
95CzeAPSE-224
**Meckling, Brent**
82MedHatT-12
83MedHatT-16
**Mede, Roger**
94GerDELE-146
**Medeiros, Brian**
93OweSouPla-19
**Medicus, Dieter**
94GerDELE-8
95GerDELE-169
**Medrik, Stanislav**
91SweSemWCS-112

❏ 94FinnJaaK-197
❏ 95CzeAPSE-33
❏ 95SloAPSNT-10
❏ 96SweSemW-225
**Medzihorsky, Branislav**
❏ 95SloPeeWT-16
**Meehan, Gerry**
❏ 69SeaTotW-15
❏ 70ColSta-20
❏ 70EssPowPla-83
❏ 70OPC-125
❏ 70SarProSta-20
❏ 70Top-125
❏ 71OPC-160
❏ 71SabPos-13
❏ 71SarProSta-17
❏ 71Top-74
❏ 71TorSun-34
❏ 72OPC-22
❏ 72SarProSta-29
❏ 72Top-16
❏ 73OPC-22
❏ 73SabPos-7
❏ 73Top-22
❏ 74CanuRoyB-12
❏ 74NHLActSta-54
❏ 74NHLActStaU-39
❏ 74OPCNHL-99
❏ 74Top-99
❏ 76OPCNHL-35
❏ 76OPCNHL-396
❏ 76Top-35
❏ 77OPCNHL-53
❏ 77Top-53
❏ 78OPC-128
❏ 78Top-128
**Meehan, Jeremy**
❏ 93DetJrRW-11
**Meehan, Pat**
❏ 91BriColJHL-68
❏ 92BriColJHL-84
**Meeker, Howie**
❏ 44BeeGro2P-432
❏ 45QuaOatP-35A
❏ 45QuaOatP-35B
❏ 45QuaOatP-35C
❏ 45QuaOatP-60A
❏ 48ExhCan-35
❏ 51Par-72
❏ 52Par-42
❏ 94ParMisL-133
**Meger, Paul**
❏ 44BeeGro2P-273
❏ 45QuaOatP-99
❏ 48ExhCan-17
❏ 51Par-2
❏ 52Par-4
❏ 53Par-21
❏ 54Par-94
❏ 55Par-51
❏ 55ParQuaO-51
**Mehalko, Brad**
❏ 93LetHur-9
❏ 94ParSE-SE265
❏ 94ParSEG-SE265
❏ 94SP-184
❏ 94SPDieCut-184
❏ 95LetHur-14
**Meighan, Ron**
❏ 82NorBayC-16
❏ 83PenHeiP-19
❏ 83PenTealP-24
**Meikle, Derek**
❏ 91AirCanSJHL-D48
**Meisenheimer, Harvey**
❏ 61HamRed-14
**Meisner, Kevin**
❏ 88SudWol-8
**Meissner, Dick**
❏ 44BeeGro2P-50
❏ 60ShiCoi-111
❏ 61ShiCoi-15
❏ 61Top-6
❏ 61Top-64
❏ 63Top-60
**Meister, Rupert**
❏ 94GerDELE-51
❏ 95GerDELE-2
❏ 96GerDELE-48
**Meitinger, Holger**
❏ 82SweSemHVS-113
**Mejzlik, Roman**
❏ 94CzeAPSE-196
❏ 95CzeAPSE-212
**Melametsa, Anssi**
❏ 85JetPol-13
**Melanovsky, Marek**
❏ 95CzeAPSE-195
❏ 95UppDec-543
❏ 95UppDecEleIce-543
❏ 95UppDecEleIceG-543
❏ 96CzeAPSE-329
**Melanson, A.J.**
❏ 93DubFigS-18
**Melanson, Bruce**
❏ 83OshGen-19
**Melanson, Dean**
❏ 907thInnSQMJHL-209
❏ 917thInnSQMJHL-21
❏ 93Cla-143
❏ 93RochAmeKod-16
❏ 94ClaProP-102
❏ 95RochAmeSS-11
**Melanson, Robert**
❏ 91KnoChe-20

❏ 92CleLum-23
❏ 93MusFur-9
❏ 95MusFur-14
**Melanson, Roland (Rollie)**
❏ 83IsITealss-9
❏ 83OPC-12
❏ 83OPCSti-88
❏ 83OPCSti-317
❏ 84IsIIsIN-22
❏ 84NorStaPos-18
❏ 84OPC-130
❏ 84OPC-387
❏ 84OPCSti-58
❏ 85NorStaPos-22
❏ 85OPC-230
❏ 86Kin20tATI-15
❏ 87KinTeal4-15
❏ 87OPC-19
❏ 87OPCSti-213
❏ 87PanSti-271
❏ 87Top-19
❏ 88OPC-160
❏ 88OPCSti-151
❏ 88PanSti-69
❏ 88Top-160
❏ 89ProAHL-213
❏ 90ProAHLIHL-579
❏ 91OPCPre-97
❏ 91UppDec-575
❏ 91UppDecF-575
❏ 92Bow-187
❏ 92StaClu-184
❏ 92Top-298
❏ 92TopGol-298G
**Melanson, Stan**
❏ 917thInnSQMJHL-28
**Melfi, Patrick**
❏ 917thInnSQMJHL-72
**Melin, Brad**
❏ 84VicCou-13
**Melin, Roger**
❏ 84SweSemE-139
**Melkersson, Tommy**
❏ 89SweSemE-35
❏ 90SweSemE-184
❏ 91SweSemE-35
❏ 92SweSemE-55
❏ 93SweSemE-31
❏ 94SweLeaE-119
❏ 94SweLeaE-180
❏ 95SweUppDE-23
**Mellanby, Scott**
❏ 86FlyPos-18
❏ 88OPC-21
❏ 88PanSti-322
❏ 88Top-21
❏ 89FlyPos-15
❏ 89OPC-253
❏ 90FlyPos-17
❏ 90OPC-173
❏ 90ProSet-220
❏ 90Sco-242
❏ 90ScoCan-242
❏ 90Top-173
❏ 90TopTif-173
❏ 91Bow-236
❏ 91OilIGA-15
❏ 91OilTeal-16
❏ 91OPC-200
❏ 91OPCPre-30
❏ 91PanSti-238
❏ 91Par-50
❏ 91ParFre-50
❏ 91Pin-45
❏ 91PinFre-45
❏ 91ProSet-172
❏ 91ProSet-383
❏ 91ProSetFre-172
❏ 91ProSetFre-383
❏ 91ProSetPla-173
❏ 91ScoAme-279
❏ 91ScoCan-575
❏ 91ScoRoo-25T
❏ 91StaClu-110
❏ 91Top-200
❏ 91UppDec-542
❏ 91UppDecF-542
❏ 92Bow-163
❏ 92DurPan-17
❏ 92OilIGA-15
❏ 92OPC-140
❏ 92Par-52
❏ 92ParEmel-52
❏ 92PinFre-346
❏ 92ProSet-54
❏ 92Sco-148
❏ 92ScoCan-148
❏ 92StaClu-462
❏ 92Top-444
❏ 92TopGol-444G
❏ 92Ult-295
❏ 92UppDec-119
❏ 93Don-126
❏ 93DurSco-46
❏ 93Lea-262
❏ 93OPCPre-249
❏ 93PanSti-243
❏ 93PanTeal-7
❏ 93Par-81
❏ 93ParEmel-81
❏ 93Pin-168
❏ 93PinCan-168
❏ 93PinExp-6

❏ 93Pow-98
❏ 93Sco-63
❏ 93Sco-503
❏ 93ScoCan-63
❏ 93ScoCan-503
❏ 93ScoGol-503
❏ 93StaClu-31
❏ 93StaClu-369
❏ 93StaCluFDI-31
❏ 93StaCluFDI-369
❏ 93StaCluFDIO-31
❏ 93StaCluO-31
❏ 93StaCluO-369
❏ 93TopPre-249
❏ 93TopPreG-249
❏ 93Ult-328
❏ 93UppDec-107
❏ 93UppDecSP-57
❏ 94BeAPSig-170
❏ 94CanGarnNHLP-108
❏ 94Don-42
❏ 94EASpo-53
❏ 94Fla-65
❏ 94Fle-80
❏ 94Lea-182
❏ 94LeaLim-103
❏ 94OPCPre-144
❏ 94OPCPreSE-144
❏ 94PanPop-3
❏ 94Par-85
❏ 94ParGol-85
❏ 94Pin-73
❏ 94PinArtP-73
❏ 94PinRinC-73
❏ 94Sco-102
❏ 94ScoGol-102
❏ 94ScoPla-102
❏ 94ScoPlaTS-102
❏ 94Sel-85
❏ 94SelGol-85
❏ 94SP-47
❏ 94SPDieCut-47
❏ 94TopPre-144
❏ 94TopPreSE-144
❏ 94Ult-298
❏ 94UppDec-92
❏ 94UppDecEleIce-92
❏ 94UppDecSPI-SP121
❏ 94UppDecSPIDC-SP121
❏ 95Bow-37
❏ 95BowAllFoi-37
❏ 95CanGamNHLP-116
❏ 95ColCho-171
❏ 95ColChoPC-171
❏ 95ColChoPCP-171
❏ 95Don-37
❏ 95DonEli-86
❏ 95DonEliDCS-86
❏ 95DonEliDCU-86
❏ 95Fin-136
❏ 95FinRef-136
❏ 95ImpSti-49
❏ 95Lea-87
❏ 95LeaLim-114
❏ 95Met-60
❏ 95ParInt-355
❏ 95ParIntEl-355
❏ 95Pin-78
❏ 95PinArtP-78
❏ 95PinRinC-78
❏ 95PlaOneoOne-154
❏ 95ProMag-88
❏ 95Sco-134
❏ 95ScoBlaIce-134
❏ 95ScoBlaIceAP-134
❏ 95SelCer-3
❏ 95SelCerMG-3
❏ 95SP-55
❏ 95StaClu-170
❏ 95StaCluMOMS-170
❏ 95Sum-57
❏ 95SumArtP-57
❏ 95SumIce-57
❏ 95Top-260
❏ 95TopOPCI-260
❏ 95Ult-242
❏ 95UltCreCra-10
❏ 95UppDec-399
❏ 95UppDecEleIce-399
❏ 95UppDecEleIceG-399
❏ 95UppDecSpeE-SE34
❏ 95UppDecSpeEdiG-SE34
❏ 95Zen-25
❏ 96BeAPAut-171
❏ 96BeAPAutSil-171
❏ 96BeAPla-171
❏ 96ColCho-102
❏ 96Don-49
❏ 96DonCanI-107
❏ 96DonCanIGPP-107
❏ 96DonCanIRPP-107
❏ 96DonEli-32
❏ 96DonEliDCS-32
❏ 96DonPrePro-49
❏ 96Fle-40
❏ 96Lea-132
❏ 96LeaLim-50
❏ 96LeaLimG-50
❏ 96LeaLimStu-17
❏ 96LeaPre-111
❏ 96LeaPreP-132
❏ 96LeaPrePP-111
❏ 96LeaPreSG-8
❏ 96LeaPreSte-8
❏ 96MetUni-60

❏ 96NHLProSTA-88
❏ 96Pin-126
❏ 96PinArtP-126
❏ 96PinPreS-126
❏ 96PinRinC-126
❏ 96PlaOneoOne-387
❏ 96Sco-31
❏ 96ScoArtPro-31
❏ 96ScoDeaCAP-31
❏ 96ScoGolB-31
❏ 96ScoSpeAP-31
❏ 96ScoSup-13
❏ 96SelCer-84
❏ 96SelCerAP-84
❏ 96SelCerBlu-84
❏ 96SelCerMB-84
❏ 96SelCerMG-84
❏ 96SelCerMR-84
❏ 96SelCerRed-84
❏ 96SkyImp-46
❏ 96SP-65
❏ 96StaCluMO-32
❏ 96Sum-8
❏ 96SumArtP-8
❏ 96SumIce-8
❏ 96SumMet-8
❏ 96SumPreS-8
❏ 96TeaOut-5
❏ 96TopNHLP-101
❏ 96TopPicOI-101
❏ 96Ult-66
❏ 96UltGolM-66
❏ 96UppDec-200
❏ 96UppDec-265
❏ 96UppDecBD-127
❏ 96UppDecBDG-127
❏ 96UppDecGN-X25
❏ 96Zen-16
❏ 96ZenArtP-16
❏ 97ColCho-100
❏ 97ColChoSta-SQ37
❏ 97Don-171
❏ 97DonEli-76
❏ 97DonEliAsp-76
❏ 97DonEliS-76
❏ 97DonLim-110
❏ 97DonLimExp-110
❏ 97DonPre-135
❏ 97DonPreCttC-135
❏ 97DonPreProG-171
❏ 97DonPreProS-171
❏ 97DonPri-129
❏ 97DonPriSoA-129
❏ 97Kat-62
❏ 97KatGol-62
❏ 97KatSil-62
❏ 97Lea-110
❏ 97LeaFraMat-110
❏ 97LeaFraMDC-110
❏ 97LeaInt-110
❏ 97LeaIntUI-110
❏ 97Pac-321
❏ 97PacCop-321
❏ 97PacCroR-59
❏ 97PacCroREG-59
❏ 97PacCroRIB-59
❏ 97PacCroRS-59
❏ 97PacDyn-54
❏ 97PacDynC-54
❏ 97PacDynDG-54
❏ 97PacDynIB-54
❏ 97PacDynR-54
❏ 97PacDynSil-54
❏ 97PacDynTan-54
❏ 97PacEmeGre-321
❏ 97PacIceB-321
❏ 97PacInv-61
❏ 97PacInvC-61
❏ 97PacInvEG-61
❏ 97PacInvIB-61
❏ 97PacInvR-61
❏ 97PacInvS-61
❏ 97PacOme-100
❏ 97PacOmeC-100
❏ 97PacOmeDG-100
❏ 97PacOmeEG-100
❏ 97PacOmeG-100
❏ 97PacOmeIB-100
❏ 97PacPar-81
❏ 97PacParC-81
❏ 97PacParDG-81
❏ 97PacParEG-81
❏ 97PacParIB-81
❏ 97PacParRed-81
❏ 97PacRed-321
❏ 97PacSil-321
❏ 97PinCer-107
❏ 97PinCerMB-107
❏ 97PinCerMG-107
❏ 97PinCerMR-107
❏ 97PinCerR-107
❏ 97PinIns-165
❏ 97PinTotCMPG-107
❏ 97PinTotCPB-107
❏ 97PinTotCPG-107
❏ 97PinTotCPR-107
❏ 97Sco-177
❏ 97SPAut-68
❏ 97Stu-41
❏ 97StuPrePG-41
❏ 97StuPrePS-41
❏ 97UppDec-282

❏ 97UppDec-92
❏ 97UppDecBDD-92
❏ 97UppDecBDQD-92
❏ 97UppDecBDTD-92
❏ 97UppDecGDM-282
❏ 98Be A PPA-58
❏ 98Be A PPAA-58
❏ 98Be A PPAAF-58
❏ 98Be A PPTBASG-58
❏ 98Be APG-58
❏ 98O-Pchr-13
❏ 98O-PChrR-13
❏ 98Pac-226
❏ 98PacAur-83
❏ 98PacIceB-226
❏ 98PacPar-99
❏ 98PacParC-99
❏ 98PacParEG-99
❏ 98PacParH-99
❏ 98PacParIB-99
❏ 98PacParS-99
❏ 98PacRed-226
❏ 98Top-13
❏ 98TopO-P-13
❏ 98UC-90
❏ 98UD ChoPCR-90
❏ 98UD ChoR-90
❏ 98UDCP-90
❏ 98UppDec-279
❏ 98UppDecE-279
❏ 98UppDecE1o1-279
❏ 98UppDecGR-279
❏ 99Pac-178
❏ 99PacCop-178
❏ 99PacGol-178
❏ 99PacIceB-178
❏ 99PacPreD-178
❏ 99UppDecM-90
❏ 99UppDecMGS-90
❏ 99UppDecMSS-90
**Mellbin, Bo**
❏ 71SweHocS-356
**Mellinger, Hasse**
❏ 65SweCorI-210
❏ 67SweHoc-272
❏ 69SweHocS-325
**Mellios, Loui**
❏ 91BriColJHL-117
❏ 92BriColJHL-180
❏ 92BriColJHL-184
**Mellor, Tom**
❏ 72SweSemWC-121
❏ 73RedWinMP-13
**Mellstrom, Johan**
❏ 83SweSemE-210
❏ 84SweSemE-235
**Melnechuk, Jeff**
❏ 93SudWol-2
❏ 93SudWolP-23
**Melyakov, Igor**
❏ 94Cla95DP-DP6
**Menard, Carl**
❏ 907thInnSQMJHL-80
❏ 917thInnSQMJHL-19
**Menard, Daniel**
❏ 77GraVic-15
**Menard, Derry**
❏ 94CenHocL-64
**Menard, Howie**
❏ 61HamRed-15
❏ 69OPC-73
❏ 70OPC-124
❏ 70Top-124
**Menard, Martin**
❏ 95SlaMernC-68
❏ 95BowCHL-54
❏ 97BowCHLOPC-54
**Menard, Stephane**
❏ 907thInnSQMJHL-235
❏ 917thInnSQMJHL-5
❏ 94KnoChe-5
**Menard, Terry**
❏ 93ThuBayS-19
❏ 94ThuBayS-9
❏ 95ThuBayS-12
❏ 96ForWorF-12
**Mende, Karsten**
❏ 94FinnJaaK-278
❏ 94GerDELE-211
❏ 95GerDELE-203
❏ 96GerDELE-344
**Mendel, Rob (Bob)**
❏ 90ProAHLIHL-198
❏ 91ProAHLCHL-335
❏ 95GerDELE-6
❏ 96GerDELE-5
**Menges, Greg**
❏ 91GreMon-10
❏ 92GreMon-19
**Menhart, Marian**
❏ 95PriAlbR-15
❏ 96PriAlbR-12
❏ 96PriAlbROC-14
**Menicci, Tom**
❏ 94HamRoaA-11
**Mentis, Jim**
❏ 84VicCou-14
**Mercer, Lee**
❏ 96FitFly-20
❏ 97FitFly-16
**Mercer, Randy**
❏ 96St.JohnML-20
**Mercier, Chad**
❏ 96RegPat-7
**Mercier, Don**
❏ 86MonGolF-15

**Mercier, Martin**
❏ 92MaiBlaB-32
**Meredith, Greg**
❏ 83OPC-88
**Merinov, Vladimir**
❏ 74SweHocS-39
**Merk, Klaus**
❏ 93SweSemWCS-150
❏ 94FinnJaaK-271
❏ 94GerDELE-70
❏ 95GerDELE-50
❏ 95GerDELE-440
❏ 95SweGloWC-217
❏ 96GerDELE-247
❏ 96SweSemW-192
❏ 98GerDELE-273
❏ 98GerDELE-327
**Merkosky, Glenn**
❏ 88ProAHL-4
❏ 89ProAHL-323
❏ 90ProAHLIHL-470
❏ 91ProAHLCHL-141
❏ 94SudWol-24
**Merra, Martti**
❏ 93FinnJyvHS-193
❏ 93FinnSIS-255
**Merrell, Barry**
❏ 71RocAme-13
**Merrick, Wayne**
❏ 72BluWhiBor-11
❏ 73BluWhiBor-12
❏ 74NHLActSta-248
❏ 74OPCNHL-66
❏ 74Top-66
❏ 75OPCNHL-228
❏ 75Top-228
❏ 76OPCNHL-18
❏ 76OPCNHL-383
❏ 76Top-18
❏ 77OPCNHL-176
❏ 77Top-176
❏ 78OPC-258
❏ 78Top-258
❏ 79IsITrans-11
❏ 79OPC-169
❏ 79Top-169
❏ 80OPC-345
❏ 81OPC-216
❏ 82OPC-205
❏ 82PosCer-12
❏ 83IsITealss-10
❏ 84IsIIsIN-10
❏ 93IsICheBA-5
**Merritt, Ryan**
❏ 89WinSpi-11
❏ 907thInnSOHL-187
❏ 917thInnSOHL-61
**Mersch, Mike**
❏ 87FliSpi-15
❏ 88FliSpi-19
❏ 88FliSpi-19
❏ 89ProIHL-161
❏ 90ProAHLIHL-386
**Mertzig, Jan**
❏ 95SweLeaE-253
❏ 95SweLeaER-6
❏ 95SweUppDE-117
**Merz, Suzanne**
❏ 94ClaWomOH-W28
**Mesicek, Radek**
❏ 94CzeAPSE-234
❏ 96CzeAPSE-103
**Messier, Kevin**
❏ 91AirCanSJHL-D6
❏ 92MPSPhoSJHL-120
**Messier, Doug**
❏ 83MonAlp-1
**Messier, Eric**
❏ 917thInnSQMJHL-111
❏ 97Be A PPAD-204
❏ 97Be A PPAPD-204
❏ 97BePla-204
❏ 97BePlaAut-204
❏ 97DonLim-125
❏ 97DonLimExp-125
❏ 97Kat-167
❏ 97KatGol-167
❏ 97KatSil-167
❏ 97PacInvNRB-55
❏ 97PacOme-61
❏ 97PacOmeC-61
❏ 97PacOmeDG-61
❏ 97PacOmeEG-61
❏ 97PacOmeG-61
❏ 97PacOmeIB-61
❏ 97PacRev-36
❏ 97PacRevC-36
❏ 97PacRevE-36
❏ 97PacRevIB-36
❏ 97PacRevR-36
❏ 97PacRevS-36
❏ 97SPAut-178
❏ 97UppDec-45
❏ 97UppDecBD-13
❏ 97UppDecBDD-13
❏ 97UppDecBDQD-13
❏ 97UppDecBDTD-13
❏ 97Zen5x7-70
❏ 97ZenGolImp-70
❏ 98Pac-165
❏ 98PacAur-49
❏ 98PacIceB-165
❏ 98PacPar-58
❏ 98PacParC-58
❏ 98PacParEG-58

❑ 98PacParH-58
❑ 98PacParIB-58
❑ 98PacParS-58
❑ 98PacRed-165
❑ 98UC-53
❑ 98UD ChoPCR-53
❑ 98UD ChoR-53
❑ 98UDCP-53
❑ 98UppDec-70
❑ 98UppDecE-70
❑ 98UppDecE1o1-70
❑ 98UppDecGR-70

**Messier, Joby**

❑ 92BinRan-12
❑ 92Cla-72
❑ 92ClaLPs-LP10
❑ 93ClaProPBC-BC13
❑ 93ClaProPro-76
❑ 93ClaProPro-127
❑ 93Lea-298
❑ 93OPCPre-522
❑ 93OPCPreG-522
❑ 93Par-399
❑ 93ParEmel-399
❑ 93Pow-161
❑ 93StaClu-339
❑ 93StaCluFDI-339
❑ 93StaCluO-339
❑ 93TopPre-522
❑ 93TopPreG-522
❑ 93Ult-170
❑ 93UltAllRoo-6
❑ 93UppDec-73
❑ 94BinRan-13
❑ 94Lea-375
❑ 94OPCPre-476
❑ 94OPCPreSE-476
❑ 94Pin-497
❑ 94PinArtP-497
❑ 94PinRinC-497
❑ 94TopPre-476
❑ 94TopPreSE-476
❑ 96ClaGol-72

**Messier, Mark**

❑ 79OilPos-17
❑ 80OPC-289
❑ 80PepCap-34
❑ 81OilRedR-11
❑ 81OPC-118
❑ 81OPCSti-210
❑ 81PosSta-15
❑ 82McDSti-15
❑ 82NeiGre-45
❑ 82OilRedR-11
❑ 82OPC-117
❑ 82OPCSti-94
❑ 82OPCSti-159
❑ 82PosCer-6
❑ 83Ess-13
❑ 83OilDol-H20
❑ 83OilMcD-18
❑ 83OPC-23
❑ 83OPC-39
❑ 83OPCSti-97
❑ 83OPCSti-98
❑ 83OPCSti-157
❑ 83PufSti-4
❑ 83Vac-36
❑ 847EDis-21
❑ 84OilRedR-11
❑ 84OilTeal-19
❑ 84OPC-213
❑ 84OPC-254
❑ 84OPCSti-5
❑ 84OPCSti-261
❑ 84Top-159
❑ 85OilRedR-11
❑ 85OPC-177
❑ 85OPCSti-228
❑ 86KraDra-43
❑ 86OilRedR-11
❑ 86OilTeal-11
❑ 86OPC-186
❑ 86OPCSti-79
❑ 86Top-186
❑ 87OilTeal-11
❑ 87OPC-112
❑ 87OPCMin-28
❑ 87OPCSti-92
❑ 87PanSti-194
❑ 87PanSti-263
❑ 87ProAll-13
❑ 87Top-112
❑ 88EssAllSta-30
❑ 88FriLayS-35
❑ 88OilTeal-21
❑ 88OilTenAnn-89
❑ 88OPC-93
❑ 88OPCMin-25
❑ 88OPCSti-230
❑ 88PanSti-61
❑ 88Top-93
❑ 89Kra-15
❑ 89OilTeal-17
❑ 89OPC-65
❑ 89OPCSti-227
❑ 89PanSti-74
❑ 89SweSemWCS-69
❑ 89Top-65
❑ 90Bow-199
❑ 90BowHatTri-4
❑ 90BowTif-199
❑ 90Kra-32
❑ 90Kra-71
❑ 90OilIGA-16
❑ 90OPC-130
❑ 90OPC-193
❑ 90OPC-519
❑ 90OPCPre-71
❑ 90PanSti-219
❑ 90ProSet-91
❑ 90ProSet-349
❑ 90ProSet-381
❑ 90ProSet-386
❑ 90ProSet-397
❑ 90Sco-100
❑ 90Sco-315
❑ 90Sco-331
❑ 90Sco-360
❑ 90ScoCan-100
❑ 90ScoCan-315
❑ 90ScoCan-360
❑ 90ScoHotRS-33
❑ 90ScoPro-100A
❑ 90ScoPro-100B
❑ 90Top-130
❑ 90Top-193
❑ 90TopTeaSL-16
❑ 90TopTif-130
❑ 90TopTif-193
❑ 90UppDec-44
❑ 90UppDec-206
❑ 90UppDec-321
❑ 90UppDec-494
❑ 90UppDecF-44
❑ 90UppDecF-206
❑ 90UppDecF-321
❑ 90UppDecF-494
❑ 90UppDecHol-6
❑ 90UppDecHol-6
❑ 90UppDecHol-7
❑ 91Bow-114
❑ 91Gil-31
❑ 91Kra-16
❑ 91OilPanTS-14
❑ 91OilPanTS-G
❑ 91OPC-346
❑ 91OPCPre-51
❑ 91PanSti-124
❑ 91Par-121
❑ 91Par-213
❑ 91Par-468
❑ 91Par-475
❑ 91ParFre-121
❑ 91ParFre-213
❑ 91ParFre-468
❑ 91ParFre-475
❑ 91ParPHC-PHC8
❑ 91ParPHCF-PHC8
❑ 91Pin-50
❑ 91Pin-390
❑ 91PinFre-50
❑ 91PinFre-390
❑ 91ProSet-74
❑ 91ProSet-282
❑ 91ProSet-439
❑ 91ProSet-579
❑ 91ProSetFre-74
❑ 91ProSetFre-282
❑ 91ProSetFre-439
❑ 91ProSetFre-579
❑ 91ProSetPC-19
❑ 91ProSetPla-81
❑ 91ProSetPlaPC-PC20
❑ 91ScoAme-285
❑ 91ScoAme-373
❑ 91ScoAme-420
❑ 91ScoCan-263
❑ 91ScoCan-310
❑ 91ScoCan-505
❑ 91ScoCan-635
❑ 91ScoRoo-85T
❑ 91StaClu-111
❑ 91SweSemWCS-63
❑ 91Top-346
❑ 91TopBowPS-6
❑ 91UppDec-14
❑ 91UppDec-246
❑ 91UppDec-545
❑ 91UppDec-610
❑ 91UppDec-620
❑ 91UppDecBB-3
❑ 91UppDecBB-4
❑ 91UppDecF-14
❑ 91UppDecF-246
❑ 91UppDecF-545
❑ 91UppDecF-610
❑ 91UppDecF-620
❑ 92Bow-113
❑ 92Bow-234
❑ 92EnoMarM-1
❑ 92EnoMarM-2
❑ 92EnoMarM-3
❑ 92EnoMarM-4
❑ 92EnoMarM-5
❑ 92EnoMarM-6
❑ 92EnoMarM-7
❑ 92EnoMarM-8
❑ 92EnoMarM-9
❑ 92EnoMarM-10
❑ 92Hig5Pre-P4
❑ 92HumDum2-15
❑ 92KelPos-2
❑ 92Kra-45
❑ 92McDUppD-H1
❑ 92OPC-208
❑ 92OPC-258
❑ 92OPC25AI-13
❑ 92OPCPreSP-15
❑ 92OPCTroW-3
❑ 92PanSti-233
❑ 92PanStiFre-233
❑ 92Par-111
❑ 92ParCheP-CP4
❑ 92ParEmel-111
❑ 92Pin-1
❑ 92PinFre-1
❑ 92ProSet-111
❑ 92ProSetAW-CC1
❑ 92Sco-300
❑ 92Sco-431
❑ 92Sco-493
❑ 92Sco-521
❑ 92ScoCan-300
❑ 92ScoCan-431
❑ 92ScoCan-493
❑ 92ScoCan-521
❑ 92SeaPat-26
❑ 92StaClu-241
❑ 92StaClu-443
❑ 92Top-258
❑ 92Top-274
❑ 92TopGol-258G
❑ 92TopGol-274G
❑ 92Ult-139
❑ 92UltAwaW-1
❑ 92UltAwaW-10
❑ 92UppDec-34
❑ 92UppDec-242
❑ 92UppDec-432
❑ 92UppDec-437
❑ 92UppDec-453
❑ 93Don-222
❑ 93DonSpeP-O
❑ 93KenStaLA-9
❑ 93KenStaLC-8
❑ 93Kra-43
❑ 93Lea-158
❑ 93OPCPre-430
❑ 93OPCPreG-430
❑ 93PanSti-I
❑ 93Par-127
❑ 93ParChePH-D4
❑ 93ParEmel-127
❑ 93Pin-125
❑ 93Pin-238
❑ 93PinCan-125
❑ 93PinCan-238
❑ 93PinCap-15
❑ 93PinCapC-15
❑ 93Pow-162
❑ 93PowPoiL-9
❑ 93Sco-200
❑ 93ScoCan-200
❑ 93ScoDynDUS-5
❑ 93StaClu-35
❑ 93StaCluFDI-35
❑ 93StaCluFDIO-35
❑ 93StaCluO-35
❑ 93SweSemWCS-202
❑ 93TopPre-430
❑ 93TopPreG-430
❑ 93TopPrePS-601
❑ 93Ult-183
❑ 93UltPreP-6
❑ 93UppDec-51
❑ 93UppDec-298
❑ 93UppDecGGO-GG5
❑ 93UppDecLAS-7
❑ 93UppDecSP-103
❑ 94CanGamNHLP-166
❑ 94Don-9
❑ 94DonDom-1
❑ 94DonIceMas-7
❑ 94EASpo-87
❑ 94Fin-16
❑ 94FinBowB-B2
❑ 94FinBowBR-B2
❑ 94FinnJaaK-94
❑ 94FinnJaaK-350
❑ 94FinRef-16
❑ 94FinRinL-1
❑ 94FinSupTW-16
❑ 94Fla-115
❑ 94FlaCenS-8
❑ 94Fle-136
❑ 94FleHea-7
❑ 94HocWit-102
❑ 94KenStaLA-13
❑ 94Kra-22
❑ 94Lea-11
❑ 94LeaGolS-5
❑ 94LeaLim-89
❑ 94LeaLimI-15
❑ 94OPCPre-1
❑ 94OPCPre-278
❑ 94OPCPreSE-1
❑ 94OPCPreSE-278
❑ 94ParCratGB-27
❑ 94ParCratGG-27
❑ 94ParCratGR-27
❑ 94ParSE-SE113
❑ 94ParSEG-SE113
❑ 94ParVin-V33
❑ 94Pin-300
❑ 94PinArtP-300
❑ 94PinGam-GR9
❑ 94PinRinC-300
❑ 94PinTeaP-TP9
❑ 94PinTeaPDP-TP9
❑ 94ScoDreTea-DT16
❑ 94ScoFra-TF15
❑ 94Sel-1
❑ 94SelGol-1
❑ 94SP-73
❑ 94SPDieCut-73
❑ 94SPPre-28
❑ 94SPPreDC-28
❑ 94StaClu-1
❑ 94StaCluDD-2
❑ 94StaCluDDMO-2
❑ 94StaCluFDI-1
❑ 94StaCluFI-3
❑ 94StaCluFIMO-3
❑ 94StaCluMO-27
❑ 94StaCluMOMS-1
❑ 94StaCluST-15
❑ 94StaCluSTWC-1
❑ 94TopFinB-15
❑ 94TopPre-1
❑ 94TopPre-120
❑ 94TopPre-278
❑ 94TopPreGTG-15
❑ 94TopPreSE-1
❑ 94TopPreSE-278
❑ 94Ult-140
❑ 94UltAllS-4
❑ 94UltPreP-7
❑ 94UppDec-62
❑ 94UppDec-234
❑ 94UppDec-563
❑ 94UppDecElelce-62
❑ 94UppDecElelce-234
❑ 94UppDecElelce-563
❑ 94UppDecPC-C22
❑ 94UppDecPCEG-C22
❑ 94UppDecPH-H4
❑ 94UppDecPHEG-H4
❑ 94UppDecPHES-H4
❑ 94UppDecPHG-H4
❑ 94UppDecPR-R34
❑ 94UppDecPR-R54
❑ 94UppDecPRE-R34
❑ 94UppDecPRE-R54
❑ 94UppDecPreRG-R34
❑ 94UppDecPreRG-R54
❑ 94UppDecSPI-SP51
❑ 94UppDecSPIDC-SP51
❑ 95Bow-8
❑ 95BowAllFoi-8
❑ 95BowBes-BB6
❑ 95BowBesRef-BB6
❑ 95CanGamNHLP-6
❑ 95CanGamNHLP-24
❑ 95CanGamNHLP-180
❑ 95ColCho-220
❑ 95ColChoCTG-C6
❑ 95ColChoCTG-C6B
❑ 95ColChoCTG-C6C
❑ 95ColChoCTGGB-C6
❑ 95ColChoCTGGR-C6
❑ 95ColChoCTGSB-C6
❑ 95ColChoCTGSR-C6
❑ 95ColChoPC-220
❑ 95ColChoPCP-220
❑ 95Don-271
❑ 95DonEli-46
❑ 95DonEliCE-8
❑ 95DonEliDCS-46
❑ 95DonEliDCU-46
❑ 95DonIgn-5
❑ 95Emo-116
❑ 95EmoNteP-3
❑ 95Fin-50
❑ 95Fin-99
❑ 95FinnSemWC-97
❑ 95FinRef-50
❑ 95FinRef-99
❑ 95ImpSti-80
❑ 95Lea-193
❑ 95Lea-68
❑ 95LeaLim-75
❑ 95McDPin-MCD-5
❑ 95Met-97
❑ 95MetIW-8
❑ 95NHLAcePC-11C
❑ 95NHLCooT-5
❑ 95NHLCooT-RP5
❑ 95ParInt-136
❑ 95ParIntCCGS2-7
❑ 95ParIntCCSS2-7
❑ 95ParIntEl-136
❑ 95ParIntPTP-PP6
❑ 95ParIntPTP-PP12
❑ 95Pin-5
❑ 95PinArtP-5
❑ 95PinFan-18
❑ 95PinFirS-1
❑ 95PinFulC-12
❑ 95PinRinC-5
❑ 95PlaOneoOne-175
❑ 95PlaOneoOne-284
❑ 95ProMag-98
❑ 95Sco-50
❑ 95ScoBlaIce-50
❑ 95ScoBlaIceAP-50
❑ 95ScoDreTea-4
❑ 95ScoGolBla-15
❑ 95SelCer-14
❑ 95SelCerDS-15
❑ 95SelCerDSG-15
❑ 95SelCerMG-14
❑ 95SkyImp-111
❑ 95SkyImpCI-5
❑ 95SkyImpIQ-5
❑ 95SP-92
❑ 95SPHol-FX14
❑ 95SPHolSpFX-FX14
❑ 95SPStaEto-E19
❑ 95SPStaEtoG-E19
❑ 95StaClu-178
❑ 95StaCluM-M9
❑ 95StaCluMO-19
❑ 95StaCluMOMS-178
❑ 95StaCluNem-N8
❑ 95Sum-1
❑ 95SumArtP-1
❑ 95SumGM-16
❑ 95SumIce-1
❑ 95SweGloWC-84
❑ 95Top-5
❑ 95Top-240
❑ 95TopHomGC-HGC29
❑ 95TopMarMPB-5
❑ 95TopMysF-M3
❑ 95TopMysFR-M3
❑ 95TopOPCI-5
❑ 95TopOPCI-240
❑ 95TopPowL-3PL
❑ 95TopRinL-1RL
❑ 95TopSupSki-60
❑ 95TopSupSkiPla-60
❑ 95Ult-105
❑ 95Ult-393
❑ 95UltCreCra-11
❑ 95UltGolM-105
❑ 95UltPrePiv-5
❑ 95UltPrePivGM-5
❑ 95UppDec-169
❑ 95UppDec-217
❑ 95UppDecAGPRW-19
❑ 95UppDecElelce-169
❑ 95UppDecElelce-217
❑ 95UppDecElelceG-169
❑ 95UppDecElelceG-217
❑ 95UppDecFreFra-F7
❑ 95UppDecFreFraJ-F7
❑ 95UppDecNHLAS-AS16
❑ 95UppDecPHE-H9
❑ 95UppDecPRE-R39
❑ 95UppDecPRE-R56
❑ 95UppDecPreR-R39
❑ 95UppDecPreR-R56
❑ 95UppDecSpeE-SE141
❑ 95UppDecSpeEdiG-SE141
❑ 95UppPreHV-H9
❑ 95UppPreRP-R39
❑ 95UppPreRP-R56
❑ 95Zen-18
❑ 95ZenZT-5
❑ 96BeAPAut-111
❑ 96BeAPAutSil-111
❑ 96BeAPBisITB-19
❑ 96BeAPla-111
❑ 96ColCho-166
❑ 96ColCho-296
❑ 96ColCho-335
❑ 96ColChoCTG-C30A
❑ 96ColChoCTG-C30B
❑ 96ColChoCTG-C30C
❑ 96ColChoCTGE-CR30
❑ 96ColChoCTGEG-CR30
❑ 96ColChoCTGG-C30A
❑ 96ColChoCTGG-C30B
❑ 96ColChoCTGG-C30C
❑ 96ColChoSti-S10
❑ 96Don-16
❑ 96DonCanI-87
❑ 96DonCanIGPP-87
❑ 96DonCanIOC-3
❑ 96DonCanIRPP-87
❑ 96DonEli-22
❑ 96DonEliDCS-22
❑ 96DonEliIns-5
❑ 96DonEliInsG-5
❑ 96DonEliP-2
❑ 96DonHitLis-8
❑ 96DonPrePro-16
❑ 96Fla-61
❑ 96FlaBluI-61
❑ 96FlaHotN-9
❑ 96FlaNowAT-1
❑ 96Fle-71
❑ 96FleArtRos-15
❑ 96FlePCC-5
❑ 96FlePicF5-29
❑ 96HocGreC-15
❑ 96HocGreCG-15
❑ 96Lea-180
❑ 96LeaFirOI-15
❑ 96LeaLim-65
❑ 96LeaLimBTB-2
❑ 96LeaLimBTBLE-2
❑ 96LeaLimBTBP-P2
❑ 96LeaLimG-65
❑ 96LeaPre-66
❑ 96LeaPreP-180
❑ 96LeaPrePP-66
❑ 96LeaPreSG-42
❑ 96LeaPreSP-4
❑ 96LeaPreSte-42
❑ 96LeaSwe-8
❑ 96LeaSwe(-8
❑ 96MetUni-99
❑ 96MetUniCS-8
❑ 96MetUniCSSP-8
❑ 96MetUniLW-13
❑ 96MetUniLWSP-13
❑ 96NHLACEPC-32
❑ 96NHLProSTA-98
❑ 96Pin-2
❑ 96PinArtP-2
❑ 96PinByTN-12
❑ 96PinByTNP-12
❑ 96PinFan-FC6
❑ 96PinFoi-2
❑ 96PinMcD-22
❑ 96PinMin-16
❑ 96PinMinB-16
❑ 96PinMinCoiB-16
❑ 96PinMinCoiGP-16
❑ 96PinMinCoiN-16
❑ 96PinMinCoiS-16
❑ 96PinMinCoiSG-16
❑ 96PinMinG-16
❑ 96PinMinS-16
❑ 96PinPreS-2
❑ 96PinRinC-2
❑ 96PinTeaP-4
❑ 96PlaOneoOne-424
❑ 96Sco-24
❑ 96ScoArtPro-24
❑ 96ScoDeaCAP-24
❑ 96ScoDreTea-5
❑ 96ScoGolB-24
❑ 96ScoSpeAP-24
❑ 96ScoSudDea-10
❑ 96SelCer-36
❑ 96SelCerAP-36
❑ 96SelCerBlu-36
❑ 96SelCerCor-5
❑ 96SelCerMB-36
❑ 96SelCerMG-36
❑ 96SelCerMR-36
❑ 96SelCerRed-36
❑ 96SkyImp-82
❑ 96SkyImpB-14
❑ 96SP-98
❑ 96SPCleWin-CW11
❑ 96SPGamFil-GF10
❑ 96SPx-27
❑ 96SPxGol-27
❑ 96SPxHolH-HH5
❑ 96StaCluMO-40
❑ 96Sum-111
❑ 96SumArtP-111
❑ 96SumHigV-1
❑ 96SumHigVM-1
❑ 96SumIce-111
❑ 96SumMet-111
❑ 96SumPreS-111
❑ 96SweSemW-86
❑ 96TeaOut-20
❑ 96TopNHLP-25
❑ 96TopPic5C-FC6
❑ 96TopPicOI-25
❑ 96TopPicTS-TS5
❑ 96Ult-109
❑ 96UltCleTheIce-7
❑ 96UltGolM-110
❑ 96UltMr.Mom-8
❑ 96UppDec-299
❑ 96UppDecBD-100
❑ 96UppDecBDG-100
❑ 96UppDecBDRFTC-RC11
❑ 96UppDecGJ-GJ11
❑ 96UppDecHH-HH2
❑ 96UppDecHHG-HH2
❑ 96UppDecHHS-HH2
❑ 96UppDecIce-111
❑ 96UppDecIceDF-S1
❑ 96UppDecIcePar-111
❑ 96UppDecIceSCF-S1
❑ 96UppDecLSH-LS2
❑ 96UppDecLSHF-LS2
❑ 96UppDecLSHS-LS2
❑ 96UppDecSS-SS9A
❑ 96Zen-94
❑ 96ZenArtP-94
❑ 96ZenChaS-1
❑ 96ZenChaSD-1
❑ 97BeAPlaTAN-17
❑ 97BeAPMesDC-1
❑ 97BeAPMesDC-2
❑ 97ColCho-168
❑ 97ColChoSta-SQ49
❑ 97ColChoWD-W2
❑ 97Don-4
❑ 97DonCanI-50
❑ 97DonCanIDS-50
❑ 97DonCanINP-2
❑ 97DonCanIPS-50
❑ 97DonCanISCS-23
❑ 97DonEli-5
❑ 97DonEli-127
❑ 97DonEli-150
❑ 97DonEliAsp-5
❑ 97DonEliAsp-127
❑ 97DonEliAsp-150
❑ 97DonEliC-4
❑ 97DonEliMC-4
❑ 97DonEliPN-3A
❑ 97DonEliPN-3B
❑ 97DonEliPN-3C
❑ 97DonEliPNDC-3A
❑ 97DonEliPNDC-3B
❑ 97DonEliPNDC-3C
❑ 97DonEliS-5
❑ 97DonEliS-127
❑ 97DonEliS-150
❑ 97DonLim-25
❑ 97DonLim-84
❑ 97DonLim-187
❑ 97DonLimExp-25
❑ 97DonLimExp-84
❑ 97DonLimExp-187
❑ 97DonLimFOTG-44
❑ 97DonLimFOTG-59
❑ 97DonLin2L-23
❑ 97DonLin2LDC-23
❑ 97DonPre-7
❑ 97DonPre-177
❑ 97DonPreCttC-7
❑ 97DonPreCttC-177
❑ 97DonPreDWT-8
❑ 97DonPreLotT-7C
❑ 97DonPrePM-4
❑ 97DonPreProG-4
❑ 97DonPreProS-4
❑ 97DonPreT-15
❑ 97DonPreTB-15
❑ 97DonPreTBC-15
❑ 97DonPreTPC-15
❑ 97DonPreTPG-15
❑ 97DonPri-16
❑ 97DonPri-189
❑ 97DonPriDD-7
❑ 97DonPriODI-14
❑ 97DonPriP-6
❑ 97DonPriS-6
❑ 97DonPriSB-6
❑ 97DonPriSG-6
❑ 97DonPriSoA-16
❑ 97DonPriSoA-189
❑ 97DonPriSS-6
❑ 97EssOlyHH-20
❑ 97EssOlyHHF-20
❑ 97Kat-148
❑ 97KatGol-148
❑ 97KatSil-148
❑ 97Lea-9
❑ 97Lea-176
❑ 97LeaFirOnIce-11
❑ 97LeaFraMat-9
❑ 97LeaFraMat-176
❑ 97LeaFraMDC-9
❑ 97LeaFraMDC-176
❑ 97LeaInt-9
❑ 97LeaIntUI-9
❑ 97Pac-11
❑ 97Pac-CM1
❑ 97PacCarSup-13
❑ 97PacCarSupM-13
❑ 97PacCop-11
❑ 97PacCraChoAwa-8
❑ 97PacCroR-136
❑ 97PacCroRBoSDC-20
❑ 97PacCroREG-136
❑ 97PacCroRHTDC-19
❑ 97PacCroRIB-136
❑ 97PacCroRLCDC-20
❑ 97PacCroRS-136
❑ 97PacDyn-81
❑ 97PacDyn-140
❑ 97PacDynBKS-63
❑ 97PacDynC-81
❑ 97PacDynC-140
❑ 97PacDynDD-10B
❑ 97PacDynDG-81
❑ 97PacDynDG-140
❑ 97PacDynEG-81
❑ 97PacDynEG-140
❑ 97PacDynIB-81
❑ 97PacDynIB-140
❑ 97PacDynKotN-7
❑ 97PacDynR-81
❑ 97PacDynR-140
❑ 97PacDynSil-81
❑ 97PacDynSil-140
❑ 97PacDynTan-3
❑ 97PacDynTan-19
❑ 97PacEmeGre-11
❑ 97PacGolCroDC-16
❑ 97PacIceB-11
❑ 97PacInv-89
❑ 97PacInvAZ-16
❑ 97PacInvC-89
❑ 97PacInvEG-89
❑ 97PacInvFP-22
❑ 97PacInvIB-89
❑ 97PacInvNRB-131
❑ 97PacInvOTG-13
❑ 97PacInvR-89
❑ 97PacInvS-89
❑ 97PacOme-231
❑ 97PacOmeC-231
❑ 97PacOmeDG-231
❑ 97PacOmeEG-231
❑ 97PacOmeG-231
❑ 97PacOmeGFDCC-19
❑ 97PacOmeIB-231
❑ 97PacOmeSil-12
❑ 97PacOmeSLC-20
❑ 97PacOmeTL-20
❑ 97PacPar-190
❑ 97PacParBNDC-20
❑ 97PacParC-190
❑ 97PacParCG-12
❑ 97PacParDG-190
❑ 97PacParEG-190
❑ 97PacParIB-190
❑ 97PacParP-20
❑ 97PacParRed-190
❑ 97PacParSil-190
❑ 97PacRed-11
❑ 97PacRev-142
❑ 97PacRev1AGD-19
❑ 97PacRevC-142
❑ 97PacRevE-142
❑ 97PacRevIB-142
❑ 97PacRevR-142
❑ 97PacRevS-142
❑ 97PacSil-11
❑ 97PacSlaSDC-5B
❑ 97Pin-27

❑ 97Pin-194
❑ 97PinArtP-27
❑ 97PinBee-30
❑ 97PinBeeGP-30
❑ 97PinBeeGT-2
❑ 97PinBeeT-2
❑ 97PinCer-43
❑ 97PinCerGT-12
❑ 97PinCerMB-43
❑ 97PinCerMG-43
❑ 97PinCerMR-43
❑ 97PinCerR-43
❑ 97PinCerT-12
❑ 97PinEpiGO-12
❑ 97PinEpiGP-12
❑ 97PinEpiME-12
❑ 97PinEpiMO-12
❑ 97PinEpiMP-12
❑ 97PinEpiPE-12
❑ 97PinEpiPO-12
❑ 97PinEpiPP-12
❑ 97PinEpiSE-12
❑ 97PinEpiSO-12
❑ 97PinEpiSP-12
❑ 97PinIns-50
❑ 97PinInsC-21
❑ 97PinInsCC-50
❑ 97PinInsCG-21
❑ 97PinInsEC-50
❑ 97PinInsT-18
❑ 97PinMin-13
❑ 97PinMinB-13
❑ 97PinMinCBP-13
❑ 97PinMinCGPP-13
❑ 97PinMinCNSP-13
❑ 97PinMinCoiB-13
❑ 97PinMinCoiGP-13
❑ 97PinMinCoiN-13
❑ 97PinMinCoiSG-13
❑ 97PinMinCoiSS-13
❑ 97PinMinGolTea-13
❑ 97PinMinSilTea-13
❑ 97PinPowPac-9
❑ 97PinPrePBB-27
❑ 97PinPrePBB-194
❑ 97PinPrePBC-27
❑ 97PinPrePBC-194
❑ 97PinPrePBM-27
❑ 97PinPrePBM-194
❑ 97PinPrePBY-27
❑ 97PinPrePBY-194
❑ 97PinPrePFC-27
❑ 97PinPrePFC-194
❑ 97PinPrePFM-27
❑ 97PinPrePFM-194
❑ 97PinPrePFY-27
❑ 97PinPrePFY-194
❑ 97PinPrePla-27
❑ 97PinPrePla-194
❑ 97PinRinC-27
❑ 97PinTeaP-5
❑ 97PinTeaPM-5
❑ 97PinTeaPP-5
❑ 97PinTeaPPM-5
❑ 97PinTotCMPG-43
❑ 97PinTotCPB-43
❑ 97PinTotCPG-43
❑ 97PinTotCPR-43
❑ 97PosPin-5
❑ 97Sco-85
❑ 97ScoArtPro-85
❑ 97ScoCanPla-3
❑ 97ScoCanPre-3
❑ 97ScoCanu-3
❑ 97ScoGolBla-85
❑ 97SP AutI-I16
❑ 97SPAut-157
❑ 97SPAutID-I16
❑ 97SPAutIE-I16
❑ 97SPx-32
❑ 97SPxBro-32
❑ 97SPxDim-SPX3
❑ 97SPxGol-32
❑ 97SPxGraF-32
❑ 97SPxSil-32
❑ 97SPxSte-32
❑ 97Stu-9
❑ 97StuPor-9
❑ 97StuPrePG-9
❑ 97StuPrePS-9
❑ 97StuSil-6
❑ 97StuSil8-6
❑ 97TopHocMC-19
❑ 97TopHocMC-20
❑ 97UppDec-374
❑ 97UppDecBD-7
❑ 97UppDecBDDD-7
❑ 97UppDecBDPC-PC23
❑ 97UppDecBDPCDD-PC23
❑ 97UppDecBDPCM-PC23
❑ 97UppDecBDPCQD-PC23
❑ 97UppDecBDPCTD-PC23
❑ 97UppDecBDQD-7
❑ 97UppDecBDTD-7
❑ 97UppDecCtAG-14
❑ 97UppDecCtAG-AR14
❑ 97UppDecGDM-374
❑ 97UppDecIC-IC11
❑ 97UppDecIC2-IC11
❑ 97UppDecIce-71
❑ 97UppDecIceP-71
❑ 97UppDecILL-L3B
❑ 97UppDecILL2-L3B
❑ 97UppDecIPS-71
❑ 97UppDecSG-SG11
❑ 97UppDecSSM-SS11
❑ 97UppDecSSW-SS11
❑ 97UppDecTS-5
❑ 97UppDecTSL2-5
❑ 97UppDecTSS-11B
❑ 97Zen-16
❑ 97Zen5x7-64
❑ 97ZenGolImp-64
❑ 97ZenSilImp-64
❑ 97ZenZGol-16
❑ 97ZenZSil-16
❑ 98Be A PPA-290
❑ 98Be A PPAA-290
❑ 98Be A PPAAF-290
❑ 98Be A PPAGUSC-S10
❑ 98Be A PPAJ-AS10
❑ 98Be A PPAM-M2
❑ 98Be A PPAM-M8
❑ 98Be A PPPGUJC-G20
❑ 98Be A PPPH-H1
❑ 98Be A PPPPUJC-P17
❑ 98Be A PPSE-290
❑ 98Be APG-290
❑ 98BowBes-5
❑ 98BowBesAR-5
❑ 98BowBesR-5
❑ 98Fin-68
❑ 98FinDouMF-M41
❑ 98FinDouMF-M42
❑ 98FinDouMF-M43
❑ 98FinDouMF-M44
❑ 98FinDouSMFR-M41
❑ 98FinDouSMFR-M42
❑ 98FinDouSMFR-M43
❑ 98FinDouSMFR-M44
❑ 98FinNo P-68
❑ 98FinNo PR-68
❑ 98FinRedL-R18
❑ 98FinRedLR-R18
❑ 98FinRef-68
❑ 98O-PChr-138
❑ 98O-PChrBFtP-2
❑ 98O-PChrBFtPR-2
❑ 98O-PChrR-138
❑ 98Pac-11
❑ 98PacAur-189
❑ 98PacAurALC-19
❑ 98PacAurC-18
❑ 98PacAurCF-48
❑ 98PacAurCFC-48
❑ 98PacAurCFIB-48
❑ 98PacAurCFR-48
❑ 98PacAurCFS-48
❑ 98PacAurMAC-19
❑ 98PacCroR-135
❑ 98PacCroRLS-135
❑ 98PacCroRMP-19
❑ 98PacCroRPotG-24
❑ 98PacCroRPP-23
❑ 98PacDynI-189
❑ 98PacDynI-18
❑ 98PacDynIFT-19
❑ 98PacDynIIB-189
❑ 98PacDynIR-189
❑ 98PacDynITC-26
❑ 98PacEO P-20
❑ 98PacGolCD-34
❑ 98PacIceB-11
❑ 98PacOmeEP1o1-20
❑ 98PacOmeFtF-10
❑ 98PacOmeH-236
❑ 98PacOmeO-34
❑ 98PacOmeODI-236
❑ 98PacOmeP-20
❑ 98PacOmePI-10
❑ 98PacOmePIB-10
❑ 98PacOmeR-236
❑ 98PacPar-236
❑ 98PacParC-236
❑ 98PacParEG-236
❑ 98PacParH-236
❑ 98PacParHoFB-10
❑ 98PacParHoFBPP-10
❑ 98PacParIB-236
❑ 98PacParS-236
❑ 98PacParSDDC-19
❑ 98PacParTCD-26
❑ 98PacRed-11
❑ 98PacRev-141
❑ 98PacRevCTL-19
❑ 98PacRevIS-141
❑ 98PacRevR-141
❑ 98PacRevS-35
❑ 98PacTim-20
❑ 98PacTitI-18
❑ 98PinEpiGE-12
❑ 98SP Aut-85
❑ 98SP AutSM-S12
❑ 98SPxFin-160
❑ 98SPxFinR-160
❑ 98SPxFinS-160
❑ 98SPXTopP-57
❑ 98SPXTopPF-57
❑ 98SPXTopPPS-PS30
❑ 98SPXTopPR-57
❑ 98Top-138
❑ 98TopBlaFTP-2
❑ 98TopGolLC1-6
❑ 98TopGolLC1B-6
❑ 98TopGolLC1BOoO-6
❑ 98TopGolLC1OoO-6
❑ 98TopGolLC1R-6
❑ 98TopGolLC1ROoO-6
❑ 98TopGolLC2-6
❑ 98TopGolLC2B-6
❑ 98TopGolLC2BOoO-6
❑ 98TopGolLC2OoO-6
❑ 98TopGolLC2R-6
❑ 98TopGolLC2ROoO-6
❑ 98TopGolLC3-6
❑ 98TopGolLC3B-6
❑ 98TopGolLC3BOoO-6
❑ 98TopGolLC3OoO-6
❑ 98TopGolLC3R-6
❑ 98TopGolLC3ROoO-6
❑ 98TopLocL-L11
❑ 98TopMysFB-M19
❑ 98TopMysFBR-M19
❑ 98TopMysFG-M19
❑ 98TopMysFGR-M19
❑ 98TopMysFS-M19
❑ 98TopMysFSR-M19
❑ 98TopO-P-138
❑ 98UC-211
❑ 98UCMBH-BH9
❑ 98UCSB-SQ29
❑ 98UCSG-SQ29
❑ 98UCSG-SQ29
❑ 98UCSR-SQ29
❑ 98UD ChoPCR-211
❑ 98UD ChoR-211
❑ 98UD3-53
❑ 98UD3-113
❑ 98UD3-173
❑ 98UD3DieC-53
❑ 98UD3DieC-113
❑ 98UD3DieC-173
❑ 98UDCP-211
❑ 98UppDec-195
❑ 98UppDecBD-85
❑ 98UppDecDD-85
❑ 98UppDecE-195
❑ 98UppDecE1o1-195
❑ 98UppDecGR-195
❑ 98UppDecLSH-LS11
❑ 98UppDecLSHQ1-LS11
❑ 98UppDecLSHQ2-LS11
❑ 98UppDecLSHQ3-LS11
❑ 98UppDecM-201
❑ 98UppDecMGS-201
❑ 98UppDecMPG-PG7
❑ 98UppDecMSS-201
❑ 98UppDecMSS-201
❑ 98UppDecQD-85
❑ 98UppDecTD-85
❑ 98UppDecWFG-WF24
❑ 98UppDecWFP-WF24
❑ 99AurSty-20
❑ 99Pac-426
❑ 99PacAur-140
❑ 99PacAurPD-140
❑ 99PacCop-426
❑ 99PacGol-426
❑ 99PacGolCD-36
❑ 99PacIceB-426
❑ 99PacPreD-426
❑ 99PacTeaL-27
❑ 99RetHoc-77
❑ 99SP AutPS-85
❑ 99UppDecCL-12
❑ 99UppDecCLCLC-12
❑ 99UppDecM-204
❑ 99UppDecMGS-204
❑ 99UppDecMSS-204
❑ 99UppDecMSS-204
❑ 99UppDecRDR-DR6
❑ 99UppDecRDRI-DR6
❑ 99UppDecRG-77
❑ 99UppDecRP-77

**Messier, Mitch**
❑ 88ProIHL-66
❑ 89ProIHL-98
❑ 90ProAHLIHL-102
❑ 91ProAHLCHL-154
❑ 93ClaProPro-76

**Messuri, John**
❑ 89JohChi-21
❑ 91ProAHLCHL-439

**Meszaros, Dave**
❑ 84MonGolF-21
❑ 85MonGolF-5

**Metcalfe, Jason**
❑ 95Sla-244

**Metcalfe, Scott**
❑ 83KinCan-10
❑ 84KinCan-6
❑ 85KinCan-6
❑ 86KinCan-10
❑ 88OilTenAnn-127
❑ 88ProAHL-258
❑ 89ProAHL-262
❑ 90ProAHLIHL-267
❑ 93KnoChe-10
❑ 95RochAmeSS-12
❑ 98GerDELE-190

**Methot, Francois**
❑ 95BowDraPro-P25
❑ 95UppDec-521
❑ 95UppDecEleIce-521
❑ 95UppDecEleIceG-521
❑ 97BowCHL-57
❑ 97BowCHLOPC-57
❑ 98BowCHL-95
❑ 98BowCHLGA-95
❑ 98BowCHLOI-95
❑ 98BowChrC-95
❑ 98BowChrCGA-95
❑ 98BowChrCGAR-95
❑ 98BowChrCOI-95
❑ 98BowChrCOIR-95
❑ 98BowChrCR-95

**Metlicka, Pavel**
❑ 95CzeAPSE-259

**Metlyuk, Denis**
❑ 91UppDec-653
❑ 91UppDecCWJC-14
❑ 91UppDecF-653
❑ 92Cla-45
❑ 94Cla-91
❑ 94ClaDraGol-91
❑ 94ClaProP-215
❑ 94ClaTri-T49
❑ 96ClaGol-45

**Metro, Rich**
❑ 93WatBlaH-19

**Metro, Terry**
❑ 91AirCanSJHL-C22

**Mettavainio, Jan Ove**
❑ 85SwePanS-52
❑ 86SwePanS-39
❑ 87SwePanS-51
❑ 89SweSemE-149
❑ 90SweSemE-232

**Mettovaara, Sami**
❑ 93FinnJyvHS-177
❑ 93FinnSIS-176
❑ 94FinnSIS-44
❑ 95FinnSIS-337

**Metz, Don**
❑ 34BeeGro1P-339
❑ 39OPCV3011-8
❑ 40OPCV3012-111
❑ 44BeeGro2P-433
❑ 45QuaOatP-36A
❑ 45QuaOatP-36B
❑ 45QuaOatP-36C

**Metz, Nick**
❑ 34BeeGro1P-340
❑ 35OPCV304C-84
❑ 36TriPos-6
❑ 36V356WorG-28
❑ 37OPCV304E-144
❑ 38QuaOatP-25
❑ 39OPCV3011-51
❑ 40OPCV3012-133
❑ 40OPCV3012-141
❑ 44BeeGro2P-434
❑ 45QuaOatP-37A
❑ 45QuaOatP-37B
❑ 45QuaOatP-37C

**Meulenbroeks, John**
❑ 83BraAle-28
❑ 85MonGolF-21

**Meunier, Yves**
❑ 907thInnSQMJHL-204
❑ 917thInnSQMJHL-22
❑ 917thInnSQMJHL-59

**Meurer, Peter**
❑ 24CreSel-13

**Mews, Harry**
❑ 90HamRoaA-56
❑ 91ProAHLCHL-565
❑ 92HamRoaA-15

**Meyer, D.**
❑ 95GerDELE-72
❑ 95GerDELE-432

**Meyer, Fritz**
❑ 94GerDELE-14
❑ 95GerDELE-5

**Meyer, Jayson**
❑ 81RegPat-11
❑ 82RegPat-21
❑ 83RegPat-21
❑ 94FinnJaaK-276
❑ 95FinnSemWC-167
❑ 95GerDELE-202
❑ 96GerDELE-343
❑ 96SweSemW-195
❑ 98GerDELE-30

**Meyers, Dan**
❑ 91AirCanSJHL-A2

**Mezin, Andrei**
❑ 95FliGen-13
❑ 98GerDELE-249

**Micalef, Corrado**
❑ 83OPC-116
❑ 83OPC-126
❑ 83OPCSti-147
❑ 85OPC-200

**Michaels, J.J.**
❑ 96AncAce-7

**Michalchuk, Chad**
❑ 917thInnSWHL-114
❑ 91SasBla-15

**Michalek, Vladimir**
❑ 95CzeAPSE-238

**Michaud, Dany**
❑ 917thInnSQMJHL-229

**Michaud, Mark**
❑ 87BroBra-7
❑ 93HamRoaA-1
❑ 94BirBul-18

**Michayluk, Dave**
❑ 81RegPat-20
❑ 83SprInd-11
❑ 88ProIHL-57
❑ 89ProIHL-153
❑ 90ProAHLIHL-389
❑ 91ProAHLCHL-288
❑ 92CleLum-13
❑ 93ClaProPro-123
❑ 93CleLum-19
❑ 93CleLumPos-14
❑ 95CleLum-18
❑ 96CleLum-17

**Michel, Steffen**
❑ 94GerDELE-278
❑ 95GerDELE-269

**Micheletti, Joe**
❑ 81RocPos-19
❑ 82PosCer-11

**Michelin, Leon**
❑ 52JunBluT-36

**Micheller, Klaus**
❑ 94GerDELE-239
❑ 95GerDELE-223
❑ 96GerDELE-74

**Michie, Jack**
❑ 69SeaTotW-9

**Michon, Michel**
❑ 907thInnSWHL-332

**Miciak, Darren**
❑ 89HamRoaA-16
❑ 91ProAHLCHL-435
❑ 94CenHocL-53

**Mick, Troy**
❑ 86PorWinH-14
❑ 87PorWinH-15
❑ 88PorWinH-15
❑ 89RegPat-12
❑ 90KnoChe-113
❑ 91KnoChe-16
❑ 92NasKni-21

**Mickey, Larry**
❑ 68OPC-195
❑ 69MapLeaWBG-23
❑ 70DadCoo-85
❑ 70EssPowPla-154
❑ 70OPC-162
❑ 70SarProSta-74
❑ 71OPC-167
❑ 71SarProSta-149
❑ 71TorSun-204
❑ 73SabPos-8
❑ 74NHLActSta-44

**Mickolajak, Todd**
❑ 93MinDul-20

**Mickoski, Nick**
❑ 44BeeGro2P-345
❑ 51Par-97
❑ 52Par-101
❑ 53Par-62
❑ 54Par-75
❑ 54Top-29
❑ 57Top-32
❑ 58Top-27
❑ 59Top-37
❑ 59Top-53
❑ 94ParMisL-25

**Micuda, Miroslav**
❑ 95SloPeeWT-17

**Miculinic, Jeremy**
❑ 94SarSti-7
❑ 95Cla-82
❑ 95Sla-28

**Middendorf, Max**
❑ 84SudWol-12
❑ 85SudWol-22
❑ 86SudWol-22
❑ 87NordGenF-21
❑ 88ProAHL-113
❑ 89HalCit-15
❑ 89ProAHL-172
❑ 91ProAHLCHL-217

**Middlebrook, Lindsay**
❑ 88OilTenAnn-102

**Middleton, Marcus**
❑ 89SudWol-12
❑ 907thInnSOHL-40

**Middleton, Rick**
❑ 74NHLActStaU-26
❑ 74OPCNHL-304
❑ 75OPCNHL-37
❑ 75Top-37
❑ 76OPCNHL-127
❑ 76Top-127
❑ 77OPCNHL-246
❑ 77Top-246
❑ 78OPC-113
❑ 78Top-113
❑ 79OPC-10
❑ 79Top-10
❑ 80OPC-94
❑ 80OPC-251
❑ 80Top-94
❑ 80Top-251
❑ 81OPC-2
❑ 81OPC-18
❑ 81OPC-19
❑ 81OPCSti-45
❑ 81Top-22
❑ 81Top-46
❑ 81Top-E129
❑ 82McDSti-9
❑ 82OPC-6
❑ 82OPC-15
❑ 82OPCSti-78
❑ 82OPCSti-79
❑ 82OPCSti-262
❑ 82PosCer-1
❑ 83BruTeaIss-11
❑ 83OPC-43
❑ 83OPC-54
❑ 83OPC-214
❑ 83OPCSti-14
❑ 83OPCSti-45
❑ 83OPCSti-329
❑ 83OPCSti-330
❑ 83PufSti-10
❑ 847EDis-2
❑ 84KelAccD-3A
❑ 84KelAccD-3B
❑ 84OPC-9
❑ 84OPC-352
❑ 84OPCSti-142
❑ 84OPCSti-181
❑ 84OPCSti-182
❑ 84Top-8
❑ 857ECreCar-1
❑ 85OPC-64
❑ 85OPCSti-159
❑ 85Top-64
❑ 86OPC-157
❑ 86OPCSti-35
❑ 86Top-157
❑ 87OPC-115
❑ 87OPCSti-138
❑ 87PanSti-12
❑ 87Top-115
❑ 88BruPos-12
❑ 88BruSpoA-13
❑ 88OPC-87
❑ 88OPCSti-26
❑ 88Top-87
❑ 91BruSpoAL-17

**Midgley, Jim**
❑ 95Sla-213

**Miehm, Kevin**
❑ 89ProIHL-11
❑ 90ProAHLIHL-93
❑ 91ProAHLCHL-28
❑ 92PeoRivC-17
❑ 92UppDec-543
❑ 93ClaProPro-63
❑ 93Par-447
❑ 93ParEmeI-447
❑ 93TopPreG-264G
❑ 93Ult-205
❑ 93UltPro-6
❑ 95ColEdgI-128

**Mielczarek, Ted**
❑ 86SudWol-1
❑ 87SudWol-2
❑ 88SudWol-3

**Mielko, Brian**
❑ 917thInnSOHL-118

**Miettinen, Tommi**
❑ 93FinnJyvHS-173
❑ 93Par-522
❑ 93ParEmeI-522
❑ 94Fin-133
❑ 94FinnSIS-86
❑ 94FinnSISJ-3
❑ 94FinnSISND-7
❑ 94FinRef-133
❑ 94FinSupTW-133
❑ 94ParSE-SE221
❑ 94ParSEG-SE221
❑ 95FinnSemWC-236
❑ 95FinnSIS-330
❑ 96FinnSISR-144

**Migay, Rudy**
❑ 44BeeGro2P-435
❑ 45QuaOatP-38
❑ 52Par-96
❑ 53Par-17
❑ 54Par-21
❑ 55Par-12
❑ 55ParQuaO-12
❑ 57Par-T6
❑ 60ShiCoi-18
❑ 94ParMisL-111

**Migdal, Thomas**
❑ 99WicThu-16

**Mignacca, Sonny**
❑ 907thInnSWHL-23
❑ 917thInnSWHL-314

**Migneault, John**
❑ 75RoaPhoWHA-18

**Mihalik, Tomas**
❑ 95SloPeeWT-18

**Miikkulainen, Jarno**
❑ 93FinnJyvHS-351
❑ 93FinnSIS-213
❑ 94FinnSIS-80
❑ 95FinnSIS-152
❑ 95FinnSIS-300

**Mikaelsson, Par**
❑ 89SweSemE-214

**Mikesch, Jeff**
❑ 93MicTecH-16

**Mikesch, Pat**
❑ 93MicTecH-1
❑ 96KenTho-13
❑ 98FloEve-15

**Mikhailov, Boris**
❑ 69SweHocS-9
❑ 69SweWorC-128
❑ 69SweWorC-131
❑ 70SweHocS-119
❑ 70SweHocS-326
❑ 71SweHocS-37
❑ 72SweSemWC-13
❑ 73SweHocS-86
❑ 73SweWorCS-86
❑ 74SweHocS-7
❑ 74SweSemHVS-33
❑ 79PanSti-150
❑ 80USSOlyTMP-6
❑ 91FutTreC72-43
❑ 95SweGloWC-243

**Mikhailovsky, Maxim**
❑ 90OPCRedA-9R
❑ 91OPCIns-22R
❑ 92RusStaRA-20

**Mikita, Stan**
❑ 44BeeGro2P-125
❑ 60ShiCoi-71
❑ 60Top-14
❑ 60TopSta-36
❑ 61ShiCoi-22
❑ 61Top-36
❑ 62ShiMetC-46
❑ 62Top-34
❑ 62TopHocBuc-17
❑ 63ChePho-39
❑ 63Top-36
❑ 63TorSta-26
❑ 64BeeGro3P-49
❑ 64CocCap-35
❑ 64Top-31
❑ 64Top-106
❑ 64TorSta-33
❑ 65Coc-35
❑ 65Top-60
❑ 66Top-62
❑ 66Top-124
❑ 66TopUSAT-62
❑ 67GenMil-4
❑ 67Top-64
❑ 67Top-114
❑ 67Top-126
❑ 68Bla-5
❑ 68OPC-155
❑ 68OPC-202
❑ 68OPC-211
❑ 68OPCPucSti-1
❑ 68ShiCoi-25
❑ 68Top-20
❑ 69OPC-76
❑ 69OPCFou-13
❑ 69OPCSta-21
❑ 69Top-76
❑ 70BlaBor-3
❑ 70BlaBor-9
❑ 70DadCoo-86
❑ 70EssPowPla-125
❑ 70OPC-20
❑ 70OPC-240
❑ 70SarProSta-48
❑ 70Top-20
❑ 70TopStiS-23
❑ 71Baz-35
❑ 71ColHea-2
❑ 71LetActR-10
❑ 71OPC-125
❑ 71SarProSta-33
❑ 71Top-125
❑ 71TorSun-76
❑ 72KellroT-6
❑ 72OPC-156
❑ 72OPC-177
❑ 72OPCPlaC-5
❑ 72OPCTeaC-19
❑ 72SarProSta-63
❑ 72SweSemWC-227
❑ 72Top-56
❑ 73OPC-6
❑ 73Top-145
❑ 74NHLActSta-81
❑ 74OPCNHL-20
❑ 74OPCNHL-69
❑ 74Top-20
❑ 74Top-69
❑ 75OPCNHL-30
❑ 75OPCNHL-317
❑ 75Top-30
❑ 75Top-317
❑ 76OPCNHL-225
❑ 76Top-225
❑ 77OPCNHL-195
❑ 77Spo-4
❑ 77Top-195
❑ 78OPC-75
❑ 78Top-75
❑ 79OPC-155
❑ 79Top-155
❑ 81TCMA-13
❑ 83HalFP-O11
❑ 85HalFC-226
❑ 88EssAllSta-31
❑ 90ProSet-405
❑ 90ProSet-665
❑ 91FutTreC72-61
❑ 92HalFL-15
❑ 92ZelMasH-5
❑ 92ZelMasoHS-5
❑ 93AmeLicSPC-4
❑ 93UppDecLAS-46
❑ 94HocWit-39
❑ 94ParMisLFS-FS3
❑ 94ParTalB-26
❑ 94ParTalB-138
❑ 94ParTalB-147
❑ 94ParTalB-170
❑ 94ParTalBM-SL2
❑ 94ParTalBM-TW3
❑ 95Par66-24
❑ 95Par66-125
❑ 95Par66-PR125
❑ 95Par66Coi-24
❑ 95Par66P-4
❑ 97PinBee-59
❑ 97PinBeeGOA-59
❑ 97PinBeeGP-59
❑ 98O-PChrBFtP-8
❑ 98O-PChrBFtPR-8
❑ 98TopBlaFTP-8
❑ 98TopBlaFTPA-8

□ 99RetHoc-91
□ 99UppDecCL-18
□ 99UppDecCLCLC-18
□ 99UppDecES-11
□ 99UppDecRG-G7A
□ 99UppDecRG-91
□ 99UppDecRGI-G7A
□ 99UppDecRII-SM
□ 99UppDecRIL1-SM
□ 99UppDecRP-91
**Mikkelson, Bill**
□ 72OPC-79
□ 72Top-118
□ 74CapWhiB-20
□ 74NHLActSta-307
□ 74OPCNHL-23
□ 74Top-23
□ 75OPCNHL-207
□ 75Top-207
**Mikko, Ingemar**
□ 84SweSemE-187
**Mikko, Roger**
□ 84SweSemE-188
□ 85SwePanS-163
□ 86SwePanS-182
**Mikkola, Iikka**
□ 98SPXTopP-71
□ 98SPXTopPF-71
□ 98SPXTopPR-71
□ 98UppDecDD-98
□ 98UppDecDD-98
□ 98UppDecQD-98
□ 98UppDecTD-98
**Mikkola, Niko**
□ 93FinnSIS-50
□ 94FinnSIS-88
□ 95FinnSemWC-240
**Mikkolainen, Reijo**
□ 89SweSemWCS-38
□ 93FinnSIS-53
□ 94FinnSIS-206
□ 95FinnSIS-37
□ 95FinnSIS-187
**Miklenda, Jaroslav**
□ 93Par-519
□ 93ParEmel-519
□ 93UppDec-573
**Mikol, Jim**
□ 44BeeGro2P-436
□ 60CleBar-14
□ 64BeeGro3P-142
□ 64CocCap-82
□ 64Top-36
□ 94ParTalB-99
**Mikolasek, Tomas**
□ 94CzeAPSE-66
□ 95CzeAPSE-92
□ 96CzeAPSE-88
**Mikulchik, Oleg**
□ 95UppDec-471
**Mikus, Tomas**
□ 96SloPeeWT-18
**Milani, Tom**
□ 77KalWin-9
□ 82SweSemHVS-138
**Milanovic, Ryan**
□ 96KitRan-19
**Milbury, Mike**
□ 77OPCNHL-134
□ 77Top-134
□ 78OPC-59
□ 78Top-59
□ 79OPC-114
□ 79Top-114
□ 80OPC-191
□ 80Top-191
□ 81OPC-16
□ 82PosCer-1
□ 83BruTealss-12
□ 83OPC-55
□ 84OPC-10
□ 87PanSti-8
□ 90ProSet-560
□ 92FutTrePS-1
□ 96IslPos-15
**Mild, Hans**
□ 65SweCorI-127
**Milford, Jake (John C)**
□ 85HalFC-253
**Milhench, Keith**
□ 97KinHaw-1
**Mill, Jim**
□ 92RalIce-8
□ 92RalIce-29
□ 93HunBli-17
□ 93RoaExp-13
**Millar, Aaron**
□ 95MedHatT-10
□ 96MedHatT-12
**Millar, Al**
□ 56QueAce-11
□ 66TulOil-8
**Millar, Craig**
□ 95SwiCurB-10
□ 97Be A PPAD-239
□ 97Be A PPAPD-239
□ 97BeAPla-239
□ 97SPAut-182
□ 98Pac-215
□ 98PacIceB-215
□ 98PacOmeH-98
□ 98PacOmeODI-98
□ 98PacOmeR-98
□ 98PacRed-215

□ 98UppDec-95
□ 98UppDecE-95
□ 98UppDecE1o1-95
□ 98UppDecGR-95
**Millar, Mike**
□ 83BraAle-20
□ 88ProAHL-47
□ 89BruSpoAU-6
□ 89ProAHL-67
□ 90NewSai-15
□ 90ProAHLIHL-168
□ 94GerDELE-159
□ 95GerDELE-159
□ 96GerDELE-235
**Millen, Corey**
□ 89ProIHL-44
□ 89RanMarMB-23
□ 91Bow-60
□ 91OPC-461
□ 91Par-292
□ 91ParFre-292
□ 91ProSetPla-185
□ 91ScoAme-318
□ 91ScoCan-348
□ 91StaClu-71
□ 91Top-461
□ 91UppDec-604
□ 91UppDecF-110
□ 91UppDecF-604
□ 92Bow-57
□ 92OPC-334
□ 92PanSti-70
□ 92ParStiFre-70
□ 92Par-306
□ 92ParEmel-306
□ 92Pin-138
□ 92PinFre-138
□ 92Sco-111
□ 92ScoCan-111
□ 92ScoSha-26
□ 92ScoShaCan-26
□ 92StaClu-296
□ 92Top-326
□ 92TopGol-326G
□ 92Ult-86
□ 92UppDec-48
□ 93Don-181
□ 93Lea-361
□ 93OPCPre-493
□ 93OPCPreG-493
□ 93PanSti-207
□ 93Par-381
□ 93ParEmel-381
□ 93Pin-350
□ 93PinCan-350
□ 93Pow-379
□ 93Sco-62
□ 93ScoCan-62
□ 93ScoCan-519
□ 93ScoGol-519
□ 93StaClu-437
□ 93StaCluFDI-437
□ 93StaCluO-437
□ 93TopPre-493
□ 93TopPreG-493
□ 93Ult-361
□ 93UppDec-483
□ 93UppDecSP-84
□ 94CanGamNHLP-147
□ 94Don-148
□ 94Lea-187
□ 94Par-122
□ 94ParGol-122
□ 94Pin-425
□ 94PinArtP-425
□ 94PinRinC-425
□ 94Sco-99
□ 94ScoGol-99
□ 94ScoPla-99
□ 94ScoPlaTS-99
□ 94StaPos-18
□ 94Ult-120
□ 94UppDec-25
□ 94UppDecEleIce-25
□ 95CanGamNHLP-84
□ 95ColCho-274
□ 95ColChoPC-274
□ 95ColChoPCP-274
□ 95ParInt-304
□ 95ParIntEI-304
□ 95Sco-172
□ 95ScoBlaIce-172
□ 95ScoBlaIceAP-172
□ 95UppDec-105
□ 95UppDecEleIce-105
□ 95UppDecEleIceG-105
□ 96UppDec-231
□ 97Pac-107
□ 97PacCop-107
□ 97PacEmeGre-107
□ 97PacIceB-107
□ 97PacRed-107
□ 97PacSil-107
□ 98GerDELE-87
**Millen, Greg**
□ 79OPC-281
□ 80OPC-158
□ 80Top-158
□ 81OPC-134
□ 81Top-E115
□ 82OPC-126
□ 82OPCSti-130
□ 82PosCer-7

□ 82WhaJunHC-12
□ 83OPC-143
□ 83OPCSti-262
□ 83PufSti-16
□ 84OPC-75
□ 84OPCSti-198
□ 84Top-58
□ 84WhaJunW-12
□ 85OPC-221
□ 85OPCSti-51
□ 87BluKod-18
□ 87BluTealss-15
□ 88BluKod-29
□ 88BluTealss-15
□ 88OPC-117
□ 88PanSti-100
□ 88Top-117
□ 89Nord-31
□ 89OPC-137
□ 89OPC-314
□ 89PanSti-129
□ 89Top-137
□ 90BlaCok-18
□ 90Bow-3
□ 90BowTif-3
□ 90OPC-335
□ 90PanSti-188
□ 90ProSet-56
□ 90Sco-42
□ 90ScoCan-42
□ 90Top-335
□ 90TopTif-335
□ 90UppDec-213
□ 90UppDecF-213
**Miller, Aaron**
□ 94ClaProP-105
□ 95ColEdgI-29
□ 97Be A PPAD-75
□ 97Be A PPAPD-75
□ 97BeAPla-75
□ 97BeAPlaAut-75
□ 97Pac-317
□ 97PacCop-317
□ 97PacEmeGre-317
□ 97PacIceB-317
□ 97PacRed-317
□ 97PacSil-317
□ 97UppDec-258
□ 99Pac-111
□ 99PacCop-111
□ 99PacGol-111
□ 99PacIceB-111
□ 99PacPreD-111
**Miller, Al**
□ 51LavDaiQSHL-57
□ 51LavDaiS-7
**Miller, Aren**
□ 95SpoChi-30
□ 97BeeAutA-70
□ 97PinBee-70
□ 97PinBeeGP-70
**Miller, Bobby (Bob)**
□ 79OPC-196
□ 79Top-196
□ 80OPC-236
□ 80Top-236
□ 81RocPos-20
□ 82PosCer-11
□ 84KinSmo-20
**Miller, Brad**
□ 86RegPat-19
□ 87RegPat-20
□ 88RegPat-16
□ 88SabWonBH-17
□ 89ProAHL-264
□ 90ProAHLIHL-272
□ 90ProSet-591
□ 90SabCam-17
□ 91Par-243
□ 91ParFre-243
□ 91ProSet-354
□ 91ProSetFre-354
□ 91RochAmeKod-19
□ 91SabBluS-13
□ 91SabPepC-13
□ 92St.JohML-14
□ 92StaClu-475
□ 93Par-306
□ 93ParEmel-306
□ 98LasVegT-14
**Miller, Colin**
□ 88NiaFalT-13
□ 89SauSteMG-11
□ 907thInnSOHL-169
□ 917thInnSMC-20
□ 917thInnSOHL-321
□ 95DayBom-13
□ 96DayBom-24
**Miller, Cory**
□ 96MinGolGCAS-20
**Miller, Dennis**
□ 91ProAHLICHL-434
□ 95ForWorFT-17
**Miller, Gary**
□ 897thInnSOHL-160
□ 907thInnSOHL-312
□ 917thInnSOHL-89
**Miller, Gus**
□ 92BriColJHL-228
**Miller, Jason**
□ 907thInnSWHL-28
□ 90UppDec-335
□ 90UppDecF-335
□ 90OPC-163
□ 91ProAHLCHL-420

□ 91ScoAme-312
□ 91ScoCan-342
□ 91Top-163
□ 91ClaProPro-13
□ 95FinnSIS-222
□ 95FinnSIS-377
□ 95PeoRiv-11
□ 98GerDELE-254
**Miller, Jay**
□ 85MonGolF-23
□ 87PanSti-18
□ 88BruSpoA-14
□ 88PanSti-212
□ 89KinSmo-15
□ 90KinSmo-16
□ 90UppDec-414
□ 90UppDecF-414
□ 91Bow-198
□ 91OPC-467
□ 91ProSet-402
□ 91ProSetFre-402
□ 91ScoCan-543
□ 91StaClu-63
□ 91Top-467
**Miller, Keith**
□ 88ProAHL-107
□ 89ProIHL-137
**Miller, Kelly**
□ 86CapKod-17
□ 87CapKod-10
□ 87CapTealss-16
□ 87OPC-189
□ 87PanSti-186
□ 87Top-189
□ 88CapBor-14
□ 88CapSmo-14
□ 88OPC-130
□ 88PanSti-373
□ 88Top-130
□ 89CapKod-10
□ 89CapTealss-17
□ 89OPC-131
□ 89OPCSti-74
□ 89PanSti-348
□ 89Top-131
□ 90Bow-76
□ 90BowTif-76
□ 90CapKod-17
□ 90CapPos-17
□ 90CapSmo-17
□ 90OPC-81
□ 90OPCPre-72
□ 90PanSti-156
□ 90ProSet-318
□ 90Sco-168
□ 90ScoCan-168
□ 90Top-81
□ 90TopTif-81
□ 90UppDec-130
□ 90UppDecF-130
□ 91Bow-292
□ 91CapJun5-21
□ 91CapKod-21
□ 91OPC-342
□ 91PanSti-202
□ 91Par-414
□ 91ParFre-414
□ 91Pin-23
□ 91PinFre-23
□ 91Pin-372
□ 91PinFre-372
□ 91ProSet-611
□ 91ProSetFre-611
□ 91ProSetFre-615
□ 91ScoAme-81
□ 91ScoAme-309
□ 91ScoCan-81
□ 91ScoCan-339
□ 91StaClu-106
□ 91Top-342
□ 91UppDec-133
□ 91UppDecF-133
□ 92Bow-338
□ 92CapKod-21
□ 92OPC-142
□ 92PanSti-166
□ 92PanStiFre-166
□ 92Pin-160
□ 92PinFre-160
□ 92Sco-55
□ 92ScoCan-55
□ 92ScoUSAG-14
□ 92StaClu-361
□ 92Top-429
□ 92TopGol-479G
□ 92Ult-236
□ 92UppDec-179
□ 93Don-365
□ 93Lea-254
□ 93OPCPre-474
□ 93OPCPreG-474
□ 93PanSti-30
□ 93Par-491
□ 93ParEmel-491
□ 93Pin-284
□ 93Pow-468
□ 93Sco-30
□ 93ScoCan-30
□ 93StaClu-17
□ 93StaCluFDI-17
□ 93StaCluFDIO-17

□ 93StaCluO-17
□ 93TopPre-474
□ 93TopPreG-474
□ 93Ult-88
□ 93UppDec-384
□ 94CanGamNHLP-247
□ 94Don-52
□ 94Lea-519
□ 94OPCPre-222
□ 94OPCPreSE-222
□ 94Par-256
□ 94ParGol-256
□ 94Pin-158
□ 94PinArtP-158
□ 94PinRinC-158
□ 94Sco-63
□ 94ScoGol-63
□ 94ScoPla-63
□ 94ScoPlaTS-63
□ 94TopPre-222
□ 94TopPreSE-222
□ 94Ult-390
□ 94UppDec-151
□ 94UppDecEleIce-151
□ 95CanGamNHLP-280
□ 95Cap-18
□ 95ColCho-82
□ 95ColChoPC-82
□ 95ColChoPCP-82
□ 95Don-159
□ 95ParInt-219
□ 95ParIntEI-219
□ 95PlaOneoOne-324
□ 95Sco-271
□ 95ScoBlaIce-271
□ 95ScoBlaIceAP-271
□ 95Top-126
□ 95TopOPCI-126
□ 95UppDec-346
□ 95UppDecEleIce-346
□ 95UppDecEleIceG-346
□ 96BeAPAut-46
□ 96BeAPAutSil-46
□ 96BeAPla-46
□ 97PacInvNRB-211
□ 98PacIceB-444
□ 98PacRed-444
**Miller, Kevin**
□ 89ProIHL-29
□ 90OPCPre-73
□ 90ProSet-493
□ 90ScoRoo-18T
□ 90UppDec-444
□ 90UppDecF-444
□ 91Bow-57
□ 91OPC-125
□ 91Par-40
□ 91ParFre-40
□ 91Pin-133
□ 91PinFre-133
□ 91ProSet-60
□ 91ProSetFre-60
□ 91ProSetPla-168
□ 91ScoAme-126
□ 91ScoAme-309
□ 91ScoCan-126
□ 91ScoCan-339
□ 91ScoYouS-40
□ 91StaClu-286
□ 91Top-125
□ 91UppDec-142
□ 91UppDecF-142
□ 92Bow-391
□ 92OPC-291
□ 92PanSti-115
□ 92PanStiFre-115
□ 92Pin-313
□ 92PinFre-313
□ 92Sco-229
□ 92ScoCan-229
□ 92StaClu-229
□ 92Top-129
□ 92TopGol-129G
□ 92Ult-396
□ 92UppDec-482
□ 93Don-298
□ 93Lea-192
□ 93OPCPre-8
□ 93OPCPreG-8
□ 93Par-178
□ 93ParEmel-178
□ 93Pin-126
□ 93PinCan-126
□ 93Sco-89
□ 93ScoCan-89
□ 93StaClu-193
□ 93StaCluFDI-193
□ 93StaCluFDIO-193
□ 93StaCluO-193
□ 93TopPre-8
□ 93TopPreG-8
□ 93Ult-218
□ 93UppDec-408
□ 94CanGamNHLP-205
□ 94Don-11
□ 94FinnJaaK-116
□ 94Lea-129
□ 94OPCPre-21
□ 94OPCPreSE-21
□ 94ParSE-SE150
□ 94ParSEG-SE150
□ 94Pin-289
□ 94PinArtP-289

□ 94PinRinC-289
□ 94Sco-25
□ 94ScoGol-25
□ 94ScoPla-25
□ 94ScoPlaTS-25
□ 94TopPre-21
□ 94TopPreSE-21
□ 94Ult-186
□ 94UppDec-451
□ 94UppDecEleIce-451
□ 95CanGamNHLP-224
□ 95ColCho-275
□ 95ColChoPC-275
□ 95ColChoPCP-275
□ 95Pin-146
□ 95PinArtP-146
□ 95PinRinC-146
□ 95SweGloWC-119
□ 96BeAPAut-165
□ 96BeAPAutSil-165
□ 96BeAPla-165
□ 96Pin-15
□ 96PinArtP-15
□ 96PinFoi-15
□ 96PinPreS-15
□ 96PinRinC-15
□ 96UppDec-236
□ 97ColCho-50
□ 97Pac-46
□ 97PacCop-46
□ 97PacEmeGre-46
□ 97PacIceB-46
□ 97PacRed-46
□ 97PacSil-46
**Miller, Kip**
□ 90HalCit-17
□ 90ProAHLIHL-452
□ 90Sco-330A
□ 90Sco-330B
□ 90ScoCan-330A
□ 90ScoCan-330B
□ 90UppDec-522
□ 90UppDecF-522
□ 91Bow-139
□ 91NordPet-19
□ 91OPC-387
□ 91OPCPre-42
□ 91Par-142
□ 91ParFre-142
□ 91Pin-306
□ 91PinFre-306
□ 91ProSet-555
□ 91ProSetFre-555
□ 91ScoAme-384
□ 91ScoCan-274
□ 91Top-387
□ 91UppDec-431
□ 91UppDecF-431
□ 92UppDec-35
□ 92UppDec-247
□ 93UppDec-421
□ 95ColEdgI-138
□ 95IndIce-15
□ 99Pac-343
□ 99PacGol-343
□ 99PacIceB-343
□ 99PacPreD-343
**Miller, Kris**
□ 91ProAHLCHL-394
□ 92RalIce-9
□ 92RalIce-26
**Miller, Kurt**
□ 91LakSupSL-19
□ 95AdiRedW-15
**Miller, Lucas**
□ 94KitRan-23
**Miller, Mark**
□ 97LouRivF-25
**Miller, Nate**
□ 96MinGolGCAS-21
**Miller, Paul**
□ 83MonAlp-15
**Miller, Perry**
□ 75OPCWHA-6
□ 78OPC-16
□ 78Top-16
□ 79OPC-157
□ 79Top-157
□ 81OPC-101
**Miller, Rod**
□ 93MinDul-21
**Miller, Scott**
□ 92WinSpi-23
**Miller, Todd**
□ 95Sla-343
**Miller, Tom**
□ 72OPC-32
□ 72SarProSta-137
□ 72Top-76
□ 73OPC-249
□ 73Top-8
**Miller, Warren**
□ 81OPC-130
□ 81Top-E84
□ 82OPC-127
□ 82PosCer-7
**Millette, Andre**
□ 88RivDu R-18
**Milley, Norm**
□ 96SudWol-14
□ 96SudWolP-17
□ 97SudWolP-7
□ 97OPCPre-414
□ 98BowCHL-38

□ 98BowCHL-129
□ 98BowCHLAuB-A16
□ 98BowCHLAuG-A16
□ 98BowCHLAuS-A16
□ 98BowCHLGA-38
□ 98BowCHLGA-129
□ 98BowCHLOI-38
□ 98BowCHLOI-129
□ 98BowChrC-38
□ 98BowChrC-129
□ 98BowChrCGA-38
□ 98BowChrCGA-129
□ 98BowChrCGAR-38
□ 98BowChrCGAR-129
□ 98BowChrCOI-38
□ 98BowChrCOI-129
□ 98BowChrCOIR-38
□ 98BowChrCOIR-129
□ 98BowChrCR-38
□ 98BowChrCR-129
**Millham, Mike**
□ 92WheThu-10
**Millie, Les**
□ 93SheSte-12
□ 94SheSte-12
□ 97SheSte-12
**Millier, Pierre**
□ 84ChiSag-19
**Milliken, Rob**
□ 92BriColJHL-232
**Mills, Craig**
□ 95Bow-99
□ 95BowAllFoi-99
□ 95Don-292
□ 95DonEliWJ-19
□ 95ParInt-497
□ 95ParIntEI-497
□ 95Sla-52
□ 95UppDec-527
□ 95UppDecEleIce-527
□ 95UppDecEleIceG-527
□ 97SPAut-176
□ 97UppDec-251
**Mills, Kelly**
□ 90RicRen-6
**Mills, Mark**
□ 98CinCyc-25
**Milton, Kjell-Rune**
□ 67SweHoc-208
□ 69SweHocS-192
□ 69SweWorC-43
□ 69SweWorC-109
□ 70SweHocS-86
□ 70SweHocS-279
□ 71SweHocS-8
□ 71SweHocS-179
□ 72SweHocS-6
□ 72SweHocS-169
□ 72SweSemWC-62
□ 73SweHocS-21
□ 73SweHocS-143
□ 73SweWorCS-21
□ 73SweWorCS-143
□ 74SweHocS-22
□ 74SweHocS-176
□ 74SweSemHVS-16
**Minard, Chris**
□ 95Sla-56
□ 96WheNai-35
**Mindjimba, Antoine**
□ 94FreNatT-19
**Miner, John**
□ 82RegPat-5
□ 83RegPat-5
□ 85NovScoO-14
□ 88OilTenAnn-30
□ 93SwiHNL-270
□ 95SwiHNL-167
□ 98GerDELE-97
**Minge, Leszek**
□ 89SweSemWCS-147
**Minichiello, Mike**
□ 94DubFigs-19
**Minkhorst, Bill**
□ 95Sla-126
**Minnis, Mike**
□ 92BriColJHL-83
**Minor, Doug**
□ 89SauSteMG-9
□ 907thInnSOHL-188
**Minor, Gerry (Gerald)**
□ 80CanuSilD-18
□ 80CanuTeal-17
□ 80PepCap-115
□ 81CanuSilD-9
□ 81CanuTeal-16
□ 81OPC-342
□ 82Canu-15
□ 82OPC-352
**Mio, Eddie (Ed)**
□ 79OilPos-18A
□ 79OilPos-18B
□ 80OPC-341
□ 80PepCap-35
□ 81OPC-119
□ 81OPCSti-216
□ 82OPC-230
□ 82OPCSti-142
□ 83OPC-127
□ 83OPCSti-209
□ 84OPC-51
□ 84Top-45
□ 88OilTenAnn-51
□ 91OPC-639
□ 91UppDecF-639

**Mirabile, Steve**
❑ 92HamRoaA-7
**Mirao, Silverio**
❑ 91BriColJHL-39
❑ 92BriColJHL-46
**Mireau, Brent**
❑ 84BraWheK-2
❑ 85BraWheK-2
**Mironov, Boris**
❑ 91UppDec-662
❑ 91UppDecCWJC-23
❑ 91UppDecF-662
❑ 92Cla-44
❑ 92RusStaRA-15
❑ 92RusStaRA-21
❑ 92TriFroRWP-21
❑ 92TriFroRWP-22
❑ 93Don-384
❑ 93Don-429
❑ 93DonRatR-9
❑ 93JetRuf-16
❑ 93Lea-364
❑ 93OPCPre-394
❑ 93OPCPreG-394
❑ 93Par-264
❑ 93ParEmel-264
❑ 93Pow-474
❑ 93PowRooS-6
❑ 93Sco-607
❑ 93ScoCan-607
❑ 93ScoGol-607
❑ 93StaClu-338
❑ 93StaCluFDI-338
❑ 93StaCluO-338
❑ 93TopPre-394
❑ 93TopPreG-394
❑ 93Ult-454
❑ 93UltWavF-8
❑ 93UppDec-492
❑ 93UppDecSP-176
❑ 94CanGamNHLP-102
❑ 94Don-218
❑ 94Lea-179
❑ 94LeaGolR-8
❑ 94OPCFinIns-17
❑ 94OPCPre-288
❑ 94OPCPreSE-288
❑ 94ParSE-SE57
❑ 94ParSEG-SE57
❑ 94Pin-188
❑ 94PinArtP-188
❑ 94PinRinC-188
❑ 94Sco-255
❑ 94ScoGol-255
❑ 94ScoPla-255
❑ 94ScoPlaTS-255
❑ 94StaClu-85
❑ 94StaCluFDI-85
❑ 94StaCluMOMS-85
❑ 94StaCluSTWC-85
❑ 94TopPre-288
❑ 94TopPreSE-288
❑ 94Ult-73
❑ 94UltAllRoo-5
❑ 94UppDec-172
❑ 94UppDecElelce-172
❑ 95ParInt-75
❑ 95ParIntEl-75
❑ 95PlaOneoOne-150
❑ 95Ult-239
❑ 96BeAPAut-88
❑ 96BeAPAutSil-88
❑ 96BeAPla-88
❑ 96ClaGol-44
❑ 96Fla-34
❑ 96FlaBlul-34
❑ 96OilPos-2
❑ 97PacInvNRB-81
❑ 97PacOme-94
❑ 97PacOmeC-94
❑ 97PacOmeDG-94
❑ 97PacOmeEG-94
❑ 97PacOmeG-94
❑ 97PacOmeIB-94
❑ 97UppDec-276
❑ 98Be A PPA-51
❑ 98Be A PPAA-51
❑ 98Be A PPAAF-51
❑ 98Be A PPTBASG-51
❑ 98Be APG-51
❑ 98Fin-60
❑ 98FinNo P-60
❑ 98FinNo PR-60
❑ 98FinRef-60
❑ 98Pac-216
❑ 98PacAur-74
❑ 98PacIceB-216
❑ 98PacPar-90
❑ 98PacParC-90
❑ 98PacParEG-90
❑ 98PacParH-90
❑ 98PacParIB-90
❑ 98PacParS-90
❑ 98PacRed-216
❑ 98UC-83
❑ 98UD ChoPCR-83
❑ 98UD ChoR-83
❑ 98UDCP-83
❑ 98UppDec-273
❑ 98UppDecE-273
❑ 98UppDecE1o1-273
❑ 98UppDecGR-273
❑ 99Pac-94
❑ 99PacCop-94
❑ 99PacGol-94
❑ 99PacIceB-94
❑ 99PacPreD-94
**Mironov, Dmitri**
❑ 90OPC-514
❑ 91OPC-515
❑ 91OPCIns-23R
❑ 91Par-391
❑ 91ParFre-391
❑ 91StaPicH-58
❑ 91SweSemWCS-84
❑ 91Top-515
❑ 92MapLeaK-17
❑ 92OPC-71
❑ 92Par-417
❑ 92ParEmel-417
❑ 92Pin-247
❑ 92Pin-419
❑ 92PinFre-247
❑ 92PinFre-419
❑ 92RusStaRA-22
❑ 92RusStaRA-22
❑ 92Sco-468
❑ 92ScoCan-468
❑ 92StaClu-5
❑ 92Top-144
❑ 92TopGol-144G
❑ 92Ult-422
❑ 92UltImp-15
❑ 92UppDec-83
❑ 93OPCPre-419
❑ 93OPCPreG-419
❑ 93Par-477
❑ 93ParEmel-477
❑ 93Pow-245
❑ 93Sco-209
❑ 93ScoBla-8
❑ 93ScoCan-209
❑ 93TopPre-419
❑ 93TopPreG-419
❑ 93Ult-127
❑ 93UppDec-513
❑ 94BeAPSig-19
❑ 94CanGamNHLP-241
❑ 94Don-58
❑ 94Fla-183
❑ 94Fle-217
❑ 94Lea-254
❑ 94MapLeaG-13
❑ 94MapLeaK-20
❑ 94MapLeaP-3
❑ 94MapLeaPP-20
❑ 94OPCPre-165
❑ 94OPCPreSE-165
❑ 94Par-232
❑ 94ParGol-232
❑ 94Pin-229
❑ 94PinArtP-229
❑ 94PinRinC-229
❑ 94SP-120
❑ 94SPDieCut-120
❑ 94TopPre-165
❑ 94TopPreSE-165
❑ 94Ult-218
❑ 94UppDec-222
❑ 94UppDecElelce-222
❑ 94UppDecSPI-SP79
❑ 94UppDecSPIDC-SP79
❑ 95CanGamNHLP-219
❑ 95ColCho-125
❑ 95ColChoPC-125
❑ 95ColChoPCP-125
❑ 95Emo-139
❑ 95Lea-96
❑ 95ParInt-437
❑ 95ParIntEl-437
❑ 95PenFoo-25
❑ 95PlaOneoOne-189
❑ 95Sco-180
❑ 95ScoBlaIce-180
❑ 95ScoBlaIceAP-180
❑ 95Ult-290
❑ 95UppDec-322
❑ 95UppDecElelce-322
❑ 95UppDecElelceG-322
❑ 96ColCho-221
❑ 96Duc-7
❑ 96SweSemW-133
❑ 96TopNHLP-167
❑ 96TopPicOI-167
❑ 96UppDec-138
❑ 97Be A PPAD-170
❑ 97Be A PPAPD-170
❑ 97BeAPla-170
❑ 97BeAPlaAut-170
❑ 97ColCho-3
❑ 97Don-130
❑ 97DonPreProG-130
❑ 97DonPreProS-130
❑ 97Pac-234
❑ 97PacCop-234
❑ 97PacEmeGre-234
❑ 97PacIceB-234
❑ 97PacOme-4
❑ 97PacOmeC-4
❑ 97PacOmeDG-4
❑ 97PacOmeEG-4
❑ 97PacOmeG-4
❑ 97PacOmeIB-4
❑ 97PacPar-4
❑ 97PacParC-4
❑ 97PacParDG-4
❑ 97PacParEG-4
❑ 97PacParIB-4
❑ 97PacParRed-4
❑ 97PacParSil-4
❑ 97PacRed-234
❑ 97PacRev-3
❑ 97PacRevC-3
❑ 97PacRevE-3
❑ 97PacRevIB-3
❑ 97PacRevR-3
❑ 97PacRevS-3
❑ 97PacSil-234
❑ 97Pin-125
❑ 97PinPrePBB-125
❑ 97PinPrePBC-125
❑ 97PinPrePBM-125
❑ 97PinPrePBY-125
❑ 97PinPrePFC-125
❑ 97PinPrePFM-125
❑ 97PinPrePFY-125
❑ 97PinPrePla-125
❑ 97Sco-240
❑ 97ScoMigDPla-4
❑ 97ScoMigDPre-4
❑ 97ScoMigDuc-4
❑ 97UppDec-213
❑ 98Be A PPA-295
❑ 98Be A PPAA-295
❑ 98Be A PPAAF-295
❑ 98Be A PPSE-295
❑ 98Be APG-295
❑ 98Pac-202
❑ 98PacIceB-202
❑ 98PacRed-202
❑ 98SPxFin-31
❑ 98SPxFinR-31
❑ 98SPxFinS-31
❑ 98UppDec-385
❑ 98UppDecE-385
❑ 98UppDecE1o1-385
❑ 98UppDecGR-385
**Misek, Petr**
❑ 82SweSemHVS-85
**Mishakov, Yevgeny**
❑ 69SweHocS-10
❑ 69SweWorC-21
❑ 69SweWorC-64
❑ 70SweHocS-327
❑ 71SweHocS-38
❑ 72SweSemWC-12
❑ 73SweHocS-104
❑ 73SweWorCS-104
❑ 74SweSemHVS-48
❑ 91FutTreC72-75
**Miskolczi, Ted**
❑ 897thInnSOHL-78
❑ 907thInnSOHL-290
❑ 91JohChi-14
❑ 94BraSmo-18
**Mistrik, Stanislav**
❑ 95SloPeeWT-19
**Miszuk, John**
❑ 68OPC-93
❑ 68ShiCoi-123
❑ 68Top-93
❑ 69OPC-124
❑ 69OPCFou-3
❑ 69Top-124
❑ 76OPCWHA-57
**Mitani, Darcy**
❑ 92NorDakFS-21
**Mitchell, Dan**
❑ 95SpoChi-29
**Mitchell, Daryll**
❑ 91NasKni-5
**Mitchell, David (Dave)**
❑ 92WesMic-19
❑ 92WinSpi-30
❑ 93WesMic-22
**Mitchell, Greg**
❑ 91ArIce-14
❑ 92ArIce-11
**Mitchell, Herbie**
❑ 24C144ChaCig-40
❑ 24V1452-29
**Mitchell, Jeff**
❑ 93DetJrRW-14
❑ 94DetJrRW-15
❑ 94Fin-121
❑ 94FinRef-121
❑ 94FinSupTW-121
❑ 94LeaLimWJUSA-8
❑ 94SP-195
❑ 94SPDieCut-195
❑ 95Cla-84
❑ 95SlaMemC-89
**Mitchell, Kevin**
❑ 97GueSto-5
**Mitchell, Red**
❑ 34BeeGro1P-70
**Mitchell, Roy**
❑ 86PorWinH-15
❑ 87PorWinH-16
❑ 88PorWinH-16
❑ 89ProAHL-192
❑ 90ProAHLIHL-65
❑ 91ProAHLCHL-144
**Mitchell, Tote**
❑ 24CreFal-8
**Mitew, T.**
❑ 95GerDELE-47
**Mitrovic, Savo**
❑ 93GreMon-8
**Mittelsteadt, Joey**
❑ 87PorWinH-17
❑ 88PorWinH-17
❑ 907thInnSMC-17
❑ 907thInnSWHL-295
❑ 92DalFre-13
❑ 93DalFre-13
**Mitterfellner, V.**
❑ 95GerDELE-370
**Mittleholt, Craig**
❑ 96AncAce-9
**Mitton, Paul**
❑ 897thInnSOHL-107
❑ 907thInnSOHL-110
❑ 94BraSmo-12
**Mix, Holger**
❑ 94GerDELE-42
❑ 95GerDELE-39
**Mix, Tom**
❑ 92BriColJHL-74
**Mizerek, Josh**
❑ 95NorlowH-20
**Mjoberg, Lars**
❑ 69SweHocS-158
❑ 70SweHocS-116
❑ 71SweHocS-206
❑ 72SweHocS-192
**Moberg, Dan**
❑ 82VicCou-17
**Moberg, Larry**
❑ 96RoaExp-35
**Modano, Mike**
❑ 90Bow-188
❑ 90BowTif-188
❑ 90Kra-32
❑ 90OPC-348
❑ 90OPCBoxB-F
❑ 90OPCPre-74
❑ 90PanSti-253
❑ 90PanSti-340
❑ 90ProSet-142
❑ 90Sco-120
❑ 90Sco-327
❑ 90ScoCan-120
❑ 90ScoCan-327
❑ 90ScoHotRS-97
❑ 90ScoYouS-20
❑ 90Top-348
❑ 90TopBoxB-F
❑ 90TopTif-348
❑ 90UppDec-46
❑ 90UppDec-346
❑ 90UppDecF-46
❑ 90UppDecF-346
❑ 91Bow-125
❑ 91Bow-415
❑ 91Gil-15
❑ 91Kra-48
❑ 91OPC-367
❑ 91PanSti-116
❑ 91Par-81
❑ 91ParFre-81
❑ 91Pin-5
❑ 91PinFre-5
❑ 91ProSet-105
❑ 91ProSetFre-105
❑ 91ProSetPla-55
❑ 91ProSetPla-143
❑ 91ScoAme-247
❑ 91ScoAme-423
❑ 91ScoCan-313
❑ 91ScoCan-467
❑ 91ScoKel-4
❑ 91ScoYouS-35
❑ 91StaClu-187
❑ 91SweSemWCS-141
❑ 91Top-367
❑ 91UppDec-32
❑ 91UppDec-160
❑ 91UppDecF-32
❑ 91UppDecF-160
❑ 92Bow-151
❑ 92OPC-313
❑ 92PanSti-93
❑ 92PanStiFre-91
❑ 92Par-75
❑ 92ParEmel-75
❑ 92Pin-155
❑ 92Pin-260
❑ 92PinFre-155
❑ 92PinFre-260
❑ 92PinTea2-2
❑ 92PinTea2F-2
❑ 92ProSet-76
❑ 92ProSetGTL-7
❑ 92Sco-139
❑ 92Sco-427
❑ 92ScoCan-139
❑ 92ScoCan-427
❑ 92ScoUSAG-5
❑ 92ScoYouS-40
❑ 92SeaPat-65
❑ 92StaClu-4
❑ 92Top-441
❑ 92TopGol-441G
❑ 92Ult-96
❑ 92UppDec-9
❑ 92UppDec-305
❑ 93Don-76
❑ 93DonSpeP-F
❑ 93Lea-202
❑ 93McDUppD-10
❑ 93OPCPre-46
❑ 93OPCPreF-6
❑ 93OPCPreG-46
❑ 93PanSti-X
❑ 93Par-49
❑ 93ParEmel-49
❑ 93ParFirO-F6
❑ 93Pin-40
❑ 93PinAllS-28
❑ 93PinAllSC-28
❑ 93PinCan-40
❑ 93PinTea2-17
❑ 93PinTea2C-17
❑ 93Pow-63
❑ 93PowSlaA-8
❑ 93Sco-142
❑ 93ScoCan-142
❑ 93ScoFra-5
❑ 93StaClu-130
❑ 93StaCluAS-21
❑ 93StaCluFDI-130
❑ 93StaCluFDIO-130
❑ 93StaCluO-130
❑ 93SweSemWCS-182
❑ 93TopPre-46
❑ 93TopPreF-6
❑ 93TopPreG-46
❑ 93Ult-194
❑ 93UppDec-294
❑ 93UppDec-397
❑ 93UppDecLAS-31
❑ 93UppDecNR-24
❑ 93UppDecSP-38
❑ 94ActPacBHP-3
❑ 94BeAPla-R8
❑ 94BeAPla-R114
❑ 94CanGamNHLP-81
❑ 94Don-193
❑ 94DonIceMas-8
❑ 94EASpo-33
❑ 94Fin-106
❑ 94FinBowB-B6
❑ 94FinBowBR-B6
❑ 94FinnJaaK-125
❑ 94FinRef-106
❑ 94FinSupTW-106
❑ 94Fla-43
❑ 94FlaCenS-9
❑ 94FlaScoP-7
❑ 94Fle-55
❑ 94FleSlaA-6
❑ 94HocWit-60
❑ 94Kra-23
❑ 94Lea-9
❑ 94LeaGolS-10
❑ 94LeaLim-60
❑ 94LeaLimI-6
❑ 94OPCPre-230
❑ 94OPCPreSE-230
❑ 94Par-308
❑ 94ParCratGB-6
❑ 94ParCratGG-6
❑ 94ParCratGR-6
❑ 94ParGol-308
❑ 94ParSE-SE47
❑ 94ParSEG-SE47
❑ 94ParVin-V2
❑ 94Pin-3
❑ 94Pin1HS-3
❑ 94PinArtP-3
❑ 94PinBoo-BR5
❑ 94PinGam-GR8
❑ 94PinRinC-3
❑ 94PinWorEdi-WE9
❑ 94Sco-188
❑ 94Sco90PC-16
❑ 94ScoDreTea-DT17
❑ 94ScoFra-TF6
❑ 94ScoGol-188
❑ 94ScoPla-188
❑ 94ScoPlaTS-188
❑ 94Sel-38
❑ 94Sel-NNO
❑ 94SelGol-38
❑ 94SP-28
❑ 94SPDieCut-28
❑ 94StaCluST-6
❑ 94StaHoc-21
❑ 94StaPinS-3
❑ 94StaPinS-NNO
❑ 94StaPos-19
❑ 94StaScoS-188
❑ 94TopFinI-9
❑ 94TopPre-230
❑ 94TopPreGTG-4
❑ 94TopPreSE-230
❑ 94Ult-55
❑ 94UltPreP-8
❑ 94UltSpeM-7
❑ 94UppDec-58
❑ 94UppDecElelce-58
❑ 94UppDecIG-IG8
❑ 94UppDecNBAP-31
❑ 94UppDecPR-R37
❑ 94UppDecPRE-R37
❑ 94UppDecPreRG-R37
❑ 94UppDecSPI-SP21
❑ 94UppDecSPIDC-SP21
❑ 95BeAPla-153
❑ 95BeAPSig-S153
❑ 95BeAPSigDC-S153
❑ 95Bow-35
❑ 95BowAllFoi-35
❑ 95CanGamNHLP-85
❑ 95ColCho-238
❑ 95ColChoCTG-C16
❑ 95ColChoCTG-C16B
❑ 95ColChoCTG-C16C
❑ 95ColChoCTGGB-C16
❑ 95ColChoCTGGR-C16
❑ 95ColChoCTGSB-C16
❑ 95ColChoCTGSR-C16
❑ 95ColChoPC-238
❑ 95ColChoPCP-238
❑ 95Don-62
❑ 95DonEli-32
❑ 95DonEliDCS-32
❑ 95DonEliDCU-32
❑ 95DonProPoi-8
❑ 95Emo-49
❑ 95EmoXci-3
❑ 95Fin-128
❑ 95FinnSemWC-116
❑ 95FinRef-128
❑ 95ImpSti-33
❑ 95KenStaLA-11
❑ 95KenStaLC-9
❑ 95Lea-227
❑ 95LeaLim-51
❑ 95Met-42
❑ 95MetHM-10
❑ 95NHLAcePC-3D
❑ 95ParInt-55
❑ 95ParIntEl-55
❑ 95Pin-108
❑ 95PinArtP-108
❑ 95PinFan-14
❑ 95PinRinC-108
❑ 95PinRoa2-5
❑ 95PlaOneoOne-31
❑ 95PlaOneoOne-142
❑ 95PlaOneoOne-250
❑ 95ProMag-124
❑ 95Sco-120
❑ 95ScoBlaIce-120
❑ 95ScoBlaIceAP-120
❑ 95ScoBorBat-9
❑ 95ScoGolBla-6
❑ 95SelCer-17
❑ 95SelCerMG-17
❑ 95SelCerP-17
❑ 95SkyImp-48
❑ 95SP-36
❑ 95SPStaEto-E11
❑ 95SPStaEtoG-E11
❑ 95StaClu-168
❑ 95StaCluMO-25
❑ 95StaCluMOMS-168
❑ 95StaScoS-120
❑ 95Sum-14
❑ 95SumArtP-14
❑ 95SumIce-14
❑ 95SweGloWC-111
❑ 95Top-80
❑ 95TopHomGUSA-HGA3
❑ 95TopOPCI-80
❑ 95TopSupSki-46
❑ 95TopSupSkiPla-46
❑ 95Ult-41
❑ 95Ult-394
❑ 95UltExtAtt-14
❑ 95UltGolM-41
❑ 95UppDec-220
❑ 95UppDec-420
❑ 95UppDecAGPRW-14
❑ 95UppDecElelce-220
❑ 95UppDecElelce-420
❑ 95UppDecElelceG-220
❑ 95UppDecElelceG-420
❑ 95UppDecPRE-R59
❑ 95UppDecPreR-R59
❑ 95UppDecSpeE-SE26
❑ 95UppDecSpeEdiG-SE26
❑ 95Zen-24
❑ 95ZenZT-10
❑ 96BeAPBisITB-8
❑ 96ColCho-69
❑ 96ColCho-315
❑ 96ColChoBlo-69
❑ 96ColChoMVP-UD17
❑ 96ColChoMVPG-UD17
❑ 96ColChoSti-S15
❑ 96Don-22
❑ 96DonCanI-25
❑ 96DonCanIGPP-25
❑ 96DonCanIRPP-25
❑ 96DonDom-9
❑ 96DonEli-116
❑ 96DonEliDCS-116
❑ 96DonGoTS-7
❑ 96DonPrePro-22
❑ 96Fla-23
❑ 96FlaBlul-23
❑ 96Fle-27
❑ 96FlePicDL-7
❑ 96FlePicF5-30
❑ 96FlePicJE-11
❑ 96KraUppD-35
❑ 96Lea-12
❑ 96LeaFirOI-14
❑ 96LeaLeaAL-15
❑ 96LeaLeaALP-P15
❑ 96LeaLim-13
❑ 96LeaLimG-13
❑ 96LeaLimStu-8
❑ 96LeaPre-44
❑ 96LeaPre-150
❑ 96LeaPreP-12
❑ 96LeaPrePP-44
❑ 96LeaPrePP-150
❑ 96LeaPreSG-28
❑ 96LeaPreSte-28
❑ 96MetUni-40
❑ 96NHLACEPC-33
❑ 96NHLProSTA-124
❑ 96Pin-154
❑ 96PinArtP-154
❑ 96PinFoi-154
❑ 96PinPreS-154
❑ 96PinRinC-154
❑ 96PlaOneoOne-352
❑ 96Sco-72
❑ 96ScoArtPro-72
❑ 96ScoDeaCAP-72
❑ 96ScoGolB-72
❑ 96ScoSpeAP-72
❑ 96ScoSup-4
❑ 96SelCer-2
❑ 96SelCerAP-2
❑ 96SelCerBlu-2
❑ 96SelCerMB-2
❑ 96SelCerMG-2
❑ 96SelCerMR-2
❑ 96SelCerRed-2
❑ 96SkyImp-30
❑ 96SP-40
❑ 96SPHolCol-HC25
❑ 96SPx-11
❑ 96SPxGol-11
❑ 96StaPos-21
❑ 96StaScoS-72
❑ 96Sum-23
❑ 96SumArtP-23
❑ 96SumIce-23
❑ 96SumMet-23
❑ 96SumPreS-23
❑ 96SweSemW-166
❑ 96TeaOut-25
❑ 96TopNHLP-51
❑ 96TopPicOI-51
❑ 96Ult-44
❑ 96UltGolM-44
❑ 96UppDec-43
❑ 96UppDec-363
❑ 96UppDecBD-99
❑ 96UppDecBDG-99
❑ 96UppDecBDRFTC-RC16
❑ 96UppDecGJ-GJ9
❑ 96UppDecGN-X21
❑ 96UppDecIce-82
❑ 96UppDecIcePar-82
❑ 96UppDecSS-SS19A
❑ 96Zen-1
❑ 96ZenArtP-1
❑ 96ZenAss-2
❑ 97BeAPlaPOT-10
❑ 97ColCho-65
❑ 97ColChoCTG-C2A
❑ 97ColChoCTG-C2B
❑ 97ColChoCTG-C2C
❑ 97ColChoCTGE-CR2
❑ 97ColChoSta-SQ82
❑ 97ColChoSti-S8
❑ 97Don-104
❑ 97DonCanI-13
❑ 97DonCanIDS-13
❑ 97DonCanIPS-13
❑ 97DonCanISCS-1
❑ 97DonEli-2
❑ 97DonEli-129
❑ 97DonEliAsp-2
❑ 97DonEliAsp-129
❑ 97DonEliC-18
❑ 97DonEliMC-18
❑ 97DonEliS-2
❑ 97DonEliS-129
❑ 97DonLim-19
❑ 97DonLim-42
❑ 97DonLim-193
❑ 97DonLimExp-19
❑ 97DonLimExp-42
❑ 97DonLimExp-193
❑ 97DonLimFOTG-67
❑ 97DonLin2L-14
❑ 97DonLin2LDC-14
❑ 97DonPre-8
❑ 97DonPre-176
❑ 97DonPreCttC-8
❑ 97DonPreCttC-176
❑ 97DonPreDWT-5
❑ 97DonPreLotT-5A
❑ 97DonPreProG-104
❑ 97DonPreProS-104
❑ 97DonPreT-7
❑ 97DonPreTB-7
❑ 97DonPreTBC-7
❑ 97DonPreTPC-7
❑ 97DonPreTPG-7
❑ 97DonPri-11
❑ 97DonPri-192
❑ 97DonPriDD-13
❑ 97DonPriODI-11
❑ 97DonPriP-12
❑ 97DonPriS-12
❑ 97DonPriSB-12
❑ 97DonPriSG-12
❑ 97DonPriSoA-11
❑ 97DonPriSoA-192
❑ 97DonPriSS-12
❑ 97EssOlyHH-24
❑ 97EssOlyHHF-24
❑ 97Kat-46
❑ 97KatGol-46
❑ 97KatSil-46
❑ 97Lea-15
❑ 97Lea-181
❑ 97LeaBanSea-9
❑ 97LeaFirOnIce-6
❑ 97LeaFraMat-15
❑ 97LeaFraMat-181
❑ 97LeaFraMDC-15
❑ 97LeaFraMDC-181
❑ 97LeaInt-15
❑ 97LeaIntUI-15

97Pac-4
97PacCarSup-5
97PacCarSupM-5
97PacCop-4
97PacCroR-41
97PacCroRBoSDC-7
97PacCroREG-41
97PacCroRHTDC-6
97PacCroRIB-41
97PacCroRLCDC-7
97PacCroRS-41
97PacDyn-37
97PacDynBKS-30
97PacDynC-37
97PacDynDG-37
97PacDynEG-37
97PacDynIB-37
97PacDynR-37
97PacDynSil-37
97PacDynTan-42
97PacEmeGre-4
97PacIceB-4
97PacInv-41
97PacInvAZ-8
97PacInvC-41
97PacInvEG-41
97PacInvFP-11
97PacInvIB-41
97PacInvNRB-63
97PacInvR-41
97PacInvS-41
97PacOme-73
97PacOme-246
97PacOme-S73
97PacOmeC-73
97PacOmeC-246
97PacOmeDG-73
97PacOmeDG-246
97PacOmeEG-73
97PacOmeEG-246
97PacOmeG-73
97PacOmeG-246
97PacOmeGFDCC-5
97PacOmeIB-73
97PacOmeIB-246
97PacOmeSLC-7
97PacPar-60
97PacPar-P60
97PacParC-60
97PacParDG-60
97PacParEG-60
97PacParIB-60
97PacParP-8
97PacParRed-60
97PacParSil-60
97PacRed-4
97PacRev-43
97PacRev1AGD-10
97PacRevC-43
97PacRevE-43
97PacRevIB-43
97PacRevR-43
97PacRevS-43
97PacRevTCL-8
97PacSil-4
97PacTeaCCC-8
97Pin-91
97PinArtP-91
97PinBee-26
97PinBeeGP-26
97PinBeeGT-3
97PinBeeT-3
97PinCer-33
97PinCerMB-33
97PinCerMG-33
97PinCerMR-33
97PinCerR-33
97PinIns-15
97PinInsCC-15
97PinInsEC-15
97PinPrePBB-91
97PinPrePBC-91
97PinPrePBM-91
97PinPrePBY-91
97PinPrePFC-91
97PinPrePFM-91
97PinPrePFY-91
97PinPrePla-91
97PinRinC-91
97PinTotCMPG-33
97PinTotCPB-33
97PinTotCPG-33
97PinTotCPR-33
97Sco-92
97Sco-262
97ScoArtPro-92
97ScoGolBla-92
97SP Autl-I37
97SPAut-43
97SPAutID-I37
97SPAutIE-I37
97SPx-13
97SPxBro-13
97SPxGol-13
97SPxGraF-13
97SPxSil-13
97SPxSte-13
97Stu-13
97StuPor-13
97StuPrePG-13
97StuPrePS-13
97StuSil-19
97StuSil8-19
97UppDec-56
97UppDecBD-80
97UppDecBDDD-80
97UppDecBDPC-PC25
97UppDecBDPCM-PC25
97UppDecBDPCDD-PC25
97UppDecBDPCQD-PC25
97UppDecBDPCTD-PC25
97UppDecBDQD-80
97UppDecBDTD-80
97UppDecIce-62
97UppDecIceP-62
97UppDecILL-L8B
97UppDecILL2-L8B
97UppDecIPS-62
97UppDecSG-SG29
97UppDecSSM-SS29
97UppDecSSW-SS29
97UppDecTS-26
97UppDecTSL2-26
97UppDecTSS-16B
97Zen-37
97Zen5x7-58
97ZenChaTC-5
97ZenGolImp-58
97ZenSilImp-58
97ZenZGol-37
97ZenZSil-37
98Be A PPA-40
98Be A PPAA-40
98Be A PPAAF-40
98Be A PPAGUSC-S4
98Be A PPAJ-AS4
98Be A PPPGUJC-G17
98Be A PPPPUJC-P14
98Be A PPTBASG-40
98Be APG-40
98BowBes-48
98BowBesAR-48
98BowBesR-48
98Fin-75
98FinDouMF-M31
98FinDouMF-M32
98FinDouMF-M33
98FinDouMF-M34
98FinDouSMFR-M31
98FinDouSMFR-M33
98FinDouSMFR-M34
98FinNo P-75
98FinNo PR-75
98FinRedL-R2
98FinRedLR-R2
98FinRef-75
98O-PChr-50
98O-PChrR-50
98Pac-181
98Pac-S181
98PacAur-58
98PacAurALC-8
98PacAurC-7
98PacAurCF-15
98PacAurCFC-15
98PacAurCFIB-15
98PacAurCFR-15
98PacAurCFS-15
98PacAurMAC-7
98PacAurNC-5
98PacCraCA-5
98PacCroR-41
98PacCroRLS-41
98PacCroRMP-8
98PacCroRPotG-11
98PacCroRPP-7
98PacDynI-59
98PacDynII-8
98PacDynIFT-8
98PacDynIIB-59
98PacDynIPP-5
98PacDynIR-59
98PacDynITC-8
98PacEO P-8
98PacGolCD-12
98PacIceB-181
98PacOmeEP1o1-8
98PacOmeFtF-9
98PacOmeH-73
98PacOmeO-13
98PacOmeODI-73
98PacOmeP-7
98PacOmePI-16
98PacOmePIB-16
98PacOmeR-73
98PacPar-68
98PacParC-68
98PacParEG-68
98PacParH-68
98PacParIB-68
98PacParS-68
98PacParSDDC-6
98PacParTCD-8
98PacRed-181
98PacRev-44
98PacRevADC-20
98PacRevCTL-7
98PacRevIS-44
98PacRevNI-5
98PacRevR-44
98PacRevS-15
98PacTeaC-8
98PacTim-9
98PacTitl-8
98RevThrPA-25
98RevThrPA-25
98SP Aut-25
98SP AutSM-S14
98SP AutSS-SS12
98SPxFin-109
98SPxFin-169
98SPxFinR-109
98SPxFinR-169
98SPxFinS-109
98SPxFinS-169
98SPXTopP-18
98SPXTopPF-18
98SPXTopPPHH-H11
98SPXTopPLI-L5
98SPXTopPPS-PS24
98SPXTopPW-18
98Top-50
98TopGolLC1-2
98TopGolLC1B-2
98TopGolLC1BOoO-2
98TopGolLC1OoO-2
98TopGolLC1R-2
98TopGolLC1ROoO-2
98TopGolLC2-2
98TopGolLC2B-2
98TopGolLC2BOoO-2
98TopGolLC2OoO-2
98TopGolLC2R-2
98TopGolLC2ROoO-2
98TopGolLC3-2
98TopGolLC3B-2
98TopGolLC3BOoO-2
98TopGolLC3OoO-2
98TopGolLC3R-2
98TopGolLC3ROoO-2
98TopLocL-L12
98TopMysFB-M5
98TopMysFBR-M5
98TopMysFG-M5
98TopMysFGR-M5
98TopMysFS-M5
98TopMysFSR-M5
98TopO-P-50
98UC-69
98UCMBH-BH16
98UCSB-SQ24
98UCSG-SQ24
98UCSG-SQ24
98UCSR-SQ24
98UD ChoPCR-69
98UD ChoR-69
98UD3-39
98UD3-99
98UD3-159
98UD3DieC-39
98UD3DieC-99
98UD3DieC-159
98UppDec-30
98UppDecBD-27
98UppDecDD-27
98UppDecE-30
98UppDecE-256
98UppDecE1o1-30
98UppDecE1o1-256
98UppDecFF-FF12
98UppDecFF-FF12
98UppDecFFQ1-FF12
98UppDecFFQ2-FF12
98UppDecFIT-FT13
98UppDecFITQ1-FT13
98UppDecFITQ2-FT13
98UppDecFITQ3-FT13
98UppDecGR-30
98UppDecGR-256
98UppDecLSH-LS28
98UppDecLSHQ1-LS28
98UppDecLSHQ2-LS28
98UppDecLSHQ3-LS28
98UppDecM-61
98UppDecM1-M5
98UppDecM2-M5
98UppDECMGS-MM
98UppDecMGS-61
98UppDecMPG-PG4
98UppDecMSS-61
98UppDecMSS-61
98UppDecP-P18
98UppDecPQ1-P18
98UppDecPQ2-P18
98UppDecPQ3-P18
98UppDecQD-27
98UppDecTD-27
98UppDecWFG-WF30
98UppDecWFP-WF30
99AurSty-8
99Pac-126
99PacAur-47
99PacAurCFC-11
99PacAurCFPB-11
99PacAurCP-6
99PacAurCPP-6
99PacAurPD-47
99PacCop-126
99PacCra-6
99PacGol-126
99PacGolCD-15
99PacHomaA-8
99PacIceB-126
99PacPreD-126
99PacTeaC-8
99PacTeaL-9
99RetHoc-24
99SP AutPS-25
99UppDecCL-61
99UppDecCLCLC-61
99UppDecM-59
99UppDecMGS-59
99UppDecMSS-59
99UppDecMSS-59
99UppDecRG-24
99UppDecRP-24

**Modes, Werner**
72SweSemWC-99

**Modig, Lars**
84SweSemE-177
85SwePanS-157
86SwePanS-169
87SwePanS-176
89SweSemE-148
90SweSemE-228
91SweSemE-156
92SweSemE-177
93SweSemE-148
94SweLeaE-101
94SweLeaE-76
95SweUppDE-114

**Modin, Fredrik**
94SweLeaE-273
94SweLeaENHLD-3
94SweLeaERR-1
95SigRoo-7
95SigRooSig-11
95SweGloWC-59
95SweLeaE-19
95SweUppDE-35
95SweUppDE-220
95SweUppDETNA-NA4
96BeAPAut-216
96BeAPAutSil-216
96BeAPla-216
96DonCanI-130
96DonCanIGPP-130
96DonCanIRPP-130
96SelCer-112
96SelCerAP-112
96SelCerBlu-112
96SelCerMG-112
96SelCerMR-112
96SelCerRed-112
96SweSemW-73
96UppDec-345
97ColCho-249
97Pac-127
97PacCop-127
97PacEmeGre-127
97PacIceB-127
97PacRed-127
97PacSil-127
97ScoMapL-13
97ScoMapLPla-13
97ScoMapLPre-13
97UppDec-162
98Be A PPA-134
98Be A PPAA-134
98Be A PPAAF-134
98Be A PPTBASG-134
98Be APG-134
98Pac-419
98PacIceB-419
98PacRed-419
98UppDec-192
98UppDecE-192
98UppDecE1o1-192
98UppDecGR-192
98UppDecM-193
98UppDecMGS-193
98UppDecMSS-193

**Modry, Jaroslav**
93ClaProPro-146
93Don-455
93OPCPre-307
93OPCPreG-307
93Par-386
93ParEmel-386
93Pow-380
93Sco-616
93ScoCan-616
93ScoGol-616
93StaCluI-411
93StaCluO-411
93TopPre-307
93TopPreG-307
93Ult-362
93UltWavF-9
93UppDec-319
94ClaProP-24
94CzeApAPSE-97
94Don-197
94Lea-496
94OPCPre-512
94OPCPreSE-512
94Par-123
94Par-290
94ParGol-123
94ParGol-290
94TopPre-512
94TopPreSE-512
94UppDec-473
94UppDecEleIce-473
94ParInt-418
95ParInt-418
95SweSemWCS-218
96Top-171

**Modzelewski, Jan**
69SweWorC-195
69SweWorC-199

**Moe, Billy**
44BeeGro2P-346

**Moen, Jeff**

92MinGolG-15
93MinGolG-22
94MinGolG-21
95MinGolG-21

**Moes, Mike**
90NewSai-16
90ProAHLIHL-148

**Moeser, Duanne**
94GerDELE-9
95GerDELE-12
96GerDELE-12
98GerDELE-287

**Moffat, Corri**
91AirCanSJHL-A10
91AirCanSJHLAS-18
92MPSPhoSJHL-77

**Moffat, Lyle**
74MapLeaP-15
74DOPCNHL-379
77OPCWHA-64
78JetPos-16
79JetPos-19
79OPC-277

**Moffat, Mike**
81KinCan-23

**Moffatt, Rob**
83BraAle-7

**Moffett, Greg**
83NovScoV-24

**Moger, Sandy**
92Cla-67
92HamCan-19
92ClaProP-187
95Don-245
95Lea-272
95SelCer-140
95SelCerMG-140
95Sum-185
95SumArtP-185
95SumIce-185
95Ult-11
95UltGolM-11
95UppDec-332
95UppDecEleIce-332
95UppDecEleIceG-332
96BeAPAut-172
96BeAPAutSil-172
96BeAPla-172
96ClaGol-67
96Sum-53
96SumArtP-53
96SumIce-53
96SumMet-53
96SumPreS-53
97PacInvNRB-15
98Be A PPA-64
98Be A PPAA-64
98Be A PPAAF-64
98Be A PPTBASG-64
98Be APG-64
98O-PChr-59
98O-PChrR-59
98Pac-240
98PacIceB-240
98PacRed-240
98Top-59
98TopO-P-59

**Mogilny, Alexander**
89SabBluS-13
89SabCam-15
90Bow-240
90BowTif-240
90OPC-42
90PCBoxB-A
90PCPre-75
90PanSti-338
90ProSet-26
90SabBluS-15
90SabCam-18
90Sco-43
90ScoCan-43
90ScoYouS-26
90Top-42
90TopTif-42
90UppDec-24
90UppDecF-24
91Bow-30
91Kra-60
91OPC-32
91OPC-171
91PanSti-304
91Par-12
91ParFre-12
91Pin-163
91PinFre-163
91ProSet-16
91ProSetFre-16
91ProSetPla-283
91RusStaNHL-8
91RusStaRA-14
91SabBluS-14
91SabPepC-14
91ScoAme-236
91ScoCan-456
91ScoYouS-13
91StaClu-195
91SweSemWCS-218
91Top-171
91UppDec-267
91UppDec-618
91UppDecES-2
91UppDecESF-2
91UppDecF-267
91UppDecF-618
92Bow-34
92Bow-235
92HumDum1-16
92McDUppD-22
92OPC-279
92PanSti-248
92PanSti-299
92PanStiFre-248
92PanStiFre-299
92Par-218
92Par-218
92ParEmel-13
92ParEmel-218
92Pin-77
92PinCanPP-3
92PinFre-77
92PinTea2-28
92PinTea2F-28
92ProSet-19
92SabBluS-13
92SabJubF-9
92Sco-248
92ScoCan-248
92ScoYouS-8
92StaClu-320
92Top-382
92TopGol-382G
92Ult-18
92UltImp-16
92UppDec-167
92UppDec-456
92UppDecWJG-WG18
93Cla-122
93Cla-AU5
93ClaCraNum-N7
93Don-39
93DonEli-8
93DonSpeP-C
93Kra-16
93Lea-91
93LeaGolAS-8
93LeaHatTA-2
93McDUppD-19
93OPCPre-148
93OPCPre-172
93OPCPre-245
93OPCPreBG-10
93OPCPreG-148
93OPCPreG-172
93OPCPreG-245
93PanSti-J
93Par-21
93ParEmel-21
93Pin-10
93Pin2HS-NF9
93PinAllS-22
93PinAllSC-22
93PinCan-10
93PinNifFif-2
93PinTea2-2
93PinTea2-C
93PinTeaP-12
93PinTeaPC-12
93Pow-32
93PowGloG-5
93PowPoiL-10
93SabLimETI-4
93SabNoc-13
93Sco-222
93Sco-477
93ScoCan-222
93ScoCan-477
93ScoDynDUS-2
93ScoIntS-8
93ScoIntSC-8
93SeaPat-12
93StaClu-91
93StaCluAS-12
93StaCluFDI-91
93StaCluFDIO-91
93StaCluO-91
93TopPre-148
93TopPre-172
93TopPre-245
93TopPreG-148
93TopPreG-172
93TopPreG-245
93Ult-238
93UltAllS-5
93UltRedLS-7
93UltSpeM-7
93UppDec-234
93UppDec-488
93UppDecFH-34
93UppDecHT-HT15
93UppDecLAS-8
93UppDecNB-HB1
93UppDecSilSka-H10
93UppDecSilSkaG-H10
93UppDecSP-18
94BeAPla-R68
94CanGamNHLP-44
94Don-92
94EASpo-17
94EASpo-191
94Fin-68
94Fin-99
94FinRef-68
94FinRef-99
94FinSupTW-68
94FinSupTW-99
94Fla-20
94FlaScoP-8
94Fle-25
94HocWit-75
94KenStaLA-14
94KenStaLC-8
94Kra-24
94Lea-256
94LeaFirOlce-10
94LeaLim-36
94McDUppD-McD8
94OPCPre-50
94OPCPreSE-50
94Par-21
94ParGol-21
94ParSEES-ES14
94ParSEV-34
94Pin-125
94PinArtP-125
94PinBoo-BR17
94PinRinC-125
94PosCerBR-17
94Sco-200
94ScoGol-200
94ScoPla-200
94ScoPlaTS-200
94Sel-22
94SelGol-22
94SP-13
94SPDieCut-13
94StaCluMO-26
94TopFinIn-19
94TopPre-50
94TopPreGTG-13
94TopPreSE-50
94Ult-26
94UltAllS-5
94UltGloGre-6
94UltSpeM-8
94UppDec-334
94UppDec-552
94UppDecEleIce-334
94UppDecEleIce-552
94UppDecPH-H9
94UppDecPHEG-H9
94UppDecPHES-H9
94UppDecPHG-H9
94UppDecSPI-SP10
94UppDecSPIDC-SP10
95APLetL-LL9
95BeAPla-204
95BeAPSig-S204
95BeAPSigDC-S204
95Bow-5
95BowAllFoi-5
95BowBes-BB9
95BowBesRef-BB9
95CanGamNHLP-272
95ColCho-163
95ColChoPC-163
95ColChoPCP-163
95Don-275
95DonEli-18
95DonEliCE-7
95DonEliDCS-18
95DonEliDCU-18
95Emo-182
95Fin-140
95Fin-160
95FinRef-140
95FinRef-160
95ImpStri-124
95Kra-56
95Lea-187
95LeaFireFra-8
95LeaLim-83
95LeaLimSG-6
95McDPin-MCD-21
95Met-153
95MetIS-15
95MetWin-5
95NHLCooT-19
95NHLCooT-RP19
95ParInt-212
95ParInt-246
95ParIntCCGS2-3
95ParIntCCSS2-3
95ParIntEI-212
95ParIntEI-246
95ParIntPTP-PP18
95ParIntPTP-PP48
95PlaOneoOne-102
95PlaOneoOne-209
95PlaOneoOne-318
95ProMag-29
95Sco-21
95ScoBlaIce-21
95ScoBlaIceAP-21
95ScoGolBla-3
95SelCer-43
95SelCerMG-43
95SelCerP-43
95SkyImp-171
95SP-148
95SPStaEto-E28
95SPStaEtoG-E28
95StaClu-1
95StaCluEN-EN9
95StaCluMOMS-1
95StaCluMPT-6
95Sum-48
95SumArtP-48
95SumIce-48
95Top-225
95Top-376
95TopMarMPB-376

❑ 95TopOPCI-225
❑ 95TopOPCI-376
❑ 95TopPowL-6PL
❑ 95TopSupSki-36
❑ 95TopSupSkiPla-36
❑ 95Ult-21
❑ 95Ult-317
❑ 95UltExtAtt-15
❑ 95UltGolM-21
❑ 95UppDec-188
❑ 95UppDec-221
❑ 95UppDecAGPRW-4
❑ 95UppDecEleIce-188
❑ 95UppDecEleIce-221
❑ 95UppDecEleIceG-188
❑ 95UppDecEleIceG-221
❑ 95UppDecNHLAS-AS10
❑ 95UppDecPRE-R6
❑ 95UppDecPRE-R35
❑ 95UppDecPreR-R6
❑ 95UppDecPreR-R35
❑ 95UppDecSpeE-SE173
❑ 95UppDecSpeEdiG-SE173
❑ 95UppPreRP-R35
❑ 95Zen-31
❑ 96BeAPBisITB-24
❑ 96CanuPos-89
❑ 96ColCho-267
❑ 96ColCho-333
❑ 96ColChoBloBi-8
❑ 96ColChoCTG-C3A
❑ 96ColChoCTG-C3B
❑ 96ColChoCTG-C3C
❑ 96ColChoCTGE-CR3
❑ 96ColChoCTGEG-CR3
❑ 96ColChoCTGG-C3A
❑ 96ColChoCTGG-C3B
❑ 96ColChoCTGG-C3C
❑ 96ColChoMVP-UD4
❑ 96ColChoMVPG-UD4
❑ 96Don-181
❑ 96DonCanI-91
❑ 96DonCanIGPP-91
❑ 96DonCanIRPP-91
❑ 96DonDom-7
❑ 96DonEli-56
❑ 96DonEliDCS-56
❑ 96DonEliS-9
❑ 96DonGoTS-4
❑ 96DonPrePro-181
❑ 96Fla-96
❑ 96FlaBluI-96
❑ 96Fle-114
❑ 96Fle-138
❑ 96FleArtRos-16
❑ 96FlePicDL-4
❑ 96FlePicF5-31
❑ 96FlePicJE-3
❑ 96HocGreC-16
❑ 96HocGreCG-16
❑ 96KraUppD-24
❑ 96KraUppD-69
❑ 96Lea-162
❑ 96LeaFirOI-2
❑ 96LeaLeaAL-11
❑ 96LeaLeaALP-P11
❑ 96LeaLim-8
❑ 96LeaLimG-8
❑ 96LeaLimStu-13
❑ 96LeaPre-2
❑ 96LeaPreP-162
❑ 96LeaPrePP-2
❑ 96LeaPreSG-51
❑ 96LeaPreSte-51
❑ 96MetUni-159
❑ 96MetUniIC-11
❑ 96MetUniICSP-11
❑ 96MetUniLW-14
❑ 96MetUniLWSP-14
❑ 96NHLACEPC-34
❑ 96NHLProSTA-29
❑ 96Pin-87
❑ 96PinArtP-87
❑ 96PinFoi-87
❑ 96PinMcD-11
❑ 96PinPreS-87
❑ 96PinRinC-87
❑ 96PlaOneoOne-422
❑ 96Sco-16
❑ 96ScoArtPro-16
❑ 96ScoDeaCAP-16
❑ 96ScoDreTea-9
❑ 96ScoGolB-16
❑ 96ScoSam-16
❑ 96ScoSpeAP-16
❑ 96ScoSudDea-8
❑ 96SelCer-70
❑ 96SelCerAP-70
❑ 96SelCerBlu-70
❑ 96SelCerMB-70
❑ 96SelCerMG-70
❑ 96SelCerMR-70
❑ 96SelCerRed-70
❑ 96SkyImp-135
❑ 96SkyImpB-15
❑ 96SP-158
❑ 96SPGamFil-GF12
❑ 96SPx-47
❑ 96SPxGol-47
❑ 96StaCluMO-10
❑ 96Sum-107
❑ 96SumArtP-107
❑ 96SumHigV-11
❑ 96SumHigVM-11
❑ 96SumIce-107
❑ 96SumMet-107
❑ 96SumPreS-107
❑ 96SumUnt-9
❑ 96TeaOut-39
❑ 96TopNHLP-9
❑ 96TopPicFT-FT19
❑ 96TopPicOI-9
❑ 96TopPicTS-TS9
❑ 96Ult-170
❑ 96UltGolM-170
❑ 96UltPow-13
❑ 96UltPowRL-5
❑ 96UppDec-167
❑ 96UppDecBD-89
❑ 96UppDecBDG-89
❑ 96UppDecGN-X29
❑ 96UppDecHH-HH12
❑ 96UppDecHHG-HH12
❑ 96UppDecHHS-HH12
❑ 96UppDecIce-104
❑ 96UppDecIcePar-104
❑ 96UppDecSS-SS10B
❑ 96Zen-34
❑ 96ZenArtP-34
❑ 96ZenZT-9
❑ 97Be A PPAD-247
❑ 97Be A PPAPD-247
❑ 97BeAPla-247
❑ 97BeAPlaAut-247
❑ 97BeAPlaTAN-18
❑ 97ColCho-256
❑ 97ColChoSta-SQ69
❑ 97Don-106
❑ 97DonCanI-45
❑ 97DonCanIDS-45
❑ 97DonCanIPS-45
❑ 97DonEli-69
❑ 97DonEliAsp-69
❑ 97DonEliS-69
❑ 97DonLim-68
❑ 97DonLim-104
❑ 97DonLim-122
❑ 97DonLimExp-68
❑ 97DonLimExp-104
❑ 97DonLimExp-122
❑ 97DonLimFOTG-51
❑ 97DonPre-39
❑ 97DonPre-170
❑ 97DonPreCttC-39
❑ 97DonPreCttC-170
❑ 97DonPreProG-106
❑ 97DonPreProS-106
❑ 97DonPri-119
❑ 97DonPriSoA-119
❑ 97EssOlyHH-39
❑ 97EssOlyHHF-39
❑ 97Kat-149
❑ 97KatGol-149
❑ 97KatSil-149
❑ 97Lea-25
❑ 97LeaFraMat-25
❑ 97LeaFraMDC-25
❑ 97LeaInt-25
❑ 97LeaIntUI-25
❑ 97McDGamFil-2
❑ 97Pac-89
❑ 97PacCop-89
❑ 97PacCroR-137
❑ 97PacCroREG-137
❑ 97PacCroRIB-137
❑ 97PacCroRS-137
❑ 97PacDyn-129
❑ 97PacDynC-129
❑ 97PacDynDD-15B
❑ 97PacDynDG-129
❑ 97PacDynEG-129
❑ 97PacDynIB-129
❑ 97PacDynR-129
❑ 97PacDynSil-129
❑ 97PacDynTan-55
❑ 97PacEmeGre-89
❑ 97PacIceB-89
❑ 97PacInv-144
❑ 97PacInvAZ-24
❑ 97PacInvC-144
❑ 97PacInvEG-144
❑ 97PacInvFP-35
❑ 97PacInvIB-144
❑ 97PacInvNRB-203
❑ 97PacInvR-144
❑ 97PacInvS-144
❑ 97PacOme-232
❑ 97PacOmeC-232
❑ 97PacOmeDG-232
❑ 97PacOmeEG-232
❑ 97PacOmeG-232
❑ 97PacOmeIB-232
❑ 97PacRed-89
❑ 97PacRev-143
❑ 97PacRevC-143
❑ 97PacRevE-143
❑ 97PacRevIB-143
❑ 97PacRevR-143
❑ 97PacRevS-143
❑ 97PacSil-89
❑ 97PacSlaSDC-11C
❑ 97Pin-58
❑ 97PinArtP-58
❑ 97PinCer-60
❑ 97PinCerMB-60
❑ 97PinCerMG-60
❑ 97PinCerMR-60
❑ 97PinCerR-60
❑ 97PinIns-34
❑ 97PinInsCC-34
❑ 97PinInsEC-34
❑ 97PinInsT-27
❑ 97PinPrePBB-58
❑ 97PinPrePBC-58
❑ 97PinPrePBM-58
❑ 97PinPrePBY-58
❑ 97PinPrePFC-58
❑ 97PinPrePFM-58
❑ 97PinPrePFY-58
❑ 97PinPrePla-58
❑ 97PinRinC-58
❑ 97PinTotCMPG-60
❑ 97PinTotCPB-60
❑ 97PinTotCPG-60
❑ 97PinTotCPR-60
❑ 97Sco-129
❑ 97ScoArtPro-129
❑ 97ScoCanPla-2
❑ 97ScoCanPre-2
❑ 97ScoCanu-2
❑ 97ScoGolBla-129
❑ 97SPAut-155
❑ 97UppDecBD-97
❑ 97UppDecBDDD-97
❑ 97UppDecBDQD-97
❑ 97UppDecBDTD-97
❑ 97UppDecTSS-19B
❑ 97Zen-79
❑ 97ZenZGol-79
❑ 97ZenZSil-79
❑ 98Be A PPA-141
❑ 98Be A PPAA-141
❑ 98Be A PPAAF-141
❑ 98Be A PPAGUSC-S13
❑ 98Be A PPAJ-AS14
❑ 98Be A PPPGUJC-G21
❑ 98Be A PPPUJC-P2
❑ 98Be A PPTBASG-141
❑ 98Be APG-141
❑ 98BowBes-40
❑ 98BowBesAR-40
❑ 98BowBesR-140
❑ 98Fin-129
❑ 98FinNo P-129
❑ 98FinNo PR-129
❑ 98FinRef-129
❑ 98O-PChr-207
❑ 98O-PChrR-207
❑ 98Pac-89
❑ 98PacAur-190
❑ 98PacCroR-136
❑ 98PacCroRLS-136
❑ 98PacDynI-190
❑ 98PacDynIIB-190
❑ 98PacDynIR-190
❑ 98PacIceB-89
❑ 98PacOmeH-237
❑ 98PacOmeODI-237
❑ 98PacOmeR-237
❑ 98PacPar-237
❑ 98PacParC-237
❑ 98PacParEG-237
❑ 98PacParH-237
❑ 98PacParIB-237
❑ 98PacParS-237
❑ 98PacRed-89
❑ 98PacRev-142
❑ 98PacRevIS-142
❑ 98PacRevR-142
❑ 98SP AutSotTG-AM
❑ 98SSASotT-AM
❑ 98Top-207
❑ 98TopGolLC1-62
❑ 98TopGolLC1B-62
❑ 98TopGolLC1BOoO-62
❑ 98TopGolLC1OoO-62
❑ 98TopGolLC1R-62
❑ 98TopGolLC1ROoO-62
❑ 98TopGolLC2-62
❑ 98TopGolLC2B-62
❑ 98TopGolLC2BOoO-62
❑ 98TopGolLC2OoO-62
❑ 98TopGolLC2R-62
❑ 98TopGolLC2ROoO-62
❑ 98TopGolLC3-62
❑ 98TopGolLC3B-62
❑ 98TopGolLC3BOoO-62
❑ 98TopGolLC3OoO-62
❑ 98TopGolLC3R-62
❑ 98TopGolLC3ROoO-62
❑ 98TopO-P-207
❑ 98UC-210
❑ 98UD ChoPCR-210
❑ 98UD ChoR-210
❑ 98UppDec-376
❑ 98UppDecE-376
❑ 98UppDecE1o1-376
❑ 98UppDecGR-376
❑ 98UppDecM-204
❑ 98UppDecMGS-204
❑ 98UppDecMSS-204
❑ 98UppDecMSS-204
❑ 99Pac-427
❑ 99PacAur-142
❑ 99PacAurPD-142
❑ 99PacCop-427
❑ 99PacGol-427
❑ 99PacIceB-427
❑ 99PacPreD-427
❑ 99UppDecM-210
❑ 99UppDecMGS-210
❑ 99UppDecMSS-210
❑ 99UppDecMSS-210

**Mohagen, Tony**
❑ 95SeaThu-17
❑ 96SeaThu-17

**Mohlin, Dan**
❑ 83SweSemE-122
❑ 84SweSemE-114

**Mohlin, Ove**
❑ 91SweSemE-48

**Mohninger, Bret**
❑ 91AirCanSJHL-C26

**Mohns, Doug**
❑ 44BeeGro2P-51
❑ 52JunBluT-107
❑ 54Par-57
❑ 54Top-18
❑ 55BruPho-12
❑ 57BruTealss-14
❑ 57Top-12
❑ 58Top-50
❑ 59Top-58
❑ 60ShiCoi-106
❑ 60Top-52
❑ 60TopSta-37
❑ 61ShiCoi-10
❑ 61Top-10
❑ 62Top-6
❑ 62TopHocBuc-18
❑ 63Top-3
❑ 64BeeGro3P-50
❑ 64CocCap-20
❑ 64Top-25
❑ 65Coc-20
❑ 65Top-118
❑ 66Top-61
❑ 66TopUSAT-61
❑ 67Top-63
❑ 68OPC-19
❑ 68ShiCoi-24
❑ 68Top-19
❑ 69OPC-72
❑ 69OPCFou-14
❑ 69Top-72
❑ 70DadCoo-87
❑ 70EssPowPla-118
❑ 70OPC-16
❑ 70OPCDec-29
❑ 70SarProSta-47
❑ 70Top-16
❑ 71OPC-242
❑ 71SarProSta-84
❑ 71TorSun-137
❑ 72OPC-75
❑ 72SarProSta-102
❑ 72Top-78
❑ 73OPC-241
❑ 74CapWhiB-21
❑ 74NHLActSta-309
❑ 74OPCNHL-181
❑ 74Top-181
❑ 91BruSpoAL-18
❑ 91UltOriS-53
❑ 91UltOriSF-53
❑ 94ParMisL-18
❑ 94ParTalB-27
❑ 95Par66-35
❑ 95Par66Coi-35

**Moise, Martin**
❑ 97BowCHL-72
❑ 97BowCHLOPC-72
❑ 98BowCHL-113
❑ 98BowCHLGA-113
❑ 98BowCHLOI-113
❑ 98BowChrC-113
❑ 98BowChrCGA-113
❑ 98BowChrCGAR-113
❑ 98BowChrCOI-113
❑ 98BowChrCOIR-113
❑ 98BowChrCR-113
❑ 98QueRem-15

**Mokosak, Carl**
❑ 88ProAHL-156
❑ 89ProIHL-132
❑ 90ProAHLIHL-304
❑ 90ProAHLIHL-412

**Mokosak, John**
❑ 81VicCou-11
❑ 82VicCou-18
❑ 88ProAHL-11
❑ 90ProAHLIHL-127
❑ 91ProAHLCHL-192
❑ 92PhoRoa-15

**Mokros, Milan**
❑ 94GerDELE-153
❑ 95GerDELE-149
❑ 96GerDELE-245

**Molander, Borje**
❑ 64SweCorI-111
❑ 65SweCorI-111
❑ 67SweHoc-35
❑ 69SweHocS-48

**Molander, Lars**
❑ 64SweCorI-114
❑ 65SweCorI-114
❑ 67SweHoc-177
❑ 69SweHocS-178

**Molander, Pontus**
❑ 84SweSemE-85
❑ 86SwePanS-93
❑ 87SwePanS-77

**Molander, Urban**
❑ 90SweSemE-181
❑ 91SweSemE-37

**Molin, Lars**
❑ 81CanuSilD-24
❑ 81CanuTeal-17
❑ 81SweSemHVS-17
❑ 82Canu-16
❑ 82OPC-353
❑ 82OPCSti-245
❑ 82PosCer-19
❑ 82SweSemHVS-149
❑ 83Canu-14
❑ 83Vac-113
❑ 85SwePanS-216
❑ 86SwePanS-204
❑ 87SwePanS-203

**Molin, Ove**
❑ 92SweSemE-68
❑ 93SweSemE-44
❑ 94SweLeaE-85
❑ 95SweLeaE-20
❑ 95SweLeaEG-2
❑ 95SweUppDE-33

**Molin, Sacha**
❑ 94SweLeaE-166

**Molina, Alfio**
❑ 72SweSemWC-157

**Molleken, Lorne**
❑ 84SprInd-2
❑ 917thInnSWHL-100
❑ 91SasBla-1

**Moller, Fredrik**
❑ 93SweSemE-238

**Moller, Mike**
❑ 84SabBluS-11
❑ 85NovScoO-3
❑ 88OilTenAnn-136
❑ 89ProAHL-305
❑ 93RedDeeR-16

**Moller, Randy**
❑ 82NordPos-14
❑ 83NordPos-18
❑ 83OPC-297
❑ 83OPCSti-248
❑ 83Vac-69
❑ 84NordPos-17
❑ 84OPC-284
❑ 84OPCSti-174
❑ 85NordGenF-18
❑ 85NordMcD-14
❑ 85NordPla-6
❑ 85NordPro-17
❑ 85NordTeal-15
❑ 85OPC-240
❑ 85OPCSti-145
❑ 86KraDra-46
❑ 86NordGenF-16
❑ 86NordMcD-17
❑ 86NordTeal-15
❑ 87NordGenF-22
❑ 87OPC-251
❑ 87OPCSti-229
❑ 87PanSti-172
❑ 88NordGenF-23
❑ 88NordTeal-24
❑ 88PanSti-351
❑ 89Nord-32
❑ 89OPC-259
❑ 89OPCSti-195
❑ 89PanSti-331
❑ 89RanMarMB-24
❑ 90OPC-515
❑ 90ProSet-202
❑ 90Sco-45
❑ 90ScoCan-45
❑ 90UppDec-418
❑ 90UppDecF-418
❑ 91Bow-58
❑ 91OPC-371
❑ 91Pin-256
❑ 91PinFre-256
❑ 91ProSet-163
❑ 91ProSetFre-163
❑ 91ScoAme-79
❑ 91ScoCan-79
❑ 91StaClu-2
❑ 91Top-371
❑ 92Pin-176
❑ 92PinFre-176
❑ 92SabBluS-14
❑ 92SabJubF-10
❑ 92Sco-289
❑ 92ScoCan-289
❑ 92StaClu-484
❑ 92Top-407
❑ 92TopGol-407G
❑ 93Sco-422
❑ 93ScoCan-422
❑ 93StaClu-435
❑ 93StaCluFDI-435
❑ 93StaCluO-435
❑ 94Lea-344
❑ 94Pin-401
❑ 94PinArtP-401
❑ 94PinRinC-401

**Moller, Tommy**
❑ 83SweSemE-107
❑ 84SweSemE-107

**Molling, Jochen**
❑ 94GerDELE-55
❑ 95GerDELE-409
❑ 96GerDELE-251
❑ 98GerDELE-55

**Molloy, Mitch**
❑ 88ProAHL-151
❑ 89JohChi-29
❑ 90ProAHLIHL-283
❑ 92SanDieG-20

**Molnar, Petr**
❑ 94CzeAPSE-207
❑ 95CzeAPSE-159

**Molson, Sen.H.de M**
❑ 83HalFP-012
❑ 85HalFC-221

**Molyneaux, Larry**
❑ 34BeeGro1P-286

**Momesso, Sergio**
❑ 85CanaPos-21
❑ 85CanaPro-11
❑ 86CanaPos-14
❑ 86KraDra-45
❑ 87BluTealss-16
❑ 87CanaPos-18
❑ 87CanaVacS-55
❑ 87CanaVacS-56
❑ 88BluKod-27
❑ 88BluTealss-16
❑ 89BluKod-27
❑ 90BluKod-16
❑ 90Bow-17
❑ 90BowTif-17
❑ 90OPC-244
❑ 90PanSti-263
❑ 90ProSet-268
❑ 90Sco-224
❑ 90ScoCan-224
❑ 90Top-244
❑ 90TopTif-244
❑ 90UppDec-19
❑ 90UppDecF-19
❑ 91Bow-309
❑ 91CanuAutC-15
❑ 91CanuTeal8-15
❑ 91OPC-462
❑ 91OPCPre-55
❑ 91PanSti-44
❑ 91Par-185
❑ 91ParFre-185
❑ 91Pin-34
❑ 91PinFre-34
❑ 91ProSet-242
❑ 91ProSetFre-242
❑ 91ProSetPla-240
❑ 91ScoAme-121
❑ 91ScoCan-121
❑ 91StaClu-17
❑ 91Top-462
❑ 91UppDec-571
❑ 91UppDecF-571
❑ 92Bow-316
❑ 92CanuRoaTA-14
❑ 92DurPan-26
❑ 92OPC-377
❑ 92Par-421
❑ 92ParEmeI-421
❑ 92Pin-163
❑ 92PinFre-163
❑ 92ProSet-194
❑ 92Sco-79
❑ 92ScoCan-79
❑ 92StaClu-42
❑ 92Top-214
❑ 92TopGol-214G
❑ 92Ult-225
❑ 92UppDec-85
❑ 93Don-349
❑ 93DurSco-33
❑ 93Lea-250
❑ 93Par-212
❑ 93ParEmeI-212
❑ 93Pin-393
❑ 93PinCan-393
❑ 93Sco-255
❑ 93ScoCan-255
❑ 93StaClu-323
❑ 93StaCluFDI-323
❑ 93StaCluO-323
❑ 93Ult-47
❑ 93UppDec-104
❑ 94BeAPSig-178
❑ 94CanGamNHLP-342
❑ 94Lea-499
❑ 94OPCPre-356
❑ 94OPCPreSE-356
❑ 94Par-249
❑ 94ParGol-249
❑ 94Pin-307
❑ 94PinArtP-307
❑ 94PinRinC-307
❑ 94StaClu-65
❑ 94StaCluFDI-65
❑ 94StaCluMOMS-65
❑ 94StaCluSTWC-65
❑ 94TopPre-356
❑ 94TopPreSE-356
❑ 94Ult-384
❑ 94UppDec-65
❑ 94UppDecEleIce-65
❑ 95CanuBuiDA-12
❑ 95ColCho-99
❑ 95ColChoPC-99
❑ 95ColChoPCP-99
❑ 95Don-380
❑ 95Lea-58
❑ 95ParInt-473
❑ 95ParIntEl-473
❑ 95Sco-161
❑ 95ScoBlaIce-161
❑ 95ScoBlaIceAP-161
❑ 95StaClu-123
❑ 95StaCluMOMS-123
❑ 95Sum-163
❑ 95SumArtP-163
❑ 95SumIce-163
❑ 95Ult-313
❑ 95UppDec-125
❑ 95UppDecEleIce-125
❑ 95UppDecEleIceG-125
❑ 97PacInv-121
❑ 97PacInvC-121
❑ 97PacInvEG-121
❑ 97PacInvIB-121
❑ 97PacInvR-121
❑ 97PacInvS-121
❑ 98GerDELE-248

**Monahan, Garry**
❑ 64CanaPos-13
❑ 67CanaIGA-20
❑ 67Top-8
❑ 68CanaIGA-20
❑ 68CanaPosBW-10
❑ 69OPC-160
❑ 70ColSta-13
❑ 70EssPowPla-31
❑ 70MapLeaP-9
❑ 70OPC-112
❑ 70SarProSta-207
❑ 70Top-112
❑ 71MapLeaP-13
❑ 71SarProSta-199
❑ 71TorSun-266
❑ 72MapLeaP-21
❑ 72OPC-207
❑ 72SarProSta-202
❑ 73MapLeaP-19
❑ 73OPC-226
❑ 74CanuRoyB-13
❑ 75CanuRoyB-13
❑ 75OPCNHL-357
❑ 76CanuRoyB-11
❑ 76OPCNHL-295
❑ 77CanCanDC-10
❑ 77CanuRoyB-14
❑ 77OPCNHL-341
❑ 78MapLeaP-15
❑ 78OPC-268

**Monahan, Hartland**
❑ 76OPCNHL-203
❑ 76Top-203
❑ 77OPCNHL-96
❑ 77Top-96
❑ 78OPC-393

**Mondou, Armand**
❑ 33OPCV304A-48
❑ 33V129-44
❑ 33V357IceK-17
❑ 34BeeGro1P-169
❑ 34SweCap-12
❑ 35DiaMatT2-48
❑ 35DiaMatT3-45
❑ 35DiaMatTI-48
❑ 37OPCV304E-177
❑ 39OPCV3011-27

**Mondou, Pierre**
❑ 77CanaPos-17
❑ 78CanaPos-19
❑ 78OPC-102
❑ 78Top-102
❑ 79CanaPos-17
❑ 79OPC-211
❑ 79Top-211
❑ 80CanaPos-16
❑ 80OPC-42
❑ 80PepCap-52
❑ 80Top-42
❑ 81CanaPos-18
❑ 81OPC-188
❑ 82CanaPos-14
❑ 82CanaSte-10
❑ 82OPC-188
❑ 82OPCSti-35
❑ 82PosCer-10
❑ 83CanaPos-17
❑ 83OPC-191
❑ 83OPCSti-68
❑ 83Vac-49
❑ 84CanaPos-17
❑ 84OPC-266
❑ 84OPCSti-162
❑ 85OPC-211
❑ 85OPCSti-133
❑ 92SpoFla-11

**Mondt, Nikolaus**
❑ 95GerDELE-99
❑ 96GerDELE-287
❑ 98GerDELE-58

**Mongeau, Michel**
❑ 88FliSpi-17
❑ 89ProIHL-17
❑ 90ProAHLIHL-91
❑ 90Sco-395
❑ 90ScoCan-395
❑ 90UppDec-345
❑ 90UppDecF-345
❑ 91BluPos-15
❑ 91ProAHLCHL-26
❑ 91UppDec-213
❑ 91UppDecF-213
❑ 92Pin-388
❑ 92PinFre-388
❑ 92StaClu-415
❑ 92Ult-203
❑ 93PeoRiv-19
❑ 95ColEdgI-178
❑ 95PeoRiv-12
❑ 96MilAdmBO-18

**Mongeon, Hughes**
❑ 907thInnSQMJHL-189
❑ 917thInnSQMJHL-32

**Mononen, Erkki**
❑ 71SweHocS-68
❑ 72SweSemWC-81

**Mononen, Lauri**
❑ 69SweHocS-377
❑ 70SweHocS-306
❑ 71SweHocS-69
❑ 72SweHocS-37
❑ 72SweSemWC-82
❑ 73SweHocS-35
❑ 73SweWorCS-35
❑ 74SweSemHVS-99
❑ 75RoaPhoWHA-24
❑ 76RoaPhoWHA-13
**Monrisson, Sandy**
❑ 52JunBluT-164
**Montan, Carl-Fredrik**
❑ 67SweHoc-294
❑ 69SweHocS-340
❑ 70SweHocS-256
**Montanari, Mark**
❑ 86KitRan-18
❑ 87KitRan-19
❑ 88KitRan-19
❑ 89ProAHL-57
❑ 907thInnSMC-30
❑ 90ProAHLIHL-142
❑ 96GerDELE-102
**Montandon, Gil**
❑ 91SweSemWCS-198
❑ 93SweSemWCS-128
❑ 93SwiHNL-76
❑ 95FinnSemWC-193
❑ 95SweGloWC-215
❑ 95SwiHNL-103
**Montemurro, Carlo**
❑ 52JunBluT-92
**Montgomery, Jim**
❑ 92MaiBlaB-12
❑ 92MaiBlaB-27
❑ 93Cla-55
❑ 93Cla-AU6
❑ 93Don-300
❑ 93DonRatR-13
❑ 93MaiBlaB-61
❑ 93OPCPre-488
❑ 93OPCPreG-488
❑ 93Par-176
❑ 93ParEmel-176
❑ 93Pin-438
❑ 93PinCan-438
❑ 93Pow-431
❑ 93Sco-621
❑ 93ScoCan-621
❑ 93ScoGol-621
❑ 93TopPre-488
❑ 93TopPreG-488
❑ 93Ult-413
❑ 93UppDec-472
❑ 94CanaPos-15
❑ 94ClaProP-25
❑ 94Lea-258
❑ 94Lea-348
❑ 94OPCPre-91
❑ 94OPCPreSE-91
❑ 94Par-198
❑ 94ParGol-198
❑ 94ParSE-SE93
❑ 94ParSEG-SE93
❑ 94Pin-159
❑ 94PinArtP-159
❑ 94PinRinC-159
❑ 94TopPre-91
❑ 94TopPreSE-91
❑ 94Ult-187
❑ 94Ult-312
❑ 94UppDec-132
❑ 94UppDecElelce-132
❑ 95ColEdgI-46
❑ 96ColEdgFL-11
❑ 96GerDELE-348
**Montgomery, Scott**
❑ 86KitRan-26
❑ 87KitRan-29
**Moody, Bill**
❑ 92BriColJHL-140
❑ 97FifFly-6
**Moog, Andy**
❑ 81OilRedR-35
❑ 81OPC-120
❑ 82OilRedR-35
❑ 83OilDol-H15
❑ 83OilMcD-3
❑ 83OPC-40
❑ 83OPCSti-99
❑ 83OPCSti-155
❑ 83Vac-37
❑ 84OilRedR-35
❑ 84OilTeal-20
❑ 84OPC-255
❑ 84OPCSti-262
❑ 85OilRedR-35
❑ 85OPC-12
❑ 85OPCSti-123
❑ 85OPCSti-220
❑ 85Top-12
❑ 86KraDra-46
❑ 86OilRedR-35
❑ 86OilRedR-35
❑ 86OilTeal-35
❑ 86OPC-212
❑ 86OPCSti-66
❑ 87OPC-204
❑ 87OPCSti-93
❑ 87PanSti-255
❑ 88BruPos-13
❑ 88BruSpoA-15
❑ 88OilTenAnn-91
❑ 89BruSpoA-15
❑ 89OPC-160
❑ 89OPCSti-30
❑ 89PanSti-191
❑ 89Top-160
❑ 90Bow-35
❑ 90BowTif-35
❑ 90BruSpoA-16
❑ 90BruSpoA-26
❑ 90Kra-35
❑ 90OPC-294
❑ 90OPC-486
❑ 90OPCPre-76
❑ 90PanSti-11
❑ 90ProSet-10
❑ 90ProSet-382
❑ 90Sco-140
❑ 90Sco-365
❑ 90ScoCan-140
❑ 90ScoCan-365
❑ 90ScoHotRS-62
❑ 90Top-294
❑ 90TopTif-294
❑ 90UppDec-209
❑ 90UppDec-232
❑ 90UppDecF-209
❑ 90UppDecF-232
❑ 91Bow-361
❑ 91Bow-418
❑ 91BruSpoA-11
❑ 91BruSpoA-24
❑ 91Gil-29
❑ 91Kra-59
❑ 91McDUppD-9
❑ 91OPC-338
❑ 91OPCPre-133
❑ 91PanSti-179
❑ 91Par-8
❑ 91Par-459
❑ 91ParFre-8
❑ 91Pin-126
❑ 91Pin-379
❑ 91PinFre-126
❑ 91PinFre-379
❑ 91ProSet-10
❑ 91ProSet-299
❑ 91ProSetFre-10
❑ 91ProSetFre-299
❑ 91ProSetPC-2
❑ 91ProSetPCP-2
❑ 91ProSetPla-4
❑ 91ProSetPOTM-P4
❑ 91ScoAme-90
❑ 91ScoCan-90
❑ 91ScoKel-10
❑ 91StaClu-211
❑ 91Top-338
❑ 91UppDec-147
❑ 91UppDecF-147
❑ 92Bow-79
❑ 92BruPos-6
❑ 92Kra-32
❑ 92OPC-184
❑ 92PanSti-135
❑ 92PanStiFre-135
❑ 92Par-3
❑ 92ParEmel-3
❑ 92Pin-91
❑ 92Pin-263
❑ 92PinAmePP-1
❑ 92PinFre-91
❑ 92PinFre-263
❑ 92ProSet-7
❑ 92Sco-120
❑ 92ScoCan-120
❑ 92SeaPat-19
❑ 92StaClu-430
❑ 92Top-394
❑ 92TopGol-394G
❑ 92Ult-6
❑ 92UppDec-1
❑ 92UppDec-329
❑ 93Don-87
❑ 93Lea-369
❑ 93OPCPre-476
❑ 93OPCPreG-476
❑ 93PanSti-9
❑ 93Par-47
❑ 93ParEmel-47
❑ 93Pin-347
❑ 93PinCan-347
❑ 93Pow-64
❑ 93Sco-11
❑ 93Sco-516
❑ 93ScoCan-11
❑ 93ScoCan-516
❑ 93ScoGol-516
❑ 93StaClu-470
❑ 93StaCluFDI-470
❑ 93StaCluO-470
❑ 93TopPre-476
❑ 93TopPreG-476
❑ 93Ult-2
❑ 93Ult-301
❑ 93UppDec-478
❑ 93UppDecSP-39
❑ 94BeAPSig-30
❑ 94CanGamNHLP-277
❑ 94Don-108
❑ 94EASpo-12
❑ 94Fla-44
❑ 94Fle-56
❑ 94Kra-48
❑ 94KraGoaM-4
❑ 94Lea-47
❑ 94OPCPre-81
❑ 94OPCPre-511
❑ 94OPCPreSE-81
❑ 94OPCPreSE-511
❑ 94Par-51
❑ 94ParGol-51
❑ 94Pin-315
❑ 94PinArtP-315
❑ 94PinGoaG-GT14
❑ 94PinMas-MA8
❑ 94PinRinC-315
❑ 94Sco-173
❑ 94ScoGol-173
❑ 94ScoPla-173
❑ 94ScoPlaTS-173
❑ 94Sel-94
❑ 94SelGol-94
❑ 94SP-32
❑ 94SPDieCut-32
❑ 94StaClu-231
❑ 94StaCluFDI-231
❑ 94StaCluMOMS-231
❑ 94StaCluSTWC-231
❑ 94StaHoc-22
❑ 94StaPinS-315
❑ 94StaPinS-NNO
❑ 94StaPos-20
❑ 94StaScoS-173
❑ 94TopPre-81
❑ 94TopPre-511
❑ 94TopPreSE-81
❑ 94TopPreSE-511
❑ 94Ult-56
❑ 94UppDec-81
❑ 94UppDecElelce-81
❑ 94UppDecSPI-SP111
❑ 94UppDecSPIDC-SP111
❑ 95CanGamNHLP-92
❑ 95ColCho-62
❑ 95ColChoPC-62
❑ 95ColChoPCP-62
❑ 95Don-290
❑ 95Emo-50
❑ 95ImpSti-35
❑ 95Kra-30
❑ 95Met-43
❑ 95ParInt-59
❑ 95ParIntEl-59
❑ 95Pin-114
❑ 95PinArtP-114
❑ 95PinMas-5
❑ 95PinRinC-114
❑ 95PlaOneoOne-32
❑ 95ProMag-125
❑ 95Sco-64
❑ 95ScoBlaIce-64
❑ 95ScoBlaIceAP-64
❑ 95SelCer-77
❑ 95SelCerMG-77
❑ 95SkyImp-49
❑ 95StaScoS-64
❑ 95Sum-96
❑ 95SumArtP-96
❑ 95SumIce-96
❑ 95SumInTheCre-12
❑ 95Top-53
❑ 95TopHidGem-14HG
❑ 95TopOPCI-53
❑ 95TopSupSki-83
❑ 95TopSupSkiPla-83
❑ 95Ult-42
❑ 95UltGolM-42
❑ 95UltPrePadMen-8
❑ 95UltPrePadMenGM-8
❑ 95UppDec-191
❑ 95UppDecElelce-191
❑ 95UppDecElelceG-191
❑ 95Zen-105
❑ 96BeAPAut-7
❑ 96BeAPAutSil-7
❑ 96BeAPla-7
❑ 96BeAPStaTP-12
❑ 96Don-166
❑ 96DonCanI-90
❑ 96DonCanIGPP-90
❑ 96DonCanIRPP-90
❑ 96DonEli-3
❑ 96DonEliDCS-3
❑ 96DonPrePro-166
❑ 96Fla-24
❑ 96FlaBluI-24
❑ 96Lea-99
❑ 96LeaPreP-99
❑ 96MetUni-41
❑ 96NHLProSTA-125
❑ 96Pin-166
❑ 96PinArtP-166
❑ 96PinFoi-166
❑ 96PinPreS-166
❑ 96PinRinC-166
❑ 96PlaOneoOne-382
❑ 96Sco-104
❑ 96ScoArtPro-104
❑ 96ScoDeaCAP-104
❑ 96ScoGolB-104
❑ 96ScoSpeAP-104
❑ 96SelCer-25
❑ 96SelCerAP-25
❑ 96SelCerBlu-25
❑ 96SelCerMB-25
❑ 96SelCerMG-25
❑ 96SelCerMR-25
❑ 96SelCerRed-25
❑ 96SP-44
❑ 96StaPos-23
❑ 96StaScoS-104
❑ 96Sum-130
❑ 96SumArtP-130
❑ 96SumIce-130
❑ 96SumMet-130
❑ 96SumPreS-130
❑ 96Ult-45
❑ 96UltGolM-45
❑ 96Zen-110
❑ 96ZenArtP-110
❑ 97CanaPos-13
❑ 97ColCho-67
❑ 97ColChoSta-SQ34
❑ 97Don-40
❑ 97DonCanI-85
❑ 97DonCanIDS-85
❑ 97DonCanIPS-85
❑ 97DonEli-66
❑ 97DonEliAsp-66
❑ 97DonEliS-66
❑ 97DonLim-28
❑ 97DonLimExp-28
❑ 97DonLimFOTG-36
❑ 97DonPre-113
❑ 97DonPreCttC-113
❑ 97DonPreProG-40
❑ 97DonPreProS-40
❑ 97DonPri-108
❑ 97DonPriSoA-108
❑ 97McD-28
❑ 97Pac-35
❑ 97PacCop-35
❑ 97PacCroR-70
❑ 97PacCroREG-70
❑ 97PacCroRFODC-10
❑ 97PacCroRIB-70
❑ 97PacCroRS-70
❑ 97PacDynBKS-31
❑ 97PacEmeGre-35
❑ 97PacIceB-35
❑ 97PacInTheCLC-6
❑ 97PacInv-42
❑ 97PacInvC-42
❑ 97PacInvEG-42
❑ 97PacInvIB-42
❑ 97PacInvNRB-64
❑ 97PacInvR-42
❑ 97PacInvS-42
❑ 97PacOme-120
❑ 97PacOmeC-120
❑ 97PacOmeDG-120
❑ 97PacOmeEG-120
❑ 97PacOmeG-120
❑ 97PacOmeIB-120
❑ 97PacOmeNSZ-6
❑ 97PacPar-96
❑ 97PacParC-96
❑ 97PacParDG-96
❑ 97PacParEG-96
❑ 97PacParGSL-10
❑ 97PacParIB-96
❑ 97PacParRed-96
❑ 97PacParSil-96
❑ 97PacRed-35
❑ 97PacRev-72
❑ 97PacRevC-72
❑ 97PacRevE-72
❑ 97PacRevIB-72
❑ 97PacRevR-72
❑ 97PacRevRtSD-10
❑ 97PacRevS-72
❑ 97PacSil-35
❑ 97Pin-70
❑ 97PinArtP-70
❑ 97PinCer-5
❑ 97PinCerMB-5
❑ 97PinCerMG-5
❑ 97PinCerMR-5
❑ 97PinCerR-5
❑ 97PinIns-47
❑ 97PinInsCC-47
❑ 97PinInsEC-47
❑ 97PinPrePBB-70
❑ 97PinPrePBC-70
❑ 97PinPrePBM-70
❑ 97PinPrePBY-70
❑ 97PinPrePFC-70
❑ 97PinPrePFM-70
❑ 97PinPrePFY-70
❑ 97PinPrePla-70
❑ 97PinRinC-70
❑ 97PinTotCMPG-5
❑ 97PinTotCPB-5
❑ 97PinTotCPG-5
❑ 97PinTotCPR-5
❑ 97Sco-8
❑ 97ScoArtPro-8
❑ 97ScoCan-1
❑ 97ScoCanPla-1
❑ 97ScoGolBla-8
❑ 97SPAut-81
❑ 97UppDec-294
❑ 97UppDecBD-113
❑ 97UppDecBDDD-113
❑ 97UppDecBDQD-113
❑ 97UppDecBDTD-113
❑ 98Pac-255
❑ 98PacIceB-255
❑ 98PacRed-255
❑ 98ScoCanPre-1
❑ 98SPxFin-44
❑ 98SPxFinR-44
❑ 98SPxFinS-44
❑ 98UC-106
❑ 98UD ChoPCR-106
❑ 98UD ChoR-106
**Moon, Cam**
❑ 89SasBla-2
❑ 907thInnSWHL-87
❑ 90SasBla-3
**Mooney, Matthew (Matt)**
❑ 90RayJrC-14
❑ 91RayJrC-11
**Mooney, Mike**
❑ 89RayJrC-16
**Moore, Barrie**
❑ 917thInnSOHL-259
❑ 91SudWol-20
❑ 92SudWol-17
❑ 93SudWol-15
❑ 93SudWolP-15
❑ 94SudWol-14
❑ 94SudWolP-10
❑ 95ColEdgI-65
❑ 95RochAmeSS-13
**Moore, Blaine**
❑ 92BriColJHL-238
❑ 94RicRen-7
❑ 95LasVegThu-8
❑ 96LasVegThu-16
**Moore, Charlie**
❑ 83BelBul-13
❑ 84BelBul-8
**Moore, David**
❑ 91CinCyc-16
❑ 94CenHocL-102
**Moore, Dean**
❑ 91AirCanSJHL-A15
❑ 92MPSPhoSJHL-106
**Moore, Dickie**
❑ 44BeeGro2P-274
❑ 45QuaOatP-100
❑ 48ExhCan-18
❑ 52Par-10
❑ 53Par-28
❑ 54Par-2
❑ 55Par-38
❑ 55ParQuaO-38
❑ 57Par-M14
❑ 58Par-8
❑ 59Par-14
❑ 60Par-38
❑ 60Par-57
❑ 60ShiCoi-22
❑ 60YorPreP-24
❑ 61Par-36
❑ 61ShiCoi-107
❑ 61YorYelB-5
❑ 62Par-42
❑ 62ShiMetC-37
❑ 62YorIroOTra-22
❑ 63MapLeaWB-17
❑ 63TorSta-27
❑ 64BeeGro3P-176
❑ 64CocCap-100
❑ 83HalFP-J10
❑ 85HalFC-190
❑ 92ParParR-PR26
❑ 93OPCCanHF-59
❑ 93OPCCanHF-63
❑ 93ParParRCI-12
❑ 94ParMisL-70
❑ 94ParTalB-116
❑ 99UppDecCL-31
❑ 99UppDecCLCLC-31
**Moore, Greg**
❑ 92MPSPhoSJHL-98
**Moore, Jimmy**
❑ 51LavDaiQSHL-36
❑ 52St.LawS-3
**Moore, Kevin**
❑ 91FerStaB-24
**Moore, Mike**
❑ 87PorWinH-18
❑ 88PorWinH-18
**Moore, Scott**
❑ 90SweSemE-71
❑ 91SweSemE-241
**Moore, Skeeter**
❑ 85MinDul-1
**Moores, Tom**
❑ 917thInnSOHL-214
❑ 93NiaFalT-17
**Moraal, Arie**
❑ 83KinCan-4
❑ 84KinCan-3
❑ 85KinCan-3
❑ 86KinCan-3
❑ 87KinCan-1
**Morabito, John**
❑ 91BriColJHL-12
❑ 92BriColJHL-190
❑ 95BirBul-11
**Moran, Amby**
❑ 23V1281PauC-29
**Moran, Brad**
❑ 98BowCHL-72
❑ 98BowCHLGA-72
❑ 98BowCHLOI-72
❑ 98BowChrC-72
❑ 98BowChrCGA-72
❑ 98BowChrCGAR-72
❑ 98BowChrCOI-72
❑ 98BowChrCOIR-72
❑ 98BowChrCR-72
**Moran, Ian**
❑ 93Pow-512
❑ 93StaCluTUSA-17
❑ 93TopPreTUSA-2
❑ 93Ult-492
❑ 94Cla-101
❑ 94ClaDraGol-101
❑ 95PenFoo-20
❑ 95SkyImp-216
❑ 95StaClu-219
❑ 95StaCluMOMS-219
❑ 96CleLum-18
❑ 97Be A PPAD-93
❑ 97Be A PPAPD-93
❑ 97BeAPla-93
❑ 97BeAPlaAut-93
❑ 97PacDynBKS-79
**Moran, Paddy**
❑ 10C55SweCP-1
❑ 10C56-28
❑ 11C55-1
❑ 12C57-18
❑ 60Top-2
❑ 60TopSta-38
❑ 83HalFP-K10
❑ 85HalFC-144
**Morava, Marian**
❑ 96CzeAPSE-318
**Moravec, David**
❑ 96CzeAPSE-206
**More, Jay (Jayson)**
❑ 90ProAHLIHL-99B
❑ 91Par-387
❑ 91ParFre-387
❑ 91Pin-342
❑ 91PinFre-342
❑ 92Bow-388
❑ 92OPC-312
❑ 92Par-394
❑ 92ParEmel-394
❑ 92ProSet-169
❑ 92Sco-147
❑ 92ScoCan-147
❑ 92StaClu-60
❑ 92Top-245
❑ 92TopGol-245G
❑ 92UppDec-488
❑ 93OPCPre-227
❑ 93OPCPreG-227
❑ 93Par-452
❑ 93ParEmel-452
❑ 93StaClu-208
❑ 93StaCluFDI-208
❑ 93StaCluFDIO-208
❑ 93StaCluO-208
❑ 93TopPre-227
❑ 93TopPreG-227
❑ 94Lea-509
❑ 94StaClu-165
❑ 94StaCluFDI-165
❑ 94StaCluMOMS-165
❑ 94StaCluSTWC-165
❑ 95PlaOneoOne-303
❑ 96PlaOneoOne-417
❑ 97Be A PPAD-70
❑ 97Be A PPAPD-70
❑ 97BeAPla-70
❑ 97BeAPlaAut-70
❑ 98Pac-98
❑ 98PacIceB-98
❑ 98PacPar-126
❑ 98PacParC-126
❑ 98PacParEG-126
❑ 98PacParH-126
❑ 98PacParIB-126
❑ 98PacParS-126
❑ 98PacRed-98
**More, Paul**
❑ 83BraWheK-15
❑ 84BraWheK-23
**Moreau, Eric**
❑ 917thInnSQMJHL-191
❑ 93NiaFalT-28
**Moreau, Ethan**
❑ 917thInnSOHL-212
❑ 93NiaFalT-13
❑ 94Cla-12
❑ 94ClaDraGol-12
❑ 94ClaTri-T13
❑ 94SudWol-20
❑ 95Cla-97
❑ 95ClaCHLAS-AS12
❑ 95ColEdgI-134
❑ 95Ima-50
❑ 95ImaGol-50
❑ 95IndIce-16
❑ 95ParInt-540
❑ 95ParIntEl-540
❑ 96BeAPLH-4A
❑ 96BeAPLHAut-4A
❑ 96BeAPLHAutSil-4A
❑ 96ColCho-354
❑ 96ColEdgFL-34
❑ 96ColEdgPC-7
❑ 96Don-228
❑ 96DonCanI-127
❑ 96DonCanIGPP-127
❑ 96DonCanIRPP-127
❑ 96DonEli-136
❑ 96DonEliAsp-20
❑ 96DonEliDCS-136
❑ 96DonPrePro-228
❑ 96Fla-104
❑ 96FlaBluI-104
❑ 96LeaGolR-1
❑ 96LeaLimR-1
❑ 96LeaLimRG-1
❑ 96LeaPre-139
❑ 96LeaPrePP-139
❑ 96MetUni-187
❑ 96Pin-239
❑ 96PinArtP-239
❑ 96PinFoi-239
❑ 96PinPreS-239
❑ 96PinRinC-239
❑ 96Sco-268
❑ 96ScoArtPro-268
❑ 96ScoDeaCAP-268
❑ 96ScoGolB-268
❑ 96ScoSpeAP-268
❑ 96SelCer-116
❑ 96SelCerAP-116
❑ 96SelCerBlu-116
❑ 96SelCerMB-116
❑ 96SelCerMG-116
❑ 96SelCerMR-116
❑ 96SelCerRed-116
❑ 96SP-31
❑ 96Sum-184
❑ 96SumArtP-184
❑ 96SumIce-184
❑ 96SumMet-184
❑ 96SumPreS-184
❑ 96Ult-32
❑ 96UltGolM-32
❑ 96UltRoo-13
❑ 96UppDec-187
❑ 96UppDecBD-69
❑ 96UppDecBDG-69
❑ 96Zen-133
❑ 96ZenArtP-133
❑ 97ColCho-51
❑ 97Don-50
❑ 97DonCanI-83
❑ 97DonCanIDS-83
❑ 97DonCanIPS-83
❑ 97DonEli-52
❑ 97DonEliAsp-52
❑ 97DonEliS-52
❑ 97DonLim-60
❑ 97DonLim-87
❑ 97DonLim-94
❑ 97DonLimExp-60
❑ 97DonLimExp-87
❑ 97DonLimExp-94
❑ 97DonPre-35
❑ 97DonPreCttC-35
❑ 97DonPreProG-50
❑ 97DonPreProS-50
❑ 97DonPri-116
❑ 97DonPriSoA-116
❑ 97Kat-35
❑ 97KatGol-35
❑ 97KatSil-35
❑ 97Lea-143
❑ 97LeaFraMat-143
❑ 97LeaFraMDC-143
❑ 97LeaInt-143
❑ 97LeaIntUI-143
❑ 97PacDyn-28
❑ 97PacDynC-28
❑ 97PacDynDG-28
❑ 97PacDynEG-28
❑ 97PacDynIB-28
❑ 97PacDynR-28
❑ 97PacDynSil-28
❑ 97PacDynTan-40
❑ 97PacInv-31
❑ 97PacInvC-31
❑ 97PacInvEG-31
❑ 97PacInvIB-31
❑ 97PacInvR-31
❑ 97PacInvS-31
❑ 97PacPar-46
❑ 97PacParC-46
❑ 97PacParDG-46
❑ 97PacParEG-46
❑ 97PacParIB-46
❑ 97PacParRed-46
❑ 97PacParSil-46
❑ 97Pin-189
❑ 97PinIns-184
❑ 97PinPrePBB-189
❑ 97PinPrePBC-189
❑ 97PinPrePBM-189
❑ 97PinPrePBY-189
❑ 97PinPrePFC-189
❑ 97PinPrePFM-189
❑ 97PinPrePFY-189
❑ 97PinPrePla-189
❑ 97Sco-151
❑ 97ScoArtPro-151
❑ 97ScoGolBla-151
❑ 97Stu-83
❑ 97StuHarH-23
❑ 97StuPrePG-83
❑ 97StuPrePS-83
❑ 97UppDec-250
❑ 98Fin-71
❑ 98FinNo P-71
❑ 98FinNo PR-71
❑ 98FinRef-71
❑ 99Pac-160
❑ 99PacCop-160
❑ 99PacGol-160
❑ 99PacIceB-160
❑ 99PacPreD-160
**Moreau, Marguerite**
❑ 92DisMigDM-4
**Moreau, Sebastien**
❑ 917thInnSQMJHL-106
❑ 92MPSPhoSJHL-165
**Morel, Alexandre**
❑ 98QueRem-16
**Morel, Denis**

❑ 90ProSet-695
**Moren, Darren**
❑ 83VicCou-18
❑ 84SasBlaS-15
**Morency, Steve**
❑ 98Vald'OF-18
**Morenz, Brian**
❑ 74MarSanDW-3
**Morenz, Howie**
❑ 23V1451-15
❑ 24C144ChaCig-41
❑ 24V130MapC-12
❑ 24V1452-47
❑ 27LaPat-14
❑ 33OPCV304A-23
❑ 33V129-41
❑ 33V252CanG-38
❑ 33V288HamG-8
❑ 33V3572IceKP-4
❑ 33V357IceK-36
❑ 34BeeGro1P-170
❑ 34DiaMatS-46
❑ 34SweCap-35
❑ 35DiaMatT2-49
❑ 35DiaMatT3-46
❑ 35DiaMatTI-49
❑ 36OPCV304D-121
❑ 36V356WorG-18
❑ 55Par-57
❑ 55ParQuaO-57
❑ 60Top-59
❑ 60TopSta-39
❑ 83HalFP-H12
❑ 85HalFC-106
❑ 91ProSet-336
❑ 91ProSetFre-336
❑ 93OPCCanHF-13
❑ 94HalFT-7
❑ 94ParMisLP-P1
❑ 99UppDecCL-14
❑ 99UppDecCLCLC-14
**Morenz, Howie Jr.**
❑ 36V356WorG-100
**Moret, Leo**
❑ 28V1282PauC-44
**Morgan, Brad**
❑ 97SudWolP-20
**Morgan, Chris**
❑ 91AirCanSJHL-A18
**Morgan, Cory**
❑ 96PriAlbR-13
❑ 96PriAlbROC-15
**Morgan, Jason**
❑ 93KitRan-13
❑ 94KitRan-14
❑ 95Sla-121
❑ 98UppDec-109
❑ 98UppDecE-109
❑ 98UppDecE1o1-109
❑ 98UppDecGR-109
**Mori, Aaron**
❑ 96RegPat-10
**Moriarty, Gerald**
❑ 95Sla-333
❑ 96SudWol-15
**Morin, Derek**
❑ 897thInnSOHL-89
❑ 907thInnSOHL-13
**Morin, Guillaume**
❑ 917thInnSQMJHL-173
**Morin, Jean-Martin**
❑ 917thInnSQMJHL-138
**Morin, Jesper**
❑ 98GerDELE-9
**Morin, Joel**
❑ 87KinCan-10
❑ 897thInnSOHL-165
**Morin, Marc**
❑ 84ChiSag-20
**Morin, Mike**
❑ 84SasBlaS-16
❑ 85BraWheK-19
❑ 91LakSupSL-20
❑ 95RicRen-20
**Morin, Nathan**
❑ 90MonAAA-16
❑ 917thInnSQMJHL-158
**Morin, Olivier**
❑ 97BowCHL-74
❑ 97BowCHLOPC-74
**Morin, Pete**
❑ 34BeeGro1P-171
❑ 36V356WorG-129
❑ 52St.LawS-16
**Morin, Stephane**
❑ 89HalCit-16
❑ 89ProAHL-167
❑ 90HalCit-18
❑ 90ProAHLIHL-455
❑ 90UppDec-524
❑ 90UppDecF-524
❑ 91Bow-148
❑ 91NordPet-20
❑ 91OPC-159
❑ 91PanSti-263
❑ 91Par-147
❑ 91ParFre-147
❑ 91Pin-245
❑ 91PinFre-245
❑ 91ProSet-201
❑ 91ProSetFre-201
❑ 91ProSetPla-100
❑ 91ScoAme-361
❑ 91ScoCan-254
❑ 91ScoYouS-39
❑ 91StaClu-216
❑ 91Top-159
❑ 91UppDec-433
❑ 91UppDecF-433
❑ 92DurPan-9
❑ 92HamCan-20
❑ 92PanSti-214
❑ 92PanStiFre-214
❑ 92StaClu-469
❑ 92Top-316
❑ 92TopGol-316G
❑ 95ColEdgI-169
❑ 98GerDELE-109
**Morin, Vic**
❑ 80SauSteMG-12
**Morisette, Dave**
❑ 92HamRoaA-14
❑ 98UppDecM-106
❑ 98UppDecMGS-106
❑ 98UppDecMSS-106
❑ 98UppDecMSS-106
**Morissette, Alain**
❑ 91ProAHLCHL-303
**Morissette, Dave**
❑ 907thInnSQMJHL-199
❑ 91HamRoaA-12
❑ 93RoaExp-14
❑ 93RoaExp-23
❑ 98SP Aut-129
❑ 98SP AutSotTG-DM
❑ 98SSASotT-DM
❑ 98UppDec-406
❑ 98UppDecE-406
❑ 98UppDecE1o1-406
❑ 98UppDecGR-406
❑ 99SP AutPS-129
**Mork, Gary**
❑ 69ColChe-13
**Morley, Peter**
❑ 94GuiFla-11
❑ 97GuiFla-1
**Mormina, Bob**
❑ 83SprInd-12
**Moro, Marc**
❑ 93KinFro-4
❑ 95Cla-24
❑ 95Sla-116
❑ 96SauSteMG-12
❑ 96SauSteMGA-12
❑ 97BowCHL-17
❑ 97BowCHLOPC-17
**Morocco, Rick**
❑ 80SauSteMG-20
❑ 82NorBayC-17
**Moroney, Des**
❑ 64SweCorI-57
❑ 65SweCorI-57A
❑ 67SweHoc-273
❑ 69SweHocS-284
❑ 70SweHocS-182
❑ 71SweHocS-268
**Morozhov, Valentin**
❑ 95SigRoo-68
❑ 95SigRooSig-68
**Morozov, Alexei**
❑ 94Sel-158
❑ 94SelGol-158
❑ 95SigRooFF-FF10
❑ 95SigRooFFS-FF10
❑ 95UppDec-553
❑ 95UppDecEleIce-553
❑ 95UppDecEleIceG-553
❑ 96UppDecIce-139
❑ 97Be A PPAD-212
❑ 97Be A PPAPD-212
❑ 97BeAPla-212
❑ 97BeAPlaAut-212
❑ 97DonEli-108
❑ 97DonEliAsp-108
❑ 97DonEliS-108
❑ 97DonPre-155
❑ 97DonPreCttC-155
❑ 97DonPri-183
❑ 97DonPriSoA-183
❑ 97Kat-119
❑ 97KatGol-119
❑ 97KatSil-119
❑ 97Lea-164
❑ 97LeaFraMat-164
❑ 97LeaFraMDC-164
❑ 97McD-38
❑ 97PacCroR-111
❑ 97PacCroREG-111
❑ 97PacCroRIB-111
❑ 97PacCroRS-111
❑ 97PacOme-187
❑ 97PacOmeC-187
❑ 97PacOmeDG-187
❑ 97PacOmeEG-187
❑ 97PacOmeG-187
❑ 97PacOmeIB-187
❑ 97PacPar-152
❑ 97PacParC-152
❑ 97PacParDG-152
❑ 97PacParEG-152
❑ 97PacParIB-152
❑ 97PacParRed-152
❑ 97PacParSil-152
❑ 97Pin-6
❑ 97PinArtP-6
❑ 97PinBeeGT-24
❑ 97PinBeeT-24
❑ 97PinCerRR-H
❑ 97PinCerRRG-H
❑ 97PinCerRRMG-H
❑ 97PinMin-27
❑ 97PinMinB-27
❑ 97PinMinCBP-27
❑ 97PinMinCGPP-27
❑ 97PinMinCNSP-27
❑ 97PinMinCoiB-27
❑ 97PinMinCoiGP-27
❑ 97PinMinCoiN-27
❑ 97PinMinCoiSG-27
❑ 97PinMinCoiSS-27
❑ 97PinMinGolTea-27
❑ 97PinMinSilTea-27
❑ 97PinPrePBB-6
❑ 97PinPrePBC-6
❑ 97PinPrePBM-6
❑ 97PinPrePBY-6
❑ 97PinPrePFC-6
❑ 97PinPrePFM-6
❑ 97PinPrePFY-6
❑ 97PinPrePla-6
❑ 97PinRinC-6
❑ 97Sco-74
❑ 97ScoArtPro-74
❑ 97ScoGolBla-74
❑ 97ScoPen-18
❑ 97ScoPenPla-18
❑ 97ScoPenPre-18
❑ 97SP AutI-I15
❑ 97SPAut-190
❑ 97SPAutID-I15
❑ 97SPAutIE-I15
❑ 97UppDec-341
❑ 97UppDecBD-130
❑ 97UppDecBDDD-130
❑ 97UppDecBDPC-PC5
❑ 97UppDecBDPCDD-PC5
❑ 97UppDecBDPCM-PC5
❑ 97UppDecBDPCQD-PC5
❑ 97UppDecBDPCTD-PC5
❑ 97UppDecBDQD-130
❑ 97UppDecBDTD-130
❑ 97UppDecIce-56
❑ 97UppDecIceP-56
❑ 97UppDecILL-L7B
❑ 97UppDecILL2-L7B
❑ 97UppDecIPS-56
❑ 97Zen-94
❑ 97Zen5x7-67
❑ 97ZenGolImp-67
❑ 97ZenRooR-8
❑ 97ZenSilImp-67
❑ 97ZenZGol-94
❑ 97ZenZSil-94
❑ 97ZenZT-18
❑ 97ZenZTG-18
❑ 98Be A PPA-111
❑ 98Be A PPAA-111
❑ 98Be A PPAAF-111
❑ 98Be A PPTBASG-111
❑ 98Be APG-111
❑ 98O-PChr-70
❑ 98O-PChrR-70
❑ 98Pac-95
❑ 98PacAur-156
❑ 98PacCroR-111
❑ 98PacCroRLS-111
❑ 98PacDynI-152
❑ 98PacDynIIB-152
❑ 98PacDynIR-152
❑ 98PacIceB-95
❑ 98PacOmeH-198
❑ 98PacOmeODI-198
❑ 98PacOmeR-198
❑ 98PacPar-194
❑ 98PacParC-194
❑ 98PacParEG-194
❑ 98PacParH-194
❑ 98PacParIB-194
❑ 98PacParS-194
❑ 98PacRed-95
❑ 98SPxFin-95
❑ 98SPxFin-149
❑ 98SPxFinR-68
❑ 98SPxFinR-149
❑ 98SPxFinS-68
❑ 98SPxFinS-149
❑ 98Top-70
❑ 98TopO-P-70
❑ 98UC-166
❑ 98UD ChoPCR-166
❑ 98UD ChoR-166
❑ 98UD3-22
❑ 98UD3-82
❑ 98UD3-142
❑ 98UD3DieC-22
❑ 98UD3DieC-82
❑ 98UD3DieC-142
❑ 98UppDec-158
❑ 98UppDecBD-71
❑ 98UppDecDD-71
❑ 98UppDecE-158
❑ 98UppDecE1o1-158
❑ 98UppDecFIT-FT14
❑ 98UppDecFITQ1-FT14
❑ 98UppDecFITQ2-FT14
❑ 98UppDecFITQ3-FT14
❑ 98UppDecGR-158
❑ 98UppDecM-165
❑ 98UppDecMGS-165
❑ 98UppDecMSS-165
❑ 98UppDecMSS-165
❑ 98UppDecQD-71
❑ 98UppDecTD-71
❑ 99Pac-344
❑ 99PacCop-344
❑ 99PacGol-344
❑ 99PacIceB-344
❑ 99PacPreD-344
**Morque, Chris**
❑ 94HunBli-17
**Morris, Bernie**
❑ 23V1281PauC-64
❑ 28V1282PauC-73
**Morris, Derek**
❑ 96RegPat-16
❑ 97Be A PPAD-245
❑ 97Be A PPAPD-245
❑ 97BeAPla-245
❑ 97BeAPlaAut-245
❑ 97BowCHL-109
❑ 97BowCHLOPC-109
❑ 97DonEli-114
❑ 97DonEli-132
❑ 97DonEliAsp-114
❑ 97DonEliAsp-132
❑ 97DonEliS-114
❑ 97DonEliS-132
❑ 97DonPri-182
❑ 97DonPriSoA-182
❑ 97PacOme-31
❑ 97PacOmeC-31
❑ 97PacOmeDG-31
❑ 97PacOmeEG-31
❑ 97PacOmeG-31
❑ 97PacOmeIB-31
❑ 97SPAut-191
❑ 97UppDec-233
❑ 97UppDecBD-104
❑ 97UppDecBDDD-104
❑ 97UppDecBDQD-104
❑ 97UppDecBDTD-104
❑ 97UppDecIce-51
❑ 97UppDecIceP-51
❑ 97UppDecIPS-51
❑ 98BowBes-78
❑ 98BowBesAR-78
❑ 98BowBesR-78
❑ 98Fin-136
❑ 98FinNo P-136
❑ 98FinNo PR-136
❑ 98FinRef-136
❑ 98O-PChr-69
❑ 98O-PChrR-69
❑ 98Pac-53
❑ 98PacAur-27
❑ 98PacIceB-53
❑ 98PacPar-30
❑ 98PacParC-30
❑ 98PacParEG-30
❑ 98PacParH-30
❑ 98PacParIB-30
❑ 98PacParS-30
❑ 98PacRed-53
❑ 98SP Aut-11
❑ 98SPxFin-13
❑ 98SPxFin-136
❑ 98SPxFinR-13
❑ 98SPxFinR-136
❑ 98SPxFinS-13
❑ 98SPxFinS-136
❑ 98Top-69
❑ 98TopO-P-69
❑ 98UC-29
❑ 98UD ChoPCR-29
❑ 98UD ChoR-29
❑ 98UD3-5
❑ 98UD3-65
❑ 98UD3-125
❑ 98UD3DieC-5
❑ 98UD3DieC-65
❑ 98UD3DieC-125
❑ 98UppDec-51
❑ 98UppDecE-51
❑ 98UppDecE1o1-51
❑ 98UppDecGR-51
❑ 98UppDecM-28
❑ 98UppDecMGS-28
❑ 98UppDecMSS-28
❑ 98UppDecMSS-28
❑ 99Pac-58
❑ 99PacCop-58
❑ 99PacGol-58
❑ 99PacIceB-58
❑ 99PacPreD-58
❑ 99SP AutPS-11
❑ 99UppDecM-31
❑ 99UppDecMGS-31
❑ 99UppDecMPS-DM
❑ 99UppDecMSS-31
❑ 99UppDecMSS-31
**Morris, Elwyn**
❑ 45QuaOatP-39
**Morris, Frank**
❑ 96FifFly-18
❑ 97FifFly-19
**Morris, Jon**
❑ 89ProAHL-207
❑ 90Bow-84
❑ 90BowTif-84
❑ 90Dev-18
❑ 90OPC-457
❑ 90ProSet-621
❑ 90Sco-401
❑ 90ScoCan-401
❑ 90UppDec-65
❑ 90UppDecF-65
❑ 91Bow-286
❑ 91OPC-332
❑ 91ProAHLCHL-426
❑ 91ProSet-424
❑ 91ProSetFre-424
❑ 91ScoCan-548
❑ 91StaClu-360
❑ 91Top-332
❑ 91UppDec-216
❑ 91UppDecF-216
**Morris, Keith**
❑ 92AlbIntTC-13
**Morris, Rick**
❑ 75OPCWHA-91
**Morrison, Aaron**
❑ 907thInnSOHL-267
❑ 917thInnSOHL-106
**Morrison, Adam**
❑ 83VicCou-19
❑ 84VicCou-15
**Morrison, Andrew**
❑ 95Sla-29
**Morrison, Brendan**
❑ 92BriColJHL-117
❑ 93MicWol-16
❑ 97BeeAutA-56
❑ 97PinBee-56
❑ 97PinBeeGP-56
❑ 97SPAut-193
❑ 97Zen-90
❑ 97ZenRooR-4
❑ 97ZenZGol-90
❑ 97ZenZSil-90
❑ 98BowBes-105
❑ 98BowBesA-A7A
❑ 98BowBesA-A7B
❑ 98BowBesAAR-A7A
❑ 98BowBesAAR-A7B
❑ 98BowBesAR-105
❑ 98BowBesAR-A7A
❑ 98BowBesAR-A7B
❑ 98BowBesMIF-F15
❑ 98BowBesMIFAR-F15
❑ 98BowBesMIFR-F15
❑ 98BowBesP-BP9
❑ 98BowBesPAR-BP9
❑ 98BowBesPR-BP9
❑ 98BowBesR-105
❑ 98FinFutF-F19
❑ 98FinFutFR-F19
❑ 98McD-24
❑ 98Pac-265
❑ 98PacCroR-81
❑ 98PacCroRLS-81
❑ 98PacCroRRC-5
❑ 98PacDynI-111
❑ 98PacDynIIB-111
❑ 98PacDynIR-111
❑ 98PacDynIR-4
❑ 98PacIceB-265
❑ 98PacOmeH-139
❑ 98PacOmeO-20
❑ 98PacOmeODI-139
❑ 98PacOmeR-139
❑ 98PacRed-265
❑ 98PacRev-86
❑ 98PacRevIS-86
❑ 98PacRevR-86
❑ 98SP Aut-47
❑ 98SPxFin-48
❑ 98SPxFin-145
❑ 98SPxFinR-48
❑ 98SPxFinR-145
❑ 98SPxFinS-48
❑ 98SPxFinS-145
❑ 98TopGolLC1-82
❑ 98TopGolLC1B-82
❑ 98TopGolLC1BOoO-82
❑ 98TopGolLC1OoO-82
❑ 98TopGolLC1R-82
❑ 98TopGolLC1ROoO-82
❑ 98TopGolLC2-82
❑ 98TopGolLC2B-82
❑ 98TopGolLC2BOoO-82
❑ 98TopGolLC2OoO-82
❑ 98TopGolLC2R-82
❑ 98TopGolLC2ROoO-82
❑ 98TopGolLC3-82
❑ 98TopGolLC3B-82
❑ 98TopGolLC3BOoO-82
❑ 98TopGolLC3OoO-82
❑ 98TopGolLC3R-82
❑ 98TopGolLC3ROoO-82
❑ 98UC-120
❑ 98UD ChoPCR-120
❑ 98UD ChoR-120
❑ 98UD3-30
❑ 98UD3-90
❑ 98UD3-150
❑ 98UD3DieC-30
❑ 98UD3DieC-90
❑ 98UD3DieC-150
❑ 98UppDec-5
❑ 98UppDecBD-51
❑ 98UppDecDD-51
❑ 98UppDecE-5
❑ 98UppDecE1o1-5
❑ 98UppDecGN-GN4
❑ 98UppDecGN-GN27
❑ 98UppDecGNQ1-GN4
❑ 98UppDecGNQ1-GN27
❑ 98UppDecGNQ2-GN4
❑ 98UppDecGNQ2-GN27
❑ 98UppDecGNQ3-GN4
❑ 98UppDecGNQ3-GN27
❑ 98UppDecGR-5
❑ 98UppDecM-118
❑ 98UppDecMGS-118
❑ 98UppDecMP-BM
❑ 98UppDecMSS-118
❑ 98UppDecMSS-118
❑ 98UppDecQD-51
❑ 98UppDecTD-51
❑ 99Pac-241
❑ 99PacAur-87
❑ 99PacAurPD-87
❑ 99PacCop-241
❑ 99PacGol-241
❑ 99PacIceB-241
❑ 99PacPreD-241
❑ 99SP AutPS-47
❑ 99UppDecM-117
❑ 99UppDecMGS-117
❑ 99UppDecMSS-117
❑ 99UppDecMSS-117
**Morrison, Chris**
❑ 95VanVooRHI-15
**Morrison, Craig**
❑ 83OshGen-17
**Morrison, Crutchy**
❑ 23V1281PauC-48
**Morrison, Dave**
❑ 84FreExp-1
❑ 94GerDELE-157
❑ 95GerDELE-158
❑ 96GerDELE-233
**Morrison, Don**
❑ 44BeeGro2P-196
**Morrison, George**
❑ 70EssPowPla-243
❑ 71OPC-223
❑ 71SarProSta-191
❑ 71TorSun-241
❑ 72FigSaiPos-16
❑ 72OPC-314
**Morrison, Ikey**
❑ 28V1282PauC-50
**Morrison, Jim**
❑ 44BeeGro2P-437
❑ 45QuaOatP-40
❑ 52Par-28
❑ 53Par-15
❑ 54Par-18
❑ 54Par-94
❑ 55Par-8
❑ 55Par-76
❑ 55ParQuaO-8
❑ 55ParQuaO-76
❑ 57BruTeaIss-15
❑ 57Par-T11
❑ 59Top-36
❑ 60Par-61
❑ 60ShiCoi-95
❑ 60Top-9
❑ 62QueAce-18
❑ 63QueAceQ-16
❑ 64QueAce-13
❑ 65QueAce-13
❑ 69OPC-156
❑ 70EssPowPla-233
❑ 70OPC-90
❑ 70SarProSta-169
❑ 70Top-90
❑ 81KinCan-24
❑ 82KinCan-1
❑ 94ParMisL-115
**Morrison, Justin**
❑ 907thInnSOHL-67
❑ 917thInnSOHL-229
❑ 91StaPicH-45
❑ 91UltDra-52
❑ 93MusFur-15
❑ 94MusFur-4
**Morrison, Ken**
❑ 84PriAlbRS-19
❑ 85KamBla-15
**Morrison, Kevin**
❑ 74MarSanDW-4
❑ 75OPCWHA-63
❑ 75OPCWHA-80
❑ 76OPCWHA-10
❑ 76OPCWHA-68
❑ 76SanDieMW-7
❑ 79Roc-14
**Morrison, Lew**
❑ 70EssPowPla-205
❑ 70FlyPos-8
❑ 70OPC-197
❑ 71OPC-89
❑ 72Flam-10
❑ 72OPC-143
❑ 72SarProSta-13
❑ 72Top-58
❑ 74NHLActSta-314
❑ 74NHLActStaU-27
❑ 74OPCNHL-125
❑ 74Top-125
❑ 76OPCNHL-307
❑ 77OPCNHL-300
**Morrison, Mark**
❑ 81VicCou-12
❑ 82VicCou-19
❑ 83CanNatJ-10
❑ 84VicCou-16
❑ 96FifFly-17
❑ 97FifFly-14
**Morrison, Mike**
❑ 85KitRan-15
**Morrison, Rod**
❑ 44BeeGro2P-197
**Morrison, Scott**
❑ 94FinnJaaK-321
❑ 94HumHawP-19
**Morrison, Tavis**
❑ 96DayBom-11
**Morrissey, Dan**
❑ 91BriColJHL-78
❑ 92BriColJHL-88
**Morrone, Mike**
❑ 93OweSouPla-20
❑ 94DetJrRW-9
❑ 95Sla-65
❑ 95SlaMemC-83
❑ 96DetWha-12
**Morrow, Brenden**
❑ 97BowCHL-98
❑ 97BowCHL-147
❑ 97BowCHLAu-27
❑ 97BowCHLBB-16
❑ 97BowCHLBowBesAR-16
❑ 97BowCHLBowBesR-16
❑ 97BowCHLOPC-98
❑ 97BowCHLOPC-147
❑ 98BowCHL-60
❑ 98BowCHLGA-60
❑ 98BowCHLOI-60
❑ 98BowChrC-60
❑ 98BowChrCGA-60
❑ 98BowChrCGAR-60
❑ 98BowChrCOI-60
❑ 98BowChrCOIR-60
❑ 98BowChrCR-60
❑ 98SPXTopP-66
❑ 98SPXTopPF-66
❑ 98SPXTopPR-66
❑ 98UppDecBD-94
❑ 98UppDecDD-94
❑ 98UppDecQD-94
❑ 98UppDecTD-94
**Morrow, Ken**
❑ 80OPC-9
❑ 80Top-9
❑ 81OPC-205
❑ 81OPCSti-165
❑ 81SweSemHVS-93
❑ 81Top-E91
❑ 82OPC-206
❑ 82OPCSti-58
❑ 82PosCer-12
❑ 83IslTeaIss-11
❑ 83OPC-13
❑ 83OPCSti-73
❑ 84IslIslN-19
❑ 84OPC-131
❑ 84OPCSti-93
❑ 84Top-97
❑ 85IslIslN-23
❑ 85OPC-93
❑ 85Top-93
❑ 86OPC-65
❑ 86OPCSti-215
❑ 86Top-65
❑ 87OPC-66
❑ 87OPCSti-246
❑ 87PanSti-94
❑ 87Top-66
❑ 88OPC-53
❑ 88PanSti-285
❑ 88Top-53
❑ 91UppDec-637
❑ 91UppDecF-637
❑ 95SigRooMI-21
❑ 95SigRooMI-22
❑ 95SigRooSMIS-21
❑ 95SigRooSMIS-22
**Morrow, Scott**
❑ 94St.JohF-13
❑ 96CinCyc-28
❑ 98CinCyc-14
**Morrow, Steve**
❑ 91ProAHLCHL-284
**Morschauser, Gus**
❑ 87KitRan-6
❑ 88KitRan-10
**Morth, Tommy**
❑ 82SweSemHVS-19
❑ 83SweSemE-90
❑ 84SweSemE-90
❑ 85SwePanS-82
❑ 86SwePanS-72
❑ 87SwePanS-78
**Mortier, Darren**
❑ 94SarSti-8
❑ 95Sla-337
❑ 96SarSti-16
**Morton, Dean**
❑ 88ProAHL-17
❑ 89ProAHL-328
❑ 90ProAHLIHL-314
**Morton, Rick**
❑ 907thInnSOHL-189
❑ 917thInnSOHL-272
**Mortson, Cleland**
❑ 63QueAce-18
❑ 63QueAceQ-17
❑ 64QueAce-14
❑ 65QueAce-14
**Mortson, Gus**
❑ 44BeeGro2P-127
❑ 44BeeGro2P-438
❑ 45QuaOatP-41A
❑ 45QuaOatP-41B
❑ 48ExhCan-36
❑ 51Par-73
❑ 52Par-39
❑ 53Par-81
❑ 54Par-81
❑ 54Top-17
❑ 57Top-25

❑ 58Top-38
❑ 94ParMisL-30
**Morusyk, Wayne**
❑ 71RocAme-14
**Morz, Johann**
❑ 82SweSemHVS-117
**Moscaluk, Gary**
❑ 88ProIHL-105
❑ 89ProIHL-65
**Mosdell, Ken**
❑ 34BeeGro1P-243
❑ 44BeeGro2P-275
❑ 45QuaOatP-101A
❑ 45QuaOatP-101B
❑ 45QuaOatP-101C
❑ 45QuaOatP-101D
❑ 48ExhCan-19
❑ 51Par-11
❑ 52Par-8
❑ 53Par-33
❑ 54Par-12
❑ 55Par-39
❑ 55ParQuaO-39
❑ 94ParMisL-41
**Moser, Jay**
❑ 94MinGolG-22
❑ 95MinGolG-22
❑ 96ProBru-18
❑ 96SouCarS-29
**Mosey, Scott**
❑ 84SauSteMG-14
**Mosienko, Bill**
❑ 44BeeGro2P-128
❑ 51Par-49
❑ 52Par-27
❑ 53Par-80
❑ 54Top-54
❑ 83HalFP-A11
❑ 85HalFC-11
❑ 91UltOriS-61
❑ 91UltOriSF-61
❑ 92HalFL-22
❑ 92ParParR-PR20
**Mosjkarov, Sergei**
❑ 74SweHocS-85
**Moss, Joey**
❑ 90OilIGA-17
**Moss, Tyler**
❑ 93KinFro-3
❑ 95Cla-86
❑ 95ClaCHLAS-AS7
❑ 96GraRapG-14
❑ 97Be A PPAD-230
❑ 97Be A PPAPD-230
❑ 97BeAPla-230
❑ 97BeAPlaAut-230
❑ 97DonPri-179
❑ 97DonPriSoA-179
❑ 97Kat-23
❑ 97KatGol-23
❑ 97KatSil-23
❑ 97PacCroR-20
❑ 97PacCroREG-20
❑ 97PacCroRFODC-4
❑ 97PacCroRIB-20
❑ 97PacCroRS-20
❑ 97PacOme-32
❑ 97PacOmeC-32
❑ 97PacOmeDG-32
❑ 97PacOmeEG-32
❑ 97PacOmeG-32
❑ 97PacOmeIB-32
❑ 97SPAut-174
❑ 97UppDecBD-108
❑ 97UppDecBDDD-108
❑ 97UppDecBDQD-108
❑ 97UppDecBDTD-108
❑ 97UppDecIce-32
❑ 97UppDecIceP-32
❑ 97UppDecIPS-32
❑ 98Be A PPA-17
❑ 98Be A PPAA-17
❑ 98Be A PPAAF-17
❑ 98Be A PPTBASG-17
❑ 98Be APG-17
❑ 98BowBesMIF-F10
❑ 98BowBesMIFAR-F10
❑ 98BowBesMIFR-F10
❑ 98Pac-122
❑ 98PacIceB-122
❑ 98PacOmeH-34
❑ 98PacOmeODI-34
❑ 98PacOmeR-34
❑ 98PacRed-122
❑ 98PacRev-21
❑ 98PacRevIS-21
❑ 98PacRevR-21
❑ 98UppDec-56
❑ 98UppDecE-56
❑ 98UppDecE1o1-56
❑ 98UppDecGR-56
**Mota, Kevin**
❑ 96SarSti-17
**Motkov, Dmitri**
❑ 90OPCRedA-5R
❑ 93ClaProPro-57
**Motovilov, Anatoli**
❑ 73SweHocS-131
❑ 73SweWorCS-131
**Mott, Morris**
❑ 69SweHocS-359
❑ 69SweWorC-33
❑ 69SweWorC-94
❑ 69SweWorC-189
❑ 74NHLActStaU-7
❑ 74OPCNHL-48
❑ 74Top-48
**Mottau, Mike**
❑ 98UC-300
❑ 98UD ChoPCR-300
❑ 98UD ChoR-300
**Motter, Alex**
❑ 34BeeGro1P-25
❑ 40OPCV3012-115
**Mougenel, Ryan**
❑ 93OweSouPla-21
❑ 95Sla-133
❑ 96KitRan-20
❑ 97BowCHL-27
❑ 97BowCHLOPC-27
**Mouser, Tim**
❑ 92TolSto-5
**Mouton, Claude**
❑ 87CanaPos-19
**Movsessian, Vicki**
❑ 94ClaWomOH-W23
**Mowbray, Mike**
❑ 96GuiFla-13
**Mowers, Johnny**
❑ 34BeeGro1P-118
❑ 40OPCV3012-105
**Mowers, Mark**
❑ 99Pac-230
❑ 99PacCop-230
❑ 99PacIceB-230
❑ 99PacPreD-230
**Moxam, Darren**
❑ 84BelBul-12
❑ 86KitRan-13
**Moxam, Darryl**
❑ 93OshGen-15
❑ 93PetPet-7
❑ 95Sla-390
❑ 95SudWol-17
❑ 95SudWolP-16
**Moxey, Jim**
❑ 76OPCNHL-349
**Moxness, Rob**
❑ 91RayJrC-12
**Moylan, Corey**
❑ 93SauSteMG-26
**Moylan, David (Dave)**
❑ 84SudWol-13
❑ 85SudWol-10
❑ 86SudWol-5
❑ 90ProAHLIHL-439
❑ 91ProAHLCHL-159
**Moyon, Christophe**
❑ 94FinnJaaK-214
❑ 94FreNatT-20
**Mrazek, Radek**
❑ 94CzeAPSE-210
❑ 95CzeAPSE-160
❑ 96CzeAPSE-170
**Mrena, Andrej**
❑ 95SloPeeWT-20
**Mrhalek, Roman**
❑ 91AirCanSJHL-C28
**Mrozik, Rick**
❑ 93MinDul-22
**Mruk, Jerzy**
❑ 89SweSemWCS-128
**Mucha, Jaro**
❑ 94GerDELE-158
❑ 95GerDELE-153
**Muckalt, Bill**
❑ 91BriColJHL-82
❑ 92BriColJHL-77
❑ 98Be A PPA-291
❑ 98Be A PPAA-291
❑ 98Be A PPAAF-291
❑ 98Be A PPSE-291
❑ 98Be APG-291
❑ 98BowBes-124
❑ 98BowBesA-A6A
❑ 98BowBesA-A6B
❑ 98BowBesAAR-A6A
❑ 98BowBesAAR-A6B
❑ 98BowBesAR-124
❑ 98BowBesAR-A6A
❑ 98BowBesAR-A6B
❑ 98BowBesMIF-F14
❑ 98BowBesMIFAR-F14
❑ 98BowBesMIFR-F14
❑ 98BowBesR-124
❑ 98PacCroR-137
❑ 98PacCroRLS-137
❑ 98PacCroRRC-10
❑ 98PacDynIR-10
❑ 98PacOmeH-238
❑ 98PacOmeO-35
❑ 98PacOmeODI-238
❑ 98PacOmeR-238
❑ 98PacRev-143
❑ 98PacRevIS-143
❑ 98PacRevR-143
❑ 98SP Aut-111
❑ 98SPXTopP-59
❑ 98SPXTopPF-59
❑ 98SPXTopPR-59
❑ 98TopGolLC1-73
❑ 98TopGolLC1B-73
❑ 98TopGolLC1BOoO-73
❑ 98TopGolLC1OoO-73
❑ 98TopGolLC1R-73
❑ 98TopGolLC1ROoO-73
❑ 98TopGolLC2-73
❑ 98TopGolLC2B-73
❑ 98TopGolLC2BOoO-73
❑ 98TopGolLC2OoO-73
❑ 98TopGolLC2R-73
❑ 98TopGolLC2ROoO-73
❑ 98TopGolLC3-73
❑ 98TopGolLC3B-73
❑ 98TopGolLC3BOoO-73
❑ 98TopGolLC3OoO-73
❑ 98TopGolLC3R-73
❑ 98TopGolLC3ROoO-73
❑ 98UppDec-377
❑ 98UppDecBD-86
❑ 98UppDecDD-86
❑ 98UppDecE-377
❑ 98UppDecE1o1-377
❑ 98UppDecGR-377
❑ 98UppDecM-205
❑ 98UppDecMGS-205
❑ 98UppDecMSS-205
❑ 98UppDecMSS-205
❑ 98UppDecQD-86
❑ 98UppDecTD-86
❑ 99Pac-428
❑ 99PacAur-141
❑ 99PacAurPD-141
❑ 99PacCop-428
❑ 99PacGol-428
❑ 99PacIceB-428
❑ 99PacPreD-428
❑ 99RetHoc-78
❑ 99SP AutPS-111
❑ 99UppDecM-205
❑ 99UppDecMGS-205
❑ 99UppDecMPS-BM
❑ 99UppDecMSS-205
❑ 99UppDecMSS-205
❑ 99UppDecRG-78
❑ 99UppDecRP-78
**Muckler, John**
❑ 52JunBluT-175
❑ 82OilRedR-NNO
❑ 83OilMcD-20
❑ 84OilRedR-NNO
❑ 85OilRedR-NNO
❑ 86OilRedR-NNO
❑ 88OilTenAnn-68
❑ 90OilIGA-18
❑ 90ProSet-665
❑ 92SabBluS-15
❑ 93Kra-44
**Mueggler, Brian**
❑ 897thInnSOHL-127
❑ 89NiaFalT-13
**Mueller, Brad**
❑ 84BraWheK-6
**Mueller, Brian**
❑ 91UppDecCWJC-66
❑ 92ClaKni-11
❑ 95Cla-77
❑ 95ClaAut-14
**Mueller, Regan**
❑ 93SeaThu-15
**Muhlbauer, Thomas**
❑ 94GerDELE-115
❑ 95GerDELE-327
**Muhr, Manfred**
❑ 95AusNatTea-17
❑ 95FinnSemWC-187
**Muir, Bryan**
❑ 98UppDec-314
❑ 98UppDecE-314
❑ 98UppDecE1o1-314
❑ 98UppDecGR-314
**Muir, Jimmy**
❑ 36V356WorG-128
**Muir, Wayne**
❑ 87SauSteMG-28
❑ 89SauSteMG-21
❑ 92GreMon-8
❑ 94BraSmo-17
**Muise, Randy**
❑ 91AirCanSJHL-B33
**Mujcin, Mirsad**
❑ 917thInnSWHL-296
**Mukhometov, Ildar**
❑ 91UppDecCWJC-10
**Mulhern, Richard**
❑ 76OPCNHL-265
❑ 77OPCNHL-373
❑ 78OPC-256
❑ 78Top-256
❑ 79OPC-133
❑ 79Top-133
❑ 80JetPos-18
❑ 80OPC-350
**Mulhern, Ryan**
❑ 96HamRoaA-HRA7
❑ 98KanCitB-17
**Mulick, Robert**
❑ 95SauSteMG-12
❑ 95Sla-378
❑ 96SauSteMG-13
❑ 96SauSteMGA-13
**Mullahy, Brad**
❑ 94RalIce-13
**Mullen, Brian**
❑ 82Jet-18
❑ 83Jet-18
❑ 83OPC-389
❑ 83OPCSti-148
❑ 83PufSti-4
❑ 83Vac-134
❑ 847EDis-60
❑ 84JetPol-15
❑ 84OPC-344
❑ 85JetPol-14
❑ 85JetSilD-6
❑ 85OPC-195
❑ 86JetBor-15
❑ 86KraDra-47
❑ 86OPC-38
❑ 86OPCSti-109
❑ 86Top-38
❑ 88OPC-91
❑ 88Top-91
❑ 89OPC-24
❑ 89OPCSti-243
❑ 89PanSti-286
❑ 89RanMarMB-19
❑ 89Top-24
❑ 90Bow-217
❑ 90BowTif-217
❑ 90OPC-292
❑ 90PanSti-96
❑ 90ProSet-203
❑ 90Sco-84
❑ 90ScoCan-84
❑ 90Top-292
❑ 90TopTif-292
❑ 90UppDec-182
❑ 90UppDecF-182
❑ 91Bow-61
❑ 91OPC-129
❑ 91OPCPre-166
❑ 91PanSti-289
❑ 91Par-166
❑ 91ParFre-166
❑ 91Pin-135
❑ 91PinFre-135
❑ 91ProSet-165
❑ 91ProSetFre-165
❑ 91ProSetPla-106
❑ 91ScoAme-59
❑ 91ScoAme-379
❑ 91ScoCan-59
❑ 91ScoCan-269
❑ 91ScoCan-552
❑ 91ScoRoo-2T
❑ 91ShaSanJSA-16
❑ 91StaClu-222
❑ 91Top-129
❑ 91UppDec-57
❑ 91UppDecF-57
❑ 92Bow-139
❑ 92OPC-260
❑ 92OPCPre-111
❑ 92PanSti-125
❑ 92PanStiFre-125
❑ 92Pin-333
❑ 92PinFre-333
❑ 92Sco-278
❑ 92ScoCan-278
❑ 92ScoUSAG-12
❑ 92StaClu-420
❑ 92Top-104
❑ 92TopGol-104G
❑ 92Ult-348
❑ 92UppDec-317
❑ 92UppDec-468
❑ 93OPCPre-154
❑ 93OPCPreG-154
❑ 93PanSti-61
❑ 93Pin-122
❑ 93Pin-324
❑ 93PinCan-122
❑ 93PinCan-324
❑ 93Sco-347
❑ 93ScoCan-347
❑ 93StaClu-227
❑ 93StaCluFDI-227
❑ 93StaCluFDIO-227
❑ 93StaCluO-227
❑ 93TopPre-154
❑ 93TopPreG-154
❑ 94FinnJaaK-128
❑ 94Lea-419
❑ 94StaClu-213
❑ 94StaCluFDI-213
❑ 94StaCluMOMS-213
❑ 94StaCluSTWC-213
❑ 95FinnSemWC-120
**Mullen, Dennis**
❑ 95LetHur-15
**Mullen, Joey (Joe)**
❑ 82OPC-307
❑ 82OPCSti-200
❑ 83OPC-317
❑ 84OPC-188
❑ 84OPC-367
❑ 84OPCSti-61
❑ 84Top-133
❑ 85OPC-7
❑ 85OPCSti-47
❑ 85Top-7
❑ 86FlamRedR-15
❑ 86FlamRedR-16
❑ 86KraDra-48
❑ 86OPC-44
❑ 86OPCSti-82
❑ 86Top-44
❑ 87FlamRedRP-16
❑ 87OPC-126
❑ 87OPCBoxB-G
❑ 87OPCMin-29
❑ 87OPCSti-36
❑ 87OPCSti-186
❑ 87PanSti-210
❑ 87PanSti-384
❑ 87ProAll-8
❑ 87Top-126
❑ 87TopBoxB-G
❑ 88OPC-76
❑ 88OPCSti-95
❑ 88PanSti-11
❑ 88Top-76
❑ 89Kra-60
❑ 89OPC-196
❑ 89OPC-324
❑ 89OPCBoxB-O
❑ 89OPCSti-61
❑ 89OPCSti-90
❑ 89OPCSti-160
❑ 89OPCSti-214
❑ 89PanSti-27
❑ 89PanSti-380
❑ 89PanSti-384
❑ 89SweSemWCS-170
❑ 89Top-196
❑ 89TopBoxB-O
❑ 89TopStiIns-5
❑ 90Bow-97
❑ 90BowTif-97
❑ 90Kra-36
❑ 90Kra-72
❑ 90OPC-218
❑ 90OPCPre-77
❑ 90PanSti-183
❑ 90PenFoo-8
❑ 90ProSet-40A
❑ 90ProSet-40B
❑ 90ProSet-343
❑ 90ProSet-508
❑ 90Sco-208
❑ 90ScoCan-208
❑ 90ScoHotRS-88
❑ 90ScoRoo-7T
❑ 90Top-218
❑ 90TopTif-218
❑ 90UppDec-252
❑ 90UppDec-423
❑ 90UppDecF-252
❑ 90UppDecF-423
❑ 91Bow-79
❑ 91OPC-69
❑ 91OPCPre-153
❑ 91PanSti-278
❑ 91Par-141
❑ 91ParFre-141
❑ 91PenCokE-7
❑ 91PenFoo-6
❑ 91PenFooCS-2
❑ 91Pin-176
❑ 91PinFre-176
❑ 91ProSet-191
❑ 91ProSetFre-191
❑ 91ScoAme-268
❑ 91ScoAme-379
❑ 91ScoCan-269
❑ 91ScoCan-488
❑ 91StaClu-7
❑ 91SweSemWCS-146
❑ 91Top-69
❑ 91UppDec-201
❑ 91UppDecF-201
❑ 92BluUDBB-16
❑ 92Bow-58
❑ 92OPC-23
❑ 92PanSti-223
❑ 92PanStiFre-223
❑ 92Par-368
❑ 92ParEmel-368
❑ 92PenCokC-13
❑ 92PenFoo-6
❑ 92Pin-360
❑ 92PinFre-360
❑ 92ProSet-142
❑ 92ProSet-262
❑ 92Sco-3
❑ 92ScoCan-3
❑ 92ScoUSAG-9
❑ 92StaClu-20
❑ 92Top-113
❑ 92TopGol-113G
❑ 92Ult-166
❑ 92UppDec-144
❑ 93Don-207
❑ 93Lea-300
❑ 93OPCPre-498
❑ 93OPCPreG-498
❑ 93PanSti-83
❑ 93Par-159
❑ 93ParEmel-159
❑ 93PenFoo-25
❑ 93PenSti-7
❑ 93Pin-240
❑ 93PinCan-240
❑ 93Pow-192
❑ 93Sco-7
❑ 93ScoCan-7
❑ 93StaClu-19
❑ 93StaCluFDI-19
❑ 93StaCluFDIO-19
❑ 93StaCluO-19
❑ 93SweSemWCS-178
❑ 93TopPre-498
❑ 93TopPreG-498
❑ 93Ult-171
❑ 93UppDec-186
❑ 94CanGamNHLP-187
❑ 94FinnJaaK-118
❑ 94FinRinL-10
❑ 94Fle-165
❑ 94HocWit-78
❑ 94Lea-385
❑ 94OPCPre-517
❑ 94OPCPreSE-517
❑ 94Par-180
❑ 94ParGol-180
❑ 94PenFoo-6
❑ 94Pin-149
❑ 94PinArtP-149
❑ 94PinRinC-149
❑ 94Sco-57
❑ 94ScoGol-57
❑ 94ScoPla-57
❑ 94ScoPlaTS-57
❑ 94Sel-16
❑ 94SelGol-16
❑ 94StaClu-50
❑ 94StaCluFDI-50
❑ 94StaCluMO-33
❑ 94StaCluMOMS-50
❑ 94StaCluST-18
❑ 94StaCluSTWC-50
❑ 94TopPre-517
❑ 94TopPreSE-517
❑ 94Ult-167
❑ 94UppDec-346
❑ 94UppDecEleIce-346
❑ 95BeAPla-154
❑ 95BeAPSig-S154
❑ 95BeAPSigDC-S154
❑ 95ColCho-25
❑ 95ColChoPC-25
❑ 95ColChoPCP-25
❑ 95Don-38
❑ 95Don-251
❑ 95Emo-9
❑ 95Lea-155
❑ 95Sco-252
❑ 95ScoBlaIce-252
❑ 95ScoBlaIceAP-252
❑ 95ScoBorBat-8
❑ 95SkyImp-10
❑ 95StaCluM-M7
❑ 95Sum-92
❑ 95SumArtP-92
❑ 95SumIce-92
❑ 95SweGloWC-112
❑ 95Ult-124
❑ 95Ult-206
❑ 95UltGolM-124
❑ 95UppDec-16
❑ 95UppDecEleIce-16
❑ 95UppDecEleIceG-16
❑ 96ColCho-22
❑ 96Don-191
❑ 96DonPrePro-191
❑ 96Lea-14
❑ 96LeaPreP-14
❑ 96PenTri-2
❑ 96Pin-61
❑ 96PinArtP-61
❑ 96PinFoi-61
❑ 96PinPreS-61
❑ 96PinRinC-61
❑ 96Sco-201
❑ 96ScoArtPro-201
❑ 96ScoDeaCAP-201
❑ 96ScoGolB-201
❑ 96ScoSpeAP-201
❑ 96SP-131
❑ 96SweSemW-169
**Muller, Greg**
❑ 94GerDELE-298
❑ 95GerDELE-319
**Muller, Josef**
❑ 96GerDELE-193
**Muller, Kirk**
❑ 81KinCan-15
❑ 84DevPos-27
❑ 85DevPos-7
❑ 85OPC-84
❑ 85OPCSti-64
❑ 85Top-84
❑ 86DevPol-16
❑ 86OPC-94
❑ 86OPCSti-201
❑ 86Top-94
❑ 87OPC-157
❑ 87OPCSti-65
❑ 87PanSti-79
❑ 87Top-157
❑ 88DevCar-21
❑ 88FriLaySS-33
❑ 88OPC-84
❑ 88OPCBoxB-F
❑ 88OPCSti-75
❑ 88PanSti-275
❑ 88Top-84
❑ 88TopBoxB-F
❑ 89DevCar-17
❑ 89OPC-117
❑ 89OPCSti-83
❑ 89PanSti-251
❑ 89Top-117
❑ 90Bow-82
❑ 90BowTif-82
❑ 90Dev-19
❑ 90Kra-37
❑ 90Kra-88
❑ 90OPC-245
❑ 90OPC-394
❑ 90OPCPre-78
❑ 90PanSti-73
❑ 90ProSet-172
❑ 90ProSet-371
❑ 90Sco-160
❑ 90ScoCan-160
❑ 90ScoHotRS-71
❑ 90Top-245
❑ 90Top-394
❑ 90TopTeaSL-7
❑ 90TopTif-245
❑ 90UppDec-267
❑ 90UppDec-311
❑ 90UppDecF-267
❑ 90UppDecF-311
❑ 91Bow-274
❑ 91CanaPos-20
❑ 91Gil-21
❑ 91Kra-12
❑ 91OPC-22
❑ 91OPC-191
❑ 91OPCPre-86
❑ 91OPCPre-145
❑ 91PanSti-219
❑ 91Par-89
❑ 91ParFre-89
❑ 91Pin-3
❑ 91PinFre-3
❑ 91ProSet-134
❑ 91ProSet-412
❑ 91ProSetFre-134
❑ 91ProSetFre-412
❑ 91ProSetPla-66
❑ 91ProSetPla-281
❑ 91ScoAme-110
❑ 91ScoAme-331
❑ 91ScoCan-110
❑ 91ScoCan-361
❑ 91ScoCan-614
❑ 91ScoRoo-64T
❑ 91StaClu-193
❑ 91Top-22
❑ 91UppDec-149
❑ 91UppDec-519
❑ 91UppDecF-149
❑ 91UppDecF-519
❑ 92Bow-138
❑ 92Bow-236
❑ 92CanaPos-18
❑ 92McDUppD-23
❑ 92OPC-327
❑ 92PanSti-124
❑ 92PanStiFre-148
❑ 92Par-83
❑ 92Par-504
❑ 92ParCheP-CP5
❑ 92ParEmel-83
❑ 92ParEmel-504
❑ 92Pin-111
❑ 92PinCanPP-2
❑ 92PinFre-111
❑ 92ProSet-87
❑ 92Sco-225
❑ 92ScoCan-225
❑ 92ScoSha-29
❑ 92ScoShaCan-29
❑ 92SeaPat-25
❑ 92StaClu-387
❑ 92Top-490
❑ 92TopGol-490G
❑ 92Ult-107
❑ 92UppDec-180
❑ 93CanaMol-8
❑ 93CanaPos-16
❑ 93Don-177
❑ 93Kra-17
❑ 93Kra-59
❑ 93Lea-182
❑ 93McDUppD-20A
❑ 93McDUppD-20B
❑ 93OPCCanHF-26
❑ 93OPCPre-509
❑ 93OPCPreBG-24
❑ 93OPCPreG-509
❑ 93PanSti-14
❑ 93Par-378
❑ 93ParEmel-378
❑ 93Pin-180
❑ 93PinAllS-7
❑ 93PinAllSC-7
❑ 93PinCan-180
❑ 93Pow-131
❑ 93Sco-234
❑ 93ScoCan-234
❑ 93StaClu-67
❑ 93StaCluAS-16
❑ 93StaCluFDI-67
❑ 93StaCluFDIO-67
❑ 93StaCluO-67
❑ 93TopPre-509
❑ 93TopPreG-509
❑ 93Ult-21
❑ 93UltAllS-9
❑ 93UppDec-148
❑ 93UppDecLAS-9
❑ 93UppDecSP-80
❑ 94BeAP99A-G17
❑ 94BeAPla-R3
❑ 94BeAPSig-40
❑ 94CanaPos-16
❑ 94CanGamNHLP-137
❑ 94Don-255
❑ 94EASpo-69
❑ 94Fin-44
❑ 94FinBowB-B10
❑ 94FinBowBR-B10
❑ 94FinRef-44
❑ 94FinSupTW-44
❑ 94Fla-89
❑ 94Fle-104
❑ 94HocWit-19
❑ 94Kra-9
❑ 94Lea-163
❑ 94LeaLim-37

❑ 94OPCPre-305
❑ 94OPCPreSE-305
❑ 94ParSE-SE88
❑ 94ParSEG-SE88
❑ 94ParVin-V4
❑ 94Pin-82
❑ 94PinArtP-82
❑ 94PinGam-GR7
❑ 94PinNorLig-NL2
❑ 94PinRinC-82
❑ 94PosCerBB-18
❑ 94Sco-146
❑ 94ScoChelt-Cl10
❑ 94ScoGol-146
❑ 94ScoPla-146
❑ 94ScoPlaTS-146
❑ 94Sel-107
❑ 94SelGol-107
❑ 94SP-68
❑ 94SPDieCut-68
❑ 94StaClu-130
❑ 94StaCluFDI-130
❑ 94StaCluMOMS-130
❑ 94StaCluSTWC-130
❑ 94TopPre-305
❑ 94TopPreGTG-11
❑ 94TopPreSE-305
❑ 94Ult-313
❑ 94UppDec-66
❑ 94UppDecEleIce-66
❑ 94UppDecIcIG-IG9
❑ 94UppDecSPI-SP40
❑ 94UppDecSPIDC-SP40
❑ 95CanGamNHLP-168
❑ 95ColCho-142
❑ 95ColChoPC-142
❑ 95ColChoPCP-142
❑ 95Don-129
❑ 95DonEli-54
❑ 95DonEliDCS-54
❑ 95DonEliDCU-54
❑ 95Emo-106
❑ 95ImpSti-74
❑ 95KenStaLA-12
❑ 95Lea-41
❑ 95Met-91
❑ 95NHLAcePC-2S
❑ 95ParInt-129
❑ 95ParInt-474
❑ 95ParIntEl-129
❑ 95ParIntEl-474
❑ 95PlaOneoOne-65
❑ 95ProMag-59
❑ 95Sco-96
❑ 95ScoBlaIce-96
❑ 95ScoBlaIceAP-96
❑ 95SelCer-103
❑ 95SelCerMG-103
❑ 95SkyImp-103
❑ 95SP-142
❑ 95StaClu-177
❑ 95StaCluMOMS-177
❑ 95Sum-121
❑ 95SumArtP-121
❑ 95SumIce-121
❑ 95Top-115
❑ 95TopOPCI-115
❑ 95Ult-96
❑ 95Ult-268
❑ 95UltGolM-96
❑ 95UppDecSpeE-SE52
❑ 95UppDecSpeEdiG-SE52
❑ 95Zen-45
❑ 95ZenGifG-13
❑ 96ColCho-259
❑ 96Don-161
❑ 96DonCanI-47
❑ 96DonCanIGPP-47
❑ 96DonCanIOC-10
❑ 96DonCanIRPP-47
❑ 96DonPrePro-161
❑ 96DurAllT-DC10
❑ 96FlaNowAT-2
❑ 96FlePic-138
❑ 96Lea-72
❑ 96LeaPreP-72
❑ 96MetUni-150
❑ 96NHLProSTA-59
❑ 96Pin-147
❑ 96PinArtP-147
❑ 96PinFoi-147
❑ 96PinPreS-147
❑ 96PinRinC-147
❑ 96PlaOneoOne-344
❑ 96Sco-103
❑ 96ScoArtPro-103
❑ 96ScoDeaCAP-103
❑ 96ScoGolB-103
❑ 96ScoSpeAP-103
❑ 96SkyImp-127
❑ 96SP-156
❑ 96UppDec-165
❑ 97Be A PPAD-121
❑ 97Be A PPAPD-121
❑ 97BeAPla-121
❑ 97BeAPlaAut-121
❑ 97ColCho-98
❑ 97Don-38
❑ 97DonCanI-47
❑ 97DonCanIDS-47
❑ 97DonCanIPS-47
❑ 97DonLim-156
❑ 97DonLimExp-156
❑ 97DonPre-120
❑ 97DonPreCttC-120

❑ 97DonPreProG-38
❑ 97DonPreProS-38
❑ 97Pac-217
❑ 97PacCop-217
❑ 97PacEmeGre-217
❑ 97PacIceB-217
❑ 97PacInv-62
❑ 97PacInvEG-62
❑ 97PacInvIB-62
❑ 97PacInvR-62
❑ 97PacInvS-62
❑ 97PacPar-82
❑ 97PacParC-82
❑ 97PacParDG-82
❑ 97PacParEG-82
❑ 97PacParIB-82
❑ 97PacParRed-82
❑ 97PacParSil-82
❑ 97PacRed-217
❑ 97PacSil-217
❑ 97Pin-190
❑ 97PinCer-117
❑ 97PinCerMB-117
❑ 97PinCerMG-117
❑ 97PinCerMR-117
❑ 97PinCerR-117
❑ 97PinIns-108
❑ 97PinPrePBB-190
❑ 97PinPrePBC-190
❑ 97PinPrePBM-190
❑ 97PinPrePBY-190
❑ 97PinPrePFC-190
❑ 97PinPrePFM-190
❑ 97PinPrePFY-190
❑ 97PinPrePla-190
❑ 97PinTotCMPG-117
❑ 97PinTotCPB-117
❑ 97PinTotCPG-117
❑ 97PinTotCPR-117
❑ 97Sco-105
❑ 97ScoArtPro-105
❑ 97ScoGolBla-105
❑ 97UppDec-76
❑ 98O-PChr-145
❑ 98O-PChrR-145
❑ 98Pac-227
❑ 98PacIceB-227
❑ 98PacRed-227
❑ 98Top-145
❑ 98TopO-P-145

**Muller, Mike**
❑ 91MinGolG-17
❑ 94ClaProP-71

**Muller, Robert**
❑ 98GerDELE-297

**Muller, Zdenek**
❑ 94CzeAPSE-282
❑ 95CzeAPSE-76

**Mullin, Jim**
❑ 96DenUniPio-2

**Mullin, Kory**
❑ 917thInnSWHL-301
❑ 93TacRoc-17
❑ 95St.JohML-16

**Mullin, Matthew (Matt)**
❑ 917thInnSOHL-181
❑ 92WinSpi-29
❑ 94SudWol-21
❑ 94SudWolP-26

**Mullins, Dwight**
❑ 94CenHocL-30
❑ 95ForWorFT-12
❑ 96ForWorF-11

**Muloin, Wayne**
❑ 70DadCoo-88
❑ 70EssPowPla-94
❑ 70SarProSta-135
❑ 72CleCruWHA-10
❑ 75OPCWHA-102

**Mulroy, Terry**
❑ 74SioCitM-11

**Multanen, Jari**
❑ 93FinnJyvHS-258
❑ 93FinnSIS-299

**Mulvenna, Glenn**
❑ 87KamBla-13
❑ 88ProIHL-58
❑ 89ProIHL-162
❑ 90ProAHLIHL-387
❑ 91ProAHLCHL-289
❑ 92OPCPre-97
❑ 92UppDec-490
❑ 95PeoRiv-13

**Mulvey, Grant**
❑ 75OPCNHL-272
❑ 75Top-272
❑ 76OPCNHL-167
❑ 76Top-167
❑ 77OPCNHL-101
❑ 77Top-101
❑ 78OPC-261
❑ 78Top-261
❑ 79OPC-88
❑ 79Top-88
❑ 80BlaBroBac-7
❑ 80BlaWhiBor-9
❑ 80OPC-27
❑ 80OPC-212
❑ 80Top-27
❑ 80Top-212
❑ 81BlaBroBac-7
❑ 81BlaBorPos-17
❑ 81OPC-60
❑ 81Top-W72

❑ 82OPC-69
❑ 82OPCSti-173
❑ 82PosCer-4
❑ 92SeaPat-22

**Munck, Jari**
❑ 85SwePanS-5
❑ 93FinnJyvHS-20
❑ 93FinnSIS-92
❑ 94FinnSIS-256

**Munday, Travis**
❑ 917thInnSWHL-355

**Mundy, Buster**
❑ 36V356WorG-101

**Muni, Craig**
❑ 86OilRedR-28
❑ 86OilTeal-28
❑ 87OilTeal-28
❑ 87OPC-206
❑ 87OPCMin-30
❑ 87PanSti-258
❑ 88OilTeal-22
❑ 88OilTenAnn-33
❑ 88OPC-236
❑ 89OilTeal-18
❑ 89OPC-231
❑ 89OPCSti-229
❑ 89PanSti-80
❑ 90OilIGA-11
❑ 90OPC-423
❑ 90PanSti-217
❑ 90ProSet-92
❑ 90Sco-38A
❑ 90Sco-38B
❑ 90ScoCan-38A
❑ 90ScoCan-38B
❑ 90UppDec-21
❑ 90UppDecF-21
❑ 91OilIGA-15
❑ 91OilPanTS-15
❑ 91OilTeal-17
❑ 91OPC-479
❑ 91PanSti-133
❑ 91Par-460
❑ 91Pin-262
❑ 91PinFre-262
❑ 91ProSet-382
❑ 91ProSetFre-382
❑ 91ScoAme-67
❑ 91ScoCan-67
❑ 91Top-479
❑ 91UppDec-372
❑ 91UppDecF-372
❑ 92OilIGA-16
❑ 92Sco-81
❑ 92ScoCan-81
❑ 92Ult-296
❑ 93Par-291
❑ 93ParEmel-291
❑ 93Pin-298
❑ 93PinCan-298
❑ 93Pow-299
❑ 93Sco-266
❑ 93ScoCan-266
❑ 93ScoCan-579
❑ 93ScoGol-579
❑ 94Fla-21
❑ 94Lea-373
❑ 94OPCPre-216
❑ 94OPCPreSE-216
❑ 94Pin-143
❑ 94PinArtP-143
❑ 94PinRinC-143
❑ 94Sco-29
❑ 94ScoGol-29
❑ 94ScoPla-29
❑ 94ScoPlaTS-29
❑ 94TopPre-216
❑ 94TopPreSE-216
❑ 94Ult-265
❑ 95BeAPla-14
❑ 95BeAPlaSig-S14
❑ 95BeAPSigDC-S14
❑ 97Be A PPAD-19
❑ 97Be A PPAPD-19
❑ 97BeAPla-19
❑ 97BeAPlaAut-19

**Munro, Bryce**
❑ 92BriColJHL-30

**Munro, Dunc**
❑ 24C144ChaCig-42
❑ 24V130MapC-1
❑ 24V1452-34

**Munro, Gerald**
❑ 24C144ChaCig-43
❑ 24V1452-33

**Munther, Lars**
❑ 71SweHocS-216
❑ 72SweHocS-193

**Murano, Eric**
❑ 90ProAHLIHL-338
❑ 91ProAHLCHL-606
❑ 91UppDec-50
❑ 91UppDecF-50
❑ 92HamCan-21
❑ 92PeoRiv-14
❑ 98GerDELE-296

**Murcheson, Brent**
❑ 92BriColJHL-97

**Murdoch, Bob (Robert John)**
❑ 72CanaPos-15
❑ 74NHLActSta-115
❑ 74OPCNHL-194

❑ 74Top-194
❑ 75OPCNHL-33
❑ 75Top-33
❑ 76OPCNHL-74
❑ 76OPCNHL-383
❑ 76Top-74
❑ 77OPCNHL-39
❑ 77OPCNHL-371
❑ 77Top-39
❑ 78BluPos-15
❑ 78OPC-91
❑ 78Top-91
❑ 79FlamPos-10
❑ 79FlaTeal-11
❑ 79OPC-276
❑ 80FlamPos-11
❑ 80PepCap-10
❑ 81FlamPos-14
❑ 81OPC-48
❑ 82OPC-53
❑ 82PosCer-3
❑ 85FlamRedRP-18
❑ 86FlamRedR-17
❑ 87BlaCok-12
❑ 90ProSet-680
❑ 94GerDELE-296
❑ 95GerDELE-333
❑ 96GerDELE-336

**Murdoch, Bob (Robert Lowell)**
❑ 76OPCNHL-54
❑ 76Top-54
❑ 79OPC-351
❑ 90JetIGA-23

**Murdoch, Don**
❑ 77OPCNHL-244
❑ 77Top-244
❑ 77TopGloS-12
❑ 77TopOPCGlo-12
❑ 78OPC-11
❑ 78Top-11
❑ 79OPC-168
❑ 79Top-168
❑ 80OPC-203
❑ 80PepCap-36
❑ 80Top-203
❑ 88OilTenAnn-120

**Murdoch, Murray**
❑ 24CreFal-4
❑ 33OPCV304A-37
❑ 33V129-29
❑ 33V252CanG-39
❑ 33V357IceK-68
❑ 34DiaMatS-47
❑ 35DiaMatT2-50
❑ 35DiaMatT3-47
❑ 35DiaMatTI-50
❑ 36V356WorG-88

**Murdoch, Petr**
❑ 96CzeAPSE-152

**Murdock, Lorin**
❑ 92BriColJHL-181

**Murman, Barry**
❑ 67SweHoc-161

**Murnaghan, Kevin**
❑ 95SauSteMG-13
❑ 95Sla-359

**Murovic, Mirko**
❑ 98SP Aut-130
❑ 98SP AutSotTG-MIM
❑ 98SSASotT-MIM
❑ 98UppDec-407
❑ 98UppDecE-407
❑ 98UppDecE1o1-407
❑ 98UppDecGR-407
❑ 99SP AutPS-130

**Murphy, Al**
❑ 89HamRoaA-17
❑ 90HamRoaA-55
❑ 92-TulOil-10

**Murphy, Blake**
❑ 98GerDELE-1

**Murphy, Cory**
❑ 92Ott672A-16
❑ 95SauSteMG-14
❑ 95PinRinC-181

**Murphy, Dan**
❑ 91BriColJHL-48
❑ 92BriColJHL-11
❑ 92MaiBlaB-8
❑ 92MaiBlaB-22

**Murphy, Gord**
❑ 89FlyPos-16
❑ 89OPCSti-88
❑ 89OPCSti-229
❑ 89PanSti-303
❑ 90Bow-106
❑ 90BowTif-106
❑ 90FlyPos-18
❑ 90OPC-302
❑ 90PanSti-115
❑ 90ProSet-221
❑ 90Sco-117
❑ 90ScoCan-117
❑ 90ScoHotRS-56
❑ 90ScoYouS-13
❑ 90Top-302
❑ 90TopTif-302
❑ 90UppDec-86
❑ 90UppDecF-86
❑ 91Bow-235
❑ 91FlyJCP-19

❑ 91OPC-89
❑ 91PanSti-230
❑ 91Par-227
❑ 91ParFre-227
❑ 91Pin-140
❑ 91PinFre-140
❑ 91ProSet-171
❑ 91ProSetFre-171
❑ 91ProSetPla-156
❑ 91ProSetPre-171
❑ 91ScoAme-43
❑ 91ScoCan-43
❑ 91StaClu-248
❑ 91Top-89
❑ 91UppDec-392
❑ 91UppDecF-392
❑ 92Bow-315
❑ 92Pin-132
❑ 92PinFre-132
❑ 92ProSet-11
❑ 92Sco-29
❑ 92ScoCan-29
❑ 92StaClu-445
❑ 92Top-114
❑ 92TopGol-114G
❑ 92Ult-253
❑ 93Don-131
❑ 93Lea-284
❑ 93OPCPre-465
❑ 93OPCPreG-465
❑ 93Par-345
❑ 93ParEmel-345
❑ 93Pin-380
❑ 93PinCan-380
❑ 93PinExp-2
❑ 93Pow-99
❑ 93Sco-95
❑ 93ScoCan-95
❑ 93ScoCan-548
❑ 93ScoGol-548
❑ 93StaClu-439
❑ 93StaCluFDI-439
❑ 93StaCluO-439
❑ 93TopPre-465
❑ 93TopPreG-465
❑ 93Ult-329
❑ 93UppDec-521
❑ 94CanGamNHLP-112
❑ 94Don-55
❑ 94EASpo-50
❑ 94EASpo-197
❑ 94EASpo-207
❑ 94EASpo-210
❑ 94Fla-66
❑ 94Fle-81
❑ 94Lea-250
❑ 94OPCPre-19
❑ 94OPCPreSE-19
❑ 94Pin-141
❑ 94PinArtP-141
❑ 94PinRinC-141
❑ 94Sco-117
❑ 94ScoGol-117
❑ 94ScoPla-117
❑ 94ScoPlaTS-117
❑ 94StaClu-128
❑ 94StaCluFDI-128
❑ 94StaCluMOMS-128
❑ 94StaCluSTWC-128
❑ 94TopPre-19
❑ 94TopPreSE-19
❑ 94Ult-82
❑ 94UppDec-438
❑ 94UppDecEleIce-438
❑ 95CanGamNHLP-122
❑ 95ColCho-190
❑ 95ColChoPC-190
❑ 95ColChoPCP-190
❑ 95Don-161
❑ 95Emo-70
❑ 95Lea-146
❑ 95ParInt-357
❑ 95ParIntEl-357
❑ 95Pin-181
❑ 95PinArtP-181
❑ 95PinRinC-181
❑ 95PlaOneoOne-262
❑ 95Sco-104
❑ 95ScoBlaIce-104
❑ 95ScoBlaIceAP-104
❑ 95SkyImp-68
❑ 95Ult-61
❑ 95Ult-243
❑ 95UltGolM-61
❑ 95UppDec-21
❑ 95UppDecEleIce-21
❑ 95UppDecEleIceG-21
❑ 96BeAPAut-44
❑ 96BeAPAut-Sil-44
❑ 96BeAPla-44
❑ 96FlePic-162
❑ 96UppDec-68
❑ 97PacInvNRB-88
❑ 99UppDec-285
❑ 99UppDecRG-35
❑ 99UppDecRP-35

**Murphy, Jay**
❑ 94RicRen-11
❑ 95RicRen-3
❑ 96AlaGolKin-11

**Murphy, Jodie**
❑ 917thInnSWHL-291

❑ 93MusFur-7
❑ 93SauSteMGM-18

**Murphy, Joe**
❑ 87RedWinLC-19
❑ 89OilTeal-19
❑ 90Bow-196
❑ 90BowTif-196
❑ 90OilIGA-20
❑ 90OPC-429
❑ 90ProSet-93
❑ 90Sco-293
❑ 90ScoCan-293
❑ 90UppDec-190
❑ 90UppDecF-190
❑ 91Bow-109
❑ 91OilIGA-16
❑ 91OilPanTS-16
❑ 91OilTeal-18
❑ 91OPC-48
❑ 91Par-52
❑ 91Par-458
❑ 91ParFre-52
❑ 91Pin-206
❑ 91PinFre-206
❑ 91ProSet-68
❑ 91ProSetFre-68
❑ 91ProSetPla-171
❑ 91ScoAme-299
❑ 91ScoCan-519
❑ 91StaClu-313
❑ 91Top-48
❑ 91UppDec-474
❑ 91UppDecF-474
❑ 92Bow-174
❑ 92OPC-100
❑ 92PanSti-100
❑ 92PanStiFre-100
❑ 92Par-273
❑ 92ParEmel-273
❑ 92Pin-23
❑ 92PinFre-23
❑ 92ProSet-49
❑ 92Sco-321
❑ 92ScoCan-321
❑ 92ScoCan-34
❑ 92Top-39
❑ 92TopGol-38G
❑ 92Ult-63
❑ 92UppDec-152
❑ 93BlaCok-1
❑ 93Don-66
❑ 93Lea-179
❑ 93OPCPre-273
❑ 93OPCPreF-8
❑ 93OPCPreG-273
❑ 93Par-38
❑ 93ParEmel-38
❑ 93ParFirO-F8
❑ 93Pin-45
❑ 93PinCan-45
❑ 93Pow-53
❑ 93Sco-348
❑ 93ScoCan-348
❑ 93ScoDynDUS-6
❑ 93TopPre-273
❑ 93TopPreG-273
❑ 93Ult-163
❑ 93UppDec-47
❑ 93UppDecSP-29
❑ 94BeAPSig-87
❑ 94CanGamNHLP-67
❑ 94Don-38
❑ 94Fla-34
❑ 94Fle-42
❑ 94Lea-284
❑ 94OPCPre-34
❑ 94OPCPreSE-34
❑ 94Par-44
❑ 94ParGol-44
❑ 94Pin-68
❑ 94PinArtP-68
❑ 94PinRinC-68
❑ 94Sco-170
❑ 94ScoGol-170
❑ 94ScoPla-170
❑ 94ScoPlaTS-170
❑ 94Sel-44
❑ 94SelGol-44
❑ 94SP-27
❑ 94SPDieCut-27
❑ 94TopPre-34
❑ 94TopPreSE-34
❑ 94UppDec-416
❑ 94UppDecEleIce-416
❑ 95CanGamNHLP-66
❑ 95ColCho-156
❑ 95ColChoPC-156
❑ 95ColChoPCP-156
❑ 95Don-146
❑ 95Emo-30
❑ 95Fin-58
❑ 95FinRef-58
❑ 95ImpSti-24
❑ 95Lea-109
❑ 95Met-25
❑ 95ParInt-309
❑ 95ParIntEl-309
❑ 95Pin-8
❑ 95PinArtP-8
❑ 95PinRinC-8
❑ 95ProMag-8
❑ 95Sco-110
❑ 95ScoBlaIce-110
❑ 95ScoBlaIceAP-110

❑ 95SelCer-50
❑ 95SelCerMG-50
❑ 95SkyImp-30
❑ 95StaClu-52
❑ 95StaCluMOMS-52
❑ 95Sum-10
❑ 95SumArtP-10
❑ 95SumIce-10
❑ 95Top-280
❑ 95TopOPCI-280
❑ 95Ult-217
❑ 95UppDec-278
❑ 95UppDecEleIce-278
❑ 95UppDecEleIceG-278
❑ 95Zen-4
❑ 96BeAPAut-28
❑ 96BeAPAutSil-28
❑ 96BeAPla-28
❑ 96ColCho-48
❑ 96Don-144
❑ 96DonEli-102
❑ 96DonEliDCS-102
❑ 96DonPrePro-144
❑ 96Lea-185
❑ 96LeaPreP-185
❑ 96MetUni-134
❑ 96NHLProSTA-8
❑ 96PinPreS-200
❑ 96Sco-100
❑ 96ScoArtPro-100
❑ 96ScoDeaCAP-100
❑ 96ScoGolB-100
❑ 96ScoSpeAP-100
❑ 96SP-132
❑ 96Sum-86
❑ 96SumArtP-86
❑ 96SumIce-86
❑ 96SumMet-86
❑ 96SumPreS-86
❑ 96TopNHLP-143
❑ 96TopPicOI-143
❑ 96UppDec-325
❑ 97ColCho-231
❑ 97Pac-150
❑ 97PacCop-150
❑ 97PacEmeGre-150
❑ 97PacIceB-150
❑ 97PacPar-160
❑ 97PacParC-160
❑ 97PacParDG-160
❑ 97PacParEG-160
❑ 97PacParIB-160
❑ 97PacParSil-160
❑ 97PacRed-150
❑ 97PacSil-150
❑ 97Sco-163
❑ 97ScoBlu-3
❑ 97ScoBluPla-3
❑ 97ScoBluPre-3
❑ 97UppDec-349
❑ 98Be A PPA-271
❑ 98Be A PPAA-271
❑ 98Be A PPAAF-271
❑ 98Be A PPSE-271
❑ 98Be APG-271
❑ 99Pac-377
❑ 99PacCop-377
❑ 99PacGol-377
❑ 99PacIceB-377
❑ 99PacPreD-377

**Murphy, Jonathan**
❑ 93PetPet-2
❑ 95Sla-309

**Murphy, Keith**
❑ 91AirCanSJHL-B40
❑ 91AirCanSJHLAS-30
❑ 92NorDakFS-22

**Murphy, Ken**
❑ 73RedWinTI-16

**Murphy, Kevin**
❑ 92ClaKni-12

**Murphy, Larry**
❑ 81OPC-148
❑ 81OPC-393
❑ 81OPCSti-237
❑ 81Top-W100
❑ 82OPC-158
❑ 82OPCSti-232
❑ 82PosCer-8
❑ 83OPC-159
❑ 83OPCSti-298
❑ 83PufSti-9
❑ 84CapPizH-13
❑ 84OPC-204
❑ 84OPCSti-127
❑ 85CapPizH-12
❑ 85OPC-236
❑ 86CapPol-11
❑ 86OPC-185
❑ 86Top-185
❑ 87CapKod-8
❑ 87CapTealss-17
❑ 87OPC-133
❑ 87OPCBoxB-H
❑ 87OPCMin-91
❑ 87OPCSti-119
❑ 87PanSti-176
❑ 87Top-133
❑ 87TopBoxB-H
❑ 87TopStins-7
❑ 88CapSmo-15

88OPC-141
88OPCSti-71
88PanSti-367
88Top-141
89OPC-128
89OPCSti-199
89PanSti-108
89Top-128
90Bow-177
90BowTif-177
90OPC-47
90PanSti-251
90Sco-206
90ScoCan-206
90Top-47
90TopTif-47
90UppDec-229
90UppDecF-229
91Bow-78
91Kra-71
91OPC-277
91PanSti-270
91Par-358
91Par-456
91ParFre-358
91PenCokE-55
91PenFoo-10
91PenFooCS-3
91Pin-143
91PinFre-143
91ProSet-193
91ProSetFre-193
91ProSetPla-213
91ScoAme-31
91ScoCan-31
91StaClu-112
91Top-277
91UppDec-302
91UppDecF-302
92Bow-153
92OPC-209
92PanSti-228
92PanStiFre-228
92Par-137
92ParEmel-137
92PenCokE-14
92PenFoo-10
92Pin-292
92PinFre-292
92ProSet-146
92Sco-45
92ScoCan-45
92StaClu-375
92Top-447
92TopGol-447G
92Ult-167
92UppDec-241
93Don-263
93Lea-16
93LeaGolAS-2
93OPCPre-173
93OPCPreG-173
93OPCPreG-189
93PanSti-86
93PanSti-135
93Par-162
93ParEmel-162
93PenFoo-13
93PenSti-8
93Pin-52
93PinCan-52
93Pow-193
93Sco-23
93ScoCan-23
93StaClu-283
93StaCluFDI-283
93StaCluO-283
93SweSemWCS-191
93TopPre-173
93TopPre-189
93TopPreBG-23
93TopPreG-173
93TopPreG-189
93Ult-184
93UppDec-374
93UppDecNR-8
94BeAPla-R170
94BeAPSig-148
94CanGamNHLP-191
94Don-27
94EASpo-103
94FinnJaaK-81
94FinRinL-18
94Fla-137
94Fle-166
94HocWit-48
94Lea-249
94LeaLim-12
94OPCPre-10
94OPCPre-492
94OPCPreSE-10
94OPCPreSE-492
94Par-179
94ParGol-179
94PenFoo-24
94Pin-215
94PinArtP-215
94PinRinC-215
94Sco-5
94ScoGol-5
94ScoHobS-5
94ScoPla-5
94ScoPlaTS-5

94Sel-143
94SelGol-143
94StaCluMO-32
94TopPre-10
94TopPre-492
94TopPreSE-10
94TopPreSE-492
94Ult-168
94UppDec-99
94UppDecEleIce-99
95Bow-34
95BowAllFoi-34
95CanGamNHLP-19
95CanGamNHLP-266
95ColCho-151
95ColCho-386
95ColChoPC-151
95ColChoPC-386
95ColChoPCP-151
95ColChoPCP-386
95Don-366
95DonEli-8
95DonEliDCS-8
95DonEliDCU-8
95Emo-173
95Fin-42
95FinnSemWC-83
95FinRef-42
95ImpSti-121
95Kra-50
95Lea-186
95LeaLim-97
95Met-145
95ParInt-207
95ParIntEl-207
95ParIntPTP-PP23
95PlaOneoOne-97
95PosUppD-21
95Sco-260
95ScoBlaIce-260
95ScoBlaIceAP-260
95SelCer-90
95SelCerMG-90
95SkyImp-163
95SP-143
95StaClu-144
95StaCluMOMS-144
95Sum-126
95SumArtP-126
95SumIce-126
95Top-255
95TopOPCI-255
95Ult-125
95Ult-314
95UltGolM-125
95UppDec-86
95UppDecEleIce-86
95UppDecEleIceG-86
95UppDecPHE-H38
95UppDecPreH-H38
95UppDecSpeE-SE170
95UppDecSpeEdiG-SE170
95Zen-106
96ColCho-265
96ColChoMVP-UD32
96Don-39
96DonCanI-86
96DonCanIGPP-86
96DonCanIRPP-86
96DonPrePro-39
96Fle-108
96FleNor-9
96FlePic-52
96Lea-100
96LeaPreP-100
96MetUni-151
96Pin-189
96PinArtP-189
96PinFoi-189
96PinPreS-189
96PinRinC-189
96Sco-75
96ScoArtPro-75
96ScoDeaCAP-75
96ScoGolB-75
96ScoSpeAP-75
96SkyImp-128
96SkyImpNHLF-15
96SP-154
96StaCluMO-16
96Sum-11
96SumArtP-11
96SumIce-11
96SumMet-11
96SumPreS-11
96SweSemW-82
96TeaOut-53
96Ult-164
96UltGolM-164
96UppDec-161
96UppDecGN-X39
96Zen-111
96ZenArtP-111
97Be A PPAD-141
97Be A PPAPD-141
97BeAPla-141
97BeAPlaAut-141
97PacOme-85
97PacOmeC-85
97PacOmeDG-85
97PacOmeEG-85
97PacOmeIB-85
97PacRev-49
97PacRevC-49

97PacRevE-49
97PacRevIB-49
97PacRevR-49
97PacRevS-49
97ScoRedW-8
97ScoRedWPla-8
97ScoRedWPre-8
98Be A PPA-48
98Be A PPAA-48
98Be A PPAAF-48
98Be A PPAM-M20
98Be A PPTBASG-48
98Be APG-48
980-PChr-33
980-PChrBM-B9
980-PChrBMR-B9
980-PChrR-33
980-PChrSB-SB26
980-PChrSBR-SB26
98Pac-203
98PacIceB-203
98PacOmeH-85
98PacOmeODI-85
98PacOmeR-85
98PacPar-80
98PacParC-80
98PacParEG-80
98PacParH-80
98PacParIB-80
98PacParS-80
98PacRed-203
98Top-33
98TopBoaM-B9
98Top-O-P-33
98TopSeaB-SB26
98UC-70
98UD ChoPCR-70
98UD ChoR-70
98UppDec-265
98UppDecE-265
98UppDecE1o1-265
98UppDecGR-265
99Pac-145
99PacCop-145
99PacGol-145
99PacIceB-145
99PacPreD-145

## Murphy, Mike
71BluPos-11
72BluWhiBor-12
720PC-215
72SarProSta-195
74NHLActSta-122
740PCNHL-224
74Top-224
750PCNHL-52
75Top-52
760PCNHL-21
76Top-21
770PCNHL-22
77Top-22
780PC-229
78Top-229
790PC-31
79PanSti-69
79Top-31
80KinCanN-9
800PC-286
810PC-149
810PCSti-241
81Top-W101

## Murphy, Rob
89ProIHL-172
90CanuMoh-20
900PC-37
90ProSet-546
90Top-37
90TopTif-37
91CanuAutC-16
91CanuPanTS-16
91CanuTeal8-16
91ProAHLCHL-607
91ScoCan-397
92ProSet-121
92UppDec-108
93PhoRoa-19
98GerDELE-73

## Murphy, Ronald (Ron)
44BeeGro2P-129
44BeeGro2P-348
52JunBluT-61
54Par-76
54Par-93
57Top-29
58Top-59
59Top-66
60ShiCoi-75
60Top-41
60TopSta-40
61ShiCoi-36
61Top-34
62Top-40
63Top-40
64BeeGro3P-90
64CocCap-46
65Coc-46
65Top-111
66Top-96
66TopUSAT-33
67Top-100
680PC-139
690PC-204
94ParMisL-102

94ParTalB-48
95Par66-15
95Par66Coi-15

## Murphy, Todd
91AirCanSJHL-D22
92MPSPhoSJHL-116

## Murray, Adam
917thInnSWHL-29

## Murray, Adrian
93PetPet-26
95Sla-310

## Murray, Al
34BeeGro1P-244
35DiaMatT2-51
35DiaMatT3-48
35DiaMatTI-51
360PCV304D-104
36V356WorG-54

## Murray, Andy
89FlyPos-17
93JetRuf-17

## Murray, Bob (Robert Frederick)
74NHLActSta-5
75CanuRoyB-14
76CanuRoyB-12
760PCNHL-309
770PCNHL-12
77Top-12
780PC-89
78Top-89
790PC-55
79Top-55
800PC-181
80Top-181
810PC-61
810PCSti-119
81Top-W73
820PC-70
820PC-108
830PC-108
830PCSti-109
840PC-41
840PCSti-26
84Top-32
850PC-114
85Top-114
86BlaCok-9
860PC-64
86Top-64
87BlaCok-13
870PC-156
87PanSti-289
87Top-156
88PanSti-22
89BlaCok-5
900PC-138
90Sco-376
90ScoCan-376
90Top-138
90TopTif-138

## Murray, Bob J. (Robert John)
740PCNHL-336
750PCNHL-386
760PCNHL-363

## Murray, Bryan
82Cap-16
86CapKod-19
86CapPol-18
87CapKod-xx
88CapSmo-16
90ProSet-664
90PowPreD-193
91RedWinLC-13

## Murray, Chris
93KamBla-17
94FreCan-20
95FreCan-21
96CanaPos-18
96CanaShe-12
96ColEdgFL-12
97PacInvNRB-39

## Murray, Glen
89SudWoi-6
907thInnSOHL-388
90SudWol-13
917thInnSOHL-17
917thInnSOHL-245
91AreDraPic-14
91Cla-15
91Par-229
91ParFre-229
91StaPicH-64
91SudWol-21
91UltDra-15
91UltDra-71
91UltDra-84
91UppDec-69
91UppDecF-69
920PC-74
920PCPre-52
92PanSti-142
92PanStiFre-142
92Par-9
92ParEmel-9
92Pin-224
92PinFre-224
92ProSet-222
92Sco-484
92ScoCan-484
92StaClu-198
92Top-370
92Top-370G
92UppDec-401

93ClaProPro-89
93Don-22
93Lea-317
930PCPre-477
930PCPreG-477
93Par-16
93ParEmel-16
93StaClu-59
93StaCluFDI-59
93StaCluDIO-59
93StaCluO-59
93TopPre-477
93TopPreG-477
94CanGamNHLP-41
94Don-246
94Lea-4
940PCPre-173
940PCPreSE-173
94ParSE-SE11
94ParSEG-SE11
94Pin-169
94PinArtP-169
94PinRinC-169
94TopPre-173
94TopPreSE-173
94UppDec-23
94UppDecEleIce-23
95BeAPla-144
95BeAPSig-S144
95BeAPSigDC-S144
95ParInt-440
95ParIntEl-440
95PenFoo-2
95PlaOneoOne-299
95UppDec-394
95UppDecEleIce-394
95UppDecEleIceG-394
97PacOme-110
97PacOmeC-110
97PacOmeDG-110
97PacOmeEG-110
97PacOmeIB-110
97UppDec-81
98Fin-103
98FinNo P-103
98FinNo PR-103
98FinRef-103
98Pac-241
98PacIceB-241
98PacOmeH-111
98PacOmeODI-111
98PacOmeR-111
98PacPar-105
98PacParC-105
98PacParEG-105
98PacParH-105
98PacParIB-105
98PacParS-105
98PacRed-241
98SP Aut-40
98UC-99
98UD ChoPCR-99
98UD ChoR-99
98UppDec-284
98UppDecE-284
98UppDecE1o1-284
98UppDecGR-284
99Pac-193
99PacCop-193
99PacGol-193
99PacIceB-193
99PacPreD-193
99SP AutPS-40

## Murray, Herman
36V356WorG-113

## Murray, John
34BeeGro1P-287
91ProAHLCHL-361

## Murray, Ken
36V356WorG-109

## Murray, Marty
917thInnSWHL-206
92BraWheK-17
93DonTeaC-17
93Pin-477
93PinCan-477
94Fin-161
94FinRef-161
94FinSupTW-161
94Pin-536
94PinArtP-536
94PinRinC-536
94SP-148
94SPDieCut-148
95Bow-152
95BowAllFoi-152
95ColCho-405
95Don-284
95DonCanWJT-10
95DonRatRoo-11
95Met-185
95ParInt-530
95ParIntEl-530
95SelCer-141
95SelCerMG-141
95SkyImp-192
95SlaMemC-48
95St.JohF-15
95StaClu-198
95StaCluMOMS-198
95Sum-191
95SumArtP-191

95SumIce-191
95Top-338
95TopCanWJ-6CJ
95TopOPCI-338
95Ult-350
95UppDec-500
95UppDecElelce-500
95UppDecElelceG-500
95Zen-142
96ColEdgFL-35
96FlePic-178
96SkyImp-155
97Be A PPAD-199
97Be A PPAPD-199
97BeAPla-199
97BeAPlaAut-199
97Don-221
97DonLim-39
97DonLimExp-39
97DonPreProG-221
97DonPreProS-221

## Murray, Michael
94St.JohF-14
95St.JohF-16

## Murray, Mike
90KnoChe-108
93KnoChe-11
94Cla-114
94ClaDraGol-114
94KnoChe-9
95DayBom-16

## Murray, Pat
90OPCPre-79
90ProSet-630
91ProAHLCHL-276
91ScoAme-321
91ScoCan-351
91UppDec-451
91UppDecF-451
94KnoChe-20

## Murray, Rem
93MicSta-14
96BeAPLH-5A
96BeAPLHAut-5A
96BeAPLHAutSil-5A
96ColCho-352
96ColEdgFL-14
96DonCanI-123
96DonCanIGPP-123
96DonCanIRPP-123
96DonEli-145
96DonEliAsp-22
96DonEliDCS-145
96Fla-111
96FlaBluI-111
96HocGreC-24
96HocGreCG-24
96LeaPre-136
96LeaPrePP-136
96MetUni-188
96OilPos-17
96SelCer-119
96SelCerAP-119
96SelCerBlu-119
96SelCerMB-119
96SelCerMG-119
96SelCerMR-119
96SelCerRed-119
96SP-178
96Ult-60
96UltGolM-60
96UltRoo-14
96UppDec-261
96UppDecBD-17
96UppDecBDG-17
96UppDecIce-19
96UppDecIcePar-19
96Zen-146
96ZenArtP-146
97ColCho-91
97Don-127
97DonLim-141
97DonLimExp-141
97DonLimExp-173
97DonPre-56
97DonPreCttC-56
97DonPreProG-127
97DonPreProS-127
97Lea-140
97LeaFraMat-140
97LeaFraMDC-140
97LeaInt-140
97LeaIntUI-140
97Pac-112
97PacCop-112
97PacDyn-50
97PacDynC-50
97PacDynDG-50
97PacDynEG-50
97PacDynIB-50
97PacDynSil-50
97PacDynTan-50
97PacEmeGre-112
97PacIceB-112
97PacInv-57
97PacInvC-57
97PacInvEG-57
97PacInvIB-57
97PacInvR-57
97PacInvS-57
97PacRed-112
97PacSil-112
97Pin-133

97PinIns-94
97PinPrePBB-133
97PinPrePBC-133
97PinPrePBM-133
97PinPrePBY-133
97PinPrePFC-133
97PinPrePFM-133
97PinPrePFY-133
97PinPrePla-133
97Sco-227
97UppDec-70
98Fin-84
98FinNo P-84
98FinNo PR-84
98FinRef-84
99Pac-161
99PacCop-161
99PacGol-161
99PacIceB-161
99PacPreD-161

## Murray, Rob
88ProAHL-40
90Bow-74
90BowTif-74
90CapPos-18
90CapSmo-17
900PC-460
90ProSet-553
91JetIGA-16
91MonHaw-20
91ProAHLCHL-164
96ColEdgFL-15
96SprFal-23

## Murray, Robert
79PanSti-99
82SweSemHVS-103

## Murray, Scott
91AirCanSJHL-B38

## Murray, Terry
73OPC-259
740PCNHL-126
74Top-126
81Cap-11
82Cap-17
82PosCer-20
88ProAHL-41
89CapKod-xx
89ProAHL-92
90CapKod-18
90ProSet-679

## Murray, Tim
92MPSPhoSJHL-110

## Murray, Troy
83BlaBorPos-16
83CanNatJ-NNO
840PC-42
850PC-146
850PCSti-29
85Top-146
86BlaCok-10
860PC-25
860PCSti-154
860PCSti-189
86Top-25
87BlaCok-14
870PC-74
870PCSti-79
87PanSti-227
87Top-74
88BlaCok-13
88FriLayS-32
880PC-106
880PCSti-10
88PanSti-27
88Top-106
89BlaCok-2
890PC-219
890PCSti-11
89PanSti-48
90BlaCok-2
90Bow-13
90BowTif-13
900PC-160
90PanSti-200
90ProSet-57A
90ProSet-57B
90Sco-243
90ScoCan-243
90Top-160
90TopTif-160
90UppDec-112
90UppDecF-112
91Bow-388
91JetIGA-19
910PC-87
910PCPre-75
91PanSti-17
91Par-206
91ParFre-206
91Pin-33
91PinFre-33
91ProSet-46
91ProSet-514
91ProSet-588
91ProSetFre-46
91ProSetFre-514
91ProSetFre-588
91ProSetPla-247
91ScoAme-53
91ScoCan-53
91ScoCan-585
91ScoRoo-35T
91StaClu-167
91Top-87
91UppDec-565

☐ 91UppDecF-565
☐ 92Bow-93
☐ 92OPC-64
☐ 92PanSti-57
☐ 92PanStiFre-57
☐ 92Pin-49
☐ 92PinFre-49
☐ 92ProSet-215
☐ 92Sco-189
☐ 92ScoCan-189
☐ 92SeaPat-58
☐ 92StaClu-31
☐ 92Top-284
☐ 92TopGol-284G
☐ 92Ult-242
☐ 92Ult-443
☐ 92UppDec-129
☐ 93BlaCok-23
☐ 93OPCPre-182
☐ 93OPCPreG-182
☐ 93Pin-318
☐ 93PinCan-318
☐ 93Sco-272
☐ 93ScoCan-272
☐ 93StaClu-230
☐ 93StaCluFDI-230
☐ 93StaCluFDIO-230
☐ 93StaCluO-230
☐ 93TopPre-182
☐ 93TopPreG-182
☐ 94BeAPSig-176
☐ 94OPCPre-188
☐ 94OPCPreSE-188
☐ 94Pin-139
☐ 94PinArtP-139
☐ 94PinRinC-139
☐ 94SenBelM-23
☐ 94TopPre-188
☐ 94TopPreSE-188

**Murto, Matti**
☐ 69SweWorC-159
☐ 69SweWorC-168
☐ 70SweHocS-307
☐ 71SweHocS-70
☐ 72SweSemWC-83
☐ 74SweHocS-35
☐ 74SweSemHVS-86
☐ 96FinnSISR-197

**Murtovaara, Petri**
☐ 95FinnSIS-241

**Murzyn, Dana**
☐ 85WhaJunW-13
☐ 86OPC-58
☐ 86Top-58
☐ 86WhaJunT-17
☐ 87FlamRedRP-17
☐ 87OPC-138
☐ 87PanSti-42
☐ 87Top-138
☐ 87WhaJunBK-15
☐ 90FlamIGA-15
☐ 90OPC-304
☐ 90ProSet-41
☐ 90Sco-274
☐ 90ScoCan-274
☐ 90Top-304
☐ 90TopTif-304
☐ 90UppDec-348
☐ 90UppDecF-348
☐ 91CanuAutC-17
☐ 91CanuTeal8-17
☐ 91FlamPanTS-12
☐ 91Pin-260
☐ 91PinFre-260
☐ 91ProSet-498
☐ 91ProSetFre-498
☐ 91ScoAme-357
☐ 91ScoCan-231
☐ 92Bow-71
☐ 92CanuRoaTA-15
☐ 92OPC-241
☐ 92Pin-172
☐ 92PinFre-172
☐ 92Sco-168
☐ 92ScoCan-168
☐ 92StaClu-353
☐ 92Top-194
☐ 92TopGol-194G
☐ 93Don-348
☐ 93Lea-292
☐ 93OPCPre-311
☐ 93OPCPreG-311
☐ 93Par-486
☐ 93ParEmel-486
☐ 93Pin-273
☐ 93PinCan-273
☐ 93Sco-298
☐ 93ScoCan-298
☐ 93TopPre-311
☐ 93TopPreG-311
☐ 93Ult-441
☐ 94CanuProI-16
☐ 94Pin-198
☐ 94PinArtP-198
☐ 94PinRinC-198
☐ 94Sco-134
☐ 94ScoGol-134
☐ 94ScoPla-134
☐ 94ScoPlaTS-134
☐ 95CanuBuiDA-5
☐ 96BeAPAut-160
☐ 96BeAPAutSil-160
☐ 96BeAPla-160
☐ 96CanuPos-5

☐ 97PacDynBKS-97

**Musakka, Joakim**
☐ 93SweSemE-54
☐ 94SweLeaE-282
☐ 95SweLeaE-31

**Musial, David**
☐ 94GerDELE-292
☐ 95GerDELE-282

**Musil, Frantisek (Frank)**
☐ 87NorStaPos-22
☐ 87PanSti-22
☐ 88NorStaADA-19
☐ 88PanSti-87
☐ 89OPC-217
☐ 90FlamIGA-16
☐ 90PanSti-258
☐ 90ProSet-425
☐ 90Sco-223
☐ 90ScoRoo-19T
☐ 90UppDec-383
☐ 90UppDecF-383
☐ 91Bow-259
☐ 91FlamIGA-11
☐ 91OPC-68
☐ 91Pin-282
☐ 91PinFre-282
☐ 91ProSet-368
☐ 91ProSetFre-368
☐ 91ScoAme-142
☐ 91ScoCan-142
☐ 91StaClu-235
☐ 91Top-68
☐ 92Bow-157
☐ 92FlamIGA-16
☐ 92OPC-66
☐ 92Pin-51
☐ 92PinFre-51
☐ 92Sco-83
☐ 92ScoCan-83
☐ 92StaClu-67
☐ 92Top-142
☐ 92TopGol-142G
☐ 92Ult-270
☐ 93Lea-236
☐ 93OPCPre-229
☐ 93OPCPreG-229
☐ 93Pin-101
☐ 93PinCan-101
☐ 93Pow-307
☐ 93Sco-303
☐ 93ScoCan-303
☐ 93StaClu-169
☐ 93StaCluFDI-169
☐ 93StaCluFDIO-169
☐ 93StaCluO-169
☐ 93TopPre-229
☐ 93TopPreG-229
☐ 93Ult-283
☐ 94CzeAPSE-75
☐ 94Lea-545
☐ 94OPCPre-258
☐ 94OPCPreSE-258
☐ 94Pin-64
☐ 94PinArtP-64
☐ 94PinRinC-64
☐ 94Sco-139
☐ 94ScoGol-139
☐ 94ScoPla-139
☐ 94ScoPlaTS-139
☐ 94TopPre-258
☐ 94TopPreSE-258
☐ 94Ult-31
☐ 95FinnSemWC-162
☐ 95Sen-18
☐ 96SenPizH-15
☐ 96SweSemW-111
☐ 97PacInvNRB-136

**Mutch, Tom**
☐ 91ProAHLCHL-441

**Muukkonen, Jarmo**
☐ 93FinnSIS-267
☐ 94FinnSIS-81
☐ 95FinnSIS-90
☐ 96FinnSISR-85

**Muzzatti, Jason**
☐ 92ProAHLCHL-592
☐ 92Cla-114
☐ 93Ult-284
☐ 93UppDec-482
☐ 94Lea-470
☐ 94OPCPre-373
☐ 94OPCPreSE-373
☐ 94St.JohF-15
☐ 94TopPre-373
☐ 94TopPreSE-373
☐ 95Ima-52
☐ 95ImaGol-52
☐ 95ParInt-362
☐ 95ParIntEl-362
☐ 95UppDec-491
☐ 96BeAPAut-131
☐ 96BeAPAutSil-131
☐ 96BeAPla-131
☐ 96ClaGol-114
☐ 96ColCho-117
☐ 96Fla-42
☐ 96FlaBlul-42
☐ 96UppDec-71
☐ 96WhaBobS-18
☐ 97PacInvNRB-40
☐ 97ScoRan-17
☐ 97ScoRanPla-17
☐ 97ScoRanPre-17

**Mydan, Scott**

☐ 87PorWinH-19
☐ 88PorWinH-19
☐ 89PorWinH-17
☐ 907thInnSWHL-333

**Myers, Mike**
☐ 92AlbIntTC-14

**Myhres, Brantt**
☐ 907thInnSWHL-317
☐ 907thInnSWHL-360
☐ 94LigPhoA-19
☐ 94LigPos-13
☐ 95Don-45
☐ 95Lea-75
☐ 95Ult-154
☐ 95UltGolM-154
☐ 95UppDec-23
☐ 95UppDecEleIce-23
☐ 95UppDecEleIceG-23
☐ 97Be A PPAD-203
☐ 97Be A PPAPD-203
☐ 97BeAPla-203
☐ 97BeAPlaAut-203
☐ 97Pac-334
☐ 97PacCop-334
☐ 97PacEmeGre-334
☐ 97PacIceB-334
☐ 97PacRed-334
☐ 97PacSil-334

**Mylander, Kevin**
☐ 93SeaThu-16

**Myles, David**
☐ 89WinSpi-12
☐ 907thInnSOHL-111
☐ 907thInnSOHL-191

**Myles, Mark**
☐ 897thInnSOHL-113
☐ 907thInnSOHL-366

**Myles, Vic**
☐ 34BeeGro1P-288

**Myllari, Roy**
☐ 83Ott67-20

**Myllykoski, Mikko**
☐ 93FinnJyvHS-45
☐ 93FinnSIS-237
☐ 94FinnSIS-317
☐ 95FinnSIS-22
☐ 96FinnSISR-110

**Myllys, Jarmo**
☐ 88ProIHL-26
☐ 89ProIHL-95
☐ 900PCPre-80
☐ 910PCIns-8S
☐ 910PCPre-15
☐ 91Par-162
☐ 91ParFre-162
☐ 91ProAHLCHL-509
☐ 91ShaSanJSA-17
☐ 91UppDec-537
☐ 91UppDecF-537
☐ 92Bow-125
☐ 92StaClu-113
☐ 92Top-251
☐ 92TopGol-251G
☐ 92UppDecES-E19
☐ 93FinnJyvHS-224
☐ 93FinnSIS-183
☐ 93SweSemWCS-47
☐ 94FinnJaaK-1
☐ 94FinnJaaK-332
☐ 94FinnSIS-160
☐ 94FinnSISS-9
☐ 94SweLeaE-260
☐ 94SweLeaEFA-4
☐ 95FinnJaaKLAC-1
☐ 95FinnKarWCL-11
☐ 95FinnSemWC-35
☐ 95FinnSemWC-207
☐ 95FinnSISGC-2
☐ 95FinnSISL-28
☐ 95SweGloWC-128
☐ 95SweLeaE-74
☐ 95SweLeaE-302
☐ 95SweLeaEM-12
☐ 95SweLeaES-8
☐ 95SweUppDE-113
☐ 96SweSemW-1
☐ 96SweSemWAS-AS1
☐ 96SweSemWSG-SG3

**Mylnikov, Sergei**
☐ 87RusNatT-15
☐ 89Nord-33
☐ 89NordGenF-24
☐ 89NordPol-21
☐ 89RusNatT-20
☐ 89SweSemWCS-79
☐ 900PC-445

**Mylymok, Jeremy**
☐ 91AirCanSJHL-C5
☐ 96TolSto-29

**Myre, Phil**
☐ 69CanaPosC-19
☐ 70EssPowPla-18
☐ 70SarProSta-112
☐ 71CanaPos-16
☐ 71SarProSta-101
☐ 71TorSun-159
☐ 72Flam-11
☐ 72OPC-43
☐ 72SarProSta-2
☐ 72Top-109
☐ 730PC-77
☐ 73Top-77
☐ 74NHLActSta-10
☐ 740PCNHL-270

☐ 750PCNHL-308
☐ 75Top-308
☐ 760PCNHL-17
☐ 76Top-17
☐ 770PCNHL-193
☐ 77Top-193
☐ 78BluPos-16
☐ 780PC-87
☐ 78Top-87
☐ 790PC-189
☐ 79Top-189
☐ 800PC-8
☐ 80Top-8
☐ 81RocPos-21
☐ 93BlaCok-30
☐ 96SenPizH-16

**Myres, Johnny**
☐ 24CreFal-17

**Myrra, Jouko**
☐ 94FinnSIS-344
☐ 94FinnSIS-347

**Myrvold, Anders**
☐ 94FinnJaaK-254
☐ 95Don-228
☐ 95ParInt-517
☐ 95ParIntEl-517
☐ 96Lea-220
☐ 96LeaPreP-220
☐ 96Sum-197
☐ 96SumArtP-197
☐ 96SumIce-197
☐ 96SumMet-197
☐ 96SumPreS-197

**Myshkin, Vladimir**
☐ 81SweSemHVS-38
☐ 82SweSemHVS-52
☐ 89RusNatT-19

**Nabakov, Dimitri**
☐ 98Pac-150
☐ 98PacIceB-150
☐ 98PacRed-150
☐ 98UppDec-319
☐ 98UppDecE-319
☐ 98UppDecE1o1-319
☐ 98UppDecGN-GN29
☐ 98UppDecGNQ1-GN29
☐ 98UppDecGNQ2-GN29
☐ 98UppDecGNQ3-GN29
☐ 98UppDecGR-319
☐ 99UppDecM-127
☐ 99UppDecMGS-127
☐ 99UppDecMSS-127
☐ 99UppDecMSS-127

**Nabokov, Dimitri**
☐ 94Sel-159
☐ 94SelGol-159
☐ 95SigRooA-30
☐ 95SigRooAPC-30
☐ 95SP-177
☐ 95UppDec-552
☐ 95UppDecEleIce-552
☐ 95UppDecEleIceG-552
☐ 96RegPat-25
☐ 97BowCHL-119
☐ 97BowCHLOPC-119
☐ 97PacRev-31
☐ 97PacRevC-31
☐ 97PacRevE-31
☐ 97PacRevIB-31
☐ 97PacRevR-31
☐ 97PacRevS-31
☐ 97UppDecBD-85
☐ 97UppDecBDDD-85
☐ 97UppDecBDQD-85
☐ 97UppDecBDTD-85
☐ 98SPxFin-19
☐ 98SPxFinR-19
☐ 98SPxFinS-19
☐ 98UC-50
☐ 98UD ChoPCR-50
☐ 98UD ChoR-50
☐ 98UppDecMP-DN

**Nachbaur, Don**
☐ 810PC-138
☐ 82PosCer-7
☐ 880ilTenAnn-113
☐ 88ProAHL-141
☐ 89ProAHL-345
☐ 95SeaThu-18
☐ 96SeaThu-NNO

**Nachtmann, Markus**
☐ 96GerDELE-136

**Nadeau, Patrick**
☐ 907thInnSQMJHL-91
☐ 917thInnSQMJHL-120

**Nadjiwan, Jamie**
☐ 84SudWol-14

**Nagler, M.**
☐ 95GerDELE-13

**Nagurny, Shawn**
☐ 82MedHatT-13

**Nagy, Aaron**
☐ 897thInnSOHL-32
☐ 907thInnSOHL-137
☐ 917thInnSOHL-365

**Nagy, Ladislav**
☐ 99QuePeeWHWCCS-21

**Nagy, Richard**
☐ 91AirCanSJHL-A38
☐ 91AirCanSJHLAS-36
☐ 91AirCanSJHLAS-47

**Najda, Anatoli**
☐ 910PCIns-56R
☐ 94CzeAPSE-271
☐ 95CzeAPSE-263

**Namd, Harry**
☐ 71SweHocS-346

**Namestnikov, Yevgeny**
☐ 93Don-502
☐ 94ClaProP-153
☐ 94Par-246
☐ 94ParGol-246
☐ 94Sco-218
☐ 94ScoGol-218
☐ 94ScoPla-218
☐ 94ScoPlaTS-218
☐ 95Top-46
☐ 95TopOPCl-46
☐ 96SyrCru-18

**Nanne, Lou**
☐ 690PC-198
☐ 70EssPowPla-178
☐ 710PC-240
☐ 71SarProSta-93
☐ 71TorSun-138
☐ 720PC-10
☐ 72SarProSta-111
☐ 72Top-93
☐ 73NorStaAP-7
☐ 73NorStaP-12
☐ 730PC-246
☐ 74NHLActSta-131
☐ 740PCNHL-325
☐ 750PCNHL-143
☐ 75Top-143
☐ 760PCNHL-173
☐ 76Top-173
☐ 770PCNHL-36
☐ 77Top-36
☐ 94MinGolG-23

**Nanne, Marty**
☐ 88ProIHL-106
☐ 89ProIHL-54
☐ 90ProAHLIHL-397

**Nansen, Tomas**
☐ 95SweLeaE-276
☐ 95SweUppDE-157

**Nansen, Tord**
☐ 72SweHocS-230
☐ 83SweSemE-78
☐ 84SweSemE-78

**Nantais, Richard**
☐ 760PCNHL-357

**Nanzen, Tomas**
☐ 90SweSemE-12
☐ 91SweSemE-209
☐ 92SweSemE-232
☐ 93SweSemE-202
☐ 94SweLeaE-56

**Napier, Mark**
☐ 750PCWHA-78
☐ 760PCWHA-108
☐ 770PCWHA-12
☐ 78CanaPos-20
☐ 79CanaPos-18
☐ 790PC-222
☐ 79Top-222
☐ 80CanaPos-17
☐ 800PC-111
☐ 80PepCap-53
☐ 80Top-111
☐ 81CanaPos-19
☐ 810PC-178
☐ 810PCSti-36
☐ 81Top-23
☐ 82CanaPos-15
☐ 82CanaSte-11
☐ 820PC-178
☐ 820PC-189
☐ 820PCSti-38
☐ 820PCSti-39
☐ 82PosCer-10
☐ 83NorStaPos-21
☐ 830PC-182
☐ 830PC-192
☐ 830PCSti-64
☐ 830PCSti-65
☐ 84NorStaPos-20
☐ 840ilRedR-18
☐ 840ilTeal-21
☐ 840PC-105
☐ 850ilRedR-18
☐ 850PC-253
☐ 86KraDra-49
☐ 860ilRedR-65
☐ 860ilTeal-65
☐ 860PC-183
☐ 860PCSti-75
☐ 86Top-183
☐ 87SabBluS-18
☐ 87SabWonBH-19
☐ 880ilTenAnn-28
☐ 88SabBluS-16
☐ 88SabWonBH-18
☐ 89SabCam-16
☐ 93FinnJyvHS-320
☐ 93FinnSIS-31

**Nasato, Lucio**

☐ 94KitRan-15
☐ 95Sla-13

**Nash, Don**
☐ 52JunBluT-28

**Nash, Shane**
☐ 95Sla-194

**Nash, Tom**
☐ 89ProIHL-18

**Nash, Tyson**
☐ 93KamBla-18
☐ 95SlaMemC-14
☐ 96SyrCru-18
☐ 99Pac-368
☐ 99PacCop-368
☐ 99PacGol-368
☐ 99PacIceB-368
☐ 99PacPreD-368

**Nasheim, Richard**
☐ 93SweSemWCS-282
☐ 94FinnJaaK-244
☐ 95AusNatTea-18
☐ 96SweSemW-216

**Naslund, Bert-Roland**
☐ 85SwePanS-180
☐ 86SwePanS-117
☐ 87SwePanS-116

**Naslund, Markus**
☐ 90SweSemE-23
☐ 91AreDraPic-12
☐ 91Cla-13
☐ 91StaPicH-41
☐ 91SweSemE-214
☐ 91UltDra-13
☐ 91UltDra-69
☐ 91UltDra-76
☐ 91UltDra-83
☐ 92SweSemE-240
☐ 92UppDec-234
☐ 93Don-269
☐ 93DonRatP-8
☐ 93Lea-289
☐ 93LeaFrePhe-4
☐ 93Par-245
☐ 93ParCalC-C5
☐ 93ParCalCG-C5
☐ 93ParEmel-245
☐ 93PenFoo-20
☐ 93Pin-449
☐ 93PinCan-449
☐ 93PinSupR-8
☐ 93PinSupRC-8
☐ 93Pow-412
☐ 93Sco-597
☐ 93ScoCan-597
☐ 93ScoGol-597
☐ 93StaClu-393
☐ 93StaCluFDI-393
☐ 93StaCluO-393
☐ 93SweSemWCS-14
☐ 93Ult-395
☐ 93UltWavF-10
☐ 94UppDec-500
☐ 93UppDecSP-123
☐ 94BeAPSig-68
☐ 94ClaProP-26
☐ 94Don-51
☐ 94Lea-211
☐ 94OPCPre-44
☐ 94OPCPreSE-44
☐ 94Par-287
☐ 94ParSE-SE136
☐ 94ParSEG-SE136
☐ 94ParSEV-4
☐ 94PenFoo-15
☐ 94Pin-370
☐ 94PinArtP-370
☐ 94PinRinC-370
☐ 94TopPre-44
☐ 94TopPreSE-44
☐ 94Ult-349
☐ 94UppDec-190
☐ 94UppDecElelce-190
☐ 94UppDecSPI-SP151
☐ 94UppDecSPIDC-SP151

☐ 97PacOmeEG-233
☐ 97PacOmeG-233
☐ 97PacOmeIB-233
☐ 97PacPar-191
☐ 97PacParC-191
☐ 97PacParDG-191
☐ 97PacParEG-191
☐ 97PacParIB-191
☐ 97PacParRed-191
☐ 97PacParSil-191
☐ 97PacRed-128
☐ 97PacSil-128
☐ 97Sco-150
☐ 97ScoArtPro-150
☐ 97ScoCanPla-7
☐ 97ScoCanPre-7
☐ 97ScoCanu-7
☐ 97ScoGolBla-150
☐ 97UppDec-173
☐ 98Be A PPA-140
☐ 98Be A PPAA-140
☐ 98Be A PPAAF-140
☐ 98Be A PPTBASG-140
☐ 98Be APG-140
☐ 98Fin-90
☐ 98FinNo P-90
☐ 98FinNo PR-90
☐ 98FinRef-90
☐ 98Pac-431
☐ 98PacIceB-431
☐ 98PacOmeH-239
☐ 98PacOmeODI-239
☐ 98PacOmeR-239
☐ 98PacRed-431
☐ 98UppDec-379
☐ 98UppDecE-379
☐ 98UppDecE1o1-379
☐ 98UppDecGR-379
☐ 99Pac-429
☐ 99PacAur-143
☐ 99PacAurPD-143
☐ 99PacCop-429
☐ 99PacGol-429
☐ 99PacIceB-429
☐ 99PacPreD-429
☐ 99UppDecM-206
☐ 99UppDecMGS-206
☐ 99UppDecMSS-206
☐ 99UppDecMSS-206

**Naslund, Mats**
☐ 81SweSemHVS-11
☐ 82CanaPos-16
☐ 82CanaSte-12
☐ 82SweSemHVS-13
☐ 83CanaPos-18
☐ 830PC-193
☐ 830PCSti-71
☐ 83PufSti-1
☐ 83Vac-50
☐ 84CanaPos-18
☐ 840PC-267
☐ 840PCSti-156
☐ 840PCSti-156
☐ 85CanaPla-2
☐ 85CanaPla-7
☐ 85CanaPos-22
☐ 85CanaPro-12
☐ 850PC-102
☐ 850PCSti-131
☐ 85Top-102
☐ 86CanaPos-15
☐ 86KraDra-50
☐ 860PC-161
☐ 860PCSti-11
☐ 860PCSti-122
☐ 86Top-161
☐ 86TopStilns-8
☐ 87CanaPos-20
☐ 87CanaVacS-27
☐ 87CanaVacS-45
☐ 87CanaVacS-46
☐ 87CanaVacS-47
☐ 87CanaVacS-48
☐ 87CanaVacS-87
☐ 870PC-16
☐ 870PCBoxB-L
☐ 870PCSti-6
☐ 87PanSti-61
☐ 87ProAll-18
☐ 87Top-16
☐ 87TopBoxB-L
☐ 88CanaPos-21
☐ 88EssAllSta-32
☐ 88FriLayS-25
☐ 880PC-156
☐ 880PCMin-26
☐ 880PCBoxB-R
☐ 880PCSti-50
☐ 880PCSti-215
☐ 88PanSti-259
☐ 88PanSti-406
☐ 88Top-156
☐ 89CanaKra-17
☐ 89CanaPos-25
☐ 89CanaProF-26
☐ 89Kra-23
☐ 890PC-118
☐ 890PCBoxB-H
☐ 890PCSti-46
☐ 89PanSti-243
☐ 89Top-118
☐ 89TopBoxB-H
☐ 90PanSti-62
☐ 91Pin-389
☐ 91PinFre-389
☐ 91SweSemE-188

□ 91SweSemE-349
□ 91SweSemWCS-49
□ 92SweSemE-220
□ 93SweSemE-191
□ 94Fle-14
□ 94SweLeaEGC-14
□ 95ColCho-321
□ 95ColChoPC-321
□ 95ColChoPCP-321
□ 95Don-53
□ 95SweGloWC-72
□ 95SweGloWC-245

**Nasreddine, Alain**
□ 917thInnSQMJHL-277
□ 98BowBes-130
□ 98BowBesAR-130
□ 98BowBesR-130

**Nasreddine, Samy**
□ 97BowCHL-45
□ 97BowCHLOPC-45

**Nasstrom, Anders**
□ 92SweSemE-224

**Naster, Mario**
□ 94GerDELE-167

**Nattrass, Ralph**
□ 44BeeGro2P-130

**Nattress, Ric**
□ 82CanaPos-17
□ 82CanaSte-13
□ 83CanaPos-19
□ 84CanaPos-19
□ 87FlamRedRP-18
□ 87PanSti-307
□ 88OPC-238
□ 88OPCSti-91
□ 90FlamIGA-17
□ 90OPC-459
□ 90ProSet-426
□ 90Sco-302C
□ 90ScoCan-302C
□ 91Bow-266
□ 91FlamIGA-12
□ 91FlamPanTS-13
□ 91ProSet-363
□ 91ProSetFre-363
□ 91ScoCan-249
□ 91StaClu-217
□ 92Bow-63
□ 92FlyJCP-18
□ 92FlyUppDS-26
□ 92OPC-98
□ 92Sco-344
□ 92ScoCan-344
□ 92StaClu-328
□ 92Top-219
□ 92TopGol-219G
□ 92Ult-374
□ 93Sco-381
□ 93ScoCan-381

**Natyshak, Mike**
□ 88ProAHL-116

**Naud, Daniel**
□ 94GerDELE-10

**Naud, Eric**
□ 93AmoLesFAM-15

**Naud, Martin**
□ 92QueIntP-54

**Naud, Sylvain**
□ 907thInnSMC-63
□ 907thInnSQMJHL-52
□ 92-TulOil-11
□ 94CenHocL-103

**Naumann, Andreas**
□ 91UppDec-678
□ 91UppDecCWJC-41
□ 91UppDecF-678
□ 95GerDELE-44

**Naumenko, Gregg**
□ 95NorIowH-22

**Naumenko, Nick**
□ 92NorDakFS-23
□ 98LasVegT-15

**Naumov, Sergei**
□ 94CenHocL-65

**Nauss, Ryan**
□ 93PetPet-19

**Navratil, Milan**
□ 94CzeAPSE-12
□ 95CzeAPSE-115
□ 96CzeAPSE-257

**Naylor, Mike**
□ 95DayBom-11

**Nazarov, Andrei**
□ 92Cla-7
□ 92RusStaRA-26
□ 92RusStaRA-23
□ 93Don-490
□ 94Cla-87
□ 94ClaDraGol-87
□ 94ClaProP-180
□ 94Fle-199
□ 94Lea-328
□ 94OPCPre-461
□ 94OPCPreSE-461
□ 94Par-216
□ 94ParGol-216
□ 94Sco-239
□ 94ScoGol-239
□ 94ScoPla-239
□ 94ScoPlaTS-239
□ 94TopPre-461
□ 94TopPreSE-461
□ 94Ult-367
□ 94UppDec-270
□ 94UppDecEleIce-270


□ 95ColEdgI-146
□ 95Don-187
□ 95Ima-93
□ 95ImaGol-93
□ 95Lea-131
□ 95Met-132
□ 95ParInt-186
□ 95ParIntEI-186
□ 95Pin-190
□ 95PinArtP-190
□ 95PinRinC-190
□ 95Top-121
□ 95TopOPCI-121
□ 95Ult-303
□ 95UppDecSpeE-SE164
□ 95UppDecSpeEdiG-SE164
□ 96ClaGol-7
□ 96ColCho-242
□ 97Pac-307
□ 97PacCop-307
□ 97PacEmeGre-307
□ 97PacIceB-307
□ 97PacRed-307
□ 97PacSil-307
□ 99Pac-59
□ 99PacCop-59
□ 99PacGol-59
□ 99PacIceB-59
□ 99PacPreD-59

**Nazarov, Slava**
□ 74SweHocS-71

**Nazarov, Valeri**
□ 73SweHocS-125
□ 73SweWorCS-125

**NcWana, Llew**
□ 93ThuBayS-3
□ 94ThuBayS-13
□ 95ThuBayS-14

**Ndur, Rumun**
□ 93GueSto-25
□ 94GueSto-24
□ 95RochAmeSS-15
□ 95SigRoo-37
□ 95SigRooSig-37
□ 97UppDec-184
□ 98SP AutSotTG-RN
□ 98SSASotT-RN

**Nedved, Jaroslav**
□ 94ClaProP-6
□ 94CzeAPSE-76
□ 95CzeAPSE-278
□ 96CzeAPSE-125

**Nedved, Petr**
□ 90CanuMoh-21
□ 90Kra-38
□ 90OPCPre-81
□ 90ProSet-402
□ 90ProSet-643
□ 90ScoRoo-50T
□ 90ScoYouS-37
□ 90UppDec-351
□ 90UppDec-353
□ 90UppDecF-351
□ 90UppDecF-353
□ 91Bow-324
□ 91CanuAutC-18
□ 91CanuPanTS-17
□ 91CanuTeal8-18
□ 91Kra-11
□ 91OPC-141
□ 91PanSti-49
□ 91Par-178
□ 91ParFre-178
□ 91Pin-192
□ 91PinFre-192
□ 91ProSet-235
□ 91ProSetFre-235
□ 91ScoAme-124
□ 91ScoCan-124
□ 91StaClu-280
□ 91Top-141
□ 91UppDec-227
□ 91UppDecES-5
□ 91UppDecESF-5
□ 91UppDecF-227
□ 92Bow-396
□ 92CanuRoaTA-16
□ 92OPC-89
□ 92PanSti-31
□ 92PanSti-300
□ 92PanStiFre-31
□ 92PanStiFre-300
□ 92Par-418
□ 92Par-449
□ 92ParEmel-418
□ 92ParEmel-449
□ 92Pin-127
□ 92Pin-249
□ 92PinFre-127
□ 92PinFre-249
□ 92Sco-101
□ 92ScoCan-101
□ 92StaClu-457
□ 92Top-422
□ 92TopGol-422G
□ 92Ult-226
□ 92UltImp-17
□ 92UppDec-263
□ 93Don-356
□ 93Don-486
□ 93Lea-78
□ 93OPCPre-6
□ 93OPCPreG-6
□ 93OPCPreTC-6
□ 93PanSti-171
□ 93Pin-106
□ 93PinCan-106
□ 93Pow-234
□ 93Pow-490
□ 93Sco-231
□ 93ScoCan-231
□ 93ScoIntS-22


□ 93ScoIntSC-22
□ 93StaClu-18
□ 93StaCluFDI-18
□ 93StaCluFDIO-18
□ 93StaCluO-18
□ 93TopPre-6
□ 93TopPreG-6
□ 93Ult-68
□ 94CanGamNHLP-169
□ 94Fin-101
□ 94FinRef-101
□ 94FinSupTW-101
□ 94Fle-137
□ 94Lea-360
□ 94LeaLim-67
□ 94OPCPre-286
□ 94OPCPreSE-286
□ 94ParSE-SE116
□ 94ParSEG-SE116
□ 94ParVin-V44
□ 94Pin-58
□ 94PinArtP-58
□ 94PinRinC-58
□ 94PinWorEdi-WE18
□ 94Sel-120
□ 94SelGol-120
□ 94StaClu-205
□ 94StaCluMOMS-205
□ 94StaCluSTWC-205
□ 94TopPre-286
□ 94TopPreSE-286
□ 94Ult-141
□ 94Ult-333
□ 94UltGloGre-7
□ 94UppDec-164
□ 94UppDecEleIce-164
□ 94UppDecSPI-SP141
□ 94UppDecSPIDC-SP141
□ 95BeaPla-156
□ 95BeAPSig-S156
□ 95BeAPSigDC-S156
□ 95CanGamNHLP-212
□ 95ColCho-323
□ 95ColChoPC-323
□ 95ColChoPCP-323
□ 95Don-252
□ 95Emo-140
□ 95Lea-301
□ 95ParInt-438
□ 95ParIntEI-438
□ 95PenFoo-17
□ 95PlaOneoOne-300
□ 95Sco-220
□ 95ScoBlaIce-220
□ 95ScoBlaIceAP-220
□ 95SkyImp-143
□ 95StaClu-64
□ 95StaCluMOMS-64
□ 95Sum-91
□ 95SumArtP-91
□ 95SumIce-91
□ 95SweGloWC-97
□ 95Top-304
□ 95TopOPCI-304
□ 95Ult-292
□ 95UppDec-462
□ 95UppDecEleIce-462
□ 95UppDecEleIceG-462
□ 95UppDecSpE-SE154
□ 95UppDecSpeEdiG-SE154
□ 95Zen-103
□ 96ColCho-293
□ 96ColCho-328
□ 96Don-76
□ 96DonPrePro-76
□ 96Fla-79
□ 96FlaBluI-79
□ 96Fle-88
□ 96Fle-143
□ 96FleArtRos-17
□ 96FlePicF5-32
□ 96FlePicFF-10
□ 96FlePicJE-9
□ 96Lea-71
□ 96LeaLim-39
□ 96LeaLimG-39
□ 96LeaLimStu-12
□ 96LeaPre-82
□ 96LeaPreP-71
□ 96LeaPrePP-82
□ 96LeaPreSG-56
□ 96LeaPreSte-56
□ 96MetUni-129
□ 96Pin-108
□ 96PinArtP-108
□ 96PinFoi-108
□ 96PinPreS-108
□ 96PinRinC-108
□ 96Sco-38
□ 96ScoArtPro-38
□ 96ScoDeaCAP-38
□ 96ScoGolB-38
□ 96ScoSpeAP-38
□ 96SkyImp-103
□ 96SkyImpB-16
□ 96SP-128
□ 96Sum-148
□ 96SumArtP-148
□ 96SumIce-148
□ 96SumMet-148
□ 96SumPreS-148
□ 96TopNHLP-37
□ 96TopPicOI-37


□ 96UppDec-134
□ 96UppDecBD-95
□ 96UppDecBDG-95
□ 96UppDecIce-56
□ 96UppDecIcePar-56
□ 96UppDecSS-SS26B
□ 96Zen-54
□ 96ZenArtP-54
□ 96ZenAss-13
□ 97ColCho-209
□ 97ColChoSta-SQ3
□ 97Don-152
□ 97DonCanI-71
□ 97DonCanIDS-71
□ 97DonCanIPS-71
□ 97DonLim-156
□ 97DonLimExp-156
□ 97DonPre-33
□ 97DonPreCttC-33
□ 97DonPreProG-152
□ 97DonPreProS-152
□ 97Kat-120
□ 97KatGol-120
□ 97KatSil-120
□ 97Lea-51
□ 97LeaFraMat-51
□ 97LeaFraMDC-51
□ 97LeaInt-51
□ 97LeaIntUI-51
□ 97Pac-13
□ 97PacCop-13
□ 97PacDyn-104
□ 97PacDynDG-104
□ 97PacDynEG-104
□ 97PacDynIB-104
□ 97PacDynR-104
□ 97PacDynTan-22
□ 97PacEmeGre-13
□ 97PacIceB-13
□ 97PacInv-115
□ 97PacInvC-115
□ 97PacInvEG-115
□ 97PacInvIB-115
□ 97PacInvNRB-163
□ 97PacInvR-115
□ 97PacInvS-115
□ 97PacPar-153
□ 97PacParC-153
□ 97PacParDG-153
□ 97PacParEG-153
□ 97PacParIB-153
□ 97PacParRed-153
□ 97PacParSil-153
□ 97PacRed-13
□ 97PacSil-13
□ 97PacSlaSDC-8A
□ 97Pin-124
□ 97PinCer-95
□ 97PinCerMB-95
□ 97PinCerMG-95
□ 97PinCerMR-95
□ 97PinCerR-95
□ 97PinIns-133
□ 97PinPrePBB-124
□ 97PinPrePBC-124
□ 97PinPrePBM-124
□ 97PinPrePBY-124
□ 97PinPrePFC-124
□ 97PinPrePFM-124
□ 97PinPrePFY-124
□ 97PinPrePla-124
□ 97PinTotCMPG-95
□ 97PinTotCPB-95
□ 97PinTotCPG-95
□ 97PinTotCPR-95
□ 97Sco-143
□ 97ScoArtPro-143
□ 97ScoGolBla-143
□ 97ScoPen-6
□ 97ScoPenPla-6
□ 97ScoPenPre-6
□ 97UppDec-137
□ 98Be A PPA-243
□ 98Be A PPAA-243
□ 98Be A PPAAF-243
□ 98Be A PPSE-243
□ 98Be APG-243
□ 98LasVegT-16
□ 98PacOmeH-160
□ 98PacOmeODI-160
□ 98PacOmeR-160
□ 98PacRev-96
□ 98PacRevIS-96
□ 98PacRevR-96
□ 98SPXTopP-41
□ 98SPXTopPF-41
□ 98SPXTopPR-41
□ 99Pac-276
□ 99PacAur-96
□ 99PacAurPD-96
□ 99PacCop-276
□ 99PacGol-276
□ 99PacIceB-276
□ 99PacPreD-276
□ 99RetHoc-50
□ 99UppDecM-134
□ 99UppDecMGS-134
□ 99UppDecMSS-134
□ 99UppDecMSS-134
□ 99UppDecRG-50
□ 99UppDecRP-50

**Nedved, Zdenek**


□ 92SudWol-11
□ 93Par-518
□ 93ParEmel-518
□ 93SudWol-9
□ 93SudWolP-10
□ 94SlaPro-7
□ 94SudWol-8
□ 94SudWolP-11
□ 95Bow-91
□ 95BowAllFoi-91
□ 95Cla-97
□ 95Don-157
□ 95DonRatRoo-5
□ 95ParInt-254
□ 95ParIntEI-254
□ 95StaClu-139
□ 95StaCluMOMS-139
□ 95UppDec-441
□ 95UppDecEleIce-441
□ 95UppDecEleIceG-441
□ 96Lea-230
□ 96LeaPreP-230
□ 96Pin-243
□ 96PinArtP-243
□ 96PinFoi-243
□ 96PinPreS-243
□ 96PinRinC-243

**Needham, Bill**
□ 60CleBar-15
□ 72CleCruWHA-11
□ 72CruCleWHAL-7

**Needham, Bob**
□ 92BriColJHL-54

**Needham, Mike**
□ 87KamBla-14
□ 88KamBla-20
□ 907thInnSMC-10
□ 90ProAHLIHL-375
□ 91ProAHLCHL-297
□ 92Cla-108
□ 92OPCPre-106
□ 92Par-370
□ 92ParEmel-370
□ 92PenCokC-15
□ 92Ult-380
□ 92UppDec-489
□ 93Lea-214
□ 93OPCPre-472
□ 93OPCPreG-472
□ 93PenFoo-15
□ 93StaClu-452
□ 93StaCluFDI-452
□ 93StaCluO-452
□ 93TopPre-472
□ 93TopPreG-472
□ 95AdiRedW-16
□ 96ClaGol-108

**Neely, Bob**
□ 73MapLeaP-20
□ 74MapLeaP-16
□ 74NHLActSta-263
□ 74OPCNHL-272
□ 75MapLeaP-15
□ 75OPCNHL-245
□ 75Top-245
□ 76MapLeaP-12
□ 76OPCNHL-194
□ 76Top-194
□ 77OPCNHL-347

**Neely, Cam**
□ 84Canu-18
□ 84KelWin-43
□ 84OPC-327
□ 85Canu-17
□ 85OPC-228
□ 86OPC-250
□ 87OPC-69
□ 87OPCSti-143
□ 87PanSti-10
□ 87Top-69
□ 88BruPos-14
□ 88BruSpoA-16
□ 88BruSpoA-24
□ 88FriLayS-17
□ 88OPC-58
□ 88OPCMin-27
□ 88OPCSti-22
□ 88PanSti-213
□ 88Top-58
□ 88TopStilns-9
□ 89BruSpoA-17
□ 89BruSpoAU-12
□ 89Kra-56
□ 89OPC-15
□ 89OPCBoxB-K
□ 89OPCSti-33
□ 89PanSti-182
□ 89PanSti-192
□ 89SweSemWCS-71
□ 89Top-15
□ 89TopBoxB-K
□ 90Bow-29
□ 90BowTif-29
□ 90BruSpoA-17
□ 90Kra-39
□ 90Kra-84
□ 90OPC-69
□ 90OPCPre-82
□ 90PanSti-9
□ 90PanSti-327
□ 90ProSet-11
□ 90ProSet-358
□ 90Sco-4
□ 90Sco-323


□ 90Sco-340
□ 90ScoCan-4
□ 90ScoCan-323
□ 90ScoCan-340
□ 90ScoHotRS-67
□ 90Top-69
□ 90Top-201
□ 90TopTeaSL-3
□ 90TopTif-69
□ 90TopTif-201
□ 90UppDec-156
□ 90UppDec-493
□ 90UppDecF-156
□ 90UppDecF-493
□ 91Bow-348
□ 91Bow-366
□ 91BruSpoA-13
□ 91BruSpoA-24
□ 91McDUppD-1
□ 91McDUppD-H5
□ 91OPC-170
□ 91OPC-192
□ 91OPC-266
□ 91OPCPre-107
□ 91PanSti-176
□ 91PanSti-332
□ 91Par-248
□ 91ParFre-248
□ 91Pin-78
□ 91PinB-B6
□ 91PinBFre-B6
□ 91PinFre-78
□ 91ProSet-5
□ 91ProSet-300
□ 91ProSetFre-5
□ 91ProSetFre-300
□ 91ProSetFre-Pla-1
□ 91ScoAme-6
□ 91ScoAme-301
□ 91ScoCan-6
□ 91ScoCan-305
□ 91ScoFan-8
□ 91ScoNat-8
□ 91ScoNatCWC-8
□ 91StaClu-64
□ 91SweSemWCS-68
□ 91Top-192
□ 91Top-266
□ 91UppDec-78
□ 91UppDec-234
□ 91UppDecF-78
□ 91UppDecF-234
□ 92Bow-62
□ 92HumDum2-16
□ 92OPC-174
□ 92PanSti-143
□ 92PanStiFre-143
□ 92Par-248
□ 92ParChep-CP14
□ 92ParEmel-248
□ 92Pin-25
□ 92Pin-232
□ 92PinFre-25
□ 92PinFre-232
□ 92ProSet-8
□ 92Sco-10
□ 92ScoCan-10
□ 92StaClu-316
□ 92Top-32
□ 92TopGol-32G
□ 92Ult-7
□ 92UppDec-86
□ 93Don-29
□ 93DonEli-U4
□ 93Lea-99
□ 93OPCPre-254
□ 93OPCPreG-254
□ 93PanSti-3
□ 93Par-10
□ 93ParEmel-10
□ 93Pin-30
□ 93PinCan-30
□ 93Pow-22
□ 93Sco-342
□ 93ScoCan-342
□ 93ScoDynDUS-3
□ 93StaClu-216
□ 93StaCluFDI-216
□ 93StaCluFDIO-216
□ 93StaCluO-216
□ 93TopPre-254
□ 93TopPreG-254
□ 93Ult-138
□ 93UppDec-356
□ 93UppDecSP-10
□ 94BeAPla-R143
□ 94CanGamNHLP-39
□ 94CanGamNHLP-328
□ 94CanGamNHLP-336
□ 94Cla-AU2
□ 94ClaAut-NNO
□ 94Don-269
□ 94DonDom-4
□ 94EASpo-1
□ 94EASpo-212
□ 94Fin-22
□ 94FinBowB-B3
□ 94FinBowB-X25
□ 94FinBowB-B3
□ 94FinBowBR-X25
□ 94FinRef-22
□ 94FinSupTW-22
□ 94Fla-11
□ 94Fle-15
□ 94FleHea-8

❑ 90BowHatTri-20
❑ 90BowTif-221
❑ 90Kra-40
❑ 90Kra-73
❑ 90OPC-13
❑ 90OPCPre-83
❑ 90PanSti-106
❑ 90ProSet-204
❑ 90ProSet-352
❑ 90Sco-9
❑ 90ScoCan-9
❑ 90ScoHotRS-5
❑ 90Top-13
❑ 90TopTif-13
❑ 90UppDec-34
❑ 90UppDecF-34
❑ 91Bow-76
❑ 91OPC-174
❑ 91PanSti-288
❑ 91Par-278
❑ 91Par-458
❑ 91ParFre-278
❑ 91Pin-300
❑ 91PinFre-300
❑ 91ProSet-166
❑ 91ProSet-386
❑ 91ProSetFre-166
❑ 91ProSetFre-386
❑ 91ProSetPla-174
❑ 91ScoAme-240
❑ 91ScoCan-460
❑ 91StaClu-245
❑ 91SweSemWCS-67
❑ 91Top-174
❑ 91UppDec-356
❑ 91UppDec-566
❑ 91UppDecF-356
❑ 91UppDecF-566
❑ 92Bow-161
❑ 92OilIGA-17
❑ 92OPC-52
❑ 92PanSti-109
❑ 92PanStiFre-109
❑ 92Par-49
❑ 92Par-328
❑ 92ParEmel-49
❑ 92ParEmel-328
❑ 92Pin-120
❑ 92PinFre-120
❑ 92ProSet-52
❑ 92Sco-340
❑ 92ScoCan-340
❑ 92StaClu-448
❑ 92Top-438
❑ 92TopGol-438G
❑ 92Ult-64
❑ 92UppDec-290
❑ 92UppDec-624
❑ 93Don-188
❑ 93Lea-169
❑ 93OPCPre-274
❑ 93OPCPreG-274
❑ 93PanSti-39
❑ 93Par-117
❑ 93ParEmel-117
❑ 93Pin-165
❑ 93PinCan-165
❑ 93Pow-139
❑ 93Sco-19
❑ 93ScoCan-19
❑ 93StaClu-111
❑ 93StaCluFDI-111
❑ 93StaCluFDIO-111
❑ 93StaCluO-111
❑ 93TopPre-274
❑ 93TopPreG-274
❑ 93Ult-86
❑ 93UppDec-58
❑ 93UppDecSP-85
❑ 94CanGamNHLP-68
❑ 94Fin-87
❑ 94FinRef-87
❑ 94FinSupTW-87
❑ 94Fla-35
❑ 94Fle-43
❑ 94HocWit-64
❑ 94Lea-462
❑ 94OPCPre-403
❑ 94OPCPreSE-403
❑ 94ParSE-SE38
❑ 94ParSEG-SE38
❑ 94Pin-499
❑ 94PinArtP-499
❑ 94PinRinC-499
❑ 94Sco-74
❑ 94Sco-245
❑ 94ScoGol-74
❑ 94ScoGol-245
❑ 94ScoPla-74
❑ 94ScoPla-245
❑ 94ScoPlaTS-74
❑ 94ScoPlaTS-245
❑ 94Sel-17
❑ 94SelGol-17
❑ 94SP-25
❑ 94SPDieCut-25
❑ 94SPPre-25
❑ 94SPPreDC-25
❑ 94TopPre-403
❑ 94TopPreSE-403
❑ 94Ult-42
❑ 94Ult-275
❑ 94UppDec-83
❑ 94UppDecEleIce-83
❑ 94UppDecSPI-SP106
❑ 94UppDecSPIDC-SP106
❑ 95ColCho-169
❑ 95ColChoCTG-C17
❑ 95ColChoCTG-C17B
❑ 95ColChoCTG-C17C
❑ 95ColChoCTGGB-C17
❑ 95ColChoCTGGR-C17
❑ 95ColChoCTGSB-C17
❑ 95ColChoCTGSR-C17
❑ 95ColChoPC-169
❑ 95ColChoPCP-169
❑ 95Don-24
❑ 95Emo-31
❑ 95Kra-67
❑ 95Lea-84
❑ 95Met-26
❑ 95ParInt-37
❑ 95ParIntEI-37
❑ 95PlaOneoOne-23
❑ 95ProMag-9
❑ 95Sco-29
❑ 95ScoBlaIce-29
❑ 95ScoBlaIceAP-29
❑ 95SkyImp-31
❑ 95SP-26
❑ 95StaClu-28
❑ 95StaCluMOMS-28
❑ 95Sum-135
❑ 95SumArtP-135
❑ 95SumIce-135
❑ 95SumMadH-1
❑ 95Top-122
❑ 95TopOPCI-122
❑ 95TopSupSki-72
❑ 95TopSupSkiPla-72
❑ 95Ult-34
❑ 95UltGolM-34
❑ 95UppDec-97
❑ 95UppDecEleIce-97
❑ 95UppDecEleIceG-97
❑ 95UppDecSpeE-SE16
❑ 95UppDecSpeEdiG-SE16
❑ 95Zen-46
❑ 96ColCho-50
❑ 96Don-198
❑ 96DonCanI-106
❑ 96DonCanIGPP-106
❑ 96DonCanIRPP-106
❑ 96DonEli-75
❑ 96DonEliDCS-75
❑ 96DonPrePro-198
❑ 96Lea-50
❑ 96LeaPre-60
❑ 96LeaPreP-50
❑ 96LeaPrePP-60
❑ 96MetUni-138
❑ 96NHLProSTA-9
❑ 96Pin-41
❑ 96PinArtP-41
❑ 96PinFoi-41
❑ 96PinPreS-41
❑ 96PinRinC-41
❑ 96PlaOneoOne-355
❑ 96Sco-65
❑ 96ScoArtPro-65
❑ 96ScoDeaCAP-65
❑ 96ScoGolB-65
❑ 96ScoSpeAP-65
❑ 96SP-139
❑ 96Sum-115
❑ 96SumArtP-115
❑ 96SumIce-115
❑ 96SumMet-115
❑ 96SumPreS-115
❑ 96TopNHLP-131
❑ 96TopPicOI-131
❑ 96Ult-152
❑ 96UltGolM-152
❑ 96UppDec-334
❑ 96UppDecBD-59
❑ 96UppDecBDG-59
❑ 96UppDecGN-X31
❑ 96UppDecIce-57
❑ 96UppDecIcePar-57
❑ 96Zen-32
❑ 96ZenArtP-32
❑ 97Don-34
❑ 97DonLim-36
❑ 97DonLimExp-36
❑ 97DonPreProG-34
❑ 97DonPreProS-34
❑ 97Kat-123
❑ 97KatGol-123
❑ 97KatSil-123
❑ 97Pac-255
❑ 97PacCop-255
❑ 97PacEmeGre-255
❑ 97PacIceB-255
❑ 97PacInv-127
❑ 97PacInvC-127
❑ 97PacInvEG-127
❑ 97PacInvIB-127
❑ 97PacInvR-127
❑ 97PacInvS-127
❑ 97PacRed-255
❑ 97PacSil-255
❑ 97Pin-165
❑ 97PinCer-109
❑ 97PinCerMB-109
❑ 97PinCerMG-109
❑ 97PinCerMR-109
❑ 97PinCerR-109
❑ 97PinIns-185
❑ 97PinPrePBB-165
❑ 97PinPrePBC-165
❑ 97PinPrePBM-165
❑ 97PinPrePBY-165
❑ 97PinPrePFC-165
❑ 97PinPrePFM-165
❑ 97PinPrePFY-165
❑ 97PinPrePla-165
❑ 97PinTotCMPG-109
❑ 97PinTotCPB-109
❑ 97PinTotCPG-109
❑ 97PinTotCPR-109
❑ 97Sco-180
❑ 97ShaFleAS-4
❑ 97SPAut-132
❑ 97UppDec-150
❑ 98Be A PPAM-M11
❑ 98O-PChr-78
❑ 98O-PChrR-78
❑ 98Pac-389
❑ 98PacIceB-389
❑ 98PacRed-389
❑ 98Top-78
❑ 98TopO-P-78

**Nicholls, Dave**
❑ 82KitRan-18

**Nichols, Robbie (Rob)**
❑ 83NorBayC-20
❑ 88ProAHL-1
❑ 89ProIHL-111
❑ 90ProAHLIHL-299
❑ 91ProAHLCHL-329
❑ 92SanDieG-21
❑ 95FliGen-9

**Nicholson, Al**
❑ 61UniOilW-10

**Nicholson, Dan**
❑ 81OshGen-9
❑ 82OshGen-18

**Nickel, Hartmut**
❑ 69SweWorC-175
❑ 70SweHocS-378
❑ 94GerDELE-127

**Nickel, Stacey**
❑ 84KelWin-3
❑ 86RegPat-20

**Nicol, Brett**
❑ 907thInnSOHL-138

**Nicol, Cregg**
❑ 86RegPat-21
❑ 87RegPat-21

**Nicoletti, Martin**
❑ 88ProAHL-279

**Nicolls, Jamie**
❑ 86PorWinH-16
❑ 88ProAHL-77
❑ 92GreMon-11
❑ 93GreMon-10

**Nicolls, Paul**
❑ 92BriColJHL-33

**Nicolson, Derek**
❑ 95ThuBayS-13

**Nicolson, Graeme**
❑ 81RocPos-22

**Nieckar, Barry**
❑ 93RalIce-13
❑ 94St.JohF-16

**Niederberger, Andreas**
❑ 89SweSemWCS-106
❑ 93SweSemWCS-154
❑ 94FinnJaaK-279
❑ 94GerDELE-88
❑ 95GerDELE-82
❑ 95GerDELE-438
❑ 95SweGloWC-222
❑ 96GerDELE-273

**Niedermayer, Rob**
❑ 907thInnSWHL-29
❑ 917thInnSWHL-327
❑ 92UppDec-593
❑ 93Cla-5
❑ 93Cla-AU7
❑ 93ClaTopTen-DP5
❑ 93Don-134
❑ 93DonRatR-4
❑ 93DonSpeP-I
❑ 93Kra-68
❑ 93Lea-293
❑ 93LeaFrePhe-6
❑ 93OPCPre-270
❑ 93OPCPreG-270
❑ 93Par-246
❑ 93ParCalC-C4
❑ 93ParCalCG-C4
❑ 93ParEasWesS-E5
❑ 93ParEmel-246
❑ 93ParUSACG-G5
❑ 93Pin-439
❑ 93PinCan-439
❑ 93PinSupR-4
❑ 93PinSupRC-4
❑ 93Pow-349
❑ 93PowRooS-8
❑ 93Sco-592
❑ 93ScoCan-592
❑ 93ScoGol-592
❑ 93StaClu-449
❑ 93StaCluFDI-449
❑ 93StaCluO-449
❑ 93TopPre-270
❑ 93TopPreG-270
❑ 93Ult-330
❑ 93UltSpeM-8
❑ 93UltWavF-11
❑ 93UppDec-98
❑ 93UppDecPOE-E11
❑ 93UppDecSilSka-H4
❑ 93UppDecSilSkaG-H4
❑ 93UppDecSP-58
❑ 94BeAPla-R55
❑ 94BeAPla-R119
❑ 94CanGamNHLP-109
❑ 94ClaAut-NNO
❑ 94ClaProP-27
❑ 94Don-113
❑ 94Fla-67
❑ 94Fle-82
❑ 94Lea-225
❑ 94LeaGolR-7
❑ 94LeaLim-11
❑ 94OPCFinIns-9
❑ 94OPCPre-306
❑ 94OPCPreSE-306
❑ 94Par-294
❑ 94ParGol-294
❑ 94ParSE-SE68
❑ 94ParSEG-SE68
❑ 94ParVin-V22
❑ 94Pin-168
❑ 94Pin-469
❑ 94PinArtP-168
❑ 94PinArtP-469
❑ 94PinRinC-168
❑ 94PinRinC-469
❑ 94PosCerBB-19
❑ 94Sel-25
❑ 94SelGol-25
❑ 94StaClu-22
❑ 94StaClu-117
❑ 94StaCluFDI-22
❑ 94StaCluFDI-117
❑ 94StaCluMOMS-22
❑ 94StaCluMOMS-117
❑ 94StaCluST-9
❑ 94StaCluSTWC-22
❑ 94StaCluSTWC-117
❑ 94TopPre-306
❑ 94TopPreSE-306
❑ 94Ult-84
❑ 94UppDec-287
❑ 94UppDecEleIce-287
❑ 94UppDecNBAP-10
❑ 94UppDecSPI-SP30
❑ 94UppDecSPIDC-SP30
❑ 95BeAPla-184
❑ 95BeAPSig-S184
❑ 95BeAPSigDC-S184
❑ 95Bow-76
❑ 95BowAllFoi-76
❑ 95ColCho-40
❑ 95ColChoPC-40
❑ 95ColChoPCP-40
❑ 95Don-51
❑ 95DonEli-65
❑ 95DonEliDCS-65
❑ 95DonEliDCU-65
❑ 95Fin-98
❑ 95FinRef-98
❑ 95ImpSti-50
❑ 95Lea-197
❑ 95LeaLim-35
❑ 95Met-61
❑ 95ParInt-82
❑ 95ParIntEI-82
❑ 95Pin-100
❑ 95PinArtP-100
❑ 95PinRinC-100
❑ 95PlaOneoOne-42
❑ 95PlaOneoOne-263
❑ 95ProMag-89
❑ 95Sco-48
❑ 95ScoBlaIce-48
❑ 95ScoBlaIceAP-48
❑ 95SelCer-96
❑ 95SelCerMG-96
❑ 95SP-60
❑ 95StaClu-94
❑ 95StaCluMOMS-94
❑ 95Sum-105
❑ 95SumArtP-105
❑ 95SumIce-105
❑ 95Top-31
❑ 95TopOPCI-31
❑ 95TopSupSki-22
❑ 95TopSupSkiPla-22
❑ 95Ult-62
❑ 95UltGolM-62
❑ 95UppDec-310
❑ 95UppDecEleIce-310
❑ 95UppDecEleIceG-310
❑ 95UppDecSpeE-SE35
❑ 95UppDecSpeEdiG-SE35
❑ 95Zen-110
❑ 96ColCho-103
❑ 96ColCho-318
❑ 96Don-24
❑ 96DonCanI-13
❑ 96DonCanIGPP-13
❑ 96DonCanIRPP-13
❑ 96DonEli-15
❑ 96DonEliDCS-15
❑ 96DonPrePro-24
❑ 96Fle-41
❑ 96KraUppD-63
❑ 96Lea-22
❑ 96LeaLim-78
❑ 96LeaLimG-78
❑ 96LeaLimStu-19
❑ 96LeaPre-12
❑ 96LeaPreP-22
❑ 96LeaPrePP-12
❑ 96LeaPreSG-61
❑ 96LeaPreSte-61
❑ 96MetUni-61
❑ 96NHLProSTA-89
❑ 96Pin-32
❑ 96PinArtP-32
❑ 96PinFoi-32
❑ 96PinPreS-32
❑ 96PinRinC-32
❑ 96PlaOneoOne-435
❑ 96Sco-3
❑ 96ScoArtPro-3
❑ 96ScoDeaCAP-3
❑ 96ScoGolB-3
❑ 96ScoSpeAP-3
❑ 96SelCer-7
❑ 96SelCerAP-7
❑ 96SelCerBlu-7
❑ 96SelCerMB-7
❑ 96SelCerMG-7
❑ 96SelCerMR-7
❑ 96SelCerRed-7
❑ 96SkyImp-47
❑ 96SP-62
❑ 96Sum-147
❑ 96SumArtP-147
❑ 96SumIce-147
❑ 96SumMet-147
❑ 96SumPreS-147
❑ 96TopNHLP-99
❑ 96TopPicOI-99
❑ 96Ult-67
❑ 96UltGolM-67
❑ 96UppDec-262
❑ 96UppDecBD-140
❑ 96UppDecBDG-140
❑ 96UppDecGN-X3
❑ 96UppDecSS-SS28A
❑ 96Zen-84
❑ 96ZenArtP-84
❑ 97ColCho-105
❑ 97ColChoSta-SQ18
❑ 97Don-191
❑ 97DonLim-79
❑ 97DonLimExp-79
❑ 97DonPre-61
❑ 97DonPreCttC-61
❑ 97DonPreProG-191
❑ 97DonPreProS-191
❑ 97Kat-64
❑ 97KatGol-64
❑ 97KatSil-64
❑ 97Lea-58
❑ 97LeaFraMat-58
❑ 97LeaFraMDC-58
❑ 97LeaInt-58
❑ 97LeaIntUI-58
❑ 97Pac-269
❑ 97PacCop-269
❑ 97PacEmeGre-269
❑ 97PacIceB-269
❑ 97PacPar-83
❑ 97PacParC-83
❑ 97PacParDG-83
❑ 97PacParEG-83
❑ 97PacParIB-83
❑ 97PacParRed-83
❑ 97PacParSil-83
❑ 97PacRed-269
❑ 97PacSil-269
❑ 97Pin-157
❑ 97PinIns-182
❑ 97PinPrePBB-157
❑ 97PinPrePBC-157
❑ 97PinPrePBM-157
❑ 97PinPrePBY-157
❑ 97PinPrePFC-157
❑ 97PinPrePFM-157
❑ 97PinPrePFY-157
❑ 97PinPrePla-157
❑ 97Sco-253
❑ 97SPAut-67
❑ 97SPAutSotT-RN
❑ 97UppDec-281
❑ 97UppDecBD-22
❑ 97UppDecBDDD-22
❑ 97UppDecBDQD-22
❑ 97UppDecBDTD-22
❑ 97UppDecIce-14
❑ 97UppDecIceP-14
❑ 97UppDecIPS-14
❑ 97UppDecSG-SG44
❑ 98Be A PPA-208
❑ 98Be A PPAA-208
❑ 98Be A PPAAF-208
❑ 98Be A PPSE-208
❑ 98Be APG-208
❑ 98Fin-41
❑ 98FinNo P-41
❑ 98FinNo PR-41
❑ 98FinRef-41
❑ 98O-PChr-37
❑ 98O-PChrR-37
❑ 98PacOmeH-105
❑ 98PacOmeODI-105
❑ 98PacOmeR-105
❑ 98PacRev-63
❑ 98PacRevIS-63
❑ 98PacRevR-63
❑ 98SP Aut-36
❑ 98Top-37
❑ 98TopO-P-37
❑ 98UC-94
❑ 98UD ChoPCR-94
❑ 98UD ChoR-94
❑ 98UppDec-277
❑ 98UppDecBD-39
❑ 98UppDecDD-39
❑ 98UppDecE-277
❑ 98UppDecE1o1-277
❑ 98UppDecGR-277
❑ 98UppDecM-87
❑ 98UppDecMGS-87
❑ 98UppDecMP-RN
❑ 98UppDecMSS-87
❑ 98UppDecMSS-87
❑ 98UppDecQD-39
❑ 98UppDecTD-39
❑ 99Pac-179
❑ 99PacAur-64
❑ 99PacAurPD-64
❑ 99PacCop-179
❑ 99PacGol-179
❑ 99PacIceB-179
❑ 99PacPreD-179
❑ 99SP AutPS-36
❑ 99UppDecM-88
❑ 99UppDecMGS-88
❑ 99UppDecMSS-88
❑ 99UppDecMSS-88

**Niedermayer, Scott**
❑ 907thInnSMC-18
❑ 907thInnSWHL-289
❑ 90UppDec-461
❑ 90UppDecF-461
❑ 917thInnSCHLAW-11
❑ 917thInnSCHLAW-13
❑ 917thInnSMC-97
❑ 91AreDraPic-2
❑ 91Cla-3
❑ 91OPCPre-35
❑ 91Par-94
❑ 91ParFre-94
❑ 91Pin-349
❑ 91PinFre-349
❑ 91ProSet-547
❑ 91ProSetCC-CC4
❑ 91ProSetCCF-CC4
❑ 91ProSetFre-547
❑ 91ScoCan-577
❑ 91ScoRoo-27T
❑ 91StaPicH-13
❑ 91UltDra-3
❑ 91UltDra-56
❑ 91UltDra-59
❑ 91UltDra-75
❑ 91UltDra-79
❑ 91UltDra-80
❑ 91UppDecCWJC-53
❑ 92Bow-313
❑ 92OPCPre-113
❑ 92PanSti-179
❑ 92PanStiFre-179
❑ 92Par-95
❑ 92ParEmel-95
❑ 92Pin-241
❑ 92Pin-304
❑ 92PinFre-304
❑ 92PinTea2-12
❑ 92PinTea2F-12
❑ 92ProSet-232
❑ 92Sco-401
❑ 92ScoCan-401
❑ 92ScoYouS-33
❑ 92StaClu-209
❑ 92Top-223
❑ 92TopGol-223G
❑ 92Ult-116
❑ 92UppDec-406
❑ 92UppDec-562
❑ 92UppDecACH-5
❑ 92UppDecCC-CC5
❑ 92UppDecWJG-WG1
❑ 93Don-189
❑ 93DonSpeP-M
❑ 93Lea-80
❑ 93LeaGolR-14
❑ 93OPCPre-470
❑ 93OPCPreG-470
❑ 93PanSti-42
❑ 93Par-111
❑ 93Par-240
❑ 93ParEmel-111
❑ 93ParEmel-240
❑ 93Pin-111
❑ 93PinCan-111
❑ 93PinTea2-14
❑ 93PinTea2C-14
❑ 93Pow-140
❑ 93Sco-217
❑ 93ScoCan-217
❑ 93StaClu-403
❑ 93StaCluFDI-403
❑ 93StaCluO-403
❑ 93TopPre-470
❑ 93TopPreG-470
❑ 93Ult-95
❑ 93UppDec-25
❑ 93UppDec-284
❑ 93UppDecSP-86
❑ 94BeAPla-R37
❑ 94BeAPla-R128
❑ 94BeAPSig-88
❑ 94CanGamNHLP-351
❑ 94Don-161
❑ 94Fla-96
❑ 94Fle-115
❑ 94HocWit-54
❑ 94Lea-237
❑ 94LeaLim-40
❑ 94OPCPre-240
❑ 94OPCPre-539
❑ 94OPCPreSE-240
❑ 94OPCPreSE-539
❑ 94ParSE-SE95
❑ 94ParSEG-SE95
❑ 94ParSEV-12
❑ 94Pin-75
❑ 94PinArtP-75
❑ 94PinRinC-75
❑ 94Sco-22
❑ 94ScoGol-22
❑ 94ScoPla-22
❑ 94ScoPlaTS-22
❑ 94Sel-101
❑ 94SelGol-101
❑ 94SP-67
❑ 94SPDieCut-67
❑ 94StaClu-93
❑ 94StaCluFDI-93
❑ 94StaCluMOMS-93
❑ 94StaCluSTWC-93
❑ 94TopPre-240
❑ 94TopPre-539
❑ 94TopPreSE-240
❑ 94TopPreSE-539
❑ 94Ult-121
❑ 94UppDec-324
❑ 94UppDecEleIce-324
❑ 94UppDecIG-IG6
❑ 94UppDecNBAP-32
❑ 94UppDecPC-C34
❑ 94UppDecPCEG-C34
❑ 94UppDecSPI-SP134
❑ 94UppDecSPIDC-SP134
❑ 95Bow-64
❑ 95BowAllFoi-64
❑ 95CanGamNHLP-164
❑ 95ColCho-3
❑ 95ColChoPC-3
❑ 95ColChoPCP-3
❑ 95Don-105
❑ 95Emo-100
❑ 95Fin-103
❑ 95FinRef-103
❑ 95ImpSti-71
❑ 95Lea-150
❑ 95LeaLim-43
❑ 95LeaRoaCup-9
❑ 95Met-84
❑ 95ParInt-388
❑ 95ParIntEI-388
❑ 95PlaOneoOne-59
❑ 95ProMag-38
❑ 95Sco-52
❑ 95ScoBlaIce-52
❑ 95ScoBlaIceAP-52
❑ 95SelCer-70
❑ 95SelCerMG-70
❑ 95SkyImp-95
❑ 95SP-84
❑ 95StaClu-76
❑ 95StaCluGTSC-GT8
❑ 95StaCluMOMS-76
❑ 95Sum-50
❑ 95SumArtP-50
❑ 95SumIce-50
❑ 95Top-164
❑ 95TopOPCI-164
❑ 95TopSupSki-27
❑ 95TopSupSkiPla-27
❑ 95TopYouS-YS14
❑ 95Ult-90
❑ 95Ult-194
❑ 95UltGolM-90
❑ 95UltGolM-194
❑ 95UltRisS-5
❑ 95UltRisSGM-5
❑ 95UppDec-383
❑ 95UppDecEleIce-383
❑ 95UppDecEleIceG-383
❑ 95UppDecWJA-12
❑ 95Zen-27
❑ 96BeAPAut-59
❑ 96BeAPAutSil-59
❑ 96BeAPla-59
❑ 96ColCho-149
❑ 96Dev-27
❑ 96Don-188
❑ 96DonPrePro-188
❑ 96FlaNowAT-3
❑ 96Fle-60
❑ 96FlePic-116
❑ 96Lea-198
❑ 96LeaPreP-198
❑ 96MetUni-87
❑ 96NHLProSTA-38
❑ 96Sco-108
❑ 96ScoArtPro-108
❑ 96ScoDeaCAP-108
❑ 96ScoGolB-108
❑ 96ScoSpeAP-108
❑ 96SkyImp-70
❑ 96SP-90
❑ 96Sum-57
❑ 96SumArtP-57
❑ 96SumIce-57
❑ 96SumMet-57
❑ 96SumPreS-57
❑ 96TeaOut-52
❑ 96Ult-94
❑ 96UltGolM-95
❑ 96UppDec-92
❑ 96UppDecBD-137
❑ 96UppDecBDG-137
❑ 96UppDecIce-36

96UppDecIcePar-36
96UppDecSS-SS28B
97ColCho-148
97ColChoWD-W12
97Don-72
97DonPreProG-72
97DonPreProS-72
97DonPriSoA-37
97EssOlyHH-14
97EssOlyHHF-14
97Kat-83
97KatGol-83
97KatSil-83
97Pac-247
97PacCop-247
97PacEmeGre-247
97PacIceB-247
97PacOme-132
97PacOmeDG-132
97PacOmeEG-132
97PacOmeG-132
97PacOmeIB-132
97PacRed-247
97PacRev-79
97PacRevC-79
97PacRevE-79
97PacRevIB-79
97PacRevR-79
97PacRevS-79
97PacSil-247
97Pin-115
97PinIns-95
97PinPrePBB-115
97PinPrePBC-115
97PinPrePBM-115
97PinPrePBY-115
97PinPrePFC-115
97PinPrePFM-115
97PinPrePFY-115
97PinPrePla-115
97Sco-229
97ScoDev-7
97ScoDevPla-7
97ScoDevPre-7
97UppDec-301
98Be A PPA-232
98Be A PPAA-232
98Be A PPAAF-232
98Be A PPSE-232
98APG-232
98BowBes-99
98BowBesAR-99
98BowBesR-99
98Fin-120
98FinNo P-120
98FinNo PR-120
98FinRef-120
98O-PChr-143
98O-PChrBM-B8
98O-PChrBMR-B8
98O-PChrR-143
98Pac-266
98PacAur-112
98PacIceB-266
98PacPar-136
98PacParC-136
98PacParEG-136
98PacParH-136
98PacParIB-136
98PacParS-136
98PacRed-266
98Top-143
98TopBoaM-B8
98TopO-P-143
98UC-119
98UD ChoPCR-119
98UD ChoR-119
98UppDec-308
98UppDecE-308
98UppDecE1o1-308
98UppDecGR-308
98UppDecM-120
98UppDecMGS-120
98UppDecMSS-120
99DevPowP-NJD1
99Pac-242
99PacCop-242
99PacGol-242
99PacIceB-242
99PacPreD-242
99UppDecM-118
99UppDecMGS-118
99UppDecMSS-118
99UppDecMSS-118
**Niedomyst, Tadeusz**
72SweHocS-252
74SweHocS-253
**Niekamp, Jim (James)**
71TorSun-100
72ShaLosAW-10
75RoaPhoWHA-2
76RoaPhoWHA-14
**Nielsen, Chris**
98BowCHL-130
98BowCHLAuB-A28
98BowCHLAuG-A28
98BowCHLAuS-A28
98BowCHLGA-130
98BowCHLOI-130
98BowChrC-130
98BowChrCGA-130
98BowChrCGAR-130
98BowChrCOI-130
98BowChrCOIR-130
98BowChrCR-130
**Nielsen, Devon**
92CorBigRed-22
**Nielsen, Jeff**
91MinGolG-19
92MinGolG-17
93MinGolG-23
94BinRan-14
95BinRan-17
95BinRan-15
98Pac-61
98PacIceB-61
98PacRed-61
**Nielsen, Jens**
89SweSemE-141
90SweSemE-214
91SweSemE-142
92SweSemE-163
93SweSemE-258
94SweLeaE-287
95SweLeaE-286
95SweUppDE-184
**Nielsen, Kirk**
92HarCri-27
96ProBru-14
98CinCyc-16
**Nielson, Corey**
95SigRoo-48
55SigRooSig-48
**Nielson, Len**
86RegPat-22
87MonHaw-17
88ProAHL-172
**Niemegeers, Kyle**
91AirCanSJHL-C10
92MPSPhoSJHL-11
**Niemi, Antti-Jussi**
95FinnSIS-250
95UppDec-549
95UppDecEIeIce-549
95UppDecEIeIceG-549
**Niemi, Esko**
96FinnSISR-188
**Niemi, Lars-Goran**
84SweSemE-185
86SwePanS-179
87SwePanS-180
**Niemi, Mikko**
93FinnSIS-116
**Nieminen, Lasse**
93FinnJyvHS-138
94FinnSIS-147
94FinnSIS-57
95FinnSIS-65
**Nieminen, Mika**
89SweSemWCS-50
91SweSemWCS-17
92SweSemE-197
93SweSemE-168
93SweSemWCS-69
94FinnJaak-36
94FinnSIS-369
94FinnSIS-385
94SweLeaE-22
94SweLeaE-3
95FinnJaakKLAC-7
95FinnKarWCL-12
95FinnSemWC-40
95FinnSISGC-18
95SweGloWC-135
96SweSemW-22
**Nieminen, Ville**
95FinnSIS-113
**Nienhuis, Kraig**
86MonGolF-11
95AusNatTea-19
96GerDELE-42
**Nieuwendyk, Joe**
87FlamRedRP-19
87FlamRedRP-20
88FriLayS-36
88OPC-16
88OPCMin-29
88OPCSti-90
88OPCSti-125
88OPCSti-134
88OPCSti-205
88OPCSti-216
88OPCSti-270
88PanSti-12
88PanSti-404
88Top-16
89Kra-5
89OPC-138
89OPCSti-101
89PanSti-29
89SweSemWCS-74
89Top-138
90Bow-91
90BowTif-91
90FlamIGA-18
90Kra-41
90Kra-74
90OPC-87
90OPCPre-84
90PanSti-174
90ProSet-42A
90ProSet-42B
90ProSet-344
90Sco-30A
90Sco-30B
90ScoCan-30B
90ScoHotRS-45
90Top-87
90TopTeaSL-8
90TopTif-87
90UppDec-26
90UppDecF-26
91Bow-252
91FlamIGA-13
91FlamPanTS-14
91OPC-223
91OPCPre-48
91PanSti-53
91Par-23
91ParFre-23
91Pin-54
91PinFre-54
91ProSet-29
91ProSet-569
91ProSetFre-29
91ProSetFre-569
91ProSetPla-18
91ScoAme-170
91ScoCan-170
91StaClu-60
91SweSemWCS-69
91Top-223
91UppDec-263
91UppDecF-263
92Bow-59
92FlamIGA-17
92OPC-354
92PanSti-40
92PanStiFre-40
92Par-21
92ParEmel-21
92Pin-31
92PinFre-31
92ProSet-26
92Sco-193
92ScoCan-193
92StaClu-37
92Top-105
92TopGol-105G
92Ult-25
92UppDec-128
93Don-48
93Kra-45
93Kra-60
93Lea-126
93OPCPre-205
93OPCPreG-205
93PanSti-182
93Par-31
93ParEmel-31
93Pin-198
93PinCan-198
93PinCap-4
93PinCapC-4
93Pow-39
93Sco-199
93ScoCan-199
93StaClu-96
93StaCluFDI-96
93StaCluDIO-96
93StaCluO-96
93TopPre-205
93TopPreG-205
93Ult-130
93UppDec-396
93UppDecSP-23
94BeAPSig-96
94CanGamNHLP-56
94Don-56
94EASpo-21
94Fle-32
94HocWit-82
94Lea-228
94LeaLim-82
94McDUppD-McD21
94OPCPre-537
94OPCPreSE-537
94Par-33
94ParCratGB-4
94ParCratGG-4
94ParCratGR-4
94ParGol-33
94Pin-90
94PinArtP-90
94PinRinC-90
94Sco-159
94ScoGol-159
94ScoPla-159
94ScoPlaTS-159
94Sel-131
94SelGol-131
94SP-20
94SPDieCut-20
94StaClu-166
94StaCluFDI-166
94StaCluMO-18
94StaCluMOMS-166
94StaCluSTWC-166
94TopPre-537
94TopPreSE-537
94UppDec-276
94UppDecEIeIce-276
94UppDecSPI-SP13
94UppDecSPIDC-SP13
95CanGamNHLP-49
95ColCho-133
95ColChoPC-133
95ColChoPCP-133
95Don-40
95DonEli-50
95DonEliDCS-50
95DonEliDCU-50
95DonIgn-9
95Emo-24
95Fin-168
95FinRef-168
95ImpSti-18
95Lea-305
95LeaLim-56
95McDPin-MCD-12
95Met-21
95NHLAcePC-10C
95ParInt-33
95ParInt-329
95ParIntEl-33
95ParIntEl-329
95PlaOneoOne-18
95ProMag-48
95Sco-229
95ScoBlaIce-229
95ScoBlaIceAP-229
95SelCer-32
95SelCerDS-10
95SelCerDSG-10
95SelCerMG-32
95SkyImp-24
95SP-38
95StaClu-18
95StaCluMOMS-18
95StaScoS-229
95Sum-162
95SumArtP-162
95SumIce-162
95SumMadH-13
95Top-233
95TopOPCI-233
95UppDec-285
95UppDecSpeE-SE12
95UppDecSpeEdiG-SE12
95ZenGifG-14
96BeAPAut-53
96BeAPAutSil-53
96BeAPla-53
96BeAPla-83
96ColCho-68
96ColCho-315
96Don-195
96DonCanI-63
96DonCanIGPP-63
96DonCanIRPP-63
96DonEli-62
96DonEliDCS-62
96DonPrePro-195
96FlePicF5-33
96KraUppD-13
96Lea-34
96LeaLim-75
96LeaLimG-75
96LeaPre-27
96LeaPreP-34
96LeaPrePP-27
96LeaPreSG-45
96LeaPreSte-45
96MetUni-42
96NHLProSTA-48
96Pin-183
96PinArtP-183
96PinFoi-183
96PinPreS-183
96PinRinC-183
96PlaOneoOne-334
96Sco-152
96ScoArtPro-152
96ScoDeaCAP-152
96ScoGolB-152
96ScoSpeAP-152
97Don-186
97DonCanI-51
97DonCanIDS-51
97DonCanIPS-51
97DonEli-61
97DonEliS-61
97DonEliAsp-61
97DonLim-43
97DonLimExp-43
97DonPre-115
97DonPreCttC-115
97DonPreProG-186
97DonPreProS-186
97DonPri-140
97DonPriSoA-140
97Kat-47
97KatGol-47
97KatSil-47
97Lea-108
97LeaFraMat-108
97LeaFraMDC-108
97LeaInt-108
97Pac-266
97PacCop-266
97PacCroR-42
97PacCroREG-42
97PacCroRIB-42
97PacCroRS-42
97PacDyn-38
97PacDynDG-38
97PacDynEG-38
97PacDynIB-38
97PacDynR-38
97PacDynTan-43
97PacEmeGre-266
97PacIceB-266
97PacInv-43
97PacInvC-43
97PacInvEG-43
97PacInvIB-43
97PacInvR-43
97PacInvS-43
97PacOme-74
97PacOmeC-74
97PacOmeDG-74
97PacOmeEG-74
97PacOmeIB-74
97PacOmeTL-7
97PacPar-61
97PacParC-61
97PacParDG-61
97PacParEG-61
97PacParIB-61
97PacParRed-61
97PacParSil-61
97PacRed-266
97PacRev-44
97PacRevC-44
97PacRevE-44
97PacRevIB-44
97PacRevR-44
97PacSil-266
97Pin-110
97PinBee-20
97PinBeeGP-20
97PinCer-76
97PinCerMB-76
97PinCerMG-76
97PinCerMR-76
97PinCerR-76
97PinIns-115
97PinPrePBB-110
97PinPrePBC-110
97PinPrePBM-110
97PinPrePBY-110
97PinPrePFC-110
97PinPrePFM-110
97PinPrePFY-110
97PinPrePla-110
97PinTotCMPG-76
97PinTotCPB-76
97PinTotCPG-76
97PinTotCPR-76
97Sco-135
97ScoArtPro-135
97ScoGolBla-135
97SPAut-49
97Stu-55
97StuPrePG-55
97StuPrePS-55
97UppDec-50
97UppDecBD-16
97UppDecBDDD-16
97UppDecBDOD-16
97UppDecBDTD-16
97Zen-63
97Zen5x7-15
97ZenGolImp-15
97ZenSilImp-15
97ZenZGol-63
97ZenZSil-63
98Be A PPA-193
98Be A PPAA-193
98Be A PPAAF-193
98Be A PPSE-193
98Be APG-193
98BowBes-62
98BowBesAR-62
98BowBesR-62
98DonLimAsp-16
98Fin-112
98FinNo P-112
98FinNo PR-112
98FinRedL-R14
98FinRedLR-R14
98FinRef-112
98O-PChr-161
98O-PChrR-161
98Pac-25
98PacAur-75
98PacAurMAC-8
98PacCroR-42
98PacCroRLS-42
98PacDynI-60
98PacDynIIB-60
98PacDynIR-60
98PacIceB-25
98PacOmeH-74
98PacOmeODI-74
98PacOmeR-74
98PacPar-69
98PacParC-69
98PacParEG-69
98PacParH-69
98PacParIB-69
98PacParS-69
98PacRev-45
98PacRevIS-45
98PacRevR-45
98SPxFin-26
98SPxFinR-26
98SPxFinS-26
98Top-161
98TopGolLC1-44
98TopGolLC1B-44
98TopGolLC1B0oO-44
98TopGolLC1OoO-44
98TopGolLC1R-44
98TopGolLC1ROoO-44
98TopGolLC2-44
98TopGolLC2B-44
98TopGolLC2B0oO-44
98TopGolLC2OoO-44
98TopGolLC2R-44
98TopGolLC2ROoO-44
98TopGolLC3-44
98TopGolLC3B-44
98TopGolLC3B0oO-44
98TopGolLC3OoO-44
98TopGolLC3R-44
98TopGolLC3ROoO-44
98TopO-P-161
98UC-62
98UD ChoPCR-62
98UD ChoR-62
98UppDec-78
98UppDecE-78
98UppDecE1o1-78
98UppDecFF-FF30
98UppDecFF-FF30
98UppDecFFQ1-FF30
98UppDecFFQ2-FF30
98UppDecGJ-GJ24
98UppDecGR-78
98UppDecM-63
98UppDecMGS-63
98UppDecMSS-63
98UppDecMSS-63
99Pac-127
99PacAur-48
99PacAurPD-48
99PacCop-127
99PacGol-127
99PacIceB-127
99PacPreD-127
**Nighbor, Frank**
23V1451-2
24C144ChaCig-44
24V1452-6
60Top-35
60TopSta-41
83HalFP-E12
85HalFC-72
**Nigro, Frank**
82MapLeaP-25
83MapLeaP-17
83OPC-337
83OPCSti-149
**Niinimaa, Janne**
93Cla-44
93FinnSIS-390
93Par-520
93ParEmel-520
94Cla-105
94ClaDraGol-105
94ClaTri-T49
94Fin-128
94FinnSIS-58
94FinRef-128
94FinSupTW-128
94ParSE-SE217
94ParSEG-SE217
94SP-162
94SPDieCut-162
95FinnKarWCL-13
95FinnSemWC-227
95FinnSIS-251
95FinnSIS-NNO
95FinnSISGC-8
95FinnSISL-13
96ColCho-361
96DonCanI-128
96DonCanIGPP-128
96DonCanIRPP-128
96DonEliAsp-16
96Fla-120
96FlaBluI-120
96FlyPos-16
96LeaPre-127
96LeaPrePP-127
96MetUni-189
96SelCerAP-104
96SelCerBlu-104
96SelCerMB-104
96SelCerMG-104
96SelCerMR-104
96SelCerRed-104
96SP-186
96SweSemW-6
96Ult-127
96UltGolM-127
96UltRoo-15
96UppDec-310
96UppDecBD-154
96UppDecBDG-154
96UppDecIcePar-49
96Zen-124
96ZenArtP-124
97Be A PPAd-144
97Be A PPAPD-144
97BeAPla-144
97BeAPlaAut-144
97ColCho-183
97ColChoSta-SQ26
97Don-99
97DonCanISCS-21
97DonEli-92
97DonEliAsp-92
97DonEliR-92
97DonLim-16
97DonLim-136
97DonLim-168
97DonLimExp-136
97DonLimExp-136
97DonLimExp-168
97DonLimFOTG-69
97DonPre-26
97DonPreCttC-26
97DonPreProG-99
97DonPreProS-99
97DonPri-84
97DonPriSoA-84
97Lea-75
97LeaFraMat-75
97LeaFraMDC-75
97LeaInt-75
97LeaIntUI-75
97Pac-173
97PacCop-173
97PacDyn-92
97PacDynC-92
97PacDynDG-92
97PacDynEG-92
97PacDynIB-92
97PacDynR-92
97PacDynSil-92
97PacDynTan-16
97PacEmeGre-173
97PacIceB-173
97PacInv-103
97PacInvC-103
97PacInvEG-103
97PacInvFP-26
97PacInvIB-103
97PacInvR-103
97PacInvS-103
97PacPar-135
97PacParC-135
97PacParDG-135
97PacParEG-135
97PacParIB-135
97PacParRed-135
97PacParSil-135
97PacRed-173
97PacSil-173
97PinIns-179
97Sco-165
97ScoFly-9
97ScoFlyPla-9
97ScoFlyPre-9
97SPx-37
97SPxBro-37
97SPxGol-37
97SPxGraF-37
97SPxSil-37
97SPxSte-37
97Stu-100
97StuPrePG-100
97StuPrePS-100
97UppDec-124
97UppDecGDM-124
97UppDecIce-21
97UppDecIceP-21
97UppDecIPS-21
97UppDecSG-SG41
97UppDecTSS-8A
98Fin-108
98FinNo P-108
98FinNo PR-108
98FinRef-108
98Pac-24
98PacAur-75
98PacCroR-52
98PacCroRLS-52
98PacDynI-74
98PacDynIIB-74
98PacDynIR-74
98PacIceB-24
98PacOmeH-94
98PacOmeODI-94
98PacOmeR-94
98PacPar-91
98PacParC-91
98PacParEG-91
98PacParH-91
98PacParIB-91
98PacParS-91
98PacRed-24
98SPxFin-35
98SPxFinR-35
98SPxFinS-35
98UC-86
98UD ChoPCR-86

❑ 98UD ChoR-86
❑ 98UppDec-91
❑ 98UppDecE-91
❑ 98UppDecE1o1-91
❑ 98UppDecGR-91
❑ 98UppDecM-78
❑ 98UppDecMGS-78
❑ 98UppDecMSS-78
❑ 98UppDecMSS-78
❑ 99Pac-162
❑ 99PacCop-162
❑ 99PacGol-162
❑ 99PacIceB-162
❑ 99PacPreD-162
**Niittymaki, Mika**
❑ 94FinnSIS-307
❑ 96FinnSISR-133
**Nikander, Jarkko**
❑ 93FinnJyvHS-47
❑ 93FinnSIS-247
❑ 94FinnSIS-52
❑ 95FinnSIS-317
❑ 96FinnSISR-129
**Nikitin, Valerij**
❑ 69SweWorC-132
❑ 69SweWorC-134
❑ 70SweHocS-321
❑ 74SweHocS-42
**Nikko, Jani**
❑ 93FinnJyvHS-75
❑ 93FinnSIS-111
❑ 93Par-524
❑ 93ParEmel-524
❑ 94FinnSIS-203
❑ 95FinnSemWC-226
❑ 95FinnSIS-220
❑ 95FinnSISL-84
❑ 96FinnSISR-18
**Nikolishin, Andrei**
❑ 91UppDecCWJC-7
❑ 92Cla-48
❑ 92UppDec-340
❑ 94Cla-70
❑ 94ClaDraGol-70
❑ 94ClaProPIA-IA18
❑ 94ClaROYS-R14
❑ 94ClaTri-T28
❑ 94Fin-10
❑ 94FinRef-10
❑ 94FinSupTW-10
❑ 94Fle-87
❑ 94OPCPre-421
❑ 94OPCPreSE-421
❑ 94ParSE-SE72
❑ 94ParSEG-SE72
❑ 94Pin-487
❑ 94PinArtP-487
❑ 94PinRinC-487
❑ 94Sel-184
❑ 94SelGol-184
❑ 94TopPre-421
❑ 94TopPreSE-421
❑ 94Ult-301
❑ 94UppDec-241
❑ 94UppDecEleIce-241
❑ 94UppDecPC-C9
❑ 94UppDecPCEG-C9
❑ 94UppDecPCES-C9
❑ 94UppDecSPI-SP122
❑ 94UppDecSPIDC-SP122
❑ 95ColCho-21
❑ 95ColChoPC-21
❑ 95ColChoPCP-21
❑ 95Don-124
❑ 95Emo-76
❑ 95FinnSemWC-123
❑ 95Lea-11
❑ 95ParInt-94
❑ 95ParIntEI-94
❑ 95Pin-98
❑ 95PinArtP-98
❑ 95PinRinC-98
❑ 95Sco-169
❑ 95ScoBlaIce-169
❑ 95ScoBlaIceAP-169
❑ 95SkyImp-74
❑ 95StaClu-149
❑ 95StaCluMOMS-149
❑ 95Top-361
❑ 95TopNewG-22NG
❑ 95TopOPCI-361
❑ 95Ult-68
❑ 95UltGolM-68
❑ 95UppDec-55
❑ 95UppDecEleIce-55
❑ 95UppDecEleIceG-55
❑ 95UppDecSpeE-SE38
❑ 95UppDecSpeEdiG-SE38
❑ 96BeAPAut-137
❑ 96BeAPAutSil-137
❑ 96BeAPla-137
❑ 96ClaGol-48
❑ 96ColCho-114
❑ 96FlePic-172
❑ 96Pin-179
❑ 96PinArtP-179
❑ 96PinFoi-179
❑ 96PinPreS-179
❑ 96PinRinC-179
❑ 96WhaBobS-19
❑ 97PacDynBKS-102
❑ 98Be A PPA-300
❑ 98Be A PPAA-300
❑ 98Be A PPAAF-300
❑ 98Be A PPSE-300
❑ 98Be APG-300
❑ 99Pac-445
❑ 99PacCop-445
❑ 99PacGol-445
❑ 99PacIceB-445
❑ 99PacPreD-445
**Nikolov, Angel**
❑ 94CzeAPSE-206
❑ 95ClaAut-15
❑ 95CzeAPSE-153
❑ 96CzeAPSE-172
**Nilan, Chris**
❑ 80CanaPos-18
❑ 80PepCap-54
❑ 81CanaPos-20
❑ 82CanaPos-18
❑ 82CanaSte-14
❑ 83CanaPos-20
❑ 83OPC-194
❑ 83Vac-51
❑ 84CanaPos-20
❑ 84OPC-268
❑ 85CanaPla-3
❑ 85CanaPla-7
❑ 85CanaPos-23
❑ 85CanaPos-24
❑ 85CanaPro-13
❑ 85OPCSti-127
❑ 86CanaPos-16
❑ 86KraDra-51
❑ 86OPC-199
❑ 87CanaPos-21
❑ 87CanaVacS-19
❑ 87CanaVacS-20
❑ 87OPCSti-15
❑ 87PanSti-68
❑ 87ProAll-17
❑ 88OPC-31
❑ 88OPCSti-245
❑ 88Top-31
❑ 89RanMarMB-30
❑ 89SweSemWCS-175
❑ 90BruSpoA-18
❑ 90OPC-454
❑ 90OPCPre-85
❑ 90ProSet-205A
❑ 90ProSet-205B
❑ 90ProSet-409
❑ 90Sco-311A
❑ 90ScoCan-311A
❑ 90ScoRoo-22T
❑ 90UppDec-368
❑ 90UppDec-442
❑ 90UppDecF-368
❑ 90UppDecF-442
❑ 91Bow-351
❑ 91OPC-311
❑ 91PanSti-183
❑ 91Pin-289
❑ 91PinFre-289
❑ 91ScoAme-197
❑ 91ScoCan-197
❑ 91StaClu-244
❑ 91Top-311
❑ 91UppDec-237
❑ 91UppDecF-237
❑ 92Sco-76
❑ 92ScoCan-76
**Nill, Jim**
❑ 81SweSemHVS-84
❑ 82Canu-17
❑ 83Canu-15
❑ 83OPC-357
❑ 83Vac-114
❑ 84OPC-11
❑ 84JetPol-16
❑ 86JetBor-17
❑ 88RedWinLC-15
❑ 89OPC-224
❑ 90ProAHLIHL-475
**Nilsater, Olle**
❑ 67SweHoc-209
**Nilsson, Billy**
❑ 92SweSemE-250
**Nilsson, Christer**
❑ 67SweHoc-123
❑ 69SweHocS-136
❑ 70SweHocS-93
❑ 71SweHocS-187
❑ 72SweHocS-174
**Nilsson, Fredrik**
❑ 89SweSemE-252
❑ 90SweSemE-170
❑ 91SweSemE-272
❑ 92SweSemE-290
❑ 93SweSemWCS-17
❑ 94FinnJaaK-59
**Nilsson, Goran**
❑ 81SweSemHVS-4
❑ 83SweSemE-220
❑ 83SweSemE-223
**Nilsson, Hans-Ake**
❑ 67SweHoc-90
❑ 84SweSemE-206
**Nilsson, Hardy**
❑ 72SweHocS-209
❑ 74SweHocS-254
❑ 83SweSemE-171
❑ 96GerDELE-268
**Nilsson, Henrik**
❑ 90SweSemE-172
❑ 91SweSemE-267
❑ 91SweSemE-288
❑ 93SweSemE-255
❑ 94SweLeaE-59
❑ 95GerDELE-74
❑ 95SweLeaE-205
❑ 95SweUppDE-218
**Nilsson, Jan Erik**
❑ 64SweCorl-27
❑ 65SweCorl-27
❑ 67SweHoc-225
❑ 69SweHocS-265
❑ 70SweHocS-151
❑ 71SweHocS-244
❑ 72SweHocS-228
❑ 73SweHocS-229
❑ 73SweWorCS-229
❑ 74SweHocS-177
❑ 84SweSemE-193
**Nilsson, Kent**
❑ 78JetPos-17
❑ 79FlamPos-11
❑ 79FlaTeal-12
❑ 80FlamPos-13
❑ 80OPC-106
❑ 80OPC-197
❑ 80OPCSup-3
❑ 80PepCap-11
❑ 80Top-106
❑ 80Top-197
❑ 81OPC-34
❑ 81OPC-52
❑ 81OPC-53
❑ 81OPCSti-218
❑ 81PosSta-28
❑ 81Top-24
❑ 81Top-48
❑ 82FlamDol-4
❑ 82OPC-54
❑ 82OPCSti-217
❑ 82PosCer-3
❑ 82SweSemHVS-147
❑ 83OPC-89
❑ 83OPCSti-267
❑ 83OPCSti-268
❑ 83PufSti-3
❑ 83Vac-14
❑ 84OPC-232
❑ 84OPCSti-245
❑ 85OPCSti-208
❑ 87OPCSti-88
❑ 88OilTenAnn-27
❑ 89SweSemWCS-24
❑ 91SweSemWCS-50
❑ 92SweSemE-93
❑ 95SweGloWC-71
**Nilsson, Kjell**
❑ 67SweHoc-38
❑ 73SweHocS-218
❑ 73SweWorCS-218
**Nilsson, Klas Goran**
❑ 67SweHoc-162
**Nilsson, Lars-Goran**
❑ 67SweHoc-16
❑ 67SweHoc-55
❑ 69SweHocS-70
❑ 69SweHocS-193
❑ 69SweWorC-36
❑ 69SweWorC-61
❑ 69SweWorC-117
❑ 70SweHocS-17
❑ 70SweHocS-33
❑ 70SweHocS-287
❑ 71SweHocS-20
❑ 71SweHocS-110
❑ 71SweHocS-140
❑ 72SweHocS-18
❑ 72SweHocS-90
❑ 72SweSemWC-54
❑ 74SweSemHVS-19
❑ 81SweSemHVS-120
❑ 83SweSemE-104
**Nilsson, Leif**
❑ 69SweHocS-341
❑ 70SweHocS-257
❑ 71SweHocS-317
**Nilsson, Magnus**
❑ 98UC-265
❑ 98UD ChoPCR-288
❑ 98UD ChoR-288
**Nilsson, Marcus**
❑ 95ColCho-345
❑ 95ColChoPC-345
❑ 95ColChoPCP-345
❑ 95SP-185
❑ 95UppDec-560
❑ 95UppDecEleIce-560
❑ 95UppDecEleIceG-560
❑ 96CEFLAuHP-4
❑ 97UppDecBD-137
❑ 97UppDecBDDD-137
❑ 97UppDecBDQD-137
❑ 97UppDecBDTD-137
❑ 98UC-296
❑ 98UD ChoPCR-296
❑ 98UD ChoR-296
❑ 99Pac-185
❑ 99PacCop-185
❑ 99PacGol-185
❑ 99PacIceB-185
❑ 99PacPreD-185
**Nilsson, Mats**
❑ 89SweSemE-106
❑ 90SweSemE-109
**Nilsson, Mikael**
❑ 95SweLeaE-153
**Nilsson, Nils**
❑ 64SweCorl-19
❑ 65SweCorl-19
❑ 81SweSemHVS-121
**Nilsson, Nisse**
❑ 64SweCorl-55
❑ 65SweCorl-55
❑ 67SweHoc-108
❑ 69SweHocS-123
**Nilsson, Odd**
❑ 84SweSemE-22
❑ 85SwePanS-22
❑ 87SwePanS-20
❑ 89SweSemE-22
**Nilsson, Olle**
❑ 69SweHocS-88
❑ 72SweHocS-79
**Nilsson, Orjan**
❑ 91SweSemE-137
❑ 92SweSemE-157
**Nilsson, Peder**
❑ 73SweHocS-221
❑ 73SweWorCS-221
❑ 74SweHocS-148
**Nilsson, Per**
❑ 83SweSemE-163
❑ 84SweSemE-61
❑ 85SwePanS-59
❑ 86SwePanS-207
❑ 87SwePanS-201
❑ 89SweSemE-186
**Nilsson, Peter**
❑ 71SweHocS-116
❑ 83SweSemE-87
❑ 84SweSemE-87
❑ 85SwePanS-78
❑ 86SwePanS-71
❑ 87SwePanS-84
❑ 89SweSemE-64
❑ 90SweSemE-288
❑ 91SweSemE-71
❑ 92SweSemE-91
❑ 93SweSemE-64
❑ 94SweLeaE-50
❑ 95SweUppDE1DS-DS8
**Nilsson, Petter**
❑ 91SweSemE-161
❑ 92SweSemE-182
❑ 93SweSemE-153
❑ 94SweLeaE-7
❑ 95SweLeaE-254
❑ 95SweUppDE-118
❑ 96GerDELE-347
**Nilsson, Roger**
❑ 67SweHoc-259
❑ 69SweHocS-305
❑ 72SweHocS-80
**Nilsson, Ronny**
❑ 91SweSemE-127
**Nilsson, Rune**
❑ 67SweHoc-91
**Nilsson, Stefan**
❑ 83SweSemE-38
❑ 84SweSemE-38
❑ 84SweSemE-155
❑ 85SwePanS-138
❑ 86SwePanS-18
❑ 86SwePanS-130
❑ 86SwePanS-142
❑ 86SwePanS-187
❑ 87SwePanS-124
❑ 87SwePanS-152
❑ 89SweSemE-114
❑ 89SweSemE-160
❑ 90SweSemE-240
❑ 91SweSemE-167
❑ 92SweSemE-186
❑ 92SweSemE-258
❑ 93SweSemE-156
❑ 94FinnJaaK-63
❑ 94SweLeaE-18
❑ 94SweLeaE-258
❑ 94SweLeaEP-2
❑ 94SweLeaERR-10
❑ 95SweLeaE-42
❑ 95SweLeaE-252
❑ 95SweUppDE-65
❑ 95SweUppDE-122
**Nilsson, Tommy**
❑ 84SweSemE-146
❑ 91SweSemE-10
**Nilsson, Ulf**
❑ 69SweHocS-49
❑ 70SweHocS-11
❑ 71SweHocS-88
❑ 72SweHocS-63
❑ 73SweHocS-10
❑ 73SweHocS-202
❑ 73SweWorCS-10
❑ 73SweWorCS-202
❑ 74OPCWHA-4
❑ 74SweHocS-26
❑ 74SweHocS-256
❑ 74SweSemHVS-8
❑ 75OPCWHA-83
❑ 76OPCWHA-2
❑ 76OPCWHA-3
❑ 76OPCWHA-5
❑ 76OPCWHA-9
❑ 77OPCWHA-15
❑ 78OPC-255
❑ 78Top-255
❑ 79OPC-30
❑ 79Top-30
❑ 79Top-163
❑ 80OPC-116
❑ 80Top-116
❑ 81OPC-229
❑ 81OPCSti-172
❑ 81Top-E102
❑ 82SweSemHVS-145
❑ 83SweSemE-173
❑ 84SweSemE-35
❑ 84SweSemE-196
❑ 85SwePanS-31
❑ 86SwePanS-220
❑ 87SwePanS-212
❑ 91UppDec-643
❑ 91UppDecF-643
❑ 92FutTre76CC-143
❑ 96SweSemWHL-HL11
**Nimigon, Steve**
❑ 93NiaFalT-9
❑ 95Sla-188
**Niro, Dominic**
❑ 93FliGen-8
**Nises, Ulf**
❑ 67SweHoc-145
❑ 69SweHocS-159
❑ 70SweHocS-126
❑ 71SweHocS-217
❑ 72SweHocS-194
**Niskavaara, Jakko**
❑ 95ColCho-332
❑ 95ColChoPC-332
❑ 95ColChoPCP-332
**Nissinen, Tero**
❑ 96FinnSISR-86
**Nistico, Lou**
❑ 75OPCWHA-13
**Nitel, Adam**
❑ 95Sla-203
**Nixon, Danny**
❑ 51LavDaiS-15
❑ 52St.LawS-38
**Nixon, Jaret**
❑ 95Sla-324
**Nixon, Julian**
❑ 74SioCitM-13
**Noack, Rudiger**
❑ 70SweHocS-379
**Nobili, Mario**
❑ 907thInnSQMJHL-233
❑ 917thInnSQMJHL-146
❑ 91StaPicH-34
❑ 91UltDra-51
❑ 92-TulOil-12
**Noble, Jeff**
❑ 85KitRan-18
❑ 86KitRan-17
❑ 87KitRan-18
**Noble, Reg**
❑ 23V1451-26
❑ 24C144ChaCig-45
❑ 24V1452-51
❑ 83HalFP-B8
❑ 85HalFC-22
**Noctor, John**
❑ 94GuiFla-9
**Noel, Claude**
❑ 897thInnSOHL-176
❑ 92DayBom-20
**Noel, Mike**
❑ 74SioCitM-14
**Noga, Chris**
❑ 92ArlIce-17
**Noga, Matt**
❑ 95NorIowH-23
**Nogier, Pat**
❑ 85KamBla-16
**Nohel, Pavel**
❑ 94CzeAPSE-16
❑ 95CzeAPSE-112
❑ 96CzeAPSE-275
**Nokkosmaki, Nemo**
❑ 93FinnSIS-217
❑ 94FinnSIS-232
**Nolan, Billy**
❑ 90HamRoaA-51
❑ 91HamRoaA-13
**Nolan, Jeffery**
❑ 907thInnSOHL-112
**Nolan, Owen**
❑ 897thInnSOHL-180
❑ 90NordPet-19
❑ 90OPCPre-86
❑ 90ProSet-401
❑ 90ProSet-635
❑ 90Sco-435
❑ 90ScoCan-435
❑ 90ScoRoo-80T
❑ 90ScoYouS-36
❑ 90UppDec-351
❑ 90UppDec-352
❑ 90UppDecF-351
❑ 90UppDecF-352
❑ 91Bow-134
❑ 91Gil-25
❑ 91Kra-55
❑ 91NordPanTS-17
❑ 91NordPet-21
❑ 91OPC-64
❑ 91OPCPre-193
❑ 91PanSti-266
❑ 91Par-143
❑ 91ParFre-143
❑ 91Pin-156
❑ 91PinFre-156
❑ 91ProSet-196
❑ 91ProSetFre-196
❑ 91ProSetPla-101
❑ 91ScoAme-143
❑ 91ScoCan-143
❑ 91StaClu-259
❑ 91Top-64
❑ 91UppDec-367
❑ 91UppDec-619
❑ 91UppDecF-367
❑ 91UppDecF-619
❑ 92Bow-237
❑ 92Bow-328
❑ 92HumDum2-17
❑ 92McDUppD-24
❑ 92NorPet-22
❑ 92OPC-382
❑ 92PanSti-210
❑ 92PanStiFre-210
❑ 92Par-145
❑ 92Par-455
❑ 92ParCheP-CP13
❑ 92ParEmel-145
❑ 92ParEmel-455
❑ 92Pin-6
❑ 92PinAmePP-1
❑ 92PinFre-6
❑ 92PinTea2-10
❑ 92PinTea2F-10
❑ 92ProSet-153
❑ 92Sco-286
❑ 92ScoCan-286
❑ 92ScoSha-12
❑ 92ScoShaCan-12
❑ 92ScoYouS-37
❑ 92SeaPat-46
❑ 92StaClu-78
❑ 92Top-349
❑ 92TopGol-349G
❑ 92Ult-177
❑ 92UppDec-17
❑ 92UppDec-321
❑ 93Don-279
❑ 93Lea-42
❑ 93OPCPre-267
❑ 93OPCPreF-4
❑ 93OPCPreG-267
❑ 93PanSti-70
❑ 93Par-163
❑ 93ParEmel-163
❑ 93ParFirO-F4
❑ 93Pin-151
❑ 93PinCan-151
❑ 93PinTea2-28
❑ 93PinTea2C-28
❑ 93Pow-201
❑ 93Sco-32
❑ 93ScoCan-32
❑ 93StaClu-397
❑ 93StaCluFDI-397
❑ 93StaCluO-397
❑ 93SweSemWCS-207
❑ 93TopPre-267
❑ 93TopPreF-4
❑ 93TopPreG-267
❑ 93Ult-154
❑ 93UppDec-175
❑ 93UppDecHT-HT16
❑ 93UppDecSP-128
❑ 94BeAPla-R51
❑ 94BeAPSig-59
❑ 94CanGamNHLP-197
❑ 94Don-45
❑ 94EASpo-113
❑ 94Fle-181
❑ 94HocWit-57
❑ 94Lea-144
❑ 94LeaLim-41
❑ 94NordBurK-19
❑ 94OPCPre-457
❑ 94OPCPreSE-457
❑ 94ParSE-SE143
❑ 94ParSEG-SE143
❑ 94ParVin-V43
❑ 94Pin-76
❑ 94PinArtP-76
❑ 94PinRinC-76
❑ 94Sel-4
❑ 94SelGol-4
❑ 94SP-95
❑ 94SPDieCut-95
❑ 94StaClu-102
❑ 94StaCluFDI-102
❑ 94StaCluMOMS-102
❑ 94StaCluSTWC-102
❑ 94TopPre-457
❑ 94TopPreSE-457
❑ 94Ult-177
❑ 94UppDec-103
❑ 94UppDecEleIce-103
❑ 94UppDecNBAP-33
❑ 94UppDecSPI-SP63
❑ 94UppDecSPIDC-SP63
❑ 95Bow-58
❑ 95BowAllFoi-58
❑ 95CanGamNHLP-76
❑ 95ColCho-259
❑ 95ColChoCTG-C12
❑ 95ColChoCTG-C12B
❑ 95ColChoCTG-C12C
❑ 95ColChoCTGGB-C12
❑ 95ColChoCTGGR-C12
❑ 95ColChoCTGSB-C12
❑ 95ColChoCTGSR-C12
❑ 95ColChoPC-259
❑ 95ColChoPCP-259
❑ 95Don-153
❑ 95Don-268
❑ 95DonEli-26
❑ 95DonEliDCS-26
❑ 95DonEliDCU-26
❑ 95DonMar-2
❑ 95Emo-40
❑ 95EmoNteP-6
❑ 95Fin-142
❑ 95FinRef-142
❑ 95ImpSti-110
❑ 95Lea-240
❑ 95LeaLim-93
❑ 95McDPin-MCD-10
❑ 95Met-133
❑ 95ParInt-49
❑ 95ParInt-453
❑ 95ParIntEI-49
❑ 95ParIntEI-453
❑ 95Pin-12
❑ 95PinArtP-12
❑ 95PinFulC-3
❑ 95PinRinC-12
❑ 95PlaOneoOne-27
❑ 95PlaOneoOne-241
❑ 95Sco-83
❑ 95ScoBlaIce-83
❑ 95ScoBlaIceAP-83
❑ 95ScoChelt-2
❑ 95ScoLam-4
❑ 95SelCer-19
❑ 95SelCerMG-19
❑ 95SelCerP-19
❑ 95SkyImp-150
❑ 95SkyImp-240
❑ 95SkyImpIQ-11
❑ 95SP-129
❑ 95StaClu-65
❑ 95StaCluMOMS-65
❑ 95Sum-12
❑ 95SumArtP-12
❑ 95SumIce-12
❑ 95SumMadH-1
❑ 95Top-305
❑ 95TopOPCI-305
❑ 95Ult-134
❑ 95Ult-304
❑ 95UltCreCra-13
❑ 95UltGolM-134
❑ 95UltRedLS-8
❑ 95UltRedLSGM-8
❑ 95UppDec-176
❑ 95UppDec-225
❑ 95UppDec-246
❑ 95UppDec-495
❑ 95UppDecEleIce-176
❑ 95UppDecEleIce-225
❑ 95UppDecEleIce-246
❑ 95UppDecEleIce-495
❑ 95UppDecEleIceG-176
❑ 95UppDecEleIceG-225
❑ 95UppDecEleIceG-246
❑ 95UppDecEleIceG-495
❑ 95UppDecNHLAS-AS13
❑ 95UppDecPRE-R7
❑ 95UppDecPreR-R7
❑ 95UppDecSpeE-SE163
❑ 95UppDecSpeEdiG-SE163
❑ 95Zen-16
❑ 95ZenGifG-9
❑ 96BeAPBisITB-25
❑ 96ColCho-233
❑ 96ColCho-330
❑ 96ColChoMVP-UD42
❑ 96ColChoMVPG-UD42
❑ 96ColChoSti-S25
❑ 96Don-6
❑ 96DonCanI-54
❑ 96DonCanIGPP-54
❑ 96DonCanIRPP-54
❑ 96DonEli-14
❑ 96DonEliDCS-14
❑ 96DonEliS-6
❑ 96DonHitLis-17
❑ 96DonPrePro-6
❑ 96DurAllT-DC19
❑ 96Fla-85
❑ 96FlaBluI-85
❑ 96FlaHotN-10
❑ 96Fle-100
❑ 96FlePicF5-34
❑ 96KraUppD-4
❑ 96KraUppD-36
❑ 96Lea-128
❑ 96LeaLim-20
❑ 96LeaLimBTB-3
❑ 96LeaLimBTBLE-3
❑ 96LeaLimBTBP-P3
❑ 96LeaLimG-20
❑ 96LeaPre-6
❑ 96LeaPreP-128
❑ 96LeaPrePP-6
❑ 96LeaPreSG-62
❑ 96LeaPreSte-62
❑ 96MetUni-139
❑ 96NHLACEPC-35
❑ 96Pin-186
❑ 96PinArtP-186
❑ 96PinFan-FC18
❑ 96PinFoi-186
❑ 96PinPreS-186
❑ 96PinRinC-186
❑ 96PlaOneoOne-335
❑ 96Sco-69
❑ 96ScoArtPro-69
❑ 96ScoChelt-8
❑ 96ScoDeaCAP-69
❑ 96ScoGolB-69

❑ 96ScoSpeAP-69
❑ 96SelCer-56
❑ 96SelCerAP-56
❑ 96SelCerBlu-56
❑ 96SelCerMB-56
❑ 96SelCerMG-56
❑ 96SelCerMR-56
❑ 96SelCerRed-56
❑ 96SkyImp-117
❑ 96SP-138
❑ 96SPx-41
❑ 96SPxGol-41
❑ 96StaCluMO-8
❑ 96Sum-45
❑ 96SumArtP-45
❑ 96SumIce-45
❑ 96SumMet-45
❑ 96SumPreS-45
❑ 96TeaOut-43
❑ 96TopNHLP-57
❑ 96TopPicOI-57
❑ 96Ult-153
❑ 96UltGolM-153
❑ 96UppDec-146
❑ 96UppDecBD-111
❑ 96UppDecBDG-111
❑ 96UppDecGN-X19
❑ 96UppDecIce-59
❑ 96UppDecIcePar-59
❑ 96UppDecPP-P18
❑ 96Zen-37
❑ 96ZenArtP-37
❑ 96ZenAss-14
❑ 97ColCho-214
❑ 97ColChoCTG-C30A
❑ 97ColChoCTG-C30B
❑ 97ColChoCTG-C30C
❑ 97ColChoCTGE-CR30
❑ 97ColChoSta-SQ78
❑ 97Don-84
❑ 97DonCanI-108
❑ 97DonCanIDS-108
❑ 97DonCanINP-30
❑ 97DonCanIPS-108
❑ 97DonLim-117
❑ 97DonLim-196
❑ 97DonLimExp-117
❑ 97DonLimExp-196
❑ 97DonPre-108
❑ 97DonPreCttC-108
❑ 97DonPreProG-84
❑ 97DonPreProS-84
❑ 97DonPri-46
❑ 97DonPriSoA-46
❑ 97Kat-124
❑ 97KatGol-124
❑ 97KatSil-124
❑ 97Lea-23
❑ 97LeaFraMat-23
❑ 97LeaFraMDC-23
❑ 97LeaInt-23
❑ 97LeaIntUI-23
❑ 97Pac-151
❑ 97PacCop-151
❑ 97PacCroR-121
❑ 97PacCroREG-121
❑ 97PacCroRIB-121
❑ 97PacCroRS-121
❑ 97PacDyn-114
❑ 97PacDynC-114
❑ 97PacDynDG-114
❑ 97PacDynEG-114
❑ 97PacDynIB-114
❑ 97PacDynR-114
❑ 97PacDynSil-114
❑ 97PacDynTan-50
❑ 97PacEmeGre-151
❑ 97PacIceB-151
❑ 97PacInv-128
❑ 97PacInvC-128
❑ 97PacInvEG-128
❑ 97PacInvIB-128
❑ 97PacInvR-128
❑ 97PacInvS-128
❑ 97PacOme-205
❑ 97PacOmeC-205
❑ 97PacOmeDG-205
❑ 97PacOmeEG-205
❑ 97PacOmeG-205
❑ 97PacOmeIB-205
❑ 97PacPar-169
❑ 97PacParC-169
❑ 97PacParDG-169
❑ 97PacParEG-169
❑ 97PacParIB-169
❑ 97PacParRed-169
❑ 97PacParSil-169
❑ 97PacRed-151
❑ 97PacRev-126
❑ 97PacRevC-126
❑ 97PacRevE-126
❑ 97PacRevIB-126
❑ 97PacRevR-126
❑ 97PacRevS-126
❑ 97PacSil-151
❑ 97PacTeaCCC-22
❑ 97Pin-49
❑ 97PinArtP-49
❑ 97PinBee-22
❑ 97PinBeeGP-22
❑ 97PinCer-59
❑ 97PinCerMB-59
❑ 97PinCerMG-59
❑ 97PinCerMR-59
❑ 97PinCerR-59
❑ 97PinIns-27
❑ 97PinInsCC-27
❑ 97PinInsEC-27
❑ 97PinPrePBB-49
❑ 97PinPrePBC-49
❑ 97PinPrePBM-49
❑ 97PinPrePBY-49
❑ 97PinPrePFC-49
❑ 97PinPrePFM-49
❑ 97PinPrePFY-49
❑ 97PinPrePla-49
❑ 97PinRinC-49
❑ 97PinTotCMPG-59
❑ 97PinTotCPB-59
❑ 97PinTotCPG-59
❑ 97PinTotCPR-59
❑ 97Sco-102
❑ 97ScoArtPro-102
❑ 97ScoChel-17
❑ 97ScoGolBla-102
❑ 97ShaFleAS-5
❑ 97SPAut-131
❑ 97SPx-44
❑ 97SPxBro-44
❑ 97SPxGol-44
❑ 97SPxGraF-44
❑ 97SPxSil-44
❑ 97SPxSte-44
❑ 97UppDec-147
❑ 97UppDecBD-9
❑ 97UppDecBDDD-9
❑ 97UppDecBDQD-9
❑ 97UppDecBDTD-9
❑ 97UppDecCtAG-6
❑ 97UppDecCtAG-AR6
❑ 97UppDecDV-13
❑ 97UppDecDVSM-13
❑ 97UppDecGDM-147
❑ 97UppDecIce-10
❑ 97UppDecIceP-10
❑ 97UppDecILL-L3C
❑ 97UppDecILL2-L3C
❑ 97UppDecIPS-10
❑ 97UppDecSG-SG24
❑ 97UppDecTSS-6A
❑ 97Zen-27
❑ 97Zen5x7-60
❑ 97ZenGolImp-60
❑ 97ZenSilImp-60
❑ 97ZenZGol-27
❑ 97ZenZSil-27
❑ 98BowBes-70
❑ 98BowBesAR-70
❑ 98BowBesR-70
❑ 98Fin-23
❑ 98FinNo P-23
❑ 98FinNo PR-23
❑ 98FinRef-23
❑ 980-PChr-156
❑ 980-PChrR-156
❑ 98Pac-390
❑ 98PacAur-170
❑ 98PacCroR-120
❑ 98PacCroRLS-120
❑ 98PacDynI-168
❑ 98PacDynIIB-168
❑ 98PacDynIR-168
❑ 98PacIceB-390
❑ 98PacOmeH-212
❑ 98PacOmeODI-212
❑ 98PacOmeR-212
❑ 98PacPar-214
❑ 98PacParC-214
❑ 98PacParEG-214
❑ 98PacParH-214
❑ 98PacParIB-214
❑ 98PacParS-214
❑ 98PacRed-390
❑ 98PacRev-128
❑ 98PacRevIS-128
❑ 98PacRevR-128
❑ 98SP Aut-77
❑ 98SP AutSotTG-ON
❑ 98SPxFin-71
❑ 98SPxFinR-71
❑ 98SPxFinS-71
❑ 98SSASotT-ON
❑ 98Top-156
❑ 98TopGolLC1-14
❑ 98TopGolLC1B-14
❑ 98TopGolLC1BOoO-14
❑ 98TopGolLC1OoO-14
❑ 98TopGolLC1R-14
❑ 98TopGolLC1ROoO-14
❑ 98TopGolLC2-14
❑ 98TopGolLC2B-14
❑ 98TopGolLC2BOoO-14
❑ 98TopGolLC2OoO-14
❑ 98TopGolLC2R-14
❑ 98TopGolLC2ROoO-14
❑ 98TopGolLC3-14
❑ 98TopGolLC3B-14
❑ 98TopGolLC3BOoO-14
❑ 98TopGolLC3OoO-14
❑ 98TopGolLC3R-14
❑ 98TopGolLC3ROoO-14
❑ 98TopO-P-156
❑ 98UC-175
❑ 98UD ChoPCR-175
❑ 98UD ChoR-175
❑ 98UppDec-354
❑ 98UppDecBD-75
❑ 98UppDecDD-75
❑ 98UppDecE-354
❑ 98UppDecE1o1-354
❑ 98UppDecFF-FF24
❑ 98UppDecFF-FF24
❑ 98UppDecFFQ1-FF24
❑ 98UppDecFFQ2-FF24
❑ 98UppDecFIT-FT17
❑ 98UppDecFITQ1-FT17
❑ 98UppDecFITQ2-FT17
❑ 98UppDecFITQ3-FT17
❑ 98UppDecGR-354
❑ 98UppDecM-173
❑ 98UppDecMGS-173
❑ 98UppDecMSS-173
❑ 98UppDecMSS-173
❑ 98UppDecQD-75
❑ 98UppDecTD-75
❑ 99Pac-378
❑ 99PacCop-378
❑ 99PacGol-378
❑ 99PacIceB-378
❑ 99PacPreD-378
❑ 99SP AutPS-77
❑ 99UppDecM-174
❑ 99UppDecMGS-174
❑ 99UppDecMSS-174
❑ 99UppDecMSS-174

**Nolan, Ted**
❑ 87SauSteMG-33
❑ 89SauSteMG-3
❑ 907thInnSOHL-176
❑ 917thInnSMC-24
❑ 917thInnSOHL-318
❑ 93SauSteMG-29
❑ 93SauSteMGM-30

**Nolet, Danny**
❑ 907thInnSQMJHL-266

**Nolet, Simon**
❑ 65QueAce-15
❑ 68OPC-187
❑ 70ColSta-51
❑ 70FlyPos-9
❑ 70OPC-194
❑ 70SarProSta-150
❑ 71OPC-206
❑ 71SarProSta-145
❑ 71TorSun-205
❑ 72OPC-125
❑ 72SarProSta-158
❑ 72SweSemWC-174
❑ 72Top-26
❑ 73FlyLin-12
❑ 73OPC-222
❑ 74NHLActSta-293
❑ 74OPCNHL-187
❑ 74Top-187
❑ 75OPCNHL-220
❑ 75OPCNHL-319
❑ 75Top-220
❑ 75Top-319
❑ 76OPCNHL-64
❑ 76RocCokCan-14
❑ 76RocPucBuc-13
❑ 76Top-64
❑ 84NordPos-18
❑ 85NordGenF-19
❑ 85NordTeal-16
❑ 86NordGenF-17

**Noonan, Brian**
❑ 87BlaCok-15
❑ 88BlaCok-14
❑ 88OPC-165
❑ 88OPCSti-11
❑ 88OPCSti-147
❑ 88PanSti-28
❑ 88ProIHL-107
❑ 88Top-165
❑ 90OPCPre-87
❑ 90ProSet-433
❑ 91BlaCok-19
❑ 91Par-264
❑ 91ParFre-264
❑ 91ProSetPla-165
❑ 91UppDec-380
❑ 91UppDecF-380
❑ 92Bow-98
❑ 92OPC-234
❑ 92PanSti-9
❑ 92PanStiFre-9
❑ 92Pin-194
❑ 92PinFre-194
❑ 92Sco-89
❑ 92ScoCan-89
❑ 92StaClu-400
❑ 92Top-159
❑ 92TopGol-159G
❑ 92Ult-280
❑ 92UppDec-117
❑ 93BlaCok-6
❑ 93Don-464
❑ 93Lea-398
❑ 93OPCPre-13
❑ 93OPCPreG-13
❑ 93PanSti-149
❑ 93Pin-162
❑ 93PinCan-162
❑ 93Pow-314
❑ 93Sco-411
❑ 93ScoCan-411
❑ 93TopPre-13
❑ 93TopPreG-13
❑ 93Ult-291
❑ 94CanGamNHLP-168
❑ 94Don-140
❑ 94Lea-217
❑ 94OPCPre-28
❑ 94OPCPreSE-28
❑ 94Par-143
❑ 94ParGol-143
❑ 94Pin-131
❑ 94PinArtP-131
❑ 94PinRinC-131
❑ 94TopPre-28
❑ 94TopPreSE-28
❑ 94UppDec-302
❑ 94UppDecEleIce-302
❑ 95CanGamNHLP-237
❑ 95ColCho-116
❑ 95ColChoPC-116
❑ 95ColChoPCP-116
❑ 95Don-242
❑ 95ParInt-445
❑ 95ParIntEl-445
❑ 95Sco-156
❑ 95ScoBlaIce-156
❑ 95ScoBlaIceAP-156
❑ 95StaClu-121
❑ 95StaCluMOMS-121
❑ 95Ult-301
❑ 95UppDec-272
❑ 95UppDecEleIce-272
❑ 95UppDecEleIceG-272
❑ 96BeAPAut-201
❑ 96BeAPAutSil-201
❑ 96BeAPla-201
❑ 96ColCho-232
❑ 96Pin-30
❑ 96PinArtP-30
❑ 96PinFoi-30
❑ 96PinPreS-30
❑ 96PinRinC-30
❑ 97Pac-339
❑ 97PacCop-339
❑ 97PacEmeGre-339
❑ 97PacIceB-339
❑ 97PacRed-339
❑ 97PacSil-339
❑ 97ScoCanPla-18
❑ 97ScoCanPre-18
❑ 97ScoCanu-18
❑ 98Pac-432
❑ 98PacIceB-432
❑ 98PacRed-432
❑ 98UppDec-378
❑ 98UppDecE-378
❑ 98UppDecE1o1-378
❑ 98UppDecGR-378

**Noonan, Rick**
❑ 74TeaCanLWHA-18

**Norberg, Agne**
❑ 71SweHocS-399

**Norberg, Anders**
❑ 69SweHocS-210

**Norberg, Hans**
❑ 83SweSemE-23
❑ 84SweSemE-21
❑ 85SwePanS-174
❑ 86SwePanS-180
❑ 87SwePanS-183

**Norberg, Kent**
❑ 89SweSemE-189

**Norberg, Lennart**
❑ 69SweHocS-137
❑ 69SweHocS-266
❑ 70SweHocS-94
❑ 70SweHocS-162
❑ 71SweHocS-257
❑ 72SweHocS-236
❑ 73SweHocS-232
❑ 73SweWorCS-232
❑ 81SweSemHVS-12

**Norberg, Niklas**
❑ 93SweSemE-13

**Norberg, Ulf**
❑ 83SweSemE-161
❑ 85SwePanS-208

**Nord, Bjorn**
❑ 92SweSemE-84
❑ 92UppDec-241
❑ 93SweSemE-57
❑ 94SweLeaE-133
❑ 95SweGloWC-24
❑ 95SweLeaE-192
❑ 95SweUppDE-42

**Nord, Tomas**
❑ 83SweSemE-8
❑ 84SweSemE-4
❑ 85SwePanS-140
❑ 86SwePanS-148
❑ 87SwePanS-125
❑ 89SweSemE-128
❑ 90SweSemE-205

**Nordberg, Robert**
❑ 90SweSemE-245
❑ 91SweSemE-170
❑ 92SweSemE-188
❑ 93SweSemE-160
❑ 94SweLeaE-42
❑ 95SweLeaE-82
❑ 95SweUppDE-128

**Nordenberg, Kenneth**
❑ 71SweHocS-188

**Nordfeldt, Henrik**
❑ 93SweSemE-194
❑ 94SweLeaE-281
❑ 95SweLeaE-132
❑ 95SweLeaE-132

**Nordin, Anders**
❑ 65SweCorI-177
❑ 67SweHoc-17
❑ 67SweHoc-124
❑ 69SweHocS-138
❑ 69SweWorC-119
❑ 70SweHocS-95
❑ 70SweHocS-288
❑ 71SweHocS-189
❑ 72SweHocS-175
❑ 74SweHocS-257
❑ 87SwePanS-190

**Nordin, Hakan**
❑ 83SweSemE-110
❑ 84SweSemE-101
❑ 85SwePanS-98
❑ 86SwePanS-89
❑ 87SwePanS-96
❑ 89SweSemE-272
❑ 90SweSemE-31
❑ 91SweSemE-279

**Nordin, Jan-Olof**
❑ 69SweHocS-89

**Nordin, Lars-Ake**
❑ 69SweHocS-286
❑ 70SweHocS-202
❑ 71SweHocS-298

**Nordin, Stig**
❑ 71SweHocS-169
❑ 73SweHocS-57
❑ 73SweWorCS-57

**Nordin, Urban**
❑ 89SweSemE-181
❑ 90SweSemE-15

**Nordlander, Bert-Ola**
❑ 64SweCorI-26
❑ 64SweCorI-34
❑ 65SweCorI-26
❑ 65SweCorI-34
❑ 67SweHoc-18
❑ 67SweHoc-39
❑ 69SweHocS-50
❑ 69SweHocS-194
❑ 69SweWorC-52
❑ 70SweHocS-7
❑ 71SweHocS-9
❑ 71SweHocS-81
❑ 72SweHocS-56
❑ 72SweSemWC-48
❑ 73SweHocS-195
❑ 73SweWorCS-195
❑ 81SweSemHVS-112

**Nordlinder, Per**
❑ 83SweSemE-137

**Nordlund, Birger**
❑ 67SweHoc-210

**Nordmark, Robert**
❑ 83SweSemE-60
❑ 84SweSemE-173
❑ 85SwePanS-160
❑ 86SwePanS-167
❑ 87BluKod-19
❑ 88CanuMoh-14
❑ 89CanuMoh-13
❑ 89OPCSti-66
❑ 90CanuMoh-22
❑ 90OPC-433
❑ 90ProSet-547
❑ 91CanuPanTS-18
❑ 91SweSemE-256
❑ 92SweSemE-285
❑ 93SweSemE-59
❑ 94SweLeaE-131
❑ 95FinnSIS-302
❑ 95FinnSIS-378
❑ 95FinnSISDT-4
❑ 95FinnSISL-32
❑ 96FinnSISRS-2

**Nordquist, Nicklas**
❑ 94SweLeaE-277
❑ 95SweLeaE-244

**Nordstrom, Carlin**
❑ 91AirCanSJHL-A46

**Nordstrom, Peter**
❑ 94SweLeaE-180
❑ 95SweLeaE-214
❑ 95SweUppDE-73
❑ 98PacDynI-13
❑ 98PacDynIIB-13
❑ 98PacDynIR-13
❑ 98UppDec-220
❑ 98UppDecE-220
❑ 98UppDecE1o1-220
❑ 98UppDecGR-220

**Nordstrom, Roger**
❑ 90SweSemE-126
❑ 91SweSemE-177
❑ 92SweSemE-200
❑ 93SweSemE-171
❑ 94SweLeaE-188
❑ 94SweLeaESS-8
❑ 95FinnSemWC-52
❑ 95FinnSemWC-209
❑ 95SweGloWC-2
❑ 95SweLeaE-258
❑ 95SweLeaEM-7
❑ 95SweLeaES-14
❑ 95SweUppDE-133
❑ 98GerDELE-39

**Nordstrom, Ronny**
❑ 65SweCorI-163

**Norell, Rolf**
❑ 67SweHoc-163

**Noren, Darryl**
❑ 90ProAHLIHL-525
❑ 91GreMon-11
❑ 92GreMon-12
❑ 98ChaChe-11

**Norgren, Johan**
❑ 90SweSemE-134
❑ 91SweSemE-185
❑ 92SweSemE-204
❑ 92UppDec-225
❑ 93SweSemE-173
❑ 94SweLeaE-8
❑ 98GerDELE-115

**Noris, Joe**
❑ 71PenPos-13
❑ 71TorSun-222
❑ 73SabPos-9
❑ 76OPCWHA-46
❑ 77OPCWHA-5

**Norman, Todd**
❑ 93GueSto-12
❑ 94GueSto-19
❑ 94ParSE-SE267
❑ 94ParSEG-SE267
❑ 94Sel-168
❑ 94SelGol-168
❑ 94SlaPro-4
❑ 94SP-185
❑ 94SPDieCut-185
❑ 95Cla-85
❑ 95GueSto5A-8
❑ 95SigRooA-31
❑ 95SigRooAPC-31
❑ 95Sla-99
❑ 96GueSto-15
❑ 96GueSto-32
❑ 96GueStoPC-1
❑ 97BowCHL-28
❑ 97BowCHLOPC-28

**Normand, Dean**
❑ 91AirCanSJHL-A1
❑ 92MPSPhoSJHL-29

**Normandin, Eric**
❑ 96RimOce-19
❑ 96RimOceQPP-18
❑ 97BowCHL-77
❑ 97BowCHLOPC-77
❑ 97RimOce-19

**Normandin, Mathieu**
❑ 96RimOce-20
❑ 96RimOceQPP-19

**Noronen, Mika**
❑ 97UppDecBD-26
❑ 97UppDecBDDD-26
❑ 97UppDecBDQD-26
❑ 97UppDecBDTD-26
❑ 98UC-278
❑ 98UD ChoPCR-278
❑ 98UD ChoR-278

**Norppa, Timo**
❑ 93FinnJyvHS-117
❑ 93FinnSIS-14
❑ 93SweSemWCS-70
❑ 94FinnJaaK-48
❑ 94FinnSIS-274
❑ 95FinnSIS-296
❑ 96FinnSISR-90

**Norrena, Fredrik**
❑ 94FinnSIS-97
❑ 95FinnSIS-324
❑ 95FinnSISGG-5
❑ 95FinnSISL-1
❑ 96FinnSISR-135
❑ 96FinnSISRMA-7

**Norrie, Jason**
❑ 95SeaThu-19
❑ 98ChaChe-12

**Norris, Bruce A**
❑ 83HalFP-N10
❑ 85HalFC-205

**Norris, Clayton**
❑ 907thInnSWHL-30
❑ 917thInnSWHL-318
❑ 97St.JohML-18

**Norris, Dave**
❑ 75HamFin-13

**Norris, Dwayne**
❑ 92Cla-70
❑ 93AlbIntTC-15
❑ 93ClaProPro-66
❑ 93Don-480
❑ 93OPCPreTC-13
❑ 93Pow-491
❑ 93Ult-470
❑ 94Lea-494
❑ 94Sco-238
❑ 94ScoGol-238
❑ 94ScoPla-238
❑ 94ScoPlaTS-238
❑ 94ScoTeaC-CT7
❑ 95Ima-34
❑ 95ImaGol-34
❑ 96ClaGol-70
❑ 96GerDELE-351
❑ 98GerDELE-95

**Norris, Jack**
❑ 70EssPowPla-145
❑ 70OPC-165
❑ 72SluCupWHA-16
❑ 75OPCWHA-114
❑ 75RoaPhoWHA-30

**Norris, James**
❑ 44BeeGro2P-465A
❑ 44BeeGro2P-465B
❑ 64BeeGro3P-194
❑ 72Top-172
❑ 83HalFP-D11
❑ 83HalFP-K11
❑ 85HalFC-57
❑ 85HalFC-145

**Norris, Joe**
❑ 76SanDieMW-8

**Norris, Warren**
❑ 97St.JohML-19

**Norrish, Rod**
❑ 73NorStaP-13

**Norrstrom, Rune**
❑ 69SweHocS-232
❑ 71SweHocS-374

**Norstebo, Svein Enok**
❑ 93SweSemWCS-234
❑ 94FinnJaaK-255
❑ 95SweGloWC-197
❑ 96SweSemW-205

**Norstrom, Claes**
❑ 84SweSemE-125

**Norstrom, Hakan**
❑ 71SweHocS-304
❑ 72SweHocS-260

**Norstrom, Mattias**
❑ 91SweSemE-12
❑ 92SweSemE-30
❑ 93Don-465
❑ 93Lea-426
❑ 93OPCPre-418
❑ 93OPCPreG-418
❑ 93Par-256
❑ 93ParEmel-256
❑ 93StaClu-371
❑ 93StaCluFDI-371
❑ 93StaCluO-371
❑ 93TopPre-418
❑ 93TopPreG-418
❑ 93Ult-376
❑ 93UppDec-522
❑ 94BinRan-15
❑ 94Cla-96
❑ 94ClaDraGol-96
❑ 94ClaProP-5
❑ 94Lea-57
❑ 94Par-152
❑ 94ParGol-152
❑ 94Pin-489
❑ 94PinArtP-489
❑ 94PinRinC-489
❑ 94PinRooTP-2
❑ 94Sel-194
❑ 94SelGol-194
❑ 94SelPro-194
❑ 94Ult-334
❑ 94UppDec-418
❑ 94UppDecEleIce-418
❑ 95ColEdgI-20
❑ 95Don-248
❑ 95Lea-288
❑ 95ParInt-143
❑ 95ParIntEl-143
❑ 95Ult-106
❑ 95UltGolM-106
❑ 96ColCho-130
❑ 96SP-76
❑ 96TopNHLP-171
❑ 96TopPicOI-171
❑ 96Ult-80
❑ 96UltGolM-81
❑ 96UppDec-277
❑ 97Be A PPAD-38
❑ 97Be A PPAPD-38
❑ 97BeAPla-38
❑ 97BeAPlaAut-38
❑ 97PacInvNRB-94
❑ 97UppDec-82
❑ 980-PChr-136
❑ 980-PChrR-136
❑ 98Top-136
❑ 98TopO-P-136
❑ 98UppDec-289
❑ 98UppDecE-289
❑ 98UppDecE1o1-289
❑ 98UppDecGR-289
❑ 99Pac-194
❑ 99PacCop-194
❑ 99PacGol-194
❑ 99PacIceB-194
❑ 99PacPreD-194

**Northard, Jason**
❑ 91BriColJHL-80
❑ 92BriColJHL-114

**Northcott, Baldy**
❑ 33OPCV304B-60
❑ 33V129-49
❑ 33V252CanG-40
❑ 33V357IceK-48
❑ 34BeeGro1P-201
❑ 34SweCap-23
❑ 36OPCV304D-130
❑ 36TriPos-7
❑ 36V356WorG-22
❑ 37OPCV304E-166

**Northey, William M**
❑ 83HalFP-L12
❑ 85HalFC-161

**Norton, Chris**
❑ 88ProAHL-187
❑ 89ProAHL-43
❑ 90MonHaw-18
❑ 90ProAHLIHL-252
❑ 91ProAHLCHL-386

**Norton, D'Arcy**
❑ 86KamBla-14
❑ 87KamBla-15
❑ 88ProIHL-27
❑ 89ProIHL-77
❑ 90ProAHLIHL-320
❑ 91ProAHLCHL-321

**Norton, Jeff**
❑ 89Isl-14

❑ 89OPC-120
❑ 89PanSti-273
❑ 89Top-120
❑ 90Bow-122
❑ 90BowTif-122
❑ 90OPC-166
❑ 90PanSti-93
❑ 90ProSet-189
❑ 90Sco-157
❑ 90ScoCan-157
❑ 90ScoHotRS-70
❑ 90Top-166
❑ 90TopTif-166
❑ 90UppDec-386
❑ 90UppDecF-386
❑ 91Bow-225
❑ 91OPC-243
❑ 91PanSti-248
❑ 91Par-331
❑ 91ParFre-331
❑ 91Pin-172
❑ 91PinFre-172
❑ 91ProSet-148
❑ 91ProSetFre-148
❑ 91ProSetPla-78
❑ 91ScoAme-222
❑ 91ScoCan-222
❑ 91ScoYouS-16
❑ 91StaClu-98
❑ 91Top-243
❑ 91UppDec-357
❑ 91UppDecF-357
❑ 92PanSti-205
❑ 92PanStiFre-205
❑ 92Par-337
❑ 92ParEmel-337
❑ 92Pin-102
❑ 92PinFre-102
❑ 92Sco-56
❑ 92ScoCan-56
❑ 92StaClu-324
❑ 92TopGol-526G
❑ 92Ult-349
❑ 93Don-303
❑ 93Lea-390
❑ 93OPCPre-447
❑ 93OPCPreG-447
❑ 93PanSti-64
❑ 93Par-455
❑ 93ParEmel-455
❑ 93Pin-353
❑ 93PinCan-353
❑ 93Pow-223
❑ 93Sco-69
❑ 93Sco-522
❑ 93ScoCan-69
❑ 93ScoCan-522
❑ 93ScoGol-522
❑ 93StaClu-495
❑ 93StaCluFDI-495
❑ 93StaCluO-495
❑ 93TopPre-447
❑ 93TopPreG-447
❑ 93Ult-417
❑ 93UppDec-512
❑ 94BeAPla-R57
❑ 94BeAPSig-90
❑ 94CanGamNHLP-218
❑ 94Don-132
❑ 94Fla-168
❑ 94Lea-98
❑ 94Pin-99
❑ 94PinArtP-99
❑ 94PinRinC-99
❑ 94StaClu-86
❑ 94StaCluFDI-86
❑ 94StaCluMOMS-86
❑ 94StaCluSTWC-86
❑ 94Ult-199
❑ 95CanGamNHLP-244
❑ 95ColCho-112
❑ 95ColChoPC-112
❑ 95ColChoPCP-112
❑ 95Don-117
❑ 95Lea-74
❑ 95ParInt-349
❑ 95ParIntEl-349
❑ 95Pin-188
❑ 95PinArtP-188
❑ 95PinRinC-188
❑ 95Sco-178
❑ 95ScoBlaIce-178
❑ 95ScoBlaIceAP-178
❑ 95Top-69
❑ 95TopOPCI-69
❑ 95UppDec-160
❑ 95UppDecEleIce-160
❑ 95UppDecEleIceG-160
❑ 96BeAPAut-187
❑ 96BeAPAutSil-187
❑ 96BeAPla-187
❑ 96OilPos-6
❑ 96TopNHLP-157
❑ 96TopPicOI-157
❑ 96Ult-61
❑ 96UltGolM-61
**Norton, Steve**
❑ 93MicSta-15
**Norwich, Craig**
❑ 79JetPos-20
❑ 79PanSti-209
❑ 80OPC-53
❑ 80Top-53
**Norwood, Lee**
❑ 80NordPos-19
❑ 81Cap-12
❑ 82Cap-18
❑ 87RedWinLC-20
❑ 88OPC-240
❑ 88RedWinLC-16
❑ 89OPC-75
❑ 89OPCSti-251
❑ 89PanSti-68
❑ 89RedWinLC-13
❑ 89Top-75
❑ 90Dev-20
❑ 90OPC-285
❑ 90PanSti-202
❑ 90ProSet-74
❑ 90ScoRoo-74T
❑ 90Top-285
❑ 90TopTif-285
❑ 90UppDec-78
❑ 90UppDecF-78
❑ 91PanSti-214
❑ 91Par-373
❑ 91ParFre-373
❑ 91ScoCan-528
❑ 91StaClu-317
**Nose, Virgil**
❑ 90RayJrC-15
❑ 91RayJrC-13
**Noseworthy, Dave**
❑ 897thInnSOHL-44
**Nottingham, Mike**
❑ 84KamBla-18
❑ 85KamBla-17
**Novak, Aaron**
❑ 93MinDul-23
❑ 99WicThu-17
**Novak, Eduard**
❑ 71SweHocS-57
❑ 72SweSemWC-37
❑ 74SweSemHVS-75
**Novak, Jiri**
❑ 74SweSemHVS-65
❑ 79PanSti-82
**Novak, Red (Jack)**
❑ 52JunBluT-125
**Novak, Richard**
❑ 89ProIHL-106
**Novosjolov, Waldemar**
❑ 94GerDELE-358
**Novotny, Jan**
❑ 96CzeAPSE-72
**Novotny, Jiri**
❑ 95CzeAPSE-241
❑ 95LetHur-16
❑ 96CzeAPSE-307
**Novotny, Marek**
❑ 94CzeAPSE-162
❑ 95CzeAPSE-176
❑ 96CzeAPSE-312
**Novy, Helmut**
❑ 70SweHocS-370
**Novy, Milan**
❑ 74SweSemHVS-59
❑ 79PanSti-85
❑ 81SweSemHVS-63
❑ 82Cap-19
❑ 82SweSemHVS-87
❑ 83OPCSti-187
❑ 83PufSti-19
❑ 92FutTre76CC-155
❑ 92FutTre76CC-186
❑ 92FutTre76CC-198
**Nowak, Daniel**
❑ 94GerDELE-433
❑ 96GerDELE-299
❑ 98GerDELE-211
❑ 98GerDELE-329
**Nowak, Derek**
❑ 95GerDELE-392
**Nowak, Hank**
❑ 74NHLActSta-93
❑ 74NHLActStaU-2
❑ 76OPCNHL-224
❑ 76Top-224
**Nugren, Hakan**
❑ 65SweCorI-146A
**Nummelin, Petteri**
❑ 93FinnSIS-32
❑ 94FinnJaaK-12
❑ 94FinnSIS-62
❑ 94FinnSIS-150
❑ 94FinnSISMN-2
❑ 94FinnSISS-3
❑ 95FinnKarWCL-14
❑ 95FinnSemWC-39
❑ 95FinnSISGC-9
❑ 95FinnSISL-3
❑ 95SweLeaE-206
❑ 95SweUppDE-209
❑ 96SweSemW-3
**Nummelin, Timo**
❑ 79PanSti-165
❑ 81SweSemHVS-25
❑ 82SweSemHVS-29
**Numminen, Kalevi**
❑ 74SweSemHVS-98
**Numminen, Teemu**
❑ 93FinnJyvHS-297
❑ 93FinnSIS-71
❑ 94FinnSIS-319
❑ 95FinnSIS-329
**Numminen, Teppo**
❑ 88JetPol-17
❑ 89JetSaf-22
❑ 89PanSti-172
❑ 90Bow-138
❑ 90BowTif-138
❑ 90JetIGA-24
❑ 90OPC-385
❑ 90PanSti-307
❑ 90ProSet-334
❑ 90Sco-176
❑ 90ScoCan-176
❑ 90Top-385
❑ 90TopTif-385
❑ 91Bow-201
❑ 91JetIGA-20
❑ 91JetPanTS-18
❑ 91OPC-274
❑ 91PanSti-71
❑ 91Par-200
❑ 91ParFre-200
❑ 91Pin-166
❑ 91PinFre-166
❑ 91ProSet-261
❑ 91ProSetFre-261
❑ 91ProSetPla-248
❑ 91ScoAme-101
❑ 91ScoCan-101
❑ 91StaClu-302
❑ 91SweSemWCS-201
❑ 91Top-274
❑ 91UppDec-240
❑ 91UppDecF-240
❑ 92Bow-299
❑ 92OPC-4
❑ 92PanSti-52
❑ 92PanStiFre-52
❑ 92Par-438
❑ 92ParEmel-438
❑ 92Pin-215
❑ 92PinFre-215
❑ 92ProSet-210
❑ 92Sco-102
❑ 92ScoCan-102
❑ 92StaClu-77
❑ 92Top-339
❑ 92TopGol-339G
❑ 92Ult-243
❑ 92UppDec-326
❑ 93Don-385
❑ 93JetRuf-18
❑ 93Lea-135
❑ 93OPCPre-269
❑ 93OPCPreG-269
❑ 93PanSti-197
❑ 93Par-231
❑ 93ParEmel-231
❑ 93Pin-92
❑ 93PinCan-92
❑ 93Pow-272
❑ 93Sco-132
❑ 93ScoCan-132
❑ 93StaClu-164
❑ 93StaCluFDI-164
❑ 93StaCluFDIO-164
❑ 93StaCluO-164
❑ 93SweSemWCS-57
❑ 93TopPre-269
❑ 93TopPreG-269
❑ 93Ult-455
❑ 93UppDec-53
❑ 94CanGamNHLP-346
❑ 94Don-267
❑ 94EASpo-146
❑ 94FinnJaaK-10
❑ 94FinnJaaK-335
❑ 94FinnSIS-359
❑ 94FinnSISGS-6
❑ 94Fla-208
❑ 94Lea-233
❑ 94OPCPre-376
❑ 94OPCPreSE-376
❑ 94Par-270
❑ 94ParGol-270
❑ 94ParSEES-ES10
❑ 94Pin-77
❑ 94PinArtP-77
❑ 94PinRinC-77
❑ 94Sco-91
❑ 94ScoGol-91
❑ 94ScoPla-91
❑ 94ScoPlaTS-91
❑ 94StaClu-152
❑ 94StaCluFDI-152
❑ 94StaCluMOMS-152
❑ 94StaCluSTWC-152
❑ 94TopPre-376
❑ 94TopPreSE-376
❑ 94Ult-244
❑ 94UppDec-113
❑ 94UppDecEleIce-113
❑ 95BeAPla-68
❑ 95BeAPSig-S68
❑ 95BeAPSigDC-S68
❑ 95CanGamNHLP-294
❑ 95ColCho-292
❑ 95ColChoPC-292
❑ 95ColChoPCP-292
❑ 95Don-261
❑ 95Emo-195
❑ 95Fin-167
❑ 95FinnSemWC-37
❑ 95FinnSISL-93
❑ 95FinnSISLSS-6
❑ 95FinRef-167
❑ 95JetReaC-8
❑ 95JetTeaIss-16
❑ 95Lea-247
❑ 95Met-164
❑ 95ParInt-228
❑ 95ParIntEl-228
❑ 95Pin-67
❑ 95PinArtP-67
❑ 95PinGloG-12
❑ 95PinRinC-67
❑ 95PlaOneoOne-107
❑ 95PlaOneoOne-328
❑ 95Sco-139
❑ 95ScoBlaIce-139
❑ 95ScoBlaIceAP-139
❑ 95SkyImp-183
❑ 95Sum-113
❑ 95SumArtP-113
❑ 95SumIce-113
❑ 95SweGloWC-133
❑ 95Top-67
❑ 95TopOPCI-67
❑ 95Ult-182
❑ 95UltGolM-182
❑ 95UppDec-275
❑ 95UppDecEleIce-275
❑ 95UppDecEleIceG-275
❑ 96ColCho-209
❑ 96Don-126
❑ 96DonPrePro-126
❑ 96Fle-91
❑ 96FleNor-8
❑ 96FlePic-72
❑ 96Lea-113
❑ 96LeaPreP-113
❑ 96MetUni-120
❑ 96Pin-8
❑ 96PinArtP-8
❑ 96PinFoi-8
❑ 96PinPreS-8
❑ 96PinRinC-8
❑ 96PlaOneoOne-350
❑ 96Sco-5
❑ 96ScoArtPro-5
❑ 96ScoDeaCAP-5
❑ 96ScoGolB-5
❑ 96ScoSpeAP-5
❑ 96SkyImp-143
❑ 96SkyImpNHLF-16
❑ 96SP-122
❑ 96Sum-55
❑ 96SumArtP-55
❑ 96SumIce-55
❑ 96SumMet-55
❑ 96SumPreS-55
❑ 96SweSemW-27
❑ 96Ult-134
❑ 96UltGolM-134
❑ 96UppDec-131
❑ 97ColCho-200
❑ 97Pac-122
❑ 97PacCop-122
❑ 97PacEmeGre-122
❑ 97PacIceB-122
❑ 97PacOme-175
❑ 97PacOmeC-175
❑ 97PacOmeDG-175
❑ 97PacOmeEG-175
❑ 97PacOmeG-175
❑ 97PacOmeIB-175
❑ 97PacRed-122
❑ 97PacSil-122
❑ 97SPAut-122
❑ 97UppDec-336
❑ 98Be A PPA-106
❑ 98Be A PPAA-106
❑ 98Be A PPAAF-106
❑ 98Be A PPTBASG-106
❑ 98Be APG-106
❑ 98O-PChr-57
❑ 98O-PChrR-57
❑ 98Pac-342
❑ 98PacIceB-342
❑ 98PacOmeH-186
❑ 98PacOmeODI-186
❑ 98PacOmeR-186
❑ 98PacPar-183
❑ 98PacParC-183
❑ 98PacParEG-183
❑ 98PacParH-183
❑ 98PacParIB-183
❑ 98PacParS-183
❑ 98PacRed-342
❑ 98Top-57
❑ 98TopO-P-57
❑ 98UC-157
❑ 98UD ChoPCR-157
❑ 98UD ChoR-157
❑ 98UppDec-155
❑ 98UppDecE-155
❑ 98UppDecE1o1-155
❑ 98UppDecGR-155
❑ 99Pac-323
❑ 99PacAur-110
❑ 99PacAurPD-110
❑ 99PacCop-323
❑ 99PacGol-323
❑ 99PacIceB-323
❑ 99PacPreD-323
**Nurmberg, Timo**
❑ 94FinnSIS-239
❑ 95FinnSIS-116
❑ 96FinnSISR-130
**Nurmi, Juha**
❑ 85SwePanS-169
❑ 86SwePanS-178
❑ 87SwePanS-179
❑ 89SweSemE-104
**Nurminen, Juha**
❑ 93FinnSIS-290
❑ 94FinnSIS-243
❑ 94FinnSISFI-17
❑ 95FinnSIS-10
**Nurminen, Kai**
❑ 93FinnJyvHS-329
❑ 93FinnSIS-48
❑ 94FinnSIS-101
❑ 94FinnSIS-305
❑ 94FinnSISFI-18
❑ 94FinnSISH-13
❑ 95FinnSIS-166
❑ 95FinnSISL-86
❑ 95SweLeaE-228
❑ 95SweUppDE-90
❑ 96SelCer-91
❑ 96SelCerAP-91
❑ 96SelCerBlu-91
❑ 96SelCerMB-91
❑ 96SelCerMG-91
❑ 96SelCerMR-91
❑ 96SelCerRed-91
❑ 96SP-181
❑ 96SweSemW-36
❑ 96UppDec-275
❑ 97PacInvNRB-95
**Nurro, Kimmo**
❑ 94FinnSIS-254
**Nutikka, Veli Pekka**
❑ 94Fin-135
❑ 94FinRef-135
❑ 94FinSupTW-135
❑ 94ParSE-SE222
❑ 94ParSEG-SE222
❑ 94SP-159
❑ 94SPDieCut-159
❑ 95FinnSIS-279
❑ 96FinnSISR-77
**Nuutinen, Sami**
❑ 93FinnJyvHS-195
❑ 93FinnSIS-260
❑ 93SweSemWCS-58
❑ 94FinnSIS-122
❑ 95FinnSIS-185
❑ 95FinnSISDT-6
❑ 95FinnSISL-56
**Nyberg, Lars**
❑ 83SweSemE-164
**Nyberg, Patrik**
❑ 91SweSemE-249
**Nygards, Per**
❑ 90SweSemE-280
❑ 91SweSemE-63
**Nygren, Hakan**
❑ 64SweCorI-146
❑ 65SweCorI-156B
❑ 67SweHoc-125
❑ 69SweHocS-139
❑ 69SweHocS-195
❑ 69SweWorC-39
❑ 69SweWorC-62
❑ 70SweHocS-96
❑ 71SweHocS-21
❑ 71SweHocS-190
❑ 72SweHocS-176
❑ 72SweSemWC-53
❑ 74SweHocS-179
❑ 85SwePanS-209
❑ 86SwePanS-191
❑ 93SweSemE-293
**Nykoluk, Mike**
❑ 44BeeGro2P-441
❑ 57Par-T16
❑ 81MapLeaP-16
❑ 82MapLeaP-16
❑ 83MapLeaP-18
❑ 94ParMisL-130
**Nykopp, Timo**
❑ 94FinnSIS-341
❑ 95FinnSIS-150
❑ 95FinnSIS-287
**Nykyforuk, Curtis**
❑ 88RegPat-18
❑ 89VicCou-15
**Nylander, Michael**
❑ 91Cla-47
❑ 91StaPicH-23
❑ 91SweSemE-21
❑ 91UltDra-42
❑ 91UltDra-88
❑ 92OPCPre-19
❑ 92Par-294
❑ 92ParEmel-294
❑ 92Pin-400
❑ 92PinFre-400
❑ 92SweSemE-338
❑ 92SweSemE-339
❑ 92UppDec-236
❑ 92UppDec-378
❑ 92UppDec-520
❑ 92UppDecER-ER2
❑ 92WhaDai-16
❑ 93Don-144
❑ 93Don-407
❑ 93Lea-94
❑ 93OPCPre-99
❑ 93OPCPreG-99
❑ 93PanSti-128
❑ 93Par-83
❑ 93ParEmel-83
❑ 93Pin-166
❑ 93PinCan-166
❑ 93Pow-106
❑ 93Sco-383
❑ 93ScoCan-383
❑ 93StaClu-186
❑ 93StaCluFDI-186
❑ 93StaCluFDIO-186
❑ 93StaCluO-186
❑ 93SweSemWCS-40
❑ 93TopPre-99
❑ 93TopPreG-99
❑ 93Ult-105
❑ 93UltPro-7
❑ 93UppDec-70
❑ 93UppDecHT-HT13
❑ 93UppDecNL-NL1
❑ 93UppDecSP-62
❑ 93WhaCok-12
❑ 94CanGamNHLP-57
❑ 94Don-74
❑ 94FinnSIS-352
❑ 94FinnSISGS-7
❑ 94Lea-149
❑ 94OPCPre-237
❑ 94OPCPreSE-237
❑ 94Par-32
❑ 94ParGol-32
❑ 94Pin-142
❑ 94PinArtP-142
❑ 94PinRinC-142
❑ 94Sco-59
❑ 94ScoGol-59
❑ 94ScoPla-59
❑ 94ScoPlaTS-59
❑ 94TopPre-237
❑ 94TopPreSE-237
❑ 94Ult-32
❑ 94UppDec-79
❑ 94UppDec-556
❑ 94UppDecEleIce-79
❑ 94UppDecEleIce-556
❑ 94UppDecSPI-SP103
❑ 94UppDecSPIDC-SP103
❑ 95BeAPla-148
❑ 95BeAPSig-S148
❑ 95BeAPSigDC-S148
❑ 95ColCho-311
❑ 95ColChoPC-311
❑ 95ColChoPCP-311
❑ 95Fin-172
❑ 95FinnSISL-54
❑ 95FinnSISLLG-3
❑ 95FinnSISSpe-10
❑ 95FinRef-172
❑ 95Met-22
❑ 95ParInt-34
❑ 95ParIntEl-34
❑ 95Sco-289
❑ 95ScoBlaIce-289
❑ 95ScoBlaIceAP-289
❑ 95SP-20
❑ 95StaClu-154
❑ 95StaCluMOMS-154
❑ 95SweGloWC-35
❑ 95SweUppDE-237
❑ 95Ult-213
❑ 95UppDec-454
❑ 95UppDecEleIce-454
❑ 95UppDecEleIceG-454
❑ 95UppDecSpeE-SE102
❑ 95UppDecSpeEdiG-SE102
❑ 96ColCho-38
❑ 96ColCho-312
❑ 96Lea-115
❑ 96LeaPreP-115
❑ 96Pin-151
❑ 96PinArtP-151
❑ 96PinFoi-151
❑ 96PinPreS-151
❑ 96PinRinC-151
❑ 96Sco-79
❑ 96ScoArtPro-79
❑ 96ScoDeaCAP-79
❑ 96ScoGolB-79
❑ 96ScoSpeAP-79
❑ 96SweSemW-61
❑ 96UppDec-27
❑ 97PacOme-33
❑ 97PacOmeC-33
❑ 97PacOmeDG-33
❑ 97PacOmeEG-33
❑ 97PacOmeG-33
❑ 97PacOmeIB-33
❑ 98Fin-63
❑ 98FinNo P-63
❑ 98FinNo PR-63
❑ 98FinPro-PP2
❑ 98FinRef-63
❑ 98Pac-123
❑ 98PacAur-28
❑ 98PacIceB-123
❑ 98PacPar-31
❑ 98PacParC-31
❑ 98PacParEG-31
❑ 98PacParH-31
❑ 98PacParIB-31
❑ 98PacParS-31
❑ 98PacRed-123
❑ 98UC-32
❑ 98UD ChoPCR-32
❑ 98UD ChoR-32
❑ 99Pac-393
❑ 99PacCop-393
❑ 99PacGol-393
❑ 99PacIceB-393
❑ 99PacPreD-393
**Nylander, Peter**
❑ 92SweSemE-356
❑ 95SigRoo-21
❑ 95SigRooSig-21
❑ 95UppDec-559
❑ 95UppDecEleIce-559
❑ 95UppDecEleIceG-559
**Nylund, Gary**
❑ 82MapLeaP-27
❑ 83MapLeaP-19
❑ 83Vac-94
❑ 847EDis-46
❑ 84MapLeaP-18
❑ 84OPC-307
❑ 84OPCSti-15
❑ 84OPCSti-16
❑ 85MapLeaP-23
❑ 85OPC-172
❑ 85OPCSti-14
❑ 86BlaCok-11
❑ 86OPC-243
❑ 86OPCSti-137
❑ 87BlaCok-16
❑ 87OPC-82
❑ 87OPCSti-80
❑ 87PanSti-224
❑ 87Top-82
❑ 88OPC-15
❑ 88PanSti-23
❑ 88Top-15
❑ 89Isl-15
❑ 89OPC-105
❑ 89OPCSti-114
❑ 89Top-105
❑ 90OPC-233
❑ 90PanSti-80
❑ 90ProSet-190
❑ 90Sco-86
❑ 90ScoCan-86
❑ 90Top-233
❑ 90TopTif-233
❑ 90UppDec-139
❑ 90UppDecF-139
❑ 91Bow-228
❑ 91OPC-101
❑ 91PanSti-251
❑ 91Pin-406
❑ 91PinFre-406
❑ 91ProSet-150
❑ 91ProSetFre-150
❑ 91ScoAme-192
❑ 91ScoCan-192
❑ 91StaClu-163
❑ 91Top-101
❑ 91UppDec-406
❑ 91UppDecF-406
❑ 92Sco-381
❑ 92ScoCan-381
**Nyman, Jan**
❑ 83SweSemE-153
**Nyman, Stefan**
❑ 90SweSemE-59
❑ 91SweSemE-232
❑ 93SweSemE-268
**Nyman, Tero**
❑ 96FinnSISR-11
**Nyrop, Bill**
❑ 76CanaPos-15
❑ 76OPCNHL-188
❑ 76Top-188
❑ 77CanaPos-18
❑ 77OPCNHL-91
❑ 77Top-91
❑ 78OPC-134
❑ 78Top-134
❑ 81NorStaPos-17
❑ 91KnoChe-1
❑ 92FutTre76CC-158
**Nystrom, Bob**
❑ 73OPC-202
❑ 74NHLActSta-176
❑ 74OPCNHL-123
❑ 74Top-123
❑ 75OPCNHL-259
❑ 75OPCNHL-323
❑ 75Top-259
❑ 75Top-323
❑ 76OPCNHL-153
❑ 76Top-153
❑ 77OPCNHL-62
❑ 77Top-62
❑ 78OPC-153
❑ 78Top-153
❑ 79IslTrans-12
❑ 79OPC-217
❑ 79Top-217
❑ 80OPC-102
❑ 80Top-102
❑ 81OPC-217
❑ 82OPC-208
❑ 82OPCSti-59
❑ 82PosCer-12
❑ 83IslTeaIss-12
❑ 83OPC-14
❑ 83OPCSti-85
❑ 84IslIslN-11
❑ 84KelWin-35
❑ 84OPC-132
❑ 84OPCSti-85
❑ 84Top-98
❑ 85IslIslN-12
❑ 85OPC-11
❑ 85OPCSti-69
❑ 85Top-11
❑ 86OPC-104
❑ 86OPCSti-204
❑ 86Top-104
❑ 91UppDec-641
❑ 91UppDecF-641

- 93IslCheBA-6

**Nystrom, Gert**
- 65SweCorl-116A
- 67SweHoc-178

**Nystrom, Karen**
- 94ClaWomOH-W20
- 97ColCho-295

**Nystrom, Lars Frederik**
- 72SweHocS-201
- 83SweSemE-186
- 84SweSemE-209

**Nystrom, Murray**
- 85LonKni-6
- 86LonKni-14
- 93LonKni-28

**Nystrom, Ove**
- 70SweHocS-218

**Nyyssonen, Tommi**
- 95FinnSIS-83
- 96FinnSISR-83

**O'Brien, Andy**
- 82KitRan-26

**O'Brien, Dan**
- 89NasKni-16

**O'Brien, David**
- 88ProAHL-50
- 89ProIHL-19
- 90ProAHLIHL-92

**O'Brien, Dennis**
- 71TorSun-140
- 73NorStaP-8
- 73NorStaP-14
- 730PC-88
- 73Top-177
- 74NHLActSta-128
- 740PCNHL-96
- 74Top-96
- 750PCNHL-53
- 75Top-53
- 760PCNHL-34
- 760PCNHL-387
- 76Top-34
- 770PCNHL-173
- 77Top-173
- 780PC-104
- 78Top-104
- 790PC-375

**O'Brien, J.Ambrose**
- 83HalFP-N11
- 85HalFC-206

**O'Brien, Maurice**
- 907thInnSOHL-90

**O'Brien, Sean**
- 94RicRen-17
- 95TalTigS-7

**O'Callahan, Jack**
- 80USAOlyTMP-6
- 83BlaBorPos-17
- 840PC-43
- 84Top-33
- 86BlaCok-12
- 860PC-207
- 88DevCar-22
- 95SigRooMI-23
- 95SigRooMI-24
- 95SigRooSMIS-23
- 95SigRooSMIS-24

**O'Connell, Jack**
- 36V356WorG-107

**O'Connell, John**
- 91MinGolG-20

**O'Connell, Mike**
- 800PC-61
- 80Top-61
- 810PC-6
- 81Top-E70
- 820PC-17
- 820PCSti-89
- 82PosCer-1
- 83BruTealss-13
- 830PC-56
- 830PCSti-52
- 840PC-12
- 840PCSti-185
- 84Top-9
- 850PC-2
- 850PCSti-161
- 85Top-2
- 860PC-140
- 86Top-140
- 870PC-141
- 870PCSti-107
- 87PanSti-240
- 87Top-141
- 880PC-92
- 880PCSti-248
- 88RedWinLC-18
- 88Top-92
- 890PC-223
- 890PCSti-249
- 89PanSti-69
- 89RedWinLC-14
- 900PC-114
- 90PanSti-215
- 90ProAHLIHL-296
- 90ProSet-75
- 90Top-114
- 90TopTif-114

**O'Conner, Mike**
- 93HumHawP-17
- 94SheSte-8
- 97SheSte-8

**O'Conner, Patrick**
- 94SheSte-7

**O'Connor, Buddy**
- 34BeeGro1P-172
- 36V356WorG-114
- 44BeeGro2P-349
- 45QuaOatP-102A
- 45QuaOatP-102B

**O'Connor, Eric**
- 917thInnSOMJHL-166

**O'Connor, Jeff**
- 93RenEng-19

**O'Connor, Mike**
- 94FinnJaaK-315

**O'Connor, Myles**
- 89ProAHL-206
- 90ProAHLIHL-576
- 910PC-509
- 91ProAHLCHL-425
- 91ScoAme-322
- 91Top-509
- 91UppDecF-485
- 93Par-274
- 93ParEmel-274
- 93TopPreG-527G
- 96CinCyc-6

**O'Connor, Scott**
- 94FinnJaaK-312

**O'Connor, Terry**
- 52JunBluT-161

**O'Connor, Tom**
- 93Cla-107
- 93ClaCla94-CL7

**O'Day, Dan**
- 90Arilce-9

**O'Dette, Matt**
- 93KitRan-21
- 95Sla-154
- 96RoaExp-22

**O'Donnell, Fred**
- 730PC-223
- 85KinCan-4
- 86KinCan-2

**O'Donnell, Mark**
- 917thInnSOHL-292
- 96ForWorF-15

**O'Donnell, Sean**
- 88SudWol-7
- 89SudWol-17
- 907thInnSOHL-390
- 90SudWol-6
- 91ProAHLCHL-10
- 91RochAmeKod-20
- 91RochAmePos-16
- 92RochAmeKod-12
- 92RochAmeKod-15
- 93ClaProPro-109
- 93RochAmeKod-14
- 96BeAPAut-152
- 96BeAPAutSil-152
- 96BeAPla-152
- 97PacInvNRB-96
- 98Pac-242
- 98PacIceB-242
- 98PacRed-242
- 99Pac-195
- 99PacCop-195
- 99PacGol-195
- 99PacIceB-195
- 99PacPreD-195

**O'Donoghue, Don**
- 710PC-180
- 71SarProSta-142
- 71TorSun-54

**O'Drowski, Gerry**
- 63QueAce-19
- 63QueAceQ-18

**O'Dwyer, Billy**
- 88BruPos-15
- 89ProAHL-71
- 90ProAHLIHL-420

**O'Flaherty, Gerry**
- 72CanuRoyB-15
- 720PC-278
- 73CanuRoyB-15
- 730PC-250
- 74CanuRoyB-15
- 74NHLActSta-284
- 740PCNHL-71
- 74Top-71
- 75CanuRoyB-16
- 750PCNHL-307
- 75Top-307
- 76CanuRoyB-14
- 760PCNHL-287
- 77CanuRoyB-16
- 770PCNHL-377
- 780PC-365

**O'Flaherty, James (John)**
- 34BeeGro1P-245
- 51LavDaiS-111
- 52St.LawS-71

**O'Flaherty, Patrick**
- 91BriColJHL-114
- 92BriColJHL-179

**O'Grady, Mike**
- 95Cla-51
- 95LetHur-17
- 96LetHur-11

**O'Hagan, Paul**
- 897thInnSOHL-14
- 897thInnSOHL-194
- 89oshGen-14
- 89oshGenP-24
- 907thInnSMC-78
- 907thInnSOHL-344

**O'Hagan, Sean**
- 89WinSpi-13
- 907thInnSOHL-190

**O'Handley, P.K.**

**O'Hara, Colin**
- 95SwiCurB-12
- 96MedHatT-15

**O'Hara, Mike**
- 92ForWorF-14
- 93ForWorF-13

**O'Hunter, Pat**
- 28V1282PauC-43

**O'Leary, Kelly**
- 94ClaWomOH-W39

**O'Leary, Mickey**
- 24C144ChaCig-46

**O'Malley, Terry**
- 69SweHocS-360
- 69SweWorC-18

**O'Meara, Cliff**
- 23CreSel-1
- 23V1281PauC-9
- 24CreSel-10
- 28V1282PauC-78

**O'Neil, Peggy**
- 34BeeGro1P-26
- 36V356WorG-63

**O'Neill, Don**
- 897thInnSOHL-112
- 907thInnSOHL-367
- 917thInnSOHL-138

**O'Neill, Jeff**
- 93Cla-108
- 93Cla-115
- 93Cla-AU8
- 93ClaCla94-CL1
- 93ClaCraNum-N3
- 93ClaPromo-2
- 93GueSto-2
- 93GueSto-26
- 93UppDecPOE-E4
- 94Cla-5
- 94ClaAut-5
- 94ClaCHLAS-C7
- 94ClaDraD-8
- 94ClaDraD-9
- 94ClaDraD-10
- 94ClaDraGol-5
- 94ClaProP-205
- 94ClaProP-209
- 94ClaROYS-R15
- 94ClaTri-T28
- 94Fin-162
- 94FinRef-162
- 94FinSupTW-162
- 94GueSto-25
- 94LeaLimWJC-6
- 94Pin-534
- 94PinArtP-534
- 94PinRinC-534
- 94SP-152
- 94SPDieCut-152
- 95BeAPla-166
- 95BeAPSig-S166
- 95BeAPSigDC-S166
- 95Bow-118
- 95BowAllFoi-118
- 95BowBes-BB26
- 95BowBesRef-BB26
- 95ColCho-401
- 95Don-244
- 95DonCanWJT-14
- 95DonEli-21
- 95DonEliDCS-21
- 95DonEliDCU-21
- 95DonEliR-12
- 95DonRatRoo-4
- 95Fin-96
- 95FinRef-96
- 95Ima-44
- 95ImaCleE-CE16
- 95ImaGol-44
- 95ImpSti-55
- 95LeaLim-63
- 95LeaLimRP-8
- 95Met-186
- 95ParInt-259
- 95ParIntEl-259
- 95SelCer-118
- 95SelCerFut-8
- 95SelCerMG-118
- 95SkyImp-202
- 95SkyImpNHLF-11
- 95SP-64
- 95StaClu-192
- 95StaCluMOMS-192
- 95Sum-183
- 95SumArtP-183
- 95SumIce-183
- 95Top-285
- 95TopCanWJ-20CJ
- 95TopOPCI-285
- 95TopSupSkiSR-SR3
- 95Ult-351
- 95UppDec-264
- 95UppDecEleIce-264
- 95UppDecEleIceG-264
- 95Zen-130
- 95ZenRooRC-18
- 96ColCho-343
- 96DonCanI-82
- 96DonCanIGPP-82
- 96DonCanIRPP-82
- 96DonEli-39
- 96DonEliAsp-9
- 96DonEliDCS-39
- 96FlePic-158
- 96Lea-209
- 96LeaLim-68
- 96LeaLimG-68
- 96LeaPre-9
- 96LeaPreP-209
- 96LeaPrePP-9
- 96MetUni-69
- 96Pin-210
- 96PinArtP-210
- 96PinFoi-210
- 96PinPreS-210
- 96PinRinC-210
- 96Sco-250
- 96ScoArtPro-250
- 96ScoDeaCAP-250
- 96ScoGolB-250
- 96ScoSpeAP-250
- 96SelCer-90
- 96SelCerBlu-90
- 96SelCerMB-90
- 96SelCerMG-90
- 96SelCerMR-90
- 96SelCerRed-90
- 96SP-67
- 96Sum-168
- 96SumArtP-168
- 96SumIce-168
- 96SumMet-168
- 96SumPreS-168
- 96TopPicRS-RS17
- 96UppDec-70
- 96UppDecBD-92
- 96UppDecBDG-92
- 96WhaBobS-20
- 96Zen-29
- 96ZenArtP-29
- 97Be A PPAD-130
- 97Be A PPAPD-130
- 97BeAPla-130
- 97BeAPlaAut-130
- 97CarHur-19
- 97ColCho-117
- 97Don-16
- 97DonLim-16
- 97DonLimExp-61
- 97DonPre-30
- 97DonPreProG-16
- 97DonPreProS-16
- 97DonPri-125
- 97DonPriSoA-125
- 97Pac-140
- 97PacCop-140
- 97PacEmeGre-140
- 97PacIceB-140
- 97PacRed-140
- 97PacSil-140
- 97Pin-154
- 97PinCer-128
- 97PinCerMB-128
- 97PinCerMG-128
- 97PinCerMR-128
- 97PinCerR-128
- 97PinIns-149
- 97PinPrePBB-154
- 97PinPrePBC-154
- 97PinPrePBM-154
- 97PinPrePBY-154
- 97PinPrePFC-154
- 97PinPrePFY-154
- 97PinPrePla-154
- 97PinTotCMPG-128
- 97PinTotCPB-128
- 97PinTotCPG-128
- 97PinTotCPR-128
- 97Sco-147
- 97ScoArtPro-147
- 97ScoGolBla-147
- 97SPAut-28
- 97UppDec-34
- 98Be A PPA-175
- 98Be A PPAA-175
- 98Be A PPAAF-175
- 98Be A PPSE-175
- 98Be APG-175
- 98Pac-137
- 98PacAur-36
- 98PacIceB-137
- 98PacPar-40
- 98PacParC-40
- 98PacParEG-40
- 98PacParH-40
- 98PacParIB-40
- 98PacParS-40
- 98PacRed-137
- 98UC-37
- 98UD ChoPCR-37
- 98UD ChoR-37
- 98UppDec-61
- 98UppDecE-61
- 98UppDecGR-61
- 98UppDecM-40
- 98UppDecMGS-40
- 98UppDecMSS-40
- 98UppDecMSS-40
- 99Pac-78
- 99PacCop-78
- 99PacGol-78
- 99PacIceB-78
- 99PacPreD-78

**O'Neill, Michael (Mike)**
- 90MonHaw-19
- 90ProAHLCHL-344
- 91ProAHLCHL-259
- 92Par-441
- 92ParEmel-441
- 93ClaProPro-39
- 94Par-268
- 94ParGol-268

**O'Neill, Ryan**
- 917thInnSOHL-180
- 92WinSpi-10

**O'Rear, Hayden**
- 93KnoChe-12
- 94KnoChe-7
- 97AncAce-15

**O'Ree, Willie**
- 44BeeGro2P-53
- 56QueAce-12
- 61UniOilW-4
- 97BeeAutA-75
- 97PinBee-75
- 97PinBeeGP-75
- 98UppDWO-22

**O'Regan, Tom**
- 84PenHeiP-16
- 94GerDELE-59
- 95GerDELE-54
- 96GerDELE-250

**O'Reilly, Sean**
- 897thInnSOHL-14
- 907thInnSOHL-14
- 917thInnSOHL-382
- 99WicThu-18

**O'Reilly, Terry**
- 730PC-254
- 74NHLActSta-22
- 740PCNHL-295
- 75HerSta-2
- 750PCNHL-301
- 75Top-301
- 760PCNHL-130
- 760PCNHL-381
- 76Top-130
- 770PCNHL-220
- 77Top-220
- 780PC-40
- 780PC-332
- 78Top-40
- 790PC-238
- 79Top-238
- 800PC-56
- 80Top-56
- 810PC-7
- 810PCSti-50
- 81Top-E71
- 820PC-18
- 820PCSti-85
- 82PosCer-1
- 83BruTealss-14
- 83PufSti-12
- 840PC-13
- 84Top-10
- 850PCSti-162
- 88BruSpoA-17
- 91BruSpoAL-19
- 91ProSetPla-289

**O'Rourke, Chris**
- 93FliGen-5

**O'Rourke, Dan**
- 917thInnSWHL-311
- 94CenHocL-104
- 95LouIceGP-14

**O'Shea, Danny**
- 690PC-131
- 69Top-131
- 70ColSta-16
- 70DadCoo-93
- 70EssPowPla-167
- 71SarProSta-90
- 710PC-211
- 71SarProSta-37
- 71TorSun-35
- 720PC-257
- 72SarProSta-189
- 93DayBom-10

**O'Shea, Darcy**
- 95Sla-251

**O'Shea, Kevin**
- 69SweHocS-361
- 70SarProSta-25
- 71SabPos-14
- 71SarProSta-2
- 71TorSun-35
- 720PC-257
- 72SarProSta-189

**O'Sullivan, Chris**
- 93DonTeaUSA-15
- 93Pin-484
- 93PinCan-484
- 93UppDec-565
- 96DonCanI-133
- 96DonCanIGPP-133
- 96DonCanIRPP-133
- 96LeaPre-122
- 96LeaPreP-122
- 96SelCer-111
- 96SelCerAP-111
- 96SelCerBlu-111
- 96SelCerMB-111
- 96SelCerMG-111
- 96SelCerMR-111
- 96SelCerRed-111
- 96UppDec-230
- 96UppDecBD-19
- 96UppDecBDG-19
- 96UppDecGN-X4
- 96Zen-138
- 96ZenArtP-138
- 97ColCho-35
- 97DonLim-54
- 97DonLimExp-54
- 97Lea-141
- 97LeaFraMat-141
- 97LeaFraMDC-141
- 97LeaInt-141
- 97LeaIntUI-141
- 97UppDec-235

**O'Sullivan, Kevin**
- 93Cla-71
- 93FreCan-18
- 94FreCan-21

**Oakley, Ernie**
- 51LavDaiQSHL-60

**Oates, Adam**
- 870PC-123
- 870PCSti-105
- 87PanSti-248
- 87Top-123
- 880PC-161
- 88PanSti-45
- 88RedWinLC-17
- 88Top-161
- 89BluKod-1
- 890PC-185
- 89Top-185
- 90BluKod-17
- 90Bow-16
- 90Bow-384
- 90Bow-406
- 90BruSpoA-14
- 900PC-149
- 900PCPre-88
- 90PanSti-215
- 90ProSet-269
- 90Sco-85
- 90ScoCan-85
- 90ScoHotRS-41
- 90Top-149
- 90TopTif-149
- 90UppDec-173
- 90UppDec-483
- 90UppDecF-173
- 90UppDecF-483
- 91BluPos-16
- 91Bow-384
- 91Bow-406
- 91BruSpoA-14
- 91Kra-5
- 910PC-254
- 910PC-347
- 910PC-448
- 910PCPre-7
- 91PinSti-31
- 91Par-155
- 91Par-233
- 91ParFre-155
- 91ParFre-233
- 91Pin-6
- 91Pin-378
- 91PinFre-6
- 91PinFre-378
- 91ProSet-291
- 91ProSetCC-CC7
- 91ProSetCCF-CC7
- 91ProSetFre-219
- 91ProSetPC-25
- 91ProSetPla-113
- 91ProSetSLM-1
- 91ScoAme-238
- 91ScoCan-458
- 91ScoHotC-6
- 91StaClu-108
- 91StaPicH-40
- 91Top-265
- 91Top-448
- 91UppDec-94
- 91UppDec-252
- 91UppDecF-94
- 91UppDecF-252
- 91UppDecF-627
- 92BluUDBB-17
- 92Bow-213
- 92Bow-258
- 92BruPos-7
- 92McDUppD-11
- 920PC-172
- 920PC-272
- 920PC25AI-20
- 920PCPreSP-13
- 92PanSti-136
- 92PanStiFre-136
- 92Par-4
- 92ParEmel-4
- 92Pin-40
- 92ProSet-3
- 92Sco-250
- 92ScoCan-250
- 92SeaPat-20
- 92StaClu-188
- 92StaClu-245
- 92Top-475
- 92TopGol-475G
- 92Ult-8
- 92UppDec-133
- 92UppDec-455
- 92UppDec-637
- 93ClaProPBC-BC18
- 93ClaProPro-35
- 93Don-18
- 93DonSpeP-B
- 93Lea-235
- 93LeaHatTA-8
- 93McDUppD-21
- 930PCPre-74
- 930PCPreBG-74
- 930PCPreG-50
- 930PCPreG-74
- 93PanSti-2
- 93Par-11
- 93ParEmel-11
- 93Pin-185
- 93PinAllS-9
- 93PinAllSC-9
- 93PinCan-185
- 93Pow-23
- 93PowPoiL-11
- 93Sco-125
- 93Sco-478
- 93ScoCan-125
- 93ScoCan-478
- 93ScoDreTea-17
- 93ScoDynDUS-3
- 93SeaPat-13
- 93StaClu-93
- 93StaCluAS-11
- 93StaCluFDI-93
- 93StaCluFDIO-93
- 93StaCluMasP-11
- 93StaCluMasPW-11
- 93StaCluO-93
- 93TopPre-50
- 93TopPre-74
- 93TopPreBG-5
- 93TopPreG-50
- 93TopPreG-74
- 93Ult-156
- 93UltAdaO-1
- 93UltAdaO-2
- 93UltAdaO-3
- 93UltAdaO-4
- 93UltAdaO-5
- 93UltAdaO-6
- 93UltAdaO-7
- 93UltAdaO-8
- 93UltAdaO-9
- 93UltAdaO-10
- 93UltAdaO-11
- 93UltAdaO-12
- 93UltAllS-7
- 93UltPreP-7
- 93UppDec-226
- 93UppDec-286
- 93UppDec-327
- 93UppDecHT-HT5
- 93UppDecLAS-11
- 93UppDecSilSka-H6
- 93UppDecSilSkaG-H6
- 93UppDecSP-11
- 94-ActPacM-MM4
- 94BeAPla-R45
- 94CanGamNHLP-35
- 94EASpo-9
- 94EASpo-188
- 94Fin-67
- 94FinDivFCC-3
- 94FinRef-67
- 94FinSupTW-67
- 94Fla-12
- 94FlaHotN-6
- 94Fle-16
- 94HocWit-5
- 94KenStaLA-15
- 94KenStaLC-9
- 94Kra-25
- 94Lea-305
- 94LeaGolS-14
- 94LeaLim-104
- 94LeaLimI-2
- 940PCPre-135
- 940PCPreSE-135
- 940PCPreSE-277
- 94Par-311
- 94ParGol-311
- 94ParSE-SE13
- 94ParSEG-SE13
- 94ParVin-V46
- 94Pin-120
- 94PinArtP-120
- 94PinRinC-120
- 94Sco-141
- 94Sco90PC-3
- 94ScoGol-141
- 94ScoPla-141
- 94ScoPlaTS-141
- 94Sel-58
- 94SP-8
- 94SPDieCut-8
- 94UppDecMO-37
- 94StaCluST-2

94TopPre-135
94TopPre-277
94TopPreSE-135
94TopPreSE-277
94Ult-14
94UltPreP-9
94UppDec-11
94UppDecEIeIce-11
94UppDecPH-H20
94UppDecPHEG-H20
94UppDecPHES-H20
94UppDecPHG-H20
94UppDecPR-R12
94UppDecPR-R26
94UppDecPR-R44
94UppDecPRE-R12
94UppDecPRE-R26
94UppDecPRE-R44
94UppDecPreRG-R12
94UppDecPreRG-R26
94UppDecPreRG-R44
94UppDecSPI-SP7
94UppDecSPIDC-SP7
95Bow-44
95BowAllFoi-44
95ColCho-197
95ColChoPC-197
95ColChoPCP-197
95ColEdgILL-L3
95Don-386
95DonEli-80
95DonEliDCS-80
95DonEliDCU-80
95DonIgn-1
95Emo-11
95EmoXce-1
95Fin-43
95FinRef-43
95ImpSti-8
95Kra-54
95Lea-81
95LeaLim-108
95Met-10
95MetHM-11
95NHLAcePC-10H
95ParInt-16
95ParIntEl-16
95ParIntPTP-PP53
95Pin-3
95PinArtP-3
95PinFan-5
95PinRinC-3
95PlaOneoOne-9
95PlaOneoOne-121
95PlaOneoOne-229
95ProMag-19
95Sco-119
95ScoBlaIce-119
95ScoBlaIceAP-119
95SelCer-11
95SelCerDS-5
95SelCerDSG-5
95SelCerMG-11
95SkyImp-12
95SP-7
95StaClu-40
95StaCluMO-16
95StaCluMOMS-40
95Sum-4
95SumArtP-4
95SumIce-4
95SweGloWC-90
95Top-180
95Top-381
95TopMarMPB-381
95TopOPCI-180
95TopOPCI-381
95TopPowL-7PL
95TopSupSki-2
95TopSupSkiPla-2
95Ult-13
95Ult-395
95UltExtAtt-16
95UltGolM-13
95UltPrePiv-6
95UltPrePivGM-6
95UppDec-197
95UppDecAGPRW-28
95UppDecEleIce-197
95UppDecEleIceG-197
95UppDecPRE-R16
95UppDecPreR-R16
95UppDecSpeE-SE5
95UppDecSpeEdiG-SE5
95Zen-10
96ColCho-12
96ColCho-310
96ColChoCTG-C21A
96ColChoCTG-C21B
96ColChoCTGE-CR21
96ColChoCTGEG-CR21
96ColChoCTGG-C21A
96ColChoCTGG-C21B
96ColChoMVP-UD15
96ColChoMVPG-UD15
96Don-41
96DonCanI-8
96DonCanIGPP-8
96DonCanIRPP-8
96DonEli-31
96DonEliDCS-31
96DonPrePro-41
96Fla-5
96FlaBlul-5
96Fle-6

96FleArtRos-18
96FlePic-28
96FlePicF5-35
96FlePicJE-15
96KraUppD-6
96KraUppD-46
96Lea-112
96LeaLim-5
96LeaLimG-5
96LeaPre-40
96LeaPreP-112
96LeaPrePP-40
96LeaPreSG-54
96LeaPreSte-54
96MetUni-9
96MetUniLW-15
96MetUniLWSP-15
96NHLACEPC-36
96NHLProSTA-19
96Pin-130
96PinArtP-130
96PinFoi-130
96PinPreS-130
96PinRinC-130
96Sco-162
96ScoArtPro-162
96ScoDeaCAP-162
96ScoGolB-162
96ScoSpeAP-162
96SelCer-68
96SelCerAP-68
96SelCerBlu-68
96SelCerMB-68
96SelCerMG-68
96SelCerMR-68
96SelCerRed-68
96SkyImp-7
96SkyImpB-17
96SP-11
96SPHolCol-HC29
96Sum-15
96SumArtP-15
96SumIce-15
96SumMet-15
96SumPreS-15
96SweSemW-100
96TeaOut-30
96Ult-10
96UltGolM-10
96UltPow-14
96UltPowRL-6
96UppDec-216
96UppDecBD-152
96UppDecBDG-152
96UppDecGN-X40
96UppDecIce-2
96UppDecIcePar-2
96Zen-41
96ZenArtP-41
97Be A PPAD-5
97Be A PPAPD-5
97BeAPla-5
97BeAPlaAut-5
97ColCho-266
97ColChoSta-SQ23
97ColChoSti-S28
97Don-25
97Don-228
97DonCanI-78
97DonCanIDS-78
97DonCanINP-7
97DonCanIPS-78
97DonLim-33
97DonLim-112
97DonLim-162
97DonLimExp-33
97DonLimExp-41
97DonLimExp-162
97DonPre-100
97DonPreCttC-100
97DonPreProG-25
97DonPreProGo-228
97DonPreProS-25
97DonPreProS-228
97DonPri-149
97DonPriSoA-149
97Kat-153
97KatGol-153
97KatSil-153
97Lea-130
97LeaFraMat-130
97LeaFraMDC-130
97LeaInt-130
97LeaIntUl-130
97Pac-37
97PacCop-37
97PacCroR-142
97PacCroREG-142
97PacCroRIB-142
97PacCroRS-142
97PacDyn-133
97PacDynC-133
97PacDynD-133
97PacDynEG-133
97PacDynIB-133
97PacDynR-133
97PacDynSil-133
97PacDynTan-56
97PacEmeGre-37
97PacIceB-37
97PacInv-149
97PacInvC-149
97PacInvEG-149
97PacInvIB-149
97PacInvR-149

97PacInvS-149
97PacOme-243
97PacOmeC-243
97PacOmeDG-243
97PacOmeEG-243
97PacOmeG-243
97PacOmeIB-243
97PacPar-198
97PacParC-198
97PacParDG-198
97PacParEG-198
97PacParIB-198
97PacParRed-198
97PacParSil-198
97PacRed-37
97PacRev-150
97PacRevC-150
97PacRevE-150
97PacRevIB-150
97PacRevR-150
97PacRevS-150
97PacSil-37
97PacSlaSDC-12B
97Pin-62
97PinArtP-62
97PinBee-38
97PinBeeGP-38
97PinCer-49
97PinCerMB-49
97PinCerMG-49
97PinCerMR-49
97PinCerR-49
97PinIns-28
97PinInsCC-28
97PinInsEC-28
97PinPrePBB-62
97PinPrePBC-62
97PinPrePBM-62
97PinPrePBY-62
97PinPrePFC-62
97PinPrePFM-62
97PinPrePFY-62
97PinPrePla-62
97PinRinC-62
97PinTotCMPG-49
97PinTotCPB-49
97PinTotCPG-49
97PinTotCPR-49
97Sco-117
97ScoArtPro-117
97ScoGolBla-117
97SPAut-162
97SPx-48
97SPxBro-48
97SPxDim-SPX12
97SPxGol-48
97SPxGraF-48
97SPxSil-48
97SPxSte-48
97Stu-32
97StuPreG-32
97StuPrePS-32
97UppDec-177
97UppDecBD-109
97UppDecBDDD-109
97UppDecBDQD-109
97UppDecBDTD-109
97UppDecIce-17
97UppDecIceP-17
97UppDecIPS-17
97UppDecSG-SG56
97UppDecSSM-SS12
97UppDecSSW-SS12
97UppDecTSS-18A
97Zen-32
97Zen5x7-41
97ZenGolImp-41
97ZenSilImp-41
97ZenZGol-32
97ZenZSil-32
98Be A PPA-296
98Be A PPAA-296
98Be A PPAAF-296
98Be A PPAM-M15
98Be A PPSE-296
98Be APG-296
98BowBes-72
98BowBesAR-72
98BowBesR-72
98Fin-98
98FinNo P-98
98FinNo PR-98
98FinRef-98
98O-PChr-179
98O-PChrR-179
98O-PChrSB-SB23
98O-PChrSBR-SB23
98Pac-445
98PacAur-199
98PacCroR-144
98PacCroRLS-144
98PacDynI-198
98PacDynIIB-198
98PacDynIEG-198
98PacDynIR-198
98PacIceB-445
98PacOmeH-249
98PacOmeODI-249
98PacOmeR-249
98PacPar-249
98PacParC-249
98PacParEG-249
98PacParIB-249
98PacParS-249
98PacRed-445

98PacRev-149
98PacRevIS-149
98PacRevR-149
98SP Aut-90
98Top-179
98TopGolLC1-80
98TopGolLC1B-80
98TopGolLC1BOoO-80
98TopGolLC1OoO-80
98TopGolLC1R-80
98TopGolLC1ROoO-80
98TopGolLC2B-80
98TopGolLC2BOoO-80
98TopGolLC2OoO-80
98TopGolLC2R-80
98TopGolLC2ROoO-80
98TopGolLC3-80
98TopGolLC3B-80
98TopGolLC3BOoO-80
98TopGolLC3OoO-80
98TopGolLC3ROoO-80
98TopO-P-179
98TopSeaB-SB23
98UC-217
98UD PacPCR-217
98UD DonPCR-217
98UppDec-199
98UppDecE-199
98UppDecE1o1-199
98UppDecFIT-FT20
98UppDecFITQ1-FT20
98UppDecFITQ2-FT20
98UppDecFITQ3-FT20
98UppDecGR-199
98UppDecM-212
98UppDecMGS-212
98UppDecMSS-212
98UppDecMSS-212
99Pac-446
99PacAur-150
99PacAurPD-150
99PacCop-446
99PacGol-446
99PacIceB-446
99PacPreD-446
99RetHoc-80
99SP AutPS-90
99UppDecM-214
99UppDecMGS-214
99UppDecMSS-214
99UppDecMSS-214
99UppDecRG-80
99UppDecRP-80

**Oates, Matt**
94IndIce-16
**Oatman, Ed**
10C55SweCP-5
11C55-5
12C57-47
23V1281PauC-61
**Oberg, Anders**
93SweSemE-87
**Oberg, Carl-Goran**
65SweCorI-186
67SweHoc-24
67SweHoc-79
70SweHocS-146
71SweHocS-240
72SweHocS-225
73SweHocS-66
73SweWorCS-66
81SweSemHVS-118
**Oberg, Fredrik**
92SweSemE-195
93SweSemE-165
95SweLeaE-301
95SweLeaEFF-12
95SweUppDE-193
**Oberg, Hans**
81SweSemHVS-122
**Oberg, Jan Roger**
81SweHoc-12
**Oberg, Kjell Sture**
67SweHoc-213
**Oberg, Lars**
71SweHocS-114
72SweHocS-95
73SweHocS-170
73SweWorCS-170
74SweHocS-275
**Oberrauch, Robert**
93SweSemWCS-211
95SweGloWC-228
96SweSemW-176
**Oboj, Tadeusz**
79PanSti-133
**Obresa, Peter**
89SweSemWCS-119
94GerDELE-104
95GerDELE-101
**Obsut, Jaroslav**
95SwiCurB-11
96MedHatT-14
**Oddleifson, Chris**
74CanuNoyR-14
74NHLActSta-272
740PCNHL-108
74Top-108
75CanuRoyB-15
750PCNHL-169
75Top-169
76CanuRoyB-13
760PCNHL-112

760PCNHL-395
76Top-112
77CanCanDC-11
77CanuRoyB-15
770PCNHL-209
77Top-209
78CanuRoyB-18
780PC-183
78Top-183
79CanuRoyB-17
790PC-305
800PC-295
810PCSti-246
**Odelein, Lee**
91ProAHLCHL-447
**Odelein, Lyle**
88ProHL-85
89ProAHL-185
90CanaPos-22
90ProSet-617
91CanaPos-21
910PC-350
91Top-350
91UppDec-482
91UppDecF-482
92CanaPos-19
92Par-325
92ParEmel-325
92Ult-331
93CanaPos-17
93Don-167
93Lea-283
93Par-370
93ParEmel-370
93Pin-301
93Sco-283
93ScoCan-283
93Ult-354
93UppDec-7
94CanaPos-17
94CanGamNHLP-140
94Don-272
94Fle-105
94Lea-137
940PCPre-43
940PCPreSE-43
94ParSE-SE89
94ParSEG-SE89
94Pin-132
94PinArtP-132
94PinRinC-132
94StaClu-104
94StaCluFDI-104
94StaCluMOMS-104
94StaCluSTWC-104
94TopPre-43
94TopPreSE-43
94Ult-112
95BeAPla-111
95BeAPSig-S111
95BeAPSigDC-S111
95CanaPos-10
95ColCho-6
95ColChoPC-6
95ColChoPCP-6
95Don-281
95Lea-195
95ParInt-381
95ParIntEl-381
95Pin-196
95PinArtP-196
95PinRinC-196
95PlaOneoOne-165
95UppDec-153
95UppDecEleIce-153
95UppDecEleIceG-153
96BeAPaut-148
96BeAPAutSil-148
96BeAPla-148
96Dev-24
96DurAllT-DC2
96Durl`EB-JB2
96Sco-224
96ScoArtPro-224
96ScoDeaCAP-224
96ScoGolB-224
96ScoSpeAP-224
96UppDec-289
97Be A PPAD-17
97Be A PPAPD-17
97BeAPla-17
97BeAPlaAut-17
97Pac-143
97PacCop-143
97PacEmeGre-143
97PacRed-143
97ScoDev-15
97ScoDevPla-15
97ScoDevPre-15
97UppDec-306
98Pac-243
98PacCop-243
98PacGol-243
98PacIceB-243
99Pac-243
99PacCop-243
99PacGol-243
99PacIceB-243
99PacPreD-243
**Odelein, Selmar**
87OilTeal-36
88OilTenAnn-26

88ProAHL-93
**Odeline, Selmar**
93SheSte-13
**Odgers, Jeff**
88BraWheK-12
89BraWheK-20
90KanCitBla-2
90ProAHLIHL-600
91Par-386
91ParFre-386
91UppDec-597
91UppDecF-597
92Bow-397
920PC-190
92ParSti-130
92ParStiFre-130
92Par-398
92StaClu-142
92Top-483
92TopGol-483G
930PCPre-497
930PCPreG-497
93ParSti-260
93Pow-224
93StaClu-114
93StaCluFDI-114
93StaCluFDIO-114
93StaCluO-114
93TopPre-497
93TopPreG-497
94Lea-439
94StaClu-11
94StaCluFDI-11
94StaCluMOMS-11
94StaCluSTWC-11
94Ult-368
96BeAPAut-193
96BeAPAutSil-193
96BeAPla-193
97Pac-157
97PacCop-157
97PacEmeGre-157
97PacIceB-157
97PacOme-62
97PacOmeC-62
97PacOmeDG-62
97PacOmeEG-62
97PacOmeIB-62
97PacRed-157
97PacSil-157
97ScoBru-18
97ScoBruPla-18
97ScoBruPre-18
98Pac-166
98PacIceB-166
98PacOmeH-62
98PacOmeODI-62
98PacOmeR-62
98PacRed-166
99Pac-112
99PacCop-112
99PacGol-112
99PacIceB-112
99PacPreD-112
**Odintsov, Valeri**
74SweHocS-70
**Odjick, Gino**
907hInnSMC-54
90CanuMoh-23
90ProAHLIHL-334
90UppDec-518
90UppDecF-518
910PC-203
91ProSet-505
91ProSetFre-505
91ScoCan-237
91StaClu-338
91Top-203
91UppDec-195
91UppDecF-195
92CanuRoaTA-17
92Par-422
92ParEmel-422
92Sco-540
92ScoCan-540
92Ult-427
93Don-346
93Lea-418
93Par-485
93ParEmel-485
93Pin-308
93PinCan-308
93Pow-461
93Sco-385
93ScoCan-385
93Ult-442
94CanGamNHLP-151
94CanuProI-17
94Don-241
94Fle-228
94Lea-200
94ParSE-SE186
94ParSEG-SE186
94Pin-177
94PinArtP-177
94PinRinC-177
94Sco-9
94ScoGol-9
94ScoPlaTS-9

94Ult-229
94UppDec-465
94UppDecEleIce-465
95BeAPla-222
95BeAPSig-S222
95BeAPSigDC-S222
95CanuBulDA-13
95ColCho-290
95ColChoPC-290
95ColChoPCP-290
95UppDec-338
95UppDecEleIce-338
95UppDecEleIceG-338
95CanuPos-29
96ColCho-274
97ColCho-263
97PacDynBKS-98
97ScoCanPla-16
97ScoCanPre-16
97ScoCanu-16
97UppDec-206
97UppDec-379
98PacOmeH-148
98PacOmeODI-148
98PacOmeR-148
**Odling, Sune**
73SweHocS-137
73SweWorCS-137
74SweHocS-152
**Odling, Ulf**
93SweSemE-6
**Odmark, Ulf**
83SweSemE-165
86SwePanS-210
87SwePanS-200
89SweSemE-184
90SweSemE-19
91SweSemE-221
92SweSemE-241
93SweSemE-208
**Odnokon, Mark**
85MinDul-17
917thInnSWHL-263
91PriAlbR-15
**Odnokon, Pat**
90PriAlbR-15
**Odrowski, Gerry**
44BeeGro2P-198
60ShiCoi-58
61ShiCoi-78
62Par-20
71BluPos-12
720PC-304
72ShaLosAW-11
740PCWHA-14
**Oduya, Fredrik**
96KenTho-14
**Ogilvie, Brian**
74NHLActSta-245
**Ogrodnick, John**
800PC-359
810PC-95
810PCSti-11
81Top-W95
820PC-79
820PC-92
820PCSti-179
82PosCer-5
830PC-115
830PC-128
830PCSti-137
830PCSti-138
83PufSti-16
840PC-62
840PC-356
840PCSti-34
840PCSti-35
840PCSti-137
84Top-46
850PC-70
850PCBoxB-J
850PCSti-37
850PCSti-119
85Top-70
85TopBoxB-J
85TopStilns-1
86NordTeal-16
860PC-87
860PCSti-158
86Top-87
870PC-134
870PCSti-218
87PanSti-165
87RedWinLC-23
87Top-134
880PC-153
88Top-153
89PanSti-290
89RanMarMB-25
90Bow-223
90BowTif-223
900PC-174
90PanSti-99
90ProSet-206
90Sco-113
90ScoCan-113
90Top-174
90TopTeaSL-18
90TopTif-174
90UppDec-258
90UppDecF-258
91Bow-71
910PC-365
91PanSti-293
91Par-115

❑ 91ParFre-115
❑ 91Pin-145
❑ 91PinFre-145
❑ 91ProSet-169
❑ 91ProSetFre-169
❑ 91ProSetPla-204
❑ 91ScoAme-36
❑ 91ScoCan-36
❑ 91StaClu-273
❑ 91Top-365
❑ 91UppDec-476
❑ 91UppDecF-476
❑ 92OPC-351
❑ 92Sco-329
❑ 92ScoCan-329
❑ 92StaClu-222
**Ohling, Jens**
❑ 83SweSemE-86
❑ 84SweSemE-86
❑ 85SwePanS-77
❑ 86SwePanS-70
❑ 87SwePanS-76
❑ 89SweSemE-62
❑ 90SweSemE-286
❑ 91SweSemE-69
❑ 92SweSemE-90
❑ 93SweSemE-63
❑ 94SweLeaE-38
❑ 94SweLeaESS-3
❑ 95SweLeaE-33
❑ 95SweUppDE-52
**Ohlsson, Dag**
❑ 67SweHoc-109
**Ohlsson, Eine**
❑ 67SweHoc-295
**Ohlund, Mattias**
❑ 93SweSemE-316
❑ 94ParSE-SE243
❑ 94ParSEG-SE243
❑ 94SP-172
❑ 94SPDieCut-172
❑ 94SweLeaE-288
❑ 94SweLeaENHLD-1
❑ 94SweLeaERR-4
❑ 94UppDec-520
❑ 94UppDecEleIce-520
❑ 95SigRoo-14
❑ 95SigRooSig-14
❑ 95SP-184
❑ 95SweGloWC-57
❑ 95SweLeaE-75
❑ 95SweLeaEM-8
❑ 95SweUppDE-119
❑ 95SweUppDE-229
❑ 95SweUppDE-256
❑ 95SweUppDETNA-NA16
❑ 96SweSemCDT-5
❑ 96SweSemW-52
❑ 97Be A PPAD-215
❑ 97Be A PPAPD-215
❑ 97BeAPla-215
❑ 97BeAPlaAut-215
❑ 97DonEli-98
❑ 97DonEli-139
❑ 97DonEliAsp-98
❑ 97DonEliAsp-139
❑ 97DonEliS-98
❑ 97DonEliS-139
❑ 97DonPri-171
❑ 97DonPriSoA-171
❑ 97Kat-150
❑ 97KatGol-150
❑ 97KatSil-150
❑ 97PacDyn-NNO
❑ 97PacDynC-NNO
❑ 97PacDynDG-NNO
❑ 97PacDynEG-NNO
❑ 97PacDynIB-NNO
❑ 97PacDynR-NNO
❑ 97PacDynSil-NNO
❑ 97PacOme-234
❑ 97PacOmeC-234
❑ 97PacOmeDG-234
❑ 97PacOmeEG-234
❑ 97PacOmeG-234
❑ 97PacOmeIB-234
❑ 97PacPar-192
❑ 97PacParC-192
❑ 97PacParDG-192
❑ 97PacParEG-192
❑ 97PacParIB-192
❑ 97PacParRed-192
❑ 97PacParSil-192
❑ 97PacRev-144
❑ 97PacRevC-144
❑ 97PacRevE-144
❑ 97PacRevIB-144
❑ 97PacRevR-144
❑ 97PacRevS-144
❑ 97Pin-8
❑ 97PinArtP-8
❑ 97PinPrePBB-8
❑ 97PinPrePBC-8
❑ 97PinPrePBM-8
❑ 97PinPrePBY-8
❑ 97PinPrePFC-8
❑ 97PinPrePFM-8
❑ 97PinPrePFY-8
❑ 97PinPrePla-8
❑ 97PinRinC-8
❑ 97Sco-63
❑ 97ScoArtPro-63
❑ 97ScoCanPla-6
❑ 97ScoCanPre-6
❑ 97ScoCanu-6
❑ 97ScoGolBla-63
❑ 97SPAut-196
❑ 97UppDec-380
❑ 97UppDecBD-120
❑ 97UppDecBDDD-120
❑ 97UppDecBDQD-120
❑ 97UppDecBDTD-120
❑ 97UppDecIce-42
❑ 97UppDecIceP-42
❑ 97UppDecIPS-42
❑ 97Zen-85
❑ 97Zen5x7-73
❑ 97ZenGolImp-73
❑ 97ZenRooR-13
❑ 97ZenSilImp-73
❑ 97ZenZGol-85
❑ 97ZenZSil-85
❑ 97ZenZT-11
❑ 97ZenZTG-11
❑ 98Be A PPA-142
❑ 98Be A PPAA-142
❑ 98Be A PPAAF-142
❑ 98Be A PPTBASG-142
❑ 98Be APG-142
❑ 98BowBes-73
❑ 98BowBesAR-73
❑ 98BowBesP-BP5
❑ 98BowBesPAR-BP5
❑ 98BowBesPR-BP5
❑ 98BowBesR-73
❑ 98Fin-38
❑ 98FinCen-C14
❑ 98FinCenR-C14
❑ 98FinNo P-38
❑ 98FinNo PR-38
❑ 98FinRef-38
❑ 98McD-22
❑ 98O-PChr-54
❑ 98O-PChrBM-B5
❑ 98O-PChrBMR-B5
❑ 98O-PChrR-54
❑ 98O-PChrSB-SB11
❑ 98O-PChrSBR-SB11
❑ 98Pac-2
❑ 98PacAur-191
❑ 98PacCroR-138
❑ 98PacCroRLS-138
❑ 98PacDynI-191
❑ 98PacDynIIB-191
❑ 98PacDynIR-191
❑ 98PacIceB-2
❑ 98PacOmeH-240
❑ 98PacOmeODI-240
❑ 98PacOmeR-240
❑ 98PacPar-238
❑ 98PacParC-238
❑ 98PacParEG-238
❑ 98PacParH-238
❑ 98PacParIB-238
❑ 98PacParS-238
❑ 98PacRed-2
❑ 98PacRev-144
❑ 98PacRevADC-21
❑ 98PacRevIS-144
❑ 98PacRevR-144
❑ 98SP Aut-84
❑ 98SP AutSotTG-MO
❑ 98SPxFin-127
❑ 98SPxFinR-127
❑ 98SPxFinS-127
❑ 98SSASotT-MO
❑ 98Top-54
❑ 98TopAut-A4
❑ 98TopBoaM-B5
❑ 98TopGolLC1-87
❑ 98TopGolLC1B-87
❑ 98TopGolLC1BOoO-87
❑ 98TopGolLC1OoO-87
❑ 98TopGolLC1R-87
❑ 98TopGolLC1ROoO-87
❑ 98TopGolLC2-87
❑ 98TopGolLC2B-87
❑ 98TopGolLC2BOoO-87
❑ 98TopGolLC2OoO-87
❑ 98TopGolLC2R-87
❑ 98TopGolLC2ROoO-87
❑ 98TopGolLC3-87
❑ 98TopGolLC3B-87
❑ 98TopGolLC3BOoO-87
❑ 98TopGolLC3OoO-87
❑ 98TopGolLC3R-87
❑ 98TopGolLC3ROoO-87
❑ 98TopIceA2-I12
❑ 98TopO-P-54
❑ 98TopSeaB-SB11
❑ 98UC-206
❑ 98UD ChoPCR-206
❑ 98UD ChoR-206
❑ 98UD3-14
❑ 98UD3-74
❑ 98UD3-134
❑ 98UD3DieC-14
❑ 98UD3DieC-74
❑ 98UD3DieC-134
❑ 98UppDec-197
❑ 98UppDecBD-87
❑ 98UppDecDD-87
❑ 98UppDecE-197
❑ 98UppDecE1o1-197
❑ 98UppDecGN-GN16
❑ 98UppDecGNQ1-GN16
❑ 98UppDecGNQ2-GN16
❑ 98UppDecGNQ3-GN16
❑ 98UppDecGR-197
❑ 98UppDecM-203
❑ 98UppDecMGS-203
❑ 98UppDecMSS-203
❑ 98UppDecMSS-203
❑ 98UppDecQD-87
❑ 98UppDecTD-87
❑ 99Pac-430
❑ 99PacAur-144
❑ 99PacAurPD-144
❑ 99PacCop-430
❑ 99PacGol-430
❑ 99PacIceB-430
❑ 99PacPreD-430
❑ 99SP AutPS-84
❑ 99UppDecM-207
❑ 99UppDecMGS-207
❑ 99UppDecMSS-207
❑ 99UppDecMSS-207
**Ohlzon, Bruno**
❑ 84SweSemE-127
**Ohman, Jens**
❑ 89SweSemE-183
❑ 90SweSemE-18
❑ 91SweSemE-222
**Ohman, Lars**
❑ 67SweHoc-131
❑ 69SweHocS-144
❑ 70SweHocS-98
❑ 71SweHocS-193
**Ohman, Lasse**
❑ 67SweHoc-25
❑ 72SweHocS-179
**Ohman, Mats**
❑ 84SweSemE-180
❑ 86SwePanS-176
**Ohman, Robert**
❑ 83SweSemE-176
**Ohman, Roger**
❑ 84SweSemE-179
❑ 87MonHaw-18
❑ 89SweSemE-7
❑ 90SweSemE-131
❑ 91SweSemE-182
❑ 92SweSemE-209
❑ 93SweSemE-179
❑ 94SweLeaE-272
❑ 95SweLeaE-88
❑ 95SweLeaEG-9
❑ 95SweUppDE-139
❑ 96GerDELE-232
**Ohman, Stefan**
❑ 94SweLeaE-228
**Ohman, Tore**
❑ 67SweHoc-132
❑ 69SweHocS-145
❑ 70SweHocS-99
❑ 71SweHocS-194
❑ 72SweHocS-180
**Ohrlund, Leif**
❑ 65SweCorI-206
❑ 67SweHoc-280
**Ohrlund, Torbjorn**
❑ 92SweSemE-44
**Ohrlund, Uno**
❑ 64SweCorI-7
❑ 65SweCorI-7
❑ 67SweHoc-281
❑ 69SweHocS-326
❑ 71SweHocS-380
**Oijennus, Markus**
❑ 93FinnSIS-79
❑ 94FinnSIS-114
❑ 95FinnSIS-321
**Ojanen, Janne**
❑ 88ProAHL-346
❑ 89DevCar-18
❑ 90OPC-30
❑ 90PanSti-78
❑ 90ProSet-173
❑ 90Top-30
❑ 90TopTif-30
❑ 90UppDec-290
❑ 90UppDecF-290
❑ 91UppDec-25
❑ 91UppDecF-25
❑ 92OPCPre-17
❑ 93OPCPre-16
❑ 93OPCPreG-16
❑ 93StaClu-184
❑ 93StaCluFDI-184
❑ 93StaCluFDIO-184
❑ 93StaCluO-184
❑ 93SweSemWCS-71
❑ 93TopPre-16
❑ 93TopPreG-16
❑ 94FinnJaaK-35
❑ 94FinnSIS-208
❑ 94FinnSISFI-19
❑ 94FinnSISMN-4
❑ 94FinnSISS-4
❑ 95FinnKarWCL-15
❑ 95FinnSemWC-8
❑ 95FinnSIS-322
❑ 95FinnSISGC-19
❑ 95FinnSISL-77
❑ 95FinnSISLLG-4
❑ 95FinnSISSpe-6
❑ 95SweGloWC-136
❑ 96FinnSISRMA-6
❑ 96SweSemW-8
**Ojanen, Marko**
❑ 93FinnSIS-105
❑ 94FinnSIS-132
❑ 95FinnSIS-14
**Ojerklint, Ulf**
❑ 72SweHocS-100
**Okal, Miroslav**
❑ 94CzeAPSE-194
❑ 95CzeAPSE-42
**Okal, Zdenek**
❑ 94CzeAPSE-195
❑ 95CzeAPSE-43
**Oksanen, Hannu**
❑ 84SweSemE-162
**Oksanen, Lasse**
❑ 69SweHocS-378
❑ 69SweWorC-13
❑ 69SweWorC-86
❑ 69SweWorC-162
❑ 70SweHocS-308
❑ 71SweHocS-71
❑ 72SweHocS-38
❑ 72SweSemWC-84
❑ 74SweHocS-98
❑ 74SweSemHVS-87
❑ 91SweSemWCS-229
❑ 96SweSemWHL-HL14
**Oksiuta, Roman**
❑ 91OPCIns-57R
❑ 92RusStaRA-20
❑ 92RusStaRA-24
❑ 93ClaProPro-11
❑ 93Don-111
❑ 93DonRatR-15
❑ 93Lea-411
❑ 93Par-258
❑ 93ParEmel-258
❑ 93Pin-451
❑ 93PinCan-451
❑ 93SweSemWCS-141
❑ 93UppDec-509
❑ 94CapBreO-15
❑ 94FinBowB-R5
❑ 94FinBowBR-R5
❑ 94Fle-72
❑ 95Don-66
❑ 95Emo-183
❑ 95Fin-94
❑ 95FinRef-94
❑ 95Ima-35
❑ 95ImaGol-35
❑ 95Lea-77
❑ 95LeaStuR-16
❑ 95Met-154
❑ 95ParInt-211
❑ 95ParIntEl-211
❑ 95Pin-63
❑ 95PinArtP-63
❑ 95PinRinC-63
❑ 95PlaOneoOne-210
❑ 95Sco-285
❑ 95ScoBlaIce-285
❑ 95ScoBlaIceAP-285
❑ 95SkyImp-172
❑ 95SkyImpNHLF-2
❑ 95StaClu-132
❑ 95StaCluMOMS-132
❑ 95Top-317
❑ 95TopNewG-8NG
❑ 95TopOPCI-317
❑ 95Ult-171
❑ 95UltAllRoo-9
❑ 95UltAllRooGM-9
❑ 95UltGolM-171
❑ 95UppDec-476
❑ 95UppDecEleIce-476
❑ 95UppDecEleIceG-476
❑ 96ColCho-10
❑ 96Don-44
❑ 96DonPrePro-44
❑ 96Duc-3
❑ 96MetUni-4
❑ 96Pin-139
❑ 96PinArtP-139
❑ 96PinFoi-139
❑ 96PinPreS-139
❑ 96PinRinC-139
❑ 96PlaOneoOne-397
❑ 96Sco-76
❑ 96ScoArtPro-76
❑ 96ScoDeaCAP-76
❑ 96ScoGolB-76
❑ 96ScoSpeAP-76
❑ 96SkyImp-3
❑ 96Ult-4
❑ 96UltGolM-4
❑ 97PacInvNRB-164
❑ 97ScoPen-13
❑ 97ScoPenPla-13
❑ 97ScoPenPre-13
**Oktyabrev, Arthur**
❑ 92RusStaRA-31
❑ 92RusStaRA-25
**Okvist, Tore**
❑ 83SweSemE-49
❑ 84SweSemE-186
**Olaski, Mike**
❑ 92BriColJHL-72
**Olausson, Fredrik**
❑ 84SweSemE-102
❑ 85SwePanS-97
❑ 86JetBor-18
❑ 87Jet-16
❑ 87OPC-225
❑ 87PanSti-361
❑ 88JetPol-18
❑ 89JetSaf-23
❑ 89Kra-51
❑ 89SweSemE-77
❑ 89SweSemWCS-10
❑ 90Bow-135
❑ 90BowTif-135
❑ 90JetIGA-25
❑ 90OPC-242
❑ 90PanSti-318
❑ 90ProSet-335A
❑ 90ProSet-335B
❑ 90Sco-81
❑ 90ScoCan-81
❑ 90Top-242
❑ 90TopTif-242
❑ 90UppDec-237
❑ 90UppDecF-237
❑ 91Bow-210
❑ 91JetIGA-21
❑ 91JetPanTS-19
❑ 91OPC-45
❑ 91PanSti-67
❑ 91Par-203
❑ 91ParFre-203
❑ 91Pin-74
❑ 91PinFre-74
❑ 91ProSet-264
❑ 91ProSetFre-264
❑ 91ProSetPla-133
❑ 91ScoAme-18
❑ 91ScoCan-18
❑ 91StaClu-185
❑ 91Top-45
❑ 91UppDec-383
❑ 91UppDecF-383
❑ 92Bow-295
❑ 92OPC-121
❑ 92PanSti-60
❑ 92PanStiFre-60
❑ 92Par-212
❑ 92ParEmel-212
❑ 92Pin-202
❑ 92PinFre-202
❑ 92Sco-13
❑ 92ScoCan-13
❑ 92StaClu-346
❑ 92Top-120
❑ 92TopGol-120G
❑ 92Ult-244
❑ 92UltImp-18
❑ 92UppDec-136
❑ 93Don-386
❑ 93Don-430
❑ 93JetRuf-19
❑ 93Lea-124
❑ 93OPCPre-63
❑ 93OPCPreG-63
❑ 93PanSti-198
❑ 93Par-227
❑ 93ParEmel-227
❑ 93Pin-392
❑ 93PinCan-392
❑ 93Pow-273
❑ 93Pow-342
❑ 93Sco-79
❑ 93Sco-645
❑ 93ScoCan-79
❑ 93ScoCan-645
❑ 93ScoGol-645
❑ 93SweSemWCS-26
❑ 93TopPre-63
❑ 93TopPreG-63
❑ 93Ult-147
❑ 93UppDec-209
❑ 94BeAPSig-8
❑ 94CanGamNHLP-103
❑ 94Fle-73
❑ 94Lea-327
❑ 94OPCPre-319
❑ 94OPCPreSE-319
❑ 94Pin-303
❑ 94PinArtP-303
❑ 94PinRinC-303
❑ 94Sco-147
❑ 94ScoGol-147
❑ 94ScoPla-147
❑ 94ScoPlaTS-147
❑ 94StaClu-198
❑ 94StaCluFDI-198
❑ 94StaCluMOMS-198
❑ 94StaCluSTWC-198
❑ 94TopPre-319
❑ 94TopPreSE-319
❑ 94Ult-74
❑ 94UppDec-394
❑ 94UppDecEleIce-394
❑ 95ColCho-98
❑ 95ColChoPC-98
❑ 95ColChoPCP-98
❑ 95SweGloWC-26
❑ 95SweUppDE-247
❑ 96BeAPAut-134
❑ 96BeAPAutSil-134
❑ 96BeAPla-134
❑ 97Pac-149
❑ 97PacCop-149
❑ 97PacEmeGre-149
❑ 97PacIceB-149
❑ 97PacRed-149
❑ 97PacSil-149
❑ 97UppDec-139
❑ 98Be A PPA-154
❑ 98Be A PPAA-154
❑ 98Be A PPAAF-154
❑ 98Be A PPSE-154
❑ 98Be APG-154
❑ 98O-PChr-150
❑ 98O-PChrR-150
❑ 98Pac-356
❑ 98PacIceB-356
❑ 98PacOmeH-6
❑ 98PacOmeODI-6
❑ 98PacOmeR-6
❑ 98PacPar-195
❑ 98PacParC-195
❑ 98PacParEG-195
❑ 98PacParH-195
❑ 98PacParIB-195
❑ 98PacParS-195
❑ 98PacRed-356
❑ 98Top-150
❑ 98TopO-P-150
❑ 99Pac-11
❑ 99PacCop-11
❑ 99PacGol-11
❑ 99PacIceB-11
❑ 99PacPreD-11
❑ 99UppDecM-9
❑ 99UppDecMGS-9
❑ 99UppDecMSS-9
❑ 99UppDecMSS-9
**Olberg, Dan**
❑ 90ArIIce-10
**Olbrich, Michael**
❑ 94GerDELE-175
❑ 95GerDELE-170
**Olczyk, Ed**
❑ 85OPC-86
❑ 85OPCSti-26
❑ 85Top-86
❑ 86BlaCok-13
❑ 86OPC-82
❑ 86OPCSti-156
❑ 86Top-82
❑ 87MapLeaP-14
❑ 87MapLeaPLA-9
❑ 87MapLeaPO-14
❑ 87OPC-104
❑ 87OPCSti-76
❑ 87PanSti-230
❑ 87Top-104
❑ 88FriLayS-11
❑ 88MapLeaPLA-6
❑ 88OPC-125
❑ 88OPCBoxB-G
❑ 88OPCSti-181
❑ 88PanSti-126
❑ 88Top-125
❑ 88TopBoxB-G
❑ 89Kra-38
❑ 89OPC-133
❑ 89OPCSti-172
❑ 89PanSti-132
❑ 89SweSemWCS-169
❑ 89Top-133
❑ 90Bow-161
❑ 90BowTif-161
❑ 90JetIGA-26
❑ 90OPC-206
❑ 90PanSti-283
❑ 90ProSet-286
❑ 90ProSet-563
❑ 90Sco-210
❑ 90ScoCan-210
❑ 90ScoHotRS-89
❑ 90ScoRoo-51T
❑ 90Top-206
❑ 90TopTif-206
❑ 90UppDec-222
❑ 90UppDec-431
❑ 90UppDecF-222
❑ 90UppDecF-431
❑ 91Bow-154
❑ 91JetIGA-22
❑ 91Kra-62
❑ 91MapLeaPTS-17
❑ 91OPC-182
❑ 91OPCPre-196
❑ 91PanSti-64
❑ 91Par-204
❑ 91ParFre-204
❑ 91Pin-193
❑ 91Pin-386
❑ 91PinFre-193
❑ 91PinFre-386
❑ 91ProSet-265
❑ 91ProSetFre-265
❑ 91ProSetPla-134
❑ 91ScoAme-60
❑ 91ScoCan-60
❑ 91ScoKel-18
❑ 91StaClu-57
❑ 91SweSemWCS-148
❑ 91Top-182
❑ 91UppDec-99
❑ 91UppDec-387
❑ 91UppDecF-99
❑ 91UppDecF-387
❑ 92Bow-278
❑ 92OPC-375
❑ 92PanSti-55
❑ 92PanStiFre-55
❑ 92Par-213
❑ 92Par-350
❑ 92ParEmel-213
❑ 92ParEmel-350
❑ 92Pin-145
❑ 92PinFre-145
❑ 92ProSet-213
❑ 92Sco-145
❑ 92ScoCan-145
❑ 92ScoUSAG-15
❑ 92StaClu-157
❑ 92Top-17
❑ 92TopGol-17G
❑ 92Ult-245
❑ 92Ult-357
❑ 92UppDec-211
❑ 93Lea-90
❑ 93OPCPre-398
❑ 93OPCPreG-398
❑ 93Par-402
❑ 93ParEmel-402
❑ 93Pin-154
❑ 93PinCan-154
❑ 93Pow-394
❑ 93Sco-37
❑ 93ScoCan-37
❑ 93StaClu-197
❑ 93StaCluFDI-197
❑ 93StaCluFDIO-197
❑ 93StaCluO-197
❑ 93SweSemWCS-184
❑ 93TopPre-398
❑ 93TopPreG-398
❑ 93UppDec-115
❑ 94FinnJaaK-115
❑ 94Pin-420
❑ 94PinArtP-420
❑ 94PinRinC-420
❑ 94UppDec-274
❑ 94UppDecEleIce-274
❑ 95BeAPla-141
❑ 95BeAPSig-S141
❑ 95BeAPSigDC-S141
❑ 95ColCho-106
❑ 95ColChoPC-106
❑ 95ColChoPCP-106
❑ 95JetTeaIss-17
❑ 95Sco-282
❑ 95ScoBlaIce-282
❑ 95ScoBlaIceAP-282
❑ 96Lea-117
❑ 96LeaPreP-117
❑ 96MetUni-77
❑ 96Sco-198
❑ 96ScoArtPro-198
❑ 96ScoDeaCAP-198
❑ 96ScoGolB-198
❑ 96ScoSpeAP-198
❑ 96SP-75
❑ 96Ult-81
❑ 96UltGolM-82
❑ 97Pac-92
❑ 97PacCop-92
❑ 97PacCroR-112
❑ 97PacCroREG-112
❑ 97PacCroRIB-112
❑ 97PacCroRS-112
❑ 97PacEmeGre-92
❑ 97PacIceB-92
❑ 97PacInv-116
❑ 97PacInvC-116
❑ 97PacInvEG-116
❑ 97PacInvIB-116
❑ 97PacInvR-116
❑ 97PacInvS-116
❑ 97PacOme-188
❑ 97PacOmeC-188
❑ 97PacOmeDG-188
❑ 97PacOmeEG-188
❑ 97PacOmeG-188
❑ 97PacOmeIB-188
❑ 97PacPar-154
❑ 97PacParC-154
❑ 97PacParDG-154
❑ 97PacParEG-154
❑ 97PacParIB-154
❑ 97PacParRed-154
❑ 97PacParSil-154
❑ 97PacRed-92
❑ 97PacSil-92
❑ 97PinIns-169
❑ 97Sco-206
❑ 97ScoPen-7
❑ 97ScoPenPla-7
❑ 97ScoPenPre-7
❑ 98Pac-357
❑ 98PacIceB-357
❑ 98PacRed-357
❑ 99Pac-95
❑ 99PacCop-95
❑ 99PacGol-95
❑ 99PacIceB-95
❑ 99PacPreD-95
**Oldenborger, Jeff**
❑ 95SlaMemC-2
**Oleniuk, Devon**
❑ 84SasBlaS-17
❑ 87KamBla-16
**Olenyn, Jerry**
❑ 94LasVegThu-18
**Olesehuk, Bill**
❑ 79Roc-15
**Oleson, Cory**
❑ 90ArIIce-11
❑ 91ArIIce-4
❑ 91ArIIce-18
❑ 92ArIIce-3
❑ 92ArIIce-19
**Olimb, Larry**
❑ 91MinGolG-21
❑ 92Cla-90
❑ 96ClaGol-90
**Oliveira, Mike**
❑ 95Sla-122
**Oliveira, Sam**
❑ 917thInnSOHL-7
❑ 91CorRoy-9
**Oliver, David**

91MicWol-11
93MicWol-17
94CapBreO-16
94Cla-57
94ClaAllAme-AA6
94ClaDraGol-57
94ClaROYS-R16
94ClaTri-T22
94FinBowB-R6
94FinBowBR-R6
94Fla-60
94Fle-74
94ParSE-SE60
94ParSEG-SE60
94Pin-490
94PinArtP-490
94PinRinC-490
94SPPre-13
94SPPreDC-13
94UppDec-269
94UppDecEleIce-269
94UppDecSPI-SP117
94UppDecSPIDC-SP117
95BeAPla-64
95BeAPSig-S64
95BeAPSigDC-S64
95CanGamNHLP-34
95CanGamNHLP-108
95ColCho-13
95ColChoPC-13
95ColChoPCP-13
95ColEdgI-35
95ColEdgIC-C7
95Don-8
95DonRooTea-4
95Emo-65
95Fin-62
95FinRef-62
95Ima-79
95ImaAut-79A
95ImaGol-79
95Lea-9
95LeaLim-89
95LeaStuR-4
95Met-55
95ParInt-76
95ParIntEl-76
95Pin-42
95PinArtP-42
95PinRinC-42
95PlaOneoOne-38
95Sco-60
95ScoBlaIce-60
95ScoBlaIceAP-60
95SkyImp-63
95SkyImp-231
95SkyImpNHLF-3
95StaClu-109
95StaCluMOMS-109
95Sum-98
95SumArtP-98
95SumIce-98
95Top-366
95TopHidGem-8HG
95TopNewG-14NG
95TopOPCI-366
95TopSupSki-71
95TopSupSkiPla-71
95Ult-56
95UltAllRoo-10
95UltAllRooGM-10
95UltGolM-56
95UppDec-167
95UppDecEleIce-167
95UppDecEleIceG-167
95UppDecSpeE-SE120
95UppDecSpeEdiG-SE120
96ColCho-96
96Pin-51
96PinArtP-51
96PinFoi-51
96PinPreS-51
96PinRinC-51
96PlaOneoOne-358
96Sco-193
96ScoArtPro-193
96ScoDeaCAP-193
96ScoGolB-193
96ScoSpeAP-193
96UppDec-60
**Oliver, Harold (Harry)**
23V1281PauC-69
330PCV304A-9
33V129-39
33V3357IceK-23
34DiaMatS-48
35DiaMatT2-52
35DiaMatT3-49
35DiaMatTl-52
38BruGarMS-5
83HalFP-K12
85HalFC-146
**Oliver, Lawrence**
92BriColJHL-230
**Oliver, Murray**
44BeeGro2P-52
44BeeGro2P-199
60Par-22
60ShiCoi-55
60TopSta-42
61ShiCoi-8
61Top-14
62Top-12
62TopHocBuc-19
63Top-10

64BeeGro3P-20
64CocCap-11
64Top-79
65Coc-9
65Top-34
66Top-95
67Top-82
68MapLeaWB-6
68OPC-194
68PosCerM-16
68ShiCoi-167
69MapLeaWBG-24
69OPC-52
69Top-52
70DadCoo-91
70EssPowPla-170
70OPC-167
70SarProSta-86
71OPC-239
71SarProSta-88
71TorSun-141
72SarProSta-107
73NorStaP-15
74NHLActSta-130
74OPCanHul-291
75OPCNHL-335
80NorStaPos-14
94ParTalB-2
94ParTalB-169
95Par66-9
95Par66-140
95Par66Coi-9
**Oliver, Simon**
92MPSPhoSJHL-2
**Oliverio, Mike**
83SauSteMG-17
84SauSteMG-15
87SauSteMG-17
**Olivestedt, Mattias**
93SweSemE-232
**Oliwa, Krzysztof**
94ClaProP-73
97Be A PPAD-229
97Be A PPAPD-229
97BeAPla-229
97BeAPlaAut-229
97PacOme-133
97PacOmeC-133
97PacOmeDG-133
97PacOmeEG-133
97PacOmeG-133
97PacOmeIB-133
97UppDec-302
98Pac-268
98PacIceB-268
98PacOmeH-140
98PacOmeODI-140
98PacOmeR-140
98PacPar-137
98PacParC-137
98PacParEG-137
98PacParH-137
98PacParIB-137
98PacParS-137
98PacRed-268
98UppDec-117
98UppDecE-117
98UppDecE1o1-117
98UppDecGR-117
99Pac-244
99PacCop-244
99PacGol-244
99PacIceB-244
99PacPreD-244
**Ollila, Jukka**
93FinnJyvHS-80
93FinnSIS-112
93UppDec-269
94FinnSIS-330
95FinnSIS-313
**Ollson, John**
82Ott67-15
83SprInd-5
85NovScoO-9
**Olmstead, Bert**
44BeeGro2P-132
44BeeGro2P-276
44BeeGro2P-442
45QuaOatP-103
48ExhCan-20
51Par-5
52Par-93
53Par-19
54Par-5
55Par-42
55ParQuaO-42
57Par-M19
57Par-M25
58Par-27
59Par-40
60Par-4
60ShiCoi-11
60YorPreP-26
61Par-4
61ShiCoi-52
61YorYelB-19
62ShiMetC-11
62Top-57
63MapLeaWB-19
85HalFC-248
93OPCCanHF-58
93ParParR-PR56
94ParMisL-71
94ParMisL-146
**Olofsson, Bo**

65SweCorI-214
67SweHoc-274
69SweHoc-51
70SweHoc-12
71SweHoc-89
72SweHoc-57
73SweHoc-207
73SweWorCS-207
**Olofsson, Kurt**
67SweHoc-226
69SweHoc-342
70SweHoc-258
71SweHoc-318
**Olofsson, Stefan**
93SweSemE-16
**Olofsson, Thomas**
85SwePanS-201
**Olofsson, Tony**
89SweSemE-177
90SweSemE-11
**Oloriz, Ted**
90ForSasTra-12
**Olsen, Darryl**
89ProIHL-195
90ProAHLIHL-604
91ProAHLCHL-577
**Olsen, Eric**
95Sla-108
**Olsen, Jan**
64SweCorI-94
65SweCorI-94
67SweHoc-296
69SweHocS-343
70SweHocS-248
71SweHocS-305
72SweHocS-290
**Olsen, Oystein**
93SweSemWCS-242
**Olsen, Sten**
64SweCorI-153
65SweCorI-153
67SweHoc-126
69SweHocS-140
**Olsen, Tom Erik**
93SweSemWCS-247
**Olson, Bob**
91MicTecHus-15
**Olson, Boyd**
95TriAme-19
**Olson, Eddie**
51CleBar-5
**Olson, Jarrod**
92NorDakFS-24
**Olsson, Andreas**
94SweLeaE-253
**Olsson, Bert-Ake**
69SweHocS-233
**Olsson, Bo**
67SweHoc-146
69SweHocS-160
72SweHocS-284
**Olsson, Christer**
92SweSemE-60
93SweSemE-35
94SweLeaE-97
95SweLeaEM-14
96SenPizH-18
96SweSemW-50
96SweSemWAS-AS2
97PacDayBKS-66
**Olsson, Dag**
65SweCorI-199
71SweHocS-385
**Olsson, Eine**
65SweCorI-105
**Olsson, Fredrik**
90SweSemE-218
**Olsson, Hakan**
67SweHoc-275
69SweHocS-319
70SweHocS-213
84SweSemE-167
**Olsson, Jan**
71SweHoc-90
72SweHoc-59
73SweHoc-203
73SweWorCS-203
74SweHoc-180
**Olsson, Kent**
67SweHoc-92
71SweHocS-141
83SweSemE-129
**Olsson, Leif**
71SweHocS-157
**Olsson, Mattias**
89SweSemE-82
90SweSemE-255
91SweSemE-86
92SweSemE-110
93SweSemE-83
94SweLeaE-225
95SweLeaEA-296
95SweUppDE-191
**Olsson, Nils-Olov**
73SweHoc-56
73SweWorCS-56
74SweHocS-258
79PanSti-199
**Olsson, Olle**
69SweHocS-234
**Olsson, Ove**
82SweSemHVS-20
83SweSemE-144
84SweSemE-165

85SwePanS-127
85SwePanS-128
85SwePanS-149
86SwePanS-154
**Olsson, Per-Erik**
71SweHocS-207
**Olsson, Peter**
95SweUppDE1DS-DS19
**Olsson, Roger**
65SweCorI-170
67SweHoc-19
67SweHoc-297
69SweHocS-196
69SweHocS-344
69SweWorC-108
70SweHocS-259
70SweHocS-289
71SweHocS-319
72SweHocS-299
73SweHocS-142
73SweWorCS-142
**Olsson, Stefan**
89SweSemE-231
90SweSemE-70
91SweSemE-244
**Olsson, Sten-Olov**
69SweHocS-267
**Olsson, Sven-Ove**
71SweHocS-153
**Olund, Tomas**
89SweSemE-47
90SweSemE-195
**Olvestad, Jimmie**
98SPXTopP-81
98SPXTopPF-81
98SPXTopPR-81
98UppDecBD-111
98UppDecDD-111
98UppDecQD-111
98UppDecTD-111
**Olympiev, Sergei**
93KitRan-26
94KitRan-24
96AlaGolKin-12
**Olympique, Francois**
907thInnSQMJHL-127
**Ondrejik, Viliam**
96SloPeeWT-20
**Ondrejka, Martin**
94GerDELE-215
95GerDELE-214
**Onlangs, Van**
79PanSti-280
**Onofrychuk, Darryl**
917thInnSWHL-158
**Opp, Darren**
91AirCanSJHL-D19
91AirCanSJHLAS-39
91AirCanSJHLAS-47
**Opulskis, Juris**
94CzeAPSE-127
**Oqvist, Tore**
81SweSemHVS-18
85SwePanS-43
86SwePanS-15
87SwePanS-35
**Orban, Bill**
67Top-109
**Orct, Zdenek**
94CzeAPSE-203
95CzeAPSE-150
96CzeAPSE-177
**Ordman, Rob**
83BraWheK-8
**Orekhovski, Oleg**
95Cla-65
95ClaAut-16
95SigRooFF-FF6
95SigRooFFS-FF6
**Organ, Jamie**
97GulFla-17
**Orlando, Gates**
85SabBluS-18
85SabBluSS-18
86SabBluS-20
86SabBluSSma-20
93SweSemWCS-218
94FinnJaaK-299
**Orlando, Jimmy**
34BeeGro1P-119
390PCV3011-65
76OldTim-11
**Orlov, Vladimir**
73SweHocS-126
73SweWorCS-126
**Ornskog, Stefan**
89SweSemE-115
90SweSemE-116
91SweSemE-118
92SweSemE-140
93SweSemE-110
94SweLeaE-28
95FinnSemWC-71
95SweGloWC-39
95SweLeaEC-11
95SweLeaE-G-6
95SweUppDE-83

**Orr, Bobby**
66Top-35
66TopUSAT-35
67GenMil-5
67Top-92
67Top-118
67Top-128
68OPC-200
68OPC-214
68OPCPucSti-4
68ShiCoi-5
68Top-2
69OPC-24
69OPC-209
69OPC-212
69OPCFou-11
69OPCSta-22
69Top-24
70BruPos-16
70BruTeaIss-16
70ColSta-87
70DadCoo-92
70EssPowPla-56
70OPC-3
70OPC-236
70OPC-246
70OPC-248A
70OPC-248B
70OPC-249
70OPC-252
70OPCDec-4
70PosCerS-12
70SarProSta-1
70Top-3
70TopStiS-24
71Baz-36
71ColHea-8
71LetActR-5
71LetActR-17
71MatMinRec-7
71OPC-100
71OPC-245
71OPC-251
71OPCPos-1
71OPCTBoo-24
71SarProSta-10
71SweHocS-196
71Top-2
71Top-3
71Top-100
71TorSun-15
72OPC-58
72OPC-129
72OPC-227
72OPC-280
72OPC-283
72OPCPlaC-3
72SarProSta-17
72SweHocS-113
72SweSemWC-223
72Top-62
72Top-63
72Top-100
72Top-122
73MacMil-19
73OPC-30
73OPC-150
74LipSou-8
74NHLActSta-19
74OPCNHL-2
74OPCNHL-28
74OPCNHL-100
74OPCNHL-130
74OPCNHL-248
74Top-2
74Top-28
74Top-100
74Top-130
74Top-248
75HerSta-3
75OPCNHL-100
75OPCNHL-209
75OPCNHL-210
75OPCNHL-288
75OPCNHL-314
75Top-100
75Top-209
75Top-210
75Top-288
75Top-314
76OPCNHL-213
76Top-213
76TopGlol-20
77Coc-17
77OPCNHL-251
77Top-251
78OPC-300
80OshGen-25
81TCMA-9
83HalFP-E13
85HalFC-61
88EssAllSta-33
91BayBobO-1
91BayBobO-2
91BayBobO-3
91BayBobO-NNO
91BruSpoAL-20
91Pin-392
91PinFre-392
91ScoBobO-1
91ScoBobO-2
91ScoBobO-3
91ScoBobO-4

91ScoBobO-5
91ScoBobO-6
91ScoBobO-AU
91SweSemWCS-237
92FutTre7CC-104
92FutTre7CC-126
92FutTre7CC-184
92FutTre7CC-196
92HalFL-4
95BayBobO-1
95BayBobO-2
95Par66-7
95Par66-SR1
95Par66-SR2
95Par66-SR3
95Par66-SR4
95Par66-SR5
95Par66-SRA1
95Par66-SRA2
95Par66-SRA3
95Par66-SRA4
95Par66-SRA5
95Par66Coi-7
95Par66Coi-BO1
95Par66Coi-BO2
95Par66Coi-BO3
95Par66Coi-BO4
95Par66Coi-BO5
95PinFan-31
97HigMinHLMC-3
97HigMinHLMC-4
97HigMinHMC-11
99RetHoc-81
99UppDecCA-C6
99UppDecCL-2
99UppDecCLACT-AC4
99UppDecCLCLC-2
99UppDecEotG-E2
99UppDecES-1
99UppDecRDR-DR10
99UppDecRDRI-DR10
99UppDecRG-G1A
99UppDecRG-G4B
99UppDecRGI-G1A
99UppDecRGI-G4B
99UppDecRII-BO
99UppDecRIL1-BO
99UppDecRP-81
99UppDecRTotC-TC15
**Orr, Clint**
96RegPat-19
**Orrgren, Kent**
89SweSemE-285
**Orsolini, Lionel**
94FinnJaaK-227
94FreNatT-21
**Ortiz, Sean**
95DayBom-2
**Osborne, Brad**
88BroBra-20
**Osborne, Don**
90MicTecHus-17
91MicTecHus-16
93ThuBayS-8
94ThuBayS-19
**Osborne, Keith**
88NiaFalT-15
89ProIHL-21
90ProAHLIHL-76
91ProAHLCHL-341
93ClaProPro-85
93UppDec-76
93PeoRiv-15
**Osborne, Mark**
82OPC-93
82OPCSti-182
82PosCer-5
83OPC-252
84OPC-148
84Top-110
87MapLeaP-15
87MapLeaPLA-23
87MapLeaPO-15
88MapLeaPLA-23
88OPC-241
88OPCSti-168
88PanSti-127
89OPC-274
89OPCSti-174
89PanSti-138
90Bow-156
90BowTif-156
90JetIGA-27
90OPC-227
90PanSti-278
90ProSet-287
90ProSet-564
90Sco-104
90ScoCan-104
90ScoRoo-28T
90Top-227
90TopTif-227
90UppDec-5
90UppDecF-5
91Bow-209
91JetIGA-23
91MapLeaPTS-18
91OPC-345
91PanSti-77
91Pin-96
91PinFre-96
91ProSet-270
91ProSetFre-270

91ScoAme-39
91ScoCan-39
91StaClu-21
91Top-345
91UppDec-296
91UppDecF-296
92MapLeaK-18
92Pin-305
92PinFre-305
92Sco-277
92ScoCan-277
92StaClu-379
92Top-77
92TopGol-77G
92UppDec-72
93OPCPre-268
93OPCPreG-268
93Par-476
93ParEmel-476
93Pow-452
93Sco-316
93ScoBla-7
93ScoCan-316
93TopPre-268
93TopPreG-268
93Ult-433
94BeAPla-R113
94BeAPSig-18
94Lea-503
94MapLeaG-14
94Pin-500
94PinArtP-500
94PinRinC-500
94StaClu-76
94StaCluFDI-76
94StaCluMOMS-76
94StaCluSTWC-76
94Ult-335
94UppDec-316
94UppDecEleIce-316
95CleLum-19
96CleLum-19
**Osborne, Matt**
95Cla-93
95Sla-299
95UppDec-515
95UppDecEleIce-515
95UppDecEleIceG-515
**Osburn, Randy**
72MapLeaP-29
**Osgood, Chris**
907thInnSWHL-24
917thInnSMC-123
917thInnSWHL-196
91Cla-43
91StaPicH-55
91UltDra-38
93ClaProPro-26
93Don-424
93Par-329
93ParCalC-C17
93ParCalCG-C17
93ParEmel-329
93Pin-431
93PinCan-431
93Pow-334
93PowRooS-9
93Sco-609
93ScoCan-609
93ScoGol-609
93StaClu-350
93StaCluFDI-350
93StaCluO-350
93Ult-308
93UltWavF-12
93UppDec-519
94ClaProP-28
94Don-251
94Fle-63
94Lea-315
94LeaGolR-10
94LeaLim-96
94OPCFinIns-8
94OPCPre-87
94OPCPre-199
94OPCPreSE-87
94OPCPreSE-199
94Par-283
94ParGol-283
94ParSE-SE54
94ParSEG-SE54
94Pin-199
94Pin-471
94PinArtP-199
94PinArtP-471
94PinGoaG-GT16
94PinRinC-199
94PinRinC-471
94Sco-256
94ScoGol-256
94ScoPla-256
94ScoPlaTS-256
94StaClu-138
94StaCluFDI-138
94StaCluMOMS-138
94StaCluST-7
94StaCluSTWC-138
94TopPre-87
94TopPre-199
94TopPreSE-87
94TopPreSE-199
94Ult-64
94UppDec-130
94UppDecEleIce-130
95BeAPla-193

94FinDivFCC-17
94FinRef-57
94FinSupTW-57
94Fla-169
94Fle-200
94FleFraFrut-6
94Lea-169
94LeaLim-43
94McDUppD-McD11
94OPCPre-239
94OPCPre-430
94OPCPreSE-239
94OPCPreSE-430
94Par-208
94ParCratGB-21
94ParCratGG-21
94ParCratGR-21
94ParGol-208
94ParVin-V7
94Pin-22
94PinArtP-22
94PinRinC-22
94PinWorEdi-WE11
94Sco-36
94ScoGol-36
94ScoPla-36
94ScoPlaTS-36
94Sel-63
94SelGol-63
94SP-108
94SPDieCut-108
94StaClu-177
94StaClu-204
94StaCluFDI-177
94StaCluFDI-204
94StaCluMO-11
94StaCluMOMS-177
94StaCluMOMS-204
94StaCluSTWC-177
94StaCluSTWC-204
94TopPre-239
94TopPre-430
94TopPreSE-239
94TopPreSE-430
94Ult-200
94UppDec-490
94UppDecElelce-490
94UppDecPC-C27
94UppDecPCEG-C27
94UppDecSPI-SP73
94UppDecSPIDC-SP73
95BeAPla-183
95BeAPSig-S183
95BeAPSigDC-S183
95CanGamNHLP-231
95ColCho-9
95ColChoPC-9
95ColChoPCP-9
95Don-34
95DonEli-93
95DonEliDCS-93
95DonEliDCU-93
95Emo-159
95Fin-141
95FinRef-141
95ImpSti-29
95KenStaLA-14
95Lea-183
95Met-35
95ParInt-185
95ParInt-320
95ParIntAS-2
95ParIntEI-185
95ParIntEI-320
95PlaOneoOne-193
95Sco-67
95ScoBlaIce-67
95ScoBlaIceAP-67
95SkyImp-39
95SP-32
95Sum-137
95SumArtP-137
95SumIce-137
95Ult-149
95Ult-224
95UltGolM-149
95UppDec-168
95UppDec-470
95UppDecElelce-168
95UppDecElelce-470
95UppDecElelceG-168
95UppDecElelceG-470
95UppDecSpeE-SE109
95UppDecSpeEdiG-SE109
95Zen-101
96ColCho-60
96ColChoMVP-UD35
96ColChoMVPG-UD35
96ColEdgFL-46
96Don-104
96DonPrePro-104
96Fla-19
96FlaBlul-19
96Fle-23
96FleNor-10
96FlePicDL-9
96FlePicF5-37
96FlePicJE-8
96Lea-197
96LeaPreP-197
96MetUni-36
96Pin-159
96PinArtP-159
96PinFoi-159
96PinPreS-159
96PinRinC-159
96PlaOneoOne-385
96Sco-43
96ScoArtPro-43
96ScoDeaCAP-43
96ScoGolB-43
96ScoSpeAP-43
96SkyImp-26
96SkyImpNHLF-17
96Sum-12
96SumArtP-12
96SumIce-12
96SumMet-12
96SumPreS-12
96TeaOut-54
96TopNHLP-21
96TopPicOI-21
96Ult-38
96UltGolM-38
96UppDec-37
96UppDecBD-98
96UppDecBDG-98
96UppDecGN-X9
96UppDecIce-80
96UppDecIcePar-80
96UppDecSS-SS20B
97Be A PPAD-115
97Be A PPAPD-115
97BeAPla-115
97BeAPlaAut-115
97ColCho-60
97ColChoSta-SQ38
97Don-60
97DonCanI-119
97DonCanIDS-119
97DonCanIPS-119
97DonEli-83
97DonEliAsp-83
97DonEliS-83
97DonLim-106
97DonLim-145
97DonLimExp-106
97DonLimExp-145
97DonLin2L-24
97DonLin2LDC-24
97DonPre-103
97DonPreCttC-103
97DonPreProG-60
97DonPreProS-60
97DonPri-45
97DonPriSoA-45
97Kat-40
97KatGol-40
97KatSil-40
97Lea-118
97LeaFraMat-118
97LeaFraMDC-118
97LeaInt-118
97LeaIntUI-118
97Pac-75
97PacCop-75
97PacDyn-32
97PacDynC-32
97PacDynEG-32
97PacDynIB-32
97PacDynR-32
97PacDynSil-32
97PacDynTan-41
97PacEmeGre-75
97PacIceB-75
97PacInv-37
97PacInvC-37
97PacInvEG-37
97PacInvIB-37
97PacInvR-37
97PacInvS-37
97PacOme-63
97PacOmeC-63
97PacOmeDG-63
97PacOmeEG-63
97PacOmeIB-63
97PacPar-53
97PacParDG-53
97PacParEG-53
97PacParIB-53
97PacParRed-53
97PacParSil-53
97PacRed-75
97PacRev-37
97PacRevC-37
97PacRevE-37
97PacRevIB-37
97PacRevR-37
97PacRevS-37
97PacSil-75
97Pin-128
97PinCer-89
97PinCerMB-89
97PinCerMG-89
97PinCerMR-89
97PinCerR-89
97PinIns-137
97PinPrePBB-128
97PinPrePBC-128
97PinPrePBM-128
97PinPrePBY-128
97PinPrePFC-128
97PinPrePFM-128
97PinPrePFY-128
97PinPrePla-128
97PinTotCMPG-89
97PinTotCPB-89
97PinTotCPG-89
97PinTotCPR-89
97Sco-174
97ScoAva-6
97ScoAvaPla-6
97ScoAvaPre-6
97SPAut-41
97Stu-82
97StuPrePG-82
97StuPrePS-82
97UppDec-44
97UppDecBD-27
97UppDecBDDD-27
97UppDecBDTD-27
97UppDecCtAG-10
97UppDecCtAG-AR10
97UppDecIce-24
97UppDecIceP-24
97UppDecIPS-24
97UppDecSG-SG28
97UppDecTSS-20C
98Be A PPA-188
98Be A PPAA-188
98Be A PPAAF-188
98Be A PPSE-188
98Be APG-188
98Fin-116
98FinNo P-116
98FinNo PR-116
98FinRef-116
980-PChr-121
980-PChrBM-B10
980-PChrBMR-B10
980-PChrR-121
98Pac-167
98PacAur-50
98PacIceB-167
98PacOmeH-63
98PacOmeODI-63
98PacOmeR-63
98PacPar-59
98PacParC-59
98PacParEG-59
98PacParH-59
98PacParIB-59
98PacParS-59
98PacRed-167
98Top-121
98TopBoaM-B10
98TopO-P-121
98UC-60
98UD ChoPCR-60
98UD ChoR-60
98UppDec-250
98UppDecE-250
98UppDecE1o1-250
98UppDecGR-250
99Pac-113
99PacCop-113
99PacGol-113
99PacIceB-113
99PacPreD-113
99UppDecM-56
99UppDecMGS-56
99UppDecMSS-56
99UppDecMSS-56

**Paananen, Mika**
93FinJyvHS-147
93FinnSIS-148
93FinnSIS-82
95FinnSIS-61
96FinnSISR-62

**Pacal, Tomas**
94CzeAPSE-32
94CzeAPSE-148

**Pachal, Clayton**
77RocAme-18

**Paclik, Robert**
94GerDELE-27

**Pacquet, Normand**
907thInnSQMJHL-212

**Pacula, Ireneusz**
89SweSemWCS-149
94GerDELE-160
95GerDELE-160

**Paddock, Gordon (Gord)**
83BraWheK-3
88ProAHL-127
89ProAHL-351
90ProAHLIHL-524

**Paddock, John**
80NordPos-20
80PepCap-73
88ProAHL-142
90ProAHLIHL-15
91JetIGA-24
93JetRuf-20

**Padelek, Ivan**
95CzeAPSE-13
95CzeAPSE-231

**Paden, Kevin**
94WinSpi-15
95TalTigS-8

**Paek, Jim**
88ProIHL-59
89ProIHL-158
90AlbIntTC-7
910PC-437
91Par-133
91ParFre-133
91PenCokE-2
91PenFoo-1
91Pin-344
91PinFre-344
91ProSet-554
91ProSetFre-554
91ProSetPla-266
91Top-427
91UppDec-308
91UppDecF-308
92Bow-383
920PC-328
92Par-375
92ParEmeI-375
92PenCokC-16
92PenFoo-11
92Sco-537
92ScoCan-537
92StaClu-437
92Top-243
92TopGol-243G
92Ult-168
930PCPre-243
930PCPreG-243
93PenFoo-9
93Pin-278
93PinCan-278
93Sco-334
93ScoCan-334
93StaClu-401
93StaCluO-401
93TopPre-243
93TopPreG-243
93UppDec-192
94Lea-512
940PCPre-422
940PCPreSE-422
94Pin-389
94PinArtP-389
94PinRinC-389
94SenBelM-25
94TopPre-422
94TopPreSE-422
95PlaOneoOne-288
96ColLeum-20

**Page, Alexandre**
98Vald'OF-21

**Page, Anthony**
97GuiFla-13

**Page, Fred**
93ActPacHOFI-9

**Page, Margot**
94ClaWomOH-W10

**Page, Pierre**
84MonGolF-3
85FlamRedRP-20
86FlamRedR-11
87FlamRedRP-22
91NordPet-22
92NorPet-23

**Page, Scott**
96SudWol-16
96SudWolP-18
97SudWolP-8

**Pageau, Cory**
907thInnSOHL-268

**Pagel, Rico**
96MinGolGCAS-22

**Paget, Derek**
96PriAlbR-14
96PriAlbROC-16

**Pagnutti, Rick**
71RocAme-15

**Pahlsson, Samuel**
95SP-183
95SweLeaE-273
95SweUppDE-168

**Paice, Frank**
62Top-61

**Paiement, Real**
81MilAdm-2

**Paiement, Rosaire**
70CanuRoyB-11
70ColSta-39
70DadCoo-94
70EssPowPla-48
700PC-226
70SarProSta-220
71CanuRoyB-9
710PC-233
71SarProSta-218
71Top-24
71TorSun-285
72CanuNal-4
720PC-333
730PCWHAP-5
73QuaOatWHA-3
740PCWHA-7
750PCWHA-106
760PCWHA-37
770PCWHA-36

**Paiement, Steven**
907thInnSQMJHL-126

**Paiement, Wilf**
740PCNHL-292
750PCNHL-195
750PCNHL-319
75Top-195
75Top-89
760PCNHL-37
76RocCokCan-15
76RocPucBuc-14
76Top-37
770PCNHL-130
77RocCokCan-14
77Top-130
780PC-145
78Top-145
790PC-190
79PanSti-67
79Top-190
80MapLeaP-19
800PC-225
80PepCap-93
80Top-225
81MapLeaP-17
810PC-306
810PC-311
810PC-326
810PCSti-96
810PCSti-110
81PosSta-22
81Top-25
81Top-63
82NordPos-15
820PC-288
820PCSti-22
82PosCer-16
83NordPos-19
830PC-298
83Vac-70
84NordPos-19
840PC-285
840PCSti-175
85NordPro-18
850PCSti-152
86NordMcD-18
86SabBluS-21
86SabBluSSma-21
870PC-180
87PanSti-32
87Top-180

**Paille, Marcel**
44BeeGro2P-350
50QueCit-16
52JunBluT-64
64BeeGro3P-145
64CocCap-90
64Top-92
94ParTalB-101

**Pain, Jason**
96ColCho-156

**Painchaud, Marco**
92QueIntP-43

**Paine, Greg**
91FerStaB-25

**Painter, Glenn**
95MadMon-19
96ForWorF-8

**Pajerski, ?**
69SweWorC-200

**Pajonkowski, Franck**
93SweSemWCS-264
94FinnJaaK-230
94FreNatT-22
95SweGloWC-201
96SweSemW-190

**Paladjev, Evgenij**
69SweWorC-131
69SweWorC-137
70SweHocS-317

**Palamar, Ed**
96DonCanI-58
96DonCanIGPP-58
96DonCanIRPP-58

**Paladin, ?** / **Palffy, Zigmund**
96DonEli-52
96DonEliDCS-52
96DonPrePro-45
96Fla-56
96FleBlul-56
96Fle-66
96FlePic-50
96FlePicJE-20
96IslPos-16
96KraUppD-9
96KraUppD-38
96Lea-23
96LeaFirIOl-7
96LeaLeaAL-7
96LeaLeaALP-P7
96LeaLim-57
96LeaLimG-57
96LeaPre-103
96LeaPreP-23
96LeaPrePP-103
96LeaPreSG-32
96LeaPreSte-32
96MetUni-95
96Pin-100
96PinArtP-100
96PinFoi-100
96PinMcD-18
96PinPreS-100
96PinRinC-100
96PlaOneoOne-379
96Sco-120
96ScoArtPro-120
96ScoDeaCAP-120
96ScoGolB-120
96ScoSpeAP-120
96SelCer-23
96SelCerAP-23
96SelCerBlu-23
96SelCerMB-23
96SelCerMG-23
96SelCerMR-23
96SelCerRed-23
96SkyImp-77
96SkyImpB-18
96SP-97
96SPHolCol-HC28
96SPx-29
96SPxGol-29
96Sum-20
96SumArtP-20
96SumIce-20
96SumMet-20
96SumPreS-20
96SweSemW-234
96TeaOut-15
96Ult-103
96UltGolM-103
96UppDec-97
96UppDecBD-6
96UppDecBDG-6
95BeAPla-24
95BeAPSig-S24
95BeAPSigDC-S24
95BowAllFoi-31
95CanGamNHLP-169
95ColChoPC-94
95ColChoPCP-94
95ColEdgI-195
95ColEdgIC-C24
95Don-316
95DonEli-13
95DonEliDCS-13
95DonEliDCU-13
95Fin-117
95FinRef-117
95Met-92
95ParInt-131
95ParIntEI-131
95Pin-88
95PinArtP-88
95PinGloG-14
95PinRinC-88
95PlaOneoOne-172
95Sco-267
95ScoBlaIce-267
95ScoBlaIceAP-267
95SloAPSNT-24
95SP-86
95StaClu-99
95StaCluMOMS-99
95Sum-144
95SumArtP-144
95SumIce-144
95Top-348
95TopOPCI-348
95Ult-97
95Ult-269
95UltGolM-97
95UltHigSpe-14
95UppDec-140
95UppDecElelce-140
95UppDecElelceG-140
95UppDecSpeE-SE51
95UppDecSpeEdiG-SE51
96BeAPBisITB-15
96ColCho-166
96ColCho-323
96ColChoMVP-UD24
96ColChoMVPG-UD24
96Don-45
96UppDecGN-X17
96UppDecIce-94
96UppDecIcePar-94
96UppDecSS-SS21A
96Zen-97
96ZenArtP-97
96ZenAss-7
97Be A PPAD-135
97Be A PPAPD-135
97BeAPla-135
97BeAPlaAut-135
97ColCho-150
97ColChoCTG-C16A
97ColChoCTG-C16B
97ColChoCTG-C16C
97ColChoCTG-CR16
97ColChoSta-SQ66
97ColChoSti-S16
97Don-125
97DonCanI-33
97DonCanIDS-33
97DonCanIPS-33
97DonEli-34
97DonEli-130
97DonEliAsp-34
97DonEliAsp-130
97DonEliS-34
97DonEliS-130
97DonLim-12
97DonLim-163
97DonLim-181
97DonLimExp-12
97DonLimExp-163
97DonLimExp-181
97DonLimFOTG-24
97DonPre-106
97DonPreCttC-106
97DonPreProG-125
97DonPreProS-125
97DonPri-58
97DonPri-212
97DonPriDD-22
97DonPriDD-P22
97DonPriP-32
97DonPriS-32
97DonPriSB-32
97DonPriSG-32
97DonPriSoA-58
97DonPriSoA-212
97DonPriSoA-32
97DonRedAle-8
97Kat-90
97KatGol-90
97KatSil-90
97Lea-55
97LeaBanSea-12
97LeaFraMat-55
97LeaFraMDC-55
97LeaInt-55
97LeaIntUI-55
97Pac-5
97PacCop-5
97PacCroR-79
97PacCroREG-79
97PacCroRHTDC-10
97PacCroRIB-79
97PacCroRS-79
97PacDyn-74
97PacDynBKS-57
97PacDynC-74
97PacDynDD-9B
97PacDynDG-74
97PacDynEG-74
97PacDynIB-74
97PacDynR-74
97PacDynSil-74
97PacDynTan-11
97PacEmeGre-5
97PacIceB-5
97PacInv-82
97PacInvAZ-13
97PacInvC-82
97PacInvEG-82
97PacInvFP-20
97PacInvIB-82
97PacInvNRB-119
97PacInvR-82
97PacInvS-82
97PacOme-140
97PacOmeC-140
97PacOmeDG-140
97PacOmeEG-140
97PacOmeG-140
97PacOmeIB-140
97PacOmeSLC-12
97PacPar-109
97PacParDG-109
97PacParEG-109
97PacParIB-109
97PacParRed-109
97PacParSil-109
97PacRed-5
97PacRev-82
97PacRevC-82
97PacRevE-82
97PacRevIB-82
97PacRevR-82
97PacRevS-82
97PacRevTCL-15
97PacSil-5
97PacTeaCCC-15
97Pin-56
97PinArtP-56
97PinBee-42

❑ 97PinBeeGP-42
❑ 97PinCer-94
❑ 97PinCerMB-94
❑ 97PinCerMG-94
❑ 97PinCerMR-94
❑ 97PinCerR-94
❑ 97PinIns-14
❑ 97PinInsCC-14
❑ 97PinInsEC-14
❑ 97PinInsT-22
❑ 97PinPrePBB-56
❑ 97PinPrePBC-56
❑ 97PinPrePBM-56
❑ 97PinPrePBY-56
❑ 97PinPrePFC-56
❑ 97PinPrePFM-56
❑ 97PinPrePFY-56
❑ 97PinPrePla-56
❑ 97PinRinC-56
❑ 97PinTotCMPG-94
❑ 97PinTotCPB-94
❑ 97PinTotCPG-94
❑ 97PinTotCPR-94
❑ 97Sco-106
❑ 97ScoArtPro-106
❑ 97ScoGolBla-106
❑ 97SP AutI-I38
❑ 97SPAut-91
❑ 97SPAutID-I38
❑ 97SPAutIE-I38
❑ 97SPx-28
❑ 97SPxBro-28
❑ 97SPxDim-SPX13
❑ 97SPxGol-28
❑ 97SPxGraF-28
❑ 97SPxSil-28
❑ 97SPxSte-28
❑ 97Stu-46
❑ 97StuHarH-13
❑ 97StuPor-31
❑ 97StuPrePG-46
❑ 97StuPrePS-46
❑ 97UppDec-99
❑ 97UppDecBD-18
❑ 97UppDecBDDD-18
❑ 97UppDecBDQD-18
❑ 97UppDecBDTD-18
❑ 97UppDecDV-21
❑ 97UppDecDVSM-21
❑ 97UppDecIce-16
❑ 97UppDecIceP-16
❑ 97UppDecIPS-16
❑ 97UppDecSG-SG5
❑ 97UppDecSSM-SS26
❑ 97UppDecSSW-SS26
❑ 97UppDecTS-22
❑ 97UppDecTSL2-22
❑ 97Zen-30
❑ 97Zen5x7-27
❑ 97ZenGolImp-27
❑ 97ZenSilImp-27
❑ 97ZenZGol-30
❑ 97ZenZSil-30
❑ 98Be A PPA-236
❑ 98Be A PPAA-236
❑ 98Be A PPAAF-236
❑ 98Be A PPSE-236
❑ 98Be APG-236
❑ 98BowBes-15
❑ 98BowBesAR-15
❑ 98BowBesR-15
❑ 98Fin-40
❑ 98FinCen-C6
❑ 98FinCenR-C6
❑ 98FinNo P-40
❑ 98FinNo PR-40
❑ 98FinRedL-R20
❑ 98FinRedLR-R20
❑ 98FinRef-40
❑ 98IslPowP-NYI4
❑ 98O-PChr-184
❑ 98O-PChrR-184
❑ 98O-PChrSB-SB17
❑ 98O-PChrSBR-SB17
❑ 98Pac-284
❑ 98PacAur-117
❑ 98PacAurCF-29
❑ 98PacAurCFC-29
❑ 98PacAurCFIB-29
❑ 98PacAurCFR-29
❑ 98PacAurCFS-29
❑ 98PacAurMAC-12
❑ 98PacCroR-84
❑ 98PacCroRLS-84
❑ 98PacDynI-116
❑ 98PacDynIIB-116
❑ 98PacDynIR-116
❑ 98PacGolCD-22
❑ 98PacIceB-284
❑ 98PacOmeH-149
❑ 98PacOmeO-21
❑ 98PacOmeODI-149
❑ 98PacOmeR-149
❑ 98PacPar-145
❑ 98PacParC-145
❑ 98PacParEG-145
❑ 98PacParH-145
❑ 98PacParIB-145
❑ 98PacParS-145
❑ 98PacParSDDC-11
❑ 98PacParTCD-16
❑ 98PacRed-284
❑ 98PacRev-89
❑ 98PacRevIS-89
❑ 98PacRevR-89
❑ 98PacRevS-22
❑ 98PacTeaC-16
❑ 98SP Aut-52
❑ 98SP AutSS-SS24
❑ 98SPxFin-114
❑ 98SPxFinR-114
❑ 98SPxFinS-114
❑ 98SPXTopP-36
❑ 98SPXTopPF-36
❑ 98SPXTopPHH-H19
❑ 98SPXTopPLI-L29
❑ 98SPXTopPR-36
❑ 98Top-184
❑ 98TopLocL-L3
❑ 98TopMysFB-M11
❑ 98TopMysFBR-M11
❑ 98TopMysFG-M11
❑ 98TopMysFGR-M11
❑ 98TopMysFS-M11
❑ 98TopMysFSR-M11
❑ 98TopO-P-184
❑ 98TopSeaB-SB17
❑ 98UC-121
❑ 98UCMBH-BH13
❑ 98UD ChoPCR-121
❑ 98UD ChoR-121
❑ 98UD3-44
❑ 98UD3-104
❑ 98UD3-164
❑ 98UD3DieC-44
❑ 98UD3DieC-104
❑ 98UD3DieC-164
❑ 98UDCP-121
❑ 98UppDec-315
❑ 98UppDecBD-53
❑ 98UppDecDD-53
❑ 98UppDecE-315
❑ 98UppDecE1o1-315
❑ 98UppDecFF-FF10
❑ 98UppDecFF-FF10
❑ 98UppDecFFQ1-FF10
❑ 98UppDecFFQ2-FF10
❑ 98UppDecGR-315
❑ 98UppDecM-125
❑ 98UppDecMGS-125
❑ 98UppDecMSS-125
❑ 98UppDecMSS-125
❑ 98UppDecQD-53
❑ 98UppDecTD-53
❑ 98UppDecWFG-WF17
❑ 98UppDecWFP-WF17
❑ 99Pac-261
❑ 99PacAur-69
❑ 99PacAurPD-69
❑ 99PacCop-261
❑ 99PacGol-261
❑ 99PacHomaA-16
❑ 99PacIceB-261
❑ 99PacPreD-261
❑ 99PacTeaL-17
❑ 99RetHoc-53
❑ 99SP AutPS-52
❑ 99UppDecM-123
❑ 99UppDecMGS-GU3
❑ 99UppDecMGS-123
❑ 99UppDecMGUSA-GU3
❑ 99UppDecMSS-123
❑ 99UppDecMSS-123
❑ 99UppDecRG-53
❑ 99UppDecRII-ZP
❑ 99UppDecRIL1-ZP
❑ 99UppDecRP-53

**Palichuk, Ed**
❑ 82BraWheK-13

**Palinek, Martin**
❑ 95CzeAPSE-231

**Pallante, Rob**
❑ 92NasKni-19

**Pallin, Rob**
❑ 85MinDul-4

**Palm, Jorgen**
❑ 71SweHocS-120
❑ 72SweHocS-102
❑ 73SweHocS-177
❑ 73SweWorCS-177
❑ 74SweHocS-181
❑ 85SwePanS-202
❑ 86SwePanS-198
❑ 89SweSemE-271
❑ 92SweSemE-35
❑ 93SweSemE-292

**Palm, Thomas**
❑ 71SweHocS-128

**Palmateer, Mike**
❑ 76MapLeaP-13
❑ 77MapLeaP-12
❑ 77OPCNHL-211
❑ 77Top-211
❑ 78MapLeaP-17
❑ 78OPC-70
❑ 78OPC-160
❑ 78Top-70
❑ 78Top-160
❑ 79MapLeaP-21
❑ 79MapLeaP-22
❑ 79OPC-197
❑ 79Top-197
❑ 80OPC-95
❑ 80OPCSup-23
❑ 80Top-95
❑ 81Cap-13
❑ 81OPC-351
❑ 81OPC-394
❑ 81OPCSti-194
❑ 81PosSta-9
❑ 81Top-E121
❑ 82MapLeaP-28
❑ 83MapLeaP-20
❑ 83OPC-338
❑ 83OPCSti-39
❑ 83PufSti-5
❑ 83Vac-95
❑ 84OPC-308
❑ 84OPCSti-22

**Palmer, Brad**
❑ 81NorStaPos-19
❑ 82OPC-21
❑ 82PosCer-9
❑ 82VicCou-20
❑ 83BruTeaIss-15

**Palmer, Chris**
❑ 90ProAHLIHL-565

**Palmer, Drew**
❑ 93SeaThu-17
❑ 95SeaThu-20

**Palmer, Jay**
❑ 83BraWheK-12

**Palmer, Rob**
❑ 78OPC-298
❑ 79OPC-352
❑ 80KinCarN-10
❑ 80OPC-104
❑ 80Top-104

**Palmer, Steve**
❑ 92ClaKni-14
❑ 98GerDELE-137

**Palmqvist, Bjorn**
❑ 64SweCorI-9
❑ 64SweCorI-157
❑ 65SweCorI-9
❑ 65SweCorI-157
❑ 67SweHoc-20
❑ 67SweHoc-70
❑ 69SweHocS-101
❑ 69SweHocS-197
❑ 69SweWorC-113
❑ 70SweHocS-58
❑ 70SweHocS-290
❑ 71SweHocS-22
❑ 71SweHocS-129
❑ 72SweHocS-19
❑ 72SweHocS-106
❑ 72SweSemWC-60
❑ 73SweHocS-214
❑ 73SweWorCS-214
❑ 74SweHocS-259
❑ 74SweSemHVS-20

**Palo, Marko**
❑ 93FinnJyvHS-54
❑ 93FinnSIS-244
❑ 93FinnSIS-379
❑ 94FinnJaaK-37
❑ 94FinnSIS-370
❑ 94SweLeaE-197
❑ 95FinnBecAC-8
❑ 95FinnKarWCL-16
❑ 95FinnSemWC-13
❑ 95FinnSISGC-20
❑ 95FinnSISL-88
❑ 95SweLeaE-268
❑ 95SweUppDE-140
❑ 96SweSemW-13

**Palsola, Sakari**
❑ 95FinnSIS-106
❑ 96FinnSISR-102

**Paluch, Scott**
❑ 88ProIHL-76
❑ 89ProIHL-4

**Panchartek, Frantisek**
❑ 71SweHocS-46
❑ 72SweSemWC-26
❑ 74SweSemHVS-73

**Pancoe, Don**
❑ 88NiaFalT-20
❑ 897thInnSOHL-140
❑ 89NiaFalT-14

**Pandolfo, Jay**
❑ 93DonTeaUSA-16
❑ 93Pin-497
❑ 93PinCan-497
❑ 93UppDec-556
❑ 96Dev-20
❑ 96SP-180
❑ 96UppDecBD-21
❑ 96UppDecBDG-21
❑ 97ColCho-145
❑ 97PacDynBKS-53
❑ 97UppDec-93
❑ 98UppDecM-123
❑ 98UppDecMGS-123
❑ 98UppDecMSS-123
❑ 98UppDecMSS-123
❑ 99Pac-245
❑ 99PacCop-245
❑ 99PacGol-245
❑ 99PacIceB-245
❑ 99PacPreD-245

**Panek, Chris**
❑ 88ProAHL-203
❑ 89ProAHL-19
❑ 95GerDELE-49

**Pang, Darren**
❑ 82Ott67-16
❑ 83Ott67-21
❑ 87BlaCok-17
❑ 88BlaCok-15
❑ 88OPC-51
❑ 88OPCSti-8
❑ 88OPCSti-18
❑ 88OPCSti-135
❑ 88OPCSti-151
❑ 88PanSti-21
❑ 88Top-51
❑ 89OPC-31
❑ 89OPCSti-10
❑ 89PanSti-42
❑ 89Top-31

**Panin, Mikhail**
❑ 90OPC-492

**Pankewicz, Greg**
❑ 89RegPat-13
❑ 907thInnSWHL-180
❑ 91KnoChe-9
❑ 94ClaProP-57

**Pankewicz, Trent**
❑ 94CenHocL-66

**Pankov, Dmitri**
❑ 95RicRen-11

**Pankratz, Joe**
❑ 94MinGolG-24

**Pannitto, Mark**
❑ 95NorIowH-25

**Panteleyev, Grigori**
❑ 92Par-243
❑ 92ParEmel-243
❑ 92Ult-254
❑ 92UppDec-492
❑ 93ClaProPro-130
❑ 93Sco-337
❑ 93ScoCan-337
❑ 93Ult-179

**Paolucci, Dan**
❑ 907thInnSQMJHL-144

**Paone, Pat**
❑ 93PetPet-8

**Papike, Joe**
❑ 34BeeGro1P-73

**Papineau, Justin**
❑ 97UppDec-415
❑ 98BowCHL-31
❑ 98BowCHL-149
❑ 98BowCHLAuB-A1
❑ 98BowCHLAuG-A1
❑ 98BowCHLAuS-A1
❑ 98BowCHLGA-31
❑ 98BowCHLGA-149
❑ 98BowCHLOI-31
❑ 98BowCHLOI-149
❑ 98BowChrC-31
❑ 98BowChrC-149
❑ 98BowChrCGA-31
❑ 98BowChrCGA-149
❑ 98BowChrCGAR-31
❑ 98BowChrCGAR-149
❑ 98BowChrCOI-31
❑ 98BowChrCOI-149
❑ 98BowChrCOIR-31
❑ 98BowChrCOIR-149
❑ 98BowChrCR-31
❑ 98BowChrCR-149

**Papineau, Rob**
❑ 907thInnSOHL-113

**Papista, Costa**
❑ 85SudWol-8
❑ 86SudWol-3

**Papp, Jamie**
❑ 93CorBigRed-20

**Pappas, Perry**
❑ 907thInnSOHL-170
❑ 917thInnSMC-13
❑ 917thInnSOHL-319
❑ 93SauSteMGM-11
❑ 96WheNai-18

**Pappin, Jim**
❑ 63RochAme-18
❑ 64BeeGro3P-177
❑ 64Top-64
❑ 64TorSta-35
❑ 65MapLeaWB-14
❑ 65Top-16
❑ 66Top-76
❑ 66TopUSAT-49
❑ 67PosFliB-7
❑ 67Top-78
❑ 67YorActOct-7
❑ 67YorActOct-8
❑ 67YorActOct-32
❑ 68Bla-6
❑ 68OPC-21
❑ 68ShiCoi-34
❑ 68Top-21
❑ 69MapLeaWBG-25
❑ 69OPC-133
❑ 69Top-73
❑ 70BlaBor-11
❑ 70ColSta-43
❑ 70EssPowPla-115
❑ 70OPC-13
❑ 70SarProSta-41
❑ 70Top-13
❑ 71LetActR-10
❑ 71OPC-98
❑ 71SarProSta-40
❑ 71Top-98
❑ 71TorSun-79
❑ 72OPC-42
❑ 72SarProSta-64
❑ 72Top-148
❑ 73OPC-112
❑ 73Top-112
❑ 74LipSou-36
❑ 74NHLActSta-76
❑ 74OPCNHL-69
❑ 74OPCNHL-113
❑ 74Top-69
❑ 74Top-113
❑ 75OPCNHL-234
❑ 75OPCNHL-317
❑ 75Top-234
❑ 75Top-317
❑ 91UltOriS-62
❑ 91UltOriSF-62
❑ 94ParTalB-123
❑ 95Par66-107
❑ 95Par66Coi-107

**Paquet, Dave**
❑ 907thInnSQMJHL-16
❑ 917thInnSMC-68
❑ 917thInnSQMJHL-113

**Paquet, Francois**
❑ 92QueIntP-6

**Paquet, Normand**
❑ 917thInnSQMJHL-2

**Paquet, Simon**
❑ 92QueIntP-12

**Paquette, Andy**
❑ 85SudWol-16
❑ 88SudWol-20

**Paquette, Charles**
❑ 917thInnSQMJHL-103
❑ 96ProBru-3

**Paquette, Darryl**
❑ 90SudWol-1
❑ 95HamRoaA-4
❑ 95PorPir-17
❑ 96HamRoaA-HRA1

**Paquette, Francois**
❑ 917thInnSQMJHL-199

**Paquette, Phil**
❑ 86SudWol-23

**Paquette, Rhiall**
❑ 67ColChe-10

**Paquin, Patrice**
❑ 917thInnSQMJHL-184

**Para, Kelly**
❑ 86KamBla-15

**Paradis, Daniel**
❑ 907thInnSQMJHL-42
❑ 917thInnSMC-45
❑ 917thInnSQMJHL-95

**Paradis, Stephane**
❑ 917thInnSQMJHL-140

**Paradise, Bob**
❑ 69SweWorC-89
❑ 69SweWorC-90
❑ 69SweWorC-183
❑ 72Flam-12
❑ 72SarProSta-11
❑ 74NHLActSta-227
❑ 74OPCNHL-343
❑ 74PenPos-17
❑ 75OPCNHL-21
❑ 75Top-21
❑ 76OPCNHL-368
❑ 77OPCNHL-203
❑ 78OPC-375

**Paradise, Dick**
❑ 72FigSaiPos-17
❑ 73QuaOatWHA-49

**Paradise, Jim**
❑ 95TalTigS-10

**Pare, Jean-Philippe**
❑ 98BowCHL-94
❑ 98BowCHLGA-94
❑ 98BowCHLOI-94
❑ 98BowChrC-94
❑ 98BowChrCGA-94
❑ 98BowChrCGAR-94
❑ 98BowChrCOI-94
❑ 98BowChrCOIR-94
❑ 98BowChrCR-94

**Parent, Bernie**
❑ 64BeeGro3P-21
❑ 65Coc-18
❑ 68OPC-89
❑ 68ShiCoi-122
❑ 68Top-89
❑ 69OPC-89
❑ 69OPCFou-1
❑ 69OPCSta-23
❑ 69Top-89
❑ 70ColSta-93
❑ 70DadCoo-95
❑ 70EssPowPla-216
❑ 70OPC-78
❑ 70SarProSta-146
❑ 70Top-78
❑ 71MapLeaP-14
❑ 71OPC-131
❑ 71SarProSta-205
❑ 71Top-131
❑ 71TorSun-267
❑ 72SweSemWC-175
❑ 73FlyLin-13
❑ 73OPC-66
❑ 73Top-66
❑ 74LipSou-18
❑ 74NHLActSta-202
❑ 74OPCNHL-4
❑ 74OPCNHL-60
❑ 74OPCNHL-138
❑ 74OPCNHL-249
❑ 74OPCNHL-251
❑ 74Top-4
❑ 74Top-60
❑ 74Top-138
❑ 74Top-249
❑ 74Top-251
❑ 75HerSta-24
❑ 75OPCNHL-213
❑ 75OPCNHL-291
❑ 75OPCNHL-300
❑ 75Top-213
❑ 75Top-291
❑ 75Top-300
❑ 76OPCNHL-10
❑ 76Top-10
❑ 77OPCNHL-8
❑ 77OPCNHL-65
❑ 77Top-8
❑ 77Top-65
❑ 78OPC-15
❑ 78OPC-68
❑ 78OPC-70
❑ 78Top-15
❑ 78Top-68
❑ 78Top-70
❑ 79OPC-6
❑ 79OPC-8
❑ 79Top-6
❑ 79Top-8A
❑ 79Top-8B
❑ 85FlyPos-21
❑ 85HalFC-246
❑ 86FlyPos-19
❑ 91Pin-384
❑ 91PinFre-384
❑ 92FlyUppDS-44
❑ 92OPC-217
❑ 92OPC25Al-1
❑ 92Par-470
❑ 92ParEmel-470
❑ 93HigLinGG-7
❑ 94ParTalBFS-FS4
❑ 95Par66-14
❑ 95Par66Coi-14

**Parent, Rich**
❑ 94MusFur-2
❑ 95MusFur-15
❑ 96DetVip-11

**Parent, Russ**
❑ 96FifFly-3

**Parent, Sebastien**
❑ 907thInnSQMJHL-36
❑ 917thInnSMC-41
❑ 917thInnSQMJHL-91

**Parfet, Van**
❑ 98LasVegT-27

**Pargeter, George**
❑ 51BufBis-17

**Parise, J.P.**
❑ 68OPC-149
❑ 69OPC-127
❑ 69Top-127
❑ 70DadCoo-96
❑ 70EssPowPla-171
❑ 70OPC-168
❑ 70SarProSta-94
❑ 70TopStiS-25
❑ 71OPC-243
❑ 71SarProSta-83
❑ 71TorSun-142
❑ 72OPC-199
❑ 72OPCTeaC-20
❑ 72SarProSta-101
❑ 72SweSemWC-219
❑ 73MacMil-20
❑ 73NorStaAP-9
❑ 73NorStaP-16
❑ 73OPC-46
❑ 73Top-46
❑ 74LipSou-4
❑ 74NHLActSta-133
❑ 74OPCNHL-83
❑ 74Top-83
❑ 75OPCNHL-127
❑ 75Top-127
❑ 76OPCNHL-182
❑ 76Top-182
❑ 77OPCNHL-29
❑ 77Top-29
❑ 78NorStaCD-3
❑ 78OPC-350
❑ 79OPC-118
❑ 79Top-118
❑ 80NorStaPos-14
❑ 91FutTreC72-99

**Parish, Kevin**
❑ 94GuiFla-8

**Parizeau, Mike (Michel)**
❑ 71BluPos-14
❑ 71TorSun-242
❑ 72NordPos-17
❑ 72OPC-335
❑ 73NordTeal-17
❑ 73QuaOatWHA-43
❑ 74OPCWHA-52

**Park, Brad**
❑ 70DadCoo-97
❑ 70EssPowPla-182
❑ 70OPC-67
❑ 70OPC-239
❑ 70OPCDec-43
❑ 70SarProSta-124
❑ 70Top-67
❑ 71ColHea-9
❑ 71LetActR-20
❑ 71OPC-40
❑ 71OPC-257
❑ 71SarProSta-116
❑ 71Top-40
❑ 71TorSun-178
❑ 72OPC-85A
❑ 72OPC-85B
❑ 72OPC-114
❑ 72OPC-227
❑ 72OPCPlaC-15
❑ 72OPCTeaC-21
❑ 72SarProSta-144
❑ 72SweHocS-114
❑ 72SweSemWC-194
❑ 72Top-30
❑ 72Top-123
❑ 73MacMil-21
❑ 73OPC-165
❑ 73Top-165
❑ 74LipSou-10
❑ 74NHLActSta-196
❑ 74OPCNHL-50
❑ 74OPCNHL-131
❑ 74OPCNHL-141
❑ 74Top-50
❑ 74Top-131
❑ 74Top-141
❑ 75HerSta-4
❑ 75OPCNHL-260A
❑ 75OPCNHL-260B
❑ 75Top-260
❑ 76OPCNHL-60
❑ 76Top-60
❑ 76TopGloI-2
❑ 77Coc-18
❑ 77OPCNHL-190
❑ 77Spo-5
❑ 77Top-190
❑ 77TopGloS-13
❑ 77TopOPCGlo-13
❑ 78OPC-79
❑ 78Top-79
❑ 79OPC-23
❑ 79OPC-164
❑ 79Top-23
❑ 79Top-164
❑ 80OPC-74
❑ 80OPCSup-1
❑ 80Top-74
❑ 81OPC-8
❑ 81OPCSti-48
❑ 81Top-E72
❑ 82OPC-19
❑ 82OPCSti-82
❑ 82PosCer-1
❑ 83OPC-29
❑ 83OPCSti-48
❑ 83OPCSti-178
❑ 83PufSti-15
❑ 84OPC-63
❑ 84OPC-378
❑ 84OPC-390
❑ 84OPCSti-38
❑ 84OPCSti-231
❑ 84Top-47
❑ 88EssAllSta-34
❑ 91BruSpoAL-21
❑ 91FutTreC72-95
❑ 92QueIntPWG-1
❑ 93ZelMasH-6
❑ 93ZelMasoHS-6
❑ 94HocWit-10
❑ 95SigRooCF-CF2
❑ 95SigRooCFS-CF2
❑ 99QuePeeWHWCCS-1
❑ 99RetHoc-106
❑ 99UppDecES-16
❑ 99UppDecRG-106
❑ 99UppDecRII-BP
❑ 99UppDecRIL1-BP
❑ 99UppDecRP-106

**Park, Jim**
❑ 77OPCWHA-56

**Park, Richard**
❑ 93DonTeaUSA-17
❑ 93Pin-498
❑ 93PinCan-498
❑ 93UppDec-553
❑ 94Fin-112
❑ 94FinRef-112
❑ 94FinSupTW-112
❑ 94LeaLimWJUSA-9
❑ 94ParSE-SE249
❑ 94ParSEG-SE249
❑ 94Sco-210
❑ 94ScoGol-210
❑ 94ScoPla-210
❑ 94SP-175
❑ 94SPDieCut-175
❑ 94UppDec-525
❑ 94UppDecEleIce-525
❑ 95BeAPla-185
❑ 95BeAPSig-S185
❑ 95BeAPSigDC-S185
❑ 95Bow-123
❑ 95BowAllFoi-123
❑ 95Don-331
❑ 95Fin-89
❑ 95FinRef-89
❑ 95FleMetPP-4
❑ 95Lea-221
❑ 95LeaLim-36
❑ 95Met-187
❑ 95ParInt-169
❑ 95ParIntEl-169
❑ 95PenFoo-7
❑ 95Pin-220
❑ 95PinArtP-220
❑ 95PinRinC-220
❑ 95Sco-295
❑ 95ScoBlaIce-295
❑ 95ScoBlaIceAP-295
❑ 95SigRoo-12

❑ 95SigRooSig-12
❑ 95SkyImp-217
❑ 95SP-120
❑ 95StaClu-208
❑ 95StaCluMOMS-208
❑ 95Top-119
❑ 95TopOPCI-119
❑ 95UppDec-419
❑ 95UppDecEleIce-419
❑ 95UppDecEleIceG-419
❑ 96CleLum-21
❑ 96ColCho-217
❑ 97PacInvNRB-6
❑ 97UppDec-215

**Parker, Jeff**
❑ 88ProAHL-254
❑ 88SabBluS-17
❑ 88SabWonBH-19
❑ 89SabBluS-14
❑ 89SabCam-17
❑ 90OPC-497

**Parker, Scott**
❑ 98PacOmeH-66
❑ 98PacOmeODI-66
❑ 98PacOmeR-66

**Parker, Shane**
❑ 94NorBayC-25
❑ 95Sla-230

**Parker, Stan**
❑ 52JunBluT-86

**Parkin, Danny**
❑ 94HumHawP-17

**Parks, Greg**
❑ 90OPCPre-89
❑ 91ProAHLCHL-462
❑ 92Par-491
❑ 92ParEmel-491
❑ 92SweSemE-170
❑ 93SweSemE-139
❑ 94ScoTeaC-CT11
❑ 95SweLeaE-175
❑ 95SweLeaEFF-2
❑ 95SweUppDE-32

**Parlini, Fred**
❑ 96GuiFla-6

**Parmstrom, Anders**
❑ 64SweCorI-41
❑ 65SweCorI-41
❑ 67SweHoc-40
❑ 69SweHocS-52

**Parnell, Greg**
❑ 90MicTecHus-18
❑ 91MicTecHus-17

**Parrish, Dwight**
❑ 91FerStaB-26
❑ 96DayBom-6

**Parrish, Mark**
❑ 95DonEliWJ-38
❑ 98Be A PPA-206
❑ 98Be A PPAA-206
❑ 98Be A PPAAF-206
❑ 98Be A PPSE-206
❑ 98Be APG-206
❑ 98BowBes-120
❑ 98BowBesA-A9A
❑ 98BowBesA-A9B
❑ 98BowBesAAR-A9A
❑ 98BowBesAAR-A9B
❑ 98BowBesAR-120
❑ 98BowBesAR-A9A
❑ 98BowBesAR-A9B
❑ 98BowBesMIF-F3
❑ 98BowBesMIFAR-F3
❑ 98BowBesMIFR-F3
❑ 98BowBesR-120
❑ 98PacCroR-61
❑ 98PacCroRLS-61
❑ 98PacCroRPP-12
❑ 98PacCroRRC-3
❑ 98PacDynI-85
❑ 98PacDynIIB-85
❑ 98PacDynIR-85
❑ 98PacDynIR-3
❑ 98PacOmeH-106
❑ 98PacOmeODI-106
❑ 98PacOmePI-4
❑ 98PacOmePIB-4
❑ 98PacOmeR-106
❑ 98PacRev-64
❑ 98PacRevIS-64
❑ 98PacRevR-64
❑ 98PacRevS-19
❑ 98SP Aut-97
❑ 98SPXTopP-29
❑ 98SPXTopPF-29
❑ 98SPXTopPR-29
❑ 98TopGolLC1-89
❑ 98TopGolLC1B-89
❑ 98TopGolLC1BOoO-89
❑ 98TopGolLC1OoO-89
❑ 98TopGolLC1R-89
❑ 98TopGolLC1ROoO-89
❑ 98TopGolLC2-89
❑ 98TopGolLC2B-89
❑ 98TopGolLC2BOoO-89
❑ 98TopGolLC2OoO-89
❑ 98TopGolLC2R-89
❑ 98TopGolLC2ROoO-89
❑ 98TopGolLC3-89
❑ 98TopGolLC3B-89
❑ 98TopGolLC3BOoO-89
❑ 98TopGolLC3OoO-89
❑ 98TopGolLC3R-89
❑ 98TopGolLC3ROoO-89
❑ 98UppDec-282
❑ 98UppDecBD-38
❑ 98UppDecDD-38
❑ 98UppDecE-282
❑ 98UppDecE1o1-282
❑ 98UppDecGR-282
❑ 98UppDecM-91
❑ 98UppDecM1-M20
❑ 98UppDecM2-M20
❑ 98UppDecMGS-91
❑ 98UppDecMP-MP
❑ 98UppDecMPG-PG12
❑ 98UppDecMSS-91
❑ 98UppDecMSS-91
❑ 98UppDecQD-38
❑ 98UppDecTD-38
❑ 99Pac-180
❑ 99PacAur-65
❑ 99PacAurPD-65
❑ 99PacCop-180
❑ 99PacGol-180
❑ 99PacIceB-180
❑ 99PacPreD-180
❑ 99RetHoc-37
❑ 99SP AutPS-97
❑ 99UppDecM-84
❑ 99UppDecMGS-84
❑ 99UppDecMSS-84
❑ 99UppDecMSS-84
❑ 99UppDecRG-G9C
❑ 99UppDecRG-37
❑ 99UppDecRGI-G9C
❑ 99UppDecRP-37

**Parro, Dave**
❑ 77RocAme-19
❑ 81Cap-14
❑ 82Cap-20
❑ 82OPC-371
❑ 82OPCSti-158

**Parrott, Jeff**
❑ 96DetVip-12

**Parson, Mike**
❑ 90ProAHLIHL-129
❑ 94PorPir-19

**Parson, Steven (Steve)**
❑ 907thInnSOHL-291
❑ 917thInnSOHL-283
❑ 93KinFro-20
❑ 94ThuBayS-16
❑ 95ThuBayS-15
❑ 96SouCarS-18

**Parsons, Darren**
❑ 86RegPat-23
❑ 88RegPat-19

**Parsons, Don**
❑ 92NasKni-10

**Parsons, George**
❑ 34BeeGro1P-341
❑ 38QuaOatP-26

**Parth, Elmar**
❑ 94FinnJaaK-292

**Parthenais, Pat**
❑ 96DetWha-13

**Partinen, Lalli**
❑ 69SweHocS-379
❑ 70SweHocS-298
❑ 96FinnSISR-191

**Parviainen, Jari**
❑ 93FinnJyvHS-260
❑ 93FinnSIS-283

**Pasanen, Jari**
❑ 96GerDELE-221

**Pascal, Brent**
❑ 81RegPat-19

**Pascall, Brad**
❑ 92RochAmeKod-16
❑ 93RochAmeKod-19

**Paschal, Kevin**
❑ 92BriColJHL-214

**Pasco, Ron**
❑ 93RenEng-20
❑ 94GreMon-10
❑ 95TalTigS-5
❑ 98GerDELE-240

**Pascucci, Ron**
❑ 93HamRoaA-3
❑ 94HamRoaA-5
❑ 95HamRoaA-6
❑ 96PorPir-6

**Pasek, Dusan**
❑ 82SweSemHVS-93
❑ 88NorStaADA-20
❑ 89ProIHL-82
❑ 91SweSemWCS-113
❑ 95SloAPSNT-2

**Pashulka, Steve**
❑ 92MPSPhoSJHL-43

**Pasin, Dave**
❑ 84PriAlbRS-20
❑ 86MonGolF-7
❑ 86OPC-76
❑ 86Top-76
❑ 88ProAHL-221
❑ 90ProAHLIHL-425

**Pasjkov, Alexander**
❑ 73SweHocS-120
❑ 73SweWorCS-120

**Paslawski, Greg**
❑ 83Vac-52
❑ 87BluKod-20
❑ 87BluTeaIss-17
❑ 87OPC-10
❑ 87OPCSti-23
❑ 87PanSti-314
❑ 87Top-10
❑ 88BluKod-28
❑ 88BluTeaIss-17
❑ 89JetSaf-24
❑ 89OPC-268
❑ 90JetIGA-28
❑ 90OPC-154
❑ 90PanSti-309
❑ 90ProSet-336
❑ 90Sco-249
❑ 90ScoCan-249
❑ 90Top-154
❑ 90TopTif-154
❑ 90UppDec-239
❑ 90UppDecF-239
❑ 91JetPanTS-20
❑ 91NordPet-23
❑ 91Par-365
❑ 91ParFre-365
❑ 91Pin-286
❑ 91PinFre-286
❑ 91ProSet-469
❑ 91ProSetFre-469
❑ 91ProSetPla-220
❑ 91ScoCan-579
❑ 91ScoRoo-29T
❑ 92Bow-277
❑ 92FlyJCP-19
❑ 92FlyUppDS-14
❑ 92FlyUppDS-33
❑ 92OPC-193
❑ 92Par-132
❑ 92ParEmel-132
❑ 92Pin-370
❑ 92PinFre-370
❑ 92ProSet-155
❑ 92Sco-175
❑ 92ScoCan-175
❑ 92ScoSha-16
❑ 92ScoShaCan-16
❑ 92StaClu-275
❑ 92Top-33
❑ 92TopGol-33G
❑ 92Ult-375
❑ 92UppDec-531
❑ 93Pin-337
❑ 93PinCan-337
❑ 93Sco-290
❑ 93ScoCan-290
❑ 95ColEdgI-179
❑ 95PeoRiv-16

**Pasma, Rod**
❑ 907thInnSOHL-42
❑ 917thInnSOHL-234
❑ 95LouIceG-12
❑ 95LouIceGP-15

**Passarelli, Val**
❑ 90MonAAA-17
❑ 91FerStaB-27

**Passero, Daniel**
❑ 96SauSteMG-15
❑ 96SauSteMGA-15

**Passmore, Steve**
❑ 907thInnSWHL-255
❑ 917thInnSWHL-68
❑ 93KamBla-19
❑ 94CapBreO-17
❑ 99Pac-168
❑ 99PacCop-168
❑ 99PacGol-168
❑ 99PacIceB-168
❑ 99PacPreD-168

**Pastika, Michael**
❑ 94GerDELE-421

**Pastinsky, Oliver**
❑ 93SauSteMG-4
❑ 93SauSteMGM-4

**Patafie, Brian**
❑ 81Ott67-9
❑ 83NovScoV-18
❑ 84MonGolF-1
❑ 85MonGolF-18
❑ 86MonGolF-6

**Pateman, Jerry**
❑ 90ProSet-696

**Patenaude, Rusty**
❑ 74OPCWHA-51
❑ 75OPCWHA-76
❑ 76OPCWHA-19

**Patera, Pavel**
❑ 94CzeAPSE-58
❑ 95CzeAPSE-352
❑ 96CzeAPSE-341
❑ 96SweSemW-114

**Paterson, Cory**
❑ 88RegPat-20
❑ 89RegPat-14
❑ 92WheThu-11
❑ 93WheThu-3
❑ 93WheThu-PC4

**Paterson, Craig**
❑ 96RicRen-15

**Paterson, Joe**
❑ 85FlyPos-22
❑ 86Kin20tATI-17
❑ 87KinTeal4-17
❑ 88ProAHL-207
❑ 89ProIHL-41
❑ 90ProAHLIHL-8
❑ 91ProAHLCHL-203
❑ 95SauSteMG-15
❑ 95Sla-380
❑ 96SauSteMG-14
❑ 96SauSteMGA-14

**Paterson, Mark**
❑ 82Ott67-17
❑ 83Ott67-22
❑ 86MonGolF-17
❑ 88ProIHL-108

**Paterson, Rick**
❑ 81BlaBorPos-19
❑ 82PosCer-4
❑ 83BlaBorPos-18
❑ 83OPC-109
❑ 84OPC-44
❑ 86BlaCok-14
❑ 93CleLum-2
❑ 93CleLumPos-16
❑ 95CleLum-20
❑ 96CleLum-22

**Paterson, Ron**
❑ 81SweSemHVS-74

**Patey, Doug**
❑ 79OPC-298

**Patey, Larry**
❑ 74NHLActSta-64
❑ 75OPCNHL-137
❑ 75OPCNHL-316
❑ 75Top-137
❑ 75Top-316
❑ 76OPCNHL-320
❑ 77OPCNHL-199
❑ 77Top-199
❑ 78BluPos-17
❑ 78OPC-8
❑ 78Top-8
❑ 79OPC-57
❑ 79Top-57
❑ 80OPC-310
❑ 81OPC-303
❑ 82OPC-308
❑ 82PosCer-17
❑ 84OPC-149
❑ 84Top-111

**Patoine, Remy**
❑ 88RivDu R-20

**Patrick, Craig**
❑ 71OPC-184
❑ 72OPC-221
❑ 72SarProSta-55
❑ 72SweSemWC-130
❑ 73OPC-52
❑ 73Top-52
❑ 74LipSou-46
❑ 74NHLActSta-72
❑ 74NHLActStaU-34
❑ 74OPCNHL-262
❑ 74Top-262
❑ 75OPCNHL-178
❑ 75Top-178
❑ 77OPCNHL-278
❑ 95SigRooMI-43
❑ 95SigRooMI-44
❑ 95SigRooSMIS-43
❑ 95SigRooSMIS-44

**Patrick, Frank**
❑ 10C56-1
❑ 83HalFP-B9
❑ 85HalFC-23

**Patrick, Glen**
❑ 79PanSti-210

**Patrick, James**
❑ 83CanNatJ-11
❑ 84OPC-150
❑ 84Top-112
❑ 85OPC-15
❑ 85OPCSti-83
❑ 85Top-15
❑ 86OPC-113
❑ 86OPCSti-220
❑ 86Top-113
❑ 87OPC-18
❑ 87OPCSti-30
❑ 87PanSti-107
❑ 87Top-18
❑ 88FriLaySS-30
❑ 88OPC-69
❑ 88OPCSti-246
❑ 88PanSti-303
❑ 88Top-69
❑ 89OPC-90
❑ 89OPCSti-242
❑ 89PanSti-289
❑ 89RanMarMB-3
❑ 89SweSemWCS-61
❑ 89Top-90
❑ 90Bow-225
❑ 90BowTif-225
❑ 90OPC-101
❑ 90OPC-131
❑ 90PanSti-97
❑ 90ProSet-207
❑ 90Sco-194
❑ 90ScoCan-194
❑ 90ScoHotRS-84
❑ 90Top-101
❑ 90Top-131
❑ 90TopTif-131
❑ 90UppDec-185
❑ 90UppDecF-185
❑ 91Bow-66
❑ 91OPC-253
❑ 91OPCPre-172
❑ 91PanSti-287
❑ 91Par-120
❑ 91ParFre-120
❑ 91Pin-26
❑ 91PinFre-26
❑ 91ProSet-164
❑ 91ProSetFre-164
❑ 91ProSetPla-82
❑ 91ScoAme-230
❑ 91ScoCan-230
❑ 91StaClu-277
❑ 91Top-253
❑ 91UppDec-275
❑ 91UppDecF-275
❑ 92Bow-127
❑ 92OPC-215
❑ 92PanSti-240
❑ 92PanStiFre-240
❑ 92Par-113
❑ 92ParEmel-113
❑ 92Pin-140
❑ 92PinFre-140
❑ 92ProSet-119
❑ 92Sco-203
❑ 92ScoCan-203
❑ 92StaClu-394
❑ 92Top-71
❑ 92TopGol-71G
❑ 92Ult-141
❑ 92UppDec-320
❑ 93Don-213
❑ 93Don-408
❑ 93Lea-232
❑ 93OPCPre-149
❑ 93OPCPreG-149
❑ 93Par-360
❑ 93ParEmel-360
❑ 93Pin-246
❑ 93PinCan-246
❑ 93Pow-164
❑ 93Pow-353
❑ 93Sco-73
❑ 93Sco-574
❑ 93ScoCan-73
❑ 93ScoCan-574
❑ 93ScoGol-574
❑ 93StaClu-302
❑ 93StaCluFDI-302
❑ 93StaCluO-302
❑ 93TopPre-149
❑ 93TopPreG-149
❑ 93Ult-336
❑ 93WhaCok-13
❑ 94BeAPSig-98
❑ 94CanGamNHLP-59
❑ 94Don-185
❑ 94EASpo-86
❑ 94Fla-26
❑ 94Fle-33
❑ 94Lea-281
❑ 94OPCPre-30
❑ 94OPCPreSE-30
❑ 94Par-40
❑ 94ParGol-40
❑ 94Pin-196
❑ 94PinArtP-196
❑ 94PinRinC-196
❑ 94Sco-8
❑ 94ScoGol-8
❑ 94ScoPla-8
❑ 94ScoPlaTS-8
❑ 94TopPre-30
❑ 94TopPreSE-30
❑ 94Ult-33
❑ 94UppDec-424
❑ 94UppDecEleIce-424
❑ 95ParInt-303
❑ 95ParIntEl-303
❑ 95UppDec-53
❑ 95UppDecEleIce-53
❑ 95UppDecEleIceG-53
❑ 96Don-158
❑ 96DonPrePro-158
❑ 96MetUni-21
❑ 96Sco-189
❑ 96ScoArtPro-189
❑ 96ScoDeaCAP-189
❑ 96ScoGolB-189
❑ 96ScoSpeAP-189
❑ 96TopNHLP-165
❑ 96TopPicOI-165
❑ 97PacDynBKS-14

**Patrick, Lester**
❑ 10C56-26
❑ 12C57-41
❑ 36V356WorG-94
❑ 60Top-1
❑ 83HalFP-C10
❑ 85HalFC-40
❑ 94ParMisLP-P10

**Patrick, Lynn**
❑ 34BeeGro1P-289
❑ 35DiaMatT2-54
❑ 35DiaMatT2-55
❑ 35DiaMatT3-51
❑ 35OPCV304C-79
❑ 36OPCV304D-128
❑ 36V356WorG-57
❑ 39OPCV3011-36
❑ 40OPCV3012-136
❑ 83HalFP-N12
❑ 85HalFC-207

**Patrick, Murray**
❑ 34BeeGro1P-290
❑ 39OPCV3011-38

**Patronas, Nik**
❑ 94DubFigS-21

**Patschinski, Rainer**
❑ 69SweWorC-176
❑ 70SweHocS-380

**Pattersen, Lars**
❑ 96RegPat-13

**Patterson, Colin**
❑ 83Vac-15
❑ 85FlamRedRP-21
❑ 86FlamRedR-20
❑ 87FlamRedRP-23
❑ 89Kra-7
❑ 89OPC-71
❑ 89OPCSti-102
❑ 89PanSti-36
❑ 89Top-71
❑ 90FlamIGA-20
❑ 90OPC-420
❑ 91FlamPanTS-16
❑ 91ProSet-356
❑ 91ProSetFre-356
❑ 91SabBluS-15
❑ 91SabPepC-15
❑ 91ScoCan-525
❑ 92SabBluS-16
❑ 92Sco-312
❑ 92ScoCan-312
❑ 92Top-91
❑ 92TopGol-91G

**Patterson, Dennis**
❑ 74NHLActSta-304
❑ 75OPCNHL-51
❑ 75Top-51

**Patterson, Eddie (Ed)**
❑ 907thInnSWHL-52
❑ 907thInnSWHL-291
❑ 917thInnSWHL-94
❑ 92CleLum-17
❑ 93CleLum-17
❑ 93CleLumPos-17
❑ 93Don-474
❑ 94ClaProP-159
❑ 94Don-265
❑ 94Lea-290
❑ 94StaClu-232
❑ 94StaCluFDI-232
❑ 94StaCluMOMS-232
❑ 94StaCluSTWC-232
❑ 95PenFoo-14
❑ 96CleLum-23
❑ 98CinCyc-17

**Patterson, Georges (George)**
❑ 27LaPat-20
❑ 33OPCV304A-14
❑ 33V357IceK-35
❑ 34DiaMatS-49

**Patterson, Nevin**
❑ 97SudWolP-13

**Patterson, Phil**
❑ 81Ott67-10
❑ 82Ott67-18
❑ 83Ott67-23

**Patterson, Ron**
❑ 91AirCanSJHL-C30

**Patton, Kirk**
❑ 95AlaGolKin-14

**Patuli, Arduino**
❑ 92QueIntP-38

**Paul, Jean**
❑ 56QueAce-8
❑ 70NorStaP-6
❑ 74NHLActStaU-25
❑ 80QueRem-9
❑ 89OshGenP-20

**Paul, Jeff**
❑ 95Sla-185

**Paul, John**
❑ 84KinSmo-10
❑ 96DetWha-11

**Paul, Kyle**
❑ 92MPSPhoSJHL-28

**Pauna, Matti**
❑ 83SweSemE-39
❑ 84SweSemE-39
❑ 85SwePanS-33
❑ 86SwePanS-19
❑ 87SwePanS-34
❑ 90SweSemE-131
❑ 91SweSemE-193

**Pavelec, Stanislav**
❑ 94CzeAPSE-236
❑ 95CzeAPSE-6

**Pavelek, Zdenek**
❑ 96CzeAPSE-113

**Pavelich, Mark**
❑ 81SweSemHVS-102
❑ 82OPC-231
❑ 82OPCSti-138
❑ 82PosCer-13
❑ 83OPC-238
❑ 83OPC-239
❑ 83OPC-253
❑ 83OPCSti-213
❑ 83OPCSti-214
❑ 84OPC-151
❑ 84OPCSti-97
❑ 84Top-113
❑ 85OPC-69
❑ 85OPCSti-84
❑ 85Top-69
❑ 95SigRooMI-25
❑ 95SigRooMI-26
❑ 95SigRooSMIS-25
❑ 95SigRooSMIS-26

**Pavelich, Marty**
❑ 44BeeGro2P-200
❑ 51Par-54
❑ 52Par-66
❑ 53Par-44
❑ 54Par-43
❑ 54Top-34
❑ 76OldTim-12
❑ 80USAOlyTMP-12
❑ 94ParMisL-53

**Pavelich, Matt**
❑ 85HalFC-261

**Pavels, Stig**
❑ 65SweCorI-53

**Pavese, Jim**
❑ 80SauSteMG-18
❑ 81SauSteMG-18
❑ 82PosCer-16
❑ 82PosCer-17
❑ 87PanSti-310
❑ 88RedWinLC-19
❑ 90ProAHLIHL-423

**Pavlas, Petr**
❑ 91SweSemWCS-108
❑ 94FinnSIS-205
❑ 95CzeAPSE-226
❑ 95FinnSemWC-145
❑ 96CzeAPSE-267

**Pavlik, Karel**
❑ 95CzeAPSE-223

**Pavlikovsky, Rastislav**
❑ 98CinCyc-18

**Pavlis, Libor**
❑ 96CzeAPSE-209

**Pavlu, Martin**
❑ 82SweSemHVS-139
❑ 95FinnSemWC-176
❑ 96SweSemW-182

**Pavoni, Reto**
❑ 91SweSemWCS-178
❑ 93SwiHNL-8
❑ 95SweGloWC-208
❑ 95SwiHNL-6
❑ 95SwiHNL-517
❑ 95SwiHNL-526
❑ 95SwiHNL-529
❑ 95SwiHNL-535

**Pawlaczyk, Dan**
❑ 93DetJrRW-16
❑ 94DetJrRW-19
❑ 95Sla-63
❑ 95SlaMemC-93
❑ 96SarSti-20
❑ 96TolSto-28

**Pawloski, Jerry**
❑ 92HarCri-28

**Pawluk, Jeff**
❑ 917thInnSOHL-359

**Pawluk, Mike**
❑ 92BriColJHL-148
❑ 92BriColJHL-245

**Pawluk, Ryan**
❑ 93KitRan-12
❑ 95Sla-314
❑ 95Sla-426

**Pawlyschyn, Walter**
❑ 51LavDaiS-8
❑ 52St.LawS-35

**Payan, Eugene**
❑ 10C55SweCP-43
❑ 11C55-43
❑ 12C57-9

**Payer, Serge**
❑ 95Sla-138
❑ 96KitRan-21
❑ 96UppDec-385

**Payette, Andre**
❑ 93SauSteMG-8
❑ 95Cla-95
❑ 95SauSteMG-16
❑ 95Sla-360

**Payette, Jean**
❑ 72NordPos-18
❑ 72OPC-311
❑ 73NordTeal-18

**Payne, Anthony**
❑ 93HumHawP-15
❑ 97KinHaw-9

**Payne, Davis**
❑ 90MicTecHus-19
❑ 91MicTecHus-18
❑ 91MicTecHus-34
❑ 92GreMon-7
❑ 93GreMon-11
❑ 94GreMon-9
❑ 96ProBru-11
❑ 97PacDynBKS-7

**Payne, Jason**
❑ 95Sla-14

**Payne, Steve**
❑ 78NorStaCD-7
❑ 79NorStaPos-11
❑ 79OPC-64
❑ 79Top-64
❑ 80NorStaPos-15
❑ 80OPC-139
❑ 80OPC-274
❑ 80Top-139
❑ 81NorStaPos-18
❑ 81OPC-166
❑ 81OPCSti-22
❑ 81OPCSti-92
❑ 81Top-W110
❑ 82NorStaPos-18
❑ 82OPC-172
❑ 82OPCSti-191
❑ 82PosCer-9
❑ 83NorStaPos-22
❑ 83OPC-178
❑ 83OPCSti-121
❑ 84NorSta7E-11
❑ 84NorStaPos-21
❑ 84OPC-106

840PCSti-49
84Top-80
85NorStaPos-23
85OPC-65
85OPCSti-42
85Top-65
86OPC-219
87NorStaPos-23
87OPCSti-56

**Paynter, Kent**
82KitRan-25
83KitRan-12
84KitRan-17
85NovScoO-20
88ProIHL-109
89ProAHL-101
90ProAHLIHL-196
91JetIGA-25
91MonHaw-21
91ProAHLCHL-168
94MilAdm-20
95MilAdmBO-14
96MilAdmBO-19

**Pazler, Lubos**
94CzeAPSE-263

**Peacock, Richard**
95SasBla-14

**Peacock, Shane**
89LetHur-16
907thInnSWHL-134
917thInnSWHL-343
91Cla-48
91StaPicH-33
91UltDra-43
93LetHur-10
98GerDELE-45

**Peacosh, Gene**
73QuaOatWHA-24
74MarSanDW-5
740PCWHA-27
750PCWHA-24
760PCWHA-60
760PCWHA-71

**Peake, Pat**
907thInnSOHL-114
917thInnSMC-106
917thInnSOHL-35
91AreDraPic-11
91Cla-12
91StaPicH-39
91UltDra-12
91UltDra-68
91UppDec-697
91UppDecCWJC-84
91UppDecF-697
93Cla-12
93Cla-33
93Cla-AU9
93Don-361
93Pin-436
93PinCan-436
93PinSupR-9
93PinSupRC-9
93Pow-469
93PowRooS-10
93Sco-590
93ScoCan-590
93ScoGol-590
93Ult-449
93UppDec-518
93UppDecSP-172
94ClaProP-29
94Don-318
94Fla-203
94Fle-238
94Lea-83
94LeaGolR-12
940PCPre-12
940PCPreSE-12
94Par-281
94ParGol-281
94ParSE-SE196
94ParSEG-SE196
94ParVin-V63
94Pin-136
94PinArtP-136
94PinRinC-136
94TopPre-12
94TopPreSE-12
94Ult-237
94UppDec-125
94UppDecEleIce-125
94UppDecSPI-SP176
94UppDecSPIDC-SP176
95Cap-20
95Don-230
95ParInt-488
95ParIntEI-488
95PlaOneoOne-214
95Sco-181
95ScoBlaIce-181
95ScoBlaIceAP-181
95StaClu-136
95StaCluMOMS-136
95Ult-325
95UppDec-163
95UppDecEleIce-163
95UppDecEleIceG-163
95UppDecSpeE-SE175
95UppDecSpeEdiG-SE175
96ColCho-282
96Sco-67
96ScoArtPro-67
96ScoDeaCAP-67
96ScoGolB-67

96ScoSpeAP-67
96UppDec-353
97Be A PPAD-171
97Be A PPAPD-171
97BeAPla-171
97BeAPlaAut-171
97UppDec-179

**Peal, Skip (Allen)**
52JunBluT-113

**Pearce, Barcley**
97GuiFla-18

**Pearce, Garry**
89RegPat-15
907thInnSWHL-176
917thInnSWHL-223

**Pearce, Randy**
87KitRan-23
88KitRan-23
89KitRan-23
907thInnSMC-29
91HamRoaA-14
93PorPir-1
96HamRoaA-HRA13

**Pearn, Perry**
93SwiHNL-134
95JetTeaIss-4
96SenPizH-19

**Pearson, Andy**
85KinCan-9

**Pearson, Mel**
72FigSaiPos-18

**Pearson, Rob**
897thInnSOHL-7
907thInnSOHL-15
91MapLeaP-24
910PCPre-65
91Par-169
91ParFre-169
91Pin-304
91PinFre-304
91ProSet-562
91ProSetFre-562
91ScoAme-311
91ScoCan-341
91ScoCan-385
91UppDec-598
91UppDecF-598
92Bow-381
92MapLeaK-19
920PC-136
92PanSti-80
92PanStiFre-80
92Par-414
92ParEmel-414
92Pin-245
92Pin-287
92PinFre-245
92PinFre-287
92PinTea2-23
92PinTea2F-23
92ProSet-191
92ProSetRGL-9
92Sco-333
92ScoCan-333
92ScoYouS-18
92StaClu-377
92Top-168
92TopGol-168G
92Ult-423
92UppDec-318
93Don-339
93Lea-174
930PCPre-137
930PCPreG-137
93Par-474
93ParEmel-474
93Pin-89
93PinCan-89
93Pow-453
93Sco-96
93ScoBla-6
93ScoCan-96
93StaClu-498
93StaCluFDI-498
93StaCluO-498
93TopPre-137
93TopPreG-137
93Ult-434
93UppDec-48
94BeAPSig-76
940PCPre-341
940PCPreSE-341
94Pin-375
94PinArtP-375
94PinRinC-375
94Sco-137
94ScoGol-137
94ScoPla-137
94ScoPlaTS-137
94TopPre-341
94TopPreSE-341
94UppDec-180
94UppDecEleIce-180
95ProPir-18
95UppDec-212
95UppDecEleIce-212
95UppDecEleIceG-212

**Pearson, Scott**
85KinCan-15
86KinCan-11
87KinCan-22
88NiaFalT-11
89ProAHL-119
900PC-356
90Top-356

90TopTif-356
91Bow-150
91MapLeaPTS-19
910PC-297
91ProSet-208
91ProSetFre-208
91ScoAme-138
91ScoCan-138
91StaClu-178
91Top-297
91UppDec-336
91UppDecF-336
92NorPet-24
92Par-381
92ParEmel-381
93Don-106
93Lea-297
93Pin-375
93PinCan-375
93Sco-376
93Sco-543
93ScoCan-376
93ScoCan-543
93ScoGol-543
93UppDec-389
94CanGamNHLP-100
94Don-196
94Lea-349
940PCPre-124
940PCPreSE-124
94Par-78
94ParGol-78
94Pin-213
94PinArtP-213
94PinRinC-213
94TopPre-124
94TopPreSE-124
94Ult-75
94Ult-250
94UppDec-97
94UppDecEleIce-97
95ParInt-22
95ParIntEI-22
95RochAmeSS-16
95UppDec-135
95UppDecEleIce-135
95UppDecEleIceG-135

**Pearson, Ted**
84MonGolF-14

**Peat, Stephen**
97UppDec-405
98BowCHL-136
98BowCHLAu-A4
98BowCHLAuB-A4
98BowCHLAuS-A4
98BowCHLGA-136
98BowCHLOI-136
98BowChrC-136
98BowChrCGA-136
98BowChrCGAR-136
98BowChrCOI-136
98BowChrCOIR-136
98BowChrCR-136

**Peca, David**
95Sla-40

**Peca, Justin**
91MicTecHus-30
93MicTecH-14
94EriPan-14

**Peca, Michael (Mike)**
907thInnSOHL-392
90SudWol-21
917thInnSOHL-247
91SudWol-22
92Cla-17
920tt672A-17
93Cla-25
93DonTeaC-18
93Pin-478
93PinCan-478
93UppDec-542
94BeAPSig-165
94Cla-116
94ClaDraGol-116
94ClaProP-154
94ClaTri-T70
94Don-266
94Fin-59
94FinRef-59
94FinSupTW-59
94Fle-229
94FleRooS-8
94Lea-193
940PCPreSE-275
94Par-245
94ParGol-245
94Pin-260
94PinArtP-260
94PinRinC-260
94PinRooTP-8
94Sco-237
94ScoGol-237
94ScoPla-237
94ScoPlaTS-237
94Sel-198
94SelGol-198
94TopPreSE-275
94UltPro-6
94UppDec-257
94UppDec-533
94UppDecEleIce-257
94UppDecEleIce-533
94UppDecEleIce-547
94UppDecPC-C10

94UppDecPCEG-C10
94UppDecPCES-C10
94UppDecSPI-SP173
94UppDecSPIDC-SP173
95CanGamNHLP-41
95CanuBuiDA-17
95Don-266
95Lea-114
95ParInt-290
95ParIntEI-290
95PlaOneoOne-128
95Sco-157
95ScoBlaIce-157
95ScoBlaIceAP-157
95Top-350
95TopOPCI-350
95Ult-212
95UppDec-333
95UppDecEleIce-333
95UppDecEleIceG-333
95UppDecWJA-7
96ClaGol-17
96ColCho-32
96Sco-209
96ScoArtPro-209
96ScoDeaCAP-209
96ScoGolB-209
96ScoSpeAP-209
96SkyImp-12
96UppDec-21
97Be A PPAD-44
97Be A PPADP-44
97BeAPla-44
97BeAPlaAut-44
97ColCho-26
97Don-21
97DonCanI-89
97DonCanIDS-89
97DonCanIPS-89
97DonLim-39
97DonLimExp-39
97DonPre-34
97DonPreCttC-34
97DonPreProG-21
97DonPreProS-21
97DonPri-145
97DonPriSoA-145
97Kat-16
97KatGol-16
97KatSil-16
97Lea-107
97LeaFraMat-107
97LeaFraMDC-107
97LeaInt-107
97LeaIntUI-107
97Pac-341
97PacCop-341
97PacCroR-15
97PacCroREG-15
97PacCroRIB-15
97PacCroRLCDC-4
97PacCroRS-15
97PacDyn-12
97PacDyn-136
97PacDynBKS-105
97PacDynC-12
97PacDynC-136
97PacDynDD-3B
97PacDynDG-12
97PacDynDG-136
97PacDynEG-12
97PacDynEG-136
97PacDynIB-12
97PacDynIB-136
97PacDynR-12
97PacDynR-136
97PacDynSil-12
97PacDynSil-136
97PacDynTan-21
97PacDynTan-33
97PacEmeGre-341
97PacGolCroDC-4
97PacIceB-341
97PacInv-13
97PacInvAZ-3
97PacInvC-13
97PacInvEG-13
97PacInvIB-13
97PacInvOTG-3
97PacInvR-13
97PacInvS-13
97PacOme-24
97PacOmeC-24
97PacOmeDG-24
97PacOmeEG-24
97PacOmeG-24
97PacOmeIB-24
97PacPar-21
97PacParC-21
97PacParEG-21
97PacParG-21
97PacParRed-21
97PacParSil-21
97PacRed-341
97PacRev-15
97PacRevC-15
97PacRevE-15
97PacRevR-15
97PacRevS-15
97PacRevTCL-3
97PacSil-341
97Pin-101
97PinCer-99

97PinCerMB-99
97PinCerMG-99
97PinCerMR-99
97PinCerR-99
97PinIns-128
97PinPrePBB-101
97PinPrePBC-101
97PinPrePBM-101
97PinPrePBY-101
97PinPrePFC-101
97PinPrePFM-101
97PinPrePFY-101
97PinPrePla-101
97PinTotCMPG-99
97PinTotCPB-99
97PinTotCPG-99
97PinTotCPR-99
97Sco-187
97Sco-268
97ScoChel-14
97ScoSab-11
97ScoSabPla-11
97ScoSabPre-11
97Stu-72
97StuPreG-72
97StuPrePS-72
97UppDec-227
97UppDecGDM-227
97UppDecTSS-7C
98Be A PPAA-12
98Be A PPAAA-12
98Be A PPAAF-12
98Be A PPTBASG-12
98Be APG-12
98BowBes-32
98BowBesAR-32
98BowBesR-32
98Fin-92
98FinNo P-92
98FinNo PR-92
98FinRef-92
980-PChr-94
980-PChrR-94
98Pac-27
98PacAur-19
98PacAurCF-7
98PacAurCFC-7
98PacAurCFIB-7
98PacAurCFR-7
98PacAurCFS-7
98PacAurMAC-4
98PacCroR-14
98PacCroRLS-14
98PacCroRPotG-3
98PacCroRPP-3
98PacDynI-20
98PacDynIFT-3
98PacDynIIB-20
98PacDynIR-20
98PacGolCD-5
98PacIceB-27
98PacOmeH-25
98PacOmeODI-25
98PacOmeR-25
98Par-21
98ParC-21
98ParEG-21
98ParH-21
98ParIB-21
98ParS-21
98PacRed-27
98PacRev-15
98PacRevIS-15
98PacRevR-15
98PacRevS-5
98SP Aut-9
98SPxFin-9
98SPxFinR-9
98SPxFinS-9
98Top-94
98TopGolLC1-91
98TopGolLC1B-91
98TopGolLC1BOoO-91
98TopGolLC1OoO-91
98TopGolLC1R-91
98TopGolLC1ROoO-91
98TopGolLC2-91
98TopGolLC2B-91
98TopGolLC2BOoO-91
98TopGolLC2OoO-91
98TopGolLC2ROoO-91
98TopGolLC3-91
98TopGolLC3B-91
98TopGolLC3BOoO-91
98TopGolLC3OoO-91
98TopGolLC3ROoO-91
98TopO-P-94
98UC-24
98UD ChoPCR-24
98UD ChoR-24
98UppDec-46
98UppDecE-46
98UppDecE1o1-46
98UppDecGR-46
98UppDecM-26
98UppDecMGS-26
98UppDecMSS-26
99Pac-41
99PacAur-18
99PacAurCF-5
99PacAurCF-5
99PacAurCFPB-5

99PacAurPD-18
99PacCop-41
99PacGol-41
99PacGolCD-6
99PacIceB-41
99PacPreD-41
99SP AutPS-9
99UppDecM-23
99UppDecMGS-23
99UppDecMPS-MP
99UppDecMSS-23
99UppDecMSS-23

**Peck, Jim**
74SioCitM-15

**Peddigrew, Jeff**
93SeaThu-18

**Pedersen, Al (Allen)**
82MedHatT-15
83MedHatT-9
85MonGolF-4
870PC-174
870PCSti-132
87Top-174
88BruPos-16
88BruSpoA-18
880PC-103
88Top-103
89BruSpoA-18
90BruSpoA-19
900PC-505
90ProSet-12
90Sco-181
90ScoCan-181
910PC-128
91ScoCan-599
91Top-128
92Par-300
92ParEmel-300
92WhaDai-17
930PCPre-439
93StaClu-366
93StaCluFDI-366
93StaCluO-366
93TopPre-439
93TopPreG-439

**Pedersen, Kenneth**
69SweHocS-287
70SweHocS-134

**Pedersen, Kristian**
91SweSemE-114
92SweSemE-130

**Pedersen, Barry**
820PC-20
820PCSti-92
820PCSti-93
82VicCou-21
83BruTealss-16
830PC-57
830PCSti-49
830PCSti-50
83PufSti-77
840PC-14
840PCSti-187
84Top-11
850PC-52
85Top-52
86Canu-12
86KraDra-52
860PC-34
86Top-34
87CanuSheOil-14
870PC-177
870PCSti-188
87Top-177
88CanuMoh-15
88FriLayS-39
880PC-32
880PCSti-65
88PanSti-138
88Top-32
89CanuMoh-14
890PC-281
890PCSti-60
89PanSti-153
900PC-134
90PenFoo-4
90ProSet-238
900PCPre-124
91ProSet-351
91ProSetFre-351
91ScoCan-639
92Bow-48
920PC-295
92Top-241
92TopGol-241G

**Pedersen, Denis**
93Cla-26
93PriAlbR-16
94Cla-112
94ClaDraGol-112
94ClaTri-T37
94Fin-163
94FinRef-163
94FinSupTW-163
94Pin-538
94PinArtP-538
94PinRinC-538
94PriAlbR-15

94SP-144
94SPDieCut-144
95Bow-138
95BowAllFoi-138
95Don-257
95DonCanWJT-20
95ParInt-395
95ParIntEI-395
95SkyImp-207
95TopCanWJ-12CJ
95Ult-359
95UppDec-354
95UppDecEleIce-354
95UppDecEleIceG-354
96BeAPAut-217
96BeAPAutSil-217
96BeAPla-217
96BeAPla-P217
96Dev-10
96Lea-226
96LeaPreP-226
96Pin-221
96PinArtP-221
96PinFoi-221
96PinPreS-221
96PinRinC-221
96UppDec-288
97ColCho-149
97DonLim-154
97DonLimExp-154
97Pac-221
97PacCop-221
97PacEmeGre-221
97PacIceB-221
97PacInv-79
97PacInvC-79
97PacInvEG-79
97PacInvIB-79
97PacInvR-79
97PacInvS-79
97PacRed-221
97PacSil-221
97ScoDev-11
97ScoDevPla-11
97ScoDevPre-11
97UppDec-97
98Fin-144
98FinNo P-144
98FinNo PR-144
98FinRef-144
980-PChr-214
980-PChrR-214
98Pac-269
98PacIceB-269
98PacRed-269
98Top-214
98TopIceA2-I4
98TopO-P-214
98UppDec-312
98UppDecE-312
98UppDecE1o1-312
98UppDecGR-312

**Pederson, Mark**
85MedHatT-19
88ProAHL-280
90CanaPos-23
900PC-82
90ProSet-618
90Sco-387
90ScoCan-387
90Top-82
90TopTif-82
90UppDec-532
90UppDecF-532
91Bow-242
91CanaPanTS-17
91FlyJCP-20
910PC-399
91Par-345
91ParFre-345
91ScoCan-435
91StaClu-291
91Top-399
91UppDec-363
91UppDecF-363
92Bow-390
920PC-157
92PanSti-188
92PanStiFre-188
92Pin-213
92Sco-263
92ScoCan-263
92StaClu-168
92Top-327
92TopGol-327G
92UppDec-209
98GerDELE-32

**Pederson, Todd**
82MedHatT-16

**Pederson, Tom**
920PCPre-33
92Ult-403
93ClaProPro-145
93Par-184
93ParEmel-184
93Pow-226
93UppDec-92
940PCPre-142
940PCPreSE-142
94Pin-448
94PinArtP-448
94PinRinC-448
94TopPre-142
94TopPreSE-142

❑ 95ColCho-38
❑ 95ColChoPC-38
❑ 95ColChoPCP-38
❑ 98GerDELE-191
**Peer, Brit**
❑ 83SauSteMG-18
❑ 84SauSteMG-16
**Peerless, Blaine**
❑ 81MilAdm-4
**Peet, Shaun**
❑ 92BriColJHL-108
**Peeters, Pete**
❑ 80OPC-279
❑ 81OPC-245
❑ 81OPCSti-177
❑ 81Top-E109
❑ 82OPC-22
❑ 82OPCSti-117
❑ 82PosCer-14
❑ 83BruTeaIss-17
❑ 83OPC-44
❑ 83OPC-58
❑ 83OPC-209
❑ 83OPC-221
❑ 83OPC-222
❑ 83OPCSti-41
❑ 83OPCSti-42
❑ 83OPCSti-170
❑ 83OPCSti-318
❑ 83PufSti-9
❑ 84OPC-15
❑ 84OPCSti-144
❑ 84OPCSti-184
❑ 84Top-12
❑ 85OPC-75
❑ 85OPCSti-160
❑ 85Top-75
❑ 86CapKod-20
❑ 86CapPol-19
❑ 86OPC-77
❑ 86Top-77
❑ 87CapKod-1
❑ 87CapTeaIss-18
❑ 87OPC-44
❑ 87PanSti-174
❑ 87Top-44
❑ 88CapBor-16
❑ 88CapSmo-17
❑ 88OPC-180
❑ 88OPCMin-30
❑ 88OPCSti-207
❑ 88PanSti-364
❑ 88Top-180
❑ 89FlyPos-18
❑ 89OPC-195
❑ 89Top-195
❑ 90FlyPos-19
❑ 90OPC-109
❑ 90ProSet-502
❑ 90ProSetPM-NNO
❑ 90Top-109
❑ 90TopTif-109
❑ 90UppDec-424
❑ 90UppDecF-424
❑ 91Bow-237
❑ 91OPC-29
❑ 91ProSetPlaPC-PC2
❑ 91ScoCan-544
❑ 91StaClu-88
❑ 91Top-29
❑ 91UppDec-642
❑ 91UppDecF-642
**Pegg, Jamie**
❑ 897thInnSOHL-104
❑ 907thInnSOHL-368
**Pehrson, Joakim**
❑ 85SwePanS-65
❑ 86SwePanS-47
❑ 87SwePanS-59
❑ 89SweSemE-43
❑ 90SweSemE-191
❑ 91SweSemE-46
**Peipmann, Jason**
❑ 92BriColJHL-14
**Peirson, Johnny (John)**
❑ 44BeeGro2P-54A
❑ 44BeeGro2P-54B
❑ 51Par-34
❑ 52Par-78
❑ 53Par-88
❑ 54Par-60
❑ 55BruPho-14
❑ 57BruTeaIss-16
❑ 91BruSpoAL-22
❑ 94ParMisL-5
**Peitonen, Esa**
❑ 79PanSti-170
**Pejchar, Rudolf**
❑ 94CzeAPSE-139
❑ 95CzeAPSE-244
**Pekarek, David**
❑ 907thInnSQMJHL-12
❑ 917thInnSMC-66
❑ 917thInnSQMJHL-239
**Pekkarinen, Veli-Pekka**
❑ 93FinnJyvHS-178
❑ 93FinnSIS-170
❑ 94FinnSIS-127
❑ 95FinnSIS-79
**Pekki, Semi**
❑ 94FinnSIS-70
❑ 95FinnSIS-237
❑ 95FinnSISL-108
❑ 96FinnSISR-40
**Pelchat, Patrick**
❑ 93AmoLesFAM-17
❑ 98BowCHL-88
❑ 98BowCHLGA-88
❑ 98BowCHLOI-88
❑ 98BowChrC-88
❑ 98BowChrCGA-88
❑ 98BowChrCGAR-88
❑ 98BowChrCOI-88
❑ 98BowChrCOIR-88
❑ 98BowChrCR-88
**Pelchat, Rodrigue**
❑ 51LavDaiLSJ-27
**Pelensky, Perry**
❑ 83SprInd-13
**Pell, Gordon**
❑ 897thInnSOHL-80
❑ 907thInnSOHL-213
❑ 917thInnSOHL-23
❑ 91CorRoy-4
**Pella, Dean**
❑ 87KinCan-18
❑ 88SudWol-12
**Pella, Tyler**
❑ 87KinCan-23
❑ 88SudWol-11
**Pellaers, Ryan**
❑ 917thInnSWHL-67
**Pellegrims, Mike**
❑ 96GerDELE-167
❑ 98GerDELE-237
**Pellegrino, Santino**
❑ 93SweSemWCS-228
❑ 94FinnJaaK-305
**Pellerin, Brian**
❑ 907thInnSWHL-266
❑ 90PriAlbR-16
❑ 91ProAHLCHL-45
❑ 92PeoRivC-18
❑ 93PeoRiv-20
**Pellerin, Scott**
❑ 92Cla-81
❑ 92MaiBlaB-7
❑ 93ClaProPro-18
❑ 93ClaProPro-90
❑ 93Lea-167
❑ 93Par-116
❑ 93ParEmeI-116
❑ 93Sco-373
❑ 93ScoCan-373
❑ 93StaClu-13
❑ 93StaCluFDI-13
❑ 93StaCluFDIO-13
❑ 93StaCluO-13
❑ 93Ult-142
❑ 93UppDec-52
❑ 96ClaGol-81
❑ 97Be A PPAD-50
❑ 97Be A PPAPD-50
❑ 97BeAPla-50
❑ 97BeAPlaAut-50
❑ 97Pac-95
❑ 97PacCop-95
❑ 97PacEmeGre-95
❑ 97PacIceB-95
❑ 97PacRed-95
❑ 97PacSil-95
❑ 97ScoBlu-12
❑ 97ScoBluPla-12
❑ 97ScoBluPre-12
❑ 98Pac-370
❑ 98PacIceB-370
❑ 98PacRed-370
❑ 99Pac-361
❑ 99PacCop-361
❑ 99PacGol-361
❑ 99PacIceB-361
❑ 99PacPreD-361
**Pelletier, Francois**
❑ 907thInnSMC-66
**Pelletier, Gaston**
❑ 52JunBluT-77
❑ 72SweSemWC-155
**Pelletier, Jean-Marc**
❑ 97RimOce-35
❑ 98UC-301
❑ 98UD ChoPCR-301
❑ 98UD ChoR-301
❑ 99QuePeeWHWCCS-11
❑ 99UppDecM-147
❑ 99UppDecMGS-147
❑ 99UppDecMSS-147
❑ 99UppDecMSS-147
❑ 99UppDecRG-G3C
❑ 99UppDecRGI-G3C
**Pelletier, Lloyd**
❑ 907thInnSWHL-53
❑ 917thInnSWHL-235
**Pelletier, Marcel**
❑ 51LavDaiQSHL-33
❑ 52St.LawS-90
**Peloffy, Andre**
❑ 74CapWhiB-22
**Peltola, Mikko**
❑ 93FinnJyvHS-288
❑ 93FinnSIS-69
❑ 94FinnSIS-324
❑ 95FinnSemWC-29
❑ 95FinnSIS-102
❑ 96FinnSISR-178
**Peltola, Pekka**
❑ 93FinnJyvHS-22
❑ 93FinnSIS-97
❑ 94FinnSIS-68
❑ 95FinnSIS-362
**Peltomaa, Timo**
❑ 91SweSemWCS-25
❑ 93FinnJyvHS-79
❑ 93FinnSIS-125
❑ 93SweSemWCS-72
❑ 94FinnSIS-43
❑ 94FinnSIS-158
❑ 94FinnSISH-8
❑ 95FinnSemWC-50
❑ 95FinnSIS-227
❑ 95FinnSISL-104
❑ 96FinnSISRS-7
❑ 96GerDELE-63
**Peltonen, Esa**
❑ 69SweHocS-380
❑ 69SweWorC-85
❑ 70SweHocS-309
❑ 71SweHocS-72
❑ 72SweSemWC-85
❑ 74SweHocS-33
❑ 74SweSemHVS-88
❑ 82SweSemHVS-49
**Peltonen, Jarno**
❑ 93FinnJyvHS-83
❑ 93FinnSIS-123
❑ 94FinnSIS-259
❑ 95FinnSIS-235
❑ 96FinnSISR-32
❑ 96GerDELE-267
❑ 98GerDELE-250
**Peltonen, Jorma**
❑ 69SweHocS-381
❑ 70SweHocS-310
❑ 74SweHocS-99
**Peltonen, Pasi**
❑ 93FinnSIS-211
❑ 94FinnSIS-103
❑ 95FinnSIS-153
❑ 96FinnSISR-152
**Peltonen, Ville**
❑ 92UppDec-616
❑ 93FinnJyvHS-28
❑ 93FinnSIS-101
❑ 93FinnSIS-365
❑ 93FinnSIS-391
❑ 94Cla-97
❑ 94ClaDraGol-97
❑ 94ClaTri-T61
❑ 94FinnJaaK-33
❑ 94FinnSIS-166
❑ 94FinnSIS-216
❑ 94FinnSISH-6
❑ 95Bow-133
❑ 95BowAllFoi-133
❑ 95FinnBecAC-3
❑ 95FinnKarWCL-17
❑ 95FinnSemWC-16
❑ 95FinnSemWC-230
❑ 95FinnSIS-172
❑ 95FinnSISGC-21
❑ 95FinnSISL-41
❑ 95FinnSISP-5
❑ 95ParInt-456
❑ 95ParInt-521
❑ 95ParIntEI-456
❑ 95ParIntEI-521
❑ 95UppDec-384
❑ 95UppDecEleIce-384
❑ 95UppDecEleIceG-384
❑ 96ColCho-241
❑ 96Don-224
❑ 96DonPrePro-224
❑ 96Lea-144
❑ 96LeaPreP-144
❑ 96SweSemW-16
❑ 96SweSemW-37
❑ 96SweSemWAS-AS6
❑ 96UppDec-335
**Peluso, Mike**
❑ 89ProIHL-57
❑ 90BlaCok-22
❑ 90ProSet-601
❑ 91BlaCok-20
❑ 91OPC-293
❑ 91ProAHLCHL-496
❑ 91ScoCan-529
❑ 91Top-293
❑ 91UppDec-414
❑ 91UppDecF-414
❑ 92Par-118
❑ 92ParEmeI-118
❑ 92Pin-379
❑ 92PinFre-379
❑ 92ProSet-122
❑ 92Sco-536
❑ 92ScoCan-536
❑ 92Sen-12
❑ 92Ult-365
❑ 93Lea-407
❑ 93OmaLan-18
❑ 93PanSti-116
❑ 93Pin-385
❑ 93PinCan-385
❑ 93Sco-265
❑ 93Sco-551
❑ 93ScoCan-265
❑ 93ScoCan-551
❑ 93ScoGol-551
❑ 93StaClu-497
❑ 93StaCluFDI-497
❑ 93StaCluO-497
❑ 94Lea-546
❑ 94Pin-423
❑ 94PinArtP-423
❑ 94PinRinC-423
❑ 95CanGamNHLP-161
❑ 95TopPowL-10PL
❑ 96BeAPAut-136
❑ 96BeAPAutSil-136
❑ 96BeAPla-136
❑ 97Pac-306
❑ 97PacCop-306
❑ 97PacEmeGre-306
❑ 97PacIceB-306
❑ 97PacRed-306
❑ 97PacSil-306
**Pelyk, Mike**
❑ 68MapLeaWB-7
❑ 68PosCerM-17
❑ 68ShiCoi-166
❑ 69MapLeaWBG-26
❑ 70DadCoo-98
❑ 70EssPowPla-21
❑ 70MapLeaP-10
❑ 70OPC-107
❑ 70SarProSta-203
❑ 70Top-107
❑ 71MapLeaP-15
❑ 71OPC-92
❑ 71SarProSta-197
❑ 71Top-92
❑ 71TorSun-268
❑ 72MapLeaP-23
❑ 72OPC-17
❑ 72SarProSta-200
❑ 72Top-107
❑ 73MapLeaP-21
❑ 73OPC-71
❑ 73Top-71
❑ 74OPCWHA-19
❑ 75StiKah-9
❑ 76MapLeaP-14
❑ 76OPCNHL-342
**Pelzer, James**
❑ 91BriColJHL-96
**Penelton, Paul**
❑ 85KitRan-25
**Penicka, Lubomir**
❑ 81SweSemHVS-71
❑ 82SweSemHVS-94
**Penk, Jan**
❑ 94CzeAPSE-260
❑ 95CzeAPSE-133
**Penkala, Joe**
❑ 88SasBla-1
**Penn, Josh**
❑ 98FloEve-17
**Penn, Shawn**
❑ 94TolSto-17
❑ 95TolSto-19
**Pennell, Fred**
❑ 87SudWol-10
**Pennell, Gordie**
❑ 51BufBis-18
**Pennell, Rod**
❑ 88SudWol-10
**Penner, Pat**
❑ 92ForWorF-15
**Penney, Chad**
❑ 907thInnSOHL-314
❑ 917thInnSOHL-58
❑ 93SauSteMGM-9
❑ 93UppDec-436
❑ 94Cla-68
❑ 94ClaDraGol-68
❑ 94ClaProP-65
❑ 94ClaTri-T46
❑ 94Lea-241
❑ 94OPCPre-267
❑ 94OPCPreSE-267
❑ 94TopPre-267
❑ 94TopPreSE-267
**Penney, Jackson**
❑ 90ProAHLIHL-115
❑ 92AlbIntTC-15
❑ 95GerDELE-402
❑ 96GerDELE-264
❑ 98GerDELE-232
**Penney, Ryan**
❑ 95Sla-182
**Penney, Steve**
❑ 83CanaPos-21
❑ 83NovScoV-15
❑ 84CanaPos-21
❑ 84CanaPos-22
❑ 84OPC-269
❑ 85CanaPla-4
❑ 85CanaPla-7
❑ 85CanaPos-25
❑ 85CanaPro-14
❑ 85OPC-4
❑ 85OPCSti-126
❑ 85Top-4
❑ 86JetBor-19
❑ 86KraDra-53
❑ 86OPC-222
❑ 87MonHaw-21
**Pennington, Cliff**
❑ 44BeeGro2P-55A
❑ 44BeeGro2P-55B
❑ 61ShiCoi-1
❑ 61Top-19
❑ 62Top-14
❑ 63QueAce-22
❑ 64BeeGro3P-22
**Penniston, Don**
❑ 51LavDaiQSHL-58
**Pennock, Berkley**
❑ 93RedDeeR-18
**Pennock, Trevor**
❑ 907thInnSWHL-18
❑ 91BriColJHL-126
**Pennoyer, Rob**
❑ 92BriColJHL-128
**Penstock, Byron**
❑ 907thInnSWHL-224
❑ 90BraWheK-18
❑ 917thInnSWHL-302
❑ 92BraWheK-18
❑ 95SlaMemC-26
**Penton, Scott**
❑ 93OweSouPla-22
**Penttinen, Jukka**
❑ 95FinnSIS-258
❑ 96FinnSISR-46
**Pepin, Bob**
❑ 51LavDaiS-52
❑ 52St.LawS-83
**Pepin, Rene**
❑ 51LavDaiQSHL-42
❑ 52St.LawS-82
**Peplinski, Jim**
❑ 80FlamPos-15
❑ 80PepCap-13
❑ 81FlamPos-15
❑ 81OPC-49
❑ 82FlamDol-5
❑ 82OPC-55
❑ 82OPCSti-216
❑ 82PosCer-3
❑ 83Ess-14
❑ 83OPC-90
❑ 83Vac-16
❑ 84OPC-233
❑ 85FlamRedRP-22
❑ 86FlamRedR-21
❑ 86KraDra-54
❑ 86OPC-182
❑ 86OPCSti-84
❑ 86Top-182
❑ 87FlamRedRP-24
❑ 87OPC-209
❑ 87OPCSti-46
❑ 87PanSti-213
❑ 88OPC-243
❑ 88OPCSti-88
❑ 88PanSti-14
❑ 89OPC-206
❑ 89OPCSti-99
❑ 89PanSti-37
**Pepperall, Colin**
❑ 95Sla-197
❑ 97BowCHL-30
❑ 97BowCHLOPC-30
❑ 98BowCHL-19
❑ 98BowCHLGA-19
❑ 98BowCHLOI-19
❑ 98BowChrC-19
❑ 98BowChrCGA-19
❑ 98BowChrCGAR-19
❑ 98BowChrCOI-19
❑ 98BowChrCOIR-19
❑ 98BowChrCR-19
**Pepperall, Ryan**
❑ 94KitRan-16
❑ 95Cla-46
❑ 95Cla-87
❑ 95Sla-147
❑ 95Sla-NNO
❑ 96KitRan-22
❑ 97St.JohML-20
**Perardi, Eric**
❑ 93RenEng-21
**Percival, Rob**
❑ 88BroBra-15
**Pereira, Lenny**
❑ 94RalIce-14
**Perez, Denis**
❑ 93SweSemWCS-255
❑ 94FinnJaaK-215
❑ 94FreNatT-23
❑ 96SweSemW-186
❑ 98GerDELE-242
**Perkins, Darren**
❑ 907thInnSWHL-279
❑ 90PriAlbR-17
❑ 917thInnSWHL-244
❑ 91PriAlbR-17
❑ 93HamRoaA-6
❑ 93TolSto-12
❑ 94ThuBayS-2
❑ 94TolSto-18
❑ 95ThuBayS-16
**Perkins, Ross**
❑ 74OPCWHA-39
**Perkins, Terry**
❑ 86FreExp-20
❑ 88SalLakCGE-3
**Perkovic, Steven**
❑ 93HamRoaA-14
**Perlini, Fred**
❑ 94GuiFla-4
❑ 95GuiFla-6
❑ 95GuiFla-28
**Perlstrom, Stefan**
❑ 83SweSemE-83
❑ 84SweSemE-77
❑ 85SwePanS-74
❑ 86SwePanS-62
**Perna, Dominic**
❑ 97BowCHL-49
❑ 97BowCHLOPC-49
❑ 98BowCHL-83
❑ 98BowCHL-163
❑ 98BowCHLGA-83
❑ 98BowCHLGA-163
❑ 98BowCHLOI-83
❑ 98BowCHLOI-163
❑ 98BowChrC-83
❑ 98BowChrC-163
❑ 98BowChrCGA-83
❑ 98BowChrCGA-163
❑ 98BowChrCGAR-83
❑ 98BowChrCGAR-163
❑ 98BowChrCOI-83
❑ 98BowChrCOI-163
❑ 98BowChrCOIR-83
❑ 98BowChrCOIR-163
❑ 98BowChrCR-83
❑ 98BowChrCR-163
**Perna, Mike**
❑ 93NiaFalT-24
❑ 95Sla-202
**Peronmaa, Petri**
❑ 96FinnSISR-111
**Perpich, John**
❑ 90CapKod-19
**Perras, Jean-Sebastien**
❑ 90MonAAA-18
**Perrault, Jocelyn**
❑ 88ProAHL-121
**Perrault, Kirby**
❑ 90MicTecHus-20
❑ 91MicTecHus-19
❑ 93MicTecH-9
**Perreault, Albert**
❑ 36V356WorG-115
**Perreault, Bob**
❑ 44BeeGro2P-56A
❑ 44BeeGro2P-56B
❑ 62Top-2
❑ 64BeeGro3P-23
**Perreault, Fernand**
❑ 51CleBar-14
❑ 51LavDaiQSHL-98
❑ 51LavDaiS-28
**Perreault, Gerry**
❑ 51LavDaiLSJ-7
❑ 84KelAccD-34
**Perreault, Gil (Gilbert)**
❑ 70ColSta-28
❑ 70DadCoo-99
❑ 70EssPowPla-81
❑ 70OPC-131
❑ 70SarProSta-23
❑ 70Top-131
❑ 71Baz-6
❑ 71OPC-60
❑ 71OPC-246
❑ 71OPCPos-14
❑ 71OPCTBoo-8
❑ 71SabPos-15
❑ 71SarProSta-19
❑ 71Top-60
❑ 71TorSun-36
❑ 72OPC-136
❑ 72OPCTeaC-22
❑ 72SabPepPB-5
❑ 72SabPepPB-6
❑ 72SabPepPB-7
❑ 72SarProSta-31
❑ 72Top-120
❑ 73OPC-70
❑ 73SabBel-4
❑ 73SabPos-10
❑ 73Top-70
❑ 74LipSou-2
❑ 74NHLActSta-50
❑ 74OPCNHL-25
❑ 74Top-25
❑ 75OPCNHL-10
❑ 75Top-10
❑ 76OPCNHL-2
❑ 76OPCNHL-3
❑ 76OPCNHL-180
❑ 76OPCNHL-214
❑ 76OPCNHL-380
❑ 76SabGla-3
❑ 76Top-2
❑ 76Top-3
❑ 76Top-180
❑ 76Top-214
❑ 76TopGloI-9
❑ 77OPCNHL-7
❑ 77OPCNHL-210
❑ 77Top-7
❑ 77Top-210
❑ 77TopGloS-14
❑ 77TopOPCGlo-14
❑ 78OPC-130
❑ 78Top-130
❑ 79OPC-180
❑ 79SabMilP-4
❑ 79Top-180
❑ 80OPC-80
❑ 80OPCSup-2
❑ 80SabMilP-4
❑ 80Top-80
❑ 81OPC-30
❑ 81OPCSti-60
❑ 81PosSta-2
❑ 81SabMilP-4
❑ 82OPC-25
❑ 82OPC-30
❑ 82OPCSti-118
❑ 82PosCer-2
❑ 82SabMilP-7
❑ 83OPC-67
❑ 83OPCSti-4
❑ 83OPCSti-240
❑ 83OPCSti-241
❑ 83PufSti-8
❑ 847EDis-4
❑ 84KelAccD-3A
❑ 84OPC-24
❑ 84OPCSti-201
❑ 84OPCSti-202
❑ 84SabBluS-12
❑ 84Top-19
❑ 857ECreCar-2
❑ 85OPC-160
❑ 85OPCBoxB-K
❑ 85OPCSti-188
❑ 85SabBluS-19
❑ 85SabBluSS-19
❑ 85Top-160
❑ 85TopBoxB-K
❑ 86OPC-79
❑ 86OPCSti-43
❑ 86SabBluS-22
❑ 86SabBluSSma-22
❑ 86Top-79
❑ 88EssAllSta-35
❑ 90Sco-355
❑ 90ScoCan-355
❑ 91FutTreC72-51
❑ 91Kra-80
❑ 91ProSet-596
❑ 91ProSetFre-596
❑ 92FutTre76CC-162
❑ 93SabNoc-14
❑ 95ZelMasoH-5
❑ 99UppDecCL-50
❑ 99UppDecCLCLC-50
**Perreault, Mathieu**
❑ 92QueIntP-51
**Perreault, Nicolas**
❑ 93MicSta-16
❑ 94St.JohF-17
❑ 95TolSto-2
**Perreault, Yanic**
❑ 907thInnSQMJHL-100
❑ 907thInnSQMJHL-146
❑ 917thInnSCHLAW-22
❑ 917thInnSCHLAW-30
❑ 917thInnSMC-115
❑ 91AreDraPic-31
❑ 91Cla-39
❑ 91ProAHLCHL-339
❑ 91StaPicH-22
❑ 91UltDra-34
❑ 91UltDra-54
❑ 91UltDra-87
❑ 92Sco-487
❑ 92ScoCan-487
❑ 92St.JohML-15
❑ 92UppDec-70
❑ 93St.JohML-18
❑ 94ClaProP-113
❑ 94Par-230
❑ 94ParGol-230
❑ 95BeAPla-150
❑ 95BeAPSig-S150
❑ 95BeAPSigDC-S150
❑ 95ColEdgI-184
❑ 95ColEdgI-C8
❑ 95ColEdgIQ-IR3
❑ 95Don-375
❑ 95Lea-249
❑ 95Met-73
❑ 95ParInt-372
❑ 95ParIntEI-372
❑ 95Sum-166
❑ 95SumArtP-166
❑ 95SumIce-166
❑ 95Top-223
❑ 95TopOPCI-223
❑ 95Ult-253
❑ 95UppDec-28
❑ 95UppDecEleIce-28
❑ 95UppDecEleIceG-28
❑ 95UppDecSpeE-SE130
❑ 95UppDecSpeEdiG-SE130
❑ 95Zen-113
❑ 96ColCho-126
❑ 96Don-21
❑ 96DonCanI-76
❑ 96DonCanIGPP-76
❑ 96DonCanIRPP-76
❑ 96DonEli-76
❑ 96DonEliDCS-76
❑ 96DonPrePro-21
❑ 96KraUppD-20
❑ 96Lea-7
❑ 96LeaPre-107
❑ 96LeaPreP-7
❑ 96LeaPrePP-107
❑ 96Pin-42
❑ 96PinArtP-42
❑ 96PinFoi-42
❑ 96PinPreS-42
❑ 96PinRinC-42
❑ 96Sco-25
❑ 96ScoArtPro-25
❑ 96ScoDeaCAP-25
❑ 96ScoGolB-25
❑ 96ScoSpeAP-25
❑ 96UppDec-79
❑ 96Zen-86
❑ 96ZenArtP-86
❑ 97DonPri-142
❑ 97DonPriSoA-142
❑ 97Kat-71
❑ 97KatGol-71
❑ 97KatSil-71
❑ 97PacCroR-64

❑ 97PacCroREG-64
❑ 97PacCroRIB-64
❑ 97PacCroRS-64
❑ 97PacInvNRB-97
❑ 97PacOme-111
❑ 97PacOmeC-111
❑ 97PacOmeDG-111
❑ 97PacOmeEG-111
❑ 97PacOmeG-111
❑ 97PacOmeIB-111
❑ 97PacRev-65
❑ 97PacRevC-65
❑ 97PacRevE-65
❑ 97PacRevIB-65
❑ 97PacRevR-65
❑ 97PacRevS-65
❑ 97PinBee-35
❑ 97PinBeeGP-35
❑ 97SPAut-75
❑ 97SPAutSotT-YP
❑ 97UppDecBD-127
❑ 97UppDecBDDD-127
❑ 97UppDecBDQD-127
❑ 97UppDecBDTD-127
❑ 97Zen-64
❑ 97Zen5x7-29
❑ 97ZenGolImp-29
❑ 97ZenSilImp-29
❑ 97ZenZGol-64
❑ 97ZenZSil-64
❑ 98Be A PPA-62
❑ 98Be A PPAA-62
❑ 98Be A PPAAF-62
❑ 98Be A PPTBASG-62
❑ 98Be APG-62
❑ 98KinPowP-LAK4
❑ 98Pac-243
❑ 98PacAur-87
❑ 98PacCroR-64
❑ 98PacCroRLS-64
❑ 98PacDynI-89
❑ 98PacDynIIB-89
❑ 98PacDynIR-89
❑ 98PacIceB-243
❑ 98PacPar-106
❑ 98PacParC-106
❑ 98PacParEG-106
❑ 98PacParH-106
❑ 98PacParIB-106
❑ 98PacParS-106
❑ 98PacRed-243
❑ 98UC-96
❑ 98UD ChoPCR-96
❑ 98UD ChoR-96
❑ 98UppDec-105
❑ 98UppDecE-105
❑ 98UppDecE1o1-105
❑ 98UppDecGR-105
❑ 99Pac-414
❑ 99PacAur-137
❑ 99PacAurPD-137
❑ 99PacCop-414
❑ 99PacGol-414
❑ 99PacIceB-414
❑ 99PacPreD-414

**Perrett, Craig**
❑ 91AirCanSJHL-C34

**Perrier, Bryant**
❑ 89ProIHL-100

**Perrin, Eric**
❑ 98KanCitB-7

**Perron, Jean**
❑ 84CanaPos-23
❑ 85CanaPos-26
❑ 85CanaPro-15
❑ 86CanaPos-17
❑ 87CanaPos-22
❑ 87CanaVacS-7
❑ 87CanaVacS-10

**Perrott, Nathan**
❑ 95Cla-39
❑ 95Sla-236
❑ 96SauSteMG-16
❑ 96SauSteMGA-16

**Perry, Alan**
❑ 88ProIHL-3
❑ 92OklCitB-18
❑ 94CenHocL-67

**Perry, Brian**
❑ 69OPC-84

**Perry, Jeff**
❑ 907thInnSOHL-292
❑ 94St.JohF-18
❑ 95St.JohF-18

**Perry, Randy**
❑ 93LetHur-11
❑ 95LetHur-18
❑ 96SeaThu-23
❑ 97BowCHL-96
❑ 97BowCHLOPC-96
❑ 98GerDELE-221

**Perry, Tom**
❑ 91AirCanSJHL-B10
❑ 92MPSPhoSJHL-35

**Perry, Tyler**
❑ 95SeaThu-21

**Pers, Bengt-Ake**
❑ 86SwePanS-139
❑ 87SwePanS-150

**Perschau, Dirk**
❑ 94GerDELE-44
❑ 95GerDELE-32
❑ 96GerDELE-26

**Person, Todd**
❑ 92RalIce-10
❑ 92RalIce-35

**Persson, Bengt**
❑ 65SweCorI-115
❑ 67SweHoc-260
❑ 69SweHocS-306

**Persson, Gunnar**
❑ 83SweSemE-56
❑ 84SweSemE-56
❑ 85SwePanS-53
❑ 86SwePanS-35
❑ 87SwePanS-53

**Persson, Hakan**
❑ 87SwePanS-257
❑ 92SweSemE-256

**Persson, Hans Ake**
❑ 73SweHocS-169
❑ 73SweWorCS-169

**Persson, Ingemar**
❑ 65SweCorI-120

**Persson, Jerry**
❑ 91SweSemE-294
❑ 92SweSemE-311
❑ 93SweSemE-278
❑ 94SweLeaE-257
❑ 95SweLeaE-199

**Persson, Joakim**
❑ 90SweSemE-274
❑ 91SweSemE-55
❑ 93SweSemE-42
❑ 94SweLeaE-192
❑ 94SweLeaERR-7
❑ 95SweLeaE-4
❑ 95SweLeaES-1
❑ 95SweUppDE-1
❑ 95SweUppDETNA-NA1
❑ 96GerDELE-92

**Persson, Kent**
❑ 65SweCorI-204
❑ 67SweHoc-276
❑ 69SweHocS-320
❑ 70SweHocS-224
❑ 72SweHocS-281
❑ 74SweHocS-260

**Persson, Mikael**
❑ 92SweSemE-315

**Persson, Ricard**
❑ 89SweSemE-126
❑ 90SweSemE-203
❑ 91SweSemE-132
❑ 92SweSemE-156
❑ 93SweSemE-178
❑ 94SweLeaE-55
❑ 95Don-304
❑ 95StaClu-225
❑ 95StaCluMOMS-225
❑ 96BeAPAut-210
❑ 96BeAPAutSil-210
❑ 96BeAPla-210
❑ 97PacInvNRB-172

**Persson, Stefan**
❑ 78OPC-144
❑ 78Top-144
❑ 79IslTrans-13
❑ 79OPC-32
❑ 79Top-32
❑ 80OPC-219
❑ 80Top-219
❑ 81OPC-206
❑ 81Top-E92
❑ 82OPC-209
❑ 82PosCer-12
❑ 83OPC-15
❑ 83SweSemE-116
❑ 84IslIslN-20
❑ 84OPC-133
❑ 84SweSemE-116
❑ 84Top-99
❑ 85IslIslN-24
❑ 85SwePanS-105
❑ 86SwePanS-103
❑ 87SwePanS-101
❑ 89SweSemE-112
❑ 90SweSemE-118

**Persson, Stig-Olof**
❑ 71SweHocS-338
❑ 72SweHocS-150

**Persson, Torbjorn**
❑ 90SweSemE-122
❑ 91SweSemE-123
❑ 92SweSemE-142
❑ 93SweSemE-112
❑ 94SweLeaE-132

**Perthaler, Christian**
❑ 93SweSemWCS-283
❑ 95AusNatTea-20

**Pervukhin, Vasili**
❑ 79PanSti-143
❑ 81SweSemHVS-42
❑ 82SweSemHVS-55
❑ 83RusNatT-14
❑ 87RusNatT-16

**Pesat, Ivo**
❑ 94CzeAPSE-229
❑ 94CzeAPSE-230
❑ 95CzeAPSE-4
❑ 96CzeAPSE-215

**Peschke, Frank**
❑ 94GerDELE-396
❑ 95GerDELE-417

**Pesetti, Ron**
❑ 87MonHaw-20

**Pesut, George**
❑ 75OPCNHL-360

**Petawabano, Rodney**
❑ 917thInnSQMJHL-83

**Petendra, Kevin**
❑ 82KitRan-14

**Peterek, Jan**
❑ 94CzeAPSE-137

**Peters, Andrew**
❑ 98BowCHL-150
❑ 98BowCHLAuB-A33
❑ 98BowCHLAuG-A33
❑ 98BowCHLAuS-A33
❑ 98BowCHLGA-150
❑ 98BowCHLOI-150
❑ 98BowChrC-150
❑ 98BowChrCGA-150
❑ 98BowChrCGAR-150
❑ 98BowChrCOI-150
❑ 98BowChrCOIR-150
❑ 98BowChrCR-150

**Peters, Dietmar**
❑ 70SweHocS-371

**Peters, Frank**
❑ 28V1282PauC-47

**Peters, Garry**
❑ 65Coc-88
❑ 65Top-28
❑ 68OPC-99
❑ 68Top-99
❑ 69OPC-171
❑ 70EssPowPla-210
❑ 70FlyPos-10
❑ 70OPC-196
❑ 70SarProSta-151
❑ 71BruTealss-17

**Peters, Geoff**
❑ 95BowDraPro-P26
❑ 95Cla-89
❑ 95Sla-190
❑ 95Sla-440
❑ 95UppDec-522
❑ 95UppDecElelce-522
❑ 95UppDecElelceG-522

**Peters, Jason**
❑ 89VicCou-16
❑ 907thInnSWHL-251
❑ 90SasBla-25
❑ 91BriColJHL-134

**Peters, Jim**
❑ 44BeeGro2P-57
❑ 44BeeGro2P-133
❑ 44BeeGro2P-201
❑ 45QuaOatP-104A
❑ 45QuaOatP-104B
❑ 51Par-41
❑ 52Par-35
❑ 53Par-69
❑ 61HamRed-17
❑ 76OldTim-13
❑ 81RedWinOld-6

**Peters, Jim (90s)**
❑ 92BirBul-11
❑ 93BirBul-11
❑ 93DayBom-5

**Peters, Jimmy**
❑ 69OPC-143
❑ 70SarProSta-77
❑ 72OPC-224
❑ 73OPC-231

**Peters, Rob**
❑ 95DayBom-19

**Peters, Tony**
❑ 92DayBom-21
❑ 93DayBom-27

**Peterson, Brent**
❑ 82SabMilP-17
❑ 83OPC-68
❑ 84OPC-25
❑ 84SabBluS-13
❑ 85Canu-18
❑ 85OPC-47
❑ 85OPCSti-178
❑ 85Top-47
❑ 86Canu-15
❑ 86KraDra-55
❑ 86OPC-251
❑ 86OPCSti-100
❑ 87OPC-263
❑ 87OPCSti-199
❑ 88WhaJunGR-12
❑ 917thInnSWHL-47
❑ 91MicTecHus-30
❑ 93MicTecH-8
❑ 95Cla-78
❑ 95ClaAut-17

**Peterson, Cory**
❑ 95SigRooA-32
❑ 95SigRooAPC-32

**Peterson, Kyle**
❑ 93MicTecH-3

**Peterson, Toby**
❑ 97UppDecBD-135
❑ 97UppDecBDDD-135
❑ 97UppDecBDQD-135
❑ 97UppDecBDTD-135
❑ 98UC-307
❑ 98UD ChoPCR-307
❑ 98UD ChoR-307

**Peterzen, Boo**
❑ 86SwePanS-133
❑ 87SwePanS-111

**Pethke, Marc**
❑ 94GerDELE-192
❑ 95GerDELE-171
❑ 96GerDELE-113
❑ 98GerDELE-10

**Petit, Jerome**
❑ 98Vald'OF-24

**Petit, Michel**
❑ 83Canu-16
❑ 84Canu-19
❑ 85FreExp-16
❑ 86Canu-16
❑ 87OPC-262
❑ 87OPCSti-196
❑ 87PanSti-342
❑ 88PanSti-304
❑ 89Nord-34
❑ 89NordGenF-25
❑ 89NordPol-22
❑ 89OPC-251
❑ 89PanSti-291
❑ 90Bow-170
❑ 90BowTif-170
❑ 90NordPet-20
❑ 90NordTeal-23
❑ 90OPC-271
❑ 90PanSti-148
❑ 90ProSet-256A
❑ 90ProSet-256B
❑ 90ProSet-539
❑ 90Sco-187
❑ 90ScoCan-187
❑ 90ScoRoo-54T
❑ 90Top-271
❑ 90TopTif-271
❑ 90UppDec-181
❑ 90UppDecF-181
❑ 91Bow-158
❑ 91MapLeaP-25
❑ 91OPC-166
❑ 91PanSti-98
❑ 91Par-252
❑ 91ParFre-252
❑ 91Pin-49
❑ 91PinFre-49
❑ 91ProSet-492
❑ 91ProSetFre-492
❑ 91ScoAme-103
❑ 91ScoCan-103
❑ 91StaClu-311
❑ 91Top-166
❑ 91UppDec-359
❑ 91UppDecF-359
❑ 92Bow-101
❑ 92DurPan-43
❑ 92FlamIGA-13
❑ 92OPC-185
❑ 92Pin-206
❑ 92PinFre-206
❑ 92Sco-38
❑ 92ScoCan-38
❑ 92StaClu-195
❑ 92Top-337
❑ 92TopGol-337G
❑ 93OPCPre-141
❑ 93OPCPreG-141
❑ 93Par-304
❑ 93ParEmel-304
❑ 93Pow-308
❑ 93Sco-275
❑ 93ScoCan-275
❑ 93StaClu-232
❑ 93StaCluFDI-232
❑ 93StaCluFDIO-232
❑ 93StaCluO-232
❑ 93TopPre-141
❑ 93TopPreG-141
❑ 93UppDec-66
❑ 94Lea-444
❑ 94OPCPre-406
❑ 94OPCPreSE-406
❑ 94Par-39
❑ 94ParGol-39
❑ 94TopPre-406
❑ 94TopPreSE-406

**Petitclerc, Eric**
❑ 92QueIntP-49

**Petitclerc, Maxime**
❑ 917thInnSQMJHL-291

**Petrash, Ken**
❑ 94GerDELE-231
❑ 95GerDELE-228
❑ 96GerDELE-79

**Petre, Henrik**
❑ 97UppDecBD-67
❑ 97UppDecBDDD-67
❑ 97UppDecBDQD-67
❑ 97UppDecBDTD-67
❑ 98UC-292
❑ 98UD ChoPCR-292
❑ 98UD ChoR-292

**Petrenko, Sergei**
❑ 92RusStaRA-26
❑ 92UppDec-346
❑ 93Cla-91
❑ 93Don-43
❑ 93Lea-425
❑ 93Par-292
❑ 93ParEmel-292
❑ 93RochAmeKod-20
❑ 93StaClu-373
❑ 93StaCluFDI-373
❑ 93StaCluO-373
❑ 93SweSemWCS-139
❑ 93Ult-275
❑ 93UppDec-450

**Petrilainen, Pasi**
❑ 95FinnSIS-110
❑ 95UppDec-550
❑ 95UppDecElelce-550
❑ 95UppDecElelceG-550
❑ 96FinnSISR-127
❑ 97UppDecBD-48
❑ 97UppDecBDDD-48
❑ 97UppDecBDQD-48
❑ 97UppDecBDTD-48
❑ 98UC-279
❑ 98UD ChoPCR-279
❑ 98UD ChoR-279

**Petroni, Pierre**
❑ 917thInnSQMJHL-23

**Petrov, Oleg**
❑ 92CanaPos-20
❑ 92FreCan-20
❑ 92OPCPre-96
❑ 92Par-486
❑ 92ParEmel-486
❑ 92RusStaRA-27
❑ 93ClaProPro-8
❑ 93Don-452
❑ 93FreCan-21
❑ 93Lea-260
❑ 93OPCCanHF-56
❑ 93Pin-212
❑ 93PinCan-212
❑ 93Pow-371
❑ 93Sco-459
❑ 93ScoCan-459
❑ 93UppDec-84
❑ 94CanaPos-18
❑ 94CanGamNHLP-138
❑ 94ClaAllRT-AR4
❑ 94ClaProP-177
❑ 94Don-61
❑ 94Fla-90
❑ 94Lea-354
❑ 94OPCFinIns-13
❑ 94OPCPre-377
❑ 94OPCPreSE-377
❑ 94Par-119
❑ 94Par-291
❑ 94ParGol-119
❑ 94ParGol-291
❑ 94ParSEV-40
❑ 94Pin-203
❑ 94PinArtP-203
❑ 94PinRinC-203
❑ 94Sco-260
❑ 94ScoGol-260
❑ 94ScoPla-260
❑ 94ScoPlaTS-260
❑ 94StaClu-241
❑ 94StaCluFDI-241
❑ 94StaCluMOMS-241
❑ 94StaCluSTWC-241
❑ 94TopPre-377
❑ 94TopPreSE-377
❑ 94Ult-314
❑ 94UppDec-137
❑ 94UppDecElelce-137
❑ 94UppDecSPI-SP41
❑ 94UppDecSPIDC-SP41
❑ 95CanaPos-11
❑ 95UppDec-343
❑ 95UppDecElelce-343
❑ 95UppDecElelceG-343

**Petrov, Sergei**
❑ 93MinDul-25

**Petrov, Vladimir**
❑ 69SweHocS-11
❑ 69SweWorC-21
❑ 69SweWorC-28
❑ 69SweWorC-70
❑ 69SweWorC-71
❑ 69SweWorC-132
❑ 70SweHocS-328
❑ 71SweHocS-39
❑ 72SweSemWC-16
❑ 73SweHocS-88
❑ 73SweWorCS-88
❑ 74SweHocS-6
❑ 74SweSemHVS-35
❑ 79PanSti-147
❑ 80USSOlyTMP-8
❑ 91FutTreC72-52
❑ 95SweGloWC-242

**Petrovicky, Robert**
❑ 91UppDecCWJC-93
❑ 92Cla-6
❑ 92OPCPre-36
❑ 92Par-61
❑ 92ParEmel-61
❑ 92Pin-402
❑ 92PinFre-402
❑ 92Ult-302
❑ 92UppDec-569
❑ 92UppDecER-ER20
❑ 92WhaDai-18
❑ 93Cla-144
❑ 93Don-145
❑ 93Lea-187
❑ 93Par-89
❑ 93ParEmel-89
❑ 93Pow-107
❑ 93Sco-277
❑ 93ScoCan-277
❑ 93SweSemWCS-106
❑ 93Ult-337
❑ 93UppDec-37
❑ 93UppDecSP-63
❑ 94BeAPla-R84
❑ 94FinnJaaK-210
❑ 94Lea-387
❑ 94Par-94
❑ 94ParGol-94
❑ 94UppDec-361
❑ 94UppDecElelce-361
❑ 95SloAPSNT-26
❑ 96ClaGol-6
❑ 96SweSemW-233
❑ 97PacDynBKS-82
❑ 97ScoBlu-9
❑ 97ScoBluPla-9
❑ 97ScoBluPre-9
❑ 97UppDec-350

**Petrovicky, Ronald**
❑ 98BowCHL-78
❑ 98BowCHLGA-78
❑ 98BowCHLOI-78
❑ 98BowChrC-78
❑ 98BowChrCGA-78
❑ 98BowChrCGAR-78
❑ 98BowChrCOI-78
❑ 98BowChrCOIR-78
❑ 98BowChrCR-78

**Petrovka, Vladimir**
❑ 91SweSemWCS-124

**Petruic, Jeff**
❑ 907thInnSWHL-151
❑ 917thInnSWHL-281
❑ 95DayBom-20

**Petruk, Randy**
❑ 95BowDraPro-P27
❑ 95SlaMemC-23
❑ 95UppDec-524
❑ 95UppDecElelce-524
❑ 95UppDecElelceG-524
❑ 96KamBla-17
❑ 97BowCHL-82
❑ 97BowCHLOPC-82
❑ 98BowCHL-42
❑ 98BowCHLGA-42
❑ 98BowCHLOI-42
❑ 98BowCHLSC-SC10
❑ 98BowChrC-42
❑ 98BowChrCGA-42
❑ 98BowChrCGAR-42
❑ 98BowChrCOI-42
❑ 98BowChrCOIR-42
❑ 98BowChrCR-42
❑ 98FloEve-18

**Petrunin, Andrei**
❑ 94SP-190
❑ 94SPDieCut-190
❑ 95Cla-66
❑ 95ClaAut-18
❑ 95SP-178
❑ 95UppDec-556
❑ 95UppDecElelce-556
❑ 95UppDecElelceG-556
❑ 96UppDecIce-143

**Petterle, Brian**
❑ 80SauSteMG-2

**Pettersson, Anders**
❑ 89SweSemE-132

**Pettersson, Daniel**
❑ 86SwePanS-241
❑ 89SweSemE-208

**Pettersson, Dennis**
❑ 72SweHocS-276
❑ 74SweHocS-182

**Pettersson, Hakan**
❑ 69SweHocS-268
❑ 70SweHocS-163
❑ 71SweHocS-23
❑ 71SweHocS-258
❑ 72SweHocS-238
❑ 72SweSemWC-66
❑ 73SweHocS-242
❑ 73SweWorCS-242
❑ 74SweHocS-261

**Pettersson, Hans**
❑ 86SwePanS-257
❑ 89SweSemE-222
❑ 90SweSemE-58

**Pettersson, Henrik**
❑ 92SweSemE-292

**Pettersson, Janne**
❑ 69SweHocS-211

**Pettersson, John**
❑ 87SwePanS-232

**Pettersson, Jorgen**
❑ 81OPC-296
❑ 81OPCSti-135
❑ 81Top-W121
❑ 82OPC-309
❑ 82OPCSti-202
❑ 82PosCer-17
❑ 82SweSemHVS-152
❑ 83OPC-318
❑ 83OPCSti-123
❑ 83PufSti-15
❑ 84OPC-189
❑ 84OPCSti-59
❑ 85WhaJunW-15
❑ 86CapPol-20
❑ 89SweSemE-280
❑ 92BluUDBB-18

**Pettersson, Kjell-Ronnie**
❑ 64SweCorI-100
❑ 65SweCorI-100
❑ 67SweHoc-298
❑ 69SweHocS-345
❑ 70SweHocS-260
❑ 71SweHocS-320
❑ 72SweHocS-300
❑ 73SweHocS-144
❑ 73SweWorCS-144

**Pettersson, Lars-Gunnar**
❑ 83SweSemE-47
❑ 84SweSemE-47
❑ 85SwePanS-41
❑ 86SwePanS-20
❑ 87SwePanS-182
❑ 89SweSemE-157
❑ 89SweSemWCS-25
❑ 90SweSemE-236
❑ 91SweSemE-166
❑ 92SweSemE-191
❑ 93SweSemE-162

**Pettersson, Lennart**
❑ 71SweHocS-82

**Pettersson, Martin**
❑ 83SweSemE-192
❑ 84SweSemE-215
❑ 86SwePanS-231
❑ 87SwePanS-226
❑ 89SweSemE-206

**Pettersson, Mikael**
❑ 86SwePanS-214
❑ 92SweSemE-237
❑ 92SweSemE-289
❑ 93SweSemE-256
❑ 94SweLeaE-239
❑ 95SweLeaE-134
❑ 95SweUppDE-196

**Pettersson, Ove**
❑ 83SweSemE-132
❑ 84SweSemE-154
❑ 85SwePanS-137
❑ 86SwePanS-141
❑ 87SwePanS-207
❑ 89SweSemE-176
❑ 90SweSemE-9

**Pettersson, Peter**
❑ 83SweSemE-222
❑ 95SweUppDE1DS-DS15

**Pettersson, Ronald**
❑ 64SweCorI-14
❑ 64SweCorI-101
❑ 65SweCorI-14
❑ 65SweCorI-101
❑ 67SweHoc-299
❑ 81SweSemHVS-126
❑ 90SweSemE-283

**Pettersson, Stefan**
❑ 69SweHocS-269
❑ 70SweHocS-152
❑ 71SweHocS-245
❑ 72SweHocS-229
❑ 73SweHocS-243
❑ 73SweWorCS-243
❑ 74SweHocS-183

**Pettersson, Tommy**
❑ 71SweHocS-270
❑ 72SweHocS-246
❑ 90SweSemE-22
❑ 91SweSemE-223

**Pettie, Jim**
❑ 77RocAme-20

**Pettinger, Gordon**
❑ 34BeeGro1P-120
❑ 36V356WorG-76

**Petz, Ryan**
❑ 917thInnSWHL-323

**Phair, Lyle**
❑ 88ProAHL-214

**Phalsson, Samuel**
❑ 95ColCho-350
❑ 95ColChoPC-350
❑ 95ColChoPCP-350

**Phelps, Chris**
❑ 907thInnSOHL-115
❑ 917thInnSOHL-27
❑ 94HamRoaA-10
❑ 95HamRoaA-17
❑ 96HamRoaA-HRA3

**Philipoff, Hal**
❑ 79OPC-27
❑ 79Top-27

**Philipp, Rainer**
❑ 72SweSemWC-109
❑ 79PanSti-108

**Phillips, Bill**
❑ 33OPCV304A-43

**Phillips, Chris**
❑ 95BowDraPro-P28
❑ 95DonEliWJ-7
❑ 95PriAlbR-16
❑ 95SP-176
❑ 95UppDec-517
❑ 95UppDecElelce-517
❑ 95UppDecElelceG-517
❑ 96CEFLAuHP-1
❑ 96PriAlbROC-17
❑ 96UppDecBD-57
❑ 96UppDecBDG-57
❑ 96UppDecIce-137
❑ 97Be A PPAD-219
❑ 97Be A PPAPD-219
❑ 97BeAPla-219
❑ 97BeAPlaAut-219
❑ 97BowCHL-105
❑ 97BowCHLOPC-105
❑ 97ColCho-301
❑ 97DonEli-64
❑ 97DonEliAsp-64
❑ 97DonEliS-64
❑ 97DonLim-80
❑ 97DonLimExp-80
❑ 97DonLimFOTG-42
❑ 97DonPre-149
❑ 97DonPre-197
❑ 97DonPreCttC-149
❑ 97DonPreCttC-197
❑ 97DonPri-180
❑ 97DonPriSoA-180

❑ 97Kat-99
❑ 97KatGol-99
❑ 97KatSil-99
❑ 97Lea-156
❑ 97Lea-198
❑ 97LeaFraMat-156
❑ 97LeaFraMat-198
❑ 97LeaFraMDC-156
❑ 97LeaFraMDC-198
❑ 97LeaInt-148
❑ 97LeaIntUI-148
❑ 97McD-37
❑ 97PacCroR-92
❑ 97PacCroREG-92
❑ 97PacCroRIB-92
❑ 97PacCroRS-92
❑ 97PacDyn-NNO
❑ 97PacDynC-NNO
❑ 97PacDynDG-NNO
❑ 97PacDynEG-NNO
❑ 97PacDynIB-NNO
❑ 97PacDynR-NNO
❑ 97PacDynSil-NNO
❑ 97PacPar-127
❑ 97PacParC-127
❑ 97PacParDG-127
❑ 97PacParEG-127
❑ 97PacParIB-127
❑ 97PacParRed-127
❑ 97PacParSil-127
❑ 97Pin-5
❑ 97PinArtP-5
❑ 97PinCerRR-B
❑ 97PinCerRRG-B
❑ 97PinCerRRMG-B
❑ 97PinPrePBB-5
❑ 97PinPrePBC-5
❑ 97PinPrePBM-5
❑ 97PinPrePBY-5
❑ 97PinPrePFC-5
❑ 97PinPrePFM-5
❑ 97PinPrePFY-5
❑ 97PinPrePla-5
❑ 97PinRinC-5
❑ 97Sco-71
❑ 97ScoArtPro-71
❑ 97ScoGolBla-71
❑ 97SP AutI-I22
❑ 97SPAut-187
❑ 97SPAutID-I22
❑ 97SPAutIE-I22
❑ 97Stu-103
❑ 97StuPrePG-103
❑ 97StuPrePS-103
❑ 97UppDec-325
❑ 97UppDecBD-28
❑ 97UppDecBDDD-28
❑ 97UppDecBDQD-28
❑ 97UppDecBDTD-28
❑ 97UppDecGDM-325
❑ 97UppDecIce-47
❑ 97UppDecIceP-47
❑ 97UppDecIPS-47
❑ 97Zen-89
❑ 97ZenZGol-89
❑ 97ZenZSil-89
❑ 98Pac-314
❑ 98PacAur-132
❑ 98PacIceB-314
❑ 98PacPar-165
❑ 98PacParC-165
❑ 98PacParEG-165
❑ 98PacParH-165
❑ 98PacParIB-165
❑ 98PacParS-165
❑ 98PacRed-314
❑ 98UC-143
❑ 98UD ChoPCR-143
❑ 98UD ChoR-143
❑ 98UD3-13
❑ 98UD3-73
❑ 98UD3-133
❑ 98UD3DieC-13
❑ 98UD3DieC-73
❑ 98UD3DieC-133
❑ 98UDCP-143
❑ 98UppDec-22
❑ 98UppDec-140
❑ 98UppDecE-22
❑ 98UppDecE-140
❑ 98UppDecE1o1-22
❑ 98UppDecE1o1-140
❑ 98UppDecGR-22
❑ 98UppDecGR-140
❑ 98UppDecM-144
❑ 98UppDecMGS-144
❑ 98UppDecMSS-144
❑ 98UppDecMSS-144

**Phillips, Greg**
❑ 95SasBla-15
❑ 96SasBla-17

**Phillips, Guy**
❑ 85MedHatT-4
❑ 88ProIHL-110
❑ 90ProAHLIHL-42
❑ 93RicRen-2
❑ 98GerDELE-117

**Phillips, Jason**
❑ 85BraWheK-20

**Phillips, Marshall**
❑ 92DayBom-22
❑ 93DayBom-22

**Phillips, Rob**
❑ 91AirCanSJHL-B5
❑ 92MPSPhoSJHL-117

**Phillips, Ryan**
❑ 92TacRoc-15
❑ 93TacRoc-19

**Phillips, Tommy**
❑ 83HalFP-N13
❑ 85HalFC-208

**Picard, Michel**
❑ 89ProAHL-297
❑ 90ProAHLIHL-172
❑ 91OPCPre-20
❑ 91Par-56
❑ 91ParFre-56
❑ 91Pin-327
❑ 91PinFre-327
❑ 91ProSet-538
❑ 91ProSetFre-538
❑ 91ScoAme-317
❑ 91ScoCan-347
❑ 91UppDec-48
❑ 91UppDecF-48
❑ 91WhaJr7E-22
❑ 92Bow-437
❑ 92OPC-179
❑ 92StaClu-119
❑ 92Top-439
❑ 92TopGol-439G
❑ 92Ult-404
❑ 93PorPir-10
❑ 95ColEdgI-49
❑ 95ColEdgIQ-IR7
❑ 95Don-328
❑ 95Ima-67
❑ 95ImaGol-67
❑ 95Lea-289
❑ 96GraRapG-17

**Picard, Nathalie**
❑ 94ClaWomOH-W14

**Picard, Noel**
❑ 68ShiCoi-153
❑ 69OPC-175
❑ 70ColSta-88
❑ 70DadCoo-100
❑ 70EssPowPla-237
❑ 70OPC-212
❑ 70SarProSta-190
❑ 71BluPos-15
❑ 71OPC-224
❑ 71SarProSta-180
❑ 71TorSun-243
❑ 72Flam-13
❑ 72OPC-180
❑ 72SarProSta-185
❑ 92BluUDBB-6
❑ 94ParTalB-69

**Picard, Robert**
❑ 78OPC-39
❑ 78Top-39
❑ 79OPC-91
❑ 79PanSti-55
❑ 79Top-91
❑ 80MapLeaP-20
❑ 80OPC-255
❑ 80PepCap-94
❑ 80Top-255
❑ 81CanaPos-21
❑ 81OPC-189
❑ 82CanaPos-19
❑ 82CanaSte-15
❑ 82OPC-190
❑ 82PosCer-10
❑ 83Jet-19
❑ 83Vac-135
❑ 84JetPol-16
❑ 84OPC-345
❑ 85NordMcD-15
❑ 85NordPla-6
❑ 85NordTeal-17
❑ 85OPC-215
❑ 85OPCSti-252
❑ 86NordGenF-18
❑ 86NordTeal-17
❑ 86NordYumY-7
❑ 86OPCSti-30
❑ 87NordGenF-23
❑ 87NordYumY-7
❑ 87OPC-248
❑ 87OPCSti-230
❑ 87PanSti-160
❑ 88NordGenF-24
❑ 88NordTeal-25
❑ 89Nord-35
❑ 89NordGenF-26
❑ 89NordPol-23
❑ 89OPC-261
❑ 89OPCSti-190
❑ 89PanSti-333

**Piccarreto, Brandon**
❑ 917thInnSQMJHL-176

**Pichette, Dave**
❑ 80NordPos-21
❑ 81NordPos-12
❑ 81OPC-280
❑ 82NordPos-16
❑ 82OPC-289
❑ 83NordPos-20
❑ 83OPC-299
❑ 84DevPos-8
❑ 85OPC-21
❑ 85OPCSti-63
❑ 85Top-21
❑ 89HalCit-17
❑ 89ProAHL-169

**Pichette, Jean-Jacques**
❑ 52JunBluT-72

**Pichette, Jean-Marc**
❑ 51LavDaiLSJ-10

**Pickard, Allan W**
❑ 83HalFP-N14
❑ 85HalFC-209

**Pickell, Doug**
❑ 85KamBla-18
❑ 86KamBla-16
❑ 87KamBla-17
❑ 88SalLakCGE-15
❑ 89ProIHL-201
❑ 90RicRen-14

**Picketts, Hal**
❑ 34DiaMatS-50

**Pickford, Warren**
❑ 91AirCanSJHL-C16
❑ 92MPSPhoSJHL-115

**Pictila, Mika**
❑ 95FinnSIS-216

**Piecko, Jan**
❑ 79PanSti-134

**Pierce, Randy**
❑ 79OPC-137
❑ 79Roc-16
❑ 79Top-137
❑ 80OPC-340
❑ 84WhaJunW-14

**Piersol, Mike**
❑ 917thInnSWHL-159
❑ 92TacRoc-16
❑ 93TacRoc-20

**Pierson, Bob**
❑ 83BraAle-22

**Pietila, Mika**
❑ 96FinnSISR-15
❑ 96FinnSISRKIG-4
❑ 96FinnSISRRE-6

**Pietila, Sakari**
❑ 95FinnSIS-393
❑ 96FinnSISRATG-7

**Pietrangelo, Frank**
❑ 88PanSti-331
❑ 88ProIHL-60
❑ 90ProSet-509
❑ 90ScoRoo-55T
❑ 90UppDec-403
❑ 90UppDecF-403
❑ 91Bow-89
❑ 91OPC-114
❑ 91PenCokE-40
❑ 91PenFooCS-12
❑ 91ScoAme-440
❑ 91ScoCan-425
❑ 91StaClu-364
❑ 91Top-114
❑ 92OPC-115
❑ 92Par-296
❑ 92ParEmel-296
❑ 92Pin-309
❑ 92PinFre-309
❑ 92ProSet-64
❑ 92Sco-535
❑ 92ScoCan-535
❑ 92StaClu-96
❑ 92Top-522
❑ 92TopGol-522G
❑ 92Ult-303
❑ 92UppDec-273
❑ 92WhaDai-19
❑ 93OPCPre-287
❑ 93OPCPreG-287
❑ 93PanSti-132
❑ 93Par-352
❑ 93ParEmel-352
❑ 93Pin-343
❑ 93PinCan-343
❑ 93Sco-419
❑ 93ScoCan-419
❑ 93StaClu-272
❑ 93StaCluFDI-272
❑ 93StaCluO-272
❑ 93TopPre-287
❑ 93TopPreG-287
❑ 93Ult-338
❑ 93UppDec-401
❑ 93WhaCok-14

**Piikkila, Markku**
❑ 93FinnJyvHS-59
❑ 93FinnSIS-245

**Pike, Alf**
❑ 34BeeGro1P-291
❑ 39OPCV3011-84
❑ 60ShiCoi-100

**Pillion, Pierre**
❑ 917thInnSQMJHL-271

**Pilo, Ulf**
❑ 71SweHocS-351

**Pilon, Neil**
❑ 84KamBla-19

**Pilon, Richard (Rich)**
❑ 89Isl-16
❑ 89ProIHL-6
❑ 90ProAHLIHL-77
❑ 90ProSet-486
❑ 90ScoRoo-45T
❑ 91OPC-379
❑ 91ScoCan-417
❑ 91Top-379
❑ 92Bow-264
❑ 92Par-490
❑ 92ParEmel-490
❑ 92StaClu-230
❑ 92Top-492
❑ 92TopGol-492G
❑ 93OPCPre-417
❑ 93OPCPreG-417
❑ 93StaClu-113
❑ 93StaCluFDI-113
❑ 93StaCluFDIO-113
❑ 93StaCluO-113
❑ 93TopPre-417
❑ 93TopPreG-417
❑ 94ParSE-SE105
❑ 94ParSEG-SE105
❑ 96IslPos-18
❑ 97Be A PPAD-81
❑ 97Be A PPAPD-81
❑ 97BeAPla-81
❑ 97BeAPlaAut-81
❑ 97PacInvNRB-120
❑ 97UppDec-101
❑ 98O-PChr-91
❑ 98O-PChrR-91
❑ 98Pac-285
❑ 98PacIceB-285
❑ 98PacPar-146
❑ 98PacParC-146
❑ 98PacParEG-146
❑ 98PacParH-146
❑ 98PacParIB-146
❑ 98PacParS-146
❑ 98PacRed-285
❑ 98Top-91
❑ 98TopO-P-91
❑ 99Pac-262
❑ 99PacCop-262
❑ 99PacGol-262
❑ 99PacIceB-262
❑ 99PacPreD-262

**Pilon, Ronald**
❑ 52JunBluT-132

**Pilote, Frederick**
❑ 92QueIntP-9

**Pilote, Pierre**
❑ 44BeeGro2P-134
❑ 57Top-22
❑ 58Top-36
❑ 59Top-2
❑ 59Top-60
❑ 60ShiCoi-66
❑ 60Top-65
❑ 60TopSta-43
❑ 61ShiCoi-27
❑ 61Top-24
❑ 62ShiMetC-50
❑ 62Top-28
❑ 62TopHocBuc-20
❑ 63ChePho-41
❑ 63Top-25
❑ 64BeeGro3P-52A
❑ 64BeeGro3P-52B
❑ 64CocCap-21
❑ 64Top-59
❑ 64Top-109
❑ 64TorSta-36
❑ 65Coc-21
❑ 65Top-56
❑ 66Top-59
❑ 66Top-123
❑ 66TopUSAT-59
❑ 67Top-59
❑ 67Top-122
❑ 68MapLeaWB-8
❑ 68OPC-124
❑ 68PosCerM-18
❑ 68ShiCoi-176
❑ 68Top-124
❑ 83HalFP-J11
❑ 85HalFC-191
❑ 91UltOriS-63
❑ 91UltOriSF-63
❑ 94ParMisL-32
❑ 94ParTalB-31
❑ 94ParTalB-134
❑ 94ParTalB-145
❑ 94ParTalBM-AS2
❑ 94ParTalBM-TW1
❑ 94ZelMasH-6
❑ 94ZelMasoHS-6
❑ 95Par66-34
❑ 95Par66-123
❑ 95Par66Coi-34

**Pilous, Rudy**
❑ 61ShiCoi-40
❑ 61Top-23
❑ 62Top-23
❑ 85HalFC-247

**Pilut, Larry**
❑ 95SweUppDE1DS-DS18

**Pimple, Rick**
❑ 72CruCleWHAL-8

**Pinard, Eric**
❑ 94FreNatT-24

**Pinches, John**
❑ 907thInnSOHL-116
❑ 917thInnSOHL-32

**Pinder, Allan**
❑ 70BlaBor-12

**Pinder, Gerry**
❑ 69SweHocS-362
❑ 69SweWorC-24
❑ 69SweWorC-63
❑ 69SweWorC-190
❑ 70EssPowPla-123
❑ 70OPC-148
❑ 70SarProSta-42
❑ 71OPC-185
❑ 71SarProSta-132
❑ 71TorSun-55
❑ 72OPC-21
❑ 73OPCWHAP-7
❑ 73QuaOatWHA-11
❑ 74OPCWHA-9
❑ 76OPCWHA-11
❑ 76SanDieMW-9

**Pineau, Marcel**
❑ 93MaiBlaB-57

**Pinel, Sylvain**
❑ 90MonAAA-19

**Pineo, Gregg**
❑ 917thInnSQMJHL-194

**Pinfold, Dennis**
❑ 907thInnSWHL-108
❑ 92TacRoc-17
❑ 93TacRoc-21

**Pinnington, Norman**
❑ 97KinHaw-15

**Pion, Rick (Richard)**
❑ 91ProAHLCHL-43
❑ 92PeoRivC-24
❑ 93PeoRiv-21

**Pipa, Leos**
❑ 94CzeAPSE-172
❑ 95CzeAPSE-192
❑ 96CzeAPSE-326

**Pirie, Brad**
❑ 81SweSemHVS-76

**Pirjeta, Lasse**
❑ 917thInnSWHL-160
❑ 93FinnSIS-52
❑ 94FinnSIS-123
❑ 95FinnSIS-331

**Piros, Kamil**
❑ 96CzeAPSE-188

**Piroutek, Radim**
❑ 94CzeAPSE-219
❑ 95CzeAPSE-161

**Pirrong, Jon**
❑ 93RenEng-22

**Pirus, Alex**
❑ 77OPCNHL-204
❑ 77Top-204

**Pisa, Ales**
❑ 94CzeAPSE-33
❑ 95UppDec-545
❑ 95UppDecEleIce-545
❑ 95UppDecEleIceG-545
❑ 96CzeAPSE-149

**Pisiak, Ryan**
❑ 917thInnSWHL-259
❑ 91PriAlbR-18

**Piskor, Michal**
❑ 94CzeAPSE-133
❑ 95CzeAPSE-233

**Pistek, Miroslav**
❑ 96SloPeeWT-21

**Pisto, Jermu**
❑ 93FinnSIS-166
❑ 94FinnSIS-287
❑ 96FinnSISR-71

**Pitirri, Richard**
❑ 95Sla-169

**Pitlick, Lance**
❑ 90ProAHLIHL-27
❑ 96SenPizH-20
❑ 97Be A PPAD-109
❑ 97Be A PPAPD-109
❑ 97BeAPla-109
❑ 97BeAPlaAut-109
❑ 97PacInvNRB-137

**Pitre, Pit (Didier)**
❑ 10C55SweCP-41
❑ 10C56-23
❑ 11C55-41
❑ 12C57-45
❑ 27LaPat-18
❑ 83HalFP-I11
❑ 85HalFC-130

**Pittis, Dominic**
❑ 917thInnSWHL-347
❑ 93LetHur-12
❑ 95CleLum-21
❑ 97Don-212
❑ 97DonCanI-140
❑ 97DonCanIDS-140
❑ 97DonCanIPS-140
❑ 97DonMed-5
❑ 97DonPreProG-212
❑ 97DonPreProS-212
❑ 97DonRatR-5
❑ 97ScoPen-20
❑ 97ScoPenPla-20
❑ 97ScoPenPre-20

**Pittman, Chris**
❑ 93KitRan-11
❑ 94KitRan-12
❑ 95Sla-279
❑ 96RicRen-16

**Pittman, Mike**
❑ 93GueSto-13
❑ 94GueSto-17
❑ 95GueSto5A-9
❑ 95Sla-97

**Pivetz, Mark**
❑ 92MPSPhoSJHL-140

**Pivonka, Michal**
❑ 86CapKod-21
❑ 86CapPol-21
❑ 87CapKod-20
❑ 87CapTealss-19
❑ 88CapBor-17
❑ 88CapSmo-18
❑ 89CapKod-20
❑ 89CapTealss-18
❑ 90Bow-68
❑ 90BowTif-68
❑ 90CapKod-20
❑ 90CapPos-19
❑ 90CapSmo-18
❑ 90OPC-68
❑ 90PanSti-154
❑ 90ProSet-319
❑ 90Sco-268
❑ 90ScoCan-268
❑ 90Top-68
❑ 90TopTif-68
❑ 90UppDec-80
❑ 90UppDecF-80
❑ 91Bow-291
❑ 91Bow-413
❑ 91CapJun5-22
❑ 91CapKod-22
❑ 91OPC-327
❑ 91PanSti-206
❑ 91Par-412
❑ 91ParFre-412
❑ 91Pin-277
❑ 91PinFre-277
❑ 91ProSet-252
❑ 91ProSetFre-252
❑ 91ProSetPla-132
❑ 91ScoAme-193
❑ 91ScoCan-193
❑ 91StaClu-44
❑ 91SweSemWCS-222
❑ 91Top-327
❑ 91UppDec-229
❑ 91UppDecF-229
❑ 92Bow-294
❑ 92CapKod-22
❑ 92OPC-30
❑ 92PanSti-161
❑ 92PanStiFre-161
❑ 92Par-432
❑ 92ParEmel-432
❑ 92Pin-151
❑ 92PinFre-151
❑ 92ProSet-201
❑ 92Sco-253
❑ 92ScoCan-253
❑ 92StaClu-382
❑ 92Top-107
❑ 92TopGol-107G
❑ 92Ult-237
❑ 92UppDec-261
❑ 93Don-374
❑ 93Lea-178
❑ 93OPCPre-321
❑ 93OPCPre-360
❑ 93OPCPreG-321
❑ 93OPCPreG-360
❑ 93PanSti-27
❑ 93Par-487
❑ 93ParEmel-487
❑ 93Pin-67
❑ 93PinCan-67
❑ 93Pow-265
❑ 93Sco-118
❑ 93ScoCan-118
❑ 93ScoIntS-15
❑ 93ScoIntSC-15
❑ 93StaClu-405
❑ 93StaCluFDI-405
❑ 93StaCluO-405
❑ 93TopPre-321
❑ 93TopPre-360
❑ 93TopPreG-321
❑ 93TopPreG-360
❑ 93Ult-101
❑ 93UppDec-154
❑ 94BeAPSig-160
❑ 94CanGamNHLP-248
❑ 94Don-292
❑ 94FinnJaaK-178
❑ 94Lea-114
❑ 94OPCPre-259
❑ 94OPCPreSE-259
❑ 94Pin-323
❑ 94PinArtP-323
❑ 94PinRinC-323
❑ 94TopPre-259
❑ 94TopPreSE-259
❑ 94Ult-238
❑ 95Cap-21
❑ 95ColCho-260
❑ 95ColChoPC-260
❑ 95ColChoPCP-260
❑ 95ColEdgI-124
❑ 95ColEdgIC-C23
❑ 95Don-197
❑ 95Fin-147
❑ 95FinRef-147
❑ 95Lea-162
❑ 95ParInt-487
❑ 95ParIntEl-487
❑ 95Sco-258
❑ 95ScoBlaIce-258
❑ 95ScoBlaIceAP-258
❑ 95SkyImp-180
❑ 95SP-157
❑ 95Sum-147
❑ 95SumArtP-147
❑ 95SumIce-147
❑ 95SweGloWC-156
❑ 95Top-330
❑ 95TopOPCI-330
❑ 95Ult-177
❑ 95UltGolM-177
❑ 95UppDec-392
❑ 95UppDecEleIce-392
❑ 95UppDecEleIceG-392
❑ 96BeAPAut-13
❑ 96BeAPAutSil-13
❑ 96BeAPla-13
❑ 96ColCho-280
❑ 96Don-60
❑ 96DonCanI-50
❑ 96DonCanIGPP-50
❑ 96DonCanIRPP-50
❑ 96DonEli-35
❑ 96DonEliDCS-35
❑ 96DonPrePro-60
❑ 96Fle-119
❑ 96KraUppD-12
❑ 96LeaLim-36
❑ 96LeaLimG-36
❑ 96LeaPre-100
❑ 96LeaPrePP-100
❑ 96MetUni-167
❑ 96Pin-173
❑ 96PinArtP-173
❑ 96PinFoi-173
❑ 96PinPreS-173
❑ 96PinRinC-173
❑ 96Sco-33
❑ 96ScoArtPro-33
❑ 96ScoDeaCAP-33
❑ 96ScoGolB-33
❑ 96ScoSpeAP-33
❑ 96SelCer-52
❑ 96SelCerAP-52
❑ 96SelCerBlu-52
❑ 96SelCerMB-52
❑ 96SelCerMG-52
❑ 96SelCerMR-52
❑ 96SelCerRed-52
❑ 96SkyImp-142
❑ 96Sum-25
❑ 96SumArtP-25
❑ 96SumIce-25
❑ 96SumMet-25
❑ 96SumPreS-25
❑ 96SweSemW-126
❑ 96TopNHLP-55
❑ 96TopPicOI-55
❑ 96Ult-178
❑ 96UltGolM-178
❑ 96UppDec-355
❑ 96Zen-62
❑ 96ZenArtP-62
❑ 97Pac-285
❑ 97PacCop-285
❑ 97PacEmeGre-285
❑ 97PacIceB-285
❑ 97PacRed-285
❑ 97PacSil-285
❑ 98Be A PPA-150
❑ 98Be A PPAA-150
❑ 98Be A PPAAF-150
❑ 98Be A PPTBASG-150
❑ 98Be APG-150

**Placatka, Tomas**
❑ 94CzeAPSE-274

**Plachta, Jacek**
❑ 94GerDELE-253
❑ 95GerDELE-251
❑ 96GerDELE-140
❑ 98GerDELE-11

**Plager, Barclay**
❑ 68OPC-177
❑ 68ShiCoi-154
❑ 69OPC-176
❑ 70DadCoo-101
❑ 70EssPowPla-241
❑ 70OPC-99
❑ 70SarProSta-184
❑ 70Top-99
❑ 71BluPos-16
❑ 71LetActR-12
❑ 71OPC-66
❑ 71SarProSta-182
❑ 71Top-66
❑ 71TorSun-244
❑ 72BluWhiBor-14
❑ 72OPC-35
❑ 72SarProSta-187
❑ 72SweSemWC-186
❑ 72Top-136
❑ 73BluWhiBor-13
❑ 73OPC-47
❑ 73Top-47
❑ 74NHLActSta-241
❑ 74OPCNHL-87
❑ 74OPCNHL-107
❑ 74Top-87
❑ 74Top-107
❑ 75OPCNHL-205
❑ 75Top-205
❑ 78BluPos-18
❑ 92BluUDBB-24

**Plager, Bill**
❑ 70SarProSta-187
❑ 71BluPos-17
❑ 71SarProSta-190
❑ 72Flam-14
❑ 72OPC-122
❑ 72SarProSta-7
❑ 72Top-12
❑ 89NewHavN-9

**Plager, Bob**
❑ 68OPC-112
❑ 68ShiCoi-148
❑ 68Top-112
❑ 69OPC-13
❑ 69Top-13
❑ 70EssPowPla-238

❑ 95ZenZT-17
❑ 96BeAPStaTP-6
❑ 96ColCho-257
❑ 96ColCho-332
❑ 96ColChoBlo-257
❑ 96ColChoBloBi-7
❑ 96ColChoMVP-UD20
❑ 96ColChoMVPG-UD20
❑ 96ColChoSti-S11
❑ 96Don-96
❑ 96DonBetPip-10
❑ 96DonCanI-67
❑ 96DonCanIGPP-67
❑ 96DonCanILG-3
❑ 96DonCanIRPP-67
❑ 96DonEli-5
❑ 96DonEliDCS-5
❑ 96DonEliPW-6
❑ 96DonEliPW-P6
❑ 96DonPrePro-96
❑ 96DurL'EB-JB12
❑ 96Fla-91
❑ 96FlaBluI-91
❑ 96FlaHotG-8
❑ 96Fle-109
❑ 96FleVez-7
❑ 96FroFlaMas-1
❑ 96KraUppD-61
❑ 96Lea-156
❑ 96LeaLim-80
❑ 96LeaLimG-80
❑ 96LeaPre-36
❑ 96LeaPreMM-5
❑ 96LeaPreP-156
❑ 96LeaPrePP-36
❑ 96LeaPreVP-10
❑ 96LeaPreVPG-10
❑ 96LeaShuDow-8
❑ 96MapLeaP-2
❑ 96MetUni-152
❑ 96MetUniAP-7
❑ 96MetUniAPSP-7
❑ 96NHLProSTA-79
❑ 96Pin-96
❑ 96PinArtP-96
❑ 96PinFoi-96
❑ 96PinMcD-38
❑ 96PinMin-24
❑ 96PinMinB-24
❑ 96PinMinCoiB-24
❑ 96PinMinCoiGP-24
❑ 96PinMinCoiN-24
❑ 96PinMinCoiS-24
❑ 96PinMinCoiSG-24
❑ 96PinMinG-24
❑ 96PinMinS-24
❑ 96PinPreS-96
❑ 96PinRinC-96
❑ 96PlaOneoOne-364
❑ 96PosUppD-14
❑ 96Sco-172
❑ 96ScoArtPro-172
❑ 96ScoDeaCAP-172
❑ 96ScoGolB-172
❑ 96ScoSpeAP-172
❑ 96ScoSudDea-12
❑ 96ScoSup-5
❑ 96SelCer-31
❑ 96SelCerAP-31
❑ 96SelCerBlu-31
❑ 96SelCerFre-8
❑ 96SelCerMB-31
❑ 96SelCerMG-31
❑ 96SelCerMR-31
❑ 96SelCerRed-31
❑ 96SkyImp-129
❑ 96SkyImpZH-7
❑ 96SP-153
❑ 96SPGamFil-GF7
❑ 96SPInsInf-IN7
❑ 96SPInsInfG-IN7
❑ 96SPx-44
❑ 96SPxGol-44
❑ 96StaCluMO-13
❑ 96Sum-72
❑ 96SumArtP-72
❑ 96SumIce-72
❑ 96SumInTheCre-9
❑ 96SumInTheCrePS-9
❑ 96SumMet-72
❑ 96SumPreS-72
❑ 96SumUnt-17
❑ 96TeaOut-74
❑ 96TopPicID-ID14
❑ 96Ult-165
❑ 96UltGolM-165
❑ 96UppDec-341
❑ 96UppDec-360
❑ 96UppDecBD-129
❑ 96UppDecBDG-129
❑ 96UppDecGN-X33
❑ 96UppDecIce-67
❑ 96UppDecIcePar-67
❑ 96UppDecSS-SS11A
❑ 96Zen-31
❑ 96ZenArtP-31
❑ 96ZenZT-16
❑ 97Be A PPAD-4
❑ 97Be A PPAPD-4
❑ 97BeAPla-4
❑ 97BeAPlaAut-4
❑ 97BeAPlaSTP-3
❑ 97ColCho-252
❑ 97ColChoSta-SQ29
❑ 97Don-154
❑ 97DonBetTP-9
❑ 97DonCanI-56
❑ 97DonCanIDS-56
❑ 97DonCanILG-2
❑ 97DonCanILGP-2
❑ 97DonCanIPS-56
❑ 97DonEli-100
❑ 97DonEli-131
❑ 97DonEliAsp-100
❑ 97DonEliAsp-131
❑ 97DonEliC-13
❑ 97DonEliMC-13
❑ 97DonEliS-100
❑ 97DonEliS-131
❑ 97DonLim-29
❑ 97DonLim-57
❑ 97DonLim-77
❑ 97DonLimExp-29
❑ 97DonLimExp-57
❑ 97DonLimExp-77
❑ 97DonLimFOTG-15
❑ 97DonPre-99
❑ 97DonPreCG-5
❑ 97DonPreCGP-5
❑ 97DonPreCttC-99
❑ 97DonPreProG-154
❑ 97DonPreProS-154
❑ 97DonPri-101
❑ 97DonPri-198
❑ 97DonPriODI-25
❑ 97DonPriP-29
❑ 97DonPriPG-3
❑ 97DonPriPGP-3
❑ 97DonPriS-29
❑ 97DonPriSB-29
❑ 97DonPriSG-29
❑ 97DonPriSoA-101
❑ 97DonPriSoA-198
❑ 97DonPriSS-29
❑ 97Kat-142
❑ 97KatGol-142
❑ 97KatSil-142
❑ 97Lea-24
❑ 97Lea-P5
❑ 97LeaFraMat-24
❑ 97LeaFraMDC-24
❑ 97LeaInt-24
❑ 97LeaIntUI-24
❑ 97LeaPipDre-5
❑ 97McD-31
❑ 97Pac-29
❑ 97PacCarSup-19
❑ 97PacCarSupM-19
❑ 97PacCop-29
❑ 97PacCroR-131
❑ 97PacCroREG-131
❑ 97PacCroRFODC-19
❑ 97PacCroRIB-131
❑ 97PacCroRS-131
❑ 97PacDyn-122
❑ 97PacDynBKS-92
❑ 97PacDynC-122
❑ 97PacDynDG-122
❑ 97PacDynEG-122
❑ 97PacDynIB-122
❑ 97PacDynR-122
❑ 97PacDynSil-122
❑ 97PacDynSto-20
❑ 97PacDynTan-17
❑ 97PacEmeGre-29
❑ 97PacIceB-29
❑ 97PacInTheCLC-20
❑ 97PacInv-137
❑ 97PacInvC-137
❑ 97PacInvEG-137
❑ 97PacInvFP-33
❑ 97PacInvIB-137
❑ 97PacInvNRB-195
❑ 97PacInvR-137
❑ 97PacInvS-137
❑ 97PacOme-223
❑ 97PacOmeC-223
❑ 97PacOmeDG-223
❑ 97PacOmeEG-223
❑ 97PacOmeG-223
❑ 97PacOmeIB-223
❑ 97PacOmeNSZ-10
❑ 97PacOmeTL-18
❑ 97PacPar-183
❑ 97PacParC-183
❑ 97PacParDG-183
❑ 97PacParEG-183
❑ 97PacParGSL-20
❑ 97PacParIB-183
❑ 97PacParRed-183
❑ 97PacParSil-183
❑ 97PacRed-29
❑ 97PacRev-136
❑ 97PacRevC-136
❑ 97PacRevE-136
❑ 97PacRevIB-136
❑ 97PacRevR-136
❑ 97PacRevRtSD-19
❑ 97PacRevS-136
❑ 97PacSil-29
❑ 97PacTeaCCC-24
❑ 97Pin-95
❑ 97PinArtP-95
❑ 97PinBee-16
❑ 97PinBeeGP-16
❑ 97PinCer-11
❑ 97PinCerMB-11
❑ 97PinCerMG-11
❑ 97PinCerMR-11
❑ 97PinCerR-11
❑ 97PinEpiGO-11
❑ 97PinEpiGP-11
❑ 97PinEpiME-11
❑ 97PinEpiMO-11
❑ 97PinEpiMP-11
❑ 97PinEpiPE-11
❑ 97PinEpiPO-11
❑ 97PinEpiPP-11
❑ 97PinEpiSE-11
❑ 97PinEpiSO-11
❑ 97PinEpiSP-11
❑ 97PinIns-46
❑ 97PinInsCC-46
❑ 97PinInsEC-46
❑ 97PinInsSto-21
❑ 97PinInsT-20
❑ 97PinPrePBB-95
❑ 97PinPrePBC-95
❑ 97PinPrePBM-95
❑ 97PinPrePBY-95
❑ 97PinPrePFC-95
❑ 97PinPrePFM-95
❑ 97PinPrePFY-95
❑ 97PinPrePla-95
❑ 97PinRinC-95
❑ 97PinTotCMPG-11
❑ 97PinTotCPB-11
❑ 97PinTotCPG-11
❑ 97PinTotCPR-11
❑ 97Sco-29
❑ 97ScoArtPro-29
❑ 97ScoGolBla-29
❑ 97ScoMapL-1
❑ 97ScoMapLPla-1
❑ 97ScoMapLPre-1
❑ 97ScoNetW-16
❑ 97SPAut-151
❑ 97Stu-66
❑ 97StuPor-34
❑ 97StuPrePG-66
❑ 97StuPrePS-66
❑ 97StuSil-20
❑ 97StuSil8-20
❑ 97TopHocMC-21
❑ 97TopHocMC-22
❑ 97UppDec-367
❑ 97UppDecBD-5
❑ 97UppDecBDDD-5
❑ 97UppDecBDQD-5
❑ 97UppDecBDTD-5
❑ 97UppDecIce-29
❑ 97UppDecIceP-29
❑ 97UppDecIPS-29
❑ 97Zen-38
❑ 97Zen5x7-42
❑ 97ZenGolImp-42
❑ 97ZenSilImp-42
❑ 97ZenZGol-38
❑ 97ZenZSil-38
❑ 98Fin-70
❑ 98FinNo P-70
❑ 98FinNo PR-70
❑ 98FinRef-70
❑ 98O-PChr-29
❑ 98O-PChrR-29
❑ 98Pac-29
❑ 98PacGolCD-31
❑ 98PacIceB-29
❑ 98PacOmeH-150
❑ 98PacOmeO-22
❑ 98PacOmeODI-150
❑ 98PacOmePI-5
❑ 98PacOmePIB-5
❑ 98PacOmeR-150
❑ 98PacRed-29
❑ 98PinEpiGE-11
❑ 98SPXTopPWM-FP
❑ 98Top-29
❑ 98TopO-P-29
❑ 98UppDec-371
❑ 98UppDecE-371
❑ 98UppDecE1o1-371
❑ 98UppDecGR-371
❑ 98UppDecM-126
❑ 98UppDecMGS-126
❑ 98UppDecMSS-126
❑ 98UppDecMSS-126
❑ 99Pac-263
❑ 99PacAur-91
❑ 99PacAurGU-12
❑ 99PacAurPD-91
❑ 99PacCop-263
❑ 99PacGol-263
❑ 99PacGolCD-22
❑ 99PacIceB-263
❑ 99PacIn tCN-11
❑ 99PacPreD-263

**Potvin, Jean**
❑ 71TorSun-122
❑ 74NHLActSta-172
❑ 74OPCNHL-101
❑ 74Top-101
❑ 75OPCNHL-36
❑ 75Top-36
❑ 76OPCNHL-93
❑ 76Top-93
❑ 77OPCNHL-144
❑ 77Top-144
❑ 78OPC-287
❑ 79IslTrans-15
❑ 79OPC-334

**Potvin, Marc**
❑ 90ProAHLIHL-486
❑ 91UppDec-405
❑ 91UppDecF-405
❑ 93WhaCok-15
❑ 94Lea-541
❑ 94Ult-259
❑ 96PorPir-9

**Potvin, Rick**
❑ 89RayJrC-17

**Potvin, Steve**
❑ 92SudWol-23
❑ 93SudWol-20
❑ 93SudWolP-19
❑ 95Cla-89

**Potyok, Shawn**
❑ 91BriColJHL-11

**Potz, Jerzy**
❑ 79PanSti-124
❑ 89SweSemWCS-135

**Poudrier, Daniel**
❑ 85FreExp-22
❑ 86FreExp-21
❑ 87NordGenF-24
❑ 94GerDELE-75
❑ 95GerDELE-34

**Poudrier, Serge**
❑ 93SweSemWCS-252
❑ 94FinnJaaK-220
❑ 94FreNatT-25
❑ 95SweGloWC-204
❑ 96GerDELE-6
❑ 96SweSemW-185

**Pouget, Christian**
❑ 94FreNatT-26
❑ 96GerDELE-177
❑ 96SweSemW-189
❑ 98GerDELE-231

**Poukar, Jiri**
❑ 94CzeAPSE-173
❑ 95CzeAPSE-190
❑ 96CzeAPSE-325

**Poulin, Charles**
❑ 907thInnSQMJHL-220
❑ 917thInnSQMJHL-12
❑ 92FreCan-19
❑ 93ClaProPro-27
❑ 93FreCan-22

**Poulin, Daniel**
❑ 77KalWin-6

**Poulin, Dave**
❑ 83FlyJCP-17
❑ 84OPC-165
❑ 84OPCSti-110
❑ 84Top-120
❑ 85FlyPos-23
❑ 85OPC-128
❑ 85OPCSti-89
❑ 85Top-128
❑ 86FlyPos-20
❑ 86OPC-71
❑ 86OPCSti-241
❑ 86Top-71
❑ 87OPC-39
❑ 87OPCMin-32
❑ 87OPCSti-98
❑ 87OPCSti-179
❑ 87PanSti-130
❑ 87PanSti-386
❑ 87Top-39
❑ 88FriLayS-27
❑ 88OPC-100
❑ 88PanSti-323
❑ 88Top-100
❑ 89BruSpoAU-7
❑ 89FlyPos-19
❑ 89OPC-115
❑ 89PanSti-305
❑ 89Top-115
❑ 90Bow-36
❑ 90BowTif-36
❑ 90BruSpoA-20
❑ 90OPC-362
❑ 90PanSti-4
❑ 90ProSet-13
❑ 90Sco-217
❑ 90ScoCan-217
❑ 90Top-362
❑ 90TopTif-362
❑ 90UppDec-177
❑ 90UppDecF-177
❑ 91Bow-359
❑ 91BruSpoA-15
❑ 91OPC-507
❑ 91ProSet-12
❑ 91ProSetFre-12
❑ 91ProSetPla-5
❑ 91ScoAme-232
❑ 91ScoCan-452
❑ 91StaClu-253
❑ 91Top-507
❑ 92Bow-19
❑ 92BruPos-8
❑ 92OPC-367
❑ 92PanSti-137
❑ 92PanStiFre-137
❑ 92Par-242
❑ 92ParEmel-242
❑ 92Pin-116
❑ 92PinFre-116
❑ 92ProSet-9
❑ 92Sco-359
❑ 92ScoCan-359
❑ 92StaClu-13
❑ 92Top-155
❑ 92TopGol-155G
❑ 92Ult-9
❑ 93Don-362
❑ 93Lea-332
❑ 93OPCPre-228
❑ 93OPCPreG-228
❑ 93PanSti-4
❑ 93Par-488
❑ 93ParEmel-488
❑ 93Pin-229
❑ 93Pin-387
❑ 93PinCan-229
❑ 93PinCan-387
❑ 93Pow-470
❑ 93Sco-228
❑ 93Sco-552
❑ 93ScoCan-228
❑ 93ScoCan-552
❑ 93ScoGol-552
❑ 93StaClu-142
❑ 93StaClu-301
❑ 93StaCluFDI-142
❑ 93StaCluFDI-301
❑ 93StaCluO-142
❑ 93StaCluO-301
❑ 93TopPre-228
❑ 93TopPreG-228
❑ 93Ult-193
❑ 93Ult-450
❑ 93UltAwaW-5
❑ 93UppDec-355
❑ 93UppDecAW-AW8
❑ 94BeAPSig-124
❑ 94OPCPre-236
❑ 94OPCPreSE-236
❑ 94Par-253
❑ 94ParGol-253
❑ 94Pin-179
❑ 94PinArtP-179
❑ 94PinRinC-179
❑ 94Sco-38
❑ 94ScoGol-38
❑ 94ScoPla-38
❑ 94ScoPlaTS-38
❑ 94TopPre-236
❑ 94TopPreSE-236
❑ 94Ult-391

**Poulin, George**
❑ 10C55SweCP-44
❑ 11C55-44
❑ 12C57-8

**Poulin, Pat (Patrick)**
❑ 907thInnSQMJHL-1
❑ 907thInnSQMJHL-152
❑ 917thInnSMC-98
❑ 917thInnSQMJHL-10
❑ 91AreDraPic-7
❑ 91Cla-8
❑ 91UltDra-8
❑ 91UltDra-64
❑ 91UppDec-65
❑ 91UppDecCWJC-51
❑ 91UppDecF-65
❑ 92OPCPre-85
❑ 92Par-60
❑ 92ParEmel-60
❑ 92Pin-418
❑ 92PinFre-418
❑ 92PinTea2-14
❑ 92PinTea2F-14
❑ 92ProSet-227
❑ 92Sco-478
❑ 92ScoCan-478
❑ 92ScoYouS-31
❑ 92StaClu-211
❑ 92Top-328
❑ 92TopGol-328G
❑ 92Ult-304
❑ 92UppDec-416
❑ 92UppDec-557
❑ 92UppDecCC-CC18
❑ 92UppDecGHS-G16
❑ 92WhaDai-20
❑ 93BlaCok-10
❑ 93Don-146
❑ 93DurSco-50
❑ 93Lea-113
❑ 93LeaGolR-10
❑ 93PanSti-126
❑ 93Par-307
❑ 93ParEmel-307
❑ 93Pin-61
❑ 93PinCan-61
❑ 93PinTea2-8
❑ 93PinTea2C-8
❑ 93Pow-108
❑ 93Pow-315
❑ 93PowSecYS-9
❑ 93Sco-202
❑ 93Sco-571
❑ 93ScoCan-202
❑ 93ScoCan-571
❑ 93ScoGol-571
❑ 93StaClu-157
❑ 93StaCluFDI-157
❑ 93StaCluFDIO-157
❑ 93StaCluO-157
❑ 93Ult-122
❑ 93Ult-292
❑ 93UppDec-138
❑ 93UppDecNL-NL2
❑ 93UppDecSP-30
❑ 94BeAPSig-168
❑ 94CanGamNHLP-69
❑ 94Don-144
❑ 94Fle-44
❑ 94Lea-390
❑ 94OPCPre-316
❑ 94OPCPreSE-316
❑ 94ParSE-SE32
❑ 94ParSEG-SE32
❑ 94Pin-283
❑ 94PinArtP-283
❑ 94PinRinC-283
❑ 94Sco-6
❑ 94ScoGol-6
❑ 94ScoHobS-6
❑ 94ScoPla-6
❑ 94ScoPlaTS-6
❑ 94StaClu-13
❑ 94StaCluFDI-13
❑ 94StaCluMOMS-13
❑ 94StaCluSTWC-13
❑ 94TopPre-316
❑ 94TopPreSE-316
❑ 94Ult-43
❑ 94UppDec-36
❑ 94UppDecEleIce-36
❑ 95CanGamNHLP-67
❑ 95ColCho-187
❑ 95ColChoPC-187
❑ 95ColChoPCP-187
❑ 95Don-269
❑ 95Emo-32
❑ 95ImpSti-25
❑ 95Lea-237
❑ 95Met-27
❑ 95ParInt-42
❑ 95ParIntEI-42
❑ 95Pin-135
❑ 95PinArtP-135
❑ 95PinRinC-135
❑ 95PlaOneoOne-133
❑ 95Sco-158
❑ 95ScoBlaIce-158
❑ 95ScoBlaIceAP-158
❑ 95SkyImp-32
❑ 95StaClu-212
❑ 95StaCluMOMS-212
❑ 95Sum-99
❑ 95SumArtP-99
❑ 95SumIce-99
❑ 95Top-326
❑ 95TopOPCI-326
❑ 95TopPowL-4PL
❑ 95UppDec-208
❑ 95UppDecEleIce-208
❑ 95UppDecEleIceG-208
❑ 95UppDecSpeE-SE106
❑ 95UppDecSpeEdiG-SE106
❑ 96PlaOneoOne-369
❑ 97ColCho-242
❑ 97Pac-230
❑ 97PacCop-230
❑ 97PacEmeGre-230
❑ 97PacIceB-230
❑ 97PacRed-230
❑ 97PacSil-230
❑ 97UppDec-366

**Poulin, Patrick**
❑ 80OshGen-6
❑ 98Be A PPA-69
❑ 98Be A PPAA-69
❑ 98Be A PPAAF-69
❑ 98Be A PPTBASG-69
❑ 98Be APG-69
❑ 99Pac-207
❑ 99PacCop-207
❑ 99PacGol-207
❑ 99PacIceB-207
❑ 99PacPreD-207

**Poulin, Rick**
❑ 89RayJrC-18

**Poulin, Skinner**
❑ 10C56-24

**Pouliot, Mario**
❑ 917thInnSQMJHL-24

**Poulsen, Marco**
❑ 93FinnJyvHS-27
❑ 93FinnSIS-98
❑ 94FinnSIS-346
❑ 95FinnSIS-345
❑ 95FinnSISL-94

**Pound, Ian**
❑ 84KitRan-12
❑ 85KitRan-11
❑ 86LonKni-17

**Pounder, Cheryl**
❑ 94ClaWomOH-W3

**Pousaz, Jacques**
❑ 72SweSemWC-148

**Pousse, Pierre**
❑ 93SweSemWCS-265
❑ 94FreNatT-27

**Pouzar, Jaroslav**
❑ 79PanSti-87
❑ 81SweSemHVS-64
❑ 82OilRedR-10
❑ 83OilMcD-23
❑ 83OPC-41
❑ 83OPCSti-151
❑ 83OPCSti-159
❑ 83Vac-38
❑ 84OilRedR-10
❑ 84OilTeal-22
❑ 84OPC-256
❑ 86OilTeal-20
❑ 88OilTenAnn-18

**Powell, Kevin**
❑ 91AirCanSJHL-D16
❑ 92NorDakFS-26
❑ 92TacRoc-18
❑ 99WicThu-19

**Power, Andrew**
❑ 93OshGen-12

**Power, Larry**
❑ 82Ott67-19

**Power, Rocket (R.)**
❑ 10C55SweCP-40
❑ 11C55-40

**Power, Ryan**
❑ 95Sla-229

**Powers, Andy**
❑ 94DubFigS-22

**Powers, Buddy**
❑ 93RenEng-23

**Powers, Jim**
❑ 92RalIce-12
❑ 92RalIce-23
❑ 93RalIce-14
❑ 94RalIce-15

**Powis, Geoffrey**
❑ 67Top-110

**Powis, Lynn**
❑ 73OPC-209
❑ 74NHLActSta-296
❑ 74OPCNHL-227
❑ 74Top-227
❑ 76OPCWHA-86

**Pozzo, Kevin**
❑ 95SlaMemC-30

**Pracey, Rick**
❑ 88BroBra-12
❑ 89SauSteMG-10

**Prachar, Kamil**
❑ 94CzeAPSE-208
❑ 94FinnJaaK-167
❑ 95CzeAPSE-152
❑ 96CzeAPSE-169

**Pracher, Dan**
❑ 95SolBar-9

**Prajsler, Petr**
❑ 88ProAHL-213
❑ 89KinSmo-11
❑ 90OPC-481
❑ 90ProAHLIHL-347
❑ 91ProAHLCHL-57

**Pratt, Babe**
❑ 34BeeGro1P-292
❑ 34BeeGro1P-343
❑ 39OPCV3011-85
❑ 45QuaOatP-44
❑ 55Par-31
❑ 55ParQuaO-31
❑ 83HalFP-L13
❑ 85HalFC-162
❑ 92HalFL-29
❑ 94ParTalBG-3

**Pratt, Harlan**
❑ 95RedDeeR-14
❑ 96PriAlbR-15
❑ 96PriAlbROC-18

**Pratt, Jon**
❑ 95PeoRiv-17
❑ 96PeoRiv-17
❑ 96PeoRivPA-18

**Pratt, Kelly**
❑ 74PenPos-18

**Pratt, Nolan**
❑ 96SprFal-34
❑ 97CarHur-20
❑ 98UppDec-239
❑ 98UppDecE-239
❑ 98UppDecE1o1-239
❑ 98UppDecGR-239

**Pratt, Stan**
❑ 36V356WorG-126

**Pratt, Tom**
❑ 88ProAHL-199

**Pratt, Tracy**
❑ 68ShiCoi-119
❑ 69OPC-111
❑ 69Top-111
❑ 70DadCoo-103
❑ 70EssPowPla-75
❑ 70OPC-146
❑ 70SarProSta-19
❑ 71LetActR-3
❑ 71OPC-107
❑ 71SabPos-16
❑ 71SarProSta-25
❑ 71Top-107
❑ 71TorSun-37
❑ 72OPC-69
❑ 72SarProSta-30
❑ 72Top-84
❑ 73OPC-54
❑ 73Top-54
❑ 74CanuRoyB-16
❑ 74NHLActSta-281
❑ 74OPCNHL-41
❑ 74Top-41
❑ 75CanuRoyB-17
❑ 75OPCNHL-133
❑ 75Top-133
❑ 76OPCNHL-275
❑ 76RocCokCan-17
❑ 76RocPucBuc-16

**Praznik, Jody**
❑ 88SasBla-6
❑ 89HamRoaA-18
❑ 90HamRoaA-44
❑ 92-TulOil-13
❑ 94CenHocL-105

**Precechtel, Jaromir**
❑ 94CzeAPSE-278
❑ 95CzeAPSE-100

**Prefontaine, Brad**
❑ 91AirCanSJHL-C2

❑ 95BirBul-5
**Premak, Garth**
❑ 87KamBla-18
❑ 92AlbIntTC-16
**Prendergast, Mike**
❑ 91UppDecCWJC-69
**Prentice, Dean**
❑ 44BeeGro2P-58
❑ 44BeeGro2P-354A
❑ 44BeeGro2P-354B
❑ 54Par-74
❑ 57Top-62
❑ 58Top-32
❑ 59Top-17
❑ 60Top-37
❑ 60TopSta-44
❑ 61ShiCoi-84
❑ 61Top-54
❑ 62Top-53
❑ 62TopHocBuc-21
❑ 63Top-13
❑ 64BeeGro3P-24
❑ 64BeeGro3P-91
❑ 64CocCap-12
❑ 64Top-19
❑ 65Coc-10
❑ 65Top-102
❑ 66Top-45
❑ 66TopUSAT-45
❑ 67Top-45
❑ 68OPC-32
❑ 68ShiCoi-38
❑ 68Top-32
❑ 69OPC-115
❑ 69Top-115
❑ 70DadCoo-104
❑ 70EssPowPla-232
❑ 70OPC-201
❑ 70SarProSta-165
❑ 71SarProSta-89
❑ 71TorSun-143
❑ 72OPC-289
❑ 72SweSemWC-218
❑ 73NorStaP-17
❑ 91UltOriS-27
❑ 91UltOriSF-27
❑ 93ParParRCI-9
❑ 94ParMisL-91
❑ 94ParTalB-5
❑ 95Par66-51
❑ 95Par66Coi-51
**Presley, Wayne**
❑ 82KitRan-12
❑ 83KitRan-16
❑ 84KitRan-20
❑ 84SauSteMG-17
❑ 85NovScoO-16
❑ 86BlaCok-15
❑ 87BlaCok-18
❑ 87OPC-179
❑ 87PanSti-228
❑ 87Top-179
❑ 88BlaCok-16
❑ 88OPC-185
❑ 88Top-185
❑ 89BlaCok-20
❑ 89OPC-98
❑ 89PanSti-52
❑ 89Top-98
❑ 90BlaCok-20
❑ 90OPC-456
❑ 90ProSet-434
❑ 90ScoRoo-92T
❑ 90UppDec-339
❑ 90UppDecF-339
❑ 91Bow-402
❑ 91OPC-385
❑ 91OPCPre-89
❑ 91PanSti-19
❑ 91Par-163
❑ 91ParFre-163
❑ 91Pin-68
❑ 91PinFre-68
❑ 91ProSet-44
❑ 91ProSet-488
❑ 91ProSetFre-44
❑ 91ProSetFre-488
❑ 91ProSetPla-228
❑ 91ScoAme-221
❑ 91ScoCan-221
❑ 91ScoCan-559
❑ 91ScoRoo-9T
❑ 91ShaSanJSA-18
❑ 91StaClu-215
❑ 91Top-385
❑ 91UppDec-371
❑ 91UppDecF-371
❑ 92Bow-76
❑ 92SabBluS-17
❑ 92SabJubF-11
❑ 92Sco-213
❑ 92ScoCan-213
❑ 92StaClu-24
❑ 92Top-424
❑ 92TopGol-424G
❑ 93OPCPre-162
❑ 93OPCPreG-162
❑ 93PanSti-107
❑ 93Par-294
❑ 93ParEmel-294
❑ 93Pin-425
❑ 93PinCan-425
❑ 93Sco-296
❑ 93ScoCan-296
❑ 93StaClu-233
❑ 93StaCluFDI-233
❑ 93StaCluFDIO-233
❑ 93StaCluO-233
❑ 93TopPre-162
❑ 93TopPreG-162
❑ 94Lea-521
❑ 94Par-27
❑ 94ParGol-27
❑ 94Pin-321
❑ 94PinArtP-321
❑ 94PinRinC-321
❑ 94StaClu-196
❑ 94StaCluFDI-196
❑ 94StaCluMOMS-196
❑ 94StaCluSTWC-196
❑ 95BeAPla-45
❑ 95BeAPSig-S45
❑ 95BeAPSigDC-S45
❑ 95ColCho-179
❑ 95ColChoPC-179
❑ 95ColChoPCP-179
❑ 95Sco-223
❑ 95ScoBlaIce-223
❑ 95ScoBlaIceAP-223
❑ 96DetVip-13
**Prest, Trevor**
❑ 91BriColJHL-42
**Preston, Brian**
❑ 92BriColJHL-23
**Preston, Dan**
❑ 917thInnSOHL-103
❑ 95Sla-73
**Preston, Rich**
❑ 76OPCWHA-115
❑ 78JetPos-18
❑ 80BlaBroBac-8
❑ 80BlaWhiBor-10
❑ 80OPC-41
❑ 80Top-41
❑ 81BlaBorPos-20
❑ 81BlaBroBac-9
❑ 82OPC-71
❑ 82PosCer-4
❑ 83BlaBorPos-19
❑ 83OPC-110
❑ 84DevPos-19
❑ 84OPC-118
❑ 84Top-34
❑ 85OPC-139
❑ 85Top-139
❑ 86BlaCok-16
❑ 86OPC-61
❑ 86OPCSti-199
❑ 86Top-61
❑ 91BlaCok-21
❑ 93BlaCok-29
❑ 96RegPat-23
**Preston, Yves**
❑ 81MilAdm-6
**Pretty, David**
❑ 80QueRem-17
**Preuss, Gunther**
❑ 94GerDELE-143
❑ 95GerDELE-141
**Prevost, Stacy**
❑ 91AirCanSJHL-B12
❑ 92MPSPhoSJHL-168
**Priakin, Sergei**
❑ 89Kra-8
❑ 90Bow-103
❑ 90BowTif-103
❑ 90FlamIGA-21
❑ 90ProSet-594
❑ 91FlamPanTS-17
❑ 93SwiHNL-178
❑ 94FinnSIS-214
❑ 95FinnSIS-91
❑ 95FinnSIS-380
❑ 95FinnSISL-61
❑ 96FinnSISR-93
**Pribyla, Kamil**
❑ 94CzeAPSE-125
**Price, Gerry**
❑ 52JunBluT-12
**Price, Matt**
❑ 95Sla-119
**Price, Noel**
❑ 52JunBluT-149
❑ 58Par-6
❑ 59Par-42
❑ 65QueAce-16
❑ 68OPC-110
❑ 68ShiCoi-138
❑ 68Top-110
❑ 70EssPowPla-149
❑ 70OPC-163
❑ 72Flam-15
❑ 72OPC-163
❑ 72SarProSta-8
❑ 73OPC-256
❑ 74NHLActSta-17
❑ 74OPCNHL-356
❑ 75OPCNHL-331
❑ 94ParMisL-131
**Price, Pat**
❑ 76OPCNHL-318
❑ 77OPCNHL-308
❑ 78OPC-368
❑ 79OilPos-19
❑ 79OPC-347
❑ 80OPC-299
❑ 80PepCap-37
❑ 81OPC-265
❑ 82OPC-274
❑ 82PosCer-15
❑ 83NordPos-21
❑ 83Vac-71
❑ 84NordPos-20
❑ 84OPC-286
❑ 85NordGenF-20
❑ 85NordMcD-16
❑ 85NordPla-4
❑ 85NordPla-6
❑ 85NordPro-19
❑ 85NordTeal-18
❑ 86KraDra-56
❑ 86NordGenF-19
❑ 86NordMcD-19
❑ 86NordTeal-18
❑ 87NorStaPos-24
❑ 88OilTenAnn-82
**Priddle, Phil**
❑ 83BraAle-23
**Priest, Merv**
❑ 89BraWheK-22
❑ 907thInnSWHL-220
❑ 90BraWheK-2
❑ 917thInnSWHL-207
❑ 95VanVooRHI-19
**Priestlay, Ken**
❑ 84VicCou-18
❑ 87SabBluS-19
❑ 88ProAHL-247
❑ 89ProAHL-257
❑ 89SabBluS-16
❑ 90AlbIntTC-16
❑ 91Par-359
❑ 91ParFre-359
❑ 91PenCokE-18
❑ 91ProSet-460
❑ 91ProSetFre-460
❑ 91ScoCan-658
❑ 91UppDec-525
❑ 91UppDecF-525
❑ 92CleLum-21
❑ 93SwiHNL-283
❑ 97SheSte-3
❑ 97SheSte-4
**Prilepskij, Alexander**
❑ 74SweHocS-95
**Prillo, Eric**
❑ 907thInnSQMJHL-90
**Primeau, Eric**
❑ 84RicRiv-11
**Primeau, Joe**
❑ 320'KeeMapL-10
❑ 33OPCV304A-12
❑ 33V129-7
❑ 33V288HamG-2
❑ 33V357IceK-40
❑ 34BeeGro1P-344
❑ 34SweCap-48
❑ 55Par-24
❑ 55ParQuaO-24
❑ 83HalFP-I12
❑ 85HalFC-131
❑ 91ProSet-338
❑ 91ProSetFre-338
**Primeau, Keith**
❑ 88NiaFalT-4
❑ 897thInnSOHL-130
❑ 897thInnSOHL-189
❑ 89NiaFalT-15
❑ 90OPCPre-91
❑ 90ProSet-606
❑ 90Sco-436
❑ 90ScoCan-436
❑ 90ScoRoo-90T
❑ 90ScoYouS-38
❑ 90UppDec-351
❑ 90UppDec-354
❑ 90UppDecF-351
❑ 90UppDecF-354
❑ 91Bow-46
❑ 91OPC-309
❑ 91ProAHLCHL-126
❑ 91RedWinLC-14
❑ 91ScoAme-144
❑ 91ScoCan-144
❑ 91StaClu-305
❑ 91Top-309
❑ 91UppDec-258
❑ 91UppDecF-258
❑ 92PanSti-117
❑ 92PanStiFre-117
❑ 92Par-277
❑ 92ParEmel-277
❑ 92Sco-316
❑ 92ScoCan-316
❑ 92StaClu-485
❑ 92Top-99
❑ 92TopGol-99G
❑ 92Ult-286
❑ 93Don-425
❑ 93Lea-276
❑ 93OPCPre-256
❑ 93OPCPreG-256
❑ 93PanSti-250
❑ 93Par-327
❑ 93ParEmel-327
❑ 93Pin-420
❑ 93PinCan-420
❑ 93Pow-75
❑ 93PowRisS-4
❑ 93Sco-364
❑ 93ScoCan-364
❑ 93StaClu-217
❑ 93StaCluFDI-217
❑ 93StaCluFDIO-217
❑ 93StaCluO-217
❑ 93TopPre-256
❑ 93TopPreG-256
❑ 93Ult-239
❑ 93UppDec-413
❑ 93UppDecSP-45
❑ 94CanGamNHLP-90
❑ 94Don-46
❑ 94Fla-51
❑ 94Fle-64
❑ 94HocWit-67
❑ 94Lea-266
❑ 94LeaLim-110
❑ 94OPCPre-330
❑ 94OPCPreSE-330
❑ 94Par-67
❑ 94ParGol-67
❑ 94ParVin-V66
❑ 94Pin-40
❑ 94PinArtP-40
❑ 94PinRinC-40
❑ 94Sel-15
❑ 94SelGol-15
❑ 94SP-37
❑ 94SPDieCut-37
❑ 94StaClu-16
❑ 94StaCluFDI-16
❑ 94StaCluMOMS-16
❑ 94StaCluSTWC-16
❑ 94TopPre-330
❑ 94TopPreSE-330
❑ 94Ult-65
❑ 94UppDec-337
❑ 94UppDecEleIce-337
❑ 94UppDecSPI-SP24
❑ 94UppDecSPIDC-SP24
❑ 95BeAPla-115
❑ 95BeAPSig-S115
❑ 95BeAPSigDC-S115
❑ 95CanGamNHLP-93
❑ 95ColCho-161
❑ 95ColChoPC-161
❑ 95ColChoPCP-161
❑ 95ColEdgILL-L4
❑ 95Don-42
❑ 95Emo-57
❑ 95EmoNteP-2
❑ 95EmoXci-12
❑ 95ImpSti-40
❑ 95Lea-170
❑ 95LeaLim-92
❑ 95Met-50
❑ 95MetIW-10
❑ 95ParInt-72
❑ 95ParIntEl-72
❑ 95Pin-197
❑ 95PinArtP-197
❑ 95PinRinC-197
❑ 95PlaOneoOne-35
❑ 95Sco-264
❑ 95ScoBlaIce-264
❑ 95ScoBlaIceAP-264
❑ 95SelCer-71
❑ 95SelCerDS-16
❑ 95SelCerDSG-16
❑ 95SelCerMG-71
❑ 95SkyImp-57
❑ 95SkyImp-241
❑ 95SP-47
❑ 95StaClu-66
❑ 95StaCluFea-F3
❑ 95StaCluMOMS-66
❑ 95Sum-140
❑ 95SumArtP-140
❑ 95SumIce-140
❑ 95Top-54
❑ 95TopHomGC-HGC21
❑ 95TopOPCI-54
❑ 95TopSupSki-47
❑ 95TopSupSkiPla-47
❑ 95Ult-48
❑ 95UltCreCra-14
❑ 95UltGolM-48
❑ 95UltRisS-6
❑ 95UltRisSGM-6
❑ 95UppDec-159
❑ 95UppDec-223
❑ 95UppDecEleIce-159
❑ 95UppDecEleIce-223
❑ 95UppDecEleIceG-159
❑ 95UppDecEleIceG-223
❑ 95UppDecSpeE-SE27
❑ 95UppDecSpeEdiG-SE27
❑ 95Zen-83
❑ 96ColCho-87
❑ 96Don-138
❑ 96DonCanI-27
❑ 96DonCanIGPP-27
❑ 96DonCanIRPP-27
❑ 96DonEli-73
❑ 96DonEliDCS-73
❑ 96DonPrePro-138
❑ 96Fla-43
❑ 96FlaBluI-43
❑ 96Fle-34
❑ 96Lea-154
❑ 96LeaPre-84
❑ 96LeaPreP-154
❑ 96LeaPrePP-84
❑ 96MetUni-70
❑ 96Pin-168
❑ 96PinArtP-168
❑ 96PinFoi-168
❑ 96PinPreS-168
❑ 96PinRinC-168
❑ 96Sco-54
❑ 96ScoArtPro-54
❑ 96ScoDeaCAP-54
❑ 96ScoGolB-54
❑ 96ScoSpeAP-54
❑ 96SelCer-40
❑ 96SelCerAP-40
❑ 96SelCerBlu-40
❑ 96SelCerMB-40
❑ 96SelCerMG-40
❑ 96SelCerMR-40
❑ 96SelCerRed-40
❑ 96SkyImp-39
❑ 96SP-68
❑ 96Sum-16
❑ 96SumArtP-16
❑ 96SumIce-16
❑ 96SumMet-16
❑ 96SumPreS-16
❑ 96TopNHLP-109
❑ 96TopPicOI-109
❑ 96Ult-75
❑ 96UltGolM-76
❑ 96UppDec-203
❑ 96UppDec-271
❑ 96UppDecBD-5
❑ 96UppDecBDG-5
❑ 96UppDecGN-X34
❑ 96UppDecIce-27
❑ 96UppDecIcePar-27
❑ 96UppDecPP-P4
❑ 96UppDecSS-SS29A
❑ 96Zen-101
❑ 96ZenArtP-101
❑ 97BeAPlaTAN-15
❑ 97CarHur-21
❑ 97ColCho-110
❑ 97ColChoCTG-C6A
❑ 97ColChoCTG-C6B
❑ 97ColChoCTG-C6C
❑ 97ColChoCTGE-CR6
❑ 97ColChoSta-SQ55
❑ 97ColChoWD-W9
❑ 97Don-185
❑ 97DonCanI-22
❑ 97DonCanIDS-22
❑ 97DonCanIPS-22
❑ 97DonEli-23
❑ 97DonEliAsp-23
❑ 97DonEliS-23
❑ 97DonLim-126
❑ 97DonLimExp-126
❑ 97DonPre-18
❑ 97DonPreCttC-18
❑ 97DonPreProG-185
❑ 97DonPreProS-185
❑ 97DonPri-38
❑ 97DonPriSoA-38
❑ 97EssOlyHH-19
❑ 97EssOlyHHF-19
❑ 97Kat-29
❑ 97KatGol-29
❑ 97KatSil-29
❑ 97Lea-119
❑ 97LeaFraMat-119
❑ 97LeaFraMDC-119
❑ 97LeaInt-119
❑ 97LeaIntUI-119
❑ 97Pac-52
❑ 97PacCop-52
❑ 97PacCroR-25
❑ 97PacCroREG-25
❑ 97PacCroRIB-25
❑ 97PacCroRS-25
❑ 97PacDyn-22
❑ 97PacDynBKS-17
❑ 97PacDynC-22
❑ 97PacDynDG-22
❑ 97PacDynEG-22
❑ 97PacDynIB-22
❑ 97PacDynR-22
❑ 97PacDynSil-22
❑ 97PacDynTan-30
❑ 97PacEmeGre-52
❑ 97PacIceB-52
❑ 97PacInv-25
❑ 97PacInvC-25
❑ 97PacInvEG-25
❑ 97PacInvIB-25
❑ 97PacInvR-25
❑ 97PacInvS-25
❑ 97PacOme-44
❑ 97PacOmeC-44
❑ 97PacOmeDG-44
❑ 97PacOmeEG-44
❑ 97PacOmeG-44
❑ 97PacOmeIB-44
❑ 97PacPar-37
❑ 97PacParC-37
❑ 97PacParDG-37
❑ 97PacParEG-37
❑ 97PacParIB-37
❑ 97PacParRed-37
❑ 97PacParSil-37
❑ 97PacRed-52
❑ 97PacRev-25
❑ 97PacRevC-25
❑ 97PacRevE-25
❑ 97PacRevIB-25
❑ 97PacRevR-25
❑ 97PacRevS-25
❑ 97PacRevTCL-5
❑ 97PacSil-52
❑ 97PacTeaCCC-5
❑ 97Pin-109
❑ 97PinCer-57
❑ 97PinCerMB-57
❑ 97PinCerMG-57
❑ 97PinCerMR-57
❑ 97PinCerR-57
❑ 97PinIns-189
❑ 97PinPrePBB-109
❑ 97PinPrePBC-109
❑ 97PinPrePBM-109
❑ 97PinPrePBY-109
❑ 97PinPrePFC-109
❑ 97PinPrePFM-109
❑ 97PinPrePFY-109
❑ 97PinPrePla-109
❑ 97PinTotCMPG-57
❑ 97PinTotCPB-57
❑ 97PinTotCPG-57
❑ 97PinTotCPR-57
❑ 97Sco-98
❑ 97ScoArtPro-98
❑ 97ScoGolBla-98
❑ 97SPAut-24
❑ 97Stu-42
❑ 97StuPrePG-42
❑ 97StuPrePS-42
❑ 97UppDec-29
❑ 97UppDecBD-3
❑ 97UppDecBDDD-3
❑ 97UppDecBDQD-3
❑ 97UppDecBDTD-3
❑ 97UppDecIce-25
❑ 97UppDecIceP-25
❑ 97UppDecIPS-25
❑ 97UppDecSG-SG55
❑ 97Zen-54
❑ 97Zen5x7-13
❑ 97ZenGolImp-13
❑ 97ZenSilImp-13
❑ 97ZenZGol-54
❑ 97ZenZSil-54
❑ 98Be A PPA-23
❑ 98Be A PPAA-23
❑ 98Be A PPAAF-23
❑ 98Be A PPTBASG-23
❑ 98Be APG-23
❑ 98BowBes-64
❑ 98BowBesAR-64
❑ 98BowBesR-64
❑ 98Fin-42
❑ 98FinNo P-42
❑ 98FinNo PR-42
❑ 98FinRef-42
❑ 98O-PChr-124
❑ 98O-PChrR-124
❑ 98Pac-138
❑ 98PacAur-37
❑ 98PacAurCF-9
❑ 98PacAurCFC-9
❑ 98PacAurCFIB-9
❑ 98PacAurCFR-9
❑ 98PacAurCFS-9
❑ 98PacCroR-26
❑ 98PacCroRLS-26
❑ 98PacDynI-37
❑ 98PacDynIIB-37
❑ 98PacDynIR-37
❑ 98PacDynITC-5
❑ 98PacIceB-138
❑ 98PacOmeH-45
❑ 98PacOmeODI-45
❑ 98PacOmeR-45
❑ 98PacPar-41
❑ 98PacParC-41
❑ 98PacParEG-41
❑ 98PacParH-41
❑ 98PacParIB-41
❑ 98PacParS-41
❑ 98PacParTCD-5
❑ 98PacRed-138
❑ 98PacRev-26
❑ 98PacRevADC-22
❑ 98PacRevIS-26
❑ 98PacRevR-26
❑ 98PacTeaC-5
❑ 98SP Aut-15
❑ 98SPXTopP-8
❑ 98SPXTopPF-8
❑ 98SPXTopPR-8
❑ 98Top-124
❑ 98TopGolLC1-56
❑ 98TopGolLC1B-56
❑ 98TopGolLC1BOoO-56
❑ 98TopGolLC1OoO-56
❑ 98TopGolLC1R-56
❑ 98TopGolLC1ROoO-56
❑ 98TopGolLC2-56
❑ 98TopGolLC2B-56
❑ 98TopGolLC2BOoO-56
❑ 98TopGolLC2OoO-56
❑ 98TopGolLC2R-56
❑ 98TopGolLC2ROoO-56
❑ 98TopGolLC3-56
❑ 98TopGolLC3B-56
❑ 98TopGolLC3BOoO-56
❑ 98TopGolLC3OoO-56
❑ 98TopGolLC3R-56
❑ 98TopGolLC3ROoO-56
❑ 98TopO-P-124
❑ 98UC-39
❑ 98UD ChoPCR-39
❑ 98UD ChoR-39
❑ 98UppDec-237
❑ 98UppDecBD-16
❑ 98UppDecDD-16
❑ 98UppDecE-237
❑ 98UppDecE1o1-237
❑ 98UppDecGR-237
❑ 98UppDecM-37
❑ 98UppDecMGS-37
❑ 98UppDecMPG-PG11
❑ 98UppDecMSS-37
❑ 98UppDecMSS-37
❑ 98UppDecQD-16
❑ 98UppDecTD-16
❑ 99Pac-79
❑ 99PacAur-28
❑ 99PacAurPD-28
❑ 99PacCop-79
❑ 99PacGol-79
❑ 99PacIceB-79
❑ 99PacPreD-79
❑ 99RetHoc-14
❑ 99SP AutPS-15
❑ 99UppDecM-38
❑ 99UppDecMGS-38
❑ 99UppDecMSS-38
❑ 99UppDecMSS-38
❑ 99UppDecRG-14
❑ 99UppDecRII-KP
❑ 99UppDecRIL1-KP
❑ 99UppDecRP-14
**Primeau, Kevin**
❑ 80CanuSilD-19
❑ 81SweSemHVS-90
❑ 91OilIGA-29
❑ 92OilIGA-29
**Primeau, Wayne**
❑ 93OweSouPla-23
❑ 93UppDecPOE-E9
❑ 94Cla-15
❑ 94ClaCHLP-CP1
❑ 94ClaDraGol-15
❑ 94ClaTri-T7
❑ 95Bow-157
❑ 95BowAllFoi-157
❑ 95Cla-93
❑ 95Ima-47
❑ 95ImaGol-47
❑ 95ParInt-26
❑ 95ParIntEl-26
❑ 95SkyImp-191
❑ 95Sla-240
❑ 95Sla-301
❑ 95Top-222
❑ 95TopOPCI-222
❑ 95UppDec-433
❑ 95UppDecEleIce-433
❑ 95UppDecEleIceG-433
❑ 96ColCho-25
❑ 96ColEdgFL-36
❑ 96Fle-132
❑ 96Lea-231
❑ 96LeaPre-131
❑ 96LeaPreP-231
❑ 96LeaPrePP-131
❑ 96MetUni-17
❑ 96Pin-220
❑ 96PinArtP-220
❑ 96PinFoi-220
❑ 96PinPreS-220
❑ 96PinRinC-220
❑ 96SkyImp-156
❑ 96Ult-20
❑ 96UltGolM-20
❑ 96UltRoo-16
❑ 96UppDec-20
❑ 96UppDecBD-76
❑ 96UppDecBDG-76
❑ 97Don-67
❑ 97DonLim-101
❑ 97DonLimExp-101
❑ 97DonPreProG-67
❑ 97DonPreProS-67
❑ 97DonPri-72
❑ 97DonPriSoA-72
❑ 97Pac-43
❑ 97PacCop-43
❑ 97PacEmeGre-43
❑ 97PacIceB-43
❑ 97PacRed-43
❑ 97PacSil-43
❑ 97ScoSab-13
❑ 97ScoSabPla-13
❑ 97ScoSabPre-13
❑ 97UppDec-17
❑ 98O-PChr-146
❑ 98O-PChrR-146
❑ 98Top-146
❑ 98TopO-P-146
**Prince, Guy**
❑ 91BriColJHL-71
❑ 92BriColJHL-75
❑ 93DayBom-12
❑ 95AlaGolKin-15
**Prince, Martin**
❑ 92QueIntP-46
**Prior, Craig**
❑ 907thInnSQMJHL-214
**Prior, Dave**
❑ 91JetIGA-26
❑ 91MonHaw-23
❑ 91ProAHLCHL-188
**Prior, Gary**
❑ 94GerDELE-6
❑ 95GerDELE-1
❑ 96GerDELE-1
**Prior, Steve**
❑ 89RayJrC-19
**Pritchard, Bruce**
❑ 84VicCou-19
**Pritchett, Grant**

❑ 917thInnSOHL-343
❑ 93GueSto-24
**Probert, Bob**
❑ 83BraAle-3
❑ 84SauSteMG-18
❑ 87RedWinLC-24
❑ 88FriLayS-41
❑ 88OPC-181
❑ 88OPCSti-247
❑ 88PanSti-46
❑ 88RedWinLC-20
❑ 88Top-181
❑ 90ProSet-76
❑ 90Sco-143
❑ 90ScoCan-143
❑ 90UppDec-448
❑ 90UppDecF-448
❑ 91Bow-55
❑ 91OPC-198
❑ 91PanSti-146
❑ 91Par-272
❑ 91ParFre-272
❑ 91Pin-183
❑ 91PinFre-183
❑ 91ProSet-61
❑ 91ProSetFre-61
❑ 91ProSetPla-34
❑ 91RedWinLC-15
❑ 91ScoAme-73
❑ 91ScoCan-73
❑ 91StaClu-59
❑ 91Top-198
❑ 91UppDec-239
❑ 91UppDecF-239
❑ 92Bow-85
❑ 92OPC-252
❑ 92Par-41
❑ 92ParCheP-CP9
❑ 92ParEmel-41
❑ 92Pin-56
❑ 92PinFre-56
❑ 92ProSet-46
❑ 92Sco-52
❑ 92ScoCan-52
❑ 92ScoSha-17
❑ 92ScoShaCan-17
❑ 92SeaPat-8
❑ 92StaClu-355
❑ 92Top-63
❑ 92TopGol-63G
❑ 92Ult-53
❑ 92UppDec-248
❑ 93Don-104
❑ 93Lea-186
❑ 93OPCPre-177
❑ 93OPCPreG-177
❑ 93PanSti-249
❑ 93Par-333
❑ 93ParEmel-333
❑ 93Pin-7
❑ 93PinCan-7
❑ 93Pow-335
❑ 93Sco-59
❑ 93ScoCan-59
❑ 93StaClu-137
❑ 93StaCluFDI-137
❑ 93StaCluFDIO-137
❑ 93StaCluO-137
❑ 93TopPre-177
❑ 93TopPreG-177
❑ 93Ult-309
❑ 93UppDec-200
❑ 93UppDecSP-46
❑ 94Par-71
❑ 94ParGol-71
❑ 94Pin-404
❑ 94PinArtP-404
❑ 94PinRinC-404
❑ 95BeAPla-221
❑ 95BeAPSig-S221
❑ 95BeAPSigDC-S221
❑ 95CanGamNHLP-68
❑ 95Don-247
❑ 95ParInt-312
❑ 95ParIntEl-312
❑ 95PlaOneoOne-134
❑ 95StaClu-152
❑ 95StaCluMOMS-152
❑ 95Top-299
❑ 95TopOPCI-299
❑ 95Ult-218
❑ 95UppDec-469
❑ 95UppDecElelce-469
❑ 95UppDecElelceG-469
❑ 95UppDecSpeE-SE105
❑ 95UppDecSpeEdiG-SE105
❑ 96Don-8
❑ 96DonPrePro-8
❑ 96Pin-84
❑ 96PinArtP-84
❑ 96PinFoi-84
❑ 96PinPreS-84
❑ 96PinRinC-84
❑ 96Sco-156
❑ 96ScoArtPro-156
❑ 96ScoDeaCAP-156
❑ 96ScoGolB-156
❑ 96ScoSpeAP-156
❑ 96UppDec-33
❑ 96UppDecSS-SS29B
❑ 97ColCho-49
❑ 97Kat-36
❑ 97KatGol-36
❑ 97KatSil-36
❑ 97Pac-290
❑ 97PacCop-290
❑ 97PacEmeGre-290
❑ 97PacIceB-290
❑ 97PacRed-290
❑ 97PacSil-290
❑ 97UppDec-39
❑ 97UppDec-197
❑ 98Be A PPA-181
❑ 98Be A PPAA-181
❑ 98Be A PPAAF-181
❑ 98Be A PPSE-181
❑ 98Be APG-181
❑ 98O-PChr-97
❑ 98O-PChrR-97
❑ 98PacDynI-44
❑ 98PacDynIB-44
❑ 98PacDynIR-44
❑ 98PacOmeH-54
❑ 98PacOmeODI-54
❑ 98PacOmeR-54
❑ 98Top-97
❑ 98TopO-P-97
❑ 98UppDecM-46
❑ 98UppDecMGS-46
❑ 98UppDecMSS-46
❑ 98UppDecMSS-46
❑ 99Pac-96
❑ 99PacCop-96
❑ 99PacGol-96
❑ 99PacIceB-96
❑ 99PacPreD-96
**Probst, Paul**
❑ 72SweSemWC-151
**Probst, Skip**
❑ 88ProIHL-88
❑ 91ProAHLCHL-450
**Proceviat, Dick**
❑ 67ColChe-11
**Proceviat, Steve**
❑ 90RayJrC-17
**Prochazka, Frantisek**
❑ 93SweSemWCS-94
❑ 94FinnJaaK-172
❑ 95GerDELE-410
**Prochazka, Libor**
❑ 94CzeAPSE-49
❑ 94CzeAPSE-52
❑ 95CzeAPSE-84
❑ 96CzeAPSE-78
❑ 96SweSemW-109
**Prochazka, Martin**
❑ 91UppDecCWJC-96
❑ 94CzeAPSE-57
❑ 95CzeAPSE-94
❑ 95FinnSemWC-155
❑ 96SweSemW-116
❑ 97PacPar-184
❑ 97PacParC-184
❑ 97PacParDG-184
❑ 97PacParEG-184
❑ 97PacParIB-184
❑ 97PacParRed-184
❑ 97PacParSil-184
❑ 97Sco-62
❑ 97ScoArtPro-62
❑ 97ScoGolBla-62
❑ 97ScoMapL-20
❑ 97ScoMapLPla-20
❑ 97ScoMapLPre-20
❑ 98Pac-420
❑ 98PacIceB-420
❑ 98PacRed-420
**Prochazka, Milan**
❑ 96CzeAPSE-163
**Prochazka, Radek**
❑ 96CzeAPSE-279
**Prochazka, Stanislav**
❑ 94CzeAPSE-36
❑ 96CzeAPSE-155
**Procyshyn, Jeremy**
❑ 92MPSPhoSJHL-88
**Prodgers, Goldie**
❑ 12C57-37
❑ 23V1451-32
❑ 24C144ChaCig-47
**Proffitt, Rob**
❑ 95AlaGolKin-16
**Proft, Paris**
❑ 96GerDELE-202
**Prokepetz, Jason**
❑ 98FloEve-19
**Prokhorov, Vitali**
❑ 92Cla-51
❑ 92OPCPre-64
❑ 92Par-157
❑ 92ParEmel-157
❑ 92Pin-404
❑ 92PinFre-404
❑ 92RusStaRA-5
❑ 92RusStaRA-29
❑ 92Ult-397
❑ 92UppDec-486
❑ 93Don-290
❑ 93Lea-326
❑ 93OPCPre-452
❑ 93OPCPreG-452
❑ 93Par-450
❑ 93ParEmel-450
❑ 93PeoRiv-22
❑ 93Pow-432
❑ 93TopPre-452
❑ 93TopPreG-452
❑ 93UppDec-363
❑ 94CanGamNHLP-206
❑ 94ClaProP-92
❑ 94Don-126
❑ 94Lea-295
❑ 94Par-206
❑ 94ParGol-206
❑ 94Pin-367
❑ 94PinArtP-367
❑ 94PinRinC-367
❑ 94StaClu-19
❑ 94StaCluFDI-19
❑ 94StaCluMOMS-19
❑ 94StaCluSTWC-19
❑ 94Ult-188
❑ 94UppDec-173
❑ 94UppDecElelce-173
❑ 95SweLeaE-221
❑ 95SweUppDE-66
❑ 96ClaGol-51
**Prokopec, Mike**
❑ 917thInnSOHL-13
❑ 91CorRoy-17
❑ 93GueSto-16
❑ 94IndIce-18
❑ 95IndIce-17
❑ 95ParInt-308
❑ 95ParIntEl-308
❑ 96ColEdgFL-50
❑ 96Zen-149
❑ 96ZenArtP-149
**Prokopetz, Jason**
❑ 91AirCanSJHL-E22
❑ 92MPSPhoSJHL-82
**Prokopjev, Alexander**
❑ 91OPCIns-25R
❑ 96CzeAPSE-207
**Prokupek, Ladislav**
❑ 93Par-514
❑ 93ParEmel-514
❑ 94CzeAPSE-176
❑ 95CzeAPSE-193
❑ 96CzeAPSE-327
**Pronger, Chris**
❑ 917thInnSOHL-134
❑ 91PetPet-2
❑ 92UppDec-591
❑ 92UppDec-SP3
❑ 93Cla-2
❑ 93ClaTopTen-DP2
❑ 93Don-150
❑ 93Don-393
❑ 93DonRatR-3
❑ 93DonSpeP-J
❑ 93Kra-69
❑ 93Lea-257
❑ 93LeaFrePhe-2
❑ 93OPCPre-485
❑ 93OPCPreG-485
❑ 93Par-249
❑ 93ParCalC-C2
❑ 93ParCalCG-C2
❑ 93ParChePH-D13
❑ 93ParEmel-249
❑ 93PetPet-29
❑ 93Pin-456
❑ 93PinCan-456
❑ 93PinSupR-2
❑ 93PinSupRC-2
❑ 93Pow-354
❑ 93PowRooS-12
❑ 93Sco-586
❑ 93ScoCan-586
❑ 93ScoGol-586
❑ 93StaClu-290
❑ 93StaCluFDI-290
❑ 93StaCluO-290
❑ 93TopPre-485
❑ 93TopPreG-485
❑ 93Ult-339
❑ 93UltWavF-14
❑ 93UppDec-190
❑ 93UppDecSilSka-H5
❑ 93UppDecSilSkaG-H5
❑ 93UppDecSP-64
❑ 93WhaCok-16
❑ 94BeAPla-R43
❑ 94CanGamNHLP-121
❑ 94ClaAllRT-AR5
❑ 94ClaProP-31
❑ 94ClaProP-AU6
❑ 94Don-215
❑ 94Fin-62
❑ 94FinRef-62
❑ 94FinSupTW-62
❑ 94Fla-73
❑ 94Fle-88
❑ 94Lea-268
❑ 94LeaGolR-9
❑ 94LeaLim-22
❑ 94LeaLimI-10
❑ 94OPCFinIns-11
❑ 94OPCPre-198
❑ 94OPCPre-381
❑ 94OPCPre-484
❑ 94OPCPreSE-198
❑ 94OPCPreSE-381
❑ 94OPCPreSE-484
❑ 94Par-274
❑ 94ParGol-274
❑ 94ParSE-SE73
❑ 94ParSEG-SE73
❑ 94ParVin-V40
❑ 94Pin-11
❑ 94Pin-466
❑ 94PinArtP-11
❑ 94PinArtP-466
❑ 94PinRinC-11
❑ 94PinRinC-466
❑ 94Sco-252
❑ 94ScoGol-252
❑ 94ScoPla-252
❑ 94ScoPlaTS-252
❑ 94Sel-111
❑ 94SelGol-111
❑ 94SP-48
❑ 94SPDieCut-48
❑ 94StaClu-111
❑ 94StaClu-235
❑ 94StaCluFDI-111
❑ 94StaCluFDI-235
❑ 94StaCluMOMS-111
❑ 94StaCluMOMS-235
❑ 94StaCluSTWC-111
❑ 94StaCluSTWC-235
❑ 94TopPre-198
❑ 94TopPre-381
❑ 94TopPre-484
❑ 94TopPreSE-198
❑ 94TopPreSE-381
❑ 94TopPreSE-484
❑ 94Ult-91
❑ 94UltAllRoo-7
❑ 94UppDec-52
❑ 94UppDecElelce-52
❑ 94UppDecNBAP-35
❑ 94UppDecSPI-SP33
❑ 94UppDecSPIDC-SP33
❑ 95BeAPla-18
❑ 95BeAPSig-S18
❑ 95BeAPSigDC-S18
❑ 95Bow-62
❑ 95BowAllFoi-62
❑ 95CanGamNHLP-243
❑ 95ColCho-232
❑ 95ColChoPC-232
❑ 95ColChoPCP-232
❑ 95Don-63
❑ 95Don-319
❑ 95DonProPoi-17
❑ 95Emo-151
❑ 95ImpSti-104
❑ 95Lea-242
❑ 95LeaLim-107
❑ 95Met-127
❑ 95ParInt-175
❑ 95ParIntEl-175
❑ 95PlaOneoOne-309
❑ 95ProMag-14
❑ 95Sco-6
❑ 95ScoBlaIce-6
❑ 95ScoBlaIceAP-6
❑ 95ScoChelt-5
❑ 95SkyImp-144
❑ 95SP-124
❑ 95StaClu-69
❑ 95StaCluMOMS-69
❑ 95Sum-30
❑ 95SumArtP-30
❑ 95SumIce-30
❑ 95Top-308
❑ 95TopHomGC-HGC15
❑ 95TopOPCI-308
❑ 95TopSupSki-54
❑ 95TopSupSkiPla-54
❑ 95Ult-69
❑ 95Ult-302
❑ 95UltGolM-69
❑ 95UppDec-174
❑ 95UppDecElelce-174
❑ 95UppDecElelceG-174
❑ 95UppDecSpeE-SE160
❑ 95UppDecSpeEdiG-SE160
❑ 95Zen-28
❑ 96ColCho-226
❑ 96Don-63
❑ 96DonPrePro-63
❑ 96Fle-99
❑ 96FlePic-114
❑ 96Lea-5
❑ 96LeaPreP-5
❑ 96MetUni-135
❑ 96NHLProSTA-14
❑ 96Pin-58
❑ 96PinArtP-58
❑ 96PinFoi-58
❑ 96PinPreS-58
❑ 96PinRinC-58
❑ 96Sco-166
❑ 96ScoArtPro-166
❑ 96ScoDeaCAP-166
❑ 96ScoGolB-166
❑ 96ScoSpeAP-166
❑ 96SkyImp-115
❑ 96SP-135
❑ 96SPHolCol-HC10
❑ 96UppDec-144
❑ 96UppDecBD-150
❑ 96UppDecBDG-150
❑ 96UppDecGN-X36
❑ 96UppDecIce-63
❑ 96UppDecIcePar-63
❑ 96UppDecPP-P24
❑ 96UppDecSS-SS27B
❑ 97ColCho-233
❑ 97ColChoWD-W14
❑ 97Don-100
❑ 97DonCanI-90
❑ 97DonCanIDS-90
❑ 97DonCanIPS-90
❑ 97DonLim-85
❑ 97DonLimExp-85
❑ 97DonPre-109
❑ 97DonPreCttC-109
❑ 97DonPreProG-100
❑ 97DonPreProS-100
❑ 97DonPri-91
❑ 97DonPriSoA-91
❑ 97EssOlyHH-15
❑ 97EssOlyHHF-15
❑ 97Lea-90
❑ 97LeaFraMat-90
❑ 97LeaFraMDC-90
❑ 97LeaInt-90
❑ 97LeaIntUI-90
❑ 97Pac-124
❑ 97PacCop-124
❑ 97PacEmeGre-124
❑ 97PacIceB-124
❑ 97PacOme-196
❑ 97PacOmeC-196
❑ 97PacOmeDG-196
❑ 97PacOmeEG-196
❑ 97PacOmeG-196
❑ 97PacOmeIB-196
❑ 97PacOmeTL-17
❑ 97PacRed-124
❑ 97PacSil-124
❑ 97PinIns-175
❑ 97ScoBlu-7
❑ 97ScoBluPla-7
❑ 97ScoBluPre-7
❑ 97SPAut-139
❑ 97UppDec-142
❑ 97UppDec-398
❑ 97UppDecBD-83
❑ 97UppDecBDDD-83
❑ 97UppDecBDQD-83
❑ 97UppDecBDTD-83
❑ 98Be A PPA-123
❑ 98Be A PPAA-123
❑ 98Be A PPAAF-123
❑ 98Be A PPTBASG-123
❑ 98Be APG-123
❑ 98BowBes-18
❑ 98BowBesAR-18
❑ 98BowBesMIF-F18
❑ 98BowBesMIFAR-F18
❑ 98BowBesMIFR-F18
❑ 98BowBesR-18
❑ 98Fin-22
❑ 98FinNo P-22
❑ 98FinNo PR-22
❑ 98FinRef-22
❑ 98O-PChr-181
❑ 98O-PChrBM-B1
❑ 98O-PChrBMR-B1
❑ 98O-PChrR-181
❑ 98O-PChrSB-SB25
❑ 98O-PChrSBR-SB25
❑ 98Pac-44
❑ 98PacAur-163
❑ 98PacCroR-116
❑ 98PacCroRLS-116
❑ 98PacDynI-161
❑ 98PacDynIB-161
❑ 98PacDynIR-161
❑ 98PacIceB-44
❑ 98PacOmeH-205
❑ 98PacOmeODI-205
❑ 98PacOmeR-205
❑ 98PacPar-206
❑ 98PacParC-206
❑ 98PacParEG-206
❑ 98PacParH-206
❑ 98PacParIB-206
❑ 98PacParS-206
❑ 98PacRed-44
❑ 98PacRevADC-23
❑ 98PacRevIS-124
❑ 98PacRevR-124
❑ 98SP Aut-71
❑ 98SPxFin-75
❑ 98SPxFinR-75
❑ 98SPxFinS-75
❑ 98SPXTopP-52
❑ 98SPXTopPF-52
❑ 98SPXTopPR-52
❑ 98Top-181
❑ 98TopBoaM-B1
❑ 98TopGolLC1-49
❑ 98TopGolLC1B-49
❑ 98TopGolLC1BOoO-49
❑ 98TopGolLC1OoO-49
❑ 98TopGolLC1R-49
❑ 98TopGolLC1ROoO-49
❑ 98TopGolLC2-49
❑ 98TopGolLC2B-49
❑ 98TopGolLC2BOoO-49
❑ 98TopGolLC2OoO-49
❑ 98TopGolLC2R-49
❑ 98TopGolLC2ROoO-49
❑ 98TopGolLC3-49
❑ 98TopGolLC3B-49
❑ 98TopGolLC3BOoO-49
❑ 98TopGolLC3OoO-49
❑ 98TopGolLC3R-49
❑ 98TopGolLC3ROoO-49
❑ 98TopIceA2-I7
❑ 98TopO-P-181
❑ 98TopSeaB-SB25
❑ 98UC-185
❑ 98UD ChoPCR-185
❑ 98UD ChoR-185
❑ 98UppDec-174
❑ 98UppDecBD-78
❑ 98UppDecDD-78
❑ 98UppDecE-174
❑ 98UppDecE1o1-174
❑ 98UppDecGR-174
❑ 98UppDecLSH-LS20
❑ 98UppDecLSHQ1-LS20
❑ 98UppDecLSHQ2-LS20
❑ 98UppDecLSHQ3-LS20
❑ 98UppDecM-180
❑ 98UppDecMGS-180
❑ 98UppDecMSS-180
❑ 98UppDecMSS-180
❑ 98UppDecQD-78
❑ 98UppDecTD-78
❑ 99Pac-362
❑ 99PacAur-127
❑ 99PacAurPD-127
❑ 99PacCop-362
❑ 99PacGol-362
❑ 99PacIceB-362
❑ 99PacPreD-362
❑ 99SP AutPS-71
❑ 99UppDecM-186
❑ 99UppDecMGS-186
❑ 99UppDecMSS-186
❑ 99UppDecMSS-186
**Pronger, Sean**
❑ 94Cla-93
❑ 94ClaDraGol-93
❑ 94KnoChe-11
❑ 95Bow-153
❑ 95BowAllFoi-153
❑ 96Duc-20
❑ 96PinPreS-223
❑ 97Be A PPAD-132
❑ 97Be A PPAPD-132
❑ 97BeAPla-132
❑ 97BeAPlaAut-132
❑ 97ColCho-2
❑ 97Don-98
❑ 97DonLim-101
❑ 97DonLimExp-101
❑ 97DonPre-123
❑ 97DonPreCttC-123
❑ 97DonPreProG-98
❑ 97DonPreProS-98
❑ 97DonPri-109
❑ 97DonPriSoA-109
❑ 97Pac-156
❑ 97PacCop-156
❑ 97PacEmeGre-156
❑ 97PacIceB-156
❑ 97PacRed-156
❑ 97PacSil-156
❑ 97ScoMigDPla-18
❑ 97ScoMigDPre-18
❑ 97ScoMigDuc-18
❑ 97SPAut-124
❑ 97UppDec-7
**Pronin, Nikolai**
❑ 98ChaChe-13
**Pronovost, Andre**
❑ 44BeeGro2P-59
❑ 44BeeGro2P-203
❑ 44BeeGro2P-279
❑ 57Par-M7
❑ 58Par-3
❑ 59Par-35
❑ 60Par-55
❑ 60ShiCoi-32
❑ 60TopSta-45
❑ 61Par-51
❑ 61ShiCoi-3
❑ 61Top-5
❑ 62Top-19
❑ 62YorIroOTra-30A
❑ 63Par-45
❑ 63YorWhiB-43
❑ 64BeeGro3P-92
❑ 94ParMisL-75
❑ 94ParTalB-62
**Pronovost, Claude**
❑ 94ParMisL-15
**Pronovost, Jean**
❑ 60Par-58
❑ 69OPC-155
❑ 70ColSta-50
❑ 70DadCoo-105
❑ 70EssPowPla-231
❑ 70OPC-202
❑ 70SarProSta-162
❑ 71LetActR-23
❑ 71OPC-118
❑ 71PenPos-15
❑ 71SarProSta-168
❑ 71Top-118
❑ 71TorSun-224
❑ 72OPC-64
❑ 72SarProSta-176
❑ 72SweSemWC-216
❑ 72Top-143
❑ 73OPC-11
❑ 73Top-11
❑ 74NHLActSta-217
❑ 74OPCNHL-110
❑ 74PenPos-19
❑ 74Top-110
❑ 75OPCNHL-280
❑ 75OPCNHL-326
❑ 75Top-280
❑ 75Top-326
❑ 76OPCNHL-14
❑ 76OPCNHL-218
❑ 76Top-14
❑ 76Top-218
❑ 77OPCNHL-261
❑ 77PenPucB-19
❑ 77Top-261
❑ 78OPC-184
❑ 78Top-184
❑ 79FlamPos-13
❑ 79FlaTeal-14
❑ 79OPC-77
❑ 79PanSti-64
❑ 79Top-77
❑ 81OPC-355
❑ 81OPCSti-196
**Pronovost, Marcel**
❑ 44BeeGro2P-204
❑ 51Par-68
❑ 52Par-61
❑ 53Par-41
❑ 54Par-34
❑ 54Top-27
❑ 57Top-43
❑ 58Top-24
❑ 59Top-44
❑ 60Par-29
❑ 60ShiCoi-56
❑ 61Par-29
❑ 61ShiCoi-68
❑ 62Par-33
❑ 62YorIroOTra-23
❑ 63ChePho-42
❑ 63Par-46
❑ 63TorSta-29
❑ 63YorWhiB-38
❑ 64BeeGro3P-93
❑ 64BeeGro3P-178A
❑ 64BeeGro3P-178B
❑ 64CocCap-39
❑ 64Top-39
❑ 64TorSta-38
❑ 65Coc-92
❑ 65MapLeaWB-15
❑ 65Top-80
❑ 66Top-20
❑ 66TopUSAT-20
❑ 67PosFliB-4
❑ 67Top-81
❑ 67YorActOct-33
❑ 67YorActOct-34
❑ 68OPC-125
❑ 68PosCerM-19
❑ 68ShiCoi-171
❑ 68Top-125
❑ 69MapLeaWBG-27
❑ 76OldTim-14
❑ 81RedWinOld-8
❑ 83HalFP-K14
❑ 85HalFC-148
❑ 91UltOriS-71
❑ 91UltOriSBB-3
❑ 91UltOriSF-71
❑ 93ParParR-PR65
❑ 94ParMisL-58
❑ 94ParTalB-55
❑ 95Par66-108
❑ 95Par66Coi-108
**Pronovost, Rene**
❑ 51LavDaiLSJ-35
**Propp, Brian**
❑ 80OPC-39
❑ 80Top-39
❑ 81OPC-246
❑ 81OPCSti-180
❑ 81Top-E110
❑ 82OPC-256
❑ 82OPCSti-111
❑ 82PosCer-14
❑ 83FlyJCP-18
❑ 83OPC-218
❑ 83OPC-271
❑ 83OPCSti-199
❑ 83PufSti-11
❑ 84KelWin-34
❑ 84OPC-166
❑ 84OPCSti-112
❑ 85FlyPos-24
❑ 85OPC-151
❑ 85OPCSti-90
❑ 85Top-141
❑ 86FlyPos-21
❑ 86OPC-86
❑ 86OPCSti-239
❑ 86Top-86
❑ 87OPC-158
❑ 87OPCMin-33
❑ 87OPCSti-97
❑ 87PanSti-131
❑ 87PanSti-193
❑ 87Top-158
❑ 88OPC-168
❑ 88OPCSti-97
❑ 88PanSti-324
❑ 88Top-168
❑ 89BruSpoAU-8
❑ 89FlyPos-20
❑ 89OPC-139
❑ 89OPCSti-106
❑ 89PanSti-306
❑ 89Top-139
❑ 90Bow-37
❑ 90BowTif-37
❑ 90OPC-8
❑ 90OPCPre-92
❑ 90PanSti-5
❑ 90PanSti-325
❑ 90ProSet-14
❑ 90ProSet-360
❑ 90ProSet-460

90Sco-269
90ScoCan-269
90ScoRoo-34T
90Top-8
90TopTif-8
90UppDec-2
90UppDec-409
90UppDecF-2
90UppDecF-409
91Bow-123
91Bow-424
91OPC-227
91PanSti-115
91Par-82
91ParFre-82
91Pin-184
91PinFre-184
91ProSet-113
91ProSetFre-113
91ProSetPla-187
91ProSetPlaPC-PC17
91ScoAme-223
91ScoCan-223
91StaClu-237
91Top-227
91UppDec-260
91UppDecF-260
92Bow-272
92OPC-350
92PanSti-93
92PanStiFre-93
92Pin-178
92PinFre-178
92ProSet-257
92Sco-72
92ScoCan-72
92StaClu-374
92Top-65
92TopGol-65G
92UppDec-177
93Don-441
93PanSti-267
93Par-85
93ParEmel-85
93Pin-342
93PinCan-342
93Sco-513
93ScoCan-513
93ScoGol-513
93Ult-340
93UppDec-368
93WhaCok-17
94Sco-247
94ScoGol-247
94ScoPla-247
94ScoPlaTS-247
94Ult-92
**Prorok, Ivo**
94CzeAPSE-223
95CzeAPSE-137
**Proskurnicki, Andrew**
95Sla-348
96SarSti-21
**Prosofsky, Garrett**
95SasBla-16
96SasBla-18
97UppDec-416
**Prosofsky, Jason**
907thInnSWHL-31
91ProAHLCHL-325
91UppDec-432
91UppDecF-432
**Prosofsky, Tyler**
92TacRoc-19
93TacRoc-22
**Prospal, Vaclav**
94Cla-29
94ClaDraGol-29
94ClaProP-174
97Be A PPAD-213
97Be A PPAPD-213
97BeAPla-213
97BeAPlaAut-213
97BeeAutA-52
97ColCho-185
97Don-219
97DonCanI-135
97DonCanIDS-135
97DonCanIPS-135
97DonEli-80
97DonEliAsp-80
97DonEliS-80
97DonLim-38
97DonLim-91
97DonLim-100
97DonLimExp-38
97DonLimExp-91
97DonLimExp-100
97DonMed-3
97DonPre-105
97DonPreCttC-105
97DonPreProG-219
97DonPreProS-219
97DonPri-165
97DonPri-190
97DonPriSoA-165
97DonPriSoA-190
97DonRatR-3
97Kat-165
97KatGol-165
97KatSil-165
97Lea-132
97Lea-165
97LeaFraMat-132
97LeaFraMat-165

97LeaFraMDC-132
97LeaFraMDC-165
97LeaInt-132
97LeaIntUI-132
97McD-39
97PacCroR-100
97PacCroREG-100
97PacCroRIB-100
97PacCroRS-100
97PacPar-136
97PacParB-136
97PacParDG-136
97PacParEG-136
97PacParIB-136
97PacParRed-136
97PacParSil-136
97Pin-19
97PinArtP-19
97PinBee-52
97PinBeeGP-52
97PinBeeGT-21
97PinBeeT-21
97PinIns-143
97PinMin-30
97PinMinB-30
97PinMinCBP-30
97PinMinCGPP-30
97PinMinCNSP-30
97PinMinCoiB-30
97PinMinCoiGP-30
97PinMinCoiN-30
97PinMinCoiSG-30
97PinMinCoiSS-30
97PinMinGolTea-30
97PinMinSilTea-30
97PinPrePBB-19
97PinPrePBC-19
97PinPrePBM-19
97PinPrePBY-19
97PinPrePFC-19
97PinPrePFM-19
97PinPrePFY-19
97PinPrePla-19
97PinRin-19
97Sco-51
97ScoArtPro-51
97ScoFly-18
97ScoFlyPla-18
97ScoFlyPre-18
97ScoGolBla-51
97SPAut-188
97UppDec-125
97UppDecBDPC-PC21
97UppDecBDPCDD-PC21
97UppDecBDPCM-PC21
97UppDecBDPCQD-PC21
97UppDecBDPCTD-PC21
97UppDecIce-45
97UppDecIceP-45
97UppDecILL-L7C
97UppDecILL2-L7C
97UppDecIPS-45
97UppDecSG-SG27
97Zen-91
97ZenRooR-6
97ZenZGol-91
97ZenZSil-91
97ZenZT-13
97ZenZTG-13
98Fin-49
98FinNo P-49
98FinNo PR-49
98FinRef-49
98PacDynI-129
98PacDynIIB-129
98PacDynIR-129
98UC-145
98UD ChoPCR-145
98UD ChoR-145
98UppDec-328
98UppDecE-328
98UppDecGR-328
98UppDecM-145
98UppDecMGS-145
98UppDecMSS-145
98UppDecMSS-145
99Pac-292
99PacCop-292
99PacGol-292
99PacIceB-292
99PacPreD-292
**Protsenko, Boris**
95BowDraPro-P29
**Proulx, Christian**
907thInnSQMJHL-218
917thInnSQMJHL-167
93FreCan-23
94ClaProP-8
94FreCan-23
94Par-121
94ParGol-121
96MilAdmBO-20
**Proulx, Hugo**
917thInnSMC-57
917thInnSQMJHL-282
94GreMon-8
**Provari, Jukko**
79PanSti-177
**Provaznik, Jiri**
94CzeAPSE-46
**Provencal, Jacques**
88RivDu R-24
**Provencher, Jimmy**
96LouRiv-21

**Provenzano, Mark**
95Sla-220
**Provost, Claude**
44BeeGro2P-280
52JunBluT-138
57Par-M12
58Par-43
59Par-18
60Par-54
60Par-58
60ShiCoi-33
60YorPreP-28
61Par-50
61ShiCoi-105
61YorYelB-17
62Par-41
62ShiMetC-35
62YorIroOTra-14
63ChePho-43
63Par-36
63Par-95
63TorSta-30
63YorWhiB-28
64BeeGro3P-111
64CanaPos-14
64CocCap-64
64Top-23
64TorSta-39
65CanaSteG-6
65Coc-64
65Top-8
66Top-9
66TopUSAT-9
67CanalGA-14
67Top-71
67YorActOct-4
67YorActOct-6
67YorActOct-20
67YorActOct-36
68CanalGA-14
68CanaPosBW-11
68OPC-163
68OPC-216
68ShiCoi-90
69CanaPosC-21
69OPC-167
70CanaPin-19
930PCCanHF-43
94ParMisL-73
94ParMisL-162
94Par66-61
95Par66Coi-61
**Prpic, Tony**
93FreCan-24
**Prpich, Dave**
917thInnSOHL-193
**Prtt, Stacy**
83BraWheK-16
**Prud'Homme, Carl**
95SlaMemC-58
**Pruneau, Martial**
51LavDaiQSHL-13
51LavDaiS-56
52St.LawS-79
**Prusa, Peter**
70SweHocS-381
**Prusa, Sven**
94GerDELE-346
**Prusek, Martin**
96CzeAPSE-191
**Pryl, Stanislav**
70SweHocS-363
**Pryor, Chris**
84SprInd-16
87NorStaPos-25
88ProAHL-311
89ProAHL-254
90ProAHLIHL-499
91ProAHLCHL-475
**Prystai, Metro**
44BeeGro2P-135
44BeeGro2P-205
51Par-65
52Par-60
53Par-42
54Par-35
54Top-24
94ParMisL-57
**Psenka, Tomas**
96SloPeeWT-23
**Ptacek, Frantisek**
94CzeAPSE-77
95CzeAPSE-275
96CzeAPSE-129
**Pucher, Rene**
94FinnJaaK-205
95SloAPSNT-18
**Puchniak, Rob**
89BraWheK-16
907thInnSWHL-231
90BraWheK-19
917thInnSWHL-197
**Pudas, Albert**
23V1281PauC-21
**Puga, Duane**
92BriColJHL-79
**Puhakka, Mika**
94FinnSIS-282
95FinnSIS-226
96FinnSISR-25
**Puhalski, Greg**
82KitRan-21
83KitRan-15

84KitRan-19
85LonKni-13
92TolSto-17
93TolSto-19
94TolSto-19
95TolSto-22
96TolSto-NNO
**Pulente, Gino**
91LakSupSL-22
**Pulford, Bob**
44BeeGro2P-443
57Par-T4
58Par-1
58Par-45
59Par-28
60Par-19
60ShiCoi-13
60YorPreP-29
61Par-8
61ShiCoi-46
61YorYelB-14
62Par-11
62ShiMetC-6
62YorIroOTra-15
63ChePho-44
63Par-12
63Par-72
63TorSta-31
63YorWhiB-18
64BeeGro3P-180A
64BeeGro3P-180B
64CocCap-103
64Top-60
64TorSta-40
65Coc-102
65Top-18
66Top-19
67PosFliB-11
67Top-19
67YorActOct-5
67YorActOct-6
67YorActOct-10
67YorActOct-14
67YorActOct-24
67YorActOct-32
68OPC-129
68PosCerM-20
68ShiCoi-162
68Top-129
69MapLeaWBG-28
69MapLeaWBG-29
69OPC-53
69OPCFou-16
69Top-53
70ColSta-2
70DadCoo-106
70EssPowPla-159
700PC-36
70SarProSta-72
70Top-36
710PC-94
710PCPos-2
71SarProSta-66
71Top-94
71TorSun-123
72SweSemWC-203
740PCNHL-229
74Top-229
81BlaBorPos-21
81BlaBorBac-8
91ProSetHI-3
93BlaCok-26
94ParMisL-113
94ParTalB-110
95Par66-114
95Par66Coi-114
**Pulford, Harvey**
83HalFP-B10
85HalFC-24
**Pulkkinen, Petri**
93FinnJyvHS-200
93FinnSIS-258
**Pulliainen, Jari**
94FinnSIS-322
94LigHeaP-1
94LigPos-14
940PCPre-410
940PCPreSE-410
94Par-225
94ParGol-225
94Pin-71
94PinArtP-71
94PinGoaG-GT15
94PinRinC-71
94Sco-72
94ScoFra-TF22
94ScoGol-72
94ScoPla-72
94ScoPlaTS-72
94Sel-45
94SelGol-45
94StaClu-162
94StaClu-183
94StaCluFDI-162
94StaCluFDI-183
94TopPre-410
94TopPreSE-410
94Ult-209
94UppDec-204
94UppDecEleIce-204
95BeAPla-85

90Kra-43
900PC-204
900PC-238
90PanSti-31
90ProSet-27
90ProSet-365
90SabBluS-16
90SabCam-19
90Sco-60
90Sco-318
90ScoCan-60
90ScoCan-318
90ScoHotRS-26
90Top-204
90Top-238
90TopTif-204
90TopTif-238
90UppDec-166
90UppDecF-166
91Bow-37
910PC-333
91PanSti-298
91Par-14
91ParFre-14
91Pin-137
91PinFre-137
91ProSet-21
91ProSetFre-21
91ProSetPla-9
91SabBluS-16
91SabPepC-16
91ScoAme-106
91ScoCan-106
91StaClu-231
91Top-333
91UppDec-248
91UppDecF-248
920PC-53
92Par-412
92ParEmel-412
92Pin-327
92PinFre-327
92TopGol-457G
92Zen-120
92Sco-47
92ScoCan-47
92StaClu-370
92Top-457
92TopGol-457G
92Ult-261
93Don-316
93Lea-403
93LigSealR-23
930PCPre-364
930PCPreG-364
93Par-468
93ParEmel-468
93Pin-361
93PinCan-361
93Pow-234
93Sco-273
93Sco-530
93ScoCan-273
93ScoCan-530
93ScoGol-530
93StaClu-275
93StaCluFDI-275
93StaCluO-275
93TopPre-364
93TopPreG-364
93Ult-247
93UppDec-473
94CanGamNHLP-295
94Don-100
94Fin-53
94FinRef-53
94FinSupTW-53
94Fla-175
94Fle-209
94Kra-50
94Lea-224
94LeaLim-109
94LigPhoA-22
94LigPos-14
940PCPre-410
940PCPreSE-410
94Par-225

95BeAPSig-S85
95BeAPSigDC-S85
95CanGamNHLP-256
95ColCho-117
95ColChoPC-117
95ColChoPCP-117
95Don-84
95Emo-166
95Fin-11
95FinRef-11
95Kra-29
95Lea-243
95LigTeal-5
95Met-139
95ParInt-195
95ParIntEl-195
95Pin-105
95PinArtP-105
95PinRinC-105
95PlaOneoOne-198
95Sco-210
95ScoBlaIce-210
95ScoBlaIceAP-210
95SelCer-58
95SelCerMG-58
95Skylmp-157
95SP-137
95StaClu-6
95StaCluMOMS-6
95Sum-85
95SumArtP-85
95SumIce-85
95Top-226
95TopOPCI-226
95Ult-155
95Ult-376
95UppDec-205
95UppDecEleIce-205
95UppDecEleIceG-205
95UppDecSpeE-SE78
95UppDecSpeEdiG-SE78
95Zen-112
96ColCho-247
96ColCho-331
96Don-34
96DonCanI-102
96DonCanIGPP-102
96DonCanIRPP-102
96DonEli-114
96DonEliDCS-114
96DonPrePro-34
96Fle-105
96Fle-146
96Fle-147
96FleVez-8
96KraUppD-26
96Lea-73
96LeaLim-58
96LeaLimG-58
96LeaPre-69
96LeaPreP-73
96LeaPrePP-69
96LeaPreSG-17
96LeaPreSte-17
96LeaShuDow-15
96MetUni-146
96MetUniAP-8
96MetUniAPSP-8
96NHLACEPC-38
96Pin-97
96PinArtP-97
96PinFoi-97
96PinPreS-97
96PinRinC-97
96Sco-118
96ScoArtPro-118
96ScoDeaCAP-118
96ScoGolB-118
96ScoNetW-13
96ScoSpeAP-118
96ScoSudDea-11
96SelCer-69
96SelCerAP-69
96SelCerBlu-69
96SelCerMB-69
96SelCerMG-69
96SelCerMR-69
96SelCerRed-69
96Skylmp-123
96SkylmpZH-8
96Sum-77
96SumArtP-77
96SumIce-77
96SumInTheCre-4
96SumInTheCrePS-4
96SumMet-77
96SumPreS-77
96Ult-159
96UltGolM-159
96UppDec-338
96Zen-43
96ZenArtP-43
97Be A PPAD-76
97Be A PPAPD-76
97BeAPla-76
97BeAPlaAut-76
97BeAPlaTAN-16
97ColCho-235

97DonEli-79
97DonEliAsp-79
97DonEliS-79
97DonLim-170
97DonLim-192
97DonLimExp-170
97DonLimExp-192
97DonPre-110
97DonPreCttC-110
97DonPreProG-123
97DonPreProS-123
97DonPri-136
97DonPriSoA-136
97Kat-137
97KatGol-137
97KatSil-137
97Lea-50
97LeaFraMat-50
97LeaFraMDC-50
97LeaInt-50
97LeaIntUI-50
97PacCroR-126
97PacCroREG-126
97PacCroRIB-126
97PacCroRS-126
97PacInvNRB-187
97PacOme-212
97PacOmeC-212
97PacOmeDG-212
97PacOmeEG-212
97PacOmeG-212
97PacOmeIB-212
97PacRev-129
97PacRevC-129
97PacRevE-129
97PacRevIB-129
97PacRevR-129
97PacRevS-129
97Pin-84
97PinArtP-84
97PinCer-22
97PinCerMB-22
97PinCerMG-22
97PinCerMR-22
97PinCerR-22
97PinIns-45
97PinInsCC-45
97PinInsEC-45
97PinPrePBB-84
97PinPrePBC-84
97PinPrePBM-84
97PinPrePBY-84
97PinPrePFC-84
97PinPrePFM-84
97PinPrePFY-84
97PinPrePla-84
97PinRinC-84
97PinTotCMPG-22
97PinTotCPB-22
97PinTotCPG-22
97PinTotCPR-22
97Sco-18
97ScoArtPro-18
97ScoGolBla-18
97SPAut-147
97Stu-44
97StuPrePG-44
97StuPrePS-44
97UppDec-362
97UppDecBD-74
97UppDecBDDD-74
97UppDecBDQD-74
97UppDecBDTD-74
98Be A PPA-281
98Be A PPAA-281
98Be A PPAAF-281
98Be A PPSE-281
98Be APG-281
98Pac-403
98PacIceB-403
98PacRed-403
98PacRev-132
98PacRevIS-132
98PacRevR-132
98UC-191
98UD ChoPCR-191
98UD ChoR-191
98UDCP-191
98UppDec-367
98UppDecE-367
98UppDecE101-367
98UppDecGR-367
98UppDecM-186
98UppDecMGS-186
98UppDecMSS-186
98UppDecMSS-186
**Purcell, Bill**
90NewSai-17
**Purcell, Tom**
897thInnSOHL-164
**Purdie, Brad**
91AirCanSJHL-D36
92MaiBlaB-28
93MaiBlaB-47
96PeoRiv-18
96PeoRivPA-19
97Be A PPAD-76
97Be A PPAPD-76
97BeAPla-76
97BeAPlaAut-76
97BeAPlaTAN-16
97ColCho-235
**Purdie, Dennis**
897thInnSOHL-36
907thInnSOHL-140
917thInnSMC-120
917thInnSOHL-362
92WinSpi-24
93JohChi-12
94JohChi-15
95TolSto-11

96TolSto-19

**Purdon, Neal**
94ThuBayS-15
95ThuBayS-18

**Purdy, Brian**
89BraWheK-21
907thInnSWHL-216A
907thInnSWHL-216B
90BraWheK-14
917thInnSWHL-202

**Purinton, Dale**
96LetHur-12

**Purola, Lavi**
52JunBluT-62

**Purpur, Cliff**
34BeeGro1P-75

**Purschel, Diter**
70SweHocS-366

**Purves, John**
84BelBul-7
89ProAHL-78
90ProAHLIHL-212
91BalSki-11
91ProAHLCHL-551
95ColEdgI-190
96ColEdgFL-37

**Puschacher, Michael**
95AusNatTea-21
95FinnSemWC-183
95SweGloWC-182
96SweSemW-211

**Puschnik, Andreas**
93SweSemWCS-284
93SweSemWCS-285
94FinnJaaK-240
94FinnJaaK-242
95AusNatTea-23
95FinnSemWC-188
95SweGloWC-185

**Puschnik, Gerhard**
95AusNatTea-22

**Pusey, Chris**
83BraAle-19

**Pushkov, Sergei**
94FinnJaaK-153
94SweLeaE-291

**Pushor, Jamie**
907thInnSWHL-128
917thInnSMC-122
917thInnSWHL-342
91AreDraPic-23
91Cla-28
91StaPicH-3
91UltDra-24
91UppDec-63
91UppDec-73
91UppDecF-63
91UppDecF-73
94Lea-459
94OPCPre-478
94OPCPreSE-478
94TopPre-478
94TopPreSE-478
95AdiRedW-19
95Bow-103
95BowAllFoi-103
95Don-337
95StaClu-224
95StaCluMOMS-224
96BeAPAut-102
96BeAPAutSil-102
96BeAPla-102
96DonCanI-118
96DonCanIGPP-118
96DonCanIRPP-118
96SkyImp-157
96Sum-196
96SumArtP-196
96SumIce-196
96SumMet-196
96SumPreS-196
96UppDec-54
96Zen-147
96ZenArtP-147
97Don-52
97DonLim-136
97DonLimExp-136
97DonPreProG-52
97DonPreProS-52
97Pac-215
97PacCop-215
97PacEmeGre-215
97PacIceB-215
97PacRed-215
97PacSil-215
97ScoRedW-19
97ScoRedWPla-19
97ScoRedWPre-19
98O-PChr-51
98O-PChrR-51
98Top-51
98TopO-P-51

**Pusie, Jean**
35DiaMatTI-53
35OPCV304C-91

**Puskas, Chris**
90RayJrC-18

**Putjkov, Victor**
69SweHocS-13
69SweWorC-21
69SweWorC-22

**Putnik, Walter**
93SweSemWCS-286

**Pyatt, Nelson**
74NHLActSta-96

76OPCNHL-98
76OPCNHL-396
76RocCokCan-18
76RocPucBuc-17
76Top-98
77OPCNHL-252
77RocCokCan-16
77Top-252
78OPC-354

**Pyatt, Taylor**
97SudWolP-11
98SP Aut-131
98SP AutSotTG-TP
98SSASotT-TP
98UppDec-408
98UppDecE-408
98UppDecE1o1-408
98UppDecGR-408
99SP AutPS-131

**Pycha, Pavel**
91SweSemWCS-118
94CzeAPSE-114
95CzeAPSE-86
96CzeAPSE-251

**Pye, Bill**
92RochAmeDD-13
92RochAmeKod-17

**Pyka, Nico**
98GerDELE-166

**Pyka, Reemt**
94FinnJaaK-285
94GerDELE-233
95GerDELE-230
95GerDELE-432
96GerDELE-82
98GerDELE-31
98GerDELE-317

**Pyliotis, John**
93AmoLesFAM-18

**Pylypow, Kevin**
81RegPat-17
82BraWheK-2

**Pylypuik, Pat**
88LetHur-18
89LetHur-17
907thInnSWHL-139
92TolSto-10
93TolSto-9

**Pysz, Patrik**
94GerDELE-280
95GerDELE-317

**Pytel, Henryk**
79PanSti-130

**Quackenbush, Bill**
44BeeGro2P-60
44BeeGro2P-206
51Par-26
52Par-68
53Par-100
54Par-51
54Top-49
55BruPho-13
83HalFC-11
85HalFC-235
91BruSpoAL-23
91BruSpoAL-35

**Quapp, Vladimir**
94GerDELE-105

**Quenneville, Chad**
95Cla-79
95ClaAut-19

**Quenneville, Joel**
79MapLeaP-23
79OPC-336
79Roc-18
80OPC-19
80Top-19
81OPC-78
81OPCSti-234
81RocPos-24
81Top-W83
83OPC-145
83OPCSti-225
83WhaJunHC-14
84OPC-77
84Top-60
84WhaJunW-15
85OPC-103
85OPCSti-170
85Top-103
85WhaJunW-16
86OPC-118
86OPCSti-55
86Top-118
86WhaJunT-18
87WhaJunBK-16
88OPC-3
88Top-3
88WhaJunGR-13
89OPC-211
89WhaJunM-16
90OPC-418
91ProAHLCHL-356
92St.JohML-17

**Quenneville, Yvon**
90RayJrC-19

**Quessy, Anthony**
98Vald'OF-S1

**Quigley, Dave**
87MonHaw-19

**Quilty, Johnny**
34BeeGro1P-176
40OPCV3012-106
45QuaOatP-106

**Quinn, Dan**

83BelBul-3
84OPC-234
85FlamRedRP-23
85OPC-176
86OPC-204
86OPCSti-87
86PenKod-18
87OPC-171
87OPCSti-147
87PenKod-21
87PenMask-8
87Top-171
88OPC-41
88OPCSti-236
88PanSti-342
88Top-41
89OPC-152
89OPCSti-234
89PanSti-314
89PenFoo-6A
89Top-152
90Bow-65
90BowTif-65
90CanuMoh-25
90OPC-272
90OPCPre-93
90PanSti-305
90ProSet-303
90Sco-55
90ScoCan-55
90ScoHotRS-24
90Top-272
90TopTif-272
90UppDec-260
90UppDecF-260
91Bow-376
91CanuPanTS-20
91FlyJCP-21
91OPC-393
91OPCPre-27
91PanSti-27
91Par-351
91ParFre-351
91Pin-84
91Pin-408
91PinFre-84
91PinFre-408
91ProSet-209
91ProSetFre-209
91ProSetPla-209
91ScoAme-62
91ScoCan-62
91ScoCan-615
91ScoRoo-65T
91StaClu-243
91Top-393
91UppDec-358
91UppDec-563
91UppDecF-358
91UppDecF-563
92Bow-289
92OPC-264
92StaClu-22
92Top-143
92TopGol-143G
93SwiHNL-77
94BeAPSig-89
94Lea-61
94Lea-413
94Pin-504
94PinArtP-504
94PinRinC-504
94Ult-307
95CanGamNHLP-192
95ColCho-70
95ColChoPC-70
95ColChoPCP-70
95Don-240
95Emo-126
95ImpSti-85
95Lea-258
95Met-106
95Sco-175
95ScoBlaIce-175
95ScoBlaIceAP-175
95SkyImp-120
95StaClu-142
95StaCluMOMS-142
95Sum-116
95SumArtP-116
95SumIce-116
95SwiHNL-541
95Top-261
95TopOPCI-261
95Ult-281
95UppDecEleIce-483
95UppDecEleIceG-483
95UppDecSpeE-SE145
95UppDecSpeEdiG-SE145
96ColCho-198
96Don-92
96DonPrePro-92
96Sco-228
96ScoArtPro-228
96ScoDeaCAP-228
96ScoGolB-228
96ScoSpeAP-228
97ScoPen-14
97ScoPenPla-14
97ScoPenPre-14

**Quinn, David**
92CleLum-9

**Quinn, Jim**
82KitRan-16

83KitRan-2

**Quinn, Kevin**
94JohChi-16

**Quinn, Pat**
69MapLeaWBG-30
69OPC-85
69OPCFou-8
70CanuRoyB-13
70ColSta-72
70DadCoo-107
70EssPowPla-39
70OPC-120
70OPCDec-1
70SarProSta-209
70Top-120
71CanuRoyB-5
71SarProSta-219
71Top-122
71TorSun-287
72CanuNal-5
72Flam-16
72OPC-183
72OPCPlaC-1
72SarProSta-6
73OPC-61
73Top-61
74NHLActSta-7
74OPCNHL-286
75OPCNHL-172
75Top-172
76OPCNHL-289
76OPCNHL-379
84KinSmo-23

**Quinnell, Bob**
91BriColJHL-132
92BriColJHL-101

**Quinney, Ken**
85FreExp-14
85NordTeal-19
86NordGenF-20
87NordGenF-25
88ProAHL-112
89HalCit-18
89ProAHL-162
90HalCit-19
90ProAHLIHL-458
91ProAHLCHL-127
91UppDec-419
91UppDecF-419
93LasVegThu-20
94LasVegThu-19
95LasVegThu-15
96LasVegThu-16
98GerDELE-152

**Quint, Deron**
93Cla-109
93ClaGla94-CL5
93DonTeaUSA-18
93Pin-485
93PinCan-485
93SeaThu-20
93UppDec-561
94ClaProP-206
94ClaTri-T46
94Fin-116
94FinRef-116
94FinSupTW-116
94LeaLimWJUSA-10
94ParSE-SE247
94ParSEG-SE247
94Sco-208
94ScoGol-208
94ScoPla-208
94SP-193
94SPDieCut-193
94UppDec-524
94UppDecEleIce-524
95Bow-107
95BowAllFoi-107
95DonEli-89
95DonEliDCS-89
95DonEliDCU-89
95Fin-101
95FinRef-101
95Ima-74
95ImaAut-74A
95ImaGol-74
95Met-188
95ParIntEl-269
95SelCer-129
95SelCerMG-129
95SigRoo-26
95SigRooSig-26
95SkyImp-227
95SP-165
95StaClu-197
95StaCluMOMS-197
95Sum-181
95SumArtP-181
95SumIce-181
95Top-258
95TopOPCI-258
95Ult-352
95UppDec-498
95UppDecEleIce-498
95UppDecEleIceG-498
96ColCho-206
96Don-225
96DonPrePro-225
96Lea-143
96LeaPreP-143

96SprFal-4
96UppDec-128
97ColCho-202
97Pac-304
97PacCop-304
97PacEmeGre-304
97PacIceB-304
97PacRed-304
97PacSil-304

**Quintal, Stephane**
84RicRiv-12
88BruPos-17
88ProAHL-153
89BruSpoA-19
90BruSpoA-21
90ProSet-410
91ProSet-350
91ProSetFre-350
91ScoCan-437
92Bow-337
92Par-384
92ParEmel-384
92Sco-242
92ScoCan-242
92StaClu-350
92Top-484
92TopGol-484G
93JetRuf-21
93Par-500
93ParEmel-500
93Pin-326
93PinCan-326
93Pow-475
93Sco-412
93Sco-509
93ScoCan-412
93ScoCan-509
93ScoGol-509
93StaClu-242
93StaCluFDI-242
93StaCluFDIO-242
93StaCluO-242
93Ult-456
93UppDec-529
94CanGamNHLP-258
94Fle-244
94Lea-293
94OPCPre-6
94OPCPreSE-6
94Pin-501
94PinArtP-501
94PinRinC-501
94TopPre-6
94TopPreSE-6
94Ult-245
95CanaPos-13
95CanaShe-8
95ColCho-280
95ColChoPC-280
95ColChoPCP-280
95Don-314
95Emo-89
95ParInt-117
95ParIntEl-117
95Ult-257
96CanaPos-20
96CanaShe-14
96TeaOut-87
97Be A PPAD-9
97Be A PPAPD-94
97BeAPla-94
97BeAPlaAut-94
97CanaPos-15
97Pac-324
97PacCop-324
97PacEmeGre-324
97PacIceB-324
97PacRed-324
97PacSil-324
99Pac-208
99PacCop-208
99PacGol-208
99PacIceB-208
99PacPreD-208
99RetHoc-41
99UppDecRG-41
99UppDecRP-41

**Quintin, J.F.**
89ProIHL-97
90ProAHLIHL-117
92Cla-107
92OPCPre-37
92Sco-488
92ScoCan-488
92UppDec-483
93Ult-192
93UltPro-8
93UppDec-21
94CanaPos-20
94Lea-388
94OPCPre-176
94OPCPre-426
94OPCPreSE-176
94OPCPreSE-426
94Par-168
94ParGol-168
94Pin-391
94PinArtP-391
94PinRinC-391
94Sco-162
94ScoGol-162
94ScoPla-162
94ScoPlaTS-162
94StaClu-239
94StaCluFDI-239
94StaCluMOMS-239
94StaCluSTWC-239

91ScoAme-395
91ScoCan-285
91StaClu-377
91Top-450
91UppDec-377
91UppDecF-377
92CanaPos-21
92DurPan-49
92OPCPre-11
92Par-321
92ParEmel-321
92Ult-332
92UppDec-430
93CanaPos-19
93DurSco-15
93Lea-294
93OPCPre-313
93OPCPreG-313
93Pin-332
93PinCan-332
93Sco-437
93ScoCan-437
93StaClu-26
93StaCluFDI-26
93StaCluFDIO-26
93StaCluO-26
93TopPre-313
93TopPreG-313
93Ult-355
94PorPir-21
95IndIce-18

**Racicot, Paolo**
917thInnSQMJHL-105

**Racine, Bruce**
88ProIHL-61
89ProIHL-152
90ProAHLIHL-517
91ProAHLCHL-295
92CleLum-14
93St.JohML-19
93St.JohML-21

**Racine, Yves**
89ProAHL-317
90Bow-230
90BowTif-230
90OPC-361
90ProAHLIHL-474
90Top-361
90TopTif-361
91Bow-44
91OPC-228
91PanSti-141
91Par-265
91ParFre-265
91Pin-233
91PinFre-233
91ProSet-54
91ProSetFre-54
91ScoAme-158
91ScoYouS-37
91StaClu-198
91Top-228
91UppDec-498
91UppDecF-498
92Bow-331
92OPC-297
92PanSti-119
92PanStiFre-119
92Pin-332
92PinFre-332
92Sco-74
92ScoCan-74
92StaClu-6
92Top-277
92TopGol-277G
92Ult-287
92UppDec-142
93Don-246
93DurSco-34
93Lea-115
93Par-422
93ParEmel-422
93Pin-372
93PinCan-372
93Pow-406
93Sco-264
93Sco-540
93ScoCan-264
93ScoCan-540
93ScoGol-540
93StaClu-304
93StaCluFDI-304
93StaCluO-304
93UppDec-194
94CanaPos-20
94Lea-388
94OPCPre-176
94OPCPre-426
94OPCPreSE-176
94OPCPreSE-426
94Par-168

94TopPre-176
94TopPre-426
94TopPreSE-176
94TopPreSE-426
94Ult-316
94UppDec-171
94UppDecEleIce-171
95CanaPos-14
95CanGamNHLP-154
95FinnSemWC-80
95Pin-178
95PinArtP-178
95PinRinC-178
95Sco-221
95ScoBlaIce-221
95ScoBlaIceAP-221
95Top-138
95TopOPCI-138
95UppDecEleIce-485
95UppDecEleIceG-485
97Be A PPAD-27
97Be A PPAPD-27
97BeAPla-27
97BeAPlaAut-27
97PacInvNRB-30

**Radbjer, Ulf**
84SweSemE-137

**Radevic, Radim**
94CzeAPSE-17
96CzeAPSE-109

**Radke, Al**
91BriColJHL-152

**Radlein, Peter**
87BroBra-25

**Raeder, Cap**
88KinSmo-20

**Rafalski, Brian**
91UppDecCWJC-78
95SweLeaE-172

**Raglan, Herb**
84KinCan-24
87BluKod-21
87BluTealss-18
88BluKod-25
88BluTealss-18
89BluKod-25
90ProSet-525
91NordPet-24
91ProSet-470
91ProSetFre-470
91ScoCan-536
92NorPet-25

**Raglan, Rags (Clare)**
44BeeGro2P-137
51Par-36
53Par-79

**Ragnarsson, Marcus**
89SweSemE-59
90SweSemE-281
91SweSemE-62
92SweSemE-80
93SweSemE-53
94SweLeaE-224
95BeAPla-164
95BeAPSig-S164
95BeAPSigDC-S164
95Bow-111
95BowAllFoi-111
95BowBes-BB29
95BowBesRef-BB29
95Don-264
95DonEli-38
95DonEliDCS-38
95DonEliDCU-38
95DonEliR-7
95DonRatRoo-13
95Fin-76
95FinRef-76
95LeaLim-78
95LeaLimRP-1
95Met-189
95ParInt-519
95ParInt-531
95ParIntEl-519
95ParIntEl-531
95ParIntPTP-PP41
95SelCer-138
95SelCerMG-138
95SkyImp-220
95SP-132
95StaClu-148
95StaCluMOMS-148
95Sum-195
95SumArtP-195
95SumIce-195
95SweGloWC-18
95Top-287
95TopOPCI-287
95Ult-353
95UltHigSpe-15
95UppDec-439
95UppDecEleIce-439
95UppDecEleIceG-439
95Zen-141
95ZenRooRC-8
96ColCho-236
96Don-234
96DonCanI-83
96DonCanIGPP-83
96DonCanIRPP-83
96DonPrePro-234
96Fle-101
96FlePic-126
96FleRooSen-8
96Lea-183

□ 96LeaLim-42
□ 96LeaLimG-42
□ 96LeaPre-52
□ 96LeaPreP-183
□ 96LeaPreP-52
□ 96LeaPreSG-13
□ 96LeaPrePP-52
□ 96LeaPreSte-13
□ 96MetUni-140
□ 96Pin-207
□ 96PinArtP-207
□ 96PinFoi-207
□ 96PinPreS-207
□ 96PinRinC-207
□ 96Sco-242
□ 96ScoArtPro-242
□ 96ScoDeaCAP-242
□ 96ScoGolB-242
□ 96ScoSpeAP-242
□ 96SkyImp-118
□ 96SkyImpINHLF-18
□ 96Sum-165
□ 96SumArtP-165
□ 96SumIce-165
□ 96SumMet-165
□ 96SumPreS-165
□ 96SweSemW-49
□ 96TeaOut-88
□ 96TopPicRS-RS7
□ 96UppDec-148
□ 96Zen-79
□ 96ZenArtP-79
□ 97ColCho-222
□ 97PacDynBKS-86
□ 97ShaFleAS-6
□ 97UppDec-149
□ 98Be A PPA-117
□ 98Be A PPAA-117
□ 98Be A PPAAF-117
□ 98Be A PPTBASG-117
□ 98Be APG-117
□ 98UC-178
□ 98UD ChoPCR-178
□ 98UD ChoR-178
□ 98UppDec-166
□ 98UppDecE-166
□ 98UppDecE101-166
□ 98UppDecGR-166

**Ragot, Mike**
□ 85KamBla-20

**Ragulin, Alexander**
□ 69SweHocS-14
□ 69SweWorC-21
□ 69SweWorC-23
□ 69SweWorC-31
□ 69SweWorC-66
□ 69SweWorC-126
□ 69SweWorC-129
□ 70SweHocS-318
□ 71SweHocS-32
□ 72SweSemWC-5
□ 73SweHocS-79
□ 73SweWorCS-79
□ 74SweSemHVS-27
□ 91FutTreC72-65
□ 91SweSemWCS-242

**Rahkonen, Antti**
□ 95FinnSIS-314
□ 96FinnSISR-124

**Rahm, Niklas**
□ 92SweSemE-133
□ 93SweSemE-106
□ 95SweLeaE-232
□ 95SweUppDE-77

**Raitanen, Rauli**
□ 93FinnJyvHS-358
□ 93FinnSIS-229
□ 93SweSemWCS-73
□ 94FinnJaaK-38
□ 94FinnSIS-48
□ 94FinnSIS-381
□ 95FinnSemWC-51
□ 95FinnSIS-363
□ 95FinnSISL-21

**Raiter, Mark**
□ 89SasBla-5
□ 907thInnSWHL-84
□ 90SasBla-5
□ 917thInnSWHL-103
□ 91SasBla-5
□ 95BirBul-6

**Raitinen, Pasi**
□ 97KinHaw-17

**Rajamaki, Tommi**
□ 94Fin-123
□ 94FinnSIS-315
□ 94FinnSISND-5
□ 94FinRef-123
□ 94FinnSupTW-123
□ 94ParSE-SE226
□ 94ParSEG-SE226
□ 94UppDec-512
□ 94UppDecEleIce-512
□ 95FinnSIS-355
□ 96FinnSISR-151

**Rajnoha, Pavel**
□ 94CzeAPSE-184
□ 95CzeAPSE-184

**Raleigh, Don**
□ 44BeeGro2P-355
□ 51Par-93
□ 52Par-99
□ 53Par-68
□ 54Par-68
□ 54Top-53

**Ralph, Jim**

□ 81Ott67-11
□ 83SprInd-2
□ 85NovScoO-15
□ 88ProAHL-224

**Ram, Jamie**
□ 90MicTecHus-26
□ 91MicTecHus-21
□ 91MicTecHus-34
□ 93MicTecH-12
□ 94BinRan-16
□ 94Cla-59
□ 94ClaAllAme-AA8
□ 94ClaDraGol-59
□ 95BinRan-18
□ 95ColEdgI-21
□ 96KenTho-15
□ 96Lea-235
□ 96LeaPreP-235

**Ramage, Rob**
□ 79Roc-19
□ 80OPC-213
□ 80Top-213
□ 81OPC-79
□ 81OPCSti-154
□ 81OPCSti-229
□ 81PosSta-21
□ 81RocPos-25
□ 81Top-W84
□ 82OPC-310
□ 82OPCSti-223
□ 82PosCer-11
□ 83OPC-319
□ 83OPCSti-130
□ 83PufSti-16
□ 847EDis-43
□ 84OPC-190
□ 84OPCSti-62
□ 84OPCSti-136
□ 84Top-134
□ 857ECreCar-17
□ 85OPC-196
□ 86OPC-17
□ 86OPCSti-180
□ 86Top-17
□ 87BluKod-22
□ 87OPC-160
□ 87OPCSti-20
□ 87PanSti-306
□ 87Top-160
□ 88OPC-244
□ 88OPCSti-84
□ 89Kra-39
□ 90Bow-162
□ 90BowTif-162
□ 90Kra-44
□ 90OPC-317
□ 90PanSti-280
□ 90ProSet-288
□ 90Sco-36
□ 90ScoCan-36
□ 90Top-317
□ 90TopTif-317
□ 90UppDec-62
□ 90UppDecF-62
□ 91Bow-154
□ 91MapLeaPTS-20
□ 91OPC-55
□ 91OPCPre-76
□ 91PanSti-96
□ 91Pin-228
□ 91PinFre-228
□ 91ProSet-232
□ 91ProSet-407
□ 91ProSetFre-232
□ 91ProSetFre-407
□ 91ScoAme-233
□ 91ScoCan-573
□ 91ScoRoo-237
□ 91StaClu-239
□ 91Top-55
□ 92BluUDBB-21
□ 92Par-175
□ 92ParEmel-175
□ 92Pin-389
□ 92PinFre-389
□ 92ProSet-177
□ 92Sco-351
□ 92ScoCan-351
□ 92Ult-413
□ 92UppDec-105
□ 93CanaPos-20
□ 93OPCPreF-12
□ 93Pow-407
□ 93Sco-36
□ 93Sco-653
□ 93ScoCan-36
□ 93ScoCan-653
□ 93ScoGol-653
□ 93TopPreF-12

**Rambo, Dean**
□ 89SasBla-24
□ 907thInnSWHL-76
□ 90SasBla-8

**Ramen, Marcus**
□ 94SweLeaE-167

**Ramoser, Roland**
□ 91BriColJHL-22
□ 96GerDELE-326
□ 98GerDELE-60

**Rampf, Sven**
□ 98GerDELE-243

**Rampton, Joey**
□ 83SauSteMG-19

**Ramsay, Bruce**
□ 93ThuBayS-10

□ 94ThuBayS-18
□ 95ThuBayS-19
□ 96GraRapG-18

**Ramsay, Craig**
□ 720PC-262
□ 72SarProSta-38
□ 730PC-213
□ 74NHLActSta-40
□ 740PCNHL-305
□ 750PCNHL-271
□ 75Top-271
□ 760PCNHL-78
□ 76Top-78
□ 77Coc-19
□ 770PCNHL-191
□ 77Top-191
□ 780PC-9
□ 78Top-9
□ 790PC-207
□ 79SabBel-6
□ 79Top-207
□ 80OPC-13
□ 80Top-13
□ 81OPC-31
□ 81SabMilP-1
□ 82PosCer-2
□ 82SabMilP-3
□ 83OPC-69
□ 84OPC-27
□ 84OPCSti-215
□ 84SabBluS-15
□ 84Top-21
□ 85OPC-32
□ 85OPCSti-175
□ 85OPCSti-192
□ 85SabBluS-22
□ 85SabBluSS-22
□ 85Top-32
□ 93SabNoc-15
□ 96SenPizH-21

**Ramsey, Mike**
□ 80OPC-127
□ 80Top-127
□ 80USAOlyTMP-11
□ 81SabMilP-12
□ 81SweSemHVS-94
□ 82OPC-32
□ 82PosCer-2
□ 82SabMilP-15
□ 83OPC-70
□ 83OPCSti-243
□ 84OPC-28
□ 84OPCSti-211
□ 84SabBluS-16
□ 84Top-22
□ 85OPC-77
□ 85OPCSti-180
□ 85SabBluS-23
□ 85SabBluSS-23
□ 85Top-77
□ 86OPC-115
□ 86OPCSti-44
□ 86SabBluS-24
□ 86SabBluSSma-24
□ 86Top-115
□ 87OPC-63
□ 87OPCSti-149
□ 87PanSti-25
□ 87SabBluS-21
□ 87SabWonBH-21
□ 87Top-63
□ 88OPC-133
□ 88OPCSti-260
□ 88PanSti-222
□ 88SabBluS-20
□ 88SabWonBH-22
□ 88Top-133
□ 89OPC-140
□ 89SabBluS-18
□ 89SabCam-20
□ 89SweSemWCS-158
□ 89Top-140
□ 90OPC-102
□ 90PanSti-24
□ 90ProSet-28
□ 90SabBluS-17
□ 90SabCam-20
□ 90Sco-23
□ 90ScoCan-23
□ 90ScoHotRS-13
□ 90Top-102
□ 90TopTif-102
□ 90UppDec-168
□ 90UppDecF-168
□ 91Bow-32
□ 91OPC-236
□ 91PanSti-299
□ 91Par-19
□ 91ParFre-19
□ 91Pin-64
□ 91PinFre-64
□ 91ProSet-25
□ 91ProSet-568
□ 91ProSetFre-25
□ 91ProSetFre-568
□ 91ProSetPla-13
□ 91SabBluS-17
□ 91SabPepC-17
□ 91ScoAme-64
□ 91ScoCan-61
□ 91StaClu-135
□ 91Top-236
□ 91UppDec-253
□ 92PanSti-253
□ 92PanStiFre-253
□ 92Par-256

□ 92ParEmel-256
□ 92Pin-21
□ 92PinFre-21
□ 92SabBluS-19
□ 92SabJubF-12
□ 92Sco-28
□ 92ScoCan-28
□ 92StaClu-386
□ 92Top-473
□ 92TopGol-473G
□ 92Ult-19
□ 93PenFoo-16
□ 93Pin-394
□ 93ScoCan-236
□ 93ScoCan-424
□ 93ScoCan-495
□ 93SeaPat-57
□ 93StaClu-66
□ 93Top-126
□ 93Ult-396
□ 94Lea-536
□ 94Pin-412
□ 94PinArtP-412
□ 94PinRinC-412
□ 95SigRooMI-27
□ 95SigRooMI-28
□ 95SigRooSMIS-27
□ 95SigRooSMIS-28

**Ramstedt, Johan**
□ 96ColCho-341
□ 95ColChoPC-341
□ 95ColChoPCP-341
□ 95SigRooA-33
□ 95SweRooAPC-33
□ 95SweUppDE1DS-DS5

**Rancourt, Alain**
□ 88RivDu R-25

**Randall, Bruce**
□ 88ProAHL-128

**Randall, Bryan**
□ 95MedHatT-12
□ 94RegPat-18

**Randall, Ken**
□ 23V1451-34
□ 24C144ChaCig-48
□ 24V130MapC-24
□ 24V1452-12

**Ranford, Bill**
□ 86MonGolF-5
□ 870PC-13
□ 87PanSti-5
□ 87Top-13
□ 88OilTeal-23
□ 88OilTenAnn-60
□ 89OilTeal-20
□ 89OPC-233
□ 89OPCSti-230
□ 89PanSti-81
□ 90Kra-45
□ 90OilIGA-21
□ 90OPC-226
□ 90OPC-467
□ 90OPCPre-94
□ 90PanSti-219
□ 90ProSet-94
□ 90ProSet-390
□ 90Sco-79
□ 90Sco-331
□ 90Sco-345
□ 90Sco-358
□ 90Sco-369
□ 90ScoCan-79
□ 90ScoCan-345
□ 90ScoCan-358
□ 90ScoHotRS-39
□ 90Top-226
□ 90TopTif-226
□ 90UppDec-42
□ 90UppDecF-42
□ 91Bow-101
□ 91Gil-9
□ 91Kra-44
□ 91McDUppD-21
□ 91OilIGA-17
□ 91OilPanTS-17
□ 91OilPanTS-E
□ 91OilPanTS-F
□ 91OilTeal-19
□ 91OPC-356
□ 91OPCPre-18
□ 91PanSti-125
□ 91Par-53
□ 91Par-460
□ 91ParFre-53
□ 91Pin-170
□ 91PinB-B7
□ 91PinBFre-B7
□ 91PinFre-170
□ 91ProSet-70
□ 91ProSetFre-70
□ 91ProSetFre-283
□ 91ProSetPla-36
□ 91ScoAme-30
□ 91ScoCan-30
□ 91StaClu-249
□ 91Top-356
□ 91UppDec-10
□ 91UppDec-117
□ 91UppDecF-117
□ 91UppDecF-117
□ 92Bow-106
□ 92HumDum2-18
□ 92Kra-33
□ 92OilIGA-18
□ 92OilTeal-14

□ 92OPC-137
□ 92OPCPreSP-19
□ 92PanStiFre-99
□ 92PanStiFre-99
□ 92Par-50
□ 92ParEmel-50
□ 92Pin-4
□ 92PinFre-4
□ 92ProSet-51
□ 92Sco-236
□ 92Sco-424
□ 92Sco-495
□ 92ScoCan-236
□ 92ScoCan-424
□ 92ScoCan-495
□ 92SeaPat-57
□ 92StaClu-66
□ 92Top-126
□ 92TopGol-126G
□ 92Ult-65
□ 92UppDec-262
□ 93ClaTeaCan-TC4
□ 93Don-117
□ 93Kra-18
□ 93KraRec-6
□ 93Lea-68
□ 93LeaPaiWar-10
□ 93OPCPre-258
□ 93OPCPreG-258
□ 93PanSti-U
□ 93Par-67
□ 93ParEmel-67
□ 93Pin-81
□ 93PinCan-81
□ 93Pow-85
□ 93PowNet-6
□ 93Sco-155
□ 93ScoCan-155
□ 93ScoFra-7
□ 93StaClu-131
□ 93StaCluFDI-131
□ 93StaCluFDIO-131
□ 93StaCluO-131
□ 93TopPre-258
□ 93TopPreG-258
□ 93Ult-158
□ 93UppDec-180
□ 93UppDecSP-52
□ 94BeAPla-R28
□ 94BeAPSig-16
□ 94CanGarmNHLP-279
□ 94Don-171
□ 94EASpo-48
□ 94FinnJaaK-79
□ 94FinnJaaK-331
□ 94FinRinL-17
□ 94Fla-61
□ 94Fle-75
□ 94HocWit-76
□ 94Kra-51
□ 94Lea-60
□ 94LeaCreP-10
□ 94LeaLim-9
□ 94OPCPre-435
□ 94OPCPreSE-435
□ 94Par-72
□ 94ParGol-72
□ 94ParVin-V75
□ 94Pin-285
□ 94PinArtP-285
□ 94PinGoaG-GT6
□ 94PinNorLig-NL13
□ 94PinRinC-285
□ 94Sel-5
□ 94SelGol-5
□ 94SP-41
□ 94SPDieCut-41
□ 94StaClu-29
□ 94StaCluFDI-29
□ 94StaCluMOMS-29
□ 94StaCluST-8
□ 94StaCluSTWC-29
□ 94TopPre-435
□ 94TopPreSE-435
□ 94Ult-76
□ 94UppDec-21
□ 94UppDecEleIce-21
□ 94UppDecSPI-SP27
□ 94UppDecSPIDC-SP27
□ 95Bow-24
□ 95BowAllFoi-24
□ 95CanGarmNHLP-113
□ 95ColCho-246
□ 95ColChoPC-246
□ 95ColChoPCP-246
□ 95ColEdgILL-L5
□ 95Don-323
□ 95DonEli-12
□ 95DonEliDCS-12
□ 95DonEliDCU-12
□ 95Emo-66
□ 95Fin-51
□ 95FinnSemWC-77
□ 95FinnSemWC-201
□ 95FinnSemWC-208
□ 95FinRef-51
□ 95ImpSti-45
□ 95Kra-33
□ 95Lea-86
□ 95LeaLim-103
□ 95Met-56
□ 95NHLAcePC-3C
□ 95ParInt-78
□ 95ParInt-282
□ 95ParIntEI-78

□ 95ParIntEI-282
□ 95ParIntGP-9
□ 95PlaOneoOne-151
□ 95PlaOneoOne-258
□ 95ProMag-84
□ 95Sco-239
□ 95ScoBlaIce-239
□ 95ScoBlaIceAP-239
□ 95SelCer-55
□ 95SelCerMG-55
□ 95SkyImp-64
□ 95SP-9
□ 95StaClu-21
□ 95StaCluEN-EN6
□ 95StaCluMOMS-21
□ 95Sum-71
□ 95SumArtP-71
□ 95SumIce-71
□ 95SweGloWC-75
□ 95Top-241
□ 95TopHomGC-HGC8
□ 95TopOPCI-241
□ 95TopSupSki-86
□ 95TopSupSkiPla-86
□ 95Ult-57
□ 95UltGolM-57
□ 95UppDecEleIce-285
□ 95UppDecEleIceG-285
□ 95UppDecSpeE-SE32
□ 95UppDecSpeEdiG-SE32
□ 95Zen-47
□ 96BeAPAut-16
□ 96BeAPAutSil-16
□ 96BeAPla-16
□ 96ColCho-17
□ 96Don-87
□ 96DonCanI-75
□ 96DonCanIGPP-75
□ 96DonCanIRPP-75
□ 96DonEli-97
□ 96DonEliDCS-97
□ 96DonPrePro-87
□ 96Fla-6
□ 96FlaBluI-6
□ 96Fle-7
□ 96Lea-2
□ 96LeaLim-22
□ 96LeaLimG-22
□ 96LeaPre-3
□ 96LeaPreP-2
□ 96LeaPreP-3
□ 96LeaPreSG-40
□ 96LeaPreSte-40
□ 96MetUni-10
□ 96NHLProSTA-84
□ 96Pin-89
□ 96PinArtP-89
□ 96PinFoi-89
□ 96PinPreS-89
□ 96PinRinC-89
□ 96PlaOneoOne-374
□ 96Sco-40
□ 96ScoArtPro-40
□ 96ScoDeaCAP-40
□ 96ScoGolB-40
□ 96ScoNetW-15
□ 96ScoSpeAP-40
□ 96SkyImp-8
□ 96SP-9
□ 96SweSemW-76
□ 96TopNHLP-85
□ 96TopPicO-85
□ 96Ult-11
□ 96UltGolM-11
□ 96UppDec-8
□ 96UppDecBD-80
□ 96UppDecBDG-80
□ 96UppDecIce-3
□ 96UppDecIcePar-3
□ 96UppDecSS-SS30A
□ 96Zen-72
□ 96ZenArtP-72
□ 97ColCho-267
□ 97Don-172
□ 97DonCanI-46
□ 97DonCanIDS-46
□ 97DonCanIPS-46
□ 97DonLim-14
□ 97DonLimExp-14
□ 97DonPre-52
□ 97DonPreCttC-52
□ 97DonPreProG-172
□ 97DonPreProS-172
□ 97DonPri-55
□ 97DonPriSoA-55
□ 97Kat-154
□ 97KatGol-154
□ 97KatSil-154
□ 97Lea-33
□ 97LeaFraMat-33
□ 97LeaFraMDC-33
□ 97LeaInt-33
□ 97LeaIntUI-33
□ 97Pac-233
□ 97PacCop-233
□ 97PacDyn-134
□ 97PacDynEG-134
□ 97PacDynDG-134
□ 97PacDynIB-134
□ 97PacDynR-134
□ 97PacDynSil-134
□ 97PacDynTan-51
□ 97PacEmeGre-233
□ 97PacIceB-233

□ 97PacInv-150
□ 97PacInvC-150
□ 97PacInvEG-150
□ 97PacInvIB-150
□ 97PacInvR-150
□ 97PacInvS-150
□ 97PacPar-199
□ 97PacParC-199
□ 97PacParDG-199
□ 97PacParEG-199
□ 97PacParIB-199
□ 97PacParRed-199
□ 97PacParSil-199
□ 97PacRed-233
□ 97PacSil-233
□ 97Pin-46
□ 97PinArtP-46
□ 97PinCer-12
□ 97PinCerMB-12
□ 97PinCerMG-12
□ 97PinCerMR-12
□ 97PinCerR-12
□ 97PinIns-35
□ 97PinInsCC-35
□ 97PinInsEC-35
□ 97PinInsSto-23
□ 97PinPrePBB-46
□ 97PinPrePBC-46
□ 97PinPrePBM-46
□ 97PinPrePBY-46
□ 97PinPrePFC-46
□ 97PinPrePFM-46
□ 97PinPrePFY-46
□ 97PinPrePla-46
□ 97PinPrePRinC-46
□ 97PinTotCMPG-12
□ 97PinTotCPB-12
□ 97PinTotCPG-12
□ 97PinTotCPR-12
□ 97Sco-13
□ 97ScoArtPro-13
□ 97ScoGolBla-13
□ 97SPAut-165
□ 97UppDec-178
□ 98BowBes-87
□ 98BowBesAR-87
□ 98BowBesR-87
□ 98Pac-446
□ 98PacCroR-125
□ 98PacCroRLS-125
□ 98PacIceB-446
□ 98PacRed-446
□ 98SP Aut-78
□ 98UppDec-364
□ 98UppDecE-364
□ 98UppDecE101-364
□ 98UppDecGR-364
□ 98UppDecM-188
□ 98UppDecMGS-188
□ 98UppDecMSS-188
□ 98UppDecMSS-188
□ 99Pac-147
□ 99PacCop-147
□ 99PacGol-147
□ 99PacIceB-147
□ 99PacPreD-147
□ 99SP AutPS-78

**Ranger, Joe**
□ 85LonKni-2
□ 87KitRan-25

**Ranheim, Paul**
□ 89Kra-9
□ 90Bow-100
□ 90BowTif-100
□ 90FlamIGA-22
□ 90OPC-20
□ 90PanSti-181
□ 90PanSti-342
□ 90ProSet-44
□ 90Sco-248
□ 90ScoCan-248
□ 90Top-20
□ 90TopTif-20
□ 90UppDec-104
□ 90UppDecF-104
□ 91Bow-251
□ 91FlamIGA-16
□ 91FlamPanTS-18
□ 91OPC-15
□ 91PanSti-54
□ 91Par-249
□ 91ParFre-249
□ 91Pin-252
□ 91PinFre-252
□ 91ProSet-31
□ 91ProSetFre-31
□ 91ScoAme-21
□ 91ScoCan-21
□ 91StaClu-50
□ 91Top-15
□ 91UppDec-472
□ 91UppDecF-472
□ 92Bow-96
□ 92FlamIGA-14
□ 92OPC-36
□ 92PanSti-44
□ 92PanStiFre-44
□ 92Par-260
□ 92ParEmel-260
□ 92Pin-67
□ 92PinFre-67
□ 92ProSet-29
□ 92Sco-149
□ 92ScoCan-149
□ 92StaClu-144

❑ 92Top-486
❑ 92TopGol-486G
❑ 92Ult-27
❑ 92UppDec-328
❑ 93Don-50
❑ 93Don-442
❑ 93Lea-170
❑ 93OPCPre-481
❑ 93OPCPreG-481
❑ 93PanSti-184
❑ 93Par-32
❑ 93ParEmel-32
❑ 93Pin-265
❑ 93PinCan-265
❑ 93Pow-309
❑ 93Sco-165
❑ 93ScoCan-165
❑ 93StaClu-151
❑ 93StaCluFDI-151
❑ 93StaCluFDIO-151
❑ 93StaCluO-151
❑ 93TopPre-481
❑ 93TopPreG-481
❑ 93Ult-286
❑ 93UppDec-131
❑ 94CanGamNHLP-116
❑ 94Lea-370
❑ 94OPCPre-96
❑ 94OPCPreSE-96
❑ 94Pin-138
❑ 94PinArtP-138
❑ 94PinRinC-138
❑ 94TopPre-96
❑ 94TopPreSE-96
❑ 94UppDec-430
❑ 94UppDecEleIce-430
❑ 95BeAPla-87
❑ 95BeAPSig-S87
❑ 95BeAPSigDC-S87
❑ 95CanGamNHLP-127
❑ 95ColCho-78
❑ 95ColChoPC-78
❑ 95ColChoPCP-78
❑ 95ParInt-361
❑ 95ParIntEl-361
❑ 95PlaOneoOne-265
❑ 95Top-232
❑ 95TopOPCI-232
❑ 95UppDec-13
❑ 95UppDecEleIce-13
❑ 95UppDecEleIceG-13
❑ 96WhaBobS-21
❑ 97CarHur-22
❑ 98Be A PPA-176
❑ 98Be A PPAA-176
❑ 98Be A PPAAF-176
❑ 98Be A PPSE-176
❑ 98Be APG-176
❑ 98O-PChr-102
❑ 98O-PChrR-102
❑ 98Pac-139
❑ 98PacIceB-139
❑ 98PacRed-139
❑ 98Top-102
❑ 98TopO-P-102
**Raninen, Juha**
❑ 71SweHocS-382
**Rankin, Frank**
❑ 83HalFP-I13
❑ 85HalFC-132
**Rantanen, Jarmo**
❑ 93FinnJyvHS-146
❑ 93FinnSIS-145
**Rantanen, Marko**
❑ 93FinnSIS-4
❑ 94FinnSIS-295
❑ 95FinnSIS-247
**Rantasila, Juha**
❑ 69SweHocS-382
❑ 69SweWorC-88
❑ 69SweWorC-166
❑ 70SweHocS-299
❑ 72SweSemWC-92
❑ 74SweHocS-29
**Rantasila, Valtonen**
❑ 69SweWorC-123
**Rapp, Anders**
❑ 67SweHoc-243
❑ 69SweHocS-288
❑ 70SweHocS-185
**Rappana, Kevin**
❑ 92NorDakFS-27
**Rasmussen, Erik**
❑ 94Cla95DP-DP7
❑ 94Sel-152
❑ 94SelGol-152
❑ 95DonEliWJ-39
❑ 95MinGolG-24
❑ 96MinGolGCAS-23
❑ 96UppDecIce-146
❑ 97Be A PPAD-217
❑ 97Be A PPAPD-217
❑ 97BeAPla-217
❑ 97BeAPlaAut-217
❑ 97Lea-153
❑ 97LeaFraMat-153
❑ 97LeaFraMDC-153
❑ 97PacDyn-NNO
❑ 97PacDynC-NNO
❑ 97PacDynDG-NNO
❑ 97PacDynEG-NNO
❑ 97PacDynIB-NNO
❑ 97PacDynR-NNO
❑ 97PacDynSil-NNO
❑ 97PacPar-23
❑ 97PacParC-23
❑ 97PacParDG-23
❑ 97PacParEG-23
❑ 97PacParIB-23
❑ 97PacParRed-23
❑ 97PacParSil-23
❑ 97Pin-3
❑ 97PinArtP-3
❑ 97PinPrePBB-3
❑ 97PinPrePBC-3
❑ 97PinPrePBM-3
❑ 97PinPrePBY-3
❑ 97PinPrePFC-3
❑ 97PinPrePFM-3
❑ 97PinPrePFY-3
❑ 97PinPrePla-3
❑ 97PinRinC-3
❑ 97Sco-58
❑ 97ScoArtPro-58
❑ 97ScoGolBla-58
❑ 97ScoSab-16
❑ 97ScoSabPla-16
❑ 97ScoSabPre-16
❑ 97SPAut-173
❑ 97UppDec-226
❑ 97UppDecIce-57
❑ 97UppDecIceP-57
❑ 97UppDecIPS-57
❑ 97ZenRooR-3
❑ 98FinFutF-F20
❑ 98FinFutFR-F20
❑ 98SPxFin-10
❑ 98SPxFin-142
❑ 98SPxFinR-10
❑ 98SPxFinR-142
❑ 98SPxFinS-10
❑ 98SPxFinS-142
❑ 98UC-25
❑ 98UD ChoPCR-25
❑ 98UD ChoR-25
❑ 98UDCP-25
❑ 98UppDec-43
❑ 98UppDecE-43
❑ 98UppDecE1o1-43
❑ 98UppDecGR-43
❑ 98UppDecM-23
❑ 98UppDecMGS-23
❑ 98UppDecMP-ER
❑ 98UppDecMSS-23
❑ 98UppDecMSS-23
❑ 99Pac-42
❑ 99PacCop-42
❑ 99PacGol-42
❑ 99PacIceB-42
❑ 99PacPreD-42
**Ratchford, Mike**
❑ 52JunBluT-150
**Ratchuk, Peter**
❑ 95Cla-68
❑ 98BowCHL-99
❑ 98BowCHLGA-99
❑ 98BowCHLOI-99
❑ 98BowCHLSC-SC14
❑ 98BowChrC-99
❑ 98BowChrCGA-99
❑ 98BowChrCGAR-99
❑ 98BowChrCOI-99
❑ 98BowChrCOIR-99
❑ 98BowChrCR-99
**Ratelle, Jean**
❑ 44BeeGro2P-356A
❑ 44BeeGro2P-356B
❑ 61ShiCoi-98
❑ 61Top-60
❑ 62Top-58
❑ 63Top-63
❑ 64BeeGro3P-147
❑ 65Coc-86
❑ 65Top-25
❑ 66Top-29
❑ 66TopUSAT-29
❑ 67Top-31
❑ 68OPC-77
❑ 68ShiCoi-94
❑ 68Top-77
❑ 69OPC-42
❑ 69OPCFou-17
❑ 69OPCSta-24
❑ 69Top-42
❑ 70ColSta-25
❑ 70DadCoo-108
❑ 70EssPowPla-194
❑ 70OPC-181
❑ 70OPCDec-40
❑ 70PosCerS-14
❑ 70SarProSta-118
❑ 70TopStiS-26
❑ 71ColHea-11
❑ 71LetActR-14
❑ 71OPC-97
❑ 71OPCPos-19
❑ 71SarProSta-114
❑ 71Top-97
❑ 71TorSun-179
❑ 72OPC-12
❑ 72OPC-48A
❑ 72OPC-48B
❑ 72OPC-250
❑ 72OPC-280
❑ 72OPC-283
❑ 72OPCTeaC-23
❑ 72SarProSta-142
❑ 72SweHocS-120
❑ 72SweSemWC-214
❑ 72Top-50
❑ 72Top-62
❑ 72Top-63
❑ 72Top-130
❑ 73MacMil-23
❑ 73OPC-141
❑ 73Top-73
❑ 74NHLActSta-186
❑ 74OPCNHL-145
❑ 74Top-145
❑ 75HerSta-5
❑ 75OPCNHL-243A
❑ 75OPCNHL-243B
❑ 75OPCNHL-324
❑ 75Top-243
❑ 75Top-324
❑ 76OPCNHL-2
❑ 76OPCNHL-80
❑ 76OPCNHL-381
❑ 76Top-2
❑ 76Top-80
❑ 76TopGlol-22
❑ 77OPCNHL-40
❑ 77Top-40
❑ 77TopGloS-16
❑ 77TopOPCGlo-16
❑ 78OPC-155
❑ 78Top-155
❑ 79OPC-225
❑ 79Top-225
❑ 80OPC-6
❑ 80Top-6
❑ 85HalFC-249
❑ 91BruSpoAL-24
❑ 91FutTreC72-66
❑ 93ZelMasH-7
❑ 93ZelMasoHS-7
❑ 94ParTalB-89
❑ 94ParTalB-152
❑ 95Par66-88
❑ 95Par66Coi-88
**Rath, Marius**
❑ 93SweSemWCS-246
❑ 94FinnJaaK-266
❑ 95FinnSemWC-182
❑ 95SweGloWC-195
❑ 96SweSemW-209
**Rathbone, Jason**
❑ 92HamRoaA-10
**Rathje, Mike**
❑ 907thInnSWHL-41
❑ 917thInnSWHL-330
❑ 92Cla-3
❑ 92Cla-60
❑ 92ClaLPs-LP3
❑ 92UppDec-589
❑ 93Cla-145
❑ 93Don-314
❑ 93Lea-419
❑ 93OPCPre-427
❑ 93OPCPreG-427
❑ 93Par-458
❑ 93ParEmel-458
❑ 93Pin-442
❑ 93PinCan-442
❑ 93Pow-437
❑ 93Sco-595
❑ 93ScoCan-595
❑ 93ScoGol-595
❑ 93StaClu-322
❑ 93StaCluFDI-322
❑ 93StaCluO-322
❑ 93TopPre-427
❑ 93TopPreG-427
❑ 93Ult-418
❑ 93UltWavF-15
❑ 93UppDec-460
❑ 93UppDecSP-147
❑ 94ClaProP-32
❑ 94Don-170
❑ 94Lea-139
❑ 94ParSE-SE160
❑ 94ParSEG-SE160
❑ 94Pin-363
❑ 94PinArtP-363
❑ 94PinRinC-363
❑ 94Sco-261
❑ 94ScoGol-261
❑ 94ScoPla-261
❑ 94ScoPlaTS-261
❑ 94StaClu-215
❑ 94StaCluFDI-215
❑ 94StaCluMOMS-215
❑ 94StaCluSTWC-215
❑ 94Ult-201
❑ 94UppDec-168
❑ 94UppDecEleIce-168
❑ 95Don-305
❑ 95Emo-160
❑ 95Pin-155
❑ 95PinArtP-155
❑ 95PinRinC-155
❑ 95SkyImp-151
❑ 95Top-191
❑ 95TopOPCI-191
❑ 96ClaGol-3
❑ 96ClaGol-60
❑ 97PacInvNRB-180
❑ 99Pac-379
❑ 99PacCop-379
❑ 99PacGol-379
❑ 99PacIceB-379
❑ 99PacPreD-379
**Ratliff, Elden**
❑ 92DisMigDM-5
**Ratushny, Dan**
❑ 91AlbIntTC-18
❑ 93UppDec-245
❑ 95PeoRiv-18
❑ 98KanCitB-3
**Raty, Tuomo**
❑ 94FinnSIS-299
**Rau, Thorsten**
❑ 94GerDELE-180
**Raubal, A.**
❑ 95GerDELE-110
❑ 95GerDELE-341
**Raubal, Michael**
❑ 94GerDELE-119
**Raubal, Toni**
❑ 94GerDELE-124
**Rauch, Gunther**
❑ 71SweHocS-375
**Rauch, Martin**
❑ 91SweSemWCS-186
❑ 93SwiHNL-66
❑ 95SwiHNL-92
**Rauhala, Reine**
❑ 91SweSemE-146
❑ 92SweSemE-161
❑ 92UppDec-598
**Raunio, Matti**
❑ 95FinnSIS-304
**Rautakallio, Pekka**
❑ 74SweSemHVS-79
❑ 75RoaPhoWHA-19
❑ 76OPCWHA-114
❑ 76RoaPhoWHA-15
❑ 79FlamPos-14
❑ 79FlaTeal-15
❑ 79PanSti-164
❑ 80FlamPos-16
❑ 80OPC-356
❑ 80PepCap-14
❑ 81FlamPos-17
❑ 81OPC-108
❑ 81OPCSti-223
❑ 82OPCSti-218
❑ 82PosCer-3
❑ 82SweSemHVS-161
❑ 91SweSemWCS-228
❑ 93SwiHNL-363
❑ 95SwiHNL-213
❑ 96SweSemWHL-HL15
**Rautakorpi, Jukka**
❑ 95FinnSIS-394
**Rautiainen, Matti**
❑ 79PanSti-179
**Rautio, Jani**
❑ 93FinnJyvHS-167
❑ 93FinnSIS-173
**Rautio, Kai**
❑ 94FinnSIS-261
❑ 95FinnSIS-72
❑ 95FinnSIS-219
❑ 96GerDELE-53
**Rautio, Mika**
❑ 94FinnSIS-118
❑ 94FinnSISNP-6
❑ 95FinnSIS-283
❑ 95FinnSISL-55
**Rautio, Samuli**
❑ 93FinnJyvHS-286
❑ 93FinnSIS-78
❑ 94FinnSIS-126
**Ravlich, Matt**
❑ 64BeeGro3P-53
❑ 65Coc-23
❑ 65Top-115
❑ 66Top-58
❑ 66TopUSAT-58
❑ 68OPC-152
❑ 68ShiCoi-29
❑ 69OPC-161
❑ 70ColSta-69
❑ 70DadCoo-109
❑ 70EssPowPla-160
❑ 70OPC-32
❑ 70SarProSta-71
❑ 70Top-32
❑ 94ParTalB-35
❑ 95Par66-22
❑ 95Par66Coi-22
**Rawles, Bill**
❑ 94GuiFla-16
**Rawson, Geoff**
❑ 897thInnSOHL-129
❑ 89NiaFalT-16
❑ 907thInnSOHL-269
❑ 917thInnSOHL-215
**Ray, Jean-Michel**
❑ 84RicRiv-13
**Ray, Martin**
❑ 907thInnSQMJHL-118
**Ray, Robert (Rob)**
❑ 88ProAHL-265
❑ 89ProAHL-256
❑ 89SabCam-21
❑ 90ProAHLIHL-277
❑ 90ProSet-419
❑ 90SabBluS-18
❑ 90SabCam-21
❑ 90UppDec-516
❑ 90UppDecF-516
❑ 91ProSet-355
❑ 91ProSetFre-355
❑ 91SabBluS-18
❑ 91SabPepC-18
❑ 91ScoCan-610
❑ 91UppDec-349
❑ 91UppDecF-349
❑ 92Par-252
❑ 92ParEmel-252
❑ 92SabBluS-20
❑ 92SabJubF-3
❑ 93Sco-433
❑ 93ScoCan-433
❑ 94Par-30
❑ 94ParGol-30
❑ 94Pin-514
❑ 94PinArtP-514
❑ 94PinRinC-514
❑ 95BeAPla-56
❑ 95BeAPSig-S56
❑ 95BeAPSigDC-S56
❑ 95ColCho-198
❑ 95ColChoPC-198
❑ 95ColChoPCP-198
❑ 96Sco-200
❑ 96ScoArtPro-200
❑ 96ScoDeaCAP-200
❑ 96ScoGolB-200
❑ 96ScoSpeAP-200
❑ 96UppDecBD-32
❑ 96UppDecBDG-32
❑ 97ColCho-23
❑ 97Kat-17
❑ 97KatGol-17
❑ 97KatSil-17
❑ 97PacInvNRB-21
❑ 97Sco-242
❑ 97ScoSab-14
❑ 97ScoSabPla-14
❑ 97ScoSabPre-14
❑ 97UppDec-228
❑ 98Be A PPA-165
❑ 98Be A PPAA-165
❑ 98Be A PPAAF-165
❑ 98Be A PPSE-165
❑ 98Be APG-165
❑ 98Pac-108
❑ 98PacIceB-108
❑ 98PacOmeH-26
❑ 98PacOmeODI-26
❑ 98PacOmeR-26
❑ 98PacRed-108
❑ 99Pac-43
❑ 99PacCop-43
❑ 99PacGol-43
❑ 99PacIceB-43
❑ 99PacPreD-43
**Ray, Vern**
❑ 93ThuBayS-17
❑ 95ForWorF-4
❑ 96ForWorF-13
**Raycroft, Andrew**
❑ 97SudWolP-24
**Raymond, Alain**
❑ 82NorBayC-18
❑ 89HamRoaA-19
❑ 90ProAHLIHL-78
❑ 91ProAHLCHL-38
**Raymond, Eric**
❑ 907thInnSMC-55
❑ 907thInnSQMJHL-73
❑ 917thInnSQMJHL-241
❑ 93WheThu-8
**Raymond, Jacques**
❑ 93OPCCanHF-18
**Raymond, Paul**
❑ 33V357IceK-18
❑ 35DiaMatTI-54
**Raymond, Richard**
❑ 907thInnSOHL-43
❑ 917thInnSOHL-4
❑ 91CorRoy-3
**Raymond, Sen. Donat**
❑ 83HalFP-E14
❑ 85HalFC-73
**Raynak, Geoff**
❑ 92CorBigRed-23
**Rayner, Chuck**
❑ 34BeeGro1P-246
❑ 44BeeGro2P-357
❑ 48ExhCan-51
❑ 51Par-104
❑ 52Par-22
❑ 52RoyDesH-2
❑ 53Par-59
❑ 83HalFP-L14
❑ 85HalFC-163
❑ 92SpoFla-3
**Razin, Gennady**
❑ 96KamBla-19
**Read, Mel**
❑ 51LavDaiQSHL-65
**Reade, Mark**
❑ 81KinCan-4
❑ 82KinCan-12
**Reader, Alan**
❑ 98GerDELE-283
**Ready, Ryan**
❑ 95Sla-45
**Reardon, Kenny (Ken)**
❑ 34BeeGro1P-177
❑ 40OPCV3012-116
❑ 44BeeGro2P-281
❑ 45QuaOatP-107A
❑ 45QuaOatP-107B
❑ 45QuaOatP-107C
❑ 48ExhCan-21
❑ 55Par-64
❑ 55ParQuaO-64
❑ 59Par-22
❑ 83HalFP-B11
❑ 85HalFC-25
❑ 93OPCCanHF-42
**Reardon, Terry**
❑ 34BeeGro1P-178
**Reasoner, Marty**
❑ 94Cla95DP-DP8
❑ 94Sel-150
❑ 94SelGol-150
❑ 95DonEliWJ-40
❑ 95UppDec-566
❑ 95UppDecEleIce-566
❑ 95UppDecEleIceG-566
❑ 96UppDecIce-150
❑ 98BowBes-113
❑ 98BowBesAR-113
❑ 98BowBesMIF-F16
❑ 98BowBesMIFAR-F16
❑ 98BowBesMIFR-F16
❑ 98BowBesR-113
❑ 98PacDynI-162
❑ 98PacDynIIB-162
❑ 98PacDynIR-162
❑ 98PacDynIR-7
❑ 98PacOmeH-208
❑ 98PacOmeODI-208
❑ 98PacOmeR-208
❑ 98SP Aut-107
❑ 98TopGolLC1-72
❑ 98TopGolLC1B-72
❑ 98TopGolLC1BOoO-72
❑ 98TopGolLC1OoO-72
❑ 98TopGolLC1R-72
❑ 98TopGolLC1ROoO-72
❑ 98TopGolLC2-72
❑ 98TopGolLC2B-72
❑ 98TopGolLC2BOoO-72
❑ 98TopGolLC2OoO-72
❑ 98TopGolLC2R-72
❑ 98TopGolLC2ROoO-72
❑ 98TopGolLC3-72
❑ 98TopGolLC3B-72
❑ 98TopGolLC3BOoO-72
❑ 98TopGolLC3OoO-72
❑ 98TopGolLC3R-72
❑ 98TopGolLC3ROoO-72
❑ 98UppDec-419
❑ 98UppDecBD-76
❑ 98UppDecDD-76
❑ 98UppDecE-419
❑ 98UppDecE1o1-419
❑ 98UppDecGN-GN5
❑ 98UppDecGNQ1-GN5
❑ 98UppDecGNQ2-GN5
❑ 98UppDecGNQ3-GN5
❑ 98UppDecGR-419
❑ 98UppDecM-178
❑ 98UppDecMGS-178
❑ 98UppDecMSS-178
❑ 98UppDecMSS-178
❑ 98UppDecP-P1
❑ 98UppDecPQ1-P1
❑ 98UppDecPQ2-P1
❑ 98UppDecPQ3-P1
❑ 98UppDecQD-76
❑ 98UppDecTD-76
❑ 99Pac-368
❑ 99PacCop-368
❑ 99PacGol-368
❑ 99PacIceB-368
❑ 99PacPreD-368
❑ 99SP AutPS-107
**Reaugh, Daryl**
❑ 84KamBla-21
❑ 85NovScoO-13
❑ 87OilTeal-29
❑ 88OilTenAnn-62
❑ 88ProAHL-80
❑ 89ProAHL-291
❑ 90ProAHLIHL-184
❑ 90UppDec-541
❑ 90UppDecF-541
❑ 90WhaJr7E-20
❑ 91Bow-19
❑ 91OPC-391
❑ 91ProAHLCHL-93
❑ 91StaClu-326
❑ 91Top-391
**Reaume, Marc**
❑ 44BeeGro2P-444
❑ 52JunBluT-146
❑ 55Par-7
❑ 55ParQuaO-7
❑ 57Par-T12
❑ 58Par-20
❑ 59Par-11
❑ 60Par-25
❑ 60ShiCoi-52
❑ 63ChePho-45
❑ 63Par-37
❑ 63Par-96
❑ 63YorWhiB-32
❑ 66TulOil-9
❑ 70CanuRoyB-14
❑ 70EssPowPla-42
❑ 70OPC-119
❑ 70Top-119
❑ 76OldTim-15
❑ 94ParMisL-114
**Reay, Billy**
❑ 44BeeGro2P-282
❑ 45QuaOatP-108A
❑ 45QuaOatP-108B
❑ 45QuaOatP-108C
❑ 45QuaOatP-108D
❑ 48ExhCan-22
❑ 51Par-13
❑ 52Par-2
❑ 55Par-66
❑ 55ParQuaO-66
❑ 57Par-T25
❑ 58Par-25
❑ 63Top-22
❑ 64Top-38
❑ 65Top-54
❑ 66Top-53
❑ 70BlaBor-5
❑ 74OPCNHL-204
❑ 74Top-204
❑ 94ParTalB-43
**Rebek, Jeremy**
❑ 93OweSouPla-24
❑ 95Sla-297
**Recchi, Mark**
❑ 86KamBla-18
❑ 87KamBla-19
❑ 88ProIHL-62
❑ 90Bow-206
❑ 90BowTif-206
❑ 90OPC-280
❑ 90PanSti-130
❑ 90PanSti-341
❑ 90PenFoo-6
❑ 90ProSet-239
❑ 90Sco-186
❑ 90ScoCan-186
❑ 90ScoHotRS-81
❑ 90ScoYouS-35
❑ 90Top-280
❑ 90TopTif-280
❑ 90UppDec-178
❑ 90UppDec-487
❑ 90UppDecF-178
❑ 90UppDecF-487
❑ 91Bow-83
❑ 91Kra-2
❑ 91McDUppD-4
❑ 91OPC-196
❑ 91PanSti-280
❑ 91Par-134
❑ 91Par-347
❑ 91ParFre-134
❑ 91ParFre-347
❑ 91PenCokE-8
❑ 91PenFooCS-10
❑ 91Pin-151
❑ 91Pin-360
❑ 91PinFre-151
❑ 91PinFre-360
❑ 91ProSet-184
❑ 91ProSet-313
❑ 91ProSetCC-CC8
❑ 91ProSetCCF-CC8
❑ 91ProSetFre-184
❑ 91ProSetFre-313
❑ 91ProSetPla-97
❑ 91ProSetPla-144
❑ 91ScoAme-145
❑ 91ScoCan-145
❑ 91ScoKel-9
❑ 91ScoYouS-22
❑ 91StaClu-256
❑ 91SweSemWCS-74
❑ 91Top-196
❑ 91TopTeaSL-5
❑ 91UppDec-92
❑ 91UppDec-346
❑ 91UppDecF-92
❑ 91UppDecF-346
❑ 92Bow-314
❑ 92FlyJCP-20
❑ 92FlyUppDS-3
❑ 92FlyUppDS-22
❑ 92FlyUppDS-36
❑ 92FlyUppDS-42
❑ 92OPC-373
❑ 92PanSti-185
❑ 92PanStiFre-185
❑ 92Par-130
❑ 92ParEmel-130
❑ 92Pin-80
❑ 92PinCanPP-1
❑ 92PinFre-80
❑ 92ProSet-131
❑ 92Sco-180
❑ 92ScoCan-180
❑ 92ScoSha-18
❑ 92ScoShaCan-18
❑ 92ScoYouS-7
❑ 92SeaPat-41
❑ 92StaClu-183
❑ 92Top-267
❑ 92Top-410
❑ 92TopGol-267G
❑ 92TopGol-410G
❑ 92Ult-158
❑ 92UppDec-327
❑ 93Cla-AU10
❑ 93ClaProPBC-BC20
❑ 93ClaProPro-34
❑ 93ClaTeaCan-TC5
❑ 93Don-252
❑ 93Lea-205
❑ 93McDUppD-22
❑ 93OPCPre-230
❑ 93OPCPreG-230
❑ 93PanSti-46
❑ 93Par-149
❑ 93ParEmel-149
❑ 93Pin-50
❑ 93PinAllS-6
❑ 93PinAllSC-6

**Renberg, Mikael • 643**


❑ 94Lea-437
❑ 94OPCPre-167
❑ 94OPCPreSE-167
❑ 94Pin-351
❑ 94PinArtP-351
❑ 94PinRinC-351
❑ 94TopPre-167
❑ 94TopPreSE-167
❑ 95BeAPla-66
❑ 95BeAPSig-S66
❑ 95BeAPSigDC-S66
❑ 95Cap-22
❑ 95Emo-191
❑ 97Be A PPAD-136
❑ 97Be A PPAPD-136
❑ 97BeAPla-136
❑ 97BeAPlaAut-136
❑ 97PacInvNRB-212
**Reese, Jeff**
❑ 85LonKni-27
❑ 88ProAHL-242
❑ 90OPC-349
❑ 90PanSti-281
❑ 90ProSet-540
❑ 90Top-349
❑ 90TopTif-349
❑ 91MapLeaP-26
❑ 91MapLeaPTS-21
❑ 91OPC-81
❑ 91Par-250
❑ 91ParFre-250
❑ 91ScoCan-410
❑ 91Top-81
❑ 92Bow-412
❑ 92FlamIGA-9
❑ 92OPC-77
❑ 92Par-264
❑ 92ParEmel-264
❑ 92StaClu-322
❑ 92Top-385
❑ 92TopGol-385G
❑ 92UppDec-442
❑ 93Don-443
❑ 93OPCPre-302
❑ 93OPCPreG-302
❑ 93PanSti-187
❑ 93Pow-355
❑ 93Sco-394
❑ 93Sco-650
❑ 93ScoCan-394
❑ 93ScoCan-650
❑ 93ScoGol-650
❑ 93StaClu-22
❑ 93StaCluFDI-22
❑ 93StaCluFDIO-22
❑ 93StaCluO-22
❑ 93TopPre-302
❑ 93TopPreG-302
❑ 93WhaCok-18
❑ 94Lea-59
❑ 94OPCPre-27
❑ 94OPCPreSE-27
❑ 94ParSE-SE74
❑ 94ParSEG-SE74
❑ 94TopPre-27
❑ 94TopPreSE-27
❑ 94UppDec-476
❑ 94UppDecElelce-476
❑ 95ParInt-460
❑ 95ParIntEl-460
❑ 96DetVip-14
❑ 96Don-31
❑ 96DonPrePro-31
❑ 96Sco-213
❑ 96ScoArtPro-213
❑ 96ScoDeaCAP-213
❑ 96ScoGolB-213
❑ 96ScoSpeAP-213
**Reesor, Jason**
❑ 93NiaFalT-16
**Reeve, Jamie**
❑ 82RegPat-3
❑ 83RegPat-3
❑ 93TacRoc-23
**Reeves, Kyle**
❑ 907thInnSWHL-109
❑ 91ProAHLCHL-39
❑ 92PeoRivC-20
❑ 93TolSto-26
❑ 94FliGen-18
❑ 95ForWorFT-13
**Regan, Larry**
❑ 44BeeGro2P-61
❑ 44BeeGro2P-445
❑ 52St.LawS-103
❑ 57BruTealss-17
❑ 57Top-6
❑ 58Top-10
❑ 59Par-17
❑ 60Par-13
❑ 60ShiCoi-16
❑ 60YorPreP-30
❑ 94ParMisL-16
**Regan, Tim**
❑ 93RenEng-24
**Regehr, Robyn**
❑ 96KamBla-20
❑ 97UppDec-406
❑ 98BowCHL-137
❑ 98BowCHLAuB-A14
❑ 98BowCHLAuG-A14
❑ 98BowCHLAuS-A14
❑ 98BowCHLGA-137
❑ 98BowCHLOI-137
❑ 98BowChrC-137
❑ 98BowChrCGA-137
❑ 98BowChrCGAR-137
❑ 98BowChrCOI-137
❑ 98BowChrCOIR-137
❑ 98BowChrCR-137
❑ 98FinFutF-F15
❑ 98FinFutFR-F15
**Regier, Darcey**
❑ 81IndChe-16
❑ 82IndChe-16
**Regnier, Curtis (Curt)**
❑ 907thInnSWHL-264
❑ 90PriAlbR-18
❑ 917thInnSWHL-253
❑ 91PriAlbR-20
**Rehnberg, Henrik**
❑ 93SweSemE-315
❑ 95ColCho-347
❑ 95ColChoPC-347
❑ 95ColChoPCP-347
❑ 95SweUppDE-61
**Rehnstrom, Kjell**
❑ 69SweHocS-90
**Rehnstrom, Peder**
❑ 69SweHocS-91
**Reibel, Earl**
❑ 44BeeGro2P-62
❑ 44BeeGro2P-207
❑ 53Par-36
❑ 54Par-37
❑ 54Par-97
❑ 54Top-52
❑ 57Top-45
❑ 58Top-57
❑ 94ParMisL-49
❑ 94ParMisL-147
**Reich, Chad**
❑ 95MedHatT-13
**Reich, Dory**
❑ 90ForSasTra-14
**Reich, Jeremy**
❑ 95SeaThu-24
❑ 96SeaThu-23
❑ 96UppDec-386
❑ 97BowCHL-143
❑ 97BowCHLAu-39
❑ 97BowCHLOPC-143
**Reich, Shawn**
❑ 90ForSasTra-15
**Reichart, Chris**
❑ 94LigPos-15
**Reichel, Martin**
❑ 92Cla-28
❑ 94GerDELE-378
❑ 95GerDELE-376
❑ 96ClaGol-28
❑ 96GerDELE-378
❑ 96SweSemW-199
❑ 98GerDELE-251
❑ 98GerDELE-332
**Reichel, Robert**
❑ 90FlamIGA-23
❑ 90OPCPre-95
❑ 90ProSet-595
❑ 90ScoRoo-30T
❑ 90ScoYouS-29
❑ 90UppDec-533
❑ 90UppDecF-533
❑ 91Bow-267
❑ 91FlamIGA-17
❑ 91OPC-411
❑ 91PanSti-63
❑ 91PanSti-343
❑ 91Par-21
❑ 91ParFre-21
❑ 91Pin-56
❑ 91PinFre-56
❑ 91ProSet-361
❑ 91ProSetFre-361
❑ 91ProSetPla-163
❑ 91ScoAme-263
❑ 91ScoCan-483
❑ 91ScoYouS-24
❑ 91StaClu-393
❑ 91SweSemWCS-223
❑ 91Top-411
❑ 91UppDec-223
❑ 91UppDecF-223
❑ 92Bow-401
❑ 92FlamIGA-5
❑ 92OPC-93
❑ 92PanSti-42
❑ 92PanSti-301
❑ 92PanStiFre-42
❑ 92PanStiFre-301
❑ 92Par-26
❑ 92ParEmel-26
❑ 92Pin-101
❑ 92PinFre-101
❑ 92Sco-106
❑ 92ScoCan-106
❑ 92StaClu-180
❑ 92Top-157
❑ 92TopGol-157G
❑ 92Ult-28
❑ 92UppDec-42
❑ 93Don-51
❑ 93Lea-59
❑ 93OPCPre-404
❑ 93OPCPreG-404
❑ 93PanSti-180
❑ 93Par-300
❑ 93ParEmel-300
❑ 93Pin-35
❑ 93PinCan-35
❑ 93Pow-41
❑ 93PowRisS-5
❑ 93Sco-204
❑ 93ScoCan-204
❑ 93ScoIntS-6
❑ 93ScoIntSC-6
❑ 93ScoIntSC-198
❑ 93StaClu-198
❑ 93StaCluFDI-198
❑ 93StaCluFDIO-198
❑ 93StaCluO-198
❑ 93TopPre-404
❑ 93TopPreG-404
❑ 93Ult-164
❑ 93UppDec-313
❑ 93UppDecHT-HT4
❑ 94CanGamNHLP-60
❑ 94Don-169
❑ 94FinnJaaK-184
❑ 94Fla-27
❑ 94Fle-34
❑ 94Kra-26
❑ 94Lea-243
❑ 94LeaLim-39
❑ 94LeaLimI-4
❑ 94OPCPre-213
❑ 94OPCPreSE-213
❑ 94Par-34
❑ 94ParGol-34
❑ 94ParVin-V47
❑ 94Pin-12
❑ 94PinArtP-12
❑ 94PinRinC-12
❑ 94PinWorEdi-WE13
❑ 94Sco90PC-17
❑ 94Sel-138
❑ 94SelGol-138
❑ 94TopFinI-20
❑ 94TopPre-213
❑ 94TopPreSE-213
❑ 94Ult-34
❑ 94UppDec-357
❑ 94UppDecElelce-357
❑ 94UppDecSPI-SP104
❑ 94UppDecSPIDC-SP104
❑ 95GerDELE-116
❑ 95GerDELE-439
❑ 95GerDELE-445
❑ 95SweGloWC-159
❑ 96BeAPAut-81
❑ 96BeAPAutSil-81
❑ 96BeAPla-81
❑ 96CzeAPSE-349
❑ 96MetUni-22
❑ 96SweSemW-128
❑ 96Ult-26
❑ 96UltGolM-26
❑ 96UppDec-228
❑ 97ColCho-151
❑ 97Pac-326
❑ 97PacCop-326
❑ 97PacCroR-80
❑ 97PacCroREG-80
❑ 97PacCroRIB-80
❑ 97PacCroRS-80
❑ 97PacEmeGre-326
❑ 97PacIceB-326
❑ 97PacOme-141
❑ 97PacOmeC-141
❑ 97PacOmeDG-141
❑ 97PacOmeEG-141
❑ 97PacOmeG-141
❑ 97PacOmeIB-141
❑ 97PacPar-110
❑ 97PacParC-110
❑ 97PacParDG-110
❑ 97PacParEG-110
❑ 97PacParIB-110
❑ 97PacParRed-110
❑ 97PacParSil-110
❑ 97PacRed-326
❑ 97PacRev-83
❑ 97PacRevC-83
❑ 97PacRevE-83
❑ 97PacRevIB-83
❑ 97PacRevR-83
❑ 97PacRevS-83
❑ 97PacSil-326
❑ 97Sco-218
❑ 97SPAut-97
❑ 97UppDec-104
❑ 97UppDecBD-49
❑ 97UppDecBDDD-49
❑ 97UppDecBDQD-49
❑ 97UppDecBDTD-49
❑ 97Zen-70
❑ 97ZenZGol-70
❑ 97ZenZSil-70
❑ 98Be A PPA-86
❑ 98Be A PPAA-86
❑ 98Be A PPAAF-86
❑ 98Be A PPTBASG-86
❑ 98Be APG-86
❑ 98BowBes-95
❑ 98BowBesAR-95
❑ 98BowBesR-95
❑ 98Pac-286
❑ 98PacAur-118
❑ 98PacCroR-85
❑ 98PacCroRLS-85
❑ 98PacDynI-117
❑ 98PacDynIIB-117
❑ 98PacDynIR-117
❑ 98PacIceB-286
❑ 98PacOmeH-151
❑ 98PacOmeODI-151
❑ 98PacOmeR-151
❑ 98PacPar-147
❑ 98PacParC-147
❑ 98PacParEG-147
❑ 98PacParH-147
❑ 98PacParIB-147
❑ 98PacParS-147
❑ 98PacRed-286
❑ 98SP Aut-54
❑ 98TopGolLC1-19
❑ 98TopGolLC1B-19
❑ 98TopGolLC1BOoO-19
❑ 98TopGolLC1OoO-19
❑ 98TopGolLC1R-19
❑ 98TopGolLC1ROoO-19
❑ 98TopGolLC2-19
❑ 98TopGolLC2B-19
❑ 98TopGolLC2BOoO-19
❑ 98TopGolLC2OoO-19
❑ 98TopGolLC2R-19
❑ 98TopGolLC2ROoO-19
❑ 98TopGolLC3-19
❑ 98TopGolLC3B-19
❑ 98TopGolLC3BOoO-19
❑ 98TopGolLC3OoO-19
❑ 98TopGolLC3R-19
❑ 98TopGolLC3ROoO-19
❑ 98UC-126
❑ 98UD ChoPCR-126
❑ 98UD ChoR-126
❑ 98UppDecM-127
❑ 98UppDecMGS-127
❑ 98UppDecMSS-127
❑ 98UppDecMSS-127
❑ 99Pac-324
❑ 99PacCop-324
❑ 99PacGol-324
❑ 99PacIceB-324
❑ 99PacPreD-324
❑ 99SP AutPS-54
❑ 99UppDecM-157
❑ 99UppDecMGS-157
❑ 99UppDecMSS-157
❑ 99UppDecMSS-157
**Reichenberg, Ronny**
❑ 86SwePanS-161
❑ 89SweSemE-139
❑ 90SweSemE-217
**Reichert, Craig**
❑ 917thInnSWHL-18
❑ 93RedDeeR-20
**Reichmuth, Craig**
❑ 74MarSanDW-7
**Reid, Bill**
❑ 92MPSPhoSJHL-126
**Reid, Charlie**
❑ 23V1281PauC-68
**Reid, Dave (50s)**
❑ 44BeeGro2P-446
**Reid, Dave (80s)**
❑ 85MonGolF-22
❑ 86MonGolF-24
❑ 88MapLeaPLA-24
❑ 89OPCSti-170
❑ 90OPC-290
❑ 90ProSet-541
❑ 90ScoRoo-109T
❑ 90Top-290
❑ 90TopTif-290
❑ 90UppDec-364
❑ 90UppDecF-364
❑ 91Bow-153
❑ 91BruSpoA-16
❑ 91MapLeaPTS-22
❑ 91OPC-423
❑ 91PanSti-104
❑ 91ProAHLCHL-66
❑ 91ProSet-229
❑ 91ProSet-348
❑ 91ProSetFre-229
❑ 91ProSetFre-348
❑ 91ProSetPre-229
❑ 91ScoAme-173
❑ 91ScoCan-173
❑ 91StaClu-78
❑ 91Top-423
❑ 91UppDec-217
❑ 91UppDec-531
❑ 91UppDecF-217
❑ 91UppDecF-531
❑ 92Par-249
❑ 92ParEmel-249
❑ 92Sco-380
❑ 92ScoCan-380
❑ 92Top-521
❑ 92TopGol-521G
❑ 93Don-403
❑ 93OPCPre-67
❑ 93OPCPreG-67
❑ 93Pin-191
❑ 93PinCan-191
❑ 93Pow-290
❑ 93Sco-371
❑ 93ScoCan-371
❑ 93StaClu-100
❑ 93StaCluFDI-100
❑ 93StaCluFDIO-100
❑ 93StaCluO-100
❑ 93TopPre-67
❑ 93TopPreG-67
❑ 93Ult-269
❑ 94BeAPla-R88
❑ 94BeAPSig-103
❑ 94Lea-501
❑ 94OPCPre-51
❑ 94OPCPreSE-51
❑ 94ParSE-SE12
❑ 94ParSEG-SE12
❑ 94Pin-234
❑ 94PinArtP-234
❑ 94PinRinC-234
❑ 94Sco-80
❑ 94ScoGol-80
❑ 94ScoPla-80
❑ 94ScoPlaTS-80
❑ 94TopPre-51
❑ 94TopPreSE-51
❑ 95ParInt-281
❑ 95ParIntEl-281
❑ 95PlaOneoOne-122
❑ 95Top-76
❑ 95TopOPCI-76
❑ 96BeAPAut-121
❑ 96BeAPAutSil-121
❑ 96BeAPla-121
❑ 96FlePic-176
❑ 96Pin-182
❑ 96PinFoi-182
❑ 96PinPreS-182
❑ 96PlaOneoOne-386
❑ 96Sco-220
❑ 96ScoArtPro-220
❑ 96ScoDeaCAP-220
❑ 96ScoGolB-220
❑ 96ScoSpeAP-220
❑ 96StaPos-24
❑ 96Sum-146
❑ 96SumMet-146
❑ 96SumPreS-146
❑ 97ColCho-73
❑ 97PacInvNRB-65
❑ 97UppDec-264
**Reid, Grayden**
❑ 907thInnSOHL-293
❑ 917thInnSOHL-294
❑ 91UltDra-53
**Reid, Jarret**
❑ 907thInnSOHL-171
❑ 917thInnSMC-12
❑ 917thInnSOHL-324
❑ 93SauSteMGM-15
**Reid, Jay**
❑ 82MedHatT-17
**Reid, Jeff**
❑ 907thInnSOHL-44
❑ 917thInnSOHL-18
❑ 91CorRoy-22
❑ 93KnoChe-13
❑ 94LasVegThu-21
**Reid, Jerry**
❑ 51CleBar-6
**Reid, John**
❑ 84BelBul-20
❑ 88ProIHL-111
❑ 89NasKni-18
❑ 89NasKni-19
❑ 91ProAHLCHL-449
❑ 96FifFly-2
**Reid, Kelly**
❑ 97KinHaw-6
**Reid, Kevin**
❑ 907thInnSOHL-172
❑ 917thInnSOHL-355
**Reid, Reg**
❑ 24V1452-55
**Reid, Shawn**
❑ 94Cla-60
❑ 94ClaAllAme-AA9
❑ 94ClaDraGol-60
❑ 95BinRan-19
**Reid, Steve**
❑ 96SudWol-17
**Reid, Ted (Edward)**
❑ 52JunBluT-4
**Reid, Tom**
❑ 70EssPowPla-175
❑ 70NorStaP-7
❑ 70OPC-43
❑ 70SarProSta-85
❑ 70Top-43
❑ 71OPC-21
❑ 71SarProSta-82
❑ 71TorSun-144
❑ 72SarProSta-99
❑ 73NorStaAP-10
❑ 73NorStaP-18
❑ 73OPC-109
❑ 73Top-109
❑ 74NHLActSta-134
❑ 74OPCNHL-52
❑ 74Top-52
❑ 75OPCNHL-277
❑ 75Top-277
❑ 76OPCNHL-123
❑ 76Top-123
❑ 77OPCNHL-306
**Reier, Michael**
❑ 907thInnSOHL-214
❑ 92DayBom-23
**Reierson, Dave**
❑ 88SalLakCGE-9
❑ 94GerDELE-141
❑ 95GerDELE-129
**Reigle, Ed**
❑ 51CleBar-3
**Reijonen, Tuomas**
❑ 95ColCho-336
❑ 95ColChoPC-336
❑ 95ColChoPCP-336
❑ 96FinnSISR-131
**Reil, Joachim**
❑ 82SweSemHVS-107
❑ 94GerDELE-376
**Reilly, Gary**
❑ 89LetHur-18
**Reimann, Dan**
❑ 97LouRivF-19
**Reimer, Andrew**
❑ 917thInnSWHL-142
**Reimer, Mark**
❑ 88ProAHL-8
❑ 89ProAHL-325
❑ 90ProAHLIHL-311
❑ 91ProAHLCHL-121
**Reimer, Rob**
❑ 907thInnSWHL-150A
❑ 907thInnSWHL-150B
**Reindl, Franz**
❑ 79PanSti-110
❑ 82SweSemHVS-118
**Reinhard, Francis**
❑ 72SweSemWC-139
**Reinhart, Paul**
❑ 79FlamPos-15
❑ 79FlaTeal-16
❑ 80FlamPos-17
❑ 80OPC-157
❑ 80PepCap-15
❑ 80Top-157
❑ 81FlamPos-18
❑ 81OPC-36
❑ 81OPCSti-224
❑ 81Top-28
❑ 82FlamDol-6
❑ 82OPC-56
❑ 82OPCSti-219
❑ 82PosCer-3
❑ 83Ess-15
❑ 83OPC-91
❑ 83OPCSti-264
❑ 83PufSti-5
❑ 83Vac-17
❑ 847EDis-7
❑ 84KelAccD-1
❑ 84OPC-235
❑ 857ECreCar-3
❑ 85FlamRedRP-24
❑ 85OPC-48
❑ 85OPCSti-209
❑ 85Top-48
❑ 86FlamRedR-22
❑ 86FlamRedR-23
❑ 86KraDra-57
❑ 86OPC-205
❑ 87FlamRedRP-25
❑ 87OPC-143
❑ 87OPCMin-34
❑ 87OPCSti-39
❑ 87PanSti-206
❑ 87Top-143
❑ 88CanuMoh-16
❑ 89CanuMoh-15
❑ 89Kra-44
❑ 89KraAllSS-1
❑ 89OPC-148
❑ 89OPCSti-65
❑ 89Top-148
❑ 90Bow-60
❑ 90BowTif-60
❑ 90OPC-293
❑ 90PanSti-293
❑ 90ProSet-304
❑ 90Sco-173
❑ 90ScoCan-173
❑ 90Top-293
❑ 90TopTeaSL-5
❑ 90TopTif-293
❑ 90UppDec-110
❑ 90UppDecF-110
**Reirden, Todd**
❑ 94RalIce-18
**Reis, Shawn**
❑ 91AirCanSJHL-B14
**Reise, Leo**
❑ 23V1281PauC-36
❑ 23V1451-33
❑ 44BeeGro2P-208
❑ 44BeeGro2P-358
❑ 51Par-69
❑ 52Par-49
❑ 52RoyDesH-6
❑ 53Par-65
❑ 54Par-67
❑ 76OldTim-16
❑ 91UltOriS-28
❑ 91UltOriSF-28
**Reisinger, Ralf**
❑ 94GerDELE-312
❑ 95GerDELE-211
**Reiter, Jody**
❑ 91AirCanSJHL-C4
❑ 92MPSPhoSJHL-97
**Reja, Daniel**
❑ 93LonKni-14
❑ 93LonKni-24
❑ 95Sla-50
❑ 96LouRiv-7
❑ 97LouRivF-17
**Remackel, Chad**
❑ 96GraRapG-20
**Rempel, Nathan**
❑ 95SasBla-17
❑ 96SasBla-19
**Renard, Jason**
❑ 917thInnSWHL-246
❑ 91PriAlbR-21
❑ 93RicRen-9
**Renaud, Mark**
❑ 82WhaJunHC-15
**Renaud, Phil**
❑ 51LavDaiQSHL-18
❑ 52St.LawS-40
**Renberg, Mikael**
❑ 90SweSemE-241
❑ 91SweSemE-171
❑ 92SweSemE-190
❑ 92UppDec-233
❑ 93Don-255
❑ 93DonEli-U1
❑ 93DonRatR-5
❑ 93Lea-323
❑ 93LeaFrePhe-5
❑ 93Par-251
❑ 93ParCalC-C12
❑ 93ParCalCG-C12
❑ 93ParEmel-251
❑ 93Pin-454
❑ 93PinCan-454
❑ 93PinSupR-6
❑ 93PinSupRC-6
❑ 93Pow-408
❑ 93PowGloG-6
❑ 93PowRooS-13
❑ 93Sco-602
❑ 93ScoCan-602
❑ 93ScoGol-602
❑ 93StaClu-269
❑ 93StaCluFDI-269
❑ 93StaCluO-269
❑ 93SweSemE-310
❑ 93SweSemWCS-12
❑ 93Ult-391
❑ 93UltWavF-16
❑ 93UppDec-486
❑ 93UppDecSP-118
❑ 94BeAPla-R74
❑ 94BeAPSig-24
❑ 94CanGamNHLP-181
❑ 94ClaProP-33
❑ 94Don-236
❑ 94DonDom-4
❑ 94FinnJaaK-67
❑ 94Fla-131
❑ 94Fle-158
❑ 94FleFraFut-7
❑ 94Lea-54
❑ 94LeaGolR-6
❑ 94LeaGolS-9
❑ 94LeaLim-33
❑ 94McDUppD-McD39
❑ 94OPCFinIns-16
❑ 94OPCPre-191
❑ 94OPCPre-294
❑ 94OPCPre-383
❑ 94OPCPreSE-191
❑ 94OPCPreSE-294
❑ 94OPCPreSE-383
❑ 94Par-272
❑ 94ParGol-272
❑ 94ParSE-SE129
❑ 94ParSEES-ES3
❑ 94ParSEG-SE129
❑ 94ParVin-V78
❑ 94Pin-79
❑ 94Pin-464
❑ 94PinArtP-79
❑ 94PinArtP-464
❑ 94PinRinC-79
❑ 94PinRinC-464
❑ 94PinWorEdi-WE10
❑ 94Sco-249
❑ 94ScoGol-249
❑ 94ScoPla-249
❑ 94ScoPlaTS-249
❑ 94Sel-61
❑ 94SelGol-61
❑ 94SP-83
❑ 94SPDieCut-83
❑ 94StaClu-145
❑ 94StaCluDD-4
❑ 94StaCluDDMO-4
❑ 94StaCluFDI-145
❑ 94StaCluMO-47
❑ 94StaCluMOMS-145
❑ 94StaCluSTWC-145
❑ 94SweLeaE-199
❑ 94SweLeaEGS-5
❑ 94TopFinB-22
❑ 94TopPre-191
❑ 94TopPre-294
❑ 94TopPre-383
❑ 94TopPreSE-191
❑ 94TopPreSE-294
❑ 94TopPreSE-383
❑ 94Ult-159
❑ 94UltAllRoo-8
❑ 94UltGloGre-8
❑ 94UltPow-7
❑ 94UppDec-271
❑ 94UppDec-561
❑ 94UppDecElelce-271
❑ 94UppDecElelce-561
❑ 94UppDecSPI-SP59
❑ 94UppDecSPIDC-SP59
❑ 95Bow-83
❑ 95BowAllFoi-83
❑ 95ColCho-222
❑ 95ColChoPC-222
❑ 95ColChoPCP-222
❑ 95Don-80

❑ 95DonDom-2
❑ 95DonEli-94
❑ 95DonEliDCS-94
❑ 95DonEliDCU-94
❑ 95DonEliIns-3
❑ 95Emo-134
❑ 95EmoNteP-5
❑ 95Fin-120
❑ 95FinRef-120
❑ 95ImpSti-91
❑ 95ImpStiDCS-18
❑ 95Lea-128
❑ 95LeaFirOIce-12
❑ 95LeaFreFra-3
❑ 95LeaGolS-6
❑ 95LeaLim-119
❑ 95McDPin-MCD-22
❑ 95Met-113
❑ 95MetIS-16
❑ 95NHLAcePC-12C
❑ 95ParInt-161
❑ 95ParInt-243
❑ 95ParInt-NNO1
❑ 95ParIntAS-6
❑ 95ParIntCCGS1-7
❑ 95ParIntCCSS1-7
❑ 95ParIntEl-161
❑ 95ParIntEl-243
❑ 95Pin-41
❑ 95PinArtP-41
❑ 95PinGloG-5
❑ 95PinRinC-41
❑ 95PinRoa2-12
❑ 95PlaOneoOne-183
❑ 95ProMag-55
❑ 95Sco-35
❑ 95ScoBlaIce-35
❑ 95ScoBlaIceAP-35
❑ 95ScoLam-8
❑ 95SelCer-31
❑ 95SelCerDS-12
❑ 95SelCerDSG-12
❑ 95SelCerMG-31
❑ 95SkyImp-128
❑ 95SkyImp-245
❑ 95SP-107
❑ 95StaClu-110
❑ 95StaCluGTSC-GT7
❑ 95StaCluMOMS-110
❑ 95StaCluPS-PS5
❑ 95Sum-44
❑ 95SumArtP-44
❑ 95SumIce-44
❑ 95SweGloWC-29
❑ 95SweGloWC-259
❑ 95SweGloWC-260
❑ 95SweGloWC-261
❑ 95SweGloWC-268
❑ 95SweUppDE-235
❑ 95Top-18
❑ 95Top-353
❑ 95TopMarMPB-18
❑ 95TopMysF-M12
❑ 95TopMysFR-M12
❑ 95TopOPCI-18
❑ 95TopOPCI-353
❑ 95TopPowL-1PL
❑ 95TopSupSki-8
❑ 95TopSupSkiPla-8
❑ 95TopYouS-YS3
❑ 95Ult-120
❑ 95UltGolM-120
❑ 95UltHigSpe-16
❑ 95UltRisS-7
❑ 95UltRisSGM-7
❑ 95UppDec-194
❑ 95UppDecEleIce-194
❑ 95UppDecEleIceG-194
❑ 95UppDecSpeE-SE149
❑ 95UppDecSpeEdiG-SE149
❑ 95Zen-42
❑ 95ZenGifG-8
❑ 96BeAPAut-91
❑ 96BeAPAutSil-91
❑ 96BeAPla-91
❑ 96BeAPla-P91
❑ 96ColCho-189
❑ 96ColCho-326
❑ 96ColChoCTG-C25A
❑ 96ColChoCTG-C25B
❑ 96ColChoCTG-C25C
❑ 96ColChoCTGG-C25A
❑ 96ColChoCTGG-C25B
❑ 96ColChoCTGG-C25C
❑ 96Don-125
❑ 96DonCanI-77
❑ 96DonCanIGPP-77
❑ 96DonCanIRPP-77
❑ 96DonEli-33
❑ 96DonEliDCS-33
❑ 96DonPrePro-125
❑ 96Fle-83
❑ 96FlePic-46
❑ 96FlyPos-19
❑ 96Lea-108
❑ 96LeaLim-79
❑ 96LeaLimG-79
❑ 96LeaPre-58
❑ 96LeaPreP-108
❑ 96LeaPrePP-58
❑ 96LeaPreSG-58
❑ 96LeaPreSte-58
❑ 96MetUni-115
❑ 96NHLProSTA-55
❑ 96Pin-55
❑ 96PinArtP-55
❑ 96PinFoi-55
❑ 96PinPreS-55
❑ 96PinRinC-55
❑ 96Sco-177
❑ 96ScoArtPro-177
❑ 96ScoDeaCAP-177
❑ 96ScoGolB-177
❑ 96ScoSpeAP-177
❑ 96SkyImp-98
❑ 96SP-115
❑ 96Sum-73
❑ 96SumArtP-73
❑ 96SumIce-73
❑ 96SumMet-73
❑ 96SumPreS-73
❑ 96SweSemCDT-9
❑ 96SweSemW-58
❑ 96SweSemW-237
❑ 96SweSemW-238
❑ 96SweSemW-239
❑ 96SweSemW-240
❑ 96SweSemW-NNO
❑ 96TeaOut-45
❑ 96Ult-128
❑ 96UltGolM-128
❑ 96UppDec-307
❑ 96UppDecBD-49
❑ 96UppDecBDG-49
❑ 96UppDecIce-46
❑ 96UppDecIcePar-46
❑ 96UppDecPP-P2
❑ 96UppDecSS-SS23B
❑ 96Zen-109
❑ 96ZenArtP-109
❑ 96ZenAss-4
❑ 97ColCho-184
❑ 97ColChoSta-SQ9
❑ 97Don-151
❑ 97DonCanI-96
❑ 97DonCanIDS-96
❑ 97DonCanIPS-96
❑ 97DonLim-64
❑ 97DonLimExp-64
❑ 97DonPre-68
❑ 97DonPreCttC-68
❑ 97DonPreProG-151
❑ 97DonPreProS-151
❑ 97DonPri-75
❑ 97DonPriSoA-75
❑ 97Kat-138
❑ 97KatGol-138
❑ 97KatSil-138
❑ 97Lea-38
❑ 97LeaFraMat-38
❑ 97LeaFraMDC-38
❑ 97LeaInt-38
❑ 97LeaIntUI-38
❑ 97Pac-59
❑ 97PacCop-59
❑ 97PacEmeGre-59
❑ 97PacIceB-59
❑ 97PacInv-104
❑ 97PacInvC-104
❑ 97PacInvEG-104
❑ 97PacInvIB-104
❑ 97PacInvR-104
❑ 97PacInvS-104
❑ 97PacOme-213
❑ 97PacOmeC-213
❑ 97PacOmeDG-213
❑ 97PacOmeEG-213
❑ 97PacOmeG-213
❑ 97PacOmeIB-213
❑ 97PacPar-175
❑ 97PacParC-175
❑ 97PacParDG-175
❑ 97PacParEG-175
❑ 97PacParIB-175
❑ 97PacParRed-175
❑ 97PacParSil-175
❑ 97PacRed-59
❑ 97PacRev-130
❑ 97PacRevC-130
❑ 97PacRevE-130
❑ 97PacRevIB-130
❑ 97PacRevR-130
❑ 97PacRevS-130
❑ 97PacSil-59
❑ 97Pin-144
❑ 97PinIns-119
❑ 97PinPrePBB-144
❑ 97PinPrePBC-144
❑ 97PinPrePBM-144
❑ 97PinPrePBY-144
❑ 97PinPrePFC-144
❑ 97PinPrePFM-144
❑ 97PinPrePFY-144
❑ 97PinPrePla-144
❑ 97Sco-138
❑ 97ScoArtPro-138
❑ 97ScoGolBla-138
❑ 97Stu-49
❑ 97StuPrePG-49
❑ 97StuPrePS-49
❑ 97UppDec-119
❑ 97UppDec-361
❑ 97Zen-45
❑ 97Zen5x7-31
❑ 97ZenGolImp-31
❑ 97ZenSilImp-31
❑ 97ZenZGol-45
❑ 97ZenZSil-45
❑ 98Be A PPA-131
❑ 98Be A PPAA-131
❑ 98Be A PPAAF-131
❑ 98Be A PPTBASG-131
❑ 98Be APG-131
❑ 98Fin-87
❑ 98FinNo P-87
❑ 98FinNo PR-87
❑ 98FinRef-87
❑ 98O-PChr-16
❑ 98O-PChrR-16
❑ 98Pac-404
❑ 98PacAur-174
❑ 98PacIceB-404
❑ 98PacOmeH-178
❑ 98PacOmeODI-178
❑ 98PacOmeR-178
❑ 98PacPar-219
❑ 98PacParC-219
❑ 98PacParEG-219
❑ 98PacParH-219
❑ 98PacParIB-219
❑ 98PacParS-219
❑ 98PacRed-404
❑ 98Top-16
❑ 98TopO-P-16
❑ 98UC-197
❑ 98UD ChoPCR-197
❑ 98UD ChoR-197
❑ 98UppDec-179
❑ 98UppDecE-179
❑ 98UppDecE1o1-179
❑ 98UppDecGR-179
❑ 99Pac-311
❑ 99PacCop-311
❑ 99PacGol-311
❑ 99PacIceB-311
❑ 99PacPreD-311

**Rene, Patrice**
❑ 907thInnSQMJHL-94

**Renfrew, Brian**
❑ 92WesMic-20
❑ 93WesMic-23
❑ 95DayBom-18
❑ 97AncAce-16

**Rennette, Tyler**
❑ 97BowCHL-6
❑ 97BowCHL-131
❑ 97BowCHLAu-11
❑ 97BowCHLOPC-6
❑ 97BowCHLOPC-131

**Renney, Tommy (Tom)**
❑ 907thInnSWHL-287
❑ 917thInnSCHLAW-17
❑ 917thInnSWHL-75
❑ 92AlbIntTC-17
❑ 93AlbIntTC-16

**Rentzsch, Marco**
❑ 94GerDELE-63
❑ 95GerDELE-56
❑ 96GerDELE-253

**Renz, Andreas**
❑ 94GerDELE-438
❑ 95GerDELE-393
❑ 96GerDELE-300
❑ 98GerDELE-223

**Repnjov, Vladimir**
❑ 74SweHocS-64

**Repo, Seppo**
❑ 72SweSemWC-86
❑ 73SweHocS-38
❑ 73SweWorCS-38
❑ 74SweHocS-32
❑ 74SweSemHVS-89
❑ 76RoaPhoWHA-16
❑ 79PanSti-173

**Repp, Carl**
❑ 89ProAHL-8

**Repps, Juri**
❑ 73SweHocS-132
❑ 73SweWorCS-132

**Resare, Bjorn**
❑ 71SweHocS-386

**Resch, Chico (Glenn)**
❑ 74NHLActSta-169
❑ 74OPCNHL-353
❑ 75HerSta-17
❑ 75OPCNHL-145
❑ 75Top-145
❑ 76OPCNHL-6
❑ 76OPCNHL-250
❑ 76Top-6
❑ 76Top-250
❑ 76TopGloI-6
❑ 77OPCNHL-6
❑ 77OPCNHL-50
❑ 77Top-6
❑ 77Top-50
❑ 77TopGloS-17
❑ 77TopOPCGlo-17
❑ 78OPC-105
❑ 78Top-105
❑ 79IslTrans-17
❑ 79OPC-6
❑ 79OPC-20
❑ 79Top-6
❑ 79Top-20
❑ 80OPC-235
❑ 80Top-235
❑ 81OPC-80
❑ 81OPC-389
❑ 81OPCSti-230
❑ 81RocPos-26
❑ 81Top-W85
❑ 82OPC-145
❑ 82OPC-146
❑ 82OPCSti-222
❑ 82PosCer-11
❑ 83OPC-236
❑ 83OPCSti-222
❑ 83OPCSti-223
❑ 83PufSti-12
❑ 847EDis-32
❑ 84DevPos-1
❑ 84KelAccD-6
❑ 84OPC-119
❑ 84OPCSti-68
❑ 84OPCSti-69
❑ 84Top-89
❑ 857ECreCar-11
❑ 85DevPos-8
❑ 85OPC-36
❑ 85OPCBoxB-L
❑ 85OPCSti-61
❑ 85Top-36
❑ 85TopBoxB-L
❑ 86FlyPos-22
❑ 86OPC-158
❑ 86OPCSti-234
❑ 86Top-158
❑ 90UppDec-507
❑ 90UppDecF-507

**Ressmann, Gerald**
❑ 95AusNatTea-24

**Rettew, Scott**
❑ 84ChiSag-21

**Rettschlag, Adam**
❑ 917thInnSWHL-299

**Rettschlag, Gus**
❑ 92BriColJHL-3

**Retzer, Stephan**
❑ 94GerDELE-255
❑ 95GerDELE-253
❑ 96GerDELE-142

**Reusse, Wes**
❑ 92BriColJHL-13

**Reuta, Viktor**
❑ 93GueSto-15

**Reuter, Rene**
❑ 94GerDELE-139
❑ 95GerDELE-139

**Reuthie, Christian**
❑ 71SweHocS-400

**Revell, Dan**
❑ 80OshGen-4
❑ 81OshGen-5
❑ 82IndChe-17

**Revenberg, Jim**
❑ 89ProIHL-180
❑ 90ProAHLIHL-339

**Rexe, Steve**
❑ 69SweHocS-363

**Reynard, Ryan**
❑ 95AlaGolKin-17

**Reynolds, Bobby**
❑ 89ProAHL-126
❑ 90NewSai-18
❑ 90ProAHLIHL-152
❑ 91BalSki-4
❑ 91ProAHLCHL-552
❑ 95GerDELE-331
❑ 96GerDELE-105

**Reynolds, Peter**
❑ 98SP Aut-120
❑ 98SSASotT-PRE
❑ 98UppDec-397
❑ 98UppDecE-397
❑ 98UppDecE1o1-397
❑ 98UppDecGR-397
❑ 99SP AutPS-120

**Reynolds, Todd**
❑ 88BroBra-21

**Rezansoff, Jesse**
❑ 95SwiCurB-17

**Reznicek, Josef**
❑ 91SweSemWCS-107
❑ 95GerDELE-411
❑ 96CzeAPSE-291

**Rheaume, Dominic**
❑ 907thInnSQMJHL-232
❑ 917thInnSQMJHL-128

**Rheaume, Manon**
❑ 92Cla-59
❑ 92ClaManRCP-1
❑ 92ClaManRP-NNO
❑ 92QueIntPWG-2
❑ 93Ble23KMR-1
❑ 93Ble23KMR-2
❑ 93Ble23KMR-3
❑ 93Ble23KMR-NNO
❑ 93Cla-112
❑ 93Cla-146
❑ 93Cla-149
❑ 93Cla-150
❑ 93Cla-MR1
❑ 93Cla-AU11
❑ 93ClaCraNum-N8
❑ 93ClaDraMRP-NNO
❑ 93ClaPre-HK2
❑ 93ClaProPLP-BC10
❑ 93ClaProPLP-LP1
❑ 93ClaProPProt-PR2
❑ 93ClaProPro-1
❑ 93ClaProPro-2
❑ 93ClaProPro-3
❑ 93ClaProPro-4
❑ 93ClaProPro-5
❑ 93ClaProPro-6
❑ 93ClaProPro-7
❑ 93ClaProPro-100
❑ 93ClaProPro-AU2
❑ 93KnoChe-14
❑ 94Cla-120
❑ 94Cla-AU3
❑ 94ClaAut-NNO
❑ 94ClaDraGol-120
❑ 94ClaPic-CP15
❑ 94ClaPre-HK4
❑ 94ClaProP-129
❑ 94ClaProP-239
❑ 94ClaProP-250
❑ 94ClaProP-AU7
❑ 94ClaWomOH-W1
❑ 94ClaWomOH-W21
❑ 94LasVegThu-22
❑ 95ClaAut-NNO
❑ 95ColEdgI-155
❑ 95Ima-72
❑ 95ImaCleE-CE20
❑ 95ImaGol-72
❑ 95SweGloWC-250
❑ 96ClaGol-59
❑ 96ColEdgFL-38
❑ 99QuePeeWHWCCS-3

**Rheaume, Pascal**
❑ 917thInnSQMJHL-115
❑ 94ClaProP-129
❑ 94ClaProP-145
❑ 97Be A PPAD-227
❑ 97Be A PPAPD-227
❑ 97BeAPla-227
❑ 97BeAPlaAut-227
❑ 97Don-215
❑ 97DonLim-53
❑ 97DonLim-66
❑ 97DonLimExp-53
❑ 97DonLimExp-66
❑ 97DonPreProG-215
❑ 97DonPreProS-215
❑ 97PacOme-197
❑ 97PacOmeC-197
❑ 97PacOmeDG-197
❑ 97PacOmeEG-197
❑ 97PacOmeG-197
❑ 97PacOmeIB-197
❑ 98Pac-371
❑ 98PacIceB-371
❑ 98PacRed-371
❑ 98UppDec-175
❑ 98UppDecE-175
❑ 98UppDecE1o1-175
❑ 98UppDecGR-175
❑ 99Pac-363
❑ 99PacCop-363
❑ 99PacGol-363
❑ 99PacIceB-363
❑ 99PacPreD-363

**Rhinehart, Dwayne**
❑ 91AirCanSJHL-C46
❑ 91AirCanSJHLAS-40

**Rhiness, Brad**
❑ 76SanDieMW-10

**Rhodes, Damian**
❑ 90MicTecHus-22
❑ 90NewSai-19
❑ 90ProAHLIHL-167
❑ 91ProAHLCHL-355
❑ 92St.JohML-18
❑ 93ClaProPro-111
❑ 93Lea-367
❑ 93Par-470
❑ 93ParEmeI-470
❑ 93Pow-454
❑ 93Sco-604
❑ 93ScoCan-604
❑ 93ScoGol-604
❑ 93St.JohML-20
❑ 93Ult-435
❑ 93UppDec-364
❑ 94ClaProP-34
❑ 94MapLeaG-16
❑ 94MapLeaK-22
❑ 94MapLeaPP-11
❑ 94OPCFinIns-18
❑ 94OPCPre-269
❑ 94OPCPreSE-269
❑ 94TopPre-269
❑ 94TopPreSE-269
❑ 94UppDec-154
❑ 94UppDecEleIce-154
❑ 95Don-274
❑ 95ParInt-200
❑ 95ParInt-417
❑ 95ParIntEl-200
❑ 95ParIntEl-417
❑ 95SP-104
❑ 95UppDec-337
❑ 95UppDecEleIce-337
❑ 95UppDecEleIceG-337
❑ 96BeAPAut-202
❑ 96BeAPAutSil-202
❑ 96BeAPla-202
❑ 96ColCho-186
❑ 96ColCho-325
❑ 96Don-156
❑ 96DonCanI-16
❑ 96DonCanIGPP-16
❑ 96DonCanIRPP-16
❑ 96DonEli-113
❑ 96DonEliDCS-113
❑ 96DonPrePro-156
❑ 96Fla-64
❑ 96FlaBluI-64
❑ 96Fle-76
❑ 96Lea-47
❑ 96LeaLim-55
❑ 96LeaLimG-55
❑ 96LeaPre-109
❑ 96LeaPreP-47
❑ 96LeaPrePP-109
❑ 96LeaPreSG-50
❑ 96LeaPreSte-50
❑ 96LeaShuDow-7
❑ 96MetUni-107
❑ 96MetUniAP-9
❑ 96MetUniAPSP-9
❑ 96Pin-150
❑ 96PinArtP-150
❑ 96PinFoi-150
❑ 96PinMcD-39
❑ 96PinPreS-150
❑ 96PinRinC-150
❑ 96Sco-136
❑ 96ScoArtPro-136
❑ 96ScoDeaCAP-136
❑ 96ScoGolB-136
❑ 96ScoNetW-17
❑ 96ScoSpeAP-136
❑ 96SelCer-28
❑ 96SelCerAP-28
❑ 96SelCerBlu-28
❑ 96SelCerFre-15
❑ 96SelCerMB-28
❑ 96SelCerMG-28
❑ 96SelCerMR-28
❑ 96SelCerRed-28
❑ 96SenPizH-23
❑ 96SkyImp-90
❑ 96SP-110
❑ 96Sum-21
❑ 96SumArtP-21
❑ 96SumIce-21
❑ 96SumInTheCre-7
❑ 96SumInTheCrePS-7
❑ 96SumMet-21
❑ 96SumPreS-21
❑ 96Ult-119
❑ 96UltGolM-120
❑ 96UppDec-112
❑ 96UppDecBD-71
❑ 96UppDecBDG-71
❑ 96UppDecIce-45
❑ 96UppDecIcePar-45
❑ 96Zen-53
❑ 96ZenArtP-53
❑ 97ColCho-178
❑ 97Don-166
❑ 97DonCanI-125
❑ 97DonCanIDS-125
❑ 97DonCanIPS-125
❑ 97DonEli-42
❑ 97DonEliAsp-42
❑ 97DonEliS-42
❑ 97DonLim-57
❑ 97DonLim-186
❑ 97DonLimExp-57
❑ 97DonLimExp-186
❑ 97DonLimFOTG-60
❑ 97DonPre-37
❑ 97DonPreCG-18
❑ 97DonPreCG-P18
❑ 97DonPreCGP-18
❑ 97DonPreCGP-P18
❑ 97DonPreCttC-37
❑ 97DonPreProG-166
❑ 97DonPreProS-166
❑ 97DonPri-57
❑ 97DonPriSoA-57
❑ 97Kat-101
❑ 97KatGol-101
❑ 97KatSil-101
❑ 97Lea-45
❑ 97LeaFraMat-45
❑ 97LeaFraMDC-45
❑ 97LeaInt-45
❑ 97LeaIntUI-45
❑ 97LeaPipDre-11
❑ 97McD-30
❑ 97Pac-146
❑ 97PacCop-146
❑ 97PacDyn-86
❑ 97PacDynC-86
❑ 97PacDynDG-86
❑ 97PacDynEG-86
❑ 97PacDynIB-86
❑ 97PacDynR-86
❑ 97PacDynSil-86
❑ 97PacDynTan-69
❑ 97PacEmeGre-146
❑ 97PacIceB-146
❑ 97PacOme-157
❑ 97PacOmeC-157
❑ 97PacOmeDG-157
❑ 97PacOmeEG-157
❑ 97PacOmeG-157
❑ 97PacOmeIB-157
❑ 97PacPar-128
❑ 97PacParC-128
❑ 97PacParDG-128
❑ 97PacParEG-128
❑ 97PacParIB-128
❑ 97PacParRed-128
❑ 97PacParSil-128
❑ 97PacRed-146
❑ 97PacRev-94
❑ 97PacRevC-94
❑ 97PacRevE-94
❑ 97PacRevIB-94
❑ 97PacRevR-94
❑ 97PacRevS-94
❑ 97PacSil-146
❑ 97Pin-44
❑ 97PinArtP-44
❑ 97PinCer-20
❑ 97PinCerMB-20
❑ 97PinCerMG-20
❑ 97PinCerMR-20
❑ 97PinCerR-20
❑ 97PinIns-65
❑ 97PinInsCC-65
❑ 97PinInsEC-65
❑ 97PinPrePBB-44
❑ 97PinPrePBC-44
❑ 97PinPrePBM-44
❑ 97PinPrePBY-44
❑ 97PinPrePFC-44
❑ 97PinPrePFM-44
❑ 97PinPrePFY-44
❑ 97PinPrePla-44
❑ 97PinRinC-44
❑ 97PinTotCMPG-20
❑ 97PinTotCPB-20
❑ 97PinTotCPG-20
❑ 97PinTotCPR-20
❑ 97Sco-16
❑ 97ScoArtPro-16
❑ 97ScoGolBla-16
❑ 97ScoNetW-7
❑ 97Stu-71
❑ 97StuPrePG-71
❑ 97StuPrePS-71
❑ 97UppDec-322
❑ 98Be A PPA-96
❑ 98Be A PPAA-96
❑ 98Be A PPAAF-96
❑ 98Be A PPTBASG-96
❑ 98Be APG-96
❑ 98BowBes-54
❑ 98BowBesAR-54
❑ 98BowBesR-54
❑ 98Fin-146
❑ 98FinNo P-146
❑ 98FinNo PR-146
❑ 98FinRef-146
❑ 98LunGoaG-6
❑ 98LunGoaGS-6
❑ 98O-PChr-74
❑ 98O-PChrR-74
❑ 98Pac-1
❑ 98PacAur-133
❑ 98PacAurCF-33
❑ 98PacAurCFC-33
❑ 98PacAurCFIB-33
❑ 98PacAurCFR-33
❑ 98PacAurCFS-33
❑ 98PacCroR-95
❑ 98PacCroRLS-95
❑ 98PacDynI-130
❑ 98PacDynIIB-130
❑ 98PacDynIR-130
❑ 98PacIceB-1
❑ 98PacOmeH-168
❑ 98PacOmeODI-168
❑ 98PacOmeR-168
❑ 98PacPar-166
❑ 98PacParC-166
❑ 98PacParEG-166
❑ 98PacParGSLC-13
❑ 98PacParH-166
❑ 98PacParIB-166
❑ 98PacParS-166
❑ 98PacRed-1
❑ 98PacRev-101
❑ 98PacRevIS-101
❑ 98PacRevR-101
❑ 98Top-74
❑ 98TopGolLC1-97
❑ 98TopGolLC1B-97
❑ 98TopGolLC1BOoO-97
❑ 98TopGolLC1OoO-97
❑ 98TopGolLC1R-97
❑ 98TopGolLC1ROoO-97
❑ 98TopGolLC2-97
❑ 98TopGolLC2B-97
❑ 98TopGolLC2BOoO-97
❑ 98TopGolLC2OoO-97
❑ 98TopGolLC2R-97
❑ 98TopGolLC2ROoO-97
❑ 98TopGolLC3-97
❑ 98TopGolLC3B-97
❑ 98TopGolLC3BOoO-97
❑ 98TopGolLC3OoO-97
❑ 98TopGolLC3R-97
❑ 98TopGolLC3ROoO-97
❑ 98TopO-P-74
❑ 98UC-139
❑ 98UD ChoPCR-139
❑ 98UD ChoR-139
❑ 98UppDec-137
❑ 98UppDecE-137
❑ 98UppDecE1o1-137
❑ 98UppDecGR-137
❑ 98UppDecM-140
❑ 98UppDecMGS-140
❑ 98UppDecMSS-140
❑ 98UppDecMSS-140
❑ 99Pac-294
❑ 99PacAur-8
❑ 99PacAurPD-8
❑ 99PacCop-294
❑ 99PacGol-294
❑ 99PacIceB-294
❑ 99PacPreD-294

**Rhodin, Thomas**
❑ 90SweSemE-258
❑ 91SweSemE-87
❑ 92SweSemE-109

- 93SweSemE-82
- 94SweLeaE-15
- 95SweLeaE-41
- 95SweUppDE-60
- 98GerDELE-165

**Ribble, Jerry**
- 907thInnSOHL-45

**Ribble, Pat**
- 790PC-199
- 79Top-199
- 800PC-393
- 810PC-339

**Ribeiro, Mike**
- 97UppDec-417
- 98BowCHL-85
- 98BowCHL-132
- 98BowCHLAuB-A38
- 98BowCHLAuG-A38
- 98BowCHLAuS-A38
- 98BowCHLGA-85
- 98BowCHLGA-132
- 98BowCHLOI-85
- 98BowCHLOI-132
- 98BowChrC-85
- 98BowChrC-132
- 98BowChrCGA-85
- 98BowChrCGA-132
- 98BowChrCGAR-132
- 98BowChrCOI-85
- 98BowChrCOI-132
- 98BowChrCOIR-85
- 98BowChrCOIR-132
- 98BowChrCR-85
- 98BowChrCR-132
- 99QuePeeWHWCCS-29

**Ribiero, Mike**
- 98BowBes-143
- 98BowBesAR-143
- 98BowBesR-143

**Ricard, Eric**
- 89ProAHL-16
- 90ProAHLIHL-434
- 91ProAHLCHL-371
- 94CenHocL-31
- 98FloEve-21

**Ricci, Mike**
- 897thInnSOHL-100
- 897thInnSOHL-183
- 897thInnSOHL-190
- 90FlyPos-20
- 900PCPre-96
- 90ProSet-631
- 90Sco-433
- 90ScoCan-433
- 90ScoRoo-60T
- 90ScoYouS-39
- 90UppDec-351
- 90UppDecF-351
- 90UppDecF-355
- 91Bow-246
- 91FlyJCP-22
- 91Gil-32
- 91Kra-52
- 910PC-13
- 910PC-194
- 910PCPre-23
- 91PanSti-231
- 91PanSti-338
- 91Par-123
- 91ParFre-123
- 91Pin-32
- 91PinFre-32
- 91ProSet-170
- 91ProSetFre-170
- 91ProSetPla-85
- 91ScoAme-28
- 91ScoCan-28
- 91ScoYouS-10
- 91StaClu-386
- 91StaPicH-60
- 91Top-13
- 91Top-194
- 91UppDec-143
- 91UppDecF-143
- 92Bow-406
- 92NorPet-26
- 920PC-329
- 920PCPre-91
- 92PanSti-184
- 92PanStiFre-184
- 92Par-146
- 92ParEmel-146
- 92Pin-314
- 92PinFre-314
- 92ProSet-133
- 92Sco-84
- 92ScoCan-84
- 92StaClu-408
- 92Top-86
- 92TopGol-86G
- 92Ult-178
- 92Ult-389
- 92UppDec-477
- 92UppDec-627
- 93Don-280
- 93Kra-19
- 93KraRec-7
- 93Lea-23
- 930PCPre-62
- 930PCPreG-62
- 93PanSti-69
- 93Par-439
- 93ParEmel-439
- 93Pin-110
- 93PinCan-110
- 93PinTea2-22
- 93PinTea2C-22
- 93Pow-202
- 93Sco-120
- 93ScoCan-120
- 93StaClu-176
- 93StaCluDI-176
- 93StaCluDIO-176
- 93StaCluO-176
- 93TopPre-62
- 93TopPreG-62
- 93Ult-168
- 93UppDec-352
- 93UppDecNR-10
- 93UppDecSP-129
- 94BeAPla-R49
- 94BeAPla-R108
- 94BeAPSig-37
- 94CanGamNHLP-198
- 94Don-104
- 94Fla-150
- 94Fle-182
- 94HocWit-79
- 94Lea-240
- 94NordBurK-20
- 940PCPre-548
- 940PCPreSE-548
- 94Par-186
- 94ParGol-186
- 94Pin-280
- 94PinArtP-280
- 94PinRinC-280
- 94Sel-114
- 94SelGol-114
- 94SP-98
- 94SPDieCut-98
- 94StaClu-3
- 94StaCluFDI-3
- 94StaCluMOMS-3
- 94StaCluSTWC-3
- 94TopPre-548
- 94TopPreSE-548
- 94Ult-178
- 94UppDec-284
- 94UppDecEleIce-284
- 94UppDecSPI-SP64
- 94UppDecSPIDC-SP64
- 95CanGamNHLP-73
- 95ColCho-282
- 95ColChoPC-282
- 95ColChoPCP-282
- 95Don-120
- 95Emo-41
- 95FinnSemWC-92
- 95ImpSti-30
- 95Lea-156
- 95ParInt-318
- 95ParIntEl-318
- 95ProMag-4
- 95Sco-234
- 95ScoBlaIce-234
- 95ScoBlaIceAP-234
- 95ScoChelt-12
- 95SelCerDS-6
- 95SelCerDSG-6
- 95SkyImp-40
- 95StaClu-71
- 95StaCluMOMS-71
- 95Sum-109
- 95SumArtP-109
- 95SumIce-109
- 95Ult-135
- 95UltGolM-135
- 95UppDecEleIce-457
- 95UppDecEleIceG-457
- 95Zen-91
- 96BeAPAut-116
- 96BeAPAutSil-116
- 96BeAPla-116
- 96Don-177
- 96DonCanI-99
- 96DonCanIGPP-99
- 96DonCanIRPP-99
- 96DonPrePro-177
- 96Lea-141
- 96LeaPreP-141
- 96LeaPrePP-78
- 96NHLProSTA-4
- 96Sco-106
- 96ScoArtPro-106
- 96ScoDeaCAP-106
- 96ScoGolB-106
- 96ScoSpeAP-106
- 96SP-37
- 96Sum-70
- 96SumArtP-70
- 96SumIce-70
- 96SumMet-70
- 96SumPreS-70
- 96UppDec-36
- 96UppDecBD-109
- 96UppDecBDG-109
- 96UppDecPP-P25
- 97ColCho-61
- 97Don-180
- 97DonLim-58
- 97DonLimExp-58
- 97DonPreProG-180
- 97DonPreProS-180
- 97DonPri-107
- 97DonPriSoA-107
- 97Lea-65
- 97LeaFraMat-65
- 97LeaFraMDC-65
- 97LeaInt-65
- 97LeaIntUI-65
- 97Pac-109
- 97PacCop-109
- 97PacEmeGre-109
- 97PacIceB-109
- 97PacRed-109
- 97PacSil-109
- 97ScoAva-17
- 97ScoAvaPla-17
- 97ScoAvaPre-17
- 97SPAut-136
- 97UppDec-48
- 97UppDecBD-64
- 97UppDecBDD-64
- 97UppDecBDQD-64
- 97UppDecBDTD-64
- 98Be A PPA-270
- 98Be A PPAA-270
- 98Be A PPAAF-270
- 98Be A PPSE-270
- 98Be APG-270
- 98Fin-145
- 98FinNo P-145
- 98FinNo PR-145
- 98FinRef-145
- 98Pac-391
- 98PacIceB-391
- 98PacOmeH-213
- 98PacOmeODI-213
- 98PacOmeR-213
- 98PacRed-391
- 98UC-180
- 98UD ChoPCR-180
- 98UD ChoR-180
- 98UppDec-170
- 98UppDecE-170
- 98UppDecE1o1-170
- 98UppDecBD-170
- 98UppDecM-177
- 98UppDecMGS-177
- 98UppDecMSS-177
- 98UppDecMSS-177
- 99Pac-380
- 99PacCop-380
- 99PacIceB-380
- 99PacPreD-380
- 99UppDecM-178
- 99UppDecMGS-178
- 99UppDecMSS-178
- 99UppDecMSS-178

**Ricciardi, Jeff**
- 897thInnSOHL-61
- 907thInnSOHL-91
- 917thInnSOHL-304
- 94IndIce-19
- 95LasVegThu-11
- 98GerDELE-106

**Rice, Murray**
- 84BraWheK-10
- 85BraWheK-10

**Rice, Steven (Steve)**
- 87KitRan-16
- 88KitRan-16
- 897thInnSOHL-181
- 897thInnSOHL-187
- 89KitRan-17
- 907thInnSMC-38
- 907thInnSOHL-249
- 90KitRan-29
- 900PCPre-97
- 90ProSet-626
- 90Sco-390
- 90ScoCan-390
- 90UppDec-462
- 90UppDec-473
- 90UppDecF-462
- 90UppDecF-473
- 910ilIGA-18
- 910ilTeal-21
- 91Pin-334
- 91PinFre-334
- 91ProAHLCHL-227
- 91ScoCan-440
- 91ScoCan-440
- 91UppDec-440
- 91UppDec-441
- 91UppDecF-440
- 91UppDecF-441
- 920ilTeal-15
- 92Sco-545
- 92ScoCan-545
- 92UppDec-98
- 93ClaProPro-150
- 93Don-107
- 93Par-72
- 93ParEmel-72
- 93Pow-86
- 93StaClu-446
- 93StaCluFDI-446
- 93StaCluO-446
- 93Ult-181
- 93UppDec-367
- 94BeAPSig-49
- 94Lea-324
- 94Lea-477
- 94Pin-154
- 94PinArtP-154
- 94PinRinC-154
- 94SlaPro-5
- 94StaCluFDI-54
- 94StaCluMOMS-54
- 94StaCluSTWC-54
- 94Ult-302
- 94UppDec-294
- 94UppDecEleIce-294
- 95CanGamNHLP-128
- 95ColChoPC-218
- 95ColChoPCP-218
- 95ColEdgIC-C13
- 95Don-81
- 95Lea-198
- 95ParInt-95
- 95ParIntEl-95
- 95Pin-166
- 95PinArtP-166
- 95PinRinC-166
- 95PlaOneoOne-156
- 95Sco-167
- 95ScoBlaIce-167
- 95ScoBlaIceAP-167
- 95Top-109
- 95TopOPCI-109
- 95UppDec-210
- 95UppDecEleIce-210
- 95UppDecEleIceG-210
- 96BeAPAut-8
- 96BeAPAutSil-8
- 96BeAPla-8
- 96WhaBobS-22
- 97CarHur-23
- 97Kat-28
- 97KatGol-28
- 97KatSil-28
- 97PacDynBKS-18
- 97PacPar-38
- 97PacParC-38
- 97PacParDG-38
- 97PacParG-38
- 97PacParIB-38
- 97PacParRed-38
- 97PacParSil-38
- 97Sco-76
- 97ScoArtPro-76
- 97ScoGolBla-76
- 97UppDec-32

**Rice, Tyler**
- 91AirCanSJHLAS-34
- 91AirCanSJHLAS-49

**Rich, D.**
- 95GerDELE-325

**Richard, Chad**
- 96AncAce-12

**Richard, Henri**
- 44BeeGro2P-283
- 52JunBluT-139
- 57Par-M4
- 58Par-2
- 59Par-39
- 60Par-47
- 60Par-57
- 60ShiCoi-34
- 60YorPreP-31
- 61Par-43
- 61ShiCoi-10
- 61YorYelB-18
- 62EIProDis-6
- 62Par-38
- 62ShiMetC-41
- 62YorIroOTra-10
- 63ChePho-46
- 63Par-23
- 63Par-82
- 63TorSta-32
- 63YorWhiB-19
- 64BeeGro3P-112
- 64CanaPos-16
- 64CocCap-66
- 64Top-48
- 64TorSta-41
- 65CanaSteG-7
- 65Coc-66
- 65CocBoo-D
- 65CocBoo-71
- 66Top-8
- 66TopUSAT-8
- 67CanalGA-16
- 67PosFliB-5
- 67Top-72
- 68CanalGA-16
- 68CanaPosBW-13
- 680PC-165
- 680PCPucSti-124
- 68PosCerM-21
- 68ShiCoi-89
- 68Top-64
- 69CanaPosC-23
- 690PC-163
- 690PCFou-16
- 69Top-11
- 70CanaPin-12
- 70DadCoo-111
- 70EssPowPla-11
- 700PC-176
- 700PCDec-24
- 70SarProSta-98
- 71Baz-5
- 71CanaPos-19
- 71FriLay-4
- 71LetActR-15
- 710PC-120
- 710PCTBoo-6
- 71SarProSta-103
- 71Top-120
- 71TorSun-161
- 72CanaPos-17
- 720PC-251
- 72SarProSta-119
- 72SweSemWC-198
- 73CanaPos-18
- 730PC-87
- 73Top-87
- 74CanaPos-17
- 74NHLActSta-156
- 740PCNHL-243
- 740PCNHL-321
- 74Top-243
- 81TCMA-7
- 82CanaPos-20
- 83HalFP-G11
- 85HalFC-91
- 91Kra-88

**Richard, Jacques**
- 72Flam-17
- 720PC-279
- 730PC-169
- 73Top-169
- 740PCNHL-14
- 740PCNHL-139
- 74Top-14
- 74Top-139
- 750PCNHL-117
- 75Top-117
- 760PCNHL-8
- 76Top-8
- 770PCNHL-366
- 80NordPos-23
- 80PepCap-75
- 81NordPos-14
- 810PC-268
- 810PC-285
- 810PCSti-71
- 81Top-29
- 82NordPos-17
- 820PC-290
- 82PosCer-16
- 83NordPos-22

**Richard, Jason**
- 94JohChi-17

**Richard, Jean-Marc**
- 84ChiSag-22
- 88ProAHL-115
- 89HalCit-19
- 89ProAHL-173
- 90HalCit-20
- 90ProAHLIHL-457
- 91ProAHLCHL-243
- 93LasVegThu-21
- 94LasVegThu-23
- 98GerDELE-148

**Richard, Mike**
- 88ProAHL-44
- 89ProAHL-86
- 93SwiHNL-256
- 95SwiHNL-228

**Richard, Rocket (Maurice)**
- 34BeeGro1P-179
- 44BeeGro2P-284
- 45QuaOatP-109A
- 45QuaOatP-109B
- 45QuaOatP-109C
- 45QuaOatP-109D
- 48ExhCan-23
- 48ExhCan-24
- 48ExhCan-55
- 48ExhCan-60
- 51Par-4
- 52Par-1
- 53Par-24
- 53Par-30
- 54Par-7
- 55Par-37
- 55Par-72
- 55Par-73
- 55ParQuaO-37
- 55ParQuaO-72
- 55ParQuaO-73
- 57Par-M5
- 58Par-38
- 59Par-2
- 60Par-45
- 60WonBreL-4
- 60WonBrePP-4
- 64BeeGro3P-113
- 83HalFP-A12
- 85HalFC-1
- 91Kra-6
- 91Kra-65
- 91ProSet-337
- 91ProSetFre-337
- 92HalFL-3
- 92Sco-548C
- 92Sco-549C
- 92ScoCan-548C
- 92ScoCan-549C
- 92ScoCanO-NNO1
- 92ScoCanO-NNO2
- 92ScoCanO-AU
- 92SpoFla-9
- 92ZelMasH-6
- 92ZelMasoHS-6
- 93AmeLicSPC-5
- 930PCCanHF-6
- 930PCCanHF-29
- 930PCCanHF-59
- 930PCCanP-1
- 93ParChePH-D16
- 93ParParR-PR36
- 93ParParR-PR48
- 93ParParR-PR63
- 93ParParRCI-5
- 94HocWit-16
- 94ParMisL-66
- 94ParMisL-65
- 94ParMisL-139
- 94ParMisLA-2
- 94ParTalBG-5
- 95Par66-58
- 95Par66Coi-58
- 95SigRooCF-CF4
- 95SigRooCFS-CF5
- 97PinBee-61
- 97PinBeeGOA-61
- 97PinBeeGP-61
- 99RetHoc-84
- 99UppDecCL-5
- 99UppDecLACT-AC8
- 99UppDecLCLC-5
- 99UppDecEotG-E6
- 99UppDecES-7
- 99UppDecRDR-DR14
- 99UppDecRDRI-DR14
- 99UppDecRG-G6A
- 99UppDecRG-84
- 99UppDecRGI-G6A
- 99UppDecRII-MAR
- 99UppDecRIL1-MAR
- 99UppDecRP-84

**Richard, Rodney**
- 98BowCHL-13
- 98BowCHLGA-13
- 98BowCHLOI-13
- 98BowChrC-13
- 98BowChrCGA-13
- 98BowChrCGAR-13
- 98BowChrCOI-13
- 98BowChrCOIR-13
- 98BowChrCR-13

**Richard, Serge**
- 84RicRiv-14

**Richards, Brad**
- 97RimOce-39
- 97UppDec-418
- 98BowCHL-116
- 98BowCHLGA-116
- 98BowCHLOI-116
- 98BowChrC-116
- 98BowChrCGA-116
- 98BowChrCGAR-116
- 98BowChrCOI-116
- 98BowChrCOIR-116
- 98BowChrCR-116

**Richards, Mark**
- 92TolSto-25
- 95TalTigS-17
- 95TalTigS-21

**Richards, Steve**
- 95HamRoaA-15

**Richards, Todd**
- 89ProAHL-183
- 91UppDec-430
- 91UppDecF-430
- 92Top-79
- 92TopGol-79G
- 93LasVegThu-22
- 94LasVegThu-24
- 95ColEdgI-175

**Richards, Travis**
- 91MinGolG-22
- 92MinGolG-18
- 93Cla-74
- 93Pow-513
- 93TopPreTUSA-7
- 94ClaAut-NNO
- 95Ima-92
- 95ImaGol-92
- 96GraRapG-21

**Richardson, Bill**
- 51LavDaiS-113
- 52St.LawS-68

**Richardson, Bryan**
- 93RenEng-25
- 96DayBom-15

**Richardson, Dave**
- 62SudWol-19
- 94ParTalB-94

**Richardson, George**
- 83HalFP-F11
- 85HalFC-85

**Richardson, Glen**
- 75HamFin-15

**Richardson, Ken**
- 917thInnSWHL-230
- 93RedDeer-21

**Richardson, Luke**
- 87MapLeaP-16
- 87MapLeaPLA-27
- 87MapLeaPO-16
- 880PC-245
- 880PCSti-173
- 88PanSti-119
- 89PanSti-142
- 900PC-428
- 90ProSet-289
- 90Sco-236
- 90ScoCan-236
- 90UppDec-362
- 90UppDecF-362
- 91Bow-167
- 91MapLeaPTS-23
- 910ilIGA-19
- 910ilTeal-22
- 910PC-351
- 910PCPre-46
- 91Par-274
- 91ParFre-274
- 91Pin-212
- 91PinFre-212
- 91ProSet-387
- 91ProSetFre-387
- 91ScoAme-139
- 91ScoCan-139
- 91ScoCan-620
- 91ScoRoo-70T
- 91StaClu-172
- 91Top-351
- 91UppDec-418
- 91UppDec-522
- 91UppDecF-418
- 91UppDecF-522
- 92Bow-255
- 920ilIGA-19
- 920ilTeal-16
- 920PC-171
- 92Pin-41
- 92PinFre-41
- 92PinFre-235
- 92Sco-62
- 92ScoCan-62
- 92StaClu-456
- 92Top-409
- 92TopGol-409G
- 92Ult-297
- 93Don-115
- 93Pin-139
- 93PinCan-139
- 93Sco-252
- 93ScoCan-252
- 93Ult-318
- 94CanGamNHLP-338
- 940PCPre-466
- 940PCPreSE-466
- 94Pin-431
- 94PinArtP-431
- 94PinRinC-431
- 94TopPre-466
- 94TopPreSE-466
- 94UppDec-215
- 94UppDecEleIce-215
- 95BeAPla-70
- 95BeAPSig-S70
- 95BeAPSigDC-S70
- 95Top-108
- 95TopOPCI-108
- 96OilPos-22
- 96UppDec-61
- 97ColCho-96
- 97PacInvNRB-82
- 97ScoFly-10
- 97ScoFlyPla-10
- 97ScoFlyPre-10
- 97UppDec-330
- 98Be A PPA-103
- 98Be A PPAA-103
- 98Be A PPAAF-103
- 98Be A PPTBASG-103
- 980-PChr-159
- 980-PChrR-159
- 98Top-159
- 98TopO-P-159

**Richardson, Terry**
- 790PC-77

**Richer, Antoine**
- 93SweSemWCS-266
- 94FinnJaaK-224
- 94FreNatT-28
- 95FinnSemWC-200
- 95SweGloWC-207
- 96SweSemW-187

**Richer, Stephane JG**
- 88ProAHL-296
- 89ProAHLIHL-195
- 90ProAHLIHL-354
- 91ProAHLCHL-86
- 95GerDELE-270
- 96GerDELE-165
- 98GerDELE-228

**Richer, Stephane JJ**
❑ 84ChiSag-23
❑ 85CanaPos-27
❑ 85CanaPro-16
❑ 86CanaPos-18
❑ 86KraDra-58
❑ 87CanaPos-23A
❑ 87CanaPos-23B
❑ 87CanaVacS-51
❑ 87CanaVacS-52
❑ 87CanaVacS-54
❑ 87OPC-233
❑ 87PanSti-65
❑ 88CanaPos-22
❑ 88FriLayS-40
❑ 88OPC-5
❑ 88OPCMin-31
❑ 88OPCSti-49
❑ 88PanSti-260
❑ 88Top-5
❑ 89CanaKra-18
❑ 89CanaPos-26
❑ 89CanaProF-44
❑ 89Kra-24
❑ 89OPC-153
❑ 89OPCSti-51
❑ 89PanSti-239
❑ 89Top-153
❑ 90Bow-45
❑ 90BowHatTri-11
❑ 90BowTif-45
❑ 90CanaPos-24
❑ 90Kra-46
❑ 90Kra-89
❑ 90OPC-186
❑ 90OPCPre-98
❑ 90PanSti-53
❑ 90ProSet-156
❑ 90ProSet-370
❑ 90Sco-75
❑ 90ScoCan-75
❑ 90ScoHotRS-38
❑ 90Top-186
❑ 90TopTeaSL-4
❑ 90TopTif-186
❑ 90UppDec-276
❑ 90UppDecF-276
❑ 91Bow-330
❑ 91CanaPanTS-18
❑ 91Kra-21
❑ 91OPC-298
❑ 91OPC-369
❑ 91OPCPre-113
❑ 91PanSti-193
❑ 91Par-100
❑ 91ParFre-100
❑ 91Pin-14
❑ 91PinFre-14
❑ 91ProSet-122
❑ 91ProSet-420
❑ 91ProSetFre-122
❑ 91ProSetFre-420
❑ 91ProSetPla-67
❑ 91ScoAme-234
❑ 91ScoCan-581
❑ 91ScoRoo-31T
❑ 91StaClu-86
❑ 91Top-369
❑ 91UppDec-244
❑ 91UppDec-536
❑ 91UppDecF-244
❑ 91UppDecF-536
❑ 92Bow-46
❑ 92DurPan-18
❑ 92OPC-76
❑ 92OPCPreSP-18
❑ 92PanSti-173
❑ 92PanStiFre-173
❑ 92Par-91
❑ 92ParEmel-91
❑ 92Pin-361
❑ 92PinFre-361
❑ 92ProSet-93
❑ 92Sco-140
❑ 92ScoCan-140
❑ 92StaClu-9
❑ 92Top-160
❑ 92TopGol-160G
❑ 92Ult-117
❑ 92UppDec-56
❑ 93Don-190
❑ 93DurSco-48
❑ 93Lea-138
❑ 93OPCPre-158
❑ 93OPCPre-327
❑ 93OPCPreG-158
❑ 93OPCPreG-327
❑ 93PanSti-37
❑ 93Par-113
❑ 93ParEmel-113
❑ 93Pin-143
❑ 93PinCan-143
❑ 93Pow-141
❑ 93Sco-34
❑ 93ScoCan-34
❑ 93StaClu-61
❑ 93StaClu-347
❑ 93StaCluFDI-61
❑ 93StaCluFDI-347
❑ 93StaCluFDIO-61
❑ 93StaCluO-61
❑ 93StaCluO-347
❑ 93TopPre-158
❑ 93TopPre-327
❑ 93TopPreG-158
❑ 93TopPreG-327
❑ 93Ult-152
❑ 93UppDec-403
❑ 93UppDecSP-87
❑ 94CanGamNHLP-148
❑ 94Don-79
❑ 94EASpo-76
❑ 94Fin-94
❑ 94FinDivFCC-10
❑ 94FinRef-94
❑ 94FinSupTW-94
❑ 94Fla-97
❑ 94Fle-116
❑ 94FleSlaA-7
❑ 94Lea-24
❑ 94OPCPre-105
❑ 94OPCPreSE-105
❑ 94ParSE-SE100
❑ 94ParSEG-SE100
❑ 94ParVin-V50
❑ 94Pin-166
❑ 94PinArtP-166
❑ 94PinBoo-BR14
❑ 94PinRinC-166
❑ 94Sel-108
❑ 94SelGol-108
❑ 94SelPro-108
❑ 94SP-64
❑ 94SPDieCut-64
❑ 94TopPre-105
❑ 94TopPreSE-105
❑ 94Ult-122
❑ 94UppDec-388
❑ 94UppDecEleIce-388
❑ 94UppDecSPI-SP44
❑ 94UppDecSPIDC-SP44
❑ 95Bow-14
❑ 95BowAllFoi-14
❑ 95CanGamNHLP-163
❑ 95ColCho-250
❑ 95ColChoPC-250
❑ 95ColChoPCP-250
❑ 95Don-178
❑ 95Emo-101
❑ 95ImpSti-69
❑ 95Kra-71
❑ 95Lea-91
❑ 95LeaLim-68
❑ 95Met-85
❑ 95ParInt-118
❑ 95ParIntEl-118
❑ 95Pin-35
❑ 95PinArtP-35
❑ 95PinRinC-35
❑ 95PlaOneoOne-60
❑ 95ProMag-39
❑ 95Sco-130
❑ 95ScoBlaIce-130
❑ 95ScoBlaIceAP-130
❑ 95ScoGolBla-14
❑ 95SelCer-39
❑ 95SelCerMG-39
❑ 95SkyImp-96
❑ 95SP-85
❑ 95StaClu-176
❑ 95StaCluMOMS-176
❑ 95StaCluPS-PS10
❑ 95Sum-52
❑ 95SumArtP-52
❑ 95SumIce-52
❑ 95Top-231
❑ 95TopHomGC-HGC28
❑ 95TopOPCI-231
❑ 95TopSupSki-41
❑ 95TopSupSkiPla-41
❑ 95Ult-91
❑ 95Ult-195
❑ 95UltGolM-91
❑ 95UltGolM-195
❑ 95UppDec-426
❑ 95UppDecEleIce-426
❑ 95UppDecEleIceG-426
❑ 95UppDecSpeE-SE47
❑ 95UppDecSpeEdiG-SE47
❑ 95Zen-39
❑ 96BeAPAut-50
❑ 96BeAPAutSil-50
❑ 96BeAPla-50
❑ 96CanaPos-22
❑ 96CanaShe-16
❑ 96Don-108
❑ 96DonCanI-98
❑ 96DonCanIGPP-98
❑ 96DonCanIRPP-98
❑ 96DonEli-36
❑ 96DonEliDCS-36
❑ 96DonPrePro-108
❑ 96FlePic-128
❑ 96Lea-18
❑ 96LeaPre-76
❑ 96LeaPreP-18
❑ 96LeaPrePP-76
❑ 96MetUni-82
❑ 96NHLProSTA-39
❑ 96Pin-33
❑ 96PinArtP-33
❑ 96PinFoi-33
❑ 96PinPreS-33
❑ 96PinRinC-33
❑ 96PlaOneoOne-342
❑ 96Sco-232
❑ 96ScoArtPro-232
❑ 96ScoDeaCAP-232
❑ 96ScoGolB-232
❑ 96ScoSpeAP-232
❑ 96SP-83
❑ 96Sum-99
❑ 96SumArtP-99
❑ 96SumIce-99
❑ 96SumMet-99
❑ 96SumPreS-99
❑ 96TeaOut-35
❑ 96Ult-89
❑ 96UltGolM-90
❑ 96UppDec-94
❑ 96Zen-42
❑ 96ZenArtP-42
❑ 97CanaPos-17
❑ 97ColCho-138
❑ 97DonCanI-104
❑ 97DonCanIDS-104
❑ 97DonCanIPS-104
❑ 97Pac-44
❑ 97PacCop-44
❑ 97PacCroR-72
❑ 97PacCroREG-72
❑ 97PacCroRIB-72
❑ 97PacCroRS-72
❑ 97PacDyn-65
❑ 97PacDynBKS-50
❑ 97PacDynC-65
❑ 97PacDynDG-65
❑ 97PacDynEG-65
❑ 97PacDynIB-65
❑ 97PacDynR-65
❑ 97PacDynSil-65
❑ 97PacDynTan-48
❑ 97PacEmeGre-44
❑ 97PacIceB-44
❑ 97PacInv-73
❑ 97PacInvC-73
❑ 97PacInvEG-73
❑ 97PacInvIB-73
❑ 97PacInvNRB-105
❑ 97PacInvR-73
❑ 97PacInvS-73
❑ 97PacPar-98
❑ 97PacParC-98
❑ 97PacParDG-98
❑ 97PacParEG-98
❑ 97PacParIB-98
❑ 97PacParRed-98
❑ 97PacParSil-98
❑ 97PacRed-44
❑ 97PacSil-44
❑ 97PacSlaSDC-4C
❑ 97PacTeaCCC-13
❑ 97Pin-160
❑ 97PinPrePBB-160
❑ 97PinPrePBC-160
❑ 97PinPrePBM-160
❑ 97PinPrePBY-160
❑ 97PinPrePFC-160
❑ 97PinPrePFM-160
❑ 97PinPrePFY-160
❑ 97PinPrePla-160
❑ 97Sco-213
❑ 97ScoCan-8
❑ 97ScoCanPla-8
❑ 98Be A PPA-133
❑ 98Be A PPAA-133
❑ 98Be A PPAAF-133
❑ 98Be A PPTBASG-133
❑ 98Be APG-133
❑ 98Pac-405
❑ 98PacAur-175
❑ 98PacCroR-126
❑ 98PacCroRLS-126
❑ 98PacDynI-174
❑ 98PacDynIIB-174
❑ 98PacDynIR-174
❑ 98PacIceB-405
❑ 98PacOmeH-221
❑ 98PacOmeODI-221
❑ 98PacOmeR-221
❑ 98PacPar-220
❑ 98PacParC-220
❑ 98PacParEG-220
❑ 98PacParH-220
❑ 98PacParIB-220
❑ 98PacParS-220
❑ 98PacRed-405
❑ 98PacRev-134
❑ 98PacRevIS-134
❑ 98PacRevR-134
❑ 98ScoCanPre-8
❑ 98SPxFin-78
❑ 98SPxFinR-78
❑ 98SPxFinS-78
❑ 98UC-193
❑ 98UD ChoPCR-193
❑ 98UD ChoR-193
❑ 98UDCP-193
❑ 98UppDec-183
❑ 98UppDecE-183
❑ 98UppDecE1o1-183
❑ 98UppDecGR-183
❑ 99Pac-394
❑ 99PacCop-394
❑ 99PacIceB-394
❑ 99PacPreD-394

**Richey, Steve**
❑ 81KinCan-22
❑ 82KinCan-23

**Richison, Grant**
❑ 89ProAHL-46
❑ 90MonHaw-20
❑ 90ProAHLIHL-255
❑ 91ProAHLCHL-244
❑ 98KanCitB-19

**Richmond, Steve**
❑ 86OPC-208
❑ 88ProAHL-218

**Richter, Barry**
❑ 93Cla-75
❑ 93ClaPre-HK3
❑ 93Pow-514
❑ 93StaCluTUSA-19
❑ 93TopPreTUSA-18
❑ 93Ult-494
❑ 94BinRan-17
❑ 94ClaAut-NNO
❑ 95BinRan-20
❑ 96ColEdgFL-39
❑ 96TopNHLP-177
❑ 96TopPicOI-177
❑ 96UppDec-219
❑ 99Pac-264
❑ 99PacCop-264
❑ 99PacGol-264
❑ 99PacIceB-264
❑ 99PacPreD-264

**Richter, Dave**
❑ 83NorStaPos-24
❑ 84NorStaPos-23
❑ 86Canu-17
❑ 87BluTeaIss-19
❑ 87CanuSheOil-15
❑ 87OPC-261
❑ 87OPCSti-190
❑ 87PanSti-344
❑ 88BluKod-5
❑ 88BluTeaIss-19
❑ 90ProAHLIHL-522

**Richter, Mike**
❑ 89ProIHL-48
❑ 89RanMarMB-35
❑ 90Bow-218
❑ 90BowTif-218
❑ 90OPC-330
❑ 90PanSti-98
❑ 90PanSti-345
❑ 90ProSet-398
❑ 90ProSet-627
❑ 90Sco-74
❑ 90ScoCan-74
❑ 90ScoYouS-27
❑ 90Top-330
❑ 90TopTif-330
❑ 90UppDec-32
❑ 90UppDecF-32
❑ 91Bow-70
❑ 91Gil-39
❑ 91Kra-88
❑ 91OPC-11
❑ 91OPC-91
❑ 91OPCPre-78
❑ 91PanSti-290
❑ 91Par-117
❑ 91ParFre-117
❑ 91Pin-164
❑ 91Pin-384
❑ 91PinFre-164
❑ 91PinFre-384
❑ 91ProSet-161
❑ 91ProSetFre-161
❑ 91ProSetNHLAS-AC2
❑ 91ProSetPla-83
❑ 91ProSetPla-279
❑ 91ScoAme-120
❑ 91ScoCan-120
❑ 91ScoYouS-2
❑ 91StaClu-2
❑ 91SweSemWCS-128
❑ 91Top-11
❑ 91Top-91
❑ 91UppDec-34
❑ 91UppDec-175
❑ 91UppDec-610
❑ 91UppDec-634
❑ 91UppDecF-34
❑ 91UppDecF-175
❑ 91UppDecF-610
❑ 91UppDecF-634
❑ 92Bow-238
❑ 92Bow-354
❑ 92McDUppD-25
❑ 92OPC-259
❑ 92PanSti-231
❑ 92PanStiFre-231
❑ 92Par-112
❑ 92ParEmel-112
❑ 92Pin-75
❑ 92Pin-270
❑ 92PinFre-75
❑ 92PinFre-270
❑ 92PinTeaP-1
❑ 92PinTeaPF-1
❑ 92ProSet-116
❑ 92Sco-5
❑ 92ScoCan-5
❑ 92ScoCanPS-2
❑ 92ScoUSAG-6
❑ 92ScoYouS-9
❑ 92SeaPat-29
❑ 92StaClu-242
❑ 92StaClu-266
❑ 92Top-367
❑ 92TopGol-367G
❑ 92Ult-142
❑ 92UppDec-34
❑ 92UppDec-145
❑ 93Don-223
❑ 93Lea-185
❑ 93OPCPre-135
❑ 93OPCPreG-135
❑ 93PanSti-99
❑ 93Par-129
❑ 93Par-132
❑ 93ParEmel-129
❑ 93ParEmel-132
❑ 93Pin-242
❑ 93PinCan-242
❑ 93Pow-165
❑ 93Sco-99
❑ 93ScoCan-99
❑ 93StaClu-64
❑ 93StaCluFDI-64
❑ 93StaCluFDIO-64
❑ 93StaCluO-64
❑ 93SweSemWCS-170
❑ 93TopPre-135
❑ 93TopPreG-135
❑ 93Ult-228
❑ 93UppDec-42
❑ 94CanGamNHLP-288
❑ 94CanGamNHLP-337
❑ 94Don-165
❑ 94DonMasM-8
❑ 94EASpo-90
❑ 94Fin-86
❑ 94FinBowB-B13
❑ 94FinBowBR-B13
❑ 94FinDivFCC-6
❑ 94FinnJaaK-107
❑ 94FinRef-86
❑ 94FinSupTW-86
❑ 94Fla-117
❑ 94Fle-139
❑ 94FleNet-8
❑ 94HocWit-1
❑ 94KenStaLA-16
❑ 94KenStaLC-10
❑ 94Kra-52
❑ 94Lea-18
❑ 94LeaCreP-8
❑ 94LeaGolS-3
❑ 94LeaLim-17
❑ 94McDUppD-NNO
❑ 94OPCPre-70
❑ 94OPCPre-155
❑ 94OPCPre-314
❑ 94OPCPreSE-70
❑ 94OPCPreSE-155
❑ 94OPCPreSE-314
❑ 94ParSE-SE110
❑ 94ParSEG-SE110
❑ 94ParVin-V5
❑ 94Pin-10
❑ 94PinArtP-10
❑ 94PinGoaG-GT2
❑ 94PinRinC-10
❑ 94PinTeaP-TP2
❑ 94PinTeaPDP-TP2
❑ 94Sco-130
❑ 94ScoGol-130
❑ 94ScoPla-130
❑ 94ScoPlaTS-130
❑ 94Sel-133
❑ 94SelFirLin-7
❑ 94SelGol-133
❑ 94SP-75
❑ 94SPDieCut-75
❑ 94StaClu-181
❑ 94StaCluFDI-181
❑ 94StaCluMO-45
❑ 94StaCluMOMS-181
❑ 94StaCluST-15
❑ 94StaCluSTWC-181
❑ 94TopPre-70
❑ 94TopPre-155
❑ 94TopPre-314
❑ 94TopPreSE-70
❑ 94TopPreSE-155
❑ 94TopPreSE-314
❑ 94Ult-143
❑ 94UltPrePM-5
❑ 94UppDec-78
❑ 94UppDecEleIce-78
❑ 94UppDecPH-H30
❑ 94UppDecPHEG-H30
❑ 94UppDecPHES-H30
❑ 94UppDecPHG-H30
❑ 94UppDecSPI-SP52
❑ 94UppDecSPIDC-SP52
❑ 95BeAPla-191
❑ 95BeAPSig-S191
❑ 95BeAPSigDC-S191
❑ 95CanGamNHLP-189
❑ 95ColCho-306
❑ 95ColChoPC-306
❑ 95ColChoPCP-306
❑ 95Don-59
❑ 95Emo-117
❑ 95Fin-169
❑ 95FinnSemWC-218
❑ 95FinRef-169
❑ 95ImpSti-83
❑ 95Kra-22
❑ 95Lea-42
❑ 95Met-98
❑ 95ParInt-138
❑ 95ParIntEl-138
❑ 95ParIntGP-12
❑ 95ParIntPTP-PP31
❑ 95Pin-47
❑ 95PinArtP-47
❑ 95PinRinC-47
❑ 95PlaOneoOne-69
❑ 95ProMag-99
❑ 95Sco-140
❑ 95Sco-321
❑ 95ScoBlaIce-140
❑ 95ScoBlaIce-321
❑ 95ScoBlaIceAP-140
❑ 95ScoBlaIceAP-321
❑ 95SelCer-73
❑ 95SelCerMG-73
❑ 95SkyImp-112
❑ 95SP-95
❑ 95StaClu-49
❑ 95StaCluMOMS-49
❑ 95StaCluNem-N4
❑ 95Sum-115
❑ 95SumArtP-115
❑ 95SumIce-115
❑ 95SumInTheCre-11
❑ 95SweGloWC-100
❑ 95Top-212
❑ 95TopHomGUSA-HGA10
❑ 95TopOPCI-212
❑ 95TopSupSki-74
❑ 95TopSupSkiPla-74
❑ 95Ult-276
❑ 95UppDec-438
❑ 95UppDecEleIce-438
❑ 95UppDecEleIceG-438
❑ 95UppDecPHE-H12
❑ 95UppDecSpeE-SE58
❑ 95UppDecSpeEdiG-SE58
❑ 95UppPreHV-H12
❑ 95Zen-53
❑ 96BeAPStaTP-10
❑ 96ColCho-167
❑ 96ColCho-324
❑ 96Don-184
❑ 96DonCanI-26
❑ 96DonCanIGPP-26
❑ 96DonCanIRPP-26
❑ 96DonEli-96
❑ 96DonEliDCS-96
❑ 96DonEliPW-2
❑ 96DonEliPW-P2
❑ 96DonPrePro-184
❑ 96Fla-62
❑ 96FlaBluI-62
❑ 96FlaHotG-9
❑ 96FlePic-84
❑ 96FlePicDL-2
❑ 96KraUppD-52
❑ 96Lea-178
❑ 96LeaLim-41
❑ 96LeaLimG-41
❑ 96LeaPre-55
❑ 96LeaPreMM-11
❑ 96LeaPreP-178
❑ 96LeaPrePP-55
❑ 96LeaPreSG-46
❑ 96LeaPreSte-46
❑ 96LeaShuDow-11
❑ 96MetUni-100
❑ 96MetUniAP-10
❑ 96MetUniAPSP-10
❑ 96NHLProSTA-99
❑ 96Pin-112
❑ 96PinArtP-112
❑ 96PinFan-FC10
❑ 96PinFoi-112
❑ 96PinMas-9
❑ 96PinMasDC-9
❑ 96PinPreS-112
❑ 96PinRinC-112
❑ 96Sco-150
❑ 96ScoArtPro-150
❑ 96ScoDeaCAP-150
❑ 96ScoGolB-150
❑ 96ScoSpeAP-150
❑ 96ScoSudDea-9
❑ 96ScoSup-12
❑ 96SelCer-39
❑ 96SelCerAP-39
❑ 96SelCerBlu-39
❑ 96SelCerFre-11
❑ 96SelCerMB-39
❑ 96SelCerMG-39
❑ 96SelCerMR-39
❑ 96SelCerRed-39
❑ 96SkyImp-83
❑ 96SP-100
❑ 96SPHolCol-HC27
❑ 96SPSPxFor-3
❑ 96SPx-28
❑ 96SPxGol-28
❑ 96Sum-145
❑ 96SumArtP-145
❑ 96SumIce-145
❑ 96SumInTheCre-2
❑ 96SumInTheCrePS-2
❑ 96SumMet-145
❑ 96SumPreS-145
❑ 96SweSemW-158
❑ 96TeaOut-62
❑ 96TopPicID-ID13
❑ 96Ult-110
❑ 96UltGolM-111
❑ 96UppDec-109
❑ 96UppDecBD-35
❑ 96UppDecBDG-35
❑ 96UppDecIce-41
❑ 96UppDecIcePar-41
❑ 96Zen-66
❑ 96ZenArtP-66
❑ 96ZenChaS-14
❑ 96ZenChaSD-14
❑ 97Be A PPAD-37
❑ 97Be A PPAPD-37
❑ 97BeAPla-37
❑ 97BeAPlaAut-37
❑ 97BeAPlaSTP-10
❑ 97ColCho-161
❑ 97ColChoSta-SQ30
❑ 97Don-124
❑ 97DonCanI-107
❑ 97DonCanIDS-107
❑ 97DonCanIPS-107
❑ 97DonCanISCS-15
❑ 97DonEli-56
❑ 97DonEliAsp-56
❑ 97DonEliS-56
❑ 97DonLim-32
❑ 97DonLim-134
❑ 97DonLimExp-32
❑ 97DonLimExp-134
❑ 97DonLimFOTG-11
❑ 97DonPre-124
❑ 97DonPreCG-15
❑ 97DonPreCGP-15
❑ 97DonPreCttC-124
❑ 97DonPreProG-124
❑ 97DonPreProS-124
❑ 97DonPri-143
❑ 97DonPriPG-5
❑ 97DonPriPGP-5
❑ 97DonPriSoA-143
❑ 97EssOlyHH-33
❑ 97EssOlyHHF-33
❑ 97Kat-95
❑ 97KatGol-95
❑ 97KatSil-95
❑ 97Lea-70
❑ 97LeaFraMat-70
❑ 97LeaFraMDC-70
❑ 97LeaInt-70
❑ 97LeaIntUI-70
❑ 97LeaPipDre-8
❑ 97McD-29
❑ 97Pac-197
❑ 97PacCop-197
❑ 97PacCroR-87
❑ 97PacCroREG-87
❑ 97PacCroRFODC-12
❑ 97PacCroRIB-87
❑ 97PacCroRS-87
❑ 97PacDyn-82
❑ 97PacDynC-82
❑ 97PacDynDG-82
❑ 97PacDynEG-82
❑ 97PacDynIB-82
❑ 97PacDynR-82
❑ 97PacDynSil-82
❑ 97PacDynSto-14
❑ 97PacDynTan-70
❑ 97PacEmeGre-197
❑ 97PacIceB-197
❑ 97PacInTheCLC-13
❑ 97PacInv-90
❑ 97PacInvC-90
❑ 97PacInvEG-90
❑ 97PacInvIB-90
❑ 97PacInvR-90
❑ 97PacInvS-90
❑ 97PacOme-148
❑ 97PacOmeC-148
❑ 97PacOmeDG-148
❑ 97PacOmeEG-148
❑ 97PacOmeG-148
❑ 97PacOmeIB-148
❑ 97PacOmeNSZ-8
❑ 97PacPar-119
❑ 97PacParC-119
❑ 97PacParDG-119
❑ 97PacParEG-119
❑ 97PacParGSL-13
❑ 97PacParIB-119
❑ 97PacParRed-119
❑ 97PacParSil-119
❑ 97PacRed-197
❑ 97PacRev-90
❑ 97PacRevC-90
❑ 97PacRevE-90
❑ 97PacRevIB-90
❑ 97PacRevR-90
❑ 97PacRevRtSD-13
❑ 97PacRevS-90
❑ 97PacSil-197
❑ 97Pin-55
❑ 97PinArtP-55
❑ 97PinBee-41
❑ 97PinBeeGP-41
❑ 97PinCer-13
❑ 97PinCerMB-13
❑ 97PinCerMG-13
❑ 97PinCerMR-13
❑ 97PinCerR-13
❑ 97PinIns-81
❑ 97PinInsC-22
❑ 97PinInsCC-81
❑ 97PinInsCG-22
❑ 97PinInsEC-81
❑ 97PinInsSto-5
❑ 97PinInsT-26
❑ 97PinMas-2
❑ 97PinMasDC-2
❑ 97PinMasJ-2
❑ 97PinMasPro-2
❑ 97PinPrePBB-55
❑ 97PinPrePBC-55
❑ 97PinPrePBM-55
❑ 97PinPrePBY-55
❑ 97PinPrePFC-55

97PinPrePFM-55
97PinPrePFY-55
97PinPrePla-55
97PinRepMas-4
97PinRinC-55
97PinTin-7
97PinTotCMPG-13
97PinTotCPB-13
97PinTotCPG-13
97PinTotCPR-13
97Sco-11
97ScoArtPro-11
97ScoGolBla-11
97ScoNetW-6
97ScoRan-16
97ScoRanPla-16
97ScoRanPre-16
97SPxAut-101
97SPx-31
97SPxBro-31
97SPxGol-31
97SPxGraF-31
97SPxSil-31
97SPxSte-31
97Stu-59
97StuPor-33
97StuPrePG-59
97StuPrePS-59
97UppDec-107
97UppDecBD-4
97UppDecBDDD-4
97UppDecBDQD-4
97UppDecBDTD-4
97UppDecGDM-107
97UppDecGJ-GJ11
97UppDecIce-3
97UppDecIceP-3
97UppDecIPS-3
97UppDecSG-SG53
97UppDecTSS-10C
97Zen-18
97Zen5x7-63
97ZenGolImp-63
97ZenSillmp-63
97ZenZSil-18
98Be A PPA-89
98Be A PPAA-89
98Be A PPAAF-89
98Be A PPPH-H6
98Be A PPTBASG-89
98Bow APG-89
98BowBes-43
98BowBesAR-43
98BowBesR-43
98Fin-89
98FinNo P-89
98FinNo PR-89
98FinRef-89
98LunGoaG-7
98LunGoaGS-7
98McDGreT-T8
98O-PChr-200
98O-PChrR-200
98Pac-298
98PacAur-125
98PacAurCF-31
98PacAurCFC-31
98PacAurCFB-31
98PacAurCFR-31
98PacAurCFS-31
98PacCroR-91
98PacCroRLS-91
98PacDynI-125
98PacDynIIB-125
98PacDynIIW-6
98PacDynIR-125
98PacIceB-298
98PacOmeH-161
98PacOmeODI-161
98PacOmeR-161
98PacPar-156
98PacParC-156
98PacParEG-156
98PacParGSLC-12
98PacParH-156
98PacParIB-156
98PacParS-156
98PacRed-298
98PacRev-97
98PacRevIS-97
98PacRevR-97
98RanPowP-NYR4
98RevThrPA-16
98RevThrPH-16
98SP Aut-55
98SPXTopPPS-PS7
98SPXTopPWM-MR
98Top-200
98TopGolLC1-54
98TopGolLC1B-54
98TopGolLC1B0o0-54
98TopGolLC1O0o0-54
98TopGolLC1R-54
98TopGolLC1R0o0-54
98TopGolLC2-54
98TopGolLC2B-54
98TopGolLC2B0o0-54
98TopGolLC2O0o0-54
98TopGolLC2R-54
98TopGolLC2R0o0-54
98TopGolLC3-54
98TopGolLC3B-54
98TopGolLC3o0o0-54

98TopGolLC3R-54
98TopGolLC3R0o0-54
98TopO-P-200
98UC-135
98UC-246
98UD ChoPCR-135
98UD ChoPCR-246
98UD ChoR-135
98UD ChoR-246
98UDCP-135
98UppDec-324
98UppDecBD-58
98UppDecDD-58
98UppDecE-324
98UppDecE1o1-324
98UppDecGR-324
98UppDecM-135
98UppDecMGS-135
98UppDecMSS-135
98UppDecMSS-135
98UppDecQD-58
98UppDecTD-58
99Pac-278
99PacAur-97
99PacAurGU-13
99PacAurPD-97
99PacCop-278
99PacGol-278
99PacGolCD-23
99PacHomaA-17
99PacIceB-278
99PacIn tCN-12
99PacPreD-278
99PacTeaL-18
99RetHoc-52
99SP AutPS-55
99UppDec-133
99UppDecMGS-133
99UppDecMSS-133
99UppDecMSS-133
99UppDecRG-52
99UppDecRII-MIR
99UppDecRIL1-MIR
99UppDecRP-52
**Richter, Pavel**
79NasSti-88
94CzeAPSE-299
**Ridderwall, Rolf**
83SweSemE-75
84SweSemE-74
85SwePanS-69
86SwePanS-57
87SwePanS-68
89SweSemE-50
89SweSemWCS-4
91SweSemE-320
91SweSemE-336
91SweSemWCS-28
92SweSemE-26
94FinnJaaK-53
**Ridley, Curt**
76CanuRoyB-15
760PCNHL-197
76Top-197
77CanCanDC-12
77CanuRoyB-17
770PCNHL-395
780PC-302
79CanuRoyB-18
80MapLeaP-21
**Ridley, Mike**
86CapKod-22
860PC-66
860PCBoxB-L
860PCSti-131
860PCSti-221
86Top-66
86TopBoxB-L
87CapKod-17
87CapTealss-20
870PC-8
870PCSti-234
87PanSti-181
87Top-8
88CapBor-18
88CapSmo-20
880PC-104
880PCSti-74
88PanSti-374
88Top-104
89CapKod-17
89CapTealss-19
890PC-165
890PCBoxB-B
890PCSti-81
89PanSti-339
89Top-165
89TopBoxB-B
90Bow-77
90BowTif-77
90CapKod-22
90CapPos-20
90CapSmo-19
900PC-327
90PanSti-163
90ProSet-320A
90ProSet-320B
90Sco-33
90ScoCan-33
90Top-327
90TopTif-327
90UppDec-97
90UppDecF-97
91Bow-308
91CapJun5-23

91CapKod-23
910PC-245
91PanSti-199
91Par-192
91ParFre-192
91Pin-94
91PinFre-94
91ProSet-254
91ProSetFre-254
91ProSetPla-128
91ScoAme-283
91ScoCan-503
91StaClu-68
91Top-245
91UppDec-112
91UppDecF-112
92Bow-360
92CapKod-23
920PC-305
92PanSti-162
92PanStiFre-162
92Par-200
92ParEmel-200
92Pin-170
92PinFre-170
92Sco-187
92ScoCan-187
92ScoSha-6
92ScoShaCan-6
92StaClu-200
92Top-236
92TopGol-236G
92Ult-238
92UppDec-173
93Don-375
93Lea-102
930PCPre-78
930PCPreG-78
93PanSti-25
93Par-218
93ParEmel-218
93Pin-135
93PinCan-135
93Pow-266
93Sco-197
93ScoCan-197
93StaClu-123
93StaCluFDI-123
93StaCluFDIO-123
93StaCluO-123
93TopPre-78
93TopPreG-78
93Ult-148
93UppDec-341
93UppDecSP-173
94CanGamNHLP-236
94EASpo-153
94Fla-185
94Fle-219
94Lea-374
94MapLeaK-23
94MapLeaP-3
94MapLeaPP-12
940PCPre-301
940PCPreSE-301
94Par-250
94ParGol-250
94ParSE-SE178
94ParSEG-SE178
94ParVin-V72
94Pin-384
94PinArtP-384
94PinRinC-384
94Sco-199
94ScoGol-199
94ScoPla-199
94ScoPlaTS-199
94Sel-19
94SelGol-19
94SP-118
94SPDieCut-118
94StaClu-105
94StaCluFDI-105
94StaCluMOMS-105
94StaCluSTWC-105
94TopPre-301
94TopPreSE-301
94Ult-378
94UppDec-177
94UppDecEIeIce-177
94UppDecSPI-SP169
94UppDecSPIDC-SP169
95BeAPla-63
95BeAPSig-S63
95BeAPSigDC-S63
95CanGamNHLP-270
95ColCho-48
95ColChoPC-48
95ColChoPCP-48
95Don-250
95Emo-184
95Lea-212
95Met-155
95ParInt-214
95ParIntEl-214
95PlaOneoOne-319
95Sco-236
95ScoBlaIce-236
95ScoBlaIceAP-236
95SkyImp-173
95StaClu-51
95StaCluMOMS-51
95Ult-163
95UltGolM-163

95UppDec-75
95UppDecEIeIce-75
95UppDecEIeIceG-75
96CanuPos-17
96Don-141
96DonPrePro-141
96Pin-172
96PinArtP-172
96PinFoi-172
96PinPreS-172
96PinRinC-172
96Sco-184
96ScoArtPro-184
96ScoDeaCAP-184
96ScoGolB-184
96ScoSpeAP-184
96UppDecBD-125
96UppDecBDPro-125
97ColCho-264
97Pac-206
97PacCop-206
97PacEmeGre-206
97PacIceB-206
97PacRed-206
97PacSil-206
**Ridolfi, Brian**
96DayBom-7
**Ridpath, Bruce**
10C55SweCP-14
10C56-34
11C55-14
12C57-28
**Rieder, Dana**
907thInnSWHL-32
917thInnSWHL-317
**Riedmeier, Erwin**
72SweSemWC-98
**Riehl, Jeremy**
917thInnSWHL-179
**Riehl, Kevin**
907thInnSWHL-33
917thInnSWHL-329
93Rallce-16
94Rallce-17
95SigRooA-35
95SigRooAPC-35
**Riel, Guy**
80QueRem-18
**Riendeau, Vincent**
86SheCan-22
87BluTealss-30
88BluKod-30
88BluTealss-20
89BluKod-30
890PCSti-146
890PCSti-265
89PanSti-120
90BluKod-18
90Bow-20
90BowTif-20
900PC-177
90PanSti-268
90Sco-107
90ScoCan-107
90Top-177
90TopTif-177
90UppDec-152
90UppDecF-152
91Bow-372
910PC-370
91ProSet-213
91ProSetFre-213
91ProSetPla-112
91ScoAme-23
91ScoCan-23
91ScoRoo-43T
91StaClu-128
91Top-370
91UppDec-220
91UppDecF-220
92Bow-262
92Par-278
92ParEmel-278
92Pin-177
92PinFre-177
92Sco-396
92ScoCan-396
92StaClu-172
92Top-466
92TopGol-466G
93Ult-288
930PCPre-411
930PCPreG-411
93Pin-312
93PinCan-312
93TopPre-411
93TopPreG-411
94CanGamNHLP-272
94Fla-13
94Kra-53
94KraGoaM-6
940PCPre-324
940PCPreSE-324
94Par-14
94ParGol-14
94Pin-212
94PinArtP-212
94PinRinC-212
94StaClu-43
94StaCluFDI-43
94StaCluMOMS-43
94StaCluSTWC-43

94TopPre-324
94TopPreSE-324
94Ult-15
95GerDELE-335
**Riffel, Kevin**
91AirCanSJHL-B9
**Riggin, Dennis**
52JunBluT-1
**Riggin, Pat**
79FlamPos-16
79FlaTeal-17
80FlamPos-18
80PepCap-16
81FlamPos-19
810PC-37
810PCSti-12
810PCSti-221
81Top-30
82Cap-22
820PC-372
82PosCer-3
83PufSti-21
84CapPizH-14
840PC-205
840PC-218
840PC-386
840PCSti-65
840PCSti-233
84Top-148
84Top-164
85CapPizH-13
850PC-136
850PCSti-106
85Top-136
860PCSti-41
87PenKod-12
**Riggin, Travis**
93KitRan-7
93KitRan-29
94KitRan-9
**Rigolet, Gerald**
72SweSemWC-158
**Riha, Milos**
96CzeAPSE-142
**Riihijarvi, Heikki**
93FinnJyvHS-116
93FinnSIS-10
**Riihijarvi, Juha**
93Cla-45
93FinnSIS-369
93FinnSIS-384
93SweSemWCS-74
94ClaProP-48
94FinnJaaK-40
94FinnSIS-301
94FinnSIS-382
94FinnSISH-12
95FinnSemWC-46
95FinnSIS-99
95FinnSIS-35
95FinnSISSpo-3
96FinnSISR-179
96FinnSISR-NNO
96FinnSISRATG-2
96SweSemW-34
**Riihijarvi, Teemu**
95Cla-12
95ClaIceBre-BK11
95ColCho-331
95ColChoPC-331
95FinnSIS-92
95FinnSISDD-2
95UppDec-548
95UppDecEIeIce-548
95UppDecEIeIceG-548
96ClaIceBreDC-BK11
96FinnSISR-91
**Riihinen, Jani**
95ColCho-330
95ColChoPC-330
95ColChoPCP-330
**Riihiranta, Heikki**
69SweWorC-160
70SweHocS-300
73SweHocS-34
73SweWorCS-34
740PCWHA-31
74SweHocS-30
74SweSemHVS-80
750PCWHA-125
760PCWHA-58
**Riksson, Roland**
71SweHocS-393
**Rilcof, Kevan**
91BriColJHL-5
92BriColJHL-22
**Riley, Bill**
770PCNHL-360
780PC-292
790PC-303
83NovScoV-9
**Riley, Jack**
34SweCap-14
35DiaMatTI-55
**Riley, Ron**
72NatOttWHA-18
**Rimmel, Patrik**
94CzeAPSE-10
95CzeAPSE-107
**Rimsky, Dalibor**
96CzeAPSE-116
**Rindell, Harri**
93FinnJyvHS-13

**Ring, Tomas**
91SweSemE-138
**Ringler, Tim**
81MilAdm-15
**Rinkinen, Juha-Pekka**
96FinnSISR-115
**Rintanen, Kimmo**
92UppDec-618
93FinnJyvHS-229
93FinnSIS-203
94FinnSIS-257
94FinnSemWC-19
95FinnSemWC-229
95FinnSIS-130
96FinnSISR-145
96FinnSISRMA-1
**Riopelle, Rip (Howard)**
44BeeGro2P-285
45QuaOatP-110A
45QuaOatP-110B
51LavDaiQSHL-101
52St.LawS-55
**Rioux, Daniel**
80QueRem-19
**Rioux, Luc**
96DetWha-22
**Rioux, Pierre**
84MonGolF-25
94GerDELE-92
98GerDELE-271
**Ripley, Vic**
330PCV304B-67
33V357IceK-54
34DiaMatS-51
35DiaMatTI-56
**Riplinger, Brent**
92NorMicW-20
93NorMicW-23
**Risdale, Mike**
89RegPat-16
907thInnSWHL-166
917thInnSWHL-238
**Risebrough, Doug**
74CanaPos-18
75CanaPos-14
75HerSta-12
750PCNHL-107
75Top-107
76CanaPos-16
760PCNHL-109
760PCNHL-388
76Top-109
77CanaPos-109
770PCNHL-189
77Top-189
78CanaPos-21
780PC-249
78Top-249
79CanaPos-19
790PC-13
79Top-13
80CanaPos-19
800PC-275
80PepCap-55
81CanaPos-22
810PC-190
820PC-57
82PosCer-10
830PC-92
830PCSti-269
83PufSti-1
83Vac-18
847EDis-8
84KelAccD-2
840PC-236
840PCSti-241
85FlamRedRP-25
85FlamRedRP-26
850PC-243
86FlamRedR-24
86KraDra-59
860PC-196
86Top-196
87FlamRedRP-26
90FlamIGA-24
90ProSet-663
91FlamIGA-29
**Risidore, Ryan**
93GueSto-5
94GueSto-5
95GueSto5A-20
95Sla-85
96SprFal-28
**Rissling, Gary**
83PenTealP-25
84PenHeiP-17
**Rita, Jani**
98SPXTopP-67
98SPXTopPF-67
98SPXTopPR-67
98UppDecBD-97
98UppDecDD-97
98UppDecQD-97
98UppDecTD-97
**Ritchie, Byron**
93LetHur-12
93LetHur-19
96LetHur-13
97BowCHL-108
97BowCHLOPC-108
99Pac-83
99PacCop-83
99PacGol-83
99PacIceB-83

99PacPreD-83
**Ritchie, Darren**
92BraWheK-19
95SlaMemC-40
95SouCarS-11
95St.JohF-19
**Ritchie, Jim**
89SauSteMG-6
91NasKni-20
**Riutta, Bruce**
69SweWorC-181
72SweSemWC-120
**Riva, Dan**
93OmaLan-20
**Rivard, Fern**
74NHLActSta-142
**Rivard, Francois**
907thInnSQMJHL-102
917thInnSQMJHL-130
**Rivard, Jean-Francois**
917thInnSQMJHL-181
**Rivard, Stefan**
93NorBayC-12
94NorBayC-14
**Rivers, Andy**
84KinCan-15
86KinCan-14
**Rivers, Daryl**
93LonKin-15
95Sla-280
**Rivers, Gus**
36ProvRed-7
**Rivers, Jamie**
917thInnSOHL-257
91SudWol-8
92SudWol-9
93SudWol-8
93SudWolP-8
94Fin-152
94FinRef-152
94FinSupTW-152
94LeaLimWJC-8
94Pin-526
94PinArtP-526
94PinRinC-526
94SlaPro-6
94SlaPro-7
94SP-141
94SPDieCut-141
94SudWol-7
94SudWolP-23
94UppDec-501
94UppDecEIeIce-501
95Bow-132
95BowAllFoi-132
95Cla-97
95ColEdgI-95
95Don-342
95DonCanWJT-7
95SigRoo-36
95SigRooAB2-B1
95SigRooSig-36
95SkyImp-78
95TopCanWJ-21CJ
95UppDec-477
95UppDecEIeIce-477
95UppDecEIeIceG-477
96ColEdgFL-40
96Lea-236
96LeaPreP-236
96Pin-216
96PinArtP-216
96PinFoi-216
96PinPreS-216
96PinRinC-216
96SkyImp-158
96UppDec-145
97Be A PPAD-231
97Be A PPPAD-231
97BeAPla-231
97BeAPlaAut-231
97PacOme-198
97PacOmeC-198
97PacOmeDG-198
97PacOmeEG-198
97PacOmeIB-198
97ScoBlu-13
97ScoBluPla-13
97ScoBluPre-13
98Pac-372
98PacIceB-372
98PacRed-372
98UppDec-359
98UppDecE-359
98UppDecE1o1-359
98UppDecGR-359
**Rivers, Shawn**
907thInnSOHL-393
91SudWol-98
917thInnSOHL-260
91SudWol-9
93Sco-470
93ScoCan-490
94ClaProP-107
95ColEdgI-108
96GerDELE-8
**Rivers, Wayne**
61HamRed-15
63Top-17
64TorSta-42
720PC-315
73QuaOatWHA-44
740PCWHA-13
750PCWHA-38

❑ 76SanDieMW-11
**Rivet, Craig**
❑ 917thInnSOHL-235
❑ 93KinFro-21
❑ 94FreCan-24
❑ 95FreCan-23
❑ 95Lea-310
❑ 96CanaPos-23
❑ 96CanaShe-17
❑ 97Be A PPAD-102
❑ 97Be A PPAPD-102
❑ 97BeAPla-102
❑ 97BeAPlaAut-102
❑ 97CanaPos-18
❑ 97PacDynBKS-51
**Rjabykin, Dimitri**
❑ 95UppDec-557
❑ 95UppDecEleIce-557
❑ 95UppDecEleIceG-557
**Roach, Dave**
❑ 88ProAHL-76
**Roach, Gary**
❑ 917thInnSOHL-337
❑ 93SauSteMG-13
❑ 93SauSteMGM-14
❑ 94NorBayC-23
**Roach, John**
❑ 24C144ChaCig-50
❑ 33V357IceK-67
**Roach, Mickey**
❑ 23V1451-38
❑ 24C144ChaCig-51
❑ 24V130MapC-23
❑ 24V1452-18
**Rob, Lubos**
❑ 93SweSemWCS-97
❑ 94CzeAPSE-106
❑ 95CzeAPSE-67
❑ 96CzeAPSE-252
**Robazzo, Rino**
❑ 61Top-39
❑ 63QueAce-20
❑ 65QueAce-17
**Robb, Doug**
❑ 81MilAdm-12
**Robbins, Adam**
❑ 95Sla-41
❑ 96ForWorF-14
**Robbins, Matt**
❑ 94ClaProP-230
**Roberge, Jean**
❑ 907thInnSQMJHL-53
❑ 917thInnSQMJHL-234
**Roberge, Mario**
❑ 88ProAHL-290
❑ 89ProAHL-187
❑ 90ProAHLIHL-57
❑ 91CanaPos-23
❑ 91ProSet-415
❑ 91ProSetFre-415
❑ 92CanaPos-22
❑ 92DurPan-27
❑ 92Par-322
❑ 92ParEmel-322
❑ 93CanaPos-21
❑ 93DurSco-16
❑ 95FreCan-24
**Roberge, Roger**
❑ 51LavDaiS-44
❑ 52St.LawS-73
**Roberge, Serge**
❑ 88ProAHL-286
❑ 89ProAHL-200
❑ 90HalCit-21
❑ 90ProAHLIHL-454
❑ 91ProAHLCHL-538
❑ 95RochAmeSS-17
**Robert, Claude**
❑ 51LavDaiQSHL-17
❑ 52St.LawS-47
**Robert, Rene**
❑ 71PenPos-16
❑ 71TorSun-225
❑ 72OPC-2
❑ 72SarProSta-42
❑ 72Top-161
❑ 73OPC-139
❑ 73Top-139
❑ 74LipSou-24
❑ 74NHLActSta-49
❑ 74OPCNHL-42
❑ 74OPCNHL-142
❑ 74Top-42
❑ 74Top-142
❑ 75OPCNHL-46
❑ 75OPCNHL-296
❑ 75OPCNHL-315
❑ 75Top-46
❑ 75Top-296
❑ 75Top-315
❑ 76OPCNHL-42
❑ 76OPCNHL-214
❑ 76Top-42
❑ 76Top-214
❑ 77OPCNHL-222
❑ 77Top-222
❑ 78OPC-188
❑ 78Top-188
❑ 79OPC-12
❑ 79Roc-20
❑ 79Top-12
❑ 80OPC-239
❑ 80OPC-259
❑ 80Top-239
❑ 80Top-259
❑ 81MapLeaP-18
❑ 81OPC-322
❑ 82OPC-330
❑ 93SabNoc-17
**Robert, Ross**
❑ 51Par-18
**Roberto, Phil**
❑ 69CanaPosC-24
❑ 71BluPos-19
❑ 71CanaPos-19
❑ 71OPC-228
❑ 71SarProSta-109
❑ 71TorSun-162
❑ 72BluWhiBor-17
❑ 72OPC-82
❑ 72Top-52
❑ 73BluWhiBor-16
❑ 73OPC-3
❑ 73Top-151
❑ 74NHLActSta-235
❑ 74NHLActStaU-12
❑ 74OPCNHL-208
❑ 74Top-208
❑ 75OPCNHL-80
❑ 75Top-80
❑ 76OPCNHL-345
❑ 76RocPucBuc-18
❑ 92BirBul-20
❑ 93BirBul-20
❑ 94BirBul-20
❑ 95BirBul-2
**Roberts, Alex**
❑ 90ProAHLIHL-408
❑ 92TolSto-11
**Roberts, Bobby**
❑ 51LavDaiQSHL-103
**Roberts, David**
❑ 91MicWol-12
❑ 93Cla-76
❑ 93Pow-515
❑ 93StaCluTUSA-20
❑ 93TopPreTUSA-16
❑ 93Ult-495
❑ 94Cla-106
❑ 94ClaAut-106
❑ 94ClaDraGol-106
❑ 94ClaTri-T58
❑ 94FinnJaaK-134
❑ 94Lea-478
❑ 94Par-201
❑ 94ParGol-201
❑ 94Sco-222
❑ 94ScoGol-222
❑ 94ScoPla-222
❑ 94ScoPlaTS-222
❑ 95ColEdgIC-C1
❑ 95Emo-152
❑ 95Lea-13
❑ 95ParInt-179
❑ 95ParIntEl-179
❑ 95Pin-157
❑ 95PinArtP-157
❑ 95PinRinC-157
❑ 95Sco-286
❑ 95ScoBlaIce-286
❑ 95ScoBlaIceAP-286
❑ 95SigRooA-36
❑ 95SigRooAPC-36
❑ 95Top-43
❑ 95TopOPCI-43
❑ 96BeAPAut-93
❑ 96BeAPAutSil-93
❑ 96BeAPla-93
❑ 96CanuPos-7
❑ 97ColCho-265
❑ 97DonLim-31
❑ 97DonLimExp-31
❑ 97PacInvNRB-204
❑ 97ScoCanPla-19
❑ 97ScoCanPre-19
❑ 97ScoCanu-19
**Roberts, Doug**
❑ 67Top-50
❑ 68OPC-88
❑ 68Top-88
❑ 69OPC-81
❑ 69Top-81
❑ 70EssPowPla-92
❑ 70OPC-71
❑ 70SarProSta-138
❑ 70Top-71
❑ 71Top-83
❑ 72SarProSta-26
❑ 73OPC-207
❑ 73RedWinMP-14
❑ 74NHLActSta-103
❑ 74OPCNHL-312
❑ 92RalIce-14
❑ 94CenHocL-17
**Roberts, Gary**
❑ 82Ott67-20
❑ 83Ott67-24
❑ 84Ott67-20
❑ 86FlamRedR-25
❑ 86MonGolF-12
❑ 87FlamRedRP-27
❑ 87PanSti-217
❑ 88PanSti-15
❑ 89OPC-202
❑ 89OPCSti-98
❑ 89PanSti-35
❑ 90Bow-95
❑ 90BowTif-95
❑ 90FlamIGA-25
❑ 90OPC-161
❑ 90PanSti-179
❑ 90ProSet-45
❑ 90Sco-106
❑ 90ScoCan-106
❑ 90Top-161
❑ 90TopTif-161
❑ 90UppDec-29
❑ 90UppDecF-29
❑ 91Bow-263
❑ 91FlamIGA-18
❑ 91FlamPanTS-19
❑ 91OPC-320
❑ 91OPCPre-126
❑ 91PanSti-52
❑ 91Par-24
❑ 91Par-436
❑ 91ParFre-24
❑ 91ParFre-436
❑ 91Pin-37
❑ 91PinFre-37
❑ 91ProSet-30
❑ 91ProSetFre-30
❑ 91ProSetPla-161
❑ 91ProSetPla-280
❑ 91ScoAme-199
❑ 91ScoCan-199
❑ 91StaClu-126
❑ 91Top-320
❑ 91UppDec-190
❑ 91UppDecF-190
❑ 92Bow-109
❑ 92Bow-214
❑ 92FlamIGA-6
❑ 92OPC-72
❑ 92OPCPreSP-14
❑ 92PanSti-45
❑ 92PanStiFre-45
❑ 92Par-22
❑ 92ParCheP-CP8
❑ 92ParEmel-22
❑ 92Pin-3
❑ 92Pin-242
❑ 92PinFre-3
❑ 92PinFre-242
❑ 92ProSet-21
❑ 92ProSetGTL-1
❑ 92Sco-322
❑ 92ScoCan-322
❑ 92ScoSha-1
❑ 92ScoShaCan-1
❑ 92StaClu-48
❑ 92Top-116
❑ 92TopGol-116G
❑ 92Ult-29
❑ 92UppDec-289
❑ 93Don-52
❑ 93Lea-36
❑ 93McDUppD-11
❑ 93OPCPre-382
❑ 93OPCPre-510
❑ 93OPCPreG-382
❑ 93OPCPreG-510
❑ 93PanSti-181
❑ 93Par-302
❑ 93ParEmel-302
❑ 93Pin-55
❑ 93PinAllS-29
❑ 93PinAllSC-29
❑ 93PinCan-55
❑ 93Pow-42
❑ 93Sco-241
❑ 93ScoCan-241
❑ 93ScoDynDC-4
❑ 93StaClu-235
❑ 93StaCluFDI-235
❑ 93StaCluFDIO-235
❑ 93StaCluFin-9
❑ 93StaCluO-235
❑ 93SweSemWCS-208
❑ 93TopPre-382
❑ 93TopPre-510
❑ 93TopPreG-382
❑ 93TopPreG-510
❑ 93Ult-187
❑ 93UppDec-151
❑ 93UppDecHT-HT3
❑ 93UppDecLAS-32
❑ 93UppDecSP-25
❑ 94BeAPSig-17
❑ 94CanGamNHLP-61
❑ 94Don-143
❑ 94EASpo-22
❑ 94Fin-82
❑ 94FinDivFCC-19
❑ 94FinRef-82
❑ 94FinSupTW-82
❑ 94Fla-28
❑ 94Fle-35
❑ 94Kra-12
❑ 94Lea-326
❑ 94LeaLim-114
❑ 94OPCPre-445
❑ 94OPCPreSE-445
❑ 94ParSE-SE27
❑ 94ParSEG-SE27
❑ 94ParVin-V29
❑ 94Pin-115
❑ 94PinArtP-115
❑ 94PinNorLig-NL16
❑ 94PinRinC-115
❑ 94Sco-186
❑ 94ScoChelt-CI12
❑ 94ScoGol-186
❑ 94ScoPla-186
❑ 94ScoPlaTS-186
❑ 94Sel-147
❑ 94SelGol-147
❑ 94StaClu-230
❑ 94StaCluFDI-230
❑ 94StaCluMOMS-230
❑ 94StaCluSTWC-230
❑ 94TopFinI-16
❑ 94TopPre-445
❑ 94TopPreSE-445
❑ 94Ult-35
❑ 94UltRedLS-7
❑ 94UppDec-20
❑ 94UppDecEleIce-20
❑ 94UppDecSPI-SP14
❑ 94UppDecSPIDC-SP14
❑ 95ColCho-174
❑ 95ColChoPC-174
❑ 95ColChoPCP-174
❑ 95Don-372
❑ 95Emo-25
❑ 95Lea-277
❑ 95ParInt-301
❑ 95ParIntEl-301
❑ 95Pin-137
❑ 95PinArtP-137
❑ 95PinRinC-137
❑ 95PlaOneoOne-19
❑ 95ProMag-49
❑ 95Sco-97
❑ 95ScoBlaIce-97
❑ 95ScoBlaIceAP-97
❑ 95Sum-150
❑ 95SumArtP-150
❑ 95SumIce-150
❑ 95Top-78
❑ 95TopOPCI-78
❑ 95Ult-28
❑ 95UltGolM-28
❑ 95UppDec-19
❑ 95UppDecEleIce-19
❑ 95UppDecEleIceG-19
❑ 96ColCho-44
❑ 96NHLACEPC-39
❑ 96NHLProSTA-49
❑ 97Be A PPAD-73
❑ 97Be A PPAPD-73
❑ 97BeAPla-73
❑ 97BeAPlaAut-73
❑ 97CarHur-24
❑ 97DonPre-63
❑ 97DonPreCttC-63
❑ 97DonPri-106
❑ 97DonPriSoA-106
❑ 97PacOme-45
❑ 97PacOmeC-45
❑ 97PacOmeDG-45
❑ 97PacOmeEG-45
❑ 97PacOmeG-45
❑ 97PacOmeIB-45
❑ 97PacPar-39
❑ 97PacParC-39
❑ 97PacParDG-39
❑ 97PacParEG-39
❑ 97PacParIB-39
❑ 97PacParRed-39
❑ 97PacParSil-39
❑ 97PacRev-26
❑ 97PacRevC-26
❑ 97PacRevE-26
❑ 97PacRevIB-26
❑ 97PacRevR-26
❑ 97PacRevS-26
❑ 97Pin-170
❑ 97PinPrePBB-170
❑ 97PinPrePBC-170
❑ 97PinPrePBM-170
❑ 97PinPrePBY-170
❑ 97PinPrePFC-170
❑ 97PinPrePFM-170
❑ 97PinPrePFY-170
❑ 97PinPrePla-170
❑ 97SPAut-26
❑ 97UppDec-240
❑ 97UppDecBD-86
❑ 97UppDecBDDD-86
❑ 97UppDecBDQD-86
❑ 97UppDecBDTD-86
❑ 97UppDecGDM-240
❑ 98Pac-140
❑ 98PacIceB-140
❑ 98PacOmeH-46
❑ 98PacOmeODI-46
❑ 98PacOmeR-46
❑ 98PacPar-42
❑ 98PacParC-42
❑ 98PacParEG-42
❑ 98PacParH-42
❑ 98PacParIB-42
❑ 98PacParS-42
❑ 98PacRed-140
❑ 98UC-36
❑ 98UD ChoPCR-36
❑ 98UD ChoR-36
❑ 98UppDec-236
❑ 98UppDecBD-15
❑ 98UppDecDD-15
❑ 98UppDecE-236
❑ 98UppDecE1o1-236
❑ 98UppDecGR-236
❑ 98UppDecM-41
❑ 98UppDecMGS-41
❑ 98UppDecMSS-41
❑ 98UppDecMSS-41
❑ 98UppDecQD-15
❑ 98UppDecTD-15
❑ 99Pac-80
❑ 99PacCop-80
❑ 99PacGol-80
❑ 99PacIceB-80
❑ 99PacPreD-80
**Roberts, Gordie**
❑ 79OPC-265
❑ 80OPC-112
❑ 80Top-112
❑ 81NorStaPos-20
❑ 81OPC-167
❑ 81Top-W111
❑ 82NorStaPos-20
❑ 82OPC-174
❑ 82PosCer-9
❑ 83HalFP-O13
❑ 83NorStaPos-25
❑ 83OPC-180
❑ 83OPCSti-114
❑ 83VicCou-20
❑ 84NorSta7E-5
❑ 84NorStaPos-24
❑ 84OPC-107
❑ 85NorStaPos-25
❑ 85OPC-28
❑ 85OPCSti-43
❑ 85Top-28
❑ 86NorSta7E-10
❑ 86OPC-42
❑ 86Top-42
❑ 87BluTeaIss-21
❑ 87NorStaPos-26
❑ 87OPC-41
❑ 87OPCSti-55
❑ 87Top-41
❑ 88BluKod-4
❑ 88BluTeaIss-21
❑ 88PanSti-102
❑ 89BluKod-4
❑ 90OPC-256
❑ 90PanSti-269
❑ 90ProSet-271
❑ 90ProSet-510
❑ 90Sco-245
❑ 90ScoCan-245
❑ 90ScoRoo-83T
❑ 90Top-256
❑ 90TopTif-256
❑ 91OPC-494
❑ 91PenCokE-28
❑ 91Pin-274
❑ 91PinFre-274
❑ 91ProSet-458
❑ 91ProSetFre-458
❑ 91ScoAme-439
❑ 91ScoCan-422
❑ 91Top-494
❑ 92Bow-197
❑ 92BruPos-9
❑ 92OPC-233
❑ 92OPCPre-86
❑ 92Pin-312
❑ 92PinFre-312
❑ 92Sco-201
❑ 92ScoCan-201
❑ 92StaClu-185
❑ 92Top-176
❑ 92TopGol-176G
❑ 92Ult-255
❑ 93OPCPre-275
❑ 93OPCPreG-275
❑ 93Pin-319
❑ 93PinCan-319
❑ 93Sco-274
❑ 93ScoCan-274
❑ 93StaClu-41
❑ 93StaCluFDI-41
❑ 93StaCluFDIO-41
❑ 93StaCluO-41
❑ 93TopPre-275
❑ 93TopPreG-275
**Roberts, Gordon**
❑ 10C55SweCP-33
❑ 10C56-3
❑ 11C55-33
❑ 12C57-23
❑ 85HalFC-222
**Roberts, Jim (James Wilfred)**
❑ 64BeeGro3P-114
❑ 64CocCap-72
❑ 65Coc-71
❑ 65Top-74
❑ 66Top-6
❑ 68OPC-113
❑ 68ShiCoi-152
❑ 68Top-113
❑ 69CanaPosC-25
❑ 69OPC-174
❑ 69OPCFou-9
❑ 69Top-14
❑ 70DadCoo-112
❑ 70EssPowPla-239
❑ 70OPC-213
❑ 70SarProSta-179
❑ 71CanaPos-20
❑ 71OPC-116
❑ 71SarProSta-181
❑ 71Top-116
❑ 71TorSun-246
❑ 72CanaPos-18
❑ 72OPC-269
❑ 72SarProSta-126
❑ 72SweSemWC-182
❑ 73CanaPos-19
❑ 73OPC-181
❑ 74CanaPos-19
❑ 74NHLActSta-161
❑ 74OPCNHL-78
❑ 74Top-78
❑ 75CanaPos-15
❑ 75OPCNHL-378
❑ 76CanaPos-17
❑ 76OPCNHL-119
❑ 76OPCNHL-217
❑ 76Top-119
❑ 76Top-217
❑ 77OPCNHL-281
❑ 86PenKod-19
❑ 88ProAHL-312
❑ 89ProAHL-253
❑ 90ProAHLIHL-182
❑ 94ParTalB-79
❑ 95Par66-72
❑ 95Par66Coi-72
**Roberts, Jimmy (James Drew)**
❑ 71LetActR-14
❑ 77OPCNHL-392
❑ 78OPC-342
**Roberts, Mike**
❑ 91JohChi-10
**Roberts, Minpy**
❑ 52JunBluT-22
**Roberts, Steve**
❑ 91BriColJHL-27
❑ 92BriColJHL-50
❑ 95DayBom-21
❑ 96DayBom-1
**Roberts, Tim**
❑ 92WheThu-13
❑ 93WheThu-7
❑ 94WheThu-5
**Roberts, W.**
❑ 23V1281PauC-6
❑ 24CreSel-5
**Robertson, Bobby (Bob)**
❑ 51LavDaiS-103
❑ 52St.LawS-69
**Robertson, Chris**
❑ 88BraWheK-14
**Robertson, Earl**
❑ 34BeeGro1P-247
❑ 39OPCV3011-63
**Robertson, Fred**
❑ 32O'KeeMapL-18
❑ 33V129-15
**Robertson, George**
❑ 44BeeGro2P-286
❑ 45QuaOatP-111
**Robertson, Grant**
❑ 83BelBul-23
❑ 84BelBul-19
**Robertson, Iain**
❑ 94FinnJaaK-329
**Robertson, James**
❑ 52JunBluT-103
**Robertson, Kenneth**
❑ 52JunBluT-99
**Robertson, Kevin**
❑ 89BraWheK-11
❑ 907thInnSWHL-215
❑ 90BraWheK-9
❑ 91BriColJHL-110
❑ 92BriColJHL-170
**Robertson, Roger**
❑ 84BelBul-23
**Robertson, Sean**
❑ 94PriAlbR-16
**Robertson, Torrie**
❑ 81Cap-15
❑ 83WhaJunHC-15
❑ 84VicCou-20
❑ 84WhaJunW-16
❑ 85OPC-218
❑ 85WhaJunW-17
❑ 86OPC-214
❑ 86WhaJunT-19
❑ 87WhaJunBK-17
❑ 88WhaJunGR-14
❑ 90ProAHLIHL-520
❑ 90ProSet-77
**Robertsson, Bert**
❑ 96SyrCru-27
**Robichaud, Andre**
❑ 92BriColJHL-85
**Robichaud, Ryan**
❑ 95GueSto5A-25
❑ 95Sla-91
❑ 96GueSto-10
**Robidas, Stephane**
❑ 97BowCHL-65
❑ 97BowCHLOPC-65
**Robidoux, Florent**
❑ 80BlaBroBac-9
❑ 81BlaBroBac-10
❑ 83SprInd-16
**Robillard, Marc**
❑ 917thInnSOHL-83
**Robin, Jean-Sebastien**
❑ 98UppDecE-350
**Robins, Trevor**
❑ 89SasBla-4
❑ 907thInnSWHL-88
❑ 90SasBla-2
❑ 917thInnSWHL-101
❑ 91SasBla-2
❑ 92BraWheK-20
**Robinson, Bill**
❑ 51LavDaiQSHL-107
❑ 52St.LawS-58
❑ 907thInnSOHL-68
**Robinson, Claude C**
❑ 83HalFP-J12
❑ 85HalFC-192
**Robinson, Derek**
❑ 92BriColJHL-165
**Robinson, Doug**
❑ 64CocCap-28
❑ 64Top-84
❑ 65Coc-77
❑ 65Top-26
❑ 68OPC-160
❑ 68ShiCoi-61
❑ 70EssPowPla-153
❑ 94ParTalB-34
❑ 95Par66-96
❑ 95Par66Coi-96
**Robinson, Earl**
❑ 33OPCV304B-55
❑ 33V357IceK-5
❑ 34BeeGro1P-180
❑ 34BeeGro1P-202
❑ 34SweCap-24
❑ 36OPCV304D-115
❑ 36V356WorG-85
❑ 37OPCV304E-165
**Robinson, Jane**
❑ 94ClaWomOH-W8
**Robinson, Jason**
❑ 95Sla-195
**Robinson, Justin**
❑ 94NorBayC-20
❑ 95Sla-11
**Robinson, Larry**
❑ 73CanaPos-20
❑ 73OPC-237
❑ 74CanaPos-20
❑ 74NHLActSta-153
❑ 74OPCNHL-280
❑ 75CanaPos-16
❑ 75HerSta-13
❑ 75OPCNHL-241
❑ 75Top-241
❑ 76CanaPos-18
❑ 76OPCNHL-151
❑ 76Top-151
❑ 77CanaPos-20
❑ 77Coc-20
❑ 77OPCNHL-2
❑ 77OPCNHL-30
❑ 77Top-30
❑ 77TopGloS-18
❑ 77TopOPCGlo-18
❑ 78CanaPos-22
❑ 78OPC-210
❑ 78OPC-329
❑ 78Top-210
❑ 79CanaPos-20
❑ 79OPC-50
❑ 79Top-50
❑ 80CanaPos-20
❑ 80OPC-84
❑ 80OPC-230
❑ 80OPCSup-11
❑ 80PepCap-56
❑ 80Top-84
❑ 80Top-230
❑ 81CanaPos-23
❑ 81OPC-179
❑ 81OPC-196
❑ 81OPCSti-31
❑ 81OPCSti-42
❑ 81OPCSti-148
❑ 81PosSta-16
❑ 81Top-31
❑ 82CanaPos-21
❑ 82CanaSte-16
❑ 82McDSti-17
❑ 82McDSti-34
❑ 82OPC-191
❑ 82OPCSti-31
❑ 82OPCSti-169
❑ 82PosCer-10
❑ 83CanaPos-23
❑ 83Ess-16
❑ 83OPC-195
❑ 83OPCSti-60
❑ 83OPCSti-61
❑ 83PufSti-2
❑ 83Vac-53
❑ 847EDis-30
❑ 84CanaPos-24
❑ 84KelAccD-2
❑ 84OPC-270
❑ 84OPCSti-147
❑ 84OPCSti-148
❑ 84Top-82
❑ 857ECreCar-10
❑ 85CanaPla-5
❑ 85CanaPla-7
❑ 85CanaPos-28
❑ 85CanaPro-17
❑ 85OPC-147
❑ 85OPCSti-140
❑ 85Top-147
❑ 86CanaPos-19
❑ 86KraDra-60
❑ 86OPC-62
❑ 86OPCBoxB-M
❑ 86OPCSti-8
❑ 86OPCSti-123
❑ 86Top-62
❑ 86TopBoxB-M
❑ 86TopStiIns-12

❑ 87CanaPos-24
❑ 87CanaVacS-72
❑ 87CanaVacS-73
❑ 87OPC-192
❑ 87OPCSti-16
❑ 87PanSti-57
❑ 87ProAll-1
❑ 87Top-192
❑ 88CanaPos-23
❑ 88EssAllSta-37
❑ 88OPC-246
❑ 88OPCSti-39
❑ 89KinSmo-7
❑ 89OPC-235
❑ 89OPCSti-55
❑ 89PanSti-245
❑ 90Bow-150
❑ 90BowTif-150
❑ 90KinSmo-9
❑ 90Kra-47
❑ 90OPC-261
❑ 90PanSti-244
❑ 90ProSet-125
❑ 90Sco-260
❑ 90ScoCan-260
❑ 90Top-261
❑ 90TopTif-261
❑ 90UppDec-52
❑ 90UppDecF-52
❑ 91Bow-177
❑ 91Kra-79
❑ 91Kra-80
❑ 91OPC-458
❑ 91PanSti-82
❑ 91Par-74
❑ 91ParFre-74
❑ 91Pin-208
❑ 91Pin-403
❑ 91PinFre-208
❑ 91PinFre-403
❑ 91ProSet-104
❑ 91ProSetFre-104
❑ 91ScoAme-291
❑ 91ScoCan-511
❑ 91StaClu-252
❑ 91Top-458
❑ 91UppDec-499
❑ 91UppDecF-499
❑ 92Bow-215
❑ 92FutTre76CC-182
❑ 92OPC-167
❑ 92OPC25Al-6
❑ 93OPCCanHF-59
❑ 93UppDecLAS-48
❑ 94ClaProP-53
❑ 94HocWit-92
❑ 98KinLA TC-3
❑ 99RetHoc-100
❑ 99UppDecCL-25
❑ 99UppDecCLCLC-25
❑ 99UppDecES-4
❑ 99UppDecJotC-JC3
❑ 99UppDecRG-100
❑ 99UppDecRII-LR
❑ 99UppDecRIL1-LR
❑ 99UppDecRP-100
❑ 99UppDecRTotC-TC11
**Robinson, Moe**
❑ 77NovScoV-18
**Robinson, Nick**
❑ 96SauSteMG-18
❑ 96SauSteMGA-18
**Robinson, Rob**
❑ 89ProIHL-22
❑ 90ProAHLIHL-79
❑ 91BluPos-17
❑ 92PeoRivC-21
❑ 92TopGol-527G
**Robinson, Scott**
❑ 89ProIHL-78
❑ 90ProAHLIHL-118
❑ 91ProAHLCHL-153
**Robinson, Stephane**
❑ 84RicRiv-15
**Robinson, Todd**
❑ 95UppDec-508
❑ 95UppDecElelce-508
❑ 95UppDecElelceG-508
❑ 97BowCHL-93
❑ 97BowCHLOPC-93
❑ 98BowCHL-52
❑ 98BowCHLGA-52
❑ 98BowCHLOI-52
❑ 98BowChrC-52
❑ 98BowChrCGA-52
❑ 98BowChrCGAR-52
❑ 98BowChrCOI-52
❑ 98BowChrCOIR-52
❑ 98BowChrCR-52
**Robison, Jeff**
❑ 92Rallce-15
❑ 92Rallce-22
❑ 93Rallce-17
**Robitaille, Luc**
❑ 86Kin20tATI-19
❑ 87KinTeal4-19
❑ 87OPC-42
❑ 87OPCBoxB-D
❑ 87OPCMin-35
❑ 87OPCSti-122
❑ 87OPCSti-133
❑ 87OPCSti-177
❑ 87OPCSti-187
❑ 87OPCSti-217
❑ 87PanSti-277
❑ 87PanSti-379
❑ 87Top-42
❑ 87TopBoxB-D
❑ 87TopStiIns-12
❑ 88EssAllSta-38
❑ 88FriLayS-10
❑ 88KinSmo-21
❑ 88OPC-124
❑ 88OPCBoxB-P
❑ 88OPCMin-32
❑ 88OPCSti-114
❑ 88OPCSti-157
❑ 88PanSti-78
❑ 88Top-124
❑ 88TopBoxB-P
❑ 88TopStiIns-1
❑ 89KinSmo-8
❑ 89OPC-88
❑ 89OPCSti-148
❑ 89PanSti-95
❑ 89PanSti-177
❑ 89SweSemWCS-68
❑ 89Top-88
❑ 90Bow-152
❑ 90BowHatTri-12
❑ 90BowTif-152
❑ 90KinSmo-10
❑ 90Kra-48
❑ 90Kra-75
❑ 90OPC-194
❑ 90OPC-209
❑ 90OPCPre-99
❑ 90PanSti-233
❑ 90PanSti-331
❑ 90ProSet-126
❑ 90ProSet-341
❑ 90Sco-150
❑ 90Sco-316
❑ 90ScoCan-150
❑ 90ScoCan-316
❑ 90ScoHotRS-66
❑ 90Top-194
❑ 90Top-209
❑ 90TopTif-194
❑ 90TopTif-209
❑ 90UppDec-73
❑ 90UppDecF-73
❑ 91Bow-188
❑ 91Gil-1
❑ 91Kra-70
❑ 91McDUppD-14
❑ 91OPC-260
❑ 91OPC-405
❑ 91OPCPre-34
❑ 91PanSti-91
❑ 91PanSti-324
❑ 91Par-68
❑ 91Par-224
❑ 91ParFre-68
❑ 91ParFre-224
❑ 91Pin-17
❑ 91Pin-385
❑ 91PinB-B10
❑ 91PinBFre-B10
❑ 91PinFre-17
❑ 91PinFre-385
❑ 91ProSet-95
❑ 91ProSet-286
❑ 91ProSetFre-95
❑ 91ProSetFre-286
❑ 91ProSetNHLAS-AC9
❑ 91ProSetPC-12
❑ 91ProSetPla-50
❑ 91ProSetPla-142
❑ 91ProSetPOTM-P6
❑ 91ScoAme-3
❑ 91ScoAme-345
❑ 91ScoCan-3
❑ 91ScoCan-375
❑ 91ScoFan-5
❑ 91ScoNat-5
❑ 91ScoNatCWC-5
❑ 91StaClu-159
❑ 91SweSemWCS-70
❑ 91Top-260
❑ 91Top-405
❑ 91UppDec-145
❑ 91UppDec-507
❑ 91UppDec-623
❑ 91UppDecF-145
❑ 91UppDecF-507
❑ 91UppDecF-623
❑ 92Bow-70
❑ 92Bow-216
❑ 92DurPan-28
❑ 92HumDum2-19
❑ 92KelPos-3
❑ 92McDUppD-12
❑ 92OPC-6
❑ 92PanSti-65
❑ 92PanSti-288
❑ 92PanStiFre-65
❑ 92PanStiFre-288
❑ 92Par-68
❑ 92Par-501
❑ 92ParEmel-68
❑ 92ParEmel-501
❑ 92Pin-175
❑ 92Pin-251
❑ 92PinCanPP-3
❑ 92PinFre-175
❑ 92PinFre-251
❑ 92ProSet-72
❑ 92Sco-290
❑ 92Sco-498
❑ 92ScoCan-290
❑ 92ScoCan-498
❑ 92SeaPat-10
❑ 92StaClu-44
❑ 92StaClu-247
❑ 92Top-101
❑ 92Top-266
❑ 92TopGol-101G
❑ 92TopGol-266G
❑ 92Ult-87
❑ 92UltAllS-11
❑ 92UppDec-8
❑ 92UppDec-216
❑ 92UppDecGHS-G2
❑ 92UppDecWJG-WG20
❑ 93Don-162
❑ 93Don-395
❑ 93DonSpeP-NNO
❑ 93DurSco-41
❑ 93Kra-20
❑ 93Lea-20
❑ 93LeaGolAS-9
❑ 93McDUppD-H3
❑ 93OPCPre-90
❑ 93OPCPre-180
❑ 93OPCPreG-90
❑ 93OPCPreG-180
❑ 93PanSti-201
❑ 93Par-91
❑ 93ParEmel-91
❑ 93Pin-145
❑ 93PinAllS-37
❑ 93PinAllSC-37
❑ 93PinCan-145
❑ 93PinNifFif-5
❑ 93PinTeaP-4
❑ 93PinTeaPC-4
❑ 93Pow-120
❑ 93PowPoiL-13
❑ 93Sco-245
❑ 93Sco-451
❑ 93ScoCan-245
❑ 93ScoCan-451
❑ 93ScoDreTea-24
❑ 93StaClu-87
❑ 93StaCluAS-18
❑ 93StaCluFDI-87
❑ 93StaCluFDIO-87
❑ 93StaCluFin-7
❑ 93StaCluO-87
❑ 93SweSemWCS-204
❑ 93TopPre-90
❑ 93TopPre-180
❑ 93TopPreG-90
❑ 93TopPreG-180
❑ 93Ult-208
❑ 93UltAllS-13
❑ 93UltRedLS-9
❑ 93UppDec-231
❑ 93UppDec-293
❑ 93UppDec-414
❑ 93UppDecGGO-GG8
❑ 93UppDecHT-HT17
❑ 93UppDecLAS-33
❑ 93UppDecSP-73
❑ 94BeAPla-R95
❑ 94BeAPSig-113
❑ 94DonIceMas-9
❑ 94EASpo-64
❑ 94EASpo-200
❑ 94Fin-89
❑ 94FinDivFCC-4
❑ 94FinnJaaK-92
❑ 94FinnJaaK-353
❑ 94FinRef-89
❑ 94FinSupTW-89
❑ 94Fla-138
❑ 94FlaHotN-7
❑ 94Fle-167
❑ 94HocWit-96
❑ 94KenStaLA-17
❑ 94KenStaLC-11
❑ 94Lea-20
❑ 94Lea-193
❑ 94LeaLim-88
❑ 94OPCPre-526
❑ 94OPCPre-540
❑ 94OPCPreSE-526
❑ 94OPCPreSE-540
❑ 94ParSE-SE137
❑ 94ParSEG-SE137
❑ 94ParVin-V67
❑ 94PenFoo-14
❑ 94Pin-400
❑ 94PinArtP-400
❑ 94PinRinC-400
❑ 94PinTeaP-TP7
❑ 94PinTeaPDP-TP7
❑ 94PosCerBB-21
❑ 94ScoDreTea-DT10
❑ 94Sel-32
❑ 94SelFirLin-10
❑ 94SelGol-32
❑ 94SP-93
❑ 94SPDieCut-93
❑ 94StaClu-57
❑ 94StaCluDD-4
❑ 94StaCluDDMO-4
❑ 94StaCluFDI-57
❑ 94StaCluMOMS-57
❑ 94StaCluSTWC-57
❑ 94TopFinl-13
❑ 94TopPre-526
❑ 94TopPre-540
❑ 94TopPreSE-526
❑ 94TopPreSE-540
❑ 94Ult-103
❑ 94Ult-350
❑ 94UppDec-194
❑ 94UppDecElelce-194
❑ 94UppDecNBAP-12
❑ 94UppDecSPI-SP152
❑ 94UppDecSPIDC-SP152
❑ 95Bow-23
❑ 95BowAllFoi-23
❑ 95CanGamNHLP-183
❑ 95ColCho-164
❑ 95ColChoPC-164
❑ 95ColChoPCP-164
❑ 95Don-104
❑ 95Don-348
❑ 95DonEli-105
❑ 95DonEliDCS-105
❑ 95DonEliDCU-105
❑ 95Emo-118
❑ 95Fin-24
❑ 95FinnSemWC-89
❑ 95FinRef-24
❑ 95ImpSti-82
❑ 95KenStaLA-16
❑ 95Lea-129
❑ 95LeaLim-91
❑ 95Met-99
❑ 95ParInt-140
❑ 95ParIntEl-140
❑ 95PlaOneoOne-71
❑ 95PlaOneoOne-286
❑ 95PosUppD-8
❑ 95ProMag-100
❑ 95Sco-54
❑ 95ScoBlaIce-54
❑ 95ScoBlaIceAP-54
❑ 95ScoLam-9
❑ 95SelCer-53
❑ 95SelCerMG-53
❑ 95SkyImp-113
❑ 95SkyImpIQ-14
❑ 95SP-97
❑ 95StaClu-100
❑ 95StaCluMOMS-100
❑ 95Sum-89
❑ 95SumArtP-89
❑ 95SumIce-89
❑ 95SumMadH-14
❑ 95SweGloWC-94
❑ 95SweGloWC-249
❑ 95Top-40
❑ 95Top-352
❑ 95Top-379
❑ 95TopHidGem-2HG
❑ 95TopHomGC-HGC19
❑ 95TopMarMPB-379
❑ 95TopOPCI-40
❑ 95TopOPCI-352
❑ 95TopOPCI-379
❑ 95TopSupSki-56
❑ 95TopSupSkiPla-56
❑ 95Ult-277
❑ 95UppDec-8
❑ 95UppDec-244
❑ 95UppDecElelce-8
❑ 95UppDecElelce-244
❑ 95UppDecElelceG-8
❑ 95UppDecElelceG-244
❑ 95UppDecSpeE-SE144
❑ 95UppDecSpeEdiG-SE144
❑ 95Zen-48
❑ 96BeAPAut-12
❑ 96BeAPAutSil-12
❑ 96BeAPla-12
❑ 96ColCho-171
❑ 96Don-7
❑ 96DonCanI-64
❑ 96DonCanIGPP-64
❑ 96DonCanIRPP-64
❑ 96DonEli-78
❑ 96DonEliDCS-78
❑ 96DonPrePro-7
❑ 96Lea-134
❑ 96LeaLim-27
❑ 96LeaLimG-27
❑ 96LeaPre-13
❑ 96LeaPreP-134
❑ 96LeaPrePP-13
❑ 96MetUni-101
❑ 96NHLProSTA-100
❑ 96PosUppD-16
❑ 96Sco-113
❑ 96ScoArtPro-113
❑ 96ScoDeaCAP-113
❑ 96ScoGolB-113
❑ 96ScoSpeAP-113
❑ 96SelCer-13
❑ 96SelCerAP-13
❑ 96SelCerBlu-13
❑ 96SelCerMB-13
❑ 96SelCerMG-13
❑ 96SelCerMR-13
❑ 96SelCerRed-13
❑ 96SP-102
❑ 96Sum-13
❑ 96SumArtP-13
❑ 96SumIce-13
❑ 96SumMet-13
❑ 96SumPreS-13
❑ 96SweSemW-93
❑ 96TeaOut-2
❑ 96TopNHLP-87
❑ 96TopPicOI-87
❑ 96Ult-111
❑ 96UltGolM-112
❑ 96Zen-36
❑ 96ZenArtP-36
❑ 97ColCho-170
❑ 97Don-90
❑ 97DonCanI-68
❑ 97DonCanIDS-68
❑ 97DonCanIPS-68
❑ 97DonEli-85
❑ 97DonEliAsp-85
❑ 97DonEliS-85
❑ 97DonLim-75
❑ 97DonLimExp-75
❑ 97DonPre-121
❑ 97DonPreCttC-121
❑ 97DonPreProG-90
❑ 97DonPreProS-90
❑ 97DonPri-32
❑ 97DonPriSoA-32
❑ 97Kat-72
❑ 97KatGol-72
❑ 97KatSil-72
❑ 97Lea-121
❑ 97LeaFraMat-121
❑ 97LeaFraMDC-121
❑ 97LeaInt-121
❑ 97LeaIntUI-121
❑ 97Pac-145
❑ 97PacCop-145
❑ 97PacCroR-65
❑ 97PacCroREG-65
❑ 97PacCroRIB-65
❑ 97PacCroRS-65
❑ 97PacEmeGre-145
❑ 97PacIceB-145
❑ 97PacInv-91
❑ 97PacInvC-91
❑ 97PacInvEG-91
❑ 97PacInvIB-91
❑ 97PacInvR-91
❑ 97PacInvS-91
❑ 97PacOme-112
❑ 97PacOmeC-112
❑ 97PacOmeDG-112
❑ 97PacOmeEG-112
❑ 97PacOmeG-112
❑ 97PacOmeIB-112
❑ 97PacPar-91
❑ 97PacParC-91
❑ 97PacParDG-91
❑ 97PacParEG-91
❑ 97PacParIB-91
❑ 97PacParRed-91
❑ 97PacParSil-91
❑ 97PacRed-145
❑ 97PacRev-66
❑ 97PacRevC-66
❑ 97PacRevE-66
❑ 97PacRevIB-66
❑ 97PacRevR-66
❑ 97PacRevS-66
❑ 97PacSil-145
❑ 97Pin-149
❑ 97PinBee-36
❑ 97PinBeeGP-36
❑ 97PinCer-92
❑ 97PinCerMB-92
❑ 97PinCerMG-92
❑ 97PinCerMR-92
❑ 97PinCerR-92
❑ 97PinIns-168
❑ 97PinPrePBB-149
❑ 97PinPrePBC-149
❑ 97PinPrePBM-149
❑ 97PinPrePBY-149
❑ 97PinPrePFC-149
❑ 97PinPrePFM-149
❑ 97PinPrePFY-149
❑ 97PinPrePla-149
❑ 97PinTotCMPG-92
❑ 97PinTotCPB-92
❑ 97PinTotCPG-92
❑ 97PinTotCPR-92
❑ 97Sco-149
❑ 97ScoArtPro-149
❑ 97ScoGolBla-149
❑ 97SP AutI-I18
❑ 97SPAut-77
❑ 97SPAutID-I18
❑ 97SPAutIE-I18
❑ 97Stu-53
❑ 97StuPrePG-53
❑ 97StuPrePS-53
❑ 97UppDec-290
❑ 97UppDecBD-76
❑ 97UppDecBDDD-76
❑ 97UppDecBDQD-76
❑ 97UppDecBDTD-76
❑ 97UppDecGDM-290
❑ 97Zen-41
❑ 97Zen5x7-56
❑ 97ZenGolImp-56
❑ 97ZenSilImp-56
❑ 97ZenZGol-41
❑ 97ZenZSil-41
❑ 98Be A PPA-61
❑ 98Be A PPAA-61
❑ 98Be A PPAAF-61
❑ 98Be A PPAM-M18
❑ 98Be A PPTBASG-61
❑ 98Be APG-61
❑ 98Fin-128
❑ 98FinNo P-128
❑ 98FinNo PR-128
❑ 98FinRef-128
❑ 98KinLA TC-4
❑ 98KinPowP-LAK3
❑ 98McDGreT-T13
❑ 98O-PChr-174
❑ 98O-PChrR-174
❑ 98Pac-244
❑ 98PacAur-88
❑ 98PacCroR-65
❑ 98PacCroRLS-65
❑ 98PacDynI-90
❑ 98PacDynIIB-90
❑ 98PacDynIR-90
❑ 98PacIceB-244
❑ 98PacOmeH-112
❑ 98PacOmeODI-112
❑ 98PacOmeR-112
❑ 98PacPar-107
❑ 98PacParC-107
❑ 98PacParEG-107
❑ 98PacParH-107
❑ 98PacParIB-107
❑ 98PacParS-107
❑ 98PacRed-244
❑ 98PacRev-68
❑ 98PacRevIS-68
❑ 98PacRevR-68
❑ 98SP Aut-38
❑ 98Top-174
❑ 98TopO-P-174
❑ 98UC-98
❑ 98UCMBH-BH12
❑ 98UD ChoPCR-98
❑ 98UD ChoR-98
❑ 98UppDec-104
❑ 98UppDecE-104
❑ 98UppDecE1o1-104
❑ 98UppDecGR-104
❑ 98UppDecM-97
❑ 98UppDecMGS-97
❑ 98UppDecMSS-97
❑ 98UppDecMSS-97
❑ 99Pac-196
❑ 99PacAur-70
❑ 99PacAurPD-70
❑ 99PacCop-196
❑ 99PacGol-196
❑ 99PacHomaA-12
❑ 99PacIceB-196
❑ 99PacPreD-196
❑ 99PacTeaL-13
❑ 99RetHoc-40
❑ 99SP AutPS-38
❑ 99UppDecM-96
❑ 99UppDecMGS-96
❑ 99UppDecMPS-LR
❑ 99UppDecMSS-96
❑ 99UppDecMSS-96
❑ 99UppDecRG-40
❑ 99UppDecRP-40
**Robitaille, Mike**
❑ 71OPC-8
❑ 71SabPos-17
❑ 71SarProSta-29
❑ 71Top-8
❑ 71TorSun-38
❑ 73OPC-121
❑ 73SabPos-11
❑ 73Top-121
❑ 74CanuRoyB-17
❑ 74NHLActSta-51
❑ 74NHLActStaU-40
❑ 74OPCNHL-159
❑ 74Top-159
❑ 75CanuRoyB-18
❑ 75OPCNHL-24
❑ 75Top-24
❑ 76CanuRoyB-16
❑ 76OPCNHL-359
**Robitaille, Patrice**
❑ 92ClaKni-15
❑ 95PeoRiv-19
❑ 96MilAdmBO-21
**Robitaille, Randy**
❑ 97ScoBru-12
❑ 97ScoBruPla-12
❑ 97ScoBruPre-12
❑ 97UppDec-182
❑ 99UppDecM-20
❑ 99UppDecMGS-20
❑ 99UppDecMSS-20
❑ 99UppDecMSS-20
**Robitaille, Stephane**
❑ 98GerDELE-51
**Robson, Bob**
❑ 91AirCanSJHLAS-50
**Robson, Ryan**
❑ 95SlaMemC-42
**Rocca, Tony**
❑ 84KinCan-22
**Roche, Dave**
❑ 917thInnSOHL-139
❑ 91PetPet-19
❑ 93PetPet-3
❑ 93WinSpi-18
❑ 94WinSpi-20
❑ 95Bow-144
❑ 95BowAllFoi-144
❑ 95Cla-90
❑ 95Don-287
❑ 95PenFoo-16
❑ 97Pac-253
❑ 97PacCop-253
❑ 97PacEmeGre-253
❑ 97PacIceB-253
❑ 97PacRed-253
❑ 97PacSil-253
❑ 97ScoPen-17
❑ 97ScoPenPla-17
❑ 97ScoPenPre-17
**Roche, Desse**
❑ 33V357IceK-70
❑ 35DiaMatTI-57
**Roche, Earl**
❑ 33V357IceK-62
❑ 35DiaMatTI-58
**Roche, Scott**
❑ 93NorBayC-21
❑ 94Cla95DP-DP9
❑ 94NorBayC-2
❑ 95Cla-54
❑ 95Cla-90
❑ 95SigRooFF-FF9
❑ 95SigRooFFS-FF9
❑ 95Sla-207
❑ 95Sla-NNO
**Rochefort, Danny**
❑ 84RicRiv-16
**Rochefort, Leon**
❑ 63QueAce-21
❑ 63QueAceQ-20
❑ 64QueAce-15
❑ 65QueAce-18
❑ 67YorActOct-1
❑ 68OPC-95
❑ 68ShiCoi-131
❑ 68Top-95
❑ 69OPC-105
❑ 69OPCFou-7
❑ 69Top-105
❑ 71CanaPos-21
❑ 71OPC-135
❑ 71SarProSta-63
❑ 71TorSun-102
❑ 72Flam-18
❑ 72OPC-204
❑ 72SarProSta-81
❑ 74CanuRoyB-18
❑ 75OPCNHL-374
❑ 92SpoFla-8
**Rochefort, Normand**
❑ 80NordPos-24
❑ 81NordPos-15
❑ 82McDSti-35
❑ 82NordPos-18
❑ 82OPC-291
❑ 82PosCer-16
❑ 83NordPos-23
❑ 83OPC-300
❑ 83Vac-72
❑ 84NordPos-21
❑ 84OPC-287
❑ 84OPCSti-176
❑ 85NordGenF-21
❑ 85NordMcD-17
❑ 85NordPro-20
❑ 85NordTeal-20
❑ 85OPCSti-148
❑ 86NordGenF-21
❑ 86NordMcD-20
❑ 86NordTeal-19
❑ 86NordYumY-8
❑ 87NordGenF-26
❑ 87NordYumY-8
❑ 87PanSti-161
❑ 88OPCSti-182
❑ 89RanMarMB-5
❑ 90ProSet-494
❑ 90Sco-149
❑ 90ScoCan-149
❑ 90UppDec-437
❑ 90UppDecF-437
❑ 91Bow-73
❑ 91Pin-273
❑ 91PinFre-273
❑ 91ScoAme-171
❑ 91ScoCan-171
❑ 92DurPan-44
❑ 92Sco-377
❑ 92ScoCan-377
**Rochefort, Richard**
❑ 94SudWol-15
❑ 94SudWolP-13
❑ 95Sla-399
❑ 95SudWol-24
❑ 95SudWolP-18
❑ 96SarSti-22
❑ 96SudWol-18
❑ 96SudWolP-19
❑ 97BowCHL-21
❑ 97BowCHLOPC-21
**Rocheleau, Nathan**
❑ 93OmaLan-21
**Rochette, Eric**
❑ 907thInnSQMJHL-22
❑ 917thInnSMC-35
**Rochette, Gaeton**
❑ 77NovScoV-19
**Rochon, Frank**
❑ 75OPCWHA-51
**Rochon, Patrick**
❑ 93RenEng-26
**Rodden, Mike**
❑ 85HalFC-164
**Rodden, Milt**
❑ 83HalFP-L15
**Roddis, Gareth**
❑ 95SolBar-3
**Rodek, Stan**
❑ 52JunBluT-168
**Roderick, John**

□ 93PeoRiv-24
**Rodgers, Marc**
□ 91thInnSQMJHL-45
□ 92WheThu-14
□ 93KnoChe-15
□ 93LasVegThu-23
□ 94LasVegThu-25
□ 95LasVegThu-13
**Rodman, Andy**
□ 87BroBra-24
**Rodrigue, Alex**
□ 95SlaMemC-55
**Rodrigue, Guillaume**
□ 96RimOceU-7
**Rodrigue, Sylvain**
□ 907thInnSQMJHL-20
□ 917thInnSMC-25
□ 917thInnSQMJHL-96
**Roedger, Roy**
□ 82SweSemHVS-121
□ 89SweSemWCS-122
**Roenick, Jeremy**
□ 89BlaCok-6
□ 90BlaCok-6
□ 90Bow-1
□ 90BowTif-1
□ 90OPC-7
□ 90OPCPre-100
□ 90PanSti-201
□ 90ProSet-58
□ 90Sco-179
□ 90ScoCan-179
□ 90ScoHotRS-31
□ 90ScoPro-179
□ 90ScoYouS-24
□ 90Top-7
□ 90TopTif-7
□ 90UppDec-63
□ 90UppDec-316
□ 90UppDec-481
□ 90UppDecF-63
□ 90UppDecF-316
□ 90UppDecF-481
□ 91BlaCok-22
□ 91Bow-386
□ 91Bow-403
□ 91Gil-13
□ 91Kra-56
□ 91OPC-106
□ 91OPCPre-52
□ 91OPCPre-174
□ 91PanSti-12
□ 91Par-29
□ 91Par-439
□ 91ParFre-29
□ 91ParFre-439
□ 91Pin-120
□ 91Pin-359
□ 91PinFre-120
□ 91PinFre-359
□ 91ProSet-40
□ 91ProSet-280
□ 91ProSet-605
□ 91ProSetFre-40
□ 91ProSetFre-280
□ 91ProSetFre-605
□ 91ProSetPC-6
□ 91ProSetPla-24
□ 91ProSetPla-141
□ 91ScoAme-220
□ 91ScoAme-305
□ 91ScoAme-418
□ 91ScoCan-220
□ 91ScoCan-309
□ 91ScoCan-334
□ 91ScoHotC-10
□ 91ScoKel-5
□ 91ScoYouS-21
□ 91StaClu-46
□ 91SweSemWCS-149
□ 91Top-106
□ 91UppDec-36
□ 91UppDec-166
□ 91UppDec-629
□ 91UppDecF-36
□ 91UppDecF-166
□ 91UppDecF-629
□ 92Bow-78
□ 92Bow-217
□ 92HumDum2-20
□ 92Kra-46
□ 92McDUppD-13
□ 92OPC-345
□ 92OPC-383
□ 92OPC25Al-23
□ 92OPCPreSP-5
□ 92PanSti-4
□ 92PanStiFre-4
□ 92Par-31
□ 92ParCheP-CP2
□ 92ParEmel-31
□ 92Pin-10
□ 92Pin-256
□ 92PinFre-10
□ 92PinFre-256
□ 92PinTea2-27
□ 92PinTea2F-27
□ 92ProSet-30
□ 92ProSet-252
□ 92ProSetGTL-2
□ 92Sco-200
□ 92Sco-422
□ 92Sco-499
□ 92ScoCan-200
□ 92ScoCan-422

□ 92ScoCan-499
□ 92ScoSha-10
□ 92ScoShaCan-10
□ 92ScoUSAG-3
□ 92ScoYouS-10
□ 92SeaPat-1
□ 92StaClu-167
□ 92StaClu-255
□ 92Top-400
□ 92TopGol-400G
□ 92Ult-41
□ 92UltJerR-1
□ 92UltJerR-2
□ 92UltJerR-3
□ 92UltJerR-4
□ 92UltJerR-5
□ 92UltJerR-6
□ 92UltJerR-7
□ 92UltJerR-8
□ 92UltJerR-9
□ 92UltJerR-10
□ 92UltJerR-11
□ 92UltJerR-12
□ 92UltJerR-AU
□ 92UppDec-274
□ 92UppDecGHS-G8
□ 92UppDecWJG-WG19
□ 93BlaCok-8
□ 93Don-67
□ 93DonEli-6
□ 93DonSpeP-E
□ 93KenStaLA-10
□ 93KenStaLC-9
□ 93Kra-47
□ 93Lea-27
□ 93LeaStuS-7
□ 93McDUppD-12
□ 93OPCPre-450
□ 93OPCPre-500
□ 93OPCPreG-450
□ 93OPCPreG-500
□ 93PanSti-M
□ 93Par-309
□ 93ParEasWesS-W6
□ 93ParEmel-309
□ 93Pin-140
□ 93PinAllS-39
□ 93PinAllSC-39
□ 93PinCan-140
□ 93PinNifFif-15
□ 93PinTea2-20
□ 93PinTea2C-20
□ 93PinTeaP-11
□ 93PinTeaPC-11
□ 93Pow-54
□ 93PowGam-8
□ 93PowPoiL-14
□ 93Sco-240
□ 93ScoCan-240
□ 93ScoDynDUS-6
□ 93ScoFra-4
□ 93SeaPat-15
□ 93StaClu-190
□ 93StaCluAS-20
□ 93StaCluFDI-190
□ 93StaCluFDIO-190
□ 93StaCluU-190
□ 93SweSemWCS-180
□ 93TopPre-450
□ 93TopPre-500
□ 93TopPreG-450
□ 93TopPreG-500
□ 93Ult-186
□ 93UltPreP-8
□ 93UppDec-235
□ 93UppDec-289
□ 93UppDec-314
□ 93UppDecHT-HT18
□ 93UppDecLAS-34
□ 93UppDecNR-30
□ 93UppDecSilSka-R10
□ 93UppDecSilSkaG-R10
□ 93UppDecSP-31
□ 94ActPacBPP-BP1
□ 94BAPUpCP-UC6
□ 94BeAPla-R12
□ 94BeAPla-R144
□ 94BeAPlaSig-17
□ 94CanGamNHLP-70
□ 94Don-222
□ 94DonDom-5
□ 94DonEliIns-9
□ 94EASpo-27
□ 94Fin-73
□ 94FinBowB-B5
□ 94FinBowBR-B5
□ 94FinnJaaK-122
□ 94FinnJaaK-352
□ 94FinRef-73
□ 94FinSupTW-73
□ 94Fla-36
□ 94FlaCenS-10
□ 94FlaScoP-9
□ 94Fle-8
□ 94FleSlaA-8
□ 94HocWit-103
□ 94KenStaLA-18
□ 94Kra-27
□ 94Lea-63
□ 94LeaFirOIce-2
□ 94LeaGolS-2
□ 94LeaLim-61
□ 94LeaLimG-8
□ 94LeaLimI-5
□ 94McDUppD-McD20

□ 94OPCPre-200
□ 94OPCPreSE-200
□ 94Par-302
□ 94ParCratGB-5
□ 94ParCratGG-5
□ 94ParCratGR-5
□ 94ParGol-302
□ 94ParSE-35
□ 94ParSEG-SE35
□ 94ParVin-V65
□ 94Pin-165
□ 94PinArtP-165
□ 94PinGam-GR14
□ 94PinRinC-165
□ 94PinWorEdi-WE3
□ 94Sco90PC-6
□ 94ScoDreTea-DT18
□ 94ScoFra-TF5
□ 94Sel-29
□ 94SelGol-29
□ 94SP-22
□ 94SPDieCut-22
□ 94SPPre-18
□ 94SPPreDC-18
□ 94StaClu-9
□ 94StaCluFDI-59
□ 94StaCluMO-20
□ 94StaCluMOMS-59
□ 94StaCluST-5
□ 94StaCluSTWC-59
□ 94TopFinB-13
□ 94TopFinI-11
□ 94TopPre-200
□ 94TopPreGTG-8
□ 94TopPreSE-200
□ 94Ult-44
□ 94UltPow-8
□ 94UltSpeM-9
□ 94UppDec-322
□ 94UppDecEleIce-322
□ 94UppDecIG-IG3
□ 94UppDecNBAP-13
□ 94UppDecPC-C19
□ 94UppDecPCEG-C19
□ 94UppDecPH-H13
□ 94UppDecPHEG-H13
□ 94UppDecPHES-H13
□ 94UppDecPHG-H13
□ 94UppDecPR-R8
□ 94UppDecPRE-R8
□ 94UppDecPreRG-R8
□ 94UppDecSPI-SP17
□ 94UppDecSPIDC-SP17
□ 95Bow-20
□ 95BowAllFoi-20
□ 95CanGamNHLP-26
□ 95ColCho-85
□ 95ColChoPC-85
□ 95ColChoPCP-85
□ 95Don-27
□ 95DonEli-47
□ 95DonEliCE-14
□ 95DonEliDCS-47
□ 95DonEliDCU-47
□ 95DonIgn-7
□ 95DonProPoi-1
□ 95Emo-33
□ 95Emo-NNO
□ 95Emo-NNO
□ 95EmoSam-1
□ 95EmoXce-2
□ 95EmoXci-2
□ 95Fin-25
□ 95Fin-175
□ 95FinnSemWC-118
□ 95FinRef-25
□ 95FinRef-175
□ 95FleMetPP-2
□ 95GerDELE-446
□ 95ImpSti-21
□ 95ImpStiDCS-9
□ 95Lea-116
□ 95LeaLim-80
□ 95LeaLimSG-12
□ 95McDPin-MCD-16
□ 95Met-28
□ 95MetIS-17
□ 95NHLAcePC-5D
□ 95NHLCooT-3
□ 95NHLCooT-RP3
□ 95ParInt-307
□ 95ParIntEl-307
□ 95Pin-106
□ 95PinArtP-106
□ 95PinFan-23
□ 95PinFulC-4
□ 95PinRinC-106
□ 95PinRoa2-4
□ 95PlaOneoOne-24
□ 95PlaOneoOne-135
□ 95PlaOneoOne-236
□ 95ProMag-10
□ 95Sco-55
□ 95ScoBlaIce-55
□ 95ScoBlaIceAP-55
□ 95ScoBorBat-10
□ 95ScoGolB-19
□ 95SelCer-60
□ 95SelCerDS-7
□ 95SelCerDSG-7
□ 95SelCerMG-60
□ 95SkyImp-33
□ 95SkyImpPP-1

□ 95SP-24
□ 95SPStaEto-E7
□ 95SPStaEtoG-E7
□ 95StaClu-166
□ 95StaCluMO-27
□ 95StaCluMOMS-166
□ 95Sum-82
□ 95SumArtP-82
□ 95SumIce-82
□ 95SweGloWC-117
□ 95Top-3
□ 95Top-235
□ 95TopHomGUSA-HGA2
□ 95TopOPCI-3
□ 95TopOPCI-235
□ 95TopPowL-4PL
□ 95TopPro-PP8
□ 95TopSupSki-65
□ 95TopSupSkiPla-65
□ 95Ult-135
□ 95Ult-396
□ 95UltCreCra-15
□ 95UltGolM-35
□ 95UltPrePiv-7
□ 95UltPrePivGM-7
□ 95UltUltHP-8
□ 95UltUltV-8
□ 95UppDec-227
□ 95UppDec-241
□ 95UppDec-422
□ 95UppDecAGPRW-12
□ 95UppDecEleIce-227
□ 95UppDecEleIce-241
□ 95UppDecEleIce-422
□ 95UppDecEleIceG-227
□ 95UppDecEleIceG-241
□ 95UppDecEleIceG-422
□ 95UppDecFreFra-F6
□ 95UppDecFreFraJ-F6
□ 95UppDecPRE-R47
□ 95UppDecPreR-R47
□ 95UppDecSpeE-SE104
□ 95UppDecSpeEdiG-SE104
□ 95UppPreRP-R47
□ 95Zen-72
□ 95ZenZT-6
□ 96BeAPAut-5
□ 96BeAPAutSil-5
□ 96BeAPla-5
□ 96ColCho-46
□ 96ColCho-297
□ 96ColCho-303
□ 96ColChoMVP-UD18
□ 96ColChoMVPG-UD18
□ 96ColChoSti-S6
□ 96Don-2
□ 96DonCanI-57
□ 96DonCanIGPP-57
□ 96DonCanIRPP-57
□ 96DonDom-9
□ 96DonEli-27
□ 96DonEliS-12
□ 96DonHitLis-4
□ 96DonPrePro-2
□ 96Fla-72
□ 96FlaBluI-72
□ 96Fle-18
□ 96FleArtRos-19
□ 96FlePicDL-2
□ 96FlePicF5-39
□ 96FlePicJE-10
□ 96HocGreC-17
□ 96HocGreCG-17
□ 96Lea-191
□ 96LeaFirOI-11
□ 96LeaLeaAL-13
□ 96LeaLeaALP-13
□ 96LeaLim-86
□ 96LeaLimG-86
□ 96LeaPre-4
□ 96LeaPreP-191
□ 96LeaPrePP-4
□ 96MetUni-121
□ 96NHLACEPC-40
□ 96NHLProSTA-10
□ 96Pin-98
□ 96PinArtP-98
□ 96PinFoi-98
□ 96PinMcD-12
□ 96PinMin-15
□ 96PinMinB-15
□ 96PinMinCoiB-15
□ 96PinMinCoiGP-15
□ 96PinMinCoiN-15
□ 96PinMinCoiS-15
□ 96PinMinCoiSG-15
□ 96PinMinG-15
□ 96PinMinS-15
□ 96PinPreS-98
□ 96PinTeaP-3
□ 96PosUppD-17
□ 96Sco-137
□ 96ScoArtPro-137
□ 96ScoDeaCAP-137
□ 96ScoGolB-137
□ 96ScoSpeAP-137
□ 96ScoSudDea-5
□ 96SelCer-77
□ 96SelCerAP-77
□ 96SelCerBlu-77
□ 96SelCerMB-77

□ 96SelCerMG-77
□ 96SelCerMR-77
□ 96SelCerRed-77
□ 96SkyImp-108
□ 96SkyImpB-19
□ 96SP-119
□ 96SPCleWin-CW7
□ 96SPx-7
□ 96SPxGol-7
□ 96Sum-138
□ 96SumArtP-138
□ 96SumHigV-10
□ 96SumHigVM-10
□ 96SumIce-138
□ 96SumMet-138
□ 96SumPreS-138
□ 96SweSemW-167
□ 96TopNHLP-47
□ 96TopPicFT-FT18
□ 96TopPicOI-47
□ 96Ult-135
□ 96UltGolM-135
□ 96UppDec-35
□ 96UppDec-205
□ 96UppDec-312
□ 96UppDecBD-167
□ 96UppDecBDG-167
□ 96UppDecHH-HH17
□ 96UppDecHHG-HH17
□ 96UppDecHHS-HH17
□ 96UppDecIce-51
□ 96UppDecIceDF-S8
□ 96UppDecIcePar-51
□ 96UppDecIceSCF-S8
□ 96UppDecSS-SS15A
□ 96Zen-30
□ 96ZenArtP-30
□ 96ZenZT-10
□ 97BeAPlaTAN-12
□ 97ColCho-195
□ 97ColChoSta-SQ79
□ 97ColChoSti-S13
□ 97Don-6
□ 97DonCanI-100
□ 97DonCanIDS-100
□ 97DonCanIPS-100
□ 97DonCanISCS-7
□ 97DonEli-77
□ 97DonEliAsp-77
□ 97DonEliS-77
□ 97DonLim-105
□ 97DonLim-120
□ 97DonLim-140
□ 97DonLimExp-105
□ 97DonLimExp-120
□ 97DonLimExp-140
□ 97DonLimFOTG-35
□ 97DonPre-88
□ 97DonPreProG-6
□ 97DonPreProS-6
□ 97DonPri-133
□ 97DonPriP-33
□ 97DonPriS-33
□ 97DonPriSB-33
□ 97DonPriSG-33
□ 97DonPriSoA-133
□ 97DonPriSS-33
□ 97EssOlyHH-28
□ 97EssOlyHHF-28
□ 97Kat-112
□ 97KatGol-112
□ 97KatSil-112
□ 97Lea-22
□ 97LeaFraMat-22
□ 97LeaFraMDC-22
□ 97LeaInt-22
□ 97LeaIntUI-22
□ 97LeaIntUI2-22
□ 97Pac-97
□ 97PacCarSup-16
□ 97PacCarSupM-16
□ 97PacCop-97
□ 97PacCroR-105
□ 97PacCroREG-105
□ 97PacCroRIB-105
□ 97PacCroRS-105
□ 97PacDyn-97
□ 97PacDynC-97
□ 97PacDynD-12A
□ 97PacDynDG-97
□ 97PacDynEG-97
□ 97PacDynIB-97
□ 97PacDynR-97
□ 97PacDynTan-63
□ 97PacEmeGre-97
□ 97PacIceB-97
□ 97PacInv-108
□ 97PacInvC-108
□ 97PacInvEG-108
□ 97PacInvFP-27
□ 97PacInvIB-108
□ 97PacInvR-108
□ 97PacInvS-108
□ 97PacOme-176
□ 97PacOmeH-187
□ 97PacOmeDG-176
□ 97PacOmeEG-176
□ 97PacOmeG-176
□ 97PacOmeIB-176
□ 97PacPar-142
□ 97PacParC-142
□ 97PacParDG-142
□ 97PacParEG-142

□ 97PacParIB-142
□ 97PacParRed-142
□ 97PacParSil-142
□ 97PacRed-97
□ 97PacRev-108
□ 97PacRevC-108
□ 97PacRevE-108
□ 97PacRevIB-108
□ 97PacRevR-108
□ 97PacRevS-108
□ 97PacSil-97
□ 97PacSlaSDC-7B
□ 97PacTeaCCC-19
□ 97Pin-33
□ 97Pin-197
□ 97PinArtP-33
□ 97PinCer-65
□ 97PinCerMB-65
□ 97PinCerMG-65
□ 97PinCerMR-65
□ 97PinCerR-65
□ 97PinHocMC-13
□ 97PinHocMC-14
□ 97PinIns-59
□ 97PinInsCC-59
□ 97PinInsEC-59
□ 97PinPrePBB-33
□ 97PinPrePBB-197
□ 97PinPrePBC-33
□ 97PinPrePBM-33
□ 97PinPrePBM-197
□ 97PinPrePBY-33
□ 97PinPrePBY-197
□ 97PinPrePFC-33
□ 97PinPrePFC-197
□ 97PinPrePFM-33
□ 97PinPrePFM-197
□ 97PinPrePFY-33
□ 97PinPrePFY-197
□ 97PinPrePla-33
□ 97PinPrePla-197
□ 97PinRinC-33
□ 97PinTotCMPG-65
□ 97PinTotCPB-65
□ 97PinTotCPG-65
□ 97PinTotCPR-65
□ 97Sco-107
□ 97ScoArtPro-107
□ 97ScoGolBla-107
□ 97SPAut-118
□ 97SPx-39
□ 97SPxBro-39
□ 97SPxDim-SPX2
□ 97SPxGol-39
□ 97SPxGraF-39
□ 97SPxSil-39
□ 97SPxSte-39
□ 97Stu-40
□ 97StuPor-30
□ 97StuPrePG-40
□ 97StuPrePS-40
□ 97UppDec-127
□ 97UppDecBD-59
□ 97UppDecBDD-59
□ 97UppDecBDQD-59
□ 97UppDecBDTD-59
□ 97UppDecIce-27
□ 97UppDecIceP-27
□ 97UppDecIPS-27
□ 97UppDecSG-SG57
□ 97UppDecTS-17
□ 97UppDecTSL2-17
□ 97UppDecTSS-16C
□ 97Zen-19
□ 97Zen5x7-22
□ 97ZenGolImp-22
□ 97ZenSilImp-22
□ 97ZenZGol-19
□ 97ZenZSil-19
□ 98Be A PPA-107
□ 98Be A PPAA-107
□ 98Be A PPAAF-107
□ 98Be A PPAJ-AS17
□ 98Be A PPPGUJC-G3
□ 98Be A PPPJUJC-P12
□ 98Be A PPTBASG-107
□ 98Be APG-107
□ 98BowBes-55
□ 98BowBesAR-55
□ 98BowBesR-55
□ 98Fin-30
□ 98FinNo P-30
□ 98FinNo PR-30
□ 98FinRef-30
□ 98O-PChr-171
□ 98O-PChrR-171
□ 98Pac-97
□ 98PacAur-146
□ 98PacCroR-104
□ 98PacCroRLS-104
□ 98PacDynI-144
□ 98PacDynIB-144
□ 98PacDynIR-144
□ 98PacIceB-97
□ 98PacOmeH-187
□ 98PacOmeODI-187
□ 98PacOmeR-89
□ 98PacPar-184
□ 98PacParC-142
□ 98PacParEG-184
□ 98PacParH-184
□ 98PacParIB-184
□ 98PacParS-184

□ 98PacRed-97
□ 98PacRev-111
□ 98PacRevADC-25
□ 98PacRevIS-111
□ 98PacRevR-111
□ 98PacRevS-29
□ 98SP Aut-65
□ 98SP AutSS-SS22
□ 98SPXTopP-47
□ 98SPXTopPF-47
□ 98SPXTopPHH-H24
□ 98SPXTopPLI-L20
□ 98SPXTopPR-47
□ 98Top-171
□ 98TopGolLC1-84
□ 98TopGolLC1B-84
□ 98TopGolLC1Boo0-84
□ 98TopGolLC1Oo0-84
□ 98TopGolLC1R-84
□ 98TopGolLC1ROo0-84
□ 98TopGolLC2-84
□ 98TopGolLC2B-84
□ 98TopGolLC2Boo0-84
□ 98TopGolLC2Oo0-84
□ 98TopGolLC2R-84
□ 98TopGolLC3-84
□ 98TopGolLC3B-84
□ 98TopGolLC3Boo0-84
□ 98TopGolLC3Oo0-84
□ 98TopGolLC3ROo0-84
□ 98TopDoO-P-171
□ 98UC-158
□ 98UD ChoPCR-158
□ 98UD ChoR-158
□ 98UppDec-339
□ 98UppDecBD-68
□ 98UppDecDD-68
□ 98UppDec-339
□ 98UppDecE1o1-339
□ 98UppDecFF-FF22
□ 98UppDecFFQ1-FF22
□ 98UppDecFFQ2-FF22
□ 98UppDecGR-339
□ 98UppDecM-160
□ 98UppDecMGS-160
□ 98UppDecMPG-PG15
□ 98UppDecMSS-160
□ 98UppDecMSS-160
□ 98UppDecQD-68
□ 98UppDecTD-68
□ 99Pac-325
□ 99PacAur-111
□ 99PacAurPD-111
□ 99PacCop-325
□ 99PacGol-325
□ 99PacGolCD-29
□ 99PaceIceB-325
□ 99PacPreD-325
□ 99RetHoc-63
□ 99SP AutPS-65
□ 99UppDecM-156
□ 99UppDecMGS-156
□ 99UppDecMPS-JR
□ 99UppDecMSS-156
□ 99UppDecMSS-156
□ 99UppDecRG-63
□ 99UppDecRP-63
**Roenick, Trevor**
□ 93MaiBlaB-58
□ 98LasVegT-17
**Roest, Stacy**
□ 917thInnSWHL-326
□ 95AdiRedW-20
□ 98PacOmeH-89
□ 98PacOme-89
□ 98PacOmeODI-89
□ 98PacOmeR-89
**Roff, Paul**
□ 85MinDul-11
**Roger, Sebastien**
□ 98BowBes-148
□ 98BowBesAR-148
□ 98BowBesR-148
□ 98BowCHL-106
□ 98BowCHLGA-106
□ 98BowCHLOI-106
□ 98BowChrC-106
□ 98BowChrCGA-106
□ 98BowChrCGAR-106
□ 98BowChrCOI-106
□ 98BowChrCOIR-106
□ 98BowChrCOIR-106
**Rogers, Fred**
□ 91ProSetPla-297
**Rogers, Kent**
□ 91AirCanSJHL-B17
□ 91AirCanSJHLAS-7
□ 94MPSPhoSJHL-134
**Rogers, Mike**
□ 750PCWHA-8
□ 770PCWHA-17
□ 79OPC-43
□ 79Top-43
□ 80OPC-143
□ 80Top-143
□ 810PC-127
□ 810PC-135
□ 810PC-140
□ 810PCSti-8
□ 81Top-32
□ 81Top-53
□ 81Top-E131
□ 820PC-232

Rosenberg, Edgar • 651

❑ 82OPCSti-136
❑ 82PosCer-13
❑ 83OPC-254
❑ 83OPCSti-217
❑ 84OPC-152
❑ 84OPCSti-99
❑ 84Top-114
❑ 85OilRedR-19
❑ 85OPC-39
❑ 85OPCSti-86
❑ 85Top-39
❑ 88OilTenAnn-128
**Rogers, Scott**
❑ 91AirCanSJHL-B32
❑ 91AirCanSJHL-C44
❑ 94ClaProP-241
**Rogger, Brian**
❑ 907thInnSQMJHL-154
**Rogles, Chris**
❑ 92ClaKni-16
❑ 93Cla-77
❑ 94ClaAut-NNO
❑ 94ClaProP-213
❑ 94IndIce-20
❑ 95LasVegThu-14
❑ 98GerDELE-46
**Rogov, Alexander**
❑ 74SweHocS-96
**Rohl, Dieter**
❑ 70SweHocS-383
**Rohlicek, Jeff**
❑ 84KelWin-15
❑ 86FreExp-22
❑ 89ProIHL-175
❑ 90ProAHLIHL-357
❑ 91ProAHLCHL-397
❑ 92TolSto-14
❑ 93TolSto-16
**Rohlik, Pavel**
❑ 94CzeAPSE-249
**Rohlin, Leif**
❑ 89SweSemE-245
❑ 90SweSemE-153
❑ 91SweSemE-257
❑ 92SweSemE-281
❑ 93SweSemE-246
❑ 94SweLeaE-175
❑ 94SweLeaEGC-12
❑ 94SweLeaESS-11
❑ 95Don-344
❑ 95SweGloWC-23
❑ 96CanuPos-27
**Rohloff, Jon**
❑ 93Cla-78
❑ 93MinDulCom-4
❑ 94ClaAut-NNO
❑ 94ClaProP-224
❑ 94OPCPre-516
❑ 94OPCPreSE-516
❑ 94TopPre-516
❑ 94TopPreSE-516
❑ 94Ult-260
❑ 94UppDec-378
❑ 94UppDecEleIce-378
❑ 95Don-86
❑ 95Lea-322
❑ 95Top-196
❑ 95TopOPCI-196
❑ 95UppDec-127
❑ 95UppDecEleIce-127
❑ 95UppDecEleIceG-127
❑ 96BeAPAut-207
❑ 96BeAPAutSil-207
❑ 96BeAPla-207
❑ 96ColCho-21
❑ 96UppDec-11
❑ 97PacInvNRB-16
**Rohrbach, Dirk**
❑ 94GerDELE-134
❑ 95GerDELE-135
**Rohrbach, Wilfried**
❑ 69SweWorC-175
❑ 69SweWorC-176
❑ 70SweHocS-382
**Rokama, Jouni**
❑ 93FinnJyvHS-314
❑ 93FinnSIS-29
❑ 94FinnSIS-201
❑ 94FinnSISNP-4
**Roland, Layne**
❑ 907thInnSWHL-331
❑ 917thInnSWHL-42
**Rolanti, Mike**
❑ 93RenEng-27
**Rolfe, Dale**
❑ 68OPC-41
❑ 68Top-41
❑ 69OPC-100
❑ 69OPCFou-18
❑ 69Top-100
❑ 70DadCoo-113
❑ 70EssPowPla-129
❑ 70OPC-156
❑ 70RedWinM-8
❑ 70SarProSta-55
❑ 71OPC-219
❑ 71SarProSta-118
❑ 71TorSun-180
❑ 72OPC-271
❑ 72SarProSta-146
❑ 73OPC-177
❑ 74NHLActSta-191
❑ 74OPCNHL-341
**Rolfe, Dan**
❑ 91NasKni-7
❑ 92ForWorF-17
**Rollins, Al**
❑ 44BeeGro2P-138A
❑ 44BeeGro2P-138B
❑ 44BeeGro2P-447
❑ 45QuaOatP-45
❑ 45QuaOatP-60C
❑ 48ExhCan-37
❑ 51Par-76
❑ 52Par-31
❑ 53Par-82
❑ 54Par-77
❑ 54Top-26
❑ 92ParParR-PR8
❑ 93ParParRCI-4
❑ 94ParMisL-28
**Rollins, Jerry**
❑ 76OPCWHA-43
❑ 76RoaPhoWHA-17
**Roloson, Dwayne**
❑ 94Cla-61
❑ 94ClaAllAme-AA10
❑ 94ClaDraGol-61
❑ 94St.JohF-19
❑ 95ColEdgI-73
❑ 95ColEdgIP-PR5
❑ 95ColEdgITW-G8
❑ 95Ima-41
❑ 95ImaAut-41A
❑ 95ImaGol-41
❑ 95St.JohF-20
❑ 96BeAPAut-211
❑ 96BeAPAutSil-211
❑ 96BeAPla-211
❑ 96ColEdgFL-19
❑ 97ColCho-41
❑ 97Don-148
❑ 97DonPreProG-148
❑ 97DonPreProS-148
❑ 97PacInvNRB-31
❑ 97PacOme-34
❑ 97PacOmeC-34
❑ 97PacOmeDG-34
❑ 97PacOmeEG-34
❑ 97PacOmeG-34
❑ 97PacOmeIB-34
❑ 97Pin-87
❑ 97PinArtP-87
❑ 97PinPrePBB-87
❑ 97PinPrePBC-87
❑ 97PinPrePBM-87
❑ 97PinPrePBY-87
❑ 97PinPrePFC-87
❑ 97PinPrePFM-87
❑ 97PinPrePFY-87
❑ 97PinPrePla-87
❑ 97PinRinC-87
❑ 97Sco-38
❑ 97ScoArtPro-38
❑ 97ScoGolBla-38
❑ 98Pac-124
❑ 98PacIceB-124
❑ 98PacRed-124
**Rolston, Brian**
❑ 91LakSupSL-23
❑ 91UppDec-699
❑ 91UppDecCWJC-86
❑ 91UppDecF-699
❑ 93Cla-79
❑ 93Pow-516
❑ 93StaCluTUSA-21
❑ 93TopPreTUSA-5
❑ 93Ult-496
❑ 94BeAPSig-33
❑ 94Cla-76
❑ 94ClaAut-76
❑ 94ClaDraGol-76
❑ 94ClaProP-90
❑ 94ClaProPIA-IA11
❑ 94ClaProPIH-LP10
❑ 94ClaTri-T37
❑ 94Fin-4
❑ 94FinBowB-R9
❑ 94FinBowBR-R9
❑ 94FinnJaaK-133
❑ 94FinRef-4
❑ 94FinSupTW-4
❑ 94Fla-98
❑ 94Fle-117
❑ 94Lea-441
❑ 94LeaLim-4
❑ 94OPCPre-438
❑ 94OPCPreSE-438
❑ 94ParSE-SE99
❑ 94ParSEG-SE99
❑ 94Pin-255
❑ 94Pin-473
❑ 94PinArtP-255
❑ 94PinArtP-473
❑ 94PinRinC-255
❑ 94PinRinC-473
❑ 94PinRooTP-8
❑ 94ScoTopRR-7
❑ 94Sel-177
❑ 94SelGol-177
❑ 94SelYouExp-YE10
❑ 94SPPre-12
❑ 94SPPreDC-12
❑ 94TopPre-438
❑ 94TopPreSE-438
❑ 94Ult-320
❑ 94UltPro-7
❑ 94UppDec-258
❑ 94UppDecEleIce-258
❑ 94UppDecPC-C13
❑ 94UppDecPCEG-C13
❑ 94UppDecPCES-C13
❑ 94UppDecSPI-SP135
❑ 94UppDecSPIDC-SP135
❑ 95ColCho-273
❑ 95ColCho-366
❑ 95ColChoPC-273
❑ 95ColChoPC-366
❑ 95ColChoPCP-273
❑ 95ColChoPCP-366
❑ 95ColEdgI-8
❑ 95Don-286
❑ 95DonProPoi-9
❑ 95Ima-97
❑ 95ImaGol-97
❑ 95Lea-294
❑ 95ParInt-394
❑ 95ParIntEl-394
❑ 95Pin-172
❑ 95PinArtP-172
❑ 95PinRinC-172
❑ 95Sco-80
❑ 95ScoBlaIce-80
❑ 95ScoBlaIceAP-80
❑ 95Top-362
❑ 95TopNewG-13NG
❑ 95TopOPCI-362
❑ 95UppDec-14
❑ 95UppDecEleIce-14
❑ 95UppDecEleIceG-14
❑ 96ColCho-151
❑ 96Dev-14
❑ 96Pin-7
❑ 96PinArtP-7
❑ 96PinFoi-7
❑ 96PinPreS-7
❑ 96PinRinC-7
❑ 96UppDec-285
❑ 97ColCho-144
❑ 97PacDynBKS-54
❑ 97PacPar-105
❑ 97PacParC-105
❑ 97PacParDG-105
❑ 97PacParEG-105
❑ 97PacParIB-105
❑ 97PacParRed-105
❑ 97PacParSil-105
❑ 97Sco-205
❑ 97ScoDev-6
❑ 97ScoDevPla-6
❑ 97ScoDevPre-6
❑ 97UppDec-92
❑ 97UppDecSG-SG17
❑ 98Be A PPA-230
❑ 98Be A PPAA-230
❑ 98Be A PPAAF-230
❑ 98Be A PPSE-230
❑ 98Be APG-230
❑ 98Pac-270
❑ 98PacIceB-270
❑ 98PacOmeH-141
❑ 98PacOmeODI-141
❑ 98PacOmeR-141
❑ 98PacRed-270
❑ 98UppDec-123
❑ 98UppDecE-123
❑ 98UppDecE1o1-123
❑ 98UppDecGR-123
❑ 99Pac-246
❑ 99PacCop-246
❑ 99PacGol-246
❑ 99PacIceB-246
❑ 99PacPreD-246
**Romaine, Mark**
❑ 90ProAHLIHL-578
❑ 91CinCyc-18
❑ 92BirBul-18
❑ 93BirBul-18
**Roman, Tom**
❑ 87BroBra-9
**Romanchuk, Tyler**
❑ 907thInnSWHL-34
❑ 917thInnSWHL-23
**Romanchych, Larry**
❑ 72Flam-19
❑ 72SarProSta-12
❑ 73OPC-185
❑ 73Top-185
❑ 74NHLActSta-8
❑ 74OPCNHL-157
❑ 74Top-157
❑ 75OPCNHL-153
❑ 75Top-153
❑ 76OPCNHL-281
**Romaniski, Matt**
❑ 94DubFigS-23
❑ 95NorIowH-26
**Romaniuk, Russell (Russ)**
❑ 91JetIGA-27
❑ 91OPCPre-162
❑ 91Par-198
❑ 91ParFre-198
❑ 91Pin-324
❑ 91PinFre-324
❑ 91ProSet-565
❑ 91ProSetFre-565
❑ 91ProSetPla-274
❑ 91ScoCan-627
❑ 91ScoRoo-77T
❑ 91UppDec-46
❑ 91UppDecF-46
❑ 92Bow-276
❑ 92OPC-263
❑ 92PanSti-59
❑ 92PanStiFre-59
❑ 92StaClu-164
❑ 92Top-390
❑ 92TopGol-390G
❑ 93AlbIntTC-17
❑ 93Pow-492
❑ 93Ult-471
❑ 94Par-265
❑ 94ParGol-265
❑ 94StaClu-260
❑ 94StaCluFDI-260
❑ 94StaCluMOMS-260
❑ 94StaCluSTWC-260
❑ 94Ult-394
❑ 98LasVegT-18
**Romano, Mike**
❑ 95NorIowH-27
**Romano, Roberto**
❑ 80QueRem-20
❑ 83PenTeaIP-26
❑ 84PenHeiP-18
❑ 86OPC-180
❑ 86OPCSti-229
❑ 86PenKod-20
❑ 86Top-152
**Romanov, Stanislav**
❑ 96SweSemW-150
**Rombough, Doug**
❑ 74NHLActSta-171
❑ 74NHLActStaU-21
❑ 74OPCNHL-279
❑ 75OPCNHL-161
❑ 75Top-161
**Rome, Brian**
❑ 82Ott67-21
❑ 84SauSteMG-19
**Romeiro, R.J.**
❑ 97LouRivF-24
**Romer, Andy**
❑ 94GerDELE-11
**Romer, Heinrich**
❑ 94GerDELE-18
❑ 95GerDELE-17
**Romfo, Jeff**
❑ 93MinDul-26
❑ 96SouCarS-15
**Romitjevskij, Igor**
❑ 69SweHocS-15
❑ 69SweWorC-21
❑ 69SweWorC-29
❑ 69SweWorC-127
❑ 69SweWorC-132
❑ 70SweHocS-157
❑ 70SweHocS-158
❑ 70SweHocS-319
❑ 71SweHocS-33
❑ 72SweHocS-29
❑ 72SweSemWC-6
❑ 74SweSemHVS-46
**Rommel, Wes**
❑ 91AirCanSJHL-B3
**Romnes, Doc**
❑ 34BeeGro1P-77
❑ 34BeeGro1P-248
❑ 34BeeGro1P-345
❑ 34DiaMatS-52
❑ 35DiaMatTI-59
**Ronan, Ed**
❑ 91ProAHLCHL-90
❑ 92CanaPos-23
❑ 92OPCPre-41
❑ 92Par-88
❑ 92ParEmel-88
❑ 92Ult-333
❑ 92UppDec-491
❑ 93CanaPos-22
❑ 93ClaProPro-134
❑ 93OPCCanHF-45
❑ 93StaClu-262
❑ 93StaCluFDI-262
❑ 93StaCluO-262
❑ 94CanaPos-23
❑ 95JetTeaIss-19
**Ronan, Kyle**
❑ 95MedHatT-14
**Ronan, Skene**
❑ 10C55SweCP-26
❑ 11C55-26
❑ 12C57-14
**Rondeau, Jeremy**
❑ 95SwiCurB-18
**Ronnblom, Anders**
❑ 65SweCorI-141
**Ronning, Cliff**
❑ 87BluKod-23
❑ 88BluKod-7
❑ 88ProIHL-84
❑ 89OPC-45
❑ 89OPCSti-20
❑ 89PanSti-122
❑ 89Top-45
❑ 90BluKod-19
❑ 90ProSet-526
❑ 90ScoRoo-81T
❑ 91Bow-313
❑ 91CanuAutC-21
❑ 91CanuMol-7
❑ 91CanuTeal8-21
❑ 91OPC-59
❑ 91PanSti-46
❑ 91Par-182
❑ 91ParFre-182
❑ 91Pin-106
❑ 91PinFre-106
❑ 91ProSet-241
❑ 91ProSetFre-241
❑ 91ProSetPla-236
❑ 91ScoAme-212
❑ 91ScoCan-212
❑ 91StaClu-298
❑ 91Top-59
❑ 91UppDec-208
❑ 91UppDecF-208
❑ 92Bow-411
❑ 92CanuRoaTA-19
❑ 92OPC-94
❑ 92PanSti-30
❑ 92PanStiFre-30
❑ 92Par-193
❑ 92ParEmel-193
❑ 92Pin-12
❑ 92PinFre-12
❑ 92ProSet-195
❑ 92Sco-254
❑ 92ScoCan-254
❑ 92SeaPat-32
❑ 92StaClu-373
❑ 92Top-81
❑ 92TopGol-81G
❑ 92Ult-227
❑ 92UppDec-160
❑ 93Don-357
❑ 93Lea-183
❑ 93OPCPre-81
❑ 93OPCPreG-81
❑ 93PanSti-168
❑ 93Par-210
❑ 93ParEmel-210
❑ 93Pin-69
❑ 93Pin-234
❑ 93PinCan-69
❑ 93PinCan-234
❑ 93Pow-255
❑ 93Sco-17
❑ 93Sco-443
❑ 93ScoCan-17
❑ 93ScoCan-443
❑ 93StaClu-125
❑ 93StaCluFDI-125
❑ 93StaCluFDIO-125
❑ 93StaCluO-125
❑ 93TopPre-81
❑ 93TopPreG-81
❑ 93Ult-119
❑ 93UppDec-211
❑ 94CanGamNHLP-27
❑ 94CanuProI-19
❑ 94Don-278
❑ 94EASpo-141
❑ 94Fla-194
❑ 94Fle-230
❑ 94Lea-66
❑ 94OPCPre-291
❑ 94OPCPreSE-291
❑ 94ParSE-SE188
❑ 94ParSEG-SE188
❑ 94Pin-113
❑ 94PinArtP-113
❑ 94PinRinC-113
❑ 94Sco-86
❑ 94ScoGol-86
❑ 94ScoPla-86
❑ 94ScoPlaTS-86
❑ 94Sel-122
❑ 94SelGol-122
❑ 94StaClu-200
❑ 94StaCluFDI-200
❑ 94StaCluMOMS-200
❑ 94StaCluSTWC-200
❑ 94TopPre-291
❑ 94TopPreSE-291
❑ 94Ult-230
❑ 94UppDec-358
❑ 94UppDecEleIce-358
❑ 95BeAPla-91
❑ 95BeAPSig-S91
❑ 95BeAPSigDC-S91
❑ 95CanGamNHLP-269
❑ 95CanuBuiDA-7
❑ 95ColCho-17
❑ 95ColChoPC-17
❑ 95ColChoPCP-17
❑ 95Don-79
❑ 95ParInt-479
❑ 95ParIntEl-479
❑ 95Pin-184
❑ 95PinArtP-184
❑ 95PinRinC-184
❑ 95PlaOneoOne-211
❑ 95ProMag-30
❑ 95Sco-75
❑ 95ScoBlaIce-75
❑ 95ScoBlaIceAP-75
❑ 95SP-154
❑ 95StaClu-128
❑ 95StaCluMOMS-128
❑ 95Top-99
❑ 95TopOPCI-99
❑ 95UppDec-102
❑ 95UppDecEleIce-102
❑ 95UppDecEleIceG-102
❑ 95UppDecSpeE-SE174
❑ 95UppDecSpeEdiG-SE174
❑ 96ColCho-270
❑ 96Don-47
❑ 96DonPrePro-47
❑ 96Lea-173
❑ 96LeaPreP-173
❑ 96NHLProSTA-30
❑ 96Pin-163
❑ 96PinArtP-163
❑ 96PinFoi-163
❑ 96PinPreS-163
❑ 96PinRinC-163
❑ 96PlaOneoOne-398
❑ 96Sco-163
❑ 96ScoArtPro-163
❑ 96ScoDeaCAP-163
❑ 96ScoGolB-163
❑ 96ScoSpeAP-163
❑ 96SP-124
❑ 96TopNHLP-105
❑ 96TopPicOI-105
❑ 96UppDec-315
❑ 96UppDecIce-53
❑ 96UppDecIcePar-53
❑ 97ColCho-199
❑ 97Pac-200
❑ 97PacCop-200
❑ 97PacCroR-106
❑ 97PacCroREG-106
❑ 97PacCroRIB-106
❑ 97PacCroRS-106
❑ 97PacEmeGre-200
❑ 97PacIceB-200
❑ 97PacPar-143
❑ 97PacParC-143
❑ 97PacParDG-143
❑ 97PacParEG-143
❑ 97PacParIB-143
❑ 97PacParRed-143
❑ 97PacParSil-143
❑ 97PacRed-200
❑ 97PacSil-200
❑ 97PinIns-173
❑ 97Sco-244
❑ 97UppDec-132
❑ 98Be A PPA-226
❑ 98Be A PPAA-226
❑ 98Be A PPAAF-226
❑ 98Be A PPSE-226
❑ 98Be APG-226
❑ 98BowBes-61
❑ 98BowBesAR-61
❑ 98BowBesR-61
❑ 98Fin-44
❑ 98FinNo P-44
❑ 98FinNo PR-44
❑ 98FinRef-44
❑ 98Pac-343
❑ 98PacAur-147
❑ 98PacIceB-343
❑ 98PacOmeH-132
❑ 98PacOmeODI-132
❑ 98PacOmeR-132
❑ 98PacPar-185
❑ 98PacParC-185
❑ 98PacParEG-185
❑ 98PacParH-185
❑ 98PacParIB-185
❑ 98PacParS-185
❑ 98PacRed-343
❑ 98PacRev-80
❑ 98PacRevIS-80
❑ 98PacRevR-80
❑ 98TopGolLC1-55
❑ 98TopGolLC1B-55
❑ 98TopGolLC1BOoO-55
❑ 98TopGolLC1OoO-55
❑ 98TopGolLC1R-55
❑ 98TopGolLC1ROoO-55
❑ 98TopGolLC2-55
❑ 98TopGolLC2B-55
❑ 98TopGolLC2BOoO-55
❑ 98TopGolLC2OoO-55
❑ 98TopGolLC2R-55
❑ 98TopGolLC2ROoO-55
❑ 98TopGolLC3-55
❑ 98TopGolLC3B-55
❑ 98TopGolLC3BOoO-55
❑ 98TopGolLC3OoO-55
❑ 98TopGolLC3R-55
❑ 98TopGolLC3ROoO-55
❑ 98UppDec-156
❑ 98UppDecE-156
❑ 98UppDecE1o1-156
❑ 98UppDecGR-156
❑ 98UppDecM-112
❑ 98UppDecMGS-112
❑ 98UppDecMSS-112
❑ 98UppDecMSS-112
❑ 99Pac-231
❑ 99PacAur-81
❑ 99PacAurPD-81
❑ 99PacCop-231
❑ 99PacGol-231
❑ 99PacIceB-231
❑ 99PacPreD-231
❑ 99UppDecM-108
❑ 99UppDecMGS-108
❑ 99UppDecMSS-108
❑ 99UppDecMSS-108
**Ronnkvist, Anders**
❑ 65SweCorI-213
**Ronnqvist, Petter**
❑ 91SweSemE-56
❑ 92SweSemE-76
❑ 93SweSemE-51
❑ 94SweLeaE-271
❑ 95SweLeaE-99
❑ 95SweLeaES-10
❑ 95SweUppDE-152
**Ronty, Paul**
❑ 44BeeGro2P-63
❑ 44BeeGro2P-359
❑ 48ExhCan-48
❑ 51Par-95
❑ 52Par-24
❑ 53Par-63
❑ 54Par-66
❑ 54Top-15
**Roodbol, Kees**
❑ 91BriColJHL-112
❑ 92BriColJHL-166
❑ 92BriColJHL-212
**Rooney, Larry**
❑ 91RicRen-2
**Rooney, Steve**
❑ 85CanaPos-29
❑ 85CanaPos-30
❑ 85CanaPro-18
❑ 87CanaPos-25
❑ 87Jet-18
❑ 87OPC-223
❑ 88DevCar-23
❑ 89ProAHL-210
❑ 90ProAHLIHL-364
**Rooster, Cornelius**
❑ 92KelPos-5
**Root, Bill**
❑ 82CanaPos-22
❑ 82CanaSte-17
❑ 83CanaPos-24
❑ 83OPC-196
❑ 84MapLeaP-20
❑ 84OPC-271
❑ 85MapLeaP-25
❑ 88ProAHL-229
❑ 89ProAHL-112
❑ 90NewSai-20
❑ 90ProAHLIHL-162
**Rosa, Pavel**
❑ 97BowCHL-51
❑ 97BowCHLOPC-51
❑ 98PacOmeH-117
❑ 98PacOmeODI-117
❑ 98PacOmeR-117
❑ 98PacRev-69
❑ 98PacRevIS-69
❑ 98PacRevR-69
❑ 98SPXTopP-31
❑ 98SPXTopPF-31
❑ 98SPXTopPR-31
❑ 98UppDecBD-40
❑ 98UppDecDD-40
❑ 98UppDecQD-40
❑ 98UppDecTD-40
❑ 99Pac-197
❑ 99PacCop-197
❑ 99PacGol-197
❑ 99PacIceB-197
❑ 99PacPreD-197
❑ 99RetHoc-39
❑ 99UppDecCL-79
❑ 99UppDecCLCLC-79
❑ 99UppDecM-93
❑ 99UppDecMGS-93
❑ 99UppDecMSS-93
❑ 99UppDecMSS-93
❑ 99UppDecRG-39
❑ 99UppDecRP-39
**Rosa, Stanislav**
❑ 94CzeAPSE-215
**Rosander, Ola**
❑ 89SweSemE-227
❑ 90SweSemE-69
❑ 91SweSemE-243
**Rosati, Mike**
❑ 88NiaFalT-6
❑ 93SweSemWCS-210
❑ 95FinnSemWC-171
❑ 95SweGloWC-226
❑ 96GerDELE-159
❑ 96SweSemW-174
**Roscoe, Ron**
❑ 75HamFin-16
**Rose, Arthur**
❑ 51LavDaiQSHL-94
**Rose, Jarrett**
❑ 95Sla-132
**Rose, Jay**
❑ 90CinCyc-21
❑ 91CinCyc-19
**Rosen, Anders**
❑ 71SweHocS-218
**Rosen, Johan**
❑ 93SweSemE-167
❑ 94SweLeaE-12
❑ 95SweLeaE-80
❑ 95SweLeaEG-8
❑ 95SweUppDE-132
❑ 95SweUppDETNA-NA17
❑ 98GerDELE-83
**Rosen, Roger**
❑ 95SweLeaE-297
❑ 95SweLeaER-9
❑ 95SweUppDE-201
**Rosenberg, Edgar**
❑ 74SweHocS-81
**Rosenberg, Kari**
❑ 93FinnJyvHS-44
❑ 93FinnSIS-234
❑ 94FinnSIS-34
❑ 94FinnSISJ-6
❑ 94FinnSISNP-5
❑ 95FinnSIS-16
❑ 95FinnSISGG-6
❑ 95FinnSISL-82
**Rosenblatt, Howie**
❑ 91ProAHLCHL-60
❑ 93ClaProPro-44

❑ 94GreMon-7
**Rosendahl, Hans Ake**
❑ 71SweHocS-142
❑ 72SweHocS-126
❑ 73SweHocS-183
❑ 73SweWorCS-183
**Rosenheck, Jerry**
❑ 92ClaKni-17
**Rosenqvist, Per**
❑ 92SweSemE-212
**Rosol, Petr**
❑ 89SweSemWCS-200
❑ 93SwiHNL-333
❑ 94FinnJaaK-187
❑ 95SwiHNL-480
**Ross, Andy**
❑ 94CenHocL-106
**Ross, Art**
❑ 10C55SweCP-31
❑ 10C56-8
❑ 10C56-12
❑ 11C55-31
❑ 12C57-20
❑ 36V356WorG-96
❑ 38BruGarMS-6
❑ 60Top-27
❑ 60TopSta-46
❑ 83HalFP-E15
❑ 85HalFC-74
❑ 91BruSpoAL-25
❑ 94HalFT-4
❑ 94UppDecPHG-H25
**Ross, Brian**
❑ 83KitRan-25
**Ross, Don**
❑ 72SweSemWC-122
**Ross, Gordon**
❑ 917thInnSOHL-361
❑ 93LonKni-16
**Ross, John**
❑ 23V1451-28
❑ 24V1452-52
❑ 33OPCV304B-53
❑ 33V129-18
❑ 33V252CanG-41
❑ 83HalFP-G12
❑ 85HalFC-102
**Ross, Mike**
❑ 95SouCarS-7
❑ 96SouCarS-9
**Ross, Patrik**
❑ 89SweSemE-116
❑ 90SweSemE-117
❑ 91SweSemE-120
❑ 92SweSemE-141
❑ 93SweSemE-120
**Ross, Philip D**
❑ 83HalFP-D12
❑ 85HalFC-58
**Ross, Tom**
❑ 93MicSta-17
**Rossetti, Mike**
❑ 89JohChi-25
❑ 91JohChi-18
❑ 91ProAHLCHL-56
**Rossi, Rico**
❑ 92DalFre-14
**Rossiter, Kyle**
❑ 98BowCHL-157
❑ 98BowCHLAuB-A7
❑ 98BowCHLAuG-A7
❑ 98BowCHLAuS-A7
❑ 98BowCHLGA-157
❑ 98BowCHLOI-157
❑ 98BowChrC-157
❑ 98BowChrCGA-157
❑ 98BowChrCGAR-157
❑ 98BowChrCOI-157
❑ 98BowChrCOIR-157
❑ 98BowChrCOIR-157
**Rota, Blair**
❑ 96KamBla-21
**Rota, Darcy**
❑ 74NHLActSta-82
❑ 74OPCNHL-269
❑ 75OPCNHL-66
❑ 75Top-66
❑ 76OPCNHL-47
❑ 76Top-47
❑ 77OPCNHL-117
❑ 77Top-117
❑ 78OPC-47
❑ 78Top-47
❑ 79FlaTeal-18
❑ 79OPC-360
❑ 80CanuSilD-20
❑ 80CanuTeal-18
❑ 80OPC-301
❑ 80PepCap-116
❑ 81CanuSilD-12
❑ 81CanuTeal-18
❑ 81OPC-343
❑ 82Canu-18
❑ 82OPC-355
❑ 82PosCer-19
❑ 83Canu-17
❑ 83OPC-344
❑ 83OPC-345
❑ 83OPC-358
❑ 83OPCSti-272
❑ 83PufSti-5
❑ 83Vac-115
❑ 847EDis-50
❑ 84Canu-20
❑ 84OPC-328

❑ 84OPCSti-280
❑ 84Top-139
**Rota, Randy**
❑ 74NHLActSta-305
❑ 74OPCNHL-362
❑ 75OPCNHL-237
❑ 75Top-237
❑ 76OPCNHL-353
**Rotheli, Andre**
❑ 91SweSemWCS-195
❑ 93SwiHNL-104
❑ 93SwiHNL-177
**Rothschild, Sam**
❑ 24C144ChaCig-52
❑ 24V130MapC-19
❑ 24V1452-37
**Rothwell, Nick**
❑ 95GuiFla-10
❑ 97GuiFla-14
**Rotkirch, Johann**
❑ 72SweSemWC-114
**Rouleau, Guy**
❑ 86SheCan-23
**Rouleau, Michel**
❑ 72NordPos-19
❑ 73NordTeal-19
**Roulston, Rollie**
❑ 81RedWinOld-21
**Roulston, Tom**
❑ 82OilRedR-24
❑ 82OPC-118
❑ 83OPC-42
❑ 83OPCSti-103
❑ 83Vac-39
❑ 84OPC-179
❑ 84OPCSti-123
❑ 84PenHeiP-19
❑ 88OilTenAnn-15
**Roupe, Claes**
❑ 89SweSemE-118
**Roupe, Magnus**
❑ 83SweSemE-120
❑ 84SweSemE-120
❑ 85SwePanS-107
❑ 86SwePanS-102
❑ 89SweSemE-90
❑ 90SweSemE-263
❑ 91SweSemE-94
❑ 95SweUppDE1DS-DS14
**Rourke, Alan**
❑ 96KitRan-23
**Rouse, Bob**
❑ 84NorStaPos-25
❑ 85NorStaPos-26
❑ 86NorSta7E-9
❑ 87NorStaPos-27
❑ 88NorStaADA-21
❑ 89CapKod-8
❑ 89CapTealss-20
❑ 89OPC-26
❑ 89PanSti-351
❑ 89Top-26
❑ 90PanSti-164
❑ 90ProSet-554
❑ 90Sco-147
❑ 90ScoCan-147
❑ 90UppDec-389
❑ 90UppDecF-389
❑ 91MapLeaP-27
❑ 91OPCPre-151
❑ 91PanSti-101
❑ 91Par-176
❑ 91ParFre-176
❑ 91ProSet-228
❑ 91ProSetFre-228
❑ 91ScoCan-246
❑ 92MapLeaK-21
❑ 92Pin-358
❑ 92PinFre-358
❑ 92Sco-130
❑ 92ScoCan-130
❑ 92Ult-214
❑ 93Don-333
❑ 93Lea-230
❑ 93OPCPre-207
❑ 93OPCPreG-207
❑ 93Pin-289
❑ 93PinCan-289
❑ 93Sco-304
❑ 93ScoBla-5
❑ 93ScoCan-304
❑ 93StaClu-353
❑ 93StaCluFDI-353
❑ 93StaCluO-353
❑ 93TopPre-207
❑ 93TopPreG-207
❑ 94CanGamNHLP-359
❑ 94OPCPre-393
❑ 94OPCPreSE-393
❑ 94ParSE-SE51
❑ 94ParSEG-SE51
❑ 94Pin-374
❑ 94PinArtP-374
❑ 94PinRinC-374
❑ 94StaClu-238
❑ 94StaCluFDI-238
❑ 94StaCluMOMS-238
❑ 94StaCluSTWC-238
❑ 94TopPre-393
❑ 94TopPreSE-393
❑ 94UppDec-55
❑ 94UppDecEelce-55
❑ 95BeAPla-88
❑ 95BeAPSig-S88
❑ 95BeAPSigDC-S88

❑ 95Pin-163
❑ 95PinArtP-163
❑ 95PinRinC-163
❑ 95Top-206
❑ 95TopOPCI-206
❑ 96Sco-125
❑ 96ScoArtPro-125
❑ 96ScoDeaCAP-125
❑ 96ScoGolB-125
❑ 96ScoSpeAP-125
❑ 97PacInvNRB-72
❑ 98UppDecM-175
❑ 98UppDecMGS-175
❑ 98UppDecMSS-175
❑ 98UppDecMSS-175
**Rousek, Martin**
❑ 94CzeAPSE-217
❑ 95CzeAPSE-168
❑ 96CzeAPSE-181
**Rousseau, Bobby (Bob)**
❑ 44BeeGro2P-287
❑ 61ShiCoi-117
❑ 61YorYelB-35
❑ 62Par-47
❑ 62ShiMetC-29
❑ 62ShiMetC-56
❑ 62YorIroOTra-18
❑ 63ChePho-47A
❑ 63ChePho-47B
❑ 63Par-35
❑ 63Par-94
❑ 63YorWhiB-25
❑ 64BeeGro3P-115
❑ 64CanaPos-17
❑ 64CocCap-65
❑ 64Top-80
❑ 65CanaSteG-8
❑ 65Coc-65
❑ 65Top-70
❑ 66CanaGA-6
❑ 66Top-7
❑ 66Top-132
❑ 66TopUSAT-7
❑ 67CanalGA-15
❑ 67PosFliB-12
❑ 67Top-68
❑ 67YorActOct-33
❑ 68CanalGA-15
❑ 68CanaPosBW-14
❑ 68OPC-65
❑ 68PosCerM-22
❑ 68ShiCoi-83
❑ 68Top-65
❑ 69CanaPosC-26
❑ 69OPC-9
❑ 69Top-9
❑ 70CanaPin-13
❑ 70ColSta-35
❑ 70DadCoo-114
❑ 70EssPowPla-173
❑ 70NorStaP-8
❑ 70OPC-170
❑ 70OPCDec-14
❑ 71OPC-218
❑ 71SarProSta-117
❑ 71TorSun-181
❑ 72OPC-233
❑ 72SarProSta-145
❑ 72SweSemWC-200
❑ 73OPC-233
❑ 74NHLActSta-182
❑ 74OPCNHL-326
❑ 94ParTalB-84
❑ 95Par66-77
❑ 95Par66-143
❑ 95Par66Coi-77
**Rousseau, Guy**
❑ 52JunBluT-142
❑ 55MonRoy-6
❑ 62QueAce-19
❑ 64QueAce-16
**Rousseau, Rollie (Rolland)**
❑ 51LavDaiQSHL-88
❑ 52St.LawS-8
**Roussel, Dominic**
❑ 90ProAHLIHL-31
❑ 91Par-450
❑ 91ParFre-450
❑ 91Pin-343
❑ 91PinFre-343
❑ 91ProAHLCHL-265
❑ 91ProSet-552
❑ 91ProSetFre-552
❑ 91UppDec-583
❑ 91UppDecF-583
❑ 92Bow-92
❑ 92FlyJCP-21
❑ 92FlyUppDS-7
❑ 92FlyUppDS-31
❑ 92FlyUppDS-39
❑ 92Kra-27
❑ 92OPC-198
❑ 92OPCPre-51
❑ 92OPCPreTR-3
❑ 92PanSti-183
❑ 92PanStiFre-183
❑ 92Par-129
❑ 92ParEmel-129
❑ 92Pin-96
❑ 92PinFre-96
❑ 92PinTea2-11
❑ 92PinTea2F-11
❑ 92ProSet-235
❑ 92Sco-464

❑ 92ScoCan-464
❑ 92ScoYouS-36
❑ 92SeaPat-40
❑ 92StaClu-315
❑ 92Top-10
❑ 92Top-213
❑ 92TopGol-10G
❑ 92TopGol-213G
❑ 92Ult-159
❑ 92UppDec-31
❑ 92UppDecACH-6
❑ 93Don-243
❑ 93DurSco-39
❑ 93Kra-63
❑ 93Lea-244
❑ 93OPCPre-335
❑ 93OPCPreG-335
❑ 93Par-417
❑ 93ParEmel-417
❑ 93Pin-97
❑ 93PinCan-97
❑ 93PinMas-4
❑ 93Pow-409
❑ 93Sco-82
❑ 93ScoCan-82
❑ 93StaClu-109
❑ 93StaCluFDI-109
❑ 93StaCluFDIO-109
❑ 93StaCluO-109
❑ 93TopPre-335
❑ 93TopPreG-335
❑ 93Ult-392
❑ 93UppDec-336
❑ 94CanGamNHLP-290
❑ 94ClaProP-55
❑ 94Don-263
❑ 94Lea-203
❑ 94OPCPre-56
❑ 94OPCPreSE-56
❑ 94Par-169
❑ 94ParGol-169
❑ 94Pin-208
❑ 94PinArtP-208
❑ 94PinRinC-208
❑ 94Sco-105
❑ 94ScoGol-105
❑ 94ScoPla-105
❑ 94ScoPlaTS-105
❑ 94TopPre-56
❑ 94TopPreSE-56
❑ 94UppDec-397
❑ 94UppDecEelce-397
❑ 95BeAPla-157
❑ 95BeAPSig-S157
❑ 95BeAPSigDC-S157
❑ 95Don-247
❑ 95Sco-182
❑ 95ScoBlaIce-182
❑ 95ScoBlaIceAP-182
❑ 96DonCanILG-7
❑ 96Sum-50
❑ 96SumArtP-50
❑ 96SumIce-50
❑ 96SumMet-50
❑ 96SumPreS-50
❑ 99Pac-12
❑ 99PacCop-12
❑ 99PacGol-12
❑ 99PacIceB-12
❑ 99PacPreD-12
**Rousson, Boris**
❑ 907thInnSQMJHL-64
❑ 91ProAHLCHL-200
❑ 92BinRan-17
❑ 94ClaProP-183
❑ 94FinnSIS-329
❑ 95FinnSIS-95
❑ 95FinnSIS-161
❑ 95FinnSIS-381
❑ 95FinnSISGG-2
❑ 95FinnSISL-29
❑ 95FinnSISSpe-2
❑ 95FinnSISR-95
❑ 96FinnSISR-181
❑ 96FinnSISRKIG-3
❑ 96FinnSISRMA-7
❑ 98GerDELE-98
**Rousu, Miikka**
❑ 94FinnSIS-332
❑ 94FinnSISR-142
❑ 96FinnSISRRE-9
**Routanen, Arto**
❑ 86SwePanS-115
❑ 87SwePanS-112
**Routhier, Jean-Marc**
❑ 88ProAHL-111
❑ 89HalCit-20
❑ 89NordPol-24
❑ 89ProAHL-160
**Routhier, Stephane**
❑ 93DruVol-2
**Routsalainen, Reijo**
❑ 81SweSemHVS-26
**Rouvali, Simo**
❑ 95FinnSIS-132
❑ 96FinnSISR-143
**Rowbotham, Dave**
❑ 88ProAHL-51
**Rowbotham, Ken**
❑ 897thInnSOHL-82
❑ 907thInnSOHL-17
**Rowe, Bobby**
❑ 10C55SweCP-23
❑ 11C55-23
❑ 12C57-11

**Rowe, Jon**
❑ 92MPSPhoSJHL-99
**Rowe, Sean**
❑ 93ForWorF-14
❑ 94CenHocL-32
❑ 95LouIceG-13
❑ 96AncAce-13
❑ 97AncAce-17
**Rowe, Tom**
❑ 790PC-113
❑ 79Top-113
❑ 80OPC-214
❑ 80Top-214
❑ 81OPC-139
❑ 83MonAlp-12
**Rowland, Chris**
❑ 89SpoChi-15
❑ 907thInnSWHL-310
❑ 917thInnSWHL-34
❑ 94ThuBayS-17
❑ 96LouRiv-12
**Rowland, Dean**
❑ 91BriColJHL-85
**Roworth, Kirk**
❑ 88SasBla-17
**Roy, Adam**
❑ 93MinDul-9
**Roy, Allain**
❑ 92AlbIntTC-18
❑ 94FinnSISNP-8
❑ 94ScoTeaC-CT23
**Roy, Andre**
❑ 95ColEdgI-60
❑ 96ProBru-49
**Roy, Claude**
❑ 52JunBluT-34
**Roy, Darcy T**
❑ 82Ott67-22
❑ 83Ott67-25
**Roy, Georges**
❑ 51LavDaiQSHL-30
❑ 52St.LawS-92
**Roy, Jean-Yves**
❑ 92BinRan-17
❑ 92Cla-80
❑ 92MaiBlaB-14
❑ 94BinRan-18
❑ 94ClaProP-182
❑ 94ScoTeaC-CT12
❑ 94UppDec-407
❑ 94UppDecEelce-407
❑ 95Ima-96
❑ 95ImaGol-96
❑ 96ClaGol-80
❑ 96ProBru-8
❑ 97ColCho-19
❑ 97Pac-313
❑ 97PacCop-313
❑ 97PacEmeGre-313
❑ 97PacIceB-313
❑ 97PacRed-313
❑ 97PacSil-313
❑ 97UppDec-12
**Roy, Lucien**
❑ 51LavDaiLSJ-22
**Roy, Marc Oliver**
❑ 97BowCHL-44
❑ 97BowCHLOPC-44
**Roy, Mario**
❑ 77GraVic-17
**Roy, Martin**
❑ 917thInnSQMJHL-186
❑ 95RicRen-17
**Roy, Patrick**
❑ 85CanaPos-31
❑ 85CanaPos-19
❑ 86CanaPos-20
❑ 86KraDra-61
❑ 86OPC-53
❑ 86OPCSti-5
❑ 86OPCSti-132
❑ 86Top-53
❑ 87CanaPos-26
❑ 87CanaVacS-23
❑ 87CanaVacS-42
❑ 87CanaVacS-43
❑ 87CanaVacS-69
❑ 87CanaVacS-71
❑ 87CanaVacS-74
❑ 87CanaVacS-76
❑ 87OPC-163
❑ 87OPCMin-36
❑ 87OPCSti-13
❑ 87OPCSti-185
❑ 87PanSti-56
❑ 87PanSti-376B
❑ 87Top-163
❑ 88CanaPos-24
❑ 88OPC-116
❑ 88OPCMin-33
❑ 88OPCSti-45
❑ 88OPCSti-115
❑ 88PanSti-252
❑ 88PanSti-402
❑ 88Top-116
❑ 88TopStiIns-12
❑ 89CanaKra-19
❑ 89CanaPos-27
❑ 89CanaProF-33
❑ 89Kra-25
❑ 89OPC-17
❑ 89OPC-322
❑ 89OPCSti-14

❑ 89OPCSti-57
❑ 89OPCSti-156
❑ 89OPCSti-161
❑ 89OPCSti-201
❑ 89OPCSti-211
❑ 89PanSti-235
❑ 89PanSti-376
❑ 89PanSti-383
❑ 89SweSemWCS-54
❑ 89Top-17
❑ 89TopStiIns-6
❑ 90Bow-50
❑ 90BowTif-50
❑ 90CanaPos-25
❑ 90Kra-49
❑ 90OPC-198
❑ 90OPC-219
❑ 90OPC-512
❑ 90OPCBoxB-E
❑ 90OPCPre-110
❑ 90PanSti-51
❑ 90PanSti-323
❑ 90ProSet-157
❑ 90ProSet-359
❑ 90ProSet-391
❑ 90ProSet-399
❑ 90Sco-10
❑ 90Sco-312
❑ 90Sco-344
❑ 90Sco-354
❑ 90Sco-364
❑ 90ScoCan-10
❑ 90ScoCan-312
❑ 90ScoCan-344
❑ 90ScoCan-354
❑ 90ScoCan-364
❑ 90ScoHotRS-25
❑ 90ScoPro-10
❑ 90Top-198
❑ 90Top-219
❑ 90TopBoxB-E
❑ 90TopTif-198
❑ 90TopTif-219
❑ 90UppDec-153
❑ 90UppDec-207
❑ 90UppDec-317
❑ 90UppDec-496
❑ 90UppDecF-153
❑ 90UppDecF-207
❑ 90UppDecF-317
❑ 90UppDecF-496
❑ 90UppDecP-241B
❑ 91Bow-335
❑ 91CanaPanTS-19
❑ 91CanaPanTS-G
❑ 91CanaPos-24
❑ 91Gil-28
❑ 91Kra-76
❑ 91McDUppD-8
❑ 91McDUppD-H6
❑ 91OPC-270
❑ 91OPC-413
❑ 91OPCPre-14
❑ 91OPCPre-100
❑ 91PanSti-184
❑ 91PanSti-333
❑ 91Par-90
❑ 91Par-220
❑ 91Par-442
❑ 91Par-463
❑ 91Par-470
❑ 91ParFre-90
❑ 91ParFre-220
❑ 91ParFre-442
❑ 91ParFre-463
❑ 91ParFre-470
❑ 91Pin-175
❑ 91Pin-387
❑ 91PinB-B1
❑ 91PinBFre-B1
❑ 91PinFre-175
❑ 91PinFre-387
❑ 91ProSet-125
❑ 91ProSet-304
❑ 91ProSet-599
❑ 91ProSet-613
❑ 91ProSet-AU125
❑ 91ProSet-AU599
❑ 91ProSetCC-CC2
❑ 91ProSetCCF-CC2
❑ 91ProSetFre-125
❑ 91ProSetFre-599
❑ 91ProSetFre-613
❑ 91ProSetFre-AU125
❑ 91ProSetFre-AU599
❑ 91ProSetGaz-2
❑ 91ProSetGaz-SC1
❑ 91ProSetNHLAS-AC3
❑ 91ProSetPC-14
❑ 91ProSetPla-61
❑ 91ScoAme-75
❑ 91ScoAme-342
❑ 91ScoAme-424
❑ 91ScoCan-75
❑ 91ScoCan-314
❑ 91ScoCan-372
❑ 91ScoFan-10
❑ 91ScoKel-1
❑ 91ScoNat-10
❑ 91ScoNatCWC-10
❑ 91SweSemWCS-52
❑ 91Top-270

❑ 91Top-413
❑ 91UppDec-137
❑ 91UppDec-614
❑ 91UppDecF-137
❑ 91UppDecF-614
❑ 92Bow-74
❑ 92Bow-239
❑ 92CanaPos-24
❑ 92DurPan-50
❑ 92DurPan-NNO
❑ 92HumDum1-18
❑ 92KelPos-4
❑ 92Kra-34
❑ 92Kra-47
❑ 92McDUppD-H6
❑ 92OPC-111
❑ 92OPC-164
❑ 92OPC25Al-19
❑ 92OPCTroW-4
❑ 92PanSti-147
❑ 92PanSti-277
❑ 92PanStiFre-147
❑ 92PanStiFre-277
❑ 92Par-84
❑ 92Par-463
❑ 92Par-510
❑ 92ParEmel-84
❑ 92ParEmel-463
❑ 92ParEmel-510
❑ 92Pin-130
❑ 92PinFre-130
❑ 92ProSet-2
❑ 92ProSet-85
❑ 92ProSetAW-CC2
❑ 92Sco-295
❑ 92Sco-418
❑ 92Sco-428
❑ 92Sco-489
❑ 92Sco-527
❑ 92ScoCan-295
❑ 92ScoCan-418
❑ 92ScoCan-428
❑ 92ScoCan-489
❑ 92ScoCan-527
❑ 92SeaPat-21
❑ 92StaClu-133
❑ 92StaClu-252
❑ 92Top-110
❑ 92Top-263
❑ 92Top-491
❑ 92Top-508
❑ 92TopGol-110G
❑ 92TopGol-263G
❑ 92TopGol-491G
❑ 92TopGol-508G
❑ 92Ult-108
❑ 92UltAllS-3
❑ 92UltAwaW-4
❑ 92UppDec-149
❑ 92UppDec-438
❑ 92UppDec-440
❑ 92UppDecAWT-W6
❑ 93CanaPos-23
❑ 93ClaProPro-33
❑ 93Don-178
❑ 93DonEli-9
❑ 93DonIceKin-14
❑ 93DonSpeP-L
❑ 93DurSco-17
❑ 93DurSco-NNO
❑ 93HigLinGG-1
❑ 93KenStaLA-11
❑ 93KenStaLC-10
❑ 93Kra-64
❑ 93Kra-72
❑ 93Lea-33
❑ 93Lea-100
❑ 93LeaGolAS-5
❑ 93LeaPaiWar-4
❑ 93LeaStuS-6
❑ 93McDUppD-23
❑ 93McDUppD-23L
❑ 93OPCCanHF-30
❑ 93OPCPre-1
❑ 93OPCPreBG-8
❑ 93OPCPreG-1
❑ 93PanSti-8
❑ 93Par-100
❑ 93ParChePH-D10
❑ 93ParEasWesS-E4
❑ 93ParEmel-100
❑ 93ParUSACG-G9
❑ 93Pin-150
❑ 93Pin-228
❑ 93PinAllS-18
❑ 93PinAllSC-18
❑ 93PinCan-150
❑ 93PinCan-228
❑ 93PinTeaP-1
❑ 93PinTeaP-2
❑ 93Pow-133
❑ 93PowGam-9
❑ 93PowNet-7
❑ 93Sco-315
❑ 93ScoCan-315
❑ 93ScoDreTea-2
❑ 93ScoFra-10
❑ 93SeaPat-16
❑ 93StaClu-9
❑ 93StaCluAS-1
❑ 93StaCluFDI-231
❑ 93StaCluFDIO-231
❑ 93StaCluFin-11
❑ 93StaCluMasP-7
❑ 93StaCluMasPW-7

❑ 98SP AutSS-SS2
❑ 98SPxFin-24
❑ 98SPxFin-119
❑ 98SPxFin-154
❑ 98SPxFin-171
❑ 98SPxFinR-24
❑ 98SPxFinR-119
❑ 98SPxFinR-154
❑ 98SPxFinR-171
❑ 98SPxFinS-24
❑ 98SPxFinS-119
❑ 98SPxFinS-154
❑ 98SPxFinS-171
❑ 98SPXTopP-14
❑ 98SPXTopPF-14
❑ 98SPXTopPHH-H9
❑ 98SPXTopPLI-L23
❑ 98SPXTopPPS-PS21
❑ 98SPXTopPR-14
❑ 98SPXTopPWM-PR
❑ 98SSASotT-PR
❑ 98Top-190
❑ 98TopBlaFTP-4
❑ 98TopGolLC1-77
❑ 98TopGolLC1B-77
❑ 98TopGolLC1BOoO-77
❑ 98TopGolLC1OoO-77
❑ 98TopGolLC1R-77
❑ 98TopGolLC1ROoO-77
❑ 98TopGolLC2-77
❑ 98TopGolLC2B-77
❑ 98TopGolLC2BOoO-77
❑ 98TopGolLC2OoO-77
❑ 98TopGolLC2R-77
❑ 98TopGolLC2ROoO-77
❑ 98TopGolLC3-77
❑ 98TopGolLC3B-77
❑ 98TopGolLC3BOoO-77
❑ 98TopGolLC3OoO-77
❑ 98TopGolLC3R-77
❑ 98TopGolLC3ROoO-77
❑ 98TopLocL-L8
❑ 98TopMysFB-M16
❑ 98TopMysFBR-M16
❑ 98TopMysFG-M16
❑ 98TopMysFGR-M16
❑ 98TopMysFS-M16
❑ 98TopMysFSR-M16
❑ 98TopO-P-190
❑ 98UC-54
❑ 98UC-232
❑ 98UC-243
❑ 98UC-309
❑ 98UCMBH-BH21
❑ 98UCSB-SQ3
❑ 98UCSG-SQ3
❑ 98UCSG-SQ3
❑ 98UCSR-SQ3
❑ 98UD ChoPCR-54
❑ 98UD ChoPCR-232
❑ 98UD ChoPCR-243
❑ 98UD ChoPCR-309
❑ 98UD ChoR-54
❑ 98UD ChoR-232
❑ 98UD ChoR-243
❑ 98UD ChoR-309
❑ 98UD3-46
❑ 98UD3-106
❑ 98UD3-166
❑ 98UD3DieC-46
❑ 98UD3DieC-106
❑ 98UD3DieC-166
❑ 98UppDec-74
❑ 98UppDec-208
❑ 98UppDecBD-22
❑ 98UppDecDD-22
❑ 98UppDecE-74
❑ 98UppDecE-208
❑ 98UppDecE1o1-74
❑ 98UppDecE1o1-208
❑ 98UppDecFIT-FT11
❑ 98UppDecFITQ1-FT11
❑ 98UppDecFITQ2-FT11
❑ 98UppDecFITQ3-FT11
❑ 98UppDecGN-GN7
❑ 98UppDecGN-GN8
❑ 98UppDecGN-GN9
❑ 98UppDecGNQ1-GN7
❑ 98UppDecGNQ1-GN8
❑ 98UppDecGNQ1-GN9
❑ 98UppDecGNQ2-GN7
❑ 98UppDecGNQ2-GN8
❑ 98UppDecGNQ2-GN9
❑ 98UppDecGNQ3-GN7
❑ 98UppDecGNQ3-GN8
❑ 98UppDecGNQ3-GN9
❑ 98UppDecGR-74
❑ 98UppDecGR-208
❑ 98UppDecLSH-LS10
❑ 98UppDecLSHQ1-LS10
❑ 98UppDecLSHQ2-LS10
❑ 98UppDecLSHQ3-LS10
❑ 98UppDecM-52
❑ 98UppDecM1-M23
❑ 98UppDecM2-M23
❑ 98UppDECMGS-PR
❑ 98UppDecMGS-52
❑ 98UppDecMOH-OT2
❑ 98UppDecMSF-F13
❑ 98UppDecMSS-52
❑ 98UppDecMSS-52
❑ 98UppDecP-P24
❑ 98UppDecPQ1-P24
❑ 98UppDecPQ2-P24
❑ 98UppDecPQ3-P24
❑ 98UppDecQD-22
❑ 98UppDecTD-22
❑ 98UppDecWFG-WF6
❑ 98UppDecWFP-WF6
❑ 99AurSty-6
❑ 99Pac-114
❑ 99PacAur-41
❑ 99PacAurCC-5
❑ 99PacAurCF-8
❑ 99PacAurCFC-8
❑ 99PacAurCFPB-8
❑ 99PacAurCP-5
❑ 99PacAurCPP-5
❑ 99PacAurGU-6
❑ 99PacAurPD-41
❑ 99PacCop-114
❑ 99PacCra-4
❑ 99PacGol-114
❑ 99PacGolCD-11
❑ 99PacHomaA-7
❑ 99PacIceB-114
❑ 99PacIn tCN-5
❑ 99PacPasAP-7
❑ 99PacPreD-114
❑ 99PacTeaL-8
❑ 99QuePeeWHWCCS-4
❑ 99RetHoc-20
❑ 99SP AutPS-21
❑ 99UppDecCL-35
❑ 99UppDecCL-56
❑ 99UppDecCLCLC-35
❑ 99UppDecCLCLC-56
❑ 99UppDecEotG-E5
❑ 99UppDecES-21
❑ 99UppDecM-55
❑ 99UppDecM9S-S3
❑ 99UppDecMGS-55
❑ 99UppDecMLL-LL3
❑ 99UppDecMSS-55
❑ 99UppDecMSS-55
❑ 99UppDecMT-MVP7
❑ 99UppDecRDR-DR7
❑ 99UppDecRDRI-DR7
❑ 99UppDecRG-G3B
❑ 99UppDecRG-20
❑ 99UppDecRGI-G3B
❑ 99UppDecRII-PR
❑ 99UppDecRIL1-PR
❑ 99UppDecRP-20
❑ 99UppDecRTotC-TC7

**Roy, Pierre**
❑ 72NordPos-20
❑ 73NordTeal-20
❑ 75OPCWHA-25
❑ 76NordPos-16
❑ 77NovScoV-20

**Roy, Serge**
❑ 86SwePanS-224
❑ 90ProAHLIHL-426

**Roy, Simon**
❑ 90MonAAA-21
❑ 917thInnSQMJHL-61

**Roy, Stephane**
❑ 88ProIHL-33
❑ 90AlbIntTC-17
❑ 91AlbIntTC-19
❑ 92AlbIntTC-19
❑ 95SigRoo-8
❑ 95SigRooSig-8

**Roy, Travis**
❑ 95PinFan-31

**Royal, Eric**
❑ 96WheNai-10

**Royer, Remi**
❑ 95BowDraPro-P30
❑ 98BowCHL-87
❑ 98BowCHLGA-87
❑ 98BowCHLOI-87
❑ 98BowChrC-87
❑ 98BowChrCGA-87
❑ 98BowChrCGAR-87
❑ 98BowChrCOI-87
❑ 98BowChrCOIR-87
❑ 98BowChrCR-87
❑ 98UppDec-246
❑ 98UppDecE-246
❑ 98UppDecE1o1-246
❑ 98UppDecGR-246
❑ 98UppDecM-50
❑ 98UppDecMGS-50
❑ 98UppDecMSS-50
❑ 98UppDecMSS-50
❑ 99Pac-99
❑ 99PacCop-99
❑ 99PacGol-99
❑ 99PacIceB-99
❑ 99PacPreD-99
❑ 99UppDecM-49
❑ 99UppDecMGS-49
❑ 99UppDecMSS-49
❑ 99UppDecMSS-49

**Rozon, Martin**
❑ 917thInnSQMJHL-175

**Rozsival, Michal**
❑ 98BowCHL-64
❑ 98BowCHLGA-64
❑ 98BowCHLOI-64
❑ 98BowCHLSC-SC20
❑ 98BowChrC-64
❑ 98BowChrCGA-64
❑ 98BowChrCGAR-64
❑ 98BowChrCOI-64
❑ 98BowChrCOIR-64
❑ 98BowChrCR-64

**Ruark, Mark**
❑ 907thInnSWHL-203

**Ruark, Mike**
❑ 89PorWinH-18
❑ 907thInnSWHL-311
❑ 91ProAHLCHL-393
❑ 92PhoRoa-19

**Rubachuk, Brad**
❑ 88LetHur-19
❑ 89LetHur-19
❑ 907thInnSWHL-127
❑ 91ProAHLCHL-11
❑ 91RochAmeDD-12
❑ 91RochAmeKod-21
❑ 92RochAmeDD-14
❑ 92RochAmeKod-18
❑ 93RochAmeKod-21
❑ 94BinRan-19

**Rubic, Robin**
❑ 84KitRan-16
❑ 85SudWol-9

**Rucchin, Lawrence**
❑ 98GerDELE-124

**Rucchin, Steve**
❑ 94DucCarJr-19
❑ 94UppDec-480
❑ 94UppDecEleIce-480
❑ 95Don-140
❑ 95Duc-3
❑ 95Fin-64
❑ 95FinRef-64
❑ 95Ima-56
❑ 95ImaGol-57
❑ 95Lea-54
❑ 95Met-4
❑ 95ParInt-272
❑ 95ParIntEl-272
❑ 95Pin-58
❑ 95PinArtP-58
❑ 95PinRinC-58
❑ 95SP-4
❑ 95StaClu-214
❑ 95StaCluMOMS-214
❑ 95Top-33
❑ 95TopOPCI-33
❑ 95Ult-202
❑ 95UppDec-425
❑ 95UppDecEleIce-425
❑ 95UppDecEleIceG-425
❑ 95UppDecSpeE-SE92
❑ 95UppDecSpeEdiG-SE92
❑ 96BeAPAut-186
❑ 96BeAPAutSil-186
❑ 96BeAPla-186
❑ 96ColCho-3
❑ 96Duc-11
❑ 96MetUni-5
❑ 96Pin-137
❑ 96PinArtP-137
❑ 96PinFoi-137
❑ 96PinPreS-137
❑ 96PinRinC-137
❑ 96Sco-186
❑ 96ScoArtPro-186
❑ 96ScoDeaCAP-186
❑ 96ScoGolB-186
❑ 96ScoSpeAP-186
❑ 96SP-6
❑ 96UppDec-214
❑ 96UppDecBD-20
❑ 96UppDecBDG-20
❑ 97ColCho-7
❑ 97Don-49
❑ 97DonLim-117
❑ 97DonLimExp-117
❑ 97DonPre-45
❑ 97DonPreCttC-45
❑ 97DonPreProG-49
❑ 97DonPreProS-49
❑ 97Lea-14
❑ 97LeaFraMat-101
❑ 97LeaFraMDC-101
❑ 97LeaInt-101
❑ 97LeaIntUI-101
❑ 97Pac-104
❑ 97PacCop-104
❑ 97PacCroR-3
❑ 97PacCroREG-3
❑ 97PacCroRIB-3
❑ 97PacCroRS-3
❑ 97PacDyn-4
❑ 97PacDynC-4
❑ 97PacDynDG-4
❑ 97PacDynEG-4
❑ 97PacDynIB-4
❑ 97PacDynR-4
❑ 97PacDynSil-4
❑ 97PacDynTan-30
❑ 97PacEmeGre-104
❑ 97PacIceB-104
❑ 97PacOme-5
❑ 97PacOmeC-5
❑ 97PacOmeDG-5
❑ 97PacOmeEG-5
❑ 97PacOmeG-5
❑ 97PacOmeIB-5
❑ 97PacPar-5
❑ 97PacParC-5
❑ 97PacParDG-5
❑ 97PacParEG-5
❑ 97PacParIB-5
❑ 97PacParRed-5
❑ 97PacParSil-5
❑ 97PacRed-104
❑ 97PacSil-104
❑ 97Pin-151
❑ 97PinCer-64
❑ 97PinCerMB-64
❑ 97PinCerMG-64
❑ 97PinCerMR-64
❑ 97PinCerR-64
❑ 97PinIns-188
❑ 97PinPrePBB-151
❑ 97PinPrePBC-151
❑ 97PinPrePBM-151
❑ 97PinPrePBY-151
❑ 97PinPrePFC-151
❑ 97PinPrePFM-151
❑ 97PinPrePFY-151
❑ 97PinPrePla-151
❑ 97PinTotCMPG-64
❑ 97PinTotCPB-64
❑ 97PinTotCPG-64
❑ 97PinTotCPR-64
❑ 97Sco-176
❑ 97ScoMigDPla-3
❑ 97ScoMigDPre-3
❑ 97ScoMigDuc-3
❑ 97SPAut-5
❑ 97UppDec-2
❑ 98Be A PPA-151
❑ 98Be A PPAA-151
❑ 98Be A PPAAF-151
❑ 98Be A PPSE-151
❑ 98Be APG-151
❑ 98Fin-26
❑ 98FinNo P-26
❑ 98FinNo PR-26
❑ 98FinRef-26
❑ 98Pac-62
❑ 98PacAur-4
❑ 98PacDynI-4
❑ 98PacDynIIB-4
❑ 98PacDynIR-4
❑ 98PacIceB-62
❑ 98PacOmeH-7
❑ 98PacOmeODI-7
❑ 98PacOmeR-7
❑ 98PacPar-5
❑ 98PacParC-5
❑ 98PacParEG-5
❑ 98PacParH-5
❑ 98PacParIB-5
❑ 98PacParS-5
❑ 98PacRed-62
❑ 98PacRev-4
❑ 98PacRevIS-4
❑ 98PacRevR-4
❑ 98UC-6
❑ 98UD ChoPCR-6
❑ 98UD ChoR-6
❑ 98UppDec-214
❑ 98UppDecE-214
❑ 98UppDecE1o1-214
❑ 98UppDecGR-214
❑ 98UppDecM-8
❑ 98UppDecMGS-8
❑ 98UppDecMSS-8
❑ 98UppDecMSS-8
❑ 99Pac-13
❑ 99PacAur-4
❑ 99PacAurPD-4
❑ 99PacCop-13
❑ 99PacGol-13
❑ 99PacIceB-13
❑ 99PacPreD-13
❑ 99UppDecM-8
❑ 99UppDecMGS-8
❑ 99UppDecMSS-8
❑ 99UppDecMSS-8

**Ruchar, Milan**
❑ 94CzeAPSE-67

**Ruchty, Matt**
❑ 91ProAHLCHL-410
❑ 96GraRapG-22

**Rucinski, Mike**
❑ 86MonGolF-25
❑ 88ProIHL-112
❑ 89ProIHL-61
❑ 93DetJrRW-6
❑ 94DetJrRW-5
❑ 95NorIowH-28
❑ 95Sla-61
❑ 95SlaMemC-79
❑ 96RicRen-17
❑ 98Pac-46
❑ 98PacIceB-46
❑ 98PacRed-46
❑ 98UppDec-235
❑ 98UppDecE-235
❑ 98UppDecE1o1-235
❑ 98UppDecGR-235

**Rucinsky, Martin**
❑ 91Cla-17
❑ 91OilTeal-23
❑ 91Par-366
❑ 91ParFre-366
❑ 91ProAHLCHL-230
❑ 91UppDec-19
❑ 91UppDec-70
❑ 91UppDecF-19
❑ 91UppDecF-70
❑ 92NorPet-27
❑ 92OPCPre-124
❑ 92Par-149
❑ 92ParEmel-149
❑ 92ProSet-238
❑ 92Sco-474
❑ 92ScoCan-474
❑ 92Top-523
❑ 92TopGol-523G
❑ 92Ult-390
❑ 92UppDec-556
❑ 93Don-281
❑ 93Lea-152
❑ 93OPCPre-367
❑ 93OPCPreG-367
❑ 93PanSti-74
❑ 93Par-170
❑ 93ParEmel-170
❑ 93Pin-196
❑ 93PinCan-196
❑ 93Pow-203
❑ 93Sco-254
❑ 93ScoCan-254
❑ 93StaClu-11
❑ 93StaCluFDI-11
❑ 93StaCluFDIO-11
❑ 93StaCluO-11
❑ 93TopPre-367
❑ 93TopPreG-367
❑ 93Ult-191
❑ 93UppDec-6
❑ 94CzeAPSE-221
❑ 94FinnJaaK-177
❑ 94NordBurK-21
❑ 94Par-191
❑ 94ParGol-191
❑ 94Pin-416
❑ 94PinArtP-416
❑ 94PinRinC-416
❑ 94StaClu-126
❑ 94StaCluFDI-126
❑ 94StaCluMOMS-126
❑ 94StaCluSTWC-126
❑ 94Ult-179
❑ 94UppDec-201
❑ 94UppDecEleIce-201
❑ 95FinnSemWC-152
❑ 95ParInt-379
❑ 95ParIntEl-379
❑ 95UppDec-485
❑ 96BeAPAut-124
❑ 96BeAPAutSil-124
❑ 96BeAPla-124
❑ 96CanaPos-24
❑ 96CanaShe-18
❑ 96ColCho-143
❑ 96Don-123
❑ 96DonCanI-81
❑ 96DonCanIGPP-81
❑ 96DonCanIRPP-81
❑ 96DonPrePro-123
❑ 96Fla-50
❑ 96FlaBlul-50
❑ 96Lea-96
❑ 96LeaPreP-96
❑ 96Pin-63
❑ 96PinArtP-63
❑ 96PinFoi-63
❑ 96PinPreS-63
❑ 96PinRinC-63
❑ 96Sco-134
❑ 96ScoArtPro-134
❑ 96ScoDeaCAP-134
❑ 96ScoGolB-134
❑ 96ScoSpeAP-134
❑ 96SkyImp-64
❑ 96TopNHLP-59
❑ 96TopPicOI-59
❑ 96UppDec-280
❑ 97CanaPos-19
❑ 97Pac-220
❑ 97PacCop-220
❑ 97PacEmeGre-220
❑ 97PacIceB-220
❑ 97PacOme-122
❑ 97PacOmeC-122
❑ 97PacOmeDG-122
❑ 97PacOmeEG-122
❑ 97PacOmeG-122
❑ 97PacOmeIB-122
❑ 97PacRed-220
❑ 97PacSil-220
❑ 97Pin-172
❑ 97PinIns-96
❑ 97PinPrePBB-172
❑ 97PinPrePBC-172
❑ 97PinPrePBM-172
❑ 97PinPrePBY-172
❑ 97PinPrePFC-172
❑ 97PinPrePFM-172
❑ 97PinPrePFY-172
❑ 97PinPrePla-172
❑ 97Sco-152
❑ 97ScoArtPro-152
❑ 97ScoCan-9
❑ 97ScoCanPla-9
❑ 97ScoGolBla-152
❑ 97UppDec-89
❑ 98Be A PPA-221
❑ 98Be A PPAA-221
❑ 98Be A PPAAF-221
❑ 98Be A PPSE-221
❑ 98Be APG-221
❑ 98O-PChr-15
❑ 98O-PChrR-15
❑ 98Pac-257
❑ 98PacAur-96
❑ 98PacIceB-257
❑ 98PacOmeH-125
❑ 98PacOmeODI-125
❑ 98PacOmeR-125
❑ 98PacPar-117
❑ 98PacParC-117
❑ 98PacParEG-117
❑ 98PacParH-117
❑ 98PacParIB-117
❑ 98PacParS-117
❑ 98PacRed-257
❑ 98ScoCanPre-9
❑ 98Top-15
❑ 98TopO-P-15
❑ 99Pac-209
❑ 99PacAur-76
❑ 99PacAurPD-76
❑ 99PacCop-209
❑ 99PacGol-209
❑ 99PacIceB-209
❑ 99PacPreD-209
❑ 99UppDecM-101
❑ 99UppDecMGS-101
❑ 99UppDecMSS-101
❑ 99UppDecMSS-101

**Ruck, Colin**
❑ 89RegPat-17
❑ 907thInnSWHL-181

**Rud, Eric**
❑ 98FloEve-22
❑ 98KanCitB-5

**Rudberg, Jonas**
❑ 917thInnSOHL-333

**Rudby, Lennart**
❑ 69SweHocS-179

**Rudby, Sven Ake**
❑ 69SweHocS-180
❑ 73SweHocS-180
❑ 73SweWorCS-180
❑ 74SweHocS-262

**Ruddick, Ken**
❑ 897thInnSOHL-134
❑ 89NiaFalT-17
❑ 907thInnSOHL-18

**Ruddock, Ken**
❑ 91AirCanSJHL-E16
❑ 92MPSPhoSJHL-51

**Rudenko, Bogdan**
❑ 95Sla-140
❑ 96SarSti-23

**Rudkowsky, Cody**
❑ 95SeaThu-25
❑ 96SeaThu-30

**Rudy, Wes**
❑ 92BriColJHL-20

**Ruel, Claude**
❑ 68CanaPosBW-15
❑ 69CanaPosC-27
❑ 70CanaPin-14
❑ 76CanaPos-19
❑ 77CanaPos-21
❑ 78CanaPos-23
❑ 79CanaPos-21
❑ 80CanaPos-21

**Rueter, Dirk**
❑ 81SauSteMG-19

**Rueter, Kirk**
❑ 80SauSteMG-22

**Ruff, Jason**
❑ 88LetHur-20
❑ 89LetHur-20
❑ 907thInnSWHL-138
❑ 91ProAHLCHL-46
❑ 92Cla-109
❑ 92PeoRivC-22
❑ 92UppDec-522
❑ 93ClaProPro-45
❑ 96ClaGol-109

**Ruff, Lindy**
❑ 80OPC-319
❑ 82OPC-31
❑ 82PosCer-2
❑ 82SabMilP-5
❑ 84OPC-29
❑ 84OPCSti-213
❑ 84SabBluS-17
❑ 84Top-23
❑ 85SabBluS-24
❑ 85SabBluSS-24
❑ 86OPC-4
❑ 86SabBluS-25
❑ 86SabBluSSma-25
❑ 86Top-4
❑ 87PanSti-35
❑ 87SabBluS-23
❑ 87SabWonBH-23
❑ 88OPC-40
❑ 88SabBluS-22
❑ 88SabWonBH-24
❑ 88Top-40
❑ 89RanMarMB-44
❑ 90OPC-143
❑ 90Top-143
❑ 90TopTif-143
❑ 91ProAHLCHL-6
❑ 91RochAmeDD-13
❑ 91RochAmeKod-22
❑ 91RochAmePos-17
❑ 92SanDieG-22

**Ruisma, Matti**
❑ 84SweSemE-181

**Rulik, Radim**
❑ 96CzeAPSE-287

**Rullier, Joe**
❑ 96RimOceU-8
❑ 97RimOce-7

**Rumble, Darren**
❑ 86KitRan-7
❑ 87KitRan-24
❑ 88KitRan-28
❑ 89ProAHL-342
❑ 90ProAHLIHL-34
❑ 91ProAHLCHL-271
❑ 92Par-356
❑ 92ParEmel-356
❑ 92Sen-13
❑ 92Ult-148
❑ 92UppDec-110
❑ 93OPCPre-356
❑ 93OPCPreG-356
❑ 93Par-411
❑ 93ParEmel-411
❑ 93Pow-173
❑ 93SenKraS-20
❑ 93StaClu-418
❑ 93StaCluFDI-418
❑ 93StaCluO-418
❑ 93TopPre-356
❑ 93TopPreG-356
❑ 93Ult-153

**Rumrich, Jurgen**
❑ 94FinnJaaK-286
❑ 94GerDELE-66
❑ 95GerDELE-66
❑ 95GerDELE-434
❑ 96GerDELE-262
❑ 98GerDELE-49
❑ 98GerDELE-321

**Rumrich, Michael**
❑ 93SweSemWCS-167
❑ 94GerDELE-214
❑ 95GerDELE-213
❑ 95SweGloWC-220

**Rundqvist, Thomas**
❑ 82SweSemHVS-17
❑ 83SweSemE-112
❑ 85SwePanS-100
❑ 86SwePanS-96
❑ 87SwePanS-97
❑ 89SweSemE-85
❑ 89SweSemWCS-18
❑ 90SweSemE-261
❑ 91SweSemE-90
❑ 91SweSemE-314
❑ 91SweSemE-324
❑ 91SweSemE-346
❑ 91SweSemWCS-39
❑ 92SweSemE-112
❑ 93SweSemWCS-10
❑ 94FinnJaaK-69

**Runesson, Benny**
❑ 69SweHocS-289
❑ 70SweHocS-192
❑ 71SweHocS-278
❑ 72SweHocS-253
❑ 74SweHocS-263

**Runge, Paul**
❑ 28V1282PauC-56
❑ 34BeeGro1P-203
❑ 35DiaMatT2-56
❑ 35DiaMatT3-52
❑ 36OPCV304D-106
❑ 36V356WorG-81
❑ 37OPCV304E-167

**Runyan, Eric**
❑ 93OmaLan-22

**Ruoho, Dan**
❑ 92NorMicW-21
❑ 95MadMon-7

**Ruokonen, Miikka**
❑ 93FinnJyvHS-56
❑ 94FinnSIS-298
❑ 95FinnSIS-74
❑ 96FinnSISR-74

**Ruotanen, Arto**
❑ 89SweSemE-100
❑ 90SweSemE-102
❑ 91SweSemE-110
❑ 91SweSemWCS-12
❑ 93SweSemE-225
❑ 94SweLeaE-190
❑ 95SweLeaE-114
❑ 95SweUppDE-174

**Ruotsalainen, Reijo**
❑ 82OPC-233
❑ 82PosCer-13
❑ 82SweSemHVS-155
❑ 83OPC-255
❑ 83OPCSti-216
❑ 83PufSti-19
❑ 84OPC-153
❑ 84OPCSti-101
❑ 84Top-115
❑ 857ECreCar-13
❑ 85OPC-112
❑ 85OPCBoxB-M
❑ 85OPCSti-81
❑ 85Top-112
❑ 85TopBoxB-M
❑ 86OPC-128
❑ 86OPCSti-225
❑ 86Top-128
❑ 87SwePanS-115
❑ 88OilTenAnn-22
❑ 89DevCar-20
❑ 89SweSemWCS-30
❑ 95FinnSIS-274
❑ 95FinnSISDT-7
❑ 95FinnSISL-66
❑ 95SwiHNL-524
❑ 95SwiHNL-536

**Ruotsalainen, Vesa**
❑ 93FinnJyvHS-175
❑ 93FinnSIS-168
❑ 96FinnSISR-112

**Rupnow, Mark**
❑ 95SouCarS-24

**Ruponen, Pasi**
❑ 93FinnJyvHS-256
❑ 93FinnSIS-288
**Rupp, Duane**
❑ 67Top-20
❑ 69OPC-153
❑ 69OPCFou-8
❑ 70EssPowPla-218
❑ 70OPC-89
❑ 70SarProSta-166
❑ 70Top-89
❑ 71TorSun-226
❑ 72OPC-154
❑ 72SarProSta-180
❑ 72Top-28
❑ 75OPCWHA-18
❑ 77RocAme-2
**Rupp, Michael**
❑ 98BowCHL-151
❑ 98BowCHLAuB-A3
❑ 98BowCHLAuG-A3
❑ 98BowCHLAuS-A3
❑ 98BowCHLGA-151
❑ 98BowCHLOI-151
❑ 98BowChrC-151
❑ 98BowChrCGA-151
❑ 98BowChrCGAR-151
❑ 98BowChrCOI-151
❑ 98BowChrCOIR-151
❑ 98BowChrCR-151
❑ 98FinFutF-F8
❑ 98FinFutFR-F8
❑ 98O-PChr-236
❑ 98O-PChrR-236
❑ 98Top-236
❑ 98TopO-P-236
**Ruprecht, Tomas**
❑ 95CzeAPSE-264
**Ruprecht, Vaclav**
❑ 94CzeAPSE-146
❑ 95CzeAPSE-252
❑ 96CzeAPSE-293
**Rushforth, Paul**
❑ 917thInnSOHL-67
❑ 95SouCarS-19
**Rushmer, Bart**
❑ 98SP Aut-121
❑ 98UppDec-398
❑ 98UppDecE-398
❑ 98UppDecE1o1-398
❑ 98UppDecGR-398
❑ 99SP AutPS-121
**Rushton, Jason**
❑ 92BriColJHL-195
**Rusk, Mike**
❑ 93GueSto-6
❑ 94GueSto-20
**Ruskowski, Terry**
❑ 76OPCWHA-38
❑ 77OPCWHA-37
❑ 78JetPos-19
❑ 79OPC-141
❑ 80BlaBroBac-10
❑ 80BlaWhiBor-11
❑ 80OPC-119
❑ 80Top-119
❑ 81BlaBorPos-22
❑ 81BlaBroBac-11
❑ 81OPC-62
❑ 81OPCSti-117
❑ 81Top-W74
❑ 82OPC-72
❑ 82OPCSti-178
❑ 82PosCer-4
❑ 83OPC-161
❑ 83OPCSti-291
❑ 84KinSmo-14
❑ 84OPC-89
❑ 84OPCSti-270
❑ 84Top-68
❑ 85OPC-33
❑ 85OPCSti-237
❑ 85Top-33
❑ 86OPC-111
❑ 86OPCSti-226
❑ 86PenKod-21
❑ 86Top-111
❑ 87NorStaPos-28
❑ 87OPC-73
❑ 87OPCSti-167
❑ 87PanSti-150
❑ 87Top-73
❑ 88NorStaADA-22
❑ 89SasBla-1
❑ 907thInnSWHL-92
❑ 90SasBla-1
**Rusnak, Chad**
❑ 917thInnSWHL-107
❑ 91SasBla-8
❑ 92MPSPhoSJHL-47
**Rusnak, Darius**
❑ 82SweSemHVS-92
❑ 91SweSemWCS-115
**Russell, Blaine**
❑ 95PriAlbR-17
❑ 96PriAlbROC-19
**Russell, Blair**
❑ 83HalFP-M14
❑ 85HalFC-178
**Russell, Cam**
❑ 89ProIHL-71
❑ 90ProAHLIHL-400
❑ 90Sco-408
❑ 90ScoCan-408
❑ 91ProAHLCHL-486
❑ 91UppDec-352
❑ 91UppDecF-352
❑ 93BlaCok-12
❑ 93StaClu-286
❑ 93StaCluFDI-286
❑ 93StaCluO-286
❑ 94Lea-382
❑ 95BeAPla-84
❑ 95BeAPSig-S84
❑ 95BeAPSigDC-S84
❑ 97PacInvNRB-45
**Russell, Ernie (Ernest)**
❑ 10C55SweCP-35
❑ 10C56-20
❑ 11C55-35
❑ 12C57-26
❑ 83HalFP-I14
❑ 85HalFC-133
**Russell, Kerry**
❑ 91ProAHLCHL-105
**Russell, Paul**
❑ 91ProAHLCHL-309
**Russell, Phil**
❑ 73OPC-243
❑ 74NHLActSta-89
❑ 74OPCNHL-226
❑ 74Top-226
❑ 75OPCNHL-102
❑ 75OPCNHL-211
❑ 75Top-102
❑ 75Top-211
❑ 76OPCNHL-31
❑ 76OPCNHL-382
❑ 76Top-31
❑ 77OPCNHL-235
❑ 77Top-235
❑ 78OPC-12
❑ 78Top-12
❑ 79FlamPos-17
❑ 79FlaTeal-19
❑ 79OPC-143
❑ 79Top-143
❑ 80FlamPos-19
❑ 80OPC-226
❑ 80PepCap-17
❑ 80Top-226
❑ 81FlamPos-20
❑ 81OPC-51
❑ 81OPCSti-226
❑ 82OPC-58
❑ 82PosCer-3
❑ 83OPC-237
❑ 83OPCSti-271
❑ 83PufSti-9
❑ 84DevPos-5
❑ 84KelWin-54
❑ 84OPC-120
❑ 84OPCSti-75
❑ 85OPC-30
❑ 85OPCSti-58
❑ 85Top-30
❑ 86OPC-142
❑ 86Top-142
❑ 89ProIHL-163
❑ 90ProAHLIHL-391
❑ 92CleLum-5
**Russell, Ted**
❑ 95DayBom-12
**Russell-Samways, Dean**
❑ 94GuiFla-19
❑ 95GuiFla-16
**Russo, Angelo**
❑ 91NasKni-9
**Russo, Joseph**
❑ 93OmaLan-23
**Russo, Matt**
❑ 92MPSPhoSJHL-63
**Rutherford, Jim**
❑ 70EssPowPla-127
❑ 70RedWinM-9
❑ 71LetActR-7
❑ 71PenPos-17
❑ 71SarProSta-176
❑ 72OPC-15
❑ 72SarProSta-175
❑ 72Top-97
❑ 73OPC-59
❑ 73Top-59
❑ 74NHLActSta-100
❑ 74OPCNHL-225
❑ 74Top-225
❑ 75OPCNHL-219
❑ 75Top-219
❑ 76OPCNHL-88
❑ 76Top-88
❑ 77Coc-21
❑ 77OPCNHL-239
❑ 77Top-239
❑ 78OPC-74
❑ 78Top-74
❑ 79OPC-122
❑ 79RedWinP-14
❑ 79Top-122
❑ 80OPC-125
❑ 80PepCap-95
❑ 80Top-125
❑ 917thInnSOHL-47
**Rutherford, Paul**
❑ 91RicRen-7
**Rutland, Art**
❑ 81FreExp-21
❑ 82FreExp-21
**Rutledge, Chris**
❑ 84BelBul-28
**Rutledge, Wayne**
❑ 68ShiCoi-58
❑ 72OPC-329
❑ 76OPCWHA-6
❑ 77OPCWHA-11
**Ruttan, Jack**
❑ 83HalFP-K15
❑ 85HalFC-149
**Ruuttu, Christian**
❑ 86SabBluS-26
❑ 86SabBluSSma-26
❑ 87OPC-121
❑ 87OPCMin-37
❑ 87OPCSti-134
❑ 87OPCSti-144
❑ 87PanSti-28
❑ 87SabBluS-24
❑ 87SabWonBH-24
❑ 87Top-121
❑ 88OPC-18
❑ 88OPCSti-256
❑ 88PanSti-227
❑ 88SabBluS-23
❑ 88SabWonBH-25
❑ 88Top-18
❑ 89OPC-68
❑ 89OPCSti-255
❑ 89PanSti-207
❑ 89SabBluS-19
❑ 89SabCam-22
❑ 89Top-68
❑ 90Bow-244
❑ 90BowTif-244
❑ 90OPC-182
❑ 90PanSti-20
❑ 90ProSet-29
❑ 90SabBluS-19
❑ 90SabCam-22
❑ 90Sco-77
❑ 90ScoCan-77
❑ 90Top-182
❑ 90TopTif-182
❑ 90UppDec-170
❑ 90UppDecF-170
❑ 91Bow-25
❑ 91Bow-411
❑ 91OPC-115
❑ 91PanSti-306
❑ 91Par-242
❑ 91ParFre-242
❑ 91Pin-60
❑ 91PinFre-60
❑ 91ProSet-22
❑ 91ProSetFre-22
❑ 91SabBluS-19
❑ 91SabPepC-19
❑ 91ScoAme-45
❑ 91ScoCan-45
❑ 91StaClu-33
❑ 91SweSemWCS-205
❑ 91Top-115
❑ 91UppDec-104
❑ 91UppDecES-11
❑ 91UppDecESF-11
❑ 91UppDecF-104
❑ 92Bow-341
❑ 92OPCPre-2
❑ 92PanSti-250
❑ 92PanStiFre-250
❑ 92Par-34
❑ 92ParEmel-34
❑ 92Pin-317
❑ 92PinFre-317
❑ 92Sco-334
❑ 92ScoCan-334
❑ 92StaClu-330
❑ 92Top-485
❑ 92TopGol-485G
❑ 92Ult-281
❑ 92UppDec-446
❑ 93BlaCok-17
❑ 93Don-72
❑ 93Lea-334
❑ 93OPCPre-355
❑ 93OPCPreG-355
❑ 93Par-39
❑ 93ParEmel-39
❑ 93Pin-116
❑ 93PinCan-116
❑ 93Sco-84
❑ 93ScoCan-84
❑ 93StaClu-103
❑ 93StaCluFDI-103
❑ 93StaCluFDIO-103
❑ 93StaCluO-103
❑ 93SweSemWCS-75
❑ 93TopPre-355
❑ 93TopPreG-355
❑ 93UppDec-141
❑ 94CanGamNHLP-71
❑ 94FinnJaaK-43
❑ 94FinnSIS-234
❑ 94FinnSISGS-8
❑ 94Par-42
❑ 94ParGol-42
❑ 94ParSEES-ES12
❑ 94Pin-434
❑ 94PinArtP-434
❑ 94PinRinC-434
❑ 94StaClu-131
❑ 94StaCluFDI-131
❑ 94StaCluMOMS-131
❑ 94StaCluSTWC-131
❑ 94UppDec-56
❑ 94UppDecEleIce-56
❑ 95ColCho-278
❑ 95ColChoPCP-278
❑ 95ColChoPCP-278
❑ 95FinnJaaKLAC-6
❑ 95FinnSemWC-22
❑ 95FinnSISL-42
❑ 95FinnSISLSS-2
❑ 95PlaOneoOne-103
❑ 95SweGloWC-143
❑ 95SweLeaE-207
❑ 95SweLeaE-307
❑ 95SweUppDE-210
❑ 95SweUppDE-233
❑ 95SweUppDE-258
❑ 96SweSemW-25
**Ruzicka, Vladimir**
❑ 89SweSemWCS-190
❑ 90OPC-393
❑ 90ProSet-588
❑ 90ScoRoo-44T
❑ 90Top-393
❑ 90TopTif-393
❑ 90UppDec-538
❑ 90UppDecF-538
❑ 91BruSpoA-17
❑ 91OPCPre-144
❑ 91Par-3
❑ 91ParFre-3
❑ 91Pin-181
❑ 91PinFre-181
❑ 91ProSet-353
❑ 91ProSetFre-353
❑ 91ProSetPla-152
❑ 91ScoCan-411
❑ 91ScoRoo-83T
❑ 91StaClu-383
❑ 91UppDec-288
❑ 91UppDecF-288
❑ 92Bow-431
❑ 92BruPos-10
❑ 92OPC-228
❑ 92PanSti-138
❑ 92PanStiFre-138
❑ 92Par-5
❑ 92ParEmel-5
❑ 92Pin-59
❑ 92PinFre-59
❑ 92ProSet-5
❑ 92Sco-208
❑ 92ScoCan-208
❑ 92StaClu-358
❑ 92Top-333
❑ 92TopGol-333G
❑ 92Ult-10
❑ 92UppDec-258
❑ 92UppDecES-E4
❑ 93Don-228
❑ 93Lea-438
❑ 93Pin-406
❑ 93PinCan-406
❑ 93Pow-174
❑ 93Sco-154
❑ 93Sco-562
❑ 93ScoCan-154
❑ 93ScoCan-562
❑ 93ScoGol-562
❑ 93SenKraS-21
❑ 93Ult-383
❑ 94CzeAPSE-265
❑ 95CzeAPSE-135
**Ryabchikov, Evgeny**
❑ 93Par-533
❑ 93ParEmel-533
❑ 93Pin-508
❑ 93PinCan-508
❑ 94Cla-18
❑ 94ClaDraGol-18
❑ 94ClaTri-T4
❑ 95ColEdgI-61
❑ 95Ima-70
❑ 95ImaGol-70
❑ 95SigRoo-9
❑ 95SigRooSig-9
❑ 96DayBom-23
**Ryan, Gregory (Greg)**
❑ 897thInnSOHL-33
❑ 907thInnSOHL-142
❑ 917thInnSOHL-377
❑ 92Ott672A-18
**Ryan, Terry**
❑ 92BriColJHL-201
❑ 94TriAme-8
❑ 95Cla-8
❑ 95ClaIceBre-BK8
❑ 95Ima-18
❑ 95ImaGol-18
❑ 95ImaPlaPDC-PD8
❑ 95SigRooA-37
❑ 95SigRooAB2-B2
❑ 95SigRooAPC-37
❑ 95TriAme-21
❑ 95TriAme-30
❑ 96ClaIceBreDC-BK8
❑ 96DonCanI-142
❑ 96DonCanIGPP-142
❑ 96DonCanIOC-16
❑ 96DonCanIRPP-142
❑ 96DonEliAsp-11
❑ 96LeaPre-141
❑ 96LeaPrePP-141
❑ 96Zen-144
❑ 96ZenArtP-144
❑ 97Don-24
❑ 97DonCanI-128
❑ 97DonCanIDS-128
❑ 97DonCanIPS-128
❑ 97DonLim-123
❑ 97DonLimExp-123
❑ 97DonPreProG-24
❑ 97DonPreProS-24
❑ 97Pin-11
❑ 97PinArtP-11
❑ 97PinIns-167
❑ 97PinPrePBB-11
❑ 97PinPrePBC-11
❑ 97PinPrePBM-11
❑ 97PinPrePBY-11
❑ 97PinPrePFC-11
❑ 97PinPrePFM-11
❑ 97PinPrePFY-11
❑ 97PinPrePla-11
❑ 97PinRinC-11
❑ 97ScoCan-15
❑ 97ScoCanPla-15
❑ 98McD-28
❑ 98ScoCanPre-15
❑ 98UppDec-294
❑ 98UppDecBD-45
❑ 98UppDecDD-45
❑ 98UppDecE-294
❑ 98UppDecE1o1-294
❑ 98UppDecGR-294
❑ 98UppDecM-103
❑ 98UppDecMGS-103
❑ 98UppDecMSS-103
❑ 98UppDecMSS-103
❑ 98UppDecQD-45
❑ 98UppDecTD-45
**Ryan, Terry 70s**
❑ 72FigSaiPos-19
❑ 99Pac-216
❑ 99PacCop-216
❑ 99PacGol-216
❑ 99PacIceB-216
❑ 99PacPreD-216
**Rybar, Josef**
❑ 92BriColJHL-76
❑ 94CzeAPSE-159
❑ 95CzeAPSE-260
❑ 96CzeAPSE-305
**Rybovic, Lubomir**
❑ 94FinnJaaK-195
**Rychel, Warren**
❑ 84SudWol-15
❑ 88ProIHL-113
❑ 89ProIHL-69
❑ 90ProAHLIHL-399
❑ 91MonHaw-24
❑ 91ProAHLCHL-175
❑ 92Par-309
❑ 92ParEmel-309
❑ 92UppDec-547
❑ 93Don-156
❑ 93Lea-263
❑ 93OPCPre-266
❑ 93OPCPreG-266
❑ 93Par-98
❑ 93ParEmel-98
❑ 93Pow-362
❑ 93Sco-640
❑ 93ScoCan-640
❑ 93ScoGol-640
❑ 93StaClu-258
❑ 93StaCluFDI-258
❑ 93StaCluO-258
❑ 93TopPre-266
❑ 93TopPreG-266
❑ 93Ult-346
❑ 93UppDec-93
❑ 94CanGamNHLP-128
❑ 94Don-240
❑ 94Lea-323
❑ 94MapLeaK-24
❑ 94MapLeaPP-15
❑ 94ParSE-SE84
❑ 94ParSEG-SE84
❑ 94Pin-509
❑ 94PinArtP-509
❑ 94PinRinC-509
❑ 96Duc-8
❑ 97Be A PPAD-32
❑ 97Be A PPAPD-32
❑ 97BeAPla-32
❑ 97BeAPlaAut-32
❑ 97Pac-130
❑ 97PacCop-130
❑ 97PacEmeGre-130
❑ 97PacIceB-130
❑ 97PacRed-130
❑ 97PacSil-130
❑ 97ScoMigDPla-13
❑ 97ScoMigDPre-13
❑ 97ScoMigDuc-13
❑ 98Pac-168
❑ 98PacIceB-168
❑ 98PacRed-168
**Rydberg, Ake**
❑ 65SweCorl-129
**Ryden, Jorgen**
❑ 89SweSemE-75
❑ 90SweSemE-249
❑ 91SweSemE-80
**Ryder, Colin**
❑ 92BriColJHL-134
**Ryder, Dan**
❑ 907thInnSOHL-394
❑ 90SudWol-7
❑ 917thInnSOHL-255
❑ 91SudWol-13
❑ 93RoaExp-16
❑ 94RoaExp-19
**Rydin, Ulf**
❑ 64SweCorl-135
❑ 65SweCorl-135
❑ 67SweHoc-71
❑ 69SweHocS-102
❑ 70SweHocS-59
❑ 71SweHocS-130
**Ryding, Steve**
❑ 90KnoChe-104
❑ 91KnoChe-5
**Rydman, Blaine**
❑ 72FigSaiPos-20
**Rydmark, Daniel**
❑ 86SwePanS-104
❑ 89SweSemE-93
❑ 90SweSemE-141
❑ 91SweSemE-192
❑ 92SweSemE-214
❑ 93SweSemE-185
❑ 94FinnJaaK-66
❑ 94SweLeaE-91
❑ 94SweLeaEGC-5
❑ 94SweLeaETG-7
❑ 95PhoRoa-13
❑ 95SweGloWC-33
**Ryles, Tom**
❑ 94DubFigS-24
**Rylin, Anders**
❑ 70SweHocS-52
❑ 71SweHocS-121
❑ 73SweHocS-216
❑ 73SweWorCS-216
❑ 74SweHocS-184
**Rylsma, Dan**
❑ 97Pac-323
❑ 97PacCop-323
❑ 97PacEmeGre-323
❑ 97PacIceB-323
❑ 97PacRed-323
❑ 97PacSil-323
**Ryman, Ake**
❑ 69SweHocS-291
❑ 70SweHocS-194
❑ 71SweHocS-279
❑ 72SweHocS-254
**Ryman, Jonny**
❑ 69SweHocS-290
❑ 70SweHocS-193
**Rymsha, Andy**
❑ 90ProAHLIHL-80
❑ 96GerDELE-130
❑ 98GerDELE-210
**Rysanek, Roman**
❑ 93SweSemWCS-100
❑ 94CzeAPSE-138
❑ 96CzeAPSE-201
**Saal, Jason**
❑ 93DetJrRW-2
❑ 94DetJrRW-16
❑ 95Cla-84
❑ 95ColEdgI-81
❑ 95SlaMemC-90
❑ 95St.JohML-17
❑ 96PeoRiv-20
❑ 96PeoRivPA-20
❑ 96St.JohML-21
**Saarela, Pasi**
❑ 93FinnJyvHS-227
❑ 93FinnSIS-199
❑ 94FinnSIS-277
❑ 95FinnSIS-253
❑ 96FinnSISR-54
❑ 96FinnSISRMA-2
**Saari, Timo**
❑ 74SweHocS-31
**Saarikoski, Timo**
❑ 93FinnJyvHS-113
❑ 93FinnSIS-25
❑ 93SweSemWCS-76
❑ 94FinnJaaK-47
❑ 94FinnSIS-135
❑ 94FinnSIS-380
❑ 94FinnSISH-7
❑ 95FinnSIS-54
**Saarinen, Ari**
❑ 93FinnJyvHS-354
❑ 93FinnSIS-226
❑ 94FinnSIS-94
❑ 95FinnSIS-160
**Saarinen, Pasi**
❑ 95FinnSIS-233
**Saarinen, Rod**
❑ 907thInnSOHL-239
❑ 90KitRan-27
**Saarinen, Simo**
❑ 89SweSemWCS-33
❑ 91SweSemWCS-7
❑ 93FinnJyvHS-15
❑ 93FinnSIS-88
❑ 94FinnSIS-99
❑ 95FinnSIS-4
❑ 95FinnSISL-39
**Saarinen, Toni**
❑ 95FinnSIS-228
❑ 96FinnSISR-26
**Sablik, Lukas**
❑ 95CzeAPSE-177
**Sabo, Ed**
❑ 92RicRen-14
**Sabo, Steve**
❑ 91AirCanSJHL-E49
❑ 92MPSPhoSJHL-163
**Sabol, Shaun**
❑ 88ProAHL-134
❑ 89ProAHL-333
❑ 90ProAHLIHL-46
❑ 91ProAHLCHL-202
**Sabourin, Gary**
❑ 68OPC-117
❑ 68ShiCoi-157
❑ 68Top-117
❑ 69OPC-19
❑ 69OPCFou-3
❑ 69Top-19
❑ 70ColSta-57
❑ 70DadCoo-115
❑ 70EssPowPla-244
❑ 70OPC-96
❑ 70OPCDec-28
❑ 70SarProSta-186
❑ 70Top-96
❑ 71BluPos-20
❑ 71LetActR-6
❑ 71OPC-13
❑ 71SarProSta-177
❑ 71TorSun-247
❑ 72BluWhiBor-18
❑ 72OPC-91
❑ 72SarProSta-183
❑ 72Top-163
❑ 73BluWhiBor-17
❑ 73OPC-168
❑ 73Top-184
❑ 74MapLeaP-17
❑ 74NHLActSta-253
❑ 74OPCNHL-368
❑ 75OPCNHL-299
❑ 75Top-299
❑ 76OPCNHL-266
❑ 92BluUDBB-15
**Sabourin, Ken**
❑ 82SauSteMG-18
❑ 83SauSteMG-20
❑ 84SauSteMG-20
❑ 86MonGolF-13
❑ 88SalLakCGE-19
❑ 89ProIHL-204
❑ 90CapKod-23
❑ 90ProAHLIHL-610
❑ 90ProSet-596
❑ 91CapJun5-24
❑ 91FlamPanTS-20
❑ 91OPC-43
❑ 91ScoCan-398
❑ 91StaClu-396
❑ 91Top-43
❑ 91UppDec-417
❑ 91UppDecF-417
❑ 94MilAdm-21
❑ 95MilAdmBO-15
❑ 96MilAdmBO-22
**Sacco, David**
❑ 93Cla-80
❑ 93Pow-517
❑ 93StaCluTUSA-22
❑ 93TopPreTUSA-13
❑ 93Ult-497
❑ 94ClaAut-NNO
❑ 94Don-309
❑ 94DucCarJr-20
❑ 94Lea-58
❑ 94Sco-240
❑ 94ScoGol-240
❑ 94ScoPla-240
❑ 94ScoPlaTS-240
❑ 94UppDec-328
❑ 94UppDecEleIce-328
❑ 95ColEdgI-14
❑ 96Lea-218
❑ 96LeaPreP-218
❑ 96Pin-213
❑ 96PinArtP-213
❑ 96PinFoi-213
❑ 96PinPreS-213
❑ 96PinRinC-213
**Sacco, Joe**
❑ 90NewSai-21
❑ 90ProAHLIHL-156
❑ 91Par-395
❑ 91ParFre-395
❑ 91ScoAme-319
❑ 91ScoCan-349
❑ 92Bow-417
❑ 92OPC-355
❑ 92Par-185
❑ 92ParEmel-185
❑ 92Sco-532
❑ 92ScoCan-532
❑ 92St.JohML-19
❑ 92StaClu-398
❑ 92Ult-215
❑ 92UppDec-266
❑ 92UppDec-382
❑ 93Don-2
❑ 93OPCPre-329
❑ 93OPCPreG-329
❑ 93Par-273
❑ 93ParEmel-273
❑ 93Pow-9
❑ 93StaClu-256
❑ 93StaCluFDI-256
❑ 93StaCluO-256
❑ 93TopPre-329
❑ 93TopPreG-329
❑ 93Ult-260
❑ 93UppDec-36
❑ 93UppDecSP-3
❑ 94BeAPla-R87
❑ 94BeAPSig-79
❑ 94CanGamNHLP-29

❑ 94Don-64
❑ 94DucCarJr-21
❑ 94Lea-274
❑ 94OPCPre-309
❑ 94OPCPreSE-309
❑ 94ParSE-SE5
❑ 94ParSEG-SE5
❑ 94Pin-232
❑ 94PinArtP-232
❑ 94PinRinC-232
❑ 94StaClu-161
❑ 94StaCluFDI-161
❑ 94StaCluMOMS-161
❑ 94StaCluSTWC-161
❑ 94TopPre-309
❑ 94TopPreSE-309
❑ 94Ult-6
❑ 94UppDec-166
❑ 94UppDecEleIce-166
❑ 95ColCho-68
❑ 95ColChoPC-68
❑ 95ColChoPCP-68
❑ 95Don-302
❑ 95FinnSemWC-112
❑ 95Lea-164
❑ 95Sco-68
❑ 95ScoBlaIce-68
❑ 95ScoBlaIceAP-68
❑ 95Top-86
❑ 95TopOPCI-86
❑ 95UppDec-43
❑ 95UppDecEleIce-43
❑ 95UppDecEleIceG-43
❑ 96Duc-6
❑ 96UppDec-4
❑ 97Be A PPAD-39
❑ 97Be A PPAPD-39
❑ 97BeAPla-39
❑ 97BeAPlaAut-39
❑ 97ColCho-5
❑ 97Pac-208
❑ 97PacCop-208
❑ 97PacEmeGre-208
❑ 97PacIceB-208
❑ 97PacRed-208
❑ 97PacSil-208
❑ 97ScoMigDPla-7
❑ 97ScoMigDPre-7
❑ 97ScoMigDuc-7
❑ 97SPAut-3
❑ 97UppDec-214
❑ 98Pac-287
❑ 98PacIceB-287
❑ 98PacRed-287

**Sacharuk, Larry**
❑ 74NHLActSta-249
❑ 75OPCNHL-76
❑ 75OPCNHL-327
❑ 75Top-76
❑ 75Top-327

**Sacka, Ron**
❑ 91MicWol-14
❑ 93MicWol-18

**Sadowski, John**
❑ 94DubFigS-25

**Safarik, Richard**
❑ 95SlaMemC-62

**Safronov, Kirill**
❑ 98SPXTopP-73
❑ 98SPXTopPF-73
❑ 98SPXTopPR-73
❑ 98UppDecBD-103
❑ 98UppDecDD-103
❑ 98UppDecQD-103
❑ 98UppDecTD-103

**Safsten, Gunnar**
❑ 67SweHoc-128
❑ 69SweHocS-142

**Sagala, Patrick**
❑ 92QueIntP-45

**Saganiuk, Rocky**
❑ 79MapLeaP-24
❑ 80MapLeaP-22
❑ 80OPC-64
❑ 80PepCap-96
❑ 80Top-64
❑ 81MapLeaP-19
❑ 81OPC-323
❑ 82OPC-331
❑ 82OPCSti-69
❑ 82PosCer-18
❑ 83PenTeaP-27
❑ 84PenHeiP-20

**Sagissor, Tom**
❑ 90ProAHLIHL-58
❑ 91ProAHLCHL-81

**Saharchuk, Dennis**
❑ 89SpoChi-16
❑ 907thInnSWHL-199
❑ 907thInnSWHL-327
❑ 917thInnSWHL-38

**Sahlen, Kenneth**
❑ 65SweCorI-165

**Sahlin, Anders**
❑ 67SweHoc-56

**Sahlstedt, Kalle**
❑ 93FinnJyvHS-228
❑ 93FinnSIS-195
❑ 94FinnSIS-55
❑ 94FinnSISJ-10
❑ 95FinnSemWC-21
❑ 95FinnSIS-103
❑ 96FinnSISR-101

**Sahlsten, Petter**
❑ 91SweSemE-8

**Sahlsten, Tommy**
❑ 67SweHoc-244

**Sailer, Petr**
❑ 95CzeAPSE-72
❑ 96CzeAPSE-259

**Sailynoja, Keijo**
❑ 93FinnJyvHS-112
❑ 93FinnSIS-17
❑ 94FinnSIS-124
❑ 95FinnSIS-52
❑ 96FinnSISR-48

**Saindon, Paul**
❑ 51LavDaiQSHL-70

**Saint James, Susan**
❑ 91ProSetPla-299

**Sakac, Marcel**
❑ 72SweSemWC-21
❑ 74SweSemHVS-72
❑ 92BriColJHL-118

**Sakala, Mark**
❑ 91MicWol-15
❑ 93MicWol-19

**Sakic, Brian**
❑ 907thInnSWHL-114A
❑ 907thInnSWHL-114B
❑ 917thInnSWHL-292
❑ 91UppDec-461
❑ 91UppDecF-461
❑ 92UppDec-36
❑ 93FliGen-4
❑ 94FliGen-19
❑ 95FliGen-21

**Sakic, Joe**
❑ 88NordGenF-26
❑ 88NordTeal-27
❑ 89Kra-32
❑ 89Nord-36
❑ 89NordGenF-27
❑ 89NordPol-25
❑ 89OPC-113
❑ 89OPC-313
❑ 89OPCSti-41
❑ 89OPCSti-185
❑ 89OPCSti-187
❑ 89PanSti-327
❑ 89Top-113
❑ 90Bow-169
❑ 90BowTif-169
❑ 90Kra-50
❑ 90Kra-79
❑ 90NordPet-21
❑ 90OPC-384
❑ 90OPCPre-102
❑ 90PanSti-139
❑ 90ProSet-257
❑ 90ProSet-375
❑ 90Sco-8
❑ 90ScoCan-8
❑ 90ScoHotRS-7
❑ 90ScoYouS-10
❑ 90Top-384
❑ 90TopTeaSL-14
❑ 90TopTif-384
❑ 90UppDec-164
❑ 90UppDec-301
❑ 90UppDec-490
❑ 90UppDecF-164
❑ 90UppDecF-301
❑ 90UppDecF-490
❑ 91Bow-133
❑ 91Gil-22
❑ 91Kra-41
❑ 91McDUppD-5
❑ 91NordPanTS-18
❑ 91NordPet-25
❑ 91OPC-16
❑ 91OPC-70
❑ 91PanSti-257
❑ 91PanSti-334
❑ 91Par-148
❑ 91ParFre-148
❑ 91Pin-150
❑ 91Pin-381
❑ 91PinFre-150
❑ 91PinFre-381
❑ 91ProSet-199
❑ 91ProSet-315
❑ 91ProSetFre-199
❑ 91ProSetFre-315
❑ 91ProSetNHLAS-AC5
❑ 91ProSetPC-23
❑ 91ProSetPla-102
❑ 91ScoAme-25
❑ 91ScoAme-336
❑ 91ScoCan-25
❑ 91ScoCan-366
❑ 91ScoKel-12
❑ 91ScoYouS-20
❑ 91StaClu-389
❑ 91SweSemWCS-75
❑ 91Top-16
❑ 91TopBowPS-3
❑ 91TopTeaSL-8
❑ 91UppDec-333
❑ 91UppDec-616
❑ 91UppDecF-333
❑ 91UppDecF-616
❑ 92Bow-240
❑ 92Bow-244
❑ 92HumDum1-19
❑ 92McDUppD-26
❑ 92NorPet-28
❑ 92OPC-54
❑ 92OPC-55
❑ 92OPC25AI-22
❑ 92OPCPreSP-11
❑ 92PanSti-209
❑ 92PanStiFre-209
❑ 92Par-147
❑ 92ParEmeI-147
❑ 92Pin-150
❑ 92PinFre-150
❑ 92PinTea2-21
❑ 92PinTea2F-21
❑ 92ProSet-150
❑ 92Sco-240
❑ 92Sco-434
❑ 92ScoCan-240
❑ 92ScoCan-434
❑ 92ScoYouS-20
❑ 92SeaPat-47
❑ 92StaClu-3
❑ 92Top-495
❑ 92TopGol-495G
❑ 92Ult-179
❑ 92UppDec-36
❑ 92UppDec-255
❑ 92UppDecWJG-WG8
❑ 93Don-282
❑ 93Kra-45
❑ 93Kra-65
❑ 93Lea-87
❑ 93McDUppD-24
❑ 93OPCPre-10
❑ 93OPCPreBG-15
❑ 93OPCPreG-10
❑ 93PanSti-G
❑ 93Par-169
❑ 93ParEasWesS-E9
❑ 93ParEmeI-169
❑ 93Pin-290
❑ 93PinAllS-13
❑ 93PinAllSC-13
❑ 93PinCan-290
❑ 93PinCap-19
❑ 93PinCapC-19
❑ 93PinTea2-25
❑ 93PinTea2C-25
❑ 93Pow-204
❑ 93PowPoiL-15
❑ 93Sco-135
❑ 93ScoCan-135
❑ 93ScoDreTea-14
❑ 93ScoDynDC-5
❑ 93ScoFra-17
❑ 93SeaPat-17
❑ 93StaClu-32
❑ 93StaCluAS-17
❑ 93StaCluFDI-32
❑ 93StaCluFDIO-32
❑ 93StaCluO-32
❑ 93SweSemWCS-206
❑ 93TopPre-10
❑ 93TopPreG-10
❑ 93Ult-242
❑ 93UppDec-69
❑ 93UppDec-223
❑ 93UppDecLAS-13
❑ 93UppDecNL-NL3
❑ 93UppDecNR-16
❑ 93UppDecSilSka-H9
❑ 93UppDecSilSkaG-H9
❑ 93UppDecSP-130
❑ 94BeAPla-R96
❑ 94CanGamNHLP-199
❑ 94Don-141
❑ 94EASpo-112
❑ 94Fin-69
❑ 94FinBowB-B18
❑ 94FinBowB-X23
❑ 94FinBowBR-B18
❑ 94FinBowBR-X23
❑ 94FinRef-69
❑ 94FinSupTW-69
❑ 94Fla-151
❑ 94Fle-183
❑ 94HocWit-100
❑ 94Kra-28
❑ 94Lea-165
❑ 94LeaLim-106
❑ 94LeaLimI-19
❑ 94McDUppD-McD1
❑ 94NordBurK-22
❑ 94OPCPre-480
❑ 94OPCPreSE-480
❑ 94ParCratGB-19
❑ 94ParCratGG-19
❑ 94ParCratGR-19
❑ 94ParSE-SE147
❑ 94ParSEG-SE147
❑ 94ParVin-V34
❑ 94Pin-50
❑ 94PinArtP-50
❑ 94PinNorLig-NL4
❑ 94PinRinC-50
❑ 94PosCerBB-22
❑ 94Sco90PC-19
❑ 94ScoFra-TF19
❑ 94Sel-62
❑ 94SelGol-62
❑ 94SP-94
❑ 94SPDieCut-94
❑ 94SPPre-27
❑ 94SPPreDC-27
❑ 94StaCluMO-39
❑ 94StaCluST-19
❑ 94TopPre-480
❑ 94TopPreGTG-2
❑ 94TopPreSE-480
❑ 94Ult-180
❑ 94UppDec-404
❑ 94UppDecEleIce-404
❑ 94UppDecNBAP-14
❑ 94UppDecPH-H17
❑ 94UppDecPHEG-H17
❑ 94UppDecPHES-H17
❑ 94UppDecPHG-H17
❑ 94UppDecSPI-SP65
❑ 94UppDecSPIDC-SP65
❑ 95Bow-42
❑ 95BowAllFoi-42
❑ 95BowBes-BB11
❑ 95BowBesRef-BB11
❑ 95CanGamNHLP-72
❑ 95ColCho-288
❑ 95ColCho-362
❑ 95ColChoCTG-C9
❑ 95ColChoCTG-C9B
❑ 95ColChoCTG-C9C
❑ 95ColChoCTGGB-C9
❑ 95ColChoCTGGR-C9
❑ 95ColChoCTGSB-C9
❑ 95ColChoCTGSR-C9
❑ 95ColChoPC-288
❑ 95ColChoPC-362
❑ 95ColChoPCP-288
❑ 95ColChoPCP-362
❑ 95Don-167
❑ 95DonEli-16
❑ 95DonEliDCS-16
❑ 95DonEliDCU-16
❑ 95DonEliIns-2
❑ 95Emo-42
❑ 95EmoXce-9
❑ 95EmoXci-13
❑ 95Fin-15
❑ 95Fin-80
❑ 95FinnSemWC-87
❑ 95FinRef-15
❑ 95FinRef-80
❑ 95ImpSti-27
❑ 95ImpStiDCS-4
❑ 95Kra-60
❑ 95Lea-182
❑ 95LeaLim-64
❑ 95McDPin-NNO
❑ 95Met-36
❑ 95MetHM-12
❑ 95MetIS-18
❑ 95NHLAcePC-13C
❑ 95ParInt-46
❑ 95ParIntEl-46
❑ 95ParIntPTP-PP8
❑ 95ParIntPTP-PP16
❑ 95PinRoa2-17
❑ 95PlaOneoOne-28
❑ 95PlaOneoOne-139
❑ 95PlaOneoOne-242
❑ 95ProMag-5
❑ 95Sco-5
❑ 95ScoBlaIce-5
❑ 95ScoBlaIceAP-5
❑ 95ScoBorBat-4
❑ 95ScoGolBla-1
❑ 95SelCer-45
❑ 95SelCerGT-8
❑ 95SelCerMG-45
❑ 95SkyImp-41
❑ 95SP-31
❑ 95SPStaEto-E8
❑ 95SPStaEtoG-E8
❑ 95StaClu-167
❑ 95StaCluMO-13
❑ 95StaCluMOMS-167
❑ 95Sum-61
❑ 95SumArtP-61
❑ 95SumIce-61
❑ 95Top-266
❑ 95TopMysF-M6
❑ 95TopMysFR-M6
❑ 95TopOPCI-266
❑ 95TopPro-PF20
❑ 95TopSupSki-17
❑ 95TopSupSkiPla-17
❑ 95Ult-136
❑ 95Ult-397
❑ 95UltExtAtt-17
❑ 95UltGolM-136
❑ 95UltPrePiv-8
❑ 95UltPrePivGM-8
❑ 95UltUltHP-9
❑ 95UltUltV-9
❑ 95UppDec-54
❑ 95UppDec-242
❑ 95UppDecAGPRW-5
❑ 95UppDecEleIce-54
❑ 95UppDecEleIce-242
❑ 95UppDecEleIceG-54
❑ 95UppDecEleIceG-242
❑ 95UppDecPRE-R27
❑ 95UppDecPRE-R36
❑ 95UppDecPRE-R45
❑ 95UppDecPreR-R14
❑ 95UppDecPreR-R27
❑ 95UppDecPreR-R36
❑ 95UppDecPreR-R45
❑ 95UppDecSpeE-SE111
❑ 95UppDecSpeEdiG-SE111
❑ 95UppPreRP-R36
❑ 95UppPreRP-R45
❑ 95Zen-64
❑ 95ZenZT-13
❑ 96BeAPBisITB-16
❑ 96ColCho-64
❑ 96ColCho-299
❑ 96ColCho-314
❑ 96ColCho-336
❑ 96ColChoCTG-C7A
❑ 96ColChoCTG-C7B
❑ 96ColChoCTGE-CR7
❑ 96ColChoCTGEG-CR7
❑ 96ColChoCTGG-C7A
❑ 96ColChoCTGG-C7B
❑ 96ColChoMVP-UD5
❑ 96ColChoMVPG-UD5
❑ 96Don-1
❑ 96DonCanI-74
❑ 96DonCanIGPP-74
❑ 96DonCanIOC-1
❑ 96DonCanIRPP-74
❑ 96DonEli-120
❑ 96DonEliDCS-120
❑ 96DonEliIns-7
❑ 96DonEliInsG-7
❑ 96DonEliS-11
❑ 96DonGoTS-3
❑ 96DonPrePro-1
❑ 96DurAllT-DC3
❑ 96DurL'EB-JB3
❑ 96Fla-21
❑ 96FlaBluI-21
❑ 96FlaCenIS-7
❑ 96Fle-25
❑ 96Fle-137
❑ 96FleArtRos-20
❑ 96FlePCC-6
❑ 96FlePea-10
❑ 96FlePic-2
❑ 96FlePicDL-9
❑ 96FlePicF5-41
❑ 96HocGreC-19
❑ 96HocGreCG-19
❑ 96KraUppD-39
❑ 96KraUppD-47
❑ 96Lea-139
❑ 96LeaFirOI-3
❑ 96LeaLeaAL-1
❑ 96LeaLeaALP-P1
❑ 96LeaLim-56
❑ 96LeaLimG-56
❑ 96LeaLimStu-16
❑ 96LeaPre-37
❑ 96LeaPreP-139
❑ 96LeaPrePP-37
❑ 96LeaPreSG-11
❑ 96LeaPreSP-1
❑ 96LeaPreSte-11
❑ 96MetUni-38
❑ 96MetUniC-12
❑ 96MetUniCSP-12
❑ 96MetUniLW-16
❑ 96MetUniLWSP-16
❑ 96NHLACEPC-42
❑ 96NHLProSTA-5
❑ 96Pin-201
❑ 96PinArtP-201
❑ 96PinFan-FC17
❑ 96PinFoi-201
❑ 96PinMcD-10
❑ 96PinMin-11
❑ 96PinMinB-11
❑ 96PinMinCoiB-11
❑ 96PinMinCoiGP-11
❑ 96PinMinCoiN-11
❑ 96PinMinCoiS-11
❑ 96PinMinCoiSG-11
❑ 96PinMinG-11
❑ 96PinMinS-11
❑ 96PinPreS-201
❑ 96PinRinC-201
❑ 96PinTeaP-1
❑ 96PinTro-9
❑ 96PlaOneoOne-432
❑ 96PosUppD-19
❑ 96Sco-9
❑ 96ScoArtPro-9
❑ 96ScoDeaCAP-9
❑ 96ScoDreTea-3
❑ 96ScoGolB-9
❑ 96ScoSpeAP-9
❑ 96ScoSudDea-11
❑ 96SelCer-16
❑ 96SelCerAP-16
❑ 96SelCerBlu-16
❑ 96SelCerCor-9
❑ 96SelCerMB-16
❑ 96SelCerMG-16
❑ 96SelCerMR-16
❑ 96SelCerRed-16
❑ 96SkyImp-28
❑ 96SkyImpCI-10
❑ 96SkyImpVer-9
❑ 96SP-34
❑ 96SPCleWin-CW19
❑ 96SPInsInf-IN6
❑ 96SPInsInfG-IN6
❑ 96SPx-9
❑ 96SPxGol-9
❑ 96StaCluMO-17
❑ 96Sum-1
❑ 96SumArtP-1
❑ 96SumHigV-2
❑ 96SumHigVM-2
❑ 96SumIce-1
❑ 96SumMet-1
❑ 96SumPreS-1
❑ 96SumUnt-3
❑ 96SweSemW-95
❑ 96TeaOut-18
❑ 96TopPicFT-FT20
❑ 96TopPicTS-TS12
❑ 96Ult-40
❑ 96UltGolM-40
❑ 96UltPow-15
❑ 96UltPowRL-7
❑ 96UppDec-204
❑ 96UppDec-240
❑ 96UppDecBD-169
❑ 96UppDecBDG-169
❑ 96UppDecBDRFTC-RC10
❑ 96UppDecGN-X3
❑ 96UppDecHH-HH20
❑ 96UppDecHHG-HH20
❑ 96UppDecHHS-HH20
❑ 96UppDecIce-108
❑ 96UppDecIceDF-S5
❑ 96UppDecIcePar-108
❑ 96UppDecIceSCF-S5
❑ 96UppDecLSH-LS7
❑ 96UppDecLSHF-LS7
❑ 96UppDecLSHS-LS7
❑ 96UppDecSS-SS16A
❑ 96Zen-44
❑ 96ZenArtP-44
❑ 96ZenChaS-8
❑ 96ZenChaSD-8
❑ 97AvaPin-3
❑ 97Be A PPAD-83
❑ 97Be A PPAPD-83
❑ 97BeAPla-83
❑ 97BeAPlaAut-83
❑ 97BeAPlaTAN-19
❑ 97ColCho-55
❑ 97ColChoCTG-C18A
❑ 97ColChoCTG-C18B
❑ 97ColChoCTG-C18C
❑ 97ColChoCTGE-CR18
❑ 97ColChoSta-SQ63
❑ 97ColChoSti-S19
❑ 97ColChoWD-W6
❑ 97Don-117
❑ 97DonCanI-102
❑ 97DonCanIDS-102
❑ 97DonCanINP-17
❑ 97DonCanIPS-102
❑ 97DonCanISCS-3
❑ 97DonEli-49
❑ 97DonEli-115
❑ 97DonEliAsp-49
❑ 97DonEliAsp-115
❑ 97DonEliC-3
❑ 97DonEliMC-3
❑ 97DonEliPN-11A
❑ 97DonEliPN-11B
❑ 97DonEliPN-11C
❑ 97DonEliPNDC-11A
❑ 97DonEliPNDC-11C
❑ 97DonEliS-49
❑ 97DonEliS-115
❑ 97DonLim-36
❑ 97DonLim-132
❑ 97DonLim-190
❑ 97DonLimExp-36
❑ 97DonLimExp-132
❑ 97DonLimExp-190
❑ 97DonLimFOTG-4
❑ 97DonLimFOTG-5
❑ 97DonLin2L-12
❑ 97DonLin2LDC-12
❑ 97DonPre-128
❑ 97DonPre-175
❑ 97DonPreCttC-128
❑ 97DonPreCttC-175
❑ 97DonPreDWT-3
❑ 97DonPreLotT-8A
❑ 97DonPrePM-11
❑ 97DonPreProG-117
❑ 97DonPreProS-117
❑ 97DonPreT-8
❑ 97DonPreTB-8
❑ 97DonPreTBC-8
❑ 97DonPreTPC-8
❑ 97DonPreTPG-8
❑ 97DonPri-17
❑ 97DonPri-208
❑ 97DonPriDD-11
❑ 97DonPriODI-15
❑ 97DonPriP-9
❑ 97DonPriS-9
❑ 97DonPriSB-9
❑ 97DonPriSG-9
❑ 97DonPriSoA-17
❑ 97DonPriSoA-208
❑ 97DonPriSS-9
❑ 97EssOlyHH-7
❑ 97EssOlyHHF-7
❑ 97Kat-42
❑ 97KatGol-42
❑ 97KatSil-42
❑ 97Lea-35
❑ 97LeaBanSea-24
❑ 97LeaFirOnIce-7
❑ 97LeaFraMat-35
❑ 97LeaFraMDC-35
❑ 97LeaInt-35
❑ 97LeaIntUI-35
❑ 97McD-5
❑ 97Pac-38
❑ 97PacCop-38
❑ 97PacCroR-38
❑ 97PacCroREG-38
❑ 97PacCroRHTDC-5
❑ 97PacCroRIB-38
❑ 97PacCroRLCDC-6
❑ 97PacCroRS-38
❑ 97PacDyn-34
❑ 97PacDynBKS-27
❑ 97PacDynC-34
❑ 97PacDynDD-6B
❑ 97PacDynDG-34
❑ 97PacDynEG-34
❑ 97PacDynIB-34
❑ 97PacDynKotN-4
❑ 97PacDynR-34
❑ 97PacDynSil-34
❑ 97PacDynTan-2
❑ 97PacEmeGre-38
❑ 97PacGolCroDC-9
❑ 97PacIceB-38
❑ 97PacInv-39
❑ 97PacInvAZ-7
❑ 97PacInvC-39
❑ 97PacInvEG-39
❑ 97PacInvFP-10
❑ 97PacInvIB-39
❑ 97PacInvNRB-57
❑ 97PacInvOTG-6
❑ 97PacInvR-39
❑ 97PacInvS-39
❑ 97PacOme-65
❑ 97PacOmeC-65
❑ 97PacOmeDG-65
❑ 97PacOmeEG-65
❑ 97PacOmeG-65
❑ 97PacOmeGFDCC-4
❑ 97PacOmeIB-65
❑ 97PacOmeSil-5
❑ 97PacOmeSLC-6
❑ 97PacOmeTL-5
❑ 97PacPar-55
❑ 97PacParBNDC-7
❑ 97PacParC-55
❑ 97PacParCG-5
❑ 97PacParDG-55
❑ 97PacParEG-55
❑ 97PacParIB-55
❑ 97PacParP-7
❑ 97PacParRed-55
❑ 97PacParSil-55
❑ 97PacRed-38
❑ 97PacRev-39
❑ 97PacRev1AGD-8
❑ 97PacRevC-39
❑ 97PacRevE-39
❑ 97PacRevIB-39
❑ 97PacRevR-39
❑ 97PacRevS-39
❑ 97PacSil-38
❑ 97PacSlaSDC-2B
❑ 97Pin-32
❑ 97PinArtP-32
❑ 97PinBee-4
❑ 97PinBeeGP-4
❑ 97PinBeeGT-19
❑ 97PinBeeT-19
❑ 97PinCer-50
❑ 97PinCerMB-50
❑ 97PinCerMG-50
❑ 97PinCerMR-50
❑ 97PinCerR-50
❑ 97PinEpiGO-3
❑ 97PinEpiGP-3
❑ 97PinEpiME-3
❑ 97PinEpiMO-3
❑ 97PinEpiMP-3
❑ 97PinEpiPE-3
❑ 97PinEpiPO-3
❑ 97PinEpiPP-3
❑ 97PinEpiSE-3
❑ 97PinEpiSO-3
❑ 97PinEpiSP-3
❑ 97PinIns-54
❑ 97PinInsC-8
❑ 97PinInsCC-54
❑ 97PinInsCG-8
❑ 97PinInsEC-54
❑ 97PinInsT-8
❑ 97PinMin-12
❑ 97PinMinB-12
❑ 97PinMinCBP-12
❑ 97PinMinCGPP-12
❑ 97PinMinCNSP-12
❑ 97PinMinCoiB-12
❑ 97PinMinCoiGP-12
❑ 97PinMinCoiN-12
❑ 97PinMinCoiSG-12
❑ 97PinMinCoiSS-12
❑ 97PinMinGolTea-12
❑ 97PinMinSilTea-12
❑ 97PinPowPac-12
❑ 97PinPrePBB-32
❑ 97PinPrePBC-32
❑ 97PinPrePBM-32
❑ 97PinPrePBY-32
❑ 97PinPrePFC-32
❑ 97PinPrePFM-32
❑ 97PinPrePFY-32
❑ 97PinPrePla-32
❑ 97PinRinC-32
❑ 97PinTotCMPG-50
❑ 97PinTotCPB-50
❑ 97PinTotCPG-50
❑ 97PinTotCPR-50
❑ 97PosPin-3
❑ 97Sco-125
❑ 97ScoArtPro-125
❑ 97ScoAva-18
❑ 97ScoAvaPla-18
❑ 97ScoAvaPre-18

97ScoGolBla-125
97SP Autl-I4
97SPAut-35
97SPAutID-I4
97SPAutIE-I4
97SPx-12
97SPxBro-12
97SPxDuo-10
97SPxGol-12
97SPxGraF-12
97SPxSil-12
97SPxSte-12
97Stu-23
97StuHarH-17
97StuPor-23
97StuPrePG-23
97StuPrePS-23
97StuSil-12
97StuSil8-12
97UppDec-253
97UppDecBD-96
97UppDecBDDD-96
97UppDecBDPC-PC29
97UppDecBDPCDD-PC29
97UppDecBDPCM-PC29
97UppDecBDPCQD-PC29
97UppDecBDPCTD-PC29
97UppDecBDQD-96
97UppDecBDTD-96
97UppDecDV-20
97UppDecDVDM-DM5
97UppDecDVSM-20
97UppDecGDM-253
97UppDecGJ-GJ7
97UppDecIC-IC10
97UppDecIC2-IC10
97UppDecIce-79
97UppDecIceP-79
97UppDecIPS-79
97UppDecSG-SG35
97UppDecSSM-SS19
97UppDecSSW-SS19
97UppDecTS-4
97UppDecTSL2-4
97UppDecTSS-3A
97Zen-29
97Zen5x7-7
97ZenGolImp-7
97ZenSilImp-7
97ZenZGol-29
97ZenZSil-29
98Be A PPA-37
98Be A PPAA-37
98Be A PPAGUSC-S12
98Be A PPAJ-AS13
98Be A PPGUJA-G6
98Be A PPGUJC-G6
98Be A PPPH-H10
98Be A PPPPUJC-P15
98Be A PPTBASG-37
98Be APG-37
98BowBes-49
98BowBesAR-49
98BowBesR-49
98Fin-91
98FinDouMF-M23
98FinDouMF-M26
98FinDouMF-M28
98FinDouMF-M30
98FinDouSMFR-M23
98FinDouSMFR-M26
98FinDouSMFR-M28
98FinDouSMFR-M30
98FinNo P-91
98FinNo PR-91
98FinRedL-R15
98FinRedLR-R15
98FinRef-91
98JelSpo-8
98McD-3
98O-PChr-68
98O-PChrR-68
98Pac-169
98PacAur-52
98PacAurALC-7
98PacAurC-6
98PacAurCF-13
98PacAurCFC-13
98PacAurCFIB-13
98PacAurCFR-13
98PacAurCFS-13
98PacAurFL-4
98PacAurFLIB-4
98PacAurFLR-4
98PacAurMAC-6
98PacCroR-36
98PacCroRLS-36
98PacCroRMP-6
98PacCroRPotG-8
98PacCroRPP-5
98PacDynI-52
98PacDynIAR-6
98PacDynIARB-6
98PacDynIARIB-6
98PacDynIARR-6
98PacDynIARS-6
98PacDynIFT-6
98PacDynIIB-52
98PacDynIR-52
98PacEO P-6
98PacGolCD-10
98PacIceB-169
98PacOmeEP1o1-6

98PacOmeFtF-6
98PacOmeH-65
98PacOmeO-10
98PacOmeODI-65
98PacOmeP-6
98PacOmePI-22
98PacOmePIB-22
98PacOmeR-65
98PacPar-61
98PacParC-61
98PacParEG-61
98PacParH-61
98PacParIB-61
98PacParIG-4
98PacParIGG-4
98PacParIGS-4
98PacParS-61
98PacParSDDC-5
98PacRed-169
98PacRev-39
98PacRevCTL-5
98PacRevIS-39
98PacRevR-39
98PacRevS-12
98PacTim-5
98PacTitl-7
98PinEpiGE-3
98RevThrPA-24
98RevThrPA-24
98SP Aut-22
98SP AutSM-S8
98SP AutSS-SS19
98SPxFin-22
98SPxFin-163
98SPxFinR-22
98SPxFinR-92
98SPxFinR-163
98SPxFinS-22
98SPxFinS-92
98SPxFinS-163
98SPXTopP-15
98SPXTopPF-15
98SPXTopPHH-H8
98SPXTopPLI-L13
98SPXTopPPS-PS22
98SPXTopPR-15
98SPXTopPWM-JS
98Top-68
98TopBlaLGR'-GR10
98TopGolLC1-65
98TopGolLC1B-65
98TopGolLC1Oo0-65
98TopGolLC1R-65
98TopGolLC1ROo0-65
98TopGolLC2-65
98TopGolLC2B-65
98TopGolLC2BOo0-65
98TopGolLC2Oo0-65
98TopGolLC2ROo0-65
98TopGolLC3-65
98TopGolLC3B-65
98TopGolLC3BOo0-65
98TopGolLC3Oo0-65
98TopGolLC3R-65
98TopGolLC3ROo0-65
98TopGolLGR'-GR10
98TopGolLGR'BOo0-GR10
98TopGolLGR'OoO-GR10
98TopGolLGR'ROo0-GR10
98TopLocL-L10
98TopMysFB-M20
98TopMysFBR-M20
98TopMysFGR-M20
98TopMysFGR-M20
98TopMysFS-M20
98TopMysFSR-M20
98TopO-P-68
98TopRedLGR'-GR10
98UC-59
98UC-230
98UCMBH-BH19
98UCSB-SQ11
98UCSG-SQ11
98UCSG-SQ11
98UCSR-SQ11
98UD ChoPCR-59
98UD ChoPCR-230
98UD ChoR-59
98UD ChoR-230
98UD3-59
98UD3-119
98UD3-179
98UD3DieC-59
98UD3DieC-119
98UD3DieC-179
98UppDec-248
98UppDecBD-23
98UppDecDD-23
98UppDecE-248
98UppDecE1o1-248
98UppDecFF-FF6
98UppDecFF01-FF6
98UppDecFFQ2-FF6
98UppDecFIT-FT23
98UppDecFITQ1-FT23
98UppDecFITQ2-FT23
98UppDecFITQ3-FT23
98UppDecGR-248
98UppDecLSH-LS2
98UppDecLSHQ1-LS2
98UppDecLSHQ2-LS2

98UppDecLSHQ3-LS2
98UppDecM-53
98UppDecM1-M13
98UppDecM2-M13
98UppDecMGS-53
98UppDecMOH-OT15
98UppDecMS-S10
98UppDecMSF-F15
98UppDecMSS-53
98UppDecMSS-53
98UppDecQD-23
98UppDecTD-23
98UppDecWFG-WF8
98UppDecWFP-WF8
99Pac-115
99PacAur-42
99PacAurCF-9
99PacAurCFC-9
99PacAurCFPB-9
99PacAurPD-42
99PacCop-115
99PacCra-5
99PacGol-115
99PacGolCD-12
99PacIceB-115
99PacPasAP-8
99PacPreD-115
99RetHoc-21
99SP AutPS-22
99UppDecCL-66
99UppDecCLCLC-66
99UppDecM-51
99UppDecMGS-51
99UppDecMSS-51
99UppDecMSS-51
99UppDecRG-21
99UppDecRP-21

**Salajko, Jeff**
92Ott672A-19
95Sla-331

**Salei, Ruslan**
95LasVegThu-16
96MetUni-191
96SelCer-109
96SelCerAP-109
96SelCerBlu-109
96SelCerMB-109
96SelCerMG-109
96SelCerMR-109
96SelCerRed-109
96SP-169
96Ult-5
96UltGolM-5
96UppDec-215
97Be A PPAD-124
97Be A PPAPD-124
97BeAPla-124
97BeAPlaAut-124
97PacRev-4
97PacRevC-4
97PacRevE-4
97PacRevIB-4
97PacRevR-4
97PacRevS-4
98O-PChr-99
98O-PChrR-99
98Top-99
98TopO-P-99
99Pac-14
99PacCop-14
99PacGol-14
99PacIceB-14
99PacPreD-14

**Saleski, Don**
72OPC-213
73FlyLin-14
74NHLActSta-215
75FlyCanDC-15
75OPCNHL-262
75OPCNHL-337
75Top-262
76OPCNHL-81
76Top-81
77Coc-22
77OPCNHL-233
77Top-233
78OPC-257
78Top-257
79Roc-21

**Saleva, Henry**
83SweSemE-170

**Salfi, Kent**
92MaiBlaB-13

**Salficky, Dusan**
94CzeAPSE-25
96CzeAPSE-144

**Salle, Johan**
90SweSemE-130
91SweSemE-183
92SweSemE-208
93SweSemE-177
94SweLeaE-244
95SweLeaE-265
95SweUppDE-137

**Sallin, Hans**
85SwePanS-186

**Salmelainen, Tommi**
72SweSemWC-87

**Salmi, Jorma**
65SweCorI-44A
65SweCorI-96B

**Salminen, Jussi**
95ColCho-339
95ColChoPC-339

95ColChoPCP-339
**Salminen, Kimmo**
94FinnSIS-73
94FinnSISMN-9
95FinnSIS-63
96FinnSISR-63
**Salming, Borje**
70SweHocS-23
71SweHocS-90
72SweHocS-7
72SweHocS-86
73MapLeaP-22
73SweHocS-7
73SweHocS-160
73SweWorCS-7
73SweWorCS-160
74LipSou-41A
74LipSou-41B
74MapLeaP-18
74NHLActSta-269
74OPCNHL-180
74SweHocS-314
74Top-180
75HerSta-27
75MapLeaP-16
75MapLeaP-17
75OPCNHL-283
75OPCNHL-294
75Top-283
75Top-294
76MapLeaP-15
76OPCNHL-27
76Top-22
77MapLeaP-13
77OPCNHL-2
77OPCNHL-140
77Top-2
77Top-140
78MapLeaP-18
78OPC-240
78OPC-328
78Top-240
79MapLeaP-25
79MapLeaP-26
79OPC-40
79Top-40
80MapLeaP-23
80OPC-85
80OPC-210
80OPCSup-19
80PepCap-97
80Top-85
80Top-210
81MapLeaP-20
81OPC-307
81OPCSti-98
81OPCSti-111
81PosSta-18
81Top-33
82MapLeaP-30
82MapLeaP-31
82OPC-332
82OPCSti-75
82OPCSti-76
82PosCer-18
82SweSemHVS-143
83MapLeaP-22
83OPC-341
83OPCSti-33
83OPCSti-34
83PufSti-6
83Vac-97
84KelAccD-3A
84KelAccD-3B
84MapLeaP-21
84OPC-311
84OPCSti-7
84OPCSti-8
85MapLeaP-26
85OPC-248
85OPCSti-12
86KraDra-42
86MapLeaP-17
86OPC-169
86OPCSti-136
86Top-169
87MapLeaP-17
87MapLeaPLA-8
87MapLeaP-17
87OPC-237
87OPCSti-165
87PanSti-326
87ProAl-16
88EssAllSta-39
88MapLeaPLA-5
88OPC-247
88OPCSti-174
88PanSti-120
89OPC-278
89RedWinLC-15
90SweSemE-77
91SweSemE-4
92FutTre76CC-189
92FutTre76CC-188
92FutTre76CC-197
92SweSemE-36
94HocWit-37
95SweGloWC-8

73SweWorCS-161
74SweHocS-185
79PanSti-189
83SweSemE-74
84SweSemE-73
85SwePanS-46
86SwePanS-29
**Salmon, Tim**
83KinCan-12
**Salmond, Scott**
91BriColJHL-73
**Salo, Ari**
90SweSemE-5
93FinnJyvHS-115
93FinnSIS-5
94FinnSIS-119
**Salo, Robert**
93FinnJyvHS-201
93SIS-259
93FinnSIS-93
95FinnSIS-84
**Salo, Sami**
94FinnSIS-236
95FinnSIS-124
96FinnSISR-137
96FinnSISRRE-3
98PacDynI-131
98PacDynIIB-131
98PacDynIR-131
98PacOmeH-171
98PacOmeODI-171
98PacOmeR-171
99Pac-295
99PacCop-295
99PacGol-295
99PacIceB-295
99PacPreD-295
99RetHoc-57
99UppDecM-143
99UppDecMGS-143
99UppDecMSS-143
99UppDecRG-57
99UppDecRP-57
**Salo, Tommy**
91SweSemE-254
92SweSemE-275
93SweSemE-243
94SweLeaEGC-24
95ColCho-235
95ColChoPC-235
95ColChoPCP-235
95ColEdgI-196
95ColEdgIC-C22
95ColEdgIP-PR2
95Don-196
95Emo-107
95EmoGen-5
95FinnSemWC-53
95Ima-3
95ImaCleE-CE3
95ImaGol-3
95ImaPlaPr-PR8
95Lea-177
95Met-191
95MetWin-6
95ParInt-128
95ParIntEl-128
95Pin-202
95PinArtP-202
95PinRinC-202
95PlaOneoOne-282
95Sco-314
95ScoBlalce-314
95ScoBlalceAP-314
95SelCer-112
95SelCerMG-112
95SkyImp-104
95StaClu-211
95StaCluMOMS-211
95SweGloWC-3
95SweUppDE-246
95Ult-98
95Ult-354
95UltGolM-98
95UppDec-413
95UppDecEleIce-413
95UppDecEleIceG-413
96BeAPAut-77
96BeAPAutSil-77
96BeAPla-77
96ColEdgFL-41
96Fla-57
96FlaBlul-57
96IslIsPos-19
96Lea-221
96LeaPreP-221
96Pin-244
96PinArtP-244
96PinFoi-244
96PinPreS-244
96PinRinC-244
96Sum-189
96SumArtP-189
96SumIce-189
96SumMet-189
96SumPreS-189
98PacPar-148
98PacParEG-148
98PacParGSLC-11
98PacParH-148
98PacParIB-148
98PacRed-288

97DonCanIDS-106
97DonCanIPS-106
97DonEli-101
97DonEliAsp-101
97DonEliS-101
97DonLim-130
97DonLimExp-130
97DonPre-32
97DonPreCttC-32
97DonPreProG-33
97DonPreProS-33
97DonPri-121
97DonPriPG-15
97DonPriPGP-15
97DonPriSoA-121
97Pac-56
97PacCop-56
97PacCroR-81
97PacCroREG-81
97PacCroRIB-81
97PacCroRS-81
97PacDyn-75
97PacDynC-75
97PacDynDG-75
97PacDynEG-75
97PacDynIB-75
97PacDynR-75
97PacDynSil-75
97PacDynTan-67
97PacEmeGre-56
97PacIceB-56
97PacInv-83
97PacInvC-83
97PacInvEG-83
97PacInvIB-83
97PacInvR-83
97PacInvS-83
97PacOme-142
97PacOmeC-142
97PacOmeDG-142
97PacOmeEG-142
97PacOmeG-142
97PacOmeIB-142
97PacPar-111
97PacParC-111
97PacParDG-111
97PacParEG-111
97PacParGSL-12
97PacParIB-111
97PacParRed-111
97PacParSil-111
97PacRed-56
97PacRev-84
97PacRevC-84
97PacRevE-84
97PacRevIB-84
97PacRevR-84
97PacRevRtSD-12
97PacRevS-84
97PacSil-56
97Pin-59
97PinArtP-59
97PinCer-24
97PinCerMB-24
97PinCerMG-24
97PinCerMR-24
97PinCerR-24
97PinIns-49
97PinInsCC-49
97PinInsEC-49
97PinPrePBB-59
97PinPrePBC-59
97PinPrePBM-59
97PinPrePBY-59
97PinPrePFC-59
97PinPrePFM-59
97PinPrePFY-59
97PinPrePla-59
97PinRinC-59
97PinTotCMPG-24
97PinTotCPB-24
97PinTotCPG-24
97PinTotCPR-24
97Sco-9
97ScoArtPro-9
97ScoGolBla-9
97ScoNetWrl-12
97SPAut-93
98Be A PPA-83
98Be A PPAA-83
98Be A PPAAF-83
98Be A PPTBASG-83
98Be APG-83
98O-PChr-88
98O-PChrR-88
98Pac-288
98PacAur-119
98PacCroR-86
98PacCroRLS-86
98PacDynI-118
98PacDynIIB-118
98PacDynIR-118
98PacIceB-288
98PacOmeH-152
98PacOmeODI-152
98PacOmeR-152
98PacPar-148
98PacParEG-148
98PacParH-148
98PacParIB-148
98PacRed-288

98PacRev-90
98PacRevIS-90
98PacRevR-90
98Top-88
98TopO-P-88
98UppDec-317
98UppDecE-317
98UppDecE1o1-317
98UppDecGR-317
98UppDecM-129
98UppDecMGS-129
98UppDecMSS-129
98UppDecMSS-129
99Pac-164
99PacAur-58
99PacAurGU-9
99PacAurPD-58
99PacCop-164
99PacGol-164
99PacIceB-164
99PacIn tCN-8
99PacPreD-164
99UppDecM-80
99UppDecMGS-80
99UppDecMSS-80
99UppDecMSS-80
**Salo, Vesa**
93FinnJyvHS-166
93FinnSIS-169
94FinnSIS-242
94FinnSIS-384
95FinnSIS-96
95SweLeaE-222
95SweLeaEFF-12
95SweUppDE-81
96GerDELE-151
**Salomaa, Sami-Ville**
96FinnSISR-123
**Salomaa, Timo**
84SweSemE-136
**Salomatin, Alexei**
93SweSemE-253
94SweLeaE-35
95SweLeaE-133
95SweLeaEFF-12
95SweUppDE-194
**Salomonsson, Andreas**
91SweSemE-224
92SweSemE-243
93SweSemE-211
94SweLeaE-265
95SweLeaE-108
95SweUppDE-167
96GerDELE-104
**Salomonsson, Stig**
93GreMon-12
**Salomonsson, Tord**
71SweHocS-246
**Salon, Ivan**
93SasBla-3
93SasBla-17
**Salonen, Sami**
95ColCho-328
95ColChoPC-328
95ColChoPCP-328
**Salonen, Timo**
94Fin-137
94FinnSIS-255
94FinRef-137
94FinSupTW-137
94ParSE-SE223
94ParSEG-SE223
95FinnSIS-359
95UppDec-547
95UppDecEleIce-547
95UppDecEleIceG-547
96FinnSISR-162
**Salsten, Petter**
90SweSemE-79
93SweSemWCS-231
94FinnJaaK-258
95FinnSemWC-178
96SweSemWC-204
**Saltarelli, Erasmo**
90MonAAA-22
**Salvador, Bryce**
93LetHur-14
95LetHur-20
96LetHur-14
**Salvo, Lino**
917thInnSQMJHL-156
**Salzbrunn, Jeff**
89NasKni-20
90CinCyc-27
**Samec, Jim**
83SauSteMG-21
**Samis, Phil**
51CleBar-18
52St.LawS-10
**Samotijernov, Igor**
73SweHocS-133
73SweWorCS-133
**Sampson, Gary**
86CapKod-23
**Samscartier, Alain**
907thInnSQMJHL-113
**Samsonov, Sergei**
94SP-189
94SPDieCut-189
95SP-180
95SP-GC2
95UppDec-554
95UppDecEleIce-554
95UppDecEleIceG-554
96DetVip-15

96UppDecIce-138
97Be A PPAD-220
97Be A PPAPD-220
97BeAPla-220
97BeAPlaAut-220
97DonEli-16
97DonEli-134
97DonEliAsp-16
97DonEliAsp-134
97DonEliC-12
97DonEliMC-12
97DonEliS-16
97DonEliS-134
97DonLim-131
97DonLimExp-131
97DonLimFOTG-21
97DonPre-148
97DonPre-195
97DonPreCttC-148
97DonPreCttC-195
97DonPreDWT-6
97DonPreLotT-4B
97DonPrePM-15
97DonPreTB-11
97DonPreTBC-11
97DonPreTPC-11
97DonPreTPG-11
97DonPri-178
97DonPri-200
97DonPri-218
97DonPriDD-6
97DonPriP-17
97DonPriODI-30
97DonPriS-17
97DonPriSB-17
97DonPriSG-17
97DonPriSoA-178
97DonPriSoA-200
97DonPriSoA-218
97DonPriSS-17
97Kat-12
97KatGol-12
97KatSil-12
97Lea-151
97Lea-199
97LeaFirOnIce-15
97LeaFraMat-151
97LeaFraMat-199
97LeaFraMDC-151
97LeaFraMDC-199
97LeaInt-149
97LeaIntUI-149
97McD-40
97PacDyn-NNO
97PacDynC-NNO
97PacDynDG-NNO
97PacDynEG-NNO
97PacDynIB-NNO
97PacDynR-NNO
97PacDynSil-NNO
97PacOme-18
97PacOmeC-18
97PacOmeDG-18
97PacOmeEG-18
97PacOmeIB-18
97PacPar-15
97PacParC-15
97PacParDG-15
97PacParEG-15
97PacParP-15
97PacParRed-15
97PacParSil-15
97Pin-9
97PinArtP-9
97PinBeeGT-23
97PinBeeT-23
97PinCerRR-D
97PinCerRRG-D
97PinCerRRMG-D
97PinMin-26
97PinMinB-26
97PinMinCBP-26
97PinMinCGPP-26
97PinMinCNSP-26
97PinMinCoiB-26
97PinMinCoiGP-26
97PinMinCoiN-26
97PinMinCoiSG-26
97PinMinCoiSS-26
97PinMinGolTea-26
97PinMinSilTea-26
97PinPrePBB-9
97PinPrePBC-9
97PinPrePBM-9
97PinPrePBY-9
97PinPrePFC-9
97PinPrePFM-9
97PinPrePFY-9
97PinPrePla-9
97PinRinC-9
97Sco-59
97ScoArtPro-59
97ScoBru-14
97ScoBruPla-14
97ScoBruPre-14
97ScoGolBla-59
97SPAut-172
97SPAutSotT-SS
97UppDec-219
97UppDecBD-37
97UppDecBDDD-37
97UppDecBDPC-PC28
97UppDecBDPCDD-PC28

97UppDecBDPCM-PC28
97UppDecBDPCQD-PC28
97UppDecBDPCTD-PC28
97UppDecBDQD-37
97UppDecBDTD-37
98UppDecGDM-219
97UppDecIC-IC20
97UppDecIC2-IC20
97UppDecIce-43
97UppDecIceP-43
97UppDecILL-L6A
97UppDecLL2-L6A
97UppDecIPS-43
97UppDecSG-SG30
97Zen-86
97Zen5x7-66
97ZenGolImp-66
97ZenRooR-1
97ZenSilImp-66
97ZenZGol-86
97ZenZSil-86
97ZenZT-14
97ZenZTG-14
98Be A PPA-10
98Be A PPAA-10
98Be A PPAAF-10
98Be A PPTBASG-10
98Be APG-10
98BowBes-66
98BowBesAR-66
98BowBesMIF-F11
98BowBesMIFAR-F11
98BowBesMIFR-F11
98BowBesP-BP2
98BowBesPAR-BP2
98BowBesPR-BP2
98BowBesR-66
98Fin-48
98FinCen-C20
98FinCenR-C20
98FinDouMF-M13
98FinDouMF-M16
98FinDouMF-M18
98FinDouMF-M20
98FinDouSMFR-M13
98FinDouSMFR-M16
98FinDouSMFR-M18
98FinDouSMFR-M20
98FinNo P-48
98FinNo PR-48
98FinRef-48
98McD-13
980-PChr-108
980-PChrR-108
980-PChrSB-SB8
980-PChrSBR-SB8
98Pac-87
98PacAur-14
98PacAurALC-3
98PacAurCFC-5
98PacAurCFIB-5
98PacAurCFS-5
98PacCraCA-1
98PacCroR-10
98PacCroRLS-10
98PacDynI-3
98PacDynII-14
98PacDynIIB-14
98PacDynIR-14
98PacGolCD-3
98PacIceB-87
98PacOmeH-17
98PacOmeR-17
98PacPar-16
98PacParEG-16
98PacParH-16
98PacParIB-16
98PacParS-16
98PacParSDDC-3
98PacParTCD-2
98PacRed-87
98PacRev-11
98PacRevIS-11
98PacRevR-11
98PacTeaC-2
98PacTitl-3
98PacTroW-4
98SP Aut-4
98SP AutSS-SS26
98SPxFin-5
98SPxFin-101
98SPxFin-121
98SPxFin-155
98SPxFinR-5
98SPxFinR-101
98SPxFinR-121
98SPxFinR-155
98SPxFinS-5
98SPxFinS-101
98SPxFinS-121
98SPxFinS-155
98SPXTopP-4
98SPXTopPF-4
98SPXTopPHH-H4
98SPXTopPLI-L30
98SPXTopPPS-PS2
98SPXTopPR-4
98Top-108
98TopAut-A2
98TopGolLC1-45
98TopGolLC1B-45

98TopGolLC1BOoO-45
98TopGolLC1OoO-45
98TopGolLC1R-45
98TopGolLC1RoO-45
98TopGolLC2-45
98TopGolLC2B-45
98TopGolLC2BOoO-45
98TopGolLC2OoO-45
98TopGolLC2R-45
98TopGolLC2RoO-45
98TopGolLC3-45
98TopGolLC3B-45
98TopGolLC3BoO-45
98TopGolLC3OoO-45
98TopGolLC3R-45
98TopGolLC3RoO-45
98TopIceA2-111
98TopO-P-108
98TopSeaB-SB8
98UC-13
98UCMBH-BH22
98UCSB-SQ6
98UCSG-SQ6
98UCSR-SQ6
98UD ChoPCR-13
98UD ChoR-13
98UD3-1
98UD3-61
98UD3-121
98UD3DieC-1
98UD3DieC-61
98UD3DieC-121
98UDCP-13
98UppDec-24
98UppDec-39
98UppDecBD-5
98UppDecDD-5
98UppDecE-24
98UppDecE-39
98UppDecE1o1-24
98UppDecE1o1-39
98UppDecFF-FF3
98UppDecFF-FF3
98UppDecFFQ1-FF3
98UppDecFFQ2-FF3
98UppDecFIT-FT3
98UppDecFITQ1-FT3
98UppDecFITQ2-FT3
98UppDecFITQ3-FT3
98UppDecGN-GN1
98UppDecGN-GN30
98UppDecGNQ1-GN1
98UppDecGNQ1-GN30
98UppDecGNQ2-GN1
98UppDecGNQ2-GN30
98UppDecGNQ3-GN1
98UppDecGNQ3-GN30
98UppDecGR-24
98UppDecGR-39
98UppDecLSH-LS15
98UppDecLSHQ1-LS15
98UppDecLSHQ2-LS15
98UppDecLSHQ3-LS15
98UppDecM-10
98UppDecM1-M30
98UppDecM2-M30
98UppDECMGS-SS
98UppDecMGS-10
98UppDecMOH-OT6
98UppDecMS-S3
98UppDecMSF-F2
98UppDecMSS-10
98UppDecMSS-10
98UppDecP-P13
98UppDecPQ1-P13
98UppDecPQ2-P13
98UppDecPQ3-P13
98UppDecQD-5
98UppDecTD-5
98UppDecWFG-WF3
98UppDecWFP-WF3
99Pac-28
99PacAur-13
99PacAurPD-13
99PacCop-28
99PacGol-28
99PacIceB-28
99PacPreD-28
99PeeWHWCCS-6
99RetHoc-5
99SP AutPS-4
99UppDecCL-71
99UppDecCLCLC-71
99UppDecM-12
99UppDecMGS-GU8
99UppDecMGS-12
99UppDecMGS-GU8
99UppDecMGUSA-GU8
99UppDecMHoG-H5
99UppDecMSS-12
99UppDecMSS-12
99UppDecRG-G6C
99UppDecRGI-G6C
99UppDecRII-SS
99UppDecRIL1-SS
99UppDecRP-5

**Samuel, Andy**
96FitFly-9
97FitFly-12

**Samuelsson, Kjell**
83SweSemE-130
84SweSemE-152
85SwePanS-113

85SwePanS-114
88PanSti-318
89FlyPos-21
89OPC-100
89Top-100
90Bow-111
90BowTif-111
90FlyPos-21
90OPC-61
90PanSti-110
90ProSet-222
90Sco-197
90ScoCan-197
90Top-61
90Top-80
90TopTif-61
90UppDec-116
90UppDecF-116
91Bow-240
91FlyJCP-23
910PC-211
910PC-329
91PanSti-239
91Par-356
91ParFre-356
91Pin-149
91PinFre-149
91PinFre-407
91ProSet-181
91ScoAme-207
91ScoCan-207
91StaClu-70
91SweSemE-339
91Top-211
91UppDec-396
91UppDecF-396
92Bow-165
920PC-230
92Par-373
92ParEmel-373
92PenCokC-17
92PenFoo-14
92Pin-306
92PinFre-306
92Sco-195
92ScoCan-195
92StaClu-466
92Top-352
92TopGol-352G
92Ult-169
93Don-259
93Lea-274
930PCPre-34
930PCPreG-34
93Par-432
93ParEmel-432
93PenFoo-18
93Pin-293
93PinCan-293
93Pow-414
93Sco-184
93ScoCan-184
93StaClu-251
93StaClu-426
93StaCluFDI-251
93StaCluFDI-426
93StaCluO-251
93StaCluO-426
93SweSemWCS-22
93TopPre-34
93TopPreG-34
94CanGamNHLP-192
94OPCPre-73
94OPCPreSE-73
94ParSE-SE138
94ParSEES-ES7
94ParSEG-SE138
94PenFoo-21
94Pin-277
94PinArtP-277
94PinRinC-277
94TopPre-73
94TopPreSE-73
94Ult-351
94UppDec-128
94UppDecEleIce-128
95Don-368
95ParInt-155
95ParIntEl-155
95PlaOneoOne-184
95SweGloWC-27
95Top-259
95TopOPCI-259
95Ult-189
95UppDec-350
95UppDecEleIce-350
95UppDecEleIceG-350
96BeAPAut-189
96BeAPAutSil-189
96BeAPla-189
96FlyPos-20
97Pac-329
97PacCop-329
97PacEmeGre-329
97PacIceB-329
97PacRed-329
97PacSil-329
980-PChr-205
980-PChrR-205
98Top-205
98TopO-P-205

**Samuelsson, Morgan**

89SweSemE-159
90SweSemE-63
91SweSemE-236
92SweSemE-49
94SweLeaE-172
95SweLeaE-12
95SweLeaEFF-1
95SweLeaEG-1
95SweUppDE-18

**Samuelsson, Tommy**
81SweSemHVS-6
82SweSemHVS-10
83SweSemE-103
84SweSemE-103
85SwePanS-93
86SwePanS-86
87SwePanS-91
88SweSemE-76
89SweSemWCS-8
90SweSemE-251
91SweSemE-82
91SweSemWCS-33
92SweSemE-104
93SweSemE-76
94SweLeaE-110
94SweLeaESS-4

**Samuelsson, Ulf**
83SweSemE-134
84WhaJunW-17
85WhaJunW-18
86WhaJunT-20
870PC-23
870PCSti-205
87PanSti-41
87Top-23
87WhaJunBK-18
880PC-136
880PCSti-265
88PanSti-238
88Top-136
88WhaJunGR-15
890PC-210
89PanSti-228
89WhaJunM-17
900PC-511
90ProSet-109
90Sco-152
90ScoCan-152
90ScoHotRS-64
90UppDec-287
90UppDecF-287
90WhaJr7E-21
91Bow-88
91Bow-408
910PC-323
91PanSti-277
91Par-361
91ParFre-361
91PenCokC-5
91PenFoo-2
91PenFooCS-6
91Pin-267
91PinFre-267
91ProSet-459
91ProSetFre-459
91ProSetPla-95
91ScoAme-82
91ScoAme-304
91ScoCan-82
91ScoCan-308
91StaClu-328
91Top-323
91UppDec-230
91UppDecES-17
91UppDecESF-17
91UppDecF-230
92Bow-351
920PC-270
92PanSti-229
92PanStiFre-229
92Par-369
92Par-446
92ParEmel-369
92ParEmel-446
92PenCokC-18
92PenFoo-12
92Pin-296
92PinFre-296
92ProSet-143
92Sco-90
92ScoCan-90
92StaClu-440
92Top-127
92TopGol-127G
92Ult-170
92UltImp-20
92UppDec-189
93Don-264
930PCPre-132
930PCPreG-132
93PanSti-87
93Par-155
93ParEmel-155
93PenFoo-3
93PenSti-10
93Pin-29
93PinCan-29
93Pow-194
93Sco-161
93ScoCan-161
93StaClu-356
93StaCluFDI-356
93StaCluO-356
93SweSemWCS-21

93TopPre-132
93TopPreG-132
93Ult-204
93UppDec-142
94CanGamNHLP-193
94Don-296
94EASpo-104
94Fla-139
94Fle-168
94Lea-205
94OPCPre-391
94OPCPreSE-391
94Par-183
94ParGol-183
94PenFoo-5
94Pin-46
94PinArtP-46
94PinRinC-46
94Sco-156
94ScoChelt-CI7
94ScoGol-156
94ScoPla-156
94ScoPlaTS-156
94TopPre-391
94TopPreSE-391
94Ult-169
94UppDec-209
94UppDecEleIce-209
95BeAPla-223
95BeAPSig-S223
95BeAPSigDC-S223
95CanGamNHLP-187
95ColCho-79
95ColChoPC-79
95ColChoPCP-79
95Don-89
95Don-243
95Emo-119
95Lea-206
95Met-100
95ParInt-411
95ParIntEl-411
95PlaOneoOne-176
95Sco-203
95ScoBlaIce-203
95ScoBlaIceAP-203
95SkyImp-114
95StaClu-11
95StaCluFea-F7
95StaCluMO-17
95StaCluMOMS-11
95Sum-78
95SumArtP-78
95SumIce-78
95SweGloWC-7
95Top-144
95TopOPCI-144
95Ult-126
95Ult-278
95UltGolM-126
95UppDec-448
95UppDecEleIce-448
95UppDecEleIceG-448
95UppDecSpeE-SE142
95UppDecSpeEdiG-SE142
96PenTri-3
96SkyImp-84
96SweSemW-44
96UppDec-104
97Be A PPAD-126
97Be A PPAPD-126
97BeAPla-126
97BeAPlaAut-126
97ColCho-171
97Pac-171
97PacCop-171
97PacIceB-171
97PacRed-171
97PacSil-171
97Sco-239
97ScoRan-15
97ScoRanPla-15
97ScoRanPre-15
97UppDec-204
97UppDec-313
97UppDec-395
98Be A PPA-93
98Be A PPAA-93
98Be A PPAAF-93
98Be A PPTBASG-93
98Be APG-93
980-PChr-127
980-PChrR-127
98Pac-299
98PacAur-126
98PacIceB-126
98PacPar-157
98PacParC-157
98PacParEG-157
98PacParH-157
98PacParIB-157
98PacParS-157
98PacRed-299
98Top-127
98TopO-P-127
99Pac-148
99PacCop-148
99PacGol-148
99PacIceB-148
99PacPreD-148

**Sancimino, Mike**
92CorBigRed-24
92CorBigRed-21
96LouRiv-14

97LouRivF-12

**Sanda, Dalibor**
95CzeAPSE-265
95CzeAPSE-306

**Sandalax, Alex**
51LavDaiQSHL-38

**Sandback, Darrell**
93SeaThu-21

**Sandberg, Mikael**
92SweSemE-301
93SweSemE-207
94SweLeaE-290
95SweLeaE-198
95SweLeaES-13
95SweUppDE-204

**Sandelin, Scott**
86CanaPos-21
86SheCan-24
87CanaPos-27
88ProAHL-284
89ProAHL-332
90ProAHLIHL-41

**Sanders, Frank**
72FigSaiPos-21

**Sanders, Grant**
84KitRan-28

**Sanderson, Derek**
67Top-33
680PC-6
680PC-213
68ShiCoi-7
68Top-6
690PC-201
690PCFou-8
69Top-31
70BruPos-15
70BruTealss-7
70ColSta-6
70DadCoo-116
70EssPowPla-65
700PC-136
700PCDec-5
70SarProSta-3
70TopStiS-27
71Baz-12
71BruTealss-11
71ColHea-12
710PC-65
71SarProSta-4
71Top-65
71TorSun-16
730PC-183
73Top-182
74NHLActSta-185
740PCNHL-290
750PCNHL-73
75Top-73
760PCNHL-116
76Top-20
77CanCanDC-13
770PCNHL-42
770PCNHL-46
77Top-42
77Top-46
94ParTalBFS-FS6
95Par66-19
95ParPos66-19

**Sanderson, Geoff**
907thInnSWHL-54
91Par-57
91ParFre-57
91Pin-309
91PinFre-309
91ProSet-536
91ProSetFre-536
91ProSetPla-256
91ScoAme-324
91ScoCan-354
91UppDec-588
91UppDecF-588
91WhaJr7E-23
92Bow-136
920PC-122
92PanSti-V
92PanStiFre-V
92Par-62
92ParEmel-62
92Pin-307
92PinFre-307
92ProSet-63
92ProSetRGL-11
92Sco-108
92ScoCan-108
92StaClu-111
92Top-402
92TopGol-402G
92Ult-75
92UppDec-293
92WhaDai-21
93Cla-AU12
93ClaTeaCan-TC6
93Don-147
93Kra-21
93Lea-77
930PCPre-156
930PCPreG-156
93PanSti-V
93Par-86
93ParEmel-86
93Pin-9
93PinCan-9
93Pow-109
93PowRisS-6
93Sco-213
93ScoCan-213

❑ 93StaClu-408
❑ 93StaCluFDI-408
❑ 93StaCluO-408
❑ 93TopPre-156
❑ 93TopPreG-156
❑ 93TopPrePS-156
❑ 93Ult-151
❑ 93UltSpeM-9
❑ 93UppDec-292
❑ 93UppDec-316
❑ 93UppDecHT-HT2
❑ 93UppDecSP-65
❑ 93WhaCok-19
❑ 94CanGamNHLP-117
❑ 94ClaProP-56
❑ 94Don-77
❑ 94EASpo-58
❑ 94Fin-108
❑ 94FinRef-108
❑ 94FinSupTW-108
❑ 94Fla-74
❑ 94Fle-89
❑ 94FleSlaA-9
❑ 94HocWit-6
❑ 94Lea-219
❑ 94LeaLim-54
❑ 94OPCPre-205
❑ 94OPCPre-527
❑ 94OPCPreSE-205
❑ 94OPCPreSE-527
❑ 94Par-95
❑ 94ParCratGB-10
❑ 94ParCratGG-10
❑ 94ParCratGR-10
❑ 94ParGol-95
❑ 94ParVin-V49
❑ 94Pin-63
❑ 94PinArtP-63
❑ 94PinBoo-BR8
❑ 94PinRinC-63
❑ 94Sco-144
❑ 94ScoFra-TF10
❑ 94ScoGol-144
❑ 94ScoPla-144
❑ 94ScoPlaTS-144
❑ 94Sel-68
❑ 94SelGol-68
❑ 94SP-52
❑ 94SPDieCut-52
❑ 94StaCluMO-36
❑ 94TopFinI-15
❑ 94TopPre-205
❑ 94TopPre-527
❑ 94TopPreSE-205
❑ 94TopPreSE-527
❑ 94Ult-93
❑ 94UltSpeM-10
❑ 94UppDec-6
❑ 94UppDecElelce-6
❑ 94UppDecSPI-SP34
❑ 94UppDecSPIDC-SP34
❑ 95BeAPla-62
❑ 95BeAPSig-S62
❑ 95BeAPSigDC-S62
❑ 95Bow-67
❑ 95BowAllFoi-67
❑ 95CanGamNHLP-125
❑ 95ColCho-293
❑ 95ColChoCTG-C22
❑ 95ColChoCTG-C22B
❑ 95ColChoCTG-C22C
❑ 95ColChoCTGGB-C22
❑ 95ColChoCTGGR-C22
❑ 95ColChoCTGSB-C22
❑ 95ColChoCTGSR-C22
❑ 95ColChoPC-293
❑ 95ColChoPCP-293
❑ 95Don-201
❑ 95Emo-77
❑ 95Fin-173
❑ 95FinRef-173
❑ 95ImpSti-53
❑ 95Lea-88
❑ 95Met-66
❑ 95NHLAcePC-6H
❑ 95ParInt-91
❑ 95ParIntEl-91
❑ 95Pin-38
❑ 95PinArtP-38
❑ 95PinRinC-38
❑ 95PlaOneoOne-266
❑ 95Sco-111
❑ 95ScoBlaIce-111
❑ 95ScoBlaIceAP-111
❑ 95SelCer-26
❑ 95SelCerMG-26
❑ 95SkyImp-75
❑ 95StaClu-172
❑ 95StaCluMO-8
❑ 95StaCluMOMS-172
❑ 95Sum-38
❑ 95SumArtP-38
❑ 95SumIce-38
❑ 95Top-14
❑ 95Top-318
❑ 95TopMarMPB-14
❑ 95TopOPCI-14
❑ 95TopOPCI-318
❑ 95TopSupSki-21
❑ 95TopSupSkiPla-21
❑ 95Ult-70
❑ 95UltGolM-70
❑ 95UppDec-20
❑ 95UppDecElelce-20
❑ 95UppDecElelceG-20
❑ 95UppDecSpeE-SE127
❑ 95UppDecSpeEdiG-SE127
❑ 95Zen-14
❑ 96ColCho-113
❑ 96ColCho-319
❑ 96Don-40
❑ 96DonCanI-114
❑ 96DonCanIGPP-114
❑ 96DonCanIOC-15
❑ 96DonCanIRPP-114
❑ 96DonEli-127
❑ 96DonEliDCS-127
❑ 96DonPrePro-40
❑ 96Fla-44
❑ 96FlaBluI-44
❑ 96Fle-47
❑ 96KraUppD-3
❑ 96Lea-105
❑ 96LeaPre-86
❑ 96LeaPreP-105
❑ 96LeaPrePP-86
❑ 96MetUni-71
❑ 96NHLProSTA-128
❑ 96Pin-187
❑ 96PinArtP-187
❑ 96PinFoi-187
❑ 96PinPreS-187
❑ 96PinRinC-187
❑ 96Sco-119
❑ 96ScoArtPro-119
❑ 96ScoDeaCAP-119
❑ 96ScoGolB-119
❑ 96ScoSpeAP-119
❑ 96SkyImp-54
❑ 96SP-69
❑ 96Sum-24
❑ 96SumArtP-24
❑ 96SumIce-24
❑ 96SumMet-24
❑ 96SumPreS-24
❑ 96TopNHLP-65
❑ 96TopPicOI-65
❑ 96Ult-76
❑ 96UltGolM-77
❑ 96UppDec-75
❑ 96UppDecBD-138
❑ 96UppDecBDG-138
❑ 96UppDecIce-28
❑ 96UppDecIcePar-28
❑ 96WhaBobS-23
❑ 97Be A PPAD-112
❑ 97Be A PPAPD-112
❑ 97BeAPla-112
❑ 97BeAPlaAut-112
❑ 97CarHur-25
❑ 97ColCho-116
❑ 97ColChoSta-SQ73
❑ 97Don-79
❑ 97DonCanI-41
❑ 97DonCanIDS-41
❑ 97DonCanINP-14
❑ 97DonCanIPS-41
❑ 97DonEli-67
❑ 97DonEliAsp-67
❑ 97DonEliS-67
❑ 97DonLim-119
❑ 97DonLim-135
❑ 97DonLimExp-119
❑ 97DonLimExp-135
❑ 97DonPre-85
❑ 97DonPreCttC-85
❑ 97DonPreProG-79
❑ 97DonPreProS-79
❑ 97DonPri-50
❑ 97DonPriSoA-50
❑ 97Kat-30
❑ 97KatGol-30
❑ 97KatSil-30
❑ 97Lea-28
❑ 97LeaFraMat-28
❑ 97LeaFraMDC-28
❑ 97LeaInt-28
❑ 97LeaIntUI-28
❑ 97Pac-270
❑ 97PacCop-270
❑ 97PacCroR-26
❑ 97PacCroREG-26
❑ 97PacCroRIB-26
❑ 97PacCroRS-26
❑ 97PacDyn-23
❑ 97PacDynC-23
❑ 97PacDynDG-23
❑ 97PacDynEG-23
❑ 97PacDynIB-23
❑ 97PacDynR-23
❑ 97PacDynSil-23
❑ 97PacDynTan-38
❑ 97PacEmeGre-270
❑ 97PacIceB-270
❑ 97PacInv-26
❑ 97PacInvC-26
❑ 97PacInvEG-26
❑ 97PacInvIB-26
❑ 97PacInvR-26
❑ 97PacInvS-26
❑ 97PacRed-270
❑ 97PacSil-270
❑ 97Pin-45
❑ 97PinArtP-45
❑ 97PinBee-50
❑ 97PinBeeGP-50
❑ 97PinCer-125
❑ 97PinCerMB-125
❑ 97PinCerMG-125
❑ 97PinCerMR-125
❑ 97PinCerR-125
❑ 97PinIns-78
❑ 97PinInsCC-78
❑ 97PinInsEC-78
❑ 97PinPrePBB-45
❑ 97PinPrePBC-45
❑ 97PinPrePBM-45
❑ 97PinPrePBY-45
❑ 97PinPrePFC-45
❑ 97PinPrePFM-45
❑ 97PinPrePFY-45
❑ 97PinPrePla-45
❑ 97PinRinC-45
❑ 97PinTotCMPG-125
❑ 97PinTotCPB-125
❑ 97PinTotCPG-125
❑ 97PinTotCPR-125
❑ 97Sco-110
❑ 97ScoArtPro-110
❑ 97ScoGolBla-110
❑ 97SPAut-25
❑ 97SPx-22
❑ 97SPxBro-22
❑ 97SPxGol-22
❑ 97SPxGraF-22
❑ 97SPxSil-22
❑ 97SPxSte-22
❑ 97Stu-84
❑ 97StuPrePG-84
❑ 97StuPrePS-84
❑ 97UppDec-30
❑ 97UppDecGDM-30
❑ 97UppDecIce-8
❑ 97UppDecIceP-8
❑ 97UppDecIPS-8
❑ 97UppDecSSM-SS22
❑ 97UppDecSSW-SS22
❑ 98Be A PPA-163
❑ 98Be A PPAA-163
❑ 98Be A PPAAF-163
❑ 98Be A PPSE-163
❑ 98Be APG-163
❑ 98Pac-80
❑ 98PacIceB-80
❑ 98PacOmeH-27
❑ 98PacOmeODI-27
❑ 98PacOmeR-27
❑ 98PacRed-80
❑ 98UC-27
❑ 98UD ChoPCR-27
❑ 98UD ChoR-27
❑ 98UppDec-45
❑ 98UppDecE-45
❑ 98UppDecE1o1-45
❑ 98UppDecGR-45
❑ 98UppDecM-24
❑ 98UppDecMGS-24
❑ 98UppDecMSS-24
❑ 98UppDecMSS-24
❑ 99Pac-44
❑ 99PacCop-44
❑ 99PacGol-44
❑ 99PacIceB-44
❑ 99PacPreD-44

**Sanderson, Guy**
❑ 92ClaKni-19

**Sanderson, Mike**
❑ 92ForWorF-18
❑ 93ForWorF-15
❑ 96ForWorF-3

**Sandford, Ed**
❑ 44BeeGro2P-64
❑ 51Par-22
❑ 52Par-69
❑ 53Par-90
❑ 54Par-64
❑ 54Top-48
❑ 91BruSpoAL-26

**Sandholm, Ryan**
❑ 91AirCanSJHL-A24
❑ 92MPSPhoSJHL-103

**Sandie, Joel**
❑ 907thInnSOHL-69
❑ 917thInnSOHL-244
❑ 91SudWol-10
❑ 92SudWol-4

**Sandilands, Neil**
❑ 83KitRan-6

**Sandin, Stefan**
❑ 84SweSemE-24
❑ 87SwePanS-270

**Sandke, Pierre**
❑ 907thInnSQMJHL-58
❑ 917thInnSQMJHL-275

**Sandlak, Jim**
❑ 85Canu-19
❑ 86Canu-19
❑ 87CanuSheOil-16
❑ 87OPC-264
❑ 87OPCSti-66A
❑ 87OPCSti-135
❑ 87OPCSti-194
❑ 87PanSti-352
❑ 88CanuMoh-17
❑ 88PanSti-139
❑ 89CanuMoh-16
❑ 89OPC-267
❑ 89OPC-316
❑ 89PanSti-156
❑ 90Bow-55
❑ 90BowTif-55
❑ 90CanuMoh-26
❑ 90OPC-18
❑ 90PanSti-306
❑ 90ProSet-305
❑ 90Sco-303C
❑ 90ScoCan-303C
❑ 90Top-18
❑ 90TopTif-18
❑ 91CanuAutC-22
❑ 91CanuPanTS-21
❑ 91CanuTeal8-22
❑ 91Par-405
❑ 91ParFre-405
❑ 91Pin-294
❑ 91PinFre-294
❑ 91ProSet-497
❑ 91ProSetFre-497
❑ 91ScoCan-260
❑ 91UppDec-577
❑ 91UppDecF-577
❑ 92CanuRoaTA-20
❑ 92OPC-168
❑ 92PanSti-34
❑ 92PanStiFre-34
❑ 92Pin-210
❑ 92PinFre-210
❑ 92Sco-379
❑ 92ScoCan-379
❑ 92StaClu-175
❑ 92Top-41
❑ 92TopGol-41G
❑ 92Ult-228
❑ 92UppDec-120
❑ 93Don-138
❑ 93Par-84
❑ 93ParEmel-84
❑ 93Pin-364
❑ 93PinCan-364
❑ 93Sco-397
❑ 93Sco-532
❑ 93ScoCan-397
❑ 93ScoCan-532
❑ 93ScoGol-532
❑ 93UppDec-393
❑ 93WhaCok-20
❑ 94CanGamNHLP-118
❑ 94Par-91
❑ 94ParGol-91

**Sandlin, Tommy**
❑ 83SweSemE-50
❑ 84SweSemE-49
❑ 85SwePanS-35
❑ 89SweSemWCS-2
❑ 91SweSemE-303
❑ 92SweSemE-325
❑ 92SweSemE-342
❑ 93SweSemE-290
❑ 94SweLeaE-296

**Sandner, Christopher**
❑ 94GerDELE-317
❑ 95GerDELE-354

**Sandrock, Rob**
❑ 96MedHatT-19

**Sands, Charlie**
❑ 33V129-16
❑ 33V357IceK-58
❑ 34BeeGro1P-29
❑ 34BeeGro1P-181
❑ 36V356WorG-27
❑ 39OPCV3011-56
❑ 40OPCV3012-102

**Sands, Jason**
❑ 95Sla-118
❑ 97SudWolP-14

**Sands, Mike**
❑ 83CanNatJ-12
❑ 84SprInd-1

**Sandstrom, Mikael**
❑ 83SweSemE-61

**Sandstrom, Ronny**
❑ 70SweHocS-196
❑ 71SweHocS-282

**Sandstrom, Tomas**
❑ 83SweSemE-72
❑ 85OPC-123
❑ 85Top-123
❑ 86OPC-230
❑ 87OPC-28
❑ 87OPCMin-38
❑ 87OPCSti-35
❑ 87PanSti-114
❑ 87Top-28
❑ 88OPC-121
❑ 88OPCSti-242
❑ 88PanSti-310
❑ 88Top-121
❑ 89OPC-54
❑ 89OPCBoxB-C
❑ 89OPCSti-244
❑ 89PanSti-281
❑ 89Top-54
❑ 89TopBoxB-C
❑ 90Bow-141
❑ 90BowHatTri-21
❑ 90BowTif-141
❑ 90KinSmo-6
❑ 90OPC-301
❑ 90PanSti-243
❑ 90ProSet-127
❑ 90Sco-183
❑ 90ScoCan-183
❑ 90ScoHotRS-79
❑ 90Top-301
❑ 90TopTif-301
❑ 90UppDec-251
❑ 90UppDecF-251
❑ 91Bow-174
❑ 91Bow-179
❑ 91Kra-63
❑ 91OPC-173
❑ 91OPCPre-82
❑ 91PanSti-79
❑ 91Par-70
❑ 91ParFre-70
❑ 91Pin-178
❑ 91PinFre-178
❑ 91ProSet-97
❑ 91ProSet-287
❑ 91ProSetFre-97
❑ 91ProSetFre-287
❑ 91ProSetPla-53
❑ 91ScoAme-270
❑ 91ScoCan-490
❑ 91StaClu-209
❑ 91SweSemE-319
❑ 91SweSemWCS-208
❑ 91Top-173
❑ 91UppDec-30
❑ 91UppDec-85
❑ 91UppDec-141
❑ 91UppDecES-7
❑ 91UppDecESF-7
❑ 91UppDecF-30
❑ 91UppDecF-85
❑ 91UppDecF-141
❑ 92Bow-22
❑ 92OPC-91
❑ 92PanSti-67
❑ 92PanStiFre-67
❑ 92Pin-345
❑ 92PinFre-345
❑ 92Sco-199
❑ 92ScoCan-199
❑ 92StaClu-220
❑ 92Top-421
❑ 92TopGol-421G
❑ 92Ult-88
❑ 92UppDec-424
❑ 93Don-163
❑ 93Don-475
❑ 93Lea-106
❑ 93OPCPre-434
❑ 93OPCPreG-434
❑ 93PanSti-205
❑ 93Par-362
❑ 93ParEmel-362
❑ 93Pin-263
❑ 93PinCan-263
❑ 93Pow-121
❑ 93Sco-129
❑ 93ScoCan-129
❑ 93ScoIntS-21
❑ 93ScoIntSC-21
❑ 93StaClu-25
❑ 93StaCluFDI-25
❑ 93StaCluFDIO-25
❑ 93StaCluO-25
❑ 93SweSemWCS-32
❑ 93TopPre-434
❑ 93TopPreG-434
❑ 93Ult-246
❑ 93UppDec-188
❑ 94CanGamNHLP-188
❑ 94Don-271
❑ 94EASpo-65
❑ 94FinnJaaK-354
❑ 94Fle-169
❑ 94HocWit-87
❑ 94Lea-207
❑ 94OPCPre-108
❑ 94OPCPreSE-108
❑ 94Par-175
❑ 94ParGol-175
❑ 94PenFoo-10
❑ 94Pin-313
❑ 94PinArtP-313
❑ 94PinRinC-313
❑ 94SP-90
❑ 94SPDieCut-90
❑ 94SweLeaE-286
❑ 94SweLeaEGS-2
❑ 94TopPre-108
❑ 94TopPreSE-108
❑ 94Ult-352
❑ 94UppDec-461
❑ 94UppDecElelce-461
❑ 95BeAPla-160
❑ 95BeAPSig-S160
❑ 95BeAPSigDC-S160
❑ 95Bow-10
❑ 95BowAllFoi-10
❑ 95CanGamNHLP-214
❑ 95ColCho-139
❑ 95ColChoPC-139
❑ 95ColChoPCP-139
❑ 95Don-118
❑ 95DonEli-74
❑ 95DonEliDCS-74
❑ 95DonEliDCU-74
❑ 95Emo-141
❑ 95Fin-12
❑ 95FinRef-12
❑ 95Lea-265
❑ 95LeaLim-60
❑ 95Met-119
❑ 95ParInt-166
❑ 95ParIntEl-166
❑ 95PenFoo-15
❑ 95Sco-279
❑ 95ScoBlaIce-279
❑ 95ScoBlaIceAP-279
❑ 95SelCer-107
❑ 95SelCerMG-107
❑ 95SkyImp-134
❑ 95SP-118
❑ 95StaClu-118
❑ 95StaCluMOMS-118
❑ 95Sum-94
❑ 95SumArtP-94
❑ 95SumIce-94
❑ 95SweGloWC-28
❑ 95Top-228
❑ 95TopOPCI-228
❑ 95Ult-293
❑ 95UltCreCra-16
❑ 95UppDec-185
❑ 95UppDecElelce-185
❑ 95UppDecElelceG-185
❑ 95UppDecSpeE-SE156
❑ 95UppDecSpeEdiG-SE156
❑ 95Zen-79
❑ 96ColCho-215
❑ 96Don-78
❑ 96DonPrePro-78
❑ 96FlePic-66
❑ 96Lea-81
❑ 96LeaPreP-81
❑ 96Pin-156
❑ 96PinArtP-156
❑ 96PinFoi-156
❑ 96PinPreS-156
❑ 96PinRinC-156
❑ 96Sco-126
❑ 96ScoArtPro-126
❑ 96ScoDeaCAP-126
❑ 96ScoGolB-126
❑ 96ScoSpeAP-126
❑ 96Sum-81
❑ 96SumArtP-81
❑ 96SumIce-81
❑ 96SumMet-81
❑ 96SumPreS-81
❑ 96SweSemW-59
❑ 96UppDec-137
❑ 97DonPri-117
❑ 97DonPriSoA-117
❑ 97Kat-4
❑ 97KatGol-4
❑ 97KatSil-4
❑ 97Pac-293
❑ 97PacCop-293
❑ 97PacCroR-4
❑ 97PacCroREG-4
❑ 97PacCroRIB-4
❑ 97PacCroRS-4
❑ 97PacEmeGre-293
❑ 97PacIceB-293
❑ 97PacOme-6
❑ 97PacOmeC-6
❑ 97PacOmeDG-6
❑ 97PacOmeEG-6
❑ 97PacOmeG-6
❑ 97PacOmeIB-6
❑ 97PacPar-6
❑ 97PacParC-6
❑ 97PacParDG-6
❑ 97PacParEG-6
❑ 97PacParIB-6
❑ 97PacParRed-6
❑ 97PacParSil-6
❑ 97PacRed-293
❑ 97PacSil-293
❑ 97Pin-180
❑ 97PinPrePBB-180
❑ 97PinPrePBC-180
❑ 97PinPrePBM-180
❑ 97PinPrePBY-180
❑ 97PinPrePFC-180
❑ 97PinPrePFM-180
❑ 97PinPrePFY-180
❑ 97PinPrePla-180
❑ 97Sco-258
❑ 97ScoMigDPla-12
❑ 97ScoMigDPre-12
❑ 97ScoMigDuc-12
❑ 97SPAut-4
❑ 98Be A PPA-153
❑ 98Be A PPAA-153
❑ 98Be A PPAAF-153
❑ 98Be A PPSE-153
❑ 98Be APG-153
❑ 98O-PChr-12
❑ 98O-PChrR-12
❑ 98Pac-63
❑ 98PacAur-5
❑ 98PacCroR-4
❑ 98PacCroRLS-4
❑ 98PacDynI-5
❑ 98PacDynIIB-5
❑ 98PacDynIR-5
❑ 98PacIceB-63
❑ 98PacPar-6
❑ 98PacParC-6
❑ 98PacParEG-6
❑ 98PacParH-6
❑ 98PacParIB-6
❑ 98PacParS-6
❑ 98PacRed-63
❑ 98Top-12
❑ 98TopO-P-12
❑ 98UppDecM-3
❑ 98UppDecMGS-3
❑ 98UppDecMSS-3
❑ 98UppDecMSS-3
❑ 99Pac-15
❑ 99PacCop-15
❑ 99PacGol-15
❑ 99PacIceB-15
❑ 99PacPreD-15

**Sandstrom, Ulf**
❑ 86SwePanS-213
❑ 87SwePanS-199
❑ 89SweSemE-179
❑ 89SweSemWCS-16
❑ 90SweSemE-235
❑ 91SweSemE-172
❑ 95SweUppDE1DS-DS3

**Sandwith, Terran**
❑ 917thInnSWHL-214
❑ 93ClaProPro-114

**Sanford, Jason**
❑ 91BriColJHL-138
❑ 92BriColJHL-95

**Sangster, Darryl**
❑ 92MPSPhoSJHL-104

**Sangster, Jack**
❑ 83BraWheK-18
❑ 84BraWheK-18
❑ 85BraWheK-18

**Sangster, Rob**
❑ 87KitRan-17
❑ 88KitRan-17
❑ 897thInnSOHL-58
❑ 89KitRan-18

**Sanipass, Everett**
❑ 87BlaCok-19
❑ 88BlaCok-17
❑ 88ProIHL-114
❑ 89BlaCok-22
❑ 89ProIHL-63
❑ 90NordPet-22
❑ 90Sco-28
❑ 90ScoCan-28
❑ 91Bow-135
❑ 91NordPanTS-19
❑ 91OPC-315
❑ 91PanSti-262
❑ 91StaClu-284
❑ 91Top-315

**Sanko, Ron**
❑ 82KinCan-16
❑ 83NorBayC-21
❑ 85KitRan-23

**Sanscartier, Alain**
❑ 917thInnSQMJHL-75

**Santala, Tommi**
❑ 98SPXTopP-68
❑ 98SPXTopPF-68
❑ 98SPXTopPR-68
❑ 98UppDecBD-100
❑ 98UppDecDD-100
❑ 98UppDecQD-100
❑ 98UppDecTD-100

**Santanen, Ari**
❑ 96FinnSISR-119

**Santerre, Gino**
❑ 96LouRiv-3

**Santurian, Oleg**
❑ 93RicRen-13

**Sanza, Nick**
❑ 82SweSemHVS-123

**Sapergia, Brent**
❑ 88ProIHL-18
❑ 89ProIHL-114
❑ 90ProAHLIHL-318
❑ 91ProAHLCHL-331
❑ 94CenHocL-119

**Sapjolkin, Alexander**
❑ 73SweHocS-113
❑ 73SweWorCS-113

**Sapozhnikov, Andrei**
❑ 93Cla-92
❑ 93SweSemWCS-135
❑ 96GerDELE-211

**Sarault, Yves**
❑ 907thInnSQMJHL-175
❑ 917thInnSMC-125
❑ 917thInnSQMJHL-163
❑ 91Cla-49
❑ 91UltDra-44
❑ 92FreCan-21
❑ 93FreCan-25
❑ 94FreCan-25
❑ 97ScoAva-20
❑ 97ScoAvaPla-20
❑ 97ScoAvaPre-20

**Sarda, Roger**
❑ 51LavDaiLSJ-49

**Sargant, Shane**
❑ 87SauSteMG-27

**Sargent, Gary**
❑ 77OPCNHL-113
❑ 77Top-113
❑ 78NorStaCD-1
❑ 78OPC-37
❑ 78Top-37
❑ 79NorStaPos-13
❑ 79OPC-52
❑ 79Top-52
❑ 80NorStaPos-17
❑ 80OPC-237
❑ 80Top-237
❑ 81NorStaPos-21
❑ 82NorStaPos-21
❑ 82PosCer-9
❑ 92FutTrePS-1

**Sarich, Cory**
❑ 95BowDraPro-P31
❑ 95SasBla-18
❑ 95UppDec-519
❑ 95UppDecElelce-519
❑ 95UppDecElelceG-519
❑ 96SasBla-20
❑ 96UppDecIce-132

- 97BowCHL-115
- 97BowCHLOPC-115
- 98BowCHL-68
- 98BowCHLOI-68
- 98BowChrC-68
- 98BowChrCGA-68
- 98BowChrCGAR-68
- 98BowChrCOI-68
- 98BowChrCOIR-68
- 98BowChrCR-68
- 98UC-265
- 98UD ChoPCR-265
- 98UD ChoR-265
- 99UppDecM-24
- 99UppDecMGS-24
- 99UppDecMSS-24
- 99UppDecMSS-24

**Sarjeant, Geoff**
- 90MicTecHus-23
- 91MicTecHus-22
- 91MicTecHus-23
- 91MicTecHus-34
- 92PeoRivC-23
- 93ClaProPro-71
- 93PeoRiv-25
- 94UppDec-375
- 94UppDecEleIce-375
- 95ColEdgI-147
- 96CinCyc-31
- 96Lea-228
- 96LeaPreP-228

**Sarkijarvi, Hans**
- 83SweSemE-214
- 84SweSemE-238
- 85SwePanS-237
- 86SwePanS-258
- 87SwePanS-244

**Sarnholm, Roland**
- 67SweHoc-300

**Sarno, Peter**
- 98BowCHL-16
- 98BowCHLGA-16
- 98BowCHLOI-16
- 98BowChrC-16
- 98BowChrCGA-16
- 98BowChrCGAR-16
- 98BowChrCOI-16
- 98BowChrCOIR-16
- 98BowChrCR-16

**Sasakamoose, Fred**
- 54Par-82

**Sass, Paul**
- 91LakSupSL-24

**Sasseville, Francois**
- 93DruVol-21

**Sasso, Tom**
- 90KnoChe-109
- 91ProAHLCHL-436

**Satan, Miroslav**
- 95Bow-112
- 95BowAllFoi-112
- 95ClaAut-20
- 95Ima-58
- 95ImaGol-58
- 95Met-190
- 95ParInt-348
- 95ParIntEI-348
- 95ParIntEI-509
- 95SelCer-125
- 95SelCerMG-125
- 95SkyImp-197
- 95SloAPSNT-19
- 95SP-52
- 95StaClu-122
- 95StaCluMOMS-122
- 95Top-283
- 95TopOPCI-283
- 95Ult-355
- 95UppDec-302
- 95UppDecEleIce-302
- 95UppDecEleIceG-302
- 95Zen-150
- 96BeAPAut-39
- 96BeAPAutSil-39
- 96BeAPla-39
- 96ColCho-98
- 96Don-215
- 96DonPrePro-215
- 96Lea-189
- 96LeaPreP-189
- 96MetUni-55
- 96OilPos-18
- 96Sco-249
- 96ScoArtPro-249
- 96ScoDeaCAP-249
- 96ScoGolB-249
- 96ScoSpeAP-249
- 96SkyImp-170
- 96Sum-166
- 96SumArtP-166
- 96SumIce-166
- 96SumMet-166
- 96SumPreS-166
- 96SweSemW-231
- 96TopPicRS-RS12
- 96Ult-62
- 96UltGolM-62
- 96UppDec-260
- 97Pac-132
- 97PacCop-132
- 97PacCroR-16
- 97PacCroREG-16
- 97PacCroRIB-16

- 97PacCroRS-16
- 97PacDyn-14
- 97PacDynC-14
- 97PacDynDG-14
- 97PacDynEG-14
- 97PacDynIB-14
- 97PacDynR-14
- 97PacDynSil-14
- 97PacDynTan-21
- 97PacEmeGre-132
- 97PacIceB-132
- 97PacInv-15
- 97PacInvC-15
- 97PacInvEG-15
- 97PacInvIB-15
- 97PacInvR-15
- 97PacInvS-15
- 97PacOme-26
- 97PacOmeC-26
- 97PacOmeDG-26
- 97PacOmeEG-26
- 97PacOmeG-26
- 97PacOmeIB-26
- 97PacPar-24
- 97PacParC-24
- 97PacParDG-24
- 97PacParEG-24
- 97PacParIB-24
- 97PacParRed-24
- 97PacParSil-24
- 97PacRed-132
- 97PacRev-16
- 97PacRevC-16
- 97PacRevEG-16
- 97PacRevIB-16
- 97PacRevR-16
- 97PacRevS-16
- 97PacSil-132
- 97Pin-135
- 97PinPrePBB-135
- 97PinPrePBC-135
- 97PinPrePBM-135
- 97PinPrePBY-135
- 97PinPrePFC-135
- 97PinPrePFM-135
- 97PinPrePFY-135
- 97PinPrePla-135
- 97Sco-232
- 97ScoSab-15
- 97ScoSabPla-15
- 97ScoSabPre-15
- 97SPAut-15
- 97UppDecBD-62
- 97UppDecBDDD-62
- 97UppDecBDQD-62
- 97UppDecBDTD-62
- 97Zen-51
- 97ZenZGol-51
- 97ZenZSil-51
- 98Be A PPA-164
- 98Be A PPAA-164
- 98Be A PPAAF-164
- 98Be A PPSE-164
- 98Be APG-164
- 98Fin-65
- 98FinNo P-65
- 98FinNo PR-65
- 98FinRef-65
- 98Pac-81
- 98PacAur-20
- 98PacCroR-15
- 98PacCroRLS-15
- 98PacDynI-21
- 98PacDynIR-21
- 98PacIceB-81
- 98PacOmeH-28
- 98PacOmeODI-28
- 98PacOmeR-28
- 98PacPar-22
- 98PacParC-22
- 98PacParEG-22
- 98PacParH-22
- 98PacParIB-22
- 98PacParS-22
- 98PacRed-81
- 98PacRev-16
- 98PacRevIS-16
- 98PacRevR-16
- 98UC-22
- 98UD ChoPCR-22
- 98UD ChoR-22
- 98UppDec-225
- 98UppDecBD-8
- 98UppDecDD-8
- 98UppDecE-225
- 98UppDecE1o1-225
- 98UppDecGR-225
- 98UppDecM-19
- 98UppDecMGS-19
- 98UppDecMSS-19
- 98UppDecMSS-19
- 98UppDecQD-8
- 98UppDecTD-8
- 99Pac-45
- 99PacAur-19
- 99PacAurPD-19
- 99PacCop-45
- 99PacGol-45
- 99PacIceB-45
- 99PacPreD-45
- 99RetHoc-8
- 99UppDecM-26
- 99UppDecMGS-26
- 99UppDecMSS-26

- 99UppDecMSS-26
- 99UppDecRG-8
- 99UppDecRP-8

**Saterdalen, Jeff**
- 92RicRen-15

**Sateri, Esa**
- 93FinnSIS-242
- 94FinnSIS-65

**Sather, Glen**
- 67Top-38
- 68OPC-134
- 68ShiCoi-11
- 69OPC-116
- 69Top-116
- 70DadCoo-117
- 70EssPowPla-228
- 70OPC-205
- 70SarProSta-167
- 71OPC-221
- 71TorSun-182
- 73BluWhiBor-18
- 74CanaPos-21
- 750PCNHL-222
- 75Top-222
- 760PCWHA-56
- 81OilRedR-xx
- 82OilRedR-NNO
- 83OilMcD-20
- 84OilRedR-NNO
- 84OilRedR-NNO
- 85OilRedR-NNO
- 86OilRedR-NNO
- 88OilTenAnn-49
- 88OilTenAnn-117
- 92OilIGA-26
- 93UppDecLAS-49

**Sator, Ted**
- 87SabWonBH-25
- 87SabWonBH-26

**Sattare, Lars**
- 65SweCorI-183

**Sauer, E.J.**
- 91ProAHLCHL-440
- 92-TulOil-14

**Sauirol, Claude-Charl**
- 907thInnSQMJHL-134

**Saumier, Marc**
- 88ProAHL-288
- 89ProAHL-188
- 91ProAHLCHL-392
- 94MusFur-10

**Saumier, Raymond**
- 89ProAHL-284

**Saundercock, Paul**
- 90ProAHLIHL-415

**Saunders, David (Dave)**
- 87CanuSheOil-17
- 880PC-248
- 880PCSti-61

**Saunders, Lee**
- 92MaiBlaB-29
- 93MaiBlaB-49
- 96GuiFla-19

**Saunier, Bruno**
- 94FinnJaaK-216

**Saunier, Franck**
- 94FreNatT-29

**Saurdiff, Corwin**
- 92NorMicW-22
- 94HamRoaA-21
- 95HamRoaA-23

**Sauter, Doug**
- 83SprInd-25
- 85MedHatT-8
- 86RegPat-24
- 87RegPat-22
- 88BraWheK-19
- 89BraWheK-23
- 92WheThu-22
- 93WheThu-18

**Sauter, Hardy**
- 89BraWheK-7
- 907thInnSWHL-217
- 90BraWheK-5
- 917thInnSWHL-2

**Sauve, Bob**
- 760PCNHL-308
- 780PC-265
- 790PC-49
- 79SabBel-7
- 79Top-49
- 800PC-166
- 800PC-266
- 80SabMilP-8
- 80Top-166
- 810PC-23
- 810PCSti-56
- 81SabMilP-8
- 81Top-E77
- 820PC-34
- 820PCSti-181
- 82PosCer-3
- 82SabMilP-6
- 830PC-61
- 830PC-71
- 830PCSti-242
- 840PC-209
- 840PCSti-208
- 84SabBluS-18
- 850PC-174
- 850PCSti-181
- 850PCSti-190
- 86BlaCok-17
- 860PC-124
- 860PCSti-152

- 86Top-124
- 870PC-140
- 870PCSti-75
- 87PanSti-220
- 87Top-140
- 88DevCar-24

**Sauve, J.F.**
- 820PC-33
- 82PosCer-2
- 83NordPos-24
- 84NordPos-22
- 85NordGenF-22
- 85NordPro-21
- 850PCSti-155
- 86NordMcD-21
- 860PCSti-23

**Sauve, Philippe**
- 96RimOce-14
- 96RimOceQPP-22
- 97RimOce-33
- 98BowCHL-160
- 98BowCHLAuB-A23
- 98BowCHLAuG-A23
- 98BowCHLAuS-A23
- 98BowCHLGA-160
- 98BowCHLOI-160
- 98BowChrC-160
- 98BowChrCGA-160
- 98BowChrCGAR-160
- 98BowChrCOI-160
- 98BowChrCOIR-160
- 98BowChrCR-160
- 980-PChr-241
- 980-PChrR-241
- 98Top-241
- 98TopO-P-241
- 99QuePeeWHWCCS-19

**Savage, Alain**
- 90MonAAA-23
- 917thInnSQMJHL-69
- 96HamRoaA-HRA12

**Savage, Andre**
- 99PacCop-32
- 99PacGol-32

**Savage, Brian**
- 93AlbIntTC-18
- 93Cla-81
- 93ClaTeaCan-TC3
- 93OPCPreTC-16
- 93Pow-493
- 93Ult-472
- 94CanaPos-23
- 94Cla-34
- 94ClaAut-34
- 94ClaDraGol-34
- 94ClaProPIH-LP18
- 94ClaTri-T34
- 94Don-276
- 94FinBowB-R8
- 94FinBowBR-R8
- 94Fle-108
- 94Lea-292
- 94OPCPre-16
- 94OPCPreSE-16
- 94ParSE-SE90
- 94ParSEG-SE90
- 94Pin-248
- 94PinArtP-248
- 94PinRinC-248
- 94PinTorTP-10
- 94Sco-230
- 94ScoGol-230
- 94ScoPla-230
- 94ScoPlaTS-230
- 94ScoTeaC-CT8
- 94Sel-192
- 94SelGol-192
- 94TopPre-16
- 94TopPreSE-16
- 94UppDec-244
- 94UppDecEleIce-244
- 95BeAPla-94
- 95BeAPSig-S138
- 95BeAPSigDC-S138
- 95Bow-87
- 95BowAllFoi-87
- 95CanaPos-17
- 95CanaShe-9
- 95CanGamNHLP-144
- 95Don-20
- 95DonEli-28
- 95DonEliDCS-28
- 95DonEliDCU-28
- 95Emo-92
- 95Fin-23
- 95FinRef-23
- 95Lea-175
- 95LeaLim-82
- 95LeaStuR-15
- 95Met-79
- 95MetWin-7
- 95ParInt-112
- 95ParIntEI-112
- 95Pin-94
- 95PinArtP-94
- 95PinRinC-94

- 95Sco-76
- 95SkyImp-88
- 95SkyImpNHLF-9
- 95StaClu-37
- 95StaCluMOMS-37
- 95Sum-167
- 95SumArtP-167
- 95SumIce-167
- 95Ult-84
- 95UltGolM-84
- 95UltHigSpe-17
- 95UppDec-36
- 95UppDecEleIce-36
- 95UppDecEleIceG-36
- 95UppDecSpeE-SE132
- 95UppDecSpeEdiG-SE132
- 95Zen-20
- 96CanaPos-25
- 96CanaShe-19
- 96ColCho-140
- 96Don-168
- 96DonPrePro-168
- 96Lea-111
- 96LeaPreP-111
- 96Pin-134
- 96PinArtP-134
- 96PinFoi-134
- 96PinPreS-134
- 96PinRinC-134
- 96Sco-147
- 96ScoArtPro-147
- 96ScoDeaCAP-147
- 96ScoGolB-147
- 96ScoSpeAP-147
- 96UppDecIce-34
- 96UppDecIcePar-34
- 97CanaPos-20
- 97ColCho-131
- 97Don-109
- 97DonLim-71
- 97DonLimExp-71
- 97DonPre-62
- 97DonPreCttC-62
- 97DonPreProG-109
- 97DonPreProS-109
- 97DonPri-128
- 97DonPriSoA-128
- 97Lea-68
- 97LeaFraMat-68
- 97LeaFraMDC-68
- 97LeaInt-68
- 97LeaIntUI-68
- 97Pac-142
- 97PacCop-142
- 97PacEmeGre-142
- 97PacIceB-142
- 97PacOme-123
- 97PacOmeC-123
- 97PacOmeDG-123
- 97PacOmeEG-123
- 97PacOmeG-123
- 97PacOmeIB-123
- 97PacPar-99
- 97PacParC-99
- 97PacParDG-99
- 97PacParEG-99
- 97PacParIB-99
- 97PacParRed-99
- 97PacParSil-99
- 97PacRed-142
- 97PacSil-142
- 97Pin-152
- 97PinIns-135
- 97PinPrePBB-152
- 97PinPrePBC-152
- 97PinPrePBM-152
- 97PinPrePBY-152
- 97PinPrePFC-152
- 97PinPrePFM-152
- 97PinPrePFY-152
- 97PinPrePla-152
- 97Sco-191
- 97ScoCanPla-6
- 97ScoCanPla-6
- 97UppDec-299
- 98Pac-49
- 98PacAur-97
- 98PacIceB-49
- 98PacOmeH-126
- 98PacOmeODI-126
- 98PacOmeR-126
- 98PacPar-118
- 98PacParC-118
- 98PacParEG-118
- 98PacParH-118
- 98PacParIB-118
- 98PacParS-118
- 98PacRed-49
- 98PacRev-76
- 98PacRevIS-76
- 98PacRevR-76
- 98ScoCanPre-6
- 98UC-111
- 98UD ChoPCR-111
- 98UD ChoR-111
- 98UDCP-111
- 98UppDec-115
- 98UppDecE-115
- 98UppDecE1o1-115
- 98UppDecGR-115
- 98UppDecM-108
- 98UppDecMGS-108

- 98UppDecMSS-108
- 98UppDecMSS-108
- 99Pac-210
- 99PacAur-77
- 99PacAurPD-77
- 99PacCop-210
- 99PacGol-210
- 99PacIceB-210
- 99PacPreD-210
- 99UppDecM-107
- 99UppDecMGS-107
- 99UppDecMSS-107
- 99UppDecMSS-107

**Savage, Joel**
- 89ProAHL-263
- 90ProAHLIHL-263
- 91RochAmeDD-14
- 91RochAmePos-18
- 91UppDec-423
- 91UppDecF-423
- 92RochAmeKod-19
- 95GerDELE-381
- 96GerDELE-192
- 98GerDELE-150

**Savage, Mike**
- 83BelBul-11

**Savage, Nicolas**
- 93DruVol-6

**Savage, Reggie**
- 90ProAHLIHL-199
- 91BalSki-7
- 91ProAHLCHL-570
- 91ScoAme-320
- 91ScoCan-350
- 92CapKod-24
- 920PCPre-121
- 92Par-426
- 92ParEmel-426
- 92UppDec-474
- 93DurSco-23
- 94NordBurK-23
- 94Par-194
- 94ParGol-194
- 95ColEdgI-192
- 96SprFal-33

**Savard, Andre**
- 74NHLActSta-36
- 740PCNHL-285
- 75HerSta-6
- 750PCNHL-155
- 75Top-155
- 760PCNHL-43
- 76Top-43
- 770PCNHL-118
- 77Top-118
- 780PC-253
- 78Top-253
- 790PC-25
- 79Top-25
- 800PC-375
- 810PC-24
- 810PCSti-54
- 81SabMilP-9
- 81Top-E78
- 82PosCer-2
- 83NordPos-25
- 83Vac-73
- 84NordPos-23
- 840PC-288
- 840PCSti-101
- 85FreExp-28
- 86FreExp-23
- 87NordGenF-31
- 92NorPet-29

**Savard, Denis**
- 80BlaBroBac-11
- 80BlaWhiBor-12
- 81BlaBorPos-23
- 81BlaBorBac-12
- 810PC-63
- 810PCSti-112
- 81PosSta-3
- 81Top-W75
- 82McDSti-23
- 820PC-73
- 820PCSti-171
- 82PosCer-4
- 83BlaBorPos-20
- 830PC-96
- 830PC-111
- 830PCSti-106
- 830PCSti-107
- 830PCSti-153
- 83PufSti-18
- 847EDis-9
- 840PC-45
- 840PC-355
- 840PCSti-24
- 840PCSti-25
- 84Top-35
- 857ECreCar-4
- 850PC-73
- 850PCSti-22
- 85Top-73
- 86BlaCok-18
- 860PC-7
- 860PCBoxB-N
- 860PCSti-150
- 86Top-7
- 86TopBoxB-N
- 87BlaCok-20
- 870PC-127
- 870PCBoxB-N

- 870PCMin-39
- 870PCSti-78
- 87PanSti-225
- 87Top-127
- 87TopBoxB-N
- 88BlaCok-18
- 88EssAllSta-40
- 88FriLayS-6
- 880PC-26
- 880PCBoxB-H
- 880PCMin-34
- 880PCSti-18
- 88PanSti-29
- 88Top-26
- 88TopBoxB-H
- 89BlaCok-1
- 890PC-5
- 890PCSti-16
- 89PanSti-49
- 89SweSemWCS-66
- 89Top-5
- 90Bow-6
- 90BowTif-6
- 90CanaPos-26
- 90Kra-51
- 90OPC-26
- 90OPCPre-103
- 90PanSti-198
- 90ProSet-59A
- 90ProSet-59B
- 90ProSet-473
- 90Sco-125
- 90ScoCan-125
- 90ScoHotRS-59
- 90ScoRoo-1T
- 90Top-26
- 90TopTif-26
- 90UppDec-244
- 90UppDec-426
- 90UppDecF-244
- 90UppDecF-426
- 91Bow-342
- 91CanaPanTS-20
- 91CanaPos-25
- 91Kra-77
- 910PC-330
- 910PCPre-71
- 91PanSti-187
- 91Par-93
- 91Par-211
- 91ParFre-93
- 91ParFre-211
- 91Pin-28
- 91PinFre-28
- 91ProSet-128
- 91ProSet-305
- 91ProSetFre-128
- 91ProSetFre-305
- 91ProSetPla-64
- 91ProSetPlaPC-PC18
- 91ScoAme-165
- 91ScoCan-165
- 91StaClu-213
- 91Top-330
- 91UppDec-242
- 91UppDecF-242
- 92Bow-64
- 92CanaPos-25
- 92DurPan-10
- 92JofKoh-5
- 920PC-35
- 920PCPreSP-6
- 92PanSti-152
- 92PanStiFre-152
- 92Par-85
- 92ParEmel-85
- 92Pin-61
- 92PinAmePP-1
- 92PinFre-61
- 92ProSet-84
- 92ProSet-260
- 92Sco-202
- 92ScoCan-202
- 92SeaPat-23
- 92StaClu-467
- 92Top-414
- 92TopGol-414G
- 92Ult-109
- 92UppDec-10
- 92UppDec-162
- 92UppDec-638
- 93Don-319
- 93DurSco-25
- 93Kra-37
- 93Lea-372
- 930PCCanHF-50
- 930PCPre-305
- 930PCPreG-305
- 93PanSti-17
- 93Par-193
- 93ParEmel-193
- 93Pin-391
- 93PinCan-391
- 93Pow-447
- 93Sco-105
- 93ScoCan-105
- 93ScoCan-555
- 93ScoGol-555
- 93StaClu-297
- 93StaCluFDI-297
- 93StaCluO-297
- 93TopPre-305
- 93TopPreG-305

Schneider, Matt (Mathieu) • 661


❑ 93Ult-428
❑ 93UppDec-502
❑ 93UppDecGGO-GG1
❑ 93UppDecSP-153
❑ 94BeAPSig-94
❑ 94CanGamNHLP-225
❑ 94Don-284
❑ 94HocWit-38
❑ 94Lea-166
❑ 94OPCPre-69
❑ 94OPCPreSE-69
❑ 94Par-217
❑ 94ParGol-217
❑ 94Pin-340
❑ 94PinArtP-340
❑ 94PinRinC-340
❑ 94StaCluST-22
❑ 94TopPre-69
❑ 94TopPreSE-69
❑ 94Ult-373
❑ 94UppDec-415
❑ 94UppDecElelce-415
❑ 94UppDecSPI-SP76
❑ 94UppDecSPIDC-SP76
❑ 95ColCho-132
❑ 95ColChoPC-132
❑ 95ColChoPCP-132
❑ 95Don-233
❑ 95Lea-127
❑ 95ParInt-40
❑ 95ParIntEl-40
❑ 95PlaOneoOne-237
❑ 95Sco-281
❑ 95ScoBlaIce-281
❑ 95ScoBlaIceAP-281
❑ 95Ult-219
❑ 95UppDec-434
❑ 95UppDecElelce-434
❑ 95UppDecElelceG-434
❑ 96Don-51
❑ 96DonPrePro-51
❑ 96Sco-121
❑ 96ScoArtPro-121
❑ 96ScoDeaCAP-121
❑ 96ScoGolB-121
❑ 96ScoSpeAP-121
❑ 96StaCluMO-23
❑ 96UppDecBD-58
❑ 96UppDecBDG-58
❑ 97Pac-343
❑ 97PacCop-343
❑ 97PacEmeGre-343
❑ 97PacIceB-343
❑ 97PacRed-343
❑ 97PacSil-343
❑ 98BlaLeg-5

**Savard, Frederic**
❑ 88RivDu R-27

**Savard, Marc**
❑ 907thInnSQMJHL-250
❑ 917thInnSMC-64
❑ 917thInnSMC-130
❑ 917thInnSQMJHL-74
❑ 93DayBom-9
❑ 97BowCHL-7
❑ 97PinCerRR-L
❑ 97PinCerRRG-L
❑ 97PinCerRRMG-L
❑ 97ScoArtPro-67
❑ 97ScoGolBla-67
❑ 98GerDELE-130
❑ 98PacIceB-300
❑ 98PacRed-300
❑ 98SPxFin-54
❑ 98SPxFinR-54
❑ 98SPxFinS-54
❑ 98UD3-21
❑ 98UD3-81
❑ 98UD3-141
❑ 98UD3DieC-21
❑ 98UD3DieC-81
❑ 98UD3DieC-141
❑ 98UDCP-133
❑ 99Pac-279
❑ 99PacCop-279
❑ 99PacGol-279
❑ 99PacIceB-279
❑ 99PacPreD-279
❑ 99UppDecM-137
❑ 99UppDecMGS-137
❑ 99UppDecMSS-137
❑ 99UppDecMSS-137

**Savard, Marc (NYR)**
❑ 93OshGen-22
❑ 94ParSE-SE263
❑ 94ParSEG-SE263
❑ 94SP-182
❑ 94SPDieCut-182
❑ 95Cla-91
❑ 95Sla-250
❑ 97BowCHLOPC-7
❑ 97Pin-15
❑ 97PinArtP-15
❑ 97PinPrePBB-15
❑ 97PinPrePBC-15
❑ 97PinPrePBM-15
❑ 97PinPrePBY-15
❑ 97PinPrePFC-15
❑ 97PinPrePFM-15
❑ 97PinPrePFY-15
❑ 97PinPrePla-15
❑ 97PinRinC-15
❑ 97Sco-67
❑ 97ScoRan-19
❑ 97ScoRanPla-19
❑ 97ScoRanPre-19
❑ 98Pac-300
❑ 98UC-133
❑ 98UD ChoPCR-133
❑ 98UD ChoR-133
❑ 98UppDec-132
❑ 98UppDecE-132
❑ 98UppDecE1o1-132
❑ 98UppDecGR-132

**Savard, Mike**
❑ 91AirCanSJHL-B21
❑ 92MPSPhoSJHL-154

**Savard, Ray**
❑ 86RegPat-25

**Savard, Serge**
❑ 64CanaPos-18
❑ 67CanaIGA-18
❑ 68CanaIGA-18
❑ 68CanaPosBW-16
❑ 68PosCerM-23
❑ 68ShiCoi-91
❑ 69CanaPosC-28
❑ 69OPC-4
❑ 69OPC-210
❑ 69OPCFou-10
❑ 69Top-4
❑ 70CanaPin-15
❑ 70ColSta-74
❑ 70DadCoo-118
❑ 70EssPowPla-12
❑ 70OPC-51
❑ 70SarProSta-110
❑ 70Top-51
❑ 71CanaPos-22
❑ 71OPC-143
❑ 71SarProSta-110
❑ 71TorSun-163
❑ 72CanaPos-19
❑ 72OPC-185
❑ 72OPCTeaC-25
❑ 72SarProSta-123
❑ 73CanaPos-21
❑ 73MacMil-25
❑ 73OPC-24
❑ 73Top-24
❑ 74CanaPos-22
❑ 74LipSou-11
❑ 74NHLActSta-162
❑ 74OPCNHL-53
❑ 74Top-53
❑ 75CanaPos-17
❑ 75OPCNHL-144
❑ 75Top-144
❑ 76CanaPos-20
❑ 76OPCNHL-205
❑ 76Top-205
❑ 77CanaPos-22
❑ 77OPCNHL-45
❑ 77Top-45
❑ 78CanaPos-24
❑ 78OPC-190
❑ 78OPC-335
❑ 78Top-190
❑ 79CanaPos-22
❑ 79OPC-101
❑ 79Top-101
❑ 80CanaPos-22
❑ 80OPC-26
❑ 80PepCap-57
❑ 80Top-26
❑ 81JetPos-15
❑ 82Jet-19
❑ 82OPC-390
❑ 82PosCer-21
❑ 85HalFC-256
❑ 87CanaPos-28
❑ 88CanaPos-25
❑ 88EssAllSta-41
❑ 89CanaPos-28
❑ 90CanaPos-27
❑ 90UppDec-506
❑ 90UppDecF-506
❑ 91CanaPos-26
❑ 91FutTreC72-53
❑ 91Kra-77
❑ 92FutTre76CC-117
❑ 93OPCCanHF-4
❑ 93OPCCanHF-11
❑ 94HocWit-42
❑ 95Par66-74
❑ 95Par66Coi-74
❑ 95ZelMasoH-6
❑ 99UppDecCL-47
❑ 99UppDecCLCLC-47

**Savaria, Martin**
❑ 84RicRiv-17

**Savary, Neil**
❑ 95SlaMemC-74

**Savchenkov, Alexander**
❑ 95TalTigS-15

**Savenko, Bogdan**
❑ 93NiaFalT-19
❑ 94Indlce-21
❑ 96SyrCru-25

**Savickij, Alexander**
❑ 94CzeAPSE-145

**Savijoki, Jarkko**
❑ 96FinnSISR-22

**Saville, John**
❑ 74SioCitM-17

**Savoia, Ryan**
❑ 95CleLum-22
❑ 95ColEdgl-117

**Savoie, Claude**
❑ 907thInnSQMJHL-260
❑ 917thInnSQMJHL-262
❑ 93Cla-147
❑ 94ClaProP-121

**Savoie, Michel**
❑ 917thInnSQMJHL-49

**Savolainen, Kari**
❑ 93FinnJyvHS-133
❑ 95FinnSIS-390

**Savstrom, Kjell**
❑ 65SweCorl-185
❑ 67SweHoc-42
❑ 69SweHocS-55
❑ 70SweHocS-15

**Sawchuk, Terry**
❑ 44BeeGro2P-65
❑ 44BeeGro2P-209
❑ 48ExhCan-62
❑ 51Par-61
❑ 52Par-86
❑ 53Par-46
❑ 54Par-33
❑ 54Par-96
❑ 54Par-100
❑ 54Top-58
❑ 55BruPho-15
❑ 57Top-35
❑ 58Top-2
❑ 59Top-42
❑ 60Par-31
❑ 60ShiCoi-41
❑ 61Par-31
❑ 61ShiCoi-77
❑ 62YorIroOTra-25
❑ 63Par-53
❑ 63TorSta-33
❑ 63YorWhiB-37
❑ 64BeeGro3P-181
❑ 64CocCap-106
❑ 64Top-6
❑ 65Coc-108
❑ 65Top-12
❑ 66Top-13
❑ 68OPC-34
❑ 68OPCPucSti-20
❑ 68Top-34
❑ 69OPC-189
❑ 70OPC-231
❑ 83HalFP-D13
❑ 85HalFC-46
❑ 91BruSpoAL-27
❑ 91BruSpoAL-35
❑ 91Kra-75
❑ 91ParPHC-PHC9
❑ 91ParPHCF-PHC9
❑ 91ProSet-343
❑ 91ProSetFre-343
❑ 92ParParR-PR2
❑ 93HigLinGG-11
❑ 93ParParR-PR37
❑ 93ParParR-PR53
❑ 94HalFT-11
❑ 94HocWit-83
❑ 94ParMisL-17
❑ 94ParMisL-153
❑ 94ParMisL-167
❑ 94ParMisL-168
❑ 94ParTalB-119
❑ 94ParTalB-154
❑ 94ParTalB-156
❑ 94ParTalB-163
❑ 94ParTalB-177
❑ 94ParTalBM-TW4
❑ 95Par66-120
❑ 95Par66Coi-120
❑ 99RetHoc-87
❑ 99UppDecCA-C10
❑ 99UppDecCL-13
❑ 99UppDecCLACT-AC12
❑ 99UppDecCLCLC-13
❑ 99UppDecRG-G10A
❑ 99UppDecRG-87
❑ 99UppDecRGI-G10A
❑ 99UppDecRP-87

**Sawchuk, Wayne**
❑ 95AlaGolKin-18

**Sawtell, Drew**
❑ 88SasBla-15
❑ 89SasBla-14

**Sawyer, Dan**
❑ 94JohChi-18

**Sawyer, Kevin**
❑ 96ProBru-25

**Saxby, Tony**
❑ 94HumHawP-14

**Sbrocca, Christian**
❑ 90MonAAA-24

**Scalzo, Michael**
❑ 92QueIntP-40

**Scanlan, Derek**
❑ 94ThuBayS-3

**Scanlan, Fred**
❑ 83HalFP-H13
❑ 85HalFC-118

**Scantlebury, Stuart (Stu)**
❑ 907thInnSWHL-233
❑ 90BraWheK-17
❑ 917thInnSWHL-211
❑ 92TacRoc-20

**Scantlebury, Thomas**
❑ 96KamBla-22

**Scanzano, Jason**
❑ 92MPSPhoSJHL-142

**Scanzano, Shawn**
❑ 92QueIntP-31

**Scanzano, Wesley**
❑ 92QueIntP-30
❑ 98QueRem-19

**Scapinello, Ray**
❑ 90ProSet-697

**Scardocchio, Enrico**
❑ 917thInnSQMJHL-171

**Scatchard, Dave**
❑ 95SigRoo-54
❑ 95SigRooSig-54
❑ 96SyrCru-21
❑ 97Be A PPAD-234
❑ 97Be A PPAPD-234
❑ 97BeAPla-234
❑ 97BeAPlaAut-234
❑ 97PacOme-235
❑ 97PacOmeC-235
❑ 97PacOmeDG-235
❑ 97PacOmeEG-235
❑ 97PacOmeG-235
❑ 97PacOmeIB-235
❑ 97SPAut-161
❑ 98Pac-433
❑ 98PacIceB-433
❑ 98PacPar-239
❑ 98PacParC-239
❑ 98PacParEG-239
❑ 98PacParH-239
❑ 98PacParIB-239
❑ 98PacParS-239
❑ 98PacRed-433
❑ 98UC-209
❑ 98UD ChoPCR-209
❑ 98UD ChoR-209
❑ 99Pac-431
❑ 99PacCop-431
❑ 99PacGol-431
❑ 99PacIceB-431
❑ 99PacPreD-431

**Scerban, Bedrich**
❑ 89SweSemWCS-182
❑ 91SweSemWCS-105
❑ 92SweSemE-53
❑ 93SweSemE-28
❑ 93SweSemWCS-93
❑ 94FinnJaaK-174
❑ 94SweLeaE-25
❑ 95SweLeaE-17
❑ 95SweLeaEFF-2
❑ 95SweUppDE-20
❑ 96CzeAPSE-217

**Sceviour, Darin**
❑ 85NovScoO-19

**Schaal, Jurgen**
❑ 94GerDELE-121
❑ 95GerDELE-121
❑ 96GerDELE-61

**Schachle, Trent**
❑ 96DayBom-12

**Schaden, Mario**
❑ 93SweSemWCS-288
❑ 94FinnJaaK-246
❑ 95AusNatTea-25

**Schadler, Thomas**
❑ 94GerDELE-422

**Schaefer, Jeremy**
❑ 95SasBla-19

**Schaefer, Peter**
❑ 95Cla-14
❑ 95SlaMemC-47
❑ 96UppDecBD-88
❑ 96UppDecBDG-88
❑ 96UppDecIce-135
❑ 97BowCHL-118
❑ 97BowCHLOPC-118
❑ 97ColCho-297
❑ 97DonLim-142
❑ 97DonLimExp-142
❑ 98PacOmeH-242
❑ 98PacOmeODI-242
❑ 98PacOmeR-242
❑ 98UppDecM-208
❑ 98UppDecMGS-208
❑ 98UppDecMSS-208
❑ 98UppDecMSS-208
❑ 99Pac-432
❑ 99PacCop-432
❑ 99PacGol-432
❑ 99PacIceB-432
❑ 99PacPreD-432

**Schaeffer, Jeff**
❑ 95SwiCurB-13

**Schaeffler, James**
❑ 91AirCanSJHL-B2

**Schafer, Mike**
❑ 92WesMic-21

**Schafer, Paxton**
❑ 95Cla-41
❑ 95MedHatT-17
❑ 97Don-201
❑ 97DonCanI-133
❑ 97DonCanIDS-133
❑ 97DonCanIPS-133
❑ 97DonMed-2
❑ 97DonPreProG-201
❑ 97DonPreProS-201
❑ 97DonRatR-2
❑ 97PacDynBKS-8
❑ 97UppDec-183

**Schaffer, Ryan**
❑ 92BriColJHL-169

**Schahlin, Anders**
❑ 69SweHocS-141

**Schamehorn, Kevin**
❑ 87FliSpi-17
❑ 89ProIHL-75

**Schank, Peter**
❑ 84SweSemE-96

**Scharf, Chris**
❑ 917thInnSOHL-231

**Scheidt, Tyler**
❑ 91AirCanSJHL-A34

**Scheifele, Steve**
❑ 90ProAHLIHL-44
❑ 91RicRen-15

**Schella, John**
❑ 71CanuRoyB-19
❑ 71TorSun-288
❑ 72SluCupWHA-17
❑ 73QuaOatWHA-7
❑ 75OPCWHA-21
❑ 76OPCWHA-128

**Schertz, Jan**
❑ 94GerDELE-48
❑ 95GerDELE-42
❑ 96GerDELE-41

**Scheuer, Marc**
❑ 92QueIntP-17

**Scheuer, Tyson**
❑ 92BriColJHL-225

**Schewchuk, Jack**
❑ 40OPCV3012-126

**Schichtl, Hans**
❑ 72SweSemWC-97

**Schiebel, Brian**
❑ 91BriColJHL-58
❑ 92BriColJHL-43

**Schiffl, Heinrich**
❑ 94GerDELE-387
❑ 95GerDELE-368
❑ 96GerDELE-190
❑ 98GerDELE-126

**Schill, Dave**
❑ 89KitRan-10

**Schill, Lee**
❑ 91BriColJHL-137

**Schiller, Peter**
❑ 82SweSemHVS-111

**Schillgard, Johan**
❑ 91SweSemE-50

**Schilling, Paul**
❑ 72SweSemWC-135

**Schilstrom, Bo**
❑ 71SweHocS-368

**Schilstrom, Nils-Olov**
❑ 67SweHoc-192
❑ 69SweHocS-250
❑ 70SweHocS-144
❑ 71SweHocS-238
❑ 72SweHocS-215
❑ 73SweHocS-70
❑ 73SweWorCS-70
❑ 74SweHocS-186

**Schinkel, Chris**
❑ 91AirCanSJHL-C43
❑ 92MPSPhoSJHL-32

**Schinkel, Ken**
❑ 44BeeGro2P-360
❑ 52JunBluT-26
❑ 60ShiCoi-96
❑ 60Top-50
❑ 61ShiCoi-99
❑ 63Top-62
❑ 68OPC-106
❑ 68ShiCoi-135
❑ 68Top-106
❑ 69OPC-117
❑ 69OPCFou-1
❑ 69Top-117
❑ 70ColSta-61
❑ 70DadCoo-119
❑ 70EssPowPla-227
❑ 70OPC-92
❑ 70SarProSta-174
❑ 70Top-92
❑ 71Baz-33
❑ 71OPC-64
❑ 71PenPos-18
❑ 71SarProSta-162
❑ 71Top-64
❑ 71TorSun-227
❑ 72OPC-256
❑ 72SarProSta-170

**Schinko, Marco**
❑ 94GerDELE-62

**Schinko, Thomas**
❑ 91SweSemWCS-170
❑ 94FinnJaaK-289
❑ 95GerDELE-62
❑ 96GerDELE-258
❑ 98GerDELE-121

**Schistad, Rob**
❑ 93SweSemWCS-230
❑ 94FinnJaaK-252
❑ 96CzeAPSE-121
❑ 96SweSemW-201
❑ 98GerDELE-222

**Schlegel, Brad**
❑ 85LonKni-21
❑ 86LonKni-8
❑ 90AlbIntTC-8
❑ 91AlbIntTC-20
❑ 91CapKod-24
❑ 91Par-413
❑ 91ParFre-413
❑ 92OPCPre-28
❑ 92Par-199
❑ 92ParEmel-199
❑ 92Sco-477
❑ 92ScoCan-477
❑ 92ScoCanO-9
❑ 92StaClu-29
❑ 92Top-377
❑ 92TopGol-377G
❑ 92UppDec-101
❑ 94ScoTeaC-CT18
❑ 95GerDELE-133

**Schlickenrieder, Josef**
❑ 89SweSemWCS-104
❑ 94GerDELE-148
❑ 95GerDELE-126

**Schliebener, Andy**
❑ 81FreExp-19
❑ 82FreExp-19
❑ 83FreExp-22
❑ 84FreExp-24
❑ 84OPC-329
❑ 85FreExp-18

**Schloder, Alois**
❑ 72SweSemWC-107
❑ 79PanSti-107

**Schmalz, Kevin**
❑ 89BraWheK-18
❑ 907thInnSWHL-236

**Schmautz, Bobby**
❑ 69SeaTotW-17
❑ 71CanuRoyB-12
❑ 71TorSun-289
❑ 72CanuRoyB-16
❑ 72OPC-181
❑ 72SarProSta-219
❑ 73CanuRoyB-16
❑ 73OPC-35
❑ 73Top-35
❑ 74NHLActSta-25
❑ 74OPCNHL-27
❑ 74OPCNHL-117
❑ 74Top-27
❑ 74Top-117
❑ 75OPCNHL-251
❑ 75Top-251
❑ 76OPCNHL-189
❑ 76Top-189
❑ 77OPCNHL-59
❑ 77Top-59
❑ 78OPC-248
❑ 78Top-248
❑ 79OilPos-21
❑ 79OPC-144
❑ 79Top-144
❑ 80CanuSilD-23
❑ 80CanuTeal-19
❑ 80PepCap-117
❑ 88OilTenAnn-160

**Schmautz, Cliff**
❑ 70EssPowPla-78
❑ 70OPC-142
❑ 70SarProSta-29

**Schmid, Udo**
❑ 94GerDELE-365

**Schmidt, Chris**
❑ 907thInnSWHL-152
❑ 917thInnSWHL-268
❑ 93SeaThu-22
❑ 95SeaThu-26

**Schmidt, Darren**
❑ 82BraWheK-5
❑ 91AirCanSJHL-E11
❑ 92MPSPhoSJHL-31
❑ 93KitRan-22

**Schmidt, Don**
❑ 84PriAlbRS-21
❑ 85KamBla-21
❑ 86KamBla-19
❑ 87KamBla-20
❑ 88KamBla-21

**Schmidt, Greg**
❑ 95RedDeeR-15

**Schmidt, Jack**
❑ 34BeeGro1P-30
❑ 51LavDaiQSHL-69
❑ 51LavDaiS-69
❑ 52St.LawS-17A

**Schmidt, Michael**
❑ 91SweSemWCS-158
❑ 93SweSemWCS-152
❑ 94GerDELE-299
❑ 95GerDELE-336

**Schmidt, Milt**
❑ 34BeeGro1P-31
❑ 36ProvRed-8
❑ 40OPCV3012-132
❑ 51Par-29
❑ 52Par-70
❑ 53Par-92
❑ 54Par-59
❑ 54Top-60
❑ 57BruTealss-18
❑ 60ShiCoi-120
❑ 63Top-1
❑ 64Top-70
❑ 65Top-96
❑ 74CapWhiB-23
❑ 83HalFP-L16
❑ 85HalFC-165
❑ 91BruSpoAL-28
❑ 91BruSpoAL-29
❑ 91BruSpoAL-36
❑ 92ParParR-PR23
❑ 93ParParRCI-2
❑ 94HalFT-12
❑ 94Koll-3
❑ 94ParMisL-21
❑ 94ParTalB-22
❑ 99UppDecCL-26
❑ 99UppDecCLCLC-26

**Schmidt, Moritz**
❑ 94GerDELE-40

**Schmidt, Norm**
❑ 80OshGen-13
❑ 81OshGen-7
❑ 82OshGen-21
❑ 83PenCok-17
❑ 83PenTeaIP-28
❑ 86PenKod-22

**Schmidt, Ryan**
❑ 95Sla-327

**Schmiess, Trevor**
❑ 91AirCanSJHL-A26

**Schmitz, Christian**
❑ 94GerDELE-80
❑ 95GerDELE-313
❑ 96GerDELE-96
❑ 98GerDELE-13

**Schnarr, Werner**
❑ 24C144ChaCig-53
❑ 24V1452-26

**Schneidawind, Michael**
❑ 96GerDELE-200

**Schneider, Andreas**
❑ 94GerDELE-371
❑ 95GerDELE-437

**Schneider, Andy (Andrew)**
❑ 907thInnSWHL-55
❑ 917thInnSWHL-174
❑ 91UppDecCWJC-56
❑ 93Don-468
❑ 94ClaProP-170
❑ 94SweLeaE-217
❑ 95GerDELE-369
❑ 98GerDELE-212

**Schneider, Buzz**
❑ 81SweSemHVS-106
❑ 95SigRooMI-29
❑ 95SigRooMI-30
❑ 95SigRooSMIS-29
❑ 95SigRooSMIS-30

**Schneider, Eric**
❑ 95TriAme-22

**Schneider, Geoff**
❑ 87KinCan-27

**Schneider, Jean-Alain**
❑ 907thInnSOHL-46
❑ 917thInnSOHL-10
❑ 91CorRoy-12
❑ 92BirBul-14
❑ 93BirBul-14

**Schneider, Matt (Mathieu)**
❑ 89CanaKra-20
❑ 89ProAHL-199
❑ 90Bow-52
❑ 90BowTif-52
❑ 90CanaPos-28
❑ 90OPC-372
❑ 90PanSti-60
❑ 90ProSet-158
❑ 90Sco-127
❑ 90ScoCan-127
❑ 90ScoYouS-18
❑ 90Top-372
❑ 90TopTif-372
❑ 90UppDec-334
❑ 90UppDecF-334
❑ 91Bow-343
❑ 91CanaPanTS-21
❑ 91CanaPos-27
❑ 91OPC-392
❑ 91OPCPre-181
❑ 91PanSti-195
❑ 91Par-88
❑ 91ParFre-88
❑ 91Pin-209
❑ 91PinFre-209
❑ 91ProSet-119
❑ 91ProSetFre-119
❑ 91ScoAme-105
❑ 91ScoCan-105
❑ 91StaClu-262
❑ 91SweSemWCS-137
❑ 91Top-392
❑ 91UppDec-328
❑ 91UppDecF-328
❑ 92Bow-190
❑ 92CanaPos-26
❑ 92OPC-166
❑ 92PanSti-157
❑ 92PanStiFre-157
❑ 92Par-319
❑ 92ParEmel-319
❑ 92Pin-79
❑ 92PinFre-79
❑ 92ProSet-91
❑ 92Sco-69
❑ 92ScoCan-69
❑ 92StaClu-70
❑ 92Top-253
❑ 92TopGol-253G
❑ 92Ult-110
❑ 92UppDec-545
❑ 93CanaMol-10
❑ 93CanaPos-24
❑ 93Don-179
❑ 93Lea-53
❑ 93OPCPre-163
❑ 93OPCPreG-163
❑ 93PanSti-22
❑ 93Par-373
❑ 93ParEmel-373
❑ 93Pin-37
❑ 93PinCan-37
❑ 93PinTea2-27

662 • Schneider, Rochus


❑ 93PinTea2C-27
❑ 93Pow-134
❑ 93Sco-18
❑ 93ScoCan-18
❑ 93StaClu-391
❑ 93StaCluFDI-391
❑ 93StaCluMasP-23
❑ 93StaCluMasPW-23
❑ 93StaCluO-391
❑ 93SweSemWCS-177
❑ 93TopPre-163
❑ 93TopPreG-163
❑ 93Ult-78
❑ 93UppDec-31
❑ 94CanaPos-24
❑ 94CanGamNHLP-142
❑ 94Don-233
❑ 94EASpo-68
❑ 94Fle-109
❑ 94Lea-195
❑ 94LeaLim-101
❑ 94OPCPre-181
❑ 94OPCPreSE-181
❑ 94ParSE-SE92
❑ 94ParSEG-SE92
❑ 94ParVin-V32
❑ 94Pin-56
❑ 94PinArtP-56
❑ 94PinRinC-56
❑ 94Sco-103
❑ 94ScoGol-103
❑ 94ScoPla-103
❑ 94ScoPlaTS-103
❑ 94Sel-23
❑ 94SelGol-23
❑ 94TopPre-181
❑ 94TopPreSE-181
❑ 94Ult-114
❑ 94UppDec-101
❑ 94UppDecElelce-101
❑ 95BeAPla-20
❑ 95BeAPSig-S20
❑ 95BeAPSigDC-S20
❑ 95Bow-81
❑ 95CanGamNHLP-176
❑ 95ColCho-322
❑ 95ColChoPC-322
❑ 95ColChoPCP-322
❑ 95Don-55
❑ 95Emo-108
❑ 95Fin-56
❑ 95FinRef-56
❑ 95ImpSti-75
❑ 95Lea-67
❑ 95Met-93
❑ 95ParInt-130
❑ 95ParIntEl-130
❑ 95Pin-28
❑ 95PinArtP-28
❑ 95PinRinC-28
❑ 95PlaOneoOne-64
❑ 95ProMag-60
❑ 95Sco-206
❑ 95ScoBlalce-206
❑ 95ScoBlalceAP-206
❑ 95SelCer-8
❑ 95SelCerMG-8
❑ 95SkyImp-105
❑ 95SP-89
❑ 95StaClu-59
❑ 95StaCluMOMS-59
❑ 95Sum-25
❑ 95SumArtP-25
❑ 95SumIce-25
❑ 95Top-36
❑ 95TopOPCI-36
❑ 95TopSupSki-6
❑ 95TopSupSkiPla-6
❑ 95Ult-99
❑ 95Ult-270
❑ 95UltGolM-99
❑ 95UppDec-161
❑ 95UppDecElelce-161
❑ 95UppDecElelceG-161
❑ 95Zen-21
❑ 96ColCho-262
❑ 96Don-18
❑ 96DonCanI-97
❑ 96DonCanIGPP-97
❑ 96DonCanIRPP-97
❑ 96DonEli-88
❑ 96DonEliDCS-88
❑ 96DonPrePro-18
❑ 96Lea-190
❑ 96LeaPreP-190
❑ 96MetUni-153
❑ 96NHLProSTA-60
❑ 96Pin-124
❑ 96PinArtP-124
❑ 96PinFoi-124
❑ 96PinPreS-124
❑ 96PinRinC-124
❑ 96PlaOneoOne-343
❑ 96PosUppD-20
❑ 96Sco-115
❑ 96ScoArtPro-115
❑ 96ScoDeaCAP-115
❑ 96ScoGolB-115
❑ 96ScoSpeAP-115
❑ 96SP-155
❑ 96StaCluMO-44
❑ 96Sum-30
❑ 96SumArtP-30
❑ 96SumIce-30
❑ 96SumMet-30
❑ 96SumPreS-30
❑ 96TeaOut-81
❑ 96TopNHLP-53
❑ 96TopPicOI-53
❑ 96UppDec-343
❑ 97Be A PPAD-206
❑ 97Be A PPAPD-206
❑ 97BeAPla-206
❑ 97BeAPlaAut-206
❑ 97DonCanI-116
❑ 97DonCanIDS-116
❑ 97DonCanIPS-116
❑ 97DonPri-34
❑ 97DonPriSoA-34
❑ 97Kat-143
❑ 97KatGol-143
❑ 97KatSil-143
❑ 97Pac-179
❑ 97PacCop-179
❑ 97PacEmeGre-179
❑ 97PacIceB-179
❑ 97PacOme-224
❑ 97PacOmeC-224
❑ 97PacOmeDG-224
❑ 97PacOmeEG-224
❑ 97PacOmeG-224
❑ 97PacOmeIB-224
❑ 97PacRed-179
❑ 97PacSil-179
❑ 97Pin-150
❑ 97PinPrePBB-150
❑ 97PinPrePBC-150
❑ 97PinPrePBM-150
❑ 97PinPrePBY-150
❑ 97PinPrePFC-150
❑ 97PinPrePFM-150
❑ 97PinPrePFY-150
❑ 97PinPrePla-150
❑ 97Sco-160
❑ 97ScoArtPro-160
❑ 97ScoGolBla-160
❑ 97ScoMapL-10
❑ 97ScoMapLPla-10
❑ 97ScoMapLPre-10
❑ 97UppDec-372
❑ 98Be A PPA-239
❑ 98Be A PPAA-239
❑ 98Be A PPAAF-239
❑ 98Be A PPSE-239
❑ 98Be APG-239
❑ 98Pac-72
❑ 98PacAur-184
❑ 98PacIceB-72
❑ 98PacPar-230
❑ 98PacParC-230
❑ 98PacParEG-230
❑ 98PacParH-230
❑ 98PacParIB-230
❑ 98PacParS-230
❑ 98PacRed-72
❑ 98UC-198
❑ 98UD ChoPCR-198
❑ 98UD ChoR-198
❑ 99Pac-280
❑ 99PacCop-280
❑ 99PacGol-280
❑ 99PacIceB-280
❑ 99PacPreD-280

**Schneider, Rochus**
❑ 94GerDELE-123
❑ 95GerDELE-24
❑ 96GerDELE-21

**Schneider, Scott**
❑ 87MonHaw-22
❑ 88ProAHL-177
❑ 89ProAHL-52
❑ 90MonHaw-21
❑ 90ProAHLIHL-260
❑ 91ProAHLCHL-362

**Schneider, Wes**
❑ 96LetHur-18

**Schneitberger, Otto**
❑ 72SweSemWC-105

**Schnobrich, Tim**
❑ 94GerDELE-22
❑ 95GerDELE-182

**Schock, Harold**
❑ 93MicWol-20

**Schock, Ron**
❑ 64BeeGro3P-25
❑ 64CocCap-17
❑ 65Top-36
❑ 66Top-100
❑ 68OPC-118
❑ 68ShiCoi-147
❑ 68Top-118
❑ 69OPC-120
❑ 69OPCFou-13
❑ 69Top-120
❑ 70ColSta-42
❑ 70EssPowPla-229
❑ 70OPC-91
❑ 70OPCDec-9
❑ 70SarProSta-170
❑ 70Top-91
❑ 70TopStiS-29
❑ 71LetActR-23
❑ 71OPC-56
❑ 71PenPos-19
❑ 71SarProSta-170
❑ 71Top-56
❑ 71TorSun-228
❑ 72OPC-81
❑ 72SarProSta-179
❑ 72Top-59
❑ 73OPC-200
❑ 73Top-113
❑ 74LipSou-43
❑ 74NHLActSta-226
❑ 74OPCNHL-167
❑ 74PenPos-20
❑ 74Top-167
❑ 75OPCNHL-75
❑ 75OPCNHL-326
❑ 75Top-75
❑ 75Top-326
❑ 76OPCNHL-248
❑ 76OPCNHL-392
❑ 76Top-248
❑ 77OPCNHL-51
❑ 77Top-51
❑ 78OPC-384
❑ 94ParTalB-21
❑ 95Par66-13
❑ 95Par66Coi-13

**Schoen, Brian**
❑ 93TolSto-28
❑ 94CenHocL-33
❑ 95LouIceG-14

**Schoenfeld, Jim**
❑ 72OPC-220
❑ 72SabPepPB-8
❑ 72SarProSta-41
❑ 73OPC-86
❑ 73OPC-137
❑ 73SabPos-12
❑ 73Top-5
❑ 73Top-86
❑ 74NHLActSta-37
❑ 74OPCNHL-121
❑ 74Top-121
❑ 75OPCNHL-138
❑ 75Top-138
❑ 76OPCNHL-241
❑ 76SabGla-4
❑ 76Top-241
❑ 77OPCNHL-108
❑ 77Top-108
❑ 78OPC-178
❑ 78Top-178
❑ 79OPC-171
❑ 79SabBel-8
❑ 79Top-171
❑ 80OPC-96
❑ 80Top-96
❑ 81SabMilP-6
❑ 82OPC-94
❑ 82OPCSti-183
❑ 82PosCer-5
❑ 83OPC-59
❑ 83OPCSti-136
❑ 83PufSti-8
❑ 85SabBluS-25
❑ 85SabBluSS-25
❑ 88DevCar-25
❑ 90UppDec-505
❑ 90UppDecF-505
❑ 93SabNoc-19
❑ 95Cap-23

**Schoenroth, Todd**
❑ 91AirCanSJHL-E42

**Schofield, Dave**
❑ 88ProIHL-42

**Schofield, Dwight**
❑ 84OPC-191

**Scholz, Olaf**
❑ 94GerDELE-108
❑ 95GerDELE-330
❑ 96GerDELE-108

**Schoneck, Drew**
❑ 917thInnSWHL-161
❑ 92TacRoc-21

**Schonmoser, C.**
❑ 95GerDELE-342

**Schooley, Derek**
❑ 92WesMic-22
❑ 93WesMic-25
❑ 94HunBli-18

**Schopf, Patrick**
❑ 93SweSemWCS-110
❑ 93SwiHNL-111
❑ 95SwiHNL-160

**Schraeder, Chad**
❑ 91BriColJHL-14
❑ 92BriColJHL-203

**Schramm, Josef**
❑ 72SweSemWC-94

**Schrapp, Dennis**
❑ 94GerDELE-30
❑ 95GerDELE-3

**Schraven, T.**
❑ 95GerDELE-373

**Schreiber, Wally**
❑ 81RegPat-16
❑ 94GerDELE-261
❑ 94ScoTeaC-CT22
❑ 95GerDELE-258
❑ 96GerDELE-146
❑ 98GerDELE-66

**Schriefer, R.J.**
❑ 95NorIowH-29

**Schriner, Marty**
❑ 91UppDecCWJC-68
❑ 94RoaExp-9
❑ 95RoaExp-7

**Schriner, Sweeney (Dave)**
❑ 34BeeGro1P-249
❑ 34BeeGro1P-346
❑ 35DiaMatT2-57
❑ 35DiaMatT3-53
❑ 35DiaMatTI-60
❑ 36ChaPos-4
❑ 36OPCV304D-98
❑ 36V356WorG-58
❑ 39OPCV3011-14
❑ 40OPCV3012-122
❑ 45QuaOatP-46
❑ 55Par-27
❑ 55ParQuaO-27
❑ 83HalFP-J13
❑ 85HalFC-236

**Schroder, Klaus**
❑ 94GerDELE-33

**Schubert, Andreas**
❑ 94GerDELE-56
❑ 95GerDELE-58
❑ 96GerDELE-206

**Schubert, Thomas**
❑ 91UppDec-681
❑ 91UppDecCWJC-44
❑ 91UppDecF-681
❑ 94GerDELE-397
❑ 95GerDELE-193

**Schuchuk, Gary**
❑ 91ProAHLCHL-132

**Schuler, Alan**
❑ 92RicRen-16
❑ 93RicRen-4

**Schuler, Laura**
❑ 97ColCho-294

**Schullstrom, Jan**
❑ 67SweHoc-193
❑ 69SweHocS-251
❑ 70SweHocS-136
❑ 71SweHocS-228
❑ 72SweHocS-216
❑ 73SweHocS-72
❑ 73SweWorCS-72

**Schulte, Paxton**
❑ 917thInnSWHL-13
❑ 94ClaProP-124

**Schultz, Andreas**
❑ 93SweSemE-103
❑ 94SweLeaE-165

**Schultz, Dave**
❑ 73FlyLin-15
❑ 73OPC-137
❑ 73OPC-166
❑ 73Top-5
❑ 73Top-149
❑ 74LipSou-30
❑ 74NHLActSta-206
❑ 74OPCNHL-5
❑ 74OPCNHL-154
❑ 74OPCNHL-196
❑ 74Top-5
❑ 74Top-154
❑ 74Top-196
❑ 75FlyCanDC-16
❑ 75HerSta-25
❑ 75OPCNHL-147
❑ 75OPCNHL-211
❑ 75Top-147
❑ 75Top-211
❑ 76OPCNHL-4
❑ 76OPCNHL-150
❑ 76OPCNHL-391
❑ 76Top-4
❑ 76Top-150
❑ 77OPCNHL-353
❑ 78OPC-66
❑ 78OPC-225
❑ 78Top-66
❑ 78Top-225
❑ 79OPC-4
❑ 79OPC-134
❑ 79Top-4
❑ 79Top-134
❑ 92Par-473
❑ 92ParEmel-473

**Schultz, Derek**
❑ 97BowCHL-97
❑ 97BowCHL-127
❑ 97BowCHLAu-7
❑ 97BowCHLOPC-97
❑ 97BowCHLOPC-127

**Schultz, Igor**
❑ 94GerDELE-117
❑ 95GerDELE-118
❑ 96GerDELE-64

**Schultz, Ken**
❑ 51CleBar-13

**Schultz, Martin**
❑ 94GerDELE-118
❑ 95GerDELE-119

**Schulz, Karsten**
❑ 94GerDELE-439
❑ 95GerDELE-400

**Schumperli, Bernhard**
❑ 91UppDec-667
❑ 91UppDecCWJC-28
❑ 91UppDecF-667
❑ 93SwiHNL-206
❑ 95SwiHNL-283

**Schure, Peter**
❑ 91CinCyc-22

**Schushack, Chris**
❑ 917thInnSOHL-XXX

**Schust, Ben**
❑ 95SauSteMG-18
❑ 95Sla-364
❑ 96SauSteMG-19
❑ 96SauSteMGA-19

**Schuster, Alexander**
❑ 94GerDELE-286

**Schuster, Manfred**
❑ 89SweSemWCS-110

**Schutt, Rod**
❑ 77NovScoV-23
❑ 79OPC-234
❑ 79Top-234
❑ 80OPC-307
❑ 81OPC-259
❑ 81OPCSti-186
❑ 81Top-E116
❑ 83PenTeaIP-29

**Schutz, Derek**
❑ 95SpoChi-20

**Schwab, Corey**
❑ 907thInnSWHL-19
❑ 91ProAHLCHL-416
❑ 94ClaEnf-E5
❑ 95Bow-164
❑ 95BowAllFoi-164
❑ 95ColEdgI-9
❑ 95ColEdgIQ-IR12
❑ 95ParInt-389
❑ 95ParIntEl-389
❑ 96BeAPAut-104
❑ 96BeAPAutSil-104
❑ 96BeAPla-104
❑ 96DonEli-128
❑ 96DonEliDCS-128
❑ 96LeaPre-126
❑ 96LeaPrePP-126
❑ 97ColCho-244
❑ 97Don-77
❑ 97DonLim-130
❑ 97DonLimExp-130
❑ 97DonPreProG-77
❑ 97DonPreProS-77
❑ 97Lea-96
❑ 97LeaFraMat-96
❑ 97LeaFraMDC-96
❑ 97LeaInt-96
❑ 97LeaIntUI-96
❑ 97Pac-126
❑ 97PacCop-126
❑ 97PacEmeGre-126
❑ 97PacIceB-126
❑ 97PacRed-126
❑ 97PacSil-126
❑ 97UppDec-153
❑ 99Pac-395
❑ 99PacCop-395
❑ 99PacGol-395
❑ 99PacIceB-395
❑ 99PacPreD-395

**Schwabe, Jens**
❑ 91UppDec-680
❑ 91UppDecCWJC-43
❑ 91UppDecF-680
❑ 94GerDELE-395

**Schwalb, Mike**
❑ 89NasKni-21

**Schwark, Bob**
❑ 91AirCanSJHL-D10

**Schwartz, Darren**
❑ 89JohChi-30
❑ 92WheThu-15
❑ 93WheThu-2
❑ 93WheThu-PC2
❑ 93WheThu-UD8
❑ 94ClaProP-247
❑ 95TalTigS-9

**Schwartz, Dustin**
❑ 96MedHatT-20

**Schwarz, Oliver**
❑ 94GerDELE-355

**Schwele, S.**
❑ 95GerDELE-192

**Schweyer, Rob**
❑ 93OweSouPla-25

**Scissons, Scott**
❑ 88SasBla-19
❑ 89SasBla-20
❑ 907thInnSWHL-77
❑ 90SasBla-19
❑ 90Sco-432
❑ 90ScoCan-432
❑ 90UppDec-357
❑ 90UppDecF-357
❑ 91AlbIntTC-21
❑ 91UppDec-428
❑ 91UppDecF-428
❑ 93Don-210
❑ 93Lea-243
❑ 93Par-121
❑ 93ParEmel-121
❑ 93UppDec-511
❑ 93UppDecSP-94

**Sclisizzi, Enio**
❑ 52Par-32

**Scollan, Mark**
❑ 91AirCanSJHLAS-11
❑ 91AirCanSJHLAS-47
❑ 92CorBigRed-25
❑ 93CorBigRed-22

**Scotland, Colin**
❑ 97SudWolP-15

**Scott, Blair**
❑ 89VicCou-17
❑ 917thInnSOHL-101
❑ 94ClaProP-148

**Scott, Brad**
❑ 907thInnSWHL-173

**Scott, Brian**
❑ 93KinFro-8
❑ 94KitRanU-31
❑ 94ParSE-SE268
❑ 94ParSEG-SE268
❑ 94SP-186
❑ 94SPDieCut-186
❑ 95SigRooA-38
❑ 95SigRooAPC-38
❑ 95Sla-396
❑ 96SudWol-19
❑ 96SudWolP-20

**Scott, Chubby**
❑ 23V1281PauC-52

**Scott, Dennis**
❑ 897thInnSOHL-137

**Scott, Ganton**
❑ 24C144ChaCig-54
❑ 24V130MapC-29
❑ 24V1452-38

**Scott, Greg**
❑ 917thInnSOHL-206
❑ 93HunBli-22

**Scott, Irvin**
❑ 52JunBluT-49

**Scott, Jerry**
❑ 84Ott67-31

**Scott, Kevin**
❑ 91CinCyc-21

**Scott, Laurie**
❑ 23V1281PauC-40

**Scott, Ron**
❑ 89NewHavN-10
❑ 89ProAHL-5
❑ 90ProAHLIHL-424

**Scott, Travis**
❑ 93WinSpi-3
❑ 94WinSpi-3
❑ 95Sla-231

**Scremin, Claudio**
❑ 90KanCitBla-1
❑ 90ProAHLIHL-597
❑ 91ProAHLCHL-508
❑ 98GerDELE-195

**Scruton, Howie**
❑ 81KinCan-19

**Seabrooke, Glen**
❑ 88ProAHL-129
❑ 89ProAHL-336

**Seale, Travis**
❑ 91MicTecHus-30
❑ 93MicTecH-11

**Searle, Doug**
❑ 897thInnSOHL-119
❑ 907thInnSOHL-371
❑ 917thInnSOHL-140
❑ 91PetPet-9
❑ 93KnoChe-16
❑ 94KnoChe-6
❑ 96RoaExp-14

**Searles, Steve**
❑ 907thInnSQMJHL-173
❑ 917thInnSQMJHL-119

**Sears, Sverre**
❑ 93GreMon-13
❑ 94GreMon-6
❑ 95FliGen-3

**Seaton, Bryant**
❑ 81VicCou-13

**Seaton, Mike**
❑ 89VicCou-18
❑ 907thInnSWHL-8
❑ 91NasKni-21
❑ 92NasKni-14

**Sebastian, Jeff**
❑ 88RegPat-21
❑ 89PorWinH-19
❑ 907thInnSWHL-313
❑ 917thInnSWHL-136
❑ 98GerDELE-6

**Sebek, Venci**
❑ 94GerDELE-385
❑ 95GerDELE-150

**Sebestu, Richard**
❑ 95CzeAPSE-211

**Seca, Dylan**
❑ 94KitRanU-34

**Secemski, Krystof**
❑ 94SudWol-16
❑ 94SudWolP-14

**Secord, Al**
❑ 80BlaBroBac-12
❑ 80OPC-129
❑ 80Top-129
❑ 81BlaBorPos-24
❑ 81BlaBroBac-13
❑ 81OPC-72
❑ 82OPC-60
❑ 82OPC-74
❑ 82OPCSti-175
❑ 82PosCer-4
❑ 83BlaBorPos-21
❑ 83OPC-95
❑ 83OPC-112
❑ 83OPC-219
❑ 83OPCSti-111
❑ 83OPCSti-156
❑ 83OPCSti-160
❑ 83PufSti-16
❑ 847EDis-10
❑ 84OPC-46
❑ 86BlaCok-19
❑ 86OPC-100
❑ 86OPCSti-155
❑ 86Top-100
❑ 87MapLeaP-18
❑ 87MapLeaPLA-14
❑ 87MapLeaPO-18
❑ 87OPC-111
❑ 87OPCSti-74
❑ 87PanSti-229
❑ 87Top-111
❑ 88MapLeaPLA-14
❑ 88OPC-249
❑ 88OPCSti-179
❑ 89BlaCok-18
❑ 90Bow-12
❑ 90BowTif-12
❑ 90ProSet-60A
❑ 90ProSet-60B
❑ 91UppDec-635
❑ 91UppDecF-635
❑ 95Ima-89
❑ 95ImaGol-89

**Secord, Brian**
❑ 95Cla-83
❑ 95Sla-130
❑ 96RicRen-18

**Sedin, Daniel**
❑ 97UppDecBD-114
❑ 97UppDecBDDD-114
❑ 97UppDecBDQD-114
❑ 97UppDecBDTD-114
❑ 98SPXTopP-79
❑ 98SPXTopPF-79
❑ 98SPXTopPR-79
❑ 98UC-294
❑ 98UD ChoPCR-294
❑ 98UD ChoR-294
❑ 98UppDecBD-109
❑ 98UppDecDD-109
❑ 98UppDecQD-109
❑ 98UppDecTD-109

**Sedin, Henrik**
❑ 97UppDecBD-136
❑ 97UppDecBDDD-136
❑ 97UppDecBDQD-136
❑ 97UppDecBDTD-136
❑ 98SPXTopP-80
❑ 98SPXTopPF-80
❑ 98SPXTopPR-80
❑ 98UC-295
❑ 98UD ChoPCR-295
❑ 98UD ChoR-295
❑ 98UppDecBD-110
❑ 98UppDecDD-110
❑ 98UppDecQD-110
❑ 98UppDecTD-110

**Sedlak, Zdenek**
❑ 94CzeAPSE-201
❑ 95CzeAPSE-49

**Sedlbauer, Ron**
❑ 75CanuRoyB-19
❑ 76CanuRoyB-17
❑ 76OPCNHL-271
❑ 77CanuRoyB-18
❑ 77OPCNHL-368
❑ 78CanuRoyB-19
❑ 78OPC-139
❑ 78Top-139
❑ 79CanuRoyB-19
❑ 79OPC-19
❑ 79Top-19
❑ 80BlaBroBac-13
❑ 80OPC-134
❑ 80Top-134
❑ 81BlaBroBac-14
❑ 81OPC-324

**Sedy, Petr**
❑ 94CzeAPSE-98
❑ 95CzeAPSE-59
❑ 96CzeAPSE-245

**Seeberger, Christian**
❑ 94GerDELE-177
❑ 95GerDELE-173

**Seeley, Richard**
❑ 96LetHur-15

**Seftel, Steve**
❑ 85KinCan-8
❑ 86KinCan-20
❑ 87KinCan-20
❑ 88ProAHL-42
❑ 89ProAHL-90
❑ 90ProAHLIHL-203
❑ 91BalSki-12
❑ 91ProAHLCHL-556

**Segerberg, Hans**
❑ 84SweSemE-138
❑ 85SwePanS-21
❑ 87SwePanS-19

**Segersten, Jan**
❑ 84SweSemE-159
❑ 85SwePanS-142

**Seguin, Brett**
❑ 897thInnSOHL-49
❑ 907thInnSOHL-92
❑ 917thInnSOHL-301
❑ 93MusFur-5
❑ 94MusFur-8
❑ 95MusFur-4

**Seguin, Steve**
❑ 81KinCan-13
❑ 82KinCan-10
❑ 84KinSmo-21

**Seher, Kurt**
❑ 907thInnSWHL-61
❑ 917thInnSWHL-133
❑ 98ChaChe-14

**Sehlstedt, Christer**
❑ 69SweHocS-103
❑ 72SweHocS-226
❑ 73SweHocS-226
❑ 73SweWorCS-226
❑ 74SweHocS-149

**Seibel, Chad**
❑ 88LetHur-21
❑ 907thInnSWHL-280
❑ 90PriAlbR-19
❑ 917thInnSWHL-40
❑ 94GreMon-5
**Seibert, Earl**
❑ 34BeeGro1P-78
❑ 35DiaMatT4-12
❑ 35DiaMatT5-10
❑ 35DiaMatTI-61
❑ 37DiaMatT6-10
❑ 39OPCV3011-76
❑ 83HalFP-K16
❑ 85HalFC-150
❑ 92HalFL-27
❑ 94ParMisLP-P12
**Seibert, Oliver**
❑ 83HalFP-J14
❑ 85HalFC-193
**Seiker, Shane**
❑ 907thInnSWHL-328
**Seiling, Ric**
❑ 75HamFin-17
❑ 78OPC-242
❑ 78Top-242
❑ 79OPC-119
❑ 79SabMilP-2
❑ 79Top-119
❑ 80OPC-159
❑ 80SabMilP-4
❑ 80Top-159
❑ 81OPC-32
❑ 81SabMilP-15
❑ 82OPC-35
❑ 82OPCSti-123
❑ 82PosCer-2
❑ 82SabMilP-8
❑ 83OPC-72
❑ 84OPC-31
❑ 84OPCSti-216
❑ 84SabBluS-19
❑ 85OPCSti-182
❑ 85SabBluS-26
❑ 85SabBluSS-26
❑ 86OPC-201
**Seiling, Rod**
❑ 64BeeGro3P-148
❑ 64CocCap-85
❑ 64Top-67
❑ 65Top-23
❑ 66Top-22
❑ 66TopUSAT-22
❑ 67Top-27
❑ 68OPC-71
❑ 68ShiCoi-93
❑ 68Top-71
❑ 69OPC-36
❑ 69OPCFou-13
❑ 69Top-36
❑ 70DadCoo-120
❑ 70EssPowPla-191
❑ 70OPC-184
❑ 70SarProSta-128
❑ 71OPC-53
❑ 71SarProSta-119
❑ 71Top-53
❑ 71TorSun-183
❑ 72OPC-194
❑ 72OPCTeaC-26
❑ 72SarProSta-148
❑ 72Top-149
❑ 73OPC-9
❑ 73Top-9
❑ 74MapLeaP-19
❑ 74NHLActSta-190
❑ 74NHLActStaU-37
❑ 74OPCNHL-102
❑ 74Top-102
❑ 75MapLeaP-18
❑ 75OPCNHL-229
❑ 75Top-229
❑ 76OPCNHL-280
❑ 77OPCNHL-226
❑ 77Top-226
❑ 78OPC-394
❑ 91FutTreC72-21
❑ 94ParTalB-93
❑ 95Par66-95
❑ 95Par66Coi-95
**Seiling, Scott**
❑ 95Sla-254
❑ 95Sla-296
**Seils, Jason**
❑ 94MinGolG-25
❑ 95MinGolG-25
**Seitz, David**
❑ 92ClaKni-20
❑ 96SouCarS-14
**Sejba, Jiri**
❑ 89SweSemWCS-196
❑ 90ProAHLIHL-286
❑ 90SabBluS-21
❑ 90SabCam-23
❑ 91ProAHLCHL-5
❑ 91RochAmeDD-15
❑ 91RochAmeKod-24
❑ 91RochAmePos-19
❑ 91UppDec-362
❑ 91UppDecF-362
❑ 94CzeAPSE-37
**Sejejs, Normunds**
❑ 95CzeAPSE-156
❑ 96CzeAPSE-175
**Sekera, Martin**
❑ 94CzeAPSE-44
**Sekeras, Lubomir**
❑ 94FinnJaaK-192
❑ 95CzeAPSE-227
❑ 95SloAPSNT-9
❑ 96SweSemW-222
**Selanne, Teemu**
❑ 91SweSemWCS-21
❑ 91UppDec-21
❑ 91UppDecF-21
❑ 92OPCPre-68
❑ 92Par-209
❑ 92Par-217
❑ 92Par-500
❑ 92ParEmel-209
❑ 92ParEmel-217
❑ 92ParEmel-500
❑ 92Pin-406
❑ 92PinCanPP-3
❑ 92PinFre-406
❑ 92Ult-444
❑ 92Ult-450
❑ 92UltImp-21
❑ 92UppDec-574
❑ 92UppDecCC-CC10
❑ 92UppDecER-ER6
❑ 92UppDecGHS-G15
❑ 93Cla-124
❑ 93ClaCraNum-N5
❑ 93ClaPre-HK4
❑ 93Don-387
❑ 93Don-394
❑ 93DonEli-3
❑ 93DonIceKin-10
❑ 93DonSpeP-Z
❑ 93JetRuf-22
❑ 93Kra-22
❑ 93Lea-13
❑ 93Lea-110
❑ 93LeaGolAS-3
❑ 93LeaGolR-1
❑ 93LeaHatTA-3
❑ 93McDUppD-H2
❑ 93OPCPre-92
❑ 93OPCPre-130
❑ 93OPCPre-148
❑ 93OPCPre-483
❑ 93OPCPreBG-20
❑ 93OPCPreG-92
❑ 93OPCPreG-130
❑ 93OPCPreG-148
❑ 93OPCPreG-483
❑ 93PanSti-142
❑ 93PanSti-Q
❑ 93Par-233
❑ 93Par-235
❑ 93ParEasWesS-W3
❑ 93ParEmel-233
❑ 93ParEmel-235
❑ 93ParUSACG-G8
❑ 93Pin-4
❑ 93Pin-222
❑ 93Pin1S-5
❑ 93PinAllS-32
❑ 93PinAllSC-32
❑ 93PinCan-4
❑ 93PinCan-222
❑ 93PinNifFif-3
❑ 93PinTea2-10
❑ 93PinTea2C-10
❑ 93PinTeaP-12
❑ 93PinTeaPC-12
❑ 93Pow-274
❑ 93PowGloG-7
❑ 93PowPoiL-16
❑ 93PowSecYS-10
❑ 93PowSlaA-9
❑ 93Sco-331
❑ 93Sco-477
❑ 93ScoCan-331
❑ 93ScoCan-477
❑ 93ScoDreTea-21
❑ 93ScoDynDC-2
❑ 93ScoFra-24
❑ 93ScoIntS-2
❑ 93ScoIntSC-2
❑ 93SeaPat-18
❑ 93StaClu-141
❑ 93StaClu-210
❑ 93StaCluAS-22
❑ 93StaCluFDI-141
❑ 93StaCluFDI-210
❑ 93StaCluFDIO-141
❑ 93StaCluFDIO-210
❑ 93StaCluMasP-4
❑ 93StaCluMasPW-4
❑ 93StaCluO-141
❑ 93StaCluO-210
❑ 93SweSemWCS-77
❑ 93TopPre-92
❑ 93TopPre-130
❑ 93TopPre-148
❑ 93TopPre-483
❑ 93TopPreBG-1
❑ 93TopPreBG-A
❑ 93TopPreG-92
❑ 93TopPreG-130
❑ 93TopPreG-148
❑ 93TopPreG-483
❑ 93Ult-48
❑ 93Ult-250
❑ 93UltAllS-11
❑ 93UltAwaW-6
❑ 93UltRedLS-10
❑ 93UltSpeM-10
❑ 93UppDec-281
❑ 93UppDec-309
❑ 93UppDec-448
❑ 93UppDec-SP4
❑ 93UppDecAW-AW2
❑ 93UppDecFH-32
❑ 93UppDecLAS-35
❑ 93UppDecNR-17
❑ 93UppDecSilSka-R2
❑ 93UppDecSilSkaG-R2
❑ 93UppDecSP-177
❑ 94BAPUpCP-UC4
❑ 94BeAPla-R11
❑ 94BeAPSig-11
❑ 94CanGamNHLP-253
❑ 94ClaProPIH-LP23
❑ 94Don-210
❑ 94DonDom-8
❑ 94EASpo-149
❑ 94Fin-76
❑ 94FinBowB-B14
❑ 94FinBowBR-B14
❑ 94FinnJaaK-20
❑ 94FinnJaaK-345
❑ 94FinnSIS-263
❑ 94FinnSISGS-9
❑ 94FinRef-76
❑ 94FinSupTW-76
❑ 94Fla-209
❑ 94Fle-245
❑ 94HocWit-55
❑ 94KenStaLA-19
❑ 94KenStaLC-12
❑ 94Lea-362
❑ 94LeaFirOIce-12
❑ 94LeaLim-68
❑ 94LeaLimI-26
❑ 94McDUppD-McD25
❑ 94OPCPre-95
❑ 94OPCPre-243
❑ 94OPCPre-416
❑ 94OPCPreSE-95
❑ 94OPCPreSE-243
❑ 94OPCPreSE-416
❑ 94Par-300
❑ 94ParCratGB-26
❑ 94ParCratGG-26
❑ 94ParCratGR-26
❑ 94ParGol-300
❑ 94ParSE-SE201
❑ 94ParSEES-ES13
❑ 94ParSEG-SE201
❑ 94ParVin-V81
❑ 94Pin-25
❑ 94PinArtP-25
❑ 94PinBoo-BR15
❑ 94PinGam-GR1
❑ 94PinNorLig-NL11
❑ 94PinRinC-25
❑ 94PinWorEdi-WE1
❑ 94PosCerBB-23
❑ 94Sco-178
❑ 94ScoFra-TF26
❑ 94ScoGol-178
❑ 94ScoPla-178
❑ 94ScoPlaTS-178
❑ 94Sel-74
❑ 94SelGol-74
❑ 94SP-131
❑ 94SPDieCut-131
❑ 94SPPre-22
❑ 94SPPreDC-22
❑ 94StaCluMO-10
❑ 94StaCluST-26
❑ 94TopFinB-5
❑ 94TopPre-95
❑ 94TopPre-243
❑ 94TopPre-416
❑ 94TopPreSE-95
❑ 94TopPreSE-243
❑ 94TopPreSE-416
❑ 94Ult-246
❑ 94UltGloGre-9
❑ 94UltRedLS-8
❑ 94UppDec-90
❑ 94UppDec-557
❑ 94UppDecEleIce-557
❑ 94UppDecIG-IG13
❑ 94UppDecNBAP-15
❑ 94UppDecPR-R3
❑ 94UppDecPRE-R3
❑ 94UppDecPreRG-R3
❑ 94UppDecSPI-SP88
❑ 94UppDecSPIDC-SP88
❑ 95Bow-75
❑ 95BowAllFoi-75
❑ 95BowBes-BB2
❑ 95BowBesRef-BB2
❑ 95CanGamNHLP-292
❑ 95ColCho-244
❑ 95ColChoPC-244
❑ 95ColChoPCP-244
❑ 95Don-100
❑ 95DonEli-73
❑ 95DonEliCE-15
❑ 95DonEliDCS-73
❑ 95DonEliDCU-73
❑ 95Emo-196
❑ 95Fin-35
❑ 95Fin-155
❑ 95FinnJaaKLAC-4
❑ 95FinnSemWC-41
❑ 95FinnSISL-15
❑ 95FinnSISLSS-3
❑ 95FinRef-35
❑ 95FinRef-155
❑ 95ImpSti-134
❑ 95JetReaC-9
❑ 95JetTeaIss-20
❑ 95Kra-3
❑ 95Lea-137
❑ 95LeaLim-44
❑ 95LeaLimSG-7
❑ 95McDPin-MCD-19
❑ 95Met-165
❑ 95MetIS-19
❑ 95NHLAcePC-8C
❑ 95ParInt-232
❑ 95ParInt-250
❑ 95ParInt-275
❑ 95ParInt-NNO2
❑ 95ParIntAS-5
❑ 95ParIntCCGS1-9
❑ 95ParIntCCSS1-9
❑ 95ParIntEl-232
❑ 95ParIntEl-250
❑ 95ParIntEl-275
❑ 95ParIntPTP-PP17
❑ 95ParIntPTP-PP51
❑ 95PinFan-15
❑ 95PinRoa2-19
❑ 95PlaOneoOne-108
❑ 95PlaOneoOne-219
❑ 95PlaOneoOne-329
❑ 95ProMag-63
❑ 95Sco-7
❑ 95ScoBlaIce-7
❑ 95ScoBlaIceAP-7
❑ 95ScoGolBla-2
❑ 95ScoLam-14
❑ 95SelCer-76
❑ 95SelCerMG-76
❑ 95SkyImp-184
❑ 95SkyImpIQ-15
❑ 95SP-2
❑ 95SPHol-FX1
❑ 95SPHolSpFX-FX1
❑ 95SPStaEto-E2
❑ 95SPStaEtoG-E2
❑ 95StaClu-188
❑ 95StaCluEN-EN2
❑ 95StaCluGTSC-GT2
❑ 95StaCluMO-43
❑ 95StaCluMOMS-188
❑ 95Sum-54
❑ 95SumArtP-54
❑ 95SumIce-54
❑ 95SweGloWC-140
❑ 95Top-195
❑ 95TopCanG-9CG
❑ 95TopMysF-M9
❑ 95TopMysFR-M9
❑ 95TopOPCI-195
❑ 95TopPowL-2PL
❑ 95TopPro-PF18
❑ 95TopSupSki-31
❑ 95TopSupSkiPla-31
❑ 95TopYouS-YS11
❑ 95Ult-183
❑ 95UltGolM-183
❑ 95UppDec-171
❑ 95UppDec-253
❑ 95UppDecAGPRW-7
❑ 95UppDecEleIce-171
❑ 95UppDecEleIce-253
❑ 95UppDecEleIceG-171
❑ 95UppDecEleIceG-253
❑ 95UppDecNHLAS-AS12
❑ 95UppDecPRE-R49
❑ 95UppDecPreR-R49
❑ 95UppDecSpeE-SE89
❑ 95UppDecSpeEdiG-SE89
❑ 95UppPreRP-R49
❑ 95Zen-102
❑ 96BeAPBisITB-11
❑ 96BeAPLH-1B
❑ 96BeAPLHAut-1B
❑ 96BeAPLHAutSil-1B
❑ 96ColCho-2
❑ 96ColCho-309
❑ 96ColCho-336
❑ 96ColChoCTG-C19A
❑ 96ColChoCTG-C19B
❑ 96ColChoCTG-C19C
❑ 96ColChoCTGE-CR19
❑ 96ColChoCTGEG-CR19
❑ 96ColChoCTGG-C19A
❑ 96ColChoCTGG-C19B
❑ 96ColChoCTGG-C19C
❑ 96ColChoMVP-UD7
❑ 96ColChoMVPG-UD7
❑ 96ColChoSti-S13
❑ 96Don-157
❑ 96DonCanI-85
❑ 96DonCanIGPP-85
❑ 96DonCanIRPP-85
❑ 96DonDom-8
❑ 96DonEli-59
❑ 96DonEliDCS-59
❑ 96DonEliS-10
❑ 96DonGoTS-2
❑ 96DonPrePro-157
❑ 96Duc-24
❑ 96Fla-3
❑ 96FlaBluI-3
❑ 96FlaCenIS-8
❑ 96Fle-3
❑ 96FleArtRos-21
❑ 96FlePicDL-5
❑ 96FlePicF5-42
❑ 96KraUppD-60
❑ 96Lea-52
❑ 96Lea-238
❑ 96LeaFirOI-9
❑ 96LeaLim-64
❑ 96LeaLimG-64
❑ 96LeaPre-56
❑ 96LeaPreP-52
❑ 96LeaPreP-238
❑ 96LeaPrePP-56
❑ 96LeaPreSP-10
❑ 96LeaPreVP-11
❑ 96LeaPreVPG-11
❑ 96MetUni-6
❑ 96MetUniLW-17
❑ 96MetUniLWSP-17
❑ 96NHLACEPC-43
❑ 96NHLProSTA-63
❑ 96Pin-155
❑ 96Pin-250
❑ 96PinArtP-155
❑ 96PinArtP-250
❑ 96PinByTN-1
❑ 96PinByTN-P1
❑ 96PinByTNP-1
❑ 96PinFoi-155
❑ 96PinFoi-250
❑ 96PinMcD-2
❑ 96PinMin-13
❑ 96PinMinB-13
❑ 96PinMinCoiB-13
❑ 96PinMinCoiGP-13
❑ 96PinMinCoiN-13
❑ 96PinMinCoiS-13
❑ 96PinMinCoiSG-13
❑ 96PinMinG-13
❑ 96PinMinS-13
❑ 96PinPreS-155
❑ 96PinPreS-250
❑ 96PinRinC-155
❑ 96PinRinC-250
❑ 96PlaOneoOne-428
❑ 96Sco-145
❑ 96ScoArtPro-145
❑ 96ScoDeaCAP-145
❑ 96ScoGolB-145
❑ 96ScoSpeAP-145
❑ 96ScoSudDea-15
❑ 96ScoSup-1
❑ 96SelCer-32
❑ 96SelCerAP-32
❑ 96SelCerBlu-32
❑ 96SelCerCor-12
❑ 96SelCerMB-32
❑ 96SelCerMG-32
❑ 96SelCerMR-32
❑ 96SelCerRed-32
❑ 96SkyImp-4
❑ 96SkyImpB-20
❑ 96SkyImpVer-10
❑ 96SP-2
❑ 96SPInsInf-IN4
❑ 96SPInsInfG-IN4
❑ 96SPSPxFor-2
❑ 96SPx-2
❑ 96SPxGol-2
❑ 96StaCluMO-14
❑ 96Sum-133
❑ 96SumArtP-133
❑ 96SumHigV-12
❑ 96SumHigVM-12
❑ 96SumIce-133
❑ 96SumMet-133
❑ 96SumPreS-133
❑ 96SumUnt-8
❑ 96SweSemW-31
❑ 96SweSemWNS-NS2
❑ 96TeaOut-34
❑ 96TopNHLP-7
❑ 96TopPicFT-FT21
❑ 96TopPicOI-7
❑ 96TopPicTS-TS8
❑ 96Ult-6
❑ 96UltGolM-6
❑ 96UltPow-16
❑ 96UltPowRL-8
❑ 96UppDec-211
❑ 96UppDecBD-146
❑ 96UppDecBDG-146
❑ 96UppDecBDRFTC-RC18
❑ 96UppDecGN-X16
❑ 96UppDecHH-HH15
❑ 96UppDecHHG-HH15
❑ 96UppDecHHS-HH15
❑ 96UppDecIce-77
❑ 96UppDecIceDF-S6
❑ 96UppDecIcePar-77
❑ 96UppDecIceSCF-S6
❑ 96UppDecLSH-LS16
❑ 96UppDecLSHF-LS16
❑ 96UppDecLSHS-LS16
❑ 96UppDecSS-SS10A
❑ 96Zen-28
❑ 96ZenArtP-28
❑ 96ZenZT-3
❑ 97BeAPlaPOT-8
❑ 97ColCho-8
❑ 97ColChoCTG-C8A
❑ 97ColChoCTG-C8B
❑ 97ColChoCTG-C8C
❑ 97ColChoCTGE-CR8
❑ 97ColChoSta-SQ80
❑ 97ColChoSti-S18
❑ 97Don-159
❑ 97DonCanI-74
❑ 97DonCanIDS-74
❑ 97DonCanIPS-74
❑ 97DonCanISCS-8
❑ 97DonEli-17
❑ 97DonEli-120
❑ 97DonEli-149
❑ 97DonEliAsp-17
❑ 97DonEliAsp-120
❑ 97DonEliAsp-149
❑ 97DonEliBttF-3
❑ 97DonEliBttFA-3
❑ 97DonEliC-15
❑ 97DonEliIns-12
❑ 97DonEliMC-15
❑ 97DonEliPN-7A
❑ 97DonEliPN-7B
❑ 97DonEliPN-7C
❑ 97DonEliPNDC-7A
❑ 97DonEliPNDC-7B
❑ 97DonEliPNDC-7C
❑ 97DonEliS-17
❑ 97DonEliS-120
❑ 97DonEliS-149
❑ 97DonLim-11
❑ 97DonLim-56
❑ 97DonLim-143
❑ 97DonLimExp-11
❑ 97DonLimExp-56
❑ 97DonLimExp-143
❑ 97DonLimFOTG-43
❑ 97DonLin2L-2
❑ 97DonLin2LDC-2
❑ 97DonPre-95
❑ 97DonPre-178
❑ 97DonPreCttC-95
❑ 97DonPreCttC-178
❑ 97DonPreDWT-4
❑ 97DonPreLotT-5B
❑ 97DonPrePM-9
❑ 97DonPreProG-159
❑ 97DonPreProS-159
❑ 97DonPreT-4
❑ 97DonPreTB-4
❑ 97DonPreTBC-4
❑ 97DonPreTPC-4
❑ 97DonPreTPG-4
❑ 97DonPri-6
❑ 97DonPri-187
❑ 97DonPriDD-15
❑ 97DonPriODI-6
❑ 97DonPriP-14
❑ 97DonPriS-14
❑ 97DonPriSB-14
❑ 97DonPriSG-14
❑ 97DonPriSoA-6
❑ 97DonPriSoA-187
❑ 97DonPriSS-14
❑ 97EssOlyHH-50
❑ 97EssOlyHHF-50
❑ 97HigMinHMC-15
❑ 97Kat-5
❑ 97KatGol-5
❑ 97KatSil-5
❑ 97Lea-18
❑ 97Lea-182
❑ 97LeaBanSea-8
❑ 97LeaFirOnIce-10
❑ 97LeaFraMat-18
❑ 97LeaFraMat-182
❑ 97LeaFraMDC-18
❑ 97LeaFraMDC-182
❑ 97LeaInt-18
❑ 97LeaIntUI-18
❑ 97McD-11
❑ 97Pac-8
❑ 97PacCarSup-2
❑ 97PacCarSupM-2
❑ 97PacCop-8
❑ 97PacCroR-5
❑ 97PacCroRBoSDC-2
❑ 97PacCroRCCJ-2
❑ 97PacCroRCCJG-2
❑ 97PacCroRCCJS-2
❑ 97PacCroREG-5
❑ 97PacCroRHTDC-2
❑ 97PacCroRIB-5
❑ 97PacCroRLCDC-2
❑ 97PacCroRS-5
❑ 97PacDyn-5
❑ 97PacDyn-135
❑ 97PacDynBKS-4
❑ 97PacDynC-5
❑ 97PacDynC-135
❑ 97PacDynDD-1B
❑ 97PacDynDG-5
❑ 97PacDynDG-135
❑ 97PacDynEG-5
❑ 97PacDynEG-135
❑ 97PacDynIB-5
❑ 97PacDynIB-135
❑ 97PacDynR-5
❑ 97PacDynR-135
❑ 97PacDynSil-5
❑ 97PacDynSil-135
❑ 97PacDynTan-7
❑ 97PacDynTan-24
❑ 97PacEmeGre-8
❑ 97PacGolCroDC-2
❑ 97PacIceB-8
❑ 97PacInv-4
❑ 97PacInvAZ-2
❑ 97PacInvC-4
❑ 97PacInvEG-4
❑ 97PacInvFP-2
❑ 97PacInvIB-4
❑ 97PacInvNRB-7
❑ 97PacInvOTG-2
❑ 97PacInvR-4
❑ 97PacInvS-4
❑ 97PacOme-7
❑ 97PacOme-247
❑ 97PacOmeC-7
❑ 97PacOmeC-247
❑ 97PacOmeDG-247
❑ 97PacOmeEG-7
❑ 97PacOmeEG-247
❑ 97PacOmeG-247
❑ 97PacOmeGFDCC-2
❑ 97PacOmeIB-7
❑ 97PacOmeIB-247
❑ 97PacOmeSil-2
❑ 97PacOmeSLC-2
❑ 97PacPar-7
❑ 97PacParBNDC-2
❑ 97PacParC-7
❑ 97PacParDG-7
❑ 97PacParEG-7
❑ 97PacParIB-7
❑ 97PacParP-2
❑ 97PacParRed-7
❑ 97PacParSil-7
❑ 97PacRed-8
❑ 97PacRev-5
❑ 97PacRev1AGD-1
❑ 97PacRevC-5
❑ 97PacRevE-5
❑ 97PacRevIB-5
❑ 97PacRevNID-2
❑ 97PacRevR-5
❑ 97PacRevS-5
❑ 97PacSil-8
❑ 97PacSlaSDC-1C
❑ 97PacTeaCCC-1
❑ 97Pin-86
❑ 97PinArtP-86
❑ 97PinBee-2
❑ 97PinBeeGP-2
❑ 97PinBeeGT-11
❑ 97PinBeeT-11
❑ 97PinCer-39
❑ 97PinCerGT-16
❑ 97PinCerMB-39
❑ 97PinCerMG-39
❑ 97PinCerMR-39
❑ 97PinCerR-39
❑ 97PinCerT-16
❑ 97PinEpiGO-15
❑ 97PinEpiGP-15
❑ 97PinEpiME-15
❑ 97PinEpiMO-15
❑ 97PinEpiMP-15
❑ 97PinEpiPE-15
❑ 97PinEpiPO-15
❑ 97PinEpiPP-15
❑ 97PinEpiSE-15
❑ 97PinEpiSO-15
❑ 97PinEpiSP-15
❑ 97PinIns-38
❑ 97PinInsC-19
❑ 97PinInsCC-38
❑ 97PinInsCG-19
❑ 97PinInsEC-38
❑ 97PinInsT-11
❑ 97PinMin-7
❑ 97PinMinB-7
❑ 97PinMinCBP-7
❑ 97PinMinCGPP-7
❑ 97PinMinCNSP-7
❑ 97PinMinCoiB-7
❑ 97PinMinCoiGP-7
❑ 97PinMinCoiN-7
❑ 97PinMinCoiSG-7
❑ 97PinMinCoiSS-7
❑ 97PinMinGolTea-7
❑ 97PinMinMC-4
❑ 97PinMinMin-4
❑ 97PinMinSilTea-7
❑ 97PinPowPac-24
❑ 97PinPrePBB-86
❑ 97PinPrePBC-86
❑ 97PinPrePBM-86
❑ 97PinPrePBY-86
❑ 97PinPrePFC-86
❑ 97PinPrePFM-86
❑ 97PinPrePFY-86
❑ 97PinPrePla-86
❑ 97PinRinC-86
❑ 97PinTotCMPG-39
❑ 97PinTotCPB-39
❑ 97PinTotCPG-39
❑ 97PinTotCPR-39
❑ 97PosPin-19
❑ 97Sco-113
❑ 97ScoArtPro-113
❑ 97ScoGolBla-113
❑ 97ScoMigDPla-2
❑ 97ScoMigDPre-2
❑ 97ScoMigDuc-2
❑ 97SP AutI-I19
❑ 97SPAut-1
❑ 97SPAutID-I19
❑ 97SPAutIE-I19
❑ 97SPx-2
❑ 97SPxBro-2
❑ 97SPxDim-SPX18
❑ 97SPxGol-2
❑ 97SPxGraF-2
❑ 97SPxSil-2
❑ 97SPxSte-2
❑ 97Stu-18

❑ 97Stu-107
❑ 97StuHarH-11
❑ 97StuPor-18
❑ 97StuPrePG-18
❑ 97StuPrePG-107
❑ 97StuPrePS-18
❑ 97StuPrePS-107
❑ 97StuSil-17
❑ 97StuSil8-17
❑ 97TopHocMC-25
❑ 97TopHocMC-26
❑ 97UppDec-1
❑ 97UppDecBD-95
❑ 97UppDecBDDD-95
❑ 97UppDecBDPC-PC15
❑ 97UppDecBDPCDD-PC15
❑ 97UppDecBDPCM-PC15
❑ 97UppDecBDPCQD-PC15
❑ 97UppDecBDPCTD-PC15
❑ 97UppDecBDQD-95
❑ 97UppDecBDTD-95
❑ 97UppDecCtAG-4
❑ 97UppDecCtAG-AR4
❑ 97UppDecDV-16
❑ 97UppDecDVSM-16
❑ 97UppDecGDM-1
❑ 97UppDecIC-IC8
❑ 97UppDecIC2-IC8
❑ 97UppDecIce-80
❑ 97UppDecIceP-80
❑ 97UppDecILL-L9C
❑ 97UppDecILL2-L9C
❑ 97UppDecIPS-80
❑ 97UppDecSG-SG8
❑ 97UppDecSSM-SS8
❑ 97UppDecSSW-SS8
❑ 97UppDecTS-8
❑ 97UppDecTSL2-8
❑ 97UppDecTSS-5A
❑ 97Zen-24
❑ 97Zen5x7-6
❑ 97ZenGolImp-6
❑ 97ZenSilImp-6
❑ 97ZenZGol-24
❑ 97ZenZSil-24
❑ 97ZenZT-1
❑ 97ZenZT5x7-1
❑ 97ZenZTG-1
❑ 98Be A PPA-3
❑ 98Be A PPAA-3
❑ 98Be A PPAAF-3
❑ 98Be A PPAGUSC-S3
❑ 98Be A PPAJ-AS3
❑ 98Be A PPGUJA-G11
❑ 98Be A PPPGUJC-G11
❑ 98Be A PPPUJC-P9
❑ 98Be A PPTBASG-3
❑ 98Be APG-3
❑ 98BowBes-45
❑ 98BowBesAR-45
❑ 98BowBesMIF-F4
❑ 98BowBesMIFAR-F4
❑ 98BowBesMIFR-F4
❑ 98BowBesR-45
❑ 98CroRoyCCAJG-2
❑ 98CroRoyCCAJG-2
❑ 98CroRoyCCAJLB-2
❑ 98CroRoyCCAJP-2
❑ 98CroRoyCCAJR-2
❑ 98Fin-1
❑ 98FinCen-C15
❑ 98FinCenR-C15
❑ 98FinDouMF-M11
❑ 98FinDouMF-M15
❑ 98FinDouMF-M16
❑ 98FinDouMF-M17
❑ 98FinDouSMFR-M11
❑ 98FinDouSMFR-M15
❑ 98FinDouSMFR-M16
❑ 98FinDouSMFR-M17
❑ 98FinNo P-1
❑ 98FinNo PR-1
❑ 98FinOve-1
❑ 98FinOveR-1
❑ 98FinRedL-R8
❑ 98FinRedLR-R8
❑ 98FinRef-1
❑ 98O-PChr-109
❑ 98O-PChrR-109
❑ 98O-PChrSB-SB13
❑ 98O-PChrSBR-SB13
❑ 98Pac-8
❑ 98PacAur-6
❑ 98PacAurALC-2
❑ 98PacAurC-2
❑ 98PacAurCF-2
❑ 98PacAurCFC-2
❑ 98PacAurCFIB-2
❑ 98PacAurCFR-2
❑ 98PacAurCFS-2
❑ 98PacAurMAC-2
❑ 98PacAurNC-1
❑ 98PacCroR-5
❑ 98PacCroRCCA-2
❑ 98PacCroRCCAJ-2
❑ 98PacCroRLL-2
❑ 98PacCroRLS-5
❑ 98PacCroRMP-2
❑ 98PacCroRPotG-1
❑ 98PacDynI-6
❑ 98PacDynI-2
❑ 98PacDynIAR-2
❑ 98PacDynIARB-2
❑ 98PacDynIARIB-2
❑ 98PacDynIARR-2
❑ 98PacDynIARS-2
❑ 98PacDynIFT-2
❑ 98PacDynIIB-6
❑ 98PacDynIR-6
❑ 98PacEO P-2
❑ 98PacGolCD-2
❑ 98PacIceB-8
❑ 98PacOmeEP1o1-2
❑ 98PacOmeFtF-7
❑ 98PacOmeH-8
❑ 98PacOmeO-2
❑ 98PacOmeODI-8
❑ 98PacOmeP-2
❑ 98PacOmePI-23
❑ 98PacOmePIB-23
❑ 98PacOmeR-8
❑ 98PacPar-7
❑ 98PacParC-7
❑ 98PacParEG-7
❑ 98PacParH-7
❑ 98PacParHoFB-1
❑ 98PacParHoFBPP-1
❑ 98PacParIB-7
❑ 98PacParS-7
❑ 98PacParSDDC-2
❑ 98PacParTCD-1
❑ 98PacRed-8
❑ 98PacRev-5
❑ 98PacRevADC-26
❑ 98PacRevCTL-2
❑ 98PacRevIS-5
❑ 98PacRevR-5
❑ 98PacRevS-2
❑ 98PacTim-1
❑ 98PacTitI-2
❑ 98PinEpiGE-15
❑ 98RevThrPA-22
❑ 98RevThrPA-22
❑ 98SP Aut-2
❑ 98SP AutSM-S26
❑ 98SP AutSS-SS10
❑ 98SPxFin-1
❑ 98SPxFin-104
❑ 98SPxFin-157
❑ 98SPxFinR-1
❑ 98SPxFinR-104
❑ 98SPxFinR-157
❑ 98SPxFinS-1
❑ 98SPxFinS-104
❑ 98SPxFinS-157
❑ 98SPXTopP-2
❑ 98SPXTopPF-2
❑ 98SPXTopPHH-H2
❑ 98SPXTopPLI-L7
❑ 98SPXTopPPS-PS17
❑ 98SPXTopPR-2
❑ 98Top-109
❑ 98TopBlaLGR'-GR3
❑ 98TopGolLC1-7
❑ 98TopGolLC1B-7
❑ 98TopGolLC1BOoO-7
❑ 98TopGolLC1OoO-7
❑ 98TopGolLC1R-7
❑ 98TopGolLC1ROoO-7
❑ 98TopGolLC2-7
❑ 98TopGolLC2B-7
❑ 98TopGolLC2BOoO-7
❑ 98TopGolLC2OoO-7
❑ 98TopGolLC2R-7
❑ 98TopGolLC2ROoO-7
❑ 98TopGolLC3-7
❑ 98TopGolLC3B-7
❑ 98TopGolLC3BOoO-7
❑ 98TopGolLC3OoO-7
❑ 98TopGolLC3R-7
❑ 98TopGolLC3ROoO-7
❑ 98TopGolLGR'-GR3
❑ 98TopGolLGR'BOoO-GR3
❑ 98TopGolLGR'OoO-GR3
❑ 98TopGolLGR'ROoO-GR3
❑ 98TopLocL-L15
❑ 98TopMysFB-M1
❑ 98TopMysFBR-M1
❑ 98TopMysFG-M1
❑ 98TopMysFGR-M1
❑ 98TopMysFS-M1
❑ 98TopMysFSR-M1
❑ 98TopO-P-109
❑ 98TopRedLGR'-GR3
❑ 98TopSeaB-SB13
❑ 98UC-8
❑ 98UC-242
❑ 98UCMBH-BH15
❑ 98UCSB-SQ5
❑ 98UCSG-SQ5
❑ 98UCSG-SQ5
❑ 98UCSR-SQ5
❑ 98UD ChoPCR-8
❑ 98UD ChoPCR-242
❑ 98UD ChoR-8
❑ 98UD ChoR-242
❑ 98UD3-58
❑ 98UD3-118
❑ 98UD3-178
❑ 98UD3DieC-58
❑ 98UD3DieC-118
❑ 98UD3DieC-178
❑ 98UppDec-16
❑ 98UppDec-34
❑ 98UppDecBD-2
❑ 98UppDecDD-2
❑ 98UppDecE-16
❑ 98UppDecE-34
❑ 98UppDecE1o1-16
❑ 98UppDecE1o1-34
❑ 98UppDecFF-FF23
❑ 98UppDecFF-FF23
❑ 98UppDecFFQ1-FF23
❑ 98UppDecFFQ2-FF23
❑ 98UppDecFIT-FT28
❑ 98UppDecFITQ1-FT28
❑ 98UppDecFITQ2-FT28
❑ 98UppDecFITQ3-FT28
❑ 98UppDecGR-16
❑ 98UppDecGR-34
❑ 98UppDecLSH-LS30
❑ 98UppDecLSHQ1-LS30
❑ 98UppDecLSHQ2-LS30
❑ 98UppDecLSHQ3-LS30
❑ 98UppDecM-2
❑ 98UppDecM1-M7
❑ 98UppDecM2-M7
❑ 98UppDecMGS-2
❑ 98UppDecMS-S4
❑ 98UppDecMSF-F10
❑ 98UppDecMSS-2
❑ 98UppDecMSS-2
❑ 98UppDecP-P8
❑ 98UppDecPQ1-P8
❑ 98UppDecPQ2-P8
❑ 98UppDecPQ3-P8
❑ 98UppDecQD-2
❑ 98UppDecTD-2
❑ 98UppDecWFG-WF2
❑ 98UppDecWFP-WF2
❑ 99AurSty-2
❑ 99Pac-16
❑ 99PacAur-5
❑ 99PacAurCC-2
❑ 99PacAurCF-2
❑ 99PacAurCFC-2
❑ 99PacAurCFPB-2
❑ 99PacAurCP-2
❑ 99PacAurCPP-2
❑ 99PacAurPD-5
❑ 99PacCop-16
❑ 99PacGol-16
❑ 99PacGolCD-2
❑ 99PacHomaA-2
❑ 99PacIceB-16
❑ 99PacPasAP-2
❑ 99PacPreD-16
❑ 99RetHoc-2
❑ 99SP AutPS-2
❑ 99UppDecCL-60
❑ 99UppDecCLCLC-60
❑ 99UppDecM-5
❑ 99UppDecM9S-S8
❑ 99UppDecMGS-GU2
❑ 99UppDecMGS-5
❑ 99UppDecMGUSA-GU2
❑ 99UppDecMHoG-H4
❑ 99UppDecMSS-5
❑ 99UppDecMSS-5
❑ 99UppDecRG-G8B
❑ 99UppDecRG-2
❑ 99UppDecRGI-G8B
❑ 99UppDecRII-TS
❑ 99UppDecRIL1-TS
❑ 99UppDecRP-2

**Selby, Brit**
❑ 64BeeGro3P-182
❑ 65Coc-97
❑ 66Top-18
❑ 68OPC-96
❑ 68ShiCoi-129
❑ 68Top-96
❑ 69MapLeaWBG-31
❑ 69OPC-48
❑ 69Top-48
❑ 70ColSta-37
❑ 70DadCoo-121
❑ 70EssPowPla-248
❑ 70OPC-111A
❑ 70OPC-111B
❑ 70SarProSta-202
❑ 70Top-111
❑ 71OPC-226
❑ 71SarProSta-183
❑ 73QuaOatWHA-39
❑ 94ParTalB-121
❑ 95Par66-111
❑ 95Par66-132
❑ 95Par66Coi-111

**Seliger, Marc**
❑ 91UppDec-683
❑ 91UppDecCWJC-46
❑ 91UppDecF-683
❑ 94GerDELE-384
❑ 95GerDELE-103
❑ 95SigRoo-30
❑ 95SigRooSig-30
❑ 96HamRoaA-HRA19
❑ 96SweSemW-193
❑ 98GerDELE-2

**Selinder, Lennart**
❑ 64SweCorI-42
❑ 65SweCorI-42
❑ 67SweHoc-41
❑ 69SweHocS-53
❑ 70SweHocS-13
❑ 71SweHocS-91
❑ 72SweHocS-60
❑ 73SweHocS-201
❑ 73SweWorCS-201

**Selivanov, Alexander**
❑ 94Fin-79
❑ 94FinBowB-R17
❑ 94FinBowBR-R17
❑ 94FinRef-79
❑ 94FinSupTW-79
❑ 94Fle-210
❑ 94LigPhoA-23
❑ 94LigPos-16
❑ 94SP-113
❑ 94SPDieCut-113
❑ 94UppDec-425
❑ 94UppDec-532
❑ 94UppDecEleIce-425
❑ 94UppDecEleIce-532
❑ 94UppDecSPI-SP165
❑ 94UppDecSPIDC-SP165
❑ 95BeAPla-145
❑ 95BeAPSig-S145
❑ 95BeAPSigDC-S145
❑ 95Bow-73
❑ 95BowAllFoi-73
❑ 95CanGamNHLP-252
❑ 95ColCho-165
❑ 95ColChoPC-165
❑ 95ColChoPCP-165
❑ 95Don-90
❑ 95DonEli-84
❑ 95DonEliDCS-84
❑ 95DonEliDCU-84
❑ 95Fin-32
❑ 95FinRef-32
❑ 95Ima-16
❑ 95ImaGol-16
❑ 95Lea-49
❑ 95LigTeal-16
❑ 95Met-140
❑ 95ParInt-194
❑ 95ParIntEl-194
❑ 95Pin-116
❑ 95PinArtP-116
❑ 95PinGloG-17
❑ 95PinRinC-116
❑ 95PlaOneoOne-199
❑ 95SigRooA-39
❑ 95SigRooAPC-39
❑ 95SP-140
❑ 95StaClu-111
❑ 95StaCluMOMS-111
❑ 95Top-367
❑ 95TopNewG-11NG
❑ 95TopOPCI-367
❑ 95Ult-310
❑ 95UppDec-316
❑ 95UppDecEleIce-316
❑ 95UppDecEleIceG-316
❑ 95UppDecSpeE-SE77
❑ 95UppDecSpeEdiG-SE77
❑ 96ColCho-253
❑ 96Don-32
❑ 96DonEli-95
❑ 96DonEliDCS-95
❑ 96DonPrePro-32
❑ 96Fle-106
❑ 96Lea-62
❑ 96LeaLim-45
❑ 96LeaLimG-45
❑ 96LeaPre-43
❑ 96LeaPreP-62
❑ 96LeaPrePP-43
❑ 96MetUni-147
❑ 96Pin-77
❑ 96PinArtP-77
❑ 96PinFoi-77
❑ 96PinPreS-77
❑ 96PinRinC-77
❑ 96PlaOneoOne-390
❑ 96Sco-27
❑ 96ScoArtPro-27
❑ 96ScoDeaCAP-27
❑ 96ScoGolB-27
❑ 96ScoSpeAP-27
❑ 96ScoSup-10
❑ 96SkyImp-124
❑ 96SP-148
❑ 96Sum-58
❑ 96SumArtP-58
❑ 96SumIce-58
❑ 96SumMet-58
❑ 96SumPreS-58
❑ 96TopNHLP-123
❑ 96TopPicOI-123
❑ 96Ult-160
❑ 96UltGolM-160
❑ 96UppDec-339
❑ 96Zen-21
❑ 96ZenArtP-21
❑ 97ColCho-241
❑ 97PacDynBKS-89
❑ 97PacOme-214
❑ 97PacOmeC-214
❑ 97PacOmeDG-214
❑ 97PacOmeEG-214
❑ 97PacOmeG-214
❑ 97PacOmeIB-214
❑ 97PacPar-176
❑ 97PacParC-176
❑ 97PacParDG-176
❑ 97PacParEG-176
❑ 97PacParIB-176
❑ 97PacParRed-176
❑ 97PacParSil-176
❑ 97Sco-63
❑ 97SPAut-146
❑ 97UppDec-156
❑ 97UppDecBD-121
❑ 97UppDecBDDD-121
❑ 97UppDecBDQD-121
❑ 97UppDecBDTD-121
❑ 98Be A PPA-130
❑ 98Be A PPAA-130
❑ 98Be A PPAAF-130
❑ 98Be A PPTBASG-130
❑ 98Be APG-130
❑ 98O-PChr-85
❑ 98O-PChrR-85
❑ 98Pac-406
❑ 98PacAur-176
❑ 98PacIceB-406
❑ 98PacPar-221
❑ 98PacParC-221
❑ 98PacParEG-221
❑ 98PacParH-221
❑ 98PacParIB-221
❑ 98PacParS-221
❑ 98PacRed-406
❑ 98SP AutSotTG-AS
❑ 98SPxFin-80
❑ 98SPxFinR-80
❑ 98SPxFinS-80
❑ 98SSASotT-AS
❑ 98Top-85
❑ 98TopO-P-85
❑ 98UC-195
❑ 98UD ChoPCR-195
❑ 98UD ChoR-195
❑ 98UppDec-182
❑ 98UppDecE-182
❑ 98UppDecE1o1-182
❑ 98UppDecGR-182
❑ 99Pac-165
❑ 99PacCop-165
❑ 99PacGol-165
❑ 99PacIceB-165
❑ 99PacPreD-165

**Selke, Frank**
❑ 55Par-68
❑ 55ParQuaO-68
❑ 59Par-47
❑ 81MapLeaP-26
❑ 83HalFP-C12
❑ 85HalFC-41
❑ 87PanSti-385
❑ 90UppDecF-208
❑ 94ParMisL-85

**Selkirk, Jason**
❑ 91AirCanSJHL-A5

**Selmser, Sean**
❑ 93RedDeeR-22
❑ 95HamRoaA-19

**Selvek, Jan**
❑ 95SloAPSNT-4

**Selwood, Brad**
❑ 70MapLeaP-12
❑ 71MapLeaP-17
❑ 71SarProSta-207
❑ 71TorSun-270
❑ 72WhaNewEWHA-13
❑ 74TeaCanLWHA-19
❑ 75OPCWHA-82

**Selyanin, Sergei**
❑ 91OPCIns-58R
❑ 94FinnJaaK-141

**Semak, Alexander**
❑ 91OPCIns-42R
❑ 91Par-323
❑ 91ParFre-323
❑ 91SweSemWCS-94
❑ 91UppDec-4
❑ 91UppDecF-4
❑ 92Bow-164
❑ 92PanSti-191
❑ 92PanSti-296
❑ 92PanStiFre-176
❑ 92PanStiFre-296
❑ 92Par-329
❑ 92ParEmeI-329
❑ 92RusStaRA-30
❑ 92Sco-451
❑ 92ScoCan-451
❑ 92StaClu-444
❑ 92Top-419
❑ 92TopGol-419G
❑ 92Ult-341
❑ 92UppDec-45
❑ 92UppDecERT-ERT5
❑ 93Don-191
❑ 93Lea-35
❑ 93OPCPre-102
❑ 93OPCPreG-102
❑ 93PanSti-36
❑ 93Par-109
❑ 93ParEmeI-109
❑ 93Pin-47
❑ 93PinCan-47
❑ 93Pow-142
❑ 93Sco-284
❑ 93ScoCan-284
❑ 93ScoIntS-14
❑ 93ScoIntSC-14
❑ 93StaClu-365
❑ 93StaCluFDI-365
❑ 93StaCluO-365
❑ 93TopPre-102
❑ 93TopPreG-102
❑ 93Ult-166
❑ 93UppDec-178
❑ 93UppDecSP-88
❑ 94BeAPSig-4
❑ 94EASpo-75
❑ 94FinnJaaK-158
❑ 94Fla-99
❑ 94Fle-118
❑ 94Lea-543
❑ 94LigPhoA-24
❑ 94Pin-362
❑ 94PinArtP-362
❑ 94PinRinC-362
❑ 94StaClu-245
❑ 94StaCluFDI-245
❑ 94StaCluMOMS-245
❑ 94StaCluSTWC-245
❑ 94Ult-321
❑ 94UppDec-219
❑ 94UppDecEleIce-219
❑ 95ColCho-56
❑ 95ColChoPC-56
❑ 95ColChoPCP-56
❑ 95Emo-109
❑ 95ParInt-135
❑ 95ParIntEl-135
❑ 95Top-97
❑ 95TopOPCI-97
❑ 95Ult-271
❑ 95UppDec-40
❑ 95UppDecEleIce-40
❑ 95UppDecEleIceG-40
❑ 96CanuPos-20
❑ 96ColCho-163
❑ 96Don-26
❑ 96DonPrePro-26
❑ 96Pin-188
❑ 96PinArtP-188
❑ 96PinFoi-188
❑ 96PinPreS-188
❑ 96PinRinC-188
❑ 96Sco-212
❑ 96ScoArtPro-212
❑ 96ScoDeaCAP-212
❑ 96ScoGolB-212
❑ 96ScoSpeAP-212
❑ 96UppDec-98

**Semandel, Kurt**
❑ 90KanCitBla-15
❑ 90ProAHLIHL-598

**Semchuk, Brandy**
❑ 90ProAHLIHL-430
❑ 92PhoRoa-20

**Semeniuk, Trevor**
❑ 83MedHatT-10
❑ 84VicCou-21

**Semenko, Dave**
❑ 79OilPos-20
❑ 79OPC-371
❑ 80OPC-360
❑ 80PepCap-38
❑ 81OilRedR-27
❑ 81OPC-121
❑ 82OilRedR-27
❑ 82OPC-119
❑ 82PosCer-6
❑ 83OilDol-H19
❑ 83OilMcD-2
❑ 83Vac-40
❑ 84OilRedR-27
❑ 84OilTeal-23
❑ 85OilRedR-27
❑ 87MapLeaP-19
❑ 87MapLeaPLA-26
❑ 87MapLeaPO-19
❑ 88OilTenAnn-6

**Semenov, Anatoli**
❑ 89SweSemWCS-99
❑ 90OilIGA-22
❑ 90OPC-468
❑ 90OPCPre-104
❑ 90ProSet-608
❑ 90ScoRoo-39T
❑ 90UppDec-405
❑ 90UppDecF-405
❑ 91Bow-113
❑ 91OilIGA-20
❑ 91OilPanTS-19
❑ 91OilTeal-24
❑ 91OPC-390
❑ 91PanSti-127
❑ 91Par-279
❑ 91ParFre-279
❑ 91RusStaRA-16
❑ 91RusTriSem-11
❑ 91RusTriSem-12
❑ 91RusTriSem-13
❑ 91RusTriSem-14
❑ 91RusTriSem-15
❑ 91ScoCan-258
❑ 91StaClu-366
❑ 91Top-390
❑ 91UppDec-269
❑ 91UppDecES-4
❑ 91UppDecESF-4
❑ 91UppDecF-269
❑ 92Bow-423
❑ 92OPC-83
❑ 92Par-420
❑ 92ParEmeI-420
❑ 92Pin-386
❑ 92PinFre-386
❑ 92Sco-336
❑ 92ScoCan-336
❑ 92ScoSha-28
❑ 92ScoShaCan-28
❑ 92StaClu-143
❑ 92Top-68
❑ 92TopGol-68G
❑ 92Ult-429
❑ 92UppDec-20
❑ 92UppDec-535
❑ 93Don-3
❑ 93Lea-338
❑ 93OPCPre-506
❑ 93OPCPreG-506
❑ 93PanSti-174
❑ 93Par-3
❑ 93ParEmeI-3
❑ 93Pin-368
❑ 93PinCan-368
❑ 93Pow-10
❑ 93Sco-93
❑ 93Sco-536
❑ 93ScoCan-93
❑ 93ScoCan-536
❑ 93ScoGol-536
❑ 93StaClu-368
❑ 93StaCluFDI-368
❑ 93StaCluO-368
❑ 93TopPre-506
❑ 93TopPreG-506
❑ 93Ult-261
❑ 93UppDec-46
❑ 93UppDecSP-4
❑ 94CanGamNHLP-347
❑ 94Don-326
❑ 94EASpo-5
❑ 94Fla-5
❑ 94Lea-303
❑ 94OPCPre-524
❑ 94OPCPreSE-524
❑ 94Par-1
❑ 94ParGol-1
❑ 94Pin-322
❑ 94PinArtP-322
❑ 94PinRinC-322
❑ 94Sco-16
❑ 94ScoGol-16
❑ 94ScoPla-16
❑ 94ScoPlaTS-16
❑ 94TopPre-524
❑ 94TopPreSE-524
❑ 94Ult-7
❑ 94UppDec-105
❑ 94UppDecEleIce-105
❑ 95Don-312
❑ 95Lea-238
❑ 95ParInt-429
❑ 95ParIntEl-429
❑ 96ColCho-7
❑ 97Pac-106
❑ 97PacCop-106
❑ 97PacEmeGre-106
❑ 97PacIceB-106
❑ 97PacRed-106
❑ 97PacSil-106

**Semin, Nikolai**
❑ 92UppDec-610

**Sendrey, Rastislav**
❑ 95SloPeeWT-23

**Sendt, Thorsten**
❑ 94GerDELE-217

**Senecal, Sylvain**
❑ 84RicRiv-18

**Senechal, Claude**
❑ 50QueCit-18

**Senger, Patrick**
❑ 98GerDELE-200

**Senkow, Derek**
❑ 95MedHatT-18

**Senn, Trevor**
❑ 92WheThu-16
❑ 95RicRen-15
❑ 96RicRen-19

**Sentes, Rick**
❑ 72NatOttWHA-19

**Sentner, Peter**
❑ 90ProAHLIHL-361
❑ 91GreMon-12

**Sepkowski, Todd**
❑ 84SudWol-8

**Seppanen, Leo**
❑ 74SweSemHVS-93

**Seppo, Jukka**
❑ 93FinnSIS-253
❑ 93SweSemWCS-78
❑ 94FinnSIS-246
❑ 94FinnSISH-2
❑ 95FinnSIS-343
❑ 95FinnSISL-95
❑ 95FinnSISSpe-9
❑ 96GerDELE-239
❑ 98GerDELE-48

**Serafini, Ron**
❑ 75RoaPhoWHA-6

**Sergott, Keith**
❑ 91FerStaB-28

**Serikow, Alexander**
❑ 95GerDELE-279
❑ 96GerDELE-176
❑ 98GerDELE-235
❑ 98GerDELE-333

**Sernjajev, Vladimir**
❑ 74SweHocS-77

**Seroski, Joe**
❑ 95Sla-362
❑ 96SauSteMG-20
❑ 96SauSteMGA-20

**Serowik, Jeff**
❑ 90ProAHLIHL-154
❑ 91ProAHLCHL-337
❑ 92St.JohML-20
❑ 95IndIce-19
❑ 96LasVegThu-18

**Sertich, Mike**
❑ 85MinDul-33
❑ 93MinDul-27

**Servant, Frederick**
❑ 93AmoLesFAM-20

**Servatius, Darren**
❑ 89JohChi-22
**Servatius, Ron**
❑ 89NasKni-22
**Serviss, Tom**
❑ 72ShaLosAW-12
**Setikovsky, Jindrich**
❑ 94CzeAPSE-290
❑ 95CzeAPSE-243
**Seva, Janne**
❑ 93FinnJyvHS-87
❑ 93FinnSIS-131
❑ 94FinnSIS-347
❑ 95FinnSIS-35
**Sevcik, Frantisek**
❑ 69SweHocS-37
❑ 70SweHocS-364
❑ 94CzeAPSE-111
❑ 95CzeAPSE-209
❑ 96CzeAPSE-258
**Sevcik, Jaroslav**
❑ 88ProAHL-109
❑ 89HalCit-21
❑ 89ProAHL-176
❑ 90HalCit-22
❑ 90ProAHLIHL-460
❑ 95GerDELE-332
**Sevecek, Rene**
❑ 96CzeAPSE-198
**Severson, Cam**
❑ 96LetHur-16
**Severyn, Brent**
❑ 84BraWheK-24
❑ 88ProAHL-106
❑ 89HalCit-22
❑ 89ProAHL-171
❑ 90HalCit-23
❑ 90ProAHLIHL-456
❑ 91ProAHLCHL-408
❑ 93OPCPre-392
❑ 93OPCPreG-392
❑ 93PanTeal-8
❑ 93Par-77
❑ 93ParEmel-77
❑ 93Sco-652
❑ 93ScoCan-652
❑ 93ScoGol-652
❑ 93TopPre-392
❑ 93TopPreG-392
❑ 93Ult-331
❑ 93UppDec-453
❑ 94Lea-342
❑ 94OPCPre-334
❑ 94OPCPreSE-334
❑ 94Par-90
❑ 94ParGol-90
❑ 94TopPre-334
❑ 94TopPreSE-334
❑ 95Top-243
❑ 95TopOPCI-243
❑ 96BeAPAut-185
❑ 96BeAPAutSil-185
❑ 96BeAPla-185
❑ 97PacInvNRB-58
**Sevidov, Alexander**
❑ 73SweHocS-134
❑ 73SweWorCS-134
**Sevigny, Louis Phillippe**
❑ 94ParSE-SE259
❑ 94ParSEG-SE259
❑ 94SP-180
❑ 94SPDieCut-180
**Sevigny, Pierre**
❑ 907thInnSQMJHL-226
❑ 90UppDec-456
❑ 90UppDecF-456
❑ 91ProAHLCHL-88
❑ 92FreCan-22
❑ 93CanaPos-25
❑ 93ClaProPro-51
❑ 93Don-169
❑ 93DurSco-2
❑ 93Lea-392
❑ 93Par-106
❑ 93ParCalC-C7
❑ 93ParCalCG-C7
❑ 93ParEmel-106
❑ 93Sco-634
❑ 93ScoCan-634
❑ 93ScoGol-634
❑ 93UppDec-455
❑ 93UppDecSP-82
❑ 94CanaPos-25
❑ 94Don-195
❑ 94Lea-309
❑ 94Par-117
❑ 94ParGol-117
❑ 94StaClu-193
❑ 94StaCluFDI-193
❑ 94StaCluMOMS-193
❑ 94StaCluSTWC-193
❑ 94UppDec-402
❑ 94UppDecEleIce-402
❑ 95FreCan-25
**Sevigny, Pierre (80s)**
❑ 84ChiSag-24
**Sevigny, Richard**
❑ 79CanaPos-23
❑ 80CanaPos-23
❑ 80OPC-385
❑ 81CanaPos-24
❑ 81OPC-191
❑ 81OPC-387
❑ 81OPCSti-40
❑ 81OPCSti-256
❑ 82CanaPos-23
❑ 82CanaSte-18
❑ 82PosCer-10
❑ 83CanaPos-25
❑ 83Vac-54
❑ 84NordPos-24
❑ 84OPC-289
❑ 85NordGenF-23
❑ 85NordMcD-18
❑ 85NordPro-22
❑ 85NordTeal-21
❑ 86NordGenF-22
❑ 86NordMcD-22
❑ 86NordTeal-20
❑ 87NordGenF-27
**Sevon, Jorma**
❑ 82SweSemHVS-42
**Sexsmith, Dean**
❑ 84BraWheK-5
❑ 85BraWheK-5
**Sexton, Dan**
❑ 83VicCou-21
❑ 84VicCou-22
❑ 87RegPat-23
**Sexton, William**
❑ 52JunBluT-108
**Seymour, Dean**
❑ 91AirCanSJHL-A47
❑ 91AirCanSJHLAS-26
❑ 93NorMicW-24
❑ 96LouRiv-15
**Seymour, Glen**
❑ 86PorWinH-19
**Sgualdo, Rene**
❑ 72SweSemWC-153
**Shack, Ed (Eddie)**
❑ 44BeeGro2P-361
❑ 44BeeGro2P-448A
❑ 58Top-30
❑ 59Top-57
❑ 60ShiCoi-87
❑ 60Top-7
❑ 60YorPreP-32
❑ 61Par-7
❑ 61ShiCoi-48
❑ 61YorYelB-25
❑ 62Par-14
❑ 62ShiMetC-8
❑ 62YorIroOTra-32
❑ 63ChePho-48
❑ 63MapLeaWB-20
❑ 63Par-9
❑ 63Par-69
❑ 63TorSta-34
❑ 63YorWhiB-4
❑ 64BeeGro3P-183
❑ 64CocCap-105
❑ 64Top-71
❑ 65Coc-104
❑ 65MapLeaWB-16
❑ 66Top-17
❑ 67Top-34
❑ 68OPC-137
❑ 68ShiCoi-1
❑ 69OPC-139
❑ 69OPCFou-16
❑ 69Top-106
❑ 70ColSta-31
❑ 70DadCoo-122
❑ 70EssPowPla-89
❑ 70OPC-35
❑ 70OPCDec-2
❑ 70SarProSta-69
❑ 70Top-35
❑ 71OPC-96
❑ 71SabPos-18
❑ 71SarProSta-20
❑ 71Top-96
❑ 71TorSun-39
❑ 72OPC-186
❑ 72OPC-274
❑ 72OPCPlaC-17
❑ 73MapLeaP-23
❑ 73OPC-242
❑ 74MapLeaP-20
❑ 91UltOriS-41
❑ 91UltOriSBB-4
❑ 91UltOriSF-41
❑ 94ParMisLFS-FS4
❑ 94ParTalB-117
❑ 94ParTalB-164
❑ 95Par66-113
❑ 95Par66Coi-113
**Shadrin, Vladimir**
❑ 70SweHocS-330
❑ 72SweSemWC-19
❑ 73SweHocS-90
❑ 73SweWorCS-90
❑ 74SweSemHVS-37
❑ 91FutTreC72-54
**Shaidullin, Vadim**
❑ 94FinnSIS-300
**Shakhraichuk, Vadim**
❑ 98GerDELE-260
**Shakotto, Darren**
❑ 95LetHur-21
❑ 96LetHur-17
**Shaldybin, Yevgeny**
❑ 96ProBru-23
**Shalimov, Viktor**
❑ 82SweSemHVS-65
**Shanahan, Brendan**
❑ 85LonKni-9
❑ 86LonKni-6
❑ 88DevCar-26
❑ 88OPC-122
❑ 88PanSti-276
❑ 88Top-122
❑ 89DevCar-21
❑ 89OPC-147
❑ 89OPCSti-89
❑ 89PanSti-255
❑ 89Top-147
❑ 90Bow-85
❑ 90BowTif-85
❑ 90Dev-23
❑ 90OPC-259
❑ 90OPCPre-105
❑ 90PanSti-64
❑ 90ProSet-174
❑ 90Sco-146
❑ 90ScoCan-146
❑ 90ScoYouS-23
❑ 90Top-259
❑ 90TopTif-259
❑ 90UppDec-269
❑ 90UppDecF-269
❑ 91BluPos-18
❑ 91Bow-288
❑ 91Kra-7
❑ 91OPC-140
❑ 91OPCPre-130
❑ 91PanSti-222
❑ 91Par-153
❑ 91ParFre-153
❑ 91Pin-41
❑ 91PinFre-41
❑ 91ProSet-131
❑ 91ProSet-475
❑ 91ProSetFre-131
❑ 91ProSetFre-475
❑ 91ProSetPla-111
❑ 91ScoAme-286
❑ 91ScoCan-588
❑ 91ScoRoo-38T
❑ 91StaClu-199
❑ 91Top-140
❑ 91UppDec-561
❑ 91UppDecF-561
❑ 92Bow-183
❑ 92HumDum1-20
❑ 92OPC-244
❑ 92PanSti-17
❑ 92PanStiFre-17
❑ 92Par-156
❑ 92ParCheP-CP10
❑ 92ParEmel-156
❑ 92Pin-114
❑ 92Pin-248
❑ 92PinFre-114
❑ 92PinFre-248
❑ 92ProSet-163
❑ 92Sco-392
❑ 92ScoCan-392
❑ 92SeaPat-15
❑ 92StaClu-371
❑ 92Top-295
❑ 92TopGol-295G
❑ 92Ult-189
❑ 92UppDec-122
❑ 93Don-299
❑ 93Kra-23
❑ 93Lea-30
❑ 93LeaGolAS-9
❑ 93OPCPre-247
❑ 93OPCPreG-247
❑ 93PanSti-158
❑ 93Par-172
❑ 93ParEmel-172
❑ 93Pin-205
❑ 93PinCan-205
❑ 93PinNifFif-14
❑ 93PinTea2-29
❑ 93PinTea2C-29
❑ 93Pow-216
❑ 93PowSlaA-10
❑ 93Sco-238
❑ 93ScoCan-238
❑ 93StaClu-389
❑ 93StaCluFDI-389
❑ 93StaCluO-389
❑ 93TopPre-247
❑ 93TopPreG-247
❑ 93Ult-245
❑ 93UppDecSP-140
❑ 94BeAPla-R86
❑ 94BeAPla-R104
❑ 94BeAPla-R137
❑ 94BeAPSig-86
❑ 94CanGamNHLP-207
❑ 94CanGamNHLP-265
❑ 94Don-174
❑ 94EASpo-124
❑ 94Fin-92
❑ 94FinDivFCC-14
❑ 94FinnJaaK-100
❑ 94FinRef-92
❑ 94FinSupTW-92
❑ 94Fla-158
❑ 94FlaHotN-9
❑ 94Fle-191
❑ 94FleHea-10
❑ 94HocWit-29
❑ 94Kra-71
❑ 94Lea-113
❑ 94LeaLim-97
❑ 94LeaLimI-20
❑ 94McDUppD-McD30
❑ 94OPCPre-215
❑ 94OPCPre-529
❑ 94OPCPreSE-215
❑ 94OPCPreSE-529
❑ 94Par-196
❑ 94Par-298
❑ 94ParGol-196
❑ 94ParGol-298
❑ 94Pin-32
❑ 94PinArtP-32
❑ 94PinBoo-BR6
❑ 94PinGam-GR10
❑ 94PinRinC-32
❑ 94PinTeaP-TP6
❑ 94PinTeaPDP-TP6
❑ 94Sco-155
❑ 94Sco90PC-8
❑ 94ScoCheIt-CI5
❑ 94ScoGol-155
❑ 94ScoPla-155
❑ 94ScoPlaTS-155
❑ 94Sel-129
❑ 94SelFirLin-4
❑ 94SelGol-129
❑ 94SP-101
❑ 94SPDieCut-101
❑ 94StaCluMO-16
❑ 94StaCluST-20
❑ 94TopFinI-5
❑ 94TopPre-215
❑ 94TopPre-529
❑ 94TopPreSE-215
❑ 94TopPreSE-529
❑ 94Ult-189
❑ 94UltPow-9
❑ 94UltRedLS-9
❑ 94UppDec-292
❑ 94UppDecEleIce-292
❑ 94UppDecIG-IG4
❑ 94UppDecNBAP-16
❑ 94UppDecPR-R7
❑ 94UppDecPRE-R7
❑ 94UppDecPreRG-R7
❑ 94UppDecSPI-SP69
❑ 94UppDecSPIDC-SP69
❑ 95BAPLetL-LL13
❑ 95Bow-28
❑ 95BowAllFoi-28
❑ 95CanGamNHLP-126
❑ 95ColCho-4
❑ 95ColChoPC-4
❑ 95ColChoPCP-4
❑ 95Don-180
❑ 95Don-377
❑ 95DonEli-3
❑ 95DonEliDCS-3
❑ 95DonEliDCU-3
❑ 95DonMar-8
❑ 95Emo-78
❑ 95EmoNteP-7
❑ 95Fin-39
❑ 95Fin-65
❑ 95FinnSemWC-88
❑ 95FinRef-39
❑ 95FinRef-65
❑ 95GerDELE-447
❑ 95ImpSti-52
❑ 95ImpStiDCS-22
❑ 95KenStaLA-17
❑ 95KenStaLC-12
❑ 95Lea-121
❑ 95LeaLim-94
❑ 95Met-67
❑ 95MetIW-11
❑ 95MetIW-13
❑ 95ParInt-97
❑ 95ParIntEI-97
❑ 95ParIntNHLAS-3
❑ 95PinFan-6
❑ 95PinFulC-5
❑ 95PinRoa2-18
❑ 95PlaOneoOne-47
❑ 95PlaOneoOne-157
❑ 95PosUppD-11
❑ 95ProMag-129
❑ 95Sco-20
❑ 95ScoBlaIce-20
❑ 95ScoBlaIceAP-20
❑ 95ScoGolBla-17
❑ 95SelCer-64
❑ 95SelCerDS-9
❑ 95SelCerDSG-9
❑ 95SelCerMG-64
❑ 95SkyImp-76
❑ 95SP-62
❑ 95SPStaEto-E16
❑ 95SPStaEtoG-E16
❑ 95StaClu-25
❑ 95StaCluFea-F1
❑ 95StaCluMOMS-25
❑ 95Sum-124
❑ 95SumArtP-124
❑ 95SumGM-20
❑ 95SumIce-124
❑ 95SweGloWC-86
❑ 95Top-16
❑ 95Top-370
❑ 95TopHomGC-HGC10
❑ 95TopMarMPB-16
❑ 95TopMysF-M10
❑ 95TopMysFR-M10
❑ 95TopOPCI-16
❑ 95TopOPCI-370
❑ 95TopSupSki-55
❑ 95TopSupSkiPla-55
❑ 95Ult-142
❑ 95Ult-247
❑ 95UltCreCra-17
❑ 95UltGolM-142
❑ 95UppDec-184
❑ 95UppDecAGPRW-20
❑ 95UppDecEleIce-184
❑ 95UppDecEleIceG-184
❑ 95UppDecNHLAS-AS4
❑ 95UppDecPRE-R4
❑ 95UppDecPreR-R4
❑ 95UppDecSpeE-SE125
❑ 95UppDecSpeEdiG-SE125
❑ 95Zen-86
❑ 95ZenZT-16
❑ 96BeAPBisITB-10
❑ 96BeAPLH-3B
❑ 96BeAPLHAut-3B
❑ 96BeAPLHAutSil-3B
❑ 96ColCho-112
❑ 96ColCho-319
❑ 96ColChoCTG-C14A
❑ 96ColChoCTG-C14B
❑ 96ColChoCTG-C14C
❑ 96ColChoCTGE-CR14
❑ 96ColChoCTGEG-CR14
❑ 96ColChoCTGG-C14A
❑ 96ColChoCTGG-C14B
❑ 96ColChoCTGG-C14C
❑ 96ColChoMVP-UD26
❑ 96ColChoMVPG-UD26
❑ 96ColChoSti-S12
❑ 96Don-178
❑ 96DonCanI-101
❑ 96DonCanIGPP-101
❑ 96DonCanIOC-12
❑ 96DonCanIRPP-101
❑ 96DonEli-126
❑ 96DonEliDCS-126
❑ 96DonEliIns-6
❑ 96DonEliInsG-6
❑ 96DonEliP-7
❑ 96DonHitLis-7
❑ 96DonPrePro-178
❑ 96DurAllT-DC12
❑ 96Fla-30
❑ 96FlaBluI-30
❑ 96Fle-48
❑ 96FlePCC-10
❑ 96FlePic-40
❑ 96FlePicDL-7
❑ 96FlePicF5-43
❑ 96KraUppD-57
❑ 96Lea-146
❑ 96LeaLeaAL-17
❑ 96LeaLeaALP-P17
❑ 96LeaLim-2
❑ 96LeaLimBTB-9
❑ 96LeaLimBTBLE-9
❑ 96LeaLimBTBP-P9
❑ 96LeaLimG-2
❑ 96LeaPre-31
❑ 96LeaPreP-146
❑ 96LeaPrePP-31
❑ 96LeaPreSG-29
❑ 96LeaPreSte-29
❑ 96LeaSwe-10
❑ 96LeaSwe(-10
❑ 96MetUni-50
❑ 96MetUniCS-10
❑ 96MetUniCSSP-10
❑ 96MetUniLW-18
❑ 96MetUniLWSP-18
❑ 96NHLACEPC-44
❑ 96NHLProSTA-129
❑ 96Pin-56
❑ 96PinArtP-56
❑ 96PinByTN-2
❑ 96PinByTNP-2
❑ 96PinFan-FC8
❑ 96PinFoi-56
❑ 96PinMin-18
❑ 96PinMinB-18
❑ 96PinMinCoiB-18
❑ 96PinMinCoiGP-18
❑ 96PinMinCoiN-18
❑ 96PinMinCoiS-18
❑ 96PinMinCoiSG-18
❑ 96PinMinG-18
❑ 96PinMinS-18
❑ 96PinPreS-56
❑ 96PinRinC-56
❑ 96PinTeaP-5
❑ 96PosUppD-21
❑ 96Sco-2
❑ 96ScoArtPro-2
❑ 96ScoCheIt-6
❑ 96ScoDeaCAP-2
❑ 96ScoGolB-2
❑ 96ScoSpeAP-2
❑ 96ScoSudDea-3
❑ 96SelCer-72
❑ 96SelCerAP-72
❑ 96SelCerBlu-72
❑ 96SelCerMB-72
❑ 96SelCerMG-72
❑ 96SelCerMR-72
❑ 96SelCerRed-72
❑ 96SkyImp-55
❑ 96SkyImpB-21
❑ 96SP-50
❑ 96SPCleWin-CW8
❑ 96SPInsInf-IN3
❑ 96SPInsInfG-IN3
❑ 96SPx-19
❑ 96SPxGol-19
❑ 96StaCluMO-26
❑ 96Sum-139
❑ 96SumArtP-139
❑ 96SumIce-139
❑ 96SumMet-139
❑ 96SumPreS-139
❑ 96SweSemW-90
❑ 96Ult-55
❑ 96UltCleTheIce-9
❑ 96UltGolM-55
❑ 96UppDec-252
❑ 96UppDecBD-114
❑ 96UppDecBDG-114
❑ 96UppDecGN-X14
❑ 96UppDecIce-85
❑ 96UppDecIceDF-S2
❑ 96UppDecIcePar-85
❑ 96UppDecIceSCF-S2
❑ 96UppDecPP-P1
❑ 96UppDecSS-SS6B
❑ 96WhaBobS-24
❑ 96Zen-77
❑ 96ZenArtP-77
❑ 96ZenZT-4
❑ 97BeAPlaPOT-4
❑ 97ColCho-76
❑ 97ColChoCTG-C4A
❑ 97ColChoCTG-C4B
❑ 97ColChoCTG-C4C
❑ 97ColChoCTGE-CR4
❑ 97ColChoSta-SQ74
❑ 97ColChoSti-S14
❑ 97ColChoWD-W4
❑ 97Don-181
❑ 97DonCanI-67
❑ 97DonCanIDS-67
❑ 97DonCanINP-5
❑ 97DonCanIPS-67
❑ 97DonCanISCS-33
❑ 97DonEli-18
❑ 97DonEli-133
❑ 97DonEliAsp-18
❑ 97DonEliAsp-133
❑ 97DonEliC-27
❑ 97DonEliIns-9
❑ 97DonEliMC-27
❑ 97DonEliPN-9A
❑ 97DonEliPN-9B
❑ 97DonEliPN-9C
❑ 97DonEliPNDC-9A
❑ 97DonEliPNDC-9B
❑ 97DonEliPNDC-9C
❑ 97DonEliS-18
❑ 97DonEliS-133
❑ 97DonLim-1
❑ 97DonLim-38
❑ 97DonLim-169
❑ 97DonLimExp-1
❑ 97DonLimExp-38
❑ 97DonLimExp-169
❑ 97DonLimFOTG-13
❑ 97DonLimFOTG-53
❑ 97DonLin2L-10
❑ 97DonLin2LDC-10
❑ 97DonPre-3
❑ 97DonPre-184
❑ 97DonPreCttC-3
❑ 97DonPreCttC-184
❑ 97DonPreDWT-7
❑ 97DonPreDWT-10
❑ 97DonPreLotT-2C
❑ 97DonPrePM-1
❑ 97DonPreProG-181
❑ 97DonPreProS-181
❑ 97DonPreT-12
❑ 97DonPreT-19
❑ 97DonPreTB-12
❑ 97DonPreTB-19
❑ 97DonPreTBC-12
❑ 97DonPreTBC-19
❑ 97DonPreTPC-12
❑ 97DonPreTPC-19
❑ 97DonPreTPG-12
❑ 97DonPreTPG-19
❑ 97DonPri-19
❑ 97DonPri-186
❑ 97DonPriDD-1
❑ 97DonPriODI-17
❑ 97DonPriP-2
❑ 97DonPriS-2
❑ 97DonPriSB-2
❑ 97DonPriSG-2
❑ 97DonPriSoA-19
❑ 97DonPriSoA-186
❑ 97DonPriSS-2
❑ 97EssOlyHH-10
❑ 97EssOlyHHF-10
❑ 97Kat-53
❑ 97KatGol-53
❑ 97KatSil-53
❑ 97Lea-12
❑ 97Lea-179
❑ 97LeaBanSea-6
❑ 97LeaFirOnIce-5
❑ 97LeaFraMat-12
❑ 97LeaFraMat-179
❑ 97LeaFraMDC-12
❑ 97LeaFraMDC-179
❑ 97LeaInt-12
❑ 97LeaIntUI-12
❑ 97McD-14
❑ 97Pac-14
❑ 97PacCop-14
❑ 97PacCroR-50
❑ 97PacCroRBoSDC-9
❑ 97PacCroREG-50
❑ 97PacCroRHTDC-7
❑ 97PacCroRIB-50
❑ 97PacCroRLCDC-8
❑ 97PacCroRS-50
❑ 97PacDyn-44
❑ 97PacDyn-139
❑ 97PacDynBKS-34
❑ 97PacDynC-44
❑ 97PacDynC-139
❑ 97PacDynDD-8A
❑ 97PacDynDG-44
❑ 97PacDynDG-139
❑ 97PacDynEG-44
❑ 97PacDynEG-139
❑ 97PacDynIB-44
❑ 97PacDynIB-139
❑ 97PacDynR-44
❑ 97PacDynR-139
❑ 97PacDynSil-44
❑ 97PacDynSil-139
❑ 97PacDynTan-6
❑ 97PacDynTan-26
❑ 97PacEmeGre-14
❑ 97PacGolCroDC-10
❑ 97PacIceB-14
❑ 97PacInv-51
❑ 97PacInvAZ-10
❑ 97PacInvC-51
❑ 97PacInvEG-51
❑ 97PacInvFP-14
❑ 97PacInvIB-51
❑ 97PacInvNRB-73
❑ 97PacInvOTG-8
❑ 97PacInvR-51
❑ 97PacInvS-51
❑ 97PacOme-87
❑ 97PacOmeC-87
❑ 97PacOmeDG-87
❑ 97PacOmeEG-87
❑ 97PacOmeG-87
❑ 97PacOmeGFDCC-7
❑ 97PacOmeIB-87
❑ 97PacOmeSLC-8
❑ 97PacOmeTL-8
❑ 97PacPar-70
❑ 97PacParBNDC-9
❑ 97PacParC-70
❑ 97PacParCG-6
❑ 97PacParDG-70
❑ 97PacParEG-70
❑ 97PacParIB-70
❑ 97PacParP-9
❑ 97PacParRed-70
❑ 97PacParSil-70
❑ 97PacRed-14
❑ 97PacRev-51
❑ 97PacRev1AGD-11
❑ 97PacRevC-51
❑ 97PacRevE-51
❑ 97PacRevIB-51
❑ 97PacRevR-51
❑ 97PacRevS-51
❑ 97PacSil-14
❑ 97PacSlaSDC-3A
❑ 97Pin-80
❑ 97PinArtP-80
❑ 97PinBee-3
❑ 97PinBeeGP-3
❑ 97PinBeeGT-4
❑ 97PinBeeT-4
❑ 97PinCer-61
❑ 97PinCerGT-17
❑ 97PinCerMB-61
❑ 97PinCerMG-61
❑ 97PinCerMR-61
❑ 97PinCerR-61
❑ 97PinCerT-17
❑ 97PinEpiGO-16
❑ 97PinEpiGP-16
❑ 97PinEpiME-16
❑ 97PinEpiMO-16
❑ 97PinEpiMP-16
❑ 97PinEpiPE-16
❑ 97PinEpiPO-16
❑ 97PinEpiPP-16
❑ 97PinEpiSE-16
❑ 97PinEpiSO-16
❑ 97PinEpiSP-16
❑ 97PinIns-1
❑ 97PinIns-P1
❑ 97PinInsC-1
❑ 97PinInsCC-1
❑ 97PinInsCG-1
❑ 97PinInsEC-1
❑ 97PinInsT-14
❑ 97PinMin-6
❑ 97PinMinB-6
❑ 97PinMinCBP-6
❑ 97PinMinCGPP-6
❑ 97PinMinCNSP-6
❑ 97PinMinCoiB-6
❑ 97PinMinCoiGP-6
❑ 97PinMinCoiN-6
❑ 97PinMinCoiSG-6
❑ 97PinMinCoiSS-6
❑ 97PinMinGolTea-6
❑ 97PinMinSilTea-6
❑ 97PinPowPac-20
❑ 97PinPrePBB-80
❑ 97PinPrePBC-80
❑ 97PinPrePBM-80
❑ 97PinPrePBY-80
❑ 97PinPrePFC-80
❑ 97PinPrePFM-80
❑ 97PinPrePFY-80

97PinPrePla-80
97PinRinC-80
97PinTeaP-8
97PinTeaPM-8
97PinTeaPP-8
97PinTeaPPM-8
97PinTotCMPG-61
97PinTotCPB-61
97PinTotCPG-61
97PinTotCPR-61
97Sco-80
97ScoArtPro-80
97ScoChel-3
97ScoGolBla-80
97ScoRedW-1
97ScoRedWPla-1
97ScoRedWPre-1
97SP Autl-I10
97SPAut-55
97SPAutlD-I10
97SPAutlE-I10
97SPx-16
97SPxBro-16
97SPxDim-SPX7
97SPxGol-16
97SPxGraF-16
97SPxSil-16
97SPxSte-16
97Stu-6
97Stu-105
97StuHarH-9
97StuPor-6
97StuPrePG-6
97StuPrePG-105
97StuPrePS-6
97StuPrePS-105
97StuSil-11
97StuSil8-11
97UppDec-268
97UppDecBD-149
97UppDecBDDD-149
97UppDecBDPC-PC3
97UppDecBDPCDD-PC3
97UppDecBDPCM-PC3
97UppDecBDPCQD-PC3
97UppDecBDPCTD-PC3
97UppDecBDQD-149
97UppDecBDTD-149
97UppDecCtAG-9
97UppDecCtAG-AR9
97UppDecDV-11
97UppDecDVDM-DM6
97UppDecDVSM-11
97UppDecGDM-268
97UppDecGJ-GJ13
97UppDecIC-IC14
97UppDecIC2-IC14
97UppDecIce-84
97UppDecIceP-84
97UppDecILL-L2A
97UppDecILL2-L2A
97UppDecIPS-84
97UppDecSG-SG14
97UppDecSSM-SS14
97UppDecSSW-SS14
97UppDecTS-14
97UppDecTSL2-14
97UppDecTSS-6B
97Zen-3
97Zen5x7-9
97ZenChaTC-6
97ZenGolImp-9
97ZenSillmp-9
97ZenZGol-3
97ZenZSil-3
97ZenZT-9
97ZenZT5x7-9
97ZenZTG-9
98Be A PPA-195
98Be A PPAA-195
98Be A PPAAF-195
98Be A PPAGUSC-S21
98Be A PPGUJA-G14
98Be A PPPGUJC-G14
98Be A PPPPUJC-P21
98Be A PPSE-195
98Be A APG-195
98BowBes-52
98BowBesAR-52
98BowBesR-52
98Fin-123
98FinDouMF-M33
98FinDouMF-M36
98FinDouMF-M38
98FinDouMF-M40
98FinDouSMFR-M33
98FinDouSMFR-M36
98FinDouSMFR-M38
98FinDouSMFR-M40
98FinNo P-123
98FinNo PR-123
98FinPro-PP3
98FinRedL-R10
98FinRedLR-R10
98FinRef-123
98McD-5
98O-PChr-216
98O-PChrR-216
98Pac-14
98PacAur-68
98PacAurALC-10
98PacAurC-9
98PacAurCF-19
98PacAurCFC-19

98PacAurCFIB-19
98PacAurCFR-19
98PacAurCFS-19
98PacAurMAC-9
98PacCroR-48
98PacCroRLS-48
98PacCroRMP-10
98PacCroRPotG-13
98PacCroRPP-10
98PacDynl-68
98PacDynlFT-10
98PacDynlIB-68
98PacDynlR-68
98PacEO P-10
98PacGolCD-15
98PacIceB-14
98PacOmeEP1o1-10
98PacOmeFr-5
98PacOmeH-87
98PacOmeO-15
98PacOmeODI-87
98PacOmeP-9
98PacOmePI-17
98PacOmePIB-17
98PacOmeR-87
98PacPar-82
98PacParC-82
98PacParEG-82
98PacParH-82
98PacParIB-82
98PacParS-82
98PacParSDDC-8
98PacRed-14
98PacRev-52
98PacRevADC-27
98PacRevCTL-9
98PacRevIS-52
98PacRevR-52
98PacRevS-17
98PacTim-7
98PacTroW-9
98PinEpiGE-16
98RevThrPA-5
98RevThrRA-5
98SP Aut-29
98SP AutSM-S1
98SP AutSS-SS14
98SPxFin-32
98SPxFin-96
98SPxFinR-32
98SPxFinR-96
98SPxFinR-158
98SPxFinS-32
98SPxFinS-96
98SPxFinS-158
98SPXTopP-22
98SPXTopPHH-H13
98SPXTopPLI-L9
98SPXTopPPS-PS27
98SPXTopPR-22
98Top-216
98TopBlaLGR'-GR8
98TopGolLC1-1
98TopGolLC1B-1
98TopGolLC1B0o0-1
98TopGolLC1O0o-1
98TopGolLC1R-1
98TopGolLC1RO0o-1
98TopGolLC2-1
98TopGolLC2B-1
98TopGolLC2B0o0-1
98TopGolLC2O0o0-1
98TopGolLC2R-1
98TopGolLC2RO0o-1
98TopGolLC3-1
98TopGolLC3B-1
98TopGolLC3B0o0-1
98TopGolLC3O0o-1
98TopGolLC3R-1
98TopGolLC3RO0o-1
98TopGolLGR'-GR8
98TopGolLGR'B0o0-GR8
98TopGolLGR'O0o-GR8
98TopGolLGR'RO0o-GR8
98TopO-P-216
98TopRedLGR'-GR8
98UC-76
98UCMBH-BH24
98UCSB-SQ9
98UCSG-SQ9
98UCSR-SQ9
98UD ChoPCR-76
98UD ChoR-76
98UD3-47
98UD3-107
98UD3-167
98UD3DieC-47
98UD3DieC-107
98UD3DieC-167
98UppDec-87
98UppDecBD-33
98UppDecBD-33
98UppDecE-87
98UppDecE1o1-87
98UppDecFF-FF5
98UppDecFQ1-FF5
98UppDecFQ2-FF5
98UppDecFIT-FT22
98UppDecFITQ1-FT22
98UppDecFITQ2-FT22
98UppDecFITQ3-FT22

98UppDecGJ-GJ14
98UppDecGN-GN13
98UppDecGN-GN14
98UppDecGN-GN15
98UppDecGNQ1-GN13
98UppDecGNQ1-GN14
98UppDecGNQ2-GN13
98UppDecGNQ2-GN14
98UppDecGNQ3-GN14
98UppDecGNQ3-GN15
98UppDecGR-87
98UppDecLSH-LS4
98UppDecLSHQ1-LS4
98UppDecLSHQ2-LS4
98UppDecLSHQ3-LS4
98UppDecM-72
98UppDecM1-M9
98UppDecM2-M9
98UppDECMGS-BS
98UppDecMGS-72
98UppDecMOH-OT13
98UppDecMPG-PG1
98UppDecMSF-F8
98UppDecMSS-72
98UppDecMSS-72
98UppDec-P-14
98UppDecPQ1-P14
98UppDecPQ2-P14
98UppDecPQ3-P14
98UppDecQD-33
98UppDecTD-33
98UppDecWFG-WF10
98UppDecWFP-WF10
99AurSty-9
99Pac-149
99PacCop-149
99PacGol-149
99PacGolCD-17
99PacIceB-149
99PacPasAP-12
99PacPreD-149
99RetHoc-29
99SP AutPS-29
99UppDecM-70
99UppDecMGS-S5
99UppDecMGS-GU7
99UppDecMGS-70
99UppDecMGSA-GU7
99UppDecMSS-70
99UppDecMSS-70
99UppDecRG-G9B
99UppDecRG-48
99UppDecRGI-G9B
99UppDecRP-29

**Shanahan, Chris**
96SudWol-20
96SudWolP-21

**Shanahan, Ryan**
92SudWol-12
93SudWol-10
93SudWolP-11
94SudWol-9
94SudWolP-15
95Sla-392
95SudWol-6
95SudWolP-19

**Shanahan, Sean**
76RocCokCan-19
76RocPucBuc-19
77RocAme-21

**Shand, David (Dave)**
77OPCNHL-355
78OPC-356
79FlamPos-18
79FlaTeal-20
79PanSti-57
80MapLeaP-24
800PC-282
80PepCap-98

**Shank, Daniel**
88ProAHL-23
90Bow-235
90BowTif-235
900PC-34
90ProAHLIHL-489
90ProSet-78
90Sco-377
90ScoCan-377
90Top-34
90TopTif-34
90UppDec-99
90UppDecF-99
91ProAHLCHL-119
92SanDieG-23
95LasVegThu-18

**Shannon, Darrin**
89ProAHL-275
900PC-310
90ProAHLIHL-278
90ProSet-592
90SabCam-24
90Sco-410
90ScoCan-410
90Top-310
90TopTif-310
91Bow-24

91JetIGA-28
910PC-214
910OPCPre-146
91Par-201
91ParFre-201
91Pin-243
91PinFre-243
91ProSet-14
91ProSetFre-14
91ProSetFre-515
91ProSetPla-246
91ScoCan-438
91ScoRoo-107T
91Top-214
91UppDec-322
91UppDecF-322
91UppDecF-581
92Bow-385
920PC-332
92PanSti-58
92PanStiFre-58
92Par-436
92ParEmel-436
92Pin-106
92PinFre-106
92ProSet-218
92Sco-36
92ScoCan-36
92StaClu-55
92Top-167
92TopGol-167G
92Ult-246
92UppDec-132
93Don-388
93JetRuf-23
93Lea-194
930OPCPre-261
930OPCPreG-261
93PanSti-192
93Par-499
93ParEmel-499
93Pin-266
93PinCan-266
93Sco-280
93ScoCan-280
93StaClu-191
93StaCluFDI-191
93StaCluFDIO-191
93StaCluO-191
93TopPre-261
93TopPreG-261
94CanGamNHLP-254
94Don-139
94Fla-210
94Lea-251
940OPCPre-254
940OPCPreSE-254
94ParSE-SE204
94ParSEG-SE204
94Pin-279
94PinArtP-279
94PinRinC-279
94TopPre-254
94TopPreSE-254
94Ult-395
94UppDec-483
94UppDecElelce-483
95JetReaC-10
95JetTealss-21
95Pin-69
95PinArtP-69
95PinRinC-69
95Sco-103
95ScoBlalce-103
95ScoBlalceAP-103
96BeaAPAut-183
96BeAPAutSil-183
96BeAPla-183
97PacInvNRB-154

**Shannon, Darryl**
88ProAHL-243
90NewSai-22
90ProAHLIHL-151
91MapLeaP-28
91Par-390
91ParFre-390
91ProSet-490
91ProSetFre-490
91UppDec-493
91UppDecF-493
95JetTealss-22
95UppDec-282
95UppDecElelce-282
95UppDecElelceG-282
96BeAPAut-90
96BeAPAutSil-90
96BeAPla-90
97Pac-72
97PacCop-72
97PacEmeGre-72
97PacIceB-72
97PacRed-72
97PacSil-72
97ScoSab-19
97ScoSabPla-19
97ScoSabPre-19
98Pac-109
98PacIceB-109
98PacRed-109
99Pac-46
99PacGol-46

99PacIceB-46
99PacPreD-46

**Shannon, Gerry**
34BeeGro1P-204
35DiaMatTI-62
36ProvRed-9
370OPCV304E-179

**Shannon, Ryan**
98BowCHL-63
98BowCHLGA-63
98BowCHLOI-63
98BowChrC-63
98BowChrCGA-63
98BowChrCGAR-63
98BowChrCOI-63
98BowChrCOIR-63
98BowChrCR-63

**Shantz, Brian**
88KamBla-22
907thInnSMC-11
94CenHocL-85

**Shantz, Jeff**
907thInnSWHL-174
917thInnSWHL-219
92Cla-15
93BlaCok-5
93Cla-27
93Don-75
93Lea-405
93Par-314
93ParEmel-314
93Pin-428
93Pow-316
93Sco-605
93ScoCan-605
93ScoGol-605
93StaClu-348
93StaCluFDI-348
93StaCluO-348
93UppDec-258
93UppDec-451
93UppDecSP-32
94Don-247
94Indlce-22
94Lea-196
940OPCFinIns-23
940OPCPre-342
940OPCPreSE-342
94Par-46
94Par-289
94ParGol-46
94ParGol-289
94Pin-458
94PinArtP-458
94PinRinC-458
94StaClu-92
94StaCluFDI-92
94StaCluMOMS-92
94StaCluSTWC-92
94TopPre-342
94TopPreSE-342
94UppDec-379
94UppDecElelce-379
95ColCho-124
95ColChoPC-124
95ColChoPCP-124
95Don-209
95Lea-252
95Top-179
95TopOPCI-179
95UppDec-182
95UppDecElelce-182
95UppDecElelceG-182
96ClaGol-15
96ColCho-53
97Be A PPAD-173
97Be A PPAPD-173
97BeAPla-173
97BeAPlaAut-173
97PacInvNRB-46
97UppDec-248
98Be A PPA-31
98Be A PPAA-31
98Be A PPAAF-31
98Be A PPTBASG-31
98Pac-151
98PacAur-43
98PacIceB-151
98PacRed-151
98UppDecM-33
98UppDecMGS-33
98UppDecMSS-33
98UppDecMSS-33
99Pac-60
99PacCop-60
99PacGol-60
99PacIceB-60
99PacPreD-60

**Shapovalov, Vladimir**
69SweWorC-138

**Sharifijanov, Vadim**
92UppDec-612
93Cla-110
93ClaClaGA94-CL6
93Par-527
93ParEmel-527
93Pin-503
93UppDec-574
94Cla-21
94ClaDraGol-21
94ClaProP-207
94ClaTri-T37
94Sco-212

94ScoGol-212
97Don-204
97DonCanI-134
97DonCanIDS-134
97DonCanIPS-134
97DonLim-78
97DonLimFre-78
97DonPreProG-204
97DonPreProS-204
97Lea-163
97LeaFraMat-163
97LeaFraMDC-163
97PinIns-183
97Sco-56
97ScoArtPro-56
97ScoDev-17
97ScoDevPla-17
97ScoDevPre-17
97ScoGolBla-56
98PacOmeH-142
98PacOmeODI-142
98PacOmeR-142
98UppDec-309
98UppDecE-309
98UppDecE1o1-309
98UppDecGN-GN28
98UppDecGNQ1-GN28
98UppDecGNQ2-GN28
98UppDecGNQ3-GN28
98UppDecGR-309
99Pac-247
99PacCop-247
99PacIceB-247
99PacPreD-247
99RetHoc-48
99UppDecM-121
99UppDecMGS-121
99UppDecMSS-121
99UppDecRG-48
99UppDecRP-48

**Sharples, Jeff**
84KelWin-4
86PorWinH-20
87RedWinLC-25
880OPC-48
880OPCSti-74
880OPCSti-205
880OPCSti-249
88PanSti-38
88RedWinLC-21
88Top-48
890OPC-42
89PanSti-66
89Top-42
90ProAHLIHL-559
93LasVegThu-24
94LasVegThu-26
95ColEdgI-156
95LasVegThu-17

**Sharples, Scott**
92St.JohML-21

**Sharples, Warren**
90ProAHLIHL-625
91ProAHLCHL-591

**Sharpley, Glen**
77OPCNHL-158
77Top-158
78NorStaCD-7
780OPC-175
78Top-175
79NorStaPos-14
790OPC-93
79PanSti-63
79Top-93
80BlaBroBac-14
80NorStaPos-18
800OPC-218
80Top-218
81BlaBorPos-25
81BlaBraBac-15
810OPC-64
810OPCSti-116
81Top-W76
820OPC-75

**Sharrers, Matt**
92BriColJHL-155

**Sharron, Eric**
84RicRiv-19

**Shashov, Vladimir**
900OPC-506

**Shastin, Evgeny**
900OPCRedA-6R

**Shatalov, Yuri**
91FutTreC72-29

**Shaughnessy, Scott**
88ProAHL-108
89ProIHL-124
90ProAHLIHL-385
91ProAHLCHL-247

**Shaunessy, Steve**
90CinCyc-20
91CinCyc-23

**Shaver, Al**
93ActPacHOFI-6

**Shaver, Ryan**
95Sla-427

**Shaw, Brad**
820tt67-23
830tt67-26
89WhaJunM-18
90Bow-260
90BowTif-260
900OPC-144

900OPC-279
90PanSti-48
90PanSti-344
90ProSet-110
90Sco-99
90Sco-325
90ScoCan-99
90ScoCan-325
90Top-144
90Top-279
90TopTif-279
90UppDec-90
90UppDecF-90
90UppDecF-327
90WhaJr7E-22
91Bow-7
910OPC-442
91PanSti-311
91Par-62
91ParFre-62
91Pin-88
91PinFre-88
91ProSet-87
91ProSetFre-87
91ProSetPla-45
91ScoAme-289
91ScoCan-509
91StaClu-83
91Top-442
91UppDec-297
91UppDecF-297
91WhaJr7E-24
92Bow-111
92PanSti-265
92PanStiFre-265
92Par-352
92ParEmel-352
92Pin-372
92PinFre-372
92ProSet-124
92Sco-85
92ScoCan-85
92Sen-14
92StaClu-65
92Top-99
92TopGol-99G
92Ult-366
92UppDec-109
93Don-234
93Kra-35
93KraRec-8
93Lea-11
93PanSti-120
93Pin-271
93PinCan-271
93Pow-175
93Sco-15
93ScoCan-15
93SenKraS-22
93Ult-167
94CanGamNHLP-176
94EASpo-202
94EASpo-203
940OPCPre-161
94ParSE-SE122
94ParSEG-SE122
94Pin-162
94PinArtP-162
94PinRinC-162
94Sco-76
94ScoGol-76
94ScoPla-76
94ScoPlaTS-76
94TopPre-161
94TopPreSE-161
94Ult-151
96DetVip-16

**Shaw, David (Dave)**
82KitRan-9
83KitRan-27
84FreExp-2
85NordGenF-24
85NordMcD-19
85NordPro-3
85NordTeal-22
86NordGenF-23
86NordMcD-23
86NordTeal-21
860OPC-236
860OPCSti-31
860OPCSti-133
870OPC-252
870OPCSti-223
880OPC-57
880OPCSti-243
88Top-57
890OPC-39
89RanMarMB-21
89Top-39
900OPC-403
90ProSet-495
90Sco-98
90ScoCan-98
90UppDec-15
90UppDecF-15
91Bow-64
910illGA-21
910OPC-306
91PanSti-294
91Pin-251
91PinFre-251
91ScoAme-161
91ScoCan-161

❑ 91StaClu-306
❑ 91Top-306
❑ 91UppDec-409
❑ 91UppDecF-409
❑ 92Bow-141
❑ 92Pin-343
❑ 92PinFre-343
❑ 92Sco-183
❑ 92ScoCan-183
❑ 92StaClu-162
❑ 92Top-420
❑ 92TopGol-420G
❑ 92Ult-256
❑ 93Lea-249
❑ 93OPCPre-179
❑ 93OPCPreG-179
❑ 93Pin-124
❑ 93PinCan-124
❑ 93Sco-205
❑ 93ScoCan-205
❑ 93StaClu-229
❑ 93StaCluFDI-229
❑ 93StaCluFDIO-229
❑ 93StaCluO-229
❑ 93TopPre-179
❑ 93TopPreG-179
❑ 94BeAPSig-136
❑ 94LigPos-17
❑ 94OPCPre-358
❑ 94OPCPreSE-358
❑ 94Pin-435
❑ 94PinArtP-435
❑ 94PinRinC-435
❑ 94TopPre-358
❑ 94TopPreSE-358
❑ 95LigTeal-17
❑ 97PacInvNRB-188
**Shaw, Dean**
❑ 84BraWheK-4
**Shaw, Harry**
❑ 66TulOil-10
**Shaw, Jim**
❑ 75OPCWHA-55
**Shaw, Lloyd**
❑ 93SeaThu-23
❑ 95SeaThu-27
**Shawara, Mitch**
❑ 93PriAlbR-17
❑ 94PriAlbR-17
❑ 95PriAlbR-18
**Shea, James**
❑ 907thInnSOHL-117
❑ 917thInnSOHL-45
**Shea, Michael**
❑ 93SweSemWCS-271
❑ 94CenHocL-107
❑ 94FinnJaaK-236
❑ 95AusNatTea-26
❑ 95FinnSemWC-185
❑ 95SweGloWC-189
**Shean, Tim**
❑ 92CorBigRed-26
❑ 93CorBigRed-23
**Shearer, Danny**
❑ 75HamFin-18
**Shearer, Rob**
❑ 93WinSpi-14
❑ 94WinSpi-16
❑ 95Sla-419
**Shedden, Darryl**
❑ 95LouIceG-15
❑ 95LouIceGP-16
❑ 96HamRoaA-HRA8
**Shedden, Doug**
❑ 80SauSteMG-5
❑ 82PosCer-15
❑ 83OPC-285
❑ 83OPCSti-228
❑ 83PenHeiP-20
❑ 83PenTealP-30
❑ 84OPCSti-120
❑ 84PenHeiP-21
❑ 85OPC-247
❑ 85OPCSti-102
❑ 86NordTeal-22
❑ 86OPC-153
❑ 86OPCSti-164
❑ 86Top-153
❑ 87OPC-249
❑ 87OPCSti-226
❑ 88ProAHL-238
❑ 89ProAHL-125
❑ 90NewSai-23
❑ 90ProAHLIHL-158
❑ 90ProSet-542
❑ 94CenHocL-120
❑ 95LouIceG-16
❑ 95LouIceGP-17
**Sheehan, James**
❑ 907thInnSOHL-118
❑ 917thInnSOHL-65
**Sheehan, Kevin**
❑ 90ArlIce-2
❑ 90ArlIce-12
**Sheehan, Murray**
❑ 94DetJrRW-6
❑ 95Sla-68
❑ 95SlaMemC-80
**Sheehan, Robert (Bobby)**
❑ 71OPC-177
❑ 71TorSun-57
❑ 72OPC-297
❑ 73QuaOatWHA-20
❑ 76Top-183
❑ 77OPCWHA-47
❑ 78OPC-311
❑ 89NewHavN-11
❑ 98ChaChe-15
**Sheehy, Neil**
❑ 84MonGolF-4
❑ 85FlamRedRP-27
❑ 86FlamRedR-26
❑ 87OPC-213
❑ 87OPCSti-38
❑ 87PanSti-209
❑ 88CapBor-19
❑ 88CapSmo-21
❑ 89CapKod-15
❑ 89CapTealss-21
❑ 90CapPos-21
❑ 90CapSmo-20
❑ 90OPC-188
❑ 90Top-188
❑ 90TopTif-188
❑ 91FlamIGA-19
❑ 91OPC-407
❑ 91ScoCan-636
❑ 91ScoRoo-86T
❑ 91Top-407
**Sheehy, Tim**
❑ 69SweWorC-91
❑ 72SweSemWC-128
❑ 72WhaNewEWHA-14
❑ 76OPCWHA-33
**Sheflo, Alec**
❑ 87KamBla-21
**Shelley, Jody**
❑ 97BowCHL-76
❑ 97BowCHLOPC-76
**Shelton, Doug**
❑ 67Top-53
**Shemko, Mike**
❑ 907thInnSWHL-240
**Shendelev, Sergei**
❑ 94FinnJaaK-142
❑ 94GerDELE-306
❑ 95FinnSemWC-127
❑ 95GerDELE-107
❑ 96GerDELE-52
**Shepard, Bradley**
❑ 907thInnSOHL-316
❑ 917thInnSOHL-55
**Shepard, Ken**
❑ 91OshGen-5
❑ 93OshGen-3
❑ 96BinRan-17
**Shepelev, Sergei**
❑ 82SweSemHVS-61
❑ 83RusNatT-15
**Shepherd, Craig**
❑ 92-TulOil-15
**Sheppard, Brent**
❑ 91AirCanSJHL-D40
**Sheppard, Gregg**
❑ 72OPC-240
❑ 73OPC-8
❑ 73Top-8
❑ 74LipSou-29
❑ 74NHLActSta-35
❑ 74OPCNHL-184
❑ 74Top-184
❑ 75HerSta-7
❑ 75OPCNHL-235
❑ 75Top-235
❑ 76OPCNHL-155
❑ 76Top-155
❑ 77OPCNHL-95
❑ 77Top-95
❑ 78OPC-18
❑ 78Top-18
❑ 79OPC-172
❑ 79Top-172
❑ 80OPC-325
❑ 82PosCer-15
**Sheppard, Johnny**
❑ 23V1281PauC-47
❑ 33OPCV304A-30
❑ 33V252CanG-42
❑ 34DiaMatS-53
**Sheppard, Ray**
❑ 87SabBluS-25
❑ 87SabWonBH-26
❑ 88OPC-55
❑ 88OPCMin-35
❑ 88OPCSti-126
❑ 88OPCSti-161
❑ 88OPCSti-262
❑ 88PanSti-228
❑ 88SabBluS-25
❑ 88SabWonBH-27
❑ 88Top-55
❑ 89OPC-119
❑ 89OPCSti-259
❑ 89PanSti-211
❑ 89SabBluS-20
❑ 89SabCam-23
❑ 89Top-119
❑ 90OPC-446
❑ 90OPCPre-106
❑ 90ProSet-496
❑ 90ScoRoo-97T
❑ 90UppDec-420
❑ 90UppDecF-420
❑ 91Bow-63
❑ 91OPC-289
❑ 91OPCPre-2
❑ 91PanSti-286
❑ 91Par-41
❑ 91ParFre-41
❑ 91Pin-155
❑ 91PinFre-155
❑ 91ProSet-162
❑ 91ProSet-380
❑ 91ProSetFre-162
❑ 91ProSetFre-380
❑ 91ProSetPla-169
❑ 91ScoAme-213
❑ 91ScoCan-213
❑ 91ScoCan-586
❑ 91ScoRoo-36T
❑ 91StaClu-381
❑ 91Top-289
❑ 91UppDec-390
❑ 91UppDec-573
❑ 91UppDecF-390
❑ 91UppDecF-573
❑ 92Bow-25
❑ 92OPC-154
❑ 92PanSti-121
❑ 92PanStiFre-121
❑ 92Par-280
❑ 92ParEmel-280
❑ 92Pin-119
❑ 92PinFre-119
❑ 92ProSet-47
❑ 92Sco-163
❑ 92ScoCan-163
❑ 92ScoSha-20
❑ 92ScoShaCan-20
❑ 92StaClu-85
❑ 92Top-257
❑ 92TopGol-257G
❑ 92Ult-289
❑ 92UppDec-296
❑ 93Don-105
❑ 93Lea-44
❑ 93PanSti-247
❑ 93Par-330
❑ 93ParEmel-330
❑ 93Pin-153
❑ 93PinCan-153
❑ 93Pow-76
❑ 93Sco-83
❑ 93ScoCan-83
❑ 93Ult-310
❑ 93UppDec-398
❑ 94BeAPla-R54
❑ 94CanGamNHLP-91
❑ 94Don-293
❑ 94Fin-50
❑ 94FinRef-50
❑ 94FinSupTW-50
❑ 94Fla-52
❑ 94Fle-65
❑ 94Lea-107
❑ 94LeaLim-26
❑ 94OPCPre-429
❑ 94OPCPreSE-429
❑ 94ParSE-SE49
❑ 94ParSEG-SE49
❑ 94Pin-14
❑ 94PinArtP-14
❑ 94PinRinC-14
❑ 94Sco-175
❑ 94Sco90PC-15
❑ 94ScoGol-175
❑ 94ScoPla-175
❑ 94ScoPlaTS-175
❑ 94Sel-56
❑ 94SelGol-56
❑ 94SP-38
❑ 94SPDieCut-38
❑ 94StaClu-40
❑ 94StaCluFDI-40
❑ 94StaCluMOMS-40
❑ 94StaCluSTWC-40
❑ 94TopFinl-6
❑ 94TopPre-429
❑ 94TopPreSE-429
❑ 94Ult-66
❑ 94UppDec-152
❑ 94UppDecEleIce-152
❑ 95BeAPla-60
❑ 95BeAPSig-S60
❑ 95BeAPSigDC-S60
❑ 95CanGamNHLP-98
❑ 95ColCho-177
❑ 95ColChoPC-177
❑ 95ColChoPCP-177
❑ 95Don-198
❑ 95Don-276
❑ 95DonEli-102
❑ 95DonEliDCS-102
❑ 95DonEliDCU-102
❑ 95DonMar-4
❑ 95Emo-58
❑ 95Fin-16
❑ 95FinRef-16
❑ 95Lea-118
❑ 95LeaLim-106
❑ 95Met-134
❑ 95ParInt-457
❑ 95ParIntEl-457
❑ 95PlaOneoOne-36
❑ 95ProMag-104
❑ 95Sco-127
❑ 95ScoBlaIce-127
❑ 95ScoBlaIceAP-127
❑ 95SkyImp-152
❑ 95SP-130
❑ 95StaClu-215
❑ 95StaCluMOMS-215
❑ 95Sum-77
❑ 95SumArtP-77
❑ 95SumIce-77
❑ 95Ult-49
❑ 95Ult-305
❑ 95UltGolM-49
❑ 95UltRedLS-9
❑ 95UltRedLSGM-9
❑ 95UppDec-254
❑ 95UppDec-348
❑ 95UppDecEleIce-254
❑ 95UppDecEleIce-348
❑ 95UppDecEleIceG-254
❑ 95UppDecEleIceG-348
❑ 95UppDecSpeE-SE161
❑ 95UppDecSpeEdiG-SE161
❑ 95Zen-92
❑ 96ColCho-111
❑ 96Don-210
❑ 96DonPrePro-210
❑ 96Fla-38
❑ 96FlaBluI-38
❑ 96Fle-42
❑ 96Lea-114
❑ 96LeaPre-92
❑ 96LeaPreP-114
❑ 96LeaPrePP-92
❑ 96MetUni-62
❑ 96NHLProSTA-104
❑ 96PlaOneoOne-338
❑ 96Sco-112
❑ 96ScoArtPro-112
❑ 96ScoDeaCAP-112
❑ 96ScoGolB-112
❑ 96ScoSpeAP-112
❑ 96SkyImp-48
❑ 96SP-66
❑ 96Sum-88
❑ 96SumArtP-88
❑ 96SumIce-88
❑ 96SumMet-88
❑ 96SumPreS-88
❑ 96TopNHLP-129
❑ 96TopPicOI-129
❑ 96Ult-68
❑ 96UltGolM-68
❑ 96UppDec-263
❑ 96UppDecBD-66
❑ 96UppDecBDG-66
❑ 96UppDecIce-23
❑ 96UppDecIcePar-23
❑ 97Be A PPAD-46
❑ 97Be A PPAPD-46
❑ 97BeAPla-46
❑ 97BeAPlaAut-46
❑ 97ColCho-99
❑ 97ColChoCTG-C5A
❑ 97ColChoCTG-C5B
❑ 97ColChoCTG-C5C
❑ 97ColChoCTGE-CR5
❑ 97ColChoSta-SQ60
❑ 97Don-101
❑ 97DonCanI-29
❑ 97DonCanIDS-29
❑ 97DonCanIPS-29
❑ 97DonLim-141
❑ 97DonLimExp-141
❑ 97DonPre-36
❑ 97DonPreCttC-36
❑ 97DonPreProG-101
❑ 97DonPreProS-101
❑ 97DonPri-114
❑ 97DonPriSoA-114
❑ 97Kat-65
❑ 97KatGol-65
❑ 97KatSil-65
❑ 97Lea-115
❑ 97LeaFraMat-115
❑ 97LeaFraMDC-115
❑ 97LeaInt-115
❑ 97LeaIntUI-115
❑ 97Pac-80
❑ 97PacCop-80
❑ 97PacDyn-55
❑ 97PacDynC-55
❑ 97PacDynDG-55
❑ 97PacDynEG-55
❑ 97PacDynIB-55
❑ 97PacDynR-55
❑ 97PacDynSil-55
❑ 97PacDynTan-52
❑ 97PacEmeGre-80
❑ 97PacIceB-80
❑ 97PacInv-63
❑ 97PacInvC-63
❑ 97PacInvEG-63
❑ 97PacInvIB-63
❑ 97PacInvR-63
❑ 97PacInvS-63
❑ 97PacPar-84
❑ 97PacParC-84
❑ 97PacParDG-84
❑ 97PacParEG-84
❑ 97PacParIB-84
❑ 97PacParRed-84
❑ 97PacParSil-84
❑ 97PacRed-80
❑ 97PacSil-80
❑ 97Pin-164
❑ 97PinCer-90
❑ 97PinCerMB-90
❑ 97PinCerMG-90
❑ 97PinCerMR-90
❑ 97PinCerR-90
❑ 97PinIns-139
❑ 97PinPrePBB-164
❑ 97PinPrePBC-164
❑ 97PinPrePBM-164
❑ 97PinPrePBY-164
❑ 97PinPrePFC-164
❑ 97PinPrePFM-164
❑ 97PinPrePFY-164
❑ 97PinPrePla-164
❑ 97PinTotCMPG-90
❑ 97PinTotCPB-90
❑ 97PinTotCPG-90
❑ 97PinTotCPR-90
❑ 97Sco-121
❑ 97ScoArtPro-121
❑ 97ScoGolBla-121
❑ 97UppDec-280
❑ 98PacOmeH-47
❑ 98PacOmeODI-47
❑ 98PacOmeR-47
❑ 98PacRev-27
❑ 98PacRevIS-27
❑ 98PacRevR-27
❑ 98UppDec-240
❑ 98UppDecE-240
❑ 98UppDecE1o1-240
❑ 98UppDecGR-240
❑ 99Pac-81
❑ 99PacAur-29
❑ 99PacAurPD-29
❑ 99PacCop-81
❑ 99PacGol-81
❑ 99PacIceB-81
❑ 99PacPreD-81
**Sherban, Trevor**
❑ 89SasBla-8
❑ 907thInnSWHL-85
❑ 90SasBla-6
❑ 917thInnSWHL-297
❑ 98KanCitB-4
**Sherf, John**
❑ 34BeeGro1P-121
**Sheridan, John**
❑ 75OPCWHA-107
**Shermerhorn, Danny (Dan)**
❑ 92BriColJHL-193
❑ 92BriColJHL-206
❑ 93MaiBlaB-48
**Shero, Fred**
❑ 44BeeGro2P-362
❑ 51CleBar-2
❑ 74OPCNHL-21
❑ 74Top-21
❑ 92Par-480
❑ 92ParEmel-480
**Sherry, Simon**
❑ 93SudWol-19
❑ 93SudWolP-18
❑ 94SudWol-19
❑ 94SudWolP-16
❑ 95Sla-401
❑ 95SudWol-7
❑ 95SudWolP-20
**Sherstenka, Dan**
❑ 907thInnSWHL-115
❑ 917thInnSWHL-183
**Sherven, Gord**
❑ 83CanNatJ-13
❑ 84NorStaPos-26
❑ 85NorStaPos-27
❑ 85OilRedR-8
❑ 88OilTenAnn-12
❑ 94GerDELE-302
❑ 95GerDELE-89
❑ 96GerDELE-278
❑ 98GerDELE-295
**Shevalier, Jeff**
❑ 917thInnSOHL-68
❑ 93NorBayC-20
❑ 95PhoRoa-14
❑ 97ColCho-127
❑ 97PacInvNRB-98
❑ 98CinCyc-19
**Shewchuk, Jack**
❑ 34BeeGro1P-32
**Shibicky, Alex**
❑ 34BeeGro1P-293
❑ 36OPCV304D-109
❑ 36V356WorG-90
❑ 39OPCV3011-88
❑ 74SioCitM-18
**Shick, Rob**
❑ 90ProSet-698
**Shields, Allan**
❑ 33V3572IceKP-5
❑ 34BeeGro1P-250
❑ 35OPCV304C-89
❑ 36V356WorG-60
❑ 37OPCV304E-162
**Shields, Jordan**
❑ 96DayBom-4
**Shields, Steve**
❑ 91MicWol-16
❑ 93MicWol-21
❑ 94Cla-62
❑ 94ClaDraGol-62
❑ 94ClaTri-T7
❑ 95RochAmeSS-18
❑ 97Be A PPAD-233
❑ 97Be A PPAPD-233
❑ 97BeAPla-233
❑ 97BeAPlaAut-233
❑ 97Don-51
❑ 97DonCanI-132
❑ 97DonCanIDS-132
❑ 97DonCanIPS-132
❑ 97DonCanISCS-12
❑ 97DonLim-23
❑ 97DonLim-63
❑ 97DonLimExp-23
❑ 97DonLimExp-63
❑ 97DonPre-80
❑ 97DonPreCttC-80
❑ 97DonPreProG-51
❑ 97DonPreProS-51
❑ 97DonPri-115
❑ 97DonPriSoA-115
❑ 97Lea-86
❑ 97LeaFraMat-86
❑ 97LeaFraMDC-86
❑ 97LeaInt-86
❑ 97LeaIntUI-86
❑ 97PacInvNRB-22
❑ 97PacOme-27
❑ 97PacOmeC-27
❑ 97PacOmeDG-27
❑ 97PacOmeEG-27
❑ 97PacOmeG-27
❑ 97PacOmeIB-27
❑ 97Pin-97
❑ 97PinArtP-97
❑ 97PinCer-7
❑ 97PinCerMB-7
❑ 97PinCerMG-7
❑ 97PinCerMR-7
❑ 97PinCerR-7
❑ 97PinIns-77
❑ 97PinInsCC-77
❑ 97PinInsEC-77
❑ 97PinInsSto-19
❑ 97PinPrePBB-97
❑ 97PinPrePBC-97
❑ 97PinPrePBM-97
❑ 97PinPrePBY-97
❑ 97PinPrePFC-97
❑ 97PinPrePFM-97
❑ 97PinPrePFY-97
❑ 97PinPrePla-97
❑ 97PinRinC-97
❑ 97PinTotCMPG-7
❑ 97PinTotCPB-7
❑ 97PinTotCPG-7
❑ 97PinTotCPR-7
❑ 97Sco-44
❑ 97ScoArtPro-44
❑ 97ScoGolBla-44
❑ 97ScoSab-2
❑ 97ScoSabPla-2
❑ 97ScoSabPre-2
❑ 97Stu-79
❑ 97StuPrePG-79
❑ 97StuPrePS-79
❑ 97UppDec-21
❑ 98Be A PPA-269
❑ 98Be A PPAA-269
❑ 98Be A PPAAF-269
❑ 98Be A PPSE-269
❑ 98Be APG-269
❑ 98Pac-110
❑ 98PacIceB-110
❑ 98PacOmeH-214
❑ 98PacOmeODI-214
❑ 98PacOmeR-214
❑ 98PacRed-110
❑ 99Pac-381
❑ 99PacAur-122
❑ 99PacAurGU-122
❑ 99PacAurPD-122
❑ 99PacCop-381
❑ 99PacGol-381
❑ 99PacIceB-381
❑ 99PacPreD-381
**Shier, Andrew**
❑ 94Cla-44
❑ 94ClaDraGol-44
❑ 94RicRen-1
❑ 95MilAdmBO-16
❑ 96RicRen-21
**Shill, Jack**
❑ 34BeeGro1P-251
❑ 34BeeGro1P-327
❑ 36OPCV304D-99
❑ 36V356WorG-39
**Shim, Kyuin**
❑ 92NorMicW-23
**Shinske, Rick**
❑ 78BluPos-19
**Shipley, Blake**
❑ 92MPSPhoSJHL-41
**Shires, Jim**
❑ 71TorSun-248
**Shirjaev, Valeri**
❑ 89RusNatT-22
❑ 89SweSemWCS-84
❑ 90OPCRedA-13R
❑ 91OPCIns-59R
❑ 93SwiHNL-497
❑ 95SwiHNL-377
**Shmyr, Dean**
❑ 91BriColJHL-127
❑ 92DalFre-15
❑ 93DalFre-14
❑ 94CenHocL-86
**Shmyr, Jason**
❑ 97AncAce-18
**Shmyr, Paul**
❑ 70BlaBor-13
❑ 71OPC-6
❑ 71SarProSta-140
❑ 71TorSun-58
❑ 72CleCruWHA-13
❑ 75OPCWHA-5
❑ 76OPCWHA-69
❑ 76SanDieMW-12
❑ 77OPCWHA-59
❑ 79NorStaPos-15
❑ 80NorStaPos-19
❑ 80OPC-66
❑ 80Top-66
❑ 82PosCer-7
**Shmyrko, Gord**
❑ 82MedHatT-18
❑ 83MedHatT-22
**Shockey, John**
❑ 95SpoChi-24
**Shockey, Parry**
❑ 96LetHur-19
**Shoebottom, Bruce**
❑ 88ProAHL-166
❑ 89ProAHL-63
❑ 90ProAHLIHL-130
❑ 90ProSet-411
❑ 91ProAHLCHL-36
❑ 92RochAmeDD-15
❑ 92RochAmeKod-20
**Shold, Terry**
❑ 85MinDul-2
**Shore, Eddie**
❑ 33OPCV304A-3
❑ 33V129-37
❑ 34BeeGro1P-33
❑ 34DiaMatS-54
❑ 34SweCap-29
❑ 36OPCV304D-118
❑ 36TriPos-8
❑ 36V356WorG-5
❑ 38BruGarMS-7
❑ 39OPCV3011-100
❑ 60Top-20
❑ 83HalFP-O14
❑ 85HalFC-223
❑ 91BruSpoAL-30
❑ 94ParMisLP-P7
❑ 99RetHoc-88
❑ 99UppDecCL-10
❑ 99UppDecCLCLACT-AC10
❑ 99UppDecCLCLC-10
❑ 99UppDecRG-G4A
❑ 99UppDecRG-88
❑ 99UppDecRGI-G4A
❑ 99UppDecRP-88
**Shore, Hamby**
❑ 10C55SweCP-12
❑ 11C55-12
❑ 12C57-30
**Short, Kayle**
❑ 907thInnSOHL-215
❑ 917thInnSOHL-349
❑ 92SudWol-19
❑ 93GueSto-4
**Short, Steve**
❑ 83BraAle-16
**Showalter, Chris**
❑ 94DubFigS-26
**Shrum, Steve**
❑ 96KamBla-23
**Shtalenkov, Mikhail**
❑ 91OPCIns-43R
❑ 91SweSemWCS-79
❑ 92RusStaRA-19
❑ 93Cla-148
❑ 93ClaProPro-94
❑ 94ClaProP-49
❑ 94Don-314
❑ 94DucCarJr-22
❑ 94Fle-7
❑ 94Lea-209
❑ 94OPCPre-3
❑ 94OPCPreSE-3
❑ 94Par-4
❑ 94ParGol-4
❑ 94Pin-331
❑ 94PinArtP-331
❑ 94PinRinC-331
❑ 94TopPre-3
❑ 94TopPreSE-3
❑ 94Ult-252
❑ 94UppDec-462
❑ 94UppDecEleIce-462
❑ 95BeAPla-69
❑ 95BeAPSig-S69
❑ 95BeAPSigDC-S69
❑ 95ColCho-227
❑ 95ColChoPC-227
❑ 95ColChoPCP-227
❑ 95Duc-4
❑ 95FinnSemWC-121
❑ 95FinnSemWC-211
❑ 95ParInt-6
❑ 95ParIntEl-6
❑ 95Pin-145
❑ 95PinArtP-145
❑ 95PinRinC-145
❑ 95SweGloWC-164
❑ 95Top-344
❑ 95TopOPCI-344
❑ 95UppDec-91
❑ 95UppDecEleIce-91
❑ 95UppDecEleIceG-91
❑ 96ColCho-4
❑ 96Duc-1
❑ 96UppDec-7
❑ 97Be A PPAD-66
❑ 97Be A PPAPD-66
❑ 97BeAPla-66
❑ 97BeAPlaAut-66
❑ 97PacInvNRB-8
❑ 97PacOme-8
❑ 97PacOmeC-8

❑ 97PacOmeDG-8
❑ 97PacOmeEG-8
❑ 97PacOmeG-8
❑ 97PacOmeIB-8
❑ 97Sco-21
❑ 97ScoArtPro-21
❑ 97ScoGolBla-21
❑ 97ScoMigDPla-16
❑ 97ScoMigDPre-16
❑ 97ScoMigDuc-16
❑ 98Be A PPA-204
❑ 98Be A PPAA-204
❑ 98Be A PPAAF-204
❑ 98Be A PPSE-204
❑ 98Be APG-204
❑ 98Pac-65
❑ 98PacAur-104
❑ 98PacIceB-65
❑ 98PacOmeH-95
❑ 98PacOmeODI-95
❑ 98PacOmeR-95
❑ 98PacPar-127
❑ 98PacParC-127
❑ 98PacParEG-127
❑ 98PacParH-127
❑ 98PacParIB-127
❑ 98PacParS-127
❑ 98PacRed-65
❑ 98PacRev-56
❑ 98PacRevIS-56
❑ 98PacRevR-56
❑ 98UC-2
❑ 98UD ChoPCR-2
❑ 98UD ChoR-2
❑ 99Pac-326
❑ 99PacCop-326
❑ 99PacGol-326
❑ 99PacIceB-326
❑ 99PacPreD-326
**Shuchuk, Gary**
❑ 91ScoAme-315
❑ 91ScoCan-345
❑ 91UppDec-376
❑ 91UppDecF-376
❑ 92Par-484
❑ 92ParEmel-484
❑ 93Don-157
❑ 93Lea-222
❑ 93OPCPre-499
❑ 93OPCPreG-499
❑ 93Par-95
❑ 93ParEmel-95
❑ 93StaClu-351
❑ 93StaCluFDI-351
❑ 93StaCluO-351
❑ 93TopPre-499
❑ 93TopPreG-499
❑ 93Ult-12
❑ 93UltPro-9
❑ 93UppDec-13
❑ 94BeAPSig-36
❑ 94ParSE-SE85
❑ 94ParSEG-SE85
❑ 94StaClu-47
❑ 94StaCluFDI-47
❑ 94StaCluMOMS-47
❑ 94StaCluSTWC-47
❑ 95PhoRoa-15
**Shudra, Ron**
❑ 85KamBla-22
❑ 86KamBla-20
❑ 88OilTenAnn-11
❑ 88ProAHL-91
❑ 89ProIHL-128
❑ 93SheSte-14
❑ 94SheSte-15
❑ 97SheSte-2
❑ 97SheSte-19
**Shulmistra, Richard**
❑ 94Cla-31
❑ 94ClaDraGol-31
**Shupe, Jack**
❑ 81VicCou-14
**Shurupov, Andrei**
❑ 95Sla-54
**Shute, Dave**
❑ 907thInnSWHL-35
❑ 91KnoChe-10
❑ 93RalIce-18
**Shutt, Steve**
❑ 72CanaPos-20
❑ 72CanGreWLP-6
❑ 73CanaPos-22
❑ 74CanaPos-23
❑ 74NHLActSta-151
❑ 74OPCNHL-316
❑ 75CanaPos-18
❑ 75OPCNHL-181
❑ 75Top-181
❑ 76CanaPos-21
❑ 76OPCNHL-59
❑ 76Top-59
❑ 77CanaPos-23
❑ 77Coc-23
❑ 77OPCNHL-1
❑ 77OPCNHL-3
❑ 77OPCNHL-7
❑ 77OPCNHL-120
❑ 77OPCNHL-217
❑ 77Top-1
❑ 77Top-3
❑ 77Top-7
❑ 77Top-120
❑ 77Top-217
❑ 77TopGloS-19
❑ 77TopOPCGlo-19
❑ 78CanaPos-25
❑ 78OPC-63
❑ 78OPC-67
❑ 78OPC-170
❑ 78OPC-333
❑ 78Top-63
❑ 78Top-67
❑ 78Top-170
❑ 79CanaPos-24
❑ 79OPC-90
❑ 79Top-90
❑ 80CanaPos-24
❑ 80OPC-89
❑ 80OPC-180
❑ 80PepCap-58
❑ 80Top-89
❑ 80Top-180
❑ 81CanaPos-25
❑ 81OPC-180
❑ 81OPC-197
❑ 81OPCSti-32
❑ 81OPCSti-44
❑ 81Top-34
❑ 81Top-56
❑ 82CanaPos-24
❑ 82CanaSte-19
❑ 82OPC-192
❑ 82OPCSti-32
❑ 82OPCSti-33
❑ 82PosCer-10
❑ 83CanaPos-26
❑ 83OPC-198
❑ 83OPCSti-6
❑ 83OPCSti-57
❑ 83PufSti-6
❑ 83Vac-55
❑ 84OPC-272
❑ 88EssAllSta-42
❑ 92FutTre76CC-183
❑ 93ActPacHOFI-4
❑ 95ZelMasoH-7
❑ 96CanaPos-26
**Shvidky, Denis**
❑ 97UppDecBD-116
❑ 97UppDecBDDD-116
❑ 97UppDecBDQD-116
❑ 97UppDecBDTD-116
❑ 98SPXTopP-74
❑ 98SPXTopPF-74
❑ 98SPXTopPR-74
❑ 98UC-286
❑ 98UD ChoPCR-286
❑ 98UD ChoR-286
❑ 98UppDecBD-107
❑ 98UppDecDD-107
❑ 98UppDecQD-107
❑ 98UppDecTD-107
**Shyiak, Dave**
❑ 92NorMicW-31
**Sibr, Drew**
❑ 91ArIce-5
**Siciliano, Pete**
❑ 91HamRoaA-16
**Sicinski, Bob**
❑ 73QuaOatWHA-12
**Sidelnikov, Alexander**
❑ 73SweHocS-78
❑ 73SweWorCS-78
❑ 74SweHocS-52
❑ 91FutTreC72-28
**Sideroff, Dean**
❑ 91AirCanSJHL-A35
**Sidorkiewicz, Peter**
❑ 80OshGen-21
❑ 81OshGen-3
❑ 82OshGen-3
❑ 83OshGen-1
❑ 89OPC-11
❑ 89OPCSti-42
❑ 89OPCSti-118
❑ 89PanSti-220
❑ 89Top-11
❑ 89WhaJunM-19
❑ 90Bow-255
❑ 90BowTif-255
❑ 90OPC-14
❑ 90PanSti-38
❑ 90ProSet-451
❑ 90Sco-46
❑ 90ScoCan-46
❑ 90ScoYouS-4
❑ 90Top-14
❑ 90TopTif-14
❑ 90UppDec-69
❑ 90UppDecF-69
❑ 90WhaJr7E-23
❑ 91Bow-13
❑ 91OPC-296
❑ 91PanSti-310
❑ 91Par-286
❑ 91ParFre-286
❑ 91Pin-234
❑ 91PinFre-234
❑ 91ProSet-90
❑ 91ProSetFre-90
❑ 91ScoAme-203
❑ 91ScoCan-203
❑ 91StaClu-125
❑ 91Top-296
❑ 91UppDec-325
❑ 91UppDecF-325
❑ 91WhaJr7E-25
❑ 92Bow-162
❑ 92Kra-35
❑ 92OPC-175
❑ 92OPCPre-112
❑ 92Par-120
❑ 92Par-450
❑ 92ParEmel-120
❑ 92ParEmel-450
❑ 92Pin-371
❑ 92PinFre-371
❑ 92ProSet-125
❑ 92Sco-41
❑ 92Sco-515
❑ 92ScoCan-41
❑ 92ScoCan-515
❑ 92StaClu-27
❑ 92Top-332
❑ 92TopGol-332G
❑ 92Ult-150
❑ 92Ult-367
❑ 92UppDec-14
❑ 92UppDec-480
❑ 93PanSti-121
❑ 93Pin-381
❑ 93PinAllS-17
❑ 93PinAllSC-17
❑ 93PinCan-381
❑ 93PinMas-10
❑ 93Sco-102
❑ 93ScoCan-102
❑ 93ScoFra-14
❑ 93StaCluAS-13
❑ 94EASpo-96
❑ 94EASpo-206
**Siebert, Babe**
❑ 33OPCV304B-49
❑ 33V129-28
❑ 33V252CanG-43
❑ 33V357IceK-8
❑ 34BeeGro1P-182
❑ 34SweCap-30
❑ 36V356WorG-3
❑ 37OPCV304E-150
❑ 38QuaOatP-27
❑ 55Par-62
❑ 55ParQuaO-62
❑ 83HalFP-D14
❑ 85HalFC-59
**Siekkinen, Ari-Pekka**
❑ 93FinnJyvHS-134
❑ 93FinnSIS-136
❑ 94FinnSIS-50
❑ 94FinnSISNP-7
❑ 95FinnSIS-56
❑ 95FinnSISGG-7
❑ 95FinnSISL-46
❑ 96FinnSISRMA-9
**Sigouin, Michael**
❑ 92BriColJHL-21
**Sihvonen, Toni**
❑ 93FinnJyvHS-327
❑ 93FinnSIS-45
❑ 94FinnSIS-136
❑ 95FinnSIS-211
❑ 96FinnSISR-12
**Silfver, Claes-Henrik**
❑ 83SweSemE-119
❑ 84SweSemE-119
❑ 85SwePanS-106
❑ 86SwePanS-101
❑ 87SwePanS-103
**Silfverberg, Conny**
❑ 81SweSemHVS-10
❑ 83SweSemE-66
❑ 84SweSemE-66
❑ 85SwePanS-60
❑ 86SwePanS-42
❑ 87SwePanS-5
**Silfverberg, Jan-Erik**
❑ 72SweHocS-41
❑ 72SweHocS-82
❑ 73SweHocS-157
❑ 73SweWorCS-157
❑ 74SweHocS-187
**Silk, Dave**
❑ 80USAOlyTMP-10
❑ 81SweSemHVS-98
❑ 84OPC-16
❑ 85JetPol-17
❑ 95SigRooMI-31
❑ 95SigRooMI-32
❑ 95SigRooSMIS-31
❑ 95SigRooSMIS-32
**Sillanpaa, Teemu**
❑ 93FinnJyvHS-196
❑ 93FinnSIS-261
❑ 94FinnSIS-56
❑ 95FinnSIS-286
❑ 98GerDELE-306
**Sillers, Gerry**
❑ 71RocAme-16
**Sillgren, Harri**
❑ 93FinnJyvHS-328
❑ 93FinnSIS-49
❑ 94FinnSIS-112
❑ 95FinnSIS-133
❑ 95FinnSISP-6
**Sillinger, Mike**
❑ 87RegPat-24
❑ 88RegPat-22
❑ 89RegPat-18
❑ 907thInnSWHL-186
❑ 90OPCPre-107
❑ 90UppDec-452
❑ 90UppDecF-452
❑ 91OPC-337
❑ 91ProAHLCHL-130
❑ 91ScoAme-327
❑ 91ScoCan-357
❑ 91Top-337
❑ 91UppDec-457
❑ 91UppDecF-457
❑ 92Par-38
❑ 92ParEmel-38
❑ 92Ult-290
❑ 92UppDec-524
❑ 93Don-92
❑ 93Lea-306
❑ 93Par-331
❑ 93ParEmel-331
❑ 93Pow-336
❑ 93Sco-651
❑ 93ScoCan-651
❑ 93ScoGol-651
❑ 93Ult-311
❑ 94BeAPSig-171
❑ 94Lea-394
❑ 94OPCPre-171
❑ 94OPCPreSE-171
❑ 94TopPre-171
❑ 94TopPreSE-171
❑ 94UppDec-200
❑ 94UppDecEleIce-200
❑ 95Don-219
❑ 95ParInt-274
❑ 95ParIntEl-274
❑ 95PlaOneoOne-3
❑ 95PlaOneoOne-225
❑ 95Ult-203
❑ 95UppDec-72
❑ 95UppDecEleIce-72
❑ 95UppDecEleIceG-72
❑ 95UppDecSpeE-SE91
❑ 95UppDecSpeEdiG-SE91
❑ 96CanuPos-26
❑ 96PlaOneoOne-331
❑ 96UppDec-349
❑ 97Be A PPAD-16
❑ 97Be A PPAPD-16
❑ 97BeAPla-16
❑ 97BeAPlaAut-16
❑ 97ColCho-260
❑ 97Pac-336
❑ 97PacCop-336
❑ 97PacEmeGre-336
❑ 97PacIceB-336
❑ 97PacRed-336
❑ 97PacSil-336
❑ 97UppDec-170
❑ 98Fin-28
❑ 98FinNo P-28
❑ 98FinNo PR-28
❑ 98FinRef-28
❑ 98Pac-331
❑ 98PacIceB-331
❑ 98PacRed-331
❑ 98UppDec-147
❑ 98UppDecE-147
❑ 98UppDecE1o1-147
❑ 98UppDecGR-147
❑ 99Pac-396
❑ 99PacCop-396
❑ 99PacGol-396
❑ 99PacIceB-396
❑ 99PacPreD-396
**Sills, Francois**
❑ 94GerDELE-238
❑ 95GerDELE-114
❑ 96GerDELE-59
**Siltala, Mike**
❑ 81KinCan-18
❑ 82KinCan-8
**Siltanen, Risto**
❑ 79OilPos-22
❑ 79PanSti-166
❑ 80OPC-315
❑ 80PepCap-39
❑ 81OilRedR-8
❑ 81OilWesEM-8
❑ 81OPC-122
❑ 81OPCSti-214
❑ 82OPC-129
❑ 82PosCer-6
❑ 82SweSemHVS-157
❑ 82WhaJunHC-16
❑ 83OPC-146
❑ 83OPCSti-257
❑ 83PufSti-14
❑ 83WhaJunHC-16
❑ 84OPC-78
❑ 84Top-61
❑ 84WhaJunW-18
❑ 85NordMcD-20
❑ 85NordTeal-23
❑ 85WhaJunW-19
❑ 86NordGenF-24
❑ 86NordTeal-23
❑ 86OPC-187
❑ 86OPCSti-29
❑ 86Top-187
❑ 87PanSti-159
❑ 88OilTenAnn-48
❑ 94FinnSIS-250
❑ 95FinnSIS-140
❑ 95FinnSISL-92
**Silver, Chad**
❑ 88RegPat-23
❑ 93SwiHNL-55
❑ 95SwiHNL-178
**Silver, Shawn**
❑ 93SudWol-1
❑ 93SudWolP-21
❑ 93WinSpi-2
**Silverman, Andy**
❑ 92MaiBlaB-3
❑ 93MaiBlaB-38
❑ 95BinRan-21
❑ 96BinRan-18
**Sim, Jonathan**
❑ 95Sla-340
❑ 96SarSti-24
❑ 97BowCHL-31
❑ 97BowCHLOPC-31
❑ 98BowCHL-15
❑ 98BowCHLGA-15
❑ 98BowCHLOI-15
❑ 98BowChrC-15
❑ 98BowChrCGA-15
❑ 98BowChrCGAR-15
❑ 98BowChrCOI-15
❑ 98BowChrCOIR-15
❑ 98BowChrCR-15
❑ 99Pac-133
❑ 99PacCop-133
❑ 99PacGol-133
❑ 99PacIceB-133
❑ 99PacPreD-133
❑ 99UppDecM-66
❑ 99UppDecMGS-66
❑ 99UppDecMSS-66
❑ 99UppDecMSS-66
**Sim, Mike**
❑ 95Sla-263
**Sim, Trevor**
❑ 907thInnSMC-20
❑ 90ProAHLIHL-230
❑ 92AlbIntTC-20
❑ 93AlbIntTC-19
❑ 93OPCPreTC-11
❑ 93Pow-494
❑ 93Ult-473
❑ 94MilAdm-22
**Sima, Jaroslav**
❑ 74SweHocS-112
**Simard, Martin**
❑ 88SalLakCGE-11
❑ 90ProAHLIHL-616
❑ 91FlamIGA-20
❑ 91ProSet-526
❑ 91ProSetFre-526
❑ 94MilAdm-23
❑ 96ProBru-13
**Simard, Sebastien**
❑ 96RimOce-25
**Simchuk, Konstantin**
❑ 98LasVegT-19
**Simcik, Jan**
❑ 917thInnSQMJHL-141
**Simek, Martin**
❑ 94CzeAPSE-81
**Simicek, Robert**
❑ 94CzeAPSE-130
**Simicek, Roman**
❑ 96CzeAPSE-202
**Simioni, Mario**
❑ 84MonGolF-15
**Simmer, Charlie**
❑ 79OPC-191
❑ 79Top-191
❑ 80KinCarN-11
❑ 80OPC-4
❑ 80OPC-83
❑ 80OPC-161
❑ 80OPC-165
❑ 80OPC-171
❑ 80OPC-240
❑ 80Top-4
❑ 80Top-83
❑ 80Top-161
❑ 80Top-165
❑ 80Top-171
❑ 80Top-240
❑ 81OPC-142
❑ 81OPC-151
❑ 81OPC-391
❑ 81OPCSti-144
❑ 81OPCSti-236
❑ 81OPCSti-266
❑ 81Top-35
❑ 81Top-W130
❑ 82OPC-159
❑ 82OPCSti-237
❑ 82PosCer-8
❑ 83OPC-162
❑ 83OPCSti-290
❑ 83PufSti-8
❑ 84OPC-90
❑ 84OPC-358
❑ 84OPCSti-266
❑ 84Top-69
❑ 85OPC-87
❑ 85OPCSti-158
❑ 85Top-87
❑ 86OPC-145
❑ 86OPCSti-36
❑ 86Top-145
❑ 87OPC-52
❑ 87OPCSti-137
❑ 87PanSti-11
❑ 87PenKod-23
❑ 87Top-52
❑ 88OPC-250
❑ 90ProAHLIHL-300
❑ 91ProAHLCHL-333
**Simmons, Don**
❑ 44BeeGro2P-66A
❑ 44BeeGro2P-66B
❑ 44BeeGro2P-449
❑ 57Top-14
❑ 58Top-44
❑ 59Top-11
❑ 60ShiCoi-101
❑ 60Top-43
❑ 62ShiMetC-22
❑ 63ChePho-49
❑ 63MapLeaWB-21
❑ 63Par-2
❑ 63Par-62
❑ 63YorWhiB-15
❑ 64BeeGro3P-184
❑ 65Coc-90
❑ 65Top-88
**Simmons, Gary**
❑ 74NHLActStaU-8
❑ 74OPCNHL-371
❑ 75OPCNHL-29
❑ 75Top-29
❑ 76OPCNHL-176
❑ 76Top-176
❑ 78OPC-385
**Simms, Brad**
❑ 95Sla-345
❑ 96SarSti-25
❑ 97SudWolP-22
**Simoes, Steve (Stefan)**
❑ 907thInnSQMJHL-148
❑ 917thInnSQMJHL-197
❑ 94FliGen-20
**Simon, Chris**
❑ 897thInnSOHL-56
❑ 917thInnSOHL-313
❑ 92NorPet-30
❑ 93Lea-416
❑ 93Par-171
❑ 93ParCalC-C13
❑ 93ParCalCG-C13
❑ 93ParEmel-171
❑ 93Pin-219
❑ 93PinCan-219
❑ 93Sco-473
❑ 93ScoCan-473
❑ 93Ult-224
❑ 93UltAllRoo-7
❑ 93UppDec-243
❑ 93UppDecSP-131
❑ 94BeAPSig-58
❑ 94Lea-339
❑ 94NordBurK-24
❑ 94Pin-506
❑ 94PinArtP-506
❑ 94PinRinC-506
❑ 94UppDec-299
❑ 94UppDecEleIce-299
❑ 96ColCho-66
❑ 96Fla-100
❑ 96FlaBluI-100
❑ 96Sco-190
❑ 96ScoArtPro-190
❑ 96ScoDeaCAP-190
❑ 96ScoGolB-190
❑ 96ScoSpeAP-190
❑ 96UppDecBD-67
❑ 96UppDecBDG-67
❑ 96UppDecIce-73
❑ 96UppDecIcePar-73
❑ 97Be A PPAD-65
❑ 97Be A PPAPD-65
❑ 97BeAPla-65
❑ 97BeAPlaAut-65
❑ 97ColCho-269
❑ 97PacInvNRB-213
❑ 97UppDec-205
❑ 97UppDec-387
❑ 98Fin-99
❑ 98FinNo P-99
❑ 98FinNo PR-99
❑ 98FinRef-99
**Simon, Darcy**
❑ 91ProAHLCHL-71
❑ 92FreCan-23
❑ 96GraRapG-23
**Simon, Jason**
❑ 86LonKni-11
❑ 89NasKni-23
❑ 89ProAHL-203
❑ 90ProAHLIHL-569
❑ 91ProAHLCHL-442
❑ 96LasVegThu-19
**Simon, Joey**
❑ 87SudWol-11
❑ 93MusFur-11
❑ 94BraSmo-9
**Simon, Jurgen**
❑ 94GerDELE-194
❑ 95GerDELE-188
❑ 95GerDELE-437
❑ 96GerDELE-118
**Simon, Marc**
❑ 92QueIntP-44
**Simon, Todd**
❑ 907thInnSOHL-270
❑ 917thInnSOHL-211
❑ 92RochAmeDD-16
❑ 92RochAmeKod-21
❑ 93RochAmeKod-22
❑ 94ClaProP-228
❑ 94Don-16
❑ 94OPCPre-469
❑ 94OPCPreSE-469
❑ 94Pin-491
❑ 94PinArtP-491
❑ 94PinRinC-491
❑ 94Sco-234
❑ 94ScoGol-234
❑ 94ScoPla-234
❑ 94ScoPlaTS-234
❑ 94Sel-195
❑ 94SelGol-195
❑ 94StaClu-221
❑ 94StaCluFDI-221
❑ 94StaCluMOMS-221
❑ 94StaCluSTWC-221
❑ 94TopPre-469
❑ 94TopPreSE-469
❑ 94UppDec-456
❑ 94UppDecEleIce-456
❑ 95ColEdgI-157
❑ 95LasVegThu-19
❑ 96DetVip-17
❑ 98CinCyc-20
**Simonen, Sami**
❑ 93FinnSIS-177
❑ 94FinnSIS-33
❑ 95FinnSIS-77
❑ 96FinnSISR-75
**Simoni, Steve**
❑ 83Ott67-27
❑ 84Ott67-23
❑ 92OklCitB-15
❑ 94CenHocL-70
**Simonson, Derek**
❑ 91AirCanSJHL-B32
❑ 91AirCanSJHL-E17
❑ 92MPSPhoSJHL-50
**Simonton, Reid**
❑ 98GerDELE-238
**Simpson, Bobby**
❑ 77OPCNHL-310
❑ 78OPC-372
**Simpson, Bullet (Joe)**
❑ 23V1281PauC-41
❑ 83HalFP-B12
❑ 85HalFC-26
**Simpson, Craig**
❑ 86PenKod-23
❑ 87OilTeal-18
❑ 87OPC-80
❑ 87OPCSti-166
❑ 87PanSti-149
❑ 87PenMask-9
❑ 87Top-80
❑ 88OilTeal-25
❑ 88OilTenAnn-93
❑ 88OPC-27
❑ 88OPCMin-36
❑ 88OPCSti-123
❑ 88OPCSti-228
❑ 88PanSti-62
❑ 88Top-27
❑ 89Kra-16
❑ 89OilTeal-21
❑ 89OPC-99
❑ 89OPCSti-217
❑ 89PanSti-75
❑ 89Top-99
❑ 90Bow-201
❑ 90BowTif-201
❑ 90Kra-52
❑ 90OilIGA-23
❑ 90OPC-240
❑ 90PanSti-229
❑ 90ProSet-95
❑ 90Sco-58
❑ 90ScoCan-58
❑ 90ScoHotRS-2
❑ 90Top-240
❑ 90TopTif-240
❑ 90UppDec-129
❑ 90UppDecF-129
❑ 91Bow-107
❑ 91Kra-81
❑ 91OilIGA-22
❑ 91OilPanTS-20
❑ 91OilTeal-25
❑ 91OPC-460
❑ 91PanSti-130
❑ 91Par-54
❑ 91ParFre-54
❑ 91Pin-196
❑ 91PinFre-196
❑ 91ProSet-69
❑ 91ProSetFre-69
❑ 91ProSetPC-9
❑ 91ProSetPla-40
❑ 91ScoAme-255
❑ 91ScoCan-475
❑ 91StaClu-137
❑ 91Top-460
❑ 91UppDec-286
❑ 91UppDecF-286
❑ 92Bow-150
❑ 92OilIGA-20
❑ 92OilTeal-17
❑ 92OPC-225
❑ 92PanSti-102
❑ 92PanStiFre-102
❑ 92Par-51
❑ 92ParEmel-51
❑ 92Pin-321
❑ 92PinFre-321
❑ 92ProSet-56
❑ 92Sco-260
❑ 92ScoCan-260
❑ 92ScoSha-30
❑ 92ScoShaCan-30
❑ 92StaClu-473
❑ 92Top-356

❑ 92TopGol-356G
❑ 92Ult-66
❑ 92UppDec-309
❑ 93Don-31
❑ 93Lea-344
❑ 93OPCPre-231
❑ 93OPCPre-333
❑ 93OPCPreG-231
❑ 93OPCPreG-333
❑ 93PanSti-237
❑ 93Par-19
❑ 93ParEmel-19
❑ 93Pin-396
❑ 93PinCan-396
❑ 93Pow-301
❑ 93Sco-139
❑ 93Sco-557
❑ 93ScoCan-139
❑ 93ScoCan-557
❑ 93ScoGol-557
❑ 93StaClu-305
❑ 93StaCluFDI-305
❑ 93StaCluO-305
❑ 93TopPre-231
❑ 93TopPre-333
❑ 93TopPreG-231
❑ 93TopPreG-333
❑ 93Ult-277
❑ 93UppDec-430
❑ 93UppDecSP-19
❑ 94BeAPla-R77
❑ 94BeAPla-R120
❑ 94BeAPSig-122
❑ 94Don-112
❑ 94FinRinL-7
❑ 94Lea-198
❑ 94OPCPre-349
❑ 94OPCPreSE-349
❑ 94ParSE-SE22
❑ 94ParSEG-SE22
❑ 94ParVin-V11
❑ 94Pin-294
❑ 94PinArtP-294
❑ 94PinRinC-294
❑ 94Sco-54
❑ 94ScoGol-54
❑ 94ScoPla-54
❑ 94ScoPlaTS-54
❑ 94TopPre-349
❑ 94TopPreSE-349
❑ 94Ult-266
❑ 94UppDec-50
❑ 94UppDecEleIce-50
❑ 95ColCho-231
❑ 95ColChoPC-231
❑ 95ColChoPCP-231

**Simpson, Dave**
❑ 82IndChe-18

**Simpson, Geoff**
❑ 92NorMicW-24
❑ 93HunBli-23

**Simpson, Paul**
❑ 93HumHawP-6
❑ 94HumHawP-6
❑ 97KinHaw-5

**Simpson, Regan**
❑ 91AirCanSJHL-E27
❑ 92MPSPhoSJHL-86

**Simpson, Reid**
❑ 89ProAHL-354
❑ 90ProAHLIHL-29
❑ 91ProAHLCHL-272
❑ 96Dev-33
❑ 97Be A PPAD-47
❑ 97Be A PPAPD-47
❑ 97BeAPla-47
❑ 97BeAPlaAut-47

**Simpson, Shawn**
❑ 87SauSteMG-13
❑ 88ProAHL-28
❑ 89ProAHL-98
❑ 90ProAHLIHL-215

**Simpson, Terry**
❑ 90JetIGA-29
❑ 91JetIGA-29
❑ 95JetTeaIss-4

**Simpson, Todd**
❑ 93SasBla-18
❑ 94St.JohF-20
❑ 95St.JohF-21
❑ 96BeAPAut-105
❑ 96BeAPAutSil-105
❑ 96BeAPla-105
❑ 97ColCho-36
❑ 97Pac-73
❑ 97PacCop-73
❑ 97PacEmeGre-73
❑ 97PacIceB-73
❑ 97PacRed-73
❑ 97PacSil-73
❑ 97UppDec-238
❑ 99Pac-61
❑ 99PacCop-61
❑ 99PacGol-61
❑ 99PacIceB-61
❑ 99PacPreD-61
❑ 99RetHoc-10
❑ 99UppDecRG-10
❑ 99UppDecRP-10

**Simpson, Tom**
❑ 72NatOttWHA-20
❑ 74OPCWHA-16
❑ 75OPCWHA-81

**Simpson, Wade**
❑ 897thInnSOHL-8
❑ 89OshGen-8
❑ 89OshGenP-10
❑ 907thInnSMC-83
❑ 907thInnSOHL-345
❑ 917thInnSOHL-167
❑ 91OshGen-4
❑ 91OshGenS-4
❑ 92OshGenS-1

**Sims, Al**
❑ 74NHLActSta-20
❑ 74OPCNHL-333
❑ 75OPCNHL-136
❑ 75Top-136
❑ 77RocAme-22
❑ 79OPC-272
❑ 80OPC-233
❑ 80Top-233
❑ 81OPC-131
❑ 81OPCSti-66
❑ 81Top-E85
❑ 89ProIHL-138
❑ 90ProAHLIHL-539
❑ 91ProAHLCHL-261

**Simurda, Dave**
❑ 82KinCan-19
❑ 83KinCan-23

**Sinclair, Alan**
❑ 91MicWol-17
❑ 93MicWol-22

**Sinclair, Darren**
❑ 96SyrCru-10

**Sinclair, Doug**
❑ 91JohChi-5
❑ 92DalFre-16
❑ 95SpoChi-6

**Sinclair, Reg**
❑ 44BeeGro2P-363
❑ 51Par-103
❑ 52Par-104

**Sindel, Jaromir**
❑ 81SweSemHVS-56
❑ 82SweSemHVS-78
❑ 89SweSemWCS-179
❑ 93FinnSIS-58
❑ 94CzeAPSE-70

**Sindel, Roman**
❑ 85MinDul-21
❑ 95CzeAPSE-228

**Sinden, Harry**
❑ 52JunBluT-85
❑ 66Top-31
❑ 85HalFC-241
❑ 91BruSpoAL-31
❑ 91FutTreC72-94
❑ 92HalFL-33

**Singbush, Alex**
❑ 34BeeGro1P-183
❑ 40OPCV3012-114

**Sinisalo, Ilkka**
❑ 82PosCer-14
❑ 82SweSemHVS-158
❑ 83FlyJCP-19
❑ 84OPC-167
❑ 85FlyPos-25
❑ 85OPC-188
❑ 86FlyPos-23
❑ 86OPC-36
❑ 86OPCSti-238
❑ 86Top-36
❑ 87PanSti-136
❑ 88OPC-111
❑ 88PanSti-325
❑ 88Top-111
❑ 89FlyPos-22
❑ 90Bow-112
❑ 90BowTif-112
❑ 90OPC-152
❑ 90OPCPre-108
❑ 90PanSti-123
❑ 90ProSet-223
❑ 90ProSet-461
❑ 90Sco-286
❑ 90ScoCan-286
❑ 90ScoRoo-93T
❑ 90Top-152
❑ 90TopTif-152
❑ 90UppDec-120
❑ 90UppDecF-120
❑ 91OPC-510
❑ 91SweSemWCS-206
❑ 91Top-510
❑ 94FinnSIS-90
❑ 95FinnSIS-293
❑ 95FinnSISL-59

**Sinner, Stephan**
❑ 94GerDELE-71
❑ 95GerDELE-57
❑ 96GerDELE-207

**Sioren, Olle**
❑ 67SweHoc-110

**Sip, Radek**
❑ 907thInnSWHL-141
❑ 917thInnSWHL-341
❑ 94CzeAPSE-216
❑ 96CzeAPSE-276

**Siren, Ville**
❑ 86PenKod-24
❑ 87PenKod-24
❑ 87PenMask-10
❑ 88PanSti-335
❑ 90OPC-383
❑ 90ProSet-144
❑ 90Top-383
❑ 90TopTif-383
❑ 91SweSemWCS-9
❑ 92SweSemE-181
❑ 93SweSemE-152
❑ 93SweSemWCS-59
❑ 94FinnJaaK-15
❑ 94FinnSIS-371
❑ 94SweLeaE-246
❑ 95SwiHNL-446

**Sirkka, Jeff**
❑ 85KinCan-14
❑ 86KinCan-23
❑ 87KinCan-12
❑ 89ProAHL-59
❑ 90ProAHLIHL-406
❑ 91ProAHLCHL-477
❑ 92RochAmeDD-17
❑ 92RochAmeKod-22
❑ 93PorPir-19

**Sirois, Bob**
❑ 76OPCNHL-323
❑ 77OPCNHL-351
❑ 78OPC-96
❑ 78Top-96
❑ 79OPC-29
❑ 79Top-29
❑ 80OPC-313

**Sirota, Jason**
❑ 91BriColJHL-64

**Sirvio, Arto**
❑ 89SweSemE-278
❑ 90SweSemE-41
❑ 93FinnJyvHS-179
❑ 93FinnSIS-175
❑ 94FinnSIS-92
❑ 95FinnSIS-292
❑ 96FinnSISR-78

**Siska, Randy**
❑ 83VicCou-22
❑ 84VicCou-23
❑ 85MedHatT-21

**Sissilan, Patric**
❑ 907thInnSQMJHL-34

**Sittler, Darryl**
❑ 70EssPowPla-35
❑ 70MapLeaP-13
❑ 70OPC-218
❑ 71MapLeaP-18
❑ 71OPC-193
❑ 71SarProSta-204
❑ 71TorSun-271
❑ 72MapLeaP-26
❑ 72MapLeaP-27
❑ 72OPC-188
❑ 72SarProSta-204
❑ 73MacMil-26
❑ 73MapLeaP-24
❑ 73MapLeaP-25
❑ 73OPC-132
❑ 73Top-132
❑ 74LipSou-3
❑ 74MapLeaP-21
❑ 74NHLActSta-257
❑ 74OPCNHL-40
❑ 74OPCNHL-219
❑ 74Top-40
❑ 74Top-219
❑ 75HerSta-28
❑ 75MapLeaP-19
❑ 75MapLeaP-20
❑ 75OPCNHL-150
❑ 75OPCNHL-328
❑ 75Top-150
❑ 75Top-328
❑ 76MapLeaP-16
❑ 76OPCNHL-66
❑ 76OPCNHL-207
❑ 76OPCNHL-394
❑ 76Top-66
❑ 76Top-207
❑ 76TopGloI-8
❑ 77Coc-24
❑ 77MapLeaP-14
❑ 77OPCNHL-38
❑ 77Top-38
❑ 77TopGloS-20
❑ 77TopOPCGlo-20
❑ 78MapLeaP-19
❑ 78OPC-4
❑ 78OPC-30
❑ 78OPC-64
❑ 78OPC-65
❑ 78OPC-69
❑ 78OPC-331
❑ 78Top-4
❑ 78Top-30
❑ 78Top-64
❑ 78Top-65
❑ 78Top-69
❑ 79MapLeaP-27
❑ 79MapLeaP-28
❑ 79OPC-120
❑ 79Top-120
❑ 80MapLeaP-25
❑ 80MapLeaP-26
❑ 80OPC-50
❑ 80OPC-165
❑ 80OPC-193
❑ 80OPCSup-20
❑ 80Top-50
❑ 80Top-165
❑ 80Top-193
❑ 81MapLeaP-21
❑ 81OPC-308
❑ 81OPC-312
❑ 81OPCSti-97
❑ 81OPCSti-109
❑ 81Top-36
❑ 82OPC-257
❑ 82OPCSti-114
❑ 82PosCer-14
❑ 83FlyJCP-20
❑ 83OPC-257
❑ 83OPC-258
❑ 83OPC-272
❑ 83OPCSti-3
❑ 83OPCSti-191
❑ 83PufSti-10
❑ 847EDis-38
❑ 84KelAccD-6
❑ 84OPC-168
❑ 84OPCSti-108
❑ 84Top-121
❑ 85OPCSti-36
❑ 88EssAllSta-43
❑ 90ProSet-404
❑ 90UppDec-504
❑ 90UppDecF-504
❑ 91Kra-40
❑ 92FutTre76CC-116
❑ 92FutTre76CC-173
❑ 92FutTre76CC-175
❑ 92FutTre76CC-199
❑ 92OPC-191
❑ 92OPC25AI-8
❑ 92Pin-248
❑ 92PinFre-248
❑ 94HocWit-73
❑ 95ZelMasoH-8

**Sittler, Ryan**
❑ 91UppDec-695
❑ 91UppDecCWJC-82
❑ 91UppDecF-695
❑ 93DonTeaUSA-19
❑ 93MicWol-23
❑ 93Pin-499
❑ 93PinCan-499
❑ 93UppDec-551
❑ 95Ima-65
❑ 95ImaGol-65
❑ 98ChaChe-16

**Sittlow, Chris**
❑ 93MinDul-28

**Sivertson, Daryn**
❑ 84KelWin-6

**Sivertsson, Lars-Ake**
❑ 64SweCorl-22
❑ 64SweCorl-84
❑ 65SweCorl-22
❑ 65SweCorl-84
❑ 67SweHoc-57
❑ 69SweHocS-72
❑ 70SweHocS-34
❑ 71SweHocS-112

**Sives, Dean**
❑ 90ArIlce-13
❑ 91ArIlce-11

**Sjalin, Kent**
❑ 65SweCorl-180

**Sjalin, Tommy**
❑ 83SweSemE-160

**Sjatavalov, Juri**
❑ 74SweHocS-57

**Sjerven, Grant**
❑ 96RicRen-20

**Sjervin, Grant**
❑ 94RicRen-13
❑ 95RicRen-19

**Sjilov, Viktor**
❑ 73SweHocS-135
❑ 73SweWorCS-135

**Sjoberg, Christer**
❑ 71SweHocS-339

**Sjoberg, Goran**
❑ 83SweSemE-68
❑ 89SweSemE-251
❑ 90SweSemE-161

**Sjoberg, Hans**
❑ 65SweCorl-86
❑ 67SweHoc-58

**Sjoberg, Lars-Erik**
❑ 64SweCorl-47
❑ 65SweCorl-47
❑ 67SweHoc-72
❑ 69SweHocS-124
❑ 69SweHocS-198
❑ 69SweWorC-42
❑ 69SweWorC-54
❑ 69SweWorC-55
❑ 69SweWorC-111
❑ 70SweHocS-249
❑ 70SweHocS-280
❑ 71SweHocS-1
❑ 71SweHocS-306
❑ 72SweHocS-8
❑ 72SweHocS-291
❑ 72SweSemWC-45
❑ 73SweHocS-4
❑ 73SweHocS-138
❑ 73SweWorCS-4
❑ 73SweWorCS-138
❑ 74OPCWHA-66
❑ 74SweHocS-20
❑ 74SweHocS-188
❑ 74SweSemHVS-4
❑ 75OPCWHA-109
❑ 76OPCWHA-30
❑ 76OPCWHA-63
❑ 77OPCWHA-21
❑ 78JetPos-20
❑ 79JetPos-21
❑ 79OPC-396

**Sjodin, Tommy**
❑ 86SwePanS-41
❑ 89SweSemE-30
❑ 90SweSemE-177
❑ 91SweSemE-31
❑ 92OPCPre-109
❑ 92Par-79
❑ 92Par-224
❑ 92ParEmel-79
❑ 92ParEmel-224
❑ 92Pin-401
❑ 92PinFre-401
❑ 92SweSemE-336
❑ 92SweSemE-344
❑ 92Ult-323
❑ 92UppDec-528
❑ 93Pow-65
❑ 93Sco-248
❑ 93ScoCan-248
❑ 93StaClu-106
❑ 93StaCluFDI-106
❑ 93StaCluFDIO-106
❑ 93StaCluO-106
❑ 93SweSemWCS-24
❑ 93Ult-233
❑ 94EASpo-32
❑ 95FinnSemWC-61
❑ 95SweGloWC-16
❑ 95SwiHNL-142
❑ 95SwiHNL-512
❑ 95SwiHNL-525
❑ 96SweSemW-48
❑ 96SweSemWAS-AS3

**Sjogren, Olle**
❑ 64SweCorl-59
❑ 65SweCorl-59
❑ 69SweHocS-125
❑ 70SweHocS-79
❑ 71SweHocS-170
❑ 72SweHocS-158

**Sjogren, Soren**
❑ 71SweHocS-92
❑ 72SweHocS-58
❑ 73SweHocS-197
❑ 73SweWorCS-197

**Sjogren, Thomas**
❑ 89SweSemE-229
❑ 90ProAHLIHL-204
❑ 91SweSemE-296
❑ 92SweSemE-323
❑ 93SweSemE-276
❑ 94SweLeaE-46
❑ 95FinnSIS-265
❑ 95FinnSIS-382
❑ 95FinnSISL-52
❑ 95FinnSISSpo-5
❑ 96FinnSISR-65
❑ 96FinnSISRMA-5

**Sjoholm, Bengt**
❑ 71SweHocS-307
❑ 73SweHocS-139
❑ 73SweWorCS-139

**Sjokvist, Gosta**
❑ 67SweHoc-227
❑ 69SweHocS-270

**Sjolander, Par**
❑ 83SweSemE-33

**Sjolund, Andreas**
❑ 95ColCho-340
❑ 95ColChoPC-340
❑ 95ColChoPCP-340

**Sjoo, Hasse**
❑ 83SweSemE-238
❑ 87SwePanS-123
❑ 89SweSemE-107

**Sjostrom, Bo**
❑ 69SweHocS-212

**Sjostrom, Dick**
❑ 69SweHocS-213

**Sjostrom, Lasse**
❑ 69SweHocS-214
❑ 70SweHocS-210
❑ 71SweHocS-299

**Sjtjegolev, Stanislav**
❑ 73SweHocS-127
❑ 73SweWorCS-127

**Skalde, Jarrod**
❑ 897thInnSOHL-2
❑ 897thInnSOHL-193
❑ 89OshGen-2
❑ 89OshGenP-18
❑ 907thInnSMC-91
❑ 907thInnSOHL-346
❑ 91ProAHLCHL-411
❑ 91ScoAme-392
❑ 91ScoCan-282
❑ 91UppDec-446
❑ 91UppDecF-446
❑ 92ProSet-231
❑ 92StaClu-189
❑ 92Top-84
❑ 92TopGol-84G
❑ 92UppDec-91
❑ 93Lea-333
❑ 93Pow-11
❑ 93UppDec-12
❑ 94ClaProP-192
❑ 94LasVegThu-27
❑ 95ColEdgl-15
❑ 95St.JohF-22
❑ 97Be A PPAD-198
❑ 97Be A PPAPD-198
❑ 97BeAPla-198
❑ 97BeAPlaAut-198

**Skarda, Randy**
❑ 90ProAHLIHL-81

**Skarin, Jerry Aberg**
❑ 72SweHocS-202

**Skazyk, Eddy**
❑ 93CorBigRed-24

**Skellett, Jason**
❑ 897thInnSOHL-91
❑ 907thInnSOHL-216

**Skene, Dan**
❑ 92BriColJHL-234

**Skillgard, Johan**
❑ 907thInnSWHL-223
❑ 90BraWheK-16

**Skilliter, Willie**
❑ 917thInnSOHL-275
❑ 93OweSouPla-26

**Skime, Larry**
❑ 69SweWorC-178

**Skinnari, Ville**
❑ 93FinnSIS-285

**Skinner, Alf**
❑ 24C144ChaCig-55
❑ 24V130MapC-5
❑ 24V1452-27

**Skinner, Jim**
❑ 94ParMisL-63

**Skinner, Larry**
❑ 76RocPucBuc-20

**Skjodt, Charlie**
❑ 81IndChe-17

**Skladany, Frantisek**
❑ 96SloPeeWT-25

**Skogland, Mike**
❑ 95NorlowH-30

**Skoglund, Emil**
❑ 92SweSemE-162

**Skoglund, Ulf**
❑ 83SweSemE-143
❑ 84SweSemE-164
❑ 85SwePanS-148
❑ 86SwePanS-151
❑ 87SwePanS-165

**Skogs, Borje**
❑ 71SweHocS-219
❑ 72SweHocS-195

**Skold, Joakim**
❑ 91SweSemE-250

**Skold, Leif**
❑ 65SweCorl-126A

**Skolney, Shawn**
❑ 96SeaThu-24

**Skoog, Borje**
❑ 70SweHocS-127

**Skoog, Robert**
❑ 84SweSemE-171
❑ 85SwePanS-156
❑ 86SwePanS-166
❑ 87SwePanS-171
❑ 89SweSemE-146
❑ 90SweSemE-224
❑ 91SweSemE-152
❑ 92SweSemE-175
❑ 93SweSemE-146

**Skopac, Tony**
❑ 92SweSemE-89
❑ 94SweLeaE-230
❑ 95SweUppDE1DS-DS10

**Skopintsev, Andrei**
❑ 95GerDELE-10
❑ 96SweSemW-140

**Skordaker, Lennart**
❑ 67SweHoc-164

**Skorepa, Zdenek**
❑ 94CzeAPSE-214
❑ 95Sla-120

**Skorodenski, Warren**
❑ 85NovScoO-11
❑ 85OPC-255
❑ 85OPC-264
❑ 87OilTeal-30
❑ 88OilTenAnn-131

**Skorvaga, Norbert**
❑ 95SloPeeWT-24

**Skoryna, Chris**
❑ 917thInnSOHL-36
❑ 93GueSto-18

**Skosyrev, Sergei**
❑ 90OPC-496

**Skoula, Martin**
❑ 98BowCHL-22
❑ 98BowCHL-158
❑ 98BowCHLAuB-A39
❑ 98BowCHLAuG-A39
❑ 98BowCHLAuS-A39
❑ 98BowCHLGA-22
❑ 98BowCHLGA-158
❑ 98BowCHLOI-22
❑ 98BowCHLOI-158
❑ 98BowChrC-22
❑ 98BowChrC-158
❑ 98BowChrCGA-22
❑ 98BowChrCGA-158
❑ 98BowChrCGAR-22
❑ 98BowChrCGAR-158
❑ 98BowChrCOI-22
❑ 98BowChrCOI-158
❑ 98BowChrCOIR-22
❑ 98BowChrCOIR-158
❑ 98BowChrCR-22
❑ 98BowChrCR-158
❑ 98FinFutF-F14
❑ 98FinFutFR-F14

**Skov, Elmer**
❑ 52JunBluT-10

**Skov, Glen**
❑ 44BeeGro2P-210
❑ 51Par-57
❑ 52Par-63
❑ 53Par-48
❑ 54Par-40
❑ 54Top-16
❑ 57Top-30
❑ 58Top-3
❑ 59Top-12
❑ 76OldTim-17
❑ 81RedWinOld-19
❑ 94ParMisL-23

**Skovira, Miroslav**
❑ 95CzeAPSE-237

**Skrastins, Karlis**
❑ 95FinnSIS-326
❑ 95FinnSIS-383

**Skrbek, Pavel**
❑ 96CzeAPSE-82

**Skriko, Petri**
❑ 84Canu-21
❑ 85Canu-20
❑ 86Canu-11
❑ 86KraDra-63
❑ 86OPC-252
❑ 86OPCSti-103
❑ 87CanuSheOil-18
❑ 87OPC-255
❑ 87OPCMin-40
❑ 87OPCSti-192
❑ 87PanSti-347
❑ 88CanuMoh-18
❑ 88OPC-137
❑ 88OPCSti-64
❑ 88PanSti-140
❑ 88Top-137
❑ 89CanuMoh-17
❑ 89OPC-33
❑ 89OPCBoxB-D
❑ 89OPCSti-70
❑ 89PanSti-147
❑ 89SweSemWCS-44
❑ 89Top-33
❑ 89TopBoxB-D
❑ 90Bow-54
❑ 90BowTif-54
❑ 90OPC-316
❑ 90PanSti-298
❑ 90ProSet-306
❑ 90Sco-154
❑ 90ScoCan-154
❑ 90Top-316
❑ 90TopTif-316
❑ 90UppDec-147
❑ 90UppDec-302
❑ 90UppDecF-147
❑ 90UppDecF-302
❑ 91Bow-364
❑ 91CanuPanTS-22
❑ 91OPC-30
❑ 91ProSet-8
❑ 91ProSet-517
❑ 91ProSetFre-8
❑ 91ProSetFre-517
❑ 91ScoAme-188
❑ 91ScoCan-188
❑ 91ScoRoo-72T
❑ 91StaClu-315
❑ 91SweSemWCS-204
❑ 91Top-30
❑ 91UppDec-334
❑ 91UppDecF-334
❑ 93SweSemWCS-79

**Skrlac, Rob**
❑ 96KamBla-24

**Skrudland, Brian**
❑ 81SasBla-10
❑ 83NovScoV-11
❑ 85CanaPos-32
❑ 85CanaPro-20
❑ 86CanaPos-22
❑ 86KraDra-64
❑ 87CanaPos-29
❑ 87CanaVacS-32
❑ 87CanaVacS-34
❑ 87CanaVacS-36
❑ 87OPC-235
❑ 87PanSti-67
❑ 88CanaPos-26
❑ 89CanaKra-21
❑ 89CanaPos-29
❑ 89CanaProF-39
❑ 90Bow-49
❑ 90BowTif-49
❑ 90CanaPos-29
❑ 90OPC-270
❑ 90PanSti-55
❑ 90ProSet-159
❑ 90Sco-238
❑ 90ScoCan-238
❑ 90Top-270
❑ 90TopTif-270
❑ 90UppDec-93
❑ 90UppDecF-93
❑ 91Bow-331
❑ 91CanaPanTS-22
❑ 91CanaPos-28
❑ 91OPC-349
❑ 91PanSti-194
❑ 91Par-314
❑ 91ParFre-314
❑ 91Pin-160
❑ 91PinFre-160
❑ 91ProSet-127
❑ 91ProSet-306

□ 91ProSetFre-127
□ 91ProSetFre-306
□ 91ScoAme-294
□ 91ScoCan-514
□ 91StaClu-129
□ 91Top-349
□ 91UppDec-422
□ 91UppDecF-422
□ 92CanaPos-27
□ 92OPC-45
□ 92Par-266
□ 92ParEmel-266
□ 92Pin-347
□ 92PinFre-347
□ 92Sco-136
□ 92ScoCan-136
□ 92StaClu-114
□ 92Top-408
□ 92TopGol-408G
□ 92Ult-111
□ 93Don-124
□ 93Kra-48
□ 93Lea-325
□ 93OPCPre-26
□ 93OPCPre-508
□ 93OPCPreG-26
□ 93OPCPreG-508
□ 93Par-75
□ 93ParEmel-75
□ 93Pin-188
□ 93PinCan-188
□ 93PinCap-9
□ 93PinCapC-9
□ 93PinExp-5
□ 93Pow-100
□ 93Sco-258
□ 93Sco-505
□ 93ScoCan-258
□ 93ScoCan-505
□ 93ScoGol-505
□ 93StaClu-177
□ 93StaClu-349
□ 93StaCluFDI-177
□ 93StaCluFDI-349
□ 93StaCluFDIO-177
□ 93StaCluO-177
□ 93StaCluO-349
□ 93TopPre-26
□ 93TopPre-508
□ 93TopPreG-26
□ 93TopPreG-508
□ 93Ult-332
□ 93UppDec-96
□ 93UppDecSP-59
□ 94CanGamNHLP-110
□ 94Don-130
□ 94EASpo-51
□ 94Fla-68
□ 94Lea-177
□ 94OPCPre-265
□ 94OPCPreSE-265
□ 94PanPop-1
□ 94ParSE-SE63
□ 94ParSEG-SE63
□ 94Pin-21
□ 94PinArtP-21
□ 94PinRinC-21
□ 94Sco-53
□ 94ScoGol-53
□ 94ScoPla-53
□ 94ScoPlaTS-53
□ 94Sel-126
□ 94SelGol-126
□ 94StaClu-36
□ 94StaCluFDI-36
□ 94StaCluMOMS-36
□ 94StaCluSTWC-36
□ 94TopPre-265
□ 94TopPreSE-265
□ 94Ult-85
□ 94UppDec-331
□ 94UppDecElelce-331
□ 95ParInt-358
□ 95ParIntEl-358
□ 95PlaOneoOne-43
□ 95Sco-74
□ 95ScoBlaIce-74
□ 95ScoBlaIceAP-74
□ 95Sum-136
□ 95SumArtP-136
□ 95SumIce-136
□ 95Ult-63
□ 95UltGoIM-63
□ 95UppDec-276
□ 95UppDecElelce-276
□ 95UppDecElelceG-276
□ 96BeAPAut-205
□ 96BeAPAutSil-205
□ 96BeAPla-205
□ 96Don-118
□ 96DonPrePro-118
□ 96KraUppD-39
□ 96Lea-69
□ 96LeaPreP-69
□ 96SasBla-21
□ 96Sco-133
□ 96ScoArtPro-133
□ 96ScoDeaCAP-133
□ 96ScoGoIB-133
□ 96ScoSpeAP-133
□ 96SP-64
□ 96Sum-39
□ 96SumArtP-39
□ 96SumIce-39
□ 96SumMet-39

□ 96SumPreS-39
□ 96UppDecBD-64
□ 96UppDecBDG-64
□ 97Pac-295
□ 97PacCop-295
□ 97PacEmeGre-295
□ 97PacIceB-295
□ 97PacPar-120
□ 97PacParC-120
□ 97PacParDG-120
□ 97PacParEG-120
□ 97PacParRed-120
□ 97PacParSil-120
□ 97PacRed-295
□ 97PacSil-295
□ 98Pac-182
□ 98PacIceB-182
□ 98PacRed-182

**Skrypec, Gerry**
□ 907thInnSOHL-94
□ 917thInnSOHL-296
□ 920tt672A-20
□ 93DetJrRW-19

**Skudra, Peter**
□ 94GreMon-4
□ 97PacRev-114
□ 97PacRevC-114
□ 97PacRevE-114
□ 97PacRevlB-114
□ 97PacRevR-114
□ 97PacRevS-114
□ 97SPAut-130
□ 98Be A PPA-110
□ 98Be A PPAA-110
□ 98Be A PPAAF-110
□ 98Be A PPTBASG-110
□ 98BeAPG-110
□ 98Pac-358
□ 98PacIceB-358
□ 98PacRed-358
□ 98UC-170
□ 98UD ChoPCR-170
□ 98UD ChoR-170
□ 98UppDec-165
□ 98UppDecE-165
□ 98UppDecE101-165
□ 98UppDecGR-165
□ 99Pac-345
□ 99PacCop-345
□ 99PacGol-345
□ 99PacIceB-345
□ 99PacPreD-345

**Skuta, Vitezslav**
□ 94CzeAPSE-122
□ 96CzeAPSE-196

**Skvorstsov, Alexander**
□ 81SweSemHVS-53
□ 83RusNatT-16

**Skyllqvist, Roddy**
□ 71SweHocS-340
□ 72SweHocS-146

**Slaby, Vaclav**
□ 95CzeAPSE-229

**Slaney, John**
□ 897thInnSOHL-185
□ 907thInnSOHL-47
□ 90UppDec-360
□ 90UppDec-457
□ 90UppDecF-360
□ 90UppDecF-457
□ 917thInnSOHL-1
□ 91CorRoy-24
□ 91UppDecCWJC-54
□ 93Par-494
□ 93ParEmel-494
□ 93PorPir-20
□ 93Sco-636
□ 93ScoCan-636
□ 94Don-298
□ 94Lea-96
□ 94OPCPre-402
□ 94OPCPreSE-402
□ 94Par-257
□ 94ParGol-257
□ 94Pin-214
□ 94PinArtP-214
□ 94PinRinC-214
□ 94Sco-262
□ 94ScoGol-262
□ 94ScoPla-262
□ 94ScoPlaTS-262
□ 94StaClu-39
□ 94StaCluFDI-39
□ 94StaCluFDI-113
□ 94StaCluMOMS-39
□ 94StaCluMOMS-113
□ 94StaCluSTWC-39
□ 94StaCluSTWC-113
□ 94TopPre-402
□ 94TopPreSE-402
□ 94UppDec-39
□ 94UppDecElelce-39
□ 95ParInt-47
□ 95ParIntEl-47
□ 96BeAPAut-100
□ 96BeAPAutSil-100
□ 96BeAPla-100
□ 96FlePic-154
□ 96UppDec-81

**Slanina, Peter**
□ 82SweSemHVS-99

□ 89SweSemWCS-183
□ 91SweSemWCS-109

**Slansky, Vaclav**
□ 93RedDeeR-23

**Slapke, Peter**
□ 69SweWorC-169
□ 70SweHocS-373

**Slapshot, Mascot**
□ 95Cap-24
□ 95Cap-25

**Slater, Chris**
□ 93MicSta-18

**Slater, Ken**
□ 83KinCan-27
□ 84KinCan-4

**Slater, Mark**
□ 97FifFly-5

**Slater, Peter**
□ 72ShaLosAW-13

**Slavik, Jan**
□ 96PeoRiv-21
□ 96PeoRivPA-21

**Slavik, Michal**
□ 94CzeAPSE-11
□ 95CzeAPSE-111
□ 96CzeAPSE-274

**Slavik, Robert**
□ 94CzeAPSE-95
□ 95CzeAPSE-54
□ 96CzeAPSE-240

**Slawson, Randy**
□ 82BraWheK-17

**Sleaver, John**
□ 52JunBluT-177

**Slegr, Jiri**
□ 91StaPicH-29
□ 91SweSemWCS-106
□ 91UppDec-18
□ 91UppDecF-18
□ 92CanuRoaTA-21
□ 920PCPre-54
□ 92Par-196
□ 92ParEmel-196
□ 92Ult-430
□ 92UppDec-515
□ 92UppDecER-ER9
□ 93Don-358
□ 93Lea-31
□ 930PCPre-164
□ 930PCPreG-164
□ 93Par-214
□ 93ParEmel-214
□ 93Pin-417
□ 93PinCan-417
□ 93Pow-256
□ 93Sco-378
□ 93ScoCan-378
□ 93StaClu-42
□ 93StaCluFDI-42
□ 93StaCluFDIO-42
□ 93StaCluO-42
□ 93TopPre-164
□ 93TopPreG-164
□ 93Ult-136
□ 93UppDec-18
□ 93UppDecSP-166
□ 94BeAPla-R123
□ 94BeAPSig-119
□ 94CanuProI-20
□ 94CzeAPSE-209
□ 94Don-294
□ 94FinnJaaK-182
□ 94FinnJaaK-343
□ 94Lea-290
□ 940PCPre-543
□ 940PCPreSE-543
□ 94ParSE-SE189
□ 94ParSEG-SE189
□ 94ParVin-V27
□ 94TopPre-543
□ 94TopPreSE-543
□ 94Ult-385
□ 94UppDec-95
□ 94UppDecElelce-95
□ 95CanGamNHLP-110
□ 95CanuBuiDA-11
□ 95ColCho-144
□ 95ColChoPC-144
□ 95ColChoPCP-144
□ 95ParInt-344
□ 95ParIntEl-344
□ 95SweGloWC-151
□ 95UppDec-42
□ 95UppDecElelce-42
□ 95UppDecElelceG-42
□ 96SweSemW-113
□ 98Fin-46
□ 98FinNo P-46
□ 98FinNo PR-46
□ 98FinRef-46
□ 98Pac-71
□ 98PacDynI-153
□ 98PacDynIIB-153
□ 98PacDynIR-153
□ 98PacIceB-71
□ 98PacPar-196
□ 98PacParC-196
□ 98PacParEG-196
□ 98PacParIB-196
□ 98PacParS-196
□ 98PacRed-71
□ 99Pac-346
□ 99PacCop-346
□ 99PacGol-346

□ 99PacIceB-346
□ 99PacPreD-346

**Sleigher, Louis**
□ 82NordPos-19
□ 83NordPos-26
□ 830PC-301
□ 83Vac-74
□ 840PC-290

**Slemko, Ryan**
□ 907thInnSWHL-322

**Slifka, Dave**
□ 94CenHocL-69

**Slivchenko, Vadim**
□ 93WheThu-15
□ 93WheThuUD9
□ 94WheThu-4

**Sliz, Greg**
□ 84Ott67-24

**Slizek, Ladislav**
□ 94CzeAPSE-268

**Sloan, Blake**
□ 93DonTeaUSA-20
□ 93MicWol-24
□ 93Pin-486
□ 93PinCan-486
□ 99Pac-133
□ 99PacCop-133
□ 99PacGol-133
□ 99PacIceB-133
□ 99PacPreD-133

**Sloan, Tod**
□ 44BeeGro2P-139
□ 44BeeGro2P-450
□ 45QuaOatP-47A
□ 45QuaOatP-47B
□ 48ExhCan-39
□ 51Par-87
□ 52Par-48
□ 53Par-5
□ 54Par-30
□ 54Par-98
□ 55Par-10
□ 55Par-77
□ 55ParQuaO-10
□ 55ParQuaO-77
□ 57Par-T5
□ 58Top-42
□ 59Top-13
□ 60ShiCoi-64
□ 60Top-51
□ 91UltOriS-42
□ 91UltOriSF-42
□ 94ParMisL-112
□ 94ParMisL-144
□ 94ParMisL-174

**Slobodzian, Pete**
□ 34BeeGro1P-252

**Slota, Kevin**
□ 93LonKni-17
□ 95Sla-176

**Slowakiewicz, Andr.**
□ 79PanSti-122

**Slowakiewicz, T.**
□ 79PanSti-119

**Slowinski, Ed**
□ 44BeeGro2P-364
□ 51Par-102
□ 52Par-19

**Slukynsky, Tim**
□ 91AirCanSJHL-C27
□ 92MPSPhoSJHL-166

**Slupina, Roman**
□ 96CzeAPSE-99

**Sly, Darryl**
□ 63RochAme-19
□ 68MapLeaWB-9
□ 70CanuRoyB-15
□ 70EssPowPla-41
□ 700PC-115
□ 70SarProSta-221
□ 70Top-115

**Sly, Ryan**
□ 95Sla-386
□ 95SudWol-19
□ 95SudWoIP-21
□ 95SudWol-21
□ 96SudWoIP-22

**Smagin, Vladimir**
□ 74SweHocS-92

**Smail, Doug**
□ 80JetPos-19
□ 80PepCap-136
□ 81JetPos-16
□ 82Jet-20
□ 820PC-388
□ 83Jet-20
□ 830PC-390
□ 830PCSti-287
□ 83Vac-136
□ 84JetPol-18
□ 840PC-346
□ 85JetPol-18
□ 850PC-175
□ 850PCSti-255
□ 86JetBor-19
□ 860PC-256
□ 87Jet-19
□ 870PC-181
□ 870PCSti-254
□ 87PanSti-367
□ 87Top-181
□ 88JetPol-20
□ 880PC-251
□ 880PCSti-137
□ 88PanSti-158

□ 89JetSaf-25
□ 890PC-294
□ 890PCSti-141
□ 89PanSti-171
□ 90Bow-134
□ 90BowTif-134
□ 900PC-268
□ 90PanSti-308
□ 90ProSet-462
□ 90Sco-196
□ 90ScoCan-196
□ 90ScoRoo-69T
□ 90Top-268
□ 90TopTif-268
□ 90UppDec-105
□ 90UppDecF-105
□ 91Bow-118
□ 91JetPanTS-21
□ 91NordPet-26
□ 910PC-334
□ 91PanSti-111
□ 91ProSet-117
□ 91ProSet-466
□ 91ProSetFre-117
□ 91ProSetFre-466
□ 91ScoAme-12
□ 91ScoCan-12
□ 91ScoCan-592
□ 91StaClu-255
□ 91Top-334
□ 92Bow-362
□ 920PC-196
□ 92Pin-377
□ 92PinFre-377
□ 92Sco-197
□ 92ScoCan-197
□ 92StaClu-334
□ 92Top-459
□ 92TopGol-459G
□ 92UppDec-124

**Smaill, Walter**
□ 10C55SweCP-27
□ 11C55-27A
□ 11C55-27B
□ 12C57-22

**Small, Brian**
□ 83BelBul-10

**Small, Todd**
□ 91AirCanSJHL-A30

**Smart, Cadrin**
□ 917thInnSWHL-344

**Smart, Jason**
□ 88SasBla-20
□ 89SasBla-21
□ 91ProAHLCHL-305
□ 92CleLum-20
□ 95ToISto-17

**Smart, Kelly**
□ 95SlaMemC-35
□ 97BowCHL-106
□ 97BowCHLOPC-106

**Smazal, Heiko**
□ 95GerDELE-292
□ 96GerDELE-319
□ 98GerDELE-259

**Smazal, Mike**
□ 94GerDELE-252

**Smeaton, Cooper**
□ 83HalFP-C13
□ 85HalFC-42

**Smedberg, Peter**
□ 86SwePanS-215

**Smedsmo, Dave**
□ 75StiKah-11

**Smehlik, Richard**
□ 92Cla-40
□ 920PCPre-90
□ 92Par-14
□ 92ParEmel-14
□ 92Pin-393
□ 92PinFre-393
□ 92SabBluS-21
□ 92SabJubF-13
□ 92Ult-262
□ 92UltImp-22
□ 92UppDec-564
□ 92UppDecER-ER1
□ 93Don-40
□ 93Lea-188
□ 930PCPre-521
□ 930PCPreG-521
□ 93PanSti-110
□ 93Par-20
□ 93ParEmel-20
□ 93Pin-152
□ 93PinCan-152
□ 93Pow-33
□ 93Sco-249
□ 93ScoCan-249
□ 93StaClu-107
□ 93StaCluFDI-107
□ 93StaCluFDIO-107
□ 93StaCluO-107
□ 93TopPre-521
□ 93TopPreG-521
□ 93Ult-200
□ 93UppDec-169
□ 94CanGamNHLP-52
□ 94CzeAPSE-128
□ 94Don-136
□ 94FinnJaaK-168
□ 94Fla-22
□ 94Fle-27
□ 94Lea-306
□ 940PCPre-93

□ 940PCPreSE-93
□ 94Par-28
□ 94ParGol-28
□ 94Pin-17
□ 94PinArtP-17
□ 94PinRinC-17
□ 94Sco-129
□ 94ScoGol-129
□ 94ScoPla-129
□ 94ScoPlaTS-129
□ 94TopPre-93
□ 94TopPreSE-93
□ 94Ult-28
□ 94UppDec-181
□ 94UppDecEleIce-181
□ 95Don-76
□ 95Lea-276
□ 95Pin-187
□ 95PinArtP-187
□ 95PinRinC-187
□ 95SweGloWC-147
□ 95Top-168
□ 95TopOPCI-168
□ 96ClaGol-40
□ 96UppDecIce-6
□ 96UppDecIcePar-6
□ 97Be A PPAD-74
□ 97Be A PPAPD-74
□ 97BeAPla-74
□ 97BeAPlaAut-74
□ 97PacInvNRB-23
□ 98Pac-42
□ 98PacIceB-42
□ 98PacRed-42

**Smelle, Carl**
□ 51LavDaiS-81
□ 52St.LawS-34

**Smelle, Tom**
□ 51LavDaiS-84
□ 52St.LawS-21

**Smerciak, Marian**
□ 94FinnJaaK-193
□ 95SloAPSNT-12
□ 96SweSemW-223

**Smetak, Martin**
□ 94CzeAPSE-9
□ 96CzeAPSE-203

**Smicek, Jiri**
□ 94GerDELE-349

**Smid, Karel**
□ 94CzeAPSE-142
□ 95CzeAPSE-246
□ 96CzeAPSE-292

**Smillie, Rob**
□ 92BriColJHL-176

**Smillie, Steve**
□ 917thInnSOHL-367
□ 97KinHaw-11

**Smirnov, Alexander**
□ 900PC-499
□ 910PCIns-60R
□ 93FinnJyvHS-326
□ 93FinnSIS-39
□ 94FinnJaaK-139
□ 94FinnSIS-77
□ 95FinnSemWC-125
□ 95SweGloWC-170
□ 96SweSemW-139

**Smirnov, Andrei**
□ 89SweSemWCS-83

**Smith, Adam**
□ 91BriColJHL-32
□ 92TacRoc-22
□ 93TacRoc-24
□ 93UppDecPOE-E1
□ 96BinRan-19

**Smith, Al**
□ 69MapLeaWBG-32
□ 70EssPowPla-217
□ 700PC-87
□ 70SarProSta-161
□ 70Top-87
□ 71LetActR-19
□ 710PC-27
□ 71SarProSta-61
□ 71Top-27
□ 71TorSun-103
□ 72WhaNewEWHA-15
□ 730PCWHAP-1
□ 73QuaOatWHA-2
□ 760PCNHL-152
□ 76Top-152
□ 770PCWHA-49
□ 790PC-300
□ 800PC-252
□ 80Top-252

**Smith, Alex**
□ 330PCV304B-69
□ 33V129-47
□ 33V252CanG-44
□ 35DiaMatTI-63

**Smith, Alfred**
□ 83HalFP-J15
□ 85HalFC-194

**Smith, Barry**
□ 77RocAme-23
□ 79Roc-22
□ 87SabWonBH-27
□ 88SabWonBH-28
□ 93KnoChe-19
□ 94EriPan-3
□ 94KnoChe-2

**Smith, Billy (Bill)**
□ 730PC-142
□ 73Top-162

□ 74NHLActSta-178
□ 740PCNHL-82
□ 74Top-82
□ 750PCNHL-372
□ 760PCNHL-46
□ 76Top-46
□ 77Coc-25
□ 770PCNHL-229
□ 77Top-229
□ 780PC-62
□ 78Top-62
□ 79IsITrans-18
□ 790PC-242
□ 79Top-242
□ 800PC-5
□ 800PC-60
□ 80Top-5
□ 80Top-60
□ 810PC-207
□ 810PCSti-161
□ 81Top-E93
□ 82McDSti-4
□ 82McDSti-16
□ 820PC-211
□ 820PCSti-60
□ 820PCSti-61
□ 820PCSti-251
□ 82PosCer-12
□ 83IsITealss-14
□ 830PC-17
□ 830PCSti-16
□ 830PCSti-86
□ 830PCSti-316
□ 83PufSti-19
□ 84IsIIsIIN-23
□ 84IsIIsIIN-36
□ 840PC-135
□ 840PCSti-40
□ 84Top-101
□ 85IsIIsIIN-7
□ 85IsIIsIIN-34
□ 850PCSti-76
□ 860PC-228
□ 860PCSti-213
□ 87PanSti-89
□ 88EssAIISta-44
□ 880PC-17
□ 88Top-17
□ 917thInnSOHL-96
□ 93ActPacHOFI-3
□ 93IsICheBA-8
□ 94HocWit-95
□ 97SPAutMoaL-M2
□ 97SPAutTra-T2

**Smith, Bobby**
□ 78NorStaCO-5
□ 79NorStaPos-16
□ 790PC-206
□ 79Top-206
□ 80NorStaPos-20
□ 800PC-17
□ 80Top-17
□ 81NorStaPos-22
□ 810PC-157
□ 810PC-170
□ 810PC-174
□ 810PCSti-88
□ 81PosSta-5
□ 81Top-37
□ 81Top-55
□ 81Top-W131
□ 82NorStaPos-22
□ 820PC-175
□ 820PCSti-188
□ 82PosCer-9
□ 83CanaPos-27
□ 830PC-181
□ 830PCSti-116
□ 83PufSti-14
□ 83Vac-56
□ 84CanaPos-25
□ 840PC-273
□ 840PCSti-151
□ 840PCSti-152
□ 84Top-83
□ 85CanaPla-6
□ 85CanaPla-7
□ 85CanaPos-33
□ 85CanaPos-34
□ 85CanaPos-21
□ 850PC-181
□ 850PCSti-132
□ 86CanaPos-23
□ 86KraDra-65
□ 860PC-188
□ 860PCSti-13
□ 86Top-188
□ 87CanaPos-30
□ 87CanaVacS-26
□ 87CanaVacS-28
□ 87CanaPos-21
□ 87CanaVacS-41
□ 87CanaVacS-86
□ 870PC-48
□ 870PCSti-10
□ 87PanSti-62
□ 87Top-48
□ 88CanaPos-27
□ 880PC-88
□ 880PCBoxB-D
□ 880PCSti-44
□ 88PanSti-261
□ 88Top-88
□ 88TopBoxB-D

89CanaKra-22
89CanaPos-30
89CanaProF-15
89Kra-26
89OPC-188
89OPCSti-47
89PanSti-236
89Top-188
90Bow-51
90BowTif-51
90Kra-53
90OPC-287
90OPCPre-109
90PanSti-52
90ProSet-160
90ProSet-463
90Sco-61
90ScoCan-61
90ScoRoo-75T
90Top-287
90TopTif-287
90UppDec-72
90UppDec-406
90UppDecF-72
90UppDecF-406
91Bow-117
91Kra-82
91OPC-398
91PanSti-113
91Par-83
91Par-217
91ParFre-83
91ParFre-217
91Pin-210
91PinFre-210
91ProSet-115
91ProSet-289
91ProSetFre-115
91ProSetFre-289
91ProSetPlaPC-PC13
91ScoAme-32
91ScoCan-32
91StaClu-25
91Top-398
91UppDec-293
91UppDecF-293
92Bow-54
92OPC-396
92PanSti-96
92PanStiFre-96
92Pin-142
92PinFre-142
92ProSet-81
92ProSet-259
92Sco-205
92Sco-446
92ScoCan-205
92ScoCan-446
92StaClu-427
92Top-388
92TopGol-388G
92Ult-97

**Smith, Brad**
80FlamPos-20
80PepCap-18
81OPC-103
86MapLeaP-18
87MapLeaPLA-22
87PanSti-335
89WinSpi-16
907thInnSOHL-200

**Smith, Brandon**
89PorWinH-20
907thInnSWHL-314
917thInnSWHL-27
94DayBom-17
95AdiRedW-21

**Smith, Brian**
60Par-27

**Smith, Chris**
800shGen-20
810shGen-2
83MonAlp-2

**Smith, Chris (MSU)**
93MicSta-19

**Smith, Clint**
34BeeGro1P-294
390PCV3011-35
91ProSetHI-6

**Smith, Dallas**
60ShiCoi-116
60TopSta-47
61ShiCoi-2
61Top-4
62Top-9
66Top-101
66TopUSAT-3
67Top-41
68OPC-136
68ShiCoi-13
69OPC-25
69Top-25
70BruPos-17
70BruTealss-8
70EssPowPla-69
700PC-137
70SarProSta-16
71BruTealss-15
71LetActR-5
710PC-170
71SarProSta-11
71TorSun-17
720PC-21
720PC-135
72SarProSta-19

72Top-45
730PC-167
73Top-42
74NHLActSta-33
740PCNHL-146
74Top-146
750PCNHL-118
75Top-118
760PCNHL-105
76Top-105

**Smith, Damian**
94FinnJaaK-319
96GuiFla-12

**Smith, Dan**
95TriAme-23

**Smith, Darcy**
93SeaThu-25
95MedHatT-19
96KamBla-25

**Smith, Darin**
85LonKni-12
88ProIHL-87
89ProIHL-9
90KanCitBla-8
90ProAHLIHL-591
91ProAHLCHL-248

**Smith, Darren**
90ForSasTra-16

**Smith, Dave**
94BinRan-20

**Smith, David**
97FifFly-20

**Smith, Dean**
94SheSte-8

**Smith, Denis**
51LavDaiS-12
52St.LawS-42

**Smith, Dennis**
81KinCan-21
82KinCan-2
83KinCan-2
88ProAHL-9
89ProAHL-96
91ProAHLCHL-54
95Cla-36
97BowCHL-37
97BowCHLOPC-37

**Smith, Derek**
780PC-222
78Top-222
790PC-89
79Top-89
800PC-199
80Top-199
810PC-25
810PCSti-59
81Top-E79
820PC-95
82PosCer-5

**Smith, Derrick**
85FlyPos-26
86FlyPos-24
87PanSti-135
89FlyPos-23
89PanSti-304
90FlyPos-22
900PC-463
90ProSet-503
91Bow-245
910PC-486
91PanSti-232
91ProSet-174
91ProSetFre-174
91ScoCan-444
91Top-486
920PC-363
92ColEdgI-142

**Smith, Des**
34BeeGro1P-206
370PCV304E-148
390PCV3011-77

**Smith, DJ (Denis)**
94WinSpi-7
95Cla-98
95Sla-410
97Don-206
97DonCanI-142
97DonCanIDS-142
97DonCanIPS-142
97DonLim-37
97DonLimExp-37
97DonPreProG-206
97DonPreProS-206
97St.JohML-22
97UppDec-194

**Smith, Don**
10C55SweCP-19
11C55-19
12C57-12

**Smith, Doug**
820PC-160
82PosCer-8
84KinSmo-15
840PC-91
860PC-202
86SabBluS-27
86SabBluSSma-27
87SabBluS-26
87SabWonBH-28
88OilTenAnn-69
91FerStaB-29

**Smith, Ed**
84SudWol-16

**Smith, Fiona**

97ColCho-293

**Smith, Floyd**
44BeeGro2P-211
63Par-57
63YorWhiB-42
64BeeGro3P-94A
64BeeGro3P-94B
64BeeGro3P-94C
64CocCap-50
64Top-42
64TorSta-43
65Coc-49
65Top-109
66Top-106
67Top-52
68MapLeaWB-10
680PC-130
68PosCerM-24
68ShiCoi-127
68Top-130
690PC-49
69Top-49
70DadCoo-123
70EssPowPla-85
700PC-140
70SarProSta-30
710PC-158
740PCNHL-176
74Top-176
79MapLeaP-29
94ParTalB-45
95Par66-52
95Par66Coi-52

**Smith, Frank D**
83HalFP-G13
85HalFC-103

**Smith, Gairin**
897thInnSOHL-65
907thInnSOHL-217
917thInnSOHL-100
93RoaExp-17
94WheThu-11

**Smith, Gary**
680PC-176
68ShiCoi-115
690PC-78
69Top-78
70ColSta-90
70EssPowPla-91
700PC-69
710PC-117
72SarProSta-43
71Top-124
71TorSun-80
720PC-117
72SarProSta-61
72SweSemWC-171
72Top-144
73CanuRoyB-17
730PC-126
73Top-126
74CanuRoyB-19
74LipSou-15
74NHLActSta-274
740PCNHL-22
74Top-22
75CanuRoyB-20
750PCNHL-115
75Top-115
760PCNHL-317
770PCNHL-184
77Top-184
79JetPos-22
790PC-103
79Top-103

**Smith, Geoff**
89OilTeal-22
90Bow-192
90BowTif-192
90OilIGA-24
900PC-33
90ProSet-446
90Sco-326
90Sco-373
90ScoCan-326
90ScoCan-373
90Top-33
90TopTif-33
90UppDec-326
90UppDecF-326
91Bow-112
91OilIGA-23
91OilIPanTS-21
91OilTeal-26
910PC-301
91Pin-283
91PinFre-283
91ProSet-384
91ProSetFre-384
91ScoAme-87
91ScoCan-87
91StaClu-42
91Top-301
92Bow-95
92OilIGA-21
92OilTeal-18
92OPC-338
92Pin-192
92PinFre-192
92Sco-192
92ScoCan-192

92StaClu-84
92Top-275
92TopGol-275G
93Don-112
93Don-435
93Lea-302
93Pin-416
93PinCan-416
93Sco-306
93Sco-646
93ScoCan-306
93ScoCan-646
93ScoGol-646
94Lea-366
94Par-82
94ParGol-82
94Pin-354
94PinArtP-354
94PinRinC-354
94UppDec-109
94UppDecEleIce-109
98CinCyc-21

**Smith, Gord**
74CapWhiB-24
760PCNHL-303
770PCNHL-387
780PC-347
79JetPos-23
790PC-285
82BraWheK-18

**Smith, Greg**
770PCNHL-269
78NorStaCD-3
780PC-303
79NorStaPos-17
790PC-11
79Top-11
80NorStaPos-21
810PC-168
81Top-W112
820PC-96
82PosCer-5
830PC-130
830PCSti-140
840PC-64
86CapKod-24
86CapPol-23
87CapKod-19
87CapTealss-21
87RedWinLC-26
92DalFre-17
93DalFre-15
94CenHocL-121
99WicThu-20

**Smith, Hooley (Reginald)**
24C144ChaCig-56
24V1452-5
33V3572IceKP-6
33V357IceK-31
34BeeGro1P-207
34BeeGro1P-253
34SweCap-25
350PCV304C-76
36ChaPos-3
360PCV304D-132
36V356WorG-20
390PCV3011-17
83HalFP-C14
85HalFC-43

**Smith, Jarrett**
97BowCHL-122
97BowCHLAu-2
97BowCHLBB-15
97BowCHLBowBesAR-15
97BowCHLBowBesR-15
97BowCHLOPC-122

**Smith, Jason**
907thInnSWHL-62
917thInnSWHL-226
917thInnSWHL-309
92Cla-10
93Don-182
93Lea-389
93Par-379
93ParEmel-379
93Pin-433
93PinCan-433
93Pow-381
93Sco-613
93ScoCan-613
93ScoGol-613
93Ult-363
93UltWavF-17
93UppDec-252
94ClaProP-135
94Don-256
94EriPan-13
94Lea-245
940PCPre-344
940PCPreSE-344
94Par-130
94ParGol-130
94Pin-417
94PinArtP-417
94PinRinC-417
94StaClu-83
94StaCluFDI-83
94StaCluMOMS-83
94StaCluSTWC-83
94TopPre-344
94TopPreSE-344
94Ult-322
95Don-279
96ClaGol-10
96Dev-26

97Be A PPAD-191
97Be A PPAPD-191
97BeAPla-191
97BeAPlaAut-191
97PacInvNRB-196
98Be A PPA-139
98Be A PPAA-139
98Be A PPAAF-139
98Be A PPTBASG-139
98Be APG-139
98Pac-421
98PacIceB-421
98PacRed-421

**Smith, Jeff**
907thInnSOHL-218
917thInnSOHL-290

**Smith, Jeff (80s)**
97GuiFla-19

**Smith, Jim**
87SudWol-9
88SudWol-9

**Smith, Joel**
82NorBayC-20

**Smith, John**
51LavDaiQSHL-44

**Smith, Julian**
96DetWha-14

**Smith, Kenny**
44BeeGro2P-67

**Smith, Mark**
95LetHur-22
95SasBla-20
96LetHur-20
98BowCHL-70
98BowCHLGA-70
98BowCHLOI-70
98BowChrC-70
98BowChrCGA-70
98BowChrCGAR-70
98BowChrCOI-70
98BowChrCOIR-70
98BowChrCR-70

**Smith, Martin**
91AirCanSJHL-B29
91AirCanSJHL-D15
91AirCanSJHLAS-4
92RicRen-17

**Smith, Matt**
917thInnSWHL-63

**Smith, Mike (Michael)**
91LakSupSL-25
93Cla-82
93RoaExp-18
94ClaProP-244
94RoaExp-5
95RoaExp-9
96RoaExp-5

**Smith, Neil**
92WesMic-23

**Smith, Normie**
34BeeGro1P-123
36V356WorG-74

**Smith, Randy**
83SasBla-12
88ProIHL-34
89ProIHL-87
90AlbIntTC-18
91AlbIntTC-22
92ScoCanO-4
93LasVegThu-25

**Smith, Rick**
70BruPos-18
70BruTealss-17
70EssPowPla-61
700PC-135
70SarProSta-11
71BruTealss-7
710PC-174
71SarProSta-5
720PC-23
720PC-284
72Top-34
74FigSaiWHA-20
74TeaCanLWHA-20
750PCWHA-41
760PCNHL-269
770PCNHL-104
77Top-104
780PC-164
78Top-164
790PC-59
79Top-59

**Smith, Rick (Jrs)**
83SasBla-21

**Smith, Ron**
91ProAHLCHL-212
96CinCyc-NNO

**Smith, Russell**
96RimOceU-9

**Smith, Ryan**
907thInnSWHL-131
917thInnSWHL-205
91AirCanSJHL-C11
92BraWheK-21
93LetHur-15

**Smith, Sandy**
90ProAHLIHL-373
91ProAHLCHL-299

**Smith, Scott**
92NorMicW-25
93NorMicW-25

**Smith, Sid**
44BeeGro2P-451

45QuaOatP-48A
45QuaOatP-48B
48ExhCan-38
51Par-84
52Par-45
53Par-2
54Par-22
55Par-2
55Par-75
55ParQua0-2
55ParQua0-75
57Par-T10
91UltOriS-43
91UltOriSF-43
94ParMisL-109

**Smith, Simon**
97GuiFla-19

**Smith, Steve**
80SauSteMG-8
81SauSteMG-20
82SauSteMG-19
83MonAlp-10
83SprInd-22
84NovSco0-11
85OilRedR-5
86OilRedR-5
86OilTeal-5
87OilTeal-5
87PanSti-259
88OilTeal-26
88OilTenAnn-121
880PC-252
880PCSti-225
88PanSti-55
88ProAHL-249
88SalLakCGE-7
89KitRan-28
89Kra-77
890ilTeal-23
890PC-228
890PCSti-223
89PanSti-83
89ProAHL-272
907thInnSMC-37
907thInnSOHL-199
907thInnSOHL-240
90Bow-200
90BowTif-200
90KitRan-9
900illGA-25
900PC-368
90PanSti-226
90ProAHLIHL-287
90ProSet-96
90Sco-129
90ScoCan-129
90Top-368
90TopTif-368
90UppDec-148
90UppDecF-148
917thInnSOHL-187
91BlaCok-23
91Bow-106
91Bow-417
91Kra-85
910ilPanTS-22
910PC-21
910PCPre-136
91PanSti-121
91Par-31
91ParFre-31
91Pin-18
91PinFre-18
91ProSet-73
91ProSet-370
91ProSetFre-73
91ProSetFre-284
91ProSetFre-370
91ProSetPla-27
91ScoAme-11
91ScoCan-11
91ScoCan-623
91ScoRoo-73T
91StaClu-230
91Top-21
91UppDec-350
91UppDecF-350
92Bow-24
92OPC-108
92PanSti-12
92PanStiFre-12
92Par-32
92Par-444
92ParEmel-32
92ParEmel-444
92Pin-57
92PinFre-57
92ProSet-37
92Sco-48
92ScoCan-48
92StaClu-383
92Top-315
92TopGol-315G
92Ult-42
93BlaCok-20
93Don-68
93Lea-95
930PCPre-39
930PCPreG-39
93PanSti-154
93Par-310
93ParEmel-310
93Pin-70
93PinCan-70

93Pow-55
93Sco-192
93ScoCan-192
93StaClu-218
93StaCluFDI-218
93StaCluFDIO-218
93StaClu0-218
93TopPre-39
93TopPreG-39
93Ult-231
94BeAPla-R62
94CanGamNHLP-74
94Don-183
94EASpo-26
94FinnJaaK-85
94FinRinL-12
94Fla-37
94Fle-46
94Lea-257
940PCPre-133
940PCPreSE-133
94Pin-211
94PinArtP-211
94PinRinC-211
94Sco-121
94ScoGol-121
94ScoPla-121
94ScoPlaTS-121
94TopPre-133
94TopPreSE-133
94Ult-45
95BeAPla-123
95BeAPSig-S123
95BeAPSigDC-S123
95Don-179
95FinnSemWC-81
95Lea-194
95ParInt-43
95ParIntEl-43
95Pin-191
95PinArtP-191
95PinRinC-191
95Sco-27
95ScoBlaIce-27
95ScoBlaIceAP-27
95SweGloWC-78
95Top-205
95TopOPCI-205
97PacDynBKS-22

**Smith, Stuart**
82WhaJunHC-17

**Smith, Thomas J**
85HalFC-237

**Smith, Todd**
820shGen-6

**Smith, Tommy**
83HalFP-H14
91AriIce-3
92AriIce-4

**Smith, Travis**
91AirCanSJHL-C48
92MPSPhoSJHL-152
96DenUniPio-1

**Smith, Trevor**
87KinCan-29

**Smith, Troy**
95Sla-60
96DetWha-15

**Smith, Vern**
84SprInd-7
88ProAHL-313
89ProAHL-243
90ProAHLIHL-533
91ProAHLCHL-387

**Smith, Warren**
96DenUniPio-9

**Smith, Wayne**
85MinDul-6

**Smith, Wyatt**
94Sel-156
94SelGol-156
95DonEliWJ-41
95MinGolG-26
96MinGolGCAS-24

**Smolik, Jaroslav**
95CzeAPSE-218

**Smolinski, Bryan**
92Par-481
92ParEmel-481
93Don-30
93Lea-204
93MicSta-95
930PCPre-466
930PCPreG-466
93Par-259
93ParEmel-259
93Pin-217
93PinCan-217
93Pow-291
93PowRooS-14
93Sco-472
93ScoCan-472
93StaClu-274
93StaClu0-274
93TopPre-466
93TopPreG-466
93Ult-232
93UltAllRoo-8
93UppDec-242
93UppDecSP-12
94BeAPSig-47
94CanGamNHLP-38
94Don-21
94Fle-17

- 94Lea-130
- 94LeaGoIR-14
- 94LeaLim-57
- 94OPCFinIns-2
- 94OPCPre-196
- 94OPCPre-479
- 94OPCPreSE-196
- 94OPCPreSE-479
- 94Par-12
- 94Par-276
- 94ParGoI-12
- 94ParGoI-276
- 94ParSEV-26
- 94Pin-13
- 94Pin-470
- 94PinArtP-13
- 94PinArtP-470
- 94PinRinC-13
- 94PinRinC-470
- 94Sel-132
- 94SelGoI-132
- 94SP-11
- 94SPDieCut-11
- 94StaClu-103
- 94StaCluFDI-103
- 94StaCluMOMS-103
- 94StaCluSTWC-103
- 94TopPre-196
- 94TopPre-479
- 94TopPreSE-196
- 94TopPreSE-479
- 94Ult-16
- 94UltAllRoo-9
- 94UppDec-399
- 94UppDecEleIce-399
- 94UppDecSPI-SP96
- 94UppDecSPIDC-SP96
- 95CanGamNHLP-213
- 95ColCho-178
- 95ColChoPC-178
- 95ColChoPCP-178
- 95Don-138
- 95Don-327
- 95Emo-142
- 95Lea-239
- 95Met-120
- 95ParInt-168
- 95ParIntEI-168
- 95PenFoo-24
- 95PlaOneoOne-188
- 95Sco-43
- 95ScoBIaIce-43
- 95ScoBIaIceAP-43
- 95SkyImp-135
- 95StaClu-210
- 95StaCluMOMS-210
- 95Sum-156
- 95SumArtP-156
- 95SumIce-156
- 95Ult-14
- 95Ult-294
- 95UltGoIM-14
- 95UppDec-494
- 95UppDecEleIce-494
- 95UppDecEleIceG-494
- 96BeAPAut-132
- 96BeAPAutSil-132
- 96BeAPla-132
- 96ColCho-218
- 96Don-99
- 96DonPrePro-99
- 96Fla-58
- 96FlaBIuI-58
- 96Fle-89
- 96FlePic-132
- 96IsIPos-20
- 96NHLProSTA-94
- 96Pin-125
- 96PinArtP-125
- 96PinPreS-125
- 96PinRinC-125
- 96PlaOneoOne-389
- 96Sco-88
- 96ScoArtPro-88
- 96ScoDeaCAP-88
- 96ScoGoIB-88
- 96ScoSpeAP-88
- 96SkyImp-104
- 96UppDec-322
- 96UppDecBD-120
- 96UppDecBDG-120
- 96UppDecIce-39
- 96UppDecIcePar-39
- 97ColCho-152
- 97Pac-196
- 97PacCop-196
- 97PacCroR-82
- 97PacCroREG-82
- 97PacCroRIB-82
- 97PacCroRS-82
- 97PacDyn-76
- 97PacDynC-76
- 97PacDynDG-76
- 97PacDynEG-76
- 97PacDynIB-76
- 97PacDynR-76
- 97PacDynSil-76
- 97PacDynTan-76
- 97PacEmeGre-196
- 97PacIceB-196
- 97PacInv-84
- 97PacInvC-84
- 97PacInvEG-84

- 97PacInvIB-84
- 97PacInvR-84
- 97PacInvS-84
- 97PacOme-143
- 97PacOmeC-143
- 97PacOmeDG-143
- 97PacOmeEG-143
- 97PacOmeG-143
- 97PacOmeIB-143
- 97PacPar-112
- 97PacParC-112
- 97PacParDG-112
- 97PacParEG-112
- 97PacParIB-112
- 97PacParRed-112
- 97PacParSil-112
- 97PacRed-196
- 97PacSil-196
- 97PinCer-108
- 97PinCerMB-108
- 97PinCerMG-108
- 97PinCerMR-108
- 97PinCerR-108
- 97PinIns-178
- 97PinTotCMPG-108
- 97PinTotCPB-108
- 97PinTotCPG-108
- 97PinTotCPR-108
- 97Sco-241
- 97UppDec-310
- 98Be A PPA-233
- 98Be A PPAA-233
- 98Be A PPAAF-233
- 98Be A PPSE-233
- 98Be APG-233
- 98IsIPowP-NYI2
- 98O-PChr-38
- 98O-PChrR-38
- 98Pac-289
- 98PacAur-120
- 98PacDynI-119
- 98PacDynIIB-119
- 98PacDynIR-119
- 98PacIceB-289
- 98PacPar-149
- 98PacParC-149
- 98PacParEG-149
- 98PacParH-149
- 98PacParIB-149
- 98PacParS-149
- 98PacRed-289
- 98Top-38
- 98TopO-P-38
- 98UC-12
- 98UD ChoPCR-127
- 98UD ChoPCR-127
- 98UppDec-128
- 98UppDecE-128
- 98UppDecE1o1-128
- 98UppDecGR-128
- 99Pac-265
- 99PacCop-265
- 99PacGoI-265
- 99PacIceB-265
- 99PacPreD-265

**Smrke, John**
- 78BIuPos-20
- 79OPC-340

**Smrke, Louis (Lou)**
- 51LavDaiQSHL-24
- 52St.LawS-94

**Smrke, Stan**
- 51LavDaiQSHL-23
- 52St.LawS-97
- 63RochAme-20

**Smyl, Stan**
- 78CanuRoyB-20
- 79CanuRoyB-20
- 80CanuSiID-21
- 80CanuTeal-20
- 80OPC-128
- 80OPC-208
- 80PepCap-118
- 80Top-128
- 80Top-208
- 81CanuSiID-13
- 81CanuTeal-19
- 81OPC-328
- 81PosSta-25
- 81Top-38
- 82Canu-19
- 82OPC-356
- 82OPCSti-242
- 82PosCer-19
- 83Canu-18
- 83Ess-17
- 83OPC-359
- 83OPCSti-274
- 83PufSti-2
- 83Vac-116
- 847EDis-51
- 84Canu-22
- 84KelAccD-4
- 84KelWin-28
- 84OPC-330
- 84OPCSti-281
- 84Top-140
- 857ECreCar-19
- 85Canu-21
- 850PC-68
- 850PCSti-247
- 85Top-68
- 86Canu-18
- 86KraDra-66
- 86OPC-50

- 86OPCSti-96
- 86Top-50
- 87CanuSheOil-19
- 87OPC-4
- 87OPCSti-198
- 87PanSti-349
- 87Top-4
- 88CanuMoh-19
- 88OPC-253
- 88OPCSti-60
- 88PanSti-141
- 89CanuMoh-19
- 89OPC-283
- 89OPCSti-68
- 89PanSti-159
- 90CanuMoh-27
- 90PanSti-292
- 90ProSet-548
- 90Sco-374
- 90ScoCan-374
- 90UppDec-299
- 90UppDecF-299
- 91CanuPanTS-23

**Smyth, Brad**
- 90 thlnnSOHL-143
- 94BirBul-21
- 96ColEdgFL-20
- 96SelCer-113
- 96SelCerAP-113
- 96SelCerBlu-113
- 96SelCerMB-113
- 96SelCerMG-113
- 96SelCerMR-113
- 96SelCerRed-113
- 96Zen-150
- 96ZenArtP-150
- 97PacInvNRB-99
- 98Be A PPA-75
- 98Be A PPAA-75
- 98Be A PPAAF-75
- 98Be A PPTBASG-75
- 98Be APG-75

**Smyth, Greg**
- 88NordGenF-27
- 88NordTeal-28
- 89HalCit-23
- 89ProAHL-17
- 90HalCit-25
- 90ProAHLIHL-453
- 91NordPet-27
- 91ProSet-465
- 91ProSetFre-465
- 92FlamIGA-7
- 93OPCPre-306
- 93OPCPreG-306
- 93TopPre-306
- 93TopPreG-306
- 94St.JohML-22
- 97St.JohML-23

**Smyth, Kevin**
- 90 thlnnSWHL-155
- 91 thlnnSWHL-279
- 92Cla-24
- 93Don-444
- 94Cla-47
- 94ClaDraGol-47
- 94ClaProP-225
- 94ClaTri-T28
- 94Don-59
- 94Lea-320
- 94OPCPre-68
- 94OPCPreSE-68
- 94Par-99
- 94ParGol-99
- 94Sco-225
- 94ScoGol-225
- 94ScoPla-225
- 94ScoPlaTS-225
- 94TopPre-68
- 94TopPreSE-68
- 95Ult-71
- 95UltGoIM-71
- 95UppDec-181
- 95UppDecEleIce-181
- 95UppDecEleIceG-181
- 96ClaGol-24
- 96WhaBobS-25

- 95SelCer-121
- 95SelCerMG-121
- 95SigRoo-31
- 95SigRooAB2-B3
- 95SigRooSig-31
- 95SkyImp-198
- 95Sum-176
- 95SumArtP-176
- 95SumIce-176
- 95TopCanWJ-8CJ
- 95Zen-137
- 96Don-223
- 96DonCanI-89
- 96DonCanIGPP-89
- 96DonCanIRPP-89
- 96DonEli-124
- 96DonEliDCS-124
- 96DonPrePro-223
- 96Fla-35
- 96FlaBIuI-35
- 96Lea-171
- 96LeaPre-72
- 96LeaPreP-171
- 96LeaPrePP-72
- 96OilPos-94
- 96SP-56
- 96TeaOut-10
- 96UppDec-258
- 96Zen-104
- 96ZenArtP-104
- 97ColCho-92
- 97Don-358
- 97DonCanI-52
- 97DonCanIDS-52
- 97DonCanINP-10
- 97DonCanIPS-52
- 97DonCanISCS-17
- 97DonEli-70
- 97DonEli-140
- 97DonEliAsp-70
- 97DonEliAsp-140
- 97DonEliC-21
- 97DonEliMC-21
- 97DonEliS-70
- 97DonEliS-140
- 97DonLim-26
- 97DonLim-65
- 97DonLim-99
- 97DonLimExp-26
- 97DonLimExp-65
- 97DonLimExp-99
- 97DonLimFOTG-50
- 97DonLin2L-22
- 97DonLin2LDC-22
- 97DonPre-119
- 97DonPre-189
- 97DonPreCttC-119
- 97DonPreCttC-189
- 97DonPreLotT-1A
- 97DonPreProG-158
- 97DonPreProS-158
- 97DonPri-24
- 97DonPri-201
- 97DonPriDD-5
- 97DonPriODI-18
- 97DonPriP-19
- 97DonPriS-19
- 97DonPriSB-19
- 97DonPriSB-344
- 97DonPriSoA-24
- 97DonPriSoA-201
- 97DonPriSS-19
- 97DonRedAle-2
- 97Kat-59
- 97KatGol-59
- 97KatSil-59
- 97Lea-49
- 97Lea-184
- 97LeaBanSea-10
- 97LeaFirOnIce-9
- 97LeaFraMat-49
- 97LeaFraMat-184
- 97LeaFraMDC-49
- 97LeaFraMDC-184
- 97LeaInt-49
- 97LeaIntUI-49
- 97Pac-94
- 97PacCop-94
- 97PacCroR-54
- 97PacCroRBoSDC-11
- 97PacCroREG-54
- 97PacCroRHTDC-9
- 97PacCroRIB-54
- 97PacCroRS-54
- 97PacDyn-51
- 97PacDynBKS-39
- 97PacDynC-51
- 97PacDynDG-51
- 97PacDynEG-51
- 97PacDynIB-51
- 97PacDynR-51
- 97PacDynSil-51
- 97PacDynTan-47
- 97PacEmeGre-94
- 97PacGolCroDC-12
- 97PacIceB-94
- 97PacInv-58
- 97PacInvC-58
- 97PacInvEG-58
- 97PacInvIB-58
- 97PacInvNRB-83
- 97PacInvR-58

- 97PacInvS-58
- 97PacOme-95
- 97PacOmeC-95
- 97PacOmeDG-95
- 97PacOmeEG-95
- 97PacOmeG-95
- 97PacOmeGFDCC-9
- 97PacOmeIB-95
- 97PacOmeTL-10
- 97PacPar-77
- 97PacParC-77
- 97PacParDG-77
- 97PacParEG-77
- 97PacParIB-77
- 97PacParRed-77
- 97PacParSil-77
- 97PacRed-94
- 97PacRev-56
- 97PacRevC-56
- 97PacRevE-56
- 97PacRevIB-56
- 97PacRevR-56
- 97PacRevS-56
- 97PacRevTCL-10
- 97PacSil-94
- 97PinCer-79
- 97PinCerMB-79
- 97PinCerMG-79
- 97PinCerMR-79
- 97PinCerR-79
- 97PinTotCMPG-79
- 97PinTotCPB-79
- 97PinTotCPG-79
- 97PinTotCPR-79
- 97Sco-120
- 97ScoArtPro-120
- 97ScoChel-8
- 97ScoGolBla-120
- 97SPAut-61
- 97Stu-16
- 97StuHarH-8
- 97StuPor-NNO
- 97StuPrePG-16
- 97StuPrePS-16
- 97StuSil-21
- 97StuSil8-21
- 97UppDec-274
- 97UppDecGDM-274
- 97UppDecIce-6
- 97UppDecIceP-6
- 97UppDecILL-L5A
- 97UppDecILL2-L5A
- 97UppDecIPS-6
- 97Zen-71
- 97Zen5x7-16
- 97ZenGolImp-16
- 97ZenSilImp-16
- 97ZenZGol-71
- 97ZenZSil-71
- 98BowBes-69
- 98BowBesAR-69
- 98BowBesR-69
- 98O-PChr-40
- 98O-PChrR-40
- 98Pac-94
- 98PacAur-76
- 98PacCroR-54
- 98PacCroRLS-54
- 98PacCroRPP-11
- 98PacDynI-76
- 98PacDynIIB-76
- 98PacDynIR-76
- 98PacDynITC-10
- 98PacIceB-94
- 98PacOmeH-96
- 98PacOmeODI-96
- 98PacOmeR-96
- 98PacPar-92
- 98PacParC-92
- 98PacParEG-92
- 98PacParH-92
- 98PacParIB-92
- 98PacParS-92
- 98PacParTCD-10
- 98PacRed-94
- 98PacRev-57
- 98PacRevR-57
- 98PacTeaC-10
- 98SP AutSotTG-RS
- 98SSASotT-RS
- 98Top-40
- 98TopGoILC1-32
- 98TopGoILC1B-32
- 98TopGoILC1BOoO-32
- 98TopGoILC1OoO-32
- 98TopGoILC1R-32
- 98TopGoILC1ROoO-32
- 98TopGoILC2-32
- 98TopGoILC2B-32
- 98TopGoILC2BOoO-32
- 98TopGoILC2OoO-32
- 98TopGoILC2R-32
- 98TopGoILC2ROoO-32
- 98TopGoILC3-32
- 98TopGoILC3B-32
- 98TopGoILC3BOoO-32
- 98TopGoILC3OoO-32
- 98TopGoILC3R-32
- 98TopGoILC3ROoO-32
- 98TopO-P-40
- 98UC-82
- 98UD ChoPCR-82

- 98UD ChoR-82
- 98UppDec-272
- 98UppDecE-272
- 98UppDecE1o1-272
- 98UppDecGR-272
- 98UppDecM-82
- 98UppDecMGS-82
- 98UppDecMSS-82
- 98UppDecMSS-82
- 99Pac-166
- 99PacAur-59
- 99PacAurPD-59
- 99PacCop-166
- 99PacGol-166
- 99PacIceB-166
- 99PacPreD-166

**Smythe, Connie (Conn)**
- 320 KeeMapL-19
- 36V356WorG-95
- 83HalFP-B13
- 85HalFC-27
- 90UppDecF-201
- 92HalFL-2

**Smythe, Stafford**
- 59Par-36

**Snedden, Dennis**
- 91ProAHLCHL-615
- 93TolSto-13

**Sneddon, Bob**
- 70EssPowPla-108

**Snell, Chris**
- 897 thlnnSOHL-51
- 907 thlnnSOHL-95
- 90UppDec-468
- 90UppDecF-468
- 917 thlnnSCHLAW-4
- 91ProAHLCHL-7
- 91RochAmeDD-16
- 91RochAmeKod-25
- 91RochAmePos-20
- 92RochAmeDD-18
- 92RochAmeKod-23
- 93MinDul-20
- 93St.JohML-21
- 94ClaProP-93
- 95ColEdgI-185
- 95PhoRoa-16
- 98GerDELE-133

**Snell, Ted**
- 74NHLActSta-294
- 74NHLActStaU-13
- 95SwiHNL-31

**Snepsts, Harold**
- 75CanuRoyB-21
- 75OPCNHL-396
- 76CanuRoyB-18
- 76OPCNHL-366
- 76OPCNHL-395
- 77CanuRoyB-19
- 77OPCNHL-295
- 78CanuRoyB-21
- 78OPC-380
- 79CanuRoyB-21
- 79OPC-186
- 79Top-186
- 80CanuSiID-22
- 80CanuTeal-21
- 80OPC-312
- 80PepCap-119
- 81CanuSiID-8
- 81OPC-344
- 81OPCSti-250
- 82Canu-20
- 82OPC-357
- 82OPCSti-243
- 82PosCer-19
- 83Canu-19
- 83Ess-18
- 83OPC-360
- 83Vac-117
- 847EDis-28
- 84KelWin-47
- 84NorStaPos-27
- 84OPC-108
- 85OPC-232
- 85OPCSti-44
- 87OPCSti-110
- 87PanSti-241
- 88CanuMoh-20
- 89CanuMoh-20
- 89OPC-286
- 90BluKod-20
- 90ProSet-527
- 90ScoRoo-61T
- 91ProAHLCHL-35

**Snesar, Shawn**
- 88SasBla-8
- 89SasBla-7
- 91HamRoaA-17
- 92HamRoaA-1
- 93HamRoaA-2
- 94RicRen-3

**Snesrud, Matt**
- 95NorlowH-31

**Snider, Ed**
- 92FlyUppDS-44

**Snis, Ingemar**
- 70SweHocS-80
- 71SweHocS-171
- 72SweHocS-270

**Snita, Marcin**
- 95Sla-353
- 96SarSti-26

**Snopek, Jan**

- 93OshGen-4
- 95Sla-248

**Snow, Garth**
- 92MaiBlaB-15
- 92MaiBlaB-33
- 93Cla-58
- 93Don-481
- 93Pow-425
- 93Sco-628
- 93ScoCan-628
- 93ScoGol-628
- 94Cla-84
- 94ClaDraGol-84
- 94ClaProP-35
- 94ClaROYS-R17
- 94ClaTri-T55
- 94Lea-180
- 95BeAPla-57
- 95BeAPSig-S57
- 95BeAPSigDC-S57
- 95ParInt-425
- 95ParIntEI-425
- 95SkyImp-215
- 95Ult-287
- 95UppDec-289
- 95UppDecEleIce-289
- 95UppDecEleIceG-289
- 96Don-207
- 96DonPrePro-207
- 96FlyPos-21
- 96Lea-97
- 96LeaPreP-97
- 96Sco-204
- 96ScoArtPro-204
- 96ScoDeaCAP-204
- 96ScoGoIB-204
- 96ScoSpeAP-204
- 97Be A PPAD-77
- 97Be A PPAPD-77
- 97BeAPla-77
- 97BeAPlaAut-77
- 97BeAPlaSTP-12
- 97Don-11
- 97DonBetTP-7
- 97DonCanI-38
- 97DonCanIDS-38
- 97DonCanISCS-10
- 97DonLim-170
- 97DonLimExp-170
- 97DonPre-111
- 97DonPreCttC-111
- 97DonPreProG-11
- 97DonPreProS-11
- 97DonPri-138
- 97DonPriPG-16
- 97DonPriPG-P16
- 97DonPriGP-16
- 97DonPriGP-P16
- 97DonPriSoA-138
- 97Pac-147
- 97PacCop-147
- 97PacCroRFODC-14
- 97PacDyn-93
- 97PacDynC-93
- 97PacDynDG-93
- 97PacDynEG-93
- 97PacDynIB-93
- 97PacDynR-93
- 97PacDynSil-93
- 97PacDynSto-16
- 97PacDynTan-54
- 97PacEmeGre-147
- 97PacIceB-147
- 97PacInTheCLC-15
- 97PacOme-170
- 97PacOmeC-170
- 97PacOmeDG-170
- 97PacOmeEG-170
- 97PacOmeG-170
- 97PacOmeIB-170
- 97PacPar-137
- 97PacParC-137
- 97PacParDG-137
- 97PacParEG-137
- 97PacParGSL-15
- 97PacParIB-137
- 97PacParRed-137
- 97PacParSil-137
- 97PacRed-147
- 97PacSil-147
- 97Pin-63
- 97PinArtP-63
- 97PinCer-28
- 97PinCerMB-28
- 97PinCerMG-28
- 97PinCerMR-28
- 97PinCerR-28
- 97PinIns-68
- 97PinInsCC-68
- 97PinInsEC-68
- 97PinInsSto-17
- 97PinInsSUG-4A/B
- 97PinInsSUG-4C/D
- 97PinMas-8
- 97PinMasDC-8
- 97PinMasPro-8
- 97PinPrePBB-63
- 97PinPrePBM-63
- 97PinPrePBY-63
- 97PinPrePFC-63
- 97PinPrePFM-63
- 97PinPrePFY-63

❑ 97PinPrePla-63
❑ 97PinRinC-63
❑ 97PinTin-9
❑ 97PinTotCMPG-28
❑ 97PinTotCPB-28
❑ 97PinTotCPG-28
❑ 97PinTotCPR-28
❑ 97Sco-3
❑ 97ScoArtPro-3
❑ 97ScoFly-2
❑ 97ScoFlyPla-2
❑ 97ScoFlyPre-2
❑ 97ScoGolBla-3
❑ 97ScoNetW-8
❑ 98Be A PPA-144
❑ 98Be A PPAA-144
❑ 98Be A PPAAF-144
❑ 98Be A PPTBASG-144
❑ 98Be APG-144
❑ 98O-PChr-122
❑ 98O-PChrR-122
❑ 98Pac-434
❑ 98PacAur-192
❑ 98PacCroR-139
❑ 98PacCroRLS-139
❑ 98PacDynI-192
❑ 98PacDynIIB-192
❑ 98PacDynIR-192
❑ 98PacIceB-434
❑ 98PacOmeH-241
❑ 98PacOmeODI-241
❑ 98PacOmeR-241
❑ 98PacPar-240
❑ 98PacParC-240
❑ 98PacParEG-240
❑ 98PacParH-240
❑ 98PacParIB-240
❑ 98PacParS-240
❑ 98PacRed-434
❑ 98PacRev-145
❑ 98PacRevIS-145
❑ 98PacRevR-145
❑ 98SPxFin-86
❑ 98SPxFinR-86
❑ 98SPxFinS-86
❑ 98Top-122
❑ 98TopO-P-122
❑ 98UC-207
❑ 98UD ChoPCR-207
❑ 98UD ChoR-207
❑ 98UppDec-198
❑ 98UppDecE-198
❑ 98UppDecE1o1-198
❑ 98UppDecGR-198
❑ 99Pac-433
❑ 99PacAur-145
❑ 99PacAurPD-145
❑ 99PacCop-433
❑ 99PacGol-433
❑ 99PacIceB-433
❑ 99PacPreD-433
**Snow, Jason**
❑ 89WinSpi-15
❑ 907thInnSOHL-96
**Snuggerud, Dave**
❑ 89SabBluS-21
❑ 89SabCam-24
❑ 90Bow-249
❑ 90BowTif-249
❑ 90OPC-340
❑ 90PanSti-19
❑ 90ProSet-30
❑ 90SabBluS-22
❑ 90SabCam-25
❑ 90ScoRoo-48T
❑ 90Top-340
❑ 90TopTif-340
❑ 90UppDec-189
❑ 90UppDecF-189
❑ 91Bow-29
❑ 91OPC-441
❑ 91PanSti-308
❑ 91Pin-223
❑ 91PinFre-223
❑ 91ProSet-18
❑ 91ProSetFre-18
❑ 91SabBluS-20
❑ 91SabPepC-20
❑ 91ScoAme-206
❑ 91ScoCan-206
❑ 91StaClu-320
❑ 91Top-441
❑ 91UppDec-194
❑ 91UppDecF-194
❑ 92Bow-309
❑ 92Pin-183
❑ 92PinFre-183
❑ 92Sco-182
❑ 92ScoCan-182
**Snyder, Dan**
❑ 95Sla-294
**Sobchuk, Dennis**
❑ 74OPCWHA-56
❑ 74PhoRoaWP-8
❑ 75OPCWHA-115
❑ 75StiKah-12
❑ 76OPCWHA-29
❑ 76StiKah-7
❑ 77OPCWHA-53
❑ 86RegPat-26
❑ 87RegPat-25
**Sobchuk, Gene**
❑ 71RocAme-17
❑ 75StiKah-13
**Sobek, Jeanine**
❑ 94ClaWomOH-W35
**Soberlak, Peter**
❑ 85KamBla-23
❑ 89ProAHL-134
❑ 90ProAHLIHL-226
❑ 91ProAHLCHL-229
**Sobush, Shawn**
❑ 95SudWolP-22
**Soccio, Len**
❑ 95BufStaRHI-20
❑ 96GerDELE-218
❑ 98GerDELE-181
**Soderberg, Ake**
❑ 69SweHocS-272
❑ 70SweHocS-164
❑ 71SweHocS-259
❑ 72SweHocS-239
❑ 72SweSemWC-70
❑ 73SweHocS-239
❑ 73SweWorCS-239
❑ 74SweHocS-265
**Soderberg, Anders**
❑ 91SweSemE-333
❑ 93SweSemE-205
❑ 94ParSE-SE234
❑ 94ParSEG-SE234
❑ 94SP-169
❑ 94SPDieCut-169
❑ 94SweLeaE-220
❑ 94UppDec-521
❑ 94UppDecEleIce-521
❑ 95SweLeaE-103
❑ 95SweLeaEG-10
❑ 95SweUppDE-161
❑ 95SweUppDE-221
**Soderberg, Lennart**
❑ 64SweCorI-39
❑ 65SweCorI-39
**Sodergren, Hakan**
❑ 83SweSemE-95
❑ 84SweSemE-88
❑ 85SwePanS-84
❑ 86SwePanS-69
❑ 87SwePanS-80
❑ 89SweSemE-60
❑ 89SweSemWCS-23
❑ 90SweSemE-290
**Soderholm, Patrik**
❑ 89SweSemE-190
**Soderling, Benny**
❑ 65SweCorI-40
**Soderlund, Cenneth**
❑ 86SwePanS-159
❑ 89SweSemE-140
❑ 90SweSemE-215
❑ 91SweSemE-143
❑ 92SweSemE-172
**Soderlund, Kent**
❑ 71SweHocS-123
**Soderstrom, Dan**
❑ 67SweHoc-112
❑ 69SweHocS-126
❑ 70SweHocS-81
❑ 71SweHocS-172
❑ 72SweHocS-164
❑ 72SweSemWC-68
❑ 73SweHocS-15
❑ 73SweHocS-51
❑ 73SweWorCS-15
❑ 73SweWorCS-51
❑ 74SweHocS-25
❑ 74SweHocS-266
❑ 74SweSemHVS-10
❑ 81SweSemHVS-16
❑ 84SweSemE-169
❑ 85SwePanS-132
**Soderstrom, Hans**
❑ 65SweCorI-69A
**Soderstrom, Tommy**
❑ 89SweSemE-51
❑ 90SweSemE-273
❑ 91SweSemE-54
❑ 91SweSemE-316
❑ 91SweSemE-338
❑ 91SweSemWCS-29
❑ 92FlyUppDS-28
❑ 92FlyUppDS-31
❑ 92Par-367
❑ 92Par-448
❑ 92ParEmel-367
❑ 92ParEmel-448
❑ 92SweSemE-343
❑ 92Ult-160
❑ 92UltImp-23
❑ 92UppDec-377
❑ 92UppDec-475
❑ 93Cla-125
❑ 93ClaProPBC-BC8
❑ 93ClaProPro-91
❑ 93Don-253
❑ 93Lea-37
❑ 93LeaGolR-12
❑ 93OPCPre-55
❑ 93OPCPre-122
❑ 93OPCPreG-55
❑ 93OPCPreG-122
❑ 93PanSti-55
❑ 93Par-150
❑ 93ParEmel-150
❑ 93Pin-19
❑ 93PinCan-19
❑ 93Pow-185
❑ 93PowNet-8
❑ 93PowSecYS-11
❑ 93Sco-336
❑ 93ScoCan-336
❑ 93ScoIntS-5
❑ 93ScoIntSC-5
❑ 93StaClu-340
❑ 93StaClu-430
❑ 93StaCluFDI-340
❑ 93StaCluFDI-430
❑ 93StaCluO-340
❑ 93StaCluO-430
❑ 93SweSemWCS-19
❑ 93TopPre-55
❑ 93TopPre-122
❑ 93TopPreG-55
❑ 93TopPreG-122
❑ 93Ult-217
❑ 93UppDec-182
❑ 94EASpo-102
❑ 94FinnJaaK-54
❑ 94FinnJaaK-334
❑ 94Lea-184
❑ 94Pin-309
❑ 94PinArtP-309
❑ 94PinRinC-309
❑ 94StaClu-24
❑ 94StaCluFDI-24
❑ 94StaCluMOMS-24
❑ 94StaCluSTWC-24
❑ 94Ult-160
❑ 94UppDec-474
❑ 94UppDecEleIce-474
❑ 95ColCho-28
❑ 95ColChoPC-28
❑ 95ColChoPCP-28
❑ 95FinnSemWC-54
❑ 95FinnSemWC-212
❑ 95Kra-34
❑ 95ParInt-127
❑ 95ParInt-240
❑ 95ParIntEl-127
❑ 95ParIntEl-240
❑ 95Pin-90
❑ 95PinArtP-90
❑ 95PinGloG-15
❑ 95PinRinC-90
❑ 95Sco-215
❑ 95ScoBlaIce-215
❑ 95ScoBlaIceAP-215
❑ 95Sum-46
❑ 95SumArtP-46
❑ 95SumIce-46
❑ 95SweGloWC-1
❑ 95SweUppDE-238
❑ 95Top-334
❑ 95TopOPCI-334
❑ 95Ult-100
❑ 95UltGolM-100
❑ 95UppDec-313
❑ 95UppDecEleIce-313
❑ 95UppDecEleIceG-313
❑ 95UppDecSpeE-SE140
❑ 95UppDecSpeEdiG-SE140
❑ 96Don-72
❑ 96DonPrePro-72
❑ 96Lea-51
❑ 96LeaPreP-51
❑ 96Sco-82
❑ 96ScoArtPro-82
❑ 96ScoDeaCAP-82
❑ 96ScoGolB-82
❑ 96ScoSpeAP-82
❑ 96SweSemCDT-1
❑ 96SweSemW-38
❑ 96SweSemWSG-SG4
**Sodke, Sonny**
❑ 82BraWheK-4
**Soetaert, Doug**
❑ 80OPC-324
❑ 81JetPos-17
❑ 82Jet-21
❑ 82OPC-389
❑ 82OPCSti-211
❑ 83Jet-21
❑ 83OPC-391
❑ 83OPCSti-288
❑ 83Vac-137
❑ 84CanaPos-26
❑ 84OPC-247
❑ 85CanaPos-35
❑ 85CanaPos-36
❑ 85CanaPro-22
❑ 85OPCSti-136
❑ 86OPCSti-16
❑ 89NewHavN-12
**Sogaard, Kim**
❑ 93SweSemWCS-236
**Soghomonian, J. Marc**
❑ 94FreNatT-30
**Sohlin, Stefan**
❑ 87SwePanS-255
**Sohrman, Richard**
❑ 93SweSemE-272
**Sokka, Mikko**
❑ 96FinnSISR-139
**Sokolovski, Alexander**
❑ 74SweHocS-73
**Sokolsky, Jamie**
❑ 95Sla-37
❑ 97BowCHL-38
❑ 97BowCHLOPC-38
**Solari, Kelvin**
❑ 93PetPet-23
**Solbach, Carsten**
❑ 94GerDELE-429
❑ 95GerDELE-385
❑ 96GerDELE-292
**Solderer, Erich**
❑ 93SweSemWCS-275
❑ 94FinnJaaK-238
**Soldt, Van**
❑ 79PanSti-277
**Soler, Jeremy**
❑ 92QueIntP-58
**Soleway, Jay**
❑ 80FlamPos-21
**Solf, Patrick**
❑ 94GerDELE-50
❑ 95GerDELE-33
**Solheim, Ken**
❑ 82NorStaPos-23
❑ 83OPC-131
❑ 84NorStaPos-28
❑ 85NovScoO-6
❑ 88OilTenAnn-8
**Soling, Jonas**
❑ 96SudWol-22
❑ 96SudWolP-23
❑ 97SudWolP-9
**Solinger, Robert (Bob)**
❑ 44BeeGro2P-452
❑ 45QuaOatP-49
❑ 51Par-88
❑ 52Par-50
❑ 53Par-16
❑ 61UniOilW-8
**Solinski, Jacek**
❑ 89SweSemWCS-144
**Solly, Jim**
❑ 92OklCitB-16
❑ 94HunBli-19
**Solodukhin, Vyacheslav**
❑ 91FutTreC72-28
**Somers, Art**
❑ 24HolCre-3
❑ 28V1282PauC-49
❑ 33OPCV304A-17
❑ 34DiaMatS-55
❑ 35DiaMatT2-58
**Somers, Chris**
❑ 86LonKni-29
**Somervuori, Eero**
❑ 95FinnSIS-256
❑ 97UppDecBD-139
❑ 97UppDecBDDD-139
❑ 97UppDecBDQD-139
❑ 97UppDecBDTD-139
❑ 98UC-281
❑ 98UD ChoPCR-281
❑ 98UD ChoR-281
**Sommer, Roy**
❑ 88OilTenAnn-110
❑ 92RicRen-18
❑ 93RicRen-11
❑ 94RicRen-20
❑ 95RicRen-24
**Sommers, Darb**
❑ 23V1281PauC-58
**Sonmez, Jim**
❑ 88SudWol-18
❑ 89SudWol-13
❑ 907thInnSOHL-19
**Sonmor, Glen**
❑ 72FigSaiPos-22
❑ 79NorStaPos-18
❑ 80NorStaPos-14
❑ 81NorStaPos-23
**Sonnenberg, Martin**
❑ 95SasBla-21
❑ 96SasBla-22
❑ 98BowCHL-69
❑ 98BowCHLGA-69
❑ 98BowCHLOI-69
❑ 98BowChrC-69
❑ 98BowChrCGA-69
❑ 98BowChrCGAR-69
❑ 98BowChrCOI-69
❑ 98BowChrCOIR-69
❑ 98BowChrCR-69
**Sopel, Brent**
❑ 95SwiCurB-14
**Sorenson, Kelly**
❑ 92HamRoaA-5
❑ 93HamRoaA-11
❑ 94HamRoaA-15
**Sormunen, Pasi**
❑ 93FinnJyvHS-21
❑ 93FinnSIS-89
❑ 93SweSemWCS-60
❑ 94FinnJaaK-11
❑ 94FinnSIS-238
❑ 95FinnSemWC-6
❑ 95FinnSIS-45
❑ 96FinnSISR-44
❑ 96FinnSISRS-3
**Sorochan, Jason**
❑ 907thInnSWHL-135
❑ 917thInnSWHL-350
**Sorochan, Lee**
❑ 917thInnSWHL-338
❑ 93LetHur-16
❑ 94Fin-153
❑ 94FinRef-153
❑ 94FinSupTW-153
❑ 94Pin-528
❑ 94PinArtP-528
❑ 94PinRinC-528
❑ 94SP-147
❑ 94SPDieCut-147
❑ 95BinRan-22
❑ 95DonCanWJT-9
❑ 95TopCanWJ-9CJ
❑ 96BinRan-20
**Sorokin, Sergei**
❑ 91OPCIns-44R
❑ 92UppDec-343
❑ 93Cla-93
❑ 93SweSemWCS-134
❑ 94FinnJaaK-144
❑ 95GerDELE-85
❑ 96GerDELE-274
**Sorokin, Vladimir**
❑ 74SweHocS-76
**Sorrell, John**
❑ 33OPCV304A-42
❑ 33V252CanG-45
❑ 34BeeGro1P-124
❑ 34BeeGro1P-254
❑ 36V356WorG-25
❑ 39OPCV3011-60
**Soskin, Barry**
❑ 92TolSto-4
❑ 95TolSto-21
❑ 96TolSto-NNO
**Sotropa, J.**
❑ 91AirCanSJHL-D37
❑ 92MPSPhoSJHL-139
**Souch, Mark**
❑ 90ForSasTra-17
**Souchotte, Kurtise**
❑ 91AirCanSJHL-B49
❑ 92MPSPhoSJHL-72
**Soucy, Alfred**
❑ 52JunBluT-42
**Soucy, Christian**
❑ 94ClaProP-75
❑ 94IndIce-23
❑ 94ParSE-SE33
❑ 94ParSEG-SE33
❑ 94Ult-276
❑ 94UppDec-223
❑ 94UppDecEleIce-223
❑ 95IndIce-20
**Soudek, Karel**
❑ 95CzeAPSE-58
❑ 96CzeAPSE-242
**Soukoroff, Phil**
❑ 93JohChi-9
**Soule, Russ**
❑ 83BelBul-28
**Soules, Jason**
❑ 88NiaFalT-9
❑ 907thInnSOHL-219
❑ 90UppDec-75
❑ 90UppDecF-75
❑ 91ProAHLCHL-219
**Soules, Nate**
❑ 91ArIIce-16
❑ 92ArIIce-13
**Soulier, Mathieu**
❑ 92QueIntP-27
**Soulliere, Stephane**
❑ 92OshGenS-15
❑ 93OshGen-11
❑ 94SarSti-11
**Souray, Sheldon**
❑ 95SigRoo-27
❑ 95SigRooSig-27
❑ 98Pac-271
❑ 98PacIceB-271
❑ 98PacPar-138
❑ 98PacParC-138
❑ 98PacParEG-138
❑ 98PacParH-138
❑ 98PacParIB-138
❑ 98PacParS-138
❑ 98PacRed-271
❑ 98UppDec-122
❑ 98UppDecE-122
❑ 98UppDecE1o1-122
❑ 98UppDecGR-122
**Southern, Bruce**
❑ 88JetPol-23
**Soutokorva, Osmo**
❑ 89SweSemE-150
❑ 90SweSemE-231
❑ 91SweSemE-208
**Sova, Tommi**
❑ 94Fin-138
❑ 94FinRef-138
❑ 94FinSupTW-138
❑ 94ParSE-SE224
❑ 94ParSEG-SE224
❑ 95FinnSIS-49
**Spaccucci, Nicola**
❑ 96RimOceQPP-23
**Spacek, Jaroslav**
❑ 94CzeAPSE-148
❑ 95CzeAPSE-249
❑ 96CzeAPSE-294
❑ 98UppDec-281
❑ 98UppDecE-281
❑ 98UppDecE1o1-281
❑ 98UppDecGR-281
❑ 98UppDecM-86
❑ 98UppDecMGS-86
❑ 98UppDecMSS-86
❑ 98UppDecMSS-86
❑ 99Pac-181
❑ 99PacCop-181
❑ 99PacGol-181
❑ 99PacIceB-181
❑ 99PacPreD-181
**Spadafore, Tim**
❑ 93RenEng-28
**Spangler, Ken**
❑ 88FliSpi-18
❑ 89ProIHL-118
❑ 91ProAHLCHL-446
❑ 93FliGen-12
❑ 94FliGen-21
**Sparkes, Brad**
❑ 85KitRan-28
**Sparks, Andy**
❑ 94GuiFla-5
❑ 95GuiFla-8
**Sparks, Todd**
❑ 907thInnSQMJHL-131
❑ 917thInnSQMJHL-215
❑ 95RicRen-4
**Sparrow, Spunk**
❑ 23V1281PauC-49
**Speck, Fred**
❑ 71SarProSta-220
❑ 71TorSun-290
❑ 72FigSaiPos-23
❑ 72OPC-331
**Speer, Mike (Michael)**
❑ 907thInnSOHL-185
❑ 907thInnSOHL-294
❑ 91ProAHLCHL-487
❑ 92IndIce-22
❑ 94BraSmo-20
❑ 94ClaProP-168
**Spehar, Dave**
❑ 96MinGolGCAS-25
**Speirs, Pete**
❑ 23CreSel-3
❑ 23V1281PauC-2
❑ 24CreSel-12
**Spelda, Jaroslav**
❑ 94CzeAPSE-28
**Spence, Joe**
❑ 61SudWol-16
❑ 62SudWol-20
**Spence, Wally**
❑ 92MPSPhoSJHL-21
**Spencer, Brian**
❑ 69MapLeaWBM-5
❑ 71MapLeaP-19
❑ 71OPC-198
❑ 71TorSun-272
❑ 72OPC-61
❑ 72SarProSta-132
❑ 72Top-53
❑ 73OPC-83
❑ 73Top-83
❑ 74NHLActSta-38
❑ 74OPCNHL-328
❑ 75OPCNHL-384
❑ 76OPCNHL-191
❑ 76Top-191
❑ 77OPCNHL-9
❑ 77Top-9
❑ 78OPC-137
❑ 78Top-137
**Spencer, Irv**
❑ 60ShiCoi-88
❑ 61ShiCoi-86
❑ 61Top-47
❑ 62Top-17
**Spencer, Sean**
❑ 907thInnSOHL-97
❑ 917thInnSOHL-295
❑ 92Ott672A-21
**Spenrath, Greg**
❑ 91ProAHLCHL-145
❑ 93LasVegThu-26
**Sperger, Zdenek**
❑ 94CzeAPSE-107
❑ 95CzeAPSE-74
**Spero, Kevin**
❑ 917thInnSOHL-168
❑ 91OshGen-10
❑ 91OshGenS-20
❑ 92OshGenS-11
**Speyers, Chris**
❑ 24C144ChaCig-57
❑ 34DiaMatS-56
**Spiers, Pete**
❑ 28V1282PauC-76
**Spina, Steve**
❑ 93SauSteMG-27
**Spink, Lonnie**
❑ 85KamBla-24
**Spitzig, Tim**
❑ 917thInnSOHL-79
❑ 93KitRan-1
❑ 93KitRan-9
❑ 94KitRan-10
**Splett, Jamie**
❑ 88RegPat-24
❑ 89RegPat-19
❑ 907thInnSWHL-178
**Spoltore, Fred**
❑ 95LouIceG-17
**Spoltore, John**
❑ 897thInnSOHL-149
❑ 907thInnSOHL-317
❑ 917thInnSOHL-66
❑ 95LouIceGP-18
**Spott, Steve**
❑ 90RicRen-5
**Spratt, Len**
❑ 84KinCan-9
**Sprenger, Jim**
❑ 85MinDul-22
**Spring, Don**
❑ 80JetPos-20
❑ 80PepCap-137
❑ 81JetPos-18
❑ 81OPC-375
❑ 81SweSemHVS-80
❑ 82Jet-22
❑ 82OPC-392
❑ 82PosCer-21
❑ 83OPC-392
**Spring, Frank**
❑ 75OPCNHL-341
**Spring, Jesse**
❑ 23V1451-36
❑ 24C144ChaCig-58
❑ 24V1452-20
**Sprott, Jim**
❑ 86LonKni-12
❑ 90HalCit-26
❑ 90ProAHLIHL-464
❑ 91ProAHLCHL-377
**Sproxton, Dennis**
❑ 907thInnSWHL-70
**Spruce, Andy**
❑ 76CanuRoyB-19
❑ 77RocCokCan-17
❑ 78OPC-378
❑ 84SudWol-1
**Spry, Brad**
❑ 907thInnSOHL-98
**Spry, Earl**
❑ 94GerDELE-227
❑ 95GerDELE-224
❑ 96GerDELE-75
**Spurr, Chad**
❑ 96SauSteMG-21
❑ 96SauSteMGA-21
**Srdinko, Jan**
❑ 94CzeAPSE-237
❑ 95CzeAPSE-7
❑ 96CzeAPSE-220
**Srek, Pavel**
❑ 94CzeAPSE-80
❑ 95CzeAPSE-274
**Srochenski, Darren**
❑ 94CenHocL-34
**Srsen, Tomas**
❑ 90ProAHLIHL-237
❑ 91ProAHLCHL-234
❑ 92SweSemE-166
❑ 93SweSemE-234
❑ 94SweLeaE-45
❑ 94SweLeaETG-1
❑ 95CzeAPSE-17
❑ 95FinnSemWC-156
❑ 96CzeAPSE-228
**Srubko, Andrei**
❑ 98LasVegT-20
**St-Germain, Luc**
❑ 93AmoLesFAM-19
**St-Louis, Jonathan**
❑ 97RimOce-36
**St-Onge, David**
❑ 96RimOce-26
❑ 96RimOceQPP-24
❑ 97RimOce-25
**St. Amour, Martin**
❑ 90ProAHLIHL-70
❑ 91CinCyc-20
**St. Amour, Stephane**
❑ 917thInnSQMJHL-161
❑ 93DruVol-12
**St. Aubin, Joey**
❑ 88KitRan-14
❑ 89KitRan-15
❑ 907thInnSMC-47
❑ 907thInnSOHL-241
❑ 90KitRan-13
**St. Croix, Chris**
❑ 96KamBla-26
**St. Croix, Rick**
❑ 81OPC-252
❑ 82MapLeaP-32
❑ 82OPC-258
❑ 83MapLeaP-24
❑ 83OPC-340
❑ 83OPCSti-36
❑ 83Vac-98
❑ 84OPC-310
❑ 85OPCSti-8
❑ 88JetPol-23
**St. Cyr, Gerry**
❑ 907thInnSWHL-249
❑ 917thInnSWHL-64
❑ 93ThuBayS-18
❑ 94TolSto-21
❑ 95FliGen-17
**St. Cyr, Raymond**
❑ 52JunBluT-44
**St. Germain, Matt**
❑ 917thInnSOHL-137
❑ 91PetPet-18
❑ 93PetPet-12
**St. Hilaire, Irene**
❑ 51LavDaiS-55
❑ 52St.LawS-87
**St. Jacques, Kevin**
❑ 89LetHur-21
❑ 907thInnSWHL-134
❑ 917thInnSWHL-352
❑ 92IndIce-21
❑ 93ClaProPro-136
**St. Jacques, Michel**
❑ 907thInnSQMJHL-33
❑ 917thInnSMC-30
❑ 917thInnSQMJHL-82
❑ 94CenHocL-71
**St. James, Tom**
❑ 82KitRan-7
**St. Jean, Maurice**

- 51LavDaiLSJ-25

**St. John, Mike**
- 897thInnSOHL-143

**St. Laurent, Andre**
- 750PCNHL-387
- 760PCNHL-29
- 76Top-29
- 770PCNHL-171
- 77Top-171
- 780PC-32
- 78Top-32
- 790PC-73
- 79Top-73
- 800PC-316
- 830PC-286
- 83PenHeiP-21
- 83PenTealP-31

**St. Laurent, Dollard**
- 44BeeGro2P-140
- 44BeeGro2P-288
- 45QuaOatP-112
- 48ExhCan-25
- 52Par-52
- 53Par-23
- 55Par-48
- 55ParQuaO-48
- 58Top-5
- 59Top-43
- 60ShiCoi-74
- 61ShiCoi-35
- 61Top-31
- 61Top-44
- 62QueAce-20
- 62Top-30
- 64BeeGro3P-54
- 91UltOriS-15
- 91UltOriSF-15
- 93ParParR-PR68
- 94ParMisL-69

**St. Laurent, Sam**
- 88ProAHL-7
- 89ProAHL-315
- 90ProAHLIHL-9
- 91ProAHLCHL-193

**St. Louis, France**
- 94ClaWomOH-W2
- 97ColCho-284

**St. Louis, Josh**
- 95SwiCurB-15

**St. Louis, Martin**
- 98PacCroR-20
- 98PacCroRLS-20
- 98PacDynI-28
- 98PacDynIIB-28
- 98PacDynIR-28
- 98PacOmeH-38
- 98PacOmeODI-38
- 98PacOmeR-38
- 98UppDec-234
- 98UppDecE-234
- 98UppDecE1o1-234
- 98UppDecGR-234

**St. Louis, Todd**
- 95Sla-175

**St. Marseille, Derrick**
- 77NovScoV-22

**St. Marseille, Frank**
- 690PC-177
- 70ColSta-22
- 70DadCoo-126
- 70EssPowPla-242
- 700PC-214
- 700PCDec-26
- 70SarProSta-180
- 70TopStiS-28
- 71Baz-17
- 71BluPos-21
- 710PC-38
- 710PCTBoo-15
- 71SarProSta-184
- 71Top-38
- 71TorSun-249
- 720PC-65
- 72SarProSta-188
- 72Top-71
- 730PC-262
- 74NHLActSta-110
- 740PCNHL-98
- 740PCNHL-374
- 74Top-98
- 750PCNHL-15
- 75Top-15
- 760PCNHL-276
- 77NovScoV-21
- 92BluUDBB-19

**St. Martin, Blair**
- 95MedHatT-16
- 96MedHatT-18

**St. Pierre, David**
- 907thInnSQMJHL-236
- 917thInnSQMJHL-145
- 91UppDecWCJC-49
- 93ClaProPro-108
- 95HamRoaA-14

**St. Pierre, Yan**
- 917thInnSQMJHL-243
- 93DruVol-8

**St. Sauveur, Claude**
- 730PCWHAP-18
- 740PCWHA-62
- 750PCWHA-124
- 760PCNHL-379
- 760PCWHA-90
- 770PCWHA-77

**St.Germain, David**

- 98Vald'OF-14

**St.Germain, Francois**
- 88RivDu R-26

**Stacchi, Mike**
- 95RoaExp-5

**Stacey, Brian**
- 917thInnSOHL-373
- 93LonKni-18
- 95SauSteMG-19
- 95Sla-372

**Stackhouse, Ron**
- 70EssPowPla-106
- 710PC-83
- 71SarProSta-64
- 71TorSun-59
- 720PC-287
- 72SarProSta-77
- 730PC-236
- 73RedWinMP-15
- 73RedWinTi-18
- 74NHLActSta-228
- 740PCNHL-188
- 74PenPos-21
- 74Top-188
- 750PCNHL-111
- 75Top-111
- 760PCNHL-72
- 76Top-72
- 770PCNHL-157
- 77PenPucB-3
- 77Top-157
- 780PC-72
- 78Top-72
- 790PC-154
- 79Top-154
- 800PC-228
- 80Top-228
- 810PC-266
- 810PCSti-188
- 820PC-275
- 82PosCer-15

**Stadey, Ben**
- 93WatBlaH-22

**Stadler, Walter**
- 72SweSemWC-95

**Stagg, Brian**
- 917thInnSOHL-232

**Stahan, Butch**
- 51LavDaiQSHL-105
- 52St.LawS-72

**Stahl, Christer**
- 72SweHocS-271
- 74SweHocS-151

**Stahl, Craig**
- 95TriAme-24

**Stahl, Mikael**
- 86SwePanS-216
- 87SwePanS-206
- 89SweSemE-185
- 90SweSemE-20

**Stahl, Paul**
- 65SweCorl-164
- 67SweHoc-127

**Staios, Steve**
- 907thInnSOHL-271
- 917thInnSMC-107
- 917thInnSOHL-219
- 91AreDraPic-20
- 91Cla-24
- 91StaPicH-51
- 91UltDra-22
- 92SudWol-27
- 93PeoRiv-26
- 94ClaProP-149
- 96Lea-223
- 96LeaPreP-223
- 96Pin-231
- 96PinPreS-231
- 96UppDec-218
- 97Be A PPAD-161
- 97Be A PPAPD-161
- 97BeAPla-161
- 97BeAPlaAut-161

**Stait, Bill**
- 92MPSPhoSJHL-54

**Stajduhar, Nick**
- 907thInnSOHL-144
- 917thInnSOHL-380
- 93Cla-28
- 93DonTeaC-19
- 93LonKni-19
- 93LonKni-25
- 93Par-507
- 93ParEmel-507
- 93Pin-463
- 93PinCan-463
- 93UppDec-543
- 94CapBreO-18
- 94Cla-83
- 94ClaDraGol-83
- 96UppDec-194

**Stakowski, Hartley**
- 67ColChe-12

**Stalberg, Lars**
- 67SweHoc-93

**Stalnacke, Erik**
- 84SweSemE-182
- 85SwePanS-170
- 86SwePanS-177
- 87SwePanS-177

**Stambert, Orvar**
- 83SweSemE-80
- 84SweSemE-80
- 85SwePanS-71
- 86SwePanS-60

- 87SwePanS-70
- 89SweSemE-54
- 90SweSemE-279
- 91SweSemE-60

**Stamler, Lorne**
- 78MapLeaP-20
- 780PC-301
- 79JetPos-24
- 81IndChe-18
- 82IndChe-19

**Stamp, Eric**
- 917thInnSOHL-195

**Standish, Bobby**
- 91AirCanSJHL-D3

**Standling, David**
- 94HumHawP-NNO

**Stanek, Ed**
- 93WatBlaH-23

**Stanfield, Fred**
- 64BeeGro3P-55A
- 64BeeGro3P-55B
- 64CocCap-23
- 65Coc-24
- 65Top-63
- 66Top-56
- 67Top-36
- 680PC-10
- 68ShiCoi-9
- 68Top-10
- 690PC-32
- 69Top-32
- 70BruPos-14
- 70BruTealss-18
- 700PC-5
- 700PCDec-7
- 70SarProSta-12
- 70Top-5
- 71BruTealss-12
- 710PC-7
- 71SarProSta-1
- 71Top-7
- 71TorSun-19
- 720PC-150
- 72SarProSta-15
- 72Top-135
- 73NorStaP-19
- 74NHLActSta-132
- 74NHLActStaU-5
- 740PCNHL-31
- 74Top-31
- 750PCNHL-332
- 760PCNHL-58
- 76Top-58
- 770PCNHL-161
- 77Top-161
- 780PC-352
- 91UltOriS-54
- 91UltOriSF-54
- 94ParTalB-37
- 95Par66-25
- 95Par66Coi-25

**Stanfield, Jim**
- 72SarProSta-86

**Stanfield, Rob**
- 95Sla-134
- 96KitRan-24

**Stangby, Shane**
- 907thInnSWHL-252
- 91AirCanSJHL-E47

**Stangle, Frank**
- 36V356WorG-110

**Staniforth, Kent**
- 907thInnSWHL-144
- 917thInnSWHL-272

**Staniowski, Ed**
- 760PCNHL-104
- 76Top-104
- 770PCNHL-54
- 77Top-54
- 78BluPos-21
- 790PC-361
- 800PC-328
- 81JetPos-19
- 82Jet-23
- 820PC-393
- 820PCSti-210
- 82PosCer-21

**Stankiewicz, Brian**
- 93SweSemWCS-269
- 94FinnJaaK-232

**Stanley, Allan**
- 44BeeGro2P-365
- 44BeeGro2P-453A
- 44BeeGro2P-453B
- 51Par-44
- 52Par-21
- 53Par-64
- 54Par-41
- 57Top-15
- 58Par-23
- 59Par-44
- 60Par-16
- 60ShiCoi-6
- 60YorPreP-33
- 61Par-16
- 61ShiCoi-42
- 61YorYelB-9
- 62Par-9
- 62ShiMetC-2
- 63ChePho-50
- 63MapLeaWB-22
- 63Par-1
- 63Par-61

- 63TorSta-35
- 63YorWhiB-14
- 64BeeGro3P-185
- 64CocCap-107
- 64Top-104
- 64TorSta-44
- 65Coc-106
- 65MapLeaWB-17
- 66Top-16
- 66Top-128
- 66TopUSAT-16
- 67Top-13
- 67YorActOct-1
- 67YorActOct-26
- 680PC-183
- 680PCPucSti-16
- 68ShiCoi-125
- 69MapLeaWBG-34
- 83HalFP-G14
- 85HalFC-238
- 91UltOriS-44
- 91UltOriS-75
- 91UltOriSF-44
- 91UltOriSF-75
- 92ParParR-PR11
- 94ParMisL-20
- 94ParTalB-115
- 95Par66-110
- 95Par66Coi-110

**Stanley, Barney**
- 23V1281PauC-30
- 83HalFP-A13

**Stanley, Daryl**
- 81SasBla-2
- 83SprInd-23
- 86FlyPos-25
- 87CanuSheOil-20
- 89CanuMoh-21

**Stanley, Graham**
- 89ProAHL-18
- 90ProAHLIHL-353

**Stanley, Lord**
- 83HalFP-A14
- 85HalFC-13
- 92HalFL-18

**Stanley, Russell**
- 85HalFC-12

**Stanowski, Wally**
- 34BeeGro1P-348
- 390PCV3011-11
- 400PCV3012-103
- 44BeeGro2P-366
- 44BeeGro2P-454
- 45QuaOatP-50A
- 45QuaOatP-50B

**Stansfield, Sean**
- 88SudWol-16

**Stantien, Roman**
- 94CzeAPSE-242
- 95CzeAPSE-22
- 96CzeAPSE-229

**Stanton, Paul**
- 89ProIHL-156
- 900PCPre-110
- 90ProSet-633
- 90ScoRoo-27T
- 90UppDec-404
- 90UppDecF-404
- 91Bow-91
- 910PC-339
- 91PanSti-274
- 91PenFoo-13
- 91ProSet-457
- 91ProSetFre-457
- 91ScoAme-366
- 91ScoCan-406
- 91StaClu-380
- 91Top-339
- 91UppDec-203
- 91UppDecF-203
- 92Bow-284
- 920PC-361
- 92PenCokC-19
- 92PenFoo-13
- 92Pin-308
- 92PinFre-308
- 92Sco-135
- 92ScoCan-135
- 92StaClu-52
- 92Top-460
- 92TopGol-460G
- 92Ult-381
- 92UppDec-100
- 930PCPre-5
- 930PCPreG-5
- 93Par-288
- 93ParEmel-288
- 93Pin-330
- 93PinCan-330
- 93Sco-321
- 93ScoCan-321
- 93ScoCan-510
- 93ScoGol-510
- 93StaClu-52
- 93StaCluFDI-52
- 93StaCluFDIO-52
- 93StaCluO-52
- 93TopPre-5
- 93TopPreG-5
- 95GerDELE-267
- 96GerDELE-161
- 98GerDELE-229

**Staples, Jeff**

- 92BraWheK-22
- 95SlaMemC-28

**Stapleton, Mike**
- 86BlaCok-20
- 87BlaCok-21
- 88ProIHL-115
- 90PacAHLIHL-402
- 91BlaCok-24
- 92PenCokC-20
- 93PenFoo-21
- 94Lea-147
- 94Pin-228
- 94PinArtP-228
- 94PinRinC-228
- 95JetTealss-23
- 95PlaOneoOne-39
- 96BeAPAut-92
- 96BeAPAutSil-92
- 96BeAPla-92
- 97PacInvNRB-155
- 99Pac-327
- 99PacCop-327
- 99PacGol-327
- 99PacleB-327
- 99PacPreD-327

**Stapleton, Pat**
- 44BeeGro2P-68A
- 44BeeGro2P-68B
- 61ShiCoi-13
- 61Top-9
- 62Top-8
- 64BeeGro3P-26
- 64BeeGro3P-56
- 65Top-120
- 66Top-57
- 66Top-129
- 66TopUSAT-57
- 67Top-61
- 68Ba-7
- 680PC-15
- 68ShiCoi-18
- 68Top-15
- 690PC-69
- 690PCFou-17
- 69Top-69
- 70ColSta-77
- 70DadCoo-125
- 70EssPowPla-119
- 700PC-17
- 70SarProSta-44
- 70Top-17
- 710PC-25
- 710PC-258
- 71SarProSta-45
- 71Top-25
- 71TorSun-81
- 720PC-4
- 720PC-249
- 72OPCTeaC-27
- 72SarProSta-69
- 72Top-70
- 72Top-129
- 73MacMil-27
- 730PCWHAP-4
- 740PCWHA-35
- 74TeaCanLWHA-21
- 91FutTreC72-9
- 91Kra-68
- 91Kra-69
- 95Par66-38
- 95Par66Coi-38

**Starck, Lars**
- 67SweHoc-73
- 69SweHocS-104
- 71SweHocS-357

**Starikov, Sergei**
- 81SweSemHVS-43
- 82SweSemWC-32
- 83RusNatT-17
- 87RusNatT-17
- 89DevCar-22
- 90ProAHLIHL-557
- 91ProAHLCHL-327
- 92SanDieG-24

**Stark, Jay**
- 86PorWinH-21

**Starke, Joe**
- 35DiaMatTI-64

**Starnyski, Aaron**
- 94SudWol-22

**Starostenko, Dmitri**
- 92RusStaRA-25
- 92RusStaRA-31
- 94BinRan-21
- 94ClaProP-118
- 94BinRan-23

**Starr, Harold**
- 35DiaMatT2-59
- 35DiaMatT3-54

**Starsjinov, Vyatcheslav**
- 69SweHocS-16
- 69SweWorC-35
- 69SweWorC-65
- 69SweWorC-72
- 69SweWorC-121
- 69SweWorC-129
- 69SweWorC-136
- 70SweHocS-331
- 71SweHocS-40
- 72SweSemWC-8
- 74SweSemHVS-44
- 91FutTreC72-38

**Startup, James**
- 917thInnSWHL-106

- 91SasBla-23

**Stas, Sergei**
- 94EriPan-7
- 98GerDELE-252

**Stasiuk, Jeremy**
- 95DayBom-27

**Stasiuk, Vic**
- 44BeeGro2P-69
- 44BeeGro2P-212A
- 44BeeGro2P-212B
- 44BeeGro2P-212C
- 51Par-62
- 52Par-90
- 53Par-39
- 55BruPho-16
- 57BruTealss-19
- 57Top-11
- 58Top-9
- 59Top-14
- 60ShiCoi-103
- 60Top-66
- 61Par-32
- 61ShiCoi-63
- 62Par-27
- 62YorIroOTra-30B
- 63Par-58
- 70FlyPos-11
- 93ParParR-PR64
- 94ParMisL-9
- 94ParMisL-169

**Stastny, Anton**
- 80NordPos-25
- 80PepCap-76
- 81NordPos-16
- 810PC-282
- 810PCSti-70
- 82NordPos-20
- 820PC-294
- 820PCSti-24
- 83NordPos-27
- 830PC-302
- 830PCSti-252
- 83PufSti-14
- 83Vac-75
- 84NordPos-25
- 840PC-291
- 840PCSti-178
- 85NordGenF-25
- 85NordMcD-21
- 85NordPla-6
- 85NordPro-24
- 85NordTeal-24
- 850PC-78
- 850PCSti-147
- 85Top-78
- 86KraDra-67
- 86NordGenF-25
- 86NordMcD-24
- 86NordTeal-24
- 86NordYumY-9
- 860PC-125
- 860PCSti-27
- 86Top-125
- 87NordGenF-28
- 87NordYumY-9
- 870PC-185
- 870PCSti-228
- 87PanSti-166
- 87Top-185
- 88NordGenF-28
- 88NordTeal-29
- 880PC-98
- 880PCSti-194
- 88PanSti-357
- 88Top-98
- 94FinnJaaK-202

**Stastny, Bohuslav**
- 71SweHocS-58
- 72SweSemWC-32
- 74SweHocS-16
- 74SweSemHVS-64

**Stastny, Marian**
- 79PanSti-90
- 81NordPos-18
- 82McDSti-10
- 820PC-295
- 820PCSti-20
- 82PosCer-8
- 83NordPos-28
- 830PC-303
- 830PCSti-168
- 830PCSti-251
- 83PufSti-16
- 83Vac-76
- 84NordPos-26
- 840PC-292
- 840PCSti-177
- 85MapLeaP-27
- 850PCSti-144

- 820PC-276
- 820PC-292
- 820PC-293
- 820PCSti-15
- 820PCSti-19
- 820PCSti-167
- 83NordPos-29
- 830PC-304
- 830PCSti-167
- 830PCSti-253
- 83PufSti-13
- 83Vac-77
- 847TEdis-41
- 84KelAccD-2
- 84NordPos-27
- 840PC-293
- 840PCSti-141
- 840PCSti-164
- 840PCSti-165
- 84Top-130
- 857ECreCar-16
- 85NordGenF-26
- 85NordMcD-22
- 85NordPla-5
- 85NordPla-6
- 85NordPro-25
- 85NordTeal-25
- 850PC-31
- 850PCSti-156
- 85Top-31
- 86KraDra-68
- 86NordGenF-26
- 86NordMcD-25
- 86NordTeal-25
- 86NordYumY-10
- 860PC-20
- 860PCSti-26
- 86Top-20
- 87NordGenF-29
- 87NordYumY-10
- 870PC-21
- 870PCSti-222
- 87PanSti-164
- 87ProAll-12
- 87Top-21
- 88FriLayS-21
- 88NordGenF-29
- 88NordTeal-30
- 880PC-22
- 880PCMin-37
- 880PCSti-189
- 88PanSti-358
- 88Top-22
- 89Kra-33
- 89Nord-37
- 89NordGenF-28
- 89NordPol-26
- 890PC-143
- 890PCSti-182
- 89PanSti-324
- 89Top-143
- 90Bow-86
- 90BowTif-86
- 90Dev-24
- 90Kra-54
- 90NordTeal-24
- 900PC-334
- 90PanSti-70
- 90ProSet-175A
- 90ProSet-175B
- 90Sco-96
- 90ScoCan-96
- 90ScoHotRS-48
- 90Top-334
- 90TopTif-334
- 90UppDec-163
- 90UppDecF-163
- 91Bow-287
- 91Kra-83
- 910PC-191
- 910PC-275
- 91PanSti-220
- 91Par-103
- 91Par-209
- 91ParFre-103
- 91ParFre-209
- 91Pin-266
- 91PinFre-266
- 91ProSet-143
- 91ProSetFre-143
- 91ProSetPC-16
- 91ProSetPla-194
- 91ScoAme-66
- 91ScoCan-66
- 91StaClu-263
- 91Top-275
- 91UppDec-113
- 91UppDecF-113
- 92Bow-249
- 92FutTre76CC-131
- 920PC-216
- 92PanSti-174
- 92PanStiFre-174
- 92Pin-359
- 92PinFre-359
- 92ProSet-100
- 92Sco-291
- 92ScoCan-291
- 92StaClu-140
- 92Top-469
- 92TopGol-469G
- 92Ult-118
- 92UltImp-24
- 93Don-487
- 93PanSti-41

❑ 93Sco-22
❑ 93ScoCan-22
❑ 94CanGamNHLP-208
❑ 94Don-191
❑ 94FinnJaaK-200
❑ 94Fla-159
❑ 94HocWit-70
❑ 94OPCPre-182
❑ 94OPCPreSE-182
❑ 94Par-203
❑ 94ParGol-203
❑ 94Pin-134
❑ 94PinArtP-134
❑ 94PinRinC-134
❑ 94TopPre-182
❑ 94TopPreSE-182
❑ 94Ult-190
❑ 94UppDec-60
❑ 94UppDecEleIce-60
❑ 95SloAPSNT-22
❑ 96SweSemW-227
❑ 98HaloFM-2
❑ 99UppDecCL-36
❑ 99UppDecCLCLC-36
**Stauber, Pete**
❑ 91ProAHLCHL-129
**Stauber, Robb**
❑ 90OPC-181
❑ 90ProAHLIHL-418
❑ 90Top-181
❑ 90TopTif-181
❑ 90UppDec-165
❑ 90UppDecF-165
❑ 92OPCPre-115
❑ 92Par-303
❑ 92ParEmel-303
❑ 92Ult-311
❑ 92UppDec-495
❑ 93OPCPre-109
❑ 93OPCPreG-109
❑ 93Pin-338
❑ 93PinCan-338
❑ 93PinMas-3
❑ 93Pow-363
❑ 93Sco-346
❑ 93ScoCan-346
❑ 93StaClu-327
❑ 93StaCluFDI-327
❑ 93StaCluO-327
❑ 93TopPre-109
❑ 93TopPreG-109
❑ 93Ult-347
❑ 94BeAPla-R59
❑ 94OPCPre-248
❑ 94OPCPreSE-248
❑ 94Par-109
❑ 94ParGol-109
❑ 94TopPre-248
❑ 94TopPreSE-248
❑ 95ParInt-25
❑ 95ParIntEl-25
❑ 95RochAmeSS-19
❑ 96PorPir-1
**Stavjana, Antonin**
❑ 89SweSemWCS-181
❑ 91SweSemWCS-111
❑ 92SweSemE-127
❑ 93SweSemE-100
❑ 94CzeAPSE-230
❑ 94FinnJaaK-173
❑ 95CzeAPSE-8
❑ 95SweGloWC-150
❑ 96CzeAPSE-216
❑ 96SweSemW-105
**Stavjana, Miroslav**
❑ 94CzeAPSE-240
**Stearns, Cal**
❑ 60CleBar-16
**Steblecki, Roman**
❑ 89SweSemWCS-145
**Steblyk, Brent**
❑ 82MedHatT-19
❑ 83MedHatT-12
**Stebnicki, Marek**
❑ 94GerDELE-241
❑ 95GerDELE-235
❑ 96GerDELE-86
❑ 98GerDELE-26
**Stecher, Dino**
❑ 91SweSemWCS-179
❑ 93SwiHNL-34
❑ 95SwiHNL-33
**Stecksen, Ulf**
❑ 69SweHocS-215
**Steege, Brandon**
❑ 91MinGolG-23
❑ 92MinGolG-19
❑ 93MinGolG-24
❑ 94MinGolG-26
**Steel, Andy**
❑ 93HumHawP-19
❑ 97KinHaw-12
**Steel, Greg**
❑ 78LouGea-17
**Steelers, Sheffield**
❑ 93SheSte-18
❑ 94SheSte-5
❑ 97SheSte-14
❑ 97SheSte-14
**Steen, Anders**
❑ 80JetPos-21
❑ 80PepCap-138
❑ 83SweSemE-118
**Steen, Thomas**
❑ 81JetPos-20
❑ 82Jet-24
❑ 82OPC-391
❑ 82SweSemHVS-150
❑ 83Jet-22
❑ 83OPC-393
❑ 83OPCSti-289
❑ 83Vac-138
❑ 84JetPol-19
❑ 84OPC-348
❑ 84OPCSti-292
❑ 85JetPol-19
❑ 85OPC-206
❑ 85OPCSti-253
❑ 86JetBor-22
❑ 86KraDra-69
❑ 86OPC-257
❑ 86OPCSti-110
❑ 87Jet-20
❑ 87OPC-221
❑ 87PanSti-365
❑ 88JetPol-21
❑ 88OPC-254
❑ 88OPCSti-138
❑ 88PanSti-159
❑ 89JetSaf-26
❑ 89OPC-290
❑ 89OPCSti-144
❑ 89PanSti-163
❑ 89SweSemWCS-15
❑ 90Bow-133
❑ 90BowTif-133
❑ 90JetIGA-30
❑ 90Kra-55
❑ 90OPC-283
❑ 90PanSti-316
❑ 90ProSet-356
❑ 90ProSet-565
❑ 90Sco-14
❑ 90ScoCan-14
❑ 90ScoHotRS-8
❑ 90Top-283
❑ 90TopTif-283
❑ 90UppDec-94
❑ 90UppDec-313
❑ 90UppDecF-94
❑ 90UppDecF-313
❑ 91Bow-200
❑ 91JetIGA-30
❑ 91JetPanTS-22
❑ 91OPC-218
❑ 91PanSti-68
❑ 91Pin-275
❑ 91PinFre-275
❑ 91ProSet-271
❑ 91ProSetFre-271
❑ 91ProSetPla-138
❑ 91ScoAme-198
❑ 91ScoCan-198
❑ 91StaClu-207
❑ 91SweSemWCS-209
❑ 91Top-218
❑ 91UppDec-181
❑ 91UppDecF-181
❑ 92Bow-312
❑ 92OPC-385
❑ 92PanSti-53
❑ 92PanStiFre-53
❑ 92Par-214
❑ 92ParEmel-214
❑ 92Pin-29
❑ 92PinFre-29
❑ 92ProSet-217
❑ 92Sco-80
❑ 92ScoCan-80
❑ 92Top-141
❑ 92TopGol-141G
❑ 92Ult-247
❑ 92UppDec-154
❑ 93Don-389
❑ 93JetRuf-24
❑ 93Lea-165
❑ 93OPCPre-11
❑ 93OPCPreG-11
❑ 93PanSti-191
❑ 93Par-502
❑ 93ParEmel-502
❑ 93Pin-159
❑ 93PinCan-159
❑ 93Pow-275
❑ 93Pow-476
❑ 93Sco-71
❑ 93ScoCan-71
❑ 93StaClu-282
❑ 93StaCluFDI-282
❑ 93StaCluO-282
❑ 93SweSemWCS-36
❑ 93TopPre-11
❑ 93TopPreG-11
❑ 93Ult-69
❑ 93UppDec-166
❑ 94BeAPSig-159
❑ 94CanGamNHLP-255
❑ 94Don-154
❑ 94EASpo-148
❑ 94Lea-376
❑ 94OPCPre-471
❑ 94OPCPreSE-471
❑ 94Par-263
❑ 94ParGol-263
❑ 94Pin-171
❑ 94PinArtP-171
❑ 94PinRinC-171
❑ 94Sco-65
❑ 94ScoGol-65
❑ 94ScoPla-65
❑ 94ScoPlaTS-65
❑ 94StaClu-176
❑ 94StaCluFDI-176
❑ 94StaCluMOMS-176
❑ 94StaCluSTWC-176
❑ 94TopPre-471
❑ 94TopPreSE-471
❑ 94Ult-396
❑ 94UppDec-192
❑ 94UppDecEleIce-192
❑ 95SweGloWC-40
❑ 96GerDELE-33
❑ 98GerDELE-162
**Steenbergen, Lyle**
❑ 96SasBla-23
**Steer, Jamie**
❑ 90MicTecHus-24
❑ 91MicTecHus-24
❑ 91MicTecHus-25
❑ 91MicTecHus-34
❑ 92GreMon-16
❑ 94ClaProP-240
❑ 94DayBom-8
❑ 94DayBom-22
**Stefan, Greg**
❑ 80OshGen-22
❑ 84OPC-65
❑ 84OPCSti-41
❑ 84Top-48
❑ 85OPC-157
❑ 85OPCSti-31
❑ 85Top-157
❑ 86OPC-51
❑ 86OPCSti-165
❑ 86Top-51
❑ 87OPC-186
❑ 87PanSti-237
❑ 87RedWinLC-27
❑ 87Top-186
❑ 88OPC-68
❑ 88OPCMin-38
❑ 88OPCSti-252
❑ 88PanSti-37
❑ 88RedWinLC-22
❑ 88Top-68
❑ 89OPC-23
❑ 89OPCSti-248
❑ 89PanSti-59
❑ 89RedWinLC-16
❑ 89Top-23
**Stefan, Joe**
❑ 90ProAHLIHL-519
**Stefan, Leo**
❑ 94FinnJaaK-290
❑ 94GerDELE-206
❑ 95GerDELE-208
❑ 95SweGloWC-223
❑ 96GerDELE-290
❑ 96SweSemW-200
❑ 98GerDELE-324
**Stefaniak, Josef**
❑ 69SweWorC-197
**Steffen, Jeff**
❑ 81OshGen-22
❑ 82OshGen-8
❑ 83OshGen-25
**Steffen, Todd**
❑ 82KitRan-23
**Steiger, Ewald**
❑ 94GerDELE-310
**Steiger, Helmut**
❑ 82SweSemHVS-119
❑ 89SweSemWCS-116
❑ 91SweSemWCS-174
❑ 94GerDELE-267
❑ 95GerDELE-260
❑ 96GerDELE-148
**Stein, Phil**
❑ 34BeeGro1P-349
**Steinbock, Stefan**
❑ 94GerDELE-325
❑ 95GerDELE-301
❑ 96GerDELE-328
**Steinburg, Trevor**
❑ 88NordGenF-30
❑ 88NordTeal-31
❑ 89HalCit-24
❑ 89ProAHL-154
❑ 90ProAHLIHL-462
**Steinecker, Stefan**
❑ 94GerDELE-57
❑ 95GerDELE-52
**Steiner, Ondrej**
❑ 92Cla-37
❑ 92UppDec-604
❑ 94CzeAPSE-158
❑ 95CzeAPSE-255
❑ 96ClaGol-37
**Steinmetz, Todd**
❑ 93WatBlaH-24
**Steklac, Peter**
❑ 96SloPeeWT-26
**Stelcich, Martin**
❑ 94CzeAPSE-213
**Stelljes, Matt**
❑ 92MinGolG-20
**Stelmak, Jamie**
❑ 91AirCanSJHL-B36
❑ 92MPSPhoSJHL-137
**Stelnov, Igor**
❑ 87RusNatT-18
❑ 89SweSemWCS-85
❑ 91OPCIns-26R
❑ 92SweSemE-260
**Stemkowski, Pete**
❑ 64BeeGro3P-186
❑ 65Coc-98
❑ 65Top-84
❑ 66Top-15
❑ 66TopUSAT-15
❑ 67PosFliB-10
❑ 67Top-12
❑ 67YorActOct-8
❑ 67YorActOct-9
❑ 67YorActOct-12
❑ 67YorActOct-14
❑ 68OPC-33
❑ 68ShiCoi-43
❑ 68Top-33
❑ 69OPC-65
❑ 69Top-65
❑ 70EssPowPla-196
❑ 70OPC-25
❑ 70OPC-182
❑ 70SarProSta-50
❑ 70Top-25
❑ 71OPC-217
❑ 71SarProSta-115
❑ 71TorSun-184
❑ 72OPC-78
❑ 72SarProSta-143
❑ 73OPC-217
❑ 74LipSou-42
❑ 74NHLActSta-193
❑ 74OPCNHL-77
❑ 74Top-77
❑ 75OPCNHL-303
❑ 75Top-303
❑ 76OPCNHL-166
❑ 76Top-166
❑ 77OPCNHL-272
❑ 78OPC-290
❑ 94ParTalB-113
❑ 95Par66-112
❑ 95Par66Coi-112
**Sten, Marko**
❑ 93FinnSIS-210
**Stenar, Olle**
❑ 65SweCorI-66
**Stenlund, Ola**
❑ 83SweSemE-178
❑ 84SweSemE-201
❑ 86SwePanS-223
❑ 87SwePanS-216
❑ 89SweSemE-197
**Stenlund, Ove**
❑ 64SweCorI-150
❑ 65SweCorI-150
❑ 67SweHoc-277
❑ 69SweHocS-321
❑ 70SweHocS-225
❑ 72SweHocS-283
**Stenvall, Lars**
❑ 73SweHocS-40
❑ 73SweWorCS-40
**Stepan, Brad**
❑ 87SauSteMG-25
**Stepanek, Dan**
❑ 94DubFigS-27
**Stepanek, Martin**
❑ 94CzeAPSE-65
❑ 95CzeAPSE-85
❑ 96CzeAPSE-173
**Stephan, Greg**
❑ 95Sla-79
**Stephan, Joe**
❑ 89ProIHL-127
**Stephanson, Ken**
❑ 72NatOttWHA-21
**Stephens, Charlie**
❑ 97BeeAutA-72
❑ 97PinBee-72
❑ 97PinBeeGP-72
❑ 98SP Aut-132
❑ 98SP AutSotTG-CS
❑ 98SSASotT-CS
❑ 98UppDec-409
❑ 98UppDecE-409
❑ 98UppDecE1o1-409
❑ 98UppDecGR-409
❑ 99SP AutPS-132
**Stephens, Troy**
❑ 897thInnSOHL-98
❑ 907thInnSOHL-372
❑ 95ForWorFT-10
**Stephenson, Bob**
❑ 79MapLeaP-30
❑ 79OPC-391
**Stephenson, Ken**
❑ 69SweHocS-364
**Stephenson, Slade**
❑ 917thInnSWHL-356
**Stephenson, Wayne**
❑ 69SweHocS-365
❑ 69SweWorC-188
❑ 72BluWhiBor-19
❑ 72OPC-275
❑ 72SarProSta-191
❑ 73BluWhiBor-19
❑ 73OPC-31
❑ 73Top-31
❑ 74OPCNHL-218
❑ 74Top-218
❑ 75FlyCanDC-17
❑ 75OPCNHL-355
❑ 76OPCNHL-190
❑ 76Top-190
❑ 77OPCNHL-142
❑ 77Top-142
❑ 78OPC-223
❑ 78Top-223
❑ 79OPC-38
❑ 79Top-38
❑ 80OPC-121
❑ 80Top-121
❑ 81SweSemHVS-73
**Sterflinger, Robert**
❑ 94GerDELE-99
❑ 95GerDELE-86
❑ 96GerDELE-275
**Sterflinger, Thomas**
❑ 94GerDELE-336
❑ 95GerDELE-294
❑ 96GerDELE-323
**Stern, Mike**
❑ 81OshGen-13
❑ 82OshGen-17
❑ 83OshGen-20
**Stern, Ron**
❑ 92ParEmel-265
❑ 95BeAPSigDC-S79
❑ 95CanGamNHLP-59
**Stern, Ronnie**
❑ 87FliSpi-18
❑ 88CanuMoh-21
❑ 89ProIHL-179
❑ 90CanuMoh-28
❑ 90ProSet-549
❑ 91CanuPanTS-24
❑ 91FlamIGA-21
❑ 91ProSet-362
❑ 91ProSetFre-362
❑ 91ScoCan-408
❑ 92FlamIGA-25
❑ 92Par-265
❑ 92Pin-217
❑ 92PinFre-217
❑ 92Sco-237
❑ 92ScoCan-237
❑ 92Ult-271
❑ 93DurSco-28
❑ 93Lea-261
❑ 93OPCPre-341
❑ 93OPCPreG-341
❑ 93Par-303
❑ 93ParEmel-303
❑ 93Pow-43
❑ 93Sco-409
❑ 93ScoCan-409
❑ 93StaClu-68
❑ 93StaCluFDI-68
❑ 93StaCluFDIO-68
❑ 93StaCluO-68
❑ 93TopPre-341
❑ 93TopPreG-341
❑ 94BeAPla-R122
❑ 94Lea-399
❑ 94OPCPre-71
❑ 94OPCPreSE-71
❑ 94TopPre-71
❑ 94TopPreSE-71
❑ 94UppDec-27
❑ 94UppDecEleIce-27
❑ 95BeAPla-79
❑ 95BeAPSig-S79
❑ 95Lea-204
❑ 95PlaOneoOne-131
❑ 95Top-181
❑ 95TopOPCI-181
❑ 95UppDec-368
❑ 95UppDecEleIce-368
❑ 95UppDecEleIceG-368
❑ 96UppDec-28
❑ 97Pac-346
❑ 97PacCop-346
❑ 97PacEmeGre-346
❑ 97PacIceB-346
❑ 97PacRed-346
❑ 97PacSil-346
❑ 99Pac-382
❑ 99PacCop-382
❑ 99PacGol-382
❑ 99PacIceB-382
❑ 99PacPreD-382
**Sterner, Krister**
❑ 70SweHocS-67
❑ 71SweHocS-119
❑ 72SweHocS-39
❑ 73SweHocS-152
❑ 73SweWorCS-152
❑ 74SweHocS-150
**Sterner, Ove**
❑ 65SweCorI-104B
**Sterner, Ulf**
❑ 64SweCorI-4
❑ 64SweCorI-97
❑ 65SweCorI-4
❑ 65SweCorI-97
❑ 67SweHoc-165
❑ 69SweHocS-199
❑ 69SweHocS-346
❑ 69SweWorC-41
❑ 69SweWorC-48
❑ 69SweWorC-57
❑ 69SweWorC-58
❑ 69SweWorC-115
❑ 70SweHocS-291
❑ 71SweHocS-24
❑ 71SweHocS-176
❑ 72SweSemWC-56
❑ 73SweHocS-9
❑ 73SweHocS-179
❑ 73SweWorCS-9
❑ 73SweWorCS-179
❑ 74SweHocS-317
❑ 81SweSemHVS-115
❑ 91SweSemWCS-234
❑ 95SweGloWC-69
**Stevens, John**
❑ 83OshGen-26
❑ 88ProAHL-123
❑ 89ProAHL-346
❑ 90ProAHLIHL-189
❑ 91ProAHLCHL-108
**Stevens, Kevin**
❑ 89PanSti-321
❑ 89PenCokE-4
❑ 89PenFoo-7
❑ 90Bow-208
❑ 90BowTif-208
❑ 90OPC-360
❑ 90OPCPre-111
❑ 90PanSti-131
❑ 90PenFoo-9
❑ 90ProSet-240
❑ 90Sco-53
❑ 90ScoCan-53
❑ 90ScoYouS-17
❑ 90Top-360
❑ 90TopTif-360
❑ 90UppDec-14
❑ 90UppDecF-14
❑ 91Bow-92
❑ 91Bow-418
❑ 91Bow-421
❑ 91Bow-422
❑ 91McDUppD-3
❑ 91OPC-267
❑ 91OPC-421
❑ 91OPCPre-26
❑ 91PanSti-269
❑ 91Par-135
❑ 91Par-473
❑ 91ParFre-135
❑ 91ParFre-473
❑ 91PenCokE-25
❑ 91PenFoo-8
❑ 91PenFooCS-9
❑ 91Pin-191
❑ 91PinB-B4
❑ 91PinBFre-B4
❑ 91PinFre-191
❑ 91ProSet-185
❑ 91ProSet-314
❑ 91ProSetFre-185
❑ 91ProSetFre-314
❑ 91ProSetPla-93
❑ 91ProSetPOTM-P2
❑ 91ScoAme-248
❑ 91ScoCan-468
❑ 91StaClu-234
❑ 91SweSemWCS-145
❑ 91Top-267
❑ 91Top-421
❑ 91UppDec-154
❑ 91UppDec-613
❑ 91UppDecF-154
❑ 91UppDecF-613
❑ 92Bow-241
❑ 92Bow-366
❑ 92HumDum1-21
❑ 92McDUppD-H3
❑ 92OPC-29
❑ 92PanSti-221
❑ 92PanSti-281
❑ 92PanStiFre-221
❑ 92PanStiFre-281
❑ 92Par-138
❑ 92Par-466
❑ 92ParEmel-138
❑ 92ParEmel-466
❑ 92PenCokC-21
❑ 92PenFoo-15
❑ 92Pin-288
❑ 92PinCanPP-2
❑ 92PinFre-288
❑ 92PinTeaP-4
❑ 92PinTeaPF-4
❑ 92ProSet-140
❑ 92Sco-25
❑ 92Sco-492
❑ 92Sco-518
❑ 92ScoCan-25
❑ 92ScoCan-492
❑ 92ScoCanPS-1
❑ 92ScoCanPS-2
❑ 92ScoUSAG-10
❑ 92SeaPat-66
❑ 92StaClu-110
❑ 92StaClu-257
❑ 92Top-259
❑ 92Top-343
❑ 92Top-429
❑ 92TopGol-259G
❑ 92TopGol-343G
❑ 92TopGol-429G
❑ 92Ult-171
❑ 92UltAllS-5
❑ 92UppDec-275
❑ 92UppDec-454
❑ 92UppDec-630
❑ 92UppDecGHS-G4
❑ 93ClaProPro-31
❑ 93Don-265
❑ 93Lea-69
❑ 93LeaGolAS-4
❑ 93LeaHatTA-9
❑ 93McDUppD-25
❑ 93OPCPre-170
❑ 93OPCPre-370
❑ 93OPCPreG-170
❑ 93OPCPreG-370
❑ 93PanSti-79
❑ 93Par-158
❑ 93ParEmel-158
❑ 93PenFoo-17
❑ 93PenSti-11
❑ 93Pin-149
❑ 93PinAllS-15
❑ 93PinAllSC-15
❑ 93PinCan-149
❑ 93PinNifFif-9
❑ 93PinTeaP-4
❑ 93PinTeaPC-4
❑ 93Pow-195
❑ 93PowPoiL-17
❑ 93Sco-325
❑ 93ScoCan-325
❑ 93ScoDreTea-23
❑ 93ScoDynDC-8
❑ 93SeaPat-19
❑ 93StaClu-158
❑ 93StaClu-457
❑ 93StaCluAS-6
❑ 93StaCluFDI-158
❑ 93StaCluFDI-457
❑ 93StaCluFDIO-158
❑ 93StaCluO-158
❑ 93StaCluO-457
❑ 93SweSemWCS-179
❑ 93TopPre-170
❑ 93TopPre-370
❑ 93TopPreG-170
❑ 93TopPreG-370
❑ 93Ult-229
❑ 93UltAllS-6
❑ 93UppDec-126
❑ 93UppDec-230
❑ 93UppDecHT-HT19
❑ 93UppDecLAS-14
❑ 93UppDecSP-124
❑ 94BeAPla-R82
❑ 94CanGamNHLP-189
❑ 94Don-229
❑ 94EASpo-106
❑ 94Fin-80
❑ 94FinRef-80
❑ 94FinRinL-13
❑ 94FinSupTW-80
❑ 94Fla-140
❑ 94Fle-170
❑ 94HocWit-20
❑ 94Lea-356
❑ 94LeaLim-46
❑ 94OPCPre-290
❑ 94OPCPreSE-290
❑ 94Par-177
❑ 94ParGol-177
❑ 94ParSEV-9
❑ 94PenFoo-19
❑ 94Pin-299
❑ 94PinArtP-299
❑ 94PinRinC-299
❑ 94PinTeaP-TP7
❑ 94PinTeaPDP-TP7
❑ 94Sco-182
❑ 94ScoChelt-CI4
❑ 94ScoGol-182
❑ 94ScoPla-182
❑ 94ScoPlaTS-182
❑ 94Sel-106
❑ 94SelGol-106
❑ 94TopFinI-17
❑ 94TopPre-290
❑ 94TopPreSE-290
❑ 94Ult-170
❑ 94UltRedLS-10
❑ 94UppDec-390
❑ 94UppDecEleIce-390
❑ 94UppDecSPI-SP62
❑ 94UppDecSPIDC-SP62
❑ 95BeAPla-12
❑ 95BeAPSig-S12
❑ 95BeAPSigDC-S12
❑ 95Bow-59
❑ 95BowAllFoi-59
❑ 95ColCho-219
❑ 95ColChoPC-219
❑ 95ColChoPCP-219
❑ 95ColEdgILL-L10
❑ 95Don-221
❑ 95DonEli-95
❑ 95DonEliDCS-95
❑ 95DonEliDCU-95
❑ 95Emo-12
❑ 95EmoNteP-8
❑ 95ImpSti-9
❑ 95Lea-216
❑ 95LeaLim-96
❑ 95Met-11
❑ 95ParInt-10
❑ 95ParInt-370
❑ 95ParIntEl-10
❑ 95ParIntEl-370
❑ 95PinFan-28
❑ 95PlaOneoOne-10
❑ 95PlaOneoOne-123
❑ 95ProMag-20
❑ 95Sco-44
❑ 95ScoBlaIce-44
❑ 95ScoBlaIceAP-44
❑ 95SelCer-46
❑ 95SelCerMG-46
❑ 95SkyImp-13
❑ 95StaClu-50

676 • Stevens, Mike


❑ 95StaCluFea-F6
❑ 95StaCluMOMS-50
❑ 95Sum-67
❑ 95SumArtP-67
❑ 95SumIce-67
❑ 95SweGloWC-122
❑ 95Top-282
❑ 95TopHidGem-11HG
❑ 95TopOPCI-282
❑ 95TopPowL-5PL
❑ 95TopSupSki-61
❑ 95TopSupSkiPla-61
❑ 95Ult-127
❑ 95Ult-207
❑ 95UltCreCra-18
❑ 95UltGolM-127
❑ 95UppDec-96
❑ 95UppDecEleIce-96
❑ 95UppDecEleIceG-96
❑ 95UppDecSpeE-SE96
❑ 95UppDecSpeEdiG-SE96
❑ 95Zen-52
❑ 95ZenGifG-2
❑ 96ColCho-124
❑ 96NHLProSTA-20
❑ 96PenTri-6
❑ 96PlaOneoOne-333
❑ 96SP-73
❑ 96TeaOut-12
❑ 96TopNHLP-81
❑ 96TopPicOI-81
❑ 96UppDec-78
❑ 96UppDecGN-X34
❑ 97DonPri-42
❑ 97DonPriSoA-42
❑ 97Kat-96
❑ 97KatGol-96
❑ 97KatSil-96
❑ 97Pac-115
❑ 97PacCop-115
❑ 97PacEmeGre-115
❑ 97PacIceB-115
❑ 97PacOme-149
❑ 97PacOmeC-149
❑ 97PacOmeDG-149
❑ 97PacOmeEG-149
❑ 97PacOmeG-149
❑ 97PacOmeIB-149
❑ 97PacPar-121
❑ 97PacParC-121
❑ 97PacParDG-121
❑ 97PacParEG-121
❑ 97PacParIB-121
❑ 97PacParRed-121
❑ 97PacParSil-121
❑ 97PacRed-115
❑ 97PacRev-91
❑ 97PacRevC-91
❑ 97PacRevE-91
❑ 97PacRevIB-91
❑ 97PacRevR-91
❑ 97PacRevS-91
❑ 97PacSil-115
❑ 97Pin-143
❑ 97PinIns-153
❑ 97PinPrePBB-143
❑ 97PinPrePBC-143
❑ 97PinPrePBM-143
❑ 97PinPrePBY-143
❑ 97PinPrePFC-143
❑ 97PinPrePFM-143
❑ 97PinPrePFY-143
❑ 97PinPrePla-143
❑ 97Sco-159
❑ 97ScoArtPro-159
❑ 97ScoGolBla-159
❑ 97ScoRan-6
❑ 97ScoRanPla-6
❑ 97ScoRanPre-6
❑ 98Be A PPA-88
❑ 98Be A PPAA-88
❑ 98Be A PPAAF-88
❑ 98Be A PPTBASG-88
❑ 98Be APG-88
❑ 98Fin-56
❑ 98FinNo P-56
❑ 98FinNo PR-56
❑ 98FinRef-56
❑ 98Pac-301
❑ 98PacAur-127
❑ 98PacIceB-301
❑ 98PacPar-158
❑ 98PacParC-158
❑ 98PacParEG-158
❑ 98PacParH-158
❑ 98PacParIB-158
❑ 98PacParS-158
❑ 98PacRed-301
❑ 98UppDec-130
❑ 98UppDecE-130
❑ 98UppDecE1o1-130
❑ 98UppDecGR-130
❑ 99Pac-281
❑ 99PacCop-281
❑ 99PacGol-281
❑ 99PacIceB-281
❑ 99PacPreD-281

**Stevens, Mike**
❑ 83KitRan-21
❑ 84KitRan-25
❑ 85FreExp-5
❑ 86FreExp-24
❑ 88ProAHL-301
❑ 89ProAHL-240
❑ 90NewSai-24
❑ 90ProAHLIHL-146
❑ 91ProAHLCHL-345
❑ 92BinRan-7
❑ 95CleLum-23
❑ 95ColEdgI-118
❑ 98GerDELE-236

**Stevens, P.C.**
❑ 23V1281PauC-33

**Stevens, Randy**
❑ 91MicTecHus-30
❑ 93MicTecH-7
❑ 95Cla-80
❑ 95ClaAut-21
❑ 96LouRiv-11

**Stevens, Rod**
❑ 917thInnSWHL-82
❑ 93KamBla-20
❑ 96SyrCru-38

**Stevens, Scott**
❑ 82Cap-23
❑ 83OPC-376
❑ 83OPCSti-188
❑ 84CapPizH-15
❑ 84OPC-206
❑ 84Top-149
❑ 85CapPizH-14
❑ 85OPC-62
❑ 85OPCSti-107
❑ 85Top-62
❑ 86CapKod-25
❑ 86CapPol-24
❑ 86OPC-126
❑ 86OPCSti-254
❑ 86Top-126
❑ 87CapKod-3
❑ 87CapTeaIss-22
❑ 87OPC-25
❑ 87OPCSti-233
❑ 87PanSti-177
❑ 87Top-25
❑ 88CapBor-20
❑ 88CapSmo-22
❑ 88FriLayS-15
❑ 88OPC-60
❑ 88OPCMin-39
❑ 88OPCSti-68
❑ 88PanSti-368
❑ 88Top-60
❑ 88TopStiIns-4
❑ 89CapKod-3
❑ 89CapTeaIss-22
❑ 89OPC-93
❑ 89OPCSti-76
❑ 89PanSti-341
❑ 89SweSemWCS-58
❑ 89Top-93
❑ 90BluKod-21
❑ 90Kra-56
❑ 90OPC-211
❑ 90OPC-394
❑ 90OPCPre-112
❑ 90PanSti-155
❑ 90ProSet-321
❑ 90ProSet-528
❑ 90Sco-188
❑ 90Sco-341
❑ 90ScoCan-188
❑ 90ScoCan-341
❑ 90ScoHotRS-82
❑ 90ScoRoo-40T
❑ 90Top-211
❑ 90Top-394
❑ 90TopTif-211
❑ 90UppDec-236
❑ 90UppDec-436
❑ 90UppDec-482
❑ 90UppDecF-236
❑ 90UppDecF-436
❑ 90UppDecF-482
❑ 91Bow-369
❑ 91Kra-53
❑ 91McDUppD-24
❑ 91OPC-481
❑ 91OPCPre-84
❑ 91PanSti-26
❑ 91Par-102
❑ 91ParFre-102
❑ 91Pin-81
❑ 91PinFre-81
❑ 91ProSet-216
❑ 91ProSet-292
❑ 91ProSet-423
❑ 91ProSetFre-216
❑ 91ProSetFre-292
❑ 91ProSetFre-423
❑ 91ProSetPla-72
❑ 91ProSetPla-281
❑ 91ScoAme-40
❑ 91ScoAme-303
❑ 91ScoCan-40
❑ 91ScoCan-307
❑ 91ScoCan-595
❑ 91ScoRoo-45T
❑ 91StaClu-265
❑ 91SweSemWCS-56
❑ 91Top-481
❑ 91UppDec-132
❑ 91UppDec-539
❑ 91UppDecF-132
❑ 91UppDecF-539
❑ 92BluUDBB-20
❑ 92Bow-160
❑ 92Bow-242
❑ 92HumDum1-22
❑ 92McDUppD-27
❑ 92OPC-251
❑ 92OPC-336
❑ 92OPC25AI-16
❑ 92PanSti-181
❑ 92PanStiFre-181
❑ 92Par-92
❑ 92ParCheP-CP18
❑ 92ParEmel-92
❑ 92Pin-280
❑ 92PinCanPP-1
❑ 92PinFre-280
❑ 92ProSet-95
❑ 92Sco-429
❑ 92ScoCan-429
❑ 92SeaPat-50
❑ 92StaClu-151
❑ 92Top-156
❑ 92Top-269
❑ 92TopGol-156G
❑ 92TopGol-269G
❑ 92Ult-119
❑ 92UppDec-297
❑ 93Don-192
❑ 93Kra-49
❑ 93Lea-60
❑ 93McDUppD-26
❑ 93OPCPre-80
❑ 93OPCPreG-80
❑ 93PanSti-43
❑ 93Par-114
❑ 93ParEmel-114
❑ 93Pin-25
❑ 93PinAllS-4
❑ 93PinAllSC-4
❑ 93PinCan-25
❑ 93PinCap-13
❑ 93PinCapC-13
❑ 93PinTeaP-3
❑ 93PinTeaPC-3
❑ 93Pow-143
❑ 93Sco-111
❑ 93ScoCan-111
❑ 93ScoDreTea-5
❑ 93ScoFra-11
❑ 93StaClu-383
❑ 93StaCluAS-9
❑ 93StaCluFDI-383
❑ 93StaCluO-383
❑ 93SweSemWCS-196
❑ 93TopPre-80
❑ 93TopPreG-80
❑ 93Ult-189
❑ 93UppDec-119
❑ 93UppDecLAS-15
❑ 93UppDecSP-89
❑ 94BeAPla-R146
❑ 94CanGamNHLP-152
❑ 94CanGamNHLP-262
❑ 94CanGamNHLP-345
❑ 94Don-262
❑ 94DonDom-2
❑ 94EASpo-73
❑ 94Fin-18
❑ 94FinDivFCC-7
❑ 94FinnJaaK-83
❑ 94FinRef-18
❑ 94FinSupTW-18
❑ 94Fla-100
❑ 94Fle-119
❑ 94HocWit-65
❑ 94Kra-72
❑ 94Lea-363
❑ 94LeaGolS-12
❑ 94LeaLim-85
❑ 94McDUppD-McD7
❑ 94OPCPre-126
❑ 94OPCPre-153
❑ 94OPCPre-370
❑ 94OPCPre-451
❑ 94OPCPre-494
❑ 94OPCPreSE-126
❑ 94OPCPreSE-153
❑ 94OPCPreSE-370
❑ 94OPCPreSE-451
❑ 94OPCPreSE-494
❑ 94ParCratGB-13
❑ 94ParCratGG-13
❑ 94ParCratGR-13
❑ 94ParSE-SE97
❑ 94ParSEG-SE97
❑ 94ParVin-V41
❑ 94Pin-310
❑ 94PinArtP-310
❑ 94PinRinC-310
❑ 94PinTeaP-TP5
❑ 94PinTeaPDP-TP5
❑ 94Sco-193
❑ 94ScoCheIt-CI2
❑ 94ScoDreTea-DT5
❑ 94ScoFra-TF13
❑ 94ScoGol-193
❑ 94ScoPla-193
❑ 94ScoPlaTS-193
❑ 94Sel-82
❑ 94SelFirLin-8
❑ 94SelGol-82
❑ 94SP-66
❑ 94SPDieCut-66
❑ 94StaClu-4
❑ 94StaCluFDI-4
❑ 94StaCluMO-30
❑ 94StaCluMOMS-4
❑ 94StaCluSTWC-4
❑ 94TopPre-126
❑ 94TopPre-153
❑ 94TopPre-370
❑ 94TopPre-451
❑ 94TopPre-494
❑ 94TopPreSE-126
❑ 94TopPreSE-153
❑ 94TopPreSE-370
❑ 94TopPreSE-451
❑ 94TopPreSE-494
❑ 94Ult-123
❑ 94UppDec-73
❑ 94UppDecEleIce-73
❑ 94UppDecIG-IG5
❑ 94UppDecNBAP-36
❑ 94UppDecPC-C30
❑ 94UppDecPCEG-C30
❑ 94UppDecPR-R48
❑ 94UppDecPRE-R48
❑ 94UppDecPreRG-R48
❑ 94UppDecSPI-SP45
❑ 94UppDecSPIDC-SP45
❑ 95BeAPla-219
❑ 95BeAPSig-S219
❑ 95BeAPSigDC-S219
❑ 95Bow-50
❑ 95BowAllFoi-50
❑ 95BowBes-BB4
❑ 95BowBesRef-BB4
❑ 95CanGamNHLP-165
❑ 95ColCho-223
❑ 95ColChoPC-223
❑ 95ColChoPCP-223
❑ 95Don-163
❑ 95DonEli-70
❑ 95DonEliDCS-70
❑ 95DonEliDCU-70
❑ 95Emo-102
❑ 95Fin-33
❑ 95Fin-152
❑ 95FinRef-33
❑ 95FinRef-152
❑ 95ImpSti-72
❑ 95KenStaLA-18
❑ 95KenStaLC-13
❑ 95Kra-6
❑ 95Lea-124
❑ 95Met-86
❑ 95MetIW-12
❑ 95NHLAcePC-2C
❑ 95ParInt-121
❑ 95ParIntEl-121
❑ 95ParIntNHLAS-4
❑ 95Pin-86
❑ 95PinArtP-86
❑ 95PinFulC-2
❑ 95PinRinC-86
❑ 95PlaOneoOne-61
❑ 95PlaOneoOne-167
❑ 95PosUppD-12
❑ 95ProMag-40
❑ 95Sco-160
❑ 95ScoBlaIce-160
❑ 95ScoBlaIceAP-160
❑ 95SelCer-66
❑ 95SelCerDS-18
❑ 95SelCerDSG-18
❑ 95SelCerMG-66
❑ 95SkyImp-97
❑ 95SP-81
❑ 95SPHol-FX13
❑ 95SPHolSpFX-FX13
❑ 95StaClu-45
❑ 95StaCluFea-F4
❑ 95StaCluMO-10
❑ 95StaCluMOMS-45
❑ 95StaCluNem-N1
❑ 95Sum-134
❑ 95SumArtP-134
❑ 95SumGM-8
❑ 95SumIce-134
❑ 95SweGloWC-81
❑ 95Top-275
❑ 95TopMysF-M17
❑ 95TopMysFR-M17
❑ 95TopOPCI-275
❑ 95TopPro-PF13
❑ 95TopRinL-6RL
❑ 95TopSupSki-7
❑ 95TopSupSkiPla-7
❑ 95Ult-92
❑ 95Ult-196
❑ 95UltGolM-92
❑ 95UppDec-482
❑ 95UppDecAGPRW-27
❑ 95UppDecEleIce-482
❑ 95UppDecEleIceG-482
❑ 95UppDecNHLAS-AS2
❑ 95UppDecPHE-H35
❑ 95UppDecPreH-H35
❑ 95UppDecSpeE-SE49
❑ 95UppDecSpeEdiG-SE49
❑ 95Zen-89
❑ 96ColCho-148
❑ 96ColCho-305
❑ 96ColCho-322
❑ 96ColChoMVP-UD36
❑ 96ColChoMVPG-UD36
❑ 96Dev-4
❑ 96Don-57
❑ 96DonCanI-103
❑ 96DonCanIGPP-103
❑ 96DonCanIRPP-103
❑ 96DonEli-30
❑ 96DonEliDCS-30
❑ 96DonHitLis-9
❑ 96DonPrePro-57
❑ 96DurAllT-DC16
❑ 96DurL'EB-JB16
❑ 96Fla-54
❑ 96FlaBluI-54
❑ 96Fle-61
❑ 96KraUppD-38
❑ 96Lea-175
❑ 96LeaLim-23
❑ 96LeaLimG-23
❑ 96LeaPre-38
❑ 96LeaPreP-175
❑ 96LeaPrePP-38
❑ 96MetUni-88
❑ 96NHLProSTA-40
❑ 96Pin-4
❑ 96PinArtP-4
❑ 96PinFoi-4
❑ 96PinPreS-4
❑ 96PinRinC-4
❑ 96PosUppD-22
❑ 96Sco-138
❑ 96ScoArtPro-138
❑ 96ScoDeaCAP-138
❑ 96ScoGolB-138
❑ 96ScoSpeAP-138
❑ 96SelCer-54
❑ 96SelCerAP-54
❑ 96SelCerBlu-54
❑ 96SelCerMB-54
❑ 96SelCerMG-54
❑ 96SelCerMR-54
❑ 96SelCerRed-54
❑ 96SkyImp-71
❑ 96SP-89
❑ 96SPx-24
❑ 96SPxGol-24
❑ 96StaCluMO-27
❑ 96Sum-9
❑ 96SumArtP-9
❑ 96SumIce-9
❑ 96SumMet-9
❑ 96SumPreS-9
❑ 96SweSemW-80
❑ 96TeaOut-48
❑ 96TopNHLP-115
❑ 96TopPicID-ID4
❑ 96TopPicOI-115
❑ 96Ult-95
❑ 96UltGolM-96
❑ 96UppDec-286
❑ 96UppDecBD-124
❑ 96UppDecBDG-124
❑ 96UppDecGN-X36
❑ 96UppDecPP-P9
❑ 96UppDecSS-SS9B
❑ 96Zen-73
❑ 96ZenArtP-73
❑ 97ColCho-140
❑ 97ColChoWD-W17
❑ 97Don-194
❑ 97DonCanI-114
❑ 97DonCanIDS-114
❑ 97DonCanIPS-114
❑ 97DonLim-176
❑ 97DonLimExp-176
❑ 97DonPreProG-194
❑ 97DonPreProS-194
❑ 97Kat-84
❑ 97KatGol-84
❑ 97KatSil-84
❑ 97Pac-273
❑ 97PacCop-273
❑ 97PacCroR-77
❑ 97PacCroRIB-77
❑ 97PacCroRS-77
❑ 97PacEmeGre-273
❑ 97PacIceB-273
❑ 97PacOme-134
❑ 97PacOmeC-134
❑ 97PacOmeDG-134
❑ 97PacOmeEG-134
❑ 97PacOmeG-134
❑ 97PacOmeIB-134
❑ 97PacRed-273
❑ 97PacSil-273
❑ 97Pin-158
❑ 97PinCer-115
❑ 97PinCerMB-115
❑ 97PinCerMG-115
❑ 97PinCerMR-115
❑ 97PinCerR-115
❑ 97PinIns-154
❑ 97PinPrePBB-158
❑ 97PinPrePBC-158
❑ 97PinPrePBM-158
❑ 97PinPrePBY-158
❑ 97PinPrePFC-158
❑ 97PinPrePFM-158
❑ 97PinPrePFY-158
❑ 97PinPrePla-158
❑ 97PinTotCMPG-115
❑ 97PinTotCPB-115
❑ 97PinTotCPG-115
❑ 97PinTotCPR-115
❑ 97Sco-224
❑ 97ScoDev-8
❑ 97ScoDevPla-8
❑ 97ScoDevPre-8
❑ 97SP AutI-I35
❑ 97SPAut-85
❑ 97SPAutID-I35
❑ 97SPAutIE-I35
❑ 97SPx-26
❑ 97SPxBro-26
❑ 97SPxGol-26
❑ 97SPxGraF-26
❑ 97SPxSil-26
❑ 97SPxSte-26
❑ 97UppDec-95
❑ 97UppDec-396
❑ 97UppDecBD-17
❑ 97UppDecBDDD-17
❑ 97UppDecBDQD-17
❑ 97UppDecBDTD-17
❑ 97UppDecTSS-11C
❑ 98Fin-132
❑ 98FinNo P-132
❑ 98FinNo PR-132
❑ 98FinPro-PP1
❑ 98FinRef-132
❑ 98O-PChr-23
❑ 98O-PChrBM-B12
❑ 98O-PChrBMR-B12
❑ 98O-PChrR-23
❑ 98Pac-272
❑ 98PacAur-113
❑ 98PacDynI-112
❑ 98PacDynIIB-112
❑ 98PacDynIR-112
❑ 98PacIceB-272
❑ 98PacOmeH-143
❑ 98PacOmeODI-143
❑ 98PacOmeR-143
❑ 98PacPar-139
❑ 98PacParC-139
❑ 98PacParEG-139
❑ 98PacParH-139
❑ 98PacParIB-139
❑ 98PacParS-139
❑ 98PacRed-272
❑ 98SP Aut-49
❑ 98Top-23
❑ 98TopBoaM-B12
❑ 98TopGolLC1-100
❑ 98TopGolLC1B-100
❑ 98TopGolLC1BOoO-100
❑ 98TopGolLC1OoO-100
❑ 98TopGolLC1R-100
❑ 98TopGolLC1ROoO-100
❑ 98TopGolLC2-100
❑ 98TopGolLC2B-100
❑ 98TopGolLC2BOoO-100
❑ 98TopGolLC2OoO-100
❑ 98TopGolLC2R-100
❑ 98TopGolLC2ROoO-100
❑ 98TopGolLC3-100
❑ 98TopGolLC3B-100
❑ 98TopGolLC3BOoO-100
❑ 98TopGolLC3OoO-100
❑ 98TopGolLC3R-100
❑ 98TopGolLC3ROoO-100
❑ 98TopO-P-23
❑ 98UC-113
❑ 98UC-239
❑ 98UD ChoPCR-113
❑ 98UD ChoPCR-239
❑ 98UD ChoR-113
❑ 98UD ChoR-239
❑ 98UDCP-113
❑ 98UppDec-121
❑ 98UppDecBD-49
❑ 98UppDecDD-49
❑ 98UppDecE-121
❑ 98UppDecE1o1-121
❑ 98UppDecGR-121
❑ 98UppDecM-116
❑ 98UppDecMGS-116
❑ 98UppDecMSS-116
❑ 98UppDecMSS-116
❑ 98UppDecQD-49
❑ 98UppDecTD-49
❑ 99DevPowP-NJD2
❑ 99Pac-250
❑ 99PacCop-250
❑ 99PacGol-250
❑ 99PacIceB-250
❑ 99PacPreD-250
❑ 99RetHoc-46
❑ 99SP AutPS-49
❑ 99UppDecM-114
❑ 99UppDecMGS-114
❑ 99UppDecMSS-114
❑ 99UppDecMSS-114
❑ 99UppDecRG-46
❑ 99UppDecRP-46

**Stevenson, Jason**
❑ 917thInnSOHL-90

**Stevenson, Jeremy**
❑ 907thInnSOHL-48
❑ 917thInnSOHL-8
❑ 91CorRoy-10
❑ 93SauSteMG-25
❑ 94GreMon-2

**Stevenson, Shayne**
❑ 86LonKni-15
❑ 88KitRan-20
❑ 897thInnSOHL-182
❑ 89KitRan-21
❑ 907thInnSMC-49
❑ 90ProAHLIHL-123
❑ 90Sco-405
❑ 90ScoCan-405
❑ 91OPC-121
❑ 91Top-121
❑ 91UppDec-332
❑ 91UppDecF-332

**Stevenson, Travis**
❑ 917thInnSWHL-273

**Stevenson, Turner**
❑ 907thInnSWHL-9
❑ 90Sco-426
❑ 90ScoCan-426
❑ 917thInnSWHL-125
❑ 91UppDec-691
❑ 91UppDecCWJC-65
❑ 91UppDecF-691
❑ 92FreCan-24
❑ 93FreCan-26
❑ 93UppDec-248
❑ 94CanaPos-26
❑ 94Fle-110
❑ 94FreCan-26
❑ 94Lea-492
❑ 94OPCPre-392
❑ 94OPCPreSE-392
❑ 94TopPre-392
❑ 94TopPreSE-392
❑ 94Ult-317
❑ 94UppDec-221
❑ 94UppDecEleIce-221
❑ 94UppDecSPI-SP132
❑ 94UppDecSPIDC-SP132
❑ 95CanaPos-18
❑ 95CanaShe-5
❑ 95ColCho-167
❑ 95ColChoPC-167
❑ 95ColChoPCP-167
❑ 95Don-218
❑ 95Lea-285
❑ 95ParInt-385
❑ 95ParIntEl-385
❑ 95Pin-115
❑ 95PinArtP-115
❑ 95PinRinC-115
❑ 95Top-34
❑ 95TopOPCI-34
❑ 95UppDec-202
❑ 95UppDecEleIce-202
❑ 95UppDecEleIceG-202
❑ 95UppDecWJA-6
❑ 96CanaPos-27
❑ 96CanaShe-20
❑ 96UppDec-85
❑ 97Be A PPAD-181
❑ 97Be A PPAPD-181
❑ 97BeAPla-181
❑ 97BeAPlaAut-181
❑ 97CanaPos-21
❑ 97PacInvNRB-106
❑ 97UppDec-297
❑ 98Be A PPA-71
❑ 98Be A PPAA-71
❑ 98Be A PPAAF-71
❑ 98Be A PPTBASG-71
❑ 98Be APG-71
❑ 99Pac-211
❑ 99PacCop-211
❑ 99PacGol-211
❑ 99PacIceB-211
❑ 99PacPreD-211
❑ 99UppDecM-106
❑ 99UppDecMGS-106
❑ 99UppDecMSS-106
❑ 99UppDecMSS-106

**Stewart, Adam**
❑ 96PriAlbROC-20

**Stewart, Alan**
❑ 88ProAHL-334
❑ 90Dev-25
❑ 90OPCPre-113
❑ 90ProSet-480

**Stewart, Andy**
❑ 94CenHocL-35

**Stewart, Bill**
❑ 79OPC-313
❑ 83MapLeaP-23
❑ 84MapLeaP-22
❑ 93SweSemWCS-213
❑ 95SweGloWC-238

**Stewart, Bill (30s)**
❑ 35DiaMatT5-11
❑ 36V356WorG-135
❑ 37DiaMatT6-11

**Stewart, Bill (50s)**
❑ 52JunBluT-94

**Stewart, Blair**
❑ 78OPC-355
❑ 79OPC-332

**Stewart, Bob**
❑ 72SarProSta-56
❑ 73OPC-188
❑ 73Top-159
❑ 74NHLActSta-71
❑ 74OPCNHL-92
❑ 74Top-92
❑ 75OPCNHL-47
❑ 75Top-47
❑ 76OPCNHL-291
❑ 77Coc-26
❑ 77OPCNHL-299
❑ 78BluPos-22
❑ 78OPC-46
❑ 78Top-46
❑ 79OPC-297

**Stewart, Brian**
❑ 95SauSteMG-20
❑ 95Sla-376
❑ 96SauSteMG-22
❑ 96SauSteMGA-22

**Stewart, Bryan**
❑ 90ForSasTra-18

**Stewart, Cam**
❑ 91MicWol-18

93Don-20
93Lea-337
93Par-284
93ParEmel-284
93Pin-434
93PinCan-434
93Pow-292
93Sco-588
93ScoCan-588
93ScoGol-588
93StaClu-440
93StaCluFDI-440
93StaCluO-440
93Ult-270
93UppDec-464
94ClaAut-NNO
94ClaProP-36
94Don-316
94Lea-281
940PCPre-111
940PCPreSE-111
94TopPre-111
94TopPreSE-111
94UppDec-487
94UppDecElcIce-487
**Stewart, David (Dave)**
907thInnSOHL-71
917thInnSOHL-236
92PhoRoa-21
93PhoRoa-21
94RoaExp-4
95RoaExp-2
96RoaExp-2
**Stewart, Doug**
81Ott67-12
82Ott67-24
83BraAle-11
91BriColJHL-63
**Stewart, Gary**
88ProIHL-5
**Stewart, Gaye**
34BeeGro1P-350A
34BeeGro1P-350B
44BeeGro2P-141
44BeeGro2P-213
45QuaOatP-51A
45QuaOatP-51B
51Par-99
52Par-25
91UltOriS-45
91UltOriSF-45
**Stewart, Glenn**
94GreMon-3
**Stewart, Jack**
34BeeGro1P-125
400PCV3012-124
44BeeGro2P-142
44BeeGro2P-214
51Par-53
76OldTim-18
83HalFP-N15
85HalFC-210
**Stewart, John**
72Flam-20
740PCNHL-175
74Top-175
**Stewart, Jon**
91RayJrC-15
**Stewart, Michael**
92BinRan-3
92Cla-71
94BinRan-22
96ClaGol-71
**Stewart, Nels**
330PCV304A-6
33V252CanG-46
33V357IceK-12
34BeeGro1P-255
34DiaMatS-57
34SweCap-31
35DiaMatT2-60
35DiaMatT3-55
35DiaMatTI-65
38BruGarMS-8
60Top-5
60TopSta-48
83HalFP-F12
85HalFC-86
**Stewart, Paul**
90ProSet-699
**Stewart, Ralph**
64CocCap-98
74NHLActSta-167
740PCNHL-158
740PCNHL-233
74Top-158
74Top-233
75OPCNHL-182
75Top-182
76CanuRoyB-20
760PCNHL-229
76Top-229
770PCNHL-386
**Stewart, Rob**
95VanVooRHI-13
**Stewart, Ron**
44BeeGro2P-455
45QuaOatP-52
52Par-94
53Par-9
54Par-23
54Par-92
55Par-5
55ParQuaO-5
57Par-T7

58Par-14
59Par-26
60Par-6
60ShiCoi-10
60YorPreP-34
61Par-6
61YorYelB-20
62Par-6
62ShiMetC-21
63ChePho-51
63Par-14
63Par-74
63TorSta-36
63YorWhiB-3
64BeeGro3P-27
64BeeGro3P-187A
64BeeGro3P-187B
64Top-99
64TorSta-45
65Coc-4
65Top-103
66Top-94
680PC-168
68ShiCoi-108
690PC-41
69Top-41
70EssPowPla-189
700PC-64
70SarProSta-120
70Top-64
710PC-236
94ParMisL-110
94ParTalB-128
95Par66-2
95Par66Coi-2
**Stewart, Ryan**
84KamBla-22
87MonHaw-23
93WinSpi-19
**Stewart, Scott**
91AirCanSJHL-B24
**Stickle, Leon**
90ProSet-700
**Stickney, Brent**
93FliGen-2
**Stienburg, Trevor**
85NordGenF-27
86FreExp-25
90HalCit-27
91ProAHLCHL-372
**Stiles, Tony**
84MonGolf-23
85MonGolf-12
**Still, Alastair**
88SudWol-17
89SudWol-2
907thInnSOHL-395
90SudWol-17
917thInnSOHL-230
**Stillman, Cory**
907thInnSOHL-192
917thInnSCHLAW-5
917thInnSOHL-175
92Cla-5
92Cla-8
92ClaLPs-LP5
92WinSpi-31
93Cla-29
94Cla-49
94ClaDraGol-49
94ClaProP-190
94ClaTri-T10
940PCPre-515
940PCPreSE-515
94ParSE-SE29
94ParSEG-SE29
94Pin-494
94PinArtP-494
94PinRinC-494
94St.JohF-22
94TopPre-515
94TopPreSE-515
94UppDec-268
94UppDecElcIce-268
95BeAPla-132
95BeAPSig-S132
95BeAPSigDC-S132
95Bow-131
95BowAllFoi-131
95BowBes-BB27
95BowBesRef-BB27
95CanGamNHLP-51
95ColCho-111
95ColChoPC-111
95ColChoPCP-111
95ColEdgI-74
95Don-152
95DonRatRoo-12
95Fin-61
95FinRef-61
95Ima-38
95ImaGol-38
95Lea-5
95ParInt-299
95ParIntEI-299
95Pin-212
95PinArtP-212
95PinRinC-212
95Sco-300
95ScoBlaIce-300
95ScoBlaIceAP-300
95SelCer-128
95SelCerMG-128
95SP-17
95Top-332

95TopOPCI-332
95TopSupSkiSR-SR4
95Ult-214
95UppDec-283
95UppDecElcIce-283
95UppDecElcIceG-283
95Zen-123
95ZenRooRC-16
96ClaGol-5
96ClaGol-8
96ColCho-40
96Don-231
96DonEli-106
96DonEliDCS-106
96DonPrePro-231
96Lea-138
96LeaPre-15
96LeaPreP-138
96LeaPrePP-15
96Sco-243
96ScoArtPro-243
96ScoDeaCAP-243
96ScoGolB-243
96ScoSpeAP-243
96SelCer-58
96SelCerAP-58
96SelCerBlu-58
96SelCerMB-58
96SelCerMG-58
96SelCerMR-58
96SelCerRed-58
96SkyImp-172
96TopNHLP-145
96TopPicOI-145
96TopPicRS-RS9
96UppDec-229
96Zen-113
96ZenArtP-113
97Be A PPAD-24
97Be A PPAPD-24
97BeAPla-24
97BeAPlaAut-24
97DonPri-88
97DonPriSoA-88
97Kat-24
97KatGol-24
97KatSil-24
97Pac-211
97PacCop-211
97PacCroR-21
97PacCroREG-21
97PacCroRIB-21
97PacCroRS-21
97PacEmeGre-211
97PacIceB-211
97PacOme-35
97PacOmeC-35
97PacOmeDG-35
97PacOmeEG-35
97PacOmeG-35
97PacOmeIB-35
97PacRed-211
97PacRev-20
97PacRevC-20
97PacRevE-20
97PacRevIB-20
97PacRevR-20
97PacRevS-20
97PacSil-211
97PinIns-164
97Sco-225
97SPAut-19
97Zen-52
97ZenZGol-52
97ZenZSil-52
980-PChr-191
980-PChrR-191
98Pac-125
98PacAur-29
98PacIceB-125
98PacOmeH-35
98PacOmeODI-35
98PacOmeR-35
98PacPar-32
98PacParC-32
98PacParEG-32
98PacParH-32
98PacParIB-32
98PacParS-32
98PacRed-125
98PacRev-22
98PacRevIS-22
98PacRevR-22
98Top-191
98TopO-P-191
98UC-33
98UD ChoPCR-33
98UD ChoR-33
98UDCP-33
98UppDec-54
98UppDecE-54
98UppDecE1o1-54
98UppDecGR-54
99Pac-62
99PacAur-24
99PacAurPD-24
99PacCop-62
99PacGol-62
99PacIceB-62
99PacPreD-62
**Stillman, Fredrik**
85SwePanS-183
86SwePanS-119
87SwePanS-114
89SweSemE-101

90SweSemE-103
91SweSemE-107
91SweSemE-345
91SweSemWCS-34
92SweSemE-135
93SweSemE-107
93SweSemWCS-9
93SweSemWCS-6
94FinnJaaK-57
94SweLeaE-216
94SweLeaEG-6
94SweLeaESS-5
95FinnSemWC-56
95GerDELE-55
95SweGloWC-17
**Stingh, Harkie**
95Sla-35
**Stitt, Mark**
95TolSto-10
**Stiver, Dan**
91MicWol-19
93St.JohML-22
94ClaProP-99
**Stocco, Regan**
93GueSto-7
94GueSto-8
95GueSto5A-19
95Sla-81
**Stock, Corey**
907thInnSWHL-309
917thInnSWHL-162
92TacRoc-23
93TacRoc-25
**Stock, P.J.**
98UppDec-131
98UppDecE-131
98UppDecE1o1-131
98UppDecGR-131
**Stockham, Darryl**
95SlaMemC-46
**Stoddard, Jack**
52Par-97
53Par-60
**Stojanov, Alexandar (Alek)**
907thInnSOHL-220
917thInnSMC-110
91AreDraPic-5
91Cla-6
91StaPicH-46
91UltDra-6
91UltDraP-2
95Bow-141
95BowAllFoi-141
95Don-329
95Lea-297
95Top-368
95TopOPCI-368
95UppDec-195
95UppDecElcIce-195
95UppDecElcIceG-195
96BeAPAut-80
96BeAPAutSil-80
96BeAPla-80
**Stolk, Darren**
89ProIHL-157
90ProAHLIIHL-384
91ProAHLCHL-579
**Stolp, Jeff**
91MinGolG-24
93DayBom-17
94DayBom-17
94DayBom-24
**Stolpe, Jan**
67SweHoc-228
69SweHocS-271
**Stoltz, Roland**
64SweCorI-29
64SweCorI-124
65SweCorI-29
65SweCorI-124
67SweHoc-74
69SweHocS-105
81SweSemHVS-111
83SweSemE-191
84SweSemE-219
86SwePanS-230
**Stone, Matt**
907thInnSOHL-99
917thInnSOHL-311
**Stone, Mike**
91MicWol-20
93MicWol-25
94HunBli-20
**Stone, Shawn**
917thInnSWHL-31
**Stonier, Troy**
95Sla-271
**Stopar, Rob**
897thInnSOHL-94
907thInnSOHL-242
90KitRan-10
**Storey, Red**
83HalFP-B14
85HalFC-28
**Storf, Florian**
94GerDELE-104
95GerDELE-104
96GerDELE-49
**Stork, Dean**
92BriColJHL-12
**Storm, Jay**
93MicTecH-4
**Storm, Jim**
90MicTecHus-16

91MicTecHus-26
91MicTecHus-34
93Don-445
93Par-354
93ParEmel-354
93Pow-356
93Sco-610
93ScoCan-610
93ScoGol-610
93StaCluTUSA-23
93TopPreTUSA-22
93WhaCok-21
94ClaAut-NNO
94ClaProP-37
94Don-280
94Lea-213
94Pin-237
94PinArtP-237
94PinRinC-237
94StaClu-26
94StaCluFDI-26
94StaCluMOMS-26
94StaCluSTWC-26
**Stormqvist, Jan-Erik**
89SweSemE-34
90SweSemE-182
**Storr, Jamie**
917thInnSOHL-270
93DonTeaC-20
930weSouPla-27
930weSouPla-28
930weSouPla-29
930weSouPla-30
93Par-508
93ParEmel-508
93Pin-458
93PinCan-458
93UppDec-538
94BeAPla-R157
94Cla-7
94ClaCHLAS-C9
94ClaDraGol-7
94ClaROYS-R18
94ClaTri-T31
94Fin-12
94Fin-146
94FinBowB-R7
94FinBowBR-R7
94FinRef-12
94FinRef-146
94FinSupTW-12
94FinSupTW-146
94Fle-99
94FleRooS-9
94LeaLimWJC-10
94LeaPhe-1
940PCPre-437
940PCPreSE-437
94ParSE-SE80
94ParSEG-SE80
94Pin-254
94Pin-475
94Pin-521
94PinArtP-254
94PinArtP-475
94PinRinC-254
94PinRinC-475
94PinRooTP-1
94Sco-201
94ScoGol-201
94ScoPla-201
94ScoTopRR-5
94Sel-170
94SelGol-170
94SelPro-YE1
94SelYouExp-YE1
94SP-137
94SPDieCut-137
94TopPre-437
94TopPreSE-437
94UltPro-8
94UppDec-236
94UppDec-531
94UppDec-568
94UppDecElcIce-236
94UppDecElcIce-531
94UppDecElcIce-568
94UppDecSPI-SP128
94UppDecSPIDC-SP128
94WinSpi-2
95Bow-128
95BowAllFoi-128
95ColCho-213
95ColChoPC-213
95ColChoPCP-213
95Don-67
95DonCanWJT-1
95DonProPoi-15
95Emo-84
95EmoGen-4
95Ima-75
95ImaGol-75
95Lea-12
95LeaLim-101
95LeaStuR-13
95Met-192
95ParInt-104
95ParIntEI-104
95PhoRoa-17
95PlaOneoOne-52
95ProMag-69
95SelCer-136
95SelCerMG-136
95SkyImp-204
95Top-363

790PC-356
800PC-30
800PC-59
800PC-161
800PC-167
80Top-30
80Top-59
80Top-161
80Top-167
810PC-132
810PCSti-63
81Top-E86
820PC-122
820PC-130
820PC-131
820PCSti-126
82PosCer-7
82WhaJunHC-18
830PC-135
830PC-136
830PC-147
830PCSti-258
830PCSti-259
83PufSti-15
83WhaJunHC-17
840PC-154
91CinCyc-24
**Stowe, Mark**
907thInnSWHL-263
90PriAlbR-20
**Stoyanovich, Dave**
83NovScoV-17
**Stoyanovich, Steve**
81IndChe-19
82IndChe-20
83WhaJunHC-18
93LonKni-21
**Strachan, Al**
93ActPacHOFI-10
**Strachan, Wayne**
91LakSupSL-26
**Strain, Ryan**
907thInnSWHL-90
90SasBla-24
917thInnSWHL-163
**Straka, Josef**
95CzeAPSE-165
96CzeAPSE-186
**Straka, Martin**
91UppDecCWJC-99
92Cla-33
920PCPre-21
92Par-140
92ParEmel-140
92PenCokC-22
92PenFoo-17
92Ult-382
92UppDec-559
92UppDecER-ER19
93Don-266
93Lea-220
930PCPre-155
930PCPreG-155
93Par-156
93ParEmel-156
93PenFoo-2
93Pin-204
93PinCan-204
93Pow-415
93PowRisS-7
93Sco-375
93ScoCan-375
93StaClu-415
93StaCluFDI-415
93StaCluO-415
93TopPre-155
93TopPreG-155
93Ult-244
93UppDec-40
93UppDecSP-125
94CanGamNHLP-190
94CzeAPSE-155
94Don-224
94Fla-141
94Fle-171
94Lea-36
94LeaLim-62
940PCPre-164
940PCPreSE-164
94ParSE-SE134
94ParSEG-SE134
94ParVin-V16
94PenFoo-25
94Pin-352
94PinArtP-352
94PinRinC-352
94Sco-82
94ScoGol-82
94ScoPla-82
94Sel-36
94SelGol-36
94StaClu-34
94StaCluFDI-34
94StaCluMOMS-34
94StaCluSTWC-34
94TopPre-164
94TopPreSE-164
94Ult-171
94UppDec-289
94UppDecElcIce-289
94UppDecSPI-SP153
94UppDecSPIDC-SP153
94WhaBla-106
95BeAPSig-S106

95BeAPSigDC-S106
95Bow-72
95BowAllFoi-12
95CanGamNHLP-193
95Emo-127
95Fin-92
95FinnSemWC-160
95FinRef-92
95Lea-253
95Met-107
95ParInt-145
95ParInt-397
95ParIntEl-145
95ParIntEl-397
95PlaOneoOne-289
95ProMag-115
95Sco-132
95ScoBlaIce-132
95ScoBlaIceAP-132
95SkyImp-121
95StaClu-87
95StaCluMOMS-87
95Top-246
95TopOPCI-246
95Ult-282
95UppDec-427
95UppDecEleIce-427
95UppDecEleIceG-427
95UppDecSpeE-SE146
95UppDecSpeEdiG-SE146
96ClaGol-33
96NHLProSTA-115
96PlaOneoOne-410
96UppDec-65
96UppDecIce-24
96UppDecIcePar-24
97Pac-139
97PacCop-139
97PacEmeGre-139
97PacIceB-139
97PacRed-139
97PacRev-115
97PacRevC-115
97PacRevE-115
97PacRevIB-115
97PacRevR-115
97PacRevS-115
97PacSil-139
97SPAut-129
98Be A PPA-115
98Be A PPAA-115
98Be A PPAAF-115
98Be A PPTBASG-115
98Be APG-115
98O-PChr-45
98O-PChrR-45
98Pac-82
98PacAur-157
98PacDynI-154
98PacDynIIB-154
98PacDynIR-154
98PacIceB-82
98PacOmeH-199
98PacOmeODI-199
98PacOmeR-199
98PacPar-197
98PacParC-197
98PacParEG-197
98PacParH-197
98PacParIB-197
98PacParS-197
98PacRed-82
98PacRev-120
98PacRevIS-120
98PacRevR-120
98SP Aut-69
98TopO-45
98TopO-P-45
98UppDec-349
98UppDecE-349
98UppDecE1o1-349
98UppDecGR-349
98UppDecM-168
98UppDecMGS-168
98UppDecMSS-168
98UppDecMSS-168
99Pac-347
99PacAur-118
99PacAurPD-118
99PacCop-347
99PacGol-347
99PacIceB-347
99PacPreD-347
99RetHoc-67
99SP AutPS-69
99UppDecM-166
99UppDecMGS-166
99UppDecMSS-166
99UppDecMSS-166
99UppDecRG-67
99UppDecRP-67
**Straka, Michal**
94CzeAPSE-156
95CzeAPSE-254
96CzeAPSE-303
**Strakhov, Yuri**
900PC-484
**Stramkowski, Jens**
98GerDELE-217
**Strand, Jan Roger**
71SweHocS-280
72SweHocS-255
74SweHocS-264
**Strand, Paul**
90ForSasTra-19

**Strandberg, Tomas**
89SweSemE-254
90SweSemE-167
91SweSemE-57
92SweSemE-39
94SweLeaE-48
95SweLeaE-156
95SweLeaEFF-1
95SweUppDE-13
**Stranka, G.**
95GerDELE-334
**Stratton, Art**
63YorWhiB-44
69SeaTotW-6
**Straub, Brian**
91ProAHLCHL-323
**Straub, Josef**
94CzeAPSE-199
95CzeAPSE-39
**Straube, Chris**
94GerDELE-319
95GerDELE-284
98GerDELE-258
**Strauss, Wolfgang**
95AusNatTea-27
**Strba, Martin**
95CzeAPSE-73
**Street, Keith**
89ProIHL-171
96AncAce-14
97AncAce-19
**Strelow, Warren**
90Dev-26
**Streu, Craig**
96GerDELE-15
**Striar, Rob**
93ForWorF-16
**Stridh, Jonny**
83SweSemE-67
84SweSemE-67
85SwePanS-61
86SwePanS-48
87SwePanS-56
**Striemitzer, Klaus**
94GerDELE-354
**Stringer, Rejean**
91AirCanSJHL-A9
92MPSPhoSJHL-122
**Stripp, Wayne**
89HamRoaA-20
**Strobel, Eric**
80USAOlyTMP-9
81SweSemHVS-103
95SigRooMI-35
95SigRooMI-36
95SigRooSMIS-35
95SigRooSMIS-36
**Strohack, Mark**
907thInnSOHL-295
96ForWorF-9
**Strohm, Lennart**
69SweHocS-216
71SweHocS-347
**Strom, Dennis**
90SweSemE-119
91SweSemE-122
92SweSemE-144
**Strom, Ingemar**
83SweSemE-66
85SwePanS-214
89SweSemE-187
90SweSemE-21
91SweSemE-220
**Strom, Peter**
93SweSemE-280
94ParSE-SE242
94ParSEG-SE242
94SweLeaE-233
94SweLeaENHLD-8
95SweLeaE-148
95SweLeaEG-4
95SweUppDE-212
**Stromback, Doug**
84KitRan-13
93HunBli-24
**Stromberg, Hans**
69SweHocS-54
70SweHocS-14
71SweHocS-93
**Stromberg, Mika**
93FinnJyvHS-111
93FinnSIS-9
93SweSemWCS-61
94FinnJaaK-14
94FinnSIS-313
94FinnSIS-387
94FinnSISJ-9
95FinnBecAC-7
95FinnKarWCL-18
95FinnSemWC-26
95FinnSIS-47
95FinnSIS-168
95FinnSISDT-2
95FinnSISGL-10
95FinnSISL-12
95FinnSISR-42
96FinnSISR-183
96FinnSISRATG-6
96SweSemW-18
**Strompf, Ladislav**
94GerDELE-110
95GerDELE-105
**Stromqvist, Hakan**
89SweSemE-172
**Stromsoe, Ulf**

69SweHocS-307
70SweHocS-212
**Stromvall, Johan**
84SweSemE-191
85SwePanS-168
86SwePanS-184
87SwePanS-178
89SweSemE-156
90SweSemE-234
91SweSemE-163
92SweSemE-187
93SweSemE-158
94SweLeaE-30
94SweLeaESS-7
95SweLeaE-249
95SweUppDE-125
**Strong, Ken**
95SweGloWC-183
**Strot, Brett**
90KnoChe-114
93FliGen-3
**Struch, David**
88SasBla-12
89SasBla-12
907thInnSWHL-78
90SasBla-10
91SasBla-10
94St.JohF-23
95St.JohF-23
**Strudwick, Jason**
93KamBla-21
95ColEdgI-96
95SlaMemC-21
96KenTho-17
98UppDecM-202
98UppDecMGS-202
98UppDecMSS-202
98UppDecMSS-202
**Strueby, Todd**
81SasBla-16
83MonAlp-20
84NovScoO-10
88OilTenAnn-132
90AlbIntTC-19
91ProAHLCHL-585
**Strumm, Don**
98LasVegT-24
**Strunk, Steve**
96MilAdmBO-23
**Stuart, Brad**
96RegPat-4
98BowSem-137
98BowBesAR-137
98BowBesR-137
98BowCHL-66
98BowCHL-138
98BowCHLAuB-A22
98BowCHLAuA-A22
98BowCHLAuS-A22
98BowCHLGA-66
98BowCHLGA-138
98BowCHLOI-66
98BowCHLOI-138
98BowCHLSC-SC8
98BowChrC-66
98BowChrC-138
98BowChrCGA-66
98BowChrCGA-138
98BowChrCGAR-66
98BowChrCGAR-138
98BowChrCOI-66
98BowChrCOI-138
98BowChrCOIR-66
98BowChrCOIR-138
98BowChrCR-66
98BowChrCR-138
98FinFutF-F4
98FinFutFR-F4
98O-PChr-228
98O-PChrR-228
98TopO-228
98TopO-P-228
**Stuart, Bruce**
10C555SweCP-15
10C56-17
11C55-15
83HalFP-O15
85HalFC-224
**Stuart, Hod**
83HalFP-F13
85HalFC-87
**Stuart, Ira**
28V1282PauC-61
**Stuart, Red**
23V1451-22
24V1452-31
**Stuck, Dan**
88ProAHL-144
89ProAHL-358
**Stuckey, Mark**
94GerDELE-248
**Stumpel, Jozef**
91Cla-34
91Par-231
91ParFre-231
92Pin-412
92PinFre-412
92UppDec-485
93ClaProPBC-BC16
93ClaProPro-83
93Don-23
93Lea-404
930PCPre-416
930PCPreG-416
93Par-15

93ParEmel-15
93Pow-293
93StaClu-488
93StaCluFDI-488
93StaCluO-488
93TopPre-416
93TopPreG-416
93Ult-212
93UltAllRoo-9
93UppDec-379
94Don-322
94Lea-143
94OPCPre-214
94OPCPreSE-214
94Par-19
94ParGol-19
94ParGol-293
94Pin-418
94PinArtP-418
94PinRinC-418
94TopPre-214
94TopPreSE-214
94Ult-261
94UppDec-155
94UppDecEleIce-155
95BeAPla-208
95BeAPSig-S208
95BeAPSigDC-S208
95ColCho-308
95ColChoPC-308
95ColChoPCP-308
95Don-195
95GerDELE-448
95Lea-223
95ParInt-13
95ParIntEl-13
95SloAPSNT-28
95UppDec-157
95UppDecEleIce-157
95UppDecEleIceG-157
96Fla-7
96FlaBluI-7
96Lea-116
96LeaPreP-116
96Sco-187
96ScoArtPro-187
96ScoDeaCAP-187
96ScoGolB-187
96ScoSpeAP-187
96SweSemW-230
96UppDec-12
96UppDecBD-60
96UppDecBDG-60
97ColCho-18
97ColChoSta-SQ17
97Don-134
97DonCanI-43
97DonCanIDS-43
97DonCanIPS-43
97DonEli-26
97DonEliAsp-26
97DonEliS-26
97DonLim-96
97DonLimExp-96
97DonPre-55
97DonPreCttC-55
97DonPreProG-134
97DonPreProS-134
97DonPri-60
97DonPriSoA-60
97Lea-40
97LeaFraMat-40
97LeaFraMDC-40
97LeaInt-40
97LeaIntUl-40
97Pac-71
97PacCop-71
97PacCroREG-66
97PacCroRIB-66
97PacCroRS-66
97PacDyn-9
97PacDynC-9
97PacDynDG-9
97PacDynEG-9
97PacDynIB-9
97PacDynR-9
97PacDynSil-9
97PacDynTan-31
97PacEmeGre-71
97PacIceB-71
97PacInv-10
97PacInvC-10
97PacInvEG-10
97PacInvIB-10
97PacInvR-10
97PacInvS-10
97PacOme-114
97PacOmeC-114
97PacOmeDG-114
97PacOmeEG-114
97PacOmeG-114
97PacOmeIB-114
97PacPar-92
97PacParC-92
97PacParDG-92
97PacParEG-92
97PacParIB-92
97PacParRed-92
97PacRed-71
97PacRev-71
97PacRevC-67
97PacRevE-67

97PacRevIB-67
97PacRevR-67
97PacRevS-67
97PacRevTCL-12
97PacSil-71
97Pin-138
97PinCer-97
97PinCerMB-97
97PinCerMG-97
97PinCerMR-97
97PinCerR-97
97PinIns-127
97PinPrePBB-138
97PinPrePBC-138
97PinPrePBM-138
97PinPrePBY-138
97PinPrePFC-138
97PinPrePFM-138
97PinPrePFY-138
97PinPrePla-138
97PinTotCMPG-97
97PinTotCPB-97
97PinTotCPG-97
97PinTotCPR-97
97Sco-122
97ScoArtPro-122
97ScoGolBla-122
97SPAut-71
97Zen-28
97Zen5x7-23
97ZenGolImp-23
97ZenSilImp-23
97ZenZGol-28
97ZenZSil-28
98Be A PPA-63
98Be A PPAA-63
98Be A PPAAF-63
98Be A PPTBASG-63
98Be APG-63
98BowBes-91
98BowBesAR-91
98BowBesR-91
98Fin-67
98FinNo P-67
98FinNo PR-67
98FinRef-67
98KinPowP-LAK2
98O-PChr-132
98O-PChrR-132
98O-PChrSB-SB24
98O-PChrSBR-SB24
98Pac-246
98PacAur-90
98PacCroR-66
98PacCroRLS-66
98PacDynI-91
98PacDynIIB-91
98PacDynIR-91
98PacIceB-246
98PacOmeH-114
98PacOmeODI-114
98PacOmeR-114
98PacPar-109
98PacParC-109
98PacParEG-109
98PacParH-109
98PacParIB-109
98PacParS-109
98PacRed-246
98PacRev-70
98PacRevIS-70
98PacRevR-70
98PacTeaC-12
98SP AutSotTG-JS
98SPxFin-41
98SPxFinR-41
98SPxFinS-41
98SSASotT-JS
98Top-132
98TopO-P-132
98TopSeaB-SB24
98UC-100
98UD ChoPCR-100
98UD ChoR-100
98UppDec-103
98UppDecE1o1-103
98UppDecGR-103
99Pac-199
99PacAur-72
99PacAurPD-72
99PacCop-199
99PacGol-199
99PacIceB-199
99PacPreD-199
**Stumpf, Juri**
94GerDELE-35
95GerDELE-28
**Sturgeon, Mike**
82BraWheK-19
**Sturgeon, Peter**
750PCNHL-393
**Sturm, Marco**
95GerDELE-261
96GerDELE-149
97Be A PPAD-243
97Be A PPAPD-243
97BeAPla-243
97BeAPlaAut-243
97BeAPlaPOT-10
97DonPri-168
97DonPriSoA-168
97Kat-125
97KatGol-125
97KatSil-125

97PacCroR-122
97PacCroREG-122
97PacCroRIB-122
97PacCroRS-122
97PacOme-206
97PacOmeC-206
97PacOmeDG-206
97PacOmeEG-206
97PacOmeG-206
97PacOmeIB-206
97PacRev-127
97PacRevC-127
97PacRevE-127
97PacRevIB-127
97PacRevR-127
97PacRevS-127
97PinBeeGT-25
97PinBeeT-25
97SP AutI-I40
97SPAut-192
97SPAutID-I40
97SPAutIE-I40
97UppDec-355
97UppDecBD-71
97UppDecBDDD-71
97UppDecBDPC-PC12
97UppDecBDPCD-PC12
97UppDecBDPCM-PC12
97UppDecBDPCQD-PC12
97UppDecBDPCTD-PC12
97UppDecBDQD-71
97UppDecBDTD-71
97UppDecIce-52
97UppDecIceP-52
97UppDecIPS-52
97Zen-87
97Zen5x7-68
97ZenGolImp-68
97ZenRooR-9
97ZenSilImp-68
97ZenZGol-87
97ZenZSil-87
97ZenZT-15
97ZenZTG-15
98Be A PPA-119
98Be A PPAA-119
98Be A PPAAF-119
98Be A PPTBASG-119
98Be APG-119
98BowBes-83
98BowBesAR-83
98BowBesR-83
98Fin-147
98FinNo P-147
98FinNo PR-147
98FinRef-147
98PacCroR-121
98PacCroRLS-121
98PacDynI-169
98PacDynIIB-169
98PacDynIR-169
98PacIceB-392
98PacOmeH-215
98PacOmeODI-215
98PacOmeR-215
98PacPar-215
98PacParC-215
98PacParEG-215
98PacParH-215
98PacParIB-215
98PacParS-215
98PacRed-392
98PacRev-129
98PacRevIS-129
98PacRevR-129
98SPxFin-72
98SPxFinR-72
98SPxFinS-72
98SPxFinS-150
98Top-72
98TopGolLC1-71
98TopGolLC1B-71
98TopGolLC1B0o0-71
98TopGolLC1O0o-71
98TopGolLC1R-71
98TopGolLC1R0o0-71
98TopGolLC2-71
98TopGolLC2B-71
98TopGolLC2B0o0-71
98TopGolLC2O0o-71
98TopGolLC2R-71
98TopGolLC2R0o0-71
98TopGolLC3-71
98TopGolLC3B-71
98TopGolLC3B0o0-71
98TopGolLC3O0o-71
98TopGolLC3O0o0-71
98TopGolLC3R-71
98TopGolLC3R0o0-71
98TopIceA2-I2
98TopO-P-17
98TopSeaB-SB12
98UC-181
98UD ChoPCR-181
98UD ChoR-181
98UD3-27
98UD3-87
98UD3-147
98UD3DieC-27
98UD3DieC-87
98UD3DieC-147
98UDOCP-181
98UppDec-169
98UppDecE-169
98UppDecE1o1-169
98UppDecGR-169
98UppDecM-87
98UppDecMGS-172
98UppDecMSS-172
98UppDecMSS-172
99Pac-383
99PacCop-383
99PacGol-383
99PacIceB-383
99PacPreD-383
99UppDecM-177
99UppDecMGS-177
99UppDecMSS-177
99UppDecMSS-177
**Subr, Bohuslav**
97GueSto-16
**Suchan, Greg**
897thInnSOHL-133
89NiaFalT-18
**Suchanek, Karel**
95CzeAPSE-220
96CzeAPSE-96
**Suchanek, Pavel**
91BriColJHL-30
92BriColJHL-68
**Suchanek, Rudolf**
94CzeAPSE-103
95CzeAPSE-55
96CzeAPSE-241
**Suchy, Jan**
69SweHocS-38
69SweWorC-22
69SweWorC-77
69SweWorC-143
69SweWorC-156
70SweHocS-351
71SweHocS-48
72SweSemWC-36
74SweHocS-117
74SweSemHVS-67
91SweSemWCS-247
96SweSemWHL-HL17
**Suchy, Radoslav**
97BowCHL-64
97BowCHLOPC-64
**Sugden, Brandon**
95Sla-160
**Suhonen, Alpo**
89JetSaf-29
93FinnJyvHS-103
93FinnSIS-2
95SwiHNL-3
**Suhrada, Jiri**
95CzeAPSE-217
**Suhy, Andy**
92TolSto-9
93TolSto-8
**Suk, Steve**
93MicSta-23
**Sukovic, Mil**
917thInnSQMJHL-8
**Sulander, Ari**
93FinnJyvHS-104
93FinnSIS-3
94FinnSIS-41
94FinnSIS-388
94FinnSISNP-3
94FinnSISS-8
95FinnKarWCL-19
95FinnSIS-167
95FinnSISGC-3
95FinnSISGG-3
95FinnSISL-10
95FinnSISR-41
96FinnSISR-175
96FinnSISRATG-6
96FinnSISRKIG-1
96FinnSISRMA-4
96SweSemW-10
**Sulku, Sebastian**
93FinnSIS-7
94FinnSIS-275
95FinnSIS-137
**Sulliman, Doug**
800PC-306
820PC-132
820PCSti-128
82PosCer-7
82WhaJunHC-19
830PC-148
830PCSti-256
83WhaJunHC-19
84DevPos-22
850PC-234
86DevPol-17
86OPC-121
86Top-121
870PC-116
870PCSti-59
87PanSti-82
87Top-116
880PC-172
88Top-172
89FlyPos-24
90Bow-110
90BowTif-110
90Dev-27

❑ 90OPC-473
**Sullivan, Andy**
❑ 93St.JohML-23
**Sullivan, Bob**
❑ 82WhaJunHC-20
❑ 83OPC-149
❑ 83OPCSti-189
**Sullivan, Brian**
❑ 91ProAHLCHL-412
❑ 93ClaProPro-77
**Sullivan, Chris**
❑ 93MicSta-22
❑ 96DayBom-2
❑ 97DonLim-46
❑ 97DonLimExp-46
**Sullivan, Kevin**
❑ 90KanCitBla-6
❑ 90ProAHLIHL-595
❑ 91NasKni-14
**Sullivan, Mike (Michael)**
❑ 90ProAHLIHL-307
❑ 90RayJrC-20
❑ 91Par-383
❑ 91ParFre-383
❑ 92Bow-116
❑ 92OPC-144
❑ 92Par-395
❑ 92ParEmel-395
❑ 92Sco-533
❑ 92ScoCan-533
❑ 92StaClu-262
❑ 92Top-282
❑ 92TopGol-282G
❑ 92UppDec-46
❑ 93OPCPre-21
❑ 93OPCPreG-21
❑ 93PanSti-262
❑ 93Par-454
❑ 93ParEmel-454
❑ 93Pin-287
❑ 93PinCan-287
❑ 93Sco-390
❑ 93ScoCan-390
❑ 93StaClu-139
❑ 93StaCluFDI-139
❑ 93StaCluFDIO-139
❑ 93StaCluO-139
❑ 93TopPre-21
❑ 93TopPreG-21
❑ 94BeAPSig-75
❑ 95Don-211
❑ 95Lea-167
❑ 95ParInt-300
❑ 95ParIntEl-300
❑ 96TolSto-14
❑ 97Be A PPAD-179
❑ 97Be A PPAPD-179
❑ 97BeAPla-179
❑ 97BeAPlaAut-179
❑ 97PacInvNRB-32
**Sullivan, Peter**
❑ 76OPCWHA-42
❑ 77OPCWHA-27
❑ 78JetPos-21
❑ 79JetPos-25
❑ 79OPC-378
❑ 80JetPos-22
❑ 80OPC-29
❑ 80PepCap-139
❑ 80Top-29
**Sullivan, Red (George)**
❑ 44BeeGro2P-70
❑ 44BeeGro2P-367
❑ 51Par-27
❑ 52Par-79
❑ 54Top-42
❑ 57Top-56
❑ 58Top-48
❑ 59Top-59
❑ 60ShiCoi-82
❑ 60Top-18
❑ 61ShiCoi-91
❑ 61Top-48
❑ 63Top-44
❑ 64BeeGro3P-149
❑ 64Top-29
❑ 65Top-87
❑ 91UltOriS-29
❑ 91UltOriSF-29
❑ 94ParMisL-86
❑ 94ParMisL-170
❑ 94ParTalB-108
**Sullivan, Steve**
❑ 93SauSteMG-24
❑ 93SauSteMGM-16
❑ 95ColEdgI-10
❑ 96BeAPAut-209
❑ 96BeAPAutSil-209
❑ 96BeAPla-209
❑ 96ColEdgFL-21
❑ 96ColEdgPC-4
❑ 96Dev-11
❑ 96Don-229
❑ 96DonPrePro-229
❑ 96LeaGolR-10
❑ 96LeaPre-143
❑ 96LeaPrePP-143
❑ 96Pin-226
❑ 96PinArtP-226
❑ 96PinFoi-226
❑ 96PinPreS-226
❑ 96PinRinC-226
❑ 96SkyImp-160
❑ 96Sum-180
❑ 96SumArtP-180
❑ 96SumIce-180
❑ 96SumMet-180
❑ 96SumPreS-180
❑ 96UppDec-185
❑ 96Zen-140
❑ 96ZenArtP-140
❑ 97ColCho-248
❑ 97ColChoSta-SQ4
❑ 97Don-39
❑ 97DonCanI-94
❑ 97DonCanIDS-94
❑ 97DonCanIPS-94
❑ 97DonLim-116
❑ 97DonLimExp-116
❑ 97DonPre-131
❑ 97DonPreCttC-131
❑ 97DonPreProG-39
❑ 97DonPreProS-39
❑ 97DonPri-92
❑ 97DonPriSoA-92
❑ 97Lea-84
❑ 97LeaFraMat-84
❑ 97LeaFraMDC-84
❑ 97LeaInt-84
❑ 97LeaIntUI-84
❑ 97Pac-283
❑ 97PacCop-283
❑ 97PacDyn-123
❑ 97PacDynC-123
❑ 97PacDynDG-123
❑ 97PacDynEG-123
❑ 97PacDynIB-123
❑ 97PacDynR-123
❑ 97PacDynSil-123
❑ 97PacDynTan-52
❑ 97PacEmeGre-283
❑ 97PacIceB-283
❑ 97PacInv-138
❑ 97PacInvC-138
❑ 97PacInvEG-138
❑ 97PacInvIB-138
❑ 97PacInvR-138
❑ 97PacInvS-138
❑ 97PacRed-283
❑ 97PacSil-283
❑ 97Pin-134
❑ 97PinCer-83
❑ 97PinCerMB-83
❑ 97PinCerMG-83
❑ 97PinCerMR-83
❑ 97PinCerR-83
❑ 97PinIns-102
❑ 97PinPrePBB-134
❑ 97PinPrePBC-134
❑ 97PinPrePBM-134
❑ 97PinPrePBY-134
❑ 97PinPrePFC-134
❑ 97PinPrePFM-134
❑ 97PinPrePFY-134
❑ 97PinPrePla-134
❑ 97PinTotCMPG-83
❑ 97PinTotCPB-83
❑ 97PinTotCPG-83
❑ 97PinTotCPR-83
❑ 97Sco-185
❑ 97ScoMapL-7
❑ 97ScoMapLPla-7
❑ 97ScoMapLPre-7
❑ 97SPAut-154
❑ 97UppDec-160
❑ 98Be A PPA-286
❑ 98Be A PPAA-286
❑ 98Be A PPAAF-286
❑ 98Be A PPSE-286
❑ 98Be APG-286
❑ 98Pac-422
❑ 98PacIceB-422
❑ 98PacRed-422
❑ 99Pac-415
❑ 99PacCop-415
❑ 99PacGol-415
❑ 99PacIceB-415
❑ 99PacPreD-415
**Sullivan, Steve (minors)**
❑ 91ProAHLCHL-443
❑ 92NasKni-11
**Sullivan, Todd**
❑ 95SouCarS-21
**Sullivan, Tom**
❑ 907thInnSOHL-120
❑ 917thInnSOHL-186
**Summanen, Raimo**
❑ 83OilMcD-4
❑ 84NovScoO-16
❑ 85OilRedR-25
❑ 86OilRedR-25
❑ 86OilTeal-25
❑ 88OilTenAnn-3
❑ 89SweSemWCS-40
❑ 91SweSemWCS-20
❑ 93FinnSIS-377
❑ 94FinnSIS-252
❑ 94FinnSISH-15
❑ 95FinnKarWCL-20
❑ 95FinnSISGC-22
❑ 95FinnSISL-7
❑ 96SweSemW-7
**Summerhill, Bill**
❑ 34BeeGro1P-184
**Sumner, Rob**
❑ 89VicCou-19
❑ 96SeaThu-NNO
**Sumner, Steve**
❑ 89ProAHL-310
**Sundberg, Ola**
❑ 86SwePanS-160
**Sundberg, Reino**
❑ 86SwePanS-247
❑ 87SwePanS-233
❑ 89SweSemE-217
❑ 90SweSemE-51
❑ 93SweSemE-226
**Sundblad, Erling**
❑ 69SweHocS-161
❑ 70SweHocS-128
**Sundblad, Niklas**
❑ 90SweSemE-96
❑ 91AreDraPic-15
❑ 91Cla-16
❑ 91StaPicH-8
❑ 91SweSemE-23
❑ 91UltDra-16
❑ 91UltDra-72
❑ 91UltDra-85
❑ 92SweSemE-46
❑ 92UppDec-227
❑ 94ClaProP-143
❑ 94St.JohF-24
❑ 95St.JohF-24
❑ 96Lea-234
❑ 96LeaPreP-234
❑ 96Pin-230
❑ 96PinArtP-230
❑ 96PinFoi-230
❑ 96PinPreS-230
❑ 96PinRinC-230
**Sunderland, Mathieu**
❑ 93DruVol-23
❑ 95Cla-23
❑ 96RimOce-27
**Sundin, Mats**
❑ 89SweSemE-72
❑ 90Kra-42
❑ 90NordPet-23
❑ 90OPCPre-114
❑ 90ProSet-636
❑ 90Sco-398
❑ 90ScoCan-398
❑ 90ScoRoo-100T
❑ 90ScoYouS-7
❑ 90UppDec-365
❑ 90UppDecF-365
❑ 91Bow-137
❑ 91Kra-4
❑ 91NordPanTS-20
❑ 91NordPanTS-H
❑ 91NordPet-28
❑ 91OPC-12
❑ 91OPC-219
❑ 91PanSti-255
❑ 91Par-144
❑ 91ParFre-144
❑ 91Pin-10
❑ 91Pin-389
❑ 91PinFre-10
❑ 91PinFre-389
❑ 91ProSet-197
❑ 91ProSetFre-197
❑ 91ProSetPla-99
❑ 91ScoAme-130
❑ 91ScoCan-130
❑ 91ScoYouS-3
❑ 91StaClu-300
❑ 91StaPicH-50
❑ 91SweSemE-323
❑ 91SweSemE-357
❑ 91SweSemWCS-211
❑ 91Top-12
❑ 91Top-219
❑ 91UppDec-31
❑ 91UppDec-93
❑ 91UppDec-134
❑ 91UppDecES-13
❑ 91UppDecESF-13
❑ 91UppDecF-31
❑ 91UppDecF-93
❑ 91UppDecF-134
❑ 92Bow-344
❑ 92HumDum2-21
❑ 92JofKoh-6
❑ 92NorPet-31
❑ 92OPC-110
❑ 92PanSti-212
❑ 92PanSti-302
❑ 92PanStiFre-212
❑ 92PanStiFre-302
❑ 92Par-148
❑ 92Par-221
❑ 92ParEmel-148
❑ 92ParEmel-221
❑ 92Pin-90
❑ 92PinFre-90
❑ 92PinTea2-7
❑ 92PinTea2F-7
❑ 92ProSet-149
❑ 92Sco-153
❑ 92ScoCan-153
❑ 92ScoYouS-3
❑ 92StaClu-478
❑ 92SweSemE-348
❑ 92Top-415
❑ 92TopGol-415G
❑ 92Ult-180
❑ 92UltImp-25
❑ 92UppDec-121
❑ 92UppDec-374
❑ 92UppDecES-E18
❑ 92UppDecWJG-WG17
❑ 93Don-283
❑ 93DonSpeP-S
❑ 93Lea-136
❑ 93OPCPre-460
❑ 93OPCPreBG-6
❑ 93OPCPreF-5
❑ 93OPCPreG-460
❑ 93PanSti-68
❑ 93Par-435
❑ 93ParEmel-435
❑ 93ParFirO-F5
❑ 93Pin-2
❑ 93Pin1S-6
❑ 93PinCan-2
❑ 93PinTea2-15
❑ 93PinTea2C-15
❑ 93Pow-205
❑ 93PowGloG-8
❑ 93PowPoiL-18
❑ 93Sco-9
❑ 93ScoCan-9
❑ 93ScoDynDC-5
❑ 93ScoIntS-10
❑ 93ScoIntSC-10
❑ 93StaClu-370
❑ 93StaClu-425
❑ 93StaCluFDI-370
❑ 93StaCluFDI-425
❑ 93StaCluO-370
❑ 93StaCluO-425
❑ 93SweSemE-306
❑ 93SweSemWCS-33
❑ 93TopPre-460
❑ 93TopPreF-5
❑ 93TopPreG-460
❑ 93Ult-137
❑ 93UppDec-220
❑ 93UppDec-228
❑ 93UppDec-302
❑ 93UppDec-419
❑ 93UppDecHT-HT20
❑ 93UppDecLAS-59
❑ 93UppDecSP-132
❑ 94BeAPla-R76
❑ 94CanGamNHLP-237
❑ 94EASpo-111
❑ 94Fin-110
❑ 94FinnJaaK-74
❑ 94FinRef-110
❑ 94FinSupTW-110
❑ 94Fla-186
❑ 94Fle-220
❑ 94HocWit-51
❑ 94Kra-13
❑ 94Lea-530
❑ 94LeaLim-42
❑ 94MapLeaK-25
❑ 94MapLeaP-1
❑ 94MapLeaP-2
❑ 94MapLeaP-3
❑ 94MapLeaPP-1
❑ 94OPCPre-160
❑ 94OPCPre-345
❑ 94OPCPre-412
❑ 94OPCPreSE-160
❑ 94OPCPreSE-345
❑ 94OPCPreSE-412
❑ 94Par-185
❑ 94ParGol-185
❑ 94ParSE-SE175
❑ 94ParSEES-ES2
❑ 94ParSEG-SE175
❑ 94ParSEV-37
❑ 94ParVin-V52
❑ 94Pin-386
❑ 94PinArtP-386
❑ 94PinNorLig-NL10
❑ 94PinRinC-386
❑ 94Sco-89
❑ 94ScoGol-89
❑ 94ScoPla-89
❑ 94ScoPlaTS-89
❑ 94Sel-21
❑ 94SelGol-21
❑ 94SP-116
❑ 94SPDieCut-116
❑ 94StaClu-90
❑ 94StaCluFDI-90
❑ 94StaCluMOMS-90
❑ 94StaCluSTWC-90
❑ 94SweLeaE-232
❑ 94SweLeaEGS-1
❑ 94TopFinB-11
❑ 94TopPre-160
❑ 94TopPre-345
❑ 94TopPre-412
❑ 94TopPreSE-160
❑ 94TopPreSE-345
❑ 94TopPreSE-412
❑ 94Ult-220
❑ 94Ult-379
❑ 94UppDec-51
❑ 94UppDec-548
❑ 94UppDecEleIce-51
❑ 94UppDecEleIce-548
❑ 94UppDecSPI-SP170
❑ 94UppDecSPIDC-SP170
❑ 95BeAPla-203
❑ 95BeAPSig-S203
❑ 95BeAPSigDC-S203
❑ 95Bow-49
❑ 95BowAllFoi-49
❑ 95CanGamNHLP-259
❑ 95ColCho-90
❑ 95ColChoCTG-C30
❑ 95ColChoCTG-C30B
❑ 95ColChoCTG-C30C
❑ 95ColChoCTGGB-C30
❑ 95ColChoCTGGR-C30
❑ 95ColChoCTGSB-C30
❑ 95ColChoCTGSR-C30
❑ 95ColChoPC-90
❑ 95ColChoPCP-90
❑ 95Don-176
❑ 95DonEli-72
❑ 95DonEliCE-11
❑ 95DonEliDCS-72
❑ 95DonEliDCU-72
❑ 95Emo-175
❑ 95Fin-177
❑ 95FinnSemWC-62
❑ 95FinRef-177
❑ 95ImpSti-118
❑ 95Kra-75
❑ 95Lea-244
❑ 95LeaFirOIce-8
❑ 95LeaLim-120
❑ 95LeaLimSG-9
❑ 95McDPin-MCD-18
❑ 95Met-147
❑ 95MetIS-20
❑ 95NHLAcePC-10D
❑ 95ParInt-201
❑ 95ParInt-247
❑ 95ParIntAS-6
❑ 95ParIntCCGS2-8
❑ 95ParIntCCSS2-8
❑ 95ParIntEl-201
❑ 95ParIntEl-247
❑ 95Pin-19
❑ 95PinArtP-19
❑ 95PinGloG-3
❑ 95PinRinC-19
❑ 95PinRoa2-7
❑ 95PlaOneoOne-99
❑ 95ProMag-80
❑ 95Sco-56
❑ 95ScoBlaIce-56
❑ 95ScoBlaIceAP-56
❑ 95ScoBorBat-15
❑ 95ScoGolBla-16
❑ 95SelCer-7
❑ 95SelCerMG-7
❑ 95SkyImp-165
❑ 95SP-141
❑ 95SPStaEto-E26
❑ 95SPStaEtoG-E26
❑ 95StaClu-75
❑ 95StaCluMO-26
❑ 95StaCluMOMS-75
❑ 95StaCluMPT-8
❑ 95Sum-9
❑ 95SumArtP-9
❑ 95SumIce-9
❑ 95SweGloWC-13
❑ 95SweGloWC-251
❑ 95SweGloWC-256
❑ 95SweGloWC-257
❑ 95SweGloWC-258
❑ 95SweGloWC-269
❑ 95SweUppDE-236
❑ 95Top-19
❑ 95Top-150
❑ 95TopCanG-10CG
❑ 95TopMarMPB-19
❑ 95TopOPCI-19
❑ 95TopOPCI-150
❑ 95TopSupSki-32
❑ 95TopSupSkiPla-32
❑ 95Ult-164
❑ 95UltExtAtt-19
❑ 95UltGolM-164
❑ 95UltPrePiv-9
❑ 95UltPrePivGM-9
❑ 95UppDec-147
❑ 95UppDec-219
❑ 95UppDecEleIce-147
❑ 95UppDecEleIce-219
❑ 95UppDecEleIceG-147
❑ 95UppDecEleIceG-219
❑ 95UppDecNHLAS-AS18
❑ 95UppDecSpeE-SE169
❑ 95UppDecSpeEdiG-SE169
❑ 95Zen-19
❑ 96BeAPBisITB-12
❑ 96ColCho-255
❑ 96ColCho-332
❑ 96ColChoCTG-C29A
❑ 96ColChoCTG-C29B
❑ 96ColChoCTG-C29C
❑ 96ColChoCTGE-CR29
❑ 96ColChoCTGEG-CR29
❑ 96ColChoCTGG-C29A
❑ 96ColChoCTGG-C29B
❑ 96ColChoCTGG-C29C
❑ 96ColChoMVP-UD44
❑ 96ColChoMVPG-UD44
❑ 96Don-30
❑ 96DonCanI-12
❑ 96DonCanIGPP-12
❑ 96DonCanIRPP-12
❑ 96DonEli-55
❑ 96DonEliDCS-55
❑ 96DonPrePro-30
❑ 96DurL'EB-JB13
❑ 96Fla-92
❑ 96FlaBluI-92
❑ 96FlaCenIS-9
❑ 96Fle-110
❑ 96KraUppD-7
❑ 96KraUppD-70
❑ 96Lea-53
❑ 96LeaLim-28
❑ 96LeaLimG-28
❑ 96LeaPre-14
❑ 96LeaPreP-53
❑ 96LeaPrePP-14
❑ 96LeaPreSG-33
❑ 96LeaPreSte-33
❑ 96MapLeaP-1
❑ 96MetUni-154
❑ 96NHLACEPC-45
❑ 96NHLProSTA-80
❑ 96Pin-144
❑ 96PinArtP-144
❑ 96PinFoi-144
❑ 96PinMin-17
❑ 96PinMinB-17
❑ 96PinMinCoiB-17
❑ 96PinMinCoiGP-17
❑ 96PinMinCoiN-17
❑ 96PinMinCoiS-17
❑ 96PinMinCoiSG-17
❑ 96PinMinG-17
❑ 96PinMinS-17
❑ 96PinPreS-144
❑ 96PinRinC-144
❑ 96Sco-160
❑ 96ScoArtPro-160
❑ 96ScoDeaCAP-160
❑ 96ScoGolB-160
❑ 96ScoSpeAP-160
❑ 96ScoSup-3
❑ 96SelCer-85
❑ 96SelCerAP-85
❑ 96SelCerBlu-85
❑ 96SelCerMB-85
❑ 96SelCerMG-85
❑ 96SelCerMR-85
❑ 96SelCerRed-85
❑ 96SkyImp-130
❑ 96SP-151
❑ 96SPCleWin-CW12
❑ 96SPHolCol-HC20
❑ 96SPx-43
❑ 96SPxGol-43
❑ 96StaCluMO-18
❑ 96Sum-51
❑ 96SumArtP-51
❑ 96SumIce-51
❑ 96SumMet-51
❑ 96SumPreS-51
❑ 96SweSemCDT-7
❑ 96SweSemW-56
❑ 96SweSemWNS-NS3
❑ 96TeaOut-41
❑ 96TopNHLP-43
❑ 96TopPicOI-43
❑ 96TopPicTS-TS13
❑ 96Ult-166
❑ 96UltGolM-166
❑ 96UltMr.Mom-9
❑ 96UppDec-160
❑ 96UppDecBD-163
❑ 96UppDecBDG-163
❑ 96UppDecBDRFTC-RC13
❑ 96UppDecGJ-GJ13
❑ 96UppDecGN-X38
❑ 96UppDecLSH-LS19
❑ 96UppDecLSHF-LS19
❑ 96UppDecLSHS-LS19
❑ 96UppDecPP-P28
❑ 96UppDecSS-SS23A
❑ 96Zen-64
❑ 96ZenArtP-64
❑ 97ColCho-245
❑ 97ColCho-320
❑ 97ColChoCTG-C23A
❑ 97ColChoCTG-C23B
❑ 97ColChoCTG-C23C
❑ 97ColChoCTGE-CR23
❑ 97ColChoSta-SQ83
❑ 97ColChoSti-S17
❑ 97Don-139
❑ 97DonCanI-40
❑ 97DonCanIDS-40
❑ 97DonCanIPS-40
❑ 97DonEli-58
❑ 97DonEliAsp-58
❑ 97DonEliS-58
❑ 97DonLim-9
❑ 97DonLim-13
❑ 97DonLim-128
❑ 97DonLimExp-9
❑ 97DonLimExp-13
❑ 97DonLimExp-128
❑ 97DonLimFOTG-16
❑ 97DonLimFOTG-26
❑ 97DonPre-38
❑ 97DonPreCttC-38
❑ 97DonPreProG-139
❑ 97DonPreProS-139
❑ 97DonPri-56
❑ 97DonPriSoA-56
❑ 97DonRedAle-9
❑ 97EssOlyHH-42
❑ 97EssOlyHHF-42
❑ 97Kat-144
❑ 97KatGol-144
❑ 97KatSil-144
❑ 97Lea-144
❑ 97LeaBanSea-19
❑ 97LeaFraMat-142
❑ 97LeaFraMDC-142
❑ 97LeaInt-142
❑ 97LeaIntUI-142
❑ 97McD-13
❑ 97McDGamFil-10
❑ 97Pac-205
❑ 97PacCop-205
❑ 97PacCroR-132
❑ 97PacCroREG-132
❑ 97PacCroRHTDC-17
❑ 97PacCroRIB-132
❑ 97PacCroRS-132
❑ 97PacDyn-124
❑ 97PacDyn-144
❑ 97PacDynBKS-93
❑ 97PacDynC-124
❑ 97PacDynC-144
❑ 97PacDynDG-124
❑ 97PacDynDG-144
❑ 97PacDynEG-124
❑ 97PacDynEG-144
❑ 97PacDynIB-124
❑ 97PacDynIB-144
❑ 97PacDynR-124
❑ 97PacDynR-144
❑ 97PacDynSil-124
❑ 97PacDynSil-144
❑ 97PacDynTan-16
❑ 97PacDynTan-27
❑ 97PacEmeGre-205
❑ 97PacIceB-205
❑ 97PacInv-139
❑ 97PacInvC-139
❑ 97PacInvEG-139
❑ 97PacInvFP-34
❑ 97PacInvIB-139
❑ 97PacInvR-139
❑ 97PacInvS-139
❑ 97PacOme-225
❑ 97PacOmeC-225
❑ 97PacOmeDG-225
❑ 97PacOmeEG-225
❑ 97PacOmeG-225
❑ 97PacOmeIB-225
❑ 97PacOmeSLC-18
❑ 97PacPar-185
❑ 97PacParC-185
❑ 97PacParDG-185
❑ 97PacParEG-185
❑ 97PacParIB-185
❑ 97PacParRed-185
❑ 97PacParSil-185
❑ 97PacRed-205
❑ 97PacRev-137
❑ 97PacRevC-137
❑ 97PacRevE-137
❑ 97PacRevIB-137
❑ 97PacRevR-137
❑ 97PacRevS-137
❑ 97PacRevTCL-24
❑ 97PacSil-205
❑ 97PacSlaSDC-10B
❑ 97Pin-50
❑ 97PinArtP-50
❑ 97PinBee-39
❑ 97PinBeeGP-39
❑ 97PinCer-53
❑ 97PinCerGT-15
❑ 97PinCerMB-53
❑ 97PinCerMG-53
❑ 97PinCerMR-53
❑ 97PinCerR-53
❑ 97PinCerT-15
❑ 97PinIns-21
❑ 97PinInsC-4
❑ 97PinInsCC-21
❑ 97PinInsCG-4
❑ 97PinInsEC-21
❑ 97PinInsT-23
❑ 97PinMin-10
❑ 97PinMinB-10
❑ 97PinMinCBP-10
❑ 97PinMinCGPP-10
❑ 97PinMinCNSP-10
❑ 97PinMinCoiB-10
❑ 97PinMinCoiGP-10
❑ 97PinMinCoiN-10
❑ 97PinMinCoiSG-10
❑ 97PinMinCoiSS-10
❑ 97PinMinGolTea-10
❑ 97PinMinSilTea-10
❑ 97PinPowPac-16
❑ 97PinPrePBB-50
❑ 97PinPrePBC-50
❑ 97PinPrePBM-50
❑ 97PinPrePBY-50
❑ 97PinPrePFC-50
❑ 97PinPrePFM-50
❑ 97PinPrePFY-50
❑ 97PinPrePla-50
❑ 97PinRinC-50
❑ 97PinTotCMPG-53
❑ 97PinTotCPB-53
❑ 97PinTotCPG-53
❑ 97PinTotCPR-53
❑ 97Sco-95
❑ 97ScoArtPro-95
❑ 97ScoGolBla-95
❑ 97ScoMapL-4
❑ 97ScoMapLPla-4
❑ 97ScoMapLPre-4
❑ 97SP AutI-I33
❑ 97SPAut-150
❑ 97SPAutID-I33
❑ 97SPAutIE-I33
❑ 97SPAutSotT-MS
❑ 97SPx-46
❑ 97SPxBro-46
❑ 97SPxDim-SPX17

- 97SPxGol-46
- 97SPxGraF-46
- 97SPxSil-46
- 97SPxSte-46
- 97Stu-67
- 97StuHarH-24
- 97StuPrePG-67
- 97StuPrePS-67
- 97UppDec-369
- 97UppDecBD-77
- 97UppDecBDDD-77
- 97UppDecBDPC-PC30
- 97UppDecBDPCD-PC30
- 97UppDecBDPCM-PC30
- 97UppDecBDPCQD-PC30
- 97UppDecBDPCTD-PC30
- 97UppDecBDQD-77
- 97UppDecBDTD-77
- 97UppDecCtaG-7
- 97UppDecCtaG-AR7
- 97UppDecDV-17
- 97UppDecDVSM-17
- 97UppDecGDM-369
- 97UppDecIC-IC13
- 97UppDecIC2-IC13
- 97UppDecIceP-73
- 97UppDecIce-73
- 97UppDecILL-L4C
- 97UppDecILL2-L4C
- 97UppDecIPS-73
- 97UppDecSG-SG13
- 97UppDecSSM-SS13
- 97UppDecSSW-SS13
- 97UppDecTS-13
- 97UppDecTSL2-13
- 97UppDecTSS-14B
- 97Zen-48
- 97Zen5x7-52
- 97ZenGolImp-52
- 97ZenSilImp-52
- 97ZenZGol-48
- 97ZenZSil-48
- 98Be A PPA-136
- 98Be A PPAA-136
- 98Be A PPAAF-136
- 98Be A PPAGUSC-S5
- 98Be A PPGUJA-G2
- 98Be A PPPGUJC-G2
- 98Be A PPPPUJC-P20
- 98Be A PPTBASG-136
- 98Be APG-136
- 98BowBes-39
- 98BowBesAR-39
- 98BowBesR-39
- 98Fin-106
- 98FinNo P-106
- 98FinNo PR-106
- 98FinRedL-R19
- 98FinRedLR-R19
- 98FinRef-106
- 98McD-12
- 98O-PChr-71
- 98O-PChrR-71
- 98Pac-13
- 98PacAur-185
- 98PacAurALC-17
- 98PacAurC-16
- 98PacAurCF-46
- 98PacAurCFC-46
- 98PacAurCFIB-46
- 98PacAurCFR-46
- 98PacAurCFS-46
- 98PacAurMAC-17
- 98PacCroR-132
- 98PacCroRLS-132
- 98PacCroRMP-18
- 98PacCroRPotG-23
- 98PacCroRPP-22
- 98PacDynI-184
- 98PacDynIFT-18
- 98PacDynIIB-184
- 98PacDynIR-184
- 98PacDynITC-25
- 98PacEO P-19
- 98PacGolCD-32
- 98PacIceB-13
- 98PacOmeEP101-19
- 98PacOmeFtF-8
- 98PacOmeH-231
- 98PacOmeO-33
- 98PacOmeODI-231
- 98PacOmeP-19
- 98PacOmePIB-11
- 98PacOmeR-231
- 98PacPar-231
- 98PacParC-231
- 98PacParEG-231
- 98PacParH-231
- 98PacParIB-231
- 98PacParS-231
- 98PacParSDDC-17
- 98PacParTCD-25
- 98PacRed-13
- 98PacRev-140
- 98PacRevADC-28
- 98PacRevCTL-18
- 98PacRevIS-140
- 98PacRevR-140
- 98PacRevS-34
- 98PacTeaC-25
- 98PacTim-18
- 98SP Aut-83
- 98SP AutSotTG-MS


- 98SP AutSS-SS23
- 98SPxFin-82
- 98SPxFin-118
- 98SPxFin-162
- 98SPxFinR-82
- 98SPxFinR-118
- 98SPxFinR-162
- 98SPxFinS-82
- 98SPxFinS-118
- 98SPxFinS-162
- 98SPXTopP-55
- 98SPXTopP-55
- 98SPXTopPHH-H27
- 98SPXTopPLI-L8
- 98SPXTopPPS-PS13
- 98SPXTopPR-55
- 98SPXTopPWM-MS
- 98SASaSotT-MS
- 98Top-71
- 98TopGolLC1-53
- 98TopGolLC1B-53
- 98TopGolLC1BOoO-53
- 98TopGolLC1OoO-53
- 98TopGolLC1R-53
- 98TopGolLC1ROoO-53
- 98TopGolLC2-53
- 98TopGolLC2B-53
- 98TopGolLC2BOoO-53
- 98TopGolLC2OoO-53
- 98TopGolLC2R-53
- 98TopGolLC2ROoO-53
- 98TopGolLC3-53
- 98TopGolLC3B-53
- 98TopGolLC3BOoO-53
- 98TopGolLC3OoO-53
- 98TopGolLC3R-53
- 98TopGolLC3ROoO-53
- 98TopLocL-L2
- 98TopO-P-71
- 98UC-203
- 98UCMBH-BH17
- 98UCSB-SQ19
- 98UCSG-SQ19
- 98UCSG-SQ19
- 98UCSR-SQ19
- 98UD ChoPCR-203
- 98UD ChoR-203
- 98UD3-48
- 98UD3-108
- 98UD3-168
- 98UD3DieC-48
- 98UD3DieC-108
- 98UD3DieC-168
- 98UDCP-203
- 98UppDec-370
- 98UppDecBD-84
- 98UppDecDD-84
- 98UppDecE-370
- 98UppDecE1o1-370
- 98UppDecFF-FF14
- 98UppDecFF-FF14
- 98UppDecFFQ1-FF14
- 98UppDecFFQ2-FF14
- 98UppDecGJ-GJ19
- 98UppDecGR-370
- 98UppDecLSH-LS24
- 98UppDecLSHQ1-LS24
- 98UppDecLSHQ2-LS24
- 98UppDecLSHQ3-LS24
- 98UppDecM-195
- 98UppDecMGS-195
- 98UppDecMPG-PG8
- 98UppDecMSS-195
- 98UppDecMSS-195
- 98UppDecP-P28
- 98UppDecPQ1-P28
- 98UppDecPQ2-P28
- 98UppDecPQ3-P28
- 98UppDecQD-84
- 98UppDecTD-84
- 98UppDecWFG-WF27
- 98UppDecWFP-WF27
- 99AurSty-19
- 99Pac-416
- 99PacAur-138
- 99PacAurCF-20
- 99PacAurCFC-20
- 99PacAurCFPB-20
- 99PacAurPD-138
- 99PacCop-416
- 99PacGol-416
- 99PacGolCD-35
- 99PacIceB-416
- 99PacPreD-416
- 99RetHoc-74
- 99SP AutPS-83
- 99UppDecCLC-67
- 99UppDecCLCLC-67
- 99UppDecM-196
- 99UppDecMGS-196
- 99UppDecMSS-196
- 99UppDecMSS-196
- 99UppDecRG-74
- 99UppDecRP-74

**Sundin, Sture**
- 65SweCorI-112

**Sundkvist, Kent**
- 70SweHocS-129
- 71SweHocS-220


**Sundlov, Michael**
- 87SwePanS-48
- 89SweSemE-28
- 90SweSemE-175
- 91SweSemE-28
- 92SweSemE-51
- 93SweSemE-26
- 93SweSemE-307
- 94SweLeaE-126
- 94SweLeaECS-2
- 94SweLeaEGC-15
- 95SweLeaE-15
- 95SweLeaEC-12
- 95SweLeaEM-1
- 95SweLeaES-2
- 95SweUppDE-19

**Sundquist, Christer**
- 67SweHoc-94

**Sundqvist, Karl-Johan**
- 71SweHocS-143
- 72SweHocS-9
- 72SweHocS-122
- 73SweHocS-8
- 73SweHocS-184
- 73SweWorCS-8
- 73SweWorCS-184
- 74SweHocS-189
- 74SweSemHVS-7

**Sundstrom, Billy**
- 69SweHocS-106
- 70SweHocS-53
- 71SweHocS-122
- 72SweHocS-97
- 73SweHocS-210
- 73SweWorCS-210

**Sundstrom, Kjell**
- 66SweHoc-21
- 67SweHoc-261
- 69SweHocS-308
- 70SweHocS-211
- 71SweHocS-300
- 72SweHocS-73

**Sundstrom, Niklas**
- 91SweSemE-331
- 92SweSemE-244
- 92UppDec-597
- 93Cla-8
- 93ClaTopTen-DP8
- 93Par-506
- 93ParEmeI-506
- 93SweSemE-212
- 94Cla-79
- 94ClaDraGol-79
- 94ClaTri-T43
- 94ParSE-SE237
- 94ParSEG-SE237
- 94SP-168
- 94SPDieCut-168
- 94SweLeaE-284
- 95BeAPla-177
- 95BeAPSig-S177
- 95BeAPSigDC-S177
- 95Bow-113
- 95BowAllFoi-113
- 95BowBes-BB21
- 95BowBesRef-BB21
- 95ColCho-408
- 95Don-382
- 95DonEli-60
- 95DonEliDCS-60
- 95DonEliDCU-60
- 95DonEliR-14
- 95DonRatRoo-3
- 95Fin-59
- 95FinRef-59
- 95LeaLim-104
- 95LeaLimRP-4
- 95Met-193
- 95MetIS-21
- 95ParInt-261
- 95ParInt-514
- 95ParIntEl-261
- 95ParIntEl-514
- 95SelCer-135
- 95SelCerMG-135
- 95SkyImp-213
- 95SkyImpNHLF-16
- 95SP-96
- 95StaClu-205
- 95StaCluMOMS-205
- 95Sum-187
- 95SumArtP-187
- 95SumIce-187
- 95SweGloWC-60
- 95Top-341
- 95TopOPCI-341
- 95TopSupSkiSR-SR14
- 95Ult-357
- 95UltExtAtt-18
- 95UppDec-261
- 95UppDecEelce-261
- 95UppDecEelceG-261
- 95UppDecPHE-H28
- 95UppDecPreH-H28
- 95Zen-128
- 95ZenRooRC-14
- 96ColCho-168
- 96Don-237
- 96DonEli-47
- 96DonEliDCS-47
- 96DonPrePro-237
- 96Fle-72
- 96Lea-172
- 96LeaPreP-172
- 96MetUni-102


- 96Sco-269
- 96ScoArtPro-269
- 96ScoDeaCAP-269
- 96ScoGolB-269
- 96ScoSpeAP-269
- 96SkyImp-85
- 96SPHolCol-HC26
- 96TopPicRS-RS18
- 96Ult-112
- 96UltGolM-113
- 96UppDec-107
- 96UppDecGN-X24
- 97ColCho-165
- 97ColChoSta-SQ41
- 97Don-178
- 97DonLim-64
- 97DonLimExp-64
- 97DonPreProG-178
- 97DonPreProS-178
- 97DonPri-67
- 97DonPriSoA-67
- 97Lea-36
- 97LeaFraMat-36
- 97LeaFraMDC-36
- 97LeaInt-36
- 97LeaIntUI-36
- 97Pac-86
- 97PacCop-86
- 97PacCroR-88
- 97PacCroREG-88
- 97PacCroRIB-88
- 97PacCroRS-88
- 97PacEmeGre-86
- 97PacIceB-86
- 97PacOme-150
- 97PacOmeC-150
- 97PacOmeDG-150
- 97PacOmeEG-150
- 97PacOmeIB-150
- 97PacRed-86
- 97PacSil-86
- 97PinIns-155
- 97Sco-194
- 97ScoRan-5
- 97ScoRanPla-5
- 97ScoRanPre-5
- 97SPAut-104
- 97UppDec-106
- 97UppDecTSS-7B
- 98Be A PPA-240
- 98Be A PPAAF-240
- 98Be APG-240
- 98Fin-121
- 98FinNo P-121
- 98FinNo PR-121
- 98FinRef-121
- 98O-PChr-197
- 98O-PChrR-197
- 98Pac-302
- 98PacIceB-302
- 98PacPar-159
- 98PacParC-159
- 98PacParEG-159
- 98PacParH-159
- 98PacParIB-159
- 98PacParS-159
- 98PacRed-302
- 98PacPar-282
- 98PacCop-282
- 98PacGol-282
- 98PacIceB-282
- 98PacPreD-282

**Sundstrom, Olie**
- 89SweSemE-122
- 90SweSemE-199
- 91SweSemE-129
- 92NasKni-23
- 93CleLum-24
- 93CleLumPos-18

**Sundstrom, Patrik**
- 82Canu-21
- 82SweSemHVS-15
- 83Canu-20
- 83OPC-361
- 83OPCSti-152
- 83Vac-118
- 84Canu-23
- 84OPC-331
- 84OPCSti-279
- 857ECreCar-19
- 85Canu-22
- 85OPC-115
- 85OPCSti-241
- 85Top-115
- 86Canu-20


- 86KraDra-70
- 86OPC-156
- 86OPCSti-101
- 86Top-156
- 870PC-34
- 880PCMin-40
- 87PanSti-348
- 87Top-34
- 88DevCar-27
- 88OPC-67
- 88PanSti-277
- 88Top-67
- 89DevCar-23
- 89OPC-56
- 89OPCSti-82
- 89PanSti-250
- 89SweSemWCS-21
- 89Top-56
- 90Bow-101
- 90BowTif-89
- 90Dev-28
- 90OPC-306
- 90PanSti-65
- 90ProSet-176A
- 90ProSet-176B
- 90Sco-19
- 90ScoCan-19
- 90Top-205
- 90TopTif-205
- 90UppDec-273
- 90UppDecF-273
- 91Bow-254
- 91FlamIGA-22
- 91FlamPanTS-21
- 91FlamPanTS-H
- 91OPC-451
- 91PanSti-217
- 91Pin-290
- 91PinFre-290
- 91ProSet-141
- 91ProSetFre-141
- 91ProSetPla-71
- 91ScoAme-117
- 91ScoCan-117
- 91StaClu-229
- 91Top-451
- 91UppDec-369
- 91UppDecF-369
- 93SweSemE-19

**Sundstrom, Peter**
- 82SweSemHVS-16
- 840PC-155
- 84Top-116
- 86SwePanS-23
- 87CapKod-12
- 87CapTeaIss-23
- 88CapBor-21
- 88CapSmo-23
- 89DevCar-24
- 90SweSemE-136
- 91SweSemE-191
- 92SweSemE-219
- 93SweSemE-190
- 94SweLeaE-127

**Sunesson, Ake**
- 67SweHoc-111

**Sunohara, Vicky**
- 97ColCho-280

**Suomalainen, Jukka**
- 94FinnSIS-280
- 95FinnSIS-138

**Suoniemi, Raimo**
- 74SweSemHVS-90

**Suoraniemi, Kari**
- 87SwePanS-218
- 89SweSemE-194
- 89SweSemWCS-37
- 92SweSemE-255
- 93SweSemE-221
- 94FinnSIS-372
- 94SweLeaE-116

**Suoraniemi, Seppo**
- 74SweHocS-101
- 74SweSemHVS-81
- 81SweSemHVS-34
- 82SweSemHVS-32

**Suorsa, Jari**
- 96FinnSISR-38

**Sup, Michal**
- 917thInnSWHL-90
- 91BriColJHL-16
- 94CzeAPSE-88
- 95CzeAPSE-139

**Surovy, Tomas**
- 95SloPeeWT-25

**Sushinski, Maxim**
- 93Pin-510
- 93PinCan-510

**Susi, Timo**
- 81SweSemHVS-31
- 82SweSemHVS-48

**Suter, Bob**
- 80USAOlyTMP-8
- 81SweSemHVS-92
- 95SigRooMI-33
- 95SigRooMI-34
- 95SigRooSMIS-33
- 95SigRooSMIS-34

**Suter, Gary**
- 85FlamRedRP-28
- 86FlamRedR-27
- 86KraDra-71
- 86OPC-189
- 860PCSti-134
- 860PCSti-192
- 86Top-189
- 87FlamRedRP-28


- 94ScoGol-44
- 94ScoPla-44
- 94ScoPlaTS-44
- 94TopPre-168
- 94TopPreSE-168
- 94Ult-46
- 94UppDec-74
- 94UppDecEleIce-74
- 94UppDecSPI-SP107
- 94UppDecSPIDC-SP107
- 95CanGamNHLP-69
- 95ColCho-8
- 95ColChoPC-8
- 95ColChoPCP-8
- 95Don-99
- 95DonEli-11
- 95DonEliDCS-11
- 95DonEliDCU-11
- 95Emo-34
- 95Fin-126
- 95FinRef-126
- 95Lea-219
- 95Met-29
- 95ParInt-39
- 95ParIntEl-39
- 95ParIntPTP-PP26
- 95Pin-68
- 95PinArtP-68
- 95PinRinC-68
- 95PlaOneoOne-238
- 95Sco-82
- 95ScoBalce-82
- 95ScoBalceAP-82
- 95SkyImp-34
- 95SP-25
- 95StaClu-124
- 95StaCluMOMS-124
- 95Sum-59
- 95SumArtP-59
- 95SumIce-59
- 95SweGloWC-104
- 95Top-156
- 95TopHidGem-9HG
- 95TopOPCI-156
- 95Ult-36
- 95UltGolM-36
- 95UppDec-284
- 95UppDecEelce-284
- 95UppDecEelceG-284
- 95UppDecNHLAS-AS8
- 95UppDecSpeC-SE107
- 95UppDecSpeEdiG-SE107
- 95Zen-73
- 96beAPAut-180
- 96BeAPAutSil-180
- 96beAPla-180
- 96ColCho-52
- 96Don-130
- 96DonPrePro-130
- 96Fle-19
- 96Lea-32
- 96LeaPreP-32
- 96MetUni-28
- 96Pin-195
- 96PinArtP-195
- 96PinFoi-195
- 96PinPreS-195
- 96PinRinC-195
- 96Sco-182
- 96ScoArtPro-182
- 96ScoDeaCAP-182
- 96ScoGolB-182
- 96ScoSpeAP-182
- 96SkyImp-29
- 96SP-29
- 96SweSemW-162
- 96TeaOut-82
- 96TopNHLP-41
- 96TopPicOl-41
- 96Ult-33
- 96UltGolM-33
- 96UppDec-235
- 96UppDecGN-X37
- 97ColCho-45
- 97Pac-212
- 97PacCop-212
- 97PacEmeGre-212
- 97PacIceB-212
- 97PacRed-212
- 97PacSil-212
- 98O-PChr-26
- 98O-PChrR-26
- 98Pac-152
- 98PacIceB-152
- 98PacRed-152
- 98Top-26
- 98TopO-P-26
- 98UC-47
- 98UD ChoPCR-47
- 98UD ChoR-47
- 99UppDecM-179
- 99UppDecMGS-179
- 99UppDecMGS-179
- 99UppDecMSS-179
- 99UppDecMSS-179

**Sutherland, Bill**
- 60CleBar-17
- 62QueAce-21
- 63QueAceQ-21
- 64QueAce-19
- 65QueAce-19
- 68MapLeaWB-11
- 68OPC-196
- 690PC-172
- 700PC-83
- 70Top-83

**Sundin, Ronnie**
- 92SweSemE-307
- 93SweSemE-274
- 94SweLeaE-24
- 94SweLeaE-141
- 95SweUppDE-207

- 71OPC-141
- 71SarProSta-188
- 71TorSun-250
- 79JetPos-26
- 81JetPos-21
- 82Jet-25
- 84JetPol-23
- 85JetPol-23
- 86JetBor-3
- 88JetPol-23
- 89ProAHL-75

**Sutherland, Capt.J.T.**
- 83HalFP-C15
- 85HalFC-44

**Sutherland, Steve**
- 72ShaLosAW-114
- 76NordMarA-13
- 76NordPos-17
- 76OPCWHA-127

**Sutinen, Timo**
- 74SweHocS-102
- 74SweSemHVS-91
- 96GerDELE-134

**Sutter, Brent**
- 82OPC-216
- 82OPCSti-56
- 83IslTealss-15
- 83OPC-18
- 84IslIsIN-12
- 84KelWin-29
- 84OPC-136
- 84OPCSti-88
- 84Top-102
- 85IslIsIN-13
- 85OPC-107
- 85OPCSti-71
- 85OPCSti-117
- 85Top-107
- 86OPC-117
- 86OPCSti-211
- 86Top-117
- 87OPC-27
- 87OPCSti-241
- 87PanSti-99
- 87Top-27
- 88OPC-7
- 88OPCSti-105
- 88PanSti-292
- 88Top-7
- 89Isl-14
- 89OPC-14
- 89OPCSti-115
- 89PanSti-266
- 89Top-14
- 90Bow-126
- 90BowTif-126
- 90Kra-57
- 90OPC-258
- 90OPCPre-115
- 90PanSti-90
- 90ProSet-191
- 90Sco-39
- 90ScoCan-39
- 90ScoHotRS-19
- 90Top-258
- 90TopTif-258
- 90UppDec-249
- 90UppDecF-249
- 91BlaCok-25
- 91Bow-226
- 91Kra-43
- 91OPC-165
- 91OPCPre-156
- 91PanSti-246
- 91Par-35
- 91Par-460
- 91ParFre-35
- 91Pin-79
- 91PinFre-79
- 91ProSet-154
- 91ProSet-374
- 91ProSetFre-154
- 91ProSetFre-374
- 91ProSetPla-74
- 91ProSetPla-164
- 91ScoAme-243
- 91ScoCan-463
- 91ScoRoo-103T
- 91StaClu-180
- 91Top-165
- 91UppDec-140
- 91UppDec-645
- 91UppDecF-140
- 91UppDecF-645
- 92Bow-147
- 92OPC-60
- 92Par-33
- 92ParCheP-CP3
- 92ParEmel-33
- 92Pin-39
- 92PinFre-39
- 92ProSet-36
- 92Sco-112
- 92ScoCan-112
- 92StaClu-428
- 92Top-75
- 92TopGol-75G
- 92Ult-43
- 92UppDec-199
- 93BlaCok-11
- 93Don-69
- 93Lea-142
- 93OPCPre-147
- 93OPCPreG-147
- 93PanSti-151

- 93Par-308
- 93ParEmel-308
- 93Pin-91
- 93PinCan-91
- 93Pow-56
- 93Sco-44
- 93ScoCan-44
- 93StaClu-211
- 93StaCluFDI-211
- 93StaCluFDIO-211
- 93StaCluO-211
- 93TopPre-147
- 93TopPreG-147
- 93Ult-206
- 94CanGamNHLP-72
- 94Don-290
- 94FinnJaaK-91
- 94Lea-30
- 94Pin-117
- 94PinArtP-117
- 94PinRinC-117
- 94Sco-32
- 94ScoGol-32
- 94ScoPla-32
- 94ScoPlaTS-32
- 94StaClu-218
- 94StaCluFDI-218
- 94StaCluMOMS-218
- 94StaCluSTWC-218
- 94Ult-47
- 95BeAPla-140
- 95BeAPSig-S140
- 95BeAPSigDC-S140
- 95Sco-272
- 95ScoBlaIce-272
- 95ScoBlaIceAP-272
- 97Pac-186
- 97PacEmeGre-186
- 97PacIceB-186
- 97PacRed-186
- 97PacSil-186

**Sutter, Brian**
- 78BluPos-23
- 78OPC-319
- 79OPC-84
- 79Top-84
- 80OPC-244
- 80Top-244
- 81OPC-297
- 81OPCSti-133
- 81Top-W122
- 82OPC-298
- 82OPC-311
- 82OPCSti-198
- 82PosCer-1
- 83OPC-308
- 83OPC-320
- 83OPCSti-127
- 83OPCSti-128
- 83PufSti-17
- 84OPC-192
- 84OPCSti-56
- 84Top-135
- 85?ECreCar-17
- 85OPC-135
- 85OPCBox-N
- 85OPCSti-46
- 85Top-135
- 85TopBoxB-N
- 86OPC-72
- 86OPCBoxB-O
- 86OPCSti-175
- 86Top-72
- 86TopBoxB-O
- 87BluKod-24
- 87BluTealss-22
- 88BluTealss-22
- 88OPCSti-15
- 88PanSti-111
- 89BluKod-NNO
- 90BluKod-22
- 90ProSet-676
- 91ScoAme-378
- 91ScoCan-268
- 91UppDec-645
- 91UppDecF-645
- 92BluUDBB-25

**Sutter, Darryl**
- 80BlaBroBac-15
- 80BlaWhiBor-13
- 81BlaBroBac-26
- 81BlaBroBac-16
- 81OPC-65
- 81Top-W77
- 82OPC-76
- 83BlaBorPos-22
- 83OPC-113
- 83OPCSti-105
- 84OPC-47
- 84OPCSti-30
- 84Top-36
- 85OPC-100
- 85Top-100
- 86BlaCok-21
- 86OPC-49
- 86OPCSti-151
- 86Top-49
- 87BlaCok-22
- 87PanSti-234
- 88ProHL-116
- 89ProHL-58
- 90BlaCok-26
- 91BlaCok-26
- 91UppDec-645

- 91UppDecF-645
- 93BlaCok-27

**Sutter, Doug**
- 94WheThu-20

**Sutter, Duane**
- 81OPC-211
- 82OPC-212
- 82OPCSti-52
- 83IslTealss-16
- 83OPC-19
- 84IslIsIN-13
- 84KelWin-48
- 84OPC-137
- 85IslIsIN-14
- 85OPC-227
- 85OPCSti-72
- 86OPC-39
- 86OPCSti-210
- 86Top-39
- 87BlaCok-23
- 87OPC-43
- 87PanSti-102
- 87Top-43
- 88BlaCok-19
- 89BlaCok-7
- 89OPC-221
- 90Bow-12
- 90BowTif-12
- 90OPC-466
- 90ProSet-61A
- 90ProSet-61B
- 91UppDec-645
- 91UppDecF-645
- 94IndIce-24

**Sutter, Rich**
- 83FlyJCP-21
- 83PenHeiP-22
- 84KelWin-24
- 84OPC-169
- 84OPCSti-111
- 85FlyPos-27
- 85OPC-208
- 86Canu-21
- 86OPC-29
- 86OPCSti-242
- 86Top-29
- 87CanuSheOil-21
- 87OPC-258
- 87OPCSti-193
- 87PanSti-350
- 88CanuMoh-22
- 88OPC-255
- 88OPCSti-57
- 88PanSti-142
- 89CanuMoh-22
- 89OPC-282
- 89OPCSti-62
- 89PanSti-157
- 90BluKod-23
- 90OPC-405
- 90ProSet-272
- 90Sco-281
- 90ScoCan-281
- 90UppDec-328
- 90UppDecF-328
- 91BluPos-19
- 91Bow-370
- 91OPC-143
- 91PanSti-33
- 91Par-372
- 91ParFre-372
- 91Pin-268
- 91PinFre-268
- 91ProSet-217
- 91ProSetFre-217
- 91ProSetPla-108
- 91ScoAme-63
- 91ScoAme-378
- 91ScoCan-63
- 91ScoCan-268
- 91StaClu-192
- 91Top-143
- 91UppDec-317
- 91UppDec-645
- 91UppDecF-317
- 91UppDecF-645
- 92Bow-256
- 92PanSti-19
- 92PanStiFre-19
- 92Sco-327
- 92ScoCan-327
- 92StaClu-389
- 92StaClu-488
- 92Top-434
- 92TopGol-434G
- 92Ult-398
- 92UppDec-143
- 93BlaCok-3
- 93PanSti-160
- 93Pin-108
- 93PinCan-108
- 93Pow-317
- 93Sco-323
- 93Sco-498
- 93ScoCan-323
- 93ScoCan-498
- 93StaClu-46
- 93StaCluFDI-46
- 93StaCluFDIO-46
- 93StaCluO-46
- 93Ult-293
- 94MapLeaK-26
- 94MapLeaPP-26
- 94Pin-235

- 94PinArtP-235
- 94PinRinC-235

**Sutter, Ron**
- 83FlyJCP-22
- 84KelWin-40
- 84OPC-170
- 84OPCSti-107
- 84Top-122
- 85FlyPos-28
- 85OPC-6
- 85Top-6
- 86FlyPos-26
- 86OPC-109
- 86OPCSti-243
- 86Top-109
- 87OPC-113
- 87OPCSti-102
- 87PanSti-137
- 87Top-113
- 88OPC-126
- 88Top-126
- 89FlyPos-25
- 89OPC-173
- 89OPCSti-107
- 89PanSti-299
- 89Top-173
- 90FlyPos-23
- 90OPC-45
- 90PanSti-109
- 90ProSet-224
- 90Sco-153
- 90ScoCan-153
- 90Top-45
- 90TopTif-45
- 90UppDec-68
- 90UppDecF-68
- 91Bow-238
- 91OPC-232
- 91OPCPre-95
- 91PanSti-233
- 91Par-158
- 91ParFre-158
- 91Pin-95
- 91PinFre-95
- 91ProSet-178
- 91ProSet-476
- 91ProSetFre-178
- 91ProSetFre-476
- 91ProSetPla-222
- 91ScoAme-298
- 91ScoAme-378
- 91ScoCan-283
- 91ScoCan-619
- 91ScoRoo-69T
- 91StaClu-49
- 91Top-232
- 91UppDec-309
- 91UppDec-645
- 91UppDecF-309
- 91UppDecF-645
- 92Bow-175
- 92OPC-362
- 92PanSti-20
- 92PanStiFre-20
- 92Par-389
- 92ParEmel-389
- 92ProSet-162
- 92Sco-86
- 92ScoCan-86
- 92StaClu-86
- 92StaClu-488
- 92Top-371
- 92TopGol-371G
- 92Ult-190
- 92UppDec-184
- 93Don-288
- 93Don-482
- 93Lea-275
- 93OPCPre-103
- 93OPCPreG-103
- 93PanSti-161
- 93Pin-95
- 93PinCan-95
- 93Sco-39
- 93ScoCan-39
- 93StaClu-86
- 93StaCluFDI-86
- 93StaCluFDIO-86
- 93StaCluO-86
- 93TopPre-103
- 93UppDec-33
- 94Lea-351
- 94OPCPre-428
- 94OPCPreSE-428
- 94Par-192
- 94ParGol-192
- 94Pin-383
- 94PinArtP-383
- 94PinRinC-383
- 94Sco-177
- 94ScoGol-177
- 94ScoPlaTS-177
- 94TopPre-428
- 94TopPreSE-428
- 95Sco-113
- 95ScoBlaIce-113
- 95ScoBlaIceAP-113
- 97Be A PPAPD-106
- 97BeAPla-106
- 97BeAPlaAut-106
- 97PacInvNRB-181

**Sutton, Andy**
- 98Be A PPA-268
- 98Be A PPAA-268
- 98Be A PPAAF-268
- 98Be A PPSE-268
- 98Be APG-268
- 99UppDecM-181
- 99UppDecMGS-181
- 99UppDecMSS-181

**Sutton, Blake**
- 91AirCanSJHL-E29

**Sutton, Boyd**
- 91GreMon-13
- 92OklCitB-17

**Sutton, Dave**
- 91RayJrC-17

**Sutton, Ken**
- 88SasBla-7
- 89ProAHL-260
- 90ProAHLIHL-271
- 91Par-239
- 91ParFre-239
- 91Pin-325
- 91PinFre-325
- 91SabBluS-21
- 91SabPepC-21
- 91ScoAme-393
- 91ScoCan-283
- 91UppDec-458
- 91UppDecF-458
- 92Bow-422
- 92OPC-165
- 92Par-254
- 92ParEmel-254
- 92Pin-216
- 92PinFre-216
- 92SabBluS-22
- 92SabJubF-10
- 92Sco-292
- 92ScoCan-292
- 92StaClu-292
- 92Top-59
- 92TopGol-59G
- 92Ult-20
- 93Lea-295
- 93OPCPre-89
- 93OPCPreG-89
- 93Pin-336
- 93PinCan-336
- 93Sco-410
- 93ScoCan-410
- 93StaClu-219
- 93StaCluFDI-219
- 93StaCluFDIO-219
- 93StaCluO-219
- 93TopPre-89
- 93TopPreG-89
- 94Lea-498
- 94Pin-437
- 94PinArtP-437
- 94PinRinC-437

**Sutton, Scott**
- 89RayJrC-20
- 91RayJrC-18

**Sutyla, Ken**
- 67ColChe-13

**Suvanto, Harri**
- 93FinnSIS-192
- 94FinnSIS-100
- 95FinnSIS-134

**Suzor, Mark**
- 77RocCokCan-18
- 78LouGea-18
- 78OPC-307

**Svanberg, Bo**
- 86SwePanS-105
- 87SwePanS-102
- 90SweSemE-145
- 91SweSemE-197
- 92SweSemE-213
- 93SweSemE-184
- 94SweLeaE-79
- 95SweLeaE-95
- 95SweUppDE-145

**Svangstu, Lee**
- 96MedHatT-21

**Svartvadet, Per**
- 93SweSemE-210
- 94ParSE-SE235
- 94ParSEG-SE235
- 94SweLeaE-245
- 95SweLeaE-107
- 95SweUppDE-166

**Svedberg, Hans**
- 64SweCorl-13
- 64SweCorl-139
- 65SweCorl-13
- 65SweCorl-139

**Svedberg, Lennart**
- 64SweCorl-21
- 64SweCorl-79
- 65SweCorl-21
- 65SweCorl-79
- 67SweHoc-22
- 67SweHoc-147
- 69SweHocS-162
- 69SweHocS-200
- 69SweWorC-46
- 69SweWorC-50
- 70SweHocS-118
- 70SweHocS-153
- 70SweHocS-281

- 71SweHocS-10
- 71SweHocS-247
- 72SweSemWC-46
- 81SweSemHVS-114
- 91SweSemWCS-232
- 95SweGloWC-66

**Svedberg, Mathias**
- 90SweSemE-107
- 91SweSemE-113
- 92SweSemE-132
- 93SweSemE-105
- 94SweLeaE-111

**Svedberg, Robert**
- 92SweSemE-207
- 93SweSemE-177
- 93SweSemWCS-102
- 94SweLeaE-43
- 94SweLeaETG-6
- 95BeAPla-169
- 95BeAPSig-S169
- 95BeAPSigDC-S169
- 95Don-370
- 95Fin-183
- 95FinRef-183
- 95Lea-230
- 95Met-194
- 95ParInt-84
- 95ParIntEl-84
- 95SelCer-115
- 95SelCerMG-115
- 95SloAPSNT-13
- 95StaClu-216
- 95StaCluMOMS-216
- 95Sum-196
- 95SumArtP-196
- 95SumIce-196
- 95Top-257
- 95TopOPCI-257
- 95Ult-358
- 95UltHigSpe-18
- 95UppDec-172
- 95UppDecEleIce-172
- 95UppDecEleIceG-172
- 95Zen-148
- 96ColCho-104
- 96Don-77
- 96DonPrePro-77
- 96Fla-39
- 96FlaBluI-39
- 96Fle-43
- 96FlePic-42
- 96Lea-77
- 96LeaPreP-77
- 96MetUni-63
- 96Pin-38
- 96PinArtP-38
- 96PinFoi-38
- 96PinPreS-38
- 96PinRin-38
- 96Sco-83
- 96ScoArtPro-83
- 96ScoDeaCAP-83
- 96ScoGolB-83
- 96ScoSpeAP-83
- 96SkyImp-49
- 96SP-63
- 96Sum-52
- 96SumArtP-52
- 96SumIce-52
- 96SumMet-52
- 96SumPreS-52
- 96SweSemW-221
- 96TeaOut-56
- 96Ult-69
- 96UltGolM-69
- 96UppDec-67
- 97ColCho-104
- 97ColChoSta-SQ2
- 97Pac-243
- 97PacCop-243
- 97PacDyn-56
- 97PacDynC-56
- 97PacDynDG-56
- 97PacDynEG-56
- 97PacDynR-56
- 97PacDynSil-56
- 97PacDynTan-51
- 97PacEmeGre-243
- 97PacIceB-243
- 97PacOme-101
- 97PacOmeC-101
- 97PacOmeDG-101
- 97PacOmeEG-101
- 97PacOmeG-101
- 97PacOmeIB-101
- 97PacRed-243
- 97PacSil-243
- 97Pin-141
- 97PinIns-159
- 97PinPrePBB-141
- 97PinPrePBC-141
- 97PinPrePBM-141
- 97PinPrePBY-141
- 97PinPrePFC-141
- 97PinPrePFM-141
- 97PinPrePFY-141
- 97PinPrePla-141
- 97Sco-189
- 97UppDec-73
- 98Be A PPA-59
- 98Be A PPAA-59

- 98Be A PPAAF-59
- 98Be A PPTBASG-59
- 98Be APG-59
- 98Fin-77
- 98FinNo P-77
- 98FinNo PR-77
- 98FinRef-77
- 98Pac-228
- 98PacIceB-228
- 98PacPar-100
- 98PacParC-100
- 98PacParEG-100
- 98PacParH-100
- 98PacParIB-100
- 98PacParS-100
- 98PacRed-228
- 98SPxFin-38
- 98SPxFinR-38
- 98SPxFinS-38
- 98UC-88
- 98UD ChoPCR-88
- 98UD ChoR-88
- 98UppDec-278
- 98UppDecE-278
- 98UppDecE1o1-278
- 98UppDecGR-278
- 98UppDecM-88
- 98UppDecMGS-88
- 98UppDecMSS-88
- 99Pac-182
- 99PacCop-182
- 99PacGol-182
- 99PacIceB-182
- 99PacPreD-182

**Svejkovsky, Jaroslav**
- 95BowDraPro-P32
- 95TriAme-25
- 96Fla-125
- 96FlaBluI-125
- 96PorPir-15
- 97Be A PPAD-242
- 97Be A PPAPD-242
- 97BeAPla-242
- 97BeAPlaAut-242
- 97ColCho-272
- 97Don-220
- 97DonCanI-143
- 97DonCanIDS-143
- 97DonCanIPS-143
- 97DonEli-22
- 97DonEli-141
- 97DonEliAsp-22
- 97DonEliAsp-141
- 97DonEliC-5
- 97DonEliMC-5
- 97DonEliS-22
- 97DonEliS-141
- 97DonLim-33
- 97DonLim-96
- 97DonLim-143
- 97DonLimExp-33
- 97DonLimExp-96
- 97DonLimExp-143
- 97DonLimFOTG-32
- 97DonMed-9
- 97DonPre-146
- 97DonPre-167
- 97DonPreCttC-146
- 97DonPreCttC-167
- 97DonPreLotT-8B
- 97DonPreProG-220
- 97DonPreProS-220
- 97DonPri-167
- 97DonPri-219
- 97DonPriDD-19
- 97DonPriSoA-167
- 97DonPriSoA-219
- 97DonRatR-9
- 97Kat-155
- 97KatGol-155
- 97KatSil-155
- 97Lea-67
- 97Lea-167
- 97LeaFraMat-67
- 97LeaFraMat-167
- 97LeaFraMDC-67
- 97LeaFraMDC-167
- 97LeaInt-67
- 97LeaIntUI-67
- 97McD-35
- 97PacCroR-143
- 97PacCroREG-143
- 97PacCroRIB-143
- 97PacCroRS-143
- 97PacPar-200
- 97PacParC-200
- 97PacParDG-200
- 97PacParEG-200
- 97PacParIB-200
- 97PacParRed-200
- 97PacParSil-200
- 97Pin-25
- 97PinArtP-25
- 97PinIns-125
- 97PinMin-25
- 97PinMinB-25
- 97PinMinCBP-25
- 97PinMinCGPP-25
- 97PinMinCGPP-25
- 97PinMinCNSP-25
- 97PinMinCoiB-25
- 97PinMinCoiGP-25
- 97PinMinCoiN-25
- 97PinMinCoiSG-25
- 97PinMinCoiSS-25

❑ 97PinMinGolTea-25
❑ 97PinMinSilTea-25
❑ 97PinPrePBB-25
❑ 97PinPrePBC-25
❑ 97PinPrePBM-25
❑ 97PinPrePBY-25
❑ 97PinPrePFC-25
❑ 97PinPrePFM-25
❑ 97PinPrePFY-25
❑ 97PinPrePla-25
❑ 97PinRinC-25
❑ 97Sco-53
❑ 97ScoArtPro-53
❑ 97ScoGolBla-53
❑ 97SPAutSotT-JS
❑ 97Stu-47
❑ 97StuPor-32
❑ 97StuPrePG-47
❑ 97StuPrePS-47
❑ 97UppDec-195
❑ 97UppDecIce-40
❑ 97UppDecIceP-40
❑ 97UppDecIPS-40
❑ 97UppDecSG-SG52
❑ 98Pac-447
❑ 98PacDynI-199
❑ 98PacDynIIB-199
❑ 98PacDynIR-199
❑ 98PacIceB-447
❑ 98PacRed-447
❑ 98UppDec-384
❑ 98UppDecE-384
❑ 98UppDecE1o1-384
❑ 98UppDecGR-384
❑ 98UppDecM-217
❑ 98UppDecMGS-217
❑ 98UppDecMSS-217
❑ 98UppDecMSS-217
❑ 99Pac-447
❑ 99PacCop-447
❑ 99PacGol-447
❑ 99PacIceB-447
❑ 99PacPreD-447
❑ 99UppDecM-213
❑ 99UppDecMGS-213
❑ 99UppDecMSS-213
❑ 99UppDecMSS-213
**Svensson, Anders**
❑ 84SweSemE-104
❑ 90SweSemE-132
❑ 91SweSemE-184
❑ 92SweSemE-202
**Svensson, Curt**
❑ 69SweHocS-181
**Svensson, Goran**
❑ 65SweCorI-173
**Svensson, Gunnar**
❑ 84SweSemE-98
❑ 85SwePanS-79
**Svensson, Henry**
❑ 65SweCorI-159
❑ 67SweHoc-75
❑ 69SweHocS-107
❑ 71SweHocS-360
**Svensson, Jan-Olov**
❑ 72SweHocS-84
❑ 73SweHocS-156
❑ 73SweWorCS-156
❑ 74SweHocS-190
**Svensson, Kjell**
❑ 64SweCorI-61
❑ 65SweCorI-61
❑ 67SweHoc-194
❑ 69SweHocS-252
❑ 81SweSemHVS-110
**Svensson, Kurt**
❑ 65SweCorI-132
**Svensson, Leif**
❑ 71SweHocS-358
❑ 73SweHocS-62
❑ 73SweWorCS-62
❑ 74SweHocS-191
❑ 79OPC-374
**Svensson, Magnus**
❑ 83SweSemE-131
❑ 84SweSemE-153
❑ 85SwePanS-136
❑ 86SwePanS-140
❑ 87SwePanS-151
❑ 89SweSemE-125
❑ 91SweSemE-133
❑ 92SweSemE-158
❑ 93SweSemE-128
❑ 94FinnJaaK-58
❑ 94SweLeaEGC-13
❑ 95Don-166
❑ 95Emo-71
❑ 95FinnSemWC-55
❑ 95FinnSemWC-203
❑ 95Lea-10
❑ 95ParInt-83
❑ 95ParIntEl-83
❑ 95SkyImp-69
❑ 95SweGloWC-12
❑ 95SweUppDE-243
❑ 96SweSemW-46
**Svensson, Nils-Goran**
❑ 85SwePanS-179
**Svensson, Nils-Gunnar**
❑ 86SwePanS-118
❑ 89SweSemE-103
**Svensson, Ove**
❑ 69SweHocS-108
❑ 70SweHocS-60
❑ 71SweHocS-131
❑ 73SweHocS-224
❑ 73SweWorCS-224
**Svensson, Pelle**
❑ 92SweSemE-265
❑ 93SweSemE-235
❑ 95SweUppDE-182
❑ 96GerDELE-40
❑ 98GerDELE-173
**Svensson, Per-Johan**
❑ 94SweLeaE-57
❑ 95SweLeaE-120
**Svensson, Stefan**
❑ 83SweSemE-127
❑ 84SweSemE-150
❑ 86SwePanS-227
❑ 87SwePanS-217
**Svensson, Tord**
❑ 71SweHocS-208
❑ 72SweHocS-185
❑ 74SweHocS-192
**Sverztov, Alexander**
❑ 91UppDecCWJC-8
**Svetlik, Martin**
❑ 907thInnSWHL-101
**Svetlov, Sergei**
❑ 82SweSemHVS-69
❑ 87RusNatT-19
**Svoboda, Karel**
❑ 86SheCan-25
**Svoboda, Ladislav**
❑ 96CzeAPSE-87
**Svoboda, Oldrich**
❑ 93FinnJyvHS-254
❑ 93FinnSIS-280
❑ 94FinnJaaK-164
❑ 95CzeAPSE-53
❑ 96CzeAPSE-239
**Svoboda, Petr**
❑ 84CanaPos-27
❑ 85CanaPla-3
❑ 85CanaPla-7
❑ 85CanaPos-37
❑ 85CanaPro-23
❑ 85OPCSti-139
❑ 86CanaPos-24
❑ 86KraDra-72
❑ 86OPCSti-17
❑ 86OPCSti-160
❑ 87CanaPos-31
❑ 87CanaVacS-75
❑ 87CanaVacS-77
❑ 87OPCSti-18
❑ 88CanaPos-28
❑ 88OPC-256
❑ 88OPCMin-41
❑ 88OPCSti-44
❑ 88PanSti-255
❑ 89CanaKra-23
❑ 89CanaPos-31
❑ 89CanaProF-25
❑ 89Kra-27
❑ 89OPC-238
❑ 89OPCSti-54
❑ 89PanSti-244
❑ 90Bow-46
❑ 90BowTif-46
❑ 90CanaPos-30
❑ 90OPC-246
❑ 90PanSti-50
❑ 90ProSet-161
❑ 90Sco-191
❑ 90ScoCan-191
❑ 90Top-246
❑ 90TopTif-246
❑ 90UppDec-193
❑ 90UppDecF-193
❑ 91Bow-341
❑ 91CanaPanTS-23
❑ 91CanaPos-29
❑ 91OPC-76
❑ 91OPCPre-168
❑ 91PanSti-185
❑ 91Par-237
❑ 91ParFre-237
❑ 91Pin-197
❑ 91PinFre-197
❑ 91ProSet-123
❑ 91ProSetFre-123
❑ 91ProSetPla-65
❑ 91ScoAme-95
❑ 91ScoCan-95
❑ 91StaClu-127
❑ 91Top-76
❑ 91UppDec-285
❑ 91UppDecF-285
❑ 92Bow-47
❑ 92OPC-109
❑ 92Pin-117
❑ 92PinFre-117
❑ 92ProSet-16
❑ 92SabBluS-23
❑ 92SabJubF-14
❑ 92Sco-114
❑ 92ScoCan-114
❑ 92StaClu-227
❑ 92Top-312
❑ 92TopGol-312G
❑ 92Ult-263
❑ 93Don-41
❑ 93Lea-131
❑ 93OPCPre-308
❑ 93OPCPre-324
❑ 93OPCPreG-308
❑ 93OPCPreG-324
❑ 93Pin-32
❑ 93PinCan-32
❑ 93Sco-110
❑ 93ScoCan-110
❑ 93StaClu-132
❑ 93StaCluFDI-132
❑ 93StaCluFDIO-132
❑ 93StaCluO-132
❑ 93TopPre-308
❑ 93TopPre-324
❑ 93TopPreG-308
❑ 93TopPreG-324
❑ 93UppDec-465
❑ 94CzeAPSE-205
❑ 94EASpo-14
❑ 94Lea-393
❑ 94ParSE-SE21
❑ 94ParSEG-SE21
❑ 94Pin-424
❑ 94PinArtP-424
❑ 94PinRinC-424
❑ 95CanGamNHLP-208
❑ 95ColCho-93
❑ 95ColChoPC-93
❑ 95ColChoPCP-93
❑ 95Don-306
❑ 95Lea-180
❑ 95ParInt-427
❑ 95ParIntEl-427
❑ 95Pin-168
❑ 95PinArtP-168
❑ 95PinGloG-21
❑ 95PinRinC-168
❑ 95Sco-287
❑ 95ScoBlaIce-287
❑ 95ScoBlaIceAP-287
❑ 95UppDec-76
❑ 95UppDecEleIce-76
❑ 95UppDecEleIceG-76
❑ 96BeAPAut-56
❑ 96BeAPAutSil-56
❑ 96BeAPla-56
❑ 96FlyPos-22
❑ 96SP-111
❑ 97Pac-277
❑ 97PacCop-277
❑ 97PacEmeGre-277
❑ 97PacIceB-277
❑ 97PacRed-277
❑ 97PacSil-277
❑ 97ScoFly-17
❑ 97ScoFlyPla-17
❑ 97ScoFlyPre-17
❑ 98Be A PPA-104
❑ 98Be A PPAA-104
❑ 98Be A PPAAF-104
❑ 98Be A PPTBASG-104
❑ 98Be APG-104
❑ 99Pac-397
❑ 99PacCop-397
❑ 99PacGol-397
❑ 99PacIceB-397
❑ 99PacPreD-397
**Svoboda, Radek**
❑ 96CzeAPSE-280
**Svoboda, Radoslav**
❑ 81SweSemHVS-61
**Svoboda, Valeri**
❑ 95Sla-424
**Svozil, Ladislav**
❑ 81SweSemHVS-67
❑ 96CzeAPSE-190
**Svrbik, Richard**
❑ 96SloPeeWT-27
**Swain, Brad**
❑ 92BriColJHL-19
**Swain, Garry**
❑ 76OPCWHA-91
**Swan, Jim**
❑ 86PorWinH-22
**Swanjord, Scott**
❑ 93WatBlaH-25
**Swanson, Brad**
❑ 96SeaThu-5
**Swanson, Brian**
❑ 93OmaLan-24
❑ 95DonEliWJ-42
**Swanson, Scott**
❑ 93OmaLan-25
**Swarbrick, George**
❑ 68OPC-174
❑ 68ShiCoi-113
❑ 70FlyPos-12
❑ 70OPC-82
❑ 70Top-82
**Swardh, Magnus**
❑ 93SweSemE-219
❑ 94SweLeaE-89
❑ 95SweLeaE-113
❑ 95SweLeaES-11
❑ 95SweUppDE-170
**Swartz, Tim**
❑ 95Sla-383
❑ 95SudWol-15
❑ 96SudWolP-24
**Sweeney, Bob**
❑ 86MonGolF-21
❑ 88BruPos-18
❑ 88BruSpoA-20
❑ 88OPC-134
❑ 88OPCSti-28
❑ 88OPCSti-68
❑ 88OPCSti-130
❑ 88PanSti-214
❑ 88Top-134
❑ 89BruSpoA-20
❑ 89OPC-135
❑ 89Top-135
❑ 90Bow-28
❑ 90BowTif-28
❑ 90BruSpoA-22
❑ 90OPC-99
❑ 90PanSti-15
❑ 90ProSet-15
❑ 90Sco-235
❑ 90ScoCan-235
❑ 90Top-99
❑ 90TopTif-99
❑ 90UppDec-198
❑ 90UppDecF-198
❑ 91Bow-357
❑ 91BruSpoA-18
❑ 91OPC-99
❑ 91PanSti-177
❑ 91Pin-222
❑ 91PinFre-222
❑ 91ProSet-6
❑ 91ProSetFre-6
❑ 91ScoAme-176
❑ 91ScoCan-176
❑ 91StaClu-75
❑ 91Top-99
❑ 91UppDec-391
❑ 91UppDecF-391
❑ 92Bow-5
❑ 92Bow-402
❑ 92OPC-21
❑ 92OPCPre-110
❑ 92Par-251
❑ 92ParEmel-251
❑ 92SabBluS-24
❑ 92SabJubF-15
❑ 92Sco-317
❑ 92ScoCan-317
❑ 92StaClu-455
❑ 92Top-111
❑ 92TopGol-111G
❑ 92Ult-264
❑ 92UppDec-47
❑ 92UppDec-449
❑ 93OPCPre-431
❑ 93OPCPreG-431
❑ 93PanSti-104
❑ 93Par-290
❑ 93ParEmel-290
❑ 93Pin-118
❑ 93PinCan-118
❑ 93Pow-34
❑ 93Sco-146
❑ 93ScoCan-146
❑ 93StaClu-63
❑ 93StaCluFDI-63
❑ 93StaCluFDIO-63
❑ 93StaCluO-63
❑ 93TopPre-431
❑ 93TopPreG-431
❑ 93Ult-278
❑ 93UppDec-312
❑ 94Lea-417
❑ 94ParSE-SE17
❑ 94ParSEG-SE17
❑ 94Pin-411
❑ 94PinArtP-411
❑ 94PinRinC-411
❑ 94UppDec-445
❑ 94UppDecEleIce-445
❑ 95BeAPla-26
❑ 95BeAPSig-S26
❑ 95BeAPSigDC-S26
❑ 95PlaOneoOne-232
❑ 95UppDec-443
❑ 95UppDecEleIce-443
❑ 95UppDecEleIceG-443
❑ 96ColCho-37
**Sweeney, Don**
❑ 89BruSpoAU-9
❑ 89ProAHL-58
❑ 90BruSpoA-23
❑ 90ProSet-412
❑ 90Sco-51A
❑ 90Sco-51B
❑ 90ScoCan-51A
❑ 90ScoCan-51B
❑ 91Bow-365
❑ 91BruSpoA-19
❑ 91OPC-319
❑ 91PanSti-180
❑ 91Par-228
❑ 91ParFre-228
❑ 91Pin-419
❑ 91PinFre-419
❑ 91ProSetPla-153
❑ 91ScoAme-146
❑ 91ScoCan-146
❑ 91StaClu-370
❑ 91Top-319
❑ 91UppDec-338
❑ 91UppDecF-338
❑ 92Bow-5
❑ 92Bow-402
❑ 92BruPos-11
❑ 92OPC-40
❑ 92Par-244
❑ 92ParEmel-244
❑ 92Pin-179
❑ 92PinFre-179
❑ 92Sco-186
❑ 92ScoCan-186
❑ 92StaClu-337
❑ 92Top-417
❑ 92TopGol-417G
❑ 92Ult-257
❑ 92UppDec-391
❑ 93Don-21
❑ 93Lea-281
❑ 93OPCPre-334
❑ 93OPCPreG-334
❑ 93PanSti-11
❑ 93Par-13
❑ 93ParEmel-13
❑ 93Pin-269
❑ 93PinCan-269
❑ 93Pow-24
❑ 93Sco-169
❑ 93ScoCan-169
❑ 93StaClu-117
❑ 93StaCluFDI-117
❑ 93StaCluFDIO-117
❑ 93StaCluO-117
❑ 93TopPre-334
❑ 93TopPreG-334
❑ 93Ult-271
❑ 93UppDec-101
❑ 94BeAPSig-60
❑ 94CanGamNHLP-40
❑ 94Don-281
❑ 94EASpo-8
❑ 94Fla-14
❑ 94Fle-18
❑ 94Lea-518
❑ 94OPCPre-262
❑ 94OPCPreSE-262
❑ 94ParSE-SE15
❑ 94ParSEG-SE15
❑ 94Pin-91
❑ 94PinArtP-91
❑ 94PinRinC-91
❑ 94Sco-101
❑ 94ScoGol-101
❑ 94ScoPla-101
❑ 94ScoPlaTS-101
❑ 94TopPre-262
❑ 94TopPreSE-262
❑ 94Ult-17
❑ 94UppDec-446
❑ 94UppDecEleIce-446
❑ 95ColCho-91
❑ 95ColChoPC-91
❑ 95ColChoPCP-91
❑ 95Don-101
❑ 95Emo-13
❑ 95Lea-191
❑ 95ParInt-283
❑ 95ParIntEl-283
❑ 95Pin-141
❑ 95PinArtP-141
❑ 95PinRinC-141
❑ 95Sco-163
❑ 95ScoBlaIce-163
❑ 95ScoBlaIceAP-163
❑ 95SP-11
❑ 95StaClu-146
❑ 95StaCluMOMS-146
❑ 95Top-127
❑ 95TopOPCI-127
❑ 95TopSupSki-26
❑ 95TopSupSkiPla-26
❑ 95Ult-208
❑ 95UppDec-35
❑ 95UppDecEleIce-35
❑ 95UppDecEleIceG-35
❑ 96BeAPAut-97
❑ 96BeAPAutSil-97
❑ 96BeAPla-97
❑ 96ColCho-14
❑ 96SP-10
❑ 96UppDec-217
❑ 97PacInvNRB-17
❑ 97ScoBru-20
❑ 97ScoBruPla-20
❑ 97ScoBruPre-20
❑ 97UppDec-14
❑ 98O-PChr-141
❑ 98O-PChrR-141
❑ 98Top-141
❑ 98TopO-P-141
❑ 98UppDec-40
❑ 98UppDecE-40
❑ 98UppDecE1o1-40
❑ 98UppDecGR-40
**Sweeney, Tim**
❑ 89ProIHL-203
❑ 90FlamIGA-27
❑ 90OPCPre-116
❑ 90ProSet-597
❑ 90ScoRoo-13T
❑ 90UppDec-531
❑ 90UppDecF-531
❑ 91Bow-261
❑ 91FlamIGA-23
❑ 91FlamPanTS-22
❑ 91ProSet-364
❑ 91ProSetFre-364
❑ 91StaClu-394
❑ 91UppDec-375
❑ 91UppDecF-375
❑ 92UppDec-95
❑ 93Don-11
❑ 93DucMilCap-1
❑ 93OPCPre-426
❑ 93OPCPreG-426
❑ 93Par-7
❑ 93ParEmel-7
❑ 93Pow-12
❑ 93StaClu-473
❑ 93StaCluFDI-473
❑ 93StaCluO-473
❑ 93TopPre-426
❑ 93TopPreG-426
❑ 93Ult-262
❑ 93UppDec-385
❑ 94CanGamNHLP-34
❑ 94Don-214
❑ 94Fla-6
❑ 94Lea-21
❑ 94OPCPre-147
❑ 94OPCPreSE-147
❑ 94Par-9
❑ 94ParGol-9
❑ 94Pin-93
❑ 94PinArtP-93
❑ 94PinRinC-93
❑ 94TopPre-147
❑ 94TopPreSE-147
❑ 94Ult-8
❑ 94UppDec-38
❑ 94UppDecEleIce-38
❑ 95FinnSemWC 108
❑ 96ProBru-21
❑ 97Be A PPAD-156
❑ 97Be A PPAPD-156
❑ 97BeAPla-156
❑ 97BeAPlaAut-156
❑ 97Pac-183
❑ 97PacCop-183
❑ 97PacEmeGre-183
❑ 97PacIceB-183
❑ 97PacOme-151
❑ 97PacOmeC-151
❑ 97PacOmeDG-151
❑ 97PacOmeEG-151
❑ 97PacOmeG-151
❑ 97PacOmeIB-151
❑ 97PacRed-183
❑ 97PacSil-183
❑ 98Pac-303
❑ 98PacIceB-303
❑ 98PacRed-303
**Sweet, Troy**
❑ 907thInnSOHL-347
❑ 917thInnSOHL-159
❑ 91OshGenS-8
**Sweitzer, Jason**
❑ 95Sla-252
**Swenson, Barkley**
❑ 917thInnSWHL-257
❑ 91PriAlbR-22
❑ 92TacRoc-24
**Swenson, Greg**
❑ 92CorBigRed-27
**Swiatek, Andrezej**
❑ 89SweSemWCS-136
**Swibenko, Marco**
❑ 94GerDELE-41
❑ 95GerDELE-38
**Swinson, Wes**
❑ 93KitRan-20
❑ 94KitRan-22
❑ 95Sla-127
**Switzer, Derek**
❑ 897thInnSOHL-150
❑ 907thInnSOHL-318
**Switzer, Jason**
❑ 91BriColJHL-23
❑ 92BriColJHL-199
**Sychra, Martin**
❑ 93KinFro-14
❑ 94FreCan-27
❑ 98ChaChe-17
**Sydor, Darryl**
❑ 88KamBla-23
❑ 907thInnSMC-12
❑ 907thInnSWHL-307
❑ 90Sco-425
❑ 90ScoCan-425
❑ 90UppDec-358
❑ 90UppDecF-358
❑ 917thInnSCHLAW-14
❑ 91OPCPre-90
❑ 91Pin-321
❑ 91PinFre-321
❑ 91ProSet-542
❑ 91ProSetFre-542
❑ 91ScoCan-631
❑ 91ScoRoo-81T
❑ 91UppDec-549
❑ 91UppDecF-549
❑ 92Bow-321
❑ 92OPC-11
❑ 92OPCPre-16
❑ 92PanSti-F
❑ 92PanStiFre-F
❑ 92Par-69
❑ 92ParEmel-69
❑ 92ProSet-228
❑ 92Sco-410
❑ 92ScoCan-410
❑ 92StaClu-72
❑ 92Top-39
❑ 92TopGol-39G
❑ 92Ult-312
❑ 92UppDec-63
❑ 93Don-164
❑ 93Lea-206
❑ 93LeaGolR-15
❑ 93OPCPre-226
❑ 93OPCPreG-226
❑ 93Par-96
❑ 93ParEmel-96
❑ 93Pin-113
❑ 93PinCan-113
❑ 93Pow-122
❑ 93Sco-311
❑ 93ScoCan-311
❑ 93StaClu-225
❑ 93StaCluFDI-225
❑ 93StaCluFDIO-225
❑ 93StaCluO-225
❑ 93TopPre-226
❑ 93TopPreG-226
❑ 93Ult-60
❑ 93UppDec-83
❑ 93UppDecSP-74
❑ 94BeAPla-R90
❑ 94BeAPSig-26
❑ 94Don-70
❑ 94Lea-136
❑ 94OPCPre-86
❑ 94OPCPreSE-86
❑ 94ParSE-SE82
❑ 94ParSEG-SE82
❑ 94Pin-328
❑ 94PinArtP-328
❑ 94PinRinC-328
❑ 94Sco-97
❑ 94ScoGol-97
❑ 94ScoPla-97
❑ 94ScoPlaTS-97
❑ 94StaClu-164
❑ 94StaCluFDI-164
❑ 94StaCluMOMS-164
❑ 94StaCluST-11
❑ 94StaCluSTWC-164
❑ 94TopPre-86
❑ 94TopPreSE-86
❑ 94Ult-308
❑ 94UppDec-104
❑ 94UppDecEleIce-104
❑ 95CanGamNHLP-141
❑ 95ColCho-83
❑ 95ColChoPC-83
❑ 95ColChoPCP-83
❑ 95Don-73
❑ 95Emo-85
❑ 95Lea-199
❑ 95ParInt-371
❑ 95ParIntEl-371
❑ 95Pin-96
❑ 95PinArtP-96
❑ 95PinRinC-96
❑ 95PlaOneoOne-160
❑ 95Sco-26
❑ 95ScoBlaIce-26
❑ 95ScoBlaIceAP-26
❑ 95SkyImp-82
❑ 95Ult-78
❑ 95UltGolM-78
❑ 95UppDec-5
❑ 95UppDecEleIce-5
❑ 95UppDecEleIceG-5
❑ 96BeAPAut-176
❑ 96BeAPAutSil-176
❑ 96BeAPla-176
❑ 96BeAPla-P176
❑ 96PlaOneoOne-375
❑ 96StaPos-25
❑ 96Sum-33
❑ 96SumArtP-33
❑ 96SumIce-33
❑ 96SumMet-33
❑ 96SumPreS-33
❑ 97ColCho-72
❑ 97DonLim-6
❑ 97DonLimExp-6
❑ 97Kat-48
❑ 97KatGol-48
❑ 97KatSil-48
❑ 97Pac-48
❑ 97PacCop-48
❑ 97PacDyn-39
❑ 97PacDynC-39
❑ 97PacDynDG-39
❑ 97PacDynEG-39
❑ 97PacDynIB-39
❑ 97PacDynR-39
❑ 97PacDynSil-39
❑ 97PacDynTan-34
❑ 97PacEmeGre-48
❑ 97PacIceB-48
❑ 97PacOme-75
❑ 97PacOmeC-75
❑ 97PacOmeDG-75
❑ 97PacOmeEG-75
❑ 97PacOmeG-75
❑ 97PacOmeIB-75
❑ 97PacPar-62
❑ 97PacParC-62
❑ 97PacParDG-62
❑ 97PacParEG-62
❑ 97PacParIB-62
❑ 97PacParRed-62
❑ 97PacParSil-62
❑ 97PacRed-48
❑ 97PacSil-48
❑ 97Pin-139
❑ 97PinPrePBB-139
❑ 97PinPrePBC-139
❑ 97PinPrePBM-139
❑ 97PinPrePBY-139
❑ 97PinPrePFC-139
❑ 97PinPrePFM-139
❑ 97PinPrePFY-139
❑ 97PinPrePla-139
❑ 97Sco-238
❑ 97UppDec-54
❑ 98Be A PPA-191

- 98Be A PPAA-191
- 98Be A PPAAF-191
- 98Be A PPSE-191
- 98Be APG-191
- 98Fin-148
- 98FinNo P-148
- 98FinNo PR-148
- 98FinRef-148
- 98Pac-183
- 98PacAur-60
- 98PacCroR-43
- 98PacCroRLS-43
- 98PacIceB-183
- 98PacOmeH-75
- 98PacOmeODI-75
- 98PacOmeR-75
- 98PacPar-70
- 98PacParC-70
- 98PacParEG-70
- 98PacParH-70
- 98PacParIB-70
- 98PacParS-70
- 98PacRed-183
- 98PacRev-46
- 98PacRevIS-46
- 98PacRevR-46
- 98UC-67
- 98UD ChoPCR-67
- 98UD ChoR-67
- 98UppDec-79
- 98UppDecBD-28
- 98UppDecDD-28
- 98UppDecE-79
- 98UppDecE101-79
- 98UppDecGJ-GJ20
- 98UppDecGR-79
- 98UppDecM-62
- 98UppDecMGS-62
- 98UppDecMSS-62
- 98UppDecMSS-62
- 98UppDecQD-28
- 98UppDecTD-28
- 99Pac-129
- 99PacCop-129
- 99PacGol-129
- 99PacIceB-129
- 99PacPreD-129
- 99UppDecM-61
- 99UppDecMGS-61
- 99UppDecMSS-61
- 99UppDecMSS-61

**Sykes, Phil**
- 84KinSmo-22
- 86Kin20tATI-20
- 86OPC-216
- 87KinTeal4-20
- 87PanSti-285
- 88ProAHL-197
- 89ProAHL-4
- 90JetIGA-31
- 91Bow-194
- 91JetIGA-31
- 91JetPanTS-23
- 91OPC-189
- 91ScoCan-534
- 91StaClu-271
- 91Top-189

**Sykora, Michal**
- 91ThInnSWHL-164
- 92TacRoc-25
- 92TacRoc-29
- 93Cla-30
- 93Don-307
- 93Lea-431
- 93Par-257
- 93ParEmel-257
- 93Pin-452
- 93PinCan-452
- 93Sco-600
- 93ScoCan-600
- 93ScoGol-600
- 93UppDec-489
- 94ClaProP-38
- 94Don-204
- 94Fle-201
- 94Lea-122
- 94OPCPre-362
- 94OPCPreSE-362
- 94TopPre-362
- 94TopPreSE-362
- 94Ult-369
- 94UppDec-195
- 94UppDecEleIce-195
- 95CanGamNHLP-230
- 95ParInt-181
- 95ParIntEI-181
- 95Top-105
- 95TopOPCI-105
- 96BeAPAut-113
- 96BeAPAutSil-113
- 96BeAPla-113
- 96CzeAPSE-345
- 96UppDec-151
- 96UppDecPacInvNRB-47

**Sykora, Michal (PeeWee)**
- 96SloPeeWT-28

**Sykora, Otto**
- 94GerDELE-341
- 95GerDELE-307
- 96GerDELE-334

**Sykora, Petr**
- 94Cla95DP-DP10
- 95Bow-116
- 95BowAllFoi-116
- 95Cla-18

- 95ClaAut-22
- 95ClaIceBre-BK16
- 95ColEdgI-11
- 95DonRatRoo-16
- 95Fin-134
- 95FinRef-134
- 95Ima-81
- 95ImaAut-81A
- 95ImaCleE-CE11
- 95ImaGol-81
- 95ImaPlaPDC-PD4
- 95Met-195
- 95ParInt-512
- 95ParInt-523
- 95ParIntEI-512
- 95ParIntEI-523
- 95ParIntPTP-PP43
- 95SelCer-144
- 95SelCerMG-144
- 95SP-83
- 95UppDec-318
- 96ClaIceBreDC-BK16
- 96ColCho-147
- 96ColCho-339
- 96ColEdgFL-22
- 96Dev-17
- 96DonCanI-72
- 96DonCanIGPP-72
- 96DonCanIRPP-72
- 96DonEli-122
- 96DonEliAsp-3
- 96DonEliDCS-122
- 96DonRatR-2
- 96FlePic-74
- 96FleRooSen-9
- 96Lea-206
- 96LeaLim-54
- 96LeaLimG-54
- 96LeaPre-21
- 96LeaPreP-206
- 96LeaPrePP-21
- 96LeaPreSG-12
- 96LeaPreSte-12
- 96MetUni-89
- 96Pin-200
- 96PinArtP-200
- 96PinFoi-200
- 96PinRinC-200
- 96Sco-237
- 96ScoArtPro-237
- 96ScoDeaCAP-237
- 96ScoGolB-237
- 96ScoSpeAP-237
- 96SkyImp-72
- 96SkyImp-171
- 96SkyImpNHLF-19
- 96SP-88
- 96SPx-23
- 96SPxGol-23
- 96StaCluMO-49
- 96Sum-170
- 96SumArtP-170
- 96SumIce-170
- 96SumMet-170
- 96SumPreS-170
- 96TopPicRS-RS6
- 96Ult-96
- 96UltGolM-97
- 96UppDec-98
- 96UppDecGN-X26
- 96UppDecSS-SS21B
- 96Zen-56
- 96ZenArtP-56
- 97Be A PPAD-134
- 97Be A PPAPD-134
- 97BeAPla-134
- 97BeAPlaAut-134
- 97PacOme-135
- 97PacOmeC-135
- 97PacOmeDG-135
- 97PacOmeEG-135
- 97PacOmeG-135
- 97PacOmeIB-135
- 97ScoDev-14
- 97ScoDevPla-14
- 97ScoDevPre-14
- 97SPAut-90
- 98O-PChr-2
- 98O-PChrR-2
- 98Pac-273
- 98PacIceB-273
- 98PacOmeH-144
- 98PacOmeODI-144
- 98PacOmeR-144
- 98PacRed-273
- 98Top-2
- 98TopO-P-2
- 98UC-112
- 98UD ChoPCR-112
- 98UD ChoR-112
- 98UppDec-310
- 98UppDecE-310
- 98UppDecE1o1-310
- 98UppDecGR-310
- 99Pac-248
- 99PacAur-88
- 99PacCop-248
- 99PacGol-248
- 99PacIceB-248
- 99PacPreD-248

**Sykora, Petr (DET)**
- 96CzeAPSE-162

**Sykora, Vaclav**
- 93FinnJyvHS-223
- 93FinnSIS-182

- 94FinnSIS-396
- 95FinnSIS-388
- 96CzeAPSE-120

**Sylvegard, Patrik**
- 92SweSemE-215
- 93SweSemE-186
- 94SweLeaE-103
- 94SweLeaE-90
- 95SweUppDE-146

**Sylvester, Derek**
- 93NiaFaIT-21

**Sylvia, Mike**
- 95DonEliWJ-43
- 95UppDec-565
- 95UppDecEleIce-565
- 95UppDecEleIceG-565

**Symes, Brad**
- 95SigRoo-64A
- 95SigRoo-64B
- 95SigRooSig-64
- 96WheNai-17

**Synish, Doug**
- 89ThInnSOHL-42

**Synowietz, Heinrich**
- 96GerDELE-208

**Synowietz, Paul**
- 96GerDELE-209

**Sysela, Robert**
- 96CzeAPSE-339

**Syvasalmi, Kari**
- 93FinnSIS-227
- 95FinnSIS-365

**Szabo, Dave**
- 91ThInnSOHL-64

**Szabo, Tony**
- 93RoaExp-19

**Szadkowski, Nick**
- 96SeaThu-19

**Szatmary, Rob**
- 92BriColJHL-82

**Szeryk, Jeff**
- 89SauSteMG-25
- 90KitRan-16

**Szoke, Mark**
- 90ThInnSWHL-213
- 91ThInnSMC-81
- 91ThInnSWHL-6
- 93LetHur-17

**Szopinski, Robert**
- 89SweSemWCS-134

**Szturm, Pat**
- 94ThuBayS-4
- 95ThuBayS-20

**Szura, Joe**
- 68OPC-73
- 70OPC-73
- 70Top-73
- 72OPC-313
- 72ShaLosAW-15

**Szysky, Chris**
- 95SwiCurB-16

**Taavola, Ulf**
- 86SwePanS-188

**Tabara, Zdislav**
- 94CzeAPSE-298
- 95CzeAPSE-2
- 96CzeAPSE-213

**Tabaracci, Rick**
- 89ProAHL-45
- 90JetIGA-32
- 90MonHaw-23
- 90ProAHLIHL-343
- 90ProSet-649
- 90UppDec-520
- 90UppDecF-520
- 91Bow-207
- 91JetIGA-32
- 91MonHaw-26
- 91OPC-158
- 91OPC-375
- 91ProAHLCHL-185
- 91ScoCan-244
- 91StaClu-395
- 91Top-375
- 91UppDec-339
- 91UppDecF-339
- 92Bow-324
- 92Sco-529
- 92ScoCan-529
- 92StaClu-135
- 92Top-453
- 92TopGol-453G
- 92Ult-445
- 92UppDec-58
- 92UppDec-358
- 93Don-363
- 93Lea-241
- 93OPCPre-239
- 93OPCPreG-239
- 93Pin-299
- 93PinCan-299
- 93Pow-267
- 93Sco-403
- 93ScoCan-403
- 93StaClu-378
- 93StaCluFDI-378
- 93StaCluMasP-19
- 93StaCluMasPW-19
- 93StaCluO-378
- 93TopPre-239
- 93TopPreG-239
- 94CanGamNHLP-299

**Tabarin, Dimitri**
- 95SigRoo-32
- 95SigRooSig-32

**Tabobondung, Barry**
- 80OshGen-8

**Tabor, Jan**
- 94GerDELE-404
- 95GerDELE-423

**Taborsky, Pavel**
- 94CzeAPSE-78
- 95CzeAPSE-9

**Tabuchie, Nick**
- 56QueAce-13

**Taglianetti, Peter**
- 86SheCan-26
- 87Jet-21
- 88JetPol-22
- 88OPC-257
- 88PanSti-152
- 89JetSaf-297
- 89OPC-299
- 89OPCSti-146

- 94OPCPre-367
- 94OPCPreSE-367
- 94Par-255
- 94ParGol-255
- 94Pin-444
- 94PinArtP-444
- 94PinMas-MA5
- 94PinRinC-444
- 94StaClu-74
- 94StaCluFDI-74
- 94StaCluMOMS-74
- 94StaCluSTWC-74
- 94TopPre-367
- 94TopPreSE-367
- 94Ult-239
- 94UppDec-187
- 94UppDecEleIce-187
- 95Don-214
- 95ParInt-32
- 95ParIntEI-32
- 95StaClu-119
- 95StaCluMOMS-119
- 95UppDec-196
- 95UppDecEleIce-196
- 95UppDecEleIceG-196
- 95UppDecSpE-SE103
- 95UppDecSpeEdiG-SE103
- 96BeAPAut-164
- 96BeAPAutSil-164
- 96BeAPla-164
- 96Don-10
- 96DonPrePro-10
- 96Lea-149
- 96LeaPreP-149
- 96Pin-66
- 96PinArtP-66
- 96PinFoi-66
- 96PinPreS-66
- 96PinRinC-66
- 96Sco-23
- 96ScoArtPro-23
- 96ScoDeaCAP-23
- 96ScoGolB-23
- 96ScoSpeAP-23
- 97DonPri-105
- 97DonPriSoA-105
- 97Pac-256
- 97PacCop-256
- 97PacEmeGre-256
- 97PacIceB-256
- 97PacOme-36
- 97PacOmeDG-36
- 97PacOmeEG-36
- 97PacOmeG-36
- 97PacOmeIB-36
- 97PacPar-31
- 97PacParC-31
- 97PacParDG-31
- 97PacParIB-31
- 97PacParRed-31
- 97PacParSil-31
- 97PacRed-256
- 97PacRev-21
- 97PacRevC-21
- 97PacRevEI-21
- 97PacRevIB-21
- 97PacRevR-21
- 97PacRevS-21
- 97PacSil-256
- 97Sco-28
- 97ScoArtPro-28
- 97ScoGolBla-28
- 97UppDec-236
- 98O-PChr-77
- 98O-PChrR-77
- 98Pac-126
- 98PacIceB-126
- 98PacPar-33
- 98PacParC-33
- 98PacParEG-33
- 98PacParIB-33
- 98PacParS-33
- 98PacRed-126
- 98Top-77
- 98TopO-P-77
- 99Pac-448
- 99PacCop-448
- 99PacGol-448
- 99PacIceB-448
- 99PacPreD-448

**Talafous, Dean**
- 75OPCNHL-197
- 75Top-197
- 76OPCNHL-103
- 76Top-103
- 77OPCNHL-49
- 77Top-49
- 78OPC-149
- 78Top-149
- 79OPC-54
- 79Top-54
- 80OPC-132
- 80Top-132
- 81OPC-235
- 95AHC-8

**Talakowski, Ron**
- 95ThuBayS-13

**Talbot, Jean-Guy**
- 44BeeGro2P-289
- 55Par-53
- 55ParQuaO-53
- 57Par-M9
- 57Par-M10
- 58Par-41
- 59Par-49
- 60Par-52
- 60ShiCoi-35
- 60YorPreP-35
- 61Par-48
- 61ShiCoi-109
- 61YorYelB-12
- 62Par-51
- 62ShiMetC-39
- 62ShiMetC-44
- 62YorIrooTra-4
- 63ChePho-52
- 63Par-22
- 63Par-81
- 63TorSta-37

- 89PanSti-174
- 90OPC-435
- 90OPCPre-117
- 90ProSet-505
- 90ScoRoo-16T
- 91PenCokE-32
- 91PenFoo-14
- 91ScoCan-448
- 92Pin-383
- 92PinFre-383
- 92Ult-204
- 93OPCPre-248
- 93OPCPreG-248
- 93Par-430
- 93ParEmel-430
- 93PenFoo-22
- 93Sco-295
- 93ScoCan-295
- 93StaClu-243
- 93StaCluFDI-243
- 93StaCluFDIO-243
- 93StaCluO-243
- 93TopPre-248
- 93TopPreG-248
- 93Ult-397
- 93UppDec-100
- 94Don-89
- 94ParSE-SE141
- 94ParSEG-SE141
- 94PenFoo-18
- 94Pin-505
- 94PinArtP-505
- 94PinRinC-505
- 94ParMisL-80
- 94ParMisL-88
- 94ParTalB-76
- 95Par66-68
- 95Par66Coi-68

**Tallackson, Trevor**
- 94DubFigS-28

**Tallaire, Gerald**
- 91AirCanSJHL-B19
- 91AirCanSJHLAS-35
- 91AirCanSJHLAS-48
- 92MPSPhoSJHL-3

**Tallaire, Sean**
- 91AirCanSJHL-C18
- 91LakSupSL-27

**Tallas, Rob**
- 91ThInnSWHL-126
- 91BriColJHL-106
- 91BriColJHL-119
- 93SeaThu-26
- 96ProBru-29
- 97ScoBru-3
- 97ScoBruPla-3
- 97ScoBruPre-3
- 97UppDec-223
- 98Be A PPA-158
- 98Be A PPAA-158
- 98Be A PPAAF-158
- 98Be A PPSE-158
- 98Be APG-158
- 98Pac-100
- 98PacIceB-100
- 98PacOmeH-18
- 98PacOmeODI-18
- 98PacOmeR-18
- 98PacRed-100
- 99Pac-29
- 99PacCop-29
- 99PacGol-29
- 99PacIceB-29
- 99PacPreD-29

**Tallberg, Gunnar**
- 65SweCorl-70B
- 67SweHoc-195
- 69SweHocS-253

**Tallberg, Thomas**
- 86SwePanS-107
- 91SweSemE-44
- 92SweSemE-62
- 93SweSemE-36
- 94SweLeaE-1
- 95SweLeaE-22

**Tallon, Dale**
- 70CanuRoyB-16
- 70ColSta-81
- 70DadCoo-127
- 70EssPowPla-50
- 70OPC-225
- 70PosCerS-15
- 70SarProSta-215
- 71CanuRoyB-11
- 71ColHea-13
- 71OPC-234
- 71OPCPos-5
- 71OPCTBoo-3
- 71SarProSta-209
- 71Top-95
- 71TorSun-291
- 72CanuRoyB-17
- 72OPC-121
- 72OPCPlaC-21
- 72Top-15
- 73MacMil-28
- 73OPC-211
- 73Top-129
- 74LipSou-22
- 74NHLActSta-74
- 74OPCNHL-360
- 75OPCNHL-351
- 76OPCNHL-89
- 76OPCNHL-382
- 76Top-89
- 77OPCNHL-124
- 77Top-124
- 78OPC-146
- 78Top-146
- 79FutTreC72-22
- 79ProSet-595
- 91ProSetFre-595

**Tambellini, Steve**
- 79IsITrans-19

- 80OPC-365
- 81OPC-81
- 81RocPos-27
- 81Top-W86
- 82OPC-134
- 82OPC-147
- 82OPCSti-226
- 82PosCer-11
- 83OPC-93
- 83OPC-223
- 83OPCSti-219
- 83PufSti-4
- 83Vac-19
- 84OPC-237
- 84OPCSti-239
- 85Canu-23
- 86Canu-22
- 87CanuSheOil-22
- 87OPC-259
- 87PanSti-351
- 88OPC-258
- 88OPCSti-62

**Tamburro, Mike**
- 93RenEng-29
- 96CleLum-24

**Tamer, Chris**
- 91MicWol-21
- 93Cla-83
- 93CleLum-7
- 93CleLumPos-19
- 94Cla-94
- 94ClaAut-94
- 94ClaDraGol-94
- 94ClaProP-119
- 94Lea-513
- 94OPCPre-224
- 94OPCPreSE-224
- 94PenFoo-12
- 94Pin-259
- 94PinArtP-259
- 94PinRinC-259
- 94PinRooTP-4
- 94TopPre-224
- 94TopPreSE-224
- 94UppDec-318
- 94UppDecEleIce-318
- 95ColEdgI-119
- 95ParInt-436
- 95ParIntEI-436
- 95PenFoo-18
- 95Top-169
- 95TopOPCI-169
- 96BeAPAut-182
- 96BeAPAutSil-182
- 96BeAPla-182
- 97PacInvNRB-165
- 97UppDec-345
- 98Pac-359
- 98PacIceB-359
- 98PacRed-359

**Tamer, John**
- 84BelBul-25

**Tammi, Jukka**
- 89SweSemWCS-28
- 91SweSemWC-43
- 93FinnJyvHS-74
- 93FinnSIS-109
- 94FinnJaaK-3
- 94FinnSIS-38
- 94FinnSISMN-10
- 95FinnSemWC-30
- 95FinnSemWC-216
- 95FinnSIS-339
- 95FinnSISGG-4
- 95FinnSISGG-3
- 95FinnSISLG-91
- 96GerDELE-47
- 96SweSemWC-12
- 98GerDELE-132

**Tamminen, Joe**
- 93MinDul-29

**Tamminen, Juhani**
- 70SweHocS-311
- 71SweHocS-73
- 72SweSemWC-88
- 74SweHocS-34
- 74SweSemHVS-92
- 76RoaPhoWHA-18
- 79PanSti-175
- 81SweSemHVS-34
- 82SweSemHVS-50
- 94FreNatT-31
- 96FinnSISR-198

**Tamminen, Teemu**
- 93FinnSIS-252

**Tamminen, Tiny**
- 51LavDaiLSJ-37

**Tanabe, Dave**
- 98SPXTopP-90
- 98SPXTopPF-90
- 98SPXTopPP-90
- 98UppDecBD-120
- 98UppDecDD-120
- 98UppDecQD-120
- 98UppDecTD-120

**Tancili, Chris**
- 90ProAHLIHL-179
- 91ProAHLCHL-104
- 91ProSet-539
- 91ProSetFre-539
- 91UppDec-455
- 91UppDecF-455
- 91ClaProPro-20
- 93Don-84

93OPCPre-429
93OPCPreG-429
93Par-318
93ParEmel-318
93TopPre-429
93TopPreG-429
96KenTho-16
96Pin-71
96PinArtP-71
96PinFoi-71
96PinPreS-71
96PinRinC-71

**Tanevski, Dan**
907thInnSOHL-221
917thInnSOHL-347B
93SauSteMGM-2

**Tanguay, Alex**
97UppDecBD-105
97UppDecBDDD-105
97UppDecBDQD-105
97UppDecBDTD-105
97Zen-99
97Zen5x7-99
97ZenGolImp-79
97ZenSilImp-79
97ZenZGol-99
97ZenZSil-99
98BowCHL-108
98BowCHL-152
98BowCHLAuB-A35
98BowCHLAuG-A35
98BowCHLAuS-A35
98BowCHLGA-108
98BowCHLGA-152
98BowCHLOI-108
98BowCHLOI-152
98BowCHLSC-SC15
98BowChrC-108
98BowChrC-152
98BowChrCGA-108
98BowChrCGA-152
98BowChrCGAR-108
98BowChrCGAR-152
98BowChrCOI-108
98BowChrCOI-152
98BowChrCOIR-108
98BowChrCOIR-152
98BowChrCR-108
98BowChrCR-152
98FinFutF-F10
98FinFutFR-F10
98O-PChr-237
98O-PChrR-237
98Top-237
98TopO-P-237
98UC-257
98UD ChoPCR-257
98UD ChoR-257
98UppDecGJ-GJ13
99QuePeeWHWCCS-10

**Tanguay, Christian**
81FreExp-20
82FreExp-20
83FreExp-10

**Tanguay, Martin**
88RivDu R-28
917thInnSQMJHL-135
93KnoChe-18
94ClaProP-132

**Tannahill, Don**
72CanuRoyB-18
72OPC-238
73CanuRoyB-18
73OPC-69
73Top-69
74OPCNHL-117
74Top-117

**Tanner, John**
897thInnSOHL-38
907thInnSOHL-145
907thInnSOHL-377
90NordPet-24
90OPCPre-118
90ProSet-637
91NordPanTS-21
91ProAHLCHL-366
91UppDec-119
91UppDecF-119
92NorPet-32
92Sco-452
92ScoCan-452
96WheNai-1

**Tano, Lars-Goran**
69SweHocS-73

**Tansowny, Steve**
92MPSPhoSJHL-53

**Tanti, Tony**
80OshGen-16
81BlaBorPos-27
81OshGen-18
82OshGen-11
83CanNatJ-14
83Canu-21
83OPC-362
83Vac-119
847EDis-52
84Canu-24
84OPC-332
84OPC-369
84OPCSti-274
84Top-141
85Canu-24
85OPCSti-245

85Top-153
86Canu-23
86KraDra-73
86OPC-120
86OPCSti-99
86Top-120
87CanuSheOil-23
87OPC-97
87OPCSti-195
87PanSti-345
87ProAll-15
87Top-97
88CanuMoh-23
88FriLayS-42
88OPC-82
88OPCSti-59
88PanSti-143
88Top-82
89CanuMoh-23
89Kra-45
89OPC-280
89OPCSti-71
89PanSti-149
90Bow-213
90BowTif-213
90OPC-157
90PanSti-124
90PenFoo-14
90ProSet-241
90Sco-137
90ScoCan-137
90Top-157
90TopTif-157
90UppDec-197
90UppDecF-197
91Bow-34
91OPC-133
91Par-236
91ParFre-236
91SabBluS-22
91SabPepC-22
91ScoAme-49
91ScoCan-49
91StaClu-285
91Top-133
92Bow-172
92OPC-34
92Sco-116
92ScoCan-116
92StaClu-312
92Top-235
92TopGol-235G
92UppDec-182
94GerDELE-54
95GerDELE-256

**Tarasov, Anatoli V**
83HalFP-D15
85HalFC-239
91FutTreC72-4

**Tarasov, Yevgeny**
96SweSemW-131

**Tarasuk, Allan**
82BraWheK-15
83BraWheK-21

**Tarasuk, Rick**
917thInnSOHL-269

**Tardif, Christian**
907thInnSQMJHL-71
917thInnSQMJHL-33
94ClaProP-223
95SouCarS-13
95SouCarS-17

**Tardif, Marc**
907thInnSQMJHL-109
917thInnSQMJHL-207
917thInnSQMJHL-73
94ClaProP-223

**Tardif, Marc (Habs)**
69CanaPosC-29
70ColSta-17
70EssPowPla-8
70OPC-179
71CanaPos-23
71OPC-29
71SarProSta-111
71Top-29
71TorSun-164
72CanaPos-21
72OPC-11
72SarProSta-118
72Top-105
73OPCWHAP-20
740PCWHA-43
750PCWHA-30
750PCWHA-71
76NordMarA-11
76NordPos-18
760PCWHA-1
760PCWHA-2
760PCWHA-3
760PCWHA-5
760PCWHA-118
770PCWHA-20
790PC-108
79Top-108
80NordPos-27
800PC-256
800PCSup-17
80PepCap-78
80Top-256
81NordPos-19
810PC-283
810PCSti-76
82NordPos-23

820PC-296
820PCSti-21
82PosCer-16
83Ess-19
83NordPos-30
830PC-305
830PCSti-247

**Tardif, Patrice**
92MaiBlaB-10
93MaiBlaB-46
94ClaTri-T58
94Fle-192
94UppDec-470
94UppDecEIeIce-470
95ColEdgI-97
95Don-87
95Ima-27
95ImaCleE-CE14
95ImaGol-27
95Lea-22
95Sco-88
95Top-172
95TopOPCI-172
96DetVip-18

**Tardif, Steve**
93DruVol-22
98FloEve-23

**Tarnowski, Chris**
84VicCou-4
85KamBla-25
86KamBla-21
86RegPat-27

**Tarnstrom, Dick**
92SweSemE-31
94ParSE-SE239
94ParSEG-SE239
94SweLeaE-211
95SweLeaE-9
95SweUppDE-3
95SweUppDETNA-NA2
98UD ChoS-4

**Tarrant, Jerry**
89ProIHL-27
91ProAHLCHL-373

**Tartari, Stephan**
907thInnSQMJHL-115

**Tarvainen, Jussi**
93FinnSIS-180
94Fin-142
94FinnSIS-71
94FinnSISJ-8
94FinnSISND-3
94FinRef-142
94FinSupTW-142
94ParSE-SE225
94ParSEG-SE225
95FinnSIS-75
96FinnSISR-81

**Tasker, Michael**
97KinHaw-20

**Tatarinov, Mikhail**
90CapKod-24
90CapSmo-21
90ProSet-647
90ScoRoo-53T
90UppDec-401
90UppDecF-401
91Bow-298
91NordPet-29
910PC-465
91OPCPre-62
91PanSti-210
91Par-145
91ParFre-145
91Pin-97
91PinFre-97
91ProSet-462
91ProSetFre-462
91ProSetPla-218
91RusStaNHL-9
91RusStaRA-17
91ScoAme-37
91ScoCan-37
91ScoCan-562
91ScoRoo-12T
91StaClu-390
91SweSemWCS-215
91Top-465
92Bow-395
92NorPet-33
92OPC-253
92PanSti-208
92PanStiFre-208
92Pin-35
92Sco-107
92ScoCan-107
92StaClu-47
92Top-180
92TopGol-180G
92Ult-181
92UppDec-183
93Lea-342
93Sco-328
93ScoCan-328
93UppDec-386
94FinnJaaK-336

**Tattner, Michael**
94GerDELE-373

**Taubert, Kristian**
94FinnSIS-353

**Taugher, Johnny**

36V356WorG-116

**Tavi, Mikko**
92ClaKni-21
93FinnJyvHS-176
93FinnSIS-165

**Taylor, Andrew**
93KitRan-18
93KitRan-29
94DetJrRW-13
94KitRan-20
95SigRoo-65
95SigRooSig-65
95Sla-70
95SlaMemC-87
96DetWha-16
98FloEve-24

**Taylor, Bart**
91BriColJHL-121
92BriColJHL-172

**Taylor, Billy**
34BeeGro1P-351
39OPCV3011-15
40OPCV3012-107
45QuaOatP-54

**Taylor, Bob (Bobby)**
73OPC-238
75FlyCanDC-18
92Par-475
92ParEmel-475

**Taylor, Chris**
897thInnSOHL-26
907thInnSOHL-14
917thInnSOHL-370
91UppDec-454
91UppDecF-454
93ClaProPro-113
95Sco-303
95ScoBlaIce-303
95ScoBlaIceAP-303

**Taylor, Cyclone**
10C55SweCP-20
10C56-15
11C55-20
12C57-43
60Top-46
60TopSta-46
83HalFP-A15
85HalFC-14

**Taylor, Dave**
780PC-353
790PC-232
79Top-232
80KinCarN-12
800PC-137
80Top-137
810PC-143
810PC-152
810PC-391
810PCSti-149
810PCSti-268
81Top-40
81Top-W132
820PC-161
820PCSti-164
820PCSti-231
82PosCer-8
830PC-163
83PufSti-12
84KinSmo-16
840PC-92
840PCSti-267
857ECreCar-8
850PC-214
850PCSti-238
86Kin20tATI-21
860PC-63
860PCSti-90
86Top-63
87KinTeal4-21
870PC-118
870PCSti-215
87PanSti-280
87Top-118
88KinSmo-20
880PC-46
880PCSti-155
88PanSti-79
88Top-46
88KinSmo-6
890PC-58
890PCSti-151
89PanSti-98
89Top-58
90Bow-149
90BowHatTri-22
90BowTif-149
90KinSmo-8
900PC-314
90PanSti-236
90ProSet-128
90Sco-166
90ScoCan-166
90Top-314
90TopTif-314
90UppDec-214
90UppDecF-214
91Bow-186
910PC-138
91PanSti-89
91Par-67
91Par-214
91ParFre-67
91ParFre-214

91Pin-249
91Pin-373
91PinFre-249
91PinFre-373
91ProSet-103
91ProSet-325
91ProSetFre-103
91ProSetFre-325
91ProSetNHLAS-AC16
91ScoAme-214
91ScoAme-374
91ScoAme-435
91ScoCan-214
91ScoCan-264
91ScoCan-325
91StaClu-232
91Top-138
91UppDec-270
91UppDecF-270
92Bow-37
92Par-307
92ParEmel-307
92Pin-367
92PinFre-367
92ProSet-258
92Sco-49
92ScoCan-49
92StaClu-234
92Top-446
92TopGol-446G
92Ult-313
93Lea-374
93PanSti-206
93Par-367
93ParEmel-367
93Pin-412
93PinCan-412
93Pow-364
93Sco-389
93ScoCan-389
93Ult-348
94StaCluMO-14
95LetHur-23
96LetHur-21
98KinLA TC-5

**Taylor, Dylan**
95Sla-124

**Taylor, Gary**
907thInnSOHL-222

**Taylor, Greg**
91AirCanSJHL-D28

**Taylor, Harry**
44BeeGro2P-456
45QuaOatP-53

**Taylor, Jack**
51LavDaiQSHL-67

**Taylor, Jason**
92DalFre-18
93DalFre-16
94CenHocL-18

**Taylor, Jim**
89ProAHL-80

**Taylor, Karl**
897thInnSOHL-45
907thInnSOHL-319

**Taylor, Mark**
830PC-273
830PCSti-190
83PenCok-18
840PC-180
840PCSti-121
84PenHeiP-22
84Top-127
92CorBigRed-30
93CorBigRed-30

**Taylor, Matt**
84BelBul-29

**Taylor, Mike**
94RicRen-16
95RicRen-2
96RicRen-22

**Taylor, Paul**
91BriColJHL-49
92NorMicW-26
93NorMicW-26
94DayBom-2
95PeoRiv-20

**Taylor, Randy**
88ProIHL-6
89ProIHL-151

**Taylor, Rod**
92HamRoaA-11
93HamRoaA-10
94HamRoaA-8
95HamRoaA-12
96HamRoaA-HRA10

**Taylor, Ryan**
95Sla-184

**Taylor, Scott**
85KitRan-13
86KitRan-12
89HamRoaA-21
91NasKni-18

**Taylor, Ted**
61SudWol-17
62SudWol-21
65Top-95
70CanuRoyB-17
71CanuRoyB-17
71SarProSta-223
720PC-312
73QuaOatWHA-28

**Taylor, Tim**
90ProAHLIHL-211

91BalSki-1
91ProAHLCHL-563
94Ult-286
94UppDec-325
94UppDecEIeIce-325
95BeAPla-101
95BeAPSig-S101
95BeAPSigDC-S101
95Don-349
95Top-132
95TopOPCI-132
95UppDec-295
95UppDecEIeIce-295
95UppDecEIeIceG-295
97Be A PPAD-114
97Be A PPAPD-114
97BeAPla-114
97BeAPlaAut-114
97PacDynBKS-35
97SPAut-9
98Pac-101
98PacIceB-101
98PacRed-101
98UppDec-37
98UppDecE-37
98UppDecE1o1-37
98UppDecGR-37

**Teal, Gordon**
28V1282PauC-65
56QueAce-14

**Teal, Jeff**
83NovScoV-22

**Tebbutt, Greg**
83PenCok-19

**Tedenby, Robert**
86SwePanS-211

**Teevens, Mark**
88ProIHL-4
94GerDELE-69
95GerDELE-70
96GerDELE-265

**Teichmann, Brad**
907thInnSOHL-20
917thInnSOHL-46

**Teimonen, Miikka**
95FinnSIS-288

**Tejkl, Petr**
94CzeAPSE-4
95CzeAPSE-105
96CzeAPSE-101

**Temple, Jeff**
96MedHatT-22

**Templeton, Bert**
82NorBayC-21
83NorBayC-25
897thInnSOHL-173
907thInnSOHL-323
917thInnSOHL-72
93NorBayC-23

**Tenisi, Guido**
82SweSemHVS-124

**Tenkrat, Petr**
96CzeAPSE-93

**Tennant, Ken**
52JunBluT-126

**Tepper, Stephen**
93RoaExp-20
94CenHocL-36

**Terbenche, Paul**
67Top-58
700PC-123
70Top-123
730PC-229
73SabPos-13
750PCWHA-112
78JetPos-22

**Terechin, Juri**
74SweHocS-55

**Terreri, Chris**
88ProAHL-344
89DevCar-25
90Dev-29
900PC-284
900PC-375
90PanSti-68
90ProSet-481
90Sco-239
90ScoCan-239
90Top-284
90Top-375
90TopTif-375
90UppDec-183
90UppDecF-183
91Bow-283
91Gil-38
910PC-422
910PCPre-197
91PanSti-221
91Par-98
91ParFre-98
91Pin-247
91PinFre-247
91ProSet-137
91ProSetFre-137
91ProSetPla-68
91ProSetPla-288
91ScoAme-151
91ScoCan-151
91ScoYouS-15
91StaClu-297
91SweSemWCS-129
91Top-422
91UppDec-115
91UppDecF-115

92Bow-386
92HumDum2-22
92Kra-30
92OPC-282
92PanSti-171
92PanStiFre-171
92Par-93
92ParEmel-93
92Pin-274
92PinFre-274
92ProSet-97
92Sco-270
92ScoCan-270
92SeaPat-51
92StaClu-74
92Top-303
92TopGol-303G
92Ult-120
92UppDec-43
93Don-194
93Lea-430
930PCPre-213
930PCPreG-213
93PanSti-D
93Par-112
93ParEmel-112
93Pin-267
93PinCan-267
93Pow-144
93Sco-237
93ScoCan-237
93StaClu-328
93StaCluFDI-328
93StaCluO-328
93TopPre-213
93TopPreG-213
93Ult-209
93UppDec-110
94CanGamNAHLP-285
94Don-285
94EASpo-78
94HocWit-31
94Lea-134
94OPCPre-13
94OPCPreSE-13
94ParSE-SE94
94ParSEG-SE94
94Pin-335
94PinArtP-335
94PinRinC-335
94TopPre-13
94TopPre-83
94TopPreSE-13
94Ult-33
95BeAPla-27
95BeAPSig-S27
95BeAPSigDC-S27
95Fin-149
95FinRef-149
95ParInt-451
95ParIntEI-451
95Sco-243
95ScoBlaIce-243
95ScoBlaIceAP-243
95SP-131
95Ult-306
95UppDec-450
95UppDecEIeIce-450
95UppDecEIeIceG-450
96ColCho-239
96ColCho-330
96Don-38
96DonPenPro-38
96Fle-102
96Lea-94
96LeaPreP-94
96Pin-103
96PinArtP-103
96PinFoi-103
96PinPreS-103
96PinRinC-103
96ScoArtPro-28
96ScoDeaCAP-28
96ScoGolB-28
96ScoSepAP-28
96SkyImp-119
96Sum-89
96SumArtP-89
96SumIce-89
96SumMet-89
96SumPreS-89
96UppDec-147
97Be A PPAD-30
97Be A PPAPD-30
97BeAPla-30
97BeAPlaAut-30
97PacCroR-31
97PacCroREG-31
97PacCroRIB-31
97PacCroRS-31
97PacInvNRB-48
97Sco-48
97ScoArtPro-48
97ScoGolBla-48
97ShaFleAS-7
97SPAut-33
97UppDec-40
98Pac-40
98PacIceB-40
98PacRed-40
98UppDec-307
98UppDecE-307
98UppDecE1o1-307
98UppDecGR-307

❑ 99Pac-249
❑ 99PacCop-249
❑ 99PacGol-249
❑ 99PacIceB-249
❑ 99PacPreD-249
**Terrien, Benoit**
❑ 907thInnSQMJHL-68
**Terrion, Greg**
❑ 81OPC-155
❑ 82MapLeaP-33
❑ 82MapLeaP-34
❑ 82OPC-333
❑ 82OPCSti-234
❑ 83MapLeaP-25
❑ 83OPC-342
❑ 83OPCSti-37
❑ 83Vac-99
❑ 84MapLeaP-23
❑ 84OPC-312
❑ 84OPCSti-19
❑ 85MapLeaP-28
❑ 85OPCSti-18
❑ 86KraDra-74
❑ 86MapLeaP-19
❑ 86OPC-244
❑ 86OPCSti-147
❑ 87MapLeaPLA-21
❑ 87OPC-241
❑ 87OPCSti-153
❑ 88ProAHL-240
**Terris, Marc**
❑ 96PeoRiv-22
❑ 96PeoRivPA-22
**Tertyshny, Dimitri**
❑ 98BowBes-118
❑ 98BowBesAR-118
❑ 98BowBesR-118
❑ 98PacOmeH-179
❑ 98PacOmeODI-179
❑ 98PacOmeR-179
❑ 98UppDec-336
❑ 98UppDecE-336
❑ 98UppDecE1o1-336
❑ 98UppDecGR-336
**Tertyshny, Sergei**
❑ 94PorPir-22
❑ 95PorPir-21
**Tervonen, Kai**
❑ 93FinnJyvHS-25
❑ 93FinnSIS-93
**Terzo, Anthony**
❑ 96DetWha-17
**Tesarik, Daniel**
❑ 96CzeAPSE-235
**Tesarik, Radim**
❑ 94CzeAPSE-187
❑ 95CzeAPSE-36
**Tessier, Brian**
❑ 86KinCan-6
**Tessier, Orval**
❑ 52JunBluT-104
❑ 56QueAce-15
❑ 60ShiCoi-114
❑ 83BlaBorPos-23
**Tessier, Patrick**
❑ 917thInnSQMJHL-34
**Tessier, Tommy**
❑ 92QueIntP-50
**Tetarenko, Joey**
❑ 95UppDec-523
❑ 95UppDecEleIce-523
❑ 95UppDecEleIceG-523
❑ 97BowCHL-86
❑ 97BowCHLOPC-86
**Tetrault, Alain**
❑ 77GraVic-18
**Tetrault, Daniel**
❑ 96UppDec-376
❑ 97BowCHL-134
❑ 97BowCHLAu-14
❑ 97BowCHLOPC-134
**Tetzlaff, Jeff**
❑ 95Sla-25
**Teui, Mikko**
❑ 94FinnSIS-113
**Texeira, Chuck**
❑ 92MaiBlaB-31
❑ 93MaiBlaB-51
**Tezikov, Alexei**
❑ 98BowCHL-118
❑ 98BowCHLGA-118
❑ 98BowCHLOI-118
❑ 98BowChrC-118
❑ 98BowChrCGA-118
❑ 98BowChrCGAR-118
❑ 98BowChrCOI-118
❑ 98BowChrCOIR-118
❑ 98BowChrCR-118
❑ 99Pac-450
❑ 99PacCop-450
❑ 99PacGol-450
❑ 99PacIceB-450
❑ 99PacPreD-450
**Thachuk, Keith**
❑ 96PinMcD-13
**Thacker, Rod**
❑ 87SauSteMG-32
**Thaler, Alexander**
❑ 94FinnJaaK-297
**Thawley, Mark**
❑ 92ArlIce-15
**Thayer, W.**
❑ 85HalFC-134
**Theander, Bo**
❑ 71SweHocS-173
❑ 73SweHocS-58
❑ 73SweWorCS-58
**Theberge, Gerry**
❑ 51LavDaiLSJ-14
**Theberge, Greg**
❑ 81Cap-16
❑ 82PosCer-20
**Theel, Justin**
❑ 93OmaLan-26
**Thelander, Anders**
❑ 71SweHocS-328
**Thelin, Goran**
❑ 65SweCorI-205
❑ 67SweHoc-278
❑ 69SweHocS-322
❑ 70SweHocS-226
**Thelin, Mats**
❑ 82SweSemHVS-8
❑ 83SweSemE-3
❑ 87SwePanS-11
❑ 89SweSemE-4
❑ 90SweSemE-78
❑ 91SweSemE-6
❑ 92SweSemE-29
**Thelin, Ove**
❑ 67SweHoc-279
❑ 69SweHocS-323
❑ 70SweHocS-227
❑ 72SweHocS-277
**Thelven, Michael**
❑ 83SweSemE-84
❑ 84SweSemE-76
❑ 85SwePanS-123
❑ 85SwePanS-124
❑ 87OPC-24
❑ 87PanSti-9
❑ 87Top-24
❑ 88BruPos-19
❑ 88BruSpoA-21
❑ 88PanSti-206
❑ 89BruSpoA-21
**Theodore, Jose**
❑ 95DonEliWJ-2
❑ 95SigRoo-10
❑ 95SigRooAB2-B5
❑ 95SigRooSig-10
❑ 96SlaMemC-73
❑ 95UppDec-530
❑ 95UppDecEleIce-530
❑ 95UppDecEleIceG-530
❑ 96CanaPos-28
❑ 96CanaShe-21
❑ 96ColCho-351
❑ 96Don-227
❑ 96DonCanILG-10
❑ 96DonEli-139
❑ 96DonEliDCS-139
❑ 96DonPrePro-227
❑ 96Fla-112
❑ 96FlaBluI-112
❑ 96Fle-134
❑ 96FleCalCan-9
❑ 96LeaGolR-3
❑ 96Pin-217
❑ 96PinArtP-217
❑ 96PinFoi-217
❑ 96PinPreS-217
❑ 96PinRinC-217
❑ 96Sco-267
❑ 96ScoArtPro-267
❑ 96ScoDeaCAP-267
❑ 96ScoGolB-267
❑ 96ScoSpeAP-267
❑ 96SkyImp-161
❑ 96SP-174
❑ 96Sum-182
❑ 96SumArtP-182
❑ 96SumIce-182
❑ 96SumMet-182
❑ 96SumPreS-182
❑ 96UppDec-279
❑ 96UppDecBD-116
❑ 96UppDecBDG-116
❑ 96UppDecIce-90
❑ 96UppDecIcePar-90
❑ 97ColCho-135
❑ 97Don-81
❑ 97DonBetTP-6
❑ 97DonCanILG-6
❑ 97DonCanILGP-6
❑ 97DonCanISCS-14
❑ 97DonLim-81
❑ 97DonLim-151
❑ 97DonLim-152
❑ 97DonLimExp-81
❑ 97DonLimExp-151
❑ 97DonLimExp-152
❑ 97DonLimFOTG-71
❑ 97DonPre-102
❑ 97DonPreCG-11
❑ 97DonPreCGP-11
❑ 97DonPreCttC-102
❑ 97DonPreProG-81
❑ 97DonPreProS-81
❑ 97Lea-122
❑ 97LeaFraMat-122
❑ 97LeaFraMDC-122
❑ 97LeaInt-122
❑ 97LeaIntUI-122
❑ 97LeaPipDre-9
❑ 97PacInvNRB-107
❑ 97PinIns-56
❑ 97PinInsCC-56
❑ 97PinInsEC-56
❑ 97PinInsSto-14
❑ 97Sco-42
❑ 97ScoArtPro-42
❑ 97ScoCan-3
❑ 97ScoCanPla-3
❑ 97ScoGolBla-42
❑ 97SPAutSotT-JTH
❑ 97Stu-24
❑ 97StuPrePG-24
❑ 97StuPrePS-24
❑ 97UppDec-85
❑ 97UppDecGDM-85
❑ 97UppDecIce-36
❑ 97UppDecIceP-36
❑ 97UppDecIPS-36
❑ 97UppDecSG-SG60
❑ 97UppDecTSS-12C
❑ 98Be A PPA-219
❑ 98Be A PPAA-219
❑ 98Be A PPAAF-219
❑ 98Be A PPSE-219
❑ 98Be APG-219
❑ 98BowBesMIF-F19
❑ 98BowBesMIFAR-F19
❑ 98BowBesMIFR-F19
❑ 98ScoCanPre-3
❑ 98UppDec-114
❑ 98UppDecE-114
❑ 98UppDecE1o1-114
❑ 98UppDecGN-GN8
❑ 98UppDecGNQ1-GN8
❑ 98UppDecGNQ2-GN8
❑ 98UppDecGNQ3-GN8
❑ 98UppDecGR-114
❑ 98UppDecMP-JT
❑ 99Pac-212
❑ 99PacCop-212
❑ 99PacGol-212
❑ 99PacIceB-212
❑ 99PacPreD-212
**Theoret, Luc**
❑ 95LetHur-24
❑ 96LetHur-22
❑ 96UppDec-377
❑ 98BowCHL-65
❑ 98BowCHLGA-65
❑ 98BowCHLOI-65
❑ 98BowChrC-65
❑ 98BowChrCGA-65
❑ 98BowChrCGAR-65
❑ 98BowChrCOI-65
❑ 98BowChrCOIR-65
❑ 98BowChrCR-65
**Theriault, Joel**
❑ 96HamRoaA-HRA5
**Theriault, Michel**
❑ 92QueIntP-8
**Theriault, Patrick**
❑ 92ClaKni-22
**Theriault, Paul**
❑ 81OshGen-23
❑ 82OshGen-23
❑ 83OshGen-14
**Therien, Chris**
❑ 93AlbIntTC-20
❑ 93Cla-84
❑ 93OPCPreTC-9
❑ 93Pow-495
❑ 93Ult-474
❑ 94ClaProPIA-IA6
❑ 94ClaProPIH-LP19
❑ 94Fin-13
❑ 94FinRef-13
❑ 94FinSupTW-13
❑ 94Fla-132
❑ 94Fle-159
❑ 94Lea-480
❑ 94OPCPre-322
❑ 94OPCPreSE-322
❑ 94ParSE-SE127
❑ 94ParSEG-SE127
❑ 94Pin-495
❑ 94PinArtP-495
❑ 94PinRinC-495
❑ 94ScoTeaC-CT19
❑ 94TopPre-322
❑ 94TopPreSE-322
❑ 94Ult-347
❑ 94UppDec-248
❑ 94UppDecEleIce-248
❑ 95BeAPla-21
❑ 95BeAPSig-S21
❑ 95BeAPSigDC-S21
❑ 95ColCho-184
❑ 95ColCho-374
❑ 95ColChoPC-184
❑ 95ColChoPC-374
❑ 95ColChoPCP-184
❑ 95ColChoPCP-374
❑ 95ColEdgI-47
❑ 95ColEdgIC-C9
❑ 95Don-72
❑ 95Emo-135
❑ 95Ima-32
❑ 95ImaGol-32
❑ 95Lea-18
❑ 95Met-114
❑ 95ParInt-156
❑ 95ParIntEl-156
❑ 95Pin-165
❑ 95PinArtP-165
❑ 95PinRinC-165
❑ 95PlaOneoOne-296
❑ 95Sco-98
❑ 95ScoBlaIce-98
❑ 95ScoBlaIceAP-98
❑ 95SkyImp-129
❑ 95SkyImpNHLF-8
❑ 95Top-364
❑ 95TopNewG-12NG
❑ 95TopOPCI-364
❑ 95Ult-121
❑ 95UltGolM-121
❑ 95UppDec-107
❑ 95UppDecEleIce-107
❑ 95UppDecEleIceG-107
❑ 96ColCho-197
❑ 96FlyPos-23
❑ 96Sco-28
❑ 97PacInvNRB-148
❑ 97Sco-256
❑ 97ScoFly-15
❑ 97ScoFlyPla-15
❑ 97ScoFlyPre-15
❑ 98O-PChr-144
❑ 98O-PChrR-144
❑ 98Pac-332
❑ 98PacIceB-332
❑ 98PacRed-332
❑ 98SPxFin-63
❑ 98SPxFinR-63
❑ 98SPxFinS-63
❑ 98Top-144
❑ 98TopO-P-144
❑ 98UC-154
❑ 98UD ChoPCR-154
❑ 98UD ChoR-154
❑ 98UppDec-338
❑ 98UppDecE-338
❑ 98UppDecE1o1-338
❑ 98UppDecGJ-GJ21
❑ 98UppDecGR-338
❑ 99Pac-312
❑ 99PacCop-312
❑ 99PacGol-312
❑ 99PacIceB-312
❑ 99PacPreD-312
**Therien, Gaston**
❑ 98Vald'OF-12
**Thermell, Tobias**
❑ 93SweSemE-320
**Therrien, Benoit**
❑ 917thInnSQMJHL-47
**Therrien, Gaston**
❑ 81FreExp-18
❑ 82FreExp-18
❑ 96RimOce-28
**Therrien, Mario**
❑ 907thInnSQMJHL-86
❑ 917thInnSQMJHL-36
**Therrien, Michel**
❑ 80QueRem-21
❑ 83NovScoV-16
**Therrien, Pierre-Luc**
❑ 96UppDec-372
❑ 97BowCHL-140
❑ 97BowCHLAu-20
❑ 97BowCHLBB-20
❑ 97BowCHLBowBesAR-20
❑ 97BowCHLBowBesR-20
❑ 97BowCHLOPC-140
**Thibaudeau, Gilles**
❑ 86SheCan-27
❑ 87CanaPos-32
❑ 88CanaPos-39
❑ 89Isl-18
❑ 90PanSti-288
❑ 90ProSet-290
❑ 93SwiHNL-233
❑ 95SwiHNL-232
**Thibault, Daniel**
❑ 907thInnSQMJHL-87
❑ 917thInnSQMJHL-110
**Thibault, Etienne**
❑ 917thInnSQMJHL-13
**Thibault, Gilles**
❑ 52JunBluT-76
**Thibault, Jocelyn**
❑ 917thInnSQMJHL-123
❑ 93Cla-10
❑ 93ClaTopTen-DP10
❑ 93Don-275
❑ 93DonRatR-11
❑ 93DurSco-3
❑ 93DurSco-NNO
❑ 93Lea-428
❑ 93LeaFrePhe-10
❑ 93OPCPre-393
❑ 93OPCPreG-393
❑ 93Par-247
❑ 93ParCalC-C16
❑ 93ParCalCG-C16
❑ 93ParEmel-247
❑ 93Pin-440
❑ 93PinCan-440
❑ 93Pow-426
❑ 93PowRooS-15
❑ 93Sco-593
❑ 93ScoCan-593
❑ 93ScoGol-593
❑ 93StaClu-479
❑ 93StaCluFDI-479
❑ 93StaCluO-479
❑ 93TopPre-393
❑ 93TopPreG-393
❑ 93Ult-406
❑ 93UltWavF-18
❑ 93UppDec-394
❑ 93UppDecSP-133
❑ 94ClaProP-39
❑ 94Don-71
❑ 94Lea-231
❑ 94LeaGolR-15
❑ 94LeaLim-15
❑ 94NordBurK-25
❑ 94OPCPre-123
❑ 94OPCPreSE-123
❑ 94Par-189
❑ 94Par-275
❑ 94ParGol-189
❑ 94ParGol-275
❑ 94ParVin-V61
❑ 94Pin-205
❑ 94PinArtP-205
❑ 94PinGoaG-GT18
❑ 94PinRinC-205
❑ 94Sco-250
❑ 94ScoGol-250
❑ 94ScoPla-250
❑ 94ScoPlaTS-250
❑ 94StaClu-114
❑ 94StaCluFDI-114
❑ 94StaCluMOMS-114
❑ 94StaCluSTWC-114
❑ 94TopPre-123
❑ 94TopPreSE-123
❑ 94Ult-361
❑ 94UppDec-147
❑ 94UppDecEleIce-147
❑ 95BeAPla-199
❑ 95BeAPSig-S199
❑ 95BeAPSigDC-S199
❑ 95ColCho-316
❑ 95ColChoPC-316
❑ 95ColChoPCP-316
❑ 95Don-97
❑ 95DonEli-1
❑ 95DonEliDCS-1
❑ 95DonEliDCU-1
❑ 95DonEliPW-7
❑ 95Emo-43
❑ 95Ima-6
❑ 95ImaAut-6A
❑ 95ImaCleE-CE6
❑ 95ImaGol-6
❑ 95Lea-97
❑ 95LeaLim-79
❑ 95ParInt-53
❑ 95ParInt-384
❑ 95ParIntEl-53
❑ 95ParIntEl-384
❑ 95Pin-158
❑ 95PinArtP-158
❑ 95PinMas-10
❑ 95PinRinC-158
❑ 95PlaOneoOne-29
❑ 95Sco-131
❑ 95ScoBlaIce-131
❑ 95ScoBlaIceAP-131
❑ 95SelCer-30
❑ 95SelCerFut-4
❑ 95SelCerMG-30
❑ 95SkyImp-42
❑ 95SkyImpD-7
❑ 95SP-76
❑ 95StaClu-98
❑ 95StaCluMOMS-98
❑ 95Sum-29
❑ 95SumArtP-29
❑ 95SumIce-29
❑ 95SumInTheCre-7
❑ 95Top-343
❑ 95TopOPCI-343
❑ 95Ult-258
❑ 95UltHigSpe-19
❑ 95UltRisS-8
❑ 95UltRisSGM-8
❑ 95UppDec-369
❑ 95UppDecEleIceG-369
❑ 95UppDecSpeEdiG-SE131
❑ 95Zen-34
❑ 96BeAPStaTP-15
❑ 96CanaPos-29
❑ 96CanaShe-22
❑ 96ColCho-136
❑ 96ColCho-321
❑ 96Don-101
❑ 96DonBetPip-7
❑ 96DonCanI-2
❑ 96DonCanIGPP-2
❑ 96DonCanILG-2
❑ 96DonCanIRPP-2
❑ 96DonDom-2
❑ 96DonEli-6
❑ 96DonEliDCS-6
❑ 96DonEliPW-5
❑ 96DonEliPW-P5
❑ 96DonPrePro-101
❑ 96Fla-51
❑ 96FlaBluI-51
❑ 96FlaHotG-11
❑ 96Fle-56
❑ 96FlePic-82
❑ 96KraUppD-53
❑ 96Lea-182
❑ 96LeaLim-44
❑ 96LeaLimG-44
❑ 96LeaPre-73
❑ 96LeaPreMM-8
❑ 96LeaPreP-182
❑ 96LeaPrePP-73
❑ 96LeaPreSG-55
❑ 96LeaPreSte-55
❑ 96LeaShuDow-3
❑ 96LeaTheBO.-9
❑ 96MetUni-83
❑ 96NHLACEPC-46
❑ 96Pin-142
❑ 96PinArtP-142
❑ 96PinByTN-13
❑ 96PinByTNP-13
❑ 96PinFoi-142
❑ 96PinMas-5
❑ 96PinMasDC-5
❑ 96PinMcD-36
❑ 96PinMin-27
❑ 96PinMinB-27
❑ 96PinMinCoiB-27
❑ 96PinMinCoiGP-27
❑ 96PinMinCoiN-27
❑ 96PinMinCoiS-27
❑ 96PinMinCoiSG-27
❑ 96PinMinG-27
❑ 96PinMinS-27
❑ 96PinPreS-142
❑ 96PinRinC-142
❑ 96PlaOneoOne-336
❑ 96Sco-96
❑ 96ScoArtPro-96
❑ 96ScoDeaCAP-96
❑ 96ScoGolB-96
❑ 96ScoNetW-9
❑ 96ScoSpeAP-96
❑ 96ScoSudDea-8
❑ 96SelCer-3
❑ 96SelCerAP-3
❑ 96SelCerBlu-3
❑ 96SelCerFre-12
❑ 96SelCerMB-3
❑ 96SelCerMG-3
❑ 96SelCerMR-3
❑ 96SelCerRed-3
❑ 96SkyImp-65
❑ 96SP-81
❑ 96SPHolCol-HC11
❑ 96Sum-102
❑ 96SumArtP-102
❑ 96SumIce-102
❑ 96SumInTheCre-11
❑ 96SumInTheCrePS-11
❑ 96SumMet-102
❑ 96SumPreS-102
❑ 96Ult-90
❑ 96UltGolM-91
❑ 96UppDec-83
❑ 96UppDecBD-41
❑ 96UppDecBDG-41
❑ 96UppDecGN-X5
❑ 96UppDecIce-91
❑ 96UppDecIceDF-S4
❑ 96UppDecIcePar-91
❑ 96UppDecIceSCF-S4
❑ 96UppDecSS-SS11B
❑ 96Zen-69
❑ 96ZenArtP-69
❑ 96ZenZT-11
❑ 97Be A PPAD-10
❑ 97Be A PPAPD-10
❑ 97BeAPla-10
❑ 97BeAPlaAut-10
❑ 97BeAPlaSTP-9
❑ 97CanaPos-22
❑ 97ColCho-134
❑ 97Don-35
❑ 97DonBetTP-10
❑ 97DonCanI-15
❑ 97DonCanIDS-15
❑ 97DonCanILG-7
❑ 97DonCanILGP-7
❑ 97DonCanIPS-15
❑ 97DonEli-88
❑ 97DonEliAsp-88
❑ 97DonEliBttF-2
❑ 97DonEliBttFA-2
❑ 97DonEliS-88
❑ 97DonLim-44
❑ 97DonLim-123
❑ 97DonLimExp-44
❑ 97DonLimExp-123
❑ 97DonLimFOTG-62
❑ 97DonPre-87
❑ 97DonPreCG-9
❑ 97DonPreCGP-9
❑ 97DonPreCttC-87
❑ 97DonPreProG-35
❑ 97DonPreProS-35
❑ 97DonPri-78
❑ 97DonPriODI-21
❑ 97DonPriP-36
❑ 97DonPriPG-6
❑ 97DonPriPGP-6
❑ 97DonPriS-36
❑ 97DonPriSB-36
❑ 97DonPriSG-36
❑ 97DonPriSoA-78
❑ 97DonPriSS-36
❑ 97Kat-78
❑ 97KatGol-78
❑ 97KatSil-78
❑ 97Lea-42
❑ 97LeaFraMat-42
❑ 97LeaFraMDC-42
❑ 97LeaInt-42
❑ 97LeaIntUI-42
❑ 97LeaPipDre-12
❑ 97Pac-168
❑ 97PacCop-168
❑ 97PacDyn-66
❑ 97PacDynC-66
❑ 97PacDynDG-66
❑ 97PacDynEG-66
❑ 97PacDynIB-66
❑ 97PacDynR-66
❑ 97PacDynSil-66
❑ 97PacDynSto-11
❑ 97PacDynTan-13
❑ 97PacEmeGre-168
❑ 97PacIceB-168
❑ 97PacInTheCLC-11
❑ 97PacInv-74
❑ 97PacInvC-74
❑ 97PacInvEG-74
❑ 97PacInvIB-74
❑ 97PacInvR-74
❑ 97PacInvS-74
❑ 97PacOme-124
❑ 97PacOmeC-124
❑ 97PacOmeDG-124
❑ 97PacOmeEG-124
❑ 97PacOmeG-124
❑ 97PacOmeIB-124
❑ 97PacRed-168
❑ 97PacRev-74
❑ 97PacRevC-74
❑ 97PacRevE-74
❑ 97PacRevIB-74
❑ 97PacRevR-74
❑ 97PacRevS-74
❑ 97PacSil-168
❑ 97Pin-98
❑ 97PinArtP-98
❑ 97PinBee-32
❑ 97PinBeeGP-32
❑ 97PinCer-26
❑ 97PinCerMB-26
❑ 97PinCerMG-26
❑ 97PinCerMR-26
❑ 97PinCerR-26
❑ 97PinIns-43
❑ 97PinInsC-14
❑ 97PinInsCC-43
❑ 97PinInsCG-14
❑ 97PinInsEC-43
❑ 97PinInsSto-15
❑ 97PinInsSUG-3A/B
❑ 97PinInsSUG-3C/D
❑ 97PinInsT-17
❑ 97PinPrePBB-98
❑ 97PinPrePBC-98
❑ 97PinPrePBM-98
❑ 97PinPrePBY-98
❑ 97PinPrePFC-98
❑ 97PinPrePFM-98
❑ 97PinPrePFY-98
❑ 97PinPrePla-98
❑ 97PinRinC-98
❑ 97PinTotCMPG-26
❑ 97PinTotCPB-26
❑ 97PinTotCPG-26
❑ 97PinTotCPR-26
❑ 97Sco-41
❑ 97ScoArtPro-41
❑ 97ScoCan-2
❑ 97ScoCanPla-2
❑ 97ScoGolBla-41
❑ 97ScoNetW-11
❑ 97Stu-77
❑ 97StuPrePG-77
❑ 97StuPrePS-77
❑ 97UppDec-90
❑ 97Zen-65
❑ 97Zen5x7-33
❑ 97ZenChaTC-9
❑ 97ZenGolImp-33
❑ 97ZenSilImp-33
❑ 97ZenZGol-65
❑ 97ZenZSil-65
❑ 98Be A PPA-66
❑ 98Be A PPAA-66
❑ 98Be A PPAAF-66
❑ 98Be A PPTBASG-66
❑ 98Be APG-66
❑ 98BowBes-92
❑ 98BowBesAR-92
❑ 98BowBesR-92
❑ 98FinCen-C18
❑ 98FinCenR-C18
❑ 98McD-19
❑ 98O-PChr-217
❑ 98O-PChrR-217
❑ 98Pac-258
❑ 98PacAur-98
❑ 98PacCroR-31
❑ 98PacCroRLS-31
❑ 98PacDynI-98
❑ 98PacDynIIB-98
❑ 98PacDynIR-98
❑ 98PacIceB-258
❑ 98PacOmeH-55
❑ 98PacOmeODI-55
❑ 98PacOmeR-55
❑ 98PacPar-119
❑ 98PacParC-119
❑ 98PacParEG-119
❑ 98PacParH-119
❑ 98PacParIB-119
❑ 98PacParS-119
❑ 98PacRed-258
❑ 98PacRev-32
❑ 98PacRevIS-32
❑ 98PacRevR-32
❑ 98ScoCanPre-2
❑ 98Top-217
❑ 98TopO-P-217
❑ 98UppDec-295

98UppDecE-295
98UppDecE1o1-295
98UppDecGR-295
98UppDecM-42
98UppDecMGS-42
98UppDecMSS-42
98UppDecMSS-42
99Pac-97
99PacAur-33
99PacAurGU-5
99PacAurPD-33
99PacCop-97
99PacGol-97
99PacIceB-97
99PacPreD-97
99UppDecM-47
99UppDecMGS-47
99UppDecMSS-47
99UppDecMSS-47
**Thibault, Larry**
52JunBluT-102
**Thibeault, David**
97BowCHL-78
97BowCHLOPC-78
98BowCHL-96
98BowCHLGA-96
98BowCHLOI-96
98BowChrC-96
98BowChrCGA-96
98BowChrCGAR-96
98BowChrCOI-96
98BowChrCOIR-96
98BowChrCR-96
**Thibeault, Marc**
917thInnSQMJHL-254
**Thibert, Paul**
77GraVic-19
**Thiel, Rob**
87KitRan-9
88KitRan-9
**Thiessen, Kelly**
89BraWheK-3
907thInnSWHL-64
**Thiessen, Travis**
907thInnSWHL-145
917thInnSWHL-277
92CleLum-4
93CleLum-5
93CleLumPos-20
94IndIce-25
95PeoRiv-21
**Thietke, Mark**
83SasBla-24
84KamBla-23
**Thiffault, Charles**
81NordPos-20
82NordPos-24
85NordTeal-26
86NordGenF-27
90CanaPos-31
91CanaPos-30
**Thiffault, Maurice**
51LavDaiLSJ-33
**Thivierge, Sebastien**
95GerDELE-286
**Thomas, Bill**
90HamRoaA-52
**Thomas, Conrade**
94CenHocL-122
**Thomas, Cy**
45QuaOatP-55
**Thomas, Reg**
760PCWHA-82
770PCWHA-84
**Thomas, Scott**
907thInnSWHL-143
917thInnSWHL-165
92Cla-74
92RochAmeD-199
92RochAmeKod-24
93ClaProPro-19
93ClaProPro-125
93Lea-360
930PCPre-336
930PCPreG-336
93Par-25
93ParEmel-25
93Pow-302
93RochAmeKod-23
93Sco-469
93ScoCan-469
93StaClu-471
93StaCluFDI-471
93StaCluO-471
93TopPre-336
93TopPreG-336
93UppDec-247
96CinCyc-19
96ClaGol-74
**Thomas, Steve**
85MapLeaP-29
86KraDra-75
86MapLeaP-20
860PC-245
860PCSti-135
860PCSti-140
87BlaCok-24
870PC-188
870PCSti-154
87PanSti-329
87Top-188
88BlaCok-20
880PC-259
88PanSti-30
89BlaCok-13

890PC-82
890PCSti-15
89PanSti-50
89Top-82
90BlaCok-7
90Bow-4
90BowHatTri-13
90BowTif-4
900PC-92
90ProSet-62
90Sco-66
90ScoCan-66
90ScoHotRS-30
90Top-92
90TopTif-92
90UppDec-221
90UppDecF-221
91Bow-391
910PC-210
910PCPre-195
91PanSti-14
91Par-105
91ParFre-105
91Pin-116
91PinFre-116
91ProSet-45
91ProSet-438
91ProSetFre-45
91ProSetFre-438
91ProSetPla-203
91ScoAme-94
91ScoCan-94
91ScoRoo-51T
91StaClu-109
91Top-210
91UppDec-162
91UppDec-534
91UppDecF-162
91UppDecF-534
92Bow-117
92HumDum2-23
920PC-395
92PanSti-203
92PanStiFre-203
92Par-338
92Par-454
92ParEmel-338
92ParEmel-454
92Pin-128
92PinFre-128
92ProSet-106
92Sco-12
92ScoCan-12
92StaClu-369
92Top-222
92TopGol-222G
92Ult-131
92UppDec-171
93AmeLicSPC-6
93Don-208
93Lea-81
930PCPre-300
930PCPreG-300
93PanSti-57
93Par-124
93ParEmel-124
93Pin-173
93PinCan-173
93Pow-154
93Sco-141
93ScoCan-141
93StaClu-195
93StaCluFDI-195
93StaCluFDIO-195
93StaCluO-195
93TopPre-300
93TopPreG-300
93Ult-216
93UppDec-122
93UppDecSP-95
94BeAPla-R171
94BeAPSig-145
94CanGamNHLP-159
94Don-142
94EASpo-82
94Fin-37
94FinRef-37
94FinSupTW-37
94Fla-108
94FleSlaA-10
94Lea-67
94LeaLim-6
940PCPre-495
940PCPreSE-495
94ParSE-SE102
94ParSEG-SE102
94ParVin-V68
94Pin-52
94PinArtP-52
94PinBoo-BR11
94PinRinC-52
94Sco-37
94ScoGol-37
94ScoPla-37
94ScoPlaTS-37
94Sel-105
94SelGol-105
94SP-71
94SPDieCut-71
94StaClu-80
94StaCluFDI-80
94StaCluMOMS-80
94StaCluSTWC-80
94TopFinI-14

94TopPre-495
94TopPreSE-495
94Ult-132
94UppDec-275
94UppDecElce-275
94UppDecSPI-SP139
94UppDecSPIDC-SP139
95Bow-19
95BowAllFoi-19
95CanGamNHLP-158
95ColCho-248
95ColChoPC-248
95ColChoPCP-248
95Don-32
95Don-363
95DonEli-71
95DonEliDCS-71
95DonEliDCU-71
95Fin-14
95FinRef-14
95Lea-125
95LeaLim-84
95Met-87
95ParInt-390
95ParIntEl-390
95PlaOneoOne-169
95Sco-226
95ScoBlaIce-226
95ScoBlaIceAP-226
95SkyImp-98
95SP-80
95StaClu-16
95StaCluMOMS-16
95Sum-161
95SumArtP-161
95SumIce-161
95SweGloWC-248
95Top-256
95TopOPCI-256
95Ult-263
95UppDec-472
95UppDecElce-472
95UppDecEIceG-472
95UppDecSpeE-SE136
95UppDecSpeEdiG-SE136
95Zen-114
95ZenGifG-18
96ColCho-145
96ColCho-322
96ColChoCTG-C16A
96ColChoCTG-C16B
96ColChoCTG-C16C
96ColChoCTGE-CR16
96ColChoCTGEG-CR16
96ColChoCTGG-C16A
96ColChoCTGG-C16B
96ColChoCTGG-C16C
96Dev-32
96Don-193
96DonPrePro-193
96Fle-62
96Lea-25
96LeaPreP-25
96MetUni-90
96Pin-53
96PinArtP-53
96PinFoi-53
96PinPreS-53
96PinRinC-53
96Sco-64
96ScoArtPro-64
96ScoDeaCAP-64
96ScoGolB-64
96ScoSpeAP-64
96SkyImp-73
96Sum-31
96SumArtP-31
96SumIce-31
96SumMet-31
96SumPreS-31
96Top-161
96TopNHLP-75
96TopPicOI-75
96Ult-97
96UltGolM-98
96UppDec-284
96UppDecIce-37
96UppDecIcePar-37
96Zen-33
96ZenArtP-33
97Be A PPAD-71
97Be A PPAPD-71
97BeAPla-71
97BeAPlaAut-71
97Pac-195
97PacCop-195
97PacEmeGre-195
97PacIceB-195
97PacRed-195
97PacSil-195
97ScoDev-10
97ScoDevPla-10
97ScoDevPre-10
98Pac-274
98PacIceB-274
98PacOmeH-232
98PacOmeODI-232
98PacRed-274
98UppDec-374
98UppDecE1o1-374
98UppDecGR-374
98UppDecM-196
98UppDecMGS-196
98UppDecMSS-196

98UppDecMSS-196
99Pac-417
99PacAur-139
99PacAurPD-139
99PacCop-417
99PacGol-417
99PacIceB-417
99PacPreD-417
99UppDecM-200
99UppDecMGS-200
99UppDecMSS-200
99UppDecMSS-200
**Thomas, Wayne**
73CanaPos-23
730PC-221
74CanaPos-24
74NHLActStaU-23
75HerSta-29
75MapLeaP-22
75MapLeaP-23
750PCNHL-347
76MapLeaP-17
760PCNHL-84
76Top-84
770PCNHL-19
77Top-19
780PC-166
78Top-166
790PC-126
79Top-126
87BlaCok-25
88ProIHL-27
89ProIHL-23
**Thomerson, Bob**
74SioCitM-19
**Thomlinson, Dave**
83BraWheK-10
84BraWheK-22
85BraWheK-22
88ProIHL-78
89BluKod-40
89ProIHL-15
90Bow-21
90BowTif-21
90ProAHLIHL-82
91ProAHLCHL-53
91UppDec-557
91UppDecF-557
92BinRan-6
93PhoRoa-22
95PhoRoa-18
**Thompson, Adam**
91AirCanSJHL-D17
91LakSupSL-28
94CenHocL-87
**Thompson, Adam (80s)**
81SasBla-8
**Thompson, Brent**
907thInnSWHL-43
91ProAHLCHL-402
91UppDec-608
91UppDecF-608
92ScoCan-455
92ScoCan-455
92StaClu-489
92Top-161
92TopGol-161G
930PCPre-406
930PCPreG-406
93StaClu-489
93StaCluFDI-489
93StaCluO-489
93TopPre-406
93TopPreG-406
96SprFal-3
**Thompson, Briane**
917thInnSOHL-317
93SauSteMG-19
93SauSteMGM-21
**Thompson, Chad**
91KnoChe-7
**Thompson, Chris**
95SeaThu-28
95Sla-8
96SeaThu-11
97GueSto-2
**Thompson, Corey**
91AirCanSJHL-B4
**Thompson, Dallas**
92TacRoc-26
93TacRoc-26
**Thompson, Danny**
94HumHawP-20
**Thompson, Derek**
87SudWol-13
88SudWol-14
**Thompson, Dewar**
51LavDaiS-53
52St.LawS-88
**Thompson, Errol**
72MapLeaP-28
73MapLeaP-26
74MapLeaP-23
74NHLActSta-266
75HerSta-30
75MapLeaP-24
750PCNHL-114
75Top-114
76MapLeaP-18
760PCNHL-259

760PCNHL-394
76Top-259
77MapLeaP-15
770PCNHL-293
780PC-57
78Top-57
790PC-106
79Top-106
800PC-234
80Top-234
**Thompson, Jamie**
92MaiBlaB-36
93OmaLan-27
**Thompson, Jean-Guy**
51LavDaiLSJ-54
**Thompson, Jeremy**
95TriAme-26
**Thompson, Paul**
33V129-50
34BeeGro1P-81
35DiaMatT2-61
35DiaMatT3-56
35DiaMatT4-13
35DiaMatT5-12
35DiaMatTI-66
36TriPos-9
36V356WorG-6
37DiaMatT6-12
94GuiFla-15
95GuiFla-9
95GuiFla-27
96GuiFla-7
97GuiFla-8
**Thompson, Rhys**
34BeeGro1P-352
91AirCanSJHL-D17
**Thompson, Rocky**
95MedHatT-20
96MedHatT-23
97Be A PPAD-232
97Be A PPAPD-232
97BeAPla-232
97BeAPlaAut-232
97BeAPlaPOT-20
97BeeAutA-51
**Thompson, Shawn**
91AirCanSJHL-B15
**Thompson, Tim**
93NiaFalT-6
**Thompson, Tiny (Cecil)**
330PCV304B-68
33V357IceK-57
34BeeGro1P-35
34DiaMatS-58
34SweCap-32
36V356WorG-12
38BruGarMS-9
390PCV3011-75
60Top-55
83HalFP-A16
85HalFC-15
91BruSpoAL-32
94ParTalBG-9
**Thompson, Wayne**
83NovScoV-20
**Thoms, Bill**
320'KeeMapL-NNO
33V129-10
33V288HamG-7
33V357IceK-50
34BeeGro1P-353
350PCV304C-85
370PCV304E-143
38QuaOatP-28
390PCV3011-44
**Thomson, Bruce**
82BraWheK-8
**Thomson, Floyd**
71BluPos-22
72BluWhiBor-21
73BluWhiBor-21
74NHLActSta-236
740PCNHL-298
750PCNHL-149
75Top-149
760PCNHL-356
770PCNHL-358
**Thomson, Greg**
94GerDELE-232
95GerDELE-106
96GerDELE-50
**Thomson, Jim**
44BeeGro2P-457
45QuaOatP-56A
45QuaOatP-56B
45QuaOatP-56C
45QuaOatP-56D
48ExhCan-41
51Par-82
52Par-43
53Par-8
54Par-32
55Par-11
55ParQuaO-11
57Top-23
89ProAHL-225
90ProAHLIHL-422
92Top-67
92TopGol-67G
94DucCarJr-23
94ParMisL-119
**Thomson, Tom**
91AirCanSJHL-C32
91AirCanSJHL-E23
92MPSPhoSJHL-131
**Thony, Roger**
93SweSemWCS-126
93SwiHNL-179
95SwiHNL-233
**Thoresen, Petter**

93SweSemWCS-239
94FinnJaaK-270
**Thoreus, Lars**
71SweHocS-387
72SweHocS-261
**Thorn, H.**
95GerDELE-311
**Thornberg, Ove**
86SwePanS-127
87SwePanS-126
89SweSemE-109
90SweSemE-113
91SweSemE-117
92SweSemE-137
93SweSemE-108
94SweLeaE-76
94SweLeaETG-8
**Thornbury, Tom**
84FreExp-21
94CenHocL-72
**Thornton, Bob**
93NorBayC-18
**Thornton, Erin**
907thInnSWHL-187
91BriColJHL-129
92BriColJHL-35
**Thornton, Joe**
95Cla-95
95SauSteMG-21
95Sla-363
96SauSteMG-23
96SauSteMG-24
96SauSteMGA-23
96SauSteMGA-24
96UppDec-370
96UppDecBD-160
96UppDecBDG-160
96UppDecIce-116
97Be A PPAD-232
97Be A PPAPD-232
97BeAPla-232
97BeAPlaAut-232
97BeAPlaPOT-20
97BowCHL-32
97BowCHL-125
97BowCHLAu-125
97BowCHLBB-1
97BowCHLBowBesAR-1
97BowCHLBowBesR-1
97BowCHLOPC-32
97BowCHLOPC-125
97ColCho-296
97DonEli-6
97DonEli-138
97DonEli-148
97DonEliAsp-6
97DonEliAsp-138
97DonEliAsp-148
97DonEliBttF-1
97DonEliBttFA-1
97DonEliC-24
97DonEliMC-24
97DonEliS-6
97DonEliS-138
97DonEliS-148
97DonLim-92
97DonLim-187
97DonLimExp-92
97DonLimExp-187
97DonPre-151
97DonPre-200
97DonPreCttC-151
97DonPreCttC-200
97DonPreDWT-1
97DonPreLotT-2B
97DonPrePM-2
97DonPreT-16
97DonPreTB-16
97DonPreTBC-16
97DonPreTPC-16
97DonPreTPG-16
97DonPri-173
97DonPri-207
97DonPri-215
97DonPriDD-25
97DonPriODI-28
97DonPriP-16
97DonPriS-16
97DonPriSA-173
97DonPriSoA-173
97DonPriSoA-215
97DonPriSS-16
97Kat-164
97KatGol-164
97KatSil-164
97Lea-41
97Lea-150
97LeaFirOnIce-14
97LeaFraMat-41
97LeaFraMat-150
97LeaFraMDC-41
97LeaFraMDC-150
97LeaInt-41
97LeaIntUI-41
97McD-33
97PacCroBoSDC-3
97PacCroCJ-3
97PacCroCJG-3
97PacCroREG-11
97PacCroRHTDC-3

97PacCroRIB-11
97PacCroRLCDC-3
97PacCroRS-11
97PacDyn-NNO
97PacDynC-NNO
97PacDynDG-NNO
97PacDynEG-NNO
97PacDynIB-NNO
97PacDynR-NNO
97PacDynSil-NNO
97PacOme-19
97PacOmeC-19
97PacOmeDG-19
97PacOmeEG-19
97PacOmeG-19
97PacOmeIB-19
97PacPar-16
97PacParBNDC-3
97PacParCG-2
97PacParDG-16
97PacParEG-16
97PacParIB-16
97PacParP-3
97PacParRed-16
97PacParSil-16
97PacRev-11
97PacRevC-11
97PacRevE-11
97PacRevIB-11
97PacRevR-11
97PacRevS-11
97PacRevTCL-11
97Pin-23
97PinArtP-23
97PinBee-51
97PinBeeGP-51
97PinBeeGT-22
97PinBeeT-22
97PinCerRR-A
97PinCerRRG-A
97PinCerRRMG-A
97PinMin-29
97PinMinB-29
97PinMinCBP-29
97PinMinCGPP-29
97PinMinCNSP-29
97PinMinCoiB-29
97PinMinCoiGP-29
97PinMinCoiN-29
97PinMinCoiSS-29
97PinMinCoiSS-29
97PinMinGolTea-29
97PinMinSilTea-29
97PinPowPac-3
97PinPrePBB-23
97PinPrePBC-23
97PinPrePBM-23
97PinPrePBY-23
97PinPrePFC-23
97PinPrePFM-23
97PinPrePFY-23
97PinPrePla-23
97PinRinC-23
97Sco-54
97ScoArtPro-54
97ScoBru-17
97ScoBruPla-17
97ScoBruPre-17
97ScoGolBa-54
97SP Autl-I9
97SPAut-171
97SPAutID-I9
97SPAutIE-I9
97SPAutSotT-JT
97SPAutTra-T3
97Stu-54
97StuPor-22
97StuPrePG-54
97StuPrePS-54
97UppDec-218
97UppDecBD-112
97UppDecBDDD-112
97UppDecBDPC-PC17
97UppDecBDPCDD-PC17
97UppDecBDPCM-PC17
97UppDecBDPCQD-PC17
97UppDecBDPCTD-PC17
97UppDecBDQD-112
97UppDecBDTD-112
97UppDecGDM-218
97UppDecIC-IC6
97UppDecIC2-IC6
97UppDecIce-46
97UppDecIceP-46
97UppDecILL-L1C
97UppDecILL2-L1C
97UppDecIPS-46
97UppDecSG-SG6
97UppDecSSM-SS6
97UppDecSSW-SS6
97Zen-61
97Zen5x7-74
97ZenGolImp-74
97ZenRooR-2
97ZenZGol-92
97ZenZSil-92
97ZenZT-10
97ZenZTG-10
98Be A PPA-9
98Be A PPAA-9
98Be A PPAAF-9
98Be A PPTBASG-9
98Be APG-9

98BowBes-84
98BowBesAR-84
98BowBesR-84
98FinCen-C17
98FinCenR-C17
98O-PChr-112
98O-PChrR-112
98Pac-102
98PacDynI-15
98PacDynIIB-15
98PacDynIR-15
98PacIceB-102
98PacOmeH-19
98PacOmeODI-19
98PacOmeR-19
98PacRed-102
98SP Aut-5
98SP AutSotTG-JT
98SPxFin-133
98SPxFinR-133
98SPxFinS-133
98SPXTopP-5
98SPXTopPF-5
98SPXTopPR-5
98SSASotT-JT
98Top-112
98TopGolIC1-81
98TopGolIC1B-81
98TopGolIC1BOoO-81
98TopGolIC1ROoO-81
98TopGolIC1R-81
98TopGolIC1ROoO-81
98TopGolIC2-81
98TopGolIC2B-81
98TopGolIC2BOoO-81
98TopGolIC2OoO-81
98TopGolIC2R-81
98TopGolIC2ROoO-81
98TopGolIC3-81
98TopGolIC3B-81
98TopGolIC3BOoO-81
98TopGolIC3OoO-81
98TopGolIC3R-81
98TopGolIC3ROoO-81
98TopIceA2-I13
98TopO-P-112
98UC-19
98UD ChoPCR-19
98UD ChoR-19
98UD3-15
98UD3-75
98UD3-135
98UD3DieC-15
98UD3DieC-75
98UD3DieC-135
98UppDec-19
98UppDecBD-7
98UppDecDD-7
98UppDecE-19
98UppDecE-218
98UppDecE1o1-19
98UppDecE1o1-219
98UppDecGN-GN12
98UppDecGNQ1-GN12
98UppDecGNQ2-GN12
98UppDecGNQ3-GN12
98UppDecGR-19
98UppDecGR-218
98UppDecM-12
98UppDecMGS-12
98UppDecMSS-12
98UppDecMSS-12
98UppDecQD-7
98UppDecTD-7
99Pac-30
99PacAur-14
99PacAurPD-14
99PacCop-30
99PacGol-30
99PacIceB-30
99PacPreD-30
99RetHoc-6
99SP AutPS-5
99UppDecCL-78
99UppDecCLCLC-78
99UppDecM-13
99UppDecMPS-13
99UppDecMPS-JT
99UppDecMSS-13
99UppDecMSS-13
99UppDecRG-6
99UppDecRP-6
**Thornton, Scott**
897thInnSOHL-83
90ProSet-640
90UppDec-459
90UppDecF-459
91Bow-168
91OilIGA-24
91OilTeal-27
91ScoCan-605
91ScoRoo-55T
91StaClu-378
91UppDec-353
91UppDecF-353
91UppDecF-521
94Lea-431
94Par-73
94ParGol-73
94UppDec-426
94UppDecEIeIce-426
94CanGamNHLP-112
95Don-262

95Pin-162
95PinArtP-162
95PinRinC-162
95Top-82
95TopOPCI-82
96BeAPAut-153
96BeAPAutSil-153
96BeAPla-153
96CanaPos-30
96CanaShe-23
97CanaPos-23
98Fin-93
98FinNo P-93
98FinNo PR-93
98FinRef-93
**Thornton, Shawn**
95Sla-316
97St.JohML-24
**Thornton, Steven**
95PeoRiv-22
96GerDELE-180
**Thorp, Matt**
96ColChe-14
**Thorpe, Robert**
907thInnSOHL-122
917thInnSOHL-69
96TolSto-33
**Thors, Ulf**
71SweHocS-191
72SweHocS-177
**Thudium, Calvin**
87PorWinH-20
88PorWinH-20
907thInnSWHL-212
917thInnSMC-91
**Thulin, Kurt**
64SweCorl-30
64SweCorl-128
65SweCorl-30
65SweCorl-128
67SweHoc-76
**Thuresson, Marcus**
89SweSemE-142
90SweSemE-213
91SweSemE-140
92SweSemE-164
93SweSemE-133
94SweLeaE-29
95SweLeaE-226
95SweUppDE-92
**Thurier, Fred**
34BeeGro1P-256
51CleBar-7
**Thurlby, Tom**
61UniOilW-12
**Thurstan, Trevor**
91AirCanSJHL-A19
**Thurston, Brent**
907thInnSWHL-204
917thInnSMC-78
95VanVooRHl-7
**Thurston, Eric**
81VicCou-15
82VicCou-22
83VicCou-23
**Thuss, Chuck**
95LouIceGP-19
**Thyer, Mario**
89ProIHL-85
90ProAHLIHL-119
90Sco-382
90ScoCan-382
91ProAHLCHL-160
**Tiainen, Tero**
95FinnSIS-289
96FinnSISR-87
**Tiala, Harri**
84SweSemE-16
**Tibbatts, Derek**
89SasBla-13
907thInnSWHL-79
90SasBla-12
917thInnSWHL-111
91SasBla-12
93SasBla-19
93SasBla-20
**Tibbatts, Trent**
92MPSPhoSJHL-96
**Tibbetts, Bill**
93LonKni-20
**Tichy, Marek**
94CzeAPSE-235
96CzeAPSE-269
**Tichy, Milan**
91ProAHLCHL-485
92IndIce-23
93ClaProPro-25
93Pow-101
93Sco-461
93ScoCan-461
93Ult-247
93UltAilRoo-10
**Tidey, Alex**
88OilTenAnn-163
**Tidsbury, Shane**
92BriColJHL-175
**Tie, Jussi**
95ColCho-325
95ColChoPC-325
95ColChoPCP-325
**Tiilikainen, Jukka**
93FinnJyvHS-199
93FinnSIS-265
94FinnSIS-227
95FinnSemWC-228

95FinnSIS-129
**Tikhonov, Viktor**
74SweHocS-80
83RusNatT-18
87RusNatT-20
89RusNatT-23
89SweSemWCS-77
900PCRedA-17R
**Tikkanen, Esa**
85OilRedR-10
86OilRedR-10
86OilTeal-10
90OilTeal-10
87OPC-7
87OPCSti-83
87PanSti-264
87Top-7
88OilTeal-27
88OilTenAnn-29
88OPC-260
88OPCSti-220
88PanSti-63
89Kra-18
89OilTeal-24
89OPC-12
89OPC-328
89OPCSti-219
89Top-12
90Bow-194
90BowTif-194
90OilIGA-27
90OPC-156
90PanSti-223
90ProSet-97
90Sco-13
90Sco-342
90ScoCan-13
90ScoCan-342
90ScoHotRS-6
90Top-156
90UppDec-167
90UppDecF-167
91Bow-98
91Gil-2
91OilIGA-25
91OilPanTS-23
91OilTeal-28
91OPC-378
91OPCPre-121
91PanSti-123
91Par-55
91ParFre-55
91Pin-57
91Pin-24
91PinFre-24
91ProSet-71
91ProSetFre-71
91ProSetNHLAS-AC14
91ProSetPla-39
91ScoAme-241
91ScoCan-461
91StaClu-69
91SweSemWCS-203
91Top-378
91TopTeaSL-6
91UppDec-83
91UppDec-182
91UppDecES-10
91UppDec-83
91UppDecF-182
92Bow-144
92OilIGA-23
92OPC-319
92PanSti-103
92PanStiFre-103
92Par-46
92ParEmel-46
92Pin-336
92PinFre-336
92ProSet-53
92Sco-16
92ScoCan-16
92ScoCanPS-1
92StaClu-104
92Top-476
92TopGol-476G
92Ult-67
92UppDec-188
93Don-215
93Lea-288
930PCPre-282
930PCPreG-282
93PanSti-95
93Par-135
93ParEmel-135
93Pin-279
93PinCan-279
93Pow-395
93PowGloG-9
93Sco-97
93ScoCan-97
93StaClu-477
93StaCluFDI-477
93StaCluMasP-13
93StaCluMasPW-13
93StaCluO-477
93SweSemWCS-80
93TopPre-282
93TopPreG-282
93Ult-377
93UppDecSP-104
94CanGamNHLP-209
94FinnJaaK-34

94FinnJaaK-349
94FinnSIS-276
94FinnSISGS-10
94Fla-160
94Fle-193
940PCPre-504
940PCPreSE-504
940PCPreSE-528
94ParSE-SE157
94ParSEES-ES11
94ParSEG-SE157
94Pin-174
94PinArtP-174
94PinRinC-174
94Sco-136
94ScoGol-136
94ScoPlaTS-136
94SP-103
94SPDieCut-103
94StaClu-258
94StaCluFDI-258
94StaCluMOMS-258
94StaCluSTWC-258
94TopPre-504
94TopPre-528
94TopPreSE-504
94TopPreSE-528
94Ult-191
94UppDec-42
94UppDecEIeIce-42
94UppDecSPI-SP160
94UppDecSPIDC-SP160
95CanGamNHLP-239
95ColCho-268
95ColChoPC-268
95ColChoPCP-268
95Don-17
95Emo-153
95FinnJaaKLAC-5
95FinnSemWC-43
95FinnSISL-40
95FinnSISLSS-8
95Lea-319
95Met-380
95ParInt-173
95ParInt-235
95ParIntEl-173
95ParIntEl-235
95ParIntEl-478
95Pin-57
95PinArtP-57
95PinGloG-10
95PinRinC-57
95PlaOneoOne-196
95ProMag-15
95Sco-123
95ScoBlaIce-123
95ScoBlaIceAP-123
95SkyImp-145
95SP-153
95SweGloWC-138
95Ult-140
95Ult-264
95UppDec-126
95UppDecEIeIce-126
95UppDecEIceG-126
95UppDecSpeI-SE70
95UppDecSpeG-SE137
95UppDecSpeEdiG-SE70
95UppDecSpeEdiG-SE137
96BeAPAut-31
96BeAPAutSii-31
96BeAPla-31
96CanuPos-10
96ColCho-273
96MetUni-160
96NHLProSTA-15
96Pin-46
96PinArtP-46
96PinFoi-46
96PinPreS-46
96PinRinC-46
96PlaOneoOne-392
96SweSemW-28
96SweSemWNS-NS6
96TeaOut-7
96Ult-171
96UltGolM-171
96UppDec-352
97EssOlyHH-49
97EssOlyHHF-49
97Pac-249
97PacCop-249
97PacEmeGre-249
97PacIceB-249
97PacParC-85
97PacParDG-85
97PacParEG-85
97PacParIB-85
97PacParRed-85
97PacParSil-85
97PacSil-249
97Sco-236
97UppDec-111
98McdGreT-T6
98Pac-448
98PacIceB-448
98PacOmeH-162
98PacOmeODI-162

98PacOmeR-162
98PacRed-448
**Tiley, Brad**
89SauSteMG-20
907thInnSWHL-173
917thInnSMC-6
91ProAHLCHL-95
92PhoRoa-22
93ClaProPro-129
93PhoRoa-23
**Tillander, Kurt**
69SweHocS-217
**Tilley, Tom**
87BluTealss-23
88BluTealss-23
89BluKod-20
89BluKod-20
89PanSti-128
900PC-498
90ProAHLIHL-83
91Bow-307
93Par-442
93ParEmel-442
93UppDec-491
95MilAdmBO-17
96ColEdgFL-43
96MilAdmBO-24
**Tilson, Michael**
95Sla-110
97SudWolP-19
**Tiltgen, Dean**
907thInnSWHL-104
917thInnSWHL-289
**Timander, Mattias**
92SweSemE-233
93SweSemE-197
94SweLeaE-29
95SweLeaE-101
95SweLeaEFF-10
95SweUppDE-153
95SweUppDETNA-NA19
96DonCanI-138
96DonCanIGPP-138
96DonCanIRPP-138
96DonEli-135
96DonEliDCS-135
96Fla-101
96FlaBlul-101
96LeaPre-120
96LeaPrePP-120
96SelCer-99
96SelCerAP-99
96SelCerBlu-99
96SelCerMB-99
96SelCerMG-99
96SelCerMR-99
96SelCerRed-99
96SP-170
96UppDec-220
96UppDecBD-47
96UppDecBDG-47
96Zen-134
96ZenArtP-134
97Be A PPAD-151
97Be A PPAPD-151
97BeAPla-151
97BeAPlaAut-151
97Pac-235
97PacCop-235
97PacEmeGre-235
97PacIceB-235
97PacRed-235
97PacSil-235
97UppDec-224
**Timchenko, Oleg**
98BowCHL-105
98BowCHLGA-105
98BowCHLOI-105
98BowChrC-105
98BowChrCGA-105
98BowChrCGAR-105
98BowChrCOI-105
98BowChrCOIR-105
98BowChrCR-105
**Timewell, Jason**
91BriColJHL-67
**Timgren, Ray**
44BeeGro2P-458
45QuaOatP-57A
45QuaOatP-57B
48ExhCan-40
51Par-78
54Top-13
**Timmins, Sean**
94AirCanSJHL-D26
**Timonen, Kimmo**
93FinnJyvHS-165
93FinnSIS-163
93FinnSIS-396
93UppDec-268
94Fin-129
94FinnSIS-304
94FinRef-129
94FinSupTW-129
94ParSE-SE218
94ParSEG-SE218
94SP-160
94SPDieCut-160
94UppDecEIeIce-510
95FinnSemWC-10
95FinnSemWC-233
95FinnSIS-123
95FinnSISDT-1
95FinnSISL-65

96FinnSISR-182
98PacOmeH-134
98PacOmeODI-134
98PacOmeR-134
99UppDecM-111
99UppDecMGS-111
99UppDecMSS-111
99UppDecMSS-111
**Timoschuk, Roland**
94GerDELE-186
95GerDELE-186
96GerDELE-125
**Tinordi, Mark**
90ProSet-145
90Sco-304A
90ScoCan-304A
91Bow-124
91Kra-22
910PC-308
91PanSti-109
91Par-304
91ParFre-304
91Pin-199
91PinFre-199
91ProSet-107
91ProSetFre-107
91ProSetFre-575
91ProSetPla-58
91ScoAme-93
91ScoCan-93
91ScoYouS-18
91StaClu-392
91Top-308
91UppDec-295
91UppDecF-295
92Bow-218
92Bow-399
92HumDum1-23
92OPC-17
92PanSti-97
92PanStiFre-97
92Par-76
92ParEmel-76
92Pin-18
92Pin-252
92PinFre-18
92PinFre-252
92ProSet-78
92Sco-7
92ScoCan-7
92StaClu-435
92Top-4
92TopGol-4G
92Ult-98
92UppDec-73
93Don-79
93Kra-40
93Lea-146
930PCPre-24
930PCPreG-24
93PanSti-275
93Par-320
93ParEmel-320
93Pin-16
93PinCan-16
93PinCapC-6
93Pow-66
93Sco-53
93ScoCan-53
93StaClu-384
93StaCluFDI-384
93StaCluO-384
93TopPre-24
93TopPreG-24
93Ult-213
93UppDec-89
94CanGamNHLP-85
94Don-206
94EASpo-31
94Fin-25
94FinnJaaK-82
94FinRef-25
94FinSupTW-25
94Fla-45
94Fle-239
94Lea-91
940PCPre-24
940PCPre-452
940PCPreSE-24
940PCPreSE-452
94Par-59
94ParGol-59
94Pin-29
94PinArtP-29
94PinRinC-29
94Sco-68
94ScoGol-68
94ScoPla-68
94ScoPlaTS-68
94StaHoc-23
94StaScoS-68
94TopPre-24
94TopPre-452
94TopPreSE-24
94TopPreSE-452
94Ult-57
94UppDec-369
94UppDecEIeIce-369
94UppDecSPI-SP177
94UppDecSPIDC-SP177
95BeAPla-220
95BeAPSig-220
95BeAPSigDC-S220

95CanGamNHLP-284
95Cap-26
95ColCho-141
95ColChoPC-141
95ColChoPCP-141
95Don-255
95FinnSemWC-84
95ParInt-224
95ParIntEl-224
95PinFulC-10
95PlaOneoOne-215
95Sco-144
95ScoBlaIce-144
95ScoBlaIceAP-144
95StaClu-67
95StaCluMO-21
95StaCluMOMS-67
95Sum-93
95SumArtP-93
95SumIce-93
95SweGloWC-60
95Top-198
95TopOPCI-198
95Ult-178
95UltGolM-178
95UppDec-94
95UppDecEIeIce-94
95UppDecEIeIceG-94
96Don-153
96DonPrePro-153
96Lea-31
96LeaPreP-31
96Sco-11
96ScoArtPro-11
96ScoDeaCAP-11
96ScoGolB-11
96ScoSpeAP-11
96UppDecIce-74
96UppDecIcePar-74
97Pac-181
97PacCop-181
97PacEmeGre-181
97PacIceB-181
97PacRed-181
97PacSil-181
97UppDec-385
98O-PChr-157
98O-PChrR-157
98Pac-449
98PacIceB-449
98PacRed-449
98Top-157
98TopO-P-157
**Tipler, Curtis**
95BowDraPro-P33
96RegPat-2
**Tipler, Travis**
99WicThu-21
**Tippett, Brad**
907thInnSWHL-182
917thInnSWHL-241
**Tippett, Dave**
84WhaJunW-19
85WhaJunW-20
860PC-148
86Top-148
86WhaJunT-21
870PC-86
87PanSti-51
87Top-86
87WhaJunBK-19
880PC-85
88PanSti-244
88Top-85
88WhaJunGR-16
890PC-134
890PCSti-268
89PanSti-226
89Top-134
89WhaJunM-20
90CapKod-25
90CapPos-22
90CapSmo-22
900PC-183
900PCPre-119
90PanSti-37
90ProSet-111
90ProSet-555
90Sco-192
90ScoCan-192
90ScoRoo-29T
90Top-183
90TopTif-183
90UppDec-270
90UppDecF-270
91CapJun5-25
91CapKod-20
91ScoAme-437
91ScoCan-409
91UppDec-480
91UppDecF-480
92Par-372
92ParEmel-372
92PenCokC-23
92PenFoo-16
93Lea-349
930PCPre-387
930PCPreG-387
93PanSti-89
93Pow-410
93Sco-584
93ScoCan-584
93ScoGol-584
93StaClu-124
93StaCluFDI-124

93StaCluFDIO-124
93StaCluO-124
93TopPre-387
93TopPreG-387
**Tirkkonen, Antti**
95FinnSIS-342
**Tirkkonen, Pekka**
93FinnJyvHS-168
93FinnSIS-178
94FinnJaaK-25
94FinnSIS-40
94FinnSIS-171
95FinnSIS-80
95FinnSISL-70
96GerDELE-197
**Tisdale, Tim**
89ProAHL-142
90ProAHLIHL-227
92WheThu-17
93WheThu-PC3
93WheThu-UD2
94FreCan-28
94WheThu-2
**Titov, German**
93Cla-94
93Don-56
93FinnSIS-376
93Lea-309
93Par-255
93ParEmel-255
93Pow-310
93Sco-614
93ScoCan-614
93ScoGol-614
93StaClu-364
93StaCluFDI-364
93StaCluO-364
93UppDec-476
94Don-228
94Fin-75
94FinnSIS-361
94FinnSISGS-11
94FinRef-75
94FinnSupTW-75
94Fla-29
94Fle-36
94Lea-261
94OPCPre-9
94OPCPreSE-9
94ParSE-SE26
94ParSEG-SE26
94Pin-167
94PinArtP-167
94PinRinC-167
94Sco-95
94ScoGol-95
94ScoPla-95
94ScoPlaTS-95
94SP-18
94SPDieCut-18
94TopPre-9
94TopPreSE-9
94Ult-36
94UppDec-2
94UppDecEleIce-2
95CanGamNHLP-50
95ColCho-15
95ColChoPC-15
95ColChoPCP-15
95Don-229
95DonEli-41
95DonEliDCS-41
95DonEliDCU-41
95Lea-31
95ParInt-28
95ParIntEI-28
95Pin-52
95PinGloG-9
95PinRinC-52
95PlaOneoOne-20
95ProMag-50
95Sco-71
95ScoBlaIce-71
95ScoBlaIceAP-71
95SkyImp-25
95SP-18
95UppDec-207
95UppDecEleIce-207
95UppDecEleIceG-207
95UppDecSpe-SE14
95UppDecSpeEdiG-SE14
96BeAPAut-49
96BeAPAutSil-49
96BeAPla-49
96ColCho-39
96Don-58
96DonPrePro-58
96Fle-14
96FlePic-106
96MetUni-23
96NHLProSTA-50
96Pin-36
96PinArtP-36
96PinFoi-36
96PinPreS-36
96PinRinC-36
96PlaOneoOne-354
96Sco-165
96ScoArtPro-165
96ScoDeaCAP-165
96ScoGolB-165
96ScoSpeAP-165
96SkyImp-15
96SP-24

96Sum-108
96SumArtP-108
96SumIce-108
96SumMet-108
96SumPreS-108
96SweSemW-154
96Ult-27
96UltGolM-27
96UppDec-227
97ColCho-39
97Pac-263
97PacCop-263
97PacDyn-19
97PacDynC-19
97PacDynDG-19
97PacDynEG-19
97PacDynIB-19
97PacDynR-19
97PacDynSil-19
97PacDynTan-34
97PacEmeGre-263
97PacIceB-263
97PacInv-21
97PacInvC-21
97PacInvEG-21
97PacInvIB-21
97PacInvR-21
97PacInvs-21
97PacOme-37
97PacOmeC-37
97PacOmeDG-37
97PacOmeEG-37
97PacOmeG-37
97PacOmeIB-37
97PacPar-32
97PacParC-32
97PacParDG-32
97PacParEG-32
97PacParIB-32
97PacParRed-32
97PacParSil-32
97PacRed-263
97PacSil-263
97PinCer-88
97PinCerMB-88
97PinCerMG-88
97PinCerMR-88
97PinCerR-88
97PinTotCMPG-88
97PinTotCPB-88
97PinTotCPG-88
97PinTotCPR-88
97Sco-199
97SPAut-22
98Be A PPA-262
98Be A PPAA-262
98Be A PPAAF-262
98Be A PPSE-262
98Be APG-262
98Pac-127
98PacCroR-112
98PacCroRLS-112
98PacIceB-127
98PacRed-127
98SP Aut-68
98UC-30
98UD ChoPCR-30
98UD ChoR-30
98UppDecBD-70
98UppDecDD-70
98UppDecE1o1-346
98UppDecGR-346
98UppDecM-169
98UppDecMGS-169
98UppDecMSS-169
98UppDecMSS-169
98UppDecQD-70
98UppDecTD-70
99Pac-348
99PacCop-348
99PacGol-348
99PacIceB-348
99PacPreD-348
99SP AutPS-68
99UppDecM-167
99UppDecMGS-167
99UppDecMSS-167
99UppDecMSS-167
**Titus, Stephen**
86LonKni-27
**Tiumenev, Viktor**
81SweSemHVS-48
87RusNatT-21
**Tjallden, Mikael**
92SweSemE-352
**Tjarnqvist, Daniel**
93SweSemE-226
93SweSemE-314
94SweLeaE-209
94SweLeaERR-6
95SigRoo-49
95SigRooSig-49
95SP-186
95SweLeaE-116
95SweUppDE-175
**Tjarnqvist, Mathias**
98SPXTopP-83
98SPXTopPF-83
98SPXTopPR-83
98UppDecBD-113
98UppDecDD-113
98UppDecQD-113
98UppDecTD-113

**Tjernstrom, Leif**
69SweHocS-92
**Tjitjurin, Juri**
73SweWorCS-136
73SweWorCS-136
74SweWorCS-56
**Tkach, Stanislav**
92NasKni-9
95MadMon-18
**Tkachenko, Sergei**
97AncAce-20
**Tkachuck, Pete**
51LavDaiQSHL-34
**Tkachuk, Grant**
84SasBlaS-18
88ProAHL-251
89ProIHL-105
90ProAHLIHL-281
**Tkachuk, Keith**
91Par-424
91ParFre-424
91UppDec-698
91UppDecCWJC-85
91UppDecF-698
92OPC-346
92OPCPre-43
92Par-206
92ParEmel-206
92Pin-222
92PinFre-222
92ProSet-243
92Sco-450
92ScoCan-450
92ScoYouS-29
92StaClu-116
92Top-102
92TopGol-102G
92Ult-446
92UppDec-364
92UppDec-398
92UppDec-419
92UppDecACH-2
92UppDecCC-CC15
92UppDecGHS-G18
93Don-390
93Lea-105
93LeaGolR-11
93OPCPre-27
93OPCPre-502
93OPCPreG-27
93OPCPreG-502
93PanSti-193
93Par-228
93ParEmel-228
93Pin-33
93PinCan-33
93PinCap-26
93PinCapC-26
93Pow-276
93PowRisS-8
93Sco-195
93ScoCan-195
93StaClu-135
93StaCluFDI-135
93StaCluFDIO-135
93StaCluO-135
93TopPre-27
93TopPre-502
93TopPreG-27
93TopPreG-502
93Ult-111
93UppDec-195
93UppDecNL-NL5
93UppDecSP-178
94BeAPla-R36
94CanGamNHLP-256
94Don-192
94Fin-19
94FinBowB-B17
94FinBowBR-B17
94FinRef-19
94FinSupTW-19
94Fla-211
94Fle-246
94FleFraFut-8
94Kra-29
94Lea-94
94LeaLim-108
94OPCPre-242
94OPCPre-300
94OPCPreSE-242
94OPCPreSE-300
94Par-264
94ParGol-264
94ParSEV-38
94Pin-103
94PinArtP-103
94PinGam-GR18
94PinNorLig-NL12
94PinRinC-103
94ScoChelt-CI14
94Sel-75
94SelGol-75
94SP-132
94SPDieCut-132
94StaCluFDI-5
94StaCluMOMS-5
94StaCluSTWC-5
94TopFinI-18
94TopPre-242
94TopPre-300
94TopPreSE-242
94TopPreSE-300

94Ult-247
94UltPow-10
94UppDec-145
94UppDecEleIce-145
94UppDecSPI-SP89
94UppDecSPIDC-SP89
95BAPLetL-LL1
95BeAPla-215
95BeAPSig-S215
95BeAPSigDC-S215
95Bow-69
95BowAllFoi-69
95CanGamNHLP-16
95CanGamNHLP-293
95ColCho-168
95ColCho-356
95ColCho-382
95ColChoPC-168
95ColChoPC-356
95ColChoPC-382
95ColChoPCP-168
95ColChoPCP-356
95ColChoPCP-382
95Don-78
95DonEli-81
95DonEliDCS-81
95DonEliDCU-81
95DonProPoi-7
95Emo-197
95EmoNteP-9
95Fin-123
95FinRef-123
95ImpSti-136
95JetReaC-11
95JetTealss-24
95Kra-48
95Lea-79
95LeaLim-57
95Met-166
95MetIW-14
95NHLAcePC-11S
95ParInt-501
95ParIntEI-501
95PinFulC-11
95PlaOneoOne-109
95PlaOneoOne-220
95PosUppD-23
95ProMag-64
95Sco-33
95ScoBlaIce-33
95ScoBlaIceAP-33
95ScoChelt-11
95ScoPro-33
95SelCer-37
95SelCerDS-17
95SelCerDSG-17
95SelCerMG-37
95SkyImp-185
95SkyImp-239
95SP-164
95SPStaEto-E30
95SPStaEtoG-E30
95StaClu-90
95StaCluFea-F9
95StaCluMO-39
95StaCluMOMS-90
95Sum-152
95SumArtP-152
95SumGM-6
95SumIce-152
95Top-152
95TopHomGUSA-HGA5
95TopMysF-M14
95TopMysFR-M14
95TopOPCI-152
95TopPowL-PL7
95TopRinL-7RL
95TopSupSki-51
95TopSupSkiPla-51
95Ult-184
95UltCreCra-20
95UltGolM-184
95UppDec-243
95UppDec-464
95UppDecEleIce-243
95UppDecEleIce-464
95UppDecEleIceG-243
95UppDecEleIceG-464
95UppDecSpE-SE88
95UppDecSpeEdiG-SE88
95Zen-74
95ZenGifG-1
96BeAPBisITB-6
96ColCho-201
96ColCho-295
96ColCho-327
96ColChoCTG-C26A
96ColChoCTG-C26B
96ColChoCTG-C26C
96ColChoCTGE-CR26
96ColChoCTGEG-CR26
96ColChoCTGG-C26A
96ColChoCTGG-C26B
96ColChoCTGG-C26C
96ColChoMVP-UD16
96ColChoMVPG-UD16
96Don-134
96DonCanI-22
96DonCanIRP-22
96DonCanIRPP-22
96DonDom-8
96DonEli-61
96DonEliDCS-61
96DonEliS-2
96DonHitLis-10

96DonPrePro-134
96DurAllT-DC18
96DurL'EB-JB18
96Fla-73
96FlaBluI-73
96Fle-92
96Fle-141
96FleArtRos-22
96FlePePCC-7
96FlePic-18
96FlePicDL-5
96FlePicF5-44
96KraUppD-2
96Lea-133
96LeaLeaAL-2
96LeaLeaALP-P2
96LeaLim-3
96LeaLimBTB-5
96LeaLimBTBLE-5
96LeaLimBTBP-P5
96LeaLimG-3
96LeaPre-89
96LeaPre-148
96LeaPreP-133
96LeaPrePP-89
96LeaPrePP-148
96LeaPreVP-12
96LeaPreVPG-12
96LeaTheBO.-5
96MetUni-122
96MetUniCS-11
96MetUniCSSP-11
96MetUniLW-19
96MetUniLWSP-19
96NHLACEPC-47
96NHLProSTA-64
96Pin-114
96PinArtP-114
96PinFoi-114
96PinMin-19
96PinMinB-19
96PinMinCoiB-19
96PinMinCoiGP-19
96PinMinCoiN-19
96PinMinCoiS-19
96PinMinCoiSG-19
96PinMinG-19
96PinMinS-19
96PinPreS-114
96PinRinC-114
96PlaOneoOne-351
96Sco-47
96ScoArtPro-47
96ScoChelt-3
96ScoDeaCAP-47
96ScoGolB-47
96ScoSpeAP-47
96SelCer-24
96SelCerAP-24
96SelCerBlu-24
96SelCerC-10
96SelCerMB-24
96SelCerMG-24
96SelCerMR-24
96SelCerRed-24
96SkyImp-107
96SkyImpB-22
96SP-118
96SPGamFil-GF5
96SPInsInf-IN2
96SPInsInfG-IN2
96SPx-35
96SPxGol-35
96Sum-104
96SumArtP-104
96SumIce-104
96SumMet-104
96SumPreS-104
96SweSemW-168
96TeaOut-14
96Ult-136
96UltCleTheIce-10
96UltGolM-136
96UppDec-313
96UppDecBD-153
96UppDecBDG-153
96UppDecGN-X15
96UppDecHH-HH8
96UppDecHHG-HH8
96UppDecHHS-HH8
96UppDecIce-100
96UppDecIceDF-S8
96UppDecIcePar-100
96UppDecIceSCF-S8
96UppDecLSH-LS17
96UppDecLSHF-LS17
96UppDecLSHS-LS17
96UppDecSS-SS6A
96Zen-6
96ZenArtP-6
96ZenZT-12
97b Be A PPAD-22
97be A PPAPD-22
97BeAPla-22
97BeAPlaAut-22
97BeAPlaPOT-2
97ColCho-194
97ColChoCTG-C27A
97ColChoCTG-C27B
97ColChoCTG-C27C
97ColChoCTGE-CR27
97ColChoSta-SQ87
97Don-83
97Don-207
97DonCanI-16

97DonCanIDS-16
97DonCanIPS-16
97DonEli-112
97DonEliAsp-112
97DonEliC-28
97DonEliS-112
97DonLim-83
97DonLim-133
97DonLim-138
97DonLim-140
97DonLimExp-83
97DonLimExp-133
97DonLimExp-138
97DonLimExp-140
97DonLimFOTG-18
97DonPre-6
97DonPre-191
97DonPreCttC-6
97DonPreCttC-191
97DonPreLotT-3B
97DonPreProG-83
97DonPreProS-83
97DonPreProS-227
97DonPri-3
97DonPri-202
97DonPriDD-17
97DonPriODI-3
97DonPriP-26
97DonPriS-26
97DonPriSB-26
97DonPriSG-26
97DonPriSoA-3
97DonPriSoA-202
97DonPriSS-26
97DonRedAle-4
97EssOlyHH-23
97EssOlyHHF-23
97Kat-113
97KatGol-113
97KatSil-113
97Lea-73
97Lea-185
97LeaBanSea-14
97LeaFraMat-73
97LeaFraMat-185
97LeaFraMDC-73
97LeaFraMDC-185
97LeaInt-73
97LeaIntUI-73
97McD-7
97Pac-28
97PacCarSup-17
97PacCarSupM-17
97PacCop-28
97PacCroR-107
97PacCroREG-107
97PacCroRHTDC-14
97PacCroRIB-107
97PacCroRLCDC-16
97PacCroRS-107
97PacDyn-98
97PacDynBKS-76
97PacDynC-98
97PacDynDD-12B
97PacDynDG-98
97PacDynEG-98
97PacDynIB-98
97PacDynR-98
97PacDynSil-98
97PacDynTan-6
97PacEmeGre-28
97PacIceB-28
97PacInv-109
97PacInvC-109
97PacInvEG-109
97PacInvIB-109
97PacInvNRB-156
97PacInvOTG-16
97PacInvS-109
97PacOme-177
97PacOmeC-177
97PacOmeDG-177
97PacOmeEG-177
97PacOmeG-177
97PacOmeGFDCC-15
97PacOmeIB-177
97PacPar-144
97PacParBNDC-16
97PacParC-144
97PacParDG-144
97PacParEG-144
97PacParIB-144
97PacParP-16
97PacParRed-144
97PacParSil-144
97PacRed-28
97PacRev-109
97PacRevC-109
97PacRevEG-109
97PacRevIB-109
97PacRevR-109
97PacRevS-109
97PacRevTCL-19
97PacSil-28
97PacSlaSDC-7A
97Pin-40
97PinArtP-40
97PinBee-14
97PinBeeG-14
97PinBeeGT-17
97PinBeeT-17
97PinCer-37

97PinCerGT-11
97PinCerMB-37
97PinCerMG-37
97PinCerMR-37
97PinCerR-37
97PinCerT-11
97PinEpiGo-6
97PinEpiGP-6
97PinEpiME-6
97PinEpiMO-6
97PinEpiMP-6
97PinEpiPE-6
97PinEpiPO-6
97PinEpiSE-6
97PinEpiSO-6
97PinEpiSP-6
97PinIns-5
97PinInsC-7
97PinInsCC-5
97PinInsCG-7
97PinInsEC-5
97PinInsT-24
97PinMin-21
97PinMinB-21
97PinMinCBP-21
97PinMinCGPP-21
97PinMinCNSP-21
97PinMinCoiB-21
97PinMinCoiGP-21
97PinMinCoiN-21
97PinMinCoiSG-21
97PinMinCoiSS-21
97PinMinGolTea-21
97PinMinSilTea-21
97PinPowPac-6
97PinPrePBB-40
97PinPrePBC-40
97PinPrePBM-40
97PinPrePBY-40
97PinPrePFC-40
97PinPrePFM-40
97PinPrePFY-40
97PinPrePla-40
97PinRinC-40
97PinTeaP-6
97PinTeaPM-6
97PinTeaPP-6
97PinTeaPPM-6
97PinTotCMPG-37
97PinTotCPB-37
97PinTotCPG-37
97PinTotCPR-37
97Sco-87
97ScoArtPro-87
97ScoChel-4
97ScoGolBla-87
97SP AutI-I23
97SPAutID-I23
97SPAutIE-I23
97SPx-40
97SPxBro-40
97SPxDim-SPX15
97SPxGol-40
97SPxGraF-40
97SPxSil-40
97SPxSte-40
97Stu-8
97StuHarH-7
97StuPor-8
97StuPrePG-8
97StuPrePS-8
97StuSil-18
97StuSil8-18
97UppDec-126
97UppDecBD-110
97UppDecBDDD-110
97UppDecBDPCDD-PC14
97UppDecBDPCDDD-PC14
97UppDecBDPCQD-PC14
97UppDecBDPCTD-PC14
97UppDecBDQD-110
97UppDecBDTD-110
97UppDecCtAG-AR11
97UppDecDV-18
97UppDecDVSM-18
97UppDecGDM-126
97UppDecIC-IC15
97UppDecIC2-IC15
97UppDecIce-70
97UppDecIceP-70
97UppDecILL-L3A
97UppDecILL2-L3A
97UppDecIPS-70
97UppDecSG-SG37
97UppDecSSM-SS23
97UppDecSSW-SS23
97UppDecTS-15
97UppDecTSL2-15
97UppDecTSS-6C
97Zen-7
97Zen5x7-18
97ZenGolImp-18
97ZenZGol-7
97ZenZSil-7
98Be A PPA-256
98Be A PPAA-256
98Be A PPAAF-256
98Be A PPSE-256
98Be APG-256
98BowBes-6

98BowBesAR-6
98BowBesMIF-F12
98BowBesMIFAR-F12
98BowBesMIFR-F12
98BowBesR-6
98Fin-80
98FinDouMF-M42
98FinDouMF-M45
98FinDouMF-M48
98FinDouMF-M50
98FinDouSMFR-M42
98FinDouSMFR-M45
98FinDouSMFR-M48
98FinDouSMFR-M50
98FinNo P-80
98FinNo PR-80
98FinRedL-R17
98FinRedLR-R17
98FinRef-80
98O-PChr-154
98O-PChrR-154
98O-PChrSB-SB18
98O-PChrSBR-SB18
98Pac-344
98PacAur-148
98PacAurCF-38
98PacAurCFC-38
98PacAurCFIB-38
98PacAurCFR-38
98PacAurCFS-38
98PacCroR-105
98PacCroRLS-105
98PacCroRPotG-20
98PacCroRPP-20
98PacDynI-145
98PacDynIIB-145
98PacDynIR-145
98PacDynITC-20
98PacEO P-17
98PacGolCD-27
98PacIceB-344
98PacOmeEP1o1-17
98PacOmeFtF-5
98PacOmeH-188
98PacOmeO-29
98PacOmeODI-188
98PacOmeP-17
98PacOmePI-18
98PacOmePIB-18
98PacOmeR-188
98PacPar-186
98PacParC-186
98PacParEG-186
98PacParH-186
98PacParIB-186
98PacParS-186
98PacParSDDC-15
98PacParTCD-20
98PacRed-344
98PacRev-112
98PacRevADC-29
98PacRevCTL-15
98PacRevIS-112
98PacRevR-112
98PacRevS-30
98PacTeaC-20
98PacTim-15
98PinEpiGE-6
98RevThrPA-7
98WRevThrPA-7
98SP Aut-66
98SP AutA-13
98SP AutA-14
98SP AutSM-S11
98SP AutSotTG-KT
98SP AutSS-SS25
98SPxFinR-64
98SPxFinS-64
98SPXTopP-46
98SPXTopPF-46
98SPXTopPHH-H23
98SPXTopPLI-L4
98SPXTopPPS-PS29
98SPXTopPR-46
98SSASotT-KT
98Top-154
98TopAut-A6
98TopGolLC1-12
98TopGolLC1B-12
98TopGolLC1BOo0-12
98TopGolLC1Oo0-12
98TopGolLC1R-12
98TopGolLC1ROo0-12
98TopGolLC2-12
98TopGolLC2B-12
98TopGolLC2BOo0-12
98TopGolLC2Oo0-12
98TopGolLC2R-12
98TopGolLC2ROo0-12
98TopGolLC3-12
98TopGolLC3B-12
98TopGolLC3BOo0-12
98TopGolLC3R-12
98TopGolLC3ROo0-12
98TopGolLGR'-GR6
98TopGolLGR'BOo0-GR6
98TopGolLGR'Oo0-GR6
98TopGolLGR'ROo0-GR6
98TopMysFBR-M13
98TopMysFG-M13
98TopMysFGR-M13
98TopMysFS-M13
98TopMysFSR-M13
98TopO-P-154
98TopRedLGR'-GR6
98TopSeaB-SB18
98UC-160
98UCMBH-BH2
98UCSB-SQ30
98UCSG-SQ30
98UCSR-SQ30
98UD ChoPCR-160
98UD ChoR-160
98UD3-52
98UD3-112
98UD3-172
98UD3DieC-52
98UD3DieC-112
98UD3DieC-172
98UppDec-154
98UppDecBD-66
98UppDecDD-66
98UppDecE-154
98UppDecE1o1-154
98UppDecFF-FF9
98UppDecFF-FF9
98UppDecFQ1-FF9
98UppDecFQ2-FF9
98UppDecFIT-FT19
98UppDecFIT1-FT19
98UppDecFIT2-FT19
98UppDecFIT3-FT19
98UppDecGR-154
98UppDecLSH-LS21
98UppDecLSHQ1-LS21
98UppDecLSHQ2-LS21
98UppDecLSHQ3-LS21
98UppDecM-156
98UppDecM1-M4
98UppDecM2-M4
98UppDecMGS-156
98UppDecMOH-OT12
98UppDecMPG-PG2
98UppDecMSS-156
98UppDecMSS-156
98UppDecGU-66
98UppDecTD-66
98UppDecWFG-WF23
98UppDecWFP-WF23
99AurSty-16
99Pac-328
99PacAur-113
99PacAurPD-113
99PacCop-328
99PacGol-328
99PacGolCD-30
99PacHomaA-20
99PacIceB-328
99PacPreD-328
99PacTeaL-21
99RetHoc-64
99SP AutPS-66
99UppDecCL-65
99UppDecCLCLC-65
99UppDecEotG-E8
99UppDecM-158
99UppDecMGS-GU10
99UppDecMGS-158
99UppDecMGUSA-GU10
99UppDecMSS-158
99UppDecMSS-158
99UppDecRG-G2C
99UppDecRG-64
99UppDecRGI-G2C
99UppDecRII-KT
99UppDecRIL1-KT
99UppDecRP-64

**Tkacz, Andrzej**
69SweWorC-194

**Tkaczuk, Daniel**
95Sla-17
96UppDec-387
96UppDecBD-38
96UppDecBDG-38
97BeeAutA-65
97BowCHL-8
97BowCHL-152
97BowCHLBowBesAR-4
97BowCHLBowBesR-4
97BowCHLOPC-8
97BowCHLOPC-152
97ColCho-298
97PinBee-65
97PinBeeGP-65
97UppDecBD-55
97UppDecBDDD-55
97UppDecBDQD-55
97UppDecBDTD-55
98BowBes-146
98BowBesAR-146
98BowBesR-146
98BowCHL-34
98BowCHLGA-34
98BowCHLOI-34
98BowCHLSC-SC3
98BowChrC-34
98BowChrCGA-34
98BowChrCGAR-34
98BowChrCOI-34
98BowChrCOIR-34
98BowChrCR-34
98O-PChr-227
98O-PChrR-227
98SPXTopP-65
98SPXTopPF-65
98SPXTopPR-65
98Top-227
98TopO-P-227
98UC-254
98UD ChoPCR-254
98UD ChoR-254
98UppDecBD-93
98UppDecDD-93
98UppDecGJ-GJ10
98UppDecQD-93
98UppDecTD-93
99QuePeeWHWCCS-9

**Toal, Mike**
88OilTenAnn-111

**Tocchet, Rick**
81SauSteMG-22
82SauSteMG-21
83SauSteMG-22
85FlyPos-29
86FlyPos-27
87OPC-2
87PanSti-134
87SauSteMG-26
87Top-2
88OPC-177
88OPCSti-99
88PanSti-326
88Top-177
89FlyPos-26
89Kra-57
89KraAllSS-2
89OPC-80
89OPCSti-108
89PanSti-295
89Top-80
90Bow-108
90BowHatTri-14
90BowTif-108
90FlyPos-24
90Kra-58
90OPC-26
90OPCPre-120
90PanSti-121
90ProSet-225
90ProSet-374
90Sco-80
90ScoCan-80
90ScoHotRS-40
90Top-26
90TopTeaSL-9
90TopTif-26
90UppDec-263
90UppDec-488
90UppDecF-263
90UppDecF-488
91Bow-230
91FlyJCP-24
91Kra-45
91McDUppD-2
91OPC-160
91OPCPre-64
91PanSti-229
91PanSti-331
91Par-129
91Par-354
91ParFre-129
91ParFre-354
91PenFoo-5
91Pin-20
91PinFre-20
91ProSet-177
91ProSet-311
91ProSet-580
91ProSetFre-177
91ProSetFre-311
91ProSetFre-580
91ProSetPla-88
91ScoAme-9
91ScoAme-302
91ScoAme-334
91ScoCan-9
91ScoCan-306
91ScoCan-364
91ScoKel-2
91StaClu-35
91Top-160
91TopTeaSL-13
91UppDec-91
91UppDec-122
91UppDec-503
91UppDecF-91
91UppDecF-122
91UppDecF-503
92Bow-159
92OPC-148
92PanSti-226
92PanStiFre-226
92Par-139
92ParCheP-CP12
92ParEmel-139
92PenCokC-24
92PenFoo-4
92Pin-282
92PinFre-282
92ProSet-138
92Sco-245
92ScoCan-245
92SeaPat-37
92StaClu-76
92Top-70
92TopGol-70G
92Ult-172
92UppDec-238
92UppDec-454
93Don-267
93Lea-109
93OPCPre-72
93OPCPreG-72
93PanSti-80
93Par-428
93ParEmel-428
93PenFoo-4
93PenSti-12
93Pin-174
93PinAllS-14
93PinAllSC-14
93PinCan-174
93Pow-196
93Sco-340
93ScoCan-340
93StaClu-329
93StaCluAS-20
93StaCluFDI-329
93StaCluO-329
93SweSemWCS-200
93TopPre-72
93TopPreG-72
93Ult-225
93UppDec-179
93UppDec-233
93UppDecHT-HT12
93UppDecLAS-16
93UppDecSP-126
94BeAPA99A-G18
94Fin-52
94FinnJaaK-95
94FinnJaaK-358
94FinRef-52
94FinSupTW-52
94Fla-83
94Fle-100
94HocWit-58
94Lea-100
94Lea-474
94LeaLim-117
94OPCPre-281
94OPCPreSE-281
94OPCPreSE-346
94ParSE-SE79
94ParSEG-SE79
94ParVin-V75
94Pin-371
94PinArtP-371
94PinBoo-BR18
94PinGam-GR12
94PinRinC-371
94ScoChelt-CI11
94Sel-2
94SelGol-2
94SP-55
94SPDieCut-55
94StaClu-160
94StaCluFDI-160
94StaCluMOMS-160
94StaCluSTWC-160
94TopPre-281
94TopPreSE-281
94TopPreSE-346
94Ult-309
94UppDec-224
94UppDecElelce-224
94UppDecSPI-SP129
94UppDecSPIDC-SP129
95BeAPla-82
95BeAPSig-S82
95BeAPSigSDC-S82
95Bow-36
95BowAllFoi-36
95CanGamNHLP-137
95ColCho-254
95ColChoPC-254
95ColChoPCP-254
95Don-41
95Emo-86
95EmoNteP-10
95Fin-133
95FinnSemWC-98
95FinRef-133
95ImpSti-59
95Lea-29
95LeaLim-112
95Met-74
95MetIW-15
95ParInt-287
95ParIntEI-287
95PlaOneoOne-161
95ProMag-70
95Sco-37
95ScoBlaIce-37
95ScoBlaIceAP-37
95SelCer-98
95SelCerMG-98
95SkyImp-83
95SkyImp-247
95StaClu-32
95StaCluFea-F5
95StaCluMOMS-32
95Sum-103
95SumArtP-103
95SumIce-103
95SweGloWC-92
95Top-264
95TopHidGem-15HG
95TopOPCI-264
95TopSupSki-64
95TopSupSkiPla-64
95Ult-79
95UltCreCra-19
95UltGoIM-79
95UppDec-274
95UppDecEleIce-274
95UppDecEleIceG-274
95UppDecSpeE-SE40
95UppDecSpeEdiG-SE40
95Zen-118
95ZenGifG-5
96ColCho-18
96Don-122
96DonPrePro-122
96DurAllT-DC14
96Fle-8
96Lea-90
96LeaPreP-90
96MetUni-11
96NHLProSTA-70
96Pin-23
96PinArtP-23
96PinFoi-23
96PinPreS-23
96PinRinC-23
96PlaOneoOne-376
96Sco-92
96ScoArtPro-92
96ScoDeaCAP-92
96ScoIceB-92
96ScoSpeAP-92
96SkyImp-9
96SP-12
96SweSemW-89
96TeaOut-38
96TopNHLP-111
96TopPicOI-111
96Ult-12
96UltGoIM-12
96UppDec-10
96UppDecBD-55
96UppDecBDG-55
96UppDecGN-X32
96UppDecIce-4
96UppDecIcePar-4
97Be A PPAD-127
97Be A PPAPD-127
97BeAPla-127
97BeAPlaaut-127
97Don-45
97DonLim-83
97DonLimExp-83
97DonPreProG-45
97DonPreProS-45
97DonPri-148
97DonPriSoA-148
97Pac-311
97PacCop-311
97PacEmeGre-311
97PacIceB-311
97PacOme-178
97PacOmeC-178
97PacOmeDG-178
97PacOmeEG-178
97PacOmeG-178
97PacOmeIB-178
97PacPar-145
97PacParC-145
97PacParDG-145
97PacParEG-145
97PacParIB-145
97PacParRed-145
97PacRed-311
97PacSil-311
97PinIns-174
97Sco-246
97UppDec-339
98Be A PPA-105
98Be A PPAA-105
98Be A PPAAF-105
98Be A PPTBASG-105
98Be APG-105
98BowBes-38
98BowBesAR-38
98BowBesR-38
98O-PChr-34
98O-PChrR-34
98Pac-92
98PacAur-149
98PacCroR-106
98PacCroRLS-106
98PacDynI-146
98PacDynIIB-146
98PacDynIR-146
98PacIceB-92
98PacOmeH-189
98PacOmeR-189
98PacPar-187
98PacParC-187
98PacParEG-187
98PacParH-187
98PacParIB-187
98PacParS-187
98PacRed-92
98PacRev-113
98PacRevR-113
98Top-34
98TopGolLC1-48
98TopGolLC1B-48
98TopGolLC1BOo0-48
98TopGolLC1Oo0-48
98TopGolLC1R-48
98TopGolLC1ROo0-48
98TopGolLC2-48
98TopGolLC2B-48
98TopGolLC2BOo0-48
98TopGolLC2Oo0-48
98TopGolLC2R-48
98TopGolLC2ROo0-48
98TopGolLC3-48
98TopGolLC3B-48
98TopGolLC3BOo0-48
98TopGolLC3Oo0-48
98TopGolLC3R-48
98TopGolLC3ROo0-48
98TopO-P-34
98UppDec-341
98UppDecE-341
98UppDecE1o1-341
98UppDecGR-341
98UppDecM-162
98UppDecMGS-162
98UppDecMSS-162
99Pac-329
99PacAur-112
99PacAurPD-112
99PacCop-329
99PacGol-329
99PacPreD-329
99UppDecM-159
99UppDecMGS-159
99UppDecMSS-159
99UppDecMSS-159

**Tocher, Ryan**
917thInnSOHL-204
95Sla-235

**Todd, Dick**
897thInnSOHL-123
907thInnSOHL-376
917thInnSOHL-123
91PetPet-23

**Todd, Kevin**
88ProAHL-329
89ProAHL-205
90ProAHLIHL-570
91Gil-40
91OPC-400
91OPCPre-22
91Par-97
91Par-444
91ParFre-97
91ParFre-444
91Pin-308
91PinFre-308
91ProSet-548
91ProSetFre-548
91ScoAme-397
91ScoCan-287
91Top-400
91UppDec-401
91UppDecF-401
92Bow-21
92OilTeal-19
92OPC-1
92PanSti-275
92PanSti-O
92PanStiFre-275
92PanStiFre-O
92Par-94
92Par-238
92Par-285
92ParEmel-94
92ParEmel-238
92ParEmel-285
92Pin-272
92PinFre-272
92PinTea2-272
92PinTea2F-22
92ProSet-94
92ProSetRGL-7
92Sco-162
92ScoCan-162
92ScoYouS-19
92StaClu-465
92Top-15
92Top-228
92TopGol-15G
92TopGol-228G
92Ult-121
92UppDec-11
92UppDec-303
92UppDec-365
92UppDecART-AR3
92UppDecART-AR7
93BlaCok-18
93Lea-15
93Par-37
93ParEmel-37
93Pin-270
93PinCan-270
93Pow-318
93Sco-338
93Sco-507
93ScoCan-338
93ScoCan-507
93ScoGol-507
93StaClu-8
93StaCluFDI-8
93StaCluFDIO-8
93StaCluO-8
93Ult-294
93UppDec-88
93UppDec-440
93UppDecSP-33
94BeAPSig-74
94Lea-350
94Par-108
94ParGol-108
94UppDec-120
94UppDecEleIce-120
95ParInt-374
95ParIntEI-374
95UppDec-364
95UppDecEleIce-364
95UppDecEleIceG-364
96BeAPAut-101
96BeAPAutSil-101
96BeAPla-101
96ColCho-127
96Duc-4
96UppDecIce-1
96UppDecIcePar-1
97ColCho-11
97Pac-182
97PacCop-182
97PacEmeGre-182
97PacIceB-182
97PacRed-182
97PacSil-182
97ScoMigDPla-6
97ScoMigDPlu-6
97ScoMigDuc-6
97UppDec-3

**Toews, Lorne**
907thInnSWHL-36
917thInnSWHL-316
94WheThu-17

**Toffolo, Mark**
78LouGae-19

**Toivola, Marko**
94FinnSIS-303
95FinnSIS-119

**Toivola, Tero**
93FinnSIS-75

**Tokarczyk, Trevor**
95SauSteMG-22
95Sla-367
96SauSteMG-25
96SauSteMGA-25

**Tokarz, Leszek**
79PanSti-135

**Toljanich, Mark**
917thInnSWHL-300
93RedDeeR-24

**Tolkunov, Dmitri**
98BowCHL-117
98BowCHLGA-117
98BowCHLOI-117
98BowChrC-117
98BowChrCGA-117
98BowChrCGAR-117
98BowChrCOI-117
98BowChrCOIR-117
98QueRem-21

**Tolvanen, J.**
95GerDELE-168

**Tomajko, Jan**
95CzeAPSE-122
95UppDec-544
95UppDecEleIce-544
95UppDecEleIceG-544
96CzeAPSE-277

**Toman, Ilmar**
94GerDELE-419

**Tomasek, Ales**
96CzeAPSE-6
96CzeAPSE-194

**Tomasoni, Dick**
72SweSemWC-137

**Tomassoni, Dave**

82SweSemHVS-128
**Tomassoni, Ron**
92HarCri-29
**Tomberlin, Justin**
92MaiBlaB-30
93MaiBlaB-50
94RalIce-19
**Tomek, Michal**
94CzeAPSE-245
95CzeAPSE-23
96CzeAPSE-225
**Tomilin, Vitali**
92Cla-53
93UppDec-278
96ClaGol-53
**Tomlak, Mike**
89WhaJunM-21
900PC-95
90PanSti-46
90ProAHLIHL-176
90ProSet-452
90Top-95
90TopTif-95
90UppDec-343
90UppDecF-343
90WhaJr7E-24
91Bow-14
910PC-410
91PanSti-319
91ProAHLCHL-114
91ScoCan-538
91StaClu-266
91Top-410
91UppDec-310
91UppDecF-310
94MilAdm-24
95MilAdmBO-18
96MilAdmBO-25
**Tomlinson, Dave**
91ProAHLCHL-346
92St.JohML-22
93ClaProPro-12
95ColEdgI-114
96GerDELE-170
98GerDELE-227
**Tomlinson, Jeff**
92RalIce-16
**Tomlinson, Kirk**
88KitRan-22
88ProIHL-40
91ProAHLCHL-122
93LasVegThu-28
95PeoRiv-23
**Tomlinson, Mike**
897thInnSOHL-108
907thInnSOHL-373
917thInnSOHL-126
91PetPet-10
**Tomlinson, Shayne**
93NorMicW-27
**Tommila, Esa**
93FinnJyvHS-89
93FinnSIS-126
94FinnSIS-285
95FinnSIS-188
**Tompkins, Dan**
95SeaThu-29
**Toms, C.**
10C56-29
**Toms, Jeff**
917thInnSOHL-334
93SauSteMG-23
93SauSteMGM-25
97Pac-342
97PacCop-342
97PacEmeGre-342
97PacIceB-342
97PacRed-342
97PacSil-342
**Ton, Andy**
91SweSemWCS-190
93SweSemWCS-118
93SwiHNL-180
95SwiHNL-153
95SwiHNL-520
**Ton, Petr**
94CzeAPSE-62
95CzeAPSE-95
96CzeAPSE-89
**Tonelli, John**
79IslTrans-20
790PC-146
79Top-146
800PC-305
810PC-218
820PC-213
820PCSti-49
82PosCer-12
83IslTealss-17
830PC-20
830PCSti-74
830PCSti-75
83PufSti-21
84IslIsIN-14
840PC-138
840PCSti-80
840PCSti-81
84Top-103
85IslIsIN-15
850PC-41
850PCBoxB-O
850PCSti-80
850PCSti-116
85Top-41
85TopBoxB-O

85TopStiIns-7
86FlamRedR-28
860PC-132
860PCSti-81
86Top-132
87FlamRedRP-29
870PC-84
870PCSti-47
87Top-84
88EssAllSta-45
88KinSmo-23
880PCSti-87
89KinSmo-13
890PC-8
89PanSti-90
89Top-8
90Bow-148
90BowTif-148
90KinSmo-14
900PC-281
90PanSti-235
90ProSet-129A
90ProSet-129B
90Sco-89
90ScoCan-89
90Top-281
90TopTif-281
90UppDec-95
90UppDecF-95
91BlaCok-27
91Bow-175
910PC-161
910PCPre-37
910PCPre-159
91PanSti-90
91Pin-284
91PinFre-284
91ProSet-373
91ProSetFre-373
91ProSetP-22
91ProSetPla-142
91ScoAme-172
91ScoCan-172
91ScoCan-540
91ScoRoo-17T
91StaClu-189
91Top-161
92ProSet-263
92ScoCan-342
92StaClu-159
92Top-119
92TopGol-119G
93IslCheBA-9
**Toninato, Jim**
85MinDul-12
**Tookey, Tim**
81FreExp-8
82FreExp-8
88ProAHL-191
89ProAHL-353
90ProAHLIHL-51
91ProAHLCHL-281
94ClaProP-84
**Toomey, Dick**
72SweSemWC-134
**Toomey, Sean**
85MinDul-24
**Toor, Gary**
95TriAme-27
**Topatigh, Lucio**
93SweSemWCS-221
95FinnSemWC-175
**Topazzini, Ted**
52JunBluT-145
**Topolnisky, Craig**
94GerDELE-147
**Toporowski, Brad**
917thInnSWHL-14
**Toporowski, Kerry**
89SpoChi-17
907thInnSWHL-206
917thInnSMC-85
91ProAHLCHL-499
91UltDra-48
92IndIce-24
93LasVegThu-29
94LasVegThu-29
95AdiRedW-22
**Toporowski, Shayne**
93PriAlbR-18
94PriAlbR-18
95ColEdgI-84
95St.JohML-18
96St.JohML-23
97Don-224
97DonPreProG-224
97DonPreProS-224
**Toppazzini, Jerry**
44BeeGro2P-71
53Par-98
54Top-21
55BruPho-17
55BruTealss-20
57Top-5
58Top-45
59Top-38
60ShiCoi-110
60Top-28
61ShiCoi-9
61Top-9
62Top-13
62TopHocBuc-22
63Top-18
91UltOriS-55

91UltOriSF-55
92ParParR-PR27
94ParMisL-1
**Toppazzini, Zellio**
44BeeGro2P-72
52Par-73
**Torchetti, John**
94CenHocL-88
**Torchia, Mike**
88KitRan-6
897thInnSOHL-191
897thInnSOHL-192
89KitRan-6
907thInnSMC-31
907thInnSOHL-244
90KitRan-6
917thInnSCHLAW-2
917thInnSOHL-75
91StaPicH-26
91UltDra-50
91UltDraP-3
93ClaProPro-119
95Don-143
95Lea-213
95Sco-311
95ScoBlaIce-311
95ScoBlaIceAP-311
95Ult-43
95UltGoIM-43
**Torgajev, Pavel**
93FinnSIS-46
94FinnSIS-309
95ParInt-302
95ParIntEI-302
95Ult-215
**Torkki, Jari**
88ProIHL-117
89ProIHL-55
91SweSemWCS-22
93FinnJyvHS-239
94FinnSIS-194
94FinnSIS-13
94FinnSISFI-20
95FinnSIS-104
95FinnSIS-189
95FinnSISL-34
96FinnSISR-107
96GerDELE-194
**Tormanen, Antti**
93FinnSIS-16
94FinnJaaK-28
94FinnSIS-63
94FinnSISMN-7
94FinnSISND-8
95Bow-117
95BowAllFoi-117
95Don-347
95DonRatRoo-15
95Fin-118
95FinnKarWCL-22
95FinnSemWC-49
95FinnSISGC-23
95FinnSISL-17
95FinnRef-118
95Met-196
95ParInt-415
95ParInt-522
95ParIntEI-415
95ParIntEI-522
95SelCer-111
95SelCerMG-111
95Sen-20
95SP-105
95StaClu-156
55StaCluMOMS-156
95Sum-174
95SumArtP-174
95SumIce-174
95TopSupSkiSR-SR13
95Ult-360
95UppDec-347
95UppDecEleIce-347
95UppDecEleIceG-347
95Zen-135
95ZenRooRC-4
96ColCho-184
96Sco-265
96ScoArtPro-265
96ScoDeaCAP-265
96ScoGolB-265
96ScoSpeAP-265
96Sum-161
96SumArtP-161
96SumIce-161
96SumMet-161
96SumPreS-161
96SweSemW-15
96UppDec-114
96Zen-78
96ZenArtP-78
**Tornberg, Johan**
93SweSemE-30
94SweLeaE-212
95SweLeaE-294
95SweUppDE-190
**Tornberg, Ove**
85SwePanS-189
**Tornlund, Inge**
67SweHoc-211
**Tornqvist, Alf**
84SweSemE-126
**Tornqvist, Johan**
86SwePanS-16
**Toropchenko, Leonid**

93ClaProPro-95
93CleLum-14
93CleLumPos-21
94ClaProP-212
**Torrel, Doug**
92HamCan-26
**Torrey, Bill**
84IslIsIN-28
85IslIsIN-28
**Torrey, Jeff**
91BriColJHL-88
92RicRen-19
**Torstensson, Sverker**
69SweSemHoc-182
73SweHoc-63
73SweWorCS-63
74SweHoc-193
**Torstensson, Ulf**
65SweCorI-178
67SweHoc-129
69SweHoc-109
70SweHoc-87
71SweHoc-192
72SweHoc-178
74SweWCS-267
**Torti, Sloan**
86KinCan-27
**Tortorella, John**
88ProAHL-202
89SabCam-25
90SabCam-26
95RochAmeSS-25
**Tory, Jeff**
91BriColJHL-159
92BriColJHL-138
**Tosio, Renato**
91SweSemWCS-177
93SweSemWCS-109
94SwiHNL-60
95SweGloWC-209
95SwiHNL-87
**Toskala, Vesa**
95ColCho-335
95ColChoPC-335
95ColChoPCP-335
95FinnSIS-230
95FinnSISDD-7
95FinnSISL-100
96FinnSISR-27
96FinnSISRMA-6
96FinnSISRRE-8
**Toth, Kaleb**
94PriAlbR-19
**Toth, Radek**
94CzeAPSE-251
95CzeAPSE-126
**Toth, Tony (Anthony)**
91AirCanSJHL-E50
92MPSPhoSJHL-164
**Tottle, Scott**
85FreExp-1
**Touhey, Bill**
330PCV304A-26
33V252CanG-48
**Toujikov, Rouslan**
94RoaExp-10
**Toupal, Kamil**
94CzeAPSE-31
95CzeAPSE-61
96CzeAPSE-244
**Toupal, Radek**
91SweSemWCS-117
94GerDELE-377
95CzeAPSE-65
95FinnSemWC-149
96CzeAPSE-250
**Toupin, Simon**
907thInnSQMJHL-19
917thInnSQMJHL-177
**Tousignant, Dan**
85MinDul-23
**Touzimsky, Zdenek**
94CzeAPSE-73
95CzeAPSE-182
96CzeAPSE-316
**Tovall, Trevor**
89SpoChi-18
907thInnSWHL-192
917thInnSMC-86
**Townsend, Scott**
907thInnSWHL-37
917thInnSWHL-325
93LetHur-18
**Townshend, Graeme**
89BruSpoAU-10
89ProAHL-70
90ProAHLIHL-133
91ProAHLCHL-456
93SenKraS-23
**Toye, Randy**
917thInnSWHL-20
**Trachta, David**
94CzeAPSE-161
95CzeAPSE-262
**Trachta, Karel**
94CzeAPSE-289
95CzeAPSE-242
**Trachta, Tomas**
96CzeAPSE-83
**Tracy, Joe**
91SweSemE-247
**Tracy, Tripp**
92HarCri-30
96RicRen-23

**Tracze, Steve**
95Sla-42
**Trader, Larry**
83CanNatJ-15
87CanaPos-33
87CanaVacS-44
88ProAHL-71
**Trainer, Chris**
83KitRan-28
**Trampuh, Robbie**
92BriColJHL-131
**Trapp, Barry**
82RegPat-24
83RegPat-24
**Trapp, Bob**
23V1281PauC-42
**Trapp, Doug**
82RegPat-6
83RegPat-6
**Trattner, Jurgen**
98GerDELE-197
**Traub, Puss**
23V1281PauC-23
**Traverse, Patrick**
90MonAAA-25
917thInnSQMJHL-63
98PacOmeH-171
98PacOmeODI-171
98PacOmeR-171
**Travis, Shannon**
89ProIHL-174
**Travnicek, Zdenek**
94GerDELE-300
95GerDELE-389
96GerDELE-72
**Traynor, Paul**
94KitRan-8
95Sla-139
96KitRan-25
97BowCHL-39
97BowCHLOPC-39
**Trboyevich, Dean**
96AncAce-15
**Trebil, Dan**
92MinGolG-21
93MinGolG-25
94MinGolG-27
95MinGolG-27
97Don-105
97DonPreProG-105
97DonPreProS-105
**Trebil, Ryan**
96MinGolGGAS-26
**Trefilov, Andrei**
910PCIns-45R
91StaPicH-49
92RusStaRA-4
92UppDec-345
92UppDec-514
93ClaProPBC-BC2
93ClaProPro-30
93Don-409
93Par-29
93ParEmel-29
93Pow-311
93Sco-599
93ScoCan-599
93ScoGol-599
94Don-244
94FinnJaaK-136
94Lea-87
94OPCPre-166
94OPCPreSE-166
94Par-36
94ParGol-36
94St.JohF-25
94TopPreSE-166
94Ult-271
95Don-273
95ParInt-296
95ParIntEI-296
95SweGloWC-163
95UppDec-277
95UppDecEleIce-277
95UppDecEleIceG-277
96UppDec-225
**Tremblay, Dave**
907thInnSQMJHL-29
917thInnSQMJHL-80
**Tremblay, Didier**
98BowCHL-84
98BowCHLGA-84
98BowCHLOI-84
98BowChrC-84
98BowChrCGA-84
98BowChrCGAR-84
98BowChrCOI-84
98BowChrCOIR-84
98BowChrCR-84
98Vald'OF-7
**Tremblay, Frank**
85LonKni-16
**Tremblay, Gilles**
44BeeGro2P-290A
44BeeGro2P-290B
60YorPreP-36
61ShiCoi-112
61YorYelB-4
62Par-46
62ShiMetC-24
62YorIroOTra-34
63ChePho-53

63Par-21
63Par-80
63TorSta-38
63YorWhiB-21
64BeeGro3P-117A
64BeeGro3P-117B
64CanaPos-19
64CocCap-70
64Top-2
65CanaSteG-10
65Coc-69
66CanalGA-8
66Top-4
66TopUSAT-4
67CanalGA-5
67PosFliB-9
67Top-5
68CanalGA-5
68CanaPosBW-17
680PC-66
68PosCerM-25
68Top-66
690PC-168
800QueRem-22
94ParTalB-77
95Par66-71
95Par66Coi-71
**Tremblay, J.C.**
44BeeGro2P-291A
44BeeGro2P-291B
60ShiCoi-36
61ShiCoi-118
61YorYelB-34
62Par-54
62ShiMetC-30
62YorIroOTra-6
63ChePho-54
63Par-31
63Par-90
63TorSta-39
63YorWhiB-24
64BeeGro3P-118
64CanaPos-20
64CocCap-57
64TorSta-46
65CanaSteG-11
65Coc-57
65Top-69
66CanalGA-1
66Top-5
66TopUSAT-5
67CanalGA-3
67PosFliB-3
67PosFliB-10
67Top-73
67YorActOct-9
67YorActOct-12
67YorActOct-13
67YorActOct-19
67YorActOct-24
68CanalGA-3
68CanaPosBW-18
680PC-59
680PC-206
68PosCerM-26
68ShiCoi-79
68Top-59
69CanaPosC-30
690PC-5
69Top-5
70CanaPin-16
70ColSta-64
70DadCoo-129
70EssPowPla-3
700PC-170
70PosCerS-16
70SarProSta-99
71CanaPos-24
71FriLay-5
710PC-130
710PC-252
71SarProSta-97
71Top-130
71TorSun-165
72NordPos-21
720PC-293
72SluCupWHA-18
73NordTeal-21
730PCWHAP-2
73QuaOatWHA-30
740PCWHA-18
750PCWHA-62
750PCWHA-130
76NordMarA-12
76NordPos-19
760PCWHA-2
760PCWHA-40
760PCWHA-42
770PCWHA-44
81TCMA-3
94ParTalB-74
95Par66-67
95Par66Coi-67
**Tremblay, J.F.**
96RoaExp-11
**Tremblay, Jacques**
87KinCan-4
**Tremblay, Jean**
50QueCit-19
**Tremblay, Jerome**
97BowCHL-75
97BowCHLOPC-75
**Tremblay, Jules**

51LavDaiLSJ-42
**Tremblay, Ludger**
51LavDaiQSHL-11
52St.LawS-49
56QueAce-16
**Tremblay, Marc-Aurele**
51LavDaiLSJ-34
**Tremblay, Mario**
74CanaPos-25
75CanaPos-19
750PCNHL-223
75Top-223
76CanaPos-22
760PCNHL-97
76Top-97
77CanaPos-24
770PCNHL-163
77Top-163
78CanaPos-26
780PC-376
79CanaPos-25
790PC-123
79Top-123
80CanaPos-25
800PC-297
80PepCap-29
81CanaPos-26
810PC-192
81PosSta-23
82CanaPos-25
82CanaSte-20
820PC-193
820PCSti-30
82PosCer-10
83CanaPos-28
83Ess-20
830PC-199
830PCSti-69
83PufSti-5
83Vac-57
84CanaPos-28
84KelAccD-5A
84KelAccD-5B
840PC-274
840PCSti-161
85CanaPa-6
85CanaPla-7
85CanaPos-38
85CanaPos-39
85CanaPos-24
850PC-245
850PCSti-134
860PC-223
860PCSti-9
95CanaPos-19
96CanaPos-31
**Tremblay, Michel**
98BowCHL-93
98BowCHLGA-93
98BowCHLOI-93
98BowChrC-93
98BowChrCGA-93
98BowChrCGAR-93
98BowChrCOI-93
98BowChrCOIR-93
98BowChrCR-93
**Tremblay, Nelson**
67ColChe-14
**Tremblay, Nils**
51LavDaiQSHL-51
51LavDaiS-51
52St.LawS-90
**Tremblay, Paul**
51LavDaiLSJ-29
**Tremblay, Philippe**
93AmoLesFAM-21
**Tremblay, Regis**
907thInnSMC-65
**Tremblay, Sebastien**
907thInnSQMJHL-246
917thInnSQMJHL-269
96RimOceQPP-25
**Tremblay, Simon**
98QueRem-20
**Tremblay, Trevor**
90RayJrC-21
91RayJrC-19
**Tremblay, Vincent**
81MapLeaP-22
82MapLeaP-35
820PC-334
820PCSti-70
83PenTealP-32
93DruVol-13
**Tremblay, Yannick**
96St.JohML-24
97PacOme-226
97PacOmeC-226
97PacOmeDG-226
97PacOmeEG-226
97PacOmeG-226
97PacOmeNB-226
98Pac-423
98PacIceB-423
98PacRed-423
98UppDec-190
98UppDecE-190
98UppDecE101-190
98UppDecGR-190
**Trepanier, Pascal**
917thInnSQMJHL-107
98BowBes-128
98BowBesAR-128
98BowBesR-128
**Trepanier, Serge**

Tuer, Al • 691


❑ 93AmoLesFAM-22
**Tresl, Ladislav**
❑ 88ProAHL-102
❑ 89HalCit-26
❑ 89ProAHL-175
❑ 90ProAHLIHL-433
❑ 91ProAHLCHL-614
**Tretiak, Doug**
❑ 92HamCan-27
**Tretiak, Vladislav**
❑ 69SweWorC-131
❑ 70SweHocS-160
❑ 70SweHocS-161
❑ 70SweHocS-230
❑ 70SweHocS-314
❑ 71SweHocS-27
❑ 72SweHocS-27
❑ 72SweSemWC-20
❑ 73SweHocS-77
❑ 73SweWorCS-77
❑ 74SweHocS-1
❑ 74SweSemHVS-26
❑ 79PanSti-140
❑ 80USSOlyTMP-9
❑ 81SweSemHVS-37
❑ 82SweSemHVS-51
❑ 83RusNatT-19
❑ 90AlbIntTC-20
❑ 90BlaCok-28
❑ 91FutTreC72-5
❑ 91FutTreC72-11
❑ 91FutTreC72-31
❑ 91FutTreC72-71
❑ 91RusStaNHL-10
❑ 91SweSemWCS-241
❑ 92AlbIntTC-21
❑ 92FutTre76CC-103
❑ 92FutTre76CC-109
❑ 92FutTre76CC-110
❑ 92FutTre76CC-163
❑ 92FutTrePS-1
❑ 95SweGloWC-235
❑ 99RetHoc-102
❑ 99UppDecRDR-DR15
❑ 99UppDecRDRI-DR15
❑ 99UppDecRG-102
❑ 99UppDecRII-VT
❑ 99UppDecRIL1-VT
❑ 99UppDecRP-102
**Tretowicz, Dave**
❑ 92Cla-112
❑ 92PhoRoa-23
❑ 96ClaGol-112
**Trihey, Harry**
❑ 83HalFP-F14
❑ 85HalFC-88
**Trim, Lee**
❑ 84BraWheK-13
❑ 85BraWheK-13
**Trimper, Tim**
❑ 80BlaWhiBor-14
❑ 80JetPos-23
❑ 80OPC-357
❑ 81JetPos-22
❑ 81OPC-376
❑ 82OPC-394
❑ 82PosCer-21
❑ 84SprInd-12
**Trineer, Neil**
❑ 81KinCan-8
**Tripp, John**
❑ 95Cla-55
❑ 95Cla-91
❑ 95Sla-238
❑ 97BowCHL-9
❑ 97BowCHLOPC-9
**Triulzi, Roberto**
❑ 95FinnSemWC-194
**Trnka, Pavel**
❑ 97PacOme-9
❑ 97PacOmeC-9
❑ 97PacOmeDG-9
❑ 97PacOmeEG-9
❑ 97PacOmeG-9
❑ 97PacOmeIB-9
❑ 97SPAut-170
❑ 98UppDec-35
❑ 98UppDecE-35
❑ 98UppDecE1o1-35
❑ 98UppDecGR-35
**Trofimenkoff, David**
❑ 917thInnSWHL-353
❑ 93LetHur-19
**Trojan, Richard**
❑ 94GerDELE-418
❑ 95GerDELE-390
❑ 96GerDELE-298
**Trombley, Rhett**
❑ 917thInnSWHL-99
❑ 91SasBla-7
❑ 93SauSteMG-16
❑ 94TolSto-22
❑ 95LasVegThu-20
❑ 96LasVegThu-21
**Troschinsky, Alexei**
❑ 91UppDecCWJC-6
**Trottier, Bryan**
❑ 75HerSta-18
❑ 76OPCNHL-67
❑ 76OPCNHL-115
❑ 76OPCNHL-216
❑ 76Top-67
❑ 76Top-115
❑ 76Top-216
❑ 76TopGlol-15
❑ 77OPCNHL-105
❑ 77Top-105
❑ 78OPC-10
❑ 78OPC-64
❑ 78OPC-65
❑ 78OPC-325
❑ 78Top-10
❑ 78Top-64
❑ 78Top-65
❑ 79IslTrans-21
❑ 79OPC-2
❑ 79OPC-3
❑ 79OPC-7
❑ 79OPC-100
❑ 79OPC-165
❑ 79Top-2
❑ 79Top-3
❑ 79Top-7
❑ 79Top-100
❑ 79Top-165
❑ 80OPC-40
❑ 80Top-40
❑ 81OPC-200
❑ 81OPC-210
❑ 81OPCSti-152
❑ 81OPCSti-160
❑ 81Top-41
❑ 81Top-E132
❑ 82McDSti-25
❑ 82OPC-5
❑ 82OPC-214
❑ 82OPC-215
❑ 82OPCSti-47
❑ 82OPCSti-48
❑ 82PosCer-12
❑ 83IslTeaIss-18
❑ 83OPC-21
❑ 83OPCSti-76
❑ 83OPCSti-77
❑ 83PufSti-21
❑ 847EDis-34
❑ 84IslIslN-15
❑ 84IslIslN-37
❑ 84KelWin-26
❑ 84OPC-139
❑ 84OPC-214
❑ 84OPCSti-86
❑ 84OPCSti-87
❑ 84Top-104
❑ 84Top-160
❑ 857ECreCar-12
❑ 85IslIslN-16
❑ 85IslIslN-35
❑ 85IslIslNT-1
❑ 85IslIslNT-2
❑ 85IslIslNT-3
❑ 85IslIslNT-4
❑ 85IslIslNT-5
❑ 85IslIslNT-6
❑ 85IslIslNT-7
❑ 85IslIslNT-8
❑ 85IslIslNT-9
❑ 85IslIslNT-10
❑ 85IslIslNT-11
❑ 85IslIslNT-12
❑ 85IslIslNT-13
❑ 85IslIslNT-14
❑ 85IslIslNT-15
❑ 85IslIslNT-16
❑ 85IslIslNT-17
❑ 85IslIslNT-18
❑ 85IslIslNT-19
❑ 85IslIslNT-20
❑ 85IslIslNT-21
❑ 85IslIslNT-22
❑ 85IslIslNT-23
❑ 85IslIslNT-24
❑ 85IslIslNT-25
❑ 85IslIslNT-26
❑ 85IslIslNT-27
❑ 85IslIslNT-28
❑ 85IslIslNT-29
❑ 85IslIslNT-30
❑ 85IslIslNT-31
❑ 85IslIslNT-32
❑ 85IslIslNT-33
❑ 85OPC-60
❑ 85OPCSti-65
❑ 85Top-60
❑ 86OPC-155
❑ 86OPCBoxB-P
❑ 86OPCSti-216
❑ 86Top-155
❑ 86TopBoxB-P
❑ 87OPC-60
❑ 87OPCBoxB-O
❑ 87OPCMin-41
❑ 87OPCSti-240
❑ 87PanSti-96
❑ 87Top-60
❑ 87TopBoxB-O
❑ 88EssAllSta-46
❑ 88FriLayS-2
❑ 88OPC-97
❑ 88OPCSti-112
❑ 88PanSti-293
❑ 88Top-97
❑ 89Isl-19
❑ 89OPC-149
❑ 89OPCSti-118
❑ 89PanSti-269
❑ 89PanSti-382
❑ 89Top-149
❑ 90OPC-6
❑ 90OPC-291
❑ 90OPCPre-121
❑ 90PanSti-83
❑ 90PenFoo-15
❑ 90ProSet-192
❑ 90ProSet-511
❑ 90Sco-270
❑ 90ScoCan-270
❑ 90ScoRoo-106T
❑ 90Top-6
❑ 90Top-291
❑ 90TopTif-6
❑ 90TopTif-291
❑ 90UppDec-137
❑ 90UppDec-425
❑ 90UppDecF-137
❑ 90UppDecF-425
❑ 91Bow-93
❑ 91OPC-472
❑ 91Par-208
❑ 91Par-360
❑ 91Par-431
❑ 91Par-461
❑ 91ParFre-208
❑ 91ParFre-360
❑ 91ParFre-431
❑ 91PenCokE-19
❑ 91PenFoo-12
❑ 91PenFooCS-1
❑ 91Pin-241
❑ 91PinFre-241
❑ 91ProSet-192
❑ 91ProSet-319
❑ 91ProSetFre-192
❑ 91ProSetPla-216
❑ 91ProSetPlaPC-PC19
❑ 91ScoAme-229
❑ 91ScoCan-229
❑ 91StaClu-91
❑ 91Top-472
❑ 91UppDec-329
❑ 91UppDecF-329
❑ 92Bow-152
❑ 92Bow-243
❑ 92OPC-107
❑ 92OPC-130
❑ 92OPC25Al-9
❑ 92PanSti-227
❑ 92PanStiFre-227
❑ 92Sco-157
❑ 92Sco-518
❑ 92ScoCan-157
❑ 92StaClu-26
❑ 92Top-416
❑ 92TopGol-416G
❑ 93Don-268
❑ 93Lea-318
❑ 93OPCPre-296
❑ 93OPCPreG-296
❑ 93Par-431
❑ 93ParEmel-431
❑ 93PenFoo-12
❑ 93Pin-411
❑ 93PinCan-411
❑ 93Pow-416
❑ 93Sco-567
❑ 93ScoCan-567
❑ 93ScoGol-567
❑ 93TopPre-296
❑ 93TopPreG-296
❑ 93Ult-398
❑ 93UppDecLAS-50
❑ 94HocWit-44
❑ 96PenTri-4
❑ 96SweSemWHL-HL9
❑ 97SPAutMoaL-M4
❑ 97SPAutTra-T4
❑ 99UppDecCL-30
❑ 99UppDecCLCLC-30
**Trottier, Dave**
❑ 33OPCV304B-62
❑ 33V252CanG-47
❑ 34BeeGro1P-208
❑ 34SweCap-26
❑ 36OPCV304D-126
❑ 36V356WorG-70
❑ 37OPCV304E-168
**Trottier, Eric**
❑ 92QueIntP-52
**Trottier, Guy**
❑ 70EssPowPla-25
❑ 70MapLeaP-14
❑ 71Baz-23
❑ 71MapLeaP-20
❑ 71OPC-5
❑ 71TorSun-273
❑ 72NatOttWHA-22
❑ 72OPC-326
❑ 73QuaOatWHA-40
**Trottier, Joel**
❑ 95Sla-273
❑ 97BowCHL-10
❑ 97BowCHLOPC-10
❑ 98BowCHL-40
❑ 98BowCHLGA-40
❑ 98BowCHLOI-40
❑ 98BowChrC-40
❑ 98BowChrCGA-40
❑ 98BowChrCGAR-40
❑ 98BowChrCOI-40
❑ 98BowChrCOIR-40
❑ 98BowChrCR-40
**Trottier, Monty**
❑ 81IndChe-20
❑ 82IndChe-21
❑ 84SprInd-19
**Trottier, Rocky**
❑ 82MedHatT-20
❑ 83MedHatT-13
❑ 89ProAHL-356
**Trotz, Barry**
❑ 81RegPat-21
❑ 90ProAHLIHL-218
❑ 91ProAHLCHL-572
❑ 93PorPir-3
❑ 95PorPir-22
❑ 96PorPir-NNO
**Trudel, Jean-Guy**
❑ 917thInnSQMJHL-190
❑ 95SlaMemC-64
❑ 96PeoRiv-23
❑ 96PeoRivPA-23
❑ 98KanCitB-14
**Trudel, Louis**
❑ 34BeeGro1P-83
❑ 34BeeGro1P-185
❑ 34DiaMatS-59
❑ 35DiaMatT2-62
❑ 35DiaMatT3-57
❑ 35DiaMatT4-14
❑ 35DiaMatT5-13
❑ 35DiaMatTI-67
❑ 36V356WorG-71
❑ 37DiaMatT6-13
**Trudel, Martin**
❑ 907thInnSQMJHL-65
❑ 917thInnSQMJHL-11
**True, Mads**
❑ 92MPSPhoSJHL-5
**True, Soren**
❑ 89ProIHL-47
❑ 90ProAHLIHL-530
❑ 91ProAHLCHL-311
**True, Stuart**
❑ 90ProAHLIHL-531
**Trukhno, Leonid**
❑ 91OPCIns-61R
**Trumbley, Rob**
❑ 96WheNai-36
**Trunchion, Wayne**
❑ 94GuiFla-2
❑ 95GuiFla-2
**Trunov, Vladimir**
❑ 73SweHocS-105
❑ 73SweWorCS-105
**Truntschka, Bernd**
❑ 89SweSemWCS-120
❑ 91SweSemWCS-164
❑ 93SweSemWCS-162
❑ 94GerDELE-95
❑ 96GerDELE-285
**Truntschka, Gerd**
❑ 89SweSemWCS-115
❑ 91SweSemWCS-163
❑ 93SweSemWCS-157
❑ 95GerDELE-96
**Trzcinski, Jason**
❑ 91LakSupSL-29
**Tschumi, Rick**
❑ 91SweSemWCS-181
❑ 93SweSemWCS-114
❑ 93SwiHNL-145
❑ 95SweGloWC-216
❑ 95SwiHNL-144
**Tschupp, Chris**
❑ 94EriPan-12
**Tselios, Nikos**
❑ 97BowCHL-138
❑ 97BowCHLAu-18
❑ 97BowCHLOPC-138
❑ 97UppDecBD-91
❑ 97UppDecBDDD-91
❑ 97UppDecBDQD-91
❑ 97UppDecBDTD-91
❑ 98UC-304
❑ 98UD ChoPCR-304
❑ 98UD ChoR-304
**Tsujiura, Steve**
❑ 83SprInd-6
❑ 88ProAHL-159
❑ 93SwiHNL-234
**Tsulygin, Nikolai**
❑ 92UppDec-614
❑ 93Cla-46
❑ 93Par-526
❑ 93ParEmel-526
❑ 93Pin-507
❑ 93PinCan-507
❑ 94Cla-78
❑ 94ClaDraGol-78
❑ 94ClaTri-T1
❑ 95ColEdgI-16
❑ 95SigRoo-33
❑ 95SigRooSig-33
❑ 96Duc-14
**Tsybouk, Evgeni**
❑ 96LetHur-23
**Tsygankov, Gennady**
❑ 71SweHocS-28
❑ 72SweHocS-28
❑ 72SweSemWC-7
❑ 73SweHocS-81
❑ 73SweWorCS-81
❑ 74SweHocS-2
❑ 74SweSemHVS-29
❑ 79PanSti-145
❑ 91FutTreC72-67
**Tsygurov, Denis**
❑ 94Don-200
❑ 94Fla-23
❑ 94Lea-161
❑ 94OPCPre-29
❑ 94OPCPreSE-29
❑ 94Pin-258
❑ 94PinArtP-258
❑ 94PinRinC-258
❑ 94PinRooTP-3
❑ 94TopPre-29
❑ 94TopPreSE-29
❑ 94Ult-307
❑ 96CzeAPSE-106
**Tsyplakov, Alexander**
❑ 96CzeAPSE-151
**Tsyplakov, Vladimir**
❑ 94ClaProP-103
❑ 95LasVegThu-21
❑ 95ParInt-377
❑ 95ParIntEl-377
❑ 96UppDecBD-8
❑ 96UppDecBDG-8
❑ 97Be A PPAD-197
❑ 97Be A PPAPD-197
❑ 97BeAPla-197
❑ 97BeAPlaAut-197
❑ 97ColCho-122
❑ 97Pac-82
❑ 97PacCop-82
❑ 97PacDyn-61
❑ 97PacDynC-61
❑ 97PacDynDG-61
❑ 97PacDynEG-61
❑ 97PacDynIB-61
❑ 97PacDynR-61
❑ 97PacDynSil-61
❑ 97PacDynTan-43
❑ 97PacEmeGre-82
❑ 97PacIceB-82
❑ 97PacInv-69
❑ 97PacInvC-69
❑ 97PacInvEG-69
❑ 97PacInvIB-69
❑ 97PacInvR-69
❑ 97PacInvS-69
❑ 97PacOme-115
❑ 97PacOmeC-115
❑ 97PacOmeDG-115
❑ 97PacOmeEG-115
❑ 97PacOmeG-115
❑ 97PacOmeIB-115
❑ 97PacRed-82
❑ 97PacRev-68
❑ 97PacRevC-68
❑ 97PacRevE-68
❑ 97PacRevIB-68
❑ 97PacRevR-68
❑ 97PacRevS-68
❑ 97PacSil-82
❑ 97SPAut-74
❑ 97UppDec-289
❑ 98Be A PPA-213
❑ 98Be A PPAA-213
❑ 98Be A PPAAF-213
❑ 98Be A PPSE-213
❑ 98Be APG-213
❑ 98O-PChr-14
❑ 98O-PChrR-14
❑ 98Pac-247
❑ 98PacAur-91
❑ 98PacDynI-92
❑ 98PacDynIIB-92
❑ 98PacDynIR-92
❑ 98PacIceB-247
❑ 98PacOmeH-115
❑ 98PacOmeODI-115
❑ 98PacOmeR-115
❑ 98PacPar-110
❑ 98PacParC-110
❑ 98PacParEG-110
❑ 98PacParH-110
❑ 98PacParIB-110
❑ 98PacParS-110
❑ 98PacRed-247
❑ 98SPxFin-40
❑ 98SPxFinR-40
❑ 98SPxFinS-40
❑ 98Top-14
❑ 98TopO-P-14
❑ 98UC-101
❑ 98UD ChoPCR-101
❑ 98UD ChoR-101
❑ 98UDCP-101
❑ 98UppDec-287
❑ 98UppDecE-287
❑ 98UppDecE1o1-287
❑ 98UppDecGR-287
❑ 99Pac-200
❑ 99PacCop-200
❑ 99PacGol-200
❑ 99PacIceB-200
❑ 99PacPreD-200
❑ 99UppDecM-98
❑ 99UppDecMGS-98
❑ 99UppDecMSS-98
❑ 99UppDecMSS-98
**Tsyrkunov, Oleg**
❑ 95Sla-287
**Tucker, Chris**
❑ 91UppDecCWJC-67
❑ 94RicRen-18
**Tucker, Darcy**
❑ 917thInnSWHL-88
❑ 93KamBla-22
❑ 94Fin-164
❑ 94FinRef-164
❑ 94FinSupTW-164
❑ 94Pin-537
❑ 94PinArtP-537
❑ 94PinRinC-537
❑ 94UppDec-503
❑ 94UppDecEleIce-503
❑ 95ColEdgI-42
❑ 95DonCanWJT-13
❑ 95FreCan-27
❑ 95SlaMemC-12
❑ 95TopCanWJ-16CJ
❑ 96CanaPos-32
❑ 96CanaShe-24
❑ 96ColEdgFL-23
❑ 96ColEdgPC-5
❑ 96DonCanI-143
❑ 96DonCanIGPP-143
❑ 96DonCanIRPP-143
❑ 96FlePic-148
❑ 96LeaGolR-8
❑ 96LeaPre-134
❑ 96LeaPrePP-134
❑ 96Pin-223
❑ 96PinArtP-223
❑ 96PinFoi-223
❑ 96PinRinC-223
❑ 96Sum-176
❑ 96SumArtP-176
❑ 96SumIce-176
❑ 96SumMet-176
❑ 96SumPreS-176
❑ 96UppDec-281
❑ 96UppDecIce-33
❑ 96UppDecIcePar-33
❑ 96Zen-130
❑ 96ZenArtP-130
❑ 97Be A PPAD-119
❑ 97Be A PPAPD-119
❑ 97BeAPla-119
❑ 97BeAPlaAut-119
❑ 97CanaPos-24
❑ 97Don-182
❑ 97DonCanI-111
❑ 97DonCanIDS-111
❑ 97DonCanIPS-111
❑ 97DonLim-34
❑ 97DonLim-53
❑ 97DonLimExp-34
❑ 97DonLimExp-53
❑ 97DonPre-28
❑ 97DonPreCttC-28
❑ 97DonPreProG-182
❑ 97DonPreProS-182
❑ 97Lea-77
❑ 97LeaFraMat-77
❑ 97LeaFraMDC-77
❑ 97LeaInt-77
❑ 97LeaIntUI-77
❑ 97Pac-83
❑ 97PacCop-83
❑ 97PacEmeGre-83
❑ 97PacIceB-83
❑ 97PacRed-83
❑ 97PacSil-83
❑ 97Pin-140
❑ 97PinPrePBB-140
❑ 97PinPrePBC-140
❑ 97PinPrePBM-140
❑ 97PinPrePBY-140
❑ 97PinPrePFC-140
❑ 97PinPrePFM-140
❑ 97PinPrePFY-140
❑ 97PinPrePla-140
❑ 97Sco-202
❑ 97ScoCan-13
❑ 97ScoCanPla-13
❑ 97UppDec-88
❑ 98O-PChr-183
❑ 98O-PChrR-183
❑ 98Pac-407
❑ 98PacIceB-407
❑ 98PacOmeH-222
❑ 98PacOmeODI-222
❑ 98PacOmeR-222
❑ 98PacRed-407
❑ 98ScoCanPre-13
❑ 98Top-183
❑ 98TopO-P-183
❑ 99Pac-398
❑ 99PacAur-133
❑ 99PacAurPD-133
❑ 99PacCop-398
❑ 99PacGol-398
❑ 99PacIceB-398
❑ 99PacPreD-398
❑ 99UppDecM-192
❑ 99UppDecMGS-192
❑ 99UppDecMSS-192
❑ 99UppDecMSS-192
**Tucker, Gib**
❑ 89KitRan-22
❑ 907thInnSMC-43
❑ 907thInnSOHL-245
❑ 90KitRan-20
❑ 917thInnSOHL-85
**Tucker, John**
❑ 82KitRan-24
❑ 83KitRan-20
❑ 84SabBluS-20
❑ 85OPCSti-184
❑ 85SabBluS-27
❑ 85SabBluSS-27
❑ 86OPC-67
❑ 86OPCSti-48
❑ 86SabBluS-28
❑ 86SabBluSSma-28
❑ 86Top-67
❑ 87OPC-154
❑ 87OPCSti-145
❑ 87PanSti-30
❑ 87SabBluS-27
❑ 87SabWonBH-29
❑ 87Top-154
❑ 88OPC-74
❑ 88PanSti-229
❑ 88SabBluS-26
❑ 88SabWonBH-29
❑ 88Top-74
❑ 89CapKod-12
❑ 89OPC-37
❑ 89PanSti-212
❑ 89Top-37
❑ 90OPC-374
❑ 90OPCPre-122
❑ 90PanSti-157
❑ 90ProSet-322
❑ 90ProSet-420
❑ 90SabBluS-23
❑ 90SabCam-27
❑ 90Top-374
❑ 90TopTif-374
❑ 90UppDec-387
❑ 90UppDecF-387
❑ 91StaClu-335
❑ 92LigShe-23
❑ 92Par-405
❑ 92ParEmel-405
❑ 92Ult-414
❑ 92UppDec-548
❑ 93Don-328
❑ 93Lea-21
❑ 93LigSealR-26
❑ 93OPCPre-473
❑ 93OPCPreG-473
❑ 93PanSti-212
❑ 93Par-462
❑ 93ParEmel-462
❑ 93Pin-144
❑ 93PinCan-144
❑ 93Pow-235
❑ 93Sco-354
❑ 93ScoCan-354
❑ 93StaClu-38
❑ 93StaCluFDI-38
❑ 93StaCluFDIO-38
❑ 93StaCluO-38
❑ 93TopPre-473
❑ 93TopPreG-473
❑ 93Ult-211
❑ 93UppDec-409
❑ 94CanGamNHLP-226
❑ 94Don-87
❑ 94Lea-38
❑ 94LigPhoA-25
❑ 94OPCPre-132
❑ 94OPCPreSE-132
❑ 94ParSE-SE170
❑ 94ParSEG-SE170
❑ 94Pin-226
❑ 94PinArtP-226
❑ 94PinRinC-226
❑ 94Sco-23
❑ 94ScoGol-23
❑ 94ScoPla-23
❑ 94ScoPlaTS-23
❑ 94TopPre-132
❑ 94TopPreSE-132
❑ 94Ult-210
❑ 95BeAPla-120
❑ 95BeAPSig-S120
❑ 95BeAPSigDC-S120
❑ 95CanGamNHLP-249
❑ 95ColCho-104
❑ 95ColChoPC-104
❑ 95ColChoPCP-104
❑ 95Don-311
❑ 95Lea-269
❑ 95LigTeaI-18
❑ 95ParInt-192
❑ 95ParIntEl-192
❑ 95PlaOneoOne-312
❑ 95Sco-191
❑ 95ScoBlaIce-191
❑ 95ScoBlaIceAP-191
❑ 95UppDec-78
❑ 95UppDecEleIce-78
❑ 95UppDecEleIceG-78
**Tuckwell, Harry**
❑ 23V1281PauC-51
**Tudin, Dan**
❑ 95Sla-266
**Tuer, Al**
❑ 81RegPat-22
❑ 82RegPat-9
❑ 83RegPat-9
❑ 88ProAHL-66
❑ 89ProAHL-289
❑ 90ProAHLIHL-313
❑ 91ProAHLCHL-367
**Tugnutt, Ron**
❑ 87NordGenF-30
❑ 88ProAHL-117
❑ 89Nord-38
❑ 89NordGenF-29
❑ 89NordPol-27
❑ 89OPC-263
❑ 89PanSti-332
❑ 90NordPet-25
❑ 90NordTeal-25
❑ 90OPC-367
❑ 90PanSti-142
❑ 90ProSet-258

❑ 90Sco-126
❑ 90ScoCan-126
❑ 90Top-367
❑ 90TopTif-367
❑ 90UppDec-27
❑ 90UppDecF-27
❑ 91Bow-151
❑ 91NordPanTS-22
❑ 91NordPet-30
❑ 91OPC-181
❑ 91PanSti-267
❑ 91Par-149
❑ 91Par-277
❑ 91ParFre-149
❑ 91ParFre-277
❑ 91Pin-124
❑ 91PinFre-124
❑ 91ProSet-202
❑ 91ProSetFre-202
❑ 91ProSetPla-98
❑ 91ScoAme-41
❑ 91ScoCan-41
❑ 91ScoYouS-33
❑ 91StaClu-115
❑ 91Top-181
❑ 91UppDec-277
❑ 91UppDecF-277
❑ 92OilIGA-24
❑ 92OPC-211
❑ 92Par-290
❑ 92ParEmel-290
❑ 92Pin-366
❑ 92PinFre-366
❑ 92Sco-387
❑ 92ScoCan-387
❑ 92Ult-298
❑ 93Don-12
❑ 93Don-453
❑ 93DonSpeP-A
❑ 93Lea-277
❑ 93OPCPre-286
❑ 93OPCPreG-286
❑ 93Pin-187
❑ 93PinCan-187
❑ 93Pow-13
❑ 93Sco-368
❑ 93Sco-504
❑ 93ScoCan-368
❑ 93ScoCan-504
❑ 93ScoGol-504
❑ 93StaClu-325
❑ 93StaCluFDI-325
❑ 93StaCluO-325
❑ 93TopPre-286
❑ 93TopPreG-286
❑ 93Ult-263
❑ 93UppDec-426
❑ 93UppDecSP-5
❑ 94CanaPos-27
❑ 94Don-69
❑ 94Lea-46
❑ 94OPCPre-523
❑ 94OPCPreSE-523
❑ 94Pin-172
❑ 94PinArtP-172
❑ 94PinRinC-172
❑ 94Sco-21
❑ 94ScoGol-21
❑ 94ScoPla-21
❑ 94ScoPlaTS-21
❑ 94TopPre-523
❑ 94TopPreSE-523
❑ 94UppDec-321
❑ 94UppDecElelce-321
❑ 95ColEdgI-57
❑ 95PorPir-23
❑ 95Sco-70
❑ 95ScoBlaIce-70
❑ 95ScoBlaIceAP-70
❑ 96SenPizH-24
❑ 97Be A PPAD-36
❑ 97Be A PPAPD-36
❑ 97BeAPla-36
❑ 97BeAPlaAut-36
❑ 97ColCho-181
❑ 97Don-103
❑ 97DonCanI-63
❑ 97DonCanIDS-63
❑ 97DonCanIPS-63
❑ 97DonPreProG-103
❑ 97DonPreProS-103
❑ 97DonPri-76
❑ 97DonPriSoA-76
❑ 97Pac-87
❑ 97PacCop-87
❑ 97PacCroR-93
❑ 97PacCroREG-93
❑ 97PacCroRIB-93
❑ 97PacCroRS-93
❑ 97PacEmeGre-87
❑ 97PacIceB-87
❑ 97PacInv-96
❑ 97PacInvC-96
❑ 97PacInvEG-96
❑ 97PacInvIB-96
❑ 97PacInvR-96
❑ 97PacInvS-96
❑ 97PacOme-158
❑ 97PacOmeC-158
❑ 97PacOmeDG-158
❑ 97PacOmeEG-158
❑ 97PacOmeG-158
❑ 97PacOmeIB-158
❑ 97PacRed-87
❑ 97PacRev-95
❑ 97PacRevC-95
❑ 97PacRevE-95
❑ 97PacRevIB-95
❑ 97PacRevR-95
❑ 97PacRevS-95
❑ 97PacSil-87
❑ 97Pin-99
❑ 97PinArtP-99
❑ 97PinCer-29
❑ 97PinCerMB-29
❑ 97PinCerMG-29
❑ 97PinCerMR-29
❑ 97PinCerR-29
❑ 97PinIns-82
❑ 97PinInsCC-82
❑ 97PinInsEC-82
❑ 97PinPrePBB-99
❑ 97PinPrePBC-99
❑ 97PinPrePBM-99
❑ 97PinPrePBY-99
❑ 97PinPrePFC-99
❑ 97PinPrePFM-99
❑ 97PinPrePFY-99
❑ 97PinPrePla-99
❑ 97PinRinC-99
❑ 97PinTotCMPG-29
❑ 97PinTotCPB-29
❑ 97PinTotCPG-29
❑ 97PinTotCPR-29
❑ 97Sco-49
❑ 97ScoArtPro-49
❑ 97ScoGolBla-49
❑ 97UppDec-113
❑ 98Be A PPA-244
❑ 98Be A PPAA-244
❑ 98Be A PPAAF-244
❑ 98Be A PPSE-244
❑ 98Be APG-244
❑ 98Pac-316
❑ 98PacIceB-316
❑ 98PacOmeH-169
❑ 98PacOmeODI-169
❑ 98PacOmeR-169
❑ 98PacPar-167
❑ 98PacParC-167
❑ 98PacParEG-167
❑ 98PacParH-167
❑ 98PacParIB-167
❑ 98PacParS-167
❑ 98PacRed-316
❑ 99Pac-296
❑ 99PacAur-101
❑ 99PacAurGU-14
❑ 99PacAurPD-101
❑ 99PacCop-296
❑ 99PacGol-296
❑ 99PacIceB-296
❑ 99PacIn tCN-13
❑ 99PacPreD-296
❑ 99UppDecM-142
❑ 99UppDecMGS-142
❑ 99UppDecMPS-RT
❑ 99UppDecMSS-142
❑ 99UppDecMSS-142

**Tulik, Brian**
❑ 92RalIce-17
❑ 92RalIce-31

**Tully, Brent**
❑ 907thInnSOHL-374
❑ 917thInnSOHL-130
❑ 91PetPet-5
❑ 92UppDec-592
❑ 93Cla-31
❑ 93DonTeaC-21
❑ 93PetPet-9
❑ 93Pin-464
❑ 93PinCan-464
❑ 93UppDec-530
❑ 95UppDecWJA-9
❑ 96SyrCru-44
❑ 96GerDELE-184

**Tumbach, Troy**
❑ 94GerDELE-144
❑ 95GerDELE-41

**Tuohimaa, Juha**
❑ 83SweSemE-158
❑ 85SwePanS-205
❑ 86SwePanS-173
❑ 87SwePanS-172

**Tuomainen, Marko**
❑ 91UppDec-675
❑ 91UppDecCWJC-38
❑ 91UppDecF-675
❑ 92ClaKni-23
❑ 95ColCho-121
❑ 95ColChoPC-121
❑ 95ColChoPCP-121
❑ 95ColEdgI-36
❑ 95Don-56
❑ 95Lea-171
❑ 95Top-189
❑ 95TopOPCI-189
❑ 95UppDec-12
❑ 95UppDecElelce-12
❑ 95UppDecElelceG-12

**Tuomenoksa, Antti**
❑ 93FinnJyvHS-170
❑ 93FinnSIS-167
❑ 94FinnSIS-89
❑ 94FinnSISH-3
❑ 95FinnSIS-190

**Tuominen, Jouni**
❑ 94FinnSIS-331
❑ 95FinnSIS-144

**Tuominen, Pasi**
❑ 95FinnSIS-364
❑ 96FinnSISR-158

**Tuomisto, Pekka**
❑ 93FinnJyvHS-24
❑ 93FinnSIS-102
❑ 93SweSemWCS-81
❑ 94FinnSIS-18
❑ 95FinnSIS-214

**Tupa, Martin**
❑ 95CzeAPSE-185
❑ 96CzeAPSE-317

**Turcer, Michal**
❑ 95SloPeeWT-26

**Turcotte, Alfie**
❑ 83CanaPos-29
❑ 84CanaPos-29
❑ 84CanaPos-30
❑ 84KelWin-25
❑ 89ProAHL-81
❑ 90ProAHLIHL-200
❑ 94GerDELE-440

**Turcotte, Darren**
❑ 89RanMarMB-8
❑ 90Bow-216
❑ 90BowTif-216
❑ 90OPC-48
❑ 90OPCBoxB-K
❑ 90OPCPre-123
❑ 90PanSti-107
❑ 90ProSet-208
❑ 90ProSet-400
❑ 90Sco-241
❑ 90ScoCan-241
❑ 90ScoYouS-16
❑ 90Top-48
❑ 90TopBoxB-K
❑ 90TopTif-48
❑ 90UppDec-274
❑ 90UppDec-475
❑ 90UppDecF-274
❑ 90UppDecF-475
❑ 91Bow-62
❑ 91McDUppD-7
❑ 91OPC-71
❑ 91PanSti-285
❑ 91Par-118
❑ 91ParFre-118
❑ 91Pin-47
❑ 91PinFre-47
❑ 91ProSet-160
❑ 91ProSet-310
❑ 91ProSetFre-160
❑ 91ProSetFre-310
❑ 91ScoAme-196
❑ 91ScoCan-196
❑ 91ScoYouS-28
❑ 91StaClu-346
❑ 91SweSemWCS-139
❑ 91Top-71
❑ 91UppDec-90
❑ 91UppDec-155
❑ 91UppDec-513
❑ 91UppDecF-90
❑ 91UppDecF-155
❑ 91UppDecF-513
❑ 92Bow-156
❑ 92OPC-387
❑ 92PanSti-235
❑ 92PanStiFre-235
❑ 92Par-345
❑ 92ParEmel-345
❑ 92Pin-33
❑ 92PinFre-33
❑ 92ProSet-114
❑ 92Sco-224
❑ 92ScoCan-224
❑ 92StaClu-360
❑ 92Top-203
❑ 92TopGol-203G
❑ 92Ult-143
❑ 92UppDec-169
❑ 93Don-224
❑ 93Lea-45
❑ 93OPCPre-246
❑ 93OPCPreG-246
❑ 93PanSti-94
❑ 93Par-356
❑ 93ParEmel-356
❑ 93Pin-386
❑ 93PinCan-386
❑ 93Pow-166
❑ 93Pow-357
❑ 93Sco-24
❑ 93Sco-570
❑ 93ScoCan-24
❑ 93ScoCan-570
❑ 93ScoGol-570
❑ 93StaClu-476
❑ 93StaCluFDI-476
❑ 93StaCluO-476
❑ 93TopPre-246
❑ 93TopPreG-246
❑ 93Ult-341
❑ 93UppDecSP-66
❑ 93WhaCok-22
❑ 94BeAPla-R14
❑ 94BeAPla-R124
❑ 94BeAPSig-35
❑ 94CanGamNHLP-119
❑ 94Don-286
❑ 94Fla-75
❑ 94Fle-90
❑ 94HocWit-30
❑ 94Lea-210
❑ 94OPCPre-2
❑ 94OPCPreSE-2
❑ 94ParSE-SE75
❑ 94ParSEG-SE75
❑ 94Pin-161
❑ 94PinArtP-161
❑ 94PinRinC-161
❑ 94Sco-169
❑ 94ScoGol-169
❑ 94ScoPla-169
❑ 94ScoPlaTS-169
❑ 94SP-49
❑ 94SPDieCut-49
❑ 94StaClu-201
❑ 94StaCluFDI-201
❑ 94StaCluMOMS-201
❑ 94StaCluSTWC-201
❑ 94TopPre-2
❑ 94TopPreSE-2
❑ 94Ult-94
❑ 94UppDec-84
❑ 94UppDecElelce-84
❑ 94UppDecSPI-SP123
❑ 94UppDecSPIDC-SP123
❑ 95ColCho-24
❑ 95ColChoPC-24
❑ 95ColChoPCP-24
❑ 95Don-43
❑ 95Don-295
❑ 95DonProPoi-10
❑ 95Emo-79
❑ 95JetTealss-25
❑ 95Lea-173
❑ 95Met-167
❑ 95ParInt-93
❑ 95ParInt-498
❑ 95ParIntEl-93
❑ 95ParIntEl-498
❑ 95Pin-20
❑ 95PinArtP-20
❑ 95PinRinC-20
❑ 95PlaOneoOne-267
❑ 95ProMag-130
❑ 95Sco-224
❑ 95ScoBlaIce-224
❑ 95ScoBlaIceAP-224
❑ 95SkyImp-186
❑ 95StaClu-27
❑ 95StaCluMOMS-27
❑ 95Sum-22
❑ 95SumArtP-22
❑ 95SumIce-22
❑ 95SweGloWC-123
❑ 95Top-251
❑ 95TopHomGUSA-HGA7
❑ 95TopOPCI-251
❑ 95Ult-72
❑ 95Ult-328
❑ 95UltGolM-72
❑ 95UppDec-481
❑ 95UppDecElelce-481
❑ 95UppDecElelceG-481
❑ 95UppDecSpeE-SE37
❑ 95UppDecSpeE-SE180
❑ 95UppDecSpeEdiG-SE37
❑ 95UppDecSpeEdiG-SE180
❑ 96BeAPAut-70
❑ 96BeAPAutSil-70
❑ 96BeAPla-70
❑ 96ColCho-235
❑ 96ColCho-330
❑ 96Don-59
❑ 96DonPrePro-59
❑ 96Lea-184
❑ 96LeaPreP-184
❑ 96MetUni-141
❑ 96NHLProSTA-130
❑ 96Pin-165
❑ 96PinArtP-165
❑ 96PinFoi-165
❑ 96PinPreS-165
❑ 96PinRinC-165
❑ 96PlaOneoOne-413
❑ 96Sco-219
❑ 96ScoArtPro-219
❑ 96ScoDeaCAP-219
❑ 96ScoGolB-219
❑ 96ScoSpeAP-219
❑ 96SP-142
❑ 96Sum-54
❑ 96SumArtP-54
❑ 96SumIce-54
❑ 96SumMet-54
❑ 96SumPreS-54
❑ 96Ult-154
❑ 96UltGolM-154
❑ 96UppDec-333
❑ 97ColCho-219
❑ 97Don-176
❑ 97DonLim-191
❑ 97DonLimExp-191
❑ 97DonPreProG-176
❑ 97DonPreProS-176
❑ 97Pac-229
❑ 97PacCop-229
❑ 97PacEmeGre-229
❑ 97PacIceB-229
❑ 97PacRed-229
❑ 97PacSil-229
❑ 97Sco-251
❑ 97ScoBlu-8
❑ 97ScoBluPla-8
❑ 97ScoBluPre-8
❑ 98Be A PPA-74
❑ 98Be A PPAA-74
❑ 98Be A PPAAF-74
❑ 98Be A PPTBASG-74
❑ 98Be APG-74
❑ 98Pac-373
❑ 98PacAur-105
❑ 98PacDynI-105
❑ 98PacDynIIB-105
❑ 98PacDynIR-105
❑ 98PacIceB-373
❑ 98PacPar-128
❑ 98PacParC-128
❑ 98PacParEG-128
❑ 98PacParH-128
❑ 98PacParIB-128
❑ 98PacParS-128
❑ 98PacRed-373
❑ 98UppDec-297
❑ 98UppDecE-297
❑ 98UppDecE1o1-297
❑ 98UppDecGR-297

**Turek, Filip**
❑ 94CzeAPSE-109
❑ 95CzeAPSE-68
❑ 96CzeAPSE-253

**Turek, Matt**
❑ 917thInnSOHL-341

**Turek, Roman**
❑ 93SweSemWCS-90
❑ 93SweSemWCS-96
❑ 94CzeAPSE-93
❑ 95FinnSemWC-142
❑ 95GerDELE-289
❑ 96ColCho-358
❑ 96CzeAPSE-338
❑ 96Fla-106
❑ 96FlaBlul-106
❑ 96SP-175
❑ 96SweSemW-102
❑ 96SweSemWAS-AS1
❑ 96SweSemWSG-SG6
❑ 96UppDecBD-1
❑ 96UppDecBDG-1
❑ 96UppDecGN-X28
❑ 97Be A PPAD-35
❑ 97Be A PPAPD-35
❑ 97BeAPla-35
❑ 97BeAPlaAut-35
❑ 97Don-64
❑ 97DonLim-42
❑ 97DonLim-113
❑ 97DonLimExp-42
❑ 97DonLimExp-113
❑ 97DonPreProG-64
❑ 97DonPreProS-64
❑ 97DonPri-29
❑ 97DonPriSoA-29
❑ 97Lea-56
❑ 97LeaFraMat-56
❑ 97LeaFraMDC-56
❑ 97LeaInt-56
❑ 97LeaIntUI-56
❑ 97PacInvNRB-66
❑ 97PinIns-79
❑ 97PinInsCC-79
❑ 97PinInsEC-79
❑ 97PinInsSto-9
❑ 97Sco-36
❑ 97ScoArtPro-36
❑ 97ScoGolBla-36
❑ 97UppDec-53
❑ 97UppDecIce-35
❑ 97UppDecIceP-35
❑ 97UppDecIPS-35
❑ 98Be A PPA-41
❑ 98Be A PPAA-41
❑ 98Be A PPAAF-41
❑ 98Be A PPTBASG-41
❑ 98Be APG-41
❑ 98Pac-184
❑ 98PacIceB-184
❑ 98PacOmeH-76
❑ 98PacOmeODI-76
❑ 98PacOmeR-76
❑ 98PacPar-71
❑ 98PacParC-71
❑ 98PacParEG-71
❑ 98PacParH-71
❑ 98PacParIB-71
❑ 98PacParS-71
❑ 98PacRed-184
❑ 99Pac-130
❑ 99PacCop-130
❑ 99PacGol-130
❑ 99PacIceB-130
❑ 99PacPreD-130

**Turgeon, Luc**
❑ 77GraVic-20

**Turgeon, Pierre**
❑ 87SabBluS-28
❑ 87SabWonBH-30
❑ 88OPC-194
❑ 88OPCSti-69
❑ 88OPCSti-133
❑ 88OPCSti-198
❑ 88PanSti-230
❑ 88SabBluS-27
❑ 88SabWonBH-30
❑ 88Top-194
❑ 89OPC-25
❑ 89OPCBoxB-P
❑ 89OPCSti-262
❑ 89PanSti-204
❑ 89SabBluS-23
❑ 89SabCam-26
❑ 89Top-25
❑ 89TopBoxB-P
❑ 90Bow-241
❑ 90BowTif-241
❑ 90Kra-59
❑ 90Kra-91
❑ 90OPC-66
❑ 90OPCBoxB-M
❑ 90OPCPre-124
❑ 90PanSti-28
❑ 90ProSet-31
❑ 90ProSet-366
❑ 90SabBluS-24
❑ 90SabCam-28
❑ 90Sco-110
❑ 90ScoCan-110
❑ 90ScoHotRS-53
❑ 90ScoYouS-1
❑ 90Top-66
❑ 90TopBoxB-M
❑ 90TopTeaSL-20
❑ 90TopTif-66
❑ 90UppDec-43
❑ 90UppDec-318
❑ 90UppDecF-43
❑ 90UppDecF-318
❑ 91Bow-27
❑ 91Gil-35
❑ 91OPC-416
❑ 91OPCPre-59
❑ 91PanSti-303
❑ 91Par-106
❑ 91ParFre-106
❑ 91Pin-30
❑ 91PinFre-30
❑ 91ProSet-15
❑ 91ProSet-433
❑ 91ProSetFre-15
❑ 91ProSetFre-433
❑ 91ProSetPla-10
❑ 91ScoAme-4
❑ 91ScoAme-377
❑ 91ScoAme-416
❑ 91ScoCan-4
❑ 91ScoCan-267
❑ 91ScoCan-332
❑ 91ScoKel-6
❑ 91ScoRoo-101T
❑ 91StaClu-77
❑ 91SweSemWCS-66
❑ 91Top-416
❑ 91UppDec-176
❑ 91UppDec-554
❑ 91UppDecF-176
❑ 91UppDecF-554
❑ 92Bow-23
❑ 92DurPan-11
❑ 92OPC-47
❑ 92PanSti-196
❑ 92PanStiFre-196
❑ 92Par-103
❑ 92ParEmel-103
❑ 92Pin-165
❑ 92PinCanPP-2
❑ 92PinFre-165
❑ 92PinTea2-17
❑ 92PinTea2F-17
❑ 92ProSet-104
❑ 92Sco-325
❑ 92Sco-430
❑ 92ScoCan-325
❑ 92ScoCan-430
❑ 92ScoSha-25
❑ 92ScoShaCan-25
❑ 92ScoYouS-27
❑ 92SeaPat-53
❑ 92StaClu-276
❑ 92Top-289
❑ 92TopGol-289G
❑ 92Ult-132
❑ 92UppDec-175
❑ 93Don-209
❑ 93DonSpeP-N
❑ 93DurSco-30
❑ 93Kra-24
❑ 93Lea-25
❑ 93LeaHatTA-5
❑ 93McDUppD-27
❑ 93OPCPre-190
❑ 93OPCPreF-7
❑ 93OPCPreG-190
❑ 93PanSti-F
❑ 93Par-389
❑ 93ParEasWesS-E10
❑ 93ParEmel-389
❑ 93ParFirO-F7
❑ 93Pin-160
❑ 93Pin-225
❑ 93PinAllS-5
❑ 93PinAllSC-5
❑ 93PinCan-160
❑ 93PinCan-225
❑ 93PinNifFif-7
❑ 93PinTea2-13
❑ 93PinTea2C-13
❑ 93Pow-155
❑ 93PowPoiL-19
❑ 93Sco-6
❑ 93ScoCan-6
❑ 93ScoDreTea-15
❑ 93ScoDynDC-9
❑ 93ScoFra-12
❑ 93ScoSam-6
❑ 93StaClu-145
❑ 93StaClu-380
❑ 93StaCluAS-21
❑ 93StaCluFDI-145
❑ 93StaCluFDI-380
❑ 93StaCluFDIO-145
❑ 93StaCluMasP-20
❑ 93StaCluMasPW-20
❑ 93StaCluO-145
❑ 93StaCluO-380
❑ 93TopPre-190
❑ 93TopPreBG-20
❑ 93TopPreF-7
❑ 93TopPreG-190
❑ 93Ult-197
❑ 93UltAllS-3
❑ 93UltPreP-9
❑ 93UltScoK-5
❑ 93UppDec-224
❑ 93UppDec-297
❑ 93UppDec-347
❑ 93UppDecAW-AW7
❑ 93UppDecHT-HT11
❑ 93UppDecLAS-17
❑ 93UppDecSilSka-H7
❑ 93UppDecSilSkaG-H7
❑ 93UppDecSP-96
❑ 94BeAPla-R80
❑ 94CanGamNHLP-160
❑ 94Don-23
❑ 94EASpo-81
❑ 94Fin-78
❑ 94FinBowB-B9
❑ 94FinBowBR-B9
❑ 94FinRef-78
❑ 94FinSupTW-78
❑ 94Fla-109
❑ 94Fle-130
❑ 94HocWit-27
❑ 94Lea-367
❑ 94LeaLim-52
❑ 94LeaLimI-14
❑ 94McDUppD-McD26
❑ 94OPCPre-115
❑ 94OPCPreSE-115
❑ 94Par-135
❑ 94ParCratGB-14
❑ 94ParCratGG-14
❑ 94ParCratGR-14
❑ 94ParGol-135
❑ 94ParSEV-31
❑ 94Pin-78
❑ 94PinArtP-78
❑ 94PinRinC-78
❑ 94Sco-166
❑ 94Sco90PC-14
❑ 94ScoFra-TF14
❑ 94ScoGol-166
❑ 94ScoPla-166
❑ 94ScoPlaTS-166
❑ 94Sel-46
❑ 94SelGol-46
❑ 94SP-61
❑ 94SPDieCut-61
❑ 94StaCluMO-38
❑ 94TopPre-115
❑ 94TopPreSE-115
❑ 94Ult-133
❑ 94UppDec-77
❑ 94UppDecElelce-77
❑ 94UppDecNBAP-37
❑ 94UppDecSPI-SP48
❑ 94UppDecSPIDC-SP48
❑ 95BeAPla-152
❑ 95BeAPSig-S152
❑ 95BeAPSigDC-S152
❑ 95Bow-6
❑ 95BowAllFoi-6
❑ 95CanaPos-20
❑ 95CanaShe-12
❑ 95CanGamNHLP-145
❑ 95ColCho-131
❑ 95ColChoCTG-C15
❑ 95ColChoCTG-C15B
❑ 95ColChoCTG-C15C
❑ 95ColChoCTGGB-C15
❑ 95ColChoCTGGR-C15
❑ 95ColChoCTGSB-C15
❑ 95ColChoCTGSR-C15
❑ 95ColChoPC-131
❑ 95ColChoPCP-131
❑ 95Don-61
❑ 95DonEli-90
❑ 95DonEliCE-10
❑ 95DonEliDCS-90
❑ 95DonEliDCU-90
❑ 95DonIgn-4
❑ 95Emo-93
❑ 95Fin-46
❑ 95Fin-182
❑ 95FinRef-46
❑ 95FinRef-182
❑ 95ImpSti-63
❑ 95ImpStiDCS-1
❑ 95KenStaLA-19
❑ 95Kra-4
❑ 95Lea-90
❑ 95LeaFreFra-2
❑ 95LeaLim-102
❑ 95McDPin-MCD-13
❑ 95Met-80
❑ 95NHLAcePC-8H
❑ 95ParInt-109
❑ 95ParIntEl-109
❑ 95ParIntPTP-PP50
❑ 95Pin-34
❑ 95PinArtP-34
❑ 95PinCleS-14
❑ 95PinRinC-34

❑ 95PinRoa2-20
❑ 95PlaOneoOne-56
❑ 95ProMag-25
❑ 95Sco-90
❑ 95ScoBlaIce-90
❑ 95ScoBlaIceAP-90
❑ 95ScoBorBat-1
❑ 95ScoLam-6
❑ 95SelCer-49
❑ 95SelCerMG-49
❑ 95SkyImp-89
❑ 95SP-71
❑ 95SPStaEto-E15
❑ 95SPStaEtoG-E15
❑ 95StaClu-175
❑ 95StaCluEN-EN7
❑ 95StaCluMO-20
❑ 95StaCluMOMS-175
❑ 95StaCluPS-PS1
❑ 95Sum-43
❑ 95SumArtP-43
❑ 95SumIce-43
❑ 95Top-21
❑ 95Top-224
❑ 95TopCanG-7CG
❑ 95TopHomGC-HGC3
❑ 95TopMarMPB-21
❑ 95TopOPCI-21
❑ 95TopOPCI-224
❑ 95TopPowL-9PL
❑ 95TopSupSki-9
❑ 95TopSupSkiPla-9
❑ 95Ult-85
❑ 95UltGolM-85
❑ 95UppDec-389
❑ 95UppDecEleIce-389
❑ 95UppDecEleIceG-389
❑ 95UppDecNHLAS-AS15
❑ 95UppDecSpeE-SE44
❑ 95UppDecSpeEdiG-SE44
❑ 95Zen-38
❑ 96CanaShe-25
❑ 96ColCho-133
❑ 96ColCho-321
❑ 96ColChoBlo-133
❑ 96ColChoBloBi-5
❑ 96ColChoSti-S19
❑ 96Don-17
❑ 96DonCanI-110
❑ 96DonCanIGPP-110
❑ 96DonCanIRPP-110
❑ 96DonDom-6
❑ 96DonEli-112
❑ 96DonEliDCS-112
❑ 96DonPrePro-17
❑ 96DurL'EB-JB14
❑ 96Fle-57
❑ 96FleArtRos-23
❑ 96FlePic-32
❑ 96FlePicF5-45
❑ 96Lea-186
❑ 96LeaLeaAL-18
❑ 96LeaLeaALP-P18
❑ 96LeaLim-38
❑ 96LeaLimG-38
❑ 96LeaPre-70
❑ 96LeaPreP-186
❑ 96LeaPrePP-70
❑ 96LeaPreSG-26
❑ 96LeaPreSte-26
❑ 96MetUni-84
❑ 96NHLACEPC-48
❑ 96NHLProSTA-25
❑ 96Pin-22
❑ 96PinArtP-22
❑ 96PinFoi-22
❑ 96PinMcD-19
❑ 96PinPreS-22
❑ 96PinRinC-22
❑ 96Sco-71
❑ 96ScoArtPro-71
❑ 96ScoDeaCAP-71
❑ 96ScoGolB-71
❑ 96ScoSpeAP-71
❑ 96ScoSudDea-1
❑ 96SelCer-82
❑ 96SelCerAP-82
❑ 96SelCerBlu-82
❑ 96SelCerMB-82
❑ 96SelCerMG-82
❑ 96SelCerMR-82
❑ 96SelCerRed-82
❑ 96SkyImp-66
❑ 96SkyImpB-23
❑ 96SP-137
❑ 96SPx-22
❑ 96SPxGol-22
❑ 96StaCluMO-39
❑ 96Sum-90
❑ 96SumArtP-90
❑ 96SumIce-90
❑ 96SumMet-90
❑ 96SumPreS-90
❑ 96TeaOut-24
❑ 96Ult-148
❑ 96UltGolM-148
❑ 96UppDecBD-135
❑ 96UppDecBDG-135
❑ 96UppDecIce-61
❑ 96UppDecIcePar-61
❑ 96Zen-39
❑ 96ZenArtP-39
❑ 96ZenAss-12
❑ 97BeAPlaTAN-14
❑ 97ColCho-226
❑ 97ColChoSta-SQ56
❑ 97Don-28
❑ 97DonCanI-24
❑ 97DonCanIDS-24
❑ 97DonCanINP-24
❑ 97DonCanIPS-24
❑ 97DonEli-105
❑ 97DonEliAsp-105
❑ 97DonEliS-105
❑ 97DonLim-158
❑ 97DonLim-172
❑ 97DonLimExp-158
❑ 97DonLimExp-172
❑ 97DonPre-117
❑ 97DonPreCttC-117
❑ 97DonPreProG-28
❑ 97DonPreProS-28
❑ 97DonPri-41
❑ 97DonPriSoA-41
❑ 97Kat-131
❑ 97KatGol-131
❑ 97KatSil-131
❑ 97Lea-43
❑ 97LeaFraMat-43
❑ 97LeaFraMDC-43
❑ 97LeaInt-43
❑ 97LeaIntUI-43
❑ 97Pac-32
❑ 97PacCop-32
❑ 97PacCroR-118
❑ 97PacCroREG-118
❑ 97PacCroRIB-118
❑ 97PacCroRS-118
❑ 97PacDyn-108
❑ 97PacDynBKS-83
❑ 97PacDynC-108
❑ 97PacDynDG-108
❑ 97PacDynEG-108
❑ 97PacDynIB-108
❑ 97PacDynR-108
❑ 97PacDynSil-108
❑ 97PacDynTan-59
❑ 97PacEmeGre-32
❑ 97PacIceB-32
❑ 97PacInv-122
❑ 97PacInvC-122
❑ 97PacInvEG-122
❑ 97PacInvIB-122
❑ 97PacInvNRB-173
❑ 97PacInvR-122
❑ 97PacInvS-122
❑ 97PacOme-199
❑ 97PacOmeC-199
❑ 97PacOmeDG-199
❑ 97PacOmeEG-199
❑ 97PacOmeG-199
❑ 97PacOmeIB-199
❑ 97PacPar-161
❑ 97PacParC-161
❑ 97PacParDG-161
❑ 97PacParEG-161
❑ 97PacParIB-161
❑ 97PacParRed-161
❑ 97PacParSil-161
❑ 97PacRed-32
❑ 97PacRev-122
❑ 97PacRevC-122
❑ 97PacRevE-122
❑ 97PacRevIB-122
❑ 97PacRevR-122
❑ 97PacRevS-122
❑ 97PacSil-32
❑ 97PacSlaSDC-9B
❑ 97Pin-75
❑ 97PinArtP-75
❑ 97PinCer-62
❑ 97PinCerMB-62
❑ 97PinCerMG-62
❑ 97PinCerMR-62
❑ 97PinCerR-62
❑ 97PinIns-122
❑ 97PinPrePBB-75
❑ 97PinPrePBC-75
❑ 97PinPrePBM-75
❑ 97PinPrePBY-75
❑ 97PinPrePFC-75
❑ 97PinPrePFM-75
❑ 97PinPrePFY-75
❑ 97PinPrePla-75
❑ 97PinRinC-75
❑ 97PinTotCMPG-62
❑ 97PinTotCPB-62
❑ 97PinTotCPG-62
❑ 97PinTotCPR-62
❑ 97Sco-118
❑ 97ScoArtPro-118
❑ 97ScoBlu-2
❑ 97ScoBluPla-2
❑ 97ScoBluPre-2
❑ 97ScoGolBla-118
❑ 97SPAut-141
❑ 97Stu-64
❑ 97StuPrePG-64
❑ 97StuPrePS-64
❑ 97UppDec-353
❑ 97UppDecBD-100
❑ 97UppDecBDDD-100
❑ 97UppDecBDQD-100
❑ 97UppDecBDTD-100
❑ 97UppDecGDM-353
❑ 97Zen-23
❑ 97Zen5x7-61
❑ 97ZenGolImp-61
❑ 97ZenSilImp-61
❑ 97ZenZGol-23
❑ 97ZenZSil-23
❑ 98Be A PPA-275
❑ 98Be A PPAA-275
❑ 98Be A PPAAF-275
❑ 98Be A PPSE-275
❑ 98Be APG-275
❑ 98BowBes-86
❑ 98BowBesAR-86
❑ 98BowBesR-86
❑ 98Fin-125
❑ 98FinNo P-125
❑ 98FinNo PR-125
❑ 98FinRef-125
❑ 98O-PChr-208
❑ 98O-PChrR-208
❑ 98Pac-374
❑ 98PacAur-164
❑ 98PacAurCF-42
❑ 98PacAurCFC-42
❑ 98PacAurCFIB-42
❑ 98PacAurCFR-42
❑ 98PacAurCFS-42
❑ 98PacCroR-117
❑ 98PacCroRLS-117
❑ 98PacDynI-163
❑ 98PacDynIIB-163
❑ 98PacDynIR-163
❑ 98PacIceB-374
❑ 98PacOmeH-206
❑ 98PacOmeODI-206
❑ 98PacOmeR-206
❑ 98PacPar-207
❑ 98PacParC-207
❑ 98PacParEG-207
❑ 98PacParH-207
❑ 98PacParIB-207
❑ 98PacParS-207
❑ 98PacRed-374
❑ 98PacRev-125
❑ 98PacRevIS-125
❑ 98PacRevR-125
❑ 98SP Aut-73
❑ 98SPxFin-74
❑ 98SPxFinR-74
❑ 98SPxFinS-74
❑ 98Top-208
❑ 98TopGolLC1-30
❑ 98TopGolLC1B-30
❑ 98TopGolLC1BOoO-30
❑ 98TopGolLC1OoO-30
❑ 98TopGolLC1R-30
❑ 98TopGolLC1ROoO-30
❑ 98TopGolLC2-30
❑ 98TopGolLC2B-30
❑ 98TopGolLC2BOoO-30
❑ 98TopGolLC2OoO-30
❑ 98TopGolLC2R-30
❑ 98TopGolLC2ROoO-30
❑ 98TopGolLC3-30
❑ 98TopGolLC3B-30
❑ 98TopGolLC3BOoO-30
❑ 98TopGolLC3OoO-30
❑ 98TopGolLC3R-30
❑ 98TopGolLC3ROoO-30
❑ 98TopO-P-208
❑ 98UC-184
❑ 98UD ChoPCR-184
❑ 98UD ChoR-184
❑ 98UppDec-172
❑ 98UppDecE-172
❑ 98UppDecE1o1-172
❑ 98UppDecGR-172
❑ 98UppDecM-181
❑ 98UppDecMGS-181
❑ 98UppDecMSS-181
❑ 98UppDecMSS-181
❑ 99Pac-364
❑ 99PacAur-128
❑ 99PacAurPD-128
❑ 99PacCop-364
❑ 99PacGol-364
❑ 99PacIceB-364
❑ 99PacPreD-364
❑ 99SP AutPS-73
❑ 99UppDecM-184
❑ 99UppDecMGS-184
❑ 99UppDecMSS-184
❑ 99UppDecMSS-184

**Turgeon, Sylvain**
❑ 83CanNatJ-16
❑ 83WhaJunHC-20
❑ 847EDis-23
❑ 84OPC-79
❑ 84OPC-372
❑ 84OPCSti-191
❑ 84OPCSti-192
❑ 84Top-62
❑ 84WhaJunW-20
❑ 85OPC-43
❑ 85OPCSti-165
❑ 85Top-43
❑ 85WhaJunW-21
❑ 86OPC-103
❑ 86OPCSti-53
❑ 86Top-103
❑ 86WhaJunT-22
❑ 87OPC-70
❑ 87OPCSti-203
❑ 87PanSti-50
❑ 87Top-70
❑ 87WhaJunBK-20
❑ 88OPC-24
❑ 88PanSti-245
❑ 88Top-24
❑ 88WhaJunGR-17
❑ 89DevCar-26
❑ 90Bow-81
❑ 90BowTif-81
❑ 90CanaPos-32
❑ 90OPC-73
❑ 90PanSti-71
❑ 90ProSet-177
❑ 90ProSet-474
❑ 90Sco-116
❑ 90ScoCan-116
❑ 90ScoRoo-108T
❑ 90Top-73
❑ 90TopTif-73
❑ 90UppDec-70
❑ 90UppDecF-70
❑ 91CanaPos-31
❑ 91OPC-231
❑ 91OPCPre-184
❑ 91Par-91
❑ 91ParFre-91
❑ 91Pin-226
❑ 91PinFre-226
❑ 91ProSet-416
❑ 91ProSetFre-416
❑ 91ScoAme-208
❑ 91ScoAme-377
❑ 91ScoCan-208
❑ 91ScoCan-267
❑ 91Top-231
❑ 91UppDec-579
❑ 91UppDecF-579
❑ 92Bow-167
❑ 92DurPan-29
❑ 92OPC-315
❑ 92OPCPre-116
❑ 92Par-121
❑ 92ParEmeI-121
❑ 92Pin-373
❑ 92PinFre-373
❑ 92ProSet-123
❑ 92Sco-367
❑ 92Sco-516
❑ 92ScoCan-367
❑ 92ScoCan-516
❑ 92Sen-15
❑ 92StaClu-59
❑ 92Top-375
❑ 92TopGol-375G
❑ 92Ult-149
❑ 92UppDec-107
❑ 93Don-235
❑ 93DurSco-36
❑ 93Lea-74
❑ 93OPCPre-97
❑ 93OPCPreG-97
❑ 93PanSti-K
❑ 93Par-136
❑ 93ParEmeI-136
❑ 93Pin-64
❑ 93PinCan-64
❑ 93Pow-176
❑ 93Sco-46
❑ 93ScoCan-46
❑ 93SenKraS-24
❑ 93StaClu-482
❑ 93StaCluFDI-482
❑ 93StaCluO-482
❑ 93TopPre-97
❑ 93TopPreG-97
❑ 93Ult-190
❑ 93UppDec-44
❑ 94BeAPla-R60
❑ 94CanGamNHLP-173
❑ 94Don-105
❑ 94EASpo-94
❑ 94Fle-148
❑ 94Lea-191
❑ 94OPCPre-23
❑ 94OPCPreSE-23
❑ 94Par-153
❑ 94ParGol-153
❑ 94ParVin-V51
❑ 94Pin-288
❑ 94PinArtP-288
❑ 94PinRinC-288
❑ 94SenBelM-26
❑ 94TopPre-23
❑ 94TopPreSE-23
❑ 94Ult-341
❑ 94UppDec-336
❑ 94UppDecEleIce-336
❑ 94UppDecSPI-SP146
❑ 94UppDecSPIDC-SP146
❑ 95Lea-33
❑ 95ParInt-146
❑ 95ParIntEI-146
❑ 95PlaOneoOne-290
❑ 95UppDec-177
❑ 95UppDecEleIce-177
❑ 95UppDecEleIceG-177

**Turikov, Vladimir**
❑ 91SweSemWCS-85

**Turkiewicz, Jim**
❑ 76OPCWHA-18

**Turler, Michel**
❑ 72SweSemWC-161

**Turmel, Nicolas**
❑ 917thInnSQMJHL-114

**Turmel, Richard**
❑ 83FreExp-15

**Turnbull, Dale**
❑ 87SauSteMG-9
❑ 89SauSteMG-17

**Turnbull, Ian**
❑ 73MapLeaP-27
❑ 74MapLeaP-24
❑ 74NHLActSta-259
❑ 74OPCNHL-289
❑ 75MapLeaP-25
❑ 75MapLeaP-26
❑ 75OPCNHL-41
❑ 75Top-41
❑ 76MapLeaP-19
❑ 76MapLeaP-20
❑ 76OPCNHL-39
❑ 76Top-39
❑ 77MapLeaP-16
❑ 77OPCNHL-186
❑ 77OPCNHL-215
❑ 77Top-186
❑ 77Top-215
❑ 78MapLeaP-21
❑ 78OPC-127
❑ 78Top-127
❑ 79MapLeaP-31
❑ 79OPC-228
❑ 79Top-228
❑ 80MapLeaP-27
❑ 80OPC-133
❑ 80OPCSup-21
❑ 80PepCap-99
❑ 80Top-133
❑ 81OPC-309
❑ 81OPCSti-100
❑ 81Top-42

**Turnbull, Perry**
❑ 80OPC-169
❑ 80Top-169
❑ 81OPC-298
❑ 81Top-W123
❑ 82OPC-312
❑ 82OPCSti-203
❑ 82PosCer-17
❑ 83CanaPos-30
❑ 83OPC-321
❑ 83OPCSti-124
❑ 84JetPol-20
❑ 84OPC-349
❑ 85JetPol-20
❑ 85OPC-254
❑ 86JetBor-23
❑ 86KraDra-76
❑ 86OPC-170
❑ 86Top-170
❑ 87BluKod-25
❑ 92BluUDBB-26

**Turner, Bart**
❑ 93MicSta-24

**Turner, Bob**
❑ 44BeeGro2P-143A
❑ 44BeeGro2P-143B
❑ 44BeeGro2P-292
❑ 55Par-54
❑ 55ParQuaO-54
❑ 57Par-M13
❑ 58Par-40
❑ 59Par-43
❑ 60Par-43
❑ 60ShiCoi-37
❑ 60YorPreP-37
❑ 61Par-41
❑ 61ShiCoi-37
❑ 61Top-41
❑ 62Top-29
❑ 63Top-32
❑ 64BeeGro3P-57
❑ 94ParMisL-81

**Turner, Brad**
❑ 90RicRen-1
❑ 91ProAHLCHL-381
❑ 93OPCPreTC-10
❑ 93Ult-475
❑ 94FinnSIS-302

**Turner, Dan**
❑ 82MedHatT-21
❑ 83MedHatT-11

**Turner, Jack**
❑ 67ColChe-15
❑ 69ColChe-15

**Turner, Lloyd**
❑ 83HalFP-B15
❑ 85HalFC-29

**Turner, Mark**
❑ 85SudWol-18
❑ 86SudWol-18
❑ 87KinCan-11
❑ 88SudWol-21
❑ 90CinCyc-31
❑ 91ProAHLCHL-245
❑ 93MusFur-19
❑ 95MusFur-8

**Turner, Scott**
❑ 917thInnSOHL-124
❑ 91PetPet-3

**Turunen, Timo**
❑ 73SweHocS-36
❑ 73SweWorCS-36

**Turunen, Tommi**
❑ 95FinnSIS-305
❑ 96FinnSISR-103

**Turvey, Ward**
❑ 23CreSel-10

**Tustian, Rob**
❑ 90MicTecHus-25
❑ 91ProAHLCHL-42

**Tustin, Norm**
❑ 34BeeGro1P-295

**Tuten, Audley**
❑ 34BeeGro1P-84

**Tutt, Brian**
❑ 89ProAHL-91
❑ 93FinnSIS-363
❑ 93SweSemE-80
❑ 94FinnSIS-318
❑ 96GerDELE-297
❑ 98GerDELE-245

**Tutt, Thayer**
❑ 83HalFP-I15

**Tuttle, Steve**
❑ 87BluTeaIss-24
❑ 88BluKod-35
❑ 88BluTeaIss-24
❑ 89BluKod-35
❑ 89OPC-157
❑ 89PanSti-126
❑ 89Top-157
❑ 90BluKod-24
❑ 90OPC-278
❑ 90ProAHLIHL-84
❑ 90ProSet-273
❑ 90Top-278
❑ 90TopTif-278
❑ 90UppDec-195
❑ 90UppDecF-195
❑ 91ProAHLCHL-41
❑ 92Ult-205
❑ 94MilAdm-25
❑ 95MilAdmBO-19
❑ 96MilAdmBO-26

**Tuulola, Marko**
❑ 93FinnJyvHS-235
❑ 93FinnSIS-187
❑ 94FinnJaaK-7
❑ 94FinnSIS-6
❑ 95FinnSemWC-25
❑ 95FinnSIS-248
❑ 96FinnSISR-43

**Tuyl, Clyde**
❑ 93SheSte-16
❑ 94SheSte-2
❑ 97SheSte-22
❑ 97SheSte-25

**Tuzzolino, Tony**
❑ 93MicSta-25

**Tverdovsky, Oleg**
❑ 93Cla-111
❑ 93Par-531
❑ 93ParEmeI-531
❑ 93Pin-506
❑ 93PinCan-506
❑ 94BeAPla-R160
❑ 94Cla-2
❑ 94ClaDraGol-2
❑ 94ClaPic-CP12
❑ 94ClaPre-HK5
❑ 94ClaProP-208
❑ 94ClaROYS-R19
❑ 94ClaTri-T1
❑ 94DucCarJr-24
❑ 94Fin-2
❑ 94FinBowB-R2
❑ 94FinBowB-X24
❑ 94FinBowBR-R2
❑ 94FinBowBR-X24
❑ 94FinRef-2
❑ 94FinSupTW-2
❑ 94Fle-8
❑ 94FleRooS-10
❑ 94LeaLim-24
❑ 94LeaPhe-6
❑ 94OPCPre-464
❑ 94OPCPreSE-464
❑ 94Pin-261
❑ 94PinArtP-261
❑ 94PinRinC-261
❑ 94PinRooTP-2
❑ 94Sco-214
❑ 94ScoGol-214
❑ 94ScoPla-214
❑ 94ScoTopRR-4
❑ 94Sel-169
❑ 94SelGol-169
❑ 94SelYouExp-YE2
❑ 94SP-2
❑ 94SPDieCut-2
❑ 94SPPre-5
❑ 94SPPreDC-5
❑ 94TopPre-464
❑ 94TopPreSE-464
❑ 94UltPro-9
❑ 94UppDec-243
❑ 94UppDec-540
❑ 94UppDecEleIce-243
❑ 94UppDecEleIce-540
❑ 94UppDecPC-C14
❑ 94UppDecPCEG-C14
❑ 94UppDecPCES-C14
❑ 94UppDecSPI-SP93
❑ 94UppDecSPIDC-SP93
❑ 95BeAPla-61
❑ 95BeAPSig-S61
❑ 95BeAPSigDC-S61
❑ 95Bow-88
❑ 95BowAllFoi-88
❑ 95ColCho-81
❑ 95ColChoPC-81
❑ 95ColChoPCP-81
❑ 95Don-3
❑ 95DonEli-6
❑ 95DonEliDCS-6
❑ 95DonEliDCU-6
❑ 95DonRooTea-6
❑ 95Emo-4
❑ 95ImpSti-4
❑ 95Lea-28
❑ 95LeaLim-46
❑ 95LeaStuR-6
❑ 95McDPin-MCD-35
❑ 95Met-5
❑ 95ParInt-9
❑ 95ParInt-496
❑ 95ParIntEI-9
❑ 95ParIntEI-496
❑ 95Pin-60
❑ 95PinArtP-60
❑ 95PinGloG-11
❑ 95PinRinC-60
❑ 95PlaOneoOne-4
❑ 95ProMag-44
❑ 95Sco-16
❑ 95ScoBlaIce-16
❑ 95ScoBlaIceAP-16
❑ 95SelCer-79
❑ 95SelCerFut-9
❑ 95SelCerMG-79
❑ 95SkyImp-5
❑ 95SkyImp-236
❑ 95SP-166
❑ 95StaClu-113
❑ 95StaCluMOMS-113
❑ 95Sum-37
❑ 95SumArtP-37
❑ 95SumIce-37
❑ 95Top-365
❑ 95TopNewG-4NG
❑ 95TopOPCI-365
❑ 95TopSupSki-12
❑ 95TopSupSkiPla-12
❑ 95TopYouS-YS7
❑ 95Ult-6
❑ 95UltGolM-6
❑ 95UppDec-408
❑ 95UppDecEleIce-408
❑ 95UppDecEleIceG-408
❑ 95UppDecSpeE-SE2
❑ 95UppDecSpeEdiG-SE2
❑ 95Zen-71
❑ 96ColCho-199
❑ 96ColCho-327
❑ 96Don-105
❑ 96DonPrePro-105
❑ 96Fla-74
❑ 96FlaBlul-74
❑ 96Fle-93
❑ 96Lea-3
❑ 96LeaPre-71
❑ 96LeaPreP-3
❑ 96LeaPrePP-71
❑ 96MetUni-123
❑ 96NHLProSTA-44
❑ 96Pin-145
❑ 96PinArtP-145
❑ 96PinFoi-145
❑ 96PinPreS-145
❑ 96PinRinC-145
❑ 96PlaOneoOne-332
❑ 96Sco-89
❑ 96ScoArtPro-89
❑ 96ScoDeaCAP-89
❑ 96ScoGolB-89
❑ 96ScoSpeAP-89
❑ 96SkyImp-109
❑ 96SP-121
❑ 96Sum-129
❑ 96SumArtP-129
❑ 96SumIce-129
❑ 96SumMet-129
❑ 96SumPreS-129
❑ 96TopNHLP-97
❑ 96TopPicOI-97
❑ 96Ult-137
❑ 96UltGolM-137
❑ 96UppDec-129
❑ 96UppDecBD-102
❑ 96UppDecBDG-102
❑ 96UppDecIce-99
❑ 96UppDecIcePar-99
❑ 96UppDecSS-SS25A
❑ 96Zen-70
❑ 96ZenArtP-70
❑ 97ColCho-198
❑ 97ColChoSta-SQ28
❑ 97Don-54
❑ 97DonCanI-62
❑ 97DonCanIDS-62
❑ 97DonCanIPS-62
❑ 97DonEli-109
❑ 97DonEliAsp-109
❑ 97DonEliS-109
❑ 97DonLim-93
❑ 97DonLimExp-93
❑ 97DonLin2L-6
❑ 97DonLin2LDC-6
❑ 97DonPre-137
❑ 97DonPreCttC-137
❑ 97DonPreProG-54
❑ 97DonPreProS-54
❑ 97DonPri-53
❑ 97DonPriSoA-53
❑ 97Kat-114
❑ 97KatGol-114
❑ 97KatSil-114
❑ 97Lea-92
❑ 97LeaFraMat-92
❑ 97LeaFraMDC-92
❑ 97LeaInt-92
❑ 97LeaIntUI-92
❑ 97Pac-252
❑ 97PacCop-252
❑ 97PacDyn-99

- 97PacDynC-99
- 97PacDynDG-99
- 97PacDynEG-99
- 97PacDynIB-99
- 97PacDynR-99
- 97PacDynSil-99
- 97PacDynTan-66
- 97PacEmeGre-252
- 97PacIceB-252
- 97PacInv-110
- 97PacInvC-110
- 97PacInvEG-110
- 97PacInvIB-110
- 97PacInvR-110
- 97PacInvS-110
- 97PacOme-179
- 97PacOmeC-179
- 97PacOmeDG-179
- 97PacOmeEG-179
- 97PacOmeG-179
- 97PacOmeIB-179
- 97PacPar-146
- 97PacParC-146
- 97PacParDG-146
- 97PacParEG-146
- 97PacParIB-146
- 97PacParRed-146
- 97PacParSil-146
- 97PacRed-252
- 97PacSil-252
- 97Pin-166
- 97PinCer-103
- 97PinCerMB-103
- 97PinCerMG-103
- 97PinCerMR-103
- 97PinCerR-103
- 97PinIns-132
- 97PinPrePBB-166
- 97PinPrePBC-166
- 97PinPrePBM-166
- 97PinPrePBY-166
- 97PinPrePFC-166
- 97PinPrePFM-166
- 97PinPrePFY-166
- 97PinPrePla-166
- 97PinTotCMPG-103
- 97PinTotCPB-103
- 97PinTotCPG-103
- 97PinTotCPR-103
- 97Sco-195
- 97Stu-38
- 97StuPrePG-38
- 97StuPrePS-38
- 97UppDec-335
- 97UppDecGDM-335
- 97UppDecSG-SG42
- 98Be A PPA-258
- 98Be A PPAA-258
- 98Be A PPAAF-258
- 98Be A PPSE-258
- 98Be APG-258
- 98Fin-104
- 98FinNo P-104
- 98FinNo PR-104
- 98FinRef-104
- 98Pac-345
- 98PacAur-150
- 98PacCroR-107
- 98PacCroRLS-107
- 98PacDynI-147
- 98PacDynIIB-147
- 98PacDynIR-147
- 98PacIceB-345
- 98PacOmeH-190
- 98PacOmeODI-190
- 98PacOmeR-190
- 98PacPar-188
- 98PacParC-188
- 98PacParEG-188
- 98PacParH-188
- 98PacParIB-188
- 98PacParS-188
- 98PacRed-345
- 98UC-159
- 98UD ChoPCR-159
- 98UD ChoR-159
- 98UppDec-153
- 98UppDecE-153
- 98UppDecE1o1-153
- 98UppDecGR-153
- 98UppDecM-161
- 98UppDecMGS-161
- 98UppDecMP-OT
- 98UppDecMSS-161
- 98UppDecMSS-161
- 99Pac-330
- 99PacCop-330
- 99PacGol-330
- 99PacIceB-330
- 99PacPreD-330
- 99UppDecM-163
- 99UppDecMGS-163
- 99UppDecMSS-163
- 99UppDecMSS-163

**Twist, Tony**
- 88ProIHL-79
- 89BluKod-8
- 90ProAHLIHL-85
- 91NordPet-31
- 91ScoCan-396
- 92NorPet-34
- 93Sco-400
- 93ScoCan-400
- 94Lea-13
- 94Lea-454

- 95BeAPla-214
- 95BeAPSig-S214
- 95BeAPSigDC-S214
- 95Top-203
- 95TopOPCI-203
- 96ColCho-231
- 96Sco-207
- 96ScoArtPro-207
- 96ScoDeaCAP-207
- 96ScoGolB-207
- 96ScoSpeAP-207
- 97ColCho-230
- 97Kat-132
- 97KatGol-132
- 97KatSil-132
- 97Pac-254
- 97PacCop-254
- 97PacEmeGre-254
- 97PacIceB-254
- 97PacPar-162
- 97PacParC-162
- 97PacParDG-162
- 97PacParEG-162
- 97PacParIB-162
- 97PacParRed-162
- 97PacParSil-162
- 97PacRed-254
- 97PacSil-254
- 97Sco-157
- 97ScoArtPro-157
- 97ScoBlu-10
- 97ScoBluPla-10
- 97ScoBluPre-10
- 97ScoGolBla-157
- 97UppDec-201
- 98Pac-375
- 98PacAur-165
- 98PacIceB-375
- 98PacOmeH-207
- 98PacOmeODI-207
- 98PacOmeR-207
- 98PacPar-208
- 98PacParC-208
- 98PacParEG-208
- 98PacParH-208
- 98PacParIB-208
- 98PacParS-208
- 98PacRed-375
- 98RevThrPA-8
- 98RevThrPA-8
- 98UppDec-177
- 98UppDecE-177
- 98UppDecE1o1-177
- 98UppDecGR-177
- 98UppDecM-184
- 98UppDecMGS-184
- 98UppDecMSS-184
- 98UppDecMSS-184
- 99Pac-365
- 99PacCop-365
- 99PacGol-365
- 99PacIceB-365
- 99PacPreD-365

**Twomey, Christian**
- 92BriColJHL-209

**Tyers, Shawn**
- 85KitRan-19

**Tymchuk, Greg**
- 95Sla-200

**Tymchyshyn, Darren**
- 91BriColJHL-40
- 92BriColJHL-56

**Tysk, Evert**
- 67SweHoc-148
- 69SweHocS-163

**Tyznych, Alexander**
- 89ProAHL-144
- 90ProAHLIHL-236

**Tyznych, Sergei**
- 74SweHocS-40

**Ubriaco, Gene**
- 69OPC-149
- 83HalFP-N16
- 85HalFC-240

**Udvari, Frank**

**Udvari, Steve**
- 87SauSteMG-12
- 897thInnSOHL-138
- 89NiaFaIT-20

**Uens, Jim**
- 81OshGen-20

**Uher, Zdenek**
- 96CzeAPSE-336

**Ujcik, Viktor**
- 91UppDecCWJC-92
- 94CzeAPSE-175
- 95CzeAPSE-136
- 96CzeAPSE-347

**Ujvary, Lubomir**
- 69SweWorC-144
- 70SweHocS-352

**Ulander, Mats**
- 82SweSemHVS-18
- 83SweSemE-15

**Ulanov, Igor**
- 91OPCIns-62R
- 91Par-421
- 91ParFre-421
- 91UppDec-590
- 91UppDecF-590
- 92Bow-392
- 92OPC-229
- 92Par-440
- 92ParEmel-440
- 92ProSet-216

- 92Sco-467
- 92ScoCan-467
- 92StaClu-366
- 92Top-468
- 92TopGol-468G
- 92UppDec-300
- 92UppDecES-E15
- 93JetRuf-26
- 93Pow-477
- 94BeAPSig-70
- 94Lea-416
- 94OPCPre-179
- 94OPCPreSE-179
- 94TopPre-179
- 94TopPreSE-179
- 94Ult-397
- 95FinnSemWC-129
- 96ColCho-252
- 97Be A PPAD-209
- 97Be A PPAPD-209
- 97BeAPla-209
- 97BeAPlaAut-209
- 97ColCho-239

**Ulin, Patrik**
- 92SweSemE-297

**Ulion, Gretchen**
- 94ClaWomOH-W29

**Ullman, Norm**
- 44BeeGro2P-215
- 57Top-46
- 58Top-65
- 59Top-45
- 60Par-26
- 60ShiCoi-45
- 61Par-26
- 61ShiCoi-76
- 62Par-21
- 62YorIroOTra-29
- 63ChePho-55
- 63Par-52
- 63TorSta-40
- 63YorWhiB-47
- 64BeeGro3P-95
- 64CocCap-42
- 64Top-15
- 64TorSta-47
- 65Coc-42
- 65Top-49
- 66Top-52
- 66TopUSAT-52
- 67Top-101
- 67Top-132
- 68OPC-131
- 68PosCerM-27
- 68ShiCoi-68
- 68Top-131
- 69MapLeaWBG-35
- 69MapLeaWBM-6
- 69OPC-54
- 69OPCSta-25
- 69Top-54
- 70ColSta-12
- 70DadCoo-130
- 70EssPowPla-24
- 70OPC-110
- 70OPCDec-48
- 70SarProSta-204
- 70Top-110
- 71Baz-18
- 71ColHea-15A
- 71ColHea-15B
- 71FriLay-10
- 71LetActR-17
- 71MapLeaP-16
- 71OPC-30
- 71OPCPos-11
- 71SarProSta-193
- 71Top-30
- 71TorSun-274
- 72MapLeaP-29
- 72MapLeaP-30
- 72OPC-147
- 72SarProSta-197
- 72SweSemWC-163
- 72Top-168
- 73MacMil-29
- 73MapLeaP-28
- 73OPC-27
- 73Top-148
- 74LipSou-1
- 74MapLeaP-25
- 74NHLActSta-261
- 740PCNHL-219
- 740PCNHL-236
- 74Top-219
- 74Top-236
- 760PCWHA-126
- 81TCMA-1
- 83HalFP-G15
- 85HalFC-104
- 88EssAllSta-47
- 91UltOriS-72
- 91UltOriS-78
- 91UltOriSF-72
- 91UltOriSF-78
- 92HalFL-17
- 92ParParR-PR25
- 94ParMisL-45
- 94ParTalB-58
- 94ParTalBM-AS4
- 94ParTalBM-SL3
- 94ZelMasH-8
- 94ZelMasoHS-8
- 95Par66-45
- 95Par66Coi-45

**Ulrich, Martin**
- 93SweSemWCS-273
- 94FinnJaaK-237
- 95AusNatTea-28
- 95SweGloWC-184
- 96GerDELE-166

**Ulrich, Shawn**
- 95AlaGolKin-19
- 96AlaGolKin-14

**Ulweback, Borje**
- 69SweHocS-254

**Underhill, Jason**
- 907thInnSQMJHL-206

**Unger, Garry**
- 68OPC-142
- 68ShiCoi-42
- 69OPC-159
- 70ColSta-7
- 70DadCoo-131
- 70EssPowPla-132
- 70OPC-26
- 70OPCDec-16
- 70RedWinM-10
- 70SarProSta-61
- 70Top-26
- 70TopStiS-30
- 71Baz-19
- 71BluPos-23
- 71ColHea-16
- 71LetActR-6
- 710PC-26
- 710PCPos-20
- 710PCTBop-14
- 71SarProSta-178
- 71Top-26
- 72BluWhiBor-22
- 72OPC-120
- 72SarProSta-184
- 72SweSemWC-191
- 72Top-35
- 73BluWhiBor-22
- 73BluWhiBor-23
- 730PC-15
- 73Top-15
- 74LipSou-5
- 74NHLActSta-252
- 740PCNHL-197
- 740PCNHL-237
- 74Top-197
- 74Top-237
- 750PCNHL-40
- 750PCNHL-327
- 75Top-40
- 75Top-327
- 760PCNHL-68
- 760PCNHL-260
- 760PCNHL-393
- 76Top-68
- 76Top-260
- 770PCNHL-35
- 77Top-7
- 77Top-35
- 78BluPos-24
- 78OPC-5
- 78OPC-110
- 78Top-5
- 78Top-110
- 79FlamPos-19
- 79OPC-33
- 79Top-33
- 80KinCarN-13
- 80OPC-273
- 81OilRedR-77
- 81OPC-123
- 82OilRedR-77
- 82OPC-120
- 88OilTenAnn-1
- 89ProIHL-112
- 90ProAHLIHL-368
- 92-TulOil-16
- 92BluUDBB-27
- 94CenHocL-108

**Uniac, John**
- 87SudWol-14
- 88KitRan-8
- 89KitRan-8
- 907thInnSMC-36
- 907thInnSOHL-246
- 90KitRan-8
- 92WheThu-18
- 95TalTigS-11

**Uniacke, Richard**
- 93SauSteMG-10
- 95SauSteMG-23
- 95Sla-361
- 96SauSteMG-26
- 96SauSteMG-26

**Unsinn, Xavier**
- 89SweSemWCS-102

**Urkewicz, Terry**
- 61HamRed-20

**Usjmakov, Slava**
- 74SweHocS-86

**Uski, Jani**
- 93FinnJyvHS-269
- 93FinnSIS-298

**Usov, Alexander**
- 74SweHocS-93

**Ustorf, Peter**
- 96GerDELE-246

**Ustorf, Stefan**
- 92Cla-29
- 92UppDec-371

- 93SweSemWCS-159
- 94PorPir-23
- 95Bow-147
- 95BowAllFoi-147
- 95Cap-27
- 95ColEdgl-55
- 95Don-294
- 95ParInt-520
- 95ParIntEl-538
- 95ParIntEl-520
- 95ParIntEl-538
- 95PorPir-24
- 95SigRoo-28
- 95SigRooCP-2
- 95SweGloWC-224
- 95UppDec-502
- 95UppDecElelce-502
- 95UppDecElelceG-502
- 96ClaGol-29
- 96ColCho-284
- 96LasVegT-21

**Vadenberghe, Mike**
- 907thInnSWHL-225A
- 907thInnSWHL-225B

**Vadnais, Carol**
- 64CanaPos-21
- 67CanalGA-17
- 67Top-9
- 68OPC-81
- 68ShiCoi-114
- 68Top-81
- 69OPC-82
- 69OPCFou-4
- 69OPCSta-26
- 69Top-82
- 70ColSta-86
- 70DadCoo-133
- 70EssPowPla-95
- 70OPC-70
- 70OPCDec-36
- 70SarProSta-130
- 70Top-70
- 70TopStiS-31
- 710PC-46
- 71SarProSta-137
- 71Top-46
- 71TorSun-60
- 72OPC-39
- 72SarProSta-25
- 72SweSemWC-181
- 72Top-85
- 730PC-58
- 73Top-58
- 74NHLActSta-23
- 740PCNHL-165
- 74Top-165
- 750PCNHL-27A
- 750PCNHL-27B
- 75Top-27
- 760PCNHL-257
- 760PCNHL-390
- 76Top-257
- 770PCNHL-154
- 77Top-154
- 780PC-85
- 78Top-85
- 790PC-145
- 79Top-145
- 800PC-57
- 80Top-57
- 810PC-236
- 820PC-148
- 820PCSti-224

**Vahanen, Kim**
- 93FinnSIS-238

**Vail, Eric**
- 74NHLActSta-1
- 740PCNHL-391
- 750PCNHL-135
- 750PCNHL-313
- 75Top-135
- 75Top-313
- 760PCNHL-51
- 770PCNHL-168
- 77Top-168
- 780PC-129
- 78Top-129
- 790PC-188
- 79Top-188
- 80FlamPos-22
- 800PC-15
- 80PepCap-19
- 80Top-15
- 810PC-38
- 810PCSti-220
- 81Top-43
- 820PC-97

**Vair, Steve**
- 10C55SweCP-18
- 11C55-18
- 12C57-10

**Vaive, Jeff**
- 82Ott67-25

**Vaive, Rick**
- 79CanuRoyB-22
- 80MapLeaP-28
- 800PC-242
- 80PepCap-100
- 80Top-242
- 81MapLeaP-23
- 810PC-310
- 810PCSti-101
- 81Top-44
- 82MapLeaP-36
- 82MapLeaP-37
- 820PC-314
- 820PC-335
- 820PC-336
- 820PCSti-62
- 820PCSti-63
- 82PosCer-18
- 83Ess-21
- 83MapLeaP-26

- 830PC-323
- 830PC-324
- 830PC-343
- 830PCSti-25
- 830PCSti-26
- 83PufSti-2
- 83Vac-100
- 847EDis-47
- 84KelAccD-6
- 84MapLeaP-24
- 840PC-313
- 840PC-368
- 840PCSti-11
- 840PCSti-12
- 840PCSti-139
- 84Top-138
- 857ECreCar-18
- 85MapLeaP-30
- 85MapLeaP-31
- 850PC-106
- 850PCSti-6
- 85Top-106
- 86KraDra-77
- 86MapLeaP-21
- 860PC-191
- 860PCSti-138
- 86Top-191
- 87BaCok-26
- 870PC-155
- 870PCSti-155
- 87PanSti-328
- 87ProAll-9
- 87Top-155
- 88BaCok-21
- 880PC-77
- 880PCSti-9
- 88PanSti-31
- 88SabBluS-28
- 88Top-77
- 890PC-125
- 890PCSti-256
- 89PanSti-206
- 89SabBluS-24
- 89SabCam-27
- 89Top-125
- 90Bow-250
- 90BowTif-250
- 900PC-148
- 90PanSti-23
- 90ProSet-32
- 90SabBluS-25
- 90SabCam-29
- 90Sco-103
- 90ScoCan-103
- 90Top-148
- 90TopTif-148
- 90UppDec-376
- 90UppDecF-376
- 91Bow-39
- 910PC-457
- 91PanSti-297
- 91ProSet-26
- 91ProSetFre-26
- 91SabBluS-23
- 91SabPepC-23
- 91ScoAme-26
- 91ScoCan-26
- 91StaClu-13
- 91Top-457
- 91UppDec-179
- 91UppDecF-179
- 92HamCan-28
- 95SouCarS-1
- 96SouCarS-NNO

**Valasek, Horst**
- 94CzeAPSE-297
- 95CzeAPSE-1

**Valek, Oldrich**
- 89SweSemWCS-197
- 93FinnSIS-289
- 94CzeAPSE-179

**Valenta, Peter**
- 907thInnSQMJHL-6
- 917thInnSQMJHL-224

**Valenti, Maren**
- 98GerDELE-157

**Valenti, Sven**
- 94GerDELE-294
- 95GerDELE-285
- 98GerDELE-86

**Valentine, Chris**
- 81Cap-17
- 82Cap-24
- 820PC-373
- 820PCSti-155
- 82PosCer-20
- 94GerDELE-82
- 95GerDELE-286
- 98GerDELE-86

**Valicevic, Chris**
- 93GreMon-14

**Valicevic, Rob**
- 91LakSupSL-30
- 95LouIceG-19
- 95LouIceGP-20

**Valila, Mika**
- 93FinnJyvHS-238
- 93FinnSIS-197
- 95FinnSemWC-34

**Valimont, Carl**
- 89ProIHL-184
- 90ProAHLIHL-325
- 91ProAHLCHL-603

**Valiots, Jaak**

□ 91RayJrC-20
**Valiquette, Jack**
□ 76MapLeaP-21
□ 76OPCNHL-294
□ 77MapLeaP-17
□ 77OPCNHL-64
□ 77Top-64
□ 78OPC-391
□ 79OPC-229
□ 79Top-229
□ 80OPC-108
□ 80Top-108
**Valiquette, Steve**
□ 94SudWolP-27
□ 95Sla-382
□ 95SudWol-18
□ 95SudWolP-23
□ 96SudWol-23
□ 96SudWolP-25
□ 97SudWolP-23
**Valis, Lindsay**
□ 907thInnSWHL-10
**Valk, Garry**
□ 90CanuMoh-29
□ 90ProAHLIHL-322
□ 90UppDec-530
□ 90UppDecF-530
□ 91Bow-314
□ 91OPC-117
□ 91Pin-291
□ 91PinFre-291
□ 91ProSet-499
□ 91ProSetFre-499
□ 91ScoAme-195
□ 91ScoCan-195
□ 91StaClu-318
□ 91Top-117
□ 91UppDec-152
□ 91UppDecF-152
□ 92CanuRoaTA-22
□ 92Pin-181
□ 92PinFre-181
□ 92Sco-355
□ 92ScoCan-355
□ 92StaClu-493
□ 92Top-383
□ 92TopGol-383G
□ 92UppDec-114
□ 93Don-401
□ 93OPCPre-354
□ 93OPCPreG-354
□ 93Par-4
□ 93ParEmel-4
□ 93Pow-286
□ 93Sco-641
□ 93ScoCan-641
□ 93ScoGol-641
□ 93StaClu-407
□ 93StaCluFDI-407
□ 93StaCluO-407
□ 93TopPre-354
□ 93TopPreG-354
□ 93UppDec-515
□ 94BeAPla-R116
□ 94BeAPSig-118
□ 94CanGamNHLP-370
□ 94Don-198
□ 94DucCarJr-8
□ 94Fla-7
□ 94Lea-206
□ 94OPCPre-372
□ 94OPCPreSE-372
□ 94ParSE-SE7
□ 94ParSEG-SE7
□ 94ParVin-V19
□ 94Pin-119
□ 94PinArtP-119
□ 94PinRinC-119
□ 94StaClu-89
□ 94StaCluFDI-89
□ 94StaCluMOMS-89
□ 94StaCluSTWC-89
□ 94TopPre-372
□ 94TopPreSE-372
□ 94Ult-253
□ 94UppDec-282
□ 94UppDecEleIce-282
□ 94UppDecIcIG-IG12
□ 94UppDecSPI-SP3
□ 94UppDecSPIDC-SP3
□ 95Duc-5
□ 95ParInt-5
□ 95ParIntEl-5
□ 95ProMag-45
□ 96BeAPAut-155
□ 96BeAPAutSil-155
□ 96BeAPla-155
□ 96Duc-XXX
□ 96NHLProSTA-45
□ 97ScoPen-12
□ 97ScoPenPla-12
□ 97ScoPenPre-12
□ 99Pac-418
□ 99PacCop-418
□ 99PacGol-418
□ 99PacIceB-418
□ 99PacPreD-418
**Valk, Phil**
□ 91BriColJHL-92
□ 91BriColJHL-115
**Valkeapaa, Pertti**
□ 74SweSemHVS-95
**Vallee, Sebastien**
□ 95SigRoo-55

□ 95SigRooSig-55
**Valliere, Michel**
□ 93SweSemWCS-250
□ 94FinnJaaK-211
□ 94FreNatT-32
□ 95SweGloWC-200
□ 96GerDELE-316
□ 96SweSemW-184
□ 98GerDELE-263
**Vallieres, David**
□ 98KanCitB-21
**Vallis, Lindsay**
□ 91ProAHLCHL-82
□ 92FreCan-26
□ 93ClaProPro-41
□ 93FreCan-28
**Valois, Richard**
□ 88RivDu R-29
**Valois, Stephane**
□ 88RivDu R-30
**Valtonen, Jorma**
□ 69SweWorC-157
□ 69SweWorC-163
□ 70SweHocS-294
□ 71SweHocS-59
□ 72SweHocS-33
□ 72SweSemWC-90
□ 74SweHocS-103
□ 74SweSemHVS-76
**Van Allen, Shaun**
□ 88ProAHL-87
□ 89ProAHL-151
□ 90ProAHLIHL-223
□ 91OPC-414
□ 91ProAHLCHL-221
□ 91Top-414
□ 91UppDec-52
□ 91UppDecF-52
□ 92OilIGA-25
□ 92Par-288
□ 92ParEmel-288
□ 92Ult-299
□ 93ClaProPro-64
□ 93ClaProPro-150
□ 93Don-14
□ 93OPCPre-396
□ 93OPCPreG-396
□ 93Par-278
□ 93ParEmel-278
□ 93Pow-15
□ 93StaClu-361
□ 93StaCluO-361
□ 93TopPre-396
□ 93TopPreG-396
□ 93Ult-284
□ 93UppDec-506
□ 94CanGamNHLP-31
□ 94DucCarJr-7
□ 94Lea-338
□ 94OPCPre-432
□ 94OPCPreSE-432
□ 94StaClu-207
□ 94StaCluFDI-207
□ 94StaCluMOMS-207
□ 94StaCluSTWC-207
□ 94TopPre-432
□ 94TopPreSE-432
□ 94UppDec-312
□ 94UppDecEleIce-312
□ 95ColCho-173
□ 95Don-26
□ 95Emo-5
□ 95Lea-248
□ 95ParInt-8
□ 95ParIntEl-8
□ 95Pin-102
□ 95PinArtP-102
□ 95PinRinC-102
□ 95PlaOneOne-115
□ 95Sco-166
□ 95ScoBlaIce-166
□ 95ScoBlaIceAP-166
□ 95SkyImp-6
□ 95Top-297
□ 95TopOPCI-297
□ 95Ult-7
□ 95UltGolM-7
□ 95UppDec-488
□ 95UppDecEleIce-488
□ 95UppDecEleIceG-488
□ 96BeAPAut-163
□ 96BeAPAutSil-163
□ 96BeAPla-163
□ 96ColCho-6
□ 96Don-86
□ 96DonPrePro-86
□ 96Sco-227
□ 96ScoArtPro-227
□ 96ScoDeaCAP-227
□ 96ScoGolB-227
□ 96ScoSpeAP-227
□ 96SenPizH-25
□ 97PacInvNRB-138
□ 98Be A PPA-245
□ 98Be A PPAA-245
□ 98Be A PPAAF-245
□ 98Be A PPSE-245
□ 98Be APG-245
□ 98Pac-317
□ 98PaIceB-317
□ 98PacRed-317
**Van Amburg, Sean**
□ 90RayJrC-22
□ 91RayJrC-21
**Van Boxmeer, John**

□ 74CanaPos-26
□ 76OPCNHL-330
□ 76RocCokCan-20
□ 77OPCNHL-315
□ 77RocCokCan-19
□ 78OPC-224
□ 78Top-224
□ 79OPC-96
□ 79SabBel-9
□ 79Top-96
□ 80OPC-183
□ 80Top-183
□ 81OPC-26
□ 81OPCSti-58
□ 81SabMilP-2
□ 81Top-E80
□ 82OPC-36
□ 82OPC-37
□ 82OPCSti-121
□ 82PosCer-2
□ 82SabMilP-4
□ 83OPC-73
□ 83OPCSti-244
□ 83PufSti-9
□ 83Vac-78
□ 88ProAHL-268
□ 89ProAHL-266
□ 90SabCam-30
□ 92RochAmeKod-1
□ 93RochAmeKod-1
**van den Thillart, Leo**
□ 98GerDELE-36
**Van Der Horst, Jamie**
□ 95SolBar-1
□ 97SheSte-16
**Van Der Sloot, Adrian**
□ 88NiaFalT-18
**Van Dorp, Wayne**
□ 87PenKod-25
□ 88OilTenAnn-164
□ 88ProAHL-260
□ 89BlaCok-15
□ 90OPC-527
□ 91NordPet-32
□ 92NorPet-35
**Van Drunen, David**
□ 93PriAlbR-19
□ 94PriAlbR-20
□ 95PriAlbR-19
□ 96PriAlbR-16
□ 96PriAlbROC-21
**Van Dyk, Chris**
□ 94WinSpi-6
□ 95Sla-409
**van Hellemond, Andy**
□ 90ProSet-701
**Van Impe, Darren**
□ 907thInnSWHL-268
□ 90PriAlbR-21
□ 917thInnSMC-117
□ 917thInnSWHL-258
□ 91PriAlbR-23
□ 93RedDeeR-25
□ 95ColEdgI-12
□ 95Lea-138
□ 96Duc-16
□ 96MetUni-193
□ 96SP-4
□ 96Ult-7
□ 96UltGolM-7
□ 96UppDec-213
□ 97ColCho-4
□ 97Pac-286
□ 97PacCop-286
□ 97PacEmeGre-286
□ 97PacIceB-286
□ 97PacInv-5
□ 97PacInvC-5
□ 97PacInvEG-5
□ 97PacInvIB-5
□ 97PacInvR-5
□ 97PacInvS-5
□ 97PacRed-286
□ 97PacSil-286
□ 97ScoMigDPla-9
□ 97ScoMigDPre-9
□ 97ScoMigDuc-9
□ 97UppDec-4
□ 98Be A PPA-159
□ 98Be A PPAA-159
□ 98Be A PPAAF-159
□ 98Be A PPSE-159
□ 98Be APG-159
**Van Impe, Ed**
□ 63Top-30
□ 64BeeGro3P-58
□ 68OPC-91
□ 68Top-91
□ 69OPC-92
□ 69OPCFou-18
□ 69Top-92
□ 70ColSta-78
□ 70DadCoo-134
□ 70EssPowPla-200
□ 70OPC-80
□ 70OPCDec-34
□ 70SarProSta-159
□ 70Top-80
□ 70TopStiS-32
□ 71Baz-3
□ 71LetActR-11
□ 71OPC-126
□ 71SarProSta-150
□ 71Top-126
□ 71TorSun-207

□ 72FlyMigM-7
□ 72OPC-93
□ 72SarProSta-160
□ 72Top-9
□ 73OPC-206
□ 74NHLActSta-207
□ 74OPCNHL-85
□ 74Top-85
□ 75FlyCanDC-19
□ 75OPCNHL-38
□ 75Top-38
□ 76OPCNHL-157
□ 76Top-157
□ 92Par-479
□ 92ParEmel-479
□ 95Par66-36
□ 95Par66Coi-36
**Van Kessel, John**
□ 897thInnSOHL-162
□ 89ProAHL-26
□ 90ProAHLIHL-348
□ 91ProAHLCHL-400
□ 93WheThu-UD3
□ 94CapBreO-19
□ 98GerDELE-28
**Van Leyen, Thorsten**
□ 94GerDELE-90
**Van Oene, Darren**
□ 95BowDraPro-P34
□ 95SlaMemC-44
□ 95UppDec-511
□ 95UppDecEleIce-511
□ 95UppDecEleIceG-511
**Van Rooyen, Keith**
□ 85SudWol-23
**Van Ryn, Mike**
□ 96UppDec-378
□ 98SPXTopP-63
□ 98SPXTopPF-63
□ 98SPXTopPR-63
□ 98UC-266
□ 98UD ChoPCR-266
□ 98UD ChoR-266
□ 98UppDecBD-95
□ 98UppDecDD-95
□ 98UppDecQD-95
□ 98UppDecTD-95
**Van Slooten, Mike**
□ 86RegPat-28
□ 87RegPat-27
**Van Tassel, Miles**
□ 93WatBlaH-26
**Van Volsen, Joe**
□ 93SauSteMG-17
□ 95SauSteMGM-26
□ 95SauSteMG-24
□ 95Sla-51
**Van Volsen, Mike**
□ 95Sla-33
**Vanbiesbrouck, John**
□ 80SauSteMG-13
□ 81SauSteMG-23
□ 82SauSteMG-22
□ 850PCSti-8
□ 86OPC-9
□ 860PCSti-114
□ 860PCSti-190
□ 860PCSti-218
□ 86Top-9
□ 86TopStiIns-1
□ 870PC-36
□ 870PCSti-33
□ 87PanSti-106
□ 87SauSteMG-16
□ 87Top-36
□ 880PC-102
□ 880PCMin-42
□ 880PCSti-244
□ 88PanSti-300
□ 88Top-102
□ 890PC-114
□ 890PCSti-246
□ 89PanSti-282
□ 89RanMarMB-34
□ 89SweSemWCS-154
□ 89Top-114
□ 90Bow-222
□ 90BowTif-222
□ 90OPC-175
□ 90PanSti-108
□ 90Sco-175
□ 90ScoCan-175
□ 90ScoHotRS-76
□ 90Top-75
□ 90TopTif-75
□ 90UppDec-279
□ 90UppDecF-279
□ 91Bow-68
□ 91OPC-353
□ 91PanSti-282
□ 91Par-338
□ 91ParFre-338
□ 91Pin-121
□ 91Pin-367
□ 91PinFre-121
□ 91PinFre-367
□ 91ProSet-447
□ 91ProSetFre-447
□ 91ProSetPlaPC-PC1
□ 91ScoAme-10
□ 91ScoCan-10
□ 91StaClu-323

□ 91SweSemWCS-127
□ 91Top-353
□ 91UppDec-324
□ 91UppDecF-324
□ 92Bow-132
□ 92Kra-34
□ 92OPC-275
□ 92PanSti-232
□ 92PanStiFre-232
□ 92Par-349
□ 92ParEmel-349
□ 92Pin-186
□ 92PinFre-186
□ 92Sco-160
□ 92ScoCan-160
□ 92ScoUSAG-7
□ 92Top-169
□ 92TopGol-169G
□ 92UppDec-44
□ 93Don-132
□ 93HigLinGG-5
□ 93Kra-25
□ 93Lea-371
□ 93LeaPaiWar-8
□ 930PCPre-160
□ 93OPCPre-314
□ 93OPCPreG-160
□ 93OPCPreG-314
□ 93PanSti-98
□ 93Par-73
□ 93ParEmel-73
□ 93Pin-148
□ 93PinCan-148
□ 93PinExp-1
□ 93PinMas-9
□ 93Pow-102
□ 93Sco-162
□ 93Sco-445
□ 93Sco-492
□ 93Sco-501
□ 93ScoCan-162
□ 93ScoCan-445
□ 93ScoCan-492
□ 93ScoCan-501
□ 93ScoGol-501
□ 93StaClu-85
□ 93StaClu-330
□ 93StaCluFDI-85
□ 93StaCluFDI-330
□ 93StaCluFDIO-85
□ 93StaCluMasP-10
□ 93StaCluMasPW-10
□ 93StaCluO-85
□ 93StaCluO-330
□ 93TopPre-160
□ 93TopPre-314
□ 93TopPreG-160
□ 93TopPreG-314
□ 93Ult-333
□ 93UppDec-8
□ 93UppDecNR-27
□ 93UppDecSP-60
□ 94ActPacBPP-BP2
□ 94BeAPla-R20
□ 94BeAPla-R135
□ 94BeAPSig-20
□ 94CanGamNHLP-261
□ 94CanGamNHLP-280
□ 94Don-176
□ 94DonDom-3
□ 94DonIceMas-10
□ 94DonMasM-10
□ 94EASpo-54
□ 94Fin-40
□ 94FinBowB-B8
□ 94FinBowBR-B8
□ 94FinRef-40
□ 94FinSupTW-40
□ 94Fla-69
□ 94Fle-83
□ 94FleNet-10
□ 94Kra-55
□ 94KraGoaM-8
□ 94Lea-70
□ 94LeaCreP-5
□ 94LeaGolS-13
□ 94LeaLim-72
□ 94LeaLimI-9
□ 94OPCPre-82
□ 94OPCPre-360
□ 94OPCPreSE-82
□ 94OPCPreSE-360
□ 94PanPop-2
□ 94ParCratGB-9
□ 94ParCratGG-9
□ 94ParCratGR-9
□ 94ParSE-SE67
□ 94ParSEG-SE67
□ 94ParVin-V13
□ 94Pin-100
□ 94PinArtP-100
□ 94PinGoaG-GT3
□ 94PinMas-MA2
□ 94PinRinC-100
□ 94ScoFra-TF9
□ 94Sel-7
□ 94SelGol-7
□ 94SelPro-7
□ 94SP-44
□ 94SPDieCut-44
□ 94StaClu-95
□ 94StaCluFDI-95
□ 94StaCluMO-40

□ 94StaCluMOMS-95
□ 94StaCluSTWC-95
□ 94TopPre-82
□ 94TopPre-360
□ 94TopPreSE-82
□ 94TopPreSE-360
□ 94Ult-860
□ 94UppDec-46
□ 94UppDecEleIce-46
□ 94UppDecPC-C20
□ 94UppDecPCEG-C20
□ 94UppDecPH-H32
□ 94UppDecPHEG-H32
□ 94UppDecPHES-H32
□ 94UppDecPHG-H32
□ 94UppDecSPI-SP31
□ 94UppDecSPIDC-SP31
□ 95Bow-30
□ 95BowAllFoi-30
□ 95CanGamNHLP-123
□ 95ColCho-253
□ 95ColCho-368
□ 95ColChoPC-253
□ 95ColChoPC-368
□ 95ColChoPCP-253
□ 95ColChoPCP-368
□ 95Don-106
□ 95DonEli-83
□ 95DonEliDCS-83
□ 95DonEliDCU-83
□ 95DonEliPW-6
□ 95Emo-72
□ 95Fin-20
□ 95Fin-188
□ 95FinnSemWC-102
□ 95FinnSemWC-217
□ 95FinRef-20
□ 95FinRef-188
□ 95ImpSti-47
□ 95Kra-32
□ 95Lea-172
□ 95LeaLim-47
□ 95LeaLimSS-6
□ 95Met-62
□ 95NHLAcePC-7S
□ 95ParInt-85
□ 95ParIntCCGS2-12
□ 95ParIntCCSS2-12
□ 95ParIntEI-85
□ 95ParIntG-7
□ 95ParIntPTP-PP5
□ 95ParIntPTP-PP29
□ 95PinFan-16
□ 95PlaOneoOne-44
□ 95ProMag-90
□ 95Sco-241
□ 95Sco-322
□ 95ScoBlaIce-241
□ 95ScoBlaIce-322
□ 95ScoBlaIceAP-241
□ 95ScoBlaIceAP-322
□ 95SelCer-85
□ 95SelCerMG-85
□ 95SkyImp-70
□ 95SkyImpD-6
□ 95SP-56
□ 95StaClu-35
□ 95StaCluMO-7
□ 95StaCluMOMS-35
□ 95Sum-130
□ 95SumArtP-130
□ 95SumIce-130
□ 95SumInTheCre-15
□ 95SweGloWC-101
□ 95Top-252
□ 95TopHomGUSA-HGA8
□ 95TopOPCI-252
□ 95TopPro-PF9
□ 95TopSupSki-78
□ 95TopSupSkiPla-78
□ 95Ult-64
□ 95Ult-378
□ 95UltGolM-64
□ 95UltPrePadMen-11
□ 95UltPrePadMenGM-11
□ 95UppDec-321
□ 95UppDecEleIce-321
□ 95UppDecEleIceG-321
□ 95UppDecNHLAS-AS19
□ 95UppDecPHE-H19
□ 95UppDecSpeE-SE122
□ 95UppDecSpeEdiG-SE122
□ 95UppDecPHeV-H19
□ 95Zen-36
□ 96BeAPLH-10B
□ 96BeAPLHAut-10B
□ 96BeAPLHAutSil-10B
□ 96BeAPStaTP-4
□ 96ColCho-101
□ 96ColCho-318
□ 96ColChoMVP-UD12
□ 96ColChoMVPG-UD12
□ 96Don-187
□ 96DonBetPip-4
□ 96DonCanG-GPP-84
□ 96DonCanI-RPP-84
□ 96DonDom-1
□ 96DonEli-74
□ 96DonEliDCS-74
□ 96DonEliPW-4
□ 96DonEliPW-P4
□ 96DonPrePro-187
□ 96Fla-40
□ 96FlaBluI-40

□ 96FlaHotG-12
□ 96Fle-44
□ 96FlePic-88
□ 96FlePicDL-8
□ 96FlePicF5-46
□ 96FleVez-10
□ 96KraUppD-19
□ 96Lea-193
□ 96LeaLim-30
□ 96LeaLimG-30
□ 96LeaPre-41
□ 96LeaPreMM-3
□ 96LeaPreP-193
□ 96LeaPrePP-41
□ 96LeaPreVP-2
□ 96LeaPreVPG-2
□ 96LeaShuDow-2
□ 96LeaSwe-4
□ 96LeaSwe-(4
□ 96MetUni-84
□ 96MetUniAP-12
□ 96MetUniAPSP-12
□ 96MetUniCS-12
□ 96MetUniCSSP-12
□ 96NHLProSTA-90
□ 96Pin-203
□ 96PinArtP-203
□ 96PinFan-FC9
□ 96PinFoi-203
□ 96PinMas-3
□ 96PinMasDC-3
□ 96PinMcD-35
□ 96PinMin-26
□ 96PinMinB-26
□ 96PinMinCoiB-26
□ 96PinMinCoiGP-26
□ 96PinMinCoiN-26
□ 96PinMinCoiS-26
□ 96PinMinCoiSG-26
□ 96PinMinG-26
□ 96PinMinS-26
□ 96PinPreS-203
□ 96PinRinC-203
□ 96PinTeaP-8
□ 96PlaOneoOne-425
□ 96PosUppD-23
□ 96Sco-63
□ 96ScoArtPro-63
□ 96ScoDeaCAP-63
□ 96ScoGolB-63
□ 96ScoNetW-8
□ 96ScoSam-63
□ 96ScoSpeAP-63
□ 96ScoSudDea-7
□ 96SelCer-59
□ 96SelCerAP-59
□ 96SelCerBlu-59
□ 96SelCerFre-4
□ 96SelCerMB-59
□ 96SelCerMG-59
□ 96SelCerMR-59
□ 96SelCerRed-59
□ 96SkyImp-50
□ 96SkyImpZH-10
□ 96SP-61
□ 96SPCleWin-CW9
□ 96SPGamFil-GF8
□ 96StaCluMO-34
□ 96Sum-66
□ 96SumArtP-66
□ 96SumIce-66
□ 96SumInTheCre-10
□ 96SumInTheCrePS-10
□ 96SumMet-66
□ 96SumPreS-66
□ 96SweSemW-156
□ 96TeaOut-63
□ 96TopPicID-ID12
□ 96Ult-70
□ 96UltGolM-70
□ 96UppDec-63
□ 96UppDecBD-165
□ 96UppDecBDG-165
□ 96UppDecBDRFTC-RC6
□ 96UppDecGJ-GJ7
□ 96UppDecGN-X7
□ 96UppDecHH-HH6
□ 96UppDecHHG-HH6
□ 96UppDecHHS-HH6
□ 96UppDecIce-110
□ 96UppDecIceDF-S3
□ 96UppDecIcePar-110
□ 96UppDecIceSCF-S3
□ 96UppDecSS-SS2B
□ 96Zen-91
□ 96ZenArtP-91
□ 96ZenZT-17
□ 97BeAPlaSTP-8
□ 97BeAPlaTAN-6
□ 97ColCho-102
□ 97ColCho-317
□ 97ColChoSta-SQ84
□ 97ColChoSti-S2
□ 97Don-58
□ 97DonBetTP-3
□ 97DonCanI-7
□ 97DonCanIDS-7
□ 97DonCanISCS-16
□ 97DonEli-126
□ 97DonEliAsp-3
□ 97DonEliAsp-126
□ 97DonEliC-1

□ 97DonEliIns-8
□ 97DonEliMC-1
□ 97DonEliPN-8A
□ 97DonEliPN-8B
□ 97DonEliPN-8C
□ 97DonEliPNDC-8A
□ 97DonEliPNDC-8B
□ 97DonEliPNDC-8C
□ 97DonEliS-3
□ 97DonEliS-126
□ 97DonLim-5
□ 97DonLim-62
□ 97DonLim-113
□ 97DonLimExp-5
□ 97DonLimExp-62
□ 97DonLimExp-113
□ 97DonLimFOTG-7
□ 97DonPre-9
□ 97DonPre-182
□ 97DonPreCG-4
□ 97DonPreCGP-4
□ 97DonPreCttC-9
□ 97DonPreCttC-182
□ 97DonPreDWT-8
□ 97DonPrePM-13
□ 97DonPreProG-58
□ 97DonPreProS-58
□ 97DonPreT-6
□ 97DonPreTB-6
□ 97DonPreTBC-6
□ 97DonPreTPC-6
□ 97DonPreTPG-6
□ 97DonPri-5
□ 97DonPri-193
□ 97DonPriODI-5
□ 97DonPriP-11
□ 97DonPriPG-2
□ 97DonPriPGP-2
□ 97DonPriS-11
□ 97DonPriSB-11
□ 97DonPriSG-11
□ 97DonPriSoA-5
□ 97DonPriSoA-193
□ 97DonPriSS-11
□ 97EssOlyHH-34
□ 97EssOlyHHF-34
□ 97HigMinHMC-16
□ 97Kat-66
□ 97KatGol-66
□ 97KatSil-66
□ 97Lea-5
□ 97Lea-172
□ 97LeaFraMat-5
□ 97LeaFraMat-172
□ 97LeaFraMDC-5
□ 97LeaFraMDC-172
□ 97LeaInt-5
□ 97LeaIntUI-5
□ 97LeaPipDre-2
□ 97McD-24
□ 97Pac-34
□ 97PacCarSup-9
□ 97PacCarSupM-9
□ 97PacCop-34
□ 97PacCroR-60
□ 97PacCroREG-60
□ 97PacCroRFODC-9
□ 97PacCroRIB-60
□ 97PacCroRS-60
□ 97PacDyn-57
□ 97PacDynBKS-43
□ 97PacDynC-57
□ 97PacDynDG-57
□ 97PacDynEG-57
□ 97PacDynIB-57
□ 97PacDynKotN-5
□ 97PacDynR-57
□ 97PacDynSil-57
□ 97PacDynSto-10
□ 97PacDynTan-13
□ 97PacEmeGre-34
□ 97PacGolCroDC-13
□ 97PacIceB-34
□ 97PacInTheCLC-10
□ 97PacInv-64
□ 97PacInvC-64
□ 97PacInvEG-64
□ 97PacInvFP-17
□ 97PacInvIB-64
□ 97PacInvNRB-89
□ 97PacInvR-64
□ 97PacInvS-64
□ 97PacOme-102
□ 97PacOmeC-102
□ 97PacOmeDG-102
□ 97PacOmeEG-102
□ 97PacOmeG-102
□ 97PacOmeIB-102
□ 97PacOmeNSZ-5
□ 97PacPar-86
□ 97PacParBNDC-11
□ 97PacParC-86
□ 97PacParDG-86
□ 97PacParEG-86
□ 97PacParGSL-9
□ 97PacParIB-86
□ 97PacParP-11
□ 97PacParRed-86
□ 97PacParSil-86
□ 97PacRed-34
□ 97PacRev-62
□ 97PacRevC-62
□ 97PacRevE-62
□ 97PacRevIB-62
□ 97PacRevR-62
□ 97PacRevRtSD-9
□ 97PacRevS-62
□ 97PacRevTCL-11
□ 97PacSil-34
□ 97PacTeaCCC-11
□ 97Pin-37
□ 97Pin-NNO
□ 97PinArtP-37
□ 97PinBee-27
□ 97PinBeeGP-27
□ 97PinBeeGT-5
□ 97PinBeeT-5
□ 97PinCer-6
□ 97PinCerGT-3
□ 97PinCerMB-6
□ 97PinCerMG-6
□ 97PinCerMR-6
□ 97PinCerR-6
□ 97PinCerT-3
□ 97PinEpiGO-2
□ 97PinEpiGP-2
□ 97PinEpiME-2
□ 97PinEpiMO-2
□ 97PinEpiMP-2
□ 97PinEpiPE-2
□ 97PinEpiPO-2
□ 97PinEpiPP-2
□ 97PinEpiSE-2
□ 97PinEpiSO-2
□ 97PinEpiSP-2
□ 97PinIns-19
□ 97PinInsC-20
□ 97PinInsCC-19
□ 97PinInsCG-20
□ 97PinInsEC-19
□ 97PinInsSto-2
□ 97PinInsSUG-2A/B
□ 97PinInsSUG-2C/D
□ 97PinInsT-7
□ 97PinMas-1
□ 97PinMasDC-1
□ 97PinMasJ-1
□ 97PinMasPro-1
□ 97PinMin-4
□ 97PinMinB-4
□ 97PinMinCBP-4
□ 97PinMinCGPP-4
□ 97PinMinCNSP-4
□ 97PinMinCoiB-4
□ 97PinMinCoiGP-4
□ 97PinMinCoiN-4
□ 97PinMinCoiSG-4
□ 97PinMinCoiSS-4
□ 97PinMinGolTea-4
□ 97PinMinSilTea-4
□ 97PinPowPac-13
□ 97PinPowPac-P13
□ 97PinPrePBB-37
□ 97PinPrePBC-37
□ 97PinPrePBM-37
□ 97PinPrePBY-37
□ 97PinPrePFC-37
□ 97PinPrePFM-37
□ 97PinPrePFY-37
□ 97PinPrePla-37
□ 97PinRepMas-6
□ 97PinRinC-37
□ 97PinTeaP-10
□ 97PinTeaPM-10
□ 97PinTeaPP-10
□ 97PinTeaPPM-10
□ 97PinTin-10
□ 97PinTotCMPG-6
□ 97PinTotCPB-6
□ 97PinTotCPG-6
□ 97PinTotCPR-6
□ 97Sco-34
□ 97ScoArtPro-34
□ 97ScoGolBla-34
□ 97ScoNetW-15
□ 97SP AutI-I5
□ 97SPAut-69
□ 97SPAutID-I5
□ 97SPAutIE-I5
□ 97SPx-20
□ 97SPxBro-20
□ 97SPxDuo-8
□ 97SPxGol-20
□ 97SPxGraF-20
□ 97SPxSil-20
□ 97SPxSte-20
□ 97Stu-17
□ 97StuPor-17
□ 97StuPrePG-17
□ 97StuPrePS-17
□ 97StuSil-16
□ 97StuSil8-16
□ 97UppDec-72
□ 97UppDecBD-42
□ 97UppDecBDDD-42
□ 97UppDecBDQD-42
□ 97UppDecBDTD-42
□ 97UppDecDV-7
□ 97UppDecDVSM-7
□ 97UppDecGDM-72
□ 97UppDecIC-IC17
□ 97UppDecIC2-IC17
□ 97UppDecIce-74
□ 97UppDecIceP-74
□ 97UppDecIPS-74
□ 97UppDecSG-SG54
□ 97UppDecTS-7
□ 97UppDecTSL2-7
□ 97UppDecTSS-2C
□ 97Zen-9
□ 97Zen5x7-4
□ 97ZenGolImp-4
□ 97ZenSilImp-4
□ 97ZenZGol-9
□ 97ZenZSil-9
□ 98Be A PPA-252
□ 98Be A PPAA-252
□ 98Be A PPAAF-252
□ 98Be A PPPH-H11
□ 98Be A PPSE-252
□ 98Be APG-252
□ 98BowBes-82
□ 98BowBesAR-82
□ 98BowBesR-82
□ 98Fin-55
□ 98FinNo P-55
□ 98FinNo PR-55
□ 98FinRef-55
□ 980-PChr-215
□ 980-PChrR-215
□ 98Pac-34
□ 98PacAur-142
□ 98PacCroR-101
□ 98PacCroRLS-101
□ 98PacCroRPotG-19
□ 98PacCroRPP-19
□ 98PacDynI-140
□ 98PacDynIIB-140
□ 98PacDynIIW-7
□ 98PacDynIR-140
□ 98PacIceB-34
□ 98PacOmeH-180
□ 98PacOmeO-27
□ 98PacOmeODI-180
□ 98PacOmePI-12
□ 98PacOmePIB-12
□ 98PacOmeR-180
□ 98PacPar-178
□ 98PacParC-178
□ 98PacParEG-178
□ 98PacParH-178
□ 98PacParIB-178
□ 98PacParS-178
□ 98PacRed-34
□ 98PacRev-107
□ 98PacRevIS-107
□ 98PacRevR-107
□ 98PacRevS-27
□ 98PacTeaC-11
□ 98PinEpiGE-2
□ 98RevThrPA-17
□ 98RevThrPA-17
□ 98SP Aut-62
□ 98SP AutSM-S10
□ 98SP AutSS-SS16
□ 98SPXTopP-45
□ 98SPXTopPF-45
□ 98SPXTopPHH-H20
□ 98SPXTopPLI-L2
□ 98SPXTopPPS-PS10
□ 98SPXTopPR-45
□ 98SPXTopPWM-JV
□ 98Top-215
□ 98TopGolLC1-59
□ 98TopGolLC1B-59
□ 98TopGolLC1BOoO-59
□ 98TopGolLC1OoO-59
□ 98TopGolLC1R-59
□ 98TopGolLC1ROoO-59
□ 98TopGolLC2-59
□ 98TopGolLC2B-59
□ 98TopGolLC2BOoO-59
□ 98TopGolLC2OoO-59
□ 98TopGolLC2R-59
□ 98TopGolLC2ROoO-59
□ 98TopGolLC3-59
□ 98TopGolLC3B-59
□ 98TopGolLC3BOoO-59
□ 98TopGolLC3OoO-59
□ 98TopGolLC3R-59
□ 98TopGolLC3ROoO-59
□ 98TopO-P-215
□ 98UC-89
□ 98UC-247
□ 98UCMBH-BH10
□ 98UD ChoPCR-89
□ 98UD ChoPCR-247
□ 98UD ChoR-89
□ 98UD ChoR-247
□ 98UD3-54
□ 98UD3-114
□ 98UD3-174
□ 98UD3DieC-54
□ 98UD3DieC-114
□ 98UD3DieC-174
□ 98UppDec-148
□ 98UppDecBD-64
□ 98UppDecDD-64
□ 98UppDecE-148
□ 98UppDecE1o1-148
□ 98UppDecGR-148
□ 98UppDecM-149
□ 98UppDecM1-M2
□ 98UppDecM2-M2
□ 98UppDecMGS-149
□ 98UppDecMSS-149
□ 98UppDecMSS-149
□ 98UppDecP-P7
□ 98UppDecPQ1-P7
□ 98UppDecPQ2-P7
□ 98UppDecPQ3-P7
□ 98UppDecQD-64
□ 98UppDecTD-64
□ 99Pac-313
□ 99PacAur-108
□ 99PacAurGU-15
□ 99PacAurPD-108
□ 99PacCop-313
□ 99PacGol-313
□ 99PacGolCD-28
□ 99PacIceB-313
□ 99PacIn tCN-14
□ 99PacPasAP-18
□ 99PacPreD-313
□ 99RetHoc-62
□ 99SP AutPS-62
□ 99UppDecM-155
□ 99UppDecMGS-155
□ 99UppDecMLL-LL7
□ 99UppDecMSS-155
□ 99UppDecMSS-155
□ 99UppDecRG-62
□ 99UppDecRP-62

**Vanclief, Chris**
□ 89OshGenP-33

**Vandale, Duane**
□ 92MPSPhoSJHL-94

**Vandenberghe, Mike**
□ 88BraWheK-4
□ 89BraWheK-5
□ 90BraWheK-3
□ 917thInnSWHL-334
□ 94DayBom-19

**VandenBussche, Ryan**
□ 907thInnSOHL-49
□ 917thInnSOHL-22
□ 91CorRoy-7
□ 93St.JohML-24
□ 94St.JohML-22
□ 95BinRan-24
□ 96BinRan-21
□ 97Be A PPAD-223
□ 97Be A PPAPD-223
□ 97BeAPla-223
□ 97BeAPlaAut-223

**Vander Wal, Wes**
□ 95Sla-148

**Vanderkracht, Bram**
□ 89SpoChi-19
□ 907thInnSWHL-211
□ 917thInnSMC-88
□ 917thInnSWHL-194

**Vandermeer, Pete**
□ 93RedDeeR-26
□ 95RedDeeR-16

**Vanderydt, Rob**
□ 91RicRen-1

**Vanecek, Filip**
□ 96CzeAPSE-319

**VanHerzele, Larry**
□ 83BraAle-10
□ 84BelBul-14

**Vani, Carmine**
□ 81KinCan-10
□ 82KinCan-6
□ 83KitRan-17
□ 93SweSemWCS-222
□ 94FinnJaaK-310

**Vanik, Milos**
□ 94GerDELE-142
□ 95GerDELE-140
□ 96GerDELE-335

**Vankrbec, Miroslav**
□ 96CzeAPSE-264

**Vanstaalduinen, Bart**
□ 91AirCanSJHL-B37
□ 91AirCanSJHL-D17
□ 91AirCanSJHLAS-22
□ 91AirCanSJHLAS-49
□ 93MicSta-26

**Vantighem, Travis**
□ 91AirCanSJHL-D12
□ 92MPSPhoSJHL-78

**Varada, Vaclav**
□ 95SigRoo-1
□ 95SigRooSig-1
□ 96Fla-102
□ 96FlaBlul-102
□ 96SP-171
□ 96UppDec-224
□ 97Don-217
□ 97DonCanI-141
□ 97DonCanIDS-141
□ 97DonCanIPS-141
□ 97DonLim-23
□ 97DonLim-178
□ 97DonLimExp-23
□ 97DonLimExp-178
□ 97DonPre-159
□ 97DonPreCttC-159
□ 97DonPreProG-217
□ 97DonPreProS-217
□ 97Lea-48
□ 97Lea-166
□ 97LeaFraMat-48
□ 97LeaFraMat-166
□ 97LeaFraMDC-48
□ 97LeaFraMDC-166
□ 97LeaInt-48
□ 97LeaIntUI-48
□ 97UppDec-229
□ 98Pac-111
□ 98PacDynI-22
□ 98PacDynIIB-22
□ 98PacDynIR-22
□ 98PacIceB-111
□ 98PacPar-23
□ 98PacParC-23
□ 98PacParEG-23
□ 98PacParH-23
□ 98PacParIB-23
□ 98PacParS-23
□ 98PacRed-111
□ 98UC-20
□ 98UD ChoPCR-20
□ 98UD ChoR-20
□ 98UD3-24
□ 98UD3-84
□ 98UD3-144
□ 98UD3DieC-24
□ 98UD3DieC-84
□ 98UD3DieC-144
□ 98UppDec-48
□ 98UppDecE-48
□ 98UppDecE1o1-48
□ 98UppDecGR-48
□ 99Pac-47
□ 99PacCop-47
□ 99PacGol-47
□ 99PacIceB-47
□ 99PacPreD-47

**Vardale, Duane**
□ 91AirCanSJHL-D38

**Varga, Chris**
□ 907thInnSOHL-21
□ 917thInnSOHL-38

**Varga, John**
□ 917thInnSWHL-150
□ 92TacRoc-27
□ 93DonTeaUSA-21
□ 93Pin-500
□ 93PinCan-500
□ 93TacRoc-27
□ 93UppDec-559
□ 96WheNai-14

**Vargas, Ernie**
□ 86SheCan-28
□ 89ProIHL-170

**Vargo, Jamie**
□ 89WinSpi-19

**Varholik, Jan**
□ 94FinnJaaK-194
□ 95SloAPSNT-11

**Varis, Petri**
□ 93FinnJyvHS-109
□ 93FinnSIS-23
□ 93FinnSIS-393
□ 93SweSemWCS-82
□ 94FinnJaaK-46
□ 94FinnSIS-248
□ 94FinnSIS-376
□ 95FinnSemWC-28
□ 95FinnSIS-259
□ 95FinnSISL-18
□ 95FinnSISP-7
□ 95FinnSISSpe-1
□ 96FinnSISR-47
□ 96FinnSISR-180
□ 96FinnSISRATG-1
□ 98GerDELE-92

**Varitsky, I.**
□ 95GerDELE-162

**Varjanov, Nikolai**
□ 90OPC-504

**Varjonen, Tommi**
□ 93FinnJyvHS-52
□ 93FinnSIS-251
□ 94FinnSIS-74

**Varlamov, Sergei**
□ 95SwiCurB-19
□ 97BeeAutA-73
□ 97BowCHL-120
□ 97BowCHLOPC-120
□ 97PinBee-73
□ 97PinBeeGP-73
□ 98BowBes-142
□ 98BowBesAR-142
□ 98BowBesR-142
□ 98BowCHL-79
□ 98BowCHLGA-79
□ 98BowCHLOI-79
□ 98BowCHLSC-SC9
□ 98BowChrC-79
□ 98BowChrCGA-79
□ 98BowChrCGAR-79
□ 98BowChrCOI-79
□ 98BowChrCOIR-79
□ 98BowChrCR-79
□ 98O-PChr-231
□ 98O-PChrR-231
□ 98Pac-58
□ 98PacIceB-58
□ 98PacRed-58
□ 98Top-231
□ 98TopO-P-231

**Varnakov, Mikhail**
□ 81SweSemHVS-54
□ 87RusNatT-22

**Varvio, Jarkko**
□ 91UppDec-676
□ 91UppDecCWJC-39
□ 91UppDecF-676
□ 92Cla-30
□ 93Don-90
□ 93DonRatR-6
□ 93FinnSIS-371
□ 93Lea-383
□ 93LeaFrePhe-8
□ 93Par-252
□ 93ParCalC-C8
□ 93ParCalCG-C8
□ 93ParEmel-252
□ 93Pin-430
□ 93PinCan-430
□ 93Sco-620
□ 93ScoCan-620
□ 93ScoGol-620
□ 93SweSemWCS-83
□ 93Ult-302
□ 93UltWavF-19
□ 93UppDec-422
□ 93UppDecSP-40
□ 94ClaProP-125
□ 94Don-129
□ 94FinnJaaK-44
□ 94FinnSIS-349
□ 94FinnSISGS-12
□ 94Lea-199
□ 94ParSE-SE40
□ 94ParSEG-SE40
□ 94Ult-281
□ 94UppDec-429
□ 94UppDecEleIce-429
□ 95FinnSemWC-44
□ 95FinnSIS-306
□ 95FinnSISL-89
□ 96ClaGol-30
□ 96FinnSISR-108

**Vary, John**
□ 897thInnSOHL-155
□ 907thInnSOHL-75
□ 907thInnSOHL-320
□ 917thInnSOHL-237
□ 94CenHocL-123
□ 95LouIceG-20
□ 95LouIceGP-21

**Vasicek, Tomas**
□ 94CzeAPSE-116
□ 96CzeAPSE-192

**Vasie, Valeri**
□ 96GuiFla-22

**Vasilevski, Alex**
□ 95ColEdgI-98
□ 95Ima-11
□ 95ImaGol-11
□ 95SlaMemC-49

**Vasiliev, Mikhael**
□ 83RusNatT-20

**Vasiliev, Valeri**
□ 70SweHocS-320
□ 73SweHocS-85
□ 73SweWorCS-85
□ 74SweHocS-3
□ 79PanSti-144
□ 80USSOlyTMP-10
□ 82SweSemHVS-56
□ 91FutTreC72-68
□ 92FutTre76CC-132
□ 96SweSemWHL-HI 4

**Vasilijevs, Herbert**
□ 94GerDELE-230
□ 95GueSto5A-10
□ 95Sla-94

**Vasilyev, Alexei**
□ 95UppDec-555
□ 95UppDecEleIce-555
□ 95UppDecEleIceG-555

**Vasilyev, Andrei**
□ 95ParInt-513
□ 95ParIntEl-513
□ 95UppDec-412

**Vaske, Dennis**
□ 90ProAHLIHL-508
□ 91OPC-230
□ 91ProAHLCHL-460
□ 91ScoAme-310
□ 91ScoCan-340
□ 91Top-230
□ 91UppDec-49
□ 91UppDecF-49
□ 92Bow-28
□ 92Par-335
□ 92ParEmel-335
□ 92StaClu-362
□ 92Top-87
□ 92TopGol-87G
□ 92UppDec-50
□ 92UppDec-383
□ 93OPCPre-438
□ 93OPCPreG-438
□ 93Pow-387
□ 93StaClu-358
□ 93StaCluFDI-358
□ 93StaCluO-358
□ 93TopPre-438
□ 93TopPreG-438
□ 94Par-141
□ 94ParGol-141
□ 94Pin-456
□ 94PinArtP-456
□ 94PinRinC-456
□ 94Ult-134
□ 95Emo-110
□ 95PlaOneoOne-170
□ 95SkyImp-106
□ 95Ult-272
□ 96IslPos-21
□ 97Be A PPAD-120
□ 97Be A PPAPD-120
□ 97BeAPla-120
□ 97BeAPlaAut-120
□ 97PacInvNRB-122

**Vasko, Elmer**
□ 44BeeGro2P-144
□ 57Top-27
□ 58Top-12
□ 59Top-3
□ 60ShiCoi-73
□ 60Top-23
□ 60TopSta-50
□ 61ShiCoi-26
□ 61Top-25
□ 62Top-27
□ 62TopHocBuc-23
□ 63ChePho-56
□ 63Top-26
□ 63TorSta-41
□ 64BeeGro3P-59
□ 64CocCap-22
□ 64Top-5
□ 64TorSta-48
□ 65Coc-22
□ 65Top-114
□ 68OPC-147
□ 68OPCPucSti-8
□ 91UltOriS-64
□ 91UltOriSF-64
□ 94ParMisL-31
□ 94ParTalB-30
□ 94ParTalB-141

**Vassiliev, Vladimir**
□ 94GerDELE-198

**Vater, Matthias**
□ 98GerDELE-216

**Vaughan, Doug**
□ 52JunBluT-117

**Vaughan, Kevin**
□ 93OshGen-17

**Vaughan, Lyle**
□ 91AirCanSJHL-C40

**Vaughan, R.**
□ 83BelBul-8
□ 84BelBul-2

**Vauhkonen, Jouni**
□ 92UppDec-619
□ 93FinnJyvHS-262
□ 93FinnSIS-296
□ 93FinnSIS-392
□ 93FinnSIS-392
□ 93Par-525
□ 93ParEmel-525
□ 94FinnSIS-174
□ 95FinnSemWC-234
□ 96FinnSISR-105

**Vautour, Yvon**
□ 81OPC-84
□ 81RocPos-28
□ 84FreExp-26

**Vavrecka, Jan**
□ 94CzeAPSE-8
□ 95CzeAPSE-31

**Veale, Brian**
□ 91BriColJHL-105
□ 91BriColJHL-147
□ 92BriColJHL-113

**Veber, Jiri**
□ 94FinnSIS-337
□ 95CzeAPSE-10
□ 95FinnSemWC-147
□ 96CzeAPSE-218
□ 96CzeAPSE-340

**Veber, Roman**
□ 96CzeAPSE-268

**Vecchiarelli, John**
□ 93SweSemWCS-219
□ 94FinnJaaK-303
□ 95BufStaRHI-19
□ 95BufStaRHI-19

**Veccia, Rob**
□ 84SauSteMG-21

**Vehmanen, Jorma**
□ 69SweWorC-167
□ 70SweHocS-312
□ 71SweHocS-74
□ 72SweSemWC-89
□ 96FinnSISR-194

**Veilleux, Eric**
□ 917thInnSQMJHL-245
□ 94ClaProP-67

**Veilleux, Steve**
□ 89ProIHL-167
□ 90ProAHLIHL-332
□ 91ProAHLCHL-79
□ 92FreCan-27

**Veisor, Mike**
□ 75OPCNHL-385
□ 77OPCNHL-393
□ 80OPC-361
□ 82WhaJunHC-21
□ 83WhaJunHC-21

**Veitch, Darren**
□ 81Cap-18
□ 82Cap-25
□ 82PosCer-20
□ 85CapPizH-15
□ 87OPC-114
□ 87PanSti-239
□ 87RedWinLC-28
□ 87Top-114
□ 88MapLeaPLA-22
□ 88PanSti-39
□ 89ProAHL-123
□ 90NewSai-25
□ 90ProAHLIHL-155
□ 91MonHaw-28
□ 92PeoRivC-25
□ 93PeoRiv-27
□ 95ColEdgI-80

**Vejvoda, Otakar**
□ 94CzeAPSE-59
□ 95CzeAPSE-96
□ 96SweSemW-115

**Velischek, Randy**
□ 83NorStaPos-26
□ 84NorStaPos-29

- 84SprInd-4
- 85DevPos-9
- 86DevPol-18
- 88DevCar-28
- 89DevCar-27
- 89OPC-245
- 89PanSti-259
- 90OPC-453
- 90OPCPre-125
- 90ProSet-518
- 90ScoRoo-64T
- 90UppDec-392
- 90UppDecF-392
- 91Bow-152
- 91NordPanTS-23
- 91NordPet-33
- 91OPC-377
- 91PanSti-265
- 91ProSet-206
- 91ProSetFre-206
- 91ScoAme-257
- 91ScoCan-477
- 91StaClu-27
- 91Top-377
- 91UppDec-484
- 91UppDecF-484
- 92Bow-131
- 92DurPan-45
- 92OPC-288
- 92StaClu-460
- 92Top-430
- 92TopGol-430G
- 94MilAdm-26

**Vellinga, Mike**
- 95GueSto5A-21
- 95Sla-92
- 96GueSto-19
- 96GueStoPC-3
- 97GueSto-12

**Vellucci, Mike**
- 83BelBul-17
- 88ProAHL-54

**Venasky, Vic**
- 740PCNHL-389
- 750PCNHL-312
- 75Top-312
- 760PCNHL-211
- 76Top-211
- 770PCNHL-187
- 77Top-187
- 780PC-321
- 790PC-269
- 800PC-290

**Venedam, Sean**
- 93SudWol-11
- 93SudWolP-24
- 94SudWol-10
- 94SudWolP-17
- 95Sla-393
- 95SudWol-1
- 95SudWolP-24
- 96SudWol-24
- 96SudWolP-26

**Veneruzzo, Gary**
- 680PC-119
- 68Top-119
- 700PC-101
- 70Top-101
- 720PC-330
- 72ShaLosAW-16
- 73QuaOatWHA-32
- 740PCWHA-55
- 75StiKah-14
- 760PCWHA-21
- 76SanDieMW-13

**Venis, Ken**
- 94CenHocL-89

**Venne, Maxime**
- 92QueIntP-37

**Venneruzzo, Gary**
- 66TulOil-11

**Venters, Daryl**
- 96FifFly-12
- 97FifFly-10

**Vento, Jouni**
- 93FinnJyvHS-355
- 93FinnSIS-214
- 94FinnSIS-53
- 94FinnSIS-177
- 95FinnSIS-354
- 96GerDELE-231

**Verbeek, Brian**
- 84KinCan-23
- 85KinCan-23

**Verbeek, Pat**
- 83CanNatJ-17
- 84DevPos-12
- 840PC-121
- 840PCSti-73
- 84Top-90
- 850PC-56
- 85Top-56
- 86DevPol-19
- 860PC-46
- 860PCSti-202
- 86Top-46
- 870PC-6
- 870PCSti-58
- 87PanSti-81
- 87Top-6
- 88DevCar-29
- 880PC-29
- 880PCMin-43
- 880PCSti-81
- 88PanSti-278

- 88Top-29
- 890PC-32
- 89Top-32
- 89WhaJunM-22
- 90Bow-257
- 90BowTif-257
- 900PC-112
- 90PanSti-36
- 90ProSet-112
- 90Sco-35
- 90ScoCan-35
- 90ScoHotRS-18
- 90Top-112
- 90TopTif-112
- 90UppDec-172
- 90UppDecF-172
- 90WhaJr7E-25
- 91Bow-12
- 91Gil-24
- 91Kra-23
- 910PC-499
- 910PCPre-5
- 91PanSti-313
- 91Par-64
- 91ParFre-64
- 91Pin-43
- 91PinFre-43
- 91ProSet-86
- 91ProSet-303
- 91ProSetFre-86
- 91ProSetFre-303
- 91ProSetPC-10
- 91ProSetPC-3
- 91ProSetPla-44
- 91ScoAme-70
- 91ScoCan-70
- 91StaClu-70
- 91Top-499
- 91TopTeaSL-1
- 91UppDec-193
- 91UppDecF-193
- 91WhaJr7E-26
- 92Bow-112
- 92HumDum2-24
- 920PC-197
- 92PanSti-256
- 92PanStiFre-256
- 92Par-58
- 92ParEmel-58
- 92Pin-348
- 92PinFre-348
- 92ProSet-58
- 92Sco-282
- 92ScoCan-282
- 92SeaPat-44
- 92StaClu-197
- 92Top-493
- 92TopGol-493G
- 92Ult-305
- 92UppDec-7
- 92UppDec-204
- 92WhaDai-22
- 93Don-148
- 93Kra-39
- 93Lea-144
- 930PCPre-47
- 930PCPreG-47
- 93PanSti-124
- 93Par-353
- 93ParEmel-353
- 93Pin-243
- 93PinCan-243
- 93PinCap-10
- 93PinCapC-10
- 93Pow-110
- 93Sco-10
- 93ScoCan-10
- 93StaClu-36
- 93StaCluFDI-36
- 93StaCluFDIO-36
- 93StaCluO-36
- 93TopPre-47
- 93TopPreG-47
- 93Ult-175
- 93UppDec-331
- 93UppDecSP-67
- 93WhaCok-23
- 94BeAPla-R61
- 94BeAPSig-71
- 94CanGamNHLP-120
- 94Don-299
- 94EASpo-59
- 94Fla-76
- 94Fle-91
- 94Lea-192
- 94LeaLim-27
- 940PCPre-390
- 940PCPreSE-390
- 94Par-92
- 94ParGol-92
- 94ParSEV-7
- 94Pin-37
- 94PinArtP-37
- 94PinRinC-37
- 94ScoChelt-Cl18
- 94Sel-76
- 94SelGol-76
- 94SP-72
- 94SPDieCut-72
- 94StaClu-120
- 94StaCluFDI-120
- 94StaCluMOMS-120
- 94StaCluSTWC-120

- 94Ult-95
- 94UppDec-278
- 94UppDecEIeIce-278
- 94UppDecNBAP-38
- 94UppDecSPI-SP124
- 94UppDecSPIDC-SP124
- 95CanGamNHLP-182
- 95ColCho-55
- 95ColChoPC-55
- 95ColChoPCP-55
- 95Don-29
- 95DonEli-76
- 95DonEliDCS-76
- 95DonEliDCU-76
- 95Emo-120
- 95Fin-131
- 95FinRef-131
- 95Lea-16
- 95Met-101
- 95ParIntEl-407
- 95ParIntEI-407
- 95Pin-111
- 95PinArtP-111
- 95PinRinC-111
- 95PlaOneoOne-70
- 95Sco-122
- 95ScoBlaIce-122
- 95ScoBlaIceAP-122
- 95SelCer-108
- 95SelCerMG-108
- 95SkyImp-115
- 95SP-93
- 95StaClu-17
- 95StaCluMOMS-17
- 95Sum-107
- 95SumArtP-107
- 95SumIce-107
- 95Top-37
- 95TopOPCI-37
- 95TopPowL-3PL
- 95TopSupSki-43
- 95TopSupSkiPla-43
- 95Ult-107
- 95UltGoIM-107
- 95UppDec-98
- 95UppDecEIeIce-98
- 95UppDecEIeIceG-98
- 95UppDecNHLAS-AS13
- 95Zen-82
- 96BeAPAut-38
- 96BeAPAutSil-38
- 96BeAPla-38
- 96ColCho-170
- 96Don-200
- 96DonCanI-48
- 96DonCanIGPP-48
- 96DonCanIRPP-48
- 96DonEli-42
- 96DonEliDCS-42
- 96DonPrePro-200
- 96Fla-25
- 96FlaBluI-25
- 96FlePicDL-10
- 96Lea-59
- 96LeaLim-33
- 96LeaLimG-33
- 96LeaPre-8
- 96LeaPreP-59
- 96LeaPrePP-8
- 96LeaPreSG-14
- 96LeaPreSte-14
- 96MetUni-43
- 96Pin-68
- 96PinArtP-68
- 96PinFoi-68
- 96PinPreS-68
- 96PinRinC-68
- 96PlaOneoOne-359
- 96Sco-94
- 96ScoArtPro-94
- 96ScoDeaCAP-94
- 96ScoGolB-94
- 96ScoSpeAP-94
- 96SelCer-49
- 96SelCerAP-49
- 96SelCerBlu-49
- 96SelCerMB-49
- 96SelCerMG-49
- 96SelCerMR-49
- 96SelCerRed-49
- 96SP-41
- 96StaCluMO-35
- 96StaPos-26
- 96StaScoS-94
- 96Sum-5
- 96SumArtP-5
- 96SumIce-5
- 96SumMet-5
- 96SumPreS-5
- 96TopNHLP-69
- 96TopPicOI-69
- 96Ult-47
- 96UltGoIM-47
- 96UppDec-249
- 96UppDecBD-136
- 96UppDecBDG-136
- 96UppDecIce-17
- 96UppDecIcePar-17
- 96Zen-93
- 96ZenArtP-93
- 97ColCho-66
- 97ColChoSta-SQ16
- 97Don-23
- 97DonCanI-27
- 97DonCanIDS-27

- 97DonCanIPS-27
- 97DonLim-75
- 97DonLimExp-75
- 97DonPre-57
- 97DonPreCttC-57
- 97DonPreProG-23
- 97DonPreProS-23
- 97Lea-78
- 97LeaFraMat-78
- 97LeaFraMDC-78
- 97LeaInt-78
- 97LeaIntUI-78
- 97Pac-162
- 97PacCop-162
- 97PacCroR-43
- 97PacCroREG-43
- 97PacCroRIB-43
- 97PacCroRS-43
- 97PacEmeGre-162
- 97PacIceB-162
- 97PacOme-76
- 97PacOmeC-76
- 97PacOmeDG-76
- 97PacOmeEG-76
- 97PacOmeG-76
- 97PacOmeIB-76
- 97PacPar-63
- 97PacParC-63
- 97PacParDG-63
- 97PacParEG-63
- 97PacParIB-63
- 97PacParRed-63
- 97PacParSil-63
- 97PacRed-162
- 97PacSil-162
- 97Pin-173
- 97PinCer-111
- 97PinCerMB-111
- 97PinCerMG-111
- 97PinCerMR-111
- 97PinCerR-111
- 97PinIns-157
- 97PinInsCE-157
- 97PinPrePBB-173
- 97PinPrePBC-173
- 97PinPrePBM-173
- 97PinPrePBY-173
- 97PinPrePFC-173
- 97PinPrePFM-173
- 97PinPrePFY-173
- 97PinPrePla-173
- 97PinTotCMPG-111
- 97PinTotCPB-111
- 97PinTotCPG-111
- 97PinTotCPR-111
- 97Sco-124
- 97ScoArtPro-124
- 97ScoChel-18
- 97ScoGolBla-124
- 97UppDec-262
- 98Fin-69
- 98FinNo P-69
- 98FinNo PR-69
- 98FinRef-69
- 980-PChr-120
- 980-PChrR-120
- 98Pac-185
- 98PacIceB-185
- 98PacRed-185
- 98Top-120
- 98TopO-P-120
- 98UppDec-257
- 98UppDecE-257
- 98UppDecE101-257
- 98UppDecGR-257
- 99Pac-131
- 99PacCop-131
- 99PacGol-131
- 99PacIceB-131
- 99PacPreD-131

**Verbeek, Tim**
- 96KitRan-26

**Verchota, Phil**
- 80USAOlyTMP-7
- 81SweSemHVS-107
- 95SigRooMI-37
- 95SigRooSMIS-37
- 95SigRooSMIS-38

**Verizjnikov, Viktor**
- 74SweHocS-78

**Vermeire, Antoine**
- 98QueRem-22

**Vermette, Mark**
- 88NordGenF-31
- 88NordTeal-32
- 89HalCit-25
- 89ProAHL-163
- 90HalCit-28
- 90ProAHLIHL-450
- 91NordPet-34
- 91UppDec-470
- 91UppDecF-470
- 92NorPet-36
- 93LasVegThu-30

**Verner, Andrew**
- 897thInnSOHL-121
- 907thInnSOHL-375
- 907thInnSOHL-143
- 91AreDraPic-25

- 91Cla-30
- 91PetPet-12
- 91StaPicH-21
- 91UltDra-26
- 91UppDec-74
- 91UppDecF-74
- 93ClaProPro-84

**Vernon, Mike**
- 83CanNatJ-18
- 84MonGolF-20
- 85FlamRedRP-29
- 86FlamRedR-29
- 86KraDra-78
- 87FlamRedRP-30
- 870PC-215
- 870PCSti-41
- 87PanSti-203
- 880PC-261
- 880PCMin-44
- 880PCSti-86
- 88PanSti-4
- 89Kra-62
- 89KraAllSS-4
- 890PC-163
- 890PC-300
- 890PCSti-76
- 890PCSti-94
- 890PCSti-167
- 890PCSti-215
- 89PanSti-6
- 89PanSti-7
- 89PanSti-34
- 89PanSti-178
- 89Top-163
- 89TopStiIns-12
- 90Bow-94
- 90BowTif-94
- 90FlamIGA-28
- 90Kra-61
- 90Kra-76
- 900PC-351
- 900PCBoxB-L
- 900PCPre-126
- 90PanSti-175
- 90PanSti-329
- 90ProSet-47
- 90ProSet-338
- 90Sco-9
- 90ScoCan-52
- 90ScoHotRS-23
- 90Top-351
- 90TopBoxB-L
- 90TopTif-351
- 90UppDec-254
- 90UppDec-495
- 90UppDecF-254
- 90UppDecF-495
- 91Bow-253
- 91FlamIGA-24
- 91FlamPanTS-23
- 91Kra-19
- 91McDUppD-20
- 910PC-107
- 910PC-247
- 910PCPre-9
- 91PanSti-55
- 91PanSti-328
- 91Par-27
- 91ParFre-27
- 91Pin-132
- 91PinFre-132
- 91ProSet-35
- 91ProSet-277
- 91ProSetFre-35
- 91ProSetFre-277
- 91ProSetPla-21
- 91ScoAme-80
- 91ScoCan-80
- 91StaClu-269
- 91Top-107
- 91UppDec-163
- 91UppDecF-163
- 92Bow-86
- 92FlamIGA-10
- 92Kra-36
- 920PC-247
- 92PanSti-39
- 92PanStiFre-39
- 92Par-24
- 92ParEmel-24
- 92Pin-318
- 92PinFre-318
- 92ProSet-25
- 92Sco-60
- 92ScoCan-60
- 92SeaPat-61
- 92StaClu-345
- 92Top-20
- 92TopGol-20G
- 92Ult-31
- 92UppDec-112
- 93Don-54
- 93Kra-66
- 93Lea-83
- 93LeaPaiWar-7
- 930PCPre-15
- 930PCPreBG-15
- 930PCPreG-15
- 93PanSti-188
- 93Par-301
- 93ParEmel-301
- 93Pin-231
- 93PinAllS-40
- 93PinAllSC-40
- 93PinCan-231

- 93PinMas-2
- 93Pow-45
- 93Sco-43
- 93ScoCan-43
- 93StaClu-319
- 93StaCluFDI-319
- 93StaCluO-319
- 93TopPre-15
- 93TopPreG-15
- 93TopPrePS-15
- 93Ult-207
- 93UppDec-177
- 94CanGamNHLP-278
- 94EASpo-24
- 94Fin-36
- 94FinRef-36
- 94FinSupTW-36
- 94Fla-53
- 94Fle-66
- 94HocWit-45
- 94Kra-56
- 94Lea-464
- 940PCPre-302
- 940PCPre-348
- 940PCPreSE-302
- 940PCPreSE-348
- 94ParSE-SE52
- 94ParSEG-SE52
- 94Pin-377
- 94PinArtP-377
- 94PinGoaG-GT10
- 94PinRinC-377
- 94Sel-54
- 94SelGol-54
- 94StaClu-79
- 94StaCluFDI-79
- 94StaCluFDI-189
- 94StaCluMOMS-79
- 94StaCluMOMS-189
- 94StaCluSTWC-79
- 94StaCluSTWC-189
- 94TopPre-302
- 94TopPre-348
- 94TopPreSE-302
- 94TopPreSE-348
- 94Ult-287
- 94UppDec-141
- 94UppDecEIeIce-141
- 94UppDecSPI-SP115
- 94UppDecSPIDC-SP115
- 95CanGamNHLP-104
- 95ColCho-100
- 95ColChoPC-100
- 95ColChoPCP-100
- 95ColEdgILL-L8
- 95DonBetTP-3
- 95Emo-59
- 95Kra-31
- 95Lea-8
- 95ParInt-334
- 95ParIntEl-334
- 95PinMas-6
- 95PlaOneoOne-255
- 95Sco-219
- 95Sco-319
- 95ScoBlaIce-219
- 95ScoBlaIce-319
- 95ScoBlaIceAP-219
- 95ScoBlaIceAP-319
- 95SelCer-42
- 95SelCerMG-42
- 95StaClu-12
- 95StaCluMOMS-12
- 95Sum-114
- 95SumArtP-114
- 95SumIce-114
- 95Top-11
- 95Top-160
- 95TopMarMPB-11
- 95TopOPCI-11
- 95TopOPCI-160
- 95TopSupSki-84
- 95TopSupSkiPla-84
- 95Ult-50
- 95UltGoIM-50
- 95UltPrePadMen-12
- 95UltPrePadMenGM-12
- 95UppDec-4
- 95UppDecEIeIce-4
- 95UppDecEIeIceG-4
- 95Zen-60
- 96Don-52
- 96DonCanI-94
- 96DonCanIGPP-94
- 96DonCanIRPP-94
- 96DonEli-86
- 96DonEliDCS-86
- 96DonPrePro-52
- 96Fle-144
- 96KraUppD-51
- 96Lea-147
- 96LeaPreP-147
- 96LeaPreSG-57
- 96LeaPreSte-57
- 96Pin-16
- 96PinArtP-16
- 96PinFoi-16
- 96PinPreS-16
- 96PinRinC-16
- 96RedWinDNFP-3
- 96RedWinDNFP-4
- 96Sco-164
- 96ScoArtPro-164
- 96ScoDeaCAP-164

- 96ScoGolB-164
- 96ScoNetW-14
- 96ScoSpeAP-164
- 96Sum-101
- 96SumArtP-101
- 96SumIce-101
- 96SumMet-101
- 96SumPreS-101
- 97ColCho-77
- 97ColChoSta-SQ53
- 97Don-73
- 97DonCanI-118
- 97DonCanIDS-118
- 97DonCanINP-28
- 97DonCanIPS-118
- 97DonCanISCS-31
- 97DonLim-188
- 97DonLimExp-188
- 97DonLimFOTG-17
- 97DonPre-82
- 97DonPreCG-12
- 97DonPreCGP-12
- 97DonPreCttC-82
- 97DonPreProG-73
- 97DonPreProS-73
- 97DonPri-159
- 97DonPriPG-11
- 97DonPriPGP-11
- 97DonPriSoA-159
- 97Kat-126
- 97KatGol-126
- 97KatSil-126
- 97Lea-94
- 97LeaFraMat-94
- 97LeaFraMDC-94
- 97LeaInt-94
- 97LeaIntUI-94
- 97Pac-24
- 97PacCop-24
- 97PacCroR-123
- 97PacCroREG-123
- 97PacCroRFODC-18
- 97PacCroRIB-123
- 97PacCroRS-123
- 97PacDyn-45
- 97PacDynC-45
- 97PacDynDG-45
- 97PacDynEG-45
- 97PacDynIB-45
- 97PacDynR-45
- 97PacDynSto-8
- 97PacDynTan-44
- 97PacEmeGre-24
- 97PacIceB-24
- 97PacInTheCLC-8
- 97PacInv-52
- 97PacInvC-52
- 97PacInvEG-52
- 97PacInvFP-15
- 97PacInvIB-52
- 97PacInvR-52
- 97PacInvS-52
- 97PacOme-207
- 97PacOmeC-207
- 97PacOmeDG-207
- 97PacOmeEG-207
- 97PacOmeIB-207
- 97PacPar-170
- 97PacParC-170
- 97PacParDG-170
- 97PacParEG-170
- 97PacParGSL-14
- 97PacParIB-170
- 97PacParRed-170
- 97PacParSil-170
- 97PacRed-24
- 97PacRev-128
- 97PacRevC-128
- 97PacRevE-128
- 97PacRevIB-128
- 97PacRevIB-128
- 97PacRevRtSD-18
- 97PacRevS-128
- 97PacRevTCL-22
- 97PacSil-24
- 97Pin-36
- 97PinArtP-36
- 97PinCer-8
- 97PinCerMB-8
- 97PinCerMG-8
- 97PinCerMR-8
- 97PinCerR-8
- 97PinIns-84
- 97PinIns-P84
- 97PinInsC-5
- 97PinInsCC-84
- 97PinInsCE-84
- 97PinInsCG-84
- 97PinInsSto-11
- 97PinInsSUG-1A/B
- 97PinInsSUG-1C/D
- 97PinPrePBB-36
- 97PinPrePBC-36
- 97PinPrePBM-36
- 97PinPrePBY-36
- 97PinPrePFC-36
- 97PinPrePFM-36
- 97PinPrePFY-36
- 97PinPrePla-36
- 97PinRinC-36
- 97PinTotCMPG-8
- 97PinTotCPB-8
- 97PinTotCPG-8

❑ 97PinTotCPR-8
❑ 97Sco-4
❑ 97ScoArtPro-4
❑ 97ScoGolBla-4
❑ 97SPAut-133
❑ 97Stu-69
❑ 97StuPrePG-69
❑ 97StuPrePS-69
❑ 97UppDec-60
❑ 97UppDec-356
❑ 97UppDecGDM-60
❑ 98BowBes-17
❑ 98BowBesAR-17
❑ 98BowBesR-17
❑ 98Fin-135
❑ 98FinNo P-135
❑ 98FinNo PR-135
❑ 98FinRef-135
❑ 98O-PChr-86
❑ 98O-PChrR-86
❑ 98Pac-393
❑ 98PacAur-172
❑ 98PacAurCF-44
❑ 98PacAurCFC-44
❑ 98PacAurCFIB-44
❑ 98PacAurCFR-44
❑ 98PacAurCFS-44
❑ 98PacCroR-122
❑ 98PacCroRLS-122
❑ 98PacDynI-170
❑ 98PacDynIIB-170
❑ 98PacDynIR-170
❑ 98PacDynITC-23
❑ 98PacIceB-393
❑ 98PacOmeH-216
❑ 98PacOmeODI-216
❑ 98PacOmeR-216
❑ 98PacPar-216
❑ 98PacParC-216
❑ 98PacParEG-216
❑ 98PacParGSLC-18
❑ 98PacParH-216
❑ 98PacParIB-216
❑ 98PacParS-216
❑ 98PacRed-393
❑ 98PacRev-130
❑ 98PacRevIS-130
❑ 98PacRevR-130
❑ 98Top-86
❑ 98TopO-P-86
❑ 98UC-177
❑ 98UD ChoPCR-177
❑ 98UD ChoR-177
❑ 98UppDec-167
❑ 98UppDecBD-74
❑ 98UppDecDD-74
❑ 98UppDecE-167
❑ 98UppDecE1o1-167
❑ 98UppDecGR-167
❑ 98UppDecM-176
❑ 98UppDecMGS-176
❑ 98UppDecMSS-176
❑ 98UppDecMSS-176
❑ 98UppDecQD-74
❑ 98UppDecTD-74
❑ 99Pac-384
❑ 99PacAur-123
❑ 99PacAurPD-123
❑ 99PacCop-384
❑ 99PacGol-384
❑ 99PacIceB-384
❑ 99PacIn tCN-18
❑ 99PacPreD-384
❑ 99PacTeaL-24

**Vershinin, Alex**
❑ 92CorBigRed-28
❑ 93CorBigRed-25

**Vertala, Timo**
❑ 97UppDecBD-25
❑ 97UppDecBDDD-25
❑ 97UppDecBDQD-25
❑ 97UppDecBDTD-25
❑ 98UC-277
❑ 98UD ChoPCR-277
❑ 98UD ChoR-277

**Ververgaert, Dennis**
❑ 73CanuRoyB-19
❑ 74CanuRoyB-20
❑ 74NHLActSta-275
❑ 74OPCNHL-117
❑ 74OPCNHL-207
❑ 74Top-117
❑ 74Top-207
❑ 75CanuRoyB-22
❑ 75OPCNHL-42
❑ 75Top-42
❑ 76CanuRoyB-21
❑ 76OPCNHL-175
❑ 76OPCNHL-395
❑ 76Top-175
❑ 77CanCanDC-16
❑ 77CanuRoyB-20
❑ 77OPCNHL-56
❑ 77Top-56
❑ 78CanuRoyB-22
❑ 78OPC-52
❑ 78Top-52
❑ 79OPC-214
❑ 79Top-214
❑ 80OPC-99
❑ 80Top-99
❑ 81OPC-356

**Verville, Dave**
❑ 98Vald'OF-20

**Vesa, Kimmo**
❑ 93FinnSIS-184
❑ 94FinnSIS-245

**Vescio, Kevin**
❑ 82NorBayC-22
❑ 83NorBayC-22

**Veselovsky, Peter**
❑ 94CzeAPSE-149
❑ 94FinnJaaK-201

**Vesey, Jim**
❑ 88ProIHL-91
❑ 89ProIHL-16
❑ 91BruSpoA-20
❑ 93PhoRoa-24

**Vestberg, Jan**
❑ 71SweHocS-376

**Vestergaard, Chad**
❑ 91BriColJHL-115
❑ 92BriColJHL-177

**Vettraino, Scott**
❑ 90MicTecHus-26
❑ 91MicTecHus-27

**Vezina, Georges**
❑ 10C55SweCP-38
❑ 11C55-38
❑ 12C57-1
❑ 23V1451-19
❑ 24C144ChaCig-60
❑ 24V130MapC-13
❑ 24V1452-43
❑ 27LaPat-21
❑ 34BeeGro1P-365A
❑ 34BeeGro1P-365B
❑ 55Par-56
❑ 55ParQuaO-56
❑ 60Top-19
❑ 60TopSta-51
❑ 83HalFP-B16
❑ 85HalFC-30
❑ 907thInnSQMJHL-44
❑ 91ProSet-333
❑ 91ProSetFre-333
❑ 92HalFL-26
❑ 93OPCCanHF-28
❑ 94ParMisLP-P3

**Vial, Dennis**
❑ 88NiaFalT-7
❑ 89ProIHL-32
❑ 90ProSet-628
❑ 91RedWinLC-16
❑ 91ScoCan-428
❑ 93Par-406
❑ 93ParEmel-406
❑ 93SenKraS-25
❑ 94SenBelM-27
❑ 95BeAPla-131
❑ 95BeAPSig-S131
❑ 95BeAPSigDC-S131
❑ 95Sen-21
❑ 96SenPizH-26

**Vichorek, Mark**
❑ 88FliSpi-20
❑ 90ProAHLIHL-590

**Vickers, Chris**
❑ 84Ott67-26

**Vickers, Steve**
❑ 72OPC-254
❑ 73OPC-57
❑ 73Top-57
❑ 74LipSou-34
❑ 74NHLActSta-198
❑ 74OPCNHL-29
❑ 74Top-29
❑ 75OPCNHL-19
❑ 75OPCNHL-295
❑ 75OPCNHL-324
❑ 75Top-19
❑ 75Top-295
❑ 75Top-324
❑ 76OPCNHL-75
❑ 76OPCNHL-390
❑ 76Top-75
❑ 77OPCNHL-136
❑ 77Top-136
❑ 78OPC-55
❑ 78Top-55
❑ 79OPC-195
❑ 79Top-195
❑ 80OPC-23
❑ 80Top-23
❑ 82PosCer-13

**Vielonen, Jussi**
❑ 93FinnSIS-22

**Viens, Stephan**
❑ 917thInnSQMJHL-121

**Viglasi, Ron**
❑ 82VicCou-23
❑ 84KelWin-9

**Vigneault, Alain**
❑ 917thInnSQMJHL-222
❑ 97CanaPos-25

**Vignola, Rejean**
❑ 83FreExp-19

**Viinikainen, Juha**
❑ 95ColCho-329
❑ 95ColChoPC-329
❑ 95ColChoPCP-329
❑ 96FinnSISR-66

**Viitakoski, Matti**
❑ 96FinnSISR-109

**Viitakoski, Vesa**
❑ 93Cla-47
❑ 93Don-60
❑ 93Lea-433
❑ 93Par-263
❑ 93ParCalC-C20
❑ 93ParCalCG-C20
❑ 93ParEmel-263
❑ 93Pin-444
❑ 93PinCan-444
❑ 93Sco-622
❑ 93ScoCan-622
❑ 93ScoGol-622
❑ 93SweSemWCS-84
❑ 93UppDec-344
❑ 93UppDecSP-26
❑ 94Cla-45
❑ 94ClaDraGol-45
❑ 94ClaProP-42
❑ 94ClaTri-T10
❑ 94Don-295
❑ 94FinnJaaK-22
❑ 94Lea-34
❑ 94OPCPre-472
❑ 94OPCPreSE-472
❑ 94St.JohF-26
❑ 94TopPre-472
❑ 94TopPreSE-472
❑ 94Ult-272
❑ 95FinnSemWC-45
❑ 95St.JohF-25

**Viktorsson, Jan**
❑ 83SweSemE-97
❑ 84SweSemE-93
❑ 85SwePanS-87
❑ 86SwePanS-80
❑ 87SwePanS-83
❑ 89SweSemE-63
❑ 90SweSemE-285
❑ 91SweSemE-67
❑ 91SweSemE-352
❑ 91SweSemWCS-41
❑ 92SweSemE-99
❑ 95SweLeaE-191
❑ 95SweLeaEC-15
❑ 95SweUppDE-55

**Vikulov, Vladimir**
❑ 69SweHocS-17
❑ 69SweWorC-73
❑ 69SweWorC-132
❑ 69SweWorC-135
❑ 70SweHocS-332
❑ 71SweHocS-41
❑ 72SweHocS-32
❑ 72SweHocS-48
❑ 72SweSemWC-18
❑ 73SweHocS-102
❑ 73SweWorCS-102
❑ 74SweSemHVS-49
❑ 91FutTreC72-47
❑ 92FutTre76CC-164

**Vilander, Jukka**
❑ 89SweSemWCS-47
❑ 93FinnJyvHS-317
❑ 93FinnSIS-42

**Vilen, Petri**
❑ 93FinnSIS-235

**Vilgrain, Claude**
❑ 89ProAHL-211
❑ 90ProAHLIHL-558
❑ 90UppDec-250
❑ 90UppDecF-250
❑ 91Par-321
❑ 91ParFre-321
❑ 91ProSet-425
❑ 91ProSetFre-425
❑ 91ProSetPla-195
❑ 92Bow-191
❑ 92OPC-133
❑ 92Sco-326
❑ 92ScoCan-326
❑ 92ScoSha-14
❑ 92ScoShaCan-14
❑ 92StaClu-422
❑ 92Top-187
❑ 92TopGol-187G
❑ 95SwiHNL-412
❑ 98GerDELE-204

**Ville, Christophe**
❑ 93SweSemWCS-267
❑ 94FinnJaaK-225
❑ 95FinnSemWC-199
❑ 95SweGloWC-203

**Villemure, Gilles**
❑ 63Top-46
❑ 64Top-74
❑ 67Top-86
❑ 70ColSta-89
❑ 70EssPowPla-198
❑ 70OPC-183
❑ 71Baz-10
❑ 71OPC-18
❑ 71OPC-248
❑ 71SarProSta-127
❑ 71Top-18
❑ 71TorSun-186
❑ 72OPC-132
❑ 72OPC-286
❑ 72Top-64
❑ 72Top-137
❑ 73OPC-119
❑ 73Top-153
❑ 74NHLActSta-194
❑ 74OPCNHL-179
❑ 74Top-179
❑ 75OPCNHL-379
❑ 76OPCNHL-61
❑ 76Top-61

**Villeneuve, Andre**
❑ 86SheCan-29

**Villeneuve, Bruno**
❑ 907thInnSQMJHL-145
❑ 91KnoChe-15
❑ 92RalIce-18
❑ 92RalIce-21
❑ 93KnoChe-20

**Villeneuve, Dany**
❑ 93AmoLesFAM-23

**Vilneff, Mark**
❑ 907thInnSOHL-296
❑ 94MusFur-7
❑ 95MusFur-2

**Vince, Bill**
❑ 82BraWheK-10

**Vincelette, Dan**
❑ 87BlaCok-27
❑ 88BlaCok-22
❑ 89ProIHL-59
❑ 90NordPet-26
❑ 91ProAHLCHL-480

**Vincent, Pascal**
❑ 907thInnSQMJHL-70
❑ 917thInnSQMJHL-246

**Vincent, Paul**
❑ 93SeaThu-27
❑ 95ColEdgI-85
❑ 95SigRoo-34
❑ 95SigRooSig-34
❑ 95St.JohML-19
❑ 96PeoRiv-24
❑ 96PeoRivPA-24

**Vincent, Robert**
❑ 51LavDaiLSJ-30

**Vines, Mark**
❑ 90ProSet-702

**Vinet, Claude**
❑ 52JunBluT-137

**Vinokurov, Denis**
❑ 91UppDecCWJC-4

**Vipond, Kelly**
❑ 917thInnSOHL-142
❑ 91PetPet-27
❑ 92WinSpi-20

**Virag, Dustin**
❑ 94NorBayC-16
❑ 95Sla-222

**Virkgunen, Tommi**
❑ 91BriColJHL-170
❑ 91BriColJHL-NNO

**Virkkunnen, Teemu**
❑ 98SPXTopP-69
❑ 98SPXTopPF-69
❑ 98SPXTopPR-69
❑ 98UppDecBD-101
❑ 98UppDecDD-101
❑ 98UppDecQD-101
❑ 98UppDecTD-101

**Virolainen, Mikko**
❑ 93FinnSIS-55

**Virta, Hannu**
❑ 82SabMilP-16
❑ 84SabBluS-21
❑ 85SabBluS-28
❑ 85SabBluSS-28
❑ 89SweSemWCS-34
❑ 91SweSemWCS-6
❑ 93FinnJyvHS-315
❑ 93FinnSIS-37
❑ 95FinnKarWCL-23
❑ 95FinnSemWC-23
❑ 95FinnSISGC-11
❑ 95FinnSISL-2
❑ 95FinnSISLLG-7
❑ 95SweGloWC-132
❑ 95SwiHNL-295
❑ 96SweSemW-23

**Virta, Pekka**
❑ 94FinnSIS-212
❑ 94FinnSISMN-6
❑ 95FinnSIS-146
❑ 95FinnSIS-360
❑ 95FinnSISR-157

**Virta, Toni**
❑ 93FinnJyvHS-53
❑ 93FinnSIS-243
❑ 94FinnSIS-46
❑ 95FinnSIS-224
❑ 96GerDELE-56

**Virtanen, Janne**
❑ 93FinnJyvHS-348
❑ 93FinnSIS-219
❑ 94FinnSIS-67
❑ 95FinnSIS-157
❑ 95FinnSIS-281

**Virtanen, Jari**
❑ 93FinnSIS-133
❑ 94FinnSIS-72
❑ 95FinnSIS-39

**Virtanen, Juha**
❑ 94FinnSIS-264
❑ 95FinnSIS-143
❑ 95FinnSISL-98

**Virtanen, Jukka**
❑ 93FinnSIS-385

**Virtanen, Marko**
❑ 93FinnJyvHS-148
❑ 93FinnSIS-150
❑ 93SweSemWCS-85
❑ 94FinnJaaK-49
❑ 94FinnSIS-249
❑ 94FinnSISH-18
❑ 95FinnSIS-57
❑ 95FinnSISL-53
❑ 95FinnSISP-8

**Virtue, Terry**
❑ 907thInnSWHL-107
❑ 907thInnSWHL-329
❑ 93WheThu-14

**Viscovich, Peter**
❑ 84KinCan-17
❑ 85KinCan-17

**Visheau, Mark**
❑ 907thInnSOHL-147
❑ 917thInnSOHL-378
❑ 94ClaProP-101
❑ 98PacOmeH-116
❑ 98PacOmeODI-116
❑ 98PacOmeR-116

**Vishnevsky, Vitali**
❑ 97UppDecBD-93
❑ 97UppDecBDDD-93
❑ 97UppDecBDQD-93
❑ 97UppDecBDTD-93
❑ 98UC-285
❑ 98UD ChoPCR-285
❑ 98UD ChoR-285

**Viskovich, Peter**
❑ 86KinCan-18

**Vit, Pavel**
❑ 95GerDELE-425
❑ 96GerDELE-62

**Vitale, Phil**
❑ 51LavDaiS-72
❑ 52St.LawS-28

**Vitek, Jiri**
❑ 95CzeAPSE-214

**Vitolinsh, Harijs**
❑ 90OPC-521
❑ 93Par-496
❑ 93ParEmel-496
❑ 93UppDec-428
❑ 94ClaProP-197
❑ 95SweLeaE-285
❑ 95SweUppDE-183

**Vittenberg, Andre**
❑ 94FreNatT-33

**Vitucci, Nick**
❑ 91GreMon-14
❑ 92HamRoaA-17
❑ 93PeoRiv-28
❑ 93TolSto-7
❑ 94TolSto-23
❑ 95BufStaRHI-36

**Viveiros, Emanuel**
❑ 84PriAlbRS-22
❑ 88ProIHL-29
❑ 90ProAHLIHL-183
❑ 96GerDELE-314

**Vizzutti, Chad**
❑ 92BriColJHL-159

**Vlach, Rostislav**
❑ 89SweSemWCS-194
❑ 94CzeAPSE-246
❑ 95CzeAPSE-18
❑ 96CzeAPSE-224

**Vlasak, Tomas**
❑ 93Par-515
❑ 93ParEmel-515
❑ 94CzeAPSE-218
❑ 95CzeAPSE-169
❑ 96CzeAPSE-183

**Vlasov, Igor**
❑ 95SweUppDE1DS-DS2

**Vlassenkov, Dmitri**
❑ 97UppDecBD-124
❑ 97UppDecBDDD-124
❑ 97UppDecBDQD-124
❑ 97UppDecBDTD-124
❑ 98UC-287
❑ 98UD ChoPCR-287
❑ 98UD ChoR-287

**Vlcek, Ivan**
❑ 94CzeAPSE-147
❑ 96CzeAPSE-290

**Vlk, Petr**
❑ 89SweSemWCS-189
❑ 91SweSemWCS-123
❑ 93SwiHNL-359
❑ 95CzeAPSE-187
❑ 96CzeAPSE-322

**Vlzek, Ivan**
❑ 95FinnSIS-131
❑ 95FinnSIS-384
❑ 95FinnSISDT-7
❑ 96FinnSISR-72

**Vodila, Jan**
❑ 89SweSemWCS-192

**Vodrazka, Jan**
❑ 95Sla-72
❑ 96DetWha-18

**Vogel, Jason**
❑ 92CorBigRed-29

**Vogel, Tony**
❑ 81RegPat-23
❑ 82RegPat-11
❑ 83RegPat-11
❑ 94GerDELE-303
❑ 95GerDELE-183
❑ 96GerDELE-250

**Vogeltanz, Petr**
❑ 96CzeAPSE-94

**Voisard, Gaetan**
❑ 91UppDec-664
❑ 91UppDecCWJC-25
❑ 91UppDecF-664
❑ 93SwiHNL-69
❑ 95SwiHNL-95

**Vokoun, Tomas**
❑ 94CzeAPSE-48
❑ 97Don-209
❑ 97DonCanI-138
❑ 97DonCanIDS-138
❑ 97DonCanIPS-138
❑ 97DonMed-1
❑ 97DonPreProG-209
❑ 97DonPreProS-209
❑ 97DonRatR-1
❑ 97Lea-157
❑ 97LeaFraMat-157
❑ 97LeaFraMDC-157
❑ 97PinIns-72
❑ 97PinInsCC-72
❑ 97PinInsEC-72
❑ 98PacOmeH-133
❑ 98PacOmeODI-133
❑ 98PacOmeR-133
❑ 98PacRev-81
❑ 98PacRevIS-81
❑ 98PacRevR-81
❑ 99Pac-232
❑ 99PacCop-232
❑ 99PacGol-232
❑ 99PacIceB-232
❑ 99PacPreD-232

**Volak, Milan**
❑ 94CzeAPSE-151
❑ 95CzeAPSE-258
❑ 96CzeAPSE-298

**Volcan, Mickey**
❑ 82WhaJunHC-22
❑ 83OPC-94
❑ 83Vac-20
❑ 84MonGolF-13
❑ 85NovScoO-24
❑ 90ProAHLIHL-365

**Volchkov, Alexander Jr.**
❑ 95Sla-16
❑ 95Sla-431
❑ 96ColEdgSS&D-1
❑ 97BowCHL-12
❑ 97BowCHLOPC-12

**Volchkov, Alexander Sr.**
❑ 73SweHocS-96
❑ 73SweWorCS-96
❑ 91FutTreC72-59

**Volek, David (Dave)**
❑ 89Isl-20
❑ 89OPC-85
❑ 89OPC-309
❑ 89OPCSti-43
❑ 89OPCSti-113
❑ 89OPCSti-187
❑ 89PanSti-267
❑ 89Top-85
❑ 90Bow-127
❑ 90BowTif-127
❑ 90OPC-300
❑ 90ProSet-193
❑ 90Sco-12
❑ 90ScoCan-12
❑ 90Top-300
❑ 90TopTif-300
❑ 90UppDec-1
❑ 90UppDecF-1
❑ 91Bow-223
❑ 91OPC-488
❑ 91PanSti-241
❑ 91Par-104
❑ 91ParFre-104
❑ 91Pin-198
❑ 91PinFre-198
❑ 91ProSet-147
❑ 91ProSetFre-147
❑ 91ProSetPla-75
❑ 91ScoAme-88
❑ 91ScoCan-88
❑ 91StaClu-204
❑ 91SweSemWCS-221
❑ 91Top-488
❑ 91UppDec-89
❑ 91UppDec-173
❑ 91UppDecF-89
❑ 91UppDecF-173
❑ 92Bow-196
❑ 92OPC-3
❑ 92PanSti-200
❑ 92PanStiFre-200
❑ 92Par-340
❑ 92ParEmel-340
❑ 92Pin-188
❑ 92PinFre-188
❑ 92Sco-166
❑ 92ScoCan-166
❑ 92StaClu-319
❑ 92Top-204
❑ 92TopGol-204G
❑ 92Ult-350
❑ 92UppDec-313
❑ 93OPCPre-371
❑ 93OPCPreG-371
❑ 93Par-395
❑ 93ParEmel-395
❑ 93Pin-423
❑ 93PinCan-423
❑ 93Pow-388
❑ 93Sco-495
❑ 93ScoCan-495
❑ 93StaClu-324
❑ 93StaCluFDI-324
❑ 93StaCluO-324
❑ 93SweSemWCS-108
❑ 93TopPre-371
❑ 93TopPreG-371
❑ 93UppDec-370
❑ 94Par-139
❑ 94ParGol-139
❑ 95CzeAPSE-270

**Volk, Josef**
❑ 72SweSemWC-96

**Volkov, Alexei**
❑ 98SPXTopP-78
❑ 98SPXTopPF-78
❑ 98SPXTopPR-78
❑ 98UppDecBD-104
❑ 98UppDecDD-104
❑ 98UppDecQD-104
❑ 98UppDecTD-104
❑ 99UppDecRG-G10C
❑ 99UppDecRGI-G10C

**Volkov, Mikhail**
❑ 91UppDecCWJC-5
❑ 93RochAmeKod-24
❑ 94ClaProP-104
❑ 95RochAmeSS-20
❑ 95SouCarS-5

**Volland, Andreas**
❑ 94GerDELE-188
❑ 95GerDELE-188

**Vollhoffer, Troy**
❑ 84SasBlaS-19
❑ 88FliSpi-21
❑ 88ProIHL-63

**Volmar, Doug**
❑ 73OPC-215

**Vologjaninov, Ivan**
❑ 93LetHur-21
❑ 95SlaMemC-6

**Volpe, Mike**
❑ 85KitRan-10

**Volstad, Craig**
❑ 91AirCanSJHL-C17

**Von Stefenelli, Phil**
❑ 91ProAHLCHL-604
❑ 92HamCan-25
❑ 96DetVip-19
❑ 98GerDELE-145

**Von Trzcinski, A.**
❑ 95GerDELE-198

**Vopat, Jan**
❑ 91UppDecCWJC-95
❑ 92Cla-36
❑ 92UppDec-601
❑ 94CzeAPSE-211
❑ 94FinnJaaK-171
❑ 95ColEdgI-186
❑ 95FinnSemWC-143
❑ 95PhoRoa-20
❑ 96ClaGol-36
❑ 96Lea-222
❑ 96LeaPreP-222
❑ 96Pin-214
❑ 96PinArtP-214
❑ 96PinFoi-214
❑ 96PinPreS-214
❑ 96PinRinC-214
❑ 96SweSemW-108
❑ 96Ult-83
❑ 96UltGolM-84
❑ 97ColCho-126
❑ 97Pac-271
❑ 97PacCop-271
❑ 97PacEmeGre-271
❑ 97PacIceB-271
❑ 97PacRed-271
❑ 97PacSil-271
❑ 97UppDec-79
❑ 98UppDec-299
❑ 98UppDecE-299
❑ 98UppDecE1o1-299
❑ 98UppDecGR-299

**Vopat, Roman**
❑ 95Bow-139
❑ 95BowAllFoi-139
❑ 95Don-307
❑ 95ParInt-447
❑ 95ParIntEl-447
❑ 95PriAlbR-20
❑ 95SigRoo-2
❑ 95SigRooSig-2
❑ 95SkyImp-219
❑ 95UppDec-440
❑ 95UppDecEleIce-440
❑ 95UppDecEleIceG-440
❑ 96Don-216
❑ 96DonPrePro-216
❑ 96Fle-135
❑ 96FleCalCan-10
❑ 96MetUni-194
❑ 96PinArtP-231
❑ 96PinFoi-231
❑ 96PinRinC-231
❑ 96Sco-252
❑ 96ScoArtPro-252
❑ 96ScoDeaCAP-252
❑ 96ScoGolB-252
❑ 96ScoSpeAP-252
❑ 96SkyImp-162
❑ 96Sum-193
❑ 96SumArtP-193
❑ 96SumIce-193
❑ 96SumMet-193
❑ 96SumPreS-193
❑ 97Be A PPAD-103
❑ 97Be A PPAPD-103
❑ 97BeAPla-103
❑ 97BeAPlaAut-103
❑ 97ColCho-124
❑ 97Don-147
❑ 97DonLim-129
❑ 97DonLim-180
❑ 97DonLimExp-129

Walton, Mike • 699


❑ 97DonLimExp-180
❑ 97DonPreProG-147
❑ 97DonPreProS-147
❑ 97Lea-69
❑ 97LeaFraMat-69
❑ 97LeaFraMDC-69
❑ 97LeaInt-69
❑ 97LeaIntUI-69
❑ 97UppDec-78
**Vorderbruggen, Reiner**
❑ 94GerDELE-335
**Vorlicek, Frantisek**
❑ 74SweHocS-113
❑ 94CzeAPSE-295
❑ 95CzeAPSE-174
❑ 96CzeAPSE-309
**Vorobel, Slavomir**
❑ 95SloAPSNT-14
**Vorobiev, Vladimir**
❑ 96BinRan-22
❑ 97ColCho-164
❑ 97Don-210
❑ 97DonCanI-139
❑ 97DonCanIDS-139
❑ 97DonCanIPS-139
❑ 97DonLim-97
❑ 97DonLim-121
❑ 97DonLim-197
❑ 97DonLimExp-97
❑ 97DonLimExp-121
❑ 97DonLimExp-197
❑ 97DonPreProG-210
❑ 97DonPreProS-210
❑ 97Pin-188
❑ 97PinIns-123
❑ 97PinPrePBB-188
❑ 97PinPrePBC-188
❑ 97PinPrePBM-188
❑ 97PinPrePBY-188
❑ 97PinPrePFC-188
❑ 97PinPrePFM-188
❑ 97PinPrePFY-188
❑ 97PinPrePla-188
❑ 97Sco-75
❑ 97ScoArtPro-75
❑ 97ScoGolBla-75
❑ 97ScoRan-13
❑ 97ScoRanPla-13
❑ 97ScoRanPre-13
❑ 98Pac-304
❑ 98PacIceB-304
❑ 98PacRed-304
**Vorobjev, Ilja**
❑ 94GerDELE-109
❑ 96GerDELE-57
❑ 98GerDELE-136
**Vorobjev, Piotr**
❑ 94GerDELE-103
❑ 95GerDELE-100
**Voronov, Sergei**
❑ 95HamRoaA-22
**Vos, Ralph**
❑ 96GerDELE-222
**Voss, Carl**
❑ 34BeeGro1P-128
❑ 35DiaMatT2-63
❑ 35DiaMatT3-58
❑ 35DiaMatTI-68
❑ 36V356WorG-66
❑ 37OPCV304E-175
❑ 83HalFP-O16
❑ 85HalFC-225
**Vossen, Dale**
❑ 917thInnSWHL-236
**Vossen, Jamie**
❑ 95Sla-211
**Vosta, Ondrej**
❑ 94CzeAPSE-108
❑ 95CzeAPSE-69
❑ 96CzeAPSE-256
**Vostrak, Pavel**
❑ 96CzeAPSE-308
**Vostrikov, Sergei**
❑ 91OPCIns-27R
**Vozar, Patrick**
❑ 94GerDELE-122
❑ 95GerDELE-122
**Vrabec, Thomas**
❑ 91SweSemWCS-200
❑ 93SwiHNL-80
❑ 95SwiHNL-107
**Vrataric, Rich**
❑ 95Sla-196
**Vrla, Daniel**
❑ 94CzeAPSE-232
❑ 95CzeAPSE-11
**Vujtek, Vladimir**
❑ 917thInnSWHL-303
❑ 92OilIGA-22
❑ 92OilTeal-20
❑ 92Pin-396
❑ 92PinFre-396
❑ 92UppDec-417
❑ 92UppDec-496
❑ 93OPCPre-459
❑ 93OPCPreG-459
❑ 93Par-339
❑ 93ParEmel-339
❑ 93Pow-343
❑ 93Sco-465
❑ 93ScoCan-465
❑ 93StaClu-278
❑ 93StaCluFDI-278
❑ 93StaCluO-278
❑ 93TopPre-459
❑ 93TopPreG-459
❑ 93Ult-319
❑ 93UppDec-168
❑ 94CzeAPSE-131
❑ 94CzeAPSE-293
❑ 94OPCPre-503
❑ 94OPCPreSE-503
❑ 94TopPre-503
❑ 94TopPreSE-503
❑ 94Ult-293
❑ 95CzeAPSE-27
❑ 96CzeAPSE-189
❑ 97Be A PPAD-113
❑ 97Be A PPAPD-113
❑ 97BeAPla-113
❑ 97BeAPlaAut-113
**Vukonich, Mike**
❑ 91ProAHLCHL-391
❑ 92Cla-110
❑ 92PhoRoa-24
❑ 96ClaGol-110
**Vukota, Mick**
❑ 84KelWin-22
❑ 89Isl-21
❑ 90OPC-10
❑ 90ProSet-488
❑ 90Top-10
❑ 90TopTif-10
❑ 90UppDec-39
❑ 90UppDecF-39
❑ 91OPC-25
❑ 91ScoCan-387
❑ 91StaClu-309
❑ 91Top-25
❑ 91UppDec-135
❑ 91UppDecF-135
❑ 92Sco-549A
❑ 92ScoCan-549A
❑ 94ParSE-SE101
❑ 94ParSEG-SE101
❑ 95UppDec-380
❑ 95UppDecEleIce-380
❑ 95UppDecEleIceG-380
❑ 96IslPos-22
❑ 97Be A PPAD-56
❑ 97Be A PPAPD-56
❑ 97BeAPla-56
❑ 97BeAPlaAut-56
❑ 98Pac-259
❑ 98PacIceB-259
❑ 98PacRed-259
**Vuori, Ari**
❑ 89SweSemWCS-49
❑ 93FinnJyvHS-319
❑ 93FinnSIS-51
❑ 94FinnSIS-109
❑ 95FinnSIS-191
**Vuorinen, Teemu**
❑ 94FinnSIS-222
❑ 95FinnSIS-234
❑ 96FinnSISR-28
**Vuorio, Matti**
❑ 93FinnSIS-282
**Vuorivirta, Juha**
❑ 94Fin-141
❑ 94FinnSIS-290
❑ 94FinRef-141
❑ 94FinSupTW-141
❑ 95FinnSIS-120
❑ 95FinnSISDD-10
❑ 95SigRoo-29
❑ 95SigRooSig-29
**Vuoti, Arto**
❑ 94FinnSIS-204
**Vyborny, David**
❑ 92UppDec-600
❑ 93Cla-48
❑ 94CapBreO-20
❑ 94Cla-77
❑ 94ClaDraGol-77
❑ 94FinnJaaK-185
❑ 95CzeAPSE-280
❑ 95FinnSemWC-148
❑ 96CzeAPSE-135
**Vyborny, Frantisek**
❑ 94CzeAPSE-283
❑ 95CzeAPSE-267
**Vydhlidal, Michael**
❑ 94CzeAPSE-169
❑ 96CzeAPSE-315
❑ 95CzeAPSE-179
**Vykoukal, Jiri**
❑ 90ProAHLIHL-214
❑ 91ProAHLCHL-562
❑ 94SweLeaE-279
❑ 94SweLeaEFA-6
❑ 95CzeAPSE-271
❑ 95SweGloWC-152
❑ 96CzeAPSE-123
❑ 96CzeAPSE-346
❑ 96SweSemW-107
**Waddell, Don**
❑ 87FliSpi-19
❑ 88FliSpi-22
❑ 91ProAHLCHL-332
**Wadel, Jason**
❑ 917thInnSOHL-238
**Wagar, Blair**
❑ 91AirCanSJHL-A41
**Wager, Roman**
❑ 91SweSemWCS-193
❑ 93SweSemWCS-123
❑ 93SwiHNL-29
❑ 95SwiHNL-27
❑ 95SwiHNL-522
❑ 95SwiHNL-534
**Waghorn, Graham**
❑ 94FinnJaaK-317
**Waghorne, Fred C**
❑ 83HalFP-H15
❑ 85HalFC-119
**Wagner, Bernd**
❑ 91SweSemWCS-161
❑ 94GerDELE-250
**Wagner, Thomas**
❑ 94GerDELE-403
❑ 95GerDELE-422
**Wahl, Greg**
❑ 91AirCanSJHL-C33
❑ 92MPSPhoSJHL-138
**Wahlberg, Bo**
❑ 72SweHocS-278
**Wahlberg, Mikael**
❑ 92SweSemE-65
❑ 93SweSemE-38
❑ 94SweLeaE-163
❑ 95SweLeaE-21
❑ 95SweUppDE-30
❑ 98GerDELE-171
**Wahlsten, Jali**
❑ 93FinnJyvHS-118
❑ 93SweSemWCS-86
**Wahlsten, Juhani**
❑ 69SweHocS-383
❑ 69SweWorC-87
**Wahlsten, Sami**
❑ 93SweSemWCS-87
❑ 94FinnJaaK-45
❑ 94FinnSIS-308
**Waibel, Harald**
❑ 94GerDELE-308
❑ 95GerDELE-145
**Waite, Jimmy (Jim)**
❑ 88BlaCok-23
❑ 89ProIHL-73
❑ 90OPC-214
❑ 90ProAHLIHL-401
❑ 90Sco-407A
❑ 90Sco-407B
❑ 90ScoCan-407A
❑ 90ScoCan-407B
❑ 90Top-214
❑ 90TopTif-214
❑ 91BlaCok-28
❑ 91Bow-396
❑ 91OPC-127
❑ 91Pin-316
❑ 91PinFre-316
❑ 91ProSet-530
❑ 91ProSetFre-530
❑ 91ScoCan-632
❑ 91ScoRoo-82T
❑ 91Top-127
❑ 91UppDec-443
❑ 91UppDecF-443
❑ 92Bow-120
❑ 92Par-270
❑ 92ParEmel-270
❑ 92StaClu-35
❑ 92Top-100
❑ 92TopGol-100G
❑ 92UppDec-67
❑ 93Don-302
❑ 93DurSco-49
❑ 93Lea-324
❑ 93OPCPre-388
❑ 93OPCPreG-388
❑ 93Par-181
❑ 93ParEmel-181
❑ 93Pin-371
❑ 93PinCan-371
❑ 93Pow-438
❑ 93Sco-365
❑ 93Sco-539
❑ 93ScoCan-365
❑ 93ScoCan-539
❑ 93ScoGol-539
❑ 93TopPre-388
❑ 93TopPreG-388
❑ 93Ult-419
❑ 93UppDec-501
❑ 94BeAPSig-126
❑ 94Lea-405
❑ 94OPCPre-496
❑ 94OPCPreSE-496
❑ 94Par-214
❑ 94ParGol-214
❑ 94PinMas-MA9
❑ 94TopPre-496
❑ 94TopPreSE-496
❑ 95IndIce-21
❑ 98Be A PPA-260
❑ 98Be A PPAA-260
❑ 98Be A PPAAF-260
❑ 98Be A PPSE-260
❑ 98Be APG-260
❑ 98Pac-346
❑ 98PacIceB-346
❑ 98PacOmeH-191
❑ 98PacOmeODI-191
❑ 98PacOmeR-191
❑ 98PacRed-346
❑ 98PacRev-114
❑ 98PacRevIS-114
❑ 98PacRevR-114
**Wakaluk, Darcy**
❑ 84KelWin-2
❑ 88ProAHL-213
❑ 89ProAHL-258
❑ 90ProAHLIHL-288
❑ 91Bow-33
❑ 91Par-306
❑ 91ParFre-306
❑ 91ScoCan-653
❑ 92Bow-148
❑ 92OPC-93
❑ 92Par-315
❑ 92ParEmel-315
❑ 92Sco-313
❑ 92ScoCan-313
❑ 92StaClu-153
❑ 92Top-108
❑ 92TopGol-108G
❑ 92Ult-99
❑ 93Don-420
❑ 93OPCPre-399
❑ 93OPCPreG-399
❑ 93Pow-327
❑ 93Sco-432
❑ 93ScoCan-432
❑ 93StaClu-276
❑ 93StaCluFDI-276
❑ 93StaCluO-276
❑ 93TopPre-399
❑ 93TopPreG-399
❑ 94Don-17
❑ 94Lea-152
❑ 94OPCPre-424
❑ 94OPCPreSE-424
❑ 94ParSE-SE44
❑ 94ParSEG-SE44
❑ 94Pin-157
❑ 94PinArtP-157
❑ 94PinRinC-157
❑ 94StaClu-187
❑ 94StaCluFDI-187
❑ 94StaCluMOMS-187
❑ 94StaCluSTWC-187
❑ 94StaHoc-24
❑ 94StaPinS-157
❑ 94StaPinS-NNO
❑ 94StaPos-21
❑ 94TopPre-424
❑ 94TopPreSE-424
❑ 94Ult-282
❑ 94UppDec-459
❑ 94UppDecEleIce-459
❑ 95BeAPla-90
❑ 95BeAPSig-S90
❑ 95BeAPSigDC-S90
❑ 95Fin-156
❑ 95FinRef-156
❑ 95ImaPlaPl-PL9
❑ 95ParInt-331
❑ 95ParIntEl-331
❑ 95Sco-197
❑ 95ScoBlaIce-197
❑ 95ScoBlaIceAP-197
❑ 95StaScoS-197
❑ 95Top-313
❑ 95TopOPCI-313
❑ 95Ult-231
❑ 96Sco-210
❑ 96ScoArtPro-210
❑ 96ScoDeaCAP-210
❑ 96ScoGolB-210
❑ 96ScoSpeAP-210
**Wakefield, Lance**
❑ 91AirCanSJHL-D50
**Wakeham, Randy**
❑ 93MicTecH-23
**Wakely, Ernie**
❑ 70ColSta-92
❑ 70EssPowPla-252
❑ 70OPC-97
❑ 70SarProSta-181
❑ 70Top-97
❑ 71BluPos-24
❑ 71LetActR-12
❑ 71OPC-81
❑ 71SarProSta-185
❑ 71Top-81
❑ 71TorSun-252
❑ 73QuaOatWHA-41
❑ 75OPCWHA-132
❑ 76OPCWHA-92
❑ 76SanDieMW-14
**Wala, Martin**
❑ 96SloPeeWT-29
**Walby, Steffon**
❑ 92BriColJHL-61
❑ 92BriColJHL-246
❑ 93St.JohML-25
❑ 94ClaProP-97
❑ 94St.JohML-23
❑ 95St.JohML-20
**Walcot, Brad**
❑ 82KinCan-22
❑ 83OshGen-13
❑ 85SudWol-24
**Walcott, Richie**
❑ 91ProAHLCHL-564
❑ 93HamRoaA-12
**Walder, Raymond**
❑ 91SweSemWCS-191
❑ 93SwiHNL-106
**Walitalo, Gote**
❑ 82SweSemHVS-2
❑ 83SweSemE-26
❑ 84SweSemE-26
❑ 85SwePanS-26
❑ 86SwePanS-3
❑ 87SwePanS-26
**Walker, Ben**
❑ 93LonKni-21
❑ 93LonKni-24
**Walker, Darby**
❑ 917thInnSWHL-312
**Walker, Gordie**
❑ 84KamBla-24
❑ 88ProAHL-222
❑ 89ProAHL-22
**Walker, Howard**
❑ 81Cap-20
❑ 82OPC-59
**Walker, Jack**
❑ 83HalFP-E16
❑ 85HalFC-75
**Walker, Jeff**
❑ 897thInnSOHL-148
❑ 89NiaFalT-21
❑ 907thInnSOHL-272
❑ 917thInnSOHL-133
❑ 91PetPet-17
**Walker, John**
❑ 88ProAHL-325
**Walker, Johnny**
❑ 94GerDELE-242
❑ 95GerDELE-236
❑ 96GerDELE-87
❑ 98GerDELE-23
**Walker, Kelly**
❑ 90ArIice-14
❑ 91ArIice-3
❑ 91ArIice-18
❑ 92ArIice-2
**Walker, Kurt**
❑ 76MapLeaP-22
❑ 77MapLeaP-18
❑ 78OPC-282
**Walker, Scott**
❑ 917thInnSOHL-274
❑ 93OweSouPla-31
❑ 94ClaProP-165
❑ 95Bow-143
❑ 95BowAllFoi-143
❑ 95ColEdgI-90
❑ 95Don-303
❑ 95Lea-108
❑ 95ParInt-484
❑ 95ParIntEl-484
❑ 95UppDec-418
❑ 95UppDecEleIce-418
❑ 95UppDecEleIceG-418
❑ 96CanuPos-24
❑ 96UppDec-351
❑ 97Be A PPAD-33
❑ 97Be A PPAPD-33
❑ 97BeAPla-33
❑ 97BeAPlaAut-33
❑ 97PacInvNRB-205
❑ 98Be A PPA-224
❑ 98Be A PPAA-224
❑ 98Be A PPAAF-224
❑ 98Be A PPSE-224
❑ 98Be APG-224
❑ 98Pac-435
❑ 98PacIceB-435
❑ 98PacPar-129
❑ 98PacParC-129
❑ 98PacParEG-129
❑ 98PacParH-129
❑ 98PacParIB-129
❑ 98PacParS-129
❑ 98PacRed-435
❑ 99Pac-233
❑ 99PacAur-92
❑ 99PacAurPD-92
❑ 99PacCop-233
❑ 99PacGol-233
❑ 99PacIceB-233
❑ 99PacPreD-233
**Walker, Steve**
❑ 94MusFur-14
❑ 95MusFur-13
❑ 96DetVip-20
**Walker, Todd**
❑ 917thInnSOHL-9
❑ 91CorRoy-11
**Wall, Bob**
❑ 61HamRed-18
❑ 64BeeGro3P-96
❑ 66Top-49
❑ 68OPC-156
❑ 68ShiCoi-52
❑ 69OPC-140
❑ 69OPCFou-10
❑ 70DadCoo-135
❑ 70EssPowPla-236
❑ 70OPC-98
❑ 70SarProSta-191
❑ 70Top-98
❑ 71SarProSta-50
❑ 72OPC-323
**Wallace, Bruce**
❑ 52JunBluT-58
**Wallace, Greg**
❑ 85KamBla-26
**Wallen, Peter**
❑ 87SwePanS-265
❑ 89SweSemE-129
**Wallenberg, Patrik**
❑ 93SweSemE-318
❑ 95ColCho-352
❑ 95ColChoPC-352
❑ 95ColChoPCP-352
❑ 95SweUppDE-70
❑ 95UppDec-563
❑ 95UppDecEleIce-563
❑ 95UppDecEleIceG-563
**Wallin, Anders**
❑ 83SweSemE-9
**Wallin, Claes Goran**
❑ 65SweCorI-119
❑ 73SweHocS-219
❑ 73SweWorCS-219
❑ 74SweHocS-268
❑ 91SweSemE-311
**Wallin, Hans**
❑ 86SwePanS-126
❑ 87SwePanS-118
**Wallin, Jesse**
❑ 95BowDraPro-P35
❑ 95RedDeeR-17
❑ 96UppDecIce-128
❑ 97BowCHL-104
❑ 97BowCHLOPC-104
❑ 98UC-262
❑ 98UD ChoPCR-262
❑ 98UD ChoR-262
**Wallin, Magnus**
❑ 89SweSemE-257
**Wallin, Niklas**
❑ 93SweSemE-319
**Wallin, Per**
❑ 90SweSemE-24
❑ 91SweSemE-218
❑ 92SweSemE-270
❑ 93SweSemE-228
❑ 94SweLeaE-21
❑ 95SweLeaE-118
❑ 95SweUppDE-177
**Wallin, Peter**
❑ 83SweSemE-213
❑ 84SweSemE-237
❑ 85SwePanS-236
❑ 95ColCho-354
❑ 95ColChoPC-354
❑ 95ColChoPCP-354
❑ 95SigRooA-40
❑ 95SigRooAPC-40
❑ 95SweLeaE-161
❑ 95SweLeaER-1
**Walltin, Mats**
❑ 73SweHocS-24
❑ 73SweHocS-68
❑ 73SweWorCS-24
❑ 73SweWorCS-68
❑ 74SweHocS-194
**Wallwork, Bobby**
❑ 91CinCyc-25
❑ 94CenHocL-54
❑ 95MusFur-11
**Walser, Derrick**
❑ 96RimOceU-10
❑ 97BowCHL-68
❑ 97BowCHLOPC-68
❑ 97RimOce-91
❑ 98BowBes-144
❑ 98BowBesAR-144
❑ 98BowBesR-144
❑ 98BowCHL-119
❑ 98BowCHLGA-119
❑ 98BowCHLOI-119
❑ 98BowChrC-119
❑ 98BowChrCGA-119
❑ 98BowChrCGAR-119
❑ 98BowChrCOI-119
❑ 98BowChrCOIR-119
❑ 98BowChrCR-119
❑ 98O-PChr-229
❑ 98O-PChrR-229
❑ 98Top-229
❑ 98TopO-P-229
**Walsh, Brendan**
❑ 93OmaLan-28
**Walsh, Gord**
❑ 93KinFro-7
❑ 95Cla-86
❑ 95Sla-112
**Walsh, Keith**
❑ 95Sla-150
**Walsh, Kurt**
❑ 95BowDraPro-P36
❑ 95Sla-249
❑ 95Sla-304
❑ 95Sla-437
**Walsh, Marty**
❑ 10C55SweCP-11
❑ 10C56-7
❑ 11C55-11
❑ 12C57-49
❑ 83HalFP-F15
❑ 85HalFC-89
**Walsh, Mike**
❑ 88ProAHL-314
❑ 89ProAHL-230
❑ 91ProAHLCHL-52
**Walsh, Shawn**
❑ 93Cla-59
**Walsh, Trevor**
❑ 89WinSpi-20
❑ 907thInnSOHL-194
**Walter, Jaroslav**
❑ 95CzeAPSE-198
**Walter, Ryan**
❑ 79OPC-236
❑ 79Top-236
❑ 80OPC-154
❑ 80Top-154
❑ 81Cap-21
❑ 81OPC-352
❑ 81OPCSti-192
❑ 81Top-E122
❑ 82CanaPos-26
❑ 82CanaSte-21
❑ 82OPC-194
❑ 82OPCSti-152
❑ 82PosCer-20
❑ 83CanaPos-31
❑ 83OPC-200
❑ 83OPCSti-62
❑ 83OPCSti-63
❑ 83PufSti-3
❑ 83Vac-58
❑ 84CanaPos-31
❑ 84KelWin-36
❑ 84OPC-275
❑ 84OPCSti-159
❑ 85CanaPos-40
❑ 85CanaPro-25
❑ 86CanaPos-25
❑ 86KraDra-79
❑ 86OPC-224
❑ 87CanaPos-34
❑ 87CanaVacS-24
❑ 87CanaVacS-25
❑ 87OPC-231
❑ 87OPCSti-17
❑ 88CanaPos-30
❑ 88OPC-262
❑ 88OPCSti-40
❑ 88PanSti-262
❑ 89CanaKra-24
❑ 89CanaPos-32
❑ 89OPC-240
❑ 90CanaPos-33
❑ 90OPC-296
❑ 90ProSet-475
❑ 90Top-296
❑ 90TopTif-296
❑ 91CanaPanTS-24
❑ 91CanuAutC-23
❑ 91CanuTeal8-23
❑ 91Par-401
❑ 91ParFre-401
❑ 91ProSet-504
❑ 91ProSetFre-504
❑ 91ScoCan-591
❑ 91ScoRoo-41T
❑ 92CanuRoaTA-23
❑ 92Pin-255
❑ 92PinFre-255
❑ 93StaClu-185
❑ 93StaCluFDI-185
❑ 93StaCluFDIO-185
❑ 93StaCluO-185
**Walters, Greg**
❑ 897thInnSOHL-50
❑ 90NewSai-26
❑ 90ProAHLIHL-147
❑ 91ProAHLCHL-349
**Walters, Ron**
❑ 72OPC-301
**Walters, S.**
❑ 28V1282PauC-69
**Waltin, Mats**
❑ 74SweSemHVS-18
❑ 79PanSti-188
❑ 81SweSemHVS-7
❑ 82SweSemHVS-6
❑ 83SweSemE-82
❑ 89SweSemE-57
❑ 90SweSemE-56
❑ 93SwiHNL-211
❑ 95SwiHNL-110
**Walton, Mike**
❑ 64BeeGro3P-188
❑ 65Coc-100
❑ 65Top-86
❑ 66Top-14
❑ 66TopUSAT-14
❑ 67Top-15
❑ 67YorActOct-2
❑ 67YorActOct-10
❑ 67YorActOct-11
❑ 67YorActOct-12
❑ 67YorActOct-13
❑ 67YorActOct-23
❑ 68OPC-132
❑ 68PosCerM-29
❑ 68ShiCoi-163
❑ 68Top-132
❑ 69MapLeaWBG-36
❑ 69MapLeaWBG-37
❑ 69OPC-50
❑ 69OPCFou-15
❑ 69Top-50
❑ 70ColSta-3
❑ 70DadCoo-136
❑ 70EssPowPla-28
❑ 70MapLeaP-15
❑ 70OPC-109
❑ 70SarProSta-206
❑ 70Top-109
❑ 71BruTeaIss-8
❑ 71OPC-171
❑ 71SarProSta-12
❑ 71TorSun-20
❑ 72OPC-94
❑ 72SarProSta-24
❑ 73OPCWHAP-15
❑ 74FigSaiWHA-23
❑ 74OPCWHA-10
❑ 74TeaCanLWHA-23
❑ 75OPCWHA-26
❑ 76CanuRoyB-22
❑ 76OPCNHL-23
❑ 76Top-23
❑ 77CanCanDC-15

700 • Waltonen, Jorma


❑ 77CanuRoyB-21
❑ 77OPCNHL-350
❑ 78OPC-38
❑ 78Top-38
❑ 79Top-141
❑ 95Par66-101
❑ 95Par66Coi-101
**Waltonen, Jorma**
❑ 73SweHocS-33
❑ 73SweWorCS-33
**Walz, Wes**
❑ 88LetHur-22
❑ 89LetHur-22
❑ 90BruSpoA-24
❑ 90OPCPre-127
❑ 90ProSet-589
❑ 90Sco-418
❑ 90ScoCan-418
❑ 90UppDec-527
❑ 90UppDecF-527
❑ 91Bow-353
❑ 91OPC-134
❑ 91ProAHLCHL-48
❑ 91ScoCan-430
❑ 91StaClu-325
❑ 91Top-134
❑ 91UppDec-123
❑ 91UppDecF-123
❑ 93Don-57
❑ 93Lea-393
❑ 93Par-305
❑ 93ParEmel-305
❑ 93Ult-287
❑ 93UppDec-431
❑ 94CanGamNHLP-62
❑ 94Don-319
❑ 94Lea-154
❑ 94OPCPre-137
❑ 94OPCPreSE-137
❑ 94Par-38
❑ 94ParGol-38
❑ 94TopPre-137
❑ 94TopPreSE-137
❑ 94Ult-37
❑ 94UppDec-350
❑ 94UppDecElelce-350
❑ 95AdiRedW-23
**Wamsley, Rick**
❑ 81CanaPos-27
❑ 82CanaPos-27
❑ 82CanaSte-22
❑ 82McDSti-5
❑ 82OPC-195
❑ 82OPCSti-37
❑ 83CanaPos-32
❑ 83OPC-201
❑ 83OPCSti-72
❑ 83Vac-59
❑ 84OPCSti-157
❑ 86OPC-240
❑ 86OPCSti-179
❑ 87BluKod-26
❑ 87OPC-65
❑ 87OPCSti-22
❑ 87PanSti-305
❑ 87Top-65
❑ 89OPC-204
❑ 89OPCSti-93
❑ 90Bow-98
❑ 90BowTif-98
❑ 90FlamIGA-29
❑ 90OPC-409
❑ 90PanSti-186
❑ 90ProSet-48
❑ 90Sco-309C
❑ 90ScoCan-309C
❑ 90UppDec-10
❑ 90UppDecF-10
❑ 91Bow-268
❑ 91FlamIGA-25
❑ 91FlamPanTS-24
❑ 91OPC-459
❑ 91Par-394
❑ 91ParFre-394
❑ 91ProSet-367
❑ 91ProSetFre-367
❑ 91ScoCan-232
❑ 91StaClu-294
❑ 91Top-459
❑ 91UppDec-130
❑ 91UppDecF-130
❑ 92Bow-97
❑ 92OPC-310
❑ 92StaClu-53
❑ 92Top-425
❑ 92TopGol-425G
**Wanchuk, Mike**
❑ 77KalWin-10
**Wanhainen, Rolf**
❑ 92UppDec-223
**Wannstrom, Jorgen**
❑ 89SweSemE-212
**Wansborough, Shawn**
❑ 98LasVegT-22
**Wanvig, Kyle**
❑ 98SP Aut-133
❑ 98UppDec-410
❑ 98UppDecE-410
❑ 98UppDecE1o1-410
❑ 98UppDecGR-410
❑ 99SP AutPS-133
**Ward, Aaron**
❑ 91MicWol-22
❑ 93Cla-85
❑ 93Don-93
❑ 93Lea-359
❑ 93OPCPre-484
❑ 93OPCPreG-484
❑ 93Par-262
❑ 93ParEmel-262
❑ 93Pin-432
❑ 93PinCan-432
❑ 93StaClu-423
❑ 93StaCluFDI-423
❑ 93StaCluO-423
❑ 93TopPre-484
❑ 93TopPreG-484
❑ 93UppDec-479
❑ 94ClaAut-NNO
❑ 94ClaProP-120
❑ 94Lea-312
❑ 94Sco-229
❑ 94ScoGol-229
❑ 94ScoPla-229
❑ 94ScoPlaTS-229
❑ 94UppDec-153
❑ 94UppDecElelce-153
❑ 95AdiRedW-24
❑ 95ColEdgl-5
❑ 95Ima-98
❑ 95ImaAut-98A
❑ 95ImaGol-98
❑ 95ParInt-71
❑ 95ParIntEl-71
❑ 97Be A PPAD-200
❑ 97Be A PPAPD-200
❑ 97BeAPla-200
❑ 97BeAPlaAut-200
❑ 97PacInvNRB-74
❑ 97UppDec-270
❑ 99Pac-150
❑ 99PacCop-150
❑ 99PacGol-150
❑ 99PacIceB-150
❑ 99PacPreD-150
**Ward, Caleb**
❑ 94WinSpi-23
❑ 95Sla-326
**Ward, Colin**
❑ 92WesMic-24
❑ 93WesMic-26
**Ward, Dixon**
❑ 92CanuRoaTA-24
❑ 92Cla-84
❑ 92OPCPre-67
❑ 92Par-194
❑ 92ParEmel-194
❑ 92Ult-431
❑ 92UppDec-580
❑ 92UppDecCC-CC1
❑ 93Don-449
❑ 93Lea-97
❑ 93OPCPre-58
❑ 93OPCPre-127
❑ 93OPCPreG-58
❑ 93OPCPreG-127
❑ 93Par-209
❑ 93ParEmel-209
❑ 93Pin-176
❑ 93PinCan-176
❑ 93Pow-257
❑ 93Pow-365
❑ 93Sco-210
❑ 93Sco-654
❑ 93ScoCan-210
❑ 93ScoCan-654
❑ 93ScoGol-654
❑ 93StaClu-454
❑ 93StaCluFDI-454
❑ 93StaCluO-454
❑ 93TopPre-58
❑ 93TopPre-127
❑ 93TopPreG-58
❑ 93TopPreG-127
❑ 93Ult-102
❑ 93UppDec-62
❑ 93UppDecSP-167
❑ 94CanuProl-21
❑ 94MapLeaK-27
❑ 94OPCPre-112
❑ 94OPCPreSE-112
❑ 94Par-102
❑ 94ParGol-102
❑ 94Pin-239
❑ 94PinArtP-239
❑ 94PinRinC-239
❑ 94TopPre-112
❑ 94TopPreSE-112
❑ 95RochAmeSS-21
❑ 96BeAPAut-130
❑ 96BeAPAutSil-130
❑ 96BeAPla-130
❑ 96ClaGol-84
❑ 97PacInvNRB-24
❑ 97ScoSab-3
❑ 97ScoSabPla-3
❑ 97ScoSabPre-3
❑ 97UppDec-21
❑ 98Be A PPA-16
❑ 98Be A PPAA-16
❑ 98Be A PPAAF-16
❑ 98Be A PPTBASG-16
❑ 98Be APG-16
❑ 98Pac-112
❑ 98PacAur-21
❑ 98PacIceB-112
❑ 98PacOmeH-29
❑ 98PacOmeODI-29
❑ 98PacOmeR-29
❑ 98PacPar-24
❑ 98PacParC-24
❑ 98PacParEG-24
❑ 98PacParH-24
❑ 98PacParIB-24
❑ 98PacParS-24
❑ 98PacRed-112
❑ 98PacRev-17
❑ 98PacRevIS-17
❑ 98PacRevR-17
❑ 99Pac-48
❑ 99PacCop-48
❑ 99PacGol-48
❑ 99PacIceB-48
❑ 99PacPreD-48
❑ 99UppDecM-27
❑ 99UppDecMGS-27
❑ 99UppDecMSS-27
❑ 99UppDecMSS-27
**Ward, Don**
❑ 69SeaTotW-8
**Ward, Ed**
❑ 94ClaProP-196
❑ 95Bow-105
❑ 95BowAllFoi-105
❑ 95ParInt-305
❑ 95ParIntEl-305
❑ 97Be A PPAD-172
❑ 97Be A PPAPD-172
❑ 97BeAPla-172
❑ 97BeAPlaAut-172
❑ 97PacInvNRB-33
❑ 98UppDecM-31
❑ 98UppDecMGS-31
❑ 98UppDecMSS-31
❑ 98UppDecMSS-31
**Ward, Geoff**
❑ 94KitRan-27
❑ 95Sla-155
❑ 96KitRan-27
**Ward, Jason**
❑ 95Sla-186
❑ 96UppDec-388
❑ 97BowCHL-129
❑ 97BowCHLAu-129
❑ 97BowCHLBB-5
❑ 97BowCHLBowBesAR-5
❑ 97BowCHLBowBesR-5
❑ 97BowCHLOPC-129
❑ 97ColCho-303
❑ 98BowCHL-9
❑ 98BowCHLGA-9
❑ 98BowCHLOI-9
❑ 98BowChrC-9
❑ 98BowChrCGA-9
❑ 98BowChrCGAR-9
❑ 98BowChrCOI-9
❑ 98BowChrCOIR-9
❑ 98BowChrCR-9
❑ 98UC-272
❑ 98UD ChoPCR-272
❑ 98UD ChoR-272
**Ward, Jimmy**
❑ 33OPCV304B-56
❑ 33V252CanG-49
❑ 33V357IceK-37
❑ 34BeeGro1P-209
❑ 34SweCap-27
❑ 36V356WorG-2
❑ 37OPCV304E-170
❑ 38QuaOatP-29
**Ward, Lance**
❑ 95BowDraPro-P37
❑ 95RedDeeR-18
**Ward, Ron**
❑ 66TulOil-12
❑ 69MapLeaWBG-38
❑ 71CanuRoyB-8
❑ 71TorSun-292
❑ 72OPC-332
❑ 72SluCupWHA-19
❑ 73QuaOatWHA-34
❑ 74OPCWHA-21
❑ 75OPCWHA-73
❑ 76OPCWHA-35
**Ward, Spencer**
❑ 92BriColJHL-192
**Ward, Wes**
❑ 94WinSpi-13
❑ 95Sla-421
**Warden, Jim**
❑ 79PanSti-207
**Warden, Tom**
❑ 93ThuBayS-14
**Ware, Jeffrey (Jeff)**
❑ 94ParSE-SE257
❑ 94ParSEG-SE257
❑ 94Sel-163
❑ 94SelGol-163
❑ 94SP-188
❑ 94SPDieCut-188
❑ 95Cla-15
❑ 95Cla-91
❑ 95ClaIceBre-BK14
❑ 95Ima-86
❑ 95ImaGol-86
❑ 95Sla-246
❑ 96ClaIceBreDC-BK14
❑ 96UppDecIce-131
❑ 97DonCanI-129
❑ 97DonCanIDS-129
❑ 97DonCanIPS-129
❑ 97St.JohML-25
❑ 97UppDec-370
**Ware, Mike**
❑ 88OilTenAnn-151
❑ 88ProAHL-81
❑ 90ProAHLIHL-232
❑ 93MicSta-27
❑ 95St.JohML-21
❑ 97SheSte-18
❑ 98GerDELE-196
**Wares, Eddie**
❑ 34BeeGro1P-129
❑ 39OPCV3011-73
**Warming, Thomas**
❑ 65SweCorI-75B
**Warner, Jim**
❑ 79OPC-384
❑ 79PanSti-221
**Warning, Lars-Ake**
❑ 64SweCorI-148
❑ 65SweCorI-148
❑ 69SweHocS-56
❑ 70SweHocS-16
**Warr, Steve**
❑ 72NatOttWHA-23
**Warrener, Rhett**
❑ 93SasBla-21
❑ 95Bow-108
❑ 95BowAllFoi-108
❑ 95Don-358
❑ 95DonEliWJ-9
❑ 95SigRoo-35
❑ 95SigRooSig-35
❑ 95StaClu-140
❑ 95StaCluMOMS-140
❑ 95Top-272
❑ 95TopOPCI-272
❑ 95UppDec-528
❑ 95UppDecElelce-528
❑ 95UppDecElelceG-528
❑ 96BeAPAut-138
❑ 96BeAPAutSil-138
❑ 96BeAPla-138
❑ 96SasBla-24
❑ 96UppDec-266
**Warrener, Trevor**
❑ 91AirCanSJHL-B7
❑ 92MPSPhoSJHL-129
**Warriner, Mike**
❑ 92BriColJHL-146
**Warriner, Todd**
❑ 907thInnSOHL-195
❑ 917thInnSOHL-173
❑ 92WinSpi-17
❑ 92WinSpi-31
❑ 93AlbIntTC-21
❑ 93KitRan-15
❑ 93OPCPreTC-19
❑ 93Pow-496
❑ 93Ult-476
❑ 94BeAPla-R163
❑ 94Cla-109
❑ 94ClaDraGol-109
❑ 94ClaProPIA-IA7
❑ 94ClaProPIH-LP20
❑ 94MapLeaK-28
❑ 94ScoTeaC-CT3
❑ 94St.JohML-24
❑ 95Bow-106
❑ 95BowAllFoi-106
❑ 95Don-85
❑ 95Lea-101
❑ 95ParInt-472
❑ 95ParIntEl-472
❑ 95Pin-219
❑ 95PinArtP-219
❑ 95PinRinC-219
❑ 95Sco-296
❑ 95ScoBlalce-296
❑ 95ScoBlalceAP-296
❑ 95St.JohML-22
❑ 95Top-45
❑ 95TopOPCI-45
❑ 96BeAPAut-122
❑ 96BeAPAutSil-122
❑ 96BeAPla-122
❑ 96UppDec-163
❑ 96UppDecBD-93
❑ 96UppDecBDG-93
❑ 97ColCho-254
❑ 97Don-91
❑ 97DonLim-162
❑ 97DonLimExp-162
❑ 97DonPrePro G-91
❑ 97DonPreProS-91
❑ 97Pac-257
❑ 97PacCop-257
❑ 97PacEmeGre-257
❑ 97PacIceB-257
❑ 97PacRed-257
❑ 97PacSil-257
❑ 97PinIns-166
❑ 97Sco-207
❑ 97ScoMapL-9
❑ 97ScoMapLPla-9
❑ 97ScoMapLPre-9
❑ 97UppDec-163
**Warring, Jeremy**
❑ 907thInnSWHL-102
❑ 917thInnSWHL-22
**Warus, Mike**
❑ 88ProAHL-178
**Warwick, Grant**
❑ 34BeeGro1P-296
❑ 44BeeGro2P-73
❑ 44BeeGro2P-293
❑ 45QuaOatP-113
❑ 48ExhCan-26
❑ 51BufBis-19
**Wasama, Jarmo**
❑ 96FinnSISR-190
**Washburn, Steven (Steve)**
❑ 917thInnSOHL-308
❑ 92Ott672A-22
❑ 95Cla-92
❑ 95ColEdgl-25
❑ 95Ima-36
❑ 95ImaAut-36A
❑ 95ImaGol-36
❑ 96Lea-237
❑ 96LeaPre-138
❑ 96LeaPreP-237
❑ 96LeaPrePP-138
❑ 96Pin-232
❑ 96PinArtP-232
❑ 96PinFoi-232
❑ 96PinPreS-232
❑ 96PinRinC-232
❑ 96Ult-71
❑ 96UltGolM-71
❑ 97Be A PPAD-139
❑ 97Be A PPAPD-139
❑ 97BeAPla-139
❑ 97BeAPlaAut-139
❑ 97ColCho-107
❑ 97Don-115
❑ 97DonPreProG-115
❑ 97DonPreProS-115
❑ 97PacInvNRB-90
❑ 97PacOme-103
❑ 97PacOmeC-103
❑ 97PacOmeDG-103
❑ 97PacOmeEG-103
❑ 97PacOmeG-103
❑ 97PacOmeIB-103
❑ 98O-PChr-158
❑ 98O-PChrR-158
❑ 98Pac-229
❑ 98PacIceB-229
❑ 98PacRed-229
❑ 98Top-158
❑ 98TopO-P-158
**Washkurak, Joel**
❑ 907thInnSOHL-72
**Wasley, Charlie**
❑ 92MinGolG-22
❑ 93MinGolG-26
❑ 94MinGolG-28
❑ 95MinGolG-28
**Wasnie, Nick**
❑ 28V1282PauC-64
❑ 33OPCV304A-47
❑ 33V252CanG-50
❑ 33V288HamG-1
**Wassermann, Sepp**
❑ 94GerDELE-339
❑ 95GerDELE-306
**Wasylko, Steve**
❑ 95BowDraPro-P38
❑ 95Sla-71
❑ 96DetWha-19
**Wasyluk, Trevor**
❑ 95BowDraPro-P39
❑ 95MedHatT-21
❑ 95UppDec-512
❑ 95UppDecElelce-512
❑ 95UppDecElelceG-512
❑ 96MedHatT-24
**Watchorn, Jeff**
❑ 907thInnSMC-13
❑ 907thInnSWHL-292
❑ 917thInnSWHL-92
**Wathen, Trevor**
❑ 91AirCanSJHL-A16
❑ 92MPSPhoSJHL-61
**Watkins, Larry**
❑ 907thInnSWHL-258
❑ 917thInnSWHL-320
**Watson, Bill**
❑ 86BlaCok-22
❑ 86OPC-151
❑ 86Top-151
❑ 87BlaCok-28
❑ 87PanSti-232
❑ 88ProIHL-118
**Watson, Blake**
❑ 24CreFal-14
**Watson, Brent**
❑ 907thInnSOHL-223
❑ 917thInnSOHL-351
**Watson, Bryan**
❑ 64CanaPos-23
❑ 64QueAce-18
❑ 65Top-45
❑ 66Top-48
❑ 68OPC-173
❑ 69OPC-112
❑ 69Top-112
❑ 70DadCoo-137
❑ 70EssPowPla-221
❑ 70OPC-204
❑ 70SarProSta-164
❑ 71PenPos-20
❑ 71SarProSta-164
❑ 71TorSun-229
❑ 72OPC-90
❑ 72OPC-268
❑ 72SarProSta-172
❑ 72SweSemWC-217
❑ 72Top-65
❑ 72Top-116
❑ 73OPC-14
❑ 73Top-144
❑ 74NHLActSta-95
❑ 74OPCNHL-5
❑ 74OPCNHL-259
❑ 74Top-5
❑ 74Top-259
❑ 75OPCNHL-31
❑ 75Top-31
❑ 76OPCNHL-4
❑ 76OPCNHL-228
❑ 76OPCNHL-385
❑ 76Top-4
❑ 76Top-228
❑ 77OPCNHL-342
❑ 78OPC-316
❑ 88OilTenAnn-124
**Watson, Harry**
❑ 34BeeGro1P-257
❑ 44BeeGro2P-459
❑ 45QuaOatP-58A
❑ 45QuaOatP-58B
❑ 45QuaOatP-58C
❑ 45QuaOatP-60A
❑ 51Par-70
❑ 52Par-46
❑ 53Par-12
❑ 54Par-17
❑ 83HalFP-G16
❑ 85HalFC-105
❑ 91UltOriS-46
❑ 91UltOriSF-46
❑ 93ParParRCI-11
❑ 94ParMisL-36
**Watson, Jim**
❑ 67Top-107
❑ 68ShiCoi-48
❑ 70EssPowPla-74
❑ 70OPC-144
❑ 70SarProSta-32
❑ 71OPC-165
❑ 71SabPos-20
❑ 71SarProSta-21
❑ 71TorSun-40
❑ 72ShaLosAW-17
❑ 72SluCupWHA-20
❑ 73FlyLin-17
❑ 74NHLActSta-208
❑ 74OPCNHL-303
❑ 75FlyCanDC-20
❑ 75OPCNHL-202
❑ 75Top-202
❑ 77Coc-28
❑ 77OPCNHL-43
❑ 77Top-43
❑ 78OPC-247
❑ 78Top-247
❑ 79OPC-26
❑ 79Top-26
❑ 80OPC-224
❑ 80Top-224
❑ 82OPC-259
❑ 82PosCer-14
❑ 90UppDec-514
**Watson, Joe**
❑ 66Top-33
❑ 68OPC-90
❑ 68Top-90
❑ 69OPC-93
❑ 69Top-93
❑ 70DadCoo-138
❑ 70EssPowPla-209
❑ 70OPC-79
❑ 70SarProSta-156
❑ 70Top-79
❑ 71SarProSta-158
❑ 71TorSun-208
❑ 72OPC-91
❑ 72SarProSta-159
❑ 72Top-156
❑ 73FlyLin-18
❑ 73OPC-91
❑ 73Top-91
❑ 74NHLActSta-214
❑ 74OPCNHL-217
❑ 74Top-217
❑ 75FlyCanDC-21
❑ 75OPCNHL-281
❑ 75Top-281
❑ 76OPCNHL-45
❑ 76OPCNHL-247
❑ 76Top-45
❑ 76Top-247
❑ 77Coc-29
❑ 77OPCNHL-247
❑ 77Top-247
❑ 78OPC-43
❑ 78Top-43
❑ 92Par-474
❑ 92ParEmel-474
❑ 95Par66-3
❑ 95Par66Coi-3
**Watson, Phil**
❑ 34BeeGro1P-297
❑ 36V356WorG-80
❑ 39OPCV3011-83
❑ 52JunBluT-80
❑ 61ShiCoi-19
❑ 61Top-1
❑ 62Top-1
❑ 94ParMisL-108
**Watson, Ross**
❑ 52JunBluT-159
**Watt, Mike**
❑ 95DonEliWJ-21
❑ 95UppDec-536
❑ 95UppDecElelce-536
❑ 95UppDecElelceG-536
❑ 98BowBesMIF-F11
❑ 98BowBesMIFAR-F11
❑ 98BowBesMIFR-F11
❑ 98IslPowP-NYI3
❑ 98PacOmeH-153
❑ 98PacOmeODI-153
❑ 98PacOmeR-153
❑ 98PacRev-91
❑ 98PacRevIS-91
❑ 98PacRevR-91
❑ 98SP Aut-103
❑ 98SPxFin-138
❑ 98SPxFinR-138
❑ 98SPxFinS-138
❑ 98UppDec-14
❑ 98UppDec-316
❑ 98UppDecE-14
❑ 98UppDecE-316
❑ 98UppDecE1o1-14
❑ 98UppDecE1o1-316
❑ 98UppDecGN-GN15
❑ 98UppDecGNQ1-GN15
❑ 98UppDecGNQ2-GN15
❑ 98UppDecGNQ3-GN15
❑ 98UppDecGR-14
❑ 98UppDecGR-316
❑ 98UppDecM-128
❑ 98UppDecMGS-128
❑ 98UppDecMSS-128
❑ 98UppDecMSS-128
❑ 99Pac-266
❑ 99PacAur-92
❑ 99PacAurPD-92
❑ 99PacCop-266
❑ 99PacGol-266
❑ 99PacIceB-266
❑ 99PacPreD-266
❑ 99SP AutPS-103
❑ 99UppDecM-125
❑ 99UppDecMGS-125
❑ 99UppDecMSS-125
❑ 99UppDecMSS-125
**Watt, Tom**
❑ 81JetPos-23
❑ 82Jet-26
❑ 90ProSet-677
❑ 91MapLeaP-29
❑ 95St.JohML-23
❑ 97SudWolP-6
**Watters, Tim**
❑ 81JetPos-24
❑ 81SweSemHVS-78
❑ 82Jet-27
❑ 82OPC-395
❑ 82PosCer-21
❑ 83Jet-23
❑ 83OPC-394
❑ 83Vac-139
❑ 84JetPol-21
❑ 84OPC-350
❑ 85JetPol-21
❑ 86JetBor-24
❑ 87Jet-22
❑ 87OPC-219
❑ 88KinSmo-24
❑ 89KinSmo-2
❑ 89OPC-212
❑ 90KinSmo-4
❑ 90MicTecHus-27
❑ 90OPC-461
❑ 90ProSet-458
❑ 90Sco-204
❑ 90ScoCan-204
❑ 90UppDec-117
❑ 90UppDecF-117
❑ 91ScoCan-523
❑ 91UppDec-471
❑ 91UppDecF-471
❑ 92PhoRoa-25
❑ 93OPCPre-298
❑ 93OPCPreG-298
❑ 93TopPre-298
❑ 93TopPreG-298
**Watts, Morgan**
❑ 85LonKni-8
**Waver, Jeff**
❑ 84BraWheK-16
❑ 85BraWheK-16
❑ 88ProIHL-64
❑ 90ProAHLIHL-523
**Way, Jim**
❑ 86SudWol-9
**Way, Shawn**
❑ 897thInnSOHL-84
**Weaver, Dave**
❑ 92WesMic-25
**Weaver, Jason**
❑ 907thInnSOHL-348
❑ 917thInnSOHL-160
❑ 91OshGen-18
❑ 91OshGenS-11
**Weaver, Scott**
❑ 91AirCanSJHL-D23
**Webb, Stephen**
❑ 92WinSpi-22
❑ 95MusFur-10
❑ 96KenTho-18
❑ 97Pac-248
❑ 97PacCop-248
❑ 97PacEmeGre-248
❑ 97PacIceB-248
❑ 97PacRed-248
❑ 97PacSil-248
❑ 97UppDec-308
**Webber, Mike**

□ 83NorBayC-23

**Weber, Christian**
□ 91SweSemWCS-196
□ 93SweSemWCS-125
□ 93SwiHNL-181
□ 95SweGloWC-212
□ 95SwiHNL-131
□ 95SwiHNL-508

**Weber, Jason**
□ 93CorBigRed-26

**Weber, Marc**
□ 91UppDec-666
□ 91UppDecCWJC-27
□ 91UppDecF-666
□ 93SwiHNL-207
□ 95SwiHNL-234

**Weber, Patrik**
□ 94CzeAPSE-42

**Webster, Chris**
□ 87BroBra-19
□ 88BroBra-23

**Webster, Dave**
□ 82KitRan-30

**Webster, Glen**
□ 89BraWheK-14
□ 907thInnSWHL-230
□ 90BraWheK-10

**Webster, Tom**
□ 70DadCoo-139
□ 70EssPowPla-133
□ 70OPC-155
□ 70RedWinM-11
□ 70SarProSta-57
□ 71OPC-78
□ 71SarProSta-135
□ 71Top-78
□ 72WhaNewEWHA-16
□ 74OPCWHA-8
□ 74TeaCanLWHA-24
□ 75OPCWHA-95
□ 76OPCWHA-14
□ 77OPCWHA-55
□ 90ProSet-667

**Wedl, Alexander**
□ 94GerDELE-107
□ 95GerDELE-152
□ 96GerDELE-230
□ 98GerDELE-54

**Weekes, Kevin**
□ 93OweSouPla-6
□ 93OweSouPla-32
□ 93OweSouPla-33
□ 95ColEdgI-26
□ 97DonPri-177
□ 97DonPriSoA-177
□ 97PacCroR-61
□ 97PacCroREG-61
□ 97PacCroRIB-61
□ 97PacCroRS-61
□ 97PacOme-104
□ 97PacOmeC-104
□ 97PacOmeDG-104
□ 97PacOmeEG-104
□ 97PacOmeG-104
□ 97PacOmeIB-104
□ 97SPAut-183
□ 98Pac-230
□ 98PacIceB-230
□ 98PacRed-230
□ 98UppDec-100
□ 98UppDecE-100
□ 98UppDecE1o1-100
□ 98UppDecGR-100
□ 99Pac-434
□ 99PacCop-434
□ 99PacGol-434
□ 99PacIceB-434
□ 99PacPreD-434
□ 99UppDecM-208
□ 99UppDecMGS-208
□ 99UppDecMSS-208
□ 99UppDecMSS-208

**Weeks, Steve**
□ 82OPC-234
□ 82OPCSti-141
□ 82PosCer-13
□ 84WhaJunW-21
□ 85WhaJunW-22
□ 86WhaJunT-23
□ 87PanSti-39
□ 87WhaJunBK-21
□ 88CanuMoh-24
□ 89CanuMoh-24
□ 89OPC-285
□ 89PanSti-150
□ 90OPC-407
□ 90ProAHLIHL-331
□ 90UppDec-107
□ 90UppDecF-107
□ 92Bow-274
□ 92Pin-380
□ 92PinFre-380
□ 92Sco-547
□ 92ScoCan-547
□ 92StaClu-273
□ 92Top-461
□ 92TopGol-461G

**Weenk, Heath**
□ 907thInnSWHL-185
□ 917thInnSWHL-220

**Wegener, John**
□ 90ArlIce-15

**Wegleitner, Mike**
□ 84KelWin-11

**Weibel, Lars**
□ 93SwiHNL-85
□ 95SwiHNL-136
□ 95SwiHNL-510
□ 95SwiHNL-511
□ 95SwiHNL-514

**Weidenbach, Andy**
□ 907thInnSOHL-124
□ 96HamRoaA-HRA11

**Weidenbach, John**
□ 93MicSta-28

**Weight, Doug**
□ 91OPCPre-32
□ 91OPCPre-139
□ 91Par-116
□ 91ParFre-116
□ 91Pin-310
□ 91Pin-383
□ 91PinFre-310
□ 91PinFre-383
□ 91ProSet-549
□ 91ProSetFre-549
□ 91ProSetPla-263
□ 91ScoAme-396
□ 91ScoCan-286
□ 91UppDec-440
□ 91UppDec-444
□ 91UppDecF-440
□ 91UppDecF-444
□ 92Bow-36
□ 92OilTeaI-21
□ 92OPC-114
□ 92PanSti-236
□ 92PanStiFre-236
□ 92Par-115
□ 92Par-229
□ 92ParEmel-115
□ 92ParEmel-229
□ 92Pin-189
□ 92PinFre-189
□ 92Sco-314
□ 92ScoCan-314
□ 92StaClu-380
□ 92Top-477
□ 92TopGol-477G
□ 92Ult-358
□ 92UppDec-279
□ 93Don-118
□ 93Lea-184
□ 93OPCPre-136
□ 93OPCPreG-136
□ 93PanSti-235
□ 93Par-69
□ 93ParEmel-69
□ 93Pin-17
□ 93PinCan-17
□ 93Pow-87
□ 93Sco-253
□ 93ScoCan-253
□ 93StaClu-382
□ 93StaCluFDI-382
□ 93StaCluO-382
□ 93TopPre-136
□ 93TopPreG-136
□ 93Ult-195
□ 93UppDec-442
□ 93UppDecSP-53
□ 94BeAPla-R118
□ 94BeAPSig-117
□ 94CanGamNHLP-101
□ 94Don-3
□ 94EASpo-45
□ 94Fla-62
□ 94Lea-40
□ 94LeaLim-53
□ 94OPCPre-8
□ 94OPCPreSE-8
□ 94Par-74
□ 94ParGol-74
□ 94ParSEV-23
□ 94Pin-18
□ 94PinArtP-18
□ 94PinRinC-18
□ 94Sco-58
□ 94ScoGol-58
□ 94ScoPla-58
□ 94ScoPlaTS-58
□ 94Sel-27
□ 94SelGol-27
□ 94SP-39
□ 94SPDieCut-39
□ 94TopPre-8
□ 94TopPreSE-8
□ 94Ult-77
□ 94UppDec-44
□ 94UppDec-549
□ 94UppDecEleIce-44
□ 94UppDecEleIce-549
□ 94UppDecNBAP-39
□ 94UppDecSPI-SP28
□ 94UppDecSPIDC-SP28
□ 95Bow-68
□ 95BowAllFoi-68
□ 95CanGamNHLP-105
□ 95ColCho-172
□ 95ColChoPC-172
□ 95ColChoPCP-172
□ 95Don-25
□ 95DonEli-5
□ 95DonEliDCS-5
□ 95DonEliDCU-5
□ 95Emo-67
□ 95Fin-104
□ 95FinRef-104
□ 95GerDELE-449
□ 95ImpSti-43
□ 95Kra-68
□ 95Lea-145
□ 95LeaLim-110
□ 95Met-57
□ 95ParInt-346
□ 95ParIntEl-346
□ 95PlaOneoOne-259
□ 95ProMag-85
□ 95Sco-263
□ 95ScoBlaIce-263
□ 95ScoBlaIceAP-263
□ 95SelCer-109
□ 95SelCerMG-109
□ 95SkyImp-65
□ 95SP-50
□ 95SPHol-FX9
□ 95SPHolSpFX-FX9
□ 95StaClu-74
□ 95StaCluMOMS-74
□ 95Sum-110
□ 95SumArtP-110
□ 95SumIce-110
□ 95SweGloWC-125
□ 95Top-158
□ 95TopOPCI-158
□ 95Ult-58
□ 95UltGolM-58
□ 95UppDec-280
□ 95UppDecEleIce-280
□ 95UppDecEleIceG-280
□ 95UppDecNHLAS-AS16
□ 95UppDecSpeE-SE31
□ 95UppDecSpeEdiG-SE31
□ 96BeAPAut-174
□ 96BeAPAutSil-174
□ 96BeAPla-174
□ 96ColCho-91
□ 96ColCho-317
□ 96ColChoCTG-C9A
□ 96ColChoCTG-C9B
□ 96ColChoCTG-C9C
□ 96ColChoCTGE-CR9
□ 96ColChoCTGEG-CR9
□ 96ColChoCTGG-C9A
□ 96ColChoCTGG-C9B
□ 96ColChoCTGG-C9C
□ 96ColChoMVP-UD9
□ 96ColChoMVPG-UD9
□ 96Don-85
□ 96DonCanI-14
□ 96DonCanIGPP-14
□ 96DonCanIRPP-14
□ 96DonEli-25
□ 96DonEliDCS-25
□ 96DonEliIns-3
□ 96DonEliInsG-3
□ 96DonEliS-4
□ 96DonHitLis-5
□ 96DonPrePro-85
□ 96Fla-36
□ 96FlaBluI-36
□ 96Fle-38
□ 96FleArtRos-24
□ 96FlePicF5-47
□ 96FlePicJE-4
□ 96KraUppD-21
□ 96KraUppD-71
□ 96Lea-136
□ 96LeaFirOI-6
□ 96LeaLim-71
□ 96LeaLimG-71
□ 96LeaPre-54
□ 96LeaPreP-136
□ 96LeaPrePP-54
□ 96LeaPreSG-49
□ 96LeaPreSte-49
□ 96LeaTheBO.-7
□ 96MetUni-56
□ 96MetUniLW-20
□ 96MetUniLWSP-20
□ 96NHLACEPC-50
□ 96NHLProSTA-85
□ 96OilPos-39
□ 96Pin-158
□ 96PinArtP-158
□ 96PinByTN-5
□ 96PinByTNP-5
□ 96PinFoi-158
□ 96PinMcD-16
□ 96PinPreS-158
□ 96PinRinC-158
□ 96PinTeaP-4
□ 96PlaOneoOne-434
□ 96Sco-170
□ 96ScoArtPro-170
□ 96ScoChelt-14
□ 96ScoDeaCAP-170
□ 96ScoGolB-170
□ 96ScoSpeAP-170
□ 96ScoSup-2
□ 96SelCer-50
□ 96SelCerAP-50
□ 96SelCerBlu-50
□ 96SelCerMB-50
□ 96SelCerMG-50
□ 96SelCerMR-50
□ 96SelCerRed-50
□ 96SkyImp-43
□ 96SkyImpB-24
□ 96SP-57
□ 96SPCleWin-CW10
□ 96SPHolCol-HC24
□ 96SPx-17
□ 96SPxGol-17
□ 96StaCluMO-12
□ 96Sum-92
□ 96SumArtP-92
□ 96SumIce-92
□ 96SumMet-92
□ 96SumPreS-92
□ 96SumUnt-11
□ 96SweSemW-172
□ 96TopNHLP-23
□ 96TopPicOI-23
□ 96Ult-63
□ 96UltGolM-63
□ 96UppDec-58
□ 96UppDecBD-172
□ 96UppDecBDG-172
□ 96UppDecGN-X13
□ 96UppDecIce-87
□ 96UppDecIceDF-S9
□ 96UppDecIcePar-87
□ 96UppDecIceSCF-S9
□ 96UppDecSS-SS17A
□ 96Zen-12
□ 96ZenArtP-12
□ 97ColCho-87
□ 97ColCho-319
□ 97ColChoCTG-C3A
□ 97ColChoCTG-C3B
□ 97ColChoCTG-C3C
□ 97ColChoCTGE-CR3
□ 97ColChoSta-SQ68
□ 97Don-32
□ 97DonCanI-86
□ 97DonCanIDS-86
□ 97DonCanIPS-86
□ 97DonEli-103
□ 97DonEliAsp-103
□ 97DonEliS-103
□ 97DonLim-173
□ 97DonLim-191
□ 97DonLimExp-173
□ 97DonLimExp-191
□ 97DonPre-74
□ 97DonPre-181
□ 97DonPreCttC-74
□ 97DonPreCttC-181
□ 97DonPreProG-32
□ 97DonPreProS-32
□ 97DonPri-161
□ 97DonPriSoA-161
□ 97EssOlyHH-26
□ 97EssOlyHHF-26
□ 97Kat-60
□ 97KatGol-60
□ 97KatSil-60
□ 97Lea-131
□ 97LeaFraMat-131
□ 97LeaFraMDC-131
□ 97LeaInt-131
□ 97LeaIntUI-131
□ 97McD-18
□ 97Pac-138
□ 97PacCop-138
□ 97PacCroR-55
□ 97PacCroREG-55
□ 97PacCroRIB-55
□ 97PacCroRS-55
□ 97PacDyn-52
□ 97PacDynC-52
□ 97PacDynDG-52
□ 97PacDynEG-52
□ 97PacDynIB-52
□ 97PacDynR-52
□ 97PacDynSil-52
□ 97PacDynTan-46
□ 97PacEmeGre-138
□ 97PacIceB-138
□ 97PacInv-59
□ 97PacInvC-59
□ 97PacInvEG-59
□ 97PacInvIB-59
□ 97PacInvR-59
□ 97PacInvS-59
□ 97PacOme-96
□ 97PacOmeC-96
□ 97PacOmeDG-96
□ 97PacOmeEG-96
□ 97PacOmeG-96
□ 97PacOmeIB-96
□ 97PacPar-78
□ 97PacParC-78
□ 97PacParDG-78
□ 97PacParEG-78
□ 97PacParIB-78
□ 97PacParRed-78
□ 97PacParSil-78
□ 97PacRed-138
□ 97PacRev-57
□ 97PacRevC-57
□ 97PacRevE-57
□ 97PacRevIB-57
□ 97PacRevR-57
□ 97PacRevS-57
□ 97PacSil-138
□ 97Pin-54
□ 97PinArtP-54
□ 97PinBee-34
□ 97PinBeeGP-34
□ 97PinCer-66
□ 97PinCerMB-66
□ 97PinCerMG-66
□ 97PinCerMR-66
□ 97PinCerR-66
□ 97PinIns-48
□ 97PinInsCC-48
□ 97PinInsEC-48
□ 97PinPrePBB-54
□ 97PinPrePBC-54
□ 97PinPrePBM-54
□ 97PinPrePBY-54
□ 97PinPrePFC-54
□ 97PinPrePFM-54
□ 97PinPrePFY-54
□ 97PinPrePla-54
□ 97PinRinC-54
□ 97PinTotCMPG-66
□ 97PinTotCPB-66
□ 97PinTotCPG-66
□ 97PinTotCPR-66
□ 97Sco-100
□ 97ScoArtPro-100
□ 97ScoGolBla-100
□ 97SP AutI-I32
□ 97SPAut-58
□ 97SPAutID-I32
□ 97SPAutIE-I32
□ 97SPAutSotT-DW
□ 97SPx-17
□ 97SPxBro-17
□ 97SPxDuo-7
□ 97SPxDuoAut-6
□ 97SPxGol-17
□ 97SPxGraF-17
□ 97SPxSil-17
□ 97SPxSte-17
□ 97Stu-95
□ 97StuPrePG-95
□ 97StuPrePS-95
□ 97UppDec-65
□ 97UppDecBD-84
□ 97UppDecBDDD-84
□ 97UppDecBDQD-84
□ 97UppDecBDTD-84
□ 97UppDecDV-15
□ 97UppDecDVSM-15
□ 97UppDecGJ-GJ12
□ 97UppDecIce-9
□ 97UppDecIceP-9
□ 97UppDecIPS-9
□ 97UppDecSG-SG20
□ 97UppDecSSM-SS10
□ 97UppDecSSW-SS10
□ 97UppDecTSS-13B
□ 97Zen-62
□ 97Zen5x7-50
□ 97ZenGolImp-50
□ 97ZenSilImp-50
□ 97ZenZGol-62
□ 97ZenZSil-62
□ 98BowBes-46
□ 98BowBesAR-46
□ 98BowBesR-46
□ 98Fin-133
□ 98FinNo P-133
□ 98FinNo PR-133
□ 98FinRef-133
□ 98O-PChr-8
□ 98O-PChrR-8
□ 98Pac-217
□ 98PacAur-77
□ 98PacAurCF-21
□ 98PacAurCFC-21
□ 98PacAurCFIB-21
□ 98PacAurCFR-21
□ 98PacAurCFS-21
□ 98PacCroR-55
□ 98PacCroRLS-55
□ 98PacDynI-77
□ 98PacDynIIB-77
□ 98PacDynIR-77
□ 98PacIceB-217
□ 98PacOmeH-97
□ 98PacOmeODI-97
□ 98PacOmeR-97
□ 98PacPar-93
□ 98PacParC-93
□ 98PacParEG-93
□ 98PacParH-93
□ 98PacParIB-93
□ 98PacParS-93
□ 98PacRed-217
□ 98PacRev-58
□ 98PacRevIS-58
□ 98PacRevR-58
□ 98SP Aut-33
□ 98SP AutA-4
□ 98SP AutSM-S5
□ 98SP AutSotTG-DW
□ 98SPxFin-34
□ 98SPxFin-113
□ 98SPxFinR-34
□ 98SPxFinR-113
□ 98SPxFinS-34
□ 98SPxFinS-113
□ 98SPXTopP-27
□ 98SPXTopPF-27
□ 98SPXTopPPS-PS28
□ 98SPXTopPR-27
□ 98SSASotT-DW
□ 98Top-8
□ 98TopGolLC1-18
□ 98TopGolLC1B-18
□ 98TopGolLC1BOoO-18
□ 98TopGolLC1OoO-18
□ 98TopGolLC1R-18
□ 98TopGolLC1ROoO-18
□ 98TopGolLC2-18
□ 98TopGolLC2B-18
□ 98TopGolLC2BOoO-18
□ 98TopGolLC2OoO-18
□ 98TopGolLC2R-18
□ 98TopGolLC2ROoO-18
□ 98TopGolLC3-18
□ 98TopGolLC3B-18
□ 98TopGolLC3BOoO-18
□ 98TopGolLC3OoO-18
□ 98TopGolLC3R-18
□ 98TopGolLC3ROoO-18
□ 98TopO-P-8
□ 98UC-85
□ 98UD ChoPCR-85
□ 98UD ChoR-85
□ 98UDCP-85
□ 98UppDec-90
□ 98UppDecBD-34
□ 98UppDecDD-34
□ 98UppDecE-90
□ 98UppDecE1o1-90
□ 98UppDecFF-FF21
□ 98UppDecFF-FF21
□ 98UppDecFFQ1-FF21
□ 98UppDecFFQ2-FF21
□ 98UppDecGR-90
□ 98UppDecLSH-LS22
□ 98UppDecLSHQ1-LS22
□ 98UppDecLSHQ2-LS22
□ 98UppDecLSHQ3-LS22
□ 98UppDecM-77
□ 98UppDecMGS-77
□ 98UppDecMP-DW
□ 98UppDecMSS-77
□ 98UppDecMSS-77
□ 98UppDecP-P22
□ 98UppDecPQ1-P22
□ 98UppDecPQ2-P22
□ 98UppDecPQ3-P22
□ 98UppDecQD-34
□ 98UppDecTD-34
□ 99Pac-167
□ 99PacAur-60
□ 99PacAurPD-60
□ 99PacCop-167
□ 99PacGol-167
□ 99PacIceB-167
□ 99PacPreD-167
□ 99RetHoc-32
□ 99SP AutPS-33
□ 99UppDecM-79
□ 99UppDecMGS-79
□ 99UppDecMSS-79
□ 99UppDecMSS-79
□ 99UppDecRG-32
□ 99UppDecRII-DW
□ 99UppDecRIL1-DW
□ 99UppDecRP-32

**Weiland, Cooney (Ralph)**
□ 33OPCV304A-27
□ 33V129-24
□ 33V357IceK-65
□ 34BeeGro1P-36
□ 34SweCap-39
□ 36V356WorG-69
□ 39OPCV3011-92
□ 83HalFP-H16
□ 85HalFC-120
□ 91BruSpoAL-33

**Weinberger, Randy**
□ 95SasBla-22

**Weinfurter, M.**
□ 95GerDELE-295

**Weinfurther, Michael**
□ 94GerDELE-338

**Weingartner, Rob**
□ 94CenHocL-124

**Weinhandl, Mattias**
□ 98SPXTopP-82
□ 98SPXTopPF-82
□ 98SPXTopPR-82
□ 98UppDecBD-112
□ 98UppDecDD-112
□ 98UppDecQD-112
□ 98UppDecTD-112

**Weinrich, Eric**
□ 88ProAHL-345
□ 89DevCar-28
□ 89ProAHL-222
□ 90Bow-90
□ 90BowTif-90
□ 90Dev-30
□ 90OPC-416
□ 90ProSet-622
□ 90Sco-389
□ 90ScoCan-389
□ 90UppDec-245
□ 90UppDecF-245
□ 91Bow-278
□ 91OPC-10
□ 91OPC-92
□ 91PanSti-223
□ 91Par-318
□ 91ParFre-318
□ 91Pin-89
□ 91PinFre-89
□ 91ProSet-133
□ 91ProSetFre-133
□ 91ProSetPlaPC-PC10
□ 91ScoAme-131
□ 91ScoAme-350
□ 91ScoCan-131
□ 91ScoCan-380
□ 91ScoYouS-26
□ 91StaClu-339
□ 91Top-10
□ 91Top-92
□ 91UppDec-44
□ 91UppDec-344
□ 91UppDec-509
□ 91UppDecF-44
□ 91UppDecF-344
□ 91UppDecF-509
□ 92Bow-343
□ 92OPC-95
□ 92OPCPre-63
□ 92Par-56
□ 92ParEmel-56
□ 92Pin-297
□ 92PinFre-297
□ 92Sco-308
□ 92ScoCan-308
□ 92StaClu-165
□ 92Top-399
□ 92TopGol-399G
□ 92Ult-76
□ 92Ult-306
□ 92UppDec-195
□ 92UppDec-553
□ 92WhaDai-23
□ 93BlaCok-16
□ 93Don-136
□ 93Don-416
□ 93Lea-271
□ 93OPCPre-195
□ 93OPCPreG-195
□ 93PanSti-130
□ 93Par-311
□ 93ParEmel-311
□ 93Pin-281
□ 93PinCan-281
□ 93Pow-111
□ 93Pow-319
□ 93Sco-227
□ 93Sco-573
□ 93ScoCan-227
□ 93ScoCan-573
□ 93ScoGol-573
□ 93TopPre-195
□ 93TopPreG-195
□ 93Ult-295
□ 93UppDec-497
□ 94BeAPla-R19
□ 94BeAPSig-139
□ 94Don-302
□ 94EASpo-56
□ 94FinnJaaK-112
□ 94Lea-221
□ 94OPCPre-106
□ 94OPCPreSE-106
□ 94Par-43
□ 94ParGol-43
□ 94ParVin-V83
□ 94Pin-186
□ 94PinArtP-186
□ 94PinRinC-186
□ 94TopPre-106
□ 94TopPreSE-106
□ 94UppDec-119
□ 94UppDecEleIce-119
□ 95ColCho-63
□ 95ColChoPC-63
□ 95ColChoPCP-63
□ 95ParInt-310
□ 95ParIntEl-310
□ 95Pin-182
□ 95PinArtP-182
□ 95PinRinC-182
□ 95SweGloWC-108
□ 95Top-289
□ 95TopOPCI-289
□ 95UppDec-45
□ 95UppDecEleIce-45
□ 95UppDecEleIceG-45
□ 96BeAPAut-71
□ 96BeAPAutSil-71
□ 96BeAPla-71
□ 96ColCho-51
□ 96UppDec-34
□ 96UppDecGN-X4
□ 96UppDecIce-12
□ 96UppDecIcePar-12
□ 97ColCho-52
□ 97PacInvNRB-49
□ 97UppDec-246
□ 98Be A PPA-30
□ 98Be A PPAA-30
□ 98Be A PPAAF-30
□ 98Be A PPTBASG-30
□ 98Be APG-30
□ 98Pac-153
□ 98PacIceB-153
□ 98PacPar-50
□ 98PacParC-50
□ 98PacParEG-50
□ 98PacParH-50
□ 98PacParIB-50
□ 98PacParS-50
□ 98PacRed-153
□ 98UppDec-67
□ 98UppDecE-67
□ 98UppDecE1o1-67
□ 98UppDecGR-67
□ 98UppDecM-107
□ 98UppDecMGS-107
□ 98UppDecMSS-107
□ 98UppDecMSS-107
□ 99Pac-213
□ 99PacCop-213
□ 99PacGol-213
□ 99PacIceB-213
□ 99PacPreD-213
□ 99UppDecM-103
□ 99UppDecMGS-103
□ 99UppDecMSS-103

❑ 99UppDecMSS-103
**Weinrich, Jason**
❑ 92MaiBlaB-6
❑ 93MaiBlaB-39
❑ 94HunBli-21
**Weinstock, Ulf**
❑ 71SweHocS-162
❑ 72SweHocS-155
❑ 73SweHocS-44
❑ 73SweWorCS-44
❑ 74SweHocS-195
❑ 79PanSti-187
❑ 81SweSemHVS-3
❑ 83SweSemE-129
**Weir, Bert**
❑ 84Ott67-27
**Weir, Nolan**
❑ 91AirCanSJHL-C38
❑ 92MPSPhoSJHL-16
**Weir, Stan**
❑ 74NHLActSta-63
❑ 74OPCNHL-355
❑ 75MapLeaP-27
❑ 75OPCNHL-132
❑ 75OPCNHL-316
❑ 75Top-132
❑ 75Top-316
❑ 76MapLeaP-23
❑ 76OPCNHL-270
❑ 77OPCNHL-356
❑ 79OilPos-23
❑ 79OPC-331
❑ 80OPC-153
❑ 80PepCap-40
❑ 80Top-153
❑ 81OilRedR-21
❑ 81OilWesEM-9
❑ 81OPC-124
❑ 88OilTenAnn-66
**Weir, Wally**
❑ 76NordMarA-14
❑ 76NordPos-20
❑ 79OPC-388
❑ 80NordPos-28
❑ 80PepCap-79
❑ 81NordPos-21
❑ 81OPC-284
❑ 82NordPos-25
❑ 82OPC-297
❑ 82PosCer-16
❑ 83NordPos-31
❑ 83OPC-306
❑ 83Vac-79
**Weisenbach, Heinz**
❑ 72SweSemWC-106
**Weishaar, Toby**
❑ 917thInnSWHL-166
❑ 92TacRoc-28
**Weishaupt, Erich**
❑ 79PanSti-96
❑ 82SweSemHVS-101
**Weising, Rocky**
❑ 98KanCitB-13
**Weiss, David (Dave)**
❑ 84KitRan-10
❑ 85KitRan-6
❑ 86KitRan-6
❑ 87KinCan-9
**Weiss, Doug**
❑ 88ProAHL-324
❑ 89JohChi-31
❑ 91JohChi-7
**Weiss, Ken**
❑ 93RicRen-1
**Weiss, Shaun**
❑ 92DisMigDM-6
**Welch, Jason**
❑ 91LakSupSL-31
❑ 93NorMicW-28
**Weller, Jody**
❑ 91AirCanSJHL-E19
**Wells, Brad**
❑ 83BraWheK-9
**Wells, Brian**
❑ 83BraWheK-1
❑ 94CenHocL-125
**Wells, Bryan**
❑ 93ThuBayS-7
❑ 99WicThu-23
**Wells, Chris**
❑ 917thInnSWHL-141
❑ 93SeaThu-28
❑ 94Cla-20
❑ 94ClaDraGol-20
❑ 94ClaTri-T52
❑ 95Bow-136
❑ 95BowAllFoi-136
❑ 95Ima-19
❑ 95ImaGol-19
❑ 95PenFoo-3
❑ 95SigRoo-15
❑ 95SigRooSig-15
❑ 97Be A PPAD-62
❑ 97Be A PPAPD-62
❑ 97BeAPla-62
❑ 97BeAPlaAut-62
❑ 97PacInvNRB-91
**Wells, Jay**
❑ 80KinCarN-14
❑ 82PosCer-8
❑ 84KinSmo-17
❑ 85OPC-178
❑ 86Kin20tATI-22
❑ 86OPC-217
❑ 86OPCSti-92
❑ 87KinTeal4-22
❑ 87OPC-151
❑ 87OPCSti-212
❑ 87PanSti-274
❑ 87Top-151
❑ 88PanSti-72
❑ 89FlyPos-27
❑ 90SabBluS-26
❑ 90SabCam-31
❑ 91Bow-35
❑ 91SabBluS-24
❑ 91SabPepC-24
❑ 92Sco-548A
❑ 92ScoCan-548A
❑ 93Sco-416
❑ 93ScoCan-416
❑ 94OPCPre-249
❑ 94OPCPreSE-249
❑ 94Pin-507
❑ 94PinArtP-507
❑ 94PinRinC-507
❑ 94TopPre-249
❑ 94TopPreSE-249
❑ 95BeAPla-29
❑ 95BeAPSig-S29
❑ 95BeAPSigDC-S29
❑ 97PacInvNRB-189
**Wells, Jeff**
❑ 95BirBul-4
❑ 96CinCyc-5
❑ 98CinCyc-22
**Wells, Marc**
❑ 95SigRooMI-39
❑ 95SigRooMI-40
❑ 95SigRooSMIS-39
❑ 95SigRooSMIS-40
**Welsh, Keith**
❑ 94KitRan-17
❑ 96KitRan-28
**Welte, Wade**
❑ 91AirCanSJHL-D14
❑ 92MPSPhoSJHL-80
**Welter, Josh**
❑ 92MPSPhoSJHL-92
**Welz, Markus**
❑ 96GerDELE-332
**Wen, Ting**
❑ 79PanSti-355
**Wenaas, Jeff**
❑ 85MedHatT-13
❑ 88SalLakCGE-21
❑ 89ProIHL-194
**Wennberg, Peter**
❑ 92SweSemE-269
**Wensink, John**
❑ 78OPC-133
❑ 78Top-133
❑ 79OPC-182
❑ 79Top-182
❑ 80NordPos-29
❑ 80OPC-390
❑ 80PepCap-80
❑ 81RocPos-29
❑ 82PosCer-11
**Wensley, Clint**
❑ 91AirCanSJHL-E45
**Wentworth, Cy (Marvin)**
❑ 33OPCV304B-61
❑ 33V357IceK-43
❑ 34BeeGro1P-187
❑ 34BeeGro1P-210
❑ 34SweCap-28
❑ 36OPCV304D-116
❑ 36V356WorG-19
❑ 37OPCV304E-163
❑ 38QuaOatP-30
❑ 39OPCV3011-30
**Wentzell, Jamie**
❑ 95SauSteMG-25
❑ 95Sla-161
**Werenka, Brad**
❑ 92Cla-99
❑ 92OilTeal-22
❑ 92Par-289
❑ 92ParEmel-289
❑ 93Par-68
❑ 93ParEmel-68
❑ 93Sco-438
❑ 93ScoCan-438
❑ 93UppDec-41
❑ 93UppDecSP-54
❑ 94MilAdm-27
❑ 94ScoTeaC-CT21
❑ 95IndIce-22
❑ 96ClaGol-99
❑ 97Be A PPAD-41
❑ 97Be A PPAPD-41
❑ 97BeAPla-41
❑ 97BeAPlaAut-41
❑ 98Be A PPA-264
❑ 98Be A PPAA-264
❑ 98Be A PPAAF-264
❑ 98Be A PPSE-264
❑ 98Be APG-264
❑ 99Pac-349
❑ 99PacCop-349
❑ 99PacGol-349
❑ 99PacIceB-349
❑ 99PacPreD-349
**Werenka, Darcy**
❑ 89LetHur-23
❑ 907thInnSWHL-122
❑ 917thInnSMC-101
❑ 917thInnSWHL-351
❑ 91AreDraPic-28
❑ 91Cla-33
❑ 91StaPicH-54
❑ 91UltDra-29
❑ 92BraWheK-23
❑ 92UppDec-594
❑ 94BinRan-23
❑ 94ClaProP-96
**Werenka, Nigel**
❑ 91AirCanSJHL-D25
❑ 92MPSPhoSJHL-162
**Wernblom, Magnus**
❑ 91SweSemE-215
❑ 92SweSemE-235
❑ 93SweSemE-204
❑ 94SweLeaE-68
❑ 95SweLeaE-110
❑ 95SweUppDE-160
❑ 95SweUppDETNA-NA20
**Werner, Kyle**
❑ 96SasBla-25
**Werner, Thomas**
❑ 91SweSemWCS-172
❑ 94GerDELE-133
❑ 95GerDELE-134
**Wesenberg, Brian**
❑ 94GueSto-16
❑ 95Cla-26
❑ 95Cla-85
❑ 95GueSto5A-15
❑ 95Sla-96
❑ 96GueSto-14
❑ 96GueStoPC-2
❑ 97BowCHL-33
❑ 97BowCHLOPC-33
❑ 99UppDecM-154
❑ 99UppDecMGS-154
❑ 99UppDecMSS-154
❑ 99UppDecMSS-154
**Wesley, Blake**
❑ 82OPC-133
❑ 82PosCer-7
❑ 82WhaJunHC-23
❑ 83NordPos-32
❑ 83OPC-307
❑ 83Vac-80
❑ 84FreExp-28
❑ 84OPC-294
❑ 85MapLeaP-32
**Wesley, Glen**
❑ 86PorWinH-23
❑ 88BruPos-20
❑ 88BruSpoA-22
❑ 88OPC-166
❑ 88OPCSti-85
❑ 88OPCSti-215
❑ 88PanSti-207
❑ 88Top-166
❑ 89BruSpoA-22
❑ 89OPC-51
❑ 89OPCSti-27
❑ 89PanSti-200
❑ 89Top-51
❑ 90BruSpoA-25
❑ 90OPC-379
❑ 90PanSti-6
❑ 90ProSet-16
❑ 90Sco-97
❑ 90ScoCan-97
❑ 90ScoHotRS-57
❑ 90ScoYouS-8
❑ 90Top-379
❑ 90TopTif-379
❑ 90UppDec-377
❑ 90UppDecF-377
❑ 91Bow-350
❑ 91BruSpoA-21
❑ 91OPC-452
❑ 91PanSti-182
❑ 91Par-5
❑ 91ParFre-5
❑ 91Pin-112
❑ 91PinFre-112
❑ 91ProSet-1
❑ 91ProSetFre-1
❑ 91ProSetPla-7
❑ 91ScoAme-273
❑ 91ScoCan-493
❑ 91StaClu-190
❑ 91Top-452
❑ 91UppDec-370
❑ 91UppDecF-370
❑ 92Bow-15
❑ 92BruPos-12
❑ 92OPC-150
❑ 92PanSti-145
❑ 92PanStiFre-145
❑ 92Par-6
❑ 92ParEmel-6
❑ 92Pin-326
❑ 92PinFre-326
❑ 92ProSet-10
❑ 92Sco-230
❑ 92ScoCan-230
❑ 92StaClu-279
❑ 92Top-346
❑ 92TopGol-346G
❑ 92Ult-11
❑ 92UppDec-244
❑ 93Don-19
❑ 93Lea-268
❑ 93OPCPre-114
❑ 93OPCPreG-114
❑ 93PanSti-6
❑ 93Par-17
❑ 93ParEmel-17
❑ 93Pin-383
❑ 93PinCan-383
❑ 93Pow-25
❑ 93Sco-243
❑ 93ScoCan-243
❑ 93StaClu-222
❑ 93StaCluFDI-222
❑ 93StaCluFDIO-222
❑ 93StaCluO-222
❑ 93TopPre-114
❑ 93TopPreG-114
❑ 93Ult-272
❑ 93UppDec-208
❑ 94Don-232
❑ 94Fin-60
❑ 94FinRef-60
❑ 94FinSupTW-60
❑ 94Fle-92
❑ 94Lea-6
❑ 94Lea-460
❑ 94LeaLim-13
❑ 94OPCPre-357
❑ 94OPCPreSE-357
❑ 94Par-17
❑ 94ParGol-17
❑ 94Pin-388
❑ 94PinArtP-388
❑ 94PinRinC-388
❑ 94Sel-81
❑ 94SelGol-81
❑ 94StaClu-210
❑ 94StaCluFDI-210
❑ 94StaCluMOMS-210
❑ 94StaCluSTWC-210
❑ 94TopPre-357
❑ 94TopPreSE-357
❑ 94Ult-18
❑ 94Ult-303
❑ 94UppDec-89
❑ 94UppDecEleIce-89
❑ 94UppDecSPI-SP125
❑ 94UppDecSPIDC-SP125
❑ 95BeAPla-116
❑ 95BeAPSig-S116
❑ 95BeAPSigDC-S116
❑ 95CanGamNHLP-130
❑ 95ColCho-315
❑ 95ColChoPC-315
❑ 95ColChoPCP-315
❑ 95Don-186
❑ 95Lea-231
❑ 95Met-68
❑ 95ParInt-98
❑ 95ParIntEl-98
❑ 95Pin-80
❑ 95PinArtP-80
❑ 95PinRinC-80
❑ 95PlaOneoOne-158
❑ 95Sco-194
❑ 95ScoBlaIce-194
❑ 95ScoBlaIceAP-194
❑ 95SkyImp-77
❑ 95StaClu-4
❑ 95StaCluMOMS-4
❑ 95Sum-73
❑ 95SumArtP-73
❑ 95SumIce-73
❑ 95Top-213
❑ 95TopOPCI-213
❑ 95TopSupSki-39
❑ 95TopSupSkiPla-39
❑ 95Ult-248
❑ 95UppDec-137
❑ 95UppDecEleIce-137
❑ 95UppDecEleIceG-137
❑ 96TeaOut-50
❑ 96TopNHLP-155
❑ 96TopPicOI-155
❑ 96WhaBobS-26
❑ 97CarHur-26
❑ 97ColCho-114
❑ 97Pac-244
❑ 97PacCop-244
❑ 97PacEmeGre-244
❑ 97PacIceB-244
❑ 97PacRed-244
❑ 97PacSil-244
❑ 97Pin-132
❑ 97PinPrePBB-132
❑ 97PinPrePBC-132
❑ 97PinPrePBM-132
❑ 97PinPrePBY-132
❑ 97PinPrePFC-132
❑ 97PinPrePFM-132
❑ 97PinPrePFY-132
❑ 97PinPrePla-132
❑ 97SPAut-23
❑ 97UppDec-244
❑ 98Be A PPA-26
❑ 98Be A PPAA-26
❑ 98Be A PPAAF-26
❑ 98Be A PPTBASG-26
❑ 98Be APG-26
❑ 98Pac-141
❑ 98PacIceB-141
❑ 98PacRed-141
❑ 98UC-41
❑ 98UD ChoPCR-41
❑ 98UD ChoR-41
❑ 98UDCP-41
❑ 98UppDec-59
❑ 98UppDecE-59
❑ 98UppDecE1o1-59
❑ 98UppDecGR-59
❑ 99Pac-82
❑ 99PacCop-82
❑ 99PacGol-82
❑ 99PacIceB-82
❑ 99PacPreD-82
**West, Dan**
❑ 93WinSpi-21
**West, Joseph**
❑ 96GerDELE-213
❑ 98GerDELE-183
**West, Marc**
❑ 83BraAle-9
**West, Nathan**
❑ 96DetWha-20
**West, Russ**
❑ 907thInnSWHL-142
❑ 917thInnSWHL-282
**West, Steve**
❑ 78JetPos-23
**Westerby, Bob**
❑ 93KamBla-23
❑ 95RochAmeSS-22
❑ 95SlaMemC-20
**Westerlund, Gosta**
❑ 65SweCorI-133
**Westerlund, Kjell**
❑ 67SweHoc-77
❑ 67SweHoc-229
❑ 69SweHocS-273
**Westfall, Ed**
❑ 63Top-8
❑ 64BeeGro3P-28
❑ 64CocCap-13
❑ 64Top-51
❑ 65Coc-11
❑ 65Top-37
❑ 66Top-32
❑ 66TopUSAT-32
❑ 67Top-95
❑ 68OPC-135
❑ 68ShiCoi-2
❑ 69OPC-29
❑ 69Top-29
❑ 70BruPos-11
❑ 70BruTeaIss-9
❑ 70EssPowPla-67
❑ 70OPC-139
❑ 70SarProSta-7
❑ 71BruTeaIss-13
❑ 71OPC-169
❑ 71SarProSta-2
❑ 71TorSun-21
❑ 72OPC-104
❑ 72OPCPlaC-13
❑ 72SarProSta-127
❑ 72Top-159
❑ 73OPC-67
❑ 73Top-67
❑ 74LipSou-47
❑ 74NHLActSta-180
❑ 74OPCNHL-32
❑ 74Top-32
❑ 75HerSta-19
❑ 75OPCNHL-302
❑ 75Top-302
❑ 76OPCNHL-11
❑ 76Top-11
❑ 77Coc-30
❑ 77OPCNHL-153
❑ 77Top-153
❑ 78OPC-232
❑ 78Top-232
❑ 91BruSpoAL-34
❑ 91UltOriS-56
❑ 91UltOriSF-56
❑ 93IslCheBA-10
❑ 94ParTalB-6
❑ 95Par66-4
❑ 95Par66Coi-4
**Westling, Bo**
❑ 71SweHocS-289
❑ 72SweHocS-70
**Westling, Mikael**
❑ 83SweSemE-77
**Westlund, Olle**
❑ 65SweCorI-118
❑ 67SweHoc-179
**Westlund, Todd**
❑ 91MinGolG-25
❑ 92MinGolG-23
**Westner, Dave**
❑ 78LouGea-20
**Westrum, Patrick**
❑ 79PanSti-211
**Westwick, Harry**
❑ 83HalFP-I16
❑ 85HalFC-135
**Wetherill, Darren**
❑ 91LakSupSL-32
❑ 94RicRen-12
❑ 95RicRen-7
**Wetzel, Carl**
❑ 72FigSaiPos-25
❑ 72SweSemWC-117
**Wetzel, Todd**
❑ 907thInnSOHL-273
❑ 917thInnSOHL-213
❑ 95TolSto-8
❑ 98GerDELE-8
**Wetzell, Stig**
❑ 74SweHocS-28
**Wevers, Mike**
❑ 91AirCanSJHL-E25
❑ 92MPSPhoSJHL-132
**Wharram, Ken**
❑ 44BeeGro2P-145
❑ 52JunBluT-176
❑ 58Top-14
❑ 60ShiCoi-70
❑ 61ShiCoi-32
❑ 61Top-30
❑ 61Top-43
❑ 62Top-39
❑ 63ChePho-57
❑ 63Top-38
❑ 63TorSta-42
❑ 64BeeGro3P-60
❑ 64CocCap-31
❑ 64Top-28
❑ 64Top-108
❑ 65Coc-32
❑ 65Top-61
❑ 66Top-117
❑ 66TopUSAT-44
❑ 67Top-117
❑ 67Top-125
❑ 68Bla-8
❑ 68OPC-22
❑ 68ShiCoi-21
❑ 68Top-22
❑ 69OPC-74
❑ 69Top-74
❑ 94ParTalB-23
❑ 94ParTalB-137
❑ 94ParTalB-150
❑ 95Par66-29
❑ 95Par66Coi-29
**Wheat, Brandon**
❑ 83BraWheK-17
❑ 84BraWheK-17
❑ 907thInnSWHL-334
**Wheatcroft, Jim**
❑ 88LetHur-23
**Wheaton, David**
❑ 91ProSetPla-294
**Wheeldon, Simon**
❑ 83VicCou-24
❑ 89ProIHL-39
❑ 90JetIGA-33
❑ 90MonHaw-24
❑ 90ProAHLIHL-246
❑ 91BalSki-14
❑ 91ProAHLCHL-553
**Wheeler, Shawn**
❑ 91GreMon-15
❑ 92PeoRivC-27
❑ 93HamRoaA-15
❑ 94ClaProP-235
❑ 98ChaChe-19
**Whelan, Shane**
❑ 86LonKni-24
**Whidden, Robert**
❑ 72CleCruWHA-14
**Whistle, Bill**
❑ 88BraWheK-11
**Whistle, Rob**
❑ 88ProAHL-33
**Whitaker, Gord**
❑ 87MonHaw-24
**Whitcroft, Fred**
❑ 83HalFP-C16
❑ 85HalFC-45
**White, Al**
❑ 67ColChe-16
**White, Alton**
❑ 69ColChe-16
❑ 72ShaLosAW-18
**White, Alvin**
❑ 77KalWin-18
**White, Bill**
❑ 68OPC-37
❑ 68ShiCoi-53
❑ 68Top-37
❑ 69OPC-101
❑ 69Top-101
❑ 70BlaBor-14
❑ 70EssPowPla-110
❑ 71OPC-11
❑ 71SarProSta-47
❑ 71Top-11
❑ 71TorSun-82
❑ 72OPC-158
❑ 72OPC-248
❑ 72OPCPlaC-6
❑ 72OPCTeaC-28
❑ 72SarProSta-62
❑ 72Top-40
❑ 72Top-128
❑ 73MacMil-30
❑ 73OPC-78
❑ 73Top-180
❑ 74NHLActSta-75
❑ 74OPCNHL-90
❑ 74OPCNHL-129
❑ 74Top-90
❑ 74Top-136
❑ 75OPCNHL-157
❑ 75Top-157
❑ 76OPCNHL-235
❑ 76Top-235
❑ 85SudWol-26
❑ 86SudWol-33
❑ 91FutTreC72-15
**White, Clucker**
❑ 23V1281PauC-55
**White, Colin**
❑ 95SlaMemC-67
**White, Geoff**
❑ 92BriColJHL-187
**White, George**
❑ 84MonGolF-5
❑ 85MonGolF-6
**White, Jason**
❑ 907thInnSWHL-157
❑ 907thInnSWHL-234
❑ 90BraWheK-22
❑ 91BriColJHL-143
❑ 91BriColJHL-156
❑ 93DalFre-17
**White, Jim**
❑ 74SioCitM-20
**White, K.J.**
❑ 89WinSpi-21
**White, Kam**
❑ 94NorBayC-6
❑ 94SarSti-4
❑ 95Sla-208
**White, Kevin**
❑ 907thInnSOHL-321
**White, Mike**
❑ 95Sla-27
**White, Peter**
❑ 93Don-431
❑ 93Pow-344
❑ 93Sco-629
❑ 93ScoCan-629
❑ 93ScoGol-629
❑ 94CapBreO-21
❑ 95ColEdgI-37
❑ 95Ult-240
❑ 95UppDecEleIce-296
❑ 95UppDecEleIceG-296
**White, Robert**
❑ 52JunBluT-106
**White, Scott**
❑ 90KanCitBla-11
❑ 91GreMon-16
❑ 93ClaProPro-56
**White, Sherman**
❑ 51LavDaiQSHL-35
**White, Stephane**
❑ 92QueIntP-23
**White, Todd**
❑ 98Pac-154
❑ 98PacIceB-154
❑ 98PacOmeH-57
❑ 98PacOmeODI-57
❑ 98PacOmeR-57
❑ 98PacRed-154
**White, Tony**
❑ 76OPCNHL-279
❑ 76OPCNHL-396
❑ 77OPCNHL-314
**Whitfield, Trent**
❑ 95SpoChi-9
❑ 96UppDecIce-127
❑ 97BowCHL-89
❑ 97BowCHLOPC-89
❑ 98BowCHL-50
❑ 98BowCHLGA-50
❑ 98BowCHLOI-50
❑ 98BowChrC-50
❑ 98BowChrCGA-50
❑ 98BowChrCGAR-50
❑ 98BowChrCOI-50
❑ 98BowChrCOIR-50
❑ 98BowChrCR-50
**Whitley, Brian**
❑ 94NorBayC-15
❑ 95Sla-221
**Whitlock, Bob**
❑ 74OPCWHA-12
❑ 75OPCWHA-93
**Whitmore, Kay**
❑ 88ProAHL-52
❑ 89ProAHL-303
❑ 90OPC-232
❑ 90ProSet-610
❑ 90Sco-402
❑ 90ScoCan-402
❑ 90Top-232
❑ 90TopTif-232
❑ 91Bow-3
❑ 91OPCPre-182
❑ 91Par-58
❑ 91ParFre-58
❑ 91Pin-22
❑ 91PinFre-22
❑ 91ProSetPla-178
❑ 91ScoCan-625
❑ 91ScoRoo-75T
❑ 91UppDec-291
❑ 91UppDecF-291
❑ 91WhaJr7E-27
❑ 92Bow-155
❑ 92CanuRoaTA-25
❑ 92OPCPre-87
❑ 92PanSti-255
❑ 92PanStiFre-255
❑ 92Par-423
❑ 92ParEmel-423
❑ 92Sco-304
❑ 92ScoCan-304
❑ 92StaClu-459
❑ 92Top-381
❑ 92TopGol-381G
❑ 92UppDec-76
❑ 93Don-359
❑ 93OPCPre-514
❑ 93OPCPreG-514
❑ 93Par-478A
❑ 93ParEmel-478A
❑ 93Pin-138
❑ 93PinCan-138
❑ 93Pow-462
❑ 93Sco-360

□ 93ScoCan-360
□ 93StaClu-60
□ 93StaCluFDI-60
□ 93StaCluFDIO-60
□ 93StaCluO-60
□ 93TopPre-514
□ 93TopPreG-514
□ 93Ult-443
□ 94CanuProl-22
□ 94Lea-524
□ 940PCPre-134
□ 940PCPreSE-134
□ 94Pin-438
□ 94PinArtP-438
□ 94PinRinC-438
□ 94TopPre-134
□ 94TopPreSE-134
□ 95CanuBuiDA-2

**Whitmore, Keith**
□ 907thInnSOHL-297
□ 91HamRoaA-18
□ 93FliGen-11
□ 94FliGen-22

**Whitney, Dean**
□ 93PriAlbR-20

**Whitney, Mike**
□ 95RedDeeR-19

**Whitney, Ray**
□ 89SpoChi-20
□ 907thInnSWHL-201
□ 917thInnSCHLAW-20
□ 917thInnSMC-82
□ 91Cla-20
□ 91Par-454
□ 91ParFre-454
□ 92Cla-119
□ 92ClaPromo-3
□ 92Par-160
□ 92ParEmel-160
□ 92Pin-227
□ 92PinFre-227
□ 92ProSet-241
□ 92Sco-475
□ 92ScoCan-475
□ 92StaClu-490
□ 92Top-205
□ 92TopGol-205G
□ 92UppDec-407
□ 93Par-182
□ 93ParEmel-182
□ 93Pow-439
□ 93Sco-324
□ 93ScoCan-324
□ 93Ult-420
□ 93UppDec-4
□ 94Don-117
□ 94Fle-202
□ 94Lea-448
□ 940PCPreSE-33
□ 94ParSE-SE163
□ 94ParSEG-SE163
□ 94Pin-316
□ 94PinArtP-316
□ 94PinRinC-316
□ 94SP-106
□ 94SPDieCut-106
□ 94StaClu-149
□ 94StaCluFDI-149
□ 94StaCluMOMS-149
□ 94StaCluSTWC-149
□ 94TopPre-33
□ 94TopPreSE-33
□ 94UppDec-149
□ 94UppDecElcIce-149
□ 94UppDecSPI-SP163
□ 94UppDecSPIDC-SP163
□ 95BeAPla-125
□ 95BeAPSig-S125
□ 95BeAPSigDC-S125
□ 95CanGamNHLP-225
□ 95ColCho-225
□ 95ColChoPC-225
□ 95ColChoPCP-225
□ 95Don-308
□ 95Emo-161
□ 95Lea-208
□ 95LeaRoaCup-1
□ 95ParInt-183
□ 95ParIntEl-183
□ 95PlaOneoOne-304
□ 95Sco-84
□ 95ScoBlaIce-84
□ 95ScoBlaIceAP-84
□ 95StaClu-86
□ 95StaCluMOMS-86
□ 95Top-68
□ 95TopOPCI-68
□ 95Ult-150
□ 95UltGolM-150
□ 95UppDec-62
□ 95UppDecElcIce-62
□ 95UppDecElcIceG-62
□ 96ClaGol-119
□ 96ColCho-240
□ 96Pin-20
□ 96PinArtP-20
□ 96PinFoi-20
□ 96PinPreS-20
□ 96PinRinC-20
□ 96Sum-83
□ 96SumArtP-83
□ 96SumIce-83
□ 96SumMet-83
□ 96SumPreS-83

□ 96UppDec-150
□ 97Be A PPAD-105
□ 97Be A PPAPD-105
□ 97BeAPla-105
□ 97BeAPlaAut-105
□ 97PacOme-105
□ 97PacOmeC-105
□ 97PacOmeDG-105
□ 97PacOmeEG-105
□ 97PacOmeG-105
□ 97PacOmeIB-105
□ 97PacRev-63
□ 97PacRevC-63
□ 97PacRevE-63
□ 97PacRevEB-63
□ 97PacRevIB-63
□ 97PacRevR-63
□ 97PacRevS-63
□ 97SPAut-66
□ 98Be A PPA-56
□ 98Be A PPAA-56
□ 98Be A PPAAF-56
□ 98Be A PPTBASG-56
□ 98Be APG-56
□ 98Fin-138
□ 98FinNo P-138
□ 98FinNo PR-138
□ 98FinRef-138
□ 98Pac-231
□ 98PacAur-84
□ 98PacIceB-231
□ 98PacOmeH-107
□ 98PacOmeODI-107
□ 98PacOmeR-107
□ 98PacPar-101
□ 98PacParC-101
□ 98PacParEG-101
□ 98PacParH-101
□ 98PacParIB-101
□ 98PacParS-101
□ 98PacRed-231
□ 98SPxFin-37
□ 98SPxFinR-37
□ 98SPxFinR-37
□ 98TopGolLC1-26
□ 98TopGolLC1B-26
□ 98TopGolLC1BOoO-26
□ 98TopGolLC1OoO-26
□ 98TopGolLC1R-26
□ 98TopGolLC1ROoO-26
□ 98TopGolLC2-26
□ 98TopGolLC2B-26
□ 98TopGolLC2BOoO-26
□ 98TopGolLC2OoO-26
□ 98TopGolLC2ROoO-26
□ 98TopGolLC3-26
□ 98TopGolLC3B-26
□ 98TopGolLC3BOoO-26
□ 98TopGolLC3OoO-26
□ 98TopGolLC3R-26
□ 98TopGolLC3ROoO-26
□ 98UC-87
□ 98UD ChoPCR-87
□ 98UD ChoR-87
□ 98UppDec-97
□ 98UppDecE-97
□ 98UppDecE1o1-97
□ 98UppDecGR-97
□ 98UppDecM-97
□ 98UppDecMGS-89
□ 98UppDecMSS-89
□ 98UppDecMSS-89
□ 99Pac-183
□ 99PacAur-66
□ 99PacAurPD-66
□ 99PacCop-183
□ 99PacGol-183
□ 99PacIceB-183
□ 99PacPreD-183
□ 99UppDecM-87
□ 99UppDecMGS-87
□ 99UppDecMSS-87
□ 99UppDecMelB-87

**Whitten, Erin**
□ 93TolSto-27
□ 94ClaProP-249
□ 94ClaProP-AU8
□ 94ClaWomOH-W40
□ 95FliGen-1

**Whitten, Wade**
□ 89SauSteMG-16
□ 907thInnSOHL-175
□ 917thInnSMC-8
□ 917thInnSOHL-347A

**Whittle, Jeff**
□ 917thInnSWHL-167
□ 94FliGen-23
□ 95FliGen-23

**Whittom, David (Dave)**
□ 917thInnSMC-58
□ 917thInnSQMJHL-283

**Whitton, Mike**
□ 92WesMic-26
□ 93WesMic-27
□ 95TolSto-13
□ 96TolSto-25

**Whitworth, Dave**
□ 92BriColJHL-129

**Whynot, Craig**
□ 95Sla-258

**Whyte, Darryl**
□ 93KitRan-3
□ 94KitRan-3

**Whyte, Dean**
□ 84BelBul-21

**Whyte, George**
□ 52JunBluT-63

**Whyte, Sandra**
□ 94ClaWomOH-W30

**Whyte, Sean**
□ 90ProAHLIHL-346
□ 91ProAHLCHL-401
□ 92PhoRoa-26
□ 93ClaProPro-101
□ 95ForWorFT-8

**Wiberg, Jan-Ove**
□ 74SweHocS-196

**Wickberg, Hakan**
□ 64SweCorl-23
□ 64SweCorl-77
□ 65SweCorl-23
□ 65SweCorl-77
□ 67SweHoc-23
□ 67SweHoc-59
□ 69SweHocS-74
□ 69SweWorC-106
□ 70SweHocS-35
□ 70SweHocS-292
□ 71SweHocS-20
□ 72SweHocS-20
□ 72SweSemWC-52
□ 73SweHocS-13
□ 73SweHocS-163
□ 73SweWorCS-13
□ 73SweWorCS-163
□ 74SweHocS-269
□ 74SweSemHVS-9
□ 81SweSemHVS-116

**Wickberg, Jan**
□ 83SweSemE-121

**Wickenheiser, Chris**
□ 93RedDeeR-27
□ 95RedDeeR-20

**Wickenheiser, Doug**
□ 80CanaPos-26
□ 80PepCap-60
□ 81CanaPos-28
□ 810PC-193
□ 82CanaPos-28
□ 82CanaSte-23
□ 82McDSti-26
□ 820PC-196
□ 83CanaPos-33
□ 830PC-202
□ 830PCSti-67
□ 83Vac-60
□ 840PC-193
□ 840PCSti-58
□ 850PC-229
□ 850PCSti-52
□ 87CanuSheOil-24
□ 870PC-193
□ 87PanSti-318
□ 87Top-193
□ 880PC-263
□ 880PCSti-56
□ 89CapTeaIss-23
□ 92PeoRivC-26

**Wickenheiser, Hayley**
□ 94ClaWomOH-W13
□ 97ColCho-279
□ 97EssOlyHH-58
□ 97EssOlyHHF-58

**Wickenheiser, Kurt**
□ 82RegPat-16
□ 83RegPat-16

**Wicks, Ron**
□ 91UltIOriS-87
□ 91UltIOriSF-87

**Wickstrom, Kjell-Arne**
□ 67SweHoc-166
□ 69SweHocS-93
□ 71SweHocS-132
□ 72SweHocS-210
□ 73SweHocS-11
□ 73SweHocS-71
□ 73SweWorCS-11
□ 73SweWorCS-71
□ 74SweHocS-270

**Wickstrom, Per-Allan**
□ 72SweHocS-107
□ 74SweHocS-271

**Wickware, Randy**
□ 81VicCou-16

**Widing, Juha**
□ 70ColSta-11
□ 70DadCoo-140
□ 70EssPowPla-155
□ 70SarProSta-76
□ 710PC-86
□ 710PCTBoo-19
□ 71SarProSta-65B
□ 71Top-86
□ 71TorSun-124
□ 720PC-46
□ 72SarProSta-93
□ 72Top-108
□ 730PC-159
□ 73Top-156
□ 74NHLActSta-123
□ 740PCNHL-258
□ 74Top-258
□ 750PCNHL-142
□ 750PCNHL-320
□ 75Top-142
□ 75Top-320
□ 760PCNHL-354
□ 770PCWHA-33

**Widmark, Per**
□ 93SweSemE-132

**Widmer, Jason**
□ 907thInnSWHL-136
□ 917thInnSMC-129
□ 917thInnSWHL-357
□ 93LetHur-22
□ 95Lea-287
□ 96KenTho-19

**Wiebe, Art**
□ 34BeeGro1P-85
□ 35DiaMatT2-64
□ 35DiaMatT3-59
□ 35DiaMatT4-15
□ 35DiaMatT5-14
□ 35DiaMatTI-69
□ 360PCV304D-113
□ 36V356WorG-124
□ 37DiaMatT6-14
□ 390PCV3011-49

**Wiebe, Dan**
□ 92TolSto-15

**Wieckows, Krzystof**
□ 98SP Aut-134
□ 98UppDec-411
□ 98UppDecE-411
□ 98UppDecE1o1-411
□ 98UppDecGR-411
□ 99SP AutPS-134

**Wieczorek, Dariusz**
□ 89SweSemWCS-130

**Wiegand, Chuck**
□ 91NasKni-12
□ 93JohChi-13

**Wiegand, Josh**
□ 93MicSta-29

**Wieland, Markus**
□ 94GerDELE-370
□ 95GerDELE-362
□ 96GerDELE-137
□ 98GerDELE-78

**Wiemer, Jason**
□ 93UppDecPOE-E3
□ 94Cla-8
□ 94ClaDraGol-8
□ 94ClaTri-T64
□ 94FinBowB-R16
□ 94FinBowB-X25
□ 94FinBowBR-R16
□ 94FinBowBR-X25
□ 94Fla-176
□ 94Fle-211
□ 94Lea-489
□ 94LeaLim-119
□ 94LeaPhe-4
□ 94LigPhoA-26
□ 94LigPos-18
□ 940PCPre-463
□ 940PCPreSE-463
□ 94ParSE-SE172
□ 94ParSEG-SE172
□ 94Pin-484
□ 94PinArtP-484
□ 94PinRinC-484
□ 94Sel-171
□ 94SelGol-171
□ 94TopPre-463
□ 94TopPreSE-463
□ 94Ult-374
□ 94UltPro-10
□ 94UppDec-262
□ 94UppDecElcIce-262
□ 94UppDecSPI-SP166
□ 94UppDecSPIDC-SP166
□ 95Don-11
□ 95Lea-23
□ 95LeaStuR-19
□ 95LigTeal-19
□ 95ParInt-193
□ 95Pin-77
□ 95PinArtP-77
□ 95PinRinC-77
□ 95Sco-149
□ 95ScoBlaIce-149
□ 95ScoBlaIceAP-149
□ 95Ult-156
□ 95UltGolM-156
□ 95UppDec-391
□ 95UppDecElcIce-391
□ 95UppDecElcIceG-391
□ 96BeAPAut-26
□ 96BeAPAutSil-26
□ 96BeAPla-26
□ 96UppDec-157
□ 97PacDynBKS-90
□ 98Be A PPA-21
□ 98Be A PPAA-21
□ 98Be A PPAAF-21
□ 98Be A PPTBASG-21
□ 98Be APG-21
□ 98Pac-128
□ 98PacIceB-128
□ 98PacOmeH-36
□ 98PacOmeODI-36
□ 98PacOmeR-36
□ 98PacRed-128
□ 99Pac-63
□ 99PacCop-63
□ 99PacGol-63
□ 99PacIceB-63
□ 99PacPreD-63

□ 89BruSpoAU-11
□ 89NewHavN-13
□ 900PC-439
□ 90PorSet-413
□ 91Bow-363
□ 91BruSpoA-22
□ 910PC-475
□ 91ScoCan-535
□ 91StaClu-16
□ 91Top-475

**Wienke, Steve**
□ 86KamBla-22

**Wieren, Van**
□ 79PanSti-279

**Wiesel, Adam**
□ 95Cla-81
□ 95ClaAut-81
□ 95FreCan-28

**Wiest, Rich**
□ 86KamBla-23

**Wight, David**
□ 96SauSteMG-27
□ 96SauSteMGA-27

**Wigle, Dennis**
□ 84Ott67-28

**Wigren, Ulf**
□ 67SweHoc-130
□ 69SweHocS-143
□ 70SweHocS-88
□ 71SweHocS-181
□ 72SweHocS-170

**Wiita, Martin**
□ 91SweSemE-148
□ 93SweSemE-137

**Wikberg, Anders**
□ 85SwePanS-212
□ 86SwePanS-208
□ 87SwePanS-202

**Wikgren, Ulf**
□ 83SweSemE-45
□ 84SweSemE-45

**Wiklander, Lars-Goran**
□ 95SweLeaE-203
□ 95SweLeaER-4

**Wiklander, Mikael**
□ 93SweSemE-34
□ 94SweLeaE-191
□ 95SweLeaE-179
□ 95SweUppDE-22

**Wikstrom, Jorgen**
□ 93SweSemE-3

**Wikstrom, Michael**
□ 83SweSemE-19
□ 84SweSemE-17

**Wikstrom, Sami**
□ 93FinnJyvHS-264
□ 93FinnSIS-295

**Wikulow, Sergej**
□ 94GerDELE-168

**Wilchynski, Chad**
□ 96MedHatT-25

**Wilcox, Archie**
□ 330PCV304B-57
□ 33V357IceK-9

**Wilcox, George**
□ 97AncAce-21

**Wild, Martin**
□ 79PanSti-104

**Wilder, Archie**
□ 34BeeGro1P-131
□ 400PCV3012-145

**Wildfong, Jack**
□ 61HamRed-19

**Wildgoose, Lyle**
□ 92Rallce-19
□ 92Rallce-34
□ 93Rallce-19
□ 94ClaProP-242
□ 94Rallce-20

**Wilejto, Steve**
□ 96PriAlbR-17
□ 96PriAlbROC-22

**Wiley, Jim**
□ 74NHLActSta-279
□ 76CanuRoyB-23
□ 76KenTho-20

**Wilford, Marty**
□ 95Sla-233
□ 97BowCHL-18
□ 97BowCHLOPC-18

**Wilhelmy, Jonathan**
□ 98QueRem-23

**Wilkie, Bob**
□ 89ProAHL-307
□ 90ProAHLIHL-477
□ 91ScoAme-328
□ 91ScoCan-358
□ 92Par-171
□ 94ParGol-171

**Wilkie, Brian**
□ 86RegPat-29
□ 95GerDELE-11

**Wilkie, David**
□ 907thInnSWHL-11
□ 917thInnSWHL-95
□ 92Cla-11
□ 92ClaLPs-LP7
□ 93DonTeaUSA-22
□ 93KamBla-24
□ 93Pin-487
□ 93UppDec-558
□ 94FreCan-30
□ 94Lea-458
□ 940PCPre-481

□ 940PCPreSE-481
□ 94TopPre-481
□ 94TopPreSE-481
□ 95ColEdgI-43
□ 95Lea-259
□ 95SolBar-7
□ 96BeAPAut-108
□ 96BeAPAutSil-108
□ 96BeAPla-108
□ 96CanaPos-33
□ 96CanaShe-26
□ 96ClaGol-11
□ 96Fla-113
□ 96FlaBluI-113
□ 96HocGreC-25
□ 96HocGreCG-25
□ 96MetUni-195
□ 96SP-82
□ 96TopNHLP-173
□ 96TopPicOI-173
□ 96Ult-91
□ 96UltGolM-92
□ 96UltRoo-19
□ 96UppDec-282
□ 97CanaPos-26
□ 97Pac-54
□ 97PacCop-54
□ 97PacEmeGre-54
□ 97PacIceB-54
□ 97PacRed-54
□ 97PacSil-54

**Wilkins, Barry**
□ 70CanuRoyB-18
□ 70EssPowPla-40
□ 71CanuRoyB-14
□ 710PC-230
□ 71SarProSta-221
□ 71TorSun-293
□ 72CanuNal-6
□ 72CanuRoyB-19
□ 720PC-109
□ 72SarProSta-217
□ 72Top-102
□ 73CanuRoyB-20
□ 74NHLActSta-273
□ 74NHLActStaU-29
□ 740PCNHL-182
□ 74Top-182
□ 750PCNHL-148
□ 75Top-148
□ 760PCNHL-148
□ 76Top-102

**Wilkinson, Bill**
□ 92WesMic-27
□ 93WesMic-28

**Wilkinson, Derek**
□ 917thInnSOHL-48
□ 95ColEdgI-103
□ 96CleLum-25
□ 96ColEdgFL-44
□ 97Don-213
□ 97DonPreProG-213
□ 97DonPreProS-213

**Wilkinson, Neil**
□ 88ProIHL-39
□ 89ProIHL-91
□ 90Bow-184
□ 90BowTif-184
□ 900PC-443
□ 90ProSet-465
□ 90UppDec-547
□ 90UppDecF-547
□ 910PC-348
□ 910PCPre-110
□ 91Par-382
□ 91ParFre-382
□ 91Pin-108
□ 91PinFre-108
□ 91ProSet-328
□ 91ProSetFre-328
□ 91ProSetPre-483
□ 91ProSetPla-229
□ 91ScoAme-369
□ 91ScoCan-328
□ 91ScoCan-558
□ 91ScoRoo-8T
□ 91ShaSanJSA-19
□ 91StaClu-293
□ 91Top-348
□ 91UppDec-55
□ 91UppDecF-55
□ 91UppDecF-55
□ 92HumDum2-25
□ 92PanSti-128
□ 92PanStiFre-128
□ 92Par-165
□ 92ParEmel-165
□ 92Pin-27
□ 92PinFre-27
□ 92ProSet-168
□ 92Sco-235
□ 92ScoCan-235
□ 92StaClu-219
□ 92Top-76
□ 92TopGol-76G
□ 92Ult-198
□ 92UppDec-30
□ 93BlaCok-15
□ 93Don-62
□ 93Lea-357
□ 93Par-315
□ 93ParEmel-315
□ 93Pin-354
□ 93PinCan-354

□ 93Sco-138
□ 93Sco-523
□ 93ScoCan-138
□ 93ScoCan-523
□ 93ScoGol-523
□ 93UppDec-378
□ 94BeAPla-R70
□ 94BeAPSig-44
□ 94EASpo-116
□ 94UppDec-392
□ 94UppDecElcIce-392
□ 95ParInt-439
□ 95ParIntEl-439
□ 97UppDec-347

**Wilkinson, Peter**
□ 92WesMic-28
□ 93WesMic-29

**Wilks, Brian**
□ 82KitRan-15
□ 83KitRan-9
□ 84KitRan-15
□ 88ProAHL-220
□ 89ProAHL-148

**Willard, Rod**
□ 83SprInd-18

**Willett, Paul**
□ 91ProAHLCHL-368

**Williams, Barry**
□ 74PenPos-22

**Williams, Brian**
□ 86SheCan-30

**Williams, Dan**
□ 89JohChi-26

**Williams, Darryl**
□ 88ProAHL-194
□ 89ProAHL-47
□ 90ProAHLIHL-416
□ 91ProAHLCHL-369
□ 92PhoRoa-24
□ 93PhoRoa-25

**Williams, David**
□ 90KnoChe-101
□ 92Bow-377
□ 920PC-250
□ 92ProSet-172
□ 92Sco-539
□ 92ScoCan-539
□ 92StaClu-461
□ 92Top-372
□ 92TopGol-372G
□ 92UppDec-51
□ 94DucCarJr-25
□ 94Lea-538

**Williams, Gordie**
□ 83SprInd-7

**Williams, Jack**
□ 89KitRan-9
□ 907thInnSMC-48
□ 907thInnSOHL-247
□ 90KitRan-28
□ 917thInnSOHL-57
□ 94CenHocL-126

**Williams, Jeff**
□ 93GueSto-17
□ 94GueSto-19
□ 95GueSto5A-11
□ 95Sla-98

**Williams, Martin**
□ 98GerDELE-146

**Williams, Mike**
□ 90CinCyc-23
□ 93PetPet-18
□ 94CenHocL-90
□ 95Sla-322

**Williams, Paul**
□ 97AncAce-21

**Williams, Rod**
□ 84KelWin-14
□ 85BraWapH-21
□ 86RegPat-30

**Williams, Sean**
□ 88ProIHL-119
□ 89ProIHL-50
□ 90ProAHLIHL-393
□ 91ProAHLCHL-488
□ 92IndIce-25

**Williams, Steven (Steve)**
□ 91BriColJHL-95
□ 92BriColJHL-130

**Williams, Tiger (Dave)**
□ 74MapLeaP-26
□ 75HerSta-31
□ 75MapLeaP-28
□ 75MapLeaP-29
□ 76MapLeaP-24
□ 760PCNHL-373
□ 760PCNHL-394
□ 77MapLeaP-19
□ 770PCNHL-4
□ 770PCNHL-383
□ 77Top-4
□ 78MapLeaP-22
□ 780PC-66
□ 780PC-359
□ 78Top-66
□ 79MapLeaP-32
□ 790PC-4
□ 790PC-97
□ 79Top-4
□ 79Top-97
□ 80CanuSilD-24
□ 80CanuTeal-7
□ 800PC-105
□ 800PC-164
□ 80PepCap-120

❑ 80Top-105
❑ 80Top-164
❑ 81CanuSilD-16
❑ 81CanuTeal-20
❑ 81OPC-345
❑ 81OPC-385
❑ 81OPCSti-247
❑ 81PosSta-10
❑ 82Canu-22
❑ 82OPC-358
❑ 82PosCer-19
❑ 83Canu-22
❑ 83OPC-363
❑ 83PufSti-4
❑ 83Vac-120
❑ 847EDis-12
❑ 86Kin20tATI-23
❑ 86OPC-6
❑ 86OPCSti-94
❑ 86Top-6
❑ 87KinTeal4-23
❑ 87PanSti-283
❑ 95VanVooRHI-2
**Williams, Tom**
❑ 44BeeGro2P-74
❑ 51CleBar-10
❑ 60CleBar-18
❑ 61ShiCoi-17
❑ 62Top-21
❑ 63Top-12
❑ 64BeeGro3P-29
❑ 64CocCap-8
❑ 64Top-58
❑ 65Coc-7
❑ 65Top-35
❑ 66Top-38
❑ 66TopUSAT-38
❑ 67Top-40
❑ 68OPC-11
❑ 68ShiCoi-16
❑ 68Top-11
❑ 69OPC-128
❑ 69Top-128
❑ 70ColSta-5
❑ 70DadCoo-141
❑ 70EssPowPla-172
❑ 70NorStaP-9
❑ 70OPC-169
❑ 70SarProSta-83
❑ 71OPC-31
❑ 71SarProSta-130
❑ 71Top-31
❑ 71TorSun-61
❑ 72WhaNewEWHA-17
❑ 74CapWhiB-25
❑ 74NHLActSta-118
❑ 74OPCNHL-394
❑ 75OPCNHL-79
❑ 75OPCNHL-179
❑ 75OPCNHL-330
❑ 75Top-79
❑ 75Top-179
❑ 75Top-330
❑ 76OPCNHL-319
❑ 77OPCNHL-5
❑ 77OPCNHL-44
❑ 77Top-5
❑ 77Top-44
❑ 78OPC-314
❑ 94ParTalB-4
❑ 95Par66-11
❑ 95Par66Coi-11
**Williams, Warren**
❑ 75OPCNHL-217
❑ 75Top-217
**Williamson, Andrew**
❑ 95Sla-55
❑ 95Sla-199
**Williamson, Glen**
❑ 91JetIGA-33
**Williamson, Mike**
❑ 917thInnSWHL-28
**Willis, Jordan**
❑ 93LonKni-22
❑ 93LonKni-25
❑ 95ColEdgI-143
❑ 96DayBom-8
**Willis, Ralph**
❑ 52JunBluT-98
**Willis, Rick**
❑ 91MicWol-23
❑ 93MicWol-26
❑ 95BinRan-25
❑ 96BinRan-23
**Willis, Shane**
❑ 94PriAlbR-21
❑ 95Cla-48
❑ 95PriAlbR-21
❑ 96PriAlbROC-23
❑ 96UppDecBD-26
❑ 96UppDecBDG-26
❑ 96UppDecIce-126
❑ 97BowCHL-113
❑ 97BowCHLOPC-113
❑ 97ColCho-300
❑ 98BowCHL-75
❑ 98BowCHLGA-75
❑ 98BowCHLOI-75
❑ 98BowChrC-75
❑ 98BowChrCGA-75
❑ 98BowChrCGAR-75
❑ 98BowChrCOI-75
❑ 98BowChrCOIR-75
❑ 98BowChrCR-75
❑ 99UppDecM-41
❑ 99UppDecMGS-41
❑ 99UppDecMSS-41
❑ 99UppDecMSS-41
**Willis, Tyler**
❑ 92BriColJHL-71
❑ 96SeaThu-9
❑ 97BowCHL-87
❑ 97BowCHLOPC-87
**Willmann, Dieter**
❑ 94GerDELE-287
**Willner, Brad**
❑ 91LakSupSL-33
**Willsie, Brian**
❑ 95GueSto5A-14
❑ 95Sla-100
❑ 96GueSto-18
❑ 96GueStoPC-7
❑ 97GueSto-21
❑ 98BowCHL-8
❑ 98BowCHLGA-8
❑ 98BowCHLOI-8
❑ 98BowChrC-8
❑ 98BowChrCGA-8
❑ 98BowChrCGAR-8
❑ 98BowChrCOI-8
❑ 98BowChrCOIR-8
❑ 98BowChrCR-8
❑ 98UC-273
❑ 98UD ChoPCR-273
❑ 98UD ChoR-273
**Wilm, Clarke**
❑ 93SasBla-22
❑ 95SasBla-23
❑ 98BowBes-129
❑ 98BowBesAR-129
❑ 98BowBesR-129
❑ 98PacOmeH-37
❑ 98PacOmeODI-37
❑ 98PacOmeR-37
❑ 99Pac-64
❑ 99PacCop-64
❑ 99PacGol-64
❑ 99PacIceB-64
❑ 99PacPreD-64
**Wilmert, Sean**
❑ 95MadMon-5
**Wilson, Behn**
❑ 79OPC-111
❑ 79Top-111
❑ 80OPC-145
❑ 80Top-145
❑ 81OPC-239
❑ 81OPCSti-175
❑ 81Top-45
❑ 82OPC-260
❑ 82PosCer-14
❑ 83BlaBorPos-24
❑ 83PufSti-12
❑ 86BlaCok-23
❑ 87BlaCok-29
**Wilson, Bert**
❑ 74OPCNHL-384
❑ 75OPCNHL-338
❑ 76OPCNHL-378
❑ 78OPC-369
❑ 80FlamPos-23
❑ 80PepCap-20
**Wilson, Bob**
❑ 52JunBluT-171
**Wilson, Carey**
❑ 85FlamRedRP-30
❑ 85OPC-191
❑ 85OPCSti-213
❑ 86FlamRedR-30
❑ 86KraDra-80
❑ 86OPC-166
❑ 86Top-166
❑ 87OPC-211
❑ 87OPCSti-45
❑ 87PanSti-211
❑ 88OPC-75
❑ 88OPCMin-45
❑ 88OPCSti-266
❑ 88PanSti-246
❑ 88Top-75
❑ 88WhaJunGR-18
❑ 89OPC-66
❑ 89OPCSti-239
❑ 89PanSti-280
❑ 89RanMarMB-17
❑ 89Top-66
❑ 90Bow-214
❑ 90BowTif-214
❑ 90OPC-54
❑ 90OPCPre-128
❑ 90PanSti-105
❑ 90ProSet-210
❑ 90ProSet-453
❑ 90Sco-254
❑ 90ScoCan-254
❑ 90ScoRoo-42T
❑ 90Top-54
❑ 90TopTif-54
❑ 90WhaJr7E-26
❑ 91Bow-265
❑ 91FlamIGA-26
❑ 91OPC-85
❑ 91PanSti-56
❑ 91Pin-364
❑ 91PinFre-364
❑ 91ProSet-36
❑ 91ProSetFre-36
❑ 91ScoAme-227
❑ 91ScoCan-227
❑ 91StaClu-301
❑ 91Top-85
❑ 91UppDec-538
❑ 91UppDecF-538
❑ 92FlamIGA-11
❑ 92Pin-369
❑ 92PinFre-369
❑ 92Sco-127
❑ 92ScoCan-127
❑ 92Ult-272
**Wilson, Chad**
❑ 92BriColJHL-151
❑ 93CorBigRed-28
**Wilson, Colin**
❑ 917thInnSOHL-125
❑ 91PetPet-20
❑ 92WinSpi-8
**Wilson, Craig**
❑ 897thInnSOHL-69
❑ 96FifFly-11
**Wilson, Cully**
❑ 23V1281PauC-67
**Wilson, Doug**
❑ 78OPC-168
❑ 78Top-168
❑ 80OPC-12
❑ 80Top-12
❑ 81BlaBorPos-28
❑ 81OPC-66
❑ 81Top-W78
❑ 82McDSti-36
❑ 82OPC-77
❑ 82OPC-78
❑ 82OPCSti-163
❑ 82OPCSti-172
❑ 82OPCSti-254
❑ 82PosCer-4
❑ 83BlaBorPos-25
❑ 83OPC-114
❑ 83OPCSti-112
❑ 83OPCSti-165
❑ 83PufSti-14
❑ 84KelAccD-6
❑ 84OPC-48
❑ 84OPCSti-27
❑ 84Top-37
❑ 857ECreCar-4
❑ 85OPC-45
❑ 85OPCBoxB-P
❑ 85OPCSti-25
❑ 85OPCSti-122
❑ 85Top-45
❑ 85TopBoxB-P
❑ 85TopStiIns-11
❑ 86BlaCok-24
❑ 86OPC-106
❑ 86OPCSti-153
❑ 86Top-106
❑ 87BlaCok-30
❑ 87OPC-14
❑ 87OPCSti-77
❑ 87PanSti-222
❑ 87Top-14
❑ 88BlaCok-24
❑ 88OPC-89
❑ 88OPCSti-6
❑ 88PanSti-24
❑ 88Top-89
❑ 89BlaCok-4
❑ 89OPC-112
❑ 89OPCSti-14
❑ 89PanSti-45
❑ 89Top-112
❑ 90BlaCok-4
❑ 90Bow-2
❑ 90BowTif-2
❑ 90Kra-62
❑ 90Kra-77
❑ 90OPC-111
❑ 90OPC-203
❑ 90OPC-363
❑ 90OPCBoxB-N
❑ 90OPCPre-129
❑ 90PanSti-189
❑ 90ProSet-63A
❑ 90ProSet-63B
❑ 90ProSet-346
❑ 90Sco-280
❑ 90Sco-320
❑ 90ScoCan-280
❑ 90ScoCan-320
❑ 90ScoHotRS-68
❑ 90Top-111
❑ 90Top-203
❑ 90Top-363
❑ 90TopBoxB-N
❑ 90TopTif-111
❑ 90TopTif-203
❑ 90UppDec-223
❑ 90UppDecF-223
❑ 91Bow-400
❑ 91Kra-34
❑ 91OPC-49
❑ 91OPCPre-6
❑ 91PanSti-18
❑ 91Par-168
❑ 91ParFre-168
❑ 91Pin-13
❑ 91Pin-369
❑ 91PinFre-13
❑ 91PinFre-369
❑ 91ProSet-52
❑ 91ProSet-478
❑ 91ProSet-584
❑ 91ProSetFre-52
❑ 91ProSetFre-478
❑ 91ProSetFre-584
❑ 91ProSetPla-107
❑ 91ProSetPla-141
❑ 91ScoAme-35
❑ 91ScoCan-35
❑ 91ScoCan-551
❑ 91ScoKel-19
❑ 91ScoRoo-1T
❑ 91ShaSanJSA-20
❑ 91StaClu-131
❑ 91Top-49
❑ 92Bow-75
❑ 92Bow-219
❑ 92OPC-281
❑ 92PanSti-129
❑ 92PanStiFre-129
❑ 92Par-167
❑ 92ParEmel-167
❑ 92Pin-52
❑ 92PinFre-52
❑ 92ProSet-165
❑ 92Sco-15
❑ 92ScoCan-15
❑ 92SeaPat-63
❑ 92StaClu-470
❑ 92Top-482
❑ 92TopGol-482G
❑ 92Ult-199
❑ 92UppDec-150
❑ 93OPCPre-77
❑ 93OPCPreG-77
❑ 93PanSti-264
❑ 93Sco-115
❑ 93ScoCan-115
❑ 93TopPre-77
❑ 93TopPreG-77
❑ 93Ult-230
❑ 94EASpo-115
**Wilson, Dunc**
❑ 70CanuRoyB-19
❑ 70EssPowPla-54
❑ 71CanuRoyB-15
❑ 71LetActR-20
❑ 71OPC-24
❑ 71SarProSta-222
❑ 71TorSun-294
❑ 72CanuRoyB-20
❑ 72OPC-71
❑ 72SarProSta-213
❑ 72Top-91
❑ 73MapLeaP-29
❑ 73OPC-257
❑ 74MapLeaP-27
❑ 74NHLActSta-265
❑ 74OPCNHL-327
❑ 76OPCNHL-102
❑ 77OPCNHL-8
❑ 77OPCNHL-224
❑ 77PenPucB-29
❑ 77Top-8
❑ 77Top-224
**Wilson, Jeff**
❑ 87KinCan-6
❑ 907thInnSOHL-196
**Wilson, Jesse**
❑ 907thInnSWHL-12
❑ 917thInnSWHL-132
**Wilson, Johnny**
❑ 44BeeGro2P-216
❑ 44BeeGro2P-460
❑ 52Par-89
❑ 53Par-51
❑ 54Par-44
❑ 54Top-4
❑ 57Top-47
❑ 58Top-22
❑ 59Par-13
❑ 60Par-14
❑ 60ShiCoi-15
❑ 61ShiCoi-100
❑ 76RocCokCan-21
❑ 77PenPucB-NNO
❑ 81RedWinOld-17
❑ 91UltOriS-65
❑ 91UltOriSF-65
**Wilson, Landon**
❑ 95Bow-95
❑ 95BowAllFoi-95
❑ 95ColEdgI-30
❑ 95ParInt-526
❑ 95ParIntEl-526
❑ 95SelCer-134
❑ 95SelCerMG-134
❑ 95UppDec-424
❑ 96BeAPAut-106
❑ 96BeAPAutSil-106
❑ 96BeAPla-106
❑ 96ColEdgFL-24
❑ 96Lea-215
❑ 96LeaPreP-215
❑ 96MetUni-196
❑ 96Sco-257
❑ 96ScoArtPro-257
❑ 96ScoDeaCAP-257
❑ 96ScoGolB-257
❑ 96ScoSpeAP-257
❑ 96Sum-188
❑ 96SumArtP-188
❑ 96SumIce-188
❑ 96SumMet-188
❑ 96SumPreS-188
❑ 96Ult-41
❑ 96UltGolM-41
❑ 96UltRoo-20
❑ 96UppDec-242
❑ 96Zen-142
❑ 96ZenArtP-142
❑ 97Don-87
❑ 97DonPreProG-87
❑ 97DonPreProS-87
❑ 97Lea-147
❑ 97LeaFraMat-147
❑ 97LeaFraMDC-147
❑ 97LeaInt-147
❑ 97LeaIntUI-147
❑ 97Pac-105
❑ 97PacCop-105
❑ 97PacEmeGre-105
❑ 97PacIceB-105
❑ 97PacRed-105
❑ 97PacSil-105
❑ 97UppDec-10
❑ 99Pac-31
❑ 99PacCop-31
❑ 99PacGol-31
❑ 99PacIceB-31
❑ 99PacPreD-31
**Wilson, Larry**
❑ 44BeeGro2P-146
❑ 52Par-92
❑ 53Par-74
❑ 54Par-85
❑ 54Top-40
❑ 97DonLim-52
❑ 97DonLimExp-52
**Wilson, Mike**
❑ 92SudWol-6
❑ 93Cla-32
❑ 93SudWol-6
❑ 93SudWolP-6
❑ 94SudWol-4
❑ 94SudWolP-24
❑ 95Bow-94
❑ 95BowAllFoi-94
❑ 95ColEdgI-66
❑ 95ParInt-534
❑ 95ParIntEl-534
❑ 95RochAmeSS-23
❑ 96BeAPAut-23
❑ 96BeAPAutSil-23
❑ 96BeAPla-23
❑ 96ColEdgFL-45
❑ 97PacInvNRB-25
❑ 97ScoSab-20
❑ 97ScoSabPla-20
❑ 97ScoSabPre-20
❑ 98LasVegT-23
**Wilson, Mitch**
❑ 88ProIHL-65
❑ 89ProIHL-149
❑ 90ProAHLIHL-376
**Wilson, Murray**
❑ 72CanaPos-22
❑ 73CanaPos-24
❑ 74CanaPos-27
❑ 74NHLActSta-160
❑ 74OPCNHL-359
❑ 75CanaPos-20
❑ 75OPCNHL-162
❑ 75Top-162
❑ 76CanaPos-23
❑ 76OPCNHL-254
❑ 76Top-254
❑ 77CanaPos-25
❑ 77OPCNHL-69
❑ 77Top-69
**Wilson, Phat**
❑ 23V1281PauC-16
❑ 83HalFP-J16
❑ 85HalFC-195
**Wilson, Rick**
❑ 74NHLActSta-238
❑ 74OPCNHL-284
❑ 75OPCNHL-356
❑ 76OPCNHL-293
❑ 77OPCNHL-57
❑ 77Top-57
❑ 81KinCan-17
❑ 94StaHoc-25
**Wilson, Rob**
❑ 85SudWol-25
❑ 86SudWol-25
❑ 87SudWol-25
❑ 94SheSte-21
❑ 97SheSte-3
**Wilson, Ron**
❑ 77KalWin-2
❑ 77NovScoV-24
❑ 78MapLeaP-23
❑ 79JetPos-27
❑ 79MapLeaP-33
❑ 80JetPos-24
❑ 80OPC-243
❑ 80PepCap-140
❑ 80Top-243
❑ 81OPC-377
❑ 81OPCSti-140
❑ 83Jet-24
❑ 84JetPol-22
❑ 85JetPol-22
❑ 86JetBor-25
❑ 87Jet-23
❑ 87NorStaPos-30
❑ 87OPC-224
❑ 87PanSti-291
❑ 88ProAHL-175
❑ 89ProIHL-188
❑ 90BluKod-25
❑ 90ProSet-529
❑ 91BluPos-21
❑ 91Bow-382
❑ 91OPC-120
❑ 91PanSti-34
❑ 91ProSet-220
❑ 91ProSetFre-220
❑ 91ScoCan-533
❑ 91StaClu-347
❑ 91Top-120
❑ 92Bow-364
❑ 92PanSti-18
❑ 92PanStiFre-18
❑ 92Sco-365
❑ 92ScoCan-365
❑ 92StaClu-429
❑ 92Top-78
❑ 92TopGol-78G
❑ 93CanaPos-26
❑ 93Lea-316
❑ 93OPCPre-194
❑ 93OPCPreG-194
❑ 93PanSti-162
❑ 93Pow-373
❑ 93Sco-431
❑ 93Sco-657
❑ 93ScoCan-431
❑ 93ScoCan-657
❑ 93ScoGol-657
❑ 93TopPre-194
❑ 93TopPreG-194
❑ 93Ult-356
❑ 96Duc-27
**Wilson, Ross**
❑ 89ProAHL-17
❑ 90ProAHLIHL-437
❑ 91ProAHLCHL-389
**Wilson, Stacy**
❑ 94ClaWomOH-W9
❑ 97ColCho-287
❑ 97EssOlyHH-60
❑ 97EssOlyHHF-60
**Wilson, Steve**
❑ 92DayBom-24
❑ 93CorBigRed-27
❑ 93DayBom-3
❑ 94DayBom-3
❑ 94DayBom-23
❑ 95PeoRiv-24
❑ 95PhoRoa-21
❑ 98GerDELE-101
**Winborg, Jorgen**
❑ 86SwePanS-270
**Winch, Jason**
❑ 897thInnSOHL-135
❑ 89NiaFalT-22
❑ 907thInnSOHL-274
❑ 91ProAHLCHL-14
❑ 91RochAmeKod-26
❑ 92RochAmeKod-25
**Windler, Harald**
❑ 94GerDELE-68
**Wing, Johnny**
❑ 36V356WorG-102
**Wing, Wild**
❑ 94DucCarJr-26
**Winge, Goran**
❑ 67SweHoc-113
**Wingerter, Mark**
❑ 84KelWin-21
**Wingfield, Brad**
❑ 92BriColJHL-8
**Wingren, Eddie**
❑ 65SweCorI-122
❑ 67SweHoc-78
**Winkler, Chris**
❑ 92MPSPhoSJHL-127
**Winkler, Hal**
❑ 23V1281PauC-46
**Winnes, Chris**
❑ 91BruSpoA-23
❑ 91Pin-351
❑ 91PinFre-351
❑ 91ProSet-522
❑ 91ProSetFre-522
❑ 91UppDec-514
❑ 91UppDecF-514
❑ 92UppDec-380
**Winstanley, Jeff**
❑ 96GerDELE-119
**Winsth, Walter**
❑ 69SweHocS-236
❑ 71SweHocS-363
**Wirf, Torbjorn**
❑ 84SweSemE-176
**Wirtz, Arthur M**
❑ 83HalFP-F16
❑ 85HalFC-90
**Wirtz, William W**
❑ 70BlaBor-3
❑ 83HalFP-M15
❑ 85HalFC-179
**Wise, Tony**
❑ 24CreFal-10
**Wiseman, Brian**
❑ 91MicWol-24
❑ 93MicWol-27
❑ 94Cla-63
❑ 94ClaDraGol-63
❑ 96St.JohML-25
**Wiseman, Carl**
❑ 917thInnSQMJHL-100
**Wiseman, Eddie**
❑ 34BeeGro1P-258
❑ 40OPCV3012-149
**Wiseman, Lyall**
❑ 51LavDaiQSHL-63
❑ 51LavDaiS-121
❑ 52St.LawS-100
**Wishart, Gary**
❑ 97FifFly-17
**Wismer, Chris**
❑ 95Sla-302
**Wisocki, Todd**
❑ 98FloEve-25
**Wiste, Jim**
❑ 70CanuRoyB-20
❑ 70DadCoo-142
❑ 70SarProSta-223
❑ 72CleCruWHA-15
❑ 72CruCleWHAL-9
❑ 73QuaOatWHA-1
❑ 74OPCWHA-34
**Wistling, Bengt**
❑ 71SweHocS-377
**Witehall, Johan**
❑ 90SweSemE-48
**Witkowski, Byron**
❑ 92WesMic-29
**Witt, Brendan**
❑ 917thInnSWHL-129
❑ 93DonTeaC-22
❑ 93Pin-465
❑ 93PinCan-465
❑ 93SeaThu-29
❑ 93UppDec-544
❑ 94Cla-90
❑ 94ClaCHLAS-C10
❑ 94ClaDraGol-90
❑ 94ClaTri-T73
❑ 94Sco-205
❑ 94ScoGol-205
❑ 94ScoPla-205
❑ 95Bow-127
❑ 95BowAllFoi-127
❑ 95Cap-28
❑ 95ColCho-400
❑ 95Don-361
❑ 95DonProPoi-18
❑ 95EmoGen-6
❑ 95Fin-106
❑ 95FinRef-106
❑ 95LeaLim-117
❑ 95Met-197
❑ 95ParInt-258
❑ 95ParIntEl-258
❑ 95ProMag-35
❑ 95SelCer-119
❑ 95SelCerMG-119
❑ 95SkyImp-225
❑ 95SP-162
❑ 95StaClu-193
❑ 95StaCluMOMS-193
❑ 95Sum-189
❑ 95SumArtP-189
❑ 95SumIce-189
❑ 95Top-346
❑ 95TopOPCI-346
❑ 95Ult-361
❑ 95UltHigSpe-20
❑ 95UppDec-265
❑ 95UppDecEleIce-265
❑ 95UppDecEleIceG-265
❑ 95Zen-124
❑ 95ZenRooRC-3
❑ 96ColCho-283
❑ 96ColCho-345
❑ 96DonEli-83
❑ 96DonEliDCS-83
❑ 96Fle-120
❑ 96LeaPre-74
❑ 96LeaPrePP-74
❑ 96MetUni-168
❑ 96NHLProSTA-35
❑ 96Sco-270
❑ 96ScoArtPro-270
❑ 96ScoDeaCAP-270
❑ 96ScoGolB-270
❑ 96ScoSpeAP-270
❑ 96SkyImp-143
❑ 96Sum-162
❑ 96SumArtP-162
❑ 96SumIce-162
❑ 96SumMet-162
❑ 96SumPreS-162
❑ 96UppDec-177
❑ 96Zen-50
❑ 96ZenArtP-50
❑ 97Be A PPAD-162
❑ 97Be A PPAPD-162
❑ 97BeAPla-162
❑ 97BeAPlaAut-162
❑ 97PacInvNRB-214
❑ 97UppDec-384
❑ 98Pac-450
❑ 98PacIceB-450
❑ 98PacRed-450
**Witt, Jared**
❑ 92MPSPhoSJHL-136
**Wittbrock, Marc**
❑ 94GerDELE-145
❑ 95GerDELE-132
**Wittenberg, Tom**
❑ 92BriColJHL-1
**Wittliff, Phil**
❑ 95MilAdmBO-21
❑ 96MilAdmBO-27
**Wittwer, Bruno**
❑ 72SweSemWC-141
**Wiwchar, Tim**
❑ 90ForSasTra-20

**Wlasow, Leo**
☐ 93MaiBlaB-54
**Wochy, Steve**
☐ 51CleBar-8
**Wohl, Pavel**
☐ 89SweSemWCS-177
**Wohlers, Nick**
☐ 92St.JohML-23
**Woit, Benny**
☐ 94ParMisL-40
☐ 44BeeGro2P-217
☐ 51Par-58
☐ 52Par-62
☐ 53Par-45
☐ 54Par-38
☐ 54Top-9
**Wojtynek, Henryk**
☐ 79ParnSti-118
**Wolak, Casey**
☐ 96SarSti-27
**Wolak, Mike**
☐ 85KitRan-16
☐ 89ProIHL-13
**Wolanin, Chris**
☐ 91GreMon-17
☐ 92GreMon-2
**Wolanin, Craig**
☐ 84KitRan-7
☐ 85DevPos-10
☐ 86DevPol-20
☐ 87PanSti-77
☐ 88DevCar-30
☐ 88PanSti-270
☐ 89DevCar-29
☐ 90Bow-166
☐ 90BowTif-166
☐ 90NordPet-27
☐ 90OPC-40
☐ 90ProSet-519
☐ 90Sco-167
☐ 90Top-40
☐ 90TopTif-40
☐ 91Bow-138
☐ 91NordPanTS-24
☐ 91NordPet-35
☐ 91OPC-199
☐ 91PanSti-264
☐ 91Par-369
☐ 91ParFre-369
☐ 91Pin-217
☐ 91PinFre-217
☐ 91ProSet-203
☐ 91ProSetPre-203
☐ 91ScoAme-74
☐ 91ScoCan-74
☐ 91StaClu-4
☐ 91Top-199
☐ 91UppDec-486
☐ 91UppDecF-486
☐ 92Bow-41
☐ 92NorPet-37
☐ 92Pin-107
☐ 92PinFre-107
☐ 92Sco-21
☐ 92ScoCan-21
☐ 92StaClu-317
☐ 92Top-487
☐ 92TopGol-487G
☐ 93Sco-406
☐ 93ScoCan-406
☐ 94FinnJaaK-109
☐ 94NordBurK-26
☐ 94OPCPre-228
☐ 94OPCPreSE-228
☐ 94Pin-445
☐ 94PinArtP-445
☐ 94PinRinC-445
☐ 94TopPre-228
☐ 94TopPreSE-228
☐ 95BeAPla-59
☐ 95BeAPSig-S59
☐ 95BeAPSigDC-S59
☐ 95FinnSemWC-103
☐ 95SweGloWC-110
☐ 97PacDynBKS-94
☐ 97PacInvNRB-197
☐ 97UppDec-373
**Wolanski, Paul**
☐ 88NiaFalT-3
☐ 897thInnSOHL-136
☐ 89NiaFalT-23
☐ 907thInnSOHL-275
☐ 917thInnSOHL-383
**Wolf, Manfred**
☐ 82SweSemHVS-116
☐ 89SweSemWCS-121
**Wolf, Rudolf**
☐ 94CzeAPSE-119
**Wolfe, Bernie**
☐ 76OPCNHL-227
☐ 76Top-227
☐ 77OPCNHL-138
☐ 77Top-138A
☐ 77Top-138B
☐ 78OPC-81
☐ 78Top-81
**Wolfe, Dwight**
☐ 98Vald'OF-23
**Wolfe, Harry**
☐ 81SauSteMG-24
☐ 82SauSteMG-23
☐ 83SauSteMG-23
☐ 84SauSteMG-22

☐ 87SauSteMG-31
**Wolfe, John**
☐ 96GuiFla-1
**Wolitski, Sheldon**
☐ 91BriColJHL-4
**Woo, Larry**
☐ 89VicCou-20
☐ 907thInnSWHL-250
**Wood, Dan**
☐ 81KinCan-14
☐ 84FreExp-9
**Wood, Derek**
☐ 93LetHur-23
**Wood, Dody**
☐ 907thInnSWHL-13
☐ 917thInnSWHL-134
☐ 91Cla-38
☐ 91StaPicH-12
☐ 91UltDra-33
☐ 93Par-186
☐ 93ParEmel-186
☐ 93UppDec-238
☐ 95Bow-161
☐ 95BowAllFoi-161
☐ 95UppDec-415
☐ 95UppDecEleIce-415
☐ 95UppDecEleIceG-415
☐ 97PacDynBKS-87
☐ 98KanCitB-11
**Wood, Doug**
☐ 96SouCarS-19
**Wood, Fraser**
☐ 81Ott67-13
**Wood, Ian**
☐ 84NovSco0-19
☐ 95GerDELE-310
☐ 96GerDELE-310
**Wood, Jason**
☐ 92BriColJHL-109
**Wood, Martin**
☐ 81RegPat-24
**Wood, Pryce**
☐ 88BraWheK-22
☐ 89BraWheK-4
**Wood, Randy**
☐ 88OPC-140
☐ 88OPCSti-107
☐ 88OPCSti-202
☐ 88PanSti-294
☐ 88Top-140
☐ 89Isl-22
☐ 89OPC-35
☐ 89Top-35
☐ 90Bow-121
☐ 90BowTif-121
☐ 90OPC-97
☐ 90PanSti-79
☐ 90ProSet-194
☐ 90Sco-119
☐ 90ScoCan-119
☐ 90Top-97
☐ 90TopTif-97
☐ 90UppDec-16
☐ 90UppDecF-16
☐ 91Bow-227
☐ 91OPC-205
☐ 91PanSti-244
☐ 91Par-13
☐ 91ParFre-13
☐ 91Pin-104
☐ 91PinFre-104
☐ 91ProSet-151
☐ 91ProSet-359
☐ 91ProSetFre-151
☐ 91ProSetFre-359
☐ 91ProSetPla-160
☐ 91ProSetPre-151
☐ 91SabBluS-25
☐ 91SabPepC-25
☐ 91ScoAme-281
☐ 91ScoCan-501
☐ 91ScoRoo-42T
☐ 91StaClu-221
☐ 91Top-205
☐ 91UppDec-289
☐ 91UppDecF-289
☐ 92Bow-246
☐ 92PanSti-251
☐ 92PanStiFre-251
☐ 92Pin-133
☐ 92Pin-234
☐ 92PinFre-133
☐ 92PinFre-234
☐ 92ProSet-20
☐ 92SabBluS-25
☐ 92SabJubF-16
☐ 92Sco-73
☐ 92ScoCan-73
☐ 92StaClu-206
☐ 92Top-170
☐ 92TopGol-170G
☐ 92Ult-265
☐ 92UppDec-245
☐ 93Lea-226
☐ 93OPCPre-119
☐ 93OPCPreG-119
☐ 93PanSti-105
☐ 93Par-297
☐ 93ParEmel-297
☐ 93Pin-177
☐ 93PinCan-177
☐ 93Pow-35
☐ 93Sco-55
☐ 93ScoCan-55
☐ 93StaClu-89

☐ 93StaCluFDI-89
☐ 93StaCluFDIO-89
☐ 93StaCluO-89
☐ 93TopPre-119
☐ 93TopPreG-119
☐ 93Ult-279
☐ 93UppDec-22
☐ 94CanGamNHLP-51
☐ 94EASpo-196
☐ 94Lea-544
☐ 94MapLeaK-29
☐ 94MapLeaPP-16
☐ 94OPCPre-61
☐ 94OPCPreSE-61
☐ 94Par-25
☐ 94ParGol-25
☐ 94Pin-218
☐ 94PinArtP-218
☐ 94PinRinC-218
☐ 94TopPre-61
☐ 94TopPreSE-61
☐ 95BeAPla-35
☐ 95BeAPSig-S35
☐ 95BeAPSigDC-S35
☐ 95CanGamNHLP-262
☐ 95ColCho-74
☐ 95ColChoPC-74
☐ 95ColChoPCP-74
☐ 95Don-154
☐ 95Lea-168
☐ 95Pin-164
☐ 95PinArtP-164
☐ 95PinRinC-164
☐ 95PlaOneoOne-205
☐ 95Sco-63
☐ 95ScoBlaIce-63
☐ 95ScoBlaIceAP-63
☐ 96IslPos-23
☐ 96PlaOneoOne-395
**Wood, Wayne**
☐ 76OPCWHA-31
☐ 77OPCWHA-42
**Woodall, Frank**
☐ 23CreSel-12
☐ 24HolCre-4
**Woodburn, Steven**
☐ 94FreNatT-34
**Woodcock, Tom**
☐ 71BluPos-25
**Woodcroft, Craig**
☐ 91ProAHLCHL-492
☐ 92IndIce-26
☐ 93AlbIntTC-22
☐ 93OPCPreTC-5
☐ 93Pow-497
☐ 93Ult-477
☐ 94FinnJaaK-103
☐ 98GerDELE-99
**Woodgate, Peter**
☐ 82NorBayC-23
☐ 83NorBayC-24
**Woodley, Dan**
☐ 86PorWinH-24
☐ 87FliSpi-20
☐ 89ProAHL-190
☐ 90ProAHLIHL-64
☐ 90ProAHLIHL-528
☐ 93MusFur-6
**Woodley, Darrel**
☐ 95Sla-19
**Woods, Bob**
☐ 88BraWheK-2
☐ 89ProAHL-218
☐ 90ProAHLIHL-560
☐ 91JohChi-9
☐ 93JohChi-4
☐ 95HamRoaA-21
**Woods, Brad**
☐ 88BraWheK-5
**Woods, Brock**
☐ 907thInnSOHL-73
☐ 917thInnSOHL-279
☐ 92GreMon-4
☐ 93WheThu-6
☐ 93WheThu-UD10
☐ 94WheThu-3
**Woods, Martin**
☐ 917thInnSQMJHL-255
**Woods, Paul**
☐ 78OPC-159
☐ 78Top-159
☐ 79OPC-48
☐ 79RedWinP-18
☐ 79Top-48
☐ 80OPC-148
☐ 80Top-148
☐ 81OPC-104
☐ 82OPC-98
☐ 82OPCSti-187
☐ 82PosCer-5
☐ 83OPC-133
☐ 84OPC-66
**Woods, Steve**
☐ 907thInnSOHL-224
**Woog, Dan**
☐ 92MinGolG-24
☐ 93MinGolG-27
☐ 94MinGolG-29
☐ 95MinGolG-29
☐ 96MinGolGCAS-27
**Woog, Doug**
☐ 92MinGolG-25
☐ 93MinGolG-28
☐ 94MinGolG-30
☐ 95MinGolG-2

☐ 96MinGolGCAS-2
**Woog, Steve**
☐ 92NorMicW-27
☐ 93NorMicW-29
**Woolf, Mark**
☐ 907thInnSWHL-200
☐ 917thInnSMC-92
☐ 94HunBli-22
**Woollard, Chad**
☐ 96SauSteMG-28
☐ 96SauSteMGA-28
**Woolley, Jason**
☐ 91AlbIntTC-23
☐ 92CapKod-25
☐ 92OPCPre-98
☐ 92Par-429
☐ 92ParEmel-429
☐ 92Pin-415
☐ 92PinFre-415
☐ 92ScoCanO-7
☐ 92UppDec-422
☐ 93Don-364
☐ 93Par-490
☐ 93ParEmel-490
☐ 93PorPir-8
☐ 93Sco-435
☐ 93ScoCan-435
☐ 93UppDec-462
☐ 95Don-260
☐ 95Ima-90
☐ 95ImaGol-90
☐ 95Lea-307
☐ 95ParInt-89
☐ 95ParIntEl-89
☐ 95Ult-244
☐ 95UppDec-335
☐ 95UppDecEleIce-335
☐ 95UppDecEleIceG-335
☐ 95UppDecSpe-335
☐ 95UppDecSpeEd-SE124
☐ 95UppDecSpeEdiG-SE124
☐ 96BeAPAut-58
☐ 96BeAPAutSil-58
☐ 96BeAPla-58
☐ 96ClaGol-49
☐ 96FlePic-6
☐ 97ColCho-203
☐ 97Pac-279
☐ 97PacCop-279
☐ 97PacIceB-279
☐ 97PacRed-279
☐ 97PacSil-279
☐ 97ScoSab-17
☐ 97ScoSabFla-17
☐ 97ScoSabPla-17
☐ 97UppDec-138
☐ 98Be A PPA-13
☐ 98Be A PPAA-13
☐ 98Be A PPAAF-13
☐ 98Be A PPTBASG-13
☐ 98Be APG-13
☐ 98Top-9
☐ 98TopO-P-9
☐ 99Pac-49
☐ 99PacCop-49
☐ 99PacGol-49
☐ 99PacIceB-49
☐ 99PacPreD-49
**Worden, Scott**
☐ 93MicSta-30
**Wormald, Brent**
☐ 92BriColJHL-226
**Worrell, Peter**
☐ 95SlaMemC-71
☐ 97BowCHL-56
☐ 97BowCHLOPC-56
☐ 98Pac-232
☐ 98PacIceB-232
☐ 98PacOmeH-108
☐ 98PacOmeODI-108
☐ 98PacOmeNm-108
☐ 98PacRed-232
☐ 98UppDecE-99
☐ 98UppDecE1o1-99
☐ 98UppDecG-99
☐ 98UppDecM-90
☐ 98UppDecMGS-90
☐ 98UppDecMSS-90
☐ 98UppDecMSS-90
☐ 99Pac-184
☐ 99PacCop-184
☐ 99PacGol-184
☐ 99PacIceB-184
☐ 99PacPreD-184
**Worsley, Gump (Lorne)**
☐ 44BeeGro2P-294
☐ 44BeeGro2P-369
☐ 53Par-53
☐ 54Top-10
☐ 57Top-53
☐ 58Top-39
☐ 59Top-15
☐ 59Top-54
☐ 60Top-36
☐ 60TopSta-52
☐ 61ShiCoi-85
☐ 61Top-50

☐ 61Top-64
☐ 61Top-65
☐ 62Top-45
☐ 62TopHocBuc-24
☐ 63ChePho-58
☐ 63Par-39
☐ 63Par-98
☐ 63QueAce-23
☐ 63QueAceQ-22
☐ 63YorWhiB-22
☐ 64BeeGro3P-119
☐ 64CanaPos-24
☐ 64QueAce-19
☐ 65CanaSteG-12
☐ 65Coc-72
☐ 65Top-2
☐ 66CanaIGA-10
☐ 66Top-2
☐ 66Top-65
☐ 66Top-130
☐ 66TopUSAT-2
☐ 67CanaIGA-1
☐ 67PosFliB-1
☐ 67Top-1
☐ 67YorActOct-2
☐ 67YorActOct-17
☐ 67YorActOct-18
☐ 67YorActOct-21
☐ 67YorActOct-24
☐ 67YorActOct-35
☐ 68CanaIGA-1
☐ 68CanaPosBW-20
☐ 68OPC-56
☐ 68OPC-199
☐ 68OPC-212
☐ 68OPCPucSti-6
☐ 68PosCerM-30
☐ 68ShiCoi-75
☐ 68Top-56
☐ 69OPC-1
☐ 69OPCFou-9
☐ 69Top-1
☐ 70CanaPin-22
☐ 70DadCoo-143
☐ 70EssPowPla-163
☐ 70NorStaP-10
☐ 70OPC-40
☐ 70SarProSta-84
☐ 70Top-40
☐ 71LetActR-4
☐ 71OPC-241
☐ 71OPCPos-23
☐ 71SarProSta-96
☐ 71TorSun-145
☐ 72OPC-28
☐ 72OPC-189
☐ 72OPC-286
☐ 72SarProSta-105
☐ 72SweSemWC-201
☐ 72Top-55
☐ 72Top-64
☐ 73NorStaP-20
☐ 73OPC-230
☐ 77Spo-8
☐ 81TCMA-2
☐ 83HalFP-M16
☐ 85HalFC-180
☐ 88EssAllSta-48
☐ 91UltOriS-17
☐ 91UltOriSF-17
☐ 92HalFL-30
☐ 92ParParR-PR4
☐ 93OPCCanHF-64
☐ 93ParParR-PR41
☐ 93ZelMasH-8
☐ 93ZelMasoHS-8
☐ 94HocWit-14
☐ 94ParMisL-92
☐ 94ParMisL-165
☐ 94ParMisLA-4
☐ 94ParTalB-81
☐ 95Par66-76
☐ 95Par66-131
☐ 95Par66Coi-76
**Worters, Roy**
☐ 33OPCV304A-45
☐ 33V357IceK-11
☐ 34BeeGro1P-259
☐ 34DiaMatS-60
☐ 35DiaMatT2-65
☐ 35DiaMatT3-60
☐ 35DiaMatTI-70
☐ 36TriPos-10
☐ 36V356WorG-7
☐ 83HalFP-D16
☐ 85HalFC-60
☐ 94HalFT-8
**Worthman, Kevin**
☐ 91ProAHLCHL-578
**Worthy, Chris**
☐ 69SeaTotW-16
☐ 93Ult-399
**Wortman, Kevin**
☐ 92Cla-116
☐ 96ClaGol-116
☐ 94OPCPre-328
☐ 94OPCPreSE-328
☐ 94ParSE-SE139
☐ 94ParSEG-SE139
☐ 94PenFoo-16
☐ 94Pin-230
☐ 94PinArtP-230
☐ 94PinRinC-230
☐ 94SP-88
☐ 94SPDieCut-88
☐ 94StaClu-133

☐ 91AirCanSJHL-A48
**Woytowich, Bob**
☐ 61SudWol-18
☐ 62SudWol-22
☐ 65Coc-5
☐ 65Top-100
☐ 66Top-34
☐ 68OPC-49
☐ 68OPC-192
☐ 68ShiCoi-63
☐ 68Top-49
☐ 69OPC-151
☐ 69OPCFou-14
☐ 69Top-113
☐ 70DadCoo-144
☐ 70EssPowPla-219
☐ 70OPC-88
☐ 70OPCDec-8
☐ 70SarProSta-163
☐ 70TopStiS-33
☐ 71LetActR-7
☐ 71OPC-28
☐ 71PenPos-21
☐ 71SarProSta-165
☐ 71Top-28
☐ 72OPC-325
☐ 75OPCWHA-123
☐ 94ParTalB-13
☐ 95Par66-8
☐ 95Par66Coi-8
**Wozney, Paul**
☐ 90ForSasTra-21
**Wray, Dick**
☐ 51LavDaiQSHL-28
☐ 51LavDaiS-118
**Wregget, Ken**
☐ 84KelWin-53
☐ 84MapLeaP-25
☐ 85MapLeaP-33
☐ 86KraDra-81
☐ 86MapLeaP-22
☐ 87MapLeaP-20
☐ 87MapLeaPLA-29
☐ 87MapLeaPO-20
☐ 87OPC-242
☐ 87OPCSti-164
☐ 87PanSti-321
☐ 88MapLeaPLA-29
☐ 88OPC-264
☐ 88OPCSti-177
☐ 88PanSti-117
☐ 89FlyPos-28
☐ 89OPC-255
☐ 90FlyPos-25
☐ 90OPC-80
☐ 90OPC-415
☐ 90PanSti-112
☐ 90ProSet-226
☐ 90Sco-263
☐ 90ScoCan-263
☐ 90UppDec-89
☐ 90UppDecF-89
☐ 91Bow-231
☐ 91FlyJCP-25
☐ 91OPC-136
☐ 91PanSti-236
☐ 91Par-357
☐ 91ParFre-357
☐ 91ProSet-450
☐ 91ProSetFre-450
☐ 91ProSetPla-210
☐ 91ScoAme-141
☐ 91ScoCan-141
☐ 91StaClu-8
☐ 91Top-136
☐ 91UppDec-206
☐ 91UppDecF-206
☐ 92Bow-182
☐ 92Par-371
☐ 92ParEmel-371
☐ 92PenCokC-25
☐ 92Pin-356
☐ 92PinFre-356
☐ 92Sco-399
☐ 92ScoCan-399
☐ 92StaClu-130
☐ 92Top-494
☐ 92TopGol-494G
☐ 92Ult-383
☐ 93OPCPre-277
☐ 93OPCPreG-277
☐ 93PenFoo-10
☐ 93Pin-325
☐ 93PinCan-325
☐ 93Pow-417
☐ 93Sco-329
☐ 93ScoCan-329
☐ 93TopPre-277
☐ 93TopPreG-277
☐ 93Ult-399
☐ 94Fle-172
☐ 94Lea-76

☐ 94StaCluFDI-133
☐ 94StaCluMOMS-133
☐ 94StaCluSTWC-133
☐ 94TopPre-328
☐ 94TopPreSE-328
☐ 94Ult-353
☐ 94UppDec-362
☐ 94UppDecElelce-362
☐ 95BeAPla-67
☐ 95BeAPSig-S67
☐ 95BeAPSigDC-S67
☐ 95CanGamNHLP-220
☐ 95ColCho-314
☐ 95ColChoPC-314
☐ 95ColChoPCP-314
☐ 95Don-182
☐ 95Emo-143
☐ 95Lea-19
☐ 95ParInt-167
☐ 95ParIntEl-167
☐ 95PenFoo-9
☐ 95Pin-107
☐ 95PinArtP-107
☐ 95PinRinC-107
☐ 95PlaOneoOne-80
☐ 95Sco-126
☐ 95ScoBlaIce-126
☐ 95ScoBlaIceAP-126
☐ 95SkyImp-136
☐ 95Sum-112
☐ 95SumArtP-112
☐ 95SumIce-112
☐ 95Top-190
☐ 95TopOPCI-190
☐ 95Ult-128
☐ 95UltGolM-128
☐ 95UppDec-108
☐ 95UppDecElelce-108
☐ 95UppDecElelceG-108
☐ 96ColCho-220
☐ 96Don-136
☐ 96DonPrePro-136
☐ 96Lea-40
☐ 96LeaPreP-40
☐ 96Sco-183
☐ 96ScoArtPro-183
☐ 96ScoDeaCAP-183
☐ 96ScoGolB-183
☐ 96ScoSpeAP-183
☐ 96Sum-60
☐ 96SumArtP-60
☐ 96SumIce-60
☐ 96SumMet-60
☐ 96SumPreS-60
☐ 96UppDec-135
☐ 97ColCho-210
☐ 97Don-27
☐ 97DonCanI-76
☐ 97DonCanIDS-76
☐ 97DonCanIPS-76
☐ 97DonLim-188
☐ 97DonLimExp-188
☐ 97DonPre-118
☐ 97DonPreCttC-118
☐ 97DonPreProG-27
☐ 97DonPreProS-27
☐ 97Lea-82
☐ 97LeaFraMat-82
☐ 97LeaFraMDC-82
☐ 97LeaInt-82
☐ 97LeaIntUl-82
☐ 97Pac-201
☐ 97PacCop-201
☐ 97PacEmeGre-201
☐ 97PacIceB-201
☐ 97PacRed-201
☐ 97PacSil-201
☐ 97Pin-96
☐ 97PinArtP-96
☐ 97PinCer-17
☐ 97PinCerMB-17
☐ 97PinCerMG-17
☐ 97PinCerMR-17
☐ 97PinCerR-17
☐ 97PinIns-32
☐ 97PinInsCC-32
☐ 97PinInsEC-32
☐ 97PinPrePBB-96
☐ 97PinPrePBC-96
☐ 97PinPrePBM-96
☐ 97PinPrePBY-96
☐ 97PinPrePFC-96
☐ 97PinPrePFM-96
☐ 97PinPrePFY-96
☐ 97PinPrePla-96
☐ 97PinTotCMPG-17
☐ 97PinTotCPB-17
☐ 97PinTotCPG-17
☐ 97PinTotCPR-17
☐ 97Sco-32
☐ 97ScoArtPro-32
☐ 97ScoGolBla-32
☐ 97ScoPen-2
☐ 97ScoPenPre-2
☐ 97UppDec-344
☐ 98Be A PPA-169
☐ 98Be A PPAA-169
☐ 98Be A PPAAF-169
☐ 98Be A PPSE-169
☐ 98Be APG-169
☐ 98Pac-360
☐ 98PacCroR-21
☐ 98PacCroRLS-21

- 97SPxGraF-35
- 97SPxSil-35
- 97SPxSte-35
- 97Stu-31
- 97StuPrePG-31
- 97StuPrePS-31
- 97UppDec-321
- 97UppDecBD-111
- 97UppDecBDDD-111
- 97UppDecBDQD-111
- 97UppDecBDTD-111
- 97UppDecIce-28
- 97UppDecIceP-28
- 97UppDecIPS-28
- 97UppDecSG-SG23
- 97Zen-72
- 97ZenZGol-72
- 97ZenZSil-72
- 98Be A PPA-246
- 98Be A PPAA-246
- 98Be A PPAAF-246
- 98Be A PPGUJA-G22
- 98Be a PPPGUJC-G24
- 98Be a PPPPUJC-P23
- 98Be A PPSE-246
- 98Be APG-246
- 98BowBes-37
- 98BowBesAR-37
- 98BowBesR-37
- 98Fin-96
- 98FinCen-C5
- 98FinCenR-C5
- 98FinNo P-96
- 98FinNo PR-96
- 98FinRedL-R12
- 98FinRedLR-R12
- 98FinRef-96
- 98McD-9
- 98O-PChr-5
- 98O-PChrR-5
- 98Pac-318
- 98PacAur-134
- 98PacAurCF-34
- 98PacAurCFC-34
- 98PacAurCFIB-34
- 98PacAurCFR-34
- 98PacAurCFS-34
- 98PacCroR-96
- 98PacCroRLS-96
- 98PacCroRPP-17
- 98PacDynI-132
- 98PacDynIIB-132
- 98PacDynIR-132
- 98PacDynITC-18
- 98PacIceB-318
- 98PacOmeH-170
- 98PacOmeO-24
- 98PacOmeODI-170
- 98PacOmeP-14
- 98PacOmePI-6
- 98PacOmePIB-6
- 98PacOmeR-170
- 98PacPar-168
- 98PacParC-168
- 98PacParEG-168
- 98PacParH-168
- 98PacParIB-168
- 98PacParIG-8
- 98PacParIGG-8
- 98PacParIS-8
- 98PacParS-168
- 98PacParTCD-18
- 98PacRed-318
- 98PacRev-102
- 98PacRevCTL-12
- 98PacRevIS-102
- 98PacRevR-102
- 98PacRevS-24
- 98PacTeaC-18
- 98PinEpiGE-4
- 98SP Aut-59
- 98SPxFin-57
- 98SPxFinR-98
- 98SPxFinR-57
- 98SPxFinRR-57
- 98SPxFinS-57
- 98SPxFinS-98
- 98SPXTopP-42
- 98SPXTopPF-42
- 98SPXTopPR-42
- 98Top-5
- 98TopGolLC1-11
- 98TopGolLC1B-11
- 98TopGolLC1BOo0-11
- 98TopGolLC1OoO-11
- 98TopGolLC1R-11
- 98TopGolLC1ROo0-11
- 98TopGolLC2-11
- 98TopGolLC2B-11
- 98TopGolLC2BOo0-11
- 98TopGolLC2OoO-11
- 98TopGolLC2R-11
- 98TopGolLC2ROo0-11
- 98TopGolLC3-11
- 98TopGolLC3B-11
- 98TopGolLC3BOo0-11
- 98TopGolLC3OoO-11
- 98TopGolLC3R-11
- 98TopGolLC3ROo0-11
- 98TopO-P-5
- 98UC-141
- 98UCSG-SQ10
- 98UCSG-SQ10
- 98UCSR-SQ10
- 98UCSR-SQ10
- 98UD ChoPCR-141
- 98UD ChoR-141
- 98UD3-49
- 98UD3-109
- 98UD3-169
- 98UD3DieC-49
- 98UD3DieC-109
- 98UD3DieC-169
- 98UDChr-141
- 98UppDec-139
- 98UppDecBD-59
- 98UppDecDD-59
- 98UppDecE-139
- 98UppDecE1o1-139
- 98UppDecFF-FF18
- 98UppDecFF-FF18
- 98UppDecFFQ1-FF18
- 98UppDecFFQ2-FF18
- 98UppDecGR-139
- 98UppDecM-139
- 98UppDecMGS-139
- 98UppDecMSS-139
- 98UppDecMSS-139
- 98UppDecQD-59
- 98UppDecTD-59
- 98UppDecWFG-WF20
- 98UppDecWFP-WF20
- 99AurSty-13
- 99Pac-297
- 99PacAur-102
- 99PacAurPD-102
- 99PacGol-297
- 99PacGolCD-24
- 99PacHomaA-18
- 99PacIceB-297
- 99PacPreD-297
- 99PacTeaL-19
- 99RetHoc-54
- 99SP AutPS-59
- 99UppDecCL-69
- 99UppDecCLCLC-69
- 99UppDecM-138
- 99UppDecMGS-GU13
- 99UppDecMGS-138
- 99UppDecMGUSA-GU13
- 99UppDecMSS-138
- 99UppDecMSS-138
- 99UppDecRG-54
- 99UppDecRP-54

**Yashin, Oleg**
- 91OPCIns-64R
- 93RoaExp-21
- 94RoaExp-14

**Yashin, Sergei**
- 87RusNatT-23
- 89RusNatT-24
- 89SweSemWCS-88

**Yates, Joel**
- 917thInnSOHL-239
- 93NiaFalT-7

**Yates, Ross**
- 94GerDELE-151
- 96GerDELE-157

**Yawney, Trent**
- 83SasBla-2
- 84SasBlaS-20
- 88BlaCok-25
- 89BlaCok-9
- 89OPC-222
- 89PanSti-53
- 90BlaCok-9
- 90OPC-297
- 90PanSti-187
- 90ProSet-64
- 90Sco-292
- 90ScoCan-292
- 90Top-297
- 90TopTif-297
- 90UppDec-82
- 90UppDecF-49
- 91Bow-393
- 91OPC-255
- 91Par-245
- 91ParFre-245
- 91ProAHLCHL-491
- 91ScoCan-439
- 91StaClu-205
- 91Top-255
- 92FlamIGA-12
- 92Par-262
- 92ParEmel-262
- 92Pin-174
- 92PinFre-174
- 92Sco-216
- 92ScoCan-216
- 93Pin-123
- 93PinCan-123
- 93Sco-332
- 93ScoCan-332
- 93StaClu-472
- 93StaCluFDI-472
- 93StaCluO-472
- 94Pin-245
- 94PinArtP-245
- 94PinRinC-245
- 94StaClu-44
- 94StaCluFDI-44
- 94StaCluMOMS-44
- 94StaCluSTWC-44
- 95BeAPla-146
- 95BeAPSig-S146
- 95BeAPSigDC-S146
- 95UppDecEleIce-308
- 95UppDecEleIceG-308
- 97PacDynBKS-84

**Yderstrom, Dick**
- 67SweHoc-196
- 69SweHocS-201
- 69SweHocS-255
- 70SweHocS-145
- 71SweHocS-239
- 72SweHocS-224
- 73SweHocS-18
- 73SweHocS-74
- 73SweWorCS-18
- 73SweWorCS-74
- 74SweHocS-272
- 74SweSemHVS-13

**Yeatman, D.**
- 28V1282PauC-67

**Yegorov, Alexei**
- 96FlePic-174
- 96KenTho-21
- 96Lea-216
- 96LeaPreP-216
- 96SkyImp-163
- 96Sum-195
- 96SumArtP-195
- 96SumIce-195
- 96SumMet-195
- 96SumPreS-195
- 96UppDec-192
- 97ShaFleAS-8

**Yelle, Stephane**
- 917thInnSOHL-161
- 910shGen-6
- 910shGenS-7
- 920shGenS-24
- 930shGen-10
- 95Bow-124
- 95BowAllFoi-124
- 95Don-350
- 95ParInt-539
- 95ParIntEl-539
- 95Ult-363
- 96BeAPAut-15
- 96BeAPAutSil-15
- 96BeAPla-15
- 96ColCho-61
- 96Don-220
- 96DonCanI-45
- 96DonCanIGPP-45
- 96DonCanIRPP-45
- 96DonPrePro-220
- 96Lea-150
- 96LeaPreP-150
- 96Sum-156
- 96SumArtP-156
- 96SumIce-156
- 96SumMet-156
- 96SumPreS-156
- 96UppDec-40
- 97Pac-344
- 97PacCop-344
- 97PacEmeGre-344
- 97PacIceB-344
- 97PacRed-344
- 97PacSil-344
- 97ScoAva-19
- 97ScoAvaPla-19
- 97ScoAvaPre-19
- 97UppDec-49
- 98Pac-170
- 98PacIceB-170
- 98PacRed-170
- 99Pac-116
- 99PacCop-116
- 99PacGol-116
- 99PacIceB-116
- 99PacPreD-116

**Yellowaga, Kevin**
- 88SasBla-14

**Yellowhorn, Shane**
- 96LetHur-24

**Yenedam, Sean**
- 97BowCHL-11
- 97BowCHLOPC-11

**Yeo, Michael (Mike)**
- 907thInnSOHL-396
- 90SudWol-23
- 917thInnSOHL-253
- 91SudWol-23
- 92SudWol-20
- 93SudWol-22
- 93SudWolP-22

**Yeremin, Vladimir**
- 93SwiHNL-182

**Yerkovich, Sergei**
- 96LasVegThu-22

**Yesmantovich, Igor**
- 89SweSemWCS-97

**Yewchuk, Marty**
- 95LouIceG-21

**Yingst, Doug**
- 88ProAHL-143

**Yingst, Matt**
- 94JohChi-20

**Yli-Maenpaa, Kari**
- 89SweSemE-196

**Yli-Maenpaa, Mika**
- 93FinnSIS-185
- 94FinnSIS-45
- 95FinnSIS-98

**Ylonen, Juha**
- 91UppDec-673
- 91UppDecCWJC-36
- 91UppDecF-673
- 93FinnJyvHS-114
- 93FinnSIS-21
- 94FinnSIS-20
- 95FinnKarWCL-24
- 95FinnSIS-254
- 95FinnSISGC-24
- 96FinnSISR-53
- 96SprFal-15
- 96SweSemW-21
- 97Be A PPAD-240
- 97Be A PPAPD-240
- 97BeAPla-240
- 97BeAPlaAut-240
- 97PacOme-180
- 97PacOmeC-180
- 97PacOmeDG-180
- 97PacOmeG-180
- 97PacOmeIB-180
- 97UppDec-192
- 98Pac-347
- 98PacIceB-347
- 98PacRed-347
- 98UC-164
- 98UD ChoPCR-164
- 98UD ChoR-164
- 98UppDec-151
- 98UppDecE-151
- 98UppDecE1o1-151
- 98UppDecGR-151
- 99Pac-331
- 99PacCop-331
- 99PacGol-331
- 99PacIceB-331
- 99PacPreD-331

**York, Mike**
- 95DonEliWJ-44
- 96UppDecIce-147

**York, Shawn**
- 91BriColJHL-59
- 92BriColJHL-100

**Young, Adam**
- 69SweHocS-384
- 69SweWorC-14
- 69SweWorC-164
- 70SweHocS-293
- 71SweHocS-60
- 72SweSemWC-71
- 79PanSti-162
- 91SweSemWCS-226
- 96FinnSISR-192

**York, Harry**
- 96BeAPLH-2A
- 96BeAPLHAut-2A
- 96BeAPLHAutSil-2A
- 96DonEli-130
- 96DonEliCDS-130
- 96Fla-122
- 96FlaBluI-122
- 96SelCer-96
- 96SelCerAP-96
- 96SelCerBlu-96
- 96SelCerMB-96
- 96SelCerMG-96
- 96SelCerMR-96
- 96SelCerRed-96
- 96SP-134
- 96Ult-149
- 96UltGolM-149
- 96UppDec-329
- 96Zen-131
- 96ZenArtP-131
- 97ColCho-229
- 97Don-138
- 97DonLim-1
- 97DonLim-158
- 97DonLimExp-1
- 97DonLimExp-158
- 97DonPre-50
- 97DonPreCttC-50
- 97DonPreProG-138
- 97DonPreProS-138
- 97DonPri-156
- 97DonPriSoA-156
- 97Lea-133
- 97LeaFraMat-133
- 97LeaFraMDC-133
- 97LeaInt-133
- 97LeaIntUl-133
- 97Pac-176
- 97PacCop-176
- 97PacDyn-109
- 97PacDynDG-109
- 97PacDynEG-109
- 97PacDynIB-109
- 97PacDynR-109
- 97PacDynSil-109
- 97PacDynTan-61
- 97PacEmeGre-176
- 97PacIceB-176
- 97PacRed-176
- 97PacSil-176
- 97Pin-161
- 97PinPrePBB-161
- 97PinPrePBC-161
- 97PinPrePBM-161
- 97PinPrePBY-161
- 97PinPrePFC-161
- 97PinPrePFM-161
- 97PinPrePFY-161
- 97PinPrePla-161
- 97PinPrePla-161
- 97Sco-192
- 97ScoBlu-5
- 97ScoBluPla-5
- 97ScoBluPre-5
- 97UppDec-140

**York, Jason**
- 907thInnSMC-32
- 907thInnSOHL-197
- 91ProAHLCHL-139
- 98GerDELE-234

**Young, Joey**
- 917thInnSWHL-151

**Young, John**
- 90MicTecHus-28
- 90MicTecHus-29
- 91MicTecHus-28
- 93GreMon-15

**Young, Liam**
- 95SolBar-12

**Young, Matt**
- 917thInnSWHL-182

**Young, Scott**
- 890PC-209
- 890PCSti-44
- 890PCSti-96
- 890PCSti-233
- 890PCSti-264
- 89PanSti-224
- 89ProAHL-13
- 89WhaJunM-23
- 90Bow-253
- 90BowTif-253
- 900PC-84
- 90PanSti-34
- 90ProAHLIHL-438
- 90ProSet-113
- 90Sco-21
- 90ScoCan-21
- 90ScoHotRS-12
- 90ScoYouS-14
- 90Top-84
- 90TopTif-84
- 90UppDec-87
- 90UppDecF-87
- 90WhaJr7E-27
- 91Bow-86
- 910PC-235
- 91PanSti-273
- 91ProSet-195
- 91ProSetFre-195
- 91ScoAme-287
- 91ScoCan-507
- 91StaClu-74
- 91Top-235
- 92NorPet-38
- 92Par-383
- 92ParEmel-383
- 92Ult-391
- 92UppDec-397
- 93Don-284
- 93Lea-108
- 93PanSti-73
- 93Pin-129
- 93PinCan-129
- 93Pow-206
- 93Sco-56
- 93ScoCan-56
- 93StaClu-56
- 93StaCluFDI-261
- 93StaCluO-261
- 94CanGamNHLP-200
- 94Don-310
- 94HumHawP-5
- 94Lea-108
- 94NordBurK-27
- 940PCPre-519
- 940PCPreSE-519
- 94Pin-361
- 94PinArtP-361
- 94PinRinC-361
- 94StaClu-153
- 94StaCluFDI-153
- 94StaCluMOMS-153
- 94StaCluSTWC-153
- 94TopPre-519
- 94TopPreSE-519
- 94Ult-181
- 95BeAPla-107
- 95BeAPSig-S107
- 95BeAPSigDC-S107
- 95CanGamNHLP-78
- 95ColCho-271
- 95ColChoPC-271
- 95ColChoPCP-271
- 95Don-36
- 95FinnSemWC-110
- 95GerDELE-450
- 95Lea-317
- 95ParInt-322
- 95ParIntEl-322
- 95Sco-278
- 95ScoBlaIce-278
- 95ScoBlaIceAP-278
- 95StaClu-47
- 95StaCluMOMS-47
- 95SweGloWC-124
- 95Ult-226
- 96Don-129
- 96DonCanI-30
- 96DonCanIGPP-30
- 96DonCanIRPP-30
- 96DonPrePro-129
- 96Lea-181
- 96LeaPre-98
- 96LeaPreP-181
- 96LeaPrePP-98
- 96Pin-197
- 96PinArtP-197
- 96PinFoi-197
- 96PinPreS-197
- 96PinRinC-197
- 96Sco-140
- 96ScoArtPro-140
- 96ScoDeaCAP-140
- 96ScoGolB-140
- 96ScoSpeAP-140
- 96Sum-78
- 96SumArtP-78
- 96SumIce-78
- 96SumMet-78
- 96SumPreS-78
- 96SweSemW-173
- 96TopNHLP-113
- 96TopPicOI-113
- 96UppDec-42
- 96UppDecBD-48
- 96UppDecBDG-48
- 96Zen-115
- 96ZenArtP-115
- 97Be A PPAD-143
- 97Be A PPAPD-143
- 97BeAPla-143
- 97BeAPlaAut-143
- 97Kat-6
- 97KatGol-6
- 97KatSil-6
- 97Pac-187
- 97PacCop-187
- 97PacEmeGre-187
- 97PacIceB-187
- 97PacPar-8
- 97PacParC-8
- 97PacParDG-8
- 97PacParEG-8
- 97PacParIB-8
- 97PacParRed-8
- 97PacParSil-8
- 97PacRed-187
- 97PacSil-187
- 97ScoMigDPla-10
- 97ScoMigDPre-10
- 97ScoMigDuc-10
- 98Be A PPA-278
- 98Be A PPAA-278
- 98Be A PPAAF-278
- 98Be A PPSE-278
- 98Be APG-278
- 98Pac-48
- 98PacIceB-48
- 98PacRed-48
- 99Pac-366
- 99PacCop-366
- 99PacGol-366
- 99PacIceB-366
- 99PacPreD-366

**Young, Steve**
- 89PorWinH-21

**Young, Tim**
- 760PCNHL-158
- 760PCNHL-387
- 76Top-158
- 770PCNHL-223
- 77Top-223
- 77TopGloS-22
- 77TopOPCGlo-22
- 78NorStaCD-8
- 78OPC-138
- 78Top-138
- 79NorStaPos-19
- 790PC-36
- 79Top-36
- 80NorStaPos-22
- 80OPC-174
- 80Top-174
- 81NorStaPos-24
- 810PC-169
- 810PCSti-94
- 81Top-W113
- 82NorStaPos-24
- 820PC-177
- 82PosCer-9
- 83Jet-25
- 830PC-395
- 83Vac-140
- 840PC-351

**Young, Warren**
- 850PC-152
- 850PCSti-100
- 85Top-152
- 860PC-209
- 86PenKod-25
- 96LouRiv-23
- 96LouRiv-29
- 97LouRivF-23

**Young, Wendell**
- 82KitRan-8
- 84FreExp-18
- 85FreExp-12
- 86Canu-24
- 89PenFoo-14
- 90Bow-203
- 90BowTif-203
- 900PC-309
- 90PanSti-29
- 90ProSet-512
- 90Sco-298
- 90ScoCan-298
- 90Top-80
- 90Top-309
- 90TopTif-309
- 90UppDec-102
- 90UppDecF-102
- 91PenCokE-1

92Kra-25
92LigShe-24
92OPCPre-76
92Par-170
92ParEmel-170
92Pin-381
92PinFre-381
92Sco-511
92ScoCan-511
92Ult-206
93LigKasK-6
93LigSealR-27
930PCPre-166
930PCPreG-166
93PanSti-221
93PinMas-7
93Sco-341
93ScoCan-341
93TopPre-166
93TopPreG-166
94EASpo-132
95ColEdgI-109
95ColEdgITW-G6

**Younghans, Tom**
78NorStaCD-9
78OPC-295
79NorStaPos-20
790PC-177
79PanSti-218
79Top-177
80NorStaPos-23
80OPC-343
81OPC-173

**Ysebaert, Paul**
88ProAHL-326
89ProAHL-209
90OPC-49
90ProSet-607
90Sco-406
90ScoCan-406
90Top-49
90TopTif-49
90UppDec-375
90UppDecF-375
91Bow-53
91Kra-46
91OPC-248
91Par-42
91Par-435
91ParFre-42
91ParFre-435
91Pin-36
91PinFre-36
91ProSet-59
91ProSet-608
91ProSetFre-59
91ProSetFre-608
91ProSetPla-167
91RedWinLC-17
91ScoAme-166
91ScoCan-166
91StaClu-171
91Top-248
91UppDec-278
91UppDecF-278
92Bow-376
92OPC-46
92PanSti-118
92PanStiFre-118
92Par-43
92ParEmel-43
92ParPre-PV1
92Pin-93
92PinFre-93
92ProSet-41
92ProSet-248
92Sco-95
92Sco-414
92ScoCan-95
92ScoCan-414
92ScoYouS-35
92StaClu-378
92Top-58
92Top-314
92TopGol-58G
92TopGol-314G
92Ult-54
92UppDec-176
93Don-376
93Don-417
93JetRuf-27
93Lea-388
93PanSti-248
93Par-504
93ParEmel-504
93Pin-348
93PinCan-348
93Pow-277
93Sco-239
93ScoCan-239
93ScoGol-517
93StaClu-360
93StaCluFDI-360
93StaCluO-360
93Ult-457
93UppDec-365
93UppDecSP-179
94Don-2
94Lea-202
94LigPhoA-27
94LigPos-19
940PCPreSE-368

94Par-48
94ParGol-48
94Pin-301
94PinArtP-301
94PinRinC-301
94TopPre-368
94TopPreSE-368
94Ult-277
94UppDec-491
94UppDecEleIce-491
95BeAPla-139
95BeAPSig-S139
95BeAPSigDC-S139
95CanGamNHLP-250
95ColCho-27
95ColChoPC-27
95ColChoPCP-27
95Don-258
95Emo-167
95Lea-185
95LigTeal-20
95ParInt-191
95ParIntEl-191
95Pin-17
95PinArtP-17
95PinRinC-17
95PlaOneoOne-313
95ProMag-74
95Sco-116
95ScoBlaIce-116
95ScoBlaIceAP-116
95Top-320
95TopOPCI-320
95Ult-157
95UltGolM-157
95UppDec-109
95UppDecEleIce-109
95UppDecEleIceG-109
95UppDecSpeE-SE165
96ColCho-251
96KraUppD-36
96NHLProSTA-74
96UppDec-159
97Be A PPAD-163
97Be A PPAPD-163
97BeAPla-163
97BeAPlaAut-163
97Pac-178
97PacCop-178
97PacCroR-127
97PacCroREG-127
97PacCroRIB-127
97PacCroRS-127
97PacEmeGre-178
97PacIceB-178
97PacInv-134
97PacInvC-134
97PacInvEG-134
97PacInvIB-134
97PacInvR-134
97PacInvS-134
97PacOme-215
97PacOmeC-215
97PacOmeDG-215
97PacOmeEG-215
97PacOmeG-215
97PacOmeIB-215
97PacPar-177
97PacParC-177
97PacParDG-177
97PacParEG-177
97PacParIB-177
97PacParRed-177
97PacParSil-177
97PacRed-178
97PacRev-131
97PacRevC-131
97PacRevE-131
97PacRevIB-131
97PacRevR-131
97PacRevS-131
97PacSil-178
97UppDec-159
98Fin-73
98FinNo P-73
98FinNo PR-73
98FinRef-73
98Pac-408
98PacAur-177
98PacDynl-175
98PacDynlIB-175
98PacDynlR-175
98PacIceB-408
98PacPar-222
98PacParC-222
98PacParEG-222
98PacParH-222
98PacParIB-222
98PacParS-222
98PacRed-408
98UC-194
98UD ChoPCR-194
98UD ChoR-194

**Ytteldt, Fredrik**
98GerDELE-123

**Ytter, Mats**
84SweSemE-75
85SwePanS-70
89SweSemE-240
90SweSemE-150
91SweSemE-252
92SweSemE-274
93SweSemE-242
94SweLeaE-134
95SweLeaE-126

95SweLeaES-12
95SweUppDE-186

**Yubin, Ildar**
96DayBom-5

**Yudin, Alexander**
910PCIns-47R
92UppDec-336

**Yule, Steven (Steve)**
88KamBla-24
907thInnSMC-22
907thInnSWHL-286
917thInnSWHL-78

**Yushkevich, Dimitri**
92FlyJCP-22
92FlyUppDS-10
92FlyUppDS-31
92FlyUppDS-43
920PCPre-65
92Par-133
92ParEmel-133
92Pin-394
92PinFre-394
92RusStaRA-35
92RusStaRA-34
92Ult-161
92UppDec-333
92UppDec-350
92UppDec-570
92UppDecCC-CC20
92UppDecER-ER12
93Cla-97
93Don-254
93Lea-82
930PCPre-18
930PCPreG-18
93Par-145
93ParEmel-145
93Pin-146
93PinCan-146
93Pow-186
93Sco-216
93ScoCan-216
93StaCluFDI-492
93StaCluO-492
93SweSemWCS-144
93TopPre-18
93TopPreG-18
93Ult-198
93UppDec-127
93UppDecSP-119
94Don-308
94EASpo-98
94Fle-160
94Lea-37
940PCPre-468
940PCPreSE-468
94Par-163
94ParGol-163
94Pin-227
94PinArtP-227
94PinRinC-227
94StaClu-78
94StaCluFDI-78
94StaCluMOMS-78
94StaCluSTWC-78
94TopPre-468
94TopPreSE-468
94Ult-161
94UppDec-349
94UppDecEleIce-349
95BeAPla-7
95BeAPSig-S7
95BeAPSigDC-S7
95ColCho-249
95ColChoPC-249
95ColChoPCP-249
95Don-387
95FinnSemWC-126
95Lea-291
95ParInt-469
95ParIntEl-469
95SweGloWC-171
95Top-192
95TopOPCI-192
95UppDec-81
95UppDec-376
95UppDecEleIce-81
95UppDecEleIce-376
95UppDecEleIceG-81
95UppDecEleIceG-376
96ColCho-263
96SweSemW-197
96UppDec-164
97Pac-153
97PacCop-153
97PacEmeGre-153
97PacIceB-153
97PacRed-153
97PacSil-153
97ScoMapL-16
97ScoMapLPla-16
97ScoMapLPre-16
98Fin-115
98FinNo P-115
98FinNo PR-115
98FinRef-115

**Yuzda, Jason**
90ForSasTra-23

**Yves Roy, Jean**
97ScoBru-11
97ScoBruPla-11
97ScoBruPre-11

**Yzerman, Steve**
83CanNatJ-19

847EDis-11
840PC-67
840PC-385
840PCSti-37
84Top-49
857ECreCar-5
850PC-29
850PCSti-23
850PCSti-30
85Top-29
86OPC-11
86OPCSti-161
86Top-11
870PC-56
870PCBoxB-C
870PCSti-111
87PanSti-243
87RedWinLC-29
87Top-56
87TopBoxB-C
88FriLayS-3
880PC-196
880PCBoxB-L
880PCSti-253
88PanSti-47
88RedWinLC-23
88Top-196
88TopBoxB-L
89ActPacPro-4
89Kra-63
89KraAllSS-3
89OPC-83
89OPCBoxB-L
89OPCSti-254
89PanSti-57
89RedWinLC-17
89SweSemWCS-72
89Top-83
89TopBoxB-L
90Bow-233
90BowHatTri-5
90BowTif-233
90Kra-63
90Kra-78
90OPC-133
90OPC-222
90OPCBoxB-J
90OPCPre-130
90PanSti-208
90ProSet-79
90ProSet-347
90Sco-3
90Sco-339
90ScoCan-3
90ScoCan-339
90ScoHotRS-4
90Top-133
90Top-222
90TopBoxB-J
90TopTeaSL-19
90TopTif-222
90UppDec-56
90UppDec-303
90UppDec-477
90UppDecF-56
90UppDecF-303
90UppDecF-477
90UppDecHol-7
90UppDecHol-8
90UppDecHol-9
91Bow-41
91Bow-42
91Kra-68
91McDUppD-19
910PC-60
910PC-424
910PCPre-73
910PCPre-142
91PanSti-134
91Par-44
91Par-434
91ParFre-44
91ParFre-434
91Pin-75
91Pin-383
91PinFre-75
91PinFre-383
91ProSet-62
91ProSet-281
91ProSet-571
91ProSetFre-62
91ProSetFre-281
91ProSetFre-571
91ProSetPC-8
91ProSetPla-32
91RedWinLC-18
91ScoAme-190
91ScoAme-419
91ScoCan-190
91ScoCan-335
91ScoFan-7
91ScoKel-4
91ScoNat-7
91ScoNatCWC-7
91SweSemWCS-65
91Top-424
91TopBowPS-8
91TopTeaSL-3
91UppDec-146
91UppDec-626
91UppDecBB-5
91UppDecF-146
91UppDecF-626
92Bow-103

92Bow-220
92HumDum1-24
92Kra-48
92McDUppD-14
92OPC-61
920PC-321
920PC25AI-17
92PanSti-112
92PanStiFre-112
92Par-44
92Par-456
92ParEmel-44
92ParEmel-456
92Pin-241
92Pin-258
92Pin-350
92PinFre-241
92PinFre-258
92PinFre-350
92ProSet-39
92ProSet-247
92ProSetGTL-3
92Sco-400
92ScoCan-400
92ScoCan-423
92SeaPat-6
92StaClu-254
92Top-207
92TopGol-207G
92Ult-55
92UppDec-155
92UppDecGHS-G10
92UppDecWJG-WG7
93Don-95
93DonSpeP-G
93KenStaLA-12
93KenStaLC-11
93Kra-49
93Lea-162
93LeaHatTA-10
93LeaStuS-5
93McDUppD-13
930PCPre-280
930PCPreBG-23
930PCPreG-280
93PanSti-V
93Par-326
93ParEasWesS-W5
93ParEmel-326
93Pin-175
93PinAllS-36
93PinAllSC-36
93PinCan-175
93PinCap-7
93PinCapC-7
93PinNifFif-8
93Pow-77
93PowGam-10
93PowPoiL-20
93Sco-310
93Sco-448
93ScoCan-310
93ScoCan-448
93ScoDreTea-16
93ScoDynDUS-9
93ScoFra-6
93SeaPat-20
93StaClu-70
93StaCluAS-5
93StaCluFDI-70
93StaCluFDIO-70
93StaCluO-70
93SweSemWCS-203
93TopPre-280
93TopPreBG-16
93TopPreG-280
93Ult-201
93UltAllS-12
93UltPreP-10
93UltScoK-6
93UppDec-227
93UppDec-290
93UppDec-388
93UppDecHT-HT6
93UppDecLAS-36
93UppDecNL-NL3
93UppDecNR-4
93UppDecPOE-E14
93UppDecSilSka-R6
93UppDecSilSkaG-R6
93UppDecSP-47
94ActPacBP-BP4
94BAPUpCP-UC5
94BeAP99A-G19
94BeAPla-R29
94BeAPla-R115
94BeAPSig-115
94CanGamNHLP-92
94Don-1
94EASpo-39
94Fin-84
94FinHef-84
94FinSupTW-84
94Fla-55
94FlaHotN-10
94Fle-67
94HocWit-108
94KenStaLA-20
94KenStaLC-13
94Kra-14
94Lea-148
94LeaLim-120

940PCPre-235
940PCPreSE-235
94Par-299
94ParGol-299
94ParSE-SE55
94ParSEG-SE55
94ParVin-V57
94Pin-271
94PinArtP-271
94PinRinC-271
94Sco-150
94ScoDreTea-DT20
94ScoGol-150
94ScoPla-150
94ScoPlaTS-150
94Sel-35
94SelGol-35
94SP-34
94SPDieCut-34
94TopPre-235
94TopPreGTG-12
94TopPreSE-235
94Ult-67
94UltPreP-10
94UltScoK-7
94UppDec-300
94UppDec-550
94UppDecEleIce-300
94UppDecEleIce-550
94UppDecIG-IG1
94UppDecNBAP-18
94UppDecPH-H22
94UppDecPHEG-H22
94UppDecPHES-H22
94UppDecPHG-H22
94UppDecPR-R24
94UppDecPR-R43
94UppDecPRE-R24
94UppDecPRE-R43
94UppDecPreRG-R24
94UppDecPreRG-R43
94UppDecSPI-SP25
94UppDecSPIDC-SP25
95Bow-21
95BowAllFoi-21
95CanGamNHLP-96
95ColCho-266
95ColChoCTG-C26
95ColChoCTG-C26B
95ColChoCTG-C26C
95ColChoCTGGR-C26
95ColChoCTGGR-C26C
95ColChoCTGSB-C26
95ColChoCTGSR-C26
95ColChoPC-266
95ColChoPCP-266
95Don-96
95DonEli-99
95DonEliDCS-99
95DonEliDCU-99
95DonIgn-8
95Emo-60
95Fin-162
95FinRef-162
95ImpSti-37
95ImpStiDCS-25
95Lea-60
95LeaLim-105
95NHLAcePC-3S
95ParInt-70
95ParIntEl-70
95PlaOneoOne-147
95ProMag-105
95Sco-240
95ScoBlaIce-240
95ScoBlaIceAP-240
95ScoGolBla-12
95SelCer-94
95SelCerMG-94
95SkyImp-58
95SP-46
95SPHol-FX7
95SPHolSpFX-FX7
95SPStaEto-E14
95SPStaEtoG-E14
95StaClu-20
95StaCluMOMS-20
95Sum-154
95SumArtP-154
95SumIce-154
95SweGloWC-89
95Top-237
95TopHomGC-HGC16
95TopOPCI-237
95TopSupSki-10
95TopSupSkiPla-10
95Ult-51
95UltExtAtt-20
95UltGolM-51
95UppDec-113
95UppDec-218
95UppDecAGPRW-15
95UppDecEleIce-113
95UppDecEleIce-218
95UppDecEleIceG-113
95UppDecEleIceG-218
95UppDecPRE-R15
95UppDecPRE-R58
95UppDecPreR-R15
95UppDecPreR-R58
95UppDecSpeE-SE30
95UppDecSpeEdiG-SE30
95UppDecPreRP-R58
95Zen-93

96BeAPBisITB-13
96BeAPLH-9B
96BeAPLHAut-9B
96BeAPLHAutSil-9B
96ColCho-79
96ColCho-292
96ColChoCTG-C10A
96ColChoCTG-C10B
96ColChoCTG-C10C
96ColChoCTGE-CR10
96ColChoCTGG-CR10
96ColChoCTGG-C10A
96ColChoCTGG-C10B
96ColChoCTGG-C10C
96ColChoMVP-UD14
96ColChoMVPG-UD14
96ColChoSti-S22
96Don-171
96Don-240
96DonCanI-39
96DonCanIGPP-39
96DonCanIRPP-39
96DonEli-38
96DonEliDCS-38
96DonEliP-3
96DonPrePro-171
96DonPrePro-240
96DurAllT-DC15
96Fla-31
96FlaBlul-31
96FlaCenIS-10
96Fle-35
96FleArtRos-25
96FlePCC-2
96FlePicF5-49
96HocGreC-20
96HocGreCG-20
96KraUppD-38
96Lea-13
96Lea-239
96LeaFirOI-12
96LeaLim-40
96LeaLimG-40
96LeaLimStu-14
96LeaPre-102
96LeaPreP-13
96LeaPreP-239
96LeaPreV-4
96LeaPrePP-102
96LeaPreVP-4
96LeaPreVPG-4
96MetUni-51
96NHLAcEPC-52
96NHLProSTA-105
96Pin-25
96PinArtP-25
96PinFoi-25
96PinMcD-17
96PinMin-12
96PinMinB-12
96PinMinCoiB-12
96PinMinCoiGP-12
96PinMinCoiN-12
96PinMinCoiS-12
96PinMinCoiSG-12
96PinMinG-12
96PinMinS-12
96PinPreS-25
96PinRinC-25
96PlaOneoOne-366
96Sco-60
96ScoArtPro-60
96ScoDeaCAP-60
96ScoGolB-60
96ScoSpeAP-60
96ScoSudDea-2
96SelCer-41
96SelCerAP-41
96SelCerBlu-41
96SelCerCor-14
96SelCerMB-41
96SelCerMG-41
96SelCerMR-41
96SelCerRed-41
96SkyImp-40
96SkyImpB-25
96SP-47
96SPCleWin-CW15
96PinsInf-IN8
96SPInsInfG-IN8
96SPx-14
96SPxGol-14
96SPxHoIH-HH3
96Sum-76
96SumArtP-76
96SumIce-76
96SumMet-76
96SumPreS-76
96SweSemW-101
96TeaOut-28
96TopNHLP-31
96TopPic5C-FC7
96TopPicOI-31
96TopPicTS-TS15
96Ult-56
96UltGolM-56
96UltMr.Mom-10
96UppDec-50
96UppDecB-1
96UppDecBD-162
96UppDecBDG-162
96UppDecBDRFTC-RC9
96UppDecGJ-GJ1
96UppDecGN-X13
96UppDecHH-HH19
96UppDecHHG-HH19

❑ 96UppDecHHS-HH19
❑ 96UppDecIce-109
❑ 96UppDecIceDF-S2
❑ 96UppDecIcePar-109
❑ 96UppDecIceSCF-S2
❑ 96UppDecSS-SS16B
❑ 96Zen-5
❑ 96ZenArtP-5
❑ 96ZenZT-6
❑ 97ColCho-78
❑ 97ColCho-313
❑ 97ColChoCTG-C19A
❑ 97ColChoCTG-C19B
❑ 97ColChoCTG-C19C
❑ 97ColChoCTGE-CR19
❑ 97ColChoSta-SQ67
❑ 97ColChoSti-S29
❑ 97ColChoWD-W3
❑ 97Don-2
❑ 97DonCanI-4
❑ 97DonCanIDS-4
❑ 97DonCanINP-4
❑ 97DonCanIPS-4
❑ 97DonCanISCS-19
❑ 97DonEli-15
❑ 97DonEli-122
❑ 97DonEliAsp-15
❑ 97DonEliAsp-122
❑ 97DonEliBttF-8
❑ 97DonEliBttFA-8
❑ 97DonEliC-16
❑ 97DonEliIns-6
❑ 97DonEliMC-16
❑ 97DonEliPN-10A
❑ 97DonEliPN-10B
❑ 97DonEliPN-10C
❑ 97DonEliPNDC-10A
❑ 97DonEliPNDC-10B
❑ 97DonEliPNDC-10C
❑ 97DonEliS-15
❑ 97DonEliS-122
❑ 97DonLim-41
❑ 97DonLim-115
❑ 97DonLim-165
❑ 97DonLimExp-41
❑ 97DonLimExp-115
❑ 97DonLimExp-165
❑ 97DonLimFOTG-49
❑ 97DonLimFOTG-70
❑ 97DonLin2L-5
❑ 97DonLin2LDC-5
❑ 97DonPre-41
❑ 97DonPre-179
❑ 97DonPreCttC-41
❑ 97DonPreCttC-179
❑ 97DonPreDWT-6
❑ 97DonPreLotT-6B
❑ 97DonPrePM-14
❑ 97DonPreProG-2
❑ 97DonPreProS-2
❑ 97DonPreT-13
❑ 97DonPreTB-13
❑ 97DonPreTBC-13
❑ 97DonPreTPC-13
❑ 97DonPreTPG-13
❑ 97DonPri-4
❑ 97DonPri-209
❑ 97DonPriDD-2
❑ 97DonPriODI-4
❑ 97DonPriP-3
❑ 97DonPriS-3
❑ 97DonPriSB-3
❑ 97DonPriSG-3
❑ 97DonPriSoA-4
❑ 97DonPriSoA-209
❑ 97DonPriSS-3
❑ 97HigMinHMC-17
❑ 97Kat-54
❑ 97Kat-161
❑ 97KatGol-54
❑ 97KatGol-161
❑ 97KatSil-54
❑ 97KatSil-161
❑ 97Lea-4
❑ 97Lea-171
❑ 97LeaBanSea-5
❑ 97LeaFirOnIce-4
❑ 97LeaFraMat-4
❑ 97LeaFraMat-171
❑ 97LeaFraMDC-4
❑ 97LeaFraMDC-171
❑ 97LeaInt-4
❑ 97LeaIntUI-4
❑ 97McD-19
❑ 97McDGamFil-3
❑ 97Pac-19
❑ 97PacCarSup-8
❑ 97PacCarSupM-8
❑ 97PacCop-19
❑ 97PacCraChoAwa-6
❑ 97PacCroR-51
❑ 97PacCroRBoSDC-10
❑ 97PacCroRCCJ-6
❑ 97PacCroRCCJG-6
❑ 97PacCroRCCJS-6
❑ 97PacCroREG-51
❑ 97PacCroRHTDC-8
❑ 97PacCroRIB-51
❑ 97PacCroRLCDC-9
❑ 97PacCroRS-51
❑ 97PacDyn-46
❑ 97PacDyn-139
❑ 97PacDynBKS-36
❑ 97PacDynC-46
❑ 97PacDynC-139
❑ 97PacDynDD-8B
❑ 97PacDynDG-46
❑ 97PacDynDG-139
❑ 97PacDynEG-46
❑ 97PacDynEG-139
❑ 97PacDynIB-46
❑ 97PacDynIB-139
❑ 97PacDynR-46
❑ 97PacDynR-139
❑ 97PacDynSil-46
❑ 97PacDynSil-139
❑ 97PacDynTan-7
❑ 97PacDynTan-26
❑ 97PacEmeGre-19
❑ 97PacGolCroDC-11
❑ 97PacIceB-19
❑ 97PacInv-53
❑ 97PacInvAZ-11
❑ 97PacInvC-53
❑ 97PacInvEG-53
❑ 97PacInvFP-16
❑ 97PacInvIB-53
❑ 97PacInvNRB-75
❑ 97PacInvOTG-9
❑ 97PacInvR-53
❑ 97PacInvS-53
❑ 97PacOme-88
❑ 97PacOmeC-88
❑ 97PacOmeDG-88
❑ 97PacOmeEG-88
❑ 97PacOmeG-88
❑ 97PacOmeGFDCC-8
❑ 97PacOmeIB-88
❑ 97PacOmeSil-6
❑ 97PacOmeSLC-9
❑ 97PacOmeTL-9
❑ 97PacPar-71
❑ 97PacParBNDC-10
❑ 97PacParC-71
❑ 97PacParCG-7
❑ 97PacParDG-71
❑ 97PacParEG-71
❑ 97PacParIB-71
❑ 97PacParP-10
❑ 97PacParRed-71
❑ 97PacParSil-71
❑ 97PacRed-19
❑ 97PacRev-52
❑ 97PacRevC-52
❑ 97PacRevE-52
❑ 97PacRevIB-52
❑ 97PacRevNID-5
❑ 97PacRevR-52
❑ 97PacRevS-52
❑ 97PacRevTCL-9
❑ 97PacSil-19
❑ 97PacSlaSDC-3C
❑ 97PacTeaCCC-9
❑ 97Pin-71
❑ 97PinArtP-71
❑ 97PinBee-11
❑ 97PinBeeGP-11
❑ 97PinBeeGT-16
❑ 97PinBeeT-16
❑ 97PinCer-38
❑ 97PinCerGT-13
❑ 97PinCerMB-38
❑ 97PinCerMG-38
❑ 97PinCerMR-38
❑ 97PinCerR-38
❑ 97PinCerT-13
❑ 97PinEpiGO-9
❑ 97PinEpiGP-9
❑ 97PinEpiME-9
❑ 97PinEpiMO-9
❑ 97PinEpiMP-9
❑ 97PinEpiPE-9
❑ 97PinEpiPO-9
❑ 97PinEpiPP-9
❑ 97PinEpiSE-9
❑ 97PinEpiSO-9
❑ 97PinEpiSP-9
❑ 97PinIns-24
❑ 97PinInsC-9
❑ 97PinInsCC-24
❑ 97PinInsCG-9
❑ 97PinInsEC-24
❑ 97PinInsT-9
❑ 97PinMin-5
❑ 97PinMinB-5
❑ 97PinMinCBP-5
❑ 97PinMinCGPP-5
❑ 97PinMinCNSP-5
❑ 97PinMinCoiB-5
❑ 97PinMinCoiGP-5
❑ 97PinMinCoiN-5
❑ 97PinMinCoiSG-5
❑ 97PinMinCoiSS-5
❑ 97PinMinGolTea-5
❑ 97PinMinSilTea-5
❑ 97PinPowPac-18
❑ 97PinPrePBB-71
❑ 97PinPrePBC-71
❑ 97PinPrePBM-71
❑ 97PinPrePBY-71
❑ 97PinPrePFC-71
❑ 97PinPrePFM-71
❑ 97PinPrePFY-71
❑ 97PinPrePla-71
❑ 97PinRinC-71
❑ 97PinTeaP-9
❑ 97PinTeaPM-9
❑ 97PinTeaPP-9
❑ 97PinTeaPPM-9
❑ 97PinTotCMPG-38
❑ 97PinTotCPB-38
❑ 97PinTotCPG-38
❑ 97PinTotCPR-38
❑ 97PosPin-10
❑ 97Sco-86
❑ 97Sco-263
❑ 97Sco-PR86
❑ 97ScoArtPro-86
❑ 97ScoGolBla-86
❑ 97ScoRedW-2
❑ 97ScoRedWPla-2
❑ 97ScoRedWPre-2
❑ 97SP AutI-I21
❑ 97SPAut-52
❑ 97SPAutID-I21
❑ 97SPAutIE-I21
❑ 97SPAutSotT-SY
❑ 97SPx-14
❑ 97SPxBro-14
❑ 97SPxDuo-5
❑ 97SPxGol-14
❑ 97SPxGraF-14
❑ 97SPxSil-14
❑ 97SPxSte-14
❑ 97Stu-10
❑ 97Stu-106
❑ 97StuHarH-10
❑ 97StuPor-10
❑ 97StuPrePG-10
❑ 97StuPrePG-106
❑ 97StuPrePS-10
❑ 97StuPrePS-106
❑ 97StuSil-10
❑ 97StuSil8-10
❑ 97TopHocMC-27
❑ 97TopHocMC-28
❑ 97UppDec-57
❑ 97UppDecBD-123
❑ 97UppDecBDDD-123
❑ 97UppDecBDPC-PC7
❑ 97UppDecBDPCDD-PC7
❑ 97UppDecBDPCM-PC7
❑ 97UppDecBDPCQD-PC7
❑ 97UppDecBDPCTD-PC7
❑ 97UppDecBDQD-123
❑ 97UppDecBDTD-123
❑ 97UppDecCtAG-5
❑ 97UppDecCtAG-AR5
❑ 97UppDecDV-4
❑ 97UppDecDVDM-DM3
❑ 97UppDecDVSM-4
❑ 97UppDecGDM-57
❑ 97UppDecIC-IC19
❑ 97UppDecIC2-IC19
❑ 97UppDecIce-89
❑ 97UppDecIceP-89
❑ 97UppDecILL-L5B
❑ 97UppDecILL2-L5B
❑ 97UppDecIPS-89
❑ 97UppDecSG-SG19
❑ 97UppDecSSM-SS20
❑ 97UppDecSSW-SS20
❑ 97UppDecTS-19
❑ 97UppDecTSL2-19
❑ 97UppDecTSS-3B
❑ 97Zen-5
❑ 97Zen5x7-21
❑ 97ZenChaTC-15
❑ 97ZenGolImp-21
❑ 97ZenSilImp-21
❑ 97ZenZGol-5
❑ 97ZenZSil-5
❑ 98Be A PPA-46
❑ 98Be A PPAA-46
❑ 98Be A PPAAF-46
❑ 98Be A PPAGUSC-S9
❑ 98Be A PPAJ-AS9
❑ 98Be A PPAM-M4
❑ 98Be A PPAM-M10
❑ 98Be A PPGUJA-G15
❑ 98Be A PPPGUJC-G15
❑ 98Be A PPPH-H7
❑ 98Be A PPPPUJC-P5
❑ 98Be A PPTBASG-46
❑ 98Be APG-46
❑ 98BowBes-1
❑ 98BowBesAR-1
❑ 98BowBesR-1
❑ 98BowBesSBB-SB7
❑ 98BowBesSBBAR-SB7
❑ 98BowBesSBBR-SB7
❑ 98CroRoyCCAJG-6
❑ 98CroRoyCCAJG-6
❑ 98CroRoyCCAJLB-6
❑ 98CroRoyCCAJP-6
❑ 98CroRoyCCAJR-6
❑ 98Fin-72
❑ 98FinDouMF-M31
❑ 98FinDouMF-M35
❑ 98FinDouMF-M36
❑ 98FinDouMF-M37
❑ 98FinDouSMFR-M31
❑ 98FinDouSMFR-M35
❑ 98FinDouSMFR-M36
❑ 98FinDouSMFR-M37
❑ 98FinNo P-72
❑ 98FinNo PR-72
❑ 98FinOve-5
❑ 98FinOveR-5
❑ 98FinRedL-R7
❑ 98FinRedLR-R7
❑ 98FinRef-72
❑ 98McD-6
❑ 98O-PChr-175
❑ 98O-PChrR-175
❑ 98Pac-19
❑ 98PacAur-69
❑ 98PacAurALC-11
❑ 98PacAurC-10
❑ 98PacAurCF-20
❑ 98PacAurCFC-20
❑ 98PacAurCFIB-20
❑ 98PacAurCFR-20
❑ 98PacAurCFS-20
❑ 98PacAurFL-5
❑ 98PacAurFLIB-5
❑ 98PacAurFLR-5
❑ 98PacAurMAC-10
❑ 98PacAurNC-6
❑ 98PacCroR-49
❑ 98PacCroRCCA-6
❑ 98PacCroRCCAJ-6
❑ 98PacCroRLL-6
❑ 98PacCroRLS-49
❑ 98PacCroRMP-11
❑ 98PacCroRPotG-14
❑ 98PacDynI-69
❑ 98PacDynI-10
❑ 98PacDynIAR-7
❑ 98PacDynIARB-7
❑ 98PacDynIARIB-7
❑ 98PacDynIARR-7
❑ 98PacDynIARS-7
❑ 98PacDynIFT-11
❑ 98PacDynIIB-69
❑ 98PacDynIPP-6
❑ 98PacDynIR-69
❑ 98PacDynITC-9
❑ 98PacEO P-11
❑ 98PacGolCD-16
❑ 98PacIceB-19
❑ 98PacOmeCS-4
❑ 98PacOmeCSG-4
❑ 98PacOmeCSG-4
❑ 98PacOmeCSR-4
❑ 98PacOmeEP1o1-11
❑ 98PacOmeFtF-6
❑ 98PacOmeH-88
❑ 98PacOmeO-16
❑ 98PacOmeODI-88
❑ 98PacOmeP-10
❑ 98PacOmePI-24
❑ 98PacOmePIB-24
❑ 98PacOmeR-88
❑ 98PacPar-83
❑ 98PacParC-83
❑ 98PacParEG-83
❑ 98PacParH-83
❑ 98PacParHoFB-5
❑ 98PacParHoFBPP-5
❑ 98PacParIB-83
❑ 98PacParIG-5
❑ 98PacParIGG-5
❑ 98PacParIGS-5
❑ 98PacParS-83
❑ 98PacParSDDC-9
❑ 98PacParTCD-9
❑ 98PacRed-19
❑ 98PacRev-53
❑ 98PacRevADC-30
❑ 98PacRevCTL-10
❑ 98PacRevIS-53
❑ 98PacRevNI-6
❑ 98PacRevR-53
❑ 98PacRevS-18
❑ 98PacTeaC-9
❑ 98PacTim-8
❑ 98PacTitI-10
❑ 98PacTroW-10
❑ 98PinEpiGE-9
❑ 98RevThrPA-26
❑ 98RevThrPA-26
❑ 98SP Aut-31
❑ 98SP AutA-3
❑ 98SP AutA-15
❑ 98SP AutA-16
❑ 98SP AutA-17
❑ 98SP AutSM-S23
❑ 98SP AutSM-S24
❑ 98SP AutSM-S25
❑ 98SP AutSotTG-SY
❑ 98SP AutSS-SS3
❑ 98SPxFin-30
❑ 98SPxFin-93
❑ 98SPxFin-156
❑ 98SPxFin-175
❑ 98SPxFinR-30
❑ 98SPxFinR-93
❑ 98SPxFinR-156
❑ 98SPxFinR-175
❑ 98SPxFinS-30
❑ 98SPxFinS-93
❑ 98SPxFinS-156
❑ 98SPxFinS-175
❑ 98SPXTopP-21
❑ 98SPXTopPF-21
❑ 98SPXTopPHH-H14
❑ 98SPXTopPLI-L19
❑ 98SPXTopPPS-PS26
❑ 98SPXTopPR-21
❑ 98SSASotT-SY
❑ 98Top-175
❑ 98TopGolLC1-31
❑ 98TopGolLC1B-31
❑ 98TopGolLC1BOoO-31
❑ 98TopGolLC1OoO-31
❑ 98TopGolLC1R-31
❑ 98TopGolLC1ROoO-31
❑ 98TopGolLC2-31
❑ 98TopGolLC2B-31
❑ 98TopGolLC2BOoO-31
❑ 98TopGolLC2OoO-31
❑ 98TopGolLC2R-31
❑ 98TopGolLC2ROoO-31
❑ 98TopGolLC3-31
❑ 98TopGolLC3B-31
❑ 98TopGolLC3BOoO-31
❑ 98TopGolLC3OoO-31
❑ 98TopGolLC3R-31
❑ 98TopGolLC3ROoO-31
❑ 98TopO-P-175
❑ 98UC-73
❑ 98UC-310
❑ 98UCMBH-BH27
❑ 98UCSB-SQ18
❑ 98UCSG-SQ18
❑ 98UCSG-SQ18
❑ 98UCSR-SQ18
❑ 98UD ChoPCR-73
❑ 98UD ChoPCR-310
❑ 98UD ChoR-73
❑ 98UD ChoR-310
❑ 98UD3-60
❑ 98UD3-120
❑ 98UD3-180
❑ 98UD3DieC-60
❑ 98UD3DieC-120
❑ 98UD3DieC-180
❑ 98UDCP-73
❑ 98UppDec-85
❑ 98UppDec-209
❑ 98UppDec-389
❑ 98UppDec-390
❑ 98UppDecDD-30
❑ 98UppDecDD-30
❑ 98UppDecE-85
❑ 98UppDecE-209
❑ 98UppDecE-389
❑ 98UppDecE-390
❑ 98UppDecE1o1-85
❑ 98UppDecE1o1-209
❑ 98UppDecE1o1-389
❑ 98UppDecE1o1-390
❑ 98UppDecFF-FF20
❑ 98UppDecFF-FF20
❑ 98UppDecFFQ1-FF20
❑ 98UppDecFFQ2-FF20
❑ 98UppDecFIT-FT1
❑ 98UppDecFITQ1-FT1
❑ 98UppDecFITQ2-FT1
❑ 98UppDecFITQ3-FT1
❑ 98UppDecGN-GN4
❑ 98UppDecGN-GN5
❑ 98UppDecGN-GN6
❑ 98UppDecGNQ1-GN4
❑ 98UppDecGNQ1-GN5
❑ 98UppDecGNQ1-GN6
❑ 98UppDecGNQ2-GN4
❑ 98UppDecGNQ2-GN5
❑ 98UppDecGNQ2-GN6
❑ 98UppDecGNQ3-GN4
❑ 98UppDecGNQ3-GN5
❑ 98UppDecGNQ3-GN6
❑ 98UppDecGR-85
❑ 98UppDecGR-209
❑ 98UppDecGR-389
❑ 98UppDecGR-NNO
❑ 98UppDecLSH-LS14
❑ 98UppDecLSHQ1-LS14
❑ 98UppDecLSHQ2-LS14
❑ 98UppDecLSHQ3-LS14
❑ 98UppDecM-69
❑ 98UppDecM1-M19
❑ 98UppDecM2-M19
❑ 98UppDECMGS-SY
❑ 98UppDECMGS-SYA
❑ 98UppDecMGS-69
❑ 98UppDecMOH-OT1
❑ 98UppDecMP-SY
❑ 98UppDecMS-S11
❑ 98UppDecMSF-F7
❑ 98UppDecMSS-69
❑ 98UppDecMSS-69
❑ 98UppDecP-P3
❑ 98UppDecPQ1-P3
❑ 98UppDecPQ2-P3
❑ 98UppDecPQ3-P3
❑ 98UppDecQD-30
❑ 98UppDecTD-30
❑ 98UppDecWFG-WF11
❑ 98UppDecWFP-WF11
❑ 99AurSty-10
❑ 99Pac-151
❑ 99PacAur-55
❑ 99PacAurCC-6
❑ 99PacAurCF-13
❑ 99PacAurCFC-13
❑ 99PacAurCFPB-13
❑ 99PacAurCP-7
❑ 99PacAurCPP-7
❑ 99PacAurPD-55
❑ 99PacCop-151
❑ 99PacCra-7
❑ 99PacGol-151
❑ 99PacGolCD-18
❑ 99PacHomaA-9
❑ 99PacIceB-151
❑ 99PacPasAP-13
❑ 99PacPreD-151
❑ 99PacTeaL-10
❑ 99RetHoc-27
❑ 99SP AutPS-31
❑ 99UppDecCL-57
❑ 99UppDecCLCLC-57
❑ 99UppDecES-20
❑ 99UppDecM-69
❑ 99UppDecM9S-S7
❑ 99UppDecMGS-GU11
❑ 99UppDecMGS-69
❑ 99UppDecMGUSA-GU11
❑ 99UppDecMHoG-H10
❑ 99UppDecMPS-SY
❑ 99UppDecMSS-69
❑ 99UppDecMSS-69
❑ 99UppDecMT-MVP6
❑ 99UppDecRDR-DR5
❑ 99UppDecRDRI-DR5
❑ 99UppDecRG-27
❑ 99UppDecRII-SY
❑ 99UppDecRIL1-SY
❑ 99UppDecRP-27
❑ 99UppDecRTotC-TC5

**Zabawa, Andrezei**
❑ 79PanSti-131

**Zabel, Norbert**
❑ 94GerDELE-182

**Zabransky, Libor**
❑ 94CzeAPSE-104
❑ 95CzeAPSE-60
❑ 97ScoBlu-17
❑ 97ScoBluPla-17
❑ 97ScoBluPre-17
❑ 97UppDec-144

**Zabrodsky, Jan**
❑ 70SweHocS-61

**Zach, Hans**
❑ 94GerDELE-77
❑ 95GerDELE-146
❑ 98GerDELE-64
❑ 98GerDELE-339

**Zach, Johann**
❑ 79PanSti-112

**Zachary, Travis**
❑ 98QueRem-24

**Zadina, Marek**
❑ 94CzeAPSE-38
❑ 95CzeAPSE-235

**Zadrazil, Jiri**
❑ 95CzeAPSE-24
❑ 96CzeAPSE-110

**Zafrani, Andre**
❑ 92ArIIce-16

**Zaharko, Miles**
❑ 80BlaBroBac-16
❑ 81BlaBroBac-17

**Zaichkowski, Jason**
❑ 92BriColJHL-143

**Zaine, Rod**
❑ 71SabPos-21
❑ 71TorSun-41

**Zajankala, George**
❑ 917thInnSWHL-124
❑ 92CleLum-11
❑ 94KnoChe-17
❑ 95DayBom-22

**Zajic, Josef**
❑ 94CzeAPSE-35
❑ 95CzeAPSE-97
❑ 96CzeAPSE-85

**Zajicek, Jan**
❑ 79PanSti-81

**Zajonc, Petr**
❑ 95CzeAPSE-232

**Zakall, Brian**
❑ 91BriColJHL-74

**Zalapski, Zarley**
❑ 89OPC-168
❑ 89OPCSti-2
❑ 89OPCSti-45
❑ 89OPCSti-232
❑ 89PanSti-318
❑ 89PenCokE-5
❑ 89PenFoo-3
❑ 89SweSemWCS-60
❑ 89Top-168
❑ 90Bow-207
❑ 90BowTif-207
❑ 90OPC-78
❑ 90PanSti-126
❑ 90PenFoo-12
❑ 90ProSet-242
❑ 90Sco-218
❑ 90ScoCan-218
❑ 90Top-78
❑ 90TopTif-78
❑ 90UppDec-33
❑ 90UppDecF-33
❑ 91Bow-15
❑ 91OPC-344
❑ 91PanSti-322
❑ 91Par-61
❑ 91ParFre-61
❑ 91Pin-110
❑ 91PinFre-110
❑ 91ProSet-91
❑ 91ProSetFre-91
❑ 91ProSetPla-47
❑ 91ScoAme-111
❑ 91ScoCan-111
❑ 91StaClu-228
❑ 91SweSemWCS-60
❑ 91Top-344
❑ 91UppDec-231
❑ 91UppDecF-231
❑ 91WhaJr7E-28
❑ 92Bow-173
❑ 92HumDum1-25
❑ 92OPC-248
❑ 92PanSti-263
❑ 92PanStiFre-263
❑ 92Par-59
❑ 92ParEmel-59
❑ 92Pin-271
❑ 92PinFre-271
❑ 92ProSet-59
❑ 92Sco-238
❑ 92ScoCan-238
❑ 92StaClu-25
❑ 92Top-82
❑ 92TopGol-82G
❑ 92Ult-77
❑ 92UppDec-316
❑ 92WhaDai-25
❑ 93Don-149
❑ 93Don-410
❑ 93Lea-8
❑ 93OPCPre-20
❑ 93OPCPreG-20
❑ 93PanSti-129
❑ 93Par-88
❑ 93ParEmel-88
❑ 93Pin-257
❑ 93PinAllS-2
❑ 93PinAllSC-2
❑ 93PinCan-257
❑ 93Pow-112
❑ 93Sco-104
❑ 93ScoCan-104
❑ 93StaClu-102
❑ 93StaCluAS-14
❑ 93StaCluFDI-102
❑ 93StaCluFDIO-102
❑ 93StaCluO-102
❑ 93TopPre-20
❑ 93TopPreG-20
❑ 93Ult-234
❑ 93UppDec-213
❑ 93UppDecLAS-18
❑ 93WhaCok-24
❑ 94CanGamNHLP-64
❑ 94Don-248
❑ 94EASpo-55
❑ 94Fla-30
❑ 94Lea-294
❑ 94OPCPre-379
❑ 94OPCPreSE-379
❑ 94Par-31
❑ 94ParGol-31
❑ 94Pin-342
❑ 94PinArtP-342
❑ 94PinRinC-342
❑ 94Sel-140
❑ 94SelGol-140
❑ 94StaClu-141
❑ 94StaCluFDI-141
❑ 94StaCluMOMS-141
❑ 94StaCluSTWC-141
❑ 94TopPre-379
❑ 94TopPreSE-379
❑ 94Ult-38
❑ 94UppDec-110
❑ 94UppDecEleIce-110
❑ 95BeAPla-108
❑ 95BeAPSig-S108
❑ 95BeAPSigDC-S108
❑ 95ColCho-123
❑ 95ColChoPC-123
❑ 95ColChoPCP-123
❑ 95Don-177
❑ 95Emo-26
❑ 95ImpSti-19
❑ 95Lea-225
❑ 95ParInt-31
❑ 95ParIntEI-31
❑ 95PlaOneoOne-132
❑ 95Sco-69
❑ 95ScoBlaIce-69
❑ 95ScoBlaIceAP-69
❑ 95SkyImp-26
❑ 95StaClu-96
❑ 95StaCluMOMS-96
❑ 95Top-263
❑ 95TopOPCI-263
❑ 95Ult-29
❑ 95UltGolM-29
❑ 95UppDec-480
❑ 95UppDecEleIce-480
❑ 95UppDecEleIceG-480
❑ 96ColCho-41
❑ 96Don-4
❑ 96DonPrePro-4
❑ 96Lea-95
❑ 96LeaPreP-95
❑ 96Pin-119
❑ 96PinArtP-119
❑ 96PinFoi-119
❑ 96PinPreS-119
❑ 96PinRinC-119
❑ 96Sco-205
❑ 96ScoArtPro-205
❑ 96ScoDeaCAP-205
❑ 96ScoGolB-205
❑ 96ScoSpeAP-205
❑ 96SP-25
❑ 96TeaOut-89
❑ 96UppDec-24
❑ 97Be A PPAD-68
❑ 97Be A PPAPD-68
❑ 97BeAPla-68
❑ 97BeAPlaAut-68
❑ 97PacDynBKS-15
❑ 98O-PChr-196
❑ 98O-PChrR-196
❑ 98Top-196
❑ 98TopO-P-196

❑ 98UppDec-321
❑ 98UppDecE-321
❑ 98UppDecE1o1-321
❑ 98UppDecGR-321
**Zaltsev, Sergei**
❑ 90OPC-487
**Zambon, Mike**
❑ 91BriColJHL-34
**Zamojski, Jacek**
❑ 89SweSemWCS-131
**Zamuner, Rob**
❑ 89ProIHL-40
❑ 90ProAHLIHL-1
❑ 91ProAHLCHL-204
❑ 92Cla-98
❑ 92LigShe-25
❑ 92OPCPre-69
❑ 92Par-171
❑ 92ParEmel-171
❑ 92Pin-414
❑ 92PinFre-414
❑ 92StaClu-439
❑ 92Top-426
❑ 92TopGol-426G
❑ 92Ult-415
❑ 92UppDec-583
❑ 92UppDecCC-CC4
❑ 93Don-329
❑ 93Lea-173
❑ 93LigSealR-28
❑ 93OPCPre-19
❑ 93OPCPreG-19
❑ 93PanSti-214
❑ 93Par-194
❑ 93ParEmel-194
❑ 93Pin-121
❑ 93PinCan-121
❑ 93Pow-236
❑ 93Sco-291
❑ 93ScoCan-291
❑ 93StaClu-376
❑ 93StaCluFDI-376
❑ 93StaCluO-376
❑ 93TopPre-19
❑ 93TopPreG-19
❑ 93Ult-199
❑ 93UppDec-202
❑ 93UppDecSP-154
❑ 94BeAPla-R175
❑ 94BeAPSig-147
❑ 94Lea-427
❑ 94LigPhoA-28
❑ 94LigPos-20
❑ 94Par-224
❑ 94ParGol-224
❑ 94StaClu-48
❑ 94StaCluFDI-48
❑ 94StaCluMOMS-48
❑ 94StaCluSTWC-48
❑ 94UppDec-468
❑ 94UppDecEleIce-468
❑ 95LigTeal-21
❑ 95PlaOneoOne-200
❑ 95ProMag-75
❑ 96BeAPAut-114
❑ 96BeAPAutSil-114
❑ 96BeAPla-114
❑ 96ClaGol-98
❑ 96ColCho-248
❑ 96NHLProSTA-75
❑ 96UppDec-158
❑ 97ColCho-238
❑ 97DonLim-88
❑ 97DonLimExp-88
❑ 97DonPri-112
❑ 97DonPriSoA-112
❑ 97Pac-204
❑ 97PacCop-204
❑ 97PacEmeGre-204
❑ 97PacIceB-204
❑ 97PacOme-216
❑ 97PacOmeC-216
❑ 97PacOmeDG-216
❑ 97PacOmeEG-216
❑ 97PacOmeG-216
❑ 97PacOmeIB-216
❑ 97PacRed-204
❑ 97PacRev-132
❑ 97PacRevC-132
❑ 97PacRevE-132
❑ 97PacRevIB-132
❑ 97PacRevR-132
❑ 97PacRevS-132
❑ 97PacRevTCL-23
❑ 97PacSil-204
❑ 97Sco-200
❑ 97UppDec-364
❑ 98Be A PPA-132
❑ 98Be A PPAA-132
❑ 98Be A PPAAF-132
❑ 98Be A PPTBASG-132
❑ 98Be APG-132
❑ 98Fin-20
❑ 98FinNo P-20
❑ 98FinNo PR-20
❑ 98FinRef-20
❑ 98O-PChr-43
❑ 98O-PChrR-43
❑ 98Pac-409
❑ 98PacAur-178
❑ 98PacAurCF-45
❑ 98PacAurCFC-45
❑ 98PacAurCFIB-45
❑ 98PacAurCFR-45
❑ 98PacAurCFS-45
❑ 98PacCroR-127
❑ 98PacCroRLS-127
❑ 98PacDynI-176
❑ 98PacDynIIB-176
❑ 98PacDynIR-176
❑ 98PacIceB-409
❑ 98PacOmeH-223
❑ 98PacOmeODI-223
❑ 98PacOmeR-223
❑ 98PacPar-223
❑ 98PacParC-223
❑ 98PacParEG-223
❑ 98PacParH-223
❑ 98PacParIB-223
❑ 98PacParS-223
❑ 98PacParTCD-24
❑ 98PacRed-409
❑ 98PacRev-135
❑ 98PacRevIS-135
❑ 98PacRevR-135
❑ 98PacTeaC-24
❑ 98Top-43
❑ 98TopO-P-43
❑ 98UC-196
❑ 98UD ChoPCR-196
❑ 98UD ChoR-196
❑ 98UppDecM-191
❑ 98UppDecMGS-191
❑ 98UppDecMSS-191
❑ 98UppDecMSS-191
❑ 99Pac-399
❑ 99PacCop-399
❑ 99PacGol-399
❑ 99PacIceB-399
❑ 99PacPreD-399
**Zanier, Mike**
❑ 83MonAlp-4
❑ 84NovScoO-18
❑ 88OilTenAnn-4
❑ 92DalFre-19
**Zanussi, Joe**
❑ 76OPCNHL-324
**Zanussi, Ron**
❑ 78NorStaCD-9
❑ 78OPC-252
❑ 78Top-252
❑ 79NorStaPos-21
❑ 79OPC-22
❑ 79Top-22
❑ 80NorStaPos-24
❑ 80OPC-192
❑ 80Top-192
❑ 81MapLeaP-25
❑ 81OPC-325
**Zanutto, Chris**
❑ 93LonKni-23
**Zanutto, Mike**
❑ 95Sla-245
**Zaporzan, Terry**
❑ 84KelWin-12
**Zapt, Bill**
❑ 92BriColJHL-240
**Zarillo, Bruno**
❑ 94FinnJaaK-308
❑ 95SweGloWC-231
**Zarowny, Aaron**
❑ 93LetHur-24
**Zarrillo, Bruno**
❑ 93SweSemWCS-225
❑ 96GerDELE-352
❑ 98GerDELE-89
**Zaryk, Steve**
❑ 95Sla-269
**Zatopek, Libor**
❑ 95CzeAPSE-239
**Zavaroukhine, Nikolai**
❑ 94ParSE-SE230
❑ 94ParSEG-SE230
❑ 94SP-163
❑ 94SPDieCut-163
❑ 94UppDec-516
❑ 94UppDecEleIce-516
**Zavarukhin, Nikolai**
❑ 93Cla-49
❑ 93Par-530
❑ 93ParEmel-530
**Zavediuk, Tom**
❑ 95TriAme-28
**Zavisha, Bradley (Brad)**
❑ 907thInnSWHL-14
❑ 917thInnSWHL-358
❑ 94CapBreO-23
**Zawatsky, Ed**
❑ 91RochAmePos-21
**Zayonce, Dean**
❑ 907thInnSWHL-118
❑ 91GreMon-18
❑ 93GreMon-16
❑ 94GreMon-1
❑ 98ChaChe-18
**Zdunek, Piotr**
❑ 89SweSemWCS-138
**Zednik, Richard**
❑ 96DonCanI-125
❑ 96DonCanIGPP-125
❑ 96DonCanIRPP-125
❑ 96LeaPre-133
❑ 96LeaPrePP-133
❑ 96MetUni-197
❑ 96PorPir-14
❑ 96SelCer-110
❑ 96SelCerAP-110
❑ 96SelCerBlu-110
❑ 96SelCerMB-110
❑ 96SelCerMG-110
❑ 96SelCerMR-110
❑ 96SelCerRed-110
❑ 96UppDec-356
❑ 96Zen-120
❑ 96ZenArtP-120
❑ 97BeAPlaPOT-17
❑ 97Kat-156
❑ 97KatGol-156
❑ 97KatSil-156
❑ 97PacCroR-144
❑ 97PacCroREG-144
❑ 97PacCroRIB-144
❑ 97PacCroRS-144
❑ 97PacOme-244
❑ 97PacOmeC-244
❑ 97PacOmeDG-244
❑ 97PacOmeEG-244
❑ 97PacOmeG-244
❑ 97PacOmeIB-244
❑ 97SPAut-197
❑ 97UppDec-388
❑ 97UppDecBD-51
❑ 97UppDecBDDD-51
❑ 97UppDecBDQD-51
❑ 97UppDecBDTD-51
❑ 97UppDecIce-55
❑ 97UppDecIceP-55
❑ 97UppDecIPS-55
❑ 97Zen-83
❑ 97Zen5x7-72
❑ 97ZenGolImp-72
❑ 97ZenRooR-15
❑ 97ZenSilImp-72
❑ 97ZenZGol-83
❑ 97ZenZSil-83
❑ 97ZenZT-17
❑ 97ZenZTG-17
❑ 98O-PChr-92
❑ 98O-PChrR-92
❑ 98Pac-451
❑ 98PacAur-200
❑ 98PacDynI-200
❑ 98PacDynIIB-200
❑ 98PacDynIR-200
❑ 98PacIceB-451
❑ 98PacOmeH-250
❑ 98PacOmeODI-250
❑ 98PacOmeR-250
❑ 98PacPar-250
❑ 98PacParC-250
❑ 98PacParEG-250
❑ 98PacParH-250
❑ 98PacParIB-250
❑ 98PacParS-250
❑ 98PacRed-451
❑ 98PacRev-150
❑ 98PacRevIS-150
❑ 98PacRevR-150
❑ 98SPxFin-135
❑ 98SPxFinR-135
❑ 98SPxFinS-135
❑ 98Top-92
❑ 98TopO-P-92
❑ 98UC-218
❑ 98UD ChoPCR-218
❑ 98UD ChoR-218
❑ 98UD3-7
❑ 98UD3-67
❑ 98UD3-127
❑ 98UD3DieC-7
❑ 98UD3DieC-67
❑ 98UD3DieC-127
❑ 98UppDec-206
❑ 98UppDecBD-90
❑ 98UppDecDD-90
❑ 98UppDecE-206
❑ 98UppDecE1o1-206
❑ 98UppDecGN-GN23
❑ 98UppDecGNQ1-GN23
❑ 98UppDecGNQ2-GN23
❑ 98UppDecGNQ3-GN23
❑ 98UppDecGR-206
❑ 98UppDecM-215
❑ 98UppDecMGS-215
❑ 98UppDecMSS-215
❑ 98UppDecMSS-215
❑ 98UppDecQD-90
❑ 98UppDecTD-90
❑ 99Pac-449
❑ 99PacCop-449
❑ 99PacGol-449
❑ 99PacIceB-449
❑ 99PacPreD-449
**Zehr, Jeff**
❑ 95Sla-416
❑ 97BowCHL-149
❑ 97BowCHLAu-29
❑ 97BowCHLOPC-149
**Zeidel, Larry**
❑ 44BeeGro2P-219
❑ 52Par-91
❑ 53Par-73
❑ 68OPC-92
❑ 68Top-92
**Zelenka, Jiri**
❑ 94CzeAPSE-83
❑ 95CzeAPSE-279
❑ 96CzeAPSE-343
**Zelepukin, Valeri**
❑ 91OPCIns-65R
❑ 91Par-324
❑ 91ParFre-324
❑ 91Pin-354
❑ 91PinFre-354
❑ 91ProAHLCHL-427
❑ 91ProSetPla-261
❑ 91UppDec-589
❑ 91UppDecF-589
❑ 92Bow-430
❑ 92PanSti-177
❑ 92PanStiFre-177
❑ 92Par-228
❑ 92Par-327
❑ 92ParEmel-228
❑ 92ParEmel-327
❑ 92Pin-286
❑ 92PinFre-286
❑ 92ProSetRGL-10
❑ 92RusStaRA-7
❑ 92Sco-206
❑ 92ScoCan-206
❑ 92StaClu-99
❑ 92Top-462
❑ 92TopGol-462G
❑ 92TriFroRWP-15
❑ 92TriFroRWP-16
❑ 92Ult-122
❑ 92UppDec-292
❑ 92UppDecES-E12
❑ 93Don-193
❑ 93Kra-26
❑ 93Lea-104
❑ 93PanSti-38
❑ 93Par-383
❑ 93ParEmel-383
❑ 93Pin-94
❑ 93PinCan-94
❑ 93Pow-145
❑ 93Sco-278
❑ 93ScoCan-278
❑ 93StaClu-314
❑ 93StaCluFDI-314
❑ 93StaCluO-314
❑ 93Ult-222
❑ 93UppDec-369
❑ 94CanGamNHLP-149
❑ 94Don-291
❑ 94Fla-101
❑ 94Lea-17
❑ 94OPCPre-58
❑ 94OPCPreSE-58
❑ 94Par-124
❑ 94ParGol-124
❑ 94Pin-49
❑ 94PinArtP-49
❑ 94PinRinC-49
❑ 94Sco-49
❑ 94ScoGol-49
❑ 94ScoPla-49
❑ 94ScoPlaTS-49
❑ 94StaClu-225
❑ 94StaCluFDI-225
❑ 94StaCluMOMS-225
❑ 94StaCluSTWC-225
❑ 94TopPre-58
❑ 94TopPreSE-58
❑ 94Ult-124
❑ 94UppDec-143
❑ 94UppDecEleIce-143
❑ 95BeAPla-207
❑ 95BeAPSig-S207
❑ 95BeAPSigDC-S207
❑ 95Don-320
❑ 95Lea-260
❑ 95ParInt-391
❑ 95ParIntEl-391
❑ 95Pin-194
❑ 95PinArtP-194
❑ 95PinGloG-25
❑ 95PinRinC-194
❑ 95PlaOneoOne-168
❑ 95Sco-179
❑ 95ScoBlaIce-179
❑ 95ScoBlaIceAP-179
❑ 96Dev-25
❑ 96UppDecIce-38
❑ 96UppDecIcePar-38
❑ 97Pac-299
❑ 97PacCop-299
❑ 97PacEmeGre-299
❑ 97PacIceB-299
❑ 97PacRed-299
❑ 97PacSil-299
❑ 97ScoDev-9
❑ 97ScoDevPla-9
❑ 97ScoDevPre-9
❑ 97UppDec-303
❑ 98Be A PPA-254
❑ 98Be A PPAA-254
❑ 98Be A PPAAF-254
❑ 98Be A PPSE-254
❑ 98Be APG-254
❑ 98O-PChr-187
❑ 98O-PChrR-187
❑ 98Pac-218
❑ 98PacIceB-218
❑ 98PacRed-218
❑ 98Top-187
❑ 98TopO-P-187
❑ 99Pac-314
❑ 99PacCop-314
❑ 99PacGol-314
❑ 99PacIceB-314
❑ 99PacPreD-314
**Zelezny, Otto**
❑ 95CzeAPSE-199
**Zemlak, Richard**
❑ 85NordTeal-27
❑ 86NordGenF-28
❑ 87NorStaPos-31
❑ 89ProIHL-154
❑ 90ProAHLIHL-623
❑ 91ProAHLCHL-590
❑ 94ClaEnfP-PR1
**Zemlicka, Richard**
❑ 91SweSemWCS-125
❑ 93SweSemWCS-95
❑ 94FinnJaaK-180
❑ 94GerDELE-47
❑ 95FinnSemWC-151
❑ 95SweGloWC-154
❑ 96CzeAPSE-132
❑ 96SweSemW-120
**Zent, Jason**
❑ 94Cla-117
❑ 94ClaDraGol-117
❑ 95ColEdgI-50
❑ 95Ima-54
❑ 95ImaAut-54A
❑ 95ImaGol-54
❑ 96SenPizH-29
**Zerwesz, Rainer**
❑ 94GerDELE-101
❑ 95GerDELE-212
❑ 96GerDELE-356
❑ 98GerDELE-102
**Zetek, Ondrej**
❑ 94CzeAPSE-212
❑ 95CzeAPSE-154
**Zettel, Michael**
❑ 94GerDELE-223
**Zetterberg, Bo**
❑ 65SweCorI-108
❑ 67SweHoc-180
**Zetterberg, Kent**
❑ 71SweHocS-378
**Zetterberg, Patrik**
❑ 94SweLeaE-254
❑ 95SweLeaE-292
**Zetterberg, Stig-Olof**
❑ 67SweHoc-245
**Zetterholm, Peter**
❑ 84SweSemE-9
**Zetterstrom, Lars**
❑ 74SweHocS-197
❑ 78CanuRoyB-23
❑ 79PanSti-190
**Zetterstrom, Lasse**
❑ 73SweHocS-189
❑ 73SweWorCS-189
**Zettler, Rob**
❑ 84SauSteMG-23
❑ 87SauSteMG-14
❑ 88ProIHL-25
❑ 89ProIHL-81
❑ 90OPC-289
❑ 90Top-289
❑ 90TopTif-289
❑ 91OPC-272
❑ 91OPCPre-21
❑ 91Pin-213
❑ 91PinFre-213
❑ 91ProSet-330
❑ 91ProSetFre-330
❑ 91ScoAme-370
❑ 91ScoCan-643
❑ 91ScoRoo-93T
❑ 91ShaSanJSA-21
❑ 91StaClu-194
❑ 91Top-272
❑ 91UppDec-61
❑ 91UppDecF-61
❑ 92Bow-84
❑ 92OPC-366
❑ 92PanSti-127
❑ 92PanStiFre-127
❑ 92Pin-89
❑ 92PinFre-89
❑ 92Sco-191
❑ 92ScoCan-191
❑ 92StaClu-225
❑ 92Top-227
❑ 92TopGol-227G
❑ 93Sco-413
❑ 93ScoCan-413
❑ 94Par-164
❑ 94ParGol-164
❑ 94StaClu-109
❑ 94StaCluFDI-109
❑ 94StaCluMOMS-109
❑ 94StaCluSTWC-109
❑ 94UppDec-454
❑ 94UppDecEleIce-454
❑ 96BeAPAut-64
❑ 96BeAPAutSil-64
❑ 96BeAPla-64
❑ 97Pac-101
❑ 97PacCop-101
❑ 97PacEmeGre-101
❑ 97PacIceB-101
❑ 97PacRed-101
❑ 97PacSil-101
**Zettlin, Ake**
❑ 65SweCorI-109
**Zevakhi, Alexander**
❑ 98SPXTopP-77
❑ 98SPXTopPF-77
❑ 98SPXTopPR-77
❑ 98UppDecBD-106
❑ 98UppDecDD-106
❑ 98UppDecQD-106
❑ 98UppDecTD-106
**Zezel, Peter**
❑ 85FlyPos-30
❑ 85OPC-24
❑ 85OPCSti-94
❑ 85Top-24
❑ 86FlyPos-28
❑ 86OPC-190
❑ 86OPCSti-245
❑ 86Top-190
❑ 87OPC-71
❑ 87OPCSti-96
❑ 87PanSti-129
❑ 87Top-71
❑ 88BluKod-9
❑ 88OPC-146
❑ 88OPCSti-102
❑ 88Top-146
❑ 89BluKod-9
❑ 89OPC-27
❑ 89OPCSti-23
❑ 89PanSti-118
❑ 89Top-27
❑ 90Bow-19
❑ 90BowTif-19
❑ 90OPC-15
❑ 90OPCPre-131
❑ 90PanSti-264
❑ 90ProSet-274
❑ 90ProSet-556
❑ 90Sco-24
❑ 90ScoCan-24
❑ 90ScoRoo-6T
❑ 90Top-15
❑ 90TopTif-15
❑ 90UppDec-17
❑ 90UppDecF-17
❑ 91Bow-164
❑ 91MapLeaP-30
❑ 91OPC-445
❑ 91PanSti-103
❑ 91Par-174
❑ 91ParFre-174
❑ 91Pin-174
❑ 91Pin-414
❑ 91PinFre-174
❑ 91PinFre-414
❑ 91ProSet-227
❑ 91ProSetFre-227
❑ 91ProSetPla-232
❑ 91ScoAme-269
❑ 91ScoCan-489
❑ 91StaClu-104
❑ 91Top-445
❑ 91UppDec-241
❑ 91UppDecF-241
❑ 92Bow-263
❑ 92MapLeaK-22
❑ 92OPC-337
❑ 92PanSti-81
❑ 92PanStiFre-81
❑ 92Par-410
❑ 92ParEmel-410
❑ 92Pin-283
❑ 92PinFre-283
❑ 92ProSet-187
❑ 92Sco-174
❑ 92ScoCan-174
❑ 92StaClu-433
❑ 92Top-319
❑ 92TopGol-319G
❑ 92Ult-216
❑ 92UppDec-389
❑ 93Don-338
❑ 93Lea-107
❑ 93OPCPre-454
❑ 93OPCPreG-454
❑ 93Par-206
❑ 93ParEmel-206
❑ 93Pin-297
❑ 93PinCan-297
❑ 93Pow-455
❑ 93Sco-31
❑ 93ScoBla-4
❑ 93ScoCan-31
❑ 93StaClu-116
❑ 93StaCluFDI-116
❑ 93StaCluFDIO-116
❑ 93StaCluO-116
❑ 93TopPre-454
❑ 93TopPreG-454
❑ 93Ult-436
❑ 93UppDec-199
❑ 94BeAPSig-100
❑ 94Lea-533
❑ 94OPCPre-22
❑ 94OPCPreSE-22
❑ 94Pin-109
❑ 94PinArtP-109
❑ 94PinRinC-109
❑ 94StaPos-22
❑ 94TopPre-22
❑ 94TopPreSE-22
❑ 94UppDec-140
❑ 94UppDecEleIce-140
❑ 95UppDec-377
❑ 95UppDecEleIce-377
❑ 95UppDecEleIceG-377
❑ 96BeAPAut-94
❑ 96BeAPAutSil-94
❑ 96BeAPla-94
❑ 98Be A PPA-294
❑ 98Be A PPAA-294
❑ 98Be A PPAAF-294
❑ 98Be A PPSE-294
❑ 98Be APG-294
❑ 98O-PChr-56
❑ 98O-PChrR-56
❑ 98Pac-436
❑ 98PacIceB-436
❑ 98PacRed-436
❑ 98Top-56
❑ 98TopO-P-56
**Zhamnov, Alexei**
❑ 91OPCIns-48R
❑ 91SweSemWCS-95
❑ 91UppDec-2
❑ 91UppDecF-2
❑ 92OPCPre-13
❑ 92Par-210
❑ 92ParEmel-210
❑ 92Pin-416
❑ 92PinFre-416
❑ 92RusStaRA-2
❑ 92RusStaRA-35
❑ 92TriFroRWP-7
❑ 92TriFroRWP-8
❑ 92Ult-447
❑ 92UppDec-578
❑ 92UppDecER-ER8
❑ 93Don-380
❑ 93JetRuf-28
❑ 93Lea-84
❑ 93LeaGolR-5
❑ 93OPCPre-128
❑ 93OPCPre-420
❑ 93OPCPreG-128
❑ 93OPCPreG-420
❑ 93PanSti-190
❑ 93Par-243
❑ 93Par-503
❑ 93ParEmel-243
❑ 93ParEmel-503
❑ 93Pin-56
❑ 93PinCan-56
❑ 93Pow-278
❑ 93PowRisS-9
❑ 93PowSecYS-12
❑ 93Sco-256
❑ 93ScoCan-256
❑ 93ScoDynDC-2
❑ 93StaClu-56
❑ 93StaCluFDI-56
❑ 93StaCluFDIO-56
❑ 93StaCluO-56
❑ 93TopPre-128
❑ 93TopPre-420
❑ 93TopPreBG-8
❑ 93TopPreG-128
❑ 93TopPreG-420
❑ 93Ult-128
❑ 93UppDec-162
❑ 93UppDecLAS-60
❑ 93UppDecSP-180
❑ 94BeAPSig-21
❑ 94CanGamNHLP-375
❑ 94Don-73
❑ 94EASpo-147
❑ 94Fin-102
❑ 94FinnJaaK-150
❑ 94FinnJaaK-356
❑ 94FinRef-102
❑ 94FinSupTW-102
❑ 94Fla-212
❑ 94Fle-247
❑ 94Lea-97
❑ 94LeaLim-113
❑ 94McDUppD-McD27
❑ 94OPCPre-217
❑ 94OPCPreSE-217
❑ 94Par-260
❑ 94ParGol-260
❑ 94ParSEV-45
❑ 94Pin-147
❑ 94PinArtP-147
❑ 94PinRinC-147
❑ 94Sco-154
❑ 94ScoGol-154
❑ 94ScoPla-154
❑ 94ScoPlaTS-154
❑ 94Sel-51
❑ 94SelGol-51
❑ 94SP-133
❑ 94SPDieCut-133
❑ 94StaCluST-26
❑ 94TopPre-217
❑ 94TopPreSE-217
❑ 94Ult-398
❑ 94UppDec-7
❑ 94UppDecEleIce-7
❑ 94UppDecSPI-SP90
❑ 94UppDecSPIDC-SP90
❑ 95Bow-60
❑ 95BowAllFoi-60
❑ 95CanGamNHLP-15
❑ 95CanGamNHLP-289
❑ 95ColCho-49
❑ 95ColCho-383
❑ 95ColChoCTG-C8
❑ 95ColChoCTG-C8B
❑ 95ColChoCTG-C8C
❑ 95ColChoCTGGB-C8
❑ 95ColChoCTGGR-C8
❑ 95ColChoCTGSB-C8
❑ 95ColChoCTGSR-C8
❑ 95ColChoPC-49
❑ 95ColChoPC-383
❑ 95ColChoPCP-49
❑ 95ColChoPCP-383
❑ 95Don-155
❑ 95DonEli-29
❑ 95DonEliDCS-29
❑ 95DonEliDCU-29
❑ 95DonEliIns-1

- 95Met-121
- 95MetIS-24
- 95MetWin-8
- 95ParInt-434
- 95ParIntAS-3
- 95ParIntEI-434
- 95ParIntPTP-PP27
- 95PenFoo-12
- 95PlaOneoOne-187
- 95ProMag-95
- 95Sco-188
- 95ScoBlaIce-188
- 95ScoBlaIceAP-188
- 95SelCer-67
- 95SelCerMG-67
- 95SkyImp-137
- 95SP-117
- 95StaClu-92
- 95StaCluMOMS-92
- 95Sum-74
- 95SumArtP-74
- 95SumIce-74
- 95SweGloWC-165
- 95Top-333
- 95TopOPCI-333
- 95Ult-108
- 95Ult-295
- 95UltGolM-108
- 95UppDec-474
- 95UppDecEIelce-474
- 95UppDecEIelceG-474
- 95UppDecPHE-H37
- 95UppDecPreH-H37
- 95UppDecSpeE-SE155
- 95UppDecSpeEdiG-SE155
- 95Zen-66
- 96ColCho-214
- 96Don-91
- 96DonEli-111
- 96DonEliIDCS-111
- 96DonPrePro-91
- 96Fle-28
- 96FlePic-26
- 96Lea-130
- 96LeaPre-63
- 96LeaPreP-130
- 96LeaPrePP-63
- 96MetUni-44
- 96NHLProSTA-95
- 96Pin-122
- 96PinArtP-122
- 96PinFoi-122
- 96PinPreS-122
- 96PinRinC-122
- 96PlaOneoOne-383
- 96Sco-171
- 96ScoArtPro-171
- 96ScoDeaCAP-171
- 96ScoGolB-171
- 96ScoSpeAP-171
- 96SkyImp-32
- 96SP-43
- 96StaPos-27
- 96StaScoS-171
- 96Sum-119
- 96SumArtP-119
- 96SumIce-119
- 96SumMet-119
- 96SumPreS-119
- 96SweSemW-136
- 96Ult-48
- 96UltGolM-48
- 96UppDec-246
- 96UppDecBD-56
- 96UppDecBDG-56
- 96UppDecGN-X39
- 96UppDecIce-16
- 96UppDecIcePar-16
- 96Zen-38
- 96ZenArtP-38
- 97DonLim-93
- 97DonLimExp-93
- 97DonPre-91
- 97DonPreCttC-91
- 97DonPri-51
- 97DonPriSoA-51
- 97Pac-76
- 97PacCop-76
- 97PacCroR-44
- 97PacCroREG-44
- 97PacCroRIB-44
- 97PacCroRS-44
- 97PacDyn-40
- 97PacDynC-40
- 97PacDynDG-40
- 97PacDynEG-40
- 97PacDynIB-40
- 97PacDynR-40
- 97PacDynSil-40
- 97PacDynTan-44
- 97PacEmeGre-76
- 97PacIceB-76
- 97PacInv-45
- 97PacInvC-45
- 97PacInvEG-45
- 97PacInvIB-45
- 97PacInvR-45
- 97PacInvS-45
- 97PacOme-77
- 97PacOmeC-77
- 97PacOmeDG-77
- 97PacOmeEG-77
- 97PacOmeG-77
- 97PacOmeIB-77
- 97PacRed-76
- 97PacRev-45
- 97PacRevC-45
- 97PacRevE-45
- 97PacRevIB-45
- 97PacRevR-45
- 97PacRevS-45
- 97PacSil-76
- 97SPAut-46
- 97UppDec-263
- 98Be A PPA-43
- 98Be A PPAA-43
- 98Be A PPAAF-43
- 98Be A PPTBASG-43
- 98Be APG-43
- 98O-PChr-176
- 98O-PChrBM-B7
- 98O-PChrBMR-B7
- 98O-PChrR-176
- 98Pac-56
- 98PacAur-61
- 98PacDynI-61
- 98PacDynIIB-61
- 98PacDynIR-61
- 98PacIceB-56
- 98PacOmeH-77
- 98PacOmeODI-77
- 98PacOmeR-77
- 98PacPar-72
- 98PacParC-72
- 98PacParEG-72
- 98PacParH-72
- 98PacParIB-72
- 98PacParS-72
- 98PacRed-56
- 98Top-176
- 98TopBoaM-B7
- 98TopO-P-176
- 98UC-66
- 98UD ChoPCR-66
- 98UD ChoR-66
- 98UppDec-254
- 98UppDecE-254
- 98UppDecE1o1-254
- 98UppDecGR-254
- 98UppDecM-65
- 98UppDecMGS-65
- 98UppDecMSS-65
- 98UppDecMSS-65
- 99Pac-132
- 99PacCop-132
- 99PacGol-132
- 99PacIceB-132
- 99PacPreD-132

**Zubrus, Dainius**
- 96DonCanI-147
- 96DonCanIGPP-147
- 96DonCanIRPP-147
- 96DonEli-141
- 96DonEliAsp-15
- 96DonEliDCS-141
- 96Fla-119
- 96FlaBluI-119
- 96FlyPos-24
- 96LeaLimR-6
- 96LeaLimRG-6
- 96LeaPre-128
- 96LeaPrePP-128
- 96MetUni-198
- 96SelCer-120
- 96SelCerAP-120
- 96SelCerBlu-120
- 96SelCerMB-120
- 96SelCerMG-120
- 96SelCerMR-120
- 96SelCerRed-120
- 96SP-117
- 96Ult-129
- 96UltGolM-129
- 96UppDec-309
- 96UppDecBD-68
- 96UppDecBDG-68
- 96Zen-123
- 96ZenArtP-123
- 97Be A PPAD-26
- 97Be A PPAPD-26
- 97BeAPla-26
- 97BeAPlaAut-26
- 97ColCho-187
- 97Don-75
- 97DonEli-50
- 97DonEli-135
- 97DonEliAsp-50
- 97DonEliAsp-135
- 97DonEliS-50
- 97DonEliS-135
- 97DonLim-195
- 97DonLim-195
- 97DonLimExp-109
- 97DonLimExp-195
- 97DonLimFOTG-3
- 97DonPre-59
- 97DonPre-190
- 97DonPreCttC-59
- 97DonPreCttC-190
- 97DonPreLotT-8C
- 97DonPreProG-75
- 97DonPreProS-75
- 97DonPri-23
- 97DonPriDD-29
- 97DonPriP-34
- 97DonPriS-34
- 97DonPriSB-34
- 97DonPriSG-34
- 97DonPriSoA-23
- 97DonPriSS-34
- 97Kat-108
- 97KatGol-108
- 97KatSil-108
- 97Lea-124
- 97Lea-186
- 97LeaBanSea-22
- 97LeaFirOnIce-13
- 97LeaFraMat-124
- 97LeaFraMat-186
- 97LeaFraMDC-124
- 97LeaFraMDC-186
- 97LeaInt-124
- 97LeaIntUI-124
- 97Pac-303
- 97PacCop-303
- 97PacCroR-101
- 97PacCroREG-101
- 97PacCroRIB-101
- 97PacCroRLCDC-15
- 97PacCroRS-101
- 97PacDyn-94
- 97PacDynC-94
- 97PacDynDD-11B
- 97PacDynDG-94
- 97PacDynEG-94
- 97PacDynIB-94
- 97PacDynR-94
- 97PacDynSil-94
- 97PacDynTan-94
- 97PacEmeGre-303
- 97PacIceB-303
- 97PacInv-105
- 97PacInvC-105
- 97PacInvEG-105
- 97PacInvIB-105
- 97PacInvOTG-15
- 97PacInvR-105
- 97PacInvS-105
- 97PacOme-171
- 97PacOmeC-171
- 97PacOmeDG-171
- 97PacOmeEG-171
- 97PacOmeG-171
- 97PacOmeGFDCC-14
- 97PacOmeIB-171
- 97PacPar-138
- 97PacParC-138
- 97PacParDG-138
- 97PacParEG-138
- 97PacParIB-138
- 97PacParRed-138
- 97PacParSil-138
- 97PacRed-303
- 97PacRev-104
- 97PacRevC-104
- 97PacRevE-104
- 97PacRevIB-104
- 97PacRevR-104
- 97PacRevS-104
- 97PacSil-303
- 97Pin-105
- 97PinCer-116
- 97PinCerMB-116
- 97PinCerMG-116
- 97PinCerMR-116
- 97PinCerR-116
- 97PinIns-33
- 97PinInsCC-33
- 97PinInsEC-33
- 97PinInsT-30
- 97PinPrePBB-105
- 97PinPrePBC-105
- 97PinPrePBM-105
- 97PinPrePBY-105
- 97PinPrePFC-105
- 97PinPrePFM-105
- 97PinPrePFY-105
- 97PinPrePla-105
- 97PinTotCMPG-116
- 97PinTotCPB-116
- 97PinTotCPG-116
- 97PinTotCPR-116
- 97Sco-249
- 97ScoFly-12
- 97ScoFlyPla-12
- 97ScoFlyPre-12
- 97SPAut-117
- 97SPAutSotT-DZ
- 97Stu-26
- 97StuHarH-5
- 97StuPor-27
- 97StuPrePG-26
- 97StuPrePS-26
- 97UppDec-122
- 97UppDecBD-8
- 97UppDecBDDD-8
- 97UppDecBDQD-8
- 97UppDecBDTD-8
- 97UppDecIce-49
- 97UppDecIceP-49
- 97UppDecIPS-49
- 97UppDecSG-SG59
- 97UppDecTSS-15B
- 98Be A PPA-102
- 98Be A PPAA-102
- 98Be A PPAAF-102
- 98Be A PPTBASG-102
- 98Be APG-102
- 98Fin-14
- 98FinNo P-14
- 98FinNo PR-14
- 98FinRef-14
- 98O-PChrSB-SB30
- 98O-PChrSBR-SB30
- 98Pac-333
- 98PacAur-143
- 98PacAurCF-37
- 98PacAurCFC-37
- 98PacAurCFIB-37
- 98PacAurCFR-37
- 98PacAurCFS-37
- 98PacCroR-102
- 98PacCroRLS-102
- 98PacDynI-141
- 98PacDynIIB-141
- 98PacDynIR-141
- 98PacGolCD-26
- 98PacIceB-333
- 98PacOmeH-181
- 98PacOmeODI-181
- 98PacOmeR-181
- 98PacPar-179
- 98PacParC-179
- 98PacParEG-179
- 98PacParH-179
- 98PacParIB-179
- 98PacParS-179
- 98PacRed-333
- 98PacRev-108
- 98PacRevIS-108
- 98PacRevR-108
- 98TopSeaB-SB30
- 98UppDec-145
- 98UppDecE-145
- 98UppDecE1o1-145
- 98UppDecGR-145
- 98UppDecM-102
- 98UppDecMGS-102
- 98UppDecMSS-102
- 98UppDecMSS-102
- 99Pac-215
- 99PacCop-215
- 99PacGol-215
- 99PacIceB-215
- 99PacPreD-215
- 99QuePeeWHWCCS-7

**Zubyck, John**
- 96GueSto-4
- 97GueSto-22

**Zuk, Greg**
- 84KelWin-5

**Zuke, Mike**
- 80OPC-209
- 80Top-209
- 81OPC-299
- 81OPCSti-132
- 81Top-W124
- 82OPC-313
- 82PosCer-17
- 83OPC-322
- 83WhaJunHC-22
- 84OPC-80
- 84OPCSti-195
- 84Top-63
- 84WhaJunW-22
- 85OPC-19
- 85Top-19
- 85WhaJunW-23
- 89SauSteMG-26
- 93SauSteMG-30
- 93SauSteMGM-32
- 96SauSteMG-29
- 96SauSteMGA-29

**Zukiwsky, Jarret**
- 89VicCou-21
- 907thInnSWHL-247
- 917thInnSWHL-284

**Zukiwsky, Jon**
- 93RedDeeR-29
- 95BowDraPro-P40
- 95RedDeeR-22

**Zultek, Matt**
- 97BowCHL-132
- 97BowCHLAu-132
- 97BowCHLOPC-132

**Zulyniak, Shane**
- 907thInnSWHL-278
- 90PriAlbR-22
- 917thInnSWHL-264
- 91PriAlbR-24
- 93PriAlbR-22
- 94PriAlbR-23

**Zurba, Peter**
- 91BriColJHL-13
- 92BriColJHL-189

**Zwakman, Greg**
- 92MinGolG-21
- 93MinGolG-29
- 94MinGolG-31
- 95MinGolG-30

**Zwijack, Tim**
- 80SauSteMG-11

**Zwyer, Dave**
- 92MPSPhoSJHL-148

**Zygulski, Scott**
- 93ForWorF-17

**Zytynsky, Taras**
- 83Sprind-24

**Zyuzin, Andrei**
- 95Cla-69
- 95ClaAut-24
- 96ColEdgSS&D-7
- 97PacOme-208
- 97PacOmeC-208
- 97PacOmeDG-208
- 97PacOmeEG-208
- 97PacOmeG-208
- 97PacOmeIB-208
- 98Be A PPA-116
- 98Be A PPAA-116
- 98Be A PPAAF-116
- 98Be A PPTBASG-116
- 98Be APG-116
- 98Pac-394
- 98PacIceB-394
- 98PacRed-394
- 98SPxFin-134
- 98SPxFinR-134
- 98SPxFinS-134
- 98UC-179
- 98UD ChoPCR-179
- 98UD ChoR-179
- 98UD3-18
- 98UD3-78
- 98UD3-138
- 98UD3DieC-18
- 98UD3DieC-78
- 98UD3DieC-138
- 98UppDec-168
- 98UppDecBD-73
- 98UppDecGR-168
- 98UppDecE-168
- 98UppDecE1o1-168
- 98UppDecGR-168
- 98UppDecM-171
- 98UppDecMGS-171
- 98UppDecMSS-171
- 98UppDecMSS-171
- 98UppDecQD-73
- 98UppDecTD-73

**Zywitza, Sven**
- 94GerDELE-13
- 95GerDELE-14
- 96GerDELE-14

# Acknowledgments

A great deal of diligence, hard work, and dedicated effort went into this year's volume. The high standards to which we hold ourselves, however, could not have been met without the expert input and generous amount of time contributed by many people. Our sincere thanks are extended to each and every one of you.

Each year we refine the process of developing the most accurate and up-to-date information for this book. I believe this year's Price Guide is our best yet. Thanks again to all of the contributors nationwide (listed below) as well as our staff here in Dallas.

Those who have worked closely with us on this and many other books, have again proven themselves invaluable in every aspect of producing this book: Mike Aronstein, Pete Belanger, Erwin Borau, Bill Bossert, John Brenner, Milt Byron, Cartomania (Joseph E. Filion), Cartophilium (Andrew Pywowarczuk), Collection de Sport AZ (Ronald Villanueve), Bill and Diane Dodge, Gervise Ford, Steve Freedman, Larry and Jeff Fritsch, John Furniss, Gary Gagen, Dick Gariepy, Dick Gilkeson, Mike and Howard Gordon, George Grauer, Gene Guarnere, Jerry and Etta Hersh, Mike Hersh, Gerald Higgs, Sean Isaacs, Dennis Kannokko, Paul and Anna Kannokko, Andrew Kossman, Lew Lipset, Paul Marchant, Michael Moretto, Daniel Naiman, Pacific Trading Cards (Mike Cramer and Mike Monson), Jean-Guy Pichette, Jack Pollard, Gavin Riley, Rotman Productions, John Rumierz, Kevin Savage, Angelo Savelli, Mike Schechter (MSA), Richard Sherman, Brad Shimbashi, Brad Shrabin, Gary Silkstone, Ralph Slate, Gerry Sobie, John Spalding, Phil and Joan Spector, Nigel Spill, Frank Steele, Murvin Sterling, Topps (Marty Appel and Sy Berger), Upper Deck (Steve Ryan), Rob Unlus, Michel Vaillancourt, Shirl Volk, Pete Wooten, Kit Young, and Robert Zanze. Finally, we give a special acknowledgment to Dennis W. Eckes, Mr. Sport Americana, whose untimely passing in 1991 was a real loss to the hobby and to me personally. The success of the Beckett Price Guides has always been the result of a team effort.

Many other individuals have provided price input, illustrative material, checklist verifications, errata, and/or background information. At the risk of inadvertently overlooking or omitting these many contributors, we should like to personally thank Ab D Cards (Dale Wesolewski), Jerry Adamic, Bren Adams, Scott Alpaugh, Neil Armstrong, Alan Applegate, Roland J. Atlas, Art Baker, Brent Barnes, Frank and Vivian Barning, Robert Beaudoin, Al Beharrell, Todd Bellerose, Gary Benton, Beulah Sports (Jeff Blatt), Brian L. Bigelow, Ki Billy, Chad Blick, Michel Bolduc, Joseph Bonett, Peter Borkowski, Luc Boucher, B. Jack Bourland III, Tony Bouwman, Jim Boyne, Elio Brandelli, Marco Brizuela, Bob Bruner, Dan Bruner, Eric Burgoyne, Scott Burke, Jim Cappello, Danny Cariseo, Greg Caskey, Dwight Chapin, Michael Chark, Steve Chiaramonte, Susan Christensen, Scott Coates, Allan E. Cohen, Shane Cohen (Grand Slam), Barry Colla, Matt Collett, Ken Collins, Joe Conte, Dan Conway, Ryan Cope, Michael J. Cox, Taylor Crane, Wil Curtis, Allen Custer, Kenneth Daniels, Steven Danver, Leo Davis, Mary Dempster, Dee\rquotes Baseball Cards, Normand Desroches, Larry DeTienne, Dave Deveney, Karlos Diego, Leon Dill, Mario DiPastena, Marc Dixon, Gerard Dolci, Benoit Doyon, Michel Dubois, Charles Dugre, John Duplisea, Don Ellis, Danny Ellwood, Michael Esposito, Evelyn Ettinger, Stewart Ettinger, Doak Ewing, Dave Feltham, Larry Fleming, Don Forsey, Frank Fox, Craig Frank, Mark Franke, Kathryn Friedlander, Bob Frye, James Funke Jr., Neil Garvey, Jim Galusha, Ron and Dave Gibara, Michael R. Gionet, Dave Giove, Harvey Goldfarb, Brian Goldstein, Jeff Goldstein, Renvel Gonsalves, Rynel Gonsalves, Seth Gordon, Erik Gravel, Pierre-Luc Gravel, Great Canadian Sportcard Co., Hall's Nostalgia, Tom Harrett, Ron Heller, Bill Henderson, Tom Hendrickson, Wayne Hepburn, Chick Hershberger, Clay Hill, Gary Hlady, Shawn Hoagland, Keith Holtzmann, Joseph Horgan, Dan Horton, Teresa Horton, D. Howery Jr., Richard Irving, Torstein H. Jacobsen, John James, Robert Jansing, Cliff Janzen, Leslie Jezuit, Robert Kantor, Jay and Mary Kasper, Alan Kaye, John Kelly, Rick Keplinger, Larry Kerrigan, Dean Konieczka, Bob Krawetz, Chuck Kucera, Rob Kuhlman, Thomas Kunnecke,

Roger Lampert, Ted Larkins, Brent Lee, Scott LeLievre, Irv Lerner, Howie Levy, Mike Lewandoski, Stephane Lizotte, Nicholas LoCasto, The Locker Room, Tim Loop, Frank Lopez, Karoline K. Lowry, Steven J. Loy, Thierry Lubenec, Jim Macie, Joe Marasco, Adam Martin, Chris Mayhew, Michael McDonald, Blake Meyer, John Meyer, Dick Millerd, Ben Mitchell, Paul V. Mohrle, Joe Morano, Michael Moretto, Michel Morin, Brian Morris, Kevin Mudrak, Larry Murray, Todd Nelkin, Rob Nicholls, Dave Nicklas, Paul Noble, Leandre Normand, Dale Novakowski, David Nystrom, John O'Hara, John O'Mara, Glenn Olson, Nelson Paine, Andrew Pak, David Paolicelli, Tom Parker, Clay Pasternack, Alan Peace, Alan Philpot, Dale Pinney, Richard Plett, Len Pottie, Red River Coins and Cards, Randall Reese, Tom Reid, Paula Reinke, Ralph Reitsma, Dorothy Reznik, Owen Ricker, John Wayne Roman, Charles Rooke, Francis Rose, Jim Routly, Grant Rowland, Joe Rubert II, Terry Sack, Joe Sak, Cheryl Sauve, Mike Shafer, Chris Sklener, Lyle Skrapek, Slapshot Sports Collectibles, Steve Smith, Carl Specht, Cary Stephenson, Dan Stickney, Andy Stoltz, Ray Stonehouse, Dave Sularz, Walt Suski, Fred Suzman, Danny Tarquini, Paul S. Taylor, Lee Temanson, Teresa Tewell, Chuck Thomas, Joe Tomasik, Darren Turcotte, Michel Vaillancourt, Variete Sports Verville Enr., Clayton Vigent, Shirl Volk, Jonathan Waldman, Jonathan Watts, David Weiner, Andrew B. Weisenfeld, Kermit B. Wells, Brian Wentz, Bill Wesslund, Frank Wilder, Jason Wilder, Kelly Wionzek, Brian Wobbeking, Ted Woo, Thomas L. Wujek, Andre Yip Hoi, Yaz's Sports Memorabilia, Gerard Yodice, Christina Zawadzki, and Bill Zimpleman. A special thanks also goes out to those who graciously donated their knowledge and expertise (and their cards) in adding to the comprehensiveness of this year's volume: Caspar Friberg (Finnish issues), Marek Pandoscak (Slovakian issues), Jiri Peterka (Czech issues), Holger Petersen (German issues), Hockey Heaven (Lind), and Per Vedin (Swedish issues).

Every year we make active solicitations for expert input. We are particularly appreciative of the help (however extensive or cursory) provided for this volume. We receive many inquiries, comments and questions regarding material within this book. In fact, each and every one is read and digested. Time constraints, however, prevent us from personally replying. But keep sharing your knowledge. Even though we cannot respond to each letter, you are making significant contributions to the hobby through your interest and comments.

The effort to continually refine and improve this book also involves a growing number of people and types of expertise on our home team. Our company boasts a substantial Collectibles Data team, which strengthens our ability to provide comprehensive analysis of the marketplace. Our hockey analysts played a major part in compiling this years book, travelling thousands of miles during the past year to attend sports card shows and visit card shops around the United States and Canada. The Beckett hockey specialists are BHC Price Guide Editor Bill Sutherland, BHC Price Guide Analyst Scott Prusha, and BHC Senior Editor Al Muir. Their baseline analysis and careful proofreading were key contributions to the accuracy of this annual.

In the years since this guide debuted, Beckett Publications has grown beyond any rational expectation. A great many talented and hard working individuals have been instrumental in this growth and success. Our whole team is to be congratulated for what we together have accomplished.

The whole Beckett Publications team has my thanks for jobs well done. Thank you, everyone.

# In Your Face, Behind-the-back,

### Subscribe to
### *Beckett Basketball*
### *Card Monthly* today!

Looking for a reliable hoops Price Guide with up-to-the-minute info? With a subscription to *Beckett Basketball Card Monthly*, you'll get the hobby's most accurate basketball card Price Guide <u>every</u> <u>month</u>! Plus get great inside info about new product releases, superstar player coverage, off-the-court news and answers to all

# Stick With Beckett's All-Pro Hockey Coverage!

## Subscribe to Beckett Hockey Card Monthly today!

Wondering where "in-the-know" hockey collectors get their monthly Price Guide? A subscription to *Beckett Hockey Card Monthly* gives you the hobby's most accurate hockey card Price Guide <u>every month</u>! Plus great info about new product releases, superstar player coverage, off-ice news and answers to all your collecting questions too!

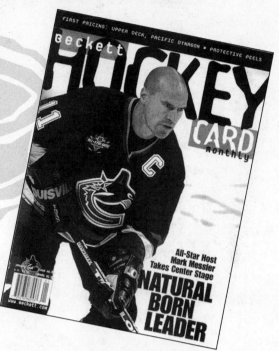

---

## Beckett Hockey Card Monthly

Name (please print) —————————————————————————

Address—————————————————————————————

City————————————————— State —————— ZIP————

Payment enclosed via: ❏ Check or Money Order ❏ Bill Me Later

Check One Please:    Price      Total

❏ 2 years (24 issues)   $44.95 = ————————
❏ 1 year (12 issues)   $24.95 = ————————

All Canadian & foreign addresses add
$12 per year for postage (includes G.S.T.).   = ————————
Payable in U.S. funds.
Please do not send cash.
Total Enclosed $

Mail to:
*Beckett Hockey Card Monthly*
P.O. Box 7647
Red Oak, IA 51591-0647
Photocopies of this coupon are acceptable.

Please allow 4-6 weeks for subscription delivery.

SHOM20

# Memorabilia, Autograph
# & Auction Action . . .

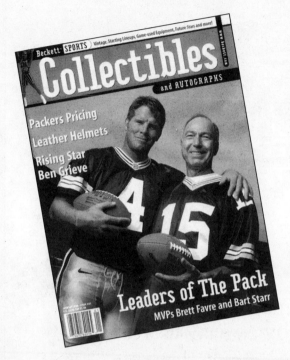

From vintage sports cards and collectibles to draft picks cards and autographed memorabilia, you won't find better coverage of today's sports collectibles hobby. With your subscription to *Beckett Sports Collectibles and Autographs*, you get regular and bonus Price Guides for the most popular collectibles.

Plus get sports auctions coverage, a figurine market watch, Kenner Starting Lineup info, autograph news and answers to your hobby questions, too!

Subscribe to *Beckett Sports Collectibles and Autographs* today!